W9-BKB-188

Latin America	**LAm**	Latinoamérica
linguistics	**Ling**	lingüística
literally	**lit**	literalmente
literary	**liter**	literario
literature	**Liter**	literatura
masculine	**m**	masculino
mathematics	**Math, Mat**	matemáticas
mechanics, mechanical	**Mec**	mecánica, mecánico
medicine	**Med**	medicina
meteorology	**Met**	meteorología
metallurgy	**Metal**	metalurgia
Mexican usage	**Mex, Méx**	uso mejicano
military	**Mil**	militar
mining	**Min**	minería
mythology	**Mit**	mitología
music	**Mus, Mús**	música
noun	**n**	nombre, sustantivo
nautical	**Naut, Náut**	náutica
negative	**neg**	negativo
optics	**Ópt**	óptica
ornithology	**Orn**	ornitología
oneself	**o.s.**	(a) sí mismo
parliament	**Parl**	parlamento
pejorative	**pej, pey**	peyorativo
for example	**p.ej.**	por ejemplo
personal	**pers**	personal
pharmacy	**Pharm**	farmacia
philosophy	**Philos**	filosofía
phonetics	**Phon**	fonética
photography	**Phot**	fotografía
physics	**Phys**	física
physiology	**Physiol**	fisiología
plural	**pl**	forma plural
poetry	**Poet**	poética
poetic	**poet, poét**	uso poético
politics	**Pol**	política
possessive	**poss, pos**	posesivo
predicative	**pred**	predicativo
prefix	**pref**	prefijo
preposition	**prep**	preposición
pronoun	**pron**	pronombre
provincial (Spain)	**prov**	provincial (España)
psychology	**Psych, Psic**	psicología
chemistry	**Quim**	química
registered trade mark	®	marca registrada
radio	**Rad**	radio
railways	**Rail**	ferrocarriles
religion	**Rel**	religión
relative	**rel**	relativo
somebody	**sb**	alguien
Southern Cone	**SC**	Cono Sur
school	**Scol**	escuela
Scotland	**Scot**	Escocia
sewing	**Sew**	costura
singular	**sing**	singular
skiing	**Ski**	esquí
slang	**sl**	argot
sociology	**Sociol**	sociología
Spanish usage	**Sp**	español de España
something	**sth**	algo
Stock Exchange	**St Ex**	Bolsa
subjunctive	**subj**	modo subjuntivo
suffix	**suf**	sufijo
superlative	**superl**	superlativo
surveying	**Survey**	agrimensura
also	**t**	también
bull fighting	**Taur**	tauromaquia
theatre	**Teat**	teatro
technical	**Tech, Téc**	técnico
telecommunications	**Telec**	telecomunicaciones
theatre	**Theat**	teatro
typography	**Tip**	tipografía
television	**TV**	televisión
typography	**Typ**	tipografía
university	**Univ**	universidad
United States	**US**	Estados Unidos
see	**V**	véase
verb	**v**	verbo
veterinary medicine	**Vet**	veterinaria
intransitive verb	**vi**	verbo intransitivo
reflexive verb	**vr**	verbo reflexivo
transitive verb	**vt**	verbo transitivo
transitive and intransitive verb	**vti**	verbo transitivo e intransitivo
zoology	**Zool**	zoología
see pages xx-xxi	*	véase págs. xx-xxi
see page xxi	†	véase pág. xxi
see page xxiii	≃	véase pág. xxiii

DICCIONARIO ESPAÑOL~INGLÉS INGLÉS~ESPAÑOL

SPANISH~ENGLISH ENGLISH~SPANISH DICTIONARY

COLLINS DICCIONARIO ESPAÑOL~INGLÉS INGLÉS~ESPAÑOL

por
Colin Smith
en colaboración con
Diarmuid Bradley Teresa de Carlos Louis Rodrigues
José Ramón Parrondo

TERCERA EDICIÓN

grijalbo

COLLINS SPANISH~ENGLISH ENGLISH~SPANISH DICTIONARY

by
Colin Smith
in collaboration with
Diarmuid Bradley **Teresa de Carlos** **Louis Rodrigues**
José Ramón Parrondo

THIRD EDITION

HarperCollins*Publishers*

third edition/tercera edición 1992

Ediciones Grijalbo, S.A.
Aragón 385, Barcelona 08013
ISBN 84-253-2401-7

HarperCollins Publishers

P.O. Box, Glasgow G4 ONB, Great Britain
ISBN 0 00 433545-7
with thumb index 0 00 433560-0

---

10 East 53rd Street, New York
New York 10022
ISBN 0-06-275504-8

First HarperCollins edition published 1990.

Library of Congress Cataloging-in-Publication Data

Smith, Colin, 1927-
Collins Spanish-English, English-Spanish dictionary / by Colin Smith in collaboration with Diarmuid Bradley, Teresa de Carlos, Louis Rodrigues, José Ramón Parrondo. — 3rd ed., Tercera ed.
p. cm.
ISBN 0-06-275504-8 (U.S.)
1. Spanish language—Dictionaries—English. 2. English language—Dictionaries—Spanish. I. Title.
PC4640.S595 1992
463'.21—dc20 91-36013
CIP

---

92 93 94 95 96 HCM 10 9 8 7 6 5 4 3 2 1

Printed in Great Britain by HarperCollins Manufacturing, Glasgow

THIRD EDITION TERCERA EDICIÓN

by

Colin Smith

in collaboration with/en colaboración con

Diarmuid Bradley Teresa de Carlos Louis Rodrigues

José Ramón Parrondo

Editorial management/Dirección editorial

Jeremy Butterfield

Coordinating editor/Coordinador de la obra

Gerard Breslin

Assistant editor/Ayudante de redacción

Lesley Johnston

SECOND EDITION SEGUNDA EDICIÓN

by

Colin Smith

in collaboration with/en colaboración con

María Boniface Hugo Pooley Arthur Montague

Mike Gonzalez

FIRST EDITION PRIMERA EDICIÓN

by

Colin Smith

in collaboration with/en colaboración con

Manuel Bermejo Marcos Eugenio Chang-Rodríguez

ACKNOWLEDGEMENTS

THIRD EDITION

In the relatively short time which has passed since the second edition of 1988, there has naturally been less opportunity for users to contribute comments and suggestions than was the case when the second edition was being prepared. However, eager and learned colleagues and users have not been altogether lacking, and thanks for contributions (in some cases extensive) are due to: the reviewers of the second edition, Jennie Bachelor, Tom Bookless, Everett L. Boyd, John Butt, Nick Gardner, María Martín, Brian Mott, Patrick Nield, Hugo Pooley, Chris Pratt, Dan Quilter, Brian Steel, Roger Wright.

SECOND EDITION

Apart from those mentioned as members of the team on the title page, who have laboured devotedly, the author's special thanks are due to Guillermo Arce, Tom Bookless, John Butt, Teresa de Carlos, Concepción and Pilar Jiménez Bautista, Daniel Quilter, and Brian Steel, who over the years have provided substantial contributions; and to the following, who in differing degrees gave additional help: Pamela Bacarisse, David Balagué, Clive Bashleigh, Peter Beardsell, William Bidgood, T.R.M. Bristow, A. Bryson Gerrard, Robert Burakoff, Trevor Chubb, G.T. Colegate, Joe Cremona, Eve Degnen, Maureen Dolan, Carmen and Pablo Domínguez, Fr Carlos Elizalde C.P., John England, G.C. Gilham, Paul Gomez, Stephen Harrison, Patrick Harvey, Tony Heathcote, David Henn, Leo Hickey, Ian Jacob, F. Killoran, Norman Lamb, Emilio Lorenzo, Rodney Mantle, Alan Morley, Brian Morris, Ana Newton, Richard Nott, Hugh O'Donnell, Brian Powell, Chris Pratt, Robert Pring-Mill, C.H. Stevenson, Diana Streeten, Ian Weetman, Richard Wharton, Roger Wright, Alan Yates.

FIRST EDITION

It is proper to retain the following from the Preface to the First Edition of 1971: 'I am greatly indebted to the following: Dr M. Bermejo Marcos, who read all the drafts; Prof. E. Chang Rodríguez, who read the first part to check information about American Spanish; Mr H.B. Hall, who advised on principles at the start and read sections of the second part; and for a variety of contributions, to Mr T.C. Bookless, Prof. R.F. Brown, Dr G.A. Davies, Miss A. Johnson, Mr A. Madigan, Mr A. McCallum, Miss G. Weston, Sr J. and Sra M. del Río, Sra A. Espinosa de Walker and Sra M.J. Fernández de Wangermann. My wife helped in all the ways that wives do. To them all, my warmest thanks.'

Colin Smith

AGRADECIMIENTOS

TERCERA EDICIÓN

En el poco tiempo transcurrido desde la publicación de la segunda edición, es natural que los usuarios no hayan tenido tantas oportunidades para enviar comentarios y sugerencias como las que tuvieron antes de la preparación de esa segunda edición. Sin embargo, no han faltado por completo colegas y usuarios entusiastas y eruditos, y ofrezco mis gracias por las aportaciones (a veces cuantiosas) de: los autores de reseñas de la segunda edición, Jennie Bachelor, Tom Bookless, Everett L. Boyd, John Butt, Nick Gardner, María Martín, Brian Mott, Patrick Nield, Hugo Pooley, Chris Pratt, Dan Quilter, Brian Steel, Roger Wright.

SEGUNDA EDICIÓN

Aparte de las personas que se mencionan en la portada, que han trabajado con devoción, quedo agradecido de manera especial por sus cuantiosas contribuciones a Guillermo Arce, Tom Bookless, John Butt, Teresa de Carlos, Concepción y Pilar Jiménez Bautista, Daniel Quilter, y Brian Steel, y a otros que de diversas maneras han aportado sus auxilios: Pamela Bacarisse, David Balagué, Clive Bashleigh, Peter Beardsell, William Bidgood, T.R.M. Bristow, A. Bryson Gerrard, Robert Burakoff, Trevor Chubb, G.T. Colegate, Joe Cremona, Eve Degnen, Maureen Dolan, Carmen and Pablo Domínguez, Fr Carlos Elizalde C.P., John England, G.C. Gilham, Paul Gomez, Stephen Harrison, Patrick Harvey, Tony Heathcote, David Henn, Leo Hickey, Ian Jacob, F. Killoran, Norman Lamb, Emilio Lorenzo, Rodney Mantle, Alan Morley, Brian Morris, Ana Newton, Richard Nott, Hugh O'Donnell, Brian Powell, Chris Pratt, Robert Pring-Mill, C.H. Stevenson, Diana Streeten, Ian Weetman, Richard Wharton, Roger Wright, Alan Yates.

PRIMERA EDICIÓN

Conservo lo siguiente del Prefacio de la Primera Edición de 1971: 'Agradezco la ayuda de: Dr M. Bermejo Marcos, que leyó todos los borradores; Prof. E. Chang-Rodríguez, que leyó la 1ª parte para mejorar lo referente al español de América; Sr H.B. Hall, que me dio consejos al principio y leyó varias letras de la 2ª parte. Han contribuido también: Sr T.C. Bookless, Prof. R.F. Brown, Dr G.A. Davies, Srta A. Johnson, Sr A. Madigan, Sr A. McCallum, Srta G. Weston, Sr J. y Sra M. del Río, Sra A. Espinosa de Walker y Sra M.J. Fernández de Wangermann. Mi esposa ha prestado su ayuda en las maneras en que suelen prestarla las esposas. Para todos, mis gracias.'

CONTENTS

ÍNDICE DE MATERIAS

PREFACE

PREFACE TO THE THIRD EDITION

The fact that this new edition appears so shortly after the second (1988) has a particular motive. While on the one hand there is a permanent need to modernize such works of reference (and the pace of neologistic creation always seems to quicken), the author and publishers have seized the opportunity offered by 1992 to salute both the Single European Act and the Spanish-speaking world, **La Hispanidad**, as it reflects on its special quincentenary of cultural achievements in which language has been both a mover and a product. The chance has been taken to improve many thousands of entries on both sides and to add (from the very extensive corpus assembled by Dairmuid Bradley, Heriot Watt University) many hundreds of neologisms of Spanish. The revision of the English side was greatly enhanced by access to the COBUILD corpora and a wealth of neologisms from Collins English Dictionaries. Many improvements have been drawn in the coverage of business and administrative language from the expert knowledge of Louis Rodrigues (Cambridge), while Teresa de Carlos' (Cambridge) acute sense of both languages has led to the refinement of many entries. We have also paid renewed attention to the lexis of computers and new technology. A new appendix on Word Formation in Spanish has been provided in order to gather together problematic aspects and to indicate solutions. The main text of the dictionary is larger by 30,000 references and 50,000 translations. The work is offered with the confidence that it will maintain and even enhance the appreciation it has enjoyed among users since its first appearance in 1971.

PREFACE TO THE SECOND EDITION

That the First Edition was so well received did not mean that the author could leave the work there and rest on any laurels. From the moment of its publication a mass of new materials began to be assembled, some of it for correction and improvement of existing entries, much relating to new items of the kind that rapid evolution of major modern languages produces. There have also been notable improvements in method devised for other books in the Collins bilingual range, now adopted here. In particular, a considerable effort has been made to improve coverage of usage in Latin America and in the United States. No doubt this second edition was already long overdue, but it is offered with some confidence that it represents a great all-round improvement.

EXTRACT FROM THE PREFACE TO THE FIRST EDITION

Given the rapidity of change in language and in its social and theoretical aspects, a new dictionary hardly needs an apology. This dictionary would be justified even if it were of the traditional type; in fact it incorporates new principles which may be of interest to linguists, and whose practical application should ease the task of users at every level.

The lexicographer who attempts to equate and harmonize two great world languages must honestly recognize that both in theory and in practice his task cannot be perfectly fulfilled. The simplest word often has such a range, such semantic potentiality and such nuances that it cannot be fully defined within a single-language dictionary; it is more difficult still to translate it in a two-language dictionary of modest size.

This is, however, an optimistic undertaking. It presupposes that the two linguistic areas are in contact for reasons of trade, diplomacy, and tourism; for cultural, literary, scientific and sporting exchanges; that each has something to learn from the other and the will to do so. It presupposes free intercommunication across the frontiers and the oceans. The dictionary is a tool of understanding and it speaks for peace, tolerance and mutual respect.

Colin Smith

PREFACIO

PREFACIO DE LA TERCERA EDICIÓN

El hecho de que esta nueva edición aparece tan pronto después de la segunda (1988) tiene un motivo bien concreto. Mientras por una parte existe la permanente necesidad de actualizar tales obras de consulta (y la rapidez de la creación neologística parece ir siempre en aumento), el autor y la editorial han aprovechado la oportunidad que ofrece 1992 para saludar tanto al Acta Única como al mundo hispanohablante, **La Hispanidad**, en el momento en que considera el quinto centenario de logros culturales en los que la lengua ha sido a la vez promotora y producto. Hemos rehecho y mejorado muchos miles de artículos en cada parte, añadiendo centenares de neologismos del español procedentes de la extensa colección de Dairmuid Bradley (Universidad de Heriot Watt). La remodelación del inglés se facilitó por el acceso a los corpora de COBUILD y los neologismos recogidos por Collins English Dictionaries. Hemos prestado atención especial a la cobertura de términos y giros del comercio y de la administración, aprovechando la pericia técnica de Louis Rodrigues (Cambridge), mientras la penetrante comprensión de Teresa de Carlos (Cambridge) en las dos lenguas ha servido para limar muchos artículos. Hemos renovado la atención concedida a la informática y las nuevas tecnologías. Presentamos un nuevo Apéndice sobre la formación de palabras en español con el propósito de reunir aspectos problemáticos para el usuario anglohablante. El texto del diccionario se aumenta en unas 30.000 referencias y 50.000 traducciones. Se ofrece la obra con la confianza de que mantendrá y aun mejorará el aprecio que viene disfrutando desde su primera aparición en 1971.

PREFACIO DE LA SEGUNDA EDICIÓN

La excelente acogida que se dio a la primera edición no quería decir que el autor pudiera dejar su trabajo en ese punto. Desde el momento de la publicación se empezó a reunir gran cantidad de materiales nuevos, en muchos casos destinados a corregir y mejorar el texto existente, en otros casos nuevos datos de los que produce la rápida evolución de las grandes lenguas modernas. En otros libros de la serie bilingüe de Collins se han realizado unos adelantos notables en cuanto al método, que he adoptado ahora. Los colaboradores se han esforzado por mejorar todo lo referente a usos lingüísticos americanos tanto para el español como para el inglés. Nadie duda que ya había llegado el momento de ofrecer esta segunda edición, y se presenta con la confianza de que supone una gran mejora.

EXTRACTO DEL PREFACIO DE LA PRIMERA EDICIÓN

El rápido desarrollo de las lenguas y de sus aspectos sociales y teóricos eximen al autor de la necesidad de disculparse al publicar un nuevo diccionario. Este libro se justificaría aun cuando fuera del tipo tradicional; se justifica más incorporando varios principios nuevos que pueden tener interés para los lingüistas, y cuya aplicación práctica podrá ayudar a los usuarios de todo tipo.

El lexicógrafo que se esfuerza por juntar y armonizar dos grandes idiomas mundiales tiene que reconocer honradamente que tanto en la teoría como en la práctica es imposible llevar perfectamente a cabo su cometido. La palabra más sencilla puede tener tal extensión, tanta potencialidad semántica y tantos matices que resulta imposible definirla en un libro monolingüe; es más difícil todavía traducirla en un diccionario bilingüe de tamaño modesto.

Con todo, esta empresa se funda en el optimismo. Ello supone que las dos áreas lingüísticas están en contacto por razones comerciales, diplomáticas y turísticas; para el intercambio cultural, literario, científico y deportivo; porque cada una tiene interés en aprender de la otra, y la voluntad de hacerlo. Ello supone que existe la libre comunicación a través de las fronteras y de los océanos. El diccionario sirve para la comprensión mutua y habla en pro de la paz.

Colin Smith

INTRODUCTION

The first edition of this dictionary contained a substantial essay on the problems of bilingual lexicography, with special reference to English and Spanish as languages whose extraordinary extension and international use increase the difficulties of adequate coverage. Parts of this essay also concerned the attempt to help the user in all possible ways with subdivisions of entries, indicators, usage examples, and so on, an attempt which at that time had its novel aspects. There is no point in reproducing this introductory essay here, partly because the principles enunciated seem now to have gained a wide acceptance and are even taken for granted.

However, it is as well to insist on certain aspects. The dictionary retains its aim of seeking to express and translate the active usage of the average educated speaker. The revised edition of 1988 thus showed a notable modernization over that of 1971 and, indeed, a considerable expansion, which has been taken further in this third edition of 1992. A few archaisms and obsolete terms are retained, since, while they are by definition not in live use, they are known and recognized in literary texts still widely read, or may have a place in humorous use. Our average educated speaker commands such technical vocabulary as he daily needs at work and at play but if faced with genuinely technical needs consults a specialist, as the user of this dictionary must for e.g. accountancy, medicine, or the oil industry. However, in acknowledgement of the growing importance of computers in our daily lives we have included a considerable number of end-user computer terms.

In line with developments since 1971, especially in public acceptability and tolerance in the mass media, there is now a proportionately greater coverage of slang terms, drug parlance, and obscenities, with the proviso that words in these classes often have a specially ephemeral existence and can cause a reference book to seem dated after only a short time.

A considerable effort was made in 1988 to improve coverage of English and Spanish as used in the New World, where speakers of both are now several times more numerous than in the European homelands and where, for English in the United States at least, so weighty a preponderance of linguistic creativity and of cultural power now resides. The problem with Spanish in the New World is of another kind, in the sheer diversity of usages among so many independent states, some with varying admixtures of elements derived from native languages: it is impossible to do complete justice to all of these in a work of this kind, perhaps in any. However, we have considerably extended coverage of Latin-American usage by a systematic examination of key linguistic areas by native speakers.

What was said in the first edition about 'Oxford' English and 'Academy' Spanish, and about 'Usage and authority', retains its validity but does not warrant repetition here. For Spanish, some account was taken in 1971 of the Academy's statutory authority and decisions about individual items, but these claims and activities have seemed increasingly unrealistic over the years (except perhaps in the very limited field of orthography), and played no part in the revisions of 1988 and 1992. This means that the dictionary surrenders even that small claim to be stating any kind of 'authority': it is simply a record of common modern usage, and makes no value-judgements. That some items recently noted in the bureaucratic, political, or sociological parlance of Spain are included even though they may have been attacked or parodied is thus true but not a matter for protest. The indications of social register of words and phrases should guide the user to some extent.

INTRODUCCIÓN

La primera edición de este diccionario incluía todo un ensayo sobre los problemas de la lexicografía bilingüe, subrayándose en especial la dificultad de abarcar adecuadamente el inglés y el español en toda su enorme extensión internacional. En este ensayo se analizaba también el esfuerzo realizado para ayudar al usuario en lo posible mediante subdivisiones de artículos, 'palabras indicadoras', ejemplos de usos, etcétera, esfuerzo que en aquel momento tenía aspectos nuevos. Hoy sería improcedente volver a imprimir este ensayo, en parte porque parece que los principios enunciados han merecido una amplia aceptación y casi se podría decir que se dan por sabidos.

Se puede sin embargo insistir en ciertos aspectos. El diccionario conserva su propósito de expresar y traducir el uso activo de la lengua de la persona culta media. La nueva edición de 1988 supuso una considerable modernización con respecto a la de 1971, y una notable expansión, que se ha extendido aún más en esta tercera edición de 1992. Unos pocos arcaísmos y términos caídos en desuso quedan incluidos, pues, si bien no siguen usándose en la lengua viva, se reconocen en los textos literarios, o pueden encontrarse en el uso humorístico. Nuestro hablante medio posee el vocabulario técnico que necesita en su trabajo o en sus ocios, pero cuando surgen necesidades realmente técnicas consulta a un especialista, así como el usuario de este diccionario tendrá que hacer para, p.ej., la contabilidad o la medicina o la industria del petróleo. No obstante, como respuesta a la creciente importancia de los ordenadores en nuestra vida diaria, hemos incluido un considerable número de términos de informática para el usuario final.

De acuerdo con la evolución desde 1971, especialmente con respecto al nivel de aceptabilidad pública y de la tolerancia en los medios de comunicación, hay ahora una mayor representación de los argots, del léxico de la droga, y de las obscenidades, siempre con la desventaja de que estas palabras tienen una existencia efímera y que pueden dar un aire 'de ayer' a cualquier obra de referencia.

Trabajamos mucho en 1988 para mejorar la cobertura del inglés y del español en el Nuevo Mundo, donde las respectivas poblaciones son ahora varias veces mayores que las de sus lugares de origen europeos y donde, en el caso del inglés de Estados Unidos por lo menos, se aprecia tanto peso de creatividad lingüística y de fuerza cultural. El problema del español de América es de otra índole, y estriba en la misma diversidad de usos de los muchos estados independientes, algunos con influencias en distinto grado de las lenguas indígenas; es imposible hacer justicia a todos en una obra de este tipo, quizás en una obra de cualquier tipo. Sin embargo, hemos aumentado mucho el espacio dedicado a los usos latinoamericanos mediante una revisión sistemática de las zonas lingüísticas más importantes por parte de personas nacidas en esas mismas zonas.

Lo que se decía en la primera edición sobre el inglés 'de Oxford' y el español 'de la Academia', y asimismo sobre 'El uso y la autoridad', sigue siendo válido pero no merece repetirse aquí. Para el español, en 1971 se prestaba atención a la autoridad y decisiones de la Real Academia, pero con el paso del tiempo estas reivindicaciones parecen cada vez menos justificadas (excepto quizás en la ortografía), y en las ediciones de 1988 y 1992 no tuvieron lugar alguno. Esto significa que el diccionario renuncia a tener 'autoridad' alguna: es sencillamente un documento del uso moderno corriente, y no hace juicios de valor. Es verdad que se incluyen palabras y giros de los lenguajes burocrático, político, y sociológico, de España, del tipo que es blanco de parodias y condenas, pero no hay motivo para formular protestas por su presencia en el diccionario. Las indicaciones del 'registro' social de estas palabras y giros servirán de guía al usuario.

Latin-American usage marked — español de América Latina

3 pisarse *vr* (*Cono Sur*) to be mistaken.
pisaverde *nm* fop.
pisca *nf* (**a**) (*Méx*) maize harvest, corn harvest (*US*). (**b**) (*And*: *prostituta*) prostitute.
piscador *nm* (*Méx*) harvester.
piscar [1g] *vi* (*Méx*) to harvest maize (*o* corn (*US*)).
piscicultura *nf* fish-farming.
piscifactoría *nf* fish-farm.
piscigranja *nf* (*LAm*) fish-farm.
piscina *nf* (**a**) (*Dep*) swimming-pool; ~ **climatizada** heated swimming-pool; ~ **cubierta** indoor swimming-pool; ~ **olímpica** Olympic-length pool. (**b**) (*tanque*) fishpond, fishtank.
Piscis *nm* (*Zodíaco*) Pisces.

superior numbers mark homographs — homógrafos señalados por números altos

pisco¹ *nm* (*And*) (**a**) (*Orn*) turkey. (**b**) (*fig*) fellow, guy* (*US*).
pisco² *nm* (*LAm*) strong liquor.
piscoiro* *nm*, **piscoira** *nf* (*Cono Sur**) bright child.
piscolabis *nm invar* (**a**) snack. (**b**) (*CAm, Méx*) money.
pisicorre *nm* (*Carib*) small bus.
piso *nm* (**a**) (*suelo*) floor; flooring.
(**b**) (*Arquit*) storey, floor; (*de autobús, barco*) deck; (*de cohete*) stage; (*de pastel*) layer; ~ **alto** top floor; ~ **bajo** ground floor, first floor (*US*); **primer** ~ first floor, second floor (*US*); **un edificio de 8 ~s** an 8-storey building; **viven en el quinto** ~ they live on the fifth floor; **autobús de dos ~s** double-decker bus; **ir en el ~ de arriba** to travel on the top deck, travel upstairs.

American English translations — inglés norteamericano señalado en las traducciones

(**c**) (*apartamento*) flat, apartment (*US*); ~ **franco** (*Esp*), ~ **de seguridad** safe house, hide-out; **poner un ~ a una** (*Esp*) to set a woman up in a flat.

peninsular usage marked — español de España

(**d**) (*Aut*: *de neumático*) tread.
(**e**) (*de zapato*) sole; **poner ~ a un zapato** to sole a shoe.
(**f**) (*Min*) set of workings; (*Geol*) layer, stratum.

field labels — indicaciones de campo semántico

(**g**) (*Cono Sur*) (*taburete*) stool; (*banco*) bench.
(**h**) (*estera*) mat; (*Cono Sur, Méx*: *tapete*) table runner; (*And, Cono Sur*: *alfombra*) long narrow rug; ~ **de baño** bathmat.
pisón *nm* (**a**) (*herramienta*) ram, rammer. (**b**) (*LAm*) = **pisotón** (**b**). (**c**) (*Cono Sur*: *mortero*) mortar.

cross references — referencias a otros artículos

pisotear [1a] *vt* (**a**) (*gen*) to tread down, trample (on, underfoot); to stamp on. (**b**) (*fig*) to trample on; *ley etc* to abuse, disregard.
pisoteo *nm* treading, trampling; stamping.
pisotón *nm* (**a**) (*gen*) stamp on the foot. (**b**) (*: *Periodismo*) newspaper scoop, reporting scoop.
pispar* [1a] **1** *vt* (‡: *robar*) to nick‡, steal. **2** *vi* (*Cono Sur*) to keep watch, spy.

all Spanish verbs referred to verb tables — códigos que remiten a paradigmas verbales

pisporra *nf* (*CAm*) wart.
pista *nf* (**a**) (*Zool y fig*) track, trail; (*fig*: *indicio*) clue; (*de cinta*) track; ~ **falsa** false trail, false clue; (*en discusión etc*) red herring; **estar sobre la** ~ to be on the scent; **estar sobre la ~ de uno** to be on sb's trail, be after sb; **seguir la ~ de uno** to be on sb's track, trail sb; to shadow sb; **la policía tiene una ~ ya** the police already have a lead (*o* clue).

numerous examples — ejemplificación de uso de la voz

(**b**) (*Dep etc*) track, course; (*cancha*) court; (*Aut*) carriageway; (*CAm*: *avenida*) avenue; (*de esquí*) run, slope; (*de circo etc*) floor, arena; (*Inform, Mús*) track; ~ **de aprendizaje** nursery slope; ~ **de aterrizaje** runway; landing-strip; ~ **de atletismo** athletics track, running track; ~ **de baile** dance-floor; ~ **de bolos** bowling-alley; ~ **de carreras** racetrack; ~ **de ceniza** dirt track; **reunión de ~ cubierta** indoor athletics meeting; ~ **de esquí** ski-run; ~ **forestal** forest trail; ~ **de hielo** ice-rink; ~ **de hierba** grass court; ~ **de patinaje** skating-rink; ~ **de tenis** tennis-court; ~ **de tierra batida** clay court; **atletismo en** ~ track events.

most common collocations — ejemplos más usados

pistacho *nm* pistachio.
pistero *adj* (*CAm*) mercenary, fond of money.
pistilo *nm* pistil.
pisto *nm* (**a**) (*Med*) chicken broth.
(**b**) (*Culin Esp*) fried vegetable hash.
(**c**) (*fig*: *revoltijo*) mixture, hotchpotch.
(**d**) **a ~s** little by little; sparingly.
(**e**) **darse ~*** to show off, swank*, shoot a line*.
(**f**) (*And, CAm*‡) dough‡, money.
(**g**) (*And*: *de revólver*) barrel.
(**h**) (*Méx*‡) shot of liquor*.

clear division into semantic categories — clara indicación del campo semántico

pistola *nf* (**a**) (*Mil*) pistol; (*Téc*) spray gun; ~ **de agua** water pistol; ~ **ametralladora** submachine-gun, tommy-gun; ~ **engrasadora**, ~ **de engrase** grease-gun; ~ **de juguete** toy pistol; ~ **de pintar**, ~ **rociadora de pintura** paint spray, spray gun. (**b**) (*Culin*) long loaf. (**c**) (**‡) prick**‡.
pistolera *nf* (**a**) holster; **salir de ~s** to get out of a tight

(**c**) (*Naut*) barco *m*, embarcación *f*.

2 *vt* hacer (a mano); **~ed products** productos *mpl* de artesanía.

phonetics in IPA

craftily [ˈkrɑːftɪlɪ] *adv* astutamente.

craftiness [ˈkrɑːftɪnɪs] *n* astucia *f*.

transcripción fonética según la notación del alfabeto fonético internacional

craftsman [ˈkrɑːftsmən] *n*, *pl* **craftsmen** [ˈkrɑːftsmən] artesano *m*; artífice *m*.

craftsmanship [ˈkrɑːftsmənʃɪp] *n* artesanía *f*.

crafty [ˈkrɑːftɪ] *adj* (**a**) *person, move etc* astuto. (**b**) (*) *gadget etc* ingenioso.

crag [kræg] *n* peñasco *m*, risco *m*.

craggy [ˈkrægɪ] *adj* peñascoso, escarpado; *face* de facciones marcadas.

indicating words pinpoint meaning

relación detallada de distintas acepciones de la voz

cram [kræm] **1** *vt* (**a**) *hen* cebar; *subject* empollar, aprender apresuradamente; *pupil* preparar apresuradamente para un examen.

(**b**) **to ~ food into one's mouth** llenarse la boca de comida; **to ~ things into a case** ir metiendo cosas apretadamente en una maleta; **we can't ~ any more in** es imposible meter más.

clear division into semantic categories

subdivisión en categorías gramaticales

(**c**) **to ~ sth with** llenar algo de, henchir algo de; **the hall is ~med** la sala está de bote en bote; **the room is ~med with furniture** el cuarto está atestado de muebles; **he had his head ~med with odd ideas** tenía la cabeza cargada de ideas raras.

2 *vi* (**a**) **to ~ in, come ~ming in** entrar en masa, amontonarse; **7 of us ~med into the Mini** los 7 logramos encajarnos en el Mini; **can I ~ in here?** ¿quepo yo aquí?

(**b**) (*for exam*) empollar.

(**c**) = **3**.

3 *vr*: **to ~ o.s. with food** darse un atracón; **to ~ o.s. with cakes** atracarse de pastas.

cram-full [ˈkræmˈfʊl] *adj* atestado (*of* de), de bote en bote.

crammer [ˈkræməʳ] *n* (*Scol*: *pupil*) empollón *m*, -ona *f*; (*teacher*) profesor *m*, -ora *f* que prepara rapidísimamente a sus alumnos para los exámenes.

superior numbers mark homographs

homógrafos señalados por números altos

cramp[1] [kræmp] *n* (*Med*) calambre *m*.

cramp[2] [kræmp] **1** *n* (*Tech*) grapa *f*; (*Archit*) pieza *f* de unión, abrazadera *f*. **2** *vt* (*hamper*) estorbar, restringir; **to ~ sb's style** cortar los vuelos a uno, cohibir a uno.

cramped [kræmpt] *adj room etc* estrecho; *writing* menudo, apretado; *position* nada cómodo; **we are very ~ for space here** estamos muy estrechos aquí.

crampon [ˈkræmpən] *n* garfio *m*; (*Mountaineering*) crampón *m*.

cramponning [ˈkræmpənɪŋ] *n* uso *m* de crampones.

cranberry [ˈkrænbərɪ] *n* arándano *m* (agrio).

crane [kreɪn] **1** *n* (*Orn*) grulla *f*; (*Tech*) grúa *f*. **2** *vt* (*also* **to ~ up**) levantar con grúa; **to ~ one's neck** estirar el cuello.

phrasal verbs

verbos preposicionales

◆**crane forward** *vi* inclinarse estirando el cuello; **to ~ forward to look at sth** estirar el cuello para mirar algo.

crane-driver [ˈkreɪnˌdraɪvəʳ] *n* gruista *mf*.

cranefly [ˈkreɪnflaɪ] *n* típula *f*.

crane operator [ˈkreɪnˌɒpəreɪtəʳ] *n* = **crane-driver**.

cranial [ˈkreɪnɪəl] *adj* craneal.

irregular plurals shown

plurales irregulares

cranium [ˈkreɪnɪəm] *n*, *pl* **crania** [ˈkreɪnɪə] cráneo *m*.

crank[1] [kræŋk] **1** *n* manivela *f*, manubrio *m*; cigüeñal *m*. **2** *vt engine* (*also* **to ~ up**) dar vuelta a, hacer arrancar con la manivela.

British English marked

inglés británico

◆**crank out*** *vt* (*US*) producir penosamente.

crank[2]* [kræŋk] *n* (*Brit*: *person*) maniático *m*, -a, *f*, chiflado *m*, -a *f*, excéntrico *m*, -a *f*; (*US*: *person*) gruñón *m*, -ona *f*.

crankcase [ˈkræŋkkeɪs] *n* cárter *m* (del cigüeñal).

crankshaft [ˈkræŋkʃɑːft] *n* (eje *m* del) cigüeñal *m*, árbol *m* del cigüeñal.

cranky* [ˈkræŋkɪ] *adj person* maniático, chiflado, excéntrico; *idea* raro, estrafalario.

asterisks mark familiar and taboo language

asteriscos señalan palabras y giros coloquiales y vulgares

cranny [ˈkrænɪ] *n* grieta *f*.

crap** [kræp] **1** *n* (*lit, fig*) mierda** *f*. **2** *vi* cagar**.

◆**crap out‡** *vi* (*US*) (**a**) (*back down*) rajarse*. (**b**) (*fail*) fracasar.

crape [kreɪp] *n* crespón *m*.

American English

inglés norteamericano

crappy** [ˈkræpɪ] *adj* (*esp US*) asqueroso.

craps [kræps] *npl* (*US*) dados *mpl*; **to shoot ~** jugar a los dados.

Spanish genders marked

indicación de género gramatical

crash [kræʃ] **1** *n* (**a**) (*noise*) estruendo *m*, estrépito *m*; (*explosion*) estallido *m*.

(**b**) (*collision*) accidente *m*, colisión *f*, choque *m*, encontronazo *m*; (*Aer*) accidente *m* de aviación.

(**c**) (*ruin*) fracaso *m*, ruina *f*; (*Comm*) quiebra *f*; crac *m*; **the 1929 ~** la crisis económica de 1929.

(**d**) (*: *drug*) mono‡ *m*, síndrome *m* de abstinencia.

2 *vt car, aircraft* estrellar (*into* contra); estropear; **he ~ed the plate to the ground** echó el plato por tierra; **he**

Using the dictionary

1 Alphabetical order is followed throughout. It must be remembered that *CH*, *LL* and *Ñ* are separate letters of the alphabet in Spanish; thus **achacar** comes after **acústico** and not after **acezar**.

2 Cross-references include alternative spellings, parts of irregular verbs, contracted forms, many prefixes and some suffixes, and parts of compound words.

3 Superior numbers are used to separate words of like spelling and pronunciation, eg **port**[1], **port**[2], **choclo**[1], **choclo**[2].

4 Noun plurals in Spanish are indicated after the headword only when irregular (eg **club**, *pl* **clubs** *o* **clubes**). In all other cases the basic rules apply: if a noun ends in a vowel it takes **-s** in the plural (eg **casa-s**, **tribu-s**); if it ends in a consonant (including for this purpose **y**) it takes **-es** in the plural (eg **pared-es**, **árbol-es**). Note the following, however:

(i) Nouns that end in stressed **í** take **-es** in the plural (eg **rubí**, **rubíes**). Exception: **esquí**, **esquís**.

(ii) Nouns that end in **-z** change this to **c** and add **-es** in the plural (eg **luz**, **luces**; **paz**, **paces**). The pronunciation is not affected.

(iii) The accent which is written on a number of endings of singular nouns is not needed in the plural (eg **nación-naciones**, **patán-patanes**, **inglés-ingleses**). Some words having no written accent in the singular need one in the plural (eg **crimen-crímenes**, **joven-jóvenes**).

(iv) There is little agreement about the plural of recent anglicisms and gallicisms, and some latinisms. Each case is treated separately in the dictionary; see eg **barman**.

5 Noun plurals in English are indicated after the headword only when they are truly irregular (eg **ox**, **oxen**), and in the few cases where a word in **-o** takes a plural in **-oes** (eg **potato-es**). In all other cases the basic rules apply:

Cómo utilizar el diccionario

1 El orden alfabético queda rigurosamente establecido. Se mantiene la costumbre de considerar la *CH*, la *LL* y la *Ñ* como letras independientes.

2 Con referencias a otros artículos figuran las variantes ortográficas, las formas de los verbos irregulares, las formas contractas, muchos prefijos y algunos sufijos, y elementos de palabras compuestas.

armor ... *n* (*US*) = **armour**.
voy *etc V* **ir**.
gave ... *pret of* **give**.

3 Los números altos sirven para distinguir las palabras que se escriben y se pronuncian iguales, p.ej. **port**[1], **port**[2], **choclo**[1], **choclo**[2].

4 Forma plural del sustantivo en español. Estas formas se hacen constar después de la voz cabeza de artículo sólo cuando son irregulares (p.ej. **club**, *pl* **clubs** *o* **clubes**). En los demás casos se aplican las siguientes reglas: si el sustantivo termina en vocal se añade **-s** para formar el plural (p.ej. **casa-s**, **tribu-s**); si termina en consonante (la **y** se considera como consonante en esta posición) se añade **-es** para formar el plural (p.ej. **pared-es**, **árbol-es**). Hay algunas excepciones:

(i) Los sustantivos que terminan en **-í** acentuada forman el plural añadiendo **-es** (p.ej. **rubí**, **rubíes**). Excepción: **esquí**, **esquís**.

(ii) Los sustantivos que terminan en **-z** la cambian en **c** al formarse el plural (p.ej. **luz**, **luces**; **paz**, **paces**). Esto no cambia la pronunciación.

(iii) El acento que se escribe en varias desinencias de los sustantivos en singular se suprime en el plural (p.ej. **nación-naciones**, **patán-patanes**). Algunas palabras que no llevan acento escrito en singular lo tienen en plural (p.ej. **crimen-crímenes**).

(iv) Reina bastante confusión acerca de la forma plural de los anglicismos y galicismos de reciente acuñación, y de algún latinismo. Se trata separadamente cada caso; véase p.ej. **barman**.

5 Forma plural del sustantivo en inglés. Estas formas se hacen constar después de la voz cabeza de artículo sólo cuando son irregulares (p.ej. **ox**, **oxen**), y en los pocos casos donde una palabra terminada en **-o** forma el plural en **-oes** (p.ej. **potato-es**). En los demás casos se aplican las siguientes reglas:

(i) Most English nouns take **-s** in the plural: **bed-s, site-s, photo-s.**

(ii) Nouns that end in **-s, -x, -z, -sh** and some in **-ch** [tʃ] take **-es** in the plural: **boss-es, box-es, dish-es, patch-es.**

(iii) Nouns that end in **-y** not preceded by a vowel change the **-y** to **-ies** in the plural: **lady-ladies, berry-berries** (but **tray-s, key-s**).

6 Spanish and English verbs. All Spanish verb headwords are referred by number and letter (eg [1a], [2e]) to the table of verb paradigms on pp.808-816. In a few cases in which verbs have slight irregularities or are defective, the fact is noted after the headword. English irregular or strong verbs have their principal parts noted in bold face after the headword; these are also listed on pp.818-819. Minor variations of spelling are listed on p.820.

7 Abbreviations and proper names. For easier reference, abbreviations, acronyms and proper names have been listed alphabetically in the wordlist, as opposed to being relegated to the appendices. **MOT** is used in every way like 'certificate' or 'permit', **IVA** like 'impuesto', and consequently these words are treated like any other noun.

8 Grammatical functions are distinguished by bold face numerals and abbreviations, eg **arder 1** *vt* ... **2** *vi* ... **3 arderse** *vr* ... . A separate division has been provided for *vr* in the English–Spanish, on the grounds that even though English has no strictly reflexive verbs this represents a convenience in translation and for the user.

9 The diverse meanings of the headword within each entry or grammatical function are separated by letters in bold face, **(a)** ... **(b)** ... . Sometimes the distinctions made are rather fine but necessary both for the compiler and the user; they are practical rather than scientific in terms of semantics. A certain order is normally followed: basic and concrete senses first, figurative and familiar ones later; *LAm* and *US* senses and highly specialized applications come last.

(i) La mayor parte de los sustantivos en inglés forman el plural añadiendo **-s**: **bed-s, site-s, photo-s.**

(ii) Los sustantivos terminados en **-s, -x, -z, -sh** y algunos en **-ch** [tʃ] forman el plural añadiendo **-es**: **boss-es, box-es, dish-es, patch-es.**

(iii) Los sustantivos terminados en **-y** no precedida por vocal forman el plural cambiando la **-y** en **-ies**: **lady-ladies, berry-berries** (pero **tray-s, key-s**).

6 Verbo español y verbo inglés. Los verbos españoles que encabezan artículo llevan una referencia por número y letra (p.ej. [1a], [2e]) al cuadro de conjugaciones en las págs. 808-816. En los casos donde el verbo es ligeramente irregular o defectivo, se nota tal hecho en el artículo. Se imprimen en negrilla inmediatamente después de la palabra cabeza de artículo el pretérito y participio de pasado de los verbos irregulares ingleses, y hay además lista de ellos en las págs. 818-819. Las ligeras variantes ortográficas de los verbos ingleses constan en la pág. 820.

7 Abreviaturas y nombres propios. Para hacer más fácil la consulta del diccionario se ha decidido insertar en el texto, por orden alfabético, las abreviaturas, siglas y nombres propios, antes que relegarlos a los apéndices del final. Efectivamente, decir **MOT** en inglés o **IVA** en español equivale exactamente a decir 'certificate' o 'impuesto' respectivamente, y por tanto esas palabras reciben el mismo tratamiento que cualquier otro sustantivo.

8 Las funciones gramaticales se señalan mediante números en negrilla y abreviaturas, p.ej. **arder 1** *vt* ... **2** *vi* ... **3 arderse** *vr* .... En la Parte 2ª hay división especial para el *vr*, por el motivo de que (aunque el verbo inglés no tiene en rigor formas reflexivas) tal sistema es muy útil en la traducción y para el usuario.

9 Los diversos significados de la palabra cabeza de artículo quedan separados por letras en negrilla, **(a)** ... **(b)** ... . Alguna vez la distinción puede parecer nimia, pero es necesaria para el autor y más para el lector; esto tiene una finalidad práctica y no pretende tener validez científica. Se ha establecido cierto orden para estas subdivisiones: primero los significados básicos y concretos, después los figurados y familiares; las acepciones (*LAm*) y (*US*) y las aplicaciones técnicas vienen en último lugar.

10 Field labels in italics: some are abbreviations (eg *Bio, Mus*), others complete words (eg *Art, Fencing*). Latin-American usage has been divided into the following five groups and labelled accordingly: Andean (Bolivia, Colombia, Ecuador, Peru); Caribbean (Cuba, Puerto Rico, Santo Domingo, Venezuela); Central American (Costa Rica, El Salvador, Guatemala, Honduras, Nicaragua, Panama); Southern Cone (Argentina, Chile, Uruguay, Paraguay); and Mexico on its own.

10 Las indicaciones de campo semántico se imprimen en cursiva. Algunas son abreviaturas (p.ej. *Bio, Mús*) y otras palabras completas (p.ej. *Arte, Esgrima*). El vocabulario latinoamericano se ha dividido e indicado de acuerdo con los siguientes grupos de países: Región Andina (Bolivia, Colombia, Ecuador, Perú); Región del Caribe (Cuba, Puerto Rico, Santo Domingo, Venezuela); Región centroamericana (Costa Rica, El Salvador, Guatemala, Honduras, Nicaragua, Panamá); Cono Sur (Argentina, Chile, Uruguay, Paraguay); y México.

11 Style labels. All words and phrases which are not standard language have been labelled according to two separate registers:

(a) formal and informal usage

(b) old-fashioned and literary usage

This labelling is given for both source and target languages and serves primarily to provide a warning to the non-native speaker. The symbols used are as follows:

(i) The abbreviation *frm* denotes formal language such as that used on an official form, in pronouncements and other formal communications.

11 Niveles lingüísticos. Las palabras y frases que se distinguen de la lengua estándar llevan un signo que indica uno de dos registros:

(a) uso 'oficial' o coloquial

(b) uso literario o arcaico

Estos signos se imprimen para las dos lenguas, y sirven sobre todo como aviso al usuario no nativo. Los símbolos utilizados son los siguientes:

(i) La abreviatura *frm* indica el lenguaje 'oficial', p.ej. el empleado en los formularios burocráticos, en los discursos políticos, en las cartas enviadas por las autoridades, etcétera.

whereto ... (*frm*, ††) adonde.

(ii) * indicates that the expression, while not forming part of standard language, is used by all educated speakers in a relaxed situation, but would not be used in a formal essay or letter, or on an occasion when the speaker wishes to impress.

(ii) * indica que la palabra o locución no forma parte de la lengua estándar, pero es empleada por todos en situación familiar o de cierta intimidad; no se emplearía en ensayo o en carta oficial, o en situación donde se quiere hacer buena impresión.

chollo* ... (*Com*) ... snip*, ...
hacer dedo* ... to thumb a lift* ...
then the band played* (*US*) y se armó la gorda*.
it costs a bomb* (*Brit*) cuesta un ojo de la cara*; ...

(iii) ‡ indicates that the expression is used by some but not all educated speakers in a very relaxed situation. Such words should be handled with extreme care by the non-native speaker unless he is very fluent in the language and is very sure of his company.

(iii) ‡ indica que la palabra o locución es de carácter marcadamente coloquial; el usuario no nativo empleará estas palabras sólo con la mayor prudencia, dominando ya la otra lengua y considerando con cuidado el contexto social en que se encuentra.

atizarse‡ ... to smoke pot
clink²‡ ... trena‡ *f*

(iv) ** means 'Danger!'. Such words are liable to offend in any situation, and therefore are to be avoided by the non-native speaker.

(iv) ** significa ¡Ojo! El usuario no nativo deberá poder reconocer estas palabras o giros, pero dado su carácter obsceno u ofensivo se guardará de emplearlos en la mayor parte de los contextos sociales.

cojón✻ ... **¡cojones!** (*rechazo*) balls!✻; (*sorpresa*) bugger me!✻; ...
dick ... (b) (✻) polla✻ *f*.

(v) † denotes old-fashioned terms which are no longer in wide current use but which the foreign user will certainly find in reading, or may encounter in humorous use.

(v) † indica palabras que ya no se emplean corrientemente pero que el usuario no nativo encontrará con frecuencia en sus lecturas, o en la actualidad con intención humorística.

merced ... (a) (†) (*favor*) favour.

(vi) †† denotes obsolete words which the user will normally find in literature, or may encounter in humorous use.

(vi) †† indica palabras más bien arcaicas que el usuario puede encontrar en sus lecturas de obras clásicas, o en la actualidad con intención humorística.

thy†† ... tu(s).
cumquibus ... (††, *hum*): **el** ~ the wherewithal.

The use of † and †† should not be confused with the label *Hist*. *Hist* does not apply to the expression itself but denotes the historical context of the object so named.

El empleo de † y †† no debe confundirse con la abreviatura *Hist*. Ésta no se aplica a la palabra o expresión sino que se refiere al hecho o a la institución etc. así llamado.

ordeal ... *n* (*Hist*) ordalías *fpl*; ...

(vii) *liter* denotes an expression which belongs to literary language.

(vii) *liter* indica que la palabra o locución pertenece a la lengua literaria o poética.

heretofore ... (*liter*) hasta ahora

(viii) The labels and symbols above are used to mark either an individual word or phrase, or a whole category, or even a complete entry.

(viii) Las indicaciones y símbolos se refieren según el caso a una palabra, una locución, parte del artículo, o al artículo en su totalidad.

The user should not confuse the style label *liter* with the field label *Liter* which indicates that the term or expression so labelled belongs to the field of literature. Similarly, the user should note that the abbreviation *lit* indicates the literal as opposed to the figurative meaning of a word.

El usuario no debe confundir la indicación estilística *liter* con *lit* que significa sentido propio o empleo literal, ni por otra parte con *Liter* que se refiere al campo de la literatura.

12 Indicators are complete words in italics placed before the translation; they aid in distinguishing meanings and help the user find that part of the headword's range which he is seeking. They have been made as brief and typical as possible, but they cannot be comprehensive and must not be taken to constitute full definitions or exact limitations. The main types of indicator are:

12 Contribuyen a hacer las distinciones semánticas las indicaciones de palabras enteras en cursiva, colocadas delante de la traducción; se proponen llamar la atención del lector hacia la parte de la extensión de la palabra con que tiene que ver. Hemos ideado estas aclaraciones para que sean breves y típicas; pero ellas no pueden ser universales, e importa mucho que no se las considere como definiciones completas ni como limitaciones exactas. Las indicaciones son de varias clases:

(i) For a **noun** headword: a variety of near-synonyms, part-definitions and hints (in parentheses), eg **poke** (*push*) ...; (*with elbow*) ...; (*jab*) ...; (*with poker*) ...

(i) Para **sustantivo** que encabeza artículo: sinónimos aproximativos, definiciones parciales, consejos (en paréntesis), p.ej. **abogado** (*notario*) ...; (*en tribunal*) ...; (*defensor*) ...

(ii) For an **adjective** headword: nouns (without parentheses) with which the adjective in its various applications might typically be used, eg **soft (b)** (*fig*) *air*, *sound* ...; *voice* ...; *step* ...; *water* ...

(iii) For a **transitive verb** headword: nouns (without parentheses) which might typically be the objects of the verb in its various applications, eg **pluck** *fruit*, *flower* ...; *bird* ...; *guitar* ...

(iv) For an **intransitive** or **reflexive verb** headword: nouns (in parentheses) which might be typical subjects of the verb, eg **rise 2 (c)** (*of sun*, *moon*) ...; (*smoke etc*) ...; (*building*, *mountain*) ...

Indicators are not repeated in derivatives but can be transferred by the user, eg adjective to adverb, adjective to abstract noun (*fair-fairness*).

13 The order of material within the entry or subdivision has been planned for convenience and does not follow a rigid pattern. However, a typical order for a lengthy noun entry is: (i) basic translations of the headword; (ii) phrases consisting of noun + adjective; (iii) the noun preceded by a preposition (often with verb as well); (iv) the noun with a verb. Alphabetical order is followed within each of these categories. No attempt is made to separate idioms from usage examples.

14 The placing of phrases in entries raises many problems. The principles generally followed are:

(i) Phrases consisting of noun + noun, verb + verb, adjective + adjective are entered under the first component, eg **'casa y comida'** under **casa**, **'black and blue'** under **black**.

(ii) Spanish collocations consisting of noun + adjective are generally entered under the noun component, eg **cabina electoral** under **cabina**. English collocations consisting of adjective + noun are generally entered under the adjective component. However, some such combinations in English now have a sufficiently independent existence to figure as main entries.

(iii) Phrases consisting of verb + noun are entered under the noun component, eg **abrir carrera** under **carrera**, **to show cause** under **cause**; but many phrases will be found in the verb entries as usage examples also.

(ii) Para **adjetivo** que encabeza artículo: sustantivos (sin paréntesis) con los que el adjetivo en sus diversas aplicaciones pudiera emplearse, p.ej. **blando** *materia*, *agua etc* ...; *pasta etc* ...; *carne* ...; *tono* ...; *clima* ...

(iii) Para **verbo transitivo** que encabeza artículo: sustantivos (sin paréntesis) que típicamente pudieran ser los objetos del verbo, p.ej. **abandonar** *lugar* ...; *persona* ...; *objeto* ...; *tentativa*, *hábito* ...

(iv) Para **verbo intransitivo** o **reflexivo** que encabeza artículo: sustantivos (entre paréntesis) que típicamente pudieran ser los sujetos del verbo, p.ej. **atascarse** (*tubo*) ...; (*motor*) ...

Estas aclaraciones no se repiten para las palabras derivadas, pero las podrá trasladar el lector, p.ej. del adjetivo al adverbio, o del adjetivo al sustantivo abstracto (*fair-fairness*).

13 El orden de material dentro del artículo o subdivisión ha sido pensado para ayudar al lector y no sigue un sistema rígido. Sin embargo, el orden normal para un artículo sobre sustantivo es: (i) las traducciones básicas de la palabra cabeza de artículo; (ii) las frases que consisten en sustantivo con adjetivo; (iii) el sustantivo precedido por preposición (muchas veces con verbo también); (iv) el sustantivo con verbo. Dentro de cada categoría se mantiene el orden alfabético. No se separan los modismos de los ejemplos que ilustran el uso.

14 La colocación de los giros en los artículos suscita muchos problemas. En general los principios son:

(i) Los giros que consisten en sustantivo + sustantivo, verbo + verbo etc figuran en el artículo del primer elemento, p.ej. **'casa y comida'** en **casa**, **'black and blue'** en **black**.

(ii) Los giros en español que consisten en sustantivo + adjetivo figuran en el artículo del elemento sustantivo, p.ej. **cabina electoral** en **cabina**. Los giros en inglés que consisten en adjetivo + sustantivo figuran en el artículo del elemento adjetivo. Pero son muchas las combinaciones inglesas de adjetivo + sustantivo que han adquirido ya una existencia bastante independiente para que figuren como palabras cabezas de artículo.

(iii) Los giros que consisten en verbo + sustantivo figuran en el artículo del sustantivo, p.ej. **to show cause** en **cause, abrir carrera** en **carrera**; pero se citan muchos giros de este tipo en los verbos, como ejemplos del uso.

(iv) Phrasal verbs are listed in the dictionary at the end of the entry for the main verb, in their own alphabetical sequence and highlighted by a lozenge.

(iv) Los verbos con partícula, o verbos frasales, aparecen en el diccionario al final del artículo del verbo principal, siguiendo el orden alfabético correspondiente y marcados por un rombo negro.

♦ **go about** ... *vt* ...
♦ **go across 1** *vt* ...

(v) Where the phrasal verb form in all its usages is identical in one meaning to one category of the main verb it is normally included in the main verb entry.

(v) Cuando el verbo frasal tiene el mismo significado que una de las categorías del verbo principal, normalmente va incluido en la entrada de este último.

bandage ... **2** *vt* (*also* **to ~ up**) vendar.

(vi) In the case of less common adverbs and prepositions the phrase may well appear under the adverb or preposition.

(vi) En el caso de los adverbios y preposiciones menos frecuentes la locución bien puede estar en el artículo del adverbio o preposición.

astern ...: **to go** ~ ciar, ir hacia atrás; ...

There is, however, intentional duplication of phrases. Thus **año bisiesto** belongs, by rule (ii) above, under **año**; but it is also the sole phrase under the headword **bisiesto**. In many other cases phrases are duplicated because they illustrate something about both headwords.

Hay, sin embargo, muchos casos donde se duplica de propósito la locución. Así **año bisiesto** pertenece, según la regla (ii) arriba, a **año**; pero también es la única locución en **bisiesto**. En otros casos se duplican las locuciones por el motivo de que en ambos lugares ilustran algo.

15 Translation by single word is obviously sufficient in many cases. Often a liberal policy has been followed in offering a number of near-synonyms separated by commas; this is especially true of the more emotive and less precise adjectives. The abbreviation (*approx*) is used where no full translation exists. Explanations in italics are given where a word has no correspondence in the other language, eg **cachetero (b)**, **cante (a)**. Where the source language headword or phrase has a cultural equivalent in the target language, the translation is preceded by the cultural equivalent sign ≃. See for instance the entry for **GCSE**. For greater precision explanations in italics and in parentheses are occasionally added after the translation, eg **camayo (c)**.

15 La traducción por una sola palabra basta en muchos casos. Pero a menudo hemos seguido una norma liberal ofreciendo varios sinónimos o casi sinónimos, separados por comas, sobre todo para los adjetivos emotivos y por lo tanto menos precisos. Donde no existe traducción adecuada se emplea la abreviatura (*aprox*). Cuando la palabra no tiene correspondencia en el otro idioma damos una explicación en cursiva, p.ej. para **cachetero (b)**, **cante (a)**. Si existe en la lengua de llegada una institución que sea equiparable, en términos aproximativos, a la de la lengua de salida, la traducción va precedida del signo ≃. Véase **RACE**. Alguna vez se añade a la traducción, en cursiva y en paréntesis, una aclaración o precisión, p.ej. para **camayo (c)**.

16 The gender of every Spanish noun is given immediately after it in both parts of the dictionary.

16 El género de todo sustantivo español consta inmediatamente después de la palabra en las dos partes del diccionario.

17 Spanish feminine forms. In the English-Spanish the typical entry '**teacher** = profesor *m*, -ora *f*' is to be read as '= profesor *m*, profesora *f*'. Often a written accent on the masculine form is not needed in the feminine, eg '**Dane** = danés *m*, -esa *f*' (to be read as '= danés *m*, danesa *f*'). The endings affected are: **-án, -ana**; **-és, -esa**; **-ón, -ona**. Where one vowel is given as the feminine ending, it replaces the **-e** or **-o** of the masculine; thus '**cook** = cocinero *m*, -a *f*' is read as '= cocinero *m*, cocinera *f*'.

17 Desinencias femeninas en español. En la Parte 2ª el artículo típico '**teacher** = profesor *m*, -ora *f*' ha de leerse '= profesor *m*, profesora *f*'. A menudo el acento que lleva el masculino se suprime en el femenino, p.ej. '**Dane** = danés *m*, -esa *f*' (ha de leerse '= danés *m*, danesa *f*'). Tales desinencias son: **-án, -ana**; **-és, esa**; **-ón, -ona**. Donde se cita una sola vocal de la forma femenina, esta vocal sustituye la **-e** o la **-o** del masculino; así '**cook** = cocinero *m*, -a *f*' ha de leerse '= cocinero *m*, cocinera *f*'.

PRONUNCIATION AND ORTHOGRAPHY

THE PRONUNCIATION OF EUROPEAN SPANISH

1 Except for a very few anomalies such as the writing of silent *h* and the existence of the two symbols *b* and *v* for the same sound, the pronunciation of Spanish is so well represented by normal orthography that it would be a waste of space to give a phonetic transcription for every Spanish word in Part I as is done for English in Part II. The general introduction given below should suffice. However, a transcription in IPA (International Phonetic Association) symbols is given for those few Spanish words in which spelling and pronunciation are not in accord, such as *reloj* [re'lo], and for those numerous anglicisms and gallicisms which retain an un-Spanish spelling or which have unexpected and unpredictable pronunciations even for those acquainted with the original languages. In some cases alternative pronunciations are given, an indication that cultured Spanish usage has not yet fixed firmly on one.

In this section the pronunciation described is that of educated Castilian, and little account is taken of that of the Spanish regions, even though some (notably Andalusia) have considerable cultural strength and a pronunciation which is socially acceptable throughout Spain. The pronunciation of Spanish in America is treated in a separate section.

It must be noted that in this attempt to describe the sounds of Spanish in terms of English, and in a limited space, one is conscious of making no more than approximations. Such comparisons have a practical end and inevitably lack the scientific exactness which trained phoneticians require.

2 Accentuation of Spanish words

For Spanish, unlike English, simple rules can be devised and stated which will enable the stress to be placed correctly on each word at sight:

(**a**) If the word ends in a vowel, or in *n* or *s* (often the signs of the plural of verbs and nouns respectively), the penultimate syllable is stressed: *zap**a**to, zap**a**tos, div**i**de, div**i**den, divid**ie**ron, antiviviseccion**i**sta, telefon**e**a, hist**o**ria, diluvi**a**ba* (such words are called *palabras llanas* or *graves*).

(**b**) If the word ends in a consonant other than *n* or *s*, the last syllable is stressed: *verd**a**d, practic**a**r, decib**e**l, virr**e**y, coñ**a**c, pesad**e**z* (such words are called *palabras agudas*).

(**c**) If the word is to be stressed in some way contrary to rules (**a**) and (**b**), an acute accent is written over the vowel to be stressed: *hablar**á**, guaran**í**, rub**í**, est**é**, rococ**ó**; m**á**quina, m**é**todos, vi**é**ndolo, paral**í**tico, h**ú**ngaro* (words of this latter type are called *palabras esdrújulas*). With only two exceptions, the same syllable is stressed in the singular and plural forms of each word, but an accent may have to be added or suppressed in the plural: *cr**i**men, cr**í**menes; naci**ó**n, naci**o**nes*. The two exceptions are *car**á**cter, caract**e**res*, and *r**é**gimen, reg**í**menes*. Only in a few verbal forms can the stress fall further back than on the antepenultimate syllable: *c**á**ntamelo, proh**í**baselo*.

3 Diphthongs, hiatus and syllable division

It will have been noted in **2**(**a**) above, in cases like *telefonea* and *historia*, that not all vowels count equally for the purposes of syllable division and stress. The convention is that *a, e* and *o* are 'strong' vowels, and *i, u* 'weak'. Four rules then apply:

(**a**) A combination of weak + strong forms a diphthong (one syllable), the stress falling on the stronger element: *b**a**ila, ci**e**rra, pu**e**sto, p**e**ine, c**a**usa*.

(**b**) A combination of weak + weak forms a diphthong (one syllable), the stress falling on the second element: *ru**i**do, fu**i**mos, vi**u**da*.

(**c**) Two strong vowels remain in hiatus as two distinct syllables, the stress falling according to rules (**a**) and (**b**) in section 2; *ma/**e**s/tro* (three syllables in all), *con/tra/**e**r* (three syllables in all), *cre/**e**r* (two syllables).

(**d**) Any word having a vowel combination whose parts are not stressed according to rules (**a**) to (**c**) above bears an acute accent on the stressed part: *cre**í**do, per**í**odo, ba**ú**l, r**í**e, t**í**o*.
Note – in those cases where IPA transcriptions are given for Spanish words, the stress mark ['] is inserted in the same way as explained for English, above in **LA PRONUNCIACIÓN DEL INGLÉS BRITÁNICO**, section 2.

4 The Spanish letters and their sounds

Note – the order in which the explanations are set out is that of the alphabet and not that of the phonetic system. The system of transcription adopted is a fairly 'broad' one; a more exact or 'narrow' system would involve, for example, division of the vowel [e] according to quality and length, and the use of two symbols instead of one [e, ɛ].

5 Vowels

Spanish vowels are clearly and rather sharply pronounced, and single vowels are free from the tendency to diphthongize which is noticeable in English (eg **side** [saɪd], **know** [nəʊ]). Moreover when they are in unstressed positions they are relaxed only slightly, again in striking contrast to English (compare English **natural** ['nætʃrəl] with Spanish **natural** [natu'ral]). Stressed vowels are somewhat more open and short before **rr** (compare **carro** with **caro, perro** with **pero**).

(*NOTE: Examples are pronounced as in British English.*)

a	[a]	Not so short as **a** in English *pat, patter,* nor so long as in English *rather, bar*	**pata** **amara**
e	[e]	In an open syllable (one which ends in a vowel) like **e** in English *they*, but without the sound of the **y**. In a closed syllable (one which ends in a consonant) is a shorter sound, like the **e** in English *set, wet*	**me** **pelo** **sangre** **peldaño**
i	[i]	Not so short as **i** in English *bit, tip,* nor so long as in English *machine*	**iris** **filo**
o	[o]	In an open syllable (one which ends in a vowel) like **o** in English *note*, but without the sound of [u] which ends the vowel in this word. In a closed syllable (one which ends in a consonant) is a shorter sound, though not quite so short as in English *pot, cot*	**poco** **cosa** **bomba** **conté**
u	[u]	Like **u** in English *rule* or **oo** in *food*. Silent after **q** and in the groups **gue, gui,** unless marked by a diaeresis (*argüir, fragüe, antigüedad*)	**luna** **pula** **aquel** **pague**
y	[i]	As a vowel – that is in the conjunction **y** 'and', and at the end of a word such as *ley, voy* – is pronounced like **i**.	

Diphthongs

(See also section 3 above)

ai, ay	[ai]	like **i** in English *side*	**baile** **estay**
au	[au]	like **ou** in English *sound*	**áureo** **causa**
ei, ey	[ei]	like **ey** in English *they*	**reina** **rey**
eu	[eu]	like the vowel sounds in English **may-you,** without the sound of the **y**	**deuda** **feudo**
oi, oy	[oi]	like **oy** in English *boy*	**oiga** **soy**

Semiconsonants

These are two, and appear in a variety of combinations as the first element; not all the combinations are listed here.

i, y	[j]	like **y** in English **y***es*, **y***acht* (See also the note under *y* in the list of consonants)	**bien** **hielo** **yunta** **apoyo**
u	[w]	like **w** in English **w***ell*	**huevo** **fuente** **agua** **guardar**

Consonants

b, v		These two letters have the same value in Spanish. There are two distinct pronunciations depending on position and context:	
	[b]	At the start of the breath-group and after written **m** and **n** (pronounced [m]) the sound is plosive like English **b**	**bomba** **boda** **enviar**
	[β]	In all other positions the sound is a bilabial fricative (unknown in English) in which the lips do not quite meet	**haba** **severo** **yo voy** **de Vigo**
c		There are two different values:	
	[k]	**c** before **a, o, u** or a consonant is like English **k** in **k***eep*, but without the slight aspiration which accompanies it	**calco** **acto** **cuco**
	[θ]	**c** before **e, i** is like English **th** in **th***in*. In parts of Andalusia and in *LAm* this is pronounced like English voiceless **s** in **s***ame*, a phenomenon known as **seseo**	**celda** **hacer** **cinco** **cecear**
		Note – in words like *acción, se***cc***ión* both types of *c*-sound are heard [kθ]	
ch	[tʃ]	like English **ch** in **ch***ur***ch**	**mucho** **chocho**
d		There are three different values depending on position and context:	
	[d]	At the start of the breath-group and after **l, n** the sound is plosive like English **d**	**dama** **aldea** **andar**
	[ð]	Between vowels and after consonants other than **l, n** the sound is relaxed and approaches English voiced **th** [ð] in **th***is*; in parts of Spain and in uneducated speech it is further relaxed and even disappears, particularly in the **-ado** ending. In the final position, the second type of [ð] is further relaxed or altogether omitted (though purists condemn this as a vulgar error). In eastern parts of Spain, however, this final **-d** may be heard as a [t]	**pide** **cada** **pardo** **sidra** **verdad** **usted** **Madrid** **callad**
f	[f]	like English **f** in **f***or*	**fama** **fofo**
g		There are three different values depending on position and context:	
	[x]	Before **e, i** it is the same as the Spanish **j** (below)	**Gijón** **general**
	[g]	At the start of the breath-group and after **n,** the sound is that of the English **g** in **g***et*	**gloria** **rango** **pingüe**
	[ɣ]	In other positions the sound is as in the second type above, but is fricative not plosive, there being no more than a close approximation of the vocal organs	**haga** **agosto** **la guerra**
		Note – in the group **gue, gui** the **u** is silent (**g***uerra*, **g***uindar*) except when marked by a diaeresis (*antig***ü***edad, arg***ü***ir*). In the group **gua** all the letters are sounded (**gua***rdia*, **gua***po*)	
h		always silent, a written convention only	**honor** **hombre** **rehacer**
j	[x]	a strong guttural sound not found in the English of England, but like the **ch** of Scots *lo***ch**, Welsh *ba***ch**, or German *Aa***ch***en, A***ch***tung*; it is silent at the end of a word (*relo***j**)	**jota** **jején** **baraja**
k	[k]	like English **k** in **k***ick*, but without the slight aspiration which accompanies it	**kilogramo**

l	[l]	like English **l** in *love*	**lelo** **panal**
ll	[ʎ]	approximating to English **lli** in *million*; in parts of Spain and most of *LAm* is pronounced as [j] and in other parts as [ʒ]; the pronunciation as [j] is condemned in Spain as a vulgar error but is extending rapidly even in Castile	**calle** **ella** **lluvia** **millón**
m	[m]	like English **m** in *made*	**mano** **mamar**
n	[n]	like English **n** in *none*; but before written **v** is pronounced as **m**, the group making [mb] (*eg* *enviar*, *sin valor*)	**nadie** **pan** **pino**
ñ	[ɲ]	approximating to English **ni** [nj] in *onion*	**uña** **ñoño**
p	[p]	like English **p** in *put*, but without the slight aspiration which accompanies it; it is often silent in *septiembre*, *séptimo*	**padre** **papa**
q	[k]	like English **k** in *kick*, but without the slight aspiration which accompanies it; it is always written in combination with **u**, which is silent	**que** **quinqué** **busqué** **quiosco**
r	[r]	a single trill or vibration stronger than any **r** in the English of England, but like the **r** in Scots; it is more relaxed in the final position and is indeed silent in parts of Spain and *LAm*; pronounced like **rr** at the start of a word and also after **l**, **n**, **s**	**coro** **quiere** **rápido** **real**
rr	[rr]	strongly trilled in a way that does not exist in English (except in parodies of Scots)	**torre** **arre burra** **irreal**
s	[s]	Two pronunciations: Except in the instances mentioned next, is a voiceless **s** like **s** in English *same*	**casa** **Isabel** **soso**
	[z]	Before a voiced consonant (**b, d, g, l, m, n**) is in most speakers a voiced **s** like **s** in English *rose*, *phase*	**desde** **asgo** **mismo** **asno**
t	[t]	like English **t** in *tame*, but without the slight aspiration which accompanies it	**título** **patata**
v		(*see* **b**)	
w		found in a few recent loanwords only; usually pronounced like Spanish **b, v** or like an English **v**, or kept as English **w**	**wáter** **week-end** **wolframio**
x		There are several possible pronunciations:	
	[ks]	Between vowels, **x** is pronounced like English **x** in *box* [ks], or	**máximo**
	[gs]	like **gs** in *big stick* [gs]	**examen**
	[s]	In a few words the **x** is pronounced between vowels like English **s** in *same* by many (but not all) speakers	**exacto** **auxilio**
	[s]	Before a consonant **x** is pronounced like English **s** in *same* by many (but not all) speakers	**extra** **sexto**
y	[j]	as a consonant or semiconsonant, is pronounced like **y** in English *yes*, *youth*; in emphatic speech in Spain and *LAm* this is heard as a voiced palatal plosive rather like the **j** in English *jam* [dʒ]; in *Argentina*, *Chile etc* this **y** is pronounced like the **s** in English *leisure* [ʒ]	**mayo** **yo** **mayor** **ya**
z	[θ]	like English **th** in *thin*; in parts of Andalusia and in *LAm* this is pronounced like English voiceless **s** in *same*, a phenomenon known as **seseo**	**zapato** **zopenco** **zumbar** **luz**

6 Additional notes on pronunciation

(**a**) The letter **b** is usually not pronounced in groups with **s** such as **obscuro, substituir,** and such words are now often written (with the Academy's sanction) **oscuro, sustituir** *etc*; they are so printed in this dictionary. A tendency to drop the **b** in pronouncing other similar groups is also noticeable, for example in **subjuntivo,** but in these cases the **b** is still always written.

(**b**) With one exception there are no real double consonants in Spanish speech; **cc** in words like **acción** is two separate sounds [kθ], while **ll** and **rr** have their own values (see the table above). The exception is the **-nn-** group found in learned words having the Latin prefix **in-**, eg **innato,** or occasionally **con-, sin-,** as in **connatural, sinnúmero.** In these cases the *n* is pronounced double [nn].

(**c**) Final **-s** of the definite and indefinite articles, plural, and of plural adjectives, is usually silent when the following noun starts with **r-**: eg **unos rábanos** [uno'rraßanos], **los romanos, varias razones, dos ratas** [do'rratas].

(**d**) Foreign sounds in Spanish hardly warrant separate treatment for our purposes; whereas the cultured Briton makes some attempt to maintain at least a vaguely French sound when he pronounces English loanwords from French, with nasal vowels and so on, the cultured Spaniard for the most part and certainly his less cultured compatriot adapts the sounds (but often not the spelling) of loanwords taken from French or English to suit his native speech habits. This is best studied in the transcriptions of individual items in the main text of the dictionary; see for example **chalet, gag, jazz, shock.**

(**e**) No old-established Spanish word begins with what is called 'impure *s*', that is, *s* plus a consonant as an initial group. When Spaniards have to pronounce a foreign name having such a group they inevitably precede it with an **e**-sound, so that **Smith** is [ez'miθ] or [ez'mis]. Very recent anglicisms tend to be written in Spanish as **slip, slogan** and so on, but must be pronounced [ez'lip], [ez'loɣan]; those that are slightly better established are written **esnob, esplín** etc, and then present no problem in pronunciation.

7 The letters of the Spanish alphabet

When the letters are cited one by one, or when a word is spelled out for greater clarity, or when an aircraft is identified by a letter and a name, and so on, the names of the letters used are:

a	[a]	**j**	['xota]	**r**	['ere]
b	[be] (in *LAm* [be'larɣa])	**k**	[ka]	**rr**	['erre]
c	[θe] [se]	**l**	['ele]	**s**	['ese]
ch	[tʃe]	**ll**	['eʎe]	**t**	[te]
d	[de]	**m**	['eme]	**u**	[u]
e	[e]	**n**	['ene]	**v**	['uße] (in *LAm* [be'korta])
f	['efe]	**ñ**	['eɲe]		
g	[xe]	**o**	[o]	**w**	['uße 'doßle] (in *LAm* ['doßle be])
h	['atʃe]	**p**	[pe]		
i	[i]	**q**	[ku]	**x**	['ekis]
				y	[i'ɣrjeɣa]
				z	['θeta] *or* ['θeða] *or* ['seta]

The letters are of the feminine gender: 'mayo se escribe con una **m** minúscula', '¿esto es una **c** o una **t**?'. One says 'una **a**' and 'la **a**,' 'una **h**' and 'la **h**' (not applying the rule as in **un ave, el agua**).

THE PRONUNCIATION OF SPANISH IN AMERICA

To generalize briefly about the vast area over which Spanish ranges in the New World is difficult; the following notes are very tentative. The upland regions (settled by Castilians from the *meseta*) tend to be linguistically conservative and to have more Castilian features; the lowland and coastal regions share many of the features of Andalusian speech. Among the vowels there is little to note. Among the consonants:

1 The Castilian [θ] sound – in writing **c** or **z** – is pronounced as various kinds of *s* [s] throughout America, a phenomenon known as *seseo*.

2 At the end of a syllable and a word, *s* is a slight aspiration, eg **las dos** [lah'doh], **mosca** ['mohka]; but in parts of the Andean region, in upland Mexico and in Peru the [s] is maintained as in Castilian.

3 Castilian written **ll** [ʎ] is pronounced in three different ways in regions of America. It survives as [ʎ] in part of Colombia, all Peru, Bolivia, N. Chile and Paraguay; in Argentina, Uruguay, upland Ecuador and part of Mexico it is pronounced [ʒ]; and in the remaining areas it is pronounced [j]. When this last kind [j] is in contact with the vowels **e** and **i** it disappears altogether and one finds in uneducated writing such forms as **gaína** (for **gallina**) and **biete** (for **billete**).

4 In uneducated speech in all parts there is much confusion of **l** and **r**: **clin** (for **crin**), **carma** (for **calma**) etc.

5 Written **h** is silent in Castilian, but in parts of Mexico and Peru this **h** is aspirated at the start of a word (when it derives from Latin initial *f*-), so that in uneducated writing one finds such forms as **jarto** (for **harto**) and **jablar** (for **hablar**). Compare **halar/jalar** and other cases in the text of the dictionary.

SPANISH ORTHOGRAPHY

The system of spelling in Spanish is extremely logical and apart from a few small anomalies it presents no problems. An excellent book for those in doubt is Manuel Seco's *Diccionario de dudas y dificultades de la lengua española*, Madrid, Espasa-Calpe, 9th ed., 1990.

1 Spelling reform in Spanish to correct the few remaining anomalies is rarely attempted. Some favour always writing **j** (not a mixture of **g** and **j**) for the [x] sound: **jeneral, Jibraltar** – quite logically, since **jirafa, jícara** and **jirón**, and many others, are so spelled by everybody. Poetic texts of Juan Ramón Jiménez are always printed with such spellings.

2 The Academy's *Nuevas Normas* of 1959 recommended spelling rare words beginning in **mn-** and rather frequent words in **ps-** with **m, s** respectively, but this is taking a long time to establish itself; we have preferred in the dictionary to give such words as **ps-** in both parts, but with a cross-reference from **s-** in the Spanish-English, in accordance with our principle of following usage rather than rules. (Note that the element **seudo-** is well established, however, and has virtually ousted **pseudo-**.)

3 Novels representing the life of the lower urban classes, peasants and the regions are numerous. In them the author may portray their speech (phonetically substandard on the purists' criteria) by such forms as:

señá *for* señora	pá *for* para
usté *for* usted	ná *for* nada
verdá *for* verdad	tó *for* todo
pué *for* puede	güevo *for* huevo
	agüela *for* abuela

4 Those who read familiar letters from less well-educated Spaniards may welcome a note on the kind of error which often appears in such documents (and is not wholly unknown in public notices and in print). The errors depend on the few anomalies of the official spelling system. Great confusion reigns over **b**, **v**; one finds **boy** for **voy**, **escrivir** for **escribir**, **tranbía** for **tranvía**, and even **vrabo** for **bravo**. **H** being silent is often omitted: **acer**, **reacer**, **ombre**; but equally it is often added where it does not belong, **hera** for **era**, **honce** for **once** and so on. Since written **ll** [ʎ] is often regionally and vulgarly pronounced [j], one sometimes finds **ll** written by hypercorrection in place of **y**: **cullo** for **cuyo**, **rallo** for **rayo**.

5 Much of the above applies also to Spanish in America, partly because of error and partly because it reflects pronunciation there (see the previous section). The confusion between written **ll** and **y** goes further than in Spain, eg with **llapa-yapa**; the same is true of initial **h-** and **j-**, eg **halar-jalar**, and of **gua-** and **hua-**, eg **guaca-huaca**; we have tried to provide cross-references to these variants in the dictionary. Forms such as **güevo** (for **huevo**) and **güeno** (for **bueno**) are common too. Newspapers and even books are more carelessly printed in parts of America than they are in Spain; examples noted from Central America include **excabar** (for **excavar**), **haya** (for **aya**), **desabitada** (for **deshabitada**); while because the regular **seseo** equates Castilian [θ] with [s] in America, one finds in print **capas** (for **capaz**), **saga** (for **zaga**), and by hypercorrection **sociego** (for **sosiego**) and **discución** (for **discusión**).

6 Use of capitals in Spanish. Capital letters are used to begin words as in English in the following cases: for the first word in the sentence; for proper names of every kind; for the names, bynames and possessive pronouns of God, Christ, the Virgin Mary etc; for ranks and authorities in the state, army, church, the professions etc.

Usage differs from English in the following cases:

(**a**) The names of the days and months do not have capitals in Spanish: **lunes, martes, abril, mayo**.

(**b**) The first person subject pronoun does not have a capital unless it begins the sentence: **yo**. In Spanish it is usual to write the abbreviations **Vd, Vds** with capitals, but **usted, ustedes** in their extended form.

(**c**) Capitals are used for the names of countries and provinces etc, but not for the names of their inhabitants, for the adjectives relating to them or for their languages: **Francia**, but **un francés, una francesa, el vino francés, hablar francés.** The same is true of adjectives and nouns formed from other types of proper names: **la teoría darviniana, los estudios cervantinos, el conocido gongorista, la escuela alfonsí.**

(**d**) In the titles of books, articles, films etc the capital is used only at the start of the first word, unless later words are proper names: **El tercer hombre, Lo que el viento se llevó** (but **Boletín de la Real Academia Española**).

e) A very few words which do not have capitals in English often have them in Spanish: **el Estado, la Iglesia** and such. This is not obligatory and may depend on the amount of respect being shown.

7 Spanish punctuation. This is as in English except for the following features:

(**a**) Exclamation and question marks are placed inverted (¡¿) at the start of the exclamation or question as well as at the end. Note that this does not always coincide with the start of the sentence: eg **Pues ¿vamos o no vamos?; Son trece en total, ¿verdad?**

(**b**) The long dash (—, called a *raya*) is often used in Spanish where English would put parentheses.

(**c**) The same dash is much used to introduce dialogue or direct speech; sometimes at the start and at the end of the quotation, but sometimes only at the start.

(**d**) The inverted commas (" ") with which English encloses passages of direct speech and uses for a variety of other purposes are often represented in Spanish by « ».

8 Word division in Spanish. There are rules, rather different from those of English, about how a word may be divided in writing at the end of a line. The main points are:

(**a**) A single consonant between vowels is grouped with the second of them: **pa-lo, Barcelo-na.**

(**b**) In a group of two consonants between vowels, the first is grouped with the preceding vowel and the second with the following vowel: **in-nato, des-mochar, paten-te.** But groups having **l** or **r** as the second element are considered as units and join the following vowel only: **re-probar, de-clarar.**

(**c**) A group consisting of consonant + **h** may be split: **ex-hibición, Al-hambra.**

(**d**) It must be remembered that **ch, ll** and **rr** are considered as individual letters and must therefore never be split: **aprove-char, aga-lla, contra-rrevolucionario.**

(**e**) In a group of three consonants, the first two join the preceding vowel and the third joins the following vowel: **trans-porte, cons-tante.** Exception: if the third consonant in the group is **l** or **r**, only the first consonant joins the preceding vowel while the second and third join the following vowel: **som-bra, des-preciar, con-clave.**

(**f**) Two vowels should never be separated, whether they form one syllable or not: **rui-do, maes-tro, pro-veer.**

(**g**) Where it can be clearly recognized that a word consists of two or more words having an independent existence of their own, the long word may be divided in ways that contravene the foregoing rules: **latino-americano, re-examinar, vos-otros.** The same applies to some prefixes: **des-animar, ex-ánime.**

9 Use of the hyphen (-, called a *guión*) in Spanish. Strictly speaking this should only be used in Spanish in the cases mentioned in the *Nuevas Normas*, *e.g.* **relaciones franco-prusianas, cuerpos técnico-administrativos.** Compound words with or without a hyphen in English should be written as single words without hyphen in Spanish; a **hotplate** is **un calientaplatos** and a **windscreen-wiper** is **un limpiaparabrisas**, while a **Latin-American** is **un hispanoamericano** or **un latinoamericano.** Nonetheless in the dictionary we have used the hyphen in a few Spanish words which have been regularly noted in that form in print.

PRONUNCIACIÓN Y ORTOGRAFÍA

LA PRONUNCIACIÓN DEL INGLÉS BRITÁNICO

Como es sabido, la ortografía del inglés se ajusta a criterios históricos y etimológicos y en muchos puntos apenas ofrece indicaciones ciertas de cómo ha de pronunciarse cada palabra. Por ello nos ha parecido aconsejable y de utilidad para los hispanohablantes dar para cada palabra inglesa una pronunciación figurada o transcripción. Al tratar de explicar en estas notas los sonidos del inglés mediante comparaciones con los sonidos del español en un espacio reducido nos damos cuenta de que realizamos una labor que no pasa de ser aproximativa. Tales comparaciones tienen una finalidad práctica y carecen del rigor científico que exigen los fonetistas especializados.

1 Sistema de signos

Se emplean los signos de la IPA (International Phonetic Association). Hemos seguido en general las transcripciones de Daniel Jones, *English Pronouncing Dictionary,* London, Dent, 14th ed., 1989. En el prólogo de esta obra el autor explica los principios que le han guiado en su trabajo.

2 Acentuación

En las transcripciones el signo [ˈ] se coloca delante de la sílaba acentuada. El signo [ˌ] se pone delante de la sílaba que lleva el acento secundario o más ligero en las palabras largas, p.ej. **acceleration** [ækˌseləˈreɪʃən]. Dos signos de acento principal [ˈ ˈ] indican que las dos sílabas, o bien dos de las sílabas, se acentúan igualmente, p.ej. **A 1** [ˈeɪˈwʌn], **able-bodied** [ˈeɪblˈbɒdɪd].

3 Signos impresos en cursiva

En la palabra *annexation* [ˌænekˈseɪʃ*ə*n], la [*ə*] en cursiva indica que este sonido puede o no pronunciarse; o porque muchos hablantes la pronuncian pero que otros muchos no la pronuncian, o bien porque es un sonido que se oye en el habla lenta y cuidada pero que no se oye en el habla corriente y en el ritmo de la frase entera.

4 Transcripciones alternativas

En los casos donde se dan dos transcripciones, ello indica que ambas pronunciaciones son igualmente aceptables en el uso de las personas cultas, p.ej. **medicine** [ˈmeds*ɪ*n, ˈmedɪs*ɪ*n], o bien que la pronunciación varía bastante según la posición de la palabra en la frase y el contexto fonético, p.ej. **an** [æn, ən, n].

5 Véase también la nota sobre la pronunciación del inglés norteamericano (pág. xxxv).

6 El orden en que se explican los signos abajo es más o menos ortográfico y no el estrictamente fonético.

Vocales

[æ]	sonido breve, bastante abierto, parecido al de **a** en *carro*	**bat** **apple**	[bæt] [ˈæpl]
[ɑː]	sonido largo parecido al de **a** en *caro*	**farm** **calm**	[fɑːm] [kɑːm]
[e]	sonido breve, bastante abierto, parecido al de **e** en *perro*	**set** **less**	[set] [les]
[ə]	‘vocal neutra’, siempre átona; parecida a la **e** del artículo francés *le* y a la **a** final del catalán (p.ej. *cas***a**, *port***a**)	**above** **porter** **convey**	[əˈbʌv] [ˈpɔːtə^{r}] [kənˈveɪ]

[ɜː]	forma larga del anterior, en sílaba acentuada; algo parecido al sonido de **eu** en la palabra francesa *l**eu**r*	**fern** **work** **murmur**	[fɜːn] [wɜːk] ['mɜːməʳ]
[ɪ]	sonido breve, abierto, parecido al de **i** en *esb**i**rro, **i**rreal*	**tip** **pity**	[tɪp] ['pɪtɪ]
[iː]	sonido largo parecido al de **i** en *v**i**no*	**see** **bean** **ceiling**	[siː] [biːn] ['siːlɪŋ]
[ɒ]	sonido breve, bastante abierto, parecido al de **o** en *c**o**rra, t**o**rre*	**rot** **wash**	[rɒt] [wɒʃ]
[ɔː]	sonido largo, bastante cerrado, algo parecido al de **o** en *p**o**r*	**ball** **board**	[bɔːl] [bɔːd]
[ʊ]	sonido muy breve, más cerrado que la **u** en *b**u**rro*	**soot** **full**	[sʊt] [fʊl]
[uː]	sonido largo, parecido al de **u** en ***u**no, s**u**pe*	**root** **fool**	[ruːt] [fuːl]
[ʌ]	sonido abierto, breve y algo oscuro, sin correspondencia en español; se pronuncia en la parte anterior de la boca sin redondear los labios	**come** **rum** **blood** **nourish**	[kʌm] [rʌm] [blʌd] ['nʌrɪʃ]

Diptongos

[aɪ]	sonido parecido al de **ai** en *fr**ai**le, v**ai**s*	**lie** **fry**	[laɪ] [fraɪ]
[aʊ]	sonido parecido al de **au** en *p**au**sa, s**au**ce*	**sow** **plough**	[saʊ] [plaʊ]
[eɪ]	sonido medio abierto, pero más cerrado que la **e** de *cas**é***; suena como si le siguiese una [i] débil, especialmente en sílaba acentuada	**fate** **say** **waiter** **straight**	[feɪt] [seɪ] ['weɪtəʳ] [streɪt]
[əʊ]	sonido que es una especie de **o** larga, sin redondear los labios ni levantar la lengua; suena como si le siguiese una [u] débil	**ago** **also** **atrocious** **note**	[ə'gəʊ] ['ɔːlsəʊ] [ə'trəʊʃəs] [nəʊt]
[ɛə]	sonido que se encuentra únicamente delante de la **r**; el primer elemento se parece a la **e** de *p**e**rro*, pero es más abierto y breve; el segundo elemento es una forma débil de la 'vocal neutra' [ə]	**there** **rare** **fair** **ne'er**	[ðɛəʳ] [rɛəʳ] [fɛəʳ] [nɛəʳ]
[ɪə]	sonido cuyo primer elemento es una **i** medio abierta; el segundo elemento es una forma débil de la 'vocal neutra' [ə]	**here** **interior** **fear** **beer**	[hɪəʳ] [ɪn'tɪərɪəʳ] [fɪəʳ] [bɪəʳ]
[ɔɪ]	sonido cuyo primer elemento es una **o** abierta, seguido de una **i** abierta pero débil; parecido al sonido de **oy** en *v**oy*** o de **oi** en *c**oi**me*	**toy** **destroy** **voice**	[tɔɪ] [dɪs'trɔɪ] [vɔɪs]
[ʊə]	sonido cuyo primer elemento es una **u** medio larga; el segundo elemento es una forma débil de la 'vocal neutra' [ə]	**allure** **sewer** **pure**	[ə'ljʊəʳ] [sjʊəʳ] [pjʊəʳ]

Consonantes

[b]	como la **b** de *tum**b**ar, um**b**río*	**bet** **able**	[bet] ['eɪbl]
[d]	como la **d** de *con**d**e, an**d**ar*	**dime** **mended**	[daɪm] ['mendɪd]

[f]	como la **f** de **f**o**f**o, *in***f***lar*	**face** **snaffle**	[feɪs] ['snæfl]
[g]	como la **g** de **g***rande, ran***g***o*	**go** **agog**	[gəʊ] [ə'gɒg]
[h]	es una aspiración fuerte, algo así como la jota castellana [x] pero sin la aspereza gutural de aquélla	**hit** **reheat**	[hɪt] ['riː'hiːt]
[j]	como la **y** de *cu***y***o, re***y***es*	**you** **pure** **million**	[juː] [pjʊəʳ] ['mɪljən]
[k]	como la **c** de **c***ama* o la **k** de **k***ilómetro*, pero acompañada por una ligera aspiración inexistente en español	**catch** **kiss** **chord** **box**	[kætʃ] [kɪs] [kɔːd] [bɔks]
[l]	como la **l** de **l***eer, pa***l***a*	**lick** **place**	[lɪk] [pleɪs]
[m]	como la **m** de **m***es, co***m***er*	**mummy** **roam**	['mʌmɪ] [rəʊm]
[n]	como la **n** de **n***ada, habla***n**	**nut** **sunny**	[nʌt] ['sʌnɪ]
[ŋ]	como el sonido que tiene la **n** en *banco, rango*	**bank** **sinker** **singer**	[bæŋk] ['sɪŋkəʳ] ['sɪŋəʳ]
[p]	como la **p** de **p***alo, ro***p***a*, pero acompañada por una ligera aspiración inexistente en español	**pope** **pepper**	[pəʊp] ['pepəʳ]
[r]	Es un sonido muy débil, casi semivocal, que no tiene la vibración fuerte que caracteriza la **r** española. Se articula elevando la punta de la lengua hacia el paladar duro. (NB: En el inglés de Inglaterra la **r** escrita se pronuncia únicamente delante de vocal; en las demás posiciones es muda. Véase la nota sobre la pronunciación del inglés norteamericano y el signo [ʳ] abajo).	**rate** **pear** **fair** **blurred** **sorrow**	[reɪt] [pɛəʳ] [fɛəʳ] [blɜːd] ['sɒrəʊ]
[ʳ]	Este signo en las transcripciones indica que la **r** escrita en posición final de palabra se pronuncia en el inglés británico en muchos casos cuando la palabra siguiente empieza con vocal. En algún dialecto inglés y sobre todo en los Estados Unidos esta **r** se pronuncia siempre, así cuando la palabra se pronuncia aislada como cuando la siguen otras (empezando con vocal o sin ella)	**bear** **humour** **after**	[bɛəʳ] ['hjuːməʳ] ['ɑːftəʳ]
[s]	como la **s** (sorda) de *ca***s***a,* **s***esión*	**sit** **scent** **cents** **pox**	[sɪt] [sent] [sents] [pɒks]
[t]	como la **t** de **t***ela, ra***t***a*, pero acompañada por una ligera aspiración inexistente en español	**tell** **strut** **matter**	[tel] [strʌt] ['mætəʳ]
[v]	Inexistente en español (aunque se encuentra en catalán y valenciano). En inglés es sonido labiodental, y se produce juntando el labio inferior con los dientes superiores	**vine** **river** **cove**	[vaɪn] ['rɪvəʳ] [kəʊv]
[w]	como la **u** de *h***u***evo,* p**u***ede*	**wine** **bewail**	[waɪn] [bɪ'weɪl]
[z]	como la **s** (sonora) de *de***s***de, mi***s***mo*	**zero** **roses** **buzzer**	['zɪərəʊ] ['rəʊzɪz] ['bʌzəʳ]
[ʒ]	Inexistente en español, pero como la **j** de las palabras francesas **j***our,* **j***alousie,* o como la **g** de las palabras portuguesas **g***ente,* **g***eral*	**rouge** **leisure** **azure**	[ruːʒ] ['leʒəʳ] ['eɪʒəʳ]
	Este sonido aparece a menudo en el grupo [dʒ], parecido al grupo **dj** de la palabra francesa *a***dj***acent*	**page** **edge** **jail**	[peɪdʒ] [edʒ] [dʒeɪl]

[ʃ]	Inexistente en español, pero como la **ch** de las palabras francesas **ch***ambre*, *fi***ch***e*, o como la **x** de la palabra portuguesa *ro***x***o*	**shame** **ocean** **ration** **sugar**	[ʃeɪm] ['əʊʃən] ['ræʃən] ['ʃʊgə^r]
	Este sonido aparece a menudo en el grupo [tʃ], parecido al grupo **ch** del español *mu***ch***o*, **ch***o***ch***o*	**much** **chuck** **natural**	[mʌtʃ] [tʃʌk] ['nætʃrəl]
[θ]	como la **z** de **z***umbar* o la **c** de **c***iento*	**thin** **maths**	[θɪn] [mæθs]
[ð]	forma sonorizada del anterior, algo parecido a la **d** de *to***d***o*, *habla***d***o*	**this** **other** **breathe**	[ðɪs] ['ʌðə^r] [bri:ð]
[x]	sonido que en rigor no pertenece al inglés de Inglaterra, pero que se encuentra en el inglés de Escocia y en palabras escocesas usadas en Inglaterra etc; es como la **j** de **j***oven*, *ro***j***o*	**loch**	[lɔx]

7 Sonidos extranjeros

El grado de corrección con que el inglés pronuncia las palabras extranjeras que acaban de incorporarse al idioma depende – como en español – del nivel cultural del hablante y de los conocimientos que pueda tener del idioma de donde se ha tomado la palabra. Las transcripciones que damos de tales palabras representan una pronunciación más bien culta. En las transcripciones la tilde [˜] indica que la vocal tiene timbre nasal (en muchas palabras de origen francés). En las pocas palabras tomadas del alemán aparece a veces la [x], para cuya explicación véase el cuadro de las consonantes.

8 Las letras del alfabeto inglés

Cuando se citan una a una, o cuando se deletrea una palabra para mayor claridad, o cuando se identifica un avión etc por una letra y su nombre, las letras suenan así:

a	[eɪ]	**j**	[dʒeɪ]	**s**	[es]
b	[bi:]	**k**	[keɪ]	**t**	[ti:]
c	[si:]	**l**	[el]	**u**	[ju:]
d	[di:]	**m**	[em]	**v**	[vi:]
e	[i:]	**n**	[en]	**w**	['dʌblju:]
f	[ef]	**o**	[əʊ]	**x**	[eks]
g	[dʒi:]	**p**	[pi:]	**y**	[waɪ]
h	[eɪtʃ]	**q**	[kju:]	**z**	[zed] (*en EEUU* [zi:])
i	[aɪ]	**r**	[ɑ:^r]		

LA PRONUNCIACIÓN DEL INGLÉS NORTEAMERICANO

Sería sin duda deseable dar aquí un resumen de las diferencias más notables que existen entre el inglés de Inglaterra y el de las regiones del Reino Unido – Escocia, Gales, Irlanda del Norte – y el de los principales países extranjeros y continentes donde se ha arraigado este idioma: Irlanda, Estados Unidos y el Canadá, las Antillas, Australia y Nueva Zelanda, Sudáfrica y los países sucesores de las antiguas colonias en el Este y Oeste de África, la India, etc. Para tal labor no disponemos ni del espacio ni mucho menos de los conocimientos necesarios. Siendo este diccionario un trabajo angloamericano, sin embargo, y considerando el predominio actual de los Estados Unidos en tantas esferas (entre ellas la lingüística), es de todos modos imprescindible apuntar algunas de las múltiples diferencias que existen entre el inglés de Inglaterra y el hablado en Estados Unidos.

Empleamos las abreviaturas (*Brit*) (British) y (*US*) (United States).

1 Acentuación

Las palabras que tienen dos sílabas o más después del acento principal llevan en (*US*) un acento secundario que no tienen en (*Brit*), p.ej. **dictionary** [(*US*) 'dɪkʃəˌnerɪ = (*Brit*) 'dɪkʃənrɪ], **secretary** [(*US*) 'sekrəˌterɪ = (*Brit*) 'sekrətrɪ]. En algunos casos se acentúa en (*US*) una sílaba distinta de la que lleva el acento en (*Brit*): p.ej. **primarily** [(*US*) praɪ'mærɪlɪ = (*Brit*) 'praɪmərɪlɪ]. Este cambio de acento se percibe ahora también, por influencia norteamericana, en el inglés de Inglaterra.

2 Entonación

El inglés de (*US*) se habla con un ritmo más lento y en un tono más monótono que en Inglaterra, debido en parte al alargamiento de las vocales que se apunta abajo.

3 Sonidos

Muchas de las vocales breves acentuadas en (*Brit*) se alargan mucho en (*US*), y alguna vocal inacentuada en (*Brit*) se oye con más claridad en (*US*), p.ej. **rapid** [(*US*) 'ræːpɪd = (*Brit*) 'ræpɪd], **capital** [(*US*) 'kæːbɪdəl = (*Brit*) 'kæpɪtl].

Peculiaridad muy notable del inglés en (*US*) es la nasalización de las vocales antes y después de las consonantes nasales [m, n, ŋ].

En las vocales individuales también hay diferencias. El sonido [ɑː] en (*Brit*) en muchas palabras se pronuncia en (*US*) como [æ] o bien [æː], p.ej. **grass** [(*US*) græs *o* græːs = (*Brit*) grɑːs], **answer** [(*US*) 'ænsər *o* 'æːnsər = (*Brit*) 'ɑːnsəʳ]. El sonido [ɒ] en (*Brit*) se pronuncia en (*US*) casi como una [ɑ] oscura, p.ej. **dollar** [(*US*) 'dɑlər = (*Brit*) 'dɒləʳ], **hot** [(*US*) hɑt = (*Brit*) hɒt], **topic** [(*US*) 'tɑpɪk = (*Brit*) 'tɒpɪk]. El diptongo que se pronuncia en (*Brit*) [juː] en sílaba acentuada se pronuncia en la mayor parte de (*US*) sin [j], p.ej. **Tuesday** [(*US*) 'tuːzdɪ = (*Brit*) 'tjuːzdɪ], **student** [(*US*) 'stuːdənt = (*Brit*) 'stjuːdənt]; pero muchas palabras de este tipo se pronuncian en (*US*) igual que en (*Brit*), p.ej. **music, pure, fuel.** En último lugar entre las vocales, se nota que la sílaba final **-ile** que se pronuncia en (*Brit*) [aɪl] es a menudo en (*US*) [əl] o bien [ɪl], p.ej. **missile** [(*US*) 'mɪsəl, 'mɪsɪl = (*Brit*) 'mɪsaɪl]. Existen otras diferencias en la pronunciación de las vocales de palabras individuales, p.ej. **tomato,** pero éstas se tratan individualmente en el texto del diccionario.

En cuanto a las consonantes, destacamos dos diferencias. La consonante sorda [t] entre vocales suele sonorizarse bastante en (*US*), p.ej. **united** [(*US*) jʊ'naɪdɪd = (*Brit*) juː'naɪtɪd], o sufre lenición [ṭ]. La *r* escrita en posición final después de vocal o entre vocal y consonante es por la mayor parte muda en (*Brit*), pero se pronuncia a menudo en (*US*), p.ej. **where** [(*US*) wɛər = (*Brit*) wɛəʳ], **sister** [(*US*) 'sɪstər = (*Brit*) 'sɪstəʳ]. Hemos tomado esto en cuenta en las transcripciones en el texto del diccionario. También en posición final de sílaba (no sólo de palabra) se nota esta pronunciación de la *r* escrita: **burden** [(*US*) 'bəːrdn = (*Brit*) 'bəːdn], **jersey** [(*US*) 'dʒəːrzɪ = (*Brit*) 'dʒəːzɪ].

Conviene advertir que aun dentro del inglés de Estados Unidos hay notables diferencias regionales; la lengua de Nueva Inglaterra difiere bastante de la del Sur, la del Medioοeste no es la de California, etc. Los datos que constan arriba no son más que indicaciones muy someras.

LA ORTOGRAFÍA DEL INGLÉS

El extranjero, mientras lucha con las muchas confusiones y rarezas de la ortografía inglesa, se consuela recordando que los propios niños ingleses, y muchas personas mayores, sostienen la misma lucha. El inglés ha de ser el único idioma para el que ha valido la pena – la cosa estuvo de moda hace unos años – organizar certámenes ortográficos, en los que se pedía que los concursantes deletreasen palabras como **parallel**, **precede** y **proceed** y **supersede**, **sylph** y **Ralph**. Ha habido muchas tentativas de reforma – siendo quizá la más conocida la de G. B. Shaw – pero ninguna se ha llevado a la práctica; las reformas norteamericanas (véase abajo) son útiles pero afectan sólo a una pequeña parte del problema.

1 En general se aplica el sistema en todo su rigor y las dudas y desviaciones permitidas son escasísimas. Es lícito escribir algunas palabras con o sin **e** muda, como **blond(e)**, **judg(e)ment**; varía la vocal en **enquiry-inquiry, encrust-incrust**, y la consonante en muchas palabras terminadas en **-ise, -ize** (pero siempre **advertise, chastise**). En casos como **spirt-spurt** se hace generalmente una distinción de sentido. Son toleradas **grandad** y **granddad, mummie** y **mummy**. Las variantes más importantes constan en el texto del diccionario.

2 En las novelas en que se presenta la vida de la clase baja urbana (p.ej. de los *Cockneys* de Londres) o de gente del campo, el autor puede representar su habla – con sus incorrecciones y barbarismos, según el criterio casticista – con formas como las siguientes:

'e	=	he	Oim	=	I'm
'ere	=	here	roit	=	right
'ope	=	hope	Lunnun	=	London
'ed	=	head	bruvver	=	brother
et	=	ate	Fursday	=	Thursday
'arf	=	half	dook	=	duke
yer	=	your	dunno	=	don't know

La **-d** final tras **n** se suprime a menudo en este lenguaje, p.ej. **an'** = **and**, y la **-g** final se suprime en la desinencia **-ing**, p.ej. **boozin'** = **boozing**. Como curiosidad apuntamos que este último fenómeno se da también en representaciones del habla de las familias aristocráticas, de los militares viejos etc: **huntin'**, **shootin'** and **fishin'**. Nótese el modo de emplear la comilla (') para indicar la supresión de una letra. Tales cambios en la escritura pueden representar una diferencia no de clase sino de región, p.ej. en escocés **awa'** = **away**, y en el inglés de las Antillas **dis** = **this**.

3 Se observan a veces deformaciones hechas con intención humorística (**luv** = **love, Injun** = **Indian**) o con afán de ultramodernidad (**nite** = **night**) o como truco publicitario en el comercio (**sox** = **socks**) o como parte de la jerga de un grupo social (**showbiz** = **show business**).

4 Son mucho más importantes las diferencias ortográficas entre el inglés británico (*Brit*) y el norteamericano (*US*):

(**a**) La **u** que se escribe en (*Brit*) en las palabras terminadas en **-our** y derivadas del latín, se suprime en (*US*): (*US*) **color** = (*Brit*) **colour**, (*US*) **labor** = (*Brit*) **labour**. (Esto no afecta a los monosílabos como **dour, flour, sour,** donde no hay diferencia). También en (*US*) se suprime la **u** del grupo **ou** [əʊ] en el interior de la palabra: (*US*) **mold** = (*Brit*) **mould**, (*US*) **smolder** = (*Brit*) **smoulder**.

(**b**) Muchas palabras que en (*Brit*) terminan en **-re** se escriben en (*US*) **-er**: *US* **center** = (*Brit*) **centre**, (*US*) **meter** = (*Brit*) **metre**, (*US*) **theater** = (*Brit*) **theatre**. (Pero no existe diferencia en **acre, lucre, massacre**).

(**c**) Ciertas vocales finales, que no tienen valor en la pronunciación, se escriben en (*Brit*) pero se suprimen en (*US*): (*US*) **catalog** = (*Brit*) **catalogue**, (*US*) **prolog** = (*Brit*) **prologue**, (*US*) **program** = (*Brit*) **programme**, (*US*) **kilogram** = (*Brit*) **kilogramme**.

(**d**) En (*US*) se suele simplificar los diptongos de origen griego y latino **ae, oe**, escribiendo sencillamente **e**: (*US*) **anemia** = (*Brit*) **anaemia**, (*US*) **anesthesia** = (*Brit*) **anaesthesia**. En (*US*) se duda entre **subpoena** y **subpena**; en (*Brit*) se mantiene siempre el primero.

(**e**) En algunos casos las palabras que en (*Brit*) terminan en **-ence** se escriben **-ense** en (*US*): (*US*) **defense** = (*Brit*) **defence**, (*US*) **offense** = (*Brit*) **offence**.

(**f**) Algunas consonantes que en (*Brit*) se escriben dobles se escriben en (*US*) sencillas: (*US*) **wagon** = (*Brit*) **waggon** (pero **wagon** se admite también en Inglaterra), y sobre todo en formas verbales: (*US*) **kidnaped** = (*Brit*) **kidnapped**, (*US*) **worshiped** = (*Brit*) **worshipped**. El caso de **l, ll** intervocálicas ofrece más complejidades. Alguna vez lo que se escribe con **ll** en (*Brit*) se encuentra con una **l** en (*US*): así (*US*) **councilor** = (*Brit*) **councillor**, (*US*) **traveler** = (*Brit*) **traveller**. Por el contrario, en posición final de sílaba o de palabra la **l** en (*Brit*) es a menudo **ll** en (*US*): así (*US*) **enroll, enrolls** = (*Brit*) **enrol, enrols**, (*US*) **skillful** = (*Brit*) **skilful**.

(**g**) En (*US*) se modifica algún otro grupo ortográfico del inglés, pero sólo en la escritura de tono familiar: (*US*) **tho** = (*Brit*) **though**, (*US*) **thru** = (*Brit*) **through**. También son más corrientes en (*US*) las formas como **Peterboro** (o bien **Peterboro'**), aunque éstas no son desconocidas en (*Brit*).

(**h**) Viene luego una serie de palabras aisladas que se escriben de modo diferente:

(*US*)	(*Brit*)	(*US*)	(*Brit*)
ax	axe	mustache	moustache
check	cheque	pajamas	pyjamas
cozy	cosy	plow	plough
gray	grey	skeptic	sceptic
gypsy	gipsy	tire	tyre

En otros casos se duda bastante; en (*US*) hay lucha entre **rime, rhyme,** mientras en (*Brit*) se escribe únicamente el segundo; en (*US*) hay lucha entre **tire, tyre,** mientras en (*Brit*) se escribe siempre el segundo.

Conviene notar que mientras la influencia del inglés norteamericano se percibe a cada paso en el inglés británico en cuanto al léxico, a la fraseología y a la sintaxis, ésta parece no haber afectado para nada la ortografía del inglés en el Reino Unido.

5 Las mayúsculas se emplean más en inglés que en español. Se emplean como en español al principio de la palabra en los siguientes casos: en la primera palabra de la frase; en los nombres propios de toda clase; en los nombres, sobrenombres y pronombres posesivos de Dios, Cristo, Nuestra Señora etc; en las graduaciones y títulos de las autoridades del estado, del ejército, de la iglesia, de las profesiones etc.

Las mayúsculas se emplean en inglés en los siguientes casos donde se escribe minúscula en español:

(**a**) Los nombres de los días y meses: **Monday, Tuesday, April, May.**

(**b**) El pronombre personal de sujeto, primera persona: **I** (**yo**). Pero el pronombre de segunda persona se escribe en inglés con minúscula: **you** (*Vd, Vds*).

(**c**) Los nombres de los habitantes de los países y provincias, los adjetivos derivados de éstos y los nombres de los idiomas: **I like the French, two Frenchwomen, French cheese, to talk French, a text in old Aragonese.** Se emplea la mayúscula también en los nombres y adjetivos derivados de otras clases de nombres propios: **a Darwinian explanation, the Bennites, two well-known Gongorists, the Alphonsine school.** Sin embargo el adjetivo de nacionalidad puede escribirse con minúscula en algún caso cuando se refiere a una cosa corriente u objeto conocido de todos, p.ej. **a french window, french beans, german measles** (en este diccionario hemos preferido escribir algunas de estas palabras con mayúscula).

(**d**) En los sustantivos y adjetivos principales en los títulos de libros, artículos, películas etc: **The Third Man, Gone with the Wind.**

6 La puntuación en inglés. Los signos y el modo de emplearlos son como en español con las siguientes excepciones:

(**a**) Los signos de admiración y de interrogación (¡¿) no se emplean en inglés en principio de frase.

(**b**) En inglés se emplea menos la doble raya (— ... —) con función parentética; se prefiere en muchos casos el paréntesis (...).

(**c**) La raya (—) que sirve a menudo en español para introducir el diálogo y la oración directa, y a veces también para cerrarlos, se sustituye en inglés por las comillas (“...”). Conviene apuntar que éstas se emplean obligatoriamente al terminar la cita u oración directa y no sólo para introducirla. Los signos « » del español se escriben siempre como comillas (“...”) en inglés.

7 La división de la palabra en inglés. Las reglas para dividir una palabra en final de renglón son menos estrictas en inglés que en español. En general se prefiere cortar la palabra tras vocal, **hori-zontal, vindi-cation,** pero se prefiere mantener como unidades ciertos sufijos comunes, **vindica-tion, glamor-ous.** De acuerdo con esto se divide la palabra dejando separada la desinencia **-ing,** p.ej. **sicken-ing,** pero si ésta está precedida por un grupo de consonantes, una de ellas va unida al **-ing,** p.ej. **tick-ling.** Se divide el grupo de dos consonantes iguales: **pat-ter, yel-low, disap-pear,** y los demás grupos consonánticos de acuerdo con los elementos separables que forman la palabra: **dis-count, per-turb.**

DICCIONARIO ESPAÑOL~INGLÉS

SPANISH~ENGLISH DICTIONARY

A

A, a¹ [a] *nf* (*letra*) A, a; **a por a y be por be** point by point, in full detail.

a² *prep* **(a)** (*lugar*: *dirección*) to; **ir a Madrid** to go to Madrid; **llegar a Madrid** to arrive in Madrid; to reach Madrid; **llegar al teatro** to arrive at the theatre; **ir al parque** to go to the park; **ir a casa** to go home; **subir a un avión** to get into a plane; **subir a un tren** to get into a train, to get on a train; **mirar al norte** to look northwards; **(de) cara al norte** facing north; **torcer a la derecha** to turn (to the) right; **caer al mar** to fall into the sea.

(b) (*lugar*: *distancia*) **está a 7 km de aquí** it is 7 km (away) from here.

(c) (*lugar*: *posición*) at; **al lado de** at the side of; **a la puerta** at the door; **estar a la mesa** to be at table; **estaba sentado a su mesa de trabajo** he was sitting at his desk; **a retaguardia** in the rear; **a orillas de** on the banks of; **al margen** in the margin.

(d) (*tiempo*) at; **a las 8** at 8 o'clock; **¿a qué hora?** at what time?; **a mediodía** at noon; **a la noche** at nightfall; (*LAm**) **a la tarde** in the afternoon; **a la mañana siguiente** the following morning; **a 3 de junio** on the third of June; **a los 55 años** at 55, at the age of 55; **al año de esto** after a year of this, a year later; **a los pocos días** within a few days, after a few days, a few days later; **a los 18 minutos** (*de un juego*) in the 18th minute; **'Cervantes a los 400 años'** (*título de estudio*) 'Cervantes after 400 years', 'Cervantes 400 years on'; **a tiempo** in time.

(e) (*manera*) **a la americana** in the American fashion, (in) the American way, American style; **a caballo** on horseback; **a escape** at full speed; **a oscuras** in the dark, in darkness; **diseño a cuadros** chequered pattern; **diseño a rayas** striped pattern; **a petición de** at the request of; **a pie** on foot; **a solicitud** on request; **tres a tres** three at a time, in threes, by threes; **beber algo a sorbos** to drink sth in sips; **mirarse a los ojos** to look into each other's eyes.

(f) (*medio, instrumento*) **funciona a pilas y a la red** it works on batteries and on the mains: **a lápiz** in pencil; **cocina a gas** gas stove; **a puñetazos** with (blows of) one's fists; **a mano** by hand; **bordado a mano** hand-embroidered; **girar algo a mano** to turn sth by hand; **despertarse al menor ruido** to wake at the least sound.

(g) (*razón*) **poco a poco** little by little; **palmo a palmo** inch by inch; **a un precio elevado** at a high price; **a 30 ptas el kilo** at 30 pesetas a kilo, for 30 pesetas a (*o* per) kilo; **al 5 por ciento** at 5%; **a 50 km por hora** at 50 km an hour.

(h) (*dativo*) to; **se lo di a él** I gave it to him; **le di dos a Pepe** I gave two to Joe, I gave Joe two; **El Toboso marcó 5 goles al Madrid** El Toboso scored 5 against Madrid.

(i) (*dativo*: *separación*) **se lo compré a él** I bought it from him.

(j) (*con objeto pers*: *no se traduce*) **vi al jefe** I saw the boss.

(k) (*construcción tras ciertos verbos*) to; **empezó a cantar** he began to sing; **voy a verle** I'm going to see him; **sabe a queso** it tastes of cheese; **huele a vino** it smells of wine.

(l) (**al** + *infin*) **al verle** on seeing him; when I saw him; *V t* **al**.

(m) (**a** + *infin*) **asuntos a tratar** agenda, items to be discussed; **el criterio a adoptar** the criterion to be adopted; **éste será el camino a recorrer** this will be the path to take.

(n) (*imperativo*) **¡a callar!** be quiet!; **¡a trabajar!** to work!, get down to it!

(o) (*si*) **a no ser esto así** if this were not so; **a decir verdad** ... to tell the truth ...; **a la que te descuides** before you know where you are ...

(p) **¡~ que ...!** I bet ...!

AA (*Aer*) *abr de* **Aerolíneas Argentinas**.

AA.AA. *abr de* **Antiguos Alumnos** Former Pupils, FPs.

AAE *nf abr de* **Asociación de Aerolíneas Europeas** Association of European Airlines, AEA.

AA.EE. *abr de* **Asuntos Exteriores**; *V* **asunto (a)**.

ab. *abr de* **abril** April, Apr.

abacá *nm* abaca, Manilla hemp.

abacado *nm* (*Carib*) avocado pear.

abacería *nf* grocer's (shop), grocery store.

abacero, -a *nm/f* grocer, provision merchant.

ábaco *nm* abacus.

abacora *nf* (*LAm*) type of tuna.

abacorar [1a] *vt* **(a)** (*And, Carib*) (*acosar*) to harass, plague, bother; (*sorprender*) to catch, surprise.

(b) (*Carib*: *acometer*) to undertake boldly; (*****: *seducir*) to entice away.

(c) (*LAm Com*) to monopolize; to corner (the market in).

abad *nm* abbot.

abadejo *nm* **(a)** (*pez*: *de mar*) cod, codfish; pollack; (*de agua dulce*) ling; (*Carib*: *pez espada*) swordfish. **(b)** (*Ent*) Spanish fly, cantharides. **(c)** (*Culin*) dried salted cod.

abadengo 1 *adj* abbatial, of an abbot. **2** *nm* abbacy.

abadesa *nf* **(a)** (*Rel*) abbess. **(b)** (*LAm**) madame, brothel-keeper.

abadía *nf* **(a)** (*edificio*) abbey. **(b)** (*rango, oficio*) abbacy.

abajadero *nm* slope, incline.

abajar [1a] *vt* (*LAm*) = **bajar**.

abajeño (*LAm*) **1** *adj* lowland (*atr*), of the lowland(s), from the lowland(s). **2** *nm*, **abajeña** *nf* lowlander; (*Méx*: *costeño*) lowlander, coastal dweller.

abajera *nf* (*Cono Sur*) saddlecloth.

abajero *adj* (*LAm*) lower, under.

abajino (*Cono Sur*) **1** *adj* northern. **2** *nm*, **abajina** *nf* northerner.

abajo 1 *adv* (*posición*) down, below, down below, underneath, (*en casa*) downstairs; (*dirección*) down, downwards, (*en casa*) downstairs; **¡~ el gobierno!** down with the government!; **aquí ~** down here; here below; **desde ~** from below; **hacia ~** down, downwards; **más ~** lower down, further down; **por ~** underneath; **cuesta ~** downhill; **río ~** downstream; **del rey (para) ~** from the king down.

2 ~ de *prep* below, under.

3 de ~ *adj*: **la parte de ~** the lower part, the underside; **el piso de ~** the downstairs flat; the floor below, the next floor down; **los de ~** the underdogs, the downtrodden, the underprivileged.

abajofirmante *nmf*: **el ~, la ~** the undersigned.

abalanzadero *nm* (*Méx*) ford, cattle crossing.

abalanzar [1f] **1** *vt* **(a)** (*pesar*) to weigh; (*equilibrar*) to balance.

(b) (*lanzar*) to hurl, throw; (*impeler*) to impel.

2 abalanzarse *vr* **(a)** to spring forward, rush forward, dash forward; (*multitud*) to surge forward; **~ a** *peligro* to rush thoughtlessly into; **~ sobre** to spring at, rush at, hurl o.s. on; to pounce on; **se abalanzaron los amantes** the lovers threw themselves at one another.

(b) (*Cono Sur*: *caballo*) to rear up.

abaldonar [1a] *vt* (*degradar*) to degrade, debase; (*insultar*) to affront.

abalear [1a] **1** *vt* (*LAm*: *disparar*) to shoot (at), fire at; (*And*: *fusilar*) to shoot, execute. **2** *vi* (*LAm*: *tirotear*) to shoot off guns, fire in the air.

abaleo *nm* (*LAm*) shooting.

abalorio *nm* glass bead; beads, beadwork; **no vale un ~** it's worthless.

abalum(b)ar* [1a] *vt* (*Méx*) to pile up, stack.
abanarse* [1a] *vr* (*Cono Sur*) to give o.s. airs, show off.
abanderado, -a *nm/f* (*Pol etc*) standard-bearer, champion, leader; (*LAm Dep*) representative; (*linier*) linesman.
abanderar [1a] *vt* (**a**) (*Náut*) to register. (**b**) *causa etc* to champion; *campaña* to take a leading role in.
abanderizar [1f] **1** *vt* to organize into bands. **2 abanderizarse** *vr* to band together; to join a band; (*Cono Sur Pol*) to take sides, adopt a position.
abandonado *adj* abandoned; *lugar etc* abandoned, deserted, godforsaken; *edificio* deserted, derelict; *piso* vacant; *aspecto* neglected; forlorn; slovenly, uncared-for; (*moralmente*) profligate; (*LAm*: *dejado*) slovenly, untidy; (*LAm**: *pervertido*) perverted.
abandonamiento *nm* = **abandono**.
abandonar [1a] **1** *vt lugar etc* to leave; *persona* to leave, abandon; to desert, forsake; (*huir de*) to flee from; *objeto* to leave behind; *tentativa, hábito* to drop, give up; (*renunciar*) to renounce, relinquish; **~ una empresa** to give up an attempt; **abandonaron a sus hijos** they deserted their children; **cuando abandonó la casa** when he left the house; **tuvo que ~ el cargo** he had to give up the post; **¡abandonado me tenías!** you'd forgotten all about me!
2 *vi* to give up; (*Inform*) to quit; (*Dep*) to withdraw, scratch, retire; (*Ajedrez*) to resign.
3 abandonarse *vr* (**a**) (*rendirse*) to give in, give up; (*desanimarse*) to lose heart, get discouraged; (*descuidarse*) to let o.s. go, get slovenly, get slack; **no te abandones** don't let yourself go.
(**b**) **~ a** to give o.s. over to, yield to, indulge in an excess of.
abandonismo *nm* defeatism.
abandonista *adj, nmf* defeatist.
abandono *nm* (*V v*) (**a**) (*acto*) abandonment; dereliction; desertion; giving up, renunciation, relinquishment; (*Dep*) withdrawal, retirement; (*Ajedrez*) resignation; **~ de la escuela** truancy, absence from school; **ganar por ~** to win by default, win thanks to an opponent's withdrawal.
(**b**) (*estado*) moral abandon; profligacy; forlornness; neglect, slovenliness; abandoned state; indulgence (*a* in); (*LAm*: *descuido*) untidiness, disorder; **darse al ~** to go morally downhill, indulge one's vices; **viven en el mayor ~** they live in utter degradation.
(**c**) (*Méx*: *ligereza*) abandon, ease.
abanicada *nf* fanning, fanning action.
abanicar [1g] **1** *vt* to fan; (*reprender*) to tell off. **2 abanicarse** *vr* to fan o.s; **~ con algo** (*Cono Sur‡*) not to give a damn about sth; to shrug one's shoulders at sth.
abanico *nm* (**a**) (*gen*) fan; fan-shaped object; (*) sword; (*ventana*) fanlight; (*Náut*) derrick; (*Carib Ferro*) points signal; **~ de chimenea** fire screen; **~ eléctrico** (*Méx*: *ventilador*) electric fan; **extender las cartas en ~** to fan out one's cards; **con hojas en ~** with leaves arranged like a fan. (**b**) (*fig*) range; spread; **~ de posibilidades** range of possibilities; **~ salarial, ~ de salarios** wage scale.
abaniquear [1a] (*LAm*) **1** *vt* to fan. **2 abaniquearse** *vr* to fan o.s.
abaniqueo *nm* fanning, fanning movement; (*manoteo*) gesticulation.
abaniquero, -a *nm/f* (*fabricante*) fan maker; (*comerciante*) dealer in fans.
abarajar* [1a] *vt* (*Cono Sur*) *golpe* to counter, parry.
abaratamiento *nm* cheapening, reduction in price; greater cheapness.
abaratar [1a] **1** *vt artículo* to make cheaper, reduce the price of; *precio* to lower. **2** *vi y* **abaratarse** *vr* to get cheaper, come down.
abarca *nf* sandal.
abarcar [1g] *vt* (*incluir*) to include, embrace, take in; to span; (*contener*) to contain, comprise; (*extenderse a*) to extend to; *trabajo* to undertake, take on; (*LAm*: *monopolizar*) to monopolize, corner (the market in); **el capítulo abarca 3 siglos** the chapter covers 3 centuries, the chapter deals with 3 centuries; **sus conocimientos abarcan todo el campo de ...** his knowledge ranges over the whole field of ...; **abarca una hectárea** it takes up a hectare, it's a hectare in size; **quien mucho abarca poco aprieta** you can bite off more than you can chew; Jack of all trades and master of none.
abarque *nm* (*And*: *huevos*) clutch.
abarquillar [1a] **1** *vt* (*arrollar*) to curl up, roll up; (*arrugar*) to wrinkle. **2 abarquillarse** *vr* (*arrollarse*) to curl up, roll up; (*arrugarse*) to crinkle.
abarraganarse [1a] *vr* to live together (as man and wife *o* though unmarried), set up house together.
abarrajado* *adj* (*Cono Sur*) (*libertino*) dissolute, free-living; (*peleonero*) quarrelsome, argumentative.
abarrajar* [1a] **1** *vi* (*Cono Sur*) to run away, flee. **2 abarrajarse** *vr* (**a**) (*And*: *caer de bruces*) to fall flat on one's face. (**b**) (*And, Cono Sur*: *prostituirse*) to prostitute o.s., sell o.s.; (*fig*) to become corrupt, be perverted.
abarrajo *nm* (*And*) fall, stumble.
abarrancadero *nm* tight spot, jam.
abarrancar [1g] **1** *vt* to make cracks in, open up fissures in.
2 abarrancarse *vr* (**a**) (*caer*) to fall into a ditch (*o* pit *etc*).
(**b**) (*atascarse*) to get stopped up.
(**c**) (*Náut*) to run aground; (*fig*) to get into a jam.
abarrotar [1a] **1** *vt* (**a**) (*atrancar*) to bar, fasten with bars.
(**b**) (*Náut*) to stow, pack tightly; (*Com*) to overstock; (*fig*) to overstock, overfill; to overcrowd; **abarrotado de** filled to bursting with, stuffed full of; **el cine estaba abarrotado (de gente)** the cinema was packed; **el orador abarrotó el aula** the speaker filled the room to overflowing.
2 abarrotarse *vr* (*LAm Com*) to become a glut on the market; **~ de** (*Méx*) to be stuffed (*o* bursting) with, be crammed full of.
abarrote *nm* (**a**) (*Náut*) packing. (**b**) (*LAm*) food item, item of food; foodstuff; **~s** food; food supplies; (*Com*) groceries; **tienda de ~s, la ~s*** grocer's (shop), grocery store, general store.
abarrotería *nf* (*Méx*: *tienda general*) grocer's (shop), grocery store; (*CAm*: *ferretería*) ironmonger's (shop), hardware store (*US*).
abarrotero, -a *nm/f* (*Méx*) grocer, owner of a general store.
abastar [1a] *vt* to supply.
abastardar [1a] **1** *vt* to degrade, debase. **2** *vi* to degenerate.
abastecedor(a) *nm/f* supplier, purveyor (*frm*); (*Méx*) wholesale butcher, meat supplier.
abastecer [2d] *vt* to supply, provide (*de* with).
abastecimiento *nm* (*acto*) supplying, provision; provisioning, catering; (*cantidad*) supply, provision; (*víveres*) provisions; **~ de agua** water supply.
abastero *nm* (*LAm*: *de ganado*) cattle-dealer; (*de comestibles*) provision merchant; (*Cono Sur, Méx*: *carnicero*) wholesale butcher, meat supplier.
abasto *nm* (**a**) supply; provisioning; **dar ~ a** to supply; **dar ~ a un pedido** to fill an order, meet an order; **no dar ~** (*fig*) to be unable to cope, be lacking in resources. (**b**) (*Cono Sur*) public meat market. (**c**) (*Carib*) grocery store, general store.
abatanado *adj* skilled, skilful.
abatanar [1a] *vt paño* to beat, full; (*fig*) to beat.
abatatado *adj* (*Cono Sur*) shy, coy.
abatatarse [1a] *vr* (*Cono Sur*) to be shy, be bashful.
abate *nm* (*Ecl*: *frec hum*) father, abbé.
abatí *nm* (*And, Cono Sur*) maize, Indian corn (*US*).
abatible *adj* folding; **asiento ~** tip-up seat; folding seat; (*Aut*) reclining seat; **mesa de alas ~s** gate-leg(ged) table, table with flaps.
abatido *adj* depressed, dejected, downcast, crestfallen; (*moralmente*) low, contemptible, despicable; (*Com, Fin*) depreciated; **estar ~ por el dolor** to be prostrate with pain; **estar muy ~** to be very depressed.
abatimiento *nm* (**a**) (*acto*) demolition, knocking down. (**b**) (*estado*) depression, dejection; (*carácter moral*) contemptible nature, despicable character.
abatir [3a] **1** *vt* (**a**) *casa etc* to demolish, knock down; to dismantle; *tienda* to take down; *árbol* to cut down, fell; *avión* to shoot down; *pájaro* to shoot, bring down; *bandera* to lower, strike; *persona* to knock down; (*enfermedad, dolor etc*) to prostrate, lay low.
(**b**) (*fig*) (*desanimar*) to depress, sadden, discourage; (*humillar*) to humble, humiliate.
2 abatirse *vr* (**a**) (*caerse*) to drop, fall; (*pájaro, avión*) to swoop, dive; **~ sobre** to swoop on, pounce on.
(**b**) (*fig*) to be depressed, get discouraged.
abayuncar [1g] (*Méx*) **1** *vt vaca etc* to throw, ground; **~ a uno*** to put sb on the spot. **2 abayuncarse*** *vr* to become countrified.
ABC, abc = **abecé**.
Abderramán *nm* Abd-al-Rahman.
abdicación *nf* abdication.
abdicar [1g] **1** *vt* to renounce, relinquish; **~ la corona** to give up the crown.

2 *vi* to abdicate; ~ **de algo** to renounce sth, relinquish sth; ~ **en uno** to abdicate in favour of sb.
abdomen *nm* abdomen.
abdominal 1 *adj* abdominal. **2** *nm* press-up.
abducción *nf* (*Med*) abduction.
abductor *nm* (*Anat*) abductor.
abecé *nm* ABC, alphabet; (*fig*) rudiments, basic elements.
abecedario *nm* alphabet; (*libro*) primer, spelling book.
abedul *nm* birch, birch-tree; ~ **plateado** silver birch.
abeja *nf* bee; ~ **asesina** killer bee; ~ **machiega,** ~ **maestra,** ~ **reina** queen bee; ~ **obrera** (*o* **neutra**) worker; (*fig*: *hormiguita*) hard worker.
abejar *nm* apiary.
abejarrón *nm* bumblebee.
abejaruco *nm* bee-eater.
abejón *nm* drone, (*Méx*) buzzing insect; **hacer ~*** (*CAm*: *cuchichear*) to whisper; (*Carib*: *silbar*) to boo, hiss.
abejonear [1a] (*And, Carib*) **1** *vt* (*fig*) to whisper (*a* to). **2** *vi* (*Carib**) to mumble, whisper.
abejorro *nm* (*abeja*) bumblebee; (*coleóptero*) cockchafer.
abejucarse [1g] *vr* (*Méx*) to twist up, climb.
abellacado *adj* villainous.
abellacar [1g] *vt* to lower, degrade.
aberenjenado *adj* violet-coloured.
aberración *nf* aberration; **es una ~ bañarse cinco veces al día** it's crazy to have a bath five times a day.
aberrante *adj* aberrant; (*disparatado*) crazy, ridiculous.
aberrar [1a] *vi* to be mistaken, err.
aberrear [1a] *vt* (*And*) to anger, annoy.
Aberri Eguna *nm* Basque national holiday (*Easter Sunday*).
abertura *nf* (**a**) (*gen*) opening; (*brecha*) gap, hole, aperture; (*grieta*) crack, cleft, slit; fissure; (*Geog*) (*cala*) cove; (*valle*) wide valley, gap; (*puerto*) pass. (**b**) (*fig*) openness, frankness.
abertzale [aβer'tʃale] **1** *adj*: **movimiento ~** (Basque) nationalist movement. **2** *nmf* Basque nationalist.
abetal *nm* fir plantation, fir wood.
abeto *nm* fir, fir-tree; ~ **blanco** silver fir; ~ **falso,** ~ **del norte,** ~ **rojo** spruce.
abetunado *adj* (*fig*) dark-skinned.
abetunar [1a] *vt* (*LAm*) to polish, clean.
abey *nm* (*Carib Bot*) jacaranda tree.
abiertamente *adv* openly.
abiertazo *adj* (*CAm*) generous, open-handed.
abierto 1 *ptp de* **abrir**.
2 *adj* open; opened; *ciudad, cara, campo, competición etc* open; *carácter* open, frank; (*LAm**: *tolerante*) generous, open; (*Carib*) conceited; **la puerta estaba abierta** the door was open, the door stood open; **muy ~, ~ de par en par** wide open; **una brecha muy abierta** a gaping hole, a wide gap; **es una carrera muy abierta** it's a very open race, the race is wide open; **dejar un grifo ~** to leave a tap running.
3 *nm* (*Dep*) open (competition).
abigarrado *adj* (*de diversos colores*) variegated, many-coloured, of many colours; *animal* piebald, brindled; mottled; *escena* motley, vivid, colourful; *habla etc* disjointed, uneven.
abigarramiento *nm* variegation; many colours; motley colouring; vividness, colourfulness.
abigarrar [1a] *vt* to paint (*etc*) in a variety of colours.
abigeato *nm* (*Méx*) (cattle) rustling.
abigeo *nm* (*Méx*: *ladrón*) (cattle) rustler.
-abilidad *V* **Aspects of Word Formation in Spanish 2.**
abintestato *adj* intestate.
abiótico *adj* abiotic.
abiselar [1a] *vt* to bevel.
Abisinia *nf* Abyssinia.
abisinio, -a *adj, nm/f* Abyssinian.
abismal *adj* abysmal; (*enorme*) vast, enormous; *diferencia* unbridgeable.
abismalmente *adv* abysmally; vastly, enormously, greatly.
abismante* *adj* (*LAm*) amazing, astonishing.
abismar [1a] **1** *vt* (*humillar*) to cast down, humble; (*arruinar*) to spoil, ruin; ~ **a uno en la tristeza** to plunge sb into sadness.
2 abismarse *vr* (**a**) (*LAm**: *asombrarse*) to be amazed, be astonished.
(**b**) (*Carib*: *arruinarse*) to be ruined.
(**c**) ~ **en** to plunge into; to sink into; ~ **en el dolor** to abandon o.s. to one's grief; **estar abismado en** to be lost in, be sunk in.
abismo *nm* (*gen*) abyss (*t fig*), chasm; (*de ola*) trough; (*Rel*) hell; **desde los ~s de la Edad Media** from the dark depths of the Middle Ages; **estar al borde del ~** to be on the brink of ruin (*o* failure *o* disaster *etc*); **de sus ideas a las mías hay un ~** our views are worlds apart.
abizcochado *adj* (*LAm*) spongy.
abjuración *nf* (*Jur*) retraction.
abjurar [1a] **1** *vt* to abjure, forswear. **2** *vi*: ~ **de** to abjure, forswear.
ablactación *nf* (*Med*) weaning.
ablactar [1a] *vt* (*Med*) to wean.
ablandabrevas* *nmf invar* useless person, good-for-nothing.
ablandador *nm*: ~ **de agua** water-softener; ~ **de carnes** (*Méx*) meat tenderizer.
ablandahigos* *nmf invar* = **ablandabrevas.**
ablandamiento *nm* (*V v* **1, 2**) softening; softening up; mitigation; soothing; moderation.
ablandar [1a] **1** *vt* (*gen*) to soften; (*Mil etc*) to soften up; (*LAm Aut*) to run in; *vientre* to loosen; *dureza* to mitigate, temper; *persona dura* to soothe, mollify, appease.
2 *vi* (*frío*) to become less severe; (*viento*) to moderate.
3 ablandarse *vr* to soften, soften up, get soft(er); (*frío*) to become less severe; (*viento*) to moderate, (*elementos*) decrease in force; (*persona*) to relent, become less harsh; (*con la edad*) to mellow.
ablande *nm* (*LAm Aut*) running-in.
ablativo *nm* ablative; ~ **absoluto** ablative absolute.
-able *V* **Aspects of Word Formation in Spanish 2.**
ablución *nf* ablution.
ablusado 1 *adj* (*no tallado*) loose. **2** *nm* (*Cono Sur*) loose garment.
abnegación *nf* self-denial, abnegation; unselfishness.
abnegado *adj* self-denying, self-sacrificing; unselfish.
abnegarse [1h *y* 1j] *vr* to deny o.s., go without, act unselfishly.
abobado *adj* silly; dim-witted; stupid-looking, bewildered; **mirar ~** to look bewildered.
abobamiento *nm* silliness, stupidity; bewilderment.
abobar [1a] **1** *vt* to make stupid; to daze, bewilder. **2 abobarse** *vr* to get stupid.
abocado *adj vino* smooth, pleasant.
abocar [1g] **1** *vt* (*tomar en la boca*) to seize (*o* catch) in one's mouth; (*acercar*) to bring nearer, bring up; *vino* to pour out, decant.
2 *vi* (**a**) (*Náut*) to enter a river, enter a channel.
(**b**) (*fig*) ~ **a** to lead to, result in, end up in; **estar abocado al desastre** to be heading for disaster; **verse abocado a un peligro** to see danger looming ahead.
(**c**) **estar abocado a** + *infin* to be designed to + *infin*; **esta medida está abocada a mejorar la situación** this measure is designed to (*o* is intended to) improve the situation.
3 abocarse *vr* (**a**) (*aproximarse*) to approach; ~ **con uno** to meet sb, have an interview with sb.
(**b**) ~ **a** (*Cono Sur*) to confront, face up to.
abocardo *nm* (*Téc*) drill.
abocastro *nm* (*And, Cono Sur*) ugly devil.
abocetar [1a] *vt* to sketch.
abocinado *adj* trumpet-shaped.
abocinar [1a] **1** *vt* to shape like a trumpet; (*Cos*) to flare. **2 abocinarse*** *vr* to fall flat on one's face.
abochornado *adj* embarrassed.
abochornante *adj* = **bochornoso** (**b**).
abochornar [1a] **1** *vt* (*sobrecalentar*) to make flushed, overheat; (*avergonzar*) to shame, embarrass.
2 abochornarse *vr* to get flushed, get overheated; (*Bot*) to wilt; ~ **de** to feel ashamed at, get embarrassed about.
abodocarse [1g] *vr* (*CAm*) (*líquido etc*) to go lumpy; (*Méx* ††) to come out in boils.
abofado *adj* (*Carib, Méx*) swollen.
abofarse [1g] *vr* (*Méx*) to stuff o.s.
abofetear [1a] *vt* to slap, hit (in the face).
abogacía *nf* (*abogados*) legal profession; (*oficio*) the law.
abogaderas *nfpl*, **abogaderías** *nfpl* (*LAm pey*) specious (*o* false) arguments.
abogado *nmf* (**a**) (*t* **abogada** *nf*) (*gen*) lawyer; (*notario*) solicitor; (*en tribunal*) barrister, attorney-at-law (*US*); (*defensor*) counsel; ~ **auxiliar** (*Méx*) junior lawyer; ~ **criminalista** criminal lawyer; ~ **charlatán** shady lawyer; ~ **del diablo** devil's advocate; ~ **defensor** defending counsel; ~ **del Estado** public prosecutor, attorney general (*US*); ~ **laboralista** labour lawyer; ~ **matrimonialista** divorce lawyer; ~ **de oficio** (*Méx*) court-appointed counsel; ~ **penalista** (*Méx*) criminal lawyer; ~ **picapleito** pettifogging law-

yer; ~ **de secano** shady solicitor; barrack-room lawyer; ~ **trampista** shady solicitor; **constituir** ~ to brief a barrister; **ejercer de** ~ to practise law, be a lawyer; **recibirse de** ~ to qualify as a solicitor; to be called to the bar.
(**b**) (*fig*) champion, advocate.

abogar [1h] *vi* to plead; ~ **por** (*o* **en**) to plead for, defend; (*fig*) to advocate, champion, back.

abolengo *nm* ancestry, lineage; inheritance.

abolición *nf* abolition, abolishment.

abolicionismo *nm* abolitionism.

abolicionista *nmf* abolitionist.

abolir [3a; *defectivo*] *vt* to abolish; to cancel, annul, revoke.

abolsado *adj* full of pockets, baggy.

abolsarse [1a] *vr* to form pockets, be baggy.

abolladura *nf* (*en metal*) dent; (*hinchazón*) bump; (*cardenal*) bruise; (*Arte*) embossing.

abollar [1a] **1** *vt* (**a**) to dent; to raise a bump on; to bruise; (*Arte*) to emboss, do repoussé work on.
(**b**) (*Méx*) (*) *filo* to blunt; (*: *amolar*) to grind down, oppress.
2 abollarse *vr* to get dented; to get bruised.

abollonar [1a] *vt metal* to emboss.

abombachado *adj pantalón* baggy.

abombado *adj* (**a**) (*gen*) convex; domed. (**b**) **estar** ~ (*LAm fig*) (*aturdido*) to be bewildered; (*tonto*) to be silly; (*: *borracho*) to be tight*. (**c**) (*LAm*) *comida* rotten; **estar** ~ to stink, smell foul.

abombar [1a] **1** *vt* (**a**) (*hacer convexo*) to make convex.
(**b**) (*) (*ensordecer*) to deafen; (*desconcertar*) to confuse; (*aturdir*) to bewilder; to stun.
2 abombarse *vr* (*LAm*) (**a**) (*pudrirse*) to rot, decompose; to smell bad.
(**b**) (*) (*emborracharse*) to get tight*; (*enloquecer*) to go mad, lose one's head; (*atontarse*) to go soft (in the head).

abominable *adj* abominable.

abominablemente *adv* abominably.

abominación *nf* (**a**) (*sentimiento*) abomination; loathing, detestation. (**b**) (*cosa*) abomination; **es una** ~ it's an abomination, it's detestable.

abominar **1** *vt* = **2**. **2** *vi*: ~ **de** to loathe, detest, abominate.

abonable *adj* (**a**) (*pagadero*) payable; due. (**b**) (*Agr*) improvable.

abonado **1** *adj* reliable, trustworthy; **estar** ~ **a** + *infin* to be ready to + *infin*; to be inclined to + *infin*; **es** ~ **para ello** he is perfectly capable of (doing) it.
2 *nm*, **abonada** *nf* subscriber; (*Teat etc*) season-ticket holder; (*Ferro*) season-ticket holder, commuter.

abonamiento *nm* = **abono**.

abonanzar [1f] *vi y* **abonanzarse** *vr* (*Met*) to grow calm, become settled.

abonar [1a] *vt* (**a**) (*avalar*) *persona* to vouch for, support; *hecho* to guarantee, confirm, vouch for.
(**b**) (*Fin*) to pay; *compra etc* to pay for; ~ **dinero en una cuenta** to pay money into an account, credit money to an account.
(**c**) (*Agr*) to fertilize, manure.
(**d**) (*suscribir*) to subscribe (for sb); **te abonaré al teatro** I'll take out a season-ticket for you to the theatre; **te abonaré a la revista** I'll take out a subscription to the journal for you.
2 *vi* (*Met*) to grow calm, become settled.
3 abonarse *vr* to subscribe (*a* to).

abonaré *nm* promissory note, IOU.

abonero *nm* (*Méx*: *vendedor*) street vendor, door-to-door salesman; (*LAm*: *que recoge abonos*) tallyman, collector.

abono *nm* (**a**) (*fianza*) guarantee; **en** ~ **de** in support of, in justification of; as confirmation of.
(**b**) (*Fin*) (*pago*) payment; (*plazo*) instalment; (*crédito*) credit; (*LAm*: *depósito*) down payment, deposit; **pagar por** (*o* **en**) ~**s** to pay by instalments.
(**c**) (*Agr*: *material*) fertilizer, manure; (*acto*) fertilizing, manuring; ~ **químico** chemical fertilizer, artificial manure.
(**d**) (*a revista*) subscription; (*Ferro, Teat etc*) season-ticket; (*abonados*) subscribers, subscription list.
(**e**) (*Méx*) (*recibo*) receipt.

aboquillado *adj cigarrillo* tipped, filter-tipped.

abordable *adj persona* approachable, accessible; *tarea* manageable, that can be tackled; *precio* reasonable; **no es nada** ~ he's a difficult man.

abordaje *nm* (*Náut*) collision, fouling; (*ataque, subida a bordo*) boarding; (*en la calle etc*) accosting, approach; (*de problema*) approach (*de* to).

abordar [1a] **1** *vt* (**a**) (*Náut*: *chocar con*) to collide with, foul; (*llegar*) to come alongside (*en el embarcadero* at the quay); (*atacar, subir a*) to board.
(**b**) *persona* to accost, approach; to stop and speak to; *tarea, tema* to tackle; *problema* to approach, tackle; (*emprender*) to undertake, get down to, start on.
(**c**) (*Méx*) *bus* to board, get on; (*Carib Aer*) to board.
2 *vi* (*Méx Náut*) to dock.

aborigen **1** *adj* aboriginal; indigenous. **2** *nmf* aboriginal, aborigine.

aborrascarse [1g] *vr* to get stormy.

aborrecer [2d] *vt* (*detestar*) to hate, loathe, detest; (*aburrirse con*) to become bored by; *nido, hijuelos* to desert, abandon.

aborrecible *adj* hateful, loathsome, detestable; invidious; abhorrent.

aborrecido *adj* hated, loathed; boring.

aborrecimiento *nm* loathing, detestation; abhorrence; boredom.

aborregado *adj*: **cielo** ~ mackerel sky.

aborregarse [1h] *vr* (**a**) (*) to follow slavishly, tag along. (**b**) (*LAm*) to be silly, get silly.

abortadora *nf* woman who suffers repeated miscarriages.

abortar [1a] **1** *vt* (**a**) (*gen*) to abort, cause to miscarry; **hacerse** ~ to have an abortion, to have o.s. aborted. (**b**) (*Aer etc*) to abort.
2 *vi* (**a**) (*Med*: *por accidente*) to have a miscarriage; (*con intención*) to abort; **hacer** ~ **a una mujer** to procure an abortion for a woman.
(**b**) (*fig*) to miscarry, fail, go awry.

abortero, -a *nm/f* abortionist.

abortista **1** *nmf* (**a**) (*criminal*) abortionist; ~ **ilegal** back-street abortionist.
(**b**) (*partidario*) abortion campaigner, person seeking to legalize abortion.
2 *nf* woman who has had an abortion.

abortivo **1** *adj* abortive. **2** *nm* abortifacient.

aborto *nm* (**a**) (*Med*: *accidental, t* ~ **espontáneo**) miscarriage; (*provocado*) abortion; (*Jur*) (criminal) abortion; ~ **clandestino** back-street abortion; ~ **eugenésico** eugenic abortion; ~ **habitual** repeated miscarriage; ~ **ilegal** illegal abortion; ~ **libre** (**y gratuito**) free right to abortion, abortion on demand; ~ **provocado** abortion; ~ **terapéutico** therapeutic abortion.
(**b**) (*Bio*) monster, unnatural creature, freak.
(**c**) (*fig*) miscarriage, failure.
(**d**) (‡) ugly man, ugly woman; (*aplicado a mujer*) old bat‡, old cow‡.

abortón *nm* (*Vet*) premature calf.

abotagamiento *nm* swelling.

abotagarse [1h] *vr* to swell up, become bloated.

abotonador *nm* buttonhook.

abotonar [1a] **1** *vt* (**a**) (*abrochar*) to button up, do up. (**b**) (*Méx*: *tapar*) to block, obstruct. **2** *vi* (*Bot*) to bud.

abovedado **1** *adj* vaulted; domed, arched. **2** *nm* vaulting.

abovedar [1a] *vt* to vault, arch.

aboyar [1a] *vt* (**a**) (*Náut*) to buoy, mark with buoys. (**b**) (*Méx*) to float.

abozalar [1a] *vt* to muzzle.

abr. *abr de* **abril** April, Apr.

abra[1] *nf* (*Geog*: *cala*) cave, small bay, inlet; (*valle*) dale, gorge; (*Geol*) fissure; (*Cono Sur, Méx*: *claro*) clearing; (*CAm, Cono Sur*: *paso de sierra*) mountain pass.

abra[2] *nf* (*LAm*) panel, leaf (of a door).

abracadabra *nf* abracadabra; hocus-pocus.

abracadabrante *adj* (*aparatoso*) spectacular; (*atractivo*) enchanting, captivating; (*mágico*) magic-seeming; (*insólito*) unusual; (*raro*) extravagant.

abracar [1g] *vt* (*Méx*) = **abrazar**.

Abraham, Abrahán *nm* Abraham.

abrasado *adj* burnt, burnt up; **estar** ~ to burn with shame; **estar** ~ **en cólera** to be in a raging temper.

abrasador *adj*, **abrasante** *adj* burning, scorching; (*fig*) withering.

abrasar [1a] **1** *vt* (**a**) (*gen*) to burn, burn up; *plantas* (*sol*) to dry up, parch; (*viento*) to sear; (*helada*) to cut, nip.
(**b**) (*fig*: *derrochar*) to squander, waste.
(**c**) (*fig*: *avergonzar*) to fill with shame.
2 abrasarse *vr* to burn (up); to catch fire; (*tierra*) to be parched; ~ **de amores** to burn with love, be violently in love; ~ **de calor** to be dying of the heat; ~ **de sed** to have a raging thirst.

abrasión *nf* graze, abrasion.

abrasivo *adj, nm* abrasive.

abrazadera *nf* bracket; clasp, brace; (*Tip*) bracket; ~ **para papeles** paper clip.
abrazar [1f] **1** *vt* (*persona*) to embrace; to hug, take in one's arms; (*fig*) to include; comprise, take in; *oportunidad* to seize; *empresa* to take charge of; *fe* to adopt, embrace; *doctrina* to espouse; *profesión* to adopt, enter, take up.
2 abrazarse *vr* to embrace (each other); ~ **a** *persona* to embrace; to cling to, clutch.
abrazo *nm* (**a**) embrace, (*fuerte*) hug; ~ **fatal** (*Inform*) deadly embrace. (**b**) (*en carta*) **un ~ fuerte** (*o* **afectuoso**) with best wishes, with kind regards, yours; **un ~** love from.
abreboca (*LAm*) **1** *adj* absent-minded. **2** *nm* appetizer.
abrebotellas *nm invar* bottle-opener.
abrecartas *nm invar* letter-opener, paper-knife.
ábrego *nm* south-west wind.
abrelatas *nm invar* tin-opener, can-opener.
abrenuncio *interj*: ¡~! not for me!; far be it from me!
abrevadero *nm* watering place, drinking-trough.
abrevar [1a] **1** *vt animal* to water, give a drink to; *tierra* to water, irrigate; *pieles* to soak; *superficie* (*antes de pintar*) to size.
2 abrevarse *vr* (*animal*) to drink, quench its thirst; ~ **en sangre** (*fig*) to wallow in blood.
abreviación *nf* abbreviation; abridgement, shortening; reduction.
abreviadamente *adv* (*sucintamente*) briefly, succinctly; (*en forma resumida*) in an abridged form.
abreviado *adj* (*breve*) brief; short, shortened; (*resumido*) abridged; **la palabra es forma abreviada de ...** the word is a shortened form of ..., the word is short for ...
abreviar [1b] **1** *vt palabra etc* to abbreviate; *texto* to abridge, reduce; *discurso, estancia, período* to shorten, cut short; *acontecimiento* to hasten; *fecha* to advance, bring forward.
2 *vi* to be quick; to get on quickly; **bueno, para ~** well, to cut a long story short.
abreviatura *nf* abbreviation.
abriboca* *adj* (*LAm*) open-mouthed.
abridor *nm*: ~ (**de botellas**) bottle-opener; ~ (**de latas**) tin-opener, can-opener.
abrigada *nf*, **abrigadero** *nm* shelter, windbreak; **abrigadero de ladrones** (*Méx*) den of thieves.
abrigado *adj lugar* sheltered, protected; *persona* well wrapped up.
abrigador 1 *adj* (*And, Méx*) warm. **2** *nm*, **abrigadora** *nf* person who covers up for another.
abrigar [1h] **1** *vt* (**a**) (*resguardar*) to shelter, protect (*de* against, from); (*ropa etc*) to keep warm, protect, cover; to wrap up; (*ayudar*) to help, support.
(**b**) (*fig*) *duda* to retain, entertain; *esperanza* to cherish, nurse; *opinión* to hold; *sospecha* to harbour.
2 abrigarse *vr* to take shelter (*de* from), protect o.s.; (*con ropa*) to cover up (warmly), wrap o.s. up; (*And*) to warm o.s; **¡abrígate bien!** wrap up well!
abrigo *nm* (**a**) (*gen*) shelter; (*protección*) protection; (*ayuda*) help, support; (*cobertura*) covering, protection; **de ~*** tremendous*; **al ~ de** sheltered from, protected from; **ropa de mucho ~** heavy clothing, warm clothes; **escapar al ~ de la noche** to flee under cover of darkness.
(**b**) (*Náut*) harbour, haven.
(**c**) (*prenda*) coat, overcoat, outer coat; ~ **de pieles** fur coat; ~ **de visón** mink coat.
(**d**) (*Cono Sur*: *manta*) blanket, quilt.
abril *nm* April; **en el ~ de la vida** in the springtime of one's life; **en ~ aguas mil** April showers bring May flowers; **una joven de 20 ~es** a girl of 20 (summers); **estar hecho un ~** to look very handsome.
abrileño *adj* April (*atr*).
abrillantado 1 *adj* polished; (*Culin*) glazed. **2** *nm* polish(ing); (*Culin*) glaze, glazing.
abrillantadora *nf* floor-polisher.
abrillantar [1a] *vt piedra* to cut into facets; (*pulir*) to polish, burnish, brighten; (*Culin*) to glaze; (*fig*) to enhance, add lustre to.
abrir [3a; *ptp* **abierto**] **1** *vt* (*gen*) to open; to open up; (*Med*) to cut open, open up; *mapa etc* to open out, spread out, extend; *libro* to open; *camino* to clear, make, open up; (*LAm*) *bosque* to clear; *foso, cimientos* to dig; *agujero* to make, bore; *pozo* to sink; *lámina* to engrave; *grifo* to turn on; *cuenta* to open; *negociaciones* to open, start; *mercado* to open up; *apetito* to whet, stimulate; *lista* to head; *desfile* to head, lead; ~ **una puerta con llave** to unlock a door; ~ **algo cortándolo** to cut sth open; ~ **una información** (*Jur*) to begin proceedings; **volver a ~ un pleito** (*Jur*) to reopen a case; **en un ~ y cerrar de ojos** in the twinkling of an eye; ~(**se**) **el tobillo** to twist one's ankle, sprain one's ankle.
2 *vi* (**a**) (*gen*) to open; (*flor*) to open, unfold.
(**b**) (*Bridge*) to open; ~ **de 3 a un palo** to open 3 in a suit; ~ **de corazones** to open (with a bid in) hearts.
(**c**) (*Carib**: *huir*) to escape, run off.
3 abrirse *vr* (**a**) (*gen*) to open; to open out, unfold, spread (out); to expand; ~ **a uno**, ~ **con uno** to confide in sb.
(**b**) (*: *largarse*) to go away, beat it*; **¡me abro!** I'm off!; **¡ábrete!** shove off!*
(**c**) (*Méx*: *echar marcha atrás*) to backtrack, back-pedal, back out.
abrita *nf* (*CAm*) short dry spell.
abrochador *nm* buttonhook; (*LAm*) stapler, stapling machine.
abrochar [1a] **1** *vt* (**a**) (*con botones*) to button (up); (*con broche*) to do up, fasten (up); (*con hebilla*) to clasp, buckle; (*asir*) to grasp; (*LAm*) *papeles* to staple (together).
(**b**) (*And*: *reprender*) to reprimand.
(**c**) (*Méx*) (*atar*) to tie up; (*agarrar*) to grab hold of.
2 abrocharse *vr* (**a**) (*LAm*) to struggle, wrestle. (**b**) *V* **1**.
abrogación *nf* abrogation, repeal.
abrogar [1h] *vt* to abrogate, repeal.
abrojo *nm* (*Bot*) thistle, thorn, caltrop; (*Mil*) caltrop; **~s** (*Méx*: *matorral*) thorn bushes; (*Náut*) submerged rocks.
abroncar* [1g] **1** *vt* (*avergonzar*) to shame, make ashamed; (*ridiculizar*) to ridicule; (*aburrir*) to bore; (*molestar*) to annoy; *orador* to boo, heckle, barrack; (*reprender*) to give a lecture to, tick off.
2 abroncarse* *vr* to get angry.
abroquelarse [1a] *vr*: ~ **con**, ~ **de** to shield o.s. with, defend o.s. with.
abrumador *adj* crushing, burdensome; exhausting; tiresome; *mayoría* vast, overwhelming; *superioridad* crushing, overwhelming; *atenciones* embarrassingly pressing; **el trabajo es ~** the work is killing; **es una responsabilidad ~a** it is a heavy responsibility.
abrumadoramente *adv* crushingly; vastly, overwhelmingly.
abrumar [1a] **1** *vt* (*agobiar*) to crush, overwhelm; (*oprimir*) to oppress, weigh down; (*cansar*) to wear out, exhaust; ~ **a uno de trabajo** to swamp sb with work.
2 abrumarse *vr* to get foggy, get misty.
abrupto *adj pendiente* steep, abrupt; *terreno* rough, rugged; *tono* abrupt; *cambio* sudden.
abrutado *adj* brutish, brutalized.
absceso *nm* abscess.
abscisión *nf* incision.
absenta *nf* absinth(e).
absentismo *nf* absenteeism; absentee landlordism; ~ **laboral** absenteeism from work.
absentista *nmf* absentee; absentee landlord.
ábside *nm* apse.
absintio *nm* absinth(e).
absolución *nf* (*Ecl*) absolution; (*Jur*) acquittal; pardon.
absoluta *nf* (**a**) (*declaración*) dogmatic statement, authoritative assertion.
(**b**) (*Mil*) discharge; **tomar la ~** to take one's discharge, leave the service.
absolutamente *adv* (**a**) (*completamente*) absolutely, completely; definitely; positively; ~ **nada** nothing at all; **es ~ imposible** it's absolutely impossible; **está ~ prohibido** it is absolutely forbidden; **el puente estaba ~ destruido** the bridge was completely destroyed.
(**b**) (*en sentido neg*) not at all, by no means; **'¿así que no viene nadie?' ... '~'** 'so nobody is coming?' ... 'nobody at all'.
absolutismo *nm* absolutism; ~ **ilustrado** enlightened dictatorship.
absolutista 1 *adj* absolutist, absolute. **2** *nmf* absolutist.
absolutizar [1f] *vt* to pin down, be precise about.
absoluto *adj* (**a**) (*gen*) absolute (*t Filos, Pol*); utter, complete; *fe* complete, implicit; *temperamento* domineering, tyrannical; **lo ~** the absolute.
(**b**) (*en sentido neg*) **en ~** nothing at all, by no means; not in the slightest; (*Méx*) absolutely, undoubtedly; **¡en ~!** certainly not!, not at all!; no way!*; **no sabía nada en ~ de eso** I knew nothing at all about it; **no tenía miedo en ~** he wasn't a bit afraid.

absolutorio *adj*: **fallo ~** (*Jur*) verdict of acquittal, verdict of not guilty.
absolver [2h; *ptp* **absuelto**] *vt* to absolve; (*Jur*) to acquit, clear (*de una acusación* of a charge); to release (*de un empeño* from an obligation).
absorbencia *nf* absorbency.
absorbente 1 *adj* (**a**) (*Quím etc*) absorbent.
(**b**) (*fig*: *interesante*) interesting, absorbing; *tarea* demanding; *amor etc* possessive, tyrannical.
2 *nm*: **~ higiénico** sanitary towel, sanitary napkin (*US*).
absorber [2a] **1** *vt* to absorb; to soak up; to suck in; *conocimientos* to absorb, take in, acquire; *capitales, recursos* to use up; *energías* to take up; *atención* to command; *lector etc* to absorb, engross.
2 absorberse *vr*: **~ en** to become absorbed in, become engrossed in.
absorbible *adj* absorbable.
absorbidad *nf* absorbency.
absorción *nf* absorption (*t fig*); (*Com*) takeover.
absorto *adj* absorbed; engrossed; **estar ~** (*extasiado*) to be entranced; (*pasmado*) to be amazed; **estar ~** (**en meditación**) to be lost in thought; **estar ~ en un proyecto** to be engrossed in a scheme, be intent on a scheme.
abstemio 1 *adj* abstemious; (*completamente*) teetotal.
2 *nm*, **abstemia** *nf* abstainer; teetotaller.
abstención *nf* abstention; non-participation.
abstencionismo *nm* non-participation, refusal to take part, opting out.
abstencionista *nmf* non-participant, person who opts out.
abstenerse [2k] *vr* to abstain; to refrain; **~ de** + *infin* to abstain from + *ger*, refrain from + *ger*, forbear to + *infin*; '**~ medianías**' 'no dealers'; '**~ si no cumplen los requisitos**' 'do not apply unless you have the qualifications'; **en la duda, abstente** when in doubt, don't.
abstinencia *nf* abstinence; abstemiousness; (*de drogas*) withdrawal; (*Ecl*) abstinence; restraint, forbearance.
abstinente *adj* (*Ecl*) abstinent, observing abstinence.
abstracción *nf* (**a**) (*gen*) abstraction; (*despiste*) absent-mindedness, engrossment in something else; (*ensueño*) reverie.
(**b**) **~ hecha de ese libro** leaving that book aside, with the exception of that book.
abstractar [1a] *vt publicaciones* to abstract, make abstracts of.
abstracto *adj* abstract; **en ~** in the abstract.
abstraer [2o] **1** *vt* to abstract; to remove, consider separately.
2 *vi*: **~ de** to leave aside, exclude.
3 abstraerse *vr* to be absorbed, be lost in thought; to be preoccupied.
abstraído *adj* withdrawn, absent-minded; preoccupied.
abstruso *adj* abstruse.
absuelto *ptp de* **absolver**.
absurdamente *adv* absurdly.
absurdidad *nf*, **absurdidez** *nf* absurdity.
absurdo 1 *adj* absurd, ridiculous, preposterous; farcical; **teatro de lo ~** theatre of the absurd; **es ~ que ...** it is absurd that ...
2 *nm* absurdity; farce; **decir ~s** to say absurd things.
abubilla *nf* hoopoe.
abucharar* [1a] *vt* (*abuchear*) to boo, jeer; (*excluir*) to ostracize, marginalize; (*criticar*) to slate*, criticize; (*avergonzar*) to put to shame; **quedarse abuchara(d)o** to be left out, be ostracized.
abuchear [1a] *vt* to boo, hoot at; to howl down, jeer at; **ser abucheado** (*Teat etc*) to be hissed at, get the bird*.
abucheo *nm* booing, hooting; jeering; **ganarse un ~** (*Teat etc*) to be hissed at, get the bird*.
abuela *nf* grandmother; (*fig*) old woman, old lady; **¡tu ~!*** rubbish!; **¡cuéntaselo a tu ~!** go tell that to the marines!; pull the other one!*; **¡no tienes ~!** come off it!, tell us another!; **no tiene ~*** he's full of himself; **no necesita ~*** he blows his own trumpet; (**éramos pocos**) **y parió la ~*** and that was the last straw, and that was all we needed.
abuelado* *adj* (*Cono Sur*) spoiled by one's grandparents.
abuelita* *nf* (**a**) (*: *persona*) grandma*, granny*; (*Méx etc*) grandmother. (**b**) (*Cono Sur*: *gorra*) baby's bonnet. (**c**) (*And*: *cuna*) cradle.
abuelito* *nm* granddad*, grandpa*; (*Méx etc*) grandfather.
abuelo *nm* grandfather; (*fig*) old man; ancestor, forbear; **~s** grandparents; **¡tu ~!*** get away!*; **está hecho un ~** he looks like an old man.
abulense 1 *adj* of Ávila. **2** *nmf* native (*o* inhabitant) of Ávila; **los ~s** the people of Ávila.
abulia *nf* lack of willpower, spinelessness; apathy.
abúlico *adj* lacking in willpower, weakwilled, spineless; apathetic.
abulón *nm* (*Zool*) abalone.
abultado *adj* bulky, large, massive; unwieldy; *libro etc* thick; (*fig*) exaggerated.
abultamiento *nm* bulkiness, (large) size; swelling, increase; exaggeration; increased importance.
abultar [1a] **1** *vt* (*agrandar*) to enlarge; (*hacer más abultado*) to make bulky; (*aumentar*) to swell, increase; (*fig*) to exaggerate.
2 *vi* to be bulky, be big; to take up a lot of room; (*fig*) to increase in importance, loom large.
abundamiento *nm* abundance, plenty; **a** (*o* **por**) **mayor ~** furthermore; with still more justification, as if that were not enough.
abundancia *nf* abundance, plenty; **en ~** in abundance, in plenty; **nadar en la ~** to be rolling in money.
abundante *adj* abundant, plentiful; *cosecha etc* heavy, copious; *provisión etc* generous; **~ en** abounding in; productive of.
abundantemente *adv* abundantly; in abundance, in plenty.
abundar [1a] *vi* to abound, be plentiful; **~ de, ~ en** to abound in, abound with, be rich in; **~ en dinero** to be well supplied with money; **~ en la opinión de uno** to share sb's opinion (*o* view) wholeheartedly.
Abundio *V* **tonto**.
abundoso *adj* (*LAm*) abundant.
abur* *interj* so long!
aburguesado *adj*: **un barrio ~** a gentrified area; **un hombre ~** a man who has become bourgeois, a man who has adopted middle-class ways.
aburguesamiento *nm* gentrification; process of becoming bourgeois, conversion to middle-class ways.
aburguesar [1a] **1** *vt casa etc* to gentrify. **2 aburguesarse** *vr* (*persona*) to become bourgeois, adopt middle-class ways.
aburrición *nf* (*LAm*) revulsion, repugnance.
aburridamente *adv* tediously, annoyingly; in a boring manner.
aburrido *adj* (*con 'ser'*) boring, tedious, dull; monotonous, humdrum; (*con 'estar'*) bored.
aburridón *adj* (*And*) rather boring.
aburrimiento *nm* boredom, tedium, monotony.
aburrir [3a] **1** *vt* (**a**) (*gen*) to bore; to tire, weary. (**b**) (‡) *dinero* to blow*; *tiempo* to spend, waste. **2 aburrirse** *vr* to be bored, get bored (*con, de, por* with); **~ como una almeja** (*u* **ostra**) to be bored stiff.
abusado* (*Méx*) **1** *interj* look out!, careful! **2** *adj* (*cauteloso*) watchful, wary; (*astuto*) sharp, on the ball; cunning. **3** *nm*, **abusada** *nf* swot*.
abusador *adj* (*Cono Sur*) abusive.
abusar [1a] *vi* to go too far, exceed one's rights, take advantage; to ask too much; **~ de** *amistad* to presume upon, take unfair advantage of; to impose upon, make unfair demands on; *autoridad, hospitalidad, niño* to abuse; *confianza* to betray; *dinero* to misuse, misapply; **~ del tabaco** to smoke too much.
abusión *nf* abuse; superstition.
abusivamente *adv* improperly; corruptly.
abusivo *adj* improper; corrupt.
abuso *nm* abuse; imposition, unfair demand; betrayal; misuse; misapplication; **~ de autoridad** abuse of authority; **~ de confianza** betrayal of trust, breach of faith; **~ deshonesto** indecent assault; **~ sexual** sexual abuse; **~ del tabaco** excessive smoking, smoking too much.
abusón* 1 *adj* (*egoísta*) selfish; (*engreído*) big-headed*, uppish*; (*insolente*) abusive. **2** *nm*, **abusona** *nf* selfish person; bighead*; **eres un ~** you're too big for your boots.
abute‡ *adv*: **vivir de ~** to live well, live like a prince; *V t* **dabuti**.
abyección *nf* wretchedness, abjectness; degradation; servility.
abyecto *adj* wretched, abject; degraded; servile.
A.C. *nm abr de* **año de Cristo** Anno Domini, AD.
a/c. (**a**) *abr de* **a cuenta** on account. (**b**) *abr de* **al cuidado de** care of, c/o.
acá *adv* (**a**) (*lugar*) here; over here, round here; **~ y allá, ~ y acullá** here and there; hither and thither; **pasearse de ~ para allá** to walk up and down, walk to and fro; **¡más ~!** more over this way!; **más ~ de** on this side of; **tráelo más ~** move it this way, bring it closer; **está muy ~** it's right

here; **no tan ~** not so close, not so far this way; **¡ven ~!, ¡vente para ~!** come over here!

(**b**) (*tiempo*) at this time, now; **de ayer ~** since yesterday; (*LAm*) lately, recently; **¿de cuándo ~ sabes tú el francés?** since when do you know French?; **de ~ a poco** of late.

(**c**) (*LAm*: *como demostrativo*) this person (*etc*) here; **~ le contará** he'll tell you about it; **~ es mi señora** and this is my wife.

acabadero* *nm* (*Méx*): **el ~** the limit, the last straw.

acabado 1 *adj* (**a**) (*completo*) finished, complete; (*perfecto*) perfect; *producto* finished; (*fig*) consummate, masterly, polished.

(**b**) (*viejo*) old, worn out; (*Med*) ruined in health, wrecked; (*LAm*: *flaco*) thin; (*Méx*: *rendido*) exhausted; **está muy ~** (*Méx*) he's looking very old.

(**c**) **él, ~ de llegar ...**, immediately after his arrival he ...

2 *n* (*Téc*) finish; **buen ~** high finish; **~ brillo** gloss finish; **~ satinado** matt finish.

acabador(a) *nm/f* (*Téc*) finisher.

acabalar [1a] *vt* to complete.

acaballadero *nm* stud farm.

acaballado* *adj* (*Cono Sur*) clumsy, gauche.

acaballar [1a] *vt yegua* to cover.

acabamiento *nm* finishing, completion; end; death; (*Méx*: *agotamiento*) exhaustion.

acabar [1a] **1** *vt* (*gen*) to finish, complete, conclude; (*dar el toque final a*) to round off, put the finishing touches to; (*matar*) to kill, kill off, destroy; (*LAm*: *hablar mal de*) to speak ill of.

2 *vi* (**a**) (*terminar*) to finish, end, come to an end; (*morir*) to die; **y no acaba** and there's no sign of it coming to an end; **es cosa de nunca ~** there's no end to it; **¡acabáramos!** at last!; get to the point!; now I understand! *o* I get it!; **~ mal** to come to a sticky end; **la palabra acaba con Z** the word ends in a Z; **el palo acaba en punta** the stick ends in a point.

(**b**) **~ con** to put an end to, make an end of; to destroy, finish off, put paid to; *abuso* to stop, put an end to; *recursos* to exhaust, use up; **esto acabará conmigo** this will be the end of me.

(**c**) **~ de** + *infin* to have just + *ptp*; **acabo de verle** I have just seen him; **acababa de hacerlo** I had just done it; **cuando acabó de escribirlo** when he finished writing it; **cuando acabemos de pagarlo** when we finish paying for it; **¡acaba de parir!*** spit it out!*; **no lo acabo de entender** I don't fully understand it, I can't quite understand it; **no me acaba de convencer** I'm not altogether satisfied with it; **para ~ de arreglarlo** to make matters worse.

(**d**) **~** + *ger*, **~ por** + *infin* to end up by + *ger*, finish up by + *ger*; **acabó aceptándolo** he finally accepted it, eventually he accepted it, he ended up (by) accepting it.

(**e**) (*LAm*⁑: *eyacular*) to come⁑.

3 acabarse *vr* (**a**) (*terminar*) to finish, stop, come to an end; (*morir*) to die; (*fig*: *esp LAm*) to wear o.s. out; to be all over (and done with); (*existencias*) to run out, be exhausted; (*provisión*) to fail; **¡se acabó!** it's all over!; (*) that was the end of that!; it's all up; **... y se acabó** ... and that's the end of the matter; **todo se acabó para él*** he's had it*; **¡un minuto más y se acabó!** one more minute and that will be it!

(**b**) (*con pron pers indirecto*) **se me acabó el tabaco** I ran out of cigarettes; **se nos acabará la gasolina** we shall soon be out of petrol; **se me acaba la paciencia** my patience is wearing thin.

acabildar [1a] *vt* to get together, organize into a group.

acabóse* *nm* the end, the limit; **¡es el ~!** it's the absolute limit!; **la fiesta fue el ~** it was the best party ever.

acacia *nf* acacia; **~ falsa** locust-tree.

acacito *adv* (*LAm*) = **acá**.

achetear [1a] *vt* to slap, punch.

acachihuite *nm* (*Méx*) (*paja*) straw, hay; (*cesto*) straw basket.

academia *nf* (*gen*) academy; learned society; (*escuela*) (private) school; **~ de baile** school of dance; **~ de comercio** business school; **~ de conductores** driving-school; **~ gastronómica** domestic science college; **~ de idiomas** language school; **~ de interpretación** drama school; **~ militar** military academy; **~ de música** school of music, conservatoire; **la Real A~** the Spanish Academy; **la Real A~ de la Historia** the Spanish Academy of History.

académico 1 *adj* academic (*t fig*). **2** *nm*, **académica** *nf* academician, member (of an academy); fellow (of a learned society); **~ de número** full member of an academy.

acaecer [2d] *vi* to happen, occur; to take place; to befall; **acaeció que ...** it came about that ...

acaecimiento *nm* happening, occurrence.

acahual *nm* (*Méx*) (*girasol*) sunflower; (*yerba*) tall grass.

acáis⁑ *nmpl* peepers⁑, eyes.

acalambrarse [1a] *vr* to get cramp.

acalaminado *adj* (*Cono Sur*) *camino etc* rough, uneven, bumpy.

acalenturarse [1a] *vr* to get feverish.

acaloradamente *adv* (*fig*) heatedly, excitedly.

acalorado *adj* heated, hot; tired; (*fig*) *discusión, palabras* heated, excited; *defensor* passionate; (*agitado*) agitated.

acaloramiento *nm* ardour, heat; vehemence, passion; anger.

acalorar [1a] **1** *vt* (*calentar*) to make hot, warm up; (*sobrecalentar*) to overheat; (*cansar*) to tire; (*fig*) *mente* to inflame, excite; *pasiones* to inflame; *audiencia* to excite, work up; *ambición etc* to stir up, encourage.

2 acalorarse *vr* to get hot, become overheated; (*fig*: *persona*) to get excited, get worked up; to get angry, get het up* (*por* about); (*discusión*) to become heated; (*al hablar*) to speak passionately.

acalórico *adj* low-calorie (*atr*), low in calories.

acaloro *nm* anger.

acalote *nm* (*Méx*) channel.

acallamiento *nm* silencing, quietening; pacification.

acallar [1a] *vt* to silence, quieten, hush; (*fig*) *persona* to assuage, pacify; *crítica, duda* to silence.

acamar [1a] *vt cosecha etc* to beat down, lay.

acamastronarse [1a] *vr* (*LAm*) to get crafty, become artful.

acampada *nf* camp.

acampado, -a *nm/f* camper.

acampanado *adj* bell-shaped; **pantalones ~s** bell-bottomed trousers.

acampar [1a] **1** *vi* to camp; to encamp. **2 acamparse** *vr* to camp.

acampo *nm* (common) pasture.

acanalado *adj* grooved, furrowed; striated; fluted; *hierro* corrugated.

acanaladura *nf* groove, furrow; striation; fluting (*t Arquit*); corrugation.

acanalar [1a] *vt* to groove, furrow; to flute; to corrugate.

acanallado *adj* disreputable, low; worthless; degenerate.

acanelado *adj* cinnamon flavoured (*o* coloured).

acantilado 1 *adj risco* steep, sheer; *costa* (*sobre el agua*) rocky; (*debajo del agua*) shelving. **2** *nm* cliff.

acanto *nm* acanthus.

acantonamiento *nm* (**a**) (*lugar*) cantonment. (**b**) (*acto*) billeting, quartering.

acantonar [1a] *vt* to billet, quarter (*en* on).

acaparador 1 *adj* acquisitive; **instintos ~es** acquisitive instincts; **tendencia ~a** monopolizing tendency.

2 *nm*, **acaparadora** *nf* monopolizer, monopolist; profiteer; hoarder.

acaparamiento *nm* monopolizing; cornering the market (*de* in); hoarding.

acaparar [1a] *vt* (*Com*) *comercio* to monopolize; *productos* to corner, corner the market in; *víveres etc* to hoard; (*fig*) to hog, keep for o.s.; *interés* to hold, absorb; **los turistas acaparan los cafés** the tourists monopolize the cafés, the tourists take over the cafés; **ella acapara la atención** she occupies everyone's attention.

acapetate *nm* (*Méx*) straw mat.

acapillar⁑ [1a] *vt* (*Méx*) to grab, take hold of.

acapullado *adj flor* in bud.

acápite *nm* (*LAm*) (*párrafo*) paragraph; (*título*) subheading; caption; **punto ~** full stop, new paragraph.

acapulqueño (*Méx*) **1** *adj* of Acapulco. **2** *nm*, **acapulqueña** *nf* native (*o* inhabitant) of Acapulco; **los ~s** the people of Acapulco.

acaracolado *adj* spiral, winding, twisting.

acaramelado *adj* (*sabor*) toffee-flavoured; (*color*) toffee-coloured; (*fig*) sugary, over-sweet; cloying; over-polite; **estaban ~s** (*amantes*) they were besotted with each other, they had eyes only for each other.

acar(e)ar [1a] *vt personas* to bring face to face; *peligro etc* to face, face up to; to confront.

acardenalar [1a] **1** *vt* to bruise. **2 acardenalarse** *vr* to get bruised, go black and blue.

acariciador *adj* caressing.

acariciar [1b] *vt* (**a**) (*gen*) to caress, fondle, stroke; *animal* to pat, stroke; (*rozar*) to brush, touch lightly.

(**b**) (*fig*) *esperanza* to cherish, cling to; *proyecto* to have in mind; to toy with.

acaricida *nm* (*Cono Sur*) insecticide.

ácaro *nm* (*Zool*) mite.

acarraladura* *nf* (*And, Cono Sur*) run, ladder (*in stocking*).

acarreadizo *adj* transportable, that can be transported.

acarreado, -a *nm/f* (*Méx*) peasant bussed in by the government in order to vote.

acarrear [1a] *vt* (**a**) (*transportar*) to transport, haul, cart, carry; (*persona*) to lug about, lug along; (*río*) to carry along, bring down.

(**b**) (*fig*) to cause, occasion, bring with it, bring in its train (*o* wake); to result in; to give rise to; **ello le acarreó muchos disgustos** it brought him lots of troubles; **acarreó la caída del gobierno** it led to the fall of the government.

acarreo *nm* transport, haulage, cartage, carriage; **gastos de ~, precio de ~** transport charges, haulage.

acarreto *nm* (*Carib, Méx*) = **acarreo.**

acartonado *adj* (*enjuto*) wizened; (*seco*) shrivelled; (*como cartón*) like cardboard.

acartonarse [1a] *vr* to get like cardboard; (*fig*) to become wizened; to shrivel up.

acartuchado* *adj* (*Cono Sur*) stuffy, stuck-up*.

acarvamiento *nm* erosion.

acaserarse* [1a] *vr* (*And*) (††) to become attached; (*Com*) to become a regular customer (*of a shop*); (*sentar la cabeza*) to settle down; (*And, Carib*: *quedar en casa*) to stay at home.

acaso 1 *adv* (**a**) (*gen*) perhaps, maybe; by chance; **~ venga** maybe he'll come; **por si ~** just in case; **por si ~ viene** if by any chance he comes; **por si ~ viniera** just in case he should come; **si ~ se necesita, llévalo** in case it should be needed, take it; **si ~** (*Méx*) at best, at most; **si ~ llegaré a cenar** (*Méx*) at best I'll arrive in time for supper.

(**b**) (*preguntas retóricas*) **¿~ yo lo sé?** how would I know?; **¿~ no quiere?** doesn't he want to, then?; **¿~ no te lo he dicho cien veces?** haven't I told you a hundred times?

2 *nm* chance, accident, coincidence; **al ~** at random; **por ~, por un ~** by chance.

acastañado *adj* (*color*) hazel.

acatamiento *nm* respect (*a* for); awe, reverence; deference.

acatar [1a] *vt* (**a**) (*respetar*) to respect; (*reverenciar*) to hold in awe, revere; (*subordinarse a*) to defer to, treat with deference; *ley* to obey, respect, observe. (**b**) (*LAm*) to notice, observe. (**c**) (*Cono Sur, Méx*: *molestar*) to annoy.

acatarrar [1a] **1** *vt* (*Méx*‡) to harass, pester. **2 acatarrarse** *vr* to catch (a) cold; (*And**: *emborracharse*) to get tight*.

acato *nm* = **acatamiento.**

acatólico, -a *adj, nm/f* non-Catholic.

acaudalado *adj* well-off, affluent.

acaudalar [1a] *vt* to acquire, accumulate; (*pey*) to hoard.

acaudillar [1a] *vt* to lead, command, head.

acceder [2a] *vi* to accede, agree (*a* to); **~ a** to enter, gain admittance to (socially); (*Cono Sur*: *tener acceso*) to gain (*o* have) access to; **~ a una base de datos** to have access to a database; **~ a una graduación superior** to attain a higher rank, be promoted to a higher rank; **~ al trono** to succeed to the throne; **~ a** + *infin* to agree to + *infin.*

accesibilidad *nf* accessibility (*to* a).

accesible *adj* accessible; approachable; **~ a** open to, accessible to.

accesión *nf* (**a**) (*consentimiento*) assent (*a* to); acquiescence (*a* in).

(**b**) (*accesorio*) accessory.

(**c**) (*Med*) attack; onset.

accésit *nm invar* consolation prize, second prize.

acceso *nm* (**a**) (*entrada*) entry, admittance, access; **'~ prohibido', 'prohibido el ~'** 'no admittance'; **de fácil ~** of easy access, easy to approach; **éstos están al ~ de todos** these are within reach of everybody, these are available to all; **dar ~ a** to lead to.

(**b**) (*camino*) way, approach, access; (*Aer*) approach; **~s** approaches.

(**c**) (*Inform*) access; **~ aleatorio** random access; **~ directo** direct access; **~ secuencial** sequential access; **~ en serie** serial access; **de ~ múltiple** multi-access.

(**d**) (*Med*) attack, fit; (*de ira etc*) fit, outburst, explosion; (*de generosidad*) fit, surge.

accesoria *nf* annex, outbuilding.

accesorio 1 *adj* accessory; dependent, subordinate; incidental.

2 *nm* accessory, attachment, extra; (*prenda de vestir*) accessory; **~s** (*Téc*) accessories, spare parts; (*Aut*) optional extras; (*Teat*) properties.

accidentado 1 *adj superficie* uneven; *horizonte etc* broken, uneven; *terreno* hilly; rough, rugged; *vida* stormy, troubled, eventful; *historial* variable, up-and-down; *viaje* eventful; (*mentalmente*) agitated, upset; (*Med*) injured; (*Carib Aut*) broken down; (*LAm euf*) hunchbacked.

2 *nm,* **accidentada** *nf* injured person; casualty; person involved in an accident.

accidental *adj* (*gen*) accidental; (*sin querer*) unintentional; (*incidente*) incidental; (*fortuito*) casual; (*fugaz*) brief, transient; **un empleo ~** a temporary job.

accidentalidad *nf* accident rate, number of accidents.

accidentalmente *adv* accidentally, by chance; unintentionally.

accidentarse [1a] *vr* to have an accident; (*Méx Aer etc*) to crash.

accidente *nm* (**a**) (*gen*) accident; mishap, misadventure; **por ~** by accident, accidentally, by chance; **~ aéreo** plane crash; **~ de carretera** road accident; **~ de circulación** traffic accident; **~ laboral, ~ de trabajo** industrial accident; industrial injury; **~ múltiple** multiple accident, pile-up; **una vida sin ~s** an uneventful life; **hay ~s que no se pueden prever** accidents will happen; **sufrir un ~** to have an accident, meet with an accident.

(**b**) (*Med*) faint, swoon.

(**c**) (*Ling*) accidence.

(**d**) **~s** (*de superficie*) unevenness; (*de terreno*) hilliness; roughness, ruggedness.

(**e**) **~ de la cara** (*Méx*) feature.

acción *nf* (**a**) (*gen*) action; act, deed; (*de droga etc*) effect; **buena ~** good deed, kind act; **mala ~** evil deed, unkind thing (to do); **hombre de ~** man of action; **~ de gracias** thanksgiving; **mecanismo de ~ retardada** delayed-action mechanism; **por ~ química** by chemical action; **¡~ y kilometraje!*** (*Carib*) let's get some action!; **dejar sin ~** to put out of action; **estar en ~*** (*Carib*) to be busy; **ganar la ~ a uno** to forestall sb; **unir la ~ a la palabra** to suit the deed to the word.

(**b**) (*de mano*) movement, gesture.

(**c**) (*Mil*) action, engagement; **entrar en ~** to go into action.

(**d**) (*Teat*: *argumento*) action, plot, story line; **~ aparte** by-play.

(**e**) (*Teat*: *interpretación*) oratory, delivery; acting.

(**f**) (*Jur*) action, lawsuit; **~ penal** trial; **ejercitar una ~, emprender acciones judiciales** to bring an action, take legal action.

(**g**) (*Com, Fin*) share; **acciones** stock(s), shares; **~ liberada** bonus share, paid-up share; **~ ordinaria** ordinary share, common stock (*US*); **~ preferente** preference share, preferred stock (*US*); **~ primitiva** ordinary share, common stock (*US*); **~ prioritaria** priority share.

accionado *nm* shares, shareholding; **~ mayoritario** majority shareholding.

accionar [1a] **1** *vt* (*Mec*) to work, drive, propel; **bomba** to set off, detonate; (*Inform*) to drive. **2** *vi* to gesticulate; to wave one's hands about.

accionariado *nm* (**a**) (*acciones*) (total of) shares, shareholding. (**b**) (*personas*) shareholders (collectively).

accionarial *adj* share (*atr*); **paquete ~, participación ~** shareholding.

accionario *adj* share (*atr*), of (*o* relating to) stocks and shares.

accionista *nmf* shareholder, stockholder; **~ mayoritario** majority shareholder.

accisa *nf* excise duty.

ACE ['aθe] *nf abr de* **Acción Católica Española.**

acebo *nm* holly, holly tree.

acebuche *nm* (**a**) (*Bot*) wild olive-tree; (*madera*) olive wood. (**b**) (*) yokel.

acecinar [1a] **1** *vt carne* to salt, cure. **2 acecinarse** *vr* to get very thin.

acechadera *nf* ambush; hiding place; (*Caza*) hide.

acechador(a) *nm/f* spy, watcher, observer.

acechar [1a] *vt* (*espiar*) to spy on, watch, observe; (*esperar*) to lie in wait for; (*amenazar*) to threaten, beset; (*Caza*) to stalk; **~ la ocasión** to wait one's chance.

acecho *nm* spying, watching; (*Mil*) ambush; **estar al ~, estar en ~** to lie in wait, be on the watch; **cazar al ~** to stalk.

acechón* *adj* spying, prying; **hacer la acechona** to spy, pry.

acedar [1a] **1** *vt* to turn sour, make bitter; (*fig*) to sour, embitter; to vex.

2 acedarse *vr* to turn sour; (*Bot*) to wither, yellow.

acedera *nf* sorrel.

acedía[1] *nf* acidity, sourness; (*Med*) heartburn; (*fig*) sourness, unpleasantness, asperity.

acedía[2] *nf* (*pez*) plaice.

acedo *adj* acid, sour; (*fig*) sour, unpleasant, disagreeable.

acéfalo *adj* headless; (*Pol etc*) leaderless.

aceitada‡ *nf* (*Cono Sur*) bribe, backhander*.

aceitar [1a] *vt* to oil, lubricate; (*Carib, Cono Sur**: *sobornar*) to bribe, grease the palm of.

aceite *nm* (**a**) (*gen*) oil; (*de oliva*) olive-oil; (*perfume*) essence; ~ **alcanforado** camphorated oil; ~ **de algodón** cottonseed oil; ~ **de almendra** almond oil; ~ **de ballena** whale-oil; ~ **de cacahuete** peanut oil; ~ **de coco** coconut oil; ~ **de colza** rape-seed oil; ~ **combustible** fuel-oil; ~ **de girasol** sunflower oil; ~ **de hígado de bacalao** cod-liver oil; ~ **de linaza** linseed oil; ~ **lubricante** lubricating oil; ~ **de maíz** corn oil; ~ **de oliva puro** pure olive-oil; ~ **de oliva refinado** refined olive-oil; ~ **de ricino** castor oil; ~ **de soja** soya oil; ~ **vegetal** vegetable oil; ~ **virgen de oliva** pure olive-oil; **echar ~ al fuego** to add fuel to the flames.

(**b**) (‡: *droga*) hash*; (*Méx etc*) LSD.

aceitera *nf* (**a**) (*de mesa*) olive-oil dish, olive-oil bottle; **~s** oil and vinegar set.

(**b**) (*Mec*) oilcan.

aceitero 1 *adj* oil (*atr*). **2** *nm* oil merchant.

aceitón *nm* thick oil, dirty oil.

aceitoso *adj* oily.

aceituna *nf* olive; ~ **rellena** stuffed olive.

aceitunado *adj* olive, olive-coloured, olive-skinned.

aceitunero, -a *nm/f* (*Com*) dealer in olives; (*Agr*) olive-picker.

aceituno 1 *adj* (*LAm*) *color* olive, olive-coloured. **2** *nm* (**a**) (*Bot*) olive-tree. (**b**) (‡) Civil Guard.

aceleración *nf* acceleration (*t Mec*); speeding up, hastening.

acelerada *nf* acceleration, speed-up.

aceleradamente *adv* quickly, speedily.

acelerado* *adj* (*LAm*) (*nervioso*) jumpy, nervous; (*impaciente*) impatient.

acelerador *nm* accelerator, gas pedal (*US*); ~ **de partículas** particle accelerator; **apretar el ~, pisar el ~** (*fig*) to speed things up, step up the pace.

acelerar [1a] **1** *vt* to accelerate (*t Mec*); to speed up, hasten, expedite; *paso* to quicken; ~ **la marcha** to go faster, accelerate.

2 acelerarse *vr* (**a**) (*apresurarse*) to hurry, hasten.

(**b**) (*LAm*) (*excitarse*) to get agitated, get jumpy; (*enloquecer*) to lose one's head.

acelerón *nm* (*fig*) leap forward; rapid increase, rapid improvement.

acelga *nf* chard; silver-beet.

acémila *nf* beast of burden, mule; (*fig*) mule-headed person.

acemilero *nm* muleteer.

acendrado *adj* pure, unblemished, refined; **de ~ carácter español** of a typically (*o* thoroughly) Spanish nature.

acendrar [1a] *vt* to purify; (*Téc, Liter etc*) to refine.

acensuar [1d] *vt* to tax.

acento *nm* (*gen*) accent; (*énfasis*) stress, emphasis; (*modulación*) tone, inflection; (*poét*) voice, words; ~ **agudo** acute accent; ~ **ortográfico** written accent; ~ **tónico** tonic accent, stress; **con fuerte ~ andaluz** with a strong Andalusian accent; **en ~ de cierto asombro** in a somewhat surprised tone; **el ~ cae en la segunda sílaba** the stress falls on the second syllable; **poner ~ en algo** (*énfasis*) to emphasize (*o* stress) sth.

acentor *nm*: ~ **común** hedgesparrow, dunnock.

acentuación *nf* accentuation.

acentuado *adj* accented, stressed.

acentuamiento *nm* (*Cono Sur*) accent, emphasis.

acentuar [1e] **1** *vt* to accent, stress; to emphasize; (*fig*) to accentuate; (*Inform*) to highlight.

2 acentuarse *vr* (**a**) (*palabra*) to be stressed, be accented; **esta palabra se acentúa en la** *u* this word is stressed on the *u*. (**b**) (*fig*) to become more noticeable, be accentuated; **se acentúa la tendencia a la baja en la Bolsa** the slide on the Stock Exchange is accelerating.

aceña *nf* water mill.

aceñero *nm* miller.

acepción *nf* (**a**) (*Ling*) sense, meaning. (**b**) (*preferencia*) preference; **sin ~ de persona** without respect of persons, without partiality of any kind.

acepilladora *nf* planer, planing machine.

acepilladura *nf* wood-shaving.

acepillar [1a] *vt* (**a**) to brush; (*Téc*) to plane, shave. (**b**) (*adular*) to flatter.

aceptabilidad *nf* acceptability.

aceptable *adj* acceptable, passable.

aceptación *nf* (*gen*) acceptance; (*aprobación*) approval, approbation; (*status*) popularity, standing; (*Com*) acceptance; **mandar algo a la ~** to send sth on approval; **este producto tendrá una ~ enorme** this product will get a big welcome, this product is sure to be very popular; **no tener ~** to be unsuccessful.

aceptar [1a] **1** *vt* to accept; to approve; *trabajo* to accept, take on, undertake, agree to do; *hechos* to accept, face.

2 *vi*: ~ **a** + *infin* to agree to + *infin*.

acepto *adj* acceptable, agreeable (*a, de* to), welcomed (*a, de* by).

acequia *nf* (**a**) (*Agr*) irrigation ditch, irrigation channel; (*de calle*) gutter. (**b**) (*LAm*) (*arroyo*) stream; (*alcantarilla*) sewer.

acera *nf* pavement, sidewalk (*US*); row (of houses); **los de la ~ de enfrente*** the gays*.

acerado *adj* (*Téc*) steel (*atr*), steely; (*con punta*) steel-tipped; (*fig*) sharp, cutting, biting.

acerar [1a] **1** *vt* (*Téc*) to make into steel; *punta etc* to put a steel tip (*etc*) on; (*fig*) to harden; to make sharp, make biting.

2 acerarse *vr* to toughen o.s., steel o.s.

acerbamente *adv* (*fig*) harshly, scathingly.

acerbidad *nf* acerbity; sourness; harshness.

acerbo *adj sabor* sharp, bitter, sour; (*fig*) harsh, scathing; **tener un odio ~ a algo** to hate sth bitterly.

acerca de *prep* about, on, concerning.

acercamiento *nm* (**a**) (*lit*) approach, bringing near, drawing near. (**b**) (*fig*) reconciliation; (*Pol*) rapprochement.

acercar [1g] **1** *vt* to bring near(er); to bring over; **~ algo al oído** to put sth to one's ear.

2 acercarse *vr* (**a**) (*gen*) to approach, come near, draw near; ~ **a** (*lit*) to approach; to come close to; (*) to pop in, pop round (*a* to), drop in (*a* at, on); (*fig*) to approach, verge on; ~ **a uno** to go up to sb, come up to sb; (*LAm*) to approach sb, open negotiations with sb.

(**b**) (*fig*: *amantes*) to be reconciled, achieve a reconciliation; (*Pol*) to make a rapprochement.

ácere *nm* maple.

acería *nf* steelworks, steel mill.

acerico *nm* small cushion; (*Cos*) pincushion.

acero *nm* steel (*t fig*); ~ **bruto** crude steel; ~ **colado,** ~ **fundido** cast steel; **~s especiales** special steels; ~ **inoxidable** stainless steel; ~ **al manganeso** manganese steel; **tener buenos ~s** (*aguante*) to have guts; (*hambre*) to be ravenously hungry.

acerote *nm* (*holgazán*) idler, loafer.

acérrimo *adj* (*fig*) *defensor etc* very strong, staunch, out-and-out; *enemigo* bitter.

acerrojar [1a] *vt* to lock, bolt.

acertado *adj conjetura, solución* correct, right; successful; *respuesta* sensible, wise, sound; *idea* bright, good; *proyecto* well-conceived; *observación* apt, fitting, well-aimed; **eso no me parece muy ~** that doesn't seem right to me; **en eso no anduvo muy ~** that was not very sensible of him; **lo ~ es hacerlo ahora** it's best to do it now.

acertante 1 *adj*: **tarjeta ~** winning card. **2** *nmf* (*de problema etc*) solver; winner; (*en quinielas*) forecaster; **hubo 9 ~s** there were 9 successful solvers (*o* forecasters).

acertar [1j] **1** *vt blanco* to hit; *solución* to get, get right, guess correctly; *objeto perdido* to find, succeed in tracing; *resultado* to achieve, succeed in reaching; **a ver si lo acertamos esta vez** let's see if we can get it right this time; **lo has acertado** you've guessed it, that's right; **no aciertas el modo de hacerlo** you don't manage to find the proper way to do it.

2 *vi* (**a**) (*dar en el blanco*) to hit the mark; (*fig*) to hit the nail on the head; (*tener razón*) to be right, get it right; (*conjeturar*) to guess right; (*lograrlo*) to manage it, be successful.

(**b**) ~ **a** + *infin* to happen to + *infin*; to manage to + *infin*, succeed in + *ger*.

(**c**) ~ **con algo** to happen on sth, hit on sth; to find sth (without trouble).

(**d**) (*Bot*) to flourish, do well.

acertijo *nm* riddle, puzzle.

acervo *nm* (*montón*) heap, pile; (*provisión*) stock, store;

(*Jur*) undivided estate; common property; ~ **arqueológico** arch(a)eological wealth, arch(a)eological riches; ~ **comunitario** (*CEE*) community patrimony; ~ **cultural** cultural tradition; cultural wealth; **aportar algo al ~ común** to bring sth to the common stock.

acetato *nm* acetate; ~ **de vinilo** vinyl acetate.

acético *adj* acetic.

acetilénico *adj* acetylene (*atr*).

acetileno *nm* acetylene.

acetona *nf* acetone.

acetre *nm* small pail; (*Ecl*) holy water vessel, portable stoup.

acezar [1f] *vi* to puff, pant.

aciago *adj* ill-fated, ill-omened, fateful.

aciano *nm* cornflower.

acíbar *nm* aloes; (*fig*) sorrow, bitterness.

acibarar [1a] *vt* to add bitter aloes to, make bitter; (*fig*) to embitter; ~ **la vida a uno** to make sb's life a misery.

acicalado *adj metal* polished, bright and clean; *persona* smart, neat, spruce; (*pey*) dapper, overdressed.

acicalar [1a] **1** *vt metal* to polish, burnish, clean; *persona etc* to dress up, bedeck, adorn.

2 acicalarse *vr* to smarten o.s. up, spruce o.s. up; to get dressed up.

acicate *nm* spur; (*fig*) spur, incentive, stimulus.

acícula *nf* (*Bot*) needle.

acidez *nf* acidity.

acidia *nf* indolence, apathy, sloth.

acidificar [1g] **1** *vt* to acidify. **2 acidificarse** *vr* to acidify.

acidillo *adj* slightly sour.

ácido 1 *adj* (**a**) *sabor, olor* sharp, sour, acid. (**b**) **estar** ~ (*LAm**) to be great*, be fabulous*.

2 *nm* (**a**) acid; ~ **ascórbico** ascorbic acid; ~ **carbólico** carbolic acid; ~ **carbónico** carbonic acid; ~ **cianhídrico** hydrocyanic acid; ~ **clorhídrico** hydrochloric acid; ~ **graso saturado** saturated fatty acid; ~ **lisérgico** lysergic acid; ~ **nicotínico** nicotinic acid; ~ **nítrico** nitric acid; ~ **nitroso** nitrous acid; ~ **nucleico** nucleic acid; ~ **oxálico** oxalic acid; ~ **ribonucleico** ribonucleic acid; ~ **sulfúrico** sulphuric acid; ~ **úrico** uric acid. (**b**) (*: *droga*) acid*; (*pastilla*) LSD tablet.

acidófilo *adj* acidophilous.

acidulante *nm* acidulant, acidifier.

acídulo *adj* acidulous; disagreeable, sharp.

acierto *nm* (**a**) (*éxito*) success; (*tiro*) good shot, hit; (*conjetura*) good guess; (*idea*) good idea; sensible choice, wise move; **fue un ~ suyo** it was a sensible choice on his part.

(**b**) (*talento*) skill, ability; (*lo apropiado*) aptness; (*juicio*) wisdom; (*discreción*) discretion; **obrar con** ~ to act sensibly; to do well; **el periódico que con todo ~ dirige X** the paper which X edits so well.

aciguatado* *adj* (*Méx*) silly, stupid.

aciguatarse [1a] *vr* (*Carib, Méx*) to grow stupid; (*: *enloquecer*) to go crazy, lose one's head.

acitrón *nm* (**a**) (*Culin*) candied citron. (**b**) (*LAm Bot*) bishop's weed, goutweed.

acizañar* [1a] *vt* to stir things*, cause trouble.

aclamación *nf* acclamation; applause, acclaim; **entre las aclamaciones del público** amid the applause of the audience; **elegir a uno por** ~ to elect sb by acclamation.

aclamar [1a] *vt* to acclaim; to applaud; ~ **a uno por jefe** to acclaim sb (as) leader, hail sb as leader.

aclaración *nf* (**a**) (*de ropa*) rinse, rinsing. (**b**) (*explicación*) clarification, explanation, elucidation. (**c**) (*Met*) brightening, clearing up.

aclarado *nm* rinse.

aclarar [1a] **1** *vt* (**a**) *ropa* to rinse; *líquido etc* to thin, thin down; (*LAm*) to clear; *bosque* to clear, thin (out).

(**b**) (*fig*) *problema* to clarify, cast light on, explain; *duda* to resolve, remove.

2 *vi* (*Met*) to brighten, clear, clear up.

3 aclararse* *vr* to catch on, get it*; **no me aclaro** I can't work it out.

aclaratorio *adj* explanatory; illuminating.

aclayos‡ *nmpl* (*Méx*) eyes.

aclimatación *nf*, **aclimatización** *nf* acclimatization, acclimation (*US*).

aclimatar [1a], **aclimatizar** [1f] **1** *vt* to acclimatize, acclimate (*US*). **2 aclimatizarse** *vr* to acclimatize o.s., get acclimatized, acclimate (*US*), get acclimated (*US*); ~ **a algo** (*fig*) to get used to sth.

acne *nf*, **acné** *nf* acne.

ACNUR [ak'nur] *nm abr de* **Alto Comisariado de las Naciones Unidas para los Refugiados** United Nations High Commission for Refugees, UNHCR.

-aco, -aca *V* **Aspects of Word Formation in Spanish 2.**

acobardar [1a] **1** *vt* to daunt, intimidate, cow, unnerve.

2 acobardarse *vr* to be frightened, get frightened; to flinch, shrink back (*ante* from, at).

acobe* *nm* (*Carib*) iron.

acobrado *adj* copper-coloured, coppery.

acocear [1a] *vt* to kick; (*fig*: *maltratar*) to ill-treat, trample on; (*insultar*) to insult.

acocil *nm* (*Méx*) freshwater shrimp; **estar como un** ~ to be red in the face.

acochambrar* [1a] *vt* (*Méx*) to make filthy.

acocharse [1a] *vr* to squat, crouch.

acochinar‡ [1a] *vt* to bump off‡.

acodado *adj* bent; elbowed.

acodalar [1a] *vt* to shore up, prop up.

acodar [1a] **1** *vt brazo* to lean, rest; *vid etc* to layer. **2 acodarse** *vr*: ~ **en** to lean on; **acodado en** leaning on, resting on; ~ **hacia** to bend towards, curve towards.

acodiciarse [1b] *vr*: ~ **a** to covet.

acodo *nm* (*Agr*) layer.

acogedizo *adj* gathered at random.

acogedor *adj* welcoming, friendly, hospitable, warm; *cuarto* snug, cosy; **un ambiente** ~ a friendly atmosphere.

acoger [2c] **1** *vt visitante etc* to welcome, receive; *refugiado* to take in, give refuge to; *fugitivo* to harbour; *idea* to receive; *palabra nueva, hecho etc* to accept, admit.

2 acogerse *vr* to take refuge; (*fig*) ~ **a** *pretexto* to take refuge in; *recurso* to resort to; *promesa* to avail o.s. of; ~ **a la ley** to have recourse to the law; ~ **a uno** to ask sb's help.

acogible *adj* (*Cono Sur*) acceptable.

acogida *nf* (*recepción*) welcome, reception; (*aprobación*) acceptance, admittance; (*refugio*) shelter, refuge, asylum; (*de ríos*) meeting place; **dar ~ a** to accept; **tener buena** ~ to be welcomed, be well received; **¿qué ~ tuvo la idea?** how was the idea received?

acogollar [1a] (*Agr*) **1** *vt* to cover up, protect. **2** *vi* to sprout.

acogotar [1a] *vt* (*matar*) to fell, kill (with a blow on the neck); (*dejar sin sentido*) to knock down, lay out; (*LAm*) to have at one's mercy; (*agarrar*) to grab round the neck; (*) to press, put pressure on, lean on*; ~ **a uno** (*Cono Sur*) to harass sb for payment.

acohombrar [1a] *vt* (*Agr*) to earth up.

acojinar [1a] *vt* (*Téc*) to cushion.

acojonador‡ *adj* (*Esp*) = **acojonante.**

acojonamiento‡ *nm* (*Esp*) funk*, fear.

acojonante‡ *adj* (*Esp*) amazing; tremendous*, stupendous; super*, great*.

acojonar‡ [1a] (*Esp*) **1** *vt* (**a**) (*atemorizar*) to put the wind up*, intimidate. (**b**) (*impresionar*) to impress; (*asombrar*) to amaze, overwhelm.

2 acojonarse *vr* (**a**) (*acobardarse*) to back down; (*inquietarse*) to get the wind up*; **¡no te acojones!** take it easy!*

(**b**) (*asombrarse*) to be amazed, be overwhelmed.

acojono‡ *nm* (*Esp*) funk*, fear.

acolada *nf* accolade.

acolchado *adj* quilted, padded; *sobre* padded.

acolchar [1a] *vt* (**a**) (*Téc*) to quilt, pad. (**b**) (*fig*) *golpe etc* to soften.

acólito *nm* (*Ecl*) acolyte, server, altar-boy; (*fig*) acolyte, minion.

acollador *nm* (*Náut*) lanyard.

acollar [1l] *vt* (*Agr*) to earth up; (*Náut*) to caulk.

acollarar [1a] *vt bueyes* to yoke, harness; (*atar*) to tie by the neck; *perro etc* to put a collar on; (*Cono Sur*: *mujer*) to trap into marriage.

acollerar [1a] **1** *vti* to gather, herd together. **2 acollerarse** *vr* = **1.**

acomedido *adj* (*LAm*) (*generoso*) helpful, obliging; (*solícito*) concerned, solicitous.

acomedirse [3k] *vr* (*LAm*) to offer to help; ~ **a hacer algo** to do sth willingly.

acometedor *adj* energetic, enterprising; *toro* fierce.

acometer [2a] *vt* (**a**) (*violentamente*) to attack; to set upon, rush on, assail; (*toro*) to charge.

(**b**) *tarea* to undertake, attempt; *asunto* to tackle, deal with; *construcción* to begin, start on.

(**c**) (*sueño etc*) to overcome; (*temor*) to seize, take hold of; (*duda*) to assail; (*enfermedad*) to attack; **le acometieron dudas** he was assailed by doubts, he began to have doubts; **me acometió la tristeza** I was overcome with sadness.

acometida *nf* (**a**) (*violento*) attack, assault; (*de toro*) charge. (**b**) (*Elec etc*) connection.

acometimiento *nm* attack; ~ **y agresión** (*Méx Jur*) assault and battery.

acometividad *nf* (**a**) (*energía*) energy, enterprise. (**b**) (*agresividad*) aggressiveness; (*de toro*) fierceness; (*Cono Sur*) touchiness; **mostrar** ~ to show fight.

acomodable *adj* adaptable; suitable.

acomodación *nf* accommodation; adaptation; arrangement.

acomodadizo *adj* accommodating, obliging; acquiescent; (*pey*) pliable, easy-going.

acomodado *adj* (**a**) (*apropiado*) suitable, fit; *precio* moderate; *artículo* moderately priced. (**b**) *persona, familia etc* well-to-do, wealthy, well-off.

acomodador *nm* (*Teat etc*) usher.

acomodadora *nf* (*Teat etc*) usherette.

acomodamiento *nm* (**a**) (*cualidad*) suitability, convenience. (**b**) (*acto*) arrangement, agreement.

acomodar [1a] **1** *vt* (**a**) (*ajustar*) to adjust, accommodate, adapt (*a* to); ~ **a uno con algo** to supply sb with sth.

(**b**) (*encontrar sitio para*) to fit in, find room for, accommodate; *persona* to take in, lodge.

(**c**) (*adaptar*) to suit, adapt (*a* to); *colores* to match; **¿puede ~me esta lana?** can you match this wool for me?; ~ **un ejemplo a un caso** to apply an example to a case in point.

(**d**) (*Mec etc*) to repair, adjust, put right.

(**e**) *enemigos, puntos de vista* to reconcile.

(**f**) *criado etc* to place; *obrero* to give a job to, take on; (*Teat*) to show to a seat; *visitante* to make comfortable, make feel at home; *enfermo* to make comfortable; *niño* to settle; (*Cono Sur, Méx*) *amigo* to fix up (with a job); **acomodé a mi primo** I fixed my cousin up (with a job).

(**g**) (*Carib*: *estafar*) to con*, trick.

2 *vi* to suit, fit; to be suitable.

3 acomodarse *vr* (**a**) (*conformarse*) to comply, conform; (*adaptarse*) to adapt o.s.

(**b**) (*en un lugar*) to install o.s., settle down; **¡acomódese a su gusto!** make yourself comfortable!, make yourself at home!

(**c**) (*Cono Sur*) (*colocarse*) to fix o.s. up (with a job), pull strings (to get a job); (*) to marry into money.

(**d**) ~ **a** to adapt o.s. to; to settle down to; to comply with, conform with; ~ **a** + *infin* to settle down to + *infin*.

(**e**) ~ **con** to reconcile o.s. to; to come to an agreement with; to comply with, conform with.

(**f**) ~ **de** to provide o.s. with.

acomodaticio *adj* = **acomodadizo**.

acomodo *nm* (**a**) (*arreglo*) arrangement; compromise; (*acuerdo*) agreement, understanding; (*pey*) secret arrangement, secret deal.

(**b**) (*puesto*) post, job; (*LAm pey*) soft job, plum job.

(**c**) (*LAm**: *soborno*) bribe.

acompañado 1 *adj* (**a**) **estar** ~, **ir** ~ to go accompanied, go with sb.

(**b**) *lugar* busy, frequented.

(**c**) **con falda acompañada** with skirt to match, with a skirt of the same colour (*o* pattern *etc*).

(**d**) **estar** ~ (*Carib**) to be drunk.

2 *nm*, **acompañada** *nf* (*LAm*) lover; common-law husband, common-law wife.

acompañamiento *nm* (**a**) (*gen*) accompaniment; **sin** ~ unaccompanied, alone.

(**b**) (*persona*) escort; (*personas*) retinue; (*LAm*) (*entierro*) funeral procession; (*boda*) wedding reception *etc*; (*Teat*) extras.

(**c**) (*Mús*) accompaniment; **con** ~ **de piano** with piano accompaniment; **cantar sin** ~ to sing unaccompanied.

(**d**) (*consecuencias*) sequel, consequences, aftermath; **el terremoto y su** ~ the earthquake and its aftermath.

(**e**) (*Teat*) walk-on parts.

acompañanta *nf* female companion, chaperon; (*Mús*) accompanist.

acompañante *nm* companion; escort; (*Mús*) accompanist.

acompañar [1a] **1** *vt* (**a**) (*gen*) to accompany, go with; (*oficialmente*) to attend; *mujer* to escort, *mujer joven* to chaperon; **prefiero que no me acompañen** I prefer to go alone; **¿quieres que te acompañe?** do you want me to come with you?; ~ **a uno a la puerta** to see sb to the door, see sb out; **seguir acompañando a uno** to keep with sb, stay with sb, not leave sb; **este vino acompaña bien al queso** this wine goes well with the cheese.

(**b**) (*Mús*) to accompany (*a, con* on).

(**c**) (*en carta*) to enclose, attach; (*como apéndice*) to attach; **en el folleto que le acompañamos** in the enclosed brochure.

(**d**) ~ **lo que se ha dicho con** (*o* **de**) **pruebas** to support what one has said with evidence.

(**e**) ~ **a uno en** to join sb in; **le acompaño en el sentimiento** please accept my condolences, I sympathize with you (in your loss).

2 acompañarse *vr* (*Mús*) to accompany o.s. (*con, de* on).

acompaño *nm* (*CAm, Méx*) meeting, group, crowd.

acompasado *adj* rhythmic, regular, measured; (*en habla*) slow; (*de paso*) slow, deliberate, leisurely.

acompasar [1a] *vt* (**a**) (*Mat*) to measure with a compass.

(**b**) (*Mús etc*) to mark the rhythm of; ~ **la dicción** to speak with a marked rhythm.

acomplejado *adj* full of complexes; gravely embarrassed, much put out.

acomplejante *adj* (*Cono Sur*) inhibiting, embarrassing.

acomplejar [1a] **1** *vt* to cause complexes in, give a complex to; to embarrass gravely, cause to be much put out.

2 acomplejarse *vr* to get a complex (*por* about); **¡no te acomplejes!** don't get so worked up!

acompletadores* *nmpl* (*Méx*) beans.

acomunarse [1a] *vr* to join forces.

aconchabarse* [1a] *vr* to gang up*.

aconchado* *nm* (*Méx*) sponger*, scrounger*.

aconchar [1a] **1** *vt* (**a**) (*poner a salvo*) to push to safety.

(**b**) (*Náut*) to beach, run aground; (*viento*) to drive ashore.

(**c**) (*Méx**: *reprender*) to tell off*.

2 aconcharse *vr* (**a**) (*Náut*) to keel over; to run aground.

(**b**) (*Cono Sur*: *líquido*) to settle, clarify.

(**c**) (*: *vivir de otro*) to sponge*, live off somebody else.

acondicionado *adj*: **bien** ~ *persona* genial, affable, nice; *objeto* in good condition; **mal** ~ *persona* bad-tempered, difficult; *objeto* in bad condition; **un laboratorio bien** ~ a well-equipped laboratory.

acondicionador *nm* (*de pelo etc*) conditioner; ~ **de aire** air-conditioner.

acondicionamiento *nm* conditioning; ~ **de aire** air-conditioning.

acondicionar [1a] *vt* (**a**) (*arreglar*) to arrange, prepare, make suitable; (*Téc*) to condition. (**b**) *sala etc* to air-condition.

acongojado *adj* distressed, anguished.

acongojar [1a] **1** *vt* to distress, grieve. **2 acongojarse** *vr* to become distressed, get upset; **¡no te acongojes!** don't get upset!, don't worry!

acónito *nm* (*Bot*) aconite, monkshood.

aconsejable *adj* advisable; sensible, politic; **nada** ~, **poco** ~ inadvisable; **eso no es** ~ that is not advisable; **no sería** ~ **que Vd** + *subj* you would be ill-advised to + *infin*.

aconsejado *adj*: **bien** ~ sensible; well-advised; **mal** ~ ill-advised, rash, ill-considered.

aconsejar [1a] **1** *vt* (**a**) *persona* to advise, counsel; ~ **a uno hacer algo** to advise sb to do sth.

(**b**) *cuidado etc* to advise, recommend; *virtud* to preach.

2 aconsejarse *vr* to seek advice, take advice; ~ **con**, ~ **de** to consult; ~ **mejor** to think better of it.

aconsonantar [1a] *vti* to rhyme (*con* with).

acontecedero *adj* which could happen, possible.

acontecer [2d] *vi* to happen, occur, come about.

acontecimiento *nm* event, happening, occurrence; incident; (*dramático*) happening; **fue realmente un** ~ it was an event of some importance.

acopiar [1b] *vt* to gather (together), collect; (*Com*) to buy up, get a monopoly of; *miel* to collect, hive.

acopio *nm* (**a**) (*acto*) gathering, collecting. (**b**) (*cantidad*) collection; store, stock; (*de madera etc*) stack; (*Cono Sur*) abundance, wealth; **hacer** ~ to stock up (*de* with), lay in stocks (*de* of).

acoplable *adj* attachable.

acoplado 1 *adj*: **un equipo bien** ~ a well coordinated team.

2 *nm* (**a**) (*LAm Aut*) trailer. (**b**) (*Cono Sur**: *parásito*) hanger-on, sponger*; (*intruso*) gatecrasher.

acoplador *nm*: ~ **acústico** acoustic coupler.

acoplamiento *nm* (*Mec*) coupling; joint; (*Elec*) connection; hookup; (*de astronaves*) docking, link-up; (*Zool*) mating; ~ **de manguito** sleeve coupling; ~ **en serie** series connection; ~ **universal** universal joint.

acoplar [1a] **1** *vt* (*Téc*) to couple; to join, fit together; (*Elec*) to connect, join up; *astronaves* to dock, link up; *bueyes* to yoke, hitch; *animales* to mate, pair; *personas* to associate, bring together; (*LAm Ferro*) to couple (up); *opiniones* to reconcile; *proyectos, esfuerzos* to coordinate.

2 acoplarse *vr* (**a**) (*Zool*) to mate, pair.

(**b**) (*astronaves*) to dock, link up (*a* with).

(**c**) (*hacer las paces*) to make it up, be reconciled.

(**d**) (*Elec*) to cause feedback.

acoplo *nm* (*Elec*) feedback.

acoquinamiento *nm* intimidation.

acoquinar [1a] **1** *vt* to scare, intimidate, cow. **2 acoquinarse** *vr* to get scared, allow o.s. to be intimidated.

acorar [1a] *vt* to distress, afflict, upset.

acorazado 1 *adj* armour-plated; ironclad; armoured.

2 *nm* battleship; ~ **de bolsillo** pocket battleship.

acorazar [1f] **1** *vt* to armour-plate, armour. **2 acorazarse** *vr* (*fig*) to steel o.s., arm o.s. (*contra* against); to harden o.s.; ~ **contra** (*fig*) to become inured to.

acorazonado *adj* heart-shaped.

acorchado *adj* spongy, cork-like; *boca* furry.

acorchar [1a] **1** *vt* to cover with cork.

2 acorcharse *vr* to become spongy, become like cork; to wither, shrivel; (*miembro*) to go to sleep.

acordada *nf* (*Jur*) decree.

acordadamente *adv* unanimously, by common consent.

acordado *adj* agreed; **lo** ~ that which has been agreed (upon).

acordar [1l] **1** *vt* (**a**) (*decidir*) to decide, resolve, agree on; ~ **que** + *subj* to resolve that ...; to resolve to + *infin.*

(**b**) (*And, Cono Sur*: *conceder*) to grant, accord.

(**c**) *opiniones* to reconcile; (*Mús*) to tune; (*Arte*) to blend, harmonize.

(**d**) ~ **algo a uno** to remind sb of sth.

2 *vi* to agree; to correspond.

3 acordarse *vr* (**a**) (*ponerse de acuerdo*) to agree, come to an agreement (*con* with); **se acordó hacerlo** it was agreed to do it; **se ha acordado que ...** it has been agreed that ...

(**b**) (*recordar*) to remember, recall, recollect; **no me acuerdo** I don't remember; **si mal no me acuerdo** if my memory serves me right; ~ **de algo** to remember sth; **¿te acuerdas de mí?** do you remember me?; **¡te acordarás de mí!** you'll be hearing from me!; **¡te acordarás de ésta!** I'll teach you!; **no se acuerda ni del santo de su nombre** he hardly remembers his own name.

acorde 1 *adj* (**a**) **con sentimientos ~s** with identical feelings; **estar ~s** to be agreed, be in agreement.

(**b**) (*Mús*) harmonious; (*con* estar) in tune, in harmony.

2 *nm* (*Mús*) chord; **a los ~s de la marcha nupcial** to the strains of the wedding march.

acordeón *nm* accordion.

acordeonista *nmf* accordionist.

acordeón-piano *nm* piano-accordion.

acordonado *adj* (**a**) *superficie etc* ribbed; *lugar* cordoned-off; *moneda, borde* milled. (**b**) (*LAm*) *animal* thin.

acordonamiento *nm* (*V adj*) ribbing; cordoning off; milling.

acordonar [1a] *vt* (**a**) (*atar*) to tie up, tie with string; *corsé etc* to lace up.

(**b**) *lugar* to cordon off, rope off, surround with a cordon; (*policía etc*) to surround.

(**c**) *moneda, borde* to mill.

(**d**) (*LAm*) *terreno* to prepare.

acornar [1l] *vt*, **acornear** [1a] *vt* to butt; to gore.

acorralamiento *nm* enclosing; cornering, trapping.

acorralar [1a] *vt ganado* to round up, pen, corral; *animal peligroso* to corner, bring to bay; *persona* to corner; (*fig*) to intimidate.

acorrer [2a] **1** *vt* to help, go to the aid of. **2** *vi* to run up; ~ **a uno** to hasten to sb.

acortamiento *nm* shortening; reduction.

acortar [1a] **1** *vt* (**a**) (*gen*) to shorten, cut down, reduce; *velas, paso* to shorten; *narración* to cut short, abbreviate. (**b**) (*LAm*: *atenuar*) to tone down.

2 acortarse *vr* (*fig*) to be slow; to be shy, falter.

acosar [1a] *vt* (*perseguir*) to pursue relentlessly; (*fig*) to hound; to harass, badger; (*obsesionar*) to obsess; *animal* to urge on; ~ **a uno a preguntas** to pester sb with questions.

acosijar [1a] *vt* (*Méx*) = **acosar.**

acoso *nm* relentless pursuit; (*fig*) hounding, harassing; relentless questioning; ~ **sexual** sexual harassment; **operación de ~ y derribo** (*Mil*) search and destroy operation.

acostar [1l] **1** *vt* (**a**) (*tender*) to lay down.

(**b**) (*en cama*) to put to bed.

(**c**) (*Náut*) to bring alongside.

2 acostarse *vr* to lie down; to go to bed; (*LAm*: *dar a luz*) to give birth; **estar acostado** to be lying down; to be in bed; **nos acostamos tarde** we go to bed late; **A se acostó con B** A went to bed with B, A slept with B; **ella se acuesta con cualquiera** she sleeps around; **es hora de ~** it's bedtime.

acostillado *adj* ribbed, with ribs.

acostumbrado *adj* usual, customary, habitual.

acostumbrar [1a] **1** *vt*: ~ **a uno a algo** to get sb used to sth; ~ **a uno a las dificultades** to inure sb to hardships; ~ **a uno a hacer algo** to accustom sb to doing sth; to get sb used to doing sth.

2 *vi*: ~ + *infin*, ~ **a** + *infin* to be accustomed to + *infin*, be in the habit of + *ger*; **los sábados acostumbra (a) ir al cine** on Saturdays he usually goes to the cinema.

3 acostumbrarse *vr* (**a**) ~ **a algo** to accustom o.s. to sth, get accustomed to sth; to get used to sth; to get the feel of sth; **estar acostumbrado a algo** to be accustomed to sth, be used to sth; **está acostumbrado a verlas venir** he's not easily fooled.

(**b**) (*LAm*) **no se acostumbra aquí** it isn't usual here; **ya no se acostumbra la chistera** nobody wears top hats any more, top hats aren't worn nowadays.

acotación *nf* (**a**) (*mojón*) boundary mark; (*Geog*) elevation mark. (**b**) (*apunte*) marginal note; (*Teat*) stage direction.

acotado 1 *adj* enclosed, fenced. **2** *nm* (*t* ~ **de caza**) game preserve.

acotamiento *nm* (*Mex Aut*) hard shoulder, berm (*US*); emergency lane.

acotar [1a] *vt* (**a**) *tierra* to survey, mark out; to limit, set bounds to; *coto etc* to fence in, protect, preserve.

(**b**) *árboles* to lop.

(**c**) *página* to annotate; *mapa* to mark elevations on.

(**d**) (*fig*) (*aceptar*) to accept, adopt; (*elegir*) to choose; (*avalar*) to vouch for; (*comprobar*) to check, verify.

acotejar [1a] *vt* (*LAm*) to arrange, put in order.

acotillo *nm* sledgehammer.

acoyundar [1a] *vt* to yoke.

acr. *abr de* **acreedor** creditor, Cr.

acracia *nf* anarchy.

ácrata 1 *adj* non-conformist; hippy; free-and-easy, unconventional; loose-living; (*Pol*) anarchistic; anarchic.

2 *nmf* non-conformist; hippy, drop-out; unconventional person; (*Pol*) anarchist.

acrático *adj* = **ácrata 1.**

acre[1] *adj sabor* sharp, bitter, tart; *olor* acrid, pungent; *temperamento* sour; *crítica etc* biting, mordant.

acre[2] *nm* (*medida*) acre.

acrecencia *nf* (**a**) (*Jur*) accretion. (**b**) = **acrecentamiento.**

acrecentamiento *nm* increase, growth.

acrecentar [1j] **1** *vt* to increase, augment; *persona etc* to advance, promote; to further the interests of. **2 acrecentarse** *vr* to increase, grow.

acrecer [2d] *vt* to increase.

acrecimiento *nm* increase, growth.

acreditación *nf* accreditation; sanctioning, authorization; vetting, (security) clearance.

acreditado *adj* (*Com, Pol*) accredited; (*estimado*) reputable, highly-esteemed; (*influyente*) influential; **nuestro representante ~** our accredited representative, our official agent; **una casa acreditada** a reputable firm; **marca acreditada** reputable make.

acreditar [1a] **1** *vt* (*dar reputación a*) to do credit to, add to the reputation of; (*avalar*) to vouch for, guarantee; (*por seguridad*) to vet, clear, give security clearance to; (*probar*) to prove; (*sancionar*) to sanction, authorize; (*Com*) to credit; (*And*) to sell on credit; ~ **a un embajador cerca de uno** to accredit an ambassador to sb; **y virtudes que le acreditan** and qualities which do him credit; ~ **su personalidad** to establish one's identity.

2 acreditarse *vr* to justify o.s., prove one's worth; ~ **de** to get a reputation for; ~ **en** to get a reputation in.

acreditivo *adj*: **documentos ~s** supporting documents.

acreedor 1 *adj*: ~ **a** worthy of, deserving of; eligible for.

2 *nm*, **acreedora** *nf* creditor; ~ **hipotecario** mortgagee.

acreencia *nf* (*And, Méx*) (*balance*) credit balance; (*deuda*) debt, amount owing (*o* owed).

acremente *adv* sharply, bitterly; pungently; bitingly.

acribadura *nf* sifting, sieving.

acribar [1a] vt to sift, riddle.

acribillado adj superficie pitted, pockmarked; ~ a riddled with, peppered with; ~ de filled with; honeycombed with; ~ de picaduras covered with stings.

acribillar [1a] vt (a) ~ a balazos to riddle with bullets, pepper with shots; ~ a puñaladas to cover with stab wounds.

(b) (fig) to pester, badger; to harass; ~ a uno a preguntas to pester sb with questions.

acridio nm (LAm) locust.

acrílico adj, nm acrylic.

acrilonitrilo nm acrylonitrile.

acriminación nf incrimination; accusation.

acriminador **1** adj incriminating. **2** nm, **acriminadora** nf accuser.

acriminar [1a] vt to incriminate; to accuse.

acrimonia nf sharpness; acridness, pungency; sourness; (fig) acrimony, bitterness.

acrimonioso adj acrimonious.

acriollarse [1a] vr (LAm) to take on local habits (o the habits of the country); (pey*) to go native.

acrisolado adj pure; tried, tested; unquestionable; una fe acrisolada a pure faith; el patriotismo más ~ the noblest kind of patriotism; de acrisolada honradez of unquestionable honesty.

acrisolar [1a] vt (Téc) to purify, refine; (fig) to purify, purge; to bring out, clarify; verdad etc to prove, reveal.

acristalado adj glazed.

acristalamiento nm glazing; los ~s windows, glazing; doble ~ double glazing.

acristianar [1a] vt to christianize; niño to baptize.

acritud nf = acrimonia.

acrobacia nf acrobatics; ~ aérea aerobatics.

acróbata nmf acrobat.

acrobático adj acrobatic.

acrobatismo nm acrobatics.

acrónimo nm acronym.

Acrópolis nf Acropolis.

acróstico adj, nm acrostic.

acta nf (a) (de reunión) minutes, record; (publicada, de sociedad) transactions; (Pol) certificate of election; (LAm Parl) act, law; ~ de acusación bill of indictment; ~ constitutiva charter; ~ de defunción death certificate; ~ matrimonial, ~ de matrimonio (Méx) marriage certificate; ~ de nacimiento (Méx) birth certificate; ~ notarial affidavit; ~ orgánica (LAm Jur) constitution; A~ Unica Europea Single European Act; levantar ~ to take the minutes; to draw up a formal statement; levantar ~ de to take the minutes of, minute; tomar ~ (Cono Sur) to take note; tomar ~ de algo (Cono Sur) to bear sth in mind.

(b) ~s (de reunión) minutes, record; (publicadas, de sociedad) transactions; ~s de un santo life of a saint; ~s de los mártires lives of the martyrs.

actinia nf actinia, sea-anemone.

actínico adj actinic.

actinio nm actinium.

actitud nf (a) (de cuerpo) posture, position, attitude, pose.

(b) (fig) attitude; position; outlook; policy; la ~ del gobierno the government's attitude, the government's position; adoptar una ~ firme to take a firm stand, put one's foot down; en ~ de + infin (as if) ready to + infin, threatening to + infin.

activación nf activation; expediting, speeding-up; stimulation.

activador nm (Téc) activator; (fig) stimulus.

activamente adv actively.

activar [1a] vt to activate; trabajo to expedite, speed up, hurry along; fuego to brighten up, poke; mercado to stimulate.

actividad nf (a) (gen) activity; liveliness; promptness; movement, bustle; estar en ~ to be active, be in operation, (volcán) be active, be in eruption; estar en plena ~ to be in full swing.

(b) (profesional etc) occupation; activity; ~ complementaria sideline; ~ lucrativa gainful employment; ~es activities; sus ~es políticas his political activities.

activisimo nm (LAm Pol) political activity.

activista nmf activist; (esp LAm) political activist.

activo **1** adj (gen) active; (vivo) lively; (pronto) prompt; (enérgico) energetic; (ocupado) busy; (Ling) active.

2 nm (a) (Com) assets; ~ bloqueado, ~ congelado frozen assets; ~ circulante circulating assets; ~ corriente current assets; ~ fijo, ~ inmovilizado fixed assets; ~ flotante floating assets; ~ inmaterial intangible assets; ~s inmobiliarios property assets, real-estate assets; ~ intangible intangible assets; ~ invisible invisible assets; ~ líquido, ~ realizable liquid assets; ~ neto net worth; ~ oculto hidden assets; ~ operante operating assets; ~ y pasivo assets and liabilities; ~ de la quiebra bankrupt's estate; ~ tangible tangible assets.

(b) oficial en ~ (Mil) serving officer; estar en ~ to be on active service; to be on the active list (t fig).

acto nm (gen) act; action, deed; (ceremonia) ceremony, function; (Teat) act; A~s de los Apóstoles Acts (of the Apostles); ~ de desagravio act of atonement; ~ de fe act of faith; ~ de habla speech act; ~ inaugural opening ceremony; ~ reflejo reflex action; ~ religioso church service; ~ continuo, ~ seguido next, forthwith, immediately after; ~ seguido de immediately after; morir en ~ de servicio to die on active service; ocurrió en ~ de servicio it happened during working hours, it happened when he (etc) was at work; en el ~ immediately; instantaneously; on the spot, there and then; en el ~ de in the act of; 'reparaciones en el ~' 'repairs while you wait'; celebrar un ~ to hold a function; hacer ~ de presencia to attend (formally), be present; to put in an appearance, make a token appearance.

actor nm (Teat) actor; (fig) protagonist; (Jur) plaintiff; ~ cinematográfico film actor.

actora adj: parte ~ (Jur) prosecution; (demandante) plaintiff.

actriz nf actress; primera ~ leading lady.

actuación nf (a) (acción) action; (conducta) performance, conduct, behaviour; (Teat) performance; (Dep) performance; (LAm) role; ~ en vivo live performance; su ~ fue importante his role (o part) was an important one.

(b) actuaciones (Jur) legal proceedings.

(c) ~ pericial expert valuation.

actual adj (presente) present; present-day; (corriente) current; cuestión current, topical; (al día) modern, up-to-date; (a la moda) fashionable; el 6 del ~ the 6th day of this month; el rey ~ the present king.

actualidad nf (a) (presente) present, present time; en la ~ at present, at the present time; nowadays, now.

(b) (contemporaneidad) present importance, current importance; cuestión de palpitante ~ highly important current issue; highly topical question; ser de gran ~ to be current, be alive; to have great importance now (o at the time); perder (su) ~ to lose interest, get stale.

(c) ~es current events; contemporary issues; (Cine) newsreel.

actualización nf modernization, bringing up to date; (curso) refresher course, course of retraining; (Inform) update, updating; (Contabilidad) discounting.

actualizador adj influencia etc modernizing.

actualizar [1f] vt to bring up to date, update, modernize; to add topicality to; (Inform) to update; (Contabilidad) to discount.

actualmente adv at present; now, nowadays; at the moment; ~ está fuera he's away at the moment; los 50 ~ en servicio the 50 at present in service.

actuar [1e] **1** vt to work, actuate, operate; to set in motion.

2 vi (Mec) to work, operate, function; (persona) to act, perform; ~ de to act as; ~ sobre to act on; actuó bien el árbitro Sr X Mr X refereed well; actúa de manera rara he's acting strangely; ~ en justicia to institute legal proceedings.

actuarial adj actuarial.

actuario nm (Jur) clerk (of the court); (Com, Fin: t ~ de seguros) actuary.

acuache* nm, **acuachi*** nm (Méx) mate, pal*.

acuadrillar [1a] **1** vt to form into a band; (Cono Sur) to set upon (o about), gang up on. **2** **acuadrillarse** vr to band together, gang up.

acuanauta nmf deep-sea diver.

acuaplano nm surfboarding.

acuarela nf watercolour.

acuarelista nmf watercolourist.

Acuario nm (Zodíaco) Aquarius.

acuario nm, **acuárium** nm aquarium.

acuartelado adj (Her) quartered.

acuartelamiento nm (a) (Mil) quartering, billeting. (b) (Her) quartering.

acuartelar [1a] **1** vt (Mil) to quarter, billet; to confine to barracks. **2** **acuartelarse** vr to withdraw to barracks.

acuático adj aquatic, water (atr).

acuátil adj aquatic, water (atr).

acuatinta nf aquatint.

acuatizaje *nm* (*Aer*) touchdown (*o* landing) (on the sea).
acuatizar [1f] *vi* (*Aer*) to come down on the water, land on the sea.
acucia *nf* (*diligencia*) diligence, keenness; (*prisa*) haste; (*anhelo*) keen desire, longing.
acuciadamente *adv* (*V n*) diligently, keenly; hastily; longingly.
acuciador *adj*, **acuciante** *adj* pressing, urgent.
acuciar [1b] *vt* (**a**) (*instar*) to urge on, goad, prod; (*dar prisa a*) to hasten; (*acosar*) to harass; to mob; (*problema etc*) to press, worry. (**b**) (*anhelar*) to desire keenly, long for.
acucioso *adj* diligent, zealous, keen; eager.
acuclillarse [1a] *vr* to squat down.
acuchamado *adj* (*Carib*: *triste*) sad, depressed.
acuchamarse [1a] *vr* (*Carib*) to get depressed.
acuchillado *adj* (**a**) *vestido* slashed. (**b**) (*escarmentado*) wary, schooled by bitter experience.
acuchillar [1a] **1** *vt* (**a**) (*cortar*) to cut, slash, hack; (*Cos*) to slash; *persona* to stab (to death), knife.
(**b**) (*Téc*) to plane down, smooth.
2 acuchillarse *vr*: **se acuchillaron** they fought with knives, they slashed at each other.
acuchucar [1g] *vt* (*Cono Sur*) to crush, flatten; to crumple.
ACUDE [a'kuðe] *nf abr de* **Asociación de Consumidores y Usuarios de España.**
acudir [3a] *vi* (**a**) (*venir*) to come, come along, come up; (*asistir*) to turn up, present o.s.; ~ **a la puerta** to come (*o* go) to the door, answer the door; ~ **a una cita** to keep an appointment, turn up for an appointment; ~ **a una llamada** to answer a call; ~ **a la mente** to come to (one's) mind; **pero no acudió** but he didn't come, but he didn't turn up.
(**b**) (*en auxilio*) to come (*o* go) to the rescue, go to help.
(**c**) (*fig*) ~ **a** to call on, turn to, have recourse to; ~ **al médico** to consult one's doctor; ~ **a uno a pedir socorro** to turn to sb for help; **tendremos que ~ a otra solución** we shall have to seek another solution; **no tener a quien ~** to have no-one to turn to.
(**d**) (*Agr*) to produce, yield.
(**e**) (*caballo*) to answer, obey.
acueducto *nm* aqueduct.
ácueo *adj* aqueous.
acuerdo *nm* (**a**) (*gen*) agreement, accord; decision; (*tratado etc*) agreement, pact; understanding; ~ **económico social** (*Pol*) wages agreement; ~ **extrajudicial** (*esp Méx*) out-of-court settlement; ~ **marco** general framework of agreement; set of agreed guidelines; ~ **de pago respectivo** knock-for-knock agreement, no-fault agreement (*US*); ~ **salarial** wage agreement, pay settlement; ~ **verbal** verbal agreement; gentleman's agreement; **¡de ~!** I agree!, agreed!; yes of course!; **de ~ con** in accordance with; **de ~ con el artículo 2 del código** under article 2 of the code, as laid down in article 2 of the code; **de común ~** with one accord, unanimously; **estar de ~** (*persona*) to agree, be in agreement (*con* with); (*cosas*) to agree, correspond; **esto está de ~ con lo que me dijo** this is in line with what he told me; **estar en perfecto ~** to be in perfect harmony; **llegar a un ~** to reach agreement, come to an understanding (*con* with); **ponerse** (*o* **quedar**) **de ~** to reach agreement, agree.
(**b**) (*Parl etc*) resolution; **tomar un ~** to pass a resolution.
(**c**) (*Arte*) harmony, blend.
(**d**) (*Cono Sur*: *consejo*) consultative meeting.
(**e**) (*recuerdo*) memory, recollection.
(**f**) (*juicio*) sense, right mind; **estar en su ~** to be in one's right mind; **volver en su ~** to come to one's senses.
acuícola *adj* water (*atr*); underwater; marine.
acuicultor(a) *nm/f* fish-farmer.
acuicultura *nf* development of water resources, aquaculture; fish-farming.
acuidad *nf* acuity.
acuífero 1 *adj* aquiferous, water-bearing. **2** *nm* aquifer.
acuilmarse [1a] *vr* (*CAm*) to get depressed; to cower, shrink away.
acuitadamente *adv* sorrowfully, with regret.
acuitar [1a] **1** *vt* to afflict, distress, grieve. **2 acuitarse** *vr* to grieve, be grieved (*por* at, by).
acular* [1a] **1** *vt* (**a**) *caballo etc* to back (*a* against, into). (**b**) (*acorralar*) to corner, force into a corner. **2** *vi* (*And*) to back away.
aculturación *nf* acculturation.
aculturar [1a] *vt* to acculturate.
acullá *adv* over there, yonder.
acullicar [1g] *vi* (*And, Cono Sur*) to chew coca (leaves).
acumuchar [1a] *vt* (*Cono Sur*) to pile up, accumulate.
acumulación *nf* (*acto*) accumulation; (*cantidad*) accumulation; pile, stock, hoard.
acumulador 1 *adj* accumulative. **2** *nm* accumulator, storage battery.
acumular [1a] **1** *vt* to accumulate; to amass, gather, collect; to pile (up), hoard; ~ **vapor** to get steam up.
2 acumularse *vr* (**a**) (*en general*) to accumulate, gather, pile up. (**b**) (*Cono Sur*: *personas*) to gather (*o* collect) together.
acumulativo *adj* accumulative.
acunar [1a] *vt* to rock (to sleep).
acuñación *nf* coining, minting; wedging.
acuñar [1a] **1** *vt* (**a**) *moneda* to coin, mint; *medalla* to strike; *frase* to coin; *rueda etc* to wedge. (**b**) (*Carib*: *llevar a cabo*) to finish successfully. **2 acuñarse** *vr* (*CAm*) to hit o.s., sustain a blow.
acuosidad *nf* wateriness; juiciness.
acuoso *adj* watery; *fruto* juicy, runny.
acupuntor(a) *nm/f* acupuncturist.
acupuntura *nf* acupuncture.
acupunturista *nmf* acupuncturist.
acurrado *adj* (**a**) (*Carib, Méx*: *guapo*) handsome. (**b**) (*CAm*: *rechoncho*) squat, chubby.
acurrucarse [1g] *vr* to squat, crouch; to huddle up, curl up.
acusación *nf* accusation; (*Jur*) accusation, charge, indictment; **negar la ~** to deny the charge, plead not guilty.
acusado 1 *adj* (**a**) (*Jur etc*) accused.
(**b**) (*fuerte*) marked, pronounced; *característica, rasgo, personalidad* strong; *contraste* marked, striking; *color* deep.
2 *nm*, **acusada** *nf* accused, defendant.
acusador 1 *adj* accusing, reproachful; **los letrados ~es** prosecuting counsel; **la parte ~a** plaintiff; prosecution. **2** *nm*, **acusadora** *nf* accuser.
acusar [1a] **1** *vt* (**a**) (*Jur etc*) to accuse (*de* of), charge (*de* with), indict (*de* on a charge of); **¿me acusas a mí?** are you accusing me?; ~ **a uno de haber hecho algo** to accuse sb of having done sth.
(**b**) (*denunciar*) to denounce; *sospechoso* to point to, proclaim the guilt of.
(**c**) (*revelar*) to show, reveal; *emoción etc* to register, show, betray; **su rostro acusó extrañeza** his face showed (*o* registered) surprise; **su silencio acusa cierta cobardía** his silence betrays a certain cowardice; **acusamos cierto retraso** we're a bit late.
(**d**) *cartas* to declare, lay down.
(**e**) ~ **recibo** to acknowledge receipt (*de* of).
2 acusarse *vr* (**a**) (*confesar*) to confess; ~ **de negligente** to confess one's negligence, confess to being negligent; ~ **de un crimen** to confess to a crime; ~ **de haberlo hecho** to confess to having done it.
(**b**) (*hacerse más fuerte*) to become more marked, get stronger; **esta tendencia se acusa cada vez más** this tendency is becoming ever more marked, this tendency gets stronger all the time.
acusativo *nm* accusative.
acusatorio *adj* accusatory, accusing.
acuse *nm*: ~ **de recibo** acknowledgement of receipt.
acusetas* *nmf invar*, **acusete*** *nmf* (*And, Cono Sur*) telltale, sneak.
acusica* *nmf*, **acusique*** *nm* tell-tale, sneak.
acusón* 1 *adj* telltale, sneaking. **2** *nm*, **acusona** *nf* telltale, sneak; gossip.
acústica *nf* acoustics.
acústico 1 *adj* acoustic. **2** *nm* hearing-aid.
acutí *nm* (*Zool*) = **agudí.**
achacable *adj*: ~ **a** attributable to.
achacar [1g] *vt* (**a**) ~ **algo a una causa** to attribute sth to a cause, put sth down to a cause; ~ **la culpa a uno** to lay the blame on someone. (**b**) (*LAm**) (*robar*) to pinch*, nick‡; (*saquear*) to pillage, loot.
achacoso *adj* sickly, ailing.
achaflanar [1a] *vt* to chamfer, bevel.
achafranar‡‡ [1a] *vi* (*Méx*) to fuck‡‡, screw‡‡.
achahuistlarse *vr* (*Mex*) to get depressed.
achalay, achachay *interj*: (*And*) ¡~! brr!
achampañado *adj* champagne-flavoured.
achamparse [1a] *vr*: (*Cono Sur*) ~ **algo** to keep sth which does not belong to one.
achancharse* [1a] *vr* (**a**) (*And*: *ponerse perezoso*) to get lazy. (**b**) (*Cono Sur*: *engordar*) to get fat. (**c**) (*And*: *ponerse violento*) to become embarrassed.
achantado* *adj* (*CAm*) bashful, shy.

achantar* [1a] **1** *vt* (**a**) (*cerrar*) to close.
(**b**) (*intimidar*) to intimidate; (*humillar*) to take down a peg.
2 *vi* to be quiet, shut up*.
3 achantarse *vr* (**a**) (*esconderse*) to hide away.
(**b**) (*fig*) to give in, comply; ~ **por las buenas** to be easily intimidated.
achaparrado *adj* dwarf, stunted; *persona* stocky, thickset, stumpy.
achapinarse [1a] *vr* (*CAm*) to adopt the local customs.
achaque *nm* (**a**) (*Med*) sickliness, infirmity, weakness; ailment, malady; (*) period, monthlies; **~s mañaneros** morning sickness; **~s de la vejez** ailments of old age.
(**b**) (*defecto*) defect, fault, weakness.
(**c**) (*asunto*) matter, subject; **en ~ de** in the matter of, on the subject of.
(**d**) (*pretexto*) pretext; **con ~ de** under the pretext of.
achara *interj*: ¡~! (*CAm*: *lástima*) what a pity!
achares* *nmpl* jealousy; **dar ~ a uno** to make sb jealous.
acharolado *adj* patent leather (*atr*).
achatamiento *nm* (**a**) (*allanamiento*) flattening. (**b**) (*LAm*: *desmoralización*) loss of moral (*o* intellectual) fibre; **sufrieron un ~** they lost heart, they felt down.
achatar [1a] **1** *vt* to flatten.
2 achatarse *vr* (**a**) (*gen*) to get flat.
(**b**) (*Cono Sur, Méx*: *declinar*) to grow weak, decline; (*LAm*: *perder ánimo*) to lose heart, feel down.
(**c**) (*Cono Sur, Méx*: *avergonzarse*) to be overcome with shame, be embarrassed; **quedarse achatado** to feel ashamed, be embarrassed.
achicado *adj* childish, childlike.
achicador *nm* scoop, baler.
achicalado *adj* (*Méx*) sugared, honeyed.
achicalar [1a] *vt* (*Méx*) to cover (*o* soak) in honey.
achicanado *adj* Chicano, characteristic of Mexican-Americans.
achicar [1g] **1** *vt* (**a**) (*empequeñecer*) to make smaller; to dwarf; *espacios* to reduce; (*Cos*) to shorten, take in; (*quitar importancia a*) to minimize, diminish the importance of.
(**b**) (*Náut etc*) to scoop, bale (out); (*con bomba*) to pump out.
(**c**) (*fig*) (*humillar*) to humiliate; (*intimidar*) to intimidate, browbeat.
(**d**) (*And*: *matar*) to kill.
(**e**) (*And, Carib*: *sujetar*) to fasten, hold down.
2 achicarse *vr* (**a**) to get smaller; to shrink.
(**b**) (*fig*) to humble o.s., eat humble pie.
(**c**) (*LAm*: *rebajarse*) to do o.s. down, belittle o.s.
achicopalado* *adj* (*Méx*) depressed, gloomy.
achicoria *nf* chicory.
achicharradero *nm* place of oppressive heat, inferno.
achicharrante *adj*: **calor ~** sweltering heat.
achicharrar [1a] **1** *vt* (**a**) (*sobrecalentar*) to scorch, overheat; (*Culin*) to fry crisp; (*por error*) to overcook, burn, scorch; **el sol achicharraba la ciudad** the sun was roasting the city.
(**b**) (*: *fastidiar*) to bother, plague.
(**c**) (‡: *matar*) to shoot, riddle with bullets.
(**d**) (*LAm*: *allanar*) to flatten, crush.
2 achicharrarse *vr* to scorch, get burnt.
achicharronar [1a] *vt* (*LAm*) to flatten, crush.
achichiguar [1i] *vt* (*Méx*) (**a**) (*) to cosset, spoil. (**b**) (*Agr*) to shade.
achichincle* *nmf* (*Méx*) camp-follower, groupie*.
achichuncle‡ *nmf* (*Méx*) creep‡, crawler‡.
achiguado* *adj* (*Méx*) spoiled.
achiguarse [1i] *vr* (*Cono Sur*) to grow a paunch; (*muro etc*) to bulge, sag.
achilarse [1a] *vr* (*And*) to turn cowardly.
achimero *nm* (*CAm*) pedlar, peddler (*US*), hawker.
achimes *nmpl* (*CAm*) cheap goods, trinkets.
achín *nm* (*CAm*) pedlar, peddler (*US*), hawker.
achinado *adj* (**a**) (*Cono Sur*) with Indian looks; (*) coarse, common.
(**b**) (*And, Carib*) Chinese-like, oriental; **ojos ~s** almond eyes.
achinar* [1a] **1** *vt* to scare. **2 achinarse** *vr* (*Cono Sur*) to become coarse..
achique *nm* (**a**) making smaller; reduction. (**b**) baling; pumping.
achiquillado *adj* (*Méx*) childish.
achiquitar [1a] *vt* (*LAm**) to make smaller, reduce in size.
achipolarse* [1a] *vr* (*Méx*) to grow sad, get gloomy.
achirarse [1a] *vr* (*And*) (*nublarse*) to cloud over; (*oscurecerse*) to get dark.
achís *interj* atishoo!
achispado* *adj* tight*, tipsy.
achispar* [1a] *vt* (*LAm*) to cheer up, liven up. **2 achisparse** *vr* to get tight*, get tipsy.
-acho, -acha *V* **Aspects of Word Formation in Spanish 2.**
achocar [1g] *vt* (**a**) (*tirar*) to throw against a wall, dash against a wall.
(**b**) (*pegar*) to hit, bash*.
(**c**) (*: *guardar*) to hoard, stash away*.
achoclonarse [1a] *vr* (*LAm*) to crowd together.
achocolatado *adj* (**a**) (*LAm*: *cualidad*) chocolate (*atr*); like chocolate. (**b**) (*LAm*: *color*) dark brown, chocolate-coloured, tan. (**c**) **estar ~‡** (*borracho*) to be canned‡.
achocharse [1a] *vr* to get doddery, begin to dodder.
acholado *adj* (*LAm*) (**a**) (*mestizo*) racially mixed, part-Indian.
(**b**) (*acobardado*) cowed; (*avergonzado*) abashed.
acholar [1a] (*LAm*) **1** *vt* (*avergonzar*) to embarrass; (*intimidar*) to intimidate, scare.
2 acholarse *vr* (**a**) (*acriollarse*) to have (*o* adopt) half-breed ways.
(**b**) (*acobardarse*) to be cowed; (*avergonzarse*) to be abashed, become shy; (*sonrojarse*) to blush.
acholo *nm* (*LAm*) embarrassment.
-achón, -achona *V* **Aspects of Word Formation in Spanish 2.**
achoramiento‡ *nm* (*Cono Sur*) threat.
achubascarse [1g] *vr* (*cielo*) to become threatening, cloud over.
achucutado *adj* (*LAm*) (*deprimido*) gloomy, depressed; (*agobiado*) overwhelmed.
achucutarse [1a] *vr* (*LAm*) (*estar afligido*) to be (*o* look) dismayed; (*deprimirse*) to be gloomy; (*marchitarse*) to wilt; (*ser tímido*) to be timid, be shy.
achucuyarse [1a] *vr* (*CAm*) = **achucutarse.**
achuchado *adj*: **estar ~** (*Cono Sur*) (*paludismo*) to have malaria; (*tener escalofríos*) to catch a chill; (*tener fiebre*) to be feverish; (*fig*) to be scared (*o* frightened); **esta tarea está achuchada** this is a tough job.
achuchar [1a] **1** *vt* (**a**) (*estrujar*) to crush, squeeze flat.
(**b**) *persona* (*empujar*) to shove, jostle; (*acosar*) to harass, pester.
(**c**) *perro* to urge on; ~ **un perro contra uno** to set a dog on sb.
2 achucharse[1] *vr* (*amantes*) to cuddle, fondle (one another), pet* (one another).
achucharse[2] [1a] *vr* (*Cono Sur*) (*paludismo*) to catch malaria; (*acatarrarse*) to catch a chill; (*tener fiebre*) to get feverish; (*asustarse*) to get scared.
achuchón *nm* (**a**) (*empujón*) squeeze; shove, push. (**b**) **tener un ~** (*Med*) to fall ill; to have a relapse.
achuicarse [1g] *vr* (*Cono Sur*) (*avergonzarse*) to be embarrassed; (*apocarse*) to feel small.
achulado *adj*, **achulapado** *adj* (**a**) (*desenvuelto*) jaunty, cocky. (**b**) (*grosero*) common, uncouth.
achumado *adj* (*LAm*) drunk.
achumarse [1a] *vr* (*LAm*) to get drunk.
achunchar [1a] (*LAm*) **1** *vt* (**a**) (*avergonzar*) to shame, cause to blush.
(**b**) (*intimidar*) to scare.
2 achuncharse *vr* (**a**) (*avergonzarse*) to feel ashamed, blush.
(**b**) (*intimidarse*) to get scared.
achuntar [1a] (*Cono Sur*) **1** *vt* to do properly, get right, do at the right time. **2** *vi* to guess right; to hit the nail on the head.
achuñuscar* [1g] *vt* (*Cono Sur*) to squeeze.
achupalla *nf* (*LAm*) pineapple.
achura *nf* (*LAm*) offal.
achurar [1a] **1** *vt* (*LAm*) *animal* to gut; *persona* to stab to death, cut to pieces.
2 *vi* (*LAm*) to benefit from a share-out, get sth free.
achurrucarse [1g] *vr* (*CAm*: *marchitarse*) to wilt.
achurruscado* *adj* rumpled, crumpled up.
achurruscar [1g] *vt* (*And, Cono Sur*) to rumple, crumple up.
ADA ['aða] *nf abr de* **Ayuda del Automovilista** ≃ AA, RAC.
-ada *V* **Aspects of Word Formation in Spanish 2.**
ADAC *nm abr de* **avión de despegue y aterrizaje cortos** vertical take-off and landing (aircraft), VTOL.
adagio *nm* adage, proverb; (*Mús*) adagio.
adalid *nm* leader, champion.
adamado *adj hombre* effeminate, soft; *mujer* elegant, chic;

(*pey*) flashy.
adamascado *adj* damask.
adamascar [1g] *vt* to damask.
Adán *nm* Adam.
adán *nm* (*sucio*) slovenly fellow; (*vago*) lazy chap*; **estar hecho un ~** to go about in rags, be terribly shabby, look a mess.
adaptabilidad *nf* adaptability; versatility.
adaptable *adj* adaptable; versatile.
adaptación *nf* adaptation.
adaptador *nm* (*Elec, Rad*) adapter.
adaptar [1a] **1** *vt* (*gen*) to adapt; (*adecuar*) to fit, make suitable (*para* for); (*ajustar*) to adjust. **2 adaptarse** *vr* to adapt o.s. (*a* to); **saber ~ a las circunstancias** to be able to adapt o.s. to the circumstances, know how to adjust to circumstances.
adaptativo *adj* adaptive.
adaraja *nf* (*Arquit*) toothing.
adarga *nf* (oval) shield.
adarme *nm* whit, jot; **ni un ~** not a whit; **no me importa un ~** I couldn't care less; **sin un ~ de educación** without the least bit of good manners; **por ~s** in driblets.
A. de C. *abr de* **año de Cristo** Anno Domini, AD.
adecentar [1a] **1** *vt* to tidy up, clean up, make decent. **2 adecentarse** *vr* to tidy o.s. up.
adecuación *nf* adaptation; adequacy, fitness, suitability.
adecuadamente *adv* adequately, fitly, suitably.
adecuado *adj* adequate; fit, suitable (*para* for); sufficient; appropriate; satisfactory; **los documentos ~s** the appropriate documents, the relevant papers; **el hombre ~ para el puesto** the right man for the job; **lo más ~ sería ...** the most appropriate thing would be to ..., it would be best to ...
adecuamiento *nm* adjustment.
adecuar [1d] *vt* to adapt, fit, make suitable; to prepare, make ready.
adefesiero* *adj* (*And, Cono Sur*: *ridículo*) comic, ridiculous; (*torpe*) clumsy; (*en el vestido*) overdressed, camp*.
adefesio *nm* (**a**) (*disparate*) piece of nonsense, absurdity; rubbish; **hablar ~s** to talk nonsense.
(**b**) (*persona*) queer bird, ridiculous person; (*de aspecto*) scarecrow, fright; **ella estaba hecha un ~** she did look a fright.
(**c**) (*vestido*) outlandish dress, ridiculous attire.
(**d**) (*maula*) unwanted object, white elephant.
adefesioso *adj* (*And*) nonsensical, ridiculous.
adehala *nf* (*propina*) gratuity, tip; (*de pago*) bonus.
a. de J.C. *abr de* **antes de Jesucristo** before Christ, BC.
adela *nf* (*CAm*) bittersweet.
adelaida *nf* (*Méx*) fuchsia.
adelantado 1 *adj* (**a**) (*avanzado*) advanced.
(**b**) (*precoz*) well advanced, ahead of one's age, precocious; **estar ~** *reloj* to be fast.
(**c**) *pago* in advance; **pagar por ~** to pay in advance.
(**d**) (*pey*) bold, forward.
2 *nm* (*Hist*) governor (of a frontier province), captain-general.
adelantamiento *nm* advance; advancement, furtherance, promotion; progress; (*Aut*) overtaking, passing
adelantar [1a] **1** *vt* (**a**) (*avanzar*) to move forward, move on, advance; (*Dep*) *balón* to pass on, pass forward.
(**b**) *paso* to speed up, quicken; *proyecto, trabajo* to speed up, hurry along; **~ los acontecimientos** to anticipate events; **no adelantemos los acontecimientos** let's not cross our bridges before we come to them.
(**c**) *suma, dinero* to advance, pay in advance; to lend.
(**d**) *reloj* to put on, put forward.
(**e**) *competidor* to get ahead of, outstrip; (*Aut*) to overtake, pass; **no le gusta dejarse ~** he doesn't like being overtaken; **estamos a punto de que se nos adelante** we are about to be overtaken.
(**f**) (*fig*) to advance, further, promote; **~ una idea** to put forward an idea.
(**g**) **~ que ...** to suggest that ..., propose that ...; to advise that ...
2 *vi* (**a**) (*avanzar*) to go ahead, get on, make headway; to improve, progress; **el enfermo adelanta** the patient is improving.
(**b**) (*Aut*) to overtake, pass; **'prohibido ~'** 'no overtaking'.
(**c**) (*reloj*) to be fast, gain; **mi reloj adelanta 5 minutos** my watch is 5 minutes fast.
3 adelantarse *vr* (**a**) (*tomar la delantera*) to go forward, go ahead; to improve, progress.
(**b**) **~ a uno** to get ahead of sb, outstrip sb; (*fig*) to steal a march on sb, beat sb to it; (*Aut*) to overtake sb, pass sb, (*pey*) cut in on sb.
(**c**) **~ a algo** to anticipate sth; **~ a los deseos de uno** to anticipate sb's wishes.
adelante 1 *adv* (**a**) (*lugar*) forward, onward; ahead; **más ~** further on; **por el camino ~** further along the road; **ir ~** to go on, go forward; *V* **sacar** (**r**) *etc.*
(**b**) (*cantidad*) **de 100 ptas en ~** from 100 pesetas up.
(**c**) (*tiempo*) **en ~, de aquí en ~, de hoy en ~** in future, from now on, henceforth; **más ~** later, afterwards.
(**d**) **¡~!** (*interj*: *al que habla*) go on!, go ahead!, carry on!; (*contestando a llamada*) come in!; (*Mil etc*) forward!; (*Cono Sur*) bravo!, that's the way!
2 *prep* (*Cono Sur*): **~ nuestro** (*etc*) in front of us (*etc*), before us (*etc*).
adelanto *nm* (**a**) (*gen*) advancement, progress.
(**b**) (*progreso*) advance, improvement; **con todos los ~s modernos** with all the modern improvements; **los ~s de la ciencia** the advances of science; **llegar con un ~ de 15 minutos** (*LAm*) to arrive 15 minutes early.
(**c**) (*Com etc*) advance; loan.
adelfa *nf* rosebay, oleander.
adelgazador *adj* slimming.
adelgazamiento *nm* slimming.
adelgazante *adj* slimming.
adelgazar [1f] **1** *vt* to make thin, make slender; *palo* to pare, whittle; *persona, figura* to slim, reduce, slenderize (*US*); (*fig*) to purify, refine; *voz* to raise the pitch of; *entendimiento* to sharpen.
2 *vi* to grow thin, lose weight; (*con intención*) to slim, reduce, lose weight; (*fig*) to split hairs.
3 adelgazarse *vr* to grow thin.
Adelpha *nf abr de* **Asociación de Defensa Ecológica y del Patrimonio Histórico-artístico.**
ademán *nm* (**a**) (*con mano*) gesture, movement, motion; (*de cuerpo*; *t Arte*) posture, attitude, position; **en ~ de** + *infin* as if to + *infin*, getting ready to + *infin*; **hacer ~ de** + *infin* to make as if to + *infin*, make a move to + *infin*; **hacer ademanes** to gesture, make signs.
(**b**) **ademanes** (*modales*) manners.
además 1 *adv* besides; moreover, furthermore; also; **y ~ la pegó** and he also beat her; **creo ~ que ...** moreover I think that ...
2 ~ de *prep* besides, in addition to; not to mention; **~ de eso** moreover; on top of that.
Adén *nm* Aden.
ADENA [a'ðena] *nf* (*Esp*) *abr de* **Asociación para la Defensa de la Naturaleza.**
adenoideo *adj* adenoidal.
adentellar [1a] *vt* to sink one's teeth into.
adentrarse [1a] *vr*: **~ en** to go into, get into, get inside; to penetrate into; **~ en la selva** to go deep(er) into the forest; **~ en sí mismo** to become lost in thought.
adentro 1 *adv* = **dentro**; **mar ~** out at sea, out to sea; **tierra ~** inland; **¡~!*** come in!
2 *prep* (*Cono Sur*): **~ mío** inside myself; **~ de** = **dentro de.**
3 *nm* (**a**) (*Cono Sur*) indoors, inside of the house.
(**b**) **~s** innermost being, innermost thoughts; **dijo para sus ~s** he said to himself; **reírse para sus ~s** to laugh inwardly.
adepto, -a *nm/f* follower, supporter; (*de mágica etc*) adept, initiate; (*LAm**) drug-addict.
aderezado *adj* favourable, suitable.
aderezar [1f] **1** *vt* to prepare, get ready, dress; *persona* to make beautiful, dress up, deck; *objeto* to embellish, adorn; *comida* to prepare; (*con especias*) to season, garnish; *ensalada* to dress; *bebidas* to prepare, mix; *vinos* to blend; *máquina etc* to repair; *tela* to gum, size.
2 aderezarse *vr* to dress up, get ready.
aderezo *nm* (**a**) (*acto*) preparation; dressing; embellishment; seasoning; mixing; blending; repair.
(**b**) (*Culin*) seasoning, dressing; (*en vestido*) adornment; (*joyas*) set of jewels; **~ de casa** household equipment; **~ de diamantes** set of diamonds; **~ de mesa** dinner service; **dar el ~ definitivo a algo** to put the finishing touch to sth.
adeudado *adj* in debt.
adeudar [1a] **1** *vt dinero* to owe; *impuestos etc* to be liable for; **~ una suma en una cuenta** to charge a sum to an account, debit an account for a sum.
2 *vi* to become related by marriage.
3 adeudarse *vr* to run into debt.
adeudo *nm* (*deuda*) debit, indebtedness; (*de aduana*)

customs duty; *(en cuenta)* debit, charge.

adeveras *(LAm)*: **de ~** *adv* = **de veras.**

ADEVIDA [aðe'βiða] *nf (Esp) abr de* **Asociación en Defensa de la Vida Humana.**

a.D.g. *abr de* **a Dios gracias** thanks be to God, Deo gratias, D.G.

adherencia *nf* adherence, adhesion; *(fig)* bond, connection; *(Aut)* road holding, road-holding qualities; **tener ~s** to have connections.

adherente 1 *adj*: **~ a** adhering to; joining. **2** *nm/f* adherent, follower.

adherido, -a *nm/f* adherent, follower.

adherir [3i] **1** *vi* to adhere, stick *(a* to); **~ a** *(fig)* to adhere to, espouse, follow; *partido etc* to join, become a member of. **2 adherirse** *vr* = **1.**

adhesión *nf* adhesion; *(fig)* adherence, support; membership; *(mensaje)* message of support.

adhesividad *nf* adhesiveness.

adhesivo 1 *adj* adhesive, sticky; *melodía* catchy. **2** *nm* adhesive.

adicción *nf* addiction.

adición *nf* **(a)** *(gen)* addition; *(Mat)* addition; adding up. **(b)** *(Cono Sur: cuenta)* bill, check *(US)*.

adicional *adj* additional, extra, supplementary; *(Inform)* add-on.

adicionar [1a] *vt* to add *(a* to); *(Mat)* to add, add up.

adictivo *adj* addictive.

adicto 1 *adj* **(a)** *(leal)* **~ a** devoted to, attached to; **las personas adictas a él** those who follow him, his supporters.

(b) ~ a *(pey)* given to, addicted to.

2 *nm,* **adicta** *nf* supporter, follower; *(LAm Dep)* supporter, fan; *(de drogas)* addict.

adiestrado *adj* trained.

adiestramiento *nm* training; drilling; practice; **~ con armas** weapons training.

adiestrar [1a] **1** *vt animal etc* to train, teach, coach; *(Mil)* to drill; *(guiar)* to guide, lead.

2 adiestrarse *vr* to practise, train o.s.; **~ a** + *infin* to train o.s. to + *infin*; to teach o.s. to + *infin.*

adifés *adv* **(a)** *(CAm: con dificultad)* with difficulty. **(b)** *(Carib: a propósito)* on purpose, deliberately.

adinerado *adj* wealthy, moneyed, well-off.

ad infinitum *adv* ad infinitum.

adiós 1 *interj* good-bye!; *(al pasar en la calle etc)* hullo!; **¡~ Madrid, que te quedas sin gente!** good riddance! **2** *nm* good-bye, farewell; **ir a decir ~ a uno** to go to say good-bye to sb; **decir ~ a algo** *(fig)* to renounce sth, give sth up.

adiosito* *interj (esp LAm)* bye-bye!, cheerio!

adiposidad *nf,* **adiposis** *nf* adiposity.

adiposo *adj* adipose, fat.

aditamento *nm (complemento)* complement, addition; *(accesorio)* accessory.

aditivo *nm* additive; **~ alimenticio** food additive.

adivinación *nf* prophecy, divination; guessing; solving; **por ~** by guesswork; **~ de pensamientos** thought-reading, mind-reading.

adivinador(a) *nm/f* diviner.

adivinanza *nf* riddle, conundrum.

adivinar [1a] *vt* to prophesy, foretell, guess; *acertijo, puzzle* to solve; *solución* to guess correctly; *pensamientos* to read; **adivina quién lo hizo** it's anyone's guess who did it; *(nadie sabrá)* no-one will be any the wiser; *(es así de fácil)* it's as easy as that; *(juego de niños) equivale a* Guess Who; **~ a uno** to guess what sb means, see through sb.

adivino 1 *nm,* **adivina** *nf* fortune-teller. **2** *nm (Zool)* praying mantis.

adj *abr de* **adjunto** enclosure(s), enclosed, enc.

adjetivar [1a] *vt* **(a)** *(Gram)* to modify; to use adjectivally, use attributively. **(b)** *(fig)* to apply epithets to.

adjetivo 1 *adj* adjectival. **2** *nm* adjective.

adjudicación *nf* award; *(en subasta)* knocking down, sale; *(Méx Jur)* adjudication, award.

adjudicar [1g] **1** *vt* to award *(a* to); **~ algo a uno en 500 pesetas** to knock sth down to sb for 500 pesetas; **~ algo al mejor postor** to knock sth down to the highest bidder.

2 adjudicarse *vr*: **~ algo** to appropriate sth; **~ el premio** to win (the prize).

adjudicatorio, -a *nm/f* person who wins an award; *(en subasta)* successful bidder.

adjuntar [1a] *vt* to append, attach; *(en carta)* to enclose; **adjuntamos factura** we enclose our account.

adjunto 1 *adj* **(a)** *(unido)* joined on; attached *(a* to); *(en carta)* attached, enclosed; **remitir algo ~** to enclose sth.

(b) *persona* assistant; *V* **profesor.**

2 *nm* **(a)** *(añadidura)* addition, adjunct; *(en carta)* enclosure.

(b) *(persona)* assistant.

adlátere *nm* companion; associate; *(pey)* minion, minder.

adminículo *nm* accessory, gadget; **~s** emergency kit.

administración *nf* **(a)** *(gen)* administration; *(gerencia)* management; running; **en ~** in trust; **obras en ~** books handled by us, books for which we are agents; **A~ de Correos** General Post Office; **~ de empresas** *(Univ: curso)* business administration; **~ financiera** financial management; **~ de lotería** *place where lottery tickets are sold*; **~ militar** commissariat; **la A~ Pública** *(Cono Sur)* the Civil Service.

(b) *(Pol)* government, administration; **~ central** central government; **~ territorial** local government.

(c) *(oficina)* headquarters, central office; *(And: de hotel)* reception.

(d) *(Carib Ecl)* extreme unction.

administrador(a) *nm/f* administrator; manager; *(de propiedad)* steward, (land) agent; bailiff; **~ de aduanas** chief customs officer, collector of customs; **~ de correos** postmaster; **~ de fincas** land agent; **~ judicial** *(Méx Jur)* receiver; **es buena administradora** *(en casa)* she runs the house well, she's a good housekeeper.

administrar [1a] **1** *vt* to administer; to manage; to run; *justicia, sacramento* to administer. **2 administrarse** *vr* to manage one's own affairs, organize one's life; to get one's priorities right.

administrativo 1 *adj* administrative; managerial; of the administration, of the government. **2** *nm,* **administrativa** *nf* clerk; administrator, administrative officer.

admirable *adj* admirable.

admiración *nf* **(a)** *(gen)* admiration; **mi ~ por ti** my admiration for you. **(b)** *(asombro)* wonder, wonderment; amazement; **esto llenó a todos de ~** this filled everyone with wonderment. **(c)** *(Tip)* exclamation mark (¡!).

admirador(a) *nm/f* admirer.

admirar [1a] **1** *vt* **(a)** *(gen)* to admire; *(respetar)* to respect, look up to.

(b) *(asombrar)* to astonish, surprise, cause to marvel; **ser de ~** to cause admiration, surprise; **no es de ~ que ...** it's not surprising that ...; **esto admiró a todos** this astonished everyone, this filled everyone with amazement; **me admira su declaración** your statement amazes me, I am amazed at what you say.

2 admirarse *vr* to be astonished, be surprised, marvel *(de* at); **se admiró de saberlo** he was amazed to hear it.

admirativo *adj* admiring, full of admiration.

admisibilidad *nf* admissibility.

admisible *adj* admissible; acceptable; *excusa etc* plausible, credible, legitimate; **eso no es ~** that cannot be allowed.

admisión *nf* admission *(a* to); acceptance; *(Mec)* intake, inlet; **~ de aire** *(Mec)* air intake; **acto de ~** *(Jur)* validation (of a suit).

admitido *adj* accepted, allowed, agreed.

admitir [3a] *vt (gen)* to admit *(a* to, *en* into); *(aceptar)* to accept, allow; *(reconocer)* to recognize; *dudas* to leave room for; *mejora etc* to allow, be susceptible of; **esto no admite demora** this allows no delay; **no admite otra explicación** it allows no other explanation; **¿admite la Academia la palabra?** does the Academy accept the word?; **hay que ~ que ...** it must be admitted that ..., it must be confessed that ...; **'no se admiten propinas'** 'no tipping', 'tipping not allowed'; **la sala admite 500 personas** the hall holds 500 people.

admón. *abr de* **administración** administration, admin.

admonición *nf* warning.

admonitivo *adj,* **admonitorio** *adj señal, voz etc* warning.

ADN *nm abr de* **ácido desoxirribonucleico** deoxyribonucleic acid, DNA.

adnominal *adj, nm* adnominal.

-ado *V* **Aspects of Word Formation in Spanish 2.**

adobado *nm* pickled meat, pickled pork.

adobar [1a] *vt (gen)* to prepare, dress; *(cocinar)* to cook; *(sazonar)* to season; *carne* to pickle; *pieles* to tan, dress; *lámpara* to trim; *narración* to twist.

adobe *nm* **(a)** *(ladrillo)* adobe, sun-dried brick. **(b)** *(Cono Sur hum: pie)* big foot. **(c) descansar haciendo ~s** *(Méx)* to moonlight, do work on the side.

adobera *nf* **(a)** *(para ladrillos)* mould for making adobes; *(Cono Sur, Méx*) (queso)* brick-shaped cheese, *(molde)* cheese mould. **(b)** *(Cono Sur hum: pie)* big foot.

adobo *nm* **(a)** *(acto)* preparation, dressing; cooking; pickling; tanning. **(b)** *(salsa)* pickle, sauce; *(Méx)* red chili

sauce; (*para curtir*) tanning mixture.
adocenado *adj* common, ordinary, commonplace.
adocenarse [1a] *vr* (**a**) (*hacerse común*) to become commonplace. (**b**) (*decaer*) to become mediocre; (*estancarse*) to remain stagnant, become fossilized.
adoctrinación *nf* indoctrination.
adoctrinador *adj* indoctrinating, indoctrinatory.
adoctrinamiento *nm* indoctrination.
adoctrinar [1a] *vt* to teach, instruct (*en* in); to indoctrinate (*en* with).
adolecer [2d] *vi* to be ill, fall ill; **~ de** (*Med*) to be ill with, fall ill with; (*fig*) to suffer from, display.
adolescencia *nf* adolescence.
adolescente 1 *adj* adolescent. **2** *nmf* adolescent; youngster, teenager.
Adolfo *nm* Adolphus, Adolph, Adolf.
adolorido *adj* (*LAm*) = **dolorido**.
adonde *conj* where.
adónde 1 *adv interrog* where? **2** *conj* where.
Adonis *nm* Adonis.
adopción *nf* adoption; **madrileño de** (*o* **por**) **~** a citizen of Madrid by adoption.
adoptado, -a *nm/f* (*Méx*) adopted child.
adoptar [1a] *vt* to adopt.
adoptivo *adj* adoptive; *niño* adopted; **patria adoptiva** country of adoption.
adoquín *nm* (**a**) (*lit*) paving stone, flagstone, wooden paving block; **me comería hasta adoquines** I could eat a horse. (**b**) (*: *tonto*) fool, dope*.
adoquinado *nm* paving.
adoquinar [1a] *vt* to pave.
adorable *adj* adorable.
adoración *nf* adoration; worship; **A~ de los Reyes** Epiphany; **una mirada llena de ~** an adoring look.
adorador *adj* adoring.
adorar [1a] *vt* to adore; to worship.
adormecedor *adj* that sends one to sleep, soporific; *droga* sedative; *música, tono* lulling, dreamy.
adormecer [2d] **1** *vt* to make sleepy, send to sleep; (*fig*) to calm, lull.
2 adormecerse *vr* (**a**) (*amodorrarse*) to become sleepy, get drowsy; to fall asleep, go to sleep; (*miembro*) to go numb, go to sleep.
(**b**) **~ en** (*fig*) to persist in, go on with.
adormecido *adj* (*persona*) sleepy, drowsy; *miembro* numb; (*fig*) inactive.
adormecimiento *nm* sleepiness, drowsiness; numbness.
adormidera *nf* (*Bot*) opium plant, poppy; (*Med*) sleeping pill, sleeping draught.
adormilarse [1a] *vr*, **adormitarse** [1a] *vr* to doze, drowse.
adornar [1a] *vt* to adorn (*de* with); to decorate, embellish, bedeck; (*Cos*) to trim (*de* with); *comida* to garnish, decorate (*de* with); *persona* to endow, bless (*de* with); **le adornan mil virtudes** he is blessed with every virtue.
adornista *nmf* decorator.
adorno *nm* adornment; decoration, embellishment; (*Cos*) trimming; (*Culin*) garnishment, decoration; **~s** (*pey*) frills, adornments; **lo mismo sin los ~s** the same without the frills; **es el principal ~ de su ciudad** he is the chief adornment of his city, he is the city's chief claim to fame.
adosado 1 *adj*: **casa adosada** *o* **chalet ~** semi-detached house. **2** *nm* semi-detached house.
adosar [1a] *vt* (**a**) **~ algo a una pared** to lean sth against a wall; to place sth with its back against a wall.
(**b**) (*LAm*) (*juntar*) to join firmly; (*en carta*) to attach, include, enclose (with a letter).
adquirido *adj*: **mal ~** ill-gotten.
adquiriente *nmf* purchaser.
adquirir [3i] *vt* (*gen*) to acquire; to obtain; to procure; to buy, purchase; *hábito* to get into, form.
adquisición *nf* acquisition; procurement; (*compra*) purchase.
adquisitivo *adj* acquisitive; **poder ~** purchasing power.
adquisividad *nf* acquisitiveness.
adral *nm* rail, sideboard (of a cart *etc*).
adrede, adredemente *adv* on purpose, purposely, deliberately.
adrenalina *nf* adrenalin(e).
Adriano *nm* Hadrian.
Adriático *nm*: **el** (**Mar**) **~** the Adriatic (Sea).
adscribir [3a; *ptp* **adscrito**] *vt*: **~ a** to appoint to, assign to; **estuvo adscrito al servicio de** ... he was attached to ..., he was in the service of ...
aduana *nf* (**a**) (*institución*) customs; (*oficina*) customs house; (*impuesto*) customs duty; **libre de ~** duty-free; **pasar por la ~** to go through the customs. (**b**) (‡) (*escondite*) pad‡, hide-out; (*refugio*) safe house; (*Méx: burdel*) brothel.
aduanal *adj* customs (*atr*).
aduanero 1 *adj* customs (*atr*). **2** *nm*, **aduanera** *nf* customs officer.
aducir [3n] *vt* to adduce, bring forward; to offer as proof; to quote, cite; *prueba* to provide, furnish.
adueñarse [1a] *vr*: **~ de** to take possession of; to appropriate; (*fig*) to master.
adujar [1a] *vt* (*Náut*) to coil.
adulación *nf* flattery, adulation.
adulada* *nf* (*Méx*) flattery.
adulador 1 *adj* flattering, fawning. **2** *nm*, **aduladora** *nf* flatterer.
adular [1a] *vt* to flatter.
adulate *adj, nm* (*LAm*) = **adulón**.
adulón* 1 *adj* fawning, cringing, soapy*. **2** *nm*, **adulona** *nf* toady, creep‡.
adulonería *nf* (*LAm*) (**a**) (*adulación*) flattering, fawning. (**b**) (*carácter*) fawning nature, soapiness.
adúltera *nf* adulteress.
adulteración *nf* adulteration.
adulterado *adj* adulterated.
adulterar [1a] **1** *vt* to adulterate. **2** *vi* to commit adultery.
adulterino *adj* adulterous; *moneda etc* spurious, counterfeit.
adulterio *nm* adultery.
adúltero 1 *adj* adulterous. **2** *nm* adulterer.
adultez *nf* adulthood.
adulto *adj, nm*, **adulta** *nf* adult, grown-up.
adunar [1a] *vt* (*lit*) to join, unite.
adunco *adj* bent, curved.
adustez *nf* austerity, severity; grimness, sternness; sullenness.
adusto *adj* (**a**) (*caliente*) scorching hot. (**b**) (*severo*) austere, severe; (*inexorable*) grim, stern; (*hosco*) sullen.
advenedizo 1 *adj* foreign, from outside; newly arrived; (*pey*) upstart. **2** *nm*, **advenediza** *nf* foreigner, outsider; newcomer; (*pey*) upstart.
advenimiento *nm* advent, arrival; **~ al trono** accession to the throne.
adventicio *adj* adventitious.
adverbial *adj* adverbial.
adverbio *nm* adverb.
adversario, -a *nm/f* adversary, opponent, antagonist.
adversidad *nf* (*gen*) adversity; (*revés*) setback, mishap.
adverso *adj lado* opposite, facing; *resultado etc* adverse, untoward; *suerte* bad.
advertencia *nf* (*aviso*) warning; (*consejo*) piece of advice; (*recordatorio*) reminder; (*en libro*) preface, foreword; **sobre ~ no hay engaño** forewarned is forearmed.
advertido *adj* sharp, wide-awake.
advertimiento *nm* = **advertencia**.
advertir [3i] **1** *vt* (**a**) (*observar*) to notice, observe; (*darse cuenta de*) to become aware of; **~ que** ... to observe that ...
(**b**) (*indicar*) to point out, draw attention to.
(**c**) (*aconsejar*) to advise; (*prevenir*) to warn; (*amonestar*) to caution; **~ que** ... to advise that ..., recommend that ...; **les advertimos que** ... (*Com*) we would advise you that ...; **te advierto que ...*** mind you, ...
2 *vi*: **~ en** to notice, observe, become aware of; to take notice of, bear in mind.
Adviento *nm* Advent.
advocación *nf* (*Ecl*) name, dedication; **una iglesia bajo la ~ de San Felipe** a church dedicated to St Philip.
advocar [1g] *vt* (*LAm*) to advocate.
ADVP 1 *adj abr de* **adicto** (*m*) **a drogas por vía parenteral** who uses drugs intravenously. **2** *nm* intravenous drug user.
adyacencia *nf* (*Cono Sur*) nearness, proximity; **en las ~s** in the vicinity.
adyacente *adj* adjacent.
AECE [a'eθe] *nf abr de* **Asociación Española de Cooperación Europea.**
aechaduras *nfpl* chaff.
AEE *nf abr de* **Agencia Europea del Espacio** European Space Agency, ESA.
aeración *nf* aeration.
aéreo *adj* aerial; air (*atr*); *ferrocarril etc* overhead, elevated.
aero... *pref* aero...

aerobic *nm*, **aeróbica** *nf* aerobics.
aeróbico *adj* aerobic.
aerobismo *nm* (*Cono Sur*) aerobics.
aerobús *nm* (*Aer*) airbus; (*Carib*) long-distance bus, coach.
aérocar *nm* airbus.
aeroclub *nm* flying club.
aerochati* *nf* air-hostess.
aerodeslizador *nm*, **aerodeslizante** *nm* hovercraft.
aerodinámica *nf* aerodynamics.
aerodinámico *adj* aerodynamic; (*perfil etc*) streamlined.
aerodinamismo *nm* streamlining.
aerodinamizar [1f] *vt* to streamline.
aeródromo *nm*, **aerodromo** *nm* aerodrome, airdrome (*US*), airfield.
aeroenviar [1c] *vt* to send by air.
aeroespacial *adj* aerospace (*atr*).
aeroestación *nf* air terminal.
aerofaro *nm* (*Aer*) beacon.
aerofoto *nf* aerial photograph.
aerofumigación *nf* crop-dusting.
aerogenerador *nm* wind turbine.
aerograma *nm* air-letter, aerogram.
aeroligero *nm* microlight.
aerolínea *nf* airline.
aerolito *nm* meteorite.
aeromodelismo *nm* aeromodelling, making model aeroplanes.
aeromodelista *nmf* model aeroplane enthusiast.
aeromodelo *nm* model aeroplane.
aeromotor *nm* aero-engine, aircraft engine.
aeromoza *nf* (*LAm*) air hostess, stewardess, flight attendant (*US*).
aeronauta *nmf* aeronaut.
aeronáutica *nf* aeronautics.
aeronáutico *adj* aeronautical.
aeronaval *adj* air-sea (*atr*); **base** ~ air-sea base.
aeronave *nf* airship; (*Carib etc*) airliner.
aeronavegabilidad *nf* airworthiness.
aeronavegable *adj* airworthy.
aeroplano *nm* aeroplane, airplane (*US*).
aeroportuario *adj* airport (*atr*).
aeroposta *nf* (*LAm*) airmail.
aeropuerto *nm* airport.
aerosol *nm* aerosol.
aerostática *nf* ballooning.
aeróstato *nm* balloon, aerostat.
aerotaxi *nm* air taxi.
aeroterrestre *adj* air-ground *atr*.
aerotransportado *adj* airborne.
aerotransportista *nm* (air) carrier.
aeroturbina *nf* wind turbine.
aerovía *nf* (*ruta*) airway; (*compañía*) airline.
AES *nm abr de* **acuerdo económico social** wages pact.
a/f *abr de* **a favor** in favour.
afabilidad *nf* affability, good nature, geniality; pleasantness, niceness.
afable *adj* affable, good-natured, genial; easy, pleasant, nice.
afablemente *adv* affably; pleasantly.
afamado *adj* famous, noted (*por* for).
afamar [1a] **1** *vt* to make famous. **2 afamarse** *vr* to become famous, make a reputation.
afán *nm* (**a**) (*industria*) hard work, industry; (*labor*) exertion, toil.
(**b**) (*ansia*) anxiety; (*solicitud*) solicitude.
(**c**) (*deseo*) desire, urge; (*celo*) zeal, eagerness; **el ~ de** the desire for, the urge for; **~ de estudios** studiousness, keenness to study; **~ de lucro** profit motive; **~ de superación** urge to improve, will to do better; **~ de victoria** urge to win; **con** ~ zealously, keenly.
afanador *nm* (*Cono Sur*: *ladrón*) thief, burglar; (*Méx*: *obrero*) menial worker; (*de limpieza*; *t* **afanadora** *nf*) cleaner.
afanaduría *nf* (*Méx Med*) casualty ward.
afanar [1a] **1** *vt* (**a**) (*gen*) to press, harass, bother; (*LAm*: *empujar*) to hustle; to jostle.
(**b**) (*CAm*: *ganar*) to earn.
(**c**) (*) to swipe‡, pinch*, nick‡.
2 afanarse *vr* (**a**) (*trabajar duro*) to toil, labour (*en* at); to strive hard, exert o.s., go all out; **~ por** + *infin* to strive to + *infin*; to toil to + *infin*.
(**b**) (*And*: *enfadarse*) to get angry.
afanoso *adj* *trabajo* hard, heavy, laborious; *tarea* tough, uphill; *temperamento* industrious; solicitous; *actividad*, *búsqueda* feverish, hectic.
afantasmado *adj* conceited.
afarolado *adj* (*LAm*) excited, worked up.
afarolarse [1a] *vr* (*LAm*) to get excited, make a fuss, get worked up*.
afasia *nf* aphasia.
afásico *adj* (*Med*) aphasic, suffering from aphasia.
AFE ['afe] *nf abr de* **Asociación de Futbolistas Españoles** ≈ Football Association, FA.
afeamiento *nm* (**a**) (*físicamente*) defacing, disfigurement. (**b**) (*fig*) condemnation, censure.
afear [1a] *vt* (**a**) (*hacer feo*) to make ugly, deface, spoil, disfigure; **los errores que afean el texto** the mistakes which disfigure the text.
(**b**) (*fig*) to condemn, censure, decry.
afección *nf* (**a**) (*afecto*) affection, fondness; (*inclinación*) inclination; **afecciones del alma** emotions; emotional disorders.
(**b**) (*Med*) condition, trouble, disease; **~ cardíaca** heart trouble, heart disease; **~ hepática** liver complaint; **~ lumbar** back trouble.
afeccionarse [1a] *vr*: **~ a** (*Cono Sur*) to take a liking to, become fond of.
afectación *nf* affectation.
afectadamente *adv* affectedly.
afectado *adj* (**a**) (*gen*) affected; (*estilo*) stilted, precious.
(**b**) (*Med*) **estar ~ del corazón** to have heart trouble; **estar ~ (del pecho)** (*Méx*) to be consumptive; **estar ~** (*Cono Sur*) to be hurt; to be ill.
afectante *adj* (*Cono Sur*) disturbing, distressing.
afectar [1a] **1** *vt* (**a**) (*gen*) to affect, have an effect on; **nos afecta gravemente** it seriously affects us; **su muerte nos afectó mucho** we were terribly saddened by his death; **por lo que afecta a esto** with regard to this; **las lluvias afectan al sur** it's raining in the south.
(**b**) (*por emoción*) to affect, move.
(**c**) (*fingir*) to affect, pretend, feign; to put on a show of; **~ ignorancia** to feign ignorance.
(**d**) (*Jur*) to tie up, encumber.
(**e**) (*LAm*: *dañar*) to hurt, harm, damage.
(**f**) (*LAm*) *forma etc* to take on, assume.
(**g**) (*LAm*) *fondos* to set aside (*a* for); (*destinar*) to devote (*a* to).
2 afectarse *vr* (*LAm*) to fall ill.
afectísimo *adj* affectionate; **suyo** ~ yours truly.
afectividad *nf* emotional nature, emotion(alism); sensitivity.
afectivo *adj* affective; emotional.
afecto 1 *adj* (**a**) (*gen*) affectionate; **~ a** attached to, fond of; inclined towards.
(**b**) **~ a** (*Jur*) subject to, liable for.
(**c**) **~ de** (*Med*) afflicted with.
2 *nm* (**a**) (*cariño*) affection, fondness (*a* for), attachment (*a* to); **tomar ~ a** to become attached to, grow fond of.
(**b**) (*emoción*) feeling, emotion; (*instinto moral*) moral instinct.
afectuosamente *adv* affectionately; ~ (*LAm*: *en carta*) yours affectionately.
afectuosidad *nf* affection.
afectuoso *adj* affectionate.
afeitada *nf* = **afeitado** (**a**).
afeitado *nm* (**a**) shave; shaving. (**b**) (*Taur*) blunting (*o* trimming) of the horns.
afeitadora *nf* electric razor, electric shaver.
afeitar [1a] **1** *vt* (**a**) *barba* to shave; *planta*, *rabo* to trim; (*Taur*) *cuernos* to blunt, trim; *toro* to blunt (*o* trim) the horns of; **¡que te afeiten!*** get your head seen to!*
(**b**) (*mujer*) to make up, paint, apply cosmetics to.
(**c**) (*: *pasar*) to brush (past), shave.
2 afeitarse *vr* (**a**) (*hombre*) to shave, have a shave.
(**b**) (*mujer*) to make o.s. up, put one's make-up on.
afeite *nm* make-up, cosmetic(s), rouge.
afelpado *adj* plush, velvety.
afeminación *nf* effeminacy.
afeminado 1 *adj* effeminate. **2** *nm* effeminate person.
afeminamiento *nm* effeminacy.
afeminarse [1a] *vr* to become effeminate.
aferrado *adj* stubborn, obstinate; **seguir ~ a** to remain firm in, stick to, stand by.
aferrar [1j *or* 1a] **1** *vt* to grasp, seize, grapple; (*Náut*) *barco* to moor, *vela etc* furl.
2 aferrarse *vr* (**a**) (*Náut*) to grapple; to anchor, moor; (*dos personas*) to grapple (together).
(**b**) **~ a, ~ en** (*fig*) to stick to, stand by; **~ a un principio**

to stick to a principle; ~ **a una esperanza** to clutch at a hope, cling to a hope; ~ **a su opinión** to remain firm in one's opinion, stick to one's view.

afestonado *adj* festooned.

affaire *nm* (*Cono Sur*: *nf*) affair(e).

afgano *adj, nm,* **afgana** *nf* Afghan.

Afganistán *nm* Afghanistan.

afianzado, -a *nm/f* (*LAm*) fiancé(e).

afianzamiento *nm* (**a**) (*refuerzo*) strengthening, fastening, securing. (**b**) (*Fin etc*) guarantee, security; (*Jur*) surety, bond.

afianzar [1f] **1** *vt* (**a**) (*reforzar*) to strengthen, fasten, secure; (*apoyar*) to support, prop up; (*fig*) to support, back.

(**b**) (*avalar*) to guarantee, vouch for; (*salir garante por*) to stand surety for.

2 afianzarse *vr* to steady o.s.; (*fig*) to become strong, become established; to make o.s. secure; ~ **a** to catch hold of, hold fast to; **la reacción se afianzó después de la guerra** the reaction set in after the war.

afición *nf* (**a**) (*amor*) fondness, liking (*a* for); (*inclinación*) taste (*a* for), inclination (*a* towards); **cobrar ~ a, tomar ~ a** to acquire a liking for, take a liking to; **tener ~ a** to like, be fond of.

(**b**) (*pasatiempo*) hobby, pastime; (*interés*) interest; **¿qué aficiones tiene?** what are his interests?; **pinta por ~** he paints as a hobby.

(**c**) (*Dep etc*) **la ~** the experts; the fans, the supporters; the sporting fraternity; **aquí hay mucha ~** there is a large public for it here, support is strong here, the fans are terribly keen here.

aficionado 1 *adj* (**a**) (*entusiasta*) keen, enthusiastic; **es muy ~** he's very keen.

(**b**) ~ **a** keen on, fond of; with a taste for; **ser** (*o* **estar**) **muy ~ a** to be very keen on, be very fond of.

(**c**) *jugador etc* amateur.

2 *nm,* **aficionada** *nf* (*gen*) enthusiast; (*no profesional*) amateur; (*como espectador etc*: *Dep*) fan, follower, supporter, (*Cine, Teat*) fan; **gritaban los ~s** the fans were shouting; **todos los ~s a la música** all music lovers; **la cantante y sus ~s** the singer and her fans; **función de ~s** amateur performance; **partido de ~s** amateur game; **somos simples ~s** we're just amateurs; **tenis para ~s** amateur tennis.

aficionar [1a] **1** *vt*: ~ **a uno a algo** to make sb keen on sth, make sb like sth.

2 aficionarse *vr*: ~ **a algo** to get fond of sth, take a liking to sth, take to sth; to become a follower (*o* fan) of sth; ~ **a** + *infin* to get fond of + *ger*, take to + *ger*.

afiche *nm* (*cartel*) poster; (*Cono Sur*: *dibujo*) illustration, picture.

afidávit *nm* affidavit, sworn statement.

áfido *nm* aphid.

afiebrado *adj* feverish.

afijo *nm* affix.

afiladera *nf* grindstone, whetstone.

afilado *adj borde* sharp; *punta* tapering, sharp.

afilador *nm* (**a**) (*persona*) knife-grinder; (*Téc*) steel, sharpener; strop, razor strop; ~ **de lápices** pencil sharpener. (**b**) (*Cono Sur* ††) womanizer, seducer.

afiladora *nf* (*Cono Sur* ††) flirt, coquette.

afiladura *nf* sharpening.

afilalápices *nm invar* pencil sharpener.

afilar [1a] **1** *vt* (**a**) *herramienta* to sharpen, put an edge on; (*sacar punta a*) to put a point on; *cuchillo* to whet, grind; *navaja* to strop.

(**b**) (*Cono Sur* ††: *flirtear*) to court; to flirt with, seduce.

(**c**) (*Cono Sur***) to screw**, fuck**.

2 afilarse *vr* (**a**) to get sharp; (*cara*) to sharpen, grow thin, get peaked; (*dedos*) to taper.

(**b**) (*And*: *prepararse*) to get ready; to get ready to tell sb off.

afiliación *nf* affiliation.

afiliado 1 *adj* affiliated (*a* to), member ...; (*Com*) subsidiary; **los países ~s** the member countries.

2 *nm,* **afiliada** *nf* (*And, Cono Sur*) member.

afiliarse [1b] *vr*: ~ **a** to affiliate to, join.

afiligranado *adj* filigreed; (*fig*) delicate, fine; *persona* dainty.

afilón *nm* (*correa*) strop; (*chaira*) steel.

afilorar [1a] *vt* (*Carib*) to adorn.

afín 1 *adj* (**a**) (*contiguo*) bordering, adjacent. (**b**) (*conexo*) related, similar, allied; *persona* related. **2** *nmf* relation by marriage.

afinación *nf* refining, polishing; completion; (*Aut, Mús*) tuning.

afinado *adj* finished, polished; (*Mús*) in tune.

afinador *nm* (*Mús*) tuning key; (*persona*) tuner; ~ **de pianos** piano tuner.

afinar [1a] **1** *vt* (*completar*) to perfect, put the finishing touch to, complete; (*refinar*) to refine, polish; *puntería etc* to sharpen, make more precise; (*Téc*) to purify, refine; (*Aut, Mús*) to tune.

2 *vi* to sing in tune, play in tune; (*fig*) to be precise, be exact.

3 afinarse *vr* (*modales*) to become more refined.

afincado *nm* (*Cono Sur*) farmer.

afincarse [1g] *vr* to establish o.s., settle (in a town *etc*).

afinidad *nf* affinity (*t Quím*); relationship, similarity, kinship (*con* with); **parentesco por ~** relationship by marriage.

afirmación *nf* affirmation.

afirmado *nm* (*Cono Sur*) (*acera*) paving, paved surface; (*Aut*) road surface.

afirmar [1a] **1** *vt* (**a**) (*reforzar*) to make firm, steady, secure, strengthen.

(**b**) (*declarar*) to affirm, assert, state; *lealtad etc* to declare, protest; ~ **que ...** to affirm that ..., state that ...; ~ **bajo juramento** to swear under oath.

2 *vi* (*Cono Sur, Méx*: *pegar*) to deal out blows, lash out.

3 afirmarse *vr* (**a**) (*recobrar el equilibrio*) to steady o.s.; ~ **en los estribos** (*lit*) to settle one's feet firmly in the stirrups; (*Cono Sur*: *fig*) to grit one's teeth.

(**b**) ~ **en lo dicho** to repeat what one has said, maintain one's opinion.

afirmativamente *adv* affirmatively; **contestar ~** to answer in the affirmative.

afirmativo *adj* affirmative, positive; **voto ~** vote in favour, vote for.

aflatarse [1a] *vr* (*LAm*) to be sad.

aflautado *adj voz* high, fluty.

aflicción *nf* affliction; grief, sorrow.

aflictivo *adj* (*LAm*) distressing, grievous.

afligente *adj* (*CAm, Méx*) distressing, upsetting.

afligido 1 *adj* grieving, sorrowing, heartbroken; ~ **por** stricken with; **los ~s padres** the bereaved parents.

2 *nm*: **los ~s** the afflicted; (*en una muerte*) the bereaved.

afligir [3e] **1** *vt* (**a**) (*gen*) to afflict; (*angustiar*) to grieve, pain, distress. (**b**) (*LAm*: *golpear*) to beat, hit.

2 afligirse *vr* to grieve (*con, de, por* about, at); **no te aflijas** don't grieve over it; **no te aflijas tanto** you must not let it affect you like this.

aflojamiento *nm* slackening; loosening; relaxation; abatement, weakening.

aflojar [1a] **1** *vt* (**a**) *tuerca, cuerda, paso etc* to slacken; *nudo etc* to loosen, undo; *presión* to relax; *agarro* to loosen, ease, let go; *freno* to release, take off; *vientre* to ease.

(**b**) (*) *dinero* to fork out*, pay up.

2 *vi* to slacken; to relent, let up; (*fiebre etc*) to abate, weaken; (*devoción*) to grow cool; (*dedicación etc*) to get slack.

3 aflojarse *vr* (*moderarse*) to slacken (off, up); (*pieza*) to come loose, work loose; (*fiebre, calor*) to abate; (*devoción*) to cool (off), diminish; (*interés*) to flag; (*precio*) to go down, weaken; (*Carib***) to shit o.s.**.

afloración *nf* outcrop.

aflorado *adj* fine, elegant.

afloramiento *nm* = **afloración.**

aflorar [1a] *vi* (*Geol*) to crop out, outcrop, appear on the surface; (*sentimiento etc*) to show, appear; to emerge.

afluencia *nf* (**a**) (*gen*) inflow, influx, flow; (*de gente etc*) press; crowd, jam; (*en reunión*) attendance, number present; **la ~ de turistas** the influx of tourists; **la ~ de coches al estadio** the flow of cars towards the stadium; **tan grande fue la ~** so great was the rush.

(**b**) (*abundancia*) abundance, plenty.

(**c**) (*elocuencia*) eloquence, fluency.

afluente 1 *adj* (**a**) *agua etc* flowing, inflowing. (**b**) *discurso* eloquent, fluent. **2** *nm* (*Geog*) tributary.

afluir [3g] *vi* to flow (*a* into); (*personas*) to flow, flock (*a* into, to).

aflujo *nm* (*Med*) afflux, congestion; (*Mec*) inflow, influx, inlet.

aflús* *adj* (*LAm*) broke*, flat* (*US*).

afluxionarse [1a] *vr* (*LAm*) to catch a cold.

afma., afmo. *abr de* **afectísima, afectísimo** Yours.

afoetear [1a] *vt* (*And, Carib* ††) to whip, beat.

afonía *nf* hoarseness, state of having lost one's voice.

afónico *adj* (**a**) (*ronco*) hoarse, voiceless; **estar ~** to be hoarse, have lost one's voice. (**b**) *letra* silent, mute.
aforador *nm* gauger.
aforar [1a] *vt* (*Téc*) to gauge; (*fig*) to appraise, evaluate.
aforismo *nm* aphorism.
aforístico *adj* aphoristic.
aforjudo* *adj* (*Cono Sur*) silly, stupid.
aforo *nm* (**a**) (*Téc*) gauging; (*fig*) appraisal, valuation.
(**b**) (*Teat etc*) capacity; **el teatro tiene un ~ de 2.000** the theatre has a capacity of 2,000, the theatre can seat 2,000.
(**c**) (*Com*) import duty.
aforrar [1a] **1** *vt* (**a**) (*lit*) to line. (**b**) (*Cono Sur**: *golpear*) to smack, punch. **2 aforrarse** *vr* (**a**) to wrap up warm, put on warm underclothes. (**b**) (*) to stuff o.s.*, tuck it away*.
afortunadamente *adv* fortunately, luckily.
afortunado *adj* fortunate, lucky.
afrailado* *adj* (*LAm*) churchy*.
afrancesado 1 *adj* francophile; (*pey*) frenchified; (*Pol*) pro-French, supporting the French.
2 *nm*, **afrancesada** *nf* francophile; (*pey*) frenchified person; (*Pol*) pro-French person, French sympathizer.
afrancesamiento *nm* (*sentimiento*) francophilism, pro-French feeling; (*proceso*) gallicization, frenchification (*pej*).
afrancesarse [1a] *vr* to go French, become gallicized, acquire French habits; to become a francophile.
afrechillo *nm* (*Cono Sur Agr*) bran.
afrecho *nm* bran; (*LAm*) sawdust; **~ remojado** mash.
afrenta *nf* affront, insult, outrage.
afrentar [1a] **1** *vt* (*insultar*) to affront, insult, outrage; (*deshonrar*) to dishonour. **2 afrentarse** *vr* to be ashamed (*de* of).
afrentoso *adj* insulting, outrageous.
África *nf* Africa; **~ Austral** Southern Africa; **~ negra** Black Africa; **~ del Norte** North Africa; **~ del Sur** South Africa.
africaans *nm* Afrikaans.
africado *adj* (*Ling*) affricate.
africánder *nm* Afrikander.
africanista *nmf* specialist in African affairs; person interested in Africa.
africano, a *adj, nm/f* African.
afrijolar [1a] *vt* (*And*) to bother, annoy; **~ una tarea a uno** to give sb an unpleasant job to do.
afro *adj* Afro; **peinado ~** Afro hairstyle.
afroamericano *adj* Afro-American.
afroasiático *adj* Afro-Asian.
afrobrasileño *adj* Afro-Brazilian.
afrocaribeño *adj* Afro-Caribbean.
afrocubano *adj* Afro-Cuban.
afrodisiaco, afrodisíaco *adj, nm* aphrodisiac.
Afrodita *nf* Aphrodite.
afronegrismo *nm* (*LAm*) word borrowed from an African language.
afrontar [1a] *vt* (**a**) *dos personas etc* to bring face to face. (**b**) *peligro, problema etc* to confront, face; to face up to; to deal with, tackle.
afrutado 1 *adj vino* fruity. **2** *nm* fruity flavour, fruitiness.
afta *nf* (*Med*) sore.
aftosa *nf* foot-and-mouth (disease).
afuera 1 *adv* out, outside; **¡~!** out of the way!, get out!, clear the way!; **de ~** from outside; (*LAm*) outside; **por ~** on the outside; **las hojas de ~** the outer leaves, the outside leaves.
2 ~ de *prep* (*LAm*) outside.
3 ~s *nfpl* outskirts, outer suburbs, outlying areas.
afuerano, afuereño, afuerino (*LAm*) **1** *adj* foreign; strange; from elsewhere, from outside.
2 *nm*, **afuerana, afuereña, afuerina** *nf* (*extranjero*) foreigner; stranger, outsider; (*trabajador*) itinerant worker, casual worker.
afuetear [1a] *vt* (*LAm*) to whip, beat.
afufa‡ *nf* flight, escape; **tomar las ~s** to beat it*.
afufar‡ [1a] *vi*, **afufarse** *vr* to beat it*, get out quick.
afufón‡ *nm* flight, escape.
afusilar [1a] *vt* (*LAm*) to shoot.
afutrarse [1a] *vr* (*Cono Sur*) to dress up.
ag. *abr de* **agosto** August, Aug.
agachada* *nf* trick, dodge*.
agachadiza *nf* (*Orn*) snipe; **hacer la ~** to duck, try not to be seen.
agachado*, -a *nm/f* (*LAm*) down-and-out, bum (*US*).
agachar [1a] **1** *vt cabeza* to bend, bow.
2 agacharse *vr* (**a**) (*agazaparse*) to stoop, crouch, get down; (*acuclillarse*) to squat; (*bajar la cabeza*) to duck; (*encogerse*) to cower.
(**b**) (*fig*) to go into hiding, lie low.
(**c**) (*LAm*: *rendirse*) to give in, submit.
(**d**) (*LAm*: *prepararse*) to get ready.
(**e**) **~ algo** (*Méx**) to keep quiet about sth (out of spite), keep sth to o.s.
(**f**) **~ con algo** (*And, Méx*) to make off with sth, pocket sth.
agache *nm* (*And*) fib, tale; **andar de ~** to be on the run.
agachón‡ *adj* (*LAm*) weakwilled, submissive.
agafar‡ [1a] *vt* to pinch*, nick‡.
agalbanado *adj* lazy, shiftless.
agalla *nf* (**a**) (*Bot*) gall; **~ de roble** oak apple.
(**b**) (*Pez*) gill.
(**c**) (*And*: *codicia*) greed.
(**d**) **~s** (*Anat*) tonsils; (*Med*) tonsillitis.
(**e**) **~s*** pluck, guts; **es hombre de ~s** he's got guts; **tener (muchas) ~s** to be brave, have guts.
(**f**) **tener ~s** (*LAm*) (*ser glotón*) to be greedy; (*ser tacaño*) to be mean; (*ser descarado*) to have lots of cheek*; (*Cono Sur*: *ser astuto*) to be sharp, be smart.
agalludo* *adj* (*LAm*) (*atrevido*) daring, bold; (*tacaño*) mean, stingy; (*And*) greedy.
ágape *nm* (*Hist*) love feast; banquet, feast.
agareno 1 *adj* Moslem. **2** *nm*, **agarena** *nf* Moslem.
agarrada *nf* (*riña*) row, argument; (*pelea*) scrap, brawl; (*Dep*) tackle.
agarradera *nf* (*LAm*), **agarradero** *nm* (**a**) (*manija*) handle; grip; (*de cortina*) cord.
(**b**) (*amparo*) protection; **~s*** pull, influence; **tener (buenas) ~s** to have pull, have friends in the right places.
agarrado *adj* (**a**) mean, tight-fisted, stingy. (**b**) **baile ~** slow dance.
agarrador *adj* (*And, Cono Sur*) *licor* strong.
agarrafar [1a] *vt* to grab hold of.
agarrao* *nm* slow dance.
agarrar [1a] **1** *vt* (**a**) (*gen*) to grasp, grip, seize, catch hold of; to grab, clutch; to pick up; **está bien agarrado*** he's got lots of pull; (*fig*) **no sé por donde ~lo** I don't know how to take him.
(**b**) (*) to get, wangle*.
(**c**) (*Com*) to corner the market in, pile up stocks of.
(**d**) (*LAm*: *sustituye a 'coger' en muchas aplicaciones*) to take; to pick up; **~ un autobús** to catch a bus; **~ una flor** to pick a flower; **~ un resfriado** to catch a cold; **agarra el libro del estante** get the book off the shelf.
(**e**) **~la**‡ to get plastered‡, get drunk.
(**f**) (*CAm, Carib, Méx**: *captar*) to get*, understand.
(**g**) (*Cono Sur*) **~ el vuelo** (*despegar*) to take off; **~ a palos a uno** (*) to beat sb up*.
(**h**) (*Carib***) to fuck**.
2 *vi* (**a**) (*gen*) to take hold (*de* of); (*Bot*) to take root; (*pintura etc*) to stick.
(**b**) (*LAm*) **~ para** to set out for; **agarre por esta calle** take this street; **agarró y se fue*** he upped and offed*.
3 agarrarse *vr* (**a**) (*dos personas*) to fight, have a fight; (*And*) to fight it out; **se agarraron a puñetazos** they fought it out with fists.
(**b**) (*asirse*) to hold on; (*Aut*) to hold the road; **¡agárrate bien!** hold on!, hold tight!; **~ a, ~ de** to hold on to, grip, seize; **~ al camino** (*Aut*) to hold the road; **agárrate!** (*) wait for it!; listen to this!; **~la*** to burst into tears.
(**c**) **se le agarró la fiebre** the fever took hold of him; **se le agarró un fuerte catarro** he got a severe cold.
(**d**) (*LAm**) **~la con uno** (*pelear*) to come to blows with sb; (*resentir*) to have sth against sb.
agarre *nm* (**a**) (*LAm*: *agarro*) hold; (*Aut*) road-holding (quality). (**b**) (*And*: *mango*) handle. (**c**) (*fig*: *valor*) guts, toughness. (**d**) **tener ~*** to have pull, be able to pull strings.
agarrete *adj* (*And*) mean, stingy.
agarro *nm* grasp, hold, clutch.
agarroch(e)ar [1a] *vt* to jab with a goad; (*Taur*) to prick with a pike.
agarrón *nm* (*LAm*) (**a**) (*tirón*) jerk, pull, tug. (**b**) = **agarrada.**
agarroso *adj* (*CAm*) sharp, acrid, bitter.
agarrotamiento *nm* tightening; strangling; (*Aut*) seizing up.
agarrotar [1a] **1** *vt lío etc* to tie tight; *persona* to squeeze tight, press tightly; *criminal* to garrotte; **esta corbata me agarrota** this tie is strangling me; **tengo los músculos agarrotados** I'm stiff.

2 agarrotarse *vr* (*Med*) to stiffen, get numb; (*Aut etc*) to seize up.
agasajado, -a *nm/f* chief guest, guest of honour.
agasajador *adj* warm, welcoming.
agasajamiento *nm* = **agasajo**.
agasajar [1a] *vt* to treat well, fête, give a royal welcome to; to entertain royally, wine and dine.
agasajo *nm* good treatment, kindness; royal welcome, lavish hospitality, entertainment.
ágata *nf* agate.
agatas *adv* (*Cono Sur*) (**a**) (*con dificultad*) (only) with great difficulty. (**b**) (*apenas*) hardly, scarcely; ~ **llegó, empezó a cantar** no sooner had he arrived than he started to sing.
agauchado *adj* (*Cono Sur*) like a *gaucho*.
agaucharse [1a] *vr* (*Cono Sur*) to imitate (*o* dress like) a *gaucho*.
agave *nf* agave, American aloe.
agavilladora *nf* binder, reaper.
agavillar [1a] **1** *vt trigo* to bind (in sheaves); *libro* to bind.
2 agavillarse *vr* to gang up, band together.
agazapar [1a] **1** *vt* (*) to grab, grab hold of, nab*.
2 agazaparse *vr* to hide; to crouch down, duck (down); **hay otra posibilidad agazapada allí** there's another possibility concealed in it; **tras esto se agazapa otra cosa** sth else is concealed behind this.
agencia *nf* agency; office, bureau; (*Cono Sur*: *montepío*) pawnshop; ~ **de cobro** debt-collecting agency; ~ **de colocaciones** employment agency; ~ **de contactos** dating agency; ~ **de créditos** credit agency; ~ **de damas de compañía** escort agency; ~ **exclusiva** exclusive agency; ~ **de información,** ~ **de noticias,** ~ **de prensa** news agency; ~ **inmobiliaria** estate agent's; ~ **de patentes** patents office; ~ **de promoción** development agency; ~ **de publicidad** advertising agency; ~ **de seguridad** security company; ~ **de transportes** carriers, removal business; ~ **de turismo,** ~ **de viajes** travel agency; ~ **única** sole agency.
agenciar [1b] **1** *vt* (*lograr*) to bring about, effect, engineer; (*obtener*) to obtain, procure (*a uno* for sb); (*pey*) to wangle*, fiddle*; *trato* to negotiate.
2 agenciarse *vr* to manage, get along; **yo me las agenciaré para llegar allí** I'll manage to get there somehow, I'll work out how to get there; ~ **algo*** to get hold of sth, manage to obtain sth.
agenciero *nm* (*Cono Sur*) (*de lotería*) lottery agent; (*agente*) representative; (*Cono Sur*: *de montepío*) pawnbroker.
agencioso *adj* active, diligent; industrious.
agenda *nf* (**a**) (*diario*) diary, notebook; (*de direcciones*) address-book; ~ **de bolsillo** pocket diary; ~ **de despacho,** ~ **de mesa** desk-diary; ~ **de trabajo** engagement book. (**b**) (*de reunión*) agenda. (**c**) (*Telec*) telephone directory.
agente 1 *nmf* (**a**) (*gen*) agent; (*policía*) policeman, policewoman; (*LAm*) public service employee, worker in a nationalized industry; ~ **de bolsa** stockbroker; ~ **comercial** business agent, broker; ~ **especial** special agent; ~ **de exportación** export agent; ~ **extranjero** foreign agent; ~ **inmobiliario** estate agent; ~ **literario** literary agent; ~ **marítimo** shipping agent; ~ **de negocios** business agent, broker; ~ **oficial** official agent, authorized agent; ~ **del orden (público)**, ~ **de policía** policeman; ~ **de prensa** press agent; ~ **provocador** agent provocateur; ~ **de publicidad** (*Com*) advertising agent; (*Teat etc*) publicity agent; ~ **secreto** secret agent; ~ **de seguros** (*LAm*) insurance agent; ~**s sociales** social partners (*employers and unions*); ~ **de transportes** carrier; ~ **tributario** tax inspector; ~ **de turismo** travel agent, courier; ~ **único** sole agent; ~ **de ventas** sales agent, sales rep(resentative); ~ **viajero** (*LAm*) commercial traveller, salesman; ~ **de viajes** travel agent.
2 *nm* (*Quím*) agent; ~ **químico** chemical agent.
agible *adj* feasible, workable.
agigantado *adj* gigantic, huge.
agigantar [1a] **1** *vt* to enlarge, increase greatly; ~ **algo** to make sth seem huge.
2 agigantarse *vr* to become huge; to seem huge; (*crisis etc*) to get much bigger.
ágil *adj* agile, nimble, quick; (*fig*) flexible, adaptable.
agilidad *nf* agility, nimbleness, quickness; (*fig*) flexibility, adaptability.
agilipollado‡ *adj* stuck-up*.
agilipollarse‡ *vr* (**a**) (*atontarse*) to get all confused, act like an idiot.
(**b**) (*engreírse*) to get very stuck-up*.
agilitar [1a] **1** *vt* to make agile; (*fig*) to help, make it easy for; (*LAm*: *activar*) to activate, set in motion. **2 agilitarse** *vr* to limber up.
agilización *nf* speeding-up; improvement.
agilizar [1f] **1** *vt* (*acelerar*) to speed up; (*mejorar*) to improve, make more flexible. **2 agilizarse** *vr* to speed up.
ágilmente *adv* nimbly, quickly.
agio *nm* agio; speculation; (*Méx Jur*) usury.
agiotaje *nm* (stock)jobbery, jobbing; speculation.
agiotista *nm* (stock)jobber; speculator; (*Méx*: *usurero*) usurer.
agitación *nf* (**a**) (*V v*) waving, flapping, shaking, stirring. (**b**) (*Náut*) roughness. (**c**) (*fig*) agitation (*t Pol*); bustle, stir, movement; excitement; nervousness.
agitado 1 *adj* (**a**) *agua* rough, choppy; *vuelo* bumpy. (**b**) (*fig*) agitated; upset, anxious; excited; nervous; hectic. **2** *nm* stirring, mixing.
agitador *nm* (**a**) (*Mec*) agitator, shaker; (*Culin*) stirrer. (**b**) (*persona*) agitator.
agitanado *adj* gipsy-like.
agitar [1a] **1** *vt* (**a**) *brazo, bandera etc* to wave; *ala* to flap; *arma* to shake, brandish; *botella etc* to shake; *líquido* (*con mano*) to shake; (*con cuchara etc*) to stir, stir round, stir up; **agitaba un pañuelo** she was waving her handkerchief.
(**b**) (*fig*) (*excitar*) to stir up; to excite, rouse; (*perturbar*) to disturb; (*inquietar*) to worry, upset, make anxious.
2 agitarse *vr* (**a**) to wave, wave to and fro; to flutter, flap; to shake; (*mar*) to get rough; **agítese antes de usar** shake (*o* stir) well before using.
(**b**) to get excited, get worked up; to get worried, get upset, upset o.s.
aglomeración *nf* agglomeration; crowd, mass; crowding; ~ **de tráfico** traffic jam; ~ **urbana** urban sprawl.
aglomerado 1 *adj* massed together, in a mass; **viven ~s** they live crowded together, they live on top of one another. **2** *nm* (*madera*) plywood; (*Téc*) agglomeration; ~ **asfáltico** asphalt.
aglomerar [1a] **1** *vt* to agglomerate, crowd together. **2 aglomerarse** *vr* to agglomerate, form a mass; to crowd together.
aglutinación *nf* agglutination.
aglutinador *adj* agglutinative; cohesive; **fuerza ~a** unifying force, force that draws things together.
aglutinadora *nf* unifying force.
aglutinante *adj* agglutinative.
aglutinar [1a] **1** *vt* to agglutinate; (*fig*) to draw together, bring together; to make coherent. **2 aglutinarse** *vr* to agglutinate; (*fig*) to come together; to gel; to become coherent.
agnosticismo *nm* agnosticism.
agnóstico *adj, nm,* **agnóstica** *nf* agnostic.
agobiador *adj,* **agobiante** *adj cargo, calor etc* oppressive; *dolor etc* unbearable; *responsabilidad, trabajo* overwhelming; *pobreza* grinding.
agobiar [1b] **1** *vt* to weigh down, bow down; to oppress, burden, overwhelm; **sentirse agobiado por** to feel o.s. weighed down by; to be overwhelmed by; **está agobiado de trabajo** he is overloaded (*o* overburdened) with work.
2 agobiarse *vr*: ~ **con,** ~ **de** to be weighed down with, bow beneath.
agobio *nm* (*carga*) burden, weight; (*opresión*) oppression; (*agotamiento*) exhaustion; (*aburrimiento*) boredom; (*Med*) nervous strain, anxiety.
agolpamiento *nm* throng, crush, rush, crowd.
agolparse [1a] *vr* to throng, rush, crowd together; to bunch together; (*problemas etc*) to come all together, come one on top of another; (*lágrimas*) to well up; to come in a flood; ~ **en torno a uno** to crowd round sb.
agonía *nf* (**a**) (*de muerte*) agony; death agony, death throes; **en su** ~ on his (*etc*) death-bed; **acortar la ~ a un animal** to put an animal out of its misery; **la época está en su** ~ the period is in its death throes.
(**b**) (*fig*: *dolor*) anguish, agony, torment.
(**c**) (*fig*: *anhelo*) desire, yearning.
agónico *adj* dying; (*fig*) agonizing.
agonioso *adj* (*LAm*) (*egoísta*) selfish; (*fastidioso*) bothersome; **es tan** ~ he's such a pest.
agonizante 1 *adj* dying; *luz* failing. **2** *nmf* dying person.
agonizar [1f] **1** *vt* (*) to bother, pester. **2** *vi* (*t* **estar agonizando**) to be dying, be in one's death agony; ~ **por** (*fig*) + *infin* to be dying to + *infin*.
agonizos *nmpl* (*Méx*) worries, troubles.
agora *adv* (*LAm*, ††) = **ahora**.

ágora *nf* main square.
agorafobia *nf* agoraphobia.
agorafóbico, -a *nm/f* agoraphobe.
agorar [1m] *vt* to predict, prophesy.
agorero 1 *adj* prophetic; ominous; **ave agorera** bird of ill omen. **2** *nm,* **agorera** *nf* soothsayer, fortuneteller; forecaster.
agostar [1a] **1** *vt* to parch, burn up; (*fig*) to wither, kill before time; (*Méx*: *pastar*) to graze on rough ground. **2 agostarse** *vr* to dry up, shrivel; (*fig*) to die, fade away.
agosteño *adj* August (*atr*).
agosto *nm* August; (*cosecha*) harvest; (*época*) harvest-time; boom period; **hacer su ~** to feather one's nest, make one's pile; to make a killing.
agotado *adj*: **estar ~** (*persona*) to be exhausted, be worn out; (*existencias, provisión*) to be finished, be exhausted, (*Com*) be sold out; (*libro*) to be out of stock; (*pila*) to be flat, be run down.
agotador *adj* exhausting.
agotamiento *nm* exhaustion; depletion, draining; (*Med*) exhaustion; **~ por calor** heat exhaustion; **~ nervioso** nervous strain.
agotar [1a] **1** *vt* (*gen*) to exhaust, use up, finish; *reservas etc* to deplete, drain, empty; *paciencia* to exhaust; *persona* to exhaust, tire out; (*Med*) to exhaust.
2 agotarse *vr* to become exhausted; to be finished, be used up; to give out, run out; to sell out; (*libro*) to go out of print; (*persona*) to exhaust o.s., wear o.s. out.
agraceño *adj* tart, sour.
agraciado *adj* (**a**) (*atractivo*) graceful; nice, attractive; (*encantador*) charming. (**b**) (*con suerte*) lucky; **salir ~** to be lucky, be the winner; **estar ~ de** to be blessed with.
agraciar [1b] *vt* (**a**) (*adornar*) to grace, adorn; (*hacer más atractivo*) to make more attractive.
(**b**) *prisionero* to pardon.
(**c**) **~ a uno con algo** to bestow sth on sb, reward sb with sth.
agradable *adj* pleasant, agreeable, nice; enjoyable; **es un sitio ~** it's a nice place; **el cadáver no era muy ~ para la vista** the body was not a pretty sight; **ser ~ al gusto** to be nice, be tasty.
agradablemente *adv* pleasantly, agreeably; enjoyably.
agradar [1a] **1** *vt* to please, be pleasing to, be to the liking of; **esto no me agrada** I don't like this.
2 *vi* to please; **su presencia siempre agrada** it's always pleasant to have you with us, your presence is always welcome; **si le agrada le traeré más café** if you wish I'll bring you more coffee.
3 agradarse *vr* to be pleased (*de* at, with).
agradecer [2d] **1** *vt persona* to thank; *favor, regalo etc* to be grateful for; **agradezco tu ayuda** I am grateful for your help, thanks for your help; **se lo agradezco** I am grateful to you, I am much obliged to you; **un favor que él no agradecería nunca lo suficiente** a favour he can never thank you enough for; **agradecería que no lo hicieras** I should be glad if you would not do it, I should be obliged if you could avoid doing it; **eso no lo tiene que ~ a nadie** he has nobody to thank for that, he owes nobody thanks for that.
2 agradecerse *vr*: **¡se agradece!** much obliged!, thanks very much!; **una copita de jerez siempre se agradece** a glass of sherry is always welcome.
agradecido *adj* grateful; appreciative; **¡muy ~!** thanks a lot!; thanks for everything!; **me miró agradecida** she looked at me gratefully; **estamos muy ~s** we are very grateful; **le quedaría muy ~ si ...** (*en carta*) I should be very grateful if ...
agradecimiento *nm* gratitude, thanks; appreciation, gratefulness.
agrado *nm* (**a**) (*cualidad*) affability; **con ~** willingly. (**b**) (*gusto*) taste, liking; **ser del ~ de uno** to be to sb's liking; **tengo el ~ de informarle que ...** (*LAm*) I have pleasure in informing you that ..., I am glad to tell you that ...
ágrafo, -a *adj, nm/f* illiterate.
agramatical *adj* ungrammatical.
agrandar [1a] **1** *vt* to make bigger, enlarge, expand; *dificultad etc* to exaggerate, magnify. **2 agrandarse** *vr* to get bigger.
agranijado *adj* pimply.
agrario *adj* agrarian; land (*atr*); **política agraria** farming policy, agricultural policy; **reforma agraria** land reform.
agrarismo *nm* (*Méx*) agrarian reform movement.
agrarista *nmf* (*Méx*) supporter (*o* advocate) of land reform.
agravación *nf,* **agravamiento** *nm* aggravation, worsening; increase; (*Med*) decline, change for the worse.
agravado *nm*: **robo con ~** robbery with aggravation.
agravante 1 *adj* aggravating. **2** *nf* additional burden; unfortunate circumstances; **con la ~ de que ...** with the further difficulty that ...; **con la ~ de la nocturnidad** (*Jur*) made more serious by the fact that it was done at night.
agravar [1a] **1** *vt* (*pesar sobre*) to weigh down, make heavier; *pena, impuesto etc* to increase; *dolor* to make worse; *problema, situación* to aggravate, make worse; *personas* to oppress, burden (*con* with).
2 agravarse *vr* to worsen, get worse; to get more difficult.
agraviar [1b] **1** *vt* (*perjudicar*) to wrong; (*insultar*) to offend, insult. **2 agraviarse** *vr* to be offended, take offence (*de, por* at).
agravio *nm* wrong, injury; offence, insult; (*Jur*) grievance, injustice; **~ comparativo** (resentment arising from) inequality; **~s de hecho** assault and battery.
agravión *adj* (*Cono Sur*) touchy, quick to take offence.
agravioso *adj* offensive, insulting.
agraz *nm* (**a**) (*uva*) sour grape; (*jugo*) sour grape juice; **en ~** prematurely, before time. (**b**) (*fig*) bitterness, ill-feeling.
agrazar [1f] **1** *vt* (**a**) (*amargar*) to embitter. (**b**) (*fastidiar*) to vex, annoy. **2** *vi* to taste sour, have a sharp taste.
agrazón *nf* (**a**) (*uva*) wild grape; (*grosellero*) gooseberry bush. (**b**) (*fig*) vexation, annoyance.
agredir [3a; *defectivo*] *vt* to attack, assault, set upon.
agregado 1 *nm* (**a**) (*Téc etc*) aggregate.
(**b**) (*Téc*: *bloque*) concrete block.
2 *nm,* **agregada** *nf* (**a**) (*Pol*) attaché; (*Univ*) assistant professor; **~ comercial** commercial attaché; **~ cultural** cultural attaché; **~ militar** military attaché; **~ de prensa** press attaché.
(**b**) (*LAm*) person newly added to a group; thing newly added to a collection; (*Cono Sur*: *inquilino*) paying guest; (*And, Carib*: *aparcero*) sharecropper, tenant farmer paying rent in kind; (*Carib*: *jornalero*) (agricultural) day labourer.
agregar [1h] *vt* (**a**) (*añadir*) to add (*a* to); (*unir*) to join (*a* to). (**b**) (*recoger*) to gather, collect. (**c**) *persona* to appoint, attach (*a* to, to the staff of).
agremiar [1b] **1** *vt* to form into a union, unionize. **2 agremiarse** *vr* to form a union.
agresión *nf* aggression; (*contra persona etc*) attack, assault.
agresivamente *adv* aggressively.
agresividad *nf* aggressiveness; drive, punch, vigour.
agresivo *adj* (*violento*) aggressive; (*vigoroso*) forceful, vigorous.
agresor 1 *adj*: **país ~** agressor country. **2** *nm,* **agresora** *nf* aggressor; attacker, assailant.
agreste *adj* (**a**) (*gen*) rural, country (*atr*). (**b**) *flor, paisaje etc* wild. (**c**) (*fig*) rough, uncouth.
agrete *adj* sourish.
agriado *adj* (*Cono Sur*) (**a**) sour, sharp. (**b**) (*fig*) (*resentido*) sour, resentful; (*exasperado*) angry, irritated.
agriar [1b *o* 1c] **1** *vt* (**a**) *sabor* to sour, turn sour. (**b**) (*fig*) (*amargar*) to sour; (*fastidiar*) to vex, annoy. **2 agriarse** *vr* (**a**) *sabor* to turn sour. (**b**) (*fig*: *fastidiarse*) to get cross, get exasperated; to become embittered.
agrícola *adj* agricultural, farming (*atr*).
agricultor 1 *adj* agricultural, farming (*atr*). **2** *nm,* **agricultora** *nf* farmer; **~ de montaña** hill-farmer.
agricultura *nf* agriculture, farming; **~ biológica, ~ ecológica, ~ orgánica** organic farming; **~ intensiva** intensive farming; **~ de montaña** hill-farming; **~ de rozas y quema** slash-and-burn agriculture; **~ de subsistencia** subsistence farming.
agricultural *adj* (*LAm*) agricultural, farming (*atr*).
agridulce *adj* bittersweet; sweet and sour.
agriera *nf* (*LAm Med*) heartburn.
agrietado *adj* cracked; *labios, manos* chapped.
agrietar [1a] **1** *vt* to crack, crack open; to make cracks in; *labios, manos* to chap.
2 agrietarse *vr* to crack; to fissure; to get cracked, get covered in cracks; (*manos*) to get chapped.
agrifolio *nm* holly.
agrimensor(a) *nm/f* surveyor.
agrimensura *nf* surveying.
agringado *adj* (*LAm*) like (*o* imitating) a foreigner.
agringarse [1h] *vr* to act (*o* behave) like a foreigner.
agrio 1 *adj* (**a**) *sabor* sour, tart, bitter; (*fig*) sharp, sour, disagreeable.

(**b**) *camino etc* rough, uneven; *materia* brittle; *color* garish.

2 *nm* sour juice; **~s** citrus fruits.

agripado *adj* (*LAm*): **estar ~** to have flu.

agriparse *vr* (*Cono Sur*) to catch a cold; to get flu.

agriura *nf* (*LAm*) sourness, tartness.

agro *nm* farming, agriculture.

agroalimentario *adj* food and agriculture (*atr*).

agrobiología *nf* agrobiology.

agrobiológico *adj* agrobiological.

agrobiólogo, -a *nm/f* agrobiologist.

agroenergética *nf* use of agricultural products as sources of energy.

agroindustria *nf* agribusiness.

agronomía *nf* agronomy, agriculture.

agrónomo 1 *adj* agricultural, farming (*atr*). **2** *nm*, **agrónoma** *nf* agronomist, agricultural expert.

agropecuario *adj* farming (*atr*), stockbreeding (*atr*); **riqueza agropecuaria** agricultural wealth; **política agropecuaria** farming policy.

agropesquero *adj* relating to farming and fishing.

agroproducto *nm* agroproduct.

agroquímico *adj, nm* agrochemical.

agrupación *nf* (**a**) (*grupo*) group, grouping; association; (*reunión*) gathering; (*unión*) union; (*Mús*) group, ensemble. (**b**) (*acto*) grouping; gathering; coming together.

agrupar [1a] **1** *vt* (*gen*) to group (together); *datos, gente etc* to gather, assemble; (*amontonar*) to crowd together.

2 agruparse *vr* to form a group; to gather, come together; to crowd together, cluster, bunch together (*en torno a* round).

agrura *nf* sourness, tartness; **~s** (*Méx Med*) heartburn.

agua *nf* (**a**) (*gen*) water; fluid, liquid; (*lluvia*) rain; (*Náut: estela*) wake; (*Náut: vía de ~*) leak; (*Arquit*) slope of a roof, pitch; **¡~!*** look out!; **¡hombre al ~!** man overboard!; **el invierno ha sido de mucha ~** it's been a very wet winter.

(**b**) (*con adj etc*) **~ para beber** drinking water; **~ bendita** holy water; **~ blanda** soft water; **~ de colonia** eau de cologne; **~ corriente** running water; **~ cuba** (*Cono Sur*) bleach; **~ destilada** distilled water; **~ dulce** fresh water; **pez de ~ dulce** freshwater fish; **~ dura** hard water; **~ de espliego** lavender water; **~ de fregar** (*: *bebida*) ditchwater; **~ de fuego** firewater; **~ de fusión de la nieve** meltwater; **~ con gas** sparkling water; **~ sin gas** still water; **~ gorda, ~ gruesa** (*Méx*) salt water; **~ de grifo** tap-water; **~ gruesa** (*LAm*) hard water; **~ hirviendo** boiling water; **~ llovediza, ~ (de) lluvia** rainwater; **~ del mar** seawater; **~ mineral** mineral water; **~ natural** tap-water; unchilled water; **~ oxigenada** hydrogen peroxide; **~ de pera** *etc* (*LAm: jugo*) pear juice *etc*; **~ perra** (*Cono Sur*) boiled water; **~ pesada** heavy water; **~ potable** drinking-water; **~ de rosas, ~ rosada** rose-water; **~ salada, ~ salina** salt water; **~ de seltz** seltzer (water); **~ subterránea** groundwater; **~ tónica** tonic water; **~ de Vichy** Vichy water.

(**c**) (*con verbo*) **¡~, que se quema la casa!** I'm dying for a drink!; **¡~ va!** look out!, timber!; **sin decir ~ va** without any warning; **eso es ~ pasada** that's all in the past; **~ pasada no mueve molino** it's no good crying over spilt milk; **bailarle el ~ a uno** to dance attendance on sb; **bañarse en ~ de rosas** to see the world through rose-coloured spectacles; **de esta ~ no beberé** I won't have anything to do with it; **nunca digas de esta ~ no beberé** don't be too sure; **cambiar el ~ al canario** (*Esp***‡**) to take a leak**‡**; **coger ~ en cesto** to labour in vain, be wasting one's time; **¿me da para mis ~s?** (*Méx: pidiendo propina*) how about a little something for me?; **echar ~ arriba a uno** (*Méx*) to give sb a dressing down; **echar un barco al ~** to launch a boat; **echar** (*o* **llevar**) **el ~ a su molino** to bring the conversation round to one's own interests; to be on the make; **echarse al ~** to dive in; (*fig*) to take the plunge; **estar con el ~ al cuello*** to be over a barrel; **hacer ~** (*Náut*) to leak, take in water; **se me hace la boca ~** my mouth is watering; **se le hace ~ en la boca** it melts in one's mouth; **irse al ~** to be ruined; **mear ~ bendita‡** to be terribly pious; **pescar en ~ turbia** to fish in troubled waters; **quedar en ~ de borrajas** to fail, come to nothing; **retener el ~** to hold water; **seguir las ~s a uno** (*Méx**) to keep on sb's good side.

(**d**) (*comparaciones*) **como ~** like water; freely, in abundance; **estar como el ~ de un lago** to be calm; **ser como el ~ por San Juan** to be harmful, be unwelcome; **es fácil como el ~** (*Cono Sur*) it's as easy as pie*; **venir como ~ de mayo** to be a godsend, be very welcome.

(**e**) **~s** waters; (*Náut*) tide; (*Med*) water, urine; (*de joya*) water, sparkle; **las ~s del Tajo** the waters of the Tagus; **~s abajo** downstream, down-river (*de* from); **~s arriba** upstream, up-river (*de* from); **~s de consumo** water supply, drinking water; **~s de escorrentía** run-off water; **~s fecales** sewage; **~s jurisdiccionales, ~s territoriales** territorial waters; **~s litorales** coastal waters; **~s mayores** excrement, faeces; **~s menores** water, urine; **~s minerales** mineral waters; **~s negras** contaminated water; (*de cloaca*) sewage; **~s de pantoque** bilge-water; **~s residuales** sewage; **~s superficiales** surface water; **cubrir ~s** (*Arquit*) to put the roof on, top out; **hacer ~s** to make water, relieve o.s.; **estar** (*o* **nadar**) **entre dos ~s** to be undecided, sit on the fence; **tomar las ~s** to take the waters; **las ~s vuelven a su cauce** (*fig*) things return to normal.

aguacate *nm* (**a**) (*fruto*) avocado pear; (*árbol*) avocado pear tree. (**b**) (*CAm**) idiot, fool. (**c**) **~s** (*Méx***‡**) balls**‡**, bollocks**‡**.

aguacatero *nm* (*Méx*) avocado pear tree.

aguacero *nm* (heavy) shower, downpour.

aguacil *nm* (*Cono Sur*) dragonfly.

aguacola *nf* (*Méx*) fish glue.

aguacha *nf* foul water, stagnant water.

aguachacha *nf* (*CAm*) weak drink, nasty drink.

aguachado *adj* (*Cono Sur*) tame.

aguachento *adj* (*And, Cono Sur Bot*) watery, very juicy.

aguachinado *adj* (*Carib*) (*acuoso*) watery; (*blando*) soft.

aguachinarse *vr* (*Méx Agr*) to be flooded.

aguachirle *nf* (**a**) (*bebida*) weak drink, nasty drink; slops, dishwater.

(**b**) (*bagatela*) trifle, mere nothing.

aguada *nf* (**a**) (*Agr*) watering place. (**b**) (*Náut*) water supply. (**c**) (*Min*) flood, flooding. (**d**) (*Arte*) watercolour, wash.

aguadilla *nf* ducking; **hacer una ~ a uno** to duck sb, hold sb's head under water.

aguado *adj* watery, watered-down, thin; (*: *abstemio*) teetotal; (*Méx*) (*perezoso*) lazy, idle; (*flojo*) weak, simpering.

aguador *nm* water carrier, water seller.

aguaducho *nm* (**a**) (*arroyo*) freshet. (**b**) (*café*) refreshment stall, small open-air café.

aguafiestas *nmf invar* spoilsport, killjoy, wet blanket.

aguafuerte *nf* etching; **grabar algo al ~** to etch sth.

aguafuertista *nmf* etcher.

aguaitada *nf* (*LAm*) look, glance; **echar una ~** to take a look at.

aguaitar [1a] **1** *vt* (**a**) (*LAm*) (*espiar*) to spy on; (*vigilar*) to watch, keep an eye on; (*acechar*) to lie in wait for. (**b**) (*And, Carib: esperar*) to wait for. (**c**) (*Cono Sur etc: ver*) to look, see. **2** *vi* (*LAm*) to look; to watch; **~ por la ventana** to look out of the window.

aguaje *nm* (**a**) (*marea*) tide, spring tide; (*corriente*) current; (*estela*) wake. (**b**) (*provisión*) water supply; (*Agr*) watering trough. (**c**) (*And, CAm*) rainstorm. (**d**) (*CAm*: regañada*) dressing-down*.

aguajirado *adj* (*Carib*) withdrawn, timid.

aguajirarse [1a] *vr* (*Carib*) to become countrified, acquire peasant's habits (*etc*); (*ser reservado*) to be withdrawn, be reserved.

agualotal *nm* (*CAm*) swamp, marsh.

aguamala *nf* (*And etc*) jellyfish.

aguamanil *nm* (*jarro*) ewer, water jug; (*jofaina*) washstand.

aguamar *nm* jellyfish.

aguamarina *nf* aquamarine.

aguamarse [1a] *vr* (*And*) to get scared, be intimidated.

aguamiel *nf* mead; sugared water; (*CAm, Méx*) fermented maguey (*o* agave juice).

aguamuerta *nf* (*Cono Sur*) jellyfish.

aguanieve *nf* sleet.

aguano *nm* (*And*) mahogany.

aguanoso *adj* (**a**) (*gen*) wet, watery; *tierra* waterlogged. (**b**) (*Méx** *persona*) wet*.

aguantable *adj* bearable, tolerable.

aguantaderas *nfpl* (*LAm*): **tener ~** to be tolerant, be patient.

aguantadero* *nm* (*Cono Sur*) hide-out.

aguantador 1 *adj* (*LAm*) = **aguantón**. **2** *nm*, **aguantadora** *nf* (**‡**) fence*, receiver (of stolen goods).

aguantar [1a] **1** *vt* (**a**) (*gen*) to bear, endure, stand, put up with; *insulto etc* to swallow; *tormenta* to weather; *examen* to bear, stand up to; *dolor* to endure, bear; **no aguanto más** I'm not putting up with this, I can't bear it any more.

(**b**) *techo etc* to hold up, sustain; *respiración* to hold.

2 *vi* (**a**) (*resistir*) to last, hold out; to resist; **aguanta mucho** he's very patient, he has lots of endurance.

(**b**) (*cuerda etc*) to hold (fast).

3 aguantarse *vr* (**a**) to restrain o.s., hold o.s. back, sit tight; to put up with it.

(**b**) (*LAm*) (*callarse*) to keep one's mouth shut; **~ de hacer algo** to hold back from doing sth; **¡aguántate!** calm down!; **tendrá que ~** he'll just have to put up with it.

aguante *nm* (*paciencia*) patience; (*resistencia*) endurance, fortitude; (*Dep*) stamina; (*de objeto*) strength; **al ~ de uno** (*Carib**) behind sb's back.

aguantón 1 *adj* (*Carib, Méx*) long-suffering, extremely patient. **2** *nm* (*Carib**): **te darás un ~** you'll have a long wait.

aguapié *nm* weak wine, plonk*.

aguar [1i] *vt* (**a**) *vino etc* to water (down). (**b**) (*fig*) to spoil, mar; *V* **fiesta**. (**c**) (*CAm, Cono Sur*) *ganado* to water.

aguarana *nmf* (*And*) primitive jungle Indian.

aguardada *nf* wait, waiting.

aguardadero *nm*, **aguardado** *nm* (*Caza*) hide.

aguardar [1a] **1** *vt* to wait for, await; to expect. **2** *vi* to hold on; to wait; **aguarde Vd** (*en narración*) that's what I'm trying to tell you, I'm coming to that.

aguardentería *nf* liquor store.

aguardentero, -a *nm/f* liquor seller.

aguardentoso *adj* alcoholic; *voz* fruity, beery.

aguardiente *nm* brandy, liquor; **~ de caña** rum; **~ de cerezas** cherry brandy; **~ de manzana** applejack.

aguardientoso *adj* (*LAm*) = **aguardentoso**.

aguardo *nm* (*Caza*) hide.

aguarrás *nm* turpentine.

aguate *nm* (*Méx*) prickle, thorn.

aguatero *nm* (*LAm*) water-carrier, water-seller.

aguatocha *nf* pump.

aguatoso *adj* (*Méx*) prickly.

aguaturma *nf* Jerusalem artichoke.

aguaviva *nf* (*Cono Sur*) jellyfish.

aguayo *nm* (*And*) multicoloured woollen cloth (*for adornment, or carried as shoulder bag*).

aguaza *nf* (*Med*) liquid (from a tumour); (*Bot*) sap.

aguazal *nm* (*charco*) puddle; (*pantano*) fen, swamp.

aguazar [1f] **1** *vt* to flood, waterlog. **2 aguazarse** *vr* to flood, become waterlogged.

agudeza *nf* (**a**) (*gen*) acuteness, sharpness; keenness. (**b**) (*ingenio*) wit, wittiness. (**c**) (*una ~*) witticism, witty saying.

agudización *nf*, **agudizamiento** *nm* sharpening; worsening.

agudizar [1f] **1** *vt* to sharpen, make more acute.

2 agudizarse *vr* to sharpen, become more acute, worsen; **el problema se agudiza** the problem is becoming more acute; **la competencia se agudiza** competition is intensifying.

agudo *adj* (**a**) *instrumento etc* sharp, pointed; *ángulo* acute.

(**b**) *enfermedad, dolor* acute.

(**c**) (*Mús*) *nota* high, high-pitched; shrill; *sonido* piercing; (*Ling*) *acento* acute.

(**d**) *mente, sentido* sharp, keen, acute, penetrating; *observación* smart, clever; *crítica* penetrating, trenchant; *ingenio* ready, lively; *pregunta* acute, searching; *sabor etc* sharp, pungent.

(**e**) (*ingenioso*) witty.

agué *interj* (*CAm*) **¡~!** hello!

agüera *nf* irrigation ditch.

agüero *nm* omen, sign; prediction, forecast; **de buen ~** lucky, propitious; **ser de buen ~** to augur well; **de mal ~** ill-omened; **pájaro de mal ~** bird of ill omen.

agüeitar [1a] (*LAm*) = **aguaitar**.

aguerrido *adj* hardened, veteran.

aguerrir [3a; *defectivo*] *vt* to inure, harden.

agüevar⁑ [1a] **1** *vt* (*CAm, Méx*) to put down, shame. **2 agüevarse** *vr* to cower, shrink.

aguijada *nf*, **aguijadera** *nf* goad.

aguijar [1a] **1** *vt* to goad; (*fig*) to urge on, spur on, goad. **2** *vi* to hurry along, make haste.

aguijón *nm* (**a**) (*puya*) point of a goad, goad; (*Zool*) sting; (*Bot*) prickle, spine, sting; **dar coces contra el ~** to kick against the pricks, struggle in vain. (**b**) (*fig*) spur, stimulus; incitement; **el ~ de la carne** sexual desire.

aguijonazo *nm* prick (with a goad), jab; (*Zool, Bot*) sting.

aguijonear [1a] *vt* = **aguijar**.

aguijoneo *nm* goading, provocation.

águila *nf* (**a**) (*Orn*) eagle; **~ calzada** booted eagle; **~ culebrera** short-toed eagle; **~ perdicera** Bonelli's eagle; **~ pescadora** osprey; **~ ratonera** buzzard; **~ real** golden eagle. (**b**) (*fig*) **ser un ~** to be a genius, be terribly clever. (**c**) (*Cono Sur*: *estafador*) cheat, swindler; **andar a palos con el ~*** to be broke; **¿~ o sol?** (*Méx*) heads or tails?

aguileña *nf* columbine.

aguileño *adj nariz* aquiline; *cara* sharp-featured; *persona* hawk-nosed.

aguilera *nf* eagle's nest, eyrie.

aguilillo, -a *nm/f* (*LAm*) fast horse.

aguilón *nm* (*Orn*) large eagle; (*de grúa*) jib; (*Arquit*) gable, gable-end; (*And*) large heavy horse.

aguilucho *nm* (*Orn*) eaglet, young eagle; harrier; (*LAm*) hawk, falcon.

aguinaldo *nm* (**a**) (*de Navidades*) Christmas box, New Year gift; (*propina*) tip; (*plus*) (salary) bonus. (**b**) (*LAm*: *villancico*) Christmas carol.

aguita⁑ *nf* (*And*) cash, dough⁑, bread⁑.

agüita *nf* (*Cono Sur*) infusion, herb tea.

agüitado *adj* (*Méx*) depressed, gloomy.

aguja *nf* (**a**) (*Cos etc*) needle; (*de sombrero*) hatpin; **~ de arria** (*LAm*) pack needle; **~ capotera** darning needle; **~ de gancho** crochet hook; **~ de hacer calceta** (*Esp*), **~ de hacer punto** knitting-needle; **~ hipodérmica** hypodermic needle; **~ magnética, ~ de marear** compass (needle); **conocer la ~ de marear** to know one's way around; **~ de media, ~ de tejer** (*LAm*) knitting-needle; **~ de zurcir** darning needle; **buscar una ~ en un pajar** to look for a needle in a haystack; **darle a la ~*** to shoot up⁑.

(**b**) (*de reloj*) hand; pointer; **tumbar la ~*** (*Aut*) to step on the gas*, go full out.

(**c**) (*Mil*) firing pin.

(**d**) **~ de pino** (*Bot*) pine needle.

(**e**) **~ (de tranquera)** (*LAm*) fencepost.

(**f**) (*Arquit*) spire, steeple.

(**g**) **~s** (*Anat*) ribs.

(**h**) **~s** (*Ferro*) points.

(**i**) (*Esp*: *t* **~ de mar**) garfish.

(**j**) (*CAm, Méx*: *carne*) beef.

agujazo *nm* prick, jab.

agujereado *adj* full of holes, pierced with holes; perforated; leaky.

agujerear [1a] *vt* to make holes in, pierce; to perforate; (*Cono Sur*) to disrupt.

agujero *nm* (**a**) (*gen*) hole; (*Anat***) hole **; **~ de hombre** manhole; **~ negro** black hole; **~ de ozono** ozone hole, hole in the ozone layer; **hacer un ~ en, practicar un ~ en** to make a hole in. (**b**) (*Cos*) needle case; pincushion. (**c**) (⁑) pad⁑; hide-out, safe house. (**d**) (*fig*) gap; discrepancy; (*Fin*) hole, drain; deficit.

agujetas *nfpl* (**a**) (*Med*) stitch; stiffness. (**b**) (*Méx*) shoelaces.

agujetero *nm* (*LAm*: *alfiletero*) pincushion.

agujón *nm* hatpin.

agur* *interj* so long!, cheerio!

agusanado *adj* maggoty, wormy.

agusanarse [1a] *vr* to get maggoty.

Agustín *nm* Augustine.

agustiniano, agustino *adj, nm* Augustinian.

agutí *nm* (*LAm Zool*) guinea-pig.

aguzado *adj* (*LAm*) sharp, on the ball*.

aguzamiento *nm* sharpening.

aguzanieves *nf invar* wagtail.

aguzar [1f] *vt* (**a**) (*afilar*) to sharpen.

(**b**) (*fig*) to incite, stir up; *apetito* to whet; **~ las orejas** to prick up one's ears; **~ la vista** to look sharp, look more carefully.

ah *interj* (**a**) oh!; **¡~ del barco!** ship ahoy! (**b**) (*LAm*) **¿~?** what?

a.h. *abr de* **año de la Hégira** from the year of the Hegira, anno Hegirae, AH.

ahechaduras *nfpl* chaff.

ahechar [1a] *vt* to sift; to winnow.

aherrojamiento *nm* (*fig*) oppression.

aherrojar [1a] *vt* to put in irons, fetter, shackle; (*fig*) to oppress.

aherrumbrarse [1a] *vr* to rust, get rusty; to take on the taste (*o* colour) of iron.

ahí 1 *adv* there; **¿de ~?** well?; what next?, (*iró*) so what?; **¡ ~ es nada!*** imagine!, wow!*; **¡ ~ está (la madre del cordero)!** that's the trouble!; **¡ ~ está el detalle!** that's the whole point!; **~ no más** (*LAm*) right here; **¡~ no más!** that's the limit!; **de ~ se deduce que ...** from that it follows that ...; **por ~** that way; over there; **200 pesos o por ~** 200 pesos or thereabouts; **está por ~** it's round here somewhere; (*persona*) he's round about somewhere; he's knocking around somewhere; **¡hasta ~ podíamos llegar!** that's the limit!, what a nerve!; **ir por ~** (*euf*) to get around, keep dubious company; **¡~ va!** there it goes!, there he goes!; (*con sorpresa*) goodness me!; (*burlándose*) get along with you!, tell us another! **2** *conj* **de ~ que** + *subj* and so ..., so that ...; with the result that ...

ahijada *nf* goddaughter; (*fig*) protégée.

ahijado *nm* godson; (*fig*) protégé.

ahijar [1a] *vt persona* to adopt; *animal* to adopt, mother; **~ algo a uno** (*fig*) to impute sth to sb; to attribute sth to sb.

ahijuna‡ *interj* (*Cono Sur*) son of a bitch!‡

ahilar [1a] **1** *vt* to line up. **2** *vi* to go in single file. **3 ahilarse** *vr* (*Med*) to faint with hunger; (*Bot*) to grow poorly; (*vino etc*) to turn sour, go off.

ahincadamente *adv* hard, earnestly; emphatically.

ahincado *adj* earnest; emphatic.

ahincar [1g] **1** *vt* to press, urge. **2 ahincarse** *vr* to hurry up, make haste.

ahínco *nm* (*seriedad*) earnestness, intentness; (*énfasis*) emphasis; (*empeño*) effort; (*resolución*) determination, perseverance; **con ~** hard, earnestly; eagerly.

ahitar [1a] **1** *vt* to cloy, surfeit. **2 ahitarse** *vr* to stuff o.s. (*de* with), give o.s. a surfeit (*de* of); (*Med*) give o.s. indigestion.

ahíto 1 *adj* (**a**) (*repleto*) gorged, surfeited, satiated. (**b**) (*fig*: *harto*) **estar ~ de** to be fed up with. (**c**) (*lleno*) full, packed tight.

2 *nm* surfeit, satiety; (*Med*) indigestion.

AHN *nm abr de* **Archivo Histórico Nacional.**

ahogadero *nm* (**a**) (*de animal*) throatband; headstall, halter; (*de verdugo*) hangman's rope. (**b**) (*fig*) **esto es un ~** it's stifling in here.

ahogado 1 *adj* (**a**) *persona* drowned; (*asfixiado*) suffocated; **perecer ~** to drown; to suffocate.

(**b**) *cuarto* close, stifling.

(**c**) *emoción* pent-up; *grito* muffled, half-smothered.

(**d**) **estar ~, verse ~** to be in a tight spot.

2 *nm*, **ahogada** *nf* drowned person.

3 *nm* (*LAm*) (*salsa*) sauce; (*guisado*) stew.

ahogador *nm* (*Méx Aut*) choke.

ahogar [1h] **1** *vt* (**a**) (*en agua*) to drown; (*asfixiar*) to suffocate; to smother; *fuego* to put out; *proyecto, proyecto de ley etc* to kill; **~ las penas** to drown one's sorrows.

(**b**) *planta* to drown, overwater.

(**c**) *grito, sollozo etc* to choke back, stifle, hold in.

(**d**) (*fig*) to afflict, oppress, crush.

(**e**) (*Ajedrez*) to stalemate.

2 ahogarse *vr* (*por accidente*) to drown; to suffocate; (*suicidio*) to drown o.s.

ahogo *nm* (**a**) drowning; **perecer por ~** to drown.

(**b**) (*Med*) shortness of breath, tightness of the chest.

(**c**) (*fig*) distress, affliction.

(**d**) (*Fin*) embarrassment, financial difficulty; economic stringency.

ahoguío *nm* (*Med*) = **ahogo** (**b**).

ahondar [1a] **1** *vt* to deepen, make deeper, dig out.

2 *vi*: **~ en** to go deeply into, penetrate deeply into; (*fig*) to study thoroughly, examine in depth.

3 ahondarse *vr* to go (*o* sink) in more deeply.

ahora 1 *adv* (*gen*) now; (*hace poco*) just now; a moment ago; (*dentro de poco*) in a little while, very soon; **desde ~** from now on; **hasta ~** up till now; as yet; hitherto; **¡hasta ~!** see you soon!; **por ~** for the present, for the moment; **~ mismito, ~ poco*** just a moment ago; **~ mismo** right now, this very minute; at this very moment; **~ es cuando** now's your chance.

2 *conj* now; now then, well now; on the other hand; **~ bien** now then, well now; but; however; **~ pues** well then; **~ ... ~** whether ... or.

ahorcado 1 *adj* (*Cono Sur**) flat broke*. **2** *nm*, **ahorcada** *nf* hanged person; *V* **soga.**

ahorcadura *nf* hanging.

ahorcajarse [1a] *vr* to sit astride; **~ en** to sit astride, straddle.

ahorcar [1g] **1** *vt* to hang; **~ a uno** (*Méx**) to milk sb, squeeze sb dry; *V* **hábito** *etc.* **2 ahorcarse** *vr* to hang o.s.

ahorita *adv* (*esp LAm*) = **ahora**; (*ahora mismo*) right now, this very minute; (*hace poco*) a moment ago, just now; (*dentro de poco*) in a moment; **¡~ voy!** I'm just coming!, I'll be with you in a moment!

ahormar [1a] *vt* (**a**) (*ajustar*) to fit, adjust (*a* to); (*formar*) to shape, mould; *zapatos* to break in, stretch; *carácter* to mould.

(**b**) (*fig*) **~ a uno** to make sb see sense.

ahorquillado *adj* forked.

ahorquillar [1a] **1** *vt* (**a**) (*apoyar*) to prop up. (**b**) (*formar*) to shape like a fork. **2 ahorquillarse** *vr* to fork, become forked.

ahorrador *adj* thrifty.

ahorrar [1a] **1** *vt dinero* to save; to put by; *molestia* to save, avoid; *peligro* to avoid; *esclavo* to free.

2 ahorrarse *vr* (**a**) **~ molestias** to save o.s. trouble, spare o.s. effort; **no ~las con nadie** to be afraid of nobody.

(**b**) (*Carib, Agr*) to abort; (*CAm*: *cosecha*) to fail.

(**c**) (*And*: *gandulear*) to shirk, refuse to work.

ahorrativo *adj* thrifty; (*pey*) tight, stingy.

ahorrillos *nmpl* small savings.

ahorrista *nmf* saver.

ahorro *nm* (*acto*) economy, saving; (*cualidad*) thrift; **~s** savings; **~ energético** energy saving, saving in energy; (*política*) energy conservation.

ahoyar [1a] *vt* to dig holes in.

ahuchar[1] [1a] *vt* to hoard, put by.

ahuchar[2] [1a] *vt* (*And, Méx*) = **azuzar** (**b**).

ahuecar [1g] **1** *vt* (**a**) (*hacer hueco*) to hollow (out), make a hollow in; **~ la mano** to cup one's hand.

(**b**) (*Agr*) to loosen, soften; (*Cos*) to fluff out.

(**c**) *voz* to deepen, make pompous, give a solemn tone to.

(**d**) *V* **ala** (**g**).

2 *vi* **¡ahueca!*** beat it!*

3 ahuecarse* *vr* to give o.s. airs.

ahuesarse [1a] *vr* (*And, Cono Sur*) (**a**) (*) (*pasar de moda*) to go out of fashion; (*comestibles*) to go off (*o* rotten); (*pasarse*) to become unsaleable.

(**b**) (*persona*) to get thin.

ahuevado *adj* (*LAm*) silly, stupid.

ahuizote *nm* (*CAm, Méx*) (**a**) (*persona*) bore. (**b**) (*maleficio*) evil spell, curse.

ahulado *nm* (*CAm, Méx*) oilskin; **~s** rubber shoes.

ahumado 1 *adj* (**a**) *tocino etc* smoked; *sabor, superficie, ventana etc* smoky; *vidrio* tinted. (**b**) (*: *borracho*) tight*, tipsy. **2** *nm* (**a**) smoking, curing. (**b**) (*: *borracho*) drunk*.

ahumar 1 *vt* (**a**) *tocino etc* to smoke, cure.

(**b**) *superficie etc* to make smoky; *cuarto* to make smoky, fill with smoke.

(**c**) *colmena* to smoke out.

2 *vi* to smoke, give out smoke.

3 ahumarse *vr* (**a**) (*comida*) to acquire a burnt taste.

(**b**) (*cuarto*) to be smoky, get smoked up.

(**c**) (*: *emborracharse*) to get tight*.

ahusado *adj* tapering, spindle-shaped.

ahusarse [1a] *vr* to taper.

ahuyentar [1a] **1** *vt* (**a**) (*espantar*) to drive away, frighten away; to put to flight; (*mantener a distancia*) to keep off.

(**b**) *temores, dudas etc* to banish, dispel; **~ las penas con vino** to drown one's sorrows in wine.

2 ahuyentarse *vr* to run away; (*Méx*) to stay away.

AI *nf abr de* **Amnistía Internacional** Amnesty International, AI.

AIF *nf abr de* **Asociación Internacional de Fomento** International Development Association, IDA.

AIH [ai'atʃe] *nf abr de* **Asociación Internacional de Hispanistas.**

aimara 1 *adj, nmf* Aymara (Indian). **2** *nm* (*Ling*) Aymara.

aína *adv* (*liter*) speedily.

aindiado *adj* (*LAm*) like (*o* resembling) an Indian, Indian-looking; dark-skinned.

AINS *nf* (*Esp*) *abr de* **Administración Institucional Nacional de Sanidad.**

airadamente *adv* angrily.

airado *adj* (**a**) (*enojado*) angry; (*violento*) wild, violent; **joven ~** angry young man (*1950s*). (**b**) *vida* immoral, depraved.

airar [1a] **1** *vt* to anger. **2 airarse** *vr* to get angry (*de, por* at).

aire *nm* (**a**) (*gen*) air; (*corriente*) wind, draught; **misil de ~ a ~** air-to-air missile; **~ colado** cold draught; **~ comprimido** compressed air; **~ detonante** firedamp; **~ líquido** liquid air; **~ puro** clean air; **~ viciado** stale air, foul air, fug; **~s de cambio** (*Pol*) winds of change; **con ~ acondicionado** air-conditioned, with air conditioning; **al ~ libre** in the open air, outdoors, (*como adj*) open-air, outdoor; **azotar el ~** to waste one's efforts; **beber los ~s por** to sigh for, yearn for; to be madly in love with; **cambiar de ~(s)** to have a change of air; **cortarlas en el ~** to be very sharp; **darse ~** to fan o.s.; **dejar una pregunta en el ~** to leave a question unanswered *o* unsettled; **echar al ~** to bare, uncover; **estar en el ~** (*Rad*) to be on the air; (*fig*) to be up in the air; to be doubtful, be undecided; **hacer ~ a uno** to fan sb; **hacerse ~** to fan o.s.; **hace mucho ~** it's very windy; **lanzar algo al ~** to throw sth up; **mantenerse** *o* **vivir del ~** to eat very little, live on thin air; **mudarse a cualquier ~** to be fickle; **ofenderse del ~** to be terribly touchy; **salir al ~** (*Rad*) to go out on the air; **saltar por los ~s*** to go up in smoke*, go up the wall*; **tomar el ~** to go for a stroll; **¡vete a tomar el ~!*** clear off!*; **¿qué ~s te traen por aquí?** what brings you here?; **volar por los ~s** to fly through the air.

(**b**) (*fig*: *aspecto, porte*) air, appearance; **darse ~s** to give o.s. airs; **darse ~s de** to boast of being; **no te des esos ~s de suficiencia conmigo** don't get on your high horse with me; **tener ~ de salud** to look healthy.

(**c**) (*fig*: *semejanza*)) resemblance; **~ de familia** family likeness; **darse un ~ a** to resemble; **tener ~ de** to look like, resemble.

(**d**) (*fig*: *humor*) humour, mood; **dar ~ al dinero** to spend money freely; **estar de buen ~** to be in a good mood; **estar de mal ~** to be in a bad mood; **ir a su ~** to go one's own way, follow one's whim, do one's own thing*; **seguir el ~ a uno** to humour sb, follow sb's whim.

(**e**) (*fig*: *elegancia etc*) air; elegance, gracefulness.

(**f**) (*Mús*) tune, air.

(**g**) (*Cono Sur* Med*) (*cuello*) stiff neck; (*parálisis*) paralysis.

aireación *nf* ventilation.

aireado *nm* ventilation; (*de vino*) aeration.

aire-aire *atr*: **misil ~** air-to-air missile.

airear [1a] **1** *vt* (**a**) (*gen*) to air, ventilate; *ropa* to air.

(**b**) (*fig*) *idea, cuestión* to air; (*en prensa etc*) to discuss at length, give a lot of coverage to; **~ la atmósfera** to clear the air, let in fresh air.

(**c**) (*publicar*) to gossip about.

2 airearse *vr* to take the air; (*Med*) to catch a chill.

aireo *nm* ventilation.

aire-tierra *atr*: **misil ~** air-to-ground missile.

airón *nm* (**a**) (*Orn*) heron. (**b**) (*de plumas etc*) tuft, crest.

airosamente *adv* gracefully, elegantly; jauntily; successfully.

airosidad *nf* grace, elegance; jauntiness.

airoso *adj* (**a**) (*ventilado*) airy; *cuarto* draughty; *lugar expuesto* windy; *tiempo* windy, blowy.

(**b**) (*fig*) graceful, elegant; jaunty; successful; **quedar ~, salir ~** to be successful, acquit o.s. well, come out with flying colours.

aislación *nf* insulation; **~ de sonido** soundproofing.

aislacionismo *nm* isolationism.

aislacionista *adj, nmf* isolationist.

aislado *adj* (**a**) (*remoto*) isolated; cut off, shut off (*de* from); lonely; **'con inodoro ~'** (*anuncio*) 'with separate WC'. (**b**) (*Elec etc*) insulated.

aislador 1 *adj* (*Elec*) insulating. **2** *nm* (*Elec*) insulator, non-conductor.

aislamiento *nm* (**a**) (*gen*) isolation; loneliness; **~ sensorial** sensory deprivation. (**b**) (*Elec etc*) insulation; insulating material; **~ acústico** soundproofing.

aislante 1 *adj* insulating. **2** *nm* insulator, insulating material.

aislar [1a] **1** *vt* (**a**) (*gen*) to isolate; (*separar*) to separate, detach; (*cortar*) to cut off, shut off.

(**b**) (*Elec etc*) to insulate.

2 aislarse *vr* to isolate o.s., cut o.s. off (*de* from); to live in isolation, live in seclusion.

AITA *nf abr de* **Asociación Internacional del Transporte Aéreo** International Air Transport Association, IATA.

ajá, ajajá *interj* fine!, splendid!; (*sorpresa*) aha!

ajajay *interj V* **ajay.**

ajamonarse* [1a] *vr* to get plump, run to fat.

ajar¹ *nm* garlic field, garlic patch.

ajar² [1a] **1** *vt* (**a**) (*gen*) to crumple, crush, mess up; to ruffle, rumple; to tamper with, spoil.

(**b**) (*fig*) to abuse, disparage.

2 ajarse *vr* to get crumpled, get messed up; (*Bot*) to wither, fade.

ajarabezado *adj*: **vino ~** wine with syrup added.

ajarafe *nm* (*Geog*) tableland; (*Arquit*) terrace, flat roof.

ajardinar [1a] *vt* to landscape; **zona ajardinada** landscaped area.

ajay *interj* (*LAm*: *risa*) **¡~!** ha!

-aje *V* **Aspects of Word Formation in Spanish 2.**

ajedrea *nf* (*Bot*) savory.

ajedrecista *nmf* chessplayer.

ajedrez *nm* chess; **un ~** a chess set, a set of chessmen.

ajedrezado *adj* chequered.

ajenjo *nm* (*Bot*) wormwood; (*bebida*) absinth(e).

ajeno *adj* (**a**) (*de otro*) somebody else's, other people's; **un coche ~** sb else's car, a car belonging to sb else; **no meterse en lo ~** not to interfere in the affairs of others; **vivir a costa ajena** to live at sb else's expense; to live off other people.

(**b**) (*extraño*) outside; alien, foreign (*a* to); (*inconsecuente*) inconsistent (*a* with); (*impropio*) inappropriate (*a, de* for, to); **ser ~ a la muerte de uno** to have no part in someone's death; **por razones ajenas a mi voluntad** for reasons beyond my control; **eso está ~ a nuestro control** that is outside our control.

(**c**) **~ de cuidados** free from care, without a care.

(**d**) (*no enterado*) unaware (*a, de* of), unsuspecting.

(**e**) **estar ~ de sí** to remain detached.

ajerezado *adj* sherry-flavoured.

ajete *nm* spring onion.

ajetreado *adj vida* busy, tiring.

ajetrearse [1a] *vr* to bustle about, be busy; to fuss; to tire o.s. out; to work hard, slave away.

ajetreo *nm* bustle; fuss; drudgery, hard work; **es un continuo ~** it's all bustle, there's constant coming and going.

ají *nm, pl* **ajíes** *o* **ajises** (*LAm*) chili, red pepper; (*salsa*) chili sauce; **ponerse como un ~** to go bright red (in the face); **estar hecho un ~** to be hopping mad, go up the wall*; **refregarle a uno el ~*** to criticize sb.

ajiaceite *nm* sauce of garlic and olive oil.

ajiaco *nm* (*Carib*) (*Culin*) potato and chili stew; (*lío*) mess, mix-up; **meterse el ~*** to eat.

ajibararse [1a] *vr* (*Carib*) = **aguajirarse.**

ajigolones *nmpl* (*CAm, Méx*) troubles, difficulties.

ajilar [1a] *vi* (*CAm, Méx*) to set out for a place; (*Carib*) to walk quickly.

ajilimoje *nm*, **ajilimójili** *nm* sauce of garlic and pepper; **~s*** bits and pieces, things, odds and ends; **ahí está el ~*** that's the point, that's the trouble.

ajillo *nm* chopped garlic; **al ~** with garlic, cooked in garlic.

ajimez *nm* mullioned window.

ajiseco *nm* (*And*) mild red pepper.

ajises* *nmpl* (*LAm*) *de* **ají.**

ajizarse* [1f] *vr* (*Cono Sur*) to lose one's temper, get mad.

ajo *nm* (**a**) (*Bot*) garlic; (*diente de ~*) clove of garlic; (*salsa*) garlic sauce; **~ tierno** spring onion.

(**b**) (*fig*) shady deal, secret affair; **¡~ y agua!*** you've just got to put up with it!; **harto de ~s** ill-bred, common; (**tieso**) **como un ~** high and mighty, stuck-up*; **andar** (*o* **estar**) **en el ~** to be mixed up in it, be concerned in a shady affair; to be in on the secret; **estar como el ~** (*Cono Sur*) to feel miserable; **revolver el ~** to stir up trouble.

(**c**) (*: *palabrota*) swearword, oath, curse; **echar** (*o* **soltar**) **~s y cebollas** to swear horribly, let fly*.

-ajo, -aja *V* **Aspects of Word Formation in Spanish 2.**

ajoaceite *nm* sauce of garlic and oil.

ajoarriero *nm* dish of cod with oil, garlic and peppers.

ajobar [1a] *vt* to carry on one's back, hump*.

ajobo *nm* load; (*fig*) burden.

ajochar [1a] *vt* (*And*) = **azuzar.**

ajonje *nm*, **ajonjo** *nm* birdlime.

ajonjeo *nm* (*And*) nice remark, compliment.

ajonjolí *nm* sesame.

ajorca *nf* bracelet, bangle.

ajornalar [1a] *vt* to employ by the day.

ajotar [1a] *vt* (*CAm*) = **azuzar**; (*Carib*) (*desdeñar*) to scorn; (*rechazar*) to rebuff.

ajoto *nm* (*Carib*) rebuff.

ajuar *nm* (*muebles*) household furnishings; (*de novia*) trousseau; (*Hist*) dowry, bridal portion; **~ (de niño)** layette.

ajuarar [1a] *vt cuarto etc* to furnish, fit up.

ajuiciado *adj* sensible.

ajuiciar [1b] *vt* to bring to one's senses.

ajumado* 1 *adj* tight*, tipsy. **2** *nm* drunk*.

ajumarse* [1a] *vr* to get tight*.

ajuntarse [1a] *vr* to live together, live in sin; (*entre niños*) **¡no me ajunto contigo!*** I'm not your friend any more!

Ajuria Enea *nf* residence of chief minister of Basque autonomous government; (*fig*) Basque autonomous government.

ajurídico *adj* (*Cono Sur*) illegal.

ajustado *adj* (**a**) (*apropiado*) right, fitting; ~ **a la ley** in accordance with the law. (**b**) *vestido* tight, closefitting; clinging; **muy** ~ stretched tight, skintight; too tight.

ajustador *nm* (**a**) (*chaleco*) bodice, jerkin. (**b**) (*Téc*) fitter. (**c**) ~**es** (*Carib*) bra*, brassière.

ajustamiento *nm* (*Fin*) settlement.

ajustar [1a] **1** *vt* (**a**) (*Téc etc*) to fit (*a* to, into); to fasten, engage.

(**b**) *máquina etc* to adjust, regulate; (*fig*) to adjust, adapt (*a* to); *abuso, error* to put right.

(**c**) *trato* to strike; *acuerdo* to make; *matrimonio* to arrange; *diferencias* to settle, reconcile, adjust.

(**d**) *cuenta* to settle (*t fig*).

(**e**) *precio* to fix.

(**f**) *criado* to hire, engage.

(**g**) (*Tip*) to make up.

(**h**) ~ **un golpe a uno** (*And*) to strike sb, lash out at sb.

2 *vi* to fit; ~ **bien** to fit well, be a good fit.

3 ajustarse *vr* (**a**) (*encajarse*) to fit (*a* into).

(**b**) (*fig*) (*adaptarse*) to adjust o.s., get adjusted (*a* to); (*conformarse*) to conform (*a* to), comply (*a* with); ~ **a las reglas** to abide by the rules.

(**c**) (*fig: llegar a un acuerdo*) to come to an agreement (*con* with).

ajuste *nm* (**a**) (*Téc etc*) fitting; adjustment; (*Cos*) fit, fitting; (*Méx Aut*) overhaul; **mal** ~ maladjustment; ~ **de plantilla** (*euf*) redeployment of labour.

(**b**) (*Fin*) settlement; (*reconciliación*) reconciliation; (*acuerdo*) compromise; (*fig*) ~ **de cuentas** getting even, settling of scores.

(**c**) (*empleo*) hiring, engagement; contract of employment.

(**d**) (*Tip*) make-up.

(**e**) (*Jur*) retaining fee; (*sobrepaga*) bonus; ~ **por aumento del costo de la vida** cost-of-living bonus.

ajusticiable *nmf* person who may face capital punishment.

ajusticiar [1b] *vt* to execute.

ajustón *nm* (*And*) (*castigo*) punishment; (*mal trato*) ill-treatment.

al = **a** + **el**; **al entrar** on entering; **al entrar yo** when I came in; on coming in, I ...; **al verlo yo** when I saw it; on seeing it, I ...; **estar al llegar** to be about to arrive.

ala 1 *nf* (**a**) (*Orn, Ent, Zool, t fig*) wing; **de cuatro ~s** four-winged; **de ~s azules** blue-winged.

(**b**) (*Aer*) wing; ~ **delta** hang-glider; **con ~s en delta** delta-winged; **con ~s en flecha** swept-wing, with swept-back wings.

(**c**) (*de sombrero*) brim; (*Arquit: alero*) eaves; (*parte de edificio*) wing; (*Anat: de corazón*) auricle; (*Cono Sur, Méx**) arm; (*de hélice*) blade; (*de mesa*) leaf, flap; **tener bajo el** ~ to have under one's arm.

(**d**) (*Pol*) wing; **el ~ izquierda del partido** the left wing of the party.

(**e**) (*Mil*) wing, flank.

(**f**) (*Dep*) wing (*part of field*).

(**g**) (*frases*) **ser como ~ de mosca** to be paper thin, be transparent; **ahuecar el ~*** to beat it*; to keep out of the way; **arrastrar el** ~ to be courting; (*fig*) to be depressed; **se le cayeron las ~s del corazón** his heart fell; **andar con el ~ caída** to be downcast; **cortar las ~s a uno** to clip sb's wings, put sb on a tight rein; **dar ~s a uno** to encourage sb, embolden sb; **quedar tocado uno de** ~ to be a lame duck; **tomar ~s*** to get cheeky*; **volar con las propias ~s** to stand on one's own two feet; **en ~s de la fantasía** on (the) wings of fantasy; **las 1000** (*etc*) **del** ~ (*Esp**) a cool 1000 pesetas.

2 *nmf* (*Dep*) winger, wing; **medio** ~ half-back, wing-half.

alabado *nm* (**a**) **al** ~ (*Cono Sur*) at dawn. (**b**) **al** ~ (*Méx*) at nightfall.

Alá *nm* Allah.

alabador *adj* approving, eulogistic.

alabamiento *nm* praise.

alabancioso *adj* boastful.

alabanza *nf* praise (*a* of); eulogy; **~s** praise, praises; **en ~ de** in praise of; **digno de toda** ~ thoroughly praiseworthy, highly commendable; **cantar las ~s de uno** to sing sb's praises.

alabar [1a] **1** *vt* to praise; *decisión etc* to think right, approve of. **2 alabarse** *vr* (**a**) (*jactarse*) to boast; ~ **de** to boast of being. (**b**) (*pagarse*) to be pleased, be satisfied.

alabarda *nf* (*Hist*) halberd.

alabardero *nm* (*Hist*) halberdier; (*Teat*) paid applauder, member of the claque.

alabastrado *adj*, **alabastrino** *adj* alabastrine, alabaster (*atr*).

alabastro *nm* alabaster.

álabe *nm* (*Mec*) wooden cog, tooth; (*de noria*) paddle, bucket; (*Bot*) drooping branch.

alabear [1a] **1** *vt* to warp. **2 alabearse** *vr* to warp.

alabeo *nm* warp, warping; **tomar** ~ to warp.

alacalufe *nmf* (*Cono Sur*) Indian inhabitant of Tierra del Fuego.

alacena *nm* food cupboard, larder, closet (*US*).

alacrán *nm* (**a**) (*Zool*) scorpion. (**b**) (*Cono Sur: chismoso*) gossip, scandalmonger.

alacranear [1a] *vi* (*Cono Sur*) to gossip, scandalmonger.

alacraneo *nm* (*Cono Sur*) gossip, scandal; scandalmongering.

alacridad *nf* alacrity, readiness; **con** ~ with alacrity, readily.

alada *nf* flutter, fluttering; wing-beat.

ALADI [a'laði] *nf abr de* **Asociación Latinoamericana de Integración.**

Aladino *nm* Aladdin.

alado *adj* winged, with wings; (*fig*) winged, swift.

alafia *nf* (*CAm*) verbosity, wordiness.

alafre (*Carib*) **1** *adj* wretched, miserable. **2** *nm* wretch.

alagartado *adj* motley, variegated.

alalá *nm traditional song in parts of northern Spain.*

ALALC *nf abr de* **Asociación Latinoamericana de Libre Comercio** Latin-American Free Trade Association, LAFTA.

alambicado *adj* (**a**) (*destilado*) distilled. (**b**) (*fig*) given sparingly, given grudgingly. (**c**) (*fig*) *estilo* subtle, precious, refined; (*pey*) affected. (**d**) **precios ~s** rock-bottom prices, lowest possible prices.

alambicamiento *nm* (*V adj*) (**a**) (*destilación*) distilling. (**b**) (*fig*) subtlety, preciosity; (*pey*) affectation.

alambicar [1g] *vt* (**a**) (*destilar*) to distil. (**b**) (*fig*) *estilo* to subtilize, polish; (*pey*) to overrefine, exaggerate. (**c**) (*fig: escudriñar*) to scrutinize, investigate. (**d**) (*reducir*) to minimize, reduce to a minimum; (*Com*) to reduce (prices) to the minimum.

alambique *nm* still; **dar algo por** ~ to give sth sparingly; **pasar algo por** ~ to go through sth with a toothcomb.

alambiquería *nf* (*Carib*) distillery.

alambiquero *nm* (*Carib*) distiller.

alambrada *nf* (*red*) wire netting; (*cerca: t* ~ **de púas**); wire fence, barbed-wire fence; (*Mil*) barbed-wire entanglement.

alambrado *nm* (*red*) wire netting; (*cerca*) wire fence; (*Elec*) wiring, wiring system.

alambrar [1a] *vt* to wire; (*LAm*) to fence (with wire).

alambre *nm* wire; ~ **cargado** live wire; ~ **de espino,** ~ **espinoso,** ~ **de púas** barbed wire; ~ **forrado** insulated wire; ~ **de tierra** earth wire, ground wire (*US*); **estar hecho un** ~ to be as thin as a rake.

alambrera *nf* wire screen; wire cover; fireguard.

alambrista *nmf* tightrope walker.

alambrito *nm* (*LAm*) tall thin person.

alambrón *nm* wire rod.

alameda *nf* (*Bot*) poplar grove; (*calle*) avenue, boulevard, tree-lined walk.

álamo *nm* poplar; poplar-tree; ~ **blanco** white poplar; ~ **de Italia** Lombardy poplar; ~ **negro** black poplar; ~ **temblón** aspen.

alamparse [1a] *vr*: ~ **por** to crave, have a craving for.

alancear [1a] *vt* to spear.

alano[1] *nm* mastiff, wolfhound.

alano[2] (*Hist*) **1** *adj* of the Alani. **2 ~s** *nmpl* Alani.

alar *nm* (*tejado*) overhanging roof, eaves; (*LAm: acera*) pavement, sidewalk (*US*); **~es**⁑ trousers, pants.

alarde *nm* (*Mil*) review; (*fig*) show, display, parade; (*Dep*) supreme effort, sprint, dash; **~s** (*And, Cono Sur*) boasts, boasting; **en un ~ final** in a final effort; **hacer ~ de** to make a show of, make a parade of; to boast of.

alardeado *adj* vaunted, much boasted-of.

alardear [1a] *vi* to boast, brag.

alardeo *nm* boasting, bragging.

alargadera *nf* (*Quím*) adapter; (*Téc*) extension.

alargado *adj* long, extended.

alargador *nm* (*Cono Sur Elec*) extension lead.

alargamiento *nm* lengthening, prolongation, extension; increase.

alargar [1h] **1** *vt* (**a**) (*gen*) to lengthen, prolong, extend; *vestido* to lengthen, let down; *cuello* to stretch, crane; *mano* to put out, stretch out; *discurso, narración* to spin out.

(**b**) *cuerda* to pay out.

(**c**) (*alcanzar*) to reach for; to hand, pass (*a* to).
(**d**) *sueldo etc* to increase, raise.
(**e**) *paso* to hasten.
2 alargarse *vr* (**a**) (*gen*) to lengthen, get longer, extend; (*días*) to get longer, draw out; (*discurso etc*) to drag out; (*orador*) to be long-winded.
(**b**) ~ **en** to expatiate on, enlarge upon; **se alargó en la charla** he spun his talk out, he took his time in the talk.
(**c**) (*irse*) to go away, withdraw.
alargo *nm* (*Elec*) extension, lead.
alarido *nm* shriek, yell; **dar ~s** to shriek, yell.
alarife *nmf* (**a**) (*Arquit*) master-builder; bricklayer. (**b**) (*Cono Sur*) (*tipo listo*) sharp customer*; (*mujer de vida*) loose woman.
alarma *nf* alarm; ~ **aérea** air-raid warning, air alert; ~ **antiincendios** fire-alarm; **falsa** ~ false alarm; ~ **de incendios** fire-alarm; ~ **de ladrones** burglar alarm; **con creciente** ~ with growing alarm, with growing concern; **señal de** ~ alarm signal; **voz de** ~ warning note; **timbre de** ~ alarm bell; **dar la** ~ to raise alarming.
alarmantemente *adv* alarmingly.
alarmar [1a] **1** *vt* to alarm; to frighten; (*Mil etc*) to alert, rouse; to call to arms.
2 alarmarse *vr* to get alarmed, be alarmed; to take fright; **¡no te alarmes!** don't be alarmed!, there's nothing to worry about!
alarmismo *nm* alarmism; (excessive) alarm.
alarmista 1 *adj* alarmist, (excessively) alarming. **2** *nmf* alarmist.
alavense = **alavés**.
alavés 1 *adj* of Álava. **2** *nm*, **alavesa** *nf* native (*o* inhabitant) of Álava; **los alaveses** the people of Álava.
alazán 1 *adj caballo* sorrel. **2** *nm* sorrel (horse).
alba *nf* (**a**) (*amanecer*) dawn, daybreak; **al** ~ at dawn; **al rayar** (*o* **romper**) **el** ~ at daybreak. (**b**) (*Ecl*) alb.
albacea *nmf* executor, (*f*) executrix.
albacetense = **albaceteño**.
albaceteño 1 *adj* of Albacete. **2** *nm*, **albaceteña** *nf* native (*o* inhabitant) of Albacete; **los ~s** the people of Albacete.
albacora *nf* albacore, longfin tunny.
albahaca *nf* basil.
albanega *nf* hairnet.
albanés, -esa 1 *adj, nm/f* Albanian. **2** *nm* (*Ling*) Albanian.
Albania *nf* Albania.
albano = **albanés**.
albañal *nm* drain, sewer; (*Agr*) dung heap; (*fig*) mess, muck.
albañil *nm* (**a**) (*artesano*) bricklayer, mason. (**b**) (*obrero*) building worker.
albañilería *nf* (*materias*) brickwork, masonry; (*acto, oficio*) bricklaying, building.
albaquía *nf* balance due, remainder.
albar *adj* white.
albarán *nm* (*Com*) delivery note, advice note; invoice; (*señal*) 'to let' sign.
albarda *nf* packsaddle; (*LAm*: *silla de montar*) saddle; ~ **sobre** ~ piling it on, with a lot of unnecessary repetition; **¡como ahora llueven ~s!*** not on your life!
albardar [1a] *vt* to saddle, put a packsaddle on.
albardear* [1a] *vt* (*CAm*) to bother, vex.
albardilla *nf* (**a**) (*silla*) small saddle; (*cojín*) cushion, pad. (**b**) (*Arquit*) coping. (**c**) (*Culin*) lard; batter.
albareque *nm* sardine net.
albaricoque *nm* apricot.
albaricoquero *nm* apricot tree.
albarrada *nf* (**a**) (*muro*) wall. (**b**) (*And*) cistern.
albatros *nm invar* albatross (*t Golf*).
albayalde *nm* white lead.
albazo *nm* (*And, Méx*) dawn raid; (*Cono Sur*) dawn visit.
albeador *nm* (*Cono Sur* ††) early riser.
albear [1a] *vi* (*Cono Sur* ††) to get up at dawn, get up early.
albedrío *nm* (*gen*: *t* **libre** ~) free will; (*capricho*) whim, fancy; (*gusto*) pleasure; **al** ~ **de uno** at one's pleasure, just as one likes, to suit o.s.
albéitar *nm* veterinary surgeon, veterinarian (*US*).
albeitería *nf* veterinary medicine.
alberca *nf* cistern, tank, reservoir; (*LAm*) swimming pool.
albérchigo *nm* (*fruto*) (clingstone) peach; (*árbol*) (clingstone) peach tree.
albergar [1h] **1** *vt* (**a**) (*gen*) to shelter, give shelter to; to lodge, put up. (**b**) (*fig*) *esperanza* to cherish; *preocupación* to have, experience. **2 albergarse** *vr* to shelter; to lodge, stay.
albergue *nm* (*refugio*) shelter, refuge; (*alojamiento*) lodging; (*Zool*) lair, den; (*Alpinismo*) refuge, mountain hut; ~ **de carretera** roadhouse; ~ **para jóvenes,** ~ **juvenil** youth hostel; ~ **nacional** state-owned tourist hotel; **dar** ~ **a uno** to give sb lodging, take sb in.
alberguista *nmf* youth-hosteller.
albero 1 *adj* white. **2** *nm* (**a**) (*Geol*) pipeclay. (**b**) (*paño*) dishcloth, tea-towel.
Alberto *nm* Albert.
albillo *adj uva, vino* white.
albina *nf* salt lake, salt marsh.
albinismo *nm* albinism.
albino, -a *adj, nm/f* albino.
Albión *nf* Albion; **la pérfida** ~ perfidious Albion.
albis: **quedarse en** ~ not to know a thing, not have a clue; **me quedé en** ~ my mind went blank.
albo *adj* (*liter*) white.
albogue *nm* (*flauta*) rustic flute, shepherd's flute; (*gaita*) bagpipes; **~s** cymbals.
albóndiga *nf* rissole, meatball.
albondigón *nm* hamburger.
albor *nm* (**a**) (*blancura*) whiteness. (**b**) (*alba*) dawn, dawn light; ~ **de la vida** childhood, youth; **~es** dawn; **a los ~es** at dawn.
alborada *nf* dawn; (*Mil*) reveille; (*Poét, Mús*) aubade, dawn song; (*Méx Rel*) night procession.
alborear [1a] *vi* to dawn.
albornoz *nm* (**a**) (*de árabe*) burnous(e). (**b**) (*de baño*) bathing wrap, bathrobe.
alborotadamente *adv* excitedly; noisily, roughly; riotously.
alborotadizo *adj* turbulent; excitable, nervy, jumpy.
alborotado *adj* (**a**) (*excitado*) agitated, excited; (*ruidoso*) noisy, rough; (*amotinado*) mutinous, riotous; *período* disturbed, eventful. (**b**) (*precipitado*) hasty, rash; (*impetuoso*) reckless.
alborotador 1 *adj* turbulent, rebellious; boisterous, noisy; mischief-making.
2 *nm*, **alborotadora** *nf* agitator, troublemaker, mischief-maker; rioter.
alborotar [1a] **1** *vt* (**a**) (*agitar*) to disturb, agitate, stir up; (*amotinar*) to incite to rebel.
(**b**) (*excitar*) to excite, arouse the curiosity of.
2 *vi* to make a racket, make a row.
3 alborotarse *vr* (**a**) (*persona*) to get excited, get worked up; (*turba etc*) to riot, become violent; (*mar*) to get rough.
(**b**) (*CAm*: *ponerse amoroso*) to become amorous.
(**c**) (*Cono Sur*: *caballo*) to rear up.
alboroto *nm* (**a**) (*disturbio*) disturbance, (*vocerío*) racket, row, uproar; (*pelea*) brawl; (*motín*) riot; **armar un** ~ to cause a commotion. (**b**) (*susto*) scare, shock, alarm. (**c**) **~s** (*And, CAm*) popcorn.
alborotoso (*And, Carib*) **1** *adj* troublesome, riotous. **2** *nm*, **alborotosa** *nf* troublemaker.
alborozado *adj* jubilant, overjoyed.
alborozar [1f] **1** *vt* to gladden, fill with joy. **2 alborozarse** *vr* to be overjoyed, rejoice.
alborozo *nm* joy, merriment.
albricias *nfpl* (**a**) (*regalo*) gift, reward (to sb bringing good news). (**b**) (*como interj*) good news!, listen to this!; congratulations!
albufera *nf* (*Valencia y Mallorca*) lagoon.
álbum *nm* album; (*Mús*) album, (*elepé*) long-playing record; ~ **doble** double album; ~ **de recortes** scrapbook; ~ **de sellos,** ~ **de estampillas** (*LAm*) stamp album.
albumen *nm* white of egg; (*Bot*) albumen.
albúmina *nf* (*Quím*) albumin.
albuminoso *adj* albuminous.
albur *nm* (**a**) (*Esp Pez*) bleak. (**b**) (*riesgo*) chance, risk; (*Méx*: *juego de palabras*) pun, play on words; (*Carib*: *mentira*) lie.
albura *nf* (*blancura*) whiteness; (*de huevo*) white of egg.
alburear [1a] **1** *vt* (*CAm*) to disturb, upset. **2** *vi* (**a**) (*enriquecerse*) (*And*) to make money, get rich; (*Carib*) to line one's pockets. (**b**) (*Méx*) to pun, play with words.
alca *nf* razorbill.
alcabala *nf* (**a**) (*Hist*) sales tax. (**b**) (*Cono Sur*) police roadblock, checkpoint.
alcachofa *nf* (**a**) artichoke; ~ **de (la) ducha** shower head. (**b**) (*Radio**) microphone.
alcahué* *nm* = **cacahuete**; *V t* **maní**.
alcahueta *nf* (*de mujeres*) procuress; (*intermediaria*) go-

between; (*chismosa*) gossip.

alcahuete *nm* (**a**) (*chulo*) procurer, pimp; (*intermediario*) go-between; (*perista*) front man, receiver (of stolen goods). (**b**) (*Teat*) drop-curtain.

alcahuetear [1a] *vi* to procure, pimp; to act as a go-between; to act as front man, be a receiver (of stolen goods).

alcahuetería *nf* procuring, pimping; **~s** pimping.

alcaide *nm* (*Hist*: *de castillo, cárcel*) governor; (*carcelero*) warder, jailer.

alcaidía *nf* (*Hist*) governorship.

alcaldable *nmf* candidate for mayor; possible mayor, potential mayor.

alcaldada *nf* abuse of authority; arbitrary act, arbitrary decision.

alcalde *nm* (**a**) mayor; **tener el padre ~** to have influence. (**b**) (*LAm**) procurer, pimp.

alcaldear* [1a] *vi* to lord it, be bossy.

alcaldesa *nf* (woman) mayor; mayoress.

alcaldía *nf* (*oficio*) mayoralty, office of mayor; (*oficina*) mayor's office.

alcalducho* *nm* jumped-up mayor, power-mad mayor.

álcali *nm* alkali.

alcalino *adj* alkaline.

alcaloide *nm* alkaloid.

alcaloideo *adj* alkaloid.

alcamonías *nfpl* (**a**) (*Culin*) aromatic seeds (for seasoning). (**b**) (*: *alcahuetería*) pimping.

alcamonero *adj* (*Carib*: *entrometido*) meddlesome.

alcance *nm* (**a**) (*del brazo etc*) reach; **estar al ~ de uno** to be within one's reach, (*fig*) be within one's powers; **el que está más al ~** the one which is nearest, the one which is most readily accessible; **estar fuera del ~ de uno** to be out of one's reach, be beyond one's reach, (*fig*) to be over one's head, be inaccessible; **poner el coche al ~ de todos** to put the car within the reach of everybody, make the car accessible to all; **al ~ del oído** within earshot; **al ~ de la voz** within call.

(**b**) (*Mil etc*) range; (*fig*) scope; grasp; importance, significance; **el ~ del problema** the extent of the problem; **al ~** within range; **al ~ de la vista** within sight; **de gran ~** (*Mil*) long-range, (*fig*) far-reaching.

(**c**) (*persecución*) chase, pursuit; **dar ~ a** to catch up (with), overtake; **seguir el ~ a** (*Mil*) to pursue; **andar** (*o* **ir**) **a los ~s de uno** to press close on sb, be on sb's tracks; **andar** (*o* **ir**) **en los ~s a uno** to spy on sb.

(**d**) (*Fin*) adverse balance, deficit.

(**e**) (*Tip*) stop-press (news).

(**f**) (*inteligencia*) intelligence, capacity; **de cortos ~s** of limited intelligence, not very bright.

(**g**) **buzón de ~** late-collection postbox.

(**h**) **~s** (*CAm*: *calumnias*) calumnies, malicious accusations.

alcancía *nf* (**a**) (*hucha*) moneybox; (*LAm Ecl*) collection box, poorbox. (**b**) (⁑) cunt⁑. (**c**) (*Méx*‡: *cárcel*) nick‡, can‡.

alcancil *nm* (*Cono Sur*) procurer, pimp.

alcándara *nf* clothes rack; (*Orn*) perch.

alcandora *nf* beacon.

alcanfor *nm* (**a**) (*Bot*) camphor. (**b**) (*LAm*: *alcahuete*) procurer, pimp.

alcanforado 1 *adj* camphorated. **2** *nm* (*LAm*) procurer, pimp.

alcanforar [1a] **1** *vt* to camphorate. **2 alcanforarse** *vr* (*And, CAm, Carib*) to disappear, make o.s. scarce*.

alcantarilla *nf* (*boca*) drain; (*cloaca*) sewer, drain; (*conducto*) culvert, conduit; (*Carib, Méx*) public fountain; (*And*: *para goma*) *vessel for collecting latex*.

alcantarillado *nm* sewer system, drains.

alcantarillar [1a] *vt* to lay sewers in, provide drains for.

alcanzadizo *adj* easy to reach, easily reachable, accessible.

alcanzado *adj* (**a**) (*) hard up*, broke*; **salir ~** to make a loss. (**b**) (*And*) (*fatigado*) tired; (*atrasado*) slow, late.

alcanzar [1f] **1** *vt* (**a**) (*en carrera etc*) to catch, catch up (with); to overtake; *tren, correo* to catch; **cuando le alcancé** when I caught up with him; **no nos alcanzarán nunca** they'll never catch us.

(**b**) (*bala etc*) to hit, strike; **un obús alcanzó la lancha** the launch was hit by a shell; **el presidente fue alcanzado por 2 balas** the president was struck by 2 bullets.

(**c**) (*llegar a*) to reach; to amount to; **la producción ha alcanzado las 20 toneladas** production has reached 20 tons; **el libro ha alcanzado 20 ediciones** the book has run into 20 editions; **las montañas alcanzan los 5.000 m** the mountains rise to 5,000 m.

(**d**) (*sentidos*) to reach to, perceive, take in.

(**e**) (*vivir hasta*) to live into the period of, live on into the time of.

(**f**) (*agarrar*) to grasp, catch hold of; *puesto* to get, obtain.

(**g**) *problema* to grasp, understand.

(**h**) (*And, Cono Sur*: *entregar*) to pass, hand over; (*traer*) to get, bring, fetch; (*dar*) to give; **alcánzame la sal, por favor** pass me the salt, please.

2 *vi* (**a**) (*llegar*) to reach, extend (*a, hasta* to, as far as); **~ para todos** to be enough (for everybody), go round; **no me alcanza el dinero** my money won't stretch to it; **el sueldo no alcanza para nada** I can't make ends meet on my salary; **¿a cuánto alcanza?** (*LAm*) how much does it all come to?

(**b**) **~ a** + *infin* to manage to + *infin*; **no alcanzo a ver cómo ...** I can't see how ...; **no alcanza a hacerlo** he can't manage to do it.

alcanzativo *adj* (*CAm*) suspicious.

alcaparra *nf* (*Bot*) caper.

alcaraván *nm* stone-curlew.

alcaravea *nf* caraway.

alcarreño 1 *adj* of La Alcarria. **2** *nm*, **alcarreña** *nf* native (*o* inhabitant) of La Alcarria; **los ~s** the people of La Alcarria.

alcatraz *nm* gannet, solan goose.

alcaucil *nm* (**a**) (*Bot*) artichoke. (**b**) (*Cono Sur*‡) (*informador*) informer, nark‡; (*alcahuete*) pimp.

alcaudón *nm* shrike.

alcayata *nf* meat hook, spike; (*Méx*) hook.

alcayota *nf* squash, vegetable marrow.

alcazaba *nf* citadel, castle.

alcázar *nm* (*Mil*) fortress, citadel; (*palacio*) royal palace; (*Náut*) quarter-deck.

alcazuz *nm* liquorice.

alce[1] *nm* (*Zool*) elk, moose; **~ de América** moose.

alce[2] *nm* (*Naipes*) cut; **no dar ~ a uno** (*Cono Sur*) to give sb no respite (*o* rest).

alción *nm* kingfisher; (*clásico*) halcyon.

alcista (*Com, Fin*) **1** *adj*: **mercado ~** bull (*o* bullish) market, rising market; **la tendencia ~** the upward tendency, the upward trend. **2** *nm* bull, speculator.

alcoba *nf* (**a**) (*dormitorio*) bedroom; (*Méx Ferro*) sleeping compartment. (**b**) (*muebles*) suite of bedroom furniture.

alcohol *nm* alcohol; **~ absoluto** absolute alcohol, pure alcohol; **~ desnaturalizado, ~ metilado, ~ metílico, ~ de quemar** methylated spirit; **~ vínico** vinic alcohol; **lámpara de ~** spirit lamp.

alcoholemia *nf* blood-level of alcohol.

alcoholero *adj* alcohol (*atr*).

alcohólico 1 *adj* alcoholic; **no ~** *bebida* non-alcoholic, soft. **2** *nm*, **alcohólica** *nf* alcoholic.

alcoholímetro *nm* Breathalyser ®.

alcoholismo *nm* alcoholism.

alcoholista* *nmf* (*Cono Sur*) drunk*.

alcoholizado, -a *nm/f* alcoholic; **morir ~** to die of alcoholism.

alcoholizar [1f] **1** *vt* to alcoholize. **2 alcoholizarse** *vr* to drink heavily.

alcor *nm* hill.

Alcorán *nm* Koran.

alcornoque *nm* (**a**) (*Bot*) cork tree, cork oak. (**b**) (*) idiot.

alcorza *nf* (**a**) (*Culin*) icing, sugar paste. (**b**) (*Cono Sur**: *tipo sensible*) crybaby, sensitive soul.

alcorzar [1f] *vt* (*Culin*) to ice.

alcotán *nm* (*Orn*) hobby.

alcotana *nf* pickaxe, mattock.

alcubilla *nf* cistern, reservoir.

alcucero *adj* sweet-toothed; greedy.

alcurnia *nf* ancestry, lineage; **de ~** of noble family, of noble birth.

alcurniado *adj* aristocratic, noble.

alcuza *nf* (*para aceite*) olive-oil bottle; (*LAm*: *vinagreras*) cruet, cruet stand.

alcuzcuz *nm* couscous.

aldaba *nf* (**a**) (*de puerta*) (door-)knocker; (*cerrojo*) bolt, latch, crossbar; (*para caballo*) hitching ring; **tener buenas ~s** to have influence, have friends in the right places. (**b**) **~s**‡ tits‡.

aldabada *nf* knock (on the door); **dar ~s en** to knock at.

aldabilla *nf* latch.

aldabón *nm* (*de puerta*) large (door-)knocker; (*de baúl etc*)

large handle.
aldabonazo *nm* bang, loud knock (on the door); (*fig*) knock, blow; **dar ~s en** to bang at.
aldea *nf* (small) village, hamlet.
aldeanismo *nm* provincialism, parish-pump attitudes.
aldeano 1 *adj* (**a**) (*de pueblo*) village (*atr*); (*fig*) rustic, rude; **gente aldeana** country people, village people.
(**b**) (*pey*) provincial, parish-pump (*atr*); **actitud aldeana** parish-pump attitude.
2 *nm*, **aldeana** *nf* villager; peasant; **los ~s** the villagers, the village people.
aldehuela *nf* hamlet.
aldeorrio *nm* backward little place, rural backwater.
alderredor *adv* = **alrededor**.
aldosterona *nf* aldosterone.
aldrina *nf* aldrin.
aleación *nf* alloy; **~ ligera** light alloy.
aleado *adj* alloyed, alloy (*atr*).
alear[1] [1a] *vt* (*Téc*) to alloy.
alear[2] [1a] *vi* (*ave*) to flutter, flap (its wings); (*persona*) to move one's arms up and down; (*Med*) to improve; **ir aleando** to be improving.
aleatoriedad *nf* randomness.
aleatorio *adj* accidental, fortuitous; uncertain; (*Estadística*) random, aleatory.
aleatorizar [1f] *vt* to randomize.
alebrarse [1j] *vr* to lie flat, squat; (*fig*) to cower; to lose heart.
alebrestar [1a] **1** *vt* (**a**) (*LAm*) (*alterar*) to distress, disturb; (*emocionar*) to excite, stimulate. **2 alebrestarse** *vr* (**a**) (*LAm*) (*alterarse*) to get distressed, become agitated; (*emocionarse*) to get excited; to become enthusiastic. (**b**) (*Carib*: *rebelarse*) to rebel. (**c**) (*And*: *caballo*) to rear up.
aleccionador *adj* instructive, enlightening.
aleccionamiento *nm* instruction, enlightenment; training.
aleccionar [1a] *vt* (*instruir*) to instruct, enlighten, teach a lesson to; (*adiestrar*) to train; (*regañar*) to lecture.
alechado *adj* (*LAm*) milky, like milk; mixed with milk.
alechugado *adj* pleated; frilled, frilly; crimped.
alechugar [1h] *vt* to fold, pleat; to frill; to crimp.
aledaño 1 *adj* adjoining, bordering. **2** *nm* boundary, limit; **~s** outskirts; surrounding area.
alefra* *interj*: **¡~!** (*Carib*) touch wood!
alegación *nf* declaration (in court); citation; claim, counterclaim; (*Carib, Cono Sur, Méx*) argument; **~ de culpabilidad** (*Méx Jur*) plea of guilty; **~ de inocencia** (*Méx Jur*) plea of not guilty.
alegador 1 *adj* (*Cono Sur*) argumentative. **2** *nm*, **alegadora** *nf* argumentative person.
alegal *adj* (*Cono Sur Jur*) illegal.
alegar [1h] **1** *vt* (**a**) (*Jur etc*) *autoridad* to cite, invoke; to state; to bring forward as an argument; *méritos etc* to cite, adduce, produce in support; **~ que** ... to claim that ..., argue that ...; **alegando que** ... claiming that ..., on the ground that ...
(**b**) (*LAm*: *disputar*) to argue against, dispute.
2 *vi* (*LAm*: *discutir*) to argue, quarrel; (*protestar*) to complain loudly, kick up a fuss.
alegata *nf* (*LAm*) fight.
alegato *nm* (**a**) (*alegación*) claim. (**b**) (*Jur*) bill (of indictment); plea, argument.
alegoría *nf* allegory.
alegóricamente *adv* allegorically.
alegórico *adj* allegoric(al).
alegorizar [1f] *vt* to allegorize.
alegrador *adj* cheering.
alegrar [1a] **1** *vt* (**a**) *persona* to cheer (up), gladden; to make merry, make happy; **esta noticia alegró a todos** this news cheered everyone up, this news made everyone happy.
(**b**) *reunión etc* to enliven, cheer up, brighten up; *fuego* to stir up, make brighter.
(**c**) *toro* to excite, stir up.
(**d**) (*Náut*) *cuerda* to slacken.
2 alegrarse *vr* (**a**) (*estado*) to be glad, be happy, rejoice; **me alegro muchísimo** I'm delighted; **~ con, ~ de, ~ por** to be glad about, rejoice at; **~ de** + *infin* to be glad to + *infin*, be happy to + *infin*; **me alegro de saberlo** I am glad to hear it; **me alegro de que lo hayas hecho** I am glad you've done it.
(**b**) (*acto*) to cheer up (*de* at); **con esto empezó a ~** at this he began to cheer up.
(**c**) (*: *emborracharse*) to get merry*, get tight*.
alegre *adj* (**a**) *persona* (*estado*) happy, merry, glad; carefree; (*temperamento*) cheerful, gay, sunny; *cara etc* happy; *música etc* merry, gay, cheerful; *noticia* good, cheering; *color* bright; *día, período* happy; *tiempo* cheerful, bright, pleasant; **~ de corazón** light-hearted.
(**b**) (*atrevido*) bold, reckless.
(**c**) *chiste* risqué, blue.
(**d**) *vida* fast, immoral; (*) *chica* fast, free-and-easy, swinging*.
(**e**) **estar ~*** to be merry*, be tight*.
alegremente *adv* happily, merrily; cheerfully, gaily; brightly; recklessly.
alegría *nf* (**a**) (*gen*) happiness, joy; gladness; cheerfulness; gaiety, merriment; brightness; **¡qué ~!** that's great!, that's splendid!; **~ vital** joie de vivre; **saltar de ~** to jump with joy, jump for joy.
(**b**) (*pey*) recklessness, irresponsibility
(**c**) **~s** public rejoicings, festivities.
(**d**) **ser el ~s** (*iró*) to be very glum, be downcast.
(**e**) **~s‡** (*Esp*) naughty bits‡.
(**f**) (*Bot*) **~ de la casa** balsam.
alegro *nm* allegro.
alegrón *nm* (**a**) (*fig*) sudden joy. (**b**) (*de fuego*) sudden blaze, flare-up.
alegrona *nf* (*LAm*) prostitute.
alehop *interj* hup!
alejado *adj* distant, remote (*from* de).
alejamiento *nm* (**a**) (*acto*) removal; withdrawal; estrangement. (**b**) (*estado*) distance, remoteness; aloofness.
Alejandría *nf* Alexandria.
alejandrino *nm* alexandrine.
Alejandro *nm* Alexander; **~ Magno** Alexander the Great.
alejar [1a] **1** *vt* (**a**) (*gen*) to remove, move away (*de* from), move to a distance; *peligro* to remove; *persona* to remove, dismiss; *sospecha* to divert; (*deshacerse de*) to get rid of; **conviene ~ tales libros de los niños** such books should be kept away from children, such books should be kept out of children's hands.
(**b**) (*fig*) to cause a rift between, separate, estrange.
2 alejarse *vr* to move away, go away (*de* from); to move to a distance; (*ruido*) to grow fainter; (*peligro*) to recede; **alejémonos un poco más** let's go a bit further away; **~ del buen camino** to get off the right road, lose one's way.
alelado *adj* (*aturdido*) stupefied, bewildered; (*bobo*) foolish, stupid.
alelamiento *nm* bewilderment; foolishness, stupidity.
alelar [1a] **1** *vt* to stupefy; to bewilder. **2 alelarse** *vr* to be stupefied, be bewildered; to look foolish, gape stupidly.
aleluya 1 *nm o f* hallelujah.
2 *nm* Easter time.
3 *nf* Easter print; strip cartoon with rhyming couplets (*originally on religious themes*); (*Arte**) daub, bad painting; (*LAm*) frivolous excuse; (*And*) spoiled child; thing that one loves excessively; (*Poét*) **~s*** doggerel; **estar de ~** to rejoice; **ir al ~** (*Carib**) to go Dutch*, share costs.
4 *nmf* (*: *persona*) hot-gospeller, evangelical.
alelúyico* *adj* evangelical.
alemán, -ana 1 *adj, nm/f* German. **2** *nm* (*Ling*) German.
Alemania *nf* Germany.
alentada *nf* big breath, deep breath; **de una ~** in one breath.
alentado *adj* (*valiente*) brave; (*orgulloso*) proud, haughty; (*Cono Sur*: *fuerte*) strong, vigorous; (*CAm, Méx*: *mejorado*) improved, better.
alentador *adj* encouraging.
alentar [1j] **1** *vt* (**a**) (*gen*) to encourage, cheer, inspire; *resistencia* to stiffen, bolster up; *ánimos* to raise, buoy up; **~ a uno a hacer algo** to encourage sb to do sth; to inspire sb to do sth.
(**b**) (*And*: *aplaudir*) to clap, applaud.
2 *vi* (**a**) (*gen*) to breathe, take a breath.
(**b**) (*fig*) to burn, glow; **en su pecho alienta mucho patriotismo** patriotism burns strongly in his heart.
3 alentarse *vr* (**a**) (*gen*) to take heart, cheer up.
(**b**) (*Med*) to get well.
(**c**) (*And, CAm*: *dar a luz*) to give birth (*de* to).
aleonarse [1a] *vr* (*Cono Sur*) to get excited, get worked up; to cause uproar (*o* a commotion).
aleoyota *nf* (*Cono Sur Bot*) pumpkin.
alepantado *adj* (*And*) absent-minded.
alerce *nm* larch, larch tree.
alergia *nf* allergy; **~ polínica** pollen allergy, allergy to pollen; **~ a la primavera** hay-fever; **tener ~ a** to be allergic to (*t fig*).

alérgico *adj* allergic (*a* to).
alergista *nmf*, **alergólogo, -a** *nm/f* allergist, specialist in allergies.
alergológico *adj* allergy (*atr*).
alero *nm* (**a**) (*Arquit*) eaves; gable-end; (*Aut*) wing; **estar** (o **seguir**) **en el** ~ (*fig*) to be unsure, remain undecided. (**b**) (*Dep*) winger.
alerón *nm* (**a**) (*Aer*) aileron. (**b**) (*Anat**) armpit.
alerta *invar* **1** *interj* watch out!
2 *adv y adj* alert, watchful; **estar** ~, **estar ojo** ~ to be on the alert, stand by, watch out; **todos los servicios de auxilio están** ~ all the rescue services are on the alert.
3 *nm* (*a veces f*) alert; (*Mil*) ~ **previa** early warning; ~ **rojo** red alert.
alertar [1a] **1** *vt* to alert, warn, put on one's guard. **2** *vi* to be alert, keep one's eyes open.
alesnado *adj* (*Carib*) brave, intrepid.
aleta *nf* (*Orn etc*) wing, small wing; (*Aut*) wing, mudguard, fin; (*de hélice*) blade; (*de pez*) fin; (*de foca, t Dep*) flipper; (‡: *mano*) mitt‡, flipper*.
aletargado *adj* drowsy, lethargic; benumbed.
aletargamiento *nm* drowsiness, lethargy; numbness.
aletargar [1h] **1** *vt* to make drowsy, make lethargic; to numb.
2 aletargarse *vr* to grow drowsy, become lethargic; to get numb.
aletazo *nm* (**a**) (*ave*) wingbeat, flap (of the wing); (*pez etc*) movement of the fin. (**b**) (*Cono Sur*: *fig*: *bofetada*) punch, slap. (**c**) (*CAm*) (*hurto*) robbery; (*estafa*) swindle.
aletear [1a] *vi* (*ave*) to flutter, flap its wings; (*pez*) to move its fins.
aleteo *nm* fluttering, flapping (of the wings); movements of the fins; (*Med*) palpitation.
aleudar [1a] **1** *vt* to leaven, ferment with yeast. **2 aleudarse** *vr* to rise.
aleve *adj* treacherous, perfidious.
alevín *nm* young fish, fry; (*fig*) beginner, neophyte, novice.
alevino *nm* (*LAm*) young fish, alevin, fry (*for restocking rivers etc*).
alevosía *nf* treachery.
alevoso 1 *adj* treacherous. **2** *nm* traitor.
alfa[1] *nf* (*letra*) alpha.
alfa[2] *nf* (*LAm*) lucerne, alfalfa.
alfabéticamente *adv* alphabetically.
alfabético *adj* alphabetic(al).
alfabetismo *nm* literacy.
alfabetización *nf* teaching literacy (*o* reading and writing); **campaña de** ~ literacy campaign, drive to teach people to read and write.
alfabetizado *adj* literate, that can read and write.
alfabetizador(a) *nm/f* literacy tutor.
alfabetizar [1f] *vt* (**a**) (*ordenar*) to alphabetize, arrange alphabetically. (**b**) ~ **a uno** to teach sb to read and write.
alfabeto *nm* alphabet; ~ **Morse** Morse code; ~ **romano** Roman alphabet.
alfajor *nm* (**a**) (*LAm*: *dulce*) *type of fudge*; (*And*: *pasta*) puff pastry; (*Esp*: *polvorón*) *cake eaten at Christmas.* (**b**) (*Cono Sur* ††) = **facón.**
alfalfa *nf* lucerne, alfalfa.
alfalfar *nm* lucerne field.
alfandoque *nm* (**a**) (*CAm, Carib, Méx*: *pasta*) *a kind of sweet pastry.* (**b**) (*And, CAm Mús*) maraca-like instrument, cylindrical rattle. (**c**) (*And*: *dulce*) toffee-like almond paste. (**d**) (*Carib*: *pastelito*) small honey cake.
alfanje *nm* cutlass; (*Pez*) swordfish.
alfanumérico *adj* alphanumeric.
alfaque *nm y* ~**s** *pl* (*Náut*) bar, bank, shoal.
alfaquí *nm* Moslem doctor, ulema, expounder of the Law.
alfar *nm* (**a**) (*taller*) pottery, potter's workshop. (**b**) (*arcilla*) clay.
alfarería *nf* (*cerámica*) pottery; (*tienda*) pottery shop.
alfarero, -a *nm/f* potter.
alfarjía *nf* (*esp for door o window frames*) batten.
alféizar *nm* (*Arquit*) splay, embrasure; sill, windowsill, ledge.
alfeñicado* *adj* (**a**) (*débil*) weakly, delicate. (**b**) (*afectado*) affected.
alfeñicarse* [1g] *vr* (**a**) (*enflaquecerse*) to get terribly thin, look frail.
(**b**) (*remilgarse*) to act affectedly, be overnice; to be very prim and proper.
alfeñique *nm* (**a**) (*Culin*) toffee-like paste, almond-flavoured sugar paste.
(**b**) (*: *persona*) delicate person; mollycoddle, sissy*; very thin person.
(**c**) (*cualidad*) affectation; primness; excessive delicacy.
alferecía *nf* epilepsy.
alférez *nm* (*Mil*) second lieutenant, subaltern; (*LAm Ecl*) official standard-bearer (in processions); ~ **de fragata** midshipman; ~ **de navío** sub-lieutenant.
alfil *nm* (*Ajedrez*) bishop.
alfiler *nm* (*gen*) pin; (*broche*) brooch, clip; ~**es** pin-money, dress allowance; ~ **de corbata** tiepin; ~ **de gancho** (*Cono Sur*) safety-pin; ~ **de seguridad** (*LAm*) safety-pin; ~ **de sombrero** hatpin; **aquí ya no cabe ni un** ~ you can't squeeze anything else in; **pedir para** ~**es** to ask for a tip; **prendido con** ~**es** shaky, hardly hanging together; **puesto con 25** ~**es** dressed up to the nines.
alfilerar [1a] *vt* to pin together, pin up.
alfilerazo *nm* pinprick (*t fig*); **tirar** ~**s a uno** to have a dig at sb.
alfilerillo *nm* (*And, Cono Sur*) *type of spikenard used for animal feeding.*
alfiletero *nm* needle case; pincushion.
alfolí *nm* (*de granos*) granary; (*de sal*) salt warehouse.
alfombra *nf* carpet; rug, mat; ~ **de baño** bathmat; ~ **encantada,** ~ **mágica** magic carpet; ~ **de oración** prayer-mat; ~ **voladora** flying carpet.
alfombrado *nm* carpeting.
alfombrar [1a] *vt* to carpet (*t fig*).
alfombrero, -a *nm/f* carpet maker.
alfombrilla *nf* (**a**) (*alfombra*) rug, mat; ~ **roja** red carpet. (**b**) (*Med*: *sarampión*) German measles; (*Carib*: *sarpullido*) rash; (*Méx*: *viruela*) smallpox.
alfonsí *adj* Alphonsine (*esp re Alfonso X, 1252-84*).
alfonsino *adj* Alphonsine (*esp re recent kings of Spain named Alfonso*).
Alfonso *nm* Alphonso; ~ **el Sabio** Alphonso the Wise (*1252-84*).
alforfón *nm* buckwheat.
alforja *nf* (*de jinete*) saddlebag; (*mochila*) knapsack; (*de bicicleta*) pannier; ~**s** (*t fig*) provisions (for a journey); **pasarse a la otra** ~ (*Cono Sur*) to overstep the mark, go too far; **sacar los pies de las** ~**s** to go off on a different tack; **para ese viaje no hacían falta** ~**s** (*fig*) there was no point in making such elaborate preparations, you didn't have to go to such trouble.
alforjudo *adj* (*Cono Sur*) silly, stupid.
alforza *nf* pleat, tuck; (*fig*) slash, scar.
alforzar [1f] *vt* (*Cos*) to pleat, tuck.
Alfredo *nm* Alfred.
alga *nf* seaweed, alga; ~ **tóxica** toxic alga.
algaida *nf* (*Bot*) bush, undergrowth; (*Geog*) dune.
algalia[1] *nf* (*Zool*) civet.
algalia[2] *nf* (*Med*) catheter.
algara *nf* (*Hist*) raid; raiding party.
algarabía *nf* (**a**) (*Ling*) Arabic.
(**b**) (*) (*habla*) double Dutch*, gibberish; gabble; (*jaleo*) din, hullabaloo*.
(**c**) (*Bot*) cornflower.
algarada *nf* (**a**) (*griterío*) outcry; **hacer una** ~, **levantar una** ~ to kick up a tremendous fuss.
(**b**) (*Hist*) cavalry raid; cavalry troop.
Algarbe *nm*: **el** ~ the Algarve.
algarero *adj* noisy, rowdy.
algarroba *nf* carob, carob bean.
algarrobo *nm* carob tree, locust tree.
algazara *nf* din, clamour, uproar.
álgebra *nf* algebra; ~ **de Boole,** ~ **booleana** Boolean algebra.
algebraico *adj* algebraic.
algecireño 1 *adj* of Algeciras. **2** *nm*, **algecireña** *nf* native (*o* inhabitant) of Algeciras; **los** ~**s** the people of Algeciras.
álgido *adj* icy, cold, chilly; (*fig*) *punto etc* culminating, decisive; most intense.
algo 1 *pron* (**a**) (*en frases afirmativas*) something; **habrá** ~ **para ti** there will be something in it for you; **esto es** ~ **nuevo** this is something new; ~ **es** ~ something is better than nothing; **eso ya es** ~ that's something; **más vale** ~ **que nada** something is better than nothing; **¡por** ~ **será!** there must be a reason behind it, he (*etc*) can't have done it for no reason at all; **ya es** ~ it's a start; **creerse** ~ to think one is somebody; **tener un** ~ to have a certain charm; **estar en** ~ (*LAm*‡) to be high (on drugs)‡; to be involved in something; **tomar** ~ to have a drink.
(**b**) (*en frases interrog y neg*) anything; **¿pasa** ~**?** is anything the matter?; **¿hay** ~ **para mí?** is there anything for

me?

2 *adv* rather, somewhat, a bit; **es ~ difícil** it's rather hard, it's a bit awkward.

3 *nm* (*And*) snack, something to eat.

algodón *nm* cotton; wadding; (*Med*) swab; (*Bot*) cotton plant; **~ de azúcar, ~ de caramelo, ~ dulce** candy-floss, cotton candy (*US*); **~ hidrófilo** cotton wool, absorbent cotton (*US*); **~ labrado** patterned cotton; **~ pólvora** guncotton; **~ en rama** raw cotton, cotton wool; **se crió entre algodones** he was always pampered; he was brought up in luxury.

algodonal *nm* cotton plantation.

algodonar [1a] *vt* to stuff with cotton wool, wad.

algodoncillo *nm* milkweed.

algodoncito *nm* cotton-wool swab, cotton bud.

algodonero 1 *adj* cotton (*atr*). **2** *nm* (**a**) (*cultivador*) cotton grower; (*comerciante*) cotton dealer. (**b**) (*Bot*) cotton plant.

algodonosa *nf* cotton grass.

algodonoso *adj* cottony.

algorítmica *nf* algorithms.

algoritmo *nm* algorithm.

alguacil *nm* (*Hist*) governor; bailiff, constable; (*Taur*: *t* **alguacilillo**) mounted official.

alguicida *nm* algicide.

alguien *pron* someone, somebody; anybody; **si ~ viene** if somebody comes, if anybody comes; **¿viste a ~?** did you see anybody?; **para ~ que conozca la materia** for anyone who is familiar with the subject; **ser ~** to be somebody; **~ se lo habrá dicho** someone or other must have told him.

alguita‡ *nf* (*And*) money, dough‡.

alguito (*LAm*) = **algo.**

alguno 1 *adj* (**algún** *delante de nm sing*) (**a**) (*delante de n*) some, any; some ... or other; **algún obispo lo dijo** some bishop said so; **algún coche lo tiene ya** some cars already have it; **hubo algunas dificultades** there were some difficulties; there were a few difficulties; **algún que otro libro** an odd book or two; a few odd books; **leo algún libro que otro** I read an occasional book, I read a book from time to time; **por alguna que otra razón** for some reason or other.

(**b**) (*precedido por neg, tras n*) no, not ... any; **no tiene talento ~** he has no talent, he hasn't any talent, he has no talent at all; **sin interés ~** without the slightest interest.

2 *pron* (**a**) (*sing*) some; one; someone, somebody; **~ es bueno** some are good, an occasional one is good; **~ de ellos** one of them; **~ que otro** one or two, an occasional one; **~ dijo que ...** someone said that ...; **busco ~ que me ayude** I'm looking for somebody to help me.

(**b**) **~s** some; a few; **~s son buenos** some are good; **vimos ~s** we saw some; we saw a few; **~s hay que ...** there are some who...

alhaja *nf* (**a**) (*joya*) jewel, gem; (*objeto precioso*) precious object, treasure; (*mueble*) fine piece (of furniture).

(**b**) (*fig*: *persona*) treasure, gem; **¡buena ~!** (*iró*) she's a fine one!

alhajado *adj* (*And*) wealthy.

alhajar [1a] *vt cuarto* to furnish, appoint (in delicate taste).

alhajera *nf* (*Cono Sur*) jewel box.

alharaca *nf* fuss; **hacer ~s** to make a fuss, make a great song and dance about sth.

alharaquiento *adj* demonstrative, highly emotional.

alhelí *nm* wallflower, stock.

alheña *nf* (**a**) (*Bot*) (*planta*) privet; (*flor*) privet flower; (*para teñir*) henna. (**b**) (*roya*) blight, mildew.

alheñar [1a] **1** *vt* (**a**) (*teñir*) to dye with henna. (**b**) (*con roya*) to blight, cover with mildew. **2 alheñarse** *vr* to become mildewed, get covered in mildew.

alhóndiga *nf* corn exchange.

alhucema *nf* lavender.

aliacán *nm* jaundice.

aliado 1 *adj* allied. **2** *nm*, **aliada** *nf* ally; **los A~s** the Allies. **3** *nm* (*Cono Sur*) (*emparedado*) toasted sandwich; (*bebida*) mixed drink.

aliaga *nf* = **aulaga.**

aliancista (*Esp Pol Hist*) **1** *adj*: **política ~** policy of Alianza Popular. **2** *nmf* member of Alianza Popular.

alianza *nf* (**a**) (*gen*) alliance; connection; (*Bib*) **A~** Covenant; **la A~ Atlántica** the Atlantic Alliance, NATO; **A~ para el Progreso** Alliance for Progress; **Santa A~** Holy Alliance. (**b**) (*anillo*) wedding ring.

aliar [1c] **1** *vt* to ally, bring into an alliance. **2 aliarse** *vr* to ally o.s.; to become allied, form an alliance.

alias *adv, nm* alias.

alicaído *adj* (*Med*) drooping, weak; (*fig*) downcast, crestfallen; depressed.

alicantina *nf* trick, ruse.

alicantino 1 *adj* of Alicante. **2** *nm*, **alicantina** *nf* native (*o* inhabitant) of Alicante; **los ~s** the people of Alicante.

alicatar [1a] *vt azulejo* to shape, cut.

alicates *nmpl* pliers, pincers; **~ de corte** wire-cutters.

Alicia *nf* Alice; **'~ en el país de las maravillas'** 'Alice in Wonderland'; **'~ en el país del espejo'** 'Alice through the Looking-glass'.

aliciente *nm* incentive, inducement; lure; attraction; **ofrecer un ~** to hold out an inducement; **ofrece el ~ de ...** it holds out the attraction of ...

alicorarse* [1a] *vr* (*And*) to get boozed*.

alicorear [1a] *vt* (*CAm*: *adornar*) to decorate, adorn.

alicrejo *nm* (*CAm*) spider-like (*o* ugly) creature; (*hum*) old horse, nag.

alicurco *adj* (*Cono Sur*) sly, cunning.

alienación *nf* alienation; (*Med*) alienation, mental derangement.

alienado 1 *adj* alienated; (*Med*) insane, mentally ill. **2** *nm*, **alienada** *nf* alienated person; (*Med*) lunatic, mad person.

alienante *adj* inhuman, dehumanizing; alienating.

alienar [1a] *vt* = **enajenar.**

alienígena 1 *adj* foreign; alien; extraterrestrial. **2** *nmf* foreigner; alien; extraterrestrial being.

alienista *nmf* specialist in mental illness, psychiatrist, alienist (*US*).

aliento *nm* (**a**) (*un ~*) breath; (*gen*) breathing, respiration; **~ fétido** bad breath; **de un ~** (*lit*) in one breath, (*fig*) in one go; **aguantar el ~, contener el ~** to hold one's breath; **dar los últimos ~s** to breathe one's last; **estar sin ~** to be out of breath; **tiene mal ~** his breath smells; **tomar ~** to take breath; to get one's breath back.

(**b**) (*fig*: *t* **~s**) courage, spirit; strength; **cobrar ~** to take heart; **dar ~ a uno** to encourage sb, give sb courage; to support sb.

alifafe* *nm* ailment.

aligación *nf* alloy; (*fig*) bond, tie.

aligeramiento *nm* lightening; easing, alleviation.

aligerar [1a] **1** *vt* (*hacer más ligero*) to lighten; *dolor* to ease, relieve, alleviate; (*abreviar*) to shorten; *paso* to quicken.

2 aligerarse *vr* (**a**) (*carga*) to get lighter; **~ de ropa** to put on lighter clothing. (**b**) (*: *irse*) to beat it*, get out.

aligustre *nm* privet.

alijar¹ [1a] *vt* (*Téc*) to sandpaper.

alijar² [1a] *vt* to lighten; *barco* to unload; *contrabanda* to land, smuggle ashore.

alijar³ *nm* tile.

alijo *nm* (**a**) (*acto*) lightening; unloading. (**b**) (*géneros*) contraband, collection of smuggled goods; **~ de armas** consignment of smuggled arms, cache of arms; **~ de drogas** consignment of drugs (seized).

alilaya 1 *nf* (*And, Carib*: *excusa*) lame (*o* flimsy) excuse. **2** *nmf* (*Méx*) cunning person, sharp character*.

alimaña *nf* (**a**) (destructive, objectionable) animal; pest; **~s** (*frec*) vermin. (**b**) (*fig*: *persona*) brute, animal.

alimañero *nm* gamekeeper, vermin destroyer.

alimentación *nf* (**a**) (*acto*) feeding, nourishment; (*comida*) food; (*fig*) nurture, fostering; **el coste de la ~** the cost of food; **la ~ de los niños** the feeding of children, the nourishment of children; **~ insuficiente** malnutrition, undernourishment; **~ natural** natural food, health foods.

(**b**) (*Téc*) feed; supply; **bomba de ~** feed pump; **~ por fricción** friction feed; **~ a la red** mains supply.

alimentador *nm* (*Téc*) feed, feeder; **~ automático de hojas, ~ de documentos, ~ de papel** (automatic) paper-feeder.

alimentar [1a] **1** *vt* (**a**) (*dar de comer a*) to feed, (*en sentido más general*) nourish.

(**b**) (*fig*) *familia* to maintain, support; to bring up, nurture; *esperanza* to nourish, encourage; to cherish; *sentimiento* to foster; *pasión* to feed, add fuel to.

(**c**) (*Téc*) to feed; *horno* to feed, stoke (*de* with); **~ una máquina de algo** to feed sth into a machine.

2 alimentarse *vr* to feed (*con, de* on); **~ de** to live on.

alimentario *adj* food (*atr*); **la industria alimentaria** the food industry.

alimenticio *adj* (**a**) (*nutritivo*) nourishing, nutritive. (**b**) (*relativo a comida*) food (*atr*); **artículos ~s** foodstuffs; **valor ~** food value, nutritional value.

alimento *nm* (**a**) (*gen*) food; nourishment; (*Méx*) meal; **~s integrales** whole foods; **~s naturales** health foods; **~ de primera necesidad** staple food. (**b**) (*fig*) encouragement,

support; incentive; (*de pasión*) fuel. (**c**) **~s** (*Jur*) alimony.
alimentoso *adj* nourishing.
alimoche *nm* Egyptian vulture.
alimón: al ~ *adv* together, jointly, in collaboration.
alindado *adj* foppish, dandified.
alindar¹ [1a] *vt* (*adornar*) to embellish, make pretty, make look nice; *persona* to doll up, prettify.
alindar² [1a] **1** *vt tierra* to mark off, mark out. **2** *vi* to adjoin, be adjacent.
alinderar [1a] *vt* (*CAm, Cono Sur*) to mark out the boundaries of.
alineación *nf* (**a**) (*Téc*) alignment; **estar fuera de ~** to be out of alignment, be out of true. (**b**) (*Dep etc*) line-up.
alineado *adj*: **está ~ con el partido** he is in line with the party; **los países no ~s** the non-aligned countries.
alineamiento *nm*: **no ~** non-alignment; *V t* **alineación.**
alinear [1a] **1** *vt* to align; to line up, put into line; (*Mil*) to form up; (*Dep*) *equipo* to play, field; (*fig*) to bring into line (*con* with).
2 alinearse *vr* to line up; (*Mil*) to fall in, form up; (*Inform*) to justify; **se alinearon a lo largo de la calle** they lined up along the street.
aliñador *nm* (*Cono Sur*) bonesetter.
aliñar [1a] *vt* (**a**) (*adornar*) to adorn, embellish. (**b**) (*preparar*) to prepare; (*Culin*) to dress, season. (**c**) (*Cono Sur*) *hueso* to set.
aliño *nm* (**a**) (*adorno*) adornment, embellishment; preparation. (**b**) (*Culin*) dressing, seasoning.
alioli *nm* (*Culin*) sauce of garlic and oil.
alionar [1a] *vt* (*Cono Sur*) to stir up.
alionín *nm* blue tit.
alipego *nm* (*CAm*) extra, bonus (*added as part of a sale*); (*) gatecrasher, intruder, person who comes uninvited.
aliquebrado *adj* crestfallen.
alirón 1 *excl* hurray! **2** *nm victory song of supporters of Real Madrid*; (*fig*) victory, triumph; victory celebration.
alisado 1 *adj* smooth; polished. **2** *nm* smoothing; polishing; finishing.
alisador *nm* (*persona*) polisher; (*herramienta*) smoothing blade, smoothing tool.
alisadura *nf* smoothing; polishing; **~s** cuttings, shavings.
alisar¹ [1a] *vt* to smooth (down); to polish, burnish; *pelo* to smooth, sleek; (*Téc*) to polish, finish, surface.
alisar² *nm*, **aliseda** *nf* alder grove.
alisios *nmpl* (*t* **vientos ~**) trade winds.
aliso *nm* alder, alder tree.
alistamiento *nm* enrolment; (*Mil*) enlistment, recruitment.
alistar¹ [1a] **1** *vt* (*poner en lista*) to list, put on a list; *miembro* to enrol; (*Mil*) to enlist; (*CAm*: *zapato*) to sew (up).
2 alistarse *vr* to enrol; (*Mil*) to enlist, join up.
alistar² [1a] **1** *vt* (*disponer*) to prepare, make ready. **2 alistarse** *vr* (*LAm*) to get dressed, get ready.
aliteración *nf* alliteration.
aliterado *adj* alliterative.
alitranca *nf* (*And, Cono Sur*) brake, braking device.
aliviadero *nm* overflow channel (*on dam*).
aliviador *adj* comforting, consoling.
alivianarse* [1a] *vr* (*Méx*) to play it cool, be cool, be laid-back*.
aliviar [1b] **1** *vt* (**a**) (*aligerar*) to lighten; (*dolor*) to ease, relieve; to make more bearable; to soothe; **~ a uno de algo** (*robar*) to relieve sb of sth.
(**b**) (*acelerar*) to speed up; *paso* to quicken.
(**c**) (‡) to nick‡, pinch*.
2 aliviarse *vr* (**a**) (*dolor*) to diminish, become more bearable; (*paciente*) to gain relief; to get better, recover; **¡que se alivie!** get better soon!
(**b**) (*fig*) to unburden o.s. (*de* of).
alivio *nm* (**a**) (*gen*) alleviation, relief, easing; mitigation; improvement; (*Med*) relief; **~ de luto** half-mourning; **¡que siga el ~!** I hope you continue to improve!
(**b**) **de ~*** awful, horrible; **un susto de ~** an awful fright, a hell of a fright.
aljaba *nf* (**a**) (*para flechas*) quiver. (**b**) (*Cono Sur Bot*) fuchsia.
aljama *nf* (*Hist*) (**a**) (*barrio*) (*de moros*) Moorish quarter; (*de judíos*) Jewish quarter, ghetto. (**b**) (*mezquita*) mosque; (*sinagoga*) synagogue. (**c**) (*reunión*) gathering of Moors *o* Jews.
aljamía *nf Spanish written in Arabic characters* (*14th-16th centuries*).
aljamiado *adj*: **texto ~** *text of Spanish written in Arabic characters.*
aljibe *nm* (**a**) (*cisterna*) cistern, tank; (*Náut*) water tender; (*Aut*) oil tanker; (*And*: *pozo*) well. (**b**) (*And*: *calabozo*) dungeon, underground prison.
aljofaina *nf* washbasin, washbowl.
aljófar *nm* (small *o* irregular) pearl; (*fig*) pearl of moisture; dewdrop.
aljofarar [1a] *vt* to bedew, cover with pearls of moisture.
aljofifa *nf* floor-cloth.
aljofifar [1a] *vt* to wash, mop, mop up.
alma *nf* (**a**) (*gen*) soul; spirit; **¡hijo de mi ~!** my precious child!
(**b**) (*locuciones con verbo*) **le arrancó el ~** he was deeply shocked by it; **se le fue el ~ a los pies** he became very disheartened, his heart sank; **se echó el ~ a las espaldas** he abandoned all scruples; he wasn't in the least worried; **entregar el ~** to give up the ghost; **estar con el ~ en la boca** to be scared to death; **hablar al ~** to speak most earnestly; **se le fue el ~ tras la muñeca** she fell for the doll, she would have sold her soul for the doll; **me llegó al ~** it affected me deeply, it really struck home; **partirse el ~** (**para**) (*Méx*) to go to great lengths (to); **se le partió el ~** she was heartbroken; **no puedo con mi ~** (*Esp*) I can't stand it any more; **rendir el ~** to give up the ghost; **romper el ~ a uno‡** to do sb in‡; **rompe el ~ verlo** it breaks one's heart to see it; **lo siento en el ~** I am truly sorry; **tener el ~ en un hilo** to have one's heart in one's mouth; to be scared to death; **tener el ~ en su almario** to be up to anything, be fully up to the job; to have lots of guts*; **tener mucha ~, tener el ~ bien puesta** to be undaunted; **no tener ~** to be pitiless; **le volvió el ~ al cuerpo** he calmed down; he recovered his composure; it relieved him of a great worry (*o* fear *etc*).
(**c**) (*comparaciones*) **andar** (*o* **estar**) **como ~ en pena** to go about like a lost soul; **estar como un ~ perdida** to be completely undecided; **ir como ~ que lleva el diablo** to go like a bat out of hell, run like hell.
(**d**) (*persona*) soul, person, inhabitant; **un pueblo de 2 mil ~s** a village of 2,000 souls, a village of 2,000 inhabitants; **¡~ mía!** my precious!, darling!; **~ bendita** simple soul; **~ de caballo** twister; **~ de Caín, ~ de Judas** fiend, devil; **¡~ de cántaro!** you idiot!; **~ de Dios** good soul; **ni ~ nacida, ni ~ viviente** not a single living soul.
(**e**) (*fig*) soul, moving spirit, leading spirit; (*de asunto*) crux, heart, vital part; **él es el ~ del movimiento** he is the leading spirit of the movement; **es el ~ de la fiesta** he's the life and soul of the party.
(**f**) **con el ~, con toda el ~** with all one's heart, heart and soul; **lo haré con toda mi ~** I'll do it with all my heart; **en lo más hondo de mi ~** in my heart of hearts.
(**g**) (*And*: *cadáver*) corpse.
(**h**) (*Bot*) pith; (*Téc*) core, heart; (*de cable*) core; (*de cuerda*) central strand; (*de cañón*) bore.
almacén *nm* (**a**) (*depósito*) warehouse, store; depository; **~ de depósito** bonded warehouse; **tener algo en ~** to have sth in store, (*Com*) to stock sth.
(**b**) (*Mec, Mil etc*) magazine.
(**c**) (*tienda*) shop, store; (*LAm*) *esp* grocer's (shop), grocery shop, grocery store; **~ frigorífico** cold store; (**grandes**) **almacenes** department store; **Almacenes Pérez** Pérez Department Store.
almacenable *adj* that can be stored, storable.
almacenado *nm* storage, warehousing.
almacenaje *nm* (**a**) (*acto*) storage, storing; **~ frigorífico** cold storage; **~ de larga duración** long-term storage. (**b**) (*precio*) storage charge, storage fee.
almacenamiento *nm* (*Inform*) storage; **~ de datos** data storage; **~ primario** primary storage; **~ secundario** secondary storage; **~ temporal en disco** (disk) spooling.
almacenar [1a] *vt* (**a**) (*poner en depósito*) to store, put into storage, keep in store; *víveres etc* to stock up (with); (*Inform*) to store, save.
(**b**) (*fig*) to keep, collect, (*pey*) hoard; **~ odio** to store up hatred.
almacenero, -a *nm/f* storekeeper, warehouseman; (*LAm*) shopkeeper.
almacenista *nmf* warehouse owner; (*LAm*) shopkeeper, grocer.
almáciga *nf*, **almácigo** *nm* (*LAm*) seedbed, nursery.
almádena *nf* sledgehammer, large hammer.
almadía *nf* raft.
almadiarse [1c] *vr* to be sick, vomit.
almadraba *nf* (*acto, arte*) tunny fishing; (*lugar*) tunny fishery; (*redes*) tunny net(s).
almadreña *nf* wooden shoe, clog.

almagre *nm* red ochre.
almajara *nf* (*Agr*) hotbed, forcing frame.
alma máter *nf* alma mater.
almanaque *nm* almanac; **hacer ~s** to muse; (*And, Cono Sur*) **echar a uno vendiendo ~s** to send sb away with a flea in his ear.
almariarse [1c] *vr* (*CAm, Cono Sur*) to be sick, vomit.
almazara *nf* oil mill, oil press.
almeja *nf* (**a**) (*Zool*) shellfish, cockle, clam (*US*). (**b**) (**‡**) cunt**‡**; **mojar la ~** to have a screw**‡**.
almenado *adj* battlemented, crenellated.
almenara *nf* (*fuego*) beacon; (*araña*) chandelier.
almenas *nfpl* battlements, crenellations.
almendra *nf* (**a**) (*Bot*) almond; **~ amarga** bitter almond; **~ garapiñada** praline, sugar almond; **~ tostada** burnt almond; **ser ~** (*Carib fig*) to be a love (*o* a peach).
(**b**) (*Bot: semilla*) kernel, stone.
(**c**) (*de vidrio*) cut-glass drop (of chandelier *etc*).
almendrada *nf* almond milk shake, drink made with milk and almonds.
almendrado 1 *adj* (**a**) *forma* almond-shaped, pear-shaped; **de ojos ~s** almond-eyed. (**b**) *sabor* nutty. **2** *nm* macaroon.
almendral *nm* almond orchard.
almendrera *nf* almond tree.
almendrillo *nm* (*LAm*) almond tree.
almendro *nm* almond tree.
almendruco *nm* green almond.
almeriense 1 *adj* of Almería. **2** *nmf* native (*o* inhabitant) of Almería; **los ~s** the people of Almería.
almete *nm* (*Hist*) helmet.
almez *nm* hackberry.
almiar *nm* haycock, hayrick.
almíbar *nm* syrup; **~ de pelo** (*LAm*) heavy syrup; **estar hecho un ~** to be all sweet and kind, be especially nice, (*pey*) overdo the sweetness.
almibarado *adj* syrupy; (*fig*) honeyed, over-sweet; *estilo, tono* sugary.
almibarar [1a] *vt* to preserve (*o* serve) in syrup; **~ las palabras** to use honeyed words, overdo the sweetness.
almidón *nm* (*gen*) starch; (*Méx: engrudo*) paste.
almidonado *adj* starched; (*fig*) (*estirado*) stiff, starchy; (*pulcro*) dapper, spruce.
almidonar [1a] *vt* to starch; **los prefiero sin ~** I prefer them unstarched.
almilla *nf* (**a**) (*jubón*) bodice; undervest. (**b**) (*Téc*) tenon. (**c**) (*Culin*) breast of pork.
alminar *nm* minaret.
almirantazgo *nm* admiralty.
almirante *nm* admiral.
almirez *nm* mortar.
almizcle *nm* musk.
almizcleño *adj* musky.
almizclera *nf* muskrat, musquash.
almizclero *nm* musk deer.
almo *adj* (*poét*) nourishing; sacred, venerable.
almocafre *nm* weeding hoe.
almodrote *nm* cheese and garlic sauce; (*fig*) hotchpotch.
almofré *nm*, **almofrez** *nm* (*LAm*) sleeping bag, bedroll.
almohada *nf* (*de cama*) pillow; bolster; (*cojín*) cushion; (*funda*) pillowcase; **~ neumática** air cushion; **consultar algo con la ~** to sleep on sth, think sth over carefully.
almohade 1 *adj* Almohad. **2 ~s** *nmpl* Almohads.
almohadilla *nf* small cushion, small pillow; (*LAm*) holder (for iron *etc*); (*CAm, Carib, Méx Dep*) base, cushion; (*Cos*) pincushion; (*Arquit*) boss; (*Téc*) pad, cushion; **~ de entintar** inkpad.
almohadillado 1 *adj* padded; stuffed; *piedra* dressed (in a special way, *eg* vermiculate). **2** *nm* ashlar; dressed ashlar.
almohadón *nm* large pillow, bolster; (*Ecl*) hassock.
almohaza *nf* currycomb.
almohazar [1f] *vt caballo* to brush down, groom; *piel* to dress.
almoneda *nf* auction; clearance sale.
almoned(e)ar [1a] *vt* to auction.
almorávide 1 *adj* Almoravid. **2 ~s** *nmpl* Almoravids.
almorranas *nfpl* (*Med*) piles.
almorta *nf* (*Bot*) vetch.
almorzar [1f *y* 1l] **1** *vt* to have for lunch, lunch on; (†† *y en regiones de LAm*) to have for second breakfast, breakfast late on.
2 *vi* to lunch, have lunch; (†† *y en regiones de LAm*) to breakfast late, have second breakfast; **vengo almorzado** I've had lunch.
almuecín *nm*, **almuédano** *nm* muezzin.
almuerzo *nm* (**a**) (*a mediodía*) lunch, (*más formal*) luncheon; (*de boda*) wedding breakfast; (†† *y en regiones de LAm*) late breakfast, second breakfast; **~ de gala** official luncheon; **~ de negocios** business lunch; **~ de trabajo** working lunch.
(**b**) (*vajilla*) dinner service.
alnado, -a *nm/f* stepchild.
aló *interj* (*LAm Telec*) hullo?
alobado‡ *adj* dim*, thick*.
alocado 1 *adj* crazy, mad. **2** *nm*, **alocada** *nf* madcap.
alocar* [1g] (*LAm*) **1** *vt* to drive crazy (with pleasure); **me alocan las pizzas** I love pizzas, I'm mad on pizzas*. **2 alocarse** *vr* to go crazy.
alocución *nf* allocution; speech, address.
áloe *nm* (*Bot*) aloe; (*Farm*) aloes.
alojado, -a *nm/f* (*LAm*) guest, lodger.
alojamiento *nm* lodging(s); housing; accommodation; (*Mil: acto*) billeting, (*casa*) billet, quarters; (*And*) small hotel, boarding house; **buscarse ~** to look for lodgings.
alojar [1a] **1** *vt* to lodge, accommodate, put up, house; (*Mil*) to billet, quarter.
2 alojarse *vr* to lodge, be lodged; to stay; (*Mil*) to be billeted, be quartered; **~ en** to lodge at, put up at; **la bala se alojó en el pulmón** the bullet lodged in the lung.
alón 1 *adj* (*LAm*) large-winged; *sombrero* broad-brimmed. **2** *nm* wing (of chicken *etc*).
alondra 1 *nf* (*Orn*) lark, skylark. **2** *nm* (*) = **albañil**.
alongar [1l] **1** *vt* = **alargar**. **2 alongarse** *vr* to move away.
alopecia *nf* alopecia.
alpaca *nf* alpaca.
alpargata *nf* rope-soled sandal, canvas sandal, espadrille; **turismo de ~** travelling on the cheap*, tourism on a shoestring.
alpargatería *nf* sandal shop.
alpargatero* *adj* low-class; down-market; done (*etc*) on the cheap*.
alpargatilla *nmf* crafty person.
alpende *nm* tool shed, lean-to.
Alpes *nmpl* Alps.
alpestre *adj* Alpine; (*fig*) mountainous, rough, wild.
alpinismo *nm* mountaineering, climbing.
alpinista *nmf* mountaineer, climber.
alpinístico *adj* mountaineering (*atr*), climbing (*atr*).
alpino *adj* Alpine.
alpiste *nm* (**a**) (*semillas*) birdseed, canary seed. (**b**) (*LAm*: dinero*) brass*; (**: alcohol*) drink, booze*.
alquería *nf* farmhouse, farmstead.
alquiladizo 1 *adj* for rent, for hire, that can be rented (*o* hired); (*pey*) hireling. **2** *nm*, **alquiladiza** *nf* hireling.
alquilado, -a *nm/f* (*Carib*) tenant.
alquilador(a) *nm/f* renter, hirer; tenant, lessee.
alquilar [1a] **1** *vt* (**a**) (*sujeto: propietario*) *casa* to rent (out), let; *coche, autocar etc* to hire (out); *garaje, TV* to rent (out).
(**b**) (*sujeto: alquilador*) *casa* to rent; *coche, autocar etc* to hire; *garaje, TV* to rent; **'por ~'** 'to let', 'for rent' (*US*); **turba alquilada** rent-a-mob.
2 alquilarse *vr* (**a**) (*casa*) to be let (*en* at, for); **'se alquila'** (*anuncio*) 'to let', 'for rent' (*US*); **aquí no se alquila casa alguna** there is no house to let here.
(**b**) (*taxi etc*) to be on hire, be out for hire.
(**c**) (*persona*) to hire o.s. out; (*Carib*) to go into service.
alquiler *nm* (**a**) (*acto*) letting, renting; hire, hiring; **de ~** for hire, on hire; **'~ sin chófer'** (*Esp*) 'drive yourself' 'self-drive'; **~ de úteros** surrogate motherhood.
(**b**) (*precio*) rent, rental; hire charge; **control de ~es** rent control; **exento de ~es** rent-free; **pagar el ~** to pay the rent; **subir el ~ a uno** to raise sb's rent.
alquimia *nf* alchemy.
alquimista *nm* alchemist.
alquitara *nf* still.
alquitarar [1a] *vt* to distil.
alquitrán *nm* tar; **~ de hulla, ~ mineral** coal tar.
alquitranado 1 *adj* tarred, tarry. **2** *nm* (*materia*) tarmac; (*tela*) tarpaulin.
alquitranar [1a] *vt* to tar.
alrededor 1 *adv* (**a**) around, about; **todo ~** all around. (**b**) **~ mío** (*etc*) (*Cono Sur*) around me (*etc*).
2 ~ de *prep* (**a**) (*gen*) around, about; **todo ~ de la iglesia** all around the church; **mirar ~ de sí, mirar ~ suyo** to look about one.
(**b**) (*fig*) about, in the region of; **~ de 200** about 200.
3 *nm*: **mirar a su ~** to look about one; **~es** surroundings,

neighbourhood; (*de ciudad*) outskirts, environs; (*de escena, lugar*) setting; **en los ~es de Londres** on the outskirts of London; in the area round London.

Alsacia *nf* Alsace.

Alsacia-Lorena *nf* Alsace-Lorraine.

alsaciano 1 *adj* Alsatian. **2** *nm*, **alsaciana** *nf* Alsatian.

alt. *abr de* **altura** height, ht.

alta *nf* (*Med*) (certificate of) discharge from hospital; (*Téc etc*) installation, fitting up, making ready; **el ~ de la línea telefónica** putting in the phone, the connecting up of the phone; **dar a uno de ~** to discharge sb from hospital, (*Mil*) to pass sb (as) fit; **darse de ~** to join, become a member; (*Med*) to return to duty; **dar una propiedad de ~** (*Jur*) to register a property (for taxation purposes); **estar de ~** to be back on duty; to be up and about again; to be back to normal; to have got over it.

altamente *adv* highly, extremely.

altanería *nf* (**a**) (*altivez*) haughtiness, disdain, arrogance. (**b**) (*Caza*) hawking, falconry. (**c**) (*Met*) upper air.

altanero *adj* (**a**) (*altivo*) haughty, disdainful, arrogant. (**b**) *ave* high-flying.

altar *nm* altar; **~ mayor** high altar; **llevar a una al ~** to lead sb to the altar; **poner a una en un ~** to put sb on a pedestal; **quedarse para adornar ~es** to be left on the shelf; **subir a los ~es** to be beatified (*o* canonized).

altaricón* *adj* big-built, large.

altavoz *nm* (*Rad*) loudspeaker; (*Elec*) amplifier.

altea *nf* mallow.

altear [1a] *vt* (*Cono Sur Hist*) to order to stop (*o* halt).

al-tec* *abr de* **alta tecnología** high technology, high-tech*.

alterabilidad *nf* changeability.

alterable *adj* changeable.

alteración *nf* (**a**) (*cambio*) alteration, change.

(**b**) (*aturdimiento*) upset, disturbance; (*Med*) irregularity of the pulse; **~ digestiva** digestive upset; **~ del orden público** breach of the peace.

(**c**) (*agitación*) strong feeling, agitation.

(**d**) (*disputa*) quarrel, dispute.

alterado *adj* agitated, upset, disturbed; angry; (*Med*) upset, disordered.

alterar [1a] **1** *vt* (**a**) (*cambiar*) to alter, change; to change for the worse; *verdad* to distort, twist.

(**b**) (*perturbar*) to upset, disturb; to cause a commotion in; *paz, silencio etc* to disturb.

(**c**) (*agitar*) to stir up, excite, agitate; to irritate, anger.

2 alterarse *vr* (**a**) (*cambiar*) to alter, change.

(**b**) (*comida*) to go bad, go off; (*leche etc*) to go sour.

(**c**) (*voz*) to falter.

(**d**) (*persona*: *agitarse*) to get upset, become agitated, become disturbed; (*enfadarse*) to get angry; (*ofenderse*) to be put out; (*distraerse*) to be put off one's stroke; **siguió sin ~** he went on unabashed, he went on unmoved; **no ~** to keep a stiff upper lip, show no emotion, not turn a hair; **¡no te alteres!** don't upset yourself!, keep calm!; **~ por algo** to get angry (*o* excited *etc*) about sth.

altercación *nf*, **altercado** *nm* argument, altercation.

altercar [1g] *vi* to argue, quarrel, wrangle.

álter ego *nm* alter ego.

alteridad *nf* otherness.

alternación *nf* alternation.

alternadamente *adv* alternately.

alternado *adj* alternate.

alternador *nm* (*Elec*) alternator.

alternancia *nf* alternation; **~ de cultivos** crop rotation; **~ en el poder** taking turns in office.

alternante *adj* alternating.

alternar [1a] **1** *vt* to alternate; to vary.

2 *vi* (**a**) (*gen*) to alternate (*con* with); (*Téc*) to alternate, reciprocate; (*hacer turno*) to take turns, change about; (*cambiar*) to vary; **alternar a los mandos** to take turns at the controls; **~ en el poder** to take turns in office.

(**b**) (*participar*) to mix, take part in the social round, socialize; (*) to go on a pub crawl*, go boozing*; to sleep around*; **~ con un grupo** to mix with a group, go around with a group; **~ con la gente bien** to hobnob with top people; to move in elevated circles; **tiene pocas ganas de ~** he doesn't want to mix, he is disinclined to be sociable; **~ de igual a igual** to be on an equal footing.

alternativa *nf* (**a**) (*opción*) alternative, option, choice; **no tener ~** to have no alternative; **tomar una ~** to make a choice.

(**b**) (*sucesión*) alternation; (*trabajo*) shift work, work done in relays; **~ de cosechas** crop rotation.

(**c**) (*Taur*) *ceremony by which a novice becomes a fully-qualified bullfighter*; **tomar la ~** to become a fully-qualified bullfighter.

(**d**) **~s** ups and downs, vicissitudes, fluctuations; **las ~s de la política** the ups and downs of politics.

alternativamente *adv* alternately.

alternativo *adj* alternating (*t Elec*); alternative, alternate; *cultura, prensa etc* alternative; **fuentes alternativas de energía** alternative energy sources.

alterne 1 *nm* mixing, socializing; (*euf*) sexual contact(s); sleeping around*; **club de ~** singles club; **estas chicas no son de ~** these girls don't sleep around*, these girls are not easy lays‡ (*V t* **chica**).

2 *nf* hostess.

alterno *adj* (*Bot, Mat etc*) alternate; **tiempo con nubes alternas** partly cloudy weather.

altero *nm* (*Méx*), **alterón** *nm* (*And*) heap, pile.

alteza *nf* (**a**) (*altura*) height.

(**b**) (*fig*) sublimity; **~ de miras** high-mindedness.

(**c**) (*título*) **A~** Highness; **Su A~ Real** His (*o* Her) Royal Highness; **sí, A~** yes, your Highness.

altibajos *nmpl* ups and downs (*t fig*).

altilocuencia *nf* grandiloquence.

altilocuente *adj*, **altílocuo** *adj* grandiloquent.

altillo *nm* (**a**) (*Geog*) small hill, hillock. (**b**) (*LAm*: *desván*) attic. (**c**) (*piso*) mezzanine.

altímetro *nm* altimeter.

altimontano *adj* high mountain (*atr*), upland (*atr*).

altinal *nm* (*Méx*) pillar, column.

altiplanicie *nf* high plateau.

altiplano *nm* high plateau; **A~** (*Geog Bol*) Altiplano.

altísimo *adj* very high; **el A~** the Almighty, the Most High.

altisonancia *nf* high-flown style (*etc*); high-sounding nature.

altisonante *adj*, **altísono** *adj* high-flown, high-sounding.

altitud *nf* height; (*Aer, Geog*) altitude, elevation; **a una ~ de** at a height of.

altivamente *adv* haughtily, arrogantly.

altivarse [1a] *vr* to give o.s. airs.

altivez *nf*, **altiveza** *nf* haughtiness, arrogance.

altivo *adj* haughty, arrogant.

alto¹ 1 *adj* (**a**) (*gen*) high; *persona* tall; *edificio, árbol, roca* high, tall; *mando, oficial, precio, relieve, traición etc* high; *ejecutivo* senior; *cámara* (*Pol*), *clase, piso* upper; **el muro tiene 5 metros de ~** the wall is 5 metres high; **él tiene 1,80 m de ~** he is 1.80 m tall; **lanzar algo de lo ~** to throw sth down (from above); **desde lo ~ del árbol** from the top of the tree; **estar en (lo) ~** to be up high, be high up, be up on top; **estar en lo ~ de la escalera** to be at the top of the stairs; **pasó por lo ~** it passed overhead; **por todo lo ~** (*fig*) in style, in the proper way.

(**b**) (*Geog*) upper; **el A~ Rin** the Upper Rhine.

(**c**) **estar ~** (*río*) to be in spate, to be swollen; (*mar*) to be rough.

(**d**) (*fig*) sublime, lofty, elevated; high; **un ~ sentido del deber** a high sense of duty; **~s pensamientos** lofty thoughts, noble thoughts.

(**e**) *hora* late, advanced; **en las altas horas** in the small hours, late at night.

(**f**) *sonido* high, loud; **en alta voz** loud(ly), in a loud voice.

(**g**) (*Mús*) *nota* sharp; *instrumento, voz* alto.

(**h**) (*Hist, Ling*) high; **~ alemán antiguo** Old High German; **la alta Edad Media** the high Middle Ages.

2 *adv* (**a**) (*gen*) high, high up; on high; **lanzar algo ~** to throw sth high.

(**b**) *sonar* loud, loudly; **hablar ~** to speak loudly, (*fig*) to speak out (frankly); **gritar ~** to shout out loud; **poner la radio más ~** to turn the radio up; **¡más ~, por favor!** louder, please!

3 *nm* (**a**) (*Geog*) hill, height; **A~s del Golán** Golan Heights.

(**b**) (*Arquit*) upper floor, upstairs flat.

(**c**) (*LAm*: *montón*) pile, stack.

(**d**) (*Mús*) alto.

(**e**) **~s y bajos** ups and downs.

(**f**) **pasar por ~** to overlook, forget, omit; to pass over, ignore.

alto² 1 *nm* halt (*t Mil*); stop; pause; **dar el ~ a uno** to order sb to halt, challenge sb; **hacer ~** to halt (*t Mil*), stop, pause; (*Méx*: *parada*) stop.

2 *interj* halt! (*t Mil*), stop!; **¡~ ahí!** halt!; **~ el fuego, ~ al fuego** ceasefire; **¡~ el fuego!** cease fire!; **echar el ~ a uno** to order sb to stop.

altocúmulo *nm* altocumulus.

altoparlante *nm* (*esp LAm*) loudspeaker.
altorrelieve *nm* high relief.
altostrato *nm* altostratus.
altozanero *nm* (*And*) porter.
altozano *nm* (**a**) (*otero*) small hill, hillock; (*de ciudad*) upper part. (**b**) (*And, Carib*) cathedral forecourt, church forecourt.
altramuz *nm* lupin.
altruísmo *nm* altruism, unselfishness.
altruísta 1 *adj* altruistic, unselfish. **2** *nmf* altruist, unselfish person.
altura *nf* (**a**) (*gen*) height; altitude; (*de agua*) depth; **~ de caída** (*de cascada etc*) fall; **~ de crucero** cruising height; **~ del suelo** ground clearance, height off the ground; **~ de la vegetación** timber line; **a una ~ de 600 m** at a height of 600 m; **sentí un dolor a la ~ de los riñones** I felt a pain in the kidney region, I felt a pain in the area of my kidneys; **tiene 5 m de ~** it is 5 m high; **él tiene 1,80 m de ~** he is 1.80 m tall; (*Aer*) **ganar ~, tomar ~** to climb, gain height.
(**b**) (*fig*: *mérito*) **poemas de ~** good poems, worthy poems; **estar a la ~ de una tarea** to be up to a task, be equal to a task; **estar a la ~ de las circunstancias** to rise to the occasion; **estar a la ~ del tiempo** to be abreast of the times; **poner a uno a la ~ del betún** (*Esp**) to make sb feel like dirt.
(**c**) (*Geog*: *latitud*) latitude; **a la ~ de** on the same latitude as; **a la ~ de Cádiz** off Cadiz; opposite Cadiz; (*Aut etc*) **a la ~ del km 8** at the 8th km (point); **a la ~ del museo** up (the street) near the museum; **la calle sale a la ~ de Correos** the street is just after the post office; **¿a qué ~ quiere?** how far along (the street)?
(**d**) (*Náut*) **barco de ~** seagoing vessel; **pesca de ~** deep-sea fishing; **remolcador de ~** deep-sea tug, ocean-going tug.
(**e**) (*Mús*) pitch.
(**f**) (*Dep*: *salto*) high jump.
(**g**) (*fig*) sublimity, loftiness; **ha sido un partido de gran ~** it has been a match of real class, it has been a really excellent game.
(**h**) **~s** (*Geog*) heights; (*Rel*) heaven; **a estas ~s** (*fig*) at this point, at this stage; at this (late) hour; (*fig*) **por estas ~s** around here; at this juncture; **estar en las ~s** to be on high.
(**i**) **una casa de 5 ~s** a 5-storey house.
alubia *nf* French bean, kidney bean.
alucinación *nf* hallucination, delusion.
alucinado *adj* (**a**) (*lit*) deluded, suffering hallucinations. (**b**) (*: *asombrado*) amazed, dumbfounded.
alucinador *adj* hallucinatory, deceptive.
alucinante 1 *adj* (**a**) (*Med*) hallucinatory. (**b**) (*Esp*: *fig*) attractive, beguiling; mysterious; (*) great*, super*. (**c**) (*Esp*: *absurdo*) absurd; fantastic; **¡es ~!*** it's mind-boggling!*
2 *nm* (*Méx*) hallucinogenic drug.
alucinar [1a] **1** *vt* (*a*) (*engañar*) to hallucinate, delude, deceive. (**b**) (*fascinar*) to fascinate, beguile; (*Esp**) to grab‡, be a hit with. **2 alucinarse** *vr* to hallucinate, be deluded; to delude o.s.
alucine* *nm* delusion; **de ~** super*, great*.
alucinógeno 1 *adj* hallucinogenic. **2** *nm* hallucinogen, hallucinogenic drug.
alucinosis *nf* hallucinosis.
alud *nm* avalanche.
aludido *adj* aforesaid, above-mentioned, this ... that has been mentioned; **darse por ~** to take it personally, take the hint; **no darse por ~** to pretend not to hear; **no te des por ~** don't take it personally.
aludir [3a] *vi*: **~ a** to allude to, mention.
aluego *adv etc* (*LAm*) = **luego.**
alujado *adj* (*CAm, Méx*) bright, shining.
alujar [1a] *vt* (*CAm, Méx*) to polish, shine.
alumbrado 1 *adj* (*) boozed*.
2 *nm* lighting, lighting system, illumination; **~ eléctrico** electric lighting; **~ de emergencia** emergency lighting; **~ fluorescente** fluorescent lighting; **~ de gas** gas lighting; **~ público** street lighting.
3 *nm*, **alumbrada** *nf* illuminist; **los A~s** the Illuminati.
alumbramiento *nm* (**a**) (*Elec etc*) lighting, illumination. (**b**) (*Med*) childbirth; **tener un feliz ~** to have a safe delivery, come safely through childbirth.
alumbrar [1a] **1** *vt* (**a**) (*Elec etc*) to light (up), illuminate, shed light on.
(**b**) *persona* to light the way for, show a light to.
(**c**) *ciego* to give sight to, restore the sight of.
(**d**) (*fig*) *persona* to enlighten.
(**e**) (*fig*) *agua* to find, strike, cause to flow.
2 *vi* (**a**) (*lit*) to give light, shed light; **esto alumbra bien** this gives a good light.
(**b**) (*Med*) to give birth, have a baby.
3 alumbrarse* *vr* to get tight*.
alumbre *nm* alum.
aluminio *nm* aluminium, aluminum (*US*); **~ doméstico, papel de ~** cooking foil, kitchen foil.
alumnado *nm* (**a**) (*personas*) (*Escol*) pupils, roll; (*Univ*) student body. (**b**) (*LAm*: *colegio*) college, school.
alumno, -a *nm/f* (**a**) (*de escuela*) pupil, (*Univ*) student; **~ externo** day pupil; **~ interno** boarder; **antiguo ~** (*de escuela*) old boy, former pupil, (*Univ*) old student, former student, alumnus (*US*).
(**b**) (*Jur*) ward, foster child.
alunarse [1a] *vr* (*CAm*) to get saddlesore (*horse*).
alunizaje *nm* (**a**) landing on the moon, moon-landing. (**b**) (*) smash-and-grab raid.
alunizar [1f] *vi* to land on the moon.
alusión *nf* allusion, mention, reference; **hacer ~ a** to allude to, mention, refer to; to hint at.
alusivo *adj* allusive.
aluvial *adj* alluvial.
aluvión *nm* (**a**) (*Geol*) alluvium; **tierras de ~** alluvial soil(s).
(**b**) (*fig*) flood; **~ de improperios** shower of insults; torrent of abuse; **llegan en incontenible ~** they come in an unstoppable flood.
aluvionado *nm* alluviation.
álveo *nm* riverbed, streambed.
alveolar *adj* alveolar.
alveolo *nm*, **alvéolo** *nm* (*Anat*) alveolus; socket; (*de panal*) cell; (*fig*) network, honeycomb.
alverja *nf* (**a**) (*arveja*) vetch. (**b**) (*LAm*: *guisante*) pea.
alverjilla *nf* sweet pea.
alza *nf* (**a**) (*de precio, temperatura*) rise; **al ~, en ~** *tendencia* upward; *precio* rising; **jugar al ~** (*Fin*) to speculate on a rising market; **revisar los precios al ~** to put prices up; **cotizarse en ~, estar en ~** (*Fin*) to rise, advance; **estar en ~** (*LAm*) to have a good name (*o* reputation); **hacer algo por la pura ~** to do sth just for the sake of it.
(**b**) (*Mil*) sight; **~s** sights; **~s fijas** fixed sights; **~s graduables** adjustable sights.
alzacristales *nm invar*: **~ eléctrico** electric windows.
alzacuello(s) *nm* clerical collar, dog-collar.
alzada *nf* (**a**) (*de caballo*) height; (*Arquit*) elevation, side view. (**b**) (*Jur*) appeal.
alzado 1 *adj* (**a**) (*elevado*) raised, elevated.
(**b**) *precio* fixed; *persona* fraudulently bankrupt; **por un tanto ~** for a lump sum.
(**c**) (*LAm*: *soberbio*) vain, stuck-up*; (*LAm*) *animal* untamed, wild; (*Pol*) mutinous; (*And*) drunk.
(**d**) **estar ~** (*Cono Sur*) to be on heat.
2 *nm* (**a**) (*Tip*) gathering. (**b**) (*Arquit*) elevation.
3 *nm*, **alzada** *nf*: **~ en armas** armed insurgent.
alzamiento *nm* (**a**) (*acto*) lifting, raising; (*de precio*) rise, increase; (*en subasta*) higher bid, raise.
(**b**) **~ de bienes** fraudulent bankruptcy.
(**c**) (*Pol*) rising, revolt.
alzaprima *nf* (**a**) (*palanca*) lever, crowbar; (*cuña*) wedge. (**b**) (*Mús*) bridge. (**c**) (*Cono Sur*: *carro pesado*) heavy trolley, flat truck.
alzaprimar [1a] *vt* to lever up, raise with a lever; (*fig*) to arouse, stir up.
alzar [1f] **1** *vt* (**a**) (*gen*) to lift (up), raise (up); to hoist (up); (*Ecl*) *hostia* to elevate; *edificio* to raise; *cosecha* to get in, gather in; (*Tip*) to gather; *mantel* to remove, put away; *prohibición, restricción* to lift; (*LAm*: *recoger*) to pick up.
(**b**) (*quitar*) to remove; (*robar*) to steal; (*ocultar*) to hide.
2 alzarse *vr* (**a**) (*persona*) to rise, get up, stand up; (*precio, temperatura etc*) to rise.
(**b**) (*Pol*) to rise, revolt.
(**c**) (*Fin*) to go fraudulently bankrupt.
(**d**) **~ algo,** (*LAm*) **~ con algo** to steal (*o* make off with*) sth; **~ con el premio** to carry off the prize.
(**e**) (*And*: *emborracharse*) to get drunk.
(**f**) (*LAm*: *animal*) to run away.
alzaválvulas *nm invar* (*Mec*) tappet.
alzo *nm* (*CAm*) theft.
allá 1 *adv* (**a**) (*lugar*) there, over there; (*dirección*) to that

place; ~ **arriba** up there; ~ **en Sevilla** down (there) in Seville; ~ **mismo** right there; **más** ~ further away, further over; further on; **más ~ de** beyond; **más ~ de los límites** outside the limits; **cualquier número más ~ de 7** any number higher than 7; **no sabe contar más ~ de 10** she can't count above (*o* beyond) 10; **muy** ~ much further on, miles away; **no tan** ~ not so far; **por** ~ thereabouts; **vamos** ~ let's go there; **¡~ voy!** I'm coming!; **¿quién va ~?** (*Mil*) who goes there?; ~ **lo veremos** (*fig*) we'll see when we get there, we'll sort that one out later.

(**b**) ~ **tú** that's up to you, that's your concern, that's for you to decide (*etc*); **¡~ él!** (*más tajante*) that's his funeral!*; ~ **cada uno** that's the concern of each one of us, that's for the individual to decide.

(**c**) (*tiempo*) ~ **en 1600** (way) back in 1600, as long ago as 1600; ~ **en mi niñez** in my childhood days; ~ **por el año 60** round about 1960 (*etc*).

2 *nm*: **el más ~** the great beyond.

allacito *adv* (*LAm*) = **allá**.

allanamiento *nm* (**a**) (*nivelación*) levelling, flattening; smoothing; razing.

(**b**) (*de obstáculos*) removal.

(**c**) (*pacificación*) pacification.

(**d**) (*Jur etc*) submission (*a* to).

(**e**) ~ **de morada** (*crimen*) housebreaking, breaking and entering, burglary; (*Jur*) search; **el juez dispuso el ~ del domicilio** the judge granted the police a search-warrant for the house.

(**f**) (*esp LAm*: *de policía*) raid, search.

allanar [1a] **1** *vt* (**a**) (*nivelar*) to level (out), flatten, make even; (*alisar*) to smooth (down); (*arrasar*) to raze, level to the ground.

(**b**) *dificultad etc* to remove, smooth away, iron out.

(**c**) *país* to pacify, subdue.

(**d**) *casa* to force an entry into, break into, burgle; (*esp LAm*: *policía*) to raid, search.

2 allanarse *vr* (**a**) (*nivelarse*) to level out, level off.

(**b**) (*edificio*) to fall down, tumble down.

(**c**) (*fig*) to submit, give way; ~ **a** to accept, conform to; **se allana a todo** he agrees to everything.

allegadizo *adj* gathered at random, put together unselectively.

allegado 1 *adj* (**a**) (*afín*) near, close; allied; **según fuentes allegadas al ministro** according to sources close to the minister.

(**b**) *persona* closely related, near; **los más ~s y queridos** one's nearest and dearest; **las personas allegadas a ...** those attached to ..., those closest to ...

2 *nm*, **allegada** *nf* (**a**) (*pariente*) relation, relative.

(**b**) (*secuaz*) follower.

allegar [1h] **1** *vt* (**a**) (*reunir*) to gather (together), collect.

(**b**) (*acercar*): ~ **una cosa a otra** to put something near something else.

(**c**) (*añadir*) to add.

2 allegarse *vr* (**a**) to arrive, approach; ~ **a uno** to go up to sb.

(**b**) (*fig*) ~ **a una opinión** to adopt a view, agree with an opinion; ~ **a una secta** to become attached to a sect.

allende (*liter*) **1** *adv* on the other side.

2 (*t* ~ **de**) *prep* beyond; ~ **los mares** overseas, beyond the seas; ~ **los Pirineos** beyond the Pyrenees, on the other side of the Pyrenees, over the Pyrenees; ~ **de eso** besides that.

allí *adv* there; ~ **arriba** up there; ~ **dentro** in there; **de** ~ from there; **de ~ a poco** shortly afterwards; **de ~ que ...** that is why ..., hence ...; **de ~ a decir que es un timo** but that's a long way from calling it a swindle; **de ~ para acá** back and forth; **hasta** ~ as far as that, up to that point; **por** ~ over there, round there; (down) that way; **una chica de por ~*** a wench, a scrubber‡; **está tirado por ~*** he's hanging around somewhere; **¡vete por ~!*** shove off!*

allicito *adv* (*LAm*) = **allí**.

A.M. *nf abr de* **amplitud modulada** amplitude modulation, AM.

a.m. (*LAm*) *abr de* **ante meridiem** ante meridiem, a.m.

ama *nf* (**a**) (*en casa*) lady of the house, mistress; ~ **de casa** housewife.

(**b**) (*dueña*) owner, proprietress; (*de pensión*) landlady; (*de soltero*) housekeeper; (*: *de burdel*) madame; ~ **de cura** priest's housekeeper; ~ **de gobierno,** ~ **de llaves** housekeeper, (*de colegio etc*) matron, bursar.

(**c**) (*de niño*) foster mother; ~ **de brazos** (*LAm*), ~ **de cría,** ~ **de leche** wet-nurse; ~ **seca** nurse, nursemaid.

amabilidad *nf* kindness; niceness; **tuvo la ~ de** + *infin* he was kind enough to + *infin*, he was good enough to + *infin*; **tenga la ~ de** + *infin* please be so kind as to + *infin*.

amable *adj* kind; nice; lovable; **¡muy ~!** thanks very much, that's very kind (of you); **es Vd muy** ~ you are very kind; **ser ~ con uno** to be kind to sb, be good to sb; **si es tan** ~ if you would be so kind; **¡qué ~ ha sido Vd en traerlo!** how kind of you to bring it!

amablemente *adv* kindly; **muy ~ me ayudó** he very kindly helped me.

amachambrarse [1a] *vr* (*Cono Sur*) *etc* = **amachinarse.**

amacharse [1a] *vr* (*LAm*) (*persona*) to dig one's heels in, refuse to be moved; (*caballo*) to refuse.

amachinarse [1a] *vr* (*LAm*) to live together, cohabit; ~ **con uno** to become sb's lover; **estar** (*o* **vivir**) **amachinado con** to live with, be the lover of.

amacho *adj* (*CAm, Cono Sur*) (*destacado*) outstanding; (*fuerte*) strong, vigorous.

amaderado *adj vino* woody.

amado 1 *adj* dear, beloved. **2** *nm*, **amada** *nf* lover, sweetheart.

amador 1 *adj* loving, fond. **2** *nm*, **amadora** *nf* lover.

amadrigar [1h] **1** *vt* to take in, give shelter to. **2 amadrigarse** *vr* (*animal*) to go into its hole, burrow; (*persona, fig*) to go into retirement, hide o.s. away; to withdraw into one's shell.

amaestrado *adj* (**a**) *animal* trained; (*en circo etc*) performing. (**b**) *plan* well-contrived, artful.

amaestrador(a) *nm/f* trainer.

amaestramiento *nm* training; drill.

amaestrar [1a] *vt persona* to train, coach; *animal* to train; *caballo* to break in.

amagar [1h] **1** *vt* (*amenazar*) to threaten, portend; (*dar indicios de*) to show signs of.

2 *vi* to threaten, be impending; to be in the offing; (*Med*) to show the first signs; (*Esgrima, Mil*) to feint; ~ **y no dar** to make empty threats; ~ **a** + *infin* to threaten to + *infin*, show signs of + *ger*.

3 amagarse *vr* (**a**) (*Cono Sur*: *tomar una postura amenazante*) to adopt a threatening posture, shape up.

(**b**) (*: *esconderse*) to hide.

amago *nm* (**a**) (*amenaza*) threat; threatening posture, threatening gesture.

(**b**) (*señal*) sign, symptom; (*indicio*) hint; ~ **tormentoso** outbreak of bad weather; **un ~ de mapa** a rough map; **con un ~ de sonrisa** with the suggestion of a smile, with a faint smile.

(**c**) (*Esgrima, Mil*) feint.

amainar [1a] **1** *vt vela* to take in, shorten; *furia etc* to calm.

2 *vi y* **amainarse** *vr* (*ira, viento etc*) to abate, moderate; (*esfuerzo etc*) to lessen, slacken; to relax.

amaine *nm* (*V v*) (**a**) shortening. (**b**) abatement, moderation; lessening, slackening; relaxation.

amaitinar [1a] *vt* to spy on.

amaizado *adj* (*And*) rich.

amalaya *interj* (*LAm*) = **ojalá.**

amalayar [1a] *vt* (*And, CAm, Méx*) to covet, long for; ~ + *infin* to long to + *infin*.

Amalia *nf* Amelia.

amalgama *nf* amalgam.

amalgamación *nf* amalgamation.

amalgamar [1a] **1** *vt* to amalgamate; to combine, mix, blend. **2 amalgamarse** *vr* to amalgamate.

amamantar [1a] *vt* (**a**) (*dar el pecho a*) to suckle, nurse.

(**b**) (*Carib*: *mimar*) to spoil.

amancebamiento *nm* illicit union, cohabitation.

amancebarse [1a] *vr* (*t* **estar amancebados, vivir amancebados**) to live together, cohabit.

amancillar [1a] *vt* to stain; (*fig*) to stain; tarnish, dishonour.

amanecer 1 *nm* dawn, daybreak; **al ~** at dawn.

2 [2d] *vi* (**a**) (*gen*) to dawn, begin to get light.

(**b**) (*aparecer*) to appear; begin to show.

(**c**) (*persona*) **amaneció en el bosque** he found himself at dawn in the wood, he woke up in the wood; **amaneció acatarrado** he woke up with a cold; **amaneció rey** he woke up to find himself king; **amaneceremos en Vigo** we'll be in Vigo by morning; **el día amaneció lloviendo** at daybreak it was raining.

(**d**) **amaneció bailando** (*LAm*) he danced all night.

(**e**) **¿cómo amaneció?** (*LAm*) how are you?, good morning!

amanecida *nf* dawn, daybreak.

amanerado *adj* mannered, affected; (*LAm*) extra polite, excessively polite.

amaneramiento *nm* affectation; (*Liter etc*) mannerism (of style).
amanerarse [1a] *vr* to become affected, fall into affectation.
amanezca *nf* (*Carib, Méx*) (*alba*) dawn; (*desayuno*) breakfast.
amanezquera *nf* (*Carib, Méx*) early morning, daybreak.
amanita *nf* amanita.
amanojar [1a] *vt* to gather by the handful, gather in bunches.
amansa *nf* (*Cono Sur*) taming; breaking-in.
amansado *adj* tame.
amansador *nm* tamer; (*Méx*) horse breaker (*o* trainer).
amansadora *nf* (*Cono Sur*) **(a)** (*sala*) waiting-room (*in public building*). **(b)** (*: *espera*) long wait (*at government office*).
amansamiento *nm* **(a)** (*acto*) taming; breaking-in; soothing. **(b)** (*cualidad*) tameness.
amansar [1a] **1** *vt animal* to tame; *caballo* to break in; *persona* to tame, subdue; *pasión etc* to soothe, appease.
2 amansarse *vr* (*persona*) to calm down; (*pasión etc*) to moderate, abate.
amanse *nm* (*And, Méx*) taming; breaking-in.
amante 1 *adj* loving, fond; **nación ~ de la paz** peace-loving nation.
2 *nm* lover; **~s** lovers.
3 *nf* lover, mistress.
amanuense *nm/f* amanuensis; scribe, copyist; secretary.
amañado *adj* **(a)** (*diestro*) skilful, clever. **(b)** (*falso*) fake, faked; (*falsificado*) fixed, rigged.
amañador 1 *adj* (*And, Carib*) having a pleasant climate. **2** *nm*, **amañadora** *nf* (*) fixer*.
amañamiento *nm* fiddling, trickery; (*Pol*) rigging, gerrymandering.
amañanar [1a] *vi* (*persona*) to wake up; (*día*) to dawn.
amañar [1a] **1** *vt* **(a)** (*gen*) to do skilfully, perform cleverly.
(b) (*pey*) to alter; to play about with, tamper with; to fiddle*; *foto etc* to fake; *partido, jurado* to fix; *cuentas* to cook*; *excusa* to cook up; *elección* to rig, rig the results of.
2 amañarse *vr* **(a)** (*ser diestro*) to be skilful, be expert; (*adquirir destreza*) to become expert, get the hang of it; (*Cono Sur*) to meet trouble head on; **~ a** + *infin* to settle down to + *infin*; **~ con** to get along with.
(b) (*Carib*: *mentir*) to tell lies, lie.
(c) (*And, Carib*: *acostumbrarse a un lugar*) to become (*o* grow) accustomed to a place (*o* person *etc*); **ya se amaña en Quito** he's settling down (*o* finding his feet) in Quito.
amaño *nm* **(a)** (*gen*) skill, expertness, cleverness; **tener ~ para** to have an apitude for.
(b) ~s (*Téc*) tools; (*fig*) tricks, cunning ways; guile; (*Cono Sur*: *mañas*) underhand means.
amapola *nf* poppy; **ponerse como una ~** to blush like a beetroot.
amar [1a] *vt* to love.
amaraje *nm* (*Aer*) landing (on the sea); splashdown, touchdown; **~ forzoso** ditching.
amarar [1a] *vi* (*Aer*) to land (on the sea); (*cápsula*) to touch down, come down, splash down; (*para evitar accidente*) to ditch.
amarchantarse [1a] *vr*: **~ en** (*LAm*) to become a (regular) customer of.
amargado *adj* bitter, embittered.
amargamente *adv* bitterly.
amargar [1h] **1** *vt* to make bitter, sour; (*fig*) *persona, relaciones* to embitter; *ocasión* to spoil, upset.
2 *vi* to be bitter, taste bitter.
3 amargarse *vr* **(a)** to get bitter.
(b) (*persona*) to get bitter, become embittered.
amargo 1 *adj* **(a)** *sabor* bitter; sharp, tart.
(b) (*fig*) bitter, embittered.
(c) (*Cono Sur*: *cobarde*) cowardly; (*Carib*: *poco servicial*) unhelpful, offhand.
2 *nm* **(a)** (*gen*) bitterness; sharpness, tartness.
(b) ~s *nmpl* bitters.
(c) (*LAm Culin*) maté tea.
3 *nm*, **amarga** *nf* (*Cono Sur**) (*de mal genio*) grouch*; (*vago*) shirker, skiver‡.
amargón *nm* dandelion.
amargor *nm*, **amargura** *nf* **(a)** (*sabor*) bitterness; sharpness, tartness. **(b)** (*fig*) bitterness; grief, distress.
amargoso *adj* (*LAm*) = **amargo**.
amaricado‡, amariconado‡ 1 *adj* effeminate, queer‡. **2** *nm* nancy-boy‡, queer‡.
Amarilis *nf* Amaryllis.
amarillear [1a] *vi* **(a)** (*volverse amarillo*) to go yellow, turn yellow.
(b) (*tirar a amarillo*) to be yellowish; (*mostrarse amarillo*) to show yellow, look yellow.
(c) (*palidecer*) to pale.
amarillecer [2d] *vi* to yellow, turn yellow.
amarillejo *adj* yellowish.
amarillento *adj* yellowish; *tez* pale, sallow.
amarillez *nf* yellow, yellowness; paleness, sallowness.
amarillismo *nm* **(a)** (*Prensa*) sensationalist journalism, sensationalism. **(b)** (*Pol**) trade unionism which is in league with the bosses.
amarillo 1 *adj* **(a)** yellow; *semáforo* amber. **(b)** *prensa* sensational, gutter (*atr*). **(c)** (*Pol**) **sindicato ~** trade union which is in league with the bosses. **2** *nm* **(a)** yellow; **~ canario** canary yellow; **~ mostaza** mustard yellow; **~ paja** straw colour. **(b)** (*Carib*) ripe banana.
amarilloso *adj* (*Cono Sur*) yellowish.
amariposado* *adj* effeminate.
amarra *nf* **(a)** (*Náut*) cable, hawser; mooring line, painter; (*LAm*: *cuerda*) rope, line, cord; (*Méx*: *rienda*) rein, lead.
(b) (*Náut*) **~s** moorings; **cortar las ~s, romper las ~s** to break loose, cut adrift; **echar las ~s** to moor.
(c) (*fig*) **soltar las ~s** to go away, vanish.
(d) (*fig*: *protección*) **~s** protection; **tener buenas ~s** to have good connections, have influence.
amarradera *nf* (*And*: *para barcos*) mooring; (*Méx*: *cuerda*) rope, line, tether.
amarradero *nm* (*poste*) post, bollard; (*amarras*) moorings; (*sitio*) berth, mooring.
amarrado *adj* (*LAm*) mean, stingy.
amarradura *nf* mooring.
amarraje *nm* mooring charges.
amarrar [1a] **1** *vt* **(a)** (*gen*) to fasten, hitch, tie up; (*Náut*) *barco* to moor, tie up; *cuerda* to lash, belay; (*LAm*) to tie; *cartas* to stack; **está de ~** he's raving mad. **(b)** (*) to swot*, mug up*.
2 *vi* (*) to swot*, cram.
3 amarrarse *vr* (*): **amarrársela** (*And, CAm*) to get tight*.
amarre *nm* (*V v* **1**) fastening, tying; mooring, berth; lashing.
amarrete (*LAm*) **1** *adj* mean, stingy. **2** *nm*, **amarreta** *nf* miser, skinflint, tightwad* (*US*).
amarro *nm* (*And*) (*cuerda*) knotted string, knotted rope; (*nudos*) mass of knots; (*paquete*) bundle, packet; **~ de cigarrillos** packet of cigarettes.
amarrocar [1g] *vi* (*Cono Sur*) to scrimp and save.
amarronado *adj* chestnut, brownish.
amarroso *adj* (*CAm*) *fruta* acrid, sharp.
amartelado *adj* lovesick; **andar ~ con, estar ~ con** to be in love with, be infatuated with; **andan muy ~s** they're deeply in love.
amartelamiento *nm* lovesickness, infatuation.
amartelar [1a] **1** *vt* **(a)** *persona* to make jealous, torment with jealousy. **(b)** *corazón* to win, conquer. **2 amartelarse** *vr* to fall in love (*de* with).
amartillar [1a] *vt* to hammer; *escopeta* to cock.
amasadera *nf* kneading trough.
amasado *adj* (*Carib*) **(a)** *sustancia* doughy. **(b)** *persona* plump.
amasador(a) 1 *nm/f* kneader, baker. **2 amasadora** *nf* kneading machine.
amasadura *nf* **(a)** (*acto*) kneading. **(b)** (*hornada*) batch.
amasamiento *nm* kneading; (*Med*) massage.
amasandería *nf* (*And, Cono Sur*) bakery, baker's shop.
amasandero, -a *nm/f* (*And, Cono Sur*) bakery worker.
amasar [1a] *vt* **(a)** *masa* to knead; *harina, argamasa* to mix, prepare; *patatas* to mash; (*Med*) to massage.
(b) (*fig**) to cook up, concoct, fix.
(c) (*) *dinero etc* to pile up, accumulate.
amasiato *nm* **(a)** (*LAm*) common-law marriage, cohabitation; **su ~ duró mucho tiempo** they lived together for a long time. **(b)** (*Méx*) casual sexual encounter, pick-up.
amasigado *adj* (*And*) dark, swarthy.
amasijar‡ [1a] *vt* (*Cono Sur*) to do in‡.
amasijo *nm* **(a)** (*acto*) kneading; mixing; mashing; (*fig*) cooking-up, concoction.
(b) (*material*) mixture, mash, batch (of dough *etc*); (*fig*) hotchpotch, medley, jumble.
(c) (*tarea*) task.
(d) (*plan*) plot, scheme.
(e) (*Carib*: *pan*) wheat bread; **~ de palos** beating,

thrashing.
amasio *nm*, **amasia** *nf* (*CAm, Méx*) lover, (*mujer*) mistress.
amate *nm* (*LAm Bot*) fig-tree.
amateur *adj, nmf* amateur.
amateurismo *nm* amateurism.
amatista *nf* amethyst.
amatorio *adj* amatory; **poesía amatoria** love poetry.
amauta *nm* (*And Hist*) Inca elder.
amayorado *adj* (*And*) *niño* precocious, forward.
amazacotado *adj* (*pesado*) heavy, clumsy, awkward; (*informe*) shapeless, formless; (*Liter etc*) ponderous, stodgy; ~ **de detalles** crammed with details.
amazona *nf* (**a**) (*Hist*) Amazon; (*jineta*) horsewoman, rider, equestrienne; (*pey*) mannish woman.
(**b**) (*vestido*) riding-habit.
Amazonas *nm*: **el río** ~ the Amazon.
Amazonia *nf* Amazonia.
amazónico *adj* Amazon (*atr*).
ambages *nmpl* circumlocutions, roundabout style; **sin** ~ in plain language, without beating about the bush.
ambagioso *adj* involved, circuitous, roundabout.
ámbar *nm* amber; ~ **gris** ambergris.
ambareado *adj* (*And* ††) *pelo* chestnut, auburn.
ambarino *adj* amber.
Amberes *nm* Antwerp.
ambición *nf* ambition; (*pey*) ambitiousness, self-seeking, egotism.
ambicionar [1a] *vt* to aspire to, seek, strive after; (*pey*) to be out for, covet; ~ **ser algo** to have an ambition to be somebody, be out to become somebody; **no ambiciona nada** he seeks nothing for himself.
ambiciosamente *adv* ambitiously.
ambicioso 1 *adj* (**a**) (*gen*) ambitious.
(**b**) (*pey*) pretentious, grandiose; *persona* over-ambitious; overweening, proud, self-seeking.
2 *nm*, **ambiciosa** *nf* ambitious person; (*en el trabajo*) careerist; ~ **de figurar** social climber.
ambidextro *adj* ambidextrous.
ambientación *nf* (**a**) (*lit*) orientation. (**b**) (*Cine, Liter etc*) setting; (*Cine: efectos*) sound-effects.
ambientado *adj* (*LAm*) (*climatizado*) air-conditioned; **estar** ~ (*persona*) to be settled in, be at home.
ambientador *nm* air-freshener.
ambientador(a) *nm/f* (*Cine, TV*) dresser.
ambiental *adj* (**a**) (*lit*) environmental, relating to one's environment; **música** ~ piped music. (**b**) (*fig*) general, pervasive.
ambientalismo *nm* environmentalism.
ambientalista *adj, nmf* environmentalist.
ambientalmente *adv* environmentally; in terms of the surroundings (*o* setting).
ambientar [1a] **1** *vt* (**a**) (*dar ambiente a*) to give an atmosphere to, add colour to; **ambienta el escenario con bailes folklóricos** he enlivens the scene with folk dances.
(**b**) (*Liter etc*) to set; **la novela está ambientada en una sociedad de ...** the novel is set in a society of ...
(**c**) (*dirigir*) to orientate, direct.
2 ambientarse *vr* to orientate o.s., get one's bearings, get a sense of direction; (*LAm*) to find one's way around; to acclimatize o.s.; **procuraré ambientarme** I'll try to get myself sorted out, I'll try to get the feel of the thing.
ambiente 1 *adj* ambient, surrounding.
2 *nm* (**a**) (*gen*) atmosphere; ~ **artificial** air-conditioning.
(**b**) (*fig*) atmosphere; (*entorno*) milieu, environment, surroundings; (*clima*) climate; (*Bio*) environment; ~ **laboral** working environment; **en ~s universitarios** in university circles, in the university world; **no me gusta el** ~ I don't like the atmosphere; **se crió en un ~ de violencia** he grew up in an atmosphere of violence; **voy a cambiar de** ~ I'm going to move to new surroundings; **había escaso ~ callejero** there was not much going on in the streets.
(**c**) (*And: cuarto*) room.
ambigú *nm* (*Esp*) buffet supper, cold supper.
ambiguamente *adv* ambiguously.
ambigüedad *nf* ambiguity.
ambiguo *adj* (*gen*) ambiguous; (*incierto*) doubtful, uncertain; (*equívoco*) noncommittal, equivocal; *género* common; (*bisexual*) bisexual.
ambilado *adj* (*Carib*): **estar** (*o* **quedar**) ~ (*boquiabierto*) to be left open-mouthed; (*embobado*) to be distracted.
ámbito *nm* (**a**) (*campo*) compass, ambit, field; (*límite*) boundary, limit; **dentro del ~ de** within the limits of; **en el ~ nacional** on a nation-wide basis, on a nation-wide scale; **en todo el ~ nacional** over the whole nation, throughout the country; **en el ~ nacional y extranjero** at home and abroad.
(**b**) (*fig*) scope, sphere, range; area; ~ **de acción** field of activity; **buscar mayor** ~ to look for greater scope.
ambivalencia *nf* ambivalence.
ambivalente *adj* ambivalent.
ambladura *nf*: **a paso de** ~ at an amble.
amblar [1a] *vi* to amble, walk in a leisurely manner.
ambo *nm* (*Cono Sur*) two-piece suit.
ambos *adj y pron* both; ~ **a dos** both (of them), both together.
ambrosía *nf* ambrosia.
Ambrosio *nm* Ambrose.
ambucia *nf* (*Cono Sur*) (*codicia*) greed, greediness; (*hambre*) voracious hunger.
ambuciento *adj* (*Cono Sur*) (*codicioso*) greedy; (*hambriento*) voracious.
ambulancia *nf* ambulance; (*Mil*) field hospital; ~ **de correos** (*Esp Ferro*) post-office coach.
ambulanciero *nm* ambulance man.
ambulante *adj* walking; roving; *músico etc* itinerant; *actor* strolling; *vendedor, exposición etc* travelling.
ambulatoriamente *adv*: **tratar un paciente** ~ to treat sb as an out-patient.
ambulatorio *nm* (*sección*) out-patients department; (*hospital*) state health-service hospital.
ameba *nf* amoeba.
amedrentador *adj* frightening, menacing.
amedrentar [1a] **1** *vt* to scare, frighten; to intimidate. **2 amedrentarse** *vr* to get scared.
amejoramiento *nm* (*LAm*) = **mejoramiento.**
amejorar [1a] *vt* (*LAm*) = **mejorar.**
amelcocharse [1a] *vr* (*Carib*) to fall in love; (*Méx*) *azúcar* to harden, set; (*ser coqueta*) to be coy, be prim.
amelonado *adj* (**a**) (*lit*) melon-shaped. (**b**) **estar ~*** to be lovesick.
amén 1 *nm* amen; **decir ~ a todo** to agree to everything; **en un decir** ~ in a trice.
2 *interj* amen!
3 ~ de *prep* (**a**) (*excepto por*) except for, aside from. (**b**) (*adémas de*) in addition to, besides; not to mention ...
4 ~ de que *conj* in spite of the fact that ...
-amen *V* **Aspects of Word Formation in Spanish 2.**
amenaza *nf* threat, menace; ~ **amarilla** yellow peril; ~ **de bomba** bomb scare; ~ **de muerte** death threat.
amenazador *adj*, **amenazante** *adj* threatening, menacing.
amenazar [1f] **1** *vt* to threaten, menace; ~ **violencia** to threaten violence; ~ **a uno de muerte** to threaten sb with death; **una especie amenazada de extinción** a species threatened with extinction; **me amenazó con despedirme** he threatened to fire me.
2 *vi* to threaten; to loom, impend; ~ + *infin*, ~ **con** + *infin* to threaten to + *infin*.
amenguar [1i] *vt* (**a**) (*lit*) to lessen, diminish. (**b**) (*fig*) (*despreciar*) to belittle; (*deshonrar*) to dishonour.
amenidad *nf* pleasantness, agreeableness; grace, elegance.
amenización *nf* improvement; enlivening; brightening up; entertainment.
amenizar [1f] *vt* to make pleasant, make more agreeable; to add charm to; *conversación* to enliven, make more entertaining; *estilo* to brighten up; *reunión* to provide entertainment for, entertain.
ameno *adj* (*agradable*) pleasant, agreeable, nice; *estilo* graceful, elegant; *libro* pleasant, readable; **es un sitio** ~ it's a nice spot; **prefiero una lectura más amena** I prefer lighter reading; **la vida aquí es más amena** life is pleasanter here.
amento *nm* catkin.
América *nf* America (*depending on context, may mean the whole continent, the United States, or Latin America*); ~ **Central** Central America; ~ **Latina** Latin America; ~ **del Norte** North America; ~ **del Sur** South America; **hacerse la** ~ (*Cono Sur*) to make a fortune.
americana *nf* coat, jacket; ~ **de sport** sports jacket.
americanada *nf* typically American thing (to do).
americanismo *nm* (*Ling*) americanism; (*LAm Pol*) Yankee imperialism; (*Carib, Méx*) liking for North American ways (*etc*).
americanista *nmf* americanist, specialist in indigenous American culture; (*liter*) specialist in American literature; (*CAm, Méx*) person with a liking for North

American ways (*etc*).

americanización *nf* americanization.

americanizar [1f] **1** *vt* to americanize; to Latin-americanize. **2 americanizarse** *vr* to become americanized; to become Latin-americanized; (*CAm, Méx*) to adopt North American ways.

americano 1 *adj* American (*depending on context, may refer to the whole continent, the United States, or Latin America*). **2** *nm*, **americana** *nf* American.

americio *nm* (*Quím*) americium.

amerindio, -a *adj, nm/f* Amerindian, American Indian.

ameritado *adj* (*LAm*) worthy.

ameritar [1a] **1** *vt* (*LAm*) to deserve. **2** *vi* to win credit, do well.

amerizaje *nm* landing (on the sea); splashdown, touchdown.

amerizar [1f] *vi* (*Aer*) to land (on the sea); (*cápsula*) to touch down, come down, splash down.

amestizado *adj* like a half-breed.

ametrallador *nm* machine gunner.

ametralladora *nf* machine gun.

ametrallar [1a] *vt* to machine-gun.

amianto *nm* asbestos.

amiba *nf*, **amibo** *nm* amoeba.

amiga *nf* (*gen*) friend; (*de chico*) girlfriend; (*amante*) lover; (*querida*) lover, mistress.

amigable *adj* friendly, amicable; (*fig*) harmonious.

amigablemente *adv* amicably.

amigacho* *nm* (*pey*) mate, buddy (*esp US*), bachelor friend; **ha salido con los ~s** he's out with the boys; **esos ~s tuyos** those cronies of yours.

amigarse [1h] *vr* to get friendly; (*amantes*) to set up house together.

amigazo* *nm* (*Cono Sur*) pal*, buddy (*esp US*), close friend.

amígdala *nf* tonsil.

amigdalitis *nf* tonsillitis.

amigdalotomía *nf* tonsillectomy.

amigo 1 *adj* friendly; (*fig*) **ser ~ de** to be fond of, be given to; **A es muy ~ de B** A is a close friend of B; **son muy ~s** they are close friends.

2 *nm* (*gen*) friend; (*de chica*) boyfriend; (*amante*) lover; **pero ¡~!** but my dear sir!, (*afectuoso*) look here, old chap!; **~ de lo ajeno** thief; **~ del alma, ~ de confianza, ~ íntimo** intimate friend, close friend; **~ de clase** schoolfriend; **~ por correspondencia** penfriend; **~ en la prosperidad** fair-weather friend; **hacerse ~s** to become friends; **hacerse ~ de** to make friends with, become a friend of; **soy ~ de hablar en franqueza** I am all for talking openly; **y todos tan ~s** and that's that, so that was that.

amigote* *nm* old pal*, old buddy (*esp US*); (*pey*) sidekick*, crony.

amiguero *adj* (*LAm*) friendly.

amiguete* *nm* buddy, mate; influential friend, friend in the right place.

amiguismo *nm* old-boy network, nepotism, jobs for the boys.

amiguita *nf* girlfriend; lover.

amiguito *nm* boyfriend; lover.

amiláceo *adj* starchy.

amilanar [1a] **1** *vt* to scare, intimidate. **2 amilanarse** *vr* to get scared, be intimidated.

aminoácido *nm* amino acid.

aminorar [1a] *vt* to lessen, diminish; *gastos etc* to cut down, reduce; *velocidad* to reduce, slacken.

amistad *nf* (**a**) (*cariño*) friendship; friendly relationship, friendly connection; **hacer** (*o* **trabar**) **~ con** to strike up a friendship with, become friends with; **llevar ~ con** to be on friendly terms with; **hacer las ~es** to make it up; **romper las ~es** to fall out, break off a friendship.

(**b**) **~es** friends, acquaintances; **invitar a las ~es** to invite one's friends.

amistar [1a] **1** *vt* (*hacer amigos*) to bring together, make friends of; (*reconciliar*) to bring about a reconciliation between, heal a breach between; (*Méx*: *hacerse amigo de*) to befriend.

2 amistarse *vr* to become friends, establish a friendship; to make it up; **~ con** to make friends with.

amistosamente *adv* amicably; in a friendly way (*o* tone *etc*).

amistoso 1 *adj* friendly, amicable; (*Dep*) friendly; (*Inform*) user-friendly. **2** *nm* (*Dep*) friendly (game).

amnesia *nf* amnesia; loss of memory; **~ temporal** blackout.

amnistía *nf* amnesty; **A~ Internacional** Amnesty International.

amnistiar [1c] *vt* to amnesty, grant an amnesty to.

amo *nm* (**a**) (*de familia etc*) master; head of the family; **~ de casa** householder; **¿está el ~?** is the master in? (**b**) (*de propiedad*) owner; proprietor. (**c**) (*en el trabajo*) boss, employer; overseer; **ser el ~** to be the boss; **ser el ~ en un juego** to be the best at a game.

amoblado 1 *adj* furnished. **2** *nm* (*CAm*) furniture, furnishings.

amoblar [1l] *vt* to furnish.

amodorramiento *nm* sleepiness, drowsiness.

amodorrarse [1a] *vr* to get sleepy, get drowsy; to fall into a stupor; to go to sleep.

amohinar [1a] **1** *vt* to vex, annoy. **2 amohinarse** *vr* to get annoyed; to sulk.

amohosado *adj* (*Cono Sur*) rusty.

amojonar [1a] *vt* to mark out, mark the boundary of.

amojosado *adj* (*Cono Sur*) rusty.

amoladera *nf* whetstone, grindstone; (*LAm**: *tipo pesado*) nuisance, pain*.

amolado *adj* (**a**) (*Cono Sur*: *fastidiado*) bothered, irritated. (**b**) (*And, Méx*) (*ofendido*) offended; (*molesto*) irritating, annoying. (**c**) (*And*: *dañado*) damaged, ruined.

amolador 1 *adj* boring, tedious. **2** *nm* knife-grinder.

amoladura *nf* grinding, sharpening.

amolar [1l *o* 1a] **1** *vt* (**a**) (*Téc*) to grind, sharpen. (**b**) (*) (*fastidiar*) to upset; to annoy, irritate; (*perseguir*) to harass, pester. (**c**) (*estropear*) to damage, ruin. (**d**) (*Méx***: *arruinar*) to screw up**, fuck up**; **¡lo amolaste!** you screwed it up!**, you fucked it up!**

2 amolarse *vr* (**a**) (**) = **joderse.** (**b**) (*Cono Sur, Méx*: *enfadarse*) to get cross, take offence. (**c**) (*enflaquecer*) to get thinner.

amoldar [1a] **1** *vt* (*formar*) to mould (*t fig*; *a, según* on); to fashion; (*ajustar*) to adapt, adjust (*a* to). **2 amoldarse** *vr* to adapt o.s., adjust o.s. (*a* to).

amonal *nm* ammonal.

amonarse* [1a] *vr* to get tight*.

amondongado *adj* fat, flabby.

amonedación *nf* coining, minting.

amonedar [1a] *vt* to coin, mint.

amonestación *nf* (**a**) (*advertencia*) warning; (*consejo*) piece of advice; (*Dep*) warning (with yellow card *etc*); (*Jur*) warning, caution. (**b**) (*Ecl*) marriage banns; **correr las amonestaciones** to publish the banns.

amonestador *adj* warning, cautionary.

amonestar [1a] *vt* (**a**) (*advertir*) to warn; (*avisar*) to advise, remind; (*reprender*) to reprove, admonish; (*Dep*) to warn (with yellow card *etc*); (*Jur*) to warn, caution. (**b**) (*Ecl*) to publish the banns of.

amoniaco, amoníaco 1 *adj* ammoniac(al). **2** *nm* ammonia; **~ líquido** liquid ammonia.

amononar [1a] *vt* (*Cono Sur*) to improve the appearance of, smarten up; (*pey*) to prettify.

amontillado *nm* amontillado (*pale dry sherry*).

amontonadamente *adv* in heaps; in confusion.

amontonado *adj* heaped (up), piled up; **viven ~s** they live on top of each other, they live in very crowded conditions.

amontonamiento *nm* heaping, piling up; banking, drifting; hoarding; accumulation; overcrowding; crowding; (*Aut*) traffic jam.

amontonar [1a] **1** *vt* (**a**) (*apilar*) to heap (up), pile (up); *nieve, nubes* etc to bank (up); *datos etc* to gather, collect, accumulate; *víveres etc* to hoard, store away; **viene amontonando fichas** he's been collecting data in large quantities; **~ alabanzas sobre uno** to heap praises on sb.

(**b**) (*And*: *insultar*) to insult.

2 amontonarse *vr* (**a**) (*apilarse*) to pile up, get piled up; (*hojas, nieve*) to drift, bank up; (*nubes*) to gather, pile up; to accumulate, collect; (*gente*) to crowd together, huddle together; (*acudir*) to come thronging; (*: *2 personas*) to shack up*; **viven amontonados*** they're shacked up together*; **la gente se amontonó en la salida** people crowded into the exit, people jammed the exit; **se amontonaron los coches** the cars got jammed.

(**b**) (*: *enfadarse*) to fly off the handle*, go up in smoke*.

(**c**) (*And*: *terreno*) to revert to scrub.

amor *nm* (**a**) (*gen*) love (*a* for, *de* of); **~ cortés** courtly love; **~ fracasado** disappointment in love, unhappy love affair; **~ interesado** cupboard love; **~ libre** free love; **~ maternal** motherly love; **~ platónico** platonic love; **~ propio** amour propre, self-respect, pride; **una relación de**

~-odio a love-hate relationship; **es cuestión de ~ propio** it's a matter of pride; **picar a uno en el ~ propio** to wound sb's pride; **~ a primera vista** love at first sight; **de** (*o* **con**) **mil ~es** with great pleasure; **¡con mil ~es!, ¡de mil ~es!** I'd love to!, I should be only too glad!; **por el ~ de** for the love of; for the sake of; **por (el) ~ de Dios** for God's sake; **por el ~ del arte** (*hum*) just for the fun of it; **por ~ al arte** (*Cono Sur*) for nothing, for love; **casarse por ~** to marry for love; **lo hizo por ~** he did it for love; **matrimonio sin ~** loveless marriage; **hacer el ~** to make love; **hacer el ~ a** to court; to make love to; **hacerse el ~** to make love; **~ con ~ se paga** one good turn deserves another, (*iró*) an eye for an eye; **tener mal de ~es** to be lovesick.

(**b**) (*persona*) love, lover; **mi ~, ~ mío** my love; **primer ~** first love; **buscar un nuevo ~** to look for a new love; **tiene un ~ en la ciudad** he's carrying on an affair in town.

(**c**) **ir al ~ del agua** to go with the current; **estar al ~ de la lumbre** to be close to the fire, be by the fireside.

(**d**) **~es** love affair, romance; **los mil ~es de don Juan** Don Juan's numberless affairs; **requebrar a una de ~es** to court sb.

amoral *adj* amoral.

amoralidad *nf* amorality.

amoratado *adj* purple, purplish; livid; (*de frío*) blue (with cold); (*LAm*: *con cardenales*) bruised, black and blue; **ojo ~** black eye.

amoratarse [1a] *vr* (*LAm*) to turn (*o* go) purple; (*por golpes*) to get bruised, go black and blue.

amorcillo *nm* (**a**) (*amorío*) flirtation, light-hearted affair.

(**b**) (*Cupido*) Cupid.

amordazar [1f] *vt persona* to gag; *perro etc* to muzzle; (*fig*) to gag, silence.

amorfo *adj* amorphous, formless, shapeless.

amorío *nm* (*t* **~s**) love affair, romance.

amorochado *adj* (*LAm*) = **morocho 1** (**a**).

amorosamente *adv* lovingly, affectionately; amorously; caressingly.

amoroso *adj* (**a**) (*gen*) loving, affectionate, tender; *mirada etc* amorous; *carta etc* love (*atr*), of love; **poesía amorosa** love-poetry; **en tono ~** in an affectionate tone; in a caressing tone; **empezar a sentirse ~** to begin to feel amorous.

(**b**) (*fig*) *tierra* workable; *metal* malleable; *tiempo* mild.

(**c**) (*Cono Sur*) sweet, pretty, cute.

amorrar [1a] *vi* to hang one's head; (*fig*) to be sullen, sulk; (*Náut*) to pitch, dip the bows under.

amortajar [1a] *vt muerto* to lay out; (*fig*) to shroud.

amortecer [2d] **1** *vt ruido* to deaden, muffle; *fuego* to damp down; *luz* to dim; (*Mús*) to tone down; *pasión* to curb, control.

2 *vi* (*ruido*) to become muffled, die away; (*Med*) to faint, swoon.

amortecido *adj*: **caer ~** to fall in a swoon, faint away.

amortecimiento *nm* (*V v* **1**) deadening, muffling; dimming; toning down; controlling; (*Med*) fainting.

amortiguación *nf* = **amortiguamiento.**

amortiguador 1 *adj* deadening, muffling; softening.

2 *nm* (*Téc*) damper, muffler; (*Mec*) shock absorber, cushion; (*Ferro*) buffer; (*Aut*) shock absorber; (*Elec*) damper; **~ de luz** dimmer; **~ de ruido** muffler, silencer.

amortiguamiento *nm* (*V v* **1**) deadening, muffling; cushioning; absorption; softening, toning down; damping; dimming.

amortiguar [1i] **1** *vt ruido* to deaden, muffle; *golpe* to cushion; *choque* to absorb; *efecto* to cushion, mitigate, diminish, reduce the force of; *fuego* to damp down; *color* to soften, tone down; (*Elec*) to damp; *luz* to dim.

2 amortiguarse *vr* (*Cono Sur*) (**a**) (*Bot*) to wither.

(**b**) (*fig*) to get depressed; to become subdued.

amortizable *adj* (*Fin*) redeemable, amortizable.

amortización *nf* (*Jur*) amortization; (*Fin*) redemption; paying-off, repayment; (*de inversión*) depreciation; (*de puesto*) suppression, abolition.

amortizar [1f] *vt* (*Jur*) to amortize; (*Fin*) *bonos etc* to redeem; *préstamo, hipoteca* to pay off, repay; to refund; *puesto* to suppress, abolish; **~ algo por desvalorización** to write sth off through depreciation.

amos‡ *interj* = **¡vamos!**; *V* **ir.**

amoscarse* [1g] *vr* (**a**) (*Esp*: *enojarse*) to get cross, get peeved*. (**b**) (*Carib, Méx*) (*aturdirse*) to get confused; (*avergonzarse*) to get embarrassed.

amostazar* [1f] **1** *vt* to make cross, peeve*. **2 amostazarse** *vr* (**a**) to get cross, get peeved*. (**b**) (*LAm*) to be embarrassed, get embarrassed.

amotinado 1 *adj* riotous, violent; (*Mil, Náut*) mutinous. **2** *nm*, **amotinada** *nf* rioter; (*Pol*) rebel, (*Mil, Náut*) mutineer.

amotinador *adj, nm* = **amotinado.**

amotinamiento *nm* (*civil*) riot; (*Pol*) rising, insurrection; (*Mil, Náut*) mutiny.

amotinar [1a] **1** *vt* to stir up, incite to riot (*o* mutiny *etc*). **2 amotinarse** *vr* to riot; to rise up, revolt, rebel; to mutiny.

amover [2h] *vt* to dismiss, remove (from office).

amovible *adj pieza* removable, detachable; *empleado* temporary.

amparador 1 *adj* helping, protecting, protective. **2** *nm*, **amparadora** *nf* protector.

amparar [1a] **1** *vt* (**a**) (*proteger*) to protect (*de* from), shelter, help; **~ a los pobres** to help the poor; **le ampara el ministro** the minister protects him. (**b**) (*Jur*) *criminal* to harbour; (*abarcar*) to cover, embrace; to apply to. (**c**) (*Carib*: *pedir prestado*) to borrow.

2 ampararse *vr* (**a**) (*buscar protección*) to seek protection, seek help; **~ a** to have recourse to; **~ con, ~ de** to seek the protection of.

(**b**) (*protegerse*) to protect o.s., defend o.s.; (*refugiarse*) to shelter.

amparo *nm* (*ayuda*) help; (*favor*) favour, protection; (*abrigo*) refuge, shelter; (*defensa*) defence; (*Jur, esp*) right of habeas corpus; **al ~ de la ley** under the protection of the law; **recurso de ~** (*Cono Sur Jur*) habeas corpus.

ampáyar *nm*, **ampáyer** *nm* (*LAm*) referee, umpire.

ampe *interj* (*And*) please!

amperímetro *nm* ammeter.

amperio *nm* ampère, amp.

ampliable *adj* extendable, which can be extended (*o* increased; *a* to); (*Inform*) expandable (*a* to).

ampliación *nf* enlargement, extension; expansion; amplification; (*Fot*) enlargement; **~ de capital(es)** increase of capital.

ampliado *nm* (*LAm Pol*) general meeting; mass meeting.

ampliadora *nf* (*Fot*) enlarger.

ampliamente *adv* amply; extensively; **satisfará ~ la demanda** it will more than meet the demand.

ampliar [1c] *vt* (*gen*) to enlarge, extend; (*Fot*) to enlarge; *comercio etc* to expand; *capital* to increase; *sonido* to amplify; *poderes* to extend, widen; *declaración* to amplify, elaborate.

amplificación *nf* amplification; (*LAm Fot*) enlargement.

amplificador *nm* (*Rad*) amplifier.

amplificar [1g] *vt* to amplify; (*LAm Fot*) to enlarge.

amplio *adj* (**a**) (*espacioso*) spacious, wide; (*extenso*) extensive; roomy; *ropa* big; *falda etc* full.

(**b**) (*fig*) broad, extensive, ample; *informe etc* detailed, full; *poderes* ample, wide; *sentido* broad.

amplitud *nf* spaciousness, extent; roominess; fullness; amplitude; **~ de banda** band width; **~ de criterio** broad-mindedness.

ampo *nm* (*blancura*) dazzling whiteness; (*copo de nieve*) snowflake; **como el ~ de la nieve** as white as the driven snow.

ampolla *nf* (*burbuja*) bubble; (*Med*) blister; (*frasco*) flask, decanter, (*Med*) ampoule; **la medida levantó ~s en la compañía** (*fig*) the measure raised a lot of bad feeling within the company.

ampollarse [1a] *vr* to blister, form blisters.

ampolleta *nf* (*botellita*) phial, small bottle; (*de arena*) hourglass, sandglass; (*de termómetro etc, t Elec*) bulb; **encendérsele a uno la ~** (*Cono Sur**) to have a brainwave.

ampón *adj* bulky; *persona* stout, tubby.

ampulosamente *adv* bombastically, pompously.

ampulosidad *nf* bombast, pomposity.

ampuloso *adj* bombastic, pompous.

amputación *nf* amputation.

amputado, -a *nm/f* amputee.

amputar [1a] *vt* to amputate, cut off.

amuchachado *adj* boyish.

amuchar* [1a] *vt* (*And, Cono Sur*) to increase, multiply.

amueblado 1 *adj* furnished (*con, de* with). **2** *nm* (*Cono Sur euf*) hotel, hotel room (*used for sexual encounters and paid for by the hour*).

amueblamiento *nm* furnishing.

amueblar [1a] *vt* to furnish (*de* with).

amuermado* *adj* boring.

amuermante* *adj* boring; dull, unexciting; mundane, banal.

amuermar* [1a] **1** *vt* to bore.

2 amuermarse *vr* (**a**) (*tener sueño*) to feel sleepy (after a meal); (*fig*) (*aburrirse*) to get bored; (*deprimirse*) to get depressed.
(**b**) (*pudrirse*) to vegetate, rot; (*ponerse pesado*) to get very dull.
amuinar [1a] (*Méx*) **1** *vt* to annoy, irritate. **2 amuinarse** *vr* to get cross.
amujerado *adj* effeminate.
amularse [1a] *vr* (*Méx*) (*persona*) to get stubborn, dig one's heels in; (*Com*) to become unsaleable, become a glut on the market.
amulatado *adj* mulatto-like.
amuleto *nm* amulet, charm.
amunicionar [1a] *vt* to supply with ammunition.
amuñecado *adj* doll-like.
amura *nf* (*Náut*) (**a**) (*proa*) bow. (**b**) (*cabo*) tack.
amurallado *adj ciudad* walled.
amurallar [1a] *vt* to wall, wall in, fortify.
amurar [1a] *vi* (*Náut*) to tack.
amurrarse [1a] *vr* (*LAm*) to get depressed, become sad.
amurriarse [1b] *vr* (*Esp*) to get sad (*o* depressed).
amurruñarse [1a] *vr* (*Carib*) (*abrazarse*) to nestle together, cuddle up; (*hacerse un ovillo*) to curl up.
amusgar [1h] **1** *vt orejas* to lay back, throw back; *ojos* to screw up, narrow. **2 amusgarse** *vr* (*CAm*) to feel ashamed.
Ana *nf* Ann(e).
anabólico *adj* anabolic.
anabolizante *nm* anabolic steroid.
anacarado *adj* pearly, mother-of-pearl (*atr*).
anacardo *nm* (*nuez*) cashew (nut); (*árbol*) cashew tree.
anaco *nm* (*And*) poncho, Indian blanket.
anacoluto *nm* anacoluthon.
anaconda *nf* anaconda.
anacoreta *nmf* anchorite.
Anacreonte *nm* Anacreon.
anacronía *nf* timelessness.
anacrónico *adj* anachronistic.
anacronismo *nm* (**a**) (*gen*) anachronism. (**b**) (*objeto*) out-of-date thing, piece of bric-a-brac.
ánade *nm* duck; ~ **friso** gadwall; ~ **rabudo** pintail; ~ **real** mallard; ~ **silbón** wigeon.
anadear [1a] *vi* to waddle.
anadeo *nm* waddle, waddling.
anadón *nm* duckling.
anaeróbico *adj*, **anaerobio** *adj* anaerobic.
anagrama *nm* anagram.
anal *adj* anal.
analcohólico *adj bebida* non-alcoholic, soft.
anales *nmpl* annals.
analfa* *adj, nmf* = **analfabeto**.
analfabetismo *nm* illiteracy.
analfabeto 1 *adj* illiterate. **2** *nm*, **analfabeta** *nf* illiterate (person).
analgesia *nf* analgesia.
analgésico 1 *adj* analgesic, pain-killing. **2** *nm* analgesic, pain-killer.
análisis *nm invar* analysis; (*explicativo*) breakdown; (*Ling*) analysis, parsing; (*Med*) test (*de* for); ~ **de costos** cost analysis; ~ **espectral** spectrum analysis; ~ **financiero** financial analysis; ~ **funcional** functional analysis; ~ **de mercados** market research; ~ **orgánico** organic analysis; ~ **de sangre** blood test; ~ **de sistemas** systems analysis; ~ **de viabilidad** feasibility study; ~ **de la voz** speech analysis.
analista *nmf* analyst; (*de historia regional*) chronicler, annalist; ~ **de inversiones** investment consultant; ~ **de sistemas** systems analyst.
analista-programador(a) *nm/f* computer analyst and programmer.
analítico *adj* analytic(al); **cuadro** ~ analytic table, table showing the breakdown by groups (*etc*).
analizable *adj* analysable; **fácilmente** ~ easy to analyse.
analizador *nm* analyst.
analizar [1f] *vt* to analyse; (*Ling*) to parse.
analogía *nf* analogy; similarity; **por** ~ **con** on the analogy of.
analógico *adj* analogical.
análogo 1 *adj* analogous, similar (*a* to). **2** *nm* analogue; **añadir frutas o** ~ add fruit or something of the kind, add fruit or something similar.
ananá(s) *nm*, **ananasa** *nf* (*And*) pineapple.
anapesto *nm* anapaest.
anaquel *nm* shelf.
anaquelería *nf* shelves, shelving.
anaranjado 1 *adj* orange(-coloured). **2** *nm* orange (colour).
anarca*, anarco* = **anarquista.**
anarcosindicalismo *nm* anarcho-syndicalism.
anarcosindicalista 1 *adj* anarcho-syndical. **2** *nmf* anarcho-syndicalist.
anarquía *nf* anarchy.
anárquico *adj* anarchic(al).
anarquismo *nm* anarchism.
anarquista 1 *adj* anarchist(ic). **2** *nmf* anarchist.
anarquizante *adj* anarchic.
anarquizar [1f] *vt* to produce anarchy in, cause utter disorder in; to sow the seeds of rebellion among.
anatema *nm* anathema.
anatematizante *adj*: **palabras** ~**s** words of condemnation.
anatematizar [1f] *vt* (*Ecl*) to anathematize; (*fig*) to curse, condemn.
anatomía *nf* anatomy.
anatómico *adj* anatomical; **asiento** ~ seat moulded to the body.
anatomizar [1f] *vt* to anatomize; (*Arte*) *huesos, músculos etc* to bring out, emphasize; (*fig*) to anatomize, dissect.
anca[1] *nf* haunch; rump, croup; ~**s*** bottom, bum‡; ~**s de rana** (*Culin*) frog's legs; **llevar a uno a las** ~**s, llevar a uno en** ~(**s**) (*LAm*) to let sb ride pillion (*o* behind one); **esto lleva el desastre en** ~(**s**) (*LAm*) this spells disaster; **no sufre** ~**s*** he can't take a joke.
anca[2] *nf* (*And*) toasted maize.
ancestral *adj* ancestral; (*fig*) ancient.
ancestro *nm* (*LAm*) (**a**) (*persona*) ancestor. (**b**) (*linaje*) ancestry.
anciana *nf* old woman, old lady, elderly lady.
ancianidad *nf* old age.
anciano 1 *adj* old, aged. **2** *nm* old man, elderly man; (*Ecl*) elder.
ancilar *adj* ancillary.
ancla *nf* anchor; ~ **de la esperanza** (*fig*) sheet anchor, last hope; **echar** ~**s** to cast anchor, drop anchor; **estar al** ~ to be (*o* lie *o* ride) at anchor; **levar** ~**s** to weigh anchor.
ancladero *nm* anchorage.
anclaje *nm* (*Naut*) anchorage; (*Aut*) catch, clamp (of a seatbelt).
anclar [1a] *vi* to anchor, drop anchor.
ancón *nm* (**a**) (*Náut*) cove. (**b**) (*And, Méx*: *rincón*) corner. (**c**) (*And*: *camino*) mountain pass.
áncora *nf* anchor; ~ **de salvación** (*fig*) sheet anchor, last hope.
anchamente *adv* widely.
ancheta *nf* (**a**) (*Com*: *lote*) small lot of goods; (*negocio*) small business; small-time affair.
(**b**) (*ganancia*) gain, profit; (*And, Méx*) (*ganga*) bargain; (*negocio*) profitable deal; (*oportunidad*) chance to make easy money; **¡vaya** (*o* **buena**) ~! some deal this turned out to be!
(**c**) (*And, Cono Sur*: *palabrería*) prattle, babble.
(**d**) (*Carib*) (*broma*) joke; (*estafa*) hoax.
ancho 1 *adj* (**a**) (*gen*) wide, broad; (*demasiado* ~) too wide; ~ **de 4 cm, 4 cm de** ~ 4 cm wide, 4 cm in width; ~ **de espaldas** broad-shouldered; **recorrer un país a lo** ~ **y a lo largo** to cross and recross a country; **por todo el** ~ **mundo** throughout the whole wide world.
(**b**) (*Cos*) big; loose, loose-fitting; *falda* full; **me viene algo** ~ it's on the big side for me; **le viene muy** ~ **el cargo** the job is too much for him, he's not up to the job.
(**c**) (*fig*) liberal, broad-minded; *vida* fast; ~ **de conciencia** not overscrupulous; ~ **de miras** broad-minded; **ponerse** ~ to be smug, get conceited; **quedarse tan** ~ to go on as if nothing had happened, remain completely unabashed.
(**d**) **estar a sus anchas** to be at one's ease, be comfortable; **aquí estoy a mis anchas** I feel at home here; **ponerse a sus anchas** to make o.s. comfortable, spread o.s.
2 *nm* width, breadth; (*Ferro*) gauge; ~ **de banda** band width; ~ **normal** standard gauge; ~ **de vía** (*Ferro*) gauge, (*Aut*) wheel track.
anchoa *nf* anchovy (*pickled, tinned*).
anchor *nm* = **anchura**.
anchote *adj persona* burly.
anchoveta *nf* (*And*) anchovy (*for fishmeal*).
anchura *nf* width, breadth; wideness; (*Cos*) bigness, looseness, fullness; (*fig*) freedom; ease, comfort; ~ **alar** wingspan; ~ **de conciencia** lack of scruple.
anchuroso *adj* wide, broad; spacious.
andadas *nfpl* (*Caza*) tracks; **volver a las** ~ to backslide, re-

vert to one's old ways.

andaderas *nfpl* baby-walker.

andadero *adj* passable, easy to traverse.

andado *adj* (*trillado*) worn, well-trodden; (*corriente*) common, ordinary; *ropa* old, worn.

andador 1 *adj* (**a**) (*rápido*) fast-walking; **es ~** he's a good walker.

(**b**) (*Cono Sur*) *caballo* well-paced, long-striding.

(**c**) (*viajero*) fond of travelling, fond of gadding about.

2 *nm*, **andadora** *nf* (*persona*) walker; gadabout.

3 *nm* (*aparato*) baby-walker; **~es** baby harness.

4 andadora *nf* (*Méx*) prostitute, streetwalker.

andadura *nf* (**a**) (*acto*) walking; (*paso*) pace, gait, walk; (*de caballo*) pace. (**b**) (*fig: camino*) path, course; (*progreso*) progress; (*avance*) advance; **comenzar nuevas ~s** to start again.

andalón *adj* (*Méx*) *caballo* well-paced, long-striding.

Andalucía *nf* Andalusia.

andalucismo *nm* (**a**) (*Ling*) andalusianism, word (*o* phrase *etc*) peculiar to Andalusia. (**b**) sense of the differentness of Andalusia; (*Pol*) doctrine of (*o* belief in) Andalusian autonomy.

andaluz, -uza 1 *adj, nm/f* Andalusian. **2** *nm* (*Ling*) Andalusian.

andaluzada* *nf* (*cuento*) tall story, piece of typical Andalusian exaggeration; (*acto*) the sort of thing one expects from an Andalusian.

andamiada *nf*, **andamiaje** *nm* scaffolding, staging.

andamio *nm* (*de edificio*) scaffold; (*tablado*) stage, stand; **~ óseo** skeleton, bone framework.

andana *nf* row, line; **llamarse ~** to go back on one's word; to wash one's hands of a matter.

andanada *nf* (**a**) (*Náut*) broadside; (*fuego artificial*) big rocket; (*fig*) reprimand, telling-off*; **~ verbal** verbal broadside; **por ~s** (*Cono Sur*) in (*o* to) excess; **soltar una ~** to say something unexpected, drop a bomb*; **soltar la ~ a uno** to give sb a telling-off*.

(**b**) (*tribuna*) covered grandstand.

(**c**) (*de ladrillos etc*) layer, row.

andante 1 *adj* walking; *caballero etc* errant. **2** *nm* (*Mús*) andante.

andanza *nf* fortune, fate; **~s** deeds, adventures.

andar [1p] **1** *vt* (**a**) *distancia* to go, cover, travel; *camino etc* to travel, go along, walk.

(**b**) (*CAm: llevar*) to wear; to carry, use, have; **yo no ando reloj** I don't wear a watch, I don't carry a watch.

2 *vi* (**a**) (*ir a pie*) to go, walk; (*moverse*) to move; (*viajar*) to go about, travel; (*caballo*) to walk, amble; **~ a caballo** to ride, go on horseback; **~ tras uno** to go after sb; to pursue sb; **~ tras una chica** to court a girl; **~ tras algo** to yearn for sth, have a keen desire for sth; **venimos andando** we walked, we came on foot.

(**b**) (*reloj*) to go; (*Mec*) to go, run, work; **el reloj anda bien** the clock keeps good time; **el reloj no anda** the clock won't go.

(**c**) (*estar*) to be; **anda por aquí** it's around here somewhere; **~ alegre** to be cheerful, feel cheerful; **hay que ~ con cuidado** one must go carefully; **anda enfermo** he's ill; **~ bien de salud** to be well, be in good health; **andamos mal de dinero** we're badly off for money; **¿cómo te anda?** how are you getting on?, how's it going?; **¿cómo anda esto?** how are things going?; **¿cómo andas de tabaco?** how are you off for cigarettes?

(**d**) **anda en los 50** he's about 50.

(**e**) **~ en** to tamper with, mess about with; **han andado en el armario** they've been rummaging in the cupboard; **no me andes en mis cosas** keep out of my things.

(**f**) **~ en** to be engaged in; **~ en pleitos** to be engaged in lawsuits, be tied up in lawsuits.

(**g**) (*tiempo*) to pass, elapse.

(**h**) **¡anda!** (*sorpresa*) get along with you!, well!, go on!; (*¡vamos!*) come on!; (*desaprobación*) get on with it!; **¡anda, anda!** don't be silly!; **¡andando!** and that's it!, now we can get on with it!; (*Méx etc*) **¡ándale (pues)!*** (*adiós*) cheerio!; (*¡apúrese!*) come on!, hurry up!; (*encontrando algo*) that's it!, that's the one!; (*gracias*) thanks!

(**i**) **anda que te anda** never letting up for a moment, without stopping at all.

(**j**) **~ haciendo algo** to be doing sth, be in the course of doing sth; **no andes criticándole todo el tiempo** don't keep criticizing him all the time.

3 andarse *vr frec = vi*; (**a**) (*irse*) to go off, go away.

(**b**) **~ con** to use, make use of, employ; **~ en** to indulge in; **Juanito se anda por el abecedario** Johnny is beginning to read.

(**c**) **todo se andará** all in good time, it will all come right in the end.

4 *nm* walk; gait, pace; **a largo ~** in the end; in the long run; **a más ~, a todo ~** at full speed, as quickly as possible; **a mejor ~** at best; **a peor ~** at worst; **estar a un ~** to be on the same level.

andaras *nm* (*And*) Indian flute.

andarica *nf* (*prov*) crab.

andariego *adj* wandering, roving; fond of travelling; restless.

andarilla *nf* (*And Mús*) type of flute.

andarín *nm* walker; **es muy ~** he is a great walker.

andarivel *nm* (**a**) (*Téc*) cableway, cable ferry; (*Náut etc*) handrope; (*Cono Sur*) (*cerco*) rope barrier; (*de piscina*) lane. (**b**) (*And: adornos*) adornments, trinkets.

andas *nfpl* (*camilla*) stretcher; (*silla*) litter, sedan chair; (*Rel*) portable platform; (*féretro*) bier; **llevar a uno en ~** (*fig*) to praise sb to the skies; to treat sb with great consideration.

ándele *interj* (*Méx*) (*¡siga!*) come on!; (*¡ya ves!*) see what I mean!; (*¡ya lo creo!*) get away!; (*correcto*) exactly!

andén *nm* (*Ferro*) platform; (*CAm: acera*) pavement, sidewalk (*US*); (*Náut*) quayside; (*And, Cono Sur Agr*) terrace; **~ de salida** departure platform; **~ de vacío** arrival platform.

Andes *nmpl* Andes.

andinismo *nm* (*LAm*) mountaineering, mountain climbing; **hacer ~** to go mountaineering, go mountain climbing.

andinista *nmf* (*LAm*) mountaineer, climber.

andino *adj* Andean, of the Andes.

ándito *nm* (*pasillo*) outer walk, corridor; (*acera*) pavement, sidewalk (*US*).

andoba* *nm* guy*, chap*.

andolina *nf* swallow.

andón *adj* (*LAm*) = **andador** (**b**).

andonear [1a] *vi* (*Carib*) (*persona*) to amble (*o* stroll) along; (*caballo*) to trot.

andorga* *nf* belly.

andorina *nf* swallow.

Andorra *nf* Andorra.

andorrano, -a *adj, nm/f* Andorran.

andorrear* [1a] *vi* (*ajetrearse*) to bustle about, fuss around; (*ir de acá para allá*) to gad about, move about a lot.

andorrero 1 *adj* bustling, busy. **2** *nm*, **andorrera** *nf* busy sort, gadabout. **3 andorrera** *nf* (*pey*) streetwalker.

andrajo *nm* (**a**) (*trapo*) rag, tatter; **~s** rags, tatters; **estar en ~s, estar hecho un ~** to be in rags; **ser un ~ humano** to be a wreck. (**b**) (*pillo*) rascal, good-for-nothing. (**c**) (*bagatela*) trifle, mere nothing.

andrajoso *adj* ragged, in tatters.

Andrés *nm* Andrew.

androcéntrico *adj* male-centred, androcentric.

androcentrismo *nm* male-centredness, androcentricity.

androfobia *nf* hatred of men.

androgénico *adj* androgenic.

andrógeno *nm* androgen.

androide *nm* android.

Andrómaca *nf* Andromache.

andrómina* *nf* fib, tale; piece of humbug; trick.

androsterona *nf* androsterone.

andullo *nm* (*Carib, Cono Sur, Méx*) plug of chewing tobacco.

andurrial *nm* (*lodazal*) bog, quagmire; (*zanja*) ditch; (*descampado*) piece of waste ground; **~es** out-of-the way place, the wilds; **en esos ~es** in that godforsaken place.

anea *nf* bulrush, reedmace.

aneblar [1j] **1** *vt* to cover with mist (*o* cloud); (*fig*) to obscure, darken, cast a cloud over. **2 aneblarse** *vr* to get misty, get cloudy; to get dark.

anécdota *nf* anecdote, story; (odd) incident, (strange) business; **este cuadro tiene una ~** there's a tale attached to this picture.

anecdotario *nm* collection of stories.

anecdótico *adj* anecdotal; trivial; **contenido ~** story content; **valor ~** story value, value as a story; **el estudio se queda en lo ~** the study does not rise above the merely superficial, the study stays on the surface.

anecdotismo *nm* anecdotal nature, (merely) anecdotal quality; triviality.

anega *nf* (*Cono Sur*) = **fanega**.

anegación *nf* drowning; flooding.

anegadizo *adj tierra* subject to flooding, frequently flooded; *madera* heavier than water.

anegar [1h] **1** *vt* (**a**) (*ahogar*) to drown. (**b**) (*inundar*) to flood; (*fig*) to overwhelm, destroy.

2 anegarse *vr* (**a**) (*ahogarse*) to drown. (**b**) (*lugar*) to flood, be flooded; ~ **en llanto** to dissolve into tears. (**c**) (*Náut*) to sink, founder.

anejo 1 *adj* attached; dependent; ~ **a** attached to; joined on to. **2** *nm* (*Arquit*) annexe, outbuilding; (*Liter, Tip*) supplement.

anemia *nf* anaemia.

anémico *adj* anaemic.

anemómetro *nm* anemometer; (*Aer*) wind gauge; ~ **registrador** wind-speed indicator.

anémona *nf*, **anémone** *nf* anemone; ~ **de mar** sea anemone.

aneroide *adj* aneroid.

anestesia *nf* anaesthesia; ~ **general** general anaesthetic; ~ **local** local anaesthetic.

anestesiante *adj, nm* anaesthetic (*t fig*).

anestesiar [1b] *vt* to anaesthetize, give an anaesthetic to; (*fig*) to blunt (the emotions of), desensitize.

anestésico *adj, nm* anaesthetic.

anestesista *nmf* anaesthetist.

anexar [1a] *vt* (*Pol*) to annex; (*Inform*) to append.

anexión *nf*, **anexionamiento** *nm* annexation.

anexionar [1a] *vt* (*Pol*) to annex.

anexo 1 *adj* attached; dependent (*t Ecl*); **llevar algo ~, tener algo ~** to have sth attached; **anexo a la presente ...** (*Méx*) please find enclosed ...

2 *nm* (*Arquit*) annexe, outbuilding; (*Ecl*) dependency; (*papel*) appendix, attached document; (*And Telec*) extension.

anfeta* *nf* = **anfetamina.**

anfetamina *nf* amphetamine.

anfetamínico, -a *nm/f* (**a**) amphetamine addict, speed freak*. (**b**) (*) bore; idiot; pain*.

anfibio 1 *adj* amphibious; amphibian (*t Aer etc*). **2** *nm* amphibian; **los ~s** (*como clase*) the amphibia.

anfibología *nf* ambiguity.

anfibológico *adj* ambiguous.

anfiteatro *nm* amphitheatre; arena; (*Teat*) dress circle; ~ **anatómico** dissecting room.

Anfitrión *nm* Amphitryon.

anfitrión *nm* host.

anfitriona *nf* hostess.

ánfora *nf* amphora; (*LAm*) ballot box; (*Cono Sur**: *de marijuana*) marijuana pouch.

anfractuosidad *nf* (*aspereza*) roughness, unevenness; (*curva*) bend; (*vuelta*) turning; (*Anat*) fold, convolution; **~es** rough places, up-and-down parts.

anfractuoso *adj* rough, uneven, up-and-down.

angarilla *nf* (*LAm*), **angarillas** *nfpl* (*carretilla*) handbarrow; (*alforjas*) panniers, packs; (*Culin*) cruet, cruet stand.

angarrio *adj* (*And, Carib*) terribly thin, thin as a rake*.

angas: por ~ o por mangas (*And*) like it or not; willy-nilly.

ángel *nm* (**a**) (*Rel*) angel; ~ **caído** fallen angel; ~ **custodio, ~ de la guarda** guardian angel; ~ **exterminador** angel of death; ~ **del infierno** hell's angel.

(**b**) (*fig*) charm, mystery; charisma; **tener** ~ to have charm, be very charming; **tener mal** ~ to be a nasty piece of work; to have an unfortunate effect (on people *etc*); **pasó un** ~ there was a sudden silence; (*en charla*) there was a lull in the conversation.

angélica *nf* angelica.

angelical *adj*, **angélico** *adj* angelic(al).

angelino 1 *adj* of Los Angeles. **2** *nm*, **angelina** *nf* native (*o* inhabitant) of Los Angeles; **los ~s** the people of Los Angeles.

angelito *nm* little angel; (*LAm*) dead child; **¡~!** (*Cono Sur*) don't play the innocent!, pull the other one!*; **¡no seas ~!** (*Cono Sur*) don't be silly!

angelón* *nm*: ~ **de retablo** fat old thing.

angelopolitano (*Méx*) **1** *adj* of Puebla. **2** *nm*, **angelopolitana** *nf* native (*o* inhabitant) of Puebla; **los ~s** the people of Puebla.

angelote *nm* (**a**) (*niño*) chubby child. (**b**) (*LAm*: *person*) decent person. (**c**) (*pez*) angel-fish.

ángelus *nm* angelus.

angina *nf* (**a**) (*Med*) angina, quinsy; (*Méx*) tonsil; **~s** tonsillitis, sore throat, pharyngitis; ~ **de pecho** angina pectoris; **tener ~s** to have a sore throat. (**b**) **~s** (*Esp*‡) tits‡.

angiosperma *nf* angiosperm.

anglicanismo *nm* Anglicanism.

anglicano, -a *adj, nm/f* Anglican.

anglicismo *nm* anglicism.

anglicista 1 *adj*: **tendencia** ~ anglicizing tendency. **2** *nmf* anglicist.

angliparla *nf* (*hum*) Spanglish.

anglo... *pref* anglo...

anglófilo, -a *nm/f* anglophile.

anglófobo 1 *adj* anglophobe, anglophobic. **2** *nm*, **anglófoba** *nf* anglophobe.

anglófono 1 *adj* English-speaking. **2** *nm*, **anglófona** *nf* English speaker.

anglohablante, angloparlante 1 *adj* English-speaking. **2** *nmf* English speaker.

anglonormando 1 *adj* Anglo-Norman; **Islas** *fpl* **Anglonormandas** Channel Isles. **2** *nm*, **anglonormanda** *nf* Anglo-Norman. **3** *nm* (*Ling*) Anglo-Norman.

anglosajón, -ona 1 *adj, nm/f* Anglo-Saxon. **2** *nm* (*Ling*) Anglo-Saxon.

Angola *nf* Angola.

angoleño, -a *adj, nm/f* Angolan.

angolés = **angoleño.**

angora *nmf* angora.

angorina *nf* artificial angora.

angostar [1a] **1** *vt* to narrow; (*Cono Sur*) to make smaller; *ropa* to take in. **2 angostarse** *vr* to narrow, get narrow(er).

angosto *adj* narrow.

angostura *nf* (**a**) (*cualidad*) narrowness. (**b**) (*Náut*) narrows, strait; (*Geog*) narrow passage, narrow defile, narrow place. (**c**) (*bebida*) angostura.

angra *nf* cove, creek.

angstrom *nm* angstrom.

anguila *nf* eel; (*Náut*) **~s** slipway.

angula *nf* elver, baby eel.

angulación *nf* (*Cine*) camera angle.

angular 1 *adj* angular; *V* **piedra. 2** *nm*: **gran** ~ wide-angle lens.

Angulema *nf* Angoulême.

angulo *nm* baby eel, elver.

ángulo *nm* (*gen, t Mat*) angle; (*esquina*) corner; (*curva*) bend, turning; (*Mec*) knee, bend; ~ **agudo** acute angle; ~ **alterno** alternate angle; ~ **de mira** angle of sight; ~ **oblicuo** oblique angle; ~ **obtuso** obtuse angle; ~ **del ojo** corner of one's eye; ~ **recto** right angle; **de ~ recto, en ~ recto** right-angled; ~ **de subida, ~ de trepada** (*Aer*) angle of climb; **de gran ~, de ~ ancho** *lente etc* wide-angle; **en ~** at an angle; **está inclinado a un ~ de 45 grados** it is leaning at an angle of 45°; **formar ~ con** to be at an angle to.

anguloso *adj cara etc* angular, sharp; *camino* tortuous, full of bends.

angurria *nf* (*And, Cono Sur*) (**a**) (*hambre*) voracious hunger, greed; (*angustia*) intense anxiety, grave worry; **comer con ~*** to scoff one's food*. (**b**) (*tacañería*) meanness, stinginess.

angurriento *adj* (*And, Cono Sur*) (**a**) (*voraz*) greedy. (**b**) (*tacaño*) mean, stingy.

angustia *nf* anguish, distress; ~ **de muerte** death-throes; **de puta ~**‡ by sheer chance.

angustiado *adj* (**a**) (*apenado*) anguished, distressed; anxious; wretched. (**b**) (*avaro*) grasping, mean.

angustiar [1b] **1** *vt* to distress, grieve, cause anguish to.

2 angustiarse *vr* to be distressed, grieve, feel anguish (*por* at, on account of); to worry, get worried.

angustiosamente *adv* in an anguished tone (*etc*); anxiously; distressingly.

angustioso *adj* (**a**) (*angustiado*) distressed, anguished; anxious. (**b**) (*doloroso*) distressing, agonizing; heartbreaking.

anhá *interj* (*Cono Sur*) = **anjá.**

anhelación *nf* (**a**) (*Med*) panting. (**b**) (*fig*) longing, yearning.

anhelante *adj* (**a**) *respiración* panting. (**b**) (*fig*) eager; longing, yearning.

anhelar [1a] **1** *vt* to be eager for; to long for, yearn for, crave.

2 *vi* (**a**) (*Med*) to gasp, pant.

(**b**) (*fig*) ~ + *infin* to be eager to + *infin*, long to + *infin*, yearn to + *infin;* ~ **por algo** to long for sth, hanker after sth; ~ **por** + *infin* to aspire to + *infin.*

anhelo *nm* eagerness; longing, yearning, desire (*de, por* for); ~ **de superación** urge to do better; **con** ~ longingly, yearningly; **tener ~s de** to be eager for, long for.

anheloso *adj* (**a**) (*Med*) gasping, panting; *respiración* heavy, difficult. (**b**) (*fig*) eager, anxious.

Aníbal *nm* Hannibal.

anidación *nf*, **anidada** *nf* (*Orn*) nesting.
anidamiento *nm* (*Inform*) nesting.
anidar [1a] **1** *vt* to take in, shelter. **2** *vi* (*Orn*) to nest, make its nest; (*fig*) to live, make one's home; (*Inform*) to nest; **la maldad anida en su alma** his heart is full of evil.
anieblar [1a] = **aneblar.**
aniego *nm* (*And, Cono Sur*), **aniegue** *nm* (*Méx*) flood.
anilina *nf* aniline.
anilla *nf* (*de cortina*) curtain ring; (*anillito*) small ring; (*de puro*) cigar band; (*Orn*) ring; (*Gimnasia*) **~s** rings.
anillado 1 *adj* ringed; ring-shaped. **2** *nm* ringing (of birds).
anillamiento *nm* ringing (of birds).
anillar [1a] *vt* (*dar forma a*) to make into a ring, make rings in; (*sujetar*) to fasten with a ring; (*Orn*) to ring.
anillejo *nm*, **anillete** *nm* small ring, ringlet.
anillo *nm* ring (*t Astron, Mec*); (*de puro*) cigar band; **~ de boda** wedding-ring; **~ de compromiso, ~ de prometida, ~ de pedida** engagement ring; **~ de crecimiento** growth ring; **~ pastoral** bishop's ring; **no creo que se me caigan los ~s por eso** I don't feel it's in any way beneath my dignity; **venir como ~ al dedo** to be just right, meet the case perfectly, be just what the doctor ordered.
ánima *nf* (**a**) (*Rel*) soul; **~ bendita, ~ en pena, ~ del purgatorio** soul in purgatory; (*Ecl*) **las ~s** evening bell, sunset bell. (**b**) (*Mil*) bore. (**c**) (*Cono Sur*: *santuario*) wayside shrine.
animación *nf* (**a**) liveliness, life; bustle, activity, movement, animation; sprightliness; **~ cultural** cultural awakening; **~ suspendida** suspended animation; **campaña de ~ social** campaign of social awakening; **experta en ~ social** social activities coordinator; **había poca ~** there wasn't much life about it; **una escena llena de ~** a scene full of life. (**b**) (*gráfica*) animation; **~ por ordenador** computer animation, computer graphics.
animadamente *adv* in lively fashion, gaily; animatedly; in sprightly fashion; merrily.
animado *adj* (**a**) *carácter, persona etc* lively, gay; (*concurrido*) bustling, busy, animated; (*enérgico*) sprightly; (*alegre*) merry, in high spirits. (**b**) *reunión* well-attended, popular. (**c**) (*Zool*) animate. (**d**) (*LAm Med*) recovering, improving.
animador *nm* compère, (*hombre*) master of ceremonies; (*TV etc*) presenter; (*LAm*) cheerleader; **~ cultural** director of cultural activities.
animadora *nf* (*cantante*) night-club singer, crooner; (*TV etc*) presenter; (*LAm*) cheerleader; **~ cultural** director of cultural activities.
animadversión *nf* ill will, animosity; animadversion.
animal 1 *adj* (**a**) (*lit*) animal.
(**b**) (*fig*) stupid.
2 *nm* (**a**) (*lit*) animal; **~ de compañía** pet; **~ de laboratorio** laboratory animal; **~ de tiro** carthorse, workhorse (*t fig*); **soy un ~ político** I am a political animal.
(**b**) (*fig*: *tonto*) fool, idiot; (*fig*: *bestia*) beast, brute; **¡~!** you brute!; **el ~ de Juan** that beast of a John; **¡qué ~ de policía!** what a brute of a policeman!; **¡no seas ~!** don't be beastly!, don't be horrid!
animalada *nf* (**a**) (*LAm*: *rebaño*) group (*o* herd) of animals.
(**b**) (*fig*) (*cualidad*) foolishness, stupidity; (*disparate*) silly thing (to do *o* say *etc*); (*grosería*) coarse thing, piece of disgraceful conduct; **hacer una ~** to do sth silly; to do sth disgraceful.
animalaje *nm* (*Cono Sur*) animals; herd (*o* group) of animals.
animalejo *nm* odd-looking creature, nasty animal; creepy-crawly*.
animalidad *nf* animality; sensuality.
animalizarse [1f] *vr* to become brutalized.
animalote *nm* big animal.
animalucho *nm* ugly brute; creepy-crawly*.
animar [1a] **1** *vt* (**a**) (*Bio*) to animate, give life to.
(**b**) *discusión, reunión etc* to enliven, liven up, add interest to; *cuarto, fuego, escena, vista etc* to brighten up; *cosa aburrida* to stimulate, give new life to, ginger up.
(**c**) *persona* (*alegrar*) to cheer up; (*alentar*) to encourage, put new heart into; **~ a uno a hacer algo** to encourage sb to do sth.
2 animarse *vr* (**a**) (*fiesta etc*) to become more lively, liven up, acquire new life; to brighten up.
(**b**) (*persona*) (*alegrarse*) to brighten up, cheer up, feel encouraged, take heart; (*decidirse*) to make up one's mind, decide; **¡anímate!** cheer up!, buck up!; (*atreverse*) go on then!; (*decidirse*) make up your mind!; **¿te animas?** do you want to have a go?, are you game?; **~ a hacer algo** to make up one's mind to do sth, resolve to do sth; **a ver si se animan** we'll wait and see if they do anything about it; **no me animo a hacerlo** I can't bring myself to do it.
anime *nm* (*Carib*) polyethylene.
anímicamente *adv* mentally.
anímico *adj* mental; **estado ~** state of mind.
animita *nf* (*Cono Sur*) roadside shrine.
ánimo *nm* (**a**) (*mente etc*) mind; soul, spirit; **eso está en el ~ de todos** everybody is aware of that; **apaciguar los ~s** to calm people down.
(**b**) (*valor*) courage, pluck; nerve; (*energía*) energy; **caer(se) de ~** to lose heart, get disheartened; **cobrar ~** to take heart, pluck up courage; **dar ~(s) a, infundir ~ a** to encourage; **dilatar el ~ a uno** to put heart into sb.
(**c**) (*intención*) intention, purpose; **con ~ de** + *infin* with the intention of + *ger*, with the idea of + *ger*; **sin ~ de ofenderle** without wishing to offend you; **sin ~ de polémica** without wishing to be controversial; **sociedad sin ~ de lucro** non-profit-making organization; **se hizo con ~ de lucro** it was done with profit in mind; **estar con ~ de** + *infin* to feel like + *ger*; **hacer ~ de** + *infin* to intend to + *infin*, mean to + *infin*; **tener ~s para algo** to be in the mood for sth, feel like sth.
(**d**) **¡~(s)!** *interj* cheer up!; (*Dep*) come on!, go it!
animosamente *adv* bravely; with spirit, in lively fashion.
animosidad *nf* animosity, ill will.
animoso *adj* brave; spirited, lively.
aniñado *adj* (**a**) childlike; (*pey*) childish, puerile. (**b**) (*Cono Sur*: *animoso*) spirited, lively. (**c**) (*Cono Sur*: *guapo*) handsome.
aniñarse [1a] *vr* to act childishly.
aniquilación *nf*, **aniquilamiento** *nm* annihilation, destruction.
aniquilar [1a] **1** *vt* to annihilate, destroy, obliterate, wipe out; to overwhelm.
2 aniquilarse *vr* (**a**) (*lit*) to be annihilated, be wiped out.
(**b**) (*fig*) to deteriorate, decline; (*Med*) to waste away; (*fortuna etc*) to disappear, be frittered away.
anís *nm* (**a**) (*Bot*) anise, aniseed. (**b**) (*bebida*) anis, anisette; **estar hecho un ~** (*And*) to be elegantly dressed; to be as clean as a new pin; **llegar a los anises** to turn up late. (**c**) (*And*: *energía*) strength, energy.
anisado *adj* flavoured with aniseed.
aniseros‡ *nmpl* (*And*): **entregar los ~** to kick the bucket‡; **vaciar los ~ a uno** to bump sb off‡.
anisete *nm* anisette.
anivelar [1a] *vt* = **nivelar.**
aniversario *nm* anniversary.
anjá *interj* (*Carib, Méx**: ¡*claro*!) of course!; that's it!; (*Carib*) (¡*bravo*!) bravo!; (*reprobación*) come off it!*
Anjeo *nm* Anjou.
Ankara *nf* Ankara.
ano *nm* anus.
anoche *adv* last night; **antes de ~** the night before last.
anochecedor(a) *nm/f* late bird, person who keeps late hours.
anochecer 1 [2d] *vi* (**a**) (*gen*) to get dark.
(**b**) (*persona*) to arrive at nightfall; **anochecimos en Toledo** we got to Toledo as night was falling.
2 *nm* nightfall, dusk; **al ~** at nightfall; **antes del ~** by nightfall, before nightfall.
anochecida *nf* nightfall, dusk.
anodino 1 *adj* anodyne; (*fig*) anodyne, harmless, inoffensive; dull. **2** *nm* anodyne.
ánodo *nm* anode.
anomalía *nf* anomaly.
anómalo *adj* anomalous.
anona *nf* (*CAm Bot*) custard apple.
anonadación *nm*, **anonadamiento** *nm* (**a**) (*destrucción*) annihilation, destruction. (**b**) (*desánimo*) discouragement, despair; humiliation.
anonadador *adj* crushing, overwhelming.
anonadar [1a] **1** *vt* (**a**) (*destruir*) to annihilate, destroy; to overwhelm. (**b**) (*desanimar*) to discourage, depress; (*humillar*) to humiliate.
2 anonadarse *vr* (**a**) (*ser derrotado*) to be crushed, be overwhelmed.
(**b**) (*desanimarse*) to get discouraged; to be humiliated.
anónimamente *adv* anonymously.
anonimato *nm*, **anonimia** *nf* anonymity; **mantenerse en el anonimato** to remain anonymous.

anónimo 1 *adj* anonymous; nameless; (*Com, Fin*) *compañía* limited.
2 *nm* (**a**) (*estado*) anonymity; **conservar** (*o* **guardar**) **el** ~ to preserve one's anonymity.
(**b**) (*persona*) anonymous person, unknown person.
(**c**) (*carta*) anonymous letter; (*documento*) anonymous document; (*Liter*) unsigned literary work.
anorac *nm*, **anorak** *nm* anorak.
anorexia *nf* anorexia; ~ **nerviosa** anorexia nervosa.
anoréxico 1 *adj* anorexic. **2** *nm*, **anoréxica** *nf* anorexic.
anormal *adj* (**a**) abnormal; irregular, unusual; *niño* subnormal, mentally handicapped. (**b**) (*) silly, cretinous.
anormalidad *nf* abnormality; irregularity; unusual nature; subnormality, mental handicap.
anormalmente *adv* abnormally, unusually.
anotación *nf* annotation; note, record, observation; (*LAm Dep*) score; (*en cuenta*) debit.
anotador(a) 1 *nm/f* (**a**) (*Liter*) annotator. (**b**) (*LAm Dep*) scorer. **2** *nm* (*LAm*) scorecard. **3 anotadora** *nf* (*Cine*) script girl, continuity girl.
anotar [1a] *vt* (**a**) (*tomar apuntes*) to annotate; to note (down), jot down, take down; to register, record; (*Com*) *pedido* to note, book. (**b**) (*Dep*) to score.
anovulatorio *nm* anovulant; contraceptive pill.
ANPE *nf abr de* **Asociación Nacional del Profesorado Estatal**.
anquilosado *adj* (*fig*) stagnant; paralyzed.
anquilosamiento *nm*, **anquilosis** *nf* (*fig*) stagnation; paralysis.
anquilosar [1a] **1** *vt* to paralyze. **2** *vi* (*Aut, Mec*) to seize up. **3 anquilosarse** *vr* to decline; to become eroded.
anquilostoma *nm* hookworm.
ánsar *nm* goose.
ansarino *nm* gosling.
Anselmo *nm* Anselm.
ansia *nf* (**a**) (*preocupación*) anxiety, worry; (*angustia*) fear, anguish. (**b**) (*anhelo*) yearning, longing (*de* for). (**c**) (*Med*) anxiety, nervous tension. (**d**) (*Med*) **~s** nausea, sick feeling.
ansiado *adj* longed-for; **el momento tan** ~ the moment which we (*etc*) had so much longed for.
ansiar [1c] **1** *vt* to long for, yearn for; to covet, crave; ~ + *infin* to long to + *infin*, yearn to + *infin*. **2** *vi*: ~ **por uno** to be madly in love with sb.
ansiedad *nf* (**a**) (*preocupación*) anxiety, worry; solicitude; suspense. (**b**) (*Med*) anxiety, nervous tension.
ansina *adv* (*LAm*) = **así**.
ansiolítico 1 *adj* sedative. **2** *nm* sedative, tranquillizer.
ansioso *adj* (**a**) (*preocupado*) anxious, uneasy, worried; solicitous; **esperamos ~s** we waited anxiously; ~ **de algo**, ~ **por algo** eager for sth, avid for sth; greedy for sth.
(**b**) (*Med*) (*tenso*) anxious, nervously tense; (*bascoso*) sick, queasy.
anta *nf* elk, moose; (*LAm*) tapir.
antagónico *adj* antagonistic; opposed, contrasting.
antagonismo *nm* antagonism.
antagonista *nmf* antagonist, opponent.
antagonístico *adj* = **antagónico**.
antagonizar [1f] *vt* to antagonize.
antañazo *adv* a long time ago.
antaño *adv* (*el año pasado*) last year; (*hace mucho*) long ago, formerly; **el** ~ **poderoso país** the once-powerful country.
antañón *adj* ancient, very old, of long ago.
antañoso *adj* (*And*) ancient, very old.
antara *nf* (*And*) pan pipes, Indian flute.
antarca *adv* (*And, Cono Sur*) on one's back; **caerse** ~ to fall flat on one's back.
antártico 1 *adj* Antarctic. **2** *nm*: **el A~** the Antarctic.
Antártida *nf* Antarctica.
ante[1] *nm* (**a**) (*Zool*) (*anta*) elk, moose; (*búfalo*) buffalo; (*Méx*: *tapir*) tapir. (**b**) (*piel*) buckskin, suede. (**c**) (*Méx*: *dulce*) macaroon.
ante[2] *prep persona* before, in the presence of; *enemigo, peligro etc* in the face of; *dificultad, duda* faced with; *asunto* with regard to; ~ **esta posibilidad** in view of this possibility; ~ **tantas posibilidades** faced with so many possibilities; ~ **todo hay que recordar que ...** first of all let's remember that ...; **estamos** ~ **un gran porvenir** we have a great future before us.
ante... *pref* ante...
-ante *V* **Aspects of Word Formation in Spanish 2**.
anteado *adj* buff-coloured, fawn.
anteanoche *adv* the night before last.
anteayer *adv* the day before yesterday.
antebrazo *nm* forearm.
anteburro *nm* (*LAm Zool*) tapir.
antecámara *nf* anteroom, antechamber; lobby.
antecedente 1 *adj* previous, preceding, foregoing; **visto lo** ~ in view of the foregoing.
2 *nm* (**a**) (*Mat, Filos, Gram*) antecedent.
(**b**) **~s** record, history, background; **¿cuáles son sus ~s?** what's his history?, what's his background like?; **~s delictivos, ~s penales, ~s policiales** criminal record; **un hombre sin ~s** a man with a clean record; **estar en ~s** to know all about it, be well informed; **poner a uno en ~s** to put sb in the picture, give sb the latest information; **tener buenos ~s** to have a good record.
anteceder [2a] *vt* to precede, go before.
antecesor 1 *adj* preceding, former. **2** *nm*, **antecesora** *nf* predecessor; (*antepasado*) ancestor, forbear.
antecomedor *nm* (*LAm*) room adjoining the dining room.
antecocina *nf* scullery.
antedatar [1a] *vt* to antedate.
antedicho *adj* aforesaid, aforementioned.
antediluviano *adj* antediluvian.
anteiglesia *nf* (*Ecl*) porch.
antejuela *nf* (*CAm*) = **lentejuela**.
antelación *nf* (*esp Esp*) precedence, priority; **con** ~ in advance, in good time, beforehand; **con mucha** ~ long in advance, long beforehand.
antelina *nf* suède, artificial buckskin.
antellevar [1a] *vt* (*Méx Aut*) to run down, knock down.
antellevón *nm* (*Méx Aut*) accident.
antemano: de ~ *adv* in advance, beforehand.
antena *nf* (**a**) (*Zool*) feeler, antenna; **tener** ~ **para** (*fig*) to have a feeling for, have a nose for.
(**b**) (*Náut*) lateen yard.
(**c**) (*Rad etc*) aerial, antenna; ~ **direccional**, ~ **dirigida** directional aerial; ~ **encerrada** built-in aerial; ~ **interior** indoor aerial; ~ **parabólica** parabolic aerial, satellite dish; ~ **de plato** dish aerial, satellite dish; ~ **de televisión** television aerial; **estar en** ~ to be on the air; **permanecer en** ~ to stay on the air; **salir en** ~ to go out on the air, be broadcast; **el programa es el sexto en duración en** ~ the programme is the sixth longest-running on TV.
(**d**) (*) **~s** ears.
antenatal *adj* antenatal, prenatal.
antenombre *nm* style, title (*preceding first name*).
anteojera[1] *nf* (**a**) (*funda*) spectacle case. (**b**) **~s** blinkers.
anteojero, -a[2] *nm/f* spectacle maker, optician.
anteojo *nm* (**a**) (*lente*) eyeglass, spyglass, (small) telescope; ~ **de larga vista** telescope.
(**b**) **~s** (*gafas*) spectacles, glasses; (*Aut, Téc etc*) goggles; (*de caballo*) blinkers; **~s ahumados** smoked glasses; **~s de concha** horn-rimmed spectacles; **~s de sol**, **~s para el sol** sunglasses.
antepagar [1h] *vt* to prepay, pay beforehand.
antepasado 1 *adj* previous, immediately past, before last. **2** *nm*, **antepasada** *nf* ancestor, forbear; **mis ~s** my forbears, my forefathers.
antepecho *nm* (*de puente etc*) rail, guardrail, parapet; (*de ventana*) ledge, sill; (*Mil*) parapet, breastwork.
antepenúltimo *adj* last but two, antepenultimate.
anteponer [2q] **1** *vt* (**a**) (*lit*) to place in front (*a* of). (**b**) (*fig*) to prefer (*a* to). **2 anteponerse** *vr* to be in front (*a* of), come in between.
anteportal *nm* porch.
anteproyecto *nm* preliminary sketch, preliminary plan; (*esp fig*) blueprint; ~ **de ley** draft bill.
antepuerto *nm* outer harbour.
antepuesto *adj* preceding, coming before.
antequerano 1 *adj* of Antequera. **2** *nm*, **antequerana** *nf* native (*o* inhabitant) of Antequera; **los ~s** the people of Antequera.
antera *nf* anther.
anterior *adj* (**a**) *pierna, parte etc* front, fore, anterior; **en la parte** ~ **del coche** on the front part of the car.
(**b**) (*en orden*) preceding, previous, former; (*Ling*) anterior; (*antedicho*) aforementioned; **cada uno mejor que el** ~ each one better than the last; **se había olvidado de todo lo** ~ he had forgotten all that had happened previously.
(**c**) (*en el tiempo*) former; previous (*a* to), earlier (*a* than); **un texto** ~ **a 1140** a text earlier than 1140; **el día** ~ the previous day, the day before.
anterioridad *nf* precedence, priority; **con** ~ previously, beforehand; earlier; **con** ~ **a esto** prior to this, before this.
anteriormente *adv* previously, before.

antes 1 *adv* (**a**) (*gen*) before; (*primero*) first; (*antaño*) once, previously, formerly; in times gone by; (*antes de ahora*) sooner, before now; **3 días ~** 3 days before, 3 days earlier; **la casa de ~** the previous house; **lo de ~** that earlier business; **en ~** (*And, Cono Sur*) in the past; **no quiso venir ~** he didn't want to come any earlier; **conviene cazar ~ la liebre** first catch your hare; **la planta existió aquí ~** the plant used to grow here; **lo vio ~ que yo** he saw it before I did; **~ hoy que mañana** the sooner the better; **lo ~ posible, cuanto ~** as soon as possible; **cuanto ~ mejor** the sooner the better; as quickly as possible; **mucho ~** long before; **poco ~** shortly before, a short time previously.

(**b**) (*preferencia*) sooner, rather; **~ (bien)** rather, on the contrary; **~ muerto que esclavo** better dead than enslaved; **~ mejor que vino** (*LAm*) it's just as well he came; **preferimos ir en tren ~ que en avión** we prefer to go by train rather than by plane; **no cederemos: ~ lo destruimos todo** we shall never give up: we would rather destroy everything.

2 ~ de *prep* before; previous to; **~ de 1900** before 1900; up to 1900; **~ de hacerlo** before doing it; **~ de terminado el discurso** before the speech was over.

3 ~ (de) que *conj* before; **~ de que te vayas** before you go.

antesala *nf* anteroom, antechamber; lobby; (*fig*) **estamos en la ~ de** we are on the verge of, we are on the threshold of; **hacer ~** to wait, wait to be received, wait to go in to see sb, (*fig*) cool one's heels.

antesalazo *nm* (*Méx*) long wait (*before admission*).

antetítulo *nm* introductory heading, prefatory heading.

anteúltimo *adj* (*Cono Sur*) penultimate.

anti... *pref* anti...; un...; non-...

antiabortista 1 *adj*: **campaña ~** anti-abortion campaign. **2** *nmf* antiabortionist.

antiácido *adj, nm* antacid.

antiadherencia *nf* non-stick properties; **prueba ~** non-stick test.

antiadherente *adj* non-stick.

antiaéreo 1 *adj* anti-aircraft. **2** *nm* (*LAm*) anti-aircraft gun.

antialcohólico (*LAm*) **1** *adj* teetotal. **2** *nm*, **antialcohólica** *nf* teetotaller.

antiamericano *adj* anti-American; un-American.

antiatómico *adj*: **refugio ~** fall-out shelter.

antiatraco(s) *adj*: **dispositivo ~** anti-theft device, security device.

antibala(s) *adj invar* bullet-proof.

antibalístico *adj* antiballistic.

antibelicista 1 *adj* anti-war; pacifist. **2** *nmf* pacifist.

antibiótico *adj, nm* antibiotic.

anticalcáreo *adj*: **dispositivo ~** anti-scaling device.

anticarro *adj invar* antitank.

anticiclón *nm* anticyclone.

anticiclonal *adj*, **anticiclónico** *adj* anticyclonic.

anticipación *nf* anticipation; foretaste; (*Com, Fin*) advance; **hacer algo con ~** to do sth well beforehand, do sth in good time; **reservar con ~** to book in advance, book early; **llegar con bastante ~** to arrive early, arrive in good time; **llegar con 10 minutos de ~** to come 10 minutes early.

anticipadamente *adv* in advance, beforehand; **le doy las gracias ~** I thank you in advance.

anticipado *adj* (*futuro*) future, prospective; (*con antelación*) early; *pago etc* advance; **por ~** in advance, beforehand.

anticipar [1a] **1** *vt* (**a**) *fecha, acontecimiento* to bring forward, advance; to hasten (the date of); **anticiparon las vacaciones** they took their holiday early; **no anticipemos los acontecimientos** let's not cross our bridges before we come to them.

(**b**) *dinero* to advance, lend, loan.

(**c**) **~ las gracias a uno** to thank sb in advance.

(**d**) (*LAm*: *prever*) to anticipate, foresee; **~ que ...** to anticipate that ...

2 anticiparse *vr* (**a**) (*acontecimiento*) to take place early, happen before the expected time.

(**b**) **~ a un acontecimiento** to anticipate an event, forestall an event; **~ a uno** to beat sb to it, steal a march on sb; **Vd se ha anticipado a mis deseos** you have anticipated my wishes; **~ a hacer algo** to do sth ahead of time, do sth before the proper time.

anticipo *nm* (**a**) (*gen*) anticipation, foretaste; **fue el ~ del fin para toda una época** it was the beginning of the end for a whole epoch; **esto es sólo un ~** this is just a foretaste.

(**b**) (*Com, Fin*) advance, loan; (*t* **~ a cuenta**) advance payment.

(**c**) (*Jur*) retaining fee.

anticlerical *adj, nmf* anticlerical.

anticlericalismo *nm* anticlericalism.

anticlinal *nm* (*LAm*) watershed; (*Geol*) anticline.

anticoagulante *adj, nm* anticoagulant.

anticoba *nf* brutal frankness, outspokenness.

anticolesterol *adj* cholesterol-free, low in cholesterol.

anticoncepción *nf* contraception, birth-control.

anticoncepcional *adj* birth-control (*atr*), family-planning (*atr*), contraceptive.

anticoncepcionismo *nm* contraception, birth-control.

anticonceptivo 1 *adj* birth-control (*atr*), family-planning (*atr*), contraceptive; **métodos ~s** birth-control methods, contraceptive devices; **píldora anticonceptiva** contraceptive pill.

2 *nm* contraceptive.

anticongelante 1 *adj* antifreeze. **2** *nm* antifreeze (solution).

anticontaminante *adj* anti-pollution.

anticorrosivo *adj* anticorrosive, antirust.

anticonstitucional *adj* unconstitutional.

anticonstitucionalidad *nf* unconstitutionality.

anticristo *nm* Antichrist.

anticuado *adj* antiquated, old-fashioned, out-of-date; obsolete.

anticuario 1 *adj* antiquarian. **2** *nm*, **anticuaria** *nf* (*erudito etc*) antiquarian, antiquary; (*Com*) antique dealer.

anticuarse [1d] *vr* to become antiquated, get out of date; to become obsolete.

anticucho *nm* (*And Culin*) (beef) kebab.

anticuerpo *nm* antibody.

antichoque(s) *adj invar*: **panel ~** shock-resistant panel.

antideportividad *nf* unsporting attitude, unsportsmanlike behaviour.

antideportivo *adj* unsporting, unsportsmanlike.

antidepresivo 1 *adj* antidepressant. **2** *nm* antidepressant (drug), stimulant.

antiderrapante *adj* non-skid.

antideslizante 1 *adj* non-slipping; (*Aut*) non-skid; *piso* non-slip. **2** *nm* (*LAm*) non-skid tyre.

antideslumbrante *adj* anti-dazzle, anti-glare.

antidetonante *adj* (*Aut*) antiknock.

antidisturbios *adj invar*: **policía ~** riot (control) police.

antidóping *adj*: **control ~** (anti-)drugs test, check for drugs.

antídoto *nm* antidote (*contra, de* against, for, to).

antidroga *adj invar*: **brigada ~** drug squad; **campaña ~** anti-drug campaign; **tratamiento ~** treatment for drug addiction.

antidúmping *adj invar* (*Com*): **medidas ~** antidumping measures, measures against dumping.

antiecológico *adj*: **producto ~** product damaging to the environment, environmentally unsafe product.

antieconómico *adj* uneconomic(al); wasteful.

antier *adv* (*LAm*) = **anteayer**.

antiestético *adj* unsightly, ugly, offensive.

antifascismo *nm* antifascism.

antifascista *adj, nmf* antifascist.

antifatiga *adj invar*: **píldora ~** anti-fatigue pill, pep pill*.

antifaz *nm* (**a**) mask; veil. (**b**) (‡) condom.

antifeminismo *nm* antifeminism.

antifeminista *adj, nmf* antifeminist.

antífona *nf* antiphony.

antifranquismo *nm* opposition to Franco.

antifranquista 1 *adj* anti-Franco. **2** *nmf* opponent of Franco, person opposed to Franco.

antifraude *adj invar*: **acción ~** action to combat fraud.

antifriccional *adj* antifriction.

antifrís *nm* (*LAm*) antifreeze (solution).

antigás *adj invar*: **careta ~** gasmask.

antigolpes *adj invar* shockproof.

Antígona *nf* Antigone.

antigripal *adj*: **vacuna ~** flu vaccine.

antigualla *nf* antique; (*pey*) old thing, relic, out-of-date object (*o* custom *etc*); (*cuento viejo*) old story; (*persona*) has-been, back number; (*trastos*) **~s** old things, junk.

antiguamente *adv* formerly, once; in ancient times, long ago.

antigüedad *nf* (**a**) (*Hist*) antiquity; **los artistas de la ~** the artists of antiquity, the artists of the ancient world; **alta ~, remota ~** high antiquity; **de toda ~** from time immemorial.

(**b**) (*edad*) antiquity, age; **la fábrica tiene una ~ de 200 años** the factory is 200 years old.
(**c**) (*objeto*) antique; **~es** antiques; antiquities; **tienda de ~es** antique shop.
(**d**) (*en escalofón*) (length of) service, seniority.
antiguerra *adj invar* anti-war.
antiguo 1 *adj* (**a**) (*viejo*) old; ancient; *coche etc* vintage, classic; **a la antigua** in the ancient manner, in the old-fashioned way; **de ~** from time immemorial, since ancient times; **en lo ~** in olden times, in ancient times.
(**b**) (*de antes*) former, old, one-time; **un ~ alumno mío** an old pupil of mine; **~ primer ministro** former prime minister.
(**c**) (*de rango*) **más ~** senior; **socio más ~** senior partner; **es más ~ que yo** he is senior to me, he is my senior.
2 *nmpl*: **los ~s** the ancients.
antihéroe *nm* antihero.
antihigiénico *adj* unhygienic, insanitary.
antihistamínico *adj, nm* antihistamine.
antihumano *adj* inhuman.
antiincendios *adj invar*: **equipo ~** fire-fighting team; **servicio ~** fire-fighting service.
antiinflacionista *adj* anti-inflationary.
antilogaritmo *nm* antilogarithm.
antilógico *adj* illogical.
antílope *nm* antelope.
antillanismo *nm* word (*o* phrase *etc*) peculiar to the Antilles.
antillano 1 *adj* West Indian, of the Antilles. **2** *nm*, **antillana** *nf* West Indian, native (*o* inhabitant) of the Antilles; **los ~s** the West Indians.
Antillas *nfpl* Antilles, West Indies; **el mar de las ~** the Caribbean (Sea).
antimacasar *nm* antimacassar.
antimanchas *adj invar*: **superficie ~** stain-resistant surface.
antimateria *nf* antimatter.
antimísil 1 *adj invar* antimissile; **mísil ~** antimissile missile. **2** *nm* antimissile.
antimonio *nm* antimony.
antimonopolio *adj invar*: **ley ~** anti-trust law.
antinatural *adj* unnatural.
antiniebla *adj invar*: **luz ~** fog-lamp.
antinomia *nf* antinomy, conflict of authority.
antinuclear *adj* antinuclear.
Antioquía *nf* Antioch.
antioxidante *adj* antirust.
antipalúdico *adj* antimalarial.
antipara *nf* screen.
antiparabólico* *adj* (*Carib*) wild, over the top.
antiparasitario 1 *adj* antiparasitic. **2** *nm* antiparasitic drug.
antiparras* *nfpl* glasses, specs*.
antipatía *nf* antipathy (*hacia* towards, *entre* between), dislike (*hacia* for); unfriendliness (*hacia* towards).
antipático *adj* disagreeable, unpleasant, antipathetic; uncongenial; **es un tipo ~** he's a disagreeable sort; **me es muy ~** I don't like him at all; **es de lo más ~** he's horrible; **en un ambiente ~** in an uncongenial atmosphere, in an unfriendly environment.
antipatizar [1f] *vi* (*LAm*) to feel unfriendly; **~ con uno** to dislike sb.
antipatriótico *adj* unpatriotic.
antiperras *nfpl* (*And*) half-moon glasses (*o* spectacles).
antípodas *nmpl* antipodes.
antipolilla *adj invar* mothproof.
antiproteccionista *adj* antiprotectionist, free-trade (*atr*).
antiproyectil *adj invar* antimissile.
antiquista (*Méx*) **1** *adj* antiquarian. **2** *nmf* antiquarian, antique dealer.
antirrábico *adj*: **vacuna antirrábica** anti-rabies vaccine.
antirracista *adj, nmf* anti-racist.
antirreglamentario *adj* illegal, unlawful; (*Dep*) foul.
antirresbaladizo *adj* (*Aut*) non-skid.
antirrino *nm* antirrhinum.
antirrobo 1 *adj invar*: **sistema ~** anti-theft system. **2** *nm* anti-theft device.
antisemita *nmf* anti-Semite.
antisemítico *adj* anti-Semitic.
antisemitismo *nm* anti-Semitism.
antiséptico *adj, nm* antiseptic.
antisocial *adj* antisocial.
antisudoral (*LAm*) *adj, nm* deodorant.
antitabaco *adj invar*: **campaña ~** anti-smoking campaign.
antitanque *adj invar* antitank.
antiterrorista *adj*: **medidas ~s** measures against terrorism; **Ley A~** ≃ Prevention of Terrorism Act.
antítesis *nf invar* antithesis.
antitético *adj* antithetic(al).
antivaho *adj invar*: **dispositivo ~** demister, demisting device.
antiviviseccionista *nmf* antivivisectionist.
antivuelco *adj invar*: **barra ~** anti-roll bar.
antofagastino (*Cono Sur*) **1** *adj* of Antofagasta. **2** *nm*, **antofagastina** *nf* native (*o* inhabitant) of Antofagasta; **los ~s** the people of Antofagasta.
antojadizo *adj* capricious; given to sudden fancies, given to whims, unpredictable.
antojado *adj*: **~ con, ~ por** taken by, hankering after; craving for.
antojarse [1a] *vr* (**a**) **~ algo** to take a fancy to sth, want sth.
(**b**) **~ que** ... to imagine that ..., fancy that ..., have a hunch that ...; **se me antoja que no estará** I have the feeling that he won't be in.
(**c**) **~** + *infin* to have a mind to + *infin*; **se me antoja comprarlo** I have a mind to buy it, I fancy buying it; **se le antojó ir al cine** he took it into his head to go to the cinema; **no se le antojó decir otra cosa** it didn't occur to him to say anything else; **no se le antoja ir** he doesn't feel like going; **¿cómo se le antoja esto?** how does this seem to you?
antojitos *nmpl* (*Cono Sur* ††) sweets, candy (*US*); (*Méx*) snacks, nibbles.
antojo *nm* (**a**) (*capricho*) caprice, whim, passing fancy, notion; **cada uno a su ~** each to his own; **hacer a su ~** to do as one pleases; **¿cuál es su ~?** what's your idea?; **no morirse de ~** (*Cono Sur*) to satisfy a whim.
(**b**) (*de embarazada*) craving; **tener ~s** to have (pregnancy) cravings.
(**c**) (*Anat*) birthmark, strawberry mark; mole.
antología *nf* anthology.
antológica *nf* (*Arte*) selective exhibition.
antológico *adj*: **exposición antológica** (*Arte*) selective exhibition; **un gol ~** a goal for the history books, a goal that will go down in history.
antónimo *nm* antonym.
Antonio *nm* Anthony.
antonomasia *nf* antonomasia; **por ~** par excellence.
antorcha *nf* torch; (*fig*) torch, lamp.
antracita *nf* anthracite.
ántrax *nm* anthrax.
antro *nm* cavern; **~ de corrupción** (*fig*) den of iniquity.
antropofagía *nf* cannibalism.
antropófago 1 *adj* man-eating, anthropophagous; cannibalistic. **2** *nm* **antropófaga** *nf* cannibal; **~s** anthropophagi.
antropoide *adj* anthropoid.
antropoideo *nm* anthropoid.
antropología *nf* anthropology; **~ social** social anthropology.
antropológico *adj* anthropological.
antropólogo, -a *nm/f* anthropologist.
antropomorfismo *nm* anthropomorphism.
antruejo *nm* carnival (*3 days before Lent*).
antucá *nm* (*Cono Sur*) sunshade, parasol.
antuviada *nf* sudden blow, bump.
antuvión *nm* sudden blow, bump; **de ~** suddenly, unexpectedly.
anual *adj, nm* (*Bot*) annual.
anualidad *nf* (**a**) (*Fin*) annuity; annual payment. (**b**) (*suceso*) annual occurrence.
anualizado *adj* (*Fin*) annual; calculated on a yearly basis.
anualmente *adv* annually, yearly.
anuario *nm* (*gen*) yearbook; annual; (*Com*) trade directory; (*manual*) reference book, handbook; **~ militar** military list; **~ telefónico** telephone directory.
anubarrado *adj* cloudy, overcast.
anublar [1a] **1** *vt* (**a**) *cielo* to cloud (over); (*oscurecer*) to dim, darken, obscure. (**b**) (*Bot*) to blight; to wither, dry up. **2 anublarse** *vr* (**a**) (*oscurecer*) to cloud over, become cloudy, become overcast; (*cielo*) to darken, get dark. (**b**) (*Bot*) to wither, dry up; (*fig*) to fade away.
anudar [1a] **1** *vt* (*atar*) to knot, tie; (*unir*) to join, link, unite; *cuento* to resume, take up again; *voz* to choke, strangle.
2 anudarse *vr* (**a**) (*enmarañarse*) to get into knots, get tied up.

(**b**) (*Bot*) to remain stunted.

(**c**) **se me anudó la voz** (**en la garganta**) I got a lump in my throat.

anuencia *nf* approval, agreement, consent.

anuente *adj* consenting, consentient.

anulación *nf* annulment, cancellation; revocation, repeal.

anular[1] [1a] **1** *vt* (*gen*) to annul, cancel; *decisión etc* to overrule, override; *ley* to revoke, repeal; *efecto* to nullify, cancel out; *gol* to disallow; (*Mat*) to cancel out; *persona* to deprive of authority, remove from office; **~ el tiempo** to put the clock back.

2 anularse *vr* (*persona*) to lose one's identity; to renounce everything.

anular[2] **1** *adj* ring-shaped, annular; **dedo ~ = 2. 2** *nm* ring finger.

anunciación *nf* announcement; **A~** (*Rel*) Annunciation; (**día de**) **la A~** the Annunciation, Lady Day (*25 March*).

anunciador *nm* announcer; (*Teat*) compère; (*Méx Rad*) announcer.

anunciante *nmf* (*Com*) advertiser.

anunciar [1b] **1** *vt* (*gen*) to announce; (*proclamar*) to proclaim; (*augurar*) to forebode, foreshadow; (*Com*) to advertise; **no nos anuncia nada bueno** it augurs ill for us, it bodes ill for us.

2 anunciarse *vr*: **el festival se anuncia animado** the festival looks like being lively, everything points to the festival being a lively one; **la cosecha se anuncia buena** the crop promises to be a good one.

anuncio *nm* (**a**) (*gen*) announcement; (*presagio*) sign, omen; (*aviso*) notice.

(**b**) (*Com etc*) advertisement; (*cartel*) placard, poster; (*Teat etc*) bill; **~s breves, ~s económicos, ~s por palabras** classified advertisements, small advertisements; **~ luminoso** illuminated sign; **~ a página completa** full-page advertisement; **~ de trabajo** job advertisement.

anuo *adj* annual.

anverso *nm* obverse.

anzuelo *nm* hook, fish hook; (*fig*) bait, lure; **echar el ~** to offer a bait, offer an inducement; **picar en el ~, tragar el ~** (*fig*) to swallow the bait, be taken in, fall for it.

añada *nf* (*Agr*) (**a**) (*año*) year, season. (**b**) (*trozo de campo*) piece of field, strip.

añadido 1 *adj* added; additional, extra; **lo ~** what is added. **2** *nm* false hair, switch, hairpiece.

añadidura *nf* addition, extra, thing added; (*Com*) extra measure, extra weight; **dar algo de ~** to give sth extra; **con algo de ~** with sth else, with sth into the bargain; **por ~** besides, in addition; on top of all that.

añadir [3a] *vt* to add (*a* to); to increase; *encanto, interés etc* to add, lend (*a* to).

añagaza *nf* (*Caza*) lure, decoy; (*fig*) lure, bait, inducement.

añal 1 *adj* (**a**) *suceso* yearly, annual. (**b**) (*Agr*) year-old. **2** *nm* year-old animal, yearling.

añangá *nm* (*Cono Sur*) the devil.

añango (*And*) **1** *adj niño* sickly. **2** *nm* small portion.

añañay* *interj* (*Cono Sur*) great!* super!*

añapar [1a] *vt* (*LAm*) to smash to bits.

añar *nm* (*LAm*): **hace ~es que ...** it's ages since ...

añascar [1g] *vt* to scrape together, get together bit by bit.

añaz *nm* (*And*) skunk.

añeja* *nf* (*Carib*) old lady*, mum*.

añejar [1a] **1** *vt* to age. **2 añejarse** *vr* to age, get old; (*vino*) to age, improve with age, mellow; (*pey*) to get stale, go musty.

añejo *adj* old; *vino* mellow, mature; (*pey*) stale, musty.

añicos *nmpl* bits, pieces, fragments; splinters; **hacer un papel ~** to tear a piece of paper into little bits; **hacer un vaso ~** to smash a glass, shatter a glass; **hacerse ~** to shatter, smash to pieces; **hacerse ~** (*fig*) to wear o.s. out.

añil *nm* **1** (*Bot*) indigo; (*color*) indigo, indigo blue; (*para lavar*) blue, bluing. **2** *adj invar* blue.

añilar [1a] *vt* to dye indigo; *ropa* to blue.

añinos *nmpl* lamb's wool.

año *nm* (**a**) (*gen*) year; **~ bisiesto** leap year; **~ civil, ~ común** calendar year; **el ~ 66 de Cristo** 66 AD; **~ económico** financial year, fiscal year; **~ escolar** school year; **~ fiscal** tax year; **~ de gracia** year of grace; **~ lectivo** school year; **~ luz** light-year; **100 ~s luz** 100 light-years; **~ natural** calendar year; **A~ Nuevo** New Year; **¡feliz ~ nuevo!** happy new year!; **día de A~ Nuevo** New Year's Day; **~ presupuestario** budget year, financial year; **~ de nuestra salud** year of Our Lord; **~ sabático** sabbatical year; **el ~ verde** (*LAm*) never; **los 40 ~s, los ~s difíciles, los ~s negros** (*Esp*) the Franco years (*1936-75*); **el ~ pasado** last year; **el ~ antepasado** the year before last; **el ~ entrante, el ~ próximo** next year; **¡mal ~ para él!** good riddance to him!, and the best of luck! (*iró*); **hace ~s** years ago; **esperamos ~s y ~s** we waited years and years; **5 toneladas al ~** 5 tons a year; **al ~ de casado** a year after his marriage, after he had been married a year; **una cosa del ~ uno** (*o* **catapún** *o* **de la pera** *o* **de la quica** *etc*) something from the year dot; **estar de buen ~** to look well-fed, be in good shape; (*****: *mujer*) to be a bit of all right‡; **en el ~ 1980** in 1980; **en los ~s 60 y 70** in the sixties and seventies; **en estos últimos ~s** in recent years, of late years; **en el ~ de la nana** (*o* **nanita** *o* **polca**) in the year dot, way back; **por los ~s de 1950** about 1950; **¡por muchos ~s!** (*brindis*) here's health!, (*cumpleaños*) many happy returns!; (*presentación*) how do you do?; **dentro de cien ~s, todos calvos** it will all be the same in a hundred years, it won't matter in the long run.

(**b**) **~s** (*de persona*) age, years; **cumplir los 21 ~s** to reach 21, have one's 21st birthday; **cumplir ~s** to have a birthday; **¿cuántos ~s tienes?** how old are you?; **tengo 9 ~s** I'm 9; **con los ~s que yo tengo** at my age; (**nunca**) **en los ~s que tengo** never before, never in my life; **de pocos ~s** young, small; **entrado en ~s** elderly, advanced in years; **quitarse ~s** to lie about one's age; **A le saca muchos ~s a B** A is much older than B.

añojal *nm* land alternatively cultivated and left fallow.

añojo, -a *nm/f* yearling.

añorante *adj* yearning, longing; nostalgic; affectionate.

añoranza *nf* longing, yearning (*de* for); hankering (*de* after); nostalgia (*de* for); sense of loss, regret (*de* for).

añorar [1a] **1** *vt* to long for, yearn for, pine for, hanker after; *muerto* to grieve for; *pérdida* to mourn. **2** *vi* to yearn, pine, grieve; to feel nostalgia, be homesick.

añoso *adj* aged, full of years.

añublar(se) [1a] = **anublar**(**se**).

añublo *nm* blight, mildew.

añudar [1a] = **anudar**.

añusgar [1h] **1** *vi* to choke; (*fig*) to get angry. **2 añusgarse** *vr* to get cross.

aojada *nf* (*And*) skylight.

aojar [1a] *vt* to put the evil eye on; to bewitch.

aojo *nm* evil eye, hoodoo; sorcery, witchcraft.

aoristo *nm* (*Ling*) aorist.

aorta *nf* aorta.

aovado *adj* oval, egg-shaped.

aovar [1a] *vi* to lay eggs.

aovillarse [1a] *vr* to roll o.s. into a ball, curl up.

AP *nf* (*Esp Pol Hist*) *abr de* **Alianza Popular.**

Ap. *nm abr de* **apartado de correos** Post Office Box, POB.

APA *nf abr de* **Asociación de Padres de Alumnos** = Parent-Teacher Association, PTA.

apa[1] *interj* (*Méx*) good God!; goodness me!

apa[2] *interj* (*ánimo*) cheer up!; (*levántate*) get up!; (*recógelo*) pick it up!; (*basta*) that's enough!

apa[3]: **al ~** *adv* (*Cono Sur*) *llevar etc* on one's back.

apabullante *adj* shattering, crushing, overwhelming.

apabullar [1a] *vt* to crush, flatten, squash (*t fig*).

apacentadero *nm* pasture, pasture land.

apacentar [1j] **1** *vt* (**a**) (*Agr*) to pasture, graze, feed.

(**b**) (*fig*) *discípulo etc* to teach, minister to; *intelecto* to feed, give food for thought to, nourish; *pasión* to gratify, pander to; *deseo* to satisfy, minister to.

2 apacentarse *vr* (**a**) (*Agr*) to graze, feed.

(**b**) (*fig*) to feed (*con, de* on).

apacibilidad *nf* gentleness, mildness; even temper, peaceable nature; calmness, quietness.

apacible *adj* gentle, mild; *temperamento* gentle, even, peaceable; *tiempo* mild, calm, quiet; *viento* gentle.

apaciblemente *adv* gently, mildly; peaceably.

apaciguador *adj* pacifying, calming, soothing.

apaciguamiento *nm* appeasement (*t Pol*), pacifying, calming.

apaciguar [1i] **1** *vt* to pacify, appease, mollify; to calm down; (*Pol*) to appease. **2 apaciguarse** *vr* to calm down, quieten down.

apache *nm* Apache (Indian); (*Esp fig*) apache, street ruffian, thug.

apacheta *nf* (**a**) (*And, Cono Sur*) (*Rel*) grotto, wayside shrine. (**b**) (*montón*) pile, heap. (**c**) (*Pol*) (political) clique; (*confabulación*) ring, gang. (**d**) (*Com*) ill-gotten gains; **hacer la ~*** to make one's pile*.

apachico *nm* (*LAm*) bundle.

apachurrar [1a] *vt* to crush, squash.

apadrinamiento *nm* sponsorship; patronage; (*fig*) back-

ing, support.
apadrinar [1a] *vt empresa* to sponsor, back; (*Dep*) to sponsor; *artista etc* to be a patron to; (*Ecl*) *niño* to act as godfather to; *novio* to be best man for; *duelista* to act as second to; (*fig*) to back, support, favour.
apadronarse [1a] *vr* to register (as a resident).
apagadizo *adj* slow to burn, difficult to ignite.
apagado 1 *adj* (**a**) *volcán* extinct; *cal* slaked; **estar ~** (*fuego etc*) to be out; (*luz, radio*) to be off.
(**b**) *sonido* muted, muffled, dull; *voz* quiet, timid.
(**c**) *color* dull, quiet, lustreless, lifeless; *persona, temperamento* listless, spiritless, colourless; *mirada* lifeless.
2 *nm* switching-off; **botón de ~** off button, off switch.
apagador *nm* (**a**) (*extintor*) extinguisher. (**b**) (*Mec*) silencer, muffler; (*Mús*) damper; (*Cono Sur, Méx Elec*) switch.
apagafuegos 1 *adj invar*: **avión ~** fire-fighting plane. **2** *nm* (**a**) fire-fighting plane. (**b**) (*persona*) trouble-shooter.
apagar [1h] **1** *vt* (**a**) *fuego* to put out, extinguish, quench; *luz* to put out, turn off, switch off; *radio etc* to switch off; *vela* to snuff; (*And, Carib*) *arma de fuego* to empty, discharge; *cal* to slake; *sed* to quench, slake.
(**b**) *sonido* to silence, muffle, deaden; (*Mús*) to mute, damp.
(**c**) *color* to dull, tone down, soften.
(**d**) *afecto, dolor etc* to kill; *ira etc* to calm, soothe.
2 apagarse *vr* (**a**) (*fuego*) to go out; (*luz*) to go out, be put out; (*volcán*) to become extinct; (*vida*) to end, come to an end; **antes de que el año se apague** before the year ends.
(**b**) (*sonido*) to die away, cease.
(**c**) (*ira etc*) to calm down, subside.
(**d**) (*persona*) to pass away.
apagavelas *nm invar* candle-snuffer.
apagón *nm* blackout; (*Elec*) power cut, electricity failure, outage; **~ informativo, ~ de noticias** news blackout.
apagoso *adj* (*LAm*) = **apagadizo**.
apaisado *adj* oblong; squat, flattened.
apajarado *adj* (*Cono Sur*) daft, scatterbrained.
apalabrar [1a] **1** *vt* (**a**) (*convenir en*) to agree to; **estar apalabrado** to be committed, have given one's word. (**b**) (*encargar*) to bespeak; (*contratar*) to engage. **2 apalabrarse** *vr* to come to a verbal agreement (*con* with).
apalabrear [1a] (*LAm*) = **apalabrar**.
Apalaches *nmpl*: **Montes ~** Appalachians.
apalancado* *adj* settled, established.
apalancamiento *nm* leverage.
apalancar [1g] **1** *vt* (**a**) (*levantar*) to lever up, move (*o* lift *etc*) with a crowbar. (**b**) (*fig*) to support; (*Cono Sur**) **~ a uno** to wangle a job for sb*. (**c**) (*guardar*) to keep; (*esconder*) to hide, stash away. **2** *vi* (‡) (*esconderse*) to hide; (*dormirse*) to settle down, kip down‡; (*encontrar lugar*) to find a place. **3 apalancarse*** *vr* to sit down, squat*; to settle in, establish o.s.
apalé *interj* (*Méx*) (**a**) (*sorpresa*) goodness me! (**b**) (*aviso*) look out!, watch it!
apaleada *nf* (*Cono Sur, Méx Agr*) winnowing.
apaleamiento *nm* beating, thrashing.
apalear [1a] *vt animal, persona* to beat, thrash; *tapiz* to beat; (*Agr*) to winnow; **~ oro, ~ plata** to be rolling in money.
apaleo *nm* (*Agr*) winnowing.
apalizar* [1f] *vt* to beat up*.
apallar [1a] *vt* (*And*) to harvest.
apamparse [1a] *vr* (*Cono Sur*) to become bewildered; to lose one's grip.
apanado 1 *adj* (*LAm*) breaded, cooked in breadcrumbs. **2** *nm* (*And*) beating.
apanalado *adj* honeycombed.
apanar [1a] *vt* (*LAm Culin*) to cover in breadcrumbs.
apancle *nm* (*Méx*) irrigation ditch.
apandar‡ [1a] *vt* to rip off‡, knock off‡.
apandillar [1a] **1** *vt* to form into a gang. **2 apandillarse** *vr* to gang up, form a gang, band together.
apandorgarse [1h] *vr* (*And*) to lose heart, get scared.
apanicar* [1g] *vt* (*Cono Sur*) to cause panic in, frighten.
apani(a)guarse [1i] *vr* (*And, Carib*) to gang up.
apantallado *adj* (*Méx*) (*impresionado*) impressed, overwhelmed; (*achatado*) overwhelmed, crushed; **quedar ~** to be left open-mouthed.
apantallar[1] [1a] *vt* to screen, shield.
apantallar[2] [1a] *vt* (*Méx*) (*impresionar*) to impress; to fill with wonder; (*achatar*) to crush, overwhelm.
apantanar [1a] *vt* to flood, make boggy, make swampy.
apañadito* *adj* neat, tidy; controlled, well-organized.
apañado *adj* (**a**) (*mañoso*) skilful, clever, handy. (**b**) (*conveniente*) suitable (*para* for). (**c**) (*) **estar ~** (*borracho*) to be tight*; **¡estás ~!*** you've had it!*; you don't have a chance!; **estar ~ para hacer algo** to have difficulty in doing sth; **estoy ~ si lo hago** I'll be in trouble if I do it; **están ~s** they're mistaken, they've got it all wrong; **~s estaríamos si confiáramos en eso** we'd be fools if we relied on that. (**d**) **los hijos quedarán bien ~s** the children will be well provided for.
apañador(a) *nm/f* (**a**) (*Dep*) catcher. (**b**) (*) fixer*.
apañar [1a] **1** *vt* (**a**) (*asir*) to take hold of, grasp, seize; (*recoger*) to pick up; (*) to pinch*.
(**b**) (*vestir*) to dress, dress up; (*envolver*) to wrap up; (*remendar*) to mend, patch up; (*arreglar*) to fix up.
(**c**) (*Cono Sur*) *crimen* to conceal, cover up; *criminal* to harbour, hide.
2 apañarse *vr* (**a**) (*ser diestro*) to be skilful, be clever; **~ para** + *infin* to contrive to + *infin*, manage to + *infin*; **apañárselas (por su cuenta)** to fend for o.s., get along without help; to manage, find a way; **apañaos como podáis** manage as best you can.
(**b**) (*Cono Sur*) **~ algo** to get one's hands on sth, get hold of sth.
apaño *nm* (**a**) (*remiendo*) patch, mend; (*fig*) fix*; shady deal, put-up job*; fiddle*, piece of juggling (with figures *etc*); **esto no tiene ~** there's no answer to this one. (**b**) (*destreza*) skill, knack, dexterity; (*pey*) craft, guile. (**c**) (‡: *amorío*) affair. (**d**) (‡: *amante*: *t* **apaña** *f*) lover.
apañuscar* [1g] *vt* (**a**) (*ajar*) to rumple; (*aplastar*) to crush. (**b**) (*: *robar*) to pinch*, steal.
apapachar [1a] *vt* (*Carib*: *abrazar*) to cuddle, hug; (*mimar*) to spoil.
apapachos *nmpl* (*Méx*) (*abrazos*) hugs, cuddles; (*caricias*) caresses.
aparador *nm* (*mueble*) sideboard; (*vitrina*) showcase; (*escaparate*) shop window; (*Téc*) workshop; **estar de ~** to be dressed up to receive visitors.
aparadorista *nmf* (*Méx*) window dresser.
aparar [1a] *vt* (**a**) (*disponer*) to arrange, prepare. (**b**) *manos etc* to stretch out (*to catch sth*). (**c**) (*Agr*) to weed, clean.
aparatarse [1a] *vr* (*And, Cono Sur*): **se aparata** it's brewing up for a storm, there's a storm coming.
aparatejo *nm* gadget.
aparato *nm* (**a**) (*Quím, Fís etc*) apparatus, piece of apparatus; (*Mec*) machine; device; piece of equipment; (*Rad, TV*) set, receiver; (*Telec*) instrument, handset; (*Aer*) machine; (*doméstico*) appliance; (*Fot*) apparatus, piece of equipment; (*Med*) dressing, bandage; surgical appliance; (*Teat*) properties; (*Anat*) system; **~ de afeitar** safety razor; **~ antirrobo** anti-theft device; **~ auditivo** hearing aid; **~ circulatorio** circulation, circulatory system; **~ crítico** (*Liter*) critical apparatus; **~ eléctrico** (*Met*) display of lightning, electrical storm; **~ de escucha** listening device; **~ fotográfico** camera; **~ lector de microfilms** microfilm reader; **~s de mando** (*Aer etc*) controls; **~ de oído** hearing aid; **~ periférico** peripheral device; **~s de pescar** fishing tackle; **~ de relojería** clockwork mechanism; **~ respiratorio** respiratory system; **~s sanitarios** bathroom fittings; **~ para sordos** hearing aid; **~ de televisión** television set; **~ para filmar, ~ tomavistas** cine-camera; **~ de uso doméstico** domestic appliance; **tengo a X en el ~** I have X on the line.
(**b**) (*boato*) display, show, ostentation; **de mucho ~** spectacular; **sin ~** unostentatiously, without ceremony, without fuss.
(**c**) (*indicios*) signs, symptoms; (*Med*) symptoms; (*Psic*) syndrome.
(**d**) (*Pol*) machine; **~ electoral** electoral machine; **~ del partido** party machine.
(**e**) (**‡) (*pene*) prick**‡; (*vagina*) cunt**‡.
aparatosamente *adv* showily, ostentatiously; pretentiously; in a spectacular way.
aparatosidad *nf* showiness, ostentation; pretentiousness; spectacular character.
aparatoso *adj* (*vistoso*) showy, ostentatious; (*exagerado*) exaggerated, pretentious; *caída, función* spectacular.
aparcacoches *nm invar* car-park attendant, parking valet.
aparcadero *nm* parking lot.
aparcamento *nm* (*CAm, Carib*), **aparcamiento** *nm* (**a**) (*acto*) parking; **~ en doble fila** double parking. (**b**) (*lugar*) car-park, parking lot (*US*), parking place; (*apartadero*) lay-by; **~ subterráneo** underground car-park.
aparcar [1g] **1** *vt* (*Aut*) to park; (*Parl**) *proyecto de ley* to

shelve; *idea* to put on the back burner. **2** *vi* to park.

aparcería *nf* (*Com*) partnership; (*Agr*) share-cropping; (*Cono Sur*) comradeship, friendship; kinship.

aparcero, -a *nm/f* (*Com*) co-owner, partner; (*Agr*) share-cropper; (*Cono Sur*) comrade, friend; (*hombre*) kinsman, (*mujer*) kinswoman.

apareamiento *nm* (**a**) (*emparejamiento*) matching; levelling. (**b**) (*emparejarse*) mating, pairing.

aparear [1a] **1** *vt* (**a**) (*emparejar*) to pair, match; (*nivelar*) to level up. (**b**) *animales* to mate, pair.

2 aparearse *vr* (**a**) to form a pair, go together. (**b**) (*animales*) to mate, pair.

aparecer [2d] *vi*, **aparecerse** *vr* (*gen*) to appear; (*presentarse*) to show up, turn up; (*revelarse*) to come into sight; to loom up; (*libro*) to come out; (*fantasma*) to appear, walk; **apareció borracho** he turned up drunk; **allí aparecen fantasmas** the place is haunted; **no ha aparecido el libro ese** that book still hasn't shown up; **Nuestra Señora se apareció a Bernadette** Our Lady appeared to Bernadette.

aparecido, -a *nm/f* ghost.

aparejado *adj* (**a**) fit, suitable, ready (*para* for). (**b**) **llevar** (*o* **traer**) **algo** ~ to entail sth.

aparejador *nm* foreman, overseer; (*Arquit*) master builder; quantity surveyor; (*Náut*) rigger.

aparejar [1a] **1** *vt* to prepare, get ready; *caballo* to saddle, harness; (*Náut*) to fit out, rig out; (*antes de pintar*) to size, prime.

2 aparejarse *vr* (**a**) (*prepararse*) to get ready; (*equiparse*) to equip o.s..

(**b**) (*CAm, Carib*) to mate, pair.

aparejo *nm* (**a**) (*acto*) preparation.

(**b**) (*avíos*) gear, equipment, tackle.

(**c**) (*Náut*) rigging; rig, type of rig.

(**d**) (*para levantar*) lifting gear, tackle, block and tackle; (*Náut*) tackle, derrick.

(**e**) (*Pesca*) tackle; ~ **de anzuelos** set of hooks.

(**f**) (*Arquit*) bond, bonding.

(**g**) (*de caballo*) (*arreos*) harness; (*CAm, Méx*: *silla*) saddle; (*And*) woman's saddle.

(**h**) (*antes de pintar*) sizing, priming.

(**i**) ~**s** gear, equipment, tools, kit.

aparellaje *nm* control gear.

aparencial *adj* apparent.

aparentar [1a] **1** *vt* (**a**) (*fingir*) to feign, affect.

(**b**) *edad* to look, seem to be; **ella no aparenta sus años** she doesn't look her age.

(**c**) ~ + *infin* to feign to + *infin*, pretend to + *infin*, make as if to + *infin*.

2 *vi* to show off, make a show.

aparente *adj* (**a**) (*que parece*) apparent, seeming; (*pey*) unreal; deceptive. (**b**) (*evidente*) visible, evident; outward. (**c**) (*conveniente*) fit, suitable, proper. (**d**) (*: *atractivo*) attractive, smart; eye-catching; (*pey*) flashy.

aparentemente *adv* (**a**) (*según parece*) seemingly. (**b**) (*evidentemente*) visibly, outwardly.

aparición *nf* (**a**) (*acto*) appearance; publication; ~ **en público** public appearance; **un libro de próxima** ~ a book soon to be published, a forthcoming book. (**b**) (*aparecido*) apparition, spectre.

apariencia *nf* (**a**) (*aspecto*) appearance, aspect, look(s).

(**b**) (*exterior*) outward appearance, semblance; **en** ~ outwardly, seemingly; **por todas las** ~**s** to all appearances; **juzgar por las** ~**s** to judge by appearances; **cubrir** ~**s, salvar las** ~**s** to keep up appearances, save one's face; **las** ~**s engañan** appearances are deceptive.

(**c**) (*probabilidad*) probability.

aparragado (*Cono Sur*) **1** *adj* stunted, dwarfish. **2** *nm* dwarf.

aparragarse [1h] *vr* (**a**) (*CAm*: *hacerse un ovillo*) to roll up, curl up.

(**b**) (*Cono Sur*: *agacharse*) to squat, crouch down.

(**c**) (*CAm, Cono Sur, Méx*: *no crecer*) to remain stunted, stay small; (*encogerse*) to shrink, grow small.

apartadero *nm* (*Aut*) lay-by; (*Ferro*) siding.

apartadijo *nm* (**a**) (*porción*) small portion, bit. (**b**) = **apartadizo 2** .

apartadizo 1 *adj* unsociable. **2** *nm* recess, alcove, nook.

apartado 1 *adj* (*separado*) separated; (*remoto*) remote, isolated, out-of-the-way.

2 *nm* (**a**) (*cuarto*) spare room; side room.

(**b**) (*t* ~ **de correos,** ~ **postal**) post-office box; box number; ~ **de localidades** (*Teat*) ticket agency.

(**c**) (*Tip*) paragraph, section; heading.

(**d**) (*Metal*) extraction.

apartahotel *nm* aparthotel.

apartamento *nm* apartment, flat.

apartamiento *nm* (**a**) (*acto*) separation; withdrawal. (**b**) (*cualidad*) seclusion, remoteness, isolation; (*lugar*) secluded spot, remote area.

apartar [1a] **1** *vt* (*separar*) to separate, divide, take away (*de* from); (*quitar*) to remove, move away, put aside; (*Min*) to extract; (*Agr*) *ganado* to separate, cut out; (*Correos*) to sort; (*Ferro*) to shunt; (*Jur*) to set aside, waive; ~ **a uno para decirle algo** to take sb aside to tell him sth; ~ **a uno de un propósito** to dissuade sb from an intention; **lograron** ~ **la discusión de ese punto** they managed to turn the discussion away from that point; **el ministro le apartó del mando** the minister removed him from the command; ~ **un pensamiento de sí** to put a thought out of one's mind; **apartó el plato con la mano** he pushed his plate aside; **¿no podemos** ~**lo un poco más?** can't we move it a bit further away?

2 apartarse *vr* (**a**) (*dos personas*) to part, separate; (*dos cosas*) to become separated.

(**b**) (*retirarse*) to move away, withdraw, retire (*de* from); (*mantenerse aparte*) to keep away (*de* from), stand aside; **¡apártate!** out of the way!; ~ **de un camino** to turn off a road; to stray from a path; **nos hemos apartado bastante de la ruta** we've got rather a long way off the route; **el cohete se está apartando de la trayectoria** the rocket is deviating from the trajectory.

(**c**) (*Jur*) to withdraw from a suit.

aparte 1 *adv* (*gen*) apart, aside; (*por separado*) separately; (*además*) besides; (*Teat*) aside; **tendremos que considerar eso** ~ we shall have to consider that separately; **hacerle a uno** ~ to exclude sb; to ignore sb; **poner algo** ~ to put sth aside, put sth on one side; **ser algo** ~ to be something superior; **eso** ~ apart from that.

2 ~ **de** *prep* apart from; ~ **de eso** apart from that; ~ **de que** ... apart from the fact that ....

3 *nm* (**a**) (*Teat*) aside.

(**b**) (*Tip*) (new) paragraph; **'(punto y)** ~**'** (*al dictar*) 'new paragraph'.

(**c**) (*LAm Agr*) separation, sorting out.

aparthotel *nm* aparthotel.

apartidismo *nm* non-political nature, non-party character.

apartidista *adj* apolitical, non-party.

apasionadamente *adv* (**a**) (*con pasión*) passionately; intensely; fervently. (**b**) (*pey*) in a biassed way, partially.

apasionado 1 *adj* (**a**) (*gen*) passionate; *denuncia etc* impassioned; (*intenso*) intense, emotional; (*ardiente*) fervent, enthusiastic; ~ **a,** ~ **por** passionately fond of, passionately attached to.

(**b**) (*pey*) biassed, partial, prejudiced.

2 *nm*, **apasionada** *nf* admirer, devotee; **los** ~**s de Góngora** devotees of Góngora, Góngora enthusiasts.

apasionamiento *nm* (**a**) passion, enthusiasm; vehemence, intensity; great fondness (*de, por* for). (**b**) (*pey*) bias, partiality, prejudice.

apasionante *adj* exciting, thrilling.

apasionar [1a] **1** *vt* (**a**) (*entusiasmar*) to fill with passion; to stir deeply, make a strong appeal to; *amante* to stir, arouse; **me apasionan las gambas** I adore prawns, I can't resist prawns; **es una lectura que apasiona** it's stirring stuff to read; **es un estudio que apasiona** it's a fascinating study; **le apasiona el fútbol** he's crazy about football, he's football-mad.

(**b**) (*afligir*) to afflict, torment.

2 apasionarse *vr* (**a**) (*excitarse*) to get excited, be roused, work o.s. up; ~ **de,** ~ **por** *persona* to fall madly in love with; *cosa* to get mad about, enthuse over, become enthusiastic about.

(**b**) (*pey*) to become biassed, give way to prejudice.

apaste *nm*, **apaxte** *nm* (*CAm*) clay pot, clay jug.

apatía *nf* apathy; (*Med*) listlessness.

apático *adj* apathetic; (*Med*) listless.

apátrida 1 *adj* stateless; (*Cono Sur*: *sin patriotismo*) unpatriotic. **2** *nmf* (*Cono Sur*) unpatriotic person.

apatronarse [1a] *vr* (*And, Cono Sur*): ~ **de uno** (*amancebarse*) to find a protector in sb; (*buscar empleo*) to seek a domestic post with sb; (*And*: *cargarse*) to take charge of sb.

apatusco *nm* (**a**) (*adornos*) frills, adornments. (**b**) (*Carib*) (*enredo*) trick; (*fingimiento*) pretence; (*intrigas*) intrigue.

APD *nf* (*Esp*) *abr de* **Asistencia Pública Domiciliaria** (*social welfare organization*).

apdo. *nm abr de* **apartado de correos** Post Office Box, PO

Box.

apeadero *nm* (**a**) (*para montar*) mounting block, step. (**b**) (*parada*) halt, stopping place; (*Ferro*) halt, wayside station. (**c**) (*alojamiento*) temporary quarters, temporary lodging, pied-à-terre.

apear [1a] **1** *vt* (**a**) *persona* to help down, help to alight (*de* from); *objeto* to take down, get down (*de* from); *árbol* to fell; **quedar apeado** (*fig*‡) to be left behind.

(**b**) *caballo* to hobble; *rueda* to chock, scotch.

(**c**) (*Arquit*) to prop up.

(**d**) (*Agrimen*) to survey, measure; to mark the boundaries of.

(**e**) *problema* to solve, work out; *dificultad* to overcome.

(**f**) ~ **a uno de su opinión** to make sb give up his view, persuade sb that his opinion is wrong; ~ **a uno de un propósito** to wean sb away from an intention, make sb give up his plan.

(**g**) ~ **el tratamiento a uno** to drop sb's title, address sb without formality.

(**h**) (*: *despedir*) to dismiss, sack*; ~ **a uno de su cargo** to remove sb from his post.

(**i**) (*And*: *matar*) to kill.

(**j**) (*CAm*: *reprender*) to dress down*, tell off*.

2 apearse *vr* (**a**) to dismount; to get down, get out (*de* of), alight (*de* from); (*Ferro*) to get off, get out.

(**b**) ~ **en** to stay at, put up at.

(**c**) *V* **burro**.

(**d**) ~ **de algo** (*And*) to get rid of sth.

(**e**) **no apeársela** (*CAm*) to be drunk all the time.

apechugar [1h] **1** *vt* (**a**) (*Cono Sur*: *hacer frente a*) to face (up to) resolutely.

(**b**) (*Cono Sur, Carib*: *agarrar*) to grab (hold of), seize.

(**c**) (*And*: *sacudir*) to shake violently.

2 *vi* (**a**) (*) to push, shove; **¡apechuga!** buck up!, come on!

(**b**) ~ **con** to put up with, swallow; *cometido* to take on.

3 apechugarse *vr*: ~ **algo** (*CAm*) to snatch sth.

apechugón *nm* violent shake, violent shove.

apedazar [1f] *vt* (**a**) (*remendar*) to mend, patch. (**b**) (*despedazar*) to tear to pieces, cut into pieces.

apedrear [1a] **1** *vt* to stone, pelt with stones; to stone to death. **2** *vi* (**a**) (*Met*) to hail. (**b**) (*Méx*‡) to stink, reek. **3 apedrearse** *vr* to be damaged by hail.

apedreo *nm* (**a**) stoning, stone throwing; stoning to death. (**b**) (*Met*) hail; damage by hail.

apegadamente *adv* devotedly.

apegado *adj*: ~ **a** attached to, devoted to, fond of.

apegarse [1h] *vr*: ~ **a** to become attached to, grow fond of.

apego *nm*: ~ **a** attachment to, devotion to, fondness for.

apelable *adj* (*Jur*) appealable, that can be appealed against, subject to appeal.

apelación *nf* (**a**) (*Jur*) appeal; **sin** ~ without appeal, final; **interponer** ~ to appeal, lodge an appeal; **presentar su** ~ to present one's appeal; **ver una** ~ to consider an appeal.

(**b**) (*fig*) help, remedy; **no hay ~, esto no tiene** ~ it's a hopeless case.

apelante *nmf* appellant.

apelar [1a] *vi* (*Jur*) to appeal (*de* against); ~ **a** (*fig*) to resort to, have recourse to, call on.

apelativo *nm* (*Ling*) common noun; (*LAm*) group (*o* collective) name.

apeldar‡ [1a] *vt*: **~las** to beat it*.

apelmazado *adj masa* compact, compressed, solid; *pelo* matted; *líquido* thick, lumpy; *escritura* clumsy.

apelmazar [1f] **1** *vt* to compress, squeeze together; (*CAm*) to roll; to firm. **2 apelmazarse** *vr* to cake, solidify; to get lumpy.

apelotonar [1a] **1** *vt* to roll into a ball. **2 apelotonarse** *vr* (*animal etc*) to roll up, curl up; (*gente*) to mass, crowd together; (*sustancia*) to get lumpy.

apellidar [1a] **1** *vt* (**a**) (*llamar*) to name, surname, call. (**b**) ~ **a uno por rey** to proclaim sb king. **2 apellidarse** *vr* to be called, call o.s., have as a surname; **¿cómo se apellida Vd?** what is your (sur)name?

apellido *nm* name; surname, family name; (*apodo*) nickname; ~ **de soltera** maiden name.

apenado *adj* (*LAm*) (*avergonzado*) ashamed, embarrassed; (*triste*) sad, sorry; (*tímido*) shy, timid.

apenar [1a] **1** *vt* to grieve, upset, trouble; to cause pain to.

2 apenarse *vr* (**a**) (*afligirse*) to grieve, sorrow, distress o.s.; ~ **de algo,** ~ **por algo** to grieve about sth, distress o.s. on account of sth.

(**b**) (*LAm*) (*avergonzarse*) to feel embarrassed, feel ashamed; (*ser triste*) to be sorry, be sad; (*ser tímido*) to be shy; (*sonrojarse*) to blush; **no se apene, no tiene importancia** (*Méx*) don't worry, it doesn't matter.

apenas 1 *adv* hardly, scarcely; ~ **nada** hardly anything; ~ **nadie** hardly anybody; ~ **si pude levantarme** I could hardly get up.

2 *conj* (**a**) ~ **hube llegado cuando** ... no sooner had I arrived than ..., I had only just arrived when ...

(**b**) (*esp LAm*: *en cuanto*) as soon as; ~ **terminó se fue** as soon as it was over she left.

apencar‡ [1g] *vi* to slog, slave.

apendectomía *nf* appendectomy.

apendejarse [1a] *vr* (*Carib*) (*hacer el tonto*) to get silly, act the fool; (*acobardarse*) to lose one's nerve.

apéndice *nm* (*Anat*) appendix; (*fig*) appendage; (*Liter etc*) appendix, supplement; (*Jur*) schedule.

apendicitis *nf* appendicitis.

Apeninos *nmpl* Apennines.

apenitas *adv* (*And, Cono Sur*) = **apenas.**

apensionado *adj* (*And, Cono Sur, Méx*) depressed, sad; grieved.

apensionar [1a] **1** *vt* (*And, Cono Sur, Méx*) to sadden, grieve. **2 apensionarse** *vr* to become sad, get depressed.

apeñuscarse [1g] *vr* (*Cono Sur*) to crowd together.

apeo *nm* (**a**) (*Agrimen*) survey. (**b**) (*soporte*) prop, support; (*andamio*) scaffolding. (**c**) (*de árboles*) felling.

apeorar [1a] *vi* to get worse.

aperado *adj* (*Cono Sur*) well-equipped.

aperar [1a] **1** *vt* (**a**) (*Agr*) to make, repair, fit up.

(**b**) (*Cono Sur*) *caballo* to harness; ~ **a uno de herramientas** to provide sb with tools, fix sb up with tools.

2 aperarse *vr*: ~ **de algo** (*Cono Sur*) to equip o.s., provide o.s. with sth; **estar bien aperado para** to be well equipped for.

apercancarse [1g] *vr* (*Cono Sur*) to go mouldy.

apercibimiento *nm* (**a**) (*acto*) preparation; provision. (**b**) (*aviso*) warning, notice. (**c**) (*Jur*) warning.

apercibir [3a] **1** *vt* (**a**) (*preparar*) to prepare, make ready; (*proveer*) to furnish, provide; **con los fusiles apercibidos** with rifles at the ready.

(**b**) (*avisar*) to warn, advise.

(**c**) (*Jur*) to warn.

(**d**) (*LAm*: *darse cuenta*) to notice, observe, see.

(**e**) *error etc* = **percibir.**

2 apercibirse *vr* to prepare o.s., get ready (*para* for); ~ **de** to provide o.s. with; ~ **de** (*Cono Sur*) to notice, perceive.

apercollar [1l] *vt* (**a**) (*agarrar*) to seize by the neck. (**b**) (*matar*) to fell, kill (with a blow on the neck). (**c**) (‡: *detener*) to knock off‡, nick‡.

aperchar [1a] *vt* (*CAm, Cono Sur*) to pile up, stack up.

apergaminado *adj* parchment-like; *piel etc* dried up, wrinkled; *cara* wizened.

apergaminarse [1a] *vr* to get like parchment; (*piel etc*) to dry up, get yellow and wrinkled.

apergollar [1a] *vt* (*LAm*) (*agarrar*) to grab by the throat; (*engañar*) to trap, ensnare.

aperital *nm* (*Cono Sur*) = **aperitivo.**

aperitivo *nm* appetizer, snack; (*bebida*) aperitif.

apero *nm* (*colectivo*: *t* **~s**) tools, gear; equipment; (*Agr*) implement; (*LAm*: *arneses*) harness, trappings; (*LAm*: *silla*) saddle; (*Méx Agr*) (*animales*) ploughing team, draught animals; **~s** (*equipo*) plough and tackle, ploughing equipment.

aperrarse* [1a] *vr* (*Cono Sur*) to dig one's heels in.

aperreado†† *adj* wretched, miserable; **llevar una vida aperreada** to have a wretched life.

aperreador *adj* bothersome, tiresome.

aperrear [1a] **1** *vt* (**a**) (*lit*) to set the dogs on. (**b**) (*fig*) (*acosar*) to harass, plague; (*cansar*) to wear out, tire out.

2 aperrearse *vr* (**a**) (*ser acosado*) to get harassed; (*trabajar demasiado*) to slave away, overwork. (**b**) (*LAm*: *insistir*) to insist.

aperreo *nm* (**a**) (*problema*) harassment, worry; toil, overwork. (**b**) (*LAm*: *molestia*) nuisance; (*ira*) rage; **¡qué ~ de vida!** it's a dog's life!

apersogar [1h] *vt* to tether, tie up; (*Carib*) to string together.

apersonado *adj*: **bien** ~ presentable, nice-looking; **mal** ~ unattractive, unprepossessing, scruffy.

apersonarse [1a] *vr* to appear in person; to appear, come, show up; (*Com*) to have a business interview; (*Jur*) to appear.

apertura 1 *nf* (**a**) (*gen*) opening; (*de un testamento*) read-

ing; (*Pol*) openness, liberalization. (**b**) (*de texto*) opening, start. **2** *nm* (*Dep*) fly-half.
aperturar [1a] *vt* to open.
aperturismo *nm* liberalization; relaxation, loosening-up; (*Pol*) (policy of) liberalization.
aperturista 1 *adj tendencia etc* liberalizing, liberal. **2** *nmf* liberalizer, liberal.
apesadumbrado *adj* grieved, sad, distressed.
apesadumbrar [1a] **1** *vt* to grieve, sadden, distress. **2 apesadumbrarse** *vr* to grieve, be grieved, distress o.s. (*con, de* about, at).
apesarar(se) [1a] = **apesadumbrar(se)**.
apescollar [1l] *vt* (*Cono Sur*) to seize by the neck.
apesgar [1h] *vt* to weigh down, overburden.
apestado *adj* (**a**) (*LAm*: *maloliente*) stinking; (*Med*) infected with the plague. (**b**) **estar ~ de** to be infested with, be full of.
apestar [1a] **1** *vt* (**a**) (*Med*) to infect (with the plague).
(**b**) (*fig*: *corromper*) to corrupt, spoil, vitiate; (*molestar*) to plague, harass; (*repugnar*) to sicken, nauseate.
(**c**) (*olor*) to stink out.
2 *vi* to stink (*a* of).
3 apestarse *vr* (**a**) (*Med*) to catch the plague.
(**b**) (*LAm Bot*) to be blighted, get blight.
(**c**) (*And*: *resfriarse*) to catch a cold.
apestillar [1a] *vt* (*Cono Sur*) (**a**) (*agarrar*) to catch, grab hold of. (**b**) (*regañar*) to tell off, reprimand.
apestoso *adj* (**a**) (*lit*) stinking; *olor* awful, pestilential. (**b**) (*****) (*molesto*) annoying; (*repugnante*) sickening, nauseating.
apetachar [1a] *vt* to patch, mend.
apetecer [2d] **1** *vt* (**a**) (*desear*) to crave, long for, yearn for.
(**b**) (*esp Esp*: *atraer*) to appeal to, attract, take one's fancy; **me apetece un helado** I feel like an ice cream, I could manage an ice cream, the idea of an ice cream appeals to me; **me apetece ir** I should like to go; **¿te apetece?** how about it?
2 *vi* to attract, have an appeal, be welcome; **la idea no apetece** the idea has no appeal; **un vaso de jerez siempre apetece** a glass of sherry is always welcome.
apetecible *adj* attractive, tempting, desirable.
apetencia *nf* hunger, appetite; (*fig*) hunger, craving, desire (*de* for); inclination.
apetente *adj* hungry, yearning, craving.
APETI *nf abr de* **Asociación Profesional Española de Traductores e Intérpretes.**
apetite *nm* appetizer; (*fig*) incentive.
apetito *nm* (**a**) (*gen*) appetite (*de* for); **abrir el ~** to whet one's appetite; **quitar el ~ de** to destroy one's appetite for.
(**b**) (*fig*) desire, relish (*de* for).
apetitoso *adj* (**a**) (*gen*) appetizing; tasty, tempting; (*fig*) tempting, attractive. (**b**) *persona* fond of good food.
API *nmf abr de* **agente de la propiedad inmobiliaria** estate agent.
apí *nm* (**a**) (*And*) *a non-alcoholic maize drink.* (**b**) (*And, Cono Sur*: *añicos*) **el vaso se hizo ~** the glass was smashed to pieces.
apiadar [1a] **1** *vt* to move to pity. **2 apiadarse** *vr*: **~ de** to take pity on, express pity for, feel sorry for.
apiado *nm* (*Cono Sur*) celery liqueur.
apicarado *adj* roguish, mischievous.
apicararse [1a] *vr* to go to the bad, pick up dishonest ways.
ápice *nm* (**a**) (*cumbre*) apex, top. (**b**) (*fig*: *de problema*) crux, knotty point; **estar en los ~s de** to be well up in, know all about. (**c**) (*fig*: *jota*) whit, iota; **ni ~** not a whit; **no ceder un ~** not to yield an inch; **no importa un ~** it doesn't matter a bit.
apichicarse [1g] *vr* (*Cono Sur*) to squat, crouch.
apicultor(a) *nm/f* beekeeper, apiarist.
apicultura *nf* beekeeping, apiculture.
apilado *nm* piling, heaping, stacking.
apilar [1a] *vt* to pile up, heap up, stack.
apilonar [1a] *vt* (*LAm*) = **apilar.**
apimplado* *adj* (*LAm*) tight*, tipsy.
apiñado *adj* (**a**) (*lleno*) crowded, packed, congested (*de* with). (**b**) *forma* cone-shaped, pyramidal.
apiñadura *nf*, **apiñamiento** *nm* crowding, congestion; crowd, squash, jam.
apiñar [1a] **1** *vt* (*agrupar, reunir*) to crowd together, bunch together; (*apretar*) to pack in, press together, squeeze together; *espacio etc* to overcrowd, congest.
2 apiñarse *vr* to crowd together, press together; to be packed tight, be squashed together; **la multitud se apiñaba alrededor de él** the crowd pressed round him.
apio *nm* (**a**) (*Bot*) celery. (**b**) (*Esp*‡) queer‡.
apiolar‡ [1a] *vt* (**a**) (*detener*) to nab*, nick‡. (**b**) (*matar*) to do in‡ bump off‡.
apio nabo *nm* celeriac.
apiparse* [1a] *vr* to stuff o.s., guzzle.
apir(i) *nm* (*LAm*) mineworker.
apirularse [1a] *vr* (*Cono Sur*) to get dressed up to the nines.
apisonadora *nf* steamroller, road roller.
apisonar [1a] *vt* to roll, roll flat; to tamp down, ram down.
apitiquarse [1a] *vr* (*And*) to get depressed; to be dismayed.
apitonar [1a] **1** *vt cáscara* to crack, pierce, break through. **2** *vi* (*cuernos*) to sprout, begin to show; (*animal*) to begin to grow horns. **3 apitonarse*** *vr* (*enfadarse*) to get into a huff; (*dos personas*) to have a slanging match*.
apizarrado *adj* slaty, slate-coloured.
aplacar [1g] *vt* to appease, placate; to soothe, calm down; *hambre etc* to satisfy.
aplanacalles *nm invar* (*LAm*) idler, layabout.
aplanador *nm*: **~ de calles** idler, layabout.
aplanamiento *nm* smoothing, levelling, flattening.
aplanar [1a] **1** *vt* (**a**) (*nivelar*) to smooth, level, make even; to roll flat, flatten; (*And*) *ropa* to iron; **~ las calles** (*LAm*) to hang about (*o* around) in the street.
(**b**) (*****) to knock out, bowl over with surprise.
2 aplanarse *vr* (**a**) (*Arquit*) to collapse, cave in, fall down.
(**b**) (*****) (*desanimarse*) to get discouraged; (*aletargarse*) to become lethargic, sink into lethargy.
aplanchar [1a] *vt* (*LAm*) = **planchar.**
aplastante *adj* overwhelming, crushing.
aplastar [1a] **1** *vt* (**a**) to flatten (out), squash, crush (flat).
(**b**) (*fig*) *enemigo etc* to crush, overwhelm; (*****) *persona* to floor, flatten, leave speechless.
2 aplastarse *vr* (**a**) to flatten o.s.; **se aplastó contra la pared** he flattened himself against the wall.
(**b**) (*Arquit etc*) to collapse.
(**c**) (*Cono Sur*) (*desanimarse*) to get discouraged, lose heart; (*atemorizarse*) to get scared, take fright.
(**d**) (*Cono Sur*: *agotarse*) to be drained, be exhausted.
(**e**) (*Cono Sur*: *atleta, caballo*) to blow up.
aplatanado *adj* (**a**) **está ~** (*Carib etc*) he has gone native.
(**b**) (*fig*) (*soso*) lumpish, lacking all ambition; (*aletargado*) weary, lethargic.
aplatanarse [1a] *vr* (**a**) (*abandonarse*) to become lethargic, sink into lethargy. (**b**) (*Carib etc*: *acriollarse*) to go native.
aplatarse [1a] *vr* (*Carib*) to get rich.
aplaudir [3a] *vt* to applaud, cheer, clap; (*fig*) to applaud, approve.
aplauso *nm* applause; (*fig*) approval, acclaim; **~s** applause, cheering, clapping.
aplazamiento *nm* (**a**) postponement, deferment; adjournment. (**b**) summons, summoning.
aplazar [1f] **1** *vt* (**a**) (*diferir*) to postpone, put off, defer; *asunto etc* to adjourn, hold over; **se ha aplazado la decisión por tiempo indefinido** the decision has been postponed indefinitely.
(**b**) (*fijar hora etc para*) to set a time for, set a date for; (*convocar*) to summon, convene.
2 *vi* (*CAm*: *suspender*) to fail (an exam).
aplebeyado *adj* coarse, coarsened.
aplebeyar [1a] **1** *vt* to coarsen, degrade; to demean. **2 aplebeyarse** *vr* to become coarse; to lower o.s., demean o.s.
aplicabilidad *nf* applicability.
aplicable *adj* applicable (*a* to).
aplicación *nf* (**a**) (*acto*) application (*t Med*); **enviar su ~** (*LAm*) to send in one's application. (**b**) (*cualidad*) industry, studiousness, application; **le falta ~** he doesn't work hard enough, he lacks steadiness. (**c**) **aplicaciones** (*Inform*) applications; **aplicaciones de gestión** management applications; **aplicaciones comerciales** business applications.
aplicado *adj* (**a**) *ciencia* applied. (**b**) *carácter* studious; diligent, industrious.
aplicador *nm* applicator.
aplicar [1g] **1** *vt* (*gen*) to apply (*a* to); *esfuerzo, dinero etc* to devote, assign (*a* to), earmark (*a* for); *hombres, recursos* to assign (*a, para* to); *crimen etc* to attribute, impute (*a* to); **~ sanciones** to impose sanctions; **~ a uno a una carrera** to enter sb for a profession, put sb in for a profession; **~ el oído a una puerta** to put one's ear to a door.
2 aplicarse *vr* (**a**) **~ algo** to attribute sth to o.s., claim sth for o.s.

(**b**) (*ley, regla etc*) ~ **a** to apply to, be applicable to, be relevant to.
(**c**) (*persona*) ~ **a** to apply o.s. to, devote o.s. to, give one's mind to; ~ **a** + *infin* to devote o.s. to + *ger*.
aplique *nm* (*lámpara*) wall lamp; (*Teat*) piece of stage décor; (*Cos*) appliqué.
aplomado *adj* self-confident.
aplomar [1a] **1** *vt* (*Arquit etc*) to plumb, test with a plumbline; to make perpendicular, make straight.
2 aplomarse *vr* (**a**) (*desplomarse*) to collapse, cave in, fall down.
(**b**) (*fig*) to gain confidence.
(**c**) (*Cono Sur*) to get embarrassed.
aplomo *nm* (*serenidad*) self-possession, assurance, aplomb; (*gravedad*) gravity, seriousness; (*pey*) nerve, cheek; **¡qué ~!** what a nerve!; **dijo con el mayor** ~ he said with the utmost assurance; **perder su** ~ to get worried, get rattled.
apocado *adj* (**a**) (*tímido*) diffident, timid; (*pusilánime*) pusillanimous; (*falto de voluntad*) spiritless, spineless. (**b**) (*humilde*) common, lowly.
apocalipsis *nm* apocalypse; **A~** (*Bib*) Revelations.
apocalíptico *adj* apocalyptic; *estilo* obscure, enigmatic.
apocamiento *nm* (**a**) (*timidez*) diffidence, pusillanimity, timidity; spinelessness. (**b**) (*depresión*) depression, depressed state.
apocar [1g] **1** *vt* (**a**) (*hacer pequeño*) to make smaller, diminish, reduce; (*fig*) to limit, restrict.
(**b**) (*denigrar*) to belittle, run down; (*humillar*) to humiliate; (*intimidar*) to intimidate; **nada me apoca** nothing scares me.
2 apocarse *vr* to feel small, feel humiliated; to humble o.s.
apocopar [1a] *vt* to apocopate.
apócope *nf* (*Ling*) apocope; **Doro es ~ de Dorotea** Doro is a shortened form of Dorotea, Doro is short for Dorotea.
apócrifo *adj* apocryphal; false, spurious.
apochongarse [1h] *vr* (*Cono Sur*) to get scared, be frightened.
apodar [1a] *vt* to nickname, dub, call; to label.
apoderado, -a *nm/f* agent, representative; (*Jur*) proxy, attorney; (*Mús, Dep*) manager.
apoderar [1a] **1** *vt* (**a**) (*autorizar*) to authorize, empower. (**b**) (*Jur*) to grant power of attorney to. **2 apoderarse** *vr*: ~ **de** to get hold of, seize, take possession of.
apodíctico *adj* apodictic, necessarily true.
apodo *nm* nickname; label; (*Jur*) false name, alias.
apódosis *nf* apodosis.
apogeo *nm* (*Astron*) apogee; (*fig*) peak, summit, top; **estar en el ~ de su fama** to be at the height of one's fame; **estar en todo su** ~ to be on top form.
apolillado *adj* moth-eaten.
apolilladura *nf* moth-hole.
apolillar [1a] **1** *vt* (*Cono Sur**): **estarla apolillando** to be snoozing*. **2 apolillarse** *vr* to get moth-eaten; (*fig*) to get old.
apolismado *adj* (*And, Carib, Méx*: *enclenque*) sickly, weak; (*CAm*: *vago*) lazy; (*Méx, Carib*: *deprimido*) gloomy, depressed; (*Carib*: *estúpido*) stupid.
apolismar [1a] **1** *vt* (*LAm*) to ruin, destroy.
2 *vi* (*CAm*) to laze about, idle.
3 apolismarse *vr* (*LAm*) (*enfermar*) to grow weak, weaken; (*deprimirse*) to get worried, get depressed; (*desanimarse*) to lose heart.
apoliticismo *nm* apolitical nature, non-political nature; non-political approach.
apolítico *adj* apolitical, non-political.
apoliyar [1a] *vt* = **apolillar.**
Apolo *nm* Apollo.
apologética *nf* apologetics.
apología *nf* defence; eulogy; (*LAm*) apology; **una ~ del terrorismo** a statement in support of terrorism.
apologista *nmf* apologist.
apoltronado *adj* lazy, idle.
apoltronarse [1a] *vr* to get lazy; to laze, loaf around, idle.
apolvillarse [1a] *vr* (*Cono Sur Agr*) to be blighted.
apoplejía *nf* apoplexy, stroke.
apoplético *adj* apoplectic.
apoquinar* [1a] *vt dinero* to fork out*, pay up.
aporcar [1g] *vt* (*Agr*) to earth up.
aporrar* [1a] **1** *vi* to dry up*, get stuck (in a speech *etc*). **2 aporrarse** *vr* to become a bore, become a nuisance.
aporreado 1 *adj vida etc* wretched, miserable; *persona* rascally. **2** *nm* (*Carib*) meat stew, chili stew.
aporrear [1a] **1** *vt* (**a**) *persona* to beat, bash*, club; to beat up*.
(**b**) *puerta, mesa etc* to thump (on), pound (on), bang away at.
(**c**) (*LAm*: *aplastar*) to crush completely (in an argument).
(**d**) (*fig*: *acosar*) to bother, pester.
2 aporrearse *vr* to slave away, slog, toil.
aporreo *nm* (**a**) (*paliza*) beating; beating-up. (**b**) (*ruido*) thumping, pounding, banging. (**c**) (*molestia*) bother, nuisance.
aportación *nf* contribution; **aportaciones de la mujer** dowry.
aportar¹ [1a] *vt* to bring; to furnish, contribute; *evidencia etc* to bring forward, adduce; (*Jur*) to contribute (to the marriage settlement).
aportar² [1a] *vi* (**a**) (*Náut*) to reach port, come into harbour. (**b**) (*aparecer*) to come out at an unexpected place. (**c**) (*llegar*) to arrive, show up, come.
aporte *nm* contribution.
aportillar [1a] **1** *vt* to break down, break open; *muro* to breach. **2 aportillarse** *vr* (*desplomarse*) to collapse, tumble down.
aposentar [1a] **1** *vt* to lodge, put up. **2 aposentarse** *vr* to lodge, put up (*en* at).
aposento *nm* room; lodging; (*Carib*) main bedroom.
aposesionarse [1a] *vr*: ~ **de** to take possession of.
aposición *nf* apposition; **en** ~ in apposition.
apósito *nm* (*Med*) application, poultice; dressing.
aposta *adv*, **apostadamente** *adv* on purpose.
apostadero *nm* (*Mil*) station, post; (*Náut*) naval station.
apostador(a) *nm/f* better, backer, punter; ~ **profesional** bookmaker.
apostar¹ [1a] **1** *vt* to station, post. **2 apostarse** *vr*: ~ **en** to station o.s. in (*o* at).
apostar² [1l] **1** *vt* (**a**) *dinero* to lay, stake, bet (*a* on).
(**b**) **~las a uno, ~las con uno** to compete with sb.
2 *vi* to bet (*a, por* on; *a que* that); **apuesto a que sí** I bet it is; ~ **por** (*fig*) *partido etc* to bet on, back; *programa etc* to put one's faith in, believe in; to advocate; ~ **fuerte por** to give strong support to.
3 apostarse *vr* to compete (*con* with), be rivals, vie; **~las a uno, ~las con uno** to compete with sb.
apostasía *nf* apostasy.
apóstata *nmf* apostate.
apostatar [1a] *vi* (*Ecl*) to apostatize (*de* from); (*fig*) to change sides.
apostema *nf* abscess.
apostilla *nf* note, comment.
apostillar [1a] *vt* to add notes to, annotate; (*fig*) to add, chime in with; *observación* to echo; **'Sí', apostilló una voz** 'Yes', a voice added.
apóstol *nm* apostle.
apostolado *nm* apostolate.
apostólico *adj* apostolic.
apostrofar [1a] *vt* (**a**) (*dirigirse a*) to apostrophize, address. (**b**) (*insultar*) to insult, shout insults at.
apóstrofe *gen nm* (**a**) (*Ling*) apostrophe. (**b**) (*insulto*) taunt, insult; (*reprensión*) rebuke, reprimand.
apóstrofo *nm* (*Tip*) inverted comma, apostrophe.
apostura *nf* (**a**) (*pulcritud*) neatness, elegance; (*hum*) nattiness. (**b**) (*belleza*) good looks.
apotegma *nm* apothegm, maxim.
apoteósico *adj* (*fig*) *éxito etc* huge, tremendous.
apoteosis *nf* apotheosis; (*fig*) climax, high point, culmination.
apoyabrazos *nm invar* armrest.
apyoacabeza(s) *nm invar* headrest.
apoyador *nm* (**a**) support, bracket. (**b**) (*Pol*) seconder.
apoyalibros *nm invar* book-ends.
apoyapié(s) *nm invar* footrest.
apoyar [1a] **1** *vt* (**a**) *codo, cabeza etc* to lean, rest (*en, sobre* on); (*Arquit, Téc*) to hold up, support; to prop up; ~ **una escalera contra una pared** to lean a ladder against a wall.
(**b**) (*fig*) *persona* to support, back; to stand by; (*pey*) to abet; *moción* to second, support; *principio* to uphold; *teoría etc* to bear out, confirm, support; **apoya su argumento en los siguientes hechos** he bases his argument on the following facts; **no apoyamos más al gobierno** we no longer support the government.
2 *vi*: ~ **en** to rest on, be supported by.
3 apoyarse *vr*: ~ **en** (**a**) *base* to rest on, be supported by; *hombro, bastón etc* to lean on; ~ **contra una pared** to lean against a wall.
(**b**) (*fig*) *persona* to rely on; to lean on; *argumento,*

evidencia etc to base o.s. on.
apoyatura *nf* (**a**) support. (**b**) (*Mús*) appoggiatura.
apoyo *nm* (**a**) (*soporte*) support; prop. (**b**) (*fig*) (*respaldo*) support, backing; (*ayuda*) help; (*aprobación*) approval, favour; ~ **económico** financial support, financial backing; **contamos con su** ~ we rely on your support.
apozarse [1f] *vr* (*And, Cono Sur*) to form a pool.
APRA ['apra] *nf* (*Perú Pol*) *abr de* **Alianza Popular Revolucionaria Americana.**
apreciable *adj* (**a**) (*gen*) appreciable, considerable; (*perceptible*) noticeable; (*mensurable*) measurable; **una cantidad** ~ an appreciable quantity; ~ **al oído** audible.
(**b**) (*fig*) worthy, estimable, esteemed; valuable; **los** ~**s esposos** the esteemed couple; **'A~ Señor ...'** (*Esp*) 'Dear Sir ...'.
apreciación *nf* (**a**) (*evaluación*) appreciation, appraisal; (*Com, Fin*) valuation; estimate; **según nuestra** ~ according to our estimation; ~ **del trabajo** job evaluation. (**b**) (*subida*) appreciation.
apreciado *adj* worthy, estimable, esteemed.
apreciar [1b] **1** *vt* (**a**) (*Com, Fin etc*) to value, assess, estimate (*en* at); to evaluate.
(**b**) (*fig*) (*estimar*) to esteem, value (*por* for); (*tener cariño a*) to like, be fond of; **aprecia mucho a los niños** she's very fond of children; ~ **algo en mucho** to value sth highly; ~ **en poco** to set little value on, attach little value to.
(**c**) (*Arte, Mús etc*) to appreciate.
(**d**) (*percibir*) to see, notice, observe; (*LAm*: *darse cuenta de*) to become aware of.
(**e**) (*LAm*: *realzar*) to add value to, enhance, improve.
(**f**) (*LAm*: *agradecer*) to be grateful for, appreciate; **lo aprecio mucho** I much appreciate it.
2 apreciarse *vr* (**a**) **se aprecia la diferencia** one can tell the difference, the difference can be appreciated. (**b**) (*valor etc*) to appreciate, rise (in value).
apreciativo *adj*: **una mirada apreciativa** an appraising look, a look of appraisal.
apreciatorio *adj*: **presión apreciatoria** upward pressure; **tendencia apreciatoria** upward tendency, tendency to rise.
aprecio *nm* (**a**) (*Com, Fin etc*) valuation, appraisal; estimate.
(**b**) (*fig*) appreciation; esteem, regard; **tener a uno en gran** ~ to hold sb in high regard; **en señal de mi** ~ as a token of my esteem; **no hacer** ~ **de algo** (*Méx*) to pay no attention to sth.
aprehender [2a] *vt* (**a**) *persona* to apprehend, detain; *mercancías* to seize. (**b**) (*Filos*) (*comprender*) to understand; (*concebir*) to conceive, think; (*concretar*) to pin down.
aprehensible *adj* understandable; conceivable; **una idea difícilmente** ~ an idea which is difficult to pin down, an idea not readily understood.
aprehensión *nf* (**a**) (*captura*) apprehension, detention, capture; seizure. (**b**) (*Filos*) understanding; conception, perception.
apremiador *adj*, **apremiante** *adj* urgent, pressing, compelling.
apremiar [1b] **1** *vt* (**a**) (*instar*) to urge (on), press; to force, compel; ~ **a uno a hacer algo,** ~ **a uno para que haga algo** to press sb to do sth.
(**b**) (*dar prisa a*) to hurry (along).
(**c**) (*oprimir*) to oppress; (*acosar*) to harass.
2 *vi* to press, be urgent; **el tiempo apremia** time presses; **apremiaba repararlo** it was an urgent task to repair it, it was urgent to get it repaired.
apremio *nm* (**a**) (*urgencia*) urgency, pressure; (*obligación*) compulsion; **por** ~ **de tiempo** because time is pressing; **por** ~ **de trabajo** because of pressure of work; ~ **de pago** demand for payment, demand note; **procedimiento de** ~ compulsory procedure.
(**b**) (*Jur*) writ, judgement; summons; judicial constraint.
(**c**) (*opresión*) oppression; (*acoso*) harassment.
aprender [2a] **1** *vti* to learn; ~ **a hacer algo** to learn to do sth. **2 aprenderse** *vr* to learn by heart.
aprendiz(a) *nm/f* (**a**) learner; beginner, novice; (*Dep*) novice, junior; ~ **de conductor** learner, learner-driver.
(**b**) (*en un oficio*) apprentice; (*Com etc*) trainee; ~ **de brujo** sorcerer's apprentice; ~ **de comercio** business trainee; **estar de** ~ **con uno** to be apprenticed to sb; **poner a A de** ~ **con B** to apprentice A to B; ~ **de todo y oficial de nada** jack of all trades and master of none.
aprendizaje *nm* (**a**) (*industrial etc*) apprenticeship; (*Com etc*) training period, period as a trainee; **hacer su** ~ to serve one's apprenticeship. (**b**) (*el aprender*) learning; **dificultades de** ~ learning difficulties.
aprensar [1a] *vt* (**a**) (*Téc*) to press, crush. (**b**) (*fig*) (*oprimir*) to oppress, crush; (*afligir*) to distress.
aprensión *nf* (*miedo*) apprehension, fear, worry; (*nerviosismo*) nervousness; (*Med*) hypochondria, fear of being ill; (*capricho*) odd idea, (*remilgos*) strange notion, idle fancy; squeamishness.
aprensivo *adj* apprehensive, worried; nervous, timid; (*Med*) hypochondriac, fearful of being ill; squeamish.
apresador(a) *nm/f* captor.
apresamiento *nm* seizure; capture.
apresar [1a] *vt* (**a**) (*agarrar*) to seize, clutch, grab, grasp. (**b**) *persona, barco* to capture. (**c**) (*Jur*) to seize.
aprestado *adj* ready; **estar** ~ **para** + *infin* to be ready to + *infin*.
aprestar [1a] **1** *vt* to prepare, get ready, make ready; *paño* to size; (*para pintar*) to prime, size.
2 aprestarse *vr* to prepare, get ready; ~ **a** + *infin*, ~ **para** + *infin* to get ready to + *infin*.
apresto *nm* (**a**) (*acto*) preparation. (**b**) (*equipo*) outfit, equipment, kit. (**c**) (*acto*: *antes de pintar*) priming, sizing. (**d**) (*materia*) size, primer.
apresuradamente *adv* hurriedly, hastily.
apresurado *adj* hurried, hasty; quick; precipitate.
apresuramiento *nm* hurry, haste, precipitation.
apresurar [1a] **1** *vt* to hurry (along); to hustle; to speed up, accelerate, expedite.
2 apresurarse *vr* to hurry, hasten, make haste; ~ **a** + *infin*, ~ **por** + *infin* to hasten to + *infin*; **me apresuré a sugerir que** ... I hastened to suggest that ..., I hastily suggested that ...
apretadamente *adv* tightly; densely, solidly.
apretadera *nf* (**a**) (*correa, cuerda*) strap, rope. (**b**) ~**s*** pressure, insistence.
apretado *adj* (**a**) *nudo, tornillo, vestido etc* tight; *V* **baile.**
(**b**) (*denso etc*) dense, thick, compact, solid; *escritura* cramped; *cuarto, espacio* full, chock-a-block; *programa etc* tight; **estaba** ~ **a presión** it was full to bursting.
(**c**) (*difícil*) difficult, dangerous; **es un caso** ~ it's a tricky business; **estar** ~ to be in a difficult situation, (*Med*) be in a bad way; **estar** ~ **de dinero** to be short of money.
(**d**) (*****: *tacaño*) tight-fisted, stingy.
(**e**) (*Méx*: *presumido*) conceited.
(**f**) (*Carib*: *sin dinero*) broke*, flat* (*US*).
apretar [1j] **1** *vt* (**a**) *cinturón, tuerca, tornillo* to tighten (up); *mano* to clasp, grip, (*al saludar*) shake; *puño* to clench; *dientes* to grit, set; *botón, pedal, gatillo etc* to press, press down; (*vestido*) to be too tight for; (*zapato*) to pinch; *persona* to hug, squeeze; (*fig*) to pressurize; ~ **a uno entre los brazos** to hug sb in one's arms; ~ **a uno contra la pared** to pin sb against the wall.
(**b**) *contenido* to pack in, pack tight; to press together, squeeze together.
(**c**) *disciplina* to tighten up; (*Mil*) *ataque* to press, intensify; *paso* to quicken.
(**d**) (*afligir*) to afflict, distress, trouble; to beset; (*Med*) to distress.
(**e**) (*importunar*) to harass, pester (*por* for).
2 *vi* (**a**) (*vestido*) to be too tight; (*zapato*) to pinch, hurt.
(**b**) (*empeorar*) to get worse, get more severe; **cuando el calor aprieta** when the heat becomes oppressive; **allí donde más aprieta el calor** out there where the heat is at its worst; **el frío aprieta** (*esp Méx*) it's getting colder.
(**c**) (*insistir*) to insist, exert pressure.
(**d**) ~ **con el enemigo** to close with the enemy, to close in on the enemy.
(**e**) (*LAm*: *esforzarse*) to make an extra (*o* special) effort.
(**f**) ~ **a correr** to break into a run, start to run.
(**g**) **¡aprieta!** nonsense!; good grief!
3 apretarse *vr* (**a**) (*estrecharse*) to narrow, get narrower.
(**b**) (*agolparse*) to crowd together, squeeze up; to huddle together.
(**c**) (*afligirse*) to grieve, be distressed.
apretón *nm* (**a**) (*presión*) squeeze, pressure; (*abrazo*) hug; ~ **financiero** financial squeeze; ~ **de manos** handshake; **se dieron un** ~ **de manos** they shook hands.
(**b**) (*agolpamiento*) press, crush, jam; **el** ~ **en el metro** the crush in the underground.
(**c**) (*apuro*) difficulty, jam, fix; **estar en un** ~ to be in a

fix, be in a quandary.
(**d**) (*carrera*) dash, sprint, short run.
apretujar [1a] *vt* (*apretar*) to press hard, squeeze hard; (*abrazar*) to hug; (*estrujar*) to crush, crumple; **estar apretujado entre dos personas** to be crushed between two people, be sandwiched between two people.
apretujón *nm* (**a**) (*apretón*) hard squeeze; (*abrazo*) big hug. (**b**) (*agolpamiento*) press, crush, jam.
apretura *nf* (**a**) = **apretón, apretujón** (**a**), (**b**). (**b**) = **apretón** (**c**).
aprieto *nm* (**a**) = **apretón** (**a**), (**b**). (**b**) (*fig*) difficulty, jam, fix; distress; **estar en un ~, verse en un ~** to be in a jam; **poner a uno en un ~** to put sb in a fix; **ayudar a uno a salir de un ~** to help sb out of trouble.
apriorismo *nm* tendency to resolve matters hastily.
apriorístico *adj* (**a**) (*deductivo*) a priori, deductive.
(**b**) (*precipitado*) hasty, premature.
aprisa *adv* quickly, hurriedly.
aprisco *nm* sheepfold.
aprisionar [1a] *vt* (*encarcelar*) to imprison; (*atar*) to bind, tie; (*atrapar*) to trap; (*aherrojar*: *t fig*) to shackle.
aprismo *nm* (*And Pol*) doctrine of APRA.
aprista *nmf* (*And Pol*) follower (*o* member) of APRA.
aprobación *nf* (**a**) approval; consent; **dar su ~** to give one's consent, approve. (**b**) (*Univ etc*) pass mark.
aprobado 1 *adj* approved; worthy, excellent. **2** *nm* (*Univ etc*) pass, pass mark; pass certificate.
aprobar [1l] **1** *vt* to approve, approve of, consent to, endorse; (*Parl*) *proyecto de ley* to pass; *informe* to approve, adopt; (*Univ*) *candidato, examen, asignatura* to pass.
2 *vi* (*Univ*) to pass; **aprobé en francés** I passed in French.
aprobatorio *adj*: **una mirada aprobatoria** an approving look.
aproches *nmpl* (*Mil*) approaches; (*LAm barrio*) neighbourhood, district.
aprontamiento *nm* quick delivery, rapid service.
aprontar [1a] *vt* (*preparar*) to get ready quickly, prepare without delay; *mercancías, dinero* to deliver at once, hand over immediately; (*Méx*) (*preparar*) to prepare in advance; (*entregar*) to hand over.
apronte *nm* (*Cono Sur*) (**a**) (*Dep*) heat, preliminary race. (**b**) **~s** preparations; **irse en los ~s** to waste one's energy on unnecessary preliminaries.
apropiación *nf* appropriation; adaptation, application; giving, gift; **~ ilícita** illegal seizure, misappropriation; (*de dinero*) fraudulent conversion; **~ indebida de fondos** misappropriation of funds, embezzlement.
apropiadamente *adv* appropriately, fittingly.
apropiado *adj* appropriate (*a, para* to), suitable, fitting (*a, para* for).
apropiar [1b] **1** *vt* (**a**) (*adecuar*) to adapt, fit (*a* to), make suitable (*a* for); (*aplicar*) to apply (*a* to).
(**b**) **~ algo a uno** to give sth to sb; (*LAm*) (*asignar*) to assign sth to sb; (*otorgar*) to award sth to sb.
2 apropiarse *vr*: **~ (de) algo** to appropriate sth.
apropincuarse [1d] *vr* (*hum*) to approach.
aprovechable *adj* usable, that can be used; useful, serviceable; wearable.
aprovechadamente *adv* profitably.
aprovechado 1 *adj* (**a**) (*trabajador*) industrious, diligent, hardworking; (*ingenioso*) resourceful.
(**b**) (*frugal*) thrifty, economical.
(**c**) (*pey*) unscrupulous, selfish; grasping.
(**d**) *tiempo etc* well-spent.
2 *nm*, **aprovechada** *nf* selfish person, person who has an eye to the main chance.
aprovechamiento *nm* (**a**) (*uso*) use, development; exploitation; **~ de recursos naturales** use of natural resources. (**b**) (*progreso*) progress, improvement.
aprovechar [1a] **1** *vt* (*utilizar*) to make (good) use of, use, utilize; (*explotar*) to develop, exploit; *oferta etc* to take up, take advantage of; *experiencia, lección* to profit by, profit from; *ocasión* to seize, avail o.s. of, take; *posibilidades* to make the most of; (*pey*) to exploit, abuse, make unfair use of, get the benefit of.
2 *vi* (**a**) (*ser útil*) to be of use, be useful, be profitable; **eso aprovecha poco** that is of little use, that is of no avail; **no ~ para nada** to be completely useless; **~ a uno** to be of use to sb, profit sb, be beneficial to sb; **¡que aproveche!** (*phrase used to those at table, hoping they will enjoy their meal*) bon appétit.
(**b**) (*progresar*) to progress, improve; **~ en los estudios** to make progress in one's work.
3 aprovecharse *vr*: **~ de** = **1**.
aprovechón *adj* opportunistic, having an eye to the main chance.
aprovisionador(a) *nm/f* supplier.
aprovisionamiento *nm* supply, supplying.
aprovisionar [1a] *vt* to supply.
aproximación *nf* (**a**) (*gen*; *t Mat*) approximation (*a* to). (**b**) (*proximidad*) nearness, closeness; **no parece ni por ~ que vaya a ceder** he seems to be nowhere near giving up. (**c**) (*acercamiento*) approach (*a* to); (*Pol*) rapprochement; (*a problema, texto*) approach. (**d**) (*de lotería*) consolation prize.
aproximadamente *adv* approximately; roughly.
aproximado *adj* approximate; *estimación, conjetura* rough.
aproximamiento *nm* = **aproximación**.
aproximar [1a] **1** *vt* to bring near(er), bring up, draw up (*a* to); **~ una silla** to bring a chair nearer, bring a chair over.
2 aproximarse *vr* (**a**) (*acercarse*) to come near, come closer, approach; **~ a** to near, approach; **el tren se aproximaba a su destino** the train was nearing its destination.
(**b**) **~ a** (*fig*) to approach, approximate to.
aproximativo *adj* approximate; *estimación, conjetura* rough.
aptitud *nf* (**a**) (*conveniencia*) suitability, fitness (*para* for). (**b**) (*talento*) aptitude, ability; capacity; **~ para los negocios** business sense, business talent; **carece de ~** he hasn't got the talent; **demostrar tener ~es** to show ability, show promise.
Aptdo. *abr de* **apartado de correos** Post Office Box, POB.
apto *adj* suitable, fit; (*Escol*) pass (*atr*); **ser ~ a aprender, ser ~ para aprender** to be quick to learn; **~ para desarrollar** suitable for developing; **no es ~ para conducir** he's not fit to drive; **película no apta para menores** film for adults only; **~ para el servicio** (*Mil*) fit for military service.
Apto. *abr de* **apartamento.**
apuesta *nf* bet, wager; (*Bridge*) bid.
apuesto *adj* (**a**) (*pulcro*) neat, elegant, spruce; (*hum*) dapper, natty. (**b**) (*guapo*) handsome, nice-looking.
Apuleyo *nm* Apuleius.
apunarse [1a] *vr* (*And, Cono Sur*) to get mountain sickness.
apuntación *nf* note; (*Mús*) notation.
apuntado *adj* (**a**) (*agudo*) pointed, sharp. (**b**) (*Cono Sur**: *borracho*) merry*, tight*.
apuntador(a) *nm/f* (*Teat*) prompter; (*Méx Dep*) scorer; **murió** (*o* **no se salvó**) **hasta el ~*** no-one was spared.
apuntalamiento *nm* propping-up, underpinning.
apuntalar [1a] **1** *vt* (*Arquit, fig*) to prop up, shore up, underpin; (*Mec*) to strut. **2 apuntalarse** *vr* to have a snack.
apuntamiento *nm* (**a**) (*de arma*) aiming, pointing. (**b**) (*nota*) note. (**c**) (*Jur*) judicial report.
apuntar [1a] **1** *vt* (**a**) *fusil etc* to aim, level, point (*a* at); *cañón* to train (*a* on); **~ a un blanco** to aim at a target; **~ a uno con el revólver** to point a pistol at sb, cover sb with a pistol; (*en atraco etc*) hold sb up with a pistol.
(**b**) (*señalar*) to point at, point to; (*indicar*) to point out; (*sugerir*) to hint at; **~ que** ... to point out that ...; to hint that ...
(**c**) (*escribir*) to note, note down, make (*o* take) a note of; (*Dep*) *puntos* to score; (*en cuenta etc*) to enter, set down; (*registrar*) to record; (*bosquejar*) to sketch, outline; **~ una cantidad en la cuenta de uno** to charge a sum to sb's account; **~ a uno** (*exámenes*) to give sb the answers.
(**d**) *herramienta* to sharpen, put a point on.
(**e**) (*Cos*) to patch, mend, darn; to tack down; to fasten temporarily.
(**f**) (*Naipes*) *dinero* to stake, put up.
(**g**) (*Teat*) to prompt.
2 *vi* (**a**) (*barba etc*) to begin to show, appear; (*día*) to dawn, break; (*LAm Bot*) to sprout, show; **el maíz apunta bien este año** (*LAm*) the corn is coming on nicely this year.
(**b**) (*Teat*; *t en examen etc*) to prompt.
(**c**) **~ y no dar** to fail to keep one's word.
(**d**) (*LAm*: *apostar*) to bet, place bets.
3 apuntarse *vr* (**a**) **~ un tanto** (*Dep*) to score a point; (*fig*) to stay one up; **~ una victoria** to score a win, chalk up a win.
(**b**) (*agriarse*) to turn sour.
(**c**) (*****: *emborracharse*) to get tight*.
(**d**) (*firmar etc*) to sign on, sign up; to put one's name down (*a* for); (*Mil*) to join up; **~ a un club** to join a club.
(**e**) (*****: *estar de acuerdo*) to agree; **¿os apuntáis?** OK?*,

(is that) agreed?; **¡me apunto!** OK!*, I'm game!

(**f**) **¿te apuntas un café?** (*Esp**: *apetecer*) how about a coffee?, do you fancy a coffee?

apunte *nm* (**a**) (*nota*) note; jotting; memorandum; (*Com*) entry; (*en cuenta bancaria, esp*) debit, debiting; (*Arte*) sketch; (*Cono Sur Com*) list of debts, note of money owing; **'A~s sobre el unicornio'** 'Notes on the Unicorn'; **llevar el ~** (*Cono Sur*) to pay attention, take notice; (*mujer*) to begin to take an interest, accept sb's advances; **sacar ~s** to take notes.

(**b**) (*Teat*) (*pie*) cue; (*apuntador*) prompter; (*texto*) prompt copy, prompt book.

(**c**) (*Naipes*) stake.

(**d**) (*LAm*: *apuesta*) bet.

apuntillar [1a] *vt* (**a**) *toro* to finish off. (**b**) (*fig*) to round off.

apuñadura *nf* knob, handle.

apuñalar [1a] *vt*, **apuñalear** [1a] *vt* (*LAm*) to stab; to knife; **~ a uno por la espalda** (*fig*) to stab sb in the back; **~ a uno con la mirada** to look daggers at sb.

apuñar [1a] *vt* to seize (in one's fist); (*Cono Sur*) to knead (with the fists).

apuñear [1a] *vt*, **apuñetear** [1a] *vt* to punch, strike.

apuradamente *adv* (**a**) (*exactamente*) precisely, exactly. (**b**) (*con dificultad*) with difficulty. (**c**) (*LAm*: *de prisa*) hurriedly.

apurado *adj* (**a**) (*sin dinero*) needy, hard up.

(**b**) (*difícil etc*) difficult; dangerous; **estar ~, estar en una situación apurada** to be in a jam, be in a tight spot; (*sentir vergüenza*) to feel embarrassed.

(**c**) (*agotado*) exhausted.

(**d**) (*exacto*) precise, exact.

(**e**) (*LAm*: *apresurado*) hurried, rushed; **estar** (*o* **ir**) **~** to be in a hurry; **hacer algo a la apurada** (*Cono Sur*) to do sth hurriedly, make a botch of sth.

apuramiento *nm* (**a**) (*Téc*) purification, refinement.

(**b**) (*agotamiento*) exhaustion.

(**c**) (*aclaración*) verification; clarification.

apurar [1a] **1** *vt* (**a**) (*Téc*) to purify, refine.

(**b**) *líquido* to drain, drink up; *vaso* to drain; *provisión etc* to use up, exhaust, finish off; *proceso* to finish, conclude.

(**c**) *hechos* to check on, verify; *asunto* to study minutely, make a thorough investigation of; *misterio* to clear up, fathom, get to the bottom of.

(**d**) (*fastidiar etc*) to annoy, bother; (*impacientar*) to make impatient; (*azorar*) to embarrass; (*presionar*) to put pressure on, force; (*importunar*) to pester; (*dar prisa a*) to hurry, hustle; to press, urge on; **¡no me apures!** don't hustle me!; **si mucho me apuras** if you really press me, if you really insist; **deja que el niño haga lo que pueda sin ~le** let the child do what he can without forcing him.

2 apurarse *vr* (**a**) (*afligirse*) to worry, fret, upset o.s. (*por* about, over); **ella se apura por poca cosa** she upsets herself for no reason; **¡no te apures!** don't worry!

(**b**) (*esforzarse*) to make an effort, go hard at it, exert o.s.; **~ por hacer algo** to strive to do sth.

(**c**) to rush, hurry up; **¡apúrate!** come along!, get a move on!; **no te apures** there's no hurry.

apuro *nm* (**a**) (*económico*) want, financial need; (*penas*) hardship, distress; **pasar ~s** to suffer hardship(s); **verse en ~s** to be in trouble, be in distress.

(**b**) (*aprieto*) fix, jam, difficulty, tight spot; **colocar a uno en ~s** to put sb on the spot; **andar** (*o* **estar**) **en ~s, estar en el mayor ~** to be in a jam; **me da un ~** I'd hate to, it would be terribly awkward; **sacar a uno de ~** to get sb out of a jam.

(**c**) (*esp LAm*) haste, hurry; **tener ~** to be in a hurry.

apurón *nm* (*LAm*) great haste, great hurry; (*Cono Sur*) impatience; **andar a los apurones** (*Cono Sur*) to do things in a rush (*o* hurry).

apurruñar [1a] *vt* (*Carib*) (*maltratar*) to maltreat, handle roughly; (*manosear*) to mess up, rumple.

aquejar [1a] *vt* (**a**) (*afligir*) to distress, grieve, afflict; (*importunar*) to worry, harass; (*cansar*) to weary; **¿qué le aqueja?** what's up with him?

(**b**) (*Med*) to ail, afflict; **le aqueja una grave enfermedad** he suffers from a serious disease, he is afflicted with a serious disease.

aquel *adj dem m*, **aquella** *f* that (*remote from speaker and listener, in time etc*); **aquellos** *mpl*, **aquellas** *fpl* those.

aquél 1 *pron dem m*, **aquélla** *f* that (*remote from speaker and listener, in time etc*); **aquéllos** *mpl*, **aquéllas** *fpl* those; that one, those (ones); **éstos son negros mientras aquéllos son blancos** the latter are black whereas the former (*o* the others *o* the earlier ones) are white; **aquél que yo quiero** the one I love; **aquél que está en el escaparate** the one that's in the window; **todo aquél que ...** each one who ...; **como aquél que dice** so to speak.

2 (*) *nm* (**a**) (*Esp*) charm; sex appeal; **tiene mucho ~** she's got it*, she certainly has sex appeal.

(**b**) **esto tiene su ~** this has its awkward points.

aquelarre *nm* witches' sabbath; (*fig*) uproar, din.

aquello *pron dem* (*'neuter'*) that; that affair, that business, that matter; **~ no tiene importancia** that's not important; **no me gusta ~** I don't care for that; **¡no se te olvide ~!** see you don't forget what I told you about (*o* what I told you to do *etc*)!; **~ de mi hermano** that business about my brother; **~ fue de miedo*** that was awful, wasn't that awful?

aquerenciado *adj* (*Cono Sur, Méx*) in love, loving.

aquerenciarse [1b] *vr* (**a**) **~ a un lugar** to become fond of a place, become attached to a place. (**b**) (*Cono Sur, Méx*: *enamorarse*) to fall in love.

aqueridarse [1a] *vr* (*Carib*) to set up house together, move in together.

aquí *adv* (**a**) (*lugar*) here; **~ dentro** in here; **~ mismo** right here, on this very spot; **a 2 km de ~** 2 km from here; (*presentando 2 personas*) **~ Pepe, ~ Manolo** this is Pepe and this is Manolo; **hubo un lío de ~ te espero*** there was a tremendous fuss*; **andar de ~ para allá** to walk up and down, walk to and fro; **hasta ~** so far, as far as here; **pase** *o* **venga por ~** come this way; **no pasó por ~** he didn't come this way; **vive por ~** (**cerca**) he lives round here, he lives hereabouts; **... y ~ no ha pasado nada** and we'll say no more about it.

(**b**) (*tiempo*) **de ~ en adelante** from now on, henceforth; **de ~ a un mes** in a month's time; a month from now; **de ~ a 1999** from now till 1999; **hasta ~** up till now.

(**c**) **de ~ que ...** *conj* and so ..., hence ..., that's why ...; *V* **ahí 2**.

aquiescencia *nf* acquiescence.

aquiescente *adj* acquiescent.

aquietar [1a] *vt* to quieten (down), calm (down); to pacify; *temores* to calm, allay.

aquijotado *adj* quixotic.

aquilatar [1a] **1** *vt* (**a**) *metal* to assay; *joya* to value, grade. (**b**) (*fig*) to weigh up, test, examine; to appreciate. **2 aquilatarse** *vr* (*Cono Sur*) to improve.

Aquiles *nm* Achilles.

aquilón *nm* (*poét*) (*viento*) north wind; (*norte*) north.

Aquisgrán *nm* Aachen, Aix-la-Chapelle.

aquisito* *adv* (*LAm*) = **aquí**.

aquistar [1a] *vt* to win, gain, acquire.

Aquitania *nf* Aquitaine.

A.R. *abr de* **Alteza Real** Royal Highness, R.H.

ara[1] *nf* altar; altar stone; **en ~s de** on the altars of, in honour of; for the sake of; **en ~s de la exactitud** in the interests of precision.

ara[2] *nm* (*LAm*) parrot.

árabe 1 *adj* Arab, Arabian, Arabic; **estilo ~** (*Arquit*) Moresque; **lengua ~** Arabic; **palabra ~** Arabic word.

2 *nmf* Arab; (*Méx*) hawker, street vendor.

3 *nm* (*Ling*) Arabic.

arabesco 1 *adj* Arabic; *estilo* arabesque. **2** *nm* arabesque.

Arabia *nf* Arabia; **~ Saudí, ~ Saudita** Saudi Arabia.

arábigo 1 *adj* Arab, Arabian, Arabic; *número* Arabic. **2** *nm* Arabic; **está en ~*** it's Greek to me; **hablar en ~*** to talk double Dutch*.

arábigoandaluz *adj* of Al-Andalus, of Muslim (southern) Spain.

arabismo *nm* (*Ling*) arabism.

arabista *nmf* Arabist.

arabizar [1f] *vt* to arabize.

arable *adj* (*esp LAm*) arable.

arácnido *nm* arachnid.

arada *nf* (**a**) (*acto*) ploughing. (**b**) (*tierra*) ploughed land. (**c**) (*extensión*) day's ploughing, yoke, area of land that can be ploughed in one day.

arado *nm* (**a**) (*apero*) plough. (**b**) (*reja*) ploughshare. (**c**) (*And*: *tierra*) ploughland, tilled land; (*huerto*) orchard.

arador *nm* ploughman.

Aragón *nm* Aragon.

aragonés, -esa 1 *adj, nm/f* Aragonese. **2** *nm* (*Ling*) Aragonese.

aragonesismo *nm* aragonesism, word (*o* phrase *etc*) peculiar to Aragon.

araguato 1 *adj* (*Carib*) dark, tawny-coloured. **2** *nm* (*And, Carib, Méx*) howler monkey.

arambel *nm* (**a**) (*Cos*) patchwork hangings, patchwork

quilt. (**b**) (*triza*) rag, shred, tatter.
arana *nf* (*trampa*) trick, swindle; (*mentira*) lie.
araná *nm* (*Carib*) straw hat.
arancel *nm* tariff, duty; ~ **protector** protective tariff.
arancelario *adj* tariff (*atr*), customs (*atr*); **barrera arancelaria** tariff barrier; **protección arancelaria** tariff protection.
arándano *nm* bilberry, whortleberry; ~ **agrio,** ~ **colorado,** ~ **encarnado** cranberry.
arandela *nf* (**a**) (*Téc*) washer. (**b**) (*de vela*) drip-collar. (**c**) (*And, Méx*: *volante*) frill, flounce. (**d**) ~**s** (*Culin*) teacakes, buns.
araña *nf* (**a**) (*Zool*) spider; **matar la** ~* (*comer*) to take the edge off one's appetite; (*perder el tiempo*) to waste time.
(**b**) (*t* ~ **de luces**) chandelier; ~ **de mesa** candelabrum.
(**c**) (*: *persona aprovechada*) resourceful person, calculating person; (*puta*) prostitute.
(**d**) (*Mex*‡) bird‡, girl.
arañar [1a] *vt* (**a**) (*herir*) to scratch. (**b**) (*reunir*) to scrape together; (*cobrar*) to claw back (*a* from), make up (*a* on); **pasó los exámenes arañando** (*Cono Sur*) he just scraped through his exams. (**c**) (*) *beneficios* to rake off, take, cream off.
arañazo *nm*, **arañón** *nm* scratch.
arañonero *nm* spider-plant.
arao *nm* guillemot.
arar [1a] *vt* to plough; to till, cultivate.
arate‡ *nm* blood.
araucano 1 *adj* Araucanian. **2** *nm*, **araucana** *nf* Araucanian, Araucan.
araucaria *nf* araucaria, monkey-puzzle tree.
arbitrador(a) *nm/f* arbiter, arbitrator.
arbitraje *nm* (**a**) (*juicio*) arbitration; ~ **industrial,** ~ **laboral** industrial arbitration. (**b**) (*Com*) arbitrage. (**c**) (*Dep*) refereeing, umpiring.
arbitrajista *nm* arbitrageur.
arbitral *adj* arbitral; of a referee (*o* an umpire); **una decisión** ~ a referee's ruling; **el equipo** ~ the referee and his linesmen.
arbitrar [1a] **1** *vt* (**a**) *disputa* to arbitrate in; (*Dep*) *tenis etc* to umpire, *boxeo, fútbol etc* to referee.
(**b**) (*obtener*) to contrive, find; (*reunir*) to bring together; to summon up one's resources for; *fondos* to raise, collect.
2 *vi* (**a**) (*actuar como árbitro*) to arbitrate; (*Dep*) to umpire, referee; ~ **en una disputa** to arbitrate in a dispute; ~ **entre A y B** to arbitrate between A and B.
(**b**) (*Filos*) to act freely, judge freely.
3 arbitrarse *vr* to get along, manage.
arbitrariamente *adv* arbitrarily.
arbitrariedad *nf* (**a**) (*cualidad*) arbitrariness, arbitrary nature. (**b**) (*acto*) arbitrary act, outrage; (*Jur*) illegal act.
arbitrario *adj* arbitrary.
arbitrio *nm* (**a**) (*libre albedrío*) free will.
(**b**) (*medio*) means, expedient.
(**c**) (*Jur*) adjudication, decision; choice; **al** ~ **de** at the discretion of; **dejar algo al** ~ **de uno** to leave sth to sb's discretion.
(**d**) (*Fin*) ~**s** municipal taxes; ~ **municipal de plusvalía** municipal capital gains tax.
arbitrismo *nm* arbitrariness, arbitrary nature.
arbitrista *nmf* promoter of crackpot (*o* utopian) schemes; armchair politician.
árbitro *nmf* (*t* **árbitra** *nf*) arbiter, arbitrator; (*Dep*: *tenis etc*) umpire, (*boxeo, fútbol etc*) referee.
árbol *nm* (**a**) (*Bot*) tree; **el** ~ **de la ciencia** the tree of knowledge; ~ **frutal** fruit tree; ~ **genealógico** family tree; ~ **de Navidad,** ~ **navideño,** ~ **de Pascua** (*Cono Sur*) Christmas tree; **estar en el** ~ (*And*) to be in a powerful position; **los** ~**es no están dejando ver el bosque** you can't see the wood for the trees.
(**b**) (*Mec*) axle, shaft; spindle; ~ **del cigüeñal** crankshaft; ~ **de levas** camshaft; ~ **motor** drive, drive-shaft; ~ **de transmisión** transmission shaft.
(**c**) (*Náut*) mast; ~ **mayor** mainmast.
(**d**) (*Inform*) tree.
arbolado 1 *adj* (**a**) *tierra* wooded, tree-covered; *calle* tree-lined, lined with trees. (**b**) (*Náut*: *barco*) with a mast, masted. (**c**) (*Náut*) **mar arbolada** heavy sea. **2** *nm* woodland.
arboladura *nf* masts and spars.
arbolar [1a] **1** *vt* (*colocar*) to put up, place upright (*a* against); *bandera* to hoist, raise; *barco* to fit with masts. **2 arbolarse** *vr* (*caballo*) to rear up, get up on its hind legs.
arboleda *nf* grove, plantation, coppice.
arboledo *nm* woodland.
arbolejo *nm* small tree.
arbóreo *adj* (**a**) (*Zool*) arboreal, tree (*atr*). (**b**) *forma* tree-like, tree-shaped.
arborícola *adj* arboreal, tree-dwelling.
arboricultor(a) *nm/f* forester.
arboricultura *nf* forestry.
arborización *nf* replanting (of trees), reafforestation.
arborizar [1f] *vi* to plant trees, replant trees.
arbotante *nm* flying buttress.
arbustivo *adj* bushy.
arbusto *nm* shrub, bush.
arca *nf* (**a**) (*caja*) chest, box, coffer; safe; (*t* ~**s**) strong-room; ~ **de hierro** strongbox; ~**s públicas** public funds; **ser como un** ~ **abierta** to be a dreadful gossip; **ser como un** ~ **cerrada** to know how to keep a secret.
(**b**) **A**~ **de la Alianza** Ark of the Covenant; **A**~ **de Noé** Noah's Ark.
(**c**) (*depósito*) tank, reservoir; ~ **de agua** water-tower.
(**d**) (*Anat*: *t* ~**s**) flank, side.
arcabucero *nm* (*Hist*) (h)arquebusier.
arcabuco *nm* thick forest, impenetrable vegetation.
arcabuz *nm* (*Hist*) (h)arquebus.
arcada *nf* (**a**) (*Arquit*) arcade, series of arches. (**b**) (*de puente*) arch, span; ~ **dentaria** denture; **de una sola** ~ single-span. (**c**) ~**s** (*Med*) retching.
árcade *adj, nmf* Arcadian.
Arcadia *nf* Arcady.
arcádico *adj*, **arcadio** *adj* Arcadian.
arcaduz *nm* (**a**) (*conducto*) pipe, conduit; (*de noria*) bucket.
(**b**) (*fig*) channel, way, means.
arcaico *adj* archaic.
arcaísmo *nm* archaism.
arcaizante *adj* archaic; *región, habla* conservative, conserving many archaisms; *persona* fond of archaisms; *estilo* old-fashioned.
arcángel *nm* archangel.
arcano 1 *adj* arcane, recondite, enigmatic. **2** *nm* secret, mystery.
arcar [1g] = **arquear**.
arce *nm* maple, maple tree.
arcediano *nm* archdeacon.
arcén *nm* (**a**) (*borde*) border, edge, brim; (*de muro*) curb, curbstone. (**b**) (*Aut*) (*de autopista*) hard shoulder, berm (*US*); (*de carretera*) verge; ~ **de servicio** service area.
arcilla *nf* clay; ~ **de alfarería,** ~ **figulina** potter's clay; ~ **cocida** baked clay; ~ **refractaria** fire clay.
arcilloso *adj* clayey.
arcipreste *nm* archpriest.
arco *nm* (**a**) (*Arquit*) arch; archway; ~ **detector de metales** metal-detecting arch; ~ **de herradura** horseshoe arch, Moorish arch; ~ **ojival** pointed arch; ~ **redondo** round arch; ~ **triunfal** triumphal arch.
(**b**) (*Anat*) arch.
(**c**) (*Geom*) arc.
(**d**) (*Elec*) arc; spotlight; ~ **voltaico** arc lamp.
(**e**) (*Mús*) bow; ~ **de violín** violin bow, fiddlestick (*hum*).
(**f**) (*Mil*) bow; ~ **y flechas** bow and arrows.
(**g**) (*de tonel*) hoop.
(**h**) ~ **iris** rainbow.
(**i**) (*Dep*) goal.
(**j**) (*fig*) ~ **constitucional,** ~ **parlamentario** range of democratic parties represented in parliament; ~ **político** political spectrum.
arcón *nm* large chest; bin, bunker.
archi... *pref* arch...; *en palabras compuestas, p.ej.* **archiconservador** ultra-conservative; **archifresco** as fresh as one can get; **archipopular** extremely popular; **un niño archimalo** a terribly naughty child; **un hombre archiestúpido** an utterly stupid man.
archiconocido *adj* extremely well-known.
archidiácono *nm* archdeacon.
archidiócesis *nf invar* archdiocese.
archiduque *nm* archduke.
archiduquesa *nf* archduchess.
archienemigo *nm* arch-enemy.
archimillonario, -a *nm/f* multimillionaire.
archipámpano *nm* (*hum*) bigwig, tycoon; panjandrum; **el** ~ **de Sevilla** the Great Panjandrum.
archipiélago *nm* archipelago; (*fig*) mass (of troubles), sea (of difficulties).
archirrepetido *adj* hackneyed, trite, over-used.

archisabido *adj* extremely well-known; **un hecho ~** a perfectly well-known fact; **eso lo tenemos ~** we know that perfectly well, that is common knowledge.
architonto 1 *adj* utterly silly. **2** *nm*, **architonta** *nf* utter fool, complete idiot.
archivado 1 *adj* (*LAm*) out-of-date, old-fashioned. **2** *nm* filing.
archivador 1 *nm* (*mueble*) filing cabinet; (*carpeta*) file. **2** *nm*, **archivadora** *nf* filing clerk.
archivar [1a] *vt* (**a**) (*guardar en un archivo*) to file, file away; to store away; to place in the archives.
(**b**) (*: *esconder*) to hide away, pigeonhole, shelve.
(**c**) (*LAm*: *retirar*) to take out of circulation.
(**d**) (*Cono Sur, Méx*: *encarcelar*) to jail.
archivero, -a *nm/f* (*de oficina*) filing clerk; (*de archivo histórico*) archivist, keeper (of archives), record officer; (*~ público*) registrar.
archivista *nmf* (*LAm*) archivist.
archivo *nm* (**a**) (*edificio*) archive(s); registry; **A~ Nacional** Public Record Office.
(**b**) (*documentos*) file; **~s** files; archives, records, muniments; **~s policíacos** police files; **~ sonoro** sound archive; **buscaremos en los ~s** we'll look in the files.
(**c**) (*Inform*) file; **~ fuente** source file.
(**d**) (*And*: *oficina*) office.
(**e**) (*Cono Sur, Méx*: *cárcel*) jail.
ardedor *adj* (*Carib, Méx*) quick-burning, easy to light.
Ardenas *nfpl* Ardennes.
ardentía *nf* (*Med*) heartburn; (*Náut*) phosphorescence.
arder [2a] **1** *vt* (**a**) (*quemar*) to burn.
(**b**) (*LAm Med*) to sting, cause to smart.
2 *vi* (**a**) (*gen*) to burn; to blaze; **~ sin llama** to smoulder; **la casa está que arde** things are on the boil, things are coming to a head.
(**b**) (*abono etc*) to ferment; (*trigo etc*) to heat up.
(**c**) (*brillar etc*) to glow, shine, blaze; (*relampaguear*) to flash.
(**d**) (*fig*) to burn, seethe; **~ de amor, ~ en amor** to burn with love; **~ en guerra** to be ablaze with war; **está que arde** (*LAm*) it's at bursting (*o* breaking) point; **¿a ti qué te arde?** what's it got to do with you?
3 arderse *vr* to burn away, burn up; (*cosecha etc*) to parch, burn up.
ardid *nm* ruse, device, stratagem; **~es** tricks, wiles.
ardido *adj* (**a**) (*valiente*) brave, bold, daring. (**b**) (*LAm*: *enojado*) cross, angry.
ardiente *adj* (**a**) (*que quema*) burning. (**b**) (*que brilla*) glowing, shining, blazing; *color* bright, glowing; *flor* bright red. (**c**) *fiebre, interés, deseo etc* burning; *amor* ardent, passionate; *partidario* fervent, passionate.
ardientemente *adv* ardently, fervently, passionately.
ardiloso *adj* (*And, Cono Sur*: *mañoso*) crafty, wily; (*Cono Sur*: *soplón*) loose-tongued.
ardilla 1 *nf* (**a**) (*Zool*) squirrel; **~ listada** chipmunk; **~ de tierra** gopher; **estar como ~** to be always on the go, not be still for a moment.
(**b**) (*LAm*) (*hombre*) clever businessman; (*mujer*) clever businesswoman; (*pey*) untrustworthy person.
2 (*) *adj invar* sharp, clever.
ardimiento¹ *nm* (*acto*) burning.
ardimiento² *nm* (*bizarría*) courage, dash.
ardita *nf* (*And, Carib, Cono Sur*) = **ardilla**.
ardite *nm*: **no me importa un ~** I don't give a tinker's curse; **no vale un ~** it's not worth a brass farthing.
ardor *nm* (**a**) (*calor*) heat, warmth.
(**b**) (*Med*) **~ de estómago** heartburn.
(**c**) (*fig*: *celo*) ardour, eagerness, zeal; (*bizarría*) courage, dash; (*de argumento*) heat, warmth; **en el ~ de la batalla** in the heat of battle.
ardoroso *adj* (**a**) (*lit*) hot, burning; **en lo más ~ del estío** in the hottest part of the summer. (**b**) (*fig*) fiery, fervent, ardent.
arduamente *adv* arduously.
arduidad *nf* arduousness.
arduo *adj* arduous, hard, tough.
área *nf* (**a**) (*gen*) area; (*Aut*) **~ de servicio(s)** service area; **en el ~ de los impuestos** in the field of taxation. (**b**) (*Mat*) are, square decameter. (**c**) (*Dep*) **~ de castigo, ~ de penálty** penalty area; **~ de gol, ~ de meta** goal area. (**d**) **~ metropolitana** (*LAm*) metropolitan area, urban district; **~ verde** (*Carib*) green area, park area.
arena *nf* (**a**) (*Geol*) sand; grit, gravel; **~s movedizas** quicksands, shifting sands; **~s de oro** (*fig*) fine gold, gold dust; **sembrar en ~** (*fig*) to labour in vain.
(**b**) (*Med*) **~s** stones, gravel.
(**c**) (*Dep etc*) arena.
arenal *nm* (**a**) (*terreno*) sandy spot, sandy ground. (**b**) (*hoyo*) sandpit; (*Golf*) bunker. (**c**) (*Náut*) sands, quicksand.
arenar [1a] *vt* (**a**) (*restregar con arena*) to sand, sprinkle with sand. (**b**) (*Téc*) to sand, polish with sand, rub with sand.
arenga *nf* (**a**) (*discurso*) harangue, speech; (*) lecture, sermon. (**b**) (*Cono Sur*: *discusión*) argument, quarrel.
arengar [1h] *vt* to harangue.
arenguear [1a] *vi* (*Cono Sur*) to argue, quarrel.
arenillas *nfpl* (*Med*) stones, gravel.
arenisca *nf* sandstone.
arenisco *adj* sandy; gravelly, gritty.
arenoso *adj* sandy.
arenque *nm* herring; **~ ahumado** kipper.
areómetro *nm* hydrometer.
arepa *nf* (*LAm*) large tortilla (*o* maize cake); **hacer ~s**** to make love (*lesbians*).
arepera *nf* (*LAm*) (**a**) *arepa* seller. (**b**) (**) lesbian.
arepero *nm* (*Carib*) poor wretch.
arequipa *nf* (*And*) rice pudding.
arequipeño 1 *adj* of (*o* from) Arequipa. **2** *nm*, **arequipeña** *nf* native (*o* inhabitant) of Arequipa; **los ~s** the people of Arequipa.
arete *nm* earring; **ir** (*o* **estar**) **de ~** (*Carib*) to be a hanger-on.
argamandijo* *nm* set of tools, tackle.
argamasa *nf* mortar, plaster.
argamasar [1a] *vt* (**a**) *mortero* to mix. (**b**) *pared* to mortar, plaster.
árgana *nf* derrick.
árganas *nfpl* (*esp Cono Sur*) wicker baskets, panniers (*carried by horse*).
Argel *nm* Algiers.
Argelia *nf* Algeria.
argelino, -a *adj, nm/f* Algerian.
argén *nm* (*Her*) argent.
argentado *adj* silvered; (*fig*) silvery.
argentar [1a] *vt* to silver.
argénteo *adj* (**a**) (*Téc*) silver-plated. (**b**) (*poét*) silver, silvery.
argentería *nf* silver (*o* gold) embroidery, silver (*o* gold) filigree.
Argentina *nf* Argentina, the Argentine.
argentinismo *nm* argentinism, word (*o* phrase *etc*) peculiar to Argentina.
argentino¹ *adj* silvery.
argentino², -a *adj, nm/f* Argentinian, Argentine.
argento *nm* (*poét*) silver; **~ vivo** quicksilver.
argo *nm* argon.
argolla *nf* (**a**) (*aro*) (large) ring; (*para caballo*) hitching ring; (*aldaba*) door-knocker; (*de servilleta*) serviette ring; (*LAm*: *de novios*) engagement ring, (*de boda*) wedding ring; **cambio de ~s** (*Cono Sur*) engagement. (**b**) (*Dep*) *argolla* (*a game like croquet*).
argollar [1a] **1** *vt* (*And*) *cerdo* to ring; (*Méx*) to hitch to a ring; **~ a uno** (*Méx*) to have a hold over sb (because of a service rendered).
2 argollarse *vr* (*And*) to get engaged.
argón *nm* argon.
argonauta *nm* Argonaut.
Argos *nm* Argus.
argot [ar'go] *nm, pl* **argots** [ar'go] slang.
argótico *adj* slang (*atr*); slangy.
argucia *nf* subtlety, sophistry, hair-splitting; trick, subtle manoeuvre.
argüende *nm* (*LAm*) argument.
argüir [3g] **1** *vt* (**a**) (*razonar*) to argue, contend; (*indicar*) to indicate, point to, imply; (*deducir*) to infer, deduce; **de ahí arguyo su buena calidad** I deduce its good quality from that; **esto arguye su poco cuidado** this indicates his lack of care.
(**b**) (*reprochar*) to reproach; to accuse; **me argüían con vehemencia** they vehemently reproached me; **~ a uno (de) su crueldad** to reproach sb for his cruelty.
2 *vi* to argue (*contra* against, with).
argumentable *adj* arguable.
argumentación *nf* argumentation; line of argument.
argumentador *adj* argumentative.
argumental *adj* (*Liter*) plot (*atr*); **línea ~** line of the plot, story-line.
argumentar [1a] *vti* to argue; **~ que** ... to argue that ...,

contend that ...

argumento *nm* (**a**) (*gen*) argument (*t Jur*); line of argument; (*razonamiento*) reasoning, thinking.

(**b**) (*Liter, Teat*) plot, story-line; ~ **de la obra** (*como prólogo*) summary of the plot, summary of the story, outline.

(**c**) (*LAm: discusión*) argument, discussion, quarrel.

aria *nf* aria.

aridecer [2d] **1** *vt* to dry up, make arid. **2** *vi y* **aridecerse** *vr* to dry up, become arid.

aridez *nf* aridity, dryness (*t fig*).

árido 1 *adj* arid, dry (*t fig*). **2 ~s** *nmpl* (*Com*) dry goods; (*Agr*) dry grains, hard grains; (*hormigón*) sand and cement; **medida para ~s** dry measure.

Aries *nm* (*Zodíaco*) Aries.

ariete *nm* (**a**) (*Mil*) battering ram. (**b**) (*Dep*) striker.

arigua *nf* (*Carib*) wild bee.

arillo *nm* earring.

ario, -a *adj, nm/f* Aryan.

ariqueño 1 *adj* of Arica. **2** *nm*, **ariqueña** *nf* native (*o* inhabitant) of Arica; **los ~s** the people of Arica.

ariscar [1g] **1** *vt* (*CAm, Carib, Méx*) (*domar*) *animal* to pacify, control; *persona* to make suspicious. **2 ariscarse** *vr* (*CAm, Carib*) to run away.

arisco *adj animal* shy; wild, temperamental, vicious; timid; *persona* surly; unsociable, unapproachable; (*LAm*) reserved.

arista *nf* (*Bot*) beard, awn; (*Geom*) edge; (*Arquit*) arris; (*Alpinismo*) arête.

aristocracia *nf* aristocracy.

aristócrata *nmf* aristocrat.

aristocrático *adj* aristocratic.

Aristófanes *nm* Aristophanes.

aristón *nm* (*Mús*) mechanical organ.

Aristóteles *nm* Aristotle.

aristotélico *adj* Aristotelian.

aritmética *nf* arithmetic.

aritmético 1 *adj* arithmetical. **2** *nmf* arithmetician.

Arlequín *nm* Harlequin.

arlequín *nm* (**a**) (*fig*) buffoon. (**b**) (*helado*) Neapolitan ice cream.

arlequinada *nf* (*Hist*) harlequinade; (*bufonada*) (piece of) buffoonery, fooling.

arlequinesco *adj* (*fig*) grotesque, ridiculous.

Arlés *nf* Arles.

arma *nf* (**a**) (*Mil etc*) arm, weapon; (**) prick**; ~ **arrojadiza** missile; ~ **atómica** atomic weapon; ~ **biológica** biological weapon; ~ **blanca** steel blade, knife, sword; ~ **de combate** assault weapon; ~ **convencional** conventional weapon; **~s cortas** small arms; ~ **de fuego** firearm, gun; ~ **de infantería** infantry weapon; ~ **larga** shotgun; ~ **negra** fencing foil; ~ **química** chemical weapon; ~ **reglamentaria** service weapon, regulation weapon; ~ **de doble filo** (*fig*) double-edged sword; **¡a las ~s!** to arms!; **¡~s al hombro!** shoulder arms!; **alzarse en ~s** to rise up in arms, rebel; **¡descansen ~s!** order arms!; (*fig*) **estar en ~s** to be anxious; **estar sobre las ~s** to be under arms; to stand by; **limpiar el ~**** to have a screw**; **pasar a uno por las ~s** to shoot sb, execute sb; **pasar a una por las ~s**** to screw sb**; **¡presenten ~s!** present arms!; **rendir las ~s** to lay down one's arms; **tocar (al) ~** to sound the call to arms; **tomar las ~s** to take up arms; **ser de ~s tomar, ser de llevar ~s** (*LAm*) to be bold, be determined, be sb to be reckoned with; **volver el ~ contra uno** to turn the tables on sb.

(**b**) (*servicio*) arm, branch, service.

(**c**) **~s** (*Her*) arms.

armada *nf* (**a**) (*escuadra*) fleet; (*nacional*) navy; (*Hist*) armada; **la A~ Británica** the British Navy; **un oficial de la ~** a naval officer.

(**b**) (*Cono Sur: lazo*) noose, lasso.

armadía *nf* = **almadía**.

armadijo *nm* trap, snare.

armadillo *nm* armadillo.

armado *adj* (**a**) (*Mil*) armed; ~ **hasta los dientes** armed to the teeth; **ir ~** to go armed. (**b**) (*Mec*) mounted, assembled. (**c**) (*Téc*) *hormigón* reinforced; *tela* toughened. (**d**) (*LAm*) stubborn.

armador *nm* (**a**) (*Náut: dueño*) shipowner; (*constructor*) shipbuilder; (*Hist*) privateer. (**b**) (*Mec*) fitter, assembler. (**c**) (*LAm*) (*chaleco*) waistcoat; (*percha*) coathanger.

armadura *nf* (**a**) (*Mil, Hist*) armour; **una ~** a suit of armour.

(**b**) (*Téc*) frame, framework; (*de gafas*) frame; (*Anat*) skeleton; (*Bot, Elec, Zool*) armature; ~ **de la cama** bedstead.

(**c**) (*Mús*) key signature.

armaduría *nf* (*LAm*) car assembly plant.

Armagedón *nm* Armageddon.

armamentismo *nm* tendency to indulge in the arms race; reliance on abundant armaments; arms build-up.

armamentista *adj* arms (*atr*); **carrera ~** arms race.

armamento *nm* (**a**) (*Mil*) arms, armaments; (*de buque, unidad*) armament. (**b**) (*Mil: acto*) arming; (*Náut*) fitting-out. (**c**) (*Téc*) framework.

armar [1a] **1** *vt* (**a**) (*con arma*) to arm (*con, de* with).

(**b**) *bayoneta* to fix; *arco* to bend; *cañón etc* to load; *trampa* to set.

(**c**) (*disponer*) to prepare, arrange, get ready; (*Mec*) to assemble, put together; to set up; to mount; *tienda* to pitch, set up; (*Arquit*) to set (*en, sobre* on).

(**d**) (*Náut*) to fit out, equip; to put into commission.

(**e**) *hormigón* to reinforce; (*Cos*) to stiffen.

(**f**) ~ **a uno caballero** to knight sb, dub sb knight.

(**g**) *pleito* to bring; *lío* to cause, make, start, stir up; **~la** to start a row, make trouble.

2 armarse *vr* (**a**) (*con arma*) to arm o.s. (*con, de* with); ~ **de valor** to gather up one's courage; ~ **de paciencia** to arm o.s. with patience, resolve to be patient.

(**b**) (*disponerse*) to prepare, get ready; *V* **Dios** *etc*.

(**c**) (*CAm, Carib, Méx*) (*obstinarse*) to become obstinate; (*negarse*) to refuse point blank.

(**d**) (*Carib: animal*) to balk, shy.

(**e**) (*LAm: tener suerte*) to be lucky, have a stroke of luck; (*enriquecerse*) to strike it rich.

(**f**) **¡te vas a armar!** (*Cono Sur*) forget it!, no way!*

armario *nm* cupboard; ~ **(para libros)** bookcase; ~ **(ropero)** wardrobe; ~ **botiquín** medicine chest; ~ **empotrado** built-in cupboard.

armatoste *nm* (**a**) (*mueble*) unwieldy piece of furniture (*etc*); (*trasto*) large useless object; (*Mec*) contraption; (*Aut*) crock, jalopy.

(**b**) (*persona*) useless great object, clumsy sort.

armazón *nf* (*m en algunas regiones de LAm*) (*armadura*) frame, framework; (*Aer, Aut*) body, chassis; (*Arquit*) shell, skeleton; (*de mueble*) frame; (*And, Cono Sur: estante*) shelves, shelving.

armella *nf* eyebolt.

Armenia *nf* Armenia.

armenio, -a *adj, nm/f* Armenian.

armería *nf* (**a**) (*museo*) military museum, museum of arms; armoury. (**b**) (*tienda*) gunsmith's (shop), gun shop. (**c**) (*arte*) art of the gunsmith. (**d**) (*Her*) heraldry.

armero *nm* (**a**) (*persona*) gunsmith, gunmaker, armourer. (**b**) (*estante*) gun rack; stand for weapons.

armiño *nm* (*Zool*) stoat; (*piel, Her*) ermine.

armisticio *nm* armistice.

armón *nm* (*t* ~ **de artillería**) gun carriage, limber.

armonía *nf* harmony; **en ~** in harmony (*con* with), in keeping (*con* with).

armónica *nf* harmonica, mouth organ.

armónicamente *adv* harmoniously; harmonically.

armonicista *nmf* harmonica player, mouth-organist.

armónico 1 *adj* harmonious; harmonic. **2** *nm* (*Mús, Fís*) harmonic.

armonio *nm* harmonium.

armoniosamente *adv* harmoniously; tunefully.

armonioso *adj* harmonious; tuneful.

armonizable *adj* (*fig*) that can be reconciled.

armonización *nf* harmonization; (*fig*) reconciliation; coordination; **ley de ~** coordinating law, law designed to reconcile differences.

armonizador *adj*: **ley ~a**; *V n.*

armonizar [1f] **1** *vt* to harmonize; (*fig*) to harmonize, bring into harmony; *diferencias* to reconcile.

2 *vi* to harmonize (*con* with); (*fig*) ~ **con** to harmonize with, blend with, be in keeping with; ~ **con** (*colores*) to blend with, tone in with.

ARN *nm abr de* **ácido ribonucleico** ribonucleic acid, RNA.

arnaco *nm* (*And*) useless object, piece of lumber.

arnero *nm* (*LAm*) sieve.

arnés *nm* (**a**) (*Mil, Hist*) armour. (**b**) harness; ~ **de seguridad** safety harness; **arneses** harness, trappings; (*fig*) gear, tackle, outfit.

árnica *nf* arnica; (*Dep*) **pedir ~** to throw in the towel.

aro[1] *nm* ring, hoop; rim; (*Dep*) quoit; (*LAm: arete*) earring; (*LAm: anillo de boda*) wedding ring; (*de servilleta*) serviette ring; ~ **de émbolo** piston ring; ~ **de rueda** rim of

a wheel; **(juego de) ~s** quoits; **entrar por el ~** to fall into line; to knuckle under; to have no option; **hacer un ~** (*Cono Sur*) to have a break; **pasar a uno por el ~** (*LAm**) to play tricks on sb.
aro[2] *nm* (*Bot*) lords-and-ladies.
aroma *nm* aroma, scent, fragrance; (*de vino*) bouquet.
aromático *adj* aromatic, sweet-scented.
aromatizador *nm* (*LAm*) spray.
aromatizante *nm* flavouring, aromatic spice.
aromatizar [1f] *vt* to scent, give fragrance to; (*Culin*) to spice, flavour with herbs.
arpa *nf* harp; **tocar el ~*** to be a thief, live by thieving.
arpado *adj* jagged, toothed, serrated.
arpar[1] [1a] *vt* (*arañar*) to scratch, claw (at); (*hacer pedazos*) to tear, tear to pieces.
arpar[2]‡ [1a] *vt* (*LAm*) to pinch*, nick‡.
arpeo *nm* grappling iron.
arpero, -a *nm/f* (*Méx*) (*ladrón*) thief, burglar; (*arpista*) harpist.
arpía *nf* harpy; (*fig*) shrew, hag.
arpicordio *nm* harpsichord.
arpillar [1a] *vt* (*CAm*) to pile up.
arpillera *nf* sacking, sackcloth.
arpir *nm* (*And, Cono Sur*) mineworker.
arpista *nmf* (*Mús*) harpist; (*Cono Sur: ladrón*) thief, burglar.
arpón *nm* harpoon; gaff.
arponar [1a] *vt*, **arponear** [1a] *vt* to harpoon; to gaff.
arponero *adj*: **navío ~** whaler, whaling-vessel.
arquear [1a] **1** *vt* (**a**) (*doblar*) to arch; to bend.
(**b**) *lana* to beat.
(**c**) (*Náut*) to gauge.
(**d**) (*LAm Com*) to check, check the contents of.
2 *vi* (*Med*) to retch.
3 arquearse *vr* to arch; to bend; (*superficie*) to camber.
arqueo *nm* (**a**) (*Arquit etc*) arching. (**b**) (*Náut*) tonnage, burden; capacity; **~ bruto** gross tonnage. (**c**) (*Com*) checking.
arqueolítico *adj* Stone-Age (*atr*).
arqueología *nf* archaeology; **~ industrial** industrial archaeology; **~ submarina** underwater archaeology.
arqueológico *adj* archaeological.
arqueólogo, -a *nm/f* archaeologist.
arquería *nf* arcade, series of arches.
arquero *nm* (**a**) (*Mil*) bowman, archer. (**b**) (*Com*) cashier. (**c**) (*Dep*) goalkeeper.
arqueta *nf* chest.
arquetípico *adj* archetypal, archetypical.
arquetipo *nm* archetype.
Arquímedes *nm* Archimedes.
arquimesa *nf* desk, escritoire.
arquitecto, -a *nm/f* architect; **~ de jardines** landscape gardener; **~ paisajista** landscaping expert.
arquitectónico *adj* architectural.
arquitectura *nf* architecture; **~ de jardines** landscape gardening; **~ paisajista** landscaping.
arquitrabe *nm* arquitrave.
arrabal *nm* suburb; (*LAm: barrio bajo*) slums, slum quarter; **~es** outskirts, outlying area.
arrabalero 1 *adj* (**a**) (*de un arrabal*) suburban; (*pey*) of (*o* from) the poorer quarters.
(**b**) (*fig*) common, coarse.
2 *nm*, **arrabalera** *nf* (**a**) (*gen*) suburbanite, (*pey*) person from the poorer quarters.
(**b**) (*fig*) common sort, coarse person.
arrabio *nm* cast iron.
arracacha *nf* (*And*) idiocy, silliness.
arracacho *nm* (*And*) idiot.
arracada *nf* pendant earring.
arracimado *adj* clustered, clustering; crowded, packed together.
arracimarse [1a] *vr* to cluster together, hang in bunches.
arraigadamente *adv* firmly, securely.
arraigado *adj* firmly rooted, well-rooted, deep-rooted; (*fig*) established, ingrained; *persona* landed, property-owning.
arraigar [1h] **1** *vt* (**a**) (*fig*) to establish; to strengthen (*en* in).
(**b**) (*LAm Jur*): **~ a uno** to put (*o* keep) sb under a restriction order.
2 *vi* (*Bot*) to take root, strike root.
3 arraigarse *vr* (*Bot*) to take root; (*costumbre etc*) to take root, establish itself, take a hold; (*persona*) to settle, establish o.s.; to acquire property; **la costumbre se arraigó en él** the habit grew on him.
arraigo *nm* (**a**) (*Bot*) rooting; **de fácil ~** easily-rooted; **de mucho ~, de viejo ~** deep-rooted.
(**b**) (*bienes*) property, land, real estate; **hombre de ~** man of property.
(**c**) (*fig: acto*) settling, establishment.
(**d**) (*fig: influencia*) hold, influence; **tener ~** to have influence.
(**e**) **orden de ~** (*Cono Sur, Méx*) restriction order.
arralar [1a] *vt* (*Méx*) *árboles* to thin out.
arramblar* [1a] *vi*: **~ con** (**a**) (*robar*) to make off with, pinch*. (**b**) (*apartar*) to remove, relegate, push aside.
arrancaclavos *nm invar* claw hammer, nail extractor.
arrancada *nf* (*arranque*) sudden start; (*aceleración*) burst of speed; (*sacudida*) jerk, jolt; (*Dep: pesos*) snatch; (*LAm*) sudden dash, escape attempt.
arrancadero *nm* starting point.
arrancado 1 *adj* (*) broke*, penniless. **2** *nm* (*Aut*) starting, ignition.
arrancador *nm* (*Aut*) starter.
arrancamiento *nm* pulling out, extraction; snatching.
arrancar [1g] **1** *vt* (**a**) *planta etc* to pull up, root out; *diente* to extract, pull; *metal* to win, extract; *pelo etc* to pluck out; *botón etc* to tear off, tear away; *papel etc* to tear out, rip out; (*Inform*) to boot; *flema* to bring up; *suspiro* to fetch; **una historia que arranca lágrimas** a story to make one cry.
(**b**) (*arrebatar etc*) to snatch, snatch away (*a, de* from); to wrench, wrest (*a, de* from); **le arrancó el bolso** he snatched her handbag; **el viento lo arrancó de mis manos** the wind snatched it from my hands; **lograron ~le el cuchillo** they managed to wrest the knife from him.
(**c**) **~ a uno de una fiesta** to drag sb away from a party; **~ a uno de un vicio** to break sb of a bad habit.
(**d**) *adhesión* to win, get; *victoria* to snatch, wrest (*a* from); **~ una promesa a uno** to force a promise out of sb, extort a promise from sb; **~ información a uno** to worm information out of sb, extract information from sb.
(**e**) (*Aut etc*) to start.
2 *vi* (**a**) (*partir*) to start, set off; (*Aut*) to start; (*Náut*) to set sail; (*acelerarse*) to pick up speed, accelerate; (*) to leave (at last), get going; (*: *largarse*) to clear out*; (*LAm*) to escape, run off; **~ a cantar** to break into song, burst out singing; **~ a correr** to start running, break into a run.
(**b**) (*Cono Sur: lanzarse*) to launch o.s., start off with a will.
(**c**) (*Arquit: arco etc*) **~ de** to spring from.
(**d**) **~ de** (*fig*) to come from, spring from, originate in; to go back to; **esto arranca del siglo XV** this goes back to the 15th century, this began in the 15th century; **todo arranca de aquello** it all starts with that.
3 arrancarse‡ *vr* (*And, Carib, Méx*) to peg out‡, kick the bucket‡.
arrancón *nm* (*Méx*) = **arrancada.**
arranchar [1a] **1** *vt* (**a**) *velas* to brace.
(**b**) *costa* to skirt, sail close to.
(**c**) (*And: arrebatar*) to snatch away (*a* from).
2 arrancharse *vr* (**a**) (*reunirse*) to gather together; (*comer*) to eat together.
(**b**) (*Carib, Méx: acomodarse*) to settle in, make o.s. comfortable; (*Carib: adaptarse*) to make the best of it.
arranque *nm* (**a**) (*sacudida*) sudden start, jerk, jolt; wrench.
(**b**) (*Aut, Mec*) start; starting, ignition; **~ (automático)** (*Aut*) (self-)starter; **~ en frío** cold start; **~ manual** crank starting.
(**c**) (*Anat, Arquit*) starting point; base.
(**d**) (*fig: impulso*) impulse; (*arrebato*) (emotional) outburst; **~ de cólera** fit of anger, outburst of bad temper; **~ de energía** burst of energy; **en un ~** impulsively.
(**e**) (*fig: gracia*) sally, witty remark.
(**f**) (*) **estar en el ~** (*LAm*) to be completely broke*.
(**g**) **no servir ni para el ~** (*Méx*) to be completely useless.
arranquera* *nf*, **arranquitis*** *nf* (*And, CAm, Carib*) = **arranque (f).**
arrapiezo *nm* (**a**) (*trapo*) rag, tatter. (**b**) (*persona*) whippersnapper.
arras *nfpl* (**a**) (*prenda*) pledge, security, deposit. (**b**) (*Hist*) *13 coins given by bridegroom to bride.*
arrasador *adj* = **arrollador.**
arrasamiento *nm* levelling; demolishing; devastation; **bombardeo de ~** carpet bombing.

arrasar [1a] **1** *vt* (**a**) (*nivelar*) to level, flatten; *edificio etc* to raze to the ground, demolish; *ciudad, región* to devastate.
(**b**) (*colmar*) to fill up, fill to the brim.
2 *vi* (**a**) (*Met*) to clear.
(**b**) (*triunfar*) to triumph, achieve a great success; (*Pol etc*) to sweep the board.
3 arrasarse *vr* (*Met*) to clear; **se le arrasaron los ojos de** (*o* **en**) **lágrimas** her eyes filled with tears.
arrastracueros *nm invar* (*Carib*) crook; rascal, rogue.
arrastradizo *adj* dangling, trailing.
arrastrado 1 *adj* (**a**) **llevar algo** ~ to drag sth along.
(**b**) (*miserable*) poor, wretched, miserable; vile; **andar** ~ to have a wretched life.
(**c**) (*astuto*) wily, rascally.
(**d**) (*LAm*: *servil*) cringing, servile.
2 *nm* rogue, rascal; (*Méx*: *pobre diablo*) down-and-out.
arrastrar [1a] **1** *vt* (**a**) (*gen*) to drag, drag along; *carro etc* to haul, pull; (*hacia abajo*) to drag down.
(**b**) *vestido etc* to trail along the ground.
(**c**) ~ **los pies** to drag one's feet, shuffle along.
(**d**) (*agua, viento etc*) to carry away, carry down, sweep along.
(**e**) *palabras* to drawl.
(**f**) (*Bridge*) *triunfos* to draw.
(**g**) (*pasiones etc*) to carry away; *adherentes etc* to win over, carry with one; *afecto, lealtad* to command, draw, win; (*Rad etc*) *audiencia* to draw, attract; **no te dejes** ~ **por esa idea** don't get carried away by that idea, don't run away with that idea.
(**h**) (*degradar*) to drag down, degrade, debase.
(**i**) (*acarrear*) to bring with it, bring in its train, have as consequences.
(**j**) ~ **a uno a hacer algo** to lead sb to do sth.
2 *vi* to drag, trail along the ground, hang down; (*Bot*) to trail.
3 arrastrarse *vr* (**a**) (*animal, persona*) to crawl, creep; to drag o.s. along; **se arrastró hasta la puerta** he dragged himself to the door.
(**b**) (*vestido etc*) to drag, trail along the ground, hang down.
(**c**) (*tiempo, función etc*) to drag.
(**d**) (*humillarse*) to grovel, fawn, creep*.
arrastre *nm* (**a**) (*acto*) drag, dragging, pulling; haulage; (*Aer*) drag; (*Pesca*) trawling; **flota de** ~ trawling fleet, fleet of trawlers; ~ **por correa** belt-drive.
(**b**) (*Carib*: *influencia*) influence, pull; **tener mucho** ~ to have a lot of influence, have connections.
(**c**) (*Taur*) dragging away of the dead bull; **estar para el** (*o* **pal**) ~ to be finished, be done for; to be all in.
(**d**) (*Inform*): ~ **de dientes** tractor; ~ **de papel por tracción** tractor feed; ~ **de papel por fricción** friction feed.
arrastrero 1 *adj* trawler (*atr*); **flota arrastrera** trawling fleet, fleet of trawlers. **2** *nm* trawler.
arrayán *nm* myrtle.
arre *interj* get up!, gee up!; (*LAm*) hurry up!
arreada *nf* (*Cono Sur, Méx*) rustling, cattle-thieving; round-up.
arreado *adj* (*And, Cono Sur, Méx*) sluggish, ponderous.
arreador *nm* (**a**) (*capataz*) foreman; (*arriero*) muleteer. (**b**) (*Cono Sur*: *látigo*) long whip.
arrear [1a] **1** *vt* (**a**) *ganado etc* to drive, urge on. (**b**) (*caballo*) to harness. (**c**) (*CAm, Cono Sur, Méx*: *ganado*) to steal, rustle. (**d**) (*) *golpe* to give. **2** *vi* to hurry along; **¡arrea!** get moving!; (*fig*: *repulsa*) get away!; (*Esp*: *asombro*) Christ!, well I'm damned!; (*admiración*) look at that!
arrebañaduras *nfpl* scrapings, remains.
arrebañar [1a] *vt* to scrape together; *comida* to eat up, clear up.
arrebatadamente *adv* suddenly, violently; headlong; rashly; **hablar** ~ to speak in a rush.
arrebatadizo *adj* excitable, hot-tempered.
arrebatado *adj* (**a**) (*apresurado*) hasty, sudden, violent. (**b**) (*impetuoso*) rash, impetuous. (**c**) (*absorto etc*) rapt, bemused; ecstatic. (**d**) *cara* flushed.
arrebatamiento *nm* (**a**) (*acto*) snatching (away); seizure; abduction. (**b**) (*fig*) captivation; (*éxtasis*) ecstasy, rapture; (*emoción*) excitement; (*ira*) anger.
arrebatar [1a] **1** *vt* (**a**) (*gen*) to snatch, snatch away (*a* from); to seize; to wrench, wrest (*a* from); (*viento*) to blow away; *página, parte etc* to tear off, rip off; *persona* to carry away, carry off, abduct; **le arrebató el revólver** he snatched the pistol from him; **nos arrebataron la victoria** they wrested victory from us; ~ **la vida a uno** to take sb's life.
(**b**) (*fig*: *conmover*) to move deeply, stir; (*extasiar*) to captivate, enrapture; (*alegrar*) to exhilarate; **se dejó** ~ **por su entusiasmo** he got carried away by his enthusiasm.
(**c**) (*Agr*) to parch.
2 arrebatarse *vr* (**a**) (*excitarse*) to get carried away; to get excited; ~ **de cólera** to be overcome with anger.
(**b**) (*Culin*) to burn, overcook.
arrebatiña *nf* scramble (to pick sth up); rush, scrimmage; snatching; **coger algo a la** ~ to snatch sth up.
arrebato *nm* (**a**) (*ira*) fit of rage, fury. (**b**) (*éxtasis*) ecstasy, rapture; **en un** ~ **de entusiasmo** in a sudden fit of enthusiasm.
arrebiatarse [1a] *vr* (*CAm*: *unirse*) to join up, join together; (*Méx*) to follow the crowd, agree automatically (with everything).
arrebol *nm* rouge; (*de cielo*) red flush, red glow; **~es** red clouds.
arrebolar [1a] **1** *vt* to redden. **2 arrebolarse** *vr* (**a**) (*maquillarse*) to apply rouge, rouge o.s. (**b**) (*enrojecer*) to redden, flush. (**c**) (*Carib*: *vestirse*) to dress up.
arrebozar [1f] **1** *vt* (**a**) (*embozar*) to cover (with a cloak); to conceal. (**b**) (*Culin*) to cover, coat; *taza* to fill right up.
2 arrebozarse *vr* (**a**) (*embozarse*) to cover one's face; to muffle up, muffle one's face.
(**b**) (*Ent*) to swarm.
arrebujar [1a] **1** *vt* (**a**) (*objetos*) to jumble together, jumble up; to bundle together. (**b**) *niño etc* to wrap up, cover. **2 arrebujarse** *vr* to wrap o.s. up (*con* in, with).
arreciar [1b] **1** *vi* to grow worse, get more severe; (*demanda*) to intensify; (*viento*) to get stronger.
2 arreciarse *vr* (**a**) = *vi*.
(**b**) (*Med*) to get stronger, pick up.
arrecife *nm* reef; ~ **de coral,** ~ **coralina** coral reef.
arrecirse [3b] *vr* (*LAm*) to be frozen stiff.
arrechada *nf* (*CAm, Méx*) = **arrechera.**
arrechar [1a] **1** *vt* (*LAm*) to arouse, excite. **2** *vi* (**a**) (*CAm*: *animarse*) to show energy, begin to make an effort. (**b**) (*CAm, Méx**: *estar cachondo*) to feel randy*. **3 arrecharse** *vr* (*CAm, Méx*) to get angry.
arrechera *nf* (**a**) (*Cono Sur Zool*) heat, mating urge; (*Méx**) randiness*, lust. (**b**) (*Méx*: *capricho*) whim, fancy. (**c**) (*Carib*: *mal humor*) bad mood.
arrecho 1 *adj* (**a**) (*CAm, Méx*) (*vigoroso*) vigorous; (*enérgico*) energetic; (*valiente*) brave. (**b**) (*CAm*: *lascivo*) randy, lecherous; sexy; **estar** ~ (*Zool*) to be on heat; (*persona*) to be in the mood, feel randy*. (**c**) (*Carib*) **¡qué ~!** what fun! (**d**) (*CAm, Carib, Méx*: *furioso*) angry, furious. **2** *nm* (**a**) **en** ~ (*CAm, Méx Zool*) on heat. (**b**) **es un** ~ (*CAm*‡: *fastidio*) he's a bloody nuisance‡, he's a pain in the ass**.
arrechucho *nm* (**a**) (*impulso*) sudden impulse; (*arranque*) fit, outburst; (*dificultad*) unforeseen difficulty, new trouble.
(**b**) (*Med*) queer turn, sudden indisposition.
arredo *adv* (*CAm, Méx*): **¡~ vaya!**‡ get lost!‡
arredomado *adj* (*LAm*) sly, artful.
arredrar [1a] **1** *vt* (**a**) (*hacer retirarse*) to drive back; (*apartar*) to remove, separate.
(**b**) (*asustar*) to scare, daunt.
2 arredrarse *vr* (**a**) (*retirarse*) to draw back, move away (*de* from).
(**b**) (*asustarse*) to get scared, lose heart; ~ **ante algo** to shrink away from sth; **sin** ~ unmoved, nothing daunted.
arregazado *adj vestido etc* tucked up; *nariz* turned up, snub.
arregazar [1f] *vt* to tuck up.
arregionado 1 *adj* (**a**) (*And, Méx*: *de mal genio*) ill-tempered, sharp; (*And*: *irreflexivo*) impulsive; (*And*: *mohino*) sulky; (*And*) cross, angry. (**b**) (*Carib*: *estimado*) highly regarded. **2** *nm*, **arregionada** *nf* (*Carib*) highly respected person.
arreglada *nf*: ~ **de bigotes** (*Cono Sur**) dirty deal, shady business.
arregladamente *adv* regularly, in an orderly way; sensibly, reasonably.
arreglado *adj* (**a**) (*ordenado*) neat, orderly, proper; (*moderado*) moderate, sensible, reasonable; **una vida arreglada** a well-regulated life, a sensible life, a well-adjusted life; **conducta arreglada** good behaviour, orderly behaviour; **un precio** ~ a reasonable price.
(**b**) ~ **a** in accordance with, adjusted to.
arreglador(a) *nm/f* (*Mus*) arranger.
arreglar [1a] **1** *vt* (**a**) (*gen*) to arrange; (*resolver*) to settle; (*ajustar*) to adjust (*a* to), regulate; *cita, fecha, reunión etc* to arrange, fix up; *problema* to put right; *abuso* to correct;

disputa to settle, put right; (*Cono Sur, Méx*) *deuda* to settle; (*LAm*) *animal* to castrate; **yo lo arreglaré** I'll see to it, I'll arrange it; **todavía no se ha arreglado nada** nothing has been fixed up yet.

(**b**) (*Mec etc*) to fix, mend, repair.

(**c**) *aspecto, pelo, cuarto etc* to tidy up, smarten up, do; **voy a que me arreglen el pelo** I'm going to have my hair done.

(**d**) (*Mús*) to arrange.

2 arreglarse *vr* (**a**) (*ponerse de acuerdo*) to come to terms (*a, con* with), reach an understanding; **~ a** to conform to, adjust o.s. to; **por fin se arreglaron** eventually they reached an agreement.

(**b**) **~ el pelo** to have one's hair done; to do one's hair, tidy one's hair.

(**c**) (*problema etc*) to work out, be solved, be all right; **por fin el asunto se arregló** everything was finally fixed up; **todo se arreglará** things will work out, everything will be all right; (*LAm*) **ya es hora de ~** it's time to get ready.

(**d**) (*LAm*: *tener suerte*) to have a stroke of luck; (*entenderse*) to get on, hit it off.

(**e**) **arreglárselas** to get by, manage; **arreglárselas para** + *infin* to manage to + *infin*; **¿cómo se las arreglan Vds?** how do you manage?; **hay que arreglárselas** you've got to get organized; it's up to you to see to it; **sabe arreglárselas** he's well able to take care of himself.

Arreglalotodo* *nm*: **el Señor ~** Mr Fixit*.

arreglista *nmf* (*Mús*) arranger.

arreglo *nm* (**a**) (*acto*) arrangement, settlement; adjustment; regulation; **~ de cuentas** (*fig*) settling of old scores; **esto no tiene ~** there's no way of sorting this out, there's no solution to this; **ya no tiene ~** it's too late now, there's nothing to be done now; it's beyond repair.

(**b**) (*orden*) rule, order; orderliness; **vivir con ~** to live an orderly life.

(**c**) (*acuerdo*) agreement, understanding; compromise; **con ~ a** according to, in accordance with; **llegar a un ~** to reach a settlement, reach a compromise.

(**d**) (*Mús*) setting, arrangement.

(**e**) (*euf*: *de amantes*) liaison, understanding.

(**f**) (*de pelo*) trim.

arregostarse [1a] *vr*: **~ a** to take a fancy to.

arregosto *nm* fancy, taste (*de* for).

arrejarse [1a] *vr* (*Cono Sur*: *arriesgarse*) to take a risk.

arrejuntado, -a *nm/f* live-in lover; **los ~s** the couple living together.

arrejuntarse [1a] *vr* to move in together; **vivir arrejuntados** to live together.

arrejunte *nm* cohabitation, living together.

arrellanarse [1a] *vr*, **arrellenarse** [1a] *vr* (**a**) to lounge, sprawl, loll; **~ en el asiento** to settle o.s. comfortably in one's chair, (*pey*) to sit sprawled in one's chair.

(**b**) (*fig*) to be happy in one's work.

arremangado *adj* turned up, tucked up; *nariz* turned up, snub.

arremangar [1h] **1** *vt manga etc* to turn up, tuck up, roll up; *falda* to tuck up. **2 arremangarse** *vr* (**a**) (*mangas etc*) to roll up one's sleeves (*etc*). (**b**) (*fig*: *adoptar una actitud firme*) to take a firm line.

arrematar* [1a] *vt* to finish, complete.

arremeter [2a] **1** *vt* (**a**) (*atacar*) to attack, assail.

(**b**) *caballo* to spur on, spur forward.

2 *vi* (**a**) (*atacar*) to rush forth, attack; **~ contra uno** to rush at sb, attack sb, launch o.s. at sb, lash out at sb.

(**b**) (*fig*) to offend good taste, shock the eye.

arremetida *nf* (**a**) (*ataque*) attack, assault; (*ímpetu*) onrush; (*empujón*) push; lunge. (**b**) (*de caballo*) sudden start.

arremolinarse [1a] *vr* (*gente*) to crowd around, mill around, swirl; (*agua*) to swirl, eddy; (*bailadores, polvo etc*) to swirl, whirl.

arrempujar [1a] *vt* = **empujar; rempujar.**

arrendable *adj*: **casa ~** house available for letting, house to let.

arrendador(a) *nm/f* (**a**) (*propietario*) landlord, landlady; (*Jur*) lessor. (**b**) (*arrendatario*) tenant.

arrendajo *nm* (**a**) (*Orn*) jay. (**b**) (*fig*) mimic.

arrendamiento *nm* (**a**) (*acto*) letting, leasing; hiring; farming out; **~ financiero** leasing; **tomar una casa en ~** to rent a house.

(**b**) (*alquiler*) rent, rental; lease; hiring fee.

(**c**) (*contrato*) contract, agreement.

arrendar¹ [1j] *vt* (**a**) (*sujeto*: *dueño*) *casa* to let, lease; *máquina etc* to hire out.

(**b**) (*sujeto*: *inquilino etc*) *casa* to rent, lease; *máquina etc* to hire.

arrendar² [1j] *vt caballo* to tie, tether (by the reins).

arrendatario, -a *nm/f* tenant; lessee, leaseholder; hirer.

arrendero *nm* (*Cono Sur, Méx*) = **arrendatario.**

arreo *nm* (**a**) (*adorno*) adornment, dress; (*de caballo*) piece of harness. (**b**) **~s** harness, trappings; (*fig*) gear, equipment. (**c**) (*LAm Agr*) drove (*o* herd) of cattle.

arrepentidamente *adv* regretfully, repentantly.

arrepentido 1 *adj* regretful, repentant, sorry; **terrorista ~** reformed terrorist; **estar ~ de algo** to regret sth, be sorry about sth; **se mostró muy ~** he was very sorry. **2** *nm*, **arrepentida** *nf* (*Ecl*) penitent; (*Pol*) reformed terrorist (*etc*); person who has turned informer.

arrepentimiento *nm* (**a**) regret, repentance, sorrow; (*Ecl*) repentance. (**b**) (*Arte*) change (made by the artist to a picture).

arrepentirse [3i] *vr* to repent, be repentant; **~ de algo** to regret sth, repent of sth; **se arrepintió de haberlo dicho** he regretted having said it; **no me arrepiento de nada** I regret nothing.

arrequín *nm* (**a**) (*LAm*: *ayudante*) helper, assistant. (**b**) (*LAm Agr*) leading animal (of a mule train).

arrequives *nmpl* (**a**) (*ropa*) finery, best clothes; (*adornos*) frills, trimmings. (**b**) (*fig*) circumstances.

arrestado *adj* bold, daring.

arrestar [1a] **1** *vt* (*detener*) to arrest; (*encarcelar*) to imprison; **~ en el cuartel** (*Mil*) to confine to barracks.

2 arrestarse *vr*: **~ a algo** to rush boldly into sth; **~ a todo** to be afraid of nothing.

arresto *nm* (**a**) arrest; imprisonment; (*Mil*) detention, confinement; **~ domiciliario** house arrest; **~ mayor** (*Esp*) imprisonment for from one month and a day to six months; **~ menor** (*Esp*) imprisonment for from one day to thirty days; **~ preventivo** preventive detention; **estar bajo ~** to be under arrest.

(**b**) (*fig*) **~s** boldness, daring; enterprise; **tener ~s** to be bold, be daring.

arrevesado *adj* (*LAm*) = **enrevesado.**

arria *nf* (*LAm*) mule train, train of pack animals.

arriada *nf* flood.

arriado *adj* (*LAm*) = **arreado.**

arrianismo *nm* Arianism.

arriano, -a *adj, nm/f* Arian.

arriar [1c] **1** *vt* (**a**) (*inundar*) to flood. (**b**) (*Náut*) *pabellón* to lower, strike; *vela* to haul down; *cuerda* to loosen; to pay out; (*****) to let go.

2 arriarse *vr* to flood, become flooded.

arriate *nm* (**a**) (*Hort*) bed, border; trellis. (**b**) (*camino*) road, path.

arriba 1 *adv* (**a**) (*posición*) above; overhead; on top; high, on high; (*Náut*) aloft; (*en casa*) upstairs; (*dirección*) up, upwards; **'este lado ~'** 'this side up'; **lo ~ escrito** what has been said above; **la persona ~ mencionada** the aforementioned person; **de ~ abajo** from top to bottom; (*persona*) from head to foot; from beginning to end; **correr de ~ abajo** to run up and down; **desde ~** from (up) above; **hacia ~** up, upwards; **está hasta ~ del trabajo*** he's fed up with the job*; **está más ~** it's higher up; it's further up; **por la calle ~** up the street; **de 10 dólares para ~** from 10 dollars upwards; **de la cintura (para) ~** from the waist up; **llegar ~** to get to the top; *V* **agua, cuesta, río** *etc.*

(**b**) **de ~** *adj*: **la parte de ~** the upper part, the top side; **los de ~** those above; those at the top; those on top.

(**c**) (*Cono Sur*) **~ mío** (*etc*) over me (*etc*), above me (*etc*); on top of me (*etc*).

2 *interj*: **¡~!** up you get!; **¡~ España!** Spain for ever!, long live Spain!; **¡~ Toboso!** (*Dep etc*) up (with) Toboso!

3 ~ de *prep* above; higher than, further up than; (*Méx*) (*encima de*) on top of; above; (*más de*) more than; **el río ~ de la ciudad** the river above the town.

arribada *nf* (*Náut y fig*) arrival, entry into harbour; **~ forzosa** emergency call, unscheduled stop; **entrar de ~** to put into port.

arribaje *nm* (*Náut*) arrival, entry into harbour.

arribano *adj* (*Cono Sur*) upper, higher.

arribar [1a] *vi* (**a**) (*esp LAm*: *llegar*) to arrive; (*Náut*) to put into port, reach port; to make an emergency call; (*ir a la deriva*) to drift; **~ a** to reach. (**b**) (*Med, Fin*) to recover, improve. (**c**) **~ a** + *infin* to manage to + *infin.*

arribazón *nf* coastal abundance of fish, off-shore shoal; (*fig*) bonanza.

arribeño, -a *nm/f* (**a**) (*LAm*: *serrano*) highlander, inlander. (**b**) (*Cono Sur*: *forastero*) stranger.

arribismo *nm* social climbing.

arribista *nmf* go-getter, arriviste, social climber.
arribo *nm* (*esp LAm*) arrival; **hacer su ~** to arrive.
arriendo *nm* = **arrendamiento.**
arriero *nm* muleteer; (*CAm*) carrier.
arriesgadamente *adv* riskily, dangerously; daringly; boldly; rashly.
arriesgado *adj* (**a**) *acto* risky, dangerous, hazardous; daring; **unas ideas arriesgadas** some dangerous ideas; **me parece ~ prometerlo** it would be rash to promise it.
(**b**) *persona* bold, daring; (*pey*) rash, foolhardy.
arriesgar [1h] **1** *vt vida etc* to risk, hazard; to endanger; *conjetura* to hazard, venture; *posibilidades* to endanger, jeopardize; *dinero* to stake.
2 arriesgarse *vr* to take a risk, expose o.s. to danger; to put one's life (*o* chances *etc*) in danger; **~ a una multa** to risk a fine, face a fine; **~ a hacer algo** to dare to do sth, risk doing sth; **~ en una empresa** to venture upon an enterprise.
arrimadero *nm* support; (*al montar*) mounting-block, step.
arrimadillo *nm* matting (*used as wainscot*).
arrimadizo 1 *adj* (*fig*) parasitic, sycophantic. **2** *nm*, **arrimadiza** *nf* parasite, hanger-on, sycophant.
arrimado 1 *adj imitación etc* close. **2** *nm*, **arrimada** *nf* parasite; (*recién venido*) newcomer (to a group); (*And: amante*) lover; (*Carib: intruso*) unwelcome guest; (*Cono Sur**: *amancebado*) ponce, kept man.
arrimar [1a] **1** *vt* (**a**) (*acercar*) to bring close, move up, draw up (*a* to); **hay que ~lo todavía más** you'll have to bring it closer still; **lo arrimamos a la ventana** we put it against the window; **arrimó el oído a la puerta** he put his ear to the door; **~ la escalera a una pared** to put (*o* lean, place) the ladder up against a wall; **vivir arrimado a uno** (*LAm*) to live off sb; **~ la culpa a uno** (*Cono Sur*) to lay the blame on sb; **~ un golpe a uno*** to give sb a blow.
(**b**) (*arrinconar*) to put away, lay aside, shelve; (*apartar*) to move out of the way; (*tirar*) to get rid of; *persona* to ignore, push aside; **el plan quedó arrimado** the plan was shelved; **~ los libros** (*fig*) to lay aside one's books, give up studying.
(**c**) (*Náut*) *carga* to stow.
(**d**) (*Méx*) *niño* to thrash, give a hiding to.
2 arrimarse *vr* (**a**) (*acercarse*) to come close, come closer; (*reunirse*) to gather, come together; (*Taur*) to fight close to the bull; (*en baile*) to dance very close, dance cheek-to-cheek.
(**b**) **~ a** (*acercarse a*) to come close(r), to get near(er) to; (*apoyarse en*) to lean against, lean on; (*amante, niño*) to cuddle up to, snuggle up to; **se arrimó a la lumbre** she huddled over the fire; **arrímate a mí** lean on me; cuddle up to me.
(**c**) (*fig*) **~ a** to join, keep company with; to seek the protection of; **arrímate a los buenos** choose your friends among good people; cultivate the virtuous.
(**d**) (*amantes*) to set up house (*o* live) together.
(**e**) (*LAm**) to sponge*.
arrimo *nm* (**a**) (*gen*) support. (**b**) (*fig: apoyo*) support, help, protection. (**c**) (*fig: afecto*) attachment. (**d**) (*: *persona*) lover. (**e**) (*: *amorío*) affair.
arrimón *nm* loafer, idler; sponger*; **estar de ~** to hang about, loaf around.
arrinconado *adj* (*fig*) (*olvidado*) forgotten, neglected; (*remoto*) remote; (*abandonado*) abandoned; (*marginado*) out in the cold.
arrinconar [1a] **1** *vt* (**a**) *cosa* to put in a corner; *enemigo etc* to corner.
(**b**) (*fig: apartar*) to lay aside, put away; (*tirar*) to get rid of; (*dar carpetazo a*) to shelve; (*desterrar*) to banish; *persona* to push aside, push into the background, ignore; (*marginar*) to leave out in the cold.
2 arrinconarse *vr* to retire, withdraw from the world.
arriñonado *adj* kidney-shaped.
arriñonar* [1a] *vt* to wear out, exhaust; **estar arriñonado** to be knackered*.
arriscadamente *adv* boldly, resolutely.
arriscado *adj* (**a**) (*Geog*) craggy. (**b**) (*fig: resuelto*) bold, resolute; (*animoso*) spirited. (**c**) (*fig: ágil*) brisk, agile.
arriscamiento *nm* boldness, resolution.
arriscar[1] [1g] **1** *vt* to risk. **2 arriscarse** *vr* to take a risk.
arriscar[2] [1g] **1** *vt* (*And, Cono Sur, Méx: doblar*) to turn (*o* fold) up; to tuck up; (*encrespar*) to stiffen; *nariz* to wrinkle.
2 *vi* (**a**) (*And: enderezarse*) to draw o.s. up, straighten up. (**b**) **~ a** (*LAm*) to amount to.
3 arriscarse *vr* (**a**) (*engreírse*) to get conceited. (**b**) (*And, CAm: estar de punto en blanco*) to dress up to the nines.
arriscocho *adj* (*And*) restless; turbulent.
arrivista = **arribista.**
arrizar [1f] *vt* (*Náut*) to reef; to fasten, lash down.
arroba *nf* (**a**) *measure of weight = 11,502 kg (25 lbs)*.
(**b**) *a variable liquid measure.*
arrobador *adj* entrancing, enchanting.
arrobamiento *nm* ecstasy, rapture, bliss; trance; **salir de su ~** to emerge from one's state of bliss.
arrobar [1a] **1** *vt* to entrance, enchant. **2 arrobarse** *vr* to become entranced, go into ecstasies, be enraptured.
arrobo *nm* = **arrobamiento.**
arrocero 1 *adj* rice (*atr*); rice-producing; **industria arrocera** rice industry.
2 *nm*, **arrocera** *nf* (*Carib*) gatecrasher.
arrochelarse [1a] *vr* (*And: ganado*) to take a liking to a place; (*perro etc*) to refuse to go out; (*caballo*) to balk, shy.
arrodajarse [1a] *vr* (*CAm*) to sit down cross-legged.
arrodillarse [1a] *vr* to kneel, kneel down, go down on one's knees; **estar arrodillado** to kneel, be kneeling (down), be on one's knees.
arrogancia *nf* arrogance; pride.
arrogante *adj* (*gen*) arrogant, haughty; (*orgulloso*) proud; (*audaz*) bold.
arrogantemente *adv* arrogantly, haughtily; proudly; boldly.
arrogarse [1h] *vr*: **~ algo** to assume sth, take sth on o.s.
arrojadamente *adv* daringly, dashingly; boldly.
arrojadizo *adj* for throwing, that can be thrown.
arrojado *adj* (*fig: bizarro*) daring, dashing; (*audaz*) bold.
arrojallamas *nm invar* flamethrower.
arrojar [1a] **1** *vt* (**a**) (*gen*) to throw, fling, hurl, cast; (*Dep*) *pelota* to bowl, pitch; (*peso*) to put; (*Pesca*) to cast; **~ algo de sí** to cast sth from one, fling sth aside
(**b**) *humo etc* to give out, send out, emit; *luz* to give, shed; *flor, renuevo* to put out; (*) to throw up, vomit; *persona* to throw out, turn out; (*esp LAm*) to bring up, throw up; **este estudio arroja alguna luz sobre el tema** this study throws some light on the subject.
(**c**) (*Com, Fin, Mat*) to give, produce, yield; *resultado, estadística* to show, throw up; **este negocio arroja déficit** this business shows an unfavourable balance; **el accidente arrojó 80 muertos** (*LAm*) the accident left 80 dead.
2 arrojarse *vr* (**a**) to throw o.s., hurl o.s. (*a* into, on; *por* out of, through); **~ al agua** to jump into the water; **~ por una ventana** to throw o.s. out of a window.
(**b**) (*fig*) **~ a, ~ en** to rush into, fling o.s. into, plunge into.
arrojo *nm* daring, dash, fearlessness; **con ~** boldly, fearlessly.
arrollado *nm* (*Cono Sur Culin*) rolled pork.
arrollador *adj* (*fig*) sweeping, overwhelming, crushing, devastating; **por una mayoría ~a** by an overwhelming majority; **es una pasión ~a** it is a consuming passion; **un ataque ~** a crushing attack.
arrollar[1] [1a] *vt* (**a**) (*enrollar*) to roll up; (*Elec, Téc etc*) to coil, wind.
(**b**) (*agua etc*) to sweep away, wash away; *enemigo* to throw back, rout; (*Dep*) *adversario* to overwhelm, crush; (*Aut, Ferro etc*) to run over, knock down; **arrollaron a sus rivales** they crushed their rivals.
(**c**) (*fig: asombrar*) *persona* to dumbfound, leave speechless; to squash.
arrollar[2] [1a] *vt* = **arrullar.**
arromar [1a] *vt* to blunt, dull.
arropar [1a] **1** *vt* (**a**) (*vestir*) to cover; to wrap up (with clothes); (*en cama*) to tuck up (in bed). (**b**) (*fig*) to protect.
2 arroparse *vr* to wrap o.s. up; to tuck o.s. up (*o* in); **¡arrópate bien!** wrap up warm!
arrope *nm* syrup; grape syrup, honey syrup.
arrorró *nm* (*LAm*) lullaby.
arrostrado *adj*: **bien ~** nice-looking; **mal ~** ugly.
arrostrar [1a] **1** *vt* (*hacer frente a*) to face; to face up to, brave, defy; (*aguantar*) to stand up to; **~ las consecuencias** to face the consequences; **~ un peligro** to face a danger resolutely, face up to a danger.
2 *vi*: **~ a algo** to show a liking for sth; **~ con** = *vt*.
3 arrostrarse *vr* to rush into the fight, throw o.s. into the fray.
arroyada *nf* (**a**) (*barranco*) gully, stream bed. (**b**) (*inundación*) flood, flooding.

arroyo *nm* (**a**) (*gen*) stream, brook; (*cauce*) watercourse; (*LAm*: *río*) river; (*Méx*) gully, ravine.

(**b**) (*cuneta*) gutter; (*fig*) the street; **estar en el ~** (*Méx*) to be on one's uppers; (*mujer*) to be on the streets; **poner a uno en el ~** to turn sb out of the house; **sacar a uno del ~** to drag sb up from the gutter; **ser del ~** to be an orphan, be a foundling.

arroyuelo *nm* small stream, brook.

arroz *nm* rice; **~ blanco** boiled rice; **~ a la cubana** rice with banana and fried egg; **~ hinchado** puffed rice; **~ integral** brown rice; **~ con leche** rice-pudding; **hubo ~ y gallo muerto** (*Esp, Carib**) it was a slap-up do*.

arrozal *nm* ricefield.

arrufarse [1a] *vr* (*Carib*: *enojarse*) to get annoyed, get angry.

arruga *nf* (**a**) (*en piel*) wrinkle, line; (*en tela*) crease, fold; ruck. (**b**) (*And**) (*estafa*) trick, swindle; (*deuda*) debt; **hacer una ~** (*And*) to cheat.

arrugado *adj cara etc* wrinkled, lined; *papel etc* creased; *vestido etc* rucked up, crumpled.

arrugar [1h] **1** *vt cara etc* to wrinkle, line; *ceño* to knit, pucker up; *papel etc* to crease; to crumple, screw up; *vestido etc* to ruck up, crumple; **~ la cara** to screw up one's face; **~ la frente** to knit one's brow, frown.

2 arrugarse *vr* (**a**) (*piel*) to wrinkle (up), get wrinkled; (*tela*) to crease, get creased; to ruck up, get crumpled; (*Bot*) to shrivel up.

(**b**) (*: *asustarse*) to get scared, get the wind up*.

arrugue *nm* (*Carib*) = **arruga**.

arruinado *adj* (**a**) ruined. (**b**) (*Cono Sur, Méx*) (*enclenque*) sickly, stunted; (*Cono Sur*: *miserable*) wretched, down and out.

arruinamiento *nm* ruin, ruination.

arruinar [1a] **1** *vt* to ruin; to wreck, destroy; (*LAm*: *desvirgar*) to deflower. **2 arruinarse** *vr* to be ruined (*t Fin*); to go to rack and ruin; (*Arquit etc*) to fall into ruins, fall down.

arrullar [1a] **1** *vt niño* to lull to sleep, rock to sleep; (*: *amante*) to whisper endearments to, say sweet nothings to.

2 *vi* (*Orn*) to coo.

3 arrullarse *vr* to bill and coo, whisper endearments; to flirt.

arrullo *nm* (*Orn*) cooing; (*fig*) billing and cooing; (*Mús*) lullaby.

arrumaco *nm* (**a**) (*caricia*) caress. (**b**) (*vestido etc*) eccentric item of dress (*o* adornment). (**c**) (*halago*) piece of flattery; **andar con ~** to flatter. (**d**) **~s** show of affection, endearments.

arrumaje *nm* (*Náut*) stowage; ballast.

arrumar [1a] **1** *vt* (*Náut*) to stow; (*amontonar*) to pile up. **2 arrumarse** *vr* (*Náut*) to become overcast.

arrumbar[1] [1a] *vt* (**a**) *objeto* to put aside, put on one side, ignore, discard; (*olvidar*) to neglect, forget. (**b**) (*en discusión*) *persona* to silence, floor; (*apartar*) to remove.

arrumbar[2] [1a] (*Náut*) **1** *vi* to take one's bearings. **2 arrumbarse** *vr* (**a**) (*marearse*) to be seasick. (**b**) (*And, Cono Sur*: *oxidarse*) to rust; (*agriarse*) to turn sour.

arrume *nm* (*And, Carib*) pile, heap.

arruncharse [1a] *vr* (*And*) to curl up, roll up.

arrurruz *nm* arrowroot.

arrutanado *adj* (*And*) plump.

arrutinarse [1a] *vr* to get into a routine, get set in one's ways.

arsenal *nm* (*Náut*) dockyard, naval dockyard; (*Mil*) arsenal; (*fig*) storehouse, mine.

arsenalera *nf* (*Cono Sur Med*) surgeon's assistant, theatre auxiliary.

arsénico *nm* arsenic.

arte *nm y nf* (*gen m en sing, f en pl*) (**a**) (*gen*) art; **~s** (*Univ*) arts; **~ abstracto** abstract art; **bellas ~s** fine arts; **~s decorativas** decorative arts; **~s gráficas** graphic arts; **~s liberales** liberal arts; **por ~ de magia** (as if) by magic; **~s marciales** martial arts; **~ mecánico** mechanical skill, manual skill; **~s y oficios** arts and crafts; **~s plásticas** plastic arts; **~ poética** poetics; **~ pop** pop art; **el séptimo ~** the cinema, film; **~ de vivir** art of living.

(**b**) (*Liter*): **~ mayor** *Spanish verse of 8 lines each of 12 syllables (15th century)*; **~ menor** *Spanish verse usually of 4 lines each of 6 or 8 syllables.*

(**c**) (*habilidad*) craft, skill; knack.

(**d**) (*astucia*) craftiness, cunning; (*trampa*) trick; **malas ~s** trickery, guile; **por malas ~s** by trickery.

(**e**) (*hechura*) workmanship; artistry.

(**f**) **no tener ~ ni parte en algo** to have nothing whatsoever to do with a matter.

(**g**) (*Pesca*) **~** (**de pescar**) (*red*) fishing-net; (*caña etc*) fishing tackle.

artefacto *nm* (**a**) (*Téc*) appliance, device, contrivance; (*explosivo*) device; **~s de alumbrado** light fittings, light fixtures (*US*); **~ explosivo, ~ infernal** bomb, explosive device; **~ nuclear** nuclear device.

(**b**) (*esp arqueológico*) artefact.

(**c**) (*Aut**) old crock, jalopy.

artejo *nm* knuckle, joint.

arteramente *adv* cunningly, artfully.

artería *nf* cunning, artfulness.

arteria *nf* artery (*t fig*); (*Elec*) feeder; **la ~ principal de una ciudad** the main artery of a city, the main thoroughfare of a town.

arterial *adj* arterial.

arterio(e)sclerosis *nf* arteriosclerosis.

artero *adj* cunning, artful.

artesa *nf* trough, kneading trough.

artesanal *adj* craft (*atr*); **industria ~** craft industry.

artesanía *nf* craftsmanship; handicraft, skill; **objeto de ~** hand-made article; **obra de ~** piece of craftsmanship; **zapatos de ~** craft shoes, hand-made shoes.

artesano 1 *adj* home-made, home-produced. **2** *nm* craftsman.

artesiano *adj*: **pozo ~** artesian well.

artesón *nm* (**a**) (*de cocina*) kitchen tub. (**b**) (*Arquit*) coffer, caisson; (*adorno*) moulding. (**c**) (*And, Méx*: *bóveda*) vault; (*arcos*) arcade, series of arches; (*terraza*) flat roof, terrace.

artesonado *nm* coffered ceiling; stuccoed ceiling, moulded ceiling.

artesonar [1a] *vt* (**a**) (*poner paneles a*) to coffer. (**b**) (*estucar*) to stucco, mould.

ártico 1 *adj* Arctic. **2** *nm*: **el Á~** the Arctic.

articulación *nf* (**a**) (*Anat*) articulation; joint. (**b**) (*Mec*) joint; **~ esférica** ball-and-socket joint; **~ universal** universal joint. (**c**) (*Ling*) articulation.

articuladamente *adv* distinctly, articulately.

articulado *adj* (**a**) *persona* articulate. (**b**) (*Anat, Mec*) articulated, jointed; (*Aut*) *volante* collapsible.

articular [1a] **1** *vt* (**a**) (*Ling*) to articulate; (*Mec*) to articulate, join together, join up.

(**b**) (*constituir*) to make up, constitute.

(**c**) (*Jur*) to article, specify charges against.

(**d**) (*And, Cono Sur**) to tell off*, dress down*.

2 *vi* (*Cono Sur*: *reñir*) to quarrel, squabble; (*quejarse*) to grumble.

articulista *nmf* columnist, feature writer, contributor (to a paper).

artículo *nm* (**a**) (*objeto*) article, thing; (*Com*) commodity; **~s** (*Com etc*) commodities, goods; **~s alimenticios** foodstuffs; **~ de comercio** commodity; **~s de consumo** consumer goods; consumables, consumable supplies; **~s de escritorio** stationery; **~s de marca** branded goods; **~s de primera necesidad** basic commodities, essentials; **~s de plata** silverware; **~s de tocador** toilet articles, toiletries.

(**b**) (*en periódico etc*) article; feature, report, study; (*en revista erudita*) article, paper; (*en libro de referencia*) entry, article; (*de ley, documento*) article, section, item; **~ de fondo** leading article, leader, editorial; **~ de portada** front-page article.

(**c**) (*Ling*) article; **~ definido** definite article; **~ indefinido** indefinite article.

(**d**) (*Anat*) articulation, joint.

artífice *nmf* (*Arte etc*) artist, craftsman; (*hacedor*) maker; (*inventor*) inventor; (*fig*) architect; **el ~ de la victoria** the architect of (the) victory.

artificial *adj* artificial.

artificialidad *nf* artificiality.

artificializar [1f] *vt* to make artificial, give an air of artificiality to.

artificialmente *adv* artificially.

artificiero *nm* explosives expert, bomb-disposal officer.

artificio *nm* (**a**) (*arte*) art, craft, skill; (*pey*) artifice. (**b**) (*hechura*) workmanship, craftsmanship. (**c**) (*aparato*) contrivance, device, appliance. (**d**) (*astucia*) cunning, sly trick.

artificiosamente *adv* (**a**) skilfully, ingeniously; artistically. (**b**) cunningly, artfully.

artificioso *adj* (**a**) (*ingenioso*) skilful, ingenious; artistic. (**b**) (*astuto*) cunning, artful.

artilugio *nm* (**a**) (*aparato*) gadget, contraption. (**b**) (*truco*) gimmick, stunt. (**c**) (*chisme*) thingummy*, whatsit*.

artillería *nf* (**a**) (*Mil*) artillery; ~ **antiaérea** anti-aircraft guns; ~ **de campaña** field guns; ~ **pesada** heavy artillery. (**b**) (*Dep**) forward line.

artillero *nm* (**a**) (*Mil*) artilleryman, gunner; (*Aer, Náut*) gunner; (*Min*) explosives expert. (**b**) (*Dep**) forward.

artimaña *nf* (**a**) (*trampa*) trap, snare. (**b**) (*fig: ingenio*) cunning.

artista *nmf* (*Arte*) artist; (*Teat etc*) artist, artiste; ~ **de cine** film actor, film actress; ~ **comercial** commercial artist; ~ **invitado** guest artist; ~ **marcial** martial arts expert; ~ **de teatro** artist, artiste; ~ **de variedades** variety artist(e).

artísticamente *adv* artistically.

artístico *adj* artistic.

artrítico *adj* arthritic.

artritis *nf* arthritis; ~ **reumatoidea** rheumatoid arthritis.

artrópodo *nm* arthropod; ~**s** *pl* (*como clase*) arthropoda.

Arturo *nm* Arthur.

Artús *nm*: **el Rey** ~ King Arthur.

aruñón *nm* (**a**) (*And: ladrón*) thief, pickpocket. (**b**) = **arañazo.**

arveja *nf* (**a**) (*Bot*) vetch. (**b**) (*LAm: guisante*) pea.

arz. *abr de* **arzobispo** Archbishop, Abp.

arzobispado *nm* archbishopric.

arzobispal *adj* archiepiscopal; **palacio** ~ archbishop's palace.

arzobispo *nm* archbishop.

arzón *nm* saddle tree; ~ **delantero** saddlebow.

as *nm* (**a**) (*Cartas*) ace; (*fig*) ace, trump card; (*dados*) one; ~ **de espadas** ace of spades; **guardarse un** ~ **en la manga** to have an ace up one's sleeve.

(**b**) (*: *campeón*) ace, wizard*; ~ **del fútbol** wizard footballer*, star player; ~ **del tenis** star tennis player; ~ **del volante** champion driver, speed king; **es un** ~ he's a wizard*, he's the tops*.

(**c**) (*fig: Tenis*) ace, ace service.

asa[1] *nf* handle; grip; (*fig*) lever, pretext; **ser muy del** ~* to be well in.

asa[2] *nf* (*Bot*) juice.

asadera *nf* (*Cono Sur Culin*) baking tin.

asadero 1 *adj* roasting, for roasting. **2** *nm* spit; (*Méx: queso*) soft cheese.

asado 1 *adj* (**a**) (*Culin*) roast, roasted; **carne asada** roast meat; ~ **al horno** baked; ~ **a la parrilla** broiled; grilled; **bien** ~ well done; **poco** ~ underdone; rare, red.

(**b**) (*LAm: enfadado*) cross, angry.

(**c**) (*) **estar** ~ (*Carib*) to be broke*.

2 *n* (**a**) (*Culin*) roast, roast meat, joint. (**b**) (*Cono Sur: carne*) steak; ~ **al palo** barbecue.

asador *nm* (**a**) (*Culin*) spit; (*mecánico*) roasting-jack; ~ **a rotación,** ~ **rotatorio** rotary spit. (**b**) (*restaurante*) carvery.

asadura 1 *nf* (**a**) (*Anat*) ~**s** entrails, offal; (*Culin*) chitterlings; **echar las** ~**s** to make a tremendous effort, bust a gut*. (**b**) (*pachorra*) sluggishness, laziness; **tiene** ~**s** he's terribly lazy. **2** *nmf* (*) stolid person, dull sort*.

asaetear [1a] *vt* (**a**) (*tirar*) to shoot, hit (with an arrow). (**b**) (*fig: acosar*) to bother, pester.

asalariado 1 *adj* paid; wage-earning. **2** *nm,* **asalariada** *nf* (**a**) (*empleado*) wage earner; employee. (**b**) (*pey: mercenario*) hireling; **es** ~ **de Eslobodia** he's in the pay of Slobodia.

asalariar [1b] *vt* to hire, put on the pay-roll.

asalmonado *adj* salmon coloured.

asaltabancos *nmf invar* bank robber.

asaltador(a) *nm/f,* **asaltante** *nmf* attacker, assailant; raider.

asaltar [1a] *vt* (**a**) *persona* to attack, assail; to rush; (*Mil*) to storm; *banco, tienda etc* to break into, raid; (*en disturbios etc*) to loot, sack; **le asaltaron 4 bandidos** he was held up by 4 bandits; **anoche fue asaltada la joyería** the jeweller's was raided last night, last night there was a break-in at the jeweller's.

(**b**) (*desastre, muerte*) to fall upon, surprise, overtake.

(**c**) (*fig: duda*) to assail, afflict; (*pensamiento*) to cross one's mind; **le asaltó una idea** he was struck by an idea, he suddenly had an idea.

asalto *nm* (**a**) (*ataque*) attack, assault; **tomar por** ~ to take by storm. (**b**) (*Boxeo*) round; (*Esgrima*) bout, assault. (**c**) (*Carib, Méx: visita*) unexpected visit.

asamblea *nf* (*gen*) assembly; (*reunión*) meeting; (*congreso*) congress, conference; ~ **general** general assembly; **llamar a** ~ (*Mil Hist*) to assemble, muster.

asambleario, -a *nm/f,* **asambleísta** *nmf* member of an assembly; (*congresista*) conference member.

asapán *nm* (*Méx*) flying squirrel.

asar [1a] **1** *vt* (**a**) (*Culin*) to roast; ~ **al horno** to bake; ~ **a la parrilla** to broil, grill.

(**b**) (*fig: acosar*) to pester, plague (*con* with).

(**c**) (‡) to shoot, gun down.

2 asarse *vr* (*fig*) to be terribly hot, roast; **me aso de calor** I'm roasting; **aquí se asa uno vivo** it's boiling hot here, the heat is killing here.

asascuarse* [1d] *vr* (*Méx*) to roll up into a ball.

asaz *adv* (†, *lit*) very, exceedingly; **una tarea** ~ **difícil** an exceedingly difficult task.

asbesto *nm* asbestos.

ascendencia *nf* (**a**) (*linaje*) ancestry, descent, origin; **de remota** ~ **normanda** of remote Norman ancestry. (**b**) (*LAm: dominio*) ascendancy; (*influencia*) hold, influence.

ascendente *adj movimiento* ascending, upward; *tendencia* rising, increasing; **en una curva** ~ in an upward curve; **la carrera** ~ **del pistón** the up-stroke of the piston; **el tren** ~ the up train.

ascender [2g] **1** *vt* to promote; **fue ascendido a teniente** he was promoted (to) lieutenant, he was raised to the rank of lieutenant.

2 *vi* (**a**) (*subir*) to ascend, rise, go up.

(**b**) (*ser ascendido*) to be promoted (*a* to), go up; **Málaga asciende a primera división** Málaga goes up to the first division.

(**c**) ~ **a** (*Com etc*) to amount to, add up to, total.

ascendiente 1 *adj* = **ascendente. 2** *nmf* (*persona*) ancestor. **3** *nm* (*influencia*) ascendancy, influence, power (*sobre* over).

ascensión *nf* (**a**) (*subida*) ascent; ~ **en globo** balloon ride, trip in a balloon. (**b**) (*ascenso*) promotion (*a* to, to the rank of). (**c**) (*Ecl*) **la A~** the Ascension; **Día de la A~** Ascension Day.

ascensional *adj curva, movimiento etc* upward; (*Astron*) ascendant, rising.

ascensionista *nmf* balloonist.

ascenso *nm* promotion (*a* to, to the rank of).

ascensor *nm* lift, elevator (*US*); (*Téc*) elevator.

ascensorista *nmf* lift attendant, elevator operator (*US*).

ascesis *nf* asceticism; ascetic life.

asceta *nmf* ascetic.

ascético *adj* ascetic.

ascetismo *nm* asceticism.

asco *nm* (**a**) (*sentimiento*) loathing, disgust, revulsion; **¡qué ~!** how awful!, how revolting!; **¡qué ~ de gente!** what awful people!; **coger ~ a algo** to get sick of sth; **dar ~ a uno** to sicken sb, disgust sb; **me das ~** you disgust me; **me dan ~ las aceitunas** I loathe olives, olives revolt me; **hacer ~s de algo** to turn up one's nose at sth; **morirse de** ~* (*Esp*) to be bored to tears.

(**b**) (*objeto etc*) loathsome thing, disgusting thing, abomination; **es un** ~ it's disgusting; **estar hecho un** ~ to be filthy; **poner a uno de** ~ (*Méx*) to insult (*o* abuse) sb.

ascua *nf* live coal, ember; **¡~s!** ouch!; **arrimar el ~ a su sardina** to look after number one, put one's own interests first; **estar como ~ de oro** to be shining bright; **estar en ~s** to be on tenterhooks; **tener a uno sobre ~s** to keep sb on tenterhooks; **sacar el ~ con la mano del gato** (*o* **con mano ajena**) to get sb else to do the dirty work.

aseadamente *adv* cleanly, neatly, tidily; smartly.

aseado *adj* clean, neat, tidy; smart.

asear [1a] **1** *vt* (**a**) (*adornar*) to adorn, embellish. (**b**) (*limpiar*) to clean up, tidy up; (*pulir*) to smarten up. **2 asearse** *vr* to tidy o.s. up; to smarten o.s. up.

asechanza *nf* trap, snare (*t fig*).

asechar [1a] *vt* to waylay, ambush; (*fig*) to set a trap for.

asediador *nm* besieger.

asediar [1b] *vt* (**a**) (*Mil*) to besiege, lay siege to; to blockade. (**b**) (*fig*) to bother, pester; (*amante*) to chase, lay siege to.

asedio *nm* (**a**) (*Mil*) siege; blockade. (**b**) (*Fin etc*) run; ~ **de un banco** run on a bank.

asegún *adv, prep* (*LAm**) = **según.**

asegurable *adv* insurable.

aseguración *nf* insurance.

asegurado 1 *adj* insured. **2** *nm,* **asegurada** *nf*: **el ~, la asegurada** the insured, the insured person.

asegurador(a)[1] *nm/f* insurer; underwriter.

aseguradora[2] *nf* insurance company.

asegurar [1a] **1** *vt* (**a**) (*fijar*) to secure, fasten, fix; to make firm, settle securely; ~ **algo con pernos** to secure sth with bolts.

(**b**) *lugar etc* to make secure, strengthen the defences of (*contra* against).

(**c**) *derechos* to safeguard, guarantee, assure.

(**d**) (*afirmar*) to assure, affirm; **le aseguro que ...** I assure you that ...; **aseguró que ...** he affirmed that ..., he confirmed that ...; **se lo aseguro** I assure you, I promise you; take my word for it; **ella le aseguró de su inocencia** she assured him of her innocence.

(**e**) (*Com, Fin*) to insure; **~ algo contra incendios** to insure sth against fire.

2 asegurarse *vr* (**a**) (*protegerse*) to make o.s. secure (*de* from).

(**b**) (*comprobar*) to make sure (*de* of); **para asegurarnos del todo** in order to make quite sure.

(**c**) (*Com, Fin*) to insure o.s.

ASELE *nf abr de* **Asociación para la Enseñanza del Español como Lengua Extranjera.**

asemejar [1a] **1** *vt* (**a**) (*hacer parecido*) to make alike, make similar; (*copiar*) to copy. (**b**) (*comparar*) to liken, compare (*a* to). **2 asemejarse** *vr* to be alike, be similar; **~ a** to be like, resemble.

asendereado *adj* (**a**) *sendero* beaten, well-trodden. (**b**) *vida* wretched, full of hardships.

asenderear [1a] *vt*: **~ a uno** to chase sb relentlessly; to bother sb, pester sb.

asenso *nm* (**a**) (*consentimiento*) assent; **dar su ~** to assent. (**b**) (*acto de creer*) credence; **dar ~ a** to give credence to.

asentada *nf* sitting; **de una ~** at one sitting.

asentaderas *nfpl* (*) behind*, bottom.

asentado *adj* established, settled, permanent.

asentador *nm* (**a**) razor strop. (**b**) (*Com*) dealer, middleman.

asentamiento *nm* (**a**) (*pueblo*) shanty town, township. (**b**) (*industrial etc*) site; establishment.

asentar [1j] **1** *vt* (**a**) *persona* to seat, sit down; *objeto* to place, fix, set; *tienda* to pitch; *ciudad etc* to found; *cimiento* to make firm; *válvula* to seat.

(**b**) *tierra* to level, tamp down, firm.

(**c**) *golpe* to give, fetch.

(**d**) *cuchillo etc* to sharpen, hone.

(**e**) (*fig: establecer*) to settle, establish, consolidate; *principio* to lay down, establish; *impresión* to fix in the mind; *opinión* to affirm, assert.

(**f**) (*apuntar*) to note down, set down, put in writing; (*Com*) *pedido* to enter, book; *libro mayor* to enter up; **~ algo al debe de uno** to debit sth to sb; **~ algo al haber de uno** to credit sth to sb.

2 *vi* to be suitable, suit.

3 asentarse *vr* (**a**) (*pájaro*) to alight, settle; (*líquido*) to settle; (*Arquit*) to settle, sink, subside.

(**b**) (*fig: establecerse*) to settle, establish o.s.

asentimiento *nm* assent, consent.

asentir [3i] *vi* (**a**) (*consentir*) to assent, agree; **~ con la cabeza** to nod (one's head).

(**b**) **~ a** to agree to, consent to; *petición* to approve, grant; *convenio* to accept; **~ a la verdad de algo** to recognize the truth of sth.

asentista *nm* contractor, supplier.

aseñorado *adj* lordly; dressed like a gentleman, behaving like a gentleman.

aseo *nm* (**a**) (*limpieza*) cleanliness, neatness, tidiness. (**b**) **~s** (*euf*) cloakroom, toilet, powder room.

aséptico *adj* aseptic; germ-free, free from infection.

asequible *adj* (*gen*) obtainable, available; *finalidad* attainable; *plan* feasible; *precio* moderate, reasonable, within reach.

aserradero *nm* sawmill.

aserrador *nm* sawyer.

aserradora *nf* power saw.

aserradura *nf* saw cut; **~s** sawdust.

aserrar [1j] *vt* to saw, saw through; to saw up.

aserrín *nm* sawdust.

aserruchar [1a] *vt* (*LAm*) = **aserrar**.

asertar [1a] *vt* to assert, affirm.

asertividad *nf* assertiveness.

asertivo *adj* assertive.

aserto *nm* assertion.

asesina *nf* murderess.

asesinado, -a *nm/f* murder victim, murdered person.

asesinar [1a] *vt* (**a**) to murder; (*Pol*) to assassinate. (**b**) (*fig: molestar*) to pester, plague to death.

asesinato *nm* murder; (*Pol*) assassination; **~ frustrado** attempted murder; **~ legal** judicial murder; **~ moral** character assassination.

asesino 1 *adj* murderous; killer. **2** *nm* (**a**) (*asesino*) murderer, killer; (*Pol*) assassin. (**b**) (*fig: matón*) thug, cut-throat; **¡~!** you brute!

asesor(a) 1 *nm/f* adviser, consultant; **~ de cuentas, ~ fiscal** tax accountant; **~ financiero** financial adviser; **asesora (del hogar)** (*Cono Sur*) maid; **~ de imagen** public-relations adviser. **2** *adj* advisory.

asesoramiento *nm* advice.

asesorar [1a] **1** *vt* (**a**) *persona* to advise, give legal (*o* professional) advice to.

(**b**) *compañía etc* to act as consultant to.

2 asesorarse *vr* (**a**) **~ con, ~ de** to take advice from, consult.

(**b**) **~ de una situación** to take stock of a situation.

asesorato *nm* (*LAm*) (**a**) (*acto*) advising. (**b**) (*oficina*) consultant's office.

asesoría *nf* (**a**) (*acto*) advising; task of advising; **~ jurídica** legal advice. (**b**) (*derechos*) adviser's fee. (**c**) (*oficina*) consultant's office.

asestar [1a] *vt* (**a**) *arma* to aim (*a* at, in the direction of); to fire, shoot. (**b**) *golpe* to deal, give, strike; **~ una puñalada a uno** to stab sb.

aseveración *nf* assertion, contention.

aseveradamente *adv* positively.

aseverar [1a] *vt* to affirm, assert.

asexuado *adj* sexless.

asexual *adj* asexual.

asfaltado 1 *adj* asphalt, asphalted; **carrera asfaltada** made-up road. **2** *nm* (**a**) (*acto*) asphalting. (**b**) (*firme*) asphalt, asphalt pavement, asphalt surface (*etc*); (*Aer etc*) tarmac.

asfaltar [1a] *vt* to asphalt.

asfáltico *adj* asphalt (*atr*).

asfalto *nm* asphalt; (*Aer etc*) tarmac; **regar el ~‡** to kick the bucket‡.

asfixia *nf* suffocation, asphyxiation, (*Med*) asphyxia.

asfixiador *adj*, **asfixiante** *adj* suffocating, asphyxiating; **calor ~** suffocating heat; **gas ~** poison gas.

asfixiar [1b] **1** *vt* (**a**) (*ahogar*) to asphyxiate; to suffocate; (*Mil: con gas*) to gas. (**b**) **estar asfixiado** (*sin dinero*) to be broke*; (*en aprieto*) to be up the creek‡. **2 asfixiarse** *vr* to be asphyxiated, suffocate.

asgo *V* **asir**.

así 1 *adv* (**a**) (*de este modo*) so, in this way, thus; by this means, thereby; **lo hizo ~** he did it like this, he did it this way; **~ lo hace cualquiera** anybody could do it, it's easy; (*título*) **'A~ se roba'** 'How to Steal'; **¡y ~ te va!** look where it's got you!; **aun ~ no me** *etc* **resultó** even then it didn't work; **¡~!** that's right!, that's the way!; **~ ~, ~ asá, ~ asado** so-so, fair, middling; **~ o asá** one way or another; **~ que asá** it makes no odds; **~ como ~, ~ que ~** anyway; **20 dólares o ~** 20 dollars or so, 20 dollars or thereabouts; **y ~ en adelante, y ~ sucesivamente** and so on; **~ que ...** so ..., therefore ...; **~ nada más** just like that, if you please; **~ pues ...** and so ..., so then ...; **~ y todo** even so; **~ es** that is so; **~ era** that's the way it was, that's what it was like; **~ es que no fuimos** so we didn't go, that's why we didn't go; **¿no es ~?** is it not so?, isn't it?; **¡~ sea!** so be it!

(**b**) (*comparaciones*) **~ A como B** both A and B, A as well as B; **~ como Vd sabe ruso yo sé chino** in the same way as you know Russian I know Chinese; **el original ~ como una copia** the original together with a copy; **no se hace ~ como ~** it's not as easy as all that.

(**c**) **~ de pobre que ...** so poor that ...; **un baúl ~ de grande** a trunk this big, a trunk as big as this; **estaba ~ de gordo** he was that fat.

2 *como adj invar*: **un hombre ~** such a man, a man like that; **todos tenemos épocas ~** we all have spells like that, we all have spells of that sort; **~ es la vida** such is life, that's life; **los franceses son ~** the French are like that, that's the way the French are.

3 *conj* (**a**) **~ que ...** as soon as ...; no sooner than ...

(**b**) **~ se esté muriendo de dolor** (*LAm*) even though he's dying of pain; **¡~ te mueras!** and I hope you die!; **~ te mueras tienes que hacerlo** you have to do it even if it costs your life; **¡~ nomás!** (*Méx**) just like that!

Asia *nf* Asia; **~ Menor** Asia Minor.

asiático, -a *adj*, *nm/f* Asian, Asiatic.

asidero *nm* (**a**) (*agarro*) hold, grasp.

(**b**) (*asa*) handle, holder.

(**c**) (*fig*) pretext, excuse; lever.

(**d**) (*Cono Sur*) basis, support; **eso no tiene ~** there is no basis for it.

asiduamente *adv* assiduously; frequently, regularly.

asiduidad *nf* (**a**) (*cualidad*) assiduousness; regularity. (**b**)

~**es** attentions, kindnesses.

asiduo 1 *adj* assiduous; frequent, regular, persistent; *admirador* devoted; **parroquiano** ~ regular customer; **como ~ lector de su periódico** as a regular (*o* constant) reader of your newspaper.

2 *nm,* **asidua** *nf* regular customer (*etc*), habitué(e); **era un ~ del café** he was an habitué of the café; **es un ~ del museo** he is a frequent visitor to the museum.

asiento *nm* (**a**) (*silla etc*) seat, chair; place; (*de bicicleta*) saddle; ~ **de atrás,** ~ **trasero** rear seat; pillion seat; ~ **delantero** front seat; ~ **expulsor,** ~ **lanzable,** ~ **proyectable** (*Aer*) ejector seat; ~ **reservado** reserved seat; **no ha calentado el** ~ he hasn't stayed long; **tomar** ~ to take a seat.

(**b**) (*sitio*) site, location.

(**c**) (*de botella etc*) bottom, base; (*Anat**) bottom.

(**d**) (*Mec*) seating; ~ **de válvula** valve seating.

(**e**) (*gen* ~**s** *pl*) sediment, dregs.

(**f**) (*Náut*) trim.

(**g**) (*Arquit*) settling; **hacer** ~ to settle, sink.

(**h**) (*acto*) settling, settlement, establishment; **estar de** ~ to be settled (in a place); **vivir de ~ con uno** to live in sin with sb.

(**i**) ~ (**minero**) (*And*) mining town, mining settlement.

(**j**) (*Com*) contract, trading agreement; (*Pol*) (peace) treaty.

(**k**) (*Fin: en cuenta etc*) entry; ~ **de cierre** closing entry; ~ **contable** book-keeping entry.

(**l**) (*cualidad*) stability; good sense, judgement; **hombre de** ~ sensible man.

asignable *adj*: ~ **a** assignable to, which can be assigned to.

asignación *nf* (**a**) (*acto*) assignment; allocation (*t Inform*); appointment; determination; ~ **de presupuesto** (*Com*) budget appropriation. (**b**) (*porción*) share, portion; (*Fin*) allowance, salary; pocket money; ~ **semanal** weekly allowance. (**c**) ~ **presupuestaria** (*Carib*) budget.

asignado *nm* (*And Agr*) wages paid in kind.

asignar [1a] *vt* (*gen*) to assign; to allot, apportion; (*Inform*) to allocate; *persona* to appoint; *tarea* to assign, set; *causas* to determine.

asignatario *nm,* **asignataria** *nf* (*LAm*) heir, legatee.

asignatura *nf* (*Univ etc*) subject, course; ~ **pendiente** (*Univ etc*) failed subject, subject to be retaken; (*fig*) matter pending, matter still to be resolved; **aprobar una** ~ to pass (in) a subject.

asigunas* *nfpl*: **según** ~ (*Carib*) it all depends.

asilado, -a *nm/f* inmate; (*Pol*) (political) refugee.

asilar [1a] **1** *vt* (**a**) (*acoger*) to take in, give shelter to; (*LAm*) to give political asylum to.

(**b**) *viejo etc* to put into a home (*o* institution).

2 asilarse *vr* (**a**) (*refugiarse*) to take refuge (*en* in); (*Pol*) to seek political asylum.

(**b**) (*viejo etc*) to enter a home (*o* institution).

asilo *nm* (**a**) (*Pol etc*) asylum; sanctuary; (*fig*) shelter, refuge; **derecho de** ~ right of sanctuary; **pedir (el) ~ político** to ask for political asylum.

(**b**) (*de viejos etc*) home, institution; ~ **de ancianos** old people's home; ~ **para desamparados** workhouse; ~ **de huérfanos** orphanage; ~ **de locos** lunatic asylum; ~ **de niños expósitos** foundling hospital; ~ **de pobres** poorhouse.

asilvestrarse [1a] *vr* (*tierra*) to become wooded, revert to woodland; (*planta*) to establish itself in the wild.

asimetría *nf* asymmetry; irregularity, unevenness.

asimétrico *adj* asymmetric(al); irregular, uneven.

asimiento *nm* (**a**) (*acto*) seizing, grasping; hold. (**b**) (*fig*) attachment, affection.

asimilable *adj*: **fácilmente** ~ readily assimilated, easy to assimilate.

asimilación *nf* assimilation.

asimilado 1 *adj* similar, related; **establecimientos hoteleros y ~s** hotels and the like. **2** *nm* (*LAm*) professional person attached to the army.

asimilar [1a] **1** *vt* to assimilate. **2 asimilarse** *vr* (**a**) (*establecerse*) to assimilate, become assimilated. (**b**) ~ **a** to resemble.

asimismo *adv* likewise, in like manner, in the same way.

asín* *adv* = **así.**

asíncrono *adj* asynchronous.

asintomático *adj* asymptomatic.

asir [3a; *pero en presente como* **salir**] **1** *vt* to seize, grasp, catch, take hold of (*con* with, *de* by); **ir asidos del brazo** to walk along arm-in-arm.

2 *vi* (*Bot*) to take root.

3 asirse *vr* to take hold; (*2 personas*) to fight, grapple, lay hold of one another; ~ **a,** ~ **de** to seize, take hold of; to clutch on to; ~ **de** (*fig*) to avail o.s. of, take advantage of; ~ **con uno** to grapple with sb.

Asiria *nf* Assyria.

asirio, -a *adj, nm/f* Assyrian.

asisito *adv* (*And etc*) = **así.**

asísmico *adj* (*LAm*): **construcción asísmica** earthquake-resistant building; **medidas asísmicas** anti-earthquake measures.

asistencia *nf* (**a**) (*presencia*) attendance, presence (*a* at).

(**b**) (*personas*) people present, those attending; audience; **¿había mucha ~?** were there many people there?

(**c**) (*ayuda*) help, assistance; (*en casa*) domestic help, service; (*Med*) care, attendance; nursing; ~ **intensiva** intensive care; ~ **letrada** legal aid; ~ **médica** medical care, medical attendance; ~ **pública** (*Cono Sur*) state medical service; public health system; ~ **sanitaria** health care; ~ **social** welfare, welfare work, social work.

(**d**) (*Méx: cuarto*) spare room, guest room.

(**e**) (*And, Méx: pensión*) cheap boarding-house.

(**f**) ~**s** (*Fin*) allowance, maintenance.

asistencial *adj* welfare (*atr*), social security (*atr*).

asistenta *nf* assistant; (*de limpieza*) charwoman, daily help, cleaning lady; (*And, Méx*) boarding-house keeper, landlady.

asistente *nm* (*a veces* **asistenta** *nf*) (**a**) (*ayudante*) assistant; (*Mil*) orderly, batman; (*And*) servant; (*And, Méx*) boarding-house keeper, landlord; ~ **social** social worker, welfare worker.

(**b**) **los ~s** (*presentes*) those present, the people present.

asistido 1 *adj*: ~ **por ordenador** computer-assisted. **2** *nm,* **asistida** *nf* (*And, Méx*) boarder, lodger, resident.

asistir [3a] **1** *vt* (**a**) (*estar presente*) to attend; (*servir*) to serve, wait on.

(**b**) (*ayudar*) to help, assist; (*Med*) to attend, care for; **el médico que le asiste** the doctor who attends him, the doctor in whose care he is; ~ **un parto** to deliver a baby.

(**c**) (*Jur*) to represent, appear for; **asistido por su abogado** with his lawyer present.

(**d**) **le asiste la razón** he has right on his side.

2 *vi* (**a**) (*estar presente*) to be present (*a* at), attend; *suceso, proceso, escena* to witness, be a witness of; **no asistió a la clase** he did not attend the class, he did not come to the class; **¿vas a ~?** are you going?; **asistieron unas 200 personas** some 200 people were present.

(**b**) (*Naipes*) to follow suit.

askenazí *adj, nf* Ashkenazi.

asma *nf* asthma; ~ **bronquial** bronchial asthma.

asmático *adj, nm,* **asmática** *nf* asthmatic.

asna *nf* female donkey.

asnada* *nf* silly thing.

asnal* *adj* asinine, silly; beastly.

asnar *adj*: **ganado** ~ donkeys.

asnear [1a] *vi* (*LAm*) to act the fool, do sth silly; to be clumsy.

asnería* *nf* silly thing.

asno *nm* (**a**) (*Zool*) donkey. (**b**) (*fig*) ass*, fathead*; **¡soy un ~!** I'm an ass!*

asociación *nf* association; society; (*Com, Fin*) partnership; ~ **aduanera** customs union; ~ **para el delito** criminal conspiracy; ~ **libre** free association; ~ **obrera** trade union; ~ **de padres de alumnos** parent-teacher association; ~ **de vecinos** neighbourhood association, residents' association; **por ~ de ideas** by association of ideas.

asociado 1 *adj* associated; *miembro etc* associate. **2** *nm,* **asociada** *nf* associate; member; (*Com, Fin*) partner.

asociar [1b] **1** *vt* (*gen*) to associate (*a, con* with); *esfuerzos, recursos etc* to pool, put together; (*Com, Fin*) to take into partnership.

2 asociarse *vr* to associate; (*Com, Fin*) to become partners, form a partnership; ~ **con uno** to team up with sb, join forces with sb.

asocio *nm* (*LAm*): **en** ~ in association (*de* with).

asolación *nf* destruction, devastation.

asolador *adj* destructive, devastating.

asolanar [1a] *vt,* **asolar**[1] [1a] **1** *vt* to dry up, parch. **2 asolanarse** *vr,* **asolarse** *vr* to dry up, be ruined.

asolar[2] [1a] **1** *vt* to raze (to the ground), lay flat, destroy; to lay waste. **2 asolarse** *vr* (*líquido*) to settle.

asoleada *nf* (*LAm*) sunstroke.

asoleado *adj* (*CAm*) (**a**) *persona* stupid. (**b**) *animal* tired out.

asoleadura *nf* (*Cono Sur*) sunstroke.
asolear [1a] **1** *vt* to put in the sun, keep in the sun; to dry in the sun.
2 asolearse *vr* (**a**) to sun o.s., bask in the sun; to get sunburnt.
(**b**) (*Cono Sur, Méx Med*) to get sunstroke.
(**c**) (*CAm*: *atontarse*) to get stupid.
asoleo *nm* (*Méx*) sunstroke.
asomada *nf* (**a**) (*aparición*) brief appearance. (**b**) (*vislumbre*) glimpse, sudden view.
asomadero *nm* (*And*) viewing point, vantage point.
asomar [1a] **1** *vt* to show, put out, stick out; ~ **la cabeza** to put one's head out (*a la ventana* of the window); ~ **la cara** to show one's face (*t fig*); **asomó un pie** she stuck a foot out.
2 *vi* to begin to show, appear, become visible; **asoman ya las nuevas plantas** the new plants are beginning to show; **asomó el buque en la niebla** the ship loomed up out of the fog.
3 asomarse *vr* (**a**) (*objeto*) to show, appear, stick out; (*costa, en niebla etc*) to loom up; **se asomaba el árbol por encima de la tapia** the tree showed above the wall.
(**b**) (*persona*) to show up, show o.s.; ~ **a,** ~ **por** to show o.s. at, lean out of, look out of; **ella estaba asomada a la ventana** she was leaning out of the window; **¡asómate!** put your head out!; **¡asómate entonces!** let me see you sometime!; ~ **a ver algo** to take a look at sth; to peep in at sth.
(**c**) (*: *emborracharse*) to get tight*, get tipsy.
(**d**) (*And*: *acercarse*) to approach, come close (to).
asombradizo *adj* easily alarmed.
asombrador *adj* amazing, astonishing.
asombrar [1a] **1** *vt* (**a**) (*pasmar*) to amaze, astonish; to frighten; **no deja de ~me** it never ceases to amaze me.
(**b**) (*ensombrecer*) to shade, cast a shadow on; *color* to darken.
2 asombrarse *vr* (**a**) (*sorprenderse*) to be amazed, be astonished (*de* at); (*escandalizarse*) to be shocked (*de* at); (*asustarse*) to take fright; ~ **de saber algo** to be surprised to learn sth.
(**b**) (*CAm*: *desmayarse*) to faint.
asombro *nm* (**a**) (*pasmo*) amazement, astonishment, surprise; (*miedo*) fear, fright.
(**b**) (*objeto*) wonder; **es el ~ del siglo** it is the wonder of the century.
asombrosamente *adv* amazingly, astonishingly.
asombroso *adj* amazing, astonishing.
asomo *nm* (**a**) (*aparición*) appearance.
(**b**) (*indicio*) hint, sign, indication, trace; **ante cualquier ~ de discrepancia** at the slightest hint of disagreement; **sin ~ de violencia** without a trace of violence; **ni por** ~ by no means, not by a long shot; **¡ni por ~!** no chance!
asonada *nf* (**a**) (*personas*) mob, rabble. (**b**) (*motín*) riot, disturbance.
asonancia *nf* (**a**) (*Liter*) assonance. (**b**) (*fig*) harmony; correspondence, connection; **no tener ~ con** to bear no relation to.
asonantar [1a] *vti* to assonate (*con* with).
asonante 1 *adj* assonant. **2** *nf* (*gen*) assonance; (*palabra*) assonant (rhyme).
asonar [1l] *vi* to assonate, be in assonance.
asordar [1a] *vt* to deafen.
asorocharse [1a] *vr* (*And, Cono Sur*) to get mountain sickness.
asosegar [1h *y* 1j] = **sosegar.**
aspa *nf* cross, X-shaped figure (*o* design *etc*); (*Mat*) multiplication sign; (*Arquit*) crosspiece; (*de molino*) sail, arm; (*Téc*) reel, winding frame; (*Cono Sur*) horn; **ventilador de** ~ rotary fan.
aspadera *nf* reel, winder.
aspado *adj* cross-shaped, X-shaped; *persona* with arms outstretched; **estar ~ en algo** to be all trussed up in sth.
aspador *nm* reel, winder.
aspamentero *adj* (*etc*) (*Cono Sur, Méx*) = **aspaventero** (*etc*).
aspar [1a] **1** *vt* (**a**) (*Téc*) to reel, wind.
(**b**) (*fig*: *fastidiar*) to vex, annoy; **¡que te aspen!‡** get lost!‡; **lo hago aunque me aspen** wild horses wouldn't stop me doing it.
2 asparse *vr* (**a**) (*retorcerse*) to writhe.
(**b**) (*fig*: *esforzarse*) to do one's utmost, go all out (*por algo* to get sth).
aspaventero 1 *adj* excitable, emotional, given to exaggerated displays of feeling; fussy. **2** *nm*, **aspaventera** *nf* excitable person; fussy person.
aspaviento *nm* exaggerated display of feeling; fulsome expression of feeling; fuss, to-do*; **~s** exaggerated gestures; **hacer ~s** to make a great fuss.
aspecto *nm* (**a**) (*apariencia*) look, appearance; looks; aspect; (*Arquit, Geog etc*) aspect; ~ **exterior** outward appearance; **un hombre de ~ feroz** a man with a fierce look, a fierce-looking man; **tener buen ~** to look well; **¿qué ~ tenía?** what was he like?, what did he look like?
(**b**) (*fig*) aspect; side; **a(l) primer ~** at first sight; **bajo ese ~** from that point of view; **estudiar una cuestión bajo todos sus ~s** to study all aspects of a question; **ver sólo un ~ de la cuestión** to see only one side to the question.
ásperamente *adv* roughly; harshly, gruffly; **dijo ~** he said in a harsh tone.
aspereza *nf* (*V adj*) roughness; ruggedness; sourness, bitterness; toughness; harshness; surliness; **contestar con ~** to answer with asperity, answer harshly; **limar ~s** (*fig*) to smooth things over.
asperges *nm* (**a**) (*aspersión*) sprinkling; **quedarse ~** to come away empty-handed. (**b**) (*Ecl*) aspergillum; hyssop.
asperillo *nm* slight sour (*o* bitter) taste.
asperjar [1a] *vt* to sprinkle; (*Ecl*) to sprinkle with holy water.
áspero *adj* (**a**) (*al tacto*) rough; *filo* uneven, jagged, rough; *terreno* rough, rugged.
(**b**) (*al gusto*) sour, tart, bitter.
(**c**) *clima* hard, tough; *trato* rough.
(**d**) *voz* harsh, rough; rasping; *tono* harsh; surly, gruff; (*inculto*) unpolished; *temperamento* sour; *disputa etc* bad-tempered.
asperón *nm* sandstone, grit; (*Téc*) grindstone.
aspersión *nf* (*de agua etc*) sprinkling; (*Agr, Hort*) spray, spraying; **riego por ~** watering by spray, watering by sprinklers.
aspersor *nm* sprinkler.
áspid(e) *nm* asp.
aspidistra *nf* aspidistra.
aspillera *nf* (*Mil*) loophole.
aspiración *nf* (**a**) (*respiración*) breath; breathing in, inhalation; (*Ling*) aspiration; (*Mús*) (*short pause for*) breath. (**b**) (*Mec*) air intake. (**c**) **aspiraciones** (*LAm*) aspirations.
aspirada *nf* aspirate.
aspirado *adj* aspirate.
aspirador 1 *adj* suction (*atr*); **bomba ~a** suction pump. **2** *nm* (*t* **~ de polvo**) vacuum-cleaner; **pasar el ~ a la alfombra** to hoover the carpet.
aspiradora *nf* vacuum-cleaner.
aspirante 1 *adj*: **bomba ~** suction pump. **2** *nmf* aspirant; candidate, applicant (*a* for); **~ de marina** naval cadet.
aspirar [1a] **1** *vt* (**a**) *aire etc* to breathe in, inhale; *líquido* to suck in, suck up; (*Téc*) to suck in, take in; *droga* to sniff.
(**b**) (*Ling*) to aspirate.
2 *vi*: **~ a algo** to aspire to sth; **no aspiro a tanto** I do not aim so high; **A aspiró a la mano de B** A sought B's hand in marriage; **~ a hacer algo** to aspire to do sth, aim to do sth, seek to do sth; **el que no sepa eso que no aspire a aprobar** whoever doesn't know that can have no hope of passing.
aspirina *nf* aspirin.
aspudo *adj* (*Cono Sur*) big-horned.
asquear [1a] **1** *vt* to nauseate; **me asquean las ratas** I loathe rats, rats nauseate (*o* disgust) me. **2** *vi y* **asquearse** *vr* to be nauseated, feel disgusted.
asquerosamente *adv* disgustingly, sickeningly; (*) awfully.
asquerosidad *nf* (**a**) (*cualidad*) loathsomeness; squalor; awfulness; vileness. (**b**) (*una* ~) mess, filth; **hacer ~es** to make a mess. (**c**) (*trampa*) dirty trick.
asqueroso *adj* (**a**) (*repugnante*) disgusting, loathsome, sickening; squalid; *comida* revolting; (*) awful, lousy‡, vile. (**b**) (*de gusto delicado*) squeamish.
asquiento *adj* (*And*) (**a**) (*quisquilloso*) fussy. (**b**) = **asqueroso.**
asta *nf* (*arma*) lance, spear; (*palo*) pole; shaft; (*asidero*) handle; (*de bandera*) flagstaff, flagpole; (*Zool*) horn, antler; **a media ~** at half mast; **dejar a uno en las ~s del toro** to leave sb in a jam.
astabandera *nf* (*LAm*) flagstaff, flagpole.
ástaco *nm* crayfish.
astado 1 *adj* horned. **2** *nm* bull.
astear [1a] *vt* (*Cono Sur*) to gore.
aster *nf* aster.
asterisco *nm* asterisk; **señalar con un ~, poner ~ a** to asterisk.

asteroide *nm* asteroid.
astigmático *adj* astigmatic.
astigmatismo *nm* astigmatism.
astil *nm* (*de herramienta*) handle, haft; (*de flecha*) shaft; (*de balanza*) beam.
astilla *nf* (**a**) (*fragmento*) splinter, chip; **~s** (*para fuego*) firewood, kindling; **hacer algo ~s** to smash sth into little pieces, smash sth to matchwood; **hacerse ~s** to shatter into little pieces. (**b**) (*Esp**) small bribe, sweetener*; **dar ~ a uno** to give sb a cut*; **ese tío no da ~** he's a very tight-fisted so-and-so*.
astillar [1a] **1** *vt* to splinter, chip; to shatter. **2 astillarse** *vr* to splinter; to shatter.
astillero *nm* shipyard, dockyard.
astracán *nm* astrakhan.
astracanada* *nf* silly thing (to do); piece of buffoonery.
astrágalo *nm* (*Arquit, Mil*) astragal; (*Anat*) ankle bone, astragalus.
astral *adj* astral, of the stars.
astreñir [3h *y* 3i] = **astringir.**
astrilla *nf* (*Cono Sur*) = **astilla.**
astringente 1 *adj* astringent, binding. **2** *nm* astringent.
astringir [3e] *vt* (**a**) (*Anat*) to constrict, contract; (*Med*) to bind. (**b**) (*fig*) to bind, compel.
astro *nm* (**a**) (*Astron*) star, heavenly body; **el ~ Rey** the sun. (**b**) (*fig*) star, leading light; (*Cine*) star.
astrofísica[1] *nf* astrophysics.
astrofísico, -a[2] *nm/f* astrophysicist.
astrología *nf* astrology.
astrológico *adj* astrological.
astrólogo, -a *nm/f* astrologer.
astronauta *nmf* astronaut.
astronáutica *nf* astronautics.
astronave *nf* spaceship.
astronomía *nf* astronomy.
astronómico *adj* astronomical.
astrónomo, -a *nm/f* astronomer.
astroso *adj* (**a**) (*malhadado*) ill-fated, unfortunate. (**b**) (*vil*) contemptible. (**c**) (*sucio*) dirty; (*desaseado*) untidy, shabby.
astucia *nf* (**a**) (*cualidad*) cleverness; guile, cunning; **actuar con ~** to act cunningly, be crafty. (**b**) **una ~** a clever trick, a piece of cunning.
astur *adj, nm* Asturian.
asturiano, -a 1 *adj, nm/f* Asturian. **2** *nm* (*Ling*) Asturian.
Asturias *n*: (**el Principado de**) **~** Asturias.
astutamente *adv* cleverly, smartly; craftily, cunningly.
astuto *adj* clever, smart; crafty, cunning.
asueto *nm* time off, break, short holiday; **día de ~** day off; **tarde de ~** afternoon off, (*Escol*) half-holiday; **tomarse un ~ de fin de semana** to take a weekend break, take the weekend off.
asumible *adj riesgo* acceptable, permissible.
asumir [3a] **1** *vt* (**a**) *responsabilidad etc* to assume, take on; *mando etc* to take over; *cargo* to take up; *actitud* to strike, adopt. (**b**) (*suponer*) to assume, suppose; to take for granted; **~ que ...** to assume that ... **2** *vi* (*Pol etc*) to take up office.
asunceño (*Cono Sur*) **1** *adj* of Asunción. **2** *nm*, **asunceña** *nf* native (*o* inhabitant) of Asunción; **los ~s** the people of Asunción.
Asunción *nf* (**a**) (*Ecl*) Assumption. (**b**) (*Geog*) Asunción.
asunción *nf* assumption.
asunto *nm* (**a**) (*gen*) matter, subject; (*tema*) topic; (*negocio*) affair, business; (*Liter*) theme, subject; plot; (*: *ligue*) affair; **¡~ concluido!** that's an end of the matter!; **el ~ está concluido** the matter is closed; **~ de alcoba** matter involving sexual relations; **~ de honor** affair of honour; **el ~ Rumasa** the Rumasa affair; **~s exteriores** foreign affairs; **Ministerio de A~s Exteriores** Foreign Ministry, Foreign Office, State Department (*US*); **~s a tratar** agenda, items to be discussed; **es un ~ de faldas** there's a woman in it somewhere; **ausente por ~ grave** absent with good reason, absent for good cause; **es un ~ triste** it's a bad business; **ir al ~** to get down to business; **entrometerse en un ~** to meddle in an affair.
(**b**) (*Carib*: *atención*) study, attention; **poner ~** to pay attention.
(**c**) **¿a ~ de qué lo hiciste?** (*Cono Sur*) why did you do it?
asurar [1a] *vt* (**a**) (*Culin etc*) to burn; (*Agr*) to burn up, parch. (**b**) (*fig*) to worry.
asurcar [1g] *vt* = **surcar.**
asustadizo *adj* easily frightened; nervy, jumpy; *animal* shy, skittish.
asustar [1a] **1** *vt* to frighten, scare; to alarm, startle.
2 asustarse *vr* to be frightened, get scared; to get alarmed, be startled; **~ de** (*o* **por**) **algo** to be frightened at sth, get alarmed about sth; **~ de** + *infin* to be afraid to + *infin*; **¡no te asustes!** don't be alarmed!
asusto *nm* (*And*) = **susto.**
A.T. *abr de* **Antiguo Testamento** Old Testament, O.T.
-ata *V* **Aspects of Word Formation in Spanish 2.**
atabacado *adj* (**a**) (*color*) tobacco-coloured. (**b**) **con aliento ~** (*Cono Sur*) with breath smelling of tobacco.
atabal *nm* kettledrum.
atabalear [1a] *vi* (*caballo*) to stamp, drum; (*con dedos*) to drum.
atacable *adj* attackable, assailable.
atacado *adj* (**a**) (*pusilánime*) fainthearted; (*vacilante*) dithery, irresolute. (**b**) (*tacaño*) mean, stingy.
atacador 1 *nm* (*Mil*) ramrod. **2** *nm*, **atacadora** *nf* attacker, assailant.
atacadura *nf* fastener, fastening.
atacante *nmf* attacker, assailant.
atacar [1g] **1** *vt* (**a**) (*Mil etc*) to attack; to assail, assault; *teoría etc* to attack, impugn; (*en disputa*) to attack, set about, go for; to press hard.
(**b**) (*Quím, Med etc*) to attack.
(**c**) (*pegar etc*) to attach, fasten; *vestido* to button up, do up.
(**d**) *bolsa etc* to stuff, pack; (*Mil, Min*) to ram home, tamp; to wad, plug.
2 atacarse* *vr* (*LAm*) to scoff*, stuff o.s.
atachar [1a] *vt* (*Méx Elec*) to plug in.
ataché *nm* (*CAm, Carib*) paper clip.
ataderas* *nfpl* garters.
atadero *nm* (*cuerda*) rope, cord; (*cierre*) fastening; (*sitio*) place for tying; (*Méx*: *liga*) garter; **eso no tiene ~** you can't make head or tail of it, there's nothing to latch on to.
atadijo *nm* loose bundle.
atado 1 *adj* (**a**) (*lit*) tied. (**b**) (*fig*: *tímido*) shy, inhibited; (*indeciso*) irresolute. **2** *nm* bundle; bunch; **~ de cigarrillos** (*Cono Sur*) packet of cigarettes.
atadora *nf* (*Agr*) binder.
atadura *nf* (**a**) (*acto*) tying, fastening. (**b**) (*cuerda etc*) string, cord, rope; (*Agr*) rope, tether; (*fig*) bond, tie. (**c**) (*fig*: *limitación*) limitation, restriction.
atafagar [1h] *vt* (**a**) (*olor*) to stifle, suffocate. (**b**) (*fig*) to pester the life out of.
ataguía *nf* cofferdam, caisson.
atajar [1a] **1** *vt* (**a**) (*gen*) to stop, intercept; *fugitivo etc* to head off, cut off; (*LAm*: *recoger*) to catch, catch in flight; (*Dep*) to tackle; (*Arquit*) to partition off; **~ a uno** (*LAm*) to hold sb back (to stop a fight); **~ un golpe** (*LAm*) to parry a blow; **me quiso ~ al almuerzo** (*LAm*) she wanted me to stay for lunch.
(**b**) *discusión* to cut short; *discurso* to interrupt, break into; *proceso* to end, stop, call a halt to; *abuso* to put a stop to; **este mal hay que ~lo** we must put an end to this evil.
2 *vi* to take a short cut (*por* by way of, across); (*Aut*) to cut corners.
3 atajarse *vr* (*avergonzarse*) to feel ashamed of o.s.; (*aturdirse*) to be overcome by confusion, be all of a dither; (*Cono Sur*) to keep one's temper, control o.s.
atajo *nm* (**a**) (*en camino*) short cut; **echar por el ~** to take the easiest way out, seek a quick solution; **no hay ~ sin trabajo** short cuts don't help in the long run. (**b**) (*Dep*) tackle.
atalaje *nm* = **atelaje.**
atalaya 1 *nf* (**a**) (*torre*) watchtower; observation point, observation post. (**b**) (*fig*) vantage point. **2** *nm* lookout, observer, sentinel.
atalayador(a) *nm/f* look-out; (*fig*) snooper, spy.
atalayar [1a] *vt* (*observar*) to watch, observe; (*vigilar*) to watch over, guard; (*espiar*) to spy on.
atañer [2f; *defectivo*: *se usa en 3ª persona de presente*] *vi*: **~ a** to concern, have to do with; **en lo que atañe a eso** with regard to that, as to that; **eso no me atañe** it's no concern of mine.
atapuzar [1f] (*Carib*) **1** *vt* to fill, stop up. **2 atapuzarse** *vr* to stuff o.s.
ataque *nm* (**a**) (*Mil etc*) attack (*a, contra* on); strike (*a, contra* against); (*Aer*) attack, raid; **~ aéreo** air raid, air attack; **~ fingido** sham attack; **~ de flanco** flank attack; **~ de frente** frontal attack; **~ preventivo** pre-emptive strike; **~ por sorpresa** surprise attack; **~ a superficie** ground

attack; **dejarse expuesto al ~** to leave o.s. open to attack; **lanzar un ~** to launch an attack; **pasar al ~** to go on the offensive; **volver al ~** to return to the attack.

(**b**) (*Med etc*) attack (*de* of), fit; **~ cardíaco, ~ al corazón** heart-attack; **~ cerebral** brain haemorrhage; **~ epiléptico** epileptic fit; **~ fulminante** stroke, seizure; **~ de risa** fit of laughing.

atar [1a] **1** *vt* (**a**) (*gen*) to tie, tie up; *cautivo* to bind; (*abrochar*) to fasten; (*Agr*) *animal* to tether; *gavilla* to bind; **zapatos de ~** lace-up shoes; **está de ~** he's raving mad; **~ corto a uno** (*fig*) to keep sb on a close rein; **~ la lengua a uno** (*fig*) to silence sb; **~ las manos a uno** (*fig*) to limit sb's freedom of action; **verse atado de pies y manos** (*fig*) to be tied hand and foot; **dejar algo atado y bien atado** (*fig*) to leave no loose ends, leave everything properly tied up.

(**b**) (*fig*) to bind, tie; to hamper.

2 *vi*: **ni ata ni desata** this is nonsense, this is getting us nowhere.

3 atarse *vr* (**a**) (*quedar atascado*) to stick, get stuck; **~ en una dificultad** to get tied up in a difficulty.

(**b**) (*sentirse violento*) to be embarrassed, get embarrassed.

(**c**) **~ a la letra** to stick to the literal meaning; **~ a una opinión** to stick to one's opinion.

ataracea *nf* = **taracea**.

atarantar [1a] **1** *vt* (**a**) (*aturdir*) to stun, daze; **quedó atarantado** he was stunned, he was unconscious.

(**b**) (*fig*) to stun, dumbfound.

2 atarantarse *vr* (**a**) to be stunned, be dumbfounded.

(**b**) (*And*: *darse prisa*) to hurry, dash, rush.

(**c**) (*Méx*: *comiendo*) to stuff o.s.

(**d**) (*CAm*, *Méx*: *bebiendo*) to get drunk.

atarazana *nf* dockyard.

atardecer 1 [2d] *vi* to get dark; **atardecía** it was getting dark, night was falling.

2 *nm* late afternoon; dusk, evening; **al ~** at dusk.

atardecida *nf* dusk, nightfall.

atareado *adj* busy, rushed; **andar muy ~** to be very busy.

atarear [1a] **1** *vt* to give a job to, assign a task to. **2 atarearse** *vr* to work hard, keep busy; to be busy (*con*, *en* with); **~ a hacer algo** to be busy doing sth.

atarjea *nf* sewage pipe, drain; (*And*: *presa de agua*) reservoir.

atarragarse [1h] *vr* (*Carib*, *Méx*) to stuff o.s., overeat.

atarugar [1h] **1** *vt* (**a**) (*asegurar*) to fasten (with a peg *o* wedge); to peg, wedge.

(**b**) *agujero* to plug, stop, bung up.

(**c**) (*llenar*) to stuff, fill (*de* with).

(**d**) (*****) **~ a uno** to shut sb up.

2 atarugarse *vr* (**a**) (*atragantarse*) to swallow the wrong way, choke.

(**b**) (*fig*) to get confused, be in a daze.

(**c**) (*****: *tragar*) to stuff o.s., overeat.

atasajar [1a] *vt carne* to jerk.

atascadero *nm* (**a**) (*lit*) mire, bog, muddy place. (**b**) (*fig*) stumbling block, obstacle; dead end.

atascar [1g] **1** *vt fuga* to stop; *agujero* to block, plug, stop up; *tubo etc* to clog, clog up, obstruct; *proceso* to hinder.

2 atascarse *vr* (**a**) (*carro etc*) to get stuck (in the mud), get bogged down; (*Aut*) to get into a jam; (*motor*) to stall; **quedó atascado a mitad de la cuesta** he got stuck halfway up the climb.

(**b**) (*fig*) to get bogged down (*en un problema* in a problem); (*en discurso*) to get stuck, dry up*.

(**c**) (*tubo etc*) to clog, get clogged up, get stopped up; (*LAm Med*) to have an internal blockage.

atasco *nm* obstruction, blockage; (*Aut*) traffic-jam.

ataúd *nm* coffin; bier.

ataujía *nf* (**a**) (*Téc*) damascene, damascene work. (**b**) (*CAm*: *desagüe*) conduit, drain.

ataviar [1c] **1** *vt* (**a**) to deck, array (*con*, *de* in); to dress up, get up (*con*, *de* in). (**b**) (*LAm*) to adapt, adjust, accommodate. **2 ataviarse** *vr* to dress up, get o.s. up (*con*, *de* in).

atávico *adj* atavistic.

atavío *nm* attire, dress; (*hum*) rig, get-up; **~s** finery.

atavismo *nm* atavism.

ate *nm* (*CAm*, *Méx Culin*) jelly.

atediante *adj* boring, wearisome.

atediar [1b] **1** *vt* to bore, weary. **2 atediarse** *vr* to get bored.

ateísmo *nm* atheism.

ateísta *adj* atheistic.

atejonarse [1a] *vr* (*Méx*) (**a**) (*arrollarse*) to curl up into a ball. (**b**) (*hacerse más astuto*) to become sharp (*o* cunning).

atelaje *nm* (**a**) (*caballos*) team (of horses). (**b**) (*arreos*) harness; (*equipo*) equipment; (*****) trousseau.

atembado *adj* (*And*) silly, stupid; lacking in willpower.

atemorizar [1f] **1** *vt* to frighten, scare. **2 atemorizarse** *vr* to get scared (*de*, *por* at).

atempar* [1a] *vi* (*CAm*) to wait, hang around.

atemperar [1a] *vt* (**a**) (*moderar*) to temper, moderate. (**b**) (*ajustar*) to adjust, accommodate (*a* to); **~ los gastos a los ingresos** (*Com*) to balance outgoings with income.

atemporal *adj* timeless.

atemporalado *adj* stormy.

atemporalidad *nf* timelessness.

Atenas *nf* Athens.

atenazar [1f] *vt* (*fig*) to grip; (*duda etc*) to torment, beset; **el miedo me atenazaba** I was gripped by fear.

atención *nf* (**a**) (*gen*) attention; care, heed; **¡~!** attention!; (*aviso*) look out!, careful!; (*escrito en envase etc*) 'with care'; **~ domiciliaria** home help; **~ primaria** primary (health) care; **¡~ a los pies!** mind your feet!; **'¡~! frenos potentes'** 'Beware!: powerful brakes'; **'¡~ a la velocidad!'** (*Aut*) 'watch your speed!'; **'¡~ a los precios!'** (*Com*) 'look at our prices!'; **'para** (*o* **a**) **la ~ de X'** (*en sobre*) 'for the attention of X'; **llamar la ~** to attract attention, catch the eye; **llamar la ~ de uno por algo** to rebuke sb for sth, find fault with sb over sth; **no me llama la ~** it doesn't surprise me; **me llamó la ~ un detalle** I was struck by a detail; **llamar la ~ de uno sobre un detalle** to draw sb's attention to a detail; **prestar ~** to pay attention, listen (*a* to).

(**b**) (*amabilidad*) kindness, civility; **atenciones** attentions, courtesies.

(**c**) (*asuntos*) **atenciones** affairs; duties, responsibilities.

(**d**) **en ~ a esto** in view of this, having regard to this.

atencioso *adj* (*LAm*) = **atento**.

atender [2g] **1** *vt* (**a**) (*gen*) to attend to, pay attention to; *consejo*, *aviso etc* to heed; (*Mec*) to service, maintain; *niño*, *enfermo etc* to look after, care for; *petición* to comply with; **~ a un cliente** to serve a customer; **~ a uno que pregunta** to give full satisfaction to an inquirer; **~ sus compromisos** to meet one's obligations; **~ el teléfono** to mind the telephone, stay at the telephone; (*Cono Sur*, *Méx*) to answer the telephone; **~ una demanda** (*Com*) to meet a demand; **~ una tienda** (*Com*) to serve in a shop; to be in charge of a shop; **~ una orden** (*Com*) to attend to an order; **~ un giro** (*Com*) to honour a draft.

(**b**) (*LAm*: *asistir a*) to attend, be present at.

2 *vi* (**a**) **~ a** to attend to, pay attention to; *detalles* to take note of; **~ a un caso urgente** to see about an urgent matter; **¡atiende a lo tuyo!** (*Cono Sur*) mind your own business!

(**b**) **~ por** to answer to the name of.

atendible *adj* acceptable, worthy of consideration; **esa objeción no es ~** that objection is not valid, that objection is not to be entertained.

ateneo *nm* cultural association (*o* centre).

atenerse [2k] *vr*: **~ a** (**a**) *regla* to abide by, obey; *verdad*, *opinión* to hold to; *promesa* to stand by, adhere to, keep to.

(**b**) (*contar con*) to rely on; **no saber a qué ~** not to know what to expect; not to know what line to take; not to know where one stands; **lo hizo ateniéndose a que ...** he did it knowing that ..., he did it taking into account the fact that ...; **~ a las consecuencias** to bear the consequences in mind.

ateniense *adj*, *nmf* Athenian.

atentado 1 *adj* (*prudente*) prudent, cautious; (*moderado*) moderate.

2 *nm* (*ofensa*) illegal act, offence; (*crimen*) outrage, crime; (*ataque*) assault, attack; attempt (*a*, *contra la vida de uno* on sb's life); **~ terrorista** terrorist outrage; **~ contra la honra, ~ contra el pudor** indecent assault.

atentamente *adv* (*V adj*) (**a**) attentively. (**b**) politely; thoughtfully, kindly; (**le saluda**) **~** yours faithfully.

atentar [1a] **1** *vt acto* to do illegally; *crimen* to attempt, try to commit.

2 *vi*: **~ a, ~ contra** to commit an outrage against; **~ contra la honra de una** to make an indecent assault on sb; **~ contra la ley** to break the law; **~ contra la vida de uno** to make an attempt on sb's life.

atentatorio *adj* illegal, criminal; **un acto ~ a ...** an act which poses a threat to ..., an act which undermines ...

atento *adj* (**a**) (*observador*) attentive (*a* to), observant, watchful (*a* of); **estar ~ a los peligros** to be mindful of the dangers.

(**b**) (*cortés*) polite; (*amable*) thoughtful, kind; (*servicial*) obliging; **ser ~ con uno** to be kind to sb, be considerate towards sb.
(**c**) **su atenta (carta)** (*Com*) your esteemed letter.
(**d**) **~ a** *como prep* in view of, in consideration of; **~ a que ...** *como conj* considering that ..., in view of the fact that ...

atenuación *nf* (*V vt*) attenuation; lessening, diminution; understatement; (*Jur*) extenuation.

atenuante 1 *adj* extenuating; **circunstancias ~s** extenuating circumstances, mitigating circumstances. **2** *nf* (**a**) **~s** (*Jur*) extenuating circumstances. (**b**) (*LAm Jur; t nm*) excuse, plea.

atenuar [1e] **1** *vt* to attenuate; *crimen etc* to extenuate; *impacto* to cushion, lessen; *importancia* to lessen, minimize; *impresión etc* to tone down; to understate. **2 atenuarse** *vr* to weaken.

ateo 1 *adj* atheistic. **2** *nm*, **atea** *nf* atheist.

ateperetarse [1a] *vr* (*CAm, Méx*) to get confused, get bewildered.

atepocate *nm* (*Méx Zool*) tadpole.

aterciopelado *adj* velvet (*atr*), velvety.

aterido *adj* numb, stiff with cold.

aterirse [3a; *defectivo; se usan el infin y pp*] *vr* to get numb, get stiff with cold.

aterrada *nf* (*Náut*) landfall.

aterrador *adj* frightening, terrifying; appalling.

aterraje *nm* (*Aer*) landing; (*Náut*) landfall.

aterrar[1] [1j] **1** *vt* (**a**) (*derribar*) to pull down, demolish, destroy.
(**b**) (*cubrir*) to cover with earth; (*Agr*) to earth up.
(**c**) (*CAm, Méx: obstruir*) to choke, obstruct.
2 *vi* (*Aer*) to land; (*Náut*) to reach land.
3 aterrarse *vr* (*Náut*) to stand inshore; **navegar aterrado** to sail inshore.

aterrar[2] [1a] **1** *vt* (*asustar*) to terrify, frighten; to appal.
2 aterrarse *vr* to be terrified, be frightened (*de* at); to be appalled (*de* about, by); to panic.

aterrazamiento *nm* terracing.

aterrazar [1f] *vt* to terrace.

aterrizaje *nm* (*Aer*) landing; **~ duro** hard landing; **~ de emergencia, ~ forzoso** emergency landing, forced landing; **~ de panza, ~ a vientre** pancake landing; **~ suave** soft landing; **~ violento** crash landing.

aterrizar [1f] *vi* (*Aer*) to land; (*persona*) to get out (of an aeroplane).

aterronar [1a] **1** *vt* to cake, harden. **2 aterronarse** *vr* to get lumpy; to cake, harden.

aterrorizador *adj* terrifying, frightening.

aterrorizar [1f] *vt* to terrify; (*Mil, Pol etc*) to terrorize.

atersar [1a] *vt* to smooth.

atesar [1j] *vt* (*LAm*) = **atiesar**.

atesoramiento *nm* hoarding, accumulation.

atesorar [1a] *vt* to hoard, store up, accumulate; *virtudes etc* to possess.

atestación *nf* attestation.

atestado[1] *nm* (*Jur*) affidavit, sworn statement.

atestado[2] *adj* obstinate, stubborn.

atestado[3] *adj* packed, cram-full; **~ de** packed with, crammed with, full of; well-stocked with.

atestar[1] [1a] *vt* (*Jur*) to attest, testify to; (*fig*) to attest, vouch for; **una palabra no atestada** an unattested word, an unrecorded word.

atestar[2] [1j] **1** *vt* to pack, cram, stuff (*de* with); to fill up (*de* with); to crowd; **~ a uno de frutas*** to stuff sb with fruit. **2 atestarse** *vr* to stuff o.s.

atestiguación *nf* (**a**) attestation. (**b**) (*Jur*) deposition, testimony.

atestiguar [1i] *vt* (*Jur*) to testify to, bear witness to, give evidence of; (*fig*) to attest, vouch for.

atezado 1 *adj* (**a**) (*bronceado*) tanned; (*moreno*) swarthy. (**b**) (*negro*) black, blackened. **2** *nm* tanning; blackening.

atezar [1f] **1** *vt* (**a**) (*al sol*) to tan, burn. (**b**) (*ennegrecer*) to blacken, turn black. **2 atezarse** *vr* to get tanned.

atiborrado *adj*: **~ de** full of, stuffed with, crammed with.

atiborrar [1a] **1** *vt* to fill, stuff (*de* with); **~ a un niño de dulces*** to stuff a child with sweets. **2 atiborrarse*** *vr* to stuff o.s. (*de* with).

ático *nm* attic; (*apartamento*) penthouse.

atiesar [1a] **1** *vt* to stiffen; to tighten, tighten up; to tauten, stretch taut.
2 atiesarse *vr* to get stiff, stiffen (up); to tighten; to tauten; (*en la construcción*) to bind.

atigrado 1 *adj* striped, marked like a tiger; *gato* tabby. **2** *nm* tabby.

atigronarse [1a] *vr* (*Carib*) to get strong.

Atila *nm* Attila.

atildado *adj* neat, elegant, stylish.

atildar [1a] **1** *vt* (**a**) (*Tip*) to put a tilde (~) over, mark with a tilde.
(**b**) (*asear*) to tidy, clean (up); to improve the looks of; to put right.
(**c**) (*criticar*) to criticize, find fault with.
2 atildarse *vr* to spruce o.s. up, titivate o.s.

atilincar [1g] *vt* (*CAm*) to tighten, stretch.

atinadamente *adv* correctly; sensibly; pertinently; **según dijo ~** as he rightly said.

atinado *adj* (*correcto*) accurate, correct; (*juicioso*) wise, sensible, judicious; (*pertinente*) pertinent; (*agudo*) penetrating; **unas observaciones atinadas** some pertinent remarks; **una decisión poco atinada** a rather unwise decision.

atinar [1a] **1** *vt solución etc* to hit upon, find; (*acertar*) to guess right; (*encontrar*) to succeed in finding.
2 *vi* (**a**) (*gen*) to guess right; to be right, do the right thing; **siempre atina** he always gets it right, he always hits the nail on the head; **el médico no le atina** the doctor doesn't know what's wrong with him.
(**b**) **~ al blanco** to hit the target, (*fig*) hit the mark; **~ a, ~ con, ~ en** *solución etc* to hit upon, find, succeed in finding.
(**c**) **~ a hacer algo** to succeed in doing sth, manage to do sth.

atingencia *nf* (*LAm*) (**a**) (*relación*) connection, bearing. (**b**) (*obligación*) obligation. (**c**) (*reserva*) qualification; (*aclaración*) clarification; (*observación*) remark, comment.

atingido *adj* (**a**) (*And, Cono Sur: deprimido*) depressed, down-in-the-mouth; (*débil*) feeble, weak; (*tímido*) timid. (**b**) (*And: sin dinero*) penniless. (**c**) (*Méx: taimado*) sly, cunning.

atingir [3c] *vt* (**a**) (*LAm*) to concern, bear on, relate to. (**b**) (*And*) to oppress.

atiparse* [1a] *vr* to stuff o.s.*

atípicamente *adv* atypically, untypically.

atipicidad *nf* atypical nature.

atípico *adj* atypical, untypical, exceptional.

atiplado *adj voz* treble, high-pitched.

atiplar [1a] **1** *vt voz* to raise the pitch of. **2 atiplarse** *vr* (*voz*) to go higher, become shrill; to go squeaky.

atipujarse [1a] *vr* (*CAm, Méx*) to stuff o.s.

atirantar [1a] **1** *vt* (**a**) to tighten, tauten; to stretch; **estar atirantado entre dos decisiones** to be torn between two decisions. (**b**) (*And, Cono Sur, Méx*) to spreadeagle, stretch out on the ground.
2 atirantarse *vr* (*Méx‡*) to peg out‡.

atisba *nm* (*And: vigilante*) watchman, look-out; (*espía*) spy.

atisbadero *nm* peephole.

atisbador(a) *nm/f* (*observador*) observer; watcher; (*espía*) spy.

atisbar [1a] *vt* (*espiar*) to spy on, watch; (*mirar*) to peep at; (*lograr ver*) to see, discern, make out; **~ a uno a través de una grieta** to peep at sb through a crack; **atisbamos un rayo de esperanza** we can just see a glimmer of hope.

atisbo *nm* (**a**) spying; watching; look, peep. (**b**) (*fig*) inkling, slight sign, first indication.

atizadero *nm* (**a**) poker. (**b**) (*fig*) spark, stimulus.

atizador *nm* poker.

atizar [1f] **1** *vt* (**a**) *fuego* to poke, stir; *horno* to stoke; *vela* to snuff, trim.
(**b**) (*fig*) *motín etc* to stir up; *pasión* to fan, rouse.
(**c**) (*) *golpe etc* to give; **se atizó el vaso** he knocked back the glassful*.
2 (*) *vi*: **¡atiza!** gosh!
3 atizarse‡ *vr* to smoke pot‡.

atizonar [1a] *vt* (*Bot*) to blight, smut.

Atlante *nm* (*Mit*) Atlas.

Atlántico *nm*: **el (Océano) ~** the Atlantic (Ocean).

Atlántida *nf* Atlantis.

atlantista 1 *adj* relating to the Atlantic Alliance (*NATO*). **2** *nmf* supporter of the Atlantic Alliance (*NATO*).

atlas *nm* atlas.

atleta *nmf* athlete.

atlético *adj* athletic.

atletismo *nm* athletics; **~ en pista cubierta, ~ en sala** indoor athletics.

atmósfera *nf* (**a**) (*Fís y fig*) atmosphere.
(**b**) (*fig*) atmosphere; (*campo*) sphere (of influence);

(*sentimiento*) feeling (about *o* towards a person); **Juan tiene buena** ~ (*LAm*) Juan enjoys considerable social standing, Juan stands well with everybody.
atmosférico *adj* atmospheric.
atoc *nm* (*And*) fox.
atocar [1g] *vt* (*LAm*) = **tocar**.
atocinado* *adj* fat, well-upholstered*.
atocinar [1a] **1** *vt* (**a**) *cerdo* to cut up; to make into bacon; *carne* to cure. (**b**) (‡) to do in‡, carve up*.
2 atocinarse* *vr* (*sulfurarse*) to get het up; (*enamorarse*) to fall madly in love.
atocle *nm* (*Méx*) sandy soil rich in humus.
atocha *nf* esparto.
atochal *nm* esparto field.
atochamiento *nm* (*Cono Sur*) traffic jam.
atochar *nm* = **atochal**.
atol *nm* (*LAm*) *drink* (*o gruel*) *made of maize flour*.
atolada *nm* (*CAm*) party.
atole *nm* (*Méx*) = **atol**.
atoleada *nf* (*CAm*) party.
atolería *nf* (*LAm*) stall (*etc*) where *atol* is sold.
atolón *nm* atoll.
atolondrado *adj* (*casquivano*) scatterbrained; (*tonto*) silly; (*aturdido*) bewildered; (*pasmado*) stunned, amazed; (*irreflexivo*) thoughtless, reckless.
atolondramiento *nm* silliness; bewilderment; stunned state, amazement; thoughtlessness, recklessness.
atolondrar [1a] **1** *vt confundir* to bewilder; *pasmar* to stun, amaze. **2 atolondrarse** *vr* to be bewildered; to be stunned, be amazed.
atolladero *nm* (**a**) (*lodazal*) muddy place; mire, morass.
(**b**) (*fig*) (*aprieto*) awkward spot, jam*; (*situación violenta*) embarrassing situation; **estar en un** ~ to be in a jam*; **sacar a uno del** ~ to get sb out of a fix*; **salir del** ~ to get out of a jam*.
atollar(se) [1a] *vi y vr* (**a**) (*atascarse*) to get stuck in the mud, get bogged down. (**b**) (*fig*) to get into a jam*, get stuck.
atomía *nf* (*LAm*) (**a**) (*acto*) evil deed, savage act. (**b**) **decir** ~**s** to shoot one's mouth off* (*a uno* to sb).
atómico *adj* atomic.
atomizador *nm* atomizer; (*de perfume etc*) spray, scent spray.
atomizar [1f] **1** *vt* to atomize; to spray. **2 atomizarse** *vr* to break up (*en* into), fragment.
átomo *nm* atom; (*fig*) atom, particle, speck; ~ **de vida** spark of life; **ni un** ~ **de** not a trace of.
atonal *adj* atonal.
atónito *adj* amazed, astounded (*con, de, por* at, by); **me miró** ~ he looked at me in amazement.
átono *adj* atonic, unstressed.
atontadamente *adv* in a bewildered way; foolishly, sillily.
atontado *adj* (**a**) (*aturdido*) stunned, bewildered. (**b**) (*tonto*) silly, dim-witted*.
atontar [1a] **1** *vt* (**a**) to stun, stupefy. (**b**) (*fig*) to stun, bewilder. **2 atontarse** *vr* to get bewildered, get confused.
atontolinamiento *nm* bewilderment.
atontolinar [1a] *vt* to daze; to stun; **quedar atontolinado** to be in a daze.
atorafo *adj* (*Carib*) anxious.
atorar [1a] **1** *vt* (**a**) (*obstruir*) to stop up, choke, obstruct; (*inmovilizar*) to stop, immobilize.
(**b**) (*Carib, Méx*: *fig*) to block, impede.
(**c**) (*) to annoy, bother, upset; **¡no me atores!** stop bothering me!; **estoy atorado de ti** I'm fed up with you*.
2 atorarse[1] *vr* (*atragantarse*) to choke, swallow the wrong way; (*trabarse la lengua*) to get tongue-tied; to have nothing to say, be unable to respond.
atorarse[2] [1a] *vr* (*Cono Sur*) to get wild, get fierce.
atormentador(a) **1** *adj* tormenting. **2** *nm/f* tormentor.
atormentar [1a] **1** *vt* to torture; (*fig*) to torture, torment; (*acosar*) to plague, harass; (*tentar*) to tantalize. **2 atormentarse** *vr* to torment o.s., suffer agonies of mind.
atornillador *nm* screwdriver.
atornillar [1a] *vt* (**a**) (*lit*) to screw on; to screw up; to screw down; to screw together. (**b**) (*LAm**: *fastidiar*) to pester, harass.
atoro *nm* (*LAm*) destruction; (*fig*) tight spot, difficulty.
atorón *nm* (*Méx*) traffic-jam.
atorozarse [1f] *vr* (*CAm*) to choke, swallow the wrong way.
atorrante **1** *adj* (**a**) *calor* baking. (**b**) (*LAm*: *vago*) lazy. **2** *nm* tramp, bum (*US*).
atorrantear [1a] *vi* (*Cono Sur*) to live like a tramp, be on the bum (*US*).
atortolado *adj*: **están** ~**s** they're like two turtle-doves.
atortolar* [1a] *vt* (*asustar*) to rattle*, scare; (*pasmar*) to shatter, flabbergast.
atortujar [1a] **1** *vt* to squeeze flat. **2 atortujarse** *vr* (*CAm*) to be shattered, be flabbergasted.
atorunado *adj* (*Cono Sur*) stocky, bull-necked.
atosigador *adj* (**a**) poisonous. (**b**) (*fig*) pestering, worrisome; pressing.
atosigante *adj* = **atosigador** (**b**).
atosigar [1h] **1** *vt* (**a**) (*envenenar*) to poison. (**b**) (*fig*) (*importunar*) to plague, badger, harass; (*presionar*) to rush, put the pressure on. **2 atosigarse** *vr* to be in a rush, get rushed.
atóxico *adj* non-poisonous.
atrabancar [1g] **1** *vt* to rush, hurry over. **2 atrabancarse** *vr* to be in a fix, get into a jam.
atrabiliario *adj* bad-tempered, difficult, moody.
atrabilis *nf* (*fig*) bad temper, difficult temperament, moodiness.
atracadero *nm* berth, wharf, landing place.
atracado *adj* (*CAm*) mean, stingy.
atracador *nm* hold-up man, bandit, gangster.
atracar [1g] **1** *vt* (**a**) *banco etc* to hold up; *viajero* to attack, waylay; (*Aer*) to hijack.
(**b**) (*Náut*) to tie up, moor, bring alongside; *astronave* to dock (*a* with).
(**c**) (*atiborrar*) to stuff, cram (with food).
(**d**) (*Carib Aut*) to park.
2 *vi* (*Náut*) to tie up, moor, come alongside; (*astronave*) to dock (*a* with); ~ **al muelle**, ~ **en el muelle** to tie up at the quay, berth at the quay.
3 atracarse *vr* (**a**) to cram, stuff o.s. (*de* with).
(**b**) (*Carib, Cono Sur*: *acercarse*) to approach, come up; ~ **a** to approach, come up to.
(**c**) (*Carib*: *pelear*) to brawl, fight.
atracción *nf* (**a**) (*gen*) attraction; (*de persona*) attractiveness, appeal, charm; ~ **gravitatoria** gravity, gravitational attraction; ~ **sexual** sexual attraction, (*de persona*) sex-appeal. (**b**) (*diversión*) amusement; **atracciones** (*Teat*) attractions, entertainment, floor show; (*de feria*) stalls, sideshows.
atraco *nm* hold-up, robbery; (*Aer*) hijack(ing); ~ **a mano armada** armed robbery; **¡es un** ~**!** (*fig*) it's sheer robbery!
atracón* *nm* blow-out‡; **darse un** ~ to stuff o.s.; **darse un** ~ **de** to stuff o.s. with, make a pig of o.s. over.
atractivamente *adv* attractively.
atractividad *nf* attractiveness.
atractivo **1** *adj* attractive. **2** *nm* attraction; attractiveness, appeal, charm.
atraer [2p] **1** *vt* (*gen*) to attract; to draw; to lure; *atención* to attract, engage; *imaginación* to appeal to; *adhesión* to attract, win, draw; **dejarse** ~ **por** to allow o.s. to be drawn towards; **sabe** ~**(se) a la juventud** he knows how to win young people over. **2 atraerse** *vr*: **se atrajo las simpatías de todos** he won everyone's affection, everyone liked him; **se atrajo el rencor del jefe** the boss began to resent him.
atragantarse [1a] *vr* (**a**) (*al comer*) to choke (*con* on), swallow the wrong way; **se me atragantó una miga** a crumb went the wrong way.
(**b**) (*fig*: *al hablar*) to get mixed up, lose the thread of what one is saying.
(**c**) **Pepe se me ha atragantado** (*fig*) Pepe sticks in my gullet, I can't bear Pepe.
atrague *nm*: **¡que** ~**!** (*Carib*) what an idiot!
atraillar [1a] *vt* to put on a leash.
atramparse [1a] *vr* (**a**) (*persona*) to fall into a trap; (*fig*) to get stuck, get o.s. into a jam. (**b**) (*tubo*) to clog, get blocked up; (*atascarse*) to stick, catch, jam.
atrancar [1g] **1** *vt puerta* to bar, bolt; *tubo* to clog, block up; (*fig*) *escotillas* to batten down; (*Cono Sur*) to constipate.
2 *vi* to stride along, take big steps; (*fig*: *al leer*) to skip a lot.
3 atrancarse *vr* (**a**) to get stuck, get bogged down (*en* in); (*fig*) to get stuck.
(**b**) (*Cono Sur* Med*) to get constipated.
(**c**) (*Méx*: *porfiarse*) to dig one's heels in.
atranco *nm* = **atascadero**.
atrapamaridos* **1** *adj invar*: **mujer** ~ = **2**. **2** *nf* woman on the look-out for a husband.
atrapar [1a] *vt* (**a**) (*en trampa*) to trap; (*coger*) to catch, nab*, overtake; *puesto* to get, land; *catarro* to catch; **quedaron atrapados en la montaña** they were trapped on the mountainside.

(**b**) (*fig*) to take in, deceive.

atraque *nm* (**a**) (*Náut*) mooring place, berth. (**b**) (*de astronave*) link-up, docking.

atrás 1 *adv* (**a**) (*lugar*) **¡~!** back!, get back!; **estar ~** to be behind; to be in the rear; **está más ~** it's further back; **ir (hacia) ~** to go back, go backwards; to go to the rear; **rueda de ~** rear wheel, back wheel.

(**b**) (*tiempo*) previously; **días ~** days ago, days before; **4 meses ~** 4 months back; **más ~** earlier, longer ago; **desde muy ~** for a very long time.

(**c**) (*Cono Sur*) **~ mío** behind me.

2 ~ de *prep* (*LAm*) = **detrás de.**

atrasado 1 *adj* (**a**) (*con retraso*) slow, late, behind (time); *pago* overdue; (*Tip*) *número* back (*atr*); **andar ~, estar ~** (*reloj*) to be slow; **estar un poco ~** (*persona*) to be a bit behind; **estar ~ en los pagos** to be behind, be in arrears; **estar ~ de noticias** to be behind the times, lack up-to-date information; **estar ~ de medios** to be short of resources; **estar ~** (*CAm**) to be broke*.

(**b**) *país* backward; underdeveloped; *alumno etc* slow, backward.

(**c**) (*Cono Sur Med etc*) ill.

2 *nm*: **es un ~** he's behind the times.

atrasar [1a] **1** *vt progreso* to slow down, slow up, retard; *salida* to delay; *reloj* to put back.

2 *vi* (*reloj*) to lose, be slow; **mi reloj atrasa 8 minutos** my watch is 8 minutes slow.

3 atrasarse *vr* (**a**) (*quedarse atrás*) to be behind; to lag, stay back, remain behind; (*tren etc*) to be slow, be late; (*reloj*) to lose, be slow; **~ en los pagos** to be in arrears.

(**b**) (*LAm*) *proyecto etc* to suffer a setback; (*Cono Sur: lastimarse*) to hurt o.s. (*de* in); (*mujer*) to be pregnant.

atraso *nm* (**a**) (*gen*) delay, time lag; (*de reloj*) slowness; (*de país etc*) backwardness; **el tren lleva ~** the train is late; **salir del ~** to catch up, make up lost time; **llegar con 20 minutos de ~** to arrive 20 minutes late.

(**b**) **~s** (*Com, Fin*) arrears; (*de pedidos etc*) backlog, quantity pending; (*And, Carib*) setback; **cobrar ~s** to collect arrears.

(**c**) **tener un ~** (*LAm Med*) to have a period.

atravesada *nf* (*LAm*) crossing, passage.

atravesado *adj* (**a**) (*oblicuo*) crossed, laid across, oblique. (**b**) (*de vista*) squinting, cross-eyed. (**c**) *perro etc* mongrel, crossbred. (**d**) (*malo*) wicked, evil; treacherous.

atravesar [1j] **1** *vt* (**a**) (*persona*) to cross, cross over, go across, go over; to pass through; *rápidos etc* to negotiate; *período* to go through, pass through; **atravesamos un momento difícil** we are going through a difficult time.

(**b**) (*bala, espada*) to pierce, go through, transfix; **~ a uno con una espada** to run sb through with a sword; **la bala atravesó el metal** the bullet passed through the metal.

(**c**) (*puente etc*) to cross, span, bridge.

(**d**) *objeto* to lay across, put across; to put crosswise, put obliquely; **~ un tronco en el camino** to lay a tree trunk across the road.

(**e**) *dinero* to bet, lay, stake.

(**f**) (*LAm Com*) to monopolize, corner (the market in).

(**g**) **le tengo atravesado** he sticks in my gullet, I can't stand him.

2 atravesarse *vr* (**a**) (*obstáculo*) to come in between; to interfere; (*problema etc*) to arise, spring up; (*hueso etc*) to stick in one's throat.

(**b**) **~ en una conversación** to butt into a conversation; **~ en un negocio** to meddle in an affair.

(**c**) **se me atraviesa el tipo ese** I can't stand that fellow.

(**d**) (*dos personas*) to wrangle, bicker, get across each other; **se atravesaron en la calle** (*LAm*) they bumped into each other in the street.

atrayente *adj* attractive.

atrechar [1a] *vi* (*Carib*) to take a short cut.

atrecho *nm* (*Carib*) short cut.

atreguar [1i] **1** *vt* to grant a truce to. **2 atreguarse** *vr* to agree to a truce.

atrenzo *nm* (*LAm*) trouble, difficulty; **estar en un ~** to be in trouble, have a problem.

atreverse [2a] *vr* (**a**) to dare; **no me atrevo, no me atrevería** I wouldn't dare; **¿te atreves?** are you game?, will you?; **¡atrévete!** just you dare!; **~ a hacer algo** to dare to do sth, venture to do sth; **~ a una empresa** to undertake a task, dare to undertake a task; **~ con un rival** to take on a rival, (venture to) compete with a rival; **se atreve con todo** he'll tackle anything; **me atrevo con una tarta** I could manage a cake.

(**b**) **~ con uno, ~ contra uno** to be insolent to sb.

atrevidamente *adv* (**a**) boldly, daringly. (**b**) insolently, disrespectfully, impudently.

atrevido *adj* (**a**) (*audaz*) bold, daring. (**b**) (*insolente*) insolent, disrespectful; (*descarado*) impudent, forward; *chiste etc* daring, risqué.

atrevimiento *nm* (**a**) (*audacia*) boldness, daring, audacity.

(**b**) (*pey*) insolence; impudence, forwardness.

atrevismo *nm* ostentatious daring.

atrezzo *nm* (*Teat*) properties; (*fig*) kit, gear.

atribución *nf* (**a**) (*acto*) attribution. (**b**) (*de puesto*) powers, authority, functions.

atribuible *adj* attributable (*a* to); **obras ~s a Góngora** works which are attributed to Góngora, works probably by Góngora.

atribuir [3g] **1** *vt* (**a**) **~ a** to attribute to; to put down to; to ascribe to, impute to.

(**b**) **las funciones atribuidas a mi cargo** the powers conferred on me by my post, the authority which goes with the post I hold.

2 atribuirse *vr*: **~ algo** to assume sth, claim sth for o.s.; to arrogate sth to o.s.; **~ la responsabilidad de un atentado** to claim responsibility for an attack.

atribulación *nf* affliction, suffering, tribulation.

atribulado 1 *adj* afflicted, suffering. **2** *nm*: **los ~s** the afflicted, the suffering, the sufferers.

atribular [1a] **1** *vt* to grieve, afflict. **2 atribularse** *vr* to grieve, be distressed.

atributivo *adj* attributive.

atributo *nm* (*gen*) attribute; (*emblema*) emblem, sign of authority.

atril *nm* (*Ecl etc*) lectern; (*para libro*) bookrest, reading desk; (*Mús*) music stand.

atrincar [1g] **1** *vt* (*LAm*) to tie up tightly. **2 atrincarse** *vr* (*Méx*) to be stubborn, dig one's heels in.

atrincherar [1a] **1** *vt* to surround with a trench, fortify with trenches.

2 atrincherarse *vr* (**a**) to entrench (o.s.), dig in; **están muy fuertemente atrincherados** (*fig*) they are very strongly entrenched. (**b**) **~ en** (*fig*) to take one's stand on; to take refuge in.

atrio *nm* (*Hist*) atrium, inner courtyard; (*Ecl*) vestibule, porch; (*de garaje*) forecourt.

atrocidad *nf* (**a**) (*desmán*) atrocity, outrage.

(**b**) (*tontería*) silly remark, foolish thing (to do); **decir ~es** to say silly things.

(**c**) (*) enormity, crime; **¡qué ~!** how dreadful!; **la comedia es una ~** the play is awful; **como me fastidian hago ~es** if they upset me I'll do sth dreadful; **me gustan los helados una ~** I'm awfully fond of ice cream.

atrochar [1a] *vi* to go by the byways; to take a short cut.

atrofia *nf* atrophy.

atrofiar [1b] **1** *vt* to atrophy. **2 atrofiarse** *vr* to atrophy.

atrojarse [1a] *vr* (*Carib*) to find no way out, be cornered; (*Méx*) to become confused, be bewildered.

atronadamente *adv* recklessly, thoughtlessly.

atronado *adj* reckless, thoughtless.

atronador *adj* deafening; *aplausos* thunderous.

atronamiento *nm* (*fig*) bewilderment, confusion, stunned state.

atronar [1l] *vt* (**a**) (*ensordecer*) to deafen. (**b**) (*aturdir*) to stun, daze; (*acogotar*) to fell with a blow on the neck. (**c**) (*fig*) to stun; to bewilder, confuse.

atropellada *nf* (*Cono Sur*) attack, onrush.

atropelladamente *adv correr etc* pell-mell, helter-skelter; *decidir* hastily; *hablar* incoherently, in a rushed way.

atropellado *adj acto* hasty, precipitate, impetuous; *manera* brusque, abrupt; violent.

atropellador *nm* lout, hooligan.

atropellaplatos* *nm invar* clumsy servant; clumsy sort.

atropellar [1a] **1** *vt* (**a**) (*pisotear*) to trample underfoot; (*derribar*) to knock down; (*empujar*) to push violently past; (*Aut etc*) to knock down, run over, run down; *figura famosa* to mob, overwhelm.

(**b**) (*fig*) *trabajo* to do hurriedly, hurry over; *derechos* to disregard, trample; *oposición, opiniones* to ride roughshod over; *inferior* to bully, oppress; *sentimientos* to insult, outrage; *constitución* to violate.

(**c**) (*LAm*) to make love to; to seduce, dishonour.

2 *vi*: **~ por** (**a**) to push one's way violently through.

(**b**) (*fig*) to disregard, ride roughshod over; **atropella por todo** he doesn't respect anything, he doesn't give a damn for anybody.

3 atropellarse *vr* to act hastily, do things thoughtlessly.

atropello *nm* (**a**) (*Aut etc*) accident; knocking down, running over.

(**b**) (*fig*) outrage (*de* upon); abuse (*de* of); disregard (*de* for); **los ~s del dictador** the dictator's crimes, the outrages committed by the dictator.

atroz *adj* (**a**) (*gen*) atrocious; (*cruel*) cruel, inhuman; (*escandaloso*) outrageous. (**b**) (*) (*grande*) huge, terrific; (*malo*) dreadful, awful.

atrozmente *adv* (**a**) atrociously; cruelly; outrageously. (**b**) (*) dreadfully.

ATS *nmf abr de* **ayudante técnico sanitario** nursing assistant.

atta., atto. *abr de* **atenta, atento** (*in courtesy formula in letters*).

attaché *nm* attaché case.

attrezzo *nm* (*Teat*) properties; (*fig*) kit, gear.

ATUDEM *nf abr de* **Asociación Turística de Estaciones de Esquí y Montaña.**

atuendo *nm* (**a**) (*vestido*) attire; (*hum*) rig, getup*. (**b**) (*boato*) pomp, show.

atufado *adj* (**a**) (*Cono Sur**: *enojado*) angry, mad*. (**b**) (*CAm, Carib**: *vanidoso*) proud, vain, stuck-up*.

atufamiento *nm* (*fig*) irritation, vexation.

atufar [1a] **1** *vt* (**a**) to overcome (with smell *o* fumes).

(**b**) (*fig*) to irritate, vex.

2 atufarse *vr* (**a**) (*vino*) to turn sour.

(**b**) (*persona*) to be overcome (with smell *o* fumes).

(**c**) (*fig*) to get angry, get mad* (*con, de, por* at, with; *t Cono Sur*); (*And*) to get bewildered, become confused; (*CAm, Carib*) to be proud, get vain.

atufo *nm* irritation.

atulipanado *adj* tulip-shaped.

atún *nm* (**a**) (blue-fin) tuna, tunny; **querer ir por ~ y ver al duque** to want to have it both ways, want to have one's cake and eat it too. (**b**) (*) nitwit*.

aturar [1a] *vt* to close up tight.

aturdidamente *adv* (**a**) in a bewildered way. (**b**) thoughtlessly, recklessly.

aturdido *adj* (**a**) (*atolondrado*) bewildered, dazed, stunned. (**b**) (*irreflexivo*) thoughtless, reckless.

aturdidura *nf* (*Cono Sur*), **aturdimiento** *nm* (**a**) stunned state, dazed condition; bewilderment, confusion; amazement. (**b**) thoughtlessness, recklessness.

aturdir [3a] **1** *vt* (**a**) (*físicamente*: *con golpe*) to stun, daze; (*ruido*) to deafen; (*droga, vino etc*) to stupefy, fuddle; (*movimiento*) to make giddy.

(**b**) (*fig*) (*atolondrar*) to stun, dumbfound; (*dejar perplejo*) to bewilder, confuse, perplex; **la noticia nos aturdió** the news stunned us.

2 aturdirse *vr* to be stunned; to get bewildered, get confused.

aturrullado *adj* bewildered, perplexed; flustered.

aturrullar [1a] **1** *vt* to bewilder, perplex; to fluster.

2 aturrullarse *vr* to get bewildered; to get flustered, get het up; **no te aturrulles cuando surja una dificultad** don't get flustered when sth awkward comes up.

atusamiento *nm* smartness, elegance.

atusar [1a] **1** *vt* (*cortar*) to trim; (*alisar*) to comb, smooth. **2 atusarse** *vr* (*fig*) to overdress, dress in great style.

audacia *nf* boldness, audacity.

audaz *adj* bold, audacious.

audazmente *adv* boldly, audaciously.

audibilidad *nf* audibility.

audible *adj* audible.

audición *nf* (**a**) (*gen*) hearing. (**b**) (*Teat etc*) audition; **dar ~ a uno** to audition sb, give sb an audition; **le hicieron una ~ para el papel** they gave him an audition for the part.

(**c**) (*Mús*) concert; **~ radiofónica** radio concert.

(**d**) (*LAm Com, Fin*) audit.

audiencia *nf* (**a**) (*acto*) audience, hearing; (*entrevista*) formal interview; **recibir a uno en ~** to grant sb an audience, receive sb in audience.

(**b**) (*sala*) audience chamber; (*Jur*) high court.

(**c**) (*personas*) audience; (*de periódico*) readership.

audífono *nm* (*de sordo*) hearing-aid, deaf-aid; (*LAm Telec*) earpiece, receiver; **~s** headphones.

audímetro *nm* audience meter.

audio *nm* audio.

audiofrecuencia *nf* audio-frequency.

audiómetro *nm* audiometer.

audiovisual *adj* audio-visual.

auditar [1a] *vt* to audit.

auditivo 1 *adj* auditory, hearing (*atr*). **2** *nm* (*Telec*) earpiece, receiver.

audito *nm* audit, auditing.

auditor(a)[1] *nm/f* (**a**) (*t* **~ de guerra**) judge-advocate. (**b**) (*Com, Fin*) auditor. (**c**) (*Méx Ferro*) ticket inspector.

auditora[2] *nf* firm of auditors, accountancy firm.

auditoría *nf* (*Com, Fin*) audit(ing); **~ administrativa, ~ de gestión, ~ operativa** management audit; **~ externa** external audit; **~ general** general audit; **~ interna** internal audit.

auditorio *nm* (**a**) (*personas*) audience. (**b**) (*sala*: *t* **auditorium** *nm*) auditorium, hall.

auge *nm* (*cima*) peak, summit, zenith; (*Astron*) apogee; (*aumento*) increase (*de* of); (*período*) period of increase, period of prosperity; (*Com*) boom (*de* in); **estar en ~** to thrive, run at a high level, do well; (*Com*) to boom.

Augias *nm*: **establos de ~** Augean Stables.

augurar [1a] *vt* (*suceso*) to augur, portend; (*persona*) to predict; **~ que ...** to predict that ...

augurio *nm* (**a**) (*gen*) augury; (*presagio*) omen, portent; (*profecía*) prediction; **consultar los ~s** to take the auguries.

(**b**) **~s** best wishes; **con nuestros ~s para ...** with our best wishes for ...; **mensaje de buenos ~s** goodwill message.

augustal *adj* Augustan.

Augusto *nm* Augustus.

augusto *adj* august.

aula *nf* (*Escol*) classroom; (*Univ*) lecture room; **~ magna** assembly hall, main hall.

aulaga *nf* furze, gorse.

aulario *nm* (*Univ*) lecture room building, block of lecture rooms.

áulico 1 *adj* court (*atr*), palace (*atr*). **2** *nm* courtier.

aullar [1a] *vi* to howl; to yell.

aullido *nm*, **aúllo** *nm* howl; yell; **dar aullidos** to howl, yell.

aumentador *nm* (*Elec*) booster.

aumentar [1a] **1** *vt* (*gen*) to increase, add to, augment; *precio* to increase, raise, put up; *producción* to increase, step up; (*Elec*) to boost, step up; (*Ópt*) to magnify; (*Fot*) to enlarge; (*Rad*) to amplify; *detalles, impresión etc* to magnify, exaggerate; **esto viene a ~ el número de ...** this helps to swell the numbers of ...

2 *vi y* **aumentarse** *vr* to increase, be on the increase; to multiply; to rise, go up; (*valor*) to appreciate.

aumentativo *adj, nm* augmentative.

aumento *nm* (**a**) increase; (*de precio*) increase, rise; (*de sueldo*) rise, raise (*US*); (*de valor*) appreciation; (*Ópt*) magnification; (*Fot*) enlargement; (*Rad*) amplification; **~ lineal** across-the-board pay rise; **~ de población** population increase; **~ de precio** rise in price; **~ salarial** wage increase; **eso le valió un ~** that got him a rise (in salary); **ir en ~** to increase, be on the increase; to prosper, do well; **una población que va en continuo ~** an ever-growing population.

(**b**) (*CAm, Méx*: *en una carta*) postscript.

aun *adv* even; **~ los que tienen dinero** even those who have money; **ni ~ si me lo regalas** not even if you give it to me; **~ así, ~ siendo esto así** even so; **~ cuando** although, even though; **más ~** even more.

aún *adv* still, yet; **~ está aquí** he's still here; **~ no lo sabemos** we still don't know, we don't know yet; **¿no ha venido ~?** hasn't he come yet?

aunar [1a] **1** *vt* to join, unite, combine. **2 aunarse** *vr* to unite, combine.

aunque *conj* though, although, even though; **~ llueva vendremos** we'll come even if it rains; **es guapa ~ algo bajita** she's pretty but rather short, she's pretty even if she is on the short side; **~ no me creas** even though you may not believe me; **~ más ...** however much ..., no matter how much ...

aúpa* **1** *interj* up!, up you get!; up with it! (*etc*); **¡~ Toboso!** up Toboso!

2 *como adj* (*): **una función de ~** a slap-up do*, a posh affair*; **una paliza de ~** a thrashing and a half; **una tormenta de ~** a real storm, the father and mother of a storm*; (*iró*) **es de ~** it's terribly bad, it's absolutely awful.

au pair 1 *adj, adv* au pair; **chica ~ = 2. 2** *nf* au pair (girl).

aupar* [1a] *vt persona* to help up, get up; *pantalón etc* to hitch up, hoist up; (*fig*) to boost, praise up; **~ a uno al poder** to raise sb to power.

aura *nf* (**a**) gentle breeze, sweet breeze. (**b**) (*fig*) popularity, popular favour; aura.

áureo *adj* (**a**) (*liter*) golden. (**b**) (*Esp Hist*) **nuestra literatura áurea** Golden Age literature.

aureola *nf*, **auréola** *nf* halo, aureole.

aureolar†† [1a] *vt* (*esp LAm*) *persona* to praise, extol the virtues of; *reputación etc* to enhance, add lustre to.
aurícula *nf* (*Anat*) auricle.
auricular 1 *adj* auricular, aural, of the ear. **2** *nm* (**a**) (*dedo*) little finger. (**b**) (*Telec*) earpiece, receiver; **~es** headphones, earphones.
aurífero *adj* gold-bearing.
aurora *nf* (*lit, fig*) dawn; **~ boreal(is)** aurora borealis, northern lights.
auscultación *nf* sounding, auscultation.
auscultar [1a] *vt* (*Med*) *pecho etc* to sound, auscultate.
ausencia *nf* absence; **en ~ del gato se divierten los ratones** when the cat's away the mice will play; **condenar a uno en su ~** to sentence sb in his absence; **hacer buenas ~s de uno** to speak kindly of sb in his absence, remember sb with affection; **tener buenas ~s** to have a good reputation; *V* **brillar**.
ausentarse [1a] *vr* to go away, absent o.s. (*de* from); to stay away (*de* from).
ausente 1 *adj* absent (*de* from); **estar ~ de** to be absent from, be missing from; **estar ~ de su casa** to be away from home.
2 *nmf* absentee; (*Jur*) missing person.
auspiciado *adj* sponsored, backed.
auspiciador 1 *adj*: **firma ~a** sponsoring firm. **2** *nm*, **auspiciadora** *nf* sponsor.
auspiciar [1b] *vt* (**a**) (*apoyar*) to back, sponsor. (**b**) (*LAm*) (*desear éxito*) to wish good luck to.
auspicios *nmpl* (*esp LAm*) auspices; (*protección*) protection, patronage; (*patrocinio*) sponsorship; **bajo los ~ de** under the auspices of, sponsored by.
auspicioso *adj* (*LAm*) auspicious.
austeramente *adv* austerely; sternly, severely.
austeridad *nf* austerity; sternness, severity; **~ económica** economic austerity.
austero *adj* austere; stern, severe.
austral 1 *adj* (**a**) southern; **el Hemisferio A~** the Southern Hemisphere. (**b**) (*Cono Sur*) of (*o* from) southern Chile. **2** *nm* (*Cono Sur Fin*) *standard monetary unit of Argentina* (*since 1985*).
Australia *nf* Australia.
australiano, -a *adj, nm/f* Australian.
Austria *nf* Austria.
austriaco, -a, austríaco, -a *adj, nm/f* Austrian.
austro *nm* (*liter*) south; (*viento*) south wind.
austro-húngaro *adj* Austro-Hungarian.
autarquía *nf* (*Pol*) autarchy, self-government; (*Econ*) autarky, national self-sufficiency.
autazo *nm* (*LAm*) theft of a car.
auténtica *nf* certificate, certification; authorized copy.
auténticamente *adv* authentically; genuinely, really.
autenticar [1g] *vt* to authenticate.
autenticidad *nf* authenticity; genuineness.
auténtico *adj* (**a**) authentic; genuine, real; **un ~ espíritu de servicio** a true spirit of service; **es un ~ campeón** he's a real champion; **éste es copia y no el ~** this one is a copy and not the real one; **días de ~ calor** days of real heat, really hot days; **ir de ~*, ser de ~*** to be absolutely with it*. (**b**) (*) great*, brilliant*.
autentificar [1g] *vt* to authenticate.
autería *nf* (*Cono Sur: presagio*) evil omen, bad sign; (*brujería*) witchcraft.
autero[1], -a *nm/f* (*LAm*) car thief.
autero[2], -a *nm/f* (*Cono Sur*) (*pesimista*) pessimist, defeatist; (*mal augurio*) jinx*, person who brings bad luck.
autillo *nm* tawny owl.
autismo *nm* autism.
autista *adj*, **autístico** *adj* autistic.
auto[1] *nm* (*Aut*) car, automobile (*US*); **~ de choque** bumper car, dodgem.
auto[2] *nm* (**a**) (*Jur*) edict, judicial decree; writ, order; document; **~ de ejecución** writ of execution; **~ de prisión** warrant for arrest; **~ de procesamiento** charge, indictment.
(**b**) **~s** documents, proceedings, court record; **estar en ~s** to be in the know; **poner a uno en ~s** to put sb in the picture.
(**c**) (*Ecl y Teat*) mystery play, religious play, allegory; **~ del nacimiento** nativity play; **~ sacramental** eucharistic play.
(**d**) (*Ecl*) **~ de fe** auto-da-fé; **hacer un ~ de fe de** (*fig*) to burn.
auto... *pref* auto..., self...
autoabastecerse [2d] *vr* to supply o.s. (*de* with); to be self-sufficient.
autoabastecimiento *nm* self-sufficiency.
autoacusación *nf* self-accusation.
autoacusarse [1a] *vr* to accuse o.s.
autoadhesivo *adj* self-adhesive; *sobre* self-sealing.
autoadministrarse [1a] *vr* (**a**) **~ una droga** to take a drug. (**b**) (*Pol*) to govern o.s., be self-governing.
autoadulación *nf* self-praise.
autoaislarse [1a] *vr* to isolate o.s.
autoalarma *nf* car alarm.
autoalimentación *nf*: **~ de hojas** (*Inform*) automatic paper feed.
autoanálisis *nm* self-analysis.
autoaprovisionamiento *nm* self-sufficiency.
autoayuda *nf* self-help.
autobiografía *nf* autobiography.
autobiográfico *adj* autobiographic(al).
autobomba *nf* fire-engine.
autobombearse* [1a] *vr* to blow one's own trumpet, shoot a line*.
autobombo* *nm* self-advertisement, self-glorification; **hacer ~** to blow one's own trumpet.
autobronceador *nm* bronzing lotion.
autobús *nm* bus, omnibus (††); coach (*Brit*); (*LAm: de distancia*) coach (*Brit*), long-distance bus (*US*); **~ de dos pisos** double-decker bus; **~ escolar** school bus; **~ de línea** coach (*Brit*), long-distance bus (*US*).
autocalificarse [1g] *vr*: **~ de** to describe o.s. as.
autocar *nm* coach, bus.
autocaravana *nf* camper, camping vehicle.
autocargador *adj*: **camión ~** self-loading truck.
autocarril *nm* (*LAm*) railway car.
autocartera *nf* holding of its own shares (*by a company*).
autocensura *nf* self-censorship.
autocine *nm* drive-in cinema.
autoclave *nm* pressure cooker; (*Med*) sterilizing apparatus.
autoconcederse [2a] *vr*: **~ un título** to grant o.s. a title.
autoconfesado *adj* self-confessed.
autoconfesarse [1a] *vr* to confess o.s.
autoconfesión *nf* self-confession.
autoconfianza *nf* self-confidence.
autoconservación *nf* self-preservation.
autocontrol *nm* (**a**) (*autodominio*) self-control, self-restraint. (**b**) (*Téc*) self-monitoring.
autoconvencerse [2d] *vr* to convince o.s.
autocracia *nf* autocracy.
autócrata *nmf* autocrat.
autocrático *adj* autocratic.
autocremarse [1a] *vr* to set fire to o.s., burn o.s. (to death).
autocrítica *nf* self-criticism, self-examination.
autocrítico *adj* self-critical.
auto-cross *nm* autocross.
autóctono *adj* autochthonous, original, native, indigenous.
autocue *nm* autocue.
auto-choque *nm* bumper car, dodgem.
autodefensa *nf* self-defence.
autodefinirse [3a] *vr* to define o.s., state one's position.
autodegradación *nf* self-abasement.
autodenominarse [1a] *vr* to call o.s.
autodestructible *adj*, **autodestructivo** *adj* self-destructive, self-destructing.
autodestruirse [3g] *vr* to self-destruct.
autodeterminación *nf* self-determination.
autodidacta *adj, nmf* = **autodidacto**.
autodidacto 1 *adj* self-educated, self-taught. **2** *nm*, **autodidacta** *nf* autodidact, self-taught person.
autodisciplina *nf* self-discipline.
autodisciplinado *adj* self-disciplined.
autodominio *nm* self-control.
autódromo *nm* motor-racing circuit, racetrack.
autoedición *nf* desktop publishing.
autoempleo *nm* self-employment.
autoengaño *nm* self-deception, self-delusion.
autoescuela *nf* driving school.
autoestima *nf* self-esteem.
autoestop *nm* = **autostop**.
autoevaluación *nf* self-assessment.
autoexpresión *nf* self-expression.
autofelicitación *nf* self-congratulation.
autofinanciarse [1b] *vr* to finance o.s.
autógena *nf* welding.
autogestión *nf* self-management; (*esp*) worker manage-

ment.
autogiro *nm* autogiro.
autogobernarse [1j] *vr* to govern itself, be self-governing.
autogobierno *nm* self-government.
autogol *nm* own goal.
autógrafo *adj, nm* autograph.
autohipnosis *nf* autohypnosis, self-hypnosis.
autoimpuesto *adj* self-imposed.
autoinculpación *nf* self-accusation; (*Jur*) plea of guilty.
autoinducido *adj* self-induced.
autoinfligido *adj herida* self-inflicted.
autolavado *nm* car-wash.
autolesionarse [1a] *vr* to inflict injury on o.s.
autolimpiable *adj horno etc* self-cleaning.
autollamarse [1a] *vr* to call o.s.
automación *nf* automation.
automarginación *nf* dropping-out.
automarginado 1 *adj*: **persona automarginada** drop-out. **2** *nm,* **automarginada** *nf* drop-out.
automarginarse [1a] *vr* to drop out; ~ **de** to drop out of; to stay away from, keep clear of, have nothing to do with.
autómata *nm* automaton, robot; (*fig*) automaton; puppet.
automática *nf* (**a**) (*ciencia*) automation. (**b**) (*lavadora*) washing-machine. (**c**) (*Mil*) automatic.
automáticamente *adv* automatically.
automaticidad *nf* automatic nature.
automático 1 *adj* automatic; self-acting. **2** *nm* (*Cono Sur*) (**a**) self-service restaurant, automat (*US*). (**b**) (*cierre*) snap fastener.
automatismo *nm* automatism.
automatización *nf* automation; ~ **de oficinas** office automation; ~ **de fábricas** factory automation.
automatizado *adj* automated.
automatizar [1f] *vt* to automate.
automedicarse [1g] *vr* to treat o.s.
automedonte *nm* (*hum y LAm*) coachman; driver.
automercado *nm* (*Carib*) supermarket.
automoción *nf*: **la industria de la** ~ the car industry, the automobile industry (*US*).
automodelismo *nm* model-car racing.
automotor 1 *adj* (*f*: **automotriz**) self-propelled. **2** *nm* (*Ferro*) diesel train; (*LAm*) self-propelled vehicle.
automóvil 1 *adj* self-propelled.
2 *nm* car, motor car, automobile (*US*); ~ **de alquiler** hire car; ~ **de carreras** racing car; ~ **de choque** bumper car, dodgem; ~ **de importación** foreign car; **ir en** ~ to go by car, travel by car.
automovilismo *nm* (**a**) (*actividad*) motoring; ~ **deportivo** motor racing. (**b**) (*industria*) car industry, automobile industry (*US*).
automovilista *nmf* motorist, driver.
automovilístico *adj* car (*atr*); **accidente** ~ car accident.
automutilación *nf* self-mutilation.
automutilarse [1a] *vr* to mutilate o.s.
autonomía *nf* (**a**) (*Pol*: *sistema*) autonomy; home rule; self-government.
(**b**) (*Pol*: *territorio*) autonomous region, autonomy.
(**c**) (*Aer, Náut*) range; **un avión de gran** ~ a long-range aircraft; **el avión tiene una** ~ **de 5.000 km** the aircraft has a range of 5,000 km.
autonómico *adj* relating to autonomy; **elecciones autonómicas** elections for the autonomous regions; **política autonómica** policy concerning autonomies; **el proceso** ~ the process leading to autonomy.
autónomo 1 *adj* (*Pol etc*) autonomous; self-governing; independent; *persona* self-employed; (*Inform*) stand-alone; **trabajo** ~ self-employment. **2** *nm,* **autónoma** *nf* self-employed person.
autopatrulla *nm* (*Méx*) patrol car.
autopegado *adj sobre* self-sealing.
autopiano *nm* (*Carib*) pianola.
autopista *nf* motorway; expressway (*US*); ~ **de peaje** toll road, toll motorway, turnpike road (*US*); ~ **perimetral** ring road, bypass.
autopolinización *nf* self-pollination.
autopreservación *nf* self-preservation.
autoproclamado *adj* self-proclaimed.
autoproclamarse [1a] *vr* to proclaim o.s.
autoprofesor *nm* teaching machine.
autoprogramable *adj* intelligent.
autopropulsado *adj* self-propelled.
autopropulsión *nf* self-propulsion.
autoprotegerse [2c] *vr* to protect o.s.
autopsia *nf* post mortem, autopsy.
autopublicidad *nf* self-advertisement; **hacer** ~ to indulge in self-advertisement.
autor(a) *nm/f* (*Liter*) author, writer; (*de idea*) creator, originator, inventor; (*de crimen*) perpetrator (*de* of), person responsible (*de* for), person concerned (*de* in).
autoría *nf* (*Liter etc*) authorship; **la** ~ **del atentado** the responsibility for the attack.
autoridad *nf* (**a**) (*gen*) authority; jurisdiction.
(**b**) (*boato*) pomp, show, ostentation.
(**c**) (*persona*) authority; **las ~es** the authorities; **~es aduaneras** customs authorities; ~ **de sanidad** health authorities; **¡abran a la ~!** open up in the name of the law!; **entregarse a la** ~ to give o.s. up (to the police).
autoritario 1 *adj* authoritarian; peremptory; dogmatic. **2** *nm,* **autoritaria** *nf* authoritarian.
autoritarismo *nm* authoritarianism.
autoritativo *adj* authoritative.
autorización *nf* authorization; permission, licence; **tener la** ~ **de uno para** + *infin* to have sb's authorization to + *infin.*
autorizadamente *adv* officially, authoritatively.
autorizado *adj* authorized, official; authoritative; approved; **la persona autorizada** the officially designated person, the approved person.
autorizar [1f] *vt* (*dar facultad a*) to authorize, empower; (*permitir*) to approve, license; (*justificar*) to justify, give (*o* lend) authority to; ~ **a uno para** + *infin* to authorize sb to + *infin*, empower sb to + *infin*; **el futuro no autoriza optimismo alguno** the future does not justify (*o* warrant) the slightest optimism.
autorradio *nf* car radio.
autorregulación *nf* self-regulation.
autorretrato *nm* self-portrait.
autorzuelo *nm* scribbler, hack, penpusher.
autoservicio *nm* self-service (restaurant *etc*).
autosostenerse [2k] *vr* to pay one's own way, be self-supporting.
autostop *nm* hitch-hiking; **hacer ~, viajar en** ~ to hitch-hike; **fuimos haciendo** ~ **de Irún a Burgos** we hitch-hiked from Irún to Burgos, we got a lift from Irún to Burgos.
autostopismo *nm* hitch-hiking.
autostopista *nmf* hitch-hiker.
autosuficiencia *nf* (**a**) (*Econ*) self-sufficiency. (**b**) (*pey*) smugness.
autosuficiente *adj* (**a**) (*Econ*) self-sufficient. (**b**) (*pey*) smug.
autosugestión *nf* autosuggestion.
autotitularse [1a] *vr* to title o.s., call o.s.
autoventa *atr*: **vendedor** ~ travelling salesman, representative who travels by car.
autovía *nf* main road, trunk road; dual carriageway, divided highway (*US*); ~ **de circunvalación** bypass, ring road.
autovivienda *nf* caravan, trailer.
Auvernia *nf* Auvergne.
auxiliar 1 *adj* auxiliary; assistant. **2** *nmf* assistant; auxiliary; assistant teacher; (*Dep*) linesman; ~ **administrativo** administrative assistant; ~ **de cabina,** ~ **de vuelo** steward, stewardess; flight attendant (*US*); ~ **de conversación** conversation assistant; ~ **de enfermería** (*CAm*) nursing auxiliary; ~ **de lengua inglesa** English language assistant; ~ **sanitario** health worker; ~ **técnico** (*LAm Dep*) coach, trainer. **3** *vt* [1b] to help, assist; to bring aid to; *moribundo* to comfort, help to make a good end.
auxilio *nm* help, aid, assistance; relief; ~ **espiritual** consolations of religion; (*sacramentos*) last rites; ~ **social** social work, welfare (work); welfare service; **primeros ~s** (*Med*) first aid; **acudir en** ~ **de uno** to come to sb's aid.
Av. *abr de* **Avenida** Avenue, Av., Ave.
a/v (*Com*) *abr de* **a vista** at sight.
avada‡ *nm* (*Carib*) queer‡.
avahar [1a] **1** *vt* to blow on, warm with one's breath. **2** *vi y* **avaharse** *vr* to steam, give off steam, give off vapour.
aval *nm* (*Com*) guarantee, reference, backing (for a loan *etc*); (*Cono Sur*) guarantor; (*Pol*) backing, support; ~ **bancario** banker's reference.
avalancha *nf* avalanche.
avalar [1a] *vt* (*Com*) to guarantee; (*fig*) *decisión etc* to support, endorse; *persona* to answer for.
avalentado *adj,* **avalentonado** *adj* boastful, bullying, arrogant; disrespectful.
avalista *nmf* guarantor.
avalorar [1a] *vt* (**a**) (*realzar*) to enhance; to set off. (**b**) (*fig*) to encourage.
avaluación, avaluada (*LAm*) *nf* valuation, appraisal.

avaluar [1e] *vt* to value, appraise (*at* en).
avalúo *nm* valuation, appraisal.
avancarga: cañón de ~ muzzle loader.
avance *nm* (**a**) (*Mil y fig*) advance; (*de precio*) rise, advance; **en ~** in advance.
(**b**) (*Cono Sur Mil*) attack, raid.
(**c**) (*Com, Fin: pago*) advance, advance payment; (*Com: cálculo*) estimate.
(**d**) (*Com: balance*) balance; balance sheet.
(**e**) (*Elec*) lead; (*Mec*) feed.
(**f**) (*Cine*) trailer; preview; **~s** (*Méx*) trailer; (*TV*) early news programme; **~ informativo** advance notice, publicity hand-out; press-release.
(**g**) (*CAm: robo*) theft; (*Mil*) looting, sacking.
(**h**) (*Cono Sur: regalo*) tempting offer, inducement (made to secure sb's goodwill).
avante *adv* (*esp LAm*) forward; (*Náut*) forward, ahead; **¡~!** forward!; **todo ~** (*Náut*) full steam ahead; **salir ~** to get ahead, get on in the world.
avanzada *nf* (*Mil*) (**a**) (*puesto*) outpost. (**b**) (*soldados*) advance party, advance guard.
avanzadilla *nf* (*Mil: patrulla*) scout, patrol; (*avanzada*) advance party.
avanzado *adj* advanced; *ideas, tendencia* advanced, avant-garde, progressive; *diseño etc* advanced; *hora* late; *hueso etc* prominent; **de edad avanzada, ~ de edad** advanced in years; **a una hora avanzada** at a late hour.
avanzar [1f] **1** *vt* (**a**) (*adelantar*) to advance, move forward.
(**b**) *dinero* to advance.
(**c**) (*promover*) to promote.
(**d**) *propuesta* to advance, put forward.
(**e**) (*Carib*) to vomit, throw up.
2 *vi y* **avanzarse** *vr* (**a**) to advance (*t Mil*), move on, push on; to go forward; **no avanzo nada** I'm not making any headway.
(**b**) (*proyecto etc*) to go forward, progress, advance.
(**c**) (*noche, invierno etc*) to advance, draw on; (*terminar*) draw to a close.
(**d**) **~se algo** (*CAm, Méx*) to steal sth.
avanzo *nm* (*Com*) (**a**) (*balance*) balance; balance sheet. (**b**) (*cálculo*) estimate.
avaricia *nf* miserliness, avarice; greed, greediness.
avariciosamente *adv* avariciously; greedily.
avaricioso *adj*, **avariento** *adj* miserly, avaricious; greedy.
avariosis *nf* (*LAm*) syphilis.
avaro 1 *adj* miserly, mean; **ser ~ de alabanzas** to be sparing in one's praise, be mean with one's praises; **ser ~ de palabras** to be a person of few words.
2 *nm*, **avara** *nf* miser, mean person.
avasallador *adj* overwhelming; domineering.
avasallamiento *nm* subjugation.
avasallar [1a] **1** *vt* (*subyugar*) (**a**) to subdue, subjugate; to dominate; to enslave. (**b**) **~ a uno** (*fig*) to steamroller sb (into agreement *o* compliance). **2 avasallarse** *vr* to submit, yield.
avatar *nm* (*transformación*) avatar, change, transformation; (*encarnación*) incarnation; (*etapa*) phase; (*ola*) wave; **~ destructivo** wave of destruction; **~es** vicissitudes, ups and downs.
Avda. *abr de* **Avenida** Avenue, Av., Ave.
ave *nf* bird; (*esp LAm*) chicken; **~ acuática, ~ acuátil** water bird; **~ canora, ~ cantora** songbird; **~ de corral** chicken, fowl; **~s de corral** fowls, poultry; **~ marina** sea bird; **~ negra** (*Cono Sur*) crooked lawyer; **~ nocturna** night bird (*t fig*); **~ del paraíso** bird of paradise; **~ de paso** bird of passage (*t fig*), migrant; **~ de presa, ~ de rapiña** bird of prey; **~ zancuda** wader, wading bird.
avecinarse [1a] *vr* to approach, come near.
avecindarse [1a] *vr* to take up one's residence, settle.
avechuco* *nm* ragamuffin, ne'er-do-well.
avefría *nf* lapwing.
avejentar [1a] *vi y* **avejentarse** *vr* to age (before one's time).
avejigar [1h] **1** *vt* to blister. **2 avejigarse** *vr* to blister.
avellana *nf* (**a**) (*Bot*) hazelnut. (**b**) (*And*) firecracker.
avellanado *adj* (**a**) *color* nutbrown. (**b**) *piel etc* shrivelled, wizened. (**c**) *sabor* nutty.
avellanal *nm* hazel wood, hazel plantation.
avellanar 1 *nm* hazel wood, hazel plantation. **2** [1a] *vt* (*Téc*) to countersink. **3 avellanarse** *vr* to shrivel up.
avellanedo *nm* hazel wood, hazel plantation.
avellanero *nm*, **avellano** *nm* hazel, hazel tree.
avemaría *nf* (**a**) (*Ecl*) Ave Maria, Hail Mary. (**b**) **al ~** at dusk; **en un ~*** in a twinkling; **saber algo como el ~*** to know sth inside out.
avena *nf* oats; **~ loca, ~ morisca, ~ silvestre** wild oats.
avenado *adj* half-crazy, rather mad.
avenal *nm* oatfield.
avenamiento *nm* draining, drainage.
avenar [1a] *vt tierra* to drain.
avenencia *nf* agreement; compromise; (*Com*) bargain, deal.
avenida *nf* (**a**) (*calle*) avenue. (**b**) (*de río*) flood, spate.
avenir [3a] **1** *vt* to reconcile, bring together.
2 avenirse *vr* (**a**) (*2 personas: acto*) to come to an agreement, be reconciled; to reach a compromise; (*estado*) to be on good terms, get on well together; **no se avienen** they don't get on, they don't agree.
(**b**) **~ con algo** to be in agreement with sth, conform to sth; to resign o.s. to sth, come to terms with sth; **~ con uno** to reach an agreement with sb; **¡allá te las avengas!*** that's your look-out!, that's up to you!
(**c**) **~ a hacer algo** to agree to do sth.
aventado *adj* (*CAm, Méx*) brave, daring.
aventador *nm* (*para fuego*) fan, blower; (*Agr*) winnowing fork.
aventadora *nf* winnowing machine.
aventajadamente *adv* outstandingly, extremely well.
aventajado *adj* outstanding, excellent, superior; (*en grado*) advanced; **~ de estatura** exceptionally tall, having the advantage of great height.
aventajar [1a] **1** *vt* (**a**) (*sobrepasar*) to surpass, beat, excel; to outstrip; (*CAm Aut*) to overtake; **A aventaja a B por 4 puntos** A leads B by 4 points; **~ con mucho a uno** to beat sb easily, be far better than sb.
(**b**) (*mejorar*) to improve, better.
(**c**) (*preferir*) to prefer.
2 aventajarse *vr* to get ahead; **~ a** to surpass, beat, excel; to get the advantage of.
aventar [1j] **1** *vt* (**a**) *fuego* to fan, blow (on); *trigo* to winnow.
(**b**) (*lanzar al aire*) to cast to the winds; (*viento*) to blow away; (*Carib Agr*) to dry in the wind.
(**c**) (*LAm: tirar*) to throw; to chuck out, throw out.
2 aventarse *vr* (**a**) (*hincharse*) to fill with air, swell up.
(**b**) (*‡: largarse*) to beat it*.
(**c**) (*Méx*) to decide.
(**d**) (*LAm: tirarse*) to throw o.s.; (*arriesgarse*) to take risks.
aventón* *nm* (*Méx*) throw; (*Aut*) lift; **pedir ~** to hitch a lift.
aventura *nf* (**a**) (*andanza*) adventure; bold venture, daring enterprise; (*pey*) escapade; **~ sentimental** love affair, affair of the heart; (*Fin, Pol etc*) **~s** reckless gambles, adventurism.
(**b**) (*azar*) chance, contingency.
(**c**) (*peligro*) risk, danger, hazard.
aventurado *adj* risky, hazardous.
aventurar [1a] **1** *vt* to venture, risk; *capital* to risk, stake.
2 aventurarse *vr* to dare, take a chance, risk it; **~ a** + *infin* to venture to + *infin*, dare to + *infin*, risk + *ger*.
aventurera *nf* adventuress.
aventurero 1 *adj* adventurous; enterprising. **2** *nm* adventurer; (*Mil*) mercenary, soldier of fortune; (*pey*) social climber.
avergonzado *adj cara* shamefaced; embarrassed; **estar ~** to be ashamed (*de, por* about, at).
avergonzar [1f *y* 1l] **1** *vt* to shame, put to shame; to abash, embarrass.
2 avergonzarse *vr* (*sentir vergüenza*) to be ashamed; (*sentirse violento*) to be embarrassed, look embarrassed; **~ de, ~ por** to be ashamed about (*o* at, of); to be embarrassed about; **~ de** + *infin* to be ashamed to + *infin*; **se avergonzó de haberlo dicho** he was ashamed at having said it.
avería[1] *nf* (*Orn*) (*pajarera*) aviary; (*aves*) flock of birds.
avería[2] *nf* (**a**) (*Com etc*) damage; (*Mec*) breakdown, fault, failure; **el coche tiene una ~** the car has had a breakdown, there's sth wrong with the car.
(**b**) **hombre de ~s** (*Cono Sur: matón*) tough guy*, thug; (*criminal*) dangerous criminal; **ser de ~** to be dangerous.
avería[3] *nf* (*Com, Náut*) average; **~ gruesa** general average.
averiado *adj fruto etc* damaged, spoiled; (*Mec*) broken down, faulty; **los faros están ~s** the lights have failed, there's sth wrong with the lights.
averiar [1c] **1** *vt* to damage, spoil; (*Mec*) to cause a breakdown in, cause a failure in; to damage.
2 averiarse *vr* (**a**) (*dañarse*) to get damaged; (*Mec*) to

have a breakdown, have a failure, fail; **se averió el arranque** the starter failed, the starter went wrong.
(**b**) (*Méx*: *perder la virginidad*) to lose one's virginity.
averiguable *adj* ascertainable.
averiguación *nf* (**a**) (*comprobación*) ascertainment, discovery; establishment; (*investigación*) investigation; inquiry; check. (**b**) (*CAm, Méx*: *discusión*) quarrel, argument.
averiguadamente *adv* certainly.
averiguado *adj* certain, established; **es un hecho ~** it is an established fact.
averiguador(a) *nm/f* investigator; inquirer.
averiguar [1i] **1** *vt* (*descubrir*) to find out, ascertain, discover; *dato etc* to look up; (*indagar*) to investigate, inquire into, find out about; (*comprobar*) to check; **~ las señas de uno** to find out sb's address; **hay que ~ esto en la biblioteca** this must be looked up in the library, you'll have to check this in the library; **eso es todo lo que se pudo ~** that is all that could be discovered.
2 *vi* (*CAm, Méx*) to quarrel, fight.
3 averiguarse *vr* (**a**) **~ con uno*** (*obligar*) to tie sb down; (*llevarse bien*) to get along with sb.
(**b**) **~ con uno** (*CAm, Méx*) to argue (*o* fight) with sb, take sb on.
averiguata *nf* (*Méx*) argument, fight.
averigüetas *nmf invar* (*And*) snooper, busybody.
averrugado *adj* warty.
aversión *nf* aversion (*a, hacer, por* to); distaste, disgust, loathing; **cobrar ~ a** to take a strong dislike to.
avestruz *nm* (**a**) (*Orn*) ostrich; **~ de la pampa** rhea.
(**b**) (*LAm**) dimwit*, idiot.
avetado *adj* veined, grained, streaked.
avetoro *nm* bittern.
avezado *adj* accustomed; inured, experienced; **los ya ~s en estos menesteres** those already experienced in such activities.
avezar [1f] **1** *vt* to accustom, inure (*a* to). **2 avezarse** *vr* to get used (to it); to become accustomed; **~ a algo** to get used to sth, get hardened to sth.
aviación *nf* (**a**) (*gen*) aviation. (**b**) (*fuerza*) air force.
aviado *adj*: **estar ~** (**a**) (*Cono Sur*: *bien surtido*) to be well off, have everything one needs; to be properly equipped (*with tools etc*).
(**b**) (*Cono Sur*: *soñar*) to have one's head in the clouds.
(**c**) (*) to be in a mess; **¡~s estamos!** what a mess we're in!; **dejar a uno ~** to leave sb in the lurch.
aviador¹ *nm* (*Aer*) airman, aviator, flyer; (*Mil*) airman, member of the air force.
aviador² *nm* (*And, Carib, Cono Sur*) (*Com*) mining speculator (*o* financier); (*prestamista*) moneylender, loan shark*.
aviadora *nf* aviator, (woman) pilot.
aviar [1c] **1** *vt* (**a**) (*preparar*) to get ready, prepare, fit out; (*ordenar*) to tidy up; (*proveer*) to equip, supply, provide (*de* with).
(**b**) (*LAm*) to advance money to; to lend equipment to, provide with equipment; to provide with food for a journey.
(**c**) **~ a uno*** (*dar prisa*) to hurry sb up, get sb moving; (*despedir*) to see sb off.
(**d**) (*prov, LAm Agr*) to castrate.
2 *vi* (*) to hurry up, get a move on; **¡vamos aviando!** let's get a move on!
3 aviarse *vr* to get ready; **~ para hacer algo** to get ready to do sth.
aviario *nm* aviary.
aviatorio *adj* (*LAm*): **accidente ~** air crash, plane crash.
avícola *adj* chicken (*atr*), poultry (*atr*); **granja ~** chicken farm, poultry farm.
avicultor(a) *nm/f* chicken farmer, poultry farmer; bird fancier.
avicultura *nf* chicken farming, poultry farming; bird fancying.
ávidamente *adv* avidly, eagerly; (*pey*) greedily.
avidez *nf* avidity, eagerness (*de* for); (*pey*) greed, greediness (*de* for); **con ~** eagerly; greedily.
ávido *adj* avid, eager (*de* for); (*pey*) greedy (*de* for); **~ de sangre** bloodthirsty.
aviejarse [1a] *vr* to age before one's time.
avieso 1 *adj* (*torcido*) distorted, crooked; (*siniestro*) sinister; (*perverso*) perverse, wicked; (*rencoroso*) spiteful. **2** *nm* (*And*) abortion.
avifauna *nf* birds, bird life.
avilantarse [1a] *vr* to be insolent.
avilantez *nf* insolence, effrontery.
avilés 1 *adj* of Ávila. **2** *nm*, **avilesa** *nf* native (*o* inhabitant) of Ávila; **los avileses** the people of Ávila.
avilesino 1 *adj* of Avilés. **2** *nm*, **avilesina** *nf* native (*o* inhabitant) of Avilés; **los ~s** the people of Avilés.
avillanado *adj* boorish, uncouth.
avinagrado *adj* sour, acid; (*fig*) sour, jaundiced, crabbed.
avinagrar [1a] **1** *vt* to sour. **2 avinagrarse** *vr* to turn sour.
Aviñón *nm* Avignon.
avío *nm* (**a**) preparation, provision; (*de pastor*) provisions for a journey.
(**b**) (*And, Carib, Cono Sur*: *préstamo*) loan (of money *o* of equipment).
(**c**) **hacer su ~*** to make one's pile*; (*iró*) to make a mess of things.
(**d**) **¡al ~!*** get cracking!*, get on with it!
(**e**) **~s** gear, tackle, kit.
avión *nm* (**a**) (*Aer*) aeroplane, plane, aircraft, airplane (*US*); **~ ambulancia** ambulance plane; **~ de carga** freight plane, cargo plane; **~ de caza, ~ de combate** fighter, pursuit plane; **~ cisterna** tanker aircraft; **~ a** (*o* **de**) **chorro, ~ de propulsión a chorro, ~ a** (*o* **de**) **reacción** jet (plane); **~ de despegue vertical** vertical take-off plane; **~ espía** spy plane; **~ de papel** paper dart; **~ de pasajeros** passenger aircraft; **por ~** (*Correos*) by airmail; **enviar artículos por ~** to send goods by plane; **ir en ~** to go by plane, go by air, fly.
(**b**) (*Orn*) martin.
(**c**) **hacer el ~ a uno‡** to do sb down, cause harm to sb; (*esp And*: *estafar*) to cheat sb.
(**d**) (*CAm*: *juego*) hopscotch.
avionazo *nm* plane crash, accident to an aircraft.
avioncito *nm*: **~ de papel** paper dart.
avionero *nm* (*And, Cono Sur*) airman.
avioneta *nf* light aircraft.
aviónica *nf* aviation, avionics.
avionístico *adj* relating to aeroplanes, relating to flying; **miedo ~** fear of flying.
avisadamente *adv* sensibly, wisely.
avisado *adj* sensible, wise; **mal ~** rash, ill-advised.
avisador 1 *nm*, **avisadora** *nf* (**a**) informant; messenger; (*pey* †) informer. (**b**) (*Cine, Teat*) programme seller. **2** *nm* electric bell; (*Culin*) timer; **~ de incendios** fire-alarm.
avisar [1a] *vt* to warn; to inform, notify, tell; **~ a uno con una semana de anticipación** to let sb know a week in advance, give sb a week's notice; **¿por qué no me avisó?** why didn't you let me know?; **en cuanto ella llegue me avisas** tell me the moment she comes; **lo hizo sin ~** he did it without warning; **~ al médico** (*etc*) to send for the doctor (*etc*), call the doctor (*etc*); **~ un taxi** to call a cab; **'avisamos grúa'** (*Esp*) 'we will call the towing vehicle' (to remove any parked car).
aviso *nm* (**a**) (*gen*) piece of information, tip; (*advertencia*) notice; warning; (*Inform*) prompt; **~ de bomba** bomb alert, bomb warning; **~ de envío** dispatch note; **~ escrito** written notice, notice in writing; **~ de mercancías** advice note; **con 15 días de ~** at a fortnight's notice; **con poco tiempo de ~** at short notice, with little warning; **~ previo de despido** prior notice of discharge; **sin previo ~** without warning, without notice; **hasta nuevo ~** until further notice; **salvo ~ en contrario** unless otherwise informed; **según (su) ~** (*Com*) as per order, as you ordered; **dar ~ a** to notify, inform; **mandar ~** to send word.
(**b**) (*LAm*) advertisement; **'~s económicos'** 'classified advertisements'; **~ mural** poster, wall poster.
(**c**) (*cualidad*) caution; discretion, prudence; **estar sobre ~** to be on the alert, be on the look-out; **poner a uno sobre ~** to forewarn sb, put sb on his guard.
avispa *nf* wasp.
avispado *adj* (*astuto*) sharp, clever, wide-awake; (*pey*) sly, wily; (*LAm*: *nervioso*) jumpy*, nervous.
avispar [1a] **1** *vt caballo* to spur on, urge on; (*fig*) to stir up, prod, ginger up. **2 avisparse** *vr* to fret, worry; (*Méx*) to become concerned, get alarmed.
avispero *nm* (**a**) (*Ent*) wasps' nest; **meterse en un ~** to get o.s. into a jam*. (**b**) (*Med*) carbuncle. (**c**) (*) mess; (*Cono Sur*) noisy gathering.
avispón *nm* hornet.
avistar [1a] **1** *vt* to sight, make out, glimpse. **2 avistarse** *vr* to have an interview (*con* with).
avituallamiento *nm* victualling, provisioning, supply(ing).
avituallar [1a] *vt* to victual, provision, supply with food.
avivado *adj* (*Cono Sur*) forewarned, alerted.
avivar [1a] **1** *vt fuego* to stoke (up); *color, luz* to brighten,

make brighter; *dolor* to intensify; *pasión* to inflame; *disputa* to add fuel to; *interés* to stimulate, arouse; to revive; *efecto* to enhance, heighten; *combatientes* to urge on; (*LAm*: *avisar*) to warn, alert.

2 avivarse *vr* to revive, acquire new life; to cheer up, become brighter; **¡avívate!** look alive!, snap out of it!

avizor 1 *adj*: **estar ojo ~** to be on the alert, be vigilant. **2** *nm* watcher.

avizorar [1a] *vt* to watch, spy on.

avocastro *nm* (*Cono Sur*) = **abocastro.**

avorazado *adj* (*Méx*) greedy, grasping.

avutarda *nf* great bustard.

axial *adj* axial.

axila *nf* axilla, armpit.

axioma *nm* axiom.

axiomático *adj* axiomatic.

axis *nm invar* (*Anat*) axis.

ay 1 *interj* (**a**) (*dolor físico*) ow!, ouch!

(**b**) (*pena etc*) oh!, oh dear!, (*más dramático*) alas!; **¡ ~ de mí!** poor me!; it's very hard (on me)!; whatever shall I do?; (*muy dramático*) woe is me!; **¡~ del que lo haga!** woe betide the man who does it!

(**c**) (*sorpresa*) oh!, goodness!

2 *nm* (*suspiro*) sigh; (*gemido*) moan, groan; (*grito*) cry; **un ~ desgarrador** a heartrending cry.

aya *nf* (*institutriz*) governess; (*niñera*) child's nurse.

ayatolá *nm*, **ayatollah** *nm* ayatollah.

Ayax *nm* Ajax.

ayer 1 *adv* yesterday; (*fig*) formerly, in the past; **~ no más, no más que ~** only yesterday; **~ por la mañana** yesterday morning; **de ~ acá** (*fig*) very suddenly; **no es cosa de ~** it's nothing new.

2 *nm* yesterday, past; **el ~ madrileño** Madrid in the past, old Madrid.

ayllu *nm* (*And*) (*Hist*: *familia*) family, tribe; (*comunidad*) community; (*tierras*) communal lands.

aymara = **aimara.**

ayo *nm* tutor.

ayote *nm* (*Méx*: *calabaza*) small pumpkin; (*CAm*: *jícaro*) pumpkin, squash; (*hum*) nut‡, bonce‡; **dar ~s a** to jilt; **la fiesta fue un ~** (*Méx*) the party was a disaster.

ayotoste *nm* armadillo.

Ayto *abr de* **Ayuntamiento.**

ayuda 1 *nf* (**a**) help, aid, assistance; **~s audiovisuales** audiovisual aids; **~ compensatoria** ≃ income support; **~ a domicilio** home help; **~ económica** financial (*o* economic) aid; **~s familiares** family allowances; **~s a la navegación** aids to navigation, navigational aids; **~ visual** visual aid.

(**b**) (*Med*) enema; (*LAm*) laxative.

2 *nm* page; **~ de cámara** valet.

ayudado *nm* (*Taur*) *two-handed pass with the cape.*

ayudador(a) *nm/f* helper.

ayudante *nm*, **ayudanta** *nf* helper, assistant; (*Mil*: *t* **~ de campo**) adjutant; (*Téc*) mate; technician; (*colegio, Univ*) assistant; (*Golf*) caddie; **~ de dirección** production assistant; **~ ejecutivo** executive assistant; **~ de electricista** electrician's mate; **~ de laboratorio** laboratory assistant; **~ de realización** (*TV*) production assistant; **~ técnico sanitario** nursing assistant.

ayudantía *nf* assistantship; (*Mil*) adjutancy; (*Téc*) post of technician.

ayudar [1a] *vt* to help, aid, assist; to help out; to be of use to, serve; **~ a uno a hacer algo** to help sb to do sth; to help sb in doing sth; **~ a uno a bajar** to help sb down, help sb out; **me ayuda muchísimo** he's a great help (to me), he helps me a lot.

ayudista *nmf* (*Cono Sur Pol*) supporter.

ayudita* *nf* small contribution.

ayunar [1a] *vi* to fast (*a* on); **~ (de)** (*fig*) to go without.

ayunas *nfpl*: **salir en ~** to go out without any breakfast; **estar** (*o* **quedarse**) **en ~** to know nothing about it, be completely in the dark.

ayuno 1 *adj* (**a**) (*en ayunas*) fasting. (**b**) **estar ~** = **estar** *etc* **en ayunas. 2** *nm* fast; fasting; abstinence; **estar** *etc* **en ~** = **estar en ayunas.**

ayuntamiento *nm* (**a**) (*corporación*) town council, city council, corporation, municipal government.

(**b**) (*edificio*) **A~** town hall, city hall.

(**c**) (*t* **~ sexual**) sexual intercourse; **tener ~ con** to have intercourse with.

ayuntar [1a] *vt* (**a**) (*Náut*) to splice. (**b**) (*And Agr*) to yoke, yoke together.

ayuya *nf* (*Cono Sur*) flat roll, scone.

azabachado *adj* jet, jet-black.

azabache *nm* (*Min*) jet; **~s** jet trinkets.

azacán *nm*, **azacana** *nf* drudge, slave; **estar hecho un ~** to be worked to death.

azacanarse [1a] *vr* to drudge, slave away.

azada *nf* hoe.

azadón *nm* large hoe, mattock.

azadonar [1a] *vt* to hoe.

azafata *nf* (**a**) (*Aer*) air hostess, stewardess, flight attendant (*US*); (*Náut*) stewardess; (*TV*) hostess; (*compañera*) escort (*supplied by escort agency*); **~ de exposiciones y congresos** congress organizer, hostess. (**b**) (*Cono Sur*) = **azafate.** (**c**) (*Hist*) lady-in-waiting; handmaiden.

azafate *nm* flat basket, tray.

azafrán *nm* (*Bot*) saffron, crocus; (*Culin*) saffron.

azafranado *adj* saffron, saffron-coloured.

azafranar [1a] *vt* (*Culin*) to saffron.

azagaya *nf* assegai, javelin.

azahar *nm* orange blossom.

azalea *nf* azalea.

azar *nm* (**a**) (*suerte*) chance, fate; **al ~** at random; **por ~** accidentally, by chance; **juego de ~** game of chance; **los ~es de la vida** life's ups and downs; **no es un ~ que** ... it is no mere accident that ..., it is not a matter of chance that ...; **decir al ~** to say to nobody in particular. (**b**) (*percance*) misfortune, accident, piece of bad luck.

azararse[1] [1a] *vr* (*ruborizarse*) to blush, redden.

azararse[2] [1a] *vr* (**a**) (*malograrse*) to go wrong, go awry. (**b**) = **azorarse.**

azarear [1a] *vt*, **azarearse** *vr* = **azorar(se).**

azarosamente *adv* hazardously; eventfully.

azaroso *adj* (**a**) (*arriesgado*) risky, hazardous, chancy; *vida* eventful; full of ups and downs. (**b**) (*malhadado*) unlucky, accident-prone.

Azerbaiyán *nm* Azerbaijan.

azerbaiyaní *adj, nmf* Azerbaijani.

ázimo *adj pan* unleavened.

-azo, -aza *V* **Aspects of Word Formation in Spanish 2.**

azocar [1g] *vt* (*Carib*) to pack tightly.

azófar *nm* brass.

azogado 1 *adj* restless, fidgety; **temblar como un ~** to shake like a leaf, tremble all over. **2** *nm* silvering (of a mirror).

azogar [1h] **1** *vt* to coat with quicksilver; *espejo* to silver. **2 azogarse** *vr* to be restless, be fidgety; to get agitated.

azogue *nm* mercury, quicksilver; **ser un ~** to be always on the go; to be restless, be fidgety.

azolve *nm* (*Méx*) sediment, deposit.

azonzado *adj* (*Cono Sur*) silly, stupid.

azor *nm* goshawk.

azora *nf* (*LAm*) = **azoramiento.**

azorado *adj* (**a**) (*alarmado*) alarmed, upset. (**b**) (*turbado*) embarrassed, flustered. (**c**) (*emocionado*) excited.

azoramiento *nm* (*V adj*) (**a**) alarm. (**b**) embarrassment, confusion; fluster. (**c**) excitement.

azorar [1a] **1** *vt* (**a**) (*alarmar etc*) to alarm, disturb, upset; to rattle.

(**b**) (*turbar*) to embarrass, fluster.

(**c**) (*emocionar*) to excite; (*instar*) to urge on, egg on.

2 azorarse *vr* (**a**) to get alarmed, get upset; to get rattled.

(**b**) to be embarrassed, get flustered.

Azores *nfpl* Azores.

azoro *nm* (**a**) (*esp LAm*) = **azoramiento.** (**b**) (*CAm*) ghost.

azorrillarse [1a] *vr* (*Méx*) to hide away, keep out of sight.

azotacalles *nm invar* idler, loafer.

azotaina *nf* beating, spanking.

azotamiento *nm* whipping, flogging.

azotar [1a] **1** *vt* to whip, flog, beat; to scourge; *niño* to thrash, spank; (*Agr etc*) to beat; *ramas etc* to jar, shake; (*lluvia, olas*) to lash, beat, beat down upon; **un viento huracanado azota la costa** a hurricane is lashing the coast.

2 azotarse *vr* (*Méx*) to put on airs, fancy o.s.

azotazo *nm* stroke, lash; spank.

azote *nm* (**a**) (*látigo*) whip, lash, scourge.

(**b**) (*golpe*) stroke, lash; spank; **ser condenado a 100 ~s** to be sentenced to 100 lashes; **~s y galeras** (*fig*) monotonous fare, the same old stuff.

(**c**) (*fig*) scourge; calamity; **Atila, el ~ de Dios** Attila, the Scourge of God.

azotea *nf* (**a**) (*techo*) flat roof, terrace roof; (*And, Cono Sur*) flat-roofed adobe house. (**b**) (‡: *cabeza*) bonce‡, head; **estar mal de la ~** to be round the bend‡.

azotera *nf* (*LAm*) (*acto*) beating, thrashing; (*azote*) cat-o'-

nine-tails.

azteca *adj, nmf* Aztec; (*fig*) Mexican.

azúcar *nm* (*en LAm gen nf*) sugar; ~ **blanco,** ~ **extrafino,** ~ **fina** castor sugar; ~ **cande,** ~ **candi** sugar candy, rock candy; ~ **de caña,** ~ **mascabada** cane sugar; ~ **de cortadillo,** ~ **en terrón** lump sugar; ~ **flor,** (*LAm*) ~ **glas,** (*Cono Sur*) ~ **impalpable,** ~ **en polvo** icing sugar; ~ **lustre** castor sugar; ~ **morena,** ~ **negra,** ~ **terciada** brown sugar.

azucarado *adj* sugary, sweet (*t fig*).

azucarar [1a] *vt* (**a**) (*agregar azúcar*) to sugar, add sugar to; to ice with sugar, coat with sugar. (**b**) (*fig*) to soften, mitigate; *persona* to sweeten.

azucarería *nf* sugar refinery; (*Carib, Méx*) sugar shop.

azucarero 1 *adj* sugar (*atr*). **2** *nm* (*t* **azucarera** *nf*) sugar basin, sugar bowl.

azucena *nf* (white) lily, Madonna lily; ~ **rosa** belladonna lily; ~ **tigrina** tiger lily.

azud *nm*, **azuda** *nf* (*noria*) waterwheel; (*presa*) dam (for irrigation), mill dam.

azuela *nf* adze.

azufre *nm* sulphur; brimstone.

azufroso *adj* sulphurous.

azul 1 *adj* blue; (*Pol*) conservative.

2 *nm* blue; blueness; ~ **celeste** sky blue; ~ **de cobalto** cobalt blue; ~ **eléctrico** electric blue; ~ **de mar,** ~ **marino** navy blue; ~ **pavo** peacock blue; ~ **de Prusia** Prussian blue; ~ **turquesa** turquoise; ~ **de ultramar** ultramarine.

azulado *adj* blue, bluish.

azular [1a] **1** *vt* to colour blue, dye blue. **2 azularse** *vr* to turn blue.

azulear [1a] *vi* (**a**) (*volverse azul*) to go blue, turn blue. (**b**) (*tirar a azul*) to be bluish; (*mostrarse azul*) to show blue, look blue.

azulejar [1a] *vt* to tile.

azulejería *nf* (**a**) (*azulejos*) tiling. (**b**) (*industria*) tile industry.

azulejo *nm* (**a**) tile, glazed tile, ornamental tile. (**b**) (*Carib, Méx*‡) copper*. (**c**) (*Méx: color*) bluish. (**d**) (*Méx Pez*) sardine-like fish.

azulenco *adj* bluish.

azulete *nm* blue (*for washing*).

azulgrana 1 *adj invar* (**a**) (*color*) blue and scarlet. (**b**) (*Dep*) of Barcelona Football Club. **2** *nmpl*: **los A~** the Barcelona club (*o* team).

azulina *nf* cornflower.

azulino *adj* bluish.

azuloso *adj* (*LAm*) bluish.

azumagarse [1h] *vr* (*Cono Sur*) to rust, get rusty.

azumbrado* *adj* tight*.

azumbre *nm liquid measure = 2.016 litres.*

azur *nm* (*Her*) azure.

azurumbado *adj* (*CAm*) (*tonto*) silly, stupid; (*borracho*) drunk.

azuzar [1f] *vt* (**a**) ~ **a los perros a uno** to set the dogs on sb, urge the dogs to attack sb.

(**b**) (*fig*) *persona* to egg on, urge on, incite; *emoción* to stir up, fan.

B

B, b [be] *nf* (*letra*) B, b; **se escribe con ~ de Barcelona** (*o* **~ de burro,** (*LAm*) **~ alta, ~ grande, ~ larga**) it's written with a *b*; **se escribe con ~ de Valencia** (*o* **~ de vaca,** (*LAm*) **~ chica, ~ corta, ~ baja**) it's written with a *v*.

B. (**a**) *abr de* **Barcelona**. (**b**) (*Rel*) *abr de* **Beato, Beata** Blessed.

baba *nf* (**a**) spittle, saliva, slobber; (*Bio*) mucus; (*de babosa etc*) slime, slimy secretion; **echar ~** to drool, slobber; **se le cae la ~** (*fig*) he's thrilled to bits, he's delighted (*por* with); (*en amor*) he's soft (*por* on), he's drooling (*por* over); (*pey*) he's a bit soft (in the head); (*LAm*) she could hardly wait; **cambiar ~s‡** to kiss.
(**b**) **mala ~*** (*malhumor*) bad temper; (*mal genio*) nasty character.

babador *nm* bib.

babasfrías *nm invar* (*And, Méx*) fool.

babaza *nf* (**a**) slime, mucus. (**b**) (*Zool*) slug.

babear [1a] **1** *vi* (**a**) to drool, slobber.
(**b**) (*fig*) to be sloppy, drool (over women).
2 babearse *vr* (**a**) (*Cono Sur*) to feel flattered, glow with satisfaction.
(**b**) **~ por algo** (*Méx*) to yearn for sth, drool over sth.

Babel *nm* Babel; **Torre de ~** Tower of Babel.

babel *nm o f* bedlam; confusion, mess.

babeo *nm* drooling, slobbering.

babero *nm* bib.

babi* *nm* = **baby** (**b**).

Babia *nf*: **estar en ~** to be daydreaming, have one's mind somewhere else.

babieca* 1 *adj* simple-minded, stupid. **2** *nmf* idiot, dolt.

Babilonia *nf* Babylon, Babylonia.

babilonia[1] *nf* bedlam.

babilónico *adj* Babylonian.

babilonio, -a[2] *adj, nm/f* Babylonian.

babilla *nf* (*Vet*) stifle.

bable *nm* dialect of Asturias.

babor *nm* port, port side, larboard; **a ~** on the port side; **la mar a ~** the sea to port; **¡tierra a ~!** land to port!; **poner el timón a ~, virar a ~** to turn to port, port the helm; **de ~** port (*atr*).

babosa *nf* slug.

babosada *nf* (*LAm*: *disparates*) stupid thing; (*inútil*) dead loss, useless thing; (*CAm, Méx*: *comentario*) stupid comment, silly remark; (*CAm, Méx*: *acto*) stupid thing to do; **¡~s!** rubbish!

babosear [1a] **1** *vt* (**a**) to drool over, slobber over.
(**b**) (*fig*) to drool over; (*CAm*) to insult; (*Méx**: *manosear*) to manhandle; (*CAm, Méx‡*: *tratar de bobo*) to take for (*o* treat like) a fool; **muchos han baboseado este problema** (*Méx*) many have taken a superficial look at this problem.
2 *vi* (**a**) to drool. (**b**) (*Méx*: *holgazanear*) to mess about.

baboseo *nm* (**a**) drooling, slobbering. (**b**) (*fig*) infatuation, drooling.

baboso 1 *adj* (**a**) drooling, slobbering; slimy.
(**b**) (*) (*fig*: *en amor*) sloppy (about women); (*sensiblero*) mushy, foolishly sentimental; (*adulón*) fawning, snivelling; (*sucio*) dirty; (*LAm*: *tonto*) silly, foolish; (*CAm*) rotten*, caddish*.
2 *nm*, **babosa** *nf* (*LAm*) fool, idiot.

babucha *nf* slipper; (*Carib*) child's bodice; (*LAm*: *blusa*) loose blouse, smock; **~s** (*Carib*) rompers; (*Méx*) high-heeled boots; **llevar algo a ~** (*Cono Sur*) to carry sth on one's back.

babuino *nm* baboon.

babujal *nm* (*Carib*) witch, sorcerer.

baby ['beiβi] *nmf* (**a**) (*LAm*) baby; (*Aut*) small car, mini; **~ crece** babygrow; **~ fútbol** table football. (**b**) (*: *babero*) bib; (*mandil*) apron, smock.

baca *nf* (**a**) (*de autocar*) top; rainproof cover. (**b**) (*portaequipajes*) luggage rack, carrier, roof rack.

bacal *nm* (*Méx*) corncob.

bacalada‡ *nf* sweetener*, bribe.

bacaladero *adj* cod (*atr*); **flota bacaladera** cod-fishing fleet.

bacaladilla *nf* blue whiting.

bacalao *nm* (**a**) cod, codfish; **mi ~*** my other half, the wife*; **cortar el ~*** to be the boss, have the final say, run the show; **¡te conozco, ~!*** I've rumbled you!*.
(**b**) (*Cono Sur*) miser, tight-fisted person.
(**c**) (*Esp***) cunt**.

bacán* 1 *adj* posh*, classy*. **2** *nm* (*Cono Sur*: *rico*) wealthy man; (*protector*) sugar daddy*; (*señorito*) playboy; (*elegante*) toff*, dude (*US*).

bacanal 1 *adj* bacchanalian. **2** *nf* (*t* **~es**) bacchanalia; (*fig*) bacchanalia, orgy.

bacanalear [1a] *vi* (*CAm*) to have a wild time.

bacane *nm* (*Carib*) driving licence, driver's license (*US*).

bacanería *nf* (*Cono Sur**) (*elegancia*) sharp dressing, nattiness; (*ostentación*) vulgar display, ostentation.

bacante *nf* bacchante; (*fig*) drunken and noisy woman.

bacar(r)á *nm* baccarat.

bacelador* *nm* (*Carib*) con man.

bacelar [1a] *vt* (*Carib*) to con, trick.

bacenica *nf* (*LAm*) = **bacinica**.

bacía *nf* (*vasija*) basin, vessel; (*de afeitar*) barber's bowl, shaving bowl.

bacilar *adj* bacillary.

bacilarse [1a] *vr* (*And*) to have a good time.

bacilo *nm* bacillus, germ.

bacilón* 1 *adj* brilliant*, great*; *V t* **vacilón**. **2** *nm* (*And*) fun, good time.

bacín *nm* (**a**) (*orinal*) chamberpot; (*cepo*) poorbox; (*de mendigo*) beggar's bowl.
(**b**) (*persona*) wretch, cur.

bacinete *nm* (*LAm*) lavatory pan.

bacinica *nf* small chamberpot.

Baco *nm* Bacchus.

bacón ['beɪkon] *nm* bacon.

bacteria *nf* bacterium, germ; **~s** bacteria, germs.

bacterial *adj*, **bacteriano** *adj* bacterial.

bactericida 1 *adj* germ-killing. **2** *nm* germicide, germ killer.

bactérico *adj* bacterial.

bacteriología *nf* bacteriology.

bacteriológico *adj* bacteriological.

bacteriólogo, -a *nm/f* bacteriologist.

bacteriosis *nf* bacteriosis.

báculo *nm* (**a**) stick, staff; **~ pastoral** crozier, bishop's staff.
(**b**) (*fig*) prop, support, staff; **ser el ~ de la vejez de uno** to be sb's comfort in old age.

bacha *nf* (*Carib*) spree, merry outing.

bachata *nf* (*Carib*) party, good time.

bachatear [1a] *vi* (*Carib*) to go on a spree, go out for a good time.

bachatero *nm* (*Carib*) reveller, carouser.

bache *nm* (**a**) hole, pothole; (*fig*) bad patch, bad spot, rut; **~ de aire** (*Aer*) air pocket. (**b**) (*fig*) (*Econ etc*) slump; **~ económico** slump, economic depression; **salir del ~** to get out of the rut, get moving again; **salvar el ~** to get the worst over, be over the worst.

bacheado *adj carretera* bumpy, uneven, full of pot-holes.

bachicha *nm* (**a**) (*Cono Sur‡*: *italiano*) dago, Wop‡. (**b**) (*Méx*) (*restos*) leftovers; (*colilla*) cigarette end, cigar stub; (*de bebida*) dregs. (**c**) (*Méx Fin*) nest-egg, secret hoard.

bachiche *nm* (*And*) = **bachicha** (**a**).

bachiller 1 *adj* garrulous, talkative.

2 *nmf pupil who has passed the school-leaving examination or holds a certificate of higher education* (*V* **bachillerato**); (*Univ*: *Hist*) bachelor.

3 *nm* (*fig*) windbag.

4 bachillera *nf* (**a**) (*erudita*) bluestocking; (*gárrula*) talkative woman.

(**b**) (*astuta*) cunning woman, scheming woman.

bachillerato *nm* school-leaving examination, baccalaureate; (*Univ*: *Hist*) bachelor's degree; ~ **comercial** certificate in business studies; ~ **elemental** lower examination (≃ *'O' level*); ~ **laboral** certificate in agricultural (*o* technical) studies; ~ **del magisterio** certificate for students proceeding to teacher-training; ~ **superior** higher certificate (≃ *'A' level*).

bachillerear* [1a] *vi* to talk a lot, prattle away.

bachillería* *nf* (**a**) (*cotorreo*) talk, prattle; idle talk. (**b**) (*disparate*) piece of nonsense.

badajada *nf* (**a**) (*de campana*) stroke (of a bell), chime. (**b**) (*fig*) piece of idle talk, piece of gossip; rubbish, stupid remark.

badajazo *nm* stroke (of a bell), chime.

badajear [1a] *vi* to swing to and fro.

badajo *nm* (**a**) (*de campana*) clapper (of a bell). (**b**) (*) chatterbox.

badajocense 1 *adj* of Badajoz. **2** *nmf* native (*o* inhabitant) of Badajoz; **los ~s** the people of Badajoz.

badajoceño = **badajocense**.

badana *nf* dressed sheepskin; **zurrar** (*o* **calentar, sobar**) **la ~ a uno*** to tan sb's hide*, (*fig*) haul sb over the coals.

badaza *nf* (*Carib*) strap (for standing passenger).

badén *nm* (*Aut*) (*bache*) bump; dip, pothole; (*agua*) splash of water; (*señal*) '~' 'splash'.

badil *nm*, **badila** *nf* fire shovel.

badilejo *nm* (*And*) (builder's) trowel.

bádminton *nm* badminton.

badulaque *nm* (**a**) (*idiota*) idiot, nincompoop. (**b**) (*Cono Sur* ††) rogue.

badulaquear [1a] *vi* (**a**) (*ser idiota*) to be an idiot, act like an idiot. (**b**) (*Cono Sur* ††) to be a rogue, be dishonest, act like a rogue.

baf(f)le *nm* (*Elec*) speaker, loudspeaker.

bagaje *nm* (**a**) (*Mil*) baggage; equipment; (*LAm*: *equipaje*) luggage, baggage (*US*). (**b**) (*animal*) beast of burden. (**c**) (*fig*) knowledge, experience.

bagatela *nf* trinket, knick-knack; trifle, mere nothing, bagatelle; **¡una ~!** a mere trifle!; **son ~s** those are trivialities, those are things of no importance.

bagayo‡ *nm* (*Cono Sur*) (**a**) (*lío*) bundle, tramp's bundle; (*carga*) heavy (*o* awkward) burden; (*cosas robadas*) loot (from a crime); (*contrabando*) contraband goods.

(**b**) (*fig*) (*inútil*) useless lump, berk‡; (*mujer fea*) old bag*.

bagazo *nm* (**a**) (*residuo*) chaff, husks; pulp; (*LAm*: *de azúcar*) husks of sugar cane. (**b**) (*fig*) dead loss. (**c**) (*Carib*: *miserable*) down-and-out.

bagre 1 *adj* (**a**) (*And*) vulgar, coarse, loud.

(**b**) (*CAm*) clever, sharp.

2 *nm* (*LAm*: *pez*) catfish.

3 *nmf* (‡) (*LAm*) (*taimado*) unpleasant person, sly sort; (*tipo feo*) ugly mug‡; (*mujer*) old bag*; **pica el ~** (*Cono Sur**) I'm starving.

bagrero *adj* (*And*) fond of ugly women.

bagual 1 *adj* (*And, Cono Sur*) (**a**) *animal* wild, untamed.

(**b**) *persona* rough, loutish, rude.

2 *nm* (**a**) (*And, Cono Sur*) wild (*o* unbroken) horse; **ganar los ~es** (*Cono Sur Hist*) to escape, get to safety.

(**b**) (*Cono Sur*: *persona*) thug, lout.

bagualada *nf* (*Cono Sur*) (**a**) herd of wild horses. (**b**) (*fig*) stupid thing (to do).

bagualón *adj* (*Cono Sur*) half-tamed.

baguío *nm* hurricane, typhoon.

bah *interj* (*desprecio*) bah!, that's nothing!, pooh!; (*incredulidad*) hum!, never!

Bahama: Islas *nfpl* ~, *t* **Las Bahamas** the Bahamas.

bahareque *nm* = **bajareque**.

baharí *nm* sparrowhawk.

bahía *nf* (*Geog*) bay.

baho *nm* (*CAm Culin*) *dish of meat and yucca*.

bahorrina *nf* (**a**) dirt, filth; slops. (**b**) (*fig*) riffraff, scum.

bahreiní *adj, nmf* Bahreini.

bailable 1 *adj*: **música ~** dance music, music that you can dance to. **2** *nm* dance, dance number; ballet.

bailada *nf* (*LAm*) dance, dancing.

bailadero *nm* (*sala*) dance hall; (*pista*) dance floor.

bailador 1 *adj* dancing. **2** *nm*, **bailadora** *nf* dancer.

bailaor(a) *nm/f* flamenco dancer.

bailar [1a] **1** *vt* (**a**) to dance: *peonza etc* to spin.

(**b**) (*LAm**) **le bailaron la herencia** they cheated her out of her inheritance.

2 *vi* to dance; (*peonza*) to spin, spin round; (*fig*) to dance, jump about; **~ al son que tocan** to toe the line; to adapt o.s. to circumstances; **éste es otro que bien baila** here's another one (of the same kind); **¿quieres ~?** shall we dance?; **sacar a una a ~** to invite a girl to dance; **le bailaban los ojos de alegría** her eyes sparkled with happiness; **¡que nos quiten lo bailado!** nobody can take away the good times we've had!

bailarín *nm* (professional) dancer; (*de ballet*) ballet dancer; **~ de claqué** tap-dancer.

bailarina *nf* (professional) dancer; dancing-girl; (*de ballet*) ballet dancer, ballerina; **~ del vientre** belly-dancer; **primera ~** prima ballerina.

bailata‡ *nf* = **baile**.

baile *nm* (**a**) (*gen*) dance; dancing, the dance; (*Teat*) dance, ballet; **~ agarrado, ~ apretado** slow dance; **~ clásico** ballet; **~ folklórico, ~ popular, ~ regional** traditional dance; **~ de salón, ~ de sociedad** ballroom dance; **~ de San Vito** St Vitus's dance; **hacer el ~** (*Fútbol**) to pass the ball to and fro, waste time.

(**b**) (*función*) dance, (*más formal*) ball; **~ de candil, ~ de medio pelo** (*LAm*) village dance, hop*; **~ de contribución** (*CAm, Carib*) public dance; **~ de disfraces** fancy dress ball; **~ de etiqueta** ball, dress ball, formal dance; **~ de fantasía** (*LAm*), **~ de máscaras** masked ball; **~ de trajes** fancy-dress ball.

bailecito(s) *nm(pl)* (*LAm*) folk dance.

bailón *adj* fond of dancing, that dances a lot.

bailongo 1 *adj* dance (*atr*); **música bailonga** music for dancing, music you can dance to. **2** *nm* (*esp LAm*) local dance.

bailotear [1a] *vi* (*pey*) to dance about, hop around.

baivel *nm* bevel.

baja *nf* (**a**) (*de precio, temperatura etc*) drop, fall; cut; **~ repentina** (*Econ*) slump, recession; **una ~ de 5 por ciento** a fall of 5%; **una ~ de los tipos de interés** a cut in interest rates; **una ~ de temperatura** a drop in temperature; **tendencia a la ~** downward tendency, tendency to fall; **jugar a la ~** (*Fin*) to speculate on a fall in prices; **dar ~, ir de ~** (*Fin*) to decline, lose value; **seguir en ~** (*Fin*) to continue downwards; **se cotiza hoy a la ~** (*fig*) it's in decline, it's going downhill.

(**b**) (*Mil*) casualty; (*en un puesto*) vacancy; (*abono*) cancelled subscription; **~ incentivada, ~ por incentivo** voluntary severance; **~ retribuida** paid leave; **~ voluntaria** voluntary redundancy; **las ~s son grandes** the casualties are heavy, there are heavy casualties; **Pepe es ~ (por enfermedad)** Pepe is off sick; **dar a uno de ~** to mark sb absent; to strike off sb, eliminate sb (from a list); (*Mil*) to post a man as absent (from parade *etc*); **dar de ~ a un soldado** to discharge a soldier; **dar de ~ a un empleado** to give notice to an employee; **dar de ~ a un miembro** to expel a member, remove sb from the list of members; **darse de ~** to drop out, withdraw, retire; to go sick; to step down; to give up one's job, leave one's post; to cease to subscribe, give up one's membership.

bajá *nm* pasha.

bajacaliforniano (*Méx*) **1** *adj* of Baja California. **2** *nm*, **bajacaliforniana** *nf* native (*o* inhabitant) of Baja California.

bajada *nf* (**a**) (*cuesta*) slope. (**b**) (*acto*) descent, going down; **~ de bandera*** minimum (taxi) fare; **~ de pantalones*** shameful capitulation; **durante la ~** as we (*etc*) went down, on the way down. (**c**) (*de precios*) reduction, lowering.

bajamar *nf* low tide, low water.

bajante *nm* drainpipe.

bajar [1a] **1** *vt* (**a**) *objeto* to lower, let down; to bring down, carry down; *equipaje etc* to take down, get down; *bandera* to lower; *persona* to help down, help out; to lead down; **~ el telón** to lower the curtain; **~ el equipaje al taxi** to take the luggage down to the taxi; **¿me ayuda a ~ esta maleta?** would you help me to get this case down?

(**b**) *brazo, ojos etc* to drop, lower; *cabeza* to bow, bend.

(**c**) *precio* to reduce, lower, cut; *gas, radio etc* to turn down; *voz* to lower; (*Aut*) *faros* to dip.

(**d**) *cuesta, escalera* to come down, go down, descend.

(**e**) (*fig*: *humillar*) to humble, humiliate.
(**f**) (*Carib*‡: *pagar*) to pay up, cough up*.
(**g**) (*And*‡: *matar*) to do in‡.
2 *vi* (**a**) (*descender*) to come down, go down, descend.
(**b**) (*de vehículo*) to get off, get out; **~ de** to get off, get out of.
(**c**) (*precio, temperatura, agua etc*) to fall; **la venta no ha bajado nunca de mil** sales have never been less than a thousand, sales have never fallen below a thousand.
3 bajarse *vr* (**a**) (*inclinarse*) to bend down, stoop; **~ a recoger algo** to bend down to pick sth up.
(**b**) (*de vehículo*) to get off, get out; **~ de** to get off, get out of; **~ del vicio*** to kick the drug habit*.
(**c**) (*fig*) to lower o.s., humble o.s.; **~ a hacer algo vil** to lower o.s. to do sth mean.
(**d**) (*Cono Sur*: *alojarse*) to stay, put up (*en* in, at).

bajareque *nm* (**a**) (*LAm*: *tapia*) mud wall; (*Carib*: *cabaña*) hovel, shack. (**b**) (*CAm*) (*llovizna*) fine drizzle; (*caña*) bamboo.

bajativo *adj* (*Cono Sur*) digestive.

bajel *nm* (*liter*) vessel, ship.

bajera *nf* (**a**) (*Arquit*) lower ground floor, basement. (**b**) (*And, CAm, Carib*) lower leaves of the tobacco plant; rough (*o* inferior) tobacco. (**c**) (*And, CAm, Carib*: *fig*) insignificant person, nobody. (**d**) (*Cono Sur*) horse blanket.

bajero *adj* (**a**) lower, under-...; **falda bajera** underskirt. (**b**) (*CAm*: *de colina etc*) downhill, descending.

bajetón *adj* (*And*) short, small.

bajeza *nf* (**a**) (*cualidad*) lowliness; vileness, baseness, meanness. (**b**) (*una ~*) mean thing, vile deed.

bajial *nm* (*LAm*) lowland; flats, floodplain.

bajini(s)*: **por lo ~** *adv decir* very quietly, in an undertone.

bajío *nm* (**a**) (*Náut*) shoal, sandbank; shallows. (**b**) (*LAm*) lowland; (*Méx*: *t* **~s**) flat arable land on a high plateau; **el B~** (*Méx*) the fertile plateau of northern Mexico.

bajista 1 *adj* (*Fin*): **tendencia ~** tendency to lower prices, bearish tendency. **2** *nm* (*Fin*) bear. **3** *nmf* (*Mús*) bass guitar player, bassist.

bajo 1 *adj* (**a**) (*no alto*) low; *persona* short, small (*t* **~ de cuerpo, ~ de estatura**); *parte, lado* lower, under; *piso* lower, ground (*atr*); *tierra* low, low-lying; *agua* shallow; **con la cabeza baja** with bowed head, with head lowered; **con los ojos ~s** with downcast eyes, with lowered eyes; **en la parte baja de la ciudad** in the lower part of the town.
(**b**) *sonido* faint, soft; *voz* low, (*de tono*) deep; **en voz baja** in an undertone, in a low voice; **por lo ~** (*Méx*: *a lo menos*) at (the) least; **decir algo por lo ~** to say sth in an undertone; **hacer algo por lo ~** to do sth secretly.
(**c**) *color* dull; pale.
(**d**) (*t* **~ de ley**) *metal* base.
(**e**) **~ latín** Low Latin; **baja Edad Media** late Middle Ages.
(**f**) *nacimiento* low, humble; *cámara* (*Pol*), *clase* lower; *condición* lowly; *tarea* menial; *barrio* poor, working-class (*y V* **barrio**).
(**g**) (*pey*) common, ordinary; *cualidad* low, poor; (*moralmente*) vile, base, mean.
2 *nm* (**a**) deep place, depth; hollow.
(**b**) (*Náut*) = **bajío**.
(**c**) (*Cos*) hemline; **~s de la falda** lower part of the skirt; **~s del pantalón** trouser bottoms.
(**d**) (*Arquit*) **~s** ground floor, first floor (*US*), ground-floor flat (*o* rooms).
(**e**) (*Mús*: *voz*) bass; **~ profundo** basso profundo.
(**f**) (*Mús*: *guitarrista*) bass guitar player, bassist.
(**g**) **~s** (*Anat*) lower parts (of the body); (*euf*) genitals.
3 *adv* (**a**) down; below.
(**b**) *tocar, cantar* quietly; *hablar* low, in a low voice; **¡más ~, por favor!** quieter, please!
4 *prep* (**a**) under, underneath, below.
(**b**) (*fig*) under; **~ Napoleón** under Napoleon; **~ el reinado de** in the reign of.
(**c**) *V* **juramento** *etc*.

bajomedieval *adj* late medieval.

bajón *nm* (**a**) (*caída*) decline, fall, drop; (*Med*) decline, worsening; withdrawal symptoms (after drug use); (*Com, Fin*) sharp fall in price; slump; **~ en la moral** slump in morale; **dar un ~** to fall away sharply, slump, go rapidly downhill; **en 3 meses ha pegado un ~ de 5 años** in 3 months he seems to have aged 5 years.
(**b**) (*Mús*) bassoon.

bajorrelieve *nm* bas-relief.

bajuno *adj truco etc* base, underhand, sly.

bajura *nf* (**a**) (*V adj* (**a**)) lowness; shortness, smallness, small size. (**b**) (*Carib Geog*) lowland. (**c**) **pesca de ~** inshore fishing, coastal fishing.

bala *nf* (**a**) (*Mil*) bullet, shot; **~ de cañón** cannonball; **~ de fogueo** blank cartridge; **~ fría** spent bullet; **~ de goma** plastic bullet, rubber bullet; **~ perdida** stray shot; **~ trazadora** tracer bullet; **como una ~** like a bullet, like lightning; **ni a ~** (*LAm*) by no means, not on any account; **ser una ~** (*Carib**) to be a pain in the neck*; **ser un(a) ~ (perdida*)** (*raro*) to be an oddball*; (*calavera*) to be a madcap; (*malo*) to be a rotter*; **quedar con la ~ pasada** (*Cono Sur*) to have a nagging doubt; **no le entra ~** (*Cono Sur*) (*de salud*) he's never ill, he's terribly tough; (*insensible*) he's very thick-skinned.
(**b**) (*Com*) bale; **~ de algodón** bale of cotton, cotton bale.
(**c**) **~ de entintar** (*Tip*) inkball, inking ball.

balaca *nf* (*LAm*: *baladronada*) boast, piece of boasting, brag; (*And*: *boato*) show, pomp.

balacada *nf* (*Cono Sur*) = **balaca**.

balacear [1a] *vt* (*CAm, Méx*) to shoot, shoot at.

balacera *nf* (*tiroteo*) exchange of shots, shooting; (*balas*) hail of bullets; (*enfrentamiento*) shoot-out.

balada *nf* (*Liter*) ballad; (*Mús*) ballad, ballade.

baladí *adj* trivial, paltry, worthless; trashy.

baladista *nmf* ballad-maker, songwriter; ballad-singer.

baladrar [1a] *vi* to scream, howl; to shout.

baladre *nm* oleander, rosebay.

baladrero *adj* loud, noisy.

baladro *nm* scream, howl; shout.

baladrón 1 *adj* boastful. **2** *nm* braggart, bully.

baladronada *nf* boast, brag; bravado, piece of bravado.

baladronear [1a] *vi* to boast, brag; to indulge in bravado.

bálago *nm* (**a**) (*paja*) (long) straw. (**b**) (*jabón*) soapsuds, lather.

balance *nm* (**a**) (*vaivén*) to-and-fro motion, oscillation; rocking, swinging; (*Náut*) roll, rolling.
(**b**) (*fig*: *indecisión*) hesitation, vacillation.
(**c**) (*Carib*: *mecedora*) rocking chair.
(**d**) (*Com, Fin*) balance; balance-sheet; (*inventario*) stocktaking; **~ de comprobación** trial balance; **~ consolidado** consolidated balance-sheet; **~ de la situación** balance-sheet; **el ~ de víctimas en el accidente** the toll of victims in the accident, the number of dead in the accident; **hacer ~** to draw up a balance; to take an inventory; (*fig*) to take stock (of one's situation).
(**e**) **~ de pagos** *etc V* **balanza** (**c**).
(**f**) (*And*: *asunto*) affair, matter; (*negocio*) deal.

balanceado *nm* (*Boxeo*) swing.

balancear [1a] **1** *vt* to balance. **2** *vi y* **balancearse** *vr* (**a**) (*movimiento*) to move to and fro, oscillate; to rock, swing; (*Náut*) to roll. (**b**) (*fig*: *vacilar*) to hesitate, vacillate, waver.

balanceo *nm* = **balance (a), (b)**.

balancín *nm* (*de balanza*) balance beam; (*Mec*) rocker, rocker arm; (*de carro*) swingletree; (*Náut*) outrigger; (*de volatinero*) balancing pole; (*para llevar cargas*) yoke; (*columpio*) seesaw, (*juguete*) child's rocking toy; (*silla*) rocking chair.

balandra *nf* sloop; (large, sea-going) yacht.

balandrán *nm* cassock.

balandrismo *nm* yachting; sailing.

balandrista *nmf* yachtsman, yachtswoman; sailing enthusiast.

balandro *nm* yacht; (*Carib*) fishing vessel.

balanza *nf* (**a**) (*instrumento*) balance (*esp Quím*), scales, weighing machine; (*Zodíaco*) **B~** Libra, the Scales; **~ de cocina** kitchen scales; **~ de cruz** grocer's scales; **~ de laboratorio, ~ de precisión** precision balance; **~ de muelle** spring-balance; **~ romana** steelyard; **estar en la ~** to be in the balance.
(**b**) (*fig*: *juicio*) judgement; (*comparación*) comparison.
(**c**) (*Com, Fin, Pol etc*) balance; **~ comercial, ~ de comercio** balance of trade; **~ por cuenta corriente, ~ de pagos** balance of payments; **~ de poder(es), ~ política** balance of power.

balaquear [1a] *vi* to boast.

balar [1a] *vi* to bleat, baa.

balasto[1] *nm* (*Ferro*) sleeper.

balasto[2] *nm* (*Cono Sur, Méx*) ballast.

balastro *nm* = **balasto**[2].

balaustrada *nf* balustrade; bannisters.

balaustre *nm* baluster; banister.

balay *nm* (*LAm*) wicker basket.

balazo *nm* shot; bullet wound; **matar a uno de un ~** to shoot sb dead.

balboa *nf* balboa (*Panamanian unit of currency*).
balbucear [1a] *vti*, **balbucir** [3f; *defectivo*: *se usan únicamente las formas que tienen -i- en la desinencia*] *vti* to stammer, stutter; (*niño*) to lisp, make its first sounds; to babble.
balbuceo *nm* stammering, stuttering; babbling.
balbuciente *adj* stammering, stuttering; babbling.
Balcanes *nmpl*: **los** ~ the Balkans; **la Península de los** ~ the Balkan Peninsula; **los (Montes)** ~ the Balkan Mountains.
balcánico *adj* Balkan.
balcanización *nf* balkanization.
balcarrias *nfpl*, **balcarrotas** *nfpl* (*And*) sideburns.
balcón *nm* balcony; balcony window; railing (of a balcony); (*fig*) vantage point.
balconada *nf* row of balconies.
balconeador(a) *nm/f* onlooker, observer.
balconear [1a] **1** *vt* (*Cono Sur*) to watch closely (from a balcony); *juego etc* to sneak a look at. **2** *vi* (*CAm*: *amantes*) to talk at the window.
balconero *nm* cat burglar.
balda *nf* shelf.
baldada *nf* (*Cono Sur*) bucketful.
baldado **1** *adj* crippled, disabled; **estar** ~* to be knackered*. **2** *nm*, **baldada** *nf* cripple, disabled person.
baldaquín *nm*, **baldaquino** *nm* canopy, baldachin.
baldar [1a] *vt* (**a**) (*lisiar*) to cripple, maim, disable. (**b**) (*fig*: *dañar*) to harm, cripple; (*Naipes*) to trump.
balde[1] *nm* bucket, pail; ~ **de la basura** (*LAm*) trash-can.
balde[2] *nm* (**a**) **obtener algo de** ~ to get sth free, get sth for nothing; **vender algo medio de** ~ to sell sth for a song; **había muchos de** ~ there were a lot left over; **estar de** ~ (*persona*) (*estar de más*) to be de trop, be unwanted, be in the way; (*sin empleo*) to be idle, be out of work.
(**b**) **¡no de** ~! (*CAm*) goodness!, I never noticed!
(**c**) **en** ~ in vain, to no purpose; **¡ni en** ~! (*LAm*) no way!*, not on your life!
baldear [1a] *vt* (**a**) (*limpiar*) to hose down; to wash, wash down, swill with water. (**b**) (*Náut*) to bail out.
baldeo *nm* (**a**) wash, hosing down. (**b**) (‡) chiv‡, knife.
baldío **1** *adj* (**a**) *tierra* uncultivated; waste. (**b**) (*ocioso*) lazy, idle. (**c**) (*vano*) vain, useless. **2** *nm* uncultivated land; waste land; uncultivated common land.
baldón *nm* (*afrenta*) affront, insult; (*tacha*) blot, stain, disgrace.
baldonar [1a] *vt* to insult; to blot, disgrace.
baldosa *nf* floor tile; paving stone; (*LAm*: *lápida*) tombstone.
baldosado *nm* tiled floor, tiling; paving (of flagstones).
baldosar [1a] *vt suelo* to tile; *vereda etc* to pave (with flagstones).
baldoseta *nf* small tile.
balduque *nm* (official) red tape (*t fig*).
baleado, -a *nm/f* shooting victim, person who has been shot.
balear[1] [1a] **1** *vt* (*esp LAm*) (**a**) (*disparar contra*) to shoot (at); (*matar*) to shoot down (*o* dead); **morir baleado** to be shot dead. (**b**) (*estafar*) to cheat, swindle. **2 balearse** *vr* (*esp LAm*) to exchange shots, shoot at each other.
balear[2] **1** *adj* Balearic, of the Balearic Isles. **2** *nmf* native (*o* inhabitant) of the Balearic Isles; **los ~es** the people of the Balearic Isles.
Baleares *nfpl* (*t* **Islas** ~ *nfpl*) Balearics, Balearic Islands.
baleárico *adj* Balearic, of the Balearic Isles.
baleo *nm* (**a**) (*esp LAm*: *tiroteo*) shooting. (**b**) (*Méx*: *abanico*) fan.
balero *nm* (*LAm*: *juguete*) cup-and-ball toy; (*Méx Téc*) ball bearing(s); (*Cono Sur*‡) head, nut‡.
balido *nm* bleat, bleating, baa.
balín *nm* small bullet, pellet; **~es** shot.
balinera *nf* (*And*) ball-bearing(s).
balística *nf* ballistics.
balístico *adj* ballistic.
balita *nf* (**a**) (*balín*) small bullet, pellet. (**b**) (*Cono Sur*: *canica*) marble.
baliza *nf* (*Náut*) (lighted) buoy, marker; (*Aer*) beacon, marker.
balizaje *nm*, **balizamiento** *nm*: ~ **de pista** (*Aer*) runway lighting, runway beacons.
balizar [1f] *vt canal* to buoy, mark with buoys; (*Aer*) to light, mark with beacons.
balneario **1** *adj estación* thermal, medicinal; spa (*atr*), health (*atr*). **2** *nm* spa, health resort.
balneoterapia *nf* balneotherapy.
balompédico *adj* football (*atr*).
balompié *nm* football.
balón *nm* (**a**) (*Dep*) (large) ball, football; (*Quím etc*) bag (for gas); (*Met*) balloon; (*Náut*) spinnaker; (*And, Cono Sur*: *bombona*) drum, canister; ~ **de playa** beach-ball; **achicar balones*, echar balones fuera*** to dodge the issue. (**b**) (*Com*) (large) bale. (**c**) (*copa*) brandy glass.
baloncestista *nmf* basketball player.
baloncestístico *adj* basketball (*atr*).
baloncesto *nm* basketball.
balonmanear [1a] *vi* (*Dep*) to handle, handle the ball.
balonmano *nm* handball.
balonvolea *nm* volleyball.
balota *nf* ballot (*ball used in voting*).
balotaje *nm* (*Méx*) (*votación*) balloting, voting; (*recuento*) counting of votes.
balotar [1a] *vi* to ballot, vote.
balsa[1] *nf* (**a**) (*Bot*) balsa; balsa wood. (**b**) (*Náut*) raft; ferry; ~ **de salvamento,** ~ **salvavidas** life-raft; ~ **neumática** (*Aer etc*) rubber dinghy, rubber raft.
balsa[2] *nf* pool, pond; (*Méx*: *pantano*) swamp, marshy place; **el pueblo es una** ~ **de aceite** the village is as quiet as the grave.
balsadera *nf*, **balsadero** *nm* ferry(-station).
balsámico *adj* balsamic, balmy; (*fig*) balmy, soothing, healing.
bálsamo *nm* (**a**) (*Med*) balsam, balm; (*Cono Sur*: *de pelo*) hair conditioner. (**b**) (*fig*) balm, comfort.
balsar *nm* (*And, Carib*) overgrown marshy place.
balsear [1a] *vt* (**a**) *río* to cross by ferry, cross on a raft. (**b**) *personas, mercancías* to ferry across.
balsero *nm* ferryman.
balsón[1] *nm* (*Méx*) (*pantano*) swamp, bog; (*agua estancada*) stagnant pool.
balsón[2] *adj* (*And*) fat, flabby.
balsoso *adj* (*And*) soft, spongy.
Baltasar *nm* Balthasar; (*Bib*) Belshazzar; *V* **cena**.
báltico *adj* Baltic; **el Mar B~** the Baltic (Sea); **los estados ~s** the Baltic states.
baluarte *nm* bastion; (*fig*) bastion, bulwark.
balumba *nf* (**a**) (*masa*) (great) bulk, mass. (**b**) (*montón*) pile, heap. (**c**) (*LAm*: *alboroto*) noise, uproar.
balumbo *nm* bulky thing, cumbersome object.
balumoso *adj* (*And, CAm, Méx*) bulky, cumbersome.
baluquero *nm* (*Fin*) forger.
balurdo **1** *adj* (*LAm*) flashy. **2** *nm* (*Cono Sur**) crooked deal*.
ballena *nf* (**a**) (*Zool*) whale; ~ **azul** blue whale; **parece una** ~* she's as fat as a cow*. (**b**) (*hueso*) whalebone; (*de corsé*) bone, stay.
ballenear [1a] *vi* to whale, hunt whales.
ballenera *nf* whaler, whaling ship.
ballenero **1** *adj* whaling (*atr*); **industria ballenera** whaling industry. **2** *nm* (**a**) (*persona*) whaler. (**b**) (*barco*) whaler, whaling ship.
ballesta *nf* (**a**) (*Hist*) crossbow. (**b**) (*Aut, Ferro etc*) spring; **~s** springs, suspension.
ballestero *nm* (*Hist*) crossbowman.
ballestrinque *nm* clove hitch.
ballet [ba'le] *nm*, *pl* **ballets** [ba'le] ballet; (*de coristas etc*) troupe of dancers, dance troupe; ~ **acuático** synchronized swimming.
balletístico *adj* ballet (*atr*).
bamba[1] *nmf* (*Carib*) negro, negress.
bamba[2] *nf* (**a**) (*And Bot*) bole, swelling (on tree trunk). (**b**) (*And*: *gordura*) fat, flabbiness.
bamba[3]‡ *nf* (*Esp*) fuzz‡, police.
bambalear [1a] = **bambolear**.
bambalina *nf* (*Teat*) drop(-scene), cloth border; **entre ~s** behind the scenes.
bambalúa *nm* (*LAm*) clumsy fellow, lout.
bambarria* *nmf* idiot, fool.
bamboleante *adj* wobbly; unsteady; *pantalones* baggy.
bambolear [1a] *vi y* **bambolearse** *vr* to swing, sway; (*al andar*) to sway, roll, reel; (*mueble*) to wobble, be unsteady; (*tren etc*) to sway.
bamboleo *nm* swinging, swaying; rolling, reeling; wobbling, unsteadiness.
bambolla* *nf* (*ostentación*) show, ostentation; (*farsa*) sham.
bambollero* *adj* showy, flashy; sham, bogus.
bambú *nm* bamboo.
bambudal *nm* (*And*) bamboo grove.
banal *adj* banal; trivial, ordinary; *persona* ordinary, commonplace; superficial.

banalidad *nf* (**a**) (*cualidad*) banality; triviality, ordinariness; superficiality.
(**b**) (*en conversación*) banality, trivial thing; **intercambiar ~es con uno** to exchange trivialities with sb, swap small talk with sb.

banalizar [1f] *vt* to trivialize.

banana *nf* (*esp LAm*) (*fruta*) banana; (*árbol*) banana tree.

bananera *nf* banana plantation.

bananal *nm* (*LAm*) banana plantation.

bananero 1 *adj* (**a**) (*LAm*: *de bananas*) banana (*atr*); **compañía bananera** banana company; **plantación bananera** banana plantation. (**b**) (*) vulgar, coarse. (**c**) (*Pol etc*) third-world (*atr*), backward; **república bananera** banana republic. **2** *nm* banana tree.

banano *nm* (*LAm*: *árbol*) banana tree.

banas *nfpl* (*Méx Rel*) banns.

banasta *nf* large basket, hamper.

banasto *nm* large round basket.

banca *nf* (**a**) (*puesto*) stand, stall; (*LAm*) bench.
(**b**) (*Com, Fin*) **la ~** the banks, banking; **~ comercial** commercial banking; **~ industrial** merchant banking, investment banking; **horas de ~** banking hours.
(**c**) (*en juegos*) bank; **hacer saltar la ~** to break the bank; **tener la ~** to be banker, hold the bank.
(**d**) (*Cono Sur**) pull, influence; **tener (gran) ~** to have (lots of) pull.

bancada *nf* stone bench; (*Mec*) bench, bed, bedplate; (*Náut*) thwart, (oarsman's) seat; (*de remo*) **~ corrediza** sliding seat.

bancal *nm* (**a**) (*Agr*) patch, plot, bed; terrace. (**b**) (*Mec*) runner, bench-cover.

bancar [1g] **1** *vt* (*Cono Sur*) to pay for; (*fig*) to put up with. **2 bancarse** *vr*: **~ algo/a uno** to put up with sth/sb.

bancario *adj* bank (*atr*), banking (*atr*); financial.

bancarrota *nf* (*esp* fraudulent) bankruptcy; failure; **declararse en ~, hacer ~** to go bankrupt.

bancazo *nm* (*Méx*) bank robbery.

banco *nm* (**a**) (*asiento*) bench, seat; (*Náut*) thwart, (oarsman's) seat; (*Téc*) bench, work table; **~ azul** (*Parl*) ministerial benches; **~ de pruebas** testbed, (*fig*) testing-ground.
(**b**) (*Geog, Náut*) bank, shoal; (*And*: *suelo aluvial*) deposit of alluvial soil; (*Carib*: *tierra elevada*) raised ground; **~ de arena** sandbank; **~ de hielo** icefield, ice floe; **~ de nieve** snowdrift.
(**c**) (*Geol*: *estrato*) stratum, layer.
(**d**) (*de peces*) shoal, school.
(**e**) (*Com, Fin*) bank; **~ por acciones** joint-stock bank; **~ de ahorros** savings bank; **~ en casa** home banking; **~ central** central bank; **~ comercial** commercial bank; **~ de crédito** credit bank; **~ de datos** databank; **~ emisor** issuing bank; **~ de esperma(s)** sperm bank; **~ fiduciario** trust company; **~ de inversiones** investment bank; **~ de liquidación** clearing house; **~ de memoria** memory bank; **~ mercantil** merchant bank; **B~ Mundial** World Bank; **~ de sangre** bloodbank.

banda *nf* (**a**) (*franja*) band, strip; ribbon; (*de vestido*) sash, band; (*Méx Aut*) fanbelt; (*Billar*) cushion; (*de tierra*) strip, ribbon; zone; (*de pista de atletismo, de autopista*) lane; (*Rad*) band; **~ ancha** broad band; **~ de dibujos** comic strip; **~ horaria caliente** (*TV*) prime time, peak viewing time; **~ magnética** (*cinta*) magnetic tape; (*de tarjeta*) magnetic strip; **~ de rodaje, ~ de rodamiento** (*Aut*) tread; **~ salarial** wage scale; wage-rise limits; **~ de sonido, ~ sonora** (*Cine*) soundtrack; **~ transportadora** conveyor belt.
(**b**) (*Dep*) boundary; touchline; **estar fuera de ~** (*balón*) to be out; (*jugador*) to be offside; **sacar de ~** to take a throw-in, throw the ball in.
(**c**) (*Geog*: *de río*) side, bank; (*de monte*) side, edge; (*de barco*) side; **~ de Gaza** Gaza Strip; **la B~ Oriental** (*Hist*) Uruguay; **de la ~ de acá** on this side; **cerrarse a la** (*o* **en**) **~** to stand firm, be adamant; **dar un barco a la ~** to careen a ship; **encerrarse en ~** to refuse to comment, refuse to say anything more; to rule oneself out; **irse a la ~** (*Náut*) to list.
(**d**) (*personas*) band; gang; troop; party; (*Orn*) flock; **~ de los cuatro** (*Pol*) gang of four; **negociaciones a tres ~s** three-party talks, trilateral negotiations.
(**e**) (*Mús*) band, (*esp*) brass band.
(**f**) **coger a uno por ~*** to make sb do the dirty work; **¡como te cojo por ~!** I'll get even with you!

bandada *nf* (**a**) (*de aves*) flock; flight; (*de peces*) shoal. (**b**) (*LAm*) = **banda (d)**.

bandazo *nm* (*caída*) heavy fall; (*Náut*) heavy roll (of a ship); (*LAm Aer*) air pocket, sudden drop; (*fig*) marked shift (of policy *etc*); **caminar dando ~s** to stumble along; to reel from side to side, stagger.

bandear [1a] **1** *vt* (**a**) (*CAm*) (*perseguir*) to pursue, chase; (*pretender*) to court.
(**b**) (*CAm*: *herir*) to wound severely; (*Cono Sur*: *con comentario*) to hurt (with a remark).
(**c**) (*Cono Sur*: *cruzar*) to cross, go right across.
2 bandearse *vr* (**a**) (*ir de un lado a otro*) to move to and fro; (*Méx Náut*) to move to the other side of a boat.
(**b**) (*Cono Sur Pol*) to change parties.
(**c**) (*Méx*) (*vacilar*) to vacillate; (*cambiar de dirección*) to go one way and then another.
(**d**) (*Esp**) (*arreglárselas*) to shift for o.s., manage; to get wise*, get organized.

bandeja *nf* (**a**) tray, salver; (*LAm*: *platón*) large serving dish, bowl; **~ de entrada** in-tray; **~ de salida** out-tray; **~ para horno** oven tray; **servir algo a uno en ~ (de plata)** (*fig*) to hand sth to sb on a plate; **te lo han servido** (*o* **puesto**) **en ~** they've made it very easy for you. (**b**) (*Cono Sur*) central reservation (*of a road*).

bandera *nf* (**a**) (*gen*) flag; banner, standard; (*Mil*) colours; (*Inform*) marker, flag; **~ ajedrezada, ~ a cuadros** chequered flag; **~ blanca** white flag; **~ de conveniencia** flag of convenience; **~ de esquina** corner flag; **~ de parlamento** flag of truce, white flag; **~ de popa** ensign; **~ de proa** jack; **~ roja** red flag; **la ~ roja y gualda** the Spanish flag; **arriar la ~** (*Náut*) to strike one's colo(u)rs; **bajar la ~** (*taxi*) to pick up a fare; (*Carib fig*) to give in; **dar la ~ a uno** to give sb pride of place; **estar hasta la ~*** to be packed out; **hacer algo a ~s desplegadas** to do sth openly; **venir a ~s desplegadas** to come out with flying colo(u)rs.
(**b**) **de ~*** terrific*, marvel(l)ous; **una mujer de ~** (*Esp**) a woman with a smashing figure*.

banderazo *nm*: **~ de salida** starting-signal.

bandería *nf* faction; (*fig*) bias, partiality.

banderilla *nf* (**a**) (*Taur*) banderilla (*barbed dart with banderole*); **~ de fuego** banderilla with attached firecracker; **poner una ~ a uno, poner ~s a uno** to taunt sb, provoke sb, make sb cross.
(**b**) (*LAm**) swindle.
(**c**) (*Culin*) savoury appetizer (served on a cocktail stick).

banderillear [1a] *vt* (*Taur*) to thrust the banderillas into (the neck of).

banderillero *nm* (*Taur*) banderillero, bullfighter who uses the banderillas.

banderín *nm* little flag, pennant; (*Ferro*) signal flag; (*Mil*: *t* **~ de enganche**) recruiting centre, recruiting post.

banderita *nf* little flag; flag sold for charity; **día de la ~** flag day.

banderizo *adj* (**a**) factional, factionist. (**b**) (*fig*) fiery, excitable.

banderola *nf* (**a**) (*gen*) banderole; signalling flag; (*Mil*) pennant, pennon; **~ de esquina** corner flag. (**b**) (*Cono Sur*: *travesaño*) transom.

bandidaje *nm*, **bandidismo** *nm* banditry.

bandido *nm* (**a**) (*delincuente*) bandit; outlaw; desperado. (**b**) (*) rogue, rascal; **¡~!** you rogue!, you beast!

bando *nm* (**a**) (*edicto*) edict, proclamation; **~s** (*Ecl*) banns.
(**b**) (*partido*) faction, party; side; (*en juegos*) side; **uno del otro ~*** one of them*; **pasar al otro ~** to change sides.

bandola *nf* (**a**) (*Mús*) mandolin. (**b**) (*And*: *capa*) bullfighter's cape. (**c**) (*Carib*: *fuete*) knotted whip.

bandolera *nf* (**a**) bandoleer; **llevar algo en ~** to wear sth across one's chest. (**b**) (*persona*) woman bandit, moll*.

bandolerismo *nm* brigandage, banditry.

bandolero *nm* brigand, bandit; (*Hist*) highwayman.

bandolina *nf* mandolin.

bandoneón *nm* (*LAm*) large accordion.

bandullo‡ *nm* belly, guts; **llenarse el ~** to stuff o.s.*

bandurria *nf* bandurria (*Spanish instrument of the lute type*).

bangaña *nf*, **bangaño** *nm* (*LAm*: *Bot*) calabash, gourd; (*vasija*) vessel made from a gourd.

Bangladesh *nm* Bangladesh.

bangladesí *adj, nmf* Bangladeshi.

banjo *nm* banjo.

banquear [1a] *vt* (**a**) (*Aer*) to bank. (**b**) (*And*) to level, flatten out.

banqueo *nm* (**a**) terraces, terracing. (**b**) (*Aer*) bank(ing).

banquero, -a *nm/f* banker.

banqueta *nf* (**a**) (*taburete*) stool; (*banco*) low bench; **~ de piano** piano stool. (**b**) (*CAm, Méx*: *acera*) pavement, side-

walk (*US*).
banquetazo* *nm* spread*, blow-out‡.
banquete *nm* banquet, feast; formal dinner; dinner party; ~ **anual** annual dinner; ~ **de boda** wedding breakfast; ~ **de gala** state banquet.
banquetear [1a] *vti* to banquet, feast.
banquillo *nm* bench; footstool; (*Dep*) (team) bench; (*Jur*: *t* ~ **de los acusados**) prisoner's seat, dock.
banquisa *nf* ice field, ice floe.
bantam *nf* (**a**) (*t* **gallina de** ~) bantam. (**b**) (*LAm*, *fig*: *persona*) small restless person.
bantú *adj*, *nmf* Bantu.
banyo *nm* (*LAm*) banjo.
bañada *nf* (*LAm*) (*baño*) bath, dip, swim; (*de pintura*) coat (of paint).
bañadera *nf* (*Cono Sur*) bathtub.
bañado *nm* (*And*, *Cono Sur*) (*pantano*) swamp, marshland; (*charco*) flash, rain pool.
bañador 1 *nm* (**a**) (*Téc*) tub, trough. (**b**) (*traje de baño*) bathing costume, swimsuit; (*de hombre*) trunks. **2** *nm*, **bañadora** *nf* bather, swimmer.
bañar [1a] **1** *vt* (**a**) (*sumergir*) to bathe, immerse, dip; (*en baño*) to bath, bathe (*US*); (*Med*) to bathe (*con*, *de* in, with); (*Téc*) to dip; to coat; cover (*de* with); (*Culin*) to dip (*de* in), coat (*de* with).
(**b**) (*mar*) to bathe, wash.
(**c**) (*luz etc*) to bathe, suffuse, flood (*de* with).
(**d**) (*fig*) to bathe (*con*, *de*, *en* in); *V* **agua.**
2 bañarse *vr* (**a**) (*en baño*) to bath, bath o.s., take a bath, bathe (*US*); (*en mar*) to bathe, swim; **ir a** ~ to go for a bathe, have a bathe, go bathing, go swimming; **'prohibido** ~**'** 'no bathing', 'no swimming'.
(**b**) **¡anda a bañarte!** (*Cono Sur*‡) get lost!‡, go to hell!
bañata* *nm* (*Esp*) swimsuit, bathing costume.
bañera *nf* bath, bathtub.
bañista *nmf* (**a**) (*en mar etc*) bather. (**b**) (*Med*) person taking the waters at a spa, patient at a spa.
baño *nm* (**a**) (*acto*) (*gen*) bathing; (*en bañera*) bath; (*en mar etc*) swim, dip, bathe; **dar un** ~ **a** (*Dep**) to whitewash*; **tomar un** ~ (*en bañera*) to bath, bathe (*US*), take a bath; (*en mar etc*) to swim, bathe, have a swim.
(**b**) (*bañera etc*) bath, bathtub; (*Téc*) bath; (*Carib*: *lugar*) cool place; (*WC*) toilet; ~ **de asiento** hip-bath; ~ **de burbujas** bubble-bath, foam-bath; ~ **de ducha** showerbath; ~ **de espuma** bubble-bath, foam-bath; ~ **de fuego** baptism of fire; ~ **de María** bain marie, double saucepan; ~ **de masas**, ~ **de multitud(es)** walkabout, mingling with the crowd; ~ **de revelado** developing bath; ~ **ruso** (*Cono Sur*) steam bath; ~ **de sangre** (*fig*) bloodbath; ~ **de sol** sun bath; ~ **turco** Turkish bath; ~ **de vapor** steam bath.
(**c**) ~**s** (*Med*) baths; spa; **ir a** ~**s** to take the waters.
(**d**) (*Arte*) wash; (*Culin*) coating, covering.
bao *nm* (*Náut*) beam.
baptismo *nm*: **el** ~ the Baptist faith.
baptista *nmf* Baptist; **la Iglesia B**~ the Baptist church.
baptisterio *nm* baptistery, font.
baque *nm* bump, bang, thud.
baqueano *nm etc* = **baquiano.**
baquelita *nf* bakelite.
baqueta *nf* (**a**) (*Mil*) ramrod.
(**b**) (*Mús*) (*de tambor*) drumstick; (*CAm*, *Méx*: *de marimba*) hammer.
(**c**) **correr** ~**s**, **pasar por** ~**s** to run the gauntlet; **mandar a** ~ to rule tyrannically; **tratar a uno a (la)** ~ to treat sb harshly.
baquetazo *nm*: **tratar a uno a** ~ **limpio*** to treat sb harshly.
baqueteado *adj* experienced; **estar** ~ to be inured to it, be used to it; **ser un** ~ to know one's way around.
baquetear [1a] *vt* to annoy, bother.
baqueteo *nm* annoyance, bother; **es un** ~ it's an imposition, it's an awful bind*.
baquetudo *adj* (*Carib*) sluggish, slow.
baquía *nf* (**a**) (*LAm*: *conocimiento de una región*) intimate knowledge of a region, local expertise. (**b**) (*And*, *Cono Sur* †: *habilidad*) expertise, dexterity, skill.
baquiano 1 *adj* (**a**) (*LAm*: *que conoce una región*) familiar with a region.
(**b**) (*And*, *Cono Sur* †: *experto*) expert, skillful; **para hacerse** ~ **hay que perderse alguna vez** (*Cono Sur*) one learns the hard way.
2 *nm* (**a**) (*LAm* †: *guía*) pathfinder, guide; local expert, person with an intimate knowledge of a region; (*Náut*) pilot.
(**b**) (*And*, *Cono Sur*: *experto*) expert; person who knows what he is talking about.
báquico *adj* Bacchic; bacchanalian, drunken.
báquiro *nm* (*And*, *Carib*) peccary.
bar *nm* bar; snack bar; ~ **de alterne**, ~ **de citas** singles bar; ~ **suizo** open plan kitchen.
baraca *nf* (charismatic) gift of bringing good luck; blessing.
barahúnda *nf* uproar, hubbub; racket, din.
baraja *nf* (**a**) (*gen*) pack of cards; (*Méx*) cards; **jugar** ~ (*LAm*) to play cards; **jugar a** (*o* **con**) **dos** ~**s** to play a double game; **romper la** ~ (*fig*) to break off the engagement, end the conflict. (**b**) ~**s** (*fig*) fight, set-to.
barajadura *nf* shuffle, shuffling.
barajar [1a] **1** *vt* (**a**) *cartas* to shuffle.
(**b**) (*fig*: *mezclar*) to jumble up, mix up, shuffle round; (*Cono Sur*: *ofrecer*) to pass round, hand round; (*Cono Sur*, *Méx*) *asunto* to entangle, confuse; (*demorar*) to delay.
(**c**) (*Cono Sur*: *agarrar*) to catch (in the air); ~ **algo en el aire** (*fig*) to see the point of sth.
2 *vi* to quarrel, squabble.
3 barajarse *vr* (**a**) (*Cono Sur*: *pelear*) to fight, brawl.
(**b**) (*mezclarse*) to get jumbled up, get mixed up.
(**c**) **se baraja la posibilidad de que** ... there is discussion of the possibility that ..., the possibility that ... is being discussed; **las cifras que se barajan ahora** the figures now being put about, the figures now being bandied about.
barajo 1 *interj* (*LAm*: *euf*) = **carajo**. **2** *nm* (*And*) (*pretexto*) pretext, excuse; (*salida*) loophole.
barajuste *nm* (*Carib*) stampede, rush.
baranda[1] *nf* rail, railing; handrail; (*Billar*) cushion.
baranda[2]‡ *nm* chief, boss.
barandal *nm* base, support (of banisters); handrail; balustrade.
barandilla *nf* balustrade; handrail; (*And*) altar rail.
barata[1] *nf* (**a**) (*And*, *Méx*: *saldo*) sale, bargain sale.
(**b**) (*And*, *Méx*: *sección de gangas*) bargain counter; (*tienda*) cut-price store.
(**c**) (*And*) **a la** ~* (*sin orden*) any old how*; **tratar a uno a la** ~ to treat sb with scorn.
barata[2] *nf* (*Cono Sur*) cockroach.
baratear [1a] *vt* to sell cheaply; to sell at a loss.
baratejo* *adj* cheap and nasty, trashy.
baratero 1 *adj* (**a**) (*esp LAm*) (*gen*) cheap; *tendero etc* who sells cheap; **tienda baratera** shop offering bargains, cut-price store.
(**b**) (*Cono Sur*: *regateo*) haggling.
2 *nm* (**a**) (*en el juego*) person who extracts money from winning gamblers.
(**b**) (*LAm*: *tendero*) shopkeeper offering bargains, cut-price merchant.
(**c**) (*Cono Sur*: *persona que regatea*) haggler.
baratez *nf* (*Carib*), **baratía** *nf* (*And*) cheapness.
baratija *nf* trinket; (*Com*) cheap novelty; (*fig*) trifle; ~**s** (*Com*) cheap goods, inexpensive articles; ~**s** (*pey*) trash, junk.
baratillero *nm* seller of cheap goods.
baratillo *nm* (**a**) (*géneros*) secondhand goods; cheap goods.
(**b**) (*tienda*) secondhand shop, junkshop; (*sección de gangas*) bargain counter.
(**c**) (*saldo*) bargain sale; **cosa de** ~ tawdry thing, gimcrack article.
(**d**) (*Méx*) flea market.
barato 1 *adj* cheap; inexpensive, economical; **obtener algo de** ~ to get sth free; **dar algo de** ~ (*fig*) to concede sth, grant sth (for the sake of argument); **echar a** ~, **meter a** ~ to heckle, barrack, interrupt noisily.
2 *adv* cheap, cheaply; inexpensively.
3 *nm* (**a**) (*saldo*) bargain sale.
(**b**) (*en el juego*) money extracted from winning gamblers; **cobrar el** ~ (*fig*) to be a bully, wield power by intimidation.
baratón 1 *adj* (*And*, *CAm*, *Méx*) *argumento* weak, feeble; *comentario* well-worn, trite. **2** *nm* (*CAm*) (*ganga*) bargain; (*saldo*) sale.
baratura *nf* cheapness; inexpensiveness.
baraúnda *nf* = **barahúnda.**
barba 1 *nf* (**a**) (*mentón*) chin.
(**b**) (*pelos*) beard, whiskers (*t* ~**s**); ~ **cerrada**, ~ **bien poblada** thick beard, big beard; ~**s de chivo** goatee; ~ **honrada** distinguished personage; **a** ~ **regada** abundantly, fully; **decir algo en las** ~**s de uno** to say sth to sb's face; **robar algo en las** ~**s de uno** to steal sth from under sb's nose; **2 naranjas por** ~ 2 oranges apiece, 2 oranges per

head; **un hombre con toda la ~** a real man; **colgar ~s al santo** to give sb his due; **hacer la ~** to shave, have a shave; **hacer la ~ a uno** to shave sb; (*fig*) to pester sb, annoy sb; (*fig*) to fawn on sb, flatter sb; **llevar ~** to have a beard; **llevar a uno de la ~** to lead sb by the nose; **mentir por la ~** to tell a barefaced lie; **subirse a las ~s de uno** to be disrespectful to sb; **tener pocas ~s** to be green, be inexperienced; **tirarse de las ~s** to rage, tear one's hair.

(**c**) (*Orn*) wattle; **~ de ballena** whalebone.

(**d**) (*Bot*) beard.

2 *nm* (**a**) (*Teat*: *papel*) old man's part; (*actor*) performer of old men's parts; (*de melodrama*) villain.

(**b**) **~s*** guy*, bloke‡.

Barba Azul *nm* Bluebeard.

barbacana *nf* (*defensa*) barbican; (*tronera*) loophole, embrasure.

barbacoa *nf* (**a**) (*Culin*) barbecue; (*CAm, Carib, Méx*: *carne*) barbecued meat, meat.

(**b**) (*LAm*: *cama*) bed made with a hurdle supported on sticks.

(**c**) (*And*: *estante*) rack for kitchen utensils.

(**d**) (*And*: *desván*) loft.

(**e**) (*And Mús*) tap-dance.

Barbada *nf*: **la ~** Barbados.

barbado 1 *adj* bearded, with a beard. **2** *nm* (**a**) (*persona*) man with a beard; (*fig*: *adulto*) full-grown man. (**b**) (*Bot*) cutting (with roots); **plantar de ~** to transplant, plant out.

Barbados *nm* Barbados.

barbar [1a] *vi* (**a**) (*gen*) to grow a beard. (**b**) (*Bot*) to strike root.

Bárbara *nf* Barbara.

bárbaramente *adv* (**a**) (*cruelmente*) barbarously; cruelly, savagely. (**b**) (*) tremendously*; **pasarlo ~** to have a great time.

barbáricamente *adv* barbarically.

barbárico *adj* barbaric.

barbaridad *nf* (**a**) (*gen*) barbarity; barbarism; (*acto*) atrocity, outrage, barbarous act; **es capaz de hacer cualquier ~** he's capable of doing sth terrible.

(**b**) (*) **¡qué ~!** how awful!, shocking!

(**c**) **~es*** awful things, terrible things, naughty things; nonsense; **decir ~es** to say awful things; to talk nonsense.

(**d**) **una ~*** (*cantidad*) a huge amount, loads*, tons* (*de* of); **había una ~ de gente** there was an awful lot of people; **comimos una ~** we ate an awful lot; **cuesta una ~** it costs a fortune; **sabe una ~ de cosas** he knows a tremendous amount.

(**e**) **una ~** (*: *como adv*) a lot, lots; **nos gustó una ~** we liked it a lot; **me quiere una ~** he's terribly fond of me, he likes me awfully; **nos divertimos una ~** we had a tremendous time, we had a lot of fun; **habló una ~** he talked his head off; **se nota una ~** it sticks out a mile.

barbarie *nf* (**a**) (*gen*) barbarism, barbarousness. (**b**) (*crueldad*) barbarity, cruelty, savagery.

barbarismo *nm* (**a**) (*Ling*) barbarism. (**b**) = **barbarie**.

bárbaro 1 *adj* (**a**) (*Hist*) barbarian, barbarous.

(**b**) (*fig*: *cruel*) barbarous, cruel, savage; (*espantoso*) awful, frightful; (*inculto*) rough, uncouth; (*audaz*) bold, daring.

(**c**) (*: *estupendo*) tremendous*, terrific*, smashing*; **¡qué ~!** how marvellous!, terrific!*; how awful!; **un éxito ~** a tremendous success*; **es un tío ~** he's a great guy*, he's a splendid chap*; **hace un frío ~** it's terribly cold.

2 *adv* (*) marvellously; terrifically*; **lo pasamos ~** we had a tremendous time; **ella canta ~** she sings marvellously.

3 *interj* (*Cono Sur**) fine!, OK!*

4 *nm*, **bárbara** *nf* (**a**) (*lit*) barbarian.

(**b**) (*) rough sort, uncouth person; **conduce como un ~** he drives like a madman; **gritó como un ~** he gave a tremendous shout, he shouted like mad.

barbarote* *nm* brute, savage.

barbear [1a] **1** *vt* (**a**) (*LAm*: *afeitar*) to shave.

(**b**) (*CAm, Méx**) (*adular*) to fawn on, suck up to*; (*mimar*) to spoil.

(**c**) (*CAm*: *fastidiar*) to annoy, bore.

(**d**) (*LAm*) *ganado* to throw, fell.

(**e**) (*alcanzar*) to reach with one's chin, come up to, be as tall as.

(**f**) (*: *ver*) to see, spot.

(**g**) (*CAm**: *regañar*) to tell off.

2 *vi* (**a**) **~ con** = *vt* (**e**). (**b**) (*CAm**: *meterse*) to stick (*o* poke) one's nose in.

barbechar [1a] *vt* (**a**) (*dejar en barbecho*) to leave fallow.

(**b**) (*arar*) to plough for sowing.

barbechera *nf* fallow, fallow land.

barbecho *nm* (**a**) (*tierra*) fallow, fallow land; **estar en ~** (*Cono Sur*: *fig*) to be in preparation, be on its way; **firmar como en un ~** to sign without reading.

(**b**) (*tierra arada*) ploughed land ready for sowing.

(**c**) (*acto*) first ploughing.

barbería *nf* (**a**) (*tienda*) barber's (shop). (**b**) (*arte*) hairdressing.

barbero 1 *nm* (**a**) (*peluquero*) barber, hairdresser; **'El ~ de Sevilla'** 'The Barber of Seville'. (**b**) (*CAm, Méx**) flatterer. **2** *adj* (*CAm, Méx**: *adulador*) grovelling; *niño* affectionate, cuddly.

barbeta* *nmf* (*Cono Sur*) fool.

barbetear [1a] *vt* (*Méx*) *ganado* to throw, fell (by twisting the head of), throw to the ground.

barbicano *adj* grey-bearded, white-bearded.

barbihecho *adj* freshly shaven.

barbijo *nm* (**a**) (*And, Cono Sur*: *correa*) chinstrap; (*And, Carib, Cono Sur*: *pañuelo*) headscarf (knotted under the chin). (**b**) (*And, Cono Sur*: *cicatriz*) scar.

barbilampiño 1 *adj* (**a**) (*lit*) smooth-faced, beardless. (**b**) (*fig*: *novato*) inexperienced. **2** *nm* (*fig*) novice, greenhorn.

barbilindo *adj* dapper, spruce; (*pey*) dandified, foppish.

barbilla *nf* (tip of the) chin.

barbiponiente *adj* (**a**) (*lit*) beginning to grow a beard, with a youthful beard. (**b**) (*fig*: *novato*) raw, inexperienced, green.

barbiquejo *nm* (**a**) = **barbijo** (**a**). (**b**) (*Carib*: *bocal*) bit.

barbiturato *nm*, **barbitúrico** *nm* barbiturate.

barbo *nm* barbel; **~ de mar** red mullet.

barbón *nm* (**a**) (*persona*) bearded man, man with a (big) beard; (*fig*) greybeard, old hand. (**b**) (*Zool*) billy-goat.

barbot(e)ar [1a] *vti* to mutter, mumble.

barboteo *nm* mutter, muttering, mumbling.

barbudo *adj* bearded; having a big beard, long-bearded.

barbulla *nf* clamour, hullabaloo.

barbullar [1a] *vi* to jabber away, talk noisily.

barca *nf* boat, small boat; **~ de pasaje** ferry; **~ de pesca, ~ pesquera** fishing boat.

Barça *nm*: (**el**) **~** Barcelona Football Club.

barcada *nf* (**a**) (*carga*) boatload. (**b**) (*viaje*) boat trip; (*travesía*) crossing (by ferry).

barcaje *nm* toll.

barcarola *nf* barcarole.

barcaza *nf* barge, lighter; ferry; **~ de desembarco** (*Mil*) landing-craft.

Barcelona *nf* Barcelona.

barcelonés 1 *adj* of Barcelona. **2** *nm*, **barcelonesa** *nf* native (*o* inhabitant) of Barcelona; **los barceloneses** the people of Barcelona.

barcia *nf* chaff.

barcino *adj* reddish-grey.

barco *nm* (*gen*) boat; (*navío*) ship, vessel; **~ de apoyo** support ship; **~ cablero** cable-ship; **~ carbonero, ~ minero** collier; **~ de carga** cargo boat; **~ contenedor** container ship; **~ de guerra** warship; **~ meteorológico** weather-ship; **~ náufrago** wreck; **~ patrullero** patrol-boat; **~ de vela** sailing-ship; **~ vivienda** houseboat; **abandonar el ~** to abandon ship; **ir en ~** to go by boat, go by ship; **como ~ sin timón** irresolute(ly), lacking a firm purpose.

barco-madre *nm, pl* **barcos-madre** mother ship.

barchilón *nm*, **barchilona** *nf* (*And*: *enfermero*) nurse, hospital aide; (*And, Cono Sur*: *curandero*) quack doctor, quack surgeon.

barda *nf* (**a**) protective covering on a wall; (*Méx*) high hedge, fence, wall; **~s** top of a wall, walls. (**b**) (‡) jacket.

bardal *nm* wall topped with brushwood *etc*.

bardana *nf* burdock.

bardar [1a] *vt* to thatch.

bardo *nm* bard.

baré *nm* (*Esp*‡) 5-peseta coin.

baremar [1a] *vt* to calculate, reckon; to measure.

baremo *nm* (*Mat*) table(s); ready-reckoner; (*fig*) scale, schedule; yardstick, gauge, criterion; set of norms, basis for comparison.

bareo* *nm*: **ir de ~** to go drinking, go pub-crawling*.

barillero *nm* (*Méx*) hawker, street vendor.

bario *nm* barium.

barítono *nm* baritone.

barjuleta *nf* knapsack.

barloventear [1a] *vi* (**a**) (*Náut*) to tack; to beat to windward. (**b**) (*fig*: *vagar*) to wander about.

Barlovento: **Islas** *nfpl* **de ~** Windward Isles.

barlovento *nm* windward; **a ~** to windward; **de ~** windward (*atr*); **ganar el ~ a** to get to windward of.
barman *nm*, *pl* **barmans, bármanes, barmen** barman, bartender.
Barna. *abr de* **Barcelona**.
barniz *nm* (**a**) (*gen*) varnish; (*Aer*) dope; (*en cerámica*) glaze; (*en metal etc*) gloss, polish; **~ para las uñas** nail varnish, nail polish; **dar de ~ a** to varnish.
(**b**) (*fig*: *cualidad superficial*) gloss, veneer; smattering, superficial knowledge.
barnizado *nm* varnish, varnishing.
barnizar [1f] *vt* to varnish; to glaze; to polish, put a gloss on.
baró *nm* (*Esp*‡) 5-peseta coin.
barométrico *adj* barometric.
barómetro *nm* barometer; **~ aneroide** aneroid barometer.
barón *nm* (**a**) (*título*) baron; (*: *Pol etc*) chief, influential member (*etc*), high-up*.
(**b**) (*Carib**) pal*, buddy (*US*).
baronesa *nf* baroness.
baronía *nf* barony.
baronial *adj* baronial.
barquero *nm* boatman; ferryman, waterman.
barquía *nf* skiff, rowing boat.
barquilla *nf* (**a**) (*Aer*: *de globo*) basket; (*de aeronave*) gondola, nacelle, car. (**b**) (*Náut*) log. (**c**) (*Carib*: *helado*) ice-cream cornet, cone.
barquillo *nm* (*Culin*) horn, rolled wafer; (*helado*) ice-cream cornet, cone.
barquinazo *nm* (*caída*) tumble, hard fall; spill; (*Aut etc*) bump, jolt; (*And*) sudden start.
barra *nf* (**a**) (*gen*) bar; rail, railing; (*en un bar*) bar, counter; (*Mec*) rod; lever; (*pan*) French bread; (*de jabón*) bar, stick; (*de metal*) bar, ingot; **~ americana** singles bar; (**la bandera de**) **las ~s y estrellas** the Stars and Stripes; **~ antivuelco, ~ estabilizadora** anti-roll bar; **~ de carmín, ~ de labios** lipstick; **~ de chocolate** (*Cono Sur*) bar of chocolate; **~ de cortina** curtain rod; **~ de equilibrio**(**s**) beam; **~ de espaciado, ~ espaciadora** space-bar, spacing-bar; **~ fija** fixed bar; **~ libre** free bar, drinks on the house; **~s paralelas** parallel bars; **a ~s derechas** honestly; **no pararse en ~s** to stop at nothing.
(**b**) (*Her*) stripe, bar; (*Tip*: *t* **~ oblicua**) oblique stroke, slash (*US*); **~ inversa** backslash.
(**c**) (*Náut*) bar, sandbank.
(**d**) (*Jur*) bar, rail; (*aprox*) dock; **la B~** (*Méx*) the Bar, the legal profession; **llevar a uno a la ~** to bring sb to justice.
(**e**) (*LAm*: *público, Jur etc*) public, members of the public; (*Cono Sur*: *público*) spectators, audience; (*Dep*) fans, supporters; **había mucha ~** there was a big audience.
(**f**) (*Cono Sur*: *pandilla*) band, gang; (*camarilla*) clique, coterie.
(**g**) (*Carib, Cono Sur, Méx*: *ría*) river mouth, estuary.
Barrabás *nm* Barrabas; **ser un ~** to be wicked, (*niño*) be mischievous, be naughty.
barrabasada *nf* mischief; outrage, excess; dirty trick.
barraca[1] *nf* (**a**) (*cabaña*) hut, cabin; (*de obreros*) workmen's hut; (*moderna, de ciudad*) shanty, hovel; (*Valencia*) thatched farmhouse; **~s** (*Méx*) shanty town.
(**b**) (*de feria*) booth, stall; **~ persa** (*Cono Sur*) cut-price store; **~ de tiro al blanco** shooting-gallery.
(**c**) (*LAm*: *depósito*) large storage shed; (*And*: *de mercado*) market stall.
(**d**) **creerse algo a la ~** to believe sth implicitly.
barraca[2] *nf* (*LAm Mil*) barracks.
barracón *nm* (**a**) (*caseta*) big hut; (*Carib Agr*) farmworkers' living quarters.
(**b**) (*de feria*) large booth, stall; side show; **~ de espejos, ~ de la risa** hall of mirrors.
barracuda *nf* barracuda.
barragana *nf* official mistress, concubine; (††) morganatic wife.
barrajes *nmpl* (*And*) shanty-town.
barranca *nf* gully, ravine.
barrancal *nm* place full of ravines.
barranco *nm* (**a**) (*Geog*) gully, ravine. (**b**) (*LAm*) (*despeñadero*) cliff; (*de río*) steep riverbank. (**c**) (*fig*: *obstáculo*) difficulty, obstacle.
barraquismo *nm* phenomenon of shanty towns, shanty town problem.
barrar [1a] *vt* to daub, smear (*de* with).
barreal *nm* (*Cono Sur*: *tierra*) heavy clay land; (*CAm*: *pantano*) bog.
barrear [1a] *vt* to barricade, fortify; to bar, fasten with a bar.
barredera *nf* (*persona*) street sweeper; (*Aut*) street-cleaning vehicle; **~ de alfombras, ~ mecánica** carpet sweeper.
barredor *nm*: **~ de frecuencia** frequency sweeper.
barredura *nf* (**a**) (*gen*) sweep, sweeping. (**b**) **~s** sweepings; rubbish, refuse.
barreminas *nm invar* minesweeper.
barrena *nf* (**a**) (*taladro*) drill, auger; bit; (*Min*) rock drill, mining drill; **~ de mano, ~ pequeña** gimlet. (**b**) (*Aer*) spin; **entrar en ~** to go into a spin.
barrenado* *adj*: **estar ~** to be dotty*.
barrenar [1a] *vt* (**a**) (*gen*) to drill, drill through, bore; *roca* to blast; *barco* to scuttle.
(**b**) (*fig*: *frustrar*) to foil, frustrate; (*) to make a mess of; (*Jur*) to violate, infringe.
barrendero, -a *nm/f* sweeper.
barrenillo *nm* (**a**) (*Zool*) borer. (**b**) (*Carib*: *empeño*) foolish persistence; (*Cono Sur, Méx*) (*preocupación*) constant worry; (*manía*) mania, pet idea.
barreno *nm* (**a**) (*Téc*: *instrumento*) large drill, borer.
(**b**) (*perforación*) bore, borehole; **dar ~ a un barco** to scuttle a ship.
(**c**) (*fig*: *vanidad*) vanity, pride.
(**d**) (*Cono Sur, Méx*) (*preocupación*) constant worry; (*manía*) mania, pet idea.
barreño *nm* washing-up basin.
barrer [1a] **1** *vt* (**a**) (*gen*) to sweep; to sweep clean, sweep out, sweep away.
(**b**) (*Mil, Náut*) to sweep (with gunfire); **~ la mente**‡ to blow one's mind‡.
(**c**) (*fig*) *obstáculos etc* to sweep aside, sweep away; *dudas* to dispel; (*And*: *derrotar*) to beat, overwhelm; **los candidatos del partido barrieron a sus adversarios** the party's candidates swept aside their rivals.
2 *vi* (**a**) **comprar algo al ~** (*Cono Sur*) to buy sth in a job lot.
(**b**) **~ hacia dentro*** to look after Number One.
3 barrerse *vr* (**a**) (*Méx*: *caballo*) to shy, start.
(**b**) (*Méx**: *humillarse*) to grovel.
barrera[1] *nf* (**a**) (*barra*) barrier; rail, bar; (*Mil etc*) barricade; (††, *Mil*) parapet; (*Ferro*) barrier, crossing gate; (*Taur*) barrier, fence round the inside of the bullring; first row of seats; (*Dep*: *de jugadores*) wall; **~ aduanera** customs barrier; **~ arancelaria** tariff barrier; **~ de color** colour bar; **~ comercial** trade barrier; **~ de contención** containing wall; **~ coralina** coral reef; **~ generacional** generation gap; **~ de peaje, ~ de portazgo** tollgate, turnpike; **~ protectora, ~ de seguridad** safety barrier; **~ racial** racial bar, colour bar; **~ del sonido** sound barrier; **poner ~s a** to hinder.
(**b**) (*Mil*: *t* **~ de fuego**) barrage; **~ de fuego móvil** creeping barrage.
(**c**) (*fig*: *impedimento*) barrier, bar; obstacle; hindrance.
barrera[2] *nf* claypit.
barrero 1 *adj* (*Cono Sur*) *caballo* that likes heavy going.
2 *nm* (*tierra fangosa*) muddy ground; (*And, Cono Sur*: *saladar*) salt marsh.
bar-restaurante *nm* bar-cum-restaurant.
barretina *nf* Catalan cap.
barriada *nf* quarter, district; (*LAm*: *barrio pobre*) shanty-town; slum quarter.
barrial *nm* (**a**) (*Méx*: *tierra*) heavy clay land. (**b**) (*LAm*: *pantano*) bog.
barrica *nf* large barrel, cask.
barricada *nf* barricade.
barrida *nf* (*LAm*) (*acto*) sweep, sweeping; (*de policía*) sweep, raid; (*en elección*) landslide.
barrido *nm* sweep, sweeping; (*Elec*) scan, sweep; **vale** (*o* **sirve**) **tanto para un ~ como para un fregado** he can turn his hand to anything.
barriga *nf* (**a**) (*Anat*) belly; paunch, guts; **echar ~** to get middle-age spread; **la cerveza echa ~** beer makes you fat; **hacer una ~ a una*** to get a girl in the family way; **llenarse la ~** to stuff o.s*; **rascarse** (*o* **tocarse**) **la ~**‡ to do damn-all‡, be idle; **tener ~*** to be in the family way.
(**b**) (*de jarra*) belly, rounded part; (*de muro*) bulge.
barrigón 1 *adj* fat, potbellied. **2** *nm*, **barrigona** *nf* (*And, Carib**) child, kid*.
barrigudo *adj* fat, potbellied.
barriguera *nf* (horse's) girth.
barril *nm* (**a**) (*tonel*) barrel; cask, keg; **cerveza de ~** draught beer, beer on draught; **~ de petróleo** barrel of

oil; ~ **de pólvora** (*fig*) powder-keg; **comer del** ~ (*And*) to eat poor-quality food.
(**b**) (*LAm*: *cometa hexagonal*) hexagonal kite.
barrila* *nf* row, to-do; **dar la** ~ to kick up a fuss.
barrilería *nf* (**a**) (*almacén*) barrel store. (**b**) (*tienda, taller*) cooper's shop. (**c**) (*arte*) cooperage.
barrilero *nm* cooper.
barrilete 1 *nm* (**a**) (*barril*) keg.
(**b**) (*Téc*) dog, clamp.
(**c**) (*de revólver*) chamber.
(**d**) (*Méx Jur*) junior barrister.
(**e**) (*Cono Sur*: *cometa*) kite.
2 *nf* (*Cono Sur*) restless woman.
barrilla *nf* (*Bot, Quím*) barilla, saltwort.
barrillo *nm* blackhead, pimple.
barrio *nm* quarter, district, area (of a town); suburb; (*LAm*) slum quarter, shanty-town; **el otro** ~* the next world; **irse al otro** ~‡ to snuff it‡; **mandar a uno al otro** ~‡ to do sb in‡; ~**s bajos** poorer quarter, working-class district, (*pey*) slums, slum area; ~ **bruja** (*And*) shanty-town; ~ **de los calvos*** graveyard; ~ **comercial** business quarter; shopping district; ~ **chino** (*Esp*) red-light district; ~ **dormitorio** commuter suburb; ~ **exterior** outer suburb; ~ **latino** Latin quarter; ~ **miseria** slum quarter, shanty-town; ~ **residencial** residential area; ~ **de tolerancia** (*And*) red-light district.
barriobajero *adj* slum (*atr*); (*fig*) vulgar, coarse, common.
barrisco: **a** ~ *adv* jumbled together, in confusion; indiscriminately.
barritar [1a] *vi* (*elefante*) to trumpet.
barrito *nm* trumpeting.
barrizal *nm* muddy place, mire.
barro *nm* (**a**) (*lodo*) mud.
(**b**) (*arcilla*) clay, potter's clay; ~ **cocido** baked clay; **vasija de** ~ earthen vessel, earthenware vessel.
(**c**) (*vasija*) earthenware pot; mug (for beer *etc*); ~**s** earthenware, crockery.
(**d**) (‡: *dinero*) dough‡, brass*; **tener** ~ **a mano** to be in the money.
(**e**) (*Cono Sur*‡: *plancha*) clanger‡; **hacer un** ~ to drop a clanger‡.
(**f**) (*Anat*) pimple.
barroco 1 *adj* baroque (*t fig*). **2** *nm* baroque (style); baroque period.
barroquismo *nm* baroque (style); baroque taste.
barroso *adj* (**a**) (*lodoso*) muddy. (**b**) (*de color*) mud-coloured; *vaca* reddish, brownish, (*CAm*: *blancuzco*) off-white. (**c**) (*Anat*) pimply.
barrote *nm* heavy bar, thick bar; crosspiece; (*de silla etc*) rung.
barruntar [1a] *vt y* **barruntarse** *vr* to sense, feel; to guess, conjecture; to suspect; ~ **que ...** to sense that ..., have a feeling that ...
barrunte *nm* sign, indication.
barrunto *nm* (**a**) (*conjetura*) guess, conjecture; (*indicio*) sign, indication; (*sospecha*) suspicion; (*presentimiento*) foreboding. (**b**) (*Carib, Méx*: *Met*) north wind which brings rain.
Barsa *nm* = **Barça**.
bartola *nf*: **echarse** (*o* **tenderse, tumbarse**) **a la** ~ to be lazy, take it easy; to do nothing.
bartolear [1a] *vi* (*Cono Sur*) to be lazy, take it easy.
bartolina *nf* (*CAm, Carib, Méx*) jail.
Bartolo *nm forma familiar de* **Bartolomé**.
bartolo* *adj* (*Méx*) thick*, stupid.
Bartolomé *nm* Bartholomew.
bartulear [1a] *vi* (*Cono Sur*) to think hard, rack one's brains.
bártulos *nmpl* things, belongings, gear; goods; (*Téc*) tools; **liar los** ~ to pack up one's belongings; (‡) to peg out‡; **preparar los** ~ to get ready (to go).
barucho* *nm* seedy bar.
barullento *adj* (*Cono Sur*) noisy, rowdy.
barullo *nm* (**a**) (*alboroto*) row, uproar, din; confusion. (**b**) **a** ~* in abundance, by the ton*.
barzón *nm* saunter, stroll; **dar** ~**es** to stroll around.
barzonear [1a] *vi* to stroll around, wander about.
basa *nf* (**a**) (*Arquit*) base (of a column). (**b**) (*fig*: *base*) basis, foundation.
basalto *nm* basalt.
basamentar [1a] *vt* = **basar**.
basamento *nm* (*Arquit*) base.
basar [1a] **1** *vt* to base; (*fig*) to base, found, ground (*sobre* on). **2 basarse** *vr*: ~ **en** (**a**) to be based on, rest on. (**b**) (*fig*) to base o.s. on, rely on.
basca *nf* (*frec* ~**s**) (**a**) (*Med*) nausea, queasy feeling, sick feeling; **dar** ~**s a uno** to make sb feel sick, turn sb's stomach; **le entraron** ~**s, tuvo una** ~ he felt nauseated, he felt sick.
(**b**) (*fig*: *rabieta*) fit of rage, tantrum.
(**c**) (*) (*grupo*) group, set of people; (*gentío*) mob; (*pandilla*) gang; (*séquito*) followers; **toda la** ~ every last one of them.
(**d**) **le dio la** ~ (*impulso*) he had a sudden urge.
bascosidad *nf* (**a**) (*porquería*) filth, dirt. (**b**) (*And*: *obscenidad*) obscenity.
bascoso *adj* (**a**) (*delicado*) squeamish, easily upset; (*Med*) queasy. (**b**) (*And*: *vomitivo*) nauseating, sickening; (*obsceno*) obscene; *persona* vile, disgusting.
báscula *nf* (platform) scales, weighing machine; (*romana*) steelyard; ~ **de baño** bathroom scales; ~ **biestable** flip-flop, toggle; ~ **de puente** weighbridge.
basculable *adj* (*Aut etc*) *luz* directional, with swinging beam.
basculante *nm* tip-up lorry, dump truck (*US*).
báscula-puente *nf* weighbridge.
bascular [1a] *vi* (*inclinarse*) to tilt, tip up; (*columpiarse*) to seesaw; (*mecerse*) to rock to and fro; (*Pol etc*) to swing; (*Inform*) to toggle.
base 1 *nf* (**a**) (*Arquit*) base; (*Téc*) base, mounting, bed; (*Agrimen*) base, base line; ~ **de maquillaje** make-up foundation.
(**b**) (*Mil*) base; ~ **aérea** air base; ~ **aeronaval** naval air base; ~ **avanzada** forward base; ~ **espacial** space-station; ~ **naval** naval base.
(**c**) (*Béisbol*) base.
(**d**) (*fig*: *fundamento*) basis, foundation; ~ **derivativa** (*Ling*) base form; ~ **imponible** taxable income; ~ **de poder** power base; **a** ~ **de** on the basis of; by means of; **a** ~ **de no hacer nada** by doing nothing; with the idea of not doing anything; **a** ~ **de 50 toneladas al año** on a basis of 50 tons a year, at 50 tons a year; **a** ~ **de bien*** (*adj*) really good, (*adv*) really well, loads*; **en** ~ **a** (*como prep*) with regard to; with a view to; **en** ~ **a** + *infin* with a view to + *ger*; **en** ~ **a que ...** (*como conj*) in view of the fact that ..., bearing in mind that ...; **coger a uno fuera de** ~ (*CAm, Carib*: *fig*) to catch sb out; **partir de una** ~ **falsa** to start from a false assumption; **sentar las** ~**s de** to do the groundwork for, lay the foundations of.
(**e**) (*Inform, Mat*) base; ~ **de datos** database; ~ **de datos relacional** relational database; ~ **de conocimientos** knowledge base.
(**f**) (*de concurso*) ~**s** conditions, rules.
(**g**) (*Pol*) rank and file, ordinary members; **militante de** ~ rank-and-file member; **opinión de** ~ grass-roots opinion, rank-and-file opinion.
(**h**) (‡: *droga*) crack, cocaine.
2 *nm* (*Dep*) base.
3 *adj* basic, base (*atr*); **color** ~ basic colour; **salario** ~ basic wage, wage taken as a base.
baseballista *nmf* (*LAm*) baseball player.
basebolero 1 *adj* (*Carib*) baseball (*atr*). **2** *nm*, **basebolera** *nf* (*Carib*) baseball player.
básica *nf* = **EGB**.
básico *adj* basic (*t Quím*).
Basilea *nf* Basle, Basel, Bâle.
basílica *nf* basilica.
basilisco *nm* (*Mit*) basilisk; (*Méx*) iguana; **estar hecho un** ~ to be terribly angry; **ponerse como un** ~ to get terribly angry.
básket *nm* basketball.
basquear [1a] *vi* to be nauseated, feel sick; **hacer** ~ **a uno** to make sb feel sick, turn sb's stomach.
básquet *nm*, **básquetbol** *nm* basketball.
basquetbolero 1 *adj* (*LAm*) basketball (*atr*). **2** *nm*, **basquetbolera** *nf* (*LAm*) basketball player.
basquetbolista *nmf* (*LAm*) basketball player.
basquetbolístico *adj* (*LAm*) basketball (*atr*).
basquiña *nf* skirt.
basta *nf* tacking stitch, basting stitch.
bastante 1 *adj* (**a**) enough, sufficient (*para* for; *para* + *infin* to + *infin*).
(**b**) (*LAm*) (*demasiado*) too much, more than enough; **toma** ~ take plenty.
2 *adv* (**a**) (*gen*) enough, sufficiently; ~ **grande** big enough, sufficiently large; **es** ~ **alto** (**como**) **para alcanzarlo** he's tall enough to reach it.
(**b**) (*en parte pey*) ~ **bueno** fairly good, quite good, ra-

ther good, goodish.

(**c**) (*muy*) very, really; **estoy ~ cansado** I'm really tired.

bastantemente *adv* sufficiently.

bastar [1a] **1** *vti* to be enough, be sufficient, suffice; **¡basta!** that's enough!, that will do!, stop now!; **¡basta ya!** that's quite enough of that!; **basta y sobra** that's more than enough; **con eso basta** that's enough; **eso me basta** that's enough for me; **basta decir que** ... suffice it to say that ...; **nos basta saber que** ... it is enough for us to know that ...; **~ a** + *infin*, **~ para** + *infin* to be enough to + *infin*, be sufficient to + *infin*.

2 bastarse *vr*: **~ a sí mismo** to be self-sufficient.

bastardear [1a] **1** *vt* to debase; to adulterate. **2** *vi* (*Bot*) to degenerate; (*fig*) to degenerate, fall away (*de* from).

bastardía *nf* (**a**) (*calidad*) bastardy. (**b**) (*fig*: *bajeza*) meanness, baseness; wicked thing.

bastardilla *nf* (*t* **letra ~**) italic type, italics; **en ~** in italics; **poner en ~** to italicize.

bastardo 1 *adj* (**a**) (*gen*) bastard. (**b**) (*fig*: *vil*) mean, base. (**c**) (*fig*: *híbrido*) hybrid, mixed. **2** *nm*, **bastarda** *nf* bastard.

bastear [1a] *vt* to tack, stitch loosely.

bastero, -a *nm/f* (*Méx*) pickpocket.

bastes‡ *nmpl* (*Esp*) dabs‡, fingers.

bastez *nf* coarseness, vulgarity.

bastidor *nm* (**a**) (*Téc, Cos etc*) frame, framework; (*de ventana*) frame, case; (*de lienzo*) stretcher; (*de vehículo*) chassis; (*And, Cono Sur*: *ventana*) lattice window; (*Carib*: *catre*) metal bedstead; (*Carib, Méx*: *colchón*) interior sprung mattress.

(**b**) (*Teat*) wing; **entre ~es** behind the scenes (*t fig*); **estar entre ~es** to be offstage; **dirigirlo entre ~es** to pull strings, work the oracle.

bastilla *nf* hem.

bastillar [1a] *vt* to hem.

bastimentar [1a] *vt* to supply, provision.

bastimento *nm* (**a**) (*provisiones*) supply (of provisions). (**b**) (*Náut*) vessel.

bastión *nm* bastion, bulwark.

basto[1] 1 *adj* (*tosco*) coarse, rough; (*grosero*) rude, uncouth. **2** *nm* packsaddle; (*LAm*: *t* **~s**) soft leather pad (*used under the saddle*).

basto[2] *nm* (*Cartas*) ace of clubs; **~s** clubs; **pintan ~s** (*fig*) things are getting tough, the going is getting rough.

bastón *nm* stick; staff; walking stick; (*porra*) truncheon; (*Mil etc*) baton; (*Her*) vertical bar, pallet; (*fig*) control, command; **~ alpino, ~ de alpinista, ~ de montaña** alpenstock; **~ de estoque** swordstick; **~ de mando** baton, sign of authority; **empuñar el ~** to take command; **meter el ~** to intervene.

bastonazo *nm* (*golpe*) blow with a stick; (*paliza*) beating, caning.

bastonear [1a] *vt* to beat (with a stick), hit (with a stick).

bastonera *nf* umbrella stand.

bastonero *nm* (**a**) (*de bailes*) master of ceremonies (*at a dance*). (**b**) (*Carib*) scoundrel, tough*.

bastón-taburete *nm* shooting stick.

basuco* *nm* unpurified cocaine.

basura *nf* (**a**) (*gen*) rubbish, refuse, garbage (*US*); litter; dust; (*Agr*) dung, manure; **~ radioactiva** radioactive waste.

(**b**) (*fig*) trash, rubbish; **la novela es una ~** the novel is rubbish; **él es una ~*** he's a shocker*, he's a rotter*.

basural *nm* (*LAm*) rubbish dump.

basurear [1a] *vt*: **~ a uno** (*Cono Sur*) to push sb along; (*fig*) (*humillar*) to humiliate sb; (*insultar*) to be rude to sb, rubbish sb*.

basurero *nm* (**a**) (*persona*) dustman, garbage man (*US*); scavenger. (**b**) (*vertedero*) rubbish dump; (*Agr*) dung heap. (**c**) (*recipiente*) dustbin, trashcan (*US*).

basuriento *adj* (*And, Cono Sur*) dirty, full of rubbish.

Basutolandia *nf* (*Hist*) Basutoland.

bata[1] *nf* dressing gown; (*de trabajo, de estar por casa*) housecoat, smock; (*salto de cama*) negligée; (*de playa*) beachwrap; (*de laboratorio etc*) white coat, laboratory coat; **~ blanca** white coat.

bata[2]‡ *nf* mother.

batacazo *nm* (**a**) (*gen*) bump, thump; (*caída*) heavy fall. (**b**) (*fig*: *chiripa*) stroke of luck, fluke; unexpected win.

bataclán *nm* (*LAm*) burlesque show (*US*), striptease show.

bataclana *nf* (*LAm*) striptease girl, stripper.

batahola* *nf* (*ruido*) din, hullabaloo*; (*jaleo*) rumpus*.

bataholear [1a] *vi*, **batajolear** [1a] *vi* (*And*) (*pelear*) to brawl; (*ser travieso*) to be mischievous, play pranks.

batalla *nf* (**a**) (*Mil*) battle; (*fig*) battle, fight, struggle; (*fig*) inner struggle, agitation (of mind); **~ campal** pitched battle; **ropa de ~** everyday clothes, clothes not kept for best; **librar ~** to do battle; **trabar ~** to join battle.

(**b**) (*Arte*) battle piece, battle scene.

(**c**) (*Aut etc*) wheelbase.

batallador 1 *adj* battling, fighting; warlike. **2** *nm*, **batalladora** *nf* battler, fighter; (*Dep*) fencer.

batallar [1a] *vi* (**a**) (*luchar*) to battle, fight, struggle (*con* with, against; *por* about, over); (*Dep*) to fence. (**b**) (*fig*: *vacilar*) to waver, vacillate.

batallita* *nf*: **contar ~s** to shoot a line*.

batallón 1 *adj*: **cuestión batallona** vexed question. **2** *nm* battalion; **~ de castigo, ~ disciplinario** punishment squad.

batán *nm* (**a**) (*lugar*) fulling mill; (*herramienta*) fulling hammer. (**b**) (*Cono Sur*: *tintorería*) dry cleaner's. (**c**) (*And*: *espesura de tela*) thickness (*of cloth*).

batanar [1a] *vt* (**a**) (*Téc*) to full. (**b**) (*) to beat, thrash.

batanear* [1a] *vt* (*pegar*) to beat, thrash; (*sacudir*) to shake.

batanero *nm* fuller.

bataola *nf* = **batahola**.

batata 1 *nf* (**a**) (*Bot*) sweet potato, yam.

(**b**) (*And, Carib*: *pantorrilla*) calf (of the leg).

(**c**) (*Cono Sur*: *tímidez*) bashfulness, embarrassment.

(**d**) (*Cono Sur**: *coche*) car.

2 *adj* (**a**) (*Cono Sur*: *tímido*) bashful, shy, embarrassed.

(**b**) (*Carib, Cono Sur*: *simple*) simple, gullible.

(**c**) (*Carib*) (*llenito*) chubby, plump; (*rechoncho*) squat.

batatar *nm* (*LAm*) sweet potato field.

batatazo *nm* (*LAm*) = **batacazo**.

batayola *nf* (*Náut*) rail.

bate *nm* (*esp LAm*) (baseball) bat; **estar al ~ de algo** (*CAm, Carib*) to be in charge of sth.

batea *nf* (**a**) (*bandeja*) tray; small trough; round trough; (*de lavar*) washtub; (*Min*) washing pan. (**b**) (*Ferro*) flat car, low wagon. (**c**) (*Náut*) flat-bottomed boat, punt.

bateador *nm* (*esp LAm*) batter.

batear [1a] **1** *vt* (*esp LAm*) to hit. **2** *vi* (**a**) (*esp LAm Dep*) to bat. (**b**) (*Carib**: *tragar*) to overeat.

batel *nm* small boat, skiff.

batelero *nm* boatman.

batelón *nm* (*And*) canoe.

batería 1 *nf* (**a**) (*Mil, Elec, para gallinas*) battery; (*de luces*) bank, battery, set; (*Teat*) footlights; (*Mús*) percussion, drums; **~ de cocina** kitchen utensils, pots and pans; **~ seca** dry battery; **aparcar en ~** (*Aut*) to park square on (*o* obliquely) to the kerb; **(re)cargar las ~s** (*fig*) to recharge one's batteries.

(**b**) (*And*: *ronda de bebidas*) round of drinks.

(**c**) (*LAm Béisbol*) hit, stroke.

(**d**) (*Méx*) **dar ~*** to keep at it; **dar ~ a*** to make trouble for, make a lot of work for.

2 *nmf* (*persona*) drummer.

baterista *nmf* (*LAm*) drummer.

batey *nm* (*Carib*) clearing in front of a country house, forecourt.

batiburrillo *nm* hotchpotch.

baticola *nf* (*de montura*) crupper; (*And*: *taparrabo*) loincloth; (*Cono Sur*: *pañal*) nappy, diaper (*US*).

batida *nf* (**a**) (*Caza*) battue; (*Mil*) reconnaissance; (*And, Cono Sur*: *redada*) raid (by the police); (*fig*: *registro*) search; combing; (*And*: *persecución*) chase. (**b**) (*And, Carib*: *paliza*) beating, thrashing.

batido 1 *adj* (**a**) *camino* well-trodden, beaten. (**b**) *seda* shot, chatoyant. **2** *nm* (*Culin*) batter; **~ (de leche)** milk-shake.

batidor *nm* (**a**) (*Caza, Téc*) beater; (*Mil*) scout. (**b**) (*herramienta*) beater; (*peine*) wide-toothed comb; (*Culin*) beater, whisk, mixer; (*CAm, Méx*: *vasija*) wooden bowl, mixing bowl. (**c**) (*Cono Sur*: *delator*) informer.

batidora *nf* (*Culin*) beater, whisk, mixer; (*Téc*) beater; **~ eléctrica** electric mixer.

batiente *nm* (**a**) (*marco de puerta*) jamb; (*marco de ventana*) frame, case; (*hoja de puerta*) leaf, panel. (**b**) (*Mús*) damper. (**c**) (*Náut*) open coastline.

batifondo *nm* (*Cono Sur*) uproar, din.

batín *nm* (*bata*) (man's) dressing gown; (*chaqueta*) smoking jacket; (*de playa*) beach-wrap.

batintín *nm* gong.

batir [3a] **1** *vt* (**a**) (*gen*) to beat; (*martillear*) to hammer, pound (on); *tambor, metal* to beat; *moneda* to mint; *alas* to beat, flap; *manos* to clap; *pelo* to back-comb.

(**b**) *casa* to knock down; *muro etc* (*Mil*) to batter down;

tienda to take down; *privilegio* to do away with.

(**c**) (*mar*) to beat on, dash against; (*sol*) to beat down on; (*viento*) to sweep.

(**d**) (*Culin*) to beat, mix, whisk; to stir, churn; *mantequilla* to cream; *nata* to whip.

(**e**) (*Caza*) to beat; to comb, search; (*Mil*) to reconnoitre.

(**f**) *adversario, enemigo* to beat, defeat; *récord* to beat.

(**g**) (*And*) *ropa* to rinse (out).

(**h**) (*Cono Sur*: *denunciar*) to inform on.

2 *vi* (*Med*) to beat violently.

3 batirse *vr* to fight, have a fight; ~ **con uno** to fight sb; ~ **en duelo** to fight a duel.

batista *nf* cambric, batiste.

bato[1] *nm* simpleton.

bato[2]‡ *nm* father.

batonista *nf* drum majorette.

batracio *nm* batrachian.

Batuecas *nfpl*: **las** ~ *backward region of Extremadura, equivalent to* the backwoods, the hillbilly country; **estar en las** ~ (*fig*) to be daydreaming.

batueco* *adj* stupid, silly.

batuque *nm* (*Cono Sur*) rumpus, racket.

batuquear [1a] *vt* (*CAm*) to pester, annoy.

baturrillo *nm* hotchpotch.

baturro 1 *adj* uncouth, rough. **2** *nm*, **baturra** *nf* Aragonese peasant.

batusino, -a *nm/f* idiot, fool.

batuta *nf* (*Mús*) baton; **llevar la** ~ (*fig*) to be the boss, be firmly in command.

baudio *nm* baud.

baúl *nm* (**a**) (*gen*) trunk; ~ **armario,** ~ **ropero** wardrobe trunk; ~ **camarote** cabin trunk; ~ **mundo** large trunk, Saratoga trunk; ~ **de viaje** portmanteau.

(**b**) (*Aut*) boot, trunk (*US*).

(**c**) (*: *vientre*) belly.

bauprés *nm* bowsprit.

bausa *nf* (*And, Méx*) laziness, idleness.

bausán *nm*, **bausana** *nf* (*lit*) dummy; (*fig*) simpleton; (*And*: *holgazán*) good-for-nothing.

bausano *nm* (*CAm*) idler, lazy person.

bauseador *nm* (*And*) idler, lazy person.

bautismal *adj* baptismal.

bautismo *nm* (**a**) (*Rel*) baptism, christening; ~ **de fuego** baptism of fire. (**b**) **romper el** ~ **a uno**‡ to knock sb's block off‡.

Bautista *nm*: **el** ~, **San Juan** ~ St John the Baptist.

bautista *adj*: **Iglesia B**~ Baptist Church.

bautizar [1f] *vt* (**a**) (*Rel*) to baptize, christen; **le bautizaron con el nombre de Wamba** he was baptized Wamba.

(**b**) (*fig*: *nombrar*) to christen, name, give a name to.

(**c**) (*) *vino* to water (down), dilute; *persona* to drench, soak.

bautizo *nm* (**a**) (*acto*) baptism, christening. (**b**) (*fiesta*) christening party.

bauxita *nf* bauxite.

bávaro, -a *adj, nm/f* Bavarian.

Baviera *nf* Bavaria.

baya *nf* berry.

bayajá *nm* (*Carib*) headscarf.

báyer‡ *nf* (*Cono Sur*) dope‡, pot‡.

bayeta *nf* (**a**) (*tela verde*) baize. (**b**) (*para limpiar*) floorcloth, cleaning rag; washing-up cloth. (**c**) (*And*: *pañal*) nappy, diaper (*US*).

bayetón *nm* (**a**) bearskin, thick woollen cloth. (**b**) (*And*: *poncho largo*) long poncho.

bayo 1 *adj* bay. **2** *nm* bay (horse).

Bayona *nf* Bayonne.

bayoneta *nf* (**a**) (*arma*) bayonet; **con ~s caladas** with fixed bayonets. (**b**) (*LAm Bot*) yucca.

bayonetazo *nm* (*arremetida*) bayonet thrust; (*herida*) bayonet wound.

bayonetear [1a] *vt* (*LAm*) to bayonet.

bayoya *nm* (*Carib*) row, uproar; **es un** ~ **aquí** it's pandemonium here.

bayunca[1] *nf* (*CAm*) bar, saloon.

bayunco 1 *adj* (*CAm*) (*tonto*) silly, stupid; (*tímido*) shy; (*grosero*) crude, vulgar. **2** *nm*, **bayunca**[2] *nf* (*CAm*) uncouth peasant; *name applied by Guatemalans to other Central Americans.*

baza *nf* (**a**) (*Naipes*) trick; ~ **de honor** honours trick; **hacer 3 ~s** to make 3 tricks.

(**b**) (*fig*) **hacer** ~ to get on; **meter** ~ to butt in; **meter** ~ **en** interfere in; **no dejar meter** ~ **a nadie** not to let sb get a word in edgeways; **sentar** ~ to intervene decisively; to speak up dogmatically; **sentada esta** ~, ... this point being established, ...; **tiene sentada la** ~ **de discreto** he has a reputation for good sense.

bazar *nm* (*mercado*) bazaar; (*almacenes*) large retail store; (*juguetería*) toy shop; (*LAm*) bazaar, charity fair; (*Méx*) second-hand shop; (*Cono Sur*: *ferretería*) ironmonger's (shop).

bazo 1 *adj* yellowish-brown. **2** *nm* (*Anat*) spleen.

bazofia *nf* (**a**) (*sobras*) left-overs, scraps of food; (*para cerdos*) pigswill. (**b**) (*fig*: *basura*) pigswill, hogwash (*US*); vile thing, filthy thing.

bazuca *nf* bazooka.

bazucar [1g] *vt*, **bazuquear** [1a] *vt* (*agitar*) to stir; (*sacudir*) to shake, jolt.

bazuqueo *nm* stirring; shaking, jolting; ~ **gástrico** rumblings in the stomach.

BC *nf abr de* **Banda Ciudadana** Citizens' Band, CB (Radio).

be[1] *nf* the (name of the) letter *b*; **por** ~ in detail, down to the last detail; **esto tiene las tres ~s** (*'bonita, barata, y buena'*) this is really very nice, this is just perfect.

be[2] *nm* baa.

beata *nf* (**a**) (*Ecl*) lay sister.

(**b**) (*gen*) devout woman; woman who lives in pious retirement; (*pey*) excessively pious woman, sanctimonious woman, goody-goody*.

(**c**) (‡ *Fin*) one peseta.

beatería *nf* affected piety; cant, sanctimoniousness.

beaterío *nm* goody-goodies*, sanctimonious people.

beatificación *nf* beatification.

beatificar [1g] *vt* to beatify.

beatífico *adj* beatific.

beatitud *nf* beatitude; blessedness; **su B**~ His Holiness.

beatnik ['bitnik] *nm, pl* **beatniks** ['bitnik] beatnik.

beato 1 *adj* (**a**) (*feliz*) happy, blessed.

(**b**) (*Ecl*) beatified; blessed.

(**c**) (*piadoso*) devout, pious; (*pey*) excessively devout; canting, hypocritical.

2 *nm* (**a**) (*Ecl*) lay brother.

(**b**) (*pey*) over-devout man, excessively pious person.

Beatriz *nf* Beatrice.

bebe, -a *nm/f* (*LAm*) baby.

bebé *nmf* baby; (*p.ej.*) ~ **foca** baby seal; **dos ~s panda** two baby pandas.

bebecina *nf* (*And*) drunkenness; drinking spree.

bebedera *nf* (*And*: *embriaguez*) habitual drunkenness; (*CAm, Méx*: *juerga*) drinking bout, drunken spree.

bebedero 1 *adj* drinkable, good to drink.

2 *nm* (**a**) (*recipiente*) drinking trough; (*Zool*) drinking place, watering hole.

(**b**) (*de jarro*) spout.

(**c**) (*And*) (*Com*) establishment selling alcoholic drinks; (*fig*) watering place (*o* hole).

bebedizo 1 *adj* drinkable. **2** *nm* (*Med*) potion; (*Hist*) love potion, philtre.

bebedor 1 *adj* hard-drinking, bibulous, given to drinking. **2** *nm*, **bebedora** *nf* drinker; (*pey*) hard drinker, toper; ~ **fuerte** heavy drinker; ~ **social** social drinker.

bebendurria *nf* (**a**) (*Cono Sur*: *fiesta*) drinking party. (**b**) (*And, Méx*) (*embriaguez*) drunkenness; (*juerga*) drinking spree.

bebé-probeta *nmf, pl* **bebés-probeta** test-tube baby.

beber 1 *nm* drink, drinking.

2 [2a] *vti* (*gen*) to drink; to drink up; (*fig*) to drink in, absorb, imbibe; ~ **de** to drink from, drink out of; ~ **a sorbos** to sip; ~ **mucho,** ~ **a pote** to drink a lot, be a heavy drinker; **se lo bebió todo** he drank it all up.

beberaje *nm* (*Cono Sur*) drink (*esp alcoholic*).

bebercio* *nm* drink, booze*.

bebereca* *nf* (*And*) booze*.

beberecua* *nf* (*And*) (**a**) (*juerga*) boozing‡. (**b**) = **bebereca.**

beberrón *adj, nm*, **beberrona** *nf* = **bebedor.**

bebestible 1 *adj* (*LAm*) drinkable. **2 ~s** *nmpl* drinks.

bebezón *nf* (*Carib*) (**a**) (*bebida*) drink, booze*. (**b**) (*embriaguez*) drunkenness; (*juerga*) drinking spree.

bebezona* *nf* booze-up*.

bebible *adj* (just) drinkable; **no** ~ undrinkable.

bebida *nf* (**a**) (*gen*) drink; beverage.

(**b**) (*alcohólico*) (alcoholic) drink; ~ **alcohólica** alcoholic drink, liquor; ~ **no alcohólica** non-alcoholic drink, soft drink; ~ **larga** long drink; ~ **refrescante** soft drink; **dado a la** ~ given to drink, hard-drinking; **darse a la** ~ to take to drink; **tener mala** ~ (*LAm*) to get violent with drink.

(**c**) (*Cono Sur*) bib.
bebido *adj* tipsy, merry*.
bebistrajo* *nm* nasty drink, filthy drink, brew.
BEBS [beßs] *abr de* **basura entra, basura sale** garbage in, garbage out, GIGO.
beca *nf* (**a**) (*dinero*) scholarship, grant; fellowship; award. (**b**) (*vestido*) sash, hood.
becacina *nf* snipe.
becada[1] *nf* (*Orn*) woodcock.
becado 1 *adj estudiante* who holds a scholarship; *investigador* who holds an award; **está aquí ~** (*LAm*) he's here on a grant. **2** *nm*, **becada**[2] *nf* scholarship holder; award holder.
becar [1g] *vt* to award a scholarship (*o* grant *etc*) to.
becario, –a *nm/f* scholarship holder; award holder; scholar, fellow.
becerrada *nf* (*Taur*) fight with young bulls.
becerrillo *nm* calfskin.
becerro *nm* (**a**) (*animal*) yearling calf, bullock; **~ de oro** golden calf. (**b**) (*piel*) calfskin. (**c**) (*Ecl Hist*) cartulary, register, record book.
bechamel *nf* white sauce, béchamel sauce.
becuadro *nm* (*Mús*) natural (sign).
Beda *nm* Bede.
bedel, –ela *nm/f* (*Univ: aprox*) head porter; (*de edificio oficial, museo*) uniformed employee; (*de colegio*) janitor.
bedoya *nm* (*And*) idiot.
beduino 1 *adj* Bedouin. **2** *nm*, **beduina** *nf* Bedouin; (*pey*) savage.
befa *nf* jeer, taunt.
befar [1a] *vt* (*t* **befarse** *vr*) **~ de** to scoff at, jeer at, taunt.
befo 1 *adj* (**a**) (*bezudo*) thick-lipped. (**b**) (*patizambo*) knock-kneed, (*zancajoso*) splayfooted. **2** *nm* lip.
begonia *nf* begonia.
behaviorismo *nm* behaviourism.
behaviorista *adj, nmf* behaviourist.
BEI *nm abr de* **Banco Europeo de Inversiones** European Investment Bank, EIB.
beibi‡ *nf* girlfriend, bird‡.
beicon *nm* bacon.
beige [beis], **beis** *adj, nm* beige.
béisbol *nm* baseball.
beisbolero 1 *adj* (*LAm*) baseball (*atr*). **2** *nm* (*LAm*) (*jugador*) baseball player; (*aficionado*) baseball fan.
beisbolista *nm* (*LAm*) baseball player.
beisbolístico *adj* baseball (*atr*).
bejuco *nm* (*LAm Bot*) liana; **no sacar ~*** (*Carib*) to miss the boat; to come a cropper*.
bejuquear [1a] *vt* (*LAm*) to beat, thrash.
bejuquero *nm* (*And*) confused situation, mess.
bejuquillo *nm* (**a**) (*Carib, Méx Bot*) (variety of) liana. (**b**) (*And: vainilla*) vanilla.
bejuquiza *nf* (*And*) beating, thrashing.
Belcebú *nm* Beelzebub.
beldad *nf* (**a**) (*cualidad*) beauty. (**b**) (*persona*) beauty, belle.
beldar [1j] *vt* to winnow (with a fork).
belduque *nm* (*CAm, Méx*) pointed sword.
Belén *nm* Bethlehem.
belén *nm* (**a**) (*de Navidad*) nativity scene, crib.
(**b**) (*fig*) (*confusión*) confusion, bedlam; (*guirigay*) madhouse; (*riesgo*) risky venture; **meterse en belenes** (*Cono Sur*) to get involved in other people's troubles.
belenista *nmf* maker of nativity scenes.
beleño *nm* henbane.
belfo = **befo**.
belga *adj, nmf* Belgian.
Bélgica *nf* Belgium.
bélgico *adj* Belgian.
Belgrado *nm* Belgrade.
Belice *nm* Belize.
beliceño, –a *adj, nm/f* Belizean.
belicismo *nm* warmongering, militarism.
belicista 1 *adj* warmongering, militaristic, warminded. **2** *nmf* warmonger.
bélico *adj* (**a**) (*gen*) warlike, martial. (**b**) *material, juguete etc* war (*atr*).
belicosidad *nf* warlike spirit; bellicosity, aggressiveness; militancy.
belicoso *adj* warlike; bellicose, aggressive; militant.
beligerancia *nf* belligerency; militancy, warlike spirit.
beligerante 1 *adj* belligerent; militant, warlike; **no ~** non-belligerent. **2** *nmf* belligerent; **no ~** non-belligerent.
belinún *nm* (*Cono Sur*) simpleton, blockhead*.
belitre *nm* (**a**) (*granuja*) rogue, scoundrel. (**b**) (*And, CAm: niño*) shrewd child; restless child.
bellaco 1 *adj* (*malvado*) wicked; (*taimado*) cunning, sly; (*pícaro*) rascally; (*Cono Sur, Méx*) *caballo* vicious, hard to control; (*And, CAm*) brave. **2** *nm* (*esp hum*) rascal, rogue, villain.
belladona *nf* deadly nightshade, belladonna.
bellamente *adv* beautifully; finely.
bellaqueada *nf* (*Cono Sur*) bucking, rearing; shy.
bellaquear [1a] *vi* (**a**) (*engañar*) to cheat, be crooked*. (**b**) (*And, Cono Sur: caballo*) to rear up, balk; to shy; (*fig*) to dig one's heels in, be stubborn.
bellaquería *nf* (**a**) (*acto*) dirty trick, wicked thing. (**b**) (*cualidad*) wickedness; cunning, slyness.
belleza *nf* (**a**) (*gen*) beauty, loveliness; **las ~s de Mallorca** the beauties of Majorca. (**b**) (*persona*) beauty, beautiful woman (*etc*); (*objeto*) lovely thing.
bello *adj* beautiful, lovely; fine; noble; *V* **arte** *etc*.
bellota *nf* (**a**) (*Bot*) acorn; (*de clavel*) bud. (**b**) *Anat* (*) Adam's apple. (**c**) (*para perfumes*) perfume-box, pomander. (**d**) **~ de mar, ~ marina** sea urchin.
bemba‡ *nf* (*LAm*) lip.
bembo *adj*, **bembón** *adj*, **bembudo** *adj* (*LAm*) thick-lipped.
bemol *nm* (**a**) (*Mús*) flat; **esto tiene muchos** (*o* **tres**) **~es*** this is a tough one, this bristles with difficulties. (**b**) **~es** (**‡ *euf*) = **cojones**.
benceno *nm* benzene.
bencina *nf* benzine; (*Cono Sur*: *gasolina*) petrol, gasoline (*US*).
bencinera[1] *nf* (*Cono Sur*) garage, petrol-station.
bencinero, –a[2] *nm/f* (*Cono Sur*) petrol-station attendant.
bendecir [*aprox* 3o] *vt* (*gen*) to bless; (*consagrar*) to consecrate; (*loar*) to praise, call down a blessing on; **~ la comida, ~ la mesa** to say grace.
bendición *nf* (**a**) (*Rel*) blessing, benediction; **~ de la mesa** grace; **bendiciones nupciales** wedding ceremony; **echar la ~** to give one's blessing (*a* to; *t fig*); **tuvo que echar la ~ a eso** he had to say good-bye to that, he had to give up all hope of (finding) that; **será mejor echar la ~ a eso** it will be best to have nothing more to do with it.
(**b**) **... que es una ~ (de Dios)** ... and it's just marvellous; **llovió que era una ~ (de Dios)** there was such a lovely lot of rain; **lo hace que es una ~** she does it splendidly, she does it with the greatest ease.
bendito 1 *adj* (**a**) (*Rel*) blessed, holy; saintly.
(**b**) (*fig*) blessed.
(**c**) (*feliz*) happy; lucky.
(**d**) (*cándido*) simple, simple-minded.
(**e**) (*piropos*) **¡~s los ojos que te ven!** lucky eyes to be looking at you!; **¡bendita la madre que te parió!** what a daughter for a mother to have!
2 *nm* (**a**) (*Rel*) saint.
(**b**) (*fig*) simple soul, good soul; **es un ~** he's a good kind person, he's sweet; **dormir como un ~** to sleep peacefully, be fast asleep.
(**c**) (*Cono Sur*: *oración*) prayer.
(**d**) (*Cono Sur*) (*Rel*) wayside shrine; (*cabaña*) native hut.
benedícite *nm* grace.
benedictino 1 *adj* Benedictine. **2** *nm* (*Ecl, licor*) Benedictine; **es obra de ~s** it's a huge task, it's a long job.
Benedicto *nm* Benedict.
benefactor 1 *adj* salutary; beneficent; *V* **estado**. **2** *nm*, **benefactora** *nf* benefactor.
beneficencia *nf* (**a**) (*gen*) beneficence, doing good.
(**b**) (*obra etc*) charity; charitable organization; (*t* **~ social**) social welfare; **vivir a cargo de la ~** to live on charity, live on public welfare.
beneficiado *nm* (*Ecl*) incumbent, beneficiary.
beneficial *adj* relating to ecclesiastical benefices; **terreno ~** glebe, glebe land.
beneficiar [1b] **1** *vt* (**a**) (*gen*) to benefit, be of benefit to.
(**b**) (*Cono Sur*) *tierra* to cultivate; *mina* to exploit, work; *mineral* to process, refine; (*CAm*: *Agr*) to process.
(**c**) (*LAm*) *animal* (*matar*) to slaughter; (*CAm*) *persona* to shoot, kill.
(**d**) (*Com*) to sell at a discount.
(**e**) (*) *puesto* to buy one's way into.
2 *vi* to be of benefit.
3 beneficiarse *vr* (**a**) (*gen*) to benefit, profit; **~ de** to benefit from, take advantage of; (*pey*) to make a good thing out of.
(**b**) **~ a uno** (*CAm*) to shoot sb.

beneficiario, -a *nmf* beneficiary.
beneficiencia *nf* (*Méx*) welfare.
beneficio *nm* (**a**) (*provecho*) benefit, profit, gain, advantage; ~ **de justicia gratuita** legal aid; ~**s marginales** fringe benefits; **a ~ de** for the benefit of; **en ~ propio** to one's own advantage; **en su propio ~, no** ... in your own interests, do not ...
(**b**) (*donativo*) benefaction.
(**c**) (*Teat*) benefit, benefit performance.
(**d**) (*Ecl*) living, benefice.
(**e**) (*Com, Fin*) profit; earnings; ~ **bruto** gross profit; ~**s excesivos** excess profits; ~**s imprevistos** windfall profits; ~ **líquido,** ~ **neto** net profit; ~**s posimpositivos** after-tax profits, profits after tax; ~ **preimpositivos** pre-tax profits, profits before tax; ~**s previstos** anticipated profits; ~**s retenidos** retained profits; ~ **por acción** earnings per share.
(**f**) (*Agr, Min*: *producto*) yield.
(**g**) (*acto*: *Agr*) cultivation; (*Min*: *de mina*) exploitation; (*Min*: *de mineral*) processing, treatment, smelting.
(**h**) (*LAm*: *matanza*) slaughter, slaughtering.
(**i**) (*Cono Sur Agr*) manure.
(**j**) (*LAm*) (*matadero*) slaughterhouse; (*cafetal*) coffee plantation; (*ingenio*) sugar refinery.
beneficioso *adj* beneficial, profitable, useful.
benéfico *adj* (**a**) (*amable etc*) beneficent, charitable, kind (*a* to; *para, con* towards). (**b**) *trabajo, organismo etc* charitable; **función benéfica** charity performance; **obra benéfica** charity.
benemérito *adj* (**a**) (*gen*) worthy, meritorious; notable; distinguished; **el ~ hispanista** the distinguished hispanist.
(**b**) **un ~ de la patria** a national hero; **la Benemérita** the Civil Guard.
beneplácito *nm* approval, consent; **dar su ~** to give one's consent.
benevolencia *nf* benevolence, kindness, kindliness; geniality.
benevolente *adj*, **benévolo** *adj* benevolent, kind, kindly; genial; ~ **con** well-disposed towards, kind to.
Bengala *nf* Bengal; **el Golfo de ~** the Gulf of Bengal.
bengala *nf* flare; star shell.
bengalí *adj, nmf* Bengali.
Bengasi *nm* Bengazi.
benignamente *adv* kindly, benignly; graciously, gently; mildly.
benignidad *nf* kindness, kindliness; graciousness, gentleness; mildness.
benigno *adj* kind, kindly, benign; gracious; gentle; *clima* mild; (*Med*) *ataque, caso* mild; *tumor* benign, non-malignant.
Benito *nm* Benedict.
benito = **benedictino.**
Benjamín *nm* Benjamin.
benjamín 1 *nm*, **benjamina** *nf* (*t* **benjasmín** *nm*, **benjasmina** *nf Cono Sur*) baby of the family, youngest child; favourite child; (*Dep*) junior, young player. **2** *nm* (*botella*) half-bottle.
benzina *nf* (*Cono Sur*) = **bencina.**
beo** *nm* cunt**.
beocio‡ *adj* stupid.
beodez *nf* drunkenness.
beodo 1 *adj* drunk. **2** *nm* drunk, drunkard.
beorí *nm* American tapir.
beque 1 *adj* (*CAm*) stammering. **2** *nmf* (*CAm*) stammerer.
bequista *nmf* (*CAm, Carib*) = **becario.**
berbecí *nmf* (*Méx*) quick-tempered person.
berbén *nm* (*Méx*) scurvy.
berberecho *nm* cockle.
berberí *adj y nmf* = **bereber.**
Berbería *nf* Barbary.
berberisco *adj* Berber.
berbiquí *nm* carpenter's brace; ~ **y barrena** brace and bit.
berdel *nm* mackerel.
bereber, berébere, berebere *adj, nmf* Berber.
berengo (*Méx*) **1** *adj* foolish, stupid. **2** *nm*, **berenga** *nf* idiot.
berenjena *nf* (**a**) aubergine, eggplant. (**b**) (*Carib**) nuisance, bother.
berenjenal *nm* (**a**) (*lit*) aubergine bed. (**b**) (*fig*: *lío*) mess, trouble; **en buen ~ nos hemos metido** we've got ourselves into a fine mess.
bereque *adj* (*CAm*) cross-eyed.
bergante *nm* scoundrel, rascal.
bergantín *nm* brig.
Beri *n*: **andar** (*o* **ir**) **con las de ~** (*tener genio*) to have a violent temper; (*tener malas intenciones*) to have evil intentions.
beril(i)o *nm* beryl.
berkelio *nm* berkelium.
Berlín *nm* Berlin; ~ **Oeste** West Berlin.
berlina *nf* (**a**) (*Aut*) saloon car, sedan. (**b**) (*Cono Sur*) doughnut, donut (*US*).
berlinés 1 *adj* Berlin (*atr*). **2** *nm*, **berlinesa** *nf* Berliner.
berma *nf* berm; (*Cono Sur*) hard shoulder; emergency lane.
bermejo *adj* (**a**) (*de color*) red, bright red; reddish; *gato* ginger; (*Carib, Méx*) *vaca* light brown. (**b**) (*Carib*: *único*) matchless, unsurpassed.
bermellón *nm* vermilion.
bermuda *nf* (*LAm*) meadow grass.
Bermudas *nfpl* (*t* **Islas Bermuda** *nfpl*) Bermuda, the Bermudas.
bermudas *nmpl* Bermuda shorts.
Berna *nf* Berne.
bernardina* *nf* yarn, tall story.
Bernardo *nm* Bernard.
berraco* *nm* noisy brat.
berrear [1a] **1** *vi* (**a**) (*Zool*) to bellow, low; (*niño*) to howl; (*Mús*: *hum*) to bawl; to screech. (**b**) (*fig*) to fly off the handle*. **2 berrearse** *vt* to squeal‡, grass‡.
berrenchín *nm* rage, tantrum.
berreta* *adj* (*Cono Sur*) cheap, flashy.
berretín* *nm* (*Cono Sur*) (*obsesión*) obsession, mania; (*terquedad*) pigheadedness.
berrido *nm* (*Zool*) bellow, bellowing; lowing; (*niño*) howl; (*Mús*: *hum*) bawl, bawling; screech.
berrinche 1 *nm* (**a**) (*) (*rabieta*) rage, tantrum*; **coger** (*o* **llevarse**) **un ~** to fly into a rage. (**b**) (*LAm*‡: *hedor*) pong‡, stink. **2 ~s*** *nm invar* bad-tempered person, stroppy individual*.
berrinchudo* *adj* (**a**) *persona* cross, bad-tempered. (**b**) (*Méx*) *animal* on heat.
berro *nm* (*Bot*) watercress; (*Carib*: *enojo*) rage, anger.
berza 1 *nf* (*Esp*) cabbage; ~ **lombarda** red cabbage; **mezclar ~s con capachos*** to get things in a shocking mess. **2** ~**s*** *nmf invar* idiot, imbecile; **¡~s!** you idiot!
berzal *nm* (*Esp*) cabbage patch.
berzotas* *nmf invar* twit*, chump*.
besamanos *nm invar* royal audience, levée.
besamel *nf* white sauce, béchamel sauce.
besana *nf* land to be ploughed.
besar [1a] *vt* (**a**) (*gen*) to kiss; ~ **la mano,** ~ **los pies** (*fig*) to pay one's humble respects (*a* to).
(**b**) (*fig*: *tocar*) to graze, touch.
2 besarse *vr* (**a**) (*gen*) to kiss, kiss one another.
(**b**) (*fig*: *tocar*) to touch, knock against each other; to bump heads.
beso *nm* (**a**) (*gen*) kiss; ~ **lingual,** ~ **de tornillo** French kiss; ~ **de la muerte** kiss of death; ~ **de la vida** kiss of life; **dar un ~ volado a, echar** (*o* **tirar**) **un ~ a** to blow a kiss to. (**b**) (*choque*) bump, collision.
besograma *nm* kissogram.
besotear [1a] *vt* (*Méx*) = **besuquear.**
bestia 1 *nf* (*Zool*) beast, animal, (*esp*) horse, mule; ~ **de arrastre,** ~ **de carga** beast of burden; ~ **negra** (*fig*) bête noire, pet aversion; ~ **de tiro** draught animal.
2 *nmf* (**a**) (*) (*idiota*) idiot, ignoramus; (*patán*) boor; (*bruto*) beast, brute; **¡~!** you idiot!, you brute!; **¡no seas ~!** don't be an idiot!
(**b**) (*: *admirativo*) **¡estás hecho un ~!** you're great!*
3 *adj* (*) stupid; **Juan es muy ~** John is a bit stupid; **el muy ~** the great idiot; **ese tío ~** that beastly fellow; **a lo ~** (*adj*) vulgar, crude; boorish; (*adv*) vulgarly, crudely; boorishly;; **me pone ~**‡ it turns me on*.
bestiada* *nf*: **una ~ de** masses of, tons of*; **disfrutar ~s** to enjoy o.s. hugely.
bestial *adj* (**a**) (*animal*) beast-like, bestial. (**b**) (*) terrific*; tremendous*, marvellous; smashing*, super*.
bestialidad *nf* (**a**) (*cualidad*) beast-like nature, bestiality. (**b**) (*sexual*) bestiality. (**c**) (*fig*) (*estupidez*) stupidity; (*disparate*) silly thing, piece of stupidity. (**d**) **una ~ de gente*** lots and lots of people.
bestialismo *nm* bestiality.
bestialmente* *adv* marvellously; **lo pasamos ~** we had a super time*.
best-seller *nm, pl* **best-sellers** best-seller.
besucar* [1g] *vt* = **besuquear.**
besucón* *adj* free with kisses, fond of kissing.

besugo *nm* (**a**) (*pez*) red bream; **con ojos de ~** with bulging eyes; with eyes like a spaniel's. (**b**) (*: *idiota*) idiot.
besuguera *nf* (**a**) fishing-boat. (**b**) (*Pez*: *Galicia*) bream. (**c**) (*Culin*) fish pan.
besuquear* [1a] **1** *vt* to cover with kisses, keep on kissing. **2 besuquearse** *vr* to kiss (each other) a lot; (*magrearse*) to pet*, neck*.
besuqueo *nm* kissing; petting*, necking*.
beta *nf* beta.
betabel 1 *nm* (*LAm*) sugar-beet. **2** *adj* (*Méx**) old, ancient.
betarraga *nf* (*LAm*), **betarrata** *nf* beetroot, beet (*US*).
betel *nm* betel.
Bética *nf* (*liter*) Andalusia; (*Hist*) Baetica.
bético *adj* (*liter*) Andalusian.
betonera *nf* (*Cono Sur*) concrete mixer.
betún *nm* (**a**) (*Quím*) bitumen; **~ de Judea, ~ judaico** asphalt. (**b**) shoe polish, blacking; **dar de ~ a** to polish, black; **darse ~*** to swank*, show off.
betunero *nm* shoeblack, bootblack.
bezo *nm* thick lip; (*Med*) proud flesh.
bezudo *adj* thick-lipped.
bi ... *pref* bi ...
biaba *nf* (*Cono Sur*) punch, slap; **dar la ~ a** (*pegar*) to beat up; (*derrotar*) to defeat, crush.
bianual *adj, nm* (*Bot*) biennial.
bianualmente *adv* biennially, every two years.
biatlón *nm* biathlon.
Bib. *nf abr de* **Biblioteca** Library, Lib.
biberón *nm* feeding bottle.
Biblia *nf* (**a**) (*Rel*) Bible; **la Santa ~** the Holy Bible. (**b**) **es la ~ (en verso)*** it's the tops*; **saber la ~*** to know everything.
bíblico *adj* Biblical.
biblio ... *pref* biblio ...
bibliobús *nm* travelling library, mobile library, library van.
bibliofilia *nf* bibliophily, love of books.
bibliófilo, -a *nmf* bibliophile.
bibliografía *nf* bibliography.
bibliográfico *adj* bibliographic(al).
bibliógrafo, -a *nmf* bibliographer.
bibliomanía *nf* bibliomania.
bibliometría *nf* bibliometry.
bibliométrico *adj* bibliometric.
biblioratio *nm* (*Cono Sur*) box-file.
biblioteca *nf* (**a**) (*gen*) library; **~ circulante** lending library; circulating library; **~ de consulta** reference library; **~ pública** public library; **~ universitaria** university library.
(**b**) (*estante*) bookcase, bookshelves.
bibliotecario 1 *adj* library (*atr*); **servicios ~s** library services. **2** *nm*, **bibliotecaria** *nf* librarian.
bibliotecnia *nf*, **bibliotecología** *nf*, **biblioteconomía** *nf* library science, librarianship.
BIC [bik] *nf* (*Esp*) *abr de* **Brigada de Investigación Criminal** ≈ CID, FBI (*US*).
bicameral *adj* (*Pol*) two-chamber, bicameral.
bicameralismo *nm* system of two-chamber government.
bicampeón, -ona *nm/f* two-times champion, twice champion.
bicarbonatado *adj* bicarbonated, fizzy.
bicarbonato *nm*: **~ (sódico), ~ de sosa** bicarbonate of soda; (*Culin*) baking soda.
bicentenario *adj, nm* bicentenary.
bíceps *nm invar* biceps.
bici* *nf* bike*.
bicicleta *nf* bicycle, cycle; **~ de carreras** racing bicycle; **~ de ejercicio, ~ estática, ~ fija, ~ gimnástica** exercise bicycle; **~ de montaña** mountain bicycle; **andar en ~, ir en ~** to cycle; to ride a bicycle.
biciclo *nm* (††) velocipede††.
bicilíndrico *adj* two-cylinder (*atr*), twin-cylinder (*atr*).
bicimoto *nm* (*CAm*) moped.
bicoca *nf* (**a**) (*bagatela*) trifle, mere nothing. (**b**) (*ganga*) bargain; (*prebenda*) soft job, plum job. (**c**) (*And, Cono Sur Ecl*) priest's skull cap. (**d**) (*And, Cono Sur*) (*capirotazo*) snap of the fingers; (*golpe*) slap, smack.
bicolor *adj* two-colour, in two colours, (*Aut*) two-tone.
bicúspide *adj* bicuspid.
bicha *nf* (**a**) (*euf*: *serpiente*) snake; (*fig*) bogy; **~ negra** bête noire, pet aversion; **mentar la ~** to bring up an unpleasant subject. (**b**) (*CAm*: *niña*) child, little girl. (**c**) (*And*: *olla*) large cooking-pot.
bichadero *nm* (*Cono Sur*) watchtower, observation tower.
bichará *nm* (*Cono Sur*) poncho (with black and white stripes).
biche 1 *adj* (*Cono Sur*: *débil*) weak; (*de mal color*) of unhealthy colour; (*And*: *no desarrollado*) stunted, immature; (*Méx**: *fofo*) soppy*, empty-headed. **2** *nm* (*And*) large cooking-pot.
bicheadero *nm* (*Cono Sur*) = **bichadero**.
bichear [1a] *vt* (*Cono Sur*) to spy (*o* keep watch) on.
bicherío *nm* (*LAm*) insects, bugs, creepy-crawlies*.
bichero *nm* boat hook; (*Pesca*) gaff.
bichi‡ *adj* (*Méx*) naked, starkers‡.
bichicori* *adj* (*Méx*) skinny.
bichito *nm* (**a**) small creature, little insect. (**b**) (‡) LSD tablet.
bicho *nm* (**a**) (*Zool etc*: *gen*: *animal*) small animal; (*insecto*) (unpleasant) insect, bug, creepy-crawly*; (*Carib, Cono Sur*: *gusano*) maggot, grub; (*And*: *serpiente*) snake; (*LAm*: *animal extraño*) odd-looking creature; **~s** (*frec*) vermin, pests, bugs.
(**b**) (*And*: *peste aviar*) fowl pest.
(**c**) (*Taur*) bull.
(**d**) (*persona*: *t* **~ raro**) odd-looking person, queer fish; **~ raro** weirdo*, weirdy*; **mal ~** rogue, villain; **es un mal ~** he's a nasty piece of work, he's a rotter*; **todo ~ viviente** every living soul, every man-jack of them; **sí, bichito*** yes, my love.
(**e**) (*) (*pey*: *niño*) brat; (*Mil*) squaddie*, recruit; (*CAm*: *niño*) child, little boy.
(**f**) **de puro ~** (*LAm*) out of sheer pig-headedness; **tener ~** to be terribly thirsty; **matar el ~** to have a drink.
(**g**) (*Carib*: *chisme*) what's-it*, thingummy*.
bichoco *adj* (*And, Cono Sur*) past it, useless; unfit to work.
BID *nm abr de* **Banco Interamericano de Desarrollo** Inter-American Development Bank, BID.
bidé *nm*, **bidet** [bi'ðe] *nm, pl* **bidets** bidet.
bidel *nm* (*LAm*) bidet.
bidimensional *adj* two-dimensional.
bidireccional *adj* duplex, bidirectional; **~ simultáneo** full duplex.
bidón *nm* drum; can, tin; **~ de aceite** oildrum.
biela *nf* (**a**) (*Téc*) connecting rod. (**b**) (‡) leg.
bielástico *adj* with two-way stretch.
bielda *nf* winnowing fork, (kind of) pitchfork.
bieldar [1a] *vt* to winnow (with a fork).
bieldo *nm* winnowing rake.
bien 1 *adv* (**a**) (*gen*) well; (*correctamente*) properly, right; (*con éxito*) successfully; **hacer algo ~** to do sth well, do sth properly; **contestar ~** to answer right, answer correctly; **lo sé muy ~** I know that perfectly well; **no veo muy ~** I can't see all that well; **¡qué ~!** (*bravo*) jolly good!, marvellous!; (*ojalá*) now that really would be something!; (*iró*) a lot of good that would do!; **~ que mal** one way or another, by hook or by crook; **de ~ en ~, de ~ en mejor** better and better; **aquí se está ~** it's nice here; **¿estás ~?** are you all right?; are you comfortable?; **ya está ~ de quejas** we've had enough complaints, that's quite enough complaining; **¿está ~ que ...?** is it all right that ...?; **hacer ~ en** + *infin* to be right to + *infin*, do well to + *infin*; **tener a ~** + *infin* to see fit to + *infin*, deign to + *infin*; to think it proper to + *infin*.
(**b**) (*de buena gana*) willingly, gladly, readily; **yo ~ iría, pero ...** I'd gladly go, but ...; (*asentimiento poco entusiasta*) **¿quieres que vayamos al cine? - ~** shall we go to the cinema? - all right.
(**c**) (*muy*) very, much, quite, a good deal, fully; **un cuarto ~ caliente** a nice warm room; **eso es ~ tonto** that's pretty silly; **un coche ~ caro** a very expensive car; **~ temprano** very early, pretty early, quite early; **había ~ 8 toneladas** there were fully (*o* easily, at least) 8 tons.
(**d**) (*fácilmente*) easily; **~ se ve que ...** one can easily see that ..., it is easy to see that ...; **~ es verdad que ...** it is of course true that ...
(**e**) (*o ... o*) **~ por avión, ~ en tren** either by air or by train; **~ se levantó, ~ se sentó** whether he stood up or sat down.
(**f**) **~ (así) como** just as, just like; **más ~** rather; **más ~ creo que ...** on the contrary I think that ...; **más ~ bajo (que alto)** rather short, on the short side; **o ~** or else; **pues ~** well, well then.
(**g**) *interj etc* **¡~!** yes!, all right; O.K.!*; jolly good!*; well done!; **¡muy ~!** (*aprobando discurso etc*) hear hear!; **¡hizo muy ~!** and he was quite right too!; **¡muy ~ (por) usted!** good for you!
2 **adj persona* well-off; *restaurante etc* posh*, classy*;

barrio ~ posh neighbourhood*; *V* **gente, niño**.

3 *conj* (**a**) ~ **que, si** ~ although, even though.

(**b**) **no** ~ **llegó, empezó a llover** no sooner had he arrived than it started to rain, as soon as he arrived it started to rain.

4 *nm* (**a**) (*gen*) good; (*provecho*) advantage, benefit, profit; **hombre de** ~ honest man, good man; **el** ~ **público** the common good; **sumo** ~ highest good; **en** ~ **de** for the good of, for the benefit of; **para** ~ for the best; positively; **hacer** ~ to do good; to be honest, lead an honest life; **hacer algo para el** ~ **de** to do sth for the well-being of.

(**b**) **mi** ~ my dear, my darling.

(**c**) ~**es** (*Com etc*) goods; (*propiedad*) property, possessions; (*riqueza*) riches, wealth; ~**es activos** active assets; ~**es de capital** capital goods; ~**es de consumo** consumer goods; ~**es de consumo duraderos** consumer durables; ~**es duraderos** durables; ~**es de equipo** capital goods; ~**es dotales** dowry; ~**es fungibles** perishable goods; ~**es gananciales** (*Jur*) shared possessions; ~**es heredables** hereditament; ~**es inmuebles**, ~**es raíces** real estate, landed property; ~**es de inversión** capital goods; ~**es mostrencos** unclaimed property, ownerless property; ~**es muebles** personal property, goods and chattels; ~ **de producción** industrial goods; ~**es públicos** government property, state property; ~**es relictos** estate, inheritance; ~**es semovientes** livestock; ~**es de servicio** services; ~ **terrestres** worldly goods; ~**es de la tierra** produce; ~**es vinculados** entail.

(**d**) **decir mil** ~**es de uno** to speak highly of sb, talk in glowing terms of sb.

bienal 1 *adj* biennial. **2** *nf* biennial exhibition, biennial show.

bienamado *adj* beloved.

bienandante *adj* happy; prosperous.

bienandanza *nf* happiness; prosperity.

bienaventuradamente *adv* happily.

bienaventurado *adj* (**a**) (*feliz*) happy, fortunate; (*Ecl*) blessed. (**b**) (*cándido*) simple, naïve.

bienaventuranza *nf* (**a**) (*Ecl*) blessedness, (eternal) bliss; **las** ~**s** the Beatitudes. (**b**) (*felicidad*) happiness; (*bienestar*) well-being, prosperity.

bienestar *nm* wellbeing, welfare; comfort; ~ **social** social welfare.

bienhablado *adj* nicely-spoken, well-spoken.

bienhadado *adj* lucky.

bienhechor 1 *adj* beneficent, beneficial. **2** *nm* benefactor.

bienhechora *nf* benefactress.

bienhechuría *nf* (*Carib*) improvement (to property).

bienintencionado *adj* well-meaning.

bienio *nm* two years, two-year period.

bienoliente *adj* sweet-smelling, fragrant.

bienpensante 1 *adj* orthodox; conservative. **2** *nmf* orthodox person; conservative.

bienquerencia *nf* (*afecto*) affection; (*buena voluntad*) goodwill.

bienquerer 1 [2t] *vt* to like, be fond of. **2** *nm* (*afecto*) affection; (*buena voluntad*) goodwill.

bienquistar [1a] **1** *vt* to bring together, reconcile. **2 bienquistarse** *vr* to become reconciled; ~ **con uno** to gain sb's esteem.

bienquisto *adj* well-liked, well-thought-of (*con, de, por* by).

bienudo* *adj* (*Cono Sur*) well-off.

bienvenida *nf* (*gen*) welcome; (*saludo*) greeting; **dar la** ~ **a uno** to welcome sb, make sb welcome.

bienvenido *adj* welcome; **¡**~! welcome!; **¡**~**s a bordo!** welcome on board!

bienvivir [3a] *vi* to live in comfort; to live decently, lead a decent life.

bies *nm*: **al** ~ (*Cos*) cut on the cross.

bifásico *adj* (*Elec*) two-phase.

bife[1] *nm* (*LAm*: *t* **baby** ~) steak, beefsteak; cutlet, fillet.

bife[2] *nm* (*Cono Sur*) slap, smack.

bífido *adj lengua etc* forked.

bifocal 1 *adj* bifocal. **2** ~**es** *nmpl* bifocals.

bifronte *adj* two-faced.

biftec *nm* steak, beefsteak.

bifurcación *nf* fork; junction; branch.

bifurcado *adj* forked.

bifurcarse [1g] *vr* to fork, branch, bifurcate; to branch off; to diverge.

bigamia *nf* bigamy.

bígamo 1 *adj* bigamous. **2** *nm*, **bígama** *nf* bigamist.

bigardear* [1a] *vi* to loaf around.

bigardo 1 *adj* lazy, idle; licentious. **2** *nm* (*vago*) idler; (*libertino*) libertine.

bígaro *nm*, **bigarro** *nm* winkle.

bignonia *nf*: ~ **del Cabo** Cape honeysuckle.

bigornia *nf* (double-headed) anvil.

bigotazo *nm* huge moustache.

bigote *nm* (*t* ~**s**) moustache; (*de gato etc*) whiskers; ~ **de cepillo** toothbrush moustache; ~ **de morsa** walrus moustache; **de** ~* terrific*, marvellous; (*pey*) awful; **chuparse los** ~**s** (*Cono Sur*) to lick one's lips; **menear el** ~* to eat, scoff*.

bigotudo *adj* with a big moustache.

bigudí *nm* hair-curler.

bijirita *nf* (*Carib*) (**a**) (*cometa*) kite. (**b**) **empinar la** ~* (*beber*) to booze*, drink a lot; (*enriquecerse*) to make money by dubious methods.

bikini *nm* bikini.

bilateral *adj* bilateral.

bilbaíno 1 *adj* of Bilbao. **2** *nm*, **bilbaína** *nf* native (*o* inhabitant) of Bilbao; **los** ~**s** the people of Bilbao.

bilbilitano 1 *adj* of Calatayud. **2** *nm*, **bilbilitana** *nf* native (*o* inhabitant) of Calatayud; **los** ~**s** the people of Calatayud.

Bilbo* ['bılβo] *nm* = **Bilbao**.

biliar *adj* bile (*atr*), gall (*atr*).

bilingüe *adj* bilingual.

bilingüismo *nm* bilingualism.

bilioso *adj* (**a**) (*gen*) bilious. (**b**) (*fig*: *irritable*) bilious, peevish.

bilis *nf* (**a**) (*Anat*) bile.

(**b**) (*fig*: *cólera*) bile, spleen; **descargar la** ~ to vent one's spleen (*contra* on); **se le exalta la** ~ he gets very cross; **eso me revuelve la** ~ it makes my blood boil; **tragar** ~ to put up with it.

bilongo *nm* (*Carib*) evil influence, evil eye; **echar** ~ **en** to put the evil eye on; **tener** ~ to bristle with difficulties.

bilonguear [1a] *vt* (*Carib*) to cast a spell on, put the evil eye on.

billar *nm* (**a**) (*juego*) billiards; ~ **americano** pool; ~ **automático**, ~ **romano** pin table. (**b**) (*sala*) billiard room; (*mesa*) billiard table.

billete *nm* (**a**) (*Esp Ferro etc*) ticket; ~ **de abono** season-ticket, commutation ticket (*US*); ~ **de andén** platform ticket; ~ **de avión** plane ticket; ~ **azul** ticket for off-peak travel; ~ **de favor** complimentary ticket; ~ **de ida y vuelta** return ticket, round-trip ticket (*US*); ~ **kilométrico** run-about ticket, mileage book; ~ **de libre circulación** travel-card which allows unlimited travel within an area; **medio** ~ half fare; ~ **sencillo** single ticket, one-way ticket (*US*); **pagar el** ~ to pay one's fare, buy one's ticket; **sacar un** ~ to get a ticket.

(**b**) (*Fin*) banknote, note, bill (*US*); (*) 1000-peseta note (*t* ~ **verde**); ~ **de banco** banknote; **un** ~ **de 5 libras** a five-pound note; **un** ~ **de 100 dólares** a 100-dollar bill; **tener** ~ **largo** (*Cono Sur**) to be rolling in it*.

(**c**) (*carta*) note, short letter; ~ **amoroso** love letter, billet-doux.

billetera *nf*, **billetero** *nm* wallet, pocketbook (*US*), billfold (*US*).

billón *nm*: **un** ~ (**de**) a billion (*Brit*), a million million, a trillion (*US*).

billonario, -a *nm/f* billionaire.

bimba[1]* *nf* top hat, topper*.

bimba[2]‡ *nf* (*Méx*) (*embriaguez*) drunkenness; (*juerga*) drinking spree.

bimba[3]‡ *nf* wallet.

bimbalete *nm* (*Méx*) (*columpio*) swing; (*de tabla*) seesaw.

bimbollo *nm* (*Méx*) bun.

bimensual *adj* twice-monthly.

bimensuario 1 *adj* twice-monthly. **2** *nm* publication appearing twice monthly.

bimestral *adj* two-monthly.

bimestralmente *adv* every two months.

bimestre 1 *adj* bimonthly, two-monthly. **2** *nm* (**a**) (*período*) period of two months. (**b**) (*pago*) bimonthly payment.

bimilenario *adj, nm* bimillenary.

bimotor 1 *adj* twin-engined. **2** *nm* twin-engined plane.

binadera *nf*, **binador** *nm* weeding hoe.

binar [1a] *vt* to hoe, dig over.

binario *adj* binary; (*Mús*) *compás* two-four.

bincha *nf* (*And, Cono Sur*) hairband.

bingo *nm* (*juego*) bingo; (*sala*) bingo hall.

binguero, -a *nm/f* bingo-hall attendant.

binoculares *nmpl*, **binóculo** *nm* (*gen*) binoculars, field glasses; (*Teat*) opera glasses; (*quevedos*) pince-nez.

binomio *nm* (**a**) (*gen*) binomial. (**b**) **el ~ ejército-pueblo** (*fig*) the people-army relationship.
bio... *pref* bio...
bioactivo *adj* bioactive.
biodegradable *adj* biodegradable.
biodegradación *nf* biodegradation.
biodegradar [1a] *vt y* **biodegradarse** *vr* to biodegrade.
bioestadística *nf* biostatistics, vital statistics.
biofísica *nf* biophysics.
biogás *nm* biogas.
biogénesis *nf* biogenesis.
biogenética *nf* genetic engineering.
biografía *nf* biography, life.
biografiado, -a *nm/f* subject of a biography, biographee.
biografiar [1c] *vt* to write the biography of.
biográfico *adj* biographic(al).
biógrafo[1], -a *nm/f* biographer.
biógrafo[2] *nm* (*Cono Sur*) cinema.
bioingeniería *nf* bioengineering.
biología *nf* biology; **~ aplicada** applied biology; **~ celular** cell biology; **~ molecular** molecular biology.
biológico *adj* biological; *alimento* organic; **cultivo ~** organically-grown crop.
biólogo, -a *nm/f* biologist.
biomasa *nf* biomass.
biombo *nm* folding screen.
biomédico *adj* biomedical.
biometría *nf* biometry, biometrics.
biónico *adj* bionic.
bioorgánico *adj* bioorganic.
biopsia *nf* biopsy.
bioquímica[1] *nf* biochemistry.
bioquímico 1 *adj* biochemical. **2** *nm*, **bioquímica[2]** *nf* biochemist.
bioscopia *nf* bioscopy.
biosensor *nm* biosensor.
biosfera *nf* biosphere.
biosíntesis *nf* biosynthesis.
biosintético *adj* biosynthetic.
biotecnología *nf* biotechnology.
biotecnológico *adj* biotechnological.
biotecnólogo, -a *nm/f* biotechnologist.
biótico *adj* biotic.
biotipo *nm* biotype.
biotopo *nm* biotope.
bióxido *nm* dioxide; **~ de carbono** carbon dioxide.
BIP *nm abr de* **Banco Internacional de Pagos** Bank of International Settlements, BIS.
bip *nm* pip, beep.
bipartidismo *nm* two-party system.
bipartidista *adj* two-party (*atr*).
bipartido *adj* divided in two.
bipartito *adj* bipartite.
bípedo *nm* biped.
biplano *nm* biplane.
biplaza *nm* (*Aer*) two-seater.
biquini *nm* bikini.
BIRD *nm abr de* **Banco Internacional para la Reconstrucción y el Desarrollo** International Bank of Reconstruction and Development, IBRD.
birdie *nm* (*Golf*) birdie.
birimbao *nm* Jew's-harp.
birlar [1a] *vt* (**a**) (*derribar*) to knock down with a blow, bring down with a shot.
(**b**) (*: *hurtar*) *persona* to swindle out of, do out of*; *cosa* to pinch*; **Juan le birló la novia** John pinched his girl; **le birlaron el empleo** he was done out of the job*.
birlibirloque: **por arte de ~** by magic, as if by magic.
birlocha *nf* (**a**) (*cometa*) kite. (**b**) (*Méx‡ Aut*) old banger‡, old crock.
birlonga: **hacer algo a la ~** to do sth carelessly, do sth sloppily.
Birmania *nf* Burma.
birmano, -a *adj, nm/f* Burmese.
birome *nf* (*Cono Sur*) (*lápiz*) propelling pencil; (*bolígrafo*) ball-point pen.
birra* *nf* beer.
birreactor 1 *adj* twin-jet. **2** *nm* twin-jet (plane).
birreta *nf* (*Ecl*); biretta; **~ (cardenalicia)** cardinal's skull cap.
birrete *nm* (*Ecl*) biretta; (*Univ*) doctor's hat, academic cap; (*Jur*) judge's cap.
birrí *nm* (*And*) snake.
birria* *nf* (**a**) (*esp Esp*: *cosa fea*) monstrosity, ugly old thing; (*obra*) wretched piece of work; (*basura*) rubbish, trash; (*cosa inútil*) useless object; **la novela es una ~** the novel is rubbish; **entre tanta ~** among so much trash; **la casa era una ~** the house was like a pigsty.
(**b**) (*Cono Sur, Méx*: *bebida*) tasteless drink; (*Méx*: *guiso*) stew.
(**c**) (*And*: *obsesión*) set idea, mania; obstinacy.
(**d**) **jugar de ~** (*LAm*) to play half-heartedly.
(**e**) (*CAm**: *cerveza*) beer.
birriondo *adj* (*LAm*) (**a**) (*: *asustadizo*) jumpy, highly strung. (**b**) (‡: *cachondo*) randy*.
biruji *nm* (*Cono Sur*) chilly wind.
birutilla *nf* (*Cono Sur*) pot scourer.
birutillar [1a] *vt* (*Cono Sur*) to polish.
bis 1 *adv* twice; ¡~! (*Theat*) encore! **2** *nm* (*Teat*) encore. **3** *adj*: **ministro ~** deputy minister, stand-in minister.
bisabuela *nf* great-grandmother.
bisabuelo *nm* great-grandfather; **~s** great-grandparents.
bisagra 1 *nf* hinge; (*: *de caderas*) waggle, wiggle. **2** *atr* (**a**) **acontecimiento ~** decisive event, event that marks a watershed. (**b**) (*Pol*) **partido ~** party that holds the balance of power.
bisar [1a] **1** *vt* (**a**) to give as an encore, repeat. (**b**) (*Cono Sur*) to encore, demand as an encore. **2** *vi* to give an encore.
bisbis(e)ar [1a] *vt* (*murmurar*) to mutter, mumble; (*Cono Sur*) to whisper.
bisbiseo *nm* mutter, muttering, mumbling.
bisbita *nf* pipit.
biscote *nm* rusk.
biscúter *nm* (*Aut*) three-wheeler.
bisecar [1g] *vt* to bisect.
bisel *nm* bevel, bevel edge.
biselado *adj* bevel (*atr*), bevelled.
biselar [1a] *vt* to bevel.
bisemanal *adj* twice-weekly.
bisemanalmente *adv* twice-weekly.
bisexual *adj, nmf* bisexual.
bisexualidad *nf* bisexuality.
bisgra‡ *nf* (*Carib*) armpit.
bisiesto *adj*: **año ~** leap year.
bisilábico *adj*, **bisílabo** *adj* two-syllabled.
bismuto *nm* bismuth.
bisnieta *nf* great-granddaughter.
bisnieto *nm* great-grandson; **~s** great-grandchildren.
bisnis‡ *nm* (prostitute's) clients, clientèle.
bisojo *adj* cross-eyed, squinting.
bisonte *nm* bison, buffalo (*US*).
bisoñada *nf* naïve remark, naïve thing to do.
bisoñé *nm* wig, toupée.
bisoñez *nf* inexperience; rawness.
bisoño 1 *adj* green, inexperienced; *recluta* raw. **2** *nm* greenhorn; (*Mil*) raw recruit, rookie*.
bisté *nm*, **bistec** *nm*, **bisteck** *nm*, **bisteque** *nm* (**a**) (*Culin*) steak, beefsteak. (**b**) (‡) tongue; **achantar el ~** to shut one's trap‡.
bistongo *adj* (*CAm, Carib, Méx*) spoiled, indulged.
bisturí *nm* scalpel.
bisunto *adj* greasy, grubby.
bisutería *nf* imitation jewellery, costume jewellery, paste.
bit *nm, pl* **bits** (*Inform*) bit; **~ de parada** stop bit; **~ de paridad** parity bit.
bitácora *nf* (*Náut*) binnacle.
bitensional *adj* (*Elec*) equipped to work on two different voltages.
bíter *nm* bitters.
bitoque *nm* (*tapón*) bung, spigot; (*CAm*: *desagüe*) drain; (*LAm*: *de jeringa*) injection tube (of a syringe); (*Cono Sur*: *canilla*) tap; (*Cono Sur*: *bulto*) bump, swelling.
bituminoso *adj* bituminous.
bivalvo *adj, nm* bivalve.
bivio *nm* (*LAm*) road junction.
Bizancio *n* Byzantium.
bizantino 1 *adj* (**a**) (*gen*) Byzantine. (**b**) (*fig*: *decadente*) decadent. (**c**) (*fig*: *baldío*) *discusión* idle, pointless; (*irreal*) over-subtle, unreal. **2** *nm*, **bizantina** *f* Byzantine.
bizarramente *adv* (**a**) (*valientemente*) gallantly, bravely; dashingly. (**b**) (*generosamente*) generously, splendidly.
bizarría *nf* (**a**) (*valor*) gallantry, bravery; dash, verve. (**b**) (*generosidad*) generosity.
bizarro *adj* (**a**) (*valiente*) gallant, brave; dashing. (**b**) (*generoso*) generous, splendid.
bizbirindo *adj* (*Méx*) lively, bright.
bizcar [1g] **1** *vt ojo* to wink. **2** *vi* to squint, be cross-eyed.

bizco 1 *adj* cross-eyed, squinting; **mirada bizca** squint, cross-eyed look; **dejar a uno ~** to impress sb strongly, leave sb open-mouthed (with wonder); **ponerse ~** to squint, look cross-eyed; **quedarse ~** to be very impressed, be dumbfounded.
2 *adv*: **mirar ~** to squint, look cross-eyed.
bizcochera *nf* biscuit barrel, biscuit tin.
bizcocho *nm* **(a)** (*Culin*) sponge, sponge cake; sponge finger; (*Náut*) hardtack, ship's biscuit; **~ borracho** sponge soaked in wine and syrup; **embarcarse con poco ~** to set out unprepared.
(b) (*Méx*) (*galleta*) biscuit; (**) cunt**.
(c) (*Cerámica*) bisque, biscuit ware.
bizcorneado *adj* (*Carib*) = **bizco**.
bizcornear [1a] *vi* (*Carib*) to squint, be cross-eyed.
bizcorneto *adj* (*And, Méx*) = **bizco.**
Bizkaia [biθ'kaya] *nf* Biscay (*Basque province*).
bizma *nf* poultice.
bizmar [1a] *vt* to poultice.
biznieto *nm* (*etc*) = **bisnieto** (*etc*).
bizquear [1a] *vi* to squint, look cross-eyed.
bizquera *nf* (*And*) squint.
bla-bla-bla *nm* claptrap, rubbish; aimless gossip; hot air, bla-bla-bla.
blanca *nf* **(a)** (*mujer*) white woman.
(b) (*Hist*) *old Spanish copper coin*; **estar sin ~, quedarse sin ~** to be broke*.
(c) (*Mús*) minim.
(d) (‡) (*cocaína*) cocaine; (*heroína*) heroin.
(e) las ~s (*Ajedrez*) white, the white pieces.
Blancanieves *nf* Snow White.
blanco 1 *adj* **(a)** (*gen*) white; *pan, pelo, vino* white; *piel* white, light; *tez* fair; **la raza blanca** the white race; **más ~ que el jazmín** (*o* **la nieve** *etc*) whiter than white, as white as snow; **más ~ que el papel** (*o* **la cera** *etc*) as white as a sheet.
(b) *página, espacio* blank.
(c) *verso* blank.
(d) (*: *cobarde*) yellow, cowardly.
(e) estar ~* to have a clean record.
2 *nm* **(a)** (*gen*) white; whiteness; **~ de España** whiting (*chalk*); **~ del huevo** white of egg; **~ del ojo** white of the eye; **~ de plomo** white lead; **calentar al ~** to make white-hot; **poner los ojos en ~** to roll one's eyes; to look ecstatic; **poner lo ~ negro** to make out that white is black.
(b) (*persona*) white man, white person; **los ~s** the whites.
(c) (*de animal*) white spot, white patch.
(d) (*intervalo*) interval, gap.
(e) (*espacio*) blank, blank space; **con 2 páginas en ~** with two blank pages; **cheque en ~** blank cheque; **dejar un ~** to leave a space; **dejar algo en ~** to leave sth blank; **firmar en ~** to sign a blank cheque; **votar en ~** to return a blank voting paper, spoil one's vote.
(f) (*formulario*) blank, blank form.
(g) (*Mil y fig*) target; **~ móvil** moving target; **ser el ~ de las burlas** to be the target for jokes, be the object of ridicule; **dar en el ~** to hit the mark; **hacer ~** to hit the target, strike home; **hacer ~ en** to hit, strike.
(h) dejar a uno en ~ to disappoint sb; **dejar al contrario en ~** to whitewash one's opponent*; **estoy en ~** I haven't a clue; **pasar la noche en ~** to have a sleepless night; **quedarse en ~** to fail to see the point, not understand a word; to be disappointed.
(i) los B~s (*Cono Sur Pol*) Uruguayan political party.
3 *attr*: **el vehículo ~** the target vehicle.
blancón *adj* (*And*) white-skinned.
blancor *nm* whiteness.
blancote 1 *adj* **(a)** sickly white, unhealthily white. **(b)** (*: *cobarde*) yellow, cowardly. **2** *nm* (*) coward.
blancura *nf* whiteness.
blancuzco *adj* whitish.
blandamente *adv* softly; mildly, gently; tenderly; indulgently.
blandear[1] [1a] *vt* = **blandir.**
blandear[2] [1a] **1** *vt* (*fig*) to convince, persuade. **2** *vi y* **blandearse** *vr* to soften, yield, give way; **~ con uno** to humour sb.
blandengue* 1 *adj* soft, weak. **2** *nm* soft sort, softie.
blandiporno* *adj invar*: **película ~** soft-porn film.
blandir [3a; *defectivo*] **1** *vt* to brandish, flourish, wave about. **2** *vi y* **blandirse** *vr* to wave to and fro, swing.
blando 1 *adj* **(a)** *materia, droga, agua etc* soft; *pasta etc* smooth; *carne* (*pey*) flabby, slack; **~ al tacto** soft to the touch; **~ de boca** *caballo* tender-mouthed.
(b) *tono etc* mild, gentle, bland; *clima* mild; *mirada* tender; *palabras* bland; **~ de corazón** sentimental, tender-hearted.
(c) *carácter* soft, delicate; sensual; (*indulgente*) soft, indulgent; (*Pol*) soft, wet; **ser ~ con el crimen** to be soft on crime.
(d) (*cobarde*) cowardly.
2 *nm*, **blanda** *nf* (*Pol etc*) softliner, wet.
blandón *nm* (*Ecl*) wax taper; large candlestick.
blandorro* 1 *sabor* weak, tasteless, insipid; *sonrisa etc* weak, sheepish. **2** *nm*, **blandorra** *nf* weakling, wimp*; coward.
blanducho *adj* soft, softish; *carne* (*pey*) flabby, slack.
blandujo *adj* softish.
blandura *nf* **(a)** (*cualidad*) softness; smoothness; mildness; gentleness; blandness; tenderness.
(b) (*cualidad moral*) moral softness, effeminacy.
(c) (*palabra*) blandishment, flattering words; **~s** endearments, sweet nothings.
blanduzco *adj* softish.
blanqueada *nf* (*LAm*: *jalbegue*) whitewashing; (*Méx*: *: *Dep*) whitewash.
blanqueador(a) *nm/f* bleacher.
blanquear [1a] **1** *vt* **(a)** (*gen*) to whiten; *pared* to whitewash; *tela* to bleach; *metal* to blanch; *falta, persona culpable etc** to whitewash; *dinero** to launder*. **(b)** (*Carib**) (*matar*) to kill; (*ganar*) to beat, overcome. **2** *vi* **(a)** (*volverse blanco*) to go white, turn white, whiten. **(b)** (*tirar a blanco*) to be whitish; (*mostrarse blanco*) to show white, look white.
blanquecer [2d] *vt* = **blanquear 1.**
blanquecino *adj* whitish.
blanqueo *nm* whitening; whitewashing; bleaching; (*) laundering.
blanquillo 1 *adj* whitish; *pan etc* white. **2** *nm* **(a)** (*de huevo*) white of egg; (*CAm, Méx euf*: *huevo*) egg. **(b)** (*And, Cono Sur*: *melocotón*) white peach. **(c)** (*Carib, Cono Sur*: *pez*) whitefish.
blanquimiento *nm* bleach, bleaching solution.
blanquín *nm*: **~ de gallina** (*Carib*: *euf*) hen's egg.
blanquinegro *adj* white-and-black.
blanquita‡ *nf* (*Carib*) cocaine.
blasfemador 1 *adj* blasphemous, blaspheming. **2** *nm*, **blasfemadora** *nf* blasphemer.
blasfemamente *adv* blasphemously.
blasfemar [1a] *vi* (*Ecl*) to blaspheme (*contra* against); (*fig*) to curse, swear; **~ de** to curse, swear about (*o* at).
blasfemia *nf* **(a)** (*Ecl*) blasphemy; (*injuria*) insult. **(b)** (*taco*) swearword, curse, oath.
blasfemo = **blasfemador.**
blasón *nm* **(a)** (*escudo*) coat of arms, escutcheon; bearings. **(b)** (*heráldica*) heraldry. **(c)** (*fig*: *honor*) honour, glory.
blasonar [1a] **1** *vt* to emblazon; (*fig*) to praise, extol. **2** *vi* to boast, brag; **~ de** to boast about; to boast of being.
blázer *nm* blazer.
bleck *nm* (*Cono Sur*) pitch, tar; **dar una mano de ~ a uno** to discredit sb, blacken sb's name.
bledo *nm*: **(no) me importa un ~, no se me da un ~** I don't care two hoots (*de* about).
bleque *nm* (*Cono Sur*) = **bleck.**
blindado 1 *adj* (*Mil*) armoured, armour-plated; (*Mec*) shielded, protected, encased; **puertas blindadas** reinforced doors. **2** *nm* (*Mil*) armoured vehicle.
blindaje *nm* (*Mil*) armour, armour plating; (*Téc*) shield, protective plating, casing.
blindar [1a] *vt* (*Mil*) to armour, armour-plate; (*Téc*) to shield.
b.l.m. *abr de* **besa las manos** (*courtesy formula*).
bloc *nm, pl* **blocs** pad, writing pad; calendar pad; notebook; (*Escol*) exercise book; **~ de dibujos** sketching-pad; **~ de notas** pad for notes; (reporter's) notebook; **~ de taquigrafía** shorthand book.
blocaje *nm* (*Dep*) tackle; stop; (*Mil*) blockade; (*Mec*) gripping, locking.
blocao *nm* blockhouse; pillbox.
blocar [1g] *vt* (*Dep*) *jugador* to tackle; *balón* to stop, trap, catch.
blof *nm* (*LAm*) bluff; **hacer un ~ a uno** to bluff sb.
blofear [1a] (*LAm*) *vi* to boast, brag.
blofero *adj* (*LAm*) boastful, bragging.
blofista *nmf* (*LAm*) boaster, braggart; bluffer.
blonda *nf* **(a)** (*encaje*) blond lace. **(b)** (*Cono Sur*: *rizo*) curl.

blondo *adj* (**a**) (*rubio*) blond(e); fair, light; (*liter*) flaxen. (**b**) (*LAm*: *liso*) soft, smooth, silken; (*CAm*: *lacio*) lank; (*Cono Sur, Méx*: *rizado*) curly.

bloque *nm* (**a**) (*gen*) block; ~ **(de casas)** block (of houses); ~ **de hormigón** block of concrete; ~ **de sellos** block of stamps; ~ **de cilindro** cylinder block; ~ **de papel** = **bloc**; ~ **publicitario** commercial break; ~ **de viviendas** block of flats.

(**b**) (*Pol*) bloc, group; **el** ~ **comunista** (*Hist*) the communist bloc.

(**c**) (*en tubo etc*) block, blockage, obstruction.

(**d**) **en** ~ en bloc.

bloqueante 1 *adj* paralysing; inhibiting. **2** *nm* (*droga*) inhibitor, anticatalyst.

bloquear [1a] **1** *vt* (**a**) (*estorbar etc*) to block, obstruct; (*Dep*) *jugador* to tackle; *pelota* to stop, trap; (*Rad*) to jam; ~ **una ley en la cámara** to block a bill in parliament; **los manifestantes bloquearon las calles** the demonstrators blocked the streets.

(**b**) (*Mec*) to block, jam; **el mecanismo está bloqueado** the mechanism is jammed, the mechanism is stuck.

(**c**) (*aislar*) to cut off; **la inundación bloqueó el pueblo** the flood cut off the village; **quedaron bloqueados por la nieve** they were cut off by the snow.

(**d**) (*Aut*) to brake, pull up; *volante* to lock.

(**e**) (*Mil*) to blockade.

(**f**) (*Com, Fin*) to freeze, block; **fondos bloqueados** frozen assets.

(**g**) **quedar bloqueado** (*fig*) to be paralysed with fear (*etc*).

2 bloquearse *vr*: ~ **de** (*fig*) to shut o.s. off from, shield o.s. from.

bloqueo *nm* (**a**) (*Mil*) blockade; **burlar el** ~, **forzar el** ~ to run the blockade.

(**b**) (*Com, Fin*) freezing, blocking; squeeze; ~ **de fondos** freezing of assets; ~ **informativo** news blackout.

(**c**) ~ **mental** mental block.

(**d**) ~ **central de cerraduras** central locking.

b.l.p. *abr de* **besa los pies** (*courtesy formula*).

bluejean *nm* (*Cono Sur*) jeans.

blufar [1a] (*etc*) = **blofear** (*etc*).

bluff [bluf] *nm* bluff.

blumes *nmpl*: **tener** ~ (*Carib**) to be fussy, be finicky.

blusa *nf* (*de mujer*) blouse; (*mono*) overall; (*bata*) smock.

blusón *nm* smock; (*Mil*) jacket.

BN 1 *nf* (*Esp*) *abr de* **Biblioteca Nacional. 2** *nm* (*Perú*) *abr de* **Banco de la Nación.**

b/n *abr de* **blanco y negro** black-and-white, b/w.

B.º (**a**) (*Fin*) *abr de* **banco** bank, bk. (**b**) (*Com*) *abr de* **beneficiario** beneficiary.

boa *nf* boa.

boardilla *nf* = **buhardilla**.

boato *nm* show, showiness, ostentation; pomp, pageantry.

bob *nm* bobsleigh.

bobada *nf* silly thing, stupid thing; **esto es una** ~ this is nonsense; **decir ~s** to say silly things, talk nonsense; **¡no digas ~s!** come off it!

bobales* *nmf invar*, **bobalías** *nmf invar* nitwit*, dolt.

bobalicón* 1 *adj* silly. **2** *nm*, **bobalicona** *nf* nitwit*, dolt.

bobamente *adv* stupidly; naïvely.

bobático* *adj* silly, half-witted.

bobear [1a] *vi* to fool about, do silly things; to talk nonsense, say silly things.

bobelas* *nmf invar* idiot, chump*.

bobera *nf* = **bobada, bobería.**

boberá *nmf* (*Carib*) fool.

bobería *nf* (**a**) (*cualidad*) silliness, idiocy. (**b**) = **bobada.**

bobeta 1 *adj* (*Cono Sur*) silly, stupid. **2** *nmf* (*Cono Sur*; *t ~s And*) fool, idiot.

bobicomio *nm* (*And*) lunatic asylum.

bóbilis *adv* (*t* **de** ~) (*gratis*) free, for nothing; (*sin esfuerzo*) without effort, without lifting a finger.

bobina *nf* (*Téc*) bobbin, spool; reel; drum, cylinder; (*Fot*) spool, reel; (*de cinta*) reel; (*Aut, Elec*) coil; ~ **de encendido** ignition coil.

bobinado *nm* (*Elec*) winding.

bobinadora *nf* winder, winding machine.

bobinar [1a] *vt* to wind.

bobo 1 *adj* (*tonto*) silly, stupid; (*simple*) simple; (*ingenuo*) naïve.

2 *nm*, **boba** *nf* (**a**) (*tonto*) idiot, fool; greenhorn; (*Teat*) clown, funny man; **a los ~s se les aparece la madre de Dios** fortune favours fools; **entre ~s anda el juego** (*iró*) they're well matched; one's as bad as the other.

(**b**) (*) (*Carib*: *reloj*) watch; (*Cono Sur*: *corazón*) heart, ticker*.

boboliche *nm* (*And*) fool.

bobsleigh ['bobslei] *nm* bobsleigh.

boca 1 *nf* (**a**) (*Anat*) mouth; ~ **de dragón** (*Bot*) snapdragon; ~ **de escorpión** (*fig*) wicked tongue; ~ **de mar** (*Culin*) crab-stick; **a** ~ verbally, by word of mouth; ~ **a** ~ (*nm*) rumour, piece of hearsay; **respiración** ~ **a** ~ kiss of life, mouth-to-mouth resuscitation; **a pedir de** ~ as much as one wishes, to one's heart's content; for the asking; **todo salió a pedir de** ~ it all turned out perfectly; **en** ~ **de** (*LAm*) according to; ~ **abajo** face downward; **apoyó la idea de** ~ **afuera** he paid lip-service to the idea; ~ **arriba** face upward; **aceituna de** ~ eating olive; **abrir tanta** ~ (*And, Carib, Méx*) to stand amazed; **andar en** ~ **de la gente** to be talked about; **la cosa anda** (*o* **va**) **de** ~ **en** ~ the story is going the rounds; **ella anda de** ~ **en** ~ she is the subject of gossip, people are talking about her; **buscar la** ~ **a uno** to (try to) draw sb out; to provoke sb; **calentársele a uno la** ~ to talk a lot; to get worked up; **¡cállate la** ~**!*** shut up!*; **coserse la** ~* to shut up*, keep mum; **dar** ~* to gab*, chat; **decir algo con la** ~ **chica** (*o* **pequeña**) to say sth without really meaning it; **no decir esta** ~ **es mía** not to open one's mouth; **lo hizo sin decir esta** ~ **es mía** he did it without a word to anybody; **en** ~ **cerrada no entran moscas** silence is golden; mum's the word; **hablar por** ~ **de ganso** to repeat sth parrot fashion; **hacer** ~ to work up an appetite; **se me hace la** ~ **agua** my mouth is watering; **se le llena la** ~ he's just paying lip service; **se le llena la** ~ **del coche** all he can talk about is the car; **meter a uno en la** ~ **del lobo** to put sb on the spot; **meterse en la** ~ **del lobo** to put one's head in the lion's mouth; **por la** ~ **muere el pez** silence is golden; **partir la** ~ **a uno*** to smash sb's face in*; **quedarse con la** ~ **abierta** to be dumbfounded; **¡qué tu** ~ **sea santa!** (*Carib*) I hope you're right!; **tapar la** ~ **a uno** to shut sb's mouth; **torcer la** ~ to make a wry face; to sneer.

(**b**) (*fig*: *abertura*) mouth, entrance, opening; approach; ~ **de agua,** ~ **de incendios,** ~ **de riego** hydrant; ~ **del estómago** pit of the stomach; **a** ~ **de invierno** at the start of winter; **a** ~ **de jarro** *beber* excessively, immoderately; (*Mil*) point-blank, at close range; *anunciar etc* point-blank; ~ **de metro** tube station entrance, subway entrance (*US*); ~ **de mina** pithead, mine entrance; ~**(s) de río** river mouth, mouth of a river.

(**c**) (*de cañón*) muzzle, mouth; **a** ~ **de cañón** (*LAm*) at point-blank range.

(**d**) (*de bogavante etc*) pincer; (*de herramienta*) cutting edge.

(**e**) (*de barril*) bunghole.

(**f**) (*CAm*: *t* ~**s**) (*tapa*) bar snack.

(**g**) (*de vino*) flavour, taste; **tener buena** ~ to have a good flavour.

(**h**) (*Inform*) slot.

2 *nm*(‡) screw‡, warder.

bocabajear [1a] *vt* (*LAm*) to put down, crush.

bocabajo *nm* (*Carib*) beating.

bocacalle *nf* entrance to a street; intersection; **la primera** ~ the first turning.

Bocacio *nm* Boccaccio.

bocacha *nf* (**a**) (‡) bigmouth‡. (**b**) (*Mil, Hist*) blunderbuss.

bocacho *adj* (*Cono Sur*) (*t**) big-mouthed.

bocadear [1a] *vt* to cut up (for eating).

bocadillería *nf* (*Esp*) snack bar, sandwich bar.

bocadillo *nm* (**a**) (*Esp*: *tapa*) snack. (**b**) (*emparedado*) sandwich, meat (*o* cheese *etc*) roll; **tomar un** ~ to have a snack, have a bite to eat. (**c**) (*en dibujo*) balloon, bubble.

bocadito *nm* (**a**) (*mordisco*) small bite, morsel, bit; **~s** (*And*) snack, appetizer; **a ~s** (*fig*) piecemeal. (**b**) (*Carib*) (*cigarrillo*) cigarette wrapped in tobacco leaf; **~s** bar snacks.

bocado *nm* (**a**) (*mordisco*) mouthful; morsel, bite; **no hay para un** ~ that's not nearly enough; **no he pasado** (*o* **probado**) ~ **en todo el día** I've not had a bite to eat all day; **no tener para un** ~ to be completely penniless; **tomar un** ~ to have a bite to eat; ~ **exquisito,** ~ **regalado** titbit; **el** ~ **del león** the lion's share; ~ **sin hueso** sinecure, soft job.

(**b**) (*freno*) bit; bridle.

(**c**) ~ **de Adán** (*Anat*) Adam's apple.

(**d**) (*And*: *veneno*) (animal) poison.

(**e**) (*: *astilla*) sweetener*, backhander*.

bocajarro: **a** ~ *adv* (*Mil*) at close range, point-blank; **decir algo a** ~ to say sth straight out.

bocal *nm* (**a**) (*jarra*) pitcher, jar. (**b**) (*Mús*, †) mouthpiece.
bocallave *nf* keyhole.
bocamanga *nf* (**a**) (*puño*) cuff, wristband. (**b**) (*Méx: agujero*) hole for the head (in a cape).
bocamina *nf* pithead, mine entrance.
bocana *nf* (river) mouth.
bocanada *nf* (**a**) (*de vino etc*) mouthful, swallow.
(**b**) (*de humo, viento*) puff; (*de aliento*) gust, blast.
(**c**) **echar ~s** to boast, brag.
(**d**) **~ de gente** crush of people.
bocaracá *nm* (*CAm*) snake.
bocarada *nf* (*LAm*) = **bocanada**.
bocata* *nm* = **bocadillo** (**a**).
bocatero, -a *nm/f* (*Carib*) loudmouth*, braggart.
bocatoma *nf* (*LAm*) water intake, inlet pipe.
bocaza* *nmf*, **bocazas*** *nmf invar* bigmouth‡; ¡~! (*insulto*) bigmouth!‡
bocera *nf* (*gen pl*) smear on the lips.
boceras* *nmf invar* idiot, fool; bigmouth‡.
bocetista *nmf* sketcher.
boceto *nm* (*bosquejo*) sketch, outline; (*diseño*) design; (*maqueta*) model, mock-up.
bocina *nf* (*Mús*) trumpet; (*Aut, de gramófono*) horn; (*megáfono*) megaphone; speaking trumpet; (*LAm: trompetilla*) ear-trumpet; (*Méx Telec*) mouthpiece; (*Cono Sur‡: soplón*) grass‡, informer; **~ de niebla** foghorn; **tocar la ~** (*Aut*) to sound one's horn.
bocinar [1a] *vi* (*Aut*) to sound one's horn, blow the horn, hoot.
bocinazo *nm* (*Aut*) hoot, toot, blast (of the horn); **dar el ~‡** to grass‡.
bocinero, -a *nm/f* horn player.
bocio *nm* goitre.
bock [bok] *nm, pl* **bocks** [bok] beer-glass, tankard.
bocón 1 *adj* (**a**) (*lit*) big-mouthed.
(**b**) (*fig: jactancioso*) boastful, big-mouthed‡; (*Carib, Cono Sur: gritón*) loud-mouthed; (*chismoso*) backbiting, gossipy; (*Méx: poco discreto*) indiscreet.
2 *nm* braggart; ¡~! (*) bigmouth!‡
bocoy *nm* hogshead, large cask.
bocha *nf* (**a**) (*bola*) bowl; **juego de las ~s** bowls. (**b**) (*Cono Sur‡*) nut‡.
bochar [1a] *vt* (**a**) (*Carib, Méx: rechazar*) to rebuff, reject. (**b**) (*Cono Sur: no aprobar*) to fail, flunk‡.
boche *nm* (**a**) (*Cono Sur Agr*) husks, chaff.
(**b**) (*Carib*: regañada*) telling-off*, dressing-down*.
(**c**) (*Carib: rechazo*) snub, slight; **dar ~ a uno** to snub sb, cold-shoulder sb.
(**d**) (*And, Cono Sur*) (*jaleo*) uproar, din; (*pelea*) brawl.
bochinche *nm* (**a**) (*jaleo*) uproar, din; (*motín*) riot; (*disturbio*) commotion.
(**b**) (*And, Carib: chisme*) piece of gossip.
(**c**) (*Méx: baile*) rave-up*; (*fiesta*) wild party.
(**d**) (*Méx: bar*) seedy bar, dive; (*tienda*) local stores.
(**e**) (*Carib*) muddle, mess.
bochinchear [1a] *vi* (*LAm*) to kick up a din, make a racket.
bochinchero 1 *adj* (*LAm*) rowdy, brawling. **2** *nm* (*LAm*) rowdy, brawler.
bochinchoso *adj* (**a**) (*LAm: chismoso*) gossiping, telltale, gossipy. (**b**) (*And: agresivo*) rowdy, noisy. (**c**) (*quisquilloso*) fussy, finicky.
bocho *nm*: **ser un ~** (*Cono Sur*) to be brainy, be clever.
bochorno *nm* (**a**) (*Met: calor*) sultry weather, oppressive weather; (*atmósfera*) stifling atmosphere; sultriness; (*viento*) hot summer breeze.
(**b**) (*Med*) queer turn; hot flush; blush.
(**c**) (*fig: vergüenza*) embarrassment, flush, (feeling of) shame; (*tacha*) stigma, dishonour; **¡qué ~!** how embarrassing!
bochornoso *adj* (**a**) (*Met*) sultry, oppressive; thundery; stuffy, stifling.
(**b**) (*fig: violento*) embarrassing; (*vergonzoso*) humiliating, shameful, disgraceful, degrading; **es un espectáculo ~** it is a degrading spectacle, it is a shameful sight.
boda *nf* (*t ~s: acto*) wedding, marriage; (*fiesta*) wedding reception; **~s de diamante** diamond wedding, (*de club etc*) diamond jubilee; **~s de oro** golden wedding, (*de club etc*) golden jubilee; **~s de plata** silver wedding, (*de club etc*) silver jubilee; **~ de negros** rowdy party.
bodega *nf* (*depósito de vinos*) wine cellar; (*despensa*) pantry; (*almacén*) storeroom, warehouse; (*tienda*) wine shop; (*Náut*) hold; (*esp LAm: bar*) bar, tavern; (*restaurante*) restaurant; (*LAm: tienda de comestibles*) grocery store, general store; **~ de carga** (*Aer*) hold.
bodegón *nm* (**a**) cheap restaurant. (**b**) (*Arte*) still life.
bodegonista *nmf* still-life painter.
bodeguero 1 *adj* (*Carib*) coarse, common. **2** *nm* (**a**) (*productor*) wine-producer; (*Com*) vintner; (*obrero*) cellarman; (*dueño*) owner of a *bodega*. (**b**) (*And, Carib: tendero*) grocer.
bodijo* *nm* quiet wedding; (*pey*) misalliance, unequal match.
bodolle *nm* (*Cono Sur*) large pruning knife, billhook.
bodoque *nm* (**a**) (*balita*) small ball, pellet (of clay).
(**b**) (*hinchazón*) lump; (*CAm, Méx*) (*Med*) lump, swelling; (*bolita*) lump, ball; (*CAm: manojo*) bunch.
(**c**) (*Méx: cosa mal hecha*) badly-made thing.
(**d**) (*: *tonto*) dimwit*.
bodorrio *nm* (**a**) = **bodijo**. (**b**) (*Méx: fiesta*) rowdy party.
bodrio *nm* (**a**) (*confusión*) mix-up, mess. (**b**) (*cosa mal hecha*) badly-made thing; monstrosity, piece of rubbish; **un ~ de sitio** an awful place.
body ['boðɪ] *nm, pl* **bodies** ['boðɪs] body-stocking.
BOE *nm* (*Esp*) *abr de* **Boletín Oficial del Estado**.
bóer 1 *adj* Boer. **2** *nmf, pl* **bóers** Boer.
bofe *nm* (*Zool*) lung; **~s** lungs, lights; **echar el ~, echar los ~s** to slog, slave; **echar los ~s por algo** to go all out for sth.
bofetada *nf* (*palmada*) slap in the face (*t fig*); (*puñetazo*) cuff, punch; **dar de ~s a uno** to hit sb, punch sb; **darse de ~s** to come to blows; (*colores*) to clash.
bofetón* *nm* punch (in the face), hard slap.
bofia‡ 1 *nf*: **la ~** the cops*. **2** *nm* cop*, copper*.
boga¹ *nf* vogue, fashion; popularity; **la ~ de la minifalda** the fashion for the miniskirt, the popularity of the miniskirt; **estar en ~** to be in fashion, be in vogue; **poner algo en ~** to establish a fashion for sth.
boga² *nf* (*Ferro etc*) bogey.
boga³ 1 *nmf* rower; oarsman, oarswoman. **2** *nf* rowing.
bogada *nf* stroke (of an oar).
bogador *nm*, **bogadora** *nf*, **bogante** *nmf* rower; oarsman, oarswoman.
bogar [1h] *vi* to row; to sail, move.
bogavante *nm* (**a**) (*Náut*) stroke, first rower. (**b**) (*Zool*) lobster.
bogotano 1 *adj* of Bogotá. **2** *nm*, **bogotana** *nf* native (*o* inhabitant) of Bogotá; **los ~s** the people of Bogotá.
bogotazo *nm* (*And*) ruin, destruction, pillage.
bohardilla *nf* = **buhardilla**.
Bohemia *nf* Bohemia.
bohémico *adj* (*Geog*) Bohemian.
bohemio, -a, (*fig*), **bohemo, -a** (*Geog*) *adj, nm/f* Bohemian.
bohío *nm* (*LAm*) hut, shack.
boicot *nm, pl* **boicots** boycott.
boicotear [1a] *vt* (*gen*) to boycott; (*sabotear*) to sabotage.
boicoteo *nm* boycott, boycotting; sabotaging.
boicotero *nm* (*LAm*) boycott.
boina 1 *nf* beret. **2** *nm*: **~ verde** commando.
boite *nf*, **boîte** *nf* [bwat] night-club.
boj(e) *nm* (*planta*) box; (*madera*) boxwood.
boje *adj* (*Méx*) silly, stupid.
bojote *nm* (**a**) (*LAm: lío*) bundle, package. (**b**) (*CAm: trozo*) lump, chunk. (**c**) (*LAm: fig*) **un ~ de** a lot of, a great many of. (**d**) (*Carib*) fuss, row.
bol *nm* (**a**) (*gen*) bowl; punch bowl; (*LAm*) finger bowl. (**b**) (*Dep*) ninepin.
bola *nf* (**a**) (*pelota etc*) ball; (*canica*) marble; (*Náut*) signal (with discs); (*Tip*) golfball; (*LAm Dep*) ball, football; (‡: *cabeza*) nut‡; **~s** (*Mec*) ball-bearings; (*LAm Caza*) bolas; (‡‡) balls‡‡; **~ de billar** billiard ball; **estar como ~ de billar** to be as bald as a coot; **~ de contar** abacus bead; **~ de cristal** crystal ball; **~ de fuego** fireball; (*Met*) ball lightning; **~ del mundo** globe; **~ de naftalina** mothball; **~ negra** black ball; **~ de nieve** snowball; **~ de partido** (*Tenis*) match ball; **~ de tempestad, ~ de tormenta** storm signal; **juego de (las) ~s** American skittles; **tú a tu ~*** that's up to you; don't you worry about it; **cambiar la ~** (*Carib**) to change one's mind; **dar ~** (*Cono Sur**) to take notice, pay attention; **dar la ~*** to be released (from jail); **¡dale ~!** what, again!; come off it!; **dejar que ruede la ~** to let things take their course; **escurrir la ~** to take French leave; **hacerse ~s*** (*LAm*) to get o.s. tied up in knots; **ir a su ~** to go one's own way; **ir en ~s‡** to be starkers‡; **poner ~s a** to pay attention to; **pasarse de la ~** (*Carib**) to go too far; **no rasca ~‡** he doesn't do a stroke; **tragar la ~** to rise to the bait, swallow the bait; **¡qué ~s!*** (*Carib, Cono

Sur) what a nerve!*
(**b**) (*Naipes*) slam, grand slam; **media** ~ small slam.
(**c**) (*betún*) shoe polish, blacking.
(**d**) (*cuento*) fib, tale; (*rumor*) rumour.
(**e**) (*Méx: ruido*) row, hubbub; (*pelea*) brawl; (*fiesta*) noisy party.
(**f**) **una ~ de gente** (*Méx*) a (whole) crowd (of people).
bolacear [1a] *vi* (*Cono Sur*) to talk rubbish.
bolaco *nm* (*Cono Sur*) ruse, device.
bolada *nf* (**a**) (*echada*) throw (of a ball); (*Billar etc*) stroke.
(**b**) **~ de aficionado** (*Cono Sur*) intervention (by a third party).
(**c**) (*LAm: suerte*) piece of luck, lucky break; (*Com: ganga*) bargain, lucky piece of business.
(**d**) (*LAm: mentira*) fib, lie; (*Méx: chiste*) joke, witty comment; (*Méx: engaño*) trick, con*.
(**e**) (*Cono Sur: golosina*) titbit, treat.
bolado *nm* (**a**) (*CAm, Cono Sur, Méx: negocio*) (business) deal; (*Méx: amorío*) love affair, flirtation.
(**b**) (*CAm Billar*) clever stroke.
(**c**) (*CAm*) (*cuento*) fib, tale; (*chisme*) rumour, piece of gossip.
(**d**) (*LAm: locuciones*) **¡hazme un ~!*** do me a favour!*; **esta noche tengo un ~*** I've got something on tonight.
bolamen** *nm* balls**.
bolardo *nm* bollard.
bolata‡ *nm* ex-con‡, old lag‡.
bolate *nm* (*And*) = **volate**.
bolazo *nm* (**a**) (*Cono Sur*) (*disparate*) silly remark, piece of nonsense; (*noticia falsa*) false news; (*mentira*) fib, lie; (*error*) mistake, error; **mandarse un ~** to put one's foot in it. (**b**) **al** (*o* **de**) **~** (*Méx*) at random; any old way.
bolchevique *adj, nmf* Bolshevik.
bolchevismo *nm* Bolshevism.
bolea *nf* (*Dep*) volley.
boleada¹ *nf* (*Cono Sur* ††) hunt, hunting expedition (with *bolas*).
boleada² *nf* (*Méx*) shoeshine.
boleado¹ *adj* (*Cono Sur*): **estar ~** to have lost one's touch; to be up the creek‡.
boleado² *nm* (*Méx*) shoeshine.
boleador(a) *nm/f* (*Méx*) (*chico*) shoeshine boy; (*chica*) shoeshine girl.
boleadoras *nfpl* (*Cono Sur*) *bolas*, lasso with balls.
bolear¹ [1a] **1** *vt* (**a**) *pelota* to throw.
(**b**) (*LAm*††: *cazar*) to hunt; (*atrapar*) to catch with *bolas*; (*And, Cono Sur: fig*) to floor, flummox.
(**c**) (*LAm*) *candidato* to reject, blackball; (*) *obrero* to sack*, fire*; (*Univ etc*) to fail.
2 *vi* (**a**) (*jugar*) to play for fun, knock the balls about.
(**b**) (*: *mentir*) to tell fibs.
(**c**) (*jactarse*) to boast.
3 bolearse *vr* (**a**) (*Cono Sur: caballo*) to rear and fall on its back; (*Aut*) to overturn.
(**b**) (*Cono Sur**) (*quedar perplejo*) to get confused, get bewildered; (*avergonzarse*) to be shamefaced.
bolear² [1a] *vt* (*Méx*) *zapatos* to shine, polish.
boleco *adj* (*CAm*) drunk.
bolera *nf* bowling-alley, skittle-alley.
bolería *nf* (*Méx*) shoeshine shop.
bolero¹ *nm* (**a**) (*baile, chaqueta*) bolero. (**b**) (*CAm, Méx: chistera*) top hat.
bolero² *nm* (*Méx*) bootblack.
boleta *nf* (**a**) (*gen*: †) pass, permit; (*permiso*) authorization; (*billete*) ticket; (*Cono Sur*) first draft of a deed; (*LAm: borrador*) draft (document); (*And: certificado*) certificate; (*And: permiso*) authorization, permit; (*LAm: papeleta*) ballot, voting paper; (*Cono Sur Escol*) (school) report; (*Carib: multa*) fine, penalty; **~ de venta** (*Cono Sur*) sales chit, receipt.
(**b**) (*Mil*) billet.
(**c**) (*tabaco*) small packet of tobacco.
(**d**) (*Cono Sur‡*) **hacer la ~ a uno** to murder sb, knock sb off‡; **ser ~** to be condemned to death.
boletería *nf* (**a**) (*LAm: gen*) ticket agency; (*Ferro etc*) ticket office; (*Teat*) box-office. (**b**) (*LAm: recaudación*) gate, takings.
boletero, -a *nm/f* (*LAm*) ticket clerk.
boletín *nm* bulletin; (*Liter*) bulletin, journal, review; (*Teat etc*) ticket; (*Carib: Ferro*) ticket; (*Mil*) pay warrant; (*Mil*) billet; (*Escol*) report; (*Com*) cut-out coupon; **~ facultativo** medical report; **~ informativo** news bulletin, news sheet; **~ de inscripción** registration form; **~ meteorológico** weather report, weather forecast; **~ naviero** shipping register; **~ de notas** school report; **~ de noticias** news bulletin; **~ oficial** official gazette; **~ de pedido** application form; (*Com*) order form; **~ de precios** price list; **~ de prensa** press-release; **~ de suscripción** subscription form.
boleto *nm* (**a**) (*LAm: gen*) ticket; **~ de ida y vuelta, de regreso, ~ de viaje redondo** return ticket, round-trip ticket (*US*); *y compárese* **billete**.
(**b**) (*de quiniela*) coupon; **~ de apuestas** betting slip.
(**c**) **de ~** (*Mex: como adv*) at once.
boli* *nm* = **bolígrafo**.
bolichada *nf* lucky break, stroke of luck; **de una ~** at one go.
boliche¹ *nm* (**a**) (*bola*) jack.
(**b**) (*juego: bochas*) bowls; ten-pin bowling; (*bolos*) skittles.
(**c**) (*bolera*) bowling alley.
(**d**) (*juguete*) cup-and-ball toy.
(**e**) (*red*) small dragnet.
(**f**) (*horno*) small furnace, smelting furnace.
boliche² *nm* (*And, Cono Sur: tienda*) grocer's, small grocery shop (*o* store); (*Cono Sur: snack*) cheap snack bar; (*And: tahona*) low-class bakery; (*Cono Sur: garita*) gambling den.
boliche³* *nm* (*LAm*) Bolivian.
bolichero *nm* (*Cono Sur*) small shopkeeper.
bólido *nm* (**a**) (*Astron*) meteorite. (**b**) (*Aut*) racing car, hot-rod* (*US*); (*hum*) (any) car; (*Náut*) powerboat, speedboat; **iba como un ~*** he was really shifting*.
bolígrafo *nm* ball-point pen.
bolilla *nf* (**a**) (*Cono Sur: canica*) marble. (**b**) (*Cono Sur Univ*) (piece of paper bearing) examination question; **dar ~ a** to be aware of.
bolillo *nm* (**a**) (*Cos*) bobbin (for lacemaking). (**b**) (*LAm Mús*) drumstick. (**c**) (*Méx Culin*) bread roll.
bolina *nf* (**a**) (*Náut: cabo*) bowline; (*sonda*) lead, sounding line; **de ~** close-hauled; **navegar de ~** to sail close to the wind. (**b**) (*: *jaleo*) racket, row, uproar.
bolinga‡ **1** *adj invar*: **estar ~** to be canned‡. **2** *nm*: **estar de ~** to be boozing*; **ir de ~** to go on the booze*.
bolita *nf* (**a**) (*gen*) small ball; pellet; (*Cono Sur: canica*) marble. (**b**) (*Cono Sur Pol*) ballot paper.
bolívar *nm* bolívar (*Venezuelan unit of currency*); **no verle la cara a B~*** to be broke*.
Bolivia *nf* Bolivia.
bolivianismo *nm* bolivianism, word (*o* phrase *etc*) peculiar to Bolivia.
boliviano, -a *adj, nm/f* Bolivian.
bolo¹ *nm* (**a**) (*Dep*) ninepin, skittle; (**juego de**) **~s** ninepins, skittles, tenpin bowling; **andar en ~** (*And*) to be naked; **ir en ~** (*Carib*) to run off, run away; **tumbar ~** (*And*) to do well, bring it off; **echar a rodar los ~s** (*fig*) to create a disturbance.
(**b**) (*Med*) large pill.
(**c**) (*moneda*) (*Fin Esp*) 5-peseta coin; (*Carib, Méx*) one-peso coin; (*Venezuela*) one-bolívar coin.
(**d**) (*Cartas*) slam.
(**e**) (*Méx: regalo*) christening present (from godparents).
(**f**) (**) prick**.
bolo²‡ **1** *adj* (*CAm: borracho*) drunk, plastered‡. **2** *nm* drunk*.
bolo³* *nm* (*Mús*) gig, concert.
bolón *nm* (**a**) (*Cono Sur: piedra*) building stone; (*Carib*) marble. (**b**) (*Carib: muchedumbre*) mob, rabble.
Bolonia *nf* Bologna.
bolonio*, -a *nm/f* dunce, ignoramus.
boloñesa *nf* bolognese sauce, meat sauce.
bolsa *nf* (**a**) (*gen*) bag; (*morral*) pouch; (*de mujer*) handbag; (*monedero*) purse; (*LAm: bolsillo*) sack; (*And, CAm, Méx: bolsillo*) pocket; **~ de agua caliente** hot-water bottle; **~ de baño** beach bag; **~ de basura** refuse sack, rubbish bag; **~ de la compra** shopping bag; **~ de cultivo** growbag; **~ de deportes** sports bag; **~ de herramientas** toolbag; **~ de hielo** ice-pack, pack of ice; **~s de mano** hand-luggage; **~ de palos** golfing bag; **~ de papel** paper bag; **~ de patatas fritas** packet of crisps; **~ de plástico** plastic bag, carrier-bag; **~ para tabaco** tobacco pouch; **~ de té** tea bag; **¡la ~ o la vida!** your money or your life!; **no abre fácilmente la ~** he's pretty mean; **hacer algo de ~** (*Cono Sur*) to do sth at somebody else's expense; **hacer algo ~** (*Cono Sur**) (*objeto*) to tear sth to pieces; (*persona*) to do sth at somebody else's expense; **volver a uno ~** (*Méx*) to swindle sb.
(**b**) (*Cos: de vestido etc*) bag; **hacer ~** to bag, pucker up.

(**c**) (*Mil*) pocket.

(**d**) (*Geol*) pocket; ~ **de aire** (*Aer*) air pocket; **todavía hay ~s de pobreza** there are still pockets of poverty.

(**e**) (*Anat, Zool*) cavity, sac; pouch; **~s de los ojos** bags under the eyes.

(**f**) (*Com, Fin*) stock exchange; stock market; ~ **de divisas** foreign-exchange market; ~ **de granos** corn exchange; ~ **negra** (*LAm*) black market; **'B~ de la propiedad'** (*sección de periódico*) 'Property Mart', 'Property for Sale'; ~ **de trabajo** labour exchange, employment bureau; **precio en la** ~ price on the stock exchange; **jugar a la** ~ to speculate, play the market; **sacar una emisión a** ~ to float an issue on the stock market; *V* **cotizar** *etc.*

(**g**) ~ **de estudio** educational grant; ~ **de viaje** travel grant, grant for travelling.

bolsear [1a] **1** *vt*: **la bolsearon** she had her handbag stolen; ~ **a uno** (*CAm, Méx*) to pick sb's pocket. **2** *vi* (**a**) (*CAm, Méx*) to pick pockets. (**b**) (*CAm, Cono Sur, Méx*: *estafar*) to cheat, swindle.

bolsicón *nm* (*And*) thick flannel skirt.

bolsicona *nf* (*And*) peasant woman.

bolsillo *nm* (**a**) (*gen*) pocket; (*monedero*) purse, moneybag, pocketbook; **guardar algo en el** ~ to put sth in one's pocket, pocket sth; **meterse a uno en el** ~ to win sb over, have sb eating out of one's hand; **rascarse el** ~* to pay up, fork out*; **tentarse el** ~ (*fig*) to feel in one's pocket, consider one's financial circumstances; **tener a uno en el** ~ to have sb captivated.

(**b**) **de** ~ pocket (*atr*), pocket-size; **edición de** ~ pocket edition; **acorazado de** ~ pocket battleship.

bolsín *nm* kerb market (in stocks and shares).

bolsiquear [1a] *vt* (*Cono Sur*): ~ **a uno** (*registrar*) to search (*o* go through) sb's pockets; (*robar*) to pick sb's pockets.

bolsista *nmf* (**a**) (*Fin*) stockbroker. (**b**) (*CAm, Méx*: *ladrón*) pickpocket.

bolsita *nf*: ~ **de té** tea bag.

bolso *nm* bag, purse (*US*); handbag, purse (*US*); ~ **de aseo** toilet bag; ~ **de bandolera** shoulder-bag; ~ **de mano,** ~ **de mujer** handbag, purse (*US*); ~ **de viaje** travelling bag; **hacer** ~ (*vela*) to fill, belly out.

bolsón 1 *nm* (**a**) (*And*: *bolso*) handbag, purse (*US*).

(**b**) (*And Min*) lump of ore.

(**c**) (*Méx*: *lago*) lagoon.

(**d**) (*And*: *tonto*) fool.

2 *adj* (**a**) (*And*: *tonto*) silly, foolish.

(**e**) (*Carib, Méx*: *perezoso*) lazy.

bolsonada *nf* (*And, Cono Sur*) silly thing to do, act of foolishness.

boludear‡ [1a] *vi* (*Cono Sur*) to mess about.

boludez‡ *nf* (*Cono Sur*) (**a**) (*cosa fácil*) piece of cake*.

(**b**) (*acto*) stupid thing to do; **boludeces** (*palabras*) rubbish, nonsense.

boludo‡ (*And, Cono Sur*) **1** *adj* thick*, stupid. **2** *nm*, **boluda** *nf* wally‡, nerd‡.

bollera‡ *nf* lesbian, dyke‡.

bollería *nf* baker's (shop), bakery, pastry shop.

bollero, -a *nm/f* baker, pastrycook.

bollo *nm* (**a**) (*Culin*) bread roll; bun; **perdonar el ~ por el coscorrón** to realize that it's more trouble than it's worth; **no pela** ~ (*Carib*) he never gets it wrong.

(**b**) (*abolladura*) dent; (*Med*) bump, lump; (*Cos*) puff.

(**c**) (*fig*: *confusión*) confusion; mix-up; **armar(se)** ~ to make a fuss; **meter a uno en el** ~ to get sb into trouble.

(**d**) (*CAm, Cono Sur*: *puñetazo*) punch.

(**e**) **~s** (*And*) troubles, problems.

(**f**) (*CAm, Carib***) cunt**.

bollón *nm* (*tachón*) (ornamented) stud; (*de oreja*) button earring.

bomba 1 *nf* (**a**) (*Mil etc*) bomb; (*proyectil*) shell; (*carga*) charge; ~ **atómica** atomic bomb; ~ **cazabobos** booby-trap bomb; ~ **de cobalto** cobalt bomb; ~ **de dispersión,** ~ **de racimo** (*Cono Sur*) cluster-bomb; ~ **de acción retardada** time-bomb; ~ **fétida** stink-bomb; ~ **de fósforo** incendiary bomb; ~ **de fragmentación** fragmentation bomb; ~ **H** H-bomb; ~ **de hidrógeno** hydrogen bomb; ~ **de humo** smoke-bomb; ~ **incendiaria** incendiary bomb; ~ **lacrimógena** tear-gas bomb; ~ **de mano** grenade, hand-grenade; ~ **nuclear** nuclear bomb; ~ **de profundidad** depth charge; ~ **de racimo** cluster-bomb; ~ **de efecto retardado,** ~ **de relojería,** ~ **de retardo** time-bomb; ~ **revientamanzanas,** ~ **vuelamanzanas** blockbuster; ~ **volante** flying bomb; **a prueba de ~s** bombproof, shellproof; **atacar con ~s, lanzar ~s sobre** to bomb, drop bombs on; **caer como una** ~ to fall like a bombshell; **estar a tres ~s** to be very cross; **estar echando ~s** to be boiling hot.

(**b**) (*fig*: *sorpresa*) surprise; (*notición*) bombshell, surprising item of news; (*éxito*) great success; **¡~!** attention please!; **es la** ~ **del año** it's the surprise of the year; **caer como una** ~ to come as a bombshell.

(**c**) (*Téc*) pump; (*Mús*) slide; (*Cono Sur*: *Aut*) garage, petrol-station; ~ **de aire** air-pump; ~ **de alimentación** feed-pump; ~ **aspirante** suction pump; ~ **bencinera** (*Carib, Cono Sur*) petrol-station, gas station (*US*); ~ **de engrase** grease-gun; ~ **de gasolina** (*en motor*) fuel-pump; (*de garaje*) petrol-pump, gas pump (*US*); ~ **impelente,** ~ **impulsora** force pump; ~ **de incendios** fire-engine; ~ **de inyección (de combustible)** fuel-pump; ~ **de pie** footpump; ~ **de succión** suction pump; **dar a la** ~ to pump, work the pump.

(**d**) (*de lámpara*) shade; glass, globe.

(**e**) (*And*: *burbuja*) soap bubble.

(**f**) (*Carib*: *tambor*) big drum; (*baile*) dance accompanied by a drum.

(**g**) (*And, Carib*: *globo*) balloon; (*Carib, Cono Sur*: *cometa*) round kite.

(**h**) (*Carib, Méx*: *chistera*) top hat.

(**i**) (*And, CAm, Cono Sur*) (*juerga*) drinking spree; (*embriaguez*) drunkenness; **estar en** ~ to be drunk.

(**j**) (*LAm*) (*rumor*) false rumour; (*mentira*) lie; (*Carib*: *noticia*) piece of news.

2 *adj invar* (*) (**a**) sensational; **noticia** ~ shattering piece of news; **está** ~ she's smashing*.

(**b**) **estar** ~ (*And**) to be clapped-out*.

3 *adv*: **pasarlo** ~* to have a grand time, have a whale of a time*.

bombachas[1] *nfpl* (*Cono Sur*: *de mujer*) panties.

bombachas[2] *nfpl* (*And, Cono Sur*), **bombaches** *nmpl* (*Carib*) baggy trousers, peasant trousers.

bombacho 1 *adj* (*LAm*) baggy, loose-fitting. **2 bombachos** *nmpl* baggy trousers; (*de golf etc*) plus-fours.

bombardear [1a] *vt* (*Mil*) to bombard, shell; (*Aer*) to bomb, raid; (*Fís*) to bombard; (*fig*) to bombard (*de* with).

bombardeo *nm* bombardment (*t fig*), shelling; bombing; raid; ~ **aéreo** air-raid, air attack (*contra, de* on); ~ **de saturación** saturation bombing; ~ **en picado** dive-bombing.

bombardero 1 *adj* bombing. **2** *nm* (*Aer*) bomber; (*Mil*: ††) bombardier.

bombardino *nm* (*Mús*) tuba, bass saxhorn.

bombasí *nm* fustian.

bombástico *adj* bombastic; (*Carib*: *elogioso*) complimentary, eulogistic.

bomba-trampa *nf, pl* **bombas-trampa** booby-trap bomb.

bombazo *nm* bomb explosion; (*fig*) bombshell.

bombeador *nm* (**a**) (*Cono Sur Aer*) bomber. (**b**) (*Cono Sur*) (*explorador*) scout; (*espía*) spy.

bombear [1a] **1** *vt* (**a**) (*Mil*) to shell.

(**b**) *líquido* to pump; to pump out, pump up.

(**c**) (*Cos*) to pad.

(**d**) (*fig*: *alabar*) to praise up, inflate the reputation of.

(**e**) (*Cono Sur**) *plan* to sabotage, wreck; (*Univ*) to fail, flunk‡; (*And**: *despedir*) to sack*, fire*.

(**f**) (*And*) (*Hist*: *espiar*) to spy on; (*reconocer*) to reconnoitre.

(**g**) (*CAm*: *robar*) to steal.

(**h**) (*Dep*) *balón* to lob; to kick high; **balón bombeado** high ball.

2 *vi* (**a**) (*Carib*: *emborracharse*) to get drunk.

(**b**) (*CAm, Méx***) to screw**, fuck**.

3 bombearse *vr* (*Arquit*) to camber; (*madera etc*) to warp, bulge.

bombeo *nm* (**a**) (*con bomba*) pumping. (**b**) (*Arquit*) camber; warping, bulging; crown (of the road).

bombero *nm* (**a**) (*gen*) fireman; **~s, cuerpo de ~s** fire brigade. (**b**) (*fig*) trouble-shooter. (**c**) (*Cono Sur*: *espía*) spy, scout; guard. (**d**) (*LAm*: *Aut*) petrol-pump attendant.

bombilla *nf* (*Elec*) (light) bulb; (*Náut*) ship's lantern; (*LAm*: *tubo*) metal tube for drinking maté; (*paja*) drinking straw; (*Méx*: *cuchara*) ladle; ~ **de flash,** ~ **fusible** (*Fot*) flash bulb; **se le encendió la** ~ it dawned on him, the penny dropped; he had a great idea.

bombillo *nm* (*And, CAm, Carib, Elec*) (light) bulb.

bombín *nm* (**a**) (*sombrero*) bowler hat. (**b**) (*Cono Sur*: *de aire*) pump, bicycle pump.

bombo 1 *adj* (**a**) (*aturdido*) dumbfounded, stunned.

(**b**) (*Carib*) (*tibio*) lukewarm; (*aguado*) watery, insipid; *persona* stupid, thick*.

(**c**) (*Méx*) *carne* bad, off.

2 *nm* (**a**) (*Mús*) big drum, bass drum; (*Téc*) cylinder, drum; (*Carib*) dance accompanied by a drum; **anunciar algo a ~ y platillo(s)** to announce sth with a lot of hype*, go in for a lot of publicity about sth; **hacer algo a ~ y platillo(s)** to make a great song and dance about sth; **tengo la cabeza hecha un ~** I've got a splitting headache; I'm all muddled.

(**b**) (*Carib*: *sombrero*) bowler hat.

(**c**) (*Náut*) barge, lighter.

(**d**) (*: *elogio exagerado*) exaggerated praise; (*Teat etc*) hype*, ballyhoo*, big write-up; **dar ~ a uno** to give sb exaggerated praise, write sb up in a big way; to boost sb; **darse el ~ mutuo** to indulge in mutual backslapping.

(**e**) **irse al ~** (*Cono Sur*) to come to grief, blow it‡; **mandar a uno al ~** (*Cono Sur*‡) to knock sb off‡; **poner a uno ~** (*Méx**) to hurl insults at sb; to hit sb.

(**f**) (*) **estar con ~** to be in the family way; **dejar a una con ~** to put a girl in the family way.

bombón *nm* (**a**) (*chocolatina*) chocolate. (**b**) (*) (*objeto*) beauty, gem; (*chica*) peach‡, smasher‡. (**c**) (*: *chollo*) gift*, cinch‡.

bombona *nf* carboy; **~ (de gas)** canister, cylinder.

bombonera *nf* (**a**) (*caja para dulces*) sweet box; (*lata para dulces*) sweet tin. (**b**) (*: *lugar*) cosy little place.

bombonería *nf* sweetshop, confectioner's (shop).

bómper *nm* (*LAm Aut*) bumper.

bonachón *adj* good-natured, kindly; easy-going; (*pey*) simple, naïve.

bonachonamente *adv* good-naturedly, in an easy-going way; (*pey*) naïvely.

bonaerense 1 *adj* of Buenos Aires province. **2** *nmf* native (*o* inhabitant) of Buenos Aires province; **los ~s** the people of Buenos Aires province.

bonancible *adj* (*Met*) fair, calm, settled; *viento* light.

bonanza *nf* (**a**) (*Náut*) fair weather, calm conditions; **ir en ~** to have fair weather.

(**b**) (*Min*) rich pocket (*o* vein) of ore, bonanza.

(**c**) (*fig*: *prosperidad*) prosperity, boom, bonanza; **estar en ~** (*Com*) to be booming; **ir en ~** go well, prosper.

bonazo *adj* = **buenazo**.

bonchar* [1a] *vi* (*Carib*) to have a party; (*fig*) to have a good time.

bonche[1] *nm* (*LAm*: *montón*) load, bunch.

bonche[2]* *nm* (*Carib*) (**a**) (*fiesta*) party, good time. (**b**) (*cosa divertida*) amusing thing; (*persona divertida*) amusing person.

bonche[3]* *nm* petting*, necking*.

bonchón *nm*, **bonchona** *nf* fun-loving person.

bondad *nf* (*gen*) goodness; (*amabilidad*) kindness, helpfulness; **tener la ~ de** + *infin* to be so kind as to + *infin*, be good enough to + *infin*; **tenga la ~ de no fumar** please do not smoke, please be so kind as not to smoke; **tuvo la ~ de prestárnoslo** he very kindly lent it to us.

bondadosamente *adv* kindly; good-naturedly.

bondadoso *adj* kind, good; kindly, kind-hearted, good-natured.

bondi *nm* (*Cono Sur*) tram.

bonete *nm* (*Ecl*) hat, biretta; (*Univ*) cap; **¡~!** (*CAm*, *Méx**) not on your life!, no way!*; **a tente ~** doggedly, insistently.

bonetería *nf* (*Cono Sur*, *Méx*) draper's (shop), clothing store.

bóngalo *nm*, **bongaló** *nm* bungalow.

bongo *nm* (*LAm*) small boat; (*And*) small punt.

bongó *nm* (*Carib*) bongo (drum), African-type drum.

boni‡ *nm* = **boniato (b)**.

boniata 1 *adj* (*LAm*) edible, non-poisonous. **2** *nf* (*Carib*) edible yucca, cassava.

boniato *nm* (**a**) (*Carib*, *Cono Sur Bot*) sweet potato, yam. (**b**) (‡: *Esp*) 1000-peseta note.

bonificación *nf* (**a**) (*pago*) bonus; (*esp Agr*) betterment, improvement (in value); (*Dep*) allowance of points. (**b**) (*Com*) allowance, discount; rebate.

bonificar [1g] **1** *vt* (**a**) (*Agr*, *Com*) to improve. (**b**) (*Com*) to allow, discount. **2 bonificarse** *vr* to improve.

bonísimo *adj superl de* **bueno**.

bonitamente *adv* (**a**) (*con maña*) nicely, neatly; craftily. (**b**) (*poco a poco*) slowly, little by little.

bonito[1] **1** *adj* (**a**) (*guapo*) pretty; nice, nice-looking; (*esp Cono Sur*) handsome; **~ como un sol** as pretty as a picture.

(**b**) (*bueno*) pretty good, passable; **una bonita cantidad** a nice little sum; **¡qué ~!** very nice too! (*t iró*).

2 *adv* (*Cono Sur**) well, nicely; **ella canta ~** she sings nicely; **se te ve ~** it looks good on you.

bonito[2] *nm* (*Pez*) bonito.

bonitura *nf* (*LAm*) beauty, attractiveness.

bono *nm* (**a**) (*gen*) voucher, certificate; **~ alimenticio** food stamp. (**b**) (*Fin*) bond; **~ de ahorros** savings bond; **~ de caja, ~ de tesorería** debenture bond; **~ de caja de ahorros** savings certificate; **~ del estado** government bond.

bono-bus *nm, pl* **bonos-bus, bonobús** *nm, pl* **bonobuses** (*Esp*) bus pass, book of bus tickets.

bono-loto *nf* (*Esp*: *t* **bonoloto**) state-run weekly lottery.

bono-metro *nm* metro pass, book of metro tickets.

bonsai *nm* bonsai.

boñiga *nf*, **boñigo** *nm* cow pat, horse dung.

boom [bum] *nm* boom; **~ inmobiliario** property boom; **dar ~ a un problema** to exaggerate a problem, make a meal of a problem.

boomerang [bume'ran] *nm, pl* **boomerangs** [bume'ran] boomerang.

boqueada *nf* gasp; **dar la última ~** to breathe one's last, be at one's last gasp; **dar las ~s** to be dying.

boquear [1a] **1** *vt* to say, utter, pronounce.

2 *vi* (**a**) (*quedar boquiabierto*) to gape, gawp.

(**b**) (*estar expirando*) to be at one's last gasp; (*fig*) to be in its final stages; (*provisión*) to be very nearly exhausted.

boquera 1 *nf* (**a**) (*Agr*) sluice. (**b**) (*Med*) lip sore, mouth ulcer. **2** *nm*: **~s**‡ screw‡, warder.

boqueriento *adj* (**a**) (*Med*) suffering from lip sores. (**b**) (*Cono Sur*: *miserable*) wretched, miserable.

boquerón *nm* (**a**) (*abertura*) wide opening, big hole. (**b**) (*Pez*) (fresh) anchovy. (**c**) (*: *persona*) = **malagueño.**

boquete *nm* gap, opening; hole, breach.

boqui‡ *nm* screw‡, warder.

boquiabierto *adj* open-mouthed; **estar ~** to stand open-mouthed, stand gaping (in astonishment); to stand aghast.

boquiancho *adj* wide-mouthed.

boquiblando *adj caballo* tender-mouthed.

boquifresco* *adj* outspoken; cheeky*.

boquilla *nf* (**a**) (*Mús*) mouthpiece; (*de manga etc*) nozzle; (*de gas*) burner; (*de pipa*) mouthpiece; cigarette holder, cigar-holder; (*Cos*) trouser bottom; **~ de filtro** filter tip; **hablar de ~** to talk out of the side of one's mouth.

(**b**) (*And*: *chisme*) rumour, piece of gossip.

(**c**) **promesa de ~** insincere promise, promise not meant to be kept; **lo dijo de ~** he was not sincere in what he said, he was only paying lip-service to it.

boquillazo *nm* (*And*) rumour, talk.

boquillero *adj* (*Carib*) smooth-talking, sweet-talking.

boquirroto *adj* talkative, garrulous.

boquirrubio 1 *adj* (**a**) (*gárrulo*) talkative; (*de mucha labia*) glib; (*indiscreto*) indiscreet, loose-tongued. (**b**) (*simple*) simple, naïve. **2** *nm* fop, dandy.

boquitinguero *adj* (*Cono Sur*) gossipy.

boquituerto *adj* wry-mouthed.

boquiverde* *adj* foul-mouthed.

boraciar [1b] *vi* (*Cono Sur*) to boast, brag.

bórax *nm* borax.

borboll(e)ar [1a] *vi* (**a**) (*burbujear*) to bubble, boil up. (**b**) (*fig*: *chisporrotear*) to splutter.

borbollón *nm* bubbling, boiling; gushing, welling up; **hablar a ~es** to talk in a torrent; to splutter; **reírse a ~es** to bubble with laughter; **salir a ~es** (*agua*) to come out in a torrent, come out with a rush, gush forth.

borbollonear [1a] *vi* = **borboll(e)ar.**

Borbón *n* Bourbon.

borbónico *adj* Bourbon.

borbotar [1a] *vi* (*hacer burbujas*) to bubble; (*al hervir*) to boil (up), boil over; (*nacer*) to gush forth, well up.

borbotón *nm* = **borbollón.**

borceguí *nm* high shoe, laced boot; half boot; (*de bebé*) (baby's) bootee.

borda *nf* (**a**) (*Náut*: *regala*) gunwale, rail; **motor fuera (de) ~** outboard motor; **echar** (*o* **tirar**) **algo por la ~** to throw sth overboard (*t fig*).

(**b**) (*Náut*: *vela*) mainsail.

(**c**) (*choza*) hut.

bordada *nf* (*Náut*) tack; **dar ~s** to tack; (*fig*) to keep on going to and fro.

bordado *nm* embroidery, needlework.

bordadora *nf* needlewoman.

bordadura *nf* embroidery, needlework.

bordalesa *nf* (*Cono Sur* ††) *wine barrel holding 225 litres.*

bordante *nmf* (*Carib*, *Méx*) lodger.

bordar [1a] *vt* to embroider; (*fig*) to do supremely well; **ha bordado su papel** she was excellent in her part.

borde[1] *nm* (**a**) (*gen*) edge, border; (*de camino etc*) side; (*de* *plato*) brim, rim, lip; (*de ventana*) ledge; (*Cos*) edge, hem, selvage; (*Náut*) board; **~ de la acera** kerb; **~ de ataque** (*Aer*) leading edge; **~ del camino, ~ de la carretera** roadside, verge; **~ del mar** seaside, seashore; **~ de salida** (*Aer*) trailing edge; **al ~ de** at the edge of, on the border of, at the side of.

(**b**) (*fig*) **estar al ~ de una crisis nerviosa** to be on the verge of a nervous breakdown; **estar en el mismo ~ del desastre** to be on the very brink of disaster.

borde[2] *adj* (**a**) (*****) *persona* anti-social; rough, uncouth; difficult, bad-tempered, stroppy*; **ponerse ~** to get stroppy*.

(**b**) *niño* illegitimate.

(**c**) (*Bot*) wild.

bordear [1a] **1** *vt* (**a**) (*seguir el borde de*) to skirt, go along (*o* round) the edge of.

(**b**) (*lindar con*) to border on; to flank; (*fig*) to verge on.

(**c**) **~ un asunto** (*Cono Sur*) to skirt round (*o* avoid) a (tricky) subject; (*Cono Sur, Méx*) to broach a subject.

(**d**) (*Cono Sur*: *calle etc*) to border, line; **los árboles bordean el camino** trees line the road.

2 *vi* (*Náut*) to tack.

bordejada *nf* (*Carib, Cono Sur*: *Náut*) tack.

bordej(e)ar [1a] *vi* (*Carib, Cono Sur*: *Náut*) to tack.

bordillo *nm* kerb.

bordin *nm* (*And, Carib, Méx*) boarding house.

bordinguero, -a *nm/f* (*And, Carib, Méx*) (*hombre*) landlord, (*mujer*) landlady.

bordo *nm* (**a**) (*Náut*) side, board; **a ~** on board; **con ordenador de a ~** with on-board computer; **estar a ~ del barco** to be on board (the) ship; **ir a ~** to go on board; **al ~** alongside; **buque de alto ~** big ship, seagoing vessel; **personaje de alto ~** distinguished person, influential person.

(**b**) (*Náut*: *bordada*) tack; **dar ~s** to tack.

(**c**) (*CAm, Cono Sur, Méx*: *presa*) roughly-built dam; (*Cono Sur*: *dique*) raised furrow; (*CAm*: *de montaña*) peak, summit.

bordó (*Cono Sur*) **1** *adj* maroon. **2** *nm* maroon.

bordón *nm* (**a**) (*de peregrino*) pilgrim's staff; (*de ciego*) stick; (*fig*) guide, helping hand.

(**b**) (*Mús*: *cuerda*) bass string; (*registro*) bass stop, bourdon; (*Poét*) refrain; (*fig*) pet word, pet phrase.

(**c**) (*And, CAm*: *benjamín*) youngest son.

bordona *nf* (*Cono Sur*) sixth string of the guitar; **~s** bass strings of the guitar.

bordoncillo *nm* pet word, pet phrase.

bordonear [1a] **1** *vt* (*Cono Sur Mús*) to strum. **2** *vi* (*And, Carib*) to hum, buzz.

bordoneo *nm* (*Cono Sur*: *Mús*) strumming.

boreal *adj* northern; **el Hemisferio B~** the Northern Hemisphere.

borgesiano, borgiano *adj* Borgesian, characteristic of J.L. Borges.

Borgoña *nf* Burgundy.

borgoña *nm* (*t* **vino de ~**) burgundy.

bórico *adj* boric.

boricua *adj, nmf* Puerto Rican.

borinqueño, -a *adj, nm/f* Puerto Rican.

Borja *n* Borgia.

borla *nf* tassel, pompom; tuft; (*Univ*) tassel on a cap; **~ (de empolvarse)** powder puff; **tomar la ~** (*Univ*) to take one's master's (*o* doctor's) degree.

borlete *nm* (*Méx*) row, din, uproar.

borne *nm* (*Elec*) terminal.

borneadizo *adj* easily warped, flexible.

bornear [1a] **1** *vt* (**a**) (*torcer*) to twist, bend.

(**b**) (*Arquit*) to hoist into place; to put in place, align.

(**c**) (*Méx*) *pelota* to spin, turn.

2 *vi* (*Náut*) to swing at anchor.

3 bornearse *vr* to warp, bulge.

borneco *adj* (*Cono Sur*) small, short.

borneo *nm* (**a**) (*torcer*) twisting, bending. (**b**) (*Arquit*) alignment. (**c**) (*Náut*) swinging at anchor.

boro *nm* (*Quím*) boron.

borona *nf* (**a**) (*maíz*) maize, corn (*US*); (*mijo*) millet. (**b**) (*pan*) maize bread, corn bread (*US*); (*LAm*: *migaja*) crumb.

borra *nf* (**a**) (*lana*) thick wool, coarse wool, flock; stuffing.

(**b**) (*pelusa*) fluff; (*Bot*) down; **~ de algodón** cotton waste; **~ de seda** floss silk.

(**c**) (*sedimento*) sediment, lees.

(**d**) (*****: *charla insustancial*) empty talk; (*basura*) trash, rubbish.

borrachear* [1a] *vi* to booze*, get drunk habitually.

borrachera *nf* (**a**) (*estado*) drunkenness, drunken state; **despejarse la ~, espabilarse la ~, quitarse la ~** to sober up, get rid of one's hangover; **pegarse una ~, ponerse una ~** (*Méx*) to get drunk.

(**b**) (*juerga*) spree, binge, drinking expedition.

borrachez *nf* drunkenness, drunken state.

borrachín *nm* drunkard, sot, toper.

borracho 1 *adj* (**a**) (*temporalmente*) drunk, intoxicated; (*por costumbre*) drunken, hard-drinking, fond of the bottle; **estar ~ como un tronco** (*o* **una uva**), **estar más ~ que una cuba** to be as drunk as a lord.

(**b**) (*fig*: *poseído de pasión*) drunk, blind, wild (*de ira etc* with rage *etc*).

(**c**) *bizcocho* tipsy, soaked in liqueur (*o* spirit); (*de color*) violet; (*LAm*) *fruta* overripe.

(**d**) **es un negocio ~*** (*Esp*) it's a real money-spinner, it's money for old rope*.

2 *nm*, **borracha** *nf* drunkard, drunk.

borrado *nm* erasure.

borrador *nm* (**a**) (*primera versión*) first draft, preliminary sketch, rough copy.

(**b**) (*cuaderno etc*) book for rough work, scribbling pad, scratch pad (*US*); (*Com*) daybook.

(**c**) (*para borrar*) rubber, eraser; duster.

borradura *nf* erasure, crossing-out.

borraja *nf* borage.

borrajear [1a] *vti* to scribble, scrawl; to doodle.

borrar [1a] **1** *vt* (**a**) (*con borrador*) to erase, rub out; (*tachar*) to cross out, score out, obliterate; to wipe out; *cinta* to wipe (clean); (*fig*) *memoria etc* to erase, efface, wipe away; (*Pol*: *euf*) to eliminate, dispose of; **~ a uno de una lista** to cross sb off a list, delete sb from a list.

(**b**) (*manchar*) to blot, smear; (*Fot etc*) to blur.

2 borrarse *vr* to resign (from a club *etc*).

borrasca *nf* (**a**) (*Met*) storm; squall.

(**b**) (*fig*: *peligro*) peril, hazard; (*revés*) setback.

(**c**) (*****: *juerga*) orgy, spree.

borrascoso *adj* (**a**) *tiempo* stormy; *viento* squally, gusty. (**b**) (*fig*) stormy, tempestuous.

borrasquero *adj* riotous, wild.

borregada* *nf* student rag*, prank.

borregaje *nm* (*Cono Sur*) flock of lambs.

borrego 1 *nm*, **borrega** *nf* (**a**) (*Zool*) lamb, yearling lamb; **no hay tales ~s** there isn't any such thing.

(**b**) (*fig*: *persona*) simpleton.

2 *nm* (*Carib*: *trampa*) con*, hoax; (*Méx*: *mentira*) lie, tall story.

3 ~s *nmpl* (*nubes*) fleecy clouds; (*prov*: *Náut*) white horses, foamy crests of waves.

borreguil *adj* meek, like a lamb.

borrica *nf* (**a**) (*Zool*) she-donkey. (**b**) (*****) stupid woman.

borricada *nf* silly thing, piece of nonsense.

borrico *nm* (**a**) (*Zool*) donkey (*t fig*). (**b**) (*Téc*) sawhorse.

borricón* *nm*, **borricote*** *nm* long-suffering person.

borriquete *nm* (*Arte*) easel; (*Téc*) sawhorse.

borrón *nm* (**a**) (*mancha*) blot, smudge, stain; (*fig*) blemish; stain, stigma; slur; **hacer ~ y cuenta nueva** to wipe the slate clean (and start again); to let bygones be bygones.

(**b**) (*Liter*) rough draft, preliminary sketch; (*Arte*) sketch; **estos ~es** (*iró*) these humble jottings.

borronear [1a] *vt* (**a**) (*borrajear*) to scribble; to doodle*. (**b**) (*hacer borrador de*) to make a rough draft of.

borroso *adj* (**a**) (*Fot*) blurred, indistinct, fuzzy; smudgy; (*Arte*) woolly. (**b**) *líquido* muddy, thick, cloudy.

boruca* *nf* row, din.

borujo *nm* lump, pressed mass, packed mass.

borujón *nm* (*Med*) bump, lump; (*lío*) bundle.

boruquear [1a] *vt* (*Méx*) (*revolver*) to mix up, mess up; (*fig*) to stir up (trouble in).

boscaje *nm* thicket, grove, small wood; (*Arte*) woodland scene.

Bosco *nm*: **el ~** Hieronymus Bosch.

boscoso *adj* wooded.

Bósforo *nm* Bosphorus; **el Estrecho del ~** the Bosphorus (Strait).

bosorola *nf* (*CAm, Méx*) sediment, dregs.

bosque *nm* wood, woodland, forest; woods; **~ pluvial** rainforest.

bosquecillo *nm* copse, small wood.

bosquejar [1a] *vt* (*Arte*) to sketch, make a sketch of, draw in outline; to model in rough; (*fig*) to sketch, outline; *plan etc* to draft.

bosquejo *nm* sketch, outline; rough model; draft.

bosquete *nm* copse, small wood.

bosquimán *nm*, **bosquimano** *nm* African bushman.

bosta *nf* dung, droppings; manure.

bostezar [1f] *vi* to yawn.

bostezo *nm* yawn.

bota[1] *nf* boot; **~s de agua** wellingtons, gumboots; **~s de campaña**, **~s camperas** top boots; **~s de esquí** ski boots; **~s de fútbol** football boots; **~s de goma** gumboots; **~s de media caña** ankle-boots; **~s de montar** riding boots; **colgar las ~s** to hang up one's boots (*t fig*); **morir con las ~s puestas** to die in harness; **ponerse las ~s*** (*enriquecerse*) to strike it rich*, make one's pile*; (*pasarlo bien*) to enjoy o.s. immensely; (*soñar*) to indulge in fantasies; (*comer*) to have a blow-out‡.

bota[2] *nf* (**a**) (*de vino*) leather wine bottle. (**b**) = 516 litres. (**c**) (*tonel*) large barrel.

botada[1] *nf* (*LAm*) (*tirada*) throw, throwing; throwing away; (*despedida*) sacking, dismissal.

botadero *nm* (*And, Méx*: *vado*) ford; (*LAm*: *vertedero*) rubbish dump.

botado 1 *adj* (**a**) (*descarado*) cheeky.

(**b**) (*CAm*: *gastador*) spendthrift.

(**c**) (*And*: *resignado*) resigned; (*dispuesto para todo*) ready for anything, resolute.

(**d**) (*CAm, Cono Sur*: *Com*) dirt cheap.

(**e**) **niño ~** (*LAm*) = **2**.

(**f**) (*CAm, Méx*: *borracho*) blind drunk.

2 *nm*, **botada[2]** *nf* (*LAm*) abandoned child, foundling; (*And*: *vago*) good-for-nothing, bum (*US*).

botador *nm* (**a**) (*Náut*) (punt) pole. (**b**) (*sacaclavos*) nail-puller, claw-hammer. (**c**) (*LAm*: *gastador*) spendthrift.

botadura *nf* (**a**) (*Náut*) launching. (**b**) (*LAm*) = **botada[1]**.

botafuego *nm* (††) linstock; (*) quick-tempered person.

botalodo *nm* (*And, Carib*) mudguard.

botalón *nm* (**a**) (*Náut*) boom, outrigger; **~ de foque** jib-boom. (**b**) (*And, Cono Sur*: *viga*) beam, prop; (*And*: *poste*) post, stake; (*And*: *de atar*) hitching post.

botanas *nfpl* (*LAm*) snack, appetizer.

botanearse* [1a] *vr*: **~ a uno** (*LAm*) to speak ill of sb, drag sb's name through the dirt.

botaneo *nm* (*LAm*) (malicious) gossip, slander.

botánica[1] *nf* botany.

botánico 1 *adj* botanical. **2** *nm*, **botánica[2]** *nf* botanist.

botanista *nmf* botanist.

botar [1a] **1** *vt* (**a**) (*lanzar*) to throw, fling, hurl; *pelota* to bowl, pitch; *balón* to kick.

(**b**) (*Náut*) *barco* to launch (*t* **~ al agua**).

(**c**) (*Náut*) *timón* to put over.

(**d**) (*esp LAm*: *tirar*) to throw away, chuck out; *persona** to fire*, sack*; *fortuna* to fritter away, squander; **le botaron de su trabajo** they sacked him from his job.

(**e**) (*LAm*: *perder*) to lose.

2 *vi* (**a**) (*pelota*) to bounce; (*Aut etc*) to bump, bounce, jolt; (*caballo*) to buck, rear; **está que bota** he's hopping mad.

(**b**) **~ a babor** (*Náut*) to put over to port.

3 botarse *vr* (*Cono Sur*) (**a**) (*cambiar empleos*) to change jobs.

(**b**) **se bota a experto** he fancies himself as expert, he claims to be an expert.

(**c**) (*Carib*: *tomar medidas extremas*) to go to extremes, go all the way.

botaratada *nf* wild thing; wild scheme, nonsensical idea.

botarate *nm* (**a**) (*loco*) madcap, wild fellow. (**b**) (*idiota*) idiot. (**c**) (*LAm*: *gastador*) spendthrift.

botarel *nm* buttress.

botarga *nf* motley, clown's outfit.

botavara *nf* (**a**) (*Náut*) boom. (**b**) (*Carib, Cono Sur*: *de carro*) pole, shaft.

bote[1] *nm* (**a**) (*arremetida*) thrust, lunge, blow.

(**b**) (*de pelota*) bounce; (*Aut etc*) bump, bounce, jolt; (*de caballo*) buck; **a ~ pronto** (*adj*) sudden; (*adv*) *decir, preguntar* suddenly, point-blank; (*desde el comienzo*) right away, from the start; **de ~ y voleo** instantly; **dar un ~** to jump; **dar el ~ a uno*** to chuck sb out; to sack sb*; **darse el ~‡** to beat it*; **dar ~s** (*Aut etc*) to bump, bounce; **pegar un ~** to jump, start (with surprise).

(**c**) **estar de ~ en ~** to be packed, be jammed full, be crowded out.

bote[2] *nm* (**a**) (*lata*) can, tin, canister; (*tarro*) pot, jar; (*en café*: *propina*) tip, (*caja*) box (*for waiters' tips*); **~ de basura** (*Méx*) dustbin, ashcan (*US*); **~ de cerveza** beer-can; can of beer; **~ de cuestación** collecting tin; **~ de humo** smoke-bomb; **está en el ~*** it's in the bag*; **lo tiene en el ~*** he's got it all sewn up*.

(**b**) (*Naipes*) jackpot, kitty.

(**c**) (*: *Aut*) grid*, jalop(p)y; (*CAm, Méx‡*) jail, nick‡.

(**d**) (*) **chupar del ~** (*congraciarse*) to curry favour, creep*; (*gorronear*) to scrounge a meal (*o* drink *etc*); (*mirar por sí*) to look after Number One; (*enriquecerse*) to feather one's nest; **pegarse el ~ con uno** to get on like a house on fire with sb.

bote[3] *nm* (*Náut*) boat; **~ de carrera**, **~ de un remero** skiff, sculling boat; **~ neumático** rubber dinghy; **~ de a ocho** racing eight; **~ de paseo** rowing boat; **~ de paso** ferry-boat; **~ patrullero** patrol boat; **~ de remos** rowing boat; **~ de salvamento**, **~ salvavidas** lifeboat.

botella *nf* (**a**) (*gen*) bottle; **~ de Leiden** Leyden jar; **cerveza de ~**, **cerveza en ~s** bottled beer.

(**b**) (*Carib*: *prebenda*) sinecure, soft job (in government).

botellazo *nm* a blow with a bottle.

botellería *nf* (*Cono Sur*) wine shop.

botellero *nm* wine-rack.

botellín *nm* small bottle, half-bottle.

botepronto *nm* (*Dep*) half-volley; *V t* **bote[1]** (**b**).

botería *nf* (*Cono Sur*) shoeshop.

bote-vivienda *nm, pl* **botes-vivienda** houseboat.

botica *nf* (**a**) (*tienda*) chemist's (shop), pharmacy, drugstore (*US*); **de todo como en ~** everything under the sun.

(**b**) (‡) trouser fly, flies.

boticaria *nf* (woman) chemist, druggist; (*Hist*) chemist's wife, apothecary's wife.

boticario *nm* chemist, druggist, (*Hist*) apothecary.

botija 1 *nf* (**a**) (*vasija*) earthenware jug; (*) fat person; **estar como una ~**, **estar hecho una ~** to be as fat as a sow; **poner a uno como ~ verde** (*LAm*) to call sb every name under the sun.

(**b**) (*CAm, Carib*: *tesoro*) buried treasure.

2 *nmf* (*Cono Sur*) baby, child.

botijo *nm* (**a**) (*Culin*) earthenware drinking jug (*with spout and handle*); *V* **tren**. (**b**) (*: *de policía*) water-cannon.

botijón* *adj* (*Méx*) potbellied.

botijuela *nf* (*LAm*) (**a**) (*botijo*) earthenware jug. (**b**) (*tesoro*) buried treasure.

botillería *nf* refreshment stall; (*LAm*) liquor store.

botillero *nm* (*Méx*) shoemaker, cobbler.

botín[1] *nm* (*Mil etc*) booty, plunder, loot.

botín[2] *nm* (**a**) (*polaina*) half boot; legging, high boot. (**b**) (*Cono Sur*: *calcetín*) sock.

botina *nf* high shoe; (*de bebé*) bootee.

botiquín *nm* (**a**) (*Med*) medicine chest; (*enfermería*) first-aid post; (*t* **~ de emergencia**) first-aid kit. (**b**) (*Carib*: *hum*) drinks cupboard.

boto[1] *adj* dull, blunt; (*fig*) dull, dim.

boto[2] *nm* leather wine bottle.

botón *nm* (**a**) (*Cos*) button; **~ (de camisa)** stud; **¡ni un ~!*** not a sausage!*

(**b**) (*Elec etc*) button; (*Téc*) button, knob; (*Rad*) knob; **~ (de puerta)** doorknob, doorhandle; **~ de alarma** alarm, alarm button; **~ de arranque** starter, starting switch; **~ de contacto**, **~ de presión** push-button; **~ de destrucción** destruct button; **~ de muestra** sample, illustration; **empujar** (*o* **presionar** *etc*) **el ~** to press the button.

(**c**) (*Esgrima*: *de flor etc*) tip.

(**d**) (*Bot*) bud; **~ de oro** buttercup, kingcup.

botonadura *nf* (set of) buttons.

botonar [1a] (*LAm*) **1** *vt* to button (up). **2** *vi* to bud, sprout.

botones *nm invar* buttons; bellboy, bellhop (*US*).

Botsuana *nf* Botswana.

botulismo *nm* botulism.

boutique [bu'tik] *nf* boutique.

bóveda *nf* (*Arquit*) vault; dome; (*cueva*) cave, cavern; **~ de cañón** barrel vault; **~ celeste** vault of heaven, sky, firmament; **~ craneal** vault of the skull.

bovedillas* *nfpl*: **subirse a las ~*** to go up the wall*.

bovino *adj* bovine; cow (*atr*), ox (*atr*).

box[1] [boks] *nm, pl* **boxes** [boks] (*de caballo*) stall; loose box; (*en carreras de coches*) pit; (*CAm, Carib, Correos*) post-office box, P.O. Box; **entrar en ~es** to make a pit-stop, go into the pits.

box[2] [boks] *nm* (*LAm*) boxing.

boxeador *nm* boxer.

boxear [1a] *vi* to box.

boxeo *nm* boxing.

bóxer *nm* boxer (dog).

boxeril *adj* (*Cono Sur*), **boxístico** *adj* boxing (*atr*).

boya *nf* (*Náut*) buoy; (*Pesca*) float; ~ **de campana** bellbuoy.
boyada *nf* drove of oxen.
boyante *adj* (*Náut*) buoyant, light in the water; (*fig*) buoyant, prosperous.
boyar [1a] *vi* to float.
boyazo *nm* (*CAm, Cono Sur*) punch.
boyé *nm* (*Cono Sur*) snake.
boyera *nf*, **boyeriza** *nf* cattle shed.
boyero *nm* (**a**) (*persona*) oxherd, drover. (**b**) (*perro*) cattle dog. (**c**) (*And: aguijada*) goad, spike.
boyuyu* *nm* chaos, mess, confusion.
bozada *nf* (*And*) halter.
bozal 1 *adj* (**a**) (*nuevo*) new, raw, green; *animal* wild, untamed.
(**b**) (*tonto*) stupid.
(**c**) (*LAm*) *negro* pure.
(**d**) (*LAm Ling*) speaking broken Spanish.
2 *nm* (*de perro*) muzzle; (*LAm: de caballo*) halter, headstall.
bozo *nm* (**a**) (*pelos*) down (on the upper lip), youthful whiskers. (**b**) (*boca*) mouth, lips. (**c**) (*cabestro*) halter, headstall.
bracamonte *nm* (*And*) ghost.
bracear [1a] **1** *vt* (**a**) (*Náut*) to measure in fathoms.
(**b**) *horno* to tap.
2 *vi* (*mover los brazos*) to swing one's arms; (*nadar*) to swim, (*esp*) crawl; (*fig*) to wrestle, struggle.
bracero *nm* (**a**) (*peón*) labourer, navvy; (*Agr*) farmhand, farm labourer. (**b**) **ir de** ~ to walk arm-in-arm.
bracete: **ir de** ~ to walk arm-in-arm.
bracmán *nm*, **bracmana** *nf* Brahman, Brahmin.
braco 1 *adj* pug-nosed. **2** *nm* (*t* **perro** ~) pointer.
braga *nf* (**a**) (*Náut, Téc*) sling, rope (for hoisting).
(**b**) (*de niño*) nappy, diaper (*US*); **~s** (*de hombre*) breeches; (*Esp*) (*de mujer*) panties; **calzar(se) las ~s** (*mujer*) to wear the pants, be the boss; **coger** (*o* **pillar** *etc*) **a uno en ~s*** to catch sb with his pants down*; **dejar a uno en ~s*** to leave sb empty-handed; **estar hecho una ~**‡ to be knackered*; **estar en ~s*** to be flat broke*.
bragado* *adj* energetic, tough; wicked, vicious.
bragadura *nf* (*Anat, Cos*) crotch.
bragazas *nm invar* henpecked husband.
braguero *nm* (*Med*) truss.
bragueta *nf* (*Cos*) fly, flies; (*de chico*) short trousers; shorts; **gran** ~ womanizer; **estar como ~ de fraile** (*Cono Sur*) to be very solemn; **oír por la ~*** (*lerdo*) to be pretty thick*; (*sordo*) to be stone-deaf; (*entender mal*) to misunderstand; **ser hombre de** ~ to be a real man.
braguetazo* *nm* marriage for money; **dar el** ~ to marry for money.
braguetero 1 *adj* (**a**) (*lascivo*) lecherous, randy.
(**b**) (*LAm: al casarse*) who marries for money; (*And, Carib: vividor*) who lives on a woman's earnings; **todos saben que es** ~ everyone knows he married for money.
2 *nm* lecher, womanizer.
braguillas *nm invar* brat.
braguita(s) *nf(pl)* panties.
brah(a)mán *nm* Brahman, Brahmin.
brama *nf* (*Zool*) rut, rutting season.
bramadero *nm* (*LAm*) tethering (*o* hitching) post.
bramante *nm* twine, string.
bramar *vi* (**a**) (*Zool*) to roar, bellow. (**b**) (*fig: persona*) to roar; to rage, bluster; (*viento, tormenta*) to howl, roar; (*mar*) to roar, thunder; **están que braman con el alcalde*** they're hopping mad with the mayor.
bramido *nm* roar, bellow; howl, howling.
branquia *nf* gill.
brasa *nf* live coal, hot coal; **a la** ~ (*Culin*) grilled; **atizar la** ~ to stir things up, add fuel to the flames; **estar en ~s** to be on tenterhooks; **estar hecho una** ~ to be very flushed.
brasear [1a] *vt* to braise.
brasería *nf* grill.
brasero *nm* (*gen*) brazier (*esp as used for domestic heating*); (*Hist*) stake; (*LAm: chimenea*) hearth, fireplace; (*And: hoguera*) large bonfire; (*Méx: hornillo*) small stove.
Brasil *nm*: **el** ~ Brazil.
brasileño, -a, (*LAm*) **brasilero, -a** *adj, nm/f* Brazilian.
brava *nf* (**a**) (*Méx: disputa*) row, fight. (**b**) **a la** ~ like it or not, by hook or by crook; **a la ~ tendrás que ir** you'll have to go whether you like it or not. (**c**) **dar una ~ a** (*Carib*) to intimidate (*o* lean on*).
bravata *nf* (*amenaza*) threat; (*fanfarronada*) boast, brag, piece of bravado; **echar ~s** to boast, talk big; to bluster.
braveador 1 *adj* blustering, bullying. **2** *nm* bully.
bravear [1a] *vi* (**a**) (*jactarse*) to boast, talk big; to bluster. (**b**) (*aplaudir*) to applaud, shout bravo.
bravera *nf* vent, window (*in an oven*).
bravero (*Carib*) **1** *adj* bullying. **2** *nm* bully.
braveza *nf* (**a**) (*ferocidad*) ferocity, savageness; (*Met*) fury, violence. (**b**) (*valor*) bravery.
bravío 1 *adj* (**a**) (*Zool*) fierce, ferocious, savage; wild; untamed; (*Bot*) wild.
(**b**) (*fig: grosero*) uncouth, coarse.
2 *nm* fierceness, savageness.
bravo 1 *adj* (**a**) (*valiente*) brave; tough, spirited, pugnacious.
(**b**) (*excelente*) fine, excellent; *banquete etc* splendid, sumptuous.
(**c**) *animal* fierce, ferocious; *mar* rough, stormy; *paisaje* rugged, rough, wild; *persona* angry, wild; bad-tempered; **ponerse ~ con uno** to get angry with sb.
(**d**) (*jactancioso*) boastful, swaggering.
(**e**) (*LAm: picante*) hot, strong.
2 *interj* bravo!, splendid!, well done!
3 *nm* thug.
bravucón 1 *adj* boastful, swaggering. **2** *nm* boaster, braggart.
bravuconada *nf* (**a**) (*cualidad*) bluster, boastfulness. (**b**) (*acto*) boast; boasting, bragging.
bravura *nf* (**a**) (*ferocidad*) fierceness, ferocity. (**b**) (*valor*) bravery. (**c**) = **bravata**.
braza *nf* (**a**) (*Náut: medida: aprox*) fathom. (**b**) (*Náut*) brace. (**c**) (*Natación*) (*t* **~ de pecho**) breast stroke; **~ de espalda** back stroke; **~ de mariposa** butterfly stroke.
brazada *nf* (**a**) (*gen*) movement of the arms.
(**b**) (*de remo*) stroke.
(**c**) (*Natación*) stroke.
(**d**) (*cantidad*) armful.
(**e**) (*LAm Náut: medida: aprox*) fathom.
brazado *nm* armful.
brazal *nm* (**a**) (*brazalete*) armband. (**b**) (*Agr*) irrigation channel.
brazalete *nm* (**a**) (*joya*) bracelet, wristlet. (**b**) (*brazal*) armlet, armband.
brazo *nm* (**a**) (*gen*) arm; (*Zool*) foreleg; (*Téc: de silla etc*) arm; bracket; (*Bot*) limb, branch; **~ armado** military wing (*of terrorist movement etc*); **~ derecho** (*fig*) right-hand man; indispensable aid; **~ de dirección** steering arm; **~ de gitano** (*Culin*) swiss roll; **~ de lámpara** lamp bracket; **~ de lámpara de gas** gas bracket; **~ lector, ~ de lectura** pick-up arm; **~ de mar** arm of the sea, sound; **estar** (*o* **ir**) **hecho un ~ de mar** to be dressed up to the nines; **~ político** political wing (*of terrorist movement etc*); **~ de reina** (*Cono Sur Culin*) swiss roll; **~ de río** branch of a river; **~ secular** secular arm; **~ de toma de sonido** pickup arm; **ir asidos** (*o* **cogidos**) **del ~, ir del ~** (*LAm*) to walk arm-in-arm; **coger a uno por el ~** to seize sb by the arm; **cruzarse de ~s** (*lit*) to fold one's arms; (*fig*) not to do anything; **estarse con los ~s cruzados** (*fig*) to sit back and do nothing; **dar el ~ a uno** (*fig*) to give sb a helping hand; **no dar su ~ a torcer** to stand fast, not give way easily; **ir del ~** (*LAm*) to walk arm-in-arm; **luchar a ~ partido** to fight hand-to-hand, (*fig*) fight bitterly; **mover algo a ~** to move sth by hand, manhandle sth; **recibir a uno con los ~s abiertos** to receive sb with open arms.
(**b**) (*fig*) (*energía*) energy, enterprise; (*valor*) courage.
(**c**) **~s** (*fig*) (*obreros*) hands, workers; (*protectores*) backers, protectors.
brazuelo *nm* (*Zool*) shoulder.
brea *nf* tar, pitch.
break [brek] *nm* break dancing.
brear [1a] *vt* (**a**) (*maltratar*) to abuse, ill-treat; **~ a uno a golpes** to beat sb up. (**b**) (*embromar*) to make fun of, tease.
brebaje *nm* (*Farm*) potion, mixture; (*hum*) nasty drink, brew, concoction.
brecina *nf* (*Bot*) heath.
breck *nm* (*Cono Sur*) = **breque** (**b**).
brécol *nm*, **brécoles** *nmpl* broccoli.
brecha *nf* (*Mil*) breach; gap, opening; (*de tiempo*) gap; (*fig*) breach, gap; (*Med*) gash, wound; **abrir ~ en una muralla** to breach a wall; **batir en ~** (*Mil*) to breach, (*fig*) get the better of; **estar en la ~** to be in the thick of things; **hacer ~ en** (*fig*) to make an impression on; **seguir en la ~** to go on with one's work, keep at it, not give in.
brega *nf* (**a**) (*lucha*) struggle; **andar a la ~** to slog away, toil hard.
(**b**) (*riña*) quarrel, scrap*, row.

(**c**) (*broma*) trick, practical joke; **dar ~ a** to play a trick on.

bregar [1h] *vi* (**a**) (*luchar*) to struggle, fight (*con* against, with; *t fig*).
(**b**) (*reñir*) to quarrel, scrap*.
(**c**) (*trabajar*) to slog away, toil hard; **tendremos que hacerlo bregando** we shall have to do it by sheer hard work.

breguetear [1a] *vi* (*And*) to argue.

breje‡ *nm*: **¿cuántos ~s tienes?** (*Esp*) how old are you?

brejetero *adj* (*Carib*) trouble-making, mischief-making.

breke *nm* (*CAm Aut*) brake.

bren *nm* bran.

breña *nf*, **breñal** *nm* scrub, rough ground; bramble patch.

breñoso *adj* rough, scrubby; brambly.

breque *nm* (**a**) (*LAm Hist*) break (*vehicle*). (**b**) (*And, Cono Sur Ferro*) luggage van, baggage car (*US*). (**c**) (*LAm Mec*) brake.

brequear [1a] *vti* (*LAm*) to brake.

brequero *nm* (*And, CAm, Méx*) brakeman.

Bretaña *nf* Brittany.

brete *nm* (**a**) (*grilletes*) fetters, shackles.
(**b**) (*fig: apuro*) tight spot, jam*; predicament; **estar en un ~** to be in a jam*; **poner a uno en un ~** to put sb on the spot.
(**c**) (*Carib*‡*) screw‡*, lay‡*.

breteles *nmpl* (*LAm*) straps.

bretón, -ona 1 *adj, nm/f* Breton. **2** *nm* (*Ling*) Breton.

bretones *nmpl* Brussels sprouts.

breva *nf* (**a**) (*Bot*) early fig, (black) fig.
(**b**) (*puro*) flat cigar; (*Carib, Cono Sur: de calidad*) good-quality cigar; (*LAm: tabaco*) chewing tobacco.
(**c**) **¡no caerá esa ~!** (*Esp*) no such luck!; **pelar la ~** (*Cono Sur*) to steal; **poner a uno como una ~** to beat sb black and blue.
(**d**) (*: *puesto*) plum, plum job; (*gaje*) perk*; **es una ~** it's a cinch‡, it's a pushover*; **para él es una ~** it's chick-enfeed to him*.

breve 1 *adj* short, brief; (*en estilo*) terse, concise; **en ~** shortly, before long, very soon; concisely.
2 *nm* (**a**) (*Ecl*) papal brief. (**b**) (*Prensa*) short news item.
3 *nf* (*Mús*) breve.

brevedad *nf* shortness, brevity; terseness, conciseness; **con** (*o* **a**) **la mayor ~** as soon as possible, at one's earliest convenience; with all possible speed; **bueno, para mayor ~ ...** well, to be brief ...; **llamado por ~** called for short.

brevemente *adv* briefly, concisely.

brevería *nf* (*Tip*) note, short news item; snippet; **'Breverías'** (*sección de periódico*) 'News in Brief'.

brevete *nm* note, memorandum; (*LAm Aut*) driving licence, driver's licence (*US*).

breviario *nm* (*Ecl*) breviary; compendium, brief treatise; (*fig*) regular reading, daily reading.

brezal *nm* moor, moorland, heath.

brezar [1f] *vt* to rock, lull (in a cradle).

brezo *nm* (*Bot*) heather; (*de pipa*) briar.

briaga *nf* (*Méx*) drunkenness.

briago *adj* (*Méx*) drunk.

briba *nf* vagabond's life, idle life; **andar** (*o* **vivir**) **a la ~** to loaf around, be on the bum (*US*).

bribón 1 *adj* (**a**) (*vago*) idle; lazy.
(**b**) (*criminal*) dishonest, rascally.
2 *nm*, **bribona** *nf* (**a**) (*vagabundo*) vagabond, vagrant; loafer.
(**b**) (*granuja*) rascal, rogue.

bribonada *nf* dirty trick, piece of mischief.

bribonear [1a] *vi* (**a**) (*gandulear*) to idle, loaf around. (**b**) (*ser granuja*) to be a rogue, play dirty tricks.

bribonería *nf* (**a**) (*briba*) vagabond's life, idle life. (**b**) (*picardía*) roguery.

bribonesco *adj* rascally, knavish.

bricbarca *nf* large sailing ship.

bricolador(a) *nm/f* = **bricolagista.**

bricolage *nm* do-it-yourself (work).

bricolagista *nmf* do-it-yourself expert.

bricolaje *nm* = **bricolage.**

bricolero, -a *nm/f*, **bricolajista** *nmf* = **bricolagista.**

brida *nf* (**a**) (*freno*) bridle; rein; **ir a toda ~** to go at top speed; **tener a uno a ~ corta** to keep sb on a tight rein, keep sb under strict control.
(**b**) (*Téc*) clamp; flange; collar; (*Ferro*) fishplate; (*Med*) adhesion.

bridge [briʒ, britʃ] *nm* (*Cartas*) bridge.

bridgista [bri'ʒista] *nmf* bridge player.

bridgístico [bri'ʒistiko] *adj* bridge (*atr*); **el mundo ~** the bridge world.

bridón *nm* snaffle; (*Mil*) bridoon.

brigada 1 *nf* (**a**) (*Mil*) brigade.
(**b**) (*de obreros etc*) squad, gang.
(**c**) (*de policía etc*) squad; **~ antidisturbios** riot squad; **~ antidrogas, ~ de estupefacientes** drug squad; **~ de bombas** bomb-disposal unit; **~ de delitos monetarios** fraud squad; **~ fluvial** river police; **B~s Internacionales** International Brigade; **~ móvil** flying squad; **~ sanitaria** sanitation department.
2 *nm* (*Mil: aprox*) staff-sergeant, sergeant-major; warrant officer.

brigadier *nm* brigadier(-general).

brigadilla *nf* squad, detachment.

brigadista *nm*: **~ internacional** member of the International Brigade.

brigán *nm* (*CAm, Carib Hist*) brigand, bandit.

brigandaje *nm* (*Carib Hist*) brigandage, banditry.

brigantino 1 *adj* of Corunna. **2** *nm*, **brigantina** *nf* native (*o* inhabitant) of Corunna; **los ~s** the people of Corunna.

Brígida *nf* Bridget.

Briján: **saber más que ~** to be very smart, know the lot.

brik *nm* carton.

brillante 1 *adj* (**a**) (*gen*) brilliant, bright, shining; *joya* bright, sparkling; *escena* brilliant, glittering, splendid; *superficie* shining; glossy; *conversación, ingenio* sparkling, scintillating; *compañía* brilliant.
(**b**) (*fig*) brilliant.
2 *nm* brilliant, diamond.

brillantemente *adv* (**a**) (*gen*) brilliantly; brightly. (**b**) (*fig*) brilliantly.

brillantez *nf* (**a**) (*color etc*) brilliance, brightness; splendour. (**b**) (*fig*) brilliance.

brillantina *nf* brilliantine, hair cream.

brillar [1a] *vi* (**a**) (*gen*) to shine; to sparkle, glitter, gleam, glisten.
(**b**) (*fig: al sonreír*) to beam; (*de alegría etc*) to glow, light up.
(**c**) (*fig: en estudios etc*) to shine; to be outstanding; **~ por su ausencia** to be conspicuous by one's absence.

brillazón *nf* (*Cono Sur*) mirage.

brillo *nm* (**a**) (*resplandor*) brilliance; brightness, shine; sparkle, glitter; glow; (*de superficie*) lustre, sheen, gloss; radiance; **sacar ~ a** to polish, shine.
(**b**) (*fig: esplendor*) splendour, lustre, brilliance.
(**c**) **~ de labios** lip gloss.

brilloso *adj* (*And, Carib, Cono Sur*) = **brillante 1 (a).**

brin *nm* fine canvas, duck.

brincar [1g] **1** *vt* (**a**) *niño* to jump up and down, bounce, dandle.
(**b**) *pasaje* (*en lectura*) to skip, miss out.
2 *vi* (**a**) (*saltar*) to skip, hop, jump, leap about; (*cordero etc*) to skip about, gambol; (*rebotar*) to bounce.
(**b**) (*fig: t ~ de cólera*) to fly into a rage, flare up; **está que brinca** he's hopping mad.
3 brincarse *vr*: **~ a uno** (*And*‡) to bump sb off‡.

brinco *nm* hop, jump, leap, skip; bounce; **a ~s** by fits and starts; **de un ~** at one bound; **de un ~** (*LAm*), **en un ~** on the spot, right away; **dar ~s** to hop, jump *etc*; **pegar un ~** to jump, give a start; **quitar los ~s a uno** to take sb down a peg; **¿para qué son tantos ~s estando el suelo parejo?** (*: *CAm, Méx*) what's all the fuss about?

brindar [1a] **1** *vt* (**a**) (*gen*) to offer, present, afford; **~ a uno con algo** to offer sth to sb; **voy a ~te un güisqui** let me stand you a whisky, have a whisky on me; **le brinda la ocasión** it offers (*o* affords) him the opportunity; **los árboles brindaban sombra** the trees afforded shade.
(**b**) (*Taur*) to dedicate (*a* to).
(**c**) **~ a uno a hacer algo** to invite sb to do sth.
2 *vi*: **~ a, ~ por** to drink to, drink a toast to, toast; **¡brindemos por la unidad!** here's to unity!, let's drink to unity!
3 brindarse *vr*: **~ a** + *infin* to offer to + *infin*.

brindis *nm invar* (**a**) toast; (*Taur*) (ceremony of) dedication. (**b**) (*And, Carib*) official reception; cocktail party.

brío *nm* (*t ~s: ánimo*) spirit, dash, verve; (*resolución*) determination, resolution; (*elegancia*) elegance; (*alegría*) jauntiness; **es hombre de ~s** he's a man of spirit, he's a man of mettle; **cortar los ~s a uno** to clip sb's wings.

briosamente *adv* with spirit, dashingly, with verve; resolutely; elegantly; jauntily.

brioso *adj* spirited, dashing, full of verve; determined, res-

olute; elegant; jaunty.
briqueta *nf* briquette.
brisa *nf* breeze.
brisera *nf* (*LAm*), **brisero** *nm* (*LAm*) windshield (*for a lamp etc*).
brisita *nf*: **tener** (*o* **pasar**) **una** ~ to be hungry, have an empty stomach.
británico 1 *adj* British. **2** *nm*, **británica** *nf* British person, Briton, Britisher (*US*); **los ~s** the British.
britano 1 *adj* (*esp Hist*) British. **2** *nm*, **britana** *nf* (*en estilo formal, Hist y Poét etc*) Briton.
brizna *nf* (**a**) (*hebra*) strand, thread, filament; (*de hierba*) blade, wisp; (*de judía*) string.
(**b**) (*trozo*) chip, piece, fragment; scrap; **no me queda ni una** ~ I haven't a scrap left.
(**c**) (*Carib*: *llovizna*) drizzle.
briznar [1a] *vi* (*Carib*) to drizzle.
broca *nf* (**a**) (*Cos*) reel, bobbin. (**b**) (*Mec*) drill, bit. (**c**) (*de zapato*) tack.
brocado *nm* brocade.
brocal *nm* rim, mouth; (*de pozo*) curb, parapet; (*Méx*) kerb.
bróculi *nm*, **broculí** *nm* broccoli.
brocha 1 *nf* (**a**) (*pincel grande*) brush, large paintbrush; ~ **de afeitar** shaving brush; **de ~ gorda** crudely painted, (*fig*) slapdash, crude, badly done.
(**b**) (*Cono Sur*) skewer, spit.
(**c**) (*: *CAm*: *zalamero*) creep‡.
2 *adj* (*: *CAm*) meddling; creeping‡, servile; **hacerse ~** (*CAm*) to play the fool.
brochada *nf*, **brochazo** *nm* brush-stroke.
broche *nm* clip, clasp, fastener; brooch; (*de libro*) clasp, hasp; (*LAm*) cufflink; (*And, Carib, Cono Sur*: *sujetapapeles*) paper clip; ~ (**para la ropa**) (*Cono Sur*) clothes peg; **el ~ final, el ~ de oro** (*fig*) the finishing touch.
brocheta *nf* skewer.
brochón 1 *nm* whitewash brush. **2** *adj* (*Carib*) flattering.
bróder* *nm* (*CAm*) lad, fellow*.
broker *nm* (*Cono Sur Fin*) broker.
brollero *adj* (*Carib*) trouble-making, mischief-making.
broma *nf* (**a**) (*gen*) fun, gaiety, merriment; **tomar algo a ~** to take sth as a joke; **estar de ~** to be in a joking mood; to be joking, not be serious; **en ~** in fun, as a joke; **ni en ~** never, not on any account; **lo decía en ~** I was only joking, I said it as a joke.
(**b**) (*una* ~) joke; hoax, leg-pull*, prank; ~ **estudiantil** student rag; ~ **pesada** practical joke, hoax; (*pey*) poor sort of joke, unfunny joke; **pero ~s aparte ...** but joking apart ...; **entre ~s y veras** half-joking(ly); **no es ninguna ~** this is serious; **fue una ~ nada más** it was just a joke; **¡déjate de ~s!** quit fooling!, joke over!; **no está para ~s** he's in no mood for jokes; **¡para ~s estoy!** (*iró*) a fine time for joking!; **gastar una ~ a uno** to play a joke on sb; **la ~ me costó caro** the affair cost me dear; **no hay ~s con la autoridad** you can't play games with the authorities.
(**c**) (*Carib, Cono Sur*) (*decepción*) disappointment; (*molestia*) vexation, annoyance.
(**d**) (*Zool*) shipworm.
bromazo *nm* unpleasant joke, stupid practical joke.
bromear [1a] *vi*, **bromearse** *vr* to joke, crack jokes*, rag; **se estaban bromeando** they were ragging each other, they were pulling each other's legs; **creía que bromeaba** I thought he was joking.
bromista 1 *adj* fond of joking, full of fun; **es muy ~** he's full of jokes, he's a great one for jokes.
2 *nmf* joker, wag; practical joker, leg-puller*; **lo ha hecho algún ~** some joker did this.
bromuro *nm* bromide.
bronca 1 *nf* (**a**) (*follón etc*) row, scrap*, set-to*; **armar una ~** to kick up a row; make a great fuss; **se armó una tremenda ~** there was an almighty row*; **dar una ~ a** (*Taur, Teat etc*) to hiss, boo, barrack.
(**b**) (*reprimenda*) ticking-off*; **nos echó una ~ fenomenal*** he gave us a terrific ticking-off*, he came down on us like a ton of bricks*.
(**c**) (*Cono Sur*) anger, fury; **me da ~** it makes me mad*.
2 *adj invar* (*) boring, tedious.
broncamente *adv* roughly, harshly; rudely.
broncata‡ *nf* = **bronca 1 (b)**.
bronce *nm* (**a**) (*gen*) bronze; **el ~** (*Mús*) the brass; **~ de campana** bell metal; **~ de cañon** gunmetal; **~ dorado** ormolu; **ligar ~** (*Esp**) to get a suntan; **ser de ~** (*fig*) to be inflexible, be deaf to appeals.
(**b**) (*Arte*) bronze (statue).
(**c**) (*moneda*) copper coin.
(**d**) (*LAm*) bell.
bronceado 1 *adj* (**a**) (*gen*) bronze, bronze-coloured.
(**b**) *piel, persona* tanned, sunburnt.
2 *nm* (**a**) (*Téc*) bronzing, bronze finish.
(**b**) (*de piel*) tan, suntan.
bronceador *nm* suntan lotion.
broncear [1a] **1** *vt* (**a**) (*Téc*) to bronze. (**b**) *piel* to tan, bronze, brown. **2 broncearse** *vr* to brown, get a suntan.
broncería *nf* (*Cono Sur*) ironmonger's (shop), ironmongery.
bronco *adj* (**a**) *superficie* rough, coarse, unpolished.
(**b**) *metal* brittle.
(**c**) *voz* gruff, rough, harsh; (*Mús*) rough, rasping, harsh; *actitud, porte* gruff, rude; surly.
(**d**) *caballo* wild, untamed.
broncopulmonar *adj* broncho-pulmonary.
bronquedad *nf* (**a**) (*tosquedad*) roughness, coarseness. (**b**) (*delicadez*) brittleness. (**c**) (*de voz*) gruffness, harshness; roughness.
bronquial *adj* bronchial.
bronquina* *nf* = **bronca (a)**.
bronquinoso* *adj* (*Carib*) quarrelsome, brawling.
bronquios *nmpl* bronchial tubes.
bronquítico 1 *adj* bronchitic. **2** *nm*, **bronquítica** *nf* bronchitis sufferer.
bronquitis *nf* bronchitis.
broquel *nm* shield (*t fig*), buckler.
broquelarse [1a] *vr* to shield o.s.
broquero *nm* (*Méx*) brace.
broqueta *nf* skewer.
brota *nf* bud, shoot.
brotar [1a] **1** *vt* (*tierra*) to bring forth; (*planta*) to sprout, put out; (*fig*) to sprout; to pour out.
2 *vi* (**a**) (*Bot*) to sprout, bud, shoot.
(**b**) (*agua*) to spring up, gush forth, flow; (*lágrimas*) to well up, start to flow; (*río*) to rise.
(**c**) (*Med*) to break out, appear, show.
(**d**) (*aparecer*) to appear, spring up; **han brotado las manifestaciones** demonstrations have occurred; there have been outbreaks of rioting; **como princesa brotada de un cuento de hadas** like a princess out of a fairy tale.
brote *nm* (**a**) (*Bot*) bud, shoot; **~s de soja** bean shoots.
(**b**) (*Med*: *aparición*) outbreak, appearance; (*erupción cutánea*) rash, pimples; **un ~ de sarampión** an outbreak of measles.
(**c**) (*fig*: *ola*) outbreak, rash; **un ~ huelguístico** an outbreak (*o* rash, wave) of strikes.
(**d**) (*fig*: *origen*) origin; (*comienzo*) earliest beginnings, first manifestation.
broza *nf* (**a**) (*hojas etc*) dead leaves, dead wood; chaff; brushwood. (**b**) (*fig*: *en discurso etc*) padding. (**c**) (*Tip*) printer's brush.
brucelosis *nf* brucellosis.
bruces: **caer de ~** to fall headlong, fall flat; **estar de ~** to lie face downwards, lie flat on one's stomach.
bruja 1 *nf* (**a**) (*hechicera*) witch; sorceress.
(**b**) (*: *arpía*) hag, old witch, shrew; (*Méx*) woman.
(**c**) (*Carib, Cono Sur*) (*fantasma*) spook*, ghost; (*puta*) whore.
2 *adj*: **estar ~‡** (*Carib, Méx*) to be broke*, be flat* (*US*); **ando bien ~‡** I'm skint‡.
Brujas *nf* Bruges.
brujear [1a] **1** *vt* (*Carib*: *t fig*) to stalk, pursue. **2** *vi* (**a**) (*gen*) to practise witchcraft. (**b**) (*Carib, Méx*: *ir de juerga*) to go on a spree.
brujería *nf* (**a**) (*hechizo*) witchcraft, sorcery, (black) magic. (**b**) (*Carib*: *pobreza*) poverty.
brujeril *adj* witch-like.
brujo *nm* sorcerer; wizard, magician; (*LAm*) medicine man; (*Méx**) doctor.
brújula *nf* (**a**) (*compás*) compass; magnetic needle; **~ de bolsillo** pocket compass; **perder la ~** to lose one's bearings, (*fig*) lose one's touch.
(**b**) (*fig*: *mira*) guide, norm.
brujulear [1a] **1** *vt* (**a**) *cartas* to uncover (gradually); (*: *adivinar*) to guess.
(**b**) (*tratar de conseguir*) to intrigue for, try to wangle.
2 *vi* (*) (**a**) to manage, get along, keep going.
(**b**) (*And, Carib*) to go on the booze*, go on a bender‡.
brulote *nm* (*And, Cono Sur*: *comentario*) obscene remark (*o* comment); (*Cono Sur*: *escrito*) obscene letter.
bruma *nf* mist, fog; (*Náut*) sea mist; **~ del alba** morning mist.
brumoso *adj* misty, foggy.

bruno *adj* dark brown.
bruñido 1 *adj* polished, burnished. **2** *nm* (**a**) (*acto*) polish, polishing; ~ **de zapato** shoeshine. (**b**) (*brillo*) polish, shine, gloss.
bruñidor *nm*, **bruñidora** *nf* polisher, burnisher.
bruñir [3h] **1** *vt* (**a**) (*sacar brillo a*) to polish, burnish, shine.
(**b**) (*maquillar*) to make up (with cosmetics).
(**c**) (*CAm*: *molestar*) to harass, pester.
2 bruñirse *vr* to make (o.s.) up.
bruscamente *adv* (**a**) (*gen*) suddenly, brusquely, sharply. (**b**) (*rudamente*) sharply, abruptly.
brusco[1] *adj* (**a**) *ataque etc* sudden; *movimiento* sudden, brusque; *curva* sharp; *bajada* (*de temperatura etc*) sharp, sudden; *cambio* sudden, marked, violent.
(**b**) *actitud, porte* brusque, sharp, abrupt; rude.
brusco[2] *nm* (*Bot*) butcher's broom.
Bruselas *nf* Brussels.
bruselas *nfpl* tweezers; **unas** ~ a pair of tweezers.
brusquedad *nf* (**a**) (*gen*) suddenness; sharpness. (**b**) (*actitud*) brusqueness, sharpness, abruptness; rudeness; **hablar con** ~ to speak sharply.
brutal 1 *adj* (**a**) (*bruto*) brutal; brutish, beastly. (**b**) (*: *estupendo*) terrific*, tremendous*; ¡~! (*LAm*) great!*, brilliant!* (**c**) (*CAm*: *asombroso*) incredible, extraordinary. **2** *nm* brute, animal.
brutalidad *nf* (**a**) (*cualidad*) brutality; brutishness, beastliness.
(**b**) (*una* ~) brutal act, piece of brutality, crime.
(**c**) (*estupidez*) stupidity.
(**d**) **me gusta una** ~* I like it tremendously*.
brutalizar [1f] **1** *vt* to brutalize, treat brutally; *mujer* to rape. **2 brutalizarse** *vr* to become brutalized.
brutalmente *adv* brutally.
bruteza *nf* (**a**) (*gen*) brutality. (**b**) (*tosquedad*) coarseness, roughness.
Bruto *nm* Brutus.
bruto 1 *adj* (**a**) (*brutal*) brute, brutish; bestial.
(**b**) (*estúpido*) stupid, ignorant; (*inculto*) coarse, rough, uncouth; **más** ~ **que un adoquín** as dumb as an ox; **Pepe es muy** ~ Joe is pretty rough, Joe is terribly uncouth; **¡no seas** ~! don't be an idiot!
(**c**) *diamante etc* (*t* **en** ~) uncut, rough, unpolished; **en** ~ rough, raw, unworked; in a rough state; **hierro (en)** ~ crude iron, pig iron; **a la bruta** (*LAm*), **a lo** ~ (*LAm*) roughly, crudely.
(**d**) **pegar a uno en** ~ (*Carib*) to beat sb mercilessly.
(**e**) (*medidas*) gross; **peso** ~ gross weight; **producto** ~ gross product.
(**f**) (*Cono Sur*: *mala calidad*) poor-quality, inferior.
(**g**) **estar** ~‡ to be randy*, **ponerse** ~ to get randy*.
2 *nm* (**a**) (*animal*) brute, beast; ¡~! you beast! (*hum*).
(**b**) (*idiota*) idiot.
bruza *nf* coarse brush, scrubbing brush; horse brush; (*Tip*) printer's brush.
Bs.As. *abr de* **Buenos Aires** Buenos Aires, B.A.
Bta, Bto *adj* (*Rel*) *abr de* **Beata, Beato** Beatus, Blessed, B.
bu *nm* bogeyman; **hacer el** ~ **a uno** to scare sb.
búa *nf* pimple.
buba *nf*, **bubón** *nm* tumour, bubo.
bubónico *adj*: **peste bubónica** bubonic plague.
bubute *nm* (*Carib*) beetle.
bucal *adj* oral, of the mouth; **por vía** ~ through the mouth, by mouth, orally.
bucanero *nm* buccaneer.
bucarán *nm* buckram.
búcaro *nm* (**a**) (*arcilla*) (fragrant) clay. (**b**) (*jarrón*) vase.
buccino *nm* whelk.
buceador(a) *nm/f* diver; underwater swimmer, skindiver.
bucear [1a] *vi* (**a**) (*gen*) to dive; to swim under water; to skin-dive; (*trabajar como buzo*) to work as a diver. (**b**) (*fig*: *explorar*) to delve, explore, look below the surface.
buceo *nm* diving; underwater swimming, skindiving; ~ **de saturación** saturation diving.
bucle *nm* (**a**) (*pelo*) curl, ringlet. (**b**) (*fig*) curve, bend, loop; (*Inform*) loop; ~**s anidados** nested loops.
bucólica *nf* (**a**) (*Liter*) pastoral poem, bucolic. (**b**) (*) meal.
bucólico *adj* pastoral, bucolic.
buchaca *nf* (*CAm, Carib, Méx*) (*bolso*) bag; (*de caballo*) saddlebag; (*Billar*) (billiard) pocket.
buchada *nf* mouthful (of liquid).
buchante‡ *nm* shot.
buche *nm* (**a**) (*Orn*) crop; (*Zool*) maw; (*) guts, belly; **llenar el** ~* to fill one's belly.
(**b**) (*fig*: *pensamientos*) inner thoughts; bosom; **sacar el** ~* to show off; **sacar el** ~ **a uno*** to make sb talk.
(**c**) (*buchada*) mouthful (of liquid); (*And*) shot, slug* (*US*) (of drink).
(**d**) (*Cos*) bag; wrinkle, pucker; **hacer** ~ to be baggy, wrinkle up.
(**e**) (*And*: *chistera*) top hat.
(**f**) (*LAm Med*) (*bocio*) goitre, thyroid; (*paperas*) mumps.
(**g**) (*Carib*: *tonto*) fool, idiot.
buché *nm* (*CAm*) rustic, peasant.
buchinche *nm* (*Carib*) (*casa*) hovel; (*tienda*) pokey little shop.
Buda *nm* Buddha.
budín *nm* (*LAm*) (*pastel*) cake; (*postre*) trifle; ~ **de pescado** fish pie; **esa chica es un** ~ that girl's a smasher‡.
budismo *nm* Buddhism.
budista *adj, nmf* Buddhist.
budleia *nf* buddleia.
buen *adj V* **bueno**.
buenamente *adv* (**a**) (*fácilmente*) easily, freely, without difficulty. (**b**) (*voluntariamente*) willingly; voluntarily.
buenamoza *nf* (*And euf*) jaundice.
buenaventura *nf* (**a**) (*suerte*) good luck. (**b**) (*adivinación*) fortune; **decir** (*o* **echar**) **la** ~ **a uno** to tell sb's fortune.
buenazo 1 *adj* kindly, good-natured; long-suffering. **2** *nm* good-natured person; **ser un** ~ to be (too) kind-hearted, be easily imposed upon; **el** ~ **de Marcos** good old Marcos.
buenmozo *adj* (*Cono Sur*) good-looking, handsome.
bueno 1 *adj* (**buen** *delante de nm sing*) (**a**) (*gen*) good; *tiempo* fine, good, fair; *constitución* strong, sound; *doctrina* right, sound; *sociedad* good, polite; **el** ~ (*Cine etc*) the goody, the good guy; **sé** ~ be good; **la buena gente, los** ~**s** good people, decent people; **la buena*** the right hand; **el** ~ **de Manolo** good old Manolo; **lo** ~ **es que** ... the best thing about it is that ..., the best part is that ...; the funny thing is that ...; ~ **fuera que** ... it would be fine if ...; ¡~ **está!** that's enough!, that'll do!; **luego verás lo que es** ~* I'll get you!; **hacer** ~ **un refrán** to corroborate a proverb, give meaning to a proverb; **hacer algo a la buena de Dios** to do sth in a hit-or-miss way, do sth haphazardly; **tan** ~ **como el pan** as good as gold.
(**b**) (*amable*) kind, good, nice; **fue muy** ~ **conmigo** he was very nice to me; **es Vd muy** ~ you are very kind.
(**c**) (*apropiado*) fit, proper, suitable; **en el momento** ~ at the right moment, at the proper time; **por buen camino** along the right road (*y V* **camino**); **ser** ~ **para** to be suitable for, be good for; ~ **de comer** good to eat, nice to eat; fit to eat.
(**d**) (*Med*) **estar** ~ to be well; **no estar** ~ **de la cabeza** to be weak in the head.
(**e**) (*iró*) fine, pretty; **¡buen conductor!** a fine driver you are!; **¡ésa sí que es buena!** that's a good one!; **¡estaría** ~**!*** a fine thing!; I should jolly well say not!*; **estaría** ~ **que** ... a fine thing it would be if ...; **le dio un tortazo de los** ~**s** he gave him a real bash*, he really did bash him*; **le di un buen susto** I gave him a good fright.
(**f**) (*: *atractivo*) attractive; **está buena** she's hot stuff*, she's quite a girl; **¡estaba buenísima!** she looked a real treat!*, she looked great!*; *V* **mozo**.
(**g**) **¿adónde** ~**?** where are you off to?; **¿de dónde** ~**?** where did you spring from?; **¡cuánto** ~ **por aquí!** what a nice surprise to see you!
(**h**) (*locuciones con* **buenas**) **¡buenas!** hullo!; **de buenas a primeras** straight away, from the very start; suddenly, without warning; **decir una noticia a uno de buenas a primeras** to spring a piece of news on sb; **estar de buenas** to be in a good mood; to be in luck; **por las buenas** (*de buena gana*) gladly, willingly; (*por capricho*) just because he (*etc*) felt like it, quite arbitrarily; **por las buenas o por las malas** willy-nilly; by hook or by crook, by fair means or foul; **resolver algo por las buenas** to come to an amicable agreement about sth.
(**i**) (*And, Cono Sur*) **estar en la buena** (*de buen humor*) to be in a good mood; (*tener suerte*) to be in luck.
2 *adv, como interj etc*: ¡~! right!, all right!, O.K.!*; (*iró*) come off it!*, so you say!; ¿~? (*Méx Telec*) hullo?; ~, **resulta que** ... well, it happens that ...; ~, **¿y qué?** well, so what?; **pero** ¡~! well, I like that!; ~, **pues** ... well ...
buenón* *adj* nice-looking, good-looking.
buey *nm* (**a**) (*Zool*) ox; bullock, steer; ~ **almizclado** musk ox; ~ **corneta** (*And, Cono Sur*) one-horned ox; ~ **de Francia** crab; ~ **marino** manatee, sea-cow.
(**b**) (*LAm fig*: *cornudo*) cuckold.

(**c**) (*Carib fig: dineral*) big sum of money.

(**d**) (*fig: locuciones*) ~ **corneta** (*And, Cono Sur: entrometido*) busybody, noseyparker*; **nunca falta un ~ corneta** (*And, Cono Sur*) there's always someone who can't keep his mouth shut; ~ **muerto** (*Carib*) bargain; ~ **suelto** free agent; (*soltero*) bachelor; **chinches** (*etc*) **como ~es** enormous bedbugs (*etc*), bedbugs (*etc*) the size of buffaloes; **es un ~ para el trabajo** he's a tremendous worker; **hablar de ~es perdidos** (*Cono Sur*) to waste one's breath; **pegar ~es** (*CAm*) to go to sleep; **poner los ~es antes que el carro** to put the cart before the horse; **saber con los ~es que ara** (*Carib, Cono Sur*) to know who your friends are; **sacar el ~ de la barranca** (*Carib, Méx*) (*tener éxito*) to bring sth off; (*salvarse*) to get out of a hole; **cuando vuelen los ~es** when pigs learn to fly.

bueyada *nf* (*LAm*) drove of oxen.

bufa* 1 *adj* (*Carib, Méx*) tight*, drunk. **2** *nf* (**a**) (*broma*) joke, piece of clowning. (**b**) (*Carib, Méx: embriaguez*) drunkenness.

búfalo 1 *nm* buffalo. **2** *adj* (*Carib**) great*, fantastic*.

bufanda *nf* (**a**) (*prenda de vestir*) scarf, muffler. (**b**) (‡) (*soborno*) sweetener*, back-hander*; (*gaje*) perk*.

bufar [1a] *vi* (**a**) to snort; (*gato*) to spit; ~ **de ira** to snort with rage. (**b**) (*Méx*) to reek, stink.

bufarrón* *nm* (*Cono Sur*) pederast, child molester.

bufé *nm* = **bufet**.

bufeo *nm* (*CAm, Carib, Méx*) (*atún*) tunny; (*delfín*) dolphin.

bufet [bu'fe] *nm, pl* **bufets** [bu'fe] (**a**) (*mueble*) sideboard. (**b**) (*cena*) buffet supper, cold supper. (**c**) (*comedor*) dining-room (of an hotel); (*restorán*) restaurant.

bufete *nm* (**a**) (*mesa*) desk. (**b**) (*Jur*) lawyer's office; lawyer's clients, lawyer's practice; **abrir ~, establecer su ~** to set up in legal practice. (**c**) (*Culin*) = **bufet (b)**.

bufido *nm* snort (*t fig*).

bufo[1] **1** *adj* comic, farcical; slapstick, knockabout; *ópera* comic.

2 *nm* (**a**) (*payaso*) clown, funny man; (*Mús*) buffo. (**b**) (*Cono Sur*‡) queer‡.

bufo[2] *adj* (*Carib*) spongy.

bufón 1 *adj* funny, comical; clownish. **2** *nm* funny man, buffoon, clown; (*Hist*) jester.

bufonada *nf* (**a**) (*gen*) buffoonery, clowning. (**b**) (*una ~*) (*dicho*) joke, jest; (*hecho*) piece of buffoonery; (*Teat*) comic piece, farce.

bufonear [1a] *vi*, **bufonearse** *vr* to joke, jest; to clown, play the fool.

bufonesco *adj* funny, comical; clownish.

buga[1]‡ *nm* (*Aut*) car.

buga[2]‡ *nm* (*persona*) straight person‡, heterosexual.

buganvilla *nf* bougainvillea.

bugle *nm* bugle.

bugui-bugui *nm* boogie-woogie.

buharda *nf*, **buhardilla** *nf* (**a**) (*ventana*) dormer window; skylight. (**b**) (*ático*) garret, loft.

búho *nm* (**a**) (*Orn: t* ~ **real**) eagle owl. (**b**) (*fig: persona*) unsociable person, recluse.

buhonería *nf* (**a**) (*acto*) peddling, hawking. (**b**) (*mercancías*) pedlar's wares, hawker's wares.

buhonero *nm* pedlar, peddler (*US*), hawker.

buido *adj* (**a**) (*puntiagudo*) sharp, pointed. (**b**) (*estriado*) fluted, grooved.

buitre 1 *nm* (**a**) (*Orn*) vulture, (*esp*) Griffon vulture; ~ **alimoche** Egyptian vulture; ~ **leonado** Griffon vulture. (**b**) (*) go-getter*; sponger*, cadger*. **2** *adj* (*) sponging*, cadging*.

buitrear [1a] **1** *vt* (**a**) (*LAm: matar*) to kill. (**b**) (*And, Cono Sur*: vomitar*) to throw up, vomit. **2** *vi* (*And, Cono Sur*) to be sick, vomit.

buitrón *nm* fish trap.

bujarra‡ *nm*, **bujarrón**‡ *nm* queer‡.

buje *nm* axle box, bushing.

bujería *nf* trinket, knick-knack.

bujero‡ *nm* hole.

bujía *nf* (**a**) (*vela*) candle; (*candelero*) candlestick. (**b**) (*Elec*) candle-power. (**c**) (*Aut etc: t* ~ **de encendido**) sparking plug. (**d**) (*CAm: bombilla*) light bulb.

bul** *nm* arse**.

bula *nf* (papal) bull; **no poder con la ~*** to have no strength left for anything; **no me vale la ~ de Meco** I'm done for.

bulbo *nm* (*Anat, Bot, Med*) bulb; (*Méx Rad*) valve, tube (*US*); (*Cono Sur Elec*) bulb.

bulboso *adj* bulbous.

bule *nm* (*Méx*) (*Bot*) gourd; (*jarro*) water pitcher; **llenarse hasta los ~s** to stuff o.s.; **el que nace para ~ hasta jícara no para** you can't escape your destiny.

bulevar *nm* boulevard, avenue.

Bulgaria *nf* Bulgaria.

búlgaro, -a 1 *adj, nm/f* Bulgarian. **2** *nm* (*Ling*) Bulgarian.

bulimia *nf* bulimia.

bulín *nm* (*Cono Sur*) (**a**) (*de soltero*) bachelor flat (*o* pad). (**b**) (*especie de burdel*) room (used for sexual encounters).

bulo *nm* hoax, false report, canard.

bulón *nm* bolt; spring pin.

bulto *nm* (**a**) (*tamaño, volumen*) size, bulk, bulkiness, volume, massiveness; (*fig*) substance, importance; **de ~** obvious, striking; *error* gross; (*Méx: de sobra*) superfluous, excess; **de gran ~** bulky; **de mucho ~** heavy, sizeable, massive, (*fig*) important; **de poco ~** small, that does not take up much room, (*fig*) unimportant; **argumentos de ~** arguments of substance; **estar de ~, hacer ~, ir de ~** to swell the number(s), make up the number(s); **hacer ~** to take up space.

(**b**) (*forma*) shape, form; vague shape, indistinct shape; **a ~** roughly, broadly; in the mass; **estimación a ~** rough estimate; **buscar el ~ a uno** to provoke (*o* push) sb; to be out for sb's blood; **calcular a ~** to calculate roughly; **decir algo a ~** to come right out with sth, blurt sth out; **ir al ~, tirar al ~** to come straight to the point; **escurrir el ~** to dodge, duck out of it, shy away, (*fig*) dodge the issue, pass the buck*; **menear el ~ a uno** to thrash sb.

(**c**) (*paquete etc*) package, bundle; bale; bulky object; piece of luggage; (*LAm*) (*bolso*) briefcase, bag; (*de escolar*) satchel; **~s de mano** hand luggage.

(**d**) (*Med*) lump, swelling.

(**e**) (*estatua*) bust, statue.

(**f**) (*Mil*‡) squaddie*, recruit.

bululú *nm* (*Carib*) excitement, agitation.

bulla *nf* (**a**) (*follón*) noise, uproar; racket; (*bullicio*) bustle; (*confusión*) fuss, confusion; (*LAm: pelea*) quarrel, brawl, fight; (*Carib: discusión*) argument; **armar ~, meter ~** to make a row (*o* racket); **meter algo a ~** to throw sth into confusion; to obstruct sth.

(**b**) (*turba*) crowd, mob.

(**c**) **ser el hombre de la ~** (*Carib*) to be the man of the moment.

bullabesa *nf* fish soup, bouillabaisse.

bullaje *nm* noisy crowd, mob.

bullanga *nf* disturbance, riot.

bullanguero 1 *adj* riotous, rowdy. **2** *nm*, **bullanguera** *f* noisy person; rioter, troublemaker.

bullaranga *nf* (*LAm*) (*follón*) noise, row; (*disturbio*) riot.

bullarengue‡ *nm* (woman's) bottom.

bulldozer [bul'doθer] *nm, pl* **bulldozers** [bul'doθer] bulldozer.

bullebulle *nmf* busybody; mischief-maker; fusspot.

bullero *adj* (*LAm*) = **bullicioso**.

bullicio *nm* (*ruido*) uproar, din, racket, hubbub; (*actividad*) bustle, bustling movement, bustling activity; (*confusión*) confusion; (*disturbio*) disturbance, riot.

bulliciosamente *adv* noisily; boisterously; busily; restlessly; riotously.

bullicioso *adj* noisy, rowdy; boisterous; busy, bustling, full of movement; active; restless; turbulent, riotous.

bullir [3h] **1** *vt* to move, stir; **no bulló pie ni mano** he did not lift a finger.

2 *vi* (**a**) (*líquido*) (*hervir*) to boil; (*agitarse*) to bubble, bubble up; **el agua bullía ligeramente** the water rippled slightly.

(**b**) (*moverse*) to move, stir, budge; to move about; to bustle about; **no bullía** he didn't move, he never stirred.

(**c**) (*insectos*) to swarm; to teem; ~ **de** (*fig*), ~ **en** to teem with, swarm with, seethe with; **bullía de indignación** he was seething with indignation; **la ciudad bullía de actividad** the town was humming with activity; **Londres está que bulle de juventud** London is bursting with young people.

3 bullirse *vr* to move, stir, budge.

bumerán *nm* boomerang.

bumerang [bume'ran] *nm, pl* **bumerangs** [bume'ran] boomerang.

bunga *nf* (*Carib*) lie.

bungalow ['boŋgalo, buŋga'lo] *nm, pl* **bungalows** ['boŋgalo, buŋga'lo] bungalow.

bungo *nm* (*CAm*) = **bongo**.

buniato *nm* = **boniato**.

bunjo *nm*: **hacer ~** (*Carib*) to hit the jackpot.

búnker ['buŋker] *nm, pl* **búnkers** ['buŋker] (**a**) (*Golf*) bun-

ker. (**b**) (*Pol*) reactionary clique, reactionary core; entrenched interests.
búnquer *nm* = **búnker**.
buñolería *nf* bakery where *buñuelos* are made; shop where *buñuelos* are sold.
buñuelo *nm* (**a**) (*Culin*: *aprox*) doughnut, fritter. (**b**) (*: *chapuza*) botched job, mess.
BUP [bup] *nm* (*Esp Escol*) *abr de* **Bachillerato Unificado y Polivalente** (*secondary school education, 14-17 age group, and leaving certificate*).
buque *nm* (**a**) (*gen*) ship, vessel, boat; ~ **de abastecimiento** supply ship; ~ **almirante** flagship; ~ **de carga,** ~ **carguero** freighter; ~ **cisterna** tanker; water-boat; ~ **correo** mail-boat; ~ **costero** coaster; ~ **de desembarco** landing-craft; ~ **escolta** escort vessel; ~ **escuela** training ship; ~ **espía** spy ship; ~ **factoría** factory ship; ~ **fanal,** ~ **faro** lightship; ~ **granelero** bulk-carrier; ~ **de guerra** warship, (*Hist*) man-of-war; ~ **hospital** hospital ship; ~ **insignia** flagship; ~ **de línea** liner, (*Hist*) ship of the line; ~ **mercante** merchantman, merchant ship; ~ **minador** minelayer; ~ **nodriza** depot ship, mother-ship; ~ **de pasajeros** passenger ship; ~ **portacontenedores** container ship; ~ **portatrén** train ferry; ~ **de ruedas** paddle-steamer; ~ **de vapor** steamer, steamship; ~ **de vela,** ~ **velero** sailing ship; **ir en** ~ to go by ship, go by sea.
(**b**) (*tonelaje*) capacity, tonnage.
(**c**) (*casco*) hull.
buqué *nm* bouquet (*of wine*).
buraco *nm* (*Cono Sur*) hole.
burata‡ *nf* (*Carib*) cash, dough‡.
burbuja *nf* bubble; **hacer ~s** to bubble.
burbujeante *adj* bubbly, fizzy; bubbling.
burbujear [1a] *vi* to bubble; to form bubbles.
burbujeo *nm* bubbling.
burda‡ *nf* door.
burdégano *nm* hinny.
burdel *nm* brothel.
Burdeos *nm* Bordeaux.
burdeos 1 *nm* claret, Bordeaux (wine) (*t* **vino de** ~). **2** *adj* maroon, dark red.
burdo *adj* coarse, rough; (*fig*) *excusa, mentira etc* clumsy.
burear* [1a] (*And*) **1** *vt* to con*, trick. **2** *vi* to go out on the town*.
bureo *nm* (**a**) (*diversión*) entertainment, amusement; spree; **ir de** ~ to have a good time, go on a spree. (**b**) (*: *paseo*) stroll; **darse un** ~ to go for a stroll.
bureta *nf* burette.
burgalés 1 *adj* of Burgos. **2** *nm*, **burgalesa** *nf* native (*o* inhabitant) of Burgos; **los burgaleses** the people of Burgos.
burgo *nm* hamlet.
burgués 1 *adj* middle class, bourgeois (*t pey*); town (*atr*). **2** *nm*, **burguesa** *nf* member of the middle class, bourgeois(e); townsman, townswoman.
burguesía *nf* middle class, bourgeoisie; **alta** ~ upper middle class; **pequeña** ~ lower middle class.
buril *nm* burin, engraver's chisel.
burilar [1a] *vt* to engrave; to chisel.
burla *nf* (**a**) (*mofa*) gibe, taunt, jeer; **~s** mockery, ridicule; **hacer** ~ **de** to make fun of, mock; **hace** ~ **de todo** he mocks everything.
(**b**) (*broma*) joke; **~s** joking, fun; **de ~s** in fun; **~s aparte** joking aside; ~ **burlando** unawares, without noticing it; on the quiet; **~s y veras** light-hearted and serious things; **entre ~s y veras** half-jokingly; **gastar ~s con uno** to make fun of sb.
(**c**) (*broma pesada*) trick; hoax, practical joke; **fue una** ~ **cruel** it was a cruel sort of joke.
burladero *nm* (*Aut*) traffic island, refuge; (*Taur*) refuge, shelter; (*Ferro etc*) recess, refuge (*in a tunnel*).
burlador 1 *adj* mocking. **2** *nm* (**a**) (*mofador*) scoffer, mocker. (**b**) (*bromista*) practical joker, hoaxer, leg-puller*. (**c**) (*seductor*) seducer, libertine.
burlar [1a] **1** *vt* (**a**) (*engañar*) to deceive, take in, hoax, trick; *enemigo etc* to outwit, outmanoeuvre; *orden* to show no respect for; to get round, disregard; *bloqueo* to run; *vigilancia* to defeat.
(**b**) *ambición, plan etc* to frustrate; *esperanzas* to cheat, disappoint.
(**c**) *mujer* to seduce, deceive.
(**d**) (*: *saber usar*) to know how to use, be able to handle; **ya burla la moto** she can handle the bike now*.
2 *vi y* **burlarse** *vr* (**a**) (*bromear*) to joke, banter; (*mofarse*) to scoff; **yo no me burlo** I'm not joking, I'm in earnest.
(**b**) **~se de** to mock, ridicule, scoff at; to make fun of.
burlería *nf* (**a**) (*mofa*) mockery; (*bromas*) fun. (**b**) (*engaño*) trick, deceit; (*ilusión*) illusion. (**c**) (*cuento*) tall story, fairy tale.
burlesco *adj* (**a**) (*divertido*) funny, comic. (**b**) (*Liter etc*) mock, burlesque.
burlete *nm* weather strip, draught excluder.
burlisto *adj* (*Cono Sur, CAm, Méx*) = **burlón.**
burlón 1 *adj* mocking; joking, teasing, bantering; *risa etc* mocking, sardonic; **dijo** ~ he said banteringly.
2 *nm*, **burlona** *nf* (**a**) (*bromista*) joker, wag, leg-puller.
(**b**) (*mofador*) mocker, scoffer.
buró *nm* (**a**) (*mueble*) bureau, (roll-top) desk. (**b**) (*Pol etc*) bureau. (**c**) (*Méx*) bedside table.
burocracia *nf* bureaucracy; officialdom.
burócrata *nmf* civil servant, administrative official, official of the public service; (*pey*) bureaucrat.
burocrático *adj* official; civil service (*atr*); (*pey*) bureaucratic.
buromática *nf*, **burótica** *nf* office automation, office computerization.
burra *nf* (**a**) (*Zool*) (she-)donkey. (**b**) (*fig**: *mujer*) stupid woman; (*t* ~ **de carga**) hard-working woman, drudge, slave. (**c**) (*Esp*‡: *bicicleta*) bike.
burrada *nf* (**a**) (*burros*) drove of donkeys.
(**b**) (*: *disparate*) silly thing, stupid act (*o* saying *etc*); **decir ~s** to talk nonsense, say silly things.
(**c**) **una** ~ (**de cosas**) a whole heap of things, heaps of things; **sabe una** ~ he knows a hell of a lot.
(**d**) (*: *como adv*) **me gusta una** ~ I like it a lot.
burrajo *adj* (*Méx*) vulgar, rude.
burrear‡ *vt* (*robar*) to rip off‡; (*engañar*) to con*.
burrero 1 *adj* (*Cono Sur*: *hum*) horse-loving, racegoing. **2** *nm* (**a**) (*Méx*: *arriero*) mule (*o* donkey) driver. (**b**) (*CAm*: *burros*) large herd of donkeys. (**c**) (*Carib*: *malhablado*) coarse (*o* foul-mouthed) individual. (**d**) (*Cono Sur*: *hum*) horse-lover.
burricie* *nf* stupidity.
burro 1 *nm* (**a**) (*Zool*) donkey; (*fig*) ass, idiot; (*Cono Sur*: *hum*) racehorse; (*caballo*) old horse, nag; (*perdedor en carrera*) also ran; (*CAm Naipes*) old maid; ~ **de agua** (*Carib, Méx*) big wave; ~ **de carga** (*fig*) glutton for work, hard worker, (*pey*) slave, drudge; ~ **cargado de letras** pompous ass; **salto de** ~ (*Méx*: *juego*) leapfrog; **apearse de su** ~, **bajar del** ~ to back down, think better of it; **no apearse de su** ~ to stick to one's guns, persist in one's error; **caer ~s aparejados** (*Carib*) to rain cats and dogs; **caerse del** ~ to realize one's mistake; **poner a uno a caer de un** ~ to beat sb black and blue; **esto comió** ~ (*Cono Sur*) it got lost, it vanished; **no ver tres** (*etc*) **en un** ~ to be as blind as a bat; **ver ~s negros** (*Cono Sur*) to see stars.
(**b**) (*Téc*) sawhorse.
(**c**) (*LAm*: *escalera*) step ladder.
(**d**) (*And, Carib*: *columpio*) swing.
2 *adj* (**a**) (*estúpido*) stupid; **el muy** ~ the great oaf.
(**b**) (‡: *cachondo*) **estar** ~ to feel randy*; **poner** ~ **a uno** to make sb feel randy*.
burrumazo* *nm* (*Carib*) blow, thump.
bursátil *adj* stock-exchange (*atr*), stock-market (*atr*); **crisis** ~ crisis on the stock exchange; **desplome** ~ stock exchange crash.
bursitis *nf* bursitis.
burujaca *nf* (*LAm*) saddlebag.
burundanga* *nf* (*Carib*) (**a**) (*objeto*) worthless object; piece of junk; **de** ~ worthless; **es** ~ it's just a piece of junk. (**b**) (*lío*) mess, mix-up.
burujo *nm* = **borujo.**
burusca *nf* (*CAm*) kindling.
bus *nm* (**a**) bus; (*LAm*: *autocar*) coach (*Brit*), long-distance bus. (**b**) (*Inform*) bus; ~ **de expansión** expansion bus; ~ **de memoria** memory bus.
busa‡ *nf*: **tener** ~ (*Esp*) to feel hungry.
busaca *nf* (*And, Carib*) saddlebag; (*Carib*) satchel.
busca 1 *nf* search, hunt (*de* for); pursuit; **en** ~ **de** in search of. **2** *nm* (*Telec*) bleeper, pager, paging device.
buscabulla *nm* (*Carib, Méx*) brawler, troublemaker.
buscabullas* *adj invar* (*Méx*) troublemaking.
buscada *nf* = **busca 1.**
buscador(a) *nm/f* searcher, seeker; ~ **de oro** gold prospector.
buscaniguas *nm invar* (*And, CAm*) squib, cracker.
buscapersonas *nm invar* = **busca 2.**
buscapié *nm* hint; feeler.
buscapiés *nm invar* squib, cracker.

buscapleitos *nmf invar* (*LAm*) troublemaker.

buscar [1g] **1** *vt* (**a**) (*gen*) to look for, search for, seek; (*objeto perdido*) to hunt for, have a look for; *enemigo* to seek out; *camorra* to be asking for, look for; *beneficio, ganancia etc* to seek, be out for; **ir a ~** to go and look for; to bring, fetch; **ven a ~me a la oficina** come and find me at the office, come and pick me up at the office; **nadie nos buscará aquí** nobody will look for us here; **tengo que ~ la referencia** I have to look the reference up; **el terrorista más buscado** the most wanted terrorist.

(**b**) (*LAm*: *pedir*) to ask for, call for.

(**c**) (*Méx*) *riña etc* to provoke.

2 *vi* (**a**) (*gen*) to look, search, hunt; **buscó en el bolsillo** he felt in his pocket, he hunted in his pocket.

(**b**) **~** + *infin* to seek to + *infin*, try to + *infin*.

3 buscarse *vr* (*Esp*) (**a**) (*anuncio*) **'se busca coche', 'búscase coche'** 'car wanted'.

(**b**) **~la*** (*arreglárselas*) to manage, get along; (*buscar camorra*) to be looking for trouble, ask for it; **se la buscó** he brought it on himself, it serves him right.

(**c**) **~las*** to fend for o.s.

buscarruidos *nm invar* rowdy, troublemaker.

buscas* *nfpl* (*Carib, Méx, And*) perks*, profits on the side.

buscavidas *nmf invar* (**a**) (*entrometido*) snooper, meddler, busybody.

(**b**) (*ambicioso*) hustler; (*pey*) social climber, go-getter.

buscón 1 *adj* (**a**) (*gen*) thieving, crooked. (**b**) (*Méx*: *diligente*) active, diligent.

2 *nm* petty thief, small-time crook; rogue.

buscona *nf* whore.

buseta *nf* (*LAm*) small bus, microbus.

busilis* *nm* (**a**) (*pega*) difficulty, snag; **ahí está el ~** there's the snag, that's the rub.

(**b**) (*esencia*) core (of the problem); **dar en el ~** to put one's finger on the spot.

búsqueda *nf* search; inquiry, investigation; (*Inform*) search.

busto *nm* bust; **~ parlante** talking head.

butaca *nf* armchair, easy chair; (*Teat*) stall; **~ ojerera** wing-chair; **~ de platea** (*Teat*) orchestra stall.

butacón *nm* large armchair.

butano *nm* (*t* **gas ~**) butane, butane gas; **color ~** orange.

butaque *nm* (*LAm*) small armchair.

buten: **de ~*** terrific*, tremendous*.

butí* *nf* boutique.

butifarra *nf* (**a**) (*salchichón*) Catalan sausage; **hacer (la) ~ a uno*** ≈ to give sb the two-fingers sign, make an obscene gesture to sb.

(**b**) (*: *media*) badly-fitting stocking.

(**c**) (*And*: *emparedado*) long sandwich.

(**d**) (*Cono Sur*) **tomar a uno para la ~** to poke fun at sb.

butiondo *adj* lewd, lustful.

butrón* *nm* hole made to effect a break-in; burglary, break-in.

butronero* *nm* burglar.

butuco *adj* (*CAm*) short, squat.

buz *nm* respectful kiss, formal kiss; **hacer el ~** to bow and scrape.

buzamiento *nm* (*Geol*) dip.

buzar [1f] *vi* (*Geol*) to dip.

buzo¹ *nm* diver.

buzo² *nm* (*And, Cono Sur*) tracksuit, jogging suit; jumpsuit.

buzón *nm* (**a**) (*Correos*) letterbox, pillar-box, mailbox (*US*); (*Inform*) mailbox; **~ de alcance** late-collection postbox; **~ de sugerencias** suggestions box; **cerrar el ~‡** to keep one's trap shut‡; **echar una carta al ~** to post a letter; **vender un ~ a uno*** (*Cono Sur*) to sell sb a dummy, pull the wool over sb's eyes.

(**b**) (*canal*) canal, conduit.

(**c**) (*tapón*) stopper; (*tapa*) lid, cover.

buzonero *nm* (*LAm*) postal employee (*who collects from letterboxes*).

byte [bait] *nm* byte.

C

C, c [θe, se (*esp LAm*)] *nf* (*letra*) C, c; **datación por C-14** C-14 dating.
C (**a**) *abr de* **centígrado** centigrade, C. (**b**) *abr de* **Compañía** Company, Co.
c *abr de* **capítulo**; = **cap.**
C/ *abr de* **Calle** Street, St.
c/ (**a**) *abr de* **cuenta** account, a/c. (**b**) *abr de* **capítulo** chapter, ch.
ca *interj* (†) not a bit of it!, no, indeed!, oh no!
C.A. *nf* (**a**) (*Elec*) *abr de* **corriente alterna** alternating current, A.C. (**b**) (*Pol*) *abr de* **Comunidad Autónoma.**
cabal 1 *adj* (*exacto*) exact; (*apropiado*) right, proper; (*acabado*) finished, complete, consummate, full; (*perfecto*) perfect; *esfuerzo etc* thorough, all-out.
2 *adv* exactly; **¡~!** perfectly correct!, right!
3 ~es *nmpl*: **estar en sus ~es** to be in one's right mind; **hacer algo por sus ~es** to do sth properly; to do things in the right order.
cábala *nf* (**a**) (*Rel*) cab(b)ala. (**b**) **~s** (*suposición*) guess, supposition; (*intrigas*) intrigues.
cabalgada *nf* (*Hist*) troop of riders; cavalry raid.
cabalgador *nm* rider, horseman.
cabalgadura *nf* (*de montar*) mount, horse; (*de carga*) beast of burden.
cabalgar [1h] **1** *vt* (**a**) (*persona*) to ride.
(**b**) (*semental*) to cover, serve.
2 *vi* to ride; to go riding; **~ en mula** to ride (on) a mule; **~ sin montura, ~ a pelo** (*LAm*) to ride bareback.
cabalgata *nf* (*acto*) ride; (*desfile*) cavalcade, mounted procession; **~ de Reyes** Twelfth Night procession.
cabalidad *nf*: **a ~** perfectly, adequately.
cabalista *nm* schemer, intriguer.
cabalístico *adj* cabalistic; (*fig*) occult, mysterious.
cabalmente *adv* exactly; properly; completely, fully; thoroughly.
caballa *nf* (Atlantic) mackerel.
caballada *nf* (**a**) (*Zool*) drove of horses. (**b**) (*LAm*: *animalada*) gaffe, blunder; **has hecho una ~** that was a stupid thing to do.
caballaje *nm* horsepower.
caballar *adj* horse (*atr*), equine; **cara ~** horse-face; **ganado ~** horses.
caballazo *nm* (*LAm*) collision between two horsemen, accident involving a horse.
caballejo *nm* (**a**) (*poney*) pony. (**b**) (*rocín*) old horse, poor horse, nag.
caballerango *nm* (*Méx*) groom.
caballerear [1a] *vi* to give o.s. the airs of a gentleman.
caballeresco *adj* (**a**) (*Hist*) knightly, chivalric; **literatura caballeresca** chivalresque literature, books of chivalry; **orden caballeresca** order of chivalry.
(**b**) *sentimiento* fine, noble, chivalrous; *trato etc* chivalrous; *carácter* gentlemanly, noble.
caballerete *nm* dandy, fop, dude (*US*).
caballería *nf* (**a**) (*animal*) (*gen*) mount; steed; (*caballo*) horse; (*mula*) mule (*etc*); **~ de carga** beast of burden.
(**b**) (*Mil*) cavalry; **~ ligera** light horse, light cavalry.
(**c**) (*Hist*) chivalry, knighthood; (*orden*) order of chivalry, military order; **~ andante** knight-errantry.
(**d**) **andarse en ~s** to overdo the compliments.
(**e**) (*CAm, Carib, Cono Sur, Méx*: *Agr*) *a land measurement of varying sizes* (*usually 42 hectares*).
caballericero *nm* (*CAm, Carib*) groom.
caballeriza *nf* (**a**) (*cuadra*) stable; (*de cría*) stud, horse-breeding establishment; **~ de alquiler** livery stable. (**b**) (*personas*) stable hands, grooms.
caballerizo *nm* groom, stableman; (*Hist*) **~ mayor del rey** master of the king's horse; **~ del rey** equerry.
caballero 1 *n* (**a**) (*el que cabalga*) rider, horseman.
(**b**) (*señor*) gentleman; **cosas indignas de un ~** things unworthy of a gentleman; **~ de industria** swindler, adventurer, gentleman crook; **~ solitario** lone wolf; **de ~ a ~** as one gentleman to another; **ser cumplido ~, ser todo un ~** to be a real gentleman; **es un mal ~** he's no gentleman; **'C~s'** 'Gents', 'Men'.
(**c**) (*Hist*) knight; noble, nobleman; **~ andante** knight-errant; **los ~s de Malta** the Knights of Malta; **~ de Santiago** Knight of (the Order of) Santiago; (*título*) **el C~ de la Rosa** the Rosenkavalier; **el C~ de la Triste Figura** the Knight of the Doleful Countenance (*Don Quixote*); **armar ~ a uno** to knight sb, dub sb knight.
(**d**) (*en oración directa, frec iró*) sir; **¿quién es Vd, ~?** who are you, sir?
2 *adj*: **iba ~ en una mula** he was riding a mule, he was mounted on a mule; **estar ~ en su opinión** to stick firmly to one's opinion.
caballerosamente *adv* like a gentleman; chivalrously.
caballerosidad *nf* gentlemanliness; chivalry.
caballeroso *adj* gentlemanly; chivalrous; **poco ~** ungentlemanly.
caballerote *nm* (*pey*) so-called gentleman, gentleman unworthy of the name.
caballete *nm* (*Agr*) ridge; (*Arquit*) (*de techo*) ridge, (*de chimenea*) cap; (*Arte*) easel; (*Téc*) trestle; (*Anat*) bridge (of the nose); **~ de aserrar** sawhorse; **~ para bicicleta** bicycle clamp, bicycle rest; **~ de pintor** painter's easel.
caballista *nm* expert horseman; expert in horses.
caballito *nm* (**a**) (*poney*) little horse, pony; **~ de niño** hobby-horse; **~ del diablo** dragonfly; **~ de mar, ~ marino** sea horse.
(**b**) **~s** (*de verbena etc*) merry-go-round.
(**c**) (*Méx*: *compresa*) sanitary towel, sanitary napkin (*US*).
caballo *nm* (**a**) (*Zool*) horse; **~ (de) aros** vaulting horse; **~ (de) balancín** rocking horse; **~ de batalla** (*fig*) forte, speciality; (*en controversia*) main point, central issue; **es su ~ de batalla** it's a hobby-horse of his; **~ blanco*** backer; **~ de buena boca** obliging chap; **~ castrado** gelding; **~ de carga** packhorse; **~ de carrera**(**s**) racehorse; **~ de caza** hunter; **~ entero** stallion; **el ~ de Espartero, el ~ de Santiago** *symbols of virility;* **~ de guerra** warhorse, charger; **~ marino** sea horse; **~ mecedor** rocking horse; **~ padre** stallion; **~ de tiro** carthorse, draught horse; **~ de Troya** Trojan horse; **~ de vaivén** rocking horse; **a ~** on horseback; **andar** (*o* **ir** *o* **montar**) **a ~** to ride, go on horseback; **las cosas andan a ~** (*Cono Sur*) the price of things is sky-high; **bajar a uno del ~** (*Carib*) to take sb down a peg (or two); **estar a ~ de algo** to be astride sth, be on sth; **estar a ~ entre dos cosas** (*fig*) to be between two things, alternate between two things; **pararle el ~ a uno** (*Méx*) to slow sb down; **pasársele el ~** to go over the top; **ser un ~*** to be stupid; **subir a ~** to mount, get on one's horse; **ir a mata ~** to go at breakneck speed; **a ~ regalado no le mires el diente** don't look a gift horse in the mouth; **como ~ desbocado** rashly, hastily; **como un ~ en una cacharrería** like a bull in a china-shop; **una dosis** (*etc*) **de ~*** a huge dose (*etc*), a massive dose (*etc*); **tropas de a ~** mounted troops; **es de a ~** he's a good rider.
(**b**) (*Ajedrez*) knight; (*Naipes*) queen.
(**c**) (*Téc*) sawhorse.
(**d**) (*Mec*) **~ de vapor decimal** (*C.V.*) metric horsepower; **~ de fuerza, ~ de potencia, ~ de vapor inglés** horse-power (HP); **un dos ~s** a small car; **~ de vapor** horse-power; **un motor de 18 ~s** an 18 horse-power engine; **¿cuántos ~s tiene este coche?** what horse-power is this car?

(**e**) (⁑) heroin.
caballón *nm* (*Agr*) ridge.
caballuno *adj* horse-like, horsy.
cabanga *nf* (*CAm*) nostalgia, homesickness; **estar de ~** to be homesick.
cabaña *nf* (**a**) (*casita*) hut, cabin, hovel, shack; **~ de madera** log cabin.
(**b**) (*Billar*) balk.
(**c**) (*Agr*) livestock.
(**d**) (*Cono Sur*: *estancia*) cattle-breeding ranch.
cabañero *nm* herdsman.
cabañuelas *nfpl* (*LAm*) (fanciful) weather predictions; (*And*) first summer rains; (*Méx*) first twelve days of January (*used to predict the weather*).
cabaré *nm* = **cabaret.**
cabaret [kaßa're] *nm, pl* **cabarets** [kaßa're] (*show*) cabaret, floor show; (*boîte*) nightclub; **~ de desnudo** nude show, striptease show, strip club.
cabaretera *nf* cabaret dancer, cabaret entertainer; nightclub hostess; showgirl.
cabaretero *adj* of a nightclub; **con ambiente ~** with a nightclub atmosphere.
cabás *nm* schoolbag, satchel.
cabe[1] *nm*: **~ de pala** windfall, lucky break; **dar un ~ a** to harm, do harm to; **dar un ~ al bolsillo** to make a hole in one's pocket.
cabe[2]* *nm* (*Dep*) header.
cabe[3] *prep* (*liter*) near, next to.
cabeceada *nf* (*LAm*) nod, shake of the head.
cabecear [1a] **1** *vt* (**a**) (*Cos*) to bind (the edge of).
(**b**) *vino* to strengthen; *vinos* to blend.
(**c**) *balón* to head.
2 *vi* (**a**) (*estando dormido*) to nod; (*negando*) to shake one's head; (*caballo*) to toss its head.
(**b**) (*Náut*) to pitch; (*Aut etc*) to lurch; (*carga*) to shift, slip.
cabeceo *nm* (**a**) (*al dormir*) nod, nodding; (*negativa*) shake of the head; (*de caballo*) toss of the head. (**b**) (*Náut*) pitching; (*Aut etc*) lurch, lurching; shifting; slipping.
cabecera *nf* (**a**) (*de cama, mesa, puente etc*) head; (*asiento*) seat of honour; (*de sala*) upper end, far end; (*de pista de aterrizaje*) end, head; **~** (**de río**) headwaters (of a river); **~ del cartel** (*Teat*) top of the bill; **ser ~ de cartel** to top the bill.
(**b**) (*tabla: de cama*) headboard; (*almohada*) pillow, bolster; (*fig*) bedside; **libro de ~** bedside book; **médico de ~** family doctor; **estar a la ~ de uno** to be at sb's bedside; to nurse sb.
(**c**) (*Tip*) headline; headpiece, title; vignette; (*de documento*) heading.
(**d**) (*Pol*) administrative centre, chief town, capital.
(**e**) (*elemento principal*) leading member; chief unit, most important element.
cabecero *nm* bedhead.
cabeciduro *adj* (*And, Carib*) stubborn, pigheaded.
cabecilla 1 *nmf* hothead, wrong-headed person. **2** *nm* (*Mil, Pol*) ringleader; rebel leader.
cabellera *nf* (**a**) (*pelo*) hair, head of hair; (*tupé etc*) wig, false hair, switch, hairpiece; **soltarse la ~*** to act (*o* speak *etc*) in a forthright way. (**b**) (*Astron*) tail (of a comet).
cabello *nm* (**a**) (*pelo*) hair; (*t* **~s**) hair, head of hair; locks; **~ de Venus** (*Bot*) maidenhair; **estar en ~** to have one's hair down; **estar en ~s** to be bareheaded; **estar pendiente de un ~** to hang by a thread; **asirse de un ~** to latch on to any excuse; **mesarse los ~s** to tear one's hair; **sentirse como colgado de los ~s** to feel on edge; **traído por los ~s** far-fetched, irrelevant.
(**b**) **~s de ángel** (*Culin*) thin vermicelli.
cabelludo *adj* hairy, shaggy; *V* **cuero.**
caber [2l] *vi* (**a**) (*gen*) to go, fit (*en* in, into); to be contained (*en* in); to have enough room; **no cabe el libro** the book won't go in, there's no room for the book; **caben 3 más** there's room for 3 more, we (*etc*) can get 3 more in; **en esta maleta no cabe** it won't go into this case, there's no room for it in this case, this case won't take it; **en este depósito caben 20 litros** this tank holds 20 litres; **¿cabe uno más?** is there room for one more?, can you get one more in?; **¿cabemos todos?** is there room for us all?; **eso no cabe por esta puerta** that won't go through this door.
(**b**) (*Mat*) **¿cuántas veces cabe 5 en 20?** how many times does 5 go into 20?
(**c**) (*fig: ser posible*) to be possible; **los compro todos y más, si cabe** I'll buy them all and more, if (that is) possible; **no cabe en él hacerlo** it is not in him to do it; **todo cabe en ese chico** that lad is capable of any mischief, anything might be expected from that lad.
(**d**) (*locuciones*) **no cabe más** that's the lot, that's the limit; one could wish for nothing more; it leaves nothing to be desired; **no ~ en sí** to be bursting, be beside o.s.; (*pey*) to be big-headed*; **no ~ en sí de contento** (*o* **gusto**) to be overjoyed, be overwhelmed with joy; **no cabe perdón** it's inexcusable; **cabe preguntar si ...** one may ask whether ..., it is proper to ask if ...; **cabe intentar otro sistema** one might try another system.
(**e**) (*fig: tocar a uno en suerte*) **~ a uno** to happen to sb, befall sb; to fall to one's lot; **le cupieron 120 dólares** his share was 120 dollars, he got 120 dollars (as his share); *V* **duda, suerte.**
cabestrar [1a] *vt* to halter, put a halter on.
cabestrillo *nm* (*Med*) sling; **con el brazo en ~** with one's arm in a sling.
cabestro *nm* (**a**) (*ronzal*) halter; **llevar a uno del ~** to lead sb by the nose. (**b**) (*buey*) leading ox, bell-ox. (**c**) (*) (*cornudo*) cuckold; (*lerdo*) thickie*.
cabeza 1 *nf* (**a**) (*Anat y en muchos sentidos figurados*) head; (*de clavo, cohete, mesa, puente etc*) head; **~ atómica, ~ nuclear** atomic warhead; (*Mec*) **~ de biela** big end; **~ buscadora** homing head, homing device; **~ de chorlito*** scatterbrain, dimwit*; **~ de escritura** (*Tip*) golf ball; **~ explosiva, ~ de guerra** warhead; **~ grabadora, ~ de impresión** (*Inform*) head, printhead; **~ hueca, ~ sin seso** idiot; **~ pelada** (*Hist: Brit*) Roundhead; **~ de playa** beachhead; **~ de puente** bridgehead; **~ de serie** (*Dep*) seed, seeded player; **~ de serrín*** airhead*; **~ sonora** recording head; **~ de turco** scapegoat, whipping boy, fall guy (*US*); **andar de ~*** to be snowed under; **andar en ~** (*LAm**) to be hatless, be bareheaded; **echar ~ a un asunto** to give thought to a matter; **no estar bien de la ~, estar mal de ~*** to be soft in the head; **estar de ~** to be on end; **caer de ~** to fall head first, fall headlong; **ir de ~*** to be snowed under; **lanzarse de ~ a** to rush headlong at; to rush headfirst into; **marcar de ~** to score from a header; **meterse de ~ en algo** to plunge into sth; **5 dólares por ~** 5 dollars a head, 5 dollars per person; **por encima de la ~** over one's head, overhead; **ganar por una ~** (**escasa**) to win by a (short) head; **un melocotón como mi ~** a peach as big as a football; **alzar** (*o* **levantar**) **la ~** (*Com etc*) to get on one's feet again, (*Med*) be up and about, be improving; **asentir con la ~** to nod (one's head); **calentarse la ~** to get tired out; **me duele la ~** my head aches, I've got a headache; **echar de ~ a uno** (*LAm**) to inform (*o* blow the whistle*) on sb; **escarmentar en ~ ajena** to learn by sb else's mistakes; **no estar bueno de la ~** to be weak in the head; **se me fue la ~** I felt giddy; **se me fue de la ~** it went right out of my mind; **es ~ de pescado** (*Cono Sur**) it's sheer nonsense; **hablar ~s de pescado** (*Cono Sur**) to talk drivel, talk through the back of one's head*; **jugarse la ~** to risk one's life; **lavarse la ~** to wash one's hair; **levantar ~** to recover one's health; **está que no levanta ~** she's totally engrossed in her work; **por fin se lo metimos en la ~** we finally got it into his head (*que* that); **esa melodía la tengo metida en la ~** I've got that tune on the brain; **meter la ~ en la arena** to bury one's head in the sand; **mover la ~ afirmativamente** to nod (one's head); **mover la ~ negativamente** to shake one's head; **jamás se me pasó por la ~** it never entered my head; **perder la ~** to lose one's head; **quitar algo de la ~ a uno** to get sth out of sb's head; **ella me ha quitado la ~** I'm crazy about her; **romper la ~ a uno** to give sb a beating; **romperse la ~** to rack one's brains; **le saca la ~ a su hermano** he is taller by a head than his brother; **sentar la ~** to settle down; to come to one's senses; **el vino se me subió a la ~** the wine went to my head; **tener ~ de pollo** (*Cono Sur**) to have a memory like a sieve; **no tener ~ para las alturas** to have no head for heights; **estar tocado de la ~** to be weak in the head; **traer de ~ a uno** to upset sb, bother sb; **vestirse por la ~*** to be female; (*sacerdote*) to be a cleric; **volver la ~** to look round, turn one's head; **volver la ~ a uno** to look away from sb, ignore sb.
(**b**) (*de monte*) top, summit; (*de liga, lista, etc*) head, top; **con Pérez a la ~ del gobierno** with Pérez at the head of the government; **ir a la ~ de la lista** to be at the top of the list; **ir en ~** to be in the lead; **tomar la ~** to take the lead.
(**c**) (*de río*) head, headwaters.
(**d**) (*Pol*) main town, chief centre, capital; **~ de partido** county town, administrative centre.
(**e**) (*Bot*) **~ de ajo** bulb of garlic; **~ de plátanos** (*And*) bunch of bananas.

(**f**) (*fig*: *origen*) origin, beginning.

2 *nmf* (*persona*) head; chief, leader; **~ de familia** head of the household; **~ de lista** person at the head of the list; **~ visible** chief, leader, top person.

cabezada *nf* (**a**) (*golpe*) butt; blow on the head.

(**b**) (*movimiento*) nod; shake of the head; **dar una ~, dar ~s, echar una ~** to nod (sleepily), doze; **darse de ~s** to rack one's brains.

(**c**) (*Náut*) pitch, pitching; **dar ~s** to pitch.

(**d**) (*parte de arreos*) head stall; (*de bota*) instep; (*de zapato*) vamp.

(**e**) (*And, Cono Sur*) saddle-tree.

(**f**) (*Carib, Cono Sur*: *de río*) headwaters.

cabezadita* *nf*: **echar una ~** to have a snooze*, doze.

cabezal *nm* (*almohada*) pillow; bolster; (*de dentista etc*) headrest; (*Med*) pad, compress; (*Inform*) head; **~ de enganche** towbar.

cabezazo *nm* butt; (*Ftbl*) header.

cabezo *nm* (*Geog*) hillock, small hill; (*Náut*) reef.

cabezón 1 *adj* = **cabezudo**. **2** *nm* (**a**) (*cabeza*) big head. (**b**) (*Cos*) hole for the head. (**c**) (*cuello*) collar band; **llevar a uno de los cabezones** to force sb to go. (**d**) **cabezones** rapids, whirlpool.

cabezonería *nf* pig-headedness.

cabezota 1 *nf* big head. **2** *nmf* (*) pig-headed person.

cabezudo 1 *adj* (**a**) (*lit*) big-headed, with a big head. (**b**) (*fig*) pig-headed. (**c**) *vino* heady. **2** *nm carnival figure with an enormous head.*

cabezuela *nf* head (of a flower); rosebud.

cabida *nf* (**a**) (*espacio*) space, room; (*capacidad*) capacity (*t Náut*); (*extensión*) extent, area; **con ~ para 50 personas** with space for 50 people; **dar ~ a** to make room for, leave space for; **hay que dar ~ a los imponderables** one must leave room for (*o* allow for) the imponderables; **tener ~ para** to have room for, hold.

(**b**) (*fig*: *influencia*) influence; **tener ~ con uno** to have influence with sb.

cabildear [1a] *vi* to lobby; (*pey*) to intrigue.

cabildeo *nm* lobbying; (*pey*) intriguing, intrigues.

cabildero -a *nm/f* lobbyist, member of a pressure group; (*pey*) intriguer.

cabildo *nm* (**a**) (*personas*) (*Ecl*) chapter; (*Pol*) town council. (**b**) (*junta*) chapter meeting; (*Carib*: *de negros*) gathering of Negroes; (*Carib*: *reunión desordenada*) riotous assembly. (**c**) (*Parl*) lobby.

cabilla *nf*: **dar ~ a**⁂ to fuck⁂, screw⁂.

cabillo *nm* end; (*Bot*) stalk, stem.

cabina *nf* (*de camión, Náut etc*) cabin; (*Ferro*) personal compartment, sleeping compartment; (*Aer*) cabin, cockpit; (*de gimnasio*) locker; (*Cine*) projection room; **~ a presión** pressurized cabin; **~ del conductor** driver's cab; **~ electoral** voting booth; **~ de prensa** press box; **~ de teléfono, ~ telefónica** telephone box, telephone kiosk, telephone booth (*US*).

cabinada *f* cabin cruiser.

cabinera *nf* (*And*) air hostess, stewardess, flight attendant (*US*).

cabinista *nmf* projectionist.

cabio *nm* (*viga*) beam, joist; rafter; (*de puerta, ventana*) lintel, transom.

cabizbajo *adj* crestfallen, dejected, downcast.

cabla *nf* (*LAm*) trick.

cable *nm* (*Náut etc*) cable, rope, hawser; (*medida*) cable length; (*Telec*) cable; (*Elec*) cable, wire, lead; **~ aéreo** overhead cable; **~ coaxial** coaxial cable; **~ de desgarre** ripcord; **~ de remolque** towline, towrope; **se le cruzaron los ~s** he got his wires crossed; **echar un ~ a uno** to give sb a helping hand, help sb out of a jam; **se le pelaron los ~s** (*CAm**) he got all mixed up.

cableado *nm* wiring, cables.

cablear [1a] *vt* to wire up.

cablegráfico *adj* cable (*atr*); **transferencia cablegráfica** cable transfer.

cablegrafiar [1c] *vi* to cable.

cablegrama *nm* cable, cablegram.

cablero *nm* cable ship.

cablista *adj* (*LAm*) sly, cunning.

cabo *nm* (**a**) (*extremo*) end, extremity; **de ~ a ~, de ~ a rabo** from beginning to end; **leer un libro de ~ a ~** to read a book from cover to cover.

(**b**) (*de período, proceso*) end; termination, conclusion; **al ~** finally, in the end; **al ~ de 3 meses** at the end of 3 months, after (the lapse of) 3 months; **dar ~ a** to complete, finish off; **dar ~ de** to put an end to; **estar al ~** to be nearing one's end; **estar al ~ de la calle** (*fig*) to know what's going on, know what's what; to know what the score is; to be up to date; **estar al ~ de la calle de que ...** to know perfectly well that ...; **¿estamos al ~ de la calle?** do you get it now?, understand?; **llevar a ~** to carry out, execute, carry through; to implement; to transact; **ponerse al ~ de un asunto** to get to know all about a matter.

(**c**) (*resto de objeto*) end, bit; stub, stump, butt; **~ de lápiz** stub of a pencil; **~ de vela** candle-end.

(**d**) (*hilo*) strand; (*Téc*) thread; (*Náut*) rope, cable; **~ de desgarre** ripcord; **~ suelto** loose end; **atar ~s** to tie up the loose ends; to put two and two together; **no dejar ningún ~ suelto** to leave no loose ends; to take every precaution.

(**e**) (*mango*) handle, haft.

(**f**) (*Geog*) cape, point; **C~ de Buena Esperanza** Cape of Good Hope; **C~ de Hornos** Cape Horn; **Islas de C~ Verde** Cape Verde Islands.

(**g**) (*persona*) chief, head; (*Mil*) corporal; (*de policía*) sergeant; (*remador*) stroke; **~ de escuadra** corporal; **~ de mar** petty officer.

(**h**) **~s** (*Cos*) accessories; (*fig*) odds and ends.

cabotaje *nm* coasting trade, coastal traffic.

cabra *nf* (**a**) (*Zool*) goat, nanny goat; (*almizclero*) musk deer; **~ montés** wild goat; **estar como una ~** to be crazy. (**b**) (*And, Carib*: *trampa*) trick, swindle; (*dado*) loaded dice. (**c**) (*Cono Sur*) (*carro*) light carriage; (*de carpintero*) sawhorse. (**d**) (*Cono Sur**: *niña*) little girl. (**e**) (*: *moto*) motorbike*.

cabracho *nm* large-scaled scorpion fish.

cabrahigo *nm* wild fig.

cabrales *nm invar a kind of very strong Asturian cheese.*

cabreante* *adj* infuriating.

cabrear* [1a] **1** *vt* to infuriate, make livid. **2 cabrearse** *vr* (**a**) (*enojarse*) to get furious, get livid. (**b**) (*sospechar*) to get suspicious. (**c**) (*Cono Sur**: *aburrirse*) to get bored.

cabreo* *nm* fury, anger; fit of bad temper; **coger un ~** to get angry, fly into a rage.

cabreriza *nf* goat shed, goat house.

cabrerizo 1 *adj* goatish; goat (*atr*). **2** *nm* goatherd.

cabrero* 1 *adj* (*Cono Sur*) bad-tempered; **ponerse ~** to fly off the handle*. **2** *nm* goatherd.

cabrestante *nm* capstan, winch.

cabria *nf* hoist, derrick; **~ de perforación** drilling-rig.

cabrio *nm* rafter.

cabrío 1 *adj* goatish; **macho ~** he-goat, billy goat. **2** *nm* herd of goats.

cabriola *nf* (**a**) (*gen*) caper; gambol; hop, skip, prance; **hacer ~s** to caper about, prance around; **hacer ~s con** (*fig*) to weave elegant patterns around. (**b**) (*Carib*: *travesura*) prank, piece of mischief.

cabriolar [1a] *vi* to caper (about); to gambol; to skip, prance (around), frisk about.

cabriolé *nm* cab, cabriolet.

cabriolear [1a] *vi* = **cabriolar**.

cabritada* *nf* dirty trick.

cabritas *nfpl* (*Cono Sur*) popcorn.

cabritilla *nf* kid, kidskin.

cabrito *nm* (**a**) kid; **a ~** astride. (**b**) (⁑) (*cornudo*) cuckold; (*de prostituta*) client; **¡~!** you bastard!⁑

cabro *nm* (**a**) (*LAm Zool*) he-goat, billy goat. (**b**) (*Cono Sur**: *niño*) small child; (*chico*) boy; (*amante*) lover, sweetheart; (*sujeto*) guy*. (**c**) (⁑) queer⁑.

cabrón *nm* (**a**) (*cornudo*) cuckold, complaisant husband.

(**b**) (⁑: *insulto*) **¡~!** you bastard!⁑, (*hum*) you old bastard!⁑; **el muy ~ le robó el coche** the bastard stole his car⁑; **el tío ~ ese** that bastard⁑; **es un ~** he's a bastard⁑.

(**c**) (*LAm*⁑: *de burdel*) brothel-keeper; (*And, Cono Sur*⁑: *chulo*) pimp; (*CAm, Cono Sur*: *traidor*) traitor; (*And*⁑: *maricón*) queer⁑, fag⁑; **¡~!** you stupid berk⁑!

cabronada* *nf* (**a**) (*mala pasada*) dirty trick; **hacer una ~ a uno** to play a dirty trick on sb. (**b**) (*faena*) tough job, fag*.

cabronazo⁑ *nm* rotter*, villain; **¡jo, ~!** (*hum*) hey, you old bastard!⁑.

cabroncete* *nm* little twerp*.

cabruno *adj* goatish; goat (*atr*).

cábula *nf* (**a**) (*And, Cono Sur*: *amuleto*) amulet. (**b**) (*Cono Sur*: *intriga*) cabal, intrigue. (**c**) (*And, CAm, Carib*: *ardid*) trick, stratagem.

cabulear [1a] *vi* (*And, CAm, Carib*) to scheme.

cabulero (*And, CAm, Carib*) **1** *adj* tricky, cunning, scheming. **2** *nm* trickster, schemer.

cabuya *nf* (*LAm*) (*Bot*) agave, pita; (*fibra*) pita fibre, pita hemp; (*cuerda*) rope, cord (of pita *or in general*); **dar ~** (*Carib*) to put things off; **ponerse en la ~** to cotton on*; **verse a uno las ~s** to see what sb is up to, see through sb's scheme.

caca *nf* (**a**) (**) (*palabra de niños*) number two*, poo-poo*. (**b**) (‡) (*fig*) dirt, filth; **¡~!** (*desagrado*) ugh!; (*no toques*) don't touch!

caca-can* *nm* pooper-scooper*.

cacaguatal *nm* (*CAm*) cocoa field.

cacahual *nm* (*LAm*) cacao plantation.

cacahuate *nm* (*CAm, Méx*), **cacahuete** *nm* (*Esp*) (*nuez*) peanut, monkey nut; (*planta*) groundnut.

cacao *nm* (**a**) (*árbol, semilla*) cacao; (*polvo, bebida*) cocoa; **pedir ~** (*LAm*) to give in, ask for mercy; **ser gran ~** to have influence; **tener un ~ en la cabeza*** to be all mixed up; **no valer un ~** (*LAm*) to be worthless, be insignificant. (**b**) (*: *jaleo*) fuss, to-do*. (**c**) **~ mental*** mental confusion; **ser un ~** to be a mess.

cacaotal *nm* (*LAm*) cacao plantation.

cacaraña *nf* (**a**) (*señal*) pockmark. (**b**) (*CAm*: *garabato*) scribble.

cacarañado *adj* pitted, pockmarked.

cacarañar [1a] *vt* (*Méx*) to scratch, pinch; to pit, scar, pockmark.

cacarear [1a] **1** *vt* to boast about, exaggerate, make much of; **ese triunfo tan cacareado** that much trumpeted triumph, that vaunted triumph.

2 *vi* to crow; to cackle.

cacareo *nm* crowing, cackling; (*fig*) crowing, boasting, trumpeting.

cacarico *adj* (*CAm*) numb.

cacarizo *adj* (*Méx*) pitted, pockmarked.

cacastle *nm* (*CAm, Méx*) (*esqueleto*) skeleton; (*canasta*) large wicker basket; (*armazón*) wicker carrying frame.

cacatúa *nf* (**a**) (*Orn*) cockatoo. (**b**) (*: *bruja*) old bat*, old cow‡.

cacaxtle *nm* (*CAm, Méx*) = **cacastle**.

cacera *nf* ditch, irrigation channel.

cacereño 1 *adj* of Cáceres. **2** *nm*, **cacereña** *nf* native (*o* inhabitant) of Cáceres; **los ~s** the people of Cáceres.

cacería *nf* (**a**) (*gen*) hunting, shooting.

(**b**) (*personas*) hunt, shoot, shooting-party; **~ de brujas** witch-hunt; **~ de zorros** fox hunt; **organizar una ~** to organize a hunt.

(**c**) (*animales cazados*) bag, total of animals (*etc*) bagged.

(**d**) (*Arte*) hunting scene.

cacerola *nf* pan, saucepan; casserole.

cacerolazo *nm* (*Cono Sur*) banging on pots and pans (*as political protest*).

cacica *nf* (*LAm*) woman chief; chief's wife; (*Pol*) wife of a local boss (*etc*).

cacicada *nf* despotic act, high-handed act; abuse of authority.

cacillo *nm* ladle.

cacimba *nf* (**a**) (*And, Carib, Cono Sur*: *pozo*) well; (*Carib*: *de árbol*) hollow of tree where rain water is collected; (*And*) outdoor privy. (**b**) (*Carib, Méx*: *casucha*) hovel, slum.

cacique (**a**) *nm* (*LAm*: *jefe*) chief, headman, local ruler; (*Pol*) local boss, party boss; (*fig*) petty tyrant, despot; (*Cono Sur*: *vago*) person who lives idly in luxury. (**b**) (*And, CAm, Méx*: *ave*) oriole.

caciquismo *nm* (*Pol*) (system of) dominance by the local boss; petty tyranny, despotism.

cacle *nm* (*Méx*) rough leather sandal.

caco* *nm* (**a**) (*ratero*) pickpocket, thief; (*criminal de categoría*) crook*. (**b**) (*cobarde*) coward.

cacofonía *nf* cacophony.

cacofónico *adj* cacophonous.

cacto *nm*, **cactus** *nm invar* cactus.

cacumen* *nm* perspicacity; brains, insight.

cacha *nf, frec* **~s** *pl* (**a**) handle; (*de revólver*) butt; **hasta las ~s** up to the hilt, completely.

(**b**) (*And*: *cuerno*) horn.

(**c**) (*And*: *de gallo*) metal spur attached to the leg of a fighting cock.

(**d**) (*And*: *arca*) large chest.

(**e**) (*) **~s** (*culo*) bottom; (*piernas*) legs.

(**f**) (*locuciones*) **estar a medias ~s** (*Méx*) to be tipsy; **estar fuera de ~** to be out of danger; **hacer ~s** (*CAm*) to try hard; **sacar ~(s) a** (*o* **de**)* to make fun of.

(**g**) (*LAm*: *cachete*) cheek.

(**h**) (*CAm**: *negocio*) crooked deal*; **¡qué ~!** what a nuisance!; **hacer la ~** to put one's back into it.

(**i**) (*CAm*: *oportunidad*) opportunity.

cachaciento *adj* (*CAm, Cono Sur*) = **cachazudo**.

cachaco *nm* (**a**) (*And, Carib*: *petimetre*) fop, dandy. (**b**) (*And‡*) (*policía*) copper*, cop*; (*desaliñado*) scruff*. (**c**) (*Carib**: *entrometido*) busybody, nosey-parker*.

cachada *nf* (**a**) (*LAm Taur*) butt, thrust; goring. (**b**) (*Cono Sur**: *broma*) joke, leg-pull*.

cachador* (*Cono Sur*) **1** *adj* fond of practical jokes. **2** *nm* practical joker.

cachafaz* *adj* (*LAm*) (*pillo*) rascally; (*taimado*) crafty; (*fresco*) cheeky*.

cachalote *nm* sperm whale.

cachancha *nf* (*Carib*) patience; **estar de ~ con uno*** to suck up to sb*.

cachaña *nf* (*Cono Sur*) (**a**) (*Orn*) small parrot. (**b**) (*broma*) hoax, leg-pull*; (*mofas*) mockery, derision. (**c**) (*arrogancia*) arrogance. (**d**) (*estupidez*) stupidity. (**e**) (*arrebatiña*) rush, scramble (for sth).

cachañar [1a] *vt* (*Cono Sur*) = **cachar¹**; **~ a uno*** to pull sb's leg*.

cachar¹ [1a] *vt* (**a**) (*romper*) to smash, break, break in pieces; *madera* to split; (*Agr*) to plough up.

(**b**) (*And, CAm*: *Taur*) to butt, gore.

(**c**) (*And, CAm, Cono Sur*) (*ridiculizar*) to scoff at, deride, ridicule; (*fastidiar*) to annoy, irritate.

(**d**) (*And, Cono Sur***) to screw**.

(**e**) (*Méx**: *registrar*) to search.

cachar² [1a] *vt* (**a**) (*Cono Sur*) *bus etc* to catch.

(**b**) (*CAm*: *obtener*) to get, obtain; (*CAm, Cono Sur*: *robar*) to steal.

(**c**) (*Cono Sur, Méx*: *sorprender*) to surprise, catch in the act.

(**d**) (*Cono Sur*) *sentido etc* to penetrate; *persona, razón* to understand; **sí, te cacho** sure, I get it*.

(**e**) (*And, CAm, Carib*: *Dep*) *pelota* to catch.

cacharpari *nm* (*And, Cono Sur*) = **cacharpaya**.

cacharpas *nfpl* (*LAm*) useless objects, lumber, junk; odds and ends.

cacharpaya *nf* (*And, Cono Sur*) send-off, farewell party; (*Cono Sur*) farewell; minor festivity.

cacharpearse [1a] *vr* (*LAm*) to dress up.

cacharra‡ *nf* rod‡, pistol.

cacharrazo* *nm* bash*, bang.

cacharrear [1a] *vt* (*CAm, Carib*) to throw into jail, jail.

cacharrería *nf* (**a**) (*tienda*) crockery shop. (**b**) (*cacharros*) crockery, pots. (**c**) (*And*) ironmongery.

cacharro *nm* (**a**) (*vasija*) earthenware pot, crock; **~s** earthenware, crockery, pots, coarse pottery.

(**b**) (*casco*) piece of pottery, potsherd.

(**c**) (*pey*) useless object, piece of junk; (*Aut etc**) old crock, jalop(p)y; (*And*) trinket.

(**d**) (‡: *pistola*) rod‡, pistol.

(**e**) (*CAm, Carib*: *cárcel*) jail.

cachas* *adj invar* he-man*, hunk*, muscle-man*; **estar ~** to be tough, be well set-up; **está ~** (*hombre*) he's dishy*; (*mujer*) she's hot stuff*.

cachativa *nf*: **tener ~** (*Cono Sur*) to be quick on the uptake.

cachaza *nf* (**a**) (*tranquilidad*) slowness; calmness, phlegm. (**b**) (*LAm*: *licor*) rum.

cachazo *nm* (*LAm*) (*golpe*) butt, thrust; (*herida*) goring.

cachazudo 1 *adj* slow; calm, phlegmatic. **2** *nm* slow sort; phlegmatic person.

cache *nm* (*Inform*) cache, cache memory.

caché *nm* = **cachet**.

cachear [1a] *vt* (**a**) (*LAm Taur*) to butt, gore. (**b**) (*LAm*: *pegar*) to punch, slap. (**c**) (*abrir*) to split, cut open. (**d**) (*registrar*) to frisk, search (for weapons).

cachejo* *nm* (*Esp*): **un ~(de) pan** a little bit of bread; **aquel ~ de partido** that awful game.

cachemir *nm*, **cachemira** *nf* cashmere.

Cachemira *nf* Kashmir.

cacheo *nm* searching, frisking (for weapons).

cachería *nf* (**a**) (*And, CAm Com*) small business, sideline. (**b**) (*Cono Sur**) (*falta de gusto*) bad taste; (*desaseo*) slovenliness.

cachero 1 *adj* (**a**) (*CAm, Carib*: *embustero*) lying, deceitful. (**b**) (*CAm*: *trabajador*) hard-working, diligent. **2** *nm* (*LAm*) sodomite.

cachet [ka'tʃe] *nm, pl* **~s** [ka'tʃe] (**a**) (*sello distintivo*) cachet; character, temperament. (**b**) (*de artista*) appearance money, fee.

cachetada *nf* (*LAm*) (*golpe*) slap, box on the ear; (*paliza*) beating.

cachetazo *nm* (**a**) (*LAm**: *bofetada*) slap, punch; (*fig*) snub. (**b**) (*LAm*: *trago*) swig*, slug* (*US*). (**c**) **¡hazme un ~!** (*CAm, Carib**) do me a favour!
cachete *nm* (**a**) (*Anat*) (fat) cheek; (*Med*) swollen cheek. (**b**) (*golpe*) punch in the face, slap. (**c**) (*arma*) dagger. (**d**) (*CAm*: *favor*) favour. (**e**) **~s*** (*Cono Sur Anat*) bottom.
cacheteada *nf* (*Cono Sur*) slap, box on the ear.
cachetear [1a] **1** *vt* (*And, Cono Sur*) to slap (*o* smack) in the face. **2** *vi* (*Cono Sur*) to eat well.
cachetero *nm* (**a**) (*puñal*) dagger. (**b**) (*Taur*) *bullfighter who finishes the bull off with a dagger.*
cachetina* *nf* fist fight, punch-up*.
cachetón *adj* (**a**) (*LAm*: *de cara rechoncha*) plump-cheeked, fat-faced. (**b**) (*Méx*: *descarado*) impudent, barefaced; (*Cono Sur*: *orgulloso*) proud, haughty. (**c**) (*CAm*: *atractivo*) attractive, congenial.
cachicamo *nm* (*And, Carib*) armadillo.
cachicán **1** *adj* sly, crafty. **2** *nm* (**a**) (*Agr*) foreman, gaffer. (**b**) (*) sly sort, wide boy*.
cachicuerno *adj arma* with a horn handle.
cachifa *nf* (*CAm, Carib*) girl, kid*.
cachifo *nm* (*And, CAm, Carib*) lad, kid*; young boy.
cachilla *nf* (*Cono Sur*) jalop(p)y, old crock.
cachimba **1** *nf* (**a**) (*LAm*: *pipa*) pipe. (**b**) (*LAm*: *cartucho*) empty cartridge. (**c**) (*Cono Sur*: *pozo*) shallow well (*o* water hole). (**d**) (*Carib*‡: *puta*) tart‡, slut. (**e**) **fregar la ~ a uno*** to get on sb's nerves. **2** *adj* (*) fantastic*, terrific*.
cachimbazo* *nm* (*CAm*) (**a**) (*golpe*) thump, blow. (**b**) (*trago*) shot, slug* (*US*).
cachimbo *nm* (**a**) (*LAm*: *pipa*) pipe; **chupar ~** (*Carib*) to smoke a pipe; (*hum*: *niño*) to suck its thumb.
(**b**) (*Carib*: *ingenio*) small sugar mill.
(**c**) (*Carib*: *pobre*) poor man.
(**d**) (*) (*And Univ*) freshman.
(**e**) (*CAm**: *montón*) pile, heap.
(**f**) (*And*: *Mil*) soldier, squaddie*.
cachimbón* *adj* (*CAm*) smart, sharp.
cachipolla *nf* mayfly.
cachiporra *nf* (**a**) (*bastón*) truncheon; club, big stick, cosh. (**b**) (*Cono Sur*: *jactancioso*) braggart.
cachiporrazo *nm* blow with a truncheon (*etc*).
cachiporrear* [1a] **1** *vt* (*Mús etc*) to bash*, pound. **2 cachiporrearse** *vr* (*Cono Sur*) to brag, boast.
cachito *nm* (**a**) (*And*) (*juego de dados*) dice game; (*cubito*) dice cup. (**b**) (*LAm**) **espera un ~** just a minute, hang on a sec*; **un ~ de café** a drop of coffee.
cachivache *nm* (**a**) pot, utensil. (**b**) **~s** pots and pans, kitchen utensils; (*fig*) trash, junk, lumber.
cacho[1] **1** *adj* (*corvado*) bent, crooked.
2 *nm* (**a**) (*miga*) crumb; (*pedacito*) bit, small piece, slice; **¡~ de gloria!** my precious!; **¡~ de ladrón!** you thief!; **es un ~ de pan*** he's terribly kind.
(**b**) (*LAm*: *cuerno*) horn; **~s** (number of) cattle; **hombre de muchos ~s** large cattle farmer; **¿cuántos ~s tiene?** how many head of cattle does he own?; **montar ~s a uno** to cuckold sb.
(**c**) (*And, Cono Sur*) (*dados*) dice, set of dice; (*cubo de dados*) dice box (*o* cup); **jugar al ~** to play dice.
(**d**) (*Cono Sur*: *para beber*) cup (made of horn); **empinar el ~** to drink a lot.
(**e**) (*Cono Sur*: *plátanos*) bunch of bananas.
(**f**) (*Cono Sur*: *Com*) unsaleable (*o* unsold) goods.
(**g**) (*LAm*) (*chiste*) funny story, joke; (*broma*) prank, practical joke; (*Carib*: *mofa*) mockery, derision.
(**h**) (*Carib*‡: *marijuana*) joint‡.
(**i**) (*Carib***: *pene*) prick**.
(**j**) (*Cono Sur*) (*problema*) problem; (*apuro*) jam*, tricky situation; (*maula*) unwanted object, useless thing.
(**k**) (*locuciones*) **echar ~ a uno** (*And*) to do better than (*o* surpass) sb; **estar fuera de ~** to be safe, be out of danger; **pegar los ~s a uno** (*CAm**) to cheat on sb, be unfaithful to sb; **raspar el ~ a uno** (*Cono Sur*) to tell sb off*; **¡~s para arriba!** (*Cono Sur*) that's marvellous!, splendid!
cacho[2] *nm* (*Pez*) (*de río*) chub; (*de mar*) (red) surmullet.
cachón *nm* (*ola*) wave, breaker; (*cascada*) small waterfall.
cachondear* [1a] (*CAm, Méx*) **1** *vi* (*acariciar*) to pet*; (*besarse*) to snog‡ (*Brit*). **2 cachondearse** *vr* (**a**) to take things as a joke; **~ de uno** to take the mickey out of sb‡, make fun of sb. (**b**) (*LAm**) to get turned on*.
cachondeo* *nm* (**a**) (*guasa*) joking; teasing, nagging; messing about; **estar de ~** to be in a joking mood; **tomar algo a ~** to take sth as a joke; **para ella la vida es un ~ continuo** life for her is just one big joke.
(**b**) (*juerga*) **estar de ~** to live it up, have a good time.
(**c**) (*jaleo*) trouble, disturbance; **armar un ~** to make a fuss.
(**d**) (*farsa*) farce, mess; poor show*; **¡esto es un ~!** what a mess!, what a farce this is!
cachondez *nf* (**a**) (*Zool*) heat, rut, readiness to mate. (**b**) (*de persona*) sexiness; randiness*.
cachondo *adj* (**a**) (*Zool*) on heat, in rut. (**b**) (*persona*) **ser ~** to be sexy; **estar ~** to feel randy*, be in the mood. (**c**) (*juerguista*) fun-loving; high-spirited, riotous. (**d**) (*gracioso*) funny, amusing; jokey; **~ mental** crazy but likable.
cachorro, -a *nm/f* (**a**) (*perrito*) pup, puppy; (*de otro animal*) cub. (**b**) (*Carib*‡) *excl* you rat!*, you swine!‡
cachuca‡ *nf* (*And*) nick‡, prison.
cachucha‡ *nf* (*Méx*) hat, tile‡.
cachucho *nm* (**a**) (*Pez*) sea-bream. (**b**) (*alfiletero*) pin box. (**c**) (*And*) daily bread; **ganarse el ~** to make a living.
cachudo **1** *adj* (**a**) (*And, Méx*: *con cuernos*) horned, with horns.
(**b**) (*And*: *rico*) wealthy.
(**c**) (*Cono Sur*) (*receloso*) suspicious, distrustful; (*taimado*) cunning.
(**d**) (*Méx*: *triste*) long-faced, miserable.
2 *nm*: **el ~** the devil, the horned one.
cachuela *nf* (**a**) (*Culin*) stew, fricassee. (**b**) (*And*: *remolinos*) rapids.
cachupín *nm*, **cachupina** *f* (*And, Carib*: *pey*) Spanish settler (in America).
cachureo *nm* (*Cono Sur*) bric-a-brac, junk, bits and pieces.
cachuzo* *adj* (*Cono Sur*) worn-out, old.
cada *adj invar* each; (*con número*) every; **~ día** each day, every day; **~ uno** each one, every one; **~ 3 meses** every 3 months; **~ (y) cuando** every now and then; **~ y cuando que ...** whenever ...; as soon as ...; **~ y siempre que ...** as soon as ...; **~ cierta distancia por la carretera** every so often along the road, at intervals along the road; **~ cierto tiempo** every so often; **¿~ cuánto?** how often?; (*LAm*) **~ que** every time, whenever; **~ que viene** every time he comes; **¡tienes ~ idea!** what funny ideas you have!; **oye una ~ historia** one hears some very strange stories (these days).
cadalso *nm* scaffold; (*Téc*) stand, platform.
cadarzo *nm* floss, floss silk.
cadáver *nm* body, dead body, corpse, cadaver (*US*); **~ en el armario** (*fig*) skeleton in the cupboard; **¡sobre mi ~!** over my dead body!; **ingresó ~** he was dead on arrival (at hospital).
cadavérico *adj* cadaverous; death-like; ghastly, deathly pale.
caddie ['kadi] *n (Golf)* caddie.
cadena **1** *nf* (**a**) (*gen*) chain (*t Com, Inform*); (*fig*) bond, link; series, sequence; (*Rad, TV*) network; **~ de agrimensor** surveyor's chain (*10m = 22 yards*); **~ alimentaria, ~ alimenticia** food chain; **~s (antideslizantes)** tyre chains; **~ de distribución** (*Aut*) timing chain; **~ de ensamblaje** assembly line; **~ de fabricación** production line; **~ de hoteles** chain of hotels; **~ de mando** chain of command; **~ de montaje** assembly line; **~ de montañas** range of mountains; **~ de oruga** caterpillar track; **~ de producción** production line; **~ de reloj** watch chain; **~ sin fin** endless chain; **~ de sonido** sound system; **reacción en ~** chain reaction.
(**b**) (*Jur*: *Hist*) chain-gang.
(**c**) **~ perpetua** (*Jur*) life imprisonment.
(**d**) (*Arquit*) wooden frame.
2 ~s* *nm*: **ser un ~** (*Esp*) to be a boaster.
cadencia *nf* cadence, rhythm; measure; (*Mús*) cadence, cadenza.
cadencioso *adj* rhythmic(al), cadenced.
cadeneta *nf* (*Cos*) chain stitch; **~ de papel** paper chain.
cadenilla *nf*, **cadenita** *nf* small chain; (*collar*) necklace.
cadera *nf* hip.
caderamen* *nm* big hips, massive hips.
cadetada *nf* thoughtless action, irresponsible act.
cadete *nm* (*Mil etc*) cadet; (*Dep*) junior; (*LAm*) office-boy; apprentice.
cadi *nm* (*Golf*) caddie.
cadí *nm* (*Hist*) cadi.
Cádiz *nm* Cadiz.
cadmio *nm* cadmium.
caducar [1g] *vi* (**a**) (*persona*) to become senile; to dodder, be in one's dotage.
(**b**) (*permiso etc*) to get out of date, run out; (*costumbre*) to fall into disuse; (*Com, Jur*) to expire, lapse; **el**

abono ha caducado the season ticket has expired.
(**c**) (*deteriorarse*) to deteriorate.
(**d**) (*comida*) to be (*o* go) past its sell-by date.

caducidad *nf* lapse, lapsing, expiry; **fecha de ~** (*alimentos*) sell-by date.

caduco *adj* (**a**) *persona* senile, very old, decrepit; worn out.
(**b**) (*Bot*) deciduous.
(**c**) *placer etc* fleeting, perishable.
(**d**) (*Com, Jur*) lapsed, expired, invalid; **quedar ~** to lapse.

caduquez *nf* senility, decrepitude.

C.A.E. (**a**) (*Com*) *abr de* **cóbrese al entregar** cash on delivery, COD. (**b**) *nm* (*Jur*) *abr de* **Código Alimentario Español.**

caedizo 1 *adj* unsteady, about to fall; weak; (*Bot*) deciduous. **2** *nm* (*And*) (*edificio*) shed; (*techo*) sloping roof.

caer [2n] *vi y en ciertos sentidos* **caerse** *vr* (**a**) (*gen*) to fall; to fall down; (*desplomarse*) to tumble (down), collapse; (*separarse*) to fall off, fall out; (*Aer*) to crash, come down; (*cortina etc*) to hang; (*pelo, rama*) to hang down; **~ al suelo** to fall to the ground; **el edificio se está cayendo** the building is falling down; **~ sobre** to fall on, pounce on; to descend upon; **cayó un rayo en la torre** the tower was struck by lightning; **estar al ~** to be about to fall, (*fig*) be about to happen, be due to happen; (*persona*) to be about to arrive; **estar a la que cae** to be alert; **dejar ~** to drop, let fall; **dejarse ~** to let o.s. go, let o.s. fall; **hacer ~** to knock down, knock over, knock off, cause to fall; **se me cayó el guante** I dropped my glove, my glove fell off; **Eslobodia nunca cayó tan bajo** Slobodia never fell so low; **~ en cama, ~ enfermo** to fall ill; **~ en un error** to fall into error; **~ redondo** to fall in a heap; **~se de miedo** to be terrified; **~se de tonto** (*etc*) to be very silly (*etc*); **se cae de viejo** he's so old he can hardly walk; **eso (se) cae de suyo** that's obvious, that goes without saying.
(**b**) (*morir*) to fall (in battle); (*Mil: ciudad*) to fall, be captured; (*: *ser detenido*) to be arrested; **ha caído el gobierno** the government has fallen; **~ como chinches, ~ como moscas** to fall like flies.
(**c**) (*nivel, precio, temperatura*) to fall, go down; to diminish; (*conversación*) to flag; (*costumbre etc*) to lapse.
(**d**) (*sol, viento*) to go down.
(**e**) (*día*) to decline, draw to its close; (*noche*) to fall, close in; **al ~ de la noche** at nightfall.
(**f**) (*color*) to fade.
(**g**) (*lugar*) to fall, lie, be located; **cae en el segundo tomo** it comes in the second volume; **eso cae más hacia el este** that lies further to the east.
(**h**) (*ventanas etc*) **~ a, ~ hacia** to look over, look out on, look towards.
(**i**) (*suceso*) to fall; **el aniversario cae en martes** the anniversary falls on a Tuesday.
(**j**) (*Com, Fin*) to fall due.
(**k**) (*herencia*) **~ a** to fall to, come to, fall to the lot of; *V* **suerte.**
(**l**) (*darse cuenta*) to realize; **no caigo** I don't get it; **ya caigo** I see, now I understand; **~ en que ...** to realize that ...; *V* **cuenta.**
(**m**) (*vestido*) **~ bien a uno** to suit sb, look well on sb; **el traje le caía mal** the suit did not fit him, the suit was not right for him.
(**n**) (*impresión*) **no me cae bien** (*o* **me cae mal**) I don't like him at all, I really don't like him, we don't get on at all well; **no me cayó bien** he did not make a good impression on me; (*más fuerte*) I didn't take to him at all; **no les caí** (*CAm*) I didn't hit it off with them, I didn't get on well with them, they didn't take to me.
(**o**) (*comida*) **~ mal a** to disagree with.
(**p**) (*Cono Sur: hacer una visita*) to come by, visit, drop in; **él suele ~ por aquí** he usually comes here.
(**q**) (*) **ese número es de ~se** that number is a real riot*.

café *nm* (**a**) (*bebida, grano, planta*) coffee; **~ ~** real coffee, coffee that really is coffee; **~ americano** large black coffee; **~ cerrero** (*And*) strong black coffee; **~ cortado** coffee with a dash of milk; **~ exprés** expresso coffee; **~ helado** iced coffee; **~ instantáneo, ~ soluble** instant coffee; **~ irlandés** Irish coffee; **~ con leche** white coffee, coffee with milk; (⁑) queer⁑; **~ molido** ground coffee; **~ negro, ~ solo, ~ tinto** (*LAm*) black coffee; **~ pintado** (*And*), **~ quemado** (*Carib*) coffee with a drop of milk; **~ tostado** roasted coffee.
(**b**) (*establecimiento*) café; coffee-house; restaurant, bar; **~ cantante** café which provides entertainment, seedy night-club.
(**c**) (*: *reprimenda*) ticking-off*.
(**d**) **estar de mal ~** to be in a bad mood, (*CAm*) to be out of sorts; **tener mal ~** to have a nasty temper; to have evil intentions.
(**e**) (*t* **color ~**) brown; **~ avellana** (*como adj*) nut-brown.

cafecito *nm* (*LAm*) black coffee.

café-concierto *nm* café which provides entertainment.

cafeína *nf* caffein(e).

cafetal *nm* (**a**) (*plantío*) coffee plantation. (**b**) (*CAm: árbol*) coffee tree.

cafetalero (*LAm*) **1** *adj* coffee (*atr*), coffee-growing (*atr*); **industria cafetalera** coffee-growing industry. **2** *nm*, **cafetalera** *nf* coffee grower.

cafetalista *nmf* (*LAm*) coffee grower.

cafetear* [1a] *vt* (*Cono Sur*) to tick off*, tell off*.

café-teatro *nm* café which provides entertainment.

cafetera[1] *nf* (**a**) (*gen*) coffee pot; **~ automática** electric kettle; **~ filtradora** percolator. (**b**) (*) (*Aut*) old crock, jalop(p)y; (*de policía*) police car.

cafetería *nf* café, coffee house; (*Ferro*) buffet, refreshment room; (*And, Carib, Cono Sur*) retail coffee shop.

cafetero 1 *adj* (**a**) (*Com*) coffee (*atr*); **industria cafetera** coffee industry. (**b**) (*que bebe café*) coffee-drinking; fond of coffee; **soy muy ~** I drink a lot of coffee. (**c**) (*asiduo*) fond of going to cafés; **es muy ~** he spends a lot of time in cafés. **2** *nm*, **cafetera**[2] *nf* (*: *dueño*) café proprietor, café owner; (*cultivador*) coffee grower; (*comerciante*) coffee merchant.

cafetín *nm* seedy bar, small café.

cafeto *nm* (*LAm*) coffee bush.

cafetucho *nm* seedy little café.

caficultor(a) *nm/f* (*CAm*) coffee grower.

caficultura *nf* (*CAm*) coffee growing.

cafiche* *nm* pimp.

cafichear* [1a] *vi* (*Cono Sur*) to live off sb else, ponce.

caficho* *nm* (*Cono Sur*) pimp, ponce.

cáfila *nf* caravan, group, flock, large number (*esp* on the march); **una ~ de disparates** a string of nonsense.

cafiolo* *nm* (*Cono Sur*) pimp, ponce.

cafre 1 *adj* (**a**) (*lit*) Kaffir. (**b**) (*fig: cruel*) cruel, savage; uncouth, boorish. **2** *nmf* Kaffir; **como ~s** (*fig*) like savages, like beasts.

caftán *nm* caftan, kaftan.

cagaaceite *nm* missel thrush.

cagada⁂ *nf* (**a**) (*acto*) shit⁂, crap⁂.
(**b**) (*materia*) shit⁂; turd⁂.
(**c**) (*fig: lío*) cock-up⁑, fuck-up⁂; (*tonterías*) crap⁂; **decir una ~** to talk a lot of crap⁂.

cagadera⁂ *nf* (*LAm*) the shits⁂, diarrhoea.

cagadero⁂ *nm* bog⁑, john (*US*⁑).

cagado⁑ *adj* yellow, funky*.

cagajón *nm* horse-dung, mule-dung.

cagalera⁂ *nf* runs⁑, the shits⁂; (*iró*) **¡brava ~!** what a mess!

cagar [1h] **1** *vt* (**a**) (⁂: *gen*) to shit⁂, crap⁂.
(**b**) (⁂) *ropa* to dirty, soil.
(**c**) (⁑: *fig: t* **~la**) to cock (it) up⁑; **¡la cagamos!** we blew it!⁑
2 *vi* (⁂) to shit⁂, have a shit⁂.
3 cagarse *vr* (**a**) = *vi*.
(**b**) (⁂) **¡me cago!, ¡me cago en la mar!** (*etc*) well I'm damned!; damn it!; **¡me cago en el gobierno!** to hell with the government!; **... y se caga la perra ...** (*Esp*) and you never saw anything like it; **la tía estaba que te cagas** she was absolutely fantastic*.

cagarro⁑ *nm* fag⁑, ciggy*.

cagarruta *nf* (**a**) (*de animal*) sheep-droppings, goat dirt. (**b**) **es una ~ de su padre**⁑ (*Esp*) he's the spitting image of his father.

cagatintas *nm invar* penpusher, clerk; (*And*) miser.

cagón⁑ **1** *adj* = **cagado. 2** *nm*, **cagona** *nf* coward.

cagueruelas⁑ *nfpl*: **las ~** the runs⁑, the trots⁑.

cagueta⁑ *nmf*, **caguetas**⁑ *nmf invar*, **caguica**⁑ *nmf invar* coward.

caguitis⁑ *nf* fear, funk*; **le entra ~** he gets the wind up*.

Cahispa [ka'ispa] *nf abr de* **Caja Hispana de Previsión.**

cahuin *nm* (*Cono Sur*) (**a**) drunkenness, drunken spree. (**b**) rowdy gathering. (**c**) (*Cono Sur*⁑: *lío*) mess, cock-up⁑.

caída *nf* (**a**) fall; tumble, spill; falling, falling-out; (*fig*) fall, collapse, downfall; (*Teat*) flop*, failure; **la C~** (*Rel*) the Fall; **la ~ del gobierno** the fall of the government; **la ~ del imperio** the collapse of the empire; **la ~ de los dientes** the falling-out of one's teeth, the loss of one's teeth; ~ **de agua** waterfall; ~ **de cabeza** fall headfirst, header; ~ **libre** free fall; **a la** ~ **del sol** at sunset; **a la** ~ **de la tarde** in the evening; **sufrir una** ~ to have a fall, have a tumble.

(**b**) (*nivel, precio etc*) fall, drop (*de 5 grados* of 5 degrees; *de la temperatura* in temperature: *de tensión* in blood pressure); decline, diminution; ~ **de la actividad económica** downturn in the economy.

(**c**) (*terreno*) drop, fall, slope; (*Geol*) dip; (*de espaldas*) slope.

(**d**) (*de cortina etc*) fold(s); (*de vestido*) set, hang.

(**e**) ~ **radiactiva** radioactive fallout.

(**f**) **~s** (*Téc*) low-grade wool.

(**g**) **~s*** witty remarks; **¡qué ~s tiene!** isn't he witty?

caído 1 *adj* (**a**) (*gen*) fallen; *cabeza etc* drooping; *cuello* turndown; *flor etc* languid, limp, drooping; **estar** ~ **de sueño** to be dead tired.

(**b**) (*fig*) crestfallen, dejected.

(**c**) ~ **de color** pale.

2 *nm* (**a**) (*muertos*) **los ~s** the fallen; **los ~s por España** those who fell for Spain; **monumento a los ~s** war memorial.

(**b**) (*Méx*: *soborno*) backhander*, bribe.

caifán* *nm* (*Méx*) pimp, ponce.

caigo *etc V* **caer**.

caimacán *nm* (*And*) important person, big shot*; ace, star, expert.

caimán *nm* (**a**) (*LAm Zool*: *reptil parecido al cocodrilo*) cayman, caiman, alligator. (**b**) (*And Zool*: *iguana*) iguana. (**c**) (*LAm**: *estafador*) twister, swindler. (**d**) (*Méx Méc*) chain wrench. (**e**) (*And*: *gandul*) lazy fellow.

caimanear [1a] (*LAm*) **1** *vt* to swindle, cheat. **2** *vi* to hunt alligators.

caimiento *nm* (**a**) (*acto*) fall, falling; (*Med*) decline. (**b**) (*fig*) dejection; limpness.

Caín *nm* Cain; **pasar las de** ~ to have a ghastly time*; **venir con las de** ~ to have evil intentions.

cainismo *nm* fratricidal violence, fratricidal treachery.

cairel *nm* (*peluca*) wig; (*Cos*) fringe.

cairelear [1a] *vt* to trim, fringe.

Cairo *nm*: **el** ~ Cairo.

caita 1 *adj invar* (*Cono Sur*) (*montaraz*) wild, untamed; (*huraño*) unsociable, withdrawn. **2** *nm* (*Cono Sur*) migratory agricultural worker.

caite *nm* (*CAm*) rough rubber-soled sandal.

caitearse [1a] *vr*: **~las** (*CAm*) to run away, beat it*.

caja *nf* (**a**) (*gen*) box; (*arca*) chest; (*de embalaje*) case, crate; (*ataúd*) coffin, casket (*US*); ~ **acústica** loudspeaker; ~ **anidadera** nestbox, nesting-box; (*TV*) **la** ~ (**boba** *etc*)* the box*; ~ **de colores** paintbox; ~ **de cuchillería** cutlery cabinet; ~ **china** Chinese box; ~ **del cuerpo** chest, thorax; ~ **de herramientas** toolbox, tool-chest; ~ **de música** musical box; ~ **negra** (*Aer*) black box; ~ **nido** nestbox, nesting-box; ~ **de seguridad** safe-deposit box; ~ **de sorpresa**(**s**) jack-in-the-box; ~ **del tambor,** ~ **del tímpano** (*Anat*) eardrum; ~ **torácica** chest wall; **estar en** ~ (*persona*) to be in good shape, (*aparato*) to be working well.

(**b**) (*Mec*) case, casing, housing; (*de vehículo*) body; ~ **de cambios** gearbox; ~ **del cigüeñal** crankcase; ~ **de eje** axle-box; ~ **de engranajes** gearbox; ~ **de fuego** (*Ferro*) fire-box; ~ **de sebo** grease-cup; ~ **de velocidades** gearbox.

(**c**) (*Elec*) box; ~ **de empalmes** junction box; ~ **de fusibles** fuse-box.

(**d**) (*Arquit*: *de escalera*) well; (*de ascensor*) well, shaft; ~ **de registro** manhole.

(**e**) ~ (**de fusil**) stock.

(**f**) (*Bot*) seed case, capsule.

(**g**) (*Com, Fin*) (*de caudales*) cashbox, safe; (*mesa*) cashier's desk, cashdesk; (*oficina*) cashier's office; (*de supermercado*) check-out; ~ **de alquiler** safe-deposit box; ~ **de caudales** strongbox, safe; ~ **de fondo** (*Cono Sur*) safe deposit box, strongbox; ~ **fuerte** strongroom, bank vault; strongbox; ~ **de** (**gastos**) **menores** petty cash; ~ **registradora** cash register, till; **metálico en** ~ cash in hand; **hacer** ~ to make up the accounts for the day, cash up; **hicieron** ~ **de X pesetas** they took in X pesetas; **ingresar en** ~ (*persona*) to pay in, (*dinero*) be paid in.

(**h**) (*Fin*) fund; ~ **B** secret account, secret fund, slush fund; ~ **de ahorros** savings bank; ~ **postal de ahorros** post-office savings bank; ~ **de compensación** equalization fund; ~ **de construcciones** building society; ~ **de jubilaciones** pension fund; ~ **de reclutamiento** recruiting office; ~ **de resistencia** strike fund; ~ **rural** agricultural credit bank.

(**i**) **despedir** (*o* **echar**) **a uno con ~s destempladas** to send sb packing.

(**j**) (*Mús*) (*de piano etc*) case; (*de violín etc*) body, case; (*Rad*) cabinet; (*tambor*) drum; ~ **de resonancia** soundbox; (*fig*) sounding board; ~ **de ritmos** drum machine, beatbox.

(**k**) (*Tip*) case; ~ **alta** upper case; ~ **baja** lower case.

(**l**) (*Cono Sur*: *lecho de río*) (dried up) riverbed.

cajear* [1a] *vt* (*And, CAm*) to beat up*.

cajero, -a *nm/f*, cashier; (bank) teller; ~ **automático** cash-dispenser, autoteller.

cajeta *nf* (**a**) small box; (*LAm*: *para dulces*) small round sweet box; (*LAm*: *dulce de leche*) fudge, soft toffee; (*Méx*: *dulce de jalea*) jelly; (*And*: *dulce*) sweet, candy (*US*).

(**b**) (*And, CAm*: *de animal*) lip.

(**c**) **de** ~ (*CAm, Méx*: *iró*) first-class, super.

(**d**) (*) (*Méx*) coward; wimp*.

(**e**) (*Cono Sur*‡) cunt‡.

cajete *nm* (*Méx*) (**a**) (*cazuela*) earthenware pot (*o* bowl). (**b**) (*: *wáter*) toilet, loo*. (**c**) (‡: *culo*) bum‡.

cajetilla 1 *nf* small box; ~ **de cigarrillos** packet of cigarettes, pack of cigarettes (*US*); (*Carib*: *dientes*) teeth.

2 *nm* (*Cono Sur**: *pey*) toff*, dude* (*US*); city slicker (*US*); (*afeminado*) poof‡, queen‡.

cajista *nmf* compositor, typesetter.

cajita *nf* small box; ~ **de cerillas,** ~ **de fósforos** (*LAm*) box of matches, matchbox; **de** ~ (*LAm*) great*, fine.

cajón *nm* (**a**) (*caja*) big box, case; crate; chest; ~ **de embalaje** packing case.

(**b**) (*And, Cono Sur*: *ataúd*) coffin, casket (*US*).

(**c**) (*gaveta*) drawer; locker; (*Com*) till; ~ **de sastre** collection of odds and ends; mixed bag, pot pourri; (*persona*) muddle-headed sort; **estar como** ~ **de sastre** to be in utter disorder, be in a terrible mess.

(**d**) (*Com*) stall, booth; ~ **de ropa** (*Méx*) draper's (shop), dry-goods store (*US*).

(**e**) (*Téc*) ~ **hidráulico,** ~ **de suspensión** caisson.

(**f**) (*Dep*) ~ **de salida** starting-gate.

(**g**) (*CAm, Cono Sur*: *barranco*) ravine.

(**h**) **eso es de** ~ that's a matter of course, that goes without saying; that's the usual thing.

(**i**) (*And Mús*) box drum.

caju *nm* cashew (nut).

cajuela *nf* (*Méx Aut*) boot, trunk (*US*).

cal *nf* lime; ~ **apagada,** ~ **muerta** slaked lime; ~ **viva** quicklime; **cerrar algo a** ~ **y canto** to shut sth firmly (*o* securely); **de** ~ **y canto** firm, strong, tough; **dar una de** ~ **y otra de arena** to apply a policy of the carrot and the stick; to blow hot and cold.

cala[1] *nf* (*Geog*) cove; creek, inlet; (*Pesca*) fishing ground; (*Náut*) hold; ~ **de construcción** slipway.

cala[2] *nf* (*de fruta*) sample slice; (*Med*) suppository; (*Aut*) dipstick; (*Med*: *sonda*) probe; **hacer** ~ **y cata** to test for quality.

cala[3]‡ *nf* (*Esp*) one peseta.

cala[4]‡ *nm* (*Mil*) glasshouse‡, prison.

calabacear* [1a] *vt* (*Univ*) *candidato* to fail, plough*; *amante* to jilt.

calabacera *nf* pumpkin (plant), gourd (plant).

calabacín *nm* (**a**) (*Bot*) marrow, courgette. (**b**) (*fig*: *idiota*) dolt.

calabacita *nf* (*Esp*) courgette.

calabaza *nf* (**a**) (*Bot*) pumpkin; gourd, calabash.

(**b**) (*fig*: *idiota*) dolt.

(**c**) (‡: *cabeza*) bonce‡, head.

(**d**) (*) **dar ~s a** *candidato* to fail, plough*; *amante* to jilt; (*ofender*) to snub, offend; **llevarse ~s, recibir ~s** (*Univ*) to fail, plough*; (*amante*) to be jilted; **salir** ~ to be a flop*, prove a miserable failure.

calabazada *nf* butt, knock (with the head); blow on the head.

calabazazo *nm* bump on the head.

calabazo *nm* (**a**) (*Bot*) pumpkin, gourd. (**b**) (*Carib Mús*) drum.

calabobos *nm* drizzle.

calabozo *nm* prison; prison cell; (*esp Hist*) dungeon; (*Mil*) military prison.

calabrote *nm* (*Náut*) cable-laid rope, cable rope.

calache* *nm* (*CAm*) thing, thingummyjig*; **reúne tus ~s** get your things, get your bits and pieces.

calada *nf* (**a**) (*mojada*) soaking. (**b**) (*de red*) lowering. (**c**) (*: *de humo*) puff, drag*. (**d**) (*de ave*) stoop, swoop, pounce. (**e**) (*: *regañada*) ticking-off*; **dar una** ~ **a uno** to tick sb off*, haul sb over the coals.

caladero *nm* fishing-grounds.

calado 1 *adj*: **estar ~ (hasta los huesos)** to be soaked (to the skin).

2 *nm* (**a**) (*Téc*) fretwork; (*Cos*) openwork.

(**b**) (*Náut*) depth of water; (*de barco*) draught; **en iguales ~s** on an even keel.

(**c**) (*fig*) depth; scope; importance; **una razón de mayor ~** a more weighty reason; **un descubrimiento de gran ~** a very important discovery.

(**d**) (*Mec*) stall, stalling.

calafate *nm* caulker; shipwright.

calafatear [1a] *vt* (*Náut*) to caulk; to plug (up).

calaguasca *nf* (*LAm*) rum.

calagurritano 1 *adj* of Calahorra. **2** *nm*, **calagurritana** *nf* native (*o* inhabitant) of Calahorra; **los ~s** the people of Calahorra.

calamar *nm* squid.

calambrazo *nm* attack of cramp, spasm.

calambre *nm* (*t* **~s**) cramp; **~ de escribiente** writer's cramp.

calambur *nm* (*LAm*) pun.

calamidad *nf* calamity, disaster; **es una ~*** (*suceso etc*) it's a great pity; it's a nuisance; (*persona*) he's utterly useless, he's a dead loss; **estar hecho una ~** to be in a very bad way; **¡vaya ~!** what bad luck!

calamina *nf* (**a**) (*gen*) calamine. (**b**) (*LAm*) corrugated iron.

calaminado *adj* (*LAm*) firm, bumpy, uneven.

calamita *nf* lodestone; magnetic needle.

calamitosamente *adv* calamitously, disastrously.

calamitoso *adj* calamitous, disastrous.

cálamo *nm* (*Bot*) stem, stalk; (*Mús*) reed; (*Mús*: *Hist*) flute; (*poét*) pen; **empuñar el ~** to take up one's pen; **menear ~** to wield a pen.

calamocano* *adj* (**a**) (*borracho*) merry*, tipsy. (**b**) (*cariñoso*) doting.

calamoco *nm* icicle.

calamorra *nf* nut, head.

calamorrada* *nf* butt; bump on the head.

calandraco *adj* (*And, Cono Sur*) (*fastidioso*) annoying, tedious; (*casquivano*) scatterbrained.

calandria[1] *nf* (*Orn*) calandra lark.

calandria[2] **1** *nf* (**a**) (*rodillo*) mangle; (*Téc*) calender. (**b**) (*Fin*‡) one peseta. (**c**) (*argot*) underworld slang, argot. **2** *nmf* (*) (*persona*) malingerer.

calaña *nf* model, pattern; (*fig*: *gen pey*) nature, kind, stamp.

calañes *nm* (*Andalucía*) *hat with a turned-up brim.*

calar[1] **1** *adj* calcareous, lime (*atr*). **2** *nm* limestone quarry.

calar[2] [1a] **1** *vt* (**a**) *persona* to soak, drench; *materia* to soak, drench; (*empapar*) to soak into, saturate, permeate.

(**b**) (*penetrar*) to penetrate, perforate, pierce, go through.

(**c**) (*Téc*) *metal* to do fretwork on; (*Cos*) to do openwork on.

(**d**) (*penetrar, fig*) *persona* to size up; *intención* to see through; *secreto* to penetrate; **¡nos ha calado!** he's rumbled us!*; **a ésos los tengo muy calados** I've got them thoroughly weighed up (*o* sized up).

(**e**) (*fijar*) *bayoneta* to fix; *mástil* to fix, step.

(**f**) *puente* to lower, let down; *red, vela* to lower.

(**g**) *fruta* to cut a sample slice of; (*LAm*) *maíz* to take a sample of.

(**h**) (*And*: *aplastar*) to crush, flatten, sit on; (*fig*: *humillar*) to humiliate.

(**i**) (*Náut*) to draw; **el buque cala 12 metros** the ship draws 12 metres, the ship has a draught of 12 metres.

2 *vi* (**a**) (*líquido*) to sink in, soak in; (*zapato*) to leak, let in the water.

(**b**) (*fig*) **~ en** to go deeply into; **hay que ~ más hondo** this must be investigated further, one must dig more deeply into this.

(**c**) (*Mec*) to stop, stall.

(**d**) (*Orn*) = **3 (c)**.

3 calarse *vr* (**a**) (*mojarse*) to get soaked, get drenched (*hasta los huesos* to the skin).

(**b**) (*lograr entrar*) to get in, squeeze in; to sneak in.

(**c**) (*Orn*) to stoop, swoop (down), pounce (*sobre* on).

(**d**) (*Mec*) to stop, stall.

(**e**) **~ el sombrero** to pull one's hat down; to put one's hat on firmly; **~ las gafas** to stick one's glasses on; to push one's glasses back.

calarredes *nm invar* trawler.

calatear [1a] **1** *vt* (*And, Cono Sur*) to undress, strip. **2 calatearse** *vr* to get undressed, strip off.

calato *adj* (*And*) naked, bare; (*fig*) penniless, broke*.

calavera 1 *nf* (**a**) (*Anat*) skull.

(**b**) (*Ent*) death's-head moth.

(**c**) (*Méx Aut*) rear light.

2 *nm* (*juerguista*) gay dog†; (*loculeo*) madcap; (*libertino*) rake, roué; (*canalla*) rotter†, cad†, heel.

calaverada *nf* madcap escapade, foolhardy act.

calaverear [1a] *vi* to live it up*; to have one's fling; (*pey*) to lead a wild life, live recklessly.

calca *nf* (**a**) (*And Agr*) barn, granary. (**b**) (*LAm*: *copia*) copy.

calcado *nm* tracing.

calcañal *nm*, **calcañar** *nm*, **calcaño** *nm* heel.

calcar [1g] *vt* (**a**) (*Téc*) to trace, make a tracing of. (**b**) **~ A en B** (*copiar*) to model A on B, base A on B; (*pey*) to copy A slavishly from B.

calcáreo *adj* calcareous, lime (*atr*).

calce *nm* (**a**) (*llanta*) (steel) tyre; (*cuña*) wedge, shim; (*punta*) iron tip; (*And*: *empaste*) filling (*of a tooth*).

(**b**) (*CAm, Carib, Méx*: *de documento*) foot, lower margin (of a document); (*firma*) signature; **firmar al ~** to sign at the foot (*o* bottom) of the page.

(**c**) (*Cono Sur*: *oportunidad*) chance, opportunity.

calcés *nm* masthead.

calceta *nf* (**a**) (*media*) (knee-length) stocking. (**b**) (*hierro*) fetter, shackle. (**c**) **hacer ~** to knit.

calcetería *nf* (**a**) (*oficio*) hosiery. (**b**) (*tienda*) hosier's (shop).

calcetero, -a *nm/f* hosier.

calcetín *nm* sock; **~ de viaje**‡ French letter; **darle la vuelta al ~** (*fig*) to turn things upside-down.

calcícola 1 *adj* calcicolous. **2** *nf* calcicole.

calcificar [1g] **1** *vt* to calcify. **2 calcificarse** *vr* to calcify.

calcífugo *adj* calcifugous.

calcina *nf* concrete.

calcinación *nf* calcination.

calcinar [1a] **1** *vt* (**a**) (*gen*) to calcine; to burn, reduce to ashes, blacken; **las ruinas calcinadas del edificio** the blackened ruins of the building.

(**b**) (*: *fastidiar*) to bother, annoy.

2 calcinarse *vr* to calcine.

calcio *nm* calcium.

calco *nm* (**a**) (*Téc*) tracing.

(**b**) (*fig*: *acto*) imprint(ing); graft(ing); implantation; **~ a escala** scale model.

(**c**) (*Ling*) calque (*de* on), loan-translation (*de* of); semantic borrowing (*de* from).

(**d**) **~s**‡ (*pies*) plates‡, feet; (*zapatos*) shoes.

calcomanía *nf* transfer.

calculable *adj* calculable.

calculador *adj* (**a**) (*gen*) calculating. (**b**) (*LAm*: *egoísta*) selfish, mercenary; **~ solar** solar calculator.

calculadora *nf* calculating machine, calculator; **~ de bolsillo** pocket calculator.

calcular [1a] *vt* (**a**) to calculate, compute; to add up, work out. (**b**) **~ que** ... to reckon that ...; to anticipate that ..., expect that ...

cálculo *nm* (**a**) (*gen*) calculation; (*cómputo*) reckoning; estimate; (*conjetura*) conjecture; (*Mat*) calculus; **~ de costo** costing; **~ diferencial** differential calculus; **hoja de ~** spreadsheet; **libro de ~s hechos** ready reckoner; **~ mental** mental arithmetic; **~ de probabilidades** theory of probability; **según mis ~s** according to my calculations, by my reckoning; **obrar con mucho ~** to act cautiously.

(**b**) (*Med*) stone; (*biliar*) gallstone.

Calcuta *nf* Calcutta.

calcha *nf* (**a**) (*Cono Sur*) (*ropa*) clothing, (*de cama*) bedding; (*arreos*) harness. (**b**) (*Cono Sur*: *cerneja*) fetlock; (*fleco*) fringe (of hair); (*pingajos*) tatters, strands.

calchona *nf* (*Cono Sur*) ghost, bogey; (*fig*) hag.

calchudo *adj* (*Cono Sur*) shrewd, cunning.

calda *nf* (**a**) heating; stoking. (**b**) **~s** hot springs, hot mineral baths.

caldeamiento *nm* warming, heating.

caldear [1a] **1** *vt* to warm (up), heat (up); (*Téc*) to weld; **estar caldeado** to be very hot, (*fig*: *situación etc*) be very tense. **2 caldearse** *vr* to get very hot, get overheated.

caldeo *nm* warming, heating; (*Téc*) welding.

caldera *nf* (*Téc*) boiler; boiling-pan; (*Cono Sur*) pot; (*tetera*) kettle, teapot; (*And*) crater; **las ~s de Pe(d)ro Botero** hell.

calderero *nm* boilermaker; coppersmith; **~ remendón** tinker.

caldereta *nf* (**a**) (*caldera pequeña*) small boiler; stewpan.

(**b**) (*Ecl*) holy water vessel. (**c**) (*Culin*) fish stew; lamb stew. (**d**) (*Carib*: *viento*) warm wind from the sea.
calderilla *nf* (**a**) (*Ecl*) holy water vessel. (**b**) (*Fin*) small change, coppers; **en ~** in coppers.
caldero *nm* small boiler, copper.
calderón *nm* (**a**) (*caldera grande*) large boiler, cauldron. (**b**) (*Tip*) paragraph sign, section mark. (**c**) (*Mús*) pause (sign).
calderoniano *adj* relating to Calderón; **héroe ~** Calderonian hero; **estudios ~s** Calderón studies.
caldo *nm* (**a**) (*sopa*) broth, bouillon; (*consomé*) consommé, clear soup; (*salsa*) (*para asado*) gravy, (*para ensalada*) dressing, sauce; **~ de carne** (*para enfermo*) beef tea; **~ de cultivo** (*Bio*) culture medium; (*fig*) breeding ground; **~ de pollo** chicken broth; **~ de teta‡** milk; **cambiar el ~ a las aceitunas‡** to have a leak‡; **dar un ~ a uno** (*Cono Sur*) to torture sb; **estar a ~*** to be broke*; **hacer el ~ gordo** to make things easier, smooth the way; **hacer el ~ gordo a uno** to play into sb's hands, make it easy for sb; **se le hacía ~ la cabeza** (*Cono Sur*) he worried a lot about it; **poner a uno a ~*** to give sb a bashing*, (*fig*: *reprender*) to give sb a dressing-down*, (*insultar*) to lay into sb*, insult sb.
(**b**) **~s** (*aceite*) oil, (*vino*) wine, (*sidra*) cider (and other vegetable juices); **los ~s jerezanos** the wines of Jerez, sherries.
(**c**) (**‡**: *cigarrillo*) fag‡, gasper‡.
(**d**) (*Méx*) sugar cane juice.
caldoso* *adj* watery, weak.
calducho *nm* (*Cono Sur*) day off.
cale *nm* slap, smack.
calé 1 *adj* gipsy (*atr*). **2** *nmf* gipsy.
calefacción *nf* heating; **~ central** central heating; **sistema de ~** heating (system).
calefaccionable *adj*: **espejo exterior ~** heated wing mirror.
calefactor 1 *adj* heating (*atr*); **sistema ~** heating system. **2** *nm* heater.
calefán *nm* (*Cono Sur*) water heater.
calefón *nm* (*Cono Sur*) hot-water boiler, water-heater; **~ a gas** gas heater.
cal(e)idoscopio *nm* kaleidoscope.
calendar [1a] *vt* to schedule, programme.
calendario *nm* calendar; (*de reforma etc*) timetable; (*de trabajo etc*) schedule; **~ de pared** wall calendar; **~ de taco** tear-off calendar; **hacer ~s** to muse, dream.
caléndula *nf* marigold.
calentador *nm* heater; **~ de agua** water-heater; **~ de cama** (*Hist*) bed-warmer, warming-pan; **~ eléctrico** electric fire; **~ a gas** gas heater, geyser, water heater; **~ de inmersión** immersion heater; **~es de piernas** leg-warmers.
calentamiento *nm* heating, warming; (*Deporte*: *~ previo*) warm-up; **~ global, ~ del planeta** global warming.
calentar [1j] **1** *vt* (**a**) *horno, agua,* to heat (up); *cuerpo, silla, comida, cuarto etc* to warm (up); *motor* to warm up; **~ al blanco** to make white-hot; **~ al rojo** to make red-hot.
(**b**) *negocio etc* to hurry on, speed up, get moving.
(**c**) (*LAm*: *provocar*) to anger, enrage.
(**d**) (*****: *zurrar*) to warm*, tan*.
(**e**) (*****: *excitar*) to arouse (sexually), turn on*.
2 calentarse *vr* (**a**) to heat up, warm up, get hot, get warm; (*junto al fuego*) to warm o.s.; (*Deporte*) to warm up.
(**b**) (*fig*: *discusión*) to get heated; (*persona*) to get heated, get het up, get excited (*por* about).
(**c**) (*Zool*) to be on heat; (*persona*) to get randy*, feel in the mood.
(**d**) (*LAm*: *enfadarse*) to get cross (*o* mad).
calentón* 1 *adj* sexy, randy*. **2** *nm* (**a**) (*And, Cono Sur**) randy person*. (**b**) **darse el ~, tener un ~** to feel randy*, feel sexy, be in the mood.
calentura *nf* (**a**) (*Med*: *fiebre*) fever, (high) temperature; **estar con ~, tener ~** to be feverish, have a temperature; **tener ~ de pollo** to pretend to be ill, have an imaginary illness.
(**b**) (*Cono Sur*: *tuberculosis*) tuberculosis.
(**c**) (*And, Cono Sur*: *cachondez*) randiness*, sexual excitement; **tener ~** to feel randy*.
(**d**) (*And*: *rabieta*) fit of rage, tantrum.
calenturiento *adj* (**a**) (*Med*) feverish. (**b**) (*Cono Sur*: *tísico*) consumptive, tubercular. (**c**) *mente* (*indecente*) dirty, prurient; (*exaltado*) rash, impulsive; (*Pol etc*) **las mentes calenturientas** the hotheads.
calenturón *nm* high fever.
calenturoso *adj* (*Med*) feverish.
calera *nf* (*cantera*) limestone quarry; (*horno*) lime-kiln.
calero 1 *adj* lime (*atr*). **2** *nm* lime-kiln.
calés‡ *nmpl* bread‡, money.
calesa *nf* chaise, calash, buggy.
calesera *nf Andalusian jacket.*
calesín *nm* gig, fly.
calesita *nf* (*And, Cono Sur*) merry-go-round, carousel (*US*).
caleta *nf* (**a**) (*Geog*) cove, small bay, inlet. (**b**) (*And*: *Náut*) coasting vessel, coaster. (**c**) (*And**: *escondite*) hiding-place.
caletero *nm* (**a**) (*Carib*: *estibador*) docker, port worker. (**b**) (*LAm Ferro*) milk-train. (**c**) (*Carib*: *en tienda*) shop assistant.
caletre* *nm* gumption*, brains; **no le cabe en el ~** he can't get it into his thick head*.
calibración *nf* calibration.
calibrado *adj* calibrated.
calibrador *nm* gauge; calliper(s); **~ de alambre** wire gauge.
calibraje *nm* calibration.
calibrar [1a] *vt* to calibrate; to gauge, measure.
calibre *nm* (**a**) (*gen*) calibre; gauge; (*Mil*) calibre, bore; (*Ferro*) gauge; (*de alambre, tubo etc*) diameter; (*fig*) calibre; **de grueso ~** large-bore; **palabras de grueso ~** (*Cono Sur*) crude language, swearing. (**b**) = **calibrador.**
calicanto *nm* (*Carib, Cono Sur*: *muro*) stone wall; (*muelle*) jetty.
calicata‡ *nf* (*pierna*) leg; (*culo*) backside.
calicó *nm* calico.
caliche *nm* (**a**) (*And, Cono Sur*) (*salitre*) saltpetre; (*terreno*) nitrate-bearing ground. (**b**) (*Cono Sur*: *jalbegue*) crust of whitewash which flakes from a wall. (**c**) **echar un ~ **** to have a screw**.
calidad *nf* (**a**) (*gen*) quality; grade; **de ~** of quality; **de mala ~** of bad quality, bad-quality, low-quality; **~ de la vida** quality of life.
(**b**) (*posición*) position, capacity; **en ~ de** in the capacity of, as.
(**c**) (*de contrato*) stipulation, term; **a ~ de que ...** provided that ...
(**d**) (*rango*) rank, importance, quality.
(**e**) **~es** (moral) qualities; gifts; worth.
cálido *adj clima, país* hot; (*fig*) *manta, aplausos, color etc* warm.
calidoscópico *adj* kaleidoscopic.
calidoscopio *nm* kaleidoscope.
calientacamas *nm invar* electric blanket.
calientafuentes *nm invar* hotplate.
calientapiernas *nm invar* leg-warmer(s).
calientapiés *nm invar* hot-water bottle; foot warmer.
calientaplatos *nm invar* hotplate.
calientapollas** *nf invar* (*Esp*) prick-teaser**.
caliente 1 *adj* (**a**) (*gen*) warm, hot.
(**b**) (*fig*) *carácter* fiery, spirited; *discusión* heated; *batalla* raging; (*LAm*) *persona* angry, mad*; **~ de cascos** hotheaded; **un verano ~** (*Pol etc*) a long hot summer.
(**c**) **estar ~** (*Zool*) to be on heat; (*****: *persona*) to feel randy*, be in the mood; **ponerse ~** to get randy*, get in the mood.
(**d**) **en ~** in the heat of the moment; (*Téc*) hot; **persecución en ~** hot pursuit; **montar algo en ~** to assemble sth while it is hot, shrink sth on.
2 *nmf* (******) **~ mental** oversexed person.
califa *nm* caliph.
califal *adj* caliphal; **la Córdoba ~** Cordova under the Caliphs, the Cordova of the Caliphs.
califato *nm* caliphate.
calificación *nf* (**a**) (*gen*) qualification; (*evaluación*) assessment; (*descripción*) description, label. (**b**) (*posición*) rating, standing; (*Escuela*) grade, mark; **~ de sobresaliente** first-class mark.
calificado *adj* (**a**) (*capacitado*) qualified, competent; *obrero* skilled. (**b**) (*conocido*) well-known, eminent; *prueba etc* undisputed; *robo* proven, manifest. (**c**) (*Méx Jur*) qualified, conditional.
calificar [1g] **1** *vt* (**a**) (*gen*) (*t Gram*) to qualify.
(**b**) (*evaluar*) to assess; to rate; *examen* to grade, mark.
(**c**) **~ a uno** (*distinguir*) to distinguish sb, give sb his standing (*o* fame); (*ennoblecer*) to ennoble sb.
(**d**) **~ a uno de tonto** to call sb silly, describe sb as silly, label sb silly.
2 calificarse *vr* (*LAm*: *Pol*) to register as a voter.
calificativo 1 *adj* qualifying. **2** *nm* qualifier, epithet; description; **sólo merece el ~ de ...** it can only be described

as ...
california *nf* (*Cono Sur*) (**a**) (*carrera*) horse-race. (**b**) (*Téc*) wirestretcher.
californiano, -a *adj, nm/f* Californian.
calígine *nf* (*poét*) mist, darkness.
caliginoso *adj* (*poét*) misty, dark.
caligrafía *nf* calligraphy, penmanship.
caligrafiar [1c] *vt* to write in a stylish hand.
caligráfico *adj* calligraphic.
calilla *nf* (*CAm, Méx*) (**a**) (*persona*) bore, nuisance. (**b**) (*molestia*) nuisance. (**c**) (*engaño*) hoax; (*broma*) boring joke.
calima *nf* = **calina.**
calimocho *nm* drink of mixed Coca-Cola and wine.
calina *nf* haze, mist; (*industrial*) smog.
calinoso *adj* hazy, misty.
calipso *nm* calypso.
caliqueño (**a**) type of cheap cigar. (**b**) (**‡**) prick**‡**; **echar un** ~ to have a screw**‡**.
calistenia *nf* cal(l)isthenics.
cáliz *nm* (**a**) (*Bot*) calyx. (**b**) (*Ecl*) chalice, communion cup; (*poét*) cup, goblet; ~ **de amargura,** ~ **de dolor** cup of sorrow, cup of bitterness.
caliza *nf* limestone.
calizo *adj* lime (*atr*); *tierra* limy.
calma *nf* (**a**) (*Met, Náut*) calm, calm weather; ~ **chicha** dead calm; **estar en** ~ to be calm.
(**b**) (*Com, Fin*) calm, inactivity, lull (*de* in); cessation, suspension (*de* of); **estar en** ~ (*mercado*) to be steady.
(**c**) (*de temperamento*) calm, calmness; (*pey*) slowness, phlegm, laziness; **¡~!, ¡con ~!** calm down!, don't get so worked up!, take your time!; **hacer algo con** ~ to do sth calmly; **lo hizo con sus ~s*** he did it calmly, he did it slowly; **tomarlo con** ~ to take things gently; **perder la** ~ to get ruffled, lose one's composure.
calmante 1 *adj* soothing, sedative. **2** *nm* sedative, tranquillizer.
calmar [1a] **1** *vt* (*gen*) to calm; *persona* to calm (down), quieten (down), soothe; *nervios* to soothe, steady; *dolor* to relieve.
2 *vi* (*viento etc*) to abate, fall calm.
3 calmarse *vr* (*persona*) to calm down, calm o.s.; (*tiempo*) to improve, settle down; **¡cálmate!** calm down!, don't get so worked up!
calmazo *nm* dead calm.
calmécac *nm* (*Méx Hist*) *Aztec school for priests.*
calmo[1] *adj* slow, steady, measured.
calmo[2] *adj* (*esp LAm*) *tierra* barren, uncultivated.
calmosamente *adv* (**a**) calmly. (**b**) slowly, sluggishly; nonchalantly, deliberately; lazily.
calmosidad *nf* (**a**) calm, calmness. (**b**) slowness, sluggishness; nonchalance; deliberateness; laziness.
calmoso *adj* (**a**) (*gen*) calm, quiet. (**b**) (*pey: torpe*) slow, sluggish; nonchalant, deliberate; lazy.
caló *nm* gipsy language, gipsy talk; (*argot*) slang; (*jerga*) cant.
calofriarse [1c] *vr* = **escalofriarse.**
calofrío *nm* = **escalofrío.**
calor *nm* (**a**) (*gen*) heat (*t Fís, Téc etc*); warmth; **un** ~ **agradable** a pleasant warmth; **un** ~ **excesivo** an excessive heat; ~ **blanco** white heat; ~ **rojo** red heat; **¡qué ~!** isn't it hot!, how hot it is!; **entrar en** ~ to get warm, begin to feel warm; (*antes de jugar, con ejercicios*) to warm up; **hace** ~ it's hot; **hace mucho** ~ it's very hot; **tener** ~ to be hot, feel hot; **tomar algo con** ~ to work hard at sth.
(**b**) (*fig: de discusión*) warmth, heat; (*de batalla*) heat; (*de acogida etc*) warmth; (*de pasión*) ardour, fervour; excitement, passion; **dar** ~ **a** to encourage; **meter a uno en** ~ to enourage sb, incite sb.
caloría *nf* calorie.
calórico *adj* caloric.
calorífero 1 *adj* heat-producing, heat-giving. **2** *nm* (*sistema*) heating system; (*estufa*) furnace, stove; (*radiador*) heater, radiator; ~ **mural** wall radiator.
calorífico *adj* calorific.
calorifugar [1h] *vt caldera, tubo* to lag.
calorífugo *adj* (*resistente*) heat-resistant, non-conducting; (*incombustible*) fireproof.
calorro, -a *adj, nm/f* gipsy.
calote‡ *nm* (*Cono Sur*) con*, swindle; **dar** ~ to skip payments, leave without paying.
calotear [1a] *vt* (*Cono Sur*) to swindle, con*.
calta *nf* marsh marigold (*t* ~ **palustre**).
caluga *nf* (*Cono Sur*) toffee, chewy sweet.
caluma *nf* (*And*) mountain pass (*in the Andes*).
calumnia *nf* calumny; (*Jur*) (*oral*) slander, (*escrito*) libel (*de* on).
calumniador(a) *nm/f* slanderer, libeller.
calumniar [1b] *vt* to slander, libel; **calumnia, que algo queda** some of the mud sticks.
calumnioso *adj* slanderous, libellous.
calurosamente *adv* (*fig*) warmly, enthusiastically, heartily.
caluroso *adj* (**a**) (*gen*) warm, hot. (**b**) (*fig: animado*) warm, enthusiastic, hearty.
calva *nf* (*en cabeza*) bald patch; (*en vestido*) bare spot, worn place; (*de bosque etc*) clearing.
Calvados *nm invar* Calvados.
Calvario *nm* (**a**) (*Ecl*) Calvary; Stations of the Cross; **c~** wayside shrine. (**b**) (*fig*) **c~** cross, heavy burden; series of disasters; string of debts; **pasar un** ~ to suffer agonies.
calvatrueno* *nm* (**a**) (*calvo*) bald pate. (**b**) (*tarambana*) wild fellow, madcap.
calvero *nm* (**a**) (*de bosque*) glade, clearing. (**b**) (*cantera*) chalkpit, marlpit.
calvicie *nf* baldness; ~ **precoz** premature baldness.
calvinismo *nm* Calvinism.
calvinista 1 *adj* Calvinist(ic). **2** *nmf* Calvinist.
calvo 1 *adj* (**a**) *cabeza, persona* bald; *piel* bald, hairless; **quedarse** ~ to go bald. (**b**) *terreno* bare, barren; *vestido* threadbare. **2** *nm* bald man.
calza *nf* (**a**) (*Mec*) wedge; scotch, chock; **poner** ~ **a** to wedge, scotch.
(**b**) (*: *media*) stocking; **~s†** hose; (*pantalón*) breeches; (*panti*) tights; **estar en ~s prietas** to be in a fix.
(**c**) (*LAm: de diente*) filling.
calzada *nf* roadway; (paved) road; causeway; (*de casa*) drive; (*LAm: avenida*) avenue; (*Carib: acera*) pavement, sidewalk (*US*); ~ **romana** Roman road.
calzado 1 *adj* shod, wearing shoes; ~ **de** shod with, wearing; **conviene ir** ~ it's better to wear shoes, one has to wear sth on one's feet.
2 *nm* footwear.
calzador *nm* shoehorn; (*And, Cono Sur*) pen-holder.
calzar [1f] **1** *vt* (**a**) (*ponerse*) to put on; (*llevar*) to wear; **calzaba zapatos verdes** she was wearing green shoes, she had green shoes on; **¿qué número calza Vd?** what size do you take?; **el que primero llega se la calza** first come first served.
(**b**) *persona* to put shoes on; to provide with footwear, supply with shoes; **me ayudó a ~me las botas** he helped me to put my boots on.
(**c**) (*arma*) to carry, take, use.
(**d**) (*Mec*) *rueda etc* to wedge, scotch, chock; to put a wedge in (*o* under *etc*), put chocks under; (*bloquear*) to block; (*asegurar*) to secure.
(**e**) (*LAm*) *diente* to fill.
(**f**) (*poner punta a*) to tip, put an iron tip on.
2 *vi* (**a**) **calza bien** he wears good shoes.
(**b**) (*) **calza poco, no calza mucho** he's pretty dim*.
3 calzarse *vr* (**a**) ~ **los zapatos** to put on one's shoes; **¿qué zapatos calzaba?** what shoes was he wearing?
(**b**) (*) ~ **un empleo** to get a job; ~ **a uno** to keep sb under one's thumb.
(**c**) ~ **a una‡** to screw sb‡.
calzo *nm* wedge, scotch, chock; shim; (*Mec*) brake-shoe; (*Náut*) skid, chock.
calzón *nm* (*t* **calzones**) (**a**) (*de hombre*) breeches; shorts (*t Dep*); (*ropa interior*) underpants; (*LAm*) trousers, pants (*US*); ~ **de baño††** bathing trunks; **calzones rotos** (*Cono Sur Culin*) doughnuts, donuts (*US*); **amarrarse los calzones** (*LAm*) to get stuck in; **hablar a** ~ **quitado** (*sin parar*) to talk without stopping; (*con franqueza*) to open one's heart, speak openly (*o* frankly); **ponerse los calzones** (*mujer: fig*) to wear the trousers; **tener (muchos) calzones** (*Méx*) to be tough.
(**b**) (*de mujer*) shorts; (*LAm*) pants, knickers; ~ **de baño** pants part of two-piece swimsuit.
(**c**) (*LAm: de bebé*) ~ **de vinilo** plastic pants; ~ **desechable** disposable nappy.
calzonaria *nf*, **calzonario** *nm* (*LAm*) pants, knickers.
calzonazos* *nm invar* (*tonto*) stupid fellow; (*débil*) weak-willed fellow; (*marido*) henpecked husband.
calzoncillos *nmpl* pants, underpants (*US*), shorts (*US*); ~ **del 9 largo***, ~ **marianos*** long johns*.
calzoneras *nfpl* (*Carib, Méx*) side-buttoning trousers.
calzoneta *nf* (*CAm, Méx*) swimming trunks.
calzonudo *adj* (*And, CAm, Cono Sur*) (*estúpido*) stupid;

(*débil*) weak-willed, timid; (*Méx*) (*enérgico*) energetic; (*audaz*) bold, brave.

callada: **a la ~** *adv*, **de ~** *adv* on the quiet, secretly; **dar la ~ por respuesta** to say nothing.

calladamente *adv* quietly, silently; secretly.

callado *adj* (**a**) (*temperamento*) quiet, reserved, reticent.

(**b**) (*silencioso*) quiet, silent; **todo estaba muy ~** everything was very quiet; **tener algo ~** to keep quiet about sth, keep sth secret; **¡qué ~ se lo tenía Vd!** you kept pretty quiet about it!; **pagar para tener ~ a uno** to pay to keep sb quiet; **nunca te quedas ~** you always have an answer for everything.

callampa *nf* (*Cono Sur*) (*Bot*) mushroom; (*: *paraguas*) brolly*, umbrella; **~s*** (*Anat*) big ears; **~s** (*t* **población ~**) shanty-town, slum.

callana *nf* (*LAm Culin*) flat earthenware pan; (*Cono Sur hum*) pocket watch.

callandico *adv*, **callandito** *adv* softly, very quietly; stealthily.

callar [1a] **1** *vt secreto* to keep; *hecho, pasaje etc* to pass over in silence, say nothing about, not mention; *dato, información* to keep back, keep to o.s., keep secret; *asunto vergonzoso* to keep quiet about, hush up.

2 *vi y* **callarse** *vr* (*gen*) to keep quiet, be silent, remain silent; (*ruido*) to stop; (*dejar de hablar*) to become silent, stop talking (*o* playing *etc*); to become quiet; (*mar, viento*) to become still, be hushed; **¡calla!, ¡cállate!, ¡cállese!** (*orden*) shut up!*, be quiet!, hold your tongue!; **calla, calle** (*asintiendo*) say no more, enough said; **¡calla!** (*sorpresa*) you don't mean to say!, well!; **¡cállate la trompa!*** shut up!* **hacer ~ a uno** to make sb be quiet, make sb stop talking (*etc*); (*enérgicamente*) to shut sb up; **¿quieres ~?** you've said enough, that's enough now; **sería mejor ~se** it would be best to say nothing; **~ como una piedra, ~ como un muerto** to shut up like a clam; **quien calla otorga** silence gives consent; **al buen ~ llaman Sancho** silence is golden.

calle *nf* (**a**) (*gen*) street, road; **~ abajo** down the street; **~ arriba** up the street; **~ ciega** (*Carib*) cul-de-sac; **~ de dirección única, ~ de un (solo) sentido** (*Méx*) one-way street; **~ de doble sentido** two-way road; **~ mayor** high street, main street; **~ peatonal, ~ salón** pedestrian precinct; **~ de rodadura, ~ de rodaje** (*Aer*) taxiway; **precio en la ~** (*Aut*) price on the road; **dejar a uno en la ~** to put sb out of a job; **echar por la ~ de en medio** to push on, press on regardless; **echarse a la ~** to go out into the street; (*turba*) to take to the streets, riot, demonstrate; **hacer (la) ~*** (*prostituta*) to be on the streets, be on the game*; **llevarse a uno de ~** to bowl sb over; **llevar** (*o* **traer**) **a uno por la ~ de la amargura** to give sb a difficult time; **y ahora patea las ~s** now he's out on the streets; **poner a uno (de patitas) en la ~** to kick sb out, chuck sb out; to put sb out of a job; **quedarse en la ~** not to have a penny to one's name; **verse en la ~** to find oneself out of a job; *V* **aplanar, rondar**.

(**b**) (*camino para pasar*) passage, way; room; **¡~!** make way!; **abrir ~, hacer ~** to make way, clear the way.

(**c**) (*Dep: de piscina, pista*) lane; (*Golf*) fairway.

(**d**) (*fig: público*) **la ~** the public; **la presión de la ~** the pressure of public opinion.

calleja *nf* = **callejuela**.

callejear [1a] *vi* to wander about the streets, stroll around; (*pey*) to loaf, hang about idly.

callejera *nf* street-walker.

callejero 1 *adj* (**a**) (*gen*) street (*atr*); **accidente ~** street accident; **disturbios ~s** trouble in the streets, rioting in the streets; **perro ~** stray dog.

(**b**) *persona* fond of walking about the streets, fond of gadding about.

2 *nm* (**a**) (*guía*) street directory. (**b**) (*Aut*) runabout.

callejón *nm* alley, alleyway, passage; (*And*) main street; (*Taur*) space between inner and outer barriers; **~ sin salida** cul-de-sac; blind alley (*t fig*); **gente de ~** (*And*) low-class people; **las negociaciones están en un ~ sin salida** the negotiations are at an impasse, the negotiations are deadlocked.

callejuela *nf* (**a**) (*gen*) narrow street, side street; alley, passage. (**b**) (*fig: subterfugio*) subterfuge; way out (of the difficulty).

callicida *nm* corn cure.

callista *nmf* chiropodist.

callo *nm* (**a**) (*Med: de pie*) corn; callus; **criar ~s** to become inured, become hardened; **pisar los ~s a uno** to tread on sb's toes (*o* corns). (**b**) (*Esp Culin*) **~s** tripe; **~s al ajo** tripe with garlic. (**c**) (‡: *mujer*) old bat*, old cow‡; ugly woman; (*hombre*) villain, nasty piece of work*. (**d**) **dar el ~** (*Esp**) to slog, work hard.

callosidad *nf* callosity, hard patch (*on hand etc*).

calloso *adj* horny, hard, rough; calloused.

CAM *nf abr de* **Comunidad Autónoma de Madrid**.

cama *nf* (**a**) (*gen*) bed; bedstead; couch; **~ de agua** water bed; **~ camera** large single bed; (*Cono Sur*) double bed; **~ de campaña** campbed; **~ de columnas, ~ imperial** fourposter bed; **~ de cuero** (*Cono Sur*) cot; **~ elástica** trampoline; **~s gemelas** twin beds; **~ de matrimonio; ~ matrimonial** (*LAm*) double bed; **media ~, ~ de monja, ~ de soltero** single bed; **~ en petaca** apple-pie bed; **~ plegable, ~ de tijera** folding bed, campbed; **~ de rayos infrarrojos, ~ solar** sunbed; **~ redonda** group sex; **~ turca** divan bed, day bed; **~ de viento** (*And, CAm*) cot; **caer en (la) ~** to fall ill; **estar en ~** (*Med*), **guardar ~** to be ill in bed, be confined to bed; **hacer la ~** to make the bed; **hacer** (*o* **poner**) **la ~ a uno** (*fig*) to play a dirty trick on sb; **quien mala ~ hace en ella se yace** having made your bed you must lie on it; **ir a la ~** to go to bed; **levantarse por los pies de la ~** to get out of bed on the wrong side; **se la llevó a la ~** he took her to bed.

(**b**) (*de animal*) bed, bedding, litter.

(**c**) (*Zool*) den, lair.

(**d**) (*de carro*) floor.

(**e**) (*Geol*) layer, stratum; (*Culin*) layer.

camachuelo *nm* bullfinch.

camada *nf* (**a**) (*Zool*) litter; (*personas*) gang, band; *V* **lobo**. (**b**) (*Geol*) layer; (*Arquit*) course (of bricks); (*de huevos, frutas*) layer.

camafeo *nm* cameo.

camagua *nf* (*CAm*) ripening maize, ripening corn (*US*); (*Méx*) unripened maize.

camal *nm* (**a**) (*cabestro*) halter. (**b**) (*palo*) pole (from which dead pigs are hung); (*And: matadero*) slaughterhouse, abattoir.

camaleón *nm* chameleon.

camaleónico *adj* chameleon-like.

camalote *nm* camalote (*an aquatic plant*).

camama* *nf* (*mentira*) lie; (*engaño*) trick.

camamila *nf* camomile.

camanance *nm* (*CAm*) dimple.

camanchaca* *nf* (*Cono Sur*) thick fog, pea-souper*.

camándula *nf* rosary; **tener muchas ~s*** to be full of tricks, be a sly sort.

camandulear [1a] *vi* to be a hypocrite, be falsely devout; (*LAm*) (*intrigar*) to intrigue, scheme; (*vacilar*) to bumble, avoid taking decisions.

camandulería *nf* prudery, priggishness; hypocrisy, false devotion.

camandulero 1 *adj* (*remilgado*) prudish, priggish; (*hipócrita*) hypocritical; (*beato*) falsely devout; (*taimado*) sly, tricky; (*LAm*) (*enredador*) intriguing, scheming; (*zalamero*) fawning, bootlicking*.

2 *nm*, **camandulera** *nf* (*gazmoño*) prude, prig; (*hipócrita*) hypocrite; (*vividor*) sly sort, tricky person; (*LAm: intrigante*) intriguer, schemer.

cama-nido *nf, pl* **camas-nido** bunk-bed.

cámara 1 *nf* (**a**) (*cuarto, sala*) room, hall; **~ acorazada** strongroom, vault; **~ de aislamiento** isolation room; **~ ardiente, ~ mortuoria** funeral chamber; **~ congeladora** freezing compartment; **~ frigorífica** cold-storage room; **~ nupcial** bridal suite; **~ de tortura** torture chamber; **música de ~** chamber music.

(**b**) (*de reyes*) royal chamber; **médico de ~** royal doctor; **gentilhombre de ~** gentleman-in-waiting.

(**c**) (*Náut*) (*camarote*) stateroom, cabin; (*de pasajeros*) saloon; (*de oficiales de marina*) wardroom; **~ de cartas** chart house; **~ de motores** engine room.

(**d**) (*Agr*) granary.

(**e**) (*Pol etc*) chamber, house; **~ agraria** chamber of agriculture; **~ alta** upper house; **~ baja** lower house; **~ de comercio** chamber of commerce; **~ de compensación** (*Fin*) clearing house; **C~ de los Comunes** House of Commons; **~ legislativa** legislative assembly; **C~ de los Lores** House of Lords; **C~ de Representantes** House of Representatives.

(**f**) (*Mec, Fís*) chamber; **~ de aire** air chamber; **~ de combustión, ~ de explosión** combustion chamber; **~ de compresión** compression chamber; **~ de descompresión** decompression chamber; **~ de gas** (*de aeronave*) gasbag; (*de nazis etc*) gas chamber; **~ de oxígeno** oxygen tent; **~ de vacío** vacuum chamber.

(**g**) (*Aut etc*: *t* **~ de aire**) tyre, inner tube; **sin ~**

neumático tubeless.

(**h**) (*Mil*) breech, chamber.

(**i**) (*Anat*) cavity.

(**j**) (*Fot*: *t* ~ **fotográfica**) camera; ~ **de cine,** ~ **cinematográfica,** ~ **filmadora** cinecamera, film camera; **a** ~ **lenta** in slow motion; **a** ~ **rápida** speeded-up; ~ **oscura** camera obscura; ~ **de televisión,** ~ **televisora** television camera; ~ **de vídeo** video camera; **chupar** ~* to collar an unfair amount of TV time*, hog the limelight.

(**k**) ~**s** (*Med*) diarrhoea; stool; **tener ~s en la lengua*** to gossip a lot, tell tales (out of school).

2 *nm* cameraman.

camarada *nmf* comrade, companion; chum*, pal*, mate; (*Pol*) comrade.

camaradería *nf* comradeship; companionship; camaraderie; matiness*; (*Dep*) team spirit.

camarata‡ *nm* waiter.

camarera *nf* (*de restaurante*) waitress; (*de hotel*) maid, chambermaid; (*en casa*) parlourmaid; lady's maid; (*Náut*) stewardess; (*Cono Sur Aer*) stewardess, flight attendant (*US*).

camarero *nm* (*de restaurante*) waiter; (*Náut*) steward; ~ **mayor** (*Hist*) royal chamberlain; ~ **principal** head waiter.

camareta *nf* (*Náut*) cabin; messroom; ~ **alta** deckhouse.

camarico *nm* (*Cono Sur*) (**a**) (*lugar*) favourite place. (**b**) (*amor*) love affair.

camarilla *nf* (**a**) (*cuarto*) small room. (**b**) (*personas*) clique, coterie; entourage; (*Pol*) lobby, pressure group; faction.

camarín *nm* (**a**) (*Teat*) dressing room; (*tocador*) boudoir; (*cuarto pequeño*) side room; (*de ascensor*) lift car, elevator car (*US*); (*Náut*) cabin; (*LAm Ferro*) sleeping compartment.

(**b**) (*Ecl*) side-chapel (for a special image); room where jewels *etc* of an image are kept.

camarógrafo *nm* (*Cine, TV*) cameraman.

camarón *nm* (**a**) (*Zool*) shrimp, prawn. (**b**) (*CAm*: *propina*) tip, gratuity. (**c**) (*And**: *traidor*) turncoat; **hacer** ~ to change sides. (**d**) (*CAm**: *trabjo*) casual (*o* occasional) work. (**e**) (*Cono Sur*: *litera*) bunk (bed).

camaronear [1a] *vi* (**a**) (*Méx*: *pescar camarones*) to go shrimping. (**b**) (*And Pol*) to change sides.

camaronero *nm* (*And*) kingfisher.

camarote *nm* (*Náut*) cabin, stateroom; ~ **de lujo** first-class cabin.

camarotero *nm*, (*LAm*) steward, cabin servant.

camaruta* *nf* bar girl.

camastro *nm* rickety old bed.

camastrón 1 *adj* (*) sly, untrustworthy. **2** (*CAm*) large (*o* double) bed.

camayo(c) *nm* (*And*) foreman, overseer (*of a country estate*).

cambado *adj* (*And, Carib, Cono Sur*) bow-legged.

cambalache *nm* (**a**) (*cambio*) swap, exchange. (**b**) (*LAm*: *tienda*) second-hand shop, junk shop.

cambalach(e)ar [1a] *vt* to swap, exchange.

cambar [1a] *vt* (*Carib, Cono Sur*) = **combar**.

cámbaro *nm* crab.

cambiable *adj* (**a**) (*variable*) changeable; variable. (**b**) (*Com, Fin etc*) exchangeable.

cambiadiscos *nm invar* record-changer.

cambiadizo *adj* changeable.

cambiador *nm* barterer; moneychanger; (*And, Cono Sur, Méx*: *Ferro*) switchman.

cambiante 1 *adj* (**a**) (*variable*) changing; variable; *tiempo* changeable.

(**b**) (*pey*) fickle, temperamental.

2 *nm* (**a**) (*persona*) moneychanger.

(**b**) (*tela*) iridescent fabric.

(**c**) ~**s** changing colours, iridescence.

cambiar [1b] **1** *vt* (**a**) (*transformar*) to change, alter, convert, turn (en into).

(**b**) (*trocar*) to change, exchange (*con, por* for); ~ **libras en francos,** ~ **libras por francos** to change pounds into francs; ~ **saludos** to exchange greetings; ~ **sellos** to exchange stamps, swap stamps.

(**c**) (*trasladar*) to shift, move; **¿lo cambiamos a otro sitio?** shall we move it somewhere else?

2 *vi* (**a**) (*gen*) to change, alter; ((*Rad*) **¡cambio!** over!; **¡cambio y corto!** over and out!; ~ **a un nuevo sistema** to change (*o* switch) to a new system; **no ha cambiado nada** nothing has changed; **entonces, la cosa cambia** that alters matters; **está muy cambiado** he's changed a lot, he has greatly altered.

(**b**) ~ **de** to change; ~ **de casa** to move (house); ~ **de color** to change colour; ~ **de dueño** to change hands; ~ **de idea** to change one's mind; ~ **de ropa** to change one's clothes; ~ **de sitio** to shift, move; ~ **de sitio con uno** to change places with sb; **cambiamos de sombrero** we exchanged hats.

(**c**) (*viento*) to veer, change round.

(**d**) **mandarse a** ~ (*LAm*) to get out.

3 cambiarse *vr* (**a**) (*gen*) to change; (*viento*) to veer, change round.

(**b**) ~ **en** to change into, be changed into.

cambiario *adj* (*Fin*) exchange (*atr*); **estabilidad cambiaria** stability of (*o* in) the exchange rate; **liberalización cambiaria** freeing of exchange controls (*o* rates *etc*).

cambiavía *nm* (*Carib, Méx*: *Ferro*) (**a**) (*persona*) switchman. (**b**) (*agujas*) switch, points.

cambiazo *nm* (*Com*) (dishonest) switch; **dar el** ~ to switch the goods.

cambio *nm* (**a**) (*transformación*) change, alteration; changeover; substitution; (*de política etc*) change, switch, shift; (*de marea*) turn; (*de lugar*) shift, move (*a* to); **ha habido muchos ~s** there have been many changes; **el** ~ **se efectuó en 1970** the changeover took place in 1970; ~ **climático** climatic change; ~ **de decoración** (*Teat*) change of décor; ~ **de domicilio** change of address; ~ **de guardia** changing of the guard; ~ **de marchas,** ~ **de velocidades** (*Aut*) gear-change; **con** ~ **de marchas automático** with automatic transmission; ~ **de la marea** turn of the tide; ~ **de pareja** wife-swapping; ~ **radical** turning point; ~ **de tiempo** change in the weather; ~ **de vía** (*Ferro*) points.

(**b**) (*Fin*: *dinero*) change, small change; **¿tienes** ~ **encima?** have you any change on you?

(**c**) (*trueque*) exchange; barter; ~ **de impresiones** exchange of views; **libre** ~ free trade; **'admitimos su coche usado a** ~**'** 'we take your old car in part exchange'; **a** ~ **de** in exchange for, in return for; **la compañía pagó X pesetas a** ~ **de que la otra concediera ...** the company paid X pesetas in return for the other allowing ...; **en** ~ in exchange; on the other hand; instead.

(**d**) (*Fin*: *tipo*) rate of exchange; **al** ~ **de** at the rate of.

cambista *nm* moneychanger.

Camboya *nf* (*Hist*) Cambodia.

camboyano, -a *adj, nm/f* Cambodian.

cambray *nm* cambric.

cambrón *nm* buckthorn; hawthorn; bramble.

cambrona *nf* (*Cono Sur††*) tough cotton cloth.

cambucho *nm* (*Cono Sur*) (*cono*) paper cone; (*cesta*) straw basket for waste paper (*o* dirty clothes); (*envase*) straw cover (*for a bottle*); (*cuartucho*) miserable little room, hovel.

cambujo *adj* (*CAm, Méx*) *animal* black; *persona* dark, swarthy.

cambullón *nm* (*And, Cono Sur*) (*estafa*) swindle; (*compló*) plot, intrigue; (*cambio*) swap, exchange.

cambur *nm* (**a**) (*Carib*: *plátano*) banana; (*árbol*) banana tree. (**b**) (*: *prebenda*) government post, soft job, cushy number‡; (*dinero*) windfall. (**c**) public servant, state employee.

cambuto *adj* (*And*) small, squat; chubby.

camelar* [1a] *vt* (**a**) *mujer* to flirt with; to attract, get off with*; to make up to*. (**b**) (*persuadir*) to cajole, blarney; to win over; **tener camelado a uno** to have sb wrapped round one's little finger. (**c**) (*Méx*) (*mirar*) to look into, look towards (*etc*); (*perseguir*) to pursue, hound.

camelia *nf* camellia.

camelista* *nmf* flatterer, creep‡.

camelo *nm* (**a**) (*flirteo*) flirtation.

(**b**) (*broma*) joke, hoax; (*cuento*) cock-and-bull story; (*bola*) humbug; (*coba*) blarney; **dar** ~ **a uno** to make fun of sb; to put one over on sb; **me huele a** ~ it smells fishy*, there's something funny going on here; **¡esto es un** ~**!*** it's all a swindle!

camellar* [1a] *vi* (*Carib*) to work (hard).

camellear* *vi* to push drugs, be a pusher.

camelleo* *nm* drug-pushing.

camellero *nm* camel-driver.

camello *nm* (**a**) (*Zool*) camel. (**b**) (*) drug-pusher.

camellón *nm* (*bebedero*) drinking trough; (*Agr*) ridge (*between furrows*); (*Méx Aut*) central reservation, divider (*US*).

camerino *nm* (*Teat*) dressing room; (*Méx Ferro*) roomette.

camero *adj* (**a**) (*gen*) bed (*atr*); for a large single bed. (**b**) (*Carib*: *grande*) big.

Camerún *nm* Cameroon.

camilucho *nm* (*Cono Sur, Méx*) Indian day labourer.

camilla nf (sofá) sofa, couch; (cuna) cot; (mesa) table with a heater underneath; (Med) stretcher.

camillero, -a nm/f stretcher-bearer.

caminante nmf traveller, wayfarer; walker.

caminar [1a] 1 vt distancia to cover, travel, do.

2 vi (a) (gen) to walk, go; (viajar) to travel, journey; (río etc) to go, move, flow; (fig) to act, move, go; venir caminando (LAm) to come on foot; ~ derecho to behave properly; ~ con pena to trudge along, move with difficulty.

(b) (LAm Mec) to work.

caminata nf (paseo largo) long walk; (por el campo) hike, ramble; (excursión) excursion, outing, jaunt.

caminero 1 adj road (atr); V peón. 2 nm (LAm) road builder.

caminito nm: ~ de rosas (fig) primrose path.

camino nm (a) (carretera) road; (Méx) (main) road; (sendero) track, path; trail; (Inform) path; ~ de acceso, ~ de entrada approach road; ~ de Damasco road to Damascus, road to conversion; ~ sin firme unsurfaced road; ~ forestal forest track; ~ francés (Hist), ~ de Santiago pilgrims' road to Santiago de Compostela; C~ de Santiago (Astron) Milky Way; ~ de herradura bridle path; ~ de ingresos, ~ de peaje toll road; ~ real highroad (t fig); ~ de sirga towpath; ~ de tierra dirt track; ~ trillado well-trodden path; (fig) beaten track; tener el ~ trillado (fig) to have the ground prepared for one; ~ vecinal country road, lane, by-road; C~s, Canales y Puertos (Univ) Civil Engineering.

(b) (dirección, distancia etc; t fig) way, road (de to), route; journey; (fig) way, path, course; el ~ a seguir the route to follow; el ~ de La Paz the way to La Paz; the La Paz road; es el ~ del desastre that is the road to disaster, that way lies disaster; el ~ de en medio (fig) the middle way, the way of compromise; ~ de Lima on the way to Lima; vamos ~ de la muerte death awaits us all; a medio ~ halfway (there); de ~ on the way, (fig) in passing; tienen otro niño de ~ they have another child on the way; en el ~ on the way, en route; está en ~ de desaparecer it's on its way out; después de 3 horas de ~ after travelling for 3 hours; nos quedan 20 kms de ~ we still have 20 kms to go; es mucho ~ it's a long way; ¿cuánto ~ hay de aquí a San José? how far is it from here to San Jose?; por (el) buen ~ along the right road; ir por (el) buen ~ (fig) to be on the right track; ¿vamos por buen ~? are we on the right road?; traer a uno por buen ~ (fig) to put sb on the right road; to disabuse sb; abrirse ~ to make one's way; allanar el ~ to smooth the way (a uno for sb); echar ~ adelante to strike out; errar el ~ to lose one's way; ir por su ~ to go one's own sweet way; todos los ~s van a Roma all roads lead to Rome; llevar a uno por mal ~ (fig) to lead sb astray; partir el ~ con uno to meet sb halfway; ponerse en ~ to set out, set forth, start; quedarse en el ~ (fig) to be left behind, be left in the lurch.

(c) (And, Cono Sur: tira) runner, strip of carpet (o matting etc); ~ de mesa table runner.

camión nm (Aut) lorry, truck (esp US); van; (de caballos) heavy wagon, dray; (Méx: autobús) bus; ~ de agua water cart, water wagon; ~ de la basura dustcart, garbage truck (US); ~ blindado troop carrier; ~ de bomberos fire engine; ~ cisterna tanker, tank wagon; ~ frigorífico refrigerator lorry; ~ ganadero cattle truck; ~ de mudanzas removal van; ~ de reparto delivery truck; ~ de riego water cart, water wagon; ~ volquete dumper; está como un ~* she looks smashing*.

camionaje nm haulage, cartage.

camionero, -a nm/f lorry driver, truckdriver (US), teamster (US).

camioneta nf van, light truck; (LAm) station-wagon; (CAm) bus; (Carib) minibus; ~ detectora detector van; ~ de reparto delivery van; ~ de tina (CAm) pick-up (truck).

camión-grúa nm, pl camiones-grúa tow-truck, towing vehicle.

camionista nm = camionero.

camion-tanque nm, pl camiones-tanque (Aut) tanker.

camisa nf (a) (de hombre) shirt; ~ (de mujer, de señora) chemise, slip; (LAm) garment, article of clothing; ~ de deporte sports shirt, vest; ~ de dormir nightdress; ~ de fuerza straitjacket; ~ de rayas striped shirt; cambiar de ~ to turn one's coat, change one's colours; estar en (mangas de) ~ to be in one's shirt-sleeves; dejar a uno sin ~ to leave sb destitute, clean sb out*; jugarse hasta la ~ to bet one's bottom dollar; no le llegaba la ~ al cuerpo he was simply terrified; meterse en ~ de once varas to interfere in other people's affairs; to bite off more than one can chew; recibir a una mujer sin ~* to take a wife without a dowry.

(b) (Bot) skin; (Zool: de culebra) slough.

(c) (Mec) jacket; case, casing; sleeve; ~ de agua water jacket; ~ de gas gas mantle.

(d) (carpeta) folder (for papers); (Tip) jacket, dust jacket, wrapper.

camisería nf outfitter's (shop).

camisero nm (a) (persona) shirt maker; outfitter. (b) (prenda) shirt dress.

camiseta nf vest, undershirt (US); (Dep) singlet, shirt, vest; (LAm) nightdress; ~ (con dibujo) T-shirt.

camisilla nf (Carib, Cono Sur) = camiseta.

camisola nf (Méx) sports shirt.

camisolín nm stiff shirt front, dickey.

camisón nm (t ~ de noche) nightdress, nightgown; (de hombre) nightgown.

camita[1], camítico adj Hamitic.

camita[2] nf small bed, cot.

camomila nf camomile.

camón nm big bed; (Arquit) oriel window; ~ de vidrios glass partition.

camorra nf row, set-to*; armar ~ to kick up a row; buscar ~ to go looking for trouble.

camorrear* [1a] vi (CAm, Cono Sur) to have a row.

camorrero nm = camorrista.

camorrista 1 adj quarrelsome, rowdy, brawling. 2 nmf quarrelsome person, rowdy element, hooligan.

camotal nm (LAm) sweet potato field (o plot).

camote nm (a) (LAm Bot) sweet potato; (Méx: bulbo) tuber, bulb.

(b) (CAm, Cono Sur: Med) bump, swelling.

(c) (Cono Sur: piedra) large stone.

(d) (Cono Sur: persona) bore, tedious person.

(e) (CAm: de pierna) calf of the leg.

(f) (CAm*: molestia) nuisance, bother.

(g) (LAm: amor) love; crush*; tener un ~ con uno to have a crush on sb*.

(h) (And, Cono Sur*: amante) lover, sweetheart.

(i) (Cono Sur: mentirilla) fib.

(j) (And, Cono Sur: tonto) fool.

(k) (LAm*) poner a uno como ~ to give sb a telling off*; tragar ~ (tener miedo) to have one's heart in one's mouth; (balbucir) to stammer.

camotear [1a] 1 vt (a) (Cono Sur: estafar) to rob, fleece; to take for a ride*.

(b) (CAm: molestar) to annoy.

2 vi (CAm: molestar) to be trying, cause trouble.

campa 1 adj invar: tierra ~ treeless land.

2 nf open field, open space.

campal adj: batalla ~ pitched battle.

campamentista nmf camper.

campamento nm camp; encampment; ~ de base base camp; ~ para prisioneros prison camp; ~ de refugiados refugee camp; ~ de trabajo labour camp; ~ de veraneo holiday camp.

campana nf (a) (gen) bell; a ~ herida, a ~ tañida, a toque de ~ to the sound of bells; echar las ~s a vuelo to peal the bells; (fig) to proclaim sth from the rooftops; to rejoice, celebrate (prematurely); estar ~ (Carib*) to be fine; hacer ~* to play truant; oír ~s y no saber dónde to get hold of the wrong end of the stick; tañer las ~s, tocar las ~s to peal the bells; tocar la ~** to wank**.

(b) (objeto) bell-shaped object; ~ de bucear, ~ de buzo diving bell; ~ de cristal bell glass, glass cover; ~ extractora extractor hood.

(c) (LAm*: ladrón) thieves' look-out; hacer de ~ to keep watch, be look-out.

campanada nf (a) (Mús) stroke, peal (of a bell); (sound of) ringing; dar la ~ to sound the alarm (t fig).

(b) (fig: escándalo) scandal, sensation, commotion; dar una ~ to make a big stir, cause a great surprise.

campanario nm (a) (de iglesia etc) belfry, bell tower, church tower. (b) (pey) de ~ mean, narrow-minded; espíritu de ~ parochial spirit, parish-pump attitude.

campanazo nm (a) = campanada. (b) (And: advertencia) warning.

campaneado adj (fig) much talked-of.

campanear [1a] vi (a) (Mús) to ring the bells. (b) (LAm*: ladrón) to keep watch.

campaneo nm bell ringing, pealing, chimes.

campanero nm (Téc) bell founder; (Mús) bell-ringer.

campaniforme adj bell-shaped.

campanilla *nf* (**a**) (*campana*) small bell, handbell, electric bell; **de muchas ~s*** big, grand; high-class.
(**b**) (*burbuja*) bubble.
(**c**) (*Anat*) uvula.
(**d**) (*Cos*) tassel.
(**e**) (*Bot*) bellflower; harebell; **~ blanca, ~ de febrero** snowdrop.
campanillazo *nm* loud ring, sudden ring.
campanillear [1a] *vi* to ring, tinkle.
campanilleo *nm* ringing, tinkling.
campanología *nf* campanology, bell-ringing.
campanólogo, -a *nm/f* campanologist, bell-ringer.
campante *adj* (**a**) (*destacado*) outstanding.
(**b**) (*pey*) self-satisfied, smug; **siguió tan ~** he went on cheerfully, he went on as if nothing had happened; **allí estaba tan ~** there he was as large as life, there he sat (*etc*) as cool as a cucumber.
campanudo *adj* (**a**) *objeto* bell-shaped; *falda* wide, spreading. (**b**) *estilo* high-flown, bombastic, sonorous; *orador* pompous, windy; **dijo ~** he said pompously.
campánula *nf* bellflower, campanula.
campaña *nf* (**a**) (*campo*) countryside; (*llanura*) level country, plain; (*LAm*) country, countryside; **batir la ~, correr la ~** to reconnoitre.
(**b**) (*Mil, Pol, fig*) campaign; (*Com*) sales drive; **~ denigratoria** smear campaign; **~ de imagen** campaign to improve one's image; **~ publicitaria** advertising campaign, publicity campaign; **de ~** (*Mil*) field (*atr*), campaign (*atr*); **hacer ~** to campaign; **hacer ~ en contra de** to campaign against; **hacer ~ a favor de** (*o* **en pro de**) to campaign for.
(**c**) (*Náut*) cruise, expedition, trip.
(**d**) (*Agr etc*) season.
campañol *nm* vole.
campar [1a] *vi* (**a**) (*Mil etc*) to camp. (**b**) (*destacar*) to stand out, excel; *V* **respeto**.
campear [1a] *vi* (**a**) (*Agr*) (*ganado*) to go to graze, go out to pasture; (*hombre*) to work in the fields.
(**b**) (*Bot*) to show green.
(**c**) (*Mil*) to reconnoitre; (*LAm*) to scour the countryside.
(**d**) **ir campeando*** to carry on, keep going.
(**e**) (*LAm*: *ir de camping*) to camp, go camping.
(**f**) (*And*: *atravesar*) to make one's way through.
(**g**) (*And*: *fardar*) to bluster.
campechana[1] *nf* (**a**) (*Carib, Méx*: *bebida*) cocktail. (**b**) (*Méx*: *de mariscos*) seafood cocktail.
campechanería *nf* (*LAm*), **campechanía** *nf* frankness, openness; heartiness, cheerfulness, geniality; fellow feeling; generosity.
campechano *adj* (**a**) (*franco*) frank, open; (*cordial*) good-hearted, hearty, cheerful, genial; (*amigable*) comradely; (*generoso*) generous. (**b**) (*Carib**) peasant (*atr*).
campeón *nm*, **campeona** *nf* champion; **~ de venta** best seller, best-selling article.
campeonar [1a] *vi* to win the championship, emerge as champion.
campeonato *nm* championship; **de ~** (*) (*a ultranza*) absolute, out-and-out; (*enorme*) huge, really big; (*estupendo*) smashing*.
campeonísimo, -a *nm/f* undisputed champion.
campera *nf* (*Cono Sur*) windcheater.
campero 1 *adj* (**a**) (*descubierto*) unsheltered, (out) in the open; open-air (*atr*); **ganado ~** stock that sleeps out in the open.
(**b**) (*LAm*) *persona* knowledgeable about the countryside; expert in farming matters; *animal* trained to travel in difficult country, sure-footed.
2 *nm* (*And*) jeep, land rover.
camperuso* (*Carib*) **1** *adj* (**a**) rural, rustic. (**b**) (*huraño*) reserved, stand-offish. **2** *nm*, **camperusa** *nf* peasant.
campesina *nf* peasant (woman).
campesinado *nm* peasantry, peasants.
campesino 1 *adj* (**a**) country (*atr*), rural; peasant (*atr*); (*pey*) rustic. (**b**) (*Zool*) field (*atr*). **2** *nm* (**a**) (*paisano*) peasant; countryman; farmer; (*pey*) peasant. (**b**) (*And*: *indio*) Indian.
campestre *adj* (**a**) country (*atr*), rural. (**b**) (*Bot*) wild.
cámping ['kampin] *nm*, *pl* **cámpings** ['kampin] (**a**) (*acto*) camping; **estar de ~** to be on a camping holiday; **hacer ~** to go camping. (**b**) (*sitio*) campsite, camping site, camping ground.
campiña *nf* countryside, open country; flat stretch of farmland, large area of cultivated land.
campirano *nm* (*LAm*) (**a**) (*campesino*) peasant; (*pey*) rustic, country bumpkin.
(**b**) (*Agr*) (*perito*) expert in farming matters; (*guía*) guide, pathfinder; (*jinete*) skilled horseman; (*ganadero*) stockbreeding expert.
campiruso (*Carib*) = **camperuso.**
campista[1] *nmf* camper.
campista[2] **1** *adj* (**a**) (*CAm, Carib*) rural, country (*atr*). (**b**) (*LAm*) = **campero 1 (b)**. **2** *nm* (*CAm*) herdsman.
campisto 1 *adj* (*CAm*) rural, country (*atr*). **2** *nm* (**a**) (*CAm*: *campesino*) peasant. (**b**) (*CAm Agr*) amateur vet.
campo *nm* (**a**) (*gen*) country, countryside; **~ abierto, ~ raso** open country; **a ~ raso** in the open; **~ a través** cross-country (running); **ir a ~ traviesa, ir ~ travieso** to go across country, take a cross-country route; **ir al ~** to go into the country; **¿te gusta el ~?** do you like the country (side)?; **el ~ está espléndido** the countryside looks lovely.
(**b**) (*Agr*; *t Inform, Mil, Fís etc*) field; (*Dep*) field, ground, pitch; **~ alfanumérico** alphanumeric field; **~ de aterrizaje** landing field; **~ aurífero** goldfield; **~ de aviación** airfield; **~ de batalla** battlefield; **~ de deportes** sports ground, playing field; recreation ground; **~ de ejercicios** (*Mil*) drilling ground; **C~s Elíseos, C~s Elíseos** Elysian Fields; **~ de fuego** field of fire; **~ de fútbol** football ground, football pitch; **~ de golf** golf course, golf links; **~ gravitatorio** field of gravity; **~ de instrucción** (*Mil*) drilling ground; **~ de juego** playground; **~ magnético** magnetic field; **~ de minas** minefield; **~ numérico** numeric field; **~ petrolífero** oilfield; **~ de pruebas** testing ground (*t fig*); **~s de riego** (*euf*) sewage farm; **~ santo** cemetery, churchyard; **~ de tiro** firing range; **~ visual** field of vision; **~ de vuelo** flying field; **trabajo de ~, trabajo en el propio ~** fieldwork; **experiencia de ~** experience in the field, experience of fieldwork; **abandonar el ~, levantar el ~** (*Mil*) to retire from the field; (*fig*) to give up the struggle; **batir el ~, reconocer el ~** to reconnoitre; **dejar el ~ libre** to leave the field open (*para* for); **se le hizo el ~ orégano** (*Cono Sur*) it all turned out nicely for him; **quedar en el ~** to fall in battle; to be killed in a duel.
(**c**) (*And*: *estancia*) farm, ranch; farmhouse; (*Cono Sur*: *tierra pobre*) barren land; (*And, Cono Sur*: *Min*) mining concession.
(**d**) (*Arte*) ground, background; (*Her*) field.
(**e**) (*Mil etc*) camp; **~ (de) base** base camp; **~ de concentración** concentration camp; **~ de internamiento** internment camp; **~ de trabajo** labour camp.
(**f**) (*equipo, en juegos*) side.
(**g**) (*LAm*: *sitio*) space, room; **~ de maniobras** room for manoeuvre; **no hay ~** there's no room.
(**h**) (*fig*: *esfera*) scope; range, sphere; **el ~ de aplicación del invento** the scope of the invention, the range of application of the invention; **hay ~ para más** there is scope for more; **dar ~ a** to give free range to, allow ample scope for.
camposantero *nm* cemetery official.
camposanto *nm* cemetery, churchyard.
CAMPSA, Campsa ['kampsa] *nf* (*Esp*) *abr de* **Compañía Arrendataria de Monopolio de Petróleos, S.A.**
campus *nm invar* (*Univ*) campus.
campusano *nm*, **campus(i)o** *nm* (*CAm etc*) peasant.
camuesa *nf* pippin, dessert apple.
camueso *nm* (**a**) (*Bot*) pippin tree. (**b**) (*: *tonto*) dolt, blockhead.
camuflado *adj* camouflaged; *coche policial* unmarked.
camuflaje *nm* camouflage.
camuflar [1a] *vt* (*t fig*) to camouflage.
can *nm* (**a**) (*Zool*: † *o hum*) dog, hound (*hum*). (**b**) (*Mil*) trigger. (**c**) (*Arquit*) corbel.
cana[1] *nf* (*t ~s*) white hair, grey hair; **echar una ~ al aire** to let one's hair down, cut loose; **faltar a las ~s** to show a lack of respect for one's elders; **peina ~s** he's getting on.
cana[2] (*LAm**) **1** *nf* (**a**) (*cárcel*) jail; (*celda*) prison cell; **caer en ~** to land in jail. (**b**) (*policía*) police. **2** *nm* policeman.
canabis *nm* cannabis.
canaca *nmf* (**a**) (*And, Cono Sur**: *chino*) Chink*, Chinese. (**b**) (*Cono Sur*) (*dueño*) brothel-keeper; (*burdel*) brothel.
Canadá *nm*: **el ~** Canada.
canadiense 1 *adj, nmf* Canadian. **2** *nm* (*prenda*: *t* **chaqueta ~**) lumber jacket.
canal[1] *nm* (**a**) (*Náut*) canal; waterway; **C~ de Panamá** Panama Canal; **C~ de Suez** Suez Canal; **~ de navegación** ship canal; **~ de riego** irrigation channel.
(**b**) (*Náut*: *parte de río etc*) deep channel; navigation

channel.

(**c**) (*Geog*) channel, strait; **C~ de la Mancha** English Channel.

(**d**) (*Anat*) canal, duct, tract; **~ digestivo** digestive tract, alimentary canal.

(**e**) (*TV*) channel; **~ de pago** pay channel, subscription channel.

(**f**) (*de cinta*) track.

(**g**) (*Carib Aut*) lane.

canal[2] *nm o f* (**a**) (*tubo*) conduit, pipe; underground watercourse; **~ de desagüe** (*And*) sewer; **~ de humo** (*Méx*) flue; **~ inclinado** chute.

(**b**) (*Arquit*: *canalón etc*) gutter, guttering; spout; drainpipe.

(**c**) (*Arquit*: *estría*) groove, fluting.

(**d**) (*Geog*) narrow valley.

(**e**) (*carne*) dressed carcass; **abrir en ~** to cut down the middle, slit open.

(**f**) (*escote*) cleavage.

canaladura *nf* fluting; *V t* **acanaladura.**

canaleta *nf* (*Cono Sur*) pipe, conduit; roof gutter.

canalete *nm* paddle.

canalización *nf* (**a**) (*acto*) canalization, channelling. (**b**) (*Téc*) piping; (*Elec*) wiring; (*de gas etc*) mains; (*LAm*: *de cloacas*) sewerage system, drainage.

canalizar [1f] *vt río etc* to canalize; to confine between banks, rebuild the banks (*o* course) of; *agua* to harness; to pipe; *aguas de riego* to channel; (*Elec*) *impulso, mensaje* to carry; (*fig*) *intereses etc* to channel, direct.

canalizo *nm* navigable channel.

canalón *nm* (**a**) (*Arquit*) gutter, guttering; spout; drainpipe; (*de disco*) groove. (**b**) (*sombrero*) shovel hat. (**c**) **canalones** (*Culin*) cannelloni.

canalla 1 *nf* rabble, mob, riffraff. **2** *nm* swine*, rotter*; ¡~! you swine!*

canallada *nf*, **canallería** *nf* (*LAm*) (*acto*) dirty trick, mean thing (to do), despicable act; (*dicho*) nasty remark, vile thing (to say).

canallesco *adj* mean, rotten*, despicable; **diversión canallesca** low form of amusement.

canana *nf* (**a**) (*Mil*) cartridge belt. (**b**) (*LAm Med*) goitre. (**c**) (*Carib*: *mala pasada*) mean trick, low prank. (**d**) **~s** (*And*) handcuffs.

canapé *nm* (**a**) (*mueble*) sofa, settee, couch. (**b**) (*Culin*) canapé.

Canarias *nfpl, t* **Islas** *nfpl* **Canarias** Canaries, Canary Isles.

canario 1 *adj* of the Canary Isles. **2** *nm*, **canaria** *f* native (*o* inhabitant) of the Canary Isles; **los ~s** the people of the Canary Isles. **3** *nm* (**a**) (*Orn*) canary. (**b**) (**) prick**. (**c**) (*LAm*: *amarillo*) yellow. **4** *interj* (*) well I'm blowed!*

canarión, -ona *nm/f* native (*o* inhabitant) of Gran Canaria.

canasta *nf* (**a**) (*gen*) (round) basket; (*de comida*) hamper; (*Com*) crate; (*Baloncesto*) basket; **~ para papeles** wastepaper basket. (**b**) (*juego*) canasta.

canastero, -a *nm/f* basket maker.

canastilla *nf* (**a**) (*gen*) small basket; (*Méx*: *de basura*) wastepaper basket; **~ de la costura** sewing basket.

(**b**) (*de bebé*) (baby's) layette.

(**c**) (*And, Carib, Cono Sur*: *de novia*) trousseau, (*hum*) bottom drawer, (*US*) hope chest.

canastillo *nm* (**a**) (*bandeja*) wicker tray, small basket. (**b**) (*de bebé*) layette.

canasto *nm* (**a**) (*gen*) large basket; (*de comida*) hamper; (*Com*) crate. (**b**) (*And*: *criado*) servant. (**c**) **¡~s!** good heavens!

cáncamo *nm* (*Náut*) eyebolt; **~ de argolla** ringbolt.

cancamurria* *nf* blues, gloom.

cancamusa* *nf* trick; **armar una ~ a uno** to throw sand in sb's eyes.

cancán *nm* (**a**) (*Mús*) cancan. (**b**) (*Cos*) flounced petticoat.

cáncana *nf* (*Cono Sur*) (*de asar*) spit, jack; (*de vela*) candlestick; (*And*) thin person.

cancanco* *nm* (*Carib Aut*) breakdown.

cancanear [1a] *vi* (**a**) (*gandulear*) to loiter, loaf about.

(**b**) (*Cono Sur*: *bailar*) to dance the cancan.

(**c**) (*And, CAm, Méx*) (*expresarse*) to express o.s. with difficulty; (*tartamudear*) to stammer; (*leer mal*) to read haltingly, falter in reading

cancaneo *nm* (*And, CAm, Méx*) (*al leer*) faltering; (*tartamudeo*) stammering.

cáncano* *nm* louse; **andar como ~ loco** to go round in circles.

cancel *nm* windproof door, storm door; (*LAm*) (*mampara*) folding screen; (*tabique*) partition, thin wall.

cancela *nf* lattice gate, wrought-iron gate; outer door, outer gate.

cancelación *nf*, **cancelamiento** *nm* cancellation; (*Inform*) deletion.

cancelar [1a] *vt* (*gen*) to cancel; *deuda* to write off, wipe out; (*Inform*) to delete; (*LAm*) *cuenta* to pay, settle; *decisión* to cancel, annul; (*fig*) to dispel, banish (from one's mind); to do away with.

cancelaría *nf* papal chancery.

cáncer *nm* (**a**) (*Med*) cancer; **~ de cuello uterino, ~ cervical** cervical cancer; **~ de los huesos** bone cancer; **~ de mama** breast cancer; **~ de pulmón** lung cancer. (**b**) **C~** (*Zodíaco*) Cancer.

cancerado *adj* cancerous; (*fig*) corrupt.

cancerarse [1a] *vr* (**a**) (*Med*) (*órgano etc*) to become cancerous; (*persona*) to get cancer, have cancer. (**b**) (*fig*) to become corrupt.

cancerígeno *adj* carcinogenic.

cancerbero *nm* goalkeeper.

cancerología *nf* study of cancer, carcinology.

cancerólogo, -a *nm/f* cancer specialist.

canceroso 1 *adj* cancerous. **2** *nm*, **cancerosa** *nf* cancer patient, cancer sufferer.

canciller *nm* chancellor; (*LAm*) foreign minister.

cancilleresco *adj* (**a**) (*Admin*) chancellery (*atr*), chancery (*atr*); diplomatic. (**b**) (*fig*) formal, ceremonious; ruled by protocol.

cancillería *nf* (*en embajada*) chancery, chancellery; (*LAm*) ministry of foreign affairs, foreign ministry.

canción *nf* song; (*Liter*) lyric, song; **~ amatoria** lovesong; **~ de copas** drinking-song; **~ de cuna** lullaby, cradlesong; **~ infantil** nursery-rhyme; **¡siempre la misma ~!** the same old story!; **dejar como la ~ a uno*** to stand sb up*; **volvemos a la misma ~** here we go again, you're harping on the same old theme.

cancionero *nm* (*Mús*) songbook, collection of songs; (*Liter*) anthology, collection of verse.

cancionista *nmf* (**a**) (*compositor*) songwriter. (**b**) (*cantante*) ballad-singer; singer, vocalist, crooner.

canción-protesta *nf, pl* **canciones-protesta** protest song.

canco *nm* (**a**) (*Cono Sur*) (*jarro*) earthenware jug; (*tiesto*) flowerpot; (*orinal*) chamberpot. (**b**) **~s** (*And, Cono Sur*: *Anat*) buttocks; hips. (**c**) (‡: *homosexual*) queer‡, fairy‡.

cancro *nm* (*Bot*) canker; (*Med*) cancer.

cancha[1] *nf* (**a**) (*en algunos sentidos, esp LAm*) field, ground; (*descampado*) open space, tract of level ground; (*Dep*) sports-field; (*de tenis*) court; (*de fútbol*) pitch; (*de gallos*) cockpit; (*hipódromo*) racetrack; (*And, Cono Sur*) wide part of a river; (*Cono Sur*) path, road; **¡~!** (*Cono Sur*) gangway!; **~ de aterrizaje** landing ground; **~ de carreras** racecourse; racetrack; **~ de fútbol** football ground; **~ de golf** golfcourse; **~ de pelota** pelota court; **~ de tenis** tennis court; **abrir ~, dar ~, hacer ~** to make way, make room (*a* for); to provide facilities (*a* for); **estar en su ~** (*Cono Sur*) to be in one's element; **tener ~** (*Cono Sur**) (*experiencia*) to be experienced, be an expert; (*influencia*) to have clout*, have pull; **tener ~ a algo** (*Carib**) to be good at sth; **en la ~ se ven los pingos** (*LAm*) actions speak louder than words.

(**b**) (*And**: *tajada*) cut.

cancha[2] *nf* (*And*) (*maíz*) toasted maize, popcorn; (*habas*) toasted beans.

canchar [1a] *vt* (*And, Cono Sur*) to toast.

canche *adj* (**a**) (*CAm*: *rubio*) blond(e). (**b**) (*And*: *soso*) poorly seasoned, tasteless.

canchero, -a *nm/f* (**a**) (*experimentado*) experienced person. (**b**) (*Dep*: *jugador*) experienced player; (*LAm*: *cuidador*) groundsman, groundswoman. (**c**) (*Cono Sur*: *vago*) layabout, loafer.

canchón *nm* (*And*) enclosed field.

candado *nm* (**a**) (*gen*) padlock; (*de libro*) clasp; **~ digital** combination lock; **poner algo bajo siete ~s** to lock sth safely away. (**b**) (*And*: *barba*) goatee beard.

candanga *nm*: **el ~** (*Méx*) the devil.

candar [1a] *vt* to lock; to lock up, put away.

cande *adj*: **azúcar ~** sugar candy, rock candy.

candeal 1 *adj*: **pan ~** white bread; **trigo ~** bread wheat. **2** *nm* (*And, Cono Sur*) egg flip.

candela *nf* (**a**) (*vela*) candle; (*candelero*) candlestick; (*Fís*) candle power, candela; **en ~** (*Náut*) vertical; **se le acabó la ~**‡ he snuffed it‡; **arrimar ~ a uno*** to give sb a tanning*; **estar con la ~ en la mano** (*fig*) to be at death's door.

(**b**) (*esp LAm*: *fuego*) fire; (*para cigarrillo*) light; **dar ~** to be a nuisance, be trying; **echar ~** (*ojos etc*) to sparkle; **pegar ~ a, prender ~ a** to set fire to, set alight.

candelabro *nm* candelabrum.

Candelaria *nf* Candlemas.

candelaria *nf* (*Bot*) mullein.

candelejón* *adj* (*And*) simple, slow.

candelero *nm* (**a**) (*velador*) candlestick; (*lámpara*) oil lamp; **tema en ~** hot subject, subject of great current interest; **estar en (el) ~** (*persona*) to be high up, be in a position of authority; (*suceso*) to be under way, be in progress; (*tema*) to be of keen current interest; **poner a uno en (el) ~** to give sb a high post; **poner algo en ~** to bring sth into the limelight.

(**b**) (*Náut*) stanchion.

candelilla *nf* (**a**) (*vela*) small candle.

(**b**) (*Bot*) catkin.

(**c**) (*LAm*: *luciérnaga*) glow-worm; (*Cono Sur*: *libélula*) dragonfly; (*And*: *niño*) lively child.

(**d**) (*Carib, Cono Sur*: *Cos*) hem, border.

candelizo *nm* icicle.

candelo *adj* (*And*) reddish-blond(e).

candencia *nf* white heat.

candente *adj* (**a**) (*encendido*) red-hot, white-hot; glowing, burning. (**b**) (*fig*) *cuestión* burning; important, pressing, urgent; *atmósfera etc* charged, electric.

candi *adj*: **azúcar ~** sugar candy, rock candy.

candidatizar [1f] *vt* to propose, nominate.

candidato, -a *nm/f* (**a**) (*pretendiente*) candidate (*a* for); applicant (*a* for). (**b**) (*Cono Sur*‡) sucker‡.

candidatura *nf* candidature.

candidez *nf* (**a**) (*cualidad*) simplicity, ingenuousness, innocence; naïveté; stupidity. (**b**) (*una ~*) silly remark.

cándido *adj* (**a**) (*ingenuo*) simple, ingenuous, innocent; naïve; (*pey*) stupid. (**b**) (*poét*) snow-white.

candil *nm* (**a**) (*lámpara*) oil lamp, kitchen lamp, (*Méx*) chandelier; (**poder**) **arder en un ~** (*fig*) (*vino*) to be very strong; (*tema etc*) to be pretty strong stuff.

(**b**) (*Zool*) tine, point, small horn.

candileja *nf* oil reservoir of a lamp; small oil lamp; **~s** (*Teat*) footlights.

candinga[1] *nf* (*Cono Sur*) impertinence, insistence.

candinga[2] *nm*: **el ~** (*Méx*) the devil.

candiota *nf* wine cask.

candiotero *nm* cooper.

candonga *nf* (**a**) (‡: *puta*) whore. (**b**) (*Fin*‡) one peseta. (**c**) (‡ *Anat*) scrotum. (**d**) (*: *lisonjas*) blarney, flattery; (*truco*) trick; (*broma*) playful trick, hoax, practical joke; (*guasa*) teasing; **dar ~ a uno** to tease sb, kid sb*. (**e**) **~s** (*And*) earrings.

candongo* *adj* **1** (*zalamero*) smooth, oily; (*taimado*) sly, crafty; (*vago*) lazy. **2** *nm* (*cobista*) creep‡, toady, flatterer; (*taimado*) sly sort; (*vago*) shirker, idler, lazy blighter‡.

candonguear* [1a] **1** *vt* to tease, kid*. **2** *vi* to shirk, dodge work.

candonguero* *adj* = **candongo 1**.

candor *nm* (**a**) (*inocencia*) innocence, guilelessness, simplicity; frankness, candidness. (**b**) (*poét*) pure whiteness.

candorosamente *adv* innocently, guilelessly, simply; frankly, candidly.

candoroso *adj* innocent, guileless, simple; *confesión etc* frank, candid.

candungo *nm* (*And*) idiot.

canear* [1a] *vt* to bash*, hit.

caneca *nf* (**a**) (*Cono Sur*: *balde*) wooden bucket; (*Carib*: *bolsa de agua*) hot-water bottle; (*And*) can, tin; (*de petróleo etc*) drum; (*porrón*) wine bottle (with a spout); (*Méx*) glazed earthenware bottle.

(**b**) (*And, Carib*) *liquid measure = 19 litres*.

caneco *adj* (*And*) tipsy.

canela *nf* (**a**) (*Bot, Culin*) cinnamon. (**b**) (*fig*) lovely thing, exquisite object; **es ~ fina** she's wonderful; **es ~ en rama** she's a very sweet person; *V* **flor.** (**c**) (*Carib*: *mulata*) mulatto girl. (**d**) *interj* (*euf*) good gracious!

canelero *nm* cinnamon tree.

canelo 1 *adj* cinnamon, cinnamon-coloured. **2** *nm* cinnamon tree.

canelón *nm* (**a**) = **canalón**. (**b**) (*carámbano*) icicle. (**c**) (*CAm*: *rizo*) corkscrew curl. (**d**) **canelones** (*Culin*) cannelloni.

canesú *nm* (**a**) (*Cos*) yoke. (**b**) (*prenda*) underbodice, camisole.

caney *nm* (**a**) (*And, Carib*: *cabaña*) log cabin, hut; (*Carib Hist*) chief's house; (*And, Carib*: *cobertizo*) large shed. (**b**) (*LAm*: *de río*) river bend.

canfín *nm* (*CAm, Carib*) petrol, gasoline (*US*).

cangalla* *nmf* (*LAm*) coward.

cangallar* [1a] *vt* (*And, Cono Sur*) to pinch*, swipe‡.

cangilón *nm* (**a**) (*jarro*) pitcher; metal tankard; (*de noria*) bucket, scoop; (*And*) drum. (**b**) (*LAm*: *carril*) cart track, rut.

cangrejo *nm* (**a**) **~ (de mar)** (common) crab; **~ (de río)** crayfish. (**b**) (*Náut*) gaff. (**c**) (*And*: *idiota*) idiot; (*And*: *granuja*) rogue, crafty person. (**d**) (*LAm*: *misterio*) mystery, enigma. (**e**) (‡: *moneda*) 25 pesetas.

cangri‡ *nm* (**a**) (*cárcel*) nick‡, prison. (**b**) (*Ecl*) church. (**c**) (*Fin*) 25 pesetas.

cangro *nm* (*And, CAm, Méx*) cancer.

canguelo* *nm*, **canguis*** *nm* funk*.

canguro *nm* (**a**) (*Zool*) kangaroo. (**b**) (*: *persona t* **cangura** *f*) baby-sitter; **hacer de ~** to baby-sit. (**c**) (*ropa*) light jacket, light coat. (**d**) (*: *Náut*) ferry.

caníbal 1 *adj* cannibal; cannibalistic, man-eating; (*fig*) fierce, savage. **2** *nmf* cannibal.

canibalesco *adj* cannibalistic.

canibalismo *nm* cannibalism; (*fig*) fierceness, savageness.

canibalizar [1f] *vt* to cannibalize.

canica *nf* (**a**) (*bola*) marble; (*juego*) marbles. (**b**) **~s**** marbles**, balls**.

canicie *nf* (*de pelo*) greyness, whiteness.

canícula *nf* dog days, midsummer heat; (*fig*) hottest part of the day; **C~** Dog Star, Sirius.

canicular 1 *adj*: **calores ~es** midsummer heat. **2 ~es** *nmpl* dog days.

canicultura *nf* dog-breeding.

caniche *nm* poodle.

canijo *adj* (**a**) (*endeble*) weak, frail, sickly. (**b**) (*Méx**: *malvado*) sly, crafty.

canilla *nf* (**a**) (*Anat*) long bone (*of arm or leg*); (*espinilla*) shin, shinbone; (*esp LAm*: *pierna*) shank, thin leg; **~ de la pierna** shinbone, tibia; **~ del brazo** armbone, ulna.

(**b**) (*Téc*) bobbin, reel, spool.

(**c**) (*grifo*) tap; (*de barril*) spout, cock, tap; **irse como una ~*, irse de ~*** to have the trots‡.

(**d**) (*de paño*) rib.

(**e**) (*Carib*: *cobardía*) cowardice.

(**f**) (*Méx*) **a ~** by hook or by crook; **tener ~** to have great physical strength.

canillento *adj* (*And*) long-legged.

canillera *nf* (*LAm*) (*miedo*) fear; (*cobardía*) cowardice.

canillita *nm* (*LAm*) newsvendor, newspaper boy.

canillón* *adj* (*LAm*), **canilludo*** *adj* (*LAm*) long-legged.

canina *nf* dog dirt.

caninez *nf* ravenous hunger.

canino 1 *adj* (**a**) (*Zool*) canine; dog (*atr*). (**b**) **hambre canina** ravenous hunger. **2** *nm* canine (tooth).

canje *nm* exchange.

canjeable *adj* (*Fin*) exchangeable for cash, that can be cashed.

canjear [1a] *vt* (*gen*) to exchange; to swap; (*trocar*) to change over, interchange; *cupón* to cash in.

cano *adj* (**a**) (*de pelo*) grey-haired, white-haired, white-headed; **quedar ~** to go grey. (**b**) (*poét*) snow-white. (**c**) (*fig*) venerable; (*pey*) hoary, ancient.

canoa *nf* (**a**) (*Náut*) canoe; boat, launch; **~ automóvil** motor boat, launch; **~ fuera borda** outboard motorboat. (**b**) (*LAm*) (*conducto*) conduit, pipe; (*comedero*) feeding trough; (*de gallinas*) chicken coop; (*de palomas*) dovecot.

canódromo *nm* dogtrack.

canoero *nm* (*LAm*), **canoísta** *nmf* canoeist.

canólogo, -a *nm/f* expert on dogs.

canon *nm* (**a**) rule, canon; (*Arte, Ecl, Mús*) canon; (*Fin*) tax, levy; (*Min*) royalty; (*Agr*) rent; **~ de tránsito** (*Aut etc*) toll; **como mandan los cánones** as the rules require, in accordance with sound principles. (**b**) (*Ecl*) **cánones** canon law.

canonical *adj* of a canon (*o* prebendary), canonical; (*fig*) easy.

canonicato *nm* (*Ecl*) canonry; (*) sinecure, cushy job‡.

canónico *adj* canonical; **derecho ~** canon law.

canóniga* *nf* nap before lunch; **coger una ~*** to have one over the eight.

canónigo *nm* canon.

canonista *nm* canon lawyer, expert in canon law.

canonización *nf* canonization.

canonizar [1f] *vt* to canonize; (*fig*) to consecrate; to applaud, extol, show approval of.
canonjía *nf* (*Ecl*) canonry; (*) sinecure, cushy job‡.
canoro *adj* melodious, sweet, tuneful; **ave canora** songbird.
canoso *adj* grey-haired, white-haired; *barba* grizzled, hoary.
canotaje *nm* boating.
canotier *nm*, **canotié** *nm* straw hat, boater.
cansadamente *adv* (*V adj*) (**a**) wearily, in a tired way. (**b**) tediously, boringly; tiresomely.
cansado *adj* (**a**) (*fatigado*) tired, weary (*de* of); *ojos* tired, strained; (*Agr*) *tierra* exhausted; **con voz cansada** in a weary voice; **estar ~** to be tired; **estoy ~ de hacerlo** I'm tired of doing it, I'm sick of doing it.
(**b**) (*aburrido*) tedious, boring; (*molesto*) tiresome, trying.
(**c**) **a las cansadas** (*Carib, Cono Sur*) after much delay, after a long wait.
cansador *adj* (*Cono Sur*) = **cansado (b)**.
cansancio *nm* tiredness, weariness; (*Med*) fatigue, exhaustion; **estar muerto de ~** to be dead tired, be dog-tired.
cansar [1a] **1** *vt* (*gen*) to tire, tire out, weary; (*Med*) to fatigue, exhaust; *ojos* to tire, strain, try; *paciencia* to try, wear out; (*Agr*) *tierra* to exhaust; *apetito* to jade; (*fig*) (*aburrir*) to bore; (*molestar*) to badger, bother (*con* with).
2 *vi* (**a**) (*fatigar*) to tire.
(**b**) (*dar la lata*) to be trying, be tiresome.
3 cansarse *vr* to tire, get tired, grow weary (*con, de* of); to get bored (*con, de* with); to tire o.s. out; **~ de hacer algo** to get tired of doing sth, get bored with doing sth.
cansera* *nf* bother; (*LAm*) wasted effort.
cansinamente *adv* wearily; lifelessly.
cansino *adj* weary; lifeless; (*lento*) slow.
cantable 1 *adj* suitable for singing, to be sung; (*Mús*) cantabile; melodious. **2** *nm* sung part of a *zarzuela*.
cantábrico *adj* Cantabrian; **Mar C~** Bay of Biscay; **los (Montes) ~s** the Cantabrian Mountains.
cántabro, -a *adj, nm/f* Cantabrian.
cantadera *nf* (*LAm*) loud singing, prolonged singing.
cantador(a) *nm/f* folksinger, singer of popular songs.
cantal *nm* (**a**) (*piedra*) boulder; (*bloque*) stone block. (**b**) (*pedregal*) stony ground.
cantaleta *nf* (*LAm*) constant nagging; boring chorus, tedious refrain.
cantaletear [1a] *vt* (*LAm*) (**a**) (*repetir*) to repeat ad nauseam, say over and over. (**b**) (*embromar*) to laugh at, make fun of.
cantalupa *nf* (*CAm*), **cantalupo** *nm* cantaloupe.
cantante 1 *adj* singing. **2** *nmf* (professional) singer; (*de jazz etc*) vocalist; **~ de ópera** opera singer.
cantaor(a) *nm/f* = **cantador(a)** (*esp de cante flamenco*).
cantar [1a] **1** *vt* (*gen*) to sing; to chant; (*alabar*) to sing about, sing of, sing the praises of; **~ mal y porfiar** to persist in doing sth badly; **~las claras** to speak out, speak frankly; (*pey*) to be cheeky.
2 *vi* (**a**) (*Mús*) to sing; to chant; (*insecto etc*) to chirp; (*máquina, rueda, etc*) to creak, squeak, grind; **~ a dos voces** to sing a duet.
(**b**) (*: *confesar*) to squeal‡, blab, spill the beans*; **~ de plano*** to tell all one knows, make a full confession.
(**c**) **~ alto** (*Cono Sur*) to ask too high a price, overcharge.
(**d**) (‡: *oler*) to smell bad, pong‡.
(**e**) (‡: *llamar la atención*) to attract (too much) attention, stand out (in an undesirable way); **las estadísticas cantan** there's no arguing with statistics, statistics don't lie.
3 *nm* (**a**) (*acto*) singing; chanting.
(**b**) (*canción*) song; (*poesía*) poem (set to music); (*épica*) epic poem; **C~ de los C~es** Song of Songs; **~ de gesta** epic poem; **C~ de mio Cid** Poem of the Cid; **eso es otro ~** that's another story.
cántara *nf* (**a**) (*recipiente*) large pitcher. (**b**) *liquid measure = 16.13 litres.*
cantarería *nf* (**a**) (*tienda*) pottery shop, earthenware shop. (**b**) (*cerámica*) pottery.
cantarero *nm* potter, dealer in earthenware.
cantárida *nf* (*t* **polvo de ~**) Spanish fly, (*Farm*) cantharides.
cantarín 1 *adj persona* fond of singing; *arroyo* tinkling, musical; *tono* singsong, lilting. **2** *nm*, **cantarina** *nf* (professional) singer.
cántaro *nm* (**a**) (*vasija*) pitcher, jug; (*cantidad*) jugful; **a ~s** in plenty; **llover a ~s** to rain cats and dogs, rain in torrents. (**b**) **~s‡** tits‡.
cantata¹ *nf* (*Mús*) cantata.
cantata²‡ *nf* tip-off.
cante *nm* (**a**) **~ flamenco, ~ jondo** *Andalusian gipsy singing.* (**b**) (‡: *soplo*) tip-off (to the police).
cantautor(a) *nm/f* singer-songwriter.
cantegriles *nmpl* (*Cono Sur*) shanty-town.
cantera *nf* (**a**) quarry, pit; **~ de arena** sandpit; **~ de piedra** stone quarry. (**b**) (*fig*) talent, genius. (**c**) (*fig*) source of supply; (*Dep*) reserve of young players; nursery, seedbed.
canterano, -a *nm/f* junior player, novice.
cantería *nf* (**a**) (*acto*) quarrying, stone cutting. (**b**) (*Arquit*) masonry, stonework. (**c**) (*piedra*) piece of masonry, stone, ashlar.
cantero *nm* (**a**) (*persona*) quarryman; stonemason.
(**b**) (*cabo*) end, extremity; **~ de pan** crust of bread.
(**c**) (*Cono Sur*) (*sembradío*) bed, plot (*of vegetables*), (*de flores*) flowerbed; (*And, Méx: de caña*) plot of sugar cane.
cántico *nm* (*Ecl*) canticle; (*fig*) song.
cantidad 1 *nf* quantity; amount, number; (*de dinero*) amount, sum; **~ alzada** fixed price, all-in price; **~ de movimiento** (*Fís*) momentum; **en ~** in quantity; **~ de, (una) gran ~ de** a great quantity of, lots of; **¿había mucha gente? ... ¡cualquier ~!** (*LAm**) were there many people? ... loads! (*o* masses!); **tengo una ~ de cosas que hacer** I've lots of things to do, I've masses of things to do.
2 *como adv* (*) a lot, a good deal; **ese coche mola ~‡** that car is really nice; **esto está degenerando ~** this is really going downhill; **sabe ~ de eso** he knows a lot about that.
cantiga *nf*, **cántiga** *nf* song, poem.
cantil *nm* (*en roca*) shelf, ledge; (*de costa*) coastal shelf; (*risco*) cliff.
cantilena *nf* ballad, song, chant; **la misma ~** (*fig*) the same old tale; **y toda esa ~*** and all that jazz*.
cantillos *nmpl* (*juego*) jacks.
cantimplora *nf* (*para agua*) water bottle, canteen; (*para licor*) hip flask; (*Téc*) syphon; (*And*) powder flask; **¡~!** (*And**) not on your life!
cantina *nf* (**a**) (*Ferro*) buffet, refreshment room; (*Mil etc*) canteen; (*snack*) snack bar; (*LAm: bar*) bar, saloon; (*Cono Sur: restorán*) cheap restaurant.
(**b**) (*bodega*) wine cellar.
(**c**) (*caja de comida*) lunch box; (*And: de leche*) milk churn; **~s** (*Méx*) saddlebags.
cantinela *nf* = **cantilena**.
cantinero *nm* barman, publican.
cantinflismo *nm* (*Méx*) babble, empty chatter.
cantío *nm* (*Carib*) folksong, popular song.
cantiral *nm* stony ground, stony place.
canto¹ *nm* (*Mús*) (**a**) (*arte, gen*) singing; chanting.
(**b**) (*acto: gen*) singing; **el ~ de los pájaros** the singing of the birds.
(**c**) (*canción*) song; **~ llano** plainsong; **~ de sirena(s)** siren song; **al ~ del gallo** at cockcrow, at daybreak.
(**d**) (*Poét*) song, lyric; (*parte de épica*) canto.
canto² *nm* (**a**) (*borde*) edge; rim, border; (*de cuchillo*) back; (*de libro*) fore-edge; (*extremo*) end, point; (*ángulo*) corner; (*de pan*) crust; **ni un ~ de uña** absolutely nothing; **estar de ~** to be on edge, be edgeways; to be on end; **le faltó el ~ de un duro** he had a narrow shave; **tener 3 cm de ~** to be 3 cm thick.
(**b**) (*piedra*) stone, pebble; rock; (*t* **~ rodado**) boulder.
cantón¹ *nm* corner; (*Her, Pol*) canton; (*Mil*) cantonment.
cantón² *nm* (*LAm Cos*) cotton material.
cantonada *nf*: **dar ~ a uno** to dodge sb, shake sb off.
cantonal *adj* cantonal.
cantonear [1a] *vi* to loaf around.
cantonera *nf* (**a**) (*anaquel*) corner shelf; (*escuadra*) corner bracket, angle iron; (*mesita*) corner table; (*armario*) corner cupboard; (*de libro, mueble etc*) corner piece.
(**b**) (*) streetwalker.
cantonero *nm* loafer, idler, good-for-nothing.
cantonés, -esa 1 *adj, nm/f* Cantonese. **2** *nm* (*Ling*) Cantonese.
cantor 1 *adj* singing, that sings; **ave ~a** songbird.
2 *nm*, **cantora** *nf* singer; (*Orn*) songbird.
Cantórbery *nm* Canterbury.
cantorral *nm* stony ground, stony place.
cantuariense *adj* of (*o* from) Canterbury.
cantuja *nf* (*And*) slang.
cantúo‡ *adj*: **una mujer cantúa** a woman with a smashing figure*.

canturía *nf* (*canto*) singing, vocal music; (*ejercicio*) singing exercise; (*pey*) monotonous singing, droning.

canturrear [1a] *vti* to hum, croon, sing softly; to chant; to drone.

canturreo *nm* humming, crooning, soft singing; chanting; droning.

canutazo‡ *nm* telephone call.

canutero *nm* (*LAm*) barrel (*of pen*).

canuto 1 (‡) *adj* (**a**) super*, smashing*.
(**b**) **pasarlas canutas** to have a rough time of it.
2 *nm* (**a**) (*tubo*) small tube, small container.
(**b**) (*Bot*) internode.
(**c**) (*: *persona*) telltale.
(**d**) (‡: *porro*) joint‡.
(**e**) (‡: *teléfono*) telephone, blower‡.

canzonetista *nf* vocalist, crooner.

caña *nf* (**a**) (*Bot*: *especie*) reed.
(**b**) (*Bot*: *tallo*) stem, stalk, cane; (*bastón*) walking-stick, cane; ~ **de azúcar,** ~ **dulce,** ~ **melar** sugar cane; ~ **de pescar** fishing rod; ~ **del timón** tiller, helm; **las ~s se vuelven lanzas** a joke can easily turn into something unpleasant.
(**c**) (*Anat*) long bone (*of arm or leg*), (*esp*) shinbone; (*de bota, media*) leg; (*de ancla, caballo*) shank; (*de pilar*) shaft; (**‡) prick**‡; ~**s** (*Méx**) legs.
(**d**) (*vaso*) tall wineglass, long glass; ~ **de cerveza** glass of beer; beer glass; **'¡dos ~s!'** (*in bar*) 'two beers please'.
(**e**) (*LAm*) (*azúcar*) sugar cane; (*licor*) rum, brandy; **estar con la ~ mala** (*Cono Sur**) to have a hangover*.
(**f**) (*Min*) gallery.
(**g**) (*Carib**) swig*, drink.
(**h**) (*And, Carib*) (*bulo*) false rumour; (*bravata*) piece of bluff, piece of bluster.
(**i**) (*LAm*: *pajita*) (drinking) straw.
(**j**) (*) **dar ~ a, meter ~ a** to attack, go for; *tarea etc* to get stuck into.

cañabrava *nf* (*LAm*) reed; bamboo.

cañada *nf* (**a**) (*barranco*) gully, ravine; (*valle*) glen. (**b**) (*camino*) cattle track, drover's road. (**c**) (*LAm*: *arroyo*) stream; low-lying wet place.

cañadón *nm* (*Cono Sur*) low-lying part of a field.

cañamar *nm* hemp field.

cañamazo *nm* (coarse) canvas (for embroidery); burlap.

cañamelar *nm* sugar-cane plantation.

cañameno *adj* hempen.

cañamero *adj* hemp (*atr*).

cañamiel *nf* sugar cane.

cáñamo *nm* (*Bot*) hemp; (*tela*) hempen cloth; (*CAm, Carib, Cono Sur*: *cuerda*) hempen cord; ~ **agramado** dressed hemp; ~ **indio** Indian hemp, marijuana; ~ **índico** (*LAm*) marijuana plant.

cañamón *nm* hemp seed; birdseed.

cañata‡ *nf* (glass of) beer.

cañavera *nf* reed grass.

cañaveral *nm* reedbed; (*Agr*) sugar-cane plantation.

cañazo *nm* (*And*) cane liquor; **dar ~ a** to play a trick on.

cañear* [1a] *vi* to drink, carouse.

cañeo* *nm* drinking, carousal.

cañengo *adj*, **cañengue** *adj* (*And, Carib*) weak, sickly; skinny.

cañería *nf* (*tubo*) pipe, piece of piping, length of piping; (*conducto*) pipeline, conduit; (*desaguadero*) drain; (*Mús*) organ pipes; (‡: *droga*) main line‡; ~**s** pipes, piping; ~ **maestra (de gas)** (gas) main.

cañero 1 *adj* (**a**) (*LAm*) sugar-cane (*atr*); **machete ~** sugar-cane knife.
(**b**) (*And, Carib*) (*mentiroso*) lying; (*fanfarrón*) boastful.
2 *nm* (**a**) (*Téc*) plumber, pipe fitter.
(**b**) (*LAm*: *Agr*) owner (*o* manager) of a sugar-cane plantation.
(**c**) (*And, Carib*) (*mentiroso*) liar; (*fanfarrón*) bluffer, boaster.

cañete *nm* small pipe.

cañí = **calé**.

cañita *nf* (*And*) (drinking) straw.

cañiza *nf* coarse linen.

cañizal *nm*, **cañizar** *nm* (*natural*) reedbed; (*Agr*) sugar-cane plantation.

cañizo *nm* (*Agr*) hurdle (for drying fruit *etc*).

caño *nm* (**a**) (*tubo*) tube, pipe; (*Mús*) pipe; (*de fuente*) jet, spout; (*Arquit*) gutter; (*alcantarilla*) drain, (open) sewer; (*And*: *grifo*) tap.
(**b**) (*galería*) gallery.
(**c**) (*bodega*) wine cellar.
(**d**) (*Náut*) navigation channel, deep channel; (*And, Carib*: *río*) narrow navigable river.

cañón 1 *nm* (**a**) (*tubo*) tube, pipe; (*Mús*) pipe, organ pipe; (*de chimenea*) flue; shaft, stack; (*de columna, ascensor*) shaft; (*de escalera*) well; (*de arma, pluma*) barrel; (*de pipa*) stem; (*Alpinismo*) chimney; **escopeta de dos cañones** double-barrelled gun; ~ **rayado** rifled barrel; **ni a ~ rayado** (*And, Carib, Cono Sur*) by no means, not at all.
(**b**) (*Mil*) gun; (*esp Hist*) cannon; (*TV**) zoom-lens; (*luz*) spotlight; ~ **de agua** water-cannon; ~ **antiaéreo** anti-aircraft gun; ~ **antitanque** anti-tank gun; ~ **arponero** harpoon; ~ **de avancarga** muzzle-loader; ~ **de campaña** fieldgun; ~ **de nieve artificial** snow machine; ~ **obús** howitzer.
(**c**) (*de pluma*) quill; quill pen.
(**d**) (*Geog*) canyon, gorge; (*And*: *paso*) pass.
(**e**) (*And*: *Bot*) trunk.
(**f**) (*And, Méx*: *camino*) mountain path.
2 *como adj invar* (*) fabulous*, marvellous; **¡el hombre está ~!** he's fabulous!*; **¡la función estaba ~!** the show was great!*; **una noticia ~** a stunning piece of news.

cañonazo *nm* (**a**) (*Mil*) gunshot; (*Hist*) cannon shot; (*Dep**) fierce shot; ~**s** gunfire, shellfire; **salva de 21 ~s** 21-gun salute; ~ **de advertencia** (*Náut*) warning shot, shot across the bows.
(**b**) (*fig*) bombshell, bolt from the blue.

cañonear [1a] **1** *vt* to shell, bombard. **2 cañonearse** *vr* (*Cono Sur**) to get tight*.

cañoneo *nm* shelling, shellfire, gunfire; bombardment, cannonade.

cañonera *nf* (**a**) (*Mil*: *Hist*) embrasure. (**b**) (*Náut*: *t* **lancha ~**) gunboat. (**c**) (*LAm*: *pistolera*) holster.

cañonero *nm* gunboat.

cañusero *nm* (*And*) owner of a sugar-cane plantation.

cañutero *nm* pincushion.

cañuto *nm* = **canuto**.

caoba *nf* mahogany.

caolín *nm* kaolin.

caos *nm* chaos.

caótico *adj* chaotic.

caotizar [1f] *vt* to throw into disarray, cause chaos in.

cap. *abr de* **capítulo** chapter, ch.

C.A.P. *nm abr de* **Certificado de Aptitud Pedagógica** (*teaching certificate*).

capa *nf* (**a**) cloak, cape; (*Ecl*: *t* ~ **pluvial**) cape; ~ **de agua,** ~ **aguadera** raincape, waterproof cloak; ~ **del cielo** canopy of heaven; ~ **(de ladrones)** (*fig*) fence, receiver; ~ **rota** (*fig*) secret emissary; ~ **torera** bullfighter's cape; **andar de ~ caída** to be in a bad way, be on the decline; **echar una ~ a uno** to cover up for sb; **echar la ~ al toro** to make a final desperate effort; **hacer de su ~ un sayo** to do what one likes with one's own things, act freely; **comedia de ~ y espada** cloak-and-dagger play.
(**b**) (*fig*) cloak, pretence; mask, disguise; **so ~ de** under the pretext of, in the guise of.
(**c**) (*Geol*) layer, bed, stratum; (*Met, Anat etc*) layer; (*de humo*) pall; (*de polvo*) layer, film; (*de nieve*) layer, covering, mantle; (*Culin*) coating; (*de pintura*) coat; **primera ~** undercoat, first coat; ~ **freática** water table; ~ **de ozono** ozone layer; ~**s sociales** social layers, social levels; **madera de tres ~s** three-ply wood.
(**d**) (*Náut*) **estar a la ~, ponerse a la ~** to lie to.

capaburro *nm* (*LAm*) pirana.

capacidad *nf* (**a**) capacity (*t Com, Fís, Téc etc*); (*cabida*) capaciousness, size; **una sala con ~ para 900** a hall with room for 900, a hall that can hold 900; **un avión con ~ para 20 plazas** a 20-seater plane; ~ **adquisitiva,** ~ **de compra** purchasing power; ~ **de almacenaje** storage capacity; ~ **de arrastre,** ~ **de convocatoria** (*de orador etc*) drawing power, power of attraction; popular appeal; ~ **de carga** carrying capacity; ~ **de endeudamiento** (limit of) borrowing powers; ~ **financiera** financial standing; ~ **de ganancia** earning power; ~ **de pago** credit-worthiness; ~ **de repercusión** resilience; ~ **útil** effective capacity.
(**b**) (*fig*) (*talento*) (mental) capacity, ability, capability, talent; (*habilidad*) competence, efficiency; (*Jur*) capacity, legal competency; **tener ~ para** to have an aptitude for, have talent for; **no tiene ~ para los negocios** he has no business sense.
(**c**) (*LAm*: *persona hábil*) able person, talented person.

capacitación *nf* (*Jur*) capacitation; (*Téc etc*) training, education.

capacitado *adj* qualified; **estar ~ para** + *infin* to be qualified to + *infin*.

capacitar [1a] **1** *vt* (**a**) **~ a uno para algo** to fit sb for sth, qualify sb for sth; (*Téc*) to train (*o* educate) sb for sth; **~ a uno para** + *infin* to enable sb to + *infin*.

(**b**) **~ a uno para hacer algo** (*And, Cono Sur, Méx*) to empower (*o* authorize) sb to do sth.

2 capacitarse *vr*: **~ para algo** to fit o.s. for sth, qualify for sth.

capacitor *nm* capacitor.

capacha *nf* (**a**) (*espuerta*) basket. (**b**) (*And, Cono Sur**) jail, clink‡; **caer en la ~** (*Cono Sur*) to fall into the trap.

capacheca *nf* (*And, Cono Sur*) street-vendor's barrow (*o* stall).

capacho *nm* (**a**) (*espuerta*) wicker basket, big basket; (*Téc*) wickerwork hod; (*And*: *alforja*) saddlebag. (**b**) (*And, Cono Sur*: *sombrero*) old hat.

capadura *nf* castration.

capar [1a] *vt* (**a**) *animal* to castrate, geld.

(**b**) (*fig*) to reduce, cut down, curtail.

(**c**) (*Carib, Méx*: *Agr*) to cut back, prune.

(**d**) (*And, Carib*) *comida* to start on, begin to eat.

caparazón *nm* (**a**) (*Hist*) caparison; (*manta*) horse blanket; (*comedero*) nosebag. (**b**) (*Zool*) shell.

caparrón *nm* bud.

caparrosa *nf* copperas; vitriol; **~ azul** copper sulphate, blue vitriol.

capataz *nm* foreman, overseer.

capaz 1 *adj* (**a**) (*en tamaño*) capacious, roomy, large; **~ de, ~ para** with a capacity of, with room for, that holds; **un coche ~ para 4 personas** a car with room for 4 people.

(**b**) (*en competencia*) able, capable; efficient, competent; fit; (*Jur*) competent; **ser ~ de algo** to be capable of sth; **ser ~ de hacer algo** to be capable of doing sth, be up to doing sth; to be competent to do sth; **es ~ de cualquier tontería** he is capable of any stupidity, one might expect any idiocy from him; **¿serías ~?** would you dare? **¡sería ~!** one could well believe it of him, I wouldn't put it past him, I'm not surprised; **~ de funcionar** (*Téc*) operational, in working order; **ser ~ para un trabajo** to be qualified for a job, be up to a job.

(**c**) (*LAm*) (**es**) **~ que venga** (*probable*) he'll probably come, he's likely to come; (*posible*) he might come, possibly he'll come; **~ que le pasaba algo** maybe he had some problem.

2 *adv* (*LAm*) **¿vendrá? – ~ que sí** will he come? – maybe (*o* he might).

capazo *nm* large basket; (*de niño*) carrycot.

capcioso *adj* wily, deceitful.

capea *nf* bullfight with young bulls.

capeador *nm* *bullfighter who uses the cape.*

capear [1a] **1** *vt* (**a**) (*Taur*) to play with the cape, wave the cape at; (*fig*) to take in, deceive.

(**b**) (*Náut y fig*) *temporal* to ride out, weather.

(**c**) (*esquivar*) to dodge.

(**d**) (*Culin*) to cap, cover (*con* with).

2 *vi* (*Náut*) to ride out the storm; to lie to.

capelo *nm* (**a**) (*Ecl*) cardinal's hat; (*fig*) cardinalate. (**b**) (*Cono Sur, Méx*: *tapa*) bell glass, glass cover. (**c**) (*LAm Univ*) **~ de doctor** doctor's gown.

capellada *nf* (*puntera*) toecap; (*remiendo*) patch.

capellán *nm* chaplain; priest, clergyman; **~ castrense, ~ de ejército** army chaplain.

capellanía *nf* chaplaincy.

capero *nm* hallstand, hatstand.

Caperucita Roja *nf* (Little) Red Riding Hood.

caperuza *nf* (pointed) hood; (*Mec*) hood, cowling; (*de pluma etc*) top, cap; **~ de chimenea** chimney cowl.

capi[1]***** *nm* = **capitán.**

capi[2] *nf* (*And, Cono Sur*) (*harina*) white maize flour; (*maíz*) maize, corn (*US*); (*vaina*) unripe pod.

capi[3]***** *nf* capital.

capia *nf* (*And, Cono Sur*) (*harina*) white maize flour; (*maíz*) maize, corn (*US*).

capiango *nm* (*Cono Sur*) clever thief.

capicúa *nm* reversible number, symmetrical number (*p.ej.* 12321); palindrome.

capigorra *nm*, **capigorrista** *nm*, **capigorrón** *nm* idler, loafer.

capilar 1 *adj* capillary; hair (*atr*); **tubo ~** capillary. **2** *nm* capillary.

capilaridad *nf* capillarity.

capilla *nf* (**a**) (*Ecl*) chapel; **~ ardiente** funeral chapel; **~ mayor** choir, chancel; **~ de la Virgen** Lady Chapel; **estar en** (**la**) **~** (*fig*) to be awaiting execution; to be in great danger; to be in suspense, be on tenterhooks.

(**b**) (*Mús*) choir.

(**c**) (*Tip*) proof sheet; **estar en ~s** to be in proof.

(**d**) (*caperuza*) cowl; (*Téc*) hood, cowl.

(**e**) (*peña*) group of supporters, following; informal club.

capiller(o) *nm* churchwarden; sexton.

capillo *nm* (**a**) (*de bebé*) baby's bonnet; (*de halcón*) hood. (**b**) (*Bot, Zool*) = **capullo.**

capirotazo *nm* flip, flick.

capirote *nm* (**a**) (*Hist, Univ, de halcón*) hood. (**b**) (*capirotazo*) flip, flick. (**c**) **tonto de ~** prize idiot, utter fool. (**d**) (*Culin*) cloth strainer (for coffee *etc*).

capirucho *nm* hood.

capiruchu *nm* (*CAm*) *child's toy consisting of wooden cup and ball.*

capisayo *nm* (*And*) vest, undershirt (*US*).

capitación *nf* poll tax, capitation.

capital 1 *adj* (*en muchos sentidos*) capital; *ciudad, crimen* capital; *enemigo, pecado* mortal; *rasgo* main, chief, principal; *punto* essential, fundamental; *importancia* capital, supreme, paramount; (*esp LAm*) *letra* capital; **lo ~** the main thing, the essential point.

2 *nm* (*Fin*) capital; capital sum; **~ en acciones** share capital; **~ activo** working capital, (*And, Cono Sur*) capital assets; **~ arriesgado** venture capital; **~ autorizado** authorized capital; **~ circulante** circulating capital; **~ de explotación** working capital; **~ emitido** issued capital; **~ fijo** fixed capital; **~ físico** (*Cono Sur*) capital assets; **~ improductivo** idle money; **~ invertido, ~ utilizado** invested capital; **~ pagado** paid-up capital; **~ (de) riesgo** risk capital; **~ social** share capital; **inversión de ~es** capital investment.

3 *nf* (**a**) (*Pol*: *de país*) capital, capital city; (*de región*) chief town, centre; **~ de provincia** provincial capital, administrative centre of the province; **en León ~** in the city of León.

(**b**) (*Tip*) decorated initial capital.

capitalidad *nf* capital status, status as capital.

capitalino (*LAm*) **1** *adj* of the capital. **2** *nm*, **capitalina** *nf* (**a**) native (*o* inhabitant) of the capital; **los ~s** the people of the capital. (**b**) (*****) city slicker*****.

capitalismo *nm* capitalism; **~ de Estado** state capitalism; **~ monopolista** monopoly capitalism.

capitalista 1 *adj* capitalist(ic). **2** *nmf* capitalist; (*hum*) Madrilenian.

capitalización *nf* capitalization; compounding.

capitalizar [1f] *vt* (**a**) to capitalize; *interés* to compound. (**b**) (*fig*) to capitalize on, turn to account.

capitán *nm* (*Dep, Mil, Náut, etc*) captain; (*jefe*) leader, chief, commander; (*Méx*) maître d'hôtel; **~ de corbeta** lieutenant-commander; **~ de fragata** commander; **~ general** (**de ejército**) (*aprox*) field marshal; **~ general** (**de armada**) chief of naval operations; **~ de navío** captain; **~ del puerto** harbour master.

capitana *nf* (**a**) (*Dep, Mil*) (woman) captain; (*Hist*) captain's wife. (**b**) (*Náut*) flagship.

capitanear [1a] *vt* *equipo* to captain; *expedición, sublevación etc* to lead, head, command.

capitanía *nf* (**a**) (*cargo*) captaincy; (*rango*) rank of captain. (**b**) **~ del puerto** harbour master's office. (**c**) (*derechos*) harbour dues.

capitel *nm* (*Arquit*) capital.

capitolio *nm* capitol; (*edificio grande*) large edifice, imposing building; (*Pol*) statehouse, parliament building; **C~** Capitol.

capitoné *nm* (**a**) removal van, furniture van. (**b**) (*Cono Sur*) quilt, quilted blanket.

capitonear [1a] *vt* (*Cono Sur*) to quilt.

capitoste *nm* (*pey*) chief, boss; petty tyrant.

capitulación *nf* (**a**) (*Mil*) capitulation, surrender; **~ sin condiciones** unconditional surrender.

(**b**) (*acuerdo*) agreement, pact; **capitulaciones** (**de boda, matrimoniales**) marriage settlement.

capitular[1] *adj* (*Ecl*) chapter (*atr*); **sala ~** chapter house, meeting room.

capitular[2] [1a] **1** *vt* (**a**) *condiciones* to agree to, agree on.

(**b**) (*Jur*) to charge (*de* with), impeach.

2 *vi* (**a**) (*pactar*) to come to terms, make an agreement (*con* with).

(**b**) (*Mil*) to capitulate, surrender.

capitulear [1a] *vi* (*And, Cono Sur*: *Parl*) to lobby.

capituleo *nm* (*And, Cono Sur*: *Parl*) lobbying.

capítulo *nm* (**a**) (*Liter, Tip*) chapter; **eso es ~ aparte** that's another question altogether; **esto merece ~ aparte** this deserves separate treatment.

(**b**) (*reprimenda*) reproof, reprimand; ~ (**de culpas**) charge, impeachment.

(**c**) (*asunto*) subject, matter; point; **ganar** ~ to make one's point.

(**d**) **~s matrimoniales** marriage contract, marriage settlement.

(**e**) (*junta*) meeting (of a council); (*Ecl*) chapter; **llamar a uno a** ~ to take sb to task, call sb to account.

(**f**) (*Ecl*) chapter house.

cap.º *abr de* **capítulo**; = **cap.**

capo* (*Cono Sur*) **1** *adj invar* great*, fabulous*. **2** *nm* (*jefe*) boss; (*persona influyente*) bigwig; (*perito*) expert; **es un** ~ (*en arte, profesión*) he's the tops*, he's brilliant.

capó *nm* (*Aut*) bonnet, hood (*US*); (*Aer*) cowling.

capoc *nm* kapok.

capón[1] *nm* rap on the head.

capón[2] **1** *adj* castrated. **2** *nm* (**a**) (*pollo*) capon; (*eunuco*) eunuch. (**b**) (*Cono Sur*) (*: *novato*) novice, greenhorn; (*cordero*) castrated sheep, wether; (*carne*) mutton.

caponera *nf* (*Agr*) chicken coop, fattening pen; (*fig*) place of easy living, open house; (‡) clink‡.

caporal *nm* chief, leader, (*Agr etc*: *esp LAm*) foreman, head man.

capot [ka'po] *nm* (*Aut*) = **capó**.

capota *nf* (**a**) (*de mujer*) bonnet. (**b**) (*de carruaje, cochecito*) hood; (*Aut*) hood, top (*US*); ~ **plegable** folding hood, folding top (*US*).

capotar [1a] *vi* (*Aut etc*) to turn over, turn turtle; to somersault; (*fig*) to fall down, collapse.

capote *nm* (**a**) (*capa*) long cloak, cloak with sleeves; (*t* ~ **de brega**) bullfighter's cape; (*Mil*) greatcoat; ~ **de monte** poncho; **a mi** ~, **para mi** ~ to my way of thinking; **de** ~ (*Méx*) on the sly, in an underhand way; **dar un** ~ **a** = **capotear (b)**; **darse** ~ (*Méx*) to give up one's job; to acknowledge defeat; **decir para su** ~ to say to o.s.; **echar un** ~ **a uno** to give sb a helping hand.

(**b**) (*ceño*) frown, scowl; (*Met*) mass of dark clouds.

(**c**) (*Naipes*) slam.

(**d**) (*Cono Sur Naipes*) **quedar** ~ to be whitewashed*.

capotear [1a] *vt* (**a**) (*Taur*) *toro* to play with the cape. (**b**) *persona* to deceive, bamboozle*. (**c**) *dificultad etc* to shirk, duck, dodge. (**d**) (*Cono Sur Naipes*) to win all the tricks against, whitewash*.

capotera *nf* (**a**) (*CAm*: *gancho*) clothes peg. (**b**) (*Cono Sur*: *azotaina*) beating. (**c**) (*CAm*: *lona*) tarpaulin.

capotudo *adj* frowning, scowling.

Capricornio *nm* (*Zodíaco*) Capricorn.

capricho *nm* (**a**) (*noción etc*) whim, caprice, (passing) fancy; (*deseo*) keen desire, sudden urge (*de* for); (*pey*) craze, fad, silly notion; **por puro** ~ just to please o.s., out of sheer cussedness*; **es un** ~ **nada más** it's just a passing whim; **fue un** ~ **suyo** it was one of his silly notions; **tiene sus ~s** he has his little whims, he has his moods.

(**b**) (*cualidad*) whimsicality, fancifulness.

(**c**) (*Arte*) caprice; (*Mús*) capriccio.

caprichosamente *adv* capriciously; whimsically; wilfully; waywardly.

caprichoso *adj* (*gen*) capricious; full of whims, having odd fancies; full of one's own pet notions; *idea, novela, etc* fanciful, whimsical; (*pey*) wilful; moody, temperamental; wayward.

caprichudo *adj* stubborn, obstinate, unyielding (about one's odd ideas).

cápsula *nf* (*Aer, Anat, Bot, Farm etc*) capsule; (*de botella*) cap; (*de tocadiscos*) pick-up; (*de cartucho*) case; (*Carib*) cartridge; ~ **espacial** space capsule; ~ **fulminante** percussion cap; ~ **de mando** command module.

capsular *adj* capsular; **en forma** ~ in capsule form.

captación *nf*: ~ **de datos** data capture.

captador *nm* (*Téc*) sensor.

captafaros *nm invar* (*t* **placa de** ~) reflector.

captar [1a] *vt* (**a**) (*atraer*) to captivate; *apoyo* to win, gain, attract; *confianza etc* to win, get; *voluntad* to gain control over; *atención etc* to get, secure; *sentido* to grasp; *persona* to win over.

(**b**) *aguas* to collect; to dam, harness.

(**c**) (*Rad*) *emisora* to tune in to; *señal* to get, pick up, receive; (*Inform*) *datos* to capture, store.

(**d**) (*Cine, Fot*) *imagen* to shoot, take, film.

captura *nf* capture; seizure; arrest.

capturar [1a] *vt* to capture; to seize; to arrest.

capucha *nf* (**a**) (*prenda*) hood; (*Ecl*) hood, cowl; ~ **antihumo** smoke hood. (**b**) (*Tip*) circumflex accent.

capuchina *nf* (**a**) (*Ecl*) Capuchin sister. (**b**) (*Bot*) nasturtium.

capuchino *nm* (**a**) (*Ecl*) Capuchin. (**b**) (*LAm Zool*) Capuchin monkey. (**c**) (**café**) ~ capuccino (coffee).

capucho *nm* cowl, hood.

capuchón *nm* (**a**) (*prenda*) capuchin, lady's hooded cloak. (**b**) (*Fot*) hood. (**c**) ~ **de válvula** (*Aut etc*) valve cap. (**d**) (*de pluma*) top, cap.

capujar [1a] *vt* (*Cono Sur*) (*atrapar*) to catch in (*o* snatch out of) the air; (*arrebatar*) to snatch; (*decir*) to say what sb else was about to say.

capullada* *nf* silly thing, piece of nonsense.

capullo *nm* (**a**) (*Zool*) cocoon. (**b**) (*Bot*) bud; (*de bellota*) cup; ~ (**de rosa**) rosebud. (**c**) (*Anat*) prepuce; **porque no me sale del** ~* because I don't want to. (**d**) (*) (*persona*: *principiante*) novice, beginner; (*imbécil*) twit*; (*Mil*) raw recruit. (**e**) (*tela*) coarse silk cloth.

caqui[1] *nm* khaki; **marcar el** ~* to finish military service.

caqui[2] *nm* (*Cono Sur*) date plum; (*fig*) red.

caquino *nm*: **reírse a ~s, reírse a** ~ **suelto** (*Méx*) to laugh uproariously, cackle.

cara[1] *nf* (**a**) (*Anat*) face; ~ **cortada** (*como apodo*) scarface; ~ **de cuchillo** hatchet face; ~ **a** ~ face to face; (*como nm*) face-to-face encounter; **a** ~ **descubierta** openly; **de** ~ opposite, facing; **mirar a uno a la** ~ to look sb in the face; **los banqueros sin** ~ the faceless bankers; **asomar la** ~ to show one's face (*t fig*); **se le caía la** ~ **de vergüenza** he blushed with shame; **cruzar la** ~ **a uno** to slash sb across the face; **dar la** ~ to face the consequences of what one has done; **no quería dar la** ~ he didn't want to show his face (in public); **dar la** ~ **por otro** to answer for sb else; **dar** ~ **a** to face up to; **decir algo en la** ~ **de uno** to say sth to sb's face; **echar algo en** ~ **a uno** to reproach sb for sth, cast sth in sb's teeth; to allude to sth; **es lo mejor que te puedes echar a la** ~* it's the very best you could wish for; **entrar** (*o* **pasar**) **por la** ~ to gatecrash; **hacer a dos ~s** to engage in double-dealing; **hacer** ~ **a** to face; *enemigo etc* to face up to, stand up to; **huir la** ~ **a uno** to avoid meeting sb; **lavar la** ~ **a uno** to lick sb's boots; **no mirar la** ~ **a uno** (*fig*) to be at daggers drawn with sb; **plantar** ~ **a uno** to confront sb; **romper la** ~ **a uno** to smash sb's face in; **sacar la** ~ **por uno** to stick up for sb; **nos veremos las ~s** (*amenaza*) we'll meet again, we'll see; **no volver la** ~ **atrás** not to flinch.

(**b**) (*usos como adv y prep*): ~ **adelante** forwards; facing forwards; ~ **atrás** backwards; facing backwards; ~ **al sol** facing the sun; (**de**) ~ **al norte** facing north; ~ **al futuro** with an eye to the future; **de** ~ **a** (*fig*) in view of, with a view to; as an aid to, as helping towards; directed towards; in connection with; **de** ~ **a** + *infin* in order to + *infin*, with a view to + *ger*.

(**c**) (*aspecto*) look, appearance; **tener** ~ **de** to look like; **tener** ~ **de querer** + *infin* to look as if one would like to + *infin*; **tener** ~ **de aburrirse** to look bored; **tener buena** ~ to look nice, (*Med*) look well; **tener mala** ~ to look bad, (*Med*) look ill; ~ **de aleluya** cheerful look; **tener** ~ **de pocos amigos** to look black, have a hangdog look; ~ **de corcho** cheeky look; ~ **dura** shamelessness; cheek*, nerve*; **¡qué** ~ **más dura!*** what a nerve!*; ~ **de hereje** ugly face; hangdog look; ~ **de (justo) juez** stern face, grim-looking face; **mala** ~ wry face, grimace; **poner mala** ~ to pout, grimace, make a (wry) face; **poner al mal tiempo buena** ~ to put a brave face on it; **poner** ~ **de circunstancias** to look appropriately grave (*etc*), look serious; **tener** ~ **de acelga** to have a face a mile long, (*Med*) to look pale, look washed out; **tener** ~ **de estatua** to have a wooden expression; **tener** ~ **de monja boba** to look all innocent; **tener** ~ **de palo** to have a wooden expression; to be poker-faced, not let on; ~ **de pascua(s)** smiling face; **tener** ~ **de pascua(s)** to look pretty pleased; **una discusión a** ~ **de perro** a fierce argument; **tener** ~ **de roñoso** to look mean; ~ **de viernes** sad look; ~ **de vinagre** sour expression.

(**d**) (*) (*valor*) boldness, nerve*; **tener** ~ **para** + *infin* to have the nerve* to + *infin*; **tener más** ~ **que ...*** to have more nerve* than ...; **¿con qué** ~ **le voy a pedir eso?*** how would I have the nerve to ask for that?*

(**e**) (*de objeto*) face; outside, surface; (*Arquit*) face, façade, front; (*Geom*) face; (*de papel*) side; (*de paño etc*) face, right side, finished side; (*de tajada, disco etc*) side; (*al sortear*) face, obverse, (*de moneda*) heads; ~ **A** A side; ~ **B** B side, (*fig*) flip side; ~ **o cruz** heads or tails; ~ **y cruz de una cuestión** both sides of a question; **echar** (*o* **jugar, sortear**) **algo a** ~ **o cruz** to toss up for sth; **escribir**

por ambas ~s write on both sides.
cara*[2] *nmf* = **caradura.**
caraba‡ *nf*: **es la ~** it's the absolute tops‡, (*pey*) it's the last straw.
carabao *nm* Philippine buffalo.
cárabe *nm* amber.
carabela *nf* caravel.
carabina *nf* (**a**) (*Mil*) carbine, rifle; **~ de aire comprimido** airgun; **ser la ~ de Ambrosio*** to be a dead loss.
(**b**) (*) chaperon; **hacer de ~, ir de ~** to go as chaperon; to play gooseberry.
carabinero *nm* (**a**) (*Mil*) carabineer, rifleman; (*de aduana*) revenue guard; (*Cono Sur*) policeman. (**b**) (*Zool*) prawn.
cárabo *nm* tawny owl.
caracol *nm* (**a**) (*Zool*) snail; (*concha*) snail shell, sea shell; conch shell; **~ comestible** edible snail; **~ de mar** (*esp*) winkle.
(**b**) (*de pelo*) curl.
(**c**) (*de forma*) spiral; (*Cono Sur*) circular shopping-centre; **escalera de ~** spiral staircase, winding staircase; **subir en ~** (*humo etc*) to spiral up, corkscrew up; **hacer ~es** (*persona*) to weave about, zigzag; (*pey*) to reel, stagger; (*caballo*) to prance about.
(**d**) **¡~es!** (*euf**) (*sorpresa*) good heavens!; (*ira*) damn it!
caracola *nf* (*Zool*) large shell.
caracoleante *adj* winding, spiral.
caracolear [1a] *vi* (*caballo*) to prance about, caracole.
caracolillo *nm* (*pelo*) kiss-curl.
carácter *nm, pl* **caracteres** (**a**) (*naturaleza*) character; (*clase*) nature, kind, condition; **de medio ~** of an ill-defined nature; **de ~ totalmente distinto** of quite a different kind.
(**b**) (*de persona*) character; **una persona de ~** a person of character; **de ~ duro** hard-natured; **no tiene ~** he lacks firmness, he's a weak character.
(**c**) (*LAm*: *Liter, Teat*) character, personage.
(**d**) (*Bio*) character; feature, characteristic; **~ adquirido** acquired characteristic; **~ hereditario** inherited characteristic.
(**e**) (*Tip*) character; **caracteres de imprenta** type, typeface; **escribir en caracteres de imprenta** to write in block letters, print.
(**f**) (*Inform*) character; **~ alfanumérico** alphanumeric character; **~ comodín** wild character; **~ de petición** prompt.
característica *nf* (**a**) characteristic; trait, quality, attribute. (**b**) (*Teat*) character actress.
características mente *adv* characteristically.
característico 1 *adj* characteristic, typical (*de* of). **2** *nm* (*Teat*) character actor.
caracteriológico *adj* character (*atr*); **cambio ~** character change, change of character.
caracterización *nf* characterization.
caracterizado *adj* (*distinguido*) distinguished, of note; (*especial*) special, peculiar, having special characteristics, (*típico*) typical.
caracterizar [1f] **1** *vt* (**a**) (*gen*) to characterize; (*tipificar*) to typify; (*distinguir*) to distinguish, set apart.
(**b**) (*honrar*) to confer (a) distinction on, confer an honour on.
(**c**) (*Teat*) *papel* to play with great effect.
2 caracterizarse *vr* (*Teat*) to make up, dress for the part.
caracú *nm* (*LAm*) bone marrow.
caracha *nf* (*LAm* ††) mange, itch; scab.
carachento *adj*, **carachoso** *adj* (*LAm*) mangy, scabby.
caracho 1 *adj* violet-coloured. **2** *interj*: **¡~!** (*And**) good heavens!, good Lord!
caradura* 1 *nmf* rotter*, cad, shameless person; **¡~!** you swine!* **2** *nf V* **cara (c).**
caraja‡ *nf*: **tener la ~** (*agotado*) to look absolutely knackered*; (*perplejo*) to be all at sea, be just not with it*.
carajear [1a] *vt* (*Cono Sur*) to insult, swear at.
carajiento *adj* (*And*) foul-mouthed.
carajillo *nm* coffee with a dash of brandy (*o* anís *etc*).
carajito* *nm* (*LAm*) kid*, small child.
carajo⁂ *nm* (**a**) prick⁂. (**b**) (*locuciones*) **de ~** tremendous*; awful; **ese conductor del ~** that shit of a driver⁂; **en el quinto ~** miles away; **no entiende ni ~, no sabe un ~ de eso** he doesn't know a damned thing about it; **¿qué ~ quieres?** what the hell do you want?‡; **me importa un ~** I don't give a damn; **irse al ~** to fail, collapse, go down the drain*; to go to the dogs; **¡vete al ~!** fuck off!⁂; **mandar a uno al ~** to tell sb to go to hell.
(**c**) *excl* damn it!, hell!
caramanchel *nm* (*LAm*) hut, shack; (*And*) shed; (*And*) street-vendor's stall.
caramba *interj* (*sorpresa*) well!, good gracious!; (*qué raro*) very odd!, how strange!; (*protesta*) hang it all!
carámbano *nm* icicle.
carambola *nf* (*Billar*) cannon; (*fig*) trick, ruse; **por ~** by a lucky chance; indirectly, in a roundabout way.
caramel *nm* sardine.
caramelear* [1a] *vt* (*And*) (*engañar*) to con*, deceive; (*engatusar*) to suck up to*, flatter.
caramelo *nm* (**a**) sweet, toffee; candy (*US*) caramel; **es de ~** it's fine. (**b**) **~s‡** hash*, pot‡.
caramillo *nm* (**a**) (*Mús*) flageolet; rustic pipe.
(**b**) (*montón*) untidy heap.
(**c**) (*chisme*) piece of gossip; (*intriga*) intrigue; **armar un ~** to make mischief, start a gossip campaign.
(**d**) (*jaleo*) fuss, trouble.
caramilloso *adj* fussy.
caranchear [1a] *vt* (*Cono Sur*) to irritate, annoy.
carancho *nm* (*And*: *búho*) owl; (*Cono Sur*: *buitre*) vulture.
caranga *nf* (*And, CAm*), **carángano** *nm* (*LAm*) louse.
carantamaula *nf* (**a**) (*careta*) grotesque mask. (**b**) (‡: *cara*) ugly mug‡; (*persona*) ugly person; scarecrow.
carantoña *nf* (**a**) (*careta*) grotesque mask.
(**b**) (‡: *cara*) ugly mug‡.
(**c**) **ella es una ~*** she's mutton dressed up as lamb*, she's a painted hag.
(**d**) **~s*** (*magreo*) caresses; petting*, fondling; **hacer ~s a uno** (*muecas*) to make faces at sb; (*amorosamente*) to make sheep's eyes at sb; (*dar coba a*) to (try to) butter sb up.
caraota *nf* (*Carib*) bean.
carapacho *nm* shell, carapace; **meterse en su ~** to go into one's shell.
carapintado* *nm* (*Argentina*) member of an army special unit.
caraqueño 1 *adj* of Caracas. **2** *nm*, **caraqueña** *nf* native (*o* inhabitant) of Caracas; **los ~s** the people of Caracas.
caráspita *excl* (*Cono Sur*) damn!
carátula *nf* (**a**) (*careta*) mask; **la ~** (*fig*: *Teat*) the stage, the theatre. (**b**) (*CAm, Méx*: *de reloj*) face, dial. (**c**) (*LAm*: *Tip*) title page; (*LAm*) cover (of a magazine). (**d**) (*de disco*) sleeve.
caravana *nf* (**a**) (*Hist*) caravan; (*fig*: *grupo*) group, band; (*fig*: *excursionistas*) crowd of trippers, group of picnickers; **ir en ~** to go in single file.
(**b**) (*Aut*: *vehículo*) caravan, trailer.
(**c**) (*Aut*) (*coches*) stream of cars; (*cola*) jam, tailback, queue.
(**d**) (*Carib*: *trampa*) bird trap.
(**e**) (*LAm*: *cortesía*) flattering remark, compliment; **bailar** (*o* **correr, hacer**) **la ~ a uno** to overdo the courtesies; to dance attention on sb.
(**f**) **~s** (*LAm*) long earrings.
caravanismo *nm* caravaning.
caravanista *nmf* caravaner.
caravan(s)era *nf*, **caravasar** *nm* caravanserai.
caray *interj* (*sorpresa*) gosh!*, good heavens!; well I'm blowed!*; (*indignación*) damn it!; **¡~ con ...!** to hell with ...!
carbohidrato *nm* carbohydrate.
carbólico *adj* carbolic.
carbón *nm* (**a**) (*Min*) coal; **~ ardiente** (*fig*) hot potato; **~ bituminoso** soft coal; **~ de leña, ~ vegetal** charcoal; **~ menudo** small coal, slack; **~ pardo** brown coal; **~ de piedra** coal; **~ térmico** steam coal; **¡se acabó el ~!*** that's it!, all done!
(**b**) (*Tip*: *t* **papel ~**) carbon paper, carbon; **copia al ~** carbon copy.
(**c**) (*Arte*) charcoal; **dibujo al ~** charcoal drawing.
(**d**) (*Elec*) carbon.
(**e**) (*Agr*) smut.
carbonada *nf* (*And, Cono Sur*) (*guiso*) meat stew; (*carne*) chop, steak; (*Cono Sur*: *sopa*) thick soup, broth; (*Cono Sur*: *picadillo*) mince.
carbonato *nm* carbonate; **~ cálcico, ~ de calcio** calcium carbonate; **~ sódico** sodium carbonate.
carboncillo *nm* (*Arte*) charcoal; (*Min*) small coal, slack; (*Aut*) carbon, carbon deposit.
carbonear [1a] *vt* (**a**) (*hacer carbón*) to make charcoal of. (**b**) (*Cono Sur**: *incitar*) to push, egg on.
carbonera *nf* (**a**) (*mina*) coalmine. (**b**) (*depósito*) coal tip,

coal heap. **(c)** *(receptáculo)* coal bin, coal bunker. **(d)** *(horno)* charcoal kiln.
carbonería *nf* coalyard.
carbonero 1 *adj* coal *(atr)*; charcoal *(atr)*; **barco ~** collier; **estación carbonera** coaling station.
2 *nm* **(a)** *(persona)* coal merchant; charcoal burner.
(b) *(Náut)* collier, coal ship.
(c) *(Orn)* coal tit.
carbónico 1 *adj* carbonic. **2** *nm* *(Cono Sur: t* **papel ~***)* carbon (paper).
carbonífero *adj* carboniferous; **industria carbonífera** coal industry.
carbonilla *nf* **(a)** *(Min)* small coal, coaldust; cinder. **(b)** *(Aut)* carbon, carbon deposit. **(c)** *(LAm Arte)* charcoal.
carbonización *nf* *(Quím)* carbonization; charring.
carbonizar [1f] **1** *vt* *(Quím)* to carbonize; to char; *madera* to make charcoal of; **quedar carbonizado** to be charred, be burnt to a cinder; *(Elec)* to be electrocuted; *(edificio)* to be burnt down, be reduced to ashes.
2 carbonizarse *vr* *(Quím)* to carbonize; = **quedar carbonizado.**
carbono *nm* carbon; **~ 14** carbon 14.
carbonoso *adj* carbonaceous.
carborundo *nm* carborundum.
carbunclo *nm (Min)*, **carbunco** *nm (Med)*, **carbúnculo** *nm (Min)* carbuncle.
carburador *nm* carburettor.
carburante *nm* fuel; **~ fósil** fossil fuel.
carburar* [1a] *vi* **(a)** *(funcionar)* to go, work. **(b)** *(pensar)* to think, ponder.
carburo *nm* carbide; **~ de silicio** silicon carbide.
carca* 1 *adj invar* square*; narrow-minded, having a closed mind; ancient; dead-beat*; *(Pol)* reactionary. **2** *nmf* **(a)** *(persona)* square*; narrow-minded person; old fogey; *(Pol)* reactionary; *(Hist)* Carlist. **(b)** *(And: mugre)* muck, filth.
carcacha* *nf (Méx: Aut)* old crock.
carcaj *nm (para flechas)* quiver; *(LAm: de fusil)* rifle case, pistol holster.
carcajada *nf* (loud) laugh, peal of laughter, guffaw; **hubo ~s** there was loud laughter; **reírse a ~s** to laugh heartily, roar with laughter; **soltar la ~** to burst out laughing.
carcajeante *adj conducta* riotous; *abrazo* hearty; *decisión etc* ridiculous, laughable.
carcajear [1a] *vi y* **carcajearse** *vr* to roar with laughter, have a good laugh *(de* at).
carcamal* *nm* **(a)** *(vejestorio)* old crock, wreck; **es un ~** he's a wreck. **(b)** = **carca.**
carcamán 1 *nm (Náut)* tub, hulk; *(And, Carib*)* old crock*, wreck. **2** *nm,* **carcamana** *nf* **(a)** **(*)** *(Carib: persona)* low-class person; *(And, Carib: inmigrante)* poor immigrant. **(b)** *(Cono Sur Pol)* diehard, reactionary.
carcancha *nf (Méx)* bus.
carcasa *nf (Aut etc)* chassis, grid; *(de neumático)* carcass; *(Téc)* casing.
carcayú *nm* wolverine.
cárcel *nf* **(a)** prison, jail; **~ abierta, ~ de régimen abierto** open prison; **~ modelo** model prison; **~ del pueblo** people's prison; **~ transitoria** remand centre; **poner en la ~** to jail, send to jail, put in prison. **(b)** *(Téc)* clamp.
carcelario *adj* prison *(atr)*.
carcelería *nf* imprisonment, detention.
carcelero 1 *adj* prison *(atr)*. **2** *nm* warder, jailer.
carcinogénico *adj* carcinogenic.
carcinógeno *nm* carcinogen.
carcinoma *nm* carcinoma.
carcocha *nf (And)* = **carcacha.**
carcoma *nf* **(a)** *(Ent)* deathwatch beetle; woodworm. **(b)** *(fig: preocupación)* anxiety, perpetual worry; *(persona)* spendthrift.
carcomer [2a] **1** *vt* **(a)** *(gen)* to bore into, eat into, eat away.
(b) *(fig) salud etc* to undermine; *fortuna* to eat into, eat away.
2 carcomerse *vr* **(a)** to get worm-eaten.
(b) *(fig)* to decay, waste away; to be eaten away.
carcomido *adj* worm-eaten, wormy, infested with woodworm; rotten; *(fig)* rotten, decayed.
carcoso *adj (And)* dirty, mucky.
carda *nf* **(a)** *(Bot)* teasel; *(Téc)* teasel, card *(for combing wool)*. **(b)** *(acto)* carding. **(c)** **(*:** *reprimenda)* reprimand; **dar una ~ a uno** to rap sb over the knuckles.
cardamomo *nm* cardamom.
cardán *nm (Cono Sur Aut)* propellor shaft; *(LAm Aut)* axle.
cardar [1a] *vt* **(a)** *(Téc)* to card, comb; **pelo cardado** swept-back hair. **(b)** **(*:** *t* **~ la lana a)** to tell off*, rap over the knuckles.
cardenal *nm* **(a)** *(Ecl)* cardinal. **(b)** *(Med)* bruise, mark, weal. **(c)** *(Cono Sur Bot)* geranium. **(d)** *(Orn)* cardinal bird.
cardenalato *nm* cardinalate.
cardenalicio *adj*: **capelo ~** cardinal's hat.
cardencha *nf (Bot, Téc)* teasel.
cardenillo *nm* verdigris.
cárdeno *adj* purple, violet; livid; *agua* opalescent.
cardiaco, cardíaco 1 *adj* **(a)** cardiac, heart *(atr)*. **(b)** **(*)** **estar ~ con** to be enchanted with, enthuse over. **2** *nm,* **cardíaca** *nf* heart case, sufferer from a heart complaint.
cardinal *adj* cardinal.
cardio... *pref* cardio...
cardiocirculano, -a *nm/f* heart surgeon.
cardiograma *nm* cardiogram, cardiograph.
cardiología *nf* cardiology.
cardiológico *adj* cardiological.
cardiólogo, -a *nm/f,* **cardiópata** *nmf* cardiologist, heart specialist.
cardiovascular *adj* cardiovascular.
cardo *nm* thistle; **es un ~*** he's very prickly.
cardón *nm (Cono Sur)* (species of) giant cactus.
cardume(n) *nm* **(a)** *(Pez)* shoal. **(b)** *(And, Cono Sur)* great number, mass; **un ~ de gente** a lot of people, a crowd of people.
carea *nm* sheepdog.
carear [1a] **1** *vt personas* to bring face to face; *textos* to compare, collate, check against each other.
2 *vi*: **~ a** to face towards, look on to.
3 carearse *vr* **(a)** *(2 personas)* to come face to face, come together, meet.
(b) **~ con** to face, face up to; to confront.
carecer [2d] *vi* **(a)** **~ de** to lack, be in need of, be without, want for; **carece de talento** he lacks talent, he has no talent; **no carecemos de dinero** we don't lack money, we're not short of money; **eso carece de sentido** that doesn't make sense; **aquí se carece de todo** here there is a great need of everything.
(b) *(Cono Sur: hacer falta)* **carece hacerlo** it is necessary to do it; **carece no dejarla** we must not allow her to.
carecimiento *nm* lack, need.
carel *nm* side, edge.
carena *nf* **(a)** *(Náut)* careening; **dar ~ a** to careen. **(b)** **(*)** ragging*; **dar ~ a uno** to rag sb*, tease sb.
carenar [1a] *vt* to careen.
carencia *nf* lack *(de* of), shortage *(de* of), need *(de* for); scarcity; *(Med etc)* deficiency; **(periodo de) ~** period free of interest payments and debt repayments.
carencial *adj*: **estado ~** state of want; **mal ~** deficiency disease.
carente *adj*: **~ de** lacking (in), devoid of.
carentón *adj (Cono Sur)* large-faced.
careo *nm* confrontation, meeting (face to face); comparison, collation; **~ (de policía)** identity parade; **someter sospechosos a ~** to bring suspects face to face.
carero *adj tienda* expensive, dear, pricey*.
carestía *nf* scarcity, shortage, dearth; famine; *(Com)* high price(s), high cost; **~ de la vida** high cost of living; **época de ~** period of shortage, lean period, bad time.
careta *nf* mask; *(Min etc)* breathing apparatus, respirator; **~ antigás** gasmask; **~ de esgrima** fencing mask; **quitar la ~ a uno** to unmask sb.
careto‡ 1 *adj* ugly. **2** *nm* clock‡, face.
carey *nm* tortoiseshell; *(Zool)* turtle.
carga *nf* **(a)** *(cargamento)* load; *(Náut)* cargo; *(Ferro)* freight; *(peso)* burden, weight; *(Aut)* tare, permitted load; **~ cinegética** carrying capacity; **~ fiscal** tax burden; **~ del hombre blanco** white man's burden; **~ de pago** payload; **a ~s** in plenty, in abundance, galore; **en plena ~** under full load; **bestia de ~** beast of burden; **buque de ~** freighter; **tomar ~** to load up, *(Náut)* take on cargo.
(b) *(Elec)* charge; load; **hilo con ~** live wire.
(c) *(Mec)* load; **~ fija, ~ muerta** dead load; **~ de fractura, ~ de rotura** breaking load; **~ útil** payload.
(d) *(Mil; t de obús, horno etc)* charge; **~ explosiva** explosive charge; **~ de pólvora** *(Min)* blasting powder; **~ de profundidad** depth charge.
(e) *(Fin)* tax, charge, duty; **~ impositiva** tax burden; **~s sociales** social security contribution.
(f) *(deber)* duty, obligation, charge; *(responsabilidad)* onus, responsibility; **~ de familia** dependent relative; **~**

personal personal commitments; **echar la ~ a uno** to put the blame on sb, put the onus on sb; **echarse con la ~*** to throw in the sponge; **llevar la ~** to be the one responsible (*de* for).

(**g**) (*Mil: ataque*) charge, attack; (*Dep*) charge, tackle; **~ a la bayoneta** bayonet charge; **~ de caballería** cavalry charge; **~ policial** baton charge; **tocar a ~** to sound the charge; **volver a la ~** (*fig*) to return to the charge, return to the attack.

(**h**) (*acto*) loading; (*Elec, Mil*) loading; charging; **de ~ frontal** front-loading; **andén de ~** loading platform; **'permitido ~ y descarga'** 'loading and unloading'; **estar a la ~** to be loading.

cargada *nf* (**a**) (*Cono Sur*) unpleasant practical joke.
(**b**) (*Méx*) = **carga (h).**
(**c**) **ir a la ~** (*Méx*) to jump on the bandwagon.

cargaderas *nfpl* (*And*) braces, suspenders (*US*).

cargadero *nm* (**a**) loading point; (*Ferro*) goods platform, loading bay. (**b**) (*Arquit*) lintel.

cargado *adj y ptp* (**a**) (*gen*) loaded, with a load, under load; *dados* loaded; (*esp fig*) laden, burdened, weighed down (*de* with); **estar ~ (de vino)** to be drunk; **estar ~ de años** to be very old, be weighed down with age; to be out of date; **estar ~ de hijos** to have a lot of children; **estar ~ de hostias‡** (*o* **puñetas‡** *etc*) to have lots of hang-ups*; **ser ~ de espaldas** to be round-shouldered, have a stoop; **un árbol ~ de fruto** a tree laden with fruit; **tener los ojos ~s de sueño** to have eyes heavy with sleep.
(**b**) (*Elec*) *hilo* live; *pila* charged.
(**c**) **~ (con bala)** (*Mil*) live.
(**d**) *café, té* strong; *licor* large; good and strong.
(**e**) *cielo* overcast; *atmósfera* heavy, sultry, close.

cargador *nm* (**a**) (*persona*) loader; (*transportador*) carrier, haulier; (*Náut*) docker, stevedore, longshoreman (*US*); (*de horno*) stoker; (*LAm*) porter.
(**b**) (*Téc: de cañón*) chamber; (*de pluma*) filler; (*Mil: Hist*) ramrod; **~ de acumuladores, ~ de baterías** battery charger.
(**c**) **~es** (*And*) braces, suspenders (*US*).

cargadora *nf* (*And, Carib*) nursemaid.

cargamento *nm* (**a**) (*acto*) loading. (**b**) (*carga*) load; (*Náut*) cargo; shipment; **~ de retorno** return cargo.

cargante 1 *adj persona* demanding, fussy; annoying, troublesome; *niño* trying; *tarea* irksome, tedious. **2** *nmf*: **es un ~** he's a pain*.

cargar [1h] **1** *vt* (**a**) (*gen*) to load (*de* with; *a, en* on); (**~** *demasiado*) to overload, burden, weigh down (*de* with); *dados* to load; *imaginación, mente etc* to fill (*de* with); **~ a uno de deudas** to encumber sb with debts; **~ a uno de nuevas obligaciones** to burden sb with new duties.
(**b**) (*Elec*) to charge; (*Inform*) to load.
(**c**) *horno* to stoke, charge.
(**d**) (*hacer más pesado*) to increase the weight of, cause to bear down more heavily; *V* **mano.**
(**e**) *impuesto* to impose, lay (*sobre* on); to increase.
(**f**) (*Com, Fin*) to charge, debit (*en cuenta a* to, to the account of); **~ de menos a uno** to undercharge sb; **~ una factura con un porcentaje por servicio** to add a service charge to a bill.
(**g**) (*achacar*) to impute, ascribe (*a* to); *culpa* to lay (*a* on); *responsabilidad* to entrust (*a* to), place (*a* on).
(**h**) (*Jur*) to charge, accuse; **~ a uno de poco escrupuloso** to accuse sb of being unscrupulous, charge sb with being unscrupulous.
(**i**) (*Mil*) *enemigo* to charge, attack.
(**j**) (*Mil*) *cañón* to load.
(**k**) (*Náut*) *vela* to take in.
(**l**) (*Univ**) *candidato* to plough*, fail.
(**m**) (*LAm*) to carry, have, use; to wear; **~ anteojos** to wear glasses; **~ revólver** to pack a gun*; **¿cargas dinero?** have you any money on (*o* with) you?
(**n**) (*And, Cono Sur: perro etc*) to attack, go for.
(**o**) (*) (*aburrir*) to bore; (*molestar*) to annoy, vex; **esto me carga** this annoys me, I find this annoying.

2 *vi* (**a**) (*Aut etc*) to load, load up; to take on a load; (*Náut*) to take on (a) cargo; **~ (demasiado, mucho)** (*fig*) to overeat, drink too much.
(**b**) **~ con** *objeto, peso* to pick up, carry away, take away; *peso* (*fig*) to shoulder, take upon o.s.; *responsabilidad* to assume, take on; *culpa* to bear.
(**c**) (*Ling: acento*) to fall (*en, sobre* on).
(**d**) (*inclinarse*) to lean, tip, incline.
(**e**) (*apoyarse*) **~ en, ~ sobre** to lean on, lean against; (*Arquit etc*) to rest on, be supported by.
(**f**) **~ sobre uno** (*presionar*) to urge sb, press sb; to importune sb.
(**g**) (*dar la lata*) to pester, be annoying.
(**h**) (*Met*) to turn, veer (*a* to, *hacia* towards).
(**i**) (*apiñarse*) to crowd together, concentrate; to come in large numbers.

3 cargarse *vr* (**a**) **~ algo** to take sth on o.s.; **~ de algo** to be full of sth, be loaded with sth; to fill o.s. up with sth, (*fig*) get one's fill of sth; **~ de hijos** to overburden o.s. with children; **~ de años** to get very old; **el árbol se carga de manzanas** the tree produces apples in abundance.
(**b**) = *vi* (**d**), (**e**).
(**c**) (*Elec*) to become charged, become live.
(**d**) (*Met: cielo*) to become overcast; (*atmósfera*) to become heavy, become oppressive.
(**e**) (*) (*enfadarse*) to get cross; (*aburrirse*) to get bored.
(**f**) **~la*** to get into hot water, get it in the neck*.
(**g**) **~ a*** (*matar*) to do in‡, bump off‡; (*eliminar*) to get rid of, remove, suppress; **¡algún día me lo cargaré!** I'll get him one day!
(**h**) **~ algo*** to break sth, smash sth.
(**i**) **~ a⁑** to screw⁑.

cargazón *nf* (**a**) (*carga*) load; (*Náut*) cargo, shipment; (*fig*) dead weight, useless mass.
(**b**) (*Med*) heaviness (*of stomach etc*).
(**c**) (*Met*) mass of heavy cloud.
(**d**) **~ de espaldas** stoop.
(**e**) (*Cono Sur*) abundance of fruit (*on tree*).

cargo *nm* (**a**) (*carga, peso*) load, weight, burden.
(**b**) (*fig*) burden; **~ de conciencia** burden on one's conscience; remorse, guilty feeling.
(**c**) (*Com*) charge, debit; **una cantidad en ~ a uno** a sum to be charged to sb; **ser en ~ a uno** to be indebted to sb; **girar a ~ de, librar a ~ de** to draw on.
(**d**) (*puesto*) post, office; (*Teat y fig*) role, part; **un ~ casi sin responsabilidades** a post almost without duties; **desempeñar un ~** to fill an office; **jurar el ~** to take the oath of office, be sworn into office; **vestir el ~** to look the part, dress the part.
(**e**) (*persona*) office-holder; highly-placed official; **altos ~s** people in authority, top people; senior officials; **altos ~s directivos** senior management, top management.
(**f**) (*deber*) duty, obligation, responsibility; (*custodia*) charge, care; **a ~ de** in the charge of; **tener algo a su ~** to have sth in one's charge, be in charge of sth; **hacerse ~ de** to take charge of; to see about; to realize, understand; **el ejército se hizo ~ del poder** the army took over power; **apenas si pude hacerme ~ de ello** I could scarcely grasp what was going on; **parecía no hacerse ~ de la dificultad** he seemed not to understand the difficulty.
(**g**) (*Jur*) charge; (*reproche*) reproach, accusation; **hacer a uno ~ de algo** to charge sb with sth.

cargosear [1a] *vt* (*And, Cono Sur*) to pester, keep on at.

cargoso *adj* (*Cono Sur*) maddening, annoying.

carguera *nf* (*And, Carib*) nursemaid.

carguero *nm* (**a**) (*Náut*) freighter, cargo boat; (*Aer*) freight plane, transport plane; **~ militar** air-force transport plane.
(**b**) (*And, Cono Sur: bestia de carga*) beast of burden.
(**c**) (*Méx*) lorry, truck.

carguío *nm* load; cargo, freight.

cari *adj* (*Cono Sur*) grey.

cariacontecido *adj* crestfallen, down in the mouth, woebegone.

cariado *adj diente, hueso* bad, rotten, decayed, carious.

cariadura *nf* (*Med*) caries, decay.

cariancho *adj* broad-faced.

cariar [1h] **1** *vt* to cause to decay, cause decay in. **2 cariarse** *vr* to decay, become decayed.

cariátide *nf* caryatid.

caribe 1 *adj* (**a**) (*Geog etc*) Caribbean; **Mar C~** Caribbean Sea.
(**b**) (*LAm*) (*caníbal*) cannibalistic; (*fig*) savage, cruel.
2 *nmf* Carib, inhabitant of the Caribbean area.
3 *nm* (*LAm*) cannibal; (*Carib: fig:* ††) savage, wild man.

caribeño = **caribe.**

caribú *nm* caribou.

caricato *nm* (*Cono Sur, Méx*) = **caricatura.**

caricatura *nf* caricature (*t fig*); cartoon.

caricaturesco *adj* absurd, ridiculous.

caricaturista *nmf* caricaturist; cartoonist.

caricaturización *f* caricaturization, caricaturing.

caricaturizar [1f] *vt* to caricature.

caricia *nf* (**a**) caress; pat, stroke; **hacer ~s** to caress, fondle, stroke.
(**b**) (*fig*) endearment.
caricioso *adj* caressing, affectionate.
caridad *nf* charity; charitableness; **¡por ~!** for goodness sake!; **la ~ empieza por uno mismo** charity begins at home; **hacer ~ a uno** to give alms to sb; **hacer la ~ de** + *infin* to do the favour of + *ger*.
carie *nf*, **caries** *nf invar* (**a**) (*Med*) dental decay, caries. (**b**) (*Agr*) blight.
carigordo *adj* fat-faced.
carilampiño *adj* (*afeitado*) clean-shaven; *joven* smooth-faced, beardless.
carilargo *adj* long-faced; (*LAm*) annoyed.
carilla *nf* (**a**) (*careta*) bee veil. (**b**) (*Tip*) side (of a sheet of paper).
carillero *adj* round-faced, full-faced.
carillo* *adj* a bit expensive, on the dear side.
carillón *nm* carillon.
carimbo *nm* (*LAm*) branding iron.
cariño *nm* (**a**) (*afecto*) affection, love (*a, por* for); fondness, liking (*a, por* for); tenderness; **sí, ~** yes, my dear; **sentir ~ por, tener ~ a** to like, be fond of; **por el ~ que te tengo** because I'm fond of you; **tomar ~ a** to take a liking to, get fond of.
(**b**) (*LAm*) (*caricia*) caress, stroke; (*regalo*) gift, token (of affection); **hacerle ~ a uno** to caress (*o* stroke) sb.
(**c**) **~s** endearments; show of affection.
cariñosamente *adv* affectionately, lovingly, fondly; tenderly.
cariñoso *adj* affectionate, loving, fond; tender.
carioca 1 *adj* of Rio de Janeiro, of the State of Guanabara. **2** *nmf* native (*o* inhabitant) of Rio de Janeiro, native (*o* inhabitant) of the State of Guanabara.
cariparejo *adj* poker-faced, inscrutable.
carirraído *adj* brazen, shameless.
carirredondo *adj* round-faced.
carisellazo *nm* (*And*) toss of a coin; **echar un ~** to toss (*o* spin) a coin.
carisma *nm* charisma.
carismático *adj* charismatic.
carita *nf* little face; **de ~** (*And*) first-class; jolly good*; **dar** (*o* **hacer**) **~** (*Méx: mujer*) to return a smile, flirt (back); **hacer ~s** (*And*) to make faces.
caritativamente *adv* charitably.
caritativo *adj* charitable (*con, para* to).
cariz *nm* look, aspect; (*fig*) outlook; (*Met*) look of the sky; **mal ~** scowl; **poner mal ~** to scowl; **esto va tomando mal ~** this business is beginning to look bad, I don't like the look of this; **en vista del ~ que toman las cosas** in view of the way things are going.
carlanca *nf* (**a**) spiked dog-collar; (*And, CAm: grillo*) shackle, fetter.
(**b**) (*CAm, Cono Sur*) (*persona*) bore, pest, drag; (*aburrimiento*) boredom, tedium; (*enojo*) annoyance, irritation.
(**c**) **~s** tricks, cunning; **tener muchas ~s** to be full of tricks.
carlinga *nf* (*Aer*) cockpit, pilot's cabin; interior of an aeroplane.
carlismo *nm* Carlism.
carlista *adj, nmf* Carlist.
carlistada *nf* Carlist attack, Carlist uprising.
Carlitos *nm forma familiar de* **Carlos** Charlie.
Carlomagno *nm* Charlemagne.
Carlos *nm* Charles.
Carlota *nf* Charlotte.
carlota *nf* (*Culin*) charlotte.
carmelita[1] (*Ecl*) **1** *adj* Carmelite. **2** *nmf* Carmelite; **~ descalzo** discalced Carmelite.
carmelita[2] *adj*, **carmelito** *adj* (*esp LAm*) light brown, tan.
carmelitano *adj* Carmelite.
Carmelo *nm* Carmelite convent.
carmen[1] *nm* (*Granada*) villa with a garden.
carmen[2] *nm* (*Liter*) song, poem.
Carmen *nm* (*Ecl*) Carmelite Order.
carmenar [1a] *vt* (**a**) (*Téc*) *lana* to card, teasel; *seda etc* to unravel; *pelo* to disentangle; **~ el pelo a uno*** to pull sb's hair. (**b**) (*) to fleece, swindle.
carmesí *adj, nm* crimson.
carmín *nm* (**a**) carmine; rouge, lipstick. (**b**) (*Bot*) dog rose.
carminativo *adj, nm* carminative.
carmíneo *adj* carmine, crimson.
carnada *nf* bait.
carnal 1 *adj* (**a**) (*Rel*) carnal, of the flesh. (**b**) *parentesco* full, blood (*atr*); **hermano ~** full brother; **primo ~** first cousin; **tío ~** real uncle. **2** *nm* (*Méx**) pal*, buddy (*US*).
carnalidad *nf* lust, carnality.
carnaval *nm* carnival (*t fig*); (*Ecl*) Shrovetide; **martes de ~** Shrove Tuesday.
carnavalero *adj*, **carnavalesco** *adj* carnival (*atr*).
carne *nf* (**a**) (*Anat*) flesh; **~ de gallina** (*fig*) gooseflesh; **~ viciosa** (*Med*) proud flesh; **me pone la ~ de gallina** it gives me gooseflesh, (*fig*) it makes my flesh creep, it gives me the creeps; **de abundantes ~s, de muchas ~s** fat; **entrado en ~s** plump, overweight; **algo metido en ~s** somewhat plump; **de pocas ~s** thin; **en ~ viva** on the raw; **en ~s** naked, with nothing on; **se me abrieron las ~s** I was terrified; **cobrar** (*o* **criar, echar**) **~s** to put on weight; **perder ~s** to lose weight; **ser de ~ y hueso** to be only human, have the same feelings as other people; **tener ~ de perro** to have an iron constitution.
(**b**) (*Culin*) meat; **~ adobada** salt meat; **~ asada** roast meat; **~ blanca** white meat; **~s blandas** (*Cono Sur*) white meat; **~ de bovino** beef; **~ de cañón** cannon-fodder; **~ de carnero** mutton; **~ de cerdo** pork; **~ concentrada** meat extract; **~ congelada** frozen meat; **~ de cordero** lamb, mutton; **~ deshilachada** (*CAm, Méx*) stewed meat; **~ fiambre** cold meat; **~ de horca** good-for-nothing, gallows bird; **~ magra, ~ mollar** lean meat; **~ marinada** (*LAm*) salt meat; **~ molida** (*LAm*) mince, minced meat; **~ de oveja, ~ ovina, ~ de ovino** mutton, lamb; sheepmeat; **~ picada** mince, minced meat; **~ porcina, ~ de porcino** pork; pigmeat; **~ de res** (*LAm*) beef; **~ roja** red meat; **~ salvajina** game; **~ tapada** stewed meat, stew; **~ de ternera** veal; **~ de vaca, ~ de vacuno** beef; **~ de venado** venison; **no ser ~ ni pescado** to be neither fish nor fowl, be neither one thing nor the other; **poner toda la ~ en el asador** to go the whole hog, stake one's all.
(**c**) (*Bot*) flesh, fleshy part, pulp; (*LAm: de árbol*) heart, hardest part; **~ de membrillo** quince jelly.
(**d**) (*Ecl etc*) flesh, carnality.
carné *nm* = **carnet**.
carneada *nf* (*Cono Sur*) (*de animales*) slaughter(ing); (*masacre*) slaughter, massacre.
carnear [1a] *vt* (**a**) (*Cono Sur*) *animal* to slaughter (and dress); (*fig: asesinar*) to murder, butcher.
(**b**) (*Cono Sur: engañar*) to cheat, swindle.
carnecería *nf* = **carnicería**.
carnerada *nf* flock of sheep.
carnerear [1a] *vi* (*Cono Sur*) to blackleg, be a strikebreaker.
carnerero *nm* shepherd.
carnero *nm* (**a**) (*Zool*) sheep, ram; **~ marino** seal; **~ de la sierra** (*LAm*), **~ de la tierra** (*LAm*) llama, alpaca, vicuña; **~ de simiente** breeding ram; **no hay tales ~s** there's no such thing; it's nothing of the sort; **cantar para el ~‡** to kick the bucket‡, peg out‡.
(**b**) (*Culin*) mutton.
(**c**) (*piel*) sheepskin.
(**d**) (*Cono Sur**) (*débil*) weak-willed person; (*esquirol*) blackleg, strikebreaker.
(**e**) **botarse** (*o* **echarse**) **al ~** (*Cono Sur*) to chuck it all up*, throw in the towel.
carnestolendas *nfpl* Shrovetide.
carnet [kar'ne] *nm, pl* **carnets** [kar'ne] (*librito*) notebook; (*de banco*) bankbook; (*de viaje*) (tourist's) travel voucher; **~ de conducir, ~ de conductor, ~ de chófer, ~ de manejo** (*LAm*) driving licence; **~ de identidad** identity card; **~ sindical** union card; **~ de socio** membership card.
carnicería *nf* (**a**) (*tienda*) butcher's (shop); (*mercado*) meat market; (*And*) slaughterhouse.
(**b**) (*fig*) slaughter, carnage; **~ en las carreteras** carnage on the roads; **hacer una ~ de** to massacre, slaughter.
carnicero 1 *adj* (**a**) (*Zool*) carnivorous, flesh-eating; (*Orn*) of prey; (*) *persona* fond of meat.
(**b**) (*fig*) savage, cruel, bloodthirsty.
2 *nm* (**a**) butcher (*t fig*).
(**b**) (*Zool*) carnivore.
cárnico *adj* meat (*atr*); **industria cárnica** meat industry.
carnitas *nfpl* (*Méx*) barbecued pork.
carnívoro 1 *adj* carnivorous, flesh-eating; meat-eating. **2** *nm* carnivore.
carnosidad *nf* (**a**) fleshiness; corpulence, obesity. (**b**) (*Med*) proud flesh.
carnoso *adj* beefy, fat.
carnudo *adj* fleshy.
caro 1 *adj* (**a**) (*querido*) dear, beloved; **las cosas que nos son tan caras** the things which are so dear to us.

(**b**) (*Com*) dear, expensive; **un coche carísimo** a terribly expensive car.
2 *adv* dear, dearly; **le costó muy ~** it cost him dear; **eso sale bastante ~** that comes rather expensive; **vender ~** to sell at a high price.

carocas* *nfpl* (*lisonjas*) (exaggerated) flattery; (*caricias*) caresses; (*jabón*) soft soap*.

carocha* *nf* (*Méx*) old banger‡, old crock.

caroleno *nm* (*Méx*) backslang.

Carolina[1] *nf* Caroline.

Carolina[2] *nf* (*Geog*): **~ del Norte** North Carolina; **~ del Sur** South Carolina.

carolingio *adj* Carolingian.

carón 1 *adj* (*LAm*) broad-faced. **2** *nm* (‡) mug‡, face.

carona *nf* (**a**) (*paño*) saddlecloth; (*parte del caballo*) saddle; **andar con las ~s ladeadas** (*Cono Sur*) to have problems. (**b**) (*Cono Sur*) bed.

carota* 1 *adj invar* barefaced, brazen. **2** *nmf* rotter*; shameless person.

carótida *nf* carotid (artery).

carozo *nm* (**a**) cob of maize, corncob (*US*). (**b**) (*LAm*: *de fruta*) stone, core (*of fruit*).

carpa[1] *nf* (*Pez*) carp; **~ dorada** goldfish.

carpa[2] *nf* (*tienda de campaña*) tent; (*toldo*) marquee; awning; (*de circo*) big top; (*LAm*: *Com*) market stall, open-air shop.

carpanta* *nf* ravenous hunger.

Cárpatos *adj*: **Montes ~** Carpathians.

carpeta *nf* (**a**) (*para papeles*) folder, file; portfolio; (*cartera*) briefcase; (*de disco*) sleeve; **~ de información** information folder, briefing kit; **cerrar la ~** to close the file (*in an investigation*).
(**b**) (*paño*: *t* **~ de mesa**) table cover.
(**c**) (*LAm*: *pupitre*) table, desk.

carpetazo *nm*: **dar ~ a** to shelve, put on one side, do nothing about.

carpetovetónico *adj* terribly Spanish, Spanish to the core; reactionary, ultraconservative.

carpidor *nm*, **carpidora** *nf* (*LAm*) weeding hoe.

carpintear [1a] *vi* to carpenter; to do woodwork (*as a hobby*).

carpintería *nf* (**a**) (*oficio etc*) carpentry, joinery, woodwork. (**b**) (*taller*) carpenter's shop.

carpintero *nm* (**a**) (*Téc*) carpenter; woodworker; **~ de blanco** joiner; **~ de carretas, ~ de prieto** cartwright, wheelwright; **~ de buque, ~ de ribera** ship's carpenter, shipwright.
(**b**) (*Orn*) woodpecker.

carpir [3a] *vt* (*LAm*) to weed, hoe.

carraca *nf* (**a**) (*Náut*: *Hist*) carrack; (*pey*) tub, old hulk.
(**b**) (*Mús, Dep*) rattle.
(**c**) (*Téc*) ratchet brace.
(**d**) (*: *coche*) old crock.
(**e**) **echar ~** (*And*) to lie.

carraco 1 *adj* feeble, decrepit. **2** *nm* (*: *coche*) old crock*.

carrada *nf* (*Cono Sur*) = **carretada.**

carral *nm* barrel, vat.

carralero *nm* cooper.

carrasca *nf* kermes oak; **ser de ~*** = **ser de aúpa**; *V* **aúpa.**

carrascoloso‡ *adj* (*LAm*) grumpy*, touchy, irritable.

carraspear [1a] *vi* (*al hablar*) to be hoarse, have a frog in one's throat; (*aclararse*) to clear one's throat, hawk.

carraspeo *nm* sore throat.

carraspera *nf* hoarseness, frog in the throat.

carrasposo *adj* (**a**) hoarse, having a sore throat. (**b**) (*LAm*) rough, harsh.

carrera *nf* (**a**) (*acto*) run; running; chase, rush; **a ~ (abierta), a ~ tendida** at full speed, all out; **a la ~** at full speed; hastily; **de ~** hastily; rashly, without thinking; easily; **partir de ~** to proceed rashly; **dar ~ libre a** to give free rein to; **darse una ~** to rush; **hacer la ~*** (*prostituta*) to walk her beat, work, ply her trade, (*gen*) to be on the game*; **hacer el trabajo a la ~** to race through one's work; **~ de aterrizaje** landing run; **~ de despegue** take-off run; **~ del oro** gold-rush.
(**b**) (*Dep*: *béisbol etc*) run.
(**c**) (*Dep*: *concurso*) race; **~s** races, racing; **de ~(s)** racing (*atr*), race (*atr*); **caballo de ~(s)** racehorse; **coche de ~s** racing car; **~ armamentística, ~ de armamentos** arms race; **~ de caballos** horse race; **~ por carretera** road race; **~ de ensacados** (*Cono Sur*) sack race; **~ contra el reloj** race against the clock; **~ contra el tiempo** race against time; **~ corta** dash, short run, sprint; **~ espacial** space race; **~ de fondo** long-distance race; **~ de medio fondo** middle-distance race; **~ lisa** flat race; **~ hacia la luna** race for the moon, race to get to the moon; **~ de maratón** marathon; **~ de obstáculos** obstacle race; (*de caballos*) steeplechase; **~ en parada** running on the spot; **~ pedestre** walking race, foot race; **~ de relevos** relay race; **~ de resistencia** endurance race, long-distance race; **~ de ruta** road race; **~ de sacos** sack race; **~ de trotones** harness race; **~ de vallas** hurdle race, hurdles; (*de caballos*) steeplechase; **abrir ~** to lead the race, be in front; **apuntarse a la ~** to stay in the running.
(**d**) (*hilera*) row, line; (*Arquit*: *de ladrillos etc*) course; (*pista*) track; (*en pelo*) parting; (*de media*) run, ladder.
(**e**) (*Arquit*: *viga*) beam, girder, joist.
(**f**) (*Mús*) run.
(**g**) (*Náut*) run, route; (*de desfile*) route; (*de taxi*) ride, journey; (*Astron*) course; **~ de Indias** (*Hist*) the Indies run; **la ~ del sol** the course of the sun.
(**h**) (*esp LAm*: *avenida*) avenue.
(**i**) (*Mec*) (*de émbolo*) stroke; (*de válvula*) lift; **~ ascendente** upstroke; **~ descendente** downstroke.
(**j**) (*fig*) career; profession; **diplomático de ~** career diplomat; **dar ~ a uno** to give sb his education, pay for sb's professional studies; to put sb to a career; **hacer ~** to get on in one's career; to get on in the world, make headway; **no hago ~ con este niño** I can't make any headway with this child; **no tiene ~** he has no profession, he doesn't do anything serious in life.
(**k**) (*Univ*) course, studies; period of study; **cuando termine la ~** when he finishes his course, when he qualifies.
(**l**) (*de la vida*) course of human life.

carrerilla *nf*: **a ~** non-stop, continuously; **de ~** on the trot, in succession; **lo dijo de ~** he reeled it off.

carrerista 1 *adj* fond of racing; (*pey*) horsy. **2** *nmf* (**a**) (*aficionado a carreras de caballos*) racing man, racing woman, racegoer; professional punter. (**b**) (*ciclista*) racing cyclist. (**c**) (*Pol*) careerist, career politician. **3** *nf* (*) streetwalker.

carrero *nm* carter, cart driver.

carreta *nf* (long narrow) wagon, low cart; (*And, Carib*) wheelbarrow; **~ de mano** = **carretilla**; **~ de bueyes** oxcart; **tener la ~ llena** (*Carib*: *fig*) to be weighed down by problems.

carretada *nf* cart load; (*fig*) cart load, great quantity; **a ~s** in loads, galore.

carretaje *nm* cartage, haulage.

carrete *nm* (*gen*) reel, spool; (*Cos*) reel, bobbin; (*Elec*) coil; (*Fot*) cartridge, film, spool; (*Pez*) reel; **~ de encendido** (*Aut*) ignition coil; **~ de inducción** (*Elec*) induction coil; **dar ~ a uno** to keep sb guessing, keep sb in suspense.

carretear [1a] *vt* (**a**) *carga* to cart, haul. (**b**) *carro* to drive; (*Aer*) to taxi.

carretel *nm* (fishing) reel; (*Náut*) log reel.

carretela *nf* (*Hist*) coach, carriage; calash; (*CAm*: *carro*) cart.

carretera *nf* (main) road, highway; **de ~** road (*atr*); **por ~** by road; **~ de circunvalación** bypass, ring road; **~ comarcal** country road; **~ de cuota** (*LAm*) toll road, turnpike (*US*); **~ nacional** *corresponde a* A-road (*Brit*), major road; **~ radial** ring road; **~ secundaria** ≃ B-road (*Brit*).

carretero 1 *adj*: **camino ~** vehicular road. **2** *nm* (**a**) (*transportista*) carter; cart driver; (*ruedero*) cartwright, wheelwright; **fuma como un ~** he smokes like a chimney. (**b**) (*LAm*) road.

carretilla *nf* (**a**) (*carro pequeño*) truck, trolley; (*t* **~ de mano**) handcart, barrow; (*Agr, Hort*) wheelbarrow; (*de niño*) go-cart; (*de bebé*) baby-walker; (*de supermercado*) trolley; **~ elevadora, ~ de horquilla** fork-lift truck.
(**b**) (*buscapiés*) squib, cracker.
(**c**) (*Cono Sur*: *quijada*) jaw, jawbone.
(**d**) (*And*: *lote*) lot, series.
(**e**) **aprender algo de ~** to learn sth mechanically; **saber algo de ~** to know sth by heart.

carretón *nm* small cart; wagon, dray; (*Ferro*) bogey; **~ de remolque** trailer.

carricero *nm*: **~ común** reed-warbler.

carricoche *nm* covered wagon, (gipsy) caravan; (*) crock.

carricuba *nf* water cart.

carriel *nm* (*And, CAm*) leather case.

carril *nm* (**a**) (*rodada*) rut, track; (*camino*) cart track, lane; (*de carretera*) lane; (*Agr*) furrow; **~ de adelantamiento** fast lane; **~ de autobús** bus lane; **~ de bicicleta** cycleway, cycle-path.

(**b**) (*Ferro*) rail, railway; (*Carib, Cono Sur*: *tren*) train; ~ **de toma** third rail.

carrilano *nm* (*Cono Sur*) (**a**) (*atracador*) robber, hold-up man. (**b**) (*Ferro*) railwayman.

carril-bicicleta *nm, pl* **carriles-bicicleta** cycleway, cycle-path.

carril-bus *nm, pl* **carriles-bus** bus lane.

carrilera *nf* (**a**) (*rodera*) rut, track. (**b**) (*Carib Ferro*) siding.

carrilero *nm* (*And Ferro*) railwayman; (*Cono Sur*‡: *embaucador*) con man*.

carrillera *nf* (**a**) (*Zool*) jaw. (**b**) (*de casco*) chinstrap.

carrillo *nm* (**a**) (*mejilla*) cheek; jowl; **comer a dos ~s** (*comer*) to eat greedily, stuff o.s.; (*más de un empleo*) to moonlight*, have more than one well-paid job; (*fig*) to run with the hare and hunt with the hounds.

(**b**) (*Téc*) pulley.

carrindanga* *nf* (*Cono Sur*) old crock.

carriola *nf* truckle bed.

carrito *nm* (**a**) (*de supermercado*: *t* ~ **de la compra**) trolley, shopping cart (*US*); (*de hotel etc*) tea trolley, serving-trolley; ~ **de bebidas** drinks trolley; ~ **de postres** dessert trolley. (**b**) (*Carib*: *taxi*) taxi.

carrizal *nm* reedbed.

carrizo *nm* (**a**) (*Bot*) reed. (**b**) **~s** (*And, Méx*) thin (*o* spindly) legs, pins‡; **hacer** ~ (*And*) to cross one's legs. (**c**) **no nos ayudan en un** ~ (*Carib*) they do nothing at all to help us. (**d**) (*And, CAm, Carib*) = **caramba.**

carro *nm* (**a**) (*gen*) cart, wagon; (*Hist*: *t* ~ **de guerra**) chariot; (*de supermercado*) trolley, shopping cart (*US*); (*LAm*) (*any*) vehicle, (*esp*) car, automobile; (*LAm*: *taxi*) cab, taxi; (*Mil*) tank; (*LAm Ferro*) car, truck, coach; ~ **alegórico** float (*in a procession*); ~ **aljibe** water cart; ~ **blindado** armoured car; ~ **de combate** tank; ~ **comedor** (*Méx*) dining-car; ~ **correo** (*LAm Ferro*) mail van; ~ **cuba** tank truck; ~ **dormitorio** (*Méx*) sleeping-car; ~ **fuerte** heavy trolley; ~ **fúnebre** hearse; ~ **de golf** golf buggy; ~ **de mudanzas** removal van; ~ **de riego** water cart; ~ **tranvía**, ~ **urbano** (*LAm*) tramcar, streetcar (*US*); **aguantar** (*o* **pasar por**) **~s y carretas** to put up with anything, remain undismayed; **apearse del ~*** to back down; **arrimarse al ~ del que manda, subirse al** ~ to climb on the bandwagon; **era como si cantara un** ~ it was like talking to a brick wall; **poner el ~ delante de las mulas** to put the cart before the horse; **¡pare Vd el ~!** hold your horses!; **tirar del** ~ (*fig*) to do all the donkey-work; **untar el ~ a uno** to grease sb's palm; *V t* **carrito.**

(**b**) (*cantidad*) cartload; **un ~ de problemas** (*fig*) a whole load of problems.

(**c**) (*de máquina de escribir*) carriage.

carrocería *nf* (**a**) (*taller*) coachbuilder's; carriage repair shop. (**b**) (*Aut etc*) bodywork, coachwork.

carrocero *nm* coachbuilder, carriage builder.

carrocha *nf* (*Ent*) eggs, ova.

carromato *nm* covered wagon, (gipsy) caravan.

carroña *nf* carrion.

carroñero *adj* (**a**) rotten; (*fig*) vile, foul. (**b**) **animal** ~ animal which feeds on carrion.

carroño *adj* (**a**) (*putrefacto*) rotten, putrid, foul. (**b**) (*And*: *cobarde*) cowardly.

carroza 1 *nf* (**a**) (*carruaje*) (state) coach, carriage; (*en desfile*) float; ~ **fúnebre** hearse.

(**b**) (*Náut*) awning.

2 *nm* (*) (**a**) (*viejo*) old geezer‡, old boy*; old fogey*; (*carca*) square*; (*Pol*) old reactionary.

(**b**) (*homosexual*) gay*, queer‡; old queen‡.

3 *adj invar* (*) archaic, passé; square*.

carruaje *nm* carriage; vehicle.

carrujo‡ *nm* (*LAm*) joint‡, reefer‡.

carrusel *nm* (**a**) (*de verbena*) merry-go-round, roundabout. (**b**) (*Fot*) carrousel, circular slide-tray. (**c**) (*de regalos etc*) revolving display.

carry-all *nm* (*Cono Sur*) estate car, station wagon (*US*).

carta *nf* (**a**) (*gen*) letter; ~ **abierta** open letter; ~ **de acuse de recibo** letter of acknowledgement; ~ **adjunta** covering letter; ~ **aérea** air-mail letter; ~ **de ajuste** test card; ~ **de amor,** ~ **amorosa** love-letter; ~ **de asignación** letter of allotment; ~ **de aviso** letter of advice; ~ **certificada** registered letter; **~s credenciales** letters of credence; ~ **de crédito** letter of credit; ~ **de emplazamiento** (*Jur*) summons; ~ **de intenciones** letter of intent; ~ **particular,** ~ **privada** private letter, personal letter; ~ **pastoral** pastoral letter; ~ **de pedido** (*Com*) order; ~ **de pésame** letter of condolence; ~ **de porte** waybill; ~ **postal** (*LAm*) postcard; ~ **de presentación,** ~ **de recomendación** letter of introduction (*para* to); ~ **de solicitud** (letter of) application; ~ **urgente** special-delivery letter; **echar una ~ al correo** to post a letter.

(**b**) (*Jur*) document, deed; (*Hist*: *de ciudad etc*) charter; ~ **blanca** carte blanche; **dar ~ blanca a uno** to give sb carte blanche; **tener ~ blanca** to have a free hand; ~ **de ciudadanía,** ~ **de naturaleza** naturalization papers; **adquirir ~ de naturaleza** (*fig*) to come to seem native, be thoroughly accepted; ~ **ejecutoria,** ~ **de hidalguía** letters patent of nobility; **C~ Magna** (*Brit*) Magna Carta; ~ **de pago** receipt, discharge in full; ~ **partida (por ABC)** indenture; ~ **de privilegio** company charter; ~ **de trabajo** work permit; ~ **de venta** bill of sale; ~ **verde** (*Aut*) green card; **a ~ cabal** thoroughly, in every respect; one hundred per cent; loyally; **caballero a ~ cabal** a thorough gentleman; **¡~ canta!** there it is in black and white!

(**c**) (*Geog*) map (*t* ~ **geográfica**); (*Náut*) chart; ~ **acotada** contour map; ~ **astral** star chart; ~ **de flujo** flowchart; ~ **de marear,** ~ **marítima** chart; ~ **meteorológica** weather map; ~ **naval,** ~ **de navegación,** ~ **de viaje** chart; ~ **de vuelo** flight plan.

(**d**) (*Naipes*) card, playing card; ~ **de figura** court card, picture card; **a ~s vistas** openly, honestly; with inside information; **echar las ~s** to tell sb's fortune (with cards); **enseñar las ~s** (*fig*) to show one's hand; **poner las ~s boca arriba, poner las ~s sobre la mesa** to put one's cards on the table; **no saber a qué ~ quedarse** not to know what to think, be undecided; to be in a dilemma; **tener** (*o* **tomar**) **~s en un asunto** to intervene (*o* take a hand) in a matter, come in on an affair; **más vale pecar por ~ de más que por ~ de menos** better safe than sorry.

(**e**) (*Culin*) menu; ~ **de vinos** wine list; **a la** ~ à la carte.

carta-bomba *nf, pl* **cartas-bomba** letter-bomb.

cartabón *nm* (*de carpintero*) square, set-square; (*de delineante*) triangle; (*Agrimen, Mil*) quadrant.

cartagenero 1 *adj* of Cartagena. **2** *nm,* **cartagenera** *nf* native (*o* inhabitant) of Cartagena; **los ~s** the people of Cartagena.

cartaginés 1 *adj* Carthaginian. **2** *nm,* **cartaginesa** *nf* Carthaginian.

Cartago *nf* Carthage.

cartapacio *nm* (*cuaderno*) notebook; (*carpeta*) folder, briefcase; (*de colegial*) satchel.

carta-tarjeta *nf, pl* **cartas-tarjeta** letter-card.

cartear [1a] **1** *vi* (*Naipes*) to play low. **2 cartearse** *vr* to correspond (*con* with); **se cartearon durante 2 años** they wrote to each other for 2 years.

cartel *nm* (*t* **cártel** *nm LAm*) (**a**) (*gen*) poster, placard; (*Teat etc*) bill; (*Cine*) credits, list of credits; (*Escol*) wall chart; ~ **de completo** 'full up' sign; ~ **de escaparate** window card; **torero de ~** star bullfighter; **poner ~*** (*Teat*) to be sold out; **tener ~*** to be a hit, be all the rage; **'se prohibe fijar ~es'** 'post no bills'.

(**b**) (*Com, Fin*) cartel, trust.

cartela *nf* (**a**) (*papel*) slip of paper, bit of card. (**b**) (*Arquit*) console; corbel; cartouche.

cartelera *nf* (*valla*) hoarding, billboard; (*tablón*) notice board; (*en periódico*) list of plays, theatre section; **mantenerse en la ~, seguir en la ~** to run, be on; **se mantuvo en la ~ durante 3 años** it ran for 3 years.

cartelero *nm* billsticker, billposter.

cartelista *nmf* poster artist, poster designer.

cartelón *nm* large notice; sign.

carteo *nm* correspondence, exchange of letters.

cárter *nm* (*Mec*) housing, case; ~ **del cigüeñal** (*Aut*) sump; crankcase.

cartera *nf* (**a**) (*de bolsillo*) wallet, pocketbook; (*para papeles*) letterfile, portfolio; (*de mano*) briefcase; (*carpeta*) folder; (*Cos*) pocket flap; (*LAm*: *bolso*) handbag, purse (*US*); (*de motocicleta*) pannier bag; (*de colegial*) satchel; ~ **de bolsillo** wallet; ~ **de herramientas** saddle-bag, toolbag; ~ **de mano** briefcase.

(**b**) (*Com*) ~ **de clientes** client portfolio; ~ **de pedidos** order-book; ~ **de pedidos exteriores** export order-book; **proyecto en** ~ plan in the pipeline.

(**c**) (*Pol*) portfolio, ministerial post; **ministro sin** ~ minister without portfolio.

(**d**) (*Fin*: *t* ~ **de valores**) portfolio, holdings; **efectos en** ~ holdings, stocks.

carterero *nm* (*Cono Sur*) pickpocket; bagsnatcher.

carterista *nm* pickpocket.

carterita *nf*: ~ **de fósforos** book of matches.

cartero *nm* postman, mailman (*US*).
cartesiano, -a *adj, nm/f* Cartesian.
cartilaginoso *adj* cartilaginous.
cartílago *nm* cartilage.
cartilla *nf* (**a**) (*Escol*) primer, first reader; spelling book; elementary treatise; **cantar** (*o* **leer**) **la ~ a uno** to give sb a severe ticking-off; **no saber la ~*** not to know a single thing.
(**b**) **~ de ahorros** savings bank book, deposit book; **~ de identidad** identity card; **~ de racionamiento** ration book; **~ de seguro** (*o* **seguridad**) social security card; **~ de trabajo** work permit.
(**c**) (*Méx*) identity card.
(**d**) (*Ecl*) certificate of ordination; liturgical calendar.
cartografía *nf* cartography, mapmaking.
cartografiado *nm* mapping.
cartográfico *adj* cartographic(al).
cartógrafo, -a *nm/f* cartographer, mapmaker.
cartomancia *nf* fortune-telling (*with cards*).
cartomante *nmf* fortune-teller (*who uses cards*).
cartón *nm* (**a**) (*materia*) cardboard, pasteboard; (*de libro*) board; **~ alquitranado** tar paper; **~ de bingo** bingo card; **~ de embalaje** wrapping paper; **~ de encuadernar** millboard; **~ acanalado, ~ ondulado** corrugated cardboard; **~ piedra** papier mâché.
(**b**) (*Arte*) artist's cartoon.
(**c**) (*caja etc*) (cardboard) box, carton.
(**d**) (*LAm*: *dibujo*) cartoon, sketch.
cartoné *nm* (*Tip*): **en ~** (bound) in boards.
cartón-madera *nm* chipboard.
cartuchera *nf* cartridge belt.
cartuchería *nf* cartridges, ammunition.
cartucho *nm* (**a**) (*Mil*) cartridge; cartridge case; **~ sin bala, ~ de fogueo** blank cartridge; **luchar hasta quemar el último ~** to fight on to the last ditch.
(**b**) (*bolsita*) paper cone, paper cornet; (*de monedas*) roll; (*LAm*) cornucopia.
(**c**) (*Inform*) cartridge.
Cartuja *nf* (*Ecl*) Carthusian order.
cartuja *nf* Carthusian monastery.
cartujano *adj, nm* Carthusian.
cartujo *nm* Carthusian.
cartulaje‡ *nm* pack of cards.
cartulario *nm* cartulary.
cartulina *nf* (*materia*) thin cardboard, Bristol board; (*tarjeta*) card; pass; (*Golf*) card; **~ amarilla** yellow card.
carura *nf* (**a**) (*And, CAm, Cono Sur*) (*lo costoso*) high price, dearness. (**b**) (*And, CAm, Cono Sur*) (*objeto*) expensive thing; **en esta tienda sólo hay ~s** everything in this shop is dear. (**c**) (*Cono Sur*: *carestía*) lack, shortage.
CASA ['kasa] *nf* (*Esp*) *abr de* **Construcciones Aeronáuticas, S.A.**
casa *nf* (**a**) (*gen*) house; (*piso*) flat, apartment; (*edificio*) building; **~ de alquiler** block of flats, apartment block; **~ de asistencia** boarding house; **~ de azotea** penthouse; **~ baja** slum, shack; **~ de baños** public baths, bathhouse (*US*); **~s baratas** low-cost housing; **~ de bebidas** bar, saloon; **~ de beneficencia** (*Hist*) poor-house; **~ de bombas** pumphouse; **~ de campaña** (*LAm*) tent; **~ de campo** country house; **~ chica** (*Méx*) mistress's house; **~ de citas, ~ pública, ~ de putas*, ~ de tolerancia, ~ de vicio** brothel; **~ consistorial** town hall; civic centre; **~ de corrección** reformatory, remand home; **~ de correos** post office; **~ cuna** (*pl* **casas cuna**) (*Hist*) foundling home; (*moderna*) day-nursery, crèche; **~ de departamentos** (*LAm*) tenement, block of flats, apartment house (*US*); **~ de ejercicios** (religious) retreat; **~ encantada** haunted house; **~ exenta** detached house; **~ de fieras** (*Madrid*) zoo, menagerie; **~ de guarda** lodge; **~ de huéspedes** boarding house; **~ de juego** gambling house; **~ de labor, ~ de labranza** farm, farmhouse; **~ de locos, ~ de orates** asylum; **~ de maternidad** maternity hospital; **~ de muñecas** doll's house; **~ pareada** semi-detached house; **~ de pisos** block of flats; **~ religiosa** monastery; convent; **~ rodante** caravan, trailer; **~ de seguridad** (*Cono Sur Pol*) safe house; **~ de socorro** first-aid post; **~ de Tócame Roque** place where one does as one likes, Liberty Hall; **~ de vecindad** block of tenements, apartment house (*US*); **un complejo como una ~*** a massive complex; **un penalti como una ~*** a clear-cut penalty.
(**b**) (*con aplicación personal, hogar*) home; residence, house; household; **~ y comida** board and lodging; **¿dónde tienes tu ~?** where is your home?; **~ mortuoria** house of mourning; **~ paterna** parents' home; **~ solariega** family seat, ancestral home; **es una ~ alegre** it's a happy home, it's a happy household; **ir a ~** to go home; **ir hacia ~** to head for home, go homewards; **ir a ~ de Juan** to go to John's house, go to John's place, go to John's; **salir de ~** to leave home; **ir de ~ en ~** to go from house to house; **estar en ~** to be at home, be in; **¿está la señora en ~?** is the lady in?, is the lady at home?; **están en ~ de los abuelos** they're at their grandparents'; **jugar en ~** (*Dep*) to play at home; **estar fuera de ~** to be out, be away from home; **jugar fuera de ~** (*Dep*) to play away; **voy para ~** I'm off home; **estar por la ~** to be about the house; **de ~** home (*atr*), household (*atr*); *deporte, ropa* indoor; *animal* pet, family (*atr*); (*fig*) ordinary, commonplace; **estar de ~** to be in one's ordinary clothes; **zapatos de andar por ~** shoes for (wearing) around the house; **una explicación para andar por ~** a rough-and-ready explanation; **ser de la ~** to be like one of the family.
(**c**) (*hogar*: *locuciones con verbo*) **abandonar la ~** to leave home, move out; **echar la ~ por la ventana** to go to enormous expense; to roll out the red carpet for sb; **empezar la ~ por el tejado** to put the cart before the horse; **franquear la ~ a uno** to open one's house to sb; **llevar la ~** to keep house, run the house; **cada uno manda en su ~** one's home is one's castle; **poner ~** to set up house; **poner ~ a una mujer** to set a woman up in a little place; **poner a uno en ~** (*fig*) to do sb a great favour; **poner su ~ en orden** (*fig*) to put one's own house in order; **sentirse como en su ~** to feel at home; **no tener ~ ni hogar** to be homeless; **vender cosas por las ~s** to sell things from door to door.
(**d**) (*fórmulas de cortesía*) **Vd está en su ~, aquí tiene Vd su ~** you're very welcome.
(**e**) (*Com, Fin*) firm, business house (*t* **~ de comercio**); **~ de banca, ~ bancaria** banking house; **~ central** head office; **~ de discos, ~ discográfica** record company; **~ editorial** publishing house; **~ de empeños, ~ de préstamos** pawnshop; **~ matriz** head office; parent company; **~ de modas** fashion house; **~ de** (**la**) **moneda** mint.
(**f**) **C~ Blanca** White House (*Washington*); **C~ Rosada** Government House (*Buenos Aires*).
(**g**) (*linaje*) house, line, family; **~ real** royal house, royal family; **la ~ de Borbón** the house of Bourbon.
(**h**) (*en juegos*) square.
casabe *nm* (*LAm*) cassava.
casa-bote *nf, pl* **casas-bote** houseboat.
casaca *nf* (**a**) (*vestido*) frock coat; (*Cono Sur*) zip jacket; **~ de montar** riding coat; **cambiar de ~, volver la ~** to turn one's coat, be a turncoat.
(**b**) (*: *boda*) wedding, marriage.
casación *nf* cassation, annulment.
casacón *nm* greatcoat.
casa-cuartel *nf, pl* **casas-cuarteles** residential barracks (for Civil Guard).
casada *nf* married woman.
casadero *adj* marriageable, of an age to be married.
casado 1 *adj* married; **bien ~** happily married; **mal ~** unhappily married; **~ y arrepentido** marry in haste and repent at leisure; **estar ~** to be married (*con* to); **estar ~ a media carta** to live in sin.
2 *nm* (**a**) (*persona*) married man; **los ~s** married men; married people; **los recién ~s** the newlyweds.
(**b**) (*Tip*) imposition.
(**c**) (*LAm Culin*) *two separate varieties of food eaten together.*
casal *nm* (**a**) (*casa de campo*) country house; (*granja*) farmhouse; (*solar*) ancestral home. (**b**) (*Cono Sur*: *matrimonio*) married couple; (*Zool*) pair.
casamata *nf* casemate.
casamentero *nm,* **casamentera** *nf* matchmaker.
casamiento *nm* marriage, wedding (ceremony); **~ por amor** love match; **~ de conveniencia** marriage of convenience; **~ a la fuerza** forced marriage, shotgun marriage; **prometer a una joven en ~** to betroth a girl (*con* to).
casampolga *nf* (*CAm Zool*) black widow spider.
Casandra *nf* Cassandra.
casapuerta *nf* entrance hall, vestibule.
casar¹ *nm* hamlet.
casar² [1a] **1** *vt* (**a**) (*sujeto*: *cura*) to marry, join in marriage, join in wedlock.
(**b**) (*sujeto*: *padre o madre*) to marry (off), give in marriage (*con* to).
(**c**) (*fig*: *emparejar*) to pair, couple; to match; (*Tip*) to impose.
(**d**) (*Jur*) to quash, annul.

2 *vi* (**a**) = *vr*.

(**b**) (*fig*: *armonizar*) to match, harmonize.

3 casarse *vr* (**a**) (*gen*) to marry, get married; **A se casó con B** A married B; **¿cuándo te vas a casar?** when are you getting married?; **volver a ~, ~ en segundas nupcias** to marry again (*y V* **nupcias**).

(**b**) (*fig*: *armonizar*) to match, harmonize.

casa-refugio *nf, pl* **casas-refugio** refuge for battered wives.

casatienda *nf* shop with dwelling accommodation, shop with flat over.

casba(h) *nf* kasbah.

casca *nf* (**a**) (*corteza*) bark (for tanning). (**b**) (*uvas*) marc (of grapes). (**c**) **~s almibaradas** candied peel.

cascabel *nm* (**a**) (*campanita*) (little) bell; **de ~ gordo** pretentious; cheap; **ser un ~*** to be a scatterbrain; **echar** (*o* **soltar**) **el ~** to drop a hint; **poner el ~ al gato** to bell the cat. (**b**) (*LAm*: *víbora*) rattlesnake.

cascabela *nf* (*LAm*) rattlesnake.

cascabelear [1a] **1** *vt* to take in*, raise the hopes of, beguile.

2 *vi* (**a**) (*LAm*: *tintinear*) to jingle, tinkle.

(**b**) (*fig*: *ser imprudente*) to act recklessly, behave frivolously, be inconsiderate.

(**c**) (*Cono Sur*: *refunfuñar*) to moan, grumble.

cascabeleo *nm* jingle, jingling, tinkling.

cascabelero* **1** *adj* scatterbrained. **2** *nm*, **cascabelera** *nf* scatterbrain.

cascabillo *nm* (**a**) (*campanilla*) little bell. (**b**) (*Bot*) (*de granos*) husk, chaff; (*de bellota*) cup.

cascada *nf* waterfall; cascade.

cascado *adj* (**a**) (*roto*) broken (down); *persona* infirm, decrepit, worn out. (**b**) *voz* weak, unmelodious, cracked; *piano etc* tinny.

cascajo *nm* (**a**) (*grava*) (piece of) gravel; (*Arquit etc t* **~s**) rubble; (*de cerámica etc*) fragments, shards.

(**b**) (*trastos*) junk, rubbish, lumber; **estar hecho un ~*** to be a wreck.

cascajoso *adj* gritty, gravelly.

cascanueces *nm invar* nutcracker; **un ~** a pair of nutcrackers.

cascar [1g] **1** *vt* (**a**) (*romper*) to crack, split, break (open); to crunch; *nuez* to crack.

(**b**) (*fig*) *salud* to shatter, undermine.

(**c**) (*) (*pegar*) to belt*, smack; (*Dep*) to beat hollow*, wipe the floor with*.

(**d**) **~la‡** to kick the bucket‡.

2 *vi* (**a**) (*chacharear**) to chatter, talk too much.

(**b**) (‡) to kick the bucket‡.

3 cascarse *vr* (**a**) (*romperse*) to crack, split, break (open).

(**b**) (*salud*) to crack up; (*voz*) to break, crack.

(**c**) **cascársela**** to wank**.

cáscara *nf* (**a**) (*de huevo, nuez, edificio*) shell; (*de grano*) husk; (*de fruto*) rind, peel, skin; (*de árbol*) bark; **~ de huevo** eggshell; (*porcelana*) eggshell china; **~ de limón** lemon peel; **~ sagrada** (*Farm*) cascara; **patatas cocidas con ~** potatoes in their jackets; **no hay más ~s*** there's no other way; **ser de la ~ amarga*** to be wild, be mischievous; (*Pol*) have radical ideas; (*sexualmente*) to be the other sort; **dar ~s de novillo a** (*LAm*) to thrash.

(**b**) (*) (*euf*) **¡~s!** well I'm blowed!*

(**c**) **~s‡** (*And*) clothes.

(**d**) **tener ~** (*CAm**) to have a cheek*, be shameless.

cascarazo *nm* (**a**) (*And, Carib*: *puñetazo*) punch; (*And*: *azote*) lash. (**b**) (*Carib**: *trago*) swig*, slug* (*US*).

cascarear‡ [1a] **1** *vt* (*And, CAm*) to belt*, smack. **2** *vi* (*Méx**) to scrape a living.

cascarilla **1** *adj* (*Carib, Cono Sur*: *enojadizo*) touchy, quick-tempered.

2 *nf* (**a**) (*Carib, Cono Sur*: *persona*) quick-tempered person.

(**b**) (*And, Cono Sur*: *Med*) medicinal herb; dried cacao husks (*used as tea*).

cascarón *nm* (broken) eggshell.

cascarrabias* *nmf invar* quick-tempered person, irritable sort.

cascarria *nf* (*Cono Sur*: *mugre*) filth, muck; (*Agr*) sheep droppings.

cascarriento *adj* (*Cono Sur*) filthy, mucky.

cascarrón* *adj* gruff, abrupt, rough.

cascarudo **1** *adj* thick-shelled, having a thick skin. **2** *nm* (*Cono Sur*) beetles (*collectively*).

casco *nm* (**a**) (*Mil etc*) helmet; (*parte de sombrero*) crown; **~s*** (*Rad*) headset, set of headphones; **~ de acero** steel helmet; **~ azul** soldier of a UN peace-keeping force; **~ de corcho** sun helmet; **~ protector** (*de motorista*) safety helmet, crash helmet; (*de albañil etc*) hard hat; **~ sideral** space helmet.

(**b**) (*Anat*) skull; (‡) brains, head, nut‡; **alegre de ~s, ligero de ~s** scatterbrained, frivolous; flighty; **calentar los ~s a uno** to get sb worked up; **estar mal de los ~s** to be crazy; **romper los ~s a uno** to bash sb's head in*; **romperse los ~s** to rack one's brains; **sentar los ~s** to quieten down, settle down, learn to behave o.s.; **tener los ~s a la jineta** to be scatterbrained.

(**c**) (*de cerámica*) fragment, shard; (*envase*) returnable soft drink bottle, empty (bottle).

(**d**) (*de cebolla*) edible part, edible layer.

(**e**) (*barril*) cask, barrel.

(**f**) (*Náut*) hull; (*pey*) old hulk.

(**g**) (*Zool*) hoof.

(**h**) (*Mec*) casing.

(**i**) (*de ciudad*) inner part, central area; (*Méx Agr*) ranchhouse, ranch and outbuildings; (*Cono Sur*: *de hacienda*) part, section; **~ comercial** business quarter; **~ urbano** inner city, area enclosed within city limits; **el ~ antiguo de la ciudad** the old part of the city.

(**j**) (*Carib*: *de fruta*) quarter, segment.

(**k**) (*LAm*: *edificio vacío*) empty building.

cascorros* *nmpl* (*Méx*) shoes.

cascorvo* *adj* (*CAm*) bow-legged.

cascote *nm* (piece of) rubble, (piece of) debris.

cascundear [1a] *vt* (*CAm*) to beat, thrash.

cáseo **1** *adj* cheesy. **2** *nm* curd.

caseoso *adj* cheesy, like cheese.

casera[1] *nf* landlady (*owner*); (*Ecl*) (priest's) housekeeper; *V t* **casero 2**.

casería *nf* (**a**) (*casa*) country house. (**b**) (*LAm* †: *clientela*) customers, clientèle.

caserío *nm* (**a**) (*casa*) country house. (**b**) (*aldea*) hamlet, settlement, group of dwellings.

caserna *nf* (*LAm*) barracks.

casero **1** *adj* (**a**) domestic, household (*atr*); *bomba, pan etc* home-made; *paño* homespun; *remedio* household; *ropa* house (*atr*), indoor, ordinary; *reunión* family (*atr*); **conejo ~** pet rabbit, tame rabbit; **el equipo ~** (*Dep*) the home team; **una victoria casera** a home win, a win for the home side.

(**b**) *persona* home-loving.

2 *nm* (**a**) (*dueño*) landlord; (*vigilante*) caretaker; (*conserje*) porter, concierge, janitor (*US*); (*inquilino*) tenant, occupier; (*Com*) house agent (*in charge of a property*).

(**b**) (*t* **casera[2]** *nf*) stay-at-home, home-lover.

(**c**) (*LAm*: *t* **casera[3]** *nf*: *cliente*) customer, client; (*Carib*: *repartidor*) (*hombre*) delivery man; (*mujer*) delivery woman.

caserón *nm* large (ramshackle) house, barracks (of a place).

caseta *nf* (*de mercado*) stall, stand, booth; (*en exposición*) stand; (*de feria*) sideshow, booth; (*Dep*) dressing-room, changing-room; pavilion; (*de piscina*) cubicle, changing-room; (*de playa*) bathing-hut, bathing-tent; (*de campo*) cottage; **~ de perro** kennel, doghouse (*US*); **~ del timón** wheelhouse; **mandar a un jugador a la ~** to send a player for an early bath.

casetera *nf* (*LAm*) cassette deck.

caset(t)e [ka'set] **1** *nf* cassette. **2** *nm* cassette-player.

cash [katʃ] *nm, pl* **cash** [katʃ] (*t* **~ and carry**) cash-and-carry store.

casi *adv* almost, nearly; **~ ~** very nearly, as near as makes no difference; **está ~ terminado** it's almost finished, it's well-nigh finished; **~ nada** next to nothing; **100 dólares ..., ~ nada** 100 dollars, a mere trifle; **~ nunca** almost never, hardly ever; **300 o ~** some 300, 300 or thereabouts.

casilla *nf* (**a**) (*cabaña*) hut, cabin, shed; (*en parque etc*) keeper's lodge; (*de mercado etc*) booth, stall; (*Ferro*) platelayer's hut, guard's hut; **~ electoral** (*Méx*) polling-station.

(**b**) (*Aut, Ferro*: *de locomotora*) cab.

(**c**) (*Teat*) box office.

(**d**) (*para cartas*) pigeonhole; (*de caja etc*) compartment; (*de papel*) ruled column, section; (*de formulario*) box; (*Ajedrez etc*) square; (*LAm Correos*) post-office box (number).

(**e**) (*And*: *retrete*) lavatory.

(**f**) (*Carib*: *trampa*) bird trap.

(**g**) **sacar a uno de sus ~s** to shake sb up, shake sb out of his complacency; to make sb cross, get sb worked up; **salir de sus ~s** to fly off the handle*.

casillero *nm* (*para cartas*) (set of) pigeonholes; (*Ferro etc*) luggage-locker; (*Correos etc*) sorting-rack; (*Dep**) scoreboard.

casimba *nf* (*LAm*) = **cacimba**.

casimir *nm* cashmere.

casimiro *adj* (*LAm*: *hum*) cross-eyed.

casinista *nm* clubman, member of a casino.

casino *nm* (*gen*) club; social club, political club; (*de juego*) casino; (*Cono Sur*) canteen.

Casio *nm* Cassius.

casis 1 *nm invar* (*t* **~ de negro**) blackcurrant bush; **~ de rojo** redcurrant bush. **2** *nf invar* (*t* **~ de negro**) blackcurrant; **~ de rojo** redcurrant.

casita *nf* small house; (*de campo*) cottage; **los niños están jugando a las ~s** the children are playing houses.

caso *nm* (**a**) (*Ling*) case.

(**b**) (*Med*) case; **es un ~ perdido** he's a dead loss, he's a disaster.

(**c**) (*en experimento etc*) case, subject; **soy un ~ difícil** I'm a difficult subject.

(**d**) (*ejemplo*) case, instance; (*suceso*) event, happening; (*circunstancias*) circumstances; **~ fortuito** (*Jur*) act of God; unforeseen circumstance; **~ límite** extreme case; **el ~ Hess** the Hess affair, the Hess case; **el ~ Romeo-Julieta** the Romeo and Juliet affair; the trouble between Romeo and Juliet; **en el ~ de Eslobodia** in the case of Slobodia; **en uno u otro ~** one way or the other; **en ~ de** in the event of; **~ que venga, en (el) ~ de que venga** in case he should come, should he come, in the event of his coming; **en ~ afirmativo** if so, if it should be so; **en ~ negativo, en el ~ contrario** if not, if it should not be so; **en el mejor de los ~s** at best; **en el peor de los ~s** at worst; **en tal ~** in such a case; **en todo ~** in any case, at all events; **en último ~** as a last resort, in the last resort; **y en su ~ también otros** and where appropriate, others also; **ponte en mi ~** put yourself in my position; **según el ~** as the case may be; **según lo requiera el ~** as the case may require; **dado el ~ que ...** supposing (that) ...; **el ~ es que ...** the fact is that ...; **creerse en el ~ de** + *infin* to think fit to + *infin*; **hablar al ~** to speak to the point; **hacer al ~, venir al ~** to be relevant; to be appropriate; **no hacer al ~, no venir al ~** to be beside the point; **pongamos por ~ que ...** let us suppose that ...; **pongamos por ~ a X** let us take X as an example; **servir para el ~** to serve one's purpose; **no tiene ~** (*Méx*) there's no point (in it); **¡vamos al ~!** let's get to the point!; let's get down to business!; **vaya por ~ ...** to give an example, ...; **verse en el ~ de** + *infin* to be compelled to + *infin*.

(**e**) (*atención*) notice; **hacer ~ a** to heed, notice; **no me hacen ~** they don't pay me any attention; **¡no haga Vd ~!** take no notice!, don't worry!; **maldito el ~ que me hace** a fat lot of notice he takes of me; **hacer ~ de** to pay attention to; to take into account; **sin hacer ~ de eso** regardless of that; **hacer ~ omiso de** to ignore, fail to mention, deliberately pass over; **¡(pero) ni ~!*** but he took absolutely no notice; **¡ni ~!*** don't pay any attention to him! (*etc*).

casona *nf* large house.

casorio* *nm* hasty marriage, unwise marriage; (*Méx*) wedding, marriage.

caspa *nf* dandruff, scurf.

Caspio *adj*: **Mar** *m* **~** Caspian Sea.

caspiroleta *nf* (*And, Carib, Cono Sur*) eggnog, egg flip.

cáspita *interj* my goodness!; come off it!*

caspitoso *adj* (**a**) full of dandruff, scurfy. (**b**) (*fig*) shoddy, tawdry.

casquería *nf* tripe and offal shop.

casquero, -a *nm/f* seller of tripe and offal.

casquete *nm* (**a**) (*gorra*) skullcap; (*Mil*) helmet; (*Mec*) cap; **~ de hielo** icecap; **~ de nieve** snow-cap; **~ polar** polar cap. (**b**) **echar un ~‡** to have a screw‡.

casquijo *nm* gravel.

casquillo *nm* (**a**) tip, cap; (*de botella*) bottle-top; (*de bastón*) ferrule, tip; (*Mec*) sleeve, bushing; (*Mil*) cartridge case. (**b**) (*LAm*: *de caballo*) horseshoe.

casquinona *nf* (*And*) (*botella*) beer bottle; (*cerveza*) beer.

casquivano 1 *adj* scatterbrained. **2** *nm*, **casquivana** *nf* scatterbrain.

cassette = **caset(t)e**.

casta *nf* (**a**) (*Rel etc*) caste; (*raza*) breed, race; (*grupo*) privileged group; (*fig*) class; quality; **de ~** of quality, of breeding; **carecer de ~** to lack breeding, have no class; **eso le viene de ~** that comes naturally to him.

(**b**) (*Méx Tip*) fount.

castamente *adv* chastely, purely.

castaña *nf* (**a**) (*Bot*) chestnut; **~ de agua** water chestnut; **~ de Indias** horse chestnut; **dar** (*o* **meter**) **la ~ a uno** to swindle sb, make a fool out of sb; **sacar a uno las ~s del fuego** to pull sb's chestnuts out of the fire for him, to do sb's dirty work for him; **¡toma ~!*** well!; how do you like that!; just imagine!; **ser algo** (*o* **uno**) **una ~*** to be a drag.

(**b**) (*de pelo*) bun, chignon.

(**c**) (*vasija*) demijohn.

(**d**) (‡: *golpe*) bash*, blow; (*Aut etc*) collision, accident, crash; **darse una ~** to give oneself a knock.

(**e**) (*Fin*‡) one peseta.

(**f**) **cogerse una ~‡** to get canned‡, get drunk.

(**g**) (‡) **tiene 71 ~s** he's 71 (years old).

(**h**) (‡) **conducir a toda ~** to drive flat out.

castañar *nm* chestnut grove.

castañazo *nm* (*Cono Sur*) punch, thump.

castañero *nm*, **castañera** *nf* chestnut seller.

castañeta *nf* (**a**) (*con dedos*) snap (of the fingers). (**b**) (*Mús*) castanet.

castañetazo *nm* snap, crack, click.

castañetear [1a] **1** *vt* (**a**) *dedos* to snap.

(**b**) (*Mús*) to play on the castanets.

2 *vi* (**a**) (*dedos*) to snap; to click; (*platos etc*) to clatter; (*dientes*) to chatter, rattle; (*huesos*) to crack; (*rodillas*) to knock together; **~ con los dedos** to snap one's fingers.

(**b**) (*Mús*) to play the castanets.

castañeteo *nm* (**a**) (*dedos*) snap(ping); click(ing); (*platos*) clatter(ing); (*dientes*) chatter(ing); rattling; (*huesos*) crack(ing); (*gopeteo*) knocking. (**b**) (*Mús*) sound of the castanets.

castaño 1 *adj* chestnut(-coloured), brown.

2 *nm* chestnut, chestnut tree; **~ de Indias** horse chestnut tree; **esto pasa de ~ oscuro** this is really too much, this is beyond a joke; **pelar el ~** (*Carib**) to hoof it*.

castañuela *nf* castanet; **no éramos unas ~s** we were not the life and soul of the party; **estar hecho unas ~s, estar como unas ~s** to be very merry, be in high spirits.

castañuelo *adj* chestnut(-coloured), brown.

castellanizar [1f] *vt* to hispanicize, give a Spanish form to.

castellano 1 *adj* Castilian; Spanish. **2** *nm*, **castellana** *nf* Castilian; Spaniard. **3** *nm* (*Ling*) Castilian, Spanish.

castellanohablante, castellanoparlante 1 *adj* Castilian-speaking, Spanish-speaking. **2** *nmf* Castilian speaker, Spanish speaker.

castellonense 1 *adj* of Castellón de la Plana. **2** *nmf* native (*o* inhabitant) of Castellón de la Plana; **los ~s** the people of Castellón de la Plana.

castellonés, -esa *adj, nm/f* = **castellonense**.

casticidad *nf* (**a**) (*Ling*) purity, correctness. (**b**) (*casticismo*) traditional character; thoroughbred character, true-born nature; authenticity, genuineness.

casticismo *nm* (**a**) (*Ling*) purity, correctness. (**b**) (*tradicionalismo*) love of tradition, traditionalism; = **casticidad (b)**.

casticista *adj, nmf* purist.

castidad *nf* chastity, purity.

castigador *nm* (**a**) (*que castiga*) punisher. (**b**) (*en lo sexual*) ladykiller; (*pey*) seducer, libertine.

castigar [1h] *vt* (**a**) (*gen*) to punish (*de, por* for); (*Dep*) to penalize (*por* for).

(**b**) (*fig*) to castigate; *carne* to mortify; (*enfermedad etc*) to afflict, affect; (*en las emociones*) to afflict, grieve; (*físicamente*) to strain, use hard; **~ mucho a un caballo** to ride a horse hard.

(**c**) (*fig*: *corregir*) *estilo etc* to refine; *texto* to correct, revise.

(**d**) (*Com*) *gastos* to reduce.

(**e**) (*Méx Mec*) to tighten (up).

castigo *nm* (**a**) (*gen*) punishment; (*Dep etc*) penalty; fine. (**b**) (*fig*) castigation; mortification, affliction. (**c**) (*fig*) (*refinación*) refinement; (*corrección*) correction, revision.

Castilla *nf* Castile; **~ la Nueva** New Castile; **~ la Vieja** Old Castile; **¡ancha es ~!** it takes all sorts!

castilla *nf* (*Cono Sur, Méx*) (**a**) (*Ling*) Castilian, Spanish; **hablar la ~** to speak Spanish. (**b**) **de ~** (*Hist*) Spanish, from the old country.

Castilla-León *nm* Castille and León.

castillejo *nm* (**a**) (*Arquit*) scaffolding. (**b**) (*de niño*) go-cart.

castillo *nm* castle; (*de elefante*) howdah; **~s en el aire**

castles in the air; ~ **de arena** sandcastle; ~ **de fuego** firework set piece; ~ **de naipes** house of cards; ~ **de popa** aftercastle; aft awning; ~ **de proa** forecastle; **hacer un ~ de un grano de arena** to make a mountain out of a molehill.
casting ['kastɪn] *nm* (*Cine etc*) casting.
castizo *adj* (**a**) (*Ling*) pure, correct.
(**b**) (*de pura sangre*) thoroughbred; true-born; (*fig*) (*tradicional*) traditional; (*genuino*) pure, authentic; genuine; **es un tipo ~*** he's one of the best; **un aragonés ~** a true-blue Aragonese, an Aragonese through and through.
casto *adj* chaste, pure.
castor *nm* beaver.
castoreño *nm* beaver (*hat*); (*Taur*) picador's hat.
castoreo *nm* (*Farm*) castor.
castra *nf* (*Bot*) (*acto*) pruning; (*época*) pruning season.
castración *nf* (**a**) (*Bio*) castration, gelding. (**b**) (*Bot*) pruning. (**c**) (*Agr*) extraction of honeycombs.
castrado 1 *adj* castrated. **2** *nm* eunuch.
castrar [1a] *vt* (**a**) (*Bio*) to castrate, geld; *gato etc* to doctor (*euf*).
(**b**) (*Bot*) to prune, cut back.
(**c**) *colmena* to extract honeycombs from.
(**d**) (*fig*: *debilitar*) to mutilate, impair, weaken.
castrense *adj* army (*atr*), military; **las glorias ~s** military glories.
castro *nm* hill-fort; Iron-Age settlement.
casual 1 *adj* (**a**) (*fortuito*) fortuitous, accidental, chance. (**b**) (*incidente*) incidental. (**c**) (*Ling*) case (*atr*); **desinencia ~** case ending. **2** *nm*: **por un ~*** by chance.
casualidad *nf* (**a**) (*gen*) chance, accident; coincidence; **fue una pura ~** it was sheer coincidence, it was entirely a matter of chance; **por ~** by chance; **¿tienes por ~ una pluma?** do you have a pen, by any chance?, do you happen to have a pen?; **me encontraba allí por ~** I happened to be there, I chanced to be there; **un día entró por ~** one day he dropped in; **da la ~ que ...** it (so) happens that ...; **dio la ~ que ...** it happened that ..., luck had it that ...; **¡qué ~!** what a coincidence!; **¡qué ~ verle aquí!** what a coincidence meeting you here!, fancy meeting you here!
(**b**) **~es** (*CAm*) casualties.
casualmente *adv* by chance, by accident, fortuitously; **~ le vi ayer** I happened to see him yesterday, as it happens I saw him yesterday.
casuario *nm* cassowary.
casuca *nf*, **casucha** *nf* hovel, shack; slum.
casuista *nmf* casuist.
casuística *nf* casuistry.
casulla *nf* chasuble.
CAT [kat] *nf* (*Esp*) *abr de* **Comisaría de Abastecimientos y Transportes.**
cata[1] *nf* (**a**) (*gen*) tasting, testing, sampling; blending; **~ de vinos** wine-tasting.
(**b**) (*muestra*) taste, sample.
(**c**) (*LAm Min*) trial excavation, test bore; prospecting.
(**d**) **ir en ~ de algo*** to go looking for sth.
cata[2] *nf* (*And, Cono Sur, Méx* †) parrot.
catabre *nm* (*And, Carib*) gourd; basket.
catacaldos *nm invar* (**a**) (*persona inconstante*) rolling stone; quitter, person who starts things but gives up easily; (*Arte etc*) dilettante.
(**b**) (*entrometido*) busybody, meddler.
cataclismismo *nm* doomwatching.
cataclismista *nmf* doomwatcher.
cataclismo *nm* cataclysm.
catacumbas *nfpl* catacombs.
catador(a) *nm/f* (*de té, vinos etc*) taster, blender, sampler; (*fig*) connoisseur.
catadura[1] *nf* tasting, sampling, blending.
catadura[2*] *nf* looks, face; **de mala ~** nasty-looking.
catafalco *nm* catafalque.
catafotos *nmpl* (*Aut*) cat's-eyes.
catajarria *nf* (*Carib*) string, series.
catalán, -ana 1 *adj, nm/f* Catalan, Catalonian. **2** *nm* (*Ling*) Catalan.
catalanismo *nm* (**a**) (*Ling*) catalanism, word (*o* phrase *etc*) peculiar to Catalonia. (**b**) sense of the differentness of Catalonia; (*Pol*) doctrine of (*o* belief in) Catalan autonomy.
catalanista 1 *adj* that supports (*etc*) Catalan autonomy; **el movimiento ~** the movement for Catalan autonomy; **la familia es muy ~** the family strongly supports Catalan autonomy.
2 *nmf* supporter (*etc*) of Catalan autonomy.
catalanizar [1f] *vt* to make Catalan, make a Catalan version of.
catalejo *nm* spyglass, telescope.
catalepsia *nf* catalepsy.
cataléptico, -a *adj, nm/f* cataleptic.
Catalina *nf* Catherine.
catálisis *nf* catalysis.
catalítico *adj* catalytic.
catalizador *nm* catalyst; (*Aut*) catalytic converter.
catalizar [1f] *vt* to catalyse.
catalogable *adj* classifiable.
catalogación *nf* cataloguing.
catalogar [1h] *vt* to catalogue.
catálogo *nm* catalogue; **~ colectivo** union catalogue; **~ de materias** subject index; **el libro está fuera de ~** the book is out of print.
Cataluña *nf* Catalonia.
catamarán *nm* catamaran.
cataplasma *nf* (**a**) (*Med*) poultice. (**b**) (*: *persona*) bore.
cataplines‡ *nmpl* goolies‡.
cataplum *interj* bang!, crash!
catapulta *nf* catapult.
catapultar [1a] *vt* to catapult.
catapún *adj*: **una cosa del año ~** an antiquated thing, a totally obsolete thing; **películas del año ~** films of the year dot.
catar [1a] *vt* (**a**) (*probar*) to taste, sample, try; (*fig*: *examinar*) to examine, inspect, have a look at; (*fig*: *estimar*) to esteem.
(**b**) (*mirar*) to look at; to look out for; **¡cata!, ¡cátale!** just look at him!; **¡cátate eso!** you just think!
(**c**) *colmena* to extract honeycombs from.
catarata *nf* (**a**) (*Geog*) waterfall, falls; cataract; **C~ del Niágara** Niagara Falls; **C~s de Victoria** Victoria Falls.
(**b**) (*Med*) cataract.
catarral *adj* catarrhal.
catarriento *adj* (*LAm*) = **catarroso.**
catarro *nm* cold; catarrh; **~ crónico del pecho** chest trouble; **coger** (*Esp*) (*o* **pescar***) **un ~** to catch a cold.
catarroso *adj* subject to colds; having catarrh, suffering from catarrh.
catarsis *nf* catharsis.
catártico *adj* cathartic.
catasalsas *nm invar* = **catacaldos.**
catastral *adj* relating to the property register; **valores ~es** property values, land values.
catastro *nm* property register, land registry, cadastre.
catástrofe *nf* catastrophe.
catastrófico *adj* catastrophic.
catastrofismo *nm* alarmism; doomwatching; scaremongering.
catastrofista 1 *adj* alarmist. **2** *nmf* alarmist; doomwatcher; scaremonger.
catatán *nm* (*Cono Sur*) punishment.
catatar [1a] *vt* (*And*) to ill-treat.
catauro *nm* (*Carib*) basket.
catavinos *nmf invar* wine taster; (*) boozer‡.
cate[1*] *nm* (*golpe*) punch, bash*; **dar ~ a uno** (*Univ*) to plough sb*.
cate[2*] *nmf* (*profesor*) teacher.
catear [1a] *vt* (**a**) (*investigar*) to investigate; (*probar*) to try, sample.
(**b**) (*Univ**) *candidato* to plough*; *examen* to fail.
(**c**) (*Cono Sur, Méx*: *Min*) to make test borings in, explore.
(**d**) (*Méx*: *policía*) to search, make a search of.
catecismo *nm* catechism.
catecúmeno, -a *nm/f* catechumen; (*fig*) convert.
cátedra 1 *nf* (**a**) (*Univ*) chair, professorship; (*de instituto*) senior teaching post (in a grammar school); **~ del Espíritu Santo** (*Ecl*) pulpit; **explicar una ~** to hold a chair (*de* of); **poner ~, sentar ~** to set up as an expert (*de* in), lay down the law (*de* about); to spout.
(**b**) (*asignatura*) subject.
(**c**) (*aula*) lecture room.
(**d**) (*estudiantes*) group of students, class.
(**e**) (*Carib* †) wonder, marvel; **es ~, está la ~** it's marvellous.
2 *adj* (*Carib*) wonderful, marvellous, excellent.
catedral *nf* cathedral; **un complejo como una ~*** a massive complex.
catedralicio *adj* cathedral (*atr*).
catedrático, -a *nm/f* (*Univ*) professor; **~ de instituto** ≈ grammar-school teacher.

cátedro* *nm* = **catedrático**.
categoría *nf* (*gen*) category; (*clase*) class, group; (*status*) rank, standing; (*calidad*) quality; (*prestigio*) prestige; ~ **fiscal,** ~ **tributaria** tax bracket; **de** ~ important; distinguished, high-ranking, prominent; **es hombre de cierta** ~ he is a man of some standing; **servicio de primera** ~ first-class service; **de baja** ~ of low quality; of low rank; **de segunda** ~ (*pey*) second-rate; **no tiene** ~ he has no standing; **tiene** ~ **de ministro** he has the rank of minister.
categóricamente *adv* categorically.
categórico *adj* categorical; *mentira* downright, outright; *orden* strict, express.
categorización *nf* categorization.
categorizar [1f] *vt* to categorize.
catenaria *nf* (*Elec, Ferro*) overhead power cable.
catequista *nmf* (*CAm Rel*) catechizer.
catequizar [1f] *vt* (**a**) (*Ecl*) to catechize, instruct in Christian doctrine. (**b**) (*: *convencer*) to win over, talk round.
caterva *nf* host, throng, crowd; **venir en** ~ to come in a throng, come thronging.
catetada* *nf* piece of nonsense; stupid action, silly thing to do.
catéter *nm* catheter.
catetismo* *nm* slow-wittedness, boorishness, stupidity.
cateto *nm* (*pey*) peasant, country bumpkin.
catimbao *nm* (*And, Cono Sur*) clown, carnival clown.
catinga *nf* (**a**) (*And, Cono Sur*) (*olor personal*) body odour; (*de animales etc*) strong smell. (**b**) (*Cono Sur*: *palabra de marineros*) soldier.
catingoso *adj* (*And, Cono Sur*), **catingudo** *adj* (*And, Cono Sur*) stinking, foul-smelling.
catire *adj* (*Carib*), **catiro** *adj* (*LAm*) (*rubio*) blond, fair; (*pelirrojo*) reddish, red-haired.
catita *nf* (*LAm*) parrot.
catitear [1a] *vi* (*Cono Sur*) to dodder, shake (with old age).
catisumba(da) *nf* (*CAm*) lot, great number; **una** ~ **de** lots of, loads of.
catoche *nm* (*Méx*) bad mood, bad temper.
catódico *adj* cathodic, cathode (*atr*).
cátodo *nm* cathode.
catolicidad *nf* catholicity.
catolicismo *nm* (Roman) Catholicism.
católico 1 *adj* (**a**) (*Ecl*) (Roman) Catholic; **no** ~ non-Catholic.
(**b**) (*fig*: *verdadero*) *doctrina* true, infallible; certain; (*: *correcto*) right, as it should be; **no estar muy** ~ not to be quite right, be none too good, have sth up (with it); (*Med*) to be under the weather.
2 *nm*, **católica** *nf* Catholic; **no** ~ non-Catholic.
Catón *nm* Cato.
catón *nm* (**a**) (*crítico*) severe critic. (**b**) (*libro*) primer, first reading book; **eso está en el** ~ that is absolutely elementary.
catorce *adj* fourteen; (*fecha*) fourteenth.
catorrazo *nm* (*Méx*), **catorro** *nm* (*Méx*) punch, blow.
catracho* (*CAm*: *pey*) **1** *adj* of El Salvador, Salvadorean. **2** *nm*, **catracha** *nf* native (*o* inhabitant) of El Salvador, Salvadorean.
catre *nm* (**a**) (*litera*) cot; (*Cono Sur*: *cama*) bed; (*And, Cono Sur*: *cuja*) bedstead; ~ **de tijera,** ~ **de viento** camp bed, bed; (*fig*) **cambiar el** ~ to change the subject. (**b**) ~ **de balsa** (*Cono Sur*: *barquito*) raft.
catrecillo *nm* camp stool, folding seat.
catrera *nf* (*Cono Sur*) bunk, bed.
catrín *nm* (*CAm, Méx*†) toff*, dude* (*US*).
catsup *nm* ketchup, catsup (*US*).
Catulo *nm* Catullus.
caucarse [1g] *vr* (*Cono Sur*: *persona*) to get old; (*comida*) to go stale.
caucasiano, -a (*Geog*), **caucásico, -a** (*de raza*) *adj, nm/f* Caucasian.
Cáucaso *nm* Caucasus.
cauce *nm* (**a**) river bed; (*Agr*) irrigation channel. (**b**) (*fig*) channel, course, way; **por el** ~ **reglamentario** through the usual channels.
caución *nf* (**a**) (*cautela*) caution, wariness. (**b**) (*Jur*) pledge, security, bond; bail; **admitir a uno a** ~ to grant sb bail.
caucionar [1a] *vt* (**a**) (*prevenir*) to prevent, guard against. (**b**) (*Jur*) to bail, go bail for.
cauch *nm* (*CAm, Carib*) couch.
cauchal *nm* rubber plantation.
cauchar 1 *nm* (*And*) rubber plantation. **2** *vi* (*And*) to tap (trees for rubber).
cauchera *nf* (**a**) (*Bot*) rubber plant, rubber tree. (**b**) (*And*: *cauchal*) rubber plantation.
cauchero 1 *adj* rubber (*atr*); **industria cauchera** rubber industry. **2** *nm* (*LAm*) rubber tapper, rubber worker.
caucho[1] *nm* (**a**) (*gen*) rubber; ~ **esponjoso** foam rubber; ~ **en bruto,** ~ **natural** natural rubber; ~ **regenerado** reclaimed rubber; ~ **sintético** synthetic rubber.
(**b**) (*LAm*: *impermeable*) raincoat, mac; (*And*) (*manta*) waterproof blanket; (*zapato*) rubber shoe; (*LAm Aut*) tyre, tire (*US*).
caucho[2] *nm* (*Carib*) couch.
cauchutado *adj* rubberized.
cauchutar [1a] *vt* to rubberize.
caudal[1] *nm* (**a**) (*de río*) volume, flow.
(**b**) (*abundancia*) plenty, abundance, wealth; (*de persona etc*) fortune, wealth; property; ~ **social** assets of a partnership.
caudal[2] *adj* caudal.
caudaloso *adj* (**a**) *río* large, carrying much water. (**b**) (*abundante*) copious, abundant; *persona etc* wealthy, rich.
caudillaje *nm* (**a**) (*jefatura*) leadership; **bajo el** ~ **de** under the leadership of. (**b**) (*LAm Pol*: *pey*) tyranny, rule by political bosses.
caudillismo *nm* (doctrine of) government by a strong man.
caudillo, -a *nm/f* (**a**) (*jefe*) leader, chief; strong man; (*jefe de estado*) head of state; **el C~** (*Esp*) the Caudillo, Franco. (**b**) (*LAm pey*) (*tirano*) tyrant; (*líder*) political boss, leader.
caula *nf* (*CAm, Cono Sur*) plot, intrigue.
cauri *nm* cowrie.
causa[1] *nf* (**a**) (*gen*) cause; (*motivo*) reason, motive; (*de queja*) grounds; **veamos qué** ~ **tiene esto, veamos cuál es la** ~ **de esto** let us see what is the reason for this; ~ **final** final cause; ~ **primera** first cause; **a** ~ **de, por** ~ **de** on account of, because of, owing to; **por mi** ~ for my sake; **por poca** ~**, sin** ~ for no good reason; **¿por qué** ~**?** why?, for what reason?; **fuera de** ~ irrelevant.
(**b**) (*Pol etc*) cause; **hacer** ~ **común con** to make common cause with.
(**c**) (*Jur*) lawsuit; case, trial; prosecution; **instruir** ~ to take legal proceedings.
causa[2] *nf* (**a**) (*Cono Sur*: *tentempié*) snack, light meal; picnic lunch. (**b**) (*And*: *ensalada de patatas*) potato salad.
causal 1 *adj* causal. **2** *nf* reason, grounds.
causalidad *nf* causality; causation.
causante 1 *adj* causing, originating; **el coche** ~ **del accidente** the car which caused the accident, the car responsible for the accident.
2 *nmf* (**a**) (*el que causa*) causer, originator.
(**b**) (*Méx Fin*) taxpayer, person liable for tax.
3 *nf* (*LAm*: *causa*) cause.
causar [1a] *vt* (*gen*) to cause; *gasto, trabajo* to create, entail, make; *impresión* to create, make; *cólera, protesta* to provoke; ~ **risa a uno** to make sb laugh.
causativo *adj* causative.
causear [1a] *vi* (*Cono Sur*) to have a snack (*o* a light meal); to have a picnic lunch.
causeo *nm* (*Cono Sur*) = **causa**[2].
cáustico *adj* caustic (*t fig*).
cautamente *adv* cautiously, warily, carefully.
cautela *nf* (**a**) (*gen*) caution, cautiousness, caginess*, wariness; **con mucha** ~ (*prevenir*) very cautiously; **tener la** ~ **de** + *infin* to take the precaution of + *ger*. (**b**) (*pey*) cunning.
cautelar [1a] **1** *adj* precautionary. **2** *vt* (**a**) (*prevenir*) to prevent, guard against. (**b**) (*LAm*: *defender*) to protect, defend. **3 cautelarse** *vr* to be on one's guard (*de* against).
cautelosamente *adv* (**a**) (*con cautela*) cautiously, cagily*, warily, carefully. (**b**) (*pey*) cunningly, craftily.
cauteloso *adj* (**a**) (*gen*) cautious, cagey*, wary, careful. (**b**) (*pey*) cunning, crafty.
cauterio *nm* (**a**) (*Med*) cautery, cauterization. (**b**) (*fig*) drastic remedy.
cauterizar [1f] *vt* (**a**) (*Med*) to cauterize. (**b**) (*fig*) to treat drastically, apply a drastic remedy to.
cautivante *adj* captivating.
cautivar [1a] *vt* (**a**) (*Mil etc*) to capture, take prisoner. (**b**) (*fig*: *hechizar*) to charm, captivate, win over; to enthrall; *corazón* to steal, captivate.
cautiverio *nm*, **cautividad** *nf* captivity; (*fig*) bondage, serfdom.
cautivo, -a *adj, nm/f* captive.

cauto *adj* cautious, wary, careful.
cava¹ *nf* (*Agr*) digging and hoeing (*esp* of vines).
cava² *nf* (*bodega*) wine-cellar; (*de garaje*) pit; (*Carib*: *nevera*) icebox.
cava³ *nm* (*vino*) sparkling wine.
cava⁴ *nf* (*Carib*) closed truck, lorry.
cavador *nm* digger; excavator; ~ **de oro** gold digger.
cavadura *nf* digging, excavation.
cavar [1a] **1** *vt hoyo* to dig; *pozo* to sink; (*Agr*) to dig over, hoe, fork over; *cepas* to dig round.
2 *vi* (**a**) (*gen*) to dig.
(**b**) (*fig*: *investigar*) to delve (*en* into), go deeply (*en* into); (*meditar*) to meditate profoundly (*en* on).
cavazón *nf* digging, excavation.
caverna *nf* cave, cavern.
cavernícola 1 *adj* (**a**) (*lit*) cave-dwelling, cave (*atr*); **hombre** ~ caveman.
(**b**) (*Pol**) reactionary.
2 *nmf* (**a**) (*lit*) cave dweller, caveman, troglodyte.
(**b**) (*Pol**) reactionary, backwoodsman.
cavernoso *adj* (**a**) (*gen*) cavernous; cave (*atr*); *montaña* full of caves, honeycombed with caves. (**b**) *sonido, voz* resounding, deep; hollow.
caviar *nm* caviar(e).
cavidad *nf* cavity; hollow, space; ~ **nasal** nasal cavity.
cavilación *nf* (**a**) (*meditación*) deep thought, rumination. (**b**) (*sospecha*) (unfounded) suspicion, apprehension.
cavilar [1a] *vt* to ponder, consider closely; to brood over, be obsessed with.
cavilosear [1a] *vi* (*Carib*: *ilusionarse*) to harbour illusions; (*Carib*: *vacilar*) to vacillate, hesitate; (*CAm*: *chismear*) to gossip.
cavilosidad *nf* (unfounded) suspicion, apprehension.
caviloso *adj* (**a**) (*obsesionado*) brooding, obsessed; (*receloso*) suspicious, mistrustful.
(**b**) (*CAm*: *chismoso*) gossipy, backbiting.
(**c**) (*And*) (*agresivo*) quarrelsome, touchy; (*quisquilloso*) fussy, finicky.
cayado *nm* staff, stick; (*Agr*) crook; (*Ecl*) crozier.
cayena *nf* cayenne pepper.
cayo *nm* (*Carib*) islet, key; **C~ Hueso** Key West.
cayubro *adj* (*And*) reddish-blond, red-haired.
cayuca‡ *nf* (*Carib*) head, bean*.
cayuco *nm* (*Carib*) dugout canoe.
caz *nm* (*de riego*) irrigation channel; (*de molino*) millrace.
caza 1 *nf* (**a**) (*gen*) hunting; (*con escopeta*) shooting, sport; (*con trampa*) trapper; (*una* ~) hunt; shoot; chase, pursuit; ~ **de brujas** witch-hunt; ~ **de control** culling; ~ **furtiva** poaching, illegal hunting; ~ **del hombre** manhunt; ~ **con hurón** ferreting; ~ **del jabalí** boar hunt(ing); ~ **de patos** duck shoot(ing); ~ **submarina** underwater fishing; ~ **del tesoro** treasure hunt; ~ **del zorro** foxhunt(ing); **andar a (la)** ~ **de** to go hunting for; **dar** ~ to give chase, go in pursuit; **dar** ~ **a** to hunt, chase, go after; to hunt down; **dar** ~ **a un empleo** to hunt for a job; **ir a la** ~, **ir de** ~ to go hunting, go (out) shooting.
(**b**) (*animales*) game; ~ **mayor** big game; ~ **menor** small game; **levantar la** ~ to put up the game; (*fig*) to give the game away.
2 *nm* (*Aer*) fighter, fighter-plane; ~ **de escolta** escort fighter; ~ **nocturno** night-fighter.
cazaautógrafos *nmf invar* autograph-hunter.
cazabe *nm* (*Carib*) cassava cake.
caza-bombardero *nm* fighter-bomber.
cazaclavos *nm invar* nail-puller.
cazadero *nm* hunting ground.
cazador *nm* (*gen*) hunter; (*a caballo*) huntsman; (*con trampa*) trapper; ~ **de alforja**, ~ **de pieles** trapper; ~ **de autógrafos** autograph-hunter; ~ **de cabezas** headhunter; ~ **furtivo** poacher.
cazadora *nf* (**a**) (*persona*) hunter, huntress. (**b**) (*prenda*) windcheater, windbreaker (*US*); (*de caza*) hunting jacket; ~ **de piel** leather jacket.
cazador-recolector *nm, pl* **cazadores-recolectores** hunter-gatherer.
cazadotes *nm invar* fortune-hunter.
cazafortunas *nf invar* fortune-hunter, gold-digger.
cazagenios *nmf invar* talent scout, talent spotter; (*Com*) head-hunter.
cazamariposas *nm invar* butterfly-net.
cazaminas *nm invar* minesweeper.
cazamoscas *nm invar* (*Orn*) flycatcher.
cazar [1f] *vt* (**a**) (*buscar*) to hunt; to trap; to chase, pursue; to go after; (*esp fig*) to hunt down, track down, run to earth; **le cacé por fin en la tienda** I eventually ran him down in the shop.
(**b**) (*coger*) to catch; *piezas cazadas etc* to bag; *puesto etc* to land, get; (*pey*) to get hold of by trickery, wangle*; *persona* to win over (by flattery); (*pey*) to take in*; **~las al vuelo** to be pretty sharp.
(**c**) (*en un error*) to catch out.
cazarrecompensas *nm invar* bounty-hunter.
cazasubmarinos *nm invar* submarine-chaser.
cazatalentos *nmf invar* talent scout, talent spotter; head-hunter.
cazatanques *nm invar*: **avión** ~ anti-tank aircraft.
cazatesoros *nm invar* treasure-hunter.
cazaturistas *atr*: **lugar** ~ tourist trap, touristy place.
cazcalear* [1a] *vi* to fuss around, buzz about.
cazcarrias *nfpl* splashes of mud on one's clothes.
cazcarriento *adj* splashed with mud, mud-stained.
cazo *nm* (**a**) (*cacerola*) saucepan; ~ **de cola** gluepot; ~ **eléctrico** electric kettle. (**b**) (*cucharón*) ladle, dipper. (**c**) (‡: *chulo*) pimp.
cazolero *nm* milksop.
cazoleta *nf* (**a**) (*cazo*) (small) pan; (*de pipa*) bowl; (*de escudo*) boss; (*de sostén*) cup. (**b**) (*de espada*) guard. (**c**) (*Mec*) housing.
cazón *nm* dogfish, tope.
cazonete *nm* (*Náut*) toggle.
cazuela *nf* (**a**) (*Culin*) (*vasija*) pan, cooking-pot, casserole; (*guiso*) casserole; (*LAm*: *guiso*) chicken stew. (**b**) (*Teat*) gallery, gods.
cazurro *adj* surly, sullen; stubborn.
cazuz *nm* ivy.
CC *nm* (**a**) (*Aut*) *abr de* **Código de la Circulación** Highway Code. (**b**) (*Pol*) *abr de* **Comité Central** Central Committee.
c/c *abr de* **cuenta corriente** current account, C/A.
c.c. *nmpl abr de* **centímetros cúbicos** cubic centimetres, c.c.
CCOO *nfpl abr de* **Comisiones Obreras.**
C.D. *nm* (**a**) *abr de* **Cuerpo Diplomático** Diplomatic Corps, Corps Diplomatique, CD. (**b**) *abr de* **Club Deportivo** sports club.
c/d (**a**) *abr de* **en casa de** care of, c/o. (**b**) (*Com*) *abr de* **con descuento** with discount.
C. de J. *nf abr de* **Compañía de Jesús** Society of Jesus, S.J.
C.D.N. *nm* (*Esp*) *abr de* **Centro Dramático Nacional** ≃ RADA.
CDS *nm abr de* **Centro Democrático y Social.**
CDU *nf abr de* **Clasificación Decimal Universal** Dewey decimal system.
CE *nm* (**a**) *abr de* **Consejo de Europa** Council of Europe. (**b**) *abr de* **Comunidad Europea** European Community, EC.
ce¹ *interj* hey!
ce² *nf* (*name of the*) *letter* **c**; ~ **por be** down to the tiniest detail, leaving nothing whatsoever out; **por** ~ **o por be** somehow or other.
ceba *nf* (**a**) (*Agr*) fattening. (**b**) (*LAm*: *de cañón*) charge, priming. (**c**) (*de horno*) stoking.
cebada *nf* barley; ~ **perlada** pearl barley.
cebadal *nm* barley field.
cebadera *nf* (**a**) (*Agr*) food bag; barley bin. (**b**) (*Téc*) hopper.
cebadero *nm* (**a**) (*comerciante*) barley dealer.
(**b**) (*mula*) leading mule (*of a team*).
(**c**) (*sitio*) feeding place.
(**d**) (*Téc*) mouth for charging a furnace.
cebado 1 *adj* (*LAm*) *animal* man-eating. **2** *nm* (**a**) (*Agr*) fattening. (**b**) priming; stoking.
cebador *nm* (*Cono Sur Aut*) choke.
cebadura *nf* (**a**) (*Agr*) fattening.
(**b**) (*de cañón*) priming; (*de horno*) stoking.
cebar [1a] **1** *vt* (**a**) (*Agr*) to fatten (up), feed (up) (*con* on).
(**b**) *fuego, horno* to feed, stoke (up); *cañón, lámpara, bomba* to prime; *fuego artificial* to light, set off.
(**c**) *anzuelo, trampa* to bait.
(**d**) *pasión etc* to feed, nourish; *cólera* to inflame; *hope* to stimulate.
(**e**) (*LAm Culin*) *maté* to make, brew.
2 *vi* (*tuerca etc*) to grip, catch, go on; (*clavo*) to go in.
3 cebarse *vr* (**a**) (*CAm, Méx*: *tiro, fuego artificial*) to fail to go off; (*fig*) to go wrong; **se me cebó** it didn't work, I didn't manage it.
(**b**) ~ **con uno** to set upon sb, go for sb, attack sb; ~ **en** to vent one's fury on; to batten on, prey upon; (*peste etc*) to rage among; (*fuego*) to devour, rage in.
(**c**) ~ **en un estudio** to devote o.s. to a study, become absorbed in a study.
(**d**) ~ **en la sangre** to gloat over the blood(shed), revel

in the blood(shed).

cebeísmo *nm* enthusiasm for CB radio.

cebeísta *nmf* CB radio enthusiast.

cebellina *nf* (*Zool*) sable.

cebiche *nm* (*And*) *marinaded fish salad; marinaded shellfish.*

cebo *nm* (**a**) (*Agr*) feed, food.
(**b**) (*de cañón*) charge, priming; (*Téc*) fuel, oven load.
(**c**) (*Pez*) bait; (*fig*) bait, lure, incentive; ~ **vivo** live bait.

cebolla *nf* (**a**) (*Bot*) onion; (*de tulipán etc*) bulb; ~ **escalonia** shallot. (**b**) (*LAm hum*) watch. (**c**) (‡: *cabeza*) onion‡, head.

cebollado *adj* (*LAm*) cooked with onions.

cebollana *nf* chive.

cebolleta *nf* (**a**) (*Bot*) spring onion. (**b**) (**‡) prick**‡.

cebollino *nm* young onion, spring onion, onion for transplanting; (*semilla*) onion seed; (*cebollana*) chive.

cebollita *nf* (*LAm Bot*: *t* ~ **china**) spring onion.

cebollón *nm* (*Cono Sur*: *pey*) old bachelor.

cebollona *nf* (*Cono Sur*: *pey*) old maid*, spinster.

cebón 1 *adj* fat, fattened. **2** *nm* fattened animal.

ceboruco *nm* (**a**) (*Carib*: *arrecife*) reef. (**b**) (*Méx*: *terreno quebrado*) rough rocky place. (**c**) (*Carib*: *maleza*) brush, scrub(land).

cebra *nf* (**a**) (*Zool*) zebra. (**b**) ~**s** (*Aut*) zebra crossing, crosswalk (*US*).

cebú *nm* zebu.

CECA ['θeka] *nf* (**a**) *abr de* **Comunidad Europea del Carbón y del Acero** European Coal and Steel Community, ECSC. (**b**) *abr de* **Confederación Española de Cajas de Ahorro**.

ceca¹ *nf* (*Fin*) mint.

Ceca² *nf*: **andar** (*o* **ir**) **de la ~ a la Meca** to go hither and thither, chase about all over the place.

CECE [θeθe] *nf abr de* **Confederación Española de Centros de la Enseñanza**.

cecear [1a] *vi* to lisp; *to pronounce* [s] *as* [θ].

ceceo *nm* lisp; *pronunciation of* [s] *as* [θ].

ceceoso *adj* lisping, having a lisp.

Cecilia *nf* Cecily.

Cecilio *nm* Cecil.

cecina *nf* dried meat, smoked meat; corned beef; (*Cono Sur*) sausage.

CEDA [θeða] *nf* (*Esp Hist*) *abr de* **Confederación Española de Derechas Autónomas.**

ceda *nm*: ~ **el paso** (*Aut*) priority, right of way.

cedazo *nm* sieve.

cedente *nmf* (*Jur*) assignor.

ceder [2a] **1** *vt* to hand over, give up; to yield (up); to part with; *territorio* to cede; *propiedad* to transfer, make over; (*Dep*) *balón* to pass; *V* **paso** *etc.*
2 *vi* (**a**) (*rendirse*) to give in, yield (*a* to); **no ceden fácilmente a las innovaciones** they do not give in (*o* give way) easily to innovations; **no cede a nadie en experiencia** he is inferior to none in experience; ~ **de una pretensión** to give up a claim, renounce a claim.
(**b**) (*bajar*) to diminish, decline, go down; (*fiebre, viento etc*) to abate.
(**c**) (*suelo, cuerda etc*) to give, give way, sag.
(**d**) (*Dep*) to pass.

cedible *adj* transferable.

cedilla *nf* cedilla.

cedizo *adj carne* high, tainted.

cedro *nm* cedar.

cedrón *nm* (*Cono Sur*) lemon verbena.

cédula *nf* (*documento*) certificate, document; (*formulario*) form, blank, (slip of) paper; (*orden*) (official) order, decree; (*Com*) warrant; (*esp LAm*) identity card; ~ **de aduana** customs permit; ~ **en blanco** blank cheque; ~ **de cambio** bill of exchange; ~ **hipotecaria** mortgage bond; ~ **personal,** ~ **de vecindad** identity card; ~ **real** royal letters patent; **dar ~ a uno** to license sb.

cedulista *nmf* (*Fin*) holder (of a certificate *etc*).

CEE *nf abr de* **Comunidad Económica Europea** European Economic Community, EEC.

cefalea *nf* severe headache, migraine.

cefálico *adj* cephalic.

céfiro *nm* zephyr.

cegador *adj* blinding; **brillo** ~ blinding glare.

cegajoso *adj* weepy, bleary-eyed.

cegar [1h *y* 1j] **1** *vt* (**a**) *persona* to blind, make blind; **le ciega la pasión** he is blinded by passion.
(**b**) (*fig*: *tapar*) *tubo etc* to block up, stop up; *hoyo* to fill up; *puerta, ventana* to wall up.
2 *vi* to go blind, become blind(ed).
3 cegarse *vr* (*fig*) to become blinded (*de* by).

cegato *adj*, **cegatón** *adj* (*LAm*) short-sighted.

cegatoso *adj* = **cegajoso.**

ceguedad *nf*, **ceguera** *nf* blindness (*t fig*); ~ **nocturna** night blindness.

ceiba *nf* ceiba, silk-cotton tree, bombax.

Ceilán *nm* (*Hist*) Ceylon.

ceilanés, -esa *adj, nm/f* (*Hist*) Ceylonese.

ceja *nf* (**a**) (*Anat*) eyebrow; **arquear las ~s** to raise one's eyebrows; **dejarse las ~s** to give of one's best; **fruncir las ~s** to knit one's brows, frown; **meterse algo entre ~ y ~** to get sth firmly into one's head; **quemarse las ~s** to work far into the night; **tener a uno entre ~ y ~** to look askance at sb; to have a grudge against sb; **tomar a uno entre ~ y ~** to take a dislike to sb.
(**b**) (*fig*: *Téc*) rim, flange; (*Cos*) edging; (*Arquit*) projection; (*de colina*) brow, crown; (*Met*) cloud-cap; (*Mús*) bridge; (*LAm*: *vereda*) forest path.

cejar [1a] *vi* (*retroceder*) to move back, back; (*fig*) to give way, back down; (*en discusión etc*) to climb down; **no** ~ to keep it up, keep going, hold out; **sin** ~ unflinchingly, undaunted; **no ~ en sus esfuerzos** to keep up one's efforts, not let up in one's efforts; **no ~ en su trabajo** to keep on with one's work.

cejijunto *adj* with bushy eyebrows; having brows that meet; (*fig*) scowling, frowning.

cejudo *adj* beetle-browed, with bushy eyebrows.

celacanto *nm* coelacanth.

celada *nf* (**a**) (*emboscada*) ambush, trap; (*fig*) trick, ruse; **caer en la** ~ to fall into the trap. (**b**) (*Hist*: *casco*) helmet, sallet.

celador(a) *nm/f* (*de edificio etc*) watchman, guard; (*de biblioteca, museo*) attendant; (*en examen*) invigilator; (*Téc*) maintenance man; (*Elec*) linesman; (*Med*) hospital porter; (*Aut*) parking attendant; (*de cárcel*) prison warder.

celaje *nm* (**a**) (*Met*) sky with clouds of varied hue; (*Náut*) clouds; ~**s** sunset clouds, sky with scudding clouds.
(**b**) (*CAm*) (*Arte*) cloud painting; (*efecto*) cloud effect.
(**c**) (*Arquit*) skylight.
(**b**) (*fig*: *presagio*) (promising) sign, token.
(**e**) (*And, Carib*: *fantasma*) ghost; **como un** ~ in a flash.

celar¹ [1a] **1** *vt* (*vigilar*) to watch over, keep a watchful eye on, keep a check on; ~ **las leyes** to see that the laws are kept; ~ **la justicia** to see that justice is done.
2 *vi*: ~ **por,** ~ **sobre** to watch over.

celar² [1a] *vt* (*ocultar*) to conceal, cover, hide.

celda *nf* cell; ~ **de castigo** solitary confinement cell.

celdilla *nf* (*de colmena*) cell; (*hueco*) cavity, hollow; (*casilla*) pigeonhole; (*Arquit*) niche.

cele *adj* (*CAm*) (*color*) light green; (*inmaduro*) unripe.

celebérrimo *adj superl de* **célebre.**

celebración *nf* (**a**) (*acto*) celebration; holding; conclusion; solemnization. (**b**) (*elogio*) praise; (*aplausos*) applause, welcome; (*de ventajas etc*) preaching.

celebrante *nm* (*Ecl*) celebrant, officiating priest.

celebrar [1a] **1** *vt* (**a**) *aniversario, suceso etc* to celebrate; *reunión* to hold; *entrevista, charla* to have, hold (*con* with); *tratado* to conclude (*con* with); *fiesta* to keep, celebrate; *boda* to perform, solemnize; *misa* to say.
(**b**) (*elogiar*) to praise; (*aplaudir*) to applaud, welcome; *ventajas* to preach, dwell on; *chiste* to laugh at, find amusing; ~ + *infin* to be glad to + *infin*, be delighted to + *infin*; **lo celebro** I'm very glad; **lo celebro mucho por él** I'm very glad for his sake.
2 *vi* (**a**) (*Ecl*) to say mass.
(**b**) (*alegrarse*) to be glad, be delighted.
(**c**) (*Carib*: *enamorarse*) to fall in love.
3 celebrarse *vr* (*fiesta etc*) to fall, occur, be celebrated; (*reunión*) to be held, take place.

célebre *adj* (**a**) (*famoso*) famous, celebrated, noted (*por* for); remarkable.
(**b**) (*gracioso*) *persona* witty, facetious; *suceso* funny, amusing; **es ~ ¿no?** he's a scream, isn't he?*; **¡fue ~!** it was killing!

celebridad *nf* (**a**) (*gen*) celebrity, fame. (**b**) (*persona*) celebrity. (**c**) (*fiestas etc*) celebration(s); festivity; pageant.

celeque *adj* (*CAm*) green, unripe.

célere *adj* rapid, swift.

celeridad *nf* speed, swiftness; **con** ~ quickly, speedily, promptly.

celeste *adj* celestial, heavenly; (*Astron*) heavenly; (*color*) sky blue.

celestial *adj* (a) (*Rel*) celestial, heavenly. (b) (*fig: delicioso*) heavenly, delightful. (c) (*: *tonto*) silly.
celestina *nf* bawd, procuress; (*de burdel*) madame.
celestinazgo *nm* pimping, procuring.
celibato *nm* (a) (*condición*) celibacy. (b) (*: *soltero*) bachelor.
célibe 1 *adj* single, unmarried; celibate. **2** *nmf* unmarried person, bachelor, spinster; celibate.
célico *adj* (*liter*) heavenly, celestial.
celidonia *nf* celandine.
celinda *nf* (*Bot*) mock orange.
celo¹ *nm* (a) (*fervor*) zeal, fervour, ardour; (*escrupulosidad*) conscientiousness; (*Rel*) religious fervour, piety; (*pey*) envy, mistrust.
(b) (*Zool*) (*de macho*) rut; (*de hembra*) heat; **caer en ~** to come into rut, come into season; **estar en ~** to be on heat, be in rut, be in season; *V* **época.**
(c) **~s** jealousy; **dar ~s** to give grounds for jealousy; **dar ~s a uno, infundir ~s a uno** to make sb jealous; **tener ~s de uno** to be jealous of sb.
celo² *nm* (*t* **papel ~**) adhesive tape.
celofán *nm* cellophane.
celosamente *adv* (a) (*con fervor*) zealously; eagerly; fervently. (b) (*pey*) suspiciously, distrustfully. (c) (*con celos*) jealously.
celosía *nf* (a) (*reja*) lattice; (*contraventana*) slatted shutter; (*ventana*) lattice window. (b) (*celos*) jealousy.
celoso *adj* (a) (*entusiasta*) zealous (*de* for), keen (*de* about, on); eager; (*fervoroso*) fervent.
(b) (*pey*) suspicious, distrustful.
(c) (*con celos*) jealous (*de* of).
(d) (*LAm: Mec etc*) highly sensitive; (*And*) *barca* unsteady, easily upset; (*LAm*) *arma* delicate, liable to go off; **este es un fusil ~** (*LAm*) this gun is quite liable to go off.
celta 1 *adj* Celtic. **2** *nmf* Celt. **3** *nm* (*Ling*) Celtic.
Celtiberia *nf* Celtiberia.
celtibérico, -a, celtíbero, -a *adj, nm/f* Celtiberian.
céltico *adj* Celtic.
célula *nf* (a) (*Bio etc*) cell; **~ fotoeléctrica** photoelectric cell; **~ fotovoltaica** photovoltaic cell; **~ germen** germ cell; **~s grises** grey matter; **~ nerviosa** nerve cell; **~ sanguínea** blood cell; **~ de silicio** silicon chip; **~ solar** solar cell. (b) (*fig, Pol*) cell; **~ terrorista** terrorist cell. (c) (*Aer*) airframe.
celular *adj* cellular; cell (*atr*); *V* **coche** *etc.*
celulitis *nf* cellulitis.
celuloide *nm* celluloid.
celulosa *nf* celulose.
cellisca *nf* sleet; sleet storm.
cellisquear [1a] *vi* to sleet.
cello¹ *nm* (*Mus*) cello.
cello² *nm* = **celo².**
CEM *nm* (*Esp*) *abr de* **Centro de Estudios para la Mujer.**
cementación *nf* (*Téc*) case-hardening, cementation.
cementar [1a] *vt* (*Téc*) to case-harden, cement.
cementera *nf* cement works.
cementerio *nm* cemetery, graveyard; **~ de coches** used-car dump; **~ nuclear** nuclear waste dump.
cementero *adj* cement (*atr*).
cementista *nm* cement worker.
cemento *nm* (*Anat, Téc*) cement; (*hormigón*) concrete; (*LAm*) glue; **~ armado, ~ reforzado** (*And*) reinforced concrete.
cemita *nf* (*LAm*) white bread roll.
CEN *nm* (*Esp*) *abr de* **Consejo de Economía Nacional.**
cena *nf* supper; evening meal; (*formal etc*) dinner; **~ de gala** dinner-party; formal dinner; (*Pol*) state banquet; **~ de negocios** business dinner; **~ de trabajo** working dinner; **la C~, la Última C~** the Last Supper; **C~ de Baltasar** Belshazzar's Feast.
cena-bufete *nf, pl* **cenas-bufete** buffet-supper.
cenáculo *nm* group, coterie; literary group, cenacle.
cenador *nm* arbour; pavilion; summerhouse.
cenaduría *nf* (*Méx*) eating house, restaurant.
cena-espectáculo *nf, pl* **cenas-espectáculo** dinner show, dinner with a floor show.
cenagal *nm* bog, quagmire, morass; (*fig*) tricky situation, sticky business.
cenagoso *adj* muddy, boggy.
cena-homenaje *nf, pl* **cenas-homenaje** formal dinner, celebratory dinner; **ofrecer una ~ a uno** to hold a dinner for sb.
cenar [1a] **1** *vt* to have for supper (*etc*), sup on, sup off.
2 *vi* to have one's supper, have dinner, dine; **invitar a uno a ~** to invite sb to dinner; **vengo cenado** I've had dinner (*etc*).
cenceño *adj* thin, skinny; *V* **pan.**
cencerrada *nf* charivari; rowdy music, noise, din.
cencerrear [1a] *vi* to jangle; (*máquina etc*) to rattle, clatter; (*puerta, carro etc*) to creak; (*Mús*) to play terribly, make a dreadful noise.
cencerreo *nm* jangle; rattle, clatter; creak; (*Mús*) dreadful noise.
cencerro *nm* cowbell; **a ~s tapados** stealthily, on the sly; **estar como un ~*** to be crazy.
cendal *nm* gauze; fine silk stuff, sendal.
Cenebad [θene'βað] *nm* (*Esp Escol*) *abr de* **Centro Nacional de Educación Básica a Distancia.**
cenefa *nf* (*Cos*) edging, trimming, border; stripe, band; (*Arquit*) border, frieze.
cenetista 1 *adj* of the CNT; anarchosyndicalist; **política ~** policy of the CNT. **2** *nmf* member of the CNT; anarchosyndicalist.
cenicero *nm* (*de mesa*) ashtray; (*recogedor*) ash pan; (*vertedero*) ash pit, ash tip.
Cenicienta *nf*: **la ~** Cinderella; **soy la ~ de la casa** I'm always the one to be left out.
ceniciento *adj* ashen, ash-coloured.
cénit *nm*, **cenit** *nm* zenith.
ceniza *nf* ash, ashes; cinder; **~s** (*de persona*) ashes, mortal remains; **huir de las ~s y dar en las brasas** to jump out of the frying pan into the fire; **reducir algo a ~s** to reduce sth to ashes.
cenizo 1 *adj* (a) (*de color*) ashen, ash-coloured.
(b) (*de mal augurio*) ill-omened; (*alarmante*) alarming.
2 *nm* (a) (*Bot*) goosefoot.
(b) (*: *gafe*) jinx*, hoodoo; **es un avión ~** it's a plane with a jinx on it*; **entrar el ~ en casa** to have a spell of bad luck; **tener el ~** to have a jinx on one*.
(c) (*persona*) bringer of bad luck; wet blanket.
cenobio *nm* monastery.
cenobita *nmf* coenobite, monk, nun.
cenojil *nm* garter.
cenorrio* *nm* posh dinner*, slap-up do*.
cenotafio *nm* cenotaph.
cenote *nm* (*CAm, Méx*) cenote, deep rock-pool, natural well.
censal *adj* = **censual.**
censar [1a] *vt* (*Cono Sur*) to take a census of.
censista *nmf* census official, census taker.
censo *nm* (a) (*de habitantes*) census; **~ de tráfico** traffic census, traffic count; **levantar el ~ de** to take a census of.
(b) (*Fin*) tax; (annual) ground rent; mortgage; leasehold.
(c) (*Pol*) **~ electoral** electoral roll, (*fig*) electorate.
(d) **ser un ~*** to be a constant drain, be a financial burden.
censor(a) *nm/f* (a) (*Pol*) censor.
(b) (*Univ*) proctor.
(c) (*Com, Fin*) **~ de cuentas** auditor; **~ jurado de cuentas** chartered accountant.
(d) (*fig: crítico*) critic.
censual *adj* (a) (*gen*) census (*atr*), relating to a census. (b) (*Fin*) tax (*atr*), mortage (*atr*) *etc.* (c) (*Pol: de elecciones*) electoral, relating to the electoral roll.
censura *nf* (a) (*Pol: acto*) censorship; censoring; **someter a la ~** to censor.
(b) (*oficina*) censor's office.
(c) (*crítica*) censure, stricture, criticism; (*reproche*) blame, reproach; (*Liter etc*) criticism, judgement; **digno de ~** censurable, blameworthy.
(d) (*Com, Fin*) **~ de cuentas** auditing.
censurable *adj* censurable, reprehensible, blameworthy.
censurar [1a] *vt* (a) (*Pol*) to censor. (b) (*criticar*) to censure, condemn, criticize, blame, reproach; to find fault with; (*Liter etc*) to criticize, judge.
censurista 1 *adj* censorious. **2** *nmf* critic, faultfinder.
cént(s) *abr de* **céntimo(s)** cent(s), c.
centaura *nf* centaury.
centauro *nm* centaur.
centavo 1 *adj* hundredth. **2** *nm* (a) (*Mat*) hundredth (part). (b) (*Fin*) *in LAm currencies*, centavo, *one-hundredth part of a peso etc.*
centella *nf* spark (*t fig*); flash of lightning.
centelleante *adj* (a) (*gen*) sparkling; gleaming, glinting, twinkling; flashing. (b) (*fig*) sparkling.
centell(e)ar [1a] *vi* (a) (*gen*) to sparkle; to gleam, glint,

glitter; (*estrella*) to twinkle; (*relámpago*) to flash. (**b**) (*fig*) to sparkle.
centelleo *nm* sparkle, sparkling; gleam(ing); glinting; flashing.
centena *nf* hundred.
centenada *nf* hundred.
centenal *nm*, **centenar**[1] *nm* (*Agr*) rye field.
centenar[2] *nm* hundred; **a ~es** by the hundred, by hundreds.
centenario 1 *adj* centenary, centennial. **2** *nm* centenary, centennial. **3** *nm*, **centenaria** *nf* (*persona*) centenarian.
centeno *nm* rye.
centésima *nf* hundredth (part).
centesimal *adj* centesimal.
centésimo 1 *adj* hundredth. **2** *nm* hundredth (part); *in LAm currencies*, centésimo, *one-hundredth part of a balboa etc.*
centígrado *adj* centigrade.
centigramo *nm* centigram.
centilitro *nm* centilitre.
centímetro *nm* centimetre.
céntimo 1 *adj* hundredth.
2 *nm* hundredth part (*esp* of a peseta), cent; **no tiene un ~** he hasn't a penny, he hasn't a bean*; **no vale un ~** it's worthless.
centinela *nmf* (*Mil*) sentry, guard, sentinel; (*en atraco etc*) look-out man; **estar de ~** to be on guard, do sentry duty; **hacer ~** (*fig*) to keep watch, be on the look-out.
centiplicado *adj* hundredfold.
centolla *nf*, **centollo** *nm* spider crab, (large) crab.
centón *nm* (**a**) (*Cos*) patchwork quilt, crazy quilt. (**b**) (*Liter*) cento.
central 1 *adj* central; middle; **en los días ~es de la semana** in midweek, midway through the week.
2 *nf* (*Com*) head office, headquarters; (*Téc*) plant, station; (*Telec*) exchange, (*privada*) switchboard; (*sindicato*) trade union; **~ (azucarera)** (*Carib*) sugar-mill; **~ de bombeo** pumping-station; **~ de correos** head post office, general post office; **~ depuradora** waterworks; **~ eléctrica, ~ de energía** power-station; **~ lechera** dairy; **~ nuclear** nuclear power-station; **~ sindical** trade union; **~ telefónica, ~ de teléfonos** telephone exchange; **~ de teléfonos automática** automatic telephone exchange; **~ de teléfonos manual** (*o* **con servicio a mano**) manual telephone exchange; **~ térmica de fuel** oil-fired power-station.
centralidad *nf* centrality, central importance.
centralismo *nm* centralism.
centralista 1 *adj* centralist, centralizing.
2 *nmf* centralist.
3 *nm* (*Carib*) sugar-mill owner.
centralita *nf* (*Telec*) switchboard.
centralización *nf* centralization.
centralizar [1f] *vt* to centralize.
centrar [1a] **1** *vt* (**a**) (*gen*) to centre (*en* on); *atención, esfuerzos* to concentrate, focus (*en* on); *novela etc* to base, centre (*en* on). (**b**) (*Mil*) *fuego* to concentrate, aim; (*Fot*) to focus (*en* on). **2 centrarse** *vr* (**a**) **~ en** to centre on, be centred on; to focus on; to concentrate on. (**b**) (*en un empleo*) to settle in, get to know the ropes.
céntrico *adj* central, middle; **punto ~** (*fig*) focal point; **es muy ~** it's very central, it's very convenient; **un restaurante ~** a restaurant in the centre of town, a downtown restaurant.
centrífuga *nf* centrifuge.
centrifugar [1h] *vt* to centrifuge; *colada* to spin.
centrífugo *adj* centrifugal.
centrípeto *adj* centripetal.
centrismo *nm* centrism, political doctrine of the centre.
centrista 1 *adj* centrist, of a centrist party (*o* policy *etc*).
2 *nmf* centrist, member of a centrist party.
centro *nm* (**a**) (*gen*) centre, middle; (*Mat, Pol*) centre; (*de actividad*) centre, hub; (*de incendio*) seat; **~ de acogida para mujeres maltratadas** refuge for battered wives; **~ de atracción** centre of attraction, main attraction; **~ de cálculo** computer centre; **~ cívico** community centre; **~ comercial** shopping centre; shopping precinct, mall (*US*); **~ de convivencia social** social centre, community centre; **~ de coordinación** (*policía*) operations room; **~ de costos** cost centre; **~ demográfico, ~ de población** centre of population; **~ de detención** detention centre; **~ docente** teaching institution; **~ espacial** space centre; **~ de fricción** trouble spot; **~ de gravedad** centre of gravity; **~ de interés** centre of interest, main point of interest; **~ de intrigas** centre of intrigue; **~ de mesa** centrepiece; **~ neurálgico** nerve-centre (*t fig*); **~ de orientación familiar, ~ de planificación familiar** family-planning clinic; **~ recreacional** (*Carib*) sports (*o* leisure) centre; **~ de salud** health centre; **~ social** community centre; **estar en su ~** (*fig*) to be in one's element; **ser de ~** (*Pol*) to be a moderate; **ir al ~** (*de ciudad*) to go into the centre, go into town, go downtown.
(**b**) (*fig: objetivo*) goal, purpose, objective.
(**c**) (*Dep*) centre; **~ de(l) campo** midfield; **delantero ~** centre-forward; **medio ~** centre-half.
(**d**) (*Dep: golpe*) centre.
(**e**) (*CAm: juego de ropa*) trousers and waistcoat; (*Carib, Méx: juego de ropa*) matching waistcoat and jacket; (*And, Carib, Méx: enaguas*) underskirt; (*And: falda*) thick flannel skirt.
centroafricano *adj* Central African; **la República Centroafricana** the Central African Republic.
Centroamérica *nf* Central America.
centroamericano, -a *adj, nm/f* Central American.
centrocampismo *nm* midfield play.
centrocampista *nmf* midfield player.
centrocampo *nm* midfield.
centroderecha *nm* centre-right.
Centroeuropa *nf* Central Europe.
centroizquierda *nm* centre-left.
centuplicar [1g] *vt* to increase a hundredfold (*t fig*), increase enormously.
centuplo 1 *adj* hundredfold, centuple. **2** *nm* centuple.
centuria *nf* century.
centurión *nm* centurion.
cenutrio* *nm* twit*, twerp*.
cénzalo *nm* mosquito.
cenzontle *nm* (*Méx*) mockingbird.
ceñido *adj* (**a**) *vestido* tight, tight-fitting, close-fitting, clinging; narrow-waisted; *curva* sharp.
(**b**) (*fig: frugal*) sparing, frugal, thrifty; moderate; **~ al tema** keeping close to the point; **~ y corto** brief and to the point.
ceñidor *nm* sash, girdle.
ceñir [3h *y* 3k] **1** *vt* (**a**) (*rodear*) to girdle, encircle, surround; (*Mil*) to besiege; **la muralla ciñe la ciudad** the wall surrounds the city; **~ una ciudad con una muralla** to encircle a city with a wall, throw a wall round a city.
(**b**) (*ponerse*) to fasten round one's waist; *espada* to gird on; *cinturón etc* to put on; **~ espada** to wear a sword.
(**c**) *frente* to bind, encircle, wreathe (*con, de* with).
(**d**) (*ajustar*) to fit tight; (*acortar*) to tighten (up), draw in; **el vestido ciñe bien el cuerpo** the dress fits well; **habrá que ceñirlo más** we shall have to draw it in.
(**e**) (*fig: abreviar*) to shorten, cut down, condense.
2 ceñirse *vr* (**a**) **~ algo** to put sth on; **se ciñó la espada** he put his sword on; **~ la corona** to take the crown.
(**b**) (*Fin etc*) to reduce expenditure, tighten one's belt; (*al hablar*) to limit o.s., be brief; **~ a un tema** to limit o.s. to a subject, concentrate on a subject; **~ al asunto** to stick to the matter in hand; **te ciñes muy a la derecha en la carretera** you keep very close to the right when you're driving.
ceño *nm* (**a**) (*expresión*) frown, scowl; **arrugar el ~, fruncir el ~** to frown, knit one's brows; **mirar con ~** (*vt*) to frown at, scowl at, give black looks to; (*vi*) to frown, scowl, look black.
(**b**) (*Met*) threatening appearance.
CEOE *nf abr de* **Confederación Española de Organizaciones Empresariales** ≈ Confederation of British Industry, CBI.
ceñudo *adj persona* frowning, grim; *mirada* black, grim.
cepa *nf* (**a**) (*Bot*) stump; (*de vid*) stock; vine; (*Zool: de cuerno, cola*) root; (*Arquit*) pier.
(**b**) (*fig: origen*) stock; **de buena ~** (*persona*) of good stock, (*cosa*) of high quality; **de buena ~ castellana** of good Castilian stock.
(**c**) (*Méx: hoyo*) pit, trench.
CEPAL [se'pal] *nf abr de* **Comisión Económica para América Latina** Economic Commission for Latin America, ECLA.
cepero *nm* trapper.
cepillado *nm* brushing, brush (*act*); planing; **se elimina con un suave ~** it goes away with a gentle brush.
cepilladura *nf* = **cepillado**.
cepillar [1a] **1** *vt* (**a**) (*gen*) to brush; (*Téc*) to plane (down).
(**b**) (*Univ**) to plough*.
(**c**) (*LAm: lisonjear*) to flatter, butter up*.
(**d**) (‡: *robar*) to rip off‡.
(**e**) (‡: *ganar*) to win, take (*a* from).
(**f**) (‡: *matar*) to bump off‡.
(**g**) (*pegar azotes*) to spank.

2 cepillarse *vr* (**a**) ~ **a uno‡** to bump sb off‡, knock sb off‡.
(**b**) ~ **algo‡** to rip sth off‡.
(**c**) ~ **a una**** to screw sb**.

cepillo *nm* (**a**) (*gen*) brush; ~ **de baño** bath-brush; ~ **de dientes** toothbrush; ~ **para el pelo** hairbrush; ~ **de púas metálicas** wire brush; ~ **de** (*o* **para**) **la ropa** clothes-brush; ~ **para el suelo** scrubbing brush; ~ **para las uñas** nail-brush; **pelo cortado al** ~ crew-cut.
(**b**) (*Téc*) plane.
(**c**) (*Ecl*) poorbox, alms box.
(**d**) (*LAm*: *adulador*) flatterer, creep‡.

cepillón‡ 1 *adj* soapy*. **2** *nm*, **cepillona** *nf* creep‡.

cepo *nm* (**a**) (*Bot*) branch, bough.
(**b**) (*Caza*) trap, snare; (*Mil*) mantrap; stocks; (*Aut*) wheel clamp; ~ **conejero** snare; ~ **lobero** wolf-trap.
(**c**) (*Mec*) reel; (*de yunque, ancla*) stock.
(**d**) (*Ecl*) poorbox, alms box.

ceporrez* *nf* idiocy, foolishness.

ceporro* *nm* (**a**) (*idiota*) twit*. (**b**) **estar como un** ~ to be very fat.

CEPSA ['θepsa] *nf* (*Com*) *abr de* **Compañía Española de Petróleos, Sociedad Anónima.**

CEPYME [θe'pime] *nf abr de* **Confederación Española de la Pequeña y Mediana Empresa.**

cequión *nm* (*Cono Sur*) large irrigation channel.

cera *nf* (**a**) (*gen*) wax; ~ **de abejas** beeswax; ~ **depilatoria** depilatory; ~ **de lustrar** wax polish; ~ **de los oídos** ear-wax; ~ **para suelos** floorpolish; **ser como una** ~ to be as gentle as a lamb.
(**b**) ~**s** honeycomb.
(**c**) (*And, Méx*: *vela*) candle.

cerafolio *nm* chervil.

cerámica *nf* (**a**) (*Arte*) ceramics, pottery. (**b**) (*objetos*) pottery (*t* ~**s**).

cerámico *adj* ceramic.

ceramista *nmf* potter.

cerbatana *nf* (*Mil etc*) blowpipe; (*juguete*) peashooter; (*Med*) ear trumpet.

cerca¹ *nf* fence, wall; ~ **eléctrica** electrified fence.

cerca² 1 *adv* (**a**) near, nearby, close; **de** ~ closely; (*Mil*) at close range; **examinar algo de** ~ to examine sth closely; **aquí** ~ near here; **por aquí** ~ nearby, hereabouts, somewhere round here.
(**b**) (*Cono Sur*) ~ **nuestro** (*etc*) near us (*etc*).
2 ~ **de** *prep* (**a**) (*lugar*) near, close to; in the neighbourhood of; **estar** ~ **de** + *infin* to be near + *ger*, be on the point of + *ger*.
(**b**) (*cantidad*) nearly, about; (*tiempo*) nearly; **hay** ~ **de 8 toneladas** there are about 8 tons; **son** ~ **de las 6** it's nearly 6 o'clock.
(**c**) (*Pol*) to; **embajador** ~ **de la corte de Ruritania** ambassador to the court of Ruritania.
3 *nm* (**a**) **tiene buen** ~ it looks all right close up.
(**b**) (*Arte*) ~**s** objects in the foreground.

cercado *nm* (**a**) (*recinto*) enclosure; (*huerto*) enclosed garden, fenced field, orchard.
(**b**) (*cerca*) fence, wall; ~ **eléctrico** electrified fence.
(**c**) (*And*: *ejido*) communal lands.
(**d**) (*And Hist*) *state capital and surrounding towns.*

cercanía *nf* (**a**) (*proximidad*) nearness, closeness, proximity.
(**b**) ~**s** (*vecindad*) neighbourhood, vicinity; surroundings.
(**c**) ~**s** (*de ciudad*) outskirts, outer suburbs, outlying areas; **tren de** ~**s** suburban train.

cercano *adj* near, close; nearby, neighbouring, next; *pariente* close; *muerte, fin* approaching; ~ **a** near to, close to.

Cercano Oriente *nm* Near East.

cercar [1g] *vt* (**a**) (*poner valla a*) to fence in, wall in, hedge; to enclose; (*rodear*) to encircle, surround, ring (*de* with); (*enemigo, montañas etc*) to hem in.
(**b**) (*Mil*) *ciudad* to surround, besiege; *tropas* to surround, cut off, encircle.

cercén *adv*: **cortar a** ~ to extirpate, take out (*o* off) completely; **cortar un brazo a** ~ to cut an arm off completely.

cercenar [1a] *vt* (**a**) (*gen*) to clip; to cut the edge off, trim the edges of; *cabo, punta* to cut off, slice off; *miembro* to cut off, amputate; *moneda* to clip.
(**b**) (*fig*) *gastos* to cut down, reduce; *texto etc* to shorten, cut down; (*suprimir*) to delete, cut out.

cerceta *nf* teal, garganey.

cerciorar [1a] **1** *vt* to inform, assure. **2 cerciorarse** *vr* to find out; to make sure; ~ **de** to find out about, ascertain; to make sure of.

cerco *nm* (**a**) (*Agr etc*) enclosure; (*LAm*: *valla*) fence, hedge; (*And*) small walled property; **saltar el** ~ (*Cono Sur Pol*) to jump on the bandwagon.
(**b**) (*Téc*) (*de rueda*) rim; (*de barril*) hoop; (*Arquit*) casing, frame; (*de suciedad etc*) ring, rim, mark.
(**c**) (*Astron, Met*) halo.
(**d**) (*grupo*) social group, circle.
(**e**) (*Mil*) siege; **alzar** (*o* **levantar**) **el** ~ to raise the siege; **poner** ~ **a** to lay siege to.

cercón *adv* (*LAm*) rather close.

cerda *nf* (**a**) (*Zool*) sow. (**b**) (*pelo*) bristle; horsehair; (*Caza*) snare, noose. (**c**) (‡: *puta*) slut; whore.

cerdada* *nf* dirty trick; nasty thing (to do).

cerdear [1a] *vi* (**a**) (*Mús*) to scratch, rasp, grate; (*Mec*) to work badly, play up. (**b**) (*: *dudar*) to hedge, jib, hold back. (**c**) (*: *hacer trampa*) to play a dirty trick.

Cerdeña *nf* Sardinia.

cerdito *nm*, **cerdita** *nf* piglet.

cerdo 1 *nm* (**a**) (*Zool*) pig; ~ **ibérico** Iberian pig; ~ **salvaje** wild pig.
(**b**) ~ **marino** (*Zool*) porpoise.
(**c**) (*Culin*) pork.
(**d**) (*fig*: *persona*) dirty person, slovenly fellow; (*en lo moral*) swine; ~ **machista** male chauvinist pig.
2 *adj* (*) (**a**) (*sucio*) dirty, filthy.
(**b**) (*vil*) rotten*.

cerdoso *adj animal* shaggy, hairy, bristly; *barba* bristly, stubbly.

cereal 1 *adj* cereal; grain (*atr*). **2** *nm* cereal; ~**es** cereals, grain; ~**es** (*Culin*) cereals, cornflakes; ~**es forrajeros** grain used as animal feed, fodder grain.

cerealista *nmf* grain farmer.

cerealístico *adj* grain (*atr*), cereal (*atr*).

cereal-pienso *nm*, *pl* **cereales-pienso** grain used as animal feed, fodder grain.

cerebelo *nm* cerebellum.

cerebral *adj* cerebral, brain (*atr*); (*pey*) scheming, calculating; shrewd.

cerebralismo *nm* intellectualism, cerebralism.

cerebro *nm* brain; cerebrum; (*fig*) brains; intelligence; ~ **electrónico** electronic brain; ~ **gris** éminence grise; **es el** ~ **del equipo** he is the brains of the team; **estrujar el** ~ to rack one's brains; **ser un** ~ to be brilliant.

ceremonia *nf* (**a**) (*acto*) ceremony; (*Ecl*) ceremony, service; **hacer** ~**s** to stand on ceremony.
(**b**) (*cualidad*) ceremony, ceremoniousness; formality; pomp; **falta de** ~ informality; **reunión de** ~ formal meeting, ceremonial meeting; **reunirse de** ~ to meet with all due ceremony; **por** ~ as a matter of form; **hablar sin** ~ to speak informally; **hacer algo sin** ~ to do sth without fuss.

ceremonial *adj, nm* ceremonial.

ceremoniosamente *adv* ceremoniously; formally; stiffly, with an excess of politeness.

ceremonioso *adj* ceremonious; *persona, vestido, saludo, visita etc* formal; (*pey*) stiff, over-polite.

céreo *adj* wax (*atr*), waxen.

cerería *nf* wax-chandler's shop, chandlery.

cerero *nm* wax chandler.

cereza *nf* cherry; **un suéter rojo** ~ a cherry-red jumper; ~ **silvestre** wild cherry.

cerezal *nm* cherry orchard.

cerezo *nm* (*árbol*) cherry tree; (*madera*) cherry wood.

cerilla *nf* (**a**) (*fósforo*) match; (*vela*) wax taper. (**b**) (*Anat*) earwax.

cerillazo *nm*: **pegar un** ~ **a** to set a match to.

cerillera *nf*, **cerillero** *nm* (**a**) (*vendedor*) street vendor of tobacco. (**b**) (*LAm*: *cajita de cerillas*) matchbox.

cerillo *nm* (*CAm, Méx*) match.

cernedor *nm* sieve.

cernejas *nfpl* fetlock.

cerner [2g] **1** *vt* (**a**) (*Téc*) to sift, sieve.
(**b**) (*fig*: *observar*) to scan, watch.
2 *vi* (**a**) (*Bot*) to bud, blossom.
(**b**) (*Met*) to drizzle.
3 cernerse *vr* (**a**) (*Orn*: *sin moverse*) to hover; (*subir*) to soar; (*Aer*) to circle; (*helicóptero*) to hover; ~ **sobre** to be poised over, hang over; (*fig*) to threaten, hang over.
(**b**) (*persona*) to swagger.

cernícalo *nm* (**a**) (*Orn*) kestrel. (**b**) (*: *tonto*) lout, dolt. (**c**) **coger un** ~* to get tight*. (**d**) (*And Orn*) hawk, falcon.

cernidillo *nm* (**a**) (*modo de andar*) swagger, rolling gait.

(**b**) (*Met*) drizzle.
cernido *nm* (**a**) (*acto*) sifting; (*harina*) sifted flour. (**b**) (*And Met*) drizzle.
cernidor *nm* sieve.
cernidura *nf* sifting.
cero *nm* (**a**) (*gen*) nothing; nought; (*Fís etc*) zero; (*Dep*) **por 3 goles a ~** by 3 goals to nil, by 3 goals to nought; **empatar a ~(s)** to draw nil-nil, play a no-score draw; **estamos a 40 contra ~** (*Tenis*) the game stands at 40-love; **estoy a ~*** I'm broke*; **estamos a ~ de leche*** we're out of milk; **yo en eso estoy ~*** I'm no good at that; **~ absoluto** absolute zero; **8 grados bajo ~** 8 degrees below zero, 8 degrees below freezing, 8 degrees of frost; **desde las ~ horas** from the start of the day; **es un ~ a la izquierda** he's useless, he's a nobody; **tendremos que partir (nuevamente) de ~** (*fig*) we shall have to start from scratch again.
(**b**) (*: *coche-patrulla*) police car.
ceroso *adj* waxen; waxy, waxlike.
cerote *nm* (**a**) (*Téc*) (shoemaker's) wax.
(**b**) (*: *miedo*) panic, funk*.
(**c**) (*CAm, Méx*: *excremento*) piece of human excrement, stool; **estar hecho un ~** (*And*), **tener ~** (*Cono Sur, Méx*) to be covered in dirt (*o* muck).
cerotear [1a] *vt hilo* to wax.
cerquillo *nm* (**a**) (*de pelo*) fringe of hair round the tonsure; (*Méx*) (*fleco*) fringe; (*rizos*) kiss-curls. (**b**) (*Téc*) seam, welt.
cerquita *adv* quite near, close by.
cerradero 1 *adj dispositivo* locking, fastening; **caja cerradera** box that can be locked, box with a lock.
2 *nm* locking device; clasp, fastener; (*de cerradura*) strike, keeper; (*de monedero*) purse strings.
cerrado *adj* (**a**) (*gen*) closed, shut; (*con llave*) locked; *puño* clenched; **~al vacío** vacuum-packed; **~ por obras** closed for repairs (*o* alterations); **aquí huele a ~** it smells stuffy in here, it's thick in here.
(**b**) *asunto* obscure, incomprehensible.
(**c**) (*Met*) *sky* cloudy, overcast; *atmósfera* heavy; *noche* dark, black.
(**d**) *curva* sharp, tight.
(**e**) *barba* thick, full.
(**f**) *persona* (*callado*) quiet, reserved, uncommunicative; (*pey*) secretive; **~ de mollera** (*poco inteligente*) dense*, dim*; (*obstinado*) pigheaded.
(**g**) *persona* (*típico*) typical, all-too-typical; **es un eslobodio ~** he's a typical Slobodian, he has all the worst features of the Slobodian.
(**h**) (*Ling*) *vocal* close.
(**i**) (*Ling*) *persona* with a broad accent; *acento* broad, marked, strong; *habla* thick, broad; **habló con ~ acento gallego** he spoke with a strong Galician accent.
(**j**) **a precio ~** at a fixed price, at a firm price.
(**k**) (*And, Cono Sur*: *terco*) pigheaded, stubborn.
cerradura *nf* (**a**) (*acto*) closing, shutting; locking.
(**b**) (*dispositivo*) lock; **~ de combinación** combination lock; **~ de golpe, ~ de muelle** spring lock; **~ de seguridad** safety lock.
cerraja *nf* (**a**) (*cerradura*) lock. (**b**) (*Bot*) sow-thistle.
cerrajería *nf* (**a**) (*oficio*) locksmith's craft (*o* trade). (**b**) (*tienda*) locksmith's (shop).
cerrajero *nm* locksmith.
cerrar [1j] **1** *vt* (**a**) *caja, ojos, boca, puerta etc* to close, shut; *puerta* (*con llave*) to lock (up); to bolt; *puño* to clench, close; *carta* to seal; *filas* to close; (*Elec, TV etc*) to switch off; **~ algo con llave** to lock sth.
(**b**) *agujero, brecha, tubo etc* to block (up), stop (up), close, obstruct; *puerto* to close; **han cerrado la frontera** they have closed the frontier; **la carretera está cerrada por la nieve** the road is blocked by snow.
(**c**) *terreno, zona* to enclose, close off, fence (in), wall (in).
(**d**) *grifo, gas, agua etc* to turn off.
(**e**) (*Elec*) *circuito* to make, close, complete.
(**f**) *tienda, negocio* to shut, close; (*para siempre*) to shut up; *fábrica* to close (down).
(**g**) *desfile* to bring up the rear of; **~ la marcha** to come last, bring up the rear.
(**h**) *cuenta, debate, narración* to close; *programa* to end, be the final item in.
(**i**) *trato* to seal, strike.
2 *vi* (**a**) (*gen*) to close, shut; **la puerta cierra mal** the door doesn't close properly; **cerramos a las 9** we close at 9; **dejar una puerta sin ~** to leave a door open.
(**b**) (*noche*) to come down, set in; (*invierno*) to close in.
(**c**) **~ con uno** to close with sb, grapple with sb; **~ con el enemigo** to come to close quarters with the enemy.
3 cerrarse *vr* (**a**) (*gen*) to close, shut; (*herida*) to close up, heal; (*Mil*) to close ranks.
(**b**) (*Met*) to cloud over, become overcast.
(**c**) **~ en** + *infin* to persist in + *ger*, go on stubbornly + *ger*.
cerrazón *nf* (**a**) (*Met*) threatening sky, storm clouds. (**b**) (*Cono Sur*: *niebla*) thick fog, thick mist. (**c**) (*And*: *de sierra*) spur. (**d**) (*fig*: *punto muerto*) impasse. (**e**) (*cualidad*) small-mindedness, narrow-mindedness; **su ~ hacia** his blind opposition to, his unreasoning hostility to.
cerrero *adj* (**a**) *animal* wild; untamed, unbroken; *persona* rough, uncouth. (**b**) (*And, Carib*: *sin azúcar*) unsweetened; (*agrio*) bitter; *pan etc* ordinary; (*Carib*) *persona* simple, ordinary.
cerril *adj* (**a**) *terreno* rough; mountainous. (**b**) *animal* wild; untamed, unbroken; *persona* (*inculto*) rough, uncouth; (*terco*) obstinate; (*de miras estrechas*) small-minded.
cerrilismo *nm* roughness, uncouthness; obstinacy; small-mindedness.
cerrillar [1a] *vt moneda* to mill.
cerro *nm* (**a**) (*colina*) hill; **andar (*o* echarse, ir) por los ~s de Úbeda** to wander from the point; to talk a lot of rubbish.
(**b**) (*Zool*) neck; backbone, back; **en ~** bareback.
(**c**) (*Téc*) bunch of cleaned hemp (*o* flax).
(**d**) (*And*: *montón*) lot, heap; **un ~ de** a heap (*o* pile) of.
cerrojazo *nm* slamming; **dar ~** to slam the bolt; (*fig*) to end unexpectedly; (*Parl*) to close (the session) unexpectedly; **dar ~ a uno** to slam the door in sb's face.
cerrojo *nm* bolt, latch; (*Dep*: *t* **táctica de ~**) defensive play, negative play; **echar el ~** to bolt the door.
certamen *nm* competition, contest; **~ de belleza** beauty contest.
certeramente *adv* accurately, unerringly.
certero *adj* (**a**) *hecho etc* accurate, sure, certain.
(**b**) *tiro* accurate, well-aimed; telling; *puntería* excellent; *tirador* sure, good, crack.
(**c**) (*enterado*) well-informed.
certeza *nf* certainty; **tener la ~ de que ...** to know for certain that ..., have the certain knowledge that ...
certidumbre *nf* certainty; conviction.
certificable *adj* certifiable; (*Correos*) registrable, that can be registered.
certificación *nf* certification; (*Correos*) registration; (*Jur*) attestation.
certificado 1 *adj* certified; (*Correos*) registered.
2 *nm* (**a**) (*gen*) certificate; **~ de aeronavegabilidad** certificate of airworthiness; **~ de aptitud** testimonial; **~ de ciudadanía** naturalization papers; **~ de defunción** death certificate; **~ de depósito** certificate of deposit; **~ escolar, ~ de escolaridad** certificate of completion of *EGB* course (at age 14); **~ médico** medical certificate; **~ de origen** certificate of origin; **~ de penales** good-conduct certificate; **~ de vacuna** vaccination certificate.
(**b**) (*Correos*) registered packet, registered item.
certificar [1g] *vt* (**a**) to certify; to guarantee, vouch for; **~ que ...** to certify that ... (**b**) (*Correos*) to register.
certitud *nf* certainty, certitude.
cerúleo *adj* sky blue.
cerumen *nm* earwax.
cerval *adj* deer (*atr*), deer-like.
cervantino *adj* Cervantine; relating to Cervantes; **estilo ~** Cervantine style; **estudios ~s** Cervantes studies.
cervantista *nmf* Cervantes scholar, specialist in Cervantes.
cervato *nm* fawn.
cervecera *nf* brewery.
cervecería *nf* (**a**) (*fábrica*) brewery. (**b**) (*bar*) bar, public house.
cervecero 1 *adj* beer (*atr*); **la industria cervecera** the brewing industry. **2** *nm* brewer.
cerveza *nf* beer; **~ de barril, ~ (servida) al grifo** draught beer, beer on draught; **~ de botella, ~ en botellas, ~ embotellada** bottled beer; **~ clara** light beer; **~ negra** dark beer, stout; **~ de sifón** (*CAm*) draught beer.
cervical *adj* (*del cuello*) neck (*atr*), cervical; (*del útero*) cervical.
Cervino *nm*: **el Monte ~** Mont Cervin, the Matterhorn.
cerviz *nf* (**a**) (*cuello*) neck, nape of the neck; **de dura ~** stubborn, headstrong, wild; **bajar (*o* doblar) la ~** to submit, bow down; **levantar la ~** to lift one's head up (again).
(**b**) (*útero*) cervix.
cervuno *adj* deer-like; deer-coloured.

cesación *nf* cessation; suspension, stoppage; ~ **del fuego** ceasefire.

cesante 1 *adj* out of a job, out of office; discharged; retired; redundant; (*LAm*) unemployed; **el gobierno** ~ the outgoing government.

2 *nm civil* (*o public*) *servant who has been made redundant*; (*LAm*) unemployed person.

cesantear [1a] *vt* (*Cono Sur*) to dismiss, sack*.

cesantía *nf* (**a**) (*condición*) state of being a *cesante*, redundancy; (*suspensión*) suspension; (*Cono Sur*) dismissal, sacking*; unemployment. (**b**) (*pago*) retirement pension, redundancy compensation, severance pay.

César *nm* Caesar.

cesar [1a] **1** *vt* (**a**) (*gen*) to cease, stop; *pagos, trabajo* to stop, suspend.

(**b**) (*despedir*) *obrero* to dismiss, sack*, fire*; *funcionario, ministro* to remove from office; **ha sido cesado de su cargo** he has been dismissed from his post; **le cesaron en el trabajo** they sacked him from his work.

2 *vi* (**a**) (*gen*) to cease, stop; to desist; ~ **de hacer algo** to stop doing sth, leave off doing sth; **no cesa de hablar** she never stops talking; **sin** ~ ceaselessly, incessantly.

(**b**) (*empleado*) to leave, quit; (*jubilarse*) to retire; ~ **en el trabajo** to give up one's work, retire from work.

cesaraugustano = **zaragozano**.

cesáreo *adj* (**a**) Caesarean; imperial. (**b**) (*Med*) **operación cesárea** Caesarean operation.

cese *nm* (**a**) (*gen*) cessation; suspension, stoppage: ~ **de alarma** (*Mil*) all-clear signal; ~ **de fuego,** ~ **de hostilidades** ceasefire; ~ **de pagos** suspension of payments, stoppage of payments; ~ **temporal de los bombardeos** temporary halt to the bombing.

(**b**) (*de funcionario*) dismissal, compulsory retirement; (*de obrero*) sacking*, firing*; **dar el** ~ **a uno** to retire sb; to sack sb*.

Ceseden [θese'ðen] *nm* (*Esp*) *abr de* **Centro Superior de Estudios de la Defensa Nacional.**

CESID, Cesid [θe'sið] *nm* (*Esp*) *abr de* **Centro Superior de Información de la Defensa** (*military intelligence service*).

cesio *nm* caesium, cesium (*US*).

cesión *nf* (**a**) (*Pol etc*) cession. (**b**) (*Jur*) cession, granting, transfer; ~ **de bienes** surrender of property.

cesionario, -a *nm/f* grantee, assign.

cesionista *nmf* grantor, assignor.

césped *nm* (**a**) (*hierba*) grass, lawn, (stretch of) turf; (*para juegos*) pitch; (*para bolos*) green. (**b**) (*tepe*) turf, sod.

cesta *nf* (*gen*) basket; (*pelota*) long wicker racquet; ~ **de la compra,** ~ **para compras** shopping basket; ~ **de la compra** (*fig*) (weekly *etc*) cost of foodstuffs; ~ **de costura** sewing basket; ~ **de Navidad** Christmas box; ~ **para papeles,** ~ **de los papeles** wastepaper basket; ~ **de picnic** picnic hamper; **llevar la** ~* to go along as chaperon; to play gooseberry.

cestada *nf* basketful.

cestería *nf* (**a**) (*arte*) basketmaking. (**b**) (*materia; objetos*) wickerwork, basketwork; **silla de** ~ wicker(work) chair. (**c**) (*tienda*) basket shop.

cestero, -a *nm/f* (*obrero*) basketmaker; (*vendedor*) basket seller.

cestillo *nm* small basket; ~ **del polen** (*Ent*) pollen sac.

cesto *nm* (**a**) (*cesta*) (large) basket; hamper; ~ **de la colada** clothes basket; ~ **para papeles,** ~ **de los papeles** wastepaper basket.

(**b**) **estar hecho un** ~ to be very drowsy; to be fuddled with drink.

(**c**) (*: *gamberro*) lout.

cesura *nf* caesura.

cetáceo *adj, nm* cetacean.

cetárea, cetaria *nf* shellfish farm.

CETME ['θetme] *nm abr de* **Centro de Estudios Técnicos de Materiales Especiales.**

cetme *nm* rifle.

cetorrino *nm* basking shark.

cetrería *nf* falconry, hawking.

cetrero *nm* (**a**) (*Caza*) falconer. (**b**) (*Ecl*) verger.

cetrino *adj* greenish-yellow; *cara, tez* sallow; (*fig*) melancholy, jaundiced.

cetro *nm* (**a**) sceptre; (*fig*) sway, power, dominion; **empuñar el** ~ to ascend the throne, begin to reign. (**b**) (*LAm: Dep*) crown, championship.

CEU *nm* (*Esp*) *abr de* **Centro de Estudios Universitarios.**

ceutí 1 *adj* of Ceuta. **2** *nmf* native (*o* inhabitant) of Ceuta; **los ~es** the people of Ceuta.

C.F. *nm abr de* **Club de Fútbol** football club, FC.

CFC *nm abr de* **clorofluorocarbono** chlorofluorocarbon, CFC.

cfr. *abr de* **confróntese, compárese** confer, compare, cf.

cg *abr de* **centígramo** centigramme, cg.

CGC-L *nm* (*Esp*) *abr de* **Consejo General de Castilla y León.**

CGPJ *nm* (*Esp*) *abr de* **Consejo General del Poder Judicial.**

CGV *nm* (*Esp*) *abr de* **Consejo General Vasco.**

C.I. *nm abr de* **coeficiente de inteligencia** (*o* **intelectual**) intelligence quotient, IQ.

Cía. *nf abr de* **Compañía** Company, Co.

cía *nf* hip bone.

cianhídrico *adj* hydrocyanic.

cianotipia *nf,* **cianotipo** *nm* blueprint.

cianuro *nm* cyanide; ~ **potásico,** ~ **de potasio** potassium cyanide.

ciar [1c] *vi* (**a**) (*ir hacia atrás*) to go backwards; (*Náut*) to go astern, back water. (**b**) (*fig: volverse atrás*) to back down, back out.

ciática *nf* sciatica.

ciático *adj* sciatic.

cibernética *nf* cybernetics.

cibernético *adj* cybernetic.

cicatear [1a] *vi* to be stingy, be mean.

cicatería *nf* stinginess, meanness.

cicatero 1 *adj* stingy, mean. **2** *nm,* **cicatera** *nf* miser, skinflint; (*) pickpocket.

cicatriz *nf* scar (*t fig*).

cicatrización *nf* healing.

cicatrizar [1f] **1** *vt* to heal. **2 cicatrizarse** *vr* to heal (up), form a scar.

Cicerón *nm* Cicero.

cicerone *nm* guide, cicerone.

ciceroniano *adj* Ciceronian.

ciclamato *nm* cyclamate.

ciclamen *nm,* **ciclamino** *nm* cyclamen.

cíclico *adj* cyclic(al).

ciclismo *nm* cycling; (*Dep*) cycle racing; ~ **en ruta** road racing.

ciclista 1 *adj* cycle (*atr*), cycling (*atr*); **vuelta** ~ cycle race. **2** *nmf* cyclist.

ciclo *nm* cycle; (*Liter*) cycle; (*de conferencias etc*) course, series, programme; (*LAm: Univ*) year, course; ~ **circadiano** circadian cycle; ~ **de instrucción** instruction cycle; ~ **del nitrógeno** nitrogen cycle; ~ **vital** life-cycle.

ciclo-cross *nm* cyclo-cross.

ciclomoto(r) *nm* moped, autocycle.

ciclón *nm* cyclone.

cíclope *nm* Cyclops.

ciclópeo *adj* gigantic, colossal.

ciclorama *nm* cyclorama.

ciclostilado *adj* cyclostyled.

ciclostilar [1a] *vt* to cyclostyle.

ciclostil(o) *nm* cyclostyle.

ciclotrón *nm* cyclotron.

cicloturismo *nm* touring by bicycle.

cicloturista *nmf* cycling tourist, touring cyclist.

-cico, -cica (*a veces t* **-ecico, -ecica**) *V* **Aspects of Word Formation in Spanish 2.**

cicuta *nf* hemlock.

cidiano *adj* relating to the Cid; **estudios ~s** Cid studies.

cidra *nf* citron.

cidracayote *nm* (*LAm*) gourd, calabash.

cidro *nm* citron (tree).

ciega *nf* blind woman.

ciego 1 *adj* (**a**) (*gen*) blind; (*cegado*) blinded; **a ciegas** blindly; **andar a ciegas, caminar a ciegas** to grope one's way; **volar a ciegas** to fly blind; **jugar a la ciega** (*Ajedrez*) to play blindfold; **quedar** ~ to go blind; **quedó** ~ **después de la explosión** he was blinded in the explosion; **más** ~ **que un topo** as blind as a bat; **tan** ~ **el uno como el otro** it's a case of the blind leading the blind.

(**b**) (*fig*) blind; ~ **a,** ~ **para** blind to; ~ **de ira** blind with rage; **con una fe ciega** with a blind faith, with an unquestioning faith; **a ciegas** blindly; heedlessly, thoughtlessly.

(**c**) (‡) **estar** ~ (*borracho*) to be canned‡, (*drogado*) to be high‡, **ponerse** ~ to get high‡ (*de* on).

(**d**) (*Arquit*) blind; *tubo etc* blocked, stopped up, choked.

2 *nm* (**a**) (*gen: persona*) blind man, blind person; **los ~s** the blind, blind people.

(**b**) (*Cono Sur Cartas*) player who holds bad cards.

(**c**) (*Carib: claro de bosque*) forest clearing.

(**d**) (‡) junkie‡.

cielo *nm* (**a**) (*gen*) sky; (*Astron*) sky, heavens, firmament; ~ **aborregado** mackerel sky; ~ **encopetado** overcast sky;

~ **máximo** (*Aer*) ceiling; **a ~ abierto, a ~ raso** in the open air; **mina a ~ abierto** opencast mine; **a ~ descubierto** in the open; **se le juntaron el ~ con la tierra** (*LAm*) he lost his nerve; **mover ~s y tierra para** + *infin* to move heaven and earth to + *infin*; **querer tapar el ~ con las manos** to try to hide sth obvious; **se vino el ~ abajo** it rained cats and dogs, the heavens opened.

(**b**) (*Arquit*: *t* ~ **raso**) ceiling; (*de boca*) roof; (*de cama*) canopy; (*CAm*: *Aut*) roof.

(**c**) (*Rel*) heaven; **¡~s!** good heavens!; **esto clama al ~** this cries out to heaven (*to be reformed etc*); **estar en el séptimo ~** to be in seventh heaven; **ganar el ~** to win salvation; **ir al ~** to go to heaven; **poner a uno en el ~** (*o* **en los cielos,** (*LAm*) **por los cielos**) to praise sb to the skies; **tomar el ~ con las manos** to be asking for trouble, be over-optimistic; **ver el ~ abierto** to see one's way out of a difficulty; to see one's chance; *V* **llover.**

(**d**) (*palabra cariñosa*) my love, sweetheart.

(**e**) (*) **el jefe es un ~** the boss is a dear, the boss is sheer heaven*.

ciempiés *nm invar* centipede.

cien[1] *adj* (*apócope de* **ciento,** *delante n*) (**a**) (*gen*) a hundred; **~ mil** a hundred thousand; **las últimas ~ páginas** the last hundred pages; **estar a ~*** to be highly excited; **me pone a ~*** (*enoja*) it sends me up the wall*; (*encandila*) it makes me feel randy*.

(**b**) **10 por ~** ten per cent; **~ por ~** a hundred per cent (*t fig*); **es español ~ por ~** he's Spanish through and through, he's Spanish to the core; **lo apoyo ~ por ~** I support it a hundred per cent, I support it wholeheartedly; **estar hasta el ~** (*And*) to be on one's last legs.

cien[2]‡ *nm* bog‡, lavatory.

ciénaga *nf* marsh, bog, swamp.

ciencia *nf* science; (*sentido antiguo*) knowledge, learning, scholarship, erudition; **hombre de ~** scientist; **~ de la alimentación** food science; **~s económicas** economics; **~s empresariales** business studies; **~s físicas** physical science; **~s forestales** forestry; **~ del hogar** domestic science, home economics (*US*); **~s naturales** natural sciences; **~s ocultas** occult sciences; **~s políticas** political science, politics; **~ social** social science; **~s de la vida** life sciences; **a ~ y paciencia de uno** with sb's knowledge and agreement, with sb's connivance; **saber algo a ~ cierta** to know sth for certain (*o* for a fact).

ciencia-ficción *nf* science fiction.

Cienciología *nf* Scientology.

cieno *nm* (*lodo*) mud, mire; (*de río*) silt, ooze; (*limo*) slime.

cienoso *adj* muddy, miry; slimy.

científicamente *adv* scientifically.

cientificidad *nf* scientific nature.

científico 1 *adj* scientific. **2** *nm*, **científica** *nf* scientist; **~ social** social scientist.

cientifismo *nm* scientific spirit.

cientista *nmf* (*LAm*) scientist.

ciento *adj y nm* hundred, (one) hundred; **~ veinte** a hundred and twenty; **en su año ~** in its hundredth year; **15 por ~** 15 per cent; **las calles están al ~ por ~ de su capacidad** the streets are at full capacity, the streets can hold no more traffic; **estar al ~ por ~** (*Dep etc*) to be on top form; **hay un 5 por ~ de descuento** there is a 5 per cent discount; **por ~s** in hundreds, by the hundred; **de ~ en boca** tiny, insignificant; **dar ~ y raya al más pintado** to be a match for anyone; **había ~ y la madre** there were far too many; and even that was still too many.

cierne *nm* blossoming, budding; **en ~(s)** (*Bot*) in blossom; (*fig*) in its infancy; **es un ajedrecista en ~s** he's a budding chessplayer, he's a future chess champion.

cierre *nm* (**a**) (*acto*) closing, shutting; locking; (*Com etc*) closing, (*final*) closing-down; (*Rad, TV*) close-down; (*de fábrica*) shutdown; **~ centralizado** central locking; **~ de dirección** steering lock; **~ de los dueños, ~ patronal** lock-out.

(**b**) (*dispositivo*) closing device, locking device; snap fastener; (*de vestido*) fastener; (*de cinturón*) buckle, clasp; (*de libro*) clasp; (*de puerta*) catch; (*de tienda*) shutter, blind; (*Aut*) choke; **~ de cremallera, ~ relámpago** (*And, Cono Sur*) zip (fastener), zipper; **~ hidráulico** water seal; **~ metálico** roll shutter, metal blind; **echar el ~‡** to shut one's trap‡.

(**c**) **de ~** closing; **precios de ~** (*Fin*) closing prices.

cierro *nm* (**a**) = **cierre.** (**b**) (*Cono Sur*: *muro*) wall; (*sobre*) envelope.

ciertamente *adv* certainly, surely; **no era ~ de los más inteligentes** he was certainly not one of the brightest.

cierto *adj* (**a**) (*seguro*) sure, certain; *promesa etc* positive, definite; **¡~!** certainly!; **~, ...** granted, ...; **por ~** certainly; by the way; **por ~ que no era el único** and moreover he was not the only one, and what is more he wasn't the only one; **no, por ~** certainly not; **¡sí, por ~!** yes of course!; **es ~** it is true, it is correct; that's it; **¿no es ~?** isn't that so?; **¿es ~ eso?** it that really so?; **es ~ que ...** it is certain that ..., it is true that ...; **lo ~ es que ...** the fact is that ...; **lo único ~ es que ...** the only sure thing is that ...; **estar ~** to be sure; **¿estás ~?** are you sure?; **estar ~ de** + *infin* to be certain to + *infin*; **estar en lo ~** to be right; **saber algo de ~** to know sth for certain.

(**b**) (*en concreto*) a certain; **~s** some, certain; **~ día de mayo** one day in May; **cierta persona que yo conozco** a certain person I know; *V* **cada** *etc.*

cierva *nf* hind.

ciervo *nm* deer; stag; (*Culin*) venison; **~ común** red deer; **~ volante** stag beetle.

cierzo *nm* north wind.

cifra *nf* (**a**) (*número*) number, numeral; **~ arábiga** Arabic numeral; **~ romana** Roman numeral; **en ~s redondeadas** in round numbers; **escribirlo en ~s y palabras** to write it down in figures and in words.

(**b**) (*cantidad*) number, quantity, amount; sum; **~ global** lump sum; **~ de ventas** sales figures, turnover; **la ~ de este año es elevada** the quantity this year is large; **la ~ de los muertos** the number of dead.

(**c**) (*clave*) code, cipher; **en ~** in code; (*fig*) mysteriously, enigmatically.

(**d**) (*abreviatura*) abbreviation; (*monograma*) monogram; (*resumen*) abridgement, summary; **en ~** in brief, briefly, concisely; in a shortened form.

cifradamente *adv* (**a**) (*con clave*) in code. (**b**) (*resumiendo*) in brief, in a shortened form.

cifrado 1 *adj* coded, in code. **2** *nm* (en)coding, ciphering.

cifrar [1a] **1** *vt* (**a**) *mensaje* to code, write in code; (*Ling*) to encode; (*fig*) to abridge, summarize; to abbreviate. (**b**) *esperanzas* to place, concentrate (*en* on). (**c**) (*calcular*) to reckon; **una duración cifrada en miles de años** a duration reckoned in thousands of years. **2 cifrarse** *vr*: **todas las esperanzas se cifran en él** all hopes are centred on him.

cigala *nf* Norway lobster.

cigarra *nf* cicada.

cigarral *nm* (*Toledo*) *country house on the banks of the Tagus.*

cigarrera *nf* (**a**) (*estuche*) cigar case. (**b**) (*obrera*) cigar maker; (*vendedora*) cigar seller.

cigarrería *nf* (*LAm*) (*tienda*) tobacconist's (shop); (*fábrica*) tobacco factory.

cigarrero *nm* (*obrero*) cigar maker; (*vendedor*) cigar-seller.

cigarrillo *nm* cigarette.

cigarro *nm* cigar (*t* ~ **puro**); cigarette (*t* ~ **de papel**); **~ habano** Havana cigar.

cigoto *nm* zygote.

ciguato *adj* (**a**) (*Carib, Méx*: *simple*) simple, stupid. (**b**) (*Carib, Méx*: *pálido*) pale, anaemic.

cigüeña *nf* (**a**) (*Orn*) stork. (**b**) (*Mec*: *manivela*) crank, handle; (*cabrestante*) winch, capstan. (**c**) (*CAm Mús*) barrel organ. (**d**) (*Carib Ferro*) bogie, bogy. (**e**) **la ~‡** the fuzz‡.

cigüeñal *nm* crankshaft.

cija *nf* sheep shed; hayloft.

cilampa *nf* (*CAm*) drizzle.

cilampear [1a] *vi* (*CAm*) to drizzle.

cilantro *nm* (*Bot, Culin*) coriander.

cilicio *nm* hair shirt; spiked belt (*o* chain *etc*) worn by penitents.

cilindrada *nf* cylinder capacity.

cilindradora *nf* steamroller, road roller.

cilindraje *nm* cylinder capacity.

cilindrar [1a] *vt* to roll, roll flat.

cilíndrico *adj* cylindrical.

cilindrín‡ *nm* fag‡, cigarette.

cilindro *nm* (*Mat, Téc*) cylinder; (*de máquina de escribir*) roller; (*) top hat; (*Méx*) barrel-organ; **~ de caminos, ~ compresor** steamroller, roadroller.

cilla *nf* (**a**) (*granero*) tithe barn, granary. (**b**) (*diezmo*) tithe.

cima *nf* (*de árbol*) top; (*de montaña*) top, peak, summit; (*fig*) summit, height; (*fig*) completion; **dar ~ a** to complete, crown with success, carry out successfully.

cimarra *nf*: **hacer ~** (*Cono Sur*) to play truant.

cimarrón 1 *adj* (**a**) (*LAm Bot, Zool*) wild, untamed; (*fig*: *inculto*) rough, uncouth; (*vago*) lazy; **negro ~** (*Hist*) run-

away slave, fugitive slave.
(**b**) (*Cono Sur*) *maté* bitter, unsweetened.
2 *nm* (*Cono Sur*) unsweetened maté.
3 *nm*, **cimarrona** *nf* (*Hist*) runaway slave, maroon.
cimarronear [1a] *vi* (*LAm*: *esclavo*) to run away.
cimba *nf* (**a**) (*And*: *cuerda*) plaited rope of hard leather. (**b**) (*And*: *trenza*) pigtail. (**c**) (*And*: *escala*) rope ladder.
címbalo *nm* cymbal.
cimbel *nm* (**a**) (*señuelo*) decoy (*t fig*). (**b**) (**‡*) prick**‡*.
cimbor(r)io *nm* (*Arquit*) dome; base of a dome; (*Min*) roof.
cimbrar [1a] *vt* (**a**) (*agitar*) to shake, swish, swing; (*curvar*) to bend. (**b**) ~ **a uno*** to clout sb (with a stick); **le cimbró de un porrazo** he clouted him with his stick.
cimbrear [1a] **1** *vt* = **cimbrar.**
2 cimbrearse *vr* (**a**) to sway, swing; to shake; to bend; ~ **al viento** to sway in the wind.
(**b**) (*persona*) to walk gracefully.
cimbreño *adj* pliant, flexible; *talle* willowy, lithe.
cimbreo *nm* swaying, swinging; shaking; bending.
cimbrón *nm* (*And, CAm, Cono Sur*: *sacudida*) shudder; (*And*) sharp pain; (*Cono Sur, Méx*: *espadazo*) blow with the flat of a sword; (*LAm*: *de lazo etc*) crack; (*LAm*: *tirón*) jerk, yank, tug.
cimbronada *nf* (*And, Cono Sur, Méx*), **cimbronazo** *nm* (*And, Cono Sur, Méx*) = **cimbrón**; (*Carib*: *terremoto*) earthquake.
cimentación *nf* (**a**) (*cimientos*) foundation. (**b**) (*acto*) laying of foundations.
cimentar [1j] *vt* (**a**) (*Arquit*) to lay the foundations of (*o* for); (*fig*: *fundar*) to found, establish. (**b**) *oro* to refine. (**c**) (*fig*: *reforzar*) to strengthen, cement.
cimera *nf* crest (*t Her*).
cimero *adj* top, topmost, uppermost; (*fig*) crowning, finest.
cimiento *nm* foundation, groundwork; (*fig*) basis, source; ~**s** (*Arquit*) foundations; **abrir los ~s** to dig the foundations; **echar los ~s de** to lay the foundations for.
cimitarra *nf* scimitar.
cimpa *nf* (*And*) = **cimba.**
cinabrio *nm* cinnabar.
cinc *nm* zinc.
cincel *nm* chisel.
cincelado *nm* chiselling; engraving.
cincelador *nm* (**a**) (*persona*) sculptor; engraver; stone cutter. (**b**) (*herramienta*) (chipping) chisel, chipping hammer.
cincelar [1a] *vt* (**a**) to chisel; to carve, engrave, cut. (**b**) (*fig*) to be precise about, make more precise; to go into fine details about.
cinco 1 *adj* five; (*fecha*) fifth; (*Univ*) five (*the pass mark*); **las** ~ five o'clock; **estar sin ~*, no tener ni ~*** to be broke*; **no estar en sus ~*** to be off one's rocker‡; **le dije cuántas son** ~ I told him a thing or two; **saber cuántas son** ~ to know what's what, know a thing or two; **tener los ~ muy listos*** to be light-fingered; **¡vengan esos ~!*** shake (on it)!*
2 *nm* (**a**) (*número*) five.
(**b**) (*And, CAm, Carib*: *guitarra*) 5-stringed guitar.
(**c**) (*: *Méx*: *trasero*) bottom, backside*.
(**d**) (*CAm, Méx*: *moneda*) 5 peso piece.
cincuenta *adj* fifty; fiftieth; **los (años)** ~ the fifties; **cantar las ~ a uno** to haul sb over the coals.
cincuentañero 1 *adj* fiftyish, about fifty. **2** *nm*, **cincuentañera** *nf* person of about fifty, person in his (*o* her) fifties.
cincuentavo *adj, nm* fiftieth.
cincuentena *nf* fifty, about fifty.
cincuenteno *adj* fiftieth.
cincuentón 1 *adj* fifty-year-old, fiftyish. **2** *nm*, **cincuentona** *nf* person of about fifty.
cincha *nf* (**a**) (*de caballo*) girth, saddle strap; **a revienta ~s** at breakneck speed; hurriedly; (*LAm*: *con renuencia*) reluctantly.
(**b**) (*Cos*: *para sillas*) webbing.
(**c**) **tener** ~ (*And*) to have a strain of Negro (*o* Indian) blood.
cinchada *nf* (*Cono Sur, Méx*) tug-of-war.
cinchar [1a] **1** *vt caballo* to girth, secure the girth of; (*Téc*) to band, hoop, secure with hoops. **2** *vi* (*Cono Sur**) (*trabajar*) to work hard; ~ **por** (*apoyar*) to root (*o* shout) for.
cincho *nm* (*faja*) sash, belt, girdle; (*aro*) iron hoop, metal band; (*CAm, Carib, Méx*) = **cincha (a).**
cinchona *nf* (*LAm*) quinine bark.
cine *nm* (**a**) (*gen y como arte*) cinema; film(s), movies (*US*); **unos muebles** (*etc*) **de ~*** posh furniture* (*etc*), luxurious furniture; **el ~ español actual** the present-day Spanish cinema; ~ **de arte y ensayo** arts cinema; ~ **en colores** colour films; ~ **hablado,** ~ **sonoro** talkies; ~ **mudo** silent films; ~ **de terror** horror movies; **hacer** ~ to make films, be engaged in film work, be working for the cinema.
(**b**) (*edificio*) cinema, movie theater (*US*); ~ **de verano** open-air cinema; **ir al** ~ to go to the cinema, go to the pictures, go to the movies (*US*).
cine... *pref* cine...
cineasta *nmf* (*entusiasta*) film fan, movie fan (*US*); (*experto*) film buff*; (*crítico*) film critic; (*creador*) film maker, director.
cine-club *nm, pl* **cine-clubs** (*para pronunciación V* **club**) cine club, film society.
cinefilia *nf* love of the cinema.
cinéfilo, -a *nm/f* film fan, movie fan (*US*); film buff*.
cinegética *nf* hunting, the chase.
cinegético *adj* hunting (*atr*), of the chase.
cinema *nm* cinema.
cinemateca *nf* film library, film archive.
cinemático *adj* cinematic.
cinematografía *nf* films, film-making, cinematography.
cinematografiar [1a] *vt* to film.
cinematográfico *adj* cine-..., film (*atr*); cinematographic.
cinematógrafo *nm* (**a**) (*cine*) cinema. (**b**) (*aparato*) cine projector, film projector.
cineración *nf* incineration.
cinerama *nm* cinerama.
cinerario *adj* (**a**) *urna* cinerary. (**b**) = **ceniciento.**
cinéreo *adj* ashy; ash-grey, ashen.
cineteca *nf* (*LAm*) film archive.
cinética *nf* kinetics.
cinético *adj* kinetic.
cingalés, -esa 1 *adj, nm/f* Singhalese. **2** *nm* (*Ling*) Singhalese.
cíngaro 1 *adj* gipsy. **2** *nm*, **cíngara** *nf* gipsy (*esp* Hungarian).
cinguería *nf* (*Cono Sur*: *obra*) sheet-metal work; (*taller*) sheet-metal shop.
cinguero *nm* (*Cono Sur*) sheet-metal worker.
cínicamente *adv* (**a**) (*con cinismo*) cynically. (**b**) (*sinvergonzadamente*) brazenly, shamelessly, impudently; in an unprincipled way.
cínico 1 *adj* (**a**) (*escéptico*) cynical. (**b**) (*descarado*) brazen, shameless, impudent; unprincipled. **2** *nm* (**a**) (*gen*) cynic.
(**b**) (*sinvergüenza*) brazen individual; unprincipled person.
cinismo *nm* (**a**) (*gen*) cynicism. (**b**) (*desvergüenza*) brazenness, shamelessness, effrontery, impudence; lack of principle; **¡qué ~!** what a nerve!*
cinofilia *nf* (**a**) dog-fancying, dog-breeding. (**b**) (*personas*) dog-fanciers, dog-breeders.
cinólogo, -a *nm/f* canine expert.
cinta *nf* (**a**) (*tira*) band, strip; tape; (*Cos*) ribbon, tape; (*Téc*) surveyor's tape; (*Cine*) film; reel; (*de grabación*) tape; ~ **adhesiva** adhesive tape; ~ **aisladora,** ~ **aislante,** ~ **de aislar** (*CAm, Méx*) insulating tape; ~ **de cotizaciones,** ~ **de teleimpresor** ticker tape; ~ **de freno** brake lining; ~ **de goma** rubber band; ~ **de llegada** (*Dep*) (finishing) tape; ~ **para máquina de escribir** typewriter ribbon; ~ **magnética** magnetic tape, recording tape; ~ **magnetofónica** audio tape; ~ **de corto metraje** short (film); ~ **de largo metraje** full-length film; ~ **de medir** (*LAm*), ~ **métrica** tape measure; ~ **de pelo** hairband; ~ **perforada** punched tape; ~ **de producción** assembly belt; ~ **simbólica** ceremonial tape; ~ **transbordadora** travelator, people mover; ~ **transportadora,** ~ **de transporte** conveyor belt; ~ **de vídeo** videotape; ~ **virgen** blank tape.
(**b**) (*Arquit*) fillet, scroll.
(**c**) (*de acera*) kerb; (*de habitación*) tile skirting.
(**d**) (*LAm*: *lata*) tin, can.
(**e**) ~**s** (*Méx*) shoelaces.
cinteado *adj* beribboned.
cintero *nm* (**a**) (*de mujer*) girdle. (**b**) (*cuerda*) rope.
cintillo *nm* (**a**) (*de sombrero*) hatband; (*LAm*: *para pelo*) hairband. (**b**) (*anillo*) small ring with jewels. (**c**) (*Tip*) heading, collective heading. (**d**) (*Carib*: *bordillo*) kerb.
cinto *nm* (*Mil*) belt, girdle, sash; ~ **negro** black belt; **armas de** ~ side arms.
cintura *nf* (**a**) (*Anat*) waist; waistline; ~ **de avispa** wasp waist; ~ **de castidad** chastity belt; **de la ~ (para) arriba** from the waist up; **tener poca** ~ to have a slim waist.
(**b**) (*faja*) girdle; **meter a uno en** ~ to bring (*o* keep) sb

under control, keep sb under; to make sb see reason.
cinturilla *nf* waistband.
cinturón *nm* (**a**) (*ceñidor*) belt; girdle; (†) sword belt; ~ **de salvamento,** ~ **salvavidas** lifebelt; ~ **de seguridad** safety belt; **apretarse el** ~ to tighten one's belt.
(**b**) (*fig*: *zona*) belt, zone; **el** ~ **industrial de Madrid** the Madrid industrial belt; ~ **de miseria** (*Méx*) slum area; ~ **verde** green belt.
(**c**) (*Aut*: *carretera*; *t* ~ **de circunvalación,** ~ **de ronda**) ringroad, beltway (*US*).
CIP [θip] **1** *nf abr de* **Comisión Internacional de Paz. 2** *nm* (*Madrid*) *abr de* **Club Internacional de Prensa.**
cipayo *nm* (**a**) (*Brit Mil Hist*) sepoy. (**b**) (*Cono Sur Pol*) politician in the service of foreign commerce.
cipe *nm* sickly baby.
cipo *nm* (*monumento*) memorial stone; (*mojón*) milestone, signpost.
cipote 1 *adj* (**a**) (*And, Carib*: *estúpido*) stupid, thick*.
(**b**) (*CAm*: *rechoncho*) plump, chubby.
2 *nm* (**a**) (*CAm, Carib*: *chico*) lad, youngster; urchin.
(**b**) (*CAm*: *maza*) Indian club.
(**c**) (*: *idiota*) chump*, blockhead.
(**d**) (*: *And*) ~ **de chica** smashing girl*; ~ **de película** splendid film.
(**e**) (‡: *barriga*) belly, guts.
(**f**) (**‡) prick**‡.
cipotear‡ [1a] *vt* to screw**‡.
ciprés *nm* cypress (tree).
cipresal *nm* cypress grove.
CIR [θir] *nm abr de* **Centro de Instrucción de Reclutas.**
circadiano *adj* circadian.
circense *adj* circus (*atr*), of the circus.
circo *nm* (**a**) (*recinto*) circus, amphitheatre. (**b**) (*función*) circus.
circonio *nm* zirconium.
circuir [3g] *vt* to encircle, surround.
circuitería *nf* circuitry.
circuito *nm* circuit; circumference, distance round (*the outside*); (*viaje*) tour; (*Elec etc*) circuit; (*Dep*) lap; ~ **en bucle** loop; ~ **cerrado** closed circuit, loop; ~ **cerrado de TV,** ~ **interno de TV, TV por** ~ **cerrado** closed-circuit TV; **corto** ~ short circuit; ~ **impreso** printed circuit; ~ **integrado** integrated circuit; ~ **lógico** logical circuit; ~ **urbano** city circuit, town circuit.
circulación *nf* (**a**) (*gen*: *t Fin, Med*) circulation; (*fig*) circulation; propagation; ~ **fiduciaria** paper money, paper currency; ~ **sanguínea,** ~ **de la sangre** circulation of the blood; **estar fuera de** ~ to be out of circulation, be no longer current; **poner algo en** ~ to issue sth, put sth into circulation.
(**b**) (*Aut*) traffic; movement of traffic; ~ **rodada** vehicular traffic, wheeled traffic; **'cerrado a la** ~ **rodada'** 'closed to vehicles'; **la** ~ **es por la derecha** they drive on the right; **calle de gran** ~ busy street, street much used by traffic; **'**~ **única'** (*Méx*) 'one way (traffic)'.
circulante *adj biblioteca* lending, circulating.
circular 1 *adj* circular, round; *billete* return, round-trip (*atr*); *viaje* round; *carta* circular.
2 *nf* circular.
3 [1a] *vt* to circulate; to pass round, send round; to put into circulation.
4 *vi* (**a**) (*gen*) to circulate (*t Fin, Med*); (*Fin*) to be in circulation; **hacer** ~ **una carta** to circulate a letter, send round a letter.
(**b**) (*personas*) to move about, walk around (*por* in); **¡circulen!** move along!; **hacer** ~ **a la gente** to move people along.
(**c**) (*Aut*) to drive; ~ **por la izquierda** (*regla de país*) to drive on the left, (*en calle etc*) to keep to the left; **hacer** ~ **los coches** to keep the cars moving.
(**d**) (*transporte*) to run; **no circula los domingos** it does not run on Sundays; **circula entre A y B** it runs between A and B, it operates between A and B.
circularidad *nf* circularity.
circulatorio *adj* (**a**) circulatory. (**b**) (*Aut*) traffic (*atr*); **colapso** ~ traffic jam, stoppage of traffic.
círculo *nm* (**a**) (*Mat etc*) circle; ~ **de giro,** ~ **de viraje** turning circle; ~ **máximo** great circle; ~ **polar antártico** Antarctic Circle; ~ **polar ártico** Arctic Circle; ~ **vicioso** vicious circle (*t fig*).
(**b**) (*anillo etc*) circle, ring, band.
(**c**) (*grupo*) circle, club, group; (*casino*) clubhouse; (*And, Cono Sur*) social gathering; (*Pol*) political group, faction.
(**d**) (*fig*: *campo*) scope, compass, extent.
circun... *pref* circum...
circuncidar [1a] *vt* (**a**) (*Med*) to circumcise. (**b**) (*fig*: *restringir*) to curtail; to moderate.
circuncisión *nf* circumcision.
circunciso 1 *adj* circumcised. **2** *nm* (*Hist*) Jew, Moor.
circundante *adj* surrounding.
circundar [1a] *vt* to surround.
circunferencia *nf* circumference.
circunflejo *nm* circumflex.
circunlocución *nf,* **circunloquio** *nm* circumlocution, roundabout expression.
circunnavegación *nf* circumnavigation.
circunnavegar [1a] *vt* to sail round, circumnavigate.
circunscribir [3a: *ptp* **circunscrito**] **1** *vt* to circumscribe; (*fig*) to circumscribe, limit, restrict (*a* to).
2 circunscribirse *vr* (*fig*) to limit o.s., confine o.s. (*a* to).
circunscripción *nf* (*de territorio*) division, subdivision; (*Parl*) constituency, electoral district.
circunspección *nf* circumspection, caution, prudence.
circunspecto *adj* circumspect, cautious, prudent; deliberate; *palabras* carefully chosen, guarded.
circunstancia *nf* circumstance; **~s agravantes** aggravating circumstances; **~s atenuantes** extenuating circumstances; mitigating circumstances; **en las ~s** in (*o* under) the circumstances; **en las ~s actuales** in the present state of things, under present conditions; **las ~s cambian los casos** circumstances alter cases; *V* **altura.**
circunstanciado *adj* detailed, circumstantial.
circunstancial *adj* (**a**) (*gen*) circumstantial. (**b**) *arreglo etc* makeshift, emergency (*atr*); *caso etc* incidental; **mi estancia en Lima era** ~ I just happened to be in Lima.
circunstante 1 *adj* (**a**) (*que rodea*) surrounding. (**b**) *persona* present. **2** *nmf* onlooker, bystander; **los ~s** those present.
circunvalación *nf*: **carretera de** ~ bypass, ring road.
circunvecino *adj* adjacent, neighbouring, surrounding.
cirial *nm* (*Ecl*) processional candlestick.
cirílico *adj, nm* Cyrillic.
cirio *nm* (**a**) (*Ecl*) (wax) candle. (**b**) (*) row, shindy*; **montar un** ~ to kick up a row (*a uno* with sb).
cirquero, -a *nm/f* (*Méx*) circus performer, acrobat; circus impresario.
cirro *nm* cirrus.
cirrocúmulo *nm* cirrocumulus.
cirrosis *nf* cirrhosis; ~ **hepática** cirrhosis of the liver.
cirrostrato *nm* cirrostratus.
ciruela *nf* plum; ~ **claudia,** ~ **verdal** greengage; ~ **damascena** damson; ~ **pasa** prune.
ciruelo *nm* (**a**) (*Bot*) plum tree. (**b**) (*) dolt, idiot.
cirugía *nf* surgery; ~ **estética** cosmetic surgery; ~ **plástica** plastic surgery.
ciruja *nmf* (*Cono Sur*) tramp.
cirujano, -a *nm/f* surgeon; ~ **plástico** plastic surgeon.
ciscar [1g] **1** *vt* (**a**) (*ensuciar*) to dirty, soil, mess up.
(**b**) (*Carib, Méx*: *avergonzar*) to shame, put down.
(**c**) (*Carib, Méx*: *meterse con*) to provoke, needle*.
2 ciscarse *vr* (**a**) (*defecar*) to soil o.s.; to do one's business*; **los que se ciscan en las teorías** those who thumb their noses at theories; **¡me cisco en todo!*** blast it!*
(**b**) (*Carib, Méx*: *avergonzarse*) to feel ashamed.
(**c**) (*Carib, Méx*: *ofenderse*) to get upset, take offence.
cisco *nm* (**a**) (*carbón*) coaldust, slack; **hacer algo** ~ to tear sth to bits, shatter sth; **estar hecho ~*** to be a wreck, be all in.
(**b**) (*: *riña*) row, shindy*; **armar un** ~**, meter** ~ to kick up a row, make trouble.
(**c**) (*Méx*: *miedo*) fear, fright.
ciscón *adj* (*Carib, Méx*) touchy.
Cisjordania *nf* West Bank.
cisjordano *adj* West Bank (*atr*).
cisma *nm* (**a**) (*Ecl*) schism; (*Pol etc*) split; (*fig*) discord, disagreement. (**b**) (*And*: *remilgo*) prudery, over-niceness. (**c**) (*And*: *chismes*) gossip.
cismático *adj* (**a**) (*Ecl*) schismatic(al); (*fig*) troublemaking, fractious, dissident. (**b**) (*And*: *remilgado*) prudish, overnice; finicky. (**c**) (*And*) gossipy.
cisne *nm* (**a**) (*Orn*) swan. (**b**) (*Cono Sur*: *borla*) powder puff.
Císter *nm* Cistercian Order.
cisterciense *adj, nm* Cistercian.
cisterna *nf* cistern; tank; reservoir.
cistitis *nf* cystitis.

cita *nf* (**a**) (*compromiso*) appointment, engagement; (*encuentro*) meeting; (*lugar*) place of meeting, rendezvous; (*de amantes*) meeting, (*con amigo o amiga*) date; ~ **a ciegas** blind date; ~ **espacial** rendez-vous in space, space link-up; **acudir a una** ~ to keep an appointment, turn up for an appointment; **se dieron (una)** ~ **para las 8** they agreed to meet at 8; **aquí los mejores atletas se han dado** ~ the best athletes are gathered here; **las cualidades que se dan** ~ **en ella** the qualities which come together in her; **faltar a una** ~ to miss an appointment, break an appointment, not turn up for a date; **tener una** ~ **con uno** to have an appointment with sb, have a date with sb.
(**b**) (*Liter etc*) quotation (*de* from); reference; (*acto*) citation; **con largas ~s probatorias** with long quotations in support.
citable *adj* quotable.
citación *nf* (**a**) (*Liter etc*) quotation. (**b**) (*Jur*) summons, citation; ~ **judicial** summons, subpoena; ~ **a licitadores** invitation to bidders, invitation of tenders.
citadino, -a *nm/f* (*LAm*) city-dweller.
citado *adj* aforementioned; **en el** ~ **país** in the aforementioned country, in this country; in the country in question.
citar [1a] **1** *vt* (**a**) *persona* to make an appointment with; to make a date with; **la cité para las 9** I arranged to meet her at 9; **la cité para delante de Correos** I arranged to meet her in front of the post office; **¿está Vd citado?** have you an appointment?, is he *etc* expecting you?
(**b**) (*Jur*) to call, summon; **tiene facultades para** ~ **testigos** he has the power to call witnesses.
(**c**) (*Taur*) to incite, provoke, stir up; to call out to.
(**d**) (*Liter etc*) to quote, cite (*de* from).
2 citarse *vr*: ~ **con uno** to arrange to meet sb (*para las* 7 at 7); **citémonos para delante del estadio** let's meet outside the stadium.
cítara *nf* zither.
-cito, -cita (*a veces t* **-ecito, -ecita**) *V* **Aspects of Word Formation in Spanish 2.**
citología *nf* cytology.
citotóxico *adj* cytotoxic.
citrato *nm* citrate.
cítrico 1 *adj* citric. **2 ~s** *nmpl* citrus fruits.
citrícola *adj* citrus (*atr*).
citrón *nm* lemon.
CiU *nm* (*Pol: Cataluña*) *abr de* **Convergència i Unió.**
ciudad *nf* city, town; **C~ del Cabo** Cape Town; ~ **colmena,** ~ **dormitorio** commuter suburb, dormitory town; **C~ Condal** Barcelona; **C~ Encantada** Cuenca; **C~ Eterna** Eternal City (*Rome*); **C~ Imperial** (*Hist de España*) Toledo; ~ **perdida** (*Méx*) slum area, shanty-town; **C~ del Turia** Valencia; **C~ del Vaticano** Vatican City; **es el mejor café de la** ~ it's the best café in town; **hoy vamos a la** ~ we're going to (*o* into, up to) town today.
ciudadanía *nf* (**a**) (*habitantes*) citizens, citizenry.
(**b**) (*status*) citizenship; ~ **de honor** freedom of a city; **derechos de** ~ citizen's rights, rights of citizenship.
ciudadano 1 *adj* civic, city (*atr*); **el orgullo** ~ civic pride.
2 *nm*, **ciudadana** *nf* (**a**) (*habitante*) city dweller, townsman.
(**b**) (*Pol etc*) citizen; **~s** townsfolk, townspeople; inhabitants; **el** ~ **de a pie** the man in the street; ~ **de honor** freeman of city; ~ **del mundo** citizen of the world; **~s de segunda clase** second-class citizens, under-privileged persons; ~ **de la tercera edad** senior citizen.
ciudadela *nf* (**a**) (*Mil*) citadel, fortress. (**b**) (*LAm: casa pobre*) tenement block.
ciudad-estado *nf, pl* **ciudades-estado** city-state.
ciudadrealeño 1 *adj* of Ciudad Real. **2** *nm*, **ciudadrealeña** *nf* native (*o* inhabitant) of Ciudad Real; **los ~s** the people of Ciudad Real.
civeta *nf* civet cat.
civeto *nm* civet.
cívico 1 *adj* civic; domestic; (*fig*) public-spirited, patriotic. **2** *nm* (**a**) (*LAm*) policeman. (**b**) (*Cono Sur: vaso*) large glass of beer.
civil 1 *adj* (**a**) (*Pol etc*) civil; **derechos ~es** civil rights; **guerra** ~ civil war; **casarse por lo** ~ to have a civil wedding, get married in a registry office (*or equivalent*).
(**b**) (*Mil*) **población** ~ civilian population.
(**c**) (*fig: cortés*) civil, courteous, polite.
2 *nm* (**a**) Civil Guard.
(**b**) (*en lenguaje de militares*) civilian.
civilidad *nf* civility, courtesy, politeness.
civilización *nf* civilization.
civilizador *adj influencia etc* civilizing.
civilizar [1f] **1** *vt* to civilize. **2 civilizarse** *vr* to become civilized.
civilizatorio *adj* civilizing.
civismo *nm* public spirit; community spirit; patriotism.
cizalla *nf* (**a**) (*gen* **~s** *pl: herramienta*) wire-cutters, metal shears. (**b**) (*virutas*) shavings, metal clippings.
cizaña *nf* (**a**) (*Bot*) darnel; (*Bib*) tares.
(**b**) (*fig: discordia*) discord; **sembrar** ~ to sow discord (*entre* among).
(**c**) (*fig: vicio*) vice, corruption, harmful influence.
cizañar [1a] *vt* to sow discord among.
cizañero, -a *nm/f* troublemaker, mischief-maker.
cl. *abr de* **centilitro** centilitre, cl..
clac 1 *nm, pl* **claques** opera hat; cocked hat. **2** *nf* = **claque.**
clamar [1a] **1** *vt* (*liter*) *justicia, venganza* to cry out for; *inocencia* to proclaim.
2 *vi* to cry out, clamour; ~ **contra** to cry out against, protest vociferously against; ~ **por** to clamour for, demand vociferously; **esto clama al cielo** this cries out to heaven (to be reformed *etc*).
clamor *nm* (**a**) (*grito*) cry, shout; (*ruido*) noise, clamour. (**b**) (*de campana*) tolling, knell. (**c**) (*fig: protesta*) clamour, outcry, protest.
clamorear [1a] **1** *vt* = **clamar 1. 2** *vi* (*campana*) to toll.
clamoreo *nm* (**a**) (*griterío*) clamour(ing), (prolonged) shouting. (**b**) (*fig: protestas*) sustained outcry, vociferous protests; **~s de protesta** vigorous protests.
clamorosamente *adv* noisily, loudly, clamorously.
clamoroso *adj* (**a**) (*ruidoso*) noisy, loud, clamorous; screaming, shrieking. (**b**) (*fig*) *éxito* resounding, enormous.
clan *nm* clan; (*fig*) faction, group.
clandestinamente *adv* secretly, clandestinely; by stealth, stealthily.
clandestinidad *nf* secrecy; secret nature; **en la** ~ in secrecy; **movimiento en la** ~ (*Pol*) underground movement; **pasar a la** ~ to go into hiding (*o* underground).
clandestinista *nm* (*LAm*) bootlegger.
clandestino 1 *adj* (*gen*) secret, clandestine; stealthy; (*Pol*) *actividad etc* clandestine, underground; *agente* secret, undercover; *boda* secret; runaway; **andar** ~ (*LAm Pol*) to be underground, operate under cover.
2 *nmpl*: **~s** (*And*) shacks.
clánico *adj* clannish, clan (*atr*).
claque *nf* claque.
claqué *nm* tap-dancing.
claqueta *nf* (*Cine*) clapperboard.
clara *nf* (**a**) (*de huevo*) white of an egg. (**b**) (*en cabeza*) bald spot; (*de paño*) bare patch, thin place. (**c**) (*Met*) bright interval.
claraboya *nf* skylight.
claramente *adv* (**a**) (*lit*) brightly; clearly. (**b**) (*fig*) clearly, plainly.
clarea *nf white wine with cinnamon, sugar and spices added.*
clarear [1a] **1** *vt* (**a**) (*gen*) to brighten; to light up; *color* to make lighter.
(**b**) (*fig*) to clarify, make clear(er).
(**c**) (*Méx: atravesar*) to go right through, penetrate; ~ **a uno** to put a bullet through sb.
2 *vi* (**a**) (*Met*) to clear up, brighten up.
(**b**) (*día*) to dawn, break; to grow light.
3 clarearse *vr* (**a**) (*paño*) to be transparent, let the light through.
(**b**) (*: *revelar*) to give the game away.
clareo‡ *nm*: **darse un** ~ (*pasear*) to take a stroll; (*irse*) to hoof it*.
clarete *nm* mixture of red and white wine.
claridad *nf* (**a**) (*luz*) brightness; light.
(**b**) (*fig*) clearness, clarity; **lo explicó todo con mucha** ~ he explained it all very clearly.
(**c**) **~es** sharp remarks, unpleasant remarks; home truths.
claridoso *adj* (*CAm, Méx*) blunt, plain-spoken.
clarificación *nf* (**a**) (*lit*) illumination, lighting (up). (**b**) (*fig*) clarification.
clarificador *adj* illuminating, enlightening; explanatory.
clarificar [1g] *vt* (**a**) (*iluminar*) to illuminate, light (up); to brighten.
(**b**) *líquido* to clarify; to refine, purify.
(**c**) (*fig: explicar*) to clarify.
clarín *nm* (**a**) (*Mús*) bugle; (*de órgano*) clarion. (**b**) (*persona*) bugler. (**c**) (*LAm: Bot*) sweet pea.
clarinada* *nf* uncalled-for remark.

clarinazo *nm* (*fig*) trumpet call.
clarinete 1 *nm* (*instrumento*) clarinet. **2** *nmf* (*persona*) clarinettist.
clarinetista *nmf* clarinettist.
clarión *nm* chalk, white crayon.
clarisa 1 *adj*: **monja ~** = **2**. **2** *nf* nun of the Order of St Clare.
clarividencia *nf* (**a**) (*lit*) clairvoyance. (**b**) (*fig: previsión*) farsightedness; (*discernimiento*) discernment; (*intuición*) intuition.
clarividente 1 *adj* far-sighted, far-seeing; discerning; gifted with intuition. **2** *nmf* clairvoyant(e).
claro 1 *adj* (**a**) *día, luz, ojos etc* bright; *cuarto* light, bright, well-lit.
(**b**) *agua* clear, transparent; *cristal, sonido, voz* clear.
(**c**) *cerveza, color* light; **verde ~** light green; **una tela verde ~** a light-green cloth.
(**d**) *contorno, letra etc* clear, distinct; bold; **tan ~ como la luz del día** as plain as a pikestaff; **tan ~ como el agua, más ~ que el sol** as clear as daylight.
(**e**) (*en consistencia*) *líquido* thin; *té etc* weak; *pelo* thin, sparse.
(**f**) *explicación, lenguaje, prueba etc* clear; plain, evident; **todo queda muy ~** it's all very clear; **¡~!** naturally!, of course!; (*esp LAm*) yes of course!, please do!; **¡pues ~!** I quite agree with you!; **¡~ que sí!** yes of course!; **¡~ que no!** of course not!; **~ que no es verdad** of course it isn't true; **está ~ que ...** it is plain that ..., it is obvious that ...; **a las ~as** clearly, plainly; openly.
(**g**) (*fig*) (*ilustre*) famous, illustrious; (*noble*) noble.
2 *adv* clearly; **hablar ~** (*fig*) to speak plainly, speak bluntly.
3 *nm* (**a**) **poner** (*o* **sacar**) **algo en ~** to explain sth, clear up sth, clarify sth; (*LAm*: *t* **pasar algo en ~**) to copy sth out; **no sacamos nada en ~** we couldn't get anything definite; there were no concrete decisions.
(**b**) **pasar la noche en ~** to have a sleepless night.
(**c**) **tener ~** (*LAm**) to have class.
(**d**) **de ~ en ~** (*obviamente*) obviously, plainly; (*toda la noche*) from dusk to dawn; **velar de ~ en ~** to lie awake all night.
(**e**) (*abertura*) opening; (*brecha, espacio*) gap, break, space; (*en bosque*) opening, clearing, glade; (*en tráfico etc*) gap, break; (*en pelo*) bald patch.
(**f**) (*Arquit*) light, window; skylight.
(**g**) (*Arte*) highlight; light tone.
(**h**) (*Met*) break in the clouds; (*CAm*) bright interval.
(**i**) (*Carib Culin*) guava jelly.
(**j**) (*Carib: bebida*) sugar-cane brandy.
(**k**) **~ de luna** moonlight.
(**l**) **~ de huevo** (*LAm*) eggwhite.
claroscuro *nm* chiaroscuro.
clase 1 *nf* (**a**) (*gen*) class; kind, sort; **con toda ~ de** with all kinds of, with every sort of, with all manner of; **gente de toda ~** people of every kind, all sorts of people; **de esta ~** of this kind; **de otra ~** of another sort; **de una misma ~** of the same kind; **de primera ~** first-class; **os deseo toda ~ de felicidades** I wish you every kind of happiness.
(**b**) (*transportes, vehículos*) class; **primera ~** first class; **~ de cámara, ~ intermedia** (*Náut*) cabin class; **~ económica** economy class; **~ preferente** club class; **~ turista** tourist class.
(**c**) (*lección etc*) (*Escol*) class; (*Univ*) lecture, class; **~ de conducción, ~ de conducir** driving lesson; **~ de geografía** geography class, geography lesson; **~ nocturna** evening class; **~s particulares** private classes, private lessons; **dar ~s** to teach; (*Univ*) to lecture; **dar ~s con uno** to take lessons from sb, study with sb; **ella da ~s de italiano** she gives Italian lessons; **faltar a ~** to miss class, not go to class; **fumarse la ~, soplarse la ~** to play truant.
(**d**) (*aula*) (*Escol*) classroom; (*Univ*) lecture room.
(**e**) (*Pol*) class; **~ alta** upper class; **~ baja** lower class(es); **~ media** middle class(es); **~ media-alta** upper-middle class; **~ media-baja** lower-middle class; **~ obrera** working class; **de la ~ obrera** working-class (*atr*); **~s pasivas** pensioners; **~ política** politicians; **las ~s poseyentes** the property-owning classes; **las ~s pudientes** the well-to-do, the moneyed classes; **ser de la ~** (*Carib: euf*) to belong to the black race, be a half-breed.
(**f**) **~s de tropa** (*Mil*) non-commissioned officers.
(**g**) **la ~ médica** the medical profession.
2 *nm*: **un primera ~** a first-class person, an outstanding person.
3 *adj* (*And**) first-rate, classy*.
clasicismo *nm* classicism.
clásico 1 *adj* (**a**) (*Arte etc*) classical.
(**b**) (*fig*) classic; (*destacado*) outstanding, remarkable; *coche etc* vintage; *institución* traditional, typical; *costumbre* time-honoured; **le dio el ~ saludo** he gave him the time-honoured salute; **es la clásica plazuela española** it is a typical Spanish square.
2 *nm* (**a**) (*obra etc*) classic.
(**b**) (*persona*) classicist.
clasificable *adj* classifiable.
clasificación *nf* classification; (*Correos*) sorting; (*Dep*) table, league; (*Náut*) rating; **~ nacional del disco** ≃ top twenty, record hit parade.
clasificador *nm* (**a**) (*persona*) classifier. (**b**) (*mueble*) filing cabinet; **~ de cartas** letter file. (**c**) (*aparato*) collator.
clasificar [1g] **1** *vt* (*gen*) to classify (*en la B* under B); (*Com etc*) to grade, rate, class; *cartas* to sort.
2 clasificarse *vr* (**a**) (*Dep*) to win a place; to occupy a position; **Meca se clasificó después de la Ceca** Meca came after Ceca, Meca finished after Ceca; **¿dónde se clasificó el equipo local?** where did the home team come?
(**b**) (*Dep*) to qualify; **no se clasificó el equipo para la final** the team did not qualify for the final.
clasismo *nm* class feelings; class-consciousness; class structure.
clasista *adj* (*Pol*) class (*atr*); class-conscious; (*pey*) snobbish.
claudia *nf* greengage.
claudicación *nf* giving way, abandonment of one's principles, shirking one's duty, backing down; **~ moral** failure of moral duty.
claudicar [1g] *vi* (**a**) (*cojear*) to limp. (**b**) (*fig*) (*engañar*) to act deceitfully; (*hacerlo mal*) to bungle it; (*vacilar*) to waver, stall. (**c**) (*fig: cejar*) to give way, abandon one's principles, shirk one's duty, back down; **no podemos ~ de nuestro pasado** we cannot deny our past, we cannot break free from our past.
Claudio *nm* Claudius.
claustral *nmf* (*Univ*) member of the Senate.
claustro *nm* (**a**) (*Ecl etc*) cloister. (**b**) (*Univ*) staff, faculty (*US*); (*como asamblea*) staff meeting; senate. (**c**) **~ materno** (*Anat*) womb.
claustrofobia *nf* claustrophobia.
claustrofóbico *adj* claustrophobic.
cláusula *nf* clause.
clausura *nf* (**a**) (*acto*) closing, closure; (*ceremonia*) formal closing, closing ceremony; **discurso de ~** closing speech. (**b**) (*Ecl*) monastic life; cloister; inner recess, sanctuary; **convento de ~** enclosed convent, enclosed monastery. (**c**) (*Méx Jur*) closing down, suspension of business.
clausurar [1a] *vt* (**a**) (*gen*) to close, bring to a close; (*Parl etc*) to adjourn, close. (**b**) (*LAm*) *casa etc* to close (up). (**c**) (*Méx Jur*) to close (down).
clava *nf* club, cudgel.
clavada *nf* (**a**) (*salto*) dive. (**b**) (⁑) **pegar una ~ a uno** to rip sb off⁑, overcharge sb.
clavadista *nm/f* (*CAm, Méx*) diver.
clavado 1 *adj* (**a**) (*asegurado con clavo*) nailed; (*fijado*) stuck fast, firmly fixed; **quedó ~ en la pared** it stuck in the wall, it remained fixed in the wall; **estamos ~s** we're stuck.
(**b**) (*mueble*) studded with nails.
(**c**) *vestido* just right, exactly fitting.
(**d**) **dejar a uno ~** to leave sb speechless; **quedó ~** he was dumbfounded.
(**e**) **a las 5 clavadas** at 5 sharp, at 5 on the dot.
(**f**) **es Domingo ~** he's the living image of Domingo; **está ~ a su padre** (*LAm*) he's the spitting image of his father.
(**g**) **¡~!** exactly!, precisely!
2 *nm* dive; **dar un ~** to dive, take a dive.
clavar [1a] **1** *vt* (**a**) *clavo* to knock in, drive in, bang in; (*fijar*) to fasten, fix; to pin; *tablas etc* to nail together, nail up; *puñal, cuchillo etc* to stick, thrust (*en* into), bury (*en* in); *cañón* to spike; **~ un anuncio a** (*o* **en**) **la puerta** to nail an announcement to the door.
(**b**) *joya* to set, mount.
(**c**) *ojos, vista,* to fix (*en* on), rivet (*en* to).
(**d**) (*: *estafar*) to cheat, twist*; **me clavaron 50 dólares** they stung me for 50 dollars*.
(**e**) (⁂) to fuck⁂.
2 clavarse *vr* (**a**) (*clavo etc*) to penetrate, go in.
(**b**) **~ una astilla en el dedo** to get a splinter in one's finger; **~ una espina** to prick o.s. on a thorn; **se clavó el**

cuchillo en el pecho he thrust the knife into his chest.
(**c**) (*fig*: *equivocarse*) to be mistaken.
(**d**) **clavársela** to get drunk.
(**e**) ~ **algo** (*Méx*‡) to pocket sth, nick sth‡.
(**f**) (*Mex*: *Dep*) to dive.

clave 1 *nf* (**a**) (*de cifra, clasificación*) key; (*cifra*) code; **la ~ del problema** the key to the problem.
(**b**) (*Ajedrez*) key move.
(**c**) (*Mús*) clef; **~ de fa** bass clef; **~ de sol** treble clef; **en ~ de humor** in a humorous tone, on a humorous note.
(**d**) (*Arquit*) keystone.
2 *nm* (*Mús*) harpsichord.
3 *como adj invar* key (*atr*); **cuestión ~** key question; **posición ~** key position.

clavecín *nm* spinet.
clavel *nm* carnation; **no tener un ~*** to be broke*.
clavelón *nm* marigold; African marigold.
clavellina *nf* pink.
clavero *nm* (*Bot*) clove tree.
claveteado *nm* studs, studding.
clavetear [1a] *vt* (**a**) *puerta etc* to stud, decorate with studs. (**b**) *cordón etc* to put a metal tip on, tag. (**c**) (*fig*) *trato etc* to clinch, close, wind up.
clavicémbalo *nm* clavicembalo, harpsichord.
clavicordio *nm* clavichord.
clavícula *nf* collar bone, clavicle.
clavidista *nmf (Méx Dep)* diver.
clavija *nf* peg, dowel, pin; pintle; (*Mús*) peg; (*Elec*) plug; **~ hendida, ~ de dos patas** split pin, cotter pin; **apretar las ~s a uno*** to put the screws on sb*.
clavillo *nm* (**a**) (*t* **clavito** *nm*) small nail, brad, tack; ~ (**de tijeras**) pin, rivet. (**b**) (*Bot*) clove.
clavo *nm* (**a**) (*Téc*) nail; tack; stud; spike; **~ romano** brass-headed nail; **~ de rosca** screw; **de ~ pasado** (*obvio*) obvious, undeniable; (*fácil*) easy; (*anticuado*) outworn, out-of-date; **verdad de ~ pasado** platitude, truism; **agarrarse a un ~ ardiendo** to clutch at a straw; **no da** (*o* **pega**) **ni ~** he doesn't do a stroke; **dar en el ~** (*fig*) to hit the nail on the head; **entrar de ~** to squeeze in; **estar como un ~** to be terribly thin; **llegar como un ~** to arrive on the dot; **meter a uno en ~** (*And, CAm, Cono Sur*) to put sb on the spot; **meter algo de ~** to squeeze sth in; **está que parte ~s** he's furious; **remachar el ~** (*fig*) to make matters worse; **ni un ~!*** not a sausage!*
(**b**) (*Bot*) clove.
(**c**) (*Med*: *callo*) corn; (*costra*) scab.
(**d**) (*Med*: *dolor*) migraine, severe headache; sharp pain; (*de borracho*) hangover*; (*fig*) anguish, acute distress.
(**e**) (*CAm, Méx Min*) rich vein of ore.
(**f**) (*And, Cono Sur*) (*cosa desagradable*) unpleasant thing; (*situación*) nasty situation; (*Com*) unsaleable article.
(**g**) (*CAm, Méx*: *problema*) problem, snag.

claxon *nm, pl* **claxons** ['klakson] *o* **cláxones** (*Aut*) horn, hooter; **tocar el ~** to sound one's horn, hoot.
claxonar [1a] *vi* (*Aut*) to sound one's horn, hoot.
claxonazo *nm* (*Aut*) hoot, toot (on the horn).
clemátide *nf* clematis.
clemencia *nf* mercy, clemency; leniency.
clemente *adj* merciful, clement; lenient.
clementina *nf* tangerine.
Cleopatra *nf* Cleopatra.
cleptomanía *nf* kleptomania.
cleptómano, -a *nm/f* kleptomaniac.
clerecía *nf* (**a**) (*clericato*) priesthood. (**b**) (*personas*) clergy.
clergyman [klerxi'man] *adj invar*: **traje ~** *modernized form of priest's attire* (*adopted in Spain 1962*).
clerical 1 *adj* clerical. **2** *nm* (*CAm, Carib*) clergyman, minister.
clericalismo *nm* clericalism.
clericato *nm*, **clericatura** *nf* priesthood.
clericó *nm* (*Cono Sur*) mulled wine.
clérigo *nm* (*católico*) priest; (*anglicano*) clergyman, priest; (*otro*) minister.
clero *nm* clergy.
clic *nm* click.
cliché *nm* (**a**) (*Tip*) cliché, stereotype plate. (**b**) (*Liter*) cliché; = **clisé**.
cliente *nmf* (*t* **clienta** *nf*) (*Com*) client, customer; (*Jur*) client; (*Med*) patient.
clientela *nf* (*Com*) clients, clientèle, customers; (*Med*) practice; patients.
clientelismo *nm* patronage system.
clima *nm* climate; (*fig*) atmosphere, climate; **~ artificial** (*LAm*) air-conditioning.
climatérico *adj* climacteric.
climático *adj* climatic.
climatización *nf* air-conditioning.
climatizado *adj* air-conditioned.
climatizador *nm* air-conditioner.
climatología *nf* (*ciencia*) climatology; (*tiempo*) weather.
climatológico *adj* climatological.
climatólogo, -a *nm/f* climatologist.
clímax ['klimas] *nm invar* climax.
clinch [klinʃ] *nm*, **clincha** *nf* (*LAm*) clinch.
clínica *nf* (**a**) (*lugar*) clinic; private hospital, nursing-home; teaching hospital; doctor's surgery; **~ de alergias** allergy clinic; **~ de reposo** convalescent home. (**b**) (*Univ*) clinical training.
clínicamente *adv* clinically; **~ muerto** clinically dead.
clínico *adj* clinical.
clip *nm, pl* **clips** [klis] (*para papeles*) paper-clip; (*de pelo*) clip; (*de pantalón*) trouser-clip; (*joya*) clip; (*de vídeo*) videoclip; (*LAm*) earring.
clipe *nm* = **clip.**
clíper *nm* (*Náut*) clipper.
clisar [1a] *vt* to stereotype, stencil.
clisé *nm* (**a**) (*Tip*) cliché, stereotype plate; (*Fot*) plate. (**b**) (*Liter*) cliché.
clisos‡ *nmpl* peepers‡, eyes.
clítoris *nm* clitoris.
clo *nm* cluck; **hacer ~** to cluck.
cloaca *nf* sewer (*t fig*); drain.
cloacal *adj* (**a**) **sistema ~** sewage system. (**b**) *chiste etc* lavatorial.
cloche *nm* (*CAm, Carib*: *Aut*) clutch.
clon *nm* clone.
clonación *nf*, **clonado** *nm*, **clonaje** *nm* cloning.
clonar [1a] *vt* to clone.
clónico 1 *adj* clonal, cloned; identical. **2** *nm* (*Inform*) clone.
cloquear [1a] *vi* to cluck.
cloqueo *nm* clucking.
cloración *nf* chlorination.
cloral *nm* chloral.
clorar [1a] *vt* to chlorinate.
clorhídrico *adj* hydrochloric.
clorinar [1a] *vt* to chlorinate.
clorinda *nf* (*Cono Sur*) bleach.
cloro *nm* chlorine.
clorofila *nf* chlorophyl(l).
clorofluorocarbono *nm* chlorofluorocarbon.
cloroformar [1a] *vt* (*Carib, Cono Sur, Méx*), **cloroformizar** [1f] *vt* to chloroform.
cloroformo *nm* chloroform.
cloruro *nm* chloride; **~ de cal** chloride of lime; **~ cálcico** calcium chloride; **~ de hidrógeno** hydrogen chloride; **~ de polivinilo** polyvinyl chloride.
closet [klo'se] *nm* (*LAm*) built-in cupboard (*o* wardrobe).
clown [klawn] *nm, pl* **clowns** [klawn] clown.
clownesco *adj* clownish.
club [klu *o* kluß] *nm, pl* **clubs** *o* **clubes** [klus *o* 'klußes] club; **~ campestre** country club; **~ de fans** fan-club; **~ de golf** golf club; **~ náutico** yacht club; **~ nocturno** night-club.
clueca *nf* broody hen.
clueco *adj* (**a**) *gallina* broody. (**b**) (*Cono Sur*: *enfermizo*) sickly, weak. (**c**) (*Carib**: *engreído*) stuck-up*.
cluniacense *adj, nm* Cluniac.
clutch *nm* (*Méx Aut*) clutch.
cm[1] *abr de* **centímetro** centimetre, cm.
cm[2] *abr de* **centímetros cuadrados** square centimetres, sq. cm.
cm[3] *abr de* **centímetros cúbicos** cubic centimetres, c.c.
CMCC *nf abr de* **Comunidad y Mercado Común del Caribe** Caribbean Community and Common Market, CARICOM.
CN *nf abr de* **Carretera Nacional** ≃ 'A' road.
CNMV *nf abr de* **Comisión Nacional del Mercado de Valores.**
CNT *nf* (**a**) (*Esp*) *abr de* **Confederación Nacional del Trabajo.** (**b**) (*Colombia, Chile, Guatemala, Méx, Uruguay*) *abr de* **Confederación Nacional de Trabajadores.**
co... *pref* co...
coa *nf* (**a**) (*CAm, Carib, Méx*: *Agr*) (*para cavar*) long-handled narrow spade; (*para sembrar*) pointed stick for sowing seed. (**b**) (*Cono Sur*: *argot*) underworld slang.
coacción *nf* coercion, compulsion; duress.
coaccionador *adj* constraining, compelling.
coaccionar [1a] *vt* to coerce, compel, put great pressure

on.
coactivo *adj* coercive; compelling.
coadjutor(a) *nm/f* assistant, coadjutor.
coadjuvar [1a] *vt* (*t vi* ~ **a**) *persona* to help, assist; *obra* to help in, contribute to.
coagulación *nf* coagulation; clotting; curdling.
coagulante *nm* coagulant.
coagular [1a] **1** *vt* to coagulate; *sangre* to clot, congeal; *leche* to curdle. **2 coagularse** *vr* to coagulate; to clot, congeal; to curdle.
coágulo *nm* coagulated mass, coagulum; clot; congealed lump; ~ **sanguíneo** blood clot.
coalición *nf* coalition; **gobierno de** ~ coalition government.
coalicionarse [1a] *vr* to form a coalition.
coartada *nf* alibi.
coartar [1a] *vt* to limit, restrict.
coaseguro *nm* coinsurance.
coautor(a) *nm/f* co-author.
coaxial *adj* coaxial.
coba* *nf* (**a**) (*mentirilla*) fib; (*truco*) neat trick. (**b**) (*jabón*) soft soap*; (*halagos*) cajolery; **dar ~ a uno** to soap sb up*, soft-soap sb*, play up to sb.
cobalto *nm* cobalt.
cobarde 1 *adj* cowardly; fainthearted, timid. **2** *nmf* coward.
cobardear [1a] *vi* to be a coward, show cowardice, act in a cowardly way.
cobardía *nf* cowardliness; faintheartedness, timidity.
cobardón *nm* shameful coward, great coward.
cobayismo *nm* use of animals (*o* humans) in medical experiments.
cobayo *nm* (*t* **cobaya** *nf*) guinea-pig (*t fig*).
cobertera *nf* (**a**) (*tapa*) lid, cover. (**b**) (*Bot*) white water lily. (**c**) (*alcahueta*) procuress.
cobertizo *nm* (*edificio*) shed, outhouse, lean-to; (*refugio*) shelter; (*pasillo*) covered passage; ~ **de aviación** hangar; ~ **de coche** carport.
cobertor *nm* bedspread, coverlet.
cobertura *nf* (**a**) (*que cubre*) cover, covering. (**b**) (*cobertor*) bedspread. (**c**) (*por periódico etc*) coverage; ~ **aérea** air cover; ~ **informativa** news coverage; ~ **del seguro** insurance cover.
cobija *nf* (**a**) (*Arquit*) coping tile, imbrex. (**b**) (*LAm*) (*de vestir*) poncho; (*manta*) blanket; **~s** bedclothes; **pegársele a uno las ~s** to oversleep. (**c**) (*Carib*: *techo*) roof (of palm leaves).
cobijar [1a] **1** *vt* (**a**) (*cubrir*) to cover (up), close in.
(**b**) (*proteger*) to protect, shelter; (*acoger*) to take in, give shelter to, (*pey*) harbour.
(**c**) (*And, Carib*: *techar*) to thatch, roof with palms.
2 cobijarse *vr* to take shelter.
cobijo *nm* (**a**) (*lit*) shelter, lodging. (**b**) (*fig*) cover.
cobista* 1 *adj* soapy*, smarmy*. **2** *nm* soapy individual*, smarmy sort*.
cobo *nm* (*Carib*) (**a**) (*Zool*) sea snail. (**b**) (*persona*) unsociable person, shy person; **ser un** ~ to be shy, be withdrawn.
cobra[1] *nf* (*Zool*) cobra.
cobra[2] *nf* (*Caza*) retrieval.
cobrable *adj*, **cobradero** *adj* (**a**) (*que puede cobrarse*) retrievable. (**b**) (*Com*) *precio* chargeable; *suma* recoverable.
cobrador *nm* (**a**) (*Com*) collector. (**b**) (*de autobús etc*) conductor. (**c**) (*perro*) retriever.
cobradora *nf* conductress.
cobranza *nf* (**a**) = **cobro.** (**b**) (*Caza*) retrieval.
cobrar [1a] **1** *vt* (**a**) *cosa perdida* to recover; (*Caza*) to retrieve, fetch, bring back; *cuerda* to take in, pull in; *palos* to get, receive; **¡vas a ~!*** you'll cop it!*; **el accidente cobró la vida de 50 personas** the accident took the lives of 50 people.
(**b**) *precio* to charge; **cobran 200 dólares por componerlo** they charge 200 dollars to repair it; **¿me cobra, por favor?** how much do I owe you?, how much is that please?; **me han cobrado demasiado** they've charged me too much, they've overcharged me.
(**c**) *suma* to collect, receive; *cheque* to cash; *sueldo* to earn; to draw, get, collect; **¿cuánto cobras al año?** how much do you get a year?, how much do they pay you a year?; **fue a la oficina a ~ el sueldo** he went to the office to get his wages; **cantidades por** ~ sums receivable; **cuenta por** ~ unpaid bill.
(**d**) ~ **a uno** (*LAm*) to press sb for payment.
(**e**) ~ **carnes** to put on weight.
(**f**) *crédito, fama etc* to get, acquire, gain; *valor* to summon up, muster; *fuerzas* to gather; ~ **cariño a uno** to take a liking to sb, grow fond of sb; ~ **fama de** to acquire a reputation as (*o* for being).
2 *vi* (**a**) (*Fin*) to draw one's pay, get one's wages; to collect one's salary; **cobra los viernes** he gets paid on Fridays; **te pagaré en cuanto cobre** I'll pay you when I get my wages; **vino el lechero a** ~ the milkman came for his money, the milkman came to be paid.
(**b**) ~ **al número llamado** (*Telec*) to reverse the charges, call collect (*US*).
3 cobrarse *vr* (**a**) (*Med*) to recover, get well; to come to.
(**b**) ~ **de una pérdida** to make up for a loss.
cobre *nm* (**a**) (*metal*) copper.
(**b**) (*Culin*) copper pans, kitchen utensils.
(**c**) (*Mús*) brass (*t* **~s**); **batir(se) el** ~ to work hard, work with a will; to hustle; (*en discusión*) to get worked up; **batirse el ~ por** + *infin* to go all out to + *infin*.
(**d**) (*LAm*: *moneda*) cent, small copper coin.
(**e**) (*LAm*) **enseñar el** ~ to show one's true colours.
cobreado *adj* copperplated.
cobreño *adj* copper (*atr*), coppery.
cobrero *nm* coppersmith.
cobrizo *adj* coppery.
cobro *nm* (**a**) (*acto*) recovery, retrieval.
(**b**) (*Fin*) collection; payment; **cargo por** ~ collection charge; **deuda de ~ difícil** debt that is hard to collect; **~ a la entrega** collect on delivery; ~ **de morosos** debt collection; ~ **revertido automático** automatic reverse-charge dialling; **llamar a ~ revertido** to reverse the charges, call collect (*US*), call toll-free (*US*); **poner al** (*o* **en**) ~ to make payable; *factura* to send out.
(**c**) (*lugar seguro*) safe place; **poner algo en** ~ to put sth in a safe place, put sth out of harm's way; **ponerse en** ~ to take refuge, get to safety.
coca[1]* *nf* (**a**) (*: *cabeza*) head, nut‡. (**b**) (‡: golpe) rap on the nut‡. (**c**) (*de pelo*) bun, coil. (**d**) (*en cuerda*) kink.
coca[2] *nf* (**a**) (*LAm Bot*) (*árbol*) coca tree (*o* bush); (*hojas*) coca leaves; (*cocaína*) cocaine. (**b**) **de** ~ (*Méx*) free, gratis.
coca[3]* *nf* Coke*, Coca-Cola ®.
cocacolo, -a *nm/f* (*And*) frivolous teenager, idle young person.
cocacolonización *nf* (*hum*) americanization.
cocacho *nm* (*And, Cono Sur*) tap on the head.
cocada *nf* (**a**) (*CAm*) (*Culin*) sweet coconut; (*viaje*) length of a journey. (**b**) (*And Aut*) tyre grip.
cocaína *nf* cocaine.
cocaínico *adj* cocaine (*atr*).
cocainomanía *nf* addiction to cocaine.
cocainómano, -a *nm/f* cocaine addict.
cocal *nm* (*LAm*) coconut plantation.
cocción *nf* (**a**) (*Culin*) (*acto*) cooking; (*duración*) cooking time; ~ **al vapor** steam cooking, steaming. (**b**) (*Téc*) baking, firing.
cóccix *nm invar* coccyx.
cocear [1a] *vti* to kick; (*fig*) to kick (*contra* against), resist.
cocer [2b *y* 2h] **1** *vt* (**a**) (*Culin*: *gen*) to cook; (*hervir*) to boil; (*al horno*) to bake.
(**b**) (*Téc*) *ladrillos etc* to bake, fire.
2 *vi* (*gen*) to cook; (*hervir*) to boil; (*burbujear*) to bubble, seethe; (*vino*) to ferment.
3 cocerse *vr* (**a**) (*fig*: *sufrir*) to suffer intensely, be in great pain. (**b**) (‡) to get plastered‡. (**c**) (*) **no está a lo que se cuece** he's not with it*; **¿qué se cuece por ahí?** what's cooking?*
cocido 1 *adj* (**a**) (*Culin*) boiled, cooked; **bien** ~ well done.
(**b**) (*perito*) skilled, experienced; **estar ~ en** to be skilled at, be expert at.
(**c**) **estar** ~‡ to be plastered‡, be drunk.
2 *nm* stew (*in Spain*: *of meat, bacon, chickpeas etc*); **ganarse el** ~ to earn one's living; to eke out a living.
cociente *nm* quotient; ~ **intelectual** intelligence quotient.
cocina *nf* (**a**) (*cuarto*) kitchen; **de** ~ kitchen (*atr*); ~ **integral** fitted kitchen.
(**b**) (*aparato*) stove, cooker; ~ **económica** cooker, range; ~ **eléctrica** electric cooker; **~ a gas, ~ de gas** gas stove, gas cooker; ~ **de petróleo** oil stove.
(**c**) (*arte*) cooking, cookery; cuisine; **alta** ~ haute cuisine; ~ **casera** plain cooking, homely cooking; **nueva** ~ nouvelle cuisine; **la ~ valenciana** Valencian cooking, the Valencian cuisine; **libro de** ~ cookery book, cookbook (*US*).
cocinada *nf* (*LAm*) (period of) cooking, cooking time.

cocinado *nm* cooking.
cocinar [1a] **1** *vt* to cook. **2** *vi* (**a**) (*lit*) to cook, do the cooking. (**b**) (*fig*) to meddle.
cocinero, -a *nm/f* cook.
cocinilla *nf* (**a**) (*cuarto*) small kitchen, kitchenette. (**b**) (*aparato*) small cooker; (*infiernillo*) spirit stove; (*escalfador*) chafing dish.
cocker ['kokeɹ] *nm* cocker (spaniel).
coco[1] *nm* (*Med*) coccus; (*Ent*) grub, maggot.
coco[2] *nm* (**a**) (*duende*) bogeyman; **parece un ~** he's an ugly devil; **¡que viene el ~!** the bogeyman will get you!
(**b**) (*mueca*) face, grimace; **hacer ~s a uno** to make faces at sb, (*amantes*) make eyes at sb; to coax sb, wheedle sb.
coco[3] **1** *nm* (**a**) (*Bot*: *nuez*) coconut; (*árbol*) coconut palm.
(**b**) (*hum**) (*cabeza*) noddle*; (*cerebro*) brain; (*inteligencia*) brains; **comer el ~ a uno** to brainwash sb, pull the wool over sb's eyes; **comerse el ~** to think hard; to worry; **me estoy comiendo el ~** I'm trying to think; **estar hasta el ~*** to be utterly fed up*; **lavar el ~ a uno** to brainwash sb.
(**c**) (*LAm*: *vasija*) cup (*etc*) made from a coconut shell.
(**d**) (*And*: *sombrero*) derby, bowler (hat).
(**e**) (*And, Cono Sur*: *tela*) percale.
(**f**) **cortarse el cabello a ~** (*And*) to have one's head shaved.
(**g**) **~s** (*And Naipes*) diamonds.
(**h**) (*Cono Sur*) **~s** (**‡**) balls**‡**; **hinchar los ~s a uno‡** to get up sb's nose‡.
2 *adj* (*Carib*) (**a**) (*duro*) hard, strong.
(**b**) (*testarudo*) obstinate.
cococha *nf* (*de bacalao etc*) barbel.
cocodrilo *nm* crocodile.
cocoliche *nm* (*Cono Sur*: *argot*) pidgin Spanish; (*italiano*) Italian.
cócona *nf* (*Carib*) tip.
coconote *nm* (*Méx*) child; chubby child; squat person.
cócora *nmf* (**a**) (*: *pesado*) bore. (**b**) (*Cono Sur*: *machaca*) conceited person, pest.
cocoroco *adj* (*Cono Sur*) (*engreído*) vain, stuck-up*; (*descarado*) insolent, cheeky*.
cocorota‡ *nf* bonce‡, head.
cocoso *adj* maggoty, worm-eaten.
cocotal *nm* coconut grove, coconut plantation.
cocotero *nm* coconut palm.
cóctel ['koktel *o* 'kotel] *nm, pl* **coctels** *o* **cócteles** (**a**) (*bebida*) cocktail; **~ de frutas** fruit cocktail; **~ de gambas** prawn cocktail; **~ Mólotov** Molotov cocktail.
(**b**) (*fiesta*) cocktail party; **ofrecer un ~ en honor de uno** to hold a cocktail party in sb's honour.
coctelera *nf* cocktail shaker.
cocuyo *nm* (*LAm*) firefly; (*Aut*) rear light.
cocha[1] *nf* (*And, Cono Sur*) (*charca*) pool; (*pantano*) swamp; (*laguna*) lagoon.
cochambre *nmf* (*mugre*) muck, filth; (*papeles*) litter; (*objeto*) filthy thing, disgusting object; (*fig*) muck, rubbish; **caer en la ~** (*fig*) to sink very low.
cochambroso *adj* filthy, nauseating, stinking; (*fig*) vile.
cochayuyo *nm* (*And, Cono Sur*) seaweed.
cochazo* *nm* whacking great car*.
coche[1] *nm* (**a**) (*Aut*) car, motorcar, automobile (*US*); **~ ambulancia** ambulance; **~ de alquiler** taxi, cab; hire car; **~ blindado** armoured car; **~ de bomberos** fire-engine; **~ de carreras** racing car; **~ celular** prison van, patrol wagon (*US*); **~ de cortesía** courtesy car; **~ chocón, ~ de choque** dodgem car; **~ deportivo** sports car; **~ de época** vintage car; **~ fúnebre, ~ mortuorio** hearse; **~ de grúa** breakdown van, tow truck; **~ K** unmarked police-car; **~ de línea** long-distance taxi; **~ de ocasión, ~ usado** used car, second-hand car; **~ de punto** taxi; **~ radio-patrulla** radio patrol-car; **~ de serie** standard model, production model; **~ de turismo** saloon car, sedan (*US*); tourer; **~ zeta** Z-car; **ir en ~** to go by car; to drive, motor; **ir en el ~ de San Francisco** (*o* **Fernando**) to go on Shank's pony, ride Shank's mare.
(**b**) (*Ferro*) coach, car, carriage; **~ directo** through carriage; **~ de equipajes** luggage-van, baggage car (*US*); **~ de viajeros** passenger coach.
(**c**) (*Hist*) coach, carriage.
(**d**) (*Méx*: *taxi*) taxi, cab.
coche[2] *nm* (*CAm, Méx*) pig, hog; pork; **~ de monte** wild pig (*o* boar).
coche-bomba *nm, pl* **coches-bomba** car-bomb.
coche-cabina *nm, pl* **coches-cabina** bubble-car.
coche-cama *nm, pl* **coches-cama** sleeping car, sleeper.
cochecillo *nm* small carriage (*etc*); **~ de inválido** invalid carriage.
cochecito *nm* pram, perambulator, baby carriage (*US*); **~ de golf** golf buggy; **~ de niño** go-cart.
coche-comedor *nm, pl* **coches-comedor** dining-car, restaurant car.
coche-correo *nm, pl* **coches-correo** (*Ferro*) mail-van, mobile sorting-office.
coche-cuba *nm, pl* **coches-cuba** tank lorry, water wagon.
coche-habitación *nm, pl* **coches-habitación** caravan, trailer.
cochemonte *nm* (*CAm Zool*) wild pig, wild boar.
coche-patrulla *nm, pl* **coches-patrulla** patrol-car.
cochera *nf* (**a**) (*de carruajes*) coach house; **~ de alquiler** livery stable. (**b**) (*Aut*) garage, carport. (**c**) (*Ferro*) engine-shed; **~ de tranvías** tram shed, tram depot.
cocherada *nf* (*Méx*) coarse (*o* vulgar) expression.
coche-restaurante *nm, pl* **coches-restaurante** dining-car, restaurant car.
cochero **1** *adj*: **puerta cochera** carriage entrance. **2** *nm* coachman; **~ de punto** cabman, cabby*; **hablar (en) ~** (*Méx*) to swear, use obscene language.
cocherón *nm* (*Ferro*) engine-shed, locomotive depot.
coche-salón *nm, pl* **coches-salón** (*Ferro*) saloon coach.
coche-vivienda *nm, pl* **coches-vivienda** caravan, trailer, camper.
cochina *nf* sow.
cochinada *nf* (**a**) (*cualidad*) filth, filthiness.
(**b**) (*objeto*) filthy object, dirty thing.
(**c**) (*acto etc*) beastly thing (to do); filthy act, filthy word; (*canallada*) dirty trick; **eso fue una ~** that was a beastly thing to do; **hacer una ~ a uno** to play a dirty trick on sb.
cochinear* [1a] *vi* to wallow in filth.
cochinería *nf* = **cochinada**.
cochinilla *nf* (**a**) (*Zool*) woodlouse.
(**b**) (*Ent, colorante*) cochineal.
(**c**) **de ~** (*Carib, Méx*) trivial, unimportant.
cochinillo *nm* piglet, sucking-pig.
cochino **1** *adj* (**a**) (*sucio*) filthy, dirty.
(**b**) (*fig*: *miserable*) filthy, rotten*, measly*; **esta vida cochina** this wretched life.
2 *nm* (**a**) (*lit*) pig; **~ de leche** sucking-pig; **~ montés** wild pig.
(**b**) (*fig*: *bestia*) hog; swine; filthy person; **realmente es un ~** he really is a swine.
cochiquera *nf*, **cochitril** *nm* pigsty (*t fig*).
cocho* (*LAm*) **1** *adj* old, past it. **2** *nm*, **cocha[2]** *nf* old man, old woman.
cochón, -ona‡ *nm/f* (*hombre*) poof‡, queer‡; (*mujer*) dyke‡.
cochoso *adj* (*And*) filthy.
cochura *nf* (**a**) (*acto*) = **cocción**. (**b**) (*hornada*) batch of loaves (*o* cakes, bricks *etc*).
cod. *nm abr de* **código** code.
coda *nf* (**a**) (*Mús*) coda. (**b**) (*Téc*) wedge.
codal *nm* (**a**) (*Bot*) layered vine shoot. (**b**) (*Arquit*) strut, prop.
codaste *nm* stern post.
codazo *nm* (**a**) (*golpe*) jab, poke, nudge (with one's elbow).
(**b**) (*Méx*: *consejo*) tip-off.
codeador *adj* (*And, Cono Sur*) whingeing, demanding.
codear [1a] **1** *vt* (**a**) (*empujar con el codo*) to elbow, nudge, jostle.
(**b**) (*And, Cono Sur*: *insistir*) **~ a uno** to keep on at sb, pester sb.
2 *vi* (**a**) to elbow, jostle; **abrirse paso codeando** to elbow one's way through.
(**b**) (*) (*And, Cono Sur*) to sponge*, live by sponging*.
3 codearse *vr*: **~ con** to hobnob with, rub shoulders with.
codeína *nf* codeine.
codeo* *nm* (*And*: *sablazo*) sponging*; (*insistencia*) pestering.
codera *nf* elbow patch; elbow guard.
codeso *nm* laburnum.
códice *nm* manuscript, codex.
codicia *nf* greed, covetousness; **~ de** greed for, lust for.
codiciable *adj* covetable, desirable; enviable.
codiciado *adj* widely desired; much in demand; sought-after, coveted; **obtuvo el ~ título** he won the coveted title.
codiciar [1b] *vt* to covet.
codicilo *nm* codicil.

codiciosamente *adv* greedily, covetously.
codicioso *adj* greedy, covetous; **estoy ~ de verte** I am very eager to see you.
codificación *nf* codification; **~ de barras** bar coding.
codificador *nm* encoder.
codificar [1g] *vt* to codify; (*TV*) to scramble.
código *nm* (**a**) (*Jur etc*) code; law, statute; (*reglas*) rules, set of rules; **~ de (la) circulación** highway code; **~ civil** civil code; **~ de leyes** law code, statute book; **~ militar** articles of war; **~ penal** penal code, criminal code.
(**b**) (*Inform, Telec etc*) code; **mensaje en ~** message in code, coded message; **~ barrado, ~ de barras** bar-code; **~ binario** binary code; **~ de colores** colour code; **~ hexadecimal** hexadecimal code; **~ legible por máquina** machine-readable code; **~ máquina** machine code; **~ postal** postcode; **~ de señales** signal code; **~ territorial** area code.
codillo *nm* (*Zool*) elbow; top joint of the foreleg; upper foreleg; (*Bot*) stump (of a branch); (*Téc*) elbow (joint), bend; angle iron; **~ de cerdo** (*Méx Culin*) pig's trotter.
codo[1] *nm* (**a**) (*Anat*) elbow; **~ del tenista** tennis elbow; **~ a ~** (*como n*) rivalry, intense competition; needle match; close-run result; **comerse los ~s de hambre** to be utterly destitute; **dar con el ~ a uno, dar de(l) ~ a uno** to nudge sb; **empinar el ~** to booze*, drink; **hablar por los ~s** to talk too much, talk nineteen to the dozen; **llevar a uno ~ con ~** to frogmarch sb along, drag sb along with his hands tied behind his back; (*fig*) to arrest sb; **mentir por los ~s** to tell huge lies; **morderse el ~** (*Cono Sur, Méx*) to restrain o.s., bite one's lip; **romperse los ~s*** to swot*; **ser del ~, ser duro de ~** to be mean; **trabajar ~ con ~** to work side by side.
(**b**) (*Téc*) elbow (joint), bend; angle iron.
(**c**) (*fig*) elbow grease; **hacer más ~s** to put more elbow grease into it; **sacó la oposición a base de ~s** he won the post by sheer hard work; **apretar los ~s** (*estudiar*) to work hard.
codo[2]⁑ *adj* (*Méx*) mean, stingy.
codorniz *nf* quail.
COE *nm abr de* **Comité Olímpico Español** Spanish Olympic Committee.
coedición *nf* (*libro*) joint publication; (*acto*) joint publishing.
coeditar [1a] *vt* to publish jointly.
coeducación *nf* coeducation.
coeducacional *adj* coeducational.
coeficiente *nm* coefficient; **~ aerodinámico, ~ de penetración aerodinámica** drag factor; **~ de caja** cash deposit requirement; **~ intelectual, ~ de inteligencia, ~ mental** intelligence quotient.
coercer [2b] *vt* to coerce, constrain; to restrain.
coerción *nf* coercion, constraint; restraint.
coercitivamente *adv* forcibly.
coercitivo *adj* coercive, forcible.
coestrella *nf* co-star.
coetáneo, -a *adj, nm/f* contemporary (*con* with).
coevo *adj* coeval.
coexistencia *nf* coexistence; **~ pacífica** peaceful coexistence.
coexistente *adj* coexistent.
coexistir [3a] *vi* to coexist (*con* with).
cofa *nf* (*Náut*) top; **~ mayor** maintop.
cofabricar [1g] *vt* to manufacture jointly.
cofia *nf* (*de enfermera, criada etc*) cap, white cap; (††) coif; bonnet.
cofinanciación *nf* joint financing.
cofinanciar [1b] *vt* to finance jointly.
cofrade *nm* member (of a brotherhood), brother.
cofradía *nf* brotherhood, fraternity; guild, association; (*de ladrones etc*) gang.
cofre *nm* chest; case (for jewels *etc*); (*Méx Aut*) bonnet.
cofrecito *nm* casket.
cofundador(a) *nm/f* co-founder.
cogedero 1 *adj fruto* ripe, ready to be picked. **2** *nm* handle.
cogedor *nm* small shovel, ash shovel; dustpan.
coger [2c] **1** *vt* (**a**) (*agarrar*) *mango, objeto etc* to take hold of, catch hold of; to seize, grasp; to hold on to; *pelota etc* to catch; *objeto caído* to pick up; *vestido etc* to gather up, hold up; *libro etc* to pick up, take up; *herramienta* (*fig*) to hold, use; **~ a uno de la mano** to take sb by the hand; **ir cogidos de la mano** to go hand-in-hand; (*amantes*) to go along holding hands; **no ha cogido un fusil en la vida** he's never held a gun in his life.
(**b**) (*robar*) to take, pinch*; **me coge siempre las cerillas** he always takes my matches; **en la aduana le cogieron una radio** they found a radio on him in the customs, they confiscated a radio from him in the customs.
(**c**) *flor, fruto etc* to pick, pluck; (*cosechar*) to harvest; to gather, collect.
(**d**) *persona etc* to catch; (*Jur*) to arrest; (*Mil*) to take prisoner; *prisionero* to take, capture; *animal* to catch, capture, trap; *pez* to catch; *competidor etc* to catch (up with); **¡por fin te he cogido!** caught you at last!; **~ un buen marido** to catch o.s. (*o* get, acquire) a good husband; **~ a uno en una mentira** to catch sb in a lie; **la noche nos cogió todavía en el mar** the night caught us still at sea; **la guerra nos cogió en Francia** the war caught us in France; **antes que nos coja la noche** before night overtakes us (*o* comes down on us); **~ a uno en la hora tonta, ~ a uno detrás de la puerta** to catch sb at a disadvantage; **~ in fraganti** to catch red-handed; **~ de nuevas a uno** to take sb by surprise; *V t* **desprevenido** *etc.*
(**e**) (*toro*) to gore; to toss; (*coche*) to knock down, run over.
(**f**) **~ los dedos en la puerta** to catch one's fingers in the door.
(**g**) *propina etc* to take, accept; *trabajo* to take on; *noticia etc* to take, receive; **cogió la noticia sin interés** he received the news without interest.
(**h**) (*emprender*) *curso, período, trabajo etc* to begin on; **cogí la conferencia a mitad** I joined the discussion halfway through.
(**i**) (*obtener*) to get, obtain, acquire; **he cogido el billete del avión** I've got my air ticket; **cógeme un puesto en la cola** get me a place in the queue; **acabo de ~ una cocinera nueva** I've got a new cook.
(**j**) *enfermedad, resfriado etc* to catch; *polvo* to gather, collect; *hábito* to get, get into, catch, acquire; **el niño cogió sarampión** the child got (*o* caught) measles; **los perros cogen pulgas** dogs get fleas; **ha cogido la manía de las quinielas** he's caught the pools craze.
(**k**) (*emoción*) to take; **~ cariño a** to take a liking to; **~ celos a** to become jealous of; **~ aversión a** to take a strong dislike to.
(**l**) *sentido* to get, understand; *palabra hablada* to catch; *radio* to pick up, get; *frase, giro* to pick up; *acento* to catch, acquire; *técnica* to pick up, learn; **con esta radio cogemos Praga** with this set we can get Prague.
(**m**) (*apuntar*) *notas etc* to take down; **le cogieron el discurso taquigráficamente** they took his speech down in shorthand.
(**n**) (*escoger*) to choose, pick; **has cogido un mal momento** you've picked a bad time.
(**o**) *medio de transporte* to take, catch, go by; **vamos a ~ el tren** let's take the train.
(**p**) (*recipiente*) to hold, take; *área* to cover, extend over, take up.
(**q**) (*LAm*⁂) to lay⁑, screw⁂.
2 *vi* (**a**) (*Bot*) to take, strike.
(**b**) (*caber*) to fit, go, have room; **aquí no coge** it doesn't fit in here, there's no room for it here.
(**c**) **cogió y se fue*** he just upped and went*.
(**d**) (*LAm*⁂) to fuck⁂, screw⁂.
3 cogerse *vr* (**a**) (*gen*) to catch; **~ los dedos en la puerta** to catch one's fingers in the door; **~ a uno** to cling tight to sb, press close against sb.
(**b**) **~ algo*** to steal sth, pinch sth*.
(**c**) **~ con uno** (*Carib*) to get on (well) with sb; **~ en algo** to get involved in sth; to get used to sth.
cogestión *nf* co-partnership (*in industry etc*), worker participation.
cogida *nf* (**a**) (*Agr*) gathering, picking; harvesting; (*Pesca*) catch. (**b**) (*Taur*) goring, tossing; **tener una ~** to be gored, be tossed. (**c**) (⁑) (dose of) pox*.
cogido *nm* (*Cos*) fold, gather, tuck.
cogienda *nf* (**a**) (*And, Carib*) = **cogida (a)**; (*Mil*) forced enlistment. (**b**) (*Méx*⁂) fucking⁂, screwing⁂.
cognado *adj, nm* cognate.
cognición *nf* cognition.
cognitivo *adj*, **cognoscitivo** *adj* cognitive.
cogollo *nm* (**a**) (*de planta*) shoot, sprout; (*de lechuga, col*) heart; (*de árbol*) top; (*LAm: de caña de azúcar*) top of sugar cane.
(**b**) (*fig: lo mejor*) best part, cream; **el ~ de la sociedad** the cream of society.
(**c**) (*fig: núcleo*) centre, core, nucleus.
(**d**) (*Carib: sombrero*) straw hat.

cogorza‡ nf: pescar una ~ to get blotto‡, get very drunk.
cogotazo nm blow on the back of the neck; (Boxeo etc) rabbit punch.
cogote nm back of the neck, nape; scruff of the neck; de ~ (Cono Sur) animal fat; carne de ~ (Cono Sur) rubbish, trash; coger a uno por el ~ to take sb by the scruff of the neck; estar hasta el ~ (Carib) to have had it up to here; ponérselas en el ~ (CAm‡) to beat it*.
cogotudo‡ 1 adj (And, Cono Sur) well-heeled*, filthy rich*; (Carib) powerful in politics; es un ~ he's got pull, he's got friends in high places. 2 nm (LAm) self-made man, parvenu.
cogujada nf woodlark.
cogulla nf (hood of) monk's habit.
cohabitación nf cohabitation; (Pol) coexistence.
cohabitar [1a] vi to live together, cohabit (t pey); (Pol) to coexist.
cohechar [1a] vt to bribe, offer a bribe to.
cohecho nm bribe, bribery.
coheredera nf coheiress.
coheredero nm coheir, joint heir.
coherencia nf coherence; (Fís etc) cohesion.
coherente adj coherent; logical; right; no sería ~ cumplir con sus órdenes there is no sense in following his orders; ~ con in line with, in tune with.
coherentemente adv (a) coherently. (b) A ~ con B A together with B, A in conjunction with B.
cohesión nf cohesion.
cohesionado adj united, unified; solid.
cohesionador adj: elemento ~ unifying force.
cohesionar [1a] vt to unite, draw together.
cohesivo adj cohesive.
cohete 1 nm (a) (gen) rocket; ~ espacial (space) rocket; ~ luminoso, ~ de señales flare, star shell, distress signal.
(b) (CAm, Méx: pistola) pistol.
(c) (Méx: mecha) blasting fuse.
(d) al ~ (And, Cono Sur) without rhyme or reason.
2 adj (CAm, Méx) drunk, tight*.
cohetería nf rocketry.
cohibición nf restraint; inhibition.
cohibido adj restrained, restricted; (de temperamento) inhibited, full of inhibitions; shy, timid, self-conscious; ill at ease; sentirse ~ to feel shy, feel embarrassed.
cohibir [3a] 1 vt (refrenar) to restrain, check, restrict; (Med etc) to inhibit; (incomodar) to make uneasy, make shy, embarrass.
2 cohibirse vr (a) (refrenarse) to restrain o.s.
(b) (sentirse cohibido) to feel inhibited; to get uneasy, to become shy, feel embarrassed.
cohombro nm cucumber.
cohonestar [1a] vt (a) (justificar) to explain away, whitewash, make appear reasonable. (b) dos cualidades etc to blend, harmonize, reconcile.
cohorte nf cohort.
COI nm abr de Comité Olímpico Internacional International Olympic Committee, IOC.
coima nf (a) (concubina) concubine; (puta) whore. (b) (‡: en el juego) rake-off*. (c) (*: And, Cono Sur: soborno) bribe; (acto) bribing, bribery.
coime nm (a) (chulo) pimp, ponce. (b) (en el juego) gambling operator. (c) (And: camarero) waiter.
coimero adj (*: And, Cono Sur) easily bribed, brib(e)able, bent‡.
coincidencia nf (a) (gen) coincidence. (b) (acuerdo) agreement; en ~ con in agreement with.
coincidente adj coincidental.
coincidentemente adv coincidentally.
coincidir [3a] vi (a) (sucesos) to coincide (con with). (b) (personas) to coincide, agree; todos coinciden en que ... everybody agrees that ...
cointérprete nmf fellow actor.
coinversión nf joint investment.
coito nm intercourse, coitus.
cojear [1a] vi (a) (persona: al andar) to limp, hobble (along); (estado) to be lame (de in); (mueble) to wobble, rock, be rocky; cojean del mismo pie they both have the same faults; sabemos de qué pie cojea we know his weak spots (o weaknesses).
(b) (fig: equivocarse) to slip up, be at fault (de in); (moralmente) to deviate from virtue.
cojera nf lameness; limp.
cojijo nm (a) (Ent) bug, small insect. (b) (fig) peeve*, grudge, grumble.
cojijoso adj peevish, cross, grumpy.
cojín nm (a) (almohadilla) cushion. (b) (‡: euf) = cojón.
cojinete nm (a) (cojín) small cushion, pad.
(b) (Mec) ~ a bolas, ~ de bolas ball-bearing; ~ de rodillos roller-bearing.
(c) (Ferro etc) chair.
(d) ~s (And, Carib, Méx) saddlebags.
cojinillos nmpl (CAm, Méx) saddlebags.
cojo 1 adj (a) persona lame; crippled; limping; mueble wobbly, rocky; ~ de un pie lame in one foot.
(b) (fig) lame, weak, shaky; el verso queda ~ the line is defective; la frase está coja the sentence is incomplete; el ~ echa la culpa al empedrado (Cono Sur) a bad workman blames his tools.
2 nm, coja nf lame person, cripple.
cojón** nm (a) (Anat) ball**; ¡cojones! (rechazo) balls!**; (sorpresa) bugger me!**; ¡y un ~!, ¡por los cojones! no way!*, not on your life!; ¡olé sus cojones! good for him!; una película de ~ a tremendous film*, a smashing film*; ¿qué cojones haces aquí? what the bloody hell are you doing here!**; me lo paso por los cojones I just laugh at it; tocar los cojones a uno (fig) to get up sb's nose‡.
(b) cojones (fig) guts; es un tío con cojones he's got guts; he's a good sort; es un tipo sin cojones he's a gutless individual*; hace falta tener cojones you've got to have guts; hacer algo por cojones to do sth by hook or by crook, do sth at all costs; tienes que hacerlo por los cojones you've bloody well got to do it‡; echar cojones a una situación to face resolutely up to a situation.
(c) (como adv) hace un frío de cojones it's bloody cold‡; me importa un ~ I don't give a damn; sabe un ~ he knows a hell of a lot; vale un ~ it's worth a hell of a lot.
cojonudamente‡ adv marvellously, splendidly.
cojonudo‡ adj (a) (físicamente) strong; (moralmente) brave; tough; full of guts. (b) (grande) huge, colossal; very important; (destacado) outstanding. (c) (soberbio) marvellous, splendid; smashing*; un tío ~ a great bloke‡; una hembra cojonuda a smashing bird‡; ¡qué ~! great stuff!* (d) (gracioso) very funny, highly amusing. (e) (LAm: holgazán) lazy, slow; (tonto) stupid.
cojudear‡ [1a] (LAm) 1 vt to con*, swindle. 2 vi to mess about.
cojudez‡ nf silly thing, piece of stupidity; ¡déjate de cojudeces! stop your nonsense!
cojudo 1 adj (a) (Agr) animal entire, not castrated; used for stud purposes. (b) (And‡: ingenuo) gullible; hacerse el ~ to act dumb. 2 nm, cojuda nf (Méx) Simple Simon.
cok [kok] nm, coke ['koke] nm (LAm) coke.
col nf cabbage; ~es de Bruselas (Brussels) sprouts; ~ rizada curly kale; ~ roja red cabbage; ~ de Saboya savoy; entre ~ y ~, lechuga a change is a good thing, variety is the spice of life.
col, col.ª nf abr de columna column, col.
cola¹ nf (a) (Aer, Astron, Orn, Zool) tail.
(b) (de frac) tail; (de vestido) train; ~ de caballo (pelo) pony-tail.
(c) (posición) end, last place, bottom; tail end; (silla) end seat; estar a la ~ de la clase to be (at the) bottom of the class; venir a la ~ to come last, come at the back; estar arrimado a la ~ (Pol) to be a reactionary; vagón de ~ last truck, rear coach.
(d) (línea etc) queue, line; (Inform) queue; ~ de impresión print(ing) queue; ~ de trabajos job queue; guardar ~, hacer ~ to queue (up), line up; ¡a la ~!, ¡haga Vd ~! get in the queue!
(e) (Téc) ~ de milano, ~ de pato dovetail.
(f) (fig) consequence(s); aftermath; tener ~, traer ~ to have grave consequences.
(g) (**) prick**.
(h) (LAm Aut) lift; pedir ~ to ask for a lift.
(i) (Cono Sur*: trasero) bum‡, bottom.
cola² nf (a) (pegamento) glue, gum; (Arte) size; ~ de contacto glue; ~ de pescado fish glue; isinglass; ~ de retal size; pintura a la ~ distemper, (Arte) tempera; comer ~ (Cono Sur) to be let down, be disappointed; eso no pega ni con ~ that has nothing whatsoever to do with it; that's utter rubbish.
(b) (And: bebida) fizzy drink; ~ de naranja orangeade.
cola³* nf Coke*, Coca-Cola ®.
colaboración nf (a) (acto) collaboration; escrito en ~ written in collaboration.
(b) (en periódico etc) contribution (a, en to); article; (de congreso) paper, communication.
colaboracionismo nm (Pol) collaboration.
colaboracionista nmf (Pol) collaborator, collaborationist.

colaborador(a) *nm/f,* collaborator, helper, co-worker; (*Liter etc*) contributor.

colaborar [1a] *vi* (**a**) to collaborate; to help, assist; ~ **con uno en un trabajo** to collaborate with sb on a piece of work.
(**b**) ~ **a,** ~ **en** (*Liter etc*) to contribute (articles) to, write for.

colaborativo *adj* collaborative.

colación *nf* (**a**) (*comparación*) collation, comparison; **sacar a** ~ to mention, bring up; to air; (*pey*) to drag in, drag up; **traer algo a** ~ to adduce sth as proof.
(**b**) (*Culin*) collation (*t Ecl*); light meal, snack; buffet meal; reception, wedding breakfast; (*LAm*: *dulce*) sweet.

colacionar [1a] *vt* to collate, compare.

colada¹ *nf* (**a**) (*acto, ropa*) wash, washing; **día de** ~ washing day; **tender la** ~ to hang out the washing; **todo saldrá en la** ~ it will all come out in the wash. (**b**) (*Quím*) bleach, lye. (**c**) (*Agr*) sheep run, cattle run; (*Geog*) defile.

coladera *nf* (**a**) (*Culin*) strainer. (**b**) (*Méx*: *alcantarilla*) sewer.

coladero *nm,* **colador** *nm* strainer; colander.

coladicto, -a *nm/f* glue-sniffer.

colado 1 *adj* (**a**) (*molde*) *metal* cast. (**b**) **aire** ~ draught. (**c**) **estar** ~* to be in love. **2** *nm,* **colada²** *nf* intruder; uninvited guest, gatecrasher.

colador *nm* sieve.

coladura *nf* (**a**) (*acto*) straining. (**b**) ~**s** grounds, dregs. (**c**) (*) absurdity, piece of nonsense; blunder, clanger‡.

colapsar [1a] **1** *vt* (**a**) (*derribar*) to overthrow, cause to collapse. (**b**) (*Aut etc*) to jam, bring to a halt, block; to disrupt; *puerta etc* to jam, block. **2** *vi y* **colapsarse** *vr* to collapse, go to pieces.

colapso *nm* (**a**) (*Med*) collapse; breakdown; ~ **nervioso** nervous breakdown. (**b**) (*fig*) collapse; breakdown; stoppage; ruin, destruction. (**c**) (*Aut etc*) jam, blockage; disruption.

colar [1l] **1** *vt* (**a**) *café, legumbres etc* to strain (off); to filter; *metal* to cast, pour.
(**b**) *ropa* to bleach.
(**c**) (*pasar*) ~ **algo por un sitio** to slip sth through a place, squeeze sth past a place; ~ **unos géneros por la aduana** to slip goods through the customs.
(**d**) (*fig*: *pasar*) ~ **algo a uno** to foist sth off on sb, palm sth off on sb; ~ **una moneda** to pass a (false) coin; ~ **una noticia a uno** to make sb believe a (false) piece of news; **¡a mí no me la cuelas!** I'm not going to swallow that!, don't give me that stuff!
(**e**) (*Méx*: *taladrar*) to drive, bore.
(**f**) ~**la**** to screw**.
2 *vi* (**a**) (*líquido*) to ooze, seep (through), filter (through), percolate; (*aire*) to get in (*por* through).
(**b**) (*pasar*) to pass; **no cuela*** I'm not swallowing that; **y si cuela, cuela** if they swallow that they'll swallow anything; **esa noticia es demasiado sospechosa para** ~ that news item is too suspect to pass.
(**c**) (*: *beber*) to booze*, tipple.
3 colarse *vr* (**a**) (*pasar*) to slip in, slip past, squeeze in; (*en cola*) to jump the queue; (*en reunión etc*) to slip in, sneak in, get in unobserved; (*en fiesta*) to gatecrash; **la moto se cuela por entre la circulación** the motorcycle slips through the traffic; **se ha colado algún indeseable** some undesirable has slipped in.
(**b**) (*: *meter la pata*) to blunder, slip up; to put one's foot in it, drop a clanger‡.
(**c**) ~ **la a una**** to screw sb**.

colateral *adj* collateral.

colca *nf* (*And*) (*troje*) barn, granary; (*almacén*) storeroom; (*ático*) attic store, loft.

colcrén *nm* cold cream.

colcha *nf* bedspread, counterpane.

colchón *nm* (**a**) mattress; ~ **de aire** airbed; (*Téc*) air-cushion; ~ **de muelles** spring mattress, interior sprung mattress; ~ **neumático** airbed; ~ **de plumas** feather-bed; ~ **de seguridad** padding, padded protection; (*fig*) buffer; buffer zone; **servir de** ~ **a** (*fig*) to act as a buffer for. (**b**) (*Fin*: *precio*) floor price, reserve price; (*fondos*) reserve fund.

colchoneta *nf* (*Dep*) mat.

cole* *nm* = **colegio.**

colear [1a] **1** *vt* (**a**) (*Taur*) *toro* to throw by twisting the tail.
(**b**) (*And*: *regañar*) to vex, nag, harass.
(**c**) (*CAm*: *seguir*) to tail, follow.
2 *vi* (**a**) **el perro colea** the dog wags its tail.
(**b**) (*fig*) **el asunto todavía colea** the affair is still not settled; **estar vivito y coleando** to be alive and kicking.
(**c**) (*CAm, Carib*: *edad*) **colea en los 50** he's close on 50, he's knocking on 50.
3 colearse *vr* (*Carib*) (**a**) (*Aut*) to skid (out of control).
(**b**) (*huésped*) to arrive unexpectedly (*o* uninvited).

colección *nf* collection; **es de** ~ (*Méx*) it's a collector's item.

coleccionable 1 *adj* collectable, which can be collected. **2** *nm* (*objeto*) collectable; (*prensa*) pull-out section.

coleccionador(a) *nm/f* collector.

coleccionar [1a] *vti* to collect.

coleccionismo *nm* collecting.

coleccionista *nmf* collector.

colecta *nf* (**a**) (*recaudación*) collection (for charity). (**b**) (*Ecl*) collect.

colectar [1a] *vt impuestos etc* to collect.

colecticio *adj* (**a**) (*Mil*) raw, untrained. (**b**) **tomo** ~ omnibus edition, collected works.

colectivamente *adv* collectively.

colectivero *nm* (*Cono Sur*) bus driver.

colectividad *nf* (**a**) (*gen*) collectivity; (*grupo*) group as a whole, community. (**b**) (*Pol*) collective ownership.

colectivización *nf* collectivization.

colectivizar [1f] *vt* to collectivize.

colectivo 1 *adj* collective (*t Ling*); **acción colectiva** joint action, group action, communal action. **2** *nm* (**a**) group, grouping, body; (*Pol*) collective. (**b**) (*And, Cono Sur, Méx*: *autobús*) (small) bus, minibus; (*And*: *taxi*) taxi.

colector *nm* (**a**) (*persona*) collector. (**b**) (*Elec*) collector; (*Mec*) sump; trap, container; (*albañal*) sewer.

colega *nmf* colleague; (*) pal*, mate, buddy; (*en oración directa*) man*.

colegiado 1 *adj* (**a**) collegiate; **decisión colegiada** decision voted on by members. (**b**) (*LAm*) qualified. **2** *nm,* **colegiada** *nf* (*Med*) doctor; (*Dep*) referee.

colegial 1 *adj* (**a**) (*Escol*) school (*atr*), college (*atr*). (**b**) (*Ecl*) collegiate. (**c**) (*Méx*: *inexperto*) raw, green*, inexperienced. **2** *nm* schoolboy; (*fig*) inexperienced person, callow youth.

colegiala *nf* schoolgirl.

colegialidad *nf* (**a**) (*cuerpo*) college; collegiate membership. (**b**) (*cualidad*) collegiality; corporate feeling.

colegiarse [1b] *vr* to become a member of one's professional association; to form a professional association.

colegiata *nf* collegiate church.

colegiatura *nf* (*Méx*) school fees, university fees.

colegio *nm* (**a**) (*escuela*) independent secondary school, private (*o* fee-paying) high school; ~ (**de párvulos**) kindergarten, primary school; ~ **de internos** boarding school; ~ **de pago** fee-paying school; **¡cómo se ve que tú no fuiste a ~s de pago!** where were you brung up?*; **ir al** ~ to go to school.
(**b**) (*Univ*) college; ~ **mayor** (*Hist*) college (*p.ej. of Salamanca or Oxford*); (*moderno*) hall of residence.
(**c**) (*otros*) ~ **de abogados** bar association; **C~ de Cardenales** College of Cardinals; ~ **electoral** polling-station; (*p.ej. US Pol*) electoral college; ~ **de médicos** medical association.

colegir [3c *y* 3k] *vt* (**a**) (*reunir*) to collect, gather. (**b**) (*deducir*) to infer, gather, conclude (*de* from); **de lo cual colijo que ...** from which I gather that ...

coleóptero *nm* beetle.

cólera 1 *nf* (**a**) (*ira*) anger, rage; **descargar la** ~ **en** to vent one's anger on; **montar en** ~ to get angry.
(**b**) (*Anat*) bile.
2 *nm* (*Med*) cholera.

colérico *adj* (*furioso*) angry, furious, irate; (*de temperamento*) irascible, bad-tempered.

colero *nm* (*Cono Sur*) top hat.

colesterol *nm* cholesterol.

coleta *nf* (**a**) (*pelo*) pigtail; **gente de** ~ bullfighters, bullfighting people; **cortarse la** ~ to quit the ring, give up bullfighting; (*fig*) to quit, give it all up, retire; **me cortaré la** ~ **si ...*** I'll eat my hat if ...
(**b**) (*: *idea adicional*) postscript, afterthought.

coletazo *nm* (**a**) (*Zool etc*) lash, blow with the tail; **está dando los últimos ~s** (*fig*) it's on its last legs.
(**b**) (*de vehículo*) sway, swaying movement; **dar ~s** to sway about.
(**c**) (*fig*) sting in the tail; unexpected after-effect; **un** ~ **de la memoria** a trick of the memory.

coleto *nm* (**a**) (*Hist*) doublet, jerkin.
(**b**) (*: *uno mismo*) body; oneself; **decir para su** ~ to say to o.s.; **echarse algo al** ~ (*comer*) to eat sth right up;

(*beber*) to drink sth down; echarse un libro al ~ to read a book right through, devour a book.
(c) (*Carib: fregasuelos*) mop.

colgadero *nm* hook, hanger, peg.

colgadizo 1 *adj* hanging, loose. 2 *nm* (*cobertizo*) lean-to shed; (*Carib: techo*) flat roof.

colgado *adj, ptp* (a) (*dudoso*) uncertain, doubtful.
(b) dejar ~ a uno to let sb down, fail sb; quedarse ~ to be disappointed; quedar ~ en una cita to be stood up on a date*; antes le veré ~ que ... I'll see him damned before ...
(c) (*) estar ~ to have withdrawal pains (from drugs); (*Fin*) to be broke*; ¡estás ~!* rubbish!, get away!*; quedar ~ to get hooked (on drugs)*.

colgadura *nf* (*t* ~s) hangings, drapery; (*tapiz*) tapestry; ~s de cama bed hangings, bed curtains.

colgajo *nm* (a) (*trapo*) rag, tatter, shred. (b) (*Bot*) bunch (*of grapes, hung to dry*). (c) (*Med*) flap of flesh.

colgante 1 *adj* hanging; droopy, floppy; dangling; puente ~ suspension bridge.
2 *nm* (a) (*joya*) drop, pendant, earring; (*Carib, Cono Sur: de reloj*) watch chain.
(b) (*Arquit*) festoon.
(c) (*pelo*) ~s fringe.
(d) ~s** balls**.

colgar [1h *y* 1l] 1 *vt* (a) *cuadro etc* to hang (up) (*de* from, *en* on); *persona* to hang; *bandera, colada etc* to hang out; ~ los hábitos (*fig*) to leave the priesthood; ~ los libros (*etc*) to abandon one's studies (*etc*).
(b) *pared* to decorate with hangings, drape (*de* with).
(c) (*atribuir*) to attribute, impute (*a* to); ~ la culpa a uno to pin the blame on sb.
(d) (*Univ*‡) to fail, flunk‡.
2 *vi* to hang, be suspended (*de* on, from); (*orejas etc*) to hang down, droop, dangle; (*Telec*) to hang up, ring off.
3 **colgarse** *vr* (a) (‡) to get high‡ (on drugs). (b) (*Cono Sur*) to plug illegally into the mains, steal electricity.

colibrí *nm* hummingbird.

cólico *nm* (*Med*) colic.

colicuar [1d] 1 *vt* to melt, dissolve; to fuse. 2 **colicuarse** *vr* to melt, dissolve, liquefy.

colifato* (*Cono Sur*) 1 *adj* nuts‡, crazy. 2 *nm* madman, nutcase‡.

coliflor *nf* cauliflower.

coligado 1 *adj* allied, coalition (*atr*); estar ~s to be allied, be in league. 2 *nm* ally, confederate.

coligarse [1h] *vr* to unite, join together, make common cause (*con* with).

coliguacho *nm* (*Cono Sur*) horsefly.

colilla *nf* fag-end‡; butt, stub; ser una ~* to be past it, be all washed up*.

colimba* (*Cono Sur Mil*) 1 *nm* conscript. 2 *nf* military service; hacer la ~ to do military service.

colimbo[1] *nm* (*Orn*) diver.

colimbo[2] *nm* (*Cono Sur*) recruit, conscript.

colín *nm* (*Carib*) machete, cane knife.

colina *nf* hill.

colinabo *nm* kohlrabi.

colindante *adj* adjacent, adjoining, neighbouring.

colindar [1a] *vi* to adjoin, be adjacent; ~ con to adjoin, be adjacent to, border on.

colirio *nm* eye-drops.

colirrojo *nm* redstart.

colís *nm* (*And*) machete, cane knife.

Coliseo *nm* Coliseum.

colisión *nf* (a) (*Aut etc*) collision; crash, smash; ~ de frente, ~ frontal head-on collision. (b) (*fig*) clash.

colisionar [1a] *vi* to collide; ~ con, ~ contra to collide with; (*fig*) to clash with, conflict with.

colista 1 *nm* (*Dep*) bottom club (in the league). 2 *nmf* person who stands in a queue.

colita[1] *nf* (*LAm Aut*) lift; hacer ~ to hitchhike, thumb a lift.

colita[2]‡ *nf* willy‡.

colitis *nf* colitis.

colmado 1 *adj* abundant, copious; full (*de* of), overflowing (*de* with); heaped (*de* with); una cucharada colmada one heaped spoonful; una tarde colmada de incidentes an afternoon (more than) full of incident.
2 *nm* cheap seafood restaurant; (*Cataluña*) grocer's shop; (*Andalucía*) retail wine shop.

colmar [1a] *vt* (a) *vaso etc* to fill to the brim, fill right up, fill to overflowing (de *with*); *plato* to heap (*de* with).
(b) (*fig*) *esperanzas etc* to fulfil, more than satisfy, realize completely.
(c) (*fig*) ~ a uno de honores to shower honours upon sb; ~ a uno de alabanzas to heap praises on sb; ~ a uno de favores to lavish favours on sb, overwhelm sb with favours.

colmatación *nf* silting.

colmena *nf* (a) (*lugar*) beehive; (*fig*) hive. (b) (*Méx: insecto*) bee; bees.

colmenar *nm* apiary.

colmenero, -a *nm/f* beekeeper.

colmillo *nm* (a) (*Anat*) eye tooth, canine (tooth); (*Zool*) fang; (*de elefante, morsa etc*) tusk.
(b) (*fig*) enseñar los ~s to show one's teeth; escupir por el ~ to talk big, brag; tener ~s (*Méx*) to be long in the tooth*; tener el ~ torcido to be an old fox; ¡ya tengo ~s! (*Méx*) you can't fool me!

colmillón *nm* (*LAm*) greed.

colmilludo *adj* (a) (*lit*) having big teeth (*o* fangs *etc*). (b) (*fig*) sharp, alert.

colmo *nm* (*fig*) height, summit, extreme; el ~ de la elegancia the height of elegance; el ~ de lo absurdo the height of absurdity; a ~ in plenty, in abundance; con ~ heaped, to overflowing; para ~ de desgracias to make matters worse, to cap it all; ¡es el ~! it's the limit!, it's the last straw!; sería el ~ si ... it would be the last straw if ...

colocación *nf* (a) (*acto*) placing; positioning; collocation; (*Com*) investment. (b) (*empleo*) job, place, situation; no encuentro ~ I can't find a job. (c) (*situación*) place, position.

colocado *adj*: apostar para ~ to back (a horse) for a place; estar ~‡ (*drogado*) to be high (on drugs)‡, (*borracho*) to be smashed‡.

colocar [1g] 1 *vt* (a) (*gen*) to place, put, position; (*ordenar*) to arrange; *tropas etc* to position, station; (*esp LAm*) to put away, put back; ~ la quilla de un buque to lay down a ship; ~ un satélite en órbita to put (*o* place) a satellite in orbit.
(b) *persona* to place (in a job), find a post for; *hija* to marry off.
(c) (*Com, Fin*) *mercancías, pedido* to place; *dinero* to place, invest; *empréstito* to float.
(d) ~ una historia a uno to bore sb with the same old story; ~ una responsabilidad a uno to saddle sb with a responsibility.
(e) (‡) to nick‡, arrest.
2 *vi* (‡): es una sustancia que coloca it's a substance that gets you high‡.
3 **colocarse** *vr* (a) (*gen*) to place o.s., station o.s.; (*Dep*) to be placed, get a place; ~ con (*Ling*) to collocate with; el equipo se ha colocado en quinto lugar the team has climbed to fifth position; el paro se coloca en 2 millones unemployment reaches 2 million.
(b) (*obtener un puesto*) to get a job.
(c) (‡) to get high (*con* on)‡.

colocata‡ *nmf* (*borracho*) drunk*; (*drogado*) junkie*.

colocón‡ *nm*: cogerse un ~ to get high‡, go on a trip‡.

colocho (*CAm*) 1 *adj* curly(-haired). 2 ~s *nmpl* (*rizos*) curls; (*virutas*) wood shavings.

colodrillo *nm* back of the neck.

colofón *nm* (a) (*Tip*) colophon. (b) (*) culmination, climax.

colofonia *nf* rosin, colophony.

colombianismo *nm* colombianism, word (*o* phrase *etc*) peculiar to Colombia.

colombiano, -a *adj, nm/f* Colombian.

colombicultor(a) *nm/f* pigeon-breeder.

colombicultura *nf* pigeon-breeding.

colombino *adj* of Columbus, relating to Columbus.

colombofilia *nf* pigeon-fancying.

colombófilo, -a *nm/f* pigeon-fancier.

colon *nm* (*Anat*) colon.

Colón *nm* Columbus.

colón *nm* colon (*unit of currency of Costa Rica and El Salvador*).

Colonia *nf* Cologne.

colonia[1] *nf* (a) (*Bio, Pol etc*) colony; (*de ciudad*) (*barrio*) suburb; (*residencial*) residential district; housing estate; ~ escolar, ~ de vacaciones, ~ de verano summer camp for schoolchildren; ~ obrera working-class housing scheme; ~ penal penal settlement; ~ proletaria shanty-town; ~ (veraniega) holiday camp; las antiguas ~s españolas the former Spanish colonies; la ~ norteamericana en Madrid the Americans resident in Madrid, the American popula-

tion of Madrid.
(**b**) (*Cos*) silk ribbon.
(**c**) (*Carib*) sugar-cane plantation.

colonia² *nf* eau-de-Cologne.

coloniaje *nm* (*LAm*) (*período*) colonial period; (*sistema*) system of colonial government; (*pey*) slavery, slave status.

colonial *adj* colonial; *alimentos, producto* overseas (*atr*), imported.

colonialismo *nm* colonialism.

colonialista *adj, nmf* colonialist.

colonización *nf* colonization; settlement.

colonizador 1 *adj* colonizing. **2** *nm*, **colonizadora** *nf* colonist, colonizer, settler; pioneer.

colonizar [1f] *vt* to colonize; to settle; (*Bio*) to inhabit, live in.

colono *nm* (**a**) (*Pol*) colonist, settler; colonial. (**b**) (*Agr*) tenant farmer. (**c**) (*Carib*: *de azúcar*) sugar planter. (**d**) (*And*: *indio*) Indian bound to an estate.

coloqueta‡ *nf* (**a**) (*detención*) arrest; **dar una ~ a** to nick‡, arrest. (**b**) (*redada*) police sweep. (**c**) = **colocata**.

coloquial *adj* colloquial, familiar.

coloquiante *nmf* speaker; person taking part in a discussion; **mi ~** the person I was (*etc*) talking to.

coloquiar [1b] *vi* to talk, discuss.

coloquio 1 *nm* (*conversación*) conversation, talk; (*congreso*) conference; (*científico etc*) colloquium; (*Liter*) dialogue. **2** *atr*: **almuerzo ~** lunch with speakers and discussion; **charla ~** talk followed by a discussion; **mesa ~** round-table discussion.

color *nm* (**a**) (*gen*) colour; hue, shade; (*fig*) colour, colouring; **a ~, en ~es** *película* in colour, colour (*atr*); **a todo ~** in full colour; **gente de ~** coloured people; **huevos de ~** (*LAm*) brown eggs; **zapatos de ~** brown shoes; **subido de ~** blue, rude, scabrous; **so ~ de** under pretext of; **el suceso tuvo ~es trágicos** the event had its tragic aspect, the event had a sad side to it; **~ base** basic colour; **~ local** local colour; **~ muerto, ~ quebrado** dull colour; **~es pastel** pastel colours; **~ sólido** fast colour; **un vestido de ~ malva** a mauve(-coloured) dress; **un vino ~ fresa** a strawberry-coloured wine; **verlo todo ~ de rosa** to see everything through rose-coloured spectacles, be ridiculously optimistic; **cambiar de ~, mudar de ~** to change colour, turn pale; **ponerse de mil ~es** to colour up; **sacar los ~es a uno** to make sb blush; **le salieron** (*o* **subieron**) **los ~es** he blushed; **subírsele a uno el ~** (*Méx*) to blush; **hay ~*** it's O.K. here*, it's an O.K. scene*; **no hay ~*, no tienen ~*** there's no comparison, they're streets apart*; **eso no tiene ~*** that seems unlikely, that's not on*.
(**b**) (*Arte*) colour, paint; (*Téc*) dye, colouring matter; (*cosmético*) rouge.
(**c**) (*Naipes*) suit.
(**d**) **~es** (*Mil*) colours; **los ~es nacionales** the national colours, the national flag.
(**e**) (*) drug(s).

coloración *nf* coloration, colouring; (*Zool etc*) coloration, markings.

colorado 1 *adj* (**a**) (*gen*) coloured, (*esp*) red; *cara* rosy, ruddy; **poner ~ a uno** to make sb blush; **ponerse ~** to blush.
(**b**) (*fig*: *esp LAm*) *chiste* blue, rude, scabrous; *argumento* plausible.
2 *nm* (**a**) (‡: *dinero*) bread‡, money.
(**b**) (*Carib*: *enfermedad*) scarlet fever.
(**c**) **los C~s** *Uruguayan political party.*

coloradón, coloradote *adj* red-faced, ruddy.

colorante 1 *adj* colouring. **2** *nm* colouring (matter).

colorar [1a] *vt* (*gen*) to colour; (*teñir*) to dye, tint, stain; **~ algo de amarillo** to colour (*o* dye *etc*) sth yellow.

coloratura *nf* coloratura.

coloreado 1 *adj* coloured; tinted. **2** *nm* colouring; tinting.

colorear [1a] **1** *vt* (**a**) = **colorar**. (**b**) (*fig*: *justificar*) to excuse; to put in a favourable light; to gloss over, whitewash. **2** *vi* to redden, show red.

colorete *nm* rouge.

colorido *nm* colour(ing) (*t fig*); **~ local** local colour.

colorín 1 *adj* (*Cono Sur*) strawberry (*o* reddish) blond(e).
2 *nm* (**a**) (*gen* **colorines** *pl*) bright colour; **tener muchos colorines** to have vivid colours; **¡qué colorines tiene el niño!** what rosy cheeks the little fellow has!; **¡~ colorado!** hey presto!, abracadabra!, (*como n*) happy ending.
(**b**) (*Orn*) goldfinch.
(**c**) (*Med*) measles.
(**d**) (*revista*) magazine of love-stories.

colorir [3a; *defectivo*] **1** *vt* (**a**) (*gen*) to colour. (**b**) (*fig*) = **colorear (b)**. **2** *vi* to take on a colour, colour up.

colosal *adj* colossal (*t fig*); *comida etc* splendid.

coloso *nm* (**a**) (*lit*) colossus; (*esp LAm*) **el ~ del norte** the United States. (**b**) (*Cono Sur Aut*) trailer.

coludo *adj* (*Cono Sur*) long-tailed.

Columbina *nf* Columbine.

columbrar [1a] *vt* (**a**) (*divisar*) to glimpse, spy, make out. (**b**) (*fig*) to guess; *solución* to begin to see.

columna *nf* (**a**) (*Arquit*) column; pillar.
(**b**) (*Mil*) column; **~ blindada** armoured column; **quinta ~** fifth column; **~ volante** flying column.
(**c**) (*Anat*) **~ vertebral** spine, spinal column.
(**d**) (*Mec*) column; **~ de dirección** steering column.
(**e**) (*Tip*) column.
(**f**) (*fig*: *soporte*) pillar, support; **una ~ de la religión** a pillar of religion.

columnata *nf* colonnade.

columnista *nmf* columnist.

columpiar [1b] **1** *vt* to swing. **2 columpiarse** *vr* (**a**) (*mecerse*) to swing; (*cuerpo etc*) to sway; (*anadear*) to waddle; (*pavonearse*) to swagger (along). (**b**) (*fig*: *oscilar*) to swing to and fro, seesaw. (**c**) (*: *meter la pata*) to drop a clanger‡.

columpio *nm* (*gen*) swing; (*LAm*: *mecedora*) rocking chair; **~ basculante, ~ de tabla** seesaw.

colusión *nf* collusion.

colza *nf* (*Bot*) rape, colza.

collado *nm* (**a**) (*colina*) hill, height; hillock. (**b**) (*puerto*) mountain pass.

collage [ko'la:ʒ] *nm* (*Arte*) collage.

collalba *nf* (*Orn*) wheatear.

collar *nm* (**a**) (*adorno*) necklace; (*cuentas*) (string of) beads; (*insignia*) chain (of office); (*de perro*) (dog) collar; (*Orn, Zool etc*) collar, ruff; **~ de perlas** pearl necklace.
(**b**) (*Mec*) collar, ring.
(**c**) **~ de fuerza** stranglehold.

collarín *nm* surgical collar.

colleja *nf* dandelion; campion.

collera *nf* (**a**) horse-collar. (**b**) **~s** (*LAm*) cufflinks.

collie ['koli] *nm* collie.

collín *nm* (*CAm*), **collines** *nm* (*And*) cane knife, machete.

coma¹ *nm* (*Med*) coma.

coma² *nf* (*Tip*) comma; (*Mat*) (decimal) point; **~ flotante** floating point; **sin faltar una ~** right down to the last detail, with complete accuracy; **12,5** 12·5 (twelve point five).

comadre *nf* (**a**) (*madrina, madre*) kinswoman, *woman relative of godparents.*
(**b**) (*vecina*) neighbour; (*amiga*) friend, crony; (*mujer de pueblo*) village woman, peasant woman; (*chismosa*) gossip; **un grupo de ~s** a group of gossips, a gathering of gossipy women.
(**c**) (*Med*) midwife.
(**d**) (*alcahueta*) go-between, procuress.
(**e**) (‡: *maricón*) pansy‡.
(**f**) (*prov*) *en oración directa entre mujeres, no se traduce.*

comadrear [1a] *vi* to gossip.

comadreja *nf* weasel.

comadreo *nm*, **comadrería** *nf* gossip; gossiping, chattering.

comadrona *nf* midwife.

comal *nm* (*CAm, Méx*) griddle.

comandancia *nf* (**a**) (*mando*) command. (**b**) (*graduación*) rank of major. (**c**) (*cuartel*) commander's headquarters (*o* office). (**d**) (*zona*) area under a commander's jurisdiction.

comandanta *nf* (**a**) (woman) commander; (*Mil*) (woman) major; (*Hist*) major's wife. (**b**) (*Náut*) flagship.

comandante *nm* (**a**) (*jefe*) commandant, commander; **~ en jefe** commander-in-chief; (*Méx*) **~ de policía** chief of police; **~ de vuelo** pilot, captain; **segundo ~** copilot, second pilot. (**b**) (*graduación*) major.

comandar [1a] *vt* to command, lead.

comandita *nf* sleeping partnership, silent partnership (*US*).

comanditario *adj*: **socio ~** sleeping partner, silent partner (*US*).

comando *nm* (**a**) (*Mil*: *mando*) command; leadership; (*Téc*) control; (*Inform*) command; **~ a distancia** remote control; **~ vocal** speech command. (**b**) (*soldado, grupo*) commando; **~ de acción** active-service unit; **~ de información** intelligence unit; **~ suicida** suicide squad. (**c**) (*prenda*) duffel coat.

comarca *nf* region, area, part.

comarcal *adj carretera* local; *emisora* local, regional.
comarcano *adj* neighbouring, bordering.
comarcar [1g] *vi* to border (*con* on), be adjacent (*con* to).
comatoso *adj* comatose.
comba *nf* (**a**) (*curva*) bend; (*alabeo*) bulge, warp, sag. (**b**) (*cuerda*) skipping rope; **dar a la** ~ to turn the skipping rope; **saltar a la** ~ to skip. (**c**) (*juego*) skipping. (**d**) **no pierde** ~ he doesn't miss a trick.
combadura *nf* (*en carretera*) curve, camber; *V t* **comba (a)**.
combar [1a] **1** *vt* to bend, curve. **2 combarse** *vr* to bend, curve; to bulge, warp; to sag.
combate *nm* fight, combat, engagement; (*fig*) battle, struggle; ~ **naval** naval battle, sea fight; ~ **singular** single combat; **estar fuera de** ~ to be out of action (*t fig*); (*Boxeo*) to be knocked out; **poner a uno fuera de** ~ to put sb out of action; (*Boxeo*) to knock sb out; **ganar por fuera de** ~ to win by a knockout.
combatiente *nm* combatant; **no** ~ non-combatant.
combatir [1a] **1** *vt* (**a**) (*Mil*) to attack; (*fig*) *tendencia, propuesta etc* to combat, fight, oppose; *mente* to assail, harass.
(**b**) (*olas, viento*) to beat upon.
2 *vi y* **combatirse** *vr* to fight, struggle (*con, contra* against).
combatividad *nf* fighting spirit, fight; (*pey*) aggressiveness.
combativo *adj* full of fight, spirited; (*pey*) aggressive, combative.
combazo *nm* (*Cono Sur*) punch.
combés *nm* (*Náut*) waist.
combi[1]* *nf*, **combinable** *nf* (*Aut*) multi-purpose van; (*LAm*: *bus*) minibus.
combi[2]* *nf* (**a**) (*ardid*) fiddle*, wangle*. (**b**) (*prenda*) slip.
combinación *nf* (**a**) (*acto etc*) combination.
(**b**) (*Quím*) compound; (*bebida*) cocktail.
(**c**) (*Ferro etc*) connection; **hacer** ~ **con** to connect with.
(**d**) (*Mat, quinielas etc*) permutation; ~ **métrica** (*Liter*) stanza form, rhyme scheme.
(**e**) (*proyecto*) arrangement, set-up, scheme; plan; (*pey*) cunning scheme, deep-laid plan.
(**f**) (*Cos*) slip; combination, combs*.
combinacional *adj* combinatory.
combinadamente *adv* jointly (*con* with).
combinado *nm* (**a**) cocktail. (**b**) (*Cono Sur*) radiogram. (**c**) (*equipo*) selection.
combinar [1a] **1** *vt* (*gen*) to combine; to join, unite, put together; *colores etc* to blend, mix, match; *proyecto* to devise, work out.
2 combinarse *vr* to combine; (*personas*) to get together, join together (*para* + *infin* to + *infin*); (*pey*) to form a ring, gang up, conspire; (*Méx*: *alternarse*) to take it in turns.
combo 1 *adj* bent; bulging; warped. **2** *nm* (**a**) (*LAm*: *martillo*) sledgehammer. (**b**) (*And, Cono Sur*) (*golpe*) slap; (*puñetazo*) punch.
combustible 1 *adj* combustible. **2** *nm* (**a**) (*gen*) fuel, combustible; ~ **nuclear** nuclear fuel. (**b**) (*Méx*: *gasolina*) petrol, gas (*US*).
combustión *nf* combustion; ~ **espontánea** spontaneous combustion.
comebolas *nm invar* (*Carib*) simple soul, gullible individual.
comecocos* *nm invar* (**a**) (*manía*) obsession, mania; (*pasatiempo*) idle pastime, absorbing but pointless activity; (*lavacerebros*) brainwashing enthusiasm.
(**b**) (*preocupación*) nagging worry.
comedero 1 *adj* eatable, edible.
2 *nm* (**a**) (*Agr*) trough, manger; (*Orn etc*) feeding-box, feeder.
(**b**) (*comedor*) dining-room; (*de animal*) feeding place.
(**c**) (*Carib*: *prostíbulo*) brothel.
(**d**) (*And*: *sitio favorito*) haunt, hang-out*.
comedia *nf* (**a**) (*moderna*) comedy; (*Hist*) play, drama, *comedia;* **alta** ~ high comedy; ~ **en un acto** one-act play; ~ **de costumbres** comedy of manners; ~ **de capa y espada** cloak-and-dagger play; ~ **de enredos** comedy of intrigue; ~ **negra** black comedy; ~ **de situación** situation comedy.
(**b**) (*fig*) farce; pretence; **hacer la** ~ to make-believe, pretend.
comedianta *nf* (**a**) (*actriz*) actress, comedienne. (**b**) (*pey*: *hipócrita*) hypocrite.
comediante *nm* (**a**) (*actor*) actor. (**b**) (*pey*: *hipócrita*) hypocrite, humbug, fraud.
comedidamente *adv* moderately; courteously; (*LAm*) obligingly.
comedido *adj* (*moderado*) moderate, restrained; (*cortés*) courteous; (*LAm*) obliging.
comedieta *nf* light comedy.
comedimiento *nm* moderation, restraint; courtesy; (*LAm*) helpfulness.
comedio *nm* middle; interval.
comediógrafo, -a *nm/f* playwright.
comedirse [3k] *vr* (**a**) (*conducta*) to behave moderately, be restrained, restrain o.s.; to be courteous, answer (*etc*) politely.
(**b**) ~ **a** (*LAm*) + *infin* to offer to + *infin*, volunteer to + *infin*.
comedón *nm* blackhead.
comedor 1 *adj* greedy, gluttonous.
2 *nm* (**a**) (*de casa*) dining-room; (*restaurante*) restaurant; (*LAm Ferro*) dining-car; ~ **de beneficencia** soup kitchen.
(**b**) (*muebles*) dining-room suite.
3 *nm*, **comedora** *nf* glutton; **ser buen** ~ to have a good appetite; **ser mal** ~ to have a poor appetite, not eat much.
comedura* *nf*: ~ **de coco** = **comecocos**.
comefuego *nm* (*Circo*) fire-eater.
comegente‡ *nm* (*And, Carib*) glutton.
comehostias* *nmf invar* goody-goody*.
comején *nm* (**a**) (*Ent*) termite, white ant. (**b**) (*And*: *glotón*) glutton. (**c**) (*And*: *preocupación*) nagging worry, gnawing anxiety.
comelitona *nf* (*Méx*) = **comilona**.
comelón *adj* (*LAm*) = **comilón**.
comelona *nf* (*LAm*) = **comilona**.
comemierdas‡ *nmf invar* shit‡.
comendador *nm* knight commander (*of a military order*).
comendatorio *adj*: **carta comendatoria** letter of recommendation.
comensal *nmf* (**a**) (*compañero*) fellow guest, diner; **habrá 13 ~es** there will be 13 to dinner; **me lo dijo mi** ~ the man sitting next to me at dinner told me so; **mis ~es** those dining with me, those at table with me.
(**b**) (*And*: *en hotel*) guest.
comentador(a) *nm/f* commentator.
comentar [1a] *vt* (*hacer comentarios sobre*) to comment on; *teoría etc* to expound; (*) (*discutir*) to discuss; (*criticar*) to criticize, gossip about.
comentariar [1b] *vt* = **comentar**.
comentario *nm* (**a**) (*observación*) comment, remark, observation; **y ahora sin más** ~ ... and now without further ado...; **'no hay ~s'** 'no comment'.
(**b**) (*Liter*) commentary.
(**c**) (*pey*) **~s** gossip, (nasty) talk, tittle-tattle; **dar lugar a ~s** to cause gossip; **hacer ~s** to gossip, pass (nasty) remarks.
comentarista *nmf* commentator (*t Rad*); ~ **deportivo** sports commentator.
comento *nm* comment; (*Liter*) commentary; (*fig*) lie, pretence.
comenzar [1f *y* 1j] *vti* to begin, start, commence; ~ **protestando** to begin by protesting; ~ **a hacer algo** to begin to do sth, start to do sth, start doing sth; ~ **con** to begin with; ~ **por** to begin with; ~ **por** + *infin* to begin by + *ger*.
comer [2a] **1** *vt* (**a**) (*gen*) to eat; **sin ~lo ni beberlo** (*fig*) without having (had) anything to do with it, without wishing to be involved; without intervening at all; **sin ~lo ni beberlo, yo** ... before I knew where I was, ...
(**b**) (*almorzar, cenar*) to eat (*o* have) for lunch (*o* dinner); **hoy comimos truchas** today we had trout for lunch (*o* dinner).
(**c**) (*Quím*) to eat away, eat into, corrode; (*Geol*) to swallow up, erode; ~ **las uñas** to bite one's nails; **me come la pierna** my leg itches; **esto come las existencias** this devours (*o* uses up) the stocks.
(**d**) *color* to fade; ~ **los colores a uno** to take away sb's colours.
(**e**) (*fig*) **le come la envidia** she is eaten up with envy.
(**f**) (*Ajedrez etc*) to take, capture.
2 *vi* (**a**) (*gen*) to eat; ~ **de** to eat, partake of, have some of; ~ **como una vaca** (*o* **fiera**) to eat like a horse; **no** ~ **ni dejar** ~ to be a dog in the manger.
(**b**) (*tomar una comida*) to have a meal, eat; (*esp*) to have lunch; (*en algunas regiones*) to have dinner, have supper.
(**c**) (*fig*) **¡pero ~ y callar!** but I'd better say no more!; **el mismo que come y viste** the very same; **este pescado es de buen** ~ this fish is good eating; **Juan es de buen** ~ John

eats anything, John has a hearty appetite; **no tienen qué ~** they don't have enough to live on.

(**d**) **~ a una** (*And*‡) to screw sb‡.

3 comerse *vr* (**a**) (*gen*) to eat up; **se lo comió todo** he ate it all up; **está para ~la*** she looks a treat*.

(**b**) (*fig*) *recursos etc* to consume, devour, eat up.

(**c**) (*fig*) *pasaje etc* to skip; *consonante* to swallow, slur; **se come las palabras** he mumbles; **tiene muchos nombres y se come el García** she has lots of names and drops the García.

(**d**) (*locuciones*) **~ a uno por pies** to take sb in completely; **se comen unos a otros** they're at daggers drawn.

(**e**) (‡) **se comió tres atracos** he confessed to three hold-ups.

comerciabilidad *nf* marketability, saleability.

comerciable *adj* (**a**) (*Com*) marketable, saleable; **valores ~s** marketable securities. (**b**) (*fig*) sociable.

comercial 1 *adj* commercial; business (*atr*), trading (*atr*); **barrio ~** business quarter, shopping district; **centro ~** business centre. **2** *nm* (*TV*) commercial.

comercializable *adj* marketable, saleable.

comercialización *nf* (**a**) (*proceso*) commercialization. (**b**) (*marquetín*) marketing.

comercializar [1f] *vt* (**a**) (*gen*) to commercialize. (**b**) *producto* to market.

comercialmente *adv* commercially.

comerciante *nmf* (*t* **comercianta** *f*) trader, dealer, merchant; **~ al por mayor** wholesaler; **~ al por menor** retailer.

comerciar [1b] *vi* (*dos personas*) to have dealings; (*dos países*) to trade; **~ con** (*t* **~ en**) *mercancías* to deal in, handle; *persona* to do business with, have dealings with; *país* trade with.

comercio *nm* (**a**) (*gen*) commerce; trade; business; **~ de, ~ en** trade in, traffic in; dealings in; **el ~ español** Spanish trade; **~ de esclavos** slave trade; **~ de exportación** export trade; **~ exterior** foreign trade, overseas trade; **~ de importación** import trade; **~ interior** home trade.

(**b**) (*personas etc colectivamente*) business interests, business world; big business.

(**c**) (*tienda*) shop, store (*US*).

(**d**) (*fig*) intercourse; dealings, contacts (*con* with); **~ sexual** sexual intercourse; **~ social** social intercourse, social contacts.

(**e**) (‡: *comida*) grub‡.

comestible 1 *adj* eatable; *hongo etc* edible.

2 *nm* (**a**) (*alimento*) foodstuff, comestible; **~s** foods, foodstuffs.

(**b**) (*Com*) **~s** groceries, provisions; **tienda de ~s** grocer's (shop), grocery (*US*).

cometa¹ *nm* (**a**) (*Astron*) comet. (**b**) (*) sweetener*, backhander*.

cometa² *nf* kite; **~ delta, ~ voladora** (*And*) hang-glider.

cometer [2a] *vt* (**a**) *crimen etc* to commit; *error* to make, commit. (**b**) *tarea etc* to entrust, commit (*a* to). (**c**) (*Ling*) *figura retórica* to use, employ.

cometido *nm* task, assignment; commitment.

comezón *nf* (**a**) (*lit*) itch, itching; (*de calor etc*) tingle, tingling sensation; **siento ~ en el brazo** my arm itches; my arm tingles. (**b**) (*fig*) itch (*por* for); **sentir ~ de** + *infin* to feel an itch to + *infin*.

comi* *nf* = **comisaría** (**a**).

comible *adj* eatable, (just) fit to eat.

cómic ['komik] *nm, pl* **cómics** ['komik] comic.

cómica *nf* (comic) actress; comedienne.

comicastro *nm* ham (actor)*.

comicidad *nf* humour, comedy, comicalness.

comicios *nmpl* elections, voting.

cómico 1 *adj* (**a**) (*gen*) comic(al), funny, amusing. (**b**) (*Teat*) comedy (*atr*); **autor ~** playwright. **2** *nm* (comic) actor; comedian.

comida *nf* (**a**) (*gen*) food; **~ basura** junk food; **~ para perros** dogfood; **~ rápida** fast food.

(**b**) (*acto*) eating; (*una ~*) meal; (*esp*) lunch, dinner; (*LAm*) supper, evening meal, dinner; **~ de coco*** brainwashing; **~ corrida** (*LAm*) fixed-price menu; **bendecir la ~** to say grace.

(**c**) (*en pensión etc*) board, keep; **~ y casa** board and lodging; **'C~s y camas'** (*letrero*) 'Rooms and Meals'.

comidilla *nf* (**a**) (*pasatiempo*) pastime, special interest. (**b**) **ser la ~ de la ciudad** (*etc*) to be the talk of the town.

comido *adj y ptp* (**a**) **estar ~** to have had lunch (*etc*); **vengo ~** I've had lunch (before coming). (**b**) **es ~ por servido** it doesn't pay, it's not worth while.

comience *nm* (*And*) = **comienzo.**

comienzo *nm* beginning, start; (*de proyecto etc*) birth, inception; (*Med etc*) onset; **al ~** at the start, at first; **en los ~s de este siglo** at the beginning of this century; **dar ~ a un acto** to begin a ceremony; **dar ~ a una carrera** to start a race (off).

comilón 1 *adj* greedy. **2** *nm*, **comilona¹** *nf* big eater, glutton.

comilona²* *nf* spread*, blow-out‡, feast.

comillas *nfpl* quotation marks, inverted commas, quotes (*US*); **en ~, entre ~** in inverted commas, in quotes (*US*).

cominero 1 *adj* fussy. **2** *nm*, **cominera** *nf* fusspot*, fussy person, milksop.

comino *nm* cumin, cumin seed; **no vale un ~** it's not worth tuppence; **no se me da un ~, (no) me importa un ~** I don't care two hoots (*de* about).

comiquero *adj* comic.

comisaría *nf* (**a**) (*policía*) police station. (**b**) (*Mil*) administrative office; (*Náut*) purser's office.

comisariado *nm* (**a**) commission. (**b**) (*Pol*) commissary.

comisariato *nm* administrative office.

comisario, -a *nm/f* commissioner; (*Mil*) administrative officer, service corps officer; (*Náut*) purser; (*de hipódromo*) steward; (*de exposición*) organizer; (*Pol*) commissar; **~ de carreras** course steward; **~ europeo** European commissioner; **~ parlamentario** parliamentary commissioner, ombudsman; **~ de policía** police superintendent, commissioner of police; **alto ~** high commissioner.

comiscar [1g] *vt* to nibble from time to time (at).

comisión *nf* (**a**) (*cometido*) assignment, task, commission; mission.

(**b**) (*Parl etc*: *junta*) committee; board, commission; (*Com, Fin*) board; **~ de encuesta** fact-finding committee, board of inquiry; **C~ Europea** European Commission; **~ mixta** joint committee; mixed commission; **Comisiones Obreras** Workers' Unions; **~ permanente** standing committee; **~ planificadora** planning board; **~ de seguimiento** watchdog committee.

(**c**) (*Com*: *pago*) commission; **~ porcentual** percentage commission (*sobre* on); **~ sobre las ventas** sales commission; **a ~** on a commission basis.

(**d**) (*acto*) commission; (*de atentado*) perpetration; **pecado de ~** sin of commission.

(**e**) **~ de servicio(s)** secondment; leave of absence.

comisionado, -a *nm/f* commissioner; (*Parl etc*) committee member; (*Com, Fin*) board member.

comisionar [1a] *vt* to commission.

comisionista *nmf* commission agent, person working on a commission basis.

comiso *nm* (*Jur*) (**a**) (*acto*) seizure, confiscation. (**b**) (*géneros*) confiscated goods.

comisquear [1a] *vt* = **comiscar.**

comistrajo *nm* bad meal, awful food; (*fig*) mess, hotchpotch.

comisura *nf* join; corner, angle; (*Anat*) commissure; **~ de los labios** corner of the mouth.

comité *nm* committee; **~ de dirección** steering committee; **~ ejecutivo** executive board; **~ de empresa** works committee, shop stewards' committee; **C~ de No Intervención** Non-Intervention Committee; **~ de redacción** drafting committee; editorial committee.

comitiva *nf* suite, retinue; train; procession; **~ fúnebre** cortège, funeral procession.

como 1 *adv* (*semejanza*) as, like; (*por ejemplo*) such as; as it were; (*más o menos*) about, approximately; **es ~ un pez** it's like a fish; **hay peces, ~ truchas y salmones** there are fish, such as trout and salmon; **juega ~ yo** he plays like I do; **toca ~ canta** she plays in much the same way as she sings, her playing is like her singing; **asistió ~ espectador** he attended as a spectator; **lo dice ~ juez** he says it (in his capacity) as a judge; **~ éste hay pocos** there are few like this; **vale más ~ poeta** he is better as a poet; **libre ~ estaba** free as he was; **la manera ~ sucedió** the way (in which) it happened; **había ~ cincuenta** there were about fifty; **vino ~ a las dos** (*LAm*) he came at about two o'clock; **sentía una ~ tristeza** she felt a sort of sadness; **fue así ~ comenzó la cosa** that was how the thing began, the thing started in that way; **tuvo resultados ~ no se habían conocido antes** it had results such as had never been known before; **pues tocar, ~ tocar, no sabe** if you mean really play, well, he doesn't.

2 *conj* (**a**) (+ *indic*: *ya que*) as, since; **~ no tenía dinero**

as (*o* since, because) I had no money; ~ **que** ... because ..., since ...; seeing that ...; it looks as if ...; **hacía ~ que no nos veía** he pretended not to see us.

(**b**) (+ *indic*: *en cuanto*) as soon as; **así ~ nos vio lanzó un grito** as soon as he saw us he shouted.

(**c**) (+ *subj*) ~ **si** ... as if ...

(**d**) (+ *subj*: *a menos que*) if, unless; provided that; ~ **no lo haga en seguida** unless he does it at once; ~ **sea** as the case may be; ~ **no sea para** + *infin* unless it be to + *infin*, except to + *infin*; ~ **vengas tarde no comerás** (*LAm*) if you come late you won't eat; **¡~ lo pierdas!** mind you don't lose it!, there'll be hell to pay if you lose it!; *V* **así, pronto, querer** *etc*.

cómo 1 *adv interrog* how?; why?, how is it that ...?; **¿~ lo hace?** how does he do it?; **¿~ son?** what are they like?, what do they look like?; **¿~ están mis nietos?** how are my grandchildren?; **¿~ estás?** how are you?; **¿~ es de alto?** how tall is it?, what height is it?; **¿a ~ son las peras?** how much are the pears?; **¿~ así?, ¿~ es eso?** how can that be?, how come?*; **¿~ no?** why not?; what do you mean?; **no sé ~ hacerlo** I don't know how to do it; **no veo ~** I don't see how; **no había ~ alcanzarlo** there was no way of reaching it.

2 *interj etc*: **¿~?** (*no entiendo*) I beg your pardon?, what?, eh?; (*sorpresa*) what was that?; (*enojo*) how dare you!; **¡y ~!** and how!, not half!*; **¡~ no!** (*esp LAm*) certainly!, of course!, with pleasure!; **¿~ no?** why not?; **¿~ 4 libros?** how do you mean, 4 books?; **¿~ qué no?** I don't see why not; what do you mean, 'no'?

3 *nm*: **el por qué y el ~ de** the whys and wherefores of.

cómoda *nf* chest of drawers; bureau.

cómodamente *adv* comfortably; conveniently.

comodidad *nf* (**a**) (*gen*) comfort; comfortableness; convenience; **pensar en su propia ~** to consider one's own convenience; **venga a su ~** come at your convenience; **vivir con ~** to live in comfort.

(**b**) **~es** comforts, amenities, pleasant things; facilities; **~es de la vida** good things of life.

(**c**) **~es** (*LAm Com*) commodities, goods.

comodín 1 *adj* (*And, Carib, Méx*) = **comodón. 2** *nm* (**a**) (*Naipes*) joker. (**b**) (*Mec etc*) useful gadget. (**c**) (*excusa*) pretext, regular excuse, standby. (**d**) (*Ling*) catch-all, useful vague word, all-purpose word (*o* phrase *etc*). (**e**) (*Inform*) wild card.

cómodo *adj* (**a**) *silla etc* comfortable; *cuarto* comfortable; cosy, snug, comfy*; *objeto* convenient. handy; *arreglo* convenient; *trabajo, tarea* agreeable.

(**b**) *persona* comfortable; **así estarás más ~** you'll be more comfortable this way; **ponerse ~** to make o.s. comfortable.

(**c**) (*satisfecho*) smug.

comodón *adj* (*regalón*) comfort-loving; (*pasivo*) easy-going, liking a quiet life; (*mimado*) spoiled, spoilt; **es muy ~** he'll do anything for a quiet life.

comodonería *nf* love of comfort; liking for a quiet life.

comodoro *nm* commodore.

comoquiera *conj* (*liter*) (**a**) ~ **que** ... (+ *indic*) since ..., in view of the fact that .... (**b**) ~ **que** ... (+ *subj*) in whatever way ...; ~ **que sea eso** however that may be, in whatever way that may be.

comp. *abr de* **compárese** compare, cp.

compa* *nm* (**a**) (*Pol*) comrade. (**b**) (*amigo*) pal*, mate.

compacidad *nf* compactness.

compactación *nf* compacting, compression.

compactar [1a] *vt* to compact, press together (*o* down *etc*), compress.

compacto 1 *adj* compact; dense; *líneas, hilos, tipo etc* close. **2** *nm* (*Elec etc*) compact disc; (*Mús*) compact hi-fi system.

compadecer [2d] **1** *vt* to pity, be sorry for; to sympathize with. **2 compadecerse** *vr*: ~ **con** to harmonize with, blend with; to agree with, fit, square with; ~ **de** = **1**.

compadrada *nf* (*Cono Sur*) cheek, insolence.

compadrazgo *nm* (**a**) (*condición*) kinship, *relationship through one's godparents*. (**b**) (*esp LAm*: *amistad*) close friendship.

compadre *nm* (**a**) (*padrino*) godfather *o* father (*with respect to each other*). (**b**) (*: *amigo*) (*esp LAm*) friend, pal*, buddy (*esp US*); (*prov*: *en oración directa*) friend. (**c**) (*Cono Sur*) (*jactancioso*) braggart; (*engreído*) show-off*; (*matón*) bully*.

compadrear [1a] *vi* (**a**) (*: *ser amigos*) to be pals*. (**b**) (*Cono Sur*: *jactarse*) to brag, show off; (*presumir*) to put on airs; (*amenazar*) to give threatening looks.

compadreo *nm* (*LAm*) companionship; close contact.

compadrito *nm* (*LAm*) = **compadre** (**c**).

compaginable *adj* compatible; **motivos difícilmente ~s** motives which it is hard to reconcile.

compaginación *nf* (*Cine*) continuity.

compaginar [1a] **1** *vt* (**a**) (*ordenar*) to arrange, put in order.

(**b**) (*Tip*) to make up.

(**c**) ~ **A con B** to reconcile A with B, bring A into line with B, adjust A and B.

2 compaginarse *vr* to agree, tally; ~ **con** to agree with, tally with, square with; (*colores*) to blend with; **no se compagina esa conducta con su carácter** such conduct does not fit in with (*o* square with) his character.

compañerismo *nm* comradeship, fellowship; companionship; (*Dep etc*) team spirit.

compañero, -a *nm/f* (**a**) (*gen*) companion; partner (*t Naipes, Dep*); mate; ~ **de armas** comrade-in-arms; ~ **de baile** dancing-partner; ~ **de cama** bedfellow; ~ **de candidatura** running mate; ~ **de clase** schoolmate, classmate; ~ **de cuarto** roommate; ~ **de infortunio** companion in misfortune; ~ **de juego** playmate; ~ **de piso** flatmate; ~ **de rancho** messmate; ~ **de trabajo** workmate; ~ **de viaje** fellow traveller (*t fig*); **es un ~ divertido** he's good company.

(**b**) **dos calcetines que no son ~s** two socks which do not match, two socks which do not make up a pair; **¿dónde está el ~ de éste?** where is the one that goes with this?, where is the other one (of the pair)?

compañía *nf* (**a**) (*gen*) company; **hacer ~ a uno** to keep sb company; **andar en malas ~s, frecuentar malas ~s** to keep bad company, have unsavoury companions.

(**b**) (*Com, Ecl, Teat etc*) company; **C~ de Jesús** Society of Jesus; **Pérez y C~** Perez and Company; ~ **de bandera** national company; ~ **inversionista** investment trust; ~ **naviera** shipping company; ~ **pública** public company; ~ **de seguros** insurance company; ~ **tenedora** holding company.

comparabilidad *nf* comparability.

comparable *adj* comparable (*a, con* to, with).

comparación *nf* comparison; **en ~ con** in comparison with, beside; **es superior a toda ~, no tiene ~** it is beyond compare, it is incomparable.

comparado *adj* (**a**) ~ **con** compared with, in comparison with, beside. (**b**) *estudio etc* comparative.

comparar [1a] *vt* to compare (*a, con* to, with); to liken (*con* to).

comparativo *adj, nm* (*Ling*) comparative.

comparecencia *nf* (*Jur*) appearance (in court); **su no ~** his non-appearance.

comparecer [2d] *vi* (*Jur*) to appear (in court); ~ **ante un juez** to appear before a judge.

comparecimiento *nm* = **comparecencia.**

comparencia *nf* (*Cono Sur*) = **comparecencia.**

comparendo *nm* (*Jur*) summons; subpoena.

comparsa 1 *nf* (*de carnaval etc*) group, procession; masquerade; **la ~** (*Teat*) the extras. **2** *nmf* (*Teat*) extra, supernumerary; (*Carib*: *bailadores*) dance team.

comparsería *nf* (*Teat*) extras, supernumeraries.

compartible *adj* which can be shared; *opinión* acceptable, readily shared.

compartimentación *nf* compartmentalization.

compartim(i)ento *nm* (**a**) (*acto*) division, sharing; distribution.

(**b**) (*Náut, Ferro etc*) compartment; ~ **de carga** (*Aer*) hold; ~ **estanco** watertight compartment.

compartir [3a] *vi* to divide (up), share (out); *opinión, responsabilidad etc* to share (*con* with); **no comparto ese criterio** I do not share that view.

compás *nm* (**a**) (*Mús*) measure, time; (*ritmo*) beat, rhythm; (*división*) bar; ~ **de 2 por 4** 2/4 time; ~ **de vals** waltz time; **a ~** in time; **al ~ de la música** in time to the music; **martillar a ~** to hammer rhythmically; **fuera de ~** off beat; **llevar el ~** to beat time, keep time; **perder el ~** to lose the beat; **entraron a los compases de un vals** they came in to the strains of a waltz; **mantenemos el ~ de espera** we are still waiting.

(**b**) (*Mat etc*: *t* ~ **de puntas**) compasses, pair of compasses.

(**c**) (*Náut etc*) compass.

compasado *adj* measured, moderate.

compasar [1a] *vt* (**a**) (*Mat*) to measure (with a compass). (**b**) *gastos, tiempo* to adjust. (**c**) (*Mús*) to divide into bars.

compasión *nf* pity, compassion; sympathy; **¡por ~!** for pity's sake!; **mover a uno a ~** to move sb to pity; **tener ~ de** to feel sorry for, take pity on; **tener pronta ~** to be quick to pity, be easily moved to pity.

compasivamente *adv* compassionately; pityingly; sympathetically, understandingly.

compasividad *nf* = **compasión**.

compasivo *adj* compassionate, full of pity; sympathetic, understanding.

compata‡ *nmf* = **compañero**.

compatibilidad *nf* compatibility.

compatibilización *nf* harmonization.

compatibilizar [1f] *vt* to harmonize, reconcile, bring into line, make compatible (*con* with).

compatible *adj* compatible (*con* with).

compatriota *nmf* compatriot, fellow countryman, fellow countrywoman.

compeler [2a] *vt* to compel; **~ a uno a** + *infin* to compel sb to + *infin*.

compendiar [1b] *vt* to abridge, condense, summarize.

compendio *nm* abridgement, condensed version; summary, abstract; compendium; **en ~** briefly, in brief.

compendiosamente *adv* briefly, succinctly.

compendioso *adj* condensed, abridged; brief, succinct.

compenetración *nf* (*fig*) mutual understanding, fellow feeling, natural sympathy; mutual influence.

compenetrarse [1a] *vr* (**a**) (*Quím etc*) to interpenetrate, fuse.

(**b**) (*fig*) to (come to) share each other's feelings; to undergo mutual influence; **~ de** to share the feeling of; to enter into the spirit of; to absorb, take in, become permeated by, undergo the pervasive influence of.

compensación *nf* (**a**) (*gen*) compensation; (*Jur*) redress, compensation; **en ~** in exchange, as compensation; **~ por despido** severance pay, redundancy payment. (**b**) (*Fin*) clearing; **cámara de ~** clearing house.

compensador *adj* compensating, compensatory.

compensar [1a] *vt persona* to compensate (*de* for); *pérdida* to compensate for, make up (for); *error etc* to redeem, make amends for; (*Mec etc*) to balance, adjust, equalize; **le compensaron con 100 dólares por los cristales rotos** they gave him 100 dollars' compensation for the broken windows.

compensatoriamente *adv* by way of compensation.

compensatorio *adj* compensatory.

competencia *nf* (**a**) (*rivalidad*) competition (*t Com*); rivalry; competitiveness; **~ desleal** unfair competition; **~ leal** fair trading; **a ~** vying with each other, as rivals; **en ~ con** in competition with; **estar en ~** to be in competition; **hacer ~ con** to compete against.

(**b**) (*aptitud*) competence (*t Jur*); aptitude; adequacy; suitability.

(**c**) (*esfera*) domain, field, province; **y otras cosas de su ~** and other things which concern him, and other things for which he is responsible; **no es de mi ~** that is not my responsibility; that is not (in) my field; **es de la ~ de ...** (*decisión*) it is at the discretion of ...

(**d**) (*Pol*) **~s** powers; **~s transferidas a las comunidades autónomas** powers transferred to the autonomous regions.

competente *adj* (**a**) (*Jur*) competent; proper, appropriate; **esto se elevará al ministerio ~** this will be sent to the appropriate ministry.

(**b**) (*apto*) competent; fit, adequate, suitable; **de fuente ~** from a reliable source; **ser ~ para un cargo** to be suitable for a post.

(**c**) *suma etc* adequate, proper.

competentemente *adv* (**a**) (*apropiadamente*) appropriately. (**b**) (*suficientemente*) competently; adequately, suitably.

competer [2a] *vi*: **~ a** to be the responsibility of, fall to; **le compete castigarlos** it is his job to punish them, it is up to him to punish them.

competición *nf* competition (*t Dep*); contest.

competido *adj carrera etc* hard-fought, close-run.

competidor 1 *adj* competing, rival. **2** *nm*, **competidora** *nf* competitor (*t Com*); rival (*a* for); opponent; (*TV etc*) contestant.

competir [3k] *vi* (**a**) (*gen*) to compete (*t Com, Dep*; *con* against, with; *en* in; *para* for).

(**b**) **~ con** (*fig*) to rival, vie with; **los dos cuadros compiten en belleza** the two pictures vie with each other in beauty; **en cuanto a resistencia A no compite con B** A cannot compete with B for stamina.

competitivamente *adv* competitively.

competitividad *nf* competitiveness.

competitivo *adj* competitive.

compilación *nf* compilation.

compilador(a) 1 *nm/f* (*persona*) compiler. **2** *nm* (*Inform*) compiler; **~ incremental** incremental compiler.

compilar [1a] *vt* to compile.

compincharse [1a] *vr* to band together, team up.

compinche *nm* pal*, chum*, buddy (*esp US*); **estar ~s** to be in cahoots (*con* with)*.

complacencia *nf* (**a**) (*placer*) pleasure, satisfaction.

(**b**) (*agrado*) willingness; **lo hizo con ~** he did it gladly.

(**c**) (*indulgencia*) indulgence, indulgent attitude; **tiene excesivas ~s con los empleados** he is too indulgent towards his employees.

(**d**) (*LAm*: *autosatisfacción*) complacency.

complacer [2w] **1** *vt persona* to please; *cliente etc* to help, oblige; *déspota* to humour; *deseo etc* to gratify, indulge; **nos complace que sea así** we are glad it is so; **¿en qué puedo ~le?** (*Com etc*) can I help you?, what can I do for you?

2 complacerse *vr*: **~ en** + *infin* to be pleased (*o* glad) to + *infin*; to take pleasure in + *ger*; **el Banco se complace en comunicar a su clientela que ...** the Bank is glad to tell its clients that ...

complacido *adj* pleased, satisfied; **me miró complacida** she gave me a grateful look; **quedamos ~s de la visita** we were pleased with our visit.

complaciente *adj* (**a**) *persona* kind, obliging, helpful; *mirada etc* cheerful; **ser ~ con** to be helpful to, be well-disposed towards. (**b**) *marido* complaisant.

complejidad *nf* complexity.

complejo 1 *adj* complex. **2** *nm* (**a**) (*Psic*) complex; **~ de culpa, ~ de culpabilidad** guilt complex; **~ de Edipo** Oedipus complex; **~ de inferioridad** inferiority complex; **~ persecutorio** persecution complex. (**b**) (*Téc*) complex; **~ deportivo** sports complex, sports hall; **~ industrial** industrial complex.

complementar [1a] *vt* to complement; to complete, make up, round off.

complementariamente *adv* in addition (*a* to), additionally.

complementario *adj* complementary; **visita complementaria** follow-up visit.

complemento *nm* (**a**) (*Mat etc*) complement.

(**b**) (*Ling*) complement, object; **~ directo** direct object; **~ indirecto** indirect object.

(**c**) (*esencial*) essential part, natural concomitant; **el vino es un ~ de la buena comida** wine is an essential concomitant to good food.

(**d**) (*culminación*) culmination; rounding-off, perfection; **sería el ~ de su felicidad** it would complete her happiness, it would be a crowning happiness to her.

(**e**) **~s** (*Aut, ~ de mujer etc*) accessories.

(**f**) (*Cine*) short, supporting feature.

(**g**) **oficial de ~** (*Mil*) reserve officer.

(**h**) (*pago*) **~ de destino** extra allowance (attached to a post); **~ salarial, ~ de sueldo** bonus, extra pay; **~ por peligrosidad** danger money.

completa *nf* (*Carib Culin*) full (cheap) meal.

completamente *adv* completely.

completar [1a] *vt* (*gen*) to complete; to round off, make up; to perfect; *pérdida* to make good; (*acabar, terminar*) to complete, finish.

completas *nfpl* (*Ecl*) compline.

completez *nf* completeness.

completo 1 *adj* (**a**) (*gen*) complete; (*acabado*) perfect, rounded, finished; *busca etc* thorough; *pensión, precio etc* inclusive, all-in; *comida* with all the trimmings; **por ~** completely, utterly; **fue un ~ fracaso** it was a complete (*o* total, utter) failure.

(**b**) *vehículo* full (up).

2 *nm* (**a**) **en la sesión estuvo el ~** all members were present at the meeting.

(**b**) (*Cono Sur Culin*) hot dog.

complexión *nf* (**a**) (*constitución*) constitution, make-up; (*temperamento*) temperament. (**b**) (*Anat*) build; **un hombre de ~ fuerte** a well-built man. (**c**) (*LAm*: *tez*) complexion.

complexionado *adj*: **bien ~** strong, tough, robust; **mal ~** weak, frail.

complexional *adj* constitutional; temperamental.

complicación *nf* complication, complexity; **una persona sin ~** an uncomplicated person; **han surgido complicaciones** complications have arisen.

complicado *adj* complicated, complex; *fractura etc* complex; *decoración etc* elaborate; *método* complicated, involved, intricate.

complicar [1g] **1** *vt* **(a)** *(gen)* to complicate.

(b) *persona* to involve *(en* in).

2 complicarse *vr* **(a)** *(gen)* to get complicated.

(b) ~ **en un asunto** to get involved *(o* entangled) in a matter.

cómplice *nmf* accomplice.

complicidad *nf* complicity, involvement *(en* in).

compló *nm, pl* **complós, complot** [kom'plo] *nm, pl* **complots** [kom'plo] plot; conspiracy; intrigue.

complotado, -a *nm/f* plotter, conspirator.

complotar [1a] *vi* to plot, conspire.

complutense *adj* of Alcalá de Henares.

componedor(a) *nm/f*: ~ **de huesos** bonesetter.

componenda *nf* **(a)** *(acuerdo)* compromise; (provisional) settlement, (temporary) arrangement. **(b)** *(pey)* shady deal.

componente 1 *adj* component, constituent. **2** *nm* *(Quím etc)* component; *(de bebida etc)* ingredient; *(Mec)* part, component; ~**s lógicos** *(Inform)* software; **un viento de** ~ **norte** a northerly wind.

componer [2q] **1** *vt* **(a)** *colección etc* to make up, put together, compose.

(b) *(elementos)* to compose, constitute, make up; *número* to make up; **componen el jurado 12 personas** 12 persons make up the jury, the jury consists of 12 persons.

(c) *(Liter, Mús etc)* to compose, write.

(d) *(Tip)* to set (up), compose.

(e) *bebida, comida* to prepare.

(f) *objeto roto* to mend, repair, fix; to overhaul; *hueso* to set; *(Med) estómago etc* to settle; to strengthen; *espíritu* to quieten, soothe; *abuso* to set to rights, correct.

(g) *riña* to settle, compose, resolve; *diferencias* to reconcile; *personas* to reconcile.

(h) *(asear)* to arrange; to tidy up, polish up, adorn; *persona* to dress up, deck out.

(i) *(Cono Sur, Méx: castrar)* to doctor*, neuter.

(j) *(And: hechizar)* to bewitch.

2 componerse *vr* **(a)** ~ **de** to consist of, be composed of, be made up of; **se compone de 6 partes** it consists of 6 parts.

(b) *(mujer etc)* to dress up; to tidy o.s. up; *(maquillarse)* to make up.

(c) ~ **con uno** to come to terms with sb, reach an agreement with sb.

(d) **componérselas** to manage, get along; to find a way; **componérselas para** + *infin* to manage to + *infin*, contrive to + *infin*; **¡allá se las componga!*** that's his funeral!*

(e) *(LAm Med)* to recover, get better; **las cosas se compondrán** everything will be all right.

componible *adj* **(a)** *objeto roto* repairable; worth mending. **(b)** *(que se puede conciliar)* reconcilable; capable of settlement.

comportable *adj* bearable.

comportamental *adj* behavioural.

comportamiento *nm* behaviour, conduct; *(Mec etc)* performance.

comportar [1a] **1** *vt* **(a)** *(aguantar)* to bear, endure, put up with.

(b) *(acarrear)* to involve, carry with it; to mean; **ello no comporta obligación alguna** it carries no obligation.

(c) *(And, Cono Sur: causar)* to entail, bring with it.

2 comportarse *vr* to behave; to comport o.s., conduct o.s.; ~ **como es debido** to behave properly.

comporte *nm* **(a)** = **comportamiento.** **(b)** *(porte)* bearing, carriage.

composición *nf* **(a)** *(en muchos sentidos, t Liter, Mús)* composition; *(Univ)* essay; ~ **de lugar** stocktaking; **hacer una** ~ **de lugar** to take stock (of one's situation).

(b) *(de riña)* settlement; *(de personas)* reconciliation; ~ **procesal** *(Jur)* out-of-court settlement.

(c) *(arreglo)* arrangement.

(d) *(acuerdo)* agreement.

(e) *(cualidad)* composure.

(f) *(Tip)* typesetting; ~ **por ordenador** computer typesetting.

compositor(a) *nm/f* **(a)** *(Mús)* composer. **(b)** *(Tip)* compositor. **(c)** *(Cono Sur: curandero)* quack doctor, bonesetter.

compost ['kompos] *nm* compost.

compostación *nf*, **compostaje** *nm* composting.

compostelano 1 *adj* of Santiago de Compostela.

2 *nm*, **compostelana** *nf* native *(o* inhabitant) of Santiago de Compostela; **los** ~**s** the people of Santiago de Compostela.

compostura *nf* **(a)** *(constitución)* composition; structure; make-up.

(b) *(Mec etc)* mending, repair, repairing; overhauling; **estar en** ~ to be undergoing repairs.

(c) *(Culin)* condiment, seasoning.

(d) *(arreglo)* arrangement; tidying, polishing, adornment.

(e) *(acuerdo)* arrangement, agreement; settlement.

(f) *(cualidad) (serenidad)* composure; *(discreción)* discretion, good sense; *(modestia)* modesty; **perder la** ~ to lose one's composure.

compota *nf* stewed fruit, preserve, compote; ~ **de manzanas** *(etc)* stewed apples *(etc)*.

compotera *nf* dessert dish.

compra *nf* **(a)** *(acto)* purchase, buying; ~ **al contado** cash purchase; ~ **a crédito** buying on credit; ~ **a plazos** hire purchase; **ir de** ~**s, ir a la** ~ to go shopping, shop; **hacer la** ~ to do the shopping.

(b) *(artículo)* purchase; ~**s** purchases, shopping; **es una buena** ~ it's a good buy.

comprador(a) *nm/f* buyer, purchaser; *(en tienda)* shopper, customer; ~ **principal** head buyer.

comprar [1a] *vt* **(a)** *(gen)* to buy, purchase *(a, de* from); ~ **al contado** to pay cash for; ~ **al fiado** to buy on credit; ~ **a plazos,** ~ **a cuotas** *(LAm)* to buy on hire purchase, pay for in instalments.

(b) *(fig)* to buy off, bribe; to win over, secure the allegiance of.

compraventa *nf* **(a)** *(acto)* buying and selling, dealing; *(negocio de* ~) second-hand shop. **(b)** *(Jur)* contract of sale.

comprender [2a] *vti* **(a)** *(incluir)* to comprise, include; *(abarcar)* to take in; *(extenderse a)* to extend to; *(consistir en)* to consist of; **servicio no comprendido** service not included; **todo comprendido** everything included, all in.

(b) *(entender)* to understand; to see; to realize; ~ **que ...** to understand that ..., see that ...; to realize that ...; **¿comprendes?** see?, understand?; **¡comprendido!** all right!, sure!; agreed!; **¡ya comprendo!** I see!, now I get it!; **no comprendo cómo** I don't see how; **comprendo su actitud** I understand his attitude; **cuando comprendió que no iba a ayudarle** when he realized *(o* saw) I was not going to help him; **compréndase bien que ...** let it be clearly understood that ...; **compréndanme Vds** let's be clear about this; **hacerse** ~ to make o.s. understood.

comprensible *adj* understandable, comprehensible *(para* to); **no es** ~ **que ...** it is incomprehensible that ..., I *(etc)* cannot understand how ...

comprensiblemente *adv* understandably.

comprensión *nf* **(a)** *(lo inclusivo)* comprehensiveness, inclusiveness; inclusion.

(b) *(acto, facultad)* understanding, comprehension; grasp; **ejercicio de** ~ **auditiva** listening comprehension test.

(c) *(emoción)* understanding (attitude); sympathy, tolerance, kindness.

comprensivo *adj* **(a)** *(inclusivo)* comprehensive, inclusive; all-embracing; **un bloque** ~ **de 50 viviendas** a block containing 50 flats.

(b) *persona, actitud* understanding; sympathetic, tolerant, kindly.

compresa *nf* compress; ~ **higiénica** sanitary towel, sanitary napkin *(US)*.

compresibilidad *nf* compressibility.

compresible *adj* compressible.

compresión *nf* compression.

compresor *nm* compressor.

comprimible *adj* compressible.

comprimido 1 *adj* compressed. **2** *nm* *(Med)* pill, tablet; ~ **para dormir** sleeping pill.

comprimir [3a] **1** *vt* **(a)** *(gen)* to compress *(t Téc; en* into); *(prensar)* to squeeze (down *etc*), press (down *etc*); *(condensar)* to condense.

(b) *(fig)* to control, restrain; *lágrimas* to keep back.

2 comprimirse *vr* *(fig)* to control o.s., contain o.s.; **tuve que comprimirme para no reír** I had to keep myself from laughing; **tendremos que comprimirnos** *(Fin)* we shall have to restrict ourselves.

comprobable *adj* verifiable, capable of being checked; **un alegato fácilmente** ~ an allegation which is easy to check.

comprobación *nf* checking, verification; proof; **en** ~ **de ello** in proof whereof, as proof of what I *(etc)* say; **de difícil** ~ hard to check, difficult to prove.

comprobador *nm* tester; ~ **de lámparas** valve tester.

comprobante 1 *adj*: **documento ~** supporting document; **documentos ~s de ello** documents in proof thereof.

2 *nm* proof, supporting document; (*Com*) receipt, voucher.

comprobar [1l] *vt* (**a**) (*averiguar*) to check, verify; (*probar*) to prove; (*demostrar*) to confirm, show; **~ que** ... to check that ...; to show that ..., establish that ...; **~ si** ... to check whether ...

(**b**) (*Mec etc*) to check, test.

comprometedor *adj* compromising.

comprometer [2a] **1** *vt* (**a**) *persona* to compromise; to embarrass, put in an awkward situation; *cómplice etc* to involve, implicate; **aquellas cartas le comprometieron** those letters compromised him.

(**b**) (*arriesgar*) to risk; (*poner en peligro*) to endanger, imperil, jeopardize; **~ la reputación** to risk one's reputation; **~ la neutralidad del país** to imperil one's country's neutrality.

(**c**) **~ a uno a algo** to hold sb to sth, pin sb down to sth; **~ a uno a** + *infin* to force sb to + *infin*, make sb feel obliged to + *infin*.

(**d**) (*Com, Jur*) to agree formally; *habitación, plaza etc* to book, reserve.

2 comprometerse *vr* (**a**) (*gen*) to compromise o.s.; to get involved (*en* in).

(**b**) **~ a** + *infin* to undertake to + *infin*, promise to + *infin*, engage to + *infin*; **se compromete a todo** he'll say yes to anything.

comprometido *adj* (**a**) *situación etc* awkward, embarrassing.

(**b**) *escritor etc* engagé, engaged, committed; **no ~** uncommitted.

(**c**) **estar ~** to be engaged; to be involved; to be at stake; **estar ~ para** + *infin* to be engaged to + *infin*.

compromisario, -a *nm/f* convention delegate.

compromiso *nm* (**a**) (*obligación*) obligation; commitment; (*promesa*) undertaking, pledge, promise; (*cita*) engagement, date; (*Pol etc*) engagement; **por ~** out of a sense of duty; **libre de ~, sin ~** without obligation; **adquirir un ~ de** + *infin* to commit o.s. to + *infin*, take on an obligation for + *ger*; **atender** (*o* **cumplir**) **sus ~s** to meet one's obligations; **hacer honor a sus ~s** to honour one's pledges; **tener muchos ~s** to have many commitments; **¿tienes ~ para esta noche?** have you anything on this evening?, are you booked up tonight?

(**b**) (*acuerdo*) agreement; **~ histórico** epoch-making deal; **~ matrimonial** engagement (to marry); **~ verbal** verbal agreement, gentlemen's agreement.

(**c**) (*aprieto*) awkward situation, jam, fix; predicament; **estar en un fuerte ~** to be in a real difficulty; **poner a uno en un ~** to place sb in an embarrassing situation; **poner a uno en el ~ de** + *infin* to put sb in the position of + *ger*; **salir de un ~** to get out of a difficulty.

(**d**) (*transacción*) compromise.

compuerta *nf* (*de canal*) sluice, floodgate; (*en puerta etc*) hatch; (*Inform*) gate.

compuesto 1 *ptp de* **componer**; **estar ~ de** to be composed of, consist of, be made up of.

2 *adj* (**a**) (*Quím, Ling, Mat, interés etc*) compound; *flor, material* composite.

(**b**) *persona etc* elegant, dressed up; tidy, neat.

(**c**) (*fig*) composed, calm.

3 *nm* (**a**) (*t Quím*) compound; preparation; composite material; **~ químico** chemical compound.

(**b**) (*Ling*) compound (word).

compulsa *nf* (**a**) (*acto*) checking, comparison. (**b**) (*Jur*) attested copy, certified true copy.

compulsar [1a] *vt* (**a**) (*comparar*) to collate, compare. (**b**) (*Jur*) to make an attested copy of.

compulsión *nf* compulsion.

compulsivamente *adv* compulsively.

compulsivo *adj* compulsory; compulsive.

compulsorio *adj* (*LAm*) compulsory.

compunción *nf* (*arrepentimiento*) compunction, regret, remorse; (*compasión*) pity; (*tristeza*) sorrow.

compungido *adj* remorseful, contrite, sorry; sad, sorrowful.

compungir [3c] **1** *vt* to make remorseful, arouse feelings of contrition in.

2 compungirse *vr* (*arrepentirse*) to feel remorseful (*por* about, because of), feel sorry (*por* for); (*entristecerse*) to feel sad, be sorrowful.

compurgar [1h] *vt* (*And, Cono Sur, Méx*) *ofensa* to purge; (*Méx Jur*) *pena* to serve out.

computación *nf* = **cómputo**.

computacional *adj* computational.

computador *nm*, **computadora** *nf* computer; **~ central** mainframe computer; **~ digital** digital computer; **~ de (sobre)mesa** desktop computer.

computadorización *nf* computerization.

computadorizado *adj* computerized.

computadorizar [1f] *vt* to computerize.

computar [1a] *vt* to calculate, compute, reckon (*en* at).

computerización *nf* computerization.

computerizado *adj* computerized.

computerizar [1f] *vt* to computerize.

computista *nmf* computer user.

cómputo *nm* (*cálculo*) calculation, computation, reckoning; (*Méx*: *suma*) total; **según nuestros ~s** according to our calculations.

comulgante *nmf* communicant.

comulgar [1h] **1** *vt* to administer communion to. **2** *vi* (**a**) (*Ecl*) to take communion, receive communion. (**b**) **~ con** to like, accept, agree with; to sympathize with; to share; **hay varias cosas con las que ella no comulga** there are several things she doesn't agree with.

comulgatorio *nm* communion rail, altar rail.

común 1 *adj* (**a**) (*gen*) common (*a* to); (*conjunto*) joint; (*público*) public, belonging to all, held in common; *género, fosa etc* common; **los intereses comunes** common interests; **de ~ con** in common with; **A no tiene nada de ~ con B** A has nothing in common with B; **en ~** in common; joint, mutual; **hacer algo en ~** to do sth jointly (*o* together).

(**b**) *distribución etc* common; *costumbre, opinión* common, widespread, general; **es costumbre muy ~** it is a very widespread custom; **la planta es ~ en la provincia** the plant is common in the province.

(**c**) *cualidad* common, ordinary; **fuera de lo ~** out of the ordinary; **por lo ~** generally.

2 *nm* (**a**) **el ~** the community, the people (at large); **bienes del ~** communal property, public property.

(**b**) **el ~ de las gentes** most people, the common run of people.

(**c**) (*wáter*) toilet.

(**d**) **los Comunes** (*Brit Pol*) the Commons.

(**e**) **Comunes** (*Escol*) subjects taken in common during first two years of the *bachillerato* course.

comuna *nf* (**a**) (*comunidad*) commune. (**b**) (*LAm*: *municipio*) municipality, town council.

comunacho, -a *nm/f* (*Cono Sur*: *pey*) commie*.

comunal *adj* communal; community (*atr*).

comunalmente *adv* communally; as a community.

comunicable *adj* (**a**) *noticias etc* communicable, that can be communicated. (**b**) *persona* approachable; sociable.

comunicación *nf* (**a**) (*gen*) communication; contact; **las comunicaciones están rotas** communications are broken; **no hemos tenido más ~ con él** we have had no further contact with him, we have heard nothing further from him.

(**b**) (*mensaje*) message; (*informe*) report; (*de congreso etc*) paper.

(**c**) (*Telec*) connection, contact; **póngame en ~ con el Sr Q** please put me through to Mr Q.

(**d**) (*Liter*) rhetorical question.

(**e**) **no hay ~ entre los dos pueblos** (*Méx*: *camino*) there's no way of getting from one town to the other.

comunicacional *adj* communication (*atr*); of communication, for communication.

comunicado 1 *adj cuartos* connected, interconnecting. **2** *nm* communiqué; **~ final** final communiqué; **~ a la prensa** press-release.

comunicador(a) *nm/f* communicator.

comunicante *nmf* correspondent, letter-writer; informant; (*de congreso*) speaker.

comunicar [1g] **1** *vt* (**a**) *información* to communicate, tell, pass on (*a* to); *noticia* to convey, tell (*a* to); *mensaje* to give, pass (*a* to); *enfermedad etc* to carry; to give (*a* to); *costumbre* to transmit, pass on; *legado etc* to pass on (*a* to), bestow (*a* on); *temor etc* to communicate (*a* to); **nos comunicó su miedo** he affected us with his fear, his fear infected us.

(**b**) *cuartos, lagos etc* to connect, join, open a way between; **cuartos comunicados** connecting rooms.

(**c**) **¿me comunica con el Sr Gomez?** (*Telec*) may I speak to Mr Gomez?

2 *vi* (**a**) (*informar*) to send a report (*de* from); **comunican desde Lisboa que ...** it is reported from Lisbon that ...

(**b**) (*Telec*) **estar comunicando** to be engaged, be busy

(*US*).

(**c**) (*Arquit*) ~ **con** to connect with; to open into.

3 comunicarse *vr* (**a**) (*personas*) to communicate (with each other); to be in touch, correspond; **nos comunicamos nuestras impresiones** we exchanged impressions.

(**b**) (*noticia, enfermedad etc*) to pass, be transmitted; **el miedo se comunicó a todos** the fear affected everybody.

(**c**) (*Arquit*) to be connected, lead into each other, intercommunicate.

(**d**) (*Ferro etc*) **la colonia está bien comunicada por tren** the development has good train services; **pueblos bien comunicados** towns having good communications.

comunicatividad *nf* communicativeness; powers of communication.

comunicativo *adj* (**a**) *persona* communicative; approachable, sociable. (**b**) *risa etc* infectious.

comunicología *nf* communication theory.

comunicólogo, -a *nm/f* communication theorist.

comunidad *nf* (**a**) (*gen*) community; (*sociedad*) society, corporation; (*Ecl*) community; (*And*) commune (of free Indians); **C~ Europea** European Community; **C~ Europea del Carbón y del Acero** European Coal and Steel Community; **C~ Británica de Naciones** British Commonwealth; ~ **autónoma** autonomous region; ~ **lingüística** speech community; ~ **de vecinos** residents' association; **de ~, en ~** jointly, together, in common. (**b**) (*: *de piso*) service charge, charge for communal services.

comunión *nf* communion.

comunismo *nm* communism.

comunista 1 *adj* communist(ic). **2** *nmf* communist; ~ **libertario** libertarian communist.

comunitariamente *adv* communally.

comunitario 1 *adj* (**a**) (*gen*) community (*atr*); communal. (**b**) (*CE*) Community (*atr*), (of the) Common Market. **2** *nm* member nation (of the EC).

comunizar [1f] *vt* to communize.

comúnmente *adv* commonly; usually, generally; frequently.

con *prep* (**a**) (*gen*) with; **atado ~ cuerda** tied with string; ~ **su ayuda** with his help; **andar ~ muletas** to walk on (*o* with) crutches; **me escribo ~ ella** I write to her; **¡~ lo difícil que es todo esto!** what with all this being so difficult; **once ~ siete** eleven point seven (*11.7*); **un dólar ~ cincuenta** one dollar fifty cents; **murió ~ 60 años** she died at the age of 60.

(**b**) (*a pesar de*) in spite of; ~ **tantas dificultades, no se descorazonó** in spite of all the difficulties he was not discouraged; ~ **ser su madre, le odia** even though she is his mother she hates him.

(**c**) (*t* **para** ~) to, towards; **amable ~ todos** kind to everybody; **ser insolente ~ el jefe** to be disrespectful to the leader.

(**d**) (+ *infin*) ~ **llegar tan tarde** (by) arriving so late; ~ **confesarlo se libró del castigo** by owning up he escaped punishment; ~ **decirle que no voy** when I tell you I'm not going; ~ **llegar a las 6 estará bien** if you come at 6 it will be all right.

(**e**) ~ **que** (+ *indic*) and so, so then; whereupon; **¿~ que Vd es el jefe?** so you're the boss?; ~ **que fuimos a la cama** and so we went to bed.

(**f**) ~ **que** (+ *subj*) by; if; providing that.

CONADEP [ko'naðep] *nf* (*Argentina Pol*) *abr de* **Comisión Nacional sobre la Desaparición de Personas.**

conato *nm* attempt; endeavour, effort (*de* + *infin* to + *infin*); ~ **de robo** attempted robbery; **hacer un ~ de** + *infin* to make an attempt to + *infin*; **poner ~ en algo** to put an effort into a task.

concatenación *nf* concatenation, linking; ~ **de circunstancias** chain of circumstances.

concatenar [1a] *vt* to link together, concatenate.

concavidad *nf* concavity, hollow, cavity.

cóncavo 1 *adj* concave; hollow. **2** *nm* hollow, cavity.

concebible *adj* conceivable, thinkable; **no es ~ que ...** it is unthinkable that ...

concebir [3k] **1** *vt* (*gen*) to conceive; to imagine; (*comprender*) to understand; ~ **esperanzas** to nourish hopes; to become hopeful; ~ **una antipatía hacia** (*o* **por**) to take a dislike to; **no concibo que ...** I cannot understand how (*o* why) ...

2 *vi* (*Bio*) to conceive, become pregnant.

conceder [2a] *vt* (*gen*) to concede, grant, admit; *honor* to confer, bestow (*a* on); *atención etc* to pay; *descuento* to allow; *premio* to award (*a* to).

concejal(a) *nm/f* town councillor.

concejalía *nf* post of town councillor; seat on the town council.

concejil *adj* relating to a town council; municipal, public.

concejo *nm* council; ~ (**municipal**) town council.

concelebrar [1a] *vt* to concelebrate.

concentración *nf* (**a**) (*gen*) concentration; (*Pol etc*) gathering, meeting, rally; (*Dep*) team meeting, team briefing. (**b**) ~ **escolar** rural school at centre of a catchment area. (**c**) (*LAm Com*) merger.

concentrado 1 *adj* concentrated. **2** *nm* (**a**) (*Culin etc*) extract, concentrate; ~ **de carne** meat extract. (**b**) (*Pol*) demonstrator.

concentrar [1a] **1** *vt* to concentrate (*en un lugar* in a place, *en una escena* on a scene).

2 concentrarse *vr* (**a**) (*Mil etc*) to gather (together), assemble.

(**b**) ~ **a** + *infin* (*fig*) to concentrate on + *ger*; **el interés se concentra en esta lucha** the interest is centred on this fight.

concéntrico *adj* concentric.

concepción *nf* (**a**) (*Bio etc*) conception; **la Inmaculada C~** the Immaculate Conception. (**b**) (*facultad*) understanding. (**c**) (*idea*) conception, idea.

conceptismo *nm* conceptism (*witty, allusive and involved style, esp 17th century*).

conceptista 1 *adj* witty, allusive and involved. **2** *nmf* writer in the style of *conceptismo*.

concepto *nm* (**a**) (*idea*) concept, conception; idea, notion; thought; **un ~ grandioso** a bold conception, a bold plan; **formarse un ~ de algo** to get an idea of sth.

(**b**) (*opinión*) view, opinion; judgement; **en mi ~** in my view; **formarse un ~ de uno** to form an opinion of sb; **¿qué ~ has formado de él?** what do you think of him?; **tener buen ~ de uno, tener un buen ~ a uno** to think highly of sb.

(**c**) (*de narración etc*) heading, section; **bajo todos (los) ~s, por todos ~s** from every point of view; in every way, in every respect; **bajo ningún ~** in no way; **por dicho ~** for this reason; **en ~ de, por ~ de** as, by way of; under the heading of; **se le pagó esa cantidad por ~ de derechos** he was paid that amount as royalties; **deducciones por ~ de seguro** deductions for social security; **por ningún ~** in no way.

(**d**) (*Liter*) conceit.

conceptual *adj* conceptual.

conceptualización *nf* conceptualization.

conceptualizar [1f] *vt* to conceptualize.

conceptuar [1e] *vt* to think, judge, deem; **le conceptúo poco apto para eso** I think him unsuited for that; ~ **a uno de** (*o* **como, por**) ... to regard sb as ..., deem sb to be ...; **no está bien conceptuado actualmente** he is not well thought of at present.

conceptuosamente *adv* wittily; (*pey*) over-elaborately, in a mannered way.

conceptuoso *adj* witty, full of conceits; (*pey*) overelaborate, mannered.

concerniente *adj*: ~ **a** concerning, relating to; **en lo ~ a** with regard to, as for.

concernir [3i; *defectivo*] *vt* to concern.

concertación *nf* (**a**) (*acto*) harmonizing; coordination; reconciliation; ~ **social** social harmony; **política de ~** consensus politics. (**b**) (*pacto*) agreement, pact.

concertadamente *adv* methodically, systematically; in an orderly fashion; harmoniously.

concertado 1 *adj* (**a**) (*metódico*) methodical, systematic; (*ordenado*) orderly; (*armonioso*) harmonious. (**b**) (*Pol*) officially approved; state-assisted. **2** *nm*, **concertada** *nf* (*And*) contract worker.

concertar [1j] **1** *vt* (**a**) (*Mús*) to harmonize, bring into harmony; to tune (up).

(**b**) *esfuerzos* to coordinate; *diferencias* to adjust, bring into line, reconcile; *personas* to achieve agreement between; to reconcile; ~ **a varias personas para que ...** to get various people to agree to + *infin*.

(**c**) (*acordar*) to agree to; *acuerdo, tratado* to conclude (*con* with); *trato, reunión etc* to arrange, fix up; *precio* to agree, fix (*en* at); ~ **una venta en 20 dólares** to agree to sell sth for 20 dollars, agree to a sale price of 20 dollars; **hemos concertado el piso en sesenta mil pesetas** we have agreed to rent the flat for 60000 pesetas; ~ **hacer algo** to agree to do sth.

2 *vi* (**a**) (*Mús*) to harmonize, be in tune.

(**b**) (*fig*) to agree (*t Gram*).

3 concertarse *vr* (**a**) (*Mús etc*) to harmonize.

(**b**) (*personas*) to reach agreement, come to terms; ~ **para** + *infin* (*pey*) to conspire together to + *infin*, act in concert to + *infin*.

concertina[1] *nf* (*instrumento*) concertina.

concertino, -a[2] *nm/f* (*persona*) first violin, leader (of the orchestra), concertmaster (*US*).

concertista *nmf* soloist, solo performer; ~ **de guitarra** concert guitarist; ~ **de piano** concert pianist.

concesión *nf* concession; grant(ing); allowance; award; (*Com*) concession.

concesionario, -a *nm/f* concessionaire, concessionary, licensee, authorized dealer; outlet; ~ **exclusivo** sole agency, exclusive dealership.

concesivo *adj* concessive.

conciencia *nf* (**a**) (*aspecto moral*) conscience; moral sense; conscientiousness; ~ **doble** double personality; **a** ~ conscientiously; **hecho a** ~ solidly built, well built; **en** ~ with a clear conscience; honestly, in truth; **te lo digo en** ~ I say it with my hand on my heart; **obrar en** ~ to act honourably; **con** ~ **limpia, con** ~ **tranquila** with a clear conscience; **ancho de** ~ not overscrupulous; **anchura de** ~ lack of scruple; **libertad de** ~ freedom of worship; **hombre sin** ~ unscrupulous person; **empezó a remorderle la** ~ his conscience began to prick him; **tener mala** ~, **tener la** ~ **negra** to have a bad conscience; **tener la** ~ **tranquila** to have a clear conscience.

(**b**) (*conocimiento*) knowledge, awareness, consciousness; ~ **de clase** class-consciousness; **a** ~ **de que ...** fully aware that ..., in the certain knowledge that ...; **tener plena** ~ **de** to be fully aware of; **tomar** ~ **de** to become aware of; **tomar** ~ **de que ...** to become aware that ...

concienciación *nf* arousal, awakening, (process of) becoming aware; conscience-raising.

concienciado *adj* politically aware, socially aware.

concienciar [1b] **1** *vt* (*despertar*) to arouse, awaken, make aware; (*sensibilizar*) to raise the conscience of; (*condicionar*) to prepare (mentally); (*convencer*) to convince, persuade. **2 concienciarse** *vr* to be aroused (*de* to), become aware (*de* of); to convince o.s. (*de que* that).

concienzar [1f] *vt* = **concienciar**.

concienzudamente *adv* conscientiously, painstakingly, thoroughly.

concienzudo *adj* conscientious, painstaking, thorough.

concierto *nm* (**a**) (*acuerdo*) concert, agreement; order; harmony; **de** ~ **con** in concert with; **quedar de** ~ **acerca de** to be in agreement with regard to.

(**b**) (*Mús: función*) concert; ~ **de arias** song recital; ~ **de cámara** chamber concert; ~ **sinfónico** symphony concert.

(**c**) (*Mús: obra*) concerto.

conciliable *adj* reconcilable; **dos opiniones no fácilmente ~s** two opinions which it is not easy to reconcile.

conciliábulo *nm* secret meeting, secret discussion.

conciliación *nf* (**a**) (*acto*) conciliation; reconciliation. (**b**) (*afinidad*) affinity, similarity.

conciliador 1 *adj* conciliatory. **2** *nm*, **conciliadora** *nf* conciliator.

conciliar[1] [1b] **1** *vt* (**a**) *enemigos etc* to reconcile; *actitudes etc* to harmonize, bring into line, blend.

(**b**) *respeto, antipatía etc* to win, gain; ~ **el sueño** to (manage to) get to sleep.

2 conciliarse *vr* = **1**(**b**).

conciliar[2] **1** *adj* (*Ecl*) of a council, council (*atr*), conciliar. **2** *nm* council member.

conciliatorio *adj* conciliatory.

concilio *n* (*Ecl*) council; **el Segundo C~ Vaticano** the Second Vatican Council.

concisamente *adv* concisely, briefly, tersely.

concisión *nf* concision, conciseness, brevity.

conciso *adj* concise, brief, terse.

concitar [1a] *vt* (**a**) (*provocar*) to stir up, incite (*contra* against). (**b**) (*reunir*) to gather, assemble, bring together.

conciudadano, -a *nm/f* fellow citizen.

conclave *nm*, **cónclave** *nm* conclave.

concluir [3g] **1** *vt* (**a**) (*terminar*) to conclude, finish.

(**b**) (*deducir*) to infer, deduce; *consecuencia etc* to reach, arrive at.

2 *vi* to end, conclude, finish; ~ **de** + *infin* to finish + *ger*; ~ **por** + *infin* to end up by + *ger*; ~ **con,** ~ **en,** ~ **por** *palabra etc* to end in; **todo ha concluido** it's all over; **¡vamos a ~ de una vez!** let's get it over.

3 concluirse *vr* to end, conclude.

conclusión *nf* conclusion; **en** ~ in conclusion, lastly, finally; **extraiga Vd las conclusiones oportunas** draw your own conclusions; **llegar a la** ~ **de que ...** to come to the conclusion that ...

concluyente *adj* conclusive; decisive; unanswerable.

concluyentemente *adv* conclusively; decisively; unanswerably.

concolón *nm* (*LAm Culin*) scrapings.

concomitante *adj* concomitant.

conconete *nm* (*Méx*) child, little one.

concordancia *nf* (**a**) (*cualidad*) concordance; harmony. (**b**) (*Ling*) concord, agreement. (**c**) (*Mús*) harmony. (**d**) **~s** (*Liter*) concordance.

concordante *adj* concordant.

concordar [1l] **1** *vt* to reconcile; to bring into line; (*Ling*) to make agree.

2 *vi* to agree (*con* with), tally (*con* with), correspond (*con* to); (*Ling*) to agree; **esto no concuerda con los hechos** this does not square with (*o* fit in with) the facts; **los dos concuerdan en sus gustos** the two agree in their tastes, the two have the same tastes.

concordato *nm* concordat.

concorde *adj*: **estar ~(s)** to be agreed, be in agreement; **estar** ~ **en** + *infin* to agree to + *infin*; **poner a dos personas ~s** to bring about agreement between two people.

concordia *nf* (**a**) (*armonía*) concord, harmony, agreement; conformity. (**b**) (*anillo*) double finger-ring. (**c**) **Línea de la C~** (*Cono Sur*) frontier between Chile and Peru.

concreción *nf* concretion; (*Med*) stone; **la falta de** ~ **del dominio español** (*Dep*) the failure of the Spaniards to turn their dominance into goals.

concretamente *adv* particularly, specifically; exactly; to be exact; ~, ... in short ..., in a word ..., to cut a long story short ...; **se refirió** ~ **a dos** he referred specifically to two; **no es** ~ **una fiesta** it's not exactly a party; ~ **eran 39** to be exact there were 39.

concretar [1a] **1** *vt* (**a**) (*hacer más concreto*) to make concrete, make (more) specific; (*especificar*) to specify; *idea etc* to express in concrete terms; *problema, pega* to pinpoint, put one's finger on; (*reducir a lo esencial*) to reduce to essentials, boil down; **concreta sus esperanzas a ganar el premio** he is concentrating all his hopes on winning the prize; **concretemos, para** ~ let us be more specific, let's come down to details; **vamos a** ~ **los puntos esenciales** let us sum up the essential points.

(**b**) *situación* to capitalize on, turn to advantage.

2 concretarse *vr* (**a**) (*gen*) to become (more) definite; ~ **a** to come down specifically to.

(**b**) ~ **a** + *infin* to limit o.s. to + *ger*, confine o.s. to + *ger*; to concentrate on + *ger*.

concretizar [1f] *vt* = **concretar**.

concreto 1 *adj* (*gen*) concrete; (*específico*) definite, actual, particular, specific; **en este caso** ~ in this particular instance; **no me dijo ninguna hora concreta** he didn't tell me any definite (*o* particular) time; **en** ~ to sum up; exactly, specifically; to be exact (*o* precise); **en** ~ **había 7** there were 7 to be exact; **no hay nada en** ~ there's nothing you can put your finger on, there's nothing definite.

2 *nm* (**a**) (*gen*) concretion.

(**b**) (*LAm: hormigón*) concrete.

concubina *nf* concubine.

concubinato *nm* concubinage.

concúbito *nm* copulation.

conculcar [1g] *vt* to infringe (on); *ley* to break, violate.

concupiscencia *nf* (**a**) (*codicia*) greed, acquisitiveness. (**b**) (*lujuria*) lustfulness, concupiscence.

concupiscente *adj* (**a**) (*avaro*) greedy, acquisitive. (**b**) (*lujurioso*) lewd, lustful, concupiscent.

concurrencia *nf* (**a**) (*coincidencia etc*) concurrence; simultaneity, coincidence.

(**b**) (*reunión*) crowd, gathering, assembly; (*público*) spectators, public, audience; (*asistencia*) attendance, turnout; **había una numerosa** ~ there was a big attendance, there was a large crowd (present).

(**c**) (*Com*) competition.

concurrente 1 *adj* (**a**) *suceso etc* concurrent.

(**b**) (*Com etc*) competing.

2 *nm* (**a**) (*asistente*) person present, person attending; ~ **al cine** cinemagoer, moviegoer (*US*); **los ~s** those present, those in the audience (*etc*).

(**b**) (*rival*) competitor.

concurrido *adj lugar* crowded; much frequented; *calle* busy, crowded; *función* popular, well-attended, full (of people).

concurrir [3a] *vi* (**a**) (*unirse: caminos etc*) to meet, come together (*en* at).

(**b**) (*reunirse*: *personas*) to meet, gather, assemble (*a* at, *en* in); **~ a un baile** to go to a dance, attend a dance; **~ a las urnas** to go to the polls; **concurren a la misma tertulia** they go to the same group.

(**c**) (*contribuir*) to contribute; **~ a la derrota** to contribute to the defeat; **~ al éxito de una empresa** to contribute to the success of an enterprise; **~ con su dinero** to contribute one's money; **~ en una empresa** to cooperate in an undertaking.

(**d**) (*cualidades etc*) to be found, be present; **concurren en ella muchas buenas cualidades** she has many good qualities.

(**e**) **~ en una opinión** to concur in an opinion, agree with an opinion.

(**f**) (*sucesos*) to coincide (*con* with).

(**g**) (*Com*) to compete; **~ a un mercado** to compete in a market.

(**h**) (*Dep etc*) to compete (*a* in), take part (*a* in).

concursado, -a *nm/f* (*Jur*) insolvent debtor, bankrupt.

concursante *nmf* competitor, contestant, participant.

concursar [1a] **1** *vt* (**a**) (*Jur*) to declare insolvent, declare bankrupt.

(**b**) (*competir*) to compete in, compete for; **va a ~ la vacante** he is going to compete for (*o* apply for) the vacancy.

2 *vi* to compete, participate.

concurso 1 *nm* (**a**) = **concurrencia.**

(**b**) **~ de acreedores** (*Jur*) meeting of creditors.

(**c**) (*coincidencia*) coincidence, concurrence.

(**d**) (*ayuda*) help, collaboration; support; cooperation; **con el ~ de** with the help of; **prestar su ~** to help, collaborate.

(**e**) (*Dep etc*) competition, contest; meeting, match, tournament; show; (*examen*) examination, open competition; **~ de belleza** beauty contest; **~ hípico** horse show, show-jumping contest; **~ de méritos** competition for posts; **~ de pastoreo** sheepdog trials; **~ radiofónico** radio quiz (show); **~ de redacción** essay competition; **~ de saltos** show-jumping contest; **precios sin ~s** competitive prices; unbeatable prices; **ganar un puesto por ~** to win a post in open competition.

(**f**) (*Com*) tender.

2 *atr*: **corrida ~** bullfighting competition; **programa ~** TV game show; **cata ~** wine-tasting competition.

concurso-subasta *nm, pl* **concursos-subasta** competitive tendering.

concusión *nf* (**a**) (*Med*) concussion.

(**b**) (*Fin*) extortion.

concusionario, -a *nm/f* extortioner.

Concha *nf forma familiar de* **María de la Concepción.**

concha *nf* (**a**) (*Zool*) shell; shellfish, (*esp*) scallop, scallop shell; (*carey*) tortoiseshell; **~ de perla** (*And*) mother-of-pearl; **meterse en su ~** to retire into one's shell; **tener muchas ~s** to be very sharp, be a sly one; **tiene más ~s que un galápago** he's as slippery as an eel.

(**b**) (*de porcelana*) flake, chip.

(**c**) (*Teat*) prompt box.

(**d**) (*And, Carib*: *descaro*) nerve, cheek*; **¡qué ~ la tuya!** you've got a nerve!

(**e**) (*And*: *pereza*) sloth, sluggishness.

(**f**) (*Anat: euf*) = **coño.**

(**g**) (*Carib*: *cartucho*) cartridge case.

(**h**) (*Carib*: *piel*) peel; (*corteza*) bark.

(**i**) **~ de su madre** (*Cono Sur*‡*) son of a bitch‡, bastard‡.

conchabado, -a *nm/f* (*LAm*) servant.

conchabar [1a] **1** *vt* (**a**) (*mezclar*) to mix, blend.

(**b**) (*LAm*) *criado* to hire, engage, employ.

(**c**) (*And, Cono Sur*: *trocar*) to barter.

2 conchabarse *vr* (**a**) (*confabularse*) to gang up (*contra* on), plot, conspire (*para* + *infin* to + *infin*); **los dos estaban conchabados** the two were in cahoots*.

(**b**) (*LAm*: *colocarse, esp como criado*) to hire o.s. out, get a job (as a servant).

conchabo *nm* (**a**) (*LAm*: *contratación*) hiring, engagement; **oficina de ~** (*Cono Sur*) employment agency for domestics.

(**b**) (*Cono Sur*: *permuta*) barter(ing).

cónchale *interj*: **¡~!** (*Carib*) well!, goodness!

Conchita *nf* = **Concha.**

conchito *nm* (*And, Cono Sur*) youngest child, baby of the family.

concho[1] *nm* (*Carib*) taxi.

concho[2] (*CAm*) **1** *adj* crude, vulgar. **2** *nm* (*campesino*) peasant; (*pey*) rustic, country bumpkin.

concho[3] *nm* (*LAm*: *t* **~s**) (*poso*) dregs, sediment; (*residuo*) residue; (*sobras*) left-overs; **hasta el ~** to the very end; **irse al ~** (*Cono Sur*) to go down, go under, sink.

concho[4] *nm* (*And, Cono Sur*) = **conchito.**

concho[5] *nm* (*Anat*: *euf*) = **coño.**

conchudo 1 *adj* (*And, Carib, Cono Sur*) sluggish, slow.

2 *nm,* **conchuda** *nf* (**a**) (*And, Méx*‡: *sinvergüenza*) shameless person, cheeky bastard‡.

(**b**) (*LAm*: *persona terca*) stubborn person, pigheaded person.

condado *nm* county; (*Hist*) earldom.

condal *adj V* **ciudad.**

conde *nm* earl, count; **el C~ Fernán González** Count Fernán González.

condecoración *nf* (*medalla etc*) decoration, medal; (*divisa*) badge; (*insignia*) insignia.

condecorar [1a] *vt* to decorate (*con* with).

condena *nf* (*Jur*) *sentencia* sentence; conviction; (*período*) term; **~ a perpetuidad, ~ de reclusión perpetua** life sentence, sentence of life imprisonment; **el año pasado hubo X ~s por embriaguez** last year there were X convictions for drunkenness; **cumplir una ~** to serve a sentence; **ser uno la ~ de otra** (*Méx*: *fig*) to be the bane of sb's life.

condenable *adj* condemnable; blameworthy.

condenación *nf* (**a**) (*gen*) condemnation; disapproval, censure; (*Ecl*) damnation; (*Jur*) = **condena.** (**b**) **¡~!** damn!, damnation!

condenadamente* *adv*: **una mujer ~ lista** a darned clever woman*; **es un trabajo ~ duro** it's darned hard work*.

condenado 1 *adj* (**a**) (*gen*) condemned; (*Jur*) condemned, convicted; (*Ecl*) damned.

(**b**) (*fig*) doomed; **el buque ~** the doomed vessel; **una especie condenada a la extinción** a species doomed to extinction; **instituciones condenadas a desaparecer** institutions doomed to disappear.

(**c**) (*) *niño* mischievous, naughty.

(**d**) (*: *maldito*) damned, flaming‡, ruddy*; **aquel ~ teléfono** that ruddy telephone*.

(**e**) (*Cono Sur*: *listo*) clever; sharp.

2 *nm,* **condenada** *nf* (**a**) (*Jur*) convicted person, criminal; **el ~ a muerte** the condemned man.

(**b**) (*Ecl*) damned soul.

(**c**) **el ~ de mi tío*** that ruddy uncle of mine*.

condenar [1a] **1** *vt* (**a**) (*gen*) to condemn.

(**b**) (*Jur*) to condemn, convict, sentence; to find guilty; **~ a uno a 3 meses de cárcel** to sentence sb to 3 months in jail, give sb a 3 month prison sentence; **~ a uno a una multa** to sentence sb to pay a fine; **~ a uno a presidio** to sentence sb to hard labour; **le condenaron por ladrón** they found him guilty of robbery.

(**c**) (*Ecl*) to damn.

(**d**) (*Arquit*) to block up, wall up.

(**e**) (*: *fastidiar*) to vex, annoy.

2 condenarse *vr* (**a**) (*confesar*) to confess (one's guilt), own up; (*reprocharse*) to blame o.s.

(**b**) (*Ecl*) to be damned.

(**c**) (*: *enfadarse*) to get cross, get worked up.

condenatorio *adj* condemnatory; **declaración condenatoria** statement of condemnation.

condensación *nf* condensation.

condensado *adj* condensed.

condensador *nm* condenser.

condensar [1a] **1** *vt* to condense. **2 condensarse** *vr* to condense, become condensed.

condesa *nf* countess.

condescendencia *nf* helpfulness, willingness (to help); affability; acquiescence (*a* in); submissiveness; **aceptar algo por ~** to accept sth so as not to hurt feelings.

condescender [2g] *vi* to acquiesce, comply, agree, say yes; **~ a algo** to consent to sth, say yes to sth; **~ a los ruegos de uno** to agree to sb's requests; **~ a** + *infin* to deign to + *infin*; **~ en** + *infin* to agree to + *infin*.

condescendiente *adj* (*servicial*) helpful, willing (to help); obliging; (*amable*) kind; (*afable*) affable; (*conforme*) acquiescent; (*sumiso*) submissive.

condición *nf* (**a**) (*naturaleza*) nature, condition; (*temperamento*) temperament, character; **la ~ humana** the human condition; **de ~ perversa** of a perverse nature; **de ~ cruel** cruel-natured.

(**b**) (*clase*) social class, rank; (*status*) status, position; **persona de ~** person of rank; **de humilde ~** of lowly origin; **una boda de personas de distinta ~** a wedding between people of different social scale.

(**c**) (*cualidades*) **condiciones** qualities; **de excelentes condiciones** of splendid qualities; **ella no tiene condiciones para pintora** she is not cut out to be a painter.

(**d**) (*estado*) **condiciones** condition, state; **condiciones de trabajo** working conditions; **condiciones de vida, condiciones vitales** living conditions; **nuestras condiciones económicas** our economic circumstances; **estar en condiciones** (*Mec*) to be in working order; **el coche está en malas condiciones** the car is in a bad state; **no está en (buenas) condiciones** it's not in a fit state; **no estamos en condiciones de resolverlo** we are not able to resolve it; **no está en condiciones para** + *infin* it is not fit to + *infin*; **no estamos en condiciones para** + *infin* we are not in a position to + *infin*; **poner en condiciones** (*Mec*) to mend, repair, put right.

(**e**) (*Jur etc*) condition; term, provision, stipulation; **las condiciones del contrato** the terms of the contract; **condiciones de favor, condiciones favorables** concessionary terms; ~ **previa** precondition; ~ **sine qua non** essential condition; **a** ~ **de que** ... on condition that ..., provided that ...; **con esta** ~ on this condition; **ayuda sin condiciones** help with no strings attached; **rendición sin condiciones** unconditional surrender; **rendirse sin condiciones** to surrender unconditionally.

condicionado *adj* conditioned.

condicional *adj* conditional (*t Ling*).

condicionalmente *adv* conditionally.

condicionante *nm* determining factor, determinant.

condicionar [1a] *vt* (**a**) to condition; to determine; to prepare; *futuro* to shape, mould. (**b**) **X condiciona su apoyo a la retirada de Y** X makes his support conditional on the withdrawal of Y.

condigno *adj* proper, corresponding.

condimentar [1a] *vt* to flavour, season; to spice.

condimento *nm* seasoning, flavouring; dressing.

condiscípulo, -a *nm/f* fellow pupil, fellow student.

condolencia *nf* condolence, sympathy.

condolerse [2h] *vr*: ~ **de,** ~ **por** to sympathize with, feel sorry for.

condominio *nm* (**a**) (*Jur*) joint ownership; condominium. (**b**) (*LAm*: *piso*) flat, apartment (*US*) (*owned by the occupant*).

condón *nm* condom, sheath.

condonar [1a] *vt acto* to condone; *castigo* to remit; *deuda* to cancel, forgive; *criminal* to reprieve.

cóndor *nm* condor.

conducción *nf* (**a**) (*acto*) leading; guiding; management; transport(ation); conveyance; piping; (*Fís*) conduction.

(**b**) (*Aut*) drive; driving; ~ **a derecha** right-hand drive; **coche de** ~ **interior** saloon car; ~ **descuidada,** ~ **negligente** careless driving; ~ **temeraria** reckless driving.

(**c**) (*Téc*) pipe; intake; outlet; ~ **de agua** water pipe; ~ **principal de agua** water main; ~ **principal de gas** gas main.

conducente *adj*: ~ a conducive to, leading to.

conducir [3n] **1** *vt* (**a**) *líquido etc* to take, convey; to pass; *carga* to take, transport, convey; **los cables conducen la electricidad** the cables carry the electricity.

(**b**) (*Aut etc*) to drive; to steer; ~ **por la derecha** to drive on the right.

(**c**) *persona* to take, lead (*a* to); to guide, conduct (*a* to); **me condujeron por un pasillo** they led me along a passage.

(**d**) *negocio, asunto* to direct, manage, conduct; *ejército, grupo, sublevación etc* to lead.

2 *vi* (**a**) (*Aut*) to drive; **aprender a** ~ to learn to drive.

(**b**) ~ **a** (*fig*) to lead to; **esto ha de** ~ **al desastre** this is bound to lead to disaster; **¿a qué conduce?** what's the point?; **no conduce a ninguna parte** this is getting us nowhere.

3 conducirse *vr* to behave, conduct o.s.

conducta *nf* (**a**) (*de persona*) conduct, behaviour; **mala** ~ misconduct, misbehaviour; **cambiar de** ~ to mend one's ways.

(**b**) (*de negocio etc*) direction, management.

conductibilidad *nf* (*Fís*) conductivity.

conductismo *nm* behaviourism.

conductista *adj, nmf* behaviourist.

conductividad *nf* = **conductibilidad.**

conductivo *adj* conductive.

conducto *nm* (**a**) (*de agua etc*) pipe, tube, conduit; (*Anat*) duct, canal; **~s** (*Aut*) leads; ~ **alimenticio** alimentary canal; ~ **biliar** bile duct; ~ **de desagüe** drain; ~ **de humo** flue; ~ **lacrimal** tear duct.

(**b**) (*fig*) agency; channel; (*persona*) agent, intermediary; **por** ~ **de** through, by means of; **por los ~s normales** through the usual channels.

conductor 1 *adj* (**a**) (*gen*) leading, guiding.

(**b**) (*Fís*) conductive.

2 *nm* (*Fís*) conductor; (*Elec*) lead; cable, flex; **no** ~ non-conductor.

3 *nm*, **conductora** *nf* (**a**) (*jefe*) leader; (*guía*) guide; (*Dep*) leader.

(**b**) (*Aut*) driver; motorist; **aprendiz de** ~, ~ **novato** learner, learner-driver.

(**c**) (*LAm*: *Mús*) conductor; (*de autobús etc*) conductor, conductress.

conductual *adj* behavioural.

condueño, -a *nm/f* joint owner, part owner, co-owner.

condumio* *nm* food, grub⁑.

conectable *adj* connectable (*a* to).

conectado *adj* (*Elec etc*) connected; **estar** ~ (*aparato*) to be on; (*hilo etc*) to be live.

conectar [1a] **1** *vt* (**a**) (*Téc*) to connect (up); (*Elec, TV etc*) to connect (up); to switch on, plug in; (*Telec*) to put through, connect (*con* to); ~ **un aparato a tierra** (*o* **con masa**) to earth (*o* ground *US*) a piece of apparatus.

(**b**) ~ **a uno con otra persona** to put sb in touch with sb else; **yo les puedo** ~ I can put you in touch (with one another); **le conectamos con Sevilla** (*Telec*) we're putting you through to Seville.

2 *vi*: ~ **con** *persona* to communicate with; to form contacts with, enter into a relationship with; ~ **con el espíritu europeo** to become imbued with the European spirit; **ellos conectan bien** they get on well, they have a good relationship; **ahora conectamos con Londres** (*TV*) now we're going over to London.

3 conectarse⁑ *vr* to make a connection⁑, get drugs.

conectividad *nf* connectivity.

conectivo *adj* connective.

conector *nm* connector.

coneja *nf* doe rabbit.

conejar *nm* warren, burrow.

conejera *nf* (**a**) (*madriguera*) warren, burrow; (*jaula*) rabbit hutch. (**b**) (⁑: *tasca*) den, dive⁑.

conejillo *nm* young rabbit; bunny; ~ **de Indias** guinea-pig.

conejita *nf* bunny girl.

conejito *nm* young rabbit; bunny; = **conejo** (**c**).

conejo 1 *adj* (*CAm*) flat, unsweetened; bitter, sour.

2 *nm* (**a**) (*Zool*) rabbit; ~ **casero** tame rabbit, pet rabbit; ~ **de monte,** ~ **silvestre** wild rabbit.

(**b**) (*CAm*) detective; **andar de** ~ (*LAm*) to be (operating) under cover.

(**c**) (⁂*Anat*) = **coño.**

(**d**) (**Mil*) recruit, squaddie*.

conejuna *nf* rabbit fur, coney.

conexión *nf* (**a**) (*Téc*) connection; plug; coupling; joint. (**b**) (*fig*) connection; relationship.

conexionarse [1a] *vr* to get in touch; to make connections, establish contacts.

conexo *adj* connected, related.

confabulación *nf* plot; intrigue; dubious scheme; (*Com*) ring.

confabularse [1a] *vr* to plot, conspire, scheme (*para* + *infin* to + *infin*); (*Com*) to form a ring.

confección *nf* (**a**) (*acto*) making; making-up, preparation; ~ **de vestidos** dressmaking.

(**b**) (*arte*) workmanship, work; **traje de** ~ ready-to-wear suit.

(**c**) (*artículo*) manufactured article, made-up article; (*Farm*) concoction, preparation; (*Cos*) ready-made garment (*o suit etc*); **es una** ~ **Pérez** it's a Pérez creation, it's a Pérez product.

confeccionado *adj* (*Cos*) ready-made, ready-to-wear.

confeccionador *nm* (*Prensa*) layout man.

confeccionar [1a] *vt lista etc* to make out; *informe* to prepare, write up; (*Cos*) to make (up); (*Farm*) to concoct, make up.

confeccionista *nmf* ready-made clothier.

confederación *nf* confederation, confederacy, league.

confederado, -a *adj, nm/f* confederate.

confederal *adj* federal.

confederarse [1a] *vr* to confederate, form a confederation.

conferencia *nf* (**a**) (*Pol etc*) conference, meeting; ~ **cumbre** summit conference; ~ **de desarme** disarmament conference; ~ **episcopal** synod; ~ **de prensa** press conference.

(**b**) (*oración*) lecture, address; **dar una** ~ to give a lecture.

(**c**) (*Telec*) call; ~ **de cobro revertido** reversed-charge call; ~ **interurbana,** ~ **de larga distancia** long-distance call, trunk call; ~ **de persona a persona** personal call; **tiene facilidad de** ~ **múltiple** it has a follow-on call facility.

(**d**) (*Inform*) conference; conferencing.

conferenciante *nmf* lecturer.

conferenciar [1b] *vi* to confer (*con* with); to be in conference.

conferencista *nmf* (*LAm*) lecturer.

conferir [3i] *vt* (**a**) *premio* to award (*a* to); *honor* to grant (*a* to), confer (*a* on), bestow (*a* on).

(**b**) (*fig*) *cualidad* to lend, give (*a* to); **los cuadros confieren dignidad al cuarto** the pictures give the room dignity.

(**c**) *documentos etc* to compare (*con* with).

confesante *nm* (*Hist*) penitent.

confesar [1j] **1** *vt* (**a**) *error* to confess, admit, acknowledge; *crimen* to own up to; (*Ecl*) *pecado* to confess.

(**b**) (*Ecl*) *pecador* to confess, hear the confession of.

2 *vi y* **confesarse** *vr* to confess, own up; (*Ecl*) to confess (*a, con* to), make one's confession; ~ **de sus pecados** to confess one's sins; **¡que Dios nos coja confesados!** God help us!

confesión *nf* confession.

confesional *adj* (**a**) (*de la confesión*) confessional; **secreto** ~ secrecy of confession. (**b**) (*de sectas*) confessional, denominational.

confes(i)onario *nm* confessional box.

confeso 1 *adj* (**a**) (*Jur etc*) (self-)confessed. (**b**) (*Hist*) *judío* converted. **2** *nm* (*Hist*) converted Jew; (*Ecl*) lay-brother.

confesor *nm* confessor.

confeti *nm* (*t* ~**s**) confetti.

confiabilidad *nf* reliability, trustworthiness.

confiable *adj* reliable, trustworthy.

confiadamente *adv* (**a**) (*con confianza*) trustingly. (**b**) (*tranquilamente*) confidently; self-confidently; hopefully. (**c**) (*de manera presumida*) conceitedly.

confiado *adj* (**a**) (*que confía*) trusting; (*crédulo*) unsuspecting, gullible.

(**b**) (*seguro de sí mismo*) confident; ~ **en sí mismo** self-confident, self-reliant; **estar muy** ~ to be excessively hopeful, nourish false hopes.

(**c**) (*vanidoso*) vain, conceited, presumptuous.

confianza *nf* (**a**) (*en otro*) trust (*en* in), reliance (*en* on); (*confiabilidad*) trustfulness; ~ **mutua** mutual trust; **persona de (toda)** ~ reliable person, trustworthy person; **puesto de** ~ responsible post, post of responsibility; **recluso de** ~ (prison) trusty; **él es de** ~ he is all right, you can speak freely in front of him; **decir algo en** ~ to say sth in confidence; **dicho sea en** ~ let it be said in confidence (*o* strictly between ourselves); **defraudar la** ~ **de uno** to let sb down; **poner su** ~ **en** to put one's trust in.

(**b**) (*en sí mismo*) confidence; ~ **en sí mismo** self-confidence; **con toda** ~ with complete confidence, with every confidence, without hesitation; **estar lleno de** ~ to be full of confidence; **infundir** ~ **a uno** to give sb confidence.

(**c**) (*vanidad*) vanity, conceit; presumption.

(**d**) (*intimidad*) intimacy, familiarity (*con* with); **amigo de** ~ close friend, intimate friend; **reunión de** ~ intimate gathering, informal gathering; **en tono de** ~ in a confidential tone; **tener** ~ **con uno** to be on close terms with sb; **tratar a uno con** ~ to treat sb without formality, not stand on ceremony with sb; **os ruego tratarme con toda** ~ I ask you to treat me as one of yourselves.

(**e**) ~**s** confidences; (*pey*) familiarities; **se toma demasiadas** ~**s** he is too familiar, he's too fresh, he takes too many liberties.

confianzudo *adj* (**a**) (*demasiado familiar*) overfamiliar, fresh. (**b**) (*LAm*: *entrometido*) meddlesome.

confiar [1c] **1** *vt*: ~ **algo a uno,** ~ **algo en uno** to entrust sth to sb, commit sth to the care of sb; ~ **algo al azar** to leave sth to chance.

2 *vi* to trust, be trusting; ~ **en** to trust, trust in; to rely on, count on; ~ **en el éxito de algo** to feel confident about the success of sth; **confiemos en Dios** let us trust in God; ~ **en que** ... to trust that ...; to expect that ...

3 confiarse *vr* (**a**) ~ **a algo** to entrust o.s. to sth.

(**b**) ~ **a uno** (*fig*) to open one's heart to sb.

confidencia *nf* confidence, secret; confidential remark; (*a policía etc*) tip-off; **hacer** ~**s a uno** to tell secrets to sb, confide in sb.

confidencial *adj* confidential; secret.

confidencialidad *nf* confidentiality, confidential nature; secrecy; **en la más estricta** ~ in the strictest confidence.

confidencialmente *adv* confidentially; secretly.

confidente *nm*, **confidenta** *nf* (**a**) (*amigo*) confidant(e); intimate friend. (**b**) (*agente*) informer; secret agent; ~ **policial** police informer.

configuración *nf* shape, configuration; (*Inform*) configuration; **la** ~ **del futuro** the shape of things to come; **la** ~ **del terreno** the lie of the land.

configurar [1a] *vt* to shape, form, fashion.

confín *nm* (*gen* **confines** *pl*) (*límite*) limit, boundary; (*horizonte*) horizon; **confines** confines, limits (*t fig*); (*parte exterior*) remote part, outermost parts, edges.

confinar [1a] **1** *vt* (*Jur etc*) to confine (*a, en* in); (*desterrar*) to banish, exile (*a* to); (*detener*) to arrest; (*encerrar*) to shut away.

2 *vi*: ~ **con** to border on (*t fig*).

3 confinarse *vr* to shut o.s. away.

confirmación *nf* confirmation (*t Ecl*).

confirmar [1a] *vt* (*gen*) to confirm (*t Ecl*); (*Jur*) to corroborate; (*apoyar*) to endorse, bear out, prove; ~ **a uno de** (*o* **como, por**) to confirm sb as; **la excepción confirma la regla** the exception proves the rule.

confirmatorio *adj* confirmatory.

confiscación *nf* confiscation.

confiscar [1g] *vt* to confiscate.

confisgado *adj* (*CAm*) mischievous, naughty.

confitado *adj*: **fruta confitada** crystallized fruit.

confitar [1a] *vt* to preserve (in syrup); to candy; (*t fig*) to sweeten.

confite *nm* sweet, candy (*US*).

confitería *nf* (**a**) (*dulces*) confectionery, sweets, candies (*US*). (**b**) (*tienda*) confectioner's (shop), sweetshop, candy store (*US*); (*Cono Sur*) café; shop selling pastry *etc*.

confitero, -a *nm/f* confectioner.

confitura *nf* preserve; crystallized fruit; jam.

conflagración *nf* conflagration; (*fig*) flare-up, outbreak; ~ **bélica** outbreak of war.

conflictividad *nf* (**a**) (*tensiones*) tensions and disputes; strains; potentiality for conflict; ~ **laboral** industrial disputes, labour troubles; ~ **social** social unrest. (**b**) (*cualidad*) controversial nature, debatable nature.

conflictivo *adj sociedad etc* troubled, filled with conflict; *sistema* unstable; *asunto* controversial; fraught with conflict; *situación* tense, troubled; *propuesta* likely to lead to a clash; **la edad conflictiva** the age of conflict; **punto** ~ point at issue; controversial point, debatable point; **zona conflictiva** area of conflict, troubled region, trouble spot.

conflicto *nm* (**a**) (*Mil*) conflict; struggle; (*fig*) clash; ~ **de intereses** clash of interests; ~ **laboral** labour dispute. (**b**) (*fig*) difficulty, fix, jam; **estar en un** ~ to be in a jam.

conflictual *adj* = **conflictivo**.

confluencia *nf* confluence.

confluente 1 *adj* confluent. **2** *nm* confluence.

confluir [3g] *vi* (*ríos etc*) to meet, join, come together; (*personas etc*) to gather, come together; to mass.

conformación *nf* shape, form, structure.

conformado 1 *adj* (**a**) **bien** ~ well-made, well-shaped. (**b**) (*sufrido*) patient, resigned, long-suffering. **2** *nm* (*Téc*) moulding, shaping, forming

conformar [1a] **1** *vt* (**a**) (*formar*) to shape, fashion; (*Téc*) to mould, shape, form.

(**b**) (*ajustar*) to adjust (*a* to), adapt (*a* to), bring into line (*a* with); *enemigos* to reconcile.

(**c**) (*constituir*) to constitute, make up.

2 *vi* to agree (*con* with).

3 conformarse *vr* to conform; to resign o.s.; ~ **con** *original* to conform to, agree with; *regla* to comply with, abide by, observe; *política etc* to adjust to, conform to, fall into line with; *situación difícil* to resign o.s. to, accept; **se conforma con cualquier cosa** he agrees to anything; he puts up with anything; **no me conformo con hacerlo así** I do not agree to doing it that way.

conforme 1 *adj* (**a**) (*parecido*) alike, similar; **son muy** ~**s en todo** they are very similar in every respect.

(**b**) (*que corresponde*) consistent (*a* with); **un premio** ~ **a sus méritos** a prize consistent with his merits, a reward in accordance with his merits.

(**c**) (*acorde*) agreed, in agreement; **¡**~**(s)!** agreed!, all right!; **estar** ~**s** to be agreed; **estamos** ~**s en el precio** we are agreed about the price; **estamos** ~**s en que** ... we agree that ...; **declararse** ~ **con algo** to consent to sth, acquiesce in sth; **por fin se mostró** ~ finally he agreed.

(**d**) (*satisfecho*) satisfied, content (*con* with); resigned (*con* to); **no se quedó** ~ **con la propina** he was not satisfied with the tip.

2 *prep*: ~ **a** in conformity with, in accordance with; in keeping with; ~ **a la muestra** as per sample; **lo hicieron ~ a sus instrucciones** they acted according to their instructions.

3 *conj* as; in proportion as; **todo sigue ~ estaba** everything is as it was; ~ **lo iban sacando** (in proportion) as they were taking it out; ~ **trabajas, así irás cobrando** you'll be paid in accordance with your work.

4 *nm* agreement; **dar el ~** to agree, give one's agreement.

conformidad *nf* (**a**) (*parecido*) similarity; correspondence; uniformity (*entre* between).

(**b**) (*acuerdo*) agreement; (*aprobación*) approval, consent; **de ~** by common consent; **de ~ con** in accordance with; **en ~** accordingly; **en ~ con** in compliance with; **no ~** nonconformity; disagreement; **dar su ~** to consent, give one's approval.

(**c**) (*resignación*) resignation (*con* to); forbearance; **soportar algo con ~** to bear sth with resignation, resign o.s. to putting up with sth.

conformismo *nm* conformism.

conformista *adj, nmf* conformist.

confort [kon'for(t)] *nm, pl* **conforts** [kon'for(t)] (**a**) (*gen*) comfort; **'todo ~'** (*anuncio*) 'all mod cons'. (**b**) (*Cono Sur euf: papel higiénico*) toilet paper.

confortabilidad *nf* comfort.

confortable 1 *adj* comfortable. **2** *nm* (*And*) sofa.

confortablemente *adv* comfortably.

confortante *adj* (**a**) (*gen*) comforting. (**b**) (*Med*) invigorating, tonic.

confortar [1a] *vt* (**a**) (*gen*) to comfort, console; to encourage. (**b**) (*Med etc*) to strengthen, invigorate, act as a tonic to.

confortativo 1 *adj* (**a**) (*gen*) comforting, consoling; encouraging.

(**b**) (*Med etc*) invigorating, tonic.

2 *nm* (**a**) (*gen*) comfort, consolation; encouragement.

(**b**) (*Med etc*) tonic, restorative.

confraternidad *nf* fraternity, brotherhood.

confraternización *nf* fraternization.

confraternizar [1f] *vi* to fraternize (*con* with).

confrontación *nf* (**a**) (*gen*) confrontation; ~ **nuclear** nuclear confrontation. (**b**) (*de textos*) comparison.

confrontar [1a] **1** *vt* (**a**) *peligro etc* to confront, face; to face up to.

(**b**) *dos personas* to bring face to face; ~ **a uno con otro** to confront sb with sb else.

(**c**) *textos* to compare, collate.

2 *vi* to border (*con* on).

3 confrontarse *vr*: ~ **con** to confront, face.

Confucio *nm* Confucius.

confundible *adj*: **fácilmente ~** easily mistaken (*con* for), easily confused (*con* with).

confundir [3a] **1** *vt* (**a**) (*borrar*) to blur, confuse.

(**b**) (*equivocar*) to mistake (*con* for), confuse (*con* with), mix up (*con* with); **confundimos el camino** we mistook our way, we got our route wrong; **ha confundido todos los sellos** he has mixed up (*o* jumbled up) all the stamps.

(**c**) (*mezclar*) to mix, mingle (*con* with).

(**d**) (*despistar*) to confound; to confuse, put off; to bewilder, perplex; *acusador etc* to put to shame; ~ **a uno con atenciones** to bewilder (*o* overwhelm) sb with kindness.

(**e**) (*perder*) to lose; **me has confundido ese libro otra vez** you've lost that book of mine again.

2 confundirse *vr* (**a**) (*borrarse*) to become blurred, become confused.

(**b**) (*armarse un lío*) to get confused, get in a muddle; to get bewildered; to make a mistake; **Vd se ha confundido de número** you have the wrong number.

(**c**) (*mezclarse*) to mix; to blend, fuse; **se confundió con la multitud** he became lost in the crowd, he disappeared in the crowd; **los policías se confundieron con los manifestantes** the police mingled with the demonstrators.

confusamente *adv recordar etc* in a confused way, confusedly; vaguely, hazily; *retirarse* in confusion, in disorder.

confusión *nf* confusion; **no hagamos confusiones** let's be clear about this, let's get this straight.

confusional *adj*: **estado ~** confused state, state of confusion.

confusionismo *nf* confusion; uncertainty; confused state; muddle-headedness; **sembrar el ~ y desconcierto** to spread alarm and despondency.

confusionista 1 *adj* muddle-headed; given to creating confusion. **2** *nmf* muddle-headed person; person given to creating confusion.

confuso *adj* (*gen*) confused; mixed up, jumbled up, in disorder; *recuerdo* confused, vague, hazy; *imagen* blurred, cloudy; **estar ~** to be confused, be bewildered; to be embarrassed.

confutar [1a] *vt* to confute.

conga *nf* (*Mús*) conga.

congal *nm* (*Méx*) brothel.

congelación *nf* (**a**) (*acto*) freezing; congealing; ~ **de imagen** (*de vídeo*) freeze-frame. (**b**) (*Med*) frostbite. (**c**) (*Fin etc*) freeze, freezing; ~ **de créditos** credit freeze; ~ **de salarios** wage freeze.

congelado *adj* (**a**) *carne etc* frozen, chilled; *grasa* congealed. (**b**) (*Med*) frostbitten. (**c**) (*Fin etc*) frozen, blocked.

congelador *nm* (**a**) (*electrodoméstico*) deep freeze, freezer; freezing unit, ice compartment; ~ **horizontal** chest freezer; ~ **vertical** cabinet freezer. (**b**) (*Náut*) frozen-food vessel; ship for freezing fish.

congeladora *nf* deep freeze, freezer.

congelar [1a] **1** *vt* (**a**) *carne, agua etc* to freeze; *sangre, grasa* to congeal; *imagen de vídeo* to freeze.

(**b**) (*Med*) to freeze, affect with frostbite.

(**c**) (*Fin etc*) to freeze, block; *proceso etc* to suspend, freeze.

2 congelarse *vr* (**a**) (*gen*) to freeze, become frozen; to congeal.

(**b**) (*Med*) to get frostbitten.

congénere *nm* fellow, person (*etc*) of the same sort; **el criminal y sus ~s** the criminal and others like him, the criminal and people of that sort.

congeniar [1b] *vi* to get on (well; *con* with); **congeniamos con los dos hermanos** we hit it off with the two brothers.

congenital *adj* (*LAm*), **congénito** *adj* congenital.

congénitamente *adv* congenitally.

congestión *nf* congestion.

congestionado *adj* (**a**) (*gen*) congested. (**b**) (*Med*) congested, (*esp*) chesty; *cara* flushed, red.

congestionamiento *nm* (*Carib Aut*) traffic jam.

congestionar [1a] **1** *vt* to congest, produce congestion in.

2 congestionarse *vr* to become congested; **se le congestionó la cara** his face became flushed, he got red in the face.

conglomeración *nf* conglomeration.

conglomerado *nm* (*Geol, Téc*) conglomerate; (*fig*) conglomeration.

conglomerar [1a] **1** *vt* to conglomerate. **2 conglomerarse** *vr* to conglomerate.

Congo *nm*: **el ~** the Congo; **¡vete al ~!‡** get lost!‡

congo *nm* (*LAm*) Negro.

congoja *nf* anguish, distress, grief.

congola *nf* (*And*) pipe.

congoleño, -a *adj, nm/f* Congolese.

congolés = **congoleño.**

congosto *nm* narrow pass, canyon.

congraciador *adj* ingratiating.

congraciamiento *nm* ingratiation; winning over.

congraciante *adj* ingratiating.

congraciar [1b] **1** *vt* to win over. **2 congraciarse** *vr* to ingratiate o.s. (*con* with).

congratulaciones *nfpl* congratulations.

congratular [1a] **1** *vt* to congratulate (*por* on).

2 congratularse *vr* to congratulate o.s., be pleased; **de eso nos congratulamos** on that we congratulate ourselves, we are glad about that.

congregación *nf* (*asamblea*) gathering, assembly; (*sociedad*) brotherhood, guild; (*Ecl*) congregation; **la ~ de los fieles** the (Catholic) Church.

congregacionalista 1 *adj* congregational. **2** *nmf* congregationalist.

congregarse [1h] *vr* to gather, congregate.

congresal *nmf* (*LAm*) = **congresista.**

congresional *adj* congressional.

congresista *nmf* delegate, member (of a congress).

congreso *nm* congress; assembly, convention; conference; (*Pol*) parliament; **C~** Congress (*US*); ~ **anual** annual conference; (*Esp Pol*) **C~ de los Diputados** ≃ House of Commons.

congresual *adj* congress (*atr*), of (the) congress; parliamentary, congressional; **reunión ~** meeting of parliament, meeting of Congress.

congrio *nm* conger (eel).

congruencia *nf* (**a**) (*t Mat*) congruence, congruity. (**b**)

(*oportunidad*) suitability.
congruente *adj*, **congruo** *adj* (**a**) (*t Mat*) congruent, congruous (*con* with); in keeping (*con* with); related (*con* to). (**b**) (*conveniente*) suitable, fitting.
cónico *adj* conical; *sección etc* (*Mat*) conic.
conífera *nf* conifer.
conífero *adj* coniferous.
conjetura *nf* guess, conjecture, surmise; **por ~** by guesswork; **son meras ~s** it's just guesswork.
conjeturable *adj* that can be guessed at; **es ~ que** ... one may conjecture that ...
conjetural *adj* conjectural.
conjeturar [1a] *vt* to guess (at), conjecture, surmise (*de, por* from; *que* that).
conjugación *nf* conjugation.
conjugar [1h] **1** *vt* (**a**) (*Ling*) to conjugate.
(**b**) (*reunir*) to combine, bring together, fit together, blend; **la obra conjuga cualidades y defectos** the work has both qualities and defects; **es difícil ~ los deseos de los dos** it is difficult to fit their wishes together.
2 conjugarse *vr* (**a**) (*Ling*) to be conjugated.
(**b**) (*unirse*) to fit together, blend; to be as one, become indistinguishable.
conjunción *nf* conjunction.
conjuntado *adj* united, combined; in harmony.
conjuntar [1a] *vt* to unite, combine; to harmonize.
conjuntivitis *nf* conjunctivitis.
conjuntivo *adj* conjunctive.
conjuntamente *adv* jointly, together; **~ con** together with.
conjuntero, -a *nm/f* member of a musical group.
conjunto 1 *adj* (**a**) (*colaborativo*) *etc* joint; united; (*Mil*) **operaciones conjuntas** combined operations.
(**b**) (*afín*) allied, related.
2 *nm* (**a**) (*gen*) whole; **en ~** as a whole, altogether; **en su ~** in its entirety; **foto de ~** group photo; **impresión de ~** overall impression; **vista de ~** all-embracing view; **formar un ~** to form a whole.
(**b**) (*Cos*) ensemble; costume; twin-set.
(**c**) (*Mús*) (*de cámara etc*) ensemble; (*de pop*) group; (*Dep*) team.
(**d**) (*Teat*) chorus.
(**e**) (*Mec*) unit, assembly.
(**f**) (*Mat*) set.
conjura *nf*, **conjuración** *nf* plot, conspiracy.
conjurado, -a *nm/f* plotter, conspirator.
conjurar [1a] **1** *vt* (**a**) *demonio* to conjure, to exorcise.
(**b**) *peligro* to stave off, ward off.
(**c**) *pensamiento etc* to rid o.s. of, get rid of.
(**d**) *persona* to entreat, beseech.
2 *vi y* **conjurarse** *vr* to plot, conspire (together).
conjuro *nm* (**a**) (*ensalmo*) incantation, conjuration, exorcism; spell; **al ~ de sus palabras** under the magical effect of his words. (**b**) (*ruego*) entreaty.
conllevar [1a] *vt* (**a**) *sentido* to convey, carry (with it); (*acarrear*) to imply, involve, to bring with it, bring in its wake.
(**b**) (*aguantar*) *dolor* to bear, suffer (patiently), live with; *persona* to bear, put up with; **~ las penas de otro** to help sb else to bear his troubles.
conmemoración *nf* commemoration.
conmemorar [1a] *vt* to commemorate.
conmemorativo *adj* commemorative; memorial (*atr*).
conmigo *pron* with me; with myself; *V* **consigo.**
conmilitón *nm* fellow soldier.
conminación *nf* (**a**) (*amenaza*) threat. (**b**) (*Méx Jur*) judgement.
conminar [1a] *vt* (**a**) (*amenazar*) to threaten (*con* with). (**b**) **~ a uno a hacer algo** to warn sb (officially) to do sth, instruct sb to do sth. (**c**) (*Méx*: *desafiar*) to challenge.
conminatorio *adj* threatening, warning.
conmiseración *nf* pity, sympathy; commiseration.
conmoción *nf* (**a**) (*Geol*) shock; tremor, earthquake.
(**b**) **~ cerebral** (*Med*) concussion.
(**c**) (*fig*) shock; commotion, disturbance; upheaval; **una ~ social** a social upheaval; **producir una ~ desagradable a uno** to give sb a nasty shock.
conmocionado *adj* (*Med*) shocked, concussed.
conmocionar [1a] *vt* (**a**) (*conmover*) to move, affect deeply; (*sacudir*) to shake profoundly, cause an upheaval in. (**b**) (*Med*) to put into shock, concuss.
conmovedor *adj* touching, moving; poignant; exciting, stirring; disturbing.
conmovedoramente *adv* touchingly, movingly.
conmover [2h] **1** *vt* (**a**) *edificio etc* to shake, disturb.
(**b**) (*fig*) to move, touch, stir, affect; to disturb, upset.
2 conmoverse *vr* (**a**) (*Geol*) to shake, be shaken.
(**b**) (*fig*) to be moved, be stirred.
conmuta *nf* (*And, Cono Sur*) change, alteration.
conmutación *nf* commutation; **~ de paquetes** packet-switching.
conmutador *nm* (*Elec*) switch; (*LAm Telec*) (*centralita*) switchboard; (*central*) telephone exchange.
conmutar [1a] *vt* (**a**) (*trocar*) to exchange (*con, por* for); (*transformar*) to convert (*en* into). (**b**) (*Jur*) to commute (*en, por* to).
connatural *adj* innate, inherent (*a* in).
connaturalizarse [1f] *vr* to become accustomed (*con* to); to become acclimatized, become acclimated (*US*) (*con* to).
connivencia *nf* collusion; connivance; **estar en ~ con** to be in collusion with.
connotación *nf* (**a**) (*sentido*) connotation. (**b**) (*parentesco*) distant relationship.
connotado *adj* (*famoso*) notable, famous; (*destacado*) outstanding.
connotar [1a] *vt* to connote.
cono *nm* cone; **el C~ Sur** = *Argentina, Chile, Uruguay.*
conocedor 1 *adj* expert, knowledgeable; **muy ~ de** very knowledgeable about.
2 *nm*, **conocedora** *nf* expert (*de* in), judge (*de* of); connoisseur (*de* of); **es buen ~ de ganado** he's a good judge of cattle.
conocencia *nf* (*esp LAm*) girlfriend, sweetheart.
conocer [2d] **1** *vt* (**a**) (*gen*) to know; to know about, understand; (*llegar a ~*) to meet, get to know; to become acquainted with; **~ a uno de vista** to know sb by sight; **le conozco ligeramente** I know him slightly; **conozco las dificultades** I know the difficulties; **la conocí en Sevilla** I met her in Seville; **vengo a ~ Portugal** I have come to get to know Portugal; **conoce su oficio** he knows his job; **no conoce gran cosa de ciencias** he doesn't know much about science; **no se le conoce tal defecto** she isn't known to have any such shortcoming; **~ a uno como su propia mano** to read sb like an open book; **le conozco de haber trabajado juntos** I know him from having worked with him; **dar a ~** to introduce, present; *noticia etc* to release (to the press *etc*); (*filtrar*) leak; **darse a ~** to make a name for o.s.; to make one's debut; **darse a ~ a uno** to make o.s. known to sb.
(**b**) (*reconocer*) to know, tell, recognize, distinguish (*en, por* by); **~ a uno por su modo de andar** to know sb by (*o* from) his walk; **él conoce cuáles son buenos** he knows (*o* can tell) which ones are good; **conocieron el peligro** they recognized the danger; **¿de qué le conoces?** how do you recognize him?; **no me conoce de nada** he doesn't know me from Adam.
(**c**) (*Jur*) *causa* to try, judge.
2 *vi* (**a**) **~ de** to know about.
(**b**) **~ de (o en) una causa** (*Jur*) to try a case.
3 conocerse *vr* (**a**) (*persona*) to know o.s.; to attain self-knowledge.
(**b**) (*2 personas*) to know each other; to get to know each other, meet, get acquainted; **se conocieron en un baile** they met at a dance.
(**c**) **se conoce que ...** it is clear that ...; it is known that ...; it is established that ...; it is recognized that ...; apparently ...; presumably ...
conocible *adj* knowable.
conocido 1 *adj* known; well-known; (*pey*) notorious; famous, noted (*por* for); **un médico ~** a well-known doctor, a prominent doctor; **un hecho conocidísimo** a very well-known fact.
2 *nm*, **conocida** *nf* acquaintance.
conocimiento *nm* (**a**) (*gen*) knowledge; **para su ~ y archivo** for your information; **hablar con ~ de causa** to know what one is talking about, speak with full knowledge of the facts; **obrar con ~ de causa** to know what one is up to; **hacer ~ de un hecho** to learn a fact; **hacer ~ de un tema** to learn about a subject, become acquainted with a subject; **ha llegado a mi ~ que ...** it has come to my notice that ...; **poner algo en ~ a uno** to inform sb of sth; to bring sth to sb's attention; **tener ~ de** to know about, have knowledge of; **al tenerse ~ del suceso** as soon as the event became known; **venir en ~ de** to learn of, hear about.
(**b**) **~s** knowledge (*de* of); information (*de* about); **~s elementales** basic knowledge; **~s generales** general knowledge; **mis pocos ~s de filosofía** my small knowledge of philosophy.
(**c**) **~s** (*personas*) acquaintances.

(**d**) (*juicio*) good sense, understanding; **los niños no tienen** ~ children have no sense.

(**e**) (*Med*) consciousness; **estar sin** ~ to be unconscious; **perder el** ~ to lose consciousness; **recobrar el** ~ to regain consciousness.

(**f**) (*Náut*) bill of lading.

(**g**) (*Jur*) cognizance.

conorte *nm* (*LAm*) comfort.

conque 1 *conj V* **con 2. 2** *nm* (**a**) (*****: *condición*) condition, reservation; **~s** ifs and buts. (**b**) (*t* **conqué**: *LAm*: *dinero*) wherewithal, means.

conquense 1 *adj* of Cuenca. **2** *nmf* native (*o* inhabitant) of Cuenca; **los ~s** the people of Cuenca.

conquista *nf* conquest (*t fig*); **ir de** ~ (*fig*) to be dressed up to kill.

conquistador 1 *adj* conquering. **2** *nm* (**a**) (*Mil etc*) conqueror; (*s. XVI*) conquistador. (**b**) (*seductor*) wolf*, ladykiller.

conquistar [1a] *vt* (**a**) (*Mil etc*) to conquer (*a* from); to overcome.

(**b**) (*fig*) *puesto etc* to win; *mercado* to win, open up; *persona* to win round, win over; *mujer* to win, succeed in attracting.

consabido *adj* (**a**) (*conocido*) well-known, familiar; (*usual*) usual; (*traído y llevado*) old, oft-repeated, timeworn. (**b**) (*susodicho*) above-mentioned.

consagración *nf* consecration, dedication.

consagrado *adj* (**a**) (*Rel*) consecrated (*a* to); dedicated (*a* to).

(**b**) (*fig*) time-honoured, hallowed, ritual, traditional; **según la expresión consagrada** in the time-honoured phrase; **principios ~s en la constitución** principles enshrined in the constitution; **un actor** ~ an established actor.

consagrar [1a] **1** *vt* (**a**) (*Rel*) to consecrate, hallow; to dedicate (*a* to); *emperador* to deify.

(**b**) (*fig*) *esfuerzo, tiempo, vida etc* to devote, dedicate (*a* to); to put in (*a* at); *monumento, placa* to put up, dedicate (*a* to).

(**c**) (*confirmar*) to confirm; **este triunfo le consagra como un cirujano excepcional** this success confirms him as (*o* shows him to be) a really exceptional surgeon.

2 consagrarse *vr*: ~ **a** to devote o.s. to.

consanguíneo *adj* related by blood, consanguineous.

consanguinidad *nf* blood relationship, consanguinity.

consciencia *nf* consciousness; awareness; realization; = **conciencia.**

consciente 1 *adj* (**a**) (*gen*) conscious; **ser** ~ **de** to be conscious of, be aware of.

(**b**) (*Med*) **estar** ~ to be conscious.

(**c**) (*Jur*) fully responsible for one's actions, aware of what one is doing.

(**d**) (*sensato*) sensible; balanced, responsible.

2 *nm* conscious, conscious mind.

conscientemente *adv* consciously.

conscripción *nf* conscription.

conscripto, -a *nm/f* conscript.

consecución *nf* obtaining, acquisition; attainment; (*Escol etc*) achievement; **de difícil** ~ hard to obtain, difficult to get hold of; **les ayudó en la** ~ **de trabajo** he helped them in obtaining work; **para la** ~ **de estos objetos** for the attainment of these aims.

consecuencia *nf* (**a**) (*resultado*) consequence; outcome, result; (*conclusión*) deduction, conclusion; **a** ~ **de eso, en** ~ **de eso** as a result of that, as a consequence of that; **como** ~**, en** ~ in consequence, accordingly; **aceptar las ~s** to take the consequences; **¡pues aténgase a las ~s!** then you'd better watch out!; **saqué la** ~ **de que ...** I gathered that ...; I drew the conclusion that ...; **no tuvo ~s** it had no ill effects, nothing bad happened as a result; **traer algo a** ~ to bring sth up.

(**b**) (*importancia*) importance; **de** ~ of importance, of some weight; **ser de** ~ to be important.

(**c**) (*constancia*) consistency; **obrar con** ~ to act consistently.

(**d**) (*esp LAm*: *honradez*) integrity.

consecuente *adj* (**a**) (*de acuerdo*) consistent (*con* with). (**b**) (*Filos*) consequent. (**c**) (*importante*) important; **no demasiado** ~ not very important. (**d**) **una persona** ~ (*LAm*) an honourable person, a person of integrity.

consecuentemente *adv* consistently.

consecutivo *adj* (*Ling etc*) consecutive.

conseguible *adj* obtainable; attainable.

conseguido *adj* successful.

conseguir [3d *y* 3k] *vt* (**a**) (*obtener*) to get, obtain, secure; to bring about; ~ + *infin* to succeed in + *ger*, manage to + *infin*; ~ **que uno haga algo** to manage to make sb do sth, get sb to do sth; **lo consigue como mi abuela** he has as much chance of getting it as the man in the moon.

(**b**) *fin etc* to attain, achieve.

conseja *nf* story, tale, legend; old wives' tale.

consejería *nf* (**a**) (*concejo*) council, commission. (**b**) (*Pol Esp*) ministry in a regional government.

consejero, -a *nm/f* adviser; consultant; member (of a board *etc*); (*de autonomía*) minister in a regional government; ~ **delegado** managing director; ~ **militar** military adviser; ~ **de publicidad** advertising consultant.

consejillo *nm* inner cabinet, kitchen cabinet.

consejo *nm* (**a**) **un** ~ a piece of advice; a hint; **su** ~ his advice, his counsel; **agradezco el** ~ I am grateful for your advice; **pedir** ~ **a uno** to ask sb for advice, ask sb's advice; ~ **pericial** expert advice; **~s** advice.

(**b**) (*Pol etc*) council; (*Com*) board; (*Jur*) tribunal; court; (*acto*) meeting (of a council *o* board *etc*); ~ **de administración** board of directors; ~ **asesor** advisory board; ~ **de disciplina** disciplinary board; ~ **escolar** school council; ~ **de guerra** court-martial; ~ **de guerra sumarísimo** drumhead court-martial; ~ **de ministros** cabinet; cabinet meeting; ~ **de redacción** editorial board; **C~ de Seguridad** Security Council.

consenso *nm* accord; assent; consensus.

consensuado *adj texto etc* agreed; established by consensus.

consensual *adj* agreed; **unión** ~ common-law marriage.

consensuar [1e] *vt* to agree on, reach an agreement on, reach a consensus on.

consentido *adj* (**a**) *niño* spoiled, pampered. (**b**) *marido* complaisant.

consentidor *adj madre etc* indulgent; weak, compliant; *marido* complaisant.

consentimiento *nm* consent.

consentir [3i] **1** *vt* (**a**) (*asentir a*) to consent to; (*permitir*) to allow, permit; (*tolerar*) to tolerate; ~ **a uno** + *infin*, ~ **que uno** + *subj* to allow sb to + *infin*; **aquí no consienten hablar** they don't let you speak here; **¡eso no se puede** ~**!** we can't have (*o* allow) that.

(**b**) (*aceptar*) to admit; (*aguantar*) to bear, put up with; **la plataforma no consiente más peso** the platform will not bear any more weight; **el abrigo consiente un arreglo más** the overcoat will bear repairing once more.

(**c**) *niño* to pamper, spoil.

2 *vi* to agree, consent, say yes (*en* to); to give in; ~ **en hacer algo** to agree to + *infin*, consent to + *infin*.

3 consentirse *vr* to break, give (way); to split, crack (up *etc*).

conserje *nm* porter; doorman; caretaker; ~ **automático** entry phone; ~ **de noche** night porter.

conserjería *nf* porter's office.

conserva *nf* (**a**) (*acto*) preserving.

(**b**) (*alimentos*) preserved foods; preserve(s); (*mermelada*) jam; (*encurtido*) pickle; **~s alimenticias** tinned foods, canned goods; **~s de carne** canned meat; potted meat; **en** ~ preserved; pickled; tinned, canned.

(**c**) (*Náut*) convoy; **navegar en (la)** ~ to sail in convoy.

conservación *nf* conservation; preservation; (*Arquit etc*) maintenance, upkeep; ~ **de la energía** energy conservation; ~ **de la naturaleza** nature conservation; ~ **refrigerada** cold storage; ~ **de suelos** soil conservation; **gastos de** ~ upkeep costs, maintenance expenses; **instinto de** ~ instinct of self-preservation.

conservacionismo *nm* conservationism; nature conservation; conservation movement.

conservacionista 1 *adj* conservationist; conservation (*atr*).

2 *nmf* conservationist.

conservador 1 *adj* (**a**) (*Culin etc*) preservative.

(**b**) (*Pol*) conservative.

2 *nm*, **conservadora** *nf* (**a**) (*Pol*) conservative.

(**b**) (*de museo*) curator, keeper; ~ **adjunto** assistant keeper.

conservadurismo *nm* (*Pol etc*) conservatism.

conservante *nm* preservative.

conservar [1a] **1** *vt* (**a**) (*preservar*) *alimentos etc* to preserve; *carne* to tin, can; *recursos* to conserve; (*Arquit etc*) to preserve.

(**b**) (*guardar*) to keep, retain; (*mantener*) *costumbre* to keep up, maintain, retain; *propiedad etc* to keep up; *color, secreto, amigo etc* to keep; **'conserve su derecha'** (*Aut*) 'keep to the right'; **conservo varias cartas suyas** I have a few letters of his; **conserva todavía la señal** he still has (*o* bears) the mark.

2 conservarse *vr* (**a**) (*costumbre etc*) to survive, remain, still exist; to be retained, be kept; (*durar*) to last out.

(**b**) (*persona*) to keep (well); to take good care of o.s.; **~ con** (*o* **en**) **salud** to keep well; **¡consérvese bien!** look after yourself!, I hope you keep well!

conservatismo *nm* conservatism.

conservativo *adj* preservative.

conservatorio *nm* (**a**) (*Mús*) conservatoire. (**b**) (*Cono Sur*: *invernáculo*) greenhouse. (**c**) (*Cono Sur*: *escuela*) private school.

conservero *adj* canning (*atr*); **la industria conservera** the canning industry.

considerable *adj* (*importante*) considerable; substantial; sizeable; (*digno de consideración*) worthy of consideration.

consideración *nf* (**a**) (*acto*) consideration; thought; reflexion; **está en ~** it is under consideration; **tomar en ~** to take into account, take into consideration.

(**b**) (*atención*) consideration; respect, regard; **en ~ a** considering, in consideration of; **por ~ a** out of regard for; **sin ~ a** irrespective of; without regard to; **hablar sin ~** to speak disrespectfully; **tratar a uno sin ~** to treat sb without consideration; **no le tengan Vds ninguna ~** don't give him any special treatment.

(**c**) (*respeto*) respect, esteem; **tengo una gran ~ por él** I hold him in high esteem; (*LAm*: *cartas*) **'de mi ~', 'de nuestra ~'** 'Dear Sir'; **le saludo con mi más distinguida ~** Yours faithfully.

(**d**) **consideraciones** kindness; **tener consideraciones con uno** to be kind to sb.

(**e**) (*importancia*) importance; **una casa de cierta ~** a sizeable house; **una herida de ~** a serious wound; **de poca ~** unimportant, of no account; **no es de ~** it's not important.

consideradamente *adv* considerately, kindly, thoughtfully.

considerado *adj* (**a**) (*respetado*) respected, esteemed; **bien ~** well-regarded; **mal ~** ill-regarded. (**b**) (*amable*) considerate, kind (*con* to), thoughtful.

considerando *nm* (*Jur*) *word with which each item in a judgement begins* ('whereas ...'); (*en sentido lato*) point, item, statement.

considerar [1a] *vt* (**a**) (*pensar*) to consider; to think about, reflect on; **~ que ...** to consider that ..., think that ...; **bien considerado, eso es razonable** on reflection, that is reasonable.

(**b**) (*tener en cuenta*) to take into account; **considera que ...** bear in mind that ..., don't forget that ...

(**c**) (*juzgar*) to consider; to think, deem; **lo considero imposible** I consider it (to be) impossible; **le consideran como loco** they think him mad; **le consideran como futuro rey** they consider him to be a future king.

(**d**) (*respetar*) to esteem, respect; **~ poco a** to scorn, despise.

(**e**) (*tratar bien*) to be kind to, show consideration for.

consigna *nf* (**a**) (*orden*) order, instruction; (*Mil*) watchword; (*de campaña etc*) watchword, slogan, motto; catchword; **~s de un vuelo** operating instructions for a flight, operational orders for a flight.

(**b**) (*Ferro etc*) cloakroom, left-luggage office, checkroom (*US*); **~ automática** left-luggage locker.

consignación *nf* (**a**) (*envío*) consignment, shipment. (**b**) (*Fin*) appropriation; earmarked sum.

consignador(a) *nm/f* consignor.

consignar [1a] *vt* (**a**) (*Com*) to send, dispatch, remit (*a* to); to consign (*a* to); to deposit (*a* with).

(**b**) (*asignar*) to assign (*para* to, for), earmark (*para* for).

(**c**) (*registrar*) to record, register; to put, set down, state; **olvidé ~ mi nombre** I forgot to write my name in, I forgot to state my name; **el hecho no quedó consignado en ningún libro** the fact was not recorded (*o* set down) in any book.

(**d**) (*CAm, Méx*: *Jur*) to remand, hold for trial.

consignatario, -a *nm/f* (*Com*) consignee; (*Com*) agent; (*Jur*) assign(ee); (*de carta etc*) recipient, addressee.

consigo *pron* (*él*) with him; (*ella*) with her; (*usted, ustedes*) with you; (*uno mismo*) with one(self) *etc*; **no lleva nada ~** he isn't taking anything with him, he's not carrying anything on him, he doesn't have anything on him; **hablaba ~** she was talking to herself; *V* **dar** *etc*.

consiguiente *adj* consequent (*a* upon); resulting; **por ~** and so, therefore, consequently.

consistencia *nf* consistence, consistency.

consistente *adj* (**a**) *conducta, teoría etc* consistent; *persona* (*LAm*: *consecuente*) consistent; *razón etc* sound, valid.

(**b**) *materia* solid, firm, tough, durable; *pasta etc* stiff, thick; substantial.

(**c**) **~ en** consisting of.

consistir [3a] *vi*: **~ en** (*LAm*: **~ de**) (**a**) (*componerse de*) to consist of; to be made of, be composed of; **¿en qué consiste?** what does it consist of?

(**b**) (*estribar en*) to lie in, be due to; **no consiste en eso la dificultad** the difficulty does not lie in that; **su atractivo consiste en su naturalidad** her charm lies in her naturalness; **si en mí solo consistiese** if it lay with me alone, if it depended entirely on me.

consistorial *adj* (*Ecl*) consistorial; *V* **casa**.

consistorio *nm* (*Ecl*) consistory; (*Pol*) town council; (*edificio*) town hall.

consocio *nmf* fellow member; (*Com*) co-partner, associate.

consola *nf* console table; (*Arquit, Inform, Mús*) console.

consolación *nf* consolation.

consolador 1 *adj* consoling, comforting. **2** *nm*, **consoladora** *nf* consoler, comforter. **3** *nm* (*aparato*) dildo.

consolar [1l] **1** *vt* to console, comfort; **me consuela de no haber ido** it consoles me for not having gone.

2 consolarse *vr* to console o.s.; to find consolation (*con* in), take comfort (*con* from).

consolatorio *adj* consolatory.

consolidación *nf* consolidation.

consolidar [1a] *vt* to consolidate, strengthen; *muro etc* to shore up; *deuda* to fund.

consomé *nm* consommé, clear soup.

consonancia *nf* (**a**) (*gen*) consonance, harmony; **en ~ con** in accordance with, in harmony with. (**b**) (*Liter*) (full) rhyme.

consonante 1 *adj* (**a**) (*gen*) consonant, harmonious; consistent.

(**b**) (*Ling*) consonantal.

(**c**) (*Liter*) rhyming.

2 *nm* (*Liter*) rhyme, rhyming word.

3 *nf* (*Ling*) consonant.

consonántico *adj* consonantal.

consonar [1l] *vi* (**a**) (*Mús y fig*) to be in harmony, harmonize. (**b**) (*Liter*) to rhyme (*con* with).

consorciarse [1b] *vr* to form a consortium, go into partnership.

consorcio *nm* (**a**) (*Com*) consortium; association, partnership; syndicate. (**b**) (*de circunstancias etc*) conjunction.

consorte *nmf* (**a**) (*esposo*) consort, spouse; **príncipe ~** prince consort. (**b**) (*fig*: *compañero*) partner, companion. (**c**) (*Jur*) **~s** colitigants; (*pey*) partners in crime, accomplices.

conspicuo *adj* eminent, famous.

conspiración *nf* conspiracy.

conspirador(a) *nm/f* conspirator.

conspirar [1a] *vi* to conspire, plot (*con* with, *contra* against); **~ a** + *infin* to conspire to + *infin* (*t fig*).

conspirativo *adj* conspiratorial.

constancia *nf* (**a**) (*firmeza*) constancy; steadiness; firmness, steadfastness; loyalty.

(**b**) (*seguridad*) certainty; (*prueba*) proof, evidence; **no hay ~ de ello** there is no certainty of it; there is no record of it, it is not recorded; **dejar ~ de algo** to place sth on record; to show evidence of sth; **para que quede ~ de la fecha** in order to give proof of the date.

(**c**) (*LAm*: *comprobante*) documentary proof, written evidence; **dar ~** to give proof, provide evidence.

constante 1 *adj* (**a**) *viento, esfuerzo etc* constant; unchanging; steady; *persona* firm, steadfast; *amigo* loyal, faithful, staunch.

(**b**) (*que continúa*) constant; continual; unending.

2 *nf* (**a**) (*Mat, fig*) constant. (**b**) (*Med*) **~s vitales** essential life processes.

constantemente *adv* constantly.

Constantino *nm* Constantine.

Constantinopla *n* (*Hist*) Constantinople.

Constanza *nf* Constance.

constar [1a] *vi* (**a**) (*ser evidente*) **~ de** to be clear from, be evident from; **consta que ...** it is clear that ..., it is a fact that ...; it is known that ...; **me consta que ...** I know for sure that ..., I have evidence that ...; **conste que yo no lo aprobé** let it be clearly understood that I did not approve it, I should like to point out that I did not approve it; **consta por ...** as is shown by ...; **que conste que lo hice por ti** believe me, I did it for your own good.

(**b**) (*existir etc*) to be on record, exist in recorded form; **no consta** (*libro etc*) not available; **no consta en el catálogo** it is not listed in the catalogue, it does not figure in the catalogue; **en el carnet no consta su edad** his age is not stated on the licence; **hacer ~** to record; to certify; **hacer ~ que ...** to reveal that ...; **y para que así conste ...** and for the record ...; **que conste: no estoy de acuerdo** for the record: I disagree; **que consten los hechos** let us put the record straight.

(**c**) **~ de** to consist of, be composed of.

(**d**) (*Poét*) to scan.

constatable *adj* observable, evident; (easily) verifiable; **es ~ que ...** it can be observed that ...

constatación *nf* confirmation, verification; observation.

constatar [1a] *vt* (*comprobar*) to confirm, verify; to check (*que* that); (*demostrar*) to show, prove; (*observar*) to observe (*que* that), note (*que* that).

constelación *nf* constellation.

constelado *adj* starry, full of stars; (*fig*) bespangled (*de* with).

consternación *nf* consternation, dismay.

consternado *adj*: **estar ~, quedarse ~** to be dismayed, be shattered; to be aghast; **dejar ~** = **consternar.**

consternar [1a] **1** *vt* to dismay, shatter, shock. **2 consternarse** *vr* to be dismayed, be shattered; to be aghast.

constipación *nf* = **constipado 2.**

constipado 1 *adj*: **estar ~** to have a cold. **2** *nm* (*Med*) cold, catarrh; **coger un ~** to catch a cold.

constiparse [1a] *vr* to catch a cold.

constitución *nf* constitution.

constitucional 1 *adj* constitutional. **2** *nmf* constitutionalist.

constitucionalmente *adv* constitutionally.

constituir [3g] **1** *vt* (**a**) (*formar*) *familia, grupo, unidad etc* to constitute, form, make up; **lo constituyen 12 miembros** it consists of 12 members, it is made up of 12 members; **esa industria constituye su principal riqueza** that industry constitutes (*o* is *o* forms) its chief wealth.

(**b**) (*equivaler a*) to be; **eso no constituye estorbo** that isn't an obstacle; that doesn't amount to an obstacle; **para mí constituye un placer** for me it is a pleasure.

(**c**) (*crear*) to constitute, create, set up, establish; *colegio etc* to found; *beca etc* to institute, endow.

(**d**) (*hacer, erigir*) **~ una nación en república** to make a country into a republic; **~ una ciudad en capital** to make a city the capital; **~ a uno en árbitro** to set sb up as arbiter; **~ heredero a uno** to make sb one's heir; **~ algo en principio** to erect sth into a principle, set sth up as a principle.

(**e**) (*forzar*) **~ a uno en una obligación** to force sb into an obligation.

(**f**) *abogado* to brief, instruct.

2 constituirse *vr* (**a**) **~ en** (*o* **por**) **juez** to set o.s. up as a judge, constitute o.s. a judge.

(**b**) **~ en un lugar** to present o.s. at a place, appear in person in a place; (*en orden*) report at a place.

constitutivo 1 *adj* constitutive, essential; **acto ~ de delito** act constituting a crime. **2** *nm* constituent element.

constituyente *adj* (*Pol*) constituent.

constreñir [3h *y* 3k] *vt* (**a**) (*limitar*) to restrict.

(**b**) **~ a uno a hacer algo** to compel (*o* force, constrain) sb to do sth.

(**c**) (*Med*) *arteria* to constrict; *persona, vientre* to constipate.

constricción *nf* constriction.

construcción *nf* (**a**) (*gen*) construction; building; structure; **~ de buques, ~ naval** shipbuilding; **~ de carreteras** road building; **en ~, en vía de ~** under construction, in course of construction.

(**b**) (*Ling*) construction.

constructivamente *adv* constructively.

constructivismo *nm* constructivism.

constructivista *adj, nmf* constructivist.

constructivo *adj* constructive.

constructor 1 *adj* building, construction (*atr*).

2 *nm* builder (*t fig*); **~ de buques, ~ naval** shipbuilder; **~ cinematográfico** set designer, set builder.

constructora *nf* construction company.

construible *adj solar* suitable for building.

construir [3g] **1** *vt* (**a**) (*gen*) to construct; to build, erect, put up. (**b**) (*Ling*) to construe. **2 construirse** *vr* (*Ling*) **este verbo se construye con 'en'** this verb takes 'en'; **aquí el verbo se construye con subjuntivo** here the verb goes into the subjunctive.

consuegra *nf* mother-in-law of one's son *o* daughter.

consuegro *nm* father-in-law of one's son *o* daughter.

consuelda *nf* comfrey.

consuelo *nm* consolation, solace, comfort; **llorar sin ~** to weep inconsolably; **premio de ~** consolation prize.

consuetudinario *adj* (**a**) (*usual*) habitual, customary; *borracho* hardened, confirmed. (**b**) **derecho ~** common law.

cónsul *nm* consul; **~ general** consul-general.

consulado *nm* (*puesto*) consulship; (*oficina*) consulate.

consular *adj* consular.

consulta *nf* (**a**) (*acto*) consultation; **~ popular** referendum.

(**b**) (*Med: consultorio*) consulting room; **~ externa** outpatients department.

(**c**) (*Med: reconocimiento*) examination; **horas de ~** surgery hours; **la ~ es de 5 a 8** the surgery is from 5 to 8; **el doctor no pasa ~ a domicilio** the doctor does not make home visits.

(**d**) (*Hist*) opinion.

(**e**) **libro de ~, obra de ~** reference book, work of reference.

consultable *adj*: **~ por todos** which can be consulted by anybody.

consultación *nf* consultation.

consultar [1a] *vt* (**a**) *persona* to consult (*acerca de, sobre* about, on); **~ a un médico** to consult a doctor, see a doctor; **consultado si era cierto, contestó ...** asked if it was true, she replied ...

(**b**) *asunto* to discuss, raise, take up (*con* with); **lo consultaré con mi abogado** I will take the matter up with my lawyer, I will consult my lawyer about it.

(**c**) *libro* to consult, look up; *referencia, palabra* to look up; to hunt up, chase up.

consúlting [kon'sultin] *nm, pl* **consúltings** [kon'sultin] business consultancy.

consultivo *adj* consultative.

consultor(a) 1 *nm/f* (*persona*) consultant. **2** *nm* (*Inform*): **~ de ortografía** spell(ing) checker. **3** *nf* consultancy (firm).

consultoría *nf* consultancy (firm); **~ de dirección, ~ gerencial** management consultancy.

consultorio *nm* information bureau; (*Med*) surgery, consulting room; (*de revista*: *t* **~ sentimental**) agony column, problem page; (*Rad*) programme of answers to listeners' queries.

consumación *nf* consummation; end; extinction.

consumado 1 *adj* consummate, perfect; accomplished (*en* in); *bribón etc* thorough, out-and-out. **2** *nm* (‡) (**a**) (*cosas robadas*) loot, swag*. (**b**) (*droga*) hash*.

consumar [1a] *vt* (**a**) (*acabar*) to complete, accomplish, carry out; *crimen* to commit; *asalto, robo* to carry out; *trato* to close, complete; *matrimonio* to consummate; (*Jur*) *condena* to carry out.

(**b**) (*And, CAm: hundir*) to submerge.

consumición *nf* (**a**) (*acto*) consumption. (**b**) (*en bar etc*) food *o* drink; **~ mínima** minimum charge; **pagar la ~** to pay for what one has had.

consumido *adj* (**a**) *persona* skinny, wasted; *fruta etc* shrivelled, shrunken. (**b**) (*fig: tímido*) timid; fretful, easily upset; **tener ~ a uno** to keep sb in a nervous state.

consumidor(a) *nm/f* consumer; **~ de drogas** drug-taker; **productos al ~** consumer products.

consumir [3a] **1** *vt* (**a**) *comida* to consume, eat; *producto* to use, consume; *combustible* to burn, use, consume; (*en restaurante etc*) to take, have.

(**b**) *material* to wear away; *paciencia* to wear down; *contenido líquido* to dry up; *persona* to waste away, exhaust the energies of, wear out.

(**c**) (*fig*) **le consumen los celos** he is eaten up with jealousy; **ese deseo le consume** that desire is burning him up; **me consume su terquedad** his obstinacy is getting on my nerves.

(**d**) (*And, CAm: sumergir*) to submerge.

2 consumirse *vr* (**a**) (*fruta etc*) to shrink, shrivel (up), lose its substance; (*persona*) to waste away; (*sopa etc*) to boil down.

(**b**) (*con fuego*) to burn out, be consumed, be devoured; **se ha consumido la vela** the candle is finished.

(**c**) (*fig: quemarse*) to burn o.s. out; (*apenarse*) to pine away, mope (*de* because of); **~ de envidia** to be eaten up with jealousy; **~ de rabia** to fume with rage; **me consumo**

de verle así it vexes me to see him like that.
consumismo *nm* (*tendencia*) consumerism; (*sociedad*) consumer society.
consumista 1 *adj* consumer (*atr*), consumerist; **el sector ~** the consumer section. **2** *nmf* consumer.
consumo *nm* (**a**) (*gen*) consumption; **~ conspicuo, ~ ostentoso** conspicuous consumption; **~ de drogas** drug-taking; **fecha de ~ preferente** best-before date; **precios al ~** consumer prices; **sociedad de ~** consumer society. (**b**) **~s** (*Fin*) municipal tax on food.
consunción *nf* consumption.
consuno: de ~ *adv* with one accord.
consustancial *adj* consubstantial; **ser ~ con** to be inseparable from, be all of a piece with.
contabilidad *nf* accounting, book-keeping; (*como profesión*) accountancy; (*letrero*) **'C~'** 'Accounts', 'Accounts Department'; **~ creativa** creative accountancy; **~ financiera** financial accounting; **~ de inflación** inflation accounting; **~ por partida doble, doble ~** book-keeping by double entry; **~ por partida simple** book-keeping by single entry.
contabilizable *adj* eligible for inclusion.
contabilización *nf* accounting, accountancy.
contabilizadora *nf* accounting machine, adding machine.
contabilizar [1f] *vt* (**a**) (*Fin*) to enter in the accounts; to tabulate. (**b**) (*fig*) to assess; to reckon with, take into account.
contable 1 *adj* countable. **2** *nmf* accountant, book-keeper.
contactar [1a] **1** *vt* = *vi*. **2** *vi*: **~ con** to contact, get in touch with.
contacto *nm* (**a**) (*gen*) contact (*t fig*); touch; (*Aut*) ignition; **dar el ~** (*Aut*) to switch on (the ignition); **estar en ~ con** to be in touch with; **entrar en ~ con** to come into contact with; (*fig*) to get in touch with, enter into relations with; **poner a A en ~ con B** to put A in touch with B; **ponerse en ~ con** to get in touch with, contact; **lo hizo el municipio en ~ con el gobierno** the city did it in collaboration with the government.
(**b**) (*LAm*: *interruptor*) switch, contact breaker; (*Méx*: *enchufe*) plug.
contado 1 *adj* (**a**) **tiene los días ~s** his days are numbered.
(**b**) **~s** few, scarce; rare; **en contadas ocasiones** on rare occasions; **contadas veces** seldom, rarely; **son ~s los que** ... there are few who ...; **pero son contadísimos los que pueden** but those who can are very few and far between.
2 *nm* (**a**) (*Com*) **al ~, de ~** (*LAm*) for cash, cash down; **pago al ~** cash payment; **¡al ~!*** sure!, O.K.!*
(**b**) **por de ~** naturally, of course; **tomar algo por de ~** to take sth for granted.
(**c**) (*And*: *plazo*) instalment.
contador *nm* (**a**) (*Mat*) abacus, counting frame.
(**b**) (*de café*) counter.
(**c**) (*esp LAm Com*: *t* **contadora** *nf*) accountant, book-keeper; (*cajero*) cashier; (*Jur*) receiver; **~ de navío** purser.
(**d**) (*And*: *prestamista*) pawnbroker, moneylender.
(**e**) (*Téc*) meter; **~ de agua** water meter; **~ de aparcamiento** parking meter; **~ de electricidad** electricity meter; **~ de gas** gas meter; **~ Geiger** Geiger counter; **~ de revoluciones** tachometer; **~ de taxi** taximeter.
contaduría *nf* (**a**) (*como profesión*) accountancy. (**b**) (*oficina*) accountant's office; cashier's office; (*Teat*) box office; (*And*) pawnbroker's, pawnshop.
contagiar [1b] **1** *vt* (**a**) *enfermedad* to pass on, transmit, give (*a* to); to spread; *persona* to infect (*con* with).
(**b**) (*fig*) to infect, contaminate (*con* with); to corrupt.
2 contagiarse *vr* (**a**) (*Med*: *enfermedad*) to be contagious (*t fig*); **el mal ejemplo se contagia** a bad example is contagious (*o* catching); **la anarquía se contagia a otros** anarchy spreads to others.
(**b**) (*persona*) to become infected (*de* with); (*fig*) to become infected, become tainted (*de* with); **se contagió de un amigo** he caught it from a friend.
contagio *nm* infection, contagion; (*fig*) contagion, corruption; taint.
contagioso *adj enfermedad* contagious, infectious, catching; *persona* infected, infectious; (*fig*) catching; corrupting.
contáiner *nm* container.
contaje *nm* count, counting.
contaminación *nf* (**a**) (*gen*) contamination; (*de texto*) corruption; (*Liter*) influence; **~ del aire, ~ atmosférica** air pollution, atmospheric pollution; **~ ambiental** environmental pollution. (**b**) (*fig*) taint, infection; defilement.
contaminador(a) *nm/f* polluter.
contaminante *nm* pollutant.
contaminar [1a] **1** *vt* (**a**) (*gen*) to contaminate; *aire, agua* to pollute; *ropa* to soil; *texto* to corrupt; (*Liter*) to influence, affect.
(**b**) (*fig*) to taint, infect; to defile; (*Ecl*) to profane.
2 contaminarse *vr* to be(come) contaminated (*con, de* with, by).
contante *adj*: **dinero ~ (y sonante)** cash, ready money.
contar [1l] **1** *vt* (**a**) (*Mat*) to count; to number off; *dinero etc* to count (up); (*incluir*) to include, count in; **cuenta 18 años** she is 18; **~ con los dedos** to count on one's fingers; **hay 9 kms a ~ desde aquí** it's 9 kms starting from here.
(**b**) (*considerar*) to count, reckon, consider; **al niño le cuentan por medio** they count the child as half; **le cuento entre mis amigos** I reckon him among my friends; **sin ~** not counting, not including; except for; not to mention; **sin ~ con que** ... leaving aside the fact that ...
(**c**) (*recordar*) to remember, bear in mind; **cuenta que es más fuerte que tú** don't forget he's stronger than you are.
(**d**) (*narrar*) to tell; **es muy largo de ~** it's a long story; **¡cuéntaselo a tu abuela!*** (*etc*) tell that to the marines!; **¡a quien se lo cuentas!*** you're telling me!; **¿a mí me lo cuentas?*** (*iró*) so what?; **ya me contarás** you tell me your side of it, you tell me how you see things; **una obra que no te voy a ~*** an indescribably fine work.
2 *vi* (**a**) (*Mat*) to count, count up; **hay que ~ mucho para llegar con la paga al final del mes** we have to go carefully (*o* watch it) in order to get to the end of the month; **cuentan por dos** he counts for (*o* as) two.
(**b**) (*fig*: *importar*) to count, matter; **esos puntos no cuentan** those points don't count; **no cuenta para nada** he doesn't count at all; **unas pocas equivocaciones no cuentan** a few errors don't matter.
(**c**) (*fiarse*) **~ con** to rely on, count on, depend on; to have; **cuenta conmigo** trust me, you can rely on me; **contaban por segura su ayuda** they were relying absolutely on his help, they thought he was sure to help them; **cuenta con varias ventajas** it has a number of advantages; **no contábamos con eso** we had not bargained for that, that was unexpected.
3 contarse *vr* (**a**) (*incluirse*) to be counted; to be included, to figure (*entre* among); **se le cuenta entre los más famosos** he is reckoned among the most famous; **me cuento entre sus admiradores** I count myself among his admirers.
(**b**) (*narrarse*) to be told; **cuéntase que** ... it is said that ..., it is related that ...; **¿qué te cuentas?*** how's things?*; **cuenta y no acaba de hablar** he never stops talking.
contemplación *nf* (**a**) (*gen*) contemplation; meditation, reflexion.
(**b**) **contemplaciones** indulgence; leniency, gentle treatment; **no andarse con contemplaciones** not to stand on ceremony; **tener demasiadas contemplaciones con uno** to be too indulgent towards sb, be too soft on sb; **no tiene contemplaciones en eso** he makes no compromises with that sort of thing; **tratar a uno con contemplaciones** to treat sb leniently; to handle sb with kid gloves; **no me vengas con contemplaciones** don't come to me with excuses; **sin contemplaciones** without ceremony; without any explanation.
contemplar [1a] **1** *vt* (**a**) (*mirar*) to look at, gaze at, watch, contemplate; (*fig*) to contemplate.
(**b**) (*tratar bien*) to show (extra) consideration for, treat (too) indulgently, be (too) lenient with.
(**c**) (*tomar en cuenta*) to take account of, deal with; **la ley contempla los casos siguientes** the law provides for the following cases.
(**d**) **~** + *infin* to contemplate +*ger*, plan to +*infin*, foresee the possibility of +*ger*.
2 *vi* (*Rel*) to meditate.
contemplativo *adj* (**a**) *vida etc* contemplative. (**b**) (*indulgente*) indulgent (*con* towards).
contemporáneo 1 *adj* contemporary; contemporaneous. **2** *nm*, **contemporánea** *nf* contemporary.
contemporización *nf* hedging, temporizing; (*Pol*) appeasement.
contemporizador 1 *adj* excessively compliant; temporizing; lacking firm principles. **2** *nm*, **contemporizadora** *nf* timeserver, compromiser; person who lacks firm principles.
contemporizar [1f] *vi* to be compliant, show o.s. ready to compromise; (*pey*) to lack firm principles; to temporize; **~ con uno** to hedge with sb; (*Pol*) to appease sb.

contención *nf* (**a**) (*Mil etc*) containing, containment; **operación de ~** holding operation. (**b**) (*restricción*) restraint; **sin ~** freely, without restraint. (**c**) (*rivalidad*) contention; rivalry. (**d**) (*Jur*) suit.

contencioso 1 *adj* (**a**) *asunto* contentious; *persona* argumentative, captious. (**b**) (*Jur*) litigious. **2** *nm* (*disputa*) dispute; (*problema*) problem; (*punto conflictivo*) point of disagreement.

contender [2g] *vi* to contend (*con* with, *sobre* over); to compete, be rivals (*en* in); (*Mil etc*) to fight; **~ en unas oposiciones** to take part in a competitive examination.

contendiente *nmf* contestant, contender.

contenedor *nm* container; (*Náut*) container ship; **~ de escombros** (builder's) skip; **~ del vidrio** bottlebank.

contener [2k] **1** *vt* (**a**) *contenido* to hold, contain.

(**b**) (*Mil etc*) to contain; *turba* to hold back; *rebeldes* to keep down, hold down; *caballo* to hold back, restrain; *respiración* to hold; *emoción* to keep back, choke back, bottle up; *enojo* to contain; *bostezo, risa* to smother; *tendencia* to check, restrain, curb.

(**c**) (*Cono Sur*: *significar*) to mean.

2 contenerse *vr* to control o.s., restrain o.s., hold o.s. in check.

contenerización *nf* containerization.

contenerizar [1f] *vt* to containerize.

contenido 1 *adj* (**a**) *persona* restrained, controlled; moderate; equable. (**b**) *emoción* suppressed. **2** *nm* contents; content.

contenta *nf* (*Com*) endorsement; (*Mil*) good-conduct certificate; (*LAm Jur*) release, acknowledgement.

contentadizo *adj* (*t* **bien ~**) easy to please; **mal ~** hard to please.

contentamente *adv* contentedly.

contentamiento *nm* contentment, satisfaction.

contentar [1a] **1** *vt* (**a**) (*gen*) to satisfy, content; to please, make happy.

(**b**) (*Com*) to endorse.

(**c**) **~ a dos personas** (*LAm*) to reconcile two people.

2 contentarse *vr* (**a**) **~ con** to be contented with, be satisfied with; **~ con** + *infin* to content o.s. with + *ger*; **se contenta con cualquier cosita** he's satisfied with anything, any little thing keeps him happy.

(**b**) (*LAm*: *reconciliarse*) to be (*o* become) reconciled (*con* with).

contento 1 *adj* (*satisfecho*) contented, satisfied; (*alegre*) pleased; glad, happy; **estar ~ con** (*o* **de**) to be satisfied with, be happy about, be content with; **están ~s con el coche** they are pleased with the car; **no está ~ en su trabajo** he's not happy in his work; **viven muy ~s** they live very happily; **¿estás ~?** are you happy?; **estar tan ~ como unas castañuelas** to be as happy as a lark; **para dejar** (*o* **poner, tener**) **a uno ~** in order to keep sb happy; **estar** (*o* **quedar**) **~ de** + *infin* to be content to + *infin*; **estaría tan ~ de** + *infin* I would as soon + *infin*.

2 *nm* (**a**) (*alegría*) contentment; joy, happiness; **a ~** to one's satisfaction; **no caber en sí de ~** to be overjoyed, be overwhelmed with joy.

(**b**) (*Jur*) release, discharge (of a debt).

contentura *nf* (*CAm, Carib*) = **contento 2**.

conteo *nm* count, counting; (*Méx Dep*) count.

contera *nf* (**a**) (*Téc*) (metal) tip, end; ferrule. (**b**) (*fig*) small extra, small addition. (**c**) **por ~** to crown it all, as a final blow.

contertuliano *nm*, **contertulio** *nm* fellow member (*of a social set*); **~s de café** café companions, people who regularly meet in a café, members of the same coffee set.

contesta *nf* (*LAm*) answer.

contestable *adj* questionable, debatable.

contestación *nf* (**a**) (*respuesta*) answer, reply; **~ a la demanda** (*Jur*) defence plea; **mala ~** sharp retort, piece of backchat; **dejar una carta sin ~** to leave a letter unanswered. (**b**) (*Pol*) protest; **movimiento de ~** protest movement, (*fig*) rebellion.

contestador 1 *adj* (*LAm*) cheeky, saucy. **2** *nm*: **~ automático** answering machine, Ansaphone ®.

contestar [1a] **1** *vti* (**a**) (*gen*) to answer, reply; (*replicar*) to answer back; **~ una pregunta** (*Univ etc*) to answer a question; **~ una carta** to reply to a letter; **~ el teléfono** to answer the telephone; **~ a un saludo** to return a greeting, respond to a greeting; **contestó que sí** he replied that it was (*o* he would *etc*); **abstenerse de ~** to make no reply; (*encuesta*) **un 7 por 100 se abstuvo de ~** there were 7% 'don't knows'.

(**b**) (*Jur*: *t* **~ con**) to corroborate, confirm.

2 *vi* (**a**) (*Méx*) to chat, talk; to argue.

(**b**) (*Pol*) to protest.

contestatario 1 *adj* rebellious; non-conformist, anti-establishment; contentious; **movimiento ~** protest movement. **2** *nm*, **contestataria** *nf* rebel; non-conformist, person of anti-establishment views; protester.

contesto *nm* (*And, Cono Sur, Méx*††) answer, reply.

contestón* *adj* given to answering back, argumentative.

contexto *nm* (**a**) (*Liter etc*) context. (**b**) (*Téc*) web, tangle.

contextualizar [1f] *vt* to provide a context for, set in a context.

contextura *nf* (**a**) (*gen*) contexture. (**b**) (*Anat*) build, physique; constitution; make-up.

contienda *nf* contest; struggle, fight.

contigo *pron* with you; (††, *to God*) with thee; *V* **consigo.**

contigüidad *nf* nearness, closeness, contiguity.

contiguo *adj* next; adjacent (*a* to); contiguous (*a* to), adjoining; **en un cuarto ~** in an adjoining room.

continencia *nf* continence.

continental *adj* continental.

continentalidad *nf* continental nature.

continente 1 *adj* continent.

2 *nm* (**a**) (*Geog*) continent; **el viejo ~** Europe, the Old World.

(**b**) (*recipiente*) container.

(**c**) (*fig*) air, mien, bearing; **de ~ distinguido** with an air of distinction; **de ~ duro** harsh-looking.

contingencia *nf* contingency; risk; hazard, danger.

contingentación *nf* quota system.

contingentado *adj* subject to a quota system.

contingentar [1a] *vt* to make subject to quotas; to fix quotas for.

contingente 1 *adj* contingent. **2** *nm* (**a**) (*Mil etc*) contingent. (**b**) = **contingencia.** (**c**) (*Com etc*) quota; **~ de importación** import quota.

continuación *nf* continuation; sequel; **a ~** then, next; immediately after; later (on), subsequently; **según lo expuesto a ~** as set out below, as follows; **a ~ de** after, following.

continuamente *adv* continuously; continually, constantly.

continuar [1e] **1** *vt* to continue, go on with; to resume; to carry on (with); *carretera etc* to continue, prolong, extend.

2 *vi* (**a**) (*ir adelante*) to continue; to go on, carry on; **'continuará'** (*serie de TV etc*) 'to be continued'; **~ hablando** to continue talking, continue to talk, go on talking; **continúa lloviendo** it's still raining; **la puerta continúa cerrada** the door is still shut; **continuaba en Noruega** he was still in Norway; he remained in Norway; **~ con su trabajo** to continue (*o* go on) with one's work; **~ con salud** to keep in good health; **~ en su puesto** to stay at one's job, carry on with one's work.

(**b**) (*prolongarse*) to continue; **la carretera continúa más allá de la frontera** the road continues (on) beyond the frontier.

continuidad *nf* continuity.

continuismo *nm* (*Pol*) politics of continuity; wish for everything to go on as before; maintenance of the status quo.

continuista *nmf* person who maintains the status quo; loyal successor (*de* to).

continuo 1 *adj* (**a**) (*no interrumpido*) continuous; (*Téc*) *correa etc* endless; (*Elec*) *corriente* direct; *V* **acto, sesión.**

(**b**) (*constante*) continual, constant; **sus continuas quejas** his continual complaints.

(**c**) **a la continua, (de) ~** continually.

2 *nm* (*t* **contínuum**) continuum.

contonearse [1a] *vr* (*hombre*) to swagger, strut; (*mujer*) to swing one's hips, walk with a waggle; to walk affectedly, show off as one walks.

contoneo *nm* swagger, strut; hip-swinging, waggle; affected gait.

contorcerse [2b *y* 2h] *vr* to writhe, twist.

contorno *nm* (**a**) (*perfil*) outline (*t Arte*); (*Geog*) contour; (*perímetro*) perimeter; (*forma*) form, shape; (*de moneda*) edge, rim; **en ~** round about, all around.

(**b**) (*medida*) measurement round, distance round; **~ de un árbol** girth of a tree, distance round a tree's trunk; **el ~ de cintura es de 26 pulgadas** her waist measurement is 26 inches.

(**c**) **~s** environs, neighbourhood, surrounding area; **Caracas y sus ~s** Caracas and its environs; **en estos ~s** in these parts, hereabouts.

contorsión *nf* contortion.

contorsionarse [1a] *vr* to contort o.s.

contorsionista *nmf* contortionist.
contra 1 *adv* (**a**) against; **puntos en ~** points against; **hablar en ~** to speak against; **votar en ~** to vote against; **opinar en ~** to disagree, take the contrary view.
(**b**) **de ~** (*LAm*) extra, over and above.
(**c**) (*LAm*) **en ~ nuestra** (*etc*), **en nuestra ~** (*etc*) against us (*etc*).
2 *prep* (*gen*) against; (*enfrente*) opposite, facing; (*Com: giro*) on; **apoyar algo ~ la pared** to lean sth against the wall; **en ~ de** against; **hablar en ~ de un proyecto** to speak against a plan; **en ~ de lo que habíamos pensado** contrary to what we had thought; **ir en ~ de algo** to go against sth, run counter to sth.
3 *nm* (**a**) con; *V* **pro.**
(**b**) (*Nicaragua*) counter-revolutionary, Contra (guerrilla).
4 *nf* (**a**) (*Esgrima*) counter.
(**b**) (*pega*) trouble, snag; inconvenience.
(**c**) **hacer la ~** to be consistently obstructive, persist in taking an opposite view; **llevar la ~ a uno** to oppose sb, contradict sb.
(**d**) (*LAm Med*) antidote.
(**e**) (*Bridge*) double.
(**f**) **la ~** (*Nicaragua*) the Contras.
contra... *pref* counter-..., contra...; cross-...; **~manifestación** counter-demonstration; **~propaganda** counter-propaganda.
contra(a)lmirante *nm* rear admiral.
contra(a)menaza *nf* counter-threat.
contra(a)rgumento *nm* counter-argument.
contra(a)tacar [1g] *vti* to counter-attack.
contra(a)taque *nm* counter-attack.
contrabajista *nmf* double-bass player, contrabassist; (*de rock*) bass guitarist.
contrabajo *nm* (**a**) (*instrumento, músico*) double bass; (*rock*) bass guitar. (**b**) (*cantante, voz*) low bass, contrabasso.
contrabalancear [1a] *vt* to counterbalance.
contrabalanza *nf* counterbalance.
contrabandear [1a] *vi* to smuggle, live by smuggling.
contrabandista *nmf* smuggler; **~ de armas** gun-runner.
contrabando *nm* (**a**) (*acto*) smuggling; **~ de armas** gun-running.
(**b**) (*mercancías*) contraband, smuggled goods; (*artículo*) prohibited article, banned item; **géneros de ~** smuggled goods; **amores de ~** (*fig*) clandestine love affair; **pasar** (*o* **introducir**) **algo de ~** to smuggle sth in, get sth in illegally.
contracargo *nm* counter-charge.
contracarro *atr*: **defensas ~** anti-tank defences.
contracción *nf* (**a**) (*gen*) contraction; shrinkage; wasting. (**b**) (*And: aplicación*) diligence, industry.
contracepción *nf* contraception.
contraceptivo *adj, nm* contraceptive.
contracifra *nf* key (to a code).
contracorriente *nf* cross-current; undercurrent; **ir a ~** to go against the current, go upstream; (*fig*) to go against the tide.
contráctil *adj* contractile.
contractual *adj* contractual.
contractualmente *adv* contractually.
contractura *nf* muscular contraction.
contracubierta *nf* back cover (*of book*).
contracultura *nf* counter-culture; alternative society.
contracultural *adj* of the counter-culture, alternative.
contracurva *nf* (*Aut*) second bend, bend the other way.
contrachapado 1 *adj*: **madera contrachapada = 2. 2** *nm* plywood.
contradecir [3o] *vt* to contradict.
contradicción *nf* contradiction; (*fig*) incompatibility; **~ de** (*o* **en los**) **términos** contradiction in terms; **espíritu de ~** contrariness; **A y B están en ~** A and B stand in contradiction to each other.
contradictorio *adj* contradictory.
contradique *nm* outer harbour wall.
contradón *nm* reciprocal gift.
contraempuje *nm* counter-thrust.
contraer [2o] **1** *vt* (**a**) (*encoger*) *materia, sustancia etc* to contract; to shrink; to make smaller (*o* tighter *etc*); *discurso, texto* to condense, shorten; **~ la frente** to wrinkle one's brow; **la humedad contrae las cuerdas** the damp makes the ropes tauten.
(**b**) (*adquirir*) *deuda, obligación etc* to contract; *costumbre* to acquire, pick up, get into; *enfermedad* to contract, catch; **~ matrimonio** to marry (*con una* sb); **~ parentesco con** to become related to.
(**c**) (*restringir*) to restrict, limit (*a* to); **contrae su teoría a ciertos puntos** he limits his theory to certain points.
2 contraerse *vr* (**a**) (*encogerse*) to contract; to shrink; to get smaller; to tighten, tauten.
(**b**) **~ a** to limit o.s. to.
contraespionaje *nm* counter-espionage, counter-intelligence.
contraetiqueta *nf* second label, label on the back (of the bottle).
contrafallar [1a] *vt* to overtrump.
contrafuerte *nm* (*Arquit*) buttress; (*Mil*) outwork; (*Geog*) spur; foothill; (*de zapato*) heel-pad, heel-stiffener.
contragambito *nm* counter-gambit.
contragolpe *nm* counter-blow; (*fig*) backlash, reaction, kickback; (*Dep*) counter-attack.
contragolpear [1a] *vi* to strike back.
contrahacer [2r] *vt* (*copiar*) to copy, imitate; *moneda* to counterfeit; *documento, prueba* to forge, fake; *libro* to pirate; *persona* to mimic, impersonate, do an impression of.
contrahaz *nm* (*de paño*) wrong side.
contrahecho *adj* (**a**) (*gen*) counterfeit; fake, faked, forged; spurious, pirated. (**b**) (*Anat*) hunchbacked, deformed.
contrahechura *nf* counterfeit; forgery, fake; pirated edition, spurious edition.
contraído *adj* (**a**) (*encogido*) contracted; shrunken, wasted.
(**b**) (*And: trabajador*) diligent, industrious.
contraimagen *nf* mirror image; (*pey*) negative image.
contraincendios *atr*: **aparato ~** fire-prevention apparatus, fire-alarm system.
contraindicación *nf* (*Med*) counter-indication.
contrainformación *nf* disinformation.
contrainforme *nm* counter-report.
contrainsurgencia *nf* counter-insurgency.
contrainteligencia *nf* counter-intelligence.
contrairritante *nm* counterirritant.
contralor *nm* (*real*) comptroller; (*LAm*) treasury inspector.
contraloría *nf* (*LAm*) treasury inspector's office; accounts office.
contralto 1 *adj* contralto. **2** *nm* counter tenor. **3** *nf* contralto.
contraluz *nm* view against the light; **a ~** against the light.
contramaestre *nm* (*Náut*) warrant officer; boatswain; (*Téc*) foreman.
contramandar [1a] *vt* to countermand.
contramandato *nm* counter-order.
contramanifestación *nf* counter-demonstration.
contramano: **a ~** *adv* in the wrong direction, the wrong way; **eso queda a ~** that's in the other direction.
contramarcha *nf* (**a**) (*Mil*) countermarch. (**b**) (*Aut etc*) reverse; **dar ~** (**a**) to reverse, (*fig*) go into reverse.
contramarchar [1a] *vi* to countermarch.
contramatar [1a] **1** *vt*: **~ a uno** (*LAm*) to bang sb against the wall.
2 contramatarse *vr* (**a**) (*LAm*) to crash into sth, collide with sth.
(**b**) **~ de** + *infin* (*Méx*) to repent of (*o* regret) + *ger*.
contramedida *nf* counter-measure.
contranatural *adj* unnatural.
contraofensiva *nf* counter-offensive.
contraoferta *nf* counter-offer.
contraorden *nf* counter-order.
contrapartida *nf* (**a**) (*Com, Fin*) balancing entry. (**b**) (*fig*) compensation; counter-weight; **pero como ~ añade que ...** but in contrast she adds that ...; **como ~ de** as compensation for; as a counterweight to; **dar algo de ~** to give sth in return (*de* for).
contrapelo: **a ~** *adv* (**a**) **acariciar un gato a ~** to stroke a cat the wrong way.
(**b**) (*fig*) **a ~** the wrong way; against the grain; **a ~ de** against, counter to; **todo lo hace a ~** he does everything the wrong way round; **intervino muy a ~** he spoke up in a most unfortunate way, he chose quite the wrong way in which to intervene.
contrapesar [1a] *vt* to counterbalance (*con* with); to counterweigh; (*fig*) to offset; to balance, compensate for.
contrapeso *nm* (**a**) (*lit*) counterpoise, counterweight; (*Com*) makeweight; (*Circo*) balancing pole. (**b**) (*fig*) counterweight.
contrapié: **a ~** *adv* with the wrong foot; awkwardly.
contrapoder *nm* anti-establishment movement.
contraponer [2q] *vt* (**a**) *dos colores etc* to compare, set

against each other.

(**b**) ~ **A a B** to set up A against B, put up A as a barrier against B; **a esta idea ellos contraponen su teoría de que ...** against this idea they set up their theory that ...

contraportada *nf* inside cover (*of book*).

contraposición *nf* comparison; contrast, clash; **en ~ a** in contrast to; **pero en ~, ...** but on the other hand, ...

contraprestación *nf* compensation; consideration.

contraproducente *adj* self-defeating; counter-productive; **tener un resultado ~** to have a boomerang effect, boomerang; **es ~** *+infin* it is worse than useless to *+infin*, it is a mistake to *+infin*.

contrapropuesta *nf* counter-proposal.

contrapuerta *nf* inner door; second door.

contrapuntear [1a] *vi* (*And*) to compete in a verse duel; (*fig*) to compete.

contrapunteo *nm* (*And, Carib, Cono Sur: riña*) argument, quarrel; (*And, Cono Sur: liter* ††) improvised verse duel; (*And, Carib, Cono Sur: debate*) debate; **en ~** (*And*) in competition.

contrapuntístico *adj* contrapuntal; (*fig*) contrasting.

contrapunto *nm* (**a**) (*lit*) counterpoint. (**b**) (*LAm: concurso de poesía*) poetic competition with improvised verses; **de ~** in competition.

contrariado *adj* upset, annoyed, put out.

contrariamente *adv*: **~ a lo que habíamos pensado** contrary to what we had thought.

contrariar [1c] *vt* (**a**) (*oponerse a*) to oppose, be opposed to, go against; (*contradecir*) to contradict; (*estorbar*) to impede, thwart. (**b**) (*fastidiar*) to vex, upset, annoy.

contrariedad *nf* (**a**) (*obstáculo*) obstacle; (*desgracia*) setback, misfortune; (*pega*) snag, trouble.

(**b**) (*disgusto*) vexation, annoyance; **producir ~ a uno** to upset sb, cause annoyance to sb.

(**c**) (*oposición*) contrary nature; opposition.

contrario 1 *adj* (**a**) (*carácter*) opposed, different; **son ~s en sus aficiones** they have opposing tastes, they differ widely in tastes.

(**b**) *dirección, lado etc* opposite; **en sentido ~** the other way, in the other direction.

(**c**) *sentido* opposite (*de* to); **se ha interpretado en sentido ~ del que realmente tiene** it has been interpreted in the opposite sense to its true one.

(**d**) (*opuesto*) contrary (*a* to); harmful, damaging, hostile (*a* to); **~ a los intereses del país** contrary to the nation's interests.

(**e**) *viento etc* contrary; *fortuna* adverse.

(**f**) (*opinión*) opposed; **él es ~ a las reformas** he is opposed to the reforms, he is against the changes.

(**g**) (*frases*) **al ~, por el ~** on the contrary; **al ~ de** unlike; **al ~ de lo que habíamos pensado** against what we had thought; **todo salió al ~ de lo que habíamos previsto** it all turned out differently from what we had expected; **lo ~** the opposite, the reverse; **de lo ~** otherwise; were it not so; **todo lo ~** quite the reverse; **llevar la contraria** to maintain an opposite point of view; to oppose sth systematically; **llevar la contraria a uno** to oppose sb, contradict sb.

2 *nm*, **contraria** *nf* enemy, adversary; (*Dep, Jur etc*) opponent; **la contraria*** my other half, my old woman*.

3 *nm* obstacle, snag.

Contrarreforma *nf* Counter-Reformation.

contrarreloj 1 *adv* against the clock. **2** *atr*: **prueba ~ = 3.**

3 *nf* time trial; race against the clock.

contrarreplicar [1g] *vi* to answer back.

contrarrestar [1a] *vt* (**a**) (*compensar*) to counteract, offset, balance; *efectos* to counter, counteract. (**b**) *pelota* to return.

contrarrevolución *nf* counter-revolution.

contrarrevolucionario, -a *adj, nm/f* counter-revolutionary.

contrasentido *nm* (**a**) (*gen*) contradiction; (*falta de lógica*) illogicality; (*inconsecuencia*) inconsistency; (*disparate*) piece of nonsense; **aquí hay un ~** there is a contradiction here; **es un ~ que él actúe así** it doesn't make sense for him to act like that.

(**b**) (*Liter*) misinterpretation; mistranslation.

contraseña *nf* (**a**) (*gen*) countersign, secret mark; counter-mark; (*Mil etc*) watchword, password. (**b**) (*Teat*: *~ de salida*) pass-out ticket.

contrastar [1a] **1** *vt* (**a**) (*resistir*) to resist.

(**b**) *metal* to assay; to hallmark; *medidas, pesas* to verify; *radio* to monitor; *hechos* to check, confirm, document.

2 *vi* (**a**) (*hacer contraste*) to contrast, form a contrast (*con* with).

(**b**) **~ a, ~ con, ~ contra** (*resistir*) to resist; (*hacer frente a*) to face up to.

contraste *nm* (**a**) (*gen*) contrast (*t TV*); **~ de pareceres** difference of opinion; **en ~ con** in contrast to; **por ~** in contrast; **hacer ~ con** to contrast with.

(**b**) (*Téc*) assay; verification; (**marca del**) **~** hallmark; (*oficina*) assay office.

(**c**) (*persona*) inspector of weights and measures; (*oficina*) weights and measures office.

contrata *nf* contract(ing).

contratación *nf* signing-up; hiring, contracting; (†) trade.

contratante *nmf* (*Com*) contractor; (*Jur*) contracting party.

contratar [1a] **1** *vt mercancías etc* to contract for; to negotiate for; to sign a contract for; *trabajo* to put out to contract; *arriendo etc* to take on; *persona* to hire, engage; *jugador etc* to sign up.

2 contratarse *vr* (*jugador etc*) to sign on; **~ para hacer algo** to contract to do sth.

contratenor *nm* counter-tenor.

contraterrorismo *nm* counter-terrorism; campaign against terrorism.

contraterrorista *adj*: **medidas ~s** measures against terrorism, anti-terrorist measures.

contratiempo *nm* (**a**) (*revés*) setback, reverse, contretemps; (*accidente*) mishap, accident. (**b**) (*Mús*) **a ~** offbeat, syncopated.

contratista *nmf* contractor; **~ de obras** building contractor, builder.

contrato *nm* contract (*de* for), agreement; **~ de arrendamiento** rental agreement; **~ bilateral** bilateral agreement; **~ de mantenimiento** maintenance contract, service agreement; **~ de sociedad** deed of partnership; **~ verbal** verbal agreement.

contratuerca *nf* locknut.

contravalor *nm* exchange value.

contravención *nf* contravention, infringement, violation.

contraveneno *nm* antidote (*de* to).

contravenir [3r] *vi*: **~ a** to contravene, infringe, violate.

contraventana *nf* shutter.

contribución *nf* (**a**) (*gen*) contribution; **poner a ~** to make use of, put to use, draw upon.

(**b**) (*Fin*) tax; **contribuciones** taxes, taxation; **~ directa** direct tax; **~ municipal, ~ territorial urbana** rates; **exento de contribuciones** free of tax, tax-free, tax-exempt (*US*); **pagar las contribuciones** to pay one's taxes (*o* rates).

contribuir [3g] *vti* (**a**) (*gen*) to contribute (*a, para* to, towards); **~ con una cantidad** to contribute a sum; **~ al éxito de algo** to contribute to (*o* help towards) the success of sth; **~ a** + *infin* to help to + *infin*.

(**b**) (*Fin*) to pay (in taxes).

contribuyente *nmf* contributor; (*Fin*) taxpayer.

contrición *nf* contrition.

contrincante *nm* opponent, rival.

contristar [1a] **1** *vt* to sadden. **2 contristarse** *vr* to grow sad, grieve.

contrito *adj* contrite.

control *nm* (**a**) (*gen*) control; **bajo ~** under control; **fuera de ~** out of control; **perder el ~** to lose control (of o.s.); **perder ~ de** to lose control of; **~ de alquileres** rent control; **~ armamentista** arms control; **~ de cambio** exchange control; **~ de la circulación** traffic control; point duty; **~ de costos** cost control; **~ de créditos** credit control; **~ de la demanda** demand management; **~ a distancia, ~ remoto** remote control; **~ de (la) natalidad** birth control; **~ de precios** price-control; **~ presupuestario** budget control; **~ de sí mismo** self-control; **~ de tonalidad** tone control; **~ de volumen** volume control.

(**b**) (*acto*) inspection, check, checking; (*Com, Fin*) audit(ing); (*Aut: de rallye*) checkpoint; (*de policía*) roadblock; **~ antidoping** drug test, test for drugs; **~ de (la) calidad** quality control; **~ de carretera** checkpoint; **~ de frontera** frontier checkpoint; **~ nuclear** nuclear inspection; **~ de pasaportes** passport inspection; **montar un ~** to set up a roadblock.

controladamente *adv* in a controlled way.

controlador(a) *nm/f* controller; (*LAm Ferro*) inspector, ticket-collector; **~ de estacionamiento** traffic warden; **~ (de tráfico) aéreo** air-traffic controller.

controlar [1a] *vt* (**a**) (*regir*) to control. (**b**) (*comprobar*) to inspect, check; (*vigilar*) to supervise; to keep an eye on; *conversación, radio etc* to monitor; (*Com, Fin*) to audit.

controversia *nf* controversy.

controversial *adj* controversial.

controvertible *adj* controversial; debatable, disputable.

controvertido *adj* controversial.
controvertir [3i] **1** *vt* to dispute, question; to argue about. **2** *vi* to argue.
contubernio *nm* (**a**) (*confabulación*) ring, conspiracy; (*connivencia*) collusion. (**b**) (*cohabitación*) cohabitation.
contumacia *nf* obstinacy, stubborn disobedience; contumaciousness; perversity; (*Jur*) contempt (of court); contumacy.
contumaz *adj* (**a**) (*terco*) obstinate, stubbornly disobedient; *perverso etc* wayward, perverse; (*bebedor*) inveterate, hardened, incorrigible; (*Jur*) guilty of contempt (of court); contumacious.
(**b**) (*Med*) disease-carrying, germ-laden.
contumazmente *adv* obstinately; perversely; contumaciously.
contumelia *nf* contumely.
contumerioso *adj* (*CAm*) finicky, fussy.
contundencia *nf* forcefulness, power; conclusive nature; crushing nature; strictness, severity; toughness; aggressive nature.
contundente *adj* (**a**) *arma* offensive, for striking a blow with; **instrumento** ~ blunt instrument.
(**b**) (*fig*) *argumento etc* forceful, convincing, powerful; *prueba* conclusive; *tono* forceful; *derrota etc* crushing, overwhelming; *arbitraje etc* strict, severe; *juego* tough, hard; aggressive; *efecto* severe.
contundir [3a] *vt* to bruise, contuse.
conturbar [1a] **1** *vt* to trouble, dismay, perturb. **2** **conturbarse** *vr* to be troubled, be dismayed, become perturbed.
contusión *nf* bruise, bruising, contusion.
contusionar [1a] *vt* to bruise; to hurt, damage.
contuso *adj* bruised.
conuco *nm* (*And, Carib*) smallholding, small farm.
conuquero *nm* (*And, Carib*) smallholder, farmer.
conurbación *nf* conurbation.
convalecencia *nf* convalescence.
convalecer [2d] *vi* to convalesce, get better (*de* after), recover (*de* from).
convaleciente *adj, nmf* convalescent.
convalidable *adj* which can be validated.
convalidación *nf* acceptance, recognition; validation; ratification, confirmation.
convalidar [1a] *vt título* to accept, recognize; to validate; *documento* to ratify, confirm.
convección *nf* convection.
convecino, -a *nm/f* (close) neighbour.
convectivo *adj* convective.
convector *nm* convector.
convencer [2b] **1** *vt* to convince; to persuade; ~ **a uno de que algo es mejor** to convince sb sth is better; ~ **a uno para que haga algo** to persuade sb to do sth; **no me convence del todo** I'm not fully convinced; **no me convence ese tío** I don't really trust that chap.
2 *vi* to convince; **el argumento no convence** the argument does not convince (*o* is not convincing).
3 convencerse *vr* to become convinced; **¡convéncete!** believe you me!; I tell you it is so!; you'll have to get used to the idea!
convencimiento *nm* (**a**) (*acto*) convincing; persuasion.
(**b**) (*certeza*) conviction, certainty; **llegar al ~ de** to become convinced of; **llevar algo al ~ de uno** to convince sb of sth; **tener el ~ de que** ... to be convinced that ...
convención *nf* convention; **C~ de Ginebra** Geneva Convention.
convencional *adj* conventional.
convencionalismo *nm* conventionalism.
convencionero *adj* (*And, Méx*) comfort-loving, self-indulgent.
convencionista *nmf* (*Méx*) *follower of Convención movement led by Zapata and Villa (1914-15)*.
convenible *adj* (**a**) (*apropiado*) suitable; fitting; *precio* fair, reasonable. (**b**) *persona* accommodating.
conveniencia *nf* (**a**) (*aptitud*) suitability, fitness; (*provecho*) usefulness, advantageousness; expediency; advisability; **a la primera ~** at one's earliest opportunity, when convenient; **ser de la ~ de uno** to suit sb; **atender a la propia ~** to think of how sth will affect one.
(**b**) **~s** conventions (*t* **~s sociales**); proprieties, decencies.
(**c**) (*acuerdo*) agreement.
(**d**) (*puesto*) domestic post, job as a servant.
(**e**) **~s** (*Fin*) (*propiedad*) property; (*renta*) income; (*de criado*) perquisites.
conveniente *adj* (*apto*) suitable; (*correcto*) fit, fitting, proper; (*provechoso*) useful, profitable, advantageous; (*oportuno*) expedient; (*aconsejable*) advisable; **nada ~** unsuitable; **no es ~ que** ... it is not advisable that ...; it is not desirable that ...; **sería ~ que** ... it would be a good thing if ..., it would be an advantage if ...; **creer** (*o* **estimar, juzgar**) ~ to think fit, see fit; **juzgar ~** + *infin* to see fit to + *infin*, deem it wise to + *infin*.
convenio *nm* agreement, treaty, convenant; ~ **colectivo** collective bargain, general wages agreement; ~ **comercial** trade agreement; ~ **salarial** wages agreement.
convenir [3r] **1** *vi* (**a**) (*estar de acuerdo*) to agree (*con* with, *en* about); ~ (**en**) **hacer algo** to agree to do sth; ~ (**en**) **que** ... to agree that ...; **'sueldo a ~'** (*anuncio*) 'salary to be agreed'.
(**b**) (*ser adecuado*) to suit, be suited to; to be suitable for; to be good for; **si le conviene** if it suits you; **no me conviene** it's not in my interest, it's not worth my while; **me conviene quedarme aquí** it is best for me to stay here; **él no te conviene para marido** he's not the husband for you; **lo que más le conviene es un reposo completo** the best thing for him is complete rest.
(**c**) (*impers*) **conviene** + *infin* it is as well to + *infin*; it is important to + *infin*; **conviene recordar que** ... it is as well to remember that ..., it is to be remembered that ...; **no conviene que se publique eso** it is not desirable that that should be published; **conviene a saber** namely, that is.
2 convenirse *vr* to agree, come to an agreement (*en* on, about).
conventillero (*And, Cono Sur*) **1** *adj* gossipy. **2** *nm*, **conventillera** *nf* scandalmonger, gossip, telltale.
conventillo *nm* (*And, Cono Sur*) tenement, inner-city slum.
convento *nm* monastery; ~ (**de monjas**) convent, nunnery.
conventual *adj* conventual.
convergencia *nf* (**a**) (*lit*) convergence. (**b**) (*fig*) common tendency, common direction; concurrence; ~ **de izquierdas** (*Pol*) grouping (*o* coming together) of left-wing forces.
convergente *adj* (**a**) (*lit*) convergent, converging. (**b**) (*fig*) having a common tendency, tending in the same direction. (**c**) (*Pol*) of the Catalan party Convergència i Unió.
convergentemente *adv*: ~ **con** together with, jointly with.
converger [2c] *vi*, **convergir** [3c] *vi* (**a**) (*lit*) to converge (*en* on).
(**b**) (*fig*) to have a common tendency, tend in the same direction (*con* as); to concur, be in accord (*con* with); (*Pol etc*) to come together; **sus esfuerzos convergen a un fin común** their efforts have a common purpose, their efforts are directed towards the same objective.
conversa[1] *nf* (*esp LAm*) (*charla*) talk, chat; (*lisonjas*) smooth talk.
conversación *nf* conversation, talk; **cambiar de ~** to change the subject; **trabar ~ con uno** to get into conversation with sb.
conversacional *adj tono etc* conversational; *estilo* colloquial.
conversada *nf* (*LAm*) talk, chat.
conversador 1 *adj* (*LAm*) talkative, chatty. **2** *nm*, **conversadora** *nf* (**a**) (*persona locuaz*) conversationalist. (**b**) (*LAm*: *zalamero*) smooth talker.
conversar [1a] **1** *vt* (**a**) (*And, Cono Sur*) (*contar*) to tell, relate; (*informar*) to report. (**b**) (*Carib*: *ligar*) to chat up*. **2** *vi* (**a**) (*charlar*) to talk, converse. (**b**) (*Mil*) to wheel.
conversata *nf* (*Cono Sur*) talk, chat.
conversión *nf* (**a**) (*gen*) conversion. (**b**) (*Mil*) wheel.
converso 1 *adj* converted. **2** *nm*, **conversa[2]** *nf* convert; (*Hist*: *esp*) converted Jew(ess), converted Moor.
conversón (*And*) **1** *adj* talkative, gossiping. **2** *nm*, **conversona** *nf* talkative person, gossip.
conversor *nm* (*Rad*) converter.
convertibilidad *nf* convertibility.
convertible *adj* convertible.
convertidor *nm* converter; ~ **catalítico** catalytic converter.
convertir [3i] **1** *vt* (**a**) (*gen*) to convert (*t Ecl*); to transform, turn (*en* into); (*Com, Elec, Téc*) to convert; *dinero* to convert, change (*en* into); ~ **a uno al catolicismo** to convert sb to Catholicism.
(**b**) *ojos etc* to turn (*a* on).
2 convertirse *vr* to be converted, be transformed, be changed (*en* into); (*Ecl*) to be converted, convert (*a* to).
convexidad *nf* convexity.
convexo *adj* convex.
convicción *nf* conviction.
convicto 1 *adj* convicted, found guilty; condemned. **2** *nm*

(*LAm*) convict.
convidada *nf* round (*esp* of drinks); **dar una ~, pagar una ~** to stand a round.
convidado, -a *nm/f* guest.
convidar [1a] **1** *vt* (**a**) (*lit*) to invite; **~ a uno a hacer algo** to invite sb to do sth; **~ a uno a una cerveza** to stand sb a beer, treat sb to a beer, invite sb to have a beer; **~ a uno con un café** to offer sb a cup of coffee.
(**b**) (*fig*) **~ a** to stir to, move to; **el ambiente convida a la meditación** the setting invites one to indulge in meditation, the atmosphere is conducive to meditation.
2 convidarse* *vr* (**a**) (*invitarse*) to invite o.s. along.
(**b**) (*ofrecerse*) to volunteer, offer one's services.
convincente *adj* convincing.
convincentemente *adv* convincingly.
convite *nm* (**a**) (*acto*) invitation. (**b**) (*función*) banquet, feast; treat; party; **~ a escote** Dutch treat.
convivencia *nf* (**a**) living together, life together; good fellowship, socializing; **'~ en familia'** (*anuncio*) 'living with a family', 'live as family'. (**b**) (*Pol*) coexistence.
convivencial *adj* social; communal; community (*atr*).
conviviente *nmf* (*LAm*) live-in lover.
convivir [3a] *vi* to live together (*esp* amicably, in harmony); to share the same life; (*Pol*) to coexist; (*fig*) to exist side by side (*con* with).
convocación *nf* summoning, calling, convoking.
convocante *nmf* organizer; promoter.
convocar [1g] **1** *vt* to summon, call (together), convoke; *elecciones, huelga* to call. **2** *vi*: **~ a** to call for.
convocatoria *nf* (**a**) (*llamamiento*) summons, call (to a meeting); notice of a meeting; **'C~s para hoy'** (*Prensa*) 'Today's Meetings'; **~ de huelga** strike call; **~ de premio** announcement of a prize competition. (**b**) = **convocación.**
convólvulo *nm* convolvulus.
convoy *nm* (**a**) (*Náut*) convoy; (*Ferro*) train; (*****) procession; retinue. (**b**) (*vinagrera*) cruet, cruet stand. (**c**) (*Carib*: *ensalada*) salad.
convoyar [1a] **1** *vt* (**a**) (*escoltar*) to convoy; to guard, escort. (**b**) (*Cono Sur*: *financiar*) to back, sponsor. **2 convoyarse** *vr* (*Carib*) to connive together, plot.
convulsión *nf* convulsion; upheaval.
convulsionar [1a] *vt* (*Med*) to produce convulsions in; (*fig*) to convulse, cause an upheaval in.
convulsivo *adj* convulsive; disturbed, distraught.
convulso *adj* convulsed (*de* with).
conyugal *adj* conjugal; married.
conyugalidad *nf* married life.
cónyuge *nmf* spouse; partner; husband *o* wife; **~s** (*frec*) spouses; married couple, husband and wife.
cónyugues *nmfpl* spouses; married couple, husband and wife.
coña‡ *nf* (**a**) (*guasa*) humour, humorous tone, joking way; **en ~** as a joke, for a laugh; **¡ni de ~!** no way!*; **y esto no es ~** and this is no joke, and this is serious; **estar de ~** to be in a joking mood; **tomar algo a ~** to take sth as a joke.
(**b**) (*molestia*) annoyance, bind*; **¡es la ~!** it's beyond a joke!
coñá = **coñac.**
coñac [ko'ɲa] *nm, pl* **coñacs** [ko'ɲas] brandy, cognac.
coñazo‡ *nm* (**a**) (*persona, cosa*) pain*; **ponerse ~** to get stroppy*. (**b**) **dar el ~** to be a real pain*.
coñe‡ *excl* = **coño** (**b**).
coñearse‡ [1a] *vr* to speak in a joking way, adopt a humorous tone; **~ de** to make fun of.
coñete‡ *adj* (*And, Cono Sur*) stingy, tightfisted.
coño *nm* (**a**) (*** *Anat*) cunt**.
(**b**) *excl* (‡) (*t* **¡qué ~!**: *enojo*) hell!, damn!, damn it all!; (*sorpresa*) well I'm damned!, Christ!; (*alegría*) **¡esto hay que celebrarlo, ~!** we jolly well must celebrate this!*; (*a persona*) **¡ayúdeme, ~!** help me, you idiot!; **¡por fin, ~!** and it was bloody well time!‡
(**c**) (‡: *como adv*) **¿qué ~(s) haces ahí?** what in hell's name are you up to?*; **¿qué ~ te importa?** why the hell does it matter to you?
(**d**) (‡: *locuciones*) **¡ay, qué ~!** what a pain!*; **¡qué libro ni qué ~!** what bloody book!‡; **que lo haga él ... ¡qué ~!** let him do it ... no way!*; **viven en el quinto ~** they live way out (in the sticks)*, they live at the back of beyond*.
(**e**) (*Cono Sur, Méx*: *español*) *pejorative term applied to Spaniards.*
cooficial *adj*: **dos lenguas ~es** two languages equally recognized as official.
cooficialidad *nf*: **la ~ de dos lenguas** the equal official status of two languages.
cooperación *nf* cooperation.
cooperador 1 *adj* cooperative; collaborating, participating. **2** *nm,* **cooperadora** *nf* collaborator, co-worker.
cooperante *nmf* (overseas) voluntary worker.
cooperar [1a] *vi* to cooperate (*a, en* in; *con* with); **~ a** + *infin* to cooperate in + *ger*; **~ a un mismo fin** to work for a common aim, work together in a common cause; **~ en** to collaborate in, work together on, take part (together) in; **los factores que cooperaron al fracaso** the factors which together led to failure, the factors which contributed to the failure.
cooperativa *nf* cooperative, mutual association; **~ agrícola** agricultural cooperative; **~ de crédito** credit union.
cooperativista *nmf* member of a cooperative.
cooperativo *adj* cooperative.
cooptación *nf* cooption.
cooptar [1a] *vt* to coopt (*a* on to).
coordenada *nf* (*Mat*) coordinate.
coordinación *nf* coordination.
coordinado 1 *adj* coordinated; (*Mil*) *operación* combined. **2 ~s** *nmpl* (*ropa*) separates.
coordinador(a)¹ *nm/f* coordinator.
coordinadora² *nf* coordinating committee.
coordinar [1a] *vt* to coordinate.
copa *nf* (**a**) (*vaso*) glass; (*poét*) goblet; (*Dep etc*) cup, trophy; **~ balón** brandy glass; **~ flauta** champagne glass; **C~ Mundial** World Cup; **llevar una ~ de más** to have (had) one over the eight; **irse de ~s, salir de ~s** to go out for a drink; **tomarse unas ~s** to have a drink or two.
(**b**) (*fig*) **~ de la amargura** cup of sorrow; **apurar la ~** to know the utmost depths of suffering.
(**c**) (*de sombrero*) crown; (*de árbol*) top.
(**d**) **~s** hearts; **la ~** the ace of hearts.
(**e**) (*And*: *conocedor*) connoisseur, judge of wine.
(**f**) (*And Aut*) hubcap.
copado *adj árbol* thick, with dense foliage.
copal *nm* (*CAm, Méx*) resin, incense.
copante *nm* (*CAm, Méx*) **~s** stepping stones.
copar [1a] *vt* (**a**) (*Mil*) to surround, cut off; (*fig*) to corner; **quedar copado en un trabajo** to get bogged down in a piece of work.
(**b**) (*Naipes*: *t* **~ la banca**) to win (all the tricks), sweep the board; (*en el juego*) to go banco; (*Pol y fig*) to sweep the board, win hands down; *premio* to walk off with, collar*; **~ el mercado** to corner the market (*de* in).
(**c**) (*Méx*: *monopolizar*) to monopolize.
coparticipación *nf* joint participation (*en* in).
copartícipe *nmf* (*socio*) partner; (*Dep etc*) fellow participant, fellow competitor; (*condueño*) joint owner; (*colaborador*) collaborator (*en* in).
copazo* *nm* mixed drink of e.g. rum and Coke.
copear [1a] *vi* (**a**) (*: *beber*) to booze*, tipple; to go on a drinking spree. (**b**) (*Com*) to sell wine (*etc*) by the glass.
Copenhague *nm* Copenhagen.
copeo* *nm*: **ir de ~** to go drinking.
Copérnico *nm* Copernicus.
copete *nm* (**a**) (*de persona*) tuft (of hair), quiff; (*de caballo*) forelock; (*Orn*) tuft, crest; (*de bebida*) head; **estar hasta el ~** (*Carib, Méx*) to be fed up to the back teeth*.
(**b**) (*fig*) pride, haughtiness; **de alto ~** aristocratic; important, socially prominent; **tener mucho ~** to be haughty, be stuck-up*.
copetín *nm* (*And, Cono Sur*) (*copa de licor*) glass of spirits; (*cóctel*) cocktail; (*aperitivo*) aperitif; (*vasito*) liqueur glass.
copetón *adj* (**a**) (*LAm*) = **copetudo** (**a**). (**b**) (*****) (*And*) **estar ~** to be tight*. (**c**) (*Carib*) cowardly.
copetudo *adj* (**a**) (*Orn etc*) tufted; crested. (**b**) (*fig*: *linajudo*) highborn, of noble birth, blue-blooded; (*engreído*) haughty, stuck-up*.
copia¹ *nf* (*gen*) copy; (*Arte*) copy; (*reproducción*) replica, reproduction; duplicate; **~ de calco, ~ al carbón, ~ carbónica** (*Cono Sur*) carbon copy; **~ certificada** certified copy; **~ fotostática** photostat; **~ impresa** (*Inform*) hard copy; **~ en limpio** fair copy; **~ de respaldo, ~ de seguridad** back-up document; back-up; **sacar una ~ de** to make a copy of.
copia² *nf* (*abundancia*) abundance, plenty; **con gran ~ de** with an abundance of, with a great deal of.
copiado *nm* copying.
copiador(a)¹ *nm/f* (**a**) (*persona*) copier, copyist. (**b**) (*libro*) letter-book.
copiadora² *nf* copying machine, photocopier.
copiante *nmf* copyist.

copiar [1b] *vt* to copy (*de* from); *estilo etc* to imitate; *dictado* to take down.
copichuela* *nf* social drink.
copiloto *nmf* (*Aut*) co-driver; (*Aer*) co-pilot.
copiosamente *adv* copiously, abundantly, plentifully.
copioso *adj* copious, abundant, plentiful.
copista *nmf* copyist.
copita *nf* (small) glass; **una ~ de jerez** a glass of sherry; **tomarse unas ~s** to have a drink or two.
copla *nf* (**a**) (*Liter*) verse (*esp* of 4 lines); (*Mús*) popular song, folksong, ballad; **~s** verses, poetry; **~s de Calaínos** *silly story* (*etc*) *with which sb irrelevantly interrupts*; **~s de ciego** doggerel; **andar en ~s** to be the talk of the town; **es la misma ~** it's the same old story; **hacer ~s** to write verse; **no valen ~s** it's no use your arguing (*o* apologizing *etc*).
(**b**) (*CAm, Cono Sur*: *Téc*) pipe joint.
copo *nm* (**a**) (*de lino etc*) tuft, small bundle; **~ de algodón** cotton ball; **~s de avena** oatmeal, rolled oats; **~s de maíz tostado** cornflakes; **~ de nieve** snowflake.
(**b**) (*And, Carib*: *de árbol*) tree top.
(**c**) (*Cono Sur*: *nubes*) piled-up clouds.
copón* *nm* large cup; (*Rel*) pyx; **¡~!** hell's teeth!*; **y todo el ~** and all the rest, and all that stuff*; **un susto** (*etc*) **del ~** a tremendous fright* (*etc*).
coproducción *nf* (*Cine etc*) joint production.
coproducir [3n] *vt* (*Cine etc*) to co-produce, produce jointly.
copropiedad *nf* co-ownership.
copropietario, -a *nm/f* co-owner, joint owner.
copucha *nf* (*Cono Sur*) gossip.
copuchar [1a] *vi* (*Cono Sur*) to gossip.
copuchento *adj* (*Cono Sur*) lying.
copudo *adj árbol* bushy, thick.
cópula *nf* (**a**) (*Bio*) copulation; **~ carnal** copulation, sexual intercourse. (**b**) (*Ling*) conjunction; (*Gram*) copula.
copularse [1a] *vr* to copulate (*con* with).
copulativo *adj* (*Ling*) copulative.
coque *nm* coke.
coqueluche *nf* whooping cough.
coquero, -a *nm/f* cocaine addict.
coqueta 1 *adj* flirtatious, flighty, coquettish; vain. **2** *nf* (**a**) (*persona*) flirt, coquette. (**b**) (*pan*) roll, small loaf. (**c**) (*mueble*) dressing table (with a full-length mirror).
coquetear [1a] *vi* to flirt (*con* with; *t fig*).
coqueteo *nm*, **coquetería** *nf* (**a**) (*cualidad*) flirtatiousness, flightiness, coquetry; flirtatious disposition; (*fig*) affection. (**b**) (*acto*) flirtation.
coqueto, coquetón 1 *adj* (**a**) *vestido etc* smart, natty*, attractive. (**b**) *hombre* flirtatious; attractive (to women). (**c**) *mujer* = **coqueta 1. 2** *nm* ladykiller, wolf*.
coquilla *nf* (*Cono Sur*) shell.
coquitos *nmpl*: **hacer ~** to make faces (*a* at).
coracha *nf* (*esp LAm*) leather bag.
coraje *nm* (**a**) (*bríos*) fighting spirit; (*dureza*) toughness; (*valor*) courage; (*fortaleza*) fortitude. (**b**) (*enojo*) anger; **dar ~ a** to make angry, enrage.
corajina *nf* fit of temper, explosion of rage.
corajudo *adj* (**a**) (*animoso*) spirited; tough; bold; (*Cono Sur*: *valiente*) brave. (**b**) (*de genio vivo*) quick-tempered, peppery.
coral[1] (*Mús*) **1** *adj* choral. **2** *nm* chorale. **3** *nf* choir, choral group.
coral[2] *nm* (**a**) (*Zool*) coral. (**b**) (*serpiente*) coral snake.
coralina *nf* coralline.
coralino *adj* coral (*atr*), coralline.
corambre *nf* hides, skins.
Corán *nm* Koran.
corana *nf* (*And, Cono Sur*: *Hist*) sickle.
coránico *adj* Koranic.
coraza *nf* (**a**) (*Mil, Hist*) cuirass; (*fig*) breastplate, protection. (**b**) (*Náut*) armour-plating. (**c**) (*Zool*) shell. (**d**) (*Aut*) radiator cover.
corazón *nm* (**a**) (*Anat y fig*) heart; **de ~** willingly; **de todo ~** from the heart; **de buen ~** kind-hearted; **¡hijo de mi ~!** my precious child!; **revista del ~** magazine of love stories; **sección del ~ solitario** lonely hearts column; **duro de ~** hard-hearted; **sin ~** heartless; **con el ~ en la mano** frankly; sincerely; **estar enfermo del ~** to have heart trouble; **sí, mi ~** yes darling; **arrancar** (*o* **partir, romper**) **el ~ a uno** to break sb's heart; **no caberle a uno el ~ en el pecho** to be bursting with joy; to be the very soul of kindness; **le dio en el ~** she had a premonition; **encoger a uno el ~** to fill sb with fear (*o* dismay, pity); **llevar el ~ en la mano** to wear one's heart on one's sleeve; **meter a uno el ~ en un puño** (*o* **en la boca**) to give sb a scare; **tener el ~ en un puño** to have one's heart in one's mouth; **morir con el ~ destrozado** to die of a broken heart; **poner el ~ en algo** to set one's heart on sth; **no tener ~** to have no heart, be heartless; **tener el ~ para** + *infin* to have the heart to + *infin*; **no tener el ~ para algo** not to feel up to sth; *V* **íntimo** *etc*.
(**b**) (*Bot*) core.
(**c**) **corazones** (*Naipes*) hearts.
corazonada *nf* (**a**) (*pálpito*) presentiment, hunch. (**b**) (*impulso*) rash impulse, sudden impulse; (*acto*) impulsive act.
corazoncito* *nm*: **tener su ~** to have a heart.
corbata *nf* tie, necktie; cravat(e); **~ de lazo, ~ michi** (*And*) bow-tie; **~ de smoking** black tie.
corbatín *nm* bow tie.
corbeta *nf* corvette.
corca *nf* woodworm.
Córcega *nf* Corsica.
corcel *nm* steed, charger.
corcor *nm* (*CAm, Carib*) gurgle; **beber ~*** to swig*, knock it back*.
corcova *nf* (**a**) hump, hunchback. (**b**) (*And, Cono Sur*: *fiesta*) all night party.
corcovado 1 *adj* hunchbacked. **2** *nm*, **corcovada** *nf* hunchback.
corcovar [1a] *vt* to bend (over); to crook.
corcovear [1a] *vi* (**a**) to prance about, cut capers; (*caballo*) to buck, plunge. (**b**) (*And, Carib, Cono Sur*: *quejarse*) to grumble, grouse*. (**c**) (*Méx*: *tener miedo*) to be frightened, be afraid.
corcovo *nm* (**a**) (*brinco*) prance, caper; buck, plunge. (**b**) (*) crookedness*.
corcha *nf* (piece of) cork bark.
corchea *nf* (*Mús*) quaver.
corchero *adj* cork (*atr*); **industria corchera** cork industry.
corcheta *nf* (*Cos*) eye (*of hook and eye*).
corchete *nm* (**a**) (*Cos*) snap fastener; catch, clasp; hook and eye. (**b**) (*Tip*) **~s agudos** angled brackets < >; **~s rectos** square brackets [ ]. (**c**) (*Cono Sur*: *grapa*) staple.
corchetear [1a] *vt* (*Cono Sur*) to staple (together).
corchetera *nf* (*Cono Sur*) stapler.
corcho *nm* (*gen*) cork; (*corteza*) cork bark; (*estera*) cork mat; (*zueco*) cork-soled clog; (*Pesca*) float; **~ bornizo, ~ virgen** virgin cork; **sacar el ~** to draw the cork, uncork.
corcholata *nf* (*Méx*) metal bottle-top.
córcholis* *excl* good Lord!, dear me!
corchoso *adj* corklike, corky.
cordada *nf* (*Alpinismo*) team, roped team.
cordaje *nm* cordage; (*de raqueta*) strings; (*Náut*) rigging.
cordal *nm* hill range.
cordel *nm* cord, line; thin rope; **a ~** straight, in a straight line.
cordelería *nf* (**a**) (*cuerdas*) cordage, ropes; (*Náut*) rigging.
(**b**) (*fábrica*) ropeyard, ropeworks.
(**c**) (*arte*) cordmaking, ropemaking.
cordelero *nm* cordmaker, ropemaker.
cordería *nf* cordage, cords, ropes.
corderillo *nm*, **corderina** *nf* lambskin.
cordero, -a 1 *nm/f* (**a**) (*Zool*) lamb; **~ asado** roast lamb; **C~ de Dios** Lamb of God; **~ lechal** young lamb; **¡no hay tales ~s!** it's nothing of the sort.
(**b**) (*fig*) meek and mild person.
2 *nm* (*piel*) lambskin.
corderuna *nf* lambskin.
cordial 1 *adj* (**a**) (*gen*) cordial; heartfelt, hearty. (**b**) (*Farm*) tonic, invigorating. **2** *nm* cordial; tonic.
cordialidad *nf* warmth, cordiality.
cordialmente *adv* cordially; heartily; (*en carta*) sincerely.
cordillera *nf* range, chain (of mountains).
cordillerano *adj* (*Cono Sur*) Andean.
cordita *nf* cordite.
Córdoba *nf* Cordova.
córdoba *nf standard monetary unit of Nicaragua.*
cordobán *nm* cordovan (leather).
cordobana: **andar a la ~** to go around stark naked.
cordobés 1 *adj* Cordovan. **2** *nm*, **cordobesa** *nf* Cordovan.
cordón *nm* (**a**) (*cuerda*) cord, string; (*Náut*: *de cable*) strand; (*de zapato*) lace; (*Mil*) braid; (*Elec*) flex, extension wire (*US*); **cordones** (*Mil*) aiguillettes; **lana de 3 cordones** 3-ply wool; **~ detonante** (*Cono Sur*) fuse.
(**b**) (*Anat*) cord; **~ umbilical** umbilical cord.
(**c**) (*Arquit*) cordon.
(**d**) (*Mil, de policía etc*) cordon; **~ sanitario** sanitary

cordon, cordon sanitaire.

(**e**) (*Cono Sur*) kerb.

(**f**) ~ **de cerros** (*And, Carib, Cono Sur*) chain of hills.

(**g**) (*And, Carib*: *licor*) liquor, brandy.

cordoncillo *nm* (*de tela*) rib; (*Cos*) braid, piping; (*de moneda*) milling, milled edge.

cordura *nf* good sense, prudence, wisdom; **con** ~ sensibly, prudently, wisely.

Corea *nf* Korea; ~ **del Norte** North Korea; ~ **del Sur** South Korea.

coreano, -a *adj, nm/f* Korean.

corear [1a] **1** *vt* to say in a chorus; *slogan* to shout (in unison), chant; (*Mús*) to sing in chorus, sing together; (*Mús*: *componer*) to compose choral music for; (*fig*) to chorus, echo parrot-fashion; **su opinión es coreada por ...** his opinion is echoed by ... **2** *vi* to speak all together; (*Mús*) to sing all together, join in.

coreografía *nf* choreography.

coreografiar [1c] *vt* to choreograph.

coreográfico *adj* choreographic.

coreógrafo, -a *nm/f* choreographer.

Corfú *nm* Corfu.

coriana *nf* (*And*) blanket.

corifeo *nm* (**a**) (*Hist*) coryphaeus. (**b**) (*fig*) leader, spokesman.

corindón *nm* corundum.

corintio *adj* Corinthian.

Corinto *n* Corinth.

corinto 1 *adj invar* maroon, purplish. **2** *nm* maroon, purplish colour.

corista 1 *nmf* (*Ecl*) chorister; (*Mús*) member of the chorus. **2** *nf* (*Teat etc*) chorus girl.

coritatis* *adv*: **estar en** ~ to be in the buff*.

cormorán *nm* cormorant.

cornada *nf* butt, thrust (with the horns), goring; **dar una** ~ **a** to gore.

cornadura *nf* horns; (*de ciervo*) antlers.

cornalina *nf* cornelian, carnelian.

cornamenta *nf* horns; (*de ciervo*) antlers; (*hum*: *de marido*) cuckold's horns; **poner la** ~ **a uno** to cuckold sb.

cornamusa *nf* (*gaita*) bagpipe; (*cuerna*) hunting horn.

córnea *nf* cornea.

corneal *adj* corneal.

cornear [1a] *vt* to butt, gore.

corneja *nf* crow; rook; ~ **negra** carrion crow; ~ **calva** rook.

córneo *adj* horny, corneous.

córner ['korne] *nm, pl* **córners** ['korne *o* 'kornes] *o* **córneres** ['korneres] (**a**) (*Dep*) corner, corner kick; **¡~!** (*interj*) corner! (**b**) (*LAm*: *Boxeo*) corner.

cornerina *nf* cornelian, carnelian.

corneta 1 *nf* (*instrumento*) bugle; (*Carib*: *Aut*) horn; ~ **acústica** ear trumpet; ~ **de llaves** cornet; ~ **de monte** hunting horn. **2** *nmf* (*persona*) bugler; cornet player.

cornetear [1a] *vi* (*Carib Aut*) to sound one's horn.

cornetín 1 *nm* (*instrumento*) cornet. **2** *nmf* (*persona*) cornet player.

cornetista *nmf* bugler.

corneto *adj* (*CAm*) bow-legged.

cornezuelo *nm* (*Bot*) ergot.

cornflaques *nmpl*, **cornflés** *nmpl* (*LAm*) cornflakes.

cornial *adj* horn-shaped.

córnico 1 *adj* Cornish. **2** *nm* (*Ling*) Cornish.

corniforme *adj* horn-shaped.

cornisa *nf* cornice; **la C~ Cantábrica** the Cantabrian coast.

cornisamento *nm* entablature.

corno *nm* (*Mús*) horn; ~ **de caza** hunting horn; ~ **inglés** cor anglais.

Cornualles *nm* Cornwall.

cornucopia *nf* (**a**) (*Mit etc*) cornucopia, horn of plenty. (**b**) (*espejo*) small ornamental mirror.

cornudo 1 *adj* (**a**) (*Zool*) horned; antlered. (**b**) *marido* cuckolded. **2** *nm* cuckold.

cornúpeta *nm* (*t* **cornúpeto** *nm*) (*Taur*: *liter*) bull; (*hum*) cuckold.

coro *nm* (**a**) (*Mús, Teat*) chorus; **una chica del** ~ a girl from the chorus, a chorus girl; **cantar** (*etc*) **a ~s** to sing (*etc*) alternately; **decir algo a** ~ to say sth in a chorus, say sth in unison; **aprender algo de** ~ to learn sth by heart; to learn sth by rote; **hacer** ~ **de** (*o* **a**) **las palabras de uno** to echo sb's words.

(**b**) (*Mús, Ecl*) choir; ~ **celestial** celestial choir, heavenly choir; **niño de** ~ choirboy.

(**c**) (*Arquit*) choir.

corola *nf* corolla.

corolario *nm* corollary.

corona *nf* (**a**) (*de rey etc*) crown; coronet; (*aureola*) halo; ~ **de espinas** crown of thorns; ~ **de nieve** snowcap; **ceñirse la** ~ to take the crown; **rey sin** ~ **de Eslobodia** uncrowned king of Slobodia.

(**b**) (*Astron*) corona; (*Met*) halo.

(**c**) (*t* ~ **de flores**) garland; chaplet; ~ **funeraria,** ~ **mortuoria** wreath.

(**d**) (*Anat*) crown (of the head), top of the head; (*de diente*) crown; (*Ecl*) tonsure.

(**e**) (*Fin*) crown.

coronación *nf* (**a**) (*de rey*) coronation. (**b**) (*fig*) crowning, completion. (**c**) (*Arquit*) = **coronamiento** (**b**). (**d**) (*Ajedrez*) queening.

coronamiento *nm* (**a**) (*fig*) crowning, completion. (**b**) (*Arquit*) crown, coping stone; top, ornamental finish.

coronar [1a] *vt* (**a**) *persona* to crown; ~ **a uno** (**por**) **rey** to crown sb king.

(**b**) *edificio etc* to crown (*con, de* with); to top, cap.

(**c**) (*fig*) to crown; to complete, round off; ~ **algo con éxito** to crown sth with success; **para ~lo** to crown it all.

(**d**) (*Ajedrez, Damas*) to queen.

(**e**) (*And, Carib, Cono Sur*: *poner los cuernos a*) to cuckold, make a cuckold of.

coronario *adj* coronary.

coronel *nm* colonel; ~ **de aviación** group captain, colonel (*US*).

coronela *nf* (woman) colonel; (*Hist*) colonel's wife.

coronilla *nf* crown, top of the head; **andar** (*o* **bailar, ir**) **de** ~ to slog away, do one's utmost (to please sb); **dar de** ~ to bump one's head; **estar hasta la** ~ to be utterly fed up (*de* with).

coronta *nf* (*And, Cono Sur*) deseeded corncob.

corotear [1a] *vi* (*And*) to move house.

coroto *nm* (*And, CAm, Carib*) (**a**) (*vasija*) gourd, vessel. (**b**) **~s** gear, things; junk.

corpacho *nm*, **corpanchón** *nm*, **corpazo** *nm* (*) carcass*, fat body*.

corpiño *nm* bodice; (*Cono Sur*) brassière, bra.

corporación *nf* corporation; association; (*Com, Fin*) corporation, company.

corporal *adj* corporal, bodily; **ejercicio** ~ physical exercise; **higiene** ~ personal hygiene.

corporativismo *nm* corporate nature; corporate spirit.

corporativo *adj* corporate.

corporeidad *nf* corporeal nature.

corpóreo *adj* corporeal, bodily.

corpulencia *nf* burliness, heavy build; stoutness, massiveness; **cayó con toda su** ~ he fell with his full weight.

corpulento *adj persona* burly, heavily-built; *árbol etc* stout, solid, massive.

corpus *nm invar* corpus, body.

Corpus *nm* Corpus Christi.

corpúsculo *nm* corpuscle.

corral *nm* (*Agr*) yard, farmyard; stockyard, cattlepen, corral (*US*); (*de niño*) playpen; (*Carib*) small cattle farm; (††) open-air theatre; ~ **de abasto** (*Cono Sur*) slaughterhouse; ~ **de carbonera** coal dump, coalyard; ~ **de madera** timberyard; ~ **de vacas*** slum; ~ **de vecindad** tenement; **hacer ~es** to play truant.

corralillo *nm*, **corralito** *nm* playpen.

corralón *nm* large yard; (*Cono Sur*: *maderería*) timberyard, woodyard; (*And*) vacant site, vacant lot (*US*).

correa *nf* (**a**) (*gen*) strap; leather strap, thong; belt (*t Téc*); (*traílla*) leash; (*ronzal*) tether; ~ **para afilar navaja** razor strop; ~ **de seguridad** safety belt; ~ **sin fin** endless belt; ~ **de transmisión** driving belt, drive; ~ **transportadora,** ~ **de transporte** conveyor belt; ~ **de ventilador** (*Aut etc*) fan-belt; **besar la** ~ to eat humble pie.

(**b**) (*cualidad*) give, stretch, elasticity; **tener** ~ to be able to put up with a lot, know how to take it, be long-suffering.

correaje *nm* belts, straps; (*Téc*) belting.

correcalles *nf invar* streetwalker.

corrección *nf* (**a**) (*acto*) correction; adjustment; ~ **de pruebas** (*Tip*) proofreading, proof-correction.

(**b**) (*reprimenda*) rebuke, reprimand; (*castigo*) punishment.

(**c**) (*cualidad*) correctness; courtesy, politeness; good manners; propriety.

correccional *nm* reformatory.

correcorre *nm* (*Carib*) headlong rush, stampede.

correctamente *adv* (**a**) (*exactamente*) correctly; accurately; aright. (**b**) (*regularmente*) regularly. (**c**) (*decen-*

temente) correctly, politely; properly, fittingly.
correctivo *adj, nm* corrective.
correcto *adj* (**a**) *solución etc* correct; accurate; right; ¡~! right!, O.K.!*
(**b**) *rasgos etc* regular, well-formed.
(**c**) *persona* correct; courteous, polite, well-mannered; *conducta* courteous, correct; *vestido* correct, proper, fitting; **estuvo muy ~ conmigo** he was very polite to me.
corrector(a) **1** *nm/f* (*Tip*) proofreader; (*Prensa*) **~ de estilo** copy editor.
2 *nm* (**a**) (*líquido*) correcting fluid. (**b**) (*Inform*) **~ ortográfico** spell(ing) checker. (**c**) (*de dientes*) brace.
corredera *nf* (**a**) (*Téc*) slide; track, rail, runner; slide valve; (*abrochador*) zip, zipper (*US*); **puerta de ~** sliding door.
(**b**) (*Náut*) log.
(**c**) (*Téc: de molino*) upper millstone.
(**d**) (*Ent*) cockroach.
(**e**) (*Dep*) racetrack.
(**f**) (*Cono Sur: rápidos*) rapids.
corredero *nm* (**a**) (*Méx Dep*) racetrack. (**b**) (*And: lecho de río*) old riverbed.
corredizo *adj puerta etc* sliding; *grúa* travelling; *nudo* running, slip (*atr*).
corredor(a) **1** *nm/f* (**a**) (*Dep*) runner; athlete; **~ automovilista** racing driver, racing motorist; **~ ciclista** racing cyclist; **~ de cortas distancias** sprinter; **~ de fondo, ~ de larga distancia** long-distance runner; **~ de pista** track athlete.
(**b**) (*Com*) agent, broker; (*: *coime*) procurer, pimp; **~ de bienes raíces, ~ de propiedades** (*Cono Sur*) estate agent, real-estate broker (*US*); **~ de bodas** matchmaker; **~ de bolsa** stockbroker; **~ de casas** house agent; **~ de comercio** business agent; **~ de fincas rurales** land agent; **~ de oreja** gossip.
(**c**) (*Mil*) scout; (††) raider.
2 *nm* corridor, passage; **~ de popa** (*Náut*) stern gallery.
correduría *nf* brokerage.
corregible *adj* which can be corrected.
corregidor *nm* (*Hist*) chief magistrate; mayor.
corregidora *nf* (*Hist*) wife of the chief magistrate; mayoress.
corregir [3c *y* 3k] **1** *vt* (**a**) (*gen*) to correct; to put right, adjust; (*repasar*) to revise, look over; *pruebas* to correct, read.
(**b**) (*reprender*) to rebuke, reprimand; (*castigar*) to punish.
2 corregirse *vr* (*persona*) to reform, mend one's ways; **~ de su terquedad** to stop being obstinate.
correlación *nf* correlation.
correlacionar [1a] *vt* to correlate.
correlativo *adj, nm* correlative.
correligionario, -a *nm/f* (*Ecl*) co-religionist, person of the same faith; (*Pol*) fellow supporter, sympathizer, like-minded person.
correlón *adj* (**a**) (*LAm: corredor*) fast, good at running. (**b**) (*CAm, Méx: cobarde*) cowardly.
correntada *nf* (*Cono Sur*) rapids, strong current.
correntón **1** *adj* (**a**) (*activo*) busy, active. (**b**) (*bromista*) jokey, jolly, fond of a lark. **2** *nm* (*And, Carib*) strong current.
correntoso *adj* (*LAm*) *río* fast-flowing, rapid; in flood, in spate; *agua* torrential.
correo *nm* (**a**) (*persona*) courier; (*cartero*) postman, mailman (*US*); (‡) drug-pusher; **~ de gabinete** (*Pol*) Queen's Messenger, diplomatic courier (*US*).
(**b**) (*Correos*) post, mail; **~ aéreo** airmail; **~ certificado** registered post; **~ electrónico** electronic mail; **~ de primera clase** first-class mail; **~ urgente** special delivery; **echar al ~, poner en el ~** to post, mail (*esp US*); **llevar algo al ~** to take sth to the post; **¿ha llegado el ~?** has the post come?; **a vuelta de ~** by return (of post); **por ~** by post, through the post.
(**c**) (*oficina*) **~s** post office; **Administración General de C~s** General Post Office; **ir a ~s, pasar por ~s** to go to the post office.
(**d**) **el ~s** (*Ferro*) the mail train, the slow train.
correosidad *nf* toughness, leatheriness; flexibility.
correoso *adj* (*duro*) tough, leathery; (*flexible*) flexible.
correr [2a] **1** *vt* (**a**) *terreno, distancia* to traverse, cover, travel over; to pass over; **ha corrido medio mundo** he's been round half the world.
(**b**) (*Mil: Hist*) to overrun; to raid, invade; to lay waste.
(**c**) *objeto* to push along; *silla* to pull up, draw up; *cerrojo* to shoot, slide, draw; *llave* to turn; *cortina, velo* to draw; *botones etc* to move; *vela* to unfurl; *nudo* to undo, untie; *balanza* to tip.
(**d**) *caballo* to race, run; *toro* to fight; *presa* to chase, hunt, pursue.
(**e**) *riesgo* to run; *aventura* to have; *suerte* to suffer, undergo.
(**f**) *colores* to make run.
(**g**) (*Com*) to auction.
(**h**) *persona* (*t* **dejar corrido**) to embarrass, put to shame, cover with confusion.
(**i**) **~ la clase*** to cut class, play hooky.
(**j**) **~la*** to live it up*; to have one's fling; to go on a spree.
(**k**) **~ a uno*** (*CAm, Carib, Méx*) to throw sb out.
(**l**) (**‡**) to screw**‡**.
2 *vi* (**a**) (*gen*) to run; to hurry, rush; **corrió a decírselo** he ran to tell him, he hastened to tell him; **~ a la perdición** to rush headlong to disaster; **¡corre!** hurry!, hurry up!; **¡no corras tanto!** don't run so hard!, not so fast!; **~ a todo ~** to run as hard as one can; **~ como un galgo** (*o* **gamo**) to run like a hare; **echar a ~** to start to run, break into a run; to run off; **dejar ~ las cosas** to let things run on, let matters ride, let things take their course.
(**b**) (*agua, electricidad etc*) to run, flow; (*aire*) to flow, go, pass; (*grifo*) to run; (*fuente*) to play; (*Cono Sur: viento*) to blow; (*coche*) to go fast; **el río corre muy crecido** the river is running very high; **corre mucho viento** it's very windy, there's a strong wind blowing; **dejar ~ la sangre** to let the blood flow.
(**c**) (*tiempo*) to pass (quickly), elapse; (*período*) to run, extend, stretch; **el tiempo corre** time is passing, time presses; **el mes que corre** the present month, the current month; **durante lo que corre del año** during the year so far.
(**d**) (*dinero etc*) to pass, be valid, be acceptable; (*rumor*) to circulate, go round; (*creencia*) to be commonly held.
(**e**) (*Geog etc*) to run; **las montañas corren del este al oeste** the mountains run from east to west.
(**f**) (*sueldo etc*) to be payable; **su sueldo correrá desde el primer día del mes** his salary will be payable from the first of the month.
(**g**) **~ con la casa** to run the house, manage the house; **~ con los gastos** to pay (*o* meet, bear) the expenses; **él corre con eso** he is responsible for that, that is in his charge; **esto corre por tu cuenta** (*fig*) that's your problem.
(**h**) **~ a, ~ por** (*Com*) to sell at.
3 correrse *vr* (**a**) (*moverse: objeto*) to slide, move along; (*lastre, carga*) to shift; (*persona*) to move (up); **se ha corrido unos centímetros el tablero** the board has moved a few centimetres; **córrete un poco hacia este lado** move a bit this way.
(**b**) (*excederse*) to go too far, let o.s. go; **no te vayas a ~ en la propina** don't overdo it on the tip.
(**c**) (*colores*) to run; (*hielo etc*) to melt; (*vela*) to gutter; (*tinta*) to spread, make a blot.
(**d**) (*sofocarse*) to blush, to get embarrassed; (*aturdirse*) to become confused.
(**e**) **~ una juerga** *etc*: *V* **juerga.**
(**f**) (*CAm, Carib, Méx: huir*) to take flight, run away; (*acobardarse*) to get scared, take fright.
(**g**) (**‡**) to come**‡**, have an orgasm.
correría *nf* (*Mil*) raid, foray; (*fig*) trip, excursion; **~s** (*fig*) trips, travels.
correspondencia *nf* (**a**) (*gen*) correspondence.
(**b**) (*cartas*) correspondence, letters; (*Correos*) post, mail; **~ entrante** incoming mail; **~ particular** private correspondence; **curso por ~** correspondence course; **entrar en ~ con uno** to enter into correspondence with sb; **estar en ~ con uno** to be in correspondence with sb.
(**c**) (*enlaces*) communications, contact; (*Ferro etc*) connection (*con* with); (*Arquit*) communication, communicating passage.
(**d**) (*acuerdo*) agreement; (*armonía*) harmony; (*agradecimiento*) gratitude; (*de palabras*) equivalence; (*de afecto etc*) return; **mis ofertas no tuvieron ~** my offers met with no response; **yo esperaba más ~** I had expected a greater response.
corresponder [2a] **1** *vi* (**a**) (*Mat etc*) to correspond (*a* to, *con* with); to tally (*con* with); **no corresponde con sus principios** it does not fit in (*o* accord) with his principles.
(**b**) (*convenir*) to be suitable, be fitting, be right; to belong; **~ a** (*color, mueble etc*) to match; to fit, fit in with,

go with; **ese libro no corresponde aquí** that book doesn't belong here; **la llave corresponde a esta cerradura** the key fits this lock; **todavía no corresponde hacerlo** it is still not the right time to do it; **el resultado no ha correspondido a nuestras esperanzas** the result did not come up to our expectations; **con una gravedad que corresponde a su importancia** with a gravity which befits its importance.

(**c**) (*ser para*) ~ **a** to fall to the lot of, be the share of; **le dieron lo que le correspondía** they gave him his share; **correspondieron 100 ptas a cada uno** everyone got 100 ptas (as his share), each one's share amounted to 100 ptas.

(**d**) (*incumbir*) ~ **a** (*deber etc*) to concern; to rest with, devolve upon; **'a quien corresponda'** 'to whom it may concern'; **me corresponde hacerlo** it is my job to do it, it is my business to do it; **no me corresponde criticarle** it is not for me to criticize him; **me corresponde jugar a mí** it's my turn to play.

(**e**) (*contestar*) to respond, reply; ~ **a** *cariño* to return, reciprocate; *favor* to repay; ~ **dignamente a** to make a fitting reply to; **ella le correspondió con una corbata** she gave him a tie in return; **pero ella le correspondió con desprecio** but she responded scornfully, but all she gave in return was disdain; **nunca podré ~ a tanta generosidad** I can never adequately repay such generosity; **un amor no correspondido** an unrequited love, a love which was never returned.

(**f**) (*Ferro etc*) to connect (*con* with).

(**g**) (*Arquit*) to communicate (*con* with).

2 corresponderse *vr* (**a**) (*gen*) to correspond; (*armonizar*) to agree, be in harmony (*con* with); (*personas*) to have mutual affection (*etc*), have regard for one another; (*colores etc*) to match, go together.

(**b**) (*Correos*) to correspond (*con* with).

correspondiente 1 *adj* (*que corresponde*) corresponding (*a* to); (*apropiado*) appropriate; *palabra* equivalent; (*respectivo*) respective. **2** *nmf* (*de academia etc*) correspondirg member.

corresponsabilidad *nf* joint responsibility.

corresponsable *adj* jointly responsible (*de* for).

corresponsal *nm* (newspaper) correspondent; ~ **de guerra** war correspondent.

corretaje *nm* brokerage.

corretear [1a] **1** *vt* (**a**) (*LAm*: *acosar*) to pursue, harass.

(**b**) (*CAm*: *ahuyentar*) to scare off.

(**c**) (*Cono Sur Com*) to sell on behalf of, act for.

(**d**) (*Cono Sur*) *trabajo* to hurry along, push*.

2 *vi* (**a**) (*ir de prisa*) to run about, rush around.

(**b**) (*vagar*) to loiter, hang about the streets.

correteo *nm*: **andar en ~s** (*CAm*) to rush about.

corretero, -a *nm/f* busy person, gadabout.

correve(i)dile *nm* (**a**) (*acusique*) tell-tale; (*chismoso*) gossip. (**b**) (*coime*) pimp.

corrida *nf* (**a**) (*acto*) run, dash, sprint; **dar una ~** to make a dash; **decir algo de ~** to rattle off sth from memory; **en una ~** in an instant.

(**b**) ~ **(de toros)** (*Taur*) bullfight; **tener ~ de toros (en casa)** to have a big family row.

(**c**) (*Carib, Cono Sur*: *fiesta*) party, rave-up‡.

(**d**) (*Cono Sur*: *fila*) row, line, file.

(**e**) (*Méx*: *recorrido*) run, journey.

(**f**) (*Geol*) outcrop.

(**g**) (*‡*) orgasm.

corrido 1 *adj* (**a**) (*seguido*) **tres noches corridas** three nights running; **hasta muy corrida la noche** far into the night.

(**b**) *peso etc* extra (large); **un kilo ~** a good kilo, a kilo and a bit more.

(**c**) (*Arquit etc*) continuous.

(**d**) (*avergonzado*) abashed, sheepish; (*confuso*) confused; (*sofocado*) embarrassed; ~ **de vergüenza** covered with shame.

(**e**) (*perito*) experienced (in the wicked ways of the world), wise, sharp, knowing; **es una mujer corrida** she's a woman who has been around.

(**f**) *estilo* fluent, confident; **decir algo de ~** to rattle sth off; **lo sabía de ~** he knew it all right through, he could say it all from memory.

(**g**) *fiesta* excellent, splendid.

2 *nm* (**a**) (*Andalusia, And, Méx*: *balada*) ballad.

(**b**) (*And*: *fugitivo*) fugitive from justice.

corriente 1 *adj* (**a**) *agua* running; *estilo* flowing, fluent, easy, smooth; *dinero etc* current, valid, accepted; *cuenta, publicación, año etc* current; *interés, noticia* topical; **el año ~** the current year, the present year.

(**b**) (*normal*) ordinary, normal, common, everyday; standard; ~ **y moliente** ordinary, run-of-the-mill; **lo ~ es no pintarlo** the usual thing is not to paint it; **aquí es ~ ver eso** it's common to see that here, that is a common sight here; **es una chica ~** she's an ordinary sort of girl.

(**c**) (*en regla*) in order; **tiene ~ la documentación** his papers are in order; **todo está ~ para la partida** everything is fixed up for your departure.

(**d**) **ir** (*o* **estar**) ~ **en los pagos** to be up to date in one's payments.

2 *nm* (**a**) (*mes*) current month; **el 9 del ~** the 9th of the current month, the 9th inst.

(**b**) **al ~** punctually, on time; up-to-date.

(**c**) **estar al ~ de** to be informed about, be aware of, be well up with; **mantenerse al ~** to keep up to date (*de* with); **tener a uno al ~ de** to keep sb informed about, keep sb in touch with; **téngame al ~** keep me informed.

3 *nf* (**a**) (*de agua*) current; stream, flow; **C~ del Golfo** Gulf Stream; **C~ de Humboldt** Humboldt Current; ~ **de lava** stream of lava; ~ **sanguínea** bloodstream; ~ **submarina** undercurrent.

(**b**) ~ **de aire** draught; ~ **de aire caliente** flow of warm air; ~ **en chorro** jet stream; ~ **térmica** thermal.

(**c**) (*Elec*) current; ~ **alterna** alternating current; ~ **continua,** ~ **directa** direct current; **el hilo está con ~** the wire is live.

(**d**) (*tendencia*) course; tendency; drift; **dejarse llevar de la ~** to drift along, follow the crowd; **las ~s modernas del arte** modern trends in art; **una fuerte ~ innovadora** a strong innovating tendency.

corrillero, -a *nm/f* idler, person with time to gossip.

corrillo *nm* huddle, knot of people, small group; (*fig*) clique, coterie.

corrimiento *nm* (**a**) (*Geol*) slipping, sliding; ~ **de tierras** landslide.

(**b**) (*Med*) discharge; (*Carib, Cono Sur*) rheumatism; (*And*) tooth abscess.

(**c**) (*fig*) embarrassment; shyness, sheepishness.

(**d**) (*Inform*) scrolling.

corrincho *nm* (**a**) (*muchedumbre*) mob. (**b**) (*And*: *jaleo*) uproar, row. (**c**) (*And*: *emoción*) excitement; (*prisa*) haste.

corro *nm* (**a**) (*de gente*) ring, circle; huddle, knot (of people); (*Fin*) round enclosure (in the stock exchange); **la gente hizo ~** the people formed a ring.

(**b**) (*juego*) ring-a-ring-a-roses; **los niños cantan esto en ~** the children sing this in a ring.

(**c**) (*espacio*) circular space; **hacer ~** to make room, leave a circular space.

(**d**) (*trozo*) small area, part, piece (of a surface); (*Agr*) plot, small field, patch.

corroboración *nf* corroboration.

corroborar [1a] *vt* to corroborate.

corroborativo *adj* corroborative.

corroer [2a] **1** *vt* to corrode; (*Geol*) to erode; (*fig*) to corrode, eat away, eat up; **le corroen los celos** he is eaten up with jealousy.

2 corroerse *vr* to corrode, become corroded.

corromper [2a] **1** *vt* (**a**) (*pudrir*) *madera etc* to rot; *alimentos* to turn bad; (*arruinar*) to spoil, ruin, cause damage to.

(**b**) (*fig*) *costumbres, lengua, joven etc* to corrupt, pervert; *placeres* to spoil; *juez, oficial* to bribe.

(**c**) (*enviciar*) to seduce, debauch, dishonour.

(**d**) (*: *enojar*) to vex, annoy.

2 *vi* (*) to smell bad.

3 corromperse *vr* (**a**) (*lit*) to rot; to go bad, deteriorate; to be spoiled.

(**b**) (*fig*) to become corrupted, become perverted.

corrompido *adj* (**a**) rotten, putrid. (**b**) (*fig*) corrupted, corrupt; depraved, degenerate, perverted.

corroncha *nf* (*And, CAm*) crust, scale.

corroncho *adj* (**a**) (*Carib*: *torpe*) slow, sluggish. (**b**) (*And*) *persona* difficult, prickly.

corronchoso *adj* (*And, CAm, Carib*) (*burdo*) rough, coarse; (*escamoso*) crusty, scaly.

corrongo *adj* (*CAm, Carib*: *excelente*) first-rate, splendid; (*encantador*) charming, attractive.

corrosión *nf* corrosion; rust; (*Geol*) erosion.

corrosivo *adj* corrosive; (*fig*) ruinous, disastrous.

corrugación *nf* contraction, shrinkage.

corrupción *nf* (**a**) (*pudrición*) rot, decay; (*hedor*) stink, stench.

(**b**) (*fig*) corruption; perversion; (*de texto*) corruption; (*Jur*) corruption; (*soborno*) graft, bribery; (*Jur*) seduction; **en el gobierno existe mucha ~** there is a lot of

corruption in the government.
corruptela *nf* (**a**) (*gen*) corruption. (**b**) (*una* ~) corrupt practice, abuse.
corruptible *adj* (**a**) *persona* corruptible, bribable. (**b**) *alimentos etc* perishable.
corrupto *adj* corrupt.
corruptor 1 *adj* corrupting. **2** *nm*, **corruptora** *nf* corrupter, perverter.
corsario *nm* privateer, corsair.
corsé *nm* corset; (*fig*) straitjacket.
corso¹, -a *adj, nm/f* Corsican.
corso² *nm* (*Náut: Hist*) privateering, piratical enterprise.
corta *nf* felling, cutting.
cortaalambres *nm invar* wire-cutters.
cortabolsas *nm invar* pickpocket.
cortacésped *nm* lawnmower.
cortacircuitos *nm invar* circuit breaker.
cortacorriente *nm* switch.
cortacutícula *nf* cuticle scissors.
cortada *nf* (**a**) (*LAm: corte*) cut, slash; (*zanja*) trench; (*atajo*) short cut. (**b**) (*de pan etc*) slice. (**c**) (*Tenis*) stroke giving backspin.
cortadillo *nm* (**a**) (*vaso*) small glass, small tumbler. (**b**) (*azúcar*) lump of sugar. (**c**) (*: *ligue*) affair.
cortado 1 *adj* (**a**) (*gen*) cut; clipped; ~ **a pico** steep, sheer, precipitous.
(**b**) *leche* sour.
(**c**) *estilo* abrupt; disjointed.
(**d**) (*avergonzado*) shamed, shamefaced; (*tímido*) shy; (*confuso*) confused; (*sofocado*) embarrassed.
(**e**) **estar** ~ (*: *Cono Sur*) to be broke*.
(**f**) **tener** (*o* **sentir**) **el cuerpo** ~ (*Méx*) to feel off colour.
2 *nm* (**a**) (*café*) coffee with a little milk.
(**b**) (*Ballet*) caper, leap.
cortador 1 *adj* cutting.
2 *nm* (**a**) (*t Téc*) cutter; ~ **de cristal** glass cutter.
(**b**) (*Cos*) cutter.
cortadora *nf* cutter, cutting-machine; slicer; ~ **de césped** lawnmower.
cortadura *nf* (**a**) (*acto*) cut, cutting.
(**b**) (*corte*) cut; slash, slit; (*borde*) cut edge.
(**c**) (*Geog*) narrow pass, defile.
(**d**) ~**s** cuttings, clippings; (*de periódico*) newspaper cuttings, newspaper clippings (*US*).
cortafrío *nm* cold chisel.
cortafuego(s) *nm* (*invar*) firebreak, fire-lane (*US*).
cortahuevos *nm invar* egg-slicer.
cortahumedades *nm invar* damp course.
cortalápices *nm invar* pencil sharpener.
cortante 1 *adj* (**a**) (*gen*) cutting, sharp. (**b**) *viento* cutting, biting; *frío* bitter. **2** *nm* (*trinchador*) cleaver, chopper.
cortapapel *nm* (*LAm*), **cortapapeles** *nm invar* paper knife; (*Téc*) paper cutter, guillotine.
cortapicos *nm invar* earwig.
cortapisa *nf* (**a**) (*restricción*) restriction, limitation (attached to a concession), condition (attached to a gift); **sin** ~**s** without strings attached.
(**b**) (*pega*) snag, obstacle; **se pone ~s para sí mismo** he makes obstacles for himself; **hablar sin ~s** to talk freely.
(**c**) (*gracia*) charm, wit.
cortaplumas *nm invar* (**a**) penknife. (**b**) (*Ent*) earwig.
cortapuros *nm invar* cigar-cutter.
cortar [1a] **1** *vt* (**a**) (*gen*) to cut; to hack, chop, slash; *pelo* to cut, clip, trim; *rama, miembro, cabeza etc* to cut off; *garganta* to cut, slit; *árbol* to cut down, fell; *carne* to carve, cut up; *disco, tela* to cut; *recorte, dibujo, vestido* to cut out; ~ **por la mitad** to cut down the middle.
(**b**) (*Mat*) to intersect, cut; (*Geog*) to cut, cut across; **esa línea corta la provincia en dos** that line cuts the province in two.
(**c**) (*Dep*) *pelota* to cut, slice, spin.
(**d**) *aire, agua etc* to cut through.
(**e**) (*frío*) *piel* to chap, crack, split.
(**f**) (*Cartas*) to cut.
(**g**) *comunicación, enemigo, retirada etc* to cut off; (*interrumpir*) *carretera, puente* to cut; *agua etc* to cut off, turn off, shut off; (*Elec*) to switch off; *incendio etc* to prevent the spread of; **la carretera está cortada** the road is cut; **quedaron cortados por la nieve** they were cut off by snow.
(**h**) (*abreviar*) *carta, oración etc* to cut short, stop, bring to a close; *persona* to interrupt; *conversación* to interrupt, cut into, break into.
(**i**) (*suprimir*) *pasaje, detalle etc* to cut out, remove, suppress.
(**j**) (*) *droga* to cut, adulterate, dilute.
2 *vi* (**a**) (*gen*) to cut; **este cuchillo no corta** this knife doesn't cut; *V* **sano** *etc*.
(**b**) (*Cartas*) to cut.
(**c**) (*viento*) to be biting; **hace un viento que corta** there's a bitter wind.
(**d**) ~ **con el pasado** to (make a) break with the past; **ha cortado con su novia** (*LAm*) he's finished with his girlfriend, he and his girlfriend have broken up.
(**e**) **¡corta!*** get away!*
(**f**) (*Rad*) **¡corto!** over!; **¡corto y cierro!** over and out!
3 cortarse *vr* (**a**) ~ **el pelo** to have one's hair cut; **si no acepta, me la corto**‡ if he doesn't accept, I'll eat my hat.
(**b**) (*manos*) to get chapped; (*tela*) to split, come apart.
(**c**) (*leche*) to curdle, turn, turn sour.
(**d**) (*fig*) to become embarrassed, get confused, become tongue-tied; **no se corta** he isn't shy, he isn't backward in coming forward.
(**e**) (*: *Cono Sur*) (*separarse*) to become separated (from the others), get left behind; (*irse*) to clear off*; (*en trato etc*) to get left out; ~ **solo** to go off on one's own.
(**f**) (*: *Cono Sur: morir*) to die.
(**g**) (*And, Carib, Méx Med*) to shiver, get the shivers.
(**h**) (*Cono Sur: caballo*) to be out of breath.
cortauñas *nm invar* nail clippers.
cortavidrios *nm invar* glass cutter.
cortavientos *nm invar* windbreak.
corte¹ *nm* (**a**) (*acto*) cut, cutting; (*Cos*) cutting out; (*de árboles*) cutting, felling; (*Cine*) cutting; (*Golf*) cut; (*: *de droga*) cut; ~ **de carretera** closing of a road; ~ **de digestión** stomach cramp; ~ **de pelo** haircut; ~ **a lo garçon** Eton crop, shingle; **dar** ~ **a** to sharpen, put an edge on.
(**b**) (*señal*) cut.
(**c**) (*Tip etc*) cut, deletion; **el censor lo dejó sin ~s** the censor did not cut it, the censor did not delete anything.
(**d**) (*Elec etc*) cut; failure; (*Aut: en carretera*) block; ~ **de corriente,** ~ **de fluido eléctrico** power cut; power failure; **hay** ~ **de agua** the water has been cut off (*o* turned off).
(**e**) (*Téc*) section; ~ **transversal** cross section; ~ **vertical** vertical section.
(**f**) (*Min*) stint.
(**g**) (*Cos: trozo*) piece, length; ~ **de vestido** dress length.
(**h**) (*Cos: arte*) tailoring; dressmaking; (*estilo*) cut, style; **un traje de** ~ **muy moderno** a suit of very modern cut; **academia de** ~ (**y confección**) dressmaking school; ~ **de mangas** *obscene sign equivalent to* two fingers; **hacer un** ~ **de mangas a uno** to give sb the two fingers (sign); **programa de** ~ **liberal** programme with liberal leanings.
(**i**) (*Tip: de libro*) edge; **con ~s dorados** with gilt edges.
(**j**) (*Mús, de disco*) short item, individual piece; (*TV*) ~ **publicitario** commercial break.
(**k**) **darse ~s** (*Cono Sur*) to put on airs.
(**l**) (*: *susto*) start, surprise.
(**m**) (*: *desaire*) snub, rebuff; **¡qué ~!** that's one in the eye!; **no le dé** ~ don't be shy, don't be reticent.
(**n**) (*: *réplica*) sharp answer.
corte² *nf* (**a**) (*real*) (royal) court.
(**b**) (*ciudad*) capital (city); **La C~** Madrid.
(**c**) (*séquito*) suite, retinue.
(**d**) **C~s** (*Pol*) Spanish parliament; **C~s de Castilla y León** Regional Assembly of Castile and León; **C~s Constituyentes** constituent assembly, constitution-making body.
(**e**) **hacer la** ~ **a una** to woo sb, court sb.
(**f**) (*LAm: tribunal*) law court; **C~ Suprema** Supreme Court.
cortedad *nf* (**a**) (*de tamaño*) shortness, smallness; (*de tiempo*) brevity; ~ **de vista** shortsightedness.
(**b**) (*t* ~ **de ánimo**) bashfulness, timidity, shyness; diffidence.
(**c**) (*t* ~ **de alcances**) stupidity.
cortejar [1a] *vt* to court, woo (*t fig*).
cortejo *nm* (**a**) (*séquito*) entourage, suite, retinue.
(**b**) (*desfile*) procession; solemn gathering; ~ **fúnebre** funeral procession; ~ **nupcial** wedding procession, wedding party.
(**c**) (*de amante*) wooing, courting; courtship.
(**d**) (*persona*) lover, beau.
cortés *adj* (**a**) (*atento*) courteous, polite; gracious. (**b**) **amor** ~ courtly love.
cortesana *nf* courtesan.

cortesanía *nf* politeness; good manners.
cortesano **1** *adj* of the court; courtly; court (*atr*); **ceremonias cortesanas** court ceremony. **2** *nm* courtier.
cortesía *nf* **(a)** (*cualidad*) courtesy, politeness; graciousness; **visita de ~** formal visit, courtesy call; **entrada de ~** free ticket, complimentary ticket; **días de ~** (*Com*) days of grace; **por ~** as a courtesy.
(b) (*etiqueta*) social etiquette; **la ~ pide que ...** etiquette demands that ...
(c) (*regalo*) present, gift.
(d) (*título*) title.
(e) (*reverencia*) bow; curtsy; **hacer una ~ a** to bow to; to curtsy to.
(f) (*en carta*) concluding formula.
cortésmente *adv* courteously, politely; graciously.
córtex *nm* cortex.
corteza *nf* **(a)** (*de árbol*) bark; (*de fruta*) peel, skin, rind; (*Anat, Bot*) cortex; (*de pan*) crust; (*de queso*) rind; **~ cerebral** cerebral cortex; **añadir una ~ de limón** to add a bit of lemon peel.
(b) (*fig: exterior*) outside, outward appearance; hide, exterior.
(c) (*fig: grosería*) roughness, coarseness.
cortijo *nm* farm, farmhouse.
cortina *nf* curtain; screen, flap; **~ de ducha** shower curtain; **~ de fuego** artillery barrage; **~ de hierro** (*Pol*) iron curtain; **~ de humo** smoke screen (*t fig*); **~ de tienda** tent flap; **~ musical** (*Cono Sur: TV etc*) musical interlude; **correr la ~** (*fig*) to draw a veil over sth; **descorrer la ~** (*fig*) to draw back the veil.
cortinado *nm* (*Cono Sur*) curtains.
cortinilla *nf* lace curtain; thin curtain.
cortisona *nf* cortisone.
corto **1** *adj* **(a)** (*espacio*) short; (*tiempo*) brief, short; (*Com, Rad*) short; (*demasiado ~*) too short; **parece ~ it looks too** short; **a la corta o a la larga** sooner or later; **el vestido le ha quedado corto** the dress has got too short for her; **el niño va todavía de ~** the child is still wearing short trousers (*etc*); **el toro quedó ~** the bull stopped short (in its charge).
(b) *provisión etc* scant, scanty; inadequate; defective; *ración etc* small; **~ de oído** hard of hearing; **~ de resuello** short of breath, short-winded; **~ de vista** shortsighted; **pongamos 50 ptas y me quedo ~** let's say 50 ptas and that's an underestimate; **se quedó corta en la comida** she did not provide enough food, she underestimated the food that would be needed; **esta ley se queda corta** this law does not go far enough, this law is less than fully satisfactory.
(c) (*t ~ de ánimos*) bashful, timid, shy; socially backward; tongue-tied; **quedarse ~** to say less than one should say, not say nearly enough; **ni ~ ni perezoso, él ...** not to be outdone, he ...; without a moment's delay, he ...; without thinking twice, he ...
(d) (*t ~ de alcances*) dim*, not very bright; **es más ~ que las mangas de un chaleco*** he's as thick as two short planks*.
2 *nm* **(a)** (*Cine*) short.
(b) (*caña*) small glass (of beer).
cortocircuitar [1a] *vt* to short-circuit.
cortocircuito *nm* short-circuit; **poner(se) en ~** to short-circuit.
cortometraje *nm* (*Cine*) short.
cortón[1] *nm* (*Ent*) mole cricket.
cortón[2]* *adj* **(a)** (*tímido*) bashful, timid. **(b) es muy ~** (*CAm*) he's always interrupting.
cortopunzante *adj* (*Cono Sur*) sharp.
Coruña *nf*: **La ~** Corunna.
coruñés **1** *adj* of Corunna. **2** *nm*, **coruñesa** *nf* native (*o* inhabitant) of Corunna; **los coruñeses** the people of Corunna.
corva *nf* back of the knee.
corvadura *nf* curve, curvature; bend.
corvejón *nm* (*de caballo*) hock; (*de gallo*) spur.
corveta **1** *adj* (*CAm*) bow-legged. **2** *nf* curvet, prance.
corvetear [1a] *vi* to curvet, prance.
corvina *nf* sea bass, croaker.
corvo *adj* curved; bent.
corza *nf* doe.
corzo *nm* roe deer, roebuck.
cosa *nf* **(a)** (*gen*) thing; matter; **hay una ~ que no me gusta** there is something I don't like; **alguna ~** something; **¿alguna ~ más?** anything else?; **20 kilos o ~ así** 20 kilos or thereabouts; **ni ~ que le parezca** nor anything like it; **otra ~** anything else, something else; **ésa es otra ~** that's another matter (altogether); **no me queda otra ~** I have no alternative; **poca ~** nothing much; **es poca ~, no es gran ~** it's not important; it isn't up to much; **como si tal ~** as if nothing (out of the ordinary) had happened; as cool as you please; **y ~s así** and suchlike; **así las ~s ...** at this point ...; **la ~ es que ...** the trouble is that ...; **no es ~ que lo dejes todo** there's no reason for you to give it all up; **no sea ~ que ...** lest ..., in case ...; **tal como están las ~s** as things stand; **¡no hay tal ~!** nothing of the sort!; **¡vaya una ~!** well!; **¡lo que son las ~s!** just imagine!; fancy that!; **las ~s van mejor** things are going better; **pasa cada ~** anything can happen; **como quien no quiere la ~** tentatively; unobtrusively, surreptitiously; **decir una ~ por otra** (*euf*) to lie; **decir cuatro ~s a uno** to give sb a piece of one's mind.
(b) (*con adj etc*) **es ~ de nunca acabar** there's no end to it; **no es ~ de broma** (*o* **risa**) it's no laughing matter; **~(s) de comer** eatables, food; **es ~ distinta** that's another matter; **~ dura, ~ fuerte** tough business, hard thing to bear; **~s de escribir** writing things, writing materials; **es ~ fácil** it's easy; **es ~ fina*** it's top-quality gear*; **¿has visto ~ igual?** did you ever see the like?; **es ~ perdida** he's a dead loss; **~ rara** strange thing; **¡(qué) ~ más rara!** how strange!, most odd!; **y, ~ rara, nadie lo vio** and, oddly enough, nobody saw it; **es ~ de ver** it's worth seeing, one must see it; **le explicó las ~s de la vida** she told her the facts of life, she told her about the birds and the bees; **ésa es ~ vieja** that's stale, that's old history; **las ~s de palacio van despacio** (*fig*) it all takes time, the mills of God grind slowly.
(c) (*asunto*) affair, business; **ésa es ~ tuya** that's your affair, that's up to you.
(d) (*idea*) **~s** odd ideas, wild notions; **¡~s de España!** that's typical of Spain!, what else can you expect in Spain!; **¡~s de muchachos!** boys will be boys!; **¡son ~s de Juan!** that's typical of John!, that's John all over!; **¡qué ~s dices!** (*hum*) what dreadful things you say!; **¡tienes unas ~s!** the things you say!
(e) (*cantidad*) **~ de 8 días** about a week; **en ~ de 10 minutos** in about 10 minutes; **es ~ de unas 4 horas** it takes about 4 hours.
(f) (‡: *droga*) hash*.
(g) (*LAm: como conj*) **~ que: camina lento, ~ que no te canses** walk slowly so that you don't get tired (*o* so as not to get tired); **no le digas nada, ~ que no se ofenda** don't say anything to him, that way he won't get offended.
cosaco **1** *adj* Cossack. **2** *nm*, **cosaca** *nf* **(a)** Cossack. **(b)** (*Cono Sur*) mounted policeman.
coscacho *nm* (*And, Cono Sur*) rap on the head.
coscarana *nf* cracknel.
coscarse* [1g] *vr* to catch on, get it*.
coscoja *nf* kermes oak.
coscolino *adj* **(a)** (*Méx*) (*malhumorado*) peevish, touchy; *niño* naughty. **(b)** (*moralmente*) of loose morals.
coscorrón *nm* **(a)** (*lit*) bump on the head. **(b)** (*fig*) setback, disappointment, knock.
coscurro *nm* hard crust (of bread).
cosecha *nf* (*gen*) crop, harvest (*t fig*); (*acto*) harvesting, gathering; (*época*) harvest, harvest time; (*producto*) crop, yield; **la ~ de 1992** (*vino*) the 1992 vintage; **de ~ propia** *legumbres etc* home-grown, home-produced; **cosas de su propia ~** (*fig*) things of one's own invention, things out of one's own head; **no añadas nada de tu ~** don't add anything that you've made up.
cosechado *nm* harvesting.
cosechadora *nf* combine-harvester.
cosechar [1a] *vt* **(a)** (*gen*) to harvest, gather (in); (*frutas*) to pick; *cereales* to cut, reap; (*cultivar*) to grow, cultivate; **aquí no cosechan sino patatas** the only thing they grow here is potatoes.
(b) (*fig*) to reap, reap the reward of; *admiración etc* to win; **no cosechó sino disgustos** all he got was troubles.
cosechero, -a *nm/f* harvester, reaper; picker.
cosechón *nm* bumper crop.
coseno *nm* cosine.
coser [2a] **1** *vt* **(a)** (*Cos*) to sew (up); to stitch (up); *botón etc* to sew on, stitch on; (*Med*) to stitch (up).
(b) (*fig*) to unite, join closely (*con* to).
(c) es cosa de ~ y cantar it's straightforward; it's plain sailing; it's a cinch‡.
(d) ~ a uno a balazos to riddle sb with bullets; **~ a uno a puñaladas** to stab sb repeatedly, carve sb up; **le encontraron cosido a puñaladas** they found him covered with

stab wounds.

2 *vi* to sew.

3 coserse *vr*: ~ **con uno** to become closely attached to sb.

cosher *adj invar* kosher.

cosiaca *nf* (*LAm*) small thing, trifle.

cosido *nm* sewing, needlework.

cosificación *nf* reification.

cosificar [1g] *vt* to reify.

cosignatario, -a *nm/f* cosignatory.

cosijoso *adj* (**a**) (*CAm, Méx*: *molesto*) bothersome, annoying. (**b**) (*CAm, Méx*: *displicente*) peevish, irritable.

cosmética *nf* cosmetics.

cosmético *adj, nm* cosmetic.

cosmetizar *vt* to improve the appearance of.

cosmetólogo, -a *nm/f* cosmetician.

cósmico *adj* cosmic.

cosmódromo *nm* space-station.

cosmogonía *nf* cosmogony.

cosmografía *nf* cosmography.

cosmógrafo, -a *nm/f* cosmographer.

cosmología *nf* cosmology.

cosmonauta *nmf* cosmonaut, spaceman, spacewoman.

cosmopolita *adj, nmf* cosmopolitan.

cosmos *nm* cosmos.

cosmovisión *nf* world view.

coso[1] *nm* (*ruedo*) arena, enclosure; (*esp*) bullring.

coso[2] *nm* (*Ent*) deathwatch beetle, woodworm.

coso[3] *nm* (*hum*) = **cosa**.

cospel *nm* (*Téc*) planchet, blank (for a coin).

cosquillar [1a] *vt* to tickle.

cosquillas *nfpl* tickling (sensation); ticklishness; **buscar las ~ a uno** to tease sb, try to stir sb up; **me hace ~** it tickles; **hacer ~ a uno** to tickle sb; (*fig*) to tickle sb's curiosity; **siento ~ en el pie** my foot tickles; **tener ~** to be ticklish; **no sufre ~, tiene malas ~** he's touchy, he can't take a joke.

cosquillear [1a] *vt* to tickle (*t fig*).

cosquilleo *nm* tickling (sensation).

cosquilloso *adj* (**a**) (*lit*) ticklish. (**b**) (*fig*) touchy, easily offended.

costa[1] *nf* (*Fin*) cost, price; **~s** (*Jur*) costs; **a ~** (*Com*) at cost; **a ~ de** at the expense of; **a toda ~** at any price; **a ~ de lo que sea** cost what it may; **condenar a uno en ~s** (*Jur*) to order sb to pay the costs.

costa[2] *nf* (*Geog*) (**a**) coast; coastline; shore, seashore; **~ afuera** offshore.

(**b**) (*Cono Sur*: *de río*) riverbank, lake-side.

(**c**) **C~ Azul** Côte d'Azur; **C~ de Marfil** Ivory Coast; **C~ de Oro** Gold Coast.

(**d**) **C~ Blanca** *coast near Almería*; **C~ Brava** *coast north of Barcelona*; **C~ Clara** *coast near Valencia*; **C~ Dorada** *coast near Tarragona*; **C~ del Sol** *coast west of Málaga.*

costabravense *adj* of the Costa Brava.

costado *nm* (**a**) (*Anat, Náut, de objeto*) side; (*Mil*) flank; **de ~** *moverse* sideways; *tumbarse* on one's side; **neumáticos de ~ blanco** white-walled tyres.

(**b**) (*Méx*: *Ferro*) platform.

(**c**) **~s** ancestors, ancestry; **español por los 4 ~s** Spanish on both sides of the family; (*fig*) thoroughly Spanish, wholly Spanish, Spanish through and through; **es un gandul por los 4 ~s** he's an absolute idler.

costal *nm* sack, bag; **estar hecho un ~ de huesos** to be all skin and bone.

costalada *nf* = **costalazo.**

costalar [1a] *vi* (*Cono Sur*) to roll over; to fall on one's side (*o* back).

costalazo *nm* heavy fall; **darse** (*o* **pegarse**) **un ~** to come a cropper, take a knock.

costanera *nf* (**a**) (*costado*) side, flank. (**b**) (*cuesta*) slope. (**c**) (*Cono Sur*: *muelle*) jetty; promenade, paved area beside the sea (*o* river). (**d**) (*Carib*: *alrededor de un pantano*) firm ground (surrounding a swamp). (**e**) **~s** (*Arquit*) rafters.

costanero *adj* (**a**) sloping; steep. (**b**) (*Náut*) coastal.

costar [1l] *vti* (*Com, Fin*) (**a**) (*gen*) to cost; **¿cuánto cuesta?** how much does it cost?, (*en tienda*) how much is it?; **¿cuesta mucho?** is it expensive?

(**b**) (*fig*) to cost (dear, dearly); **cuesta poco** it's easy; **cuesta mucho** it's difficult; **cueste lo que cueste** cost what it may; **le ha costado caro** it has cost him dear; **eso me ha costado reñir con él** doing that has meant my falling out with him, I did that only at the cost of quarrelling with him; **es un trabajo que cuesta unos minutos** it's a job which takes a few minutes; **me costó Dios y ayuda terminarlo** I had a terrible job to finish it; *V* **trabajo** *etc.*

(**c**) ~ + *infin* to find it hard to + *infin*, have a job to + *infin*; **me cuesta hablar alemán** I find it difficult to speak German, I have trouble speaking German; **me cuesta creerlo** I find that hard to believe.

costarricense = **costarriqueño.**

costarriqueñismo *nm* word (*o* phrase *etc*) peculiar to Costa Rica.

costarriqueño, -a *adj, nm/f* Costa Rican.

costasoleño *adj* of the Costa del Sol.

coste *nm* cost, price; expense; **~ humano** human cost, cost in human terms; **~s laborales unitarios** unitary labour costs; *V t* **costo.**

costear[1] [1a] *vt* (*Fin*) to pay for, defray the cost of; to endow; (*Rad, TV etc*) to back, sponsor; **costea los estudios a su sobrino** he is paying for his nephew's education; **no lo podemos ~** we can't afford it.

costear[2] [1a] **1** *vt* (*Náut*) to sail along the coast of; (*fig*) to skirt, go along the edge of; to pass close to.

2 costearse *vr* (*Cono Sur**) to traipse around*.

costear[3] [1a] *vt* (*Cono Sur*) *ganado* to pasture.

coste-eficacia *nm* cost-efficiency.

costeño 1 *adj* coastal. **2** *nm*, **costeña** *nf* (*LAm*) coastal dweller.

costera *nf* (**a**) (*de paquete etc*) side. (**b**) (*Geog*) slope. (**c**) (*Náut*) coast; (*Pesca*) fishing season.

costero *adj* coastal; *barco, comercio* coasting.

costilla *nf* (**a**) (*Anat, Náut*) rib.

(**b**) (*carne*) chop; **~ de cerdo** pork chop, pork cutlet.

(**c**) **~s*** back, shoulders; **todo carga sobre mis ~s** I get all the burdens, everything is put on my back; **medir las ~s a uno** to beat sb.

(**d**) (*hum*: *esposa*) wife, better half.

costilludo *adj* broad-shouldered, strapping.

costo *nm* (**a**) (*Fin*) cost; **~ directo** direct cost; **~ efectivo** actual cost; **~ de expedición** shipping charges; **~s de fabricación** manufacturing costs; **~s de funcionamiento** running costs; **~, seguro y flete** (*csf*) cost, insurance and freight (*cif*); **~ de (la) vida** cost of living; **el ~ de salarios de la industria** the industry's wages bill.

(**b**) (*LAm*: *esfuerzo*) trouble, effort; **hacerse el ~ de hacer algo** (*Cono Sur*) to take the trouble (*o* make the effort) to do sth.

(**c**) (**⁑**: *drogas*) hash*.

costosamente *adv* expensively.

costoso *adj* costly, expensive.

costra *nf* (*corteza*) crust; (*Med*) scab; (*de vela*) snuff.

costroso *adj* crusty; incrusted; (*Med*) scabby.

costumbre *nf* custom, habit; **~s** customs, ways, (*fig*) morals; **las ~s de esta provincia** the customs of this province; **persona de buenas ~s** respectable person, decent person; **de ~** (*adj*) usual; (*adv*) usually; **como de ~** as usual; **más que de ~** more than usual; **he perdido la ~** I have got out of the habit, (*Dep etc*) I'm out of practice; **tener la ~ de** + *infin*, **tener por ~** + *infin* to be in the habit of + *ger*; **novela de ~s** novel of (local) customs and manners.

costumbrismo *nm literary genre of (local) customs and manners.*

costumbrista 1 *adj novela etc* of (local) customs and manners. **2** *nmf* writer about (local) customs and manners, author with a strong regional flavour.

costura *nf* (**a**) (*Cos, Náut*) seam; **sin ~** seamless; **sentar las ~s** to press the seams; **sentar las ~ a uno*** to give sb a hiding*.

(**b**) (*arte, labor*) sewing; needlework; (*confección*) dressmaking; **alta ~** haute couture, high fashion, fashion designing; **la ~ italiana** Italian fashions, the Italian fashion trade.

costur(e)ar [1a] *vti* (*LAm*) = **coser.**

costurera *nf* dressmaker, seamstress.

costurero *nm* (*caja*) sewing box, sewing case; (*cuarto*) sewing room.

cota[1] *nf* (**a**) (*Hist*) tabard; doublet; **~ de malla** coat of mail. (**b**) (*Carib*: *blusa*) blouse.

cota[2] *nf* (**a**) = **cuota.** (**b**) (*Geog*) height above sea level; (*fig*) height, level; standard; **misil de baja ~** low-flying missile; **volar a baja ~** to fly low. (**c**) (*cifra*) number, figure.

cotarro *nm* (**a**) (*Hist*) night shelter for tramps *etc*; **alborotar el ~** to stir up trouble; **andar** (*o* **ir**) **de ~ en ~** to wander about, gad about; **dirigir el ~** to be the boss. (**b**) (*Cono Sur**) mate, pal*.

coteja *nf* (*And, CAm*) equal, match.

cotejar [1a] *vt* (**a**) (*comparar*) to compare, collate; to check. (**b**) (*And, Carib*: *arreglar*) to arrange.
cotejo 1 *adj* (*LAm*) similar, same. **2** *nm* (**a**) (*comparación*) comparison, collation; check. (**b**) (*Dep*) match, game.
cotelé *nm* (*Cono Sur*) corduroy.
cotense *nm* (*And, Cono Sur, Méx*), **cotensia** *nf* (*And, Cono Sur*), **cotensio** *nm* (*Cono Sur*) coarse hemp fabric.
coterna *nf* (*And*) broad hat.
cotí *nm* ticking.
cotidianeidad *nf* daily nature, routine character; ordinariness.
cotidiano *adj* daily.
cotiledón *nm* cotyledon.
cotilla *nmf* busybody, gossip.
cotillear [1a] *vi* to gossip.
cotilleo *nm* gossip(ing).
cotillero *nm*, **cotillera** *nf* = **cotilla**.
cotín *nm* (*Dep*) backhand shot.
cotitular *nmf* joint owner.
cotiza *nf* (*And, Carib*) sandal.
cotización *nf* (**a**) (*Fin*) quotation, price; ~ **de apertura** opening price; ~ **de cierre**, ~ **de clausura** closing price. (**b**) (*de miembro*) dues, subscription. (**c**) (*impuestos*) assessment (for tax); taxation. (**d**) (*cambio*) exchange rate.
cotizado *adj* in demand, popular, sought-after; (*fig*) valued, esteemed.
cotizante *nmf* contributor; paid-up member.
cotizar [1f] **1** *vt* (**a**) (*Fin*) *acción* to quote, price (*en* at).
(**b**) *cuota* to fix; *suscripción, contribución* to pay.
(**c**) (*Carib, Cono Sur*: *tasar*) to value (*en* at).
(**d**) (*Cono Sur*: *prorratear*) to share out proportionally.
(**e**) (*And, Carib*: *vender*) to sell.
2 *vi* (**a**) (*miembro*) to pay one's dues, pay one's subscription. (**b**) (*Fin*) to be quoted; **la sociedad cotiza ahora en Bolsa** the company is now quoted on the Stock Exchange.
3 cotizarse *vr* (**a**) (*Com, Fin*) ~ **a** to sell at, sell for, fetch, stand at; (*Bolsa*) to stand at, be quoted at; **estos tomates son los que más se cotizan** these tomatoes are the ones which fetch the highest price.
(**b**) (*fig*) to be valued, be esteemed; **tales conocimientos se cotizan mucho** such knowledge is highly valued.
coto¹ *nm* (**a**) (*Agr*) enclosure, enclosed pasture; (*Caza*) preserve; reserve; ~ **de caza** game preserve; ~ **cerrado** (*fig*) closed shop; ~ **redondo** large estate.
(**b**) (*mojón*) boundary stone; (*fig*) limit; **poner** ~ **a** to put a stop to; to bring under control.
(**c**) (*Com*) price-fixing agreement.
(**d**) (*Bridge*) rubber.
coto² *nm* (*LAm Med*) goitre.
cotón *nm* (**a**) (*tela*) printed cotton, cotton fabric. (**b**) (*LAm*: *camisa*) shirt; (*Méx*: *camiseta*) vest, undervest (*US*); (*Méx*: *blusa*) blouse.
cotona *nf* (**a**) (*LAm*) (*camisa*) strongly-made shirt; (*Cono Sur*) camisole; vest, undervest (*US*); (*And, CAm, Carib*: *blusa*) blouse. (**b**) (*Méx*: *cazadora*) suede jacket. (**c**) (*Carib*: *camisón*) child's nightdress.
cotonete *nm* (*Méx*: *Med etc*) cotton bud.
cotorina *nf* (*Méx*) jerkin.
cotorra *nf* (**a**) (*Orn*: *loro*) parrot, cockatoo; (*urraca*) magpie. (**b**) (*: *parlanchina*) windbag, chatterbox. (**c**) (*Méx**: *orinal*) chamberpot. (**d**) (*Méx***) (*puta*) whore, slag‡; (*vagina*) cunt**.
cotorrear [1a] *vi* to chatter, gabble.
cotorreo *nm* (**a**) (*plática*) chatter, gabble. (**b**) (*Méx**: *diversión*) fun, good time.
cotorrera *nf* female parrot; = **cotorra** (**a**), (**b**).
cotorro* *adj* (*Méx*) (*platicón*) chatty, talkative; (*alborotado*) loud, noisy.
cototo *nm* (*Cono Sur*) bump, bruise (on the head).
cotudo *adj* (**a**) (*peludo*) hairy, cottony. (**b**) (*LAm Med*) suffering from goitre. (**c**) (*And*: *tonto*) stupid.
cotufa *nf* (**a**) (*Bot*) Jerusalem artichoke. (**b**) ~**s** (*LAm*) popcorn.
coturno *nm* buskin; **de alto** ~ (*fig*) lofty, elevated.
COU [kow] *nm* (*Esp*) *abr de* **Curso de Orientación Universitaria**.
coulis *nm* (*carne*) broth; (*fruta*) syrup.
covacha *nf* (**a**) (*cueva*) small cave. (**b**) (*And, Carib, Cono Sur*: *trastera*) lumber room. (**c**) (*CAm, Carib*: *bohío*) hut. (**d**) (*And*: *puesto*) vegetable stall. (**e**) (*Carib*: *perrera*) kennel.
covachuela *nf* (*fig*) hovel.
covadera *nf* (*And, Cono Sur*) guano deposit.
cover* *nm* (*Prensa*) cover story; (*Mús*) cover version.
covin *nm*, **covín** *nm* (*Cono Sur*) popcorn.
coxcojilla *nf*, **coxcojita** *nf* hopscotch.
coxis *nm invar* coccyx.
coy *nm* (*Náut*) hammock; (*And, Carib*) cradle, cot.
coyón* *adj* (*Méx*) cowardly.
coyote *nm* (**a**) (*Zool*) coyote, prairie wolf.
(**b**) (*: *Méx*: *astuto*) astute person; (*guía*) guide of illegal immigrants (to USA); (*Com, Fin*) speculator, dealer in shares (*etc*); (*intermediario*) middleman, (*pey*) fixer*; (*sablista*) con man*; (*encubridor*) fence*.
(**c**) (*: *Méx*: *hijo*) youngest child.
coyotear [1a] *vi* (*CAm, Méx*) (**a**) (*ser listo*) to be smart, be clever. (**b**) (*Com, Fin*) to deal (*o* speculate) in shares.
coyunda *nf* (**a**) (*CAm*) (*correa*) strap; (*dogal*) tether, halter; (*tralla*) lash. (**b**) (*hum*) yoke (of marriage).
coyuntura *nf* (**a**) (*Anat*) joint.
(**b**) (*fig*) (*momento*) moment, juncture, occasion; (*oportunidad*) opportunity; (*momento favorable*) favourable moment; (*tendencia*) trend; (*situación*) situation; ~ **crítica** critical moment; turning point; **la** ~ **política** the political situation; **esperar una** ~ **favorable** to await a favourable moment.
coyuntural *adj* relating to the (present) moment (*o* situation *etc*); **datos** ~**es** relevant data; **medidas** ~**es** immediately relevant measures; **solución** ~ *ad hoc* solution.
coyunturalismo *nm* (*Pol etc*) opportunism.
coyunturalmente *adv* in an opportunistic way, responding to the demands of the moment; in the circumstances of the moment.
coz *nf* (**a**) (*con pie*) kick; **dar coces, dar de coces a** to kick; **dar coces contra el aguijón** to kick against the pricks; **tirar coces** to lash out (*t fig*).
(**b**) (*de arma*: *movimiento*) kick; (*de agua*) backward flow.
(**c**) (*de arma*: *parte*) butt.
(**d**) (*fig*) insult, rude remark; **tratar a uno a coces** to be rude to sb, treat sb like dirt.
CP (*Esp*) *nf* (**a**) *abr de* **Caja Postal**. (**b**) (*Com*) *abr de* **contestación pagada** reply paid, RP. (**c**) (*LAm*) *abr de* **casilla postal** post-office box, POB.
C.P.A. *nf abr de* **Caja Postal de Ahorros** ≈ Post Office Savings Bank.
CPN *nm* (*Esp*) *abr de* **Cuerpo de la Policía Nacional**.
CPS *nmpl abr de* **caracteres por segundo** characters per second, cps.
crac¹ *nm* (*t* **crack**) (**a**) (*Com, Fin*) failure, crash; bankruptcy; ~ **financiero** financial crash; **el** ~ **del 29** the 1929 Stock Exchange crash. (**b**) (*fig*) crack-up.
crac² *interj* snap!, crack!; **hizo ¡~! y se abrió** it went crack! and it opened out.
crac³* *nmf* (*t* **crack**) (*persona*) star player, star performer; (*caballo*) best horse, champion horse.
crack‡ *nm* (*droga*) crack‡.
crampón *nm* crampon.
cráneo *nm* skull, cranium; **ir de** ~* (*en aprieto*) to be in a tough spot; **voy de** ~* (*me va mal*) everything's going wrong for me, (*me presionan*) I'm rushed off my feet; **ir de** ~ **con uno*** to be on bad terms with sb; **va de** ~ **si hace eso*** he's got another think coming if he does that*; **esto me lleva** (*o* **trae**) **de** ~* this is driving me crazy.
crápula 1 *nf* drunkenness; (*fig*) dissipation. **2** *nm* (*) rake.
crapuloso *adj* drunken; (*fig*) dissipated.
craquear [1a] *vt* (*Quím*) to crack.
craqueo *nm* (*Quím*) cracking.
crasitud *nf* fatness.
craso *adj* (**a**) *persona* fat. (**b**) *líquido* greasy, thick. (**c**) (*fig*) *error* gross, crass, stupid. (**d**) (*And, Cono Sur*) *persona* coarse.
cráter *nm* crater.
crawl [krol] *nm* crawl.
crayón *nm* crayon, chalk.
crayota *nf* (*And*) crayon.
creación *nf* creation; **campaña de** ~ **de imagen** image-building campaign.
creacionismo *nm* creationism.
creacionista *nmf* creationist.
creador 1 *adj* creative. **2** *nm*, **creadora** *nf* creator; inventor, originator; **el C~** the Creator.
crear [1a] *vt* (*gen*) to create; *oficial* to make; (*inventar*) to invent, originate; (*fundar*) to found, establish, institute.
creatividad *nf* creativity.
creativo 1 *adj* creative. **2** *nm*, **creativa** *nf*: ~ **de pu-**

blicidad copywriter.

crece *nm o f* (*Cono Sur*) = **crecida**.

crecepelo(s) *nm* hair-restorer.

crecer [2d] **1** *vi* (*gen*) to grow; to increase; (*precio, río*) to rise; (*días*) to get longer; (*luna*) to wax; **dejar ~ la barba** to grow a beard, let one's beard grow.

2 crecerse *vr* (**a**) (*Cos*) **'se crece un punto'** 'increase by one stitch'.

(**b**) (*cobrar ánimo*) to grow bolder, acquire greater confidence; (*pey*) to get conceited, have an exaggerated sense of one's importance.

creces *nfpl* (**a**) (*aumento*) increase.

(**b**) (*Cos*) room to let out; **para los niños se hace la ropa con ~** children's clothes are made to be let out.

(**c**) **con ~** amply, fully; (*fig*) with a vengeance; **pagar a uno con ~** to more than repay one's debt; **devolver algo con ~** to return sth with interest; **había cumplido su obligación con ~** he had amply carried out his obligation.

crecida *nf* (*de río*) rise; spate, flood.

crecido *adj* (**a**) *persona, planta etc* full-grown; grown-up; **ya eres ~ para eso** you're too big for that now.

(**b**) *número, proporción* large.

(**c**) **estar ~** (*río*) to be in flood.

(**d**) (*fig*) vain, conceited.

creciente 1 *adj* growing; increasing; rising; **luna ~** crescent moon, waxing moon; *V* **cuarto**.

2 *nm* crescent.

3 *nf* (**a**) (*de río*) flood; **~ del mar** high tide, flood tide.

(**b**) (*luna*) crescent moon.

crecientemente *adv* increasingly.

crecimiento *nm* growth; increase; rise; (*Fin*) rise in value, appreciation; **~ cero** zero growth; **~ negativo** negative growth.

credencial 1 *adj* accrediting; *V* **carta**. **2** *nf* document confirming appointment (in civil service); **~es** letters of credence.

credibilidad *nf* credibility.

crediticio *adj* (*Fin*) credit (*atr*).

crédito *nm* (**a**) (*fe*) credit; belief; credence; **dar ~ a** to believe (in), credit; **apenas daba ~ a sus oídos** he could scarcely believe his ears.

(**b**) (*buena fama*) credit; authority, standing, reputation; **persona (digna) de ~** reliable person; **tiene ~ de muy escrupuloso** he has the reputation of being thoroughly honest.

(**c**) (*Com, Fin*) credit; loan; **a ~** on credit; **~ de aceptación** acceptance credit; **~ bancario** bank credit; **~ diferido** deferred credit; **~ a la exportación** export credit; **~ hipotecario** mortgage loan; **~ puente** bridging loan; **~ de vivienda** mortgage; **abrir un ~ a** to open a credit for.

(**d**) (*Cine, TV*) **~s** credits.

credo *nm* creed; credo; **en un ~, en menos que se canta un ~** in next to no time.

credulidad *nf* credulity.

crédulo *adj* credulous.

creederas *nfpl*: **tiene buenas ~** he's terribly gullible, he'll swallow anything.

creencia *nf* belief (*en* in); **en la ~ de que ...** in the belief that ...

creencial *adj* relating to belief; ideological.

creer [2e] **1** *vt* (**a**) (*gen*) to think, believe; **~ que ...** to think that ..., believe that ...; **creo que sí, lo creo** I think so; **creo que no, no creo** I don't think so; **¡ya lo creo!** I should think so!, rather!; of course!; **¡ya lo creo que está roto!** I should jolly well say it's broken!; **créame** believe me, take my word for it; **no se vaya Vd a ~ que ...** don't go thinking that ...; **es difícil, no creas** it's hard enough, I'm telling you.

(**b**) (*considerar*) to think, deem, consider; **no le creo tan culpable** I don't think him so much to blame; **creo de él que es sincero** I consider him to be sincere; **lo creo de mi deber** I consider it (to be) my duty.

2 *vi*: **~ en** to believe in.

3 creerse *vr* (**a**) (*gen*) to believe o.s. (to be), consider o.s. (to be); **se cree muy astuto** he thinks he's pretty clever; **¿quién se cree que es?** who do you think you are?; **~ alguien** to give o.s. airs; **¿qué se ha creído?** who does he think he is?; **se lo tiene muy creído*** he's very conceited, he's full of himself.

(**b**) **no me lo creo** I don't believe it; **se cree todo lo que le dicen** he swallows everything he's told; **¿(que) te crees tú eso?*** that's what you think!*; **¡no te lo crees ni tú!*** come off it!*; **se lo tiene creído*** he fancies himself; **hace falta que yo me lo crea** I still have to be convinced.

creíble *adj* believable, credible; **¿es ~ que ...?** is it conceivable that ...?

creíblemente *adv* credibly.

creído *adj* (**a**) (*crédulo*) gullible, trusting; foolishly optimistic. (**b**) (*engreído*) vain, conceited.

crema *nf* (**a**) (*de leche*) cream; (*Culin*) cream; custard; **~ agria** sour cream; **~ batida** whipped cream; **un coche color ~** a cream-coloured car; **~ inglesa** custard; **~ pastelera** confectioner's cream (*o* custard); **dejar la ~*** (*Cono Sur*) to make a hash of things*; to put one's foot in it.

(**b**) (*cosmético*) cold cream, facecream; **~ de afeitar** shaving cream; **~ antiarrugas** anti-wrinkle cream; **~ base** foundation cream; **~ de belleza** beauty-cream; **~ bronceadora** suntan cream; **~ capilar** haircream; **~ dental** toothpaste; **~ depilatoria** hair-remover; **~ hidratante, ~ humectante** moisturizing cream; **~ de limpiar** cleansing cream; **~ de manos** handcream.

(**c**) **~ para el calzado** shoe polish.

(**d**) (*fig*) cream, best; **la ~ de la sociedad** the cream of society.

cremación *nf* cremation; incineration.

cremallera *nf* (**a**) (*t* **cierre de ~**) zip fastener, zipper (*US*); **echar la ~‡** to shut one's trap‡. (**b**) (*Téc*) rack; **~ y piñón** rack and pinion.

crematístico *adj* financial, economic.

crematorio 1 *adj*: **horno ~** = *nm*. **2** *nm* crematorium; (*de basura*) incinerator.

crémor *nm* (*t* **~ tártaro**) cream of tartar.

cremosidad *nf* creaminess.

cremoso *adj* creamy.

crencha *nf* (*de pelo*) parting.

creosota *nf* creosote.

crep[1] *nm*, **crepa** *nf* (*LAm*: *Culin*) pancake, crêpe.

crep[2] *nm*, **crepé** *nm* crêpe.

crepar‡ [1a] *vi* (*Cono Sur*) to peg out‡, kick the bucket‡.

crepería *nf* pancake bar.

crepitación *nf* crackling; sizzling.

crepitar [1a] *vi* (*leño etc*) to crackle; (*jamón*) to sizzle.

crepuscular *adj* twilight, crepuscular; **luz ~** twilight.

crepúsculo *nm* twilight, dusk.

cresa *nf* maggot; larva; (*de abeja*) eggs of the queen bee.

crescendo *nm* crescendo.

Creso *nm* Croesus.

crespo 1 *adj* (**a**) *pelo* curly; kinky; *hoja etc* curled.

(**b**) *estilo* involved, tortuous.

(**c**) *persona* cross, angry.

2 *nm* hair, head of hair; (*esp Carib*: *bucle*) curl, ringlet.

crespón *nm* crape, crêpe.

cresta *nf* (**a**) (*Orn*) crest, comb; tuft. (**b**) (*peluca*) wig, toupée. (**c**) (*de ola*) crest. (**d**) (*Geog*) crest, ridge; summit.

crestería *nf* (*Arquit*) crenellations, battlements.

crestomatía *nf* anthology, collection of texts.

crestón *nm* (**a**) (*Mil*) crest (of helmet). (**b**) (*Min*) outcrop.

Creta *nf* Crete.

creta *nf* chalk.

cretáceo *adj* cretaceous.

cretense *adj, nmf* Cretan.

cretinada *nf* silly thing, stupid act.

cretinez *nf* stupidity.

cretino 1 *adj* cretinous (*t fig*). **2** *nm*, **cretina** *nf* cretin (*t fig*).

cretona *nf* cretonne, chintz.

cretoso *adj* chalky.

creyente *nmf* believer; **no ~** non-believer, unbeliever.

CRI *nf abr de* **Cruz Roja Internacional** International Red Cross.

cría *nf* (**a**) (*acto*) rearing, keeping, breeding; **~ caballar** horse breeding; **~ de ganado** cattle breeding, stock raising; **~ de peces** fish farming; **hembra de ~** breeding female.

(**b**) (*animal*) baby animal, young creature; (*conjunto*) young; litter, brood.

criada *nf* servant, maid; **~ por horas** hourly-paid woman, daily (woman); **~ para todo** maid of all work, servant with general duties.

criadero *nm* (**a**) (*Bot*) nursery.

(**b**) (*Zool*) breeding ground, breeding place; **~ de ostras** oyster bed; **~ de peces** fish hatchery, fish farm.

(**c**) (*Geol*) vein, seam.

criadilla *nf* (**a**) (*patata*) potato, tuber; **~(s) de tierra** truffles. (**b**) (*pan*) small loaf, roll. (**c**) **~s** (*Culin*) bull's testicles; (**‡**) balls**‡**.

criado 1 *adj* bred, reared, brought up; **bien ~** well-bred;

mal ~ *V* **malcriado. 2** *nm* (**a**) (*sirviente*) servant. (**b**) (*Naipes*) jack, knave.
criador *nm* (**a**) (*Agr etc*) breeder. (**b**) **el C~** (*Rel*) the Creator.
criajo, -a* *nm/f* wretched child, urchin; spotty herbert*.
criandera *nf* (*LAm*) nursemaid, wet-nurse.
crianza *nf* (**a**) (*Agr etc*) rearing, keeping, breeding. (**b**) (*Med*) lactation. (**c**) (*de vino*) ageing, maturing. (**d**) (*fig*) breeding; **mala** ~ bad breeding, lack of breeding; **sin** ~ ill-bred.
criar [1c] **1** *vt* (**a**) *bebé, hijuelos* to suckle, feed; ~ **a los pechos** to breast-feed, nurse.
(**b**) *plantas* to grow; to tend, cultivate.
(**c**) *animales* to rear, raise; to keep, breed; to fatten.
(**d**) (*tierra etc*) to bear, grow, produce; **esta tierra no cría hierba** this land does not grow grass, this soil is not suitable for grass; **los perros crían pulgas** dogs have (*o* get) fleas; ~ **carnes** to put on weight; **está criando pelo** he's getting some hair, his hair is growing.
(**e**) *niños* to bring up, raise; to educate; *V* **algodón**.
(**f**) *vino* to age, mature.
(**g**) (*fig*) *esperanzas etc* to foster, nourish, nurture.
2 *vi* (*animal*) to have young, produce.
3 criarse *vr* to grow (up); **se criaron juntos** they were brought up together, they grew up together; ~ **en buena cuna** (*o* **en buenos pañales**) to be born with a silver spoon in one's mouth.
criatura *nf* (**a**) (*ser criado*) creature (*t fig*); being.
(**b**) (*niño*) infant, baby, small child; **¡~!** look out!; I say, do be careful!; **todavía es una** ~ she's still very young, she's only a child still; **¡no seas ~!** be your age!; **hacer una** ~ **a una** to get a girl in the family way*.
criba *nf* (**a**) (*instrumento*) sieve, screen. (**b**) (*acto: fig*) sifting, selection; screening; **hacer una** ~ (*fig*) to sort out the sheep from the goats.
cribar [1a] *vt* (**a**) to sieve, sift, screen. (**b**) (*fig*) to sift, select; to screen.
cric *nm* (*Mec*) jack.
Crimea *nf* Crimea.
crimen *nm* crime (*esp* murder); ~ **de guerra** war crime; ~ **organizado** organized crime; ~ **pasional** crime of passion; ~ **de sangre** violent crime.
criminal 1 *adj* criminal; of murder, murderous. **2** *nmf* criminal (*esp* murderer); ~ **de guerra** war criminal.
criminalidad *nf* (**a**) (*gen*) criminality; guilt. (**b**) (*índice*) crime rate.
criminalista *nmf* (**a**) (*Univ*) criminologist. (**b**) (*Jur*) criminal lawyer.
criminalística *nf* criminology; study of the criminal, study of crime.
criminalizar [1f] *vt*: ~ **un acto** to make an act a criminal offence.
criminógeno *adj* conducive to crime, encouraging criminal tendencies.
criminología *nf* criminology.
criminólogo, a *nm/f* criminologist.
crin *nf* horsehair; (*t* **~es**) mane.
crinolina *nf* crinoline.
crinudo *adj* (*LAm*) *caballo* long-maned.
crío* *nm* kid*, child; (*pey*) brat.
criollaje *nm* (*LAm*) Creoles (*collectively*); peasantry.
criollo 1 *adj* (**a**) (*gen*) Creole.
(**b**) (*LAm*) (*natural*) native (to America), indigenous; national; (*de origen español*) of Spanish extraction.
2 *nm*, **criolla** *nf* (**a**) Creole.
(**b**) (*LAm*) native (of America), native American; person of Spanish extraction.
(**c**) (*And: cobarde*) coward.
cripta *nf* crypt.
cripto... *pref* crypto...
criptocomunista *nmf* crypto-communist.
criptografía *nf* cryptography.
criptográfico *adj* cryptographic(al).
criptógrafo, -a *nm/f* cryptographer.
criptograma *nm* cryptogram.
crisálida *nf* chrysalis.
crisalidar [1a] *vi* to pupate.
crisantemo *nm* chrysanthemum.
crisis *nf invar* crisis; ~ **de los cuarenta** midlife crisis; ~ **económica** economic crisis; ~ **de la energía,** ~ **energética** energy crisis; ~ **de identidad** identity crisis; ~ **nerviosa** nervous breakdown; ~ **de la vivienda** housing shortage; **hacer** ~ to be in crisis; **llegar a la** ~ to reach crisis point, come to a head.
crisma[1] *nf* (**a**) (*Ecl*) chrism, holy oil. (**b**) (‡: *cabeza*) nut‡, head; **romper la** ~ **a uno** to knock sb's block off‡.
crisma[2] **1** *nm* (*a veces f*; *t* **~s**) Christmas card. **2** *nf* (*Méx*) Christmas present.
crisol *nm* crucible; (*fig*) melting pot.
crispación *nf* (*fig*) tension, nervousness; increase of tension; outrageous nature; **una escena de absoluta** ~ an utterly shattering scene.
crispado *adj* tense, on edge.
crispante *adj* infuriating; outrageous; shattering.
crispar [1a] **1** *vt* (**a**) *músculo* to cause to twitch (*o* contract); *nervios* to set on edge; **con el rostro crispado por la ira** with his face contorted with anger; **tengo los nervios crispados** my nerves are all on edge; **eso me crispa los nervios** that gets on my nerves; that jars (*o* grates) on me.
(**b**) ~ **a uno*** to annoy sb intensely, get on sb's nerves.
2 crisparse *vr* (*músculo*) to twitch, contract; (*cara*) to contract; (*nervios*) to get all on edge; (*situación*) to become tense, get tenser.
crispetas *nfpl* (*And*) popcorn.
cristal *nm* (**a**) (*Quím*) crystal (*t fig*); ~ **líquido** liquid crystal; ~ **de roca** rock crystal.
(**b**) (*vidrio*) glass; **un** ~ a pane of glass, a sheet of glass; **~es** (*frec*) window(s); ~ **ahumado** smoked glass; ~ **antibalas** bullet-proof glass; ~ **de aumento** lens, magnifying glass; ~ **cilindrado** plate glass; **~es emplomados** leaded lights; ~ **hilado** fibreglass; ~ **inastillable** splinter-proof glass; ~ **de patente** (*Náut*) bull's-eye; ~ **de seguridad** safety glass; ~ **soplado** blown glass; ~ **tallado** cut glass; **de** ~ glass (*atr*); **puerta de ~es** glass door.
(**c**) (*espejo*) glass, mirror.
cristalera *nf* (large) window.
cristalería *nf* (**a**) (*arte*) glasswork; glass making. (**b**) (*fábrica*) glassworks; (*tienda*) glassware shop. (**c**) (*vasos*) glasses (*collectively*), glassware.
cristalero *nm* (*Cono Sur*) glass cabinet.
cristalinamente *adv* transparently.
cristalino *adj* (*Fís*) crystalline; (*fig*) clear, limpid, translucent; transparent.
cristalizar [1f] **1** *vti* to crystallize. **2 cristalizarse** *vr* to crystallize.
cristalografía *nf* crystallography.
cristalógrafo, -a *nm/f* crystallographer.
cristianamente *adv* in a Christian way; **morir** ~ to die as a Christian, to die like a good Christian.
cristianar [1a] *vt* (**a**) (*bautizar*) to christen, baptize. (**b**) *vino* to water.
cristiandad *nf* Christendom; Christianity.
cristianismo *nm* Christianity.
cristianizar [1f] *vt* to Christianize.
cristiano 1 *adj* (**a**) (*Rel*) Christian.
(**b**) **vino** ~ watered wine.
(**c**) (*LAm: ingenuo*) simple-minded.
2 *nm*, **cristiana** *nf* Christian; ~ **nuevo** (*Hist*) convert to Christianity; ~ **viejo** (*Hist*) Christian with no Jewish or Moslem blood.
3 *nm* (**a**) (*persona*) person, (living) soul; **eso lo sabe cualquier** ~ any idiot knows that; **eso no hay** ~ **que lo entienda** that is beyond anyone's comprehension; **no hay** ~ **que lo sepa** there's nobody can tell that; **este ~*** yours truly*.
(**b**) (*Ling*) ordinary language, (*esp*) Spanish; **hablar en** ~ to speak straightforwardly, make sense with what one says; ≈ to speak the Queen's (*o* King's) English.
Cristo *nm* Christ; **el año 41 antes de** ~ 41 BC; **el año 80 después de** ~ AD 80; **con el** ~ **en la boca** (*CAm**) with one's heart in one's mouth; **armar ~*** to raise Cain; **donde** ~ **dio las tres voces*, donde** ~ **perdió la gorra*** at the back of beyond*; in the middle of nowhere; **¡ni** ~ **que lo fundó!** don't you believe it!; **ni** ~ **ni nadie** nobody at all; **no había ni** ~ there wasn't a soul; **eso no lo sabe ni** ~ nobody knows that; **todo** ~ every mortal soul, every man Jack; **ir hecho un ~*** to be a sight; **poner a uno como un ~*** to give sb a dressing-down*; to heap abuse on sb.
cristo *nm* crucifix.
Cristóbal *nm* Christopher.
criterio *nm* (**a**) (*norma*) criterion; yardstick, standard of judgement; **por cualquier** ~ by any standard.
(**b**) (*enfoque*) viewpoint, attitude, approach; **depende del** ~ **de cada uno** it depends on the individual viewpoint; **lo mira con otro** ~ he looks at it from a different point of view; **hace falta tener un** ~ **más maduro** one needs a more mature approach.

(**c**) (*juicio*) discernment, discrimination; **lo dejo a su ~** I leave it to your discretion; **tiene buen ~** his taste is admirable.
(**d**) (*opinión*) view, opinion; **en mi ~** in my opinion; **cambiar de ~** to change one's mind; **no comparto ese ~** I do not share that view; **formar un ~ sobre** to form an opinion of.
criterioso* *adj* (*Cono Sur*) level-headed, sensible.
crítica[1] *nf* (**a**) (*gen*) criticism; **~ literaria** literary criticism; **~ teatral** dramatic criticism.
(**b**) (*una ~*) criticism; (*reseña*) review, notice, critique; (*pey*) criticism; (*chismes*) gossip.
criticable *adj*: **no es ~ que se te oponga** you can't blame him for standing against you.
criticador 1 *adj* critical. **2** *nm*, **criticadora** *nf* critic.
criticar [1g] *vt* to criticize.
criticastro, -a *nm/f* hack critic, ignorant critic.
criticidad *nf* critical nature; **fase de ~** critical phase.
crítico 1 *adj* critical. **2** *nm*, **crítica**[2] *nf* critic; **~ de cine, ~ cinematográfico** film critic; **~ literario** literary critic.
criticón 1 *adj* hypercritical, overcritical, faultfinding. **2** *nm*, **criticona** *nf* carping critic, faultfinder.
critiquizar [1f] *vt* to be overcritical of, indulge in petty criticism of.
CRM *nm abr de* **Certificado de regulación monetaria**.
Croacia *nf* Croatia.
croar [1a] *vi* to croak.
croata *adj, nmf* Croat(ian).
crocitar [1a] *vi* to crow, caw.
croché *nm* (*Cos*) crochet(work); **hacer ~** to crochet.
crochet [kro'tʃe] *nm* (**a**) (*Cos*) = **croché**. (**b**) (*Boxeo*) hook.
crol *nm* (*Natación*) crawl.
cromado 1 *adj* chromium-plated; chrome. **2** *nm* chromium plating; chrome.
cromático *adj* chromatic.
cromatografía *nf* chromatography.
cromatograma *nm* chromatogram.
cromo *nm* (**a**) (*Quím*) chromium; chrome. (**b**) (*Tip*) religious card; chromolithograph; (cheap) coloured print, chromo (*US*).
cromosoma *nm* chromosome.
cromosomático *adj*, **cromosómico** *adj* chromosomal.
crónica *nf* (**a**) (*Hist*) chronicle; **C~s** (*Biblia*) Chronicles; (*fig*) chronicle, account.
(**b**) (*en periódico*) news report; feature, article; **~ deportiva** sports page; **~ literaria** literary page; **~ de sociedad** society column, gossip column; **'C~ de sucesos'** 'News in Brief'.
crónico *adj* (*Med y fig*) chronic; *vicio* ingrained.
cronista *nmf* (**a**) (*Hist*) chronicler. (**b**) (*de periódico*) reporter, feature writer, columnist; **~ deportivo** sports writer; **~ de radio** radio commentator.
crono* 1 *nm* (**a**) (*reloj*) stopwatch. (**b**) (*tiempo*) recorded time. **2** *nf* time-trial.
cronografista *nmf* (*Cono Sur*) timekeeper.
cronograma *nm* (*Cono Sur*) timetable, (*fig*) schedule.
cronología *nf* chronology.
cronológicamente *adv* chronologically, in chronological order.
cronológico *adj* chronological.
cronometrada *nf* (*Dep*) time-trial.
cronometrador(a) *nm/f* timekeeper.
cronometraje *nm* timing.
cronometrar [1a] *vt* to time.
cronómetro *nm* (*Téc etc*) chronometer; (*Dep*) stopwatch.
croquet [kro'ke] *nm* croquet.
croqueta *nf* croquette, (*aprox*) rissole.
croquis *nm invar* sketch.
cross [kros] *nm invar* cross-country race; cross-country running.
crostón *nm* crouton.
crótalo *nm* (**a**) (*Zool*) rattlesnake. (**b**) **~s** (*Mús*: *liter*) castanets.
croto* *nm* (*Cono Sur*) bum, layabout*.
cruasán *nm* croissant.
cruce *nm* (**a**) (*acto*) crossing; (*Aer*) **~ incontrolado** airmiss, near miss.
(**b**) (*Mat etc*) (point of) intersection.
(**c**) (*Aut etc*) crossing, intersection; **~ de carreteras** crossroads; **~ giratorio** roundabout, traffic circle (*US*); **~ a nivel** level crossing, grade crossing (*US*); **~ de peatones** pedestrian crossing, crosswalk (*US*).
(**d**) (*Telec*) crossing of lines; **hay un ~ en las líneas** the wires are crossed.
(**e**) (*Bio*) cross, crossing.
(**f**) (*Ling*) cross, mutual interference.
crucerista *nmf* cruise passenger.
crucero *nm* (**a**) (*Mil*) cruiser; **~ de batalla** battle cruiser; **~ pesado** heavy cruiser.
(**b**) (*Náut*) cruise; **~ de recreo** pleasure cruise.
(**c**) (*Ecl*) transept.
(**d**) (*Téc*) crosspiece.
(**e**) (*Aut etc*) crossroads; crossing; (*Ferro*) crossing.
(**f**) (*Ecl*: *persona*) crossbearer.
(**g**) (*Astron*) **C~** (**Austral**) Southern Cross.
(**h**) (*misil*) cruise missile.
cruceta *nf* (**a**) (*Téc*) crosspiece; (*Náut*) crosstree. (**b**) (*Mec*) crosshead. (**c**) (*Cono Sur*: *torniquete*) turnstile.
crucial *adj* crucial.
crucificar [1g] *vt* to crucify; (*fig*) to torment, torture; to mortify.
crucifijo *nm* crucifix.
crucifixión *nf* crucifixion.
cruciforme *adj* cruciform.
crucigrama *nm* crossword (puzzle).
crucigramista *nmf* crossword enthusiast.
cruda* *nf* (*LAm*) hangover*.
crudelísimo *adj* (*liter*: *superl de* **cruel**) most cruel, terribly cruel.
crudeza *nf* (**a**) (*Culin*) (*de carne*) rawness; (*de frutas*) unripeness. (**b**) (*de comida*) indigestibility. (**c**) (*de agua*) hardness. (**d**) (*rigor*) bleakness, harshness. (**e**) (*aspereza*) crudity, crudeness, coarseness. (**f**) (*comida*) undigested food (in the stomach).
crudo 1 *adj* (**a**) *carne* raw; (*Culin*) half-cooked, underdone, raw; *legumbres* green, uncooked; *fruta etc* unripe.
(**b**) *alimentos* hard to digest; **lo tendrán ~ si piensan que ...** they'll have a tough time of it if they think that ...
(**c**) *agua* hard.
(**d**) (*Téc*) untreated; *seda* raw; *lino* unbleached.
(**e**) *tiempo* raw, bleak, harsh.
(**f**) (*liter*) cruel, merciless.
(**g**) *frase, tema etc* crude, coarse; overrealistic.
2 *nm* (**a**) (*petróleo*) crude (oil).
(**b**) (*LAm*: *tela*) coarse cloth, sackcloth.
(**c**) (*Méx**: *resaca*) hangover*.
cruel *adj* cruel (*con, para* to).
crueldad *nf* cruelty.
cruelmente *adv* cruelly.
cruento *adj* (*liter*) bloody, gory.
crujía *nf* (*Arquit*) corridor, gallery; bay; (*Med*) ward; (*Náut*) midship gangway; (*de cárcel*) wing; **pasar ~** to have a tough time of it.
crujido *nm* rustle; creak; crack; crunch; grinding, gnashing; chattering; crackle.
crujiente *adj* rustling; creaking; crunchy; grinding; crackling.
crujir [3a] *vi* (*hojas, seda, papel*) to rustle; (*madera, mueble, rama*) to creak; (*articulación, hueso*) to crack; (*grava etc*) to crunch; (*dientes*) to grind, gnash; to chatter; (*objeto que arde*) to crackle; **hacer ~ los nudillos** to crack one's knuckles.
crupier *nm* croupier.
crustáceo *nm* crustacean.
cruz *nf* (**a**) (*gen*) cross; **~ gamada** swastika; **~ de hierro** iron cross; **~ de Malta** Maltese Cross; **~ de mayo** (*LAm*), **C~ del Sur** Southern Cross; **C~ Roja** Red Cross; **¡~ y raya!** that's quite enough!, no more!; **en ~** cross-shaped; crosswise; **con los brazos en ~** with arms crossed; **por éstas que son cruces** by all that is holy; **cargar la ~** (*Méx**) to have a hangover; **firmar con una ~** to make one's mark; **hacerse cruces** to cross o.s.; (*fig*) to show one's surprise; **hacerse cruces de que ...** to be astonished that ...; **quedar en ~** to be in an agonizing situation.
(**b**) (*de espada*) hilt; (*de ancla*) crown; (*de moneda*) tails; (*Tip*) dagger; (*Zool*) withers.
(**c**) (*fig*) cross, burden; **cada uno lleva su ~** each of us has his cross to bear.
cruza *nf* (*Cono Sur*) (**a**) (*Agr*) second ploughing. (**b**) (*Bio*) cross, crossing; hybrid.
cruzada *nf* crusade; **La C~** (*in official Spanish usage up to 1975*) *the Civil War of 1936-39*.
cruzadilla *nf* (*CAm*) level crossing, grade crossing (*US*).
cruzado 1 *adj* (**a**) *brazos, cheque etc* crossed. (**b**) (*Cos*) double-breasted. (**c**) (*Zool*) crossbred, hybrid. (**d**) (*And**) hopping mad*, furious. **2** *nm* (*Hist*) crusader.
cruzador(a)* *nm/f* (*Méx*) shoplifter.
cruzamiento *nm* (**a**) (*Bio*) crossing. (**b**) (*Ferro*) crossover.

cruzar [1f] **1** *vt* (**a**) (*gen*) to cross; to cut across, intersect; *cheque* to cross; ~ **un palo sobre otro** to place a stick across another; ~ **algo sobre una superficie** to pass (*o* draw) sth across a surface; ~ **el lago a nado** to swim across the lake.

(**b**) (*Náut*) to cruise.

(**c**) (*Bio*) to cross.

(**d**) ~ **la espada con uno** to cross swords with sb; ~ **palabras con uno** to have words with sb; ~ **a uno con una condecoración** to invest sb with a decoration.

(**e**) *dinero* to put, stake.

(**f**) (*Agr, esp LAm*) to plough a second time.

(**g**) (*And, Cono Sur*: *atacar*) to fight, attack.

2 cruzarse *vr* (**a**) (*caminos, líneas etc*) to cross, cross each other; to intersect.

(**b**) ~ **de brazos** *V* **brazo.**

(**c**) (*personas*) to pass each other; ~ **con uno en la calle** to pass sb in the street.

(**d**) ~ **con uno** (*And, Cono Sur*) to fight sb, attack sb.

(**e**) **nuestras cartas se cruzaron** our letters crossed (in the post).

CSD *nm* (*Esp*) *abr de* **Consejo Superior de Deportes** ≈ *Sports Council.*

c.s.f. *abr de* **coste, seguro, y flete** cost, insurance, and freight, c.i.f.

CSIC [θe'sik] *nm* (*Esp*) *abr de* **Consejo Superior de Investigaciones Científicas.**

CSN *nm* (*Esp*) *abr de* **Consejo de Seguridad Nuclear** *nuclear safety council.*

CSP *nm* (*Esp*) *abr de* **Cuerpo Superior de Policía.**

cta., c.ta *abr de* **cuenta** account, a/c.

cta. cte. *abr de* **cuenta corriente** current account, C/A.

cta. cto. *abr de* **carta de crédito** letter of credit, L/C.

cte. *abr de* **corriente, de los corrientes** of the present month, instant, inst.

CTNE *nf abr de* **Compañía Telefónica Nacional de España** ≈ *British Telecom.*

ctra. *abr de* **carretera.**

c/u *abr de* **cada uno** each, ea.

cu *nf* the (name of the) letter q.

cuacar [1g] *vt* (*And, Carib, Cono Sur*): **no me cuaca** (*no quiero*) I don't want to; (*no me cuadra*) it doesn't suit me; **no me cuaca aquel muchacho** I don't like that boy.

cuácara *nf* (*And*: *levita*) frock coat; (*Cono Sur*: *blusa*) workman's blouse.

cuaco* *nm* (**a**) (*Carib, Méx*) (*caballo*) nag. (**b**) (*bolsista*) bag snatcher.

cuacho (*CAm*) = **cuate.**

cuaderna *nf* (*Náut*) timber; rib, frame.

cuadernillo *nm* quinternion; (*Ecl*) liturgical calendar; ~ **de sellos** book of stamps.

cuadernito *nm* notebook.

cuaderno *nm* notebook; (*Escol etc*) exercise book; folder; (*) pack of cards; (*Náut*) ~ **de bitácora,** ~ **de trabajo** logbook; **C~ de Cortes** (*Hist*) official parliamentary record.

cuadra *nf* (**a**) (*Agr*) stable; ~ **de carreras** racing stable.

(**b**) (*de hospital etc*) ward.

(**c**) (*Mil*) hut.

(**d**) (*sala*) hall, large room; (*And*) reception room.

(**e**) (*LAm*: *manzana*) block (of houses), city block.

(**f**) (*And*: *casa etc*) small rural property (*near a town*).

(**g**) (*medida*: *And, Cono Sur*) = *125.50 metres,* (*And, CAm, Carib, Cono Sur*) = *83.5 metres.*

cuadrada *nf* (*Mús*) breve.

cuadrado 1 *adj* (**a**) (*Mat etc*) square; **tenerlos ~s*** to be real tough*.

(**b**) *diseño* with squares, chequered.

(**c**) *persona* broad, square-shouldered.

(**d**) (*Carib, Cono Sur*: *grosero*) coarse, rude.

(**e**) (*And*: *elegante*) graceful, elegant.

2 *nm* (**a**) (*forma, t Mat*) square.

(**b**) (*regla*) (parallel) rule(r).

(**c**) (*Téc*) die.

(**d**) (*Cos*) gusset.

(**e**) (*Tip*) quadrat.

(**f**) (*Carib, Cono Sur**: *persona*) boor, oaf.

Cuadragésima *nf* Quadragesima.

cuadragésimo *adj* fortieth.

cuadrangular *adj* quadrangular.

cuadrángulo *adj* quadrangular.

cuadrante *nm* (**a**) (*Mat, Náut*) quadrant. (**b**) (*de instrumento, radio*) dial; (*de reloj*) face; ~ (**solar**) sundial.

cuadrar [1a] **1** *vt* (**a**) (*Mat*) to square.

(**b**) (*Téc etc*) to square (off), make square.

(**c**) *papel V* **cuadricular.**

(**d**) (*fig*) to please; to suit; **si le cuadra** if it suits you.

(**e**) (*And Aut*) to park.

2 *vi* (**a**) ~ **con** to square with, tally with, fit, correspond to; to match; to suit, go with.

(**b**) ~ + *infin* (*Cono Sur*) to be ready to + *infin.*

3 cuadrarse *vr* (**a**) to square up, square one's shoulders; (*Mil*) to stand to attention.

(**b**) (*fig*) to dig one's heels in, refuse to budge; to take a firm line.

(**c**) ~ **con uno** to become very solemn towards sb, adopt a coldly official attitude towards sb.

(**d**) (*Carib**: *enriquecerse*) to make one's pile*; (*tener éxito*) to come out on top.

cuadratín *nm* (*Tip*) quadrat, quad, space.

cuadratura *nf* quadrature.

cuadrícula *nf* squares (ruled on paper *etc*); criss-cross pattern; (*de mapa*) grid.

cuadriculado *adj* = **cuadricular 1**; **papel** ~ squared paper.

cuadricular 1 *adj papel* ruled in squares, divided into squares; squared; *tela* chequered. **2** [1a] *vt* to rule squares on, divide into squares.

cuadrilátero 1 *adj* quadrilateral, four-sided. **2** *nm* (*Mat, Arquit*) quadrilateral; (*Boxeo*) ring.

cuadrilongo 1 *adj* oblong. **2** *nm* oblong.

cuadrilla *nf* (*grupo*) party, group; (*pandilla*) band; gang; (*Mil*) squad; (††) armed patrol; (*de obreros*) gang, squad, team; shift; (*Taur*) cuadrilla, bullfighter's team; ~ **de demolición** demolition squad; ~ **de noche** night shift, night squad.

cuadrillazo *nm* (*And, Cono Sur*) gang attack.

cuadrillero *nm* group leader; chief; gang leader; (*pey, esp And, Cono Sur*) hooligan.

cuadringentésimo *adj* four hundredth.

cuadripartido *adj* quadripartite.

cuadrito *nm* (*Culin etc*) cube; **cortar en ~s** to dice.

cuadrivio *nm* quadrivium.

cuadro 1 *nm* (**a**) (*Mat*) square; **2 metros en** ~ 2 metres square; **diseño a ~s** chequered pattern, check (pattern), checked pattern (*US*); **un vestido de ~s** a check suit; **~s escoceses** tartan (pattern).

(**b**) (*Arquit, Téc*) frame; ~ **de bicicleta** bicycle frame; ~ **de ventana** window frame.

(**c**) (*Arte*) picture, painting; **dos ~s de Velázquez** two Velazquez paintings.

(**d**) (*Teat*) scene (*t fig*); (*TV*) picture; ~ **vivo** tableau; **fue un ~*** it was some scene*, it was really quite dramatic; **fue un ~ desgarrador** it was a heart-breaking scene (*o* picture).

(**e**) (*Liter*) description, picture; ~ **de costumbres** description of (regional) customs, scene of local colour.

(**f**) (*Agr, Hort*) bed; patch; plot.

(**g**) (*Elec etc*) panel; ~ **de conexión manual** (*Telec*), ~ **de conmutadores** (*Elec*), ~ **de distribución** (*Elec*) switchboard; ~ **de instrumentos** instrument panel; (*Aut*) dashboard; ~ **de mandos** control panel.

(**h**) (*Mil*) square (formation); **formar el** ~ (*fig*) to close ranks.

(**i**) (*t* ~ **sinóptico**) table, chart, diagram.

(**j**) (*personas*) cadre; staff, establishment of officials (*etc*); (*Dep*) team; (*Pol*: *de partido*) executive.

(**k**) (*Med*) set of symptoms; **el paciente presentaba un cuadro vírico** the patient showed all the signs of a virus.

(**l**) (*Cono Sur*: *matadero*) slaughterhouse.

(**m**) (*Cono Sur*: *bragas*) knickers.

(**n**) (*And*: *pizarra*) blackboard.

2 *atr*: **programa** ~ general programme, framework programme.

cuadrúpedo *nm* quadruped; four-footed animal.

cuádruple *adj* quadruple; fourfold.

cuadruplicado *adj* quadruplicate; **por** ~ in quadruplicate.

cuadruplicar [1g] **1** *vt* to quadruple; **las pérdidas cuadruplican las del año pasado** losses are four times last year's.

2 cuadruplicarse *vr* to quadruple.

cuádruplo *adj, nm* quadruple.

cuajada *nf* curd; cottage cheese; cheese tart.

cuajado 1 *adj* (**a**) (*gen*) curdled, set, coagulated, congealed.

(**b**) ~ **de** (*fig*) full of, filled with; covered with; **una situación cuajada de peligros** a situation fraught with dangers; **un texto ~ de problemas** a text bristling with problems; **una corona cuajada de joyas** a crown covered with jewels.

(**c**) **estar** ~ (*asombrarse*) (*fig*) to be dumbfounded.

(**d**) **quedarse** ~ (*fig*: *dormido*) to fall asleep.

2 *nm*: ~ **de limón** lemon curd.

cuajaleche *nm* (**a**) (*Culin*) cheese rennet. (**b**) (*Bot*) bedstraw.

cuajar [1a] **1** *vt* (**a**) (*espesar*) to thicken; *leche* to curdle; *sangre etc* to congeal, coagulate, clot; *grasa* to congeal; *gelatina etc* to set.

(**b**) (*cubrir*) to cover, adorn (excessively; *de* with); (*llenar*) to fill (*de* with); **cuajó el tablero de cifras** he covered the board with figures.

2 *vi* (**a**) (*semilla etc*) to set; (*nieve*) to lie; *V* **3**.

(**b**) (*fig*) to become set, become firm, become established; to jell; (*proyecto etc*) to take shape; to come off, work; (*resultado*) to materialize; (*propuesta, moción*) to be received, be acceptable; **el noviazgo no cuajó** the engagement did not work, the engagement was not a success; **los eslobodios no cuajan con los ruritanios** the Slobodians don't get on with (*o* don't hit if off with) the Ruritanians.

(**c**) (*Méx*: *charlar*) to chat.

3 cuajarse *vr* (**a**) (*espesarse*) to thicken; to curdle; to congeal, coagulate; to set.

(**b**) ~ **de** (*fig*) to fill with, fill up with; to become crowded with.

(**c**) (*fig*) to go fast asleep.

cuajarón *nm* clot.

cuajo *nm* (**a**) (*Culin*) rennet; ~ **en polvo** powdered rennet.

(**b**) (*fig*) phlegm, calmness; **tiene mucho** ~ he's very phlegmatic.

(**c**) **coger un** ~* to cry one's eyes out; *V t* **llorar.**

(**d**) **arrancar algo de** ~ to tear sth out by its roots; **arrancar una puerta de** ~ to wrench a door out of its frame; **extirpar un vicio de** ~ to eradicate a vice completely.

(**e**) (*Méx**: *charla*) chat; chatter.

(**f**) (*Méx**: *mentirilla*) fib.

(**g**) (*Méx**: *proyecto*) pipe-dream.

(**h**) (*Méx**: *en escuela*) playtime.

cual 1 *adj* (*liter*) such as, of the kind (that); (*Jur*) said, aforementioned; **los ~es bienes** the said property, which property; **las ceremonias fueron ~es convenían a su importancia** the ceremonies were such as befitted his importance.

2 *pron* (**a**) **cada** ~ each one, everyone; **allá cada** ~ every man to his own taste; **cada** ~ **con su cada cuala*** like with like.

(**b**) (*relativo*) **el** ~ (*etc*) which; who; whom; **ese edificio, el** ~ **se construyó en el siglo XV** that building, which was built in the 15th century; **un policía, el** ~ **me puso una multa** a policeman, who gave me a fine.

(**c**) **lo** ~ (*relativo*) which; a fact which; **se rieron mucho, lo** ~ **me disgustó** they laughed a lot, which upset me; **con lo** ~ at which, whereupon; **por lo** ~ (and) so, and because of this, on account of which; whereby.

3 *adv y conj*: + *noun* like, as; + *verb* (just) as; **brillaba** ~ **estrella** it shone like a star; ~ ... **tal** (*o* **así**) ... like ... like ...; (*verbo*) just as ..., so ...; ~ **el padre, tal el hijo** like father like son; ~ **el otro, tal éste** this one is just like the other, this one is as bad (*etc*) as the other; ~ **llega el día tras la noche** just as day follows night; ~ **si** ... as if ...; *V* **tal.**

cuál 1 *pron interrog* (**a**) which (one)?; **¿~ quieres?** which (one) do you want?; **¿~ es el que dices?** which one are you talking about?; **tú ¿a ~ colegio vas?** (*Méx*) which school do you go to?; **si es tan malo A, ¿~ debe ser B?** if A is so bad, what must B be like?; **ignora ~ será el resultado** he does not know what the outcome will be. (**b**) (*locuciones*) **son a ~ más gandul** each is as idle as the other; **una serie de coches a ~ más rápido** a series of cars each faster than the last (*o* outdoing each other in speed); **gritar a ~ más** to see who can shout the loudest; ~ **más,** ~ **menos** some more, some less. **2** *excl*: **¡~ no sería mi asombro!** how surprised I was!; **¡~ gritan esos malditos!** how those wretched people shout! **3** *adj interrog* (*LAm*) which?; **¿~ libro dices?** which book do you mean?; **¿~es carros?** which cars?; **¿a ~ colegio vas?** which school do you go to?

cualidad *nf* (*gen*) quality; (*atributo*) attribute, trait, characteristic; (*Filos, Fís etc*) property; **tiene buenas ~es** he has good qualities.

cualificado *adj* (**a**) *obrero* skilled, qualified; **obrero no** ~ unskilled worker. (**b**) **estar** ~ **para** + *infin* to be entitled to + *infin.* (**c**) *V* **calificado.**

cualitativamente *adv* qualitatively.

cualitativo *adj* qualitative.

cualquier(a), *pl* **cualesquier(a) 1** *adj* (**a**) (*gen*) any; any ... you care to name (*o* like to mention *etc*); ~ **hombre de los de aquí** any man from these parts; **en** ~ **momento** at any time; **en** ~ **sitio donde lo busques** in whatever place you look for it, whichever place you look for it in; **con** ~ **resultado que sea** with whatever result it may be.

(**b**) **hay** ~ **cantidad** (*LAm*) there's a large quantity, there's any amount.

(**c**) (*tras n*) any; **ella no es una mujer** ~ she's not just any woman, she's not just an ordinary woman.

2 *pron* **cualquiera,** *pl* **cualesquiera** (**a**) (*gen*) anybody; whoever; whichever; **¡así ~!** anybody could manage that!; big deal!*; **te lo diría** ~ anyone would tell you the same; ~ **puede hacer eso** anybody can do that; **¡~ lo sabe!** who knows?; **yo me contento con** ~ I am happy with any (*o* either); I don't mind either (of the two).

(**b**) ~ **que sea** whoever he is; whichever it is.

(**c**) **es un** ~ he's a nobody; **yo no me caso con un** ~ I'm not marrying just anybody.

(**d**) **una** ~* a whore, a slut.

cuan *adv* (*liter*): **tan estúpidos** ~ **criminales** as much stupid as they are criminal.

cuán *adv* how; **¡~ agradable fue todo eso!** how delightful it all was!

cuando 1 *adv y conj* (**a**) (*tiempo*) when; ~ **nos veamos** when we meet again; ~ **iba allí le veía** whenever I went there I saw him; **ven** ~ **quieras** come when(ever) you like; **me acuerdo de** ~ ... I remember the time when ...; **lo dejaremos para** ~ **estés mejor** we'll leave it until you're better; **de** ~ **en** ~ from time to time; *V* **cada.**

(**b**) (*condicional, causal*) if, even if, although; since, when; ~ **lo dice él, será verdad** if he says so, it must be true; ~ **no sea así** even if it is not so; ~ **más** at (the) most; ~ **menos** at least; ~ **mucho** at (the) most; ~ **no** if not, otherwise; **¡~ no!** (*LAm*) of course!, naturally!; ~ **nos convida él, de seguro comeremos bien** since he's inviting us, we're sure to eat well; *V* **aun** *etc.*

2 *prep* at the time of; **eso fue** ~ **la guerra** that was during the war; **ocurrió** ~ **la boda** it happened at the same time as the wedding; ~ **niño** as a child, when I (*etc*) was a child.

cuándo *adv y conj interrog* when; **¿~ lo perdiste?** when did you lose it?; **no sé** ~ **será** I don't know when it will be; **¿de** ~ **acá?** since when?; (*fig*) how come?; **¿desde** ~ **es esto así?** how long has it been like this?; ~ **con A,** ~ **con B** sometimes with A, sometimes with B.

cuandoquiera *conj*: ~ **que** ... whenever ...

cuantía *nf* (*cantidad*) quantity, amount; (*alcance*) extent; (*importancia*) importance; **de mayor** ~ first-rate; important; **de menor** ~, **de poca** ~ second-rate; unimportant, of little account; **se ignora la** ~ **de las pérdidas** the extent of the losses is not known.

cuántico *adj*: **teoría cuántica** quantum theory.

cuantificable *adj* quantifiable.

cuantificación *nf* quantifying; **hacer una** ~ **de** to quantify.

cuantificar [1g] *vt* to quantify.

cuantimás: ~ **que** *conj* all the more so because ...

cuantioso *adj* (*grande*) large, substantial; (*abundante*) abundant; (*numeroso*) numerous; (*importante*) considerable; *pérdida* heavy, grave.

cuantitativamente *adv* quantitatively.

cuantitativo *adj* quantitative.

cuanto 1 *adj* all that, as much as, whatever; **daremos ~s créditos se precisen** we will give all the credits that may be necessary, we will give whatever credits are needed; **~s hombres la ven la quieren** all the men that see her fall in love with her; **unos ~s libros** a few books, some books; **~s más haya tantas más comidas habrá que preparar** the more there are the more meals will have to be cooked.

2 *pron* all that (which), as much as; **~s** all those that, as many as; **tiene** ~ **desea** he has all (that) he wants; **toma** ~ **quieras** take all you want, take as much as you want; **~s más, mejor** the more the merrier.

3 *adv y conj* (**a**) **en** ~ inasmuch as; **él, en** ~ **erudito, ...** he, as a scholar, ...; **en** ~ (*conj*) as soon as, immediately, directly; **en** ~ **lo supe me fui** as soon as I heard it I left; **en** ~ **a** as for, as to, with regard to; **en** ~ **que** ... insofar as ...; **por** ~ and so, hence; because; inasmuch as, in that ...

(**b**) ~ **más** at least; ~ **más difícil parezca** the more difficult it may seem, however difficult it seems; ~ **más trabaja menos gana** the more he works the less he earns; ~ **más que resultó ser mujer** all the more so because it turned out to be a woman; *V* **antes** *etc.*

cuánto *adj, pron y adv* **1** *excl* (**a**) (+ *verbo*) **¡~ has crecido!**

how you've grown!; ¡~ **trabajas!** how hard you work!; ¡~ **has gastado!** what a lot you've spent!; ¡~ **me alegro!** I'm so glad!

(**b**) (+ *n*) **¡cuanta gente!** what a lot of people!; ¡~ **tiempo perdido!** what a lot of time wasted!, the time you've wasted!; *V* **bueno.**

2 *interrog* (**a**) (*sing*) how much?; ¿~ **has gastado?** how much have you spent?; ¿~ (**tiempo**)? how long?; ¿~ **durará esto?** how long will this last?; ¿~ **hay de aquí a Bilbao?** how far is it from here to Bilbao?; **¿a ~ estamos?** (*Dep*) what's the score?; **¿a ~ están las peras?** how much are (the) pears?; **le dije ~ la quería** I told her how much I loved her; *V* **cada, cinco.**

(**b**) (*pl*) ¿~**s?** how many?; **¿cuantas personas había?** how many people were there?; **¿a ~s estamos?** what's the date?

(**c**) **el señor no sé ~s** Mr So-and-So; **el señor Anastasio no sé ~s** Mr Anastasius Something.

cuaquerismo *nm* Quakerism.

cuáquero, -a *adj, nm/f* Quaker.

cuarcita *nf* quartzite.

cuarenta *adj* forty; fortieth; **ésas son otras ~** (*And, Cono Sur*) that's a different story; **los (años) ~** the forties; **'Los ~ principales'** (*Rad*) ≈ 'the Top Forty' (*Spanish hit parade*); **los ~ rugientes** the Roaring Forties; **cantar las ~ a uno** to tell sb a few home truths; **hasta el ~ de mayo no te quites el sayo** ne'er cast a clout till May be out.

cuarentañero 1 *adj* fortyish, about forty. **2** *nm*, **cuarentañera** *nf* person of about forty, person in his (*o* her) forties.

cuarentena *nf* (**a**) (*gen*) forty; about forty. (**b**) (*Ecl*) Lent. (**c**) (*Med*) quarantine; **poner en ~** (*fig*) *persona* to send to Coventry, *asunto* to suspend judgement on.

cuarentón 1 *adj* forty-year old, fortyish. **2** *nm*, **cuarentona** *nf* person of about forty.

cuaresma *nf* Lent.

cuaresmal *adj* Lenten.

cuark *nm, pl* **cuarks** quark.

cuarta *nf* (**a**) (*Mat*) quarter, fourth, fourth part.

(**b**) (*de mano*) span.

(**c**) (*Náut*) point (of the compass).

(**d**) (*LAm*: *látigo*) whip, riding crop.

(**e**) (*Cono Sur Agr*) extra pair of oxen.

(**f**) (*) **andar de la ~ al pértigo** (*Cono Sur*), **vivir a la ~** (*Cono Sur, Méx*) to be on the bread line.

cuartago *nm* pony.

cuartazos* *nm invar* fat person, lump*.

cuartear [1a] **1** *vt* (**a**) (*dividir*) to quarter; to divide up, cut up; *carne* to quarter, joint.

(**b**) *carretera* to zigzag up.

(**c**) (*Náut*) **~ la aguja** to box the compass.

(**d**) (*Carib, Méx*: *azotar*) to whip, beat.

2 *vi* (**a**) (*Naipes*) to make a fourth (player), make up a four.

(**b**) (*Taur*) to dodge, step aside, swerve.

3 cuartearse *vr* (**a**) (*superficie*) to crack, split.

(**b**) (*Taur*) to dodge, step aside.

(**c**) (*Méx*: *desdecirse*) to go back on one's word.

cuartel *nm* (**a**) (*cuarta parte*) quarter, fourth part; (*de ciudad*) quarter, district.

(**b**) (*Her*) quarter.

(**c**) (*Hort*) bed.

(**d**) (*Mil*) barracks; **~es** quarters; **~ de bomberos** fire station; **~ general** headquarters; **~es de invierno** winter quarters; **vida de ~** army life, service life; **estar de ~** to be on half-pay.

(**e**) **guerra sin ~** war without mercy; **lucha sin ~** (*fig*) a fight with no holds barred; **dar ~ a** to support, encourage; **no dar ~** to give no quarter, show no mercy; **no hubo ~ para los revoltosos** no mercy was shown to the rioters.

cuartelada *nf*, **cuartelazo** *nm* military uprising, mutiny, coup, putsch.

cuartelero 1 *adj* barracks (*atr*). **2** *nm* (*And*) waiter.

cuartelillo *nm* police-station; fire station.

cuartería *nf* (*Carib, Cono Sur*) bunkhouse (*on a ranch*).

cuarterón *nm* (**a**) (*peso*) quarter; quarter pound. (**b**) (*Arquit*) door panel. (**c**) (*LAm*) quadroon.

cuarteta *nf* quatrain.

cuarteto *nm* (**a**) (*Mús*) quartet(te). (**b**) (*Liter*) quatrain.

cuartil *nm* quartile.

cuartilla *nf* (**a**) (*hoja*) sheet (of paper); **~s** (*Tip*) manuscript, copy; (*apuntes*) notes, jottings. (**b**) (*de caballo*) pastern. (**c**) (*cuarta parte*) fourth part (*of a measure*).

cuarto 1 *adj* fourth.

2 *nm* (**a**) (*cuarta parte*) quarter, fourth part; (**abrigo**) **tres ~s** three-quarter length coat; **~s de final** quarter finals; **~ de hora** quarter of an hour; **las 6 y ~** a quarter past 6; **las 7 menos ~** a quarter to seven; **tardó tres ~s de hora** he took three-quarters of an hour; **~ de luna** quarter of the moon; **~ creciente** first quarter; **~ menguante** last quarter.

(**b**) (*de carne*) joint; **~s** (*de animal*) legs, limbs; **~ trasero** hindquarters, (*Culin*) rump.

(**c**) (*Tip*) quarto; **libro en ~** quarto volume.

(**d**) (*Fin*) *an ancient coin*; **~s*** money, brass*; **de tres al ~** worthless, third-rate, tuppenny-ha'penny; **por 5 ~s** for a song; **¡qué coche ni qué ocho ~s!** car, my foot!; **es hombre de muchos ~s** he's got pots of money*; **estar sin un ~, no tener un ~** to be broke*; **dar un ~ al pregonero** to tell everyone one's private business.

(**e**) (*Arquit*) (*gen*) room; rooms; (*piso*) small flat; (*Cono Sur*) bedroom; **~ de aseo, ~ de baño** bathroom; **~ de desahogo, ~ trastero** lumber room; **~ de descanso** rest room; **~ de estar** living room; **~ de juego** playroom; **~ de los niños** nursery; **~ oscuro** (*Fot*) darkroom; **poner ~** to set up house; **poner ~ a la querida** to set one's mistress up in a little place.

(**f**) (*servidumbre*) household, establishment of servants.

(**g**) (*Mil*) watch; **estar de ~** to be on duty.

cuartofinalista *nmf* quarter-finalist.

cuartones *nmpl* dressed timber, beams, planks.

cuartucho *nm* hovel; poky little room.

cuarzo *nm* quartz.

cuás* *nm* (*Méx*) bosom pal*.

cuásar *nm* quasar.

cuasi *adv* (*liter*) = **casi.**

cuasi- ... *prefix* quasi- ...

cuate (*And, CAm, Méx*) **1** *adj* twin. **2** *nm* (**a**) (*gemelo*) twin. (**b**) (*amigo*) pal*, buddy (*esp US*). (**c**) (*escopeta*) double-barrelled gun. **3** *nf* girl.

cuaternario *adj, nm* quaternary.

cuatre(re)ar [1a] **1** *vt* (*Cono Sur*) *ganado* to rustle, steal. **2** *vi* (*Cono Sur*) to act treacherously.

cuatrero 1 *adj* (*CAm*) treacherous, disloyal. **2** *nm* (*Cono Sur*) (*de ganado*) cattle rustler; (*de caballos*) horse thief.

cuatrienal *adj* four-year (*atr*); four-yearly, quadrennial.

cuatrifónico *adj* quadraphonic.

cuatrillizo *nm*, **cuatrilliza** *nf* quadruplet.

cuatrimestral *adj* four-monthly, every four months.

cuatrimestralmente *adv* every four months.

cuatrimestre *nm* four-month period.

cuatrimotor 1 *adj* four-engined. **2** *nm* four-engined plane.

cuatriplicado *adj* quadruplicate; **por ~** in quadruplicate.

cuatro 1 *adj* (**a**) (*gen*) four; (*fecha*) fourth; **las ~** four o'clock.

(**b**) **más de ~** (*fig*) quite a few, rather a lot; **sólo había ~ muebles** there were only a few sticks of furniture; **había ~ gatos** there was hardly a soul; **cayeron ~ gotas** a few drops fell.

2 *nm* (**a**) four.

(**b**) (*And, Carib*: *Mús*) four-stringed guitar.

(**c**) (*Méx*: *trampa*) trick, fraud; (*error*) blunder.

(**d**) (*Aut*) **~ ~** four-wheel drive vehicle.

cuatrocientos *adj* four hundred.

cuatrojos* *nmf invar* person who wears glasses.

cuba¹ *nf* (**a**) (*tonel*) cask, barrel; (*tina*) tub; vat; (*Ferro*) tank car; **~ para el agua de lluvia** rainwater butt; **~ de riego** water wagon, street sprinkler.

(**b**) (*: *gordo*) pot-bellied person.

(**c**) (*: *borracho*) drunkard, boozer‡; **estar hecho una ~** to be as drunk as a lord.

cuba² *nm* (*And*) youngest child.

cubaje *nm* (*LAm*) volume, contents.

cuba-libre *nm, pl* **cubas-libres** *o* **cuba-libres** drink of rum and Coca Cola.

cubanismo *nm* cubanism, word (*o* phrase *etc*) peculiar to Cuba.

cubano, -a *adj, nm//f* Cuban.

cubata* *nm* = **cuba-libre.**

cubero *nm* cooper.

cubertería *nf* cutlery; (*Com*) table wares.

cubeta *nf* (*tonel*) keg, small cask; (*balde*) pail; (*Quím, Fot*) tray; (*de termómetro*) bulb; **~ de siembra** seed box.

cubicaje *nm* (*Aut*) cylinder capacity.

cubicar [1g] *vt* (**a**) (*Mat*) to cube. (**b**) (*Fís*) to determine the volume of.

cúbico *adj* cubic; **metro ~** cubic metre; **raíz cúbica** cube root.

cubículo *nm* cubicle.

cubierta *nf* (**a**) (*gen*) cover, covering; (*Tip*) paper cover, jacket; (*Arquit*) roof; (*Téc*) casing; (*Aut*: *capó*) bonnet, hood (*US*); (*Aut etc*: *neumático*) tyre, outer cover; (*Correos*) envelope; ~ **de cama** coverlet; ~ **sin cámara** tubeless tyre; ~ **de lona** tarpaulin, canvas; **bajo esta** ~ (*Correos*) under the same cover, enclosed herewith; **bajo** ~ **separada** (*Correos*) under separate cover.
(**b**) (*Náut*) deck; ~ **de aterrizaje,** ~ **de botes** boat-deck; ~ **de paseo** promenade deck; ~ **de sol** sun deck; ~ **de vuelo** flightdeck.
(**c**) (*And, Méx*: *funda*) sheath.
(**d**) (*fig*) cover, pretext.

cubierto 1 *ptp de* **cubrir** *y adj*: (**a**) (*gen*) covered; *cielo* overcast; *persona* with a hat, wearing a hat; **no** ~ *cheque* bad, unbacked; **poco** ~ *neumático* threadbare, worn.
(**b**) **la vacante está ya cubierta** the place has already been filled.
2 *nm* (**a**) **a** ~, **bajo** ~ under cover; **a** ~ **de** safe from, out of the way of; **ponerse a** ~ to take cover, shelter (*de* from).
(**b**) (*en mesa*) place (at table), place setting; knife, fork and spoon, set of cutlery; (*comida*) meal; meal at a fixed charge; ~**s** cutlery; ~ **de 8000 pesetas** 8000-peseta meal; **precio del** ~ cover charge.

cubil *nm* den, lair.

cubilete *nm* (**a**) (*Culin*: *cuenco*) basin, bowl; (*molde*) mould; (*copa*) goblet. (**b**) (*en juegos*) cup; (*de dados*) dice box. (**c**) (*LAm*: *intriga*) intrigue. (**d**) (*LAm*) (*chistera*) top hat; (*hongo*) bowler hat.

cubiletear [1a] *vi* (**a**) (*en el juego*) to shake the dice box. (**b**) (*fig*) to intrigue, scheme.

cubiletero, -a *nm/f* conjurer.

cubismo *nm* cubism.

cubista *adj, nmf* cubist.

cubitera *nf* ice-tray.

cubito *nm* (**a**) (*de niño*) bucket, beach pail. (**b**) ~ **de caldo** stock cube; ~ **de hielo** ice-cube.

cúbito *nm* ulna.

cubo *nm* (**a**) (*Mat*) cube; ~ **de Rubik** Rubik cube.
(**b**) (*balde*) bucket, pail; (*tina*) tub; ~ **de** (**la**) **basura** dustbin, ashcan (*US*); ~ **para el carbón** coal scuttle; **llover a** ~**s** to rain cats and dogs, rain in torrents.
(**c**) (*de reloj*) barrel, drum.
(**d**) (*de rueda*) hub.
(**e**) (*caz*) millpond.
(**f**) (*Arquit*) round turret.

cubrebocas *nm invar* (*Med*) mask.

cubrecama *nf* coverlet, bedspread.

cubrecorsé *nm* camisole.

cubremesa *nf* table cover.

cubreobjetos *nm invar* (*Bio etc*) slide cover.

cubrir [3a; *ptp* **cubierto**] **1** *vt* (**a**) (*gen*) to cover (in, over, up; *con, de* with); (*Arquit*) to roof, put a roof over; *fuego* to make up, bank up; **lo cubrieron los aguas** the waters closed over it; **el agua casi me cubría** the water almost covered me, I was almost out of my depth; **no te metas donde te cubra el agua** don't go out of your depth.
(**b**) (*Dep, Mil*) to cover; to protect, defend; ~ **su retirada** to cover one's retreat.
(**c**) (*disimular etc*) to cover; to hide, conceal, cloak; **cubre su tristeza con una falsa alegría** she covers up her sadness with a false cheerfulness.
(**d**) (*llenar*) ~ **a uno de improperios** to shower insults on sb, shower sb with insults; ~ **a uno de alabanzas** to heap praises on sb; ~ **a uno de atenciones** to overwhelm sb with kindnesses; ~ **a uno de oprobio** to cover sb in shame; ~ **a uno de besos** to smother sb with kisses.
(**e**) *proteger* to cover, protect; to cover up for.
(**f**) *distancia* to cover, travel, do; ~ **80 kms en una hora** to cover 80 kms in an hour.
(**g**) *vacante* to fill.
(**h**) (*Bio*) to cover, mate with; (**‡**) to screw **‡**.
(**i**) (*Fin etc*) *gastos, necesidades* to meet, cover; *déficit, préstamo etc* to cover; *deuda* to repay; **esto cubre todas nuestras necesidades** this meets all our needs; **ello apenas cubre los gastos** this scarcely covers the expenses.
(**j**) (*Periodismo*) *suceso* to cover.
2 cubrirse *vr* (**a**) (*persona*) to cover o.s.; (*ponerse el sombrero*) to put on one's hat.
(**b**) ~ **de gloria** (*fig*) to cover o.s. with glory.
(**c**) ~ **contra un riesgo** to cover (*o* protect) o.s. against a risk; ~ **contra una posibilidad** to take precautions against an eventuality.
(**d**) (*Met*) to become overcast.

cuca *nf* (**a**) (*jugador*) compulsive gambler. (**b**) ~**s** sweets, candy (*US*); titbits; confectionery. (**c**) (‡: *Fin*) one peseta. (**d**) (*CAm*‡) cunt‡. (**e**) (*: *cucaracha*) cockroach.

cucambé *nm* (*And*) hide-and-seek.

cucamente *adv* shrewdly; slyly, craftily.

cucamonas* *nfpl* (*palabras*) sweet nothings; (*caricias*) caresses; (*magreo*) fondling, petting*; **ella me hizo** ~ she gave me a come-hither look.

cucaña *nf* (**a**) (*) (*prebenda*) plum*, soft job*; (*ganga*) bargain; (*chollo*) cinch‡, easy thing. (**b**) (*de feria etc*) greasy pole.

cucañero, -a* *nm/f* shrewd person, fly sort; hanger-on.

cucar [1g] *vt* (**a**) (*guiñar*) to wink. (**b**) (*burlarse*) to deride, poke fun at. (**c**) (*LAm*: *instar*) to urge on, incite, provoke.

cucaracha 1 *nf* (**a**) (*Ent*) cockroach. (**b**) (*Méx* *Aut*) old crock. (**c**) (‡: *droga*) roach‡. (**d**) (*Inform*) chip. **2** *nm* (*) priest.

cucarachero *nm* (*And, Carib*: *parásito*) parasite, hanger-on; (*And*: *adulador*) flatterer, creep‡.

cuclillas *adv*: **en** ~ squatting, crouching; **ponerse en** ~, **sentarse en** ~ to squat, sit on one's heels.

cuclillo *nm* (**a**) (*Orn*) cuckoo. (**b**) (*) cuckold.

cuco 1 *adj* (**a**) (*astuto*) shrewd; sly, crafty.
(**b**) (*mono*) pretty; cute; dainty.
2 *nm* (**a**) (*Orn*) cuckoo.
(**b**) (*Ent*) grub, caterpillar.
(**c**) (*: *jugador*) gambler.
(**d**) **hacer** ~ **a uno** (*Méx*) to poke fun at sb.
(**e**) (*Cono Sur**: *sabelotodo*) smart guy*, wise guy*.
(**f**) (*Carib*‡) cunt‡.
(**g**) (*And, Cono Sur*: *fantasma*) bogeyman.

cucú *nm* (*grito*) cuckoo.

cucuche (*CAm*): **ir a** ~ to ride astride.

cucufato* *nm* (*And, Cono Sur*) (*hipócrita*) hypocrite; (*mojigato*) prude; (*loco*) nut‡.

cuculí *nm* (*And, Cono Sur*) wood pigeon.

cucurucho *nm* (**a**) (*papel*) paper cone, cornet; (*Aut*) cone. (**b**) (*Ecl etc*) hooded garment; pointed hat. (**c**) (*And, CAm, Carib*: *cumbre*) top, summit, apex. (**d**) (*Carib*: *cuchitril*) hovel, shack.

cuchara *nf* (**a**) (*gen*) spoon; scoop; (*cucharón*) ladle; (*Téc*) scoop; (*balde*) bucket; dipper; ~ **de café** coffee spoon, (*equivalente a*) teaspoon; ~ **de sopa,** ~ **sopera** soup spoon, (*como medida*) tablespoon; **militar de** ~* officer who has risen from the ranks, ranker; **meter su** ~ (*en conversación*) to butt in; (*en asunto*) to meddle, shove one's oar in; **meter algo a uno con** ~ to have a hard job getting sb to understand sth; **despacharse** (*o* **servirse**) **con la** ~ **grande** (*esp LAm*) to give o.s. a big helping, (*fig*) look after Number One; **soplar** ~* to eat; **soplar** ~ **caliente*** to eat well.
(**b**) (*LAm*: *paleta*) flat trowel; **albañil de** ~ skilled bricklayer.
(**c**) (*CAm, Carib, Cono Sur*: *puchero*) pout; **hacer** ~ to pout.
(**d**) (*Méx*: *carterista*) pickpocket.

cucharada *nf* spoonful; ~ **de café** teaspoonful; ~ **rasada** level spoonful; ~ **de sopa,** ~ **sopera** tablespoonful.

cucharadita *nf* teaspoonful.

cucharear [1a] *vt* (*Culin*) to spoon out, ladle out; (*Agr*) to pitch, pitchfork.

cucharetear [1a] *vi* (**a**) (*lit*) to stir (with a spoon). (**b**) (*fig*) to meddle.

cucharilla *nf* (**a**) (*t* **cucharita,** ~ **de café,** ~ **de té**) small spoon, teaspoon. (**b**) (*Pesca*) spoon. (**c**) (*Golf*) wedge.

cucharón *nm* (*Culin*) ladle; (*Téc*) scoop, bucket; **tener el** ~ **por el mango** to be the boss, be in control.

cuche *nm* (*CAm*), **cuchí** *nm* (*And*) pig.

cuché *nm* art paper.

cuchichear [1a] *vi* to whisper (*a* to).

cuchicheo *nm* whispering.

cuchilear* [1a] *vt* (*LAm*) to egg on.

cuchilla *nf* (**a**) (*Culin*) (large, kitchen) knife; (*de carnicero*) chopper, cleaver; (*Téc*) blade; (*de patín*) blade; (*LAm*: *cortaplumas*) penknife; ~ **de afeitar** razor blade.
(**b**) (*Geog*) ridge, crest; (*LAm*: *colinas*) line of low hills; (*Carib*: *cumbre*) mountain top.

cuchillada *nf* (**a**) (*herida*) slash, cut, gash, knife wound; ~ **de cien reales** long gash, severe wound; **dar** ~ (*Teat**) to make a hit.
(**b**) (*Cos*) slash.
(**c**) ~**s** (*fig*) fight, brawl.

cuchillazo *nm* (*LAm*) = **cuchillada** (**a**).

cuchillería *nf* (**a**) (*cubiertos*) cutlery. (**b**) (*tienda*) cutler's (shop).

cuchillero 1 *adj* (*LAm*) quarrelsome, fond of brawling. **2** *nm* cutler.

cuchillo *nm* (**a**) (*gen*) knife; **~ de caza, ~ de monte** hunting knife; **~ de cocina** kitchen knife; **~ del pan** breadknife; **~ de trinchar** carving knife; **pasar a ~** to put to the sword; **remover el ~ en la llaga** to turn the knife in the wound.
(**b**) (*Arquit*: *t* **~ de armadura**) upright, support.
(**c**) **~ de aire** sharp draught, cold draught.
(**d**) (*de jabalí etc*) fang, tusk.
(**e**) (*Cos*) gore.

cuchipanda* *nf* feed*, beano‡.

cuchitril *nm* (**a**) (*Agr*) pigsty. (**b**) (*fig*) hovel; pigsty; den, hole.

cucho[1] *nm* (**a**) (*CAm*: *jorobado*) hunchback; (*Méx*: *manco*) limbless person. (**b**) (*Cono Sur*: *gato*) puss. (**c**) (*And*) = **cuchitril** (**b**).

cucho[2]* *adj* (*Méx*) gloomy, depressed.

cuchuche *nm*: **ir a ~** (*CAm*) to ride piggyback.

cuchuflé *nm* (*Carib*) = **cuchuflí**.

cuchufleta* *nf* (**a**) (*broma*) joke, crack*. (**b**) (*Méx*: *baratija*) trinket, trifle.

cuchuflí* *nm* (*Carib*) uncomfortable place; (*celda*) cell.

cuchugos *nmpl* (*And, Carib*) saddlebags.

cuchumbo *nm* (*CAm*) (*embudo*) funnel; (*balde*) bucket, pail; (*de dados*) dice box; (*juego*) game of dice.

cueca *nf* (*Cono Sur*) handkerchief dance.

cuelga *nf* (**a**) (*acto*) hanging (of fruit *etc* to dry); (*racimo*) bunch (of drying fruit *etc*). (**b**) (*regalo*) birthday present. (**c**) (*And, Cono Sur*: *Geog*) fall (in the level of a stream *etc*).

cuelgacapas *nm invar* (*percha*) coat hanger; (*mueble*) hall-stand.

cuelgue‡ *nm* (**a**) **tener un ~** (*Fin*) to be broke*; (*confuso*) to be all at sea, be in a bad way; (*drogas*) to need a fix‡. (**b**) **¡qué ~!** how awful!, how embarrassing!

cuellicorto *adj* short-necked.

cuellilargo *adj* long-necked.

cuello *nm* (**a**) (*Anat*) neck; **~ de botella** (*fig*) bottleneck; **~ del útero, ~ uterino** cervix, neck of the womb; **apostar el ~*, jugarse el ~*** to stick one's neck out; **te cortaré el ~** I'll slit your throat; **erguir el ~** to be haughty; **levantar el ~** to get on one's feet again (*fig*).
(**b**) (*prenda*) collar; **~ alto** high collar; **de ~ blanco** white-collar (*atr*); **~ blando** soft collar; **~ (de) cisne** polo neck, turtleneck (*US*); **~ de pajarita** wing collar; **~ postizo, ~ de quita y pon** detachable collar; **~ de recambio** spare collar.

cuenca *nf* (**a**) (*hueco*) hollow; (*Anat*) eye socket.
(**b**) (*Hist*) wooden bowl, begging bowl.
(**c**) (*Geog*) bowl, deep valley; (*de río*) basin, catchment area; **la ~ del Ebro** the Ebro basin; **~ hullera, ~ minera** coalfield.

cuenco *nm* (**a**) (*concavidad*) hollow; (*de cuchara*) bowl; **~ de la mano** hollow of the hand.
(**b**) (*recipiente*) earthenware bowl, wooden bowl.

cuenta *nf* (**a**) (*Mat*) count, counting; calculation; (*esp fig*) reckoning; (*Boxeo*) count; **~ de la vieja** counting on one's fingers; **~ atrás, ~ al revés** countdown; **a esa ~** at that rate; **por la ~** apparently, as far as one can tell; **beber más de la ~** to have too much to drink, have one over the eight; **caer en la ~** to catch on (*de* to), see the point (*de* of); **habida ~ de eso** bearing that in mind; **hacer algo con su ~ y razón** to be fully aware of what one is doing; **perder la ~ de** to lose count of; **tener** (*o* **tomar**) **en ~** to bear in mind, take into account; **es otra cosa a tener en ~** that's another thing to be borne in mind.
(**b**) (*Com, Fin*: *en banco*) account; **~ de ahorros** savings account; **~ de amortización** depreciation account; **~ bancaria, ~ de banco** bank account; **~ de caja** cash account; **~ de compensación** clearing account; **~ corriente** current account; **~ de crédito** loan account; **~ de depósitos** deposit account; **~ de diversos** sundries account; **~ de gastos** expense account; **~ indistinta, ~ en participación** joint account; **~ de pérdidas y ganancias** profit and loss account; **~ personal** personal account; **~ a plazo (fijo)** fixed-term account; **~ presupuestaria** budget account; **abrir una ~** to open an account; **a (buena) ~** on account; **tomar un coche a ~** to take a car in part payment; **abonar una cantidad en ~ a uno** to credit a sum to sb's account; **cargar una cantidad en ~ a uno** to charge a sum to sb's account.
(**c**) (*Com, Fin*: *factura*) account, bill; (*en restaurante etc*) bill; (*fig*) check, tally; **la ~ del sastre** the tailor's bill; **~ pendiente** unpaid bill, outstanding account; **la ~ es la ~** business is business; **ajustar** (*o* **liquidar**) **una ~** to settle an account; **echar las ~s** to reckon up; **hacer las ~s de la lechera** to indulge in wishful thinking, count one's chickens before they are hatched; **llevar la ~ de** to keep an account of; **pasar la ~** to send the bill; **presentar las ~s del Gran Capitán** to make excessive demands; **sale más a ~** it's more economical; **vivir a ~ de** to live at the expense of.
(**d**) (*fig*: *de disputa etc*) account; **ajustar ~s** to settle up (*con* with); **ajustar ~s con uno** to settle a score with sb; **le ajusté las ~s*** I told him where to get off*; **voy a ajustar ~s con él** I'm going to have it out with him; **arreglar las ~s a uno*** (*Méx*) to punish sb; **¡vamos a ~s!** let's get down to business!; **tener ~s pendientes con uno** to have a matter to settle with sb.
(**e**) (*fig*: *relato*) account; (*informe*) report, statement; **en resumidas ~s** in short, in a nutshell; all in all; **dar ~ de** to give an account of, report on; **dar ~ a uno de sus actos** to account to sb for one's actions; **no tiene que dar ~s a nadie** he's not answerable to anyone; **dar ~ de una botella** to finish off a bottle, put paid to a bottle; **dar buena ~ de sí** to give a good account of o.s.; to give as good as one gets; **darse ~ de** to realize (*que* that); **hay que darse ~ de que ...** one must not forget that ...; **¡date ~!** just fancy!; **sin darse ~** without realizing it, without noticing; **exigir** (*o* **pedir**) **~s a uno** to call sb to account, bring sb to book; **haz ~ de que no voy** (*esp LAm*) just imagine I'm not going; **rendir ~s a uno** to report to sb; **salir de ~s** to be about to give birth (*de* to).
(**f**) (*fig*: *asunto*) affair, business; **ésa es ~ mía** that's my affair, that's up to me; **de ~ y riesgo de uno** at one's own risk; **por ~ propia, por su propia ~** on one's own account, for o.s.; **por mi ~** in my opinion; as for me; **eso corre de** (*o* **por**) **mi ~** that's my affair; **éste corre por mi ~** (*bebidas etc*) this one's on me; **no querer ~s con uno** to want nothing to do with sb; to want no trouble with sb; *V* **apañar** *etc*.
(**g**) (*proyectos*) **~s** plans; **echar ~s** to reflect, take stock; **echar ~ de** + *infin* to plan to + *infin*; **le salieron fallidas las ~s** his plans went wrong.
(**h**) (*fig*: *importancia*) importance; **de (mucha) ~** important; **no tiene ~** + *infin* there is no point in + *ger*.
(**i**) (*fig*: *beneficio*) benefit; **por la ~ que le tiene** because it is to his benefit; **no trae ~ hacerlo** it is not profitable to do it; **me sale más a ~** it suits me better; **no tiene ~** there's no point in it.
(**j**) (*Rel*) bead.
(**k**) (*: *Med*) period, curse (of Eve).

cuentacorrentista *nmf* depositor.

cuentacuentos *nmf invar* storyteller.

cuentagotas *nm invar* (*Med*) dropper; **a ~** (*fig*) drop by drop, bit by bit.

cuentakilómetros *nm invar* (*distancia*) *equivalente a* milometer; (*velocidad*) speedometer.

cuentarrevoluciones *nm invar* tachometer.

cuentear [1a] **1** *vt* (**a**) (*And*) (*pretender*) to court; (*felicitar*) to compliment. (**b**) (*Méx**) to kid*, have on. **2** *vi* (*CAm*) to gossip.

cuenterete *nm* (*CAm*) (*chisme*) piece of gossip; (*cuento*) tall story, tale.

cuentero* *nm* (*Cono Sur*) confidence trickster, con man*.

cuentista *nmf* (**a**) (*narrador*) storyteller; (*Liter*) short-story writer.
(**b**) (*chismoso*) gossip; (*soplón*) telltale.
(**c**) (*persona afectada*) affected person, person with a theatrical manner; (*presumido*) conceited person, big-mouth‡.
(**d**) (*Cono Sur*: *estafador*) con man*.

cuentística *nf* (genre of) the short story.

cuento[1] *nm* (**a**) (*relato*) story, tale; (*Liter*) short story; (*chiste*) funny story, joke; **~ de hadas** fairy-tale; **~ de la lechera** (piece of) wishful thinking; **~ del tío** (*And, Cono Sur*) confidence trick, confidence game (*US*); **~ de viejas** old wives' tale; **es un ~ largo** it's a long story; **esto es mucho ~** this is terribly tedious; **es el ~ de nunca acabar** it's an endless business; **aplicarse el ~** to take note; **estar en el ~** to be in the picture, be fully informed; **ir a uno con el ~** to go off and tell sb; **va de ~ que ...** the story goes that ..., it is said that ...; **traer algo a ~** to mention sth, bring sth up; (*pey*) to drag sth in; **eso no viene a ~** that's off the point, that's irrelevant; **vivir del ~** to live by one's wits.
(**b**) **sin ~** countless.

(**c**) (*fábula*) story, tale; (*mentira*) fib; (*pretexto*) pretext; **¡puro ~!** a likely story!; **~ chino** tall story; **¡déjese de ~s!** stop beating about the bush!, get on with it!; **se me hace ~** (*Cono Sur**) I don't believe it, come off it!*; **tener más ~ que siete viejas** (*etc*) to be given to fibbing.

(**d**) (*problemas*) **~s** trouble, difficulties; (*trastornos*) upsets; **han tenido no se qué ~s entre ellos** they've had some upset among themselves; **no quiero ~s con él** I don't want any trouble with him.

(**e**) (*jaleo*) fuss; (*exageración*) exaggeration; (*palabrería*) hot air, mere words; **tiene mucho ~** he makes a lot of fuss (about nothing), he exaggerates everything so.

cuento[2] *nm* (*punta*) point, tip; ferrule.

cuera *nf* (**a**) (*LAm*: *piel*) hide; (*correa*) leather strap. (**b**) (*Méx*: *chaqueta*) leather jacket. (**c**) **~s** (*CAm*) leggings. (**d**) (*And, CAm, Carib*: *paliza*) flogging.

cuerazo *nm* (*LAm*) lashing.

cuerda *nf* (**a**) (*de atar*) rope; (*delgada*) string, cord; (*de perro*) lead; (*Pesca*) fishing line; (*Agrimen*) measuring tape; **~ arrojadiza** lasso; **~ floja** tightrope; **~ de plomada** plumbline; **~ de presidiarios** (*Hist*) chain gang; **~ de salvamento, ~ salvavidas** lifeline; **~ de tendedero, ~ para tender la ropa** clothesline; **aflojar la ~** (*fig*) to ease up; **apretar la ~** (*fig*) to tighten up; **bailar en la ~ floja** to keep in with both parties; **estar en** (*o* **contra**) **las ~s** (*fig*) to be on the ropes, be up against it; **estirar la ~** (*fig*) to go too far, overdo it; **poner a uno contra las ~s** (*fig*) to put sb up against the ropes, put sb in a tight spot; **son de la misma ~** they're all as bad as each other; **bajo ~, por debajo de ~** in an underhand way, by stealth, on the side; behind the scenes.

(**b**) (*de reloj*) spring; (*Mec*) clockwork mechanism; **dar ~ al reloj** to wind up one's watch; **dar ~ a uno** to encourage sb (to talk); **un coche de ~** a clockwork car.

(**c**) (*Mec*: *fig*) energy; **aún le queda ~** he's still got some steam left in him; **no le duró mucho la ~** he didn't keep it up long; **tienen ~ para rato** they've something to keep them going, (*esp*) they've a lot to talk about.

(**d**) (*Mús*) string, cord; **~ de arco** bowstring; **~ de tripa** catgut; **estar en su ~** (*LAm*) to be in one's element; **estar con ~** (*LAm*) to be ready and willing.

(**e**) (*Mús*: *fig*) vocal range.

(**f**) (*Anat*) cord; tendon; **~ espinal** spinal cord; **~s vocales** vocal chords.

(**g**) (*Mat*) chord.

cuerdamente *adv* (**a**) (*sensatamente*) sanely. (**b**) (*prudentemente*) wisely, sensibly, prudently.

cuerdo *adj* (**a**) *persona* sane. (**b**) *acción etc* wise, sensible, prudent.

cuereada *nf* (*LAm*) beating, tanning*.

cuerear [1a] *vt* (**a**) (*LAm*) *animal* to skin, flay. (**b**) (*LAm*) *persona* to whip, beat. (**c**) **~ a uno** (*Carib, Cono Sur*: *regañar*) to tear a strip off sb.

cuerito: **de ~ a ~** *adv* (*LAm*) from end to end.

cueriza *nf* (*LAm*) beating, tanning*.

cuerna *nf* (**a**) (*Zool*) horns; (*de ciervo*) antlers. (**b**) (*para beber*) drinking horn. (**c**) (*Mús*) rustic horn, hunting horn.

cuerno *nm* (**a**) (*Zool*) horn; (*de ciervo*) antler; **~ de la abundancia** cornucopia, horn of plenty; **el C~ de Africa** the Horn of Africa; **estar en los ~s** (**del toro**) to be in danger; to be in a jam; **poner a uno en los ~s** (**del toro**) to place sb at risk; to get sb into a fix; **poner los ~s a uno** to cuckold sb; **oler** (*o* **saber**) **a ~ quemado** to be suspicious; to leave a nasty taste in one's mouth; **esto me sabe a ~ quemado** this upsets me, this makes my blood boil.

(**b**) (*) (*locuciones*) **¡~(s)!** gosh!*, blimey!‡; **¡(y) un ~!** my foot!; **irse al ~** (*negocio*) to fail, fall through; (*persona*) to go to the dogs; **¡que se vaya al ~!** he can go to hell!; **¡vete al ~!** go to hell!, get lost!‡; **mandar a uno al ~** to tell sb to go to hell; **mandar algo al ~** to consign sth to hell; **romperse los ~s** to work one's butt off*; **¡así te rompas los ~s!** I hope you break your neck!

(**c**) (*Culin*) roll, croissant.

(**d**) (*Mil*) wing.

(**e**) (*Mús*) horn; **~ alpino** alpenhorn.

cuero *nm* (**a**) (*Zool*) skin, hide; (*de conejo etc*) pelt; (*Dep*) ball, leather*; (*Téc, materia etc*) leather; **~ adobado** tanned skin; **~ cabelludo** scalp; **~ charolado** patent leather; **andar en ~s*** to go about stark naked; **dejar a uno en ~s** (*fig*) to rob sb of everything.

(**b**) (*odre*) wineskin; (‡) toper, old soak‡; **estar hecho un ~** to be as drunk as a lord.

(**c**) (*de grifo*) washer.

(**d**) (*LAm*: *látigo*) whip; **arrimar** (*o* **dar** *etc*) **el ~ a uno** to give sb a beating.

(**e**) (*And, Carib‡*: *puta*) whore; (*And*: *solterona*) old maid; (*Carib‡*: *vieja*) old bag‡; (*And, Méx**: *amante*) mistress.

(**f**) (*CAm, Carib**: *descaro*) cheek*, nerve*.

(**g**) (‡: *cartera*) wallet.

cuerpada* *nf*: **tiene buena ~** (*Cono Sur*) she's got a good body.

cuerpazo* *nm* huge frame, mighty bulk.

cuerpear [1a] *vi* (*Cono Sur*) to dodge.

cuerpo *nm* (**a**) (*Anat etc*) body; (*tipo*) figure; (*talle*) build; (*cadáver*) corpse; (*Dep*) length; **combate ~ a ~** hand-to-hand fight; **luchar ~ a ~** to fight hand-to-hand; **~ del delito** corpus delicti; **de ~ entero** *espejo, cuadro* full-length; *bribón etc* thoroughgoing, out-and-out; true, real; *vino* full-bodied; **coche de dos ~s** hatchback (car); **coche de tres ~s** three-box car; **a ~ limpio** unarmed; **de medio ~** half-length; **en ~ y alma** fully; **un vino de mucho ~** a full-bodied wine; **dar con el ~ en tierra** to fall down; **echar el ~ atrás** to lean suddenly backwards; **estar de ~ presente** to lie in state; **ganar por 4 ~s** to win by 4 lengths; **ganar por medio ~** to win by half a length; **hacer del ~** to relieve o.s.; **hurtar el ~** to dodge, move (one's body) out of the way; **ir a ~, ir en ~** to go without a coat; **vivir a ~ de rey** to live like a king.

(**b**) (*corporación etc*) body; corporation; **~ estatal** public body; **~ legislativo** legislative body.

(**c**) (*Jur etc*) **~ de doctrina** body of teaching; **~ de leyes** body of laws.

(**d**) (*personas*) body; brigade; force; (*Mil*) corps; **~ de baile** corps de ballet; **~ de bomberos** fire-brigade, fire department (*US*); **~ diplomático** diplomatic corps; **~ de ejército** army corps; **~ electoral** electorate; **~ de intendencia** service corps; **~ de sanidad** medical corps.

(**e**) (*Quím*) body, substance; **~ compuesto** compound; **~ simple** element; **~ extraño** foreign body.

(**f**) (*Astron*) body.

(**g**) (*Anat*: *tronco*) trunk; (*fig*) main part; mass, bulk; **el ~ de un libro** the main part of a book, the book proper; **dar ~ a un líquido** to thicken a liquid; **tomar ~** to swell, get bigger; (*proyecto etc*) to take shape.

(**h**) (*de edificio*) wing; part; (*de mueble*) part, section; (*de cohete*) stage.

(**i**) (*Cos*) bodice.

(**j**) (*Tip*: *de letra*) point; **negritas del ~ 6** 6-point black.

(**k**) (*de papel etc*) thickness.

(**l**) (*Liter*) volume; **una biblioteca de 50 mil ~s** a library of 50,000 books.

(**m**) (‡: *en oración directa*) man*, brother*.

(**n**) **este ~*** yours truly*, I myself.

cuerudo *adj* (**a**) (*LAm*) *caballo* slow, sluggish; lazy. (**b**) (*LAm*) *persona* annoying. (**c**) (*Cono Sur*: *valiente*) brave, tough. (**d**) (*CAm, Carib*: *descarado*) impudent, cheeky*.

cuervo *nm* raven; crow; **~ marino** cormorant.

cuesco *nm* (**a**) (*Bot*) stone. (**b**) (*Mec*) millstone (*of oil mill*). (**c**) (*) punch, bash*. (**d**) (*‡: *pedo*) loud fart*‡.

cuesta *nf* (**a**) (*pendiente*) slope; (*en carretera etc*) hill; **~ abajo** downhill; **ir ~ abajo** (*fig*) to decline, go downhill; **~ arriba** uphill; **se me hace ~ arriba** + *infin* I find it hard to + *infin*; **~ de enero** period of financial stringency following Christmas spending; **hemos vencido la ~ ya** we're over the hump now; we're more than halfway.

(**b**) **a ~s** on one's back; **echar algo a ~s** to put sth on one's back, (*fig*) to take on the burden of sth; **lleva también eso a ~s** he has the additional burden of that.

cuestación *nf* charity collection; flag day.

cuestión *nf* (**a**) (*asunto*) matter, question, issue; (*Mat etc*) problem; **~ batallona** vexed question; **~ clave** key question; **~ de confianza** (*Parl*) vote of confidence; **~ madre** chief problem; **~ candente, ~ palpitante** burning question; **~ de orden** (*Parl*) point of order; **~ de principio** point of principle; **la cosa en ~** the matter at issue, the thing in question; **en ~ de** about, concerning; **es ~ de** it is a matter of; **eso es otra ~** that's another matter; **otra ~ sería si** ... it would be different if ...; **llamar a uno a la ~** (*Parl*) to call sb to order.

(**b**) (*disputa*) quarrel, dispute; (*dificultad*) trouble; complication; **hay ~ sobre si** ... there's an argument about whether ...; **la ~ es que** ... the trouble is that ...; **no quiero cuestiones con los empleados** I don't want trouble with the staff; **no tengamos ~** let's not have an argument about it, let's not have a fuss about it.

(**c**) (‡: *dinero*) dough‡, money.

cuestionable *adj* questionable.

cuestionador *adj* questioning.
cuestionamiento *nm* questioning.
cuestionar [1a] **1** *vt* to question, dispute, argue about. **2** *vi* to argue.
cuestionario *nm* questionnaire; (*Escol, Univ etc*) question paper.
cuestor[1] *nm* (*Hist*) quaestor.
cuestor[2], **cuestora** *nm/f* charity collector.
cuete 1 *adj* (*Méx*) drunk. **2** *nm* (**a**) (*And, CAm, Méx*: *pistola*) pistol. (**b**) (*CAm, Méx*) = **cohete**. (**c**) (*Méx*: *embriaguez*) drunkenness. (**d**) (*Méx Culin*) steak.
cuetearse [1a] *vr* (*And*) (**a**) to go off, explode. (**b**) (‡) to kick the bucket‡.
cueva *nf* (**a**) (*caverna*) cave; (*de vino, en casa etc*) cellar, vault; **~ de ladrones** den of thieves. (**b**) (*Cono Sur***) cunt**; **tener ~** ‡ to be lucky.
cuévano *nm* pannier, deep basket.
cuezo* *nm*: **meter el ~** to drop a clanger‡, put one's foot in it.
cui *nm* (*LAm*) guinea-pig.
cuica *nf* (*And*) earthworm.
cuico 1 *adj* (*And*) thin; (*Carib*) rachitic, feeble. **2** *nm* (**a**) (*Cono Sur*: *forastero*) foreigner, outsider. (**b**) (*And, Cono Sur*: *pey*: *boliviano*) Bolivian. (**c**) (*Carib*: *mejicano*) Mexican. (**d**) (*Méx*: *policía*) policeman.
cuidadero, -a *nm/f* (*Zool*) keeper.
cuidado 1 *adj aspecto etc* soigné, elegant. **2** *nm* (**a**) (*preocupación*) care, worry, concern; solicitude; **dar ~** to cause concern; **estar con ~** to be anxious, be worried; **estar de ~** to be gravely ill, be in a bad way; **enfermar de ~** to fall seriously ill; **¡no haya ~!, ¡pierda Vd ~!** don't worry!; (*LAm*) don't mention it!; **eso me trae** (*o* **tiene**) **sin ~** I'm not worried about that; I couldn't care less.
(**b**) (*atención*) care, carefulness; **¡~!** careful!, look out!, watch out!; (*letrero*) 'Caution'; **~s intensivos** intensive care; **¡~ con el paquete!** careful with the parcel!; **¡~ con el perro!** beware of the dog!; **¡~ con los rateros!** watch out for pickpockets!; **¡~ con perderlo!** mind you don't lose it!; **andarse con ~** to go carefully, watch out; **de ~** serious; worrying; threatening; **él es de ~** he's a man to be wary of; (*Méx*) he's hard to please; **poner mucho ~ en algo** to take great care over sth; **tener ~** to be careful, take care; **tener ~ con** to be careful of, watch out for, beware of; **hay que tener ~ con él** you have to handle him carefully; **¡ten ~!** careful!
(**c**) (*asunto*) care; affair; business, concern; **¡allá ~s!** let others worry about that!, that's their funeral!*; **'al ~ del Sr A'** (*Correos*) 'care of Mr A'; **eso no es ~ mío, eso no corre de mi ~** that's not my concern; **lo dejo a su ~** I leave it to you; **está al ~ de la computadora** he's in charge of the computer; **los niños están al ~ de la abuela** the children are in their grandmother's charge.
cuidador *nm* (*Boxeo*) second; (*de caballos etc*) trainer; **~ de campo** groundsman.
cuidadora *nf* (*Méx*) nursemaid, nanny.
cuidadosamente *adv* (**a**) carefully. (**b**) anxiously; solicitously. (**c**) cautiously.
cuidadoso *adj* (**a**) (*atento*) careful (*con* about, with). (**b**) (*solícito*) anxious, concerned (*de, por* about); solicitous (*de* for). (**c**) (*prudente*) careful, cautious.
cuidar [1a] **1** *vt* (**a**) (*gen*) to take care of, look after; to pay attention to; **ella cuida a los niños** she looks after the children, she minds the children; **no cuidan la casa** they don't look after the house.
(**b**) (*Med*) to look after, care for.
2 *vi* (**a**) **~ de** to take care of, look after; **~ de una obligación** to attend to a duty; **~ de que ...** to take care that ..., see (to it) that ...; **cuidó de que todo saliera bien** he ensured that everything should go smoothly; **cuide de que no pase nadie** see that nobody gets in; **que cuide que no le pase lo mismo** let him beware lest the same thing happens to him; **cuide de no caer** take care not to fall.
(**b**) **cuida con esa gente** be wary of those people.
3 cuidarse *vr* (**a**) to look after o.s. (*t Med*); (*pey*) to look after Number One; **¡cuídate!** (*adiós*) take care!; **ella ha dejado de ~** she's let herself go.
(**b**) **~ de algo** to worry about sth; **~ de** + *infin* to be careful to + *infin*; **no se cuida del qué dirán** she doesn't worry about what people will think.
(**c**) **~ muy bien de** + *infin* to take good care not to + *infin*.
cuido *nm* care, minding; **para su ~, en su ~** for your own good.
cuita *nf* (**a**) (*preocupación*) worry, trouble; (*pena*) grief, affliction; (*civil, doméstico*) strife; **contar sus ~s a uno** to tell sb one's troubles. (**b**) (*CAm*) excrement; birdlime.
cuitado *adj* (**a**) (*preocupado*) worried, troubled; wretched. (**b**) (*tímido*) timid.
cuitlacoche *nm* (*Méx*) mushroom.
cuja *nf* (**a**) bedstead. (**b**) (*CAm, Méx*) envelope.
cujinillos *nmpl* (*Gaut, Méx*) saddlebags.
culada‡ *nf*: **darse una ~** to drop a clanger‡.
culamen‡ *nm* bottom.
culandrón‡ *nm* queer‡.
culantrillo *nm* (*Bot*) maidenhair.
culantro *nm* coriander.
culata *nf* (**a**) (*de fusil*) butt; (*de cañón*) breech; (*de cilindro*) head.
(**b**) (*Zool*) haunch, hindquarters; (*: *de persona*) backside, bottom.
(**c**) (*LAm*: *de casa*) side; rear, back, back part.
(**d**) (*Cono Sur*: *cobertizo*) hut, shelter.
culatazo *nm* kick, recoil.
culé* *nmf* supporter of Barcelona Football Club.
culear 1 *vt* (*And, Cono Sur, Méx***) to fuck**. **2** *vi* (**a**) (*: *mover el culo*) to waggle one's bottom. (**b**) (*And, Cono Sur, Méx***) to fuck**.
culebra *nf* (**a**) (*Zool*) snake; **~ de cascabel** rattlesnake; **hacer ~** to zigzag, stagger along.
(**b**) (*Mec*) worm (*of a still*).
(**c**) (*: *alboroto*) disturbance, disorder.
(**d**) (*And*: *cuenta*) debt, bill.
(**e**) (*Méx*) waterspout.
(**f**) (*Méx*: *manga*) hosepipe.
culebrear [1a] *vi* (**a**) (*culebra etc*) to wriggle (along); (*camino*) to zigzag; (*río etc*) to wind, meander. (**b**) (*Carib*) to stall, hedge.
culebreo *nm* wriggling; zigzag; winding, meandering.
culebrina *nf* (**a**) (*Hist*) culverin. (**b**) (*Met*) forked lightning.
culebrón* *nm* soap-opera*.
culeco *adj* (**a**) (*LAm*) *gallina* broody.
(**b**) (*LAm*) *persona* home-loving.
(**c**) **estar ~** (*And, Carib, Cono Sur*) to be head over heels in love.
(**d**) **estar ~ con algo** (*And, CAm, Carib, Méx**) (*satisfecho*) to be very pleased about sth, be over the moon about sth; (*orgulloso*) to be very proud of sth.
culera *nf* seat (of the trousers).
culeras* *nmf invar* coward.
culero 1 *adj* lazy. **2** *nm* (**a**) (*pañal*) nappy, diaper (*US*). (**b**) (*Méx*: *cobarde*) coward; sissy. (**c**) (*CAm‡*: *maricón*) poof‡, queer‡. **3** *nm* (*), **culera** *nf* drug courier, drug smuggler.
culí *nm* coolie.
culibajo *adj* short, dumpy.
culigordo* *adj* big-bottomed, broad in the beam*.
culillera *nf* (*CAm*), **culillo** *nm* (**a**) (*And, CAm, Carib**: *miedo*) fear, fright. (**b**) **tener ~** (*Carib**) to be in a hurry.
culín *nm* cider glass.
culinario *adj* culinary, cooking (*atr*).
culipandear [1a] *vi y* **culipandearse** *vr* (*Carib*) to stall, hedge.
culminación *nf* culmination.
culminante *adj punto etc* highest, topmost, culminating; *momento* culminating; (*fig*) outstanding.
culminar [1a] **1** *vt objetivo etc* to reach, attain; *acuerdo* to conclude, put the finishing touches to; *tarea, carrera etc* to finish. **2** *vi* to reach its highest point, reach a peak; to culminate (*en* in).
culo *nm* (**a**) (‡: ***en regiones de LAm*) bottom, backside, arse**, ass (*US***); (*ano*) anus, arsehole**; **dar a uno un puntapié en el ~** to kick sb's backside, (*fig*) to boot sb out; **dejar a uno (con el) ~ al aire** to leave sb stranded; **ser un ~ de mal asiento** to be restless, be fidgety; to chop and change, keep changing one's job (*etc*); **confunde el ~ con las témporas‡** he can't tell his arse from his elbow‡; **¡que te den por (el) ~!**** get stuffed!**; **ir con el ~ a rastras** to be in a jam*; (*Fin*) to be on one's beam ends; **ir de ~*** (*persona*) to be overloaded with work; (*precio etc*) to slide, collapse; **hacer que uno vaya de ~*** to make sb work terribly hard; **la ciudad va de ~** the city is going downhill; **les mandó a tomar por ~**** he told them to get stuffed**.
(**b**) (*: *de recipiente etc*) bottom; **ser ~ de vaso** to be false, be a fake.
culón *adj* = **culigordo**.
culote *nm* culotte(s).
culpa *nf* (**a**) (*gen*) fault; blame; (*Jur etc*) guilt; **por ~ de** through the fault of; through the negligence of; **no le**

alcanza ~ no blame attaches to him; **echar la** ~ **a uno** to blame sb (*de* for); **tener la** ~ to be to blame (*de* for); **nadie tiene la** ~ nobody is to blame; **tú tienes la** ~ it's your fault; **la** ~ **fue de los frenos** the brakes were to blame; **es** ~ **suya** it's his fault.
(**b**) (*pecado*) sin, offence; **pagar las** ~**s ajenas** to pay for sb else's sins.
culpabilidad *nf* guilt.
culpabilizar [1f] *vt* = **culpar**.
culpable 1 *adj* (**a**) **la persona** ~ the person to blame, the person at fault; (*Jur*) the guilty person, the culprit; **acusarse** ~ (*LAm*), **confesarse** ~ to plead guilty; **declarar** ~ **a uno** to find sb guilty.
(**b**) *acto* to be condemned, be blameworthy; **es** ~ **no hacerlo** it is criminal not to do it; **con descuido** ~ with culpable negligence.
2 *nmf* culprit; (*Jur etc*) offender, guilty party.
culpado 1 *adj* guilty. **2** *nm*, **culpada** *nf* culprit; (*Jur*) the accused.
culpar [1a] *vt* (*acusar*) to blame, accuse; (*condenar*) to condemn; ~ **a uno de algo** to blame sb for sth; ~ **a uno de descuidado** to blame sb for being careless, accuse sb of carelessness.
cultamente *adv* in a cultured way, in a refined tone (*etc*); elegantly; (*pey*) affectedly, in an affected way.
culteranismo *nm* (*Liter*) *latinized, precious and highly metaphorical style* (*esp 17th century*).
culterano (*Liter*) **1** *adj latinized, precious and highly metaphorical.* **2** *nm*, **culterana** *nf* writer in the style of *culteranismo*.
cultismo *nm* (*Ling*) learned word.
cultista *adj* learned.
cultivable *adj* cultivable.
cultivador(a)[1] *nm/f* farmer, grower; (*de cultivo concreto*) grower; ~ **de vino** winegrower; ~ **de café** coffee grower, coffee planter.
cultivador[2] *nm* (*Agr*) cultivator.
cultivar [1a] *vt* (**a**) *tierra* to cultivate, work, till; *cultivo etc* to grow; (*Bio*) to culture.
(**b**) (*fig*) *arte, estudio etc* to cultivate; *talento etc* to develop; *memoria* to develop, improve; *amistad* to cultivate.
cultivo *nm* (**a**) (*acto*) cultivation, growing.
(**b**) (*cosecha*) crop; **el** ~ **principal de la región** the chief crop of the area; **rotación de** ~**s** rotation of crops.
(**c**) (*Bio*) culture.
culto 1 *adj* (**a**) *persona* cultivated, cultured, refined; educated; elegant; (*pey*) affected.
(**b**) (*Ling*) learned; **palabra culta** learned word.
2 *nm* worship; cult (*a* of); (*Ecl*) divine service, worship; ~ **a la personalidad** personality cult; **rendir** ~ **a** to worship; (*fig*) to pay homage to, pay tribute to.
cultrún *nm* (*Cono Sur Mús*) drum.
cultura *nf* culture; refinement; education; elegance; ~ **física** physical culture; ~ **de masas,** ~ **popular** popular culture; **persona de** ~ cultured person; educated person; **no tiene** ~ he has no manners, he doesn't know how to behave.
cultural *adj* cultural.
culturalmente *adv* culturally.
culturismo *nm* body-building.
culturista *nmf* body-builder.
culturización *nf* education, enlightenment.
culturizar [1f] **1** *vt* to educate, enlighten. **2 culturizarse** *vr* to educate o.s., improve one's mind.
cuma *nf* (**a**) (*CAm: cuchillo*) long knife, curved *machete*. (**b**) (*And: mujer*) old crone, gossip.
cumbancha *nf* (*Carib*) spree, drinking bout.
cumbia *nf* (*And*) (*música*) Colombian dance music; (*baile*) *popular Colombian dance.*
cúmbila *nm* (*Carib*) pal*, buddy (*esp US*).
cumbo *nm* (**a**) (*CAm*) (*chistera*) top hat; (*hongo*) bowler hat. (**b**) (*CAm: taza*) narrow-mouthed cup.
cumbre 1 *nf* summit, top; (*fig*) top, height, pinnacle; (*Pol*) summit, summit meeting; **conferencia** (**en la**) ~ summit conference; **está en la** ~ **de su poderío** he is at the height of his power; **hacer** ~ to make it to the top, reach the summit. **2** *atr*: top-level; outstanding, most important; **conferencia** ~ summit conference; **momento** ~ greatest moment; culminating point; **es su libro** ~ it is his most important book.
cume *nm*, **cumiche** *nm* (*CAm*) baby of the family.
cumpa* *nm* (*LAm*) pal*, buddy (*esp US*).
cumpleañero *nm*, **cumpleañera** *nf* (*LAm*) person celebrating a birthday, person whose birthday it is.
cumpleaños *nm invar* birthday; ~ **del matrimonio** (*LAm*) wedding anniversary.
cumplido 1 *adj* (**a**) (*perfecto*) complete, perfect; full; **un** ~ **caballero** a perfect gentleman, a real gentleman.
(**b**) (*Cos etc*) full, extra large.
(**c**) *comida etc* large, plentiful.
(**d**) (*cortés*) courteous, correct; formal (in manner); (*pey*) stiff, ceremonious.
(**e**) **tiene 60 años** ~**s** he is 60 (years old).
(**f**) (*LAm*) punctual.
2 *nm* compliment; courtesy; **visita de** ~ formal visit, courtesy call; **por** ~ as a compliment; out of politeness, as a matter of courtesy; **¡sin** ~**s!** no ceremony, please!; make yourself at home!; **andarse con** ~**s, estar de** ~**, usar** ~**s** to stand on ceremony, be formal; **cambiar los** ~**s de etiqueta** to exchange formal courtesies; **he venido por** ~ I came out of a sense of duty.
cumplidor *adj* reliable, trustworthy.
cumplimentar [1a] *vt* (**a**) (*visitas*) to pay one's respects to, pay a courtesy call on; (*felicitar*) to congratulate (*por* on). (**b**) *orden etc* to carry out; *deber* to perform, do. (**c**) *formulario etc* to complete, fill in.
cumplimentero *adj* formal, ceremonious; effusive.
cumplimiento *nm* (**a**) (*acto*) fulfilment; completion; performance; **falta de** ~ non-fulfilment; non-compliance; **dar** ~ **a** to fulfil. (**b**) = **cumplido 2**.
cumplir [3a] **1** *vt* (**a**) *promesa, deseo, contrato, amenaza etc* to carry out, fulfil; *condición* to comply with; (*Naipes*) *contrato* to make; *ley etc* to observe, obey; *ambición* to fulfil, realize.
(**b**) *condena* to serve; *condena de muerte* to carry out.
(**c**) *años etc* to reach, attain, complete; **hoy cumple 8 años** she's 8 today; **cuando cumpla los 21 años** when you're 21, when you reach the age of 21; **¿cuándo cumples años?** when is your birthday?; **¡que los cumplas muy felices!** many happy returns (of the day)!
2 *vi* (**a**) (*plazo*) to end, expire; (*pago*) to fall due.
(**b**) (*Mil*) to finish one's military service.
(**c**) (*hacer su deber*) to do one's duty, carry out one's task, do what is required of one; (*) to do one's marital duty; **sólo por** ~ as a matter of form, as a mere formality.
(**d**) ~ **con** = **1** (**a**); ~ **con uno** to do one's duty by sb; ~ **con la iglesia** to fulfil one's religious obligations; ~ **por uno** to act on sb's behalf.
(**e**) **le cumple hacerlo** it behoves him to do it, it is up to him to do it; **no le cumple** + *infin* it is not his place to + *infin.*
3 cumplirse *vr* (**a**) (*plan etc*) to be fulfilled, come true.
(**b**) (*plazo*) to expire, end, be up.
(**c**) **se obedece pero no se cumple** the letter of the law is observed but not its spirit.
cumquibus *nm* (††, *hum*): **el** ~ the wherewithal, the cash.
cumucho *nm* (*Cono Sur*) (**a**) (*multitud*) gathering, mob, crowd. (**b**) (*cabaña*) hut, hovel.
cumulativo *adj* cumulative.
cúmulo *nm* (**a**) (*montón*) pile, heap; accumulation; (*fig*) pile, lot. (**b**) (*Met*) cumulus.
cumulonimbo *nm* cumulonimbus.
cuna *nf* (**a**) (*camita*) cradle; cot; ~ **portátil** carrycot.
(**b**) (*asilo*) home, foundling hospital.
(**c**) (*fig: familia*) family, stock, birth; **de** ~ **humilde** of humble origin; **criarse en buena** ~ to be born with a silver spoon in one's mouth.
(**d**) (*fig: nacimiento*) birthplace; ~ **del famoso poeta** the birthplace of the famous poet.
(**e**) (*juego*) ~**s** cat's-cradle.
cundir [3a] *vi* (**a**) (*extenderse*) to spread; (*fig*) to spread, expand, increase; (*fig y pey*) to be rampant, be rife; **cunde el rumor que ...** there's a rumour going round that ...; **¡que no cunda el pánico!** don't panic!
(**b**) (*arroz etc*) to swell, expand; (*rendir*) to produce a good (*etc*) quantity, give good (*etc*) results; **hoy no me ha cundido el trabajo** work did not go well for me today; **¿te cunde?** how's it going?; **no me cunde** I'm not making any headway.
cunear [1a] **1** *vt* to rock, cradle. **2 cunearse** *vr* to rock, sway; (*al andar*) to swing along, walk with a roll.
cuneco *nm* (*Carib*) baby of the family.
cuneiforme *adj* cuneiform.
cuneta *nf* (**a**) ditch, gutter; **A deja a B en la** ~ A leaves B standing, A leaves B far behind; **quedarse en la** ~ (*fig*) to get left behind, miss the bus*. (**b**) (*CAm, Méx: de acera*)

kerb.
cunicultura *nf* rabbit breeding.
cuña *nf* (**a**) (*Téc*) wedge; (*de rueda*) chock; (*Tip*) quoin.
(**b**) **meter** ~ to sow discord.
(**c**) (*LAm**: *pez gordo*) big shot*, influential person.
(**d**) (*: *palanca*) influence, pull; **tener ~s** to have pull, have influence.
(**e**) (*CAm, Carib*: *Aut*) two-seater car.
(**f**) (*Rad, TV*) spot, slot; (*Prensa*) space-filler, brief item; ~ **publicitaria** commercial.
cuñada *nf* sister-in-law.
cuñadismo* *nm* nepotism, old boy network.
cuñado *nm* brother-in-law.
cuñete *nm* keg.
cuño *nm* (**a**) (*Téc*) stamp, die-stamp; **de nuevo** ~ *persona* new-fledged; *palabra* newly-coined. (**b**) (*fig*) stamp, mark; official stamp.
cuota *nf* (**a**) (*proporción*) quota; share; ~ **de inmigración** immigration quota; ~ **de mercado** market share, share of the market; ~ **de pantalla** quota of screen time; ~ **patronal** employer's contribution (to national insurance). (**b**) (*derechos*) fee, dues; ~ **de enseñanza** school fees; ~ **de entrada** entry fee, admission fee; ~ **del gremio** union dues; ~ **de socio** membership fee. (**c**) (*impuesto*) tax. (**d**) (*LAm*) (*mensualidad etc*) instalment, payment; **vender a ~s** to sell on credit, give credit terms for.
cuotidiano *adj* = **cotidiano**.
cupaje *nm* blending (of wines).
cupe *etc V* **caber**.
cupé *nm* (*Aut*) coupé.
Cupido *nm* Cupid.
cuplé *nm* pop song, light lyric.
cupletista *nf* cabaret singer.
cupo *nm* (**a**) (*proporción*) quota; share; ~ **de azúcar** sugar quota; ~ **de importación** import quota, trade quota. (**b**) (*Méx*: *capacidad*) space, room, capacity; (*And, Carib, Méx*) empty seat, vacancy; **no hay** ~ there's no room; **'no hay** ~**'** (*Teat*) 'house full', 'sold out'.
cupolino *nm* hubcap.
cupón *nm* coupon; (*Com*) trading stamp; ~ **de (los) ciegos** ticket for the lottery for the blind; ~ **de dividendos** dividend voucher; ~ **de franqueo** (*o* **respuesta**) **internacional** international reply coupon; ~ **de interés** interest warrant; ~ **obsequio** gift-coupon; ~ **de racionamiento** ration coupon; ~ **de regalo** gift-coupon.
cuponazo* *nm* lottery.
cuprero *adj* (*Cono Sur*) copper (*atr*).
cúpula *nf* (**a**) (*Arquit*) dome, cupola. (**b**) (*Náut*) turret. (**c**) (*Bot*) husk, shell. (**d**) (*Pol*) party leadership, leading members; (*Com, Fin*) top management.
cuquería *nf* craftiness.
cura[1] *nm* (**a**) (*Ecl*) priest; father; ~ **obrero** worker priest; ~ **párroco** parish priest; **sí, señor** ~ yes, father. (**b**) (*: *yo mismo*) I, myself; **este** ~ yours truly*; **no se ofrece este** ~ this poor devil isn't volunteering.
cura[2] *nf* (**a**) (*Med*) cure, healing; treatment; remedy; **primera** ~ first aid; ~ **de reposo,** ~ **de sueño** rest cure; ~ **de urgencia** emergency treatment, first aid; **tiene** ~ it can be cured, it is curable; **no tiene ~*** there's no remedy, it's quite hopeless.
(**b**) ~ **de almas** (*Ecl*) cure of souls.
curable *adj* curable.
curaca *nf* (**a**) (*And*: *ama*) priest's housekeeper. (**b**) (*And*: *cacique*) Indian chief, Indian native authority.
curación *nf* cure, healing; treatment; **primera** ~ first aid.
curadillo *nm* (**a**) (*Culin*) dried cod. (**b**) (*Téc*) bleached linen.
curado 1 *adj* (**a**) (*Téc*) cured; hardened; tanned, prepared. (**b**) (*And, Cono Sur**: *borracho*) drunk, tight*. **2** *nm* (*Culin*) curing.
curador(a) *nm/f* healer; ~ **por fe** faith-healer.
curalotodo *nm* cure-all.
curanderismo *nm* folk medicine; (*pey*) quack medicine, quackery.
curandero *nm* quack; bonesetter.
curar [1a] **1** *vt* (**a**) (*Med*) *persona, enfermedad* to cure (*de* of); *herida* to treat, dress; (*con droga etc*) to treat (*con* with).
(**b**) (*fig*) *mal* to remedy, put right.
(**c**) *carne, pescado* to cure, salt; *piel* to tan; *paño* to bleach; *madera* to season.
2 *vi* (*Med*) to get well (*de* after), recover (*de* from).
3 curarse *vr* (**a**) (*Med*) to recover, get better; (*t* **curarse en salud**) (*herida etc*) to heal up; (*persona*) to be on a cure, go for a cure.
(**b**) ~ **de** to take notice of, heed; (*enfermo etc*) to look after.
(**c**) (*And, Cono Sur**: *emborracharse*) to get drunk, get tight*; (*Méx**: *para reponerse*) to take a drink to sober up.
curasao *nm* curaçao.
curativo *adj* curative.
curato *nm* curacy, parish.
curazao *nm* curaçao.
curca[1] *nf* (*And, Cono Sur*) hump.
curco (*And, Cono Sur*) **1** *adj* hunchbacked. **2** *nm,* **curca**[2] *nf* hunchback.
curcuncho 1 *adj* (**a**) (*LAm*: *jorobado*) hunchbacked. (**b**) (*And**) (*hastiado*) fed up*; (*molesto*) annoyed. **2** *nm,* **curcuncha** *nf* (*LAm*) hunchback.
curda 1 *nm* (*) drunk*, sot. **2** *nf* (*) drunkenness; **agarrar una** ~ to get tight*; **estar (con la)** ~, **estar en** ~ (*Cono Sur*) to be tight*.
cureña *nf* gun carriage; **a** ~ **rasa** out in the open, exposed to the elements.
curia *nf* (**a**) (*Ecl*: *t* ~ **romana**) Curia, papal Curia. (**b**) (*Jur*) the Bar, the legal profession.
curiana *nf* cockroach.
curiara *nf* (*Carib*) dug-out canoe.
curiche* *nm* (*Cono Sur*) Negro.
curiosamente *adv* (**a**) (*extrañamente*) curiously; oddly. (**b**) (*pulcramente*) neatly, cleanly.
curiosear [1a] **1** *vt* (*mirar*) to glance at, look over; (*visitar*) to look round; (*husmear*) to nose out.
2 *vi* to look round, wander round; to poke about, nose about; (*pey*) to snoop, pry; ~ **por las tiendas** to wander round the shops; ~ **por los escaparates** to go window-shopping.
curiosidad *nf* (**a**) (*gen*) curiosity; (*pey*) inquisitiveness; **despertar la** ~ **de uno** to arouse sb's curiosity; **la** ~ **de noticias me llevó allí** the quest for news took me there; **tenemos** ~ **de saber si ...** we are curious to know if ...; **estar muerto de** ~ to be dying of curiosity.
(**b**) (*objeto*) curiosity; curio; **~es** sights, attractions; **visitar las ~es** to see the sights.
(**c**) (*aseo*) neatness, cleanliness.
(**d**) (*cuidado*) care(fulness), conscientiousness.
curioso 1 *adj* (**a**) (*persona*) curious; eager; (*pey*) inquisitive; ~ **de noticias** eager for news; **estar** ~ **por** + *infin* to be curious to + *infin*, be eager to + *infin*.
(**b**) *acto, objeto etc* curious, odd; quaint; **¡qué ~!** how curious!, how odd!
(**c**) (*aseado*) neat, clean, tidy.
(**d**) (*cuidadoso*) careful, conscientious.
(**e**) (‡) queer‡.
2 *nm,* **curiosa** *nf* bystander, spectator, onlooker; (*pey*) busybody; **los ~s de la literatura** those interested in literature.
curiosón, -ona *nm/f* busybody.
curita *nf* (*LAm*) (sticking) plaster.
currante‡ *nmf* worker, labourer.
currar‡ [1a] *vi,* **currelar‡** [1a] *vi* to work.
curre‡ *nm,* **currele‡** *nm,* **currelo‡** *nm* work; job; activity.
currículo *nm* curriculum.
curriculum *nm* (*t* ~ **vitae**) curriculum vitae.
currinche *nm* (**a**) (*Tip*) apprentice journalist, cub reporter. (**b**) (*: *persona insignificante*) little man, nonentity.
currito‡ *nm* working man, working bloke‡.
curro* 1 *adj* (**a**) (*elegante*) smart; (*ostentoso*) showy, flashy. (**b**) (*presumido*) cocky, brashly confident. **2** *nm* (‡) (**a**) (*trabajo*) work; job. (**b**) (*golpe*) bash*, punch; (*golpes*) bashing*, beating; **dar un** ~ **a uno** to beat sb up*.
Curro *nm forma familiar de* **Francisco**.
curroadicto, -a* *nm/f* workaholic.
currutaco 1 *adj* (**a**) (*ostentoso*) loud, showy, flashy.
(**b**) (*LAm*: *bajito*) short, squat.
2 *nm* (**a**) (†: *petimetre*) toff*, dandy.
(**b**) (*hombrecito*) insignificant little man.
(**c**) **~s** (*CAm*) diarrhoea.
curry ['kuri] *nm* curry.
cursante *nmf* (*LAm*) student.
cursar [1a] **1** *vt* (**a**) *mensaje* to send, dispatch; *orden* to send out; *solicitud* to pass on, dispatch, deal with.
(**b**) *asignatura* to study; *curso* to take, attend.
(**c**) *sitio* to frequent.
2 *vi*: **el mes que cursa** the present month.
cursi 1 *adj* (*de mal gusto*) in bad taste, vulgar; (*pretencioso*) pretentious; (*ostentoso*) loud, showy, flashy; (*esnob*) posh*, genteel; pseudo-refined; (*afectado*) affected. **2** *nmf* =

cursilón.
cursilería *nf* (*V adj* **1**) bad taste, vulgarity; pretentiousness; loudness, showiness, flashiness; poshness*, gentility, pseudo-refinement; affectation.
cursilón, -ona *nm/f* (*V adj* **1**) common but pretentious person; flashy type; posh sort*, genteel individual; affected person.
cursillista *nmf* member (of a course).
cursillo *nm* short course; short series (of lectures).
cursiva *nf* (*Tip*) italics; (*escritura*) cursive writing.
cursivo *adj escritura* cursive; (*Tip*) italic.
curso *nm* (**a**) (*de río etc*) course; direction; flow; **~ de agua, ~ fluvial** watercourse.
(**b**) (*Astron*) course.
(**c**) (*fig*) course; **el ~ de la enfermedad** the course of the disease, the progress of the disease; **dejar que las cosas sigan su ~** to let matters take their course; **en el ~ de la vida** in the course of a lifetime; **en el ~ de la semana** in the course of the week; **el proceso está en ~** the process is going on, the process is under way; **el año en ~** the current year, the present year; **trabajo en ~** work in progress.
(**d**) (*Jur*) **moneda de ~ legal** legal tender.
(**e**) **dar ~ a una solicitud** to deal with an application; **dar ~ a su indignación** to give vent to one's indignation, express one's indignation; **dar ~ al llanto** to let one's tears flow.
(**f**) (*Escol, Univ*: *personas*) year; **~ escolar** school year; **~ lectivo** academic year; **los del segundo ~** those in the second year, the second years.
(**g**) (*Escol, Univ*: *asignatura*) course; subject; **he perdido 2 ~s** I failed 2 subjects, I have to repeat 2 subjects; **~ acelerado** crash course; **~ de actualización** refresher course; **~ de base** foundation course; **~ por correspondencia** correspondence course; **~ intensivo** intensive course, crash course; **~ de secretaria** secretarial course.
cursor *nm* (*Téc*) slide; (*Inform*) cursor.
curtido 1 *adj* (**a**) *cuero* tanned; *piel* hardened, leathery; *cara* (*al sol*: *t* **~ a la intemperie**) tanned, weather-beaten.
(**b**) **estar ~ en** (*fig*) to be expert at, be skilled in; *sufrimientos* to be inured to.
2 *nm* (**a**) (*acto*) tanning.
(**b**) (*cuero*) tanned leather, tanned hides.
curtidor *nm* tanner.
curtiduría *nf*, **curtiembre** *nf* (*LAm*) tannery.
curtir [3a] **1** *vt* (**a**) *cuero* to tan.
(**b**) *cara etc* to tan, bronze.
(**c**) (*avezar*) to harden, inure.
2 curtirse *vr* (**a**) (*al sol*) to become tanned, become bronzed; (*a la intemperie*) to get weather-beaten.
(**b**) (*avezarse*) to become inured.
(**c**) (*LAm*) (*ensuciarse*) to get o.s. dirty; to dirty one's clothes.
curva *nf* curve; (*Mat*) graph, curve; (*Aut etc*) curve, bend; **~ de la felicidad** paunch, beer-belly; **~ de indiferencia** indifference curve; **~ de nivel** contour line.
curvatura *nf* curvature.
curvilíneo *adj* curved, curvilinear.
curvo *adj* (**a**) (*gen*) curved; crooked, bent. (**b**) (*And*: *estevado*) bow-legged. (**c**) (*Carib*: *zurdo*) left-handed.
cusca *nf* (**a**) **hacer la ~ a uno*** to play a dirty trick on sb; to harm sb, damage sb's interests.
(**b**) (*CAm*: *coqueta*) flirt.
(**c**) (*Méx*‡: *puta*) whore, slut.
cuscurrante *adj* crunchy, crisp.
cuscurro *nm* crouton.
cuscús *nm* couscous.
cuscha *nf* (*CAm*) liquor, rum.
cusma *nf* (*And*) sleeveless shirt, tunic.
cuspa *nf* (*And Agr*) weeding.
cuspar [1a] *vt* (*And Agr*) to weed.
cúspide *nf* (**a**) (*Anat*: *de diente*) cusp. (**b**) (*Geog*) summit, peak; tip, apex; (*fig*) top, pinnacle. (**c**) (*Mat*) apex.
cusqui* *nf* = **cusca** (**a**).
custodia *nf* (**a**) care, safekeeping, custody (*t Jur*); (*policial*) police protection; **~ preventiva** protective custody; **bajo la ~ de** in the care (*o* custody) of. (**b**) (*Ecl*) monstrance.
custodiar [1b] *vt* to keep, take care of, look after; to guard, watch over.
custodio *nm* guardian, keeper, custodian; *V* **ángel**.
cususa *nf* (*CAm*) home-made liquor (*o* rum).
cutacha *nf* (*LAm*) = **cuma**.
cutama *nf* (*Cono Sur*) bag, sack.
cutáneo *adj* cutaneous, skin (*atr*).
cutaras *nfpl* (*CAm, Carib, Méx*), **cutarras** *nfpl* (*CAm*) sandals, rough shoes.
cúter *nm* (*Náut*) cutter.
cutí *nm* ticking.
cutícula *nf* cuticle.
cutis *nm* skin, complexion.
cuto *adj* (**a**) (*And, CAm*) (*tullido*) maimed, crippled; (*desdentado*) toothless; *objeto* damaged, spoiled. (**b**) (*And*: *corto*) short.
cutre* *adj* (*tacaño*) mean, stingy; (*grosero*) vulgar, coarse; tasteless; *lugar* squalid, shabby; **un sitio ~** a dive‡, a hole*.
cutrería* *nf* meanness, stinginess; vulgarity, coarseness; squalidness, shabbiness; **me parece una ~** I think it's utterly tasteless.
cuy *nm* (*LAm*) guinea-pig.
cuya *nf* (*Carib, Cono Sur*) gourd, drinking vessel.
cuyo 1 *rel adj* (**a**) (*gen*) whose; of whom, of which; **la señora en cuya casa nos hospedábamos** the lady in whose house we were staying; **el asunto ~s detalles conoces** the matter of which you know the details, the matter whose details you know about.
(**b**) **en ~ caso** in which case; **por cuya razón** for which reason, and for this reason.
2 *nm* (*) lover.
cuz: **¡~ ~!** *interj* (*a perro*) here boy!
cuzqueño 1 *adj of* Cuzco. **2** *nm*, **cuzqueña** *nf* native (*o* inhabitant) of Cuzco; **los ~s** the people of Cuzco.
C.V. *nmpl abr de* **caballos de vapor** horsepower, h.p.
czar *etc* = **zar** *etc*.

CH

Ch, ch [tʃe] *nf* (*letra*) Ch, ch.
cha *nm* Shah.
chabacanear [1a] *vi* (*LAm*) to say (*o* do) coarse things.
chabacanería *nf* (**a**) (*cualidad*) vulgarity, bad taste; commonness; shoddiness.
(**b**) (*una* ~) coarse thing (to say), vulgar remark (*etc*); platitude; shoddy piece of work.
chabacanizar [1f] *vt* to trivialize.
chabacano[1] *adj chiste, comedia etc* vulgar, coarse, in bad taste; *artículo* cheap, common; *hechura etc* shoddy, crude.
chabacano[2] *nm* (*Méx*) apricot.
chabola *nf* shack, shanty; **~s** (*esp LAm*) shanty-town.
chabolismo *nm* (problem of *o* tendency to create *etc*) shanty towns; shanty-town conditions.
chabolista *nmf* shanty-town dweller.
chabón* 1 *adj* daft, stupid. **2** *nm*, **chabona** *nf* twit*.
chaca* *nf*: **estar en la** ~ (*Carib*) to be flat broke*.
chacal *nm* jackal.
chacalín* *nm*, **chacalina*** *nf* (*CAm*) (**a**) (*chico*) kid*, child. (**b**) (*camarón*) shrimp.
chacanear [1a] *vt* (**a**) (*Cono Sur*) *caballo* to spur violently. (**b**) (*Cono Sur*: *fastidiar*) to pester, annoy. (**c**) (*And*: *usar*) to use daily.
chacaneo *nm*: **para el** ~ (*And*) for daily use, ordinary.
chácara[1] *nf* (**a**) (*And, CAm, Cono Sur*: *Med*) sore, ulcer. (**b**) (*And, CAm, Carib*: *bolso*) large leather bag; (*And*: *maleta*) case.
chácara[2] *nf* (*LAm*) = **chacra.**
chacarería *nf* (**a**) (*LAm Agr*) market gardens, truck farms (*US*). (**b**) (*And, Cono Sur*: *industria*) horticulture, market gardening, truck farming (*US*); farm work.
chacarero *nm* (**a**) (*LAm*) (*dueño*) farmer, grower; market gardener, truck farmer (*US*); (*aparcero*) sharecropper; (*mayoral*) farm overseer; (*peón*) farm labourer. (**b**) (*Cono Sur*: *sandwich*) sandwich.
chacina *nf* pork.
chacinería *nf* pork butcher's.
chacinero *adj* pork (*atr*); **industria chacinera** pigmeat industry.
chacó *nm* shako.
chacolí *nm chacolí*, sharp-tasting Basque wine.
chacolotear [1a] *vi* to clatter.
chacoloteo *nm* clatter(ing).
chacón *nm* Philippine lizard.
chacota *nf* noisy merriment, fun (and games), high jinks; **estar de** ~ to be in a joking mood; **echar algo a ~, hacer ~ de algo, tomar algo a** ~ to make fun of sth, take sth as a joke.
chacotear [1a] **1** *vi* to have fun, make merry. **2 chacotearse** *vr*: ~ **de algo** to make fun of sth, take sth as a joke.
chacoteo *nm* (*Cono Sur*) = **chacota.**
chacotería *nf* (*Cono Sur*) = **chacota.**
chacotero *adj*, **chacotón** *adj* (*Cono Sur*) fond of a laugh, merry.
chacra *nf* (*LAm*) (**a**) (*granja*) small farm, smallholding, market garden, truck farm (*US*); (*hacienda*) country estate; (*esp Cono Sur*) large orchard, fruit-farming estate; (*tierras*) cultivated land. (**b**) (*casa*) farmhouse. (**c**) (*productos*) farm produce.
chacuaco 1 *adj* (*Carib, Cono Sur*) coarse, rough; (*Carib*) clumsy. **2** *nm* (*CAm*: *cigarro*) roughly-made cigar; (*CAm, Méx*: *colilla*) cigar stub.
chacha* *nf* (*niñera*) maid, nursemaid; (*de limpieza*) cleaning lady; (*del pueblo*) low-class girl.
chachacaste *nm* (*CAm*) liquor, brandy.
cha-cha-cha *nm* (**a**) (*baile*) cha-cha. (**b**) (*juego*) solitaire.
chachal *nm* (*CAm*) charm necklace.
chachalaca* (*CAm, Méx*) **1** *adj* chatty, talkative. **2** *nmf* chatterbox.
chachar [1a] *vt* (*And*) *coca* to chew.
cháchara *nf* (**a**) (*charla*) chatter, idle talk, small talk; **estar de ~*** to have a chat. (**b**) (*And*: *chiste*) joke. (**c**) **~s** (*Cono Sur, Méx*: *cosas*) things, bits and pieces; junk.
chacharachas *nfpl* (*Cono Sur*) useless ornaments; trinkets.
chacharear [1a] **1** *vt* (*Méx*) to deal in, sell. **2** *vi* to chatter, jaw*.
chacharería *nf* (*Cono Sur, Méx*) trinkets.
chacharero 1 *adj* chattering, garrulous. **2** *nm*, **chacharera** *nf* (**a**) (*parlanchín*) chatterbox. (**b**) (*Méx*: *vendedor*) rag-and-bone man.
chache* *nm* oneself, me, the speaker; **el perjudicado es el** ~ the one that suffers is yours truly*.
chachi* 1 *adj* marvellous, smashing*, jolly good*; *chica* smashing*; **café del** ~ real good coffee*; **unos amigos ~s** real friends; **¡estás ~!** I think you're terrific!* **2** *adv* marvellously, jolly well*; **me fue ~, lo pasé** ~ I had a smashing time*; it went like a bomb*.
chachipé(n) = **chachi.**
chacho* *nm* (**a**) (*chico*) boy, lad. (**b**) (*CAm*: *gemelo*) twin. (**c**) (*Méx*: *criado*) servant.
Chad *nm* Chad.
chador *nm* chador.
chafa* *adj* (*Méx*) useless.
chafalonía *nf* (*And*) worn-out gold jewellery.
chafalote 1 *adj* (*Cono Sur*: *ordinario*) common, vulgar. **2** *nm* (**a**) = **chafarote.** (**b**) (*LAm*⁂) prick⁂.
chafallar [1a] *vt* to botch, mend clumsily, make a mess of.
chafallo *nm* botched job.
chafar [1a] *vt* (**a**) (*aplastar*) to flatten; (*ajar etc*) to crumple; to ruffle, muss up; (*arrugar*) to crease; (*Culin*) *patatas* to mash; (*Med*) to lay out.
(**b**) ~ **a uno, dejar chafado a uno** to crush sb, floor sb; to cut sb short, shut sb up; to take sb down a peg; **quedó chafado** he was speechless.
(**c**) *negocio etc* to mess up, make a hash of, spoil; **le chafaron el negocio** they messed up the deal for him.
(**d**) (*Cono Sur*: *engañar*) to hoax, deceive.
chafarote *nm* (**a**) (*Hist*) cutlass; (*) sword; (*LAm*) machete. (**b**) (*CAm*⁑: *policía*) cop*.
chafarrinada *nf* spot, stain.
chafarrinar [1a] *vt* to blot, stain.
chafarrinón *nm* spot, stain; **echar un ~ a** (*fig*) to smear, slander.
chafir(r)o *nm* (*CAm, Méx*) knife.
chaflán *nm* (**a**) (*bisel*) bevel (surface), chamfer. (**b**) (*Aut*) street corner; road junction. (**c**) (*casa*) corner house.
chaflanar [1a] *vt* to bevel, chamfer.
chagra[1] **1** *nf* (*And*) = **chacra. 2** *nm* (*And*) peasant farmer.
chagra[2] *nf* (*Carib*) = **chaira.**
chagrín *nm* shagreen.
chagua *nf* (*And*) gang; system of gang labour.
chaguar [1i] *vt* (*Cono Sur*) *vaca* to milk; *ropa* to wring out.
cháguar *nm* (*And*) agave fibre, hemp; rope of agave fibre.
cháguara *nf* (*Cono Sur*) = **cháguar.**
chagüe *nm* (*CAm*) swamp, bog.
chagüite *nm* (*CAm, Méx*) (*pantano*) swamp; (*campo*) flooded field; (*bananal*) banana plantation.
chagüitear* [1a] *vi* (*CAm, Méx*) to chat, natter*.
chah *nm* Shah.
chai⁑ *nf* bird⁑, dame*.
chai(ne) *nm* (*And, CAm*) shoeshine.
chainear [1a] *vt* (*CAm*) to shine, polish.
chaira *nf* (*de afilar*) steel; (*de zapatero*) shoemaker's knife; (⁑: *cuchillo*) chiv⁑, knife.
chairar [1a] *vt* (*Cono Sur*) to sharpen.

chal *nm* shawl; ~ **de noche** evening wrap.

chala *nf* (**a**) (*And, Cono Sur*: *de maíz*) tender leaf of maize. (**b**) (*And, Cono Sur*‡: *dinero*) money, dough‡; **pelar la ~ a uno** to fleece sb. (**c**) (*Cono Sur*: *zapato*) sandal.

chalado* **1** *adj* dotty*; cranky*; **¡estás ~!** are you mad?; **estar ~ por una** to be crazy about sb; **¡ven acá, ~!** come here, you idiot! **2** *nm*, **chalada** *nf* crazy sort.

chaladura* *nf* crankiness*.

chalán *nm* (**a**) (*traficante*) dealer, huckster, (*esp*) horse dealer; (*pey*) shady businessman, shark*. (**b**) (*LAm*) horse-breaker.

chalana *nf* barge, lighter, wherry.

chalanear [1a] **1** *vt* (**a**) *persona* to haggle successfully with, beat down; *negocio* to handle cleverly, bring off.
(**b**) (*LAm*) *caballo* to break in, tame.
(**c**) (*Cono Sur**: *acosar*) to pester.
(**d**) (*CAm*: *burlarse de*) to make fun of.
2 *vi* to bargain shrewdly.

chalaneo *nm*, **chalanería** *nf* (*trato*) hard bargaining, horse trading; (*trampas*) trickery, deception.

chalaquear* [1a] (*CAm*) **1** *vt* to trick, con*. **2** *vi* to chatter away, rabbit on*.

chalar* [1a] **1** *vt* to drive crazy, drive round the bend‡. **2** **chalarse** *vr* to go crazy, go off one's rocker‡; ~ **por** to be crazy about.

chalchihuite *nm* (*Méx*) jade.

chale‡ *nmf* (*Méx pey*) Chink*.

chalé *nm* = **chalet**.

chalecito* *nm* (*frec*) second home, little place in the country, country retreat.

chaleco *nm* waistcoat, vest (*US*); (*Cono Sur*) sweater; ~ **antibalas** bulletproof vest, flakjacket; ~ **de fuerza** straitjacket; ~ **salvavidas** life jacket; **a ~** (*CAm, Méx*) by hook or by crook; **quedar como ~ de mano** (*Cono Sur*) to lose one's credibility; to disgrace o.s.

chalecón 1 *adj* (*Méx*) tricky, deceitful. **2** *nm* con man*.

chalequear [1a] *vt* (*Cono Sur, Méx*) to trick.

chalet [tʃa'le] *nm*, *pl* **chalets** [tʃa'les] (*de campo*) villa, cottage; (*de turista*) villa; (*de costa*) bungalow; (*de montaña*) chalet; (*de ciudad*) semi-detached house, detached house (with a garden); (*Golf etc*) clubhouse; ~ **adosado** semi-detached house.

chalina *nf* (**a**) (*corbata*) cravat(e), floppy bow tie. (**b**) (*esp LAm*: *chal*) small shawl, headscarf.

chalón *nm* (*LAm*) shawl, wrap.

chalona *nf* (*LAm*) dried salted mutton.

chalote *nm* shallot.

chalupa¹ *nf* launch, boat; ship's boat, lifeboat; (*And, Carib, Méx*: *canoa*) narrow canoe.

chalupa² *nf* (*Méx Culin*) stuffed tortilla.

chalupa³* **1** *adj* crazy; **volver ~ a uno** to drive sb crazy. **2** *nm* madman, crackpot.

chamaca *nf* (*Méx etc*) (*muchacha*) girl; (*novia*) girlfriend, sweetheart.

chamaco *nm* (*Méx etc*) (*muchacho*) boy, lad; (*novio*) boyfriend.

chamada *nf* (**a**) (*leña*) brushwood. (**b**) (*incendio*) brushwood fire; (*) smoke.

chamagoso* *adj* (*Méx*) (*mugriento*) filthy; (*chabacano*) crude, rough.

chamal *nm* (*Cono Sur*) tunic.

chamar* [1a] *vti* to smoke.

chámara *nf*, **chamarasca** *nf* (*leña*) kindling, brushwood; (*incendio*) brush fire, blaze.

chamaril(l)ero *nm* secondhand dealer, junk dealer.

chamarra *nf* (**a**) sheepskin jacket; (*LAm*: *saco corto*) short jacket; (*Méx*: *saco*) jacket. (**b**) (*CAm, Carib*: *manta*) blanket, poncho. (**c**) (*CAm**: *engaño*) con*, swindle.

chamarrear* [1a] *vt* (*CAm*) to con*, swindle.

chamarrero *nm* (*Carib*) quack doctor.

chamarro *nm* (*CAm, Cono Sur, Méx*) (*manta*) coarse woollen blanket; (*serape*) poncho, woollen cape.

chamba¹ *nf* (**a**) (*And*: *tepe*) turf, sod.
(**b**) (*And*: *charca*) pond, pool; (*And*: *zanja*) ditch.
(**c**) (*CAm, Méx**: *trabajo*) work; job; (*negocio*) business; (*empleo*) occupation.
(**d**) (*Méx**) (*sueldo*) wages, pay; (*sueldo bajo*) low pay; (*chollo*) soft job*.
(**e**) (*Carib, Méx**) dough‡, bread‡ (*US*).

chamba² *nf* (*chiripa*) fluke, lucky break; **por ~** by a fluke.

chambeador* (*Méx*) **1** *adj* hard-working. **2** *nm*, **chambeadora** *nf* hard worker, slogger.

chambear [1a] (*Méx*) **1** *vt* to exchange, swap, barter. **2** *vi* to work; (*inútilmente*) to slave away.

chambelán *nm* chamberlain.

chamberga* *nf* coat.

chambergo *nm* (*Hist*) cocked hat; broad-brimmed soft hat; (*) coat.

chambero *nm* (*Méx*) draughtsman.

chambón* **1** *adj* (**a**) (*torpe*) awkward, clumsy. (**b**) (*afortunado*) lucky, jammy‡. (**c**) (*desaseado*) slovenly. **2** *nm*, **chambona** *nf* fluky player, lucky player; **hacer algo a la chambona** (*And*) to do sth in a rush.

chambonada *nf* (**a**) (*torpeza*) awkwardness, clumsiness. (**b**) (*chiripa*) fluke, stroke of luck, lucky shot. (**c**) (*plancha*) blunder.

chambonear [1a] *vi* (*esp LAm*) to have a stroke of luck, win (*etc*) by a fluke.

chamborote *adj* (*And, CAm*) long-nosed.

chambra¹ *nf* (*bata*) housecoat; (*blusa*) blouse; (*chaqueta*) loose jacket.

chambra² *nf* (*Carib*) din, hubbub.

chambra³ *nf* (*Carib*) machete, broad knife.

chambrana *nf* (*And, Carib*) row, uproar; brawl.

chambre‡ *nm* (*CAm*) tittle-tattle, gossip.

chambroso‡ *adj* (*CAm*) gossipy.

chamburgo *nm* (*And*) pool, stagnant water.

chamelicos *nmpl* (*And, Cono Sur*: *trastos*) lumber, junk; (*ropa*) old clothes.

chamiza *nf* (*de techo*) thatch, thatch palm; (*leña*) brushwood.

chamizo *nm* (**a**) (*árbol*) half-burned tree (*o* log *etc*). (**b**) (*casita*) thatched hut; (*chabola*) shack, slum; (*) den, joint‡. (**c**) (*mina*) illegal coalmine.

chamo*, **-a** *nm/f* (*LAm*) kid*, child.

chamorro 1 *adj* *cabeza* shorn, close-cropped. **2** *nm*: ~ **de cerdo** (*Méx*) leg of pork.

champa¹ *nf* (*LAm*) (**a**) (*tepe*) sod, turf; ball of earth (*left round roots*). (**b**) (*greña*) mop of hair. (**c**) (*fig*) tangled mass.

champa² *nf* (*CAm, Méx*) roughly-built hut; tent.

champán *nm* champagne.

champanero *adj* champagne (*atr*).

champanizar [1f] *vt* *vino* to add a sparkle to.

Champaña *nf* Champagne.

champaña *nm* champagne.

champañazo *nm* (*Cono Sur etc*) champagne party.

champañero *adj* champagne (*atr*).

champi* *nm* = **champiñón**.

champiñón *nm* mushroom.

champú *nm* shampoo; ~ **anticaspa** anti-dandruff shampoo.

champudo *adj* (*LAm*) *pelo* dishevelled, messy; *persona* long-haired.

champurrado *nm* mixture of liquors, cocktail; (*Carib, Méx*) mixed drink (*of various ingredients*); (*Méx*: *de chocolate*) thick chocolate drink; (*fig*) mixture, mess.

champurrar [1a] *vt* *bebidas* to mix, make a cocktail of.

champurreado *nm* (**a**) (*Cono Sur Culin*) hastily-prepared dish; (*fig*) hash, botch. (**b**) = **champurrado**.

champurrear [1a] *vt* (*Carib*) (**a**) = **champurrar**. (**b**) = **chapurr(e)ar**.

chamuchina *nf* (**a**) (*LAm*: *turba*) rabble, mob; (*niños*) crowd of small children, mob of kids*. (**b**) (*And, Carib*: *jaleo*) row, shindy*. (**c**) (*LAm*) = **chamusquina**.

chamullar* [1a] **1** *vti* to speak, talk; to burble; **yo también chamullo el caló** I can talk slang too; **chamullaban en árabe** they were jabbering away in Arabic; **¿qué chamullas tú?** what are you burbling about? **2** *vi* (*Cono Sur*) to cook up a story.

chamuscar [1g] **1** *vt* (**a**) (*quemar*) to scorch, sear, singe. (**b**) (*Méx*: *vender*) to sell cheap. **2** **chamuscarse** *vr* (**a**) to get scorched, singe. (**b**) (*And**) to fly off the handle*.

chamusquina *nf* (**a**) (*quemadura*) singeing, scorching.
(**b**) (*jaleo*) row, quarrel, shindy; **esto huele a ~** I can see there's trouble brewing, there's sth nasty coming.
(**c**) (*And, CAm**: *niños*) bunch of kids.

chan *nm* (*CAm*) local guide.

chanada* *nf* trick, swindle.

chanar‡ [1a] *vt* (*t vi*: ~ **de**) to understand.

chanca *nf* (**a**) (*And, Cono Sur*: *molienda*) grinding, crushing. (**b**) (*And, Cono Sur*: *paliza*) beating.

chancaca *nf* (**a**) (*CAm Culin*) maize cake, wheat cake. (**b**) (*And Med*) sore, ulcer. (**c**) (*LAm*: *azúcar*) brown sugar, honey mass, solidified molasses (*used in the preparation of chicha*).

chancadora *nf* (*LAm*) grinder, crusher.

chancar [1g] *vt* (**a**) (*LAm*) (*moler*) to grind, crush; (*pegar*) to beat; (*aporrear*) to beat up*; (*maltratar*) to ill-treat. (**b**)

(*And, Cono Sur*: *chapucear*) to botch, bungle.

chance 1 *nm* (*a veces nf*) (*LAm**) (**a**) (*oportunidad*) chance; prospects; **dale ~** let him have a go. (**b**) (*suerte*) good luck. **2** *conj* (*Méx*) maybe, perhaps.

chancear [1a] *vi y* **chancearse** *vr* to joke, make jokes (*de* about); to fool about, play around (*con* with); **~se de uno** to make fun of sb.

chancero *adj* joking, merry, facetious; fond of a joke.

chanciller *nm* = **canciller**.

chancillería *nf* chancery.

chancla *nf* (**a**) old shoe, broken shoe. (**b**) = **chancleta**.

chancleta 1 *nf* (**a**) (*zapatilla*) slipper; **tirar la ~** (*Cono Sur*) to have a good time. (**b**) (*LAm*: *bebé*) baby girl. (**c**) (*Carib Aut*) accelerator. **2** *nmf* (‡) muggins‡, charlie‡.

chancletero *adj* (*And, Carib*), **chancletudo** *adj* (*And, Carib, Cono Sur*) (**a**) (*ordinario*) common, low-class. (**b**) (*desaseado*) scruffy.

chanclo *nm* (*zueco*) clog; (*de goma*) rubber overshoe, galosh.

chancón, -ona* *nm/f* (*And*) swot*.

chancro *nm* chancre.

chancha *nf* (**a**) (*LAm Zool*) sow. (**b**) (*Cono Sur*) (*carro*) small wooden cart; (*: *bicicleta*) bike*. (**c**) (*And hum*) mouth; **hacer la ~** (*And, Cono Sur*) to play truant.

chanchada *nf* (*LAm*) dirty trick.

chánchamo *nm* (*Méx Culin*) tamale.

cháncharas máncharas: **andar en ~** to beat about the bush.

chanchería *nf* (*LAm*) pork-butcher's shop.

chanchero *nm* (*LAm*) pork butcher.

chanchi* = **chachi**.

chancho 1 *adj* (*LAm*) dirty, filthy.

2 *nm* (**a**) (*LAm*: *cerdo*) pig, hog; (*carne*) pork; **~ salvaje** wild boar.

(**b**) (*LAm*: *Ajedrez etc*) blocked piece.

(**c**) (*Cono Sur*) = **chancadora**.

(**d**) (*LAm fig*) **son como ~s** they're as thick as thieves; **hacerse el ~ rengo** to pretend not to notice; **quedar como ~** to come off badly.

(**e**) (*Cono Sur*: *de suelos*) floor polisher.

chanchono* *nm* lie.

chanchullero* 1 *adj* crooked*, bent‡. **2** *nm* crook*, twister.

chanchullo* *nm* fiddle*, wangle*; crooked deal*; piece of graft, dirty business; **andar en ~s** to be on the fiddle*, be engaged in sth shady.

chandal *nm*, **chándal** *nm* tracksuit.

chanelar* [1a] *vt* to catch on to, twig*.

chanfaina *nf* (**a**) (*Culin*) cheap stew. (**b**) (*And, CAm*: *enredo*) mess; (*chance*) lucky break.

chanfle[1]‡ *nm* (*Cono Sur*) bobby*, cop*.

chanfle[2] *nm* (*Méx*) = **chaflán**.

chanflón *adj* misshapen; (*fig*) crude, coarse.

changa[1] *nf* (**a**) (*And, Cono Sur*) (*transporte*) (portering) job; (*chapuz*) odd job, occasional job. (**b**) (*And*: *propina*) tip, payment (to a porter).

changa[2] *nf* (*Carib*) joke.

changador *nm* (*And, Cono Sur*) (*cargador*) porter; (*factótum*) odd-job man; (*temporero*) casual worker.

changango *nm* (*Cono Sur*) small guitar.

changarro[1]* *nm* (*Aut*) old car, jalopy.

changarro[2] *nm* (*Méx*) small shop.

changarse‡ [1h] *vr* to break (down), go wrong.

chango 1 *adj* (**a**) (*Méx*: *listo*) quick, sharp; alert; **¡ponte ~!** wake up!, get wise!*; watch out!

(**b**) (*Carib, Méx*: *juguetón*) mischievous, playful.

(**c**) (*Carib*) (*tonto*) silly, brainless; (*afectado*) affected.

(**d**) (*Cono Sur*: *molesto*) annoying.

(**e**) **la gente está changa** (*Méx etc*) there are lots of people.

2 *nm*, **changa[3]** *nf* (**a**) (*Méx Zool*) small monkey.

(**b**) (*Cono Sur, Méx*) (*niño*) child; (*criado*) young servant.

(**c**) (*Méx****) cunt***.

changuear [1a] *vi* (*And, Carib, Méx*) = **chancear**.

changüi* *nm* (**a**) (*chiste*) joke. (**b**) (*estafa*) trick, swindle; **dar ~ a** to trick, swindle.

changurro *nm* crab.

chanquete *nm* whitebait.

chanta‡ *nmf* (*Cono Sur*) (*fanfarrón*) loudmouth*; (*que no cumple*) fraud.

chantaje *nm* blackmail(ing).

chantajear [1a] *vt* to blackmail.

chantajista *nmf* blackmailer.

chantar [1a] *vt* (**a**) *vestido etc* to put on.

(**b**) *objeto* to thrust, stick; to put.

(**c**) **~ algo a uno** to tell sb sth to his face.

(**d**) (*And, Cono Sur*) *objeto* to throw, chuck.

(**e**) (*And, Cono Sur*) *persona* to put, throw; **~ a uno en la calle** to throw sb out; **~ a uno en la cárcel** to put sb in jail.

(**f**) (*And, Cono Sur*) *golpe* to give, deal.

(**g**) (*Cono Sur*) (*abandonar*) to leave in the lurch; (*engañar*) to deceive, trick.

chantre *nm* (*Ecl*) precentor.

chanza *nf* joke; piece of tomfoolery, lark; **~s** jokes, banter; tomfoolery; **de ~, en ~** in fun, as a joke; **estar de ~** to be joking.

chañaca *nf* (*Cono Sur*) (**a**) (*Med*) itch, rash. (**b**) (*fig*) bad reputation.

chao[1] *nm* chow.

chao[2]* *excl* (*esp Cono Sur*) bye-bye!, so long!

chapa *nf* (**a**) (*metal*) plate, sheet; **~ acanalada, ~ ondulada** (sheet of) corrugated iron.

(**b**) (*madera*) board, panel, sheet; veneer; **madera de 3 ~s** 3-ply wood.

(**c**) (*disco etc*) small metal plate, disc, tally; (*ficha*) counter; check; (*cápsula*) bottle-top, cap; **~s** (*juego*) game of tossing coins; **~s** (*Cono Sur Fin*) small change; **~ de identidad** identity disc; **~ de matrícula, ~ de patente** (*Cono Sur*) licence plate; **estar sin ~s*** to be broke*; **hacer ~s*** to be on the game*; **poner la ~** (*Cono Sur*) to be best at everything.

(**d**) (*LAm*: *cerradura*) lock; (*tirador*) door handle.

(**e**) (*carmín*) rouge; (*chapeta*) flush (on the cheeks).

(**f**) (*juicio*) good sense, prudence; **hombre de ~** sensible man.

chapado *adj* (**a**) *muebles, adornos* covered (*o* lined) with sheet metal (*o* veneer); **~ de roble** with an oak veneer, with an oak finish; **~ de oro** gold-plated.

(**b**) **~ a la antigua** (*fig*) old-fashioned, of the old school.

chapalear [1a] *vi* (**a**) (*persona*) to splash (about); (*agua*) to lap. (**b**) (*herraduras etc*) to clatter.

chapaleo *nm* (*V vi*) (**a**) splash(ing); lap(ping). (**b**) clatter(ing).

chapapote *nm* (*Méx*) = **chapopote**.

chapar[1] [1a] **1** *vt* (**a**) (*Téc*) to plate, cover (*o* line) with sheet metal (*o* veneer); *pared* to tile. (**b**) *observación etc* to throw out, come out with; **le chapó un 'no' como una casa** he gave him a flat 'no'. (**c**) (*: *aprender*) to learn, memorize. (**d**) (‡: *cerrar*) to shut, close. **2** *vi* (**a**) (‡) (*Univ*) to swot*. (**b**) (*dormir*) to kip‡, sleep.

chapar[2] [1a] *vt* (**a**) (*And*: *espiar*) to spy on.

(**b**) (*And*) (*atrapar*) to catch; (*alcanzar*) to catch up with, overtake; *objeto* to seize, grasp.

(**c**) (*besar*) to kiss.

chaparra[1] *nf* (*árbol*) kermes oak; (*maleza*) brush, scrub.

chaparrada *nf* = **chaparrón**.

chaparral *nm* thicket (of kermes oaks), chaparral.

chaparrear [1a] *vi* to pour in torrents.

chaparreras *nfpl* (*Méx*) leather chaps.

chaparro 1 *adj* squat, short and chubby. **2** *nm* (*Bot*) kermes oak, dwarf oak. **3** *nm*, **chaparra[2]** *nf* (*fig*) short chubby person; (*Méx*) child, kid*.

chaparrón *nm* downpour, cloudburst.

chapatal *nm* muddy place.

chape *nm* (*And, Cono Sur*) tress, pigtail.

chapear [1a] **1** *vt* (**a**) = **chapar[1]**. (**b**) (*LAm Agr*) to weed. (**c**) **~ a uno** (*Carib*) to cut sb's throat. **2** *vi* (*LAm*) to clear the ground.

chapeau [tʃa'po] **1** *excl* bravo!, well done! **2** *nm* (**a**) **hacer ~** to take off one's hat (*ante* to). (**b**) (message of) appreciation, congratulations.

chapeo‡ *nm* titfer‡, hat.

chapero‡ *nm* (*homosexual*) queer‡; (*prostituto*) male prostitute, rent boy.

chapeta *nf* flush (on the cheeks).

chapetón (*LAm*) **1** *adj* awkward, clumsy. **2** *nm* Spaniard in America.

chapetonada *nf* (**a**) (*And*) (*Med*) illness caused by a change of climate; (*sarpullido*) rash.

(**b**) (*And, Cono Sur*: *torpeza*) awkwardness, clumsiness.

(**c**) (*Carib*: *aguacero*) sudden downpour.

chapín 1 *adj* (*LAm*) with crooked legs (*o* feet). **2** *nm* (**a**) (*zueco*) clog. (**b**) (*CAm hum*) Guatemalan.

chapinada *nf* (*CAm hum*) action typical of a Guatemalan, dirty trick.

chapiri‡ *nm* titfer‡, hat.

chápiro* *nm*: **¡por vida del ~!, ¡voto al ~!** damn it!

chapisca *nf* (*CAm*) maize harvest.

chapista *nm* tinsmith; (*Aut*) car-body worker, panel-beater.
chapistería *nf* car-body works, panel-beating shop.
chapita* *nf* (*And*) cop*.
chapitel *nm* (*Arquit*: *de columna*) capital; (*de torre*) spire.
chapo¹ *adj* (*Méx*) short and chubby.
chapo² *nm* (*Méx Culin*) maize porridge.
chapodar [1a] *vt* (**a**) *árbol* to prune, trim. (**b**) (*fig*) to cut down, reduce.
chapola *nf* (*And*) butterfly.
chapolín *nm* pool (*game*).
chapo(po)te *nm* (*CAm, Carib, Méx*) (*pez*) pitch, tar; (*asfalto*) asphalt.
chapotear [1a] **1** *vt* (*lavar*) to sponge (down); (*humedecer*) to wet, moisten. **2** *vi* to splash about; to paddle; to dabble (one's hands).
chapoteo *nm* (**a**) (*limpieza con esponja*) sponging; moistening. (**b**) (*chapaleo*) splashing; paddling; dabbling.
chaptalizar [1f] *vt* to chaptalize, add sugar to.
chapucear [1a] *vt* (**a**) (*trabajo*) to botch, bungle, make a mess of; to do in a slapdash way. (**b**) (*Méx*: *estafar*) to swindle.
chapuceramente *adv* roughly, crudely, shoddily; amateurishly; clumsily.
chapucería *nf* (**a**) (*cualidad*) shoddiness. (**b**) (*una* ~) botched job, shoddy piece of work, mess.
chapucero 1 *adj objeto* rough, crude, shoddy; *trabajo* bungled, slapdash; amateurish; *persona* clumsy, bungling.
2 *nm* bungler, clumsy workman (*etc*); bungling amateur.
chapulín *nm* (*LAm*), **chapulú** *nm* (*CAm*) (**a**) (*langosta*) locust; (*cigarra*) cricket. (**b**) (*) child, kid*.
chapupa* *nf*: **me salió de pura** ~ (*CAm*) it was pure luck, it was sheer fluke.
chapuro *nm* (*CAm*) asphalt.
chapurr(e)ar [1a] *vt* (**a**) *bebidas* to mix. (**b**) *idioma* to speak badly; **chapurrea el italiano** he speaks broken (*o* bad) Italian.
chapuz *nm* (**a**) (*chapuzón*) ducking; plunge, dive, dip. (**b**) = **chapuza**.
chapuza *nf* (**a**) (*chapucería*) botched job, shoddy piece of work, mess; (*trabajillo*) odd job, spare-time job; small job (done) about the house. (**b**) (*Méx*: *estafa*) trick, swindle.
chapuzar [1f] **1** *vt* to duck, dip, plunge. **2** *vi y* **chapuzarse** *vr* to duck, dive.
chapuzas *nm invar* bungler, clumsy sort.
chapuzón *nm* (**a**) (*zambullida*) dip, swim; ducking; **darse un** ~ to go for a dip. (**b**) (*de cápsula*) splashdown. (**c**) (*LAm**) cloudburst, downpour.
chaqué *nm* morning coat.
chaquet [tʃa'ke] *nm, pl* **chaquets** [tʃa'kes] = **chaqué**.
chaqueta *nf* (**a**) (*prenda*) jacket; ~ **de cuero** leather jacket. (**b**) **cambiar la** ~ = **chaquetear**. (**c**) **volarse la** ~ (*CAm*⁑) to toss off⁑.
chaquetar [1a] (*Méx*), **chaquetear** [1a] **1** *vt* (‡) to slag off‡, criticize. **2** *vi* (*cambiar de política*) to change sides, be a turncoat, turn traitor; (*acobardarse*) to go back on one's word, chicken out*, rat*.
chaquete *nm* backgammon.
chaquetero, -a *nm/f* (*Pol*) turncoat; **es** ~ he's always changing sides.
chaquetón *nm* long jacket, reefer, shooting jacket; (*de mujer*) three-quarter coat.
charada *nf* charade.
charadrio *nm* plover.
charaludo *adj* (*Méx*) thin.
charamusca *nf* (**a**) (*LAm*: *t* ~**s**) firewood, kindling. (**b**) (*Méx*: *dulce*) candy twist. (**c**) (*Carib*: *alboroto*) noise, row.
charanga *nf* (**a**) (*Mús*) brass band; band of street musicians; (*Cono Sur Mil*) cavalry band. (**b**) (*LAm**: *baile*) informal dance, hop*.
charango *nm* (*And, Cono Sur*) *a small five-stringed guitar*.
charanguero *adj* = **chapucero 1**.
charape *nm* (*Méx*) *type of pulque*.
charca *nf* pond, pool.
charco *nm* pool, puddle; **cruzar el** ~, **pasar el** ~ to cross the water, (*esp*) to cross the herring-pond (*ie the Atlantic*).
charcón¹ *adj* (*And, Cono Sur*) thin, skinny.
charcón² *nm* pool (*in a river*).
charcutería *nf* (**a**) (*productos*) cooked pork products. (**b**) (*tienda*) delicatessen.
charchina* *nf* (*LAm*) old crock, old banger‡.
charla *nf* talk, chat; (*pey*) chatter; (*Univ etc*) talk; ~ **radiofónica** radio talk; ~ **literaria** literary talk, informal literary lecture; **es de ~ común** it's common knowledge.
charlado* *nm*: **echar un** ~ to have a chat.
charlador 1 *adj* talkative; gossipy. **2** *nm*, **charladora** *nf* chatterbox; gossip.
charladuría *nf* (*t* ~**s**) small talk, chatter, gossip.
charlar [1a] *vi* to chat, talk (*de* about); (*pey*) to chatter, gossip.
charlatán 1 *adj* talkative; gossipy.
2 *nm*, **charlatana** *nf* (**a**) (*hablador*) chatterbox; (*chismoso*) gossip; (*bocón*) bigmouth‡, indiscreet talker.
(**b**) (*timador*) (confidence) trickster; (*vendedor*) smooth-tongued salesman, clever (but untrustworthy) salesman, showman; (*Med*) quack, charlatan.
charlatanear [1a] *vi* to chatter away, babble on; (*pey*) to shoot one's mouth off*.
charlatanería *nf* (**a**) (*locuacidad*) talkativeness, garrulity. (**b**) (*arte de vender etc*) (clever) salesmanship; showmanship; (*Med*) quackery, charlatanism. (**c**) (*jerga publicitaria*) sales talk, patter; (*palabrería*) hot air.
charlatanismo *nm* = **charlatanería** (**a**).
charlestón *nm* charleston.
charleta *nmf* (*Cono Sur*) chatterbox; gossip.
charli‡ *nm* 1000-peseta note.
charlista *nmf* speaker, lecturer.
Charlot *nm* Charlie Chaplin.
charlota *nf type of frozen cream cake*.
charlotada *nf* (*Teat*) gag; (*Taur*) mock bullfight.
charlotear [1a] *vi* to chatter, talk a lot.
charnego, -a *nm/f* immigrant (*esp Andalusian or Murcian in Catalonia*).
charnela *nf*, **charneta** *nf* hinge.
charol *nm* (**a**) (*barniz*) varnish; (*cuero*) patent leather; **calzárselas de** ~ (*Cono Sur*) to make a packet*; **darse** ~* to swank*, brag. (**b**) (*LAm*: *bandeja*) tray.
charola *nf* (**a**) (*LAm*: *bandeja*) tray. (**b**) ~**s** (*CAm**: *ojos*) eyes.
charolado *adj* polished, shiny.
charolar [1a] *vt* to varnish, japan.
charolés *adj, nm* Charolais.
charpa *nf* (*CAm Mil*) pistol belt, sword belt; (*Med*) sling.
charquear [1a] *vt* (*LAm*) (**a**) *carne* to dry, jerk. (**b**) *persona* to carve up, slash, wound severely; to beat (up)*.
charquecillo *nm* (*And Culin*) dried salted fish.
charqui *nm* (*LAm*: *carne*) dried beef, jerked meat; (*Cono Sur*) (*frutas*) dried fruit, (*legumbres*) dried vegetables; **hacer ~ a uno** (*fig*) = **charquear** (**b**).
charquicán *nm* (*Cono Sur Culin*) *dish of dried meat and vegetables*.
charra *nf* (**a**) (*prov*: *Salamanca*) peasant woman; (*fig*) low-class woman, coarse woman. (**b**) (*CAm*: *sombrero*) broad-brimmed hat. (**c**) (*And*: *grano*) itch, pimple. (**d**) (*CAm*⁑) prick⁑, tool⁑.
charrada *nf* (**a**) (*dicho, acto*) coarse thing, piece of bad breeding; example of bad taste.
(**b**) (*adorno*) flashy ornament, vulgar adornment; (*objeto*) tastelessly decorated object.
(**c**) (*cualidad*) coarseness, bad breeding; bad taste; tawdriness, gaudiness.
(**d**) (*Mús*) country dance.
charral *nm* (*CAm*) scrub, scrubland.
charramasca *nf* (*CAm*) firewood, kindling.
charrán¹ *nm* (*Orn*) tern.
charrán² *nm* rascal, villain.
charranada *nf* dirty trick.
charrar‡ [1a] *vi* (*hablar*) to talk, burble; (*soplar*) to blab.
charrasca *nf* (††) trailing sword; (*And, Cono Sur, Méx*) knife, razor.
charrasquear [1a] *vt* (**a**) (*Méx*: *apuñalar*) to knife, stab. (**b**) (*And, CAm, Carib*: *rasguear*) to strum.
charré *nm* trap, dog-cart.
charrería *nf* (*Méx*) horsemanship.
charretera *nf* (*Mil etc*) epaulette; shoulder flash; (*Cos*) shoulder pad.
charro 1 *adj* (**a**) *persona* rustic; coarse, vulgar, ill-bred.
(**b**) *vestido etc* loud, gaudy; *objeto* flashy, showy; over-ornamented, decorated in bad taste.
(**c**) (*salmantino*) Salamancan.
(**d**) (*mejicano*) Mexican.
(**e**) (*Méx*) *costumbre* picturesque, quaint; traditional.
(**f**) (*Méx*) *jinete* skilled in horsemanship.
2 *nm* (**a**) (*prov*: *Salamanca*) peasant.
(**b**) (*pey*) rustic, boor, coarse individual; flashy sort, overdressed individual.
(**c**) (*Méx*) (*vaquero*) horseman, cowboy; (*mejicano*)

typical Mexican.
(**d**) (*Méx: sombrero*) wide-brimmed hat.
(**e**) (*Méx Pol**) corrupt union boss.

chárter 1 *atr*: **vuelo ~** charter flight. **2** *nm, pl* **chárters** ['tʃarter] charter (flight).

chasca *nf* (**a**) (*maleza*) brushwood. (**b**) (*LAm: pelo*) mop of hair, tangled hair; tangle.

chascar [1g] **1** *vt* (**a**) *lengua etc* to click; *dedos* to snap; *látigo* to crack; *grava etc* to crunch. (**b**) *comida* to gobble, gulp down. **2** *vi* to click, snap; to crack; to crunch.

chascarrillo *nm* funny story.

chasco[1] *adj* (*And, Cono Sur*) *pelo etc* thick and crinkly, coarse.

chasco[2] *nm* (**a**) (*desilusión*) disappointment; failure, let-down; **dar un ~ a uno** to disappoint sb; **llevarse (un) ~** to be disappointed, suffer a let-down; **¡vaya ~ que me llevé!** what a let-down!
(**b**) (*broma*) trick, joke; prank; **dar ~ a uno** to pull sb's leg*; **dar un ~ a uno** to play a trick on sb.

chascón *adj* (*And, Cono Sur*) (**a**) *pelo* dishevelled, matted, entangled; *persona* dishevelled. (**b**) (*torpe*) slow, clumsy.

chasis *nm invar* (*Aut etc*) chassis; (*Fot*) plateholder; **quedarse en el ~*** to be terribly thin.

chasque *nm* (*LAm*) = **chasqui.**

chasquear[1] [1a] *vt* (**a**) (*decepcionar*) (*t* **dejar chasqueado**) to disappoint, let down; (*faltar a*) to fail, break one's promise to.
(**b**) (*engañar*) to play a trick on, make a fool of.

chasquear[2] [1a] **1** *vt* = **chascar 1**; (*And, CAm*) *freno* to champ.
2 *vi* = **chascar 2**; (*madera etc*) to creak; to crack, crackle; **~ con la lengua** to click one's tongue.
3 *vr* **chasquearse** (*And**) to make a mess of things, mess things up*.

chasqui *nm* (*LAm Hist*) messenger, courier.

chasquido *nm* click; snap; crack; crunch; creak, crackle.

chasquilla *nf* (*LAm*) fringe of hair.

chata *nf* (**a**) (*Med*) bedpan. (**b**) (*Náut*) lighter, barge, transport. (**c**) (*Cono Sur: Aut*) lorry, truck. (**d**) (*: *escopeta*) sawn-off shotgun.

chatarra *nf* scrap iron, junk; (*: *dinero*) coppers, small change; (*Mil: hum*) gongs*, medals; **vender para ~** to sell for scrap.

chatarrero *nm* scrap dealer, scrap merchant, junkman (*US*).

chatear* [1a] *vi* to go drinking, have a few drinks.

chateo* *nm* drinking expedition; **ir de ~ = chatear.**

chati‡ *nf* girl, bird‡; **¡oye ~!** hey, beautiful!*

chato 1 *adj* (**a**) *nariz* flat, snub; *persona* snub-nosed; (*) dear, love; **¡oye, chata!*** hey, beautiful!*
(**b**) *objeto* flattened, blunt; *barca etc* flat; *torre etc* low, squat.
(**c**) (*Carib, Cono Sur: pobre*) mean, wretched.
(**d**) **dejar ~ a uno** (*LAm*) (*anonadar*) to crush sb; (*avergonzar*) to embarrass sb; (*Méx: estafar*) to swindle sb; **quedarse ~ con algo** to appropriate sth.
2 *nm* (small) wine glass; glass (of wine); **tomarse unos ~s** to have a few drinks.

chatón *nm* large mounted stone.

chatre *adj* (*And, Cono Sur*) smartly-dressed; **está hecho un ~** he's looking very smart.

chatungo* *adj* = **chato**; **¡eh, ~!** hey, lad!; **¡oye, chatunga!** hey, beautiful*!

chau* *interj* (*Cono Sur*) so long!

chaucha 1 *adj invar* (**a**) (*And, Cono Sur: Agr etc*) *papa* early; (*inmaduro*) unripe, not fully grown; *nacimiento* premature; *mujer* who gives birth prematurely.
(**b**) (*Cono Sur*) (*malo*) poor-quality; (*soso*) insipid, tasteless, characterless; (*de mal gusto*) in poor taste.
2 *nf* (**a**) (*LAm: papa*) early potato, small potato; (*And, Cono Sur: judía*) string bean; (*And: comida*) food (*gen*); **pelar la ~** (*And, Cono Sur*) to brandish (*o* use) one's knife.
(**b**) (*And, Cono Sur: moneda*) 20-cent coin; (any) small coin; (*And, Cono Sur: dinero*) dough*; (*pequeña cantidad*) small amount; **le cayó la ~** the penny dropped.
(**c**) **~s‡** (*Cono Sur*) peanuts*, trifles.

chauchau‡ *nm* (*And, Cono Sur*) grub‡, chow‡.

chauchera *nf* (*And, Cono Sur*) purse, pocket-book (*US*).

chauchero *nm* (*Cono Sur*) errand boy; odd-job man; poorly-paid worker.

chauvinismo *nm* chauvinism.

chauvinista 1 *adj* chauvinist(ic). **2** *nmf* chauvinist.

chava[1]‡ *nm* = **chaval.**

chava[2]‡ *nf* (*CAm, Méx*) lass, girl.

chaval* *nm* lad, boy, kid*; **mi ~** my bloke‡, my boyfriend; **estar hecho un ~** to feel (*o* look) very young again; **es un ~** he's only a kid (still)*.

chavala* *nf* girl, kid*; **mi ~** my bird‡, my girlfriend.

chavalería* *nf* young people, kids*.

chavalo *nm* (*CAm*) (*golfo*) street urchin; (*chico*) boy.

chavalongo *nm* (*Cono Sur: fiebre*) fever; (*insolación*) sunstroke; (*modorra*) drowsiness, drowsy feeling.

chavea* *nmf* kid*, youngster.

chaveta 1 *nf* cotter, cotter pin; (*And, Méx*) broad bladed knife; **perder la ~*** (*loco*) to go off one's rocker‡, (*indignado*) go through the roof*; **perder la ~ por una chica** to go crazy about a girl. **2** *adj invar*: **estar ~‡** to be nuts‡.

chavetear [1a] *vt* (*And, Carib*) to knife.

chavo[1]‡ *nm* five pesetas; **no tener un ~, estar sin un ~** to be stony-broke*, be stone-broke* (*US*).

chavo[2]* *nm* (*CAm, Méx*) bloke‡, guy*.

chavó* *nm* kid*, boy.

chayote *nm* chayote, fruit of the *chayotera.*

chayotera *nf* chayote (plant).

che[1] *nf* the (name of the) letter *ch.*

che[2] *interj* oh dear!; (*Cono Sur*) hey!, hi!, I say!; (*CAm*) who cares!, so what?

checa[1] *nf* (**a**) (*policía*) secret police. (**b**) (*central*) secret police headquarters; (‡) nick‡, jail.

checar [1g] *vt* (*Méx etc*) = **chequear.**

checo, -a[2] 1 *adj, nm/f* Czech. **2** *nm* (*Ling*) Czech.

checoslovaco, -a *nm/f* Czechoslovak.

Checoslovaquia *nf* Czechoslovakia.

cheche *nm* (*Carib*) bully, braggart.

chechear [1a] *vt* (*Cono Sur*) = **vosear.**

chécheres *nmpl* (*And, CAm*) things, gear; junk, lumber.

chechón *adj* (*Méx*) spoilt, pampered.

cheira *nf* = **chaira.**

Chejov *nm* Chekhov.

chele *adj* (*CAm*) fair, blond(e).

chelear [1a] *vt* (*CAm*) to whiten, whitewash.

cheli‡ *nm* (**a**) (*tío*) bloke‡, guy*; (*amigo*) boyfriend; **ven acá, ~** come here, man. (**b**) (*Ling*) *Cheli* jargon, Madrid slang of 1970s.

chelín *nm* (*Fin*) shilling.

chelista *nmf* cellist.

chelo[1] *nm* (**a**) (*Mús*) cello. (**b**) (*persona*) cellist.

chelo[2] *adj* (*Méx*) fair, blond(e).

chepa *nf* hump.

cheposo 1 *adj* hunchbacked. **2** *nm,* **cheposa** *nf* hunchback.

cheque *nm* cheque, check (*US*); **~ abierto** open cheque; **~ en blanco** blank cheque; **~ caducado** stale cheque; **~ de compensación** clearing cheque; **~ cruzado** crossed cheque; **~ en descubierto** (*Méx*), **~ sin fondos, ~ sin provisión** bad cheque; **~ al portador** bearer cheque, cheque payable to bearer; **~ de viaje, ~ de viajero** traveller's cheque; **pagar mediante ~** to pay by cheque.

chequear [1a] *vt* (*esp LAm*) *cuenta, documento, salud etc* to check; *persona* to check (up) on; (*investigar*) to investigate, examine; (*CAm, Carib*) *cheque* to issue, write; to issue a cheque for; (*And, CAm, Carib*) *equipaje* to register, check in; (*And: apuntar*) to note down, record, register; (*Méx: Aut*) to service, overhaul, check.

chequeo *nm* (*esp LAm*) check; checking-up; (*Med*) check-up; (*Aut*) service, overhaul(ing).

chequera *nf* (*LAm*) chequebook.

cherife *nm* (*LAm*) sheriff (*US*).

cherna *nf* wreck fish.

chero* *nm* (*CAm*) pal*, mate, buddy (*US*).

cheruto *nm* cheroot.

cherva *nf* castor oil plant.

cheurón *nm* (*Her*) chevron.

chévere* 1 *adj* (*And, Carib, Méx*) smashing*, super*. **2** *nm* (*Carib*) bully, braggart.

chevió *nm,* **cheviot** *nm* cheviot.

chibola *nf* (*CAm*) (**a**) (*refresco*) fizzy drink, pop*. (**b**) = **chibolo.** (**c**) (*canica*) marble.

chibolo *nm* (*And, CAm*) bump, swelling; wen.

chic 1 *adj invar* chic, smart, elegant. **2** *nm* elegance; composure.

chica[1] *nf* (*joven*) girl; (*criada*) maid, servant; **~ de alterne** bar-girl, bar-room hostess; **~ de conjunto** chorus-girl.

chica[2] *nf* (*Cono Sur*) plug of chewing tobacco.

chicana[1] *nf* (*LAm*) chicanery.

chicanear [1a] **1** *vt* to trick, take in*, con*. **2** *vi* (*LAm*) to use trickery, be cunning.

chicanería *nf* (*LAm*) chicanery.

chicanero *adj* (**a**) (*LAm*: *astuto*) tricky, crafty. (**b**) (*And*: *tacaño*) mean.

chicano **1** *adj* Chicano, Mexican-American. **2** *nm*, **chicana**[2] *nf* Chicano, Mexican immigrant in the USA.

chicar* [1g] *vi* (*And*) to booze*, drink.

chicarrón **1** *adj* strapping, sturdy. **2** *nm*, **chicarrona** *nf* strapping lad; sturdy lass.

chicato* *adj* (*Cono Sur*) short-sighted.

chicle *nm* chewing gum; ~ **de burbuja,** ~ **de globo** bubble gum.

chiclear [1a] *vi* (*CAm, Méx*) (**a**) (*cosechar*) to extract gum (*for chewing*). (**b**) (*mascar*) to chew gum.

chico **1** *adj* small, little, tiny; small-size(d); **¿tiene en ~?** do you have the smaller size?; **dejar ~ a uno** to put sb in the shade.

2 *nm* (**a**) (*persona*) boy; child, youngster, lad; (*: *en oración directa*) my boy*, old boy*, old man*; **es (un) buen ~** he's a good lad (*o* chap *o* fellow); **los ~s del equipo** the lads in the team; **los ~s de la oficina** the fellows at the office; ~ **de la calle** street urchin; ~ **de oficina,** ~ **de los recados** office-boy; ~ **prodigio** child prodigy, (*Com etc*) whizz-kid; **como ~ con zapatos nuevos** as happy as a sandboy.

(**b**) (*LAm Billar, Naipes etc*) game, round; first game.

chicolear* [1a] **1** *vi* (**a**) (*flirtear*) to flirt, murmur sweet nothings, say nice things.

(**b**) (*And*: *divertirse*) to amuse o.s., have a good time; to do childish things.

2 chicolearse *vr* (*And*) to amuse o.s.

chicoleo *nm* (**a**) (*: *dicho*) compliment, flirtatious remark; **decir ~s** to say nice things.

(**b**) (*: *acto*) flirting; **estar de ~** to be in a flirtatious mood.

(**c**) (*And*: *cosa infantil*) childish thing; **no andemos con ~s** let's be serious.

chicolero *adj* flirtatious.

chicoría *nf* chicory.

chicota *nf* fine girl; (*pey*) big girl, hefty wench.

chicotazo *nm* (*LAm*) lash, swipe.

chicote *nm* (**a**) (*: *chico*) big chap*, fine lad.

(**b**) (*Náut*) piece of rope, rope end; (*LAm*) whip, lash.

(**c**) (*) (*cigarro*) cigar; (*colilla*) cigar stub.

chicotear [1a] **1** *vt* (*LAm*: *azotar*) to whip, lash; (*LAm*: *pegar*) to beat up*; (*And*: *matar*) to kill.

2 *vi* (*LAm*: *cola etc*) to lash about.

chicha[1] *nf* (**a**) (*bebida*) chicha, maize liquor, corn liquor (*US*); ~ **de uva** (*And, Cono Sur*) unfermented grape juice; **estas cosas están como ~** (*And*) there are hundreds (*o* any number) of these things; **no es ni ~ ni limonada** it's neither one thing nor the other, it's neither fish nor fowl; **sacar la ~ a uno** to make sb sweat blood; **sacar la ~ a algo** to squeeze the last drop out of sth*.

(**b**) (*: *And, CAm*: *berrinche*) rage, bad temper; **estar de ~** to be in a bad mood.

chicha[2] *nf* (*And*) thick-soled shoe.

chicha[3]* *nf* meat; **de ~ y nabo*** insignificant; **tener poca(s) ~(s)** to be slim; (*pey*) to be skinny.

chicha[4] *adj* (*Náut*): **calma ~** dead calm.

chícharo *nm* pea, chickpea.

chicharra *nf* (**a**) (*Ent*) harvest bug, cicada; **es como ~ en verano** it's nasty, it's unpleasant; **canta la ~** it's terribly hot.

(**b**) (*: *habladora*) chatterbox.

(**c**) (*: *Elec*) bell, buzzer; (*Telec*) bug*, bugging device*.

(**d**) (*CAm, Carib*: *chicharrón*) crackling (*of pork*).

(**e**) (‡: *droga*) reefer‡.

(**f**) (‡: *monedero*) purse.

chicharrero[1] *nm* oven, hot place; (*fig*) suffocating heat.

chicharrero[2] **1** *adj* of Tenerife. **2** *nm*, **chicharrera** *nf* native (*o* inhabitant) of Tenerife; **los ~s** the people of Tenerife.

chicharro *nm* horse-mackerel.

chicharrón *nm* (**a**) (*Culin*) crackling (*of pork*); piece of burnt meat; **estar hecho un ~** (*Culin*) to be burnt to a cinder; (*persona*) to be as red as a lobster.

(**b**) (*fig*) sunburnt person.

(**c**) (*Carib*: *adulador*) flatterer.

chiche **1** *adj y adv* (*CAm*) easy, simple; easily; **está ~** it's a cinch‡.

2 *nm* (**a**) (*LAm Anat*) breast, teat.

(**b**) (*LAm*) (*objeto*) precious thing, delightful object; (*joya*) fancy jewel, trinket; (*juguete*) small toy; (*persona fiable*) trustworthy person; (*inteligente*) clever person; (*pulcro*) well-dressed person; (*sitio elegante*) elegant place, nice room (*etc*).

3 *nf* (*Méx*) nursemaid.

chichear [1a] *vti* to hiss.

chicheo *nm* hiss, hissing.

chichera‡ *nf* (*CAm*) jail, clink‡.

chichería *nf* (*LAm*) *chicha* tavern; *chicha* factory.

chichero *nm* (*LAm*) *chicha* vendor (*o* maker).

chichi **1** *nm* (‡‡) cunt‡‡. **2** *nf* (*Méx*) (**a**) (*teta*) teat. (**b**) (*niñera*) nursemaid.

chichicaste *nm* (*CAm*) (*Bot*) nettle; (*Med*) nettle rash.

chichigua *nf* (**a**) (*CAm, Méx*: *niñera*) nursemaid. (**b**) (*Carib*: *cometa*) kite. (**c**) (*Méx*) (*animal manso*) tame animal; (*hembra*) nursing animal. (**d**) (*Méx**) pimp.

chicho *nm* (**a**) (*bucle*) curl, ringlet. (**b**) (*bigudí*) curler, roller.

chichón[1]* *adj* (**a**) (*Cono Sur*: *jovial*) merry, jovial. (**b**) (*CAm*: *fácil*) easy, straightforward; **está ~** it's a piece of cake*.

chichón[2] *nm* bump, lump, swelling.

chichonear* [1a] *vi* (*Cono Sur*) to joke.

chichus *nm* (*CAm*) flea.

chifa (*And*) **1** *adj* (*pey*‡) Chinky‡, Chinese. **2** *nm* Chinese restaurant.

chifla *nf* (**a**) (*sonido*) hiss, hissing, whistling. (**b**) (*instrumento*) whistle.

chifladera* *nf* (*CAm, Méx*) crazy idea.

chiflado* *adj* **1** daft, barmy‡; cranky*, crackpot; **estar ~ con, estar ~ por** to be crazy about.

2 *nm*, **chiflada** *nf* nut‡, crank*, crackpot.

chifladura *nf* (**a**) = **chifla.**

(**b**) (*: *locura*) daftness, craziness.

(**c**) (*) (*una ~*) whim, fad, mania; crazy idea, wild scheme; **su ~ es el ajedrez** his mania is chess, he is crazy about chess; **ese amor no es más que una ~** what he calls love is just a foolish infatuation.

chiflar[1] [1a] **1** *vt* (**a**) *actor, obra etc* to hiss, boo, whistle at; *silbato* to blow.

(**b**) (*: *beber*) to drink, knock back*.

(**c**) (*: *encantar*) to entrance, captivate; to drive crazy; **me chifla ese conjunto** I rave about that group*, I think that group is smashing*; **me chiflan los helados** I just adore ice cream; **a mí no me chiflan los eslobodios** I don't exactly go overboard for the Slobodians*; **esa chica le chifla (*o* tiene chiflado)** he's crazy about that girl.

2 *vi* to whistle, hiss; (*CAm, Méx*: *aves*) to sing.

3 chiflarse *vr* (**a**) (*: *pirrarse*) to go barmy‡, go crazy; **~ con, ~ por** to be (*o* go) crazy about.

(**b**) **chiflárselas** (*CAm*‡) to peg out‡, kick the bucket‡.

chiflar[2] *vt* (*Téc*) *cuero* to pare, pare down.

chiflato *nm* whistle.

chifle *nm* (**a**) (*silbo*) whistle; (*de ave*) call, bird call. (**b**) (*Hist, t CAm, Carib*) powder horn, powder flask.

chiflete *nm* whistle.

chiflido *nm* whistle, shrill sound; hiss.

chiflón *nm* (**a**) (*And, Cono Sur*: *viento*) draught, blast (of air); (*CAm, Méx*) gale.

(**b**) (*CAm, Carib, Cono Sur*: *de río*) rapids, violent current; (*CAm*) waterfall; (*Méx*: *caz*) flume, race; (*Méx*: *tobera*) nozzle.

chiguín, -ina* *nm/f* (*CAm*) kid*.

chihuahua *nm* chihuahua.

chiíta *adj, nmf* Shi'ite.

chilaba *nf* (d)jellabah.

chilacayote *nm* (*LAm*) gourd.

chilango (*Méx*) **1** *adj* of Mexico City. **2** *nm*, **chilanga** *nf* native (*o* inhabitant) of Mexico City.

Chile *nm* Chile.

chile *nm* (**a**) (*Bot, Culin*) chili, red pepper. (**b**) (*CAm**: *broma*) joke.

chilear* [1a] *vi* (*CAm*) to tell jokes.

chilena[1] *nf* overhead kick, scissors kick.

chilenismo *nm* chilenism, word (*o* phrase *etc*) peculiar to Chile.

chileno, -a[2], **chileño, -a** *adj, nm/f* Chilean.

chilicote *nm* (*And, Cono Sur*: *Ent*) cricket.

chilindrón *nm*: **al ~** cooked with tomatoes and peppers.

chilpayate*, -a *nm/f* (*Méx*) kid*, youngster.

chilposo *adj* (*Cono Sur*) ragged, tattered.

chilla[1] *nf* thin board; weatherboard, clapboard (*US*).

chilla[2] *nf* (*Cono Sur*) fox.

chilla[3] *nf* (*Méx*) (**a**) (*Teat*) gods, gallery. (**b**) (*: *pobreza*) poverty; **estar en la ~** to be flat broke*.

chilla[4] *nf* (*Caza*) decoy, call.

chillador *adj* howling, screeching, screaming; blaring; squealing; creaking.

chillante *adj* (**a**) = **chillador**. (**b**) (*fig*) = **chillón** (**b**).

chillar [1a] **1** *vi* (**a**) (*animal salvaje, gato etc*) to howl; (*ratón*) to squeak; (*cerdo*) to squeal; (*ave*) to screech, squawk; (*persona*) to yell; to shriek, scream; (*Caza*) to call; (*radio*) to blare; (*frenos*) to screech, squeal; (*puerta*) to creak; ~ **a uno** to yell at sb, scream at sb.

(**b**) (*colores*) to scream, be loud, clash.

(**c**) (*LAm*: *fig*: *protestar*) to shout, protest; **no** ~ (*Carib, Cono Sur*: *callarse*) to keep one's mouth shut, not say a word; (*CAm, Carib*: *informar*) to squeal‡, turn informer; **el cochino chilló** (*Carib, Méx*) they (*etc*) let the cat out of the bag*.

(**d**) (*LAm*: *llorar*) to sob.

2 chillarse *vr* (**a**) (*LAm*: *quejarse*) to complain (*con* to), protest (*con* to).

(**b**) (*And, Carib, Méx**) (*enojarse*) to get cross; (*ofenderse*) to take offence, get into a huff.

(**c**) (*CAm*: *sofocarse*) to get embarrassed.

chillería *nf* row, hubbub.

chillido *nm* (*V vi*) howl; squeak; squeal; screech; squawk; yell, shriek, scream; blare; creak.

chillo *nm* (**a**) (*CAm*: *deuda*) debt. (**b**) (*Carib*: *muchedumbre*) rabble, mob. (**c**) (*And*) (*ira*) anger; (*protesta*) loud protest.

chillón1 **1** *adj* (**a**) *persona* loud, shrill, noisy; *sonido, voz* shrill, strident; harsh; piercing. (**b**) *color* loud, gaudy, lurid. (**c**) (*LAm**: *quejumbroso*) moaning, whingeing*. **2** *nm*, **chillona** *nf* (*LAm*) (**a**) (*quejón*) moaner, whiner. (**b**) (*gritón*) loudmouth*.

chillón2 *nm* (*Téc*) small nail, panel pin, finishing nail (*US*).

chillonamente *adv* loudly, shrilly; stridently; piercingly.

chimal *nm* (*Méx*) dishevelled hair, mop of hair.

chimar [1a] *vt* (**a**) (*CAm*: *arañar*) to scratch. (**b**) (*CAm, Méx*: *molestar*) to annoy, bother. (**c**) (*CAm***) to fuck**, screw**.

chimba1 *nf* (*And, Cono Sur*: *orilla*) opposite bank (of a river); (*Cono Sur*: *barrio*) poor quarter (*on other side of river*); (*And*: *vado*) ford.

chimba2 *nf* (*And*) pigtail.

chimbar [1a] *vt* (*And*) *río* to ford.

chimbero *adj* (*Cono Sur*) (*de chimba*) slum (*atr*); (*grosero*) coarse, rough.

chimbo **1** *adj* (**a**) (*And, Carib*: *gastado*) worn-out, wasted, old. (**b**) (*And*) *cheque* bad. **2** *nm* (*And*) piece of meat.

chimenea *nf* (**a**) (*de edificio etc*) chimney; (*Náut etc*) funnel; smokestack; (*Min*) shaft; (*Alpinismo*) chimney; ~ **de aire** air shaft.

(**b**) (*hogar*) hearth, fireplace; ~ (**francesa**) fireplace, mantelpiece; chimney piece.

(**c**) (‡: *cabeza*) bonce‡, head.

chimichurri *nm* barbecue sauce.

chimiscolear* [1a] *vi* (*Méx*) (*chismear*) to gossip; (*curiosear*) to poke (*o* go poking) one's nose in*.

chimiscolero, -a *nm/f* (*Méx*) gossip, busybody.

chimpancé *nm* chimpanzee.

chimpín *nm* (*And*) brandy, liquor.

chimuelo *adj* (*LAm*) toothless.

China *nf* China.

china1 *nf* (**a**) (*Culin etc*) china; chinaware; porcelain. (**b**) (*seda*) China silk.

china2 *nf* (**a**) (*Geol*) pebble; (*juego*) guessing game played with pebbles; (*de droga*) block; **poner ~s** to put obstacles in the way; **le tocó la** ~ he had bad luck; he carried the can*. (**b**) (*And*: *trompo*) spinning-top.

china3 *nf* (**a**) (*LAm*: *india*) (Indian) woman, (half-breed) girl; (*And, CAm, Cono Sur*: *niñera*) nursemaid; (*And, Cono Sur*: *criada*) servant girl; (*LAm*: *amante*) mistress, concubine; (*And*: *señorita*) elegant young lady.

(**b**) (*LAm Téc*) fan, blower.

china4 *nf* (*Carib, Méx*: *naranja*) orange.

chinaca‡ *nf*: **la** ~ (*Méx*) the plebs*, the proles.

chinado‡ *adj* crazy.

chinaloa‡ *nf* (*Méx*) heroin, smack‡.

chinar‡ [1a] *vt* to carve up*, slash.

chinarro *nm* large pebble, stone.

chinazo *nm* blow from a stone; **le tocó el** ~ he had bad luck; he carried the can*.

chinchada *nf* (*Cono Sur*) tug-of-war.

chinchal *nm* (*Carib*) tobacco stall; small shop.

chinchar* [1a] **1** *vt* to pester, bother, annoy; to upset; **me chincha tener que** + *infin* it upsets me to have to + *infin*.

2 chincharse *vr* to get cross, get upset; **¡chínchate!** get lost!‡; **¡para que te chinches!** so there!; and you can lump it!*; **¡y que se chinchen los demás!** and the rest can go chase themselves!*

chincharrero *nm* (*And*) fishing boat.

chinche **1** *nf* (**a**) (*Ent*) bug, (*esp*) bedbug; **caer** (*o* **morir**) **como ~s** to die like flies.

(**b**) (*chincheta*) drawing pin, thumbtack (*US*).

(**c**) (*Cono Sur**: *rabieta*) pique, irritation.

2 *nmf* (*fig*) nuisance; annoying person, pest, bore; (*And, CAm*) naughty child.

chincheta *nf* drawing pin, thumbtack (*US*).

chinchetear [1a] *vt* to pin up.

chinchibí *nm* (*And, CAm, Cono Sur*), **chinchibirra** *nf* (*Cono Sur*) ginger beer.

chinchilla *nf* chinchilla.

chinchín1 *nm* (**a**) street music, tinny music. (**b**) (*CAm*: *sonajero*) baby's rattle.

chinchín2 *nm* (*Carib*) drizzle.

chinchón *nm* anisette.

chinchona* *nf* quinine.

chinchorrería* *nf* (**a**) (*cualidad*) fussiness; critical nature, disrespectful manner; impertinence. (**b**) (*chisme*) piece of gossip; (*cuento*) malicious tale.

chinchorrero* *adj* (**a**) (*exigente*) fussy (about details); (*criticón*) critical, disrespectful; nit-picking*; (*fresco*) impertinent. (**b**) (*chismoso*) gossipy; (*rencoroso*) malicious.

chinchorro *nm* (**a**) (*red*) net, dragnet, trawl. (**b**) (*bote*) rowing boat, dinghy. (**c**) (*LAm*: *hamaca*) hammock; (*vivienda*) poor tenement; (*Carib*: *tienda*) little shop.

chinchoso *adj* (**a**) (*con chinches*) full of bugs. (**b**) = **chinchorrero**. (**c**) (*pesado*) tiresome, annoying; boring. (**d**) (*And, Carib*: *quisquilloso*) touchy, irritable.

chinchudo* *adj*: **estar** ~ (*Cono Sur*) to be in a huff.

chinchulines *nmpl* (*Cono Sur*) tripe.

chindar‡ [1a] *vt* to chuck out.

chinear [1a] **1** *vt* (*CAm*) *niño* to carry in one's arms; to care for; (*pey*) to spoil. **2** *vi* (*Cono Sur*) to have an affair with a half-breed girl.

chinel‡ *nm* guard.

chinela *nf* (*zapatilla*) slipper, mule; (*zueco*) clog.

chinero1 *nm* china cupboard.

chinero2 *adj* (*And, Cono Sur*) fond of the (half-breed) girls.

chinesco *adj* Chinese.

chinetero *adj* (*Cono Sur*) = **chinero2**.

chinga *nf* (**a**) (*CAm, Carib*: *colilla*) fag-end‡, cigar stub; (*fig*) drop, small amount; **una** ~ **de agua** a drop of water.

(**b**) (*Carib*: *borrachera*) drunkenness. (**c**) (*Méx**) beating-up.

chingada** *nf* (*CAm, Méx*) (*acto sexual*) fuck**, screw**; (*molestia*) bloody nuisance**.

chingadazo* *nm* (*Méx*) bash*, punch.

chingado‡ *adj* (*CAm, Méx*) lousy‡, bloody‡.

chingadura *nf* (*Cono Sur*) failure.

chingana *nf* (**a**) (*And, Cono Sur*: *local*) dive‡, tavern; (*de baile*) cheap dance-hall. (**b**) (*Cono Sur*: *fiesta*) wild party.

chinganear [1a] *vi* (*And, Cono Sur*) to go on the town, live it up*.

chinganero (*And, Cono Sur*) **1** *adj* fond of living it up*, wildly social. **2** *nm*, **chinganera** *nf* owner of a *chingana*.

chingar [1h] **1** *vt* (**a**) (*CAm*) *animal* to dock, cut off the tail of.

(**b**) (*LAm***: *joder*) to fuck**, screw**; **hijo de la chingada** bastard‡, son of a bitch‡ (*US*); **¡chinga tu madre!** fuck off!**.

(**c**) (**: *Méx etc*) (*fastidiar*) to annoy, upset; (*arruinar*) to fuck up**; **estar chingado** to be cross, be upset; **¡no chingues!** don't mess me around!*

(**d**) (*Cono Sur*) *tiro* to aim badly, miss with; *tentativa* to fail in.

(**e**) (*Carib*) to carry on one's shoulder.

(**f**) (*Méx‡*: *robar*) to nick‡, pinch*.

2 *vi* (**a**) (*beber*) to drink too much.

(**b**) (*LAm***: *joder*) to fuck**, screw**.

(**c**) (*CAm*: *contar chistes*) to joke.

(**d**) (*Méx‡*: *ganar*) to win.

3 chingarse *vr* (**a**) (*: *emborracharse*) to get tight*.

(**b**) (*LAm**: *fracasar*) to fail, fall through, come to nothing; **la fiesta se chingó** the party was a failure (*o* a flop*); **el cohete se chingó** the rocket failed to go off, the rocket was a dud*.

chingo **1** *adj* (**a**) (*CAm*) *vestido* short; *cuchillo* blunt; *animal* docked, tailless; *persona* in one's underclothes, bare.

(**b**) (*And, Carib*: *chico*) small.

(**c**) (*CAm, Carib*) *persona* snub-nosed; *nariz* flat, snub.

(**d**) **estar ~ por algo** (*Carib*) (*loco por*) to be crazy about sth; (*desear*) to be dying for sth.

2 *nm* (**a**) (*And*: *potro*) colt.

(**b**) (*And, CAm*: *barca*) small boat.

(**c**) **~s** (*CAm*) underclothes.

(**d**) **un ~ de** (*Méx**) lots of, loads of.

3 *excl* (*LAm***) fuck it!**

chingón* *nm* (*Méx*) big shot*, top man, boss.

chingue 1 *adj* (*Cono Sur*) stinking, repulsive. **2** *nm* (*Cono Sur*) skunk.

chinguear [1a] *vt etc* (*CAm*) = **chingar.**

chinguirito *nm* (*Carib, Méx*: *licor*) rough liquor, firewater; (*And, Carib*: *trago*) swig (of liquor)*.

chinita[1] *nf* small stone, pebble; **poner ~s a uno** (*fig*) to make trouble for sb.

chinita[2] *nf* (*Cono Sur*: *Ent*) ladybird.

chinito *nm*, **chinita[3]** *nf* (**a**) (*Cono Sur*: *criado*) servant. (**b**) (*LAm*: *en oración directa*) dear, dearest. (**c**) (*And, Carib, Cono Sur*: *indio*) Indian boy, Indian girl.

chino[1] 1 *adj* Chinese.

2 *nm*, **china[5]** *nf* Chinese; (*m t*) Chinaman.

3 *nm* (**a**) (*Ling*) Chinese; (*fig*) Greek, double Dutch*; **ni que hablara en ~ ...** I couldn't have understood less even if he'd been talking Chinese. (**b**) (*Culin*) Chinese restaurant.

chino[2] *nm* (*Geol*) pebble, stone.

chino[3] 1 *adj* (**a**) (*CAm*: *calvo*) bald, hairless.

(**b**) (*Méx*) *pelo* curly, kinky; *persona* curly-haired.

(**c**) (*CAm, Carib*: *furioso*) angry, furious; **estar ~** to be angry; **estar ~ por algo** to be crazy about sth.

(**d**) (*LAm*: *joven*) young.

2 *nm* (**a**) (*LAm*: *mestizo*) half-breed; (*Cono Sur, Carib*: *indio*) Indian; (*And*: *t* **~ cholo**) offspring of Indian and Negress; (*Carib*: *hijo de mulato y negra*) offspring of mulatto and Negress; (*And, Carib, Cono Sur*: *criado*) servant; (*And*: *golfo*) street urchin; (*LAm*: *en oración directa*) dear, dearest; **quedar como un ~** (*Carib, Cono Sur*) to come off badly; **trabajar como un ~** (*Carib, Cono Sur*) to work like a slave.

(**b**) (*And, CAm*: *cerdo*) pig.

(**c**) (*rizos*) **~s** curls.

(**d**) (*CAm, Carib*: *enojo*) anger; **le salió el ~** he got angry; **tener un ~** to be angry.

chino[4] *nm* (*Culin*) mincer, grinder; mixer, blender.

chinólogo, -a *nm/f* expert in Chinese affairs, Sinologist; (*hum*) China watcher.

chinorri‡ *nf* bird‡, chick*.

chip *nm, pl* **chips** [tʃip] (**a**) (*Inform*) chip; **~ de memoria** memory chip; **~ de silicio** silicon chip. (**b**) (*Culin*) crisp. (**c**) (*Golf*) chip (shot).

chipe 1 *adj* (*CAm*) (**a**) (*enfermizo*) weak, sickly. (**b**) (*llorón*) whining, snivelling. **2** *nmf* (*And, CAm, Méx*) baby of the family.

chipé(n)‡ 1 *adj* (*t* **de ~**) super*, smashing*. **2** *adv* marvellously, really well; **comer de ~** to have a super meal*. **3** *nf*: **la ~** the truth.

chipear [1a] **1** *vt* (*CAm*) to bother, pester. **2** *vi* (*And, CAm*) to moan, whine.

chipi *adj etc* = **chipe.**

chipichipi *nm* (*prov, LAm*) continuous drizzle, mist.

chipichusca* *nf* whore.

chipil* *adj* (*Méx*) sad, gloomy.

chipión* *nm* (*CAm*) telling-off*.

chipirón *nm* small cuttlefish.

chipotear [1a] *vt* (*CAm*) to slap.

Chipre *nf* Cyprus.

chipriota, chipriote 1 *adj* Cyprian, Cypriot. **2** *nmf* Cypriot.

chiquear [1a] **1** *vt* (*Carib, Méx*) (*mimar*) to spoil, indulge; (*dar coba a*) to flatter, suck up to*.

2 chiquearse *vr* (**a**) (*Méx*: *mimarse*) to be spoiled.

(**b**) (*CAm*: *contonearse*) to swagger along.

chiqueo *nm* (**a**) **~s** (*Carib, Méx*) flattery, toadying. (**b**) (*CAm*: *contoneo*) swagger.

chiquero *nm* (*pocilga*: *t fig*) pigsty; (*Taur*) bull pen; (*Cono Sur*) hen run.

chiquilín *nm* (*CAm, Cono Sur, Méx*) tiny tot, small boy.

chiquillada *nf* (**a**) childish prank; childish thing (to do); **eso son ~s** that's kid's stuff*, that's for children. (**b**) (*LAm*) kids*, youngsters.

chiquillería *nf*: **una ~** a crowd of youngsters, a mob of kids*; **llevar la ~** to take the kids*.

chiquillo, -a *nm/f* kid*, youngster, child.

chiquirín *nm* (*CAm Ent*) cricket.

chiquirritín *adj*, **chiquirrito** *adj* small, tiny, wee.

chiquitear [1a] *vi* (**a**) (*jugar*) to play like a child. (**b**) (*: *beber*) to tipple.

chiquitín 1 *adj* very small, tiny. **2** *nm*, **chiquitina** *nf* small child, tiny tot.

chiquito 1 *adj* very small, tiny.

2 *nm*, **chiquita** *nf* kid*, youngster; **andarse en chiquitas** to beat about the bush, fuss about details.

3 *nm* (**a**) small glass of wine. (**b**) (*Cono Sur*): **un ~** a bit, a little; **¡espera un ~!** wait a moment!

chiquitura *nf* (**a**) (*CAm*: *nimiedad*) small thing; insignificant detail. (**b**) (*CAm*) = **chiquillada.**

chira *nf* (**a**) (*And*: *andrajo*) rag, tatter. (**b**) (*CAm*: *llaga*) wound, sore.

chirajos *nmpl* (**a**) (*CAm*: *trastos*) lumber, junk. (**b**) (*And*: *andrajos*) rags, tatters.

chirajoso *adj* (*CAm*) ragged, tattered.

chircal *nm* (*And*) brickworks, tileworks.

chiri‡ *nm* joint‡.

chiribita *nf* (**a**) (*chispa*) spark; **echar ~s, estar que echa ~s** to be furious, blow one's top; **le hacían ~s los ojos** her eyes sparkled, her eyes lit up.

(**b**) **~s*** (*Med*) spots before the eyes.

(**c**) (*Bot*) daisy.

chiribitil *nm* attic, garret; den; cubbyhole; (*pey*) poky little room, hole.

chiribito *nm* poker.

chirigota *nf* joke; fun; **fue motivo de ~** it got a laugh, it led to some amusement; **hacer de uno una ~** to poke fun at sb.

chirigotero *adj* full of jokes, facetious.

chirimbolo *nm* thingummyjig*; strange object, odd-looking implement; **~s** (*equipo*) things, gear, equipment; (*trastos*) lumber, junk; (*Culin*) kitchen things.

chirimía *nf* (peasant-type) oboe, flageolet, shawm.

chirimiri *nm* drizzle.

chirimoya *nf* (**a**) (*Bot*) custard apple. (**b**) (‡: *cabeza*) nut‡, head.

chirimoyo* *nm* (*Cono Sur*) dud cheque*.

chirinada *nf* (**a**) (*Cono Sur*: *fracaso*) failure, disaster. (**b**) = **chirinola.**

chiringuito *nm* small shop, stall; open air restaurant, open air drinks stall; bar; night club.

chirinola *nf* (**a**) (*riña*) fight, scrap*; (*discusión*) heated discussion; (*conversación*) lengthy conversation, lively talk; **pasar la tarde de ~** to spend the afternoon deep in conversation.

(**b**) (*nimiedad*) trifle, triviality, unimportant thing.

(**c**) (*juego*) skittles.

chiripa *nf* (*Billar*) lucky break; (*fig*) lucky event, fluke, stroke of luck; **de ~, por ~** by a fluke, by chance.

chiripá *nm* (*And, Cono Sur*) *kind of blanket worn as trousers*; **gente de ~** country people, peasants.

chiripero 1 *adj* lucky, fluky. **2** *nm* lucky sort.

chirís* *nmf* (*CAm*) kid*, child.

chirivía *nf* (**a**) (*Bot*) parsnip. (**b**) (*Orn*) wagtail.

chirivisco *nm* (*CAm*) firewood, kindling.

chirla[1] *nf* mussel, clam.

chirla[2]‡ *nf* armed hold-up.

chirlata* *nf* whore.

chirle *adj* (**a**) *sopa etc* watery, wishy-washy*. (**b**) (*fig*) flat, dull, wishy-washy*; **poeta ~** mere versifier, uninspired poet.

chirlo *nm* gash, slash (in the face); long scar.

chirola‡ *nf* (*CAm, Carib*), **chirona** *nf* jug‡, jail; **estar en ~** to be in jug‡.

chiros *nmpl* (*And*) rags, tatters.

chiroso *adj* (*And, CAm*) ragged, tattered.

chirota *nf* (*CAm*) tough woman.

chirote* *adj* (*And*) daft*.

chirri‡ *nm* joint‡.

chirriado *adj* (*And*) (*gracioso*) witty; (*alegre*) merry, jovial.

chirriar [1b] *vi* (**a**) (*grillo etc*) to chirp, sing; (*pájaro*) to chirp, cheep; to screech, squawk; (*rueda, gozne, puerta*) to creak, squeak; (*frenos*) to screech, squeal; (*al freír*) to hiss, sizzle; (*persona*) to sing (*o* play) out of tune.

(**b**) (*And*: *tiritar*) to shiver (with cold *etc*).

(**c**) (*And**: *ir de juerga*) to go on a spree.

chirrido *nm* (*V vi*) shrill sound, high-pitched unpleasant sound; chirp(ing); screech(ing), squawk(ing); creak(ing), squeak(ing); squeal(ing); sizzle, sizzling.

chirrión *nm* (**a**) (*carro*) tumbrel. (**b**) (*And, CAm, Méx*: *látigo*) whip. (**c**) (*CAm*: *sarta*) string, line. (**d**) (*CAm*: *charla*) chat, conversation (*esp* between lovers).

chirrionar [1a] *vt* (*And, Méx*) to whip, lash.

chirrisco *adj* (**a**) (*CAm, Carib: diminuto*) very small, tiny. (**b**) (*Méx**) *mujer* flirtatious; **viejo ~** dirty old man.
chirumen* *nm* nous*, savvy*.
chirusa* *nf* (*Cono Sur: niña*) girl, kid*; (*mujer*) poor woman.
chis *interj* (*pidiendo silencio*) sh!; (*llamando*) hey!, psst!; (*LAm: asco*) ugh!
chiscón *nm* shack, hovel, slum.
chischís *nm* (*And, CAm, Carib*) drizzle.
chisgarabís* *nm* meddler, nosey-parker*.
chisguete* *nm* swig*, drink.
chisme *nm* (**a**) (*Téc*) gadget, contrivance, jigger*; **~s** things, gear, tackle.
(**b**) (*fig: objeto*) thing, whatnot*, thingummyjig*; **dáme el ~ ese** give me that whatsit, please*; **~s** (*fig*) paraphernalia, things, odds and ends.
(**c**) (*fig: habladuría*) piece of gossip, tale; **~s** gossip, tittletattle, tales; **no me vengas con esos ~s** don't bring those tales to me, I don't want to hear your tittle-tattle.
chismear [1a] *vi* to gossip, tell tales, spread scandal.
chismería *nf*, **chismerío** *nm* (*Carib, Cono Sur*) gossip, tittle-tattle, scandal.
chismero *adj y n* = **chismoso**.
chismografía *nf* gossip.
chismorrear [1a] *vi* = **chismear**.
chismorreo *nm* = **chismería**.
chismoso 1 *adj* gossiping, scandalmongering. **2** *nm*, **chismosa** *nf* talebearer, scandalmonger.
chispa 1 *nf* (**a**) (*centella*) spark (*t Elec*); (*fig*) sparkle, gleam; **echar ~s*, estar que echa ~s*** to be hopping mad*.
(**b**) (*gota*) drop (*esp* of rain); **~s** sprinkling (of rain); **caen ~s** there are a few drops falling.
(**c**) (*hoja*) flake; small particle, (*esp*) small diamond.
(**d**) (*fig: pizca*) bit, tiny amount; **ni ~** not the least bit, nothing at all; **eso no tiene (ni) ~ de gracia** that's not in the least bit funny; **si tuviera una ~ de inteligencia** if he had an atom of intelligence.
(**e**) (*fig: ingenio*) sparkle, wit; life; **el cuento tiene ~** the story has some wit; **dar ~s** to show o.s. to be bright (*o* lively, efficient); **no da ~** he's utterly dull; **ser una ~, tener (mucha) ~** to be a lively sort; **es de ~ retardada** he's slow on the uptake.
(**f**) (*: *borrachera*) drunkenness; **coger (*o* pillar) una ~** to get tight*; **estar con la ~, tener la ~** to be tight*.
(**g**) **dar ~** (*CAm, Méx*) to work, be successful, yield results.
(**h**) (*And: rumor*) rumour.
(**i**) (*And*: arma*) gun, weapon.
2 *adj invar* (*) (**a**) **estar ~** to be tight*.
(**b**) (*Méx: divertido*) funny, amusing.
3 *nm* (*) electrician (*t* **~s**).
chisparse* [1a] *vr* (**a**) (*And: emborracharse*) to get tight*. (**b**) (*CAm, Méx: huir*) to run away, slip off.
chispazo *nm* (**a**) spark (*t fig*); **primeros ~s** (*fig*) first signs, opening shots, intimations. (**b**) (*fig*) = **chisme (c)**. (**c**) (*: *bebida*) swig*.
chispeante *adj* (*fig*) sparkling, scintillating.
chispear [1a] **1** *vi* (**a**) to spark (*t Elec*).
(**b**) (*fig*) to sparkle, scintillate.
(**c**) (*Met*) to drizzle, spot with rain.
(**d**) (*And*) to gossip, spread scandal.
2 chispearse *vr* (*Carib, Cono Sur**) to get drunk.
chispero¹ 1 *adj* (*And, Carib*) gossiping, scandalmongering. **2** *nm* (*CAm*) (††) lighter; (*Aut*) spark(ing) plug.
chispero²* 1 *adj* of low-class Madrid. **2** *nm*, **chispera** *nf* low-class inhabitant of Madrid.
chispita* *nf*: **una ~ de vino** a drop of wine.
chisporrotear [1a] *vi* to throw out sparks; (*esp Culin: aceite etc*) to hiss, splutter; (*jamón etc*) to sizzle; (*madera*) to crackle.
chisquero *nm* pocket lighter.
chist *interj* = **chis**.
chistada *nf* bad joke.
chistar [1a] *vi* to speak, say something; **no ~** not to say a word; **lo aceptó sin ~** he took it without a word; **nadie chistó** nobody spoke up, nobody answered back.
chiste *nm* joke, funny story; (*en periódico etc*) cartoon; **~ goma** shaggy-dog story; **~ verde** blue joke, dirty story; **caer en el ~** to get the point of the story, get it; **dar en el ~** to guess right; **hacer ~ de algo, tomar algo a ~** to take sth as a joke; **¡aquello tiene ~!** (*iró*) I suppose you think that's funny?; **no veo el ~** I don't get it; what's funny about that?
chistera *nf* (**a**) (*Pesca*) fish basket; (*Dep*) long curved variety of pelota racquet. (**b**) (*: *sombrero*) top hat, topper*; **~ de encantador** magician's hat.
chistosamente *adv* funnily, amusingly; wittily.
chistoso 1 *adj* funny, amusing; witty. **2** *nm*, **chistosa** *nf* wit, amusing person.
chistu *nm* (Basque) flute.
chistulari *nm* (Basque) flute player, flautist.
chita¹: **a la ~ callando** quietly; unobtrusively; (*pey*) on the quiet, on the sly.
chita² *nf* (**a**) (*Anat*) anklebone; (*juego*) *boys' game played with an anklebone*; **dar en la ~** to hit the nail on the head; **no se me da una ~, (no) me importa una ~** I don't care two hoots (*de* about).
(**b**) (*Méx*) (*saco*) net bag; (*dinero*) money; (*ahorros*) small savings, nest egg.
chiticalla* *nmf* quiet sort; (*fig*) clam.
chiticallando = **chita¹**.
chito, chitón *interj* sh!
chiva 1 *nf* (**a**) (*Agr, Zool*) kid; (*LAm*) (*cabra*) goat, nanny-goat; (*oveja*) sheep; **estar como una ~** to be crazy.
(**b**) (*LAm: barba*) goatee (beard).
(**c**) (*And, CAm*) (*autobús*) bus; (*coche*) car.
(**d**) (*CAm: manta*) blanket, bedcover; **~s** bedclothes.
(**e**) (*Carib, Cono Sur: niña*) naughty little girl; (*CAm, Cono Sur: marimacho*) mannish woman; (*And, Carib, Cono Sur: vividora*) immoral woman.
(**f**) (*CAm, Cono Sur: rabieta*) rage, tantrum.
(**g**) (*Carib: mochila*) knapsack.
(**h**) **~s** (*Méx**) junk.
(**i**) (*Cono Sur**) fib, tall story; **meter una ~** to cook up a story.
(**j**) (*Carib*: delator*) grass‡, informer.
2 *adj* (*CAm*: despabilado*) alert, sharp.
3 *excl* (*CAm**) look out!, careful!
chivar [1a] (*prov, LAm*) **1** *vt* (*fastidiar*) to annoy, upset; (*estafar*) to swindle. **2 chivarse** *vr* (**a**) (*enojarse*) to get annoyed. (**b**) (‡) = **chivatear (a)**.
chivata‡ *nf* (**a**) (*linterna*) torch. (**b**) (*pluma*) fountain-pen.
chivatazo‡ *nm* tip-off; **dar ~** to inform, give a tip-off.
chivatear [1a] **1** *vi* (**a**) (‡: *soplar*) to grass‡ (*contra* on), inform (*contra* on); to blow the gaff‡.
(**b**) (*And, Cono Sur*) (*gritar*) to shout, make a hullabaloo; (*saltar*) to jump about; (*retozar*) to indulge in horse-play, have a noisy free-for-all.
(**c**) (*Carib: impresionar*) to create a big impression.
2 chivatearse *vr* (*Carib*) to get scared.
chivato *nm* (**a**) (*Agr, Zool*) kid.
(**b**) (*: *soplón*) stool-pigeon*, informer; (*de fábrica etc*) time-keeper.
(**c**) (*LAm: niño*) child, kid*.
(**d**) (*And: pillo*) rascal, villain.
(**e**) (*And: aprendiz*) apprentice, mate.
(**f**) (*Carib*) outstanding individual.
(**g**) (*Cono Sur: aguardiente*) cheap liquor, firewater.
(**h**) (*Aut*) indicator (light).
(**i**) (*busca*) pager, beeper.
chivearse* [1a] *vr* (*CAm*) to get embarrassed.
chivera *nf* (*And, CAm*) goatee (beard).
chivero *nm* (**a**) (*And: conductor*) busdriver. (**b**) (*And: matón*) brawler. (**c**) (*Carib: intrigante*) intriguer.
chiviroso* *adj* (*CAm*) outgoing, extrovert.
chivo 1 *nm* (**a**) (*Agr, Zool*) kid; goat; billy goat; **~ expiatorio** scapegoat; **esto huele a ~** (*Carib, Cono Sur*) this smells suspicious, there's something fishy about this*.
(**b**) (*CAm: dados*) dice; (*juego*) game of dice.
(**c**) (*Carib: estafa*) fraud; (*intriga*) plot, intrigue; (*Com: acto*) smuggling; illegal trading; (*géneros*) contraband, smuggled goods.
(**d**) (*And, CAm, Carib, Cono Sur*) rage, fit of anger; **comer ~** (*And, Carib*), **ponerse como ~** (*CAm, Carib*) to get furious.
(**e**) (*Méx*) (*jornal*) day's wages; (*anticipo*) advance; (*: *soborno*) backhander*.
(**f**) (*Carib: golpe*) punch, blow.
(**g**) (*And, CAm: niño*) naughty boy, scamp.
(**h**) (*CAm*: guatemalteco*) Guatemalan.
(**i**) (*CAm‡: chulo*) pimp.
(**j**) (‡: *maricón*) poofter‡.
2 *adj* (*CAm**) (**a**) (*guatemalteco*) Guatemalan.
(**b**) **andas bien ~** you're looking very smart.
chivón (*Carib*) **1** *adj* annoying, irritating. **2** *nm*, **chivona** *nf* bore.
chocante *adj* (**a**) (*sorprendente*) startling, striking; (*raro*) odd, strange; (*notable*) noteworthy; **es ~ que ...** it is odd

that ..., it is surprising that ...; it is noteworthy that ...; **lo ~ es que** ... the odd thing about it is that ...

(**b**) (*escandaloso*) shocking, scandalous.

(**c**) (*esp LAm*) (*pesado*) tiresome, tedious, annoying; (*fresco*) cheeky, impertinent; (*repugnante*) disgusting, repulsive; (*antipático*) unpleasant.

chocantería *nf* (*LAm*) (**a**) (*descaro*) impertinence. (**b**) (*chiste*) coarse joke.

chocar [1g] **1** *vt* (**a**) (*asombrar*) to shock; to startle, surprise; **me choca que no lo hayan hecho** I am surprised that they haven't done it; **ello me chocó bastante** it gave me rather a jolt; it did surprise me rather.

(**b**) *vasos* to clink; *mano* to shake; **¡chócala!*** put it there!*, shake (on it)!; ~ **la mano con uno** to shake hands with sb; ~ **los cinco*** to shake on it*.

(**c**) (*Méx*: *asquear*) to disgust; **me choca su actitud** I can't stand his attitude, his attitude makes me sick*.

2 *vi* (**a**) (*sorprender*) to shock; to be surprising, be startling, be odd; **no es de ~** it's not all that surprising.

(**b**) (*Aut etc*) to collide, crash; (*vasos*) to clink; (*platos*) to clatter; (*Mil*) to clash; ~ **con** to collide with, crash into, smash against; to hit, strike; **el buque chocó con una mina** the ship struck a mine; **el balón chocó con el poste** the ball crashed into the post; **por fin chocó con el jefe** finally he fell out with (*o* clashed with) the boss; **esta teoría choca con dificultades** this theory runs into (*o* up against) difficulties.

3 chocarse *vr* (*Méx Aut*) to have a crash.

chocarrear [1a] *vi* (**a**) (*tontear*) to clown, act the fool. (**b**) (*contar chistes*) to tell rude jokes.

chocarrería *nf* (**a**) (*cualidad*) coarseness, vulgarity; scurrility; clownishness. (**b**) (*una ~*: *chiste*) coarse joke, dirty story; (*acción*) clownish act.

chocarrero *adj* (*grosero*) coarse, vulgar, rude; (*escandaloso*) scurrilous; (*de payaso*) clownish.

chock *nm* (*And, Carib Aut*) choke.

choclo¹ *nm* clog; sandal; overshoe; (*Méx*) low-heeled shoe; **meter el ~** (*Méx*) to put one's foot in it.

choclo² *nm* (**a**) (*LAm Agr*) ear of (tender) maize, cob of sweet corn; (*Culin*) (*gen*) corn on the cob; (*guisado*) Indian maize stew.

(**b**) **~s** (*Cono Sur*) children's arms, children's legs.

(**c**) **un ~ de** (*And fig*) a group of, a lot of.

(**d**) (*Cono Sur*) (*dificultad*) difficulty, trouble; (*molestia*) annoyance; (*carga*) burden, task.

choclón *nm* (*Cono Sur*) crowd, mob.

choco¹ (*And, Cono Sur*) **1** *adj* curly, curly-haired. **2** *nm* poodle.

choco² *adj* (*And, Cono Sur*) (*rojo*) dark red; (*chocolate*) chocolate-coloured; (*moreno*) swarthy, dark.

choco³ **1** *adj* (*CAm, Cono Sur, Méx*: *manco*) one-armed; (*cojo*) one-legged; (*tuerto*) one-eyed; (*Cono Sur*: *rabón*) tailless. **2** *nm* (**a**) (*Cono Sur*: *cabo*) stump. (**b**) (*And*: *chistera*) top hat. (**c**) (*Méx***) cunt**.

choco⁴ *nm* (*Zool*) cuttlefish.

choco⁵‡ *nm* (*droga*) = **chocolate** (**c**).

chocolatada *nf* hot chocolate drink, cocoa.

chocolate **1** *adj* (*LAm*) chocolate-coloured; dark red.

2 *nm* (**a**) (*de comer*) chocolate; (*de beber*) drinking chocolate, cocoa; **~ con leche** milk chocolate; **~ sin leche, ~ negro** plain chocolate.

(**b**) (*LAm**: *hum*) blood; **dar a uno agua de su propio ~** (*Méx**) to give sb a taste of his own medicine; **sacar el ~ a uno** to make sb's nose bleed.

(**c**) (‡: *hachís*) hash*, pot‡; **darle al ~** to be hooked on drugs.

chocolatera *nf* (**a**) (*recipiente*) chocolate pot. (**b**) (*: *vehículo viejo*) old thing, piece of junk; (*Aut*) old crock; (*Náut*) hulk.

chocolatería *nf* chocolate factory; *café specializing in serving drinking chocolate.*

chocolatero **1** *adj* fond of chocolate. **2** *nm* (**a**) (*And*: *chcolatera*) chocolate pot. (**b**) (*Carib, Méx*: *viento*) strong northerly wind.

chocolatina *nf* (**a**) chocolate. (**b**) (‡) 100 pesetas.

chocolear [1a] (*And*) **1** *vt* to dock, cut off the tail of. **2** *vi* to get depressed.

chocha¹ *nf* (*t ~* **perdiz**) woodcock.

chochada** *nf* (**a**) (**) cunt**. (**b**) (*CAm**: *nimiedad*) triviality; **~s** bits and pieces.

chochaperdiz *nf* woodcock.

chochear [1a] *vi* (**a**) (*ser senil*) to dodder, be doddery, be senile; to be in one's dotage. (**b**) (*fig*) to be soft, go all sentimental.

chochecientos* *adj pl* umpteen*.

chochera *nf*, **chochez** *nf* (**a**) (*vejez*) dotage; senility; second childhood.

(**b**) (*una ~*) silly thing; sentimental act.

(**c**) (*And, Cono Sur*: *preferido*) favourite, pet; **tener ~ por una** to dote on sb, be crazy about sb.

chochín *nm* (**a**) (*Orn*) wren. (**b**) (‡: *amiga*) bird‡, girlfriend.

chochita *nf* wren.

chocho¹ **1** *adj* (**a**) (*senil*) doddering, doddery, senile.

(**b**) (*fig*) soft, doting, sentimental; **estar ~ por** to dote on, be soft about.

(**c**) (*Cono Sur*: *alegre*) happy.

(**d**) (*CAm**: *nicaragüense*) Nicaraguan.

2 *nm*, **chocha²** *nf* (**a**) (*: *drogadicto*) drug addict.

(**b**) (*CAm**: *nicaragüense*) Nicaraguan.

3 *excl* (*CAm**) no kidding!*, really?

chocho² *nm* cinnamon sweet; **~s** sweets, candies (*US*).

chocho³** *nm* (*Anat*) cunt**.

chocho⁴* *nm* (*lío*) rumpus*, shindy*.

chochoca‡ *nf* (*CAm*) nut‡, head.

chocholear [1a] *vt* (*And*) to spoil, pamper.

chófer *nm*, **chofer** *nm*, **choferesa** *nf* (*LAm*) driver; motorist; (*empleado*) chauffeur.

cholada *nf* (*And*: *pey*) action typical of a *cholo.*

cholar‡ [1a] *vt* to nick‡, pinch*.

cholería *nf* (*And*), **cholerío** *nm* (*And*) group of *cholos.*

cholga *nf* (*LAm*) mussel, clam.

cholo **1** *adj* (**a**) (*LAm*) half-breed, mestizo (*y V* **2**).

(**b**) (*Cono Sur*: *cobarde*) cowardly.

2 *nm*, **chola** *nf* (**a**) (*LAm*) (*mestizo*) half-breed, mestizo; (any) dark-skinned person; (*CAm*: *indio*) half-civilized Indian; (*Cono Sur*: *indio*) Indian.

(**b**) (*LAm hum*: *peruano*) Peruvian.

(**c**) (*Cono Sur*: *cobarde*) coward.

(**d**) (*And, Carib*: *en oración directa*) darling, honey (*US*).

cholla *nf* (**a**) (‡: *cabeza*) nut‡, head; (*fig*) nous*, gumption*. (**b**) (*CAm*: *herida*) wound, sore. (**c**) (*And, CAm*: *pereza*) laziness, slowness.

chollo‡ *nm* (**a**) (*Com*) bargain, snip*; (*prebenda*) plum, soft job; **¡qué ~!** what luck!; **es un ~** it's a doddle*, it's a cinch‡. (**b**) (*amorío*) love-affair.

cholludo *adj* (*And, CAm*) lazy, slow.

chomba *nf* (*Cono Sur*) = **chompa.**

chompa *nf* (*LAm*) jumper, sweater.

chompipe *nm* (*CAm*) turkey.

chonco (*CAm*) **1** *adj* = **choco³**. **2** *nm* stump.

chonchón *nm* (*Cono Sur*) lamp.

chongo *nm* (**a**) (*Cono Sur*: *cuchillo*) blunt knife, worn-out knife. (**b**) (*Carib*: *caballo*) old horse. (**c**) **~s** (*CAm, Méx*) (*trenzas*) pigtails, tresses; (*moño*) bun.

chonta *nf* (*And*) palm shoots.

chontal *adj* (**a**) (*CAm*) *indio* wild, uncivilized; (*rebelde*) rebellious; (*revoltoso*) unruly. (**b**) (*And, CAm, Carib*: *inculto*) uncivilized; (*grosero*) rough, coarse; (*Carib*: *de habla inculta*) rough-spoken.

chop *nm* (*LAm*) tankard, mug.

chopa* *nf* jacket.

chopazo* *nm* (*Cono Sur*), **chope*** *nm* (*Cono Sur*) punch, bash*.

chopera *nf* poplar grove.

chopería *nf* (*Cono Sur*) bar.

chopo *nm* (**a**) (*Bot*) black poplar; **~ de Italia, ~ lombardo** Lombardy poplar.

(**b**) (*: *Mil*) gun; **cargar con el ~** (*fig*) to join up, do one's military service.

choque *nm* (**a**) (*impacto*) impact; (*de vehículo en movimiento*) jolt, jar; (*de explosión*) blast, shock wave.

(**b**) (*ruido*) crash; (*de platos etc*) clatter; (*de vasos*) clink.

(**c**) (*Aut, Ferro etc*) crash, smash; collision; **~ de frente, ~ frontal** head-on collision; **~ de trenes** rail smash, rail accident.

(**d**) **~ eléctrico** (*Elec*) electric shock.

(**e**) (*Med*) shock.

(**f**) (*Mil y fig*) clash; conflict; **entrar en ~** to clash; **estar en abierto ~ con** to conflict openly with.

choquezuela *nf* kneecap.

chorar‡ [1a] *vt casa* to burgle; *objeto* to rip off‡.

chorba‡ *nf* bird‡, girlfriend.

chorbo‡ *nm* (**a**) (*novio*) boyfriend; (*tío*) bloke‡, guy*. (**b**) (*coime*) pimp.

chorcha *nf* (**a**) (*Méx*) (*fiesta*) noisy party; **una ~ de amigos** a group of friends (out for a good time).

(**b**) (*CAm Orn*) crest, comb.
(**c**) (*CAm Med*) goitre.
(**d**) (*CAm***: *clítoris*) clit**, clitoris.
chorchero *adj* (*Méx*) party-loving.
chorchi‡ *nm* soldier.
chorear [1a] **1** *vt* (‡) (**a**) **me chorea** it gets up my nose‡; **estar choreado** to be miffed*, be upset. (**b**) (*robar*) to pinch*, nick‡. **2** *vi* (*Cono Sur*) to grumble, complain.
choreo* *nm* (*Cono Sur*) grouse*, complaint.
chori *nm* (**a**) (*cuchillo*) chiv‡, knife. (**b**) (*ladrón*) thief.
choricear‡ [1a] *vt* to rip off‡, lift*.
choricería‡ *nf* crookedness*, corruption.
choricero‡ *nm* crook*.
chorizada‡ *nf* swindle, con*; theft.
chorizar‡ [1f] *vt* to nick‡, rip off‡.
chorizo 1 *adj* (‡) lousy‡, bloody awful‡.
2 *nm* (**a**) (*Culin*) hard pork sausage, salami.
(**b**) (*Circo*) balancing pole.
(**c**) (**: *Anat*) prick**.
(**d**) (*And, Cono Sur Culin*) rump steak.
(**e**) (*And, Cono Sur Arquit*) mixture of clay and straw used in plastering.
(**f**) (‡) (*matón*) thug, lout; (*ladrón*) small-time crook*; (*carterista*) pickpocket.
(**g**) (*And*: *idiota*) idiot.
(**h**) (*Carib pey*) mulatto.
chorlitejo *nm*, **chorlito** *nm* (*Orn*) plover.
chorlo *nm*, **chorla** *nf* (*And, CAm, Carib*) great-great-grandchild.
choro¹‡ *nm* (**a**) (*persona*) thief, burglar. (**b**) (*Ling*) thieves' slang.
choro² *nm* (*And, Cono Sur*: *Zool*) mussel.
chorote *nm* (**a**) (*bebida*) (*Carib, Méx*) drinking chocolate (with brown sugar); (*And*) thick drinking chocolate.
(**b**) (*Carib*) (any) thick drink; (*bebida aguada*) watery drink; (*café*) coffee.
(**c**) (*And*: *chocolatera*) unglazed chocolate pot.
chorra *nf* (**a**) (‡) luck, jam‡; **¡qué ~ tiene!** look at that for jam!‡ (**b**) (*Cono Sur*) underworld slang. (**c**) (**: *Anat*) prick**. (**d**) **de ~‡** (*adv*) by chance. (**e**) (‡: *idiota*) idiot.
chorrada *nf* (**a**) (*de leche etc*) extra drop; bonus; **dar algo con ~** to give sth and a bit extra. (**b**) (*adorno*) unnecessary adornment; (*detalle*) superfluous detail. (**c**) (*: *dicho*) stupid remark; **~s** nonsense, drivel. (**d**) (*objeto*) knick-knack. (**e**) (**: *meados*) piss**; **echar la ~** to have a piss**.
chorrar‡ [1a] *vt* = **chorar**.
chorrear [1a] **1** *vt* (**a**) (*: *regañar*) to tick off*, dress down*.
(**b**) (*And*: *mojar*) to soak.
(**c**) (*Cono Sur‡*) to rip off‡.
2 *vi* (**a**) (*salir a chorros*) to gush (forth), spout (out), spirt; (*gotear*) to drip, trickle; **~ de sudor** to run with sweat; **la ropa chorrea todavía** his clothes are still wringing wet.
(**b**) (*fig*) to trickle (in, away *etc*); **chorrean todavía las solicitudes** the applications are still trickling in.
3 chorrearse *vr*: **~ algo** (*And*) to pinch sth*.
chorreo *nm* (**a**) (*de agua*) gushing, spouting; dripping; trickling.
(**b**) (*fig*) constant drain (on resources *etc*).
(**c**) (‡: *reprimenda*) ticking-off*, dressing-down*.
(**d**) **~ mental‡** nonsense, rubbish.
chorreón *nm* cascade.
chorrera *nf* (**a**) (*pico*) spout; (*canal*) channel, runlet.
(**b**) (*señal*) mark (left by dripping water *etc*).
(**c**) (*de río*) rapids.
(**d**) **~s** (*Cos*) frill, lace adornment.
(**e**) (*LAm fig*) string, stream, lot; **una ~ de** a whole string of, a lot of.
(**f**) (*Carib**: *regañada*) ticking-off*.
(**g**) *V* **jamón**.
chorrero‡ *adj* jammy‡, lucky.
chorretada *nf* (**a**) (*chorro*) spirt, squirt, jet. (**b**) = **chorrada** (**a**).
chorrillo *nm* (*fig*) constant stream, steady trickle.
chorro *nm* (**a**) (*de agua etc*) jet; spirt, squirt, stream; dribble, trickle; **beber a ~** to drink a jet of wine (from a wineskin); **llover a ~s** to pour; **salir a ~s** to gush forth, come spirting out.
(**b**) (*Téc*) jet, blast; (*Aer*) jet; **~ de arena** sandblast; **~ de vapor** steam jet; **avión a ~** jet plane; **motor a ~** jet engine; **con propulsión a ~** jet-propelled.
(**c**) (*fig*) stream; **un ~ de palabras** a stream of words, a torrent of words; **un ~ de gente** (*Méx*) lots of people; **un ~ de voz** a verbal blast, an awfully loud voice; **a ~s** in plenty, in abundance; **hablar a ~s** to talk nineteen to the dozen; **soltar el ~** to burst out laughing; to produce a torrent of insults (*etc*).
(**d**) (‡: *suerte*) jam‡, luck; **¡qué ~ tiene!** look at that for jam!‡
(**e**) (*And*: *de látigo*) strand (of a whip).
(**f**) (*CAm*: *grifo*) tap, faucet.
(**g**) (*Carib**: *reprimenda*) ticking-off*.
(**h**) (*Cono Sur**: *ladrón*) thief, pickpocket.
chorva *etc* = **chorba** *etc*.
chota¹‡ *nmf* (*parásito*) hanger-on; (*pelotillero*) creep‡, toady; (*de cárcel*) trusty.
chota²‡ *nf*: **la ~** (*Méx*) the fuzz‡.
chotacabras *nm invar* nightjar.
chotear [1a] **1** *vt* (**a**) (*LAm*: *burlarse de*) to make fun of.
(**b**) (*And*: *mimar*) to spoil, pamper.
(**c**) (*CAm*) *sospechoso* to shadow, tail.
2 chotearse *vr* (**a**) (*bromear*) to joke, take things as a joke; **~ de** to make fun of, ridicule. (**b**) (‡) to cough‡, inform.
choteo *nm* joking, amusement.
chotis *nm invar* (**a**) schottische. (**b**) *traditional dance of Madrid*. (**c**) **ser más agarrado que un ~*** to be tight-fisted.
choto¹ 1 *adj* (*CAm*) abundant, plentiful; **estar ~ de** to be full of, be loaded with; **de ~** free, for nothing. **2** *nm* (*cabrito*) kid; (*ternero*) calf.
choto²** (*Cono Sur*) **1** *nm* (**a**) (*pene*) prick**, cock**. (**b**) **viejo ~** stupid old git‡. **2** *adj* (*de poco valor*) crummy‡; (*viejo*) clapped-out*.
chotuno *adj cabrito, ternero* sucking, very young; *cordero* weakly; **oler a ~** to smell bad.
chova *nf* crow, rook; **~ piquirroja** chough.
chovinismo *nm etc* = **chauvinismo** *etc*.
chow-chow ['tʃautʃau] *nm, pl* **chow-chow** chow.
choza *nf* hut, shack.
chozno *nm*, **chozna** *nf* great-great-great-grandchild.
chrisma ['krisma] *nf*, **christma(s)** ['krisma] *nm, pl* **christmas** ['krismas] Christmas card.
chubasco *nm* (**a**) (*Met*) shower, squall. (**b**) (*fig*) setback; bad patch; **aguantar el ~** (*fig*) to weather the storm.
chubascoso *adj* squally, stormy.
chubasquero *nm* (**a**) (*hule*) oilskins; (*gabardina*) light raincoat; anorak. (**b**) (‡: *hum*) French letter.
chucán *adj* (*CAm*) (*bufón*) buffoonish; (*grosero*) coarse, rude.
chúcaro *adj* (*LAm*) *animal* wild, untamed; *persona* shy.
chucear [1a] *vt* (*LAm*) to prick, goad.
chuco *adj* (*And, CAm, Méx*) *pescado etc* high, off; (*CAm*: *asqueroso*) disgusting, filthy.
chucrú *nm*, **chucrut** *nm* sauerkraut.
chucha *nf* (**a**) (*Zool*) dog, bitch; **¡~!** down! (**b**) (*: *novia*) sweetheart. (**c**) (*And*: *Zool*) opossum. (**d**) (*And*: *olor*) body odour. (**e**) (*And*: *juego*) hide-and-seek. (**f**) (*And, Cono Sur***: *Anat*) cunt**. (**g**) (‡: *Fin*) one peseta.
chuchada *nf* (*CAm*) trick, swindle.
chuchear¹ [1a] *vi* to hunt, trap, fowl.
chuchear² [1a] *vi* = **cuchichear**.
chuchería *nf* (**a**) (*adorno*) trinket, bit of jewellery, knick-knack. (**b**) (*bocado*) titbit, dainty morsel; (*dulce*) sweet.
chuchito *nm* = **chucho** (**i**).
chucho 1 *adj* (**a**) (*And*) *fruta* soft, watery; *persona* wrinkled.
(**b**) (*CAm*: *tacaño*) mean.
(**c**) (*Méx*: *chismoso*) gossipy.
2 *nm* (**a**) (*Zool*) hound, mongrel, mutt‡; **¡~!** down boy!
(**b**) (*: *novio*) sweetheart.
(**c**) (*Carib*: *Ferro*) switch; siding.
(**d**) (*Carib*: *látigo*) rawhide whip.
(**e**) (*Cono Sur**: *cárcel*) jail.
(**f**) (*LAm*) (*escalofrío*) shakes, shivers; (*fiebre*) fever; **entrarle a uno el ~*** to get the jitters*.
(**g**) (*CAm**: *ostentoso*) spiv*.
(**h**) (*LAm‡*) joint‡, reefer‡.
(**i**) (*And, CAm, Méx Culin*) tamale.
chuchoca* *nf* (*Cono Sur*): **estar en la ~** to be in the thick of it, be where the action is.
chuchumeca *nf* (*And, Cono Sur*) whore.
chuchumeco *nm* (**a**) (*tacaño*) mean person, skinflint.
(**b**) (*Cono Sur*: *enfermizo*) sickly person; (*enano*) dwarf, runt; (*derrochador*) wastrel; (*And*: *viejo*) old dodderer.
(**c**) (*And, Carib**) toff*, dude* (*US*).
(**d**) (*Carib**: *idiota*) idiot.

chueca *nf* (**a**) (*Bot*) stump.
(**b**) (*Anat*) rounded bone; round head of a bone.
(**c**) (*fig*) practical joke, hoax, prank; **gastar una ~ a uno** to play a joke on sb.

chueco *adj* (**a**) (*LAm*: *patizambo*) knock-kneed; (*And, Cono Sur*: *patituerto*) pigeon-toed; (*And*: *cojo*) lame; (*Méx*: *manco*) one-armed, (*con una sola pierna*) one-legged; (*CAm, Carib, Cono Sur, Méx*: *torcido*) crooked, twisted, bent; (*corrupto*) bent‡, crooked*; (*Méx*: *zurdo*) left-handed; **un negocio ~** a crooked deal*.
(**b**) (*Méx*: *de mala vida*) loose-living; (*sospechoso*) suspicious.

chufa *nf* (**a**) (*Bot*) chufa, tiger nut. (**b**) (*: *puñetazo*) bash*, punch. (**c**) (‡: *Fin*) one peseta.

chufeta *nf* = **chufleta**.

chufla *nf* joke, merry quip; mockery, derision; **a ~** jokingly; **tomar algo a ~** to take sth as a joke.

chuflarse [1a] *vr* to joke, make jokes; to take things as a joke.

chuflay *nm* (*Cono Sur*) punch (*drink*).

chufleta *nf* joke, merry quip; taunt.

chufletear [1a] *vi* (*bromear*) to joke, make jokes; (*mofarse*) to jeer, make taunting remarks.

chuico *nm* (*Cono Sur*) carafe.

chula *nf* (**a**) (*madrileña*) woman from the back streets (of Madrid), low-class woman, coarse woman. (**b**) (*charra*) loud wench, flashy female, brassy girl. (**c**) (*LAm*: *novia*) girlfriend.

chulada *nf* (**a**) (*grosería*) coarse thing; (*cosa graciosa*) funny thing; (*truco*) mean trick.
(**b**) = **chulería** (**a**).

chulángano‡ *nm* roughneck‡, tough*.

chulapa *nf* Madrid girl in traditional dress.

chulear* [1a] **1** *vt* to pinch*, nick‡. **2** *vi* to brag, talk big*, show off. **3 chulearse** *vr*: **~ de** to take the mickey out of‡.

chulería *nf* (**a**) (*cualidad*: *encanto*) natural charm, winning ways; (*pey*: *ordinariez*) commonness, vulgarity; (*pey*: *ostentación*) flashiness; flamboyant manner.
(**b**) (*la ~*) the *chulos* (*collectively, as a group*).
(**c**) (*una ~*) = **chulada** (**a**).

chulesco *adj* = **chulo 1**.

chuleta 1 *nf* (**a**) (*Culin*) chop, cutlet; **~ de puerco** pork chop; **~ de ternera** veal chop.
(**b**) (*Cos*) insert, piece let in; (*Téc*) filling.
(**c**) (*: *golpe*) punch, bash*.
(**d**) (*: *Univ*) crib*, trot (*US*); (*TV*) autocue, teleprompter.
(**e**) **~s** (*patillas*) side-whiskers.
(**f**) (*: *persona*) (*elegante*) toff*; (*fresco*) cheeky individual*; (*agresivo*) pushy person*; (*fachendón*) show-off*, swank*.
(**g**) (*: *Golf*) divot.
2 *nm* (*) = **chulo 3** (**b**).
3 *adj invar* (*) cheeky*, saucy; pushy*.

chuletada *nf* barbecue.

chuletón *nm* large steak, T-bone steak.

chulillo *nm* (*And*) tradesman's assistant.

chulo 1 *adj* (**a**) (*gracioso*) amusing; (*encantador*) charming, attractive, winning.
(**b**) *aspecto* smart, showy, attractive; (*pey*) flashy, vulgar, gaudy.
(**c**) *aire, porte* proud; *paso* jaunty, swaggering; **con el sombrero a lo ~** with his hat at a rakish angle; **iba muy ~** he walked with a swagger, he swaggered along.
(**d**) (*) *comportamiento* bold, free from servility, outspoken; (*pey*: *fresco*) overbold, fresh*; (*impertinente*) pert, saucy; (*revoltoso*) obstreperous; (*agresivo*) truculent; **se puso en plan ~*** he got stroppy*; **no te pongas ~ conmigo** don't get fresh with me*.
(**e**) *carácter* slick; rascally, villainous.
(**f**) (*And, CAm, Méx*) (*bonito*) pretty; (*elegante*) attractive, elegant, graceful.
(**g**) (*: *muy bueno*) brilliant*, super*.
2 *adv* (*CAm**, *Méx**) well; **jugar ~** to play well.
3 *nm* (**a**) *typical working-class Madrilenian* (≃ *Cockney*); easy-going sort, free-and-easy person.
(**b**) (*pey*: *gandul*) spiv*, layabout, ne'er-do-well; (*matón*) tough guy*, lout; (*bribón*) villain, rascal; **~ (de putas)** pimp, pander.
(**c**) (*Taur*) bullfighter's assistant.
(**d**) (*And Orn*) turkey buzzard.

chulón *adj* (*CAm*) naked.

chulleco *adj* (*Cono Sur*) twisted, crooked.

chullo *nm* (*And*) woollen hat.

chuma *nf* (*And, Cono Sur*) drunkenness.

chumacera *nf* (*Mec*) ball bearing, journal bearing; (*Náut*) rowlock, oarlock (*US*).

chumarse [1a] *vr* (*And*) to get drunk.

chumbar [1a] *vt* (**a**) (*Cono Sur*: *perro*) to attack, go for; **¡chúmbale!** at him, boy! (**b**) (*And*: *fusilar*) to shoot. (**c**) (*And*) *bebé* to swaddle.

chumbe *nm* (*LAm*) sash.

chumbera *nf*, **chumbimba** *nf* (*LAm*) prickly pear.

chumbo¹ *nm* (**a**) (*Bot*) prickly pear (*fruit*); *V* **higo**. (**b**) (*And***) prick**.

chumbo² *nm* (*Cono Sur*) shot, pellet.

chumeco *nm* (*CAm*) apprentice.

chuminada* *nf* (**a**) (*tontería*) silly thing, piece of nonsense. (**b**) (*detalle*) petty detail.

chumino** *nm* cunt**.

chumpa *nf* (*CAm*) jacket.

chumpi *nm* (*And*) = **chumbe**.

chumpipe *nm* (*CAm*) turkey.

chumpipear [1a] *vi* (*CAm*) to wander about.

chunco *adj* (*And, CAm*) = **choco³**.

chunche* *nm* (*CAm*) whatsit*, thingumabob*.

chuncho (*And*) **1** *adj* (*salvaje*) savage; (*inculto*) uncivilized; (*tímido*) bashful, shy. **2** *nm*, **chuncha** *nf* savage Indian.

chuneco*, -a (*CAm*) *adj, nm/f* Jamaican.

chunga* *nf* joke; fun, banter; **contar ~s** to crack jokes*; **estar de ~** to be in a merry mood; **decir algo de ~** to say sth banteringly; **tomar las cosas en ~** to take things as a joke.

chungo‡ *adj* (*malo*) bad, rottten; (*desagradable*) nasty; (*feo*) ugly; (*dudoso*) dicey*, dodgy*; (*falso*) *billete* dud*; (*enfermo*) poorly, under the weather.

chungón* *nm*, **chungona*** *nf* joker, tease.

chunguearse* [1a] *vr* to gag, crack jokes*, be in a merry mood; to banter; **~ de uno** to have a bit of fun with sb, make fun of sb.

chuño *nm* (*LAm*) potato starch, dried potato.

chupa¹* *nf*: **poner a uno como ~ de dómine** to give sb a tremendous ticking off*; to shower insults on sb; **en la prensa le pusieron como ~ de dómine** they gave him a tremendous pasting in the press*.

chupa² *nf* (**a**) (*LAm*: *embriaguez*) drunkenness. (**b**) (*CAm*: *bolsa*) bag. (**c**) (‡) (*chaleco*) waistcoat; (*chaqueta*) leather jacket.

chupachupa 1 *nmf* (‡) sucker‡. **2** *nf* lollipop.

chupa-chups* *nm invar* lollipop.

chupada *nf* suck; (*de pipa etc*) pull, puff; (*de bebida*) sip; **~s** sucking, suction; **dar ~s a la pipa** to puff away at one's pipe; **se cree la última ~ del mate*** (*Cono Sur*) he thinks he's the cat's pyjamas*.

chupadero* *nm* (*Argentina*: 1975-81) *secret military prison.*

chupado 1 *adj* (**a**) *persona* skinny, gaunt; emaciated; **~ de cara** with a gaunt face, lantern-jawed.
(**b**) *falda* tight.
(**c**) **estar ~** (*LAm**) to be drunk.
(**d**) **está ~‡** it's dead easy*, it's a cinch‡.
2 *nm* (*Cono Sur**: *desaparecido*) missing person.

chupador *nm* (**a**) (*aro*) teething ring; (*de biberón*) teat. (**b**) (*LAm*: *borracho*) drunkard. (**c**) (*LAm*: *fumador*) smoker.

chupaflor *nm* (*CAm, Carib*) hummingbird.

chupagasolina* 1 *adj invar* gas-guzzling*, heavy on petrol. **2** *nm invar* gas-guzzler*.

chupalla *nf* (*Cono Sur, Méx*) straw hat.

chupamangas‡ *nm invar* (*And, Cono Sur*), **chupamedias‡** *nm invar* (*And, Cono Sur*) creep‡, bootlicker*.

chupamirto *nm* (*Carib, Méx*) hummingbird.

chupandina* *nf* (*Cono Sur*) boozy party*.

chupar [1a] **1** *vt* (**a**) (*gen*) to suck; (*sacar*) to suck out, suck up; (*absorber*) to absorb, take in, take up; *bebida* to sip; *esencia etc* to extract; *pecho, caramelo etc* to suck; *pipa etc* to suck, smoke, puff at; *sello* to lick, moisten (with one's tongue).
(**b**) (*LAm*: *fumar*) to smoke.
(**c**) (*: *beber*) to drink (*esp* to excess), knock back*.
(**d**) (*fig*) to milk; to sap; **le chupan el dinero** they are milking him (of his money); **el trabajo le chupa la salud** his work is undermining his health.
(**e**) (*LAm**: *aguantar*) to put up with, take.
(**f**) **~ la pelota** (*Fútbol*) to be greedy with the ball, not to pass the ball.
2 *vi* (**a**) to suck.
(**b**) (*LAm**: *beber*) to booze*.

(**c**) (*LAm*: *fumar*) to smoke.

3 chuparse *vr* (**a**) (*) **¡chúpate ésa!** put that in your pipe and smoke it!*

(**b**) **~ el dedo** to suck one's finger; *V t* **dedo.**

(**c**) **~ un insulto** (*LAm*) to put up with an insult, swallow an insult.

(**d**) (*Med*) to waste away, decline, get thin.

chupasangres *nm invar* (*fig*) bloodsucker.

chupatintas *nm invar* penpusher; petty clerk, minor bureaucrat; (*) toady, creep‡.

chupe *nm* (*LAm*: *sopa*) *a typical spicy soup*; (*cocido*) stew; (*Cono Sur*: *tapa*) snack.

chupeta *nf* (*Náut*) roundhouse.

chupete *nm* (**a**) (*aro etc*) dummy, pacifier (*US*); (*de biberón*) teat; (*LAm*: *pirulí*) lollipop. (**b**) (*LAm*: *chupada*) suck. (**c**) **de ~** *V* **rechupete.**

chupi* 1 *adj* super*, brilliant*. **2** *adv*: **pasarlo ~** to have a great time*.

chupinazo *nm* (**a**) loud bang. (**b**) (*Dep*) hard kick, fierce shot.

chupinudo* *adj* = **chupi.**

chupo *nm* (**a**) (*LAm Med*) boil. (**b**) (*And*: *biberón*) baby's bottle.

chupón *nm* (**a**) (*Bot*) sucker.

(**b**) (*: *persona*) sponger*, hanger-on, parasite; swindler.

(**c**) (*dulce*) lollipop, sucking sweet; **~ de caramelo** toffee apple.

(**d**) (*Fútbol*) greedy player.

(**e**) (*LAm*) dummy, pacifier (*US*); (*biberón*) baby's bottle; (*Méx*) teat.

(**f**) (*And, Carib*: *de pipa etc*) puff, pull.

(**g**) (*And Med*) boil.

chupóptero* *nm* rich layabout; bloodsucker.

churdón *nm* (*fruta*) raspberry; (*planta*) raspberry cane; (*jarabe*) raspberry syrup, raspberry paste.

churi‡ *nm* chiv‡, knife.

churo¹ *adj* (*And, Cono Sur*) handsome, attractive.

churo² *nm* (**a**) (*And Mús*) *coiled wind instrument.* (**b**) (*And*: *escalera*) spiral staircase. (**c**) (*And*: *rizo*) curl. (**d**) (*And‡*: *cárcel*) nick‡, jail.

churra¹ *nf* (*And, Cono Sur*) girl.

churra² *nf* (*suerte*) luck, jam‡.

churrasco *nm* (*LAm*: *barbacoa*) barbecue, barbecued meat; (*LAm*) steak; (*Cono Sur*: *filete*) steak.

churrasquear [1a] *vi* (*Cono Sur*) to eat steak.

churrasquería *nf* barbecue stall.

churre¹ *nf* thick grease; filth.

churre² *nm* (*And*) bloke‡, guy* (*US*).

churrería *nf* fritter stall.

churrero 1 *adj* (‡) lucky, jammy‡. **2** *nm*, **churrera** *nf* fritter maker, fritter seller.

churrete *nm* grease spot, dirty mark.

churretear [1a] *vt* (*LAm*) to spot, stain, dirty.

churrias* *nfpl* (*And, CAm, Carib*) diarrhoea.

churriento *adj* (**a**) (*mugriento*) greasy; filthy. (**b**) (*LAm Med*) loose.

churrigueresco *adj* (**a**) (*Arquit*) Churrigueresque (*lavishly ornamented*). (**b**) (*fig*) excessively ornate, flowery; flashy.

churro 1 *adj lana* coarse; *oveja* coarse-wooled.

2 *nm* (**a**) (*Culin*) fritter; **venderse como ~s** to sell like hot cakes.

(**b**) (*: *chapuza*) botch, mess; **el dibujo ha salido un ~** the sketch came out all wrong, he messed up the drawing.

(**c**) (*: *chiripa*) fluke.

(**d**) (*Anat*‡‡) prick‡‡.

(**e**) **Juan es un ~** (*And, Cono Sur**) Juan is dishy*.

(**f**) (*Méx**) bad film.

churrullero *adj* talkative, gossipy.

churruscar [1g] **1** *vt* to burn, scorch. **2 churruscarse** *vr* to burn, scorch.

churrusco¹ *nm* burnt toast.

churrusco² *adj* (*And, CAm*) *pelo* kinky, curly.

churumbel* *nm* (*niño*) kid*, brat; (*tío*) bloke‡, guy*.

churumbela *nf* (**a**) (*Mús*) flageolet. (**b**) (*LAm*: *para mate*) maté cup; (*And*: *pipa*) short-stemmed pipe. (**c**) (*And*: *preocupación*) worry, care.

churumen* *nm* nous*, savvy*.

chus: **no decir ~ ni mus** not to say a word.

chuscada *nf* funny remark, joke; (*pey*) coarse joke.

chusco *adj* (**a**) (*gracioso*) funny, droll; *persona* coarse but amusing; *suceso* oddly amusing. (**b**) (*And*) *perro* mongrel; *caballo etc* ordinary; *persona* coarse, ill-mannered.

chuse *nm* (*And*) blanket.

chusma *nf* rabble, mob, riffraff.

chusmaje *nm* (*LAm*) = **chusma.**

chuspa *nf* (*LAm*) bag, pouch.

chusquero* *nm* (*Mil*) ranker.

chut *nm* (**a**) (*Dep*) shot (at goal). (**b**) (‡: *droga*) shot*, fix‡.

chuta¹‡ *nf* (**a**) (*jeringuilla*) needle. (**b**) = **chut** (**b**).

chuta²‡ *excl* ¡~! (*Cono Sur*) good God!, good heavens!

chutador(a) *nm/f* (*Dep*) shooter.

chutar [1a] **1** *vi* (**a**) (*Dep*) to shoot (at goal).

(**b**) **está que chuta*** (*persona*) he's hopping mad*; (*comida*) it's scalding hot.

(**c**) (*: *ir bien*) to go well; **esto va que chuta** it's going fine*; **y va que chuta** and he'll be perfectly happy; and that's more than enough.

2 chutarse‡ *vr* to give o.s. a shot* (of drugs), shoot up‡.

chutazo* *nm* fierce drive, fierce shot (at goal).

chute¹‡ *nm* = **chut** (**b**).

chute²* *adj* (*Cono Sur*) spruce, natty*.

chuzar [1f] *vt* (*And*) to prick; to sting, hurt.

chuzo 1 *nm* (**a**) (*Mil, Hist*) pike; (*bastón*) spiked stick, metal-tipped stick; (*aguijón*) prick, goad; (*Cono Sur*: *zapapico*) pickaxe; (*Carib, Cono Sur*: *látigo*) whip; (*CAm Orn*) beak; (*CAm*: *de alacrán*) sting; **aunque caigan ~s** whatever the weather, (*fig*) come what may; **echar ~s** (*fig*) to brag; **llover a ~s** to rain cats and dogs, rain in torrents; **nevar a ~s** to snow heavily.

(**b**) (*And*) shoe.

(**c**) (‡‡: *Anat*) prick‡‡.

2 *adj* (*CAm**) *pelo* lank.

chuzón *adj* (**a**) (*astuto*) wily, sharp, cunning. (**b**) (*gracioso*) witty, amusing.

chuzonada *nf* piece of tomfoolery, piece of buffoonery.

D

D, d [de] *nf* (*letra*) D, d.
D. (**a**) (*Fin*) *abr de* **debe** debit side. (**b**) *abr de* **Don** Esquire, Esq. (**c**) *abr de* **diciembre** December, Dec.
Da., D.ª *abr de* **Doña.**
dable *adj* possible, feasible, practicable; **no es ~ hacerlo** it is not possible to do it; **en lo que sea ~** as far as possible, as far as is feasible.
dabuti‡ 1 *adj* (*gracioso*) funny, killing; (*estupendo*) super*, smashing*. **2** *adv*: **pasarlo ~** to have a great time*.
DAC *nf abr de* **división acorazada** armoured division.
daca *interj* hand it over!; **en ~ las pajas** in a jiffy; **andar al ~ y toma** to argue back and forth, bicker.
dacrón *nm* dacron.
dactilar *adj* finger (*atr*); **huella ~, impresión ~** fingerprint.
dactílico *adj* dactylic.
dáctilo *nm* dactyl.
dactilografía *nf* typing.
dactilografiar [1c] *vt* to type.
dactilógrafo, -a *nm/f* typist.
dactilograma *nm* (*Méx*) fingerprint.
dadá *nf*, **dadaísmo** *nm* dadaism.
dadista *nm* (*Méx*) gambler.
dadito *nm* (*Culin*) small cube; **cortar en ~s** to dice.
dádiva *nf* gift, present; (*fig*) sop.
dadivosidad *nf* generosity, lavishness with gifts.
dadivoso *adj* generous, open-handed, lavish with gifts.
dado[1] *nm* (**a**) (*en juegos*) die, dice; **~s** dice; **el ~ está tirado** the die is cast. (**b**) (*Arquit*) dado. (**c**) (*Mec*) block. (**d**) (*Culin*) cube; **cortar a ~s** to dice.
dado[2] *ptp de* **dar** (**a**) **en un caso ~** in a given case; **dada su corta edad** in view of his youth; **dadas estas circunstancias** since these circumstances exist, in view of these circumstances.
(**b**) **ser ~ a** to be given to; **es muy ~ a discutir** he is much given to arguing.
(**c**) **~ que ...** (*como conj*) provided that ..., so long as ...; given that ..., granted that ...
dador(a) *nm/f* (*gen*) giver, donor; (*de carta*) bearer; (*Naipes*) dealer; (*Com*) drawer; **~ de sangre** blood donor.
Dafne *nf* Daphne.
daga *nf* dagger, stiletto; (*Carib*) machete.
dagazo *nm* (*Carib, Méx*) stab wound.
daguerrotipo *nm* daguerrotype.
daifa *nf* mistress, concubine; prostitute.
daiquiri *nm* daiquiri.
dalia *nf* dahlia.
Dalila *nf* Delilah.
daliniano *adj* Daliesque.
Dalmacia *nf* Dalmatia.
dálmata *nmf* dalmatian (dog).
daltoniano *adj* colour-blind.
daltonismo *nm* colour blindness.
dallar [1a] *vt* to scythe, mow with a scythe.
dalle *nm* scythe.
dama *nf* (**a**) (*gen*) lady; (*noble*) lady, gentlewoman; (*amante*) mistress, lover; concubine; **¡D~s y caballeros!** (*esp LAm*) Ladies and gentlemen!; **el poeta y su ~** the poet and his lady, the poet and his mistress; **primera ~** (*Teat*) leading lady; (*Pol*) first lady (*US*), president's wife; **~ de compañía** (*LAm*) (lady) companion; **~ de hierro** Iron Lady; **~ de honor** (*real*) lady-in-waiting; (*en boda*) bridesmaid, maid of honour; **~ joven** (*Teat*) ingénue; **~ regidora** carnival queen.
(**b**) (*Naipes, Ajedrez*) queen; (*Damas*) king.
(**c**) **~s** (*juego*) draughts, checkers (*US*).
damajuana *nf*, **damasana** *nf* (*LAm*) demijohn.
Damasco *nm* Damascus.
damasco *nm* (**a**) (*tela*) damask. (**b**) (*Bot*) damson; (*LAm*: *fruta*) apricot; (*árbol*) apricot tree.
damasquinado *nm* (*Téc*) damascene (work).
damasquinar [1a] *vt* (*Téc*) to damascene, damask.
damasquino *adj* (*Téc*) damask; damascene.
damesana *nf* (*LAm*) demijohn.
damisela *nf* (*Hist*) damsel; (*pey*) courtesan, prostitute.
damita *nf* (*CAm*) young lady.
damnificar [1g] *vt* (*herir*) to injure, harm; (*dejar incapacitado*) to disable; (*perjudicar*) to harm the interests of; **los damnificados** (*en accidente etc*) the victims, those affected, those who have suffered loss.
Dámocles *nm* Damocles.
dandi, dandy 1 *nm* dandy, fop. **2** *atr*: **estilo ~** dandy style.
dandismo *nm* foppishness, foppish ways; extreme elegance.
danés 1 *adj* Danish. **2** *nm*, **danesa** *nf* (**a**) (*persona*) Dane. (**b**) (*perro*) Great Dane. **3** *nm* (*Ling*) Danish.
Daniel *nm* Daniel.
danone* *nm* police-car.
danta *nf* (*And, CAm, Méx*) tapir; (*anta*) elk, moose.
dantesco *adj* (**a**) (*liter*) of Dante, relating to Dante. (**b**) (*fig*) Dantesque; horrific, weird, macabre; hellish, infernal.
dantzari [dan'sari] *nm* Basque folk-dancer.
Danubio *nm* Danube.
danza *nf* (**a**) (*gen*) dancing; (*una ~*) dance; **~ de aparamiento** courtship dance, mating display; **~ contemporánea** contemporary dance; **~ de espadas** sword dance; **~ guerrera** war dance; **~ macabra, ~ de la muerte** dance of death, danse macabre; **~ de salón** ballroom dancing; **~ de los siete velos** dance of the seven veils; **~ del vientre** belly-dance.
(**b**) (*: *asunto*) shady affair, suspect deal; mess; **meterse en la ~** to get caught up in a shady affair.
(**c**) (*: *jaleo*) row, rumpus*; **armar una ~** to kick up a row; **no metas los perros en ~** let sleeping dogs lie.
danzante *nm*, **danzanta** *nf* (**a**) (*bailarín*) dancer. (**b**) (*: *persona activa*) hustler, live wire, person who is always on the go; (*pey*) busybody. (**c**) (*casquivano*) scatterbrain.
danzar [1f] **1** *vt* to dance. **2** *vi* (**a**) (*bailar*) to dance (*t fig*). (**b**) (*: *entrometerse*) to meddle; to butt in, shove one's oar in.
danzarín, -ina *nm/f* (**a**) (*bailarín*) dancer; artistic dancer, professional dancer; **~ del vientre** belly-dancer. (**b**) = **danzante** (**b**) *y* (**c**).
dañado *adj* (**a**) (*gen*) damaged; *fruta etc* spoiled; bad. (**b**) (*fig*) bad, wicked, evil.
dañar [1a] **1** *vt objeto* to damage; *persona* to harm, hurt; (*estropear*) to spoil. **2 dañarse** *vr* to get damaged, get hurt; to spoil; to rot, go bad; (*Med*) to hurt o.s., do o.s. harm.
dañinear [1a] *vt* (**a**) (*Cono Sur*) = **dañar.** (**b**) (*Cono Sur*: *robar*) to steal.
dañino 1 *adj* harmful; damaging; injurious; **animales ~s** vermin, pests, injurious creatures. **2** *nm* (*Cono Sur*) thief.
daño *nm* (**a**) (*gen*) damage; hurt, harm, injury; **en ~ de** to the detriment of; **por mi ~** to my cost; **hacer ~ a** to damage, harm; (*Med*) to hurt, injure; *estómago* to upset; **no hace ~** it doesn't hurt; **el ajo me hace ~** garlic disagrees with me; **hacerse ~** to hurt o.s., do o.s. an injury; **se hizo ~ en el pie** he hurt his foot.
(**b**) (*Med*) trouble; **los médicos no saben dónde está el ~** the doctors cannot tell where the trouble is.
(**c**) (*Jur*) **~s y perjuicios** damages; **graves ~s corporales** grievous bodily harm.
(**d**) (*LAm*: *maleficio*) spell, curse.
dañoso *adj* harmful, bad, injurious; **~ para** harmful to,

bad for.

DAO *nm abr de* **diseño asistido por ordenador** computer-aided design, CAD.

dar [1q] **1** *vt* (**a**) (*gen*) to give; *objeto* to give, hand, pass (*a* to); *recado* to give, deliver; *aviso* to give; *permiso* to give, grant, concede; *ejemplo* to set; *paso* to take; *paseo* to take, go for; *golpe* to give, deal, fetch, strike; *paliza* to give; *grito* to give, utter; *suspiro* to fetch, heave; *batalla* to fight; *examen* to sit, take; *olor* to give off; **ir dando cuerda** to pay out a rope, let out a rope; ~ **los buenos días a uno** to wish (*o* bid) sb good-day; ~ **de comer a uno** to give sb sth to eat; **nos daban garbanzos** they gave us chickpeas (to eat); **a mí no me la das*** you can't fool me; **lo que cada uno puede ~ de sí** what each one can contribute; **ahí me las den todas** that won't bother me, I can cope with everything; **el cálculo dio 99** the sum worked out at 99; **el atleta dio positivo en el control antidoping** the athlete's drug test proved positive; **por si vienen mal dadas** in case of emergency, (*ahorrar etc*) for a rainy day.

(**b**) *cosecha, beneficio etc* to yield, bear, produce, give; **dan un 7 por 100 de interés** they yield 7% interest, they bear interest at 7%.

(**c**) (*Naipes*) to deal.

(**d**) *impresión* to give, cause, produce; *placer* to give; *compasión* to cause, excite, arouse; **le dio un fuerte dolor de costado** he felt a sharp pain in his side.

(**e**) (*Teat etc*) to do, perform, put on; (*Cine*) to show, put on, screen.

(**f**) (*hora*) to strike; **el reloj dio las 3** the clock struck 3; **han dado las 4, son las 4 dadas** it's past 4 o'clock.

(**g**) ~ **como,** ~ **por** to consider, regard, assume; **lo dio como cierto** he regarded it as certain, he considered it definite; **lo daba por bien empleado** he considered it well spent; **lo podremos ~ por terminado** we shall be able to consider it finished.

(**h**) ~ **de barniz a** to varnish; ~ **de jalbegue a** to whitewash.

(**i**) ~ **a uno de puñetazos** to punch sb.

(**j**) ~**la de** to brag of being; to set o.s. up as; **la da de poeta** he tries to make out he's a poet.

(**k**) **¡dale!** (*Boxeo etc*) hit him!; (*dando caza*) after him!; (*Dep etc*) come on!; get on with it!; (*iró*) just look at him!, what an idiot!; **¡y dale!** there he goes again!; **¡dale que dale!** you do carry on so!, stop harping on it; **estoy dale que dale a este problema** I've been bashing away at this problem*; **la vecina está dale que dale al piano** our neighbour is pounding away on her piano; ~**le al vicio** to be on drugs.

(**l**) **lo mismo da** it's all the same, it makes no difference; **lo mismo me da, me da igual** it's all the same to me; **¡qué más da!** what does it matter!; never mind!; **¡qué más da un sitio que otro!** surely one place is as good as another!

(**m**) *para muchas locuciones, V el sustantivo p.ej.* **caza, grito, paseo;** *o verbo, p.ej.* **conocer, entender** *etc.*

2 *vi* (**a**) (*gen*) to give; **a quien dan no escoge** beggars can't be choosers.

(**b**) ~ **a** (*ventana*) to look out on, look on to, overlook; (*casa*) to face, face towards; ~ **sobre** to overlook.

(**c**) ~ **a la bomba** to pump, work the pump.

(**d**) ~ **con** *persona etc* to meet, run into, find; *idea, solución etc* to hit on; ~ **con algo en el suelo** to knock sth to the ground, drop sth; **el barco dio con el puente** the ship crashed into (*o* struck) the bridge; **no doy con el nombre** I can't think of the name.

(**e**) ~ **consigo en** to end up in, land in; **dio consigo en la cárcel** he ended up in jail.

(**f**) ~ **contra** to hit (against), knock against, bang into.

(**g**) ~ **de cabeza** to fall on one's head; ~ **de narices** to fall flat on one's face; ~ **de narices contra la puerta** to bang one's face on the door.

(**h**) ~ **en** + *infin* to take to + *ger*, get into the habit of + *ger*; **han dado en llamarle Boko** they've taken to calling him Boko.

(**i**) ~ **en** *suelo etc* to hit, strike; *blanco* to hit, land on; *solución* to hit on; *error* to fall into; *chiste* to catch on to, see, get the point of; ~ **en ello** to see the point, get it; **el sol le daba en la cara** the sun was shining straight into her face.

(**j**) **le da por** + *infin* he takes it into his head to + *infin*, he decides to + *infin*; he persists in + *ger*; **le ha dado por no venir a clase** he has begun to cut classes; **al chico le daba por dormirse en clase** the boy was apt to go to sleep in class; **les dio por venir a vernos** they took it into their heads to come and see us; **la casa que a uno le dio por llamar 'Miramar'** the house that sb had the bright idea of calling 'Miramar'.

(**k**) ~ **tras uno** to pursue sb vigorously, set off after sb.

(**l**) ~ **de sí** (*tela etc*) to give, stretch; (*Agr etc*) to bear heavily, yield well, produce a lot.

3 darse *vr* (**a**) (*entregarse*) to surrender, give in; to give o.s. up (*a* to).

(**b**) ~ **a** (*dedicarse*) to take to; to devote o.s. to; (*pey*) to abandon o.s. to; ~ **a la bebida** to take to drink; ~ **a creer que ...** to take to thinking that ...

(**c**) (*suceso*) to happen; **si se da el caso** if that happens.

(**d**) (*Bio etc*) to exist, occur, be found; **la planta no se da en el sur** the plant is not found in the south.

(**e**) (*Agr*) to grow, come up; **el cultivo se da bien este año** the crop is coming on well this year.

(**f**) ~ **por** to consider o.s. (as); ~ **por ofendido** to take offence; ~ **por perdido** to give o.s. up for lost; ~ **por vencido** to give up, acknowledge defeat.

(**g**) ~**las de** to pose as, fancy o.s. as; **nunca me las di de experto** I never claimed to be an expert.

(**h**) **no se me da mal** I'm not doing too badly; **se le dan muy bien las matemáticas** she's pretty good at maths, maths comes easily to her.

(**i**) **no se me da un bledo** (*o* **higo, rábano** *etc*) I don't care two hoots (*de* about).

(**j**) (*) **dársela (con queso) a uno** to fool sb, put one over on sb*; **se la da a su marido** she's unfaithful to her husband.

(**k**) *para otras locuciones V el sustantivo, p.ej.* **prisa, tono;** *o verbo, p.ej.* **conocer.**

Dardanelos *nmpl* Dardanelles.

dardo *nm* dart, shaft; (*juego*) ~**s** darts.

dares* *nmpl*: ~ **y tomares** arguments, bickering; **andar en ~ y tomares con uno** to bicker with sb, squabble with sb.

Darío *nm* Darius.

dársena *nf* (**a**) (*Náut*) dock; basin, inner harbour; ~ **de marea** tidal basin. (**b**) (*Aut*) bus shelter.

darviniano, darwiniano *adj* Darwinian.

darvinismo, darwinismo *nm* Darwinism.

darvinista, darwinista 1 *adj* Darwinist; Darwinian. **2** *nmf* Darwinist.

data *nf* (**a**) (*gen*) date; **es de larga ~** it is old-established, it goes back a long way. (**b**) (*de cuenta*) item.

datable *adj* datable, that can be dated.

datación *nf* date, dating; **de difícil ~** hard to date.

datáfono *nm* dataphone.

datar [1a] **1** *vt* to date, put a date on. **2** *vi*: ~ **de** to date from, date back to; **esto data de muy atrás** this dates back a long time, this goes a long way back.

datero* *nm* (*Cono Sur*) tipster.

dátil *nm* (**a**) (*Bot*) date; (‡) ~**es** dabs‡, fingers. (**b**) (*Zool*) date mussel.

datilera *nf* date palm.

dativo *nm* dative.

dato *nm* (*gen*) fact, datum, piece of information; **un ~ interesante** an interesting fact; ~**s** data, facts, information; **otro ~ que tener en cuenta es ...** another thing to bear in mind is ...; **no tenemos todos los ~s** we do not have all the facts; ~**s de entrada** input data; ~**s estadísticos** statistical information, statistical data, statistics; ~**s personales** personal particulars, details about o.s.; ~ **de salida** output data.

David *nm* David.

dB *nm abr de* **decibelio** decibel, dB.

DC *nf* (*Pol*) *abr de* **Democracia Cristiana.**

dcha. *abr de* **derecha** (right hand, r.h.).

d. de J.C. *adv abr de* **después de Jesucristo** Anno Domini, in the year of our Lord, AD.

de *prep* (**a**) (*posesión*) of; **el coche ~ mi amigo** the car of my friend, my friend's car; **los coches ~ mis amigos** my friends' cars; **es ~ ellos** it's theirs; **la señora ~ Pérez** Mrs Pérez; **el interés del préstamo** the interest on the loan.

(**b**) (*superlativo*) in; **el peor alumno ~ la clase** the worst pupil in the class; **es el coche más caro del mercado** it's the dearest car on the market.

(**c**) (*valor*) **una moneda ~ a 5 pesos** a 5-peso coin; **un pan ~ a libra** a pound loaf.

(**d**) (*origen, distancia*) from; **es ~ Calatayud** she's from Calatayud; **Dolores no es ~ aquí** Dolores is not from these parts; **los ~ Madrid son los mejores** those from Madrid are the best, the Madrid ones are the best; ~ **A a B hay 5 kms** it is 5 kms from A to B; **ir ~ A a Z** to go from A to Z; **altura del suelo** height above ground; ~ **esto se deduce que**

... from this one deduces that ...; **tiene 3 hijos ~ su primera mujer** he has 3 children by his first wife; **el camino ~ Elche** the Elche road, the road to Elche.

(**e**) (*aposición*) of; **la ciudad ~ Caracas** the city of Caracas.

(**f**) (*partitivo*) of; **uno ~ nosotros** one of us.

(**g**) (*números*) **3 ~ cada 4** 3 in every 4, 3 out of every 4.

(**h**) (*tema*) **una clase ~ francés** a French class; **un libro ~ biología** a biology book, a book about (*o* on) biology; **no sé nada ~ él** I don't know anything about (*o* of, concerning) him; **hablaba ~ política** he was talking about politics.

(**i**) (*materia*) of; **una cadena ~ oro** a chain of gold, a gold(en) chain.

(**j**) (*contenido*) of; **una tacita ~ café** a cup of coffee.

(**k**) (*edad*) of; **un chico ~ 15 años** a boy of 15, a 15-year old boy.

(**l**) (*profesión*) by; **es abogado ~ profesión** he's a lawyer by profession.

(**m**) (*autoría*) by, of; **un libro ~ Cela** a book by Cela, a book of Cela's.

(**n**) (*finalidad*) **goma ~ mascar** chewing gum; **máquina ~ coser** sewing machine.

(**o**) (*que funciona con*) **cocina ~ gas** gas stove; **este modelo es ~ electricidad** this model works on electricity, this is an electric model.

(**p**) (*manera, estilo*) in; **amueblado ~ roble** furnished in oak; **vestido ~ azul** dressed in blue; **pintado ~ negro** painted (in) black; **~ puerta en puerta** from door to door; **iban entrando ~ 2 en 2** they came in 2 by 2; **bajó la escalera ~ 4 en 4** he came down 4 stairs at a time; **~ más en más** more and more.

(**q**) (*medio*) at, in, with; **~ un salto** at one bound, with one jump; **~ un trago** at a gulp, in one swallow.

(**r**) (*motivo*) with; **estar loco ~ contento** to be crazy with joy; **saltar ~ alegría** to jump for joy; **morir ~ hambre** to die of (*o* from) starvation, starve to death; **estar enfermo ~ gripe** to be ill with flu; **no poder moverse ~ miedo** to be unable to move for (*o* with) fright; **~ puro cansado** out of sheer tiredness.

(**s**) (*respecto de*) in; **mejor ~ salud** in better health, better in health; **paralizado ~ las dos piernas** paralysed in both legs.

(**t**) (*descriptivo*) with; **la niña ~ pelo largo** the girl with long hair; **ese tío del sombrero** that chap with (*o* in) the hat.

(**u**) (*en calidad de*) as; **~ niño** as a child; when a child; **'el gran actor, ~ Segismundo'** (*pie de foto*) 'the great actor as Segismundo'.

(**v**) (*agente*) by; **una persona amada ~ todos** a person loved by all, a person beloved of all.

(**w**) (*hora*) at, in, by; **a las 7 ~ la mañana** at 7 o'clock, at 7 a.m.; **muy ~ mañana** very early in the morning; **~ día** by day, during the day(time); **~ noche** at night, by night, in the night time.

(**x**) (*condicional*) if; **~ resultar esto así** if this turns out to be true; **~ no poder encontrarlo** if we can't find it; **~ no ser así** if it were not so, were it not so.

(**y**) (*tras* más, menos) than; **más ~ 7** more than 7.

(**z**) (*giros*) **aquel burro ~ ministro** that ass of a minister; **el pobre ~ Pedro** poor old Peter; **el bueno ~ Juan** good old John; *para otras locuciones, V el sustantivo, p.ej.* **pie, prisa.**

dé *V* **dar.**

deambular [1a] *vi* to saunter, stroll, wander (*por* along, about, in, through).

deambulatorio *nm* (*Ecl*) ambulatory.

deán *nm* (*Ecl*) dean.

debacle *nf* débâcle, disaster.

debajo 1 *adv* (*t* **por ~**) underneath, below; on the underside.

2 ~ de *prep* under; below, beneath; **~ de la mesa** under the table, underneath the table; **por ~ de** under; below.

debate *nm* debate (*t Parl*); discussion, argument; **estar a ~** to be under debate; **poner un tema a ~** to raise an issue for discussion.

debatir[1] [3a] *vt* to debate (*t Parl*); to discuss, argue about.

debatir[2] [3a] *vi y* **debatirse** *vr* (*luchar*) to struggle; (*forcejar*) to writhe; to flail about; **~se entre la vida y la muerte** to be fighting for life.

debe *nm* debit, debit side (*of account*); **~ y haber** debit and credit; **asentar algo al ~ de uno** to debit sth to sb.

debelador(a) *nm/f* conqueror.

debelar [1a] *vt* to conquer.

deber [2a] **1** *vt* to owe; **me debes 5 dólares** you owe me 5 dollars; **¿qué le debo?** (*bares, tiendas*) how much is it?; what's the damage?*; **el respeto que todos deben a la patria** the respect which everybody owes to his country; **esto lo debe a influencia francesa** he owes this to French influence.

2 *vi* (**a**) (*obligación*) **debo hacerlo** I must do it, I have to do it; I ought to do it; **no debes comer tanto** you shouldn't eat so much; **debiera ir** he ought to go, he should go; **deberá cambiarse cada mes** (*instrucción*) it should be changed every month; **debíamos partir ayer** we were to have left yesterday; **he debido perderlo** I must have lost it; **hubieras debido traerlo** you ought to have brought it, you should have brought it.

(**b**) (*suposición*) **debe de ser así** it must be like that; that must be it; **debe de hacer mucho frío allí** it must be pretty cold there; **debe de ser brasileño** he must be a Brazilian; **no debe de ser muy caro** it can't be very dear; **debe de haber ido** he must have gone; **debió de perderlo** he must have lost it.

3 deberse *vr*: **~ a** to be owing to, be due to, be on account of; **se debe al mal tiempo** it's on account of the bad weather; **se debe a que no hay carbón** it is because (of the fact that) there's no coal; **puede ~ a que ...** it may be because ...; **¿a qué se debe esto?** what is the explanation of this?, why is this?

4 *nm* (**a**) (*obligación*) duty, obligation; **~ cuidadano** civic duty; **últimos ~es** last rites; **cumplir con un ~** to perform a duty, carry out a duty.

(**b**) (*Fin*) debt.

(**c**) **~es** (*Escol*) homework; task, assignment.

debidamente *adv* properly, as one should (*o* as it should be *etc*); in due form, duly; **si te conduces ~** if you behave properly; **un documento ~ redactado** a properly drawn up document.

debido *adj* (**a**) (*correcto*) proper, due, just; (*justo*) right, correct; **en debida forma** duly, in due form; **con el ~ respeto** with (all) due respect; **como es ~, según es ~** as is (only) proper, as is right; **un padre como es ~ no haría eso** a true father would not do that.

(**b**) **~ a** owing to, due to, because of; **~ a ello** because of this; **~ a la falta de agua** because of the water shortage; **~ a que no hay plátanos** because (of the fact that) there are no bananas.

débil 1 *adj* (*gen*) weak; (*físicamente*) weak, feeble, frail; *salud* poor; *carácter* weak; *esfuerzo etc* feeble; half-hearted; *grito* faint, feeble, weak; *luz* dim, wan, weak; **~ mental** mentally deficient. **2** *nmf*: **~ mental** mental deficient; *V* **económicamente.**

debilidad *nf* (**a**) (*gen*) weakness; feebleness; faintness; dimness; **~ senil** senility, senile decay.

(**b**) (*una* ~) weakness; **tener una ~ por el chocolate** to have a weakness for chocolate; **tener una ~ por uno** to have a soft spot for sb.

debilitación *nf* weakening, debilitation, enfeeblement.

debilitador *adj*, **debilitante** *adj* debilitating.

debilitar [1a] **1** *vt* to weaken, debilitate; *resistencia etc* to weaken, impair, lower. **2 debilitarse** *vr* to grow weak(er), weaken.

débilmente *adv* weakly; feebly; half-heartedly; faintly; dimly, wanly.

debitar [1a] *vt* to debit.

débito *nm* (**a**) (*Com*) debit; debt. (**b**) **~ conyugal** conjugal duty, marital duty. (**c**) **~s varios (de hotel)** (*LAm*) sundries.

debocar* [1g] *vti* (*LAm*) to vomit, throw up.

Débora *nf* Deborah.

debú *nm*, **debut** [de'βu] *nm*, *pl* **~s** [de'βus] début.

debutante 1 *adj* inexperienced, novice; **jugador ~** player appearing for the first time. **2** *nmf* (*t* **debutanta** *f*) (*en sociedad*) debutante; (*Dep*) new player, new cap.

debutar [1a] *vi* to make one's début.

década *nf* (*decenio*) decade; (*serie*) set of ten, series of ten.

decadencia *nf* decadence, decline, decay; **estar en franca ~** to be in full decline.

decadente *adj* decadent; effete.

decaer [2n] *vi* (**a**) (*gen*) to decay, decline; (*esfuerzo*) to flag, weaken; (*moda*) to wane; (*negocio*) to fall off; (*en salud*) to decline, sink, fail; **~ (de ánimo)** to lose heart; **ella ha decaído en belleza** her beauty is not what it was; **decayó de poderío** his power declined.

(**b**) (*Náut*) to drift, drift off course.

decagramo *nm* decagram.

decaído *adj* (*fig: desanimado*) downcast, crestfallen; **estar ~** to be down.

decaimiento *nm* decay; decline; weakening, weakness;

warning; falling-off; ~ (**de ánimo**) discouragement, depression.

decalaje *nm* time-lag, shift of time; gap, interval, discrepancy.

decalitro *nm* decalitre, decaliter (*US*).

decálogo *nm* decalogue.

decámetro *nm* decametre, decameter (*US*).

decana *nf* doyenne.

decanato *nm* deanship; deanery.

decano *nm* (**a**) (*Univ etc*) dean. (**b**) (*de grupo, de prensa etc*) doyen, senior member.

decantación *nf* leaning, tendency, movement (*hacia* towards).

decantar[1] [1a] *vt* (*liter*) to praise, laud; **el tan decantado edificio** (*iró*) this building which has been so effusively praised.

decantar[2] [1a] **1** *vt vino etc* to decant; to pour off; *sedimento* to leave behind, form, deposit. **2 decantarse** *vr*: ~ **hacia** to move towards, evolve in the direction of; to lean towards, tend towards; ~ **por algo** (*o* **uno**) to show preference for sth (*o* sb).

decapado *nm* scaling.

decapitar [1a] *vt* to behead, decapitate.

decasílabo 1 *adj* decasyllabic, ten-syllable. **2** *nm* decasyllable.

decatlón *nm* decathlon.

decena *nf* ten; about ten; ~**s** (*Mat*) tens; **una ~ de barcos** about ten ships, some ten ships; ~**s de miles de españoles** tens of thousands of Spaniards; **contar por ~s** to count in tens; **vender por ~s** to sell in tens.

decenal *adj* decennial; **plan** ~ ten-year plan.

decencia *nf* (*V adj*) (**a**) decency; seemliness, decorum; respectability; modesty; **faltar a la** ~ to offend against decency (*o* propriety). (**b**) cleanness, tidiness.

decenio *nm* decade.

decente *adj* (**a**) (*gen*) decent; (*correcto*) seemly, proper; (*honrado*) respectable; (*modesto*) modest. (**b**) (*aseado*) clean, tidy.

decentemente *adv* (*V adj*) (**a**) decently; properly; respectably; modestly. (**b**) tidily.

decepción *nf* disappointment.

decepcionante *adj* disappointing.

decepcionar [1a] *vt* to disappoint.

decesado, -a *nm/f* (*LAm*) deceased person.

deceso *nm* (*esp LAm*) passing, death; fatality.

decibel *nm*, **decibelio** *nm* decibel.

decibélico *adj* loud, noisy.

decible *adj* expressible; communicable; **eso no es** ~ that cannot be expressed, there are no words to say it.

decididamente *adv* decidedly.

decidido *adj* decided, determined; resolute; emphatic; **de carácter** ~ firm, strong-willed.

decidir [3a] **1** *vt* (**a**) *persona* to decide, persuade, convince; **esto le decidió a dejarlo** this decided him to give it up; **esto por fin le decidió** this finally made his mind up (for him).

(**b**) *cuestión, resultado* to decide, settle, resolve.

2 *vi* to decide (*de, en* about); ~ + *infin* to decide to + *infin*; ~ **en favor de uno** to decide in sb's favour; ~ **sobre cuál conviene más** to decide which is more suitable.

3 decidirse *vr* to decide, make up one's mind (*a + infin* to + *infin*); ~ **por** to decide on, settle on, choose.

decidor 1 *adj* (**a**) (*gracioso*) witty, amusing, racy. (**b**) (*elocuente*) fluent, eloquent. **2** *nm* (**a**) (*chistoso*) wit, witty talker. (**b**) (*narrador*) fluent speaker, eloquent speaker.

decil *nm* decile.

decilitro *nm* decilitre, deciliter (*US*).

décima *nf* (**a**) (*Mat*) tenth; tenth part (*esp* of a lottery ticket). (**b**) (*Ecl*) tithe. (**c**) (*Liter Hist*) *a ten-line stanza.* (**d**) **tiene sólo unas ~s de fiebre** (*Med*) he's only got a slight fever.

decimación *nf* decimation.

decimal 1 *adj* decimal. **2** *nm* decimal. **3** *nf*: ~ **periódica** recurring decimal.

decimalización *nf* decimalization.

decimalizar [1f] *vt* to decimalize.

decímetro *nm* decimetre, decimeter (*US*).

décimo *adj, nm* tenth.

decimoctavo *adj* eighteenth.

decimocuarto *adj* fourteenth.

decimonónicamente *adv* in the style of the 19th century.

decimonónico *adj* (*hum o pey*) nineteenth-century (*atr*); Victorian; (*fig*) outdated, antiquated.

decimonono *adj*, **decimonoveno** *adj* nineteenth.

decimoprimero *adj* eleventh.

decimoquinto *adj* fifteenth.

decimosegundo *adj* twelfth.

decimoséptimo *adj* seventeenth.

decimosexto *adj* sixteenth.

decimotercio *adj*, **decimotercero** *adj* thirteenth.

decir 1 [3o] *vti* (**a**) (*gen*) to say; to tell; (*texto*) to say, read; *buenaventura* to tell; *mentira* to tell; *verdad* to speak, tell; *misa* to say; *disparates etc* to talk; (*) to ask; **le dije cuántos había** I asked him how many there were; **no dijo nada** he said nothing; **¿quién te lo dijo?** who told you?; **dicen que** ... they say that ..., people say that ...; ~ **a uno que se calle** to tell sb to be quiet; **nos dijo que fuéramos** he told us to go.

(**b**) (*locuciones*: *gen*) **¿digo algo?** have I said sth?; **eso digo** that's what I say; that's just what I'm saying; **¡digo, digo!** hey!, say!; just listen to this!; now wait a minute!; **digo** ... (*Méx*) well, er ...; **había 8, digo 9** there were 8, (no) I mean 9; **pero digo mal 'decadente'** but I am wrong to say (*o* to call them *etc*) 'decadent'; **pero dice mal** but he is wrong; **y dice bien** and he is right; **como aquel que dice** so to speak; **no lo digo por ti** I'm not referring to you, I'm not getting at you; ~ **que no** to say no; ~ **que sí** to say yes; ~ **para sí,** ~ **entre sí** to say to o.s.; ~ **digo donde dijo Diego** to take back what one said earlier; **como quien dice, como si dijéramos** so to speak; in a way, more or less; **como quien no dice nada** quite casually; as though it wasn't important; **¿cómo has dicho?** what did you say?, pardon?; **decía** (*después de interrupción*) as I was saying; **¿decía Vd?** you were saying?; **¿cómo diríamos?** how shall I put it?; **¡si te lo digo yo!** of course it's true!; **¡lo que he dicho!** I stand by what I said!; **¡quién lo diría!** would you believe it!; did you ever?*; **me dijo de todo*** he called me all the names under the sun.

(**c**) (*locuciones con infin*) **es** ~ that is to say; **es mucho ~, ya es** ~ that's saying a lot, that's a big claim to make; **me permito ~ que** ... I submit that ..., I venture to say that ...; **querer** ~ to mean; **¿qué quiere ~ 'spatha'?** what does 'spatha' mean?; **¿qué quiere Vd ~ con eso?** what do you mean by that?; **dar que ~ (a la gente)** to make people talk, set the tongues wagging; **no sé qué** ~ I don't know what to say; **no hay más que** ~ there's no more to be said about it; **no hay que ~ que ..., ni que ~ tiene que** ... it goes without saying that ...; **no hay para qué** ~ of course ...; ~ **por** ~ to talk for talking's sake; **o por mejor** ~ or rather; **por ~lo así** so to speak.

(**d**) (*locuciones con futuro*) **dirás aquel otro** you must mean that other one; **ya me dirás** you tell me your side of it, you tell me how you see things; **Vd dirá** it's for you to say; (*al preparar bebida*) how much do you like?, say when*; **ello dirá** the event will show; **el qué dirán** public opinion, what people will say; **pero no quiso por el qué dirán** but she didn't want to because of what people might say; **el maldito 'qué dirán'** the curse of concern for what people will think.

(**e**) (*locuciones con subjuntivo*) (*Telec*) **¡diga!, ¡dígame!** hullo?; **dicho sea de paso** ... by the way ..., and I (*etc*) might add that ...; **digan lo que digan** whatever they (may) say; let them say what they please; **digámoslo así** so to speak; for want of a better word; **¡no me digas!** you don't say!; well I'm blowed!*; come off it!*; so what's new?*; **¡y que lo digas!** you can say that again!; **no es que yo lo diga, pero** ... it's not because I say so, but ...; **y no digamos de** ... not to mention ...; **no estuvo muy cortés, que digamos** actually he wasn't all that polite, he wasn't what you could call polite; **no es un pintor, que digamos** he's not what you could really call a painter; **es, digamos, un comerciante** he's a sort of dealer, he's a dealer ... for want of a better word; **no es muy guapa que digamos** she's not really that pretty.

(**f**) (*locuciones con ptp*) **mejor dicho** rather; I mean ...; **no es para dicho** it's not fit to be told; **¡lo dicho dicho!** I stand by what I said!; **¡dicho y hecho!** no sooner said than done!; **dicho sea de paso** ... by the way ..., and I (*etc*) might add that ...; **¡haberlo dicho!** you might have told me!; **tragarse lo dicho** to eat one's words; **dicho de otra manera** ... in other words ...

(**g**) (*mostrar, indicar*) to show, indicate, reveal; **su cara dice lo que es** his face shows him up for what he is; **una situación que tan mal dice de nuestro gobierno** a situation which shows our government up in such a bad light.

(**h**) (*: *nombrar*) to call; **al niño le dicen Anastasio** they call the child Anastasius.

(**i**) (*convenir*) to suit; ~ **con** to go with, match; **el**

vestido le dice bien the dress suits her (nicely); **el color dice bien con su cutis** the colour goes with (*o* suits, harmonizes with) her complexion.

2 decirse *vr* (**a**) **yo sé lo que me digo** I know what I'm talking about; I know what I'm up to.

(**b**) (*llamarse*) to be called, be named; **esta plaza se dice de la Revolución** this is called Revolution Square; **¿cómo se dice en inglés 'cursi'?** what's the English for 'cursi'?, how do you say 'cursi' in English?

(**c**) **se dice** it is said, they say, people say; the story goes ...; **se me ha dicho que** ... I have been told that ...; **no se diría eso ahora** that could not be said nowadays; **y no se diga** ... not to mention ...; **no se diga que** ... never let it be said that ...; **se diría que no está** she doesn't seem to be here; **eso se dice en seguida** that's easier said than done.

(**d**) **hablar portugués, lo que se dice hablar, no sé** I can't really talk Portuguese, I don't speak Portuguese at all well; **esto es lo que se dice un queso** this is a real cheese, this is what you really call a cheese.

3 *nm* (*refrán etc*) saying; (*gracia*) witty remark; **es un ~** it's just a phrase; if I may use the expression ...; I was only thinking aloud; **a ~ de todos** by all accounts; **al ~ de X** according to X; as X has it, as X would have it.

decisión *nf* (**a**) (*una ~*) decision; (*Jur*) judgement; **~ por mayoría** majority decision; **forzar una ~** to force the issue; **tomar una ~** to make (*o* take) a decision.

(**b**) (*cualidad*) decisiveness; determination, resolution.

decisivo *adj* decisive; *argumento, consideración* over-riding.

decisorio 1 *adj*: **poderes ~s** decision-making powers; **proceso ~** decision-making process. **2** *nm* (*Méx Jur*) judgment, verdict.

declamación *nf* (**a**) (*acto*) declamation; recital, recitation; (*cualidad*) delivery. (**b**) (*pey*) ranting.

declamador(a) *nm/f* (**a**) (*orador*) orator; reciter. (**b**) (*pey*) ranter.

declamar [1a] **1** *vt* to declaim; *versos etc* to recite. **2** *vi* (**a**) (*gen*) to speak out, hold forth (*contra* against). (**b**) (*pey*) to rant, carry on.

declamatorio *adj* declamatory; (*pey*) ranting.

declaración *nf* (**a**) (*gen*) declaration; (*afirmación*) pronouncement, statement; (*explicación*) explanation; (*de amor*) proposal (of marriage); **~ conjunta** joint communiqué, joint declaration; **~ de derechos** (*Pol*) bill of rights; **~ de impuestos, ~ de ingresos, ~ de renta** income-tax return.

(**b**) (*Naipes*) bid.

(**c**) (*Jur*) statement; evidence; **~ de culpabilidad** confession of guilt; **~ inmediata** (*Méx*) verbal statement; **~ jurada** sworn statement, affidavit; **prestar ~** to make a statement; to give evidence; **tomar la ~ a uno** to take a statement from sb.

declaradamente *adv* confessedly, frankly.

declarado *adj* confessed, declared.

declarante *nmf* (**a**) (*Jur*) deponent. (**b**) (*Naipes*) bidder, declarer.

declarar [1a] **1** *vt* (**a**) (*gen*) to declare, state (*que* that); (*explicar*) to explain, expound; (*en aduana*) to declare; *guerra* to declare (*a* on).

(**b**) (*Naipes*) to bid; **~ 2 picos** to bid 2 spades.

(**c**) (*Jur*) to find; **~ culpable a uno** to find sb guilty.

2 *vi* (**a**) (*gen*) to declare; **según él mismo declara** as he himself declares.

(**b**) (*Naipes*) to bid, declare; **declaró menos de lo que tenía** he underbid.

(**c**) (*Jur*) to make a statement; to testify, give evidence.

3 declararse *vr* (**a**) (*gen*) to declare o.s.; to make one's opinion (*o* position *etc*) known; **~ a una joven** to say to a girl that one loves her; (*más formal*) to propose to a girl; **~ por** to come out in favour of, declare one's support for, side with.

(**b**) **~ culpable** (*Jur*) to plead guilty; **~ inocente** to plead not guilty.

(**c**) (*epidemia, incendio, guerra etc*) to break out.

declinable *adj* declinable.

declinación *nf* (**a**) (*gen*) decline, falling-off; decay. (**b**) (*Astron, Náut*) declination. (**c**) (*Ling*) declension.

declinar [1a] **1** *vt* (**a**) (*gen*) to decline, refuse; (*Jur*) to reject; **~ hacer algo** to decline to do sth.

(**b**) (*Ling*) to decline; to inflect.

2 *vi* (**a**) (*decaer*) to decline, fall off, fall away; to decay; to deteriorate; (*día*) to draw to a close.

(**b**) (*terreno*) to slope (away, down).

(**c**) (*Ling*) to decline.

declive *nm* (**a**) (*gen*) slope, incline, declivity; pitch; (*Ferro*) gradient; **tierra en ~** sloping ground, land on a slope; **estar en ~** to slope.

(**b**) (*fig*: *Fin etc*) (*t* **~ económico**) slump.

decocción *nf* decoction.

decodificar *etc* = **descodificar** *etc*.

decolaje *nm* (*LAm Aer*) takeoff.

decolar [1l] *vi* (*LAm Aer*) to take off.

decolorado *adj* discoloured.

decolorante *nm* bleaching agent.

decolorar [1a] **1** *vt* to discolour, affect the colour of. **2 decolorarse** *vr* to get discoloured, lose colour.

decomisar [1a] *vt* to seize, confiscate.

decomiso *nm* seizure, confiscation.

decongestionante *nm* decongestant.

deconstrucción *nf* deconstruction.

decoración *nf* (**a**) (*gen*) decoration; **~ de escaparate** window display; **~ de escaparates** window dressing; **~ del hogar, ~ de interiores** interior decorating; interior design.

(**b**) (*Teat*) scenery, set, décor.

decorado *nm* (*Cine, Teat*) scenery, set, décor.

decorador(a) *nm/f* decorator; interior designer; (*Cine, TV*) set designer.

decorar[1] [1a] *vt* (*adornar*) to decorate, adorn (*de* with).

decorar[2] [1a] *vt* (*aprender*) to learn, memorize; to learn by heart; (*recitar*) to chorus.

decorativo *adj* decorative, ornamental.

decoro *nm* (**a**) (*gen*) decorum, propriety, decency; proprieties; **~ virginal** maidenly modesty. (**b**) (*honor*) honour, respect.

decorosamente *adv* decorously.

decoroso *adj* decorous, proper, decent; seemly; modest.

decrecer [2d] *vi* to decrease, diminish; (*inundación, agua*) to go down; (*días*) to get shorter, draw in.

decreciente *adj* decreasing, diminishing.

decrecimiento *nm*, **decremento** *nm* decrease, diminution; fall; shortening.

decrépito *adj* decrepit.

decrepitud *nf* decrepitude.

decretar [1a] **1** *vt* (**a**) (*ordenar*) to decree, order, ordain; **~ que** ... to decree that ...

(**b**) *premio* to award (*a* to); *penalti* to award.

(**c**) (*Méx*) *dividendo* to declare.

2 *vi* (*Jur*) to deliver a judgment.

decreto *nm* decree, order; (*Parl*) act; **real ~** royal decree; **por real ~*** compulsorily, willy-nilly.

decreto-ley *nm, pl* **decretos-leyes** decree law, order in council (*Brit*).

decúbito *nm* (*Med*): **~ prono** prone position; **~ supino** supine position; **úlcera de ~** bedsore.

decuplar [1a] *vt*, **decuplicar** [1g] *vt* to multiply tenfold, increase tenfold.

décuplo 1 *adj* tenfold. **2** *nm*: **es el ~ de lo que era** it is ten times what it was, it has increased tenfold.

decurso *nm* (*liter*): **en el ~ de los años** over the years; **en el ~ del tiempo** in the course of time.

dechado *nm* (*Cos*) sampler; (*fig*) model, example, epitome; **es un ~ de virtudes** she's a paragon of virtue; **no es ningún ~ de perfección** it isn't a model of perfection.

dedada *nf* thimbleful; (*fig*) very small quantity, very modest amount; (*de mermelada etc*) spot, dab, drop; (*de rapé*) pinch; **dar una ~ de miel a uno** (*fig*) to give sb a crumb of comfort.

dedal *nm* (**a**) (*Cos*) thimble. (**b**) (*fig*) thimbleful.

dedalera *nf* foxglove.

dédalo *nm* (**a**) (*gen*) labyrinth. (**b**) (*fig*) tangle, mess.

dedazo *nm* fingermark.

dedicación *nf* (**a**) (*gen*) dedication; (*fig*) dedication, devotion (*a* to); **las profesiones de ~ humanitaria** the caring professions.

(**b**) (*Ecl*) consecration.

(**c**) **estar en (régimen de) ~ exclusiva** (*o* **plena**), **trabajar con ~ plena** to work full-time; **'~ plena'** (*anuncio*) 'full-time'.

dedicado *adj* (*Inform*) dedicated.

dedicar [1g] **1** *vt* (**a**) (*gen*) to dedicate (*a* to); (*Ecl*) to consecrate; *libro* to dedicate (*a* to); *ejemplar* to autograph, inscribe, write in.

(**b**) *esfuerzo, tiempo* to devote, give (*a* to); **dedico un día a la semana a pescar** I spend one day a week fishing; **tengo que ~ mucho tiempo a eso** I have to give a lot of time to that.

2 dedicarse *vr*: **~ a** to devote o.s. to; to go in for, take up; ~ **a** + *infin* to devote o.s. to + *ger*; **se dedicó a la cerámica** he devoted himself to pottery, he took up pottery; **¿a qué se dedica Vd?** what do you do?; what's your line?, what business are you in?; **¡dedícate a lo tuyo!** mind your own business!

dedicatoria *nf* inscription, dedication.

dedicatorio *adj* dedicatory.

dedil *nm* fingerstall.

dedillo *nm*: **saber algo al** ~ to have sth at one's fingertips; **saber una lección al** ~ to have a lesson off pat; **dijo la lista al** ~ he rattled off the list with complete accuracy.

dedismo* *nm* arbitrary selection, arbitrary nomination.

dedo *nm* (**a**) finger; ~ (**del pie**) toe; ~ **anular** ring finger; ~ **auricular,** ~ **meñique** little finger; ~ (**del**) **corazón,** ~ **cordial** middle finger; ~ **chico** little toe; ~ **gordo** big toe; ~ **índice** index finger, forefinger; ~ (**en**) **martillo** hammer-toe; ~ **pulgar** thumb; **comerse** (*o* **morderse**) **los ~s** to get very impatient; **contar con los ~s** to count on one's fingers; **cruzar los ~s** to cross one's fingers, keep one's fingers crossed; **chuparse los ~s** to eat with relish; (*fig*) to smack one's lips; to rub one's hands; **no se chupa el** ~ he's no fool; he doesn't waste any time; **dale un** ~ **y se toma hasta el codo** give him an inch and he'll take a yard; **se le escapó de entre los ~s** it slipped through his fingers; **hacer ~*, ir al ~*** (*LAm*), **tirar** ~ (*LAm*) to thumb a lift*, hitchhike; **hacer ~s** (*Mús*) to practise, do scales; **no se mama el** ~ he's pretty smart; **meter el** ~ **en la boca a uno** to try to get sb to talk; **no se mueve un** ~ (*fig*) he won't lift a finger; **pillarse los ~s** (*fig*) to get caught red-handed; to burn one's fingers; **poner el** ~ **en** to put one's finger on, pinpoint, identify precisely; **poner el** ~ **en la llaga** to put one's finger on the spot; **señalar algo con el** ~ to point the finger of scorn at sth; **no se ven los ~s de la mano** it's pitch-dark; **viajar a ~*** to hitch-hike; **vine a** ~ I hitched here*, I hitch-hiked here.

(**b**) (*fig*) spot, bit, drop; (*como medida*) finger; finger's breadth; **¡dos ~s nada más!** (*de bebida*) just a tiny drop!; **estar a dos ~s de** to be within an inch of, be within an ace of; to be on the verge of; **no tiene dos ~s de frente** he's pretty dim; he's a lout.

(**c**) (*fig*) (system of) arbitrary selection (*o* appointment *etc*); **entrar a** ~ to get in (*o* get a job) by pulling strings.

dedocracia* *nf* arbitrary exercise of power; system of arbitrary appointment.

deducción *nf* (**a**) (*gen*) deduction; inference. (**b**) (*suma etc*) deduction.

deducible (**a**) (*gen*) deducible, inferable (*de* from); **según es fácilmente** ~ as may readily be deduced. (**b**) (*Fin etc*) deductible; (*por razones impositivas*) allowable, deductible (*US*).

deducir [3n] *vt* (**a**) (*razonar*) to deduce, infer (*de* from); *fórmula* to deduce, derive. (**b**) *suma etc* to deduct; **deducidos los gastos** less charges.

deductivo *adj* deductive.

defalcar [1g] *vt* = **desfalcar.**

defecación *nf* defecation.

defecar [1g] *vi* to defecate.

defección *nf* defection, desertion.

defectible *adj* fallible, imperfect; faulty.

defectivo *adj* defective (*t Ling*).

defecto *nm* (*gen*) fault, defect, flaw; (*Elec, Téc*) fault; (*en fabricación, argumento*) flaw; (*moral*) shortcoming, failure; ~ **físico** physical defect; ~ **de fonación,** ~ **del habla,** ~ **de la palabra** speech defect, impediment; **en** ~ **de** for lack of, for want of; **A, o en su** ~**, B** A, or failing him, B; **por** ~ (*Inform*) default.

defectuosamente *adv* defectively, faultily.

defectuoso *adj* defective, faulty.

defender [2g] **1** *vt* (*gen*) to defend (*contra* against, *de* from); to protect; (*Jur*) to defend; *causa* to champion, uphold; **para ~los contra el frío** in order to protect them from the cold.

2 defenderse *vr* (**a**) to defend o.s. (*contra* against, *de* from); ~ **bien** to resist firmly; to give a good account of o.s.

(**b**) (*fig*) **me defiendo en inglés** I can manage in English, I can get along in English, I can keep going in English; **'¿qué tal?' ... 'hombre, nos defendemos'** 'how are things?' ... 'we're managing'; **gana poco pero se defiende** she doesn't earn much but she manages (*o* gets by); ~ **como un gato** *o* **panza arriba** to fight tooth and nail.

defendible *adj* defensible; that can be defended.

defendido, -a *nm/f* (*Jur*): **mi** ~ my client.

defenestración *nf* (*hum*) abrupt dismissal, sudden removal; sudden expulsion.

defenestrar [1a] *vt* (*hum*) to dismiss abruptly, remove suddenly; to expel suddenly.

defensa 1 *nf* (**a**) (*gen*) defence (*t Ajedrez, Jur, Dep*); protection, shelter; ~ **contra,** ~ **de** defence against; ~ **pasiva** civil defence; ~ **personal** self-defence; ~ **en profundidad** defence in depth; **en** ~ **propia** in self-defence.

(**b**) (*Náut*) fender; (*Dep*) shinpad, leg-pad; (*Méx Aut*) bumper, fender (*US*); **~s** (*Taur*) horns.

(**c**) **~s** (*Mil etc*) defences, defensive works; **~s costeras** coastal defences; ~ **marítima** (*Cono Sur*) sea-wall, coast defence.

2 *nm* (*Dep*) defender; back, fullback; ~ **escoba,** ~ **libre** sweeper.

defensiva *nf* defensive; **estar a la** ~ to be on the defensive.

defensivo 1 *adj* defensive; **política** ~ defence policy. **2** *nm* defence, safeguard.

defenso *nm* (*Méx Jur*) defendant.

defensor(a) *nm/f*, defender; protector; (*de causa*) champion, upholder; (*de teoría*) proponent; (*Jur*: *t* **abogado** ~) defending counsel; ~ **del pueblo** parliamentary commissioner, ombudsman.

deferencia *nf* deference; **por** ~ **hacia** out of deference to.

deferente *adj* deferential.

deferir [3k] **1** *vt* (*Jur*) to refer, relegate (*a* to). **2** *vi*: ~ **a** to defer to.

deficiencia *nf* deficiency, shortcoming, defect (*de* in, of); ~ **mental,** ~ **psíquico** mental deficiency; ~ **visual** visual handicap.

deficiente 1 *adj* deficient, wanting (*en* in); defective; (*mentalmente*) retarded, handicapped. **2** *nmf*: ~ **mental,** ~ **psíquico** mental defective; ~ **visual** visually handicapped person.

déficit *nm* (**a**) (*Com, Fin*) deficit; ~ **comercial** trade deficit; ~ **exterior** balance of payments deficit, trade deficit; ~ **por cuenta corriente** deficit on current account; ~ **presupuestario** budget(ary) deficit. (**b**) (*fig*) lack, shortage; shortfall.

deficitario *adj* (**a**) (*Fin*) deficit (*atr*); *cuenta* in deficit, showing a deficit; *empresa, operación* loss-making. (**b**) **ser** ~ **en** to be short of, be lacking in.

definible *adj* definable, that can be defined.

definición *nf* definition; **por** ~ by definition.

definido *adj* (**a**) (*gen*) (*t Ling*) definite; **bien** ~ well defined, clearly defined; ~ **por el usuario** (*Inform*) user defined. (**b**) *carácter* tough, manly.

definir [3a] *vt* (*gen*) to define; (*aclarar*) to clarify, explain; (*decidir*) to determine, establish.

definitivamente *adv* definitively, finally.

definitivo *adj* definitive; final, ultimate; **en definitiva** (*de una vez*) definitively; (*finalmente*) finally, once and for all; (*en resumen*) in short; in the last analysis.

definitorio *adj* defining, distinctive.

deflación *nf* deflation.

deflacionar [1a] *vt* to deflate.

deflacionario *adj*, **deflacionista** *adj* deflationary.

deflactación *nf* (*Cono Sur*) deflation.

deflactar [1a] *vt* (*Cono Sur*) to deflate.

deflector *nm* (*Téc*) baffle, baffle plate.

defoliación *nf* defoliation.

defoliante *nm* defoliant.

defoliar [1b] *vt* to defoliate.

deforestar *etc* = **desforestar** *etc.*

deformación *nf* deformation; (*Rad etc*) distortion; (*Mec*) strain; (*de madera etc*) warping.

deformante *adj*: **espejo** ~ distorting mirror.

deformar [1a] **1** *vt* (*gen*) to deform; to disfigure; (*Rad etc*) to distort; (*Mec*) to strain; *madera etc* to warp, push out of shape.

2 deformarse *vr* to become deformed; to get distorted; to warp, get out of shape, lose shape.

deforme *adj* deformed, misshapen; ugly; abnormal.

deformidad *nf* (**a**) (*lit*) deformity, malformation; abnormality. (**b**) (*fig*) (moral) shortcoming.

defraudación *nf* (*V vt*) (**a**) defrauding; deceit; ~ **fiscal,** ~ **de impuestos** tax evasion. (**b**) dashing, disappointment.

defraudador(a) *nm/f* fraudster*.

defraudar [1a] *vt* (**a**) *acreedores* to cheat, defraud; to deceive; *amigos* to let down; ~ **impuestos** to evade taxes, fiddle one's income tax*. (**b**) *esperanzas* to dash, disappoint, frustrate. (**c**) (*Fís*) *luz* to intercept, cut off.

defraudatorio *adj* fraudulent.

defuera *adv* (*t* **por** ~) outwardly, on the outside.

defunción *nf* decease, demise.

defuncionar‡ [1a] *vt* to do in‡.

DEG *nmpl abr de* **derechos especiales de giro** special drawing rights, SDR.

degeneración *nf* (**a**) (*acto*) degeneration (*en* into). (**b**) (*estado*) (moral) degeneracy.

degenerado 1 *adj* degenerate. **2** *nm* degenerate, degenerate type.

degenerar [1a] *vi* (*gen*) to degenerate (*en* into); (*decaer*) to decline, decay; (*empeorar*) to get worse, get more serious; **la manifestación degeneró en una sangrienta revuelta** the demonstration degenerated into a bloody riot.

degenerativo *adj* degenerative.

deglución *nf* swallowing.

deglutir [3a] *vti* to swallow.

degollación *nf* throat cutting; (*Jur*) beheading, execution; (*sentido más amplio*) massacre, slaughter; **D~ de los Inocentes** Slaughter of the Innocents.

degolladero *nm* (**a**) (*Anat*) throat, neck, throttle.

(**b**) (*Hist*) scaffold, block (for executions); **ir al ~** (*fig*) to expose o.s. to mortal danger, (*hum*) put one's head in the lion's mouth.

(**c**) (*matadero*) slaughterhouse.

degollador *nm* (*Hist*) executioner.

degollar [1m] *vt* (**a**) (*cortar la garganta de*) to cut (*o* slit) the throat of; (*decapitar*) to behead, decapitate; (*Taur*) to kill badly, butcher; (*fig*) to massacre, slaughter.

(**b**) (*fig: destruir*) to destroy; *comedia etc* to murder, make nonsense of; *papel* to make a dreadful hash of.

(**c**) (*Cos*) to cut low in the neck.

degradación *nf* (**a**) (*gen*) degradation; humiliation. (**b**) (*Mil etc*) demotion, reduction in rank. (**c**) (*Geol*) impoverishment; (*de calidad*) worsening, decline.

degradante *adj* degrading.

degradar [1a] **1** *vt* (**a**) (*gen*) to degrade, debase; (*humillar*) to humiliate.

(**b**) (*Mil etc*) to demote, reduce in rank.

(**c**) *suelo* to impoverish; *calidad* to lower, make worse, cause to decline.

2 degradarse *vr* to demean o.s.

degüello *nm* (**a**) = **degollación; entrar a ~ en una ciudad** to put the people of a city to the sword, give no quarter to the inhabitants of a town; **tirarse a ~ contra** to lash out against.

(**b**) (*de arma*) shaft, neck, narrow part.

degustación *nf* tasting, sampling; drinking; eating, consumption.

degustar [1a] *vt* (*probar*) to taste, sample; (*beber*) to drink, take; (*comer*) to eat, consume.

dehesa *nf* pasture, meadow; pastureland, range; (*finca*) estate.

deidad *nf* deity; divinity; **~ pagana** pagan god, pagan deity.

deificación *nf* deification; apotheosis (*t fig*).

deificar [1g] *vt* (**a**) (*Rel, t fig*) to deify; to apotheosize. (**b**) (*fig: ensalzar*) to exalt, over-praise, put on a pedestal.

deísmo *nm* deism.

deísta 1 *adj* deistic(al). **2** *nmf* deist.

dejación *nf* (**a**) (*Jur*) abandonment, relinquishment. (**b**) (*And, CAm: descuido*) carelessness.

dejada *nf* (*Tenis*) let.

dejadez *nf* (*V adj*) (**a**) untidiness, slovenliness; abandon. (**b**) carelessness, negligence, neglect, slackness; laziness; supineness, lack of willpower.

dejado *adj* (**a**) (*desaliñado*) untidy, slovenly; abandoned; unkempt.

(**b**) (*descuidado*) careless, negligent, slack; (*vago*) lazy.

(**c**) (*triste*) dejected.

(**d**) **~ de la mano de Dios** (*fig*) godforsaken; beyond all hope of redemption.

dejamiento *nm* = **dejación** (**a**); = **dejadez**.

dejar [1a] **1** *vt* (**a**) (*gen*) to leave; (*omitir*) to forget, leave out; (*abandonar*) to leave, abandon, desert, forsake; (*prestar*) to lend; *esfuerzo, trabajo etc* to give up, stop, abandon; *pasajero* to put down, set down; to drop; (*Com*) *balance etc* to show, leave; *beneficio* to produce, yield; **~ aparte** to leave aside; **~ atrás** to leave behind, outstrip, outdistance; (*fig*) to surpass; **~ a uno muy atrás** to leave sb far behind; **~ algo para mañana** to leave sth till tomorrow, postpone (*o* put off) sth till tomorrow; **~ algo para después** to leave sth till later; **lo dejamos por muy difícil** we gave it up because it was too hard; **lo dejamos por imposible** we gave it up as (being) impossible; **así que lo dejamos** so we gave it up; **¡deja eso!** stop that!, drop that!, chuck it!; **te lo dejo en la conserjería** I'll leave it for you at the porter's office; **~ así las cosas** to leave things as they are; **dejémoslo así** let's leave it at that; **como dejo dicho** as I have said; **deja escritas 3 novelas** he left 3 novels which he had written; he left 3 finished novels; **deja mucho que desear** it leaves a lot to be desired; **¿me dejas 10 dólares?** can you lend me 10 dollars?; **¿me dejas el auto?** can you (*o* will you) let me have the car?

(**b**) (*permitir*) to let, allow; **quiero pero no me dejan** I want to but they won't let me; **~ a uno** + *infin* to let sb + *infin*, allow sb to + *infin*; **~ a uno entrar** to let sb in; **~ a uno pasar** to let sb in (*o* through, past *etc*); **~ a uno salir** to let sb out; **~ que las cosas vayan de mal en peor** to let things go from bad to worse; **~ que se enfríe** (*instrucción*) leave till cold; *V* **caer, mano** (**c**) *etc*.

2 *vi*: **~ de** + *infin* (**a**) (*terminar de*) to stop + *ger*, leave off + *ger*, give up + *ger*; **dejó de cantar** she stopped singing; **cuando deje de llover** when it stops raining, when the rain stops; **no puedo ~ de fumar** I can't give up smoking; *V* **existir** *etc*.

(**b**) (*no cumplir*) to fail to + *infin*, neglect to + *infin*; **no dejes de visitarles** don't fail to visit them, on no account neglect to pay them a visit.

(**c**) (*no poder menos de*) **no puedo ~ de asombrarme** I cannot but be amazed, I cannot help being astonished; **no puedo ~ de pensar que ...** I can't help thinking that ...; **no deja de ser algo raro** all the same it's rather odd; **eso no deja de tener gracia** it's not without its amusing side; **yo había dejado de oírle tocar desde hacía 5 años** I had not heard him play for 5 years.

3 dejarse *vr* (**a**) (*abandonarse*) to neglect o.s., let o.s. go, get slovenly.

(**b**) **~ de** + *infin* (*permitirse*) to allow o.s. to be + *ptp*, let o.s. be + *ptp*; **~ persuadir** to allow o.s. to be persuaded; **no se dejó engañar** he was not to be deceived; **se dejó decir que ...** he let it slip that ...; **se dejó oír una débil voz** a weak voice made itself heard (*o* could be heard); *V* **vencer** *etc*.

(**c**) **~ de** + *infin* (*terminar*) to stop + *ger*; **¡déjate de eso!** stop that!, cut it out!; *V* **broma**.

deje *nm* = **dejo** (**c**).

dejo *nm* (**a**) (*sabor*) aftertaste, tang; **tiene un ~ raro** it leaves an odd taste.

(**b**) (*fig*) touch, smack, tang, flavour.

(**c**) (*Ling*) accent, trace of accent, special inflection.

del = **de** + **el**.

Del. *abr de* **Delegación** district office.

delación *nf* accusation; denunciation.

delantal *nm* apron; **~ de cuero** leather apron; **~ de niña** pinafore.

delante 1 *adv* (**a**) (*t* **por ~**) in front; ahead; opposite; **la parte de ~** the front part; **la casa no tiene nada ~** the house has nothing opposite; **estando otros ~** with others present; in the presence of others; **abierto por ~** open in front; **¡las damas por ~!** ladies first!; **entrar al puerto (con) la popa ~** to enter harbour stern first; **tenemos todavía 4 horas por ~** we still have 4 hours in front of us; we still have 4 hours to go.

(**b**) (*LAm*) **~ nuestro** (*etc*), **en nuestro ~** (*etc*) in front of us (*etc*).

2 ~ de *prep* in front of, before; ahead of.

delantera *nf* (**a**) (*de casa, vestido*) front, front part; (*Teat*) front row; front row seat; (*Dep*) forward line.

(**b**) (*fig: ventaja*) advantage, lead; **llevar la ~** to lead, be in the lead; **llevar la ~ a uno** to be ahead of sb; **coger la ~ a uno** to get ahead of sb; to get a start on sb; **sacar la ~ a uno** to steal a march on sb; **tomar la ~** to take the lead.

(**c**) (*Anat‡*) knockers‡, tits‡.

(**d**) **~s** (*calzones*) chaps; (*mono*) overalls.

delantero 1 *adj parte, fila, rueda etc* front; *pata* front, fore; (*Dep*) *línea, posición* forward; (*en progreso etc*) first, foremost.

2 *nm* (*Dep*) forward; **~ centro** centre-forward; **~ extremo** outside forward, wing forward; **~ interior** inside forward.

delatar [1a] *vt* (**a**) (*gen*) to denounce, inform against, accuse; to betray.

(**b**) (*fig*) to reveal, betray.

delator(a) *nm/f* informer, accuser; betrayer.

delco *nm* (*Aut*) distributor.

delectación *nf* delight, delectation.

delegación *nf* (**a**) (*acto*) delegation; **~ de poderes** (*Parl*) devolution.

(**b**) (*cuerpo*) delegation; **~ comercial** trade mission; **la ~ fue a cumplimentar al Ministro** the delegation went to pay its respects to the minister.

(**c**) (*Com etc*) local office, branch; (*estatal*) office of a government department; (*comisaría*) police station; ~ **de Hacienda** local tax office.

delegado, -a *nm/f* delegate; (*Com*) agent, representative; ~ **del Gobierno** (*Esp*) representative of central government (attached to each autonomous region); ~ **sindical** shop-steward.

delegar [1h] *vt* to delegate (*a* to).

deleitable *adj* enjoyable, delightful, delectable.

deleitación *nf*, **deleitamiento** *nm* delectation.

deleitar [1a] **1** *vt* to delight, charm. **2 deleitarse** *vr*: ~ **con,** ~ **en** to delight in, take pleasure in; ~ **en** + *infin* to delight in + *ger*.

deleite *nm* delight, pleasure; joy; ~**s** delights.

deleitosamente *adv* delightfully; deliciously.

deleitoso *adj* delightful, pleasing; delicious.

deletéreo *adj* deleterious.

deletrear [1a] *vt* (**a**) *apellido, nombre etc* to spell (out). (**b**) (*fig*) to decipher, interpret. (**c**) (*Cono Sur: escudriñar*) to observe in great detail, look minutely at.

deletreo *nm* (**a**) spelling, spelling-out. (**b**) (*fig*) decipherment, interpretation.

deleznable *adj* (**a**) *materia* fragile, brittle; crumbly; unstable; *superficie etc* slippery. (**b**) (*fig*) frail; *argumento etc* weak; (*efímero*) fleeting, ephemeral; insubstantial.

délfico *adj* Delphic.

delfín[1] *nm* (*Zool*) dolphin.

delfín[2] *nm* (*Pol*) heir apparent, designated successor.

delfinario *nm* dolphinarium.

Delfos *n* Delphi.

delgadez *nf* (**a**) (*flaqueza*) thinness; slimness. (**b**) (*delicadeza*) delicateness; tenuousness. (**c**) (*agudeza*) sharpness, cleverness.

delgado 1 *adj* (**a**) (*gen*) thin; (*flaco*) thin; (*esbelto*) slim, slender; slight; ~ **como un fideo** as thin as a rake.

(**b**) (*fig: delicado*) delicate; (*tenue*) light, tenuous.

(**c**) (*fig*) *tierra* poor, exhausted.

(**d**) (*fig: agudo*) sharp, clever.

(**e**) (*Méx: aguado*) weak, thin, watery.

2 *adv V* **hilar.**

deliberación *nf* deliberation.

deliberadamente *adv* deliberately.

deliberado *adj* deliberate.

deliberar [1a] **1** *vt* (**a**) to debate, discuss. (**b**) ~ + *infin* to decide to + *infin*. **2** *vi* to deliberate (*sobre* on), discuss (*si* whether).

deliberativo *adj* deliberative.

delicadamente *adj* delicately.

delicadez *nf* (**a**) = **delicadeza.** (**b**) (*debilidad*) weakness. (**c**) (*sensibilidad excesiva*) hypersensitiveness, touchiness, susceptibility.

delicadeza *nf* (*V adj*) (**a**) delicacy; sensitivity; daintiness; thinness; frailness; refinement.

(**b**) touchiness, hypersensitiveness; fastidiousness; squeamishness; tactfulness; subtlety; **falta de** ~ tactlessness; **¡qué ~!** how charming of you!

delicado *adj* (**a**) (*gen*) delicate; dainty; *máquina etc* delicate, sensitive; *tela* thin; slender, frail; *salud* delicate; *color* soft, delicate; *plato, rasgos* dainty; *gusto* refined, exquisite; *distinción* nice, delicate, subtle; *situación* (*difícil*) delicate, tricky; (*violento*) embarrassing; *punto* tender, sensitive; sore; **está ~ del estómago** he has a delicate stomach.

(**b**) *carácter* (*difícil*) demanding; hard to please; (*quisquilloso*) touchy, hypersensitive; (*exigente*) fastidious; (*remilgado*) squeamish; (*escrupuloso*) (over)scrupulous; (*discreto*) tactful; (*atento*) considerate; *mente* subtle; keen; **es muy ~ en el comer** he's very choosy about food; **es muy ~ para la limpieza** he's very particular about cleanliness.

delicia *nf* delight; delightfulness; **el país es una ~** the country is delightful; **tiene un jardín que es una ~** he has a delightful garden; **un libro que ha hecho las ~s de muchos niños** a book which has been the delight of many children.

deliciosamente *adj* delightfully; deliciously.

delicioso *adj* delightful; (*al gusto*) delicious.

delictivo *adj* criminal.

Delilá *nf* Delilah.

delimitación *nf* delimitation.

delimitar [1a] *vt* to delimit.

delincuencia *nf* delinquency, criminality; ~ **de guante blanco** white-collar crime; ~ **juvenil,** ~ **de menores** juvenile delinquency; ~ **menor** petty crime; **cifras de la ~** figures of crimes committed, incidence of criminality.

delincuencial *adj* criminal.

delincuente 1 *adj* delinquent; criminal; guilty. **2** *nmf* delinquent, criminal, offender; guilty person; ~ **sin antecedentes penales** first offender; ~ **común** common criminal; ~ **de guante blanco** white-collar criminal; ~ **habitual** hardened criminal; ~ **juvenil** juvenile delinquent.

delineación *nf*, **delineamiento** *nm* delineation.

delineador *nm* eyeliner.

delineante *nm* draughtsman.

delinear [1a] *vt* to delineate; to outline; to draw.

delinquimiento *nm* delinquency; guilt.

delinquir [3e] *vi* to commit an offence; to offend, transgress.

deliquio *nm* swoon, fainting fit.

delirante *adj* (**a**) (*Med*) delirious; light-headed; raving. (**b**) (*) *chiste etc* deliciously funny; *idea* crazy.

delirantemente *adv* deliriously.

delirar [1a] *vi* to be delirious, rave; (*fig*) to rave, rant, talk nonsense; **¡tú deliras!*** you must be mad!

delirio *nm* (**a**) (*Med y fig*) delirium; ravings, wanderings; (*palabras*) nonsense, nonsensical talk.

(**b**) (*frenesí*) frenzy; (*manía*) mania; ~ **de grandezas** megalomania; ~ **de persecución** persecution mania.

(**c**) (*) **con ~** madly; **me gusta con ~** I'm crazy about it; **¡fue el ~!** it was great!*; **cuando acabó de hablar fue el ~** when he finished speaking there were scenes of wild enthusiasm.

delírium *nm*: ~ **tremens** delirium tremens.

delito *nm* (**a**) (*gen*) crime, offence; ~ **de mayor cuantía** felony; ~ **de menor cuantía** misdemeanour; ~ **fiscal** tax offence; ~ **menor** minor offence; ~ **contra la propiedad** crime against property; ~ **de sangre** violent crime, crime involving bloodshed. (**b**) (*fig*) misdeed, wicked act, offence.

delta 1 *nm* (*Geog*) delta. **2** *nf* (*letra*) delta.

deltaplano *nm* (**a**) (*aparato*) hang-glider. (**b**) (*deporte*) hang-gliding.

deltoideo *adj, nm* deltoid.

deludir [3a] *vt* to delude.

delusorio *adj* delusive.

demacración *nf* emaciation.

demacrado *adj* emaciated, wasted away.

demacrarse [1a] *vr* to become emaciated, waste away.

demagogia *nf* demagogy, demagoguery.

demagógico *adj* demagogic.

demagogismo *nm* demagogy, demagoguery.

demagogo *nm* demagogue.

demanda *nf* (**a**) (*solicitud*) demand, request (*de* for); (*pregunta*) inquiry; (*reivindicación*) claim; (*petición*) petition; ~ **de extradición** request for extradition; ~ **final** final demand; ~ **de pago** demand for payment; ~ **del Santo Grial** quest for the Holy Grail; **escribir en ~ de ayuda** to write asking for help; **ir en ~ de** to go in search of, go looking for; **partir en ~ de** to go off in search of; **morir en la ~** to die in the attempt.

(**b**) (*Teat*) call.

(**c**) (*Com*) demand; **hay mucha ~ de cerillas** matches are in great demand; **tener ~** to be in demand; **ese producto no tiene ~** there is no demand for that product.

(**d**) (*Elec*) load; ~ **máxima** peak load.

(**e**) (*Jur*) action, lawsuit; ~ **civil** private prosecution; ~ **judicial** legal action; **entablar ~** to bring an action, take legal proceedings, sue; **presentar ~ de divorcio** to sue for divorce, take divorce proceedings.

demandado, -a *nm/f* defendant; (*en divorcio*) respondent.

demandante *nmf* claimant; (*Jur*) plaintiff; ~ **de trabajo** person seeking work.

demandar [1a] *vt* (**a**) (*gen*) to demand, ask for, request; to claim; to petition.

(**b**) (*Jur*) to sue, file a suit against, start proceedings against; **demandó al periódico por calumnia** he sued the paper for libel; ~ **a uno por daños y perjuicios** to sue sb for damages; **ser demandado por libelo** to be sued for libel.

demaquillador *nm* make-up remover.

demarcación *nf* (**a**) demarcation; **línea de ~** demarcation line. (**b**) (*Dep*) position.

demarcar [1g] *vt* to demarcate.

demarraje *nm* spurt, break, dash.

demarrar [1a] *vi* to spurt, break away, make a dash.

demás 1 *adj*: **los ~ libros** the other books, the rest of the books, the remaining books; **y ~ gente de ese tipo** and other people of that sort.

2 *pron*: **lo** ~ the rest (of it); **los** ~, **las** ~ the others, the rest (of them); **por lo** ~ for the rest, as to the rest; otherwise; furthermore, moreover.

3 *adv* = **además; por** ~ moreover; in vain; **y** ~ etcetera, and so on; *V* **más (estar de más)**.

demasía *nf* (**a**) (*exceso*) excess, surplus; superfluity; **con** ~, **en** ~ too much, excessively. (**b**) (*fig: atropello*) excess, outrage, wicked thing; (*tuerto*) wrong; (*ofensa*) affront. (**c**) (*fig: temeridad*) boldness; (*impertinencia*) insolence.

demasiado 1 *adj* (**a**) (*gen*) too much; (*excesivo*) overmuch, excessive; **eso es** ~ that's too much; **con** ~ **cuidado** with excessive care; **hace** ~ **calor** it's too hot; **¡esto es** ~! this is too much!, that's the limit; **¡qué** ~! great!, marvellous!

(**b**) ~**s** too many.

2 *adv* too; too much, excessively; (*LAm*) a lot, a great deal; **comer** ~ to eat too much; **es** ~ **pesado para levantar** it is too heavy to lift; ~ **lo sé** I know it only too well.

demasié‡ **1** *adj, adv* = **demasiado. 2** *nm*: **es un** ~ it's way over the top.

demediar [1b] **1** *vt* to divide in half. **2** *vi* to be divided in half.

demencia *nf* madness, insanity, dementia; ~ **senil** senile dementia.

demencial *adj* mad, crazy, demented.

dementar [1a] **1** *vt* to drive mad. **2 dementarse** *vr* to go mad, become demented.

demente 1 *adj* mad, insane, demented. **2** *nmf* mad person, lunatic.

demérito *nm* (**a**) (*defecto*) demerit, fault; disadvantage. (**b**) (*indignidad*) unworthiness. (**c**) (*LAm: menosprecio*) contempt.

demeritorio *adj* undeserving, unworthy.

demo* *nmf* (*Chile*) Christian Democrat.

democracia *nf* democracy; ~ **parlamentaria** parliamentary democracy; ~ **popular** people's democracy.

demócrata *nmf* democrat.

democráticamente *adv* democratically.

democrático *adj* democratic.

democratización *nf* democratization.

democratizador *adj* democratizing.

democratizar [1f] *vt* to democratize.

demodé* *adj* out of fashion.

demografía *nf* demography.

demográficamente *adv* demographically.

demográfico *adj* demographic; population (*atr*); **la explosión demográfica** the population explosion.

demógrafo, a *nm/f* demographer.

demoledor *adj* (*fig*) *argumento etc* powerful, overwhelming; *ataque, efecto* shattering, devastating.

demoledoramente *adv* overwhelmingly.

demoler [2h] *vt* (**a**) (*gen*) to demolish; pull down. (**b**) (*fig*) to demolish.

demolición *nf* demolition.

demonche *nm* (*euf*) = **demonio.**

demoniaco, demoníaco *adj* demoniacal, demonic.

demonio *nm* (**a**) (*gen*) devil; demon; evil spirit; ~ **familiar** familiar spirit.

(**b**) (*fig*) **ese** ~ **de sereno** that devil of a night watchman; **como el** ~ like the devil; **ir como el** ~ to go like the devil, go hell for leather; **esto pesa como el** ~ this is devilish heavy; **¡vete al** ~! go to hell!; **¡vaya con mil** ~**s!** go to blazes!; **¡que se lo lleve el** ~! to hell with it!; the devil take it!; **tener el** ~ **en el cuerpo** to be always on the go, have the devil in one; **esto sabe a** ~**(s)** this tastes awful; **un ruido de todos los** ~**s** a devil of a noise.

(**c**) (*excl etc*) **¡**~**!**, **¡qué** ~**!** (*ira*) hell!, confound it!; (*exasperación*) hang it all!; (*sorpresa*) good heavens!; what the devil ...?; the devil it is!; **¿qué** ~**s será?** what the devil can that be?; **¡qué príncipe ni qué** ~**s!** prince my foot!; **¿dónde** ~ **lo habré dejado?** where the devil can I have left it?

demonología *nf* demonology.

demontre *nm* (*euf*) = **demonio.**

demora *nf* (**a**) delay; **sin** ~ without delay. (**b**) (*Náut*) bearing.

demorar [1a] **1** *vt* to delay; to hold up, hold back.

2 *vi* (**a**) (*quedarse*) to stay on, linger on; (*tardar*) to delay, waste time; **no demores!** don't be long! (**b**) ~ **en** + *infin* (*LAm*) *V* **3.**

3 demorarse *vr* = **2; ¿cuántos días se demora para ir allá?** (*LAm*) how many days does it take to get there?; ~ **en** + *infin* (*esp LAm*) to take a long time to + *infin*, be slow in + *ger*.

demorón *adj* (*And, Cono Sur*) = **demoroso.**

demoroso *adj* (*Cono Sur*) (*lento*) slow, lazy; (*moroso*) late, overdue; **ser** ~ **en** + *infin* to take a long time to + *infin*, be slow in + *ger*.

demoscopia *nf* public opinion research.

demoscópico *adj*: **sondeo** ~ public opinion survey, survey of public opinion.

Demóstenes *nm* Demosthenes.

demostrable *adj* demonstrable, that can be demonstrated.

demostración *nf* demonstration, show, display; gesture; (*Mat*) proof; ~ **de cariño** show of affection; ~ **de cólera** display of anger; ~ **comercial** commercial display, trade exhibition.

demostrar [1l] *vt* to demonstrate, show; to show off; to prove; ~ **cómo se hace algo** to demonstrate how sth is done; ~ **que** ... to show that ..., prove that ...; **Vd no puede** ~**me nada** you can't prove anything against me.

demostrativo *adj, nm* demonstrative.

demótico *adj* demotic.

demudación *nf* change, alteration (of countenance).

demudado *adj rostro* pale.

demudar [1a] **1** *vt rostro* to change, alter.

2 demudarse *vr* (**a**) (*gen*) to change, alter.

(**b**) (*fig: perder color*) to change colour, change countenance; (*alterarse*) to look upset, show one's distress; **sin** ~ without a flicker of emotion; **continuó sin** ~ he went on quite unaffected (*o* unabashed).

denante(s) *adv* (*LAm*) earlier, a while ago; in past times.

dendrocronología *nf* dendrochronology.

denegación *nf* refusal; rejection; denial.

denegar [1h *y* 1k] *vt* (*rechazar*) to refuse; to reject; (*negar*) to deny; (*Jur*) *apelación* to reject, refuse to allow.

dengoso *adj* affected; prudish; dainty, finicky.

dengue *nm* (**a**) (*afectación*) affectation; (*coquetería*) coyness; (*remilgo*) prudery; (*delicadeza*) daintiness, finickiness; (*And: contoneo*) wiggle; **hacer** ~**s** to act coyly, simper; to be finicky; **no me vengas con esos** ~**s** I don't want to hear your silly complaints.

(**b**) (*Med*) dengue, breakbone fever.

denguero *adj* = **dengoso.**

denier *nm* denier.

denigración *nf* denigration.

denigrante *adj* insulting; degrading.

denigrar [1a] *vt* (*difamar*) to denigrate, revile, run down; (*injuriar*) to insult.

denigratorio *adj* denigratory; insulting; **campaña denigratoria** campaign of denigration, smear campaign.

denodadamente *adv* boldly, dauntlessly, intrepidly; **luchar** ~ to fight bravely.

denodado *adj* bold, dauntless, intrepid, brave.

denominación *nf* (**a**) (*acto*) naming. (**b**) (*nombre*) name, designation; denomination; **moneda de baja** ~ (*LAm*) low value coin; ~ **de origen** denomination of origin; ~ **social** (*Méx*) firm's official name.

denominado *adj* named, called; so-called.

denominador *nm* denominator; ~ **común** (*Mat*) common denominator; (*fig*) staple, constant feature.

denominar [1a] *vt* to name, call, designate.

denostar [1l] *vt* to insult, revile, abuse; to condemn.

denotación *nf* (*Ling, Filos*) denotation.

denotar [1a] *vt* (*significar*) to denote; (*indicar*) to indicate, show; (*expresar*) to express.

densamente *adv* densely; compactly; thickly; solidly.

densidad *nf* density; compactness; thickness; heaviness, dryness; solidity; (*Inform*) density; (*Inform: de caracteres*) pitch; ~ **de grabación** recording density; ~ **de población** density of population.

denso *adj* (*gen*) dense; compact; *humo, líquido etc* thick; *libro, lectura, discurso* heavy, substantial, solid; **el argumento es algo** ~ (*pey*) the reasoning is somewhat confused.

dentado 1 *adj* having teeth; *rueda* cogged, toothed; *filo* jagged; *sello* perforated; (*Bot*) dentate. **2** *nm* (*de sello*) perforation.

dentadura *nf* set of teeth, teeth (*collectively*); denture; ~ **artificial,** ~ **postiza** false teeth, denture(s); **tener mala** ~ to have bad teeth.

dental *adj, nf* dental.

dentamen* *nm* teeth.

dentar [1j] **1** *vt* to put teeth on, furnish with teeth; *filo* to make jagged; (*Téc*) to indent; *sello* to perforate; **sello sin** ~ imperforate stamp.

2 *vi* to teethe, cut one's teeth.

dentellada *nf* (**a**) (*mordisco*) bite, nip; **partir algo a** ~**s** to

sever sth with one's teeth. (**b**) (*señal*) tooth mark.
dentellar [1a] *vi* (*dientes*) to chatter; **estaba dentellando** his teeth were chattering; **el susto le hizo ~** the fright made his teeth chatter.
dentellear [1a] *vt* to bite, nibble (at), sink one's teeth into.
dentera *nf* (**a**) (*gen*) the shivers, the shudders; **dar ~ a uno** to set sb's teeth on edge, give sb the shivers.
(**b**) (*fig*: *envidia*) envy, jealousy; (*deseo*) great desire; **dar ~ a uno** to make sb jealous; to make one's mouth water; **le da ~ que hagan fiestas al niño** it makes him jealous when they make a fuss of the baby.
dentición *nf* (**a**) (*acto*) teething; **estar con la ~** to be teething. (**b**) (*Anat*) dentition; **~ de leche** milk teeth.
dentífrico 1 *adj* tooth (*atr*); **pasta dentífrica** toothpaste. **2** *nm* dentifrice, toothpaste.
dentilargo *adj* long-toothed.
dentina *nf* dentin(e), ivory.
dentista *nmf* dentist.
dentistería *nf* (*And, Carib*) (**a**) (*clínica*) dentist's, dental clinic. (**b**) (*ciencia*) dentistry.
dentística *nf* (*Cono Sur*) dentistry.
dentón *adj* large-toothed, buck-toothed, toothy.
dentradera *nf* (*And*), **dentrera** *nf* (*And*) housemaid.
dentro 1 *adv* (*estar*) inside; indoors; *sentir etc* inwardly, inside; **allí ~** in there; **de ~, desde ~** from inside; **por ~** inside, on the inside, in the interior; **meter algo para ~** to push sth in; **vamos ~** let's go in(side).
2 ~ de *prep* (**a**) (*estar*) in, inside, within; **~ de la casa** inside the house.
(**b**) (*meter etc*) into, inside; **lo metió ~ del cajón** he put it into the drawer.
(**c**) (*tiempo*) within, inside; **~ de 3 meses** inside 3 months, within 3 months; **~ de poco** shortly; soon after.
(**d**) **~ de lo posible** as far as one (*etc*) can, as far as is possible; **eso no cabe ~ de lo posible** that does not come within the bounds of possibility.
dentrodera *nf* (*And*) servant.
denudación *nf* denudation.
denudar [1a] *vt* to denude (*de* of); to lay bare.
denuedo *nm* boldness, daring; bravery.
denuesto *nm* insult; **llenar a uno de ~s** to heap insults on sb.
denuncia *nf* report; denunciation; (*a policía*) complaint; (*Jur etc*) accusation; **~ de accidente** report of an accident; **~ falsa** false accusation; **hacer una ~, poner una ~** to make an official complaint (to the police *etc*).
denunciable *adj crimen* indictable, punishable.
denunciación *nf* denunciation; accusation.
denunciador(a) *nm/f*, **denunciante** *nmf* accuser; informer; **el ~ del accidente** the person who reported the accident.
denunciar [1b] *vt delito etc* to report (*a* to); (*proclamar*) to proclaim, announce; (*presagiar*) to foretell; (*Jur etc*) to denounce (*a* to), accuse (*a* before), inform against; (*pey*) to betray, give away (*a* to); *tratado* to denounce; (*indicar*) to denote, indicate, reveal; **~ que ...** to report that ...; **denunciaron los precios abusivos a las autoridades** they reported the exorbitant prices to the authorities; **el accidente fue denunciado a la policía** the accident was reported to the police; **esto denunciaba la presencia del gas** this betrayed the presence of gas, this indicated the presence of gas.
denuncio *nm* (*LAm*) = **denuncia**.
Dep. (**a**) *abr de* **Departamento** Department, Dept. (**b**) (*Com*) *abr de* **Depósito** deposit.
D.E.P. *abr de* **descanse en paz** may he rest in peace, R.I.P.
deparar [1a] *vt* to provide, furnish with; to present, offer; **nos deparó la ocasión para ...** it gave us a chance to ...; **los placeres que el viaje nos deparó** the pleasures which the trip afforded us; **pero también nos deparó la solución** but it also furnished us with the solution; **¡Dios te la depare buena!** and the best of luck! (*iró*).
departamental *adj* departmental.
departamento *nm* (**a**) (*gen*) department, section; office; bureau; **~ jurídico** legal department; **~ de visados** visa section.
(**b**) (*de caja etc*) compartment.
(**c**) (*Ferro etc*) compartment; **~ de fumadores** smoking compartment; **~ de no fumadores** non-smoking compartment; **~ de primera** first-class compartment.
(**d**) (*esp Cono Sur, Méx*: *piso*) flat, apartment.
(**e**) (*LAm*: *distrito*) department, administrative district, province.
departir [1a] *vi* to talk, converse (*con* with, *de* about).
depauperación *nf* (**a**) impoverishment. (**b**) (*Med*) weakening, exhaustion.
depauperar [1a] *vt* (**a**) to impoverish. (**b**) (*Med*) to weaken, deplete, exhaust.
dependencia *nf* (**a**) (*gen*) dependence (*de* on); reliance (*de* on); **~ psicológica** psychological dependency.
(**b**) (*parentesco*) relationship, kinship.
(**c**) (*Pol etc*) dependency.
(**d**) (*Com*: *sección*) section, office; (*sucursal*) branch office.
(**e**) (*Arquit*: *cuarto*) room; (*anejo*) outbuilding, outhouse; **~ policial** police premises; **permanecer en ~s policiales** to remain in police custody.
(**f**) (*Com etc*: *plantilla*) personnel, sales staff, employees.
(**g**) **~s** accessories.
depender [2a] *vi* (**a**) (*gen*) to depend; **~ de** to depend on; (*contar con*) to rely on; **depende** it (all) depends; **depende de lo que haga él** it depends on what he does; **todo depende de que él esté listo** it all turns on his being ready; **no depende de mí** it does not rest with me; **todos dependemos de ti** we are all relying on you. (**b**) **~ de** *autoridad* to be (*o* come) under, be answerable to; **el museo depende de otro ministerio** the museum is run by another ministry.
dependienta *nf* salesgirl, saleswoman, shop assistant.
dependiente 1 *adj* dependent (*de* on). **2** *nm* (*empleado*) employee; (*oficinista*) clerk; (*de tienda*) salesman, shop assistant, salesperson (*US*).
depilación *nf*, **depilado** *nm* depilation.
depilar [1a] *vt* to depilate, remove the hair from; *cejas* to pluck.
depilatorio 1 *adj* depilatory. **2** *nm* depilatory, hair remover.
deplorable *adj* deplorable; lamentable, regrettable.
deplorar [1a] *vt* to deplore, regret; to condemn; **lo deploro** I greatly deplore it, I'm extremely sorry.
deponente 1 *adj* (**a**) (*Ling*) deponent. (**b**) **persona ~** (*Jur*) = **2**. **2** *nmf* (*Jur*) deponent, person making a statement.
deponer [2q] **1** *vt* (**a**) (*dejar*) to lay down; to lay aside; (*quitar*) to remove, take down; *armas* to lay down.
(**b**) *rey* to depose; *gobernante* to oust, overthrow; *ministro* to remove from office.
2 *vi* (**a**) (*Jur*) to give evidence, make a statement.
(**b**) (*CAm, Méx*: *vomitar*) to vomit.
deportación *nf* deportation.
deportar [1a] *vt* to deport.
deporte *nm* sport; game; outdoor recreation; **~s acuáticos** water sports; **~ blanco** winter sports, (*esp*) skiing; **~ de competición** competitive sport; **~ de exhibición** show event; **~ hípico** horse-riding; **~s de invierno** winter sports; **~ náutico** water sports; yachting; **~ del remo** rowing; **~ de la vela** sailing; **el fútbol es un ~** football is a game; **es muy aficionado a los ~s** he is very fond of sport.
deportista 1 *adj* sports (*atr*); sporting; **el público ~** the sporting public. **2** *nm* (*jugador*) sportsman; (*aficionado*) sporting man, sports fan. **3** *nf* sportswoman.
deportivamente *adv* (**a**) sportingly; in a good spirit. (**b**) **hablando ~** in sport, in sporting terms.
deportividad *nf* sportsmanship.
deportivo 1 *adj* (**a**) *club, periódico etc* sports (*atr*). (**b**) *actitud, conducta etc* sporting, sportsmanlike. (**c**) (*pey*) casual, breezy, (too) free-and-easy. **2** *nm* (**a**) (*Aut*) sports car. (**b**) **~s** (*zapatos*) sports shoes, trainers. (**c**) (*Prensa*) sports paper.
deposición *nf* (**a**) (*acto*) deposition, removal. (**b**) (*afirmación*) assertion, affirmation; (*Jur*) deposition, evidence, statement (**c**) **hacer sus deposiciones** (*euf*) to defecate.
depositador(a) *nm/f*, **depositante** *nmf* (*Com, Fin*) depositor.
depositar [1a] **1** *vt* (*gen*) to deposit; (*poner*) to place; (*poner aparte*) to lay aside; (*guardar*) to put away, store, put into store; (*confiar*) to entrust (*en* to), confide (*en* to). **2 depositarse** *vr* (*heces*) to settle.
depositaría *nf* depository; (*Fin etc*) trust.
depositario, -a *nm/f* depository, trustee; receiver; (*de secreto etc*) repository.
depósito *nm* (**a**) (*Quím etc*) deposit; sediment; (*Geol, Min*) deposit.
(**b**) (*Com, Fin*: *dinero*) deposit; **~ bancario** bank deposit; **~ a plazo (fijo)** fixed-term deposit; **dejar una cantidad en ~** to leave a sum as a deposit.
(**c**) (*Com etc*: *almacén*) store, storehouse, warehouse; depot; (*de objetos perdidos*) pound; (*Mil*) depot; (*vertedero*)

dump; ~ **de aduana** customs warehouse; ~ **afianzado** bonded warehouse; ~ **de alimentación** (*Inform*) feeder bin; ~ **de basura** rubbish dump, tip; ~ **de cadáveres** mortuary, morgue; ~ **de carbón** coal tip; ~ **de equipajes** cloakroom; ~ **de libros** book stack; ~ **de locomotoras** engine shed; ~ **de maderas** timber yard; ~ **de municiones** ammunition dump.

(**d**) (*de líquidos*) tank; (*de wáter*) cistern; (*alberca*) reservoir; ~ **de agua** water tank, cistern; reservoir; ~ **de combustible** fuel tank; ~ **de gasolina** petrol tank.

depravación *nf* depravity, depravation, corruption.

depravado *adj* depraved, corrupt.

depravar [1a] **1** *vt* to deprave, corrupt. **2 depravarse** *vr* to become depraved.

depre* *nf* depression; **tiene la** ~ she's feeling a bit low.

depreciación *nf* depreciation; ~ **acelerada** accelerated depreciation; ~ **acumulada** accumulated depreciation.

depreciar [1b] **1** *vt* to depreciate, reduce the value of. **2 depreciarse** *vr* to depreciate, lose value.

depredación *nf* depredation; outrage, excess; pillage; (*Bio*) predation.

depredador *nm* (*Bio*) predator.

depredar [1a] *vt* to pillage; to commit outrages against; (*Bio*) to be predatory on, take as its prey.

depresión *nf* (**a**) (*Geog etc*) depression; hollow; (*de horizonte etc*) dip; (*en muro*) recess, niche.

(**b**) (*acto*) lowering; (*baja*) drop, fall (*de* in); ~ **del mercurio** fall in temperature (*o* pressure).

(**c**) (*Met*) depression.

(**d**) (*Econ*) depression, slump, recession.

(**e**) (*mental*) depression; ~ **nerviosa** nervous depression; ~ **posparto** postnatal depression.

depresivo, -a *adj, nm/f* depressive.

deprimente 1 *adj* depressing. **2** *nm* depressant.

deprimido *adj* depressed.

deprimir [3a] **1** *vt* (**a**) (*físicamente*) to depress, press down; to flatten.

(**b**) (*mentalmente etc*) to depress.

(**c**) *nivel etc* to lower, reduce.

(**d**) (*fig: humillar*) to humiliate; (*despreciar*) to belittle, disparage.

2 deprimirse *vr* to get depressed.

depuración *nf* (**a**) (*gen*) purification; cleansing. (**b**) (*Pol etc*) purge. (**c**) (*Inform*) debugging.

depurado *adj estilo* pure, refined.

depurador *nm* water purifier.

depuradora *nf* purifying plant; water-treatment plant; ~ **de aguas residuales** sewage farm.

depurar [1a] *vt* (**a**) (*gen*) to purify; to cleanse, purge. (**b**) (*Pol etc*) to purge. (**c**) (*Inform*) to debug. (**d**) (*Carib**) *empleado* to fire*.

depurativo *nm* blood tonic.

dequeísmo *nm* tendency to use 'de que' in place of 'que' (*eg* 'pienso de que').

der., der.º *adj abr de* **derecho** right, r.

derby ['derbi] *nm, pl* **derbys** local derby.

derecha *nf* (**a**) (*mano*) right hand; (*lado*) right side, right-hand side; **estar a la** ~ **de** to be on the right of; **torcer a la** ~ to turn (to the) right; **conducción a** ~ right-hand drive; **el poste de la** ~ the post on the right; **seguir por la** ~ to keep (to the) right.

(**b**) (*Pol*) right; **es de ~s** she's on the right, she has right-wing views.

(**c**) **a ~s** rightly, aright; justly; **si le entiendo a ~s** if I understand you rightly.

derechamente *adv* (**a**) (*gen*) straight, directly. (**b**) (*fig*) properly, rightly.

derechazo *nm* (*Boxeo*) right; (*Tenis*) forehand drive; (*Taur*) *a right-handed pass with the cape.*

derechismo *nm* right-wing outlook (*o* tendencies *etc*).

derechista (*Pol*) **1** *adj* rightist, right-wing. **2** *nmf* rightist, right-winger.

derechización *nf* drift towards the right.

derechizar [1f] **1** *vt partido* to lead towards the right. **2 derechizarse** *vr* to move to the right, become right-wing.

derecho 1 *adj* (**a**) *mano* right; *lado* right hand.

(**b**) (*recto*) straight; (*vertical*) upright, erect, standing; **más** ~ **que una vela** as straight as a die; **poner algo** ~ to stand sth upright.

(**c**) (*LAm: con suerte*) lucky.

(**d**) (*LAm: honrado*) honest, straight.

2 *adv* (**a**) (*de manera recta*) straight, directly; (*verticalmente*) upright.

(**b**) (*directamente*) straight, directly; **ir** ~ **a** to go straight to; **siga** ~ carry (*o* go) straight on.

3 *nm* (**a**) (*lado, cara*) right side.

(**b**) (*gen*) right; (*título*) claim, title; (*privilegio*) privilege, exemption; ~ **de antena** broadcasting rights; **~s de autor** author's copyright; **~s cinematográficos** film rights; **~s civiles** civil rights; ~ **divino** divine right; ~ **a domicilio** right of abode; **~s humanos** human rights; **~s de la mujer** women's rights; ~ **de paso,** ~ **de tránsito** right of way; ~ **de propiedad literaria** copyright; ~ **de réplica** right of reply; ~ **de retención** (*Com*) lien; ~ **de reunión** right of assembly; ~ **de visita** right of search; ~ **de votar,** ~ **al voto** right to vote, franchise; **con** ~ rightly, justly; **con** ~ **a** with a right to, with entitlement to; **por** ~ **propio** in his own right; **según** ~ by right(s); **'reservados todos los ~s'** 'all rights reserved', 'copyright'; **¡no hay ~!** it's not fair!; it's an outrage!; **'se reserva el** ~ **de entrada'** 'the management reserves the right to exclude certain persons'; **tener** ~ **a** to have a right to, be entitled to; **tener** ~ **a** + *infin* to have a right to + *infin*.

(**c**) (*Jur*) law; justice; ~ **civil** civil law; ~ **de compañías,** ~ **de sociedades** company law; ~ **comunitario** Community law; ~ **laboral,** ~ **del trabajo** labour law; ~ **mercantil** commercial law; ~ **penal** criminal law; ~ **político** constitutional law; ~ **tributario** tax law; **Facultad de D~** Faculty of Law; **estudiante de** ~ law student; **propietario en** ~ legal owner; **lo que manda el** ~ **en este caso** what justice demands in this case.

(**d**) (*Fin*) due(s); fee(s); tax(es); (*de libro, petróleo etc*) royalties; (*profesional*) fee(s); **franco de ~s** duty-free; **sujeto a ~s** subject to duty, dutiable; **~s de aduana, ~s arancelarios** customs duty; ~ **de asesoría,** ~ **de consulta** consulting fees; **~s de autor** royalties; ~ **de enganche** (*Telec*) connection charge; **~s de entrada** import duties; **~s de exportación** export duty; **~s de matrícula** registration fee; **~s de peaje** toll; ~ **preferente** preferential duty; **~s de puerto** harbour dues; **~s reales** death duties.

derechohabiente *nmf* rightful claimant.

derechura *nf* (**a**) (*franqueza*) straightness; directness; **hablar en** ~ to speak plainly, talk straight; **hacer algo en** ~ to do sth right away.

(**b**) (*justicia*) rightness, justice.

(**c**) (*And, CAm: suerte*) (good) luck.

deriva *nf* (*Náut*) drift; leeway; (*apartamiento*) deviation; ~ **continental,** ~ **de los continentes** continental drift; **buque a la** ~ ship adrift, drifting ship; **ir a la** ~ to drift, be adrift.

derivación *nf* (**a**) (*gen*) derivation; (*origen*) origin, source. (**b**) (*Ling: etimología*) etymology, derivation; (*composición*) word formation; compounding; (*palabra*) derivative; ~ **regresiva** back-formation. (**c**) (*Elec*) shunt; **en** ~ shunt (*atr*); **hacer una** ~ **en un alambre** to tap a wire. (**d**) (*de río etc*) diversion; tapping.

derivado 1 *adj* derived; derivative (*t Ling*). **2** *nm* (**a**) derivative (*t Ling*). (**b**) (*Quím etc*) by-product; ~ **cárnico** meat product; ~ **lácteo** milk product; ~ **del petróleo** oil product.

derivar [1a] **1** *vt* (**a**) to derive (*t Ling*; *de* from).

(**b**) *agua, conversación etc* to direct, divert; *río* to tap; (*Elec*) to shunt.

2 *vi* (**a**) (*Ling etc*) ~ **de** to derive from, be derived from.

(**b**) (*Náut*) to drift; ~ **en** (*fig*) to lead to, end up as; (*pey*) to drift into, degenerate into; ~ **hacia** to incline towards.

3 derivarse *vr* (**a**) (*Ling*) = **2** (**a**).

(**b**) ~ **de** (*resultar*) to stem from, arise from.

derivativo *adj, nm* derivative.

dermatología *nf* dermatology.

dermatólogo, -a *nm/f* dermatologist.

dérmico *adj* skin (*atr*); **enfermedad dérmica** skin disease.

derogación *nf* repeal, abolition.

derogar [1h] *vt* to repeal, abolish.

derrabar [1a] *vt* to dock, cut off the tail of.

derrabe *nm* rock-fall; cave-in.

derrama *nf* (*reparto*) apportionment of (local) tax; (*sobretasa*) special levy; (*tasación*) valuation, rating; (*vale*) credit voucher; (*dividendo*) interim dividend payment.

derramadero *nm* spillway; ~ **de basura** rubbish dump.

derramamiento *nm* (**a**) (*gen*) spilling; shedding; overflowing; ~ **de sangre** bloodshed. (**b**) (*esparcimiento*) scattering, spreading. (**c**) (*fig*) squandering, wasting, lavishing.

derramar [1a] **1** *vt* (**a**) (*por accidente*) *líquido* to spill; (*verter*) to pour out, pour away; *lágrimas* to weep, shed; *sangre* to shed; *luz* to shed, cast; ~ **una taza de café** to spill a cup of coffee.

(**b**) (*esparcir*) to scatter, spread (about); *favores* to scatter, lavish, pour out; *chismes, noticias* to spread.

(**c**) *impuestos* to apportion.

(**d**) (*fig*) to squander, waste.

2 derramarse *vr* (**a**) (*líquido etc*) to spill; to pour out, overflow, run over, flow out; (*pluma, vasija*) to leak; **llenar una taza hasta ~** to fill a cup to overflowing.

(**b**) (*esparcirse*) to spread, scatter, be scattered; **la multitud se derramó por todos lados** the crowd scattered in all directions.

derrame *nm* (**a**) (*acto*) = **derramamiento.**

(**b**) (*cantidad*) loss; (*salida*) overflow; outflow; (*pérdida*) leakage; waste.

(**c**) (*Med*) discharge; excess of liquid present in the body; (*de sangre*) haemorrhage; **~ cerebral** brain haemorrhage; **~ sinovial** water on the knee.

derrapada *nf*, **derrapaje** *nm*, **derrapamiento** *nm* skid, skidding.

derrapante *adj*: **'camino ~'** (*Méx*) 'slippery road'.

derrapar [1a] **1** *vi* (*Aut*) to skid. **2 derraparse** *vr* (*Méx*) (**a**) (*patinar*) to slip. (**b**) **~ por uno*** to be mad about sb*.

derrape *nm* (**a**) (*Aut*) skid. (**b**) (*Carib*‡: *alboroto*) uproar, shindy*.

derredor: **al ~ (de)**, **en ~ (de)** *adv y prep* around, about; **en su ~** round about him.

derrelicto *nm* (*Náut*) derelict.

derrengado *adj* (**a**) (*torcido*) bent, twisted, crooked. (**b**) (*lisiado*) crippled, lame; **estar ~** (*fig*) to ache all over; to be footsore; **dejar ~ a uno** (*fig*) to wear sb out.

derrengante *adj* exhausting, crippling.

derrengar [1h] *vt* (**a**) (*torcer*) to bend, twist, make crooked. (**b**) **~ a uno** to break sb's back, cripple sb; (*fig*) to wear sb out.

derrepente *nm* (*CAm*): **en un ~ = de repente.**

derretido *adj* (**a**) *metal* melted; molten; *nieve* thawed. (**b**) **estar ~ por una*** to be crazy about sb.

derretimiento *nm* (**a**) (*gen*) melting; thawing. (**b**) (*fig: derroche*) squandering. (**c**) (*fig: pasión*) mad passion, burning love.

derretir [3k] **1** *vt* (**a**) *metal* to melt; to liquefy; *helado etc* to melt; *nieve* to thaw.

(**b**) (*fig*) to squander, throw away.

(**c**) (*) (*aburrir*) to bore to tears; (*irritar*) to exasperate.

2 derretirse *vr* (**a**) (*fundirse*) to melt; to run, liquefy.

(**b**) (*fig*) to be very susceptible to love, fall in love easily; **~ por una** to be crazy about sb.

(**c**) (*: *sulfurarse*) to get worked up, fret and fume.

(**d**) (*: *mostrarse sensible*) to come over very sentimental; to go all weak at the knees.

derribar [1a] **1** *vt* (**a**) *edificio* to knock down, pull down, demolish; *barrera* to tear down; *puerta* to batter down.

(**b**) *persona* to knock down; to floor, lay out; *luchador* to floor, throw.

(**c**) (*Aer*) to shoot down, bring down; **fue derribado sobre el Canal** he was shot down over the Channel.

(**d**) (*Caza*) to shoot, bag, bring down.

(**e**) *gobierno etc* to bring down, overthrow, topple.

(**f**) (*fig*) *pasión* to subdue.

2 derribarse *vr* (**a**) (*caer al suelo*) to fall down, collapse.

(**b**) (*tirarse al suelo*) to throw o.s. down, hurl o.s. to the ground; to prostrate o.s.

derribo *nm* (**a**) (*de edificio*) knocking down, demolition. (**b**) (*Lucha*) throw. (**c**) (*Aer*) shooting down; destruction. (**d**) (*Pol*) overthrow. (**e**) **~s** rubble, debris.

derrisco *nm* (*Carib*) gorge, ravine.

derrocadero *nm* cliff, precipice, steep place.

derrocamiento *nm* (**a**) (*derrumbamiento*) flinging down, throwing down. (**b**) (*demolición*) demolition. (**c**) (*derribo*) overthrow, toppling; ousting.

derrocar [1g] **1** *vt* (**a**) *objeto, persona* to fling down, hurl down.

(**b**) *edificio etc* to knock down, demolish.

(**c**) *gobierno* to overthrow, topple; *ministro etc* to oust (*de* from).

2 derrocarse *vr*: **~ por un precipicio** to throw o.s. over a cliff.

derrochador 1 *adj* spendthrift. **2** *nm* **derrochadora** *nf* spendthrift, wastrel.

derrochar [1a] *vt* (**a**) *dinero etc* to squander, waste; to lavish, pour out. (**b**) **~ salud** to be bursting with health; **~ mal genio** to be excessively bad-tempered.

derroche *nm* (**a**) (*despilfarro*) squandering, waste; lavish expenditure; (*exceso*) extravagance; **con un formidable ~ de recursos** with a lavish use of resources; **no se puede tolerar tal ~** such extravagance is not to be tolerated.

(**b**) (*gran cantidad*) abundance, excess; **con un ~ de buen gusto** with a fine display of good taste.

derrochón = **derrochador.**

derrota[1] *nf* (**a**) (*camino*) road, route, track. (**b**) (*Náut*) course.

derrota[2] *nf* (*Dep, Mil etc*) defeat; rout; débâcle, disaster; **sufrir una grave ~** to suffer a serious defeat, (*en proyecto etc*) to suffer a grave setback.

derrotado *adj* (**a**) (*vencido*) defeated; *equipo* defeated, beaten, losing. (**b**) *ropa, persona* shabby; **un actor ~** a shabby old actor, a down-and-out actor.

derrotar [1a] **1** *vt* (**a**) (*Mil*) to defeat; to rout, put to flight; *equipo etc* to defeat, beat. (**b**) *ropa* to tear, ruin; (*fig*) *salud* to ruin. **2 derrotarse**‡ *vr* (*delincuente*) to cough‡, sing‡; **~ de uno** to grass on sb‡.

derrotero *nm* (**a**) (*Náut*) course; (*fig*) course, plan of action; **tomar otro ~** (*fig*) to adopt a different course. (**b**) (*Carib: tesoro*) hidden treasure.

derrotismo *nm* defeatism.

derrotista *adj, nmf* defeatist.

derruir [3g] *vt* to demolish, tear down.

derrumbadero *nm* (**a**) (*precipicio*) cliff, precipice, steep place. (**b**) (*fig: peligro*) danger, hazard; pitfall.

derrumbamiento *nm* (**a**) (*caída*) plunge, headlong fall.

(**b**) (*demolición*) demolition; (*desplome*) collapse; fall, cave-in; **~ de piedras** fall of rocks; **~ de tierra** landslide.

(**c**) (*fig*) collapse, ruin, destruction; (*de precio*) sharp fall, collapse.

derrumbar [1a] **1** *vt* (**a**) *objeto, persona* to fling down, hurl down; to throw headlong.

(**b**) *edificio etc* to knock down, demolish.

(**c**) (*volcar*) to upset, overturn.

2 derrumbarse *vr* (**a**) (*persona etc*) to fling o.s., hurl o.s. (headlong; *por* down, over); to fall headlong.

(**b**) (*edificio etc*) to collapse, fall down, tumble down; (*techo*) to fall in, cave in.

(**c**) (*fig: esperanzas etc*) to collapse, be ruined; **se han derrumbado los precios** prices have tumbled; the bottom has fallen out of the market.

derrumbe *nm* (**a**) = **derrumbadero.** (**b**) = **derrumbamiento.**

derviche *nm* dervish.

des... *pref* de..., des...; un...; *p.ej.* **descolonización** decolonization; **desmilitarizado** demilitarized; **desempleo** unemployment; **desfavorable** unfavourable; **desgana** unwillingness.

desabastecido *adj*: **estar ~ de** to be out of (supplies of); **nos cogió ~s de gasolina** it caught us without petrol.

desabastecimiento *nm* shortage, scarcity.

desabillé *nm* deshabille.

desabollar [1a] *vt* to knock the dents out of.

desabonarse [1a] *vr* to stop subscribing, cancel one's subscription.

desabono *nm* (**a**) (*acto*) cancellation of one's subscription. (**b**) (*fig*) discredit; **hablar en ~ de uno** to say damaging things about sb, speak ill of sb.

desaborido *adj comida* insipid, tasteless; *persona* dull.

desabotonar [1a] **1** *vt* to unbutton, undo. **2** *vi* (*Bot*) to open, blossom. **3 desabotonarse** *vr* to come undone.

desabrido *adj* (**a**) *comida* tasteless, insipid, flat.

(**b**) *tiempo* unpleasant.

(**c**) *persona* surly, rude, disagreeable; *tono etc* harsh, rough; *respuesta etc* sharp; *debate* bitter, acrimonious.

desabrigado *adj* (**a**) (*sin abrigo*) too lightly dressed, without adequate clothing. (**b**) (*fig*) unprotected, exposed; defenceless.

desabrigar [1h] **1** *vt* (**a**) (*desarropar*) to remove the clothing of; to leave bare, uncover.

(**b**) (*fig*) to leave without shelter, deprive of protection.

2 desabrigarse *vr* to take off one's (outer) clothing; to leave o.s. bare, uncover o.s.; **~ en la cama** to throw off one's bedcovers.

desabrigo *nm* (**a**) (*acto*) uncovering. (**b**) (*estado*) bareness; exposure; lack of clothing (*o* covers). (**c**) (*fig*) unprotectedness; poverty, destitution.

desabrimiento *nm* (**a**) (*de comida*) tastelessness, insipidness.

(**b**) (*disgusto*) unpleasantness.

(**c**) (*hosquedad*) surliness, rudeness; harshness; sharpness; acrimony; **contestar con ~** to answer sharply.

(**d**) (*fig*) depression, lowness of spirits; uneasy feeling.

desabrir [3a] *vt* (**a**) *comida* to give a nasty taste to. (**b**) (*fig*) to embitter; to torment.

desabrochar [1a] **1** *vt* (**a**) *ropa* to undo, unfasten, unbutton; *persona* to loosen the clothing of.

(**b**) (*fig*) to uncover, expose.

2 desabrocharse *vr* (*fig*) to pour one's heart out (*con* to).

desaburrirse [3a] *vr* (*LAm*) to enjoy o.s., have a good time.

desacatador *adj* disrespectful, insulting.

desacatar [1a] *vt persona* to be disrespectful to, behave insultingly towards; *orden* to disobey; *norma* to be out of line with, not comply with.

desacato *nm* disrespect; insulting behaviour; (*Jur etc*) contempt, act of contempt; **~ a la autoridad, ~ a la justicia** contempt (of court).

desaceleración *nf* deceleration, slowing down, slowdown; (*Econ*) downturn, reduction.

desacelerar [1a] **1** *vt* to slow down. **2** *vi* to decelerate, slow down; (*Econ*) to slow down, decline.

desacertadamente *adv* mistakenly, erroneously, wrongly; unwisely, injudiciously.

desacertado *adj opinión etc* mistaken, erroneous, wrong; *medida etc* unwise, injudicious.

desacertar [1j] *vi* to be mistaken, be wrong; to get it wrong; to act unwisely.

desacierto *nm* (*error*) mistake, miscalculation, error; miss; (*dicho*) unfortunate remark (*etc*); **fue uno de muchos ~s suyos** it was one of his many errors; **ha sido un ~ elegir tal sitio** it was a mistake to choose such a place.

desacomedido *adj* (*And*) unhelpful, obstructive.

desacomodado *adj* (**a**) *criado* unemployed, out of a job. (**b**) (*pobre*) badly off. (**c**) (*incómodo*) awkward, troublesome, inconvenient.

desacomodar [1a] **1** *vt* (**a**) *criado* to discharge. (**b**) (*incomodar*) to put out, inconvenience. **2 desacomodarse** *vr* to lose one's post.

desacompasado *adj* = **descompasado**.

desaconsejable *adj* inadvisable.

desaconsejado *adj* ill-advised.

desaconsejar [1a] *vt persona* to dissuade, advise against; *proyecto etc* to advise against; to disapprove of; **los rigores del viaje desaconsejaron esa decisión** the rigours of the journey made that decision seem inadvisable (*o* wrong).

desacoplable *adj* detachable, removable.

desacoplar [1a] *vt* (*Elec*) to disconnect; (*Mec*) to take apart, uncouple.

desacordar [1l] **1** *vt* to put out of tune. **2 desacordarse** *vr* (**a**) (*Mús*) to get out of tune. (**b**) (*olvidar*) to be forgetful; **~ de algo** to forget sth.

desacorde *adj* (**a**) (*Mús*) discordant. (**b**) (*fig*) discordant, incongruous.

desacostumbrado *adj* unusual; unaccustomed.

desacostumbrar [1a] **1** *vt*: **~ a uno de** to break sb of the habit of, wean sb away from.

2 desacostumbrarse *vr*: **~ de** to break o.s. of the habit of.

desacralizar [1f] *vt* to demystify.

desacreditar [1a] **1** *vt* (**a**) (*desprestigiar*) to discredit, damage the reputation of, bring into disrepute.

(**b**) (*denigrar*) to cry down, disparage, run down.

2 desacreditarse *vr* to become discredited.

desactivación *nf* defusing, making safe; **~ de bombas** bomb disposal.

desactivador *nm* bomb-disposal officer.

desactivar [1a] *vt bomba* to defuse, make safe, render harmless; *alarma* to deactivate, neutralize.

desactualizado *adj* out of date.

desacuerdo *nm* (**a**) (*discrepancia*) discord, disagreement; **~ amistoso** agreement to differ; **estar en ~** to be out of keeping (*con* with), be at variance (*con* with); **la corbata está en ~ con la camisa** the tie does not go with the shirt.

(**b**) (*error*) error, blunder.

(**c**) (*desmemoria*) forgetfulness.

desachavar* [1a] *vi* (*Cono Sur*) to spill the beans*.

desadaptación *nf* maladjustment.

desadeudarse [1a] *vr* to get out of debt.

desadorno *nm* bareness, lack of ornamentation.

desadvertido *adj* careless.

desadvertir [3i] *vt* (*no ver*) to fail to notice; (*desatender*) to disregard.

desafecto 1 *adj* disaffected; hostile; **elementos ~s al régimen** those hostile to the régime, those out of sympathy with the régime.

2 *nm* disaffection; ill-will, dislike; hostility.

desaferrar [1k *o* 1a] **1** *vt* (**a**) (*soltar*) to loosen, unfasten.

(**b**) **~ a uno** to make sb change his mind, dissuade sb (from a strongly held opinion *etc*).

(**c**) **~ el áncora** (*Náut*) = **2**.

2 *vi* to weigh anchor.

desafiador 1 *adj* defiant; challenging. **2** *nm*, **desafiadora** *nf* challenger.

desafiante *adj* challenging; *actitud etc* defiant.

desafiar [1c] *vt* (**a**) *persona etc* to challenge; **~ a uno a** + *infin* to challenge sb to + *infin*, dare sb to + *infin*.

(**b**) *peligro* to defy; to face, face up to.

(**c**) (*fig*: *competir*) to challenge, compete with, measure up to.

desaficionarse [1a] *vr*: **~ de** to come to dislike, take a dislike to.

desafilado *adj* blunt.

desafilar [1a] **1** *vt* to blunt, dull. **2 desafilarse** *vr* to get blunt.

desafiliarse [1b] *vr* to disaffiliate (*de* from).

desafinadamente *adv cantar etc* out of tune, off key.

desafinado *adj* flat, out of tune.

desafinar [1a] *vi* (**a**) (*Mús*) to be (*o* play, sing) out of tune; to go out of tune. (**b**) (*fig*) to speak out of turn.

desafío *nm* (**a**) (*gen*) challenge; (*combate*) duel. (**b**) (*fig*) challenge; defiance; competition, rivalry; **es un ~ a todos nosotros** it is a challenge to us all.

desaforadamente *adv* (**a**) *comportarse etc* outrageously. (**b**) *gritar* at the top of one's voice.

desaforado *adj* (**a**) *persona* lawless, violent, disorderly; *comportamiento* outrageous; **es un ~** he's a violent sort, he's dangerously excitable.

(**b**) (*enorme*) great, huge; *grito* mighty, ear-splitting.

desaforarse [1l] *vr* to behave in an outrageous way, act violently; to get worked up, lose control.

desafortunado *adj* (**a**) (*desgraciado*) unfortunate, unlucky. (**b**) (*no oportuno*) inopportune, untimely; (*desacertado*) unwise.

desafuero *nm* outrage, excess.

desagraciado *adj* graceless, unattractive; unsightly.

desagradable *adj* disagreeable, unpleasant; **ser ~ con uno** to be rude to sb.

desagradablemente *adv* unpleasantly.

desagradar [1a] **1** *vt* to displease; to bother, upset; **me desagrada ese olor** I don't like that smell; **me desagrada tener que hacerlo** I dislike having to do it.

2 *vi* to be unpleasant.

desagradecido *adj* ungrateful.

desagradecimiento *nm* ingratitude.

desagrado *nm* displeasure; dislike; dissatisfaction; **hacer algo con ~** to do sth with distaste, do sth unwillingly.

desagraviar [1b] **1** *vt* (**a**) *persona* to make amends to; (*compensar*) to indemnify; (*disculparse con*) to apologize to.

(**b**) *ofensa etc* to make amends for, put right.

2 desagraviarse *vr* to get one's own back; to exact an apology; to restore one's honour.

desagravio *nm* amends; compensation, indemnification, satisfaction; **en ~ de** as amends for.

desagregación *nm* disintegration.

desagregar [1h] **1** *vt* to disintegrate. **2 desagregarse** *vr* to disintegrate.

desaguadero *nm* (**a**) drain (*t fig*; *de* on). (**b**) (*Méx**) lavatory, loo*.

desaguar [1i] **1** *vt* (**a**) *líquido* to drain, empty, run off. (**b**) (*fig*) to squander. (**c**) (*And*: *enjuagar*) to rinse (out). **2** *vi* (**a**) (*líquido*) to drain away, drain off. (**b**) (*río*) **~ en** to drain into, flow into.

desagüe *nm* (**a**) (*acto*) drainage, draining. (**b**) (*canal*) drainage channel; (*tubo*) drainpipe; (*salida*) outlet, drain; **tubo de ~** drainpipe, waste pipe.

desaguisado 1 *adj* illegal. **2** *nm* offence, outrage.

desahogado 1 *adj* (**a**) *vestido, casa etc* roomy, large.

(**b**) *espacio* clear, free, unencumbered.

(**c**) *situación, vida* comfortable; *persona* comfortably off, in easy circumstances.

(**d**) (*descarado*) brazen, impudent, fresh*; **el tan ~ se lo comió todo** he was brazen enough to eat it all up.

2 *nm*, **desahogada** *nf* brazen person, shameless individual.

desahogar [1h] **1** *vt* (**a**) *dolor etc* to ease, relieve; *ira* to vent (*en* on).

(**b**) *persona* to console.

2 desahogarse *vr* (**a**) (*reponerse*) to recover; to make things more comfortable for o.s.; (*relajarse*) to take it easy, relax.

(**b**) (*librarse*) to get out of a difficulty (*o* debt *etc*).

(**c**) (*desfogarse*) to relieve one's feelings; to let off steam, let o.s. go; (*hablar francamente*) to speak one's mind frankly; (*confesarse*) to confess, get sth off one's chest; **~ con uno** to pour one's heart out to sb.

desahogo *nm* (**a**) (*comodidad*) comfort, ease; comfortable circumstances; **vivir con ~** to be comfortably off.

(**b**) (*alivio*) relief; recovery; **es un ~ de tantas cosas malas** it's an outlet for so many unpleasant things, it's a way of getting rid of so many bad things.

(**c**) (*libertad*) freedom; (*pey*) excessive freedom, brazenness, impudence; **expresarse con cierto ~** to express o.s. with a certain freedom, feel free to say what one really thinks.

desahuciado *adj caso* hopeless.

desahuciar [1b] **1** *vt* (**a**) *inquilino* to evict, eject; *empleado* to oust, remove, get out; (*Cono Sur: despedir*) to dismiss.

(**b**) (*quitar esperanza a*) to deprive of hope, kill the hopes of; *enfermo* to give up hope for, declare past recovery; *plan etc* to give up as a lost cause; **con esa decisión le desahuciaron definitivamente** by that decision they finally put an end to his hopes.

2 desahuciarse *vr* to lose all hope.

desahucio *nm* eviction, ejection; (*Cono Sur: despido*) dismissal.

desairado *adj* (**a**) (*menospreciado*) spurned; disregarded. (**b**) (*sin éxito*) unsuccessful; **quedar ~** to be unsuccessful, come off badly. (**c**) (*desgarbado*) unattractive; graceless.

desairar [1a] *vt persona* to slight, snub; *asunto* to disregard; to rebuff; **lo haré por no ~** I'll do it rather than cause offence.

desaire *nm* (**a**) (*menosprecio*) slight, snub; (*desacato*) act of disrespect; (*repulsa*) rebuff; **fue un ~ sin precedentes** it was an unprecedented snub; **dar** (*o* **hacer**) **un ~ a uno** to rebuff sb, offend sb; **¿me vas a hacer ese ~?** (*acerca de invitación*) I won't take no for an answer!; **sufrir un ~** to suffer a rebuff; **no lo tomes a ~** don't be offended.

(**b**) (*falta de garbo*) unattractiveness, gracelessness, lack of charm.

desajustado *adj* ill-adjusted, poorly adjusted.

desajustar [1a] **1** *vt* to disarrange, disturb the order of. **2 desajustarse** *vr* (**a**) (*estropearse*) to get out of order; (*Mec*) to break down. (**b**) (*reñir*) to disagree, fall out.

desajuste *nm* (**a**) (*falta de orden*) disorder, disarrangement; (*Mec*) breakdown. (**b**) (*desequilibrio*) imbalance, lack of balance. (**c**) (*desacuerdo*) disagreement.

desalación *nf* desalination.

desalado[1] *adj* (*apresurado*) hasty; (*impaciente*) impatient; (*ansioso*) eager; anxious.

desalado[2] *adj* desalted.

desalar[1] [1a] *vt* to remove the salt from; *agua salada* to desalinate.

desalar[2] [1a] **1** *vt* to clip the wings of. **2 desalarse** *vr* (**a**) (*correr*) to rush, hasten along. (**b**) (*anhelar*) to long, yearn; **~ por** + *infin* to long to + *infin*; to be keen to + *infin*.

desalentador *adj* discouraging.

desalentar [1j] **1** *vt* (**a**) **~ a uno** to make sb breathless, make sb gasp for breath.

(**b**) (*fig*) to discourage.

2 desalentarse *vr* to get discouraged, lose heart.

desaliento *nm* (*fig*) discouragement; depression, dejection; dismay.

desalinización *nf* desalination.

desalinizador *adj*: **planta ~a** desalination plant.

desaliñado *adj* (**a**) (*desaseado*) slovenly, dirty, down-at-heel; (*raído*) shabby; (*desordenado*) untidy, unkempt, dishevelled. (**b**) (*negligente*) careless, slipshod, slovenly.

desaliño *nm* (**a**) (*desarreglo*) slovenliness, dirtiness; shabbiness; untidiness; dishevelled state. (**b**) (*descuido*) carelessness.

desalmado *adj* cruel, heartless.

desalmarse [1a] *vr*: **~ por** to long for, crave (for).

desalojamiento *nm* (*V vt* (*a*), (*c*)) (**a**) ejection, ousting, removal; dislodging. (**b**) evacuation; abandonment; clearing.

desalojar [1a] **1** *vt* (**a**) *ocupante* to eject, oust, remove (*from* de); to dislodge (*t Mil*; *de* from); to clear out; *inquilino* to evict.

(**b**) *contenido, gas etc* to dislodge, remove, expel.

(**c**) *sitio* to evacuate; to abandon, move out of, move away from; **~ un tribunal de público** to clear a court, to clear the public from a court; **las tropas han desalojado el pueblo** the troops have moved out of the village; **la policía desalojó el local** the police cleared people out of the place.

2 *vi* to move out.

desalojo *nm* ejection, removal; evacuation; abandonment; clearance.

desalquilado *adj* vacant, untenanted.

desalquilar [1a] **1** *vt* to vacate, move out of. **2 desalquilarse** *vr* to become vacant.

desalterar [1a] **1** *vt* to assuage, calm; to quieten down. **2 desalterarse** *vr* to calm down, quieten down.

desamar [1a] *vt* to cease to love; to dislike, detest.

desamarrar [1a] *vt* to untie; (*Náut*) to cast off.

desamarre *nm* untying; (*Náut*) casting-off.

desamor *nm* coldness, indifference; dislike; enmity.

desamorado *adj* cold-hearted.

desamortización *nf* (*Jur*) disentailment; (*Hist Esp*) *sale of Church lands.*

desamortizar [1f] *vt* to disentail.

desamparado *adj* (**a**) *niño etc* helpless, defenceless; abandoned; **los niños ~s de la ciudad** the city's waifs and strays; **sentirse ~** to feel helpless.

(**b**) *lugar* (*expuesto*) exposed.

(**c**) *lugar* (*desierto*) lonely, deserted.

desamparar [1a] *vt* (**a**) *persona* to desert, abandon, leave helpless; to forsake. (**b**) *sitio* to leave, abandon; to leave defenceless. (**c**) *actividad* to cease, abandon; to lose interest in.

desamparo *nm* (**a**) (*acto*) desertion, abandonment. (**b**) (*estado*) helplessness; defencelessness, lack of protection. (**c**) (*cesación*) cessation; loss of interest (*de* in).

desamueblado *adj* unfurnished; empty, with the furniture removed.

desamueblar [1a] *vt* to remove the furniture from, clear the furniture out of.

desandar [1p] *vt*: **~ lo andado, ~ el camino** to retrace one's steps, go back the way one has come; **no se puede ~ lo andado** one cannot undo what has been done.

desangelado *adj persona* charmless, dull, unattractive; *cosa* dull, insipid; flat; played-out; *lugar* empty, lifeless.

desangramiento *nm* bleeding; **morir de ~** to bleed to death.

desangrar [1a] **1** *vt* (**a**) *persona* to bleed; *lago* to drain. (**b**) (*fig*) to impoverish, bleed white. **2 desangrarse** *vr* to lose a lot of blood.

desangre *nm* (*LAm*) bleeding, loss of blood.

desanidar [1a] **1** *vt* to oust, dislodge. **2** *vi* to fly, begin to fly, leave the nest.

desanimado 1 *adj* (**a**) (*desalentado*) downhearted, dispirited, dejected. (**b**) (*soso*) dull, lifeless, flat; **fue una fiesta de lo más ~** it was a terribly dull party. **2** *nm*, **desanimada** *nf* dropout (from the labour market).

desanimante *adj* discouraging.

desanimar [1a] **1** *vt* to discourage; to depress, sadden. **2 desanimarse** *vr* to get discouraged, lose heart; **no hay que ~** we must not lose heart, we must keep our spirits up.

desánimo *nm* (**a**) (*desaliento*) despondency, depression, dejection. (**b**) (*flojedad*) dullness, lifelessness.

desanudar [1a] *vt* to untie, unknot; to disentangle; **~ la voz** to manage to speak again, find one's voice.

desapacible *adj* (*gen*) unpleasant, disagreeable; *sonido* sharp, jangling; nasty; discordant; *tono* harsh, rough; *sabor* unpleasant, sharp; *discusión* bitter, bad-tempered; *persona* surly, unpleasant.

desaparcar [1g] *vi* to drive off.

desaparecer [2d] **1** *vt* (*esp LAm*) to cause to disappear, eliminate. **2** *vi* to disappear, vanish; to drop out of sight; (*efecto*) to wear off; (*euf*) to pass away.

desaparecido 1 *adj* (*gen*) missing; *especie* extinct; **el libro ~** the missing book; **uno de los animales ~s** one of the extinct animals; **3 siguen ~s** 3 are still missing. **2** *nm*, **desaparecida** *nf* missing person; (*LAm*: *secuestrado*) kidnap victim, kidnapped person; (*detenido*) person improperly arrested, victim of arbitrary arrest; **los ~s** the missing, those missing; **número de muertos, heridos y ~s** the number of dead, wounded and missing.

desaparejar [1a] *vt* (**a**) (*gen*) to unharness, unhitch. (**b**) (*Náut*) to unrig.

desaparición *nf* disappearance; extinction.

desapasionadamente *adv* dispassionately, impartially.

desapasionado *adj* dispassionate, impartial.

desapego *nm* (**a**) (*frialdad*) coolness, indifference (*a* towards); (*distancia*) alienation, detachment (*a* from). (**b**) (*ecuanimidad*) detachment, impartiality.

desapercibido *adj* (**a**) (*no visto*) unnoticed; **marcharse ~** to slip away (unseen); **pasar ~** to go unnoticed. (**b**) (*des-*

prevenido) unprepared.
desaplicación *nf* slackness, laziness.
desaplicado *adj* slack, lazy.
desapoderado *adj acción, movimiento* headlong, precipitate; *pasión etc* wild, violent, uncontrollable; *avidez etc* excessive; *orgullo* overweening.
desapoderar [1a] *vt* to deprive of authority; to dispossess (*de* of).
desapolillarse [1a] *vr* (*fig*) to get rid of the cobwebs.
desaprender [2a] *vt* to forget; to unlearn.
desaprensión *nf* unscrupulousness, lack of scruple.
desaprensivamente *adv* unscrupulously.
desaprensivo *adj* unscrupulous.
desapretar [1j] *vt* to loosen, slacken, undo.
desaprobación *nf* disapproval; condemnation; rejection.
desaprobar [1l] *vt* (*no aprobar*) to disapprove of; (*condenar*) to frown on, condemn; *solicitud etc* to reject, dismiss.
desapropiarse [1b] *vr*: ~ **de** to divest o.s. of, surrender, give up.
desaprovechado *adj* (**a**) (*improductivo*) unproductive, unprofitable; (*no satisfactorio*) below expectations. (**b**) *estudiante etc* slow, backward; slack. (**c**) *oportunidad* wasted.
desaprovechar [1a] **1** *vt* to fail to take advantage of, not use, waste; *oportunidad* to waste, miss. **2** *vi* to lose ground, slip back.
desarbolado *adj paisaje* treeless; stripped of trees.
desarbolar [1a] *vt* to dismast.
desarmable *adj*: **mesa** ~ fold-away table.
desarmador *nm* (*de fusil*) trigger; (*LAm*) screwdriver.
desarmante *adj* disarming.
desarmar [1a] **1** *vt* (**a**) (*Mil*) to disarm.
(**b**) (*Mec*) to take apart, take to pieces, dismantle; to strip down; *remos* to ship; *barco* to lay up; *barrera* to remove, take down.
(**c**) (*fig*) *persona* to disarm; *ira* to calm, appease.
2 *vi* to disarm.
desarme *nm* disarmament; ~ **arancelario** removal of tariff barriers; ~ **industrial** removal of trade tariffs, lifting of protectionist barriers; ~ **unilateral** unilateral disarmament.
desarraigado *adj persona* rootless, without roots.
desarraigar [1h] *vt* (**a**) *árbol* to uproot, root out, dig up. (**b**) (*fig*) to root out, eradicate; to extirpate; *persona* to uproot; to banish, expel.
desarraigo *nm* (*fig*) eradication; extirpation; uprooting; banishment, expulsion.
desarrajar [1a] *vt* (*LAm*) to break open, force the lock of.
desarrapado *adj* = **desharrapado.**
desarrebujar [1a] *vt* (**a**) (*desenredar*) to untangle; (*descubrir*) to uncover. (**b**) (*fig*) to clarify, elucidate.
desarreglado *adj* (**a**) (*Mec etc*) out of order; *estómago etc* upset; *cuarto etc* untidy, in disorder.
(**b**) *conducta* disorderly; *aspecto* slovenly, untidy; *hábitos* irregular; unsystematic; (*en comer etc*) immoderate.
desarreglar [1a] **1** *vt* (*gen*) to disarrange; *proyectos etc* to disturb, mess up, upset; (*Mec*) to put out of order; **el viento le desarregló el peinado** the wind made a mess of her hairdo; **no desarregles la cama** don't mess up your bed.
2 desarreglarse *vr* to get disarranged, get untidy; (*Mec*) to get out of order, break down.
desarreglo *nm* disorder, confusion, chaos; untidiness; irregularity; (*Mec*) trouble; (*Med*) upset; **para evitar los ~s estomacales** in order to avoid stomach upsets; **viven en el mayor** ~ they live in complete chaos.
desarrimado* *nm* loner, lone wolf.
desarrimar [1a] *vt* (**a**) to move away, separate. (**b**) *persona* to dissuade.
desarrollado *adj* (*t* **bien** ~) well-developed.
desarrollar [1a] **1** *vt* (**a**) *rollo* to unroll, unwind; *mapa etc* to unfold, open (out).
(**b**) *abreviatura, ecuación* to expand.
(**c**) (*fig*) to develop; to evolve; *teoría, tema etc* to explain, expound; *trabajo* to carry out.
(**d**) (*Mec*) **el motor desarrolla 30 caballos** the engine develops 30 hp.
2 desarrollarse *vr* (**a**) (*gen*) to unroll, unwind; (*desplegarse*) to open (out).
(**b**) (*fig*) to develop; to evolve; (*historia etc*) to unfold; (*suceso, reunión etc*) to take place; **la industria se desarrolla rápidamente** the industry is developing rapidly; **la acción se desarrolla en Roma** (*Cine etc*) the scene is set in Rome, the action takes place in Rome.
desarrollismo *nm* policy of economic development; unimpeded development.
desarrollo *nm* (**a**) development; evolution; unfolding; expansion; growth; (*de juego*) run; ~ **en línea** ribbon development; **durante el** ~ **de** in the course of; during the development of; **un país en** (**vías de**) ~ a developing country; **la industria está en pleno** ~ the industry is making rapid growth, the industry is expanding steadily; **el niño tiene mucho ~ para su edad** the child is overdeveloped for his age.
(**b**) (*de bicicleta*) gear.
desarroparse [1a] *vr* to undress; to uncover o.s.; (*en la cama*) to sleep without any bed coverings; **todavía el tiempo no es para** ~ it's not yet weather for leaving off any clothes.
desarrugar [1h] *vt* to smooth (out), remove the wrinkles from.
desarticulación *nf* taking to pieces; separation; dislocation; breaking up.
desarticulado *adj* disjointed.
desarticular [1a] *vt* (*desmontar*) to take apart, take to pieces; to separate; *huesos* to put out, dislocate; *pandilla* to break up; ~ **un grupo terrorista** to put a terrorist group out of action.
desarzonar [1a] *vt jinete* to throw, unsaddle.
desaseado *adj* (*sucio*) slovenly, dirty; (*desaliñado*) untidy, unkempt, messy; (*raído*) shabby.
desasear [1a] *vt* to dirty, soil; to mess up.
desaseo *nm* slovenliness, dirtiness; untidiness; messiness; shabbiness.
desasimiento *nm* (**a**) (*acto*) loosening, undoing; release. (**b**) (*fig*) detachment (*de* from), disinterest; (*pey*) indifference (*de* to), remoteness (*de* from).
desasir [3a, *pero presente como* **salir**] **1** *vt* to loosen, undo, let go.
2 desasirse *vr* (**a**) (*gen*) to extricate o.s. (*de* from), get clear (*de* of).
(**b**) ~ **de** (*ceder*) to let go, give up; (*deshacerse de*) to rid o.s. of, free o.s. of; to get rid of.
desasistir [3a] *vt* to desert, abandon; to neglect.
desasnar [1a] *vt* (*civilizar*) to civilize, improve, knock the corners off; (*instruir*) to make less stupid.
desasosegado *adj* uneasy, anxious; restless.
desasosegador *adj*, **desasosegante** *adj* disturbing, upsetting.
desasosegar [1h *y* 1j] **1** *vt* to disturb, perturb, make uneasy; to make restless. **2 desasosegarse** *vr* to become uneasy, get perturbed; to become restless.
desasosiego *nm* disquiet, uneasiness, anxiety; restlessness; (*Pol etc*) unrest.
desastrado *adj* (**a**) (*sucio*) dirty; (*harapiento*) shabby, ragged. (**b**) (*desgraciado*) unlucky; wretched.
desastre *nm* disaster; **¡un ~!** (*hum*) what a calamity!; how awful!; **la boda fue un** ~ the wedding was a disaster; **la función fue un** ~ the show was a shambles.
desastroso *adj* disastrous, calamitous.
desatado *adj* (*fig*) wild, violent, uncontrolled.
desatar [1a] **1** *vt* (**a**) *nudo* to untie, undo, unfasten; *cuerda* to loosen, slacken; *pieza* to detach, separate; *perro* to unleash; (*Quím*) to dissolve.
(**b**) (*fig*) *pasión, represión etc* to unleash.
(**c**) (*fig*) *misterio* to solve, clear up, unravel.
2 desatarse *vr* (**a**) (*cuerda*) to come untied, come undone, unfasten itself; to work loose; (*perro etc*) to break away, break loose.
(**b**) ~ **de un compromiso** to get out of an agreement.
(**c**) (*fig: tormenta etc*) to break, burst; (*motín*) to break out; (*entusiasmo*) to break all bounds; (*desastre*) to fall (*sobre* on); ~ **en injurias** to let rip with a torrent of abuse.
(**d**) (*fig: persona*) to get worked up, lose self-control; to talk wildly; to go too far, forget o.s.
desatascador *nm* plunger.
desatascar [1g] *vt* (**a**) *carro etc* to pull out of the mud; ~ **a uno** (*fig*) to get sb out of a jam. (**b**) *tubo etc* to clear, free, unblock.
desatención *nf* (**a**) (*distracción*) inattention; neglect; absent-mindedness. (**b**) (*descortesía*) discourtesy.
desatender [2g] *vt* to disregard, pay no attention to; to ignore; *deber* to neglect; *persona* to slight, offend.
desatentado *adj* (**a**) (*irreflexivo*) thoughtless, rash, ill-advised; (*poco sensato*) unwise, foolish. (**b**) (*excesivo*) excessive, extreme, out of all proportion.
desatento *adj* (**a**) (*descuidado*) heedless, careless; (*negligente*) neglectful; (*distraído*) inattentive. (**b**) (*descortés*)

discourteous, unmannerly (*con* to).
desatierre *nm* (*LAm*) slag heap.
desatinadamente *adv* foolishly; wildly, recklessly.
desatinado *adj* silly, foolish; wild, reckless.
desatinar [1a] **1** *vt* to perplex, bewilder. **2** *vi* (*obrar*) to act foolishly; (*hablar*) to talk nonsense, rave; (*ponerse nervioso*) to get rattled, begin to act wildly.
desatino *nm* (**a**) (*cualidad*) foolishness, folly, silliness; tactlessness.
(**b**) (*acto etc*) silly thing, foolish act; (*error*) blunder, mistake; **~s** nonsense; **¡qué ~!** how silly!, what rubbish!; **un libro lleno de ~s** a book stuffed with nonsense; **cometer un ~** to make a blunder.
desatochar [1a] *vt* (*Cono Sur*) *tráfico* to clear.
desatornillador *nm* (*LAm*) screwdriver.
desatornillar [1a] *vt* to unscrew.
desatracar [1g] *vti* (*Náut*) to cast off.
desatraillar [1a] *vt* to unleash, let off the lead.
desatrancar [1g] *vt* (**a**) *puerta* to unbar, unbolt. (**b**) *caño etc* to clear, unblock; *pozo* to clean out.
desatraque *nm* casting-off.
desatufarse [1a] *vr* (**a**) to get some fresh air. (**b**) (*fig*) to calm down.
desautorización *nf* (**a**) discrediting; disapproval; repudiation. (**b**) denial.
desautorizado *adj* (*no aprobado*) unauthorized; (*no oficial*) unofficial; (*no justificado*) unwarranted.
desautorizar [1f] *vt* (**a**) *oficial etc* to deprive of authority, declare without authority; (*desacreditar*) to discredit; (*desaprobar*) to disapprove of; (*rechazar*) to disown, repudiate. (**b**) *noticia* to deny, issue a denial of.
desavenencia *nf* (*desacuerdo*) disagreement; (*tirantez*) friction, unpleasantness; (*riña*) rift, quarrel.
desavenido *adj* (*incompatible*) incompatible; (*opuestos*) contrary, opposing; (*reñidos*) in disagreement; **ellos están ~s** they are at odds, they disagree.
desavenir [3r] **1** *vt* to cause a rift between, make trouble between; to split, break the unity of.
2 desavenirse *vr* to disagree (*con* with), fall out (*con* with).
desaventajado *adj* (*inferior*) inferior; (*desfavorable*) unfavourable, disadvantageous.
desavisado *adj* unwary; uninformed.
desayunado *ptp*: **estar ~** to have had breakfast.
desayunar [1a] **1** *vt* (**a**) to have for breakfast, breakfast on. (**b**) **vengo desayunado** I've had breakfast. **2** *vi y* **desayunarse** *vr* to breakfast, have breakfast; **~ con** to have for breakfast, breakfast on; **ahora me desayuno de ello** this is the first I've heard of it.
desayuno *nm* breakfast; **~ a la inglesa, ~ británico** English breakfast; **~ continental** continental breakfast; **~ de trabajo** working breakfast.
desazón *nf* (**a**) (*insipidez*) tastelessness, lack of flavour.
(**b**) (*de tierra*) poorness.
(**c**) (*Med*) discomfort, indisposition, slight trouble.
(**d**) (*fig*) (*molestia*) annoyance, displeasure; (*frustración*) frustration; (*inquietud*) uneasiness.
desazonante *adj* annoying, upsetting.
desazonar [1a] **1** *vt* (**a**) *comida* to make tasteless, take the flavour out of.
(**b**) (*fig*) (*molestar*) to annoy, upset, displease; (*inquietar*) to worry, cause anxiety to.
2 desazonarse *vr* (**a**) (*Med*) to feel off-colour, be out of sorts.
(**b**) (*fig*) to be annoyed; to worry, be anxious.
desbancar [1g] **1** *vt* (**a**) (*Naipes*) *banca* to bust*; *persona* to take the bank from.
(**b**) (*fig*) to displace, oust, dislodge; to cut out, supplant (in sb's affections); **el corredor fue desbancado por el pelotón a 5 km de la meta** the group overtook the leader 5 kms from the tape.
2 *vi* (*Naipes*) to go bust*.
desbandada *nf* rush (to get away); **hubo una ~ general de turistas** there was a mass exodus of tourists, masses of tourists suddenly left; **cuando empezó a llover hubo una ~ general** when it started to rain everyone rushed for shelter; **a la ~** in disorder; helter-skelter; **retirarse a la ~** to retreat in disorder, make a disorderly retreat.
desbandar* [1a] *vt* (*Carib*) *empleado* to fire*.
desbandarse [1a] *vr* (**a**) (*Mil*) to disband. (**b**) (*fig*) to flee in disorder; to go off in all directions, disperse in confusion.
desbande* *nm* (*Cono Sur*) rush (to get away).
desbarajustar [1a] *vt* to throw into confusion.
desbarajuste *nm* confusion, chaos, disorder.
desbaratamiento *nm*, **desbarate** *nm*, **desbarato** *nm* (**a**) (*destrucción*) ruin, destruction, foiling, thwarting; disruption; debunking.
(**b**) (*Mil*) rout.
(**c**) squandering.
desbaratar [1a] **1** *vt* (**a**) (*arruinar*) to ruin, spoil, destroy; to mess up; *plan etc* to foil, thwart, frustrate; *sistema* to disrupt, cause chaos in; *teoría* to make nonsense of, debunk.
(**b**) (*Mil*) to throw into confusion, rout.
(**c**) *fortuna* to squander.
(**d**) (*Mec*) to take to pieces.
2 *vi* to rave, talk nonsense.
3 desbaratarse *vr* (**a**) (*Mec*) to get out of order, develop a defect.
(**b**) (*persona*) to fly off the handle*, go off the deep end*; to become unbalanced.
desbarbar [1a] **1** *vt* (*) *persona* to shave; *papel* to trim (the edges of); *planta* to cut back, trim (off).
2 desbarbarse *vr* (*) to shave.
desbarrancadero *nm* (*LAm*) precipice.
desbarrancar [1g] **1** *vt* (**a**) (*LAm*) to fling over a precipice. (**b**) (*And, Carib*: *arruinar*) to ruin; (*And**: *aplastar*) to crush. **2 desbarrancarse** *vr* (**a**) (*LAm*) to fall over a precipice. (**b**) (*) to come down in the world.
desbarrar [1a] *vi* to talk rubbish; to be very wide of the mark.
desbastar [1a] **1** *vt* (**a**) (*Téc*) to rough-hew; to plane (down), smooth (down).
(**b**) (*fig*) to take the rough edges off; (*refinar*) to refine, polish; *recluta etc* to knock the corners off, lick into shape.
2 desbastarse *vr* (*fig*) to acquire some polish.
desbaste *nm* (**a**) (*Téc*) planing, smoothing. (**b**) (*fig*) polishing, refinement; licking into shape.
desbeber** [2a] *vi* to piss**.
desbloquear [1a] *vt* (**a**) (*Mil*) to break the blockade of. (**b**) (*Com, Fin*) to unfreeze, unblock. (**c**) *caño etc* to unblock, free; *tráfico* to free, get moving; *negociación* to break a stalemate in, secure progress in.
desbloqueo *nm* unfreezing, unblocking, freeing.
desbocado *adj* (**a**) *taza* chipped.
(**b**) *cañon* wide-mouthed.
(**c**) *caballo* runaway.
(**d**) *herramienta* worn, defective, damaged.
(**e**) *persona* foul-mouthed, foul-spoken.
(**f**) (*LAm*) *líquido* overflowing.
desbocar [1g] **1** *vt taza* to chip.
2 *vi*: **~ en** (*río*) to run into, flow into; (*calle*) to open into, come out into.
3 desbocarse *vr* (**a**) (*caballo*) to bolt, run away; (*multitud*) to rush off, run riot, get out of control.
(**b**) (*persona*) to start to swear, let out a stream of insults.
desbolado* *adj* (*Cono Sur*) disorganized.
desbole* *nm* (*Cono Sur*) (*desorden*) mess, mix-up; (*alboroto*) row, racket.
desbordamiento *nm* (**a**) (*gen*) overflowing, flooding; spilling. (**b**) (*fig*) eruption, outburst; **un tremendo ~ de entusiasmo** a great upsurge of enthusiasm. (**c**) (*Inform*) overflow.
desbordante *adj* overflowing; (*fig*) overwhelming, excessive.
desbordar [1a] **1** *vt* to pass, go beyond; to exceed, surpass; **desbordaron las líneas enemigas** they burst through the enemy lines; **el proyecto desborda los límites señalados** the plan goes well beyond the limits which were set; **esto desborda mi tolerancia** this is more than I can tolerate.
2 *vi y* **desbordarse** *vr* (**a**) (*río*) to overflow, flood, burst its banks; (*líquido*) to overflow, spill (over).
(**b**) (*entusiasmo etc*) to erupt, burst forth.
(**c**) (*persona*) to give free rein to one's feelings; (*pasarse*) to get carried away, go over the top; (*pey*) to fly off the handle*, lose one's self-control; **~(se) de alegría** to be bursting with happiness.
desborde *nm* (*Cono Sur*) = **desbordamiento**.
desbraguetado* *adj*: **estar ~** to be broke*.
desbravador *nm* horse-breaker.
desbravar [1a] **1** *vt* to break in, tame.
2 *vi y* **desbravarse** *vr* (**a**) (*animal*) to get less wild, grow less fierce.
(**b**) (*corriente etc*) to lose its strength, diminish in force.
(**c**) (*licor*) to lose its strength.

desbrozadora *nf* weeding machine.
desbrozar [1f] *vt camino etc* to clear (of rubbish); *tierra* to clear, clear the undergrowth from; *cosecha* to weed, keep clear of weeds.
desburocratizar [1f] *vt* to make less bureaucratic.
descabal *adj*, **descabalado** *adj* incomplete.
descabalgar [1h] **1** *vt* (*fig*) to unseat, remove from office. **2** *vi* to dismount.
descabellado *adj* (*fig*) wild, crazy, preposterous.
descabellar [1a] *vt* (**a**) *persona* to dishevel; to ruffle, rumple. (**b**) *toro* to kill with a thrust in the neck, administer the coup de grâce to.
descabello *nm* (*Taur*) final thrust, coup de grâce.
descabezado *adj* (**a**) (*lit*) headless. (**b**) (*fig*) wild, crazy, light-headed.
descabezar [1f] **1** *vt* (**a**) *persona etc* to behead, cut the head off; *árbol* to lop, poll, cut the top off; *planta* to top.
(**b**) (*fig*) *dificultad* to begin to get over, get over the worst part of, surmount.
2 descabezarse *vr* (**a**) (*Bot*) to shed the grain.
(**b**) (*persona*) to rack one's brains.
descachalandrado* *adj* (*And*) shabby, scruffy.
descachalandrarse* [1a] *vr* (*And*) to dress carelessly.
descachar [1a] *vt* (*And, Carib, Cono Sur*) to de-horn.
descacharrado *adj* (*CAm*) dirty, slovenly.
descacharrante* *adj* hilarious.
descachimbarse* [1a] *vi* (*CAm*) to fall flat on one's face, come a cropper*.
descafeinado *adj* decaffeinated; (*fig*) diluted, watered-down.
descafeinar [1a] *vt* to decaffeinate; (*fig*) to dilute, water down.
descalabrado *adj*: **salir ~** to come out the loser (*de* in), come off badly.
descalabrar [1a] **1** *vt* (**a**) (*romper*) to smash, damage; *persona* to hit, hurt, (*esp*) to hit on the head.
(**b**) (*fig*) to harm, damage, injure; to attack the character of.
2 descalabrarse *vr* to hurt one's head, give o.s. a bang on the head.
descalabro *nm* (*revés*) blow, setback; (*desastre*) disaster, misfortune; (*daño*) damage; (*Mil*) defeat; **~ electoral** electoral setback, disaster at the polls.
descalcificación *nf* (*Med*) lack of calcium, calcium deficiency.
descalificación *nf* discrediting; rejection, relegation to oblivion; dismissal; (*Dep*) disqualification; **~ global** general rejection, downright condemnation.
descalificar [1g] *vt* to discredit; to write off, reject, relegate to oblivion; to dismiss (the views of); (*Dep*) to disqualify.
descalzar [1f] **1** *vt* (**a**) *zapato* to take off.
(**b**) **~ a uno** to take off sb's shoes (*etc*); **A no vale para ~ a B** A can't hold a candle to B.
(**c**) *rueda* to remove the chocks from.
(**d**) (*fig*: *minar*) to dig under, undermine.
2 descalzarse *vr* (**a**) to take off one's shoes (*etc*); **~ los guantes** to take off one's gloves.
(**b**) (*caballo*) to cast a shoe.
descalzo *adj* (**a**) (*con pies desnudos*) barefoot(ed); (*sin zapatos*) shoeless; (*sin medias*) stockingless; **estar ~, estar con los pies ~s** to be barefooted, have one's shoes off, have no shoes (*etc*) on; **ir ~** to go barefooted.
(**b**) (*Ecl*) discalced.
(**c**) (*fig*) destitute; **su padre le dejó ~** his father left him without a bean.
descamarse [1a] *vr* to flake off, scale off; (*Med*) to desquamate.
descambiar* [1b] *vt* to swap, change back; (*Com*) to exchange.
descambio *nm* swap, change back; (*Com*) exchange.
descaminado *adj* (**a**) **andar ~, ir ~** to be on the wrong road.
(**b**) (*fig*) mistaken; misguided; ill-advised; **ir ~** to be on the wrong track; **andar ~ en** to be mistaken in (*o* about); **en eso no andas muy ~** you're not far wrong there.
descaminar [1a] **1** *vt* (**a**) *persona* to misdirect, give wrong directions to, put on the wrong road; (*fig*) to mislead, lead astray.
(**b**) *mercancías* to seize as contraband.
(**c**) (*LAm*) to hold up.
2 descaminarse *vr* to get lost, go the wrong way; (*fig*) to go astray.
descamisado 1 *adj* (*fig*) ragged, shabby; wretched. **2** *nm* ragamuffin; down-and-out; poor devil, wretch; (*Argentina Pol*) Peronist.
descamisar [1a] *vt* (**a**) *persona* to strip the shirt off; *fruta* to peel. (**b**) (*fig*) to ruin; (*en el juego*) to fleece.
descampado *nm* open space, piece of empty ground; open field; **comer al ~** to eat in the open air; **vivir en ~** to live in open country; **se fue a vivir en ~** he went off to live in the wilds.
descansadero *nm* stopping place, resting place.
descansado *adj* (**a**) *persona* rested, refreshed. (**b**) *sitio etc* restful; *vida etc* tranquil, unworried, free from care.
descansapié *nm* pedal, footrest.
descansar [1a] **1** *vt* (**a**) (*apoyar*) to rest, support, lean (*sobre* on).
(**b**) (*aliviar*) to rest; **esto descansa la vista más** this rests one's eyes better.
(**c**) (*ayudar*) to help, give a hand to.
(**d**) **~ sus penas en uno** to tell one's troubles to sb, confide in sb about one's troubles.
2 *vi* (**a**) (*persona*) to rest; to take a rest, have a break (*de* from); (*dormir*) to sleep, lie down; (*cadáver*) to lie, rest; **necesito ~ un rato** I need to rest a bit; **podemos ~ aquí** we can rest here; **~ en paz** to rest in peace; **no descansé en todo el día** I didn't have a moment's rest all day; **¡descanse Vd!** don't worry!; **¡que Vd descanse!, ¡descanse bien!** sleep well!
(**b**) (*Agr*) to lie fallow.
(**c**) **~ en** (*Arquit*) to rest on, be supported by.
(**d**) **~ en** (*fig*) to rely on; to trust in; **el argumento descansa sobre los siguientes hechos** the argument is based on the following facts.
3 descansarse *vr*: **~ en uno** to rely on sb, count on sb; to confide in sb.
descansillo *nm* (*Arquit*) landing.
descanso *nm* (**a**) (*gen*) rest; repose; (*alivio etc*) relief; (*período*) rest, break; **~ maternal, ~ de maternidad** maternity leave; **tomarse unos días de ~** to take a few days' rest; **trabajar sin ~** to work without a break; **es un ~ saber que no estás solo** it's a relief to know you are not alone.
(**b**) (*Dep*) interval, half-time; (*Teat*) interval.
(**c**) (*Téc*) (*apoyo*) rest, support; (*banco*) bench; (*escuadra*) bracket; **~ de cabeza** headrest.
(**d**) (*Arquit*) landing.
descañonar [1a] *vt* (**a**) *gallina* to pluck. (**b**) *cara* to shave against the grain; to shave close. (**c**) (**Naipes*) to fleece, clean out*.
descapachar [1a] *vt* (*And*) *maíz* to husk.
descapiruzar [1f] *vt* (*And*) to rumple the hair of.
descapitalización *nf* under-capitalization.
descapitalizado *adj* undercapitalized.
descapotable *adj, nm* (*Aut*) convertible.
descapsulador *nm* bottle-opener.
descaradamente *adv* shamelessly, brazenly; cheekily, saucily; blatantly.
descarado *adj* (*desvergonzado*) shameless, brazen, barefaced; (*insolente*) cheeky, saucy; (*patente*) blatant.
descararse [1a] *vr* to behave impudently, be insolent, be cheeky (*con* to); **~ a pedir algo** to have the nerve to ask for sth.
descarburar [1a] *vt* to decarbonize.
descarga *nf* (**a**) (*Náut etc*) unloading; clearing; **~ de aduana** customs clearance.
(**b**) (*Mil*) firing, discharge; **~ (cerrada)** volley; **como una ~** suddenly, unexpectedly.
(**c**) (*Elec*) discharge.
descargadero *nm* wharf.
descargado *adj* empty, unloaded; *pila* flat.
descargador *nm* unloader; (*de puerto*) docker, stevedore.
descargar [1h] **1** *vt* (**a**) *barco, carro etc* to unload; to empty; (*Inform*) to download.
(**b**) *cañón* to fire, discharge, shoot; to unload; **~ un golpe en uno** to let fly a blow at sb, deal sb a blow; **~ golpes sobre la mesa** to beat the table, rain blows on the table; **~ un golpe contra la censura** to strike a blow against censorship.
(**c**) (*Elec*) to discharge; *pila* to flatten, run down, exhaust.
(**d**) *vientre* to evacuate.
(**e**) (*nube*) *granizo etc* to send down, let fall.
(**f**) *ira etc* to vent (*en, sobre* on).
(**g**) *conciencia* to ease, relieve; *corazón* to unburden.
(**h**) (*Com*) *letra* to take up.
(**i**) *persona* to relieve, release (*de una obligación* from an

obligation); to free (*de una deuda* from a debt); (*Jur etc*) to clear, acquit (*de* of).

2 *vi* (**a**) ~ **en** (*río*) to run into, flow into; (*calle*) to open into, come out into.

(**b**) (*Elec*) to discharge.

(**c**) (*tormenta*) to burst, break.

3 descargarse *vr* (**a**) (*gen*) to unburden o.s., disburden o.s.; ~ **de algo** to get rid of sth; ~ **con** (*o* **en**) **uno de algo** to unload sth on to sb.

(**b**) (*Jur etc*) to clear o.s., vindicate o.s. (*de* of).

(**c**) (*dimitir*) to resign.

descargo *nm* (**a**) (*descargue*) unloading; emptying.

(**b**) (*de deuda*) discharge.

(**c**) (*Com*) receipt, voucher.

(**d**) ~ **de una obligación** release from an obligation; ~ **de una acusación** acquittal on a charge.

(**e**) (*Jur*: *t* ~**s, pliego de** ~**s**) evidence, depositions (in favour of the defendant); answers, rebuttals; (*fig*) excuses, piece of special pleading; **testigo de** ~ witness for the defence.

descargue *nm* unloading; emptying.

descarnado *adj* (*flaco*) thin, lean, scrawny; emaciated; (*cadavérico*) cadaverous; (*fig*) bare; *estilo, descripción* raw, harsh.

descarnador *nm* (*de dientes*) dental scraper; (*de uñas*) cuticle remover.

descarnar [1a] **1** *vt* (**a**) *hueso* to remove the flesh from; *piel* to scrape the flesh from.

(**b**) (*fig*) to eat away, corrode, wear down.

2 descarnarse *vr* to lose flesh, get thin.

descaro *nm* shamelessness, brazenness; cheek*, sauce‡, nerve*; blatancy; **tuvo el** ~ **de decirme que ...** he had the nerve to tell me that ...; **¡qué** ~! what cheek!*, what a nerve!*

descarozado *adj* (*Cono Sur*) *fruta* dried.

descarriar [1c] **1** *vt* (**a**) (*descaminar*) to misdirect, put on the wrong road.

(**b**) (*fig*) to lead astray; **ser una oveja descarriada** to be like a lost sheep.

(**c**) *animal* to separate from the herd, single out.

2 descarriarse *vr* (**a**) (*persona*) to lose one's way; (*animal*) to stray, get separated (from the herd).

(**b**) (*fig*) to err, go astray.

descarrilamiento *nm* derailment.

descarrilar [1a] *vi* (*t* **descarrilarse** *vr* (*LAm*)) (**a**) (*Ferro*) to be derailed, run off the rails, jump the track.

(**b**) (*fig*) to get off the track, wander from the point.

descarrilo *nm* derailment.

descartable *adj* that can be done without, dispensable; (*Inform*) temporary.

descartar [1a] **1** *vt* (*gen*) to discard (*t Naipes*); (*poner a un lado*) to put aside, lay aside; (*rechazar*) to reject; *posibilidad etc* to rule out.

2 descartarse *vr* (**a**) (*Naipes*) (*t* ~ **de**) to discard.

(**b**) ~ **de** to excuse o.s. from; to shun, shirk, evade.

descarte *nm* (**a**) (*Naipes*) discard. (**b**) (*acto*) discarding, rejection, ruling out; **por** ~ by a process of elimination. (**c**) (*fig*) excuse; shirking, evasion.

descasar [1a] *vt* (**a**) to annul the marriage of. (**b**) (*fig*) (*separar*) to separate; (*desordenar*) to disarrange, upset the arrangement of.

descascar [1g] **1** *vt fruta* to peel; *nuez, huevo* to shell; *árbol* to remove the bark from. **2 descascarse** *vr* (**a**) to smash to pieces, come apart. (**b**) (*) to bluster.

descascarar [1a] **1** *vt* (**a**) *fruta* to peel; *nuez, huevo* to shell, take the shell off.

(**b**) (*And*) *animal* to flay, skin.

(**c**) (*And fig*) to dishonour.

2 descascararse *vr* to peel (off), scale (off); to chip off.

descascarillar [1a] *vt vasija etc* to chip.

descastado *adj* (**a**) (*intocable*) that has lost caste, untouchable; *palabra etc* improper. (**b**) (*enajenado*) alienated from one's family; (*frío*) cold, indifferent (to affection).

descaste *nm* culling.

descaudalado *adj* penniless.

descelerar [1a] *vi etc* = **desacelerar** *etc.*

descendedero *nm* ramp.

descendencia *nf* (**a**) (*origen*) descent, origin. (**b**) (*personas*) offspring, descendants; **morir sin dejar** ~ to die without issue, leave no children.

descendente *adj* (**a**) descending, downward; downward-sloping; *cantidad* diminishing; **tren** ~ down train. (**b**) (*Inform*) top-down.

descender [2g] **1** *vt* (**a**) (*bajar*) to lower, let down; *maleta etc* to get down, lift down, take down.

(**b**) *escalera etc* to go down, descend.

2 *vi* (**a**) (*ir abajo*) to descend, come down, go down; (*de categoría*) to be demoted; (*Dep*) to be relegated.

(**b**) (*fiebre, nivel, temperatura etc*) to drop, fall, go down (*en un 5 por cien* by 5%).

(**c**) (*líquido*) to run, flow.

(**d**) (*cortina etc*) to hang.

(**e**) (*persona, fuerza*) to fail, get weak, decay; ~ **de** (*o* **en**) **energía** to suffer a loss of energy.

(**f**) ~ **a** (*fig*) to stoop to, lower o.s. to.

(**g**) ~ **de** to descend from, be descended from; to be derived from; ~ **de linaje de reyes** to come from a line of kings; **la tribu desciende de la región central** the tribe comes from the central region; the tribe originated in the central region; **de esa palabra descienden otras muchas** many other words derive from that one.

descendiente *nmf* descendant.

descendimiento *nm* descent; lowering; **el D~ de la Cruz** the Descent from the Cross.

descenso *nm* (**a**) (*acto*) descent; going down; (*de categoría*) demotion; (*de fiebre, temperatura etc*) drop, fall; (*de producción*) downturn; (*Dep en liga*) relegation; (*esquí*) downhill race; (*de calidad*) decline, falling-off; **las cifras han experimentado un brusco** ~ the figures show a sharp fall; **hay un** ~ **de calidad** there is a falling-off in quality.

(**b**) (*Min etc*) collapse, subsidence.

(**c**) (*Med*) rupture; ~ **del útero** prolapse, fallen womb.

(**d**) (*pendiente*) slope, drop, descent; **el** ~ **hacia el río** the descent to the river, the slope down to the river.

descentración *nf* maladjustment.

descentrado *adj* (**a**) (*lit*) off-centre.

(**b**) (*fig*) out of focus; wrongly adjusted, maladjusted; **parece que el problema está** ~ the problem seems to be out of focus, it seems that the question has not been properly stated; **todavía está algo** ~ he is still somewhat out of touch, he is still not properly adjusted (to the situation).

descentralización *nf* decentralization.

descentralizar [1f] *vt* to decentralize.

descentrar [1a] *vt* to decentre.

desceñir [3h *y* 31] *vt* to loosen; to undo, unfasten.

descepar [1a] *vt* (**a**) (*Agr*) to uproot, pull up by the roots. (**b**) (*fig*) to extirpate, eradicate.

descercar [1g] *vt* (**a**) (*Agr*) to remove the fence (*o* wall) round. (**b**) (*Mil*) *city* to relieve, raise the siege of.

descerco *nm* (*Mil*) relief.

descerebrado *adj* brainless, mindless.

descerrajar [1a] *vt* (**a**) *puerta etc* to force the lock of; *cerradura* to break open, force. (**b**) *disparo* to let off, fire (*a* at).

descervigar [1h] *vt* to break the neck of.

descifrable *adj* decipherable.

descifrador(a) *nm/f* decipherer; decoder; **el** ~ **del misterio** the man who solved the mystery.

descifrar [1a] *vt escritura* to decipher, (manage to) read; *mensaje* to decode; *problema* to puzzle out, figure out; *misterio* to solve, crack.

descinchar [1a] *vt caballo* to loosen the girths of.

desclasificación *nf* (*Dep*) disqualification.

desclasificar [1g] *vt* (*Dep*) to disqualify.

desclavar [1a] *vt* to pull out the nails from, unnail.

descobijar [1a] *vt* to uncover, leave exposed.

descocado* *adj* = **descarado**; *chica* brazen, forward.

descocarse* [1g] *vr* = **descararse.**

descoco* *nm* = **descaro.**

descochollado *adj* (*Cono Sur*) (**a**) (*harapiento*) ragged, shabby. (**b**) (*malo*) wicked. (**c**) (*de mal genio*) ill-tempered.

descodificación *nf* decoding; (*TV*) unscrambling, descrambling.

descodificador *nm* decoder; (*TV*) unscrambler, descrambler.

descodificar [1g] *vt* to decode; (*TV*) to unscramble, descramble.

descoger [2c] *vt* to spread out, unfold.

descojonación‡ *nf*: **¡(es la)** ~! it's the absolute bloody end!‡.

descojonante‡ *adj* (**a**) (*gracioso*) wildly funny. (**b**) (*impresionante*) immensely impressive.

descojonarse‡ [1a] *vr* (**a**) (*reír*) to die laughing. (**b**) (*matarse*: *t* ~ **vivo**) to kill o.s., do o.s. in‡.

descolada *nf* (*Méx*) snub, rebuff.

descolar [1a] *vt* (**a**) *animal* to dock, cut the tail off. (**b**)

(*CAm*: *despedir*) to fire, sack. (**c**) (*Méx*: *desairar*) to snub, slight.
descolgado, -a *nm/f* backslider.
descolgar [1h *y* 1l] **1** *vt* (*gen*) to take down, get down; (*desenganchar*) to unhook; *cuerda etc* to lower, let down; *teléfono* to pick up.
2 descolgarse *vr* (**a**) (*bajar*) to let o.s. down (*con* by, *de* from), lower o.s.; to come down, descend, climb down; ~ **por una pared** to climb down a wall; **quedar descolgado** (*fig*) to be left behind.
(**b**) (*fig*: *persona*) to turn up unexpectedly, drop by; (*Met*) to come on suddenly, set in unexpectedly.
(**c**) ~ **con una cifra** to come up with a figure; ~ **con una estupidez** to come out with a silly remark, blurt out sth silly.
descolocado *adj criado* out of a place; *objeto* misplaced; *cosa, lugar* untidy; **sentirse** ~ to feel out of place.
descolón *nm* (*Méx*) snub, rebuff.
descolonización *nf* decolonization.
descolonizar [1f] *vt* to decolonize.
descoloramiento *nm* discolo(u)ration.
descolorar [1a] *vt* = **decolorar.**
descolorido *adj* (**a**) (*gen*) discoloured, faded; pale. (**b**) (*fig*) colourless.
descollante *adj* outstanding.
descollar [1l] *vi* to stand out, be outstanding; **descuella entre los demás** he stands out among the others; **la obra que más descuella de las suyas** his most outstanding work; **la iglesia descuella sobre los demás edificios** the church stands out above (*o* towers over) the other buildings.
descombrar [1a] *vt* to clear (of obstacles), disencumber.
descomedidamente *adv* (**a**) (*excesivamente*) excessively. (**b**) (*groseramente*) rudely, insolently, disrespectfully.
descomedido *adj* (**a**) (*excesivo*) excessive, immoderate. (**b**) *persona* rude, insolent, disrespectful (*con* to, towards).
descomedimiento *nm* rudeness, insolence, disrespect.
descomedirse [3l] *vr* to be rude, be disrespectful (*con* to, towards).
descompaginar [1a] *vt* to disarrange, disorganize, mess up.
descompasadamente *adv* excessively, disproportionately.
descompasado *adj* excessive, disproportionate, out of all proportion; **a una hora descompasada** at an unearthly hour; **de tamaño** ~ of disproportionate size, extra big.
descompasarse [1a] *vr* = **descomedirse.**
descompensar [1a] *vt* to unbalance.
descompletar [1a] *vt* (*LAm*) to make incomplete, impair the completeness of; *serie, conjunto* to break, ruin.
descomponer [2q] **1** *vt* (**a**) (*gen*) to separate into its constituent parts; (*analizar*) to break down, split up; (*Quím*) to separate into its elements; *masa, unidad etc* to split up, break down; *argumento* to break down, analyse, reduce to a series of points; (*Mat*) to break down.
(**b**) *materia orgánica* to rot, decompose.
(**c**) (*Mec*) to break; to put out of order; to tamper with, mess up; *facciones* to distort; *estómago etc* to upset; ~ **el peinado a una** to mess up sb's hair.
(**d**) *orden etc* to disarrange, disturb, upset; *calma* to ruffle, disturb; ~ **los planes de uno** to upset sb's plans, mess up sb's plans.
(**e**) *persona* to shake up, give a jolt to; to put out; to anger, provoke.
(**f**) *dos personas* to cause a rift between, set at odds.
2 descomponerse *vr* (**a**) (*pudrirse*) to rot, decompose.
(**b**) (*Mec*) to break down, get out of order, develop a fault; (*estómago*) to get upset; (*tiempo*) to break up, change for the worse; (*Cono Sur*: *vomitar*) to be sick, throw up; (*Cono Sur*: *llorar*) to burst into tears; ~ **el brazo** (*And*) to put one's arm out of joint.
(**c**) (*enojarse*) to lose one's temper, get worked up; ~ **con uno** to fall out with sb.
(**d**) **se le descompuso la cara** her face fell (*o* dropped).
descomponible *adj* separable, detachable.
descomposición *nf* (**a**) (*gen*) splitting up, breakdown; (*Quím*) decomposition; (*LAm Aut*) breakdown; ~ **estadística** statistical breakdown.
(**b**) (*putrefacción*) rotting, decomposition.
(**c**) ~ **de vientre** (*Med*) stomach upset, diarrhoea.
(**d**) (*fig*) discomposure.
descompostura *nf* (**a**) (*Mec etc*) breakdown, fault, trouble; bad working order; (*LAm Elec*) fault, failure; (*desorden*) disorder; (*desorganización*) disorganization; (*desaseo*) untidiness, slovenliness.
(**b**) (*fig*: *de cara*) discomposure.
(**c**) (*fig*: *descaro*) brazenness, forwardness.
(**d**) (*And*: *dislocación*) dislocation.
descompresión *nf* decompression.
descomprometido *adj* lacking in commitment, uncommitted.
descompuesto *adj* (**a**) (*Mec etc*) broken, out of order, faulty; *cara, facciones* twisted, distorted; *roca* loose; *sistema etc* disordered, disorganized, chaotic; *cuarto* untidy; *aspecto* slovenly; **estar** ~ (*esp LAm Aut*) to be broken down.
(**b**) (*fig*: *enojado*) angry; **ponerse** ~ to get angry, get worked up, lose one's composure.
(**c**) (*fig*: *descarado*) brazen, forward; rude.
(**d**) **estar** ~ (*LAm**: *borracho*) to be tipsy.
descomunal *adj* huge, enormous, colossal.
desconcentración *nf* (**a**) (*Pol etc*) decentralization, breaking-up. (**b**) (*defecto*) lack of concentration.
desconcentrar [1a] *vt industria etc* to decentralize, break up, distribute over a wider area.
desconceptuado *adj* discredited; not well thought-of, ill-reputed.
desconcertado *adj*: **estar** (*o* **quedar**) ~ (*fig*) to be disconcerted, be taken aback; to be bewildered.
desconcertador *adj*, **desconcertante** *adj* disconcerting, upsetting; embarrassing; baffling, bewildering, puzzling.
desconcertar [1j] **1** *vt* (**a**) (*Mec etc*) to put out of order, damage; (*Anat*) to dislocate; *orden* to disarrange, disturb; *plan* to upset, dislocate, throw out of gear.
(**b**) *persona* (*incomodar*) to disconcert, upset, put out; (*azorar*) to embarrass; (*problema etc*) to baffle, bewilder, puzzle.
2 desconcertarse *vr* (**a**) (*Mec etc*) to get out of order, develop a fault; (*Anat*) to get out of joint, be dislocated.
(**b**) (*persona*) to be disconcerted, be upset, be put out; to get embarrassed; to be bewildered; **siguió sin** ~ he went on quite unruffled; **esto basta para que se desconcierte el más sosegado** this would get even the calmest of people worked up.
desconcierto *nm* (**a**) (*Mec etc*) disorder, trouble; (*daño*) damage; (*desarreglo*) disarrangement, disturbance, chaos.
(**b**) (*fig*) (*inquietud*) uneasiness; (*desorientación*) uncertainty; (*azoramiento*) embarrassment; (*perplejidad*) bewilderment; **contribuye al** ~ **de la juventud** it increases young people's bewilderment; **sembrar el** ~ **en el partido** to sow confusion in the party, create discord in the party; **hay un** ~ **fundamental** there is a basic disagreement.
desconchabar [1a] *vt* (*LAm*) to dislocate.
desconchado *nm* (*de pared*) place where plaster (*etc*) has broken away; (*de vasija*) chip.
desconchar [1a] **1** *vt* to strip off, peel off; to chip off. **2 desconcharse** *vr* to peel off, flake off; to chip.
desconectar [1a] *vt* (*Mec*) to disconnect; to uncouple; (*Elec*) to disconnect; to switch off, turn off.
desconfiado *adj* distrustful, suspicious (*de* of).
desconfianza *nf* distrust, mistrust, lack of confidence; **voto de** ~ vote of no confidence.
desconfiar [1c] *vi* to be distrustful; to lack confidence; ~ **de** to distrust, mistrust, suspect; to have no confidence in; **desconfío de ello** I doubt it; **desconfíe de las imitaciones** (*Com*) beware of imitations; **desconfía de sus posibilidades** he has no faith in his potential; **desconfío de que llegue a tiempo** I doubt if he will get here in time, I cannot be sure that he will arrive in time.
desconformar [1a] *vi y* **desconformarse** *vr* (**a**) (*disentir*) to disagree, dissent.
(**b**) **se desconforman** they do not get on well together; they are not suited to each other.
desconforme *adj* = **disconforme.**
descongelación *nf* (*Aer*) de-icing; (*de salarios*) freeing, unfreezing.
descongelar [1a] *vt nevera* (*Culin*) to defrost; (*Aer*) to de-ice; *salarios* to free, unfreeze.
descongestión *nf* relief, relieving; **una política de** ~ a policy of relieving population pressure in the cities.
descongestionante *nm* decongestant.
descongestionar [1a] *vt* to relieve; *cabeza* to clear; *ciudad etc* to make less crowded, relieve the population pressure in; *calle* to relieve the traffic problems of, make less crowded.
desconocer [2d] *vt* (**a**) (*ignorar*) not to know, be ignorant of, be unfamiliar with; (*no estar enterado de*) to be unaware of; (*no recordar*) to fail to remember; **desconocen los principios fundamentales** they are ignorant of the basic

principles; **no desconozco que** ... I am not unaware that ...
(**b**) (*no reconocer*) not to recognize; (*fingir no conocer*) to pretend not to know; (*no hacer caso a*) to ignore, disregard.
(**c**) (*rechazar*) to disown, repudiate; **pero el poeta desconoció la obra** but the poet disowned the work.

desconocido 1 *adj* (**a**) (*gen*) unknown, not known (*de, para* to); (*poco familiar*) strange, unfamiliar; (*no reconocido*) unrecognized; **lo ~** the unknown; **por razones desconocidas** for reasons which are not known (to us *etc*); **el triunfo de un atleta ~** the success of an unknown athlete.
(**b**) (*cambiado*) much changed; **está ~** he is much altered, he is hardly recognizable.
(**c**) (*ingrato*) ungrateful.
2 *nm*, **desconocida** *nf* (*persona no conocida*) stranger; unknown person; (*recién llegado*) newcomer.

desconocimiento *nm* (**a**) (*ignorancia*) ignorance. (**b**) (*rechazo*) disregard, repudiation. (**c**) (*ingratitud*) ingratitude.

desconsideración *nf* inconsiderateness, thoughtlessness.

desconsideradamente *adv* inconsiderately, thoughtlessly.

desconsiderado *adj* inconsiderate, thoughtless.

desconsoladamente *adv* disconsolately; inconsolably.

desconsolado *adj* disconsolate; inconsolable; *cara* sad, woebegone.

desconsolador *adj* distressing, grievous.

desconsolar [1m] **1** *vt* to distress, grieve. **2 desconsolarse** *vr* to be grieved; to despair, lose hope.

desconstrucción *nf* deconstruction.

desconsuelo *nm* affliction, distress, grief; sadness; despair; **con ~** sadly, despairingly.

descontado *adj*: **por ~** of course, naturally; **eso lo podemos dar por ~** we can take that for granted, we can assume that; we can rely on that; **por ~ que ...** (*como conj*) of course ...

descontaminación *nf* decontamination.

descontaminar [1a] *vt* to decontaminate.

descontar [1m] *vt* (**a**) (*deducir*) to take away; (*Com*) to discount, deduct. (**b**) (*dar por sentado*) to discount; to assume, take for granted. (**c**) (*contar atrás*) to count down.

descontentadizo *adj* hard to please; restless, unsettled.

descontentar [1a] *vt* to displease.

descontento 1 *adj* dissatisfied, discontented (*de* with); disgruntled (*de* about, at); **estar ~ de** to be dissatisfied with, be unhappy about.
2 *nm* (**a**) (*insatisfacción*) dissatisfaction, displeasure; disgruntlement.
(**b**) (*Pol etc*) discontent, unrest; **~ social** social unrest; **hay mucho ~** there is a lot of unrest.
3 *nm*, **descontenta** *nf* (*Méx*) malcontent.

descontinuación *nf* discontinuation.

descontinuar [1e] *vt* to discontinue.

descontrol *nm* decontrol; lack of control, loss of control.

descontroladamente *adv* in an uncontrolled way.

descontrolado *adj* (**a**) (*desordenado*) wild, undisciplined, out of control; **desarrollo ~** uncontrolled development; **elementos ~s** wild elements, (*Pol*) rebellious factions. (**b**) (*LAm: perturbado*) upset, irritated.

descontrolarse [1a] *vr* (**a**) (*perder control*) to lose control, get out of control, go wild. (**b**) (*: *enojarse*) to blow one's top*, go up the wall*.

desconvenir [3s] *vi* (**a**) (*personas*) to disagree (*con* with).
(**b**) (*no corresponder*) to be incongruous; not to fit, not match; (*diferir*) to differ (*con* from).
(**c**) (*no convenir*) to be inconvenient; to be unsuitable.

desconvocación *nf* calling-off, cancellation.

desconvocar [1g] *vt huelga, reunión* to call off, cancel.

desconvocatoria *nf* calling-off, (notice of) cancellation.

descoordinación *nf* lack of coordination; disorganization.

descoque *nm* = **descaro**.

descorazonador *adj* discouraging, disheartening.

descorazonamiento *nm* discouragement; dejection, depression.

descorazonar [1a] **1** *vt* to discourage, dishearten. **2 descorazonarse** *vr* to get discouraged, lose heart.

descorbatado *adj* tieless.

descorchador *nm* (**a**) (*persona*) bark stripper. (**b**) (*sacacorchos*) corkscrew.

descorchar [1a] *vt* (**a**) *árbol* to remove the bark from; to strip. (**b**) *botella* to uncork, draw the cork of, open. (**c**) *arca etc* to force, break open.

descorche *nm* uncorking, opening (of a bottle).

descornar [1m] **1** *vt* to de-horn, poll. **2 descornarse** *vr* (*fig*) (*trabajar*) to slog away, work like a slave; (*pensar*) to rack one's brains; (*: *caer*) to have a nasty fall, break one's head.

descorrer [2a] *vt cortina, cerrojo* to draw back.

descortés *adj* discourteous, rude, impolite.

descortesía *nf* discourtesy, rudeness, impoliteness.

descortésmente *adv* discourteously, rudely, impolitely.

descortezar [1f] *vt* (**a**) *árbol* to strip the bark from, remove the bark of; *pan* to cut the crust off; *fruta etc* to peel.
(**b**) (*fig*) to polish up a bit, knock the corners off.

descoser [2a] **1** *vt* (**a**) (*Cos*) *puntos* to unstitch, unpick; (*romper*) to rip, tear.
(**b**) (*separar*) to separate, part; *V* **labio**.
2 descoserse *vr* (**a**) (*Cos*) to come apart (at the seam), burst, tear.
(**b**) (*: *revelar un secreto*) to blurt out a secret, let the cat out of the bag.
(**c**) (******: *ventosear*) to fart******.
(**d**) **~ de risa** to split one's sides with laughing, die laughing.

descosido 1 *adj* (**a**) (*Cos*) unstitched, torn; (*raído*) shabby.
(**b**) (*fig*) *narración etc* disconnected, disjointed, chaotic.
(**c**) *persona, habla etc* wild, immoderate; (*hablador*) talkative; (*indiscreto*) big-mouthed*, indiscreet, blabbing.
2 *nm* (**a**) (*Cos*) open seam; (*rasgón*) rip, tear.
(**b**) **obrar como un ~** to act wildly; **beber como un ~** to drink an awful lot; **comer como un ~** to eat to excess, stuff o.s.; **gastar como un ~** to spend money wildly; **estudiar** (*etc*) **como un ~** to study (*etc*) like mad.

descotado *adj* (*LAm*) = **escotado**.

descoyuntado *adj* (**a**) (*Anat*) dislocated, out of joint. (**b**) *narración etc* incoherent, disjointed, chaotic.

descoyuntar [1a] **1** *vt* (**a**) (*Anat*) to dislocate, put out of joint.
(**b**) (*fig*) *persona* (*cansar*) to tire out; (*molestar*) to bother; to weary, annoy.
(**c**) *hechos etc* to twist, force the sense of, adapt improperly.
2 descoyuntarse *vr* (**a**) (*Anat*) **~ un hueso** to put a bone out of joint; **los huesos se descoyuntaron** the bones became dislocated.
(**b**) **~ de risa** to split one's sides with laughing, die laughing; **~ a cortesías** to overdo the courtesies, be exaggeratedly polite.

descrecer [2d] *vi* to decrease.

descrédito *nm* discredit; disrepute; **caer en ~** to fall into disrepute; **ir en ~ de** to be to the discredit of, damage the reputation of.

descreencia *nf* (*esp LAm*) unbelief.

descreer [2e] **1** *vt* to disbelieve; to place no faith in. **2** *vi* (*Rel*) to lose one's faith.

descreído 1 *adj* unbelieving; (*pey: ateo*) godless. **2** *nm*, **descreída** *nf* unbeliever.

descreimiento *nm* unbelief.

descremado *adj leche* skimmed, low-fat.

descremar [1a] *vt leche* to skim.

describir [3a; *ptp* **descrito**] *vt* to describe.

descripción *nf* description; **supera a toda ~** it is beyond description, it is indescribable.

descriptible *adj* describable.

descriptivo *adj* descriptive.

descrismar* [1a] **1** *vt*: **~ a uno** to bash sb on the head*; **¡o eso o te descrismo!** either that or I'll bash you!*.
2 descrismarse *vr* (**a**) (*trabajar*) to slave away; (*pensar*) to rack one's brains.
(**b**) (*enojarse*) to blow one's top*.

descrispar [1a] *vt* to take the tension out of.

descrito *ptp de* **describir**; **no es para ~** it is indescribable, it beggars description.

descruzar [1f] *vt piernas* to uncross.

descuajar [1a] *vt* (**a**) *masa, sólido* to melt, dissolve.
(**b**) (*Bot*) to uproot, pull up by the root; *objeto* to pull out, tear from its place.
(**c**) (*fig: extirpar*) to eradicate.
(**d**) (*fig: desanimar*) to dishearten.

descuajaringado* *adj* (*LAm*), **descuajeringado*** *adj* (*LAm*) (*destartalado*) broken-down; dilapidated; (*desaliñado*) scruffy, shabby.

descuajaringante* *adj* side-splitting.

descuajaringar* [1a] **1** *vt* (*And*) to smash to bits (*o* pieces).
2 descuajaringarse *vr* (**a**) (*Anat*) to come apart; (*cansarse*) to become exhausted; **~ de risa** to split one's sides with laughing, die laughing; **es para ~** it's enough to make you die laughing.

(b) (*LAm*: *deshacerse*) to fall to bits.

descuartizar [1f] *vt* (a) *animal* to carve up, cut up. (b) *persona* (*Hist*) to quarter; (*fig*) to tear apart; **ni que me descuarticen** not even if they tear me apart.

descubierta *nf* (a) (*Mil*) reconnoitring, patrolling. (b) **a la ~** openly; in the open.

descubierto 1 *ptp de* **descubrir**.

2 *adj* (a) *situación* open, exposed; (*Mil*) under fire; *cuerpo* bare, uncovered; *cabeza* bare; *persona* bareheaded, hatless; *coche* open; *campo* open, bare, treeless.

(b) **al ~** in the open; exposed; in full view; **poner algo al ~** to lay sth bare, expose sth to view; **quedar al ~** to be exposed; to be manifest, be obvious.

3 *nm* (*Com*: *en cuenta*) deficit; (*saldo deudor*) overdraft; *empréstito etc* unbacked; **a ~, al ~** short; **vender al ~** to sell short; **estar en ~** to be overdrawn; **girar en ~** to overdraw.

descubretalentos *nmf invar* = **cazatalentos**.

descubridero *nm* look-out post.

descubridor 1 *nm* (*Mil*) scout. **2** *nm*, **descubridora** *nf* discoverer.

descubrimiento *nm* discovery; detection; disclosure, revelation; unveiling.

descubrir [3a; *ptp* **descubierto**] **1** *vt* (a) *país, remedio etc* to discover; *criminal, fraude etc* to find, detect, spot; (*revelar*) to bring to light; to unearth, uncover; *petróleo etc* to find, strike; *solución etc* to discover, ascertain, learn.

(b) (*divisar*) to see, make out, glimpse; **apenas lo descubría entre las nubes** I could just see it among the clouds.

(c) *estatua, placa etc* to unveil.

(d) (*poner al descubierto*) to expose to view; (*revelar*) to show, reveal, disclose; (*Naipes*) to lay down; **~ el estómago** to uncover one's stomach, bare one's stomach; **~ la cabeza** to bare one's head; **~ sus intenciones** to reveal one's intentions; **~ su pecho a uno** to open one's heart to sb; **le descubrió su escritura** his writing gave him away, his writing betrayed him; **fue la criada la que les descubrió a la policía** it was the servant who gave them away to the police.

2 descubrirse *vr* (a) (*mostrarse*) to reveal o.s., show o.s.; to disclose one's whereabouts; (*verse*) to come into sight.

(b) (*quitarse el sombrero*) to take off one's hat; (*al saludar*) to raise one's hat (in greeting).

(c) **~ a uno, ~ con uno** to confess to sb, pour one's heart out to sb.

(d) (*salir a luz*) to come out, come to light.

descuelgue *nm* removal, taking out; exception; opting out.

descuento *nm* discount; rebate, reduction; **a ~** below par; **al ~, con ~** at a discount; **~ por pago al contado** discount for cash payment; **~ por no declaración de siniestro** no claims bonus.

descuerar [1a] *vt* (*Cono Sur*) (a) (*desollar*) to flay, skin. (b) (*fig*: *infamar*) to defame; (*) to tear to pieces, tick off*.

descuernar [1a] *vt* (*And, CAm, Carib*) to de-horn.

descueve* *adj* (*Cono Sur*) great*, fantastic*.

descuidadamente *adv* (a) (*gen*) carelessly; (*negligentemente*) slackly, negligently; forgetfully. (b) (*desaliñadamente*) untidily; in a slovenly way.

descuidado *adj* (a) (*sin cuidado*) careless; (*negligente*) slack, negligent; (*olvidadizo*) forgetful.

(b) *aspecto etc* untidy, slovenly; unkempt.

(c) (*desprevenido*) unprepared; off guard; **coger** (*o* **pillar** *etc*) **a uno ~** to catch sb off his guard.

(d) (*tranquilo*) easy in one's mind, without worries; nonchalant, carefree; **puedes estar ~** you needn't worry.

(e) (*abandonado*) neglected; **con aspecto de niños ~s** with the look of neglected children; **tener algo ~** to neglect sth.

descuidar [1a] **1** *vt deber etc* to neglect; *consejo* to disregard; (*olvidar*) to overlook; **ha descuidado mucho su negocio** he has neglected his business a lot.

2 *vi y* **descuidarse** *vr* (a) (*no hacer caso*) to be careless, be negligent; to get careless; (*sentirse seguro*) to feel safe, drop one's guard; **en cuanto me descuide él me lo roba** the moment I drop my guard (*o* cease to watch out) he'll steal it from me; **a poco que te descuides te cobran el doble** you've got to watch them all the time or they'll charge you double; **a poco que te descuides ya no está** before you know where you are it's gone.

(b) (*no preocuparse*) not to worry; **¡descuida!** don't worry!, it's all right!, you can forget about that!; **~se de algo** not to bother about sth; **~se de hacer algo** not to bother to do sth, neglect to do sth.

(c) (*abandonarse*) to let o.s. go, stop taking care of o.s.

descuidero, -a *nm/f* sneak thief.

descuido *nm* (a) (*gen*) carelessness; slackness; negligence; forgetfulness; **al ~** nonchalantly; **al menor ~** if your (*etc*) attention wanders for a moment; **con ~** thoughtlessly, without thinking.

(b) (*desaseo*) untidiness, slovenliness.

(c) (*un ~*) oversight; mistake, slip; **en un ~** (*LAm*) when least expected; **por ~** by an oversight, inadvertently.

desculpabilizar [1f] *vt* to exonerate, free from blame.

desculturización *nf* cultural impoverishment.

deschachar* [1a] *vt* (*CAm*) to sack*, fire*.

deschalar [1a] *vt* (*And, Cono Sur*) *maíz* to husk.

deschapar [1a] *vt* (*LAm*) *cerradura* to break.

desde 1 *prep* (a) (*lugar etc*) from; **~ Burgos hay 30 km** it's 30 km from Burgos; **~ abajo** from below; **~ arriba** from (up) above; **~ lejos** from afar, from a long way off; **~ A hasta M** from A to M.

(b) (*tiempo*) from; since; **~ ahora** from now on; **~ entonces** since then; **~ el siglo XV para acá** from the 15th century onward; **~ 1960 no existe** it ceased to exist in 1960, it went out of existence in 1960; **~ el martes** since Tuesday, after Tuesday; **~ el 4 hasta el 16** from the 4th to the 16th; **llueve ~ hace 3 días** it's been raining for 3 days; **~ hace 2 años no le vemos** we haven't seen him for 2 years, we haven't seen him these last 2 years; **¿~ cuándo es esto así?** how long has it been like this?

(c) **~ niño** since childhood, since I (*etc*) was a child.

2 ~ que *conj* since; **~ que llovió** since it rained; **~ que puedo recordar** ever since I can remember, (for) as long as I can remember.

desdecir [3p] **1** *vi*: **~ de** (a) (*ser indigno de*) to be unworthy of, be below the standard set by; (*no convenir a*) to be unbecoming to; **desdice de su patria** he is unworthy of his country; **esta novela no desdice de las otras** this novel is well up to the standard of the others, this novel is not inferior to the others.

(b) (*no ir bien con*) to clash with, not match, not suit; **la corbata desdice del traje** the tie does not go with the suit.

2 desdecirse *vr* to retract, withdraw; to go back on what one has said; **~ de algo** to go back on sth, take back sth one has said; **~ de una promesa** to go back on a promise.

desdén *nm* scorn, disdain; **al ~** carelessly, nonchalantly.

desdentado *adj* toothless.

desdeñable *adj* contemptible; **una cantidad nada ~** a far from negligible amount.

desdeñar [1a] **1** *vt* to scorn, disdain; to turn up one's nose at; to despise. **2 desdeñarse** *vr*: **~ de** + *infin* to scorn to + *infin*, not deign to + *infin*.

desdeñosamente *adv* scornfully, disdainfully; contemptuously.

desdeñoso *adj* scornful, disdainful; contemptuous.

desdibujado *adj contorno etc* blurred; (*nada claro*) unclear; (*descolorado*) faded.

desdibujar [1a] **1** *vt to blur* (the outlines of). **2 desdibujarse** *vr* to blur, get blurred, fade (away); **el recuerdo se ha desdibujado** the memory has become blurred.

desdicha *nf* (a) (*gen*) unhappiness, wretchedness; misfortune; misery. (b) (*una ~*) misfortune, calamity. (c) (*: *persona etc inútil*) dead loss.

desdichadamente *adv* unhappily; unluckily, unfortunately.

desdichado 1 *adj* (a) (*infeliz*) unhappy; (*desgraciado*) unlucky; unfortunate; wretched; **¡qué ~ soy!** how wretched I am!

(b) (*aciago*) unlucky, ill-fated; **fue un día ~** it was an unlucky day.

2 *nm*, **desdichada** *nf* poor devil, wretch.

desdinerar [1a] **1** *vt* to impoverish. **2 desdinerarse*** *vr* to cough up*, fork out‡.

desdoblado *adj* (*fig*) *personalidad* split; *carretera* two-lane.

desdoblamiento *nm* (a) (*de carreteras*) widening. (b) (*Escol*: *de grupos*) breaking down, reduction. (c) (*explicación*) explanation, clarification. (d) **~ de la personalidad** split personality.

desdoblar [1a] **1** *vt* (a) (*desplegar*) to unfold, spread out; *alambre etc* to untwist, straighten; (*desmontar*) to take apart.

(b) (*Quím*) to break down (*en* into).

(c) (*fig*) to double, divide, make two of; to split; *carretera* to widen; **~ un cargo** to split the functions of a post.

(**d**) *tema* to expand (up)on, explain.

2 desdoblarse *vr* (**a**) to divide, split into two.

(**b**) ~ **sobre un tema** to expand upon a topic.

desdoble *nm* (*Fin*) reorganization of capital.

desdorar [1a] *vt* to tarnish (*t fig*).

desdoro *nm* (*fig*) blot, blemish, stigma, dishonour; **consideran un ~ trabajar** they think it dishonourable to work; **es un ~ para todos** it is a blot on us all; **hablar en ~ de uno** to speak disparagingly of sb, discredit sb by what one says.

desdramatizar [1f] *vt* to take the drama out of; to lower the tension of; *crisis* to defuse.

deseabilidad *nf* desirability.

deseable *adj* desirable.

desear [1a] *vt* to want, desire, wish (for); **os deseo toda clase de éxito** I wish you every success; **¿qué desea la señora?** (*Com etc*) what can I do for you, madam?; **desearía más tiempo** I should like more time; **estoy deseando que esto termine** I wish this would end; ~ + *infin* to want to + *infin*, wish to + *infin*; *V* **dejar**.

desecación *nf* desiccation; draining.

desecado *adj fruta etc* dried.

desecar [1g] **1** *vt* (*gen*) to dry up, desiccate; *estanque, terreno* to drain. **2 desecarse** *vr* to dry up.

desecha *nf* (*And*) = **desecho**.

desechable *adj* disposable, throwaway; **la oferta no es ~** the offer is not to be lightly turned down; **envases ~s** non-returnable empties; **variable ~** temporary variable.

desechar [1a] *vt* (**a**) *basura* to throw out; *objeto inútil* to scrap, get rid of, jettison; *ropa* to cast off.

(**b**) *consejo, miedo, escrúpulo* to cast aside; *petición, oferta* to reject; *idea, plan* to drop, discard.

(**c**) (*subestimar*) to underrate, underestimate; (*menospreciar*) to think little of.

(**d**) (*censurar*) to censure, reprove.

(**e**) *llave* to turn.

desecho *nm* (**a**) (*t* **~s**: *residuo*) residue; (*basura*) waste, rubbish; (*hierro etc*) scrap, junk; (*carne*) offal; (*barcia*) chaff; **~ de hierro, hierro de ~** scrap iron; **~s radiactivos** radioactive waste; **producto de ~** waste product; **vestidos de ~** cast-off clothing.

(**b**) **el ~ de la sociedad** the scum of society, the dregs of society.

(**c**) **ese tío es un ~*** that fellow is a disaster, that chap is a dead loss.

(**d**) (*desprecio*) contempt, scorn; low opinion.

(**e**) (*LAm*) (*atajo*) short cut; (*desvío*) detour; (*sendero*) path, temporary road.

desegregación *nf* desegregation.

desegregar [1h] *vt* to desegregate.

desellar [1a] *vt* to unseal, open.

desembalaje *nm* unpacking.

desembalar [1a] *vt* to unpack.

desembanastar [1a] **1** *vt* (**a**) (*sacar*) to unpack; to take out (of a basket); (*) *espada* to draw. (**b**) (*fig*) *secreto* to blurt out.

2 desembanastarse *vr* (**a**) (*animal*) to break out.

(**b**) (*bajar*) to alight.

desembarazado *adj* (**a**) *camino etc* clear, free, open; (*sin carga*) unburdened, light. (**b**) (*fig*) free and easy, free of commitments; nonchalant; **~ de trabas** free, unrestrained.

desembarazar [1f] **1** *vt* (**a**) *camino etc* to clear, free (*de* of); **~ un cuarto de trastos** to clear a room of furniture.

(**b**) *lugar, piso* to vacate, leave free, leave empty.

(**c**) **~ a uno de algo** to rid sb of sth.

(**d**) (*And, Carib, Cono Sur* ††: *dar a luz a*) to give birth to.

2 desembarazarse *vr*: **~ de algo** to get rid of sth, free o.s. of sth.

desembarazo *nm* (**a**) (*acto*) clearing, freeing, disencumbrance; unburdening.

(**b**) (*And, Carib, Cono Sur*: *parto*) birth, delivery.

(**c**) (*desenfado*) freedom; (*naturalidad*) ease, naturalness; (*libertad*) lack of restraint; **hablar con ~** to talk easily, talk freely.

desembarcadero *nm* quay, landing stage, pier.

desembarcar [1g] **1** *vt personas* to land, put ashore; *mercancías* to land, unload.

2 *vi y* **desembarcarse** *vr* (**a**) (*Náut*) to land, go ashore, disembark; (*Aer*) to leave, disembark.

(**b**) (*esp LAm*: *bajar*) to alight (*de* from), get out (*de* of).

(**c**) **estar para ~*** to be about to give birth.

desembarco *nm* (*Arquit, Náut*) landing.

desembargar [1h] *vt* to free; (*Jur*) to remove the embargo on, remove the impediments from.

desembarque *nm* landing; unloading.

desembarrancar [1g] *vt barco* to refloat, get off.

desembarrar [1a] *vt* to clear of mud, remove the silt from.

desembaular [1a] *vt* (**a**) *equipaje* to unpack; to take out, get out (of a trunk); (*fig*) to empty. (**b**) (*fig*) to unburden o.s. of.

desembocadero *nm*, **desembocadura** *nf* (*gen*) outlet, exit; (*de río*) mouth; (*de alcantarilla*) outfall; (*de calle*) opening, end.

desembocar [1a] *vi*: **~ en** (**a**) (*río*) to flow into, run into, empty into; (*calle*) to meet, join, run into, lead into.

(**b**) (*fig*) to end in, result in, produce; **esto desembocó en una tragedia** this ended in tragedy, this led to tragedy.

desembolsar [1a] *vt* (*pagar*) to pay out; (*gastar*) to lay out.

desembolso *nm* payment; disbursement; outlay, expenditure; **~ de capital** capital outlay; **~ inicial** deposit, down payment; **cubrir ~s** to cover expenses.

desembozar [1f] *vt* to unmask (*t fig*), uncover.

desembragar [1h] **1** *vt* (*Mec*) to disengage, disconnect; *embrague* to release, let out. **2** *vi* (*Aut*) to declutch, let out the clutch.

desembrague *nm* disengagement; (*Aut*: *acto*) declutching; (*pieza*) clutch release.

desembravecer [2d] **1** *vt* to tame; (*fig*) to calm, pacify. **2 desembravecerse** *vr* to calm down.

desembriagar [1h] **1** *vt* to sober up. **2 desembriagarse** *vr* to sober up.

desembrollar [1a] *vt* to unravel, disentangle.

desembuchar* [1a] **1** *vt* to disgorge; (*fig*) to tell, reveal, let out.

2 *vi* (*fig*) to reveal a secret, spill the beans*; **¡desembucha!** out with it!

3 desembucharse *vr* (*Cono Sur*) to be sick.

desemejante *adj* dissimilar, unlike; **A es ~ de B** A is unlike B, A is different from B.

desemejanza *nf* dissimilarity.

desemejar [1a] **1** *vt* to alter (the appearance of), change (for the worse); to disfigure. **2** *vi* to be dissimilar, look different, not look alike.

desempacar [1g] *vt* to unpack.

desempacharse [1a] *vr* (**a**) **se desempachó** (*Med*) he got over his sick feeling; his stomach settled down (after its upset).

(**b**) (*fig*) to cease to feel shy, stop feeling awkward.

desempacho *nm* ease, confidence; unconcern; (*pey*) forwardness.

desempadronarse‡ [1a] *vr* (*Méx*) to do o.s. in‡, commit suicide.

desempañador *nm* (*Aut*) demister.

desempañar [1a] *vt cristal* to clean, demist.

desempapelar [1a] *vt paquete* to unwrap; *pared* to remove (*o* strip) the (wall)paper from.

desempaquetar [1a] *vt* to unpack, unwrap.

desempatar [1a] *vi* to break a tie; **volvieron a jugar para ~** they held a play-off (to resolve the earlier tie).

desempate *nm* (*Fútbol etc*) play-off (to resolve an earlier tie), decider; (*Tenis*) tie break(er); **~ a penaltis** penalty shoot-out.

desempedrar [1j] *vt calle* to take up the paving stones of; **ir desempedrando la calle** (*fig*) to dash along the street.

desempeñar [1a] **1** *vt* (**a**) *propiedad empeñada* to redeem, recover, get out of pawn.

(**b**) **~ a uno** to get sb out of debt, pay sb's debts; (*fig*) to get sb out of a jam.

(**c**) *cargo* to hold, fill, occupy; *deber, función* to perform, discharge; (*Teat y fig*) *papel* to play.

2 desempeñarse *vr* (**a**) (*Fin*) to get out of debt; (*fig*) to get o.s. out of a jam.

(**b**) **~ como** (*LAm*) to act as, play as.

desempeño *nm* (**a**) (*de lo empeñado*) redeeming, redemption.

(**b**) (*de deudas*) payment.

(**c**) (*cargo*) occupation; performance, discharge; (*Teat y fig*) performance, acting, showing; **un ~ meritorio** a worthy performance; **una mujer de mucho ~** a most active and able woman.

desempleada *nf* unemployed woman.

desempleado 1 *adj* unemployed, out of work. **2** *nm* unemployed man.

desempleo *nm* (**a**) unemployment. (**b**) (*pago*) unemployment benefit; **cobrar el ~** to draw unemployment benefit.

desempolvar [1a] *vt* to dust, remove the dust from.

desencadenamiento *nf* (*fig*) unleashing; bursting; ~ **de hostilidades** outbreak of hostilities.

desencadenante 1 *adj*: **los factores ~s del accidente** the factors which caused (*o* contributed to, triggered off) the accident. **2** *nm* cause, trigger.

desencadenar [1a] **1** *vt* (**a**) (*quitar las cadenas de*) to unchain; *perro etc* to unleash, let loose.

(**b**) (*fig*) to unleash; to cause, start, set off.

2 desencadenarse *vr* (**a**) (*soltarse*) to break loose, free o.s.

(**b**) (*fig*: *tormenta etc*) to burst; (*guerra*) to break out; **se desencadenaron los aplausos** a storm of clapping broke out; **se desencadenó una violenta reacción** a violent reaction was produced.

desencajado *adj cara* twisted, contorted; *ojos* wild.

desencajar [1a] **1** *vt* (**a**) *hueso* to throw out of joint; (*Anat*) to dislocate.

(**b**) (*Mec*) to disconnect, disengage, put out of gear.

2 desencajarse *vr* (*cara*) to become distorted (with fear); (*ojos*) to look wild.

desencajonar [1a] *vt* to unpack.

desencallar [1a] *vt barco* to refloat, get off.

desencaminado *adj* headed in the wrong direction, misguided.

desencantar [1a] *vt* to disillusion, disenchant.

desencanto *nm* disillusion(ment), disenchantment.

desencoger [2c] **1** *vt* (*extender*) to spread out; (*alisar*) to smooth out, straighten out. **2 desencogerse** *vr* (*fig*) to lose one's timidity.

desenconar [1a] **1** *vt* (**a**) *inflamación* to reduce.

(**b**) (*fig*) to calm down, soothe.

2 desenconarse *vr* (**a**) (*inflamación*) to grow less, abate.

(**b**) (*fig*: *odio*) to die down, abate; (*persona*) to calm down.

desencontrarse [1n] *vr* (*grupo etc*) to become separated, get split up; to fail to meet up.

desencorvar [1a] *vt* to unbend, straighten (out).

desencuentro *nm* failure to meet up; (*fig*) mix-up.

desenchufar [1a] **1** *vt* to disconnect, unplug. **2 desenchufarse*** *vr* (*hum*) to relax, unwind, switch off.

desendeudar [1a] *vi* (*LAm*) to pay one's debts, get out of the red.

desenfadaderas *nfpl*: **tener buenas ~** to be unflappable, be slow to anger; to be good at getting out of jams.

desenfadado *adj* (**a**) *aire, carácter etc* free, uninhibited; (*despreocupado*) free-and-easy; carefree; unabashed; (*desenvuelto*) self-confident; (*pey*) forward, disrespectful; *ropa etc* casual, unconventional.

(**b**) *espacio* free, unencumbered; ample.

desenfadar [1a] **1** *vt* to pacify, calm down. **2 desenfadarse** *vr* to calm down.

desenfado *nm* freedom, lack of inhibition; free-and-easy manner; self-confidence; (*pey*) forwardness, disrespect.

desenfocado *adj* out of focus; (*intencionado*) in soft focus.

desenfoque *nm* lack of focus, state of being out of focus; (*intencionado*) soft focus.

desenfrenadamente *adv* wildly, in an uncontrolled way; immoderately; licentiously.

desenfrenado *adj* (*descontrolado*) wild, uncontrolled; (*excesivo*) immoderate; *pasión etc* unbridled, licentious.

desenfrenarse [1a] *vr* (**a**) (*persona etc*) to give free rein to one's passions, let one's feelings run wild, lose all self-control; (*multitud*) to run riot, rampage.

(**b**) (*tormenta*) to burst; (*viento*) to rage.

desenfreno *nm* wildness; lack of self-control; lack of moderation; licentiousness.

desenfundar* [1a] *vi* to flash*, expose o.s.

desenganchar [1a] **1** *vt* (*gen*) to unhook, undo, unfasten; (*Ferro*) to uncouple; (*Mec*) to disengage; *caballo* to unhitch. **2 desengancharse*** *vr* to come off drugs, free o.s. from drug addiction; ~ **de** *hábito* to give up, kick*.

desengañado *adj* (**a**) (*decepcionado*) disillusioned. (**b**) (*And, Cono Sur*: *feo*) terribly ugly.

desengañar [1a] **1** *vt* (*desilusionar*) to disillusion; (*decepcionar*) to disappoint; (*hacer ver claro*) to disabuse (*de* about, of); **es mejor no ~la** it is best not to disillusion her; it is best not to destroy her hopes.

2 desengañarse *vr* (**a**) (*desilusionarse*) to become disillusioned (*de* about); (*decepcionarse*) to be disappointed.

(**b**) (*ver claro*) to see the light, come down to earth, see things as they really are; **¡desengáñate!** don't you believe it!, don't go deceiving yourself!; make no mistake!

desengaño *nm* (**a**) (*desilusión*) disillusion(ment); disappointment; **sufrir un ~ amoroso** to be disappointed in love, have an unhappy love affair; **te enseñarán los ~s** the disillusioning experiences (of life) will teach you.

(**b**) (*reproche*) admonition, reproof; home truth.

desengranar [1a] *vt* to disengage.

desengrasado *adj* (**a**) *máquina* rusty, needing oil; (*fig*) rusty. (**b**) (*Culin*) fat-free.

desengrasar [1a] *vt* to degrease, remove the grease from; to scour.

desenhebrar *vt* to unthread.

desenjaular [1a] *vt* (**a**) (*gen*) to take out of a cage; to release from a cage. (**b**) (*) *preso* to let out of jail.

desenlace *nm* outcome; (*Liter*) ending; dénouement; ~ **fatal,** ~ **trágico** tragic ending; ~ **feliz** happy ending.

desenlatar [1a] *vt* (*LAm*) *lata* to open.

desenlazar [1f] **1** *vt* (**a**) (*desatar*) to untie, unlace, undo.

(**b**) (*fig*) *problema* to solve; *asunto* to unravel.

2 desenlazarse *vr* (**a**) (*desatarse*) to come undone.

(**b**) (*Liter*) to end, turn out.

desenmarañar [1a] *vt* to disentangle, unravel (*t fig*).

desenmascarar [1a] *vt* (*fig*) to unmask, expose.

desenojar [1a] *vt* to soothe, appease, calm down.

desenredar [1a] **1** *vt* to unravel; to straighten out; to resolve, clear up.

2 desenredarse *vr* (*fig*) to get out of a jam*; ~ **de** to get out of, extricate o.s. from.

desenredo *nm* (**a**) (*acto*) unravelling, disentanglement. (**b**) (*Liter*) dénouement.

desenrollar [1a] **1** *vt* to unroll, unwind. **2 desenrollarse** *vr* to unroll, unwind; to get unrolled.

desenroscar [1g] *vt* to unscrew; to unwind.

desensibilizar [1f] *vt* to desensitize.

desensillar [1a] *vt* to unsaddle.

desentablar [1a] (*fig*) **1** *vt* (*deshacer*) to break up. **2 desentablarse** *vr*: **una discusión se desentabló** a row broke out.

desentenderse [2g] *vr*: ~ **de** (**a**) (*fingir ignorar*) to affect ignorance of, pretend not to know about.

(**b**) (*repudiar etc*) to wash one's hands of; to repudiate; to have nothing to do with; **se ha desentendido de todo eso** he has ceased to take any part in that, he has withdrawn completely from that.

desentendido *adj*: **hacerse el ~** to pay no attention; to pretend not to be interested (*o* to hear *etc*); **no te hagas el ~** don't pretend you haven't heard.

desenterrar [1j] *vt* (**a**) *cadáver* to exhume, disinter. (**b**) (*fig*) to unearth, dig up, rake up.

desentonado *adj* (**a**) (*Mús*) out of tune. (**b**) *color* clashing, not matching.

desentonar [1a] **1** *vi* (**a**) (*Mús*) to be out of tune.

(**b**) (*fig*) to be out of tune (*con* with); (*colores*) to clash (*con* with), not match; **para no ~** so as to do the right thing, so as to fall into line.

2 desentonarse *vr* (*fig*) to behave rudely, speak disrespectfully, raise one's voice angrily.

desentono *nm* (*fig*: *cualidad*) rudeness, disrespect; (*tono*) rude (*o* angry) tone of voice.

desentorpecer [2d] *vt* (**a**) *pierna etc* to stretch, loosen up. (**b**) (*) *persona* to polish up.

desentramparse* [1a] *vr* to get out of the red*.

desentrañar [1a] *vt* (**a**) (*destripar*) to disembowel; to eviscerate. (**b**) (*fig*) *misterio* to puzzle out, get to the bottom of, unravel; *significado* to puzzle out, work out.

desentrenado *adj jugador* out of practice; off form; *soldado* untrained.

desentumecer [2d] *vt* to free from numbness, restore the feeling to, get the feeling back into; *pierna* to stretch; (*Dep*) *músculos* to loosen up.

desenvainar [1a] *vt* (**a**) *espada* to draw, unsheathe; *guisantes* to shell; *garras* to show, put out. (**b**) (*fig*) to show, reveal, expose.

desenvoltura *nf* ease, naturalness; confidence; free-and-easy manner; (*al hablar*) fluency, facility; (*pey*) forwardness, brazenness.

desenvolver [2h; *ptp* **desenvuelto**] *vt* (**a**) *paquete etc* to unwrap; *rollo* to unwind, unroll; *lana etc* to disentangle, unravel.

(**b**) *teoría etc* to develop; to expound, explain, set out.

desenvolvimiento *nm* development; exposition.

desenvuelto *adj* (*natural*) easy, natural; (*confiado*) confident; (*despreocupado*) free-and-easy; *habla* fluent, easy; (*pey*) forward, brazen.

desenyugar [1h] *vt* (*LAm*), **desenyuntar** [1a] *vt* (*LAm*) to unyoke.

deseo *nm* wish, desire; **el ~ de** the desire for; **el ~ de** + *infin* the desire to + *infin*; **~ de saber** thirst for knowledge; **buen ~** good intentions; **arder en ~s de algo** to yearn for sth; **se cumplieron sus ~s** his wishes were fulfilled; **tener ~ de, venir en ~ de** to want, yearn for.

deseoso *adj*: **~ de** anxious for, desirous of; **estar ~ de** + *infin* to be anxious to + *infin*, be eager to + *infin*.

desequilibrado *adj* (**a**) (*gen*) unbalanced; badly balanced, out of true; (*desigual*) one-sided, lop-sided. (**b**) (*Med*) (mentally) unbalanced.

desequilibrar [1a] *vt* to unbalance; to overbalance, throw off balance.

desequilibrio *nm* (**a**) (*gen*) disequilibrium; unbalance, lack of balance; (*fig*) imbalance. (**b**) (*Med*) unbalanced mental condition, instability, psychological disorder.

deserción *nf* desertion; defection.

desertar [1a] *vi* to desert; **~ de** (*Mil etc*) to desert; **~ del hogar** to abandon one's home, leave home; **~ de sus deberes** to neglect one's duties; **~ de una tertulia** to stop going to a gathering.

desértico *adj* arid, desert-like; (*vacío*) deserted.

desertificar [1g] *vt* = **desertizar**.

desertización *nf* (process of) turning land into a desert; blighting; (*fig*) depopulation.

desertizar [1f] *vt* to turn into a desert; to blight; (*fig*) to depopulate.

desertor(a) *nm/f* (*Mil*) deserter; (*Pol*) defector.

deservicio *nm* disservice.

desescalada *nf* de-escalation.

desescalar [1a] *vti* to de-escalate.

desescamar [1a] *vt* to descale.

desescarchador *nm* (*Mec*) defroster.

desescolarizado *adj*: **niños ~s** children deprived of schooling.

desescombrar [1a] *vt* to clear up, clear of rubbish (*o* debris *etc*), clean up; *cadáver etc* to dig out, extract.

desescombro *nm* clearing-up, clean-up.

desespañolizar [1f] *vt* to weaken the Spanish nature of; *persona* to cause to become less Spanish, wean away from Spanish habits (*etc*).

desesperación *nf* (**a**) (*gen*) despair, desperation; **con ~** despairingly.

(**b**) (*fig*) fury; **nadar con ~** to swim furiously.

(**c**) (*una ~*) infuriating thing; **es una ~** it's maddening; it's unbearable; **es una ~ tener que** ... it's infuriating to have to ...

desesperadamente *adv* desperately, despairingly; hopelessly.

desesperado 1 *adj* (**a**) *persona* desperate, despairing; in despair; *caso, situación* hopeless; **estar ~ de** to have despaired of, have no hope of.

(**b**) *esfuerzo etc* furious, frenzied.

2 *nm*: **como un ~** like mad.

3 *nf*: **hacer algo a la desesperada** to do sth as a last hope, try a final desperate solution.

desesperante *adj* (*enloquecedor*) maddening, infuriating; (*desesperado*) hopeless.

desesperanzar [1f] **1** *vt* to deprive of hope. **2 desesperanzarse** *vr* to lose hope, despair.

desesperar [1a] **1** *vt* to deprive of hope, drive to despair; (*) to drive to distraction, drive crazy.

2 *vi* to despair (*de* of), lose hope; **~ de** + *infin* to give up all hope of + *ger*.

3 desesperarse *vr* to despair, lose hope; to get desperate.

desespero *nm* (*esp LAm*) despair, desperation.

desespinar [1a] *vt pescado* to fillet, bone.

desestabilización *nf* destabilization; subversion.

desestabilizador *adj campaña, influencia* destabilizing; *elemento, grupo* subversive.

desestabilizar [1f] *vt* to destabilize; to subvert.

desestancar [1g] *vt producto* to remove the state monopoly from, allow a free market in.

desestiba *nf* (*Náut*) unloading.

desestibar [1a] *vt* (*Náut*) to unload.

desestimable *adj* insignificant.

desestimar [1a] *vt* (**a**) (*menospreciar*) to have a low opinion of; to scorn, belittle, disparage. (**b**) *demanda, moción etc* to reject.

desestímulo *nm* disincentive.

desestructurado *adj* badly structured; disorganized; **familia desestructurada** broken home.

desexilio *nm* (*LAm*) return from exile, return home.

desfachatado* *adj* brazen, impudent, barefaced; cheeky*.

desfachatez* *nf* (**a**) (*cualidad*) brazenness, impudence; cheek*, nerve*. (**b**) **una ~** a piece of cheek*, an impudent remark.

desfalcador(a) *nm/f* embezzler.

desfalcar [1g] *vt* to embezzle.

desfalco *nm* embezzlement.

desfallecer [2d] **1** *vt* to weaken. **2** *vi* to get weak, weaken; to faint; (*voz*) to fail, falter; **~ de ánimo** to lose heart.

desfallecido *adj* weak; faint.

desfallecimiento *nm* weakness; faintness.

desfasado *adj* (*Mec*) out of phase, badly adjusted; (*fig*) out of step; behind the times, antiquated; **estar ~** (*Aer*) to be suffering from jetlag.

desfasar [1a] *vt* (*Elec*) to change the phase of; (*fig*) to put out of phase, unbalance, upset.

desfase *nm* being out of phase; imbalance; gap, difference; lack of precise correspondence, failure to correspond; maladjustment; (*Aer*) jetlag; **hay un ~ entre A y B** A and B are out of phase.

desfavorable *adj* unfavourable.

desfavorablemente *adv* unfavourably.

desfavorecer [2d] *vt* (**a**) *persona, causa* to cease to favour, withdraw support from. (**b**) (*ropa*) to be unbecoming to, not suit, not look well on.

desfavorecido *adj* underprivileged.

desfibradora *nf* shredder, shredding machine.

desfibrar [1a] *vt papel* to shred.

desfibrilador *nm* defibrillator.

desfiguración *nf*, **desfiguramiento** *nm* disfigurement, disfiguration; defacement; alteration; distortion, misrepresentation; (*Fot etc*) blurring; (*Rad*) distortion.

desfigurado *adj* (*gen*) disfigured; deformed; *sentido etc* distorted, twisted; *contorno* (*t Fot*) blurred; (*Rad*) distorted.

desfigurar [1a] *vt cara* to disfigure; *cuerpo* to deform; *cuadro, monumento etc* to deface; *contorno* (*t Fot*) to blur; *voz* to alter, disguise; *sentido* to distort, twist; to cloud; *suceso* to misrepresent, distort the truth of, alter the details of; **una cicatriz le desfigura la cara** a scar disfigures his face; **la niebla lo desfigura todo** the fog alters everything, the fog makes everything look strange.

desfiladero *nm* defile, pass; gorge.

desfilar [1a] *vi* to parade; to march past; to file by, file out (*etc*), file past; **desfilaron ante el general** they paraded before the general, they marched past the general.

desfile *nm* (*gen*) procession; (*Mil*) parade, march-past; **~ aéreo** flypast; **~ de modas, ~ de modelos** fashion show, fashion parade; **~ naval** naval review; **~ de promoción** (*Mil*) passing-out parade; **~ de la victoria** victory parade.

desfloración *nf* (**a**) deflowering, defloration. (**b**) tarnishing, messing-up, destruction of the fine appearance of.

desflorar [1a] *vt* (**a**) *mujer* to deflower.

(**b**) (*arruinar*) to tarnish, mess up, destroy the fine appearance of.

(**c**) **~ un asunto** to touch briefly on a matter, treat a matter no more than superficially, skim over a matter.

desfogar [1h] **1** *vt* (*fig*) *cólera* to vent (*con, en* on).

2 *vi* (*Náut*: *tormenta*) to burst.

3 desfogarse *vr* (*fig*) to vent one's anger; to let o.s. go, let off steam.

desfogue *nm* (*fig*) venting.

desfondado *adj* (*Fin*) bankrupt.

desfondar [1a] **1** *vt* (**a**) to knock the bottom out of, stave in (*t Náut*). (**b**) (*Agr*) to plough deeply. **2 desfondarse** *vr* (*fig*) to go to pieces, have the bottom fall out of one's life.

desforestación *nf* deforestation.

desforestar [1a] *vt* to deforest.

desgaire *nm* (**a**) (*desaseo etc*) slovenliness, carelessness.

(**b**) (*descuido afectado*) nonchalance, affected carelessness; (*desdén*) scornful attitude, disdain.

(**c**) **vestido al ~** dressed in a slovenly way; **hacer algo al ~** to do sth with a scornful air; **mirar a uno al ~** to sneer at sb, look scornfully at sb.

desgajado *adj* separated, unconnected.

desgajar [1a] **1** *vt* (**a**) *rama* to tear off, break off, split off.

(**b**) **~ a uno de** to tear sb away from.

2 desgajarse *vr* (**a**) (*rama*) to come off, break off, split away.

(**b**) **~ de** (*persona*) to tear o.s. away from.

desgalichado *adj movimiento etc* clumsy, awkward; *vestido* shabby, slovenly, sloppy; *persona* down-at-heel, unprepossessing.

desgana *nf* (**a**) (*para comer*) lack of appetite, loss of appetite.
(**b**) (*fig*) unwillingness, disinclination, reluctance; **su ~ para hacerlo** his unwillingness to do it; **hacer algo a ~** to do sth reluctantly.
(**c**) (*Med*) weakness, faintness.
desganadamente *adv* without much interest, in a desultory fashion; without enthusiasm, reluctantly.
desganado *adj*: **estar ~, sentirse ~** to have no appetite, not be hungry, be off one's food.
desganarse [1a] *vr* (**a**) (*perder el apetito*) to lose one's appetite. (**b**) (*fig*) to lose interest, get bored, get fed up.
desgano *nm* = **desgana.**
desgañitarse [1a] *vr* to bawl, shout; to scream o.s. hoarse.
desgarbado *adj* (*movimiento*) clumsy, ungainly, gawky; graceless; (*aspecto*) slovenly, uncouth.
desgarbo *nm* clumsiness; gracelessness; slovenliness.
desgarrado *adj* (**a**) *ropa* torn; tattered, in tatters. (**b**) (*fig: descarado*) shameless, barefaced, brazen. (**c**) (*fig: vicioso*) licentious.
desgarrador *adj escena etc* heartbreaking, heartrending; *emoción* uncontrollable; *grito* piercing.
desgarrar [1a] *vt* (**a**) *tela* to tear, rip (up), rend. (**b**) (*fig*) to shatter, crush; *corazón* to break. (**c**) (*LAm*) *flema* to cough up.
desgarro *nm* (**a**) (*rasgón*) tear, rip, rent; (*acto*) tearing apart, split; break-up. (**b**) (*fig: descaro*) impudence, brazenness, effrontery; (*de mujer*) forwardness. (**c**) (*fig: jactancia*) boastfulness. (**d**) (*LAm: flema*) phlegm. (**e**) (*Cono Sur Med*) sprain.
desgarrón *nm* big tear.
desgastar [1a] **1** *vt* (**a**) (*gen*) to wear away, wear down; (*Geol*) to erode, weather; *cuerda etc* to chafe, fray; *metal* to corrode, eat away, eat into; **~ la ropa** to wear one's clothes out.
(**b**) (*fig*) to spoil, ruin.
2 desgastarse *vr* (**a**) (*gen*) to wear away; to erode; to chafe, fray; to corrode; to get worn out.
(**b**) (*Med*) to get weak, decline; to wear o.s. out.
desgaste *nm* (**a**) (*gen*) wear; wear and tear; erosion; chafing; fraying; corrosion; **aumenta el ~ del motor** it increases wear on the engine; **debido al ~ de su ropa** because his clothes were so worn.
(**b**) (*desperdicio*) waste, loss; slow wasting; (*Mil*) attrition; (*Med*) weakening, decline; **~ económico** drain on one's resources; **~ natural** natural wastage; **guerra de ~** war of attrition.
desglaciación *nf* thaw.
desglobar [1a] *vt cifras etc* to break down, analyse, split up.
desglosable *adj* separable, detachable; *cifras etc* which can be broken down.
desglosar [1a] *vt* to separate, remove, detach; (*fig*) *cifras etc* to break down.
desglose *nm* breakdown.
desgobernado *adj* uncontrollable, undisciplined; *niño* wild.
desgobernar [1j] *vt* (**a**) (*Pol*) to misgovern, misrule; *asunto* to mismanage, handle badly, make a mess of. (**b**) (*Anat*) to dislocate.
desgobierno *nm* (**a**) (*Pol*) misgovernment, misrule; mismanagement, bad handling. (**b**) (*Anat*) dislocation.
desgolletar [1a] *vt botella* to knock the neck off.
desgoznar [1a] **1** *vt* (**a**) *puerta* to take off its hinges, unhinge.
(**b**) (*quitar goznes de*) to take the hinges off.
2 desgoznarse *vr* (**a**) (*persona*) to get wild, lose control; to go off the rails.
(**b**) (*plan etc*) to be thrown out of gear.
desgrabar [1a] *vt cinta* to wipe (clean).
desgracia *nf* (**a**) (*infortunio*) misfortune; (*percance*) mishap; accident; (*mala suerte*) (piece of) bad luck; setback; **por ~** unfortunately; **¡qué ~!** what a misfortune!; what bad luck!; **estar en ~** to be unfortunate, suffer constant setbacks; **en el accidente no hay que lamentar ~s personales** there were no casualties in the accident; **la familia ha tenido una serie de ~s** the family has had a series of misfortunes.
(**b**) (*falta de favor*) disgrace; disfavour; **caer en (la) ~** to fall from grace, fall into disgrace.
desgraciadamente *adv* unfortunately, unluckily; **¡~!** more's the pity!, alas!
desgraciado 1 *adj* (**a**) (*sin suerte*) unlucky, unfortunate; luckless, hapless; wretched; (*infeliz*) unhappy, miserable; **una elección desgraciada** an unfortunate choice; **~ en sus amores** unlucky in love; **~ en el juego** unlucky at cards; **era ~ en su matrimonio** he was unhappy in his marriage; **una vida desgraciada** a wretched life, a life of misery; **¡qué ~ estoy!** how wretched I am!; **¡~ de ti si lo haces!** you'd better not!, it'll be the worse for you if you do!
(**b**) (*aciago*) ill-fated, unlucky; **ese día ~** that ill-fated day.
(**c**) (*desgarbado*) graceless, ugly, lacking charm; unappealing.
(**d**) (*desagradable*) unpleasant.
(**e**) (*LAm*) rotten, wretched.
2 *nm*, **desgraciada** *nf* wretch, poor devil, unfortunate; **lo tiene aquel ~** that wretched creature has got it; **la hizo una desgraciada** he put her in the family way.
desgraciar [1b] **1** *vt* (**a**) (*estropear*) to spoil, ruin (the appearance of).
(**b**) (*ofender*) to displease.
2 desgraciarse *vr* (**a**) (*estropearse*) to spoil, be ruined, suffer damage; (*plan etc*) to fall through, collapse, fail to mature; **se le desgració el niño antes de nacer** she had a miscarriage, she lost the baby.
(**b**) **~ con uno** to fall out with sb; to lose sb's favour.
desgranar [1a] **1** *vt* (**a**) (*gen*) to remove the grain (*o* pips *etc*) from; *trigo* to thresh; *guisantes* to shell; **~ un racimo** to pick the grapes from a bunch.
(**b**) **~ las cuentas del rosario** to tell one's beads.
(**c**) **~ imprecaciones** to let fly with a string of curses; **~ mentiras** to come out with a string of lies.
(**d**) (*fig: separar*) to sort out, distinguish between.
(**e**) (*fig*) *sentido* to spell out.
2 desgranarse *vr* (**a**) (*Bot*) to fall; (*trigo*) to shed its grain; (*otra planta*) to drop its seeds.
(**b**) (*cuentas*) to come apart.
desgrasado *adj* (*Culin*) fat-free.
desgrasar [1a] *vt* = **desengrasar.**
desgravable *adj* tax-deductible, allowable against tax.
desgravación *nf*: **~ fiscal, ~ de impuestos** tax relief; tax deduction; **~ (de impuestos) personal** personal tax relief, personal allowance.
desgravar [1a] *vt* (*reducir*) *producto* to reduce the tax (*o* duty *etc*) on; (*exentar*) to exempt from tax; **la ley les desgrava estas compras** the law allows them tax relief on these purchases.
desgreñado *adj* dishevelled, tousled.
desgreñar [1a] *vt* to dishevel, rumple, tousle.
desgreño* *nm* (*And, Cono Sur*) untidiness; (*fig: desorden*) disorder, disarray; (*fig: descuido*) carelessness.
desguace *nm* (**a**) (*acto*) breaking up; scrapping; stripping. (**b**) (*parque*) scrapyard, breaker's yard.
desguarnecer [2d] *vt* (**a**) (*Téc*) to strip down; to remove the accessories (*o* trimmings *etc*) from; *instrumento* to dismantle, put out of action; **~ un barco de velas** to remove the sails from a boat.
(**b**) *caballo* to unharness.
(**c**) (*Mil*) *ciudad* to abandon, remove the garrison from; *fortaleza* to dismantle (the fortifications of).
desguarnecido *adj* (**a**) (*gen*) bare, shorn of trimmings (*etc*). (**b**) *ciudad* undefended, unprotected; *flanco* exposed.
desguazar [1f] *vt* (**a**) *madera* to dress, rough-hew. (**b**) *barco* to break up, scrap; *coche etc* to strip, scrap.
desgubernamentalizar [1f] *vt* to remove from government control.
deshabitado *adj* uninhabited; deserted; empty, vacant.
deshabitar [1a] *vt* to move out of, leave empty; to desert, quit.
deshabituación *nf* losing the habit, breaking of the habit; conquering of one's addiction; (*Med*) treatment for drug dependency.
deshabituar [1e] **1** *vt*: **~ a uno de la droga** to break sb of the drug habit, wean sb away from his addiction. **2 deshabituarse** *vr* to lose the habit; **~ de la droga** to break o.s. of the drug habit, conquer one's drug addiction.
deshacer [2s] **1** *vt* (*gen*) to undo, unmake; (*arruinar*) to spoil, ruin, damage, destroy; (*Mec etc*) to take apart; to pull to pieces; *res, carne* to cut up, carve up; *barco* to break up; *cama* to unmake, pull to pieces; *paquete* to undo, unpack, unwrap; *maleta* to unpack; *nudo* to undo, untie; *costura* to unpick; *metal etc* to wear down, wear away; *hielo etc* to melt, dissolve; *vista* to harm, damage; *persona, economía etc* to shatter; *enemigo* to shatter, rout, put to flight; *contrario* to defeat; *tratado etc* to break, violate; *agravio* to right; **~ algo en agua** to dissolve sth in water; **la lluvia deshizo el techo** the rain damaged the roof; **~ un brazo contra algo** to hurt one's arm on sth; **~ el**

camino to go back over one's route, retrace one's steps.

2 deshacerse *vr* (**a**) (*desatarse*) to come undone; (*arruinarse*) to be spoiled, get damaged; (*descomponerse*) to come apart; to fall to pieces; to break up; (*nudo*) to come untied; (*hielo*) to melt, dissolve; (*ejército etc*) to be shattered, disintegrate; (*desaparecer*) to vanish; **se deshizo la pierna al caer** he hurt his leg when he fell; **se deshizo como el humo** it vanished into thin air, it vanished like smoke; **se deshace trabajando** he works excessively hard; **cuando se deshizo la reunión** when the meeting broke up.

(**b**) (*Med*) to get weak, grow feeble; to waste away.

(**c**) (*fig: afligirse*) to grieve; to pine; (*impacientarse*) to get impatient, get worked up.

(**d**) **~ de algo** to get rid of sth; (*Com etc*) to dump sth, unload sth; **no quiero deshacerme de eso** I don't want to part with that; **logramos deshacernos de él** we managed to get rid of him.

(**e**) **~ en lágrimas** to burst into tears; **~ en elogios de uno** to shower praises on sb; **~ en cumplidos** to pay lavish compliments, come out with extravagant courtesies; to overdo the politeness.

(**f**) **~ por los melocotones** to be crazy about peaches, adore peaches; **~ por hacer algo** to strive to do sth, struggle to do sth; **~ por complacer a uno** to do one's utmost to please sb.

desharrapado 1 *adj* ragged, tattered, shabby. **2** *nm*, **desharrapada** *nf*: **los ~s de la sociedad** (*fig*) society's outcasts.

deshebillar [1a] *vt* to unbuckle.

deshebrar [1a] *vt* to unpick.

deshechizar [1f] *vt* to remove the spell from, disenchant.

deshecho 1 *ptp de* **deshacer**.

2 *adj* (**a**) (*gen*) undone; *lazo, nudo* untied; (*roto*) broken, smashed, in pieces; (*despedazado*) shattered; **tener un brazo ~** to have a badly injured arm; **estar ~*** to be worn out.

(**b**) (*Med*) *persona* weak, emaciated; *salud* broken.

(**c**) (*fig*) *tormenta* violent.

(**d**) (*Cono Sur: desaliñado*) untidy.

3 *nm* (*And, Carib, Cono Sur*) short cut.

deshelador *nm* (*Aer*) de-icer.

deshelar [1j] **1** *vt* to thaw, melt; (*Téc*) to defrost; (*Aer*) to de-ice. **2** *vi y* **deshelarse** *vr* to thaw, melt; (*Met*) to thaw.

desherbaje *nm* weeding.

desherbar [1j] *vt* to weed.

desheredar [1a] *vt* to disinherit.

desherrarse [1k] *vr* (*caballo*) to cast a shoe.

deshidratación *nf* dehydration.

deshidratado *adj* dehydrated.

deshidratar [1a] *vt* to dehydrate.

deshielo *nm* thaw; **~ diplomático** diplomatic thaw.

deshierbe *nm* weeding.

deshilachado *adj* shabby; worn, frayed.

deshilachar [1a] **1** *vt* to pull threads out of; to wear, fray. **2 deshilacharse** *vr* to get worn, fray.

deshilada *nf*: **a la ~** (**a**) (*Mil*) in single file. (**b**) (*fig*) secretly, stealthily.

deshilado *nm* (*Cos*) openwork.

deshilar [1a] **1** *vt* (*Cos*) to unravel; *carne* to shred. **2** *vi* to get thin. **3 deshilarse** *vr* to get worn, fray, come apart.

deshilvanado *adj* (*fig*) disjointed, disconnected, incoherent.

deshilvanar [1a] *vt* (*Cos*) to untack, take the stitches out of.

deshinchar [1a] **1** *vt* (**a**) *neumático* to deflate, let down; *hinchazón* to reduce (the swelling of).

(**b**) (*fig*) *ira* to give vent to.

2 deshincharse *vr* (**a**) (*neumático*) to go flat; (*hinchazón*) to go down.

(**b**) (*) to get down off one's high horse*.

deshipotecar [1g] *vt propiedad* to pay off the mortgage on.

deshojado *adj rama etc* leafless; *flor* stripped of its petals.

deshojar [1a] **1** *vt* (**a**) *árbol* to strip the leaves off; (*Quím*) to defoliate; *flor* to pull the petals off.

(**b**) (*LAm*) *maíz* to husk; *fruta* to peel; *libro* to tear the pages out of.

2 deshojarse *vr* to lose its leaves (*etc*).

deshollejar [1a] *vt uvas etc* to peel, skin.

deshollinador *nm* (chimney) sweep.

deshollinar [1a] *vt* (**a**) *chimenea* to sweep. (**b**) (*fig*) to take a close look at.

deshonestamente *adv* (*V adj*) (**a**) indecently, lewdly. (**b**) dishonestly.

deshonestidad *nf* (*V adj*) (**a**) indecency, impropriety, lewdness. (**b**) dishonesty.

deshonesto *adj* (**a**) (*indecente*) indecent, improper, lewd. (**b**) (*no honrado*) dishonest.

deshonor *nm* (**a**) (*gen*) dishonour, disgrace. (**b**) (*un ~*) insult, affront (*de* to); **no es un ~ trabajar** it is no disgrace to work.

deshonorar [1a] *vt* (**a**) (*deshonrar*) to dishonour, disgrace; (*ser indigno de*) to be unworthy of. (**b**) (*despedir*) to dismiss, deprive of office (*o* title *etc*).

deshonra *nf* (**a**) (*gen*) dishonour, disgrace; shame; **lo tiene a ~** he thinks it shameful, he considers it beneath him; **tienen a ~ trabajar** they think it beneath them to work.

(**b**) (*una ~*) shameful act.

deshonrabuenos *nmf invar* (**a**) (*calumniador*) backbiter. (**b**) (*oveja negra*) black sheep (of the family).

deshonrar [1a] *vt* (**a**) *gen*) to dishonour, disgrace, bring disgrace on. (**b**) (*afrontar*) to insult. (**c**) *mujer* to seduce, ruin.

deshonroso *adj* dishonourable, disgraceful, ignominious.

deshora: **a ~** *adv* at the wrong time; at an inconvenient time; **llegar a ~** to come unexpectedly; **acostarse a ~** to go to bed at some unearthly hour; **hacer algo a ~** to do sth at the wrong moment, mistime sth.

deshuesado *adj carne* boned; *fruta* stoned.

deshuesar [1a] *vt carne* to bone; *fruta* to stone.

deshuevarse** [1a] *vr etc* = **descojonarse** *etc*.

deshumanizador *adj*, **deshumanizante** *adj* dehumanizing.

deshumanizar [1f] *vt* to dehumanize.

deshumedecerse [2d] *vr* to dry up, lose its moisture.

desideologizado *adj* non-ideological, free of ideological considerations.

desiderátum *nm*, *pl* **desiderátums** *o* **desiderata** desideratum; ideal, thing ideally required (*o* desired); observable lack; list of books (*etc*) to be bought.

desidia *nf* (**a**) (*pereza*) laziness, idleness. (**b**) (*desaseo*) neglect; slovenliness, carelessness.

desidioso *adj* (**a**) (*perezoso*) lazy, idle. (**b**) (*descuidado*) neglected; slovenly, careless.

desierto 1 *adj* (**a**) *isla, región etc* desert; *paisaje* empty, bleak, desolate; *casa etc* empty, deserted; **la calle estaba desierta** the street was deserted.

(**b**) **declarar ~ un premio** to declare that a prize will not be awarded (for lack of good candidates *etc*); **declarar desiertas unas oposiciones** to declare a competition void.

2 *nm* desert; wilderness; **clamar en el ~, predicar en el ~** to be a voice crying in the wilderness.

designación *nf* (**a**) (*acto*) designation, appointment. (**b**) (*nombre*) designation, name.

designar [1a] *vt* (*gen*) to designate, appoint, name; (*escoger*) to select; *fecha, lugar etc* to name, fix, decide on.

designio *nm* plan, design.

desigual *adj* (**a**) (*no igual*) unequal, different; *lucha etc* unequal; *trato* unfair, inequitable.

(**b**) *tiempo etc* variable, changeable; *carácter* unpredictable.

(**c**) *terreno, escritura etc* uneven; irregular; *borde* rough.

desigualdad *nf* (**a**) (*Econ, Pol*) inequality. (**b**) (*de carácter, tiempo*) variableness, changeableness; unpredictability. (**c**) (*de escritura*) unevenness; irregularity; (*de terreno*) roughness.

desilusión *nf* disillusion(ment), disappointment; **caer en la ~** to get disillusioned; **sufrir una ~** to suffer a disappointment.

desilusionante *adj* disillusioning, disappointing.

desilusionar [1a] **1** *vt* (*desengañar*) to disillusion; (*decepcionar*) to disappoint, let down.

2 desilusionarse *vr* to get disillusioned, lose one's illusions; to be disappointed; to have one's hopes destroyed.

desimantar [1a] *vt* to demagnetize.

desincentivar [1a] *vt* to act as a disincentive to, discourage.

desincentivo *nm* disincentive.

desincrustante *adj*: **agente ~** descaling agent; **producto ~** descaling product.

desincrustar [1a] *vt* to descale.

desinencia *nf* (*Ling*) ending.

desinfección *nf* disinfection.

desinfectante *nm* disinfectant.

desinfectar [1a] *vt* to disinfect.

desinfestar [1a] *vt* to decontaminate.

desinflación *nf* deflation.

desinflado *adj neumático* flat.
desinflar [1a] **1** *vt* to deflate, let the air out of. **2 desinflarse** *vr* (*neumático*) to go down, go flat.
desinformación *nf* (**a**) (*información engañosa*) disinformation, misleading information, black propaganda. (**b**) (*ignorancia*) ignorance, lack of information.
desinformado *adj* uninformed.
desinformador 1 *adj noticia* false, calculated to deceive. **2** *nm*, **desinformadora** *nf* spreader of disinformation.
desinformar [1a] *vt* to misinform.
desinformativo *adj* misleading, false.
desinhibición *nf* lack of inhibition(s).
desinhibido *adj* uninhibited.
desinhibir [3a] **1** *vt* to free from inhibitions. **2 desinhibirse** *vr* to lose one's inhibitions.
desinsectación *nf* protection against insect pests; **la ~ de un jardín** freeing a garden of insect pests.
desinsectar [1a] *vt* to clear of insects.
desintegrable *adj* fissile.
desintegración *nf* disintegration; **~ nuclear** nuclear fission; **la ~ del átomo** the splitting of the atom.
desintegrar [1a] **1** *vt* to disintegrate; *átomo* to split, smash. **2 desintegrarse** *vr* to disintegrate; to split, be smashed.
desinterés *nm* disinterestedness, impartiality; unselfishness, generosity.
desinteresado *adj* (*imparcial*) disinterested, impartial; (*altruista*) unselfish, generous.
desintoxicación *nf* curing of poisoning; curing of drug addiction.
desintoxicar [1g] **1** *vt* to cure of poisoning; to cure of drug addiction (*o* alcoholism). **2 desintoxicarse** *vr* to undergo treatment for drug addiction (*o* alcoholism).
desinversión *nf* disinvestment.
desinvertir [3i] *vi* to disinvest.
desistimiento *nm* (**a**) (*gen*) desisting. (**b**) (*Jur*) waiver.
desistir [3a] *vi* (**a**) (*gen*) to stop, desist; **~ de algo** to desist from sth; **~ de** + *infin* to desist from + *ger*, stop + *ger*.
(**b**) **~ de un derecho** (*Jur*) to waive a right.
desjarretar [1a] *vt animal* to hamstring; (*Med*) to weaken, debilitate.
desjuntar [1a] *vt* (*separar*) to separate, take apart; (*dividir*) to divide.
deslavado *adj* (**a**) (*gen*) half-washed. (**b**) (*fig*) brazen, barefaced. (**c**) = **deslavazado**.
deslavar [1a] *vt* (**a**) (*lavar a medias*) to half-wash, wash superficially; (*quitar lavando*) to wash away. (**b**) (*debilitar*) to weaken; (*desteñir*) to fade.
deslavazado *adj* (**a**) (*lacio*) soft, weak, limp; drooping; *persona* limp. (**b**) (*desteñido*) faded, washed-out, pale; (*fig*) colourless; unsubstantial. (**c**) (*fig*) *habla etc* disjointed, incoherent.
deslave *nm* (*Méx*) landslide, rockfall.
desleal *adj* disloyal (*a, con* to); (*Com*) *competencia* unfair; *juego* foul, dirty.
deslealmente *adv* disloyally; unfairly.
deslealtad *nf* disloyalty; unfairness.
deslegalizar [1f] *vt* to outlaw, criminalize.
deslegitimar [1a] *vt* to discredit, undermine.
desleído *adj* (**a**) (*disuelto*) dissolved; diluted. (**b**) (*fig*) *idea etc* weak, woolly.
desleír [3m] **1** *vt sólido* to dissolve; *líquido* to dilute, thin; to make weaker. **2 desleírse** *vr* to dissolve; to become diluted; to get weaker.
deslenguado *adj* foul-mouthed.
deslenguarse [1i] *vr* (*decir demasiado*) to shoot one's mouth off, talk too much, be too free in what one says; (*descaradamente*) to speak insolently; (*obscenamente*) to pour out obscenities.
desliar [1c] **1** *vt* to untie, undo. **2 desliarse** *vr* to come undone.
desligado *adj* (**a**) (*suelto*) loose, free; unfastened. (**b**) (*fig*) separate, detached; **vive ~ de todo** he lives detached from everything, he lives in a world of his own.
desligamiento *nm* (*fig*) detachment (*de* from).
desligar [1h] **1** *vt* (**a**) (*desatar*) to untie, undo, unfasten; to unbind; (*desenredar*) to extricate (*de* from).
(**b**) (*fig: separar*) to separate, detach; to consider separately; **~ el primer aspecto del segundo** to separate the first aspect from the second.
(**c**) (*fig: aclarar*) to unravel, disentangle, clarify.
(**d**) (*fig: absolver*) to absolve, free (*de* from); (*eximir*) to excuse, exempt (*de* from); **~ a uno de una promesa** to release sb from a promise.
2 desligarse *vr* to come undone, get unfastened; (*persona*) to extricate o.s. (*de* from).
deslindable *adj* definable.
deslindar [1a] *vt* (**a**) *terreno* to mark out, fix the limits (*o* boundaries) of. (**b**) (*fig*) to define, clarify.
deslinde *nm* (**a**) (*acto*) demarcation, fixing of limits (*o* boundaries). (**b**) (*fig*) definition.
desliz *nm* (**a**) (*gen*) slip, slide; (*Aut*) skid.
(**b**) (*fig*) slip; lapse; indiscretion; **~ freudiano** Freudian slip; **~ de lengua** slip of the tongue; **los deslices de la juventud** the indiscretions of youth, the minor sins of youth.
deslizadero *nm* (**a**) (*gen*) slide; (*sitio*) slippery spot. (**b**) (*Téc*) chute, slide.
deslizadizo *adj* slippery.
deslizador *nm* (**a**) (*de niño*) scooter. (**b**) (*Náut*) small speedboat. (**c**) (*Dep*) surfboard, aquaplane, water ski. (**d**) (*de patín*) runner, skid.
deslizamiento *nm* slide, sliding, slipping; (*Aut*) skid; **~ (suave)** glide; **~ salarial** (upward) drift of wages; **~ de tierra** landslide.
deslizante *adj* sliding.
deslizar [1f] **1** *vt* (**a**) (*gen*) to slide, slip (*en* into, *por* along, through); **~ una mesa por el suelo** to slide a table along the floor; **~ la mano por la pierna de una** to run (*o* slide) one's hand up (*o* along) sb's leg.
(**b**) **~ una propina a uno** to slip sb a tip; **~ una observación** to slip a remark in; to let slip a remark.
2 deslizarse *vr* (**a**) (*por accidente*) to slip (*en* on, up on), slide (*por* along); (*Aut*) to skid.
(**b**) (*secreto*) to slip out; (*error*) to slip in, creep in.
(**c**) (*movimiento: culebra etc*) to slide, glide, slither; (*barca*) to glide; (*agua*) to go (gently); pass, flow gently; (*tiempo*) to pass, glide past; (*persona*) to slip away, slip off; to slip in; **~ en un cuarto** to slip into a room; **~ en una fiesta** to slip unnoticed into a party; **el agua se desliza mansamente** the water flows along gently; **la anguila se deslizó entre mis manos** the eel slipped away between my fingers; **el insecto se deslizó fuera del agujero** the insect wriggled out of the hole.
(**d**) (*equivocarse*) to slip up, blunder; (*moralmente*) to go wrong morally, get into bad ways, backslide.
deslomar [1a] **1** *vt* to break the back of; (*fig*) to wear out, exhaust utterly; **~ a uno a garrotazos** to beat sb mercilessly.
2 deslomarse *vr* (*fig*) to get worn out; to work one's guts out.
deslucido *adj* (**a**) (*deslustrado*) tarnished; (*viejo*) worn out, old and useless.
(**b**) (*sin vida*) flat, dull, lifeless; *actuación* undistinguished, characterless; **hizo un papel ~** he was dull in the part; **el jugador estuvo muy ~** the player was far from his best form, he played in a very lifeless way.
(**c**) (*desgarbado*) graceless, inelegant, awkward.
(**d**) **quedó muy ~** he did very badly, he made a very poor showing.
deslucimiento *nm* (*V adj*) (**a**) tarnished state; useless condition.
(**b**) flatness, dullness, lifelessness; (*Teat*) lack of character.
(**c**) gracelessness, inelegance.
(**d**) poor showing, bad performance.
deslucir [3f] **1** *vt* (**a**) (*deslustrar*) to tarnish; (*estropear*) to damage, spoil, ruin; to impair the splendour of, diminish the attractiveness of, dull; **la lluvia deslució el acto** the rain ruined the ceremony.
(**b**) *persona* to discredit, damage the standing of.
2 deslucirse *vr* (*fig*) to do badly, make a poor showing.
deslumbrador *adj* (**a**) (*lit*) dazzling, brilliant; glaring. (**b**) (*fig*) dazzling; puzzling, confusing, bewildering.
deslumbramiento *nm* (**a**) (*brillo*) glare, dazzle; brilliance. (**b**) (*fig*) confusion; bewilderment.
deslumbrante *adj* dazzling.
deslumbrar [1a] *vt* (**a**) (*con luz*) to dazzle; (*cegar*) to blind.
(**b**) (*fig*) (*impresionar*) to dazzle; (*dejar perplejo*) to puzzle, confuse, bewilder; (*aturdir*) to daze; **deslumbró a todos con su oratoria** he captivated everyone with his oratory, he gave a dazzling oratorical display.
deslustrado *adj* (**a**) *vidrio* frosted, ground; *loza* unglazed. (**b**) (*esp fig*) dull, lustreless; tarnished.
deslustrar [1a] *vt* (**a**) *vidrio* to frost; *loza, paño* to remove the glaze from. (**b**) (*esp fig*) to dull, tarnish (the brilliance of), dim (the lustre of). (**c**) (*fig*) *reputación etc* to sully, stain, tarnish.
deslustre *nm* (**a**) (*de vidrio*) frosting; (*de loza, paño*) re-

moval of glaze. (**b**) (*de muebles, adornos*) tarnishing; dullness, dimness. (**c**) (*fig*) stigma, stain; disgrace.

deslustroso *adj* (**a**) unbecoming, unsuitable. (**b**) (*fig*) disgraceful.

desmadejamiento *nm* enervation, weakness.

desmadejar [1a] **1** *vt* to enervate, weaken, take it out of. **2 desmadejarse** *vr* to weaken; to go floppy, loll.

desmadrado *adj* (**a**) (*desenfrenado*) unruly, rebellious; (*desinhibido*) uninhibited; outrageous; (*excéntrico*) far out*.

(**b**) (*confuso*) confused; disoriented, lost.

desmadrarse [1a] *vr* (*rebelarse*) to rebel; (*descontrolarse*) to get out of control, go too far, run to excess, run wild; (*divertirse*) to let one's hair down; (*excederse*) to go over the top; (*perder dignidad*) to lose one's dignity; ~ **por uno** to fall madly in love with sb; **los gastos se han desmadrado** costs have gone right over the top.

desmadre *nm* (**a**) (*exceso*) excess; excess of emotion; (*descontrol*) loss of control; loss of dignity; (*conducta*) outrageous behaviour; (*en cifras*) sudden leap, excessive rise; boom; **¡es el ~!** it's the end!; **esto va de ~ total** this is really getting out of hand.

(**b**) (*confusión*) chaos, confusion; mess; (*ultraje*) outrage.

(**c**) (*: *juerga*) wild party, rave-up*.

desmalezar [1f] *vt* (*LAm*) to weed.

desmallar [1a] **1** *vt puntos* to pull out; *media* to make a ladder (*o* run) in. **2 desmallarse** *vr* (*media*) to ladder.

desmamar [1a] *vt* to wean.

desmán¹ *nm* (*exceso*) excess, outrage; (*mala conducta*) piece of bad behaviour; (*abuso*) abuse (of authority); **cometer un ~** to commit an outrage (*contra* on).

desmán² *nm* (*Zool*) muskrat.

desmanchar [1a] **1** *vt* (*LAm*) to clean, remove the spots (*o* stains *etc*) from.

2 desmancharse* *vr* (*And, CAm*) (**a**) (*salir de prisa*) to bolt out; (*retirarse*) to withdraw.

(**b**) (*Agr*) to stray from the herd.

desmandado *adj* (**a**) *persona* unruly, unbridled; wild; uncontrollable, out of hand; obstreperous. (**b**) *animal* stray; *caballo* runaway.

desmandarse [1a] *vr* (**a**) (*descontrolarse*) to get out of hand, run wild, go out of control; (*portarse mal*) to be obstreperous, behave badly; (*descararse*) to be insolent.

(**b**) (*animal*) to break loose; (*caballo*) to bolt, run away.

desmano: **a ~** *adv V* **contramano**.

desmanotado *adj* clumsy, awkward.

desmantelamiento *nm* (**a**) (*acto*) dismantling; abandonment. (**b**) (*estado*) dilapidation.

desmantelar [1a] **1** *vt* (*Mil etc*) to dismantle, raze; *máquina* to strip down; *andamio etc* to take down; *pared* to strip; *casa etc* to strip of its contents, leave bare; *pandilla* to break up; *organización* to disband; to remove the threat of, put an end to; (*Náut*) to unmast, unrig; (*fig*) to abandon, forsake.

2 desmantelarse *vr* (*casa etc*) to fall into disrepair, become dilapidated.

desmaña *nf* (*V adj*) clumsiness, awkwardness; slowness, helplessness; unpractical nature.

desmañado *adj* (*torpe*) clumsy, awkward; (*lerdo*) slow, helpless; (*poco práctico*) unpractical.

desmaquillador *nm*, **desmaquillante** *nm* make-up remover.

desmaquillarse [1a] *vr* to remove one's make-up.

desmarcado *adj* (*Dep*) unmarked.

desmarcar [1g] **1** *vt* to disassociate (*de* from).

2 desmarcarse *vr* (*Dep*) to shake off one's attacker, avoid an opponent, get clear; (*fig*) to step out of line; to distance oneself (*de* from), set down the differences (*de* from).

desmayado *adj* (**a**) (*Med*) unconscious. (**b**) (*fig*) weak, faint; languid; *carácter etc* dull, lacklustre, colourless. (**c**) *color* pale, dull.

desmayar [1a] **1** *vi* (*persona*) to lose heart, get discouraged, get depressed; (*esfuerzo etc*) to falter, flag.

2 desmayarse *vr* (**a**) (*Med*) to faint (away), swoon.

(**b**) (*planta etc*) to droop low, trail.

desmayo *nm* (**a**) (*Med: acto*) faint, fainting fit, swoon; (*estado*) unconsciousness; **salir del ~** to come to, come round; **sufrir un ~** to have a fainting fit, faint.

(**b**) (*de voz*) faltering, flagging; (*de ánimo*) dejection, depression; (*del cuerpo en general*) languidness, limpness, limp feeling, listlessness; **tenía un ~ en todo el cuerpo** he felt limp all over; **las ramas caen con ~** the branches droop low, the branches trail; **hablar con ~** to talk in a small voice, speak falteringly.

desmedido *adj* (*gen*) excessive, disproportionate, out of all proportion; *ambición, orgullo* boundless, overweening; *dolor etc* exaggerated.

desmedirse [3k] *vr* to forget o.s., go too far.

desmedrado *adj* (**a**) (*estropeado*) impaired; reduced; in decline. (**b**) (*Med*) puny, feeble.

desmedrar [1a] **1** *vt* (*perjudicar*) to impair; (*reducir*) to reduce; (*estropear*) to spoil, ruin, affect badly.

2 *vi y* **desmedrarse** *vr* (**a**) (*decaer*) to fall off, decline; to go downhill; (*deteriorarse*) to deteriorate.

(**b**) (*Med*) to get weak; to get thin; (*niño*) to be sickly, waste away; (*Bot*) to grow poorly, do badly.

desmedro *nm* (**a**) (*gen*) impairment; (*reducción*) reduction; (*decaimiento*) decline, deterioration. (**b**) (*Med*) weakness, emaciation, thinness.

desmejora *nf*, **desmejoramiento** *nm* = **desmedro (a)**, **(b)**.

desmejorado *adj*: **queda muy desmejorada** she's lost her looks, she's not as attractive as she used to be; (*Med*) she's not looking at all well.

desmejorar [1a] **1** *vt* (**a**) (*perjudicar*) to impair, spoil, damage; to cause to deteriorate.

(**b**) (*Med*) to weaken, affect the health of.

2 desmejorarse *vr* (**a**) to be impaired, be spoiled; (*decaer*) to decline, deteriorate, go downhill.

(**b**) (*persona*) to lose one's looks, look less attractive; (*Med*) to lose one's health, suffer, waste away.

desmelenado 1 *adj* dishevelled, tousled. **2** *nm*, **desmelenada** *nf* long-haired lout.

desmelenar [1a] **1** *vt* to dishevel, tousle the hair of.

2 *vr* **desmelenarse*** (**a**) (*asearse*) to spruce up, pull one's socks up.

(**b**) (*obrar*) to sail into action.

(**c**) (*ir de juerga*) to let one's hair down.

desmelene* *nm* excess; informality; **¡es el ~!** it's sheer chaos!; it's way over the top!*

desmembración *nf* dismemberment, break-up.

desmembrar [1j] *vt* to dismember, separate, break up.

desmemoria *nf* poor memory, forgetfulness.

desmemoriado *adj* forgetful, absent-minded.

desmemoriarse [1b] *vr* to grow forgetful, become absent-minded.

desmentida *nf* denial; **dar una ~ a** to deny, give the lie to.

desmentido *nm* = **desmentida**.

desmentimiento *nm* denial; refutation.

desmentir [3i] **1** *vt acusación* to deny, refute, give the lie to; *rumor* to deny, scotch, scout; *teoría etc* to refute, explode; to contradict; *carácter, orígenes etc* to belie, not fit in with, be unworthy of; **~ rotundamente una acusación** to deny a charge flatly.

2 *vi* to be out of line, not fit; **~ de** to belie, clash with, be unworthy of.

3 desmentirse *vr* (*contradecirse*) to contradict o.s.; (*desdecirse*) to go back on one's word.

desmenuzable *adj* crumbly, crumbling; flaky; friable.

desmenuzar [1f] **1** *vt* (**a**) *pan etc* to crumble (up), break into small pieces; *carne* to chop, shred, mince; *queso* to grate.

(**b**) (*fig*) to examine minutely, take a close look at.

2 desmenuzarse *vr* to crumble (up), break up.

desmerecedor(a) *nm/f* undeserving person.

desmerecer [2d] **1** *vt* to be unworthy of.

2 *vi* (**a**) (*deteriorarse*) to deteriorate, go off, be less good; (*perder valor*) to lose value.

(**b**) **~ de** to compare unfavourably with, not be comparable to, not live up to; **ésta no desmerece de sus otras películas** this is in no way inferior to his other films, this is every bit as good as his earlier films.

desmesura *nf* (**a**) (*exceso*) excess, enormity; (*desproporción*) disproportion; extra size. (**b**) (*falta de moderación*) lack of moderation.

desmesuradamente *adv* disproportionately, excessively; enormously; **abrir ~ la boca** to open one's mouth extra wide.

desmesurado *adj* (**a**) (*excesivo*) disproportionate, excessive, inordinate; (*enorme*) enormous; *ambición etc* boundless; *dimensiones* extra big, unduly large, much too big.

(**b**) (*descarado*) insolent, impudent.

desmesurarse [1a] *vr* to become insolent, forget o.s., lose all restraint.

desmigajar [1a] *vt*, **desmigar** [1h] *vt* to crumble.

desmilitarización *nf* demilitarization.

desmilitarizado *adj* demilitarized.
desmilitarizar [1f] *vt* to demilitarize.
desmineralizado *adj* (*fig*) *actuación etc* lifeless, lacklustre; *persona* run down.
desmirriado *adj* (*débil*) weak, sickly; (*flaco*) thin, weedy*.
desmitificación *nf* demythologizing.
desmitificador *adj* demythologizing.
desmitificar [1g] *vt* to demythologize.
desmochar [1a] *vt árbol* to lop, cut off the top of; to pollard; *defensas* to slight; *cuernos* to cut off the points of; *texto etc* to cut, hack about, mutilate.
desmoche *nm* (**a**) (*de árbol*) lopping, pollarding.
(**b**) (*) general slaughter, mowing down, mass removal; **hubo un ~ en el primer examen** there was a mass slaughter of candidates in the first exam.
desmocho *nm* lopped branches, cuttings.
desmodular [1a] *vt* (*Rad etc*) *mensaje* to scramble.
desmolado *adj* toothless.
desmoldar [1a] *vt* (*Culin*) to remove from its mould.
desmonetizar [1f] *vt* (**a**) (*Fin*) to demonetize. (**b**) (*Cono Sur*: *desvalorizar*) to devalue.
desmontable 1 *adj* detachable; sectional, in sections, which takes apart; collapsible; that takes down. **2** *nm* tyre lever.
desmontaje *nm* dismantling, stripping down; demolition.
desmontar [1a] **1** *vt* (**a**) (*Mec*) to dismantle, strip down; to take apart, take to pieces; (*Arquit*) to knock down, demolish; *escopeta* to uncock; *tienda* to take down; *artillería enemiga* to silence, knock out; *vela* to take down.
(**b**) *terreno* to level; to clear of trees (*etc*); *árbol* to fell; *basura* to clear away.
(**c**) *jinete* to throw, unseat, unhorse; **~ a uno de un vehículo** to help sb down from a vehicle.
2 *vi y* **desmontarse** *vr* to dismount, alight (*de* from).
desmonte *nm* (**a**) (*acto*) levelling; clearing; clearing away, removal; **los trabajos exigirán el ~ de X metros cúbicos** the work will necessitate the removal of X cubic metres.
(**b**) (*terreno*) levelled ground; (*montón*) heap of soil extracted.
(**c**) (*Ferro*) cutting, cut (*US*).
(**d**) (*madera*) felled timber.
desmoralización *nf* demoralization.
desmoralizador *adj* demoralizing.
desmoralizar [1f] **1** *vt ejército etc* to demoralize; *costumbres etc* to corrupt. **2 desmoralizarse** *vr* to lose heart, get discouraged.
desmoronadizo *adj* crumbling; rickety; dilapidated.
desmoronado *adj* tumbledown, ruinous, dilapidated.
desmoronamiento *nm* crumbling, dilapidation, decay; collapse (*t fig*).
desmoronar [1a] **1** *vt* to wear away, destroy little by little; (*fig*) to erode, affect, make inroads into.
2 desmoronarse *vr* (*Geol etc*) to crumble, fall apart; (*casa etc*) to get dilapidated, fall into disrepair; (*ladrillos etc*) to fall, come down, collapse; (*fig*) to decline, decay.
desmotivación *nf* lack of motivation.
desmotivado *adj* unmotivated, lacking motivation.
desmotivar [1a] *vt* to discourage.
desmovilización *nf* (**a**) (*Mil*) demobilization. (**b**) demoralization.
desmovilizar [1f] *vt* (**a**) (*Mil*) to demobilize. (**b**) (*desanimar*) to demoralize.
desmultiplicar [1g] *vt* (*Mec*) to gear down.
desnacionalización *nf* denationalization.
desnacionalizado *adj* (**a**) *industria etc* denationalized. (**b**) *persona* stateless.
desnacionalizar [1f] *vt* to denationalize.
desnarigada *nf* (*hum*): **la ~** the skull.
desnarigado *adj* flat-nosed; snub-nosed.
desnatado *adj leche* skimmed, low-fat (*atr*).
desnatar [1a] *vt leche* to skim, take the cream off; *metal fundido* to remove the scum from; (*fig*) to take the cream off; **leche sin ~** whole milk.
desnaturalizado *adj* (**a**) (*Quím*) denatured. (**b**) *persona etc* unnatural; cruel, inhuman.
desnaturalizar [1f] **1** *vt* (**a**) (*Quím*) to denature.
(**b**) (*fig*) to denaturalize, alter the fundamental nature of; (*pervertir*) to pervert, corrupt; *texto etc* to distort; *sentido* to misrepresent, twist.
2 desnaturalizarse *vr* to give up one's nationality; to become stateless.
desnivel *nm* (**a**) (*desigualdad*) unevenness; (*tierra alta*) high ground; (*tierra baja*) low ground. (**b**) (*fig*) inequality, difference, gap; lack of adjustment (*entre* between).
desnivelado *adj* (**a**) *terreno* uneven. (**b**) (*fig*) unbalanced, badly adjusted, unequal.
desnivelar [1a] *vt* (**a**) *terreno* to make uneven. (**b**) (*fig*) to unbalance, upset the balance of, create imbalance in.
desnucar [1g] **1** *vt* to break the neck of; to fell, poleaxe. **2 desnucarse** *vr* to break one's neck.
desnuclearizar [1f] *vt* to denuclearize; **región desnuclearizada** nuclear-free area.
desnudar [1a] **1** *vt* (**a**) (*gen*; *t Bot, fig*; *de* of) to strip; *persona* to strip, undress; *brazo etc* to bare; *espada* to draw; (*Geol*) to denude; *objeto, monumento etc* to lay bare, uncover, remove the coverings from.
(**b**) (*fig*) to ruin, break; (*) *jugador* to fleece.
2 desnudarse *vr* (**a**) (*persona*) to undress, get undressed; to strip (off); **~ hasta la cintura** to strip to the waist.
(**b**) **~ de algo** to get rid of sth, cast sth aside; **el árbol se está desnudando de sus hojas** the tree is shedding (*o* losing) its leaves.
desnudez *nf* (**a**) (*de persona*) nudity, nakedness. (**b**) (*fig*) bareness.
desnudismo *nm* nudism.
desnudista *nmf* nudist.
desnudo 1 *adj* (**a**) *cuerpo* naked, nude; unclothed, bare; *brazo, árbol etc* bare; *landscape* bare, flat, featureless; **en las paredes desnudas** on the bare walls; **la ciudad quedó desnuda** the town was flattened; **cavar con las manos desnudas** to dig with one's bare hands.
(**b**) (*fig*) *estilo etc* bare, unadorned; *verdad* naked, plain, unvarnished; **estar ~ de** to be devoid of, be bereft of, be without.
(**c**) (*fig*: *pobre*) penniless; **y ahora están ~s** and now all they've got is what they stand up in; **quedarse ~** to be ruined, be bankrupt.
2 *nm* (**a**) nudity, nakedness; (*Arte*) nude; **~ integral** full-frontal nudity; **la retrató al ~** he painted her in the nude; **llevaba los hombros al ~** her shoulders were bare, she was bare-shouldered.
(**b**) **poner algo al ~** (*fig*) to lay sth bare.
desnutrición *nf* malnutrition, undernourishment.
desnutrido *adj* undernourished.
desobedecer [2d] *vti* to disobey.
desobediencia *nf* disobedience; **~ civil** civil disobedience.
desobediente *adj* disobedient.
desobstruir [3g] *vt* to unblock, unstop, clear.
desocupación *nf* (**a**) (*tiempo libre*) leisure; (*pey*) idleness. (**b**) (*Econ*) unemployment.
desocupado *adj* (**a**) *espacio, silla etc* empty, vacant, unoccupied.
(**b**) *tiempo* spare, free; leisure (*atr*).
(**c**) *persona* free, not busy; at leisure; (*pey*) idle; (*Econ*) unemployed.
desocupar [1a] **1** *vt* (**a**) *casa etc* to vacate, move out of; to leave empty; *recipiente* to empty.
(**b**) *contenido* to remove, take out.
2 *vi* (**) to shit**.
3 desocuparse *vr* (**a**) **~ de un puesto** to give up one's job.
(**b**) (*Carib, Cono Sur*) to give birth.
desodorante *nm* deodorant.
desodorizar [1f] *vt* to deodorize.
desoír [3p] *vt* to ignore, disregard; to turn a deaf ear to.
desojarse [1a] *vr* to strain one's eyes.
desolación *nf* (**a**) (*gen*) desolation. (**b**) (*fig*) grief, distress.
desolado *adj* (**a**) (*gen*) desolate. (**b**) (*fig*) sad, distressed, disconsolate; **estoy ~ por aquello** I'm terribly grieved about that.
desolador *adj* (*doloroso*) distressing, grievous; *paisaje* bleak, cheerless; *epidemia etc* devastating.
desolar [1a] **1** *vt* to lay waste, ruin, desolate. **2 desolarse** *vr* to grieve, be distressed, be disconsolate.
desolidarizarse [1f] *vr*: **~ de** to dissociate o.s. from.
desolladero *nm* slaughterhouse.
desollado *adj* (*) brazen, barefaced.
desollador *nm* (**a**) (*Ind*) skinner; (*fig*) extortioner, robber. (**b**) (*Orn*) shrike.
desolladura *nf* (**a**) (*acto*) skinning, flaying. (**b**) (*Med*) graze, abrasion; bruise. (**c**) (*fig*) extortion, piece of robbery.
desollar [1l] *vt* (**a**) (*gen*) to skin, flay.
(**b**) **~ vivo a uno** (*fig*) (*hacer pagar*) to fleece sb, make sb pay through the nose; (*criticar*) to flay sb verbally, criticize sb unmercifully.

desopinar [1a] *vt* to denigrate.
desorbitado *adj* (**a**) (*excesivo*) disproportionate, excessive; *precio* exorbitant; *pretensión etc* exaggerated. (**b**) **con los ojos ~s** wild-eyed, pop-eyed, with bulging eyes.
desorbitante *adj* excessive, overwhelming.
desorbitar [1a] **1** *vt* (**a**) (*exagerar*) to carry to extremes; to exaggerate.
(**b**) **~ un asunto** to misinterpret a matter, get a matter out of perspective, take an unbalanced view of a matter.
2 desorbitarse *vr* (*persona*) to go to extremes, lose one's sense of proportion; (*asunto etc*) to get out of hand.
desorden *nm* (**a**) (*gen*) disorder; confusion; turmoil; disarray; (*Pol*) disorder; **en ~** in confusion, in disorder; **poner las cosas en ~** to upset things, confuse things.
(**b**) (*un ~*) mess, litter, confusion.
(**c**) (*fig*) irregular life; loose living.
(**d**) **desórdenes** (*Pol etc*) disorders; (*excesos*) excesses.
desordenadamente *adv* (*V adj*) (**a**) untidily; in disorder, in a mess. (**b**) in a disorderly fashion; irregularly; unmethodically; wildly; lawlessly.
desordenado *adj* (**a**) *cuarto etc* untidy, in disorder; *objetos* disordered, confused, in a mess.
(**b**) *conducta* disorderly; *vida* irregular; *carácter* unmethodical; *niño etc* wild, unruly; *país* lawless, unsettled.
desordenar [1a] *vt* (**a**) *pelo etc* to disarrange, mess up; *cuarto* to mess up, make a mess of; (*causar confusión en*) to throw into confusion. (**b**) (*Mec etc*) to put out of order.
desorejado *adj* (**a**) (*And, Carib, Cono Sur*: *sin mangos*) without handles.
(**b**) (*And*) (*duro de oído*) hard of hearing; (*Mús*) tone deaf; **hacerse el ~*** to turn a deaf ear.
(**c**) (*fig*) (*degradado*) abject, degraded; (*disoluto*) dissolute.
(**d**) (*Carib*: *pródigo*) lavish; wasteful.
(**e**) (*CAm*: *tonto*) silly.
desorganización *nf* disorganization, disruption.
desorganizar [1f] *vt* to disorganize, disrupt.
desorientamiento *nm*, **desorientación** *nf* disorientation.
desorientar [1a] **1** *vt*: **~ a uno** to direct sb wrongly, to make sb lose his way; to disorient sb (*t fig*); **el nuevo cruce me desorientó** the new junction made me lose my bearings.
2 desorientarse *vr* (**a**) (*despistarse*) to lose one's way, lose one's bearings.
(**b**) (*fig*) to go wrong, go astray, get off the track; to get confused, become disorientated.
desovar [1l] *vi* (*pez*) to spawn; (*insecto, anfibio etc*) to lay eggs.
desove *nm* spawning; egg-laying.
desovillar [1a] *vt* (**a**) *lana* to unravel, unwind; to disentangle. (**b**) (*fig*) to unravel, clarify.
desoxidar [1a] *vt* to remove the rust from; (*Quím*) to deoxidize.
despabiladeras *nfpl* snuffers; **unas ~** a pair of snuffers.
despabilado *adj* (**a**) (*despierto*) wide-awake. (**b**) (*fig*) wide-awake; (*alerta*) alert, watchful; (*listo*) quick, sharp.
despabilar [1a] **1** *vt* (**a**) *vela* to snuff; *lámpara, mecha* to trim.
(**b**) (*fig*) *ingenio* to sharpen; *persona* to wake up; to sharpen the wits of, liven up, brighten up.
(**c**) (*fig*) *fortuna* to squander rapidly; *comida* to dispatch; *asunto* to get through quickly.
(**d**) (*: *robar*) to pinch*.
(**e**) (‡: *matar*) **~ a uno** to do sb in‡.
2 *vi y* **despabilarse** *vr* (**a**) (*gen*) to wake up; (*fig*) to look lively, get a move on; **¡despabílate!** get a move on!, jump to it!
(**b**) (*CAm, Carib, Cono Sur*: *marcharse*) to vanish; (*escaparse*) to slip away, slope off*.
despacio 1 *adv* (**a**) (*lentamente*) slowly; (*sin esforzar*) gently; (*poco a poco*) gradually; **¡~!** gently!, not so fast!, easy there!
(**b**) (*LAm*) *hablar* softly, in a low voice.
2 *nm* (*LAm*) (**a**) (*retraso*) delay; (*lentitud*) slowness.
(**b**) (*táctica*) delaying tactic.
despaciosamente *adv* (*LAm*) slowly.
despacioso *adj* slow, deliberate; sluggish; phlegmatic.
despacito *adv* (**a**) (*lentamente*) very slowly, very gently; **¡~!** easy does it! (**b**) (*dulcemente*) softly.
despachaderas *nfpl* (**a**) (*respuesta*) surly retort, unfriendly answer.
(**b**) (*inteligencia*) resourcefulness, quickness of mind; (*sentido práctico*) business sense, practical know-how; **tener buenas ~** to be practical, be on the ball; to be good at getting rid of fools.
(**c**) (*descaro*) brazenness, insolence.
despachado *adj* (**a**) (*inteligente*) resourceful, quick; businesslike; practical; **ir bien ~ de** to be well off for, be well provided with. (**b**) (*descarado*) brazen, insolent.
despachador 1 *adj* prompt, quick. **2** *nm*, **despachadora** *nf* (**a**) (*empleado*) quick worker. (**b**) **~ de equipaje** baggage handler.
despachante *nm* (*Cono Sur*) clerk; customs agent.
despachar [1a] **1** *vt* (**a**) (*hacer*) *tarea* to complete; *negocio* to do, complete, dispatch, settle, transact; *correspondencia* to deal with, attend to; *tema etc* to deal with; to polish off, knock off; *problema* to settle; **~ asuntos con el gerente** to do business with the manager, settle matters with the manager; **medio capítulo llevo despachado ya** I've already knocked off half a chapter.
(**b**) (*) *comida etc* to dispatch, put away*; *bebida** to knock back*.
(**c**) *billete etc* to issue.
(**d**) (*enviar*) *mercancías* to send, dispatch, mail (*a* to).
(**e**) (*acelerar*) to expedite, hurry along.
(**f**) (*enviar*) *persona* to send away, send off; to send packing; *empleado* to fire*, sack*.
(**g**) (*Com*) *géneros* to sell, deal in; *cliente* to attend to; **en seguida le despacho** I'll attend to you at once.
(**i**) (*Cono Sur*) *equipaje* to register.
2 *vi* (**a**) (*Com*) to do business; to serve; (*Pol etc*) **~ con uno** to meet sb, consult sb, have an interview with sb; **no despacha los domingos** he doesn't do business on Sundays, he's not in on Sundays; **¿quién despacha?** is anybody serving?
(**b**) (*terminar*) to finish things off, get things settled; (*decidirse*) to come to a decision; **¡despacha de una vez!** settle it once and for all!, make up your mind!
(**c**) (*acelerarse*) to hurry up, get on with it; **¡despacha!** get on with it!
3 despacharse *vr* (**a**) (*terminar*) to finish off; **suelo despacharme a las 5** I finish at 5, I knock off at 5*; **~ de algo** to finish sth off; to get rid of sth, get clear of sth.
(**b**) (*darse prisa*) to hurry (up).
(**c**) **~ a su gusto con uno** to say what one really thinks to sb, speak very plainly to sb.
(**d**) **~ con el cucharón*** to help o.s. to the biggest (*o* best) portion; (*fig*) to look after Number One.
despacho *nm* (**a**) (*acto*) dispatch; sending (out); (*de negocio*) dispatch, handling, settling; **~ aduanal, ~ de aduanas** customs clearance.
(**b**) (*cualidad*) resourcefulness, quickness of mind; business sense; promptness, energy, efficiency; **tener buen ~** to be very efficient, be on top of one's job.
(**c**) (*Com*: *venta*) sale (of goods); **géneros sin ~** unsaleable goods; **tener buen ~** to find a ready sale, be in good demand.
(**d**) (*mensaje*) message; (*Mil, diplomático*) dispatch; **~ telegráfico** telegram.
(**e**) (*Com, Pol etc*: *oficina*) office; (*en casa*) study; **~ de billetes, ~ de boletos** (*LAm*) booking-office; **~ de localidades** box-office; **~ de telégrafos** telegraph office.
(**f**) (*Com*: *tienda*) shop; depot; (*Cono Sur*) general store; small village shop.
(**g**) (*muebles*) set of office furniture.
(**h**) **~ de oficial** (*Mil*) commission.
(**i**) (*Pol etc*) meeting, consultation, interview (*con* with).
despachurrar [1a] *vt* (**a**) (*aplastar*) to squash, crush; to squelch; (*Culin*) to mash.
(**b**) *cuento* to mangle, make a dreadful mess of.
(**c**) *persona* to crush, flatten, floor.
despampanante* *adj* stunning.
despampanar [1a] **1** *vt* (**a**) *vid* to prune, trim.
(**b**) (*: *asombrar*) to shatter, stun, bowl over.
2 *vi* (*) to blow one's top*, give vent to one's feelings; to speak out freely.
3 despampanarse *vr* (*) to give o.s. a nasty knock.
despancar [1g] *vt* (*And*) *maíz* to husk.
desparasitar [1a] *vt* to delouse.
desparejado *adj*, **desparejo** *adj* odd, unpaired; **son ~s** they're odd, they don't match.
desparpajar [1a] **1** *vt* (**a**) (*desmontar*) to take apart carelessly; (*estropear*) to botch, bungle, spoil, mess up.
(**b**) (*CAm, Méx*: *dispersar*) to scatter, disperse.
2 *vi* to talk wildly, rant, rave.
3 desparpajarse *vr* (**a**) = *vi*.
(**b**) (*CAm, Carib*: *despertarse*) to wake up.

desparpajo *nm* (**a**) (*desenvoltura*) ease of manner, self-confidence; (*naturalidad*) naturalness; (*simpatía*) charm; (*labia*) glibness; (*descaro*) nerve*, pertness, impudence.

(**b**) (*inteligencia*) savoir-faire, practical know-how; sharpness, quickness of mind; (*presencia de ánimo*) presence of mind.

(**c**) (*CAm: desorden*) disorder, muddle.

(**d**) (*And: comentario*) flippant remark.

desparramado *adj* scattered; wide, open.

desparramar [1a] **1** *vt* (**a**) (*esparcir*) to scatter, spread (*por* over); *líquido etc* to spill; *partes* to separate.

(**b**) *fortuna* to squander; *atención* to spread too widely, fail to concentrate.

2 desparramarse *vr* (**a**) to scatter, spread out; to spill, be spilt; (*animales*) to bolt, stampede.

(**b**) (*: *pasarlo bomba*) to have a whale of a time*.

desparrame* *nm* confusion, disorder; lack of control.

desparramo *nm* (**a**) (*Carib, Cono Sur*) (*acto*) scattering, spreading; dispersal; (*el vertir*) spilling; (*fuga*) rush, stampede. (**b**) (*Cono Sur: desorden*) confusion, disorder.

despatarrado *adj*: **quedar ~** (**a**) (*lit*) to have one's legs wide apart. (**b**) (*fig*) to be dumbfounded; to be scared to death.

despatarrante* *adj* side-splitting.

despatarrar [1a] **1** *vt* (*fig*) (*aturdir*) to amaze, dumbfound; (*asustar*) to scare to death.

2 despatarrarse *vr* (**a**) (*abrir las piernas*) to open one's legs wide; (*en suelo etc*) to do the splits; (*al caer*) to fall with one's legs spread wide.

(**b**) (*fig*) to be amazed, be dumbfounded; to be scared to death.

(**c**) (*) **~ de risa** to split one's sides laughing.

despatriar [1b] *vt* (*And, Carib*) to exile.

despavorido *adj*: **estar ~** to be utterly terrified.

despe* *nf* tag, 'he'; **dar la ~** to play tag.

despeado *adj* footsore, weary.

despearse [1a] *vr* to get footsore, get utterly weary.

despectivamente *adv* contemptuously, scornfully; in derogatory terms; (*Ling*) pejoratively.

despectivo *adj* contemptuous, scornful; derogatory; (*Ling*) pejorative.

despechado *adj* angry, indignant; spiteful.

despechar [1a] **1** *vt* (**a**) (*provocar*) to anger, enrage; (*causar pena a*) to spite; (*hacer desesperar*) to drive to despair.

(**b**) (*) *niño* to wean.

2 despecharse *vr* to get angry; to fret; to despair.

despecho *nm* (**a**) (*ojeriza*) spite, rancour; (*desesperación*) despair; **de puro ~, por ~** out of (sheer) spite.

(**b**) **a ~ de** in spite of, despite; in defiance of.

(**c**) (*de niño*) weaning.

despechugado *adj persona* with one's collar open, with one's shirt front undone; bare-chested; *camisa* open-necked, open at the neck.

despechugarse [1h] *vr* to open one's collar, unbutton one's shirt at the neck; to bare one's chest (*o* breast); to unbutton one's shirt down the front.

despedazar [1f] *vt* (**a**) (*romper*) to tear apart, tear to pieces; (*cortar*) to cut into bits; (*hacer trizas*) to lacerate, mangle, cut to shreds. (**b**) (*fig*) *corazón* to break; *honor* to ruin.

despedida *nf* (**a**) (*adiós*) farewell; leave-taking; (*antes de viaje*) send-off; (*despido*) dismissal, sacking*; **cena de ~** farewell dinner; **función de ~** (*Teat*) farewell performance; **regalo de ~** parting gift; **~ de soltera** hen night; **~ de soltero** stag party.

(**b**) (*ceremonia*) farewell ceremony.

(**c**) (*Liter etc*) envoi; (*Mús*) final verse; (*en carta*) closing formula, closing phrases, ending.

(**d**) (*Inform*) log off, log out.

despedir [3k] **1** *vt* (**a**) *invitado, amigo* to see off; *visita* to see out; (*decir adiós a*) to say goodbye to; *cliente etc* to show out; **fuimos a ~le a la estación** we went to see him off at the station.

(**b**) *empleado etc* to dismiss, sack*, discharge; *pesado* to get rid of, send away; *inquilino* to evict; to give notice to.

(**c**) **~ algo de sí** to get rid of sth; **~ un pensamiento de sí** to put a thought out of one's mind, banish a thought from one's mind.

(**d**) (*arrojar*) *objeto* to hurl, fling; to project; *flecha etc* to fire; *mísil* to launch; *chorro etc* to send up; *jinete* to throw; *olor etc* to give off, give out, emit, throw off; *calor* to give out; *zumo etc* to release, allow to come out; **~ el espíritu** to give up the ghost.

2 despedirse *vr* (*decir adiós*) to say goodbye, take one's leave; (*dejar un empleo*) to give up one's job, leave (one's work); **se despidieron** they said goodbye to each other; **~ de uno** to say goodbye to sb, take one's leave of sb; (*en estación etc*) to see sb off; **¡ya puedes despedirte de ese dinero!** you can say goodbye to that money!

despegado **1** *adj* (**a**) (*separado*) detached, loose. (**b**) *persona* cold, indifferent, unconcerned. **2** *nm*: **es un ~** he has cut himself off from his family, he has kept no roots.

despegar [1h] **1** *vt* (*cosa pegada*) to unglue, unstick; (*separar*) to detach, loosen; *sobre* to open; **sin ~ los labios** without uttering a word.

2 *vi* (*Aer*) to take off (*t fig*); (*cohete*) to lift off, blast off.

3 despegarse *vr* (**a**) (*desprenderse*) to come loose, come unstuck; (*objeto*) to come apart.

(**b**) (*persona*) to become alienated, become detached (*de* from); **~ de los amigos** to break with one's friends; **~ del mundo** to withdraw from the world, renounce worldly things.

(**c**) **~ de*** not to go well with.

despego *nm* = **desapego.**

despegue *nm* (**a**) (*Aer, tb fig*) take-off; (*de cohete*) lift-off, blast-off; **~ corto** short take-off; **~ vertical** vertical take-off. (**b**) **~ industrial** (*fig*) industrial renewal.

despeinado **1** *adj* dishevelled, tousled; unkempt. **2** *nm* tousled hair-style.

despeinar [1a] **1** *pelo, persona vt* to tousle, ruffle; *peinado* to mess up, muss. **2 despeinarse** *vr* (*fig*) to make a great effort, get really involved.

despejable *adj* explicable; **difícilmente ~** hard to explain.

despejado *adj* (**a**) *camino, espacio* clear, free, unobstructed, open; *frente* clear; *cuarto etc* unencumbered, spacious.

(**b**) *cielo* cloudless, clear.

(**c**) (*persona: estar*) wide-awake; (*Med*) free of fever; lucid.

(**d**) (*persona: ser*) sharp, bright, smart.

despejar [1a] **1** *vt* (**a**) *espacio etc* to clear, disencumber, free from obstructions; **los bomberos despejaron el teatro** the firemen cleared the theatre (of people); **los guardias obligaron a ~ el tribunal** the police ordered the court to be cleared, the police ordered people to leave the court; **¡despejen!** move along!; everybody out!

(**b**) (*Dep*) *balón* to clear.

(**c**) *misterio* to clear up, clarify, resolve; (*Mat*) *incógnita* to find.

2 *vi* (**a**) (*Dep*) to clear (the ball).

(**b**) (*Met*) to clear.

3 despejarse *vr* (**a**) (*Met*) to clear, clear up; (*misterio etc*) to become clearer.

(**b**) (*persona*) (*animarse*) to liven o.s. up; (*sentirse mejor*) to feel better, feel brighter; (*despejar la cabeza*) to clear one's head.

(**c**) (*persona: relajarse*) to relax, amuse o.s.

(**d**) (*persona: en temperamento*) to become more self-assured, gain in confidence.

despeje *nm* (**a**) (*Dep*) clearance. (**b**) (*de mente*) clarity, clearness of mind.

despejo *nm* brightness; self-confidence, ease of manner; fluency.

despelotado* *adj* half-naked, scantily clad; (*LAm*) disorganized.

despelotar* [1a] **1** *vt* to strip, undress. **2 despelotarse** *vr* (**a**) to strip (off), undress. (**b**) **~ de risa** to laugh fit to bust*.

despelote* *nm* (**a**) (*estado*) nudity, nakedness; (*acto*) strip.

(**b**) (*Carib: juerga*) big spree, grand evening out.

(**c**) (*Cono Sur*) (*alboroto*) row, racket; (*desorden*) mess, mix-up.

(**d**) **se ha comprado un coche que es un ~** (*Cono Sur*) he's bought a fantastic car*.

(**e**) **¡qué ~!, ¡vaya ~!** what a laugh!

despeluchado *adj* dishevelled, tousled.

despeluchar [1a] *vt* to dishevel, tousle.

despeluz(n)ar [1f] **1** *vt* (**a**) *pelo* to dishevel, tousle, rumple.

(**b**) **~ a uno** (*fig*) to horrify sb, make sb's hair stand on end.

(**c**) (*Carib: arruinar*) to ruin, leave penniless.

2 despeluz(n)arse *vr* (**a**) (*pelo*) to stand on end.

(**b**) (*persona*) to be horrified.

despellejar [1a] *vt* (**a**) to skin, flay. (**b**) (*fig: criticar*) to flay, criticize unmercifully. (**c**) (*: *arruinar*) **~ a uno** to fleece sb.

despenalización *nf* legalization; decriminalization.

despenalizar [1f] *vt* to legalize; to decriminalize.

despenar [1a] *vt* (**a**) (*consolar*) to console. (**b**) (‡: *matar*) to do in‡, kill.
despendedor *adj* extravagant.
despendolado* *adj* uninhibited, unrestrained, free and easy, wild.
despendole* *nm* lack of inhibitions, lack of restraint; wildness.
despensa *nf* (**a**) (*armario*) pantry, larder; food store; (*Náut*) storeroom. (**b**) (*provisión*) stock of food.
despensero *nm* butler, steward; (*Náut*) storekeeper.
despeñadero *nm* (**a**) (*Geog*) cliff, precipice. (**b**) (*fig*) risk, danger.
despeñadizo *adj* dangerously steep, sheer, precipitous.
despeñar [1a] **1** *vt* to fling down, hurl from a height, throw over a cliff.
2 despeñarse *vr* (**a**) (*tirarse al suelo*) to hurl o.s. down, throw o.s. over a cliff; (*caer*) to fall headlong.
(**b**) ~ **en el vicio** to plunge into vice.
despeño *nm* fall, drop; (*fig*) failure, collapse.
despepitar [1a] **1** *vt* to remove the pips (*etc*) from.
2 despepitarse *vr* (**a**) (*gritar*) to bawl, shriek (one's head off), shout o.s. hoarse; (*obrar*) to rave, act wildly; **salir despepitado*** to rush out, go rushing out.
(**b**) ~ **por algo** to long for sth, go overboard for sth*; ~ **por** + *infin* to long to + *infin*.
despercudir [3a] *vt* (**a**) (*limpiar*) to clean, wash. (**b**) (*LAm*: *fig*) *persona* to liven up, wake up, ginger up.
desperdiciado *adj* wasteful.
desperdiciador(a) *adj, nm/f* spendthrift.
desperdiciar [1b] *vt fortuna etc* to waste, squander, fritter away; *tiempo* to waste; *oportunidad* to throw away.
desperdicio *nm* (**a**) (*acto*) waste; wasting; squandering.
(**b**) ~**s** (*basura*) rubbish, refuse; (*restos*) scraps, leftovers; (*residuos*) waste; (*Bio, Téc*) waste products; ~**s de algodón** cotton waste; ~**s de cocina** kitchen scraps; ~**s de hierro** scrap iron, junk.
(**c**) **el cerdo es un animal que no tiene** ~ nothing from a pig is wasted, everything from a pig can be used; **el muchacho no tiene** ~ he's a fine lad; **el libro no tiene** ~ the book is excellent from start to finish.
desperdigar [1h] **1** *vt* (*esparcir*) to scatter, separate, disperse; *energías etc* to spread too widely, dissipate. **2 desperdigarse** *vr* to scatter, separate.
desperezarse [1f] *vr* to stretch (o.s.).
desperezo *nm* stretch.
desperfecto *nm* flaw, blemish, imperfection; slight damage; **sufrió algunos ~s en el accidente** it suffered slight damage in the accident.
despernado *adj* footsore, weary.
despersonalizar [1f] *vt* to depersonalize.
despertador *nm* (**a**) (*reloj*) alarm clock; ~ **de viaje** travelling clock. (**b**) (*persona*) knocker-up. (**c**) (*fig*) warning.
despertamiento *nm* awakening; (*fig*) awakening, revival, rebirth.
despertar [1j] **1** *vt* (**a**) *persona etc* to wake (up), awaken.
(**b**) (*fig*) *esperanzas etc* to awaken, raise, arouse; *memoria* to awaken, revive, recall; *sentimientos* to arouse, stir up.
2 *vi y* **despertarse** *vr* to wake up, awaken; ~ **a la realidad** to wake up to reality.
3 *nm*: **el ~ religioso** the religious awakening; **el ~ de la primavera** the awakening of spring.
despestañarse [1a] *vr* (*Cono Sur*) (**a**) (*desojarse*) to strain one's eyes. (**b**) (*fig*) to burn the midnight oil, swot*.
despiadadamente *adv* cruelly; mercilessly, relentlessly; heartlessly.
despiadado *adj* cruel; merciless, relentless; heartless.
despicarse [1g] *vr* to get even, get one's revenge.
despichar [1a] **1** *vt* (*And, Carib, Cono Sur*) (*aplastar*) to crush, flatten; (*fig*) to crush. **2** *vi* (‡) to kick the bucket‡.
despido *nm* (**a**) (*acto*) dismissal; ~ **arbitrario,** ~ **improcedente** wrongful dismissal; ~ **colectivo** wholesale redundancies, large-scale dismissals; ~ **disciplinario** dismissal on disciplinary grounds; ~ **forzoso** compulsory redundancy; ~ **incentivado** voluntary redundancy; ~ **libre** arbitrary dismissal. (**b**) (*pago*) severance pay, redundancy payment.
despiece *nm* (**a**) (*de res*) quartering, carving-up. (**b**) (*Prensa*) comment, personal note.
despierto *adj* (**a**) (*gen*) awake. (**b**) (*fig*) wide-awake; sharp; alert, watchful.
despiezar [1f] *vt* to break up, split up; *res* to quarter, carve up.
despilfarrado *adj* (**a**) *derrochador* extravagant, wasteful, spendthrift. (**b**) *desaseado* ragged, shabby.
despilfarrador 1 *adj* = **despilfarrado. 2** *nm*, **despilfarradora** *nf* spendthrift.
despilfarrar [1a] *vt* to waste, squander.
despilfarro *nm* (**a**) (*acto*) wasting, squandering. (**b**) (*cualidad*) extravagance, wastefulness. (**c**) (*desaseo*) shabbiness, slovenliness, ragged state.
despintar [1a] **1** *vt* (**a**) (*quitar pintura a*) to take the paint off.
(**b**) (*fig*) *cuento etc* to alter, distort; to spoil.
(**c**) **no ~ a uno** (*And, Carib, Cono Sur*) not to let sb out of one's sight.
2 *vi*: **éste no despinta de su casta** he is no different from the rest of his family.
3 despintarse *vr* (**a**) (*con la lluvia etc*) to wash off; (*desteñirse*) to fade, lose its colour; (*LAm*: *maquillaje*) to run, get smudged.
(**b**) ~ **algo** (*fig*) to forget sth, wipe sth from one's mind; **no se me despinta que ...** I never forget that ...; I remember vividly that ...
despiojar [1a] *vt* (**a**) (*lit*) to delouse. (**b**) ~ **a uno** (*fig*) to rescue sb from the gutter.
despiole* *nm* (*Cono Sur*) = **despelote.**
despiporrante* *adj* killingly funny.
despiporre(n)* *nm* wild disturbance; mayhem; **¡fue el ~!** it was something out of this world!, it was just about the end!; **esto es el** ~ this is the limit!
despique *nm* satisfaction, revenge.
despistado 1 *adj* (**a**) (*ser*) vague, absent-minded; unpractical; hopeless.
(**b**) (*estar*) confused, out of touch, all at sea; off the beam*; **ando muy ~ con todo esto** I'm terribly muddled about all this.
2 *nm*, **despistada** *nf* absent-minded person, vague individual; unpractical type; **es un** ~ he's hopeless, he hasn't a clue; **hacerse el** ~ to pretend not to understand.
despistaje *nm* (*Med*) early detection, early diagnosis.
despistar [1a] **1** *vt* (**a**) (*Caza*) to throw off the track (*o* scent).
(**b**) (*fig*) to put off the scent; to mislead, muddle; **esa pregunta está hecha para** ~ that question is designed to mislead people.
(**c**) (‡: *robar*) to nick‡, rip off‡.
(**d**) (*Med*) to detect (early), diagnose at an early stage.
2 despistarse *vr* (*fig*) to go wrong, take the wrong route (*o* turning *etc*); to get confused.
despiste *nm* (**a**) (*Aut etc*) swerve.
(**b**) (*error*) mistake, slip.
(**c**) (*cualidad*) absent-mindedness; (*estado*) muddle, confusion, bewilderment; **¡qué ~ tienes!** you're a bright one!, what a clot you are!‡; **tiene un terrible** ~ he's terribly absent-minded; he's hopelessly unpractical; he's hopeless, he hasn't a clue.
desplacer 1 [2w] *vt* to displease. **2** *nm* displeasure.
desplantador *nm* trowel.
desplantar [1a] *vt* (**a**) *planta* to pull up, uproot, take up. (**b**) *objeto* to move out of vertical, tilt, put out of plumb.
desplante *nm* (**a**) (*en baile etc*) wrong stance.
(**b**) (*dicho*) bold statement, outspoken remark; (*pey*) impudent remark, cutting remark (*etc*); (*LAm**: *disparate*) crazy idea; **dar un** ~ to interrupt sb rudely; **me dio un** ~ (*asombrar*) he left me stunned; **ella me hizo un** ~ (*LAm**) she stood me up*.
(**c**) (*descaro*) insolence, lack of respect.
desplazado 1 *adj* (**a**) *objeto* displaced, wrongly placed, off-centre.
(**b**) *persona* badly adjusted; out of one's depth, out of one's element; (*Pol*) displaced; **sentirse un poco** ~ to feel rather out of place.
2 *nm*, **desplazada** *nf* misfit; ill-adjusted person; outsider; (*Pol*) displaced person.
desplazamiento *nm* (**a**) (*acto*) displacement, movement; (*de casa*) removal; ~ **continental** continental drift; ~ **de tierras** landslip; **puede telefonear en pleno** ~ you can phone while on the move.
(**b**) (*Náut*) displacement.
(**c**) (*viaje*) journey, trip; (*salida*) outing; **reside en Madrid aunque con frecuentes ~s** she lives in Madrid but is often away.
(**d**) (*de opinión, votos etc*) shift, swing.
(**e**) (*Inform*) scroll(ing); ~ **hacia abajo** scroll down; ~ **hacia arriba** scroll up.
desplazar [1f] **1** *vt* (**a**) *objeto* to displace, move; to transport.

(**b**) (*Náut, Fís*) to displace.
(**c**) *persona etc* to displace, supplant, take the place of.
(**d**) (*Inform*) to scroll.
2 desplazarse *vr* (**a**) (*objeto*) to move, shift.
(**b**) (*persona, vehículo*) to go, travel; (*partir*) to move away, move out; **tiene que ~ todos los días 25 kms** he has to travel 25 kms every day; **el avión se desplaza a más de 1500 kph** the aircraft travels at more than 1500 kph.
(**c**) (*opinión, votos etc*) to shift, swing; **se ha desplazado un 4 por 100 de los votos** there has been a swing of 4% in the voting.

desplegable 1 *adj*: **menú ~** pull-down menu. **2** *nm* folder, brochure; (*Prensa*) centrefold.

desplegar [1h *y* 1j] **1** *vt* (**a**) *mapa etc* to unfold, open (out), spread (out); *alas* to spread, open; *velas* to unfurl; (*Mil etc*) to deploy; (*Inform*) to display.
(**b**) (*fig*) *energías etc* to put forth, use, display; *recursos* to deploy.
(**c**) (*fig*) *misterio* to clarify, elucidate.
2 desplegarse *vr* (*flor etc*) to open (out), unfold; to spread (out); (*Mil etc*) to deploy.

despliegue *nm* (**a**) (*acto*) unfolding, opening; (*Mil etc*) deployment. (**b**) (*fig*) display, manifestation, show, exhibition; (*Inform*) display.

desplomarse [1a] *vr* (**a**) (*inclinarse*) to lean, tilt, get out of vertical; (*combarse*) to bulge, warp.
(**b**) (*derrumbarse*) to collapse, tumble down, come crashing down; to topple over; (*precio etc*) to slump, tumble; (*gobierno, sistema*) to collapse; (*Aer*) to make a pancake landing; (*persona*) to collapse, crumple up; **se ha desplomado el techo** the ceiling has fallen in, the ceiling has collapsed; **¡se desploma el cielo!** it's incredible!; **caer desplomado** to collapse, drop dead.

desplome *nm* (**a**) (*acto*) leaning, tilting; fall, collapse; slump; (*Aer*) pancake landing; (*Fin*) collapse.
(**b**) (*Arquit, Geol etc*) overhang, projecting part; (*Alpinismo*) overhang.

desplomo *nm* = **desplome (b)**.

desplumar [1a] **1** *vt* (**a**) *ave* to pluck. (**b**) (*: *estafar*) to fleece, skin‡. **2 desplumarse** *vr* to moult.

despoblación *nf* depopulation; **~ rural, ~ del campo** rural depopulation, drift from the land.

despoblado 1 *adj* unpopulated, deserted; (*fig*) desolate. **2** *nm* deserted spot, uninhabited place; wilderness.

despoblar [1m] **1** *vt* to depopulate; to reduce the population of, clear people out of; to lay waste; **~ una zona de árboles** to clear an area of trees. **2 despoblarse** *vr* to become depopulated, lose its population.

despojar [1a] **1** *vt*: **~ de** to strip of, clear of, leave bare of; (*fig*) to divest of, denude of; (*Jur*) to dispossess of, deprive of; **habían despojado la casa de muebles** they had stripped the house of furniture, they had cleared all the furniture out of the house; **verse despojado de su autoridad** to find o.s. stripped of one's authority.
2 despojarse *vr* (*desnudarse*) to undress; **~ de** *ropa* to take off, remove, strip off; *hojas etc* to shed; *poderes etc* to divest o.s. of, relinquish, give up; *prejuicio* to get rid of, free o.s. from.

despojo *nm* (**a**) (*acto*) spoliation, despoilment; plundering.
(**b**) (*Mil etc*) plunder, loot, spoils.
(**c**) **~s** (*residuo*) waste, (*restos*) left-overs, scraps; (*de animal*) offal; (*Arquit*) rubble; secondhand building materials, usable waste; (*Geol*) debris; **~s de hierro** scrap iron; **~s mortales** mortal remains.

despolitización *nf* depoliticization.

despolitizar [1f] *vt* to depoliticize.

despolvorear [1a] *vt* to dust.

desportilladura *nf* chip; nick.

desportillar [1a] **1** *vt* to chip, nick. **2 desportillarse** *vr* to chip, chip off.

desposado *adj* newly-wed, recently married; **los ~s** the bridal couple, the newly-weds.

desposar [1a] **1** *vt* (*cura*) *pareja* to marry.
2 desposarse *vr* (**a**) (*una persona*) to become engaged (*con* to); to get married (*con* to).
(**b**) (*dos personas*) to get engaged; to marry, get married.

desposeer [2e] **1** *vt* to dispossess (*de* of); to oust (*de un puesto* from a post); **~ a uno de su autoridad** to remove sb's authority, strip sb of his authority.
2 desposeerse *vr*: **~ de algo** to give sth up, relinquish sth, divest o.s. of sth.

desposeído, -a *nm/f*: **los ~s** the deprived, those in want, the have-nots.

desposeimiento *nm* dispossession; ousting.

desposorios *nmpl* (*esponsales*) engagement, betrothal; (*boda*) marriage (ceremony).

déspota *nmf* despot; **~ ilustrado** enlightened despot.

despóticamente *adv* despotically.

despótico *adj* despotic.

despotismo *nm* despotism; **~ ilustrado** enlightened despotism.

despotorrarse* [1a] *vr* to laugh o.s. silly*.

despotricar [1g] *vi* to rave, rant, carry on (*contra* about).

despreciable *adj* (*moralmente*) despicable, contemptible; (*en calidad*) worthless, trashy, valueless; (*en cantidad*) negligible; **una suma nada ~** a far from negligible amount.

despreciar [1b] **1** *vt* (*desdeñar*) to scorn, despise, look down on; *oferta* to spurn, reject; (*ofender*) to slight; (*subestimar*) to underestimate, underrate; **~ los peligros** to scorn the dangers; **~ una oferta** to reject an offer; **no hay que ~ tal posibilidad** one should not underestimate such a possibility.
2 despreciarse *vr*: **~ de** + *infin* to think it beneath o.s. to + *infin*, not deign to + *infin*.

despreciativamente *adv* scornfully, contemptuously; in a derogatory way; cynically.

despreciativo *adj* scornful, contemptuous; *dicho etc* derogatory.

desprecintar [1a] *vt* to unseal.

desprecio *nm* (**a**) (*desdén*) scorn, contempt, disdain; disparaging attitude; **lo miró con ~** he looked at it contemptuously.
(**b**) (*ofensa*) slight, snub; **le hicieron el ~ de no acudir** they snubbed him by not coming.

desprender [2a] **1** *vt* (**a**) (*soltar*) to unfasten, loosen; (*separar*) to detach, separate.
(**b**) *gas etc* to give off; *piel etc* to shed.
2 desprenderse *vr* (**a**) (*pieza*) to become detached, work loose, fall off; to fly off.
(**b**) **~ de un estorbo** to extricate o.s. from a difficulty, get free of a difficulty; **la serpiente se desprende de la piel** the snake sheds its skin.
(**c**) **~ de algo** to give sth up, part with sth; to get rid of sth; to deprive o.s. of sth; **se desprendió de sus joyas** she parted with her jewels; **tendremos que desprendernos del coche** we shall have to get rid of the car; **se desprendió de su autoridad** he relinquished his authority.
(**d**) (*gas etc*) to be given off, issue; **de la pared se desprende humedad** there is damp coming from the wall.
(**e**) (*sentido etc*) **~ de** to follow from; to be deduced from; to be implied by; to be clear from; **se desprende que ...** one gathers that ...; **se desprende de esta declaración que ...** it is clear from this statement that ...; **por fin se desprendió que ...** finally it transpired that ...

desprendido *adj* (**a**) *pieza* loose, detached; unfastened. (**b**) (*fig*) disinterested; generous.

desprendimiento *nm* (**a**) (*acto*) loosening, detachment; unfastening; **~ de matriz** prolapse; **~ de retina** detachment of the retina; **~ de tierra(s)** landslide.
(**b**) (*de gas etc*) release, emission; (*de piel etc*) shedding.
(**c**) (*fig*) disinterestedness; generosity.

despreocupación *nf* (*V adj*) (**a**) unconcern; carefree nature; nonchalance, casualness.
(**b**) unconventional outlook (*o* style *etc*); (*pey*) sloppiness, slovenliness.
(**c**) impartiality.
(**d**) (*Rel*) indifference, apathy; broad-mindedness.
(**e**) looseness.

despreocupadamente *adv* unconcernedly; in a carefree manner; nonchalantly.

despreocupado *adj* (**a**) (*sin preocupación*) unworried, unconcerned; (*tranquilo*) carefree; (*natural*) nonchalant, casual; free and easy.
(**b**) (*en vestir etc*) unconventional, casual; (*pey*) careless, sloppy, slovenly.
(**c**) (*imparcial*) unbiassed, impartial.
(**d**) (*Rel*) (*indiferente*) indifferent, apathetic; (*tolerante*) broad-minded.
(**e**) *mujer* loose.

despreocupamiento *nm* lack of interest, apathy.

despreocuparse [1a] *vr* not to worry.

despresar [1a] *vt* (*Cono Sur*) *ave etc* to cut up, carve up.

desprestigiar [1b] **1** *vt* (*criticar*) to disparage, run down; (*tachar*) to smear; (*rebajar*) to lower the prestige of, reduce the status of; (*desacreditar*) to discredit; (*aplebeyar*) to cheapen. **2 desprestigiarse** *vr* to lose (one's)

prestige; to lose caste; to cheapen o.s.
desprestigio *nm* disparagement; discredit; loss of prestige (*o* caste, standing); unpopularity; **campaña de ~** smear campaign; **esas cosas que van en ~ nuestro** those things which are to our discredit, those things which harm our reputation.
desprevención *nf* unreadiness, unpreparedness; lack of foresight.
desprevenido *adj* unready, unprepared; **coger a uno ~** to catch sb unawares, catch sb off his guard, take sb by surprise.
desprivatizar [1f] *vt* to take into public ownership.
desprogramar [1a] *vt* to deprogramme.
desproporción *nf* disproportion, lack of proportion.
desproporcionadamente *adv* disproportionately.
desproporcionado *adj* disproportionate, out of proportion.
despropósito *nm* absurdity, silly thing (to say), piece of nonsense; **~s** nonsense.
desprotección *nf* lack of (legal) protection; vulnerability, defencelessness; (*Inform*) deprotection.
desprotegido *adj* unprotected, vulnerable, defenceless; **los ~s** (*frec*) the poor and needy.
desproveer [2a; *ptp* **desprovisto** *y* **desproveído**] *vt*: **~ a uno de algo** to deprive sb of sth.
desprovisto *adj*: **~ de** devoid of, bereft of, without; **estar ~ de** to lack, be lacking in, be devoid of; **estar ~ de medios** to be without means; **un libro no ~ de méritos** a book not without merit.
después 1 *adv* (**a**) (*tiempo*) (*gen*) afterwards, later; (*desde entonces*) since, since then; (*luego*) next; **un año ~** a year later; **años ~** years later; **¿qué pasó ~?** what happened then?; **poco ~** soon after, shortly after.
(**b**) (*orden*) next, after; **¿y ~?** and what comes next?; **nuestra casa viene ~** and then our house is next.
2 ~ de *prep* (**a**) (*tiempo*) after; since; **~ de esa fecha** (*pasado*) since that date; (*futuro*) from that date, after that date; **~ de verlo** after seeing it; **no ~ de 1998** not later than 1998; **~ de descubierta la isla** after the discovery of the island, after the island had been discovered.
(**b**) (*orden*) next (to); **mi nombre está ~ del tuyo** my name comes next to yours; my name comes after yours; **es el primero ~ de éste** it's the next one after this.
3 : **~ (de) que** *conj* after; **~ (de) que lo escribí** after (*o* since) I wrote it, after writing it.
despuesito* *adv* (*Méx*) right away, in just a moment.
despulgar [1h] = **espulgar**.
despuntado *adj* blunt.
despuntar [1a] **1** *vt* to blunt, dull (the point *o* edge of).
2 *vi* (**a**) (*Bot*) to sprout, bud, begin to show.
(**b**) (*alba*) to break, appear; (*día*) to dawn.
(**c**) (*persona etc*) (*descollar*) to excel, stand out; (*brillar*) to shine, sparkle; to show intelligence; **~ de agudo** to have a sparkling wit; **despunta en matemáticas** he shines at maths; **despunta por su talento** her talent shines out, her talent is outstanding.
desquiciado *adj* (*fig*) deranged, unhinged.
desquiciamiento *nm* (**a**) upsetting, disturbance, turning upside down. (**b**) (*turbación*) unhinging; mental unbalance; hysteria.
desquiciante *adj* maddening; disturbing, unsettling.
desquiciar [1b] *vt* (**a**) *puerta* to unhinge, take off its hinges.
(**b**) (*fig*: *descomponer*) to upset, disturb, turn upside down, make a mess of.
(**c**) *persona* (*turbar*) to disturb, upset; (*volver loco*) to unhinge, affect seriously, unbalance; (*enojar*) to anger, provoke.
(**d**) *persona* (*expulsar*) to oust, lever out.
desquicio *nm* (*CAm, Cono Sur*) confusion, disorder.
desquitar [1a] **1** *vt pérdida* to make good, make up. **2 desquitarse** *vr* (*obtener satisfacción*) *vr* to obtain satisfaction; (*Com, Fin*) to recover a debt, get one's money back; (*fig*) to get even (*con* with), get one's own back (*con* on); **~ de una pérdida** to make up for a loss, compensate o.s. for a loss; **~ de una mala pasada** to get one's own back for a dirty trick (played on one).
desquite *nm* (*satisfacción*) satisfaction; (*recompensa*) compensation for a loss, recovery of a debt; (*venganza*) revenge, retaliation; (*Dep*, *t* **partido de ~**) return match; **tomar el ~** to have one's revenge, get one's own back; **tomar el ~ de algo** to make up for sth.
desratización *nf*: **campaña de ~** anti-rodent campaign.
desratizar [1f] *vt* to clear of rats.
desrazonable *adj* unreasonable.
desregulación *nf* deregulation.
desregular [1a] *vt* to free, deregulate, remove controls from.
desrielar [1a] (*LAm*) **1** *vt* to derail. **2 desrielarse** *vr* to run off the rails, jump the track, be derailed.
desriñonar [1a] = **deslomar**.
desrizar [1f] *vt pelo* to straighten.
Dest. *abr de* **destinatario** addressee; (*Com*) payee.
destacadamente *adv* notably, outstandingly.
destacado *adj* notable, outstanding, distinguished; important.
destacamento *nm* (*Mil*) detachment; **~ de desembarco** (*Naút*) landing party.
destacar [1g] **1** *vt* (**a**) (*Arte etc*) to make stand out; (*fig*) to emphasize, show up, point up, bring out; to throw into relief; **quiero ~ que ...** I wish to emphasize that ...; **sirve para ~ su belleza** it serves to enhance her beauty, it serves to show up her beauty.
(**b**) (*Mil*) to detach, detail, assign.
(**c**) (*Inform*) to highlight.
2 *vi y* **destacarse** *vr* (**a**) to stand out; **~se contra, ~se en, ~se sobre** to stand out against, be outlined against, be silhouetted against, **~se como un pegote** to stick out like a sore thumb.
(**b**) (*fig*) to stand out, be outstanding, be exceptional.
destajar [1a] *vt* (**a**) (*Naipes*) to cut. (**b**) (*And, CAm, Méx*) *res* to cut up. (**c**) *trabajo etc* to contract for, agree conditions for; to do as piecework.
destajero, -a *nm/f*, **destajista** *nmf* pieceworker.
destajo *nm* (**a**) (*gen*) piecework; contract work; (*un ~*) job; stint; **a ~** by the job; (*fig*) eagerly, keenly; energetically; **trabajar a ~** to do piecework, be on piecework; **trabajo a ~** piecework; **hablar a ~*** to talk nineteen to the dozen.
(**b**) **a ~** (*Cono Sur**) by guesswork.
(**c**) **~ de esquí** ski-lift pass.
destapador *nm* (*LAm*) bottle opener.
destapar [1a] **1** *vt* (*descubrir*) to uncover; *botella* to open, uncork; *caja* to open, take the lid off; *recipiente* to take the lid off, raise the lid of; (*fig*) to reveal, uncover.
2 *vi* (*Méx*: *echar a correr*) to break into a run.
3 destaparse *vr* (**a**) to get uncovered; (*persona*) to undress, strip off.
(**b**) (*fig*) (*causar sorpresa*) to cause surprise, do sth unexpected; (*mostrar su carácter*) to show o.s. in one's true character; **se destapó metiéndose monja** she astounded everyone by becoming a nun.
(**c**) (*fig*: *hablar*) to speak frankly, come into the open; **~ con uno** to unbosom o.s. to sb.
(**d**) (*fig*: *perder los estribos*) to let fly, lose control.
destape *nm* (**a**) (*de persona*: *estado*) state of undress, nudity; display of flesh; (*acto*) undressing, stripping off; **~ integral** full-frontal nudity. (**b**) (*fig*) permissiveness; (*Pol*) process (*o* period *etc*) of liberalization; **el ~ español** the process of liberalization in Spain (*from 1975*).
destaponar [1a] *vt* to uncork.
destartalado *adj cuarto etc* untidy, in disorder; *casa etc* large and rambling; ruinous, tumbledown, dilapidated; *vehículo etc* rickety, shaky.
destazar [1f] *vt* to cut up.
destechar [1a] *vt* to unroof, take the roof off.
destejar [1a] *vt* (**a**) *techo* to remove the tiles from. (**b**) (*fig*) to leave unprotected.
destejer [2d] *vt* (**a**) (*deshacer*) to undo, unravel; *labor de punto* to take the stitches out of. (**b**) (*fig*) to upset; to interfere with the progress of; *V* **tejer**.
destellante *adj* sparkling.
destellar [1a] *vi* to sparkle, flash; to glint, gleam.
destello *nm* (**a**) (*gen*) sparkle; flash; glint, gleam; wink(ing).
(**b**) (*Téc*) signal light, winking light.
(**c**) (*fig*) atom, particle; **no tiene un ~ de verdad** there's not an atom of truth in it.
(**d**) **~s** (*fig*) glimmer; **tiene a veces ~s de inteligencia** he sometimes shows a glimmer (*o* glimmerings) of intelligence.
destemplado *adj* (**a**) (*Mús*) *instrumento* out of tune; *voz* harsh, unpleasant.
(**b**) (*Arte*) inharmonious, badly blended, ill-matched.
(**c**) *pulso* irregular.
(**d**) (*Med*) indisposed, out of sorts; feverish.
(**e**) *carácter, ademán etc* ill-tempered; *actitud* ill-judged, intemperate, harsh.
(**f**) (*Met*) unpleasant.
destemplanza *nf* (**a**) (*Mús*) tunelessness; harshness, un-

pleasantness.
(**b**) (*Arte*) lack of harmony.
(**c**) (*irregularidad*) irregularity.
(**d**) (*Med*) indisposition; (*fiebre*) feverish condition.
(**e**) (*actitud*) intemperance, harshness.
(**f**) (*Met*) unpleasantness, inclemency.
(**g**) (*una* ~) sharp remark, harsh comment.

destemplar [1a] **1** *vt* (**a**) (*Mús*) to untune, put out of tune, upset the pitch of.
(**b**) (*fig*) to upset, disturb (the order of); to disconcert.
2 destemplarse *vr* (**a**) (*Mús*) to get out of tune, lose its pitch.
(**b**) (*fig*) to get out of order; (*persona*) to get upset, get worked up; (*pulso*) to become irregular; (*Med*) to become indisposed, get out of sorts.
(**c**) **con eso me destemplo** (*LAm*) that sets my teeth on edge, that gives me the shivers.

destemple *nm* (**a**) (*gen*) = **destemplanza**. (**b**) (*de metal*) lack of temper, poorly-tempered nature.

destensar [1a] *vt* to slacken, loosen.

desteñido *adj* faded, discoloured.

desteñir [3k] **1** *vt* to fade, discolour, take the colour out of.
2 *vi y* **desteñirse** *vr* (**a**) (*perder color*) to fade, lose colour, discolour.
(**b**) (*colores de tela*) to run; **'esta tela no destiñe'** 'this fabric will not run'.

desternillante* *adj* hilarious, very funny.

desternillarse* [1a] *vr*: ~ **de risa** to split one's sides with laughing, die laughing.

desternille* *nm* laughter, hilarity.

desterrado, -a *nm/f* exile; outlaw; (*esp fig*) outcast.

desterrar [1j] *vt* (**a**) (*exiliar*) to exile, banish.
(**b**) (*fig*) to banish; to dismiss, put aside; ~ **una sospecha** to banish a suspicion from one's mind; ~ **el uso de las armas de fuego** to banish firearms, prohibit the use of firearms.
(**c**) (*Agr, Min*) to remove the soil from.

destetar [1a] **1** *vt* to wean. **2 destetarse** *vr* (**a**) (*niño*) to be weaned; ~ **con el vino** (*fig*) to have been brought up on wine. (**b**) (‡: *mujer*) to show her tits‡.

destete *nm* weaning.

destiempo *nm*: **a** ~ at the wrong time, at an inopportune moment.

destierro *nm* (**a**) (*exilio*) exile; banishment; **vivir en el** ~ to live in exile. (**b**) (*fig*) wilderness; remote spot.

destilación *nf* distillation.

destiladera *nf* still, distilling vessel; (*LAm*) filter.

destilado *nm* distillation.

destilador *nm* (**a**) (*aparato*) still. (**b**) (*persona*) distiller.

destilar [1a] **1** *vt* (**a**) *alcohol* to distil; *sangre etc* to exude, ooze.
(**b**) (*fig*) to exude, ooze; to reveal; **la carta destilaba odio** the letter exuded hatred; **es una orden que destila crueldad** it is an order which is steeped in cruelty.
2 *vi* (*gotear*) to drip, fall (drop by drop); (*rezumar*) to ooze (out); (*filtrarse*) to filter through.

destilatorio *nm* (*aparato*); still; (*fábrica*) distillery.

destilería *nf* distillery; ~ **de petróleo** oil refinery.

destinar [1a] *vt* (**a**) (*gen*) to destine (*a, para* for, to); (*asignar*) to assign (*a* to); (*encaminar*) to design (*a* for); (*dirigir*) to intend, mean (*a, para* for); *fondos etc* to set aside, earmark (*a* for); **me habían destinado una habitación elegante** they had assigned me an elegant room; **le destinan al sacerdocio** they intend him for the priesthood; **fabricantes de aviones destinados a Eslobodia** makers of aircraft destined for (*o* for use in) Slobodia; **una carta que viene destinada a ti** a letter for you, a letter addressed to you; (*Náut etc*) **ir destinado a** to be bound for; **estar destinado a** + *infin* to be destined to + *infin*.
(**b**) *persona* to appoint, assign (*a* to); (*Mil etc*) to post (*a* to); to station (*en* in); **le han destinado a Lima** they have appointed him to Lima.

destinatario, -a *nm/f* addressee.

destino *nm* (**a**) (*suerte*) destiny, fate; **es mi ~ no encontrarlo** I am fated not to find it; **el ~ lo quiso así** it was destiny, fate willed it thus; **rige los ~s del país** he rules the country's fate, the fate of the country is in his hands.
(**b**) (*de viajero, barco etc*) destination; **'a franquear en ~'** 'postage will be paid by the addressee'; **van con ~ a Londres** they are going to London; (*Náut*) they are bound for London; **salir con ~ a** to leave for; **¿cuál es el ~ de este cuadro?** what is the destination of this picture?, where is this picture for?
(**c**) (*puesto*) job, post, position; (*Mil*) posting; (*de funcionario*) placement; ~ **público** public appointment; **buscarse un ~ de cartero** to look for a job as a postman; **¿qué ~ tienes?** where have you been placed?
(**d**) (*uso*) use, utility; **dar ~ a algo** to put sth to good use, find a use for sth.

destitución *nf* dismissal, removal.

destituido *adj*: ~ **de** devoid of, bereft of, lacking (in).

destituir [3g] *vt* (**a**) *persona* to dismiss, remove, sack* (*de* from); *ministro etc* to remove from office; **le destituyeron por inmoral** they sacked him for immorality*.
(**b**) ~ **a uno de algo** to deprive sb of sth.

destorcer [2b *y* 2h] **1** *vt cuerda etc* to untwist, take the twists out of; *alambre etc* to straighten. **2 destorcerse** *vr* (*Náut*) to get off course.

destornillado* *adj* crazy, potty*.

destornillador *nm* (**a**) (*herramienta*) (*t* **destornilladora** *nf*) screwdriver. (**b**) (*: *bebida*) screwdriver* (*cocktail of vodka and orange juice*).

destornillar [1a] **1** *vt* to unscrew. **2 destornillarse** *vr* (**a**) (*fig*) to behave wildly; (*) to go crazy. (**b**) (*LAm*) = **desternillarse**. (**c**) (*Méx**: *rabiar*) to burble on, rave.

destrabar [1a] *vt* (*gen*) to loosen, detach; *prisionero etc* to unfetter, take the shackles off.

destral *nm* small hatchet.

destreza *nf* skill, dexterity; cleverness; handiness; **~s lingüísticas** linguistic skills.

destripacuentos *nm invar* interrupter, person who butts in.

destripador *nm* (*fig*) butcher; murderer.

destripar [1a] *vt* (**a**) *animal* to gut, draw, paunch; *persona* to disembowel; to cut open the belly of, slash the stomach of.
(**b**) (*fig*) to mangle, crush; *cuento* to spoil (by interrupting and telling its ending).

destripaterrones *nm invar* poor labourer; (*) clodhopper.

destrocar* [1g *y* 1l] *vt* to swap, change back.

destronamiento *nm* dethronement; (*fig*) overthrow.

destronar [1a] *vt* to dethrone; (*fig*) to overthrow.

destroncar [1g] *vt* (**a**) *árbol* to chop off, lop (the top off); (*Cono Sur, Méx*) *planta* to uproot.
(**b**) *persona* to maim, mutilate; (*fig*) to tire out, exhaust; *caballo* to wear out.
(**c**) (*fig*) *proyecto etc* to ruin; *desarrollo* to harm, damage, dislocate; *discurso etc* to interrupt.

destrozado *adj* smashed, shattered, ruined.

destrozar [1f] *vt* (**a**) (*romper*) to smash, shatter, ruin; to break up, break to pieces; to destroy; *ropa, zapatos* to ruin; (*Mil*) *ejército, enemigo* to smash; *carne* to mangle, lacerate, tear; *nervios* to shatter; *recursos etc* to squander, dissipate.
(**b**) (*fig*) *persona* to ruin; to shatter; *vida etc* to ruin; *corazón* to break; ~ **la armonía** to ruin the harmony; ~ **a uno en una discusión** to crush sb in an argument; **le ha destrozado el que no quisiera casarse con él** he was shattered when she wouldn't marry him, her refusal to marry him broke him up.

destrozo *nm* (*gen*) destruction; (*Mil*) smashing, annihilation, rout; (*de personas*) massacre; **~s** damage, havoc, ravages; **causar ~s en** to create havoc in, cause great damage to, ravage.

destrozón *adj*: **un niño ~** a child who is hard on his clothes; **la criada es muy destrozona** the servant is a terrible one for breaking things.

destrucción *nf* destruction.

destructible *adj* destructible.

destructividad *nf* destructiveness.

destructivo *adj* destructive.

destructor 1 *adj* destructive. **2** *nm* (*Náut*) destroyer.

destruible *adj* destructible.

destruir [3g] **1** *vt* (*gen*) to destroy; (*arruinar*) to ruin, wreck; (*dañar*) to damage; *equilibrio etc* to destroy, upset; *recursos* to squander; *proyectos* to ruin.
2 destruirse *vr* (*Mat*) to cancel (each other) out.

desubicado *adj* (*Cono Sur*) tactless, silly.

desubicar [1g] *vt* (*LAm*) to disorientate, confuse, put off.

desudar [1a] *vt* to wipe the sweat off.

desuellacaras *nm invar* (**a**) (*barbero*) clumsy barber. (**b**) (*bribón*) rogue, villain.

desuello *nm* (**a**) (*acto*) skinning, flaying. (**b**) (*descaro*) brazenness, insolence. (**c**) (*: *robo*) extortion; **¡es un ~!** it's daylight robbery!

desuncir [3b] *vt* to unyoke.

desunión *nf* (**a**) (*acto*) separation; disconnection. (**b**) (*estado*) disunity; rift.

desunir [3a] *vt* (**a**) (*separar*) to separate, sever, detach. (**b**) (*fig*) to cause a rift between.

desuñarse [1a] *vr* (**a**) (*trabajar*) to work one's fingers to the bone (*por* + *infin* to + *infin*). (**b**) (*fig*) to be always up to mischief; **se desuña por el juego** he's an inveterate gambler.

desurbanización *nf* relief of city overcrowding, dispersal of city population(s) (to satellite towns).

desusado *adj* (**a**) (*anticuado*) obsolete, antiquated, out of date.
(**b**) **esa palabra está desusada de los buenos escritores** that word is no longer in use among good writers.
(**c**) (*insólito*) unwonted, unusual.

desusar [1a] **1** *vt* to stop using, discontinue the use of, give up. **2 desusarse** *vr* to go out of use, become obsolete.

desuso *nm* disuse; **caer en ~** to fall into disuse, become obsolete; **una expresión caída en ~** an obsolete expression; **dejar algo en ~** to cease to use sth, discontinue the use of sth.

desvaído *adj* (**a**) *color* pale, dull, washed-out.
(**b**) *contorno* ill-defined, vague, blurred.
(**c**) *persona* (*de carácter*) weak, characterless; *personalidad* flat, dull.
(**d**) *talla* gangling, lanky.

desvainar [1a] *vt guisantes etc* to shell.

desvalido *adj* helpless; destitute; (*Pol*) underprivileged; **los ~s** the helpless, (*Pol*) the underprivileged; **niños ~s** waifs and strays, abandoned children.

desvalijamiento *nm* robbing, robbery; rifling; burgling.

desvalijar [1a] *vt* (*gen*) to rob, plunder; *cajón, maleta etc* to ransack, rifle; *casa, tienda* to burgle, burglarize (*US*), break into, rob.

desvalimiento *nm* helplessness; destitution, great need.

desvalorar [1a] *vt* to devaluate; *moneda* to devalue.

desvalorización *nf* devaluation.

desvalorizar [1f] *vt* to devalue.

desván *nm* (*ático*) loft, attic; garret; (*trastera*) lumber room.

desvanecer [2d] **1** *vt* (**a**) (*gen*) to cause to vanish, make disappear; *humo etc* to dissipate.
(**b**) *duda etc* to dispel; *pensamiento, memoria* to banish, dismiss.
(**c**) *color* to tone down; *contorno* to blur; (*Fot*) to mask.
(**d**) *persona* to make conceited; **el dinero le ha desvanecido** the money has gone to his head.
2 desvanecerse *vr* (**a**) (*desaparecer*) to vanish, disappear.
(**b**) (*duda etc*) to vanish, be dispelled.
(**c**) (*Quím etc*) to evaporate; to dissolve, melt away, disappear.
(**d**) (*Med*) to faint (away).
(**e**) (*sonido, t Rad*) to fade (away), fade out.

desvanecido *adj* (**a**) (*Med*) faint; giddy, dizzy; **caer ~** to fall in a faint. (**b**) (*fig*) (*engreído*) vain; (*orgulloso*) proud, haughty.

desvanecimiento *nm* (**a**) (*gen*) vanishing, disappearance; dissipation, dispelling.
(**b**) (*de contornos*) blurring; (*Fot*) masking.
(**c**) (*Quím*) evaporation; melting.
(**d**) (*Med*) fainting fit, swoon; dizzy spell, attack of giddiness.
(**e**) (*Rad etc*) fading.
(**f**) (*fig*) vanity; pride, haughtiness.

desvarar [1a] *vt* to refloat.

desvariar [1c] *vi* (**a**) (*Med*) to be delirious. (**b**) (*fig*) to rave, talk nonsense.

desvarío *nm* (**a**) (*Med*) delirium; raving. (**b**) (*fig*) (*disparate*) absurdity; (*noción*) extravagant notion, strange notion; (*capricho*) whim; **~s** ravings, ramblings.

desvede *nm* ending of the close season.

desvelado *adj* (**a**) (*lit*) sleepless, wakeful; **estar ~** to be awake, be unable to get to sleep. (**b**) (*fig*) watchful, vigilant.

desvelar [1a] **1** *vt* (**a**) *persona* to keep awake; **el café me desvela** coffee keeps me awake.
(**b**) *misterio* to solve, explain; *lo oculto* to reveal, unveil.
2 desvelarse *vr* (**a**) (*estar sin dormir*) to stay awake, keep awake; (*no poder dormir*) to go without sleep, have a sleepless night.
(**b**) (*fig*) to be watchful, be vigilant, keep one's eyes open; **~ por algo** to be anxious about sth, be much concerned about sth; to take great care over sth; **~ por** + *infin* to do everything possible to + *infin*; **se desvela porque no nos falte nada** she works hard so that we should not go short of anything.

desvelo *nm* (**a**) (*falta de sueño*) lack of sleep; (*insomnio*) sleeplessness, insomnia.
(**b**) (*fig*) watchfulness, vigilance.
(**c**) **~s** *pl* (*fig*) (*preocupación*) anxiety, care, concern; (*esfuerzo*) effort, hard work; **gracias a sus ~s** thanks to his efforts.

desvencijado *adj* ramshackle, rickety, broken-down.

desvencijar [1a] **1** *vt* (**a**) (*romper*) to break; (*soltar*) to loosen, weaken.
(**b**) *persona* to weaken, exhaust.
2 desvencijarse *vr* (**a**) (*deshacerse*) to come apart, fall to pieces, break; to become disjointed.
(**b**) (*Med*) to rupture o.s.

desventaja *nf* disadvantage; handicap, liability; **estar en ~ con respecto a otros** to be at a disadvantage compared with others.

desventajado *adj* disadvantaged.

desventajosamente *adv* disadvantageously, unfavourably.

desventajoso *adj* disadvantageous, unfavourable.

desventura *nf* misfortune.

desventuradamente *adv* unfortunately.

desventurado 1 *adj* (**a**) (*desgraciado*) unfortunate, unlucky; ill-fated.
(**b**) (*infeliz*) miserable, wretched; unhappy; **¡qué ~ estoy!** how wretched I am!
(**c**) (*tímido*) timid, shy.
(**d**) (*tacaño*) mean.
2 *nm*, **desventurada** *nf* wretch, unfortunate; **algún ~** some poor devil.

desvergonzado 1 *adj* shameless; impudent, brazen; unblushing. **2** *nm*, **desvergonzada** *nf* shameless person.

desvergonzarse [1f *y* 1l] *vr* (**a**) (*perder la vergüenza*) to lose all sense of shame.
(**b**) (*insolentarse*) to be impudent, be insolent (*con* to); to behave in a shameless way (*con* to).
(**c**) **~ a pedir algo** to have the nerve to ask for sth, dare to ask for sth.

desvergüenza *nf* shamelessness; brazenness, effrontery, impudence; **esto es una ~** this is disgraceful, this is shameful; **¡qué ~!** how shocking!; what a nerve!*, the effrontery of it!; **tener la ~ de** + *infin* to have the impudence (*o* nerve*) to + *infin*.

desvertebración *nf* dislocation; disruption.

desvertebrado *adj* lacking cohesion, disorganized.

desvertebrar [1a] *vt* (*fig*) to dislocate; to disturb, disrupt, upset, throw off balance; *pandilla etc* to break up.

desvestir [3k] **1** *vt* to undress. **2 desvestirse** *vr* to undress.

desviación *nf* (**a**) (*acto*) deviation (*de* from); deviance; deflection (*de* from), departure (*de* from); (*Mec, Fís, de brújula*) deviation; **~ estándar, ~ normal** standard deviation; **es una ~ de sus principios** it is a deviation (*o* departure) from his principles.
(**b**) (*Pol, Psic*) deviation.
(**c**) (*Aut etc*) (*rodeo*) detour; diversion; (*circunvalación*) bypass, ring road; **~ de la circulación** traffic diversion.

desviacionismo *nm* deviationism.

desviacionista *adj, nmf* deviationist.

desviadero *nm* (*Ferro*) siding.

desviado *adj* (**a**) (*oblicuo*) oblique; deflected; deviant. (**b**) *lugar* remote, off the beaten track; **~ de** remote from, away from.

desviar [1c] **1** *vt* (**a**) (*físicamente*) to turn aside; to deflect, divert (*de* from); *flecha etc* to deflect; *balón* to deflect, glance; *golpe* to parry, ward off, deflect; *pregunta* to parry; *ojos* to avert, turn away; (*Aut*) to divert, re-route (*por* through); (*Ferro*) to switch (into a siding), shunt; **~ el cauce de un río** to alter the course of a river.
(**b**) (*fig*) to turn aside (*de* from); **le desviaron de su propósito** they dissuaded him from his intention; **~ a uno de su vocación** to turn sb from his (true) vocation; **~ a uno de su pensamiento** to sidetrack sb from his theme; **~ a uno de las malas compañías** to wean sb away from evil company; **~ a uno del buen camino** to lead sb astray.
2 desviarse *vr* (*persona etc*) to turn aside, turn away, deviate (*de* from); (*camino*) to branch off, leave; (*Náut*) to sheer off; (*Náut*) to go off course; (*Aut*) to turn off; to swerve; **~ de un tema** to digress from a theme; to wander from the point.

desvincular [1a] **1** *vt* to detach (*de* from); *finca* to disentail. **2 desvincularse** *vr*: **~ con, ~ de** to break (one's links) with, sever one's connections with; to get free of.

desvío *nm* (**a**) (*acto*) deflection, deviation (*de* from); (*Aut etc*) swerve.
(**b**) (*Aut etc*: *rodeo*) diversion, detour (*US*); (*circunvalación*) bypass; (*Ferro*) siding.
(**c**) (*fig*) coldness, indifference; dislike.
desvirgar [1h] *vt* (**a**) *virgen* to deflower. (**b**) (*) = **estrenar**.
desvirtuar [1e] **1** *vt* (*afectar mal*) to impair, spoil; to detract from, adversely affect the quality of; (*cancelar*) to counteract, cancel, nullify the effect of.
2 desvirtuarse *vr* to spoil, go off, decline in quality.
desvitalizado *adj* dull, lifeless.
desvitalizar [1f] *vt* to drain the life from.
desvivirse [3a] *vr*: **~ por algo** to crave sth, yearn for sth, long for sth; to be crazy about sth; **~ por los amigos** to do one's utmost for one's friends, live only to help one's friends; **~ por** + *infin* to be very eager to + *infin*; to do one's best to + *infin*, go out of one's way to + *infin*; **se desvivió por ayudarme** she did everything possible to help me.
desyerba *nf*, **desyerbo** *nm* (*LAm*) weeding.
desyerbar [1a] *vt* = **desherbar**.
detal(l): **al ~** *adv* retail.
detalladamente *adv* in detail.
detallado *adj* detailed.
detallar [1a] *vt* (**a**) (*especificar*) to detail, list in detail, specify, itemize. (**b**) *cuento etc* to tell in detail. (**c**) (*Com*) to sell retail.
detalle *nm* (**a**) (*gen*) detail, particular; item; **~s de publicación** publication details; **esto es el ~** this is the key to it, this is the secret; **al ~** in detail; **con todo ~, con todos los ~s** in detail, with full details; with full particulars; **en ~** in detail; **hasta en sus menores ~s** down to the last detail; **para más ~s vea ...** for further details see ...; **no pierde ~** he misses nothing, he doesn't miss a trick; **me observaba sin perder ~** he was watching me very closely, he watched my every move.
(**b**) (*fig*: *atención*) token (of appreciation), gesture; (*regalo*) gift; **¡qué ~!** how sweet of you!, what a nice gesture!; **tiene muchos ~s** he is very considerate; **es el primer ~ que te veo en mucho tiempo** it's the first sign of consideration I've had from you for a long time.
(**c**) **al ~** (*Com*) retail (*adj, adv*); **vender al ~** to sell retail; **comercio al ~** retail trade.
(**d**) (*estado de cuenta*) statement; (*factura*) bill.
detallismo *nm* attention to detail, care for the details.
detallista 1 *adj* retail; **comercio ~** retail trade. **2** *nmf* retailer, retail trader.
detalloso* *adj* kind, thoughtful.
detección *nf* detection.
detectable *adj* detectable.
detectar [1a] *vt* to detect.
detective *nmf* detective; **~ de la casa** house detective; **~ privado** private detective.
detectivesco *adj* detective (*atr*); investigative; **dotes detectivescas** gifts as a detective.
detector *nm* (*Náut, Tec etc*) detector; **~ de humo** smoke-detector; **~ de incendios** fire-detector; **~ de mentiras** lie-detector; **~ de metales** metal-detector; **~ de minas** mine-detector.
detención *nf* (**a**) (*acción*) stopping; (*estancamiento*) stoppage, holdup; (*retraso*) delay; **~ de juego** (*Dep*) stoppage of play; **una ~ de 15 minutos** a 15-minute delay.
(**b**) (*Jur*) arrest, detention; **~ cautelar, ~ preventiva** preventive detention; **~ domiciliaria** house-arrest; **~ ilegal** unlawful detention, wrongful arrest; **~ sin procesamiento** imprisonment without trial.
(**c**) (*cualidad*) = **detenimiento**.
detener [2k] **1** *vt* (**a**) (*parar*) *persona, balón, vehículo, epidemia* (*etc*) to stop; (*retrasar*) to hold up, check, delay; **~ el progreso de** to hold up the progress of; **no quiero ~te** I don't want to delay you; **me detuvo en la calle** he stopped me in the street, he accosted me in the street.
(**b**) (*retener*) to keep, hold back, retain; *respiración* to hold.
(**c**) (*Jur*) to arrest, detain.
2 detenerse *vr* to stop; to pause; to delay, linger; **se detuvo a mirarlo** he stopped to look at it; **¡no te detengas!** don't hang about!, don't delay!; **se detiene mucho en eso** he's taking a long time over that.
detenidamente *adv* carefully, thoroughly; at great length.
detenido 1 *adj* (**a**) (*Jur*) arrested, under arrest.
(**b**) *narración etc* detailed; *examen* lengthy, thorough; careful; (*pey*) slow, dilatory.
(**c**) (*fig*: *tímido*) timid.
(**d**) (*fig*: *tacaño*) mean, niggardly.
2 *nm*, **detenida** *nf* person under arrest; detainee.
detenimiento *nm* care, thoroughness; **con ~** carefully, thoroughly.
detentar [1a] *vt* (**a**) *puesto, récord, título* to hold. (**b**) (*pey*) *título* to hold unlawfully; *puesto etc* to occupy unlawfully.
detentor(a) *nm/f* (*Dep*) holder; **~ de marca** record holder; **~ de trofeo** cup holder, champion.
detergente *adj, nm* detergent.
deterger [2c] *vt* to clean, clean of grease; *herida* to clean; (*Culin etc*) to clean with detergent.
deteriorado *adj* spoiled, damaged; worn; *géneros* shop-soiled, damaged.
deteriorar [1a] **1** *vt* (*estropear*) to spoil, damage; to worsen, make worse; to impair; (*Mec etc*) to cause wear on, cause wear and tear to.
2 deteriorarse *vr* to deteriorate, spoil; to get damaged; to get worse; (*Mec etc*) to wear, get worn.
deterioro *nm* deterioration; impairment; damage; worsening; (*Mec etc*) wear, wear and tear; **en caso de ~ de las mercancías** should the goods be damaged in any way; **sin ~ de sus derechos** without any loss of rights, without any impairment of his rights.
determinable *adj* determinable; **fácilmente ~** easy to determine.
determinación *nf* (**a**) (*acto*) determination; decision; **tomar una ~** to take a decision. (**b**) (*cualidad*) determination, resolution.
determinado *adj* (**a**) (*preciso*) fixed, set, certain; **un día ~** on a certain day; on a given day; **en momentos ~s** at certain times; **hay ~s límites** there are fixed limits; **no hay ningún tema ~** there is no particular theme, there is no set subject.
(**b**) (*Mat*) determinate; (*Ling*) *artículo* definite.
(**c**) *persona* determined, resolute; purposeful.
determinante *adj, nm* determinant.
determinar [1a] **1** *vt* (**a**) (*decidir*) to determine, fix, settle; *fecha, precio etc* to fix; *daños, contribución etc* to determine, assess; *rumbo* to fix, decide, shape; **~ el peso de algo** to determine (*o* calculate, work out, fix) the weight of sth; **el reglamento determina que ...** the rule lays it down that ..., the rule states that ...; **'por ~'** (*anuncio*) 'to be arranged'.
(**b**) (*provocar*) to cause, bring about; **aquello determinó la caída del gobierno** that brought about the fall of the government.
(**c**) *persona* to decide, make up the mind of; **esto le determinó** this decided him; **~ a uno a hacer algo** to determine sb to do sth, lead sb to do sth.
2 determinarse *vr* to decide, make up one's mind; **¿te has determinado?** have you made up your mind?; **~ a hacer algo** to decide to do sth, determine to do sth; **no se determina a marcharse** he can't make up his mind to go.
determinismo *nm* determinism.
determinista *adj* deterministic.
detersión *nf* cleansing.
detestable *adj* detestable; odious, hateful; damnable.
detestablemente *adv* detestably.
detestación *nf* detestation, hatred, loathing.
detestar [1a] *vt* to detest, hate, loathe.
detonación *nf* detonation; report, explosion, bang.
detonador *nm* detonator.
detonante 1 *adj* (**a**) explosive. (**b**) (*) stunning, shattering. **2** *nm* explosive; (*fig*) trigger (*de* for).
detonar [1a] *vi* to detonate, explode, go off.
detracción *nf* detraction, disparagement; knocking‡; slander; vilification.
detractor 1 *adj* disparaging; slanderous. **2** *nm*, **detractora** *nf* detractor; (*Pol etc*) knocker*; slanderer.
detraer [2o] *vt* (**a**) (*quitar*) to remove, separate, take away. (**b**) (*desviar*) to turn aside. (**c**) (*denigrar*) to disparage; (*Pol etc*) to knock‡; (*difamar*) to slander; (*vilipendiar*) to vilify.
detrás 1 *adv* (**a**) behind; at the back, in the rear; **~ la foto lleva una dedicatoria** the photo has a dedication on the back; **salir de ~** to come out from behind; **por ~** behind; **atacar a uno por ~** to attack sb from behind; **los coches de ~** the cars at the back, the cars in the rear.
(**b**) (*LAm*) **~ mío** (*etc*) behind me (*etc*).
2 ~ de *prep* behind, back of (*US*); **por ~ de uno** (*fig*) behind sb's back; **salir de ~ de un árbol** to come out from behind a tree.
detrimente *adj* detrimental.
detrimento *nm* (*daño*) harm, damage; (*de intereses etc*) detriment; **en ~ de** to the detriment of; **lo hizo sin ~ de su dignidad** he did it without detriment to (*o* loss of) his

dignity.

detrito *nm*, **detritus** *nm* (*Geol etc*) detritus; debris.

deuda *nf* (**a**) (*gen*) indebtedness, debt; **estar en ~** to be in debt, owe (*por* for); **estar en ~ con uno** to be in debt to sb, (*fig*) to be indebted to sb.

(**b**) (*una ~*) debt; **~ a corto plazo** short-term debt; **~ a largo plazo** long-term debt; **~ exterior, ~ externa** foreign debt; **~ incobrable, ~ morosa** bad debt; **~ pública** national debt; **~ sin respaldo** unsecured debt; **una ~ de gratitud** a debt of gratitude; **contraer ~s** to contract debts, get into debt; **estar lleno de ~s** to be heavily in debt, be burdened with debts.

(**c**) (*Ecl*) **perdónanos nuestras ~s** forgive us our trespasses.

deudo *nm* relative.

deudor 1 *adj* (**a**) **saldo ~** debit balance, adverse balance.

(**b**) **le soy muy ~** I am greatly indebted to you.

2 *nm*, **deudora** *nf* debtor; **~ moroso** slow payer, defaulter.

deuterio *nm* (*Quím*) deuterium.

devalar [1a] *vi* (*Náut*) to drift off course.

devaluación *nf* (*Fin*) devaluation.

devaluar [1e] *vt* (*Fin*) to devalue.

devaluatorio *adj*: **tendencia devaluatoria** tendency to depreciate, tendency to lose value.

devanadera *nf* (*Cos*) reel, spool; winding frame.

devanado *nm* (*Elec*) winding.

devanador *nm* (*Cos*) reel, spool, bobbin.

devanar [1a] **1** *vt* to wind; (*araña, gusano*) to spin.

2 devanarse *vr* (**a**) **~ los sesos** to rack one's brains.

(**b**) (*CAm, Carib, Méx*) **~ de dolor** to double up with pain; **~ de risa** to double up with laughter.

devanear [1a] *vi* to rave, talk nonsense.

devaneo *nm* (**a**) (*Med*) delirium; (*fig: disparates*) ravings, nonsense, absurd talk. (**b**) (*fruslería*) time-wasting pastime, idle pursuit. (**c**) (*amorío*) affair, flirtation.

devastación *nf* devastation.

devastador *adj* devastating (*t fig*).

devastadoramente *adv* devastatingly.

devastar [1a] *vt* to devastate.

devengar [1h] *vt sueldo* to earn; to draw, receive; *interés* to earn, bear, accrue; **interés devengado** accrued interest, earned interest.

devengo *nm* amount earned; **~s** income.

devenir [3r] **1** *vi* to develop into, become, evolve into; **~ en** to develop into, become, turn into, change into.

2 *nm* evolution, process of development, (slow) change, transformation; **una nación en perpetuo ~** a nation in a constant process of development, a nation which is changing all the time.

devoción *nf* (**a**) (*Rel etc: cualidad*) devotion; devoutness, piety; **con ~** devoutly; piously; **la ~ a esta imagen** the cult of this image, the veneration for this image.

(**b**) (*gen*) devotion (*a* to); attachment (*a* to); liking, affection (*a* for); **sienten ~ por su general** they feel devotion to their general, they are devoted to their general; **estar a la ~ de uno** to be completely under sb's thumb; **tener gran ~ a uno** to be wholly devoted to sb; **tener por ~** + *infin* to be in the habit of + *ger*.

(**c**) (*Ecl: acto*) devotion, prayer; religious observance; *V* **santo.**

devocional *adj* devotional.

devocionario *nm* prayerbook.

devolución *nf* (*gen*) return; (*Dep*) return; (*Com*) repayment, refund; **~ de derechos** (*Fin*) drawback; **pidió la ~ de los libros** he asked for the books to be given back, he asked for the return of the books; **'no se admiten devoluciones'** 'no refunds will be given', 'money cannot be refunded'.

devolver [2h; *ptp* **devuelto**] **1** *vt* (**a**) (*gen*) to return; to give back, send back; to hand back; *pelota, golpe* to return; (*Com*) to repay, refund; (*) to throw up, vomit; *favor etc* to return; **~ una carta al remitente** to return a letter to the sender; **~ un florero a su sitio** to put a vase back in its place; **~ mal por bien** to return ill for good; **el espejo devuelve la imagen** the mirror sends back (*o* reflects) the image; **~ la salud a uno** to give sb back his health, restore sb to health; **esto nos devuelve al problema de los recursos** this brings us back to the problem of resources.

(**b**) *salud, vista etc* to restore; **han devuelto el castillo a su antiguo esplendor** they have restored the castle to its former glory.

2 devolverse *vr* (*LAm*) to return, come back, go back.

devorador *adj* devouring; **fuego ~** all-consuming fire; **hambre ~a** ravenous hunger; **una mujer ~a de hombres** a man-eating woman.

devorar [1a] *vt* (**a**) (*gen*) to devour; (*comer*) to eat up, gobble up.

(**b**) (*fig*) (*gen*) to devour; (*agotar*) to consume, use up; *fortuna* to run through; **este coche devora los kilómetros** this car eats up the miles; **lo devoraba con los ojos** she was eyeing it greedily; **todo lo devoró el fuego** the fire consumed everything; **devora las novelas de amores** she laps up love stories, she devours love stories; **le devoran los celos** he is consumed with jealousy; **los chicos devoran el calzado** the kids are terribly hard on their shoes.

devotamente *adv* devoutly.

devoto 1 *adj* (**a**) (*Rel*) devout; pious; **ser muy ~ de un santo** to have a special devotion to a saint; **ser ~ de la Virgen del puño** to be tight-fisted.

(**b**) **obra devota** (*Rel*) devotional work, work of devotion.

(**c**) *amigo etc* devoted; **su ~ amigo** your devoted friend; **es ~ de ese café** he is much attached to that café.

2 *nm*, **devota** *nf* (**a**) (*Rel*) devout person; (*en iglesia*) worshipper; **los ~s** the faithful; (*en iglesia*) the worshippers, the congregation.

(**b**) (*fig*) devotee, votary; admirer; **la estrella y sus ~s** the star and her admirers (*o* fans); **los ~s del ajedrez** devotees of chess.

dextrosa *nf* dextrose.

deyección *nf* (*t* **deyecciones**) excrement; (*Med*) motion; (*Geol*) debris; (*de volcán*) lava.

deyectar [1a] *vt* (*Geol*) to deposit, leave, lay down.

DF *nm* (*Méx*) *abr de* **Distrito Federal** Federal District.

D.G. (**a**) *nf abr de* **Dirección General.**

(**b**) *nm abr de* **Director General** director-general, DG.

Dg. *abr de* **decagramo** decagram.

dg. *abr de* **decigramo** decigram, dg.

DGS *nf* (**a**) *abr de* **Dirección General de Seguridad.** (**b**) *abr de* **Dirección General de Sanidad.**

DGT *nf* (**a**) *abr de* **Dirección General de Tráfico.** (**b**) *abr de* **Dirección General de Turismo.**

dha., dho *abr de* **dicha, dicho** aforesaid.

di *etc V* **dar, decir.**

día *nm* (**a**) (*gen*) day; **el ~ 2 de mayo** (on) the second of May; **ocho ~s** week; **quince ~s** fortnight; **cuatro ~s** (*fig*) a couple of days, a few days, a day or two; **¿qué ~ es?** what's the date today?; **hace buen ~** it's a fine day, it's fine today; **¡buenos ~s!,** (*Cono Sur*) **buen ~!** good morning!, good day!; **dar los buenos ~s a uno** to wish (*o* bid) sb good day; **dar los ~s a uno** to wish sb many happy returns of the day (*birthday o saint's day*); **~ y noche** night and day; **parece que no pasan por ti los ~s** you don't look a day older; **no tener más que el ~ y la noche** to be utterly poor.

(**b**) (*frases con artículo, adj etc*) **el ~ de hoy** today; **el ~ de mañana** tomorrow; (*fig*) at some future date; **el mejor ~** some fine day, any old day; **el ~ menos pensado** when you least expect it; **un ~ de éstos** one of these days; **un ~ sí y otro no, ~ (de) por medio** (*LAm*) every other day; on alternate days; **~ tras ~** day after day; **algún ~** some day, sometime; **cada ~** each day, every day; **¡cualquier ~!** (*iró*) not on your life!; **cualquier ~ viene** (*iró*) some fine day he'll turn up; **otro ~** some other day, some other time; **dejémoslo para otro ~** let's leave it for the moment; **¡tal ~ hará un año!*** a fat lot I care!*; **todos los ~s** every day, daily; **no es cosa de todos los ~s** it's not an everyday thing; **todo el santo ~** the whole livelong day; the whole blessed day; *V* **hoy.**

(**c**) (*locuciones con prep*) **~ a ~** day in day out; **el ~ a ~** day-to-day routine; **a ~s** at times, once in a while; **a los pocos ~s** within a few days, after a few days, a few days later; **al otro ~** (on) the following day; **al ~ siguiente** on the following day; **7 veces al ~** 7 times a day, 7 times daily; **estar al ~** to be up to date; (*en la moda etc*) to be trendy; **quien quiera estar al ~ en estos estudios, lea ...** if anybody wants to keep up to date in these matters, he should read ...; **está al ~ vestir así** it's the thing to dress like that; **poner al ~** *diario* to enter up, write up; *libro mayor* to write up; **vivir al ~** to live from hand to mouth; **de ~ en ~** from day to day; **ese problema es ya de ~s** that's an old problem; **pollitos de un ~** day-old chicks; **los estilos del ~** fashionable styles, up-to-date styles, trendy styles*; **en ~s de Dios** (*o* **del mundo** *o* **de la vida**) never; **en los ~s de Victoria** in Victoria's day, in Victoria's times; **en su ~** in due time; **¡hasta otro ~!** so long!

(**d**) (*locuciones con adj etc*) **~ de asueto** day off; **~ de**

ayuno fast day; ~ **azul** (*Ferro*) cheap ticket day; ~ **de la banderita** flag day; ~ **de boda** wedding day; **cien ~s** (*Pol etc*) hundred days, honeymoon period; ~ **de diario,** ~ **de entresemana,** ~ **entre semana** weekday; ~ **de los enamorados** St Valentine's Day (*14 February*); ~ **feriado** holiday, day off; ~ **festivo,** ~ **de fiesta** holiday; ~ **franco** (*Mil*) day's leave; (*Com*) **~s de gracia** days of grace, days (allowed) to pay; ~ **hábil** working day; **D~ de la Hispanidad** Columbus Day (*12 October*); ~ **inhábil** non-working day; ~ **de inocentes** (*28 December*) ≈ All Fools' Day, April Fools' Day (*1 April*); ~ **del Juicio (Final)** Judgement Day; **estaremos aquí hasta el ~ del Juicio** we'll be here till Kingdom come; ~ **laborable** working day, weekday; ~ **lectivo** (*Escol*) working day, teaching day; ~ **libre** free day, day off; ~ **de la Madre** Mother's Day (*in Spain, 8 December*); ~ **malo,** ~ **nulo** off day; ~ **de paga** payday; ~ **de puertas abiertas** open day; **D~ de la Raza** Columbus Day (*12 October*); **D~ de Reyes** Epiphany (*6 January, on which the Magi bring presents to children*); ~ **señalado** special day, red-letter day; ~ **de trabajo,** ~ **útil** working day, weekday; ~ **de tribunales** court day; ~ **de vigilia** day of abstinence; *V* **anunciación, año** *etc.*

(**e**) (*horas de luz*) daytime; (*luz*) daylight; **antes del ~** before dawn; **de ~** by day, during the day(time); **en pleno ~** in broad daylight.

diabetes *nf* diabetes.

diabético, -a *adj, nm/f* diabetic.

diabla *nf,* **diablesa** *nf* she-devil; **a la diabla** carelessly, any old how*.

diablillo* *nm* imp, monkey.

diablo *nm* (**a**) (*demonio*) devil; fiend; **ése es el ~** that's the devil of it; **ahí será el ~** there'll be the devil to pay; **donde el ~ perdió el poncho** (*Cono Sur*) in some godforsaken spot.

(**b**) (*fig*) devil; fiend; **pobre ~** poor devil; **algún pobre ~ de cartero** some poor devil of a postman; *para muchas frases, V* **demonio.**

(**c**) **~s azules** (*LAm*) blue devils, delirium tremens.

(**d**) (*Cono Sur: carro*) heavy oxcart.

diablura *nf* devilry, devilment; prank; **~s** mischief, monkey tricks.

diabólicamente *adv* diabolically, fiendishly.

diabólico *adj* diabolical, devilish, fiendish.

diaconato *nm* deaconry, diaconate.

diaconía *nf* (*distrito*) deaconry; (*casa*) deacon's house.

diaconisa *nf* deaconess.

diácono *nm* deacon.

diacrítico *adj* diacritic(al); **signo ~** diacritic, diacritical mark.

diacrónico *adj* diachronic.

diacho* *nm* (*euf*) = **diablo.**

Diada *nf* Catalan national day (*11 September*).

diadema *nf* (*gen*) diadem; (*corona*) crown; (*joya*) tiara.

diafanidad *nf* transparency; filminess; sheerness; limpidity.

diáfano *adj* (**a**) (*gen*) diaphanous, transparent; filmy; *medias, tela* sheer; *agua* limpid, crystal-clear. (**b**) (*iluminado*) bright, well-lit. (**c**) *argumento etc* clear; **es ~ que ...** it is clear that ...

diafragma *nm* diaphragm.

diagnosis *nf invar* diagnosis.

diagnóstica *nf* diagnostics.

diagnosticar [1g] *vt* to diagnose.

diagnóstico 1 *adj* diagnostic. **2** *nm* diagnosis; ~ **precoz** early diagnosis.

diagonal *adj, nf* diagonal.

diagonalmente *adv* diagonally.

diagrama *nm* diagram; ~ **de barras** bar chart; ~ **de bloques** block diagram; ~ **circular** pie chart; ~ **de dispersión** scatter diagram; ~ **de flujo** flowchart.

dial *nm* (*Aut, Rad etc*) dial.

dialectal *adj* dialectal, dialect (*atr*).

dialectalismo *nm* (**a**) (*carácter*) dialectal nature, dialectalism; **un texto lleno de ~** a text of a strongly dialectal character.

(**b**) (*palabra etc*) dialectalism, dialect word (*o* phrase *etc*).

dialéctica *nf* dialectic(s).

dialéctico *adj* dialectical.

dialecto *nm* dialect.

dialectología *nf* dialectology.

dialectólogo, -a *nm/f* dialectologist.

diálisis *nf* dialysis.

dialogante 1 *adj* open, open-minded, willing to discuss; approachable. **2** *nmf* interlocutor; participant (in a discussion); **mi ~** the person I was (*etc*) talking to.

dialogar [1h] **1** *vt* to set down (*o* compose *etc*) as a dialogue, write in dialogue form. **2** *vi* to talk, converse; ~ **con** to engage in a dialogue with.

diálogo *nm* dialogue; ~ **para besugos** fatuous exchange; ~ **norte-sur** north-south dialogue; ~ **de sordos** dialogue of the deaf.

diamante *nm* (**a**) (*joya*) diamond; ~ **en bruto** uncut diamond; (*fig*) **ser un ~ en bruto** to be a rough diamond; ~ **falso** paste; ~ **de imitación** imitation diamond. (**b**) **~s** (*Naipes*) diamonds.

diamantífero *adj* diamond-bearing.

diamantino *adj* diamond-like, adamantine; glittering.

diamantista *nmf* (*Téc*) diamond cutter; (*Com*) diamond merchant.

diametral *adj* diametrical.

diametralmente *adv* diametrically; ~ **opuesto a** diametrically opposed to.

diámetro *nm* diameter; ~ **de giro** (*Aut*) turning circle; **faros de gran ~** wide-angle headlights.

Diana *nf* Diana.

diana *nf* (**a**) (*Mil*) reveille.

(**b**) (*de blanco*) centre, bull's-eye; **dar en la ~, hacer ~** to get a bull's-eye.

(**c**) (*juego*) dartboard.

diantre* *nm* (*euf*) = **diablo**; **¡~!** oh hell!; **los había como un ~** (*Cono Sur*) there were the devil of a lot of them, there were loads of them.

diapasón *nm* (**a**) (*Mús*) diapason; normal standard pitch; range, scale.

(**b**) (*de violín etc*) fingerboard.

(**c**) ~ **normal** tuning fork.

(**d**) (*fig: de voz*) tone; **bajar el ~** to lower one's voice; **subir el ~** to raise one's voice.

diapositiva *nf* (*Fot*) slide, transparency; (*de vidrio*) lantern slide; ~ **en color** colour slide.

diariamente *adv* daily, every day.

diario 1 *adj* daily; everyday; day-to-day; **100 dólares ~s** 100 dollars a day.

2 *adv* (*LAm*) daily, every day.

3 *nm* (**a**) (*periódico*) newspaper, daily; (*libro diario*) diary; (*Com*) day-book; ~ **de a bordo,** ~ **de navegación** logbook; ~ **hablado** (*Rad etc*) news, news bulletin; ~ **de escritorio** desk diary; ~ **dominical** Sunday paper; ~ **matinal,** ~ **de la mañana** morning paper; ~ **de la noche,** ~ **vespertino** evening paper; ~ **de sesiones** (*Parl*) parliamentary report, report of proceedings in Parliament.

(**b**) (*Fin*) daily expenses.

(**c**) **a ~** daily; **de ~, para ~** for everyday use; **nuestro mantel de ~** our tablecloth for everyday (use), our ordinary tablecloth.

diarismo *nm* (*LAm*) journalism.

diarista *nmf* (**a**) (*de libro diario*) diarist. (**b**) (*LAm: de periódico*) newspaper owner (*o* publisher).

diarrea *nf* diarrhoea.

diarrucho* *nm* (*LAm*) rag*; **los ~s** the gutter press.

diáspora *nf* (*Hist*) diaspora; (*fig*) dispersal, migration.

diatónico *adj* diatonic.

diatriba *nf* diatribe, tirade.

dibujante *nmf* (**a**) (*Arte*) sketcher; cartoonist. (**b**) (*Téc*) draughtsman; (*de modas*) designer; ~ **de publicidad** commercial artist.

dibujar [1a] **1** *vt* (**a**) (*Arte*) to draw, sketch.

(**b**) (*Téc*) to design.

(**c**) (*fig*) to sketch (in words), describe, depict.

2 dibujarse *vr* (**a**) (*perfilarse*) to be outlined (*contra* against); to loom, show up.

(**b**) (*emoción etc*) to show, appear; **el sufrimiento se dibujaba en su cara** suffering showed in his face.

dibujo *nm* (**a**) (*gen*) drawing; sketching; art of design; ~ **mecánico** mechanical drawing.

(**b**) (*un ~*) drawing, sketch (*t fig*); (*en periódico etc*) cartoon; (*caricatura*) caricature; ~ **animado, ~s animados** cartoon (film); ~ **al carbón** charcoal drawing; ~ **al natural,** ~ **del natural** drawing from life; ~ **(hecho) a pulso** freehand drawing.

(**c**) (*Téc*) design; pattern; ~ **escocés** tartan (design); **un papel con ~s a rayas** a wallpaper with a striped pattern; **sedas con ~s de última novedad** silks with the latest patterns (*o* designs).

dic., dic.ᵉ *abr de* **diciembre** December, Dec.

dicción *nf* (**a**) (*gen*) diction; style. (**b**) (*una ~*) word; expression.

diccionario *nm* dictionary; ~ **de bolsillo** pocket dictionary;

~ **bilingüe** bilingual dictionary; ~ **geográfico** gazetteer.

diccionarista *nmf* lexicographer, dictionary maker.

diciembre *nm* December.

dicotomía *nf* dichotomy.

dictablanda *nf* (*hum*) kindly dictatorship, benevolent despotism.

dictado *nm* (**a**) (*gen*) dictation; **escribir al** ~ to take dictation; **escribir algo al** ~ to take sth down (as it is dictated).

(**b**) ~**s** (*fig*) dictates; **los ~s de la conciencia** the dictates of conscience.

(**c**) (*título*) honorific title, title of honour.

dictador(a) *nm/f* dictator.

dictadura *nf* dictatorship.

dictáfono ® *nm* Dictaphone ®.

dictamen *nm* (*opinión*) opinion, dictum; (*juicio*) judgement; (*informe*) report; (*Jur*) legal opinion; ~ **contable** (*Méx*) auditor's report; ~ **facultativo** (*Med*) medical report; **emitir un** ~ to issue a report; **tomar** ~ **de** to consult with.

dictaminar [1a] **1** *vt sentencia* to pass. **2** *vi* to pass judgement, give an opinion (*en* on).

dictar [1a] **1** *vt* (**a**) *carta etc* to dictate (*a* to).

(**b**) *sentencia* to pass, pronounce; *decreto etc* to issue.

(**c**) (*indicar*) to suggest, say, dictate; **lo que dicta el sentido común** what common sense suggests.

(**d**) (*LAm*) *clase* to give; *conferencia* to deliver, give; ~ **las noticias** (*Rad, TV*) to read the news.

2 *vi*: ~ **a su secretaria** to dictate to one's secretary.

dictatorial *adj*, **dictatorio** *adj* dictatorial.

dicterio *nm* insult, taunt.

dicha *nf* (**a**) (*felicidad*) happiness; **para completar su** ~ to complete her happiness.

(**b**) (*una* ~) happy thing, happy event; **es una** ~ **poder** ... it is a happy thing to be able to ...

(**c**) (*suerte*) luck, good luck; **por** ~ by chance, fortunately.

dicharachería *nf* wittiness, raciness; slanginess; saltiness.

dicharachero 1 *adj* (*gracioso*) witty, racy, sparkling; (*que usa argot*) slangy; (*de fuerte sabor*) salty.

2 *nm* witty person, racy talker, sparkling conversationalist; slangy sort; salty individual.

dicharacho *nm* coarse remark, rude thing (to say).

dicho 1 *ptp de* **decir**.

2 *adj* (*este*) said; (*susodicho*) above-mentioned, aforementioned; ~**s animales** the said animals; **en** ~ **país** in this country, in this same country; **las avispas propiamente dichas** true wasps, wasps in the strict sense; *V t* **decir**.

3 *nm* (*proverbio*) saying, proverb; (*lugar común*) tag; (*ocurrencia*) bright remark, witty observation; (*insulto*) insult; ~ **gordo** rude remark; **del** ~ **al hecho hay gran trecho** talking is not the same as actually doing; there's many a slip 'twixt cup and lip; **es un** ~ it's just a saying; **tomarse los** ~**s** to exchange promises of marriage.

dichosamente *adv* luckily, fortunately.

dichoso *adj* (**a**) (*feliz*) happy; **hacer** ~ **a uno** to make sb happy; **me siento** ~ **de** + *infin* I feel happy to + *infin*.

(**b**) (*afortunado*) lucky, fortunate; **¡~s los ojos!** nice to see you!

(**c**) (*) blessed; **¡aquel** ~ **coche!** that blessed car!

didáctica *nf* didactics; **departamento de** ~ (*Univ*) education department.

didáctico *adj* didactic.

Dido *nf* Dido.

diecinueve *adj* nineteen; (*fecha*) nineteenth.

dieciochesco *adj* eighteenth-century (*atr*).

dieciocho *adj* eighteen; (*fecha*) eighteenth.

dieciochoañero, -a *adj, nm/f* eighteen-year-old.

dieciséis *adj* sixteen; (*fecha*) sixteenth.

diecisiete *adj* seventeen; (*fecha*) seventeenth.

Diego *nm* James.

dieldrina *nf* dieldrin.

diente *nm* (**a**) (*Anat*) tooth; (*Zool*) tusk; fang; ~ **canino** canine (tooth); ~ **cariado** decayed tooth, bad tooth; ~ **incisivo** incisor; ~ **de leche** milk tooth; ~ **molar** molar; ~**s postizos** false teeth; **de ~s afuera** (*fig*) as mere lip service, without meaning it; **decir algo para ~s afuera** to say one thing and mean another, pay lip service; **más cerca están mis ~s que mis parientes** charity begins at home; **daba** ~ **con** ~ his teeth were chattering; he was trembling like a leaf, he was all of a shiver; **enseñar los ~s** (*fig*) to show one's claws, turn nasty; **estar a** ~ to be ravenous; **hablar entre ~s** to mumble, mutter; **hincar el** ~ **en** to sink one's teeth into, bite into; **hincar el** ~ **en uno** (*fig*) to get one's knife into sb; **nunca pude hincar el** ~ **a ese libro** I could never get my teeth into that book; **pelar el** ~ (*LAm*) (*coquetear*) to flirt; (*reír*) to giggle flirtatiously; **tener buen** ~ to be a hearty eater.

(**b**) (*Mec*) cog; (*de hebilla*) tongue; (*de peine, sierra etc*) tooth.

(**c**) (*Bot*) ~ **de ajo** clove of garlic; ~ **de león** dandelion.

diéresis *nf* diaeresis.

diesel *adj, nm* (*pl* **diesel**) (*Aut*) diesel(-engined car); (**motor**) ~ diesel engine; **tren** ~ diesel train.

dieseleléctrico *adj* diesel-electric.

diestra *nf* right hand.

diestramente *adv* (**a**) (*hábilmente*) skilfully; dexterously; deftly. (**b**) (*astutamente*) shrewdly; (*pey*) cunningly.

diestro 1 *adj* (**a**) (*derecho*) right; (*Her*) dexter; **a** ~ **y siniestro** wildly, at random, all over the place; **repartir golpes a** ~ **y siniestro** to lash out wildly, throw out punches right and left.

(**b**) (*hábil*) skilful; dexterous; handy, deft.

(**c**) (*listo*) shrewd, clever; (*pey*) cunning.

2 *nm* (**a**) (*Taur*) matador, bullfighter.

(**b**) (*espadachín*) expert swordsman; (*esgrimidor*) expert fencer.

(**c**) (*correa*) bridle, halter.

(**d**) (*Dep*) right-hander.

dieta *nf* (**a**) (*Med*) diet; ~ **láctea** milk diet; **estar a** ~ to diet, be on a diet. (**b**) (*Pol*) diet, assembly. (**c**) ~**s** subsistence allowance, expense allowance; ~ **de asistencia** attendance allowance. (**d**) (*And*: *guiso*) stew.

dietario *nm* engagement book.

dietética[1] *nf* dietetics.

dietético 1 *adj* (**a**) dietetic, dietary. (**b**) **restaurante** ~ restaurant for people on a diet. **2** *nm*, **dietética**[2] *nf* dietician.

dietista *nmf*, **dietólogo, -a** *nm/f* dietician.

diez[1] **1** *adj* ten; (*fecha*) tenth; **las** ~ ten o'clock; **hacer las** ~ **de últimas** to scoop the pool, sweep the board; (*fig*) to queer one's own pitch, damage one's own cause.

2 *nm* ten; **un** ~ **para Pérez** ten out of ten for Pérez.

diez[2]‡ *nm euf de* **Dios**, *en locuciones; V* **cagar 3** (**b**).

diezmar [1a] *vt* to decimate (*t fig*).

diezmillo *nm* (*Méx*) sirloin steak.

diezmo *nm* tithe.

difamación *nf* slander, defamation (*de* of); libel (*de* on).

difamador 1 *adj* slanderous, defamatory, libellous. **2** *nm*, **difamadora** *nf* slanderer, defamer; scandalmonger.

difamar [1a] *vt* (*Jur*) to slander, defame; (*esp por escrito*) to libel; (*fig*) to slander, malign.

difamatorio *adj* slanderous, defamatory, libellous.

diferencia *nf* difference; ~ **de edades** difference in ages; **a** ~ **de** unlike; in contrast to; as distinguished from; **con corta** ~, **con poca** ~ more or less; **hacer** ~ **entre** to make a distinction between; **partir la** ~ to split the difference; **partir la** ~ **con uno** (*fig*) to meet sb halfway, agree to compromise; ~ **va de A a Z** there's a big difference between A and Z; **no veo** ~ **de A a Z** I see no difference between A and Z; I see nothing to choose between A and Z.

diferenciable *adj* distinguishable.

diferenciación *nf* differentiation.

diferenciador *adj* distinguishing.

diferencial 1 *adj* differential (*t Mat*); distinctive; *impuesto etc* discriminatory. **2** *nf* (*Mat*) differential. **3** *nm* (*a veces t f*) (*Aut*) differential.

diferenciar [1b] **1** *vt* (**a**) (*distinguir*) to differentiate between; to make a difference between; ~ **A de B** to separate A from B, distinguish between A and B.

(**b**) (*Mat*) to differentiate.

(**c**) (*variar*) to vary (the use of), alter the function of.

2 *vi* to differ (*de* from), be in disagreement (*de* with; *en* about, over).

3 diferenciarse *vr* (**a**) (*ser distinto*) to differ, be different (*de* from); to be distinctive, be distinguished; **no se diferencian en nada** they do not differ at all; **se diferencian en que** ... they differ in that ...

(**b**) (*destacar*) to distinguish o.s., stand out.

diferendo *nm* difference, disagreement.

diferente *adj* (**a**) (*gen*) different; ~ **a algo**, ~ **de algo** different from sth, unlike sth. (**b**) ~**s** several, various; **por ~s razones** for various reasons.

diferentemente *adv* differently.

diferido *adj*: **emisión diferida, emisión en** ~ (*Rad, TV*) recorded programme, repeat broadcast.

diferir [3i] **1** *vt* to defer, postpone, put off; to hold over;

(*Jur*) *sentencia* to reserve.

2 *vi* to differ, be different (*de* from, *en* in).

difícil *adj* (**a**) (*gen*) difficult, hard; awkward; **~ de vencer** hard to beat, difficult to overcome; **encuentro ~ decidir si** ... I find it hard to decide whether ..., I find difficulty in deciding whether ...; **se hizo un silencio ~** there was an awkward (*o* embarrassing) silence; **creo que lo tiene ~** I think he's got a tough job on.

(**b**) (*poco probable*) unlikely; **es ~ que** ... it is unlikely that ..., it is doubtful whether ...; **es ~ que venga** she's not likely to come.

(**c**) (*de carácter*) difficult; (*rebelde*) unruly, rebellious; (*inconformista*) non-conformist; **es un hombre ~** he's a difficult man.

(**d**) (*) *cara* odd, ugly.

difícilmente *adv* with difficulty; hardly; **~ se podrá hacer** it can hardly be done; **aquí ~ va a haber para todos** there's hardly going to be enough of this for everybody; **~ se alcanza eso** that is not likely to be reached.

dificultad *nf* (*gen*) difficulty; (*problema*) trouble; (*objeción*) objection; **sin ~ alguna** without the least difficulty; **la ~ es que** ... the difficulty is that ..., the trouble is that ...; **no hay ~ para aceptar que** ... there is no difficulty about accepting that ...; **ha tenido ~es con la policía** he's been in trouble with the police; **tuvieron algunas ~es para llegar a casa** they had some trouble getting home; **poner ~es** to raise objections; to create obstacles; **me pusieron ~es para darme el pasaporte** they made it awkward for me to get a passport.

dificultar [1a] *vt* (**a**) *camino, tráfico etc* to obstruct, impede, hinder; (*obstaculizar*) to put obstacles in the way of; (*afectar*) to interfere with, hold up; to render difficult; **las restricciones dificultan el comercio** the restrictions hinder trade, the restrictions make trade difficult.

(**b**) **~ que** + *subj* to make it unlikely that ...; (*persona*) to think (*o* consider) it unlikely that ...

dificultoso *adj* (**a**) (*difícil*) difficult, hard; awkward, troublesome. (**b**) (*) *cara* odd, ugly. (**c**) *persona* difficult, awkward, full of silly objections.

difracción *nf* diffraction.

difractar [1a] *vt* to diffract.

difteria *nf* diphtheria.

difuminadamente *adv* sketchily.

difuminado *adj voz* slurred, husky; *representación* sketchy, vague, barely outlined.

difuminar [1a] **1** *vt dibujo* to blur. **2 difuminarse** *vr* (**a**) **~ en** to shade into. (**b**) (*fig*) to fade away; to evaporate.

difundir [3a] **1** *vt color, luz* to diffuse; *noticia* to spread, disseminate; to divulge, circulate; (*Rad*) to broadcast, transmit; *gas etc* to give off, give out, emit; **~ la alegría** to spread happiness, radiate happiness.

2 difundirse *vr* to spread (out); to become diffused.

difunto 1 *adj* dead, deceased; **el ~ ministro** the late minister.

2 *nm*, **difunta** *nf* dead person, deceased person; **la familia del ~** the family of the deceased; **Día de (los) D~s** All Souls' Day.

difusión *nf* (**a**) (*acto*) diffusion; spread(ing), dissemination; divulging, circulation; (*Prensa*) circulation, readership figures; **diario de ~ nacional** newspaper distributed nationally, newspaper having a nation-wide distribution. (**b**) (*cualidad*) diffuseness.

difuso *adj* (**a**) *luz* diffused; *conocimiento etc* widespread, widely extended. (**b**) *estilo etc* diffuse, wordy, discursive.

difusor *nm* blow-drier.

digerible *adj* digestible.

digerir [3i] *vt* (**a**) *comida* to digest; (*tragar*) to swallow.

(**b**) (*Quím*) to digest, absorb, dissolve.

(**c**) (*fig*) *opiniones etc* to digest, absorb, assimilate; to ponder, think over; (*en locuciones negativas*) to swallow, stomach; **no puedo ~ a ese tío** I can't stand that chap.

digestible *adj* digestible.

digestión *nf* digestion.

digestivo *adj* digestive.

digesto *m* (*Jur etc*) digest.

digitación *nf* (*Mús*) fingering.

digital 1 *adj* (**a**) digital; finger (*atr*); **impresión ~** fingerprint. (**b**) (*hum*) *V* **dedo (a dedo)**. **2** *nf* (*Bot*) foxglove; (*droga*) digitalis.

digitalizador *nm* digitizer.

digitalizar [1f] *vt* to digitalize.

digitalmente *adv* (**a**) digitally. (**b**) (*hum*) *V* **dedo (a dedo)**.

dígito *nm* digit; **~ binario** binary digit; **~ de control** check digit.

diglosia *nf* diglossia.

dignación *nf* condescension.

dignamente *adv* (**a**) (*gen*) worthily; fittingly, properly, appropriately. (**b**) (*honradamente*) honourably. (**c**) (*con dignidad*) with dignity, in a dignified way. (**d**) (*decentemente*) decently.

dignarse [1a] *vr*: **~** + *infin* (**a**) (*condescender*) to deign to + *infin*, condescend to + *infin*.

(**b**) (*fórmulas*) please ...; **dígnese venir a esta oficina** please (be so good as to) come to this office.

dignatario, -a *nm/f* dignitary.

dignidad *nf* (**a**) (*cualidad*) dignity; honour; self-respect; **herir la ~ de uno** to offend sb's self-respect.

(**b**) (*puesto*) post, office; (*categoría*) rank; **tiene ~ de ministro** he has the rank of a minister.

(**c**) (*persona*) dignitary, worthy.

dignificar [1g] *vt* to dignify.

digno *adj* (**a**) (*merecedor*) worthy; (*conveniente*) fitting; proper, appropriate; **~ de** worthy of, deserving; **~ de elogio** praiseworthy; **~ de toda alabanza** thoroughly praiseworthy, highly commendable; **~ de mención** worth a mention, worth mentioning; **un ~ castigo** a fitting punishment; **es ~ de nuestra admiración** it deserves our admiration; **es ~ de verse** it is worth seeing.

(**b**) (*honrado*) *etc* worthy, upright, honourable.

(**c**) (*grave*) dignified.

(**d**) (*decoroso*) decent; **viviendas dignas para los obreros** decent homes for the workers.

digresión *nf* digression.

dije[1] *etc V* **decir.**

dije[2] **1** *nm* (**a**) (*medallón*) medallion; (*relicario*) locket; (*amuleto*) amulet, charm; (*pey*) trinket. (**b**) (*fig*) gem, treasure, person of sterling qualities. (**c**) **~s*** boasting, bravado. **2** *adj* (*Cono Sur*) (**a**) (*guapo*) good-looking. (**b**) (*encantador*) nice, sweet, charming.

dilación *nf* delay; **sin ~** without delay, forthwith; **esto no admite ~** this must suffer no delay, this is most urgent.

dilapidación *nf* squandering, waste.

dilapidar [1a] *vt* to squander, waste.

dilatación *nf* (**a**) (*gen*) dilation; expansion (*t Fís*), enlargement, widening, stretching; protraction, prolongation. (**b**) (*fig*) calm, calm dignity.

dilatado *adj pupila* dilated; (*extenso*) vast, extensive, spacious; (*numeroso*) numerous; *período* long-drawn-out; *discurso etc* long-winded, discursive.

dilatar [1a] **1** *vt* (**a**) *pupila* to dilate; *metal* to expand; (*ampliar*) to enlarge, widen; (*extender*) to stretch, extend; *fama etc* to spread.

(**b**) (*en tiempo*) to protract, prolong, stretch out.

(**c**) *diferir* to delay, put off.

2 *vi* (*Méx*) to be delayed, be late.

3 dilatarse *vr* (**a**) to dilate; to expand (*t Fís*); to stretch, extend; to spread; **la llanura se dilata hasta el horizonte** the plain spreads (*o* extends, rolls) right to the horizon; **el valle se dilata en aquella parte** the valley widens (*o* spreads out) at that point.

(**b**) (*al hablar*) to be long-winded, be discursive; **~ en, ~ sobre** to expatiate on; to linger over, take one's time over.

(**c**) (*LAm*: *demorarse*) to delay, be slow; (*tren etc*) to be late; **~ en** + *infin* to take a long time to + *infin*, be slow to + *infin*.

dilatorias *nfpl* procrastination; delaying tactics; **andar en ~ con uno, traer a uno en ~** to use delaying tactics with sb, hedge with sb; **no me vengas con ~** don't hedge with me.

dilatorio *adj* delaying, dilatory.

dilección *nf* affection.

dilema *nm* dilemma; **estar en un ~** to be in a dilemma.

diletante *nmf* dilettante.

diligencia *nf* (**a**) (*cualidad*) diligence, care; assiduity; speed, dispatch.

(**b**) (*negocio*) piece of business; (*encargo*) errand, job, mission; **hacer ~s** to do business; **hacer una ~** to run an errand, go on an errand; (‡) to do one's business‡; **hacer las ~s de costumbre** to take the usual steps; **practicar sus ~s** to make every possible effort, do one's utmost (*para* + *infin* to + *infin*).

(**c**) (*Jur*) **~s** formalities; inquiries; steps (of an investigation *etc*); **~s judiciales** judicial proceedings; **~s previas** inquiries; **instruir ~s** to start proceedings.

(**d**) (*Hist*) stagecoach.

diligenciado *nm*, **diligenciamiento** *nm* processing.

diligenciar [1b] *vt asunto* to see about, deal with; to further, get moving; *documento, solicitud* to process, deal with.

diligente *adj* (*aplicado*) diligent; (*asiduo*) industrious, assiduous; (*pronto*) quick, speedy, prompt; **un alumno poco ~** a slack pupil, a lazy pupil.
diligentemente *adv* diligently; industriously; assiduously; speedily.
dilucidar [1a] *vt* to elucidate, explain, clarify; *caso, misterio etc* to solve, clear up; *concurso* to decide, determine.
dilución *nf* dilution.
diluido *adj* dilute; diluted, weak; watered-down.
diluir [3g] *vt* to dilute; to water down, weaken; (*fig*) to water down.
diluvial *adj* torrential.
diluviar [1b] *vi* to pour with rain, rain in torrents.
diluvio *nm* deluge, flood (*t fig*); **el D~** the Flood; **un ~ de cartas** a deluge of letters; **¡fue el ~!** it was chaos!; **¡esto es el ~!** what a mess!
dimanar [1a] *vi* to flow; (*fig*) **~ de** to arise from, spring from, stem from.
dimensión *nf* (**a**) (*Mat*) dimension (*t fig*); size; **cuarta ~** fourth dimension; **de grandes dimensiones** of great size, of large dimensions; **tomar las dimensiones de** to take the measurements of.
(**b**) (*fig: cualidad de persona*) stature, standing; **un matemático de ~ universal** a mathematician of world stature.
dimensionado *nm* measuring; assessment.
dimes *nmpl*: **~ y diretes** (*riñas*) bickering, squabbling; (*chismes*) gossip; (*intriga*) petty intrigue; **andar en ~ y diretes con uno** to bicker (*o* squabble) with sb.
diminutivo *adj, nm* diminutive.
diminuto *adj* (**a**) (*pequeño*) tiny, minute, exceedingly small; miniature. (**b**) (*imperfecto*) defective, imperfect.
dimisión *nf* resignation; **presentar la ~** to send in (*o* tender *o* submit) one's resignation.
dimisionar [1a] = **dimitir.**
dimisionario, -a *nm/f* person resigning, person who has resigned.
dimitente 1 *adj* resigning, outgoing, retiring; **el presidente ~** the outgoing chairman, the retiring chairman. **2** *nmf* person resigning.
dimitir [3a] **1** *vt* (**a**) *cargo* to resign; to give up, relinquish; **~ la jefatura del partido** to resign (from) the party leadership. (**b**) *persona* to dismiss, sack*. **2** *vi* to resign (*de* from).
din* *nm* dough‡; **el ~ y el don** money and rank, dough and dukedom‡.
Dinamarca *nf* Denmark.
dinamarqués = **danés.**
dinámica *nf* (*la ~*) dynamics; (*una ~*) dynamic; **~ de grupo** group dynamics.
dinamicidad *nf* dynamism.
dinámico *adj* dynamic.
dinamismo *nm* dynamism.
dinamita *nf* dynamite.
dinamitar [1a] *vt* to dynamite.
dinamitazo *nm* dynamite explosion; dynamiting.
dinamizador *adj* revitalizing.
dinamizar [1f] *vt* to invigorate, put (new) energy into; to stir into action.
dínamo *nf*, **dinamo** *nf* (*a veces m en LAm*) dynamo.
dinastía *nf* dynasty.
dinástico *adj* dynastic.
dinerada *nf*, **dineral** *nm* fortune, mint of money; **habrá costado un dineral** it must have cost a fortune.
dinerario *adj* money (*atr*); **aportación no dineraria** non-cash contribution.
dinerillo* *nm* small amount of money; pocket money, pin money; **tiene sus ~s** she's got a bit of money (put by).
dinero *nm* (*gen*) money; (*de país, período etc*) currency, coinage, money; **persona de ~** moneyed person, wealthy person; **es hombre de ~** he is a man of means; **¿cuánto es en ~ americano?** how much is that in American money?; **~ de bolsillo** pocket-money; **~ en caja** cash in hand; **~ por callar** hush money*; **~ caliente** hot money; **~ contante** cash; **~ contante y sonante** cash, ready money; **~ de curso legal** legal tender; **~ negro, ~ sucio** undeclared earnings; money proceeding from crime; **~ (de) plástico** plastic money; **los ~s del sacristán cantando se vienen y cantando se van** easy come easy go; **el ~ malo echa fuera al bueno** bad money drives out good; **el ~ lo puede todo, el ~ puede mucho** money can do anything, money talks; **andar mal de ~** to be badly off, be in financial difficulties; **el negocio no da ~** the business does not pay, the business is not profitable, the business is not a paying proposition; **ganar ~ a espuertas** (*o* **a porrillo**) to make money hand over fist.
dingui *nm* dinghy.
dinosaurio 1 *nm* dinosaur. **2** *adj* dinosaurian; **un coche ~** a car from the Stone Age.
dintel *nm* lintel; (*LAm*) threshold.
diñar‡ [1a] *vt* to give; **~la** to kick the bucket‡; **diñársela a uno** to swindle sb.
diocesano *adj* diocesan.
diócesi(s) *nf, pl* **diócesis** diocese.
diodo *nm* diode.
dionisiaco *adj*, **dionisíaco** *adj* Dionysian.
Dionisio *nm* Denis; (*clásico*) Dionysius.
dioptría *nf* (*ojos, gafas*) dioptre; **~s** gradation.
Dios *nm* (**a**) (*Rel*) God; **~ delante** with God's help; **~ mediante** God willing, D.V.; **a ~ gracias** thank heaven; **a la buena de ~** at random; thoughtlessly, without preparation; trusting to luck; any old how*; **a la de ~ (es Cristo)*** rashly; **una de ~ es Cristo*** an almighty row*; **armar la de ~ es Cristo*** to raise hell, cause a tremendous fuss; **esto clama a ~** this cries out to heaven (to be reformed *etc*); **~ los cría y ellos se juntan** birds of a feather flock together; **dar a ~ lo que es de ~ y al César lo que es del César** render unto Caesar that which is Caesar's and unto God that which is God's; **lo hace como ~ le da a entender** he does it as best he can, he does it according to his lights; **como ~ manda** as is proper; properly, well; **si ~ quiere** God willing, D.V.; **donde ~ pasó de largo** a godforsaken spot; **cuando ~ quiera** all in God's good time; **a ~ rogando y con el mazo dando** trust in God but keep your powder dry; **~ sabe** God knows; **sólo ~ sabe** God alone knows; **sabe ~ que no quería ofender** God knows I did not intend to cause offence; **vaya con ~** goodbye; (*ceremonioso*) may God be with you; (*iró*) and good riddance, and the best of luck; **le vino ~ a ver** he struck lucky, he had a stroke of luck.
(**b**) (*excl*) **¡~ mío!** good gracious!, good heavens!; well!; **¡por ~!** for God's sake!; **¿puedo fumar? — pero ¡por ~!** may I smoke? — please do!; **¡~ le ampare!, ¡~ le asista!, ¡~ te la depare buena!** (*iró*) I hope it keeps fine for you!, and the best of luck!; **¡~ le ayude!** (*al estornudar*) bless you!; **¡~ te bendiga!** God bless you!; **¡~ me libre!** Heaven forbid!; **¡líbreme ~ de ...!** Heaven forbid that I ...!; **¡plegue a ~!** please God!; **¡no lo quiera ~!** God forbid!; **¡válgame ~!** bless my soul!; **¡vaya por ~!** well I never!; I ask you!; **¡vive ~!** good God!
dios *nm* (**a**) god; idol; **los ~es paganos** the pagan gods. (**b**) (*) **como todo ~** like any guy; **no hay ~ que entienda eso** nobody can understand that; **no había ni ~** there wasn't a soul.
diosa *nf* goddess.
dióxido *nm* dioxide; **~ de carbono** carbon dioxide; **~ de nitrógeno** nitrogen dioxide.
dioxina *nf* dioxin.
Dip. *abr de* **Diputación** ≈ County Council, CC.
diploma *nm* diploma.
diplomacia *nf* diplomacy; **~ de cañoneras** gunboat diplomacy.
diplomado 1 *adj* qualified, trained, having a diploma. **2** *nm*, **diplomada** *nf* qualified person, holder of a diploma.
diplomarse [1a] *vr* (*esp LAm*) to graduate (from college *etc*).
diplomática¹ *nf* (**a**) (*Hist, Jur*) diplomatics. (**b**) (*Pol: cuerpo*) diplomatic corps; (*carrera*) diplomatic career, (career in the) foreign service.
diplomáticamente *adv* diplomatically.
diplomático 1 *adj* diplomatic. **2** *nm*, **diplomática²** *nf* diplomat; (*fig*) diplomatist.
diplomatura *nf* diploma course, course leading to a diploma.
dipsomanía *nf* dipsomania.
dipsomaníaco, -a *nm/f*, **dipsómano, -a** *nm/f* dipsomaniac.
díptero *nm* fly.
díptico *nm* diptych; (*Com*) folder, brochure, leaflet.
diptongar [1h] *vti* to diphthongize.
diptongo *nm* diphthong.
diputación *nf* (**a**) (*gen*) deputation, delegation; (*Admin*) committee; **~ permanente** (*Parl*) standing committee.
(**b**) **D~ General** (*Aragón, Rioja*) regional government; **~ provincial** (*personas*) ≈ county council; (*oficina*) ≈ county council offices.
diputado, -a *nm/f* delegate, representative; (*Parl*) deputy, member of parliament, representative (*US*); **~ a Cortes**

(*Esp*) parliamentary deputy, member of the Spanish *Cortes;* **el ~ por Guadalajara** the member for Guadalajara; **~ provincial** ≈ member of a county council.

diputar [1a] *vt* (*delegar*) to delegate, depute; (*autorizar*) to empower.

dique *nm* (**a**) (*marítimo*) dike, sea wall; (*muelle*) jetty, mole; (*rompeolas*) breakwater; (*dársena*) dock; **~ de contención** dam; **~ flotante** floating dock; **~ seco** dry dock; **estar en el ~** (*fig*) to be out of action; (**hacer**) **entrar en ~** to dock.

(**b**) (*fig*) check; barrier; **es un ~ contra la expansión** it is a barrier to expansion; **poner un ~ a** to check, restrain.

diquelar‡ [1a] *vt* (**a**) (*ver*) to see; (*mirar*) to look at, watch; (*vigilar*) to watch over, keep an eye on. (**b**) (*comprender*) to twig*, catch on to.

Dir. (**a**) *abr de* **dirección.** (**b**) *abr de* **director** director, dir.

dire* *nmf* = **director, directora.**

diré *etc V* **decir.**

dirección *nf* (**a**) (*gen: sentido*) direction; way; (*fig: tendencia*) course, trend; **~ del viento** wind direction; **con ~ norte** in a northerly direction; **con ~ a, en ~ a, en la ~ de** in the direction of; towards; **'~ prohibida'** (*Aut*) 'no entry', 'no thoroughfare'; **calle de ~ obligatoria, calle de ~ única** one-way street; (*Aut: de autopista*) **~ este** eastbound; **~ oeste** westbound; **calle de 2 direcciones** street with two-way traffic; **conmutador de 2 direcciones** two-way switch; **cambiar de ~** to change direction; **¿podría Vd indicarme la ~ de ...?** could you please direct me to ...?; **salir con ~ a** to leave for, depart for; to go off in the direction of; **salir con ~ desconocida** to leave for an unknown destination.

(**b**) (*acto: gobierno etc*) direction; guidance; control; (*Com etc*) running, management; (*Pol*) leadership; **~ colectiva, ~ colegiada** collective leadership; **~ empresarial** business management; **~ escénica, ~ de escena** stage management; **bajo la ~ de** under the direction of; **asumir la ~, tomar la ~** to take (over) control; **me han confiado la ~ de la obra** I have been put in charge of the work; **la revista de su digna ~** the journal which you edit.

(**c**) (*personal*) management; (*junta*) board of directors; (*Pol*) leadership; **habrá cambios en la ~ del partido** there will be changes in the party leadership, there will be changes among the party's top people.

(**d**) (*puesto*) directorship; post of manager; (*de colegio*) headship; (*de periódico*) editorship; (*Mús*) conductorship.

(**e**) (*Aut etc*) steering; **~ asistida** power steering; **de ~** steering (*atr*).

(**f**) (*oficina*) (head) office, administrative office; **D~ General de Turismo** State Tourist Office; **D~ General de Seguridad** State Security Office (*o* Service); **~ provincial** provincial office of a government department.

(**g**) (*Correos, Inform*) address; **~ comercial** business address; **~ del remitente** return address; **ponga claramente su ~** write your address clearly.

direccional 1 *adj* directional. **2 ~es** *nmpl* indicator lights.

direccionamiento *nm* (*Inform*) addressing.

direccionar [1a] *vt* (*Inform*) to address; to operate.

directa *nf* (*Aut*) top gear.

directamente *adv* directly.

directiva *nf* board of directors; governing body.

directivo 1 *adj junta etc* managing, governing; directorial; *función* managerial, administrative; *clase* managerial, executive.

2 *nm* (**a**) (*Com etc*) manager, executive; **un congreso de los ~s de la industria** a conference of executives from the industry.

(**b**) (*norma*) directive; guideline.

directo 1 *adj* (**a**) (*gen*) direct; *línea* straight; (*inmediato*) immediate; *acción, manera, traducción etc* direct.

(**b**) (*Ferro etc*) through, non-stop; (*Aer*) non-stop.

(**c**) (*TV*) *programa, vista* live; **entrevista en ~** live interview, interview broadcast live; **transmitir en ~** to broadcast live.

2 *nm* (*Boxeo*) straight punch; (*Tenis*) forehand shot (*o* drive *etc*).

director 1 *adj* (*f:* **directriz**) leading; controlling; guiding; = **directivo.**

2 *nm* director; (*Com etc*) director; manager, executive; (*Cine, TV*) director; (*Mús*) conductor; (*de colegio*) headmaster; principal; (*de escuela normal etc*) principal; (*Univ*) (*de colegio*) master; (*de residencia*) warden; (*de cárcel*) governor; (*de periódico*) editor; (*de Academia*) president; **~ adjunto** assistant manager; **~ de cine** film director; **~ comercial, ~ de márketing** marketing manager; **~ ejecutivo** executive director; **~ de empresa** company director; **~ de escena** stage manager; producer; **~ espiritual** father confessor; **~ de exportación** export manager; **~ de finanzas** financial director; **~ de funeraria** undertaker, funeral director, mortician (*US*); **~ general** general manager; **~ gerente** managing director; **~ de hotel** hotel manager; **~ de interiores** (*TV*) studio director; **~ de orquesta** conductor; **~ de personal** personnel manager; **~ de promoción** development officer; **~ de tesis** thesis supervisor, research supervisor; **~ de ventas** sales manager.

directora *nf* director; (*Com etc*) director; manageress (*V t* **director**); (*de colegio*) headmistress; principal; (*Univ*) (*de colegio*) mistress, (*de residencia*) warden.

directorial *adj* (*Com etc*) managing, executive; directorial; **clase ~** managers, management, executive class.

directorio *nm* (**a**) (*norma*) directive, instructions.

(**b**) (*junta*) directors, board of directors, directorate.

(**c**) (*libro*) directory; **~ de teléfonos** (*Méx*) telephone directory.

(**d**) (*Inform*) directory; **~ principal** root directory.

directriz 1 *adj f V* **director 1. 2** *nf* guideline, instruction, directive.

dirigencia *nf* leadership.

dirigente 1 *adj* leading. **2** *nm* (*Pol etc*) leader.

dirigible 1 *adj* (*Aer*) dirigible; (*Náut*) navigable, capable of being steered. **2** *nm* dirigible.

dirigido *adj misil* guided.

dirigir [3c] **1** *vt* (**a**) (*gen*) to direct (*a, hacia* at, to, towards); *acusación* to level (*a* at), make (*a* against); *carta, observación, pregunta, protesta* to address (*a* to); *libro* to dedicate (*a* to); *mirada* to direct (*a* towards), turn (*a* on); *manga* to play, turn (*a* on); *cañón, telescopio etc* to aim, point (*a* at).

(**b**) (*Com etc*) *empresa* to manage; to run, operate; *expedición, partido, rebelión* to lead, head; *periódico, serie etc* to edit; *tesis, trabajo etc* to direct, supervise; *juego* to control, referee.

(**c**) (*guiar*) *persona* to direct; to guide, advise (*en* about, in); *curso de acción* to direct, shape; *esfuerzos* to direct (*a* towards), concentrate (*a* on).

(**d**) (*Aut, Náut*) to steer; (*Aut*) to drive.

(**e**) (*Mús*) to conduct.

(**f**) (*Cine, Teat*) to produce, direct.

2 dirigirse *vr*: **~ a** (**a**) (*ir hacia*) to go to, make one's way to; to head for; to turn towards; (*Náut etc*) to steer for, head for; **~ hacia** to head for.

(**b**) (*fig: hablar a*) to speak to, address; to approach; **~ a uno solicitando algo** to apply to sb for sth; **se dirigió a mí en la calle** he spoke to me in the street; he accosted me in the street; (*anuncio*) **'diríjase a ...'** 'apply to ...', 'write to ...'

dirigismo *nm* management, control; dirigisme, interventionism; **~ estatal** state control.

dirigista *adj, nmf* interventionist.

dirimente *adj argumento etc* decisive; *voto* casting; *opinión, decisión* (*en competición etc*) final.

dirimir [3a] *vt* (**a**) *contrato, matrimonio etc* to dissolve, annul, declare void. (**b**) *disputa* to settle.

discada *nf* (*LAm*) collection of records.

discado *nm* (*Telec*) dialling; **~ directo** direct dialling.

discapacidad *nf* disability, (physical) handicap.

discapacitado 1 *adj* incapacitated, (physically) handicapped, disabled. **2** *nm,* **discapacitada** *nf* handicapped person, disabled person.

discapacitar [1a] *vt* to incapacitate, handicap.

discar [1g] *vti* (*Telec*) to dial.

discernidor *adj* discerning, discriminating.

discernimiento *nm* discernment, discrimination; judgement; **edad de ~** years of discretion.

discernir [3i] **1** *vt* (**a**) (*distinguir*) to discern, distinguish; **~ A de B** to distinguish A from B.

(**b**) (*Jur*) *tutor* to appoint.

(**c**) (*esp LAm*) *premio etc* to award (*a* to), confer (*a* on).

2 *vi*: **~ entre** to distinguish between, discriminate between.

disciplina *nf* (**a**) (*gen*) discipline; **~ férrea** iron discipline; **~ de voto** party discipline, party whip; **romper la ~ de voto** to vote against one's party. (**b**) (*azote: t* **~s**) whip, scourge. (**c**) **~ inglesa** (*hum*) beating, flagellation.

disciplinante *nmf* (*Rel*) flagellant, penitent.

disciplinar [1a] *vt* (**a**) (*gen*) to discipline. (**b**) (*entrenar*) to school, train; (*Mil*) to drill, train. (**c**) (*azotar*) to whip, scourge.

disciplinario *adj* disciplinary.

discipulado *nm* (**a**) (*Rel*) discipleship. (**b**) (*personas*) pupils, student body.

discípulo, -a *nm/f* pupil, student; (*Rel*) disciple; (*Filos etc*) follower.

disco[1] *nm* (**a**) (*gen*) disk, disc; (*Dep*) discus; (*Ferro*) signal; (*Aut*) traffic-light; (*Telec*) dial; (*Mús etc*) gramophone record, phonograph record (*US*); **~ compacto** compact disc; **~ de duración extendida** extended-play record (*EP*); **~ de larga duración, ~ microsurco** long-playing record (*LP*); **~ de freno** brake disc; **~ giratorio** turntable; **~ de marcar** (*Telec*) dial; **~ de oro** golden disc; **~ de platino** platinum disc; **~ rojo** red traffic-light; **~ sencillo** single; **~ volante** flying saucer; **cambiar de ~** (*fig*) to change one's tune.

(**b**) (*Inform*) disk; **~ de arranque** boot disk; **~ de cabeza fija** fixed-head disk; **~ duro, ~ fijo** hard disk; **~ flexible** floppy disk; **~ magnético** magnetic disk; **~ óptico** optical disk; **~ rígido** hard disk; **~ virtual** RAM disk.

(**c**) (*) boring affair; boring speech; tedious tale; **es un ~** it's a bore, it's so boring; **nos soltó el ~ una vez más** he told us the whole dreary tale again.

disco[2] *nf* (*sala de baile*) disco.

discóbolo, -a *nm/f* discus thrower.

discografía *nf* (**a**) (*gen*) records; (*discos*) collection of records; **la ~ de Eccles** the complete recordings of Eccles. (**b**) (*compañía*) record company.

discográfica *nf* record company.

discográfico *adj* record (*atr*); **casa discográfica** record company; **el momento ~ actual** the present state of the record industry.

díscolo *adj* uncontrollable, unruly; rebellious; *niño* mischievous; **~ a** resistant to.

disconforme *adj* differing; **estar ~** to be in disagreement (*con* with), not agree.

disconformidad *nf* disagreement.

discontinuidad *nf* lack of continuity, discontinuity.

discontinuo *adj* discontinuous.

discordancia *nf* discord (*t fig*).

discordante *adj* discordant (*t fig*).

discordar [1l] *vi* (**a**) (*Mús*) to be out of tune. (**b**) (*personas etc*) to disagree (*de* with), differ (*de* from); (*opiniones, colores etc*) to clash.

discorde *adj* (**a**) (*Mús*) *sonido* discordant, unharmonious; *instrumento* out of tune.

(**b**) (*fig*) discordant, differing; clashing; **estar ~s** (*personas*) to disagree, be in disagreement (*de* with).

discordia *nf* discord, disagreement.

discoteca *nf* (**a**) (*colección*) record library, record collection.

(**b**) (*sala de baile*) discothèque, disco.

(**c**) (*LAm*) record shop.

discotequero 1 *adj* disco (*atr*), discothèque (*atr*). **2** *nm*, **discotequera** *nf* frequenter of discothèques.

discreción *nf* (**a**) (*cualidad*) discretion, tact, good sense; discrimination; prudence; wisdom, sagacity, shrewdness.

(**b**) (*secreto*) secrecy.

(**c**) (*gracia*) wit; (*ocurrencia*) witticism.

(**d**) **a ~** at one's discretion; **añadir azúcar a ~** (*Culin*) add sugar to taste; **comer a ~** to eat as much as one likes; **con vino a ~** with as much wine as one wants; **rendirse a ~** to surrender unconditionally.

discrecional *adj poder* discretionary; (*de opción*) optional, not prescribed, within one's judgement; **parada ~** request stop.

discrecionalidad *nf* discretional nature.

discrepancia *nf* (*diferencia*) discrepancy; divergence; (*desacuerdo etc*) disagreement.

discrepante *adj* divergent; dissenting; **hubo varias voces ~s** there were some dissenting voices, some were not in agreement.

discrepar [1a] *vi* to differ (*de* from), disagree (*de* with); **discrepamos en varios puntos** we disagree on a number of points; **discrepo de esa opinión** I disagree with that view.

discretamente *adv* (**a**) (*diplomáticamente*) discreetly, tactfully, sensibly; (*con discriminación*) with discrimination; (*prudentemente*) prudently, shrewdly. (**b**) (*sobriamente*) soberly; (*en silencio*) quietly; (*modestamente*) unobtrusively.

discretear [1a] *vi* to try to be clever, be frightfully witty.

discreto *adj* (**a**) (*diplomático etc*) discreet, tactful, sensible; (*discernidor*) discriminating; (*sagaz*) prudent, wise, sagacious; shrewd.

(**b**) *vestido etc* sober, sensible; *color* quiet, sober; *posición etc* unobtrusive; *advertencia* discreet, gentle, tactful.

(**c**) (*mediano*) fair, middling, reasonable; **de inteligencia discreta** of reasonable intelligence, reasonably intelligent; **le daremos un plazo ~** we'll allow him a reasonable time; **la película es discreta** the film is quite good.

(**d**) (*Fís etc*) discreet.

discriminación *nf* (**a**) discrimination (*contra* against); **~ positiva** positive discrimination, affirmative action; **~ racial** racial discrimination; **~ sexual** sex discrimination. (**b**) (*descuido*) neglect.

discriminado *adj*: **sentirse ~** to feel that one has been unfairly treated, feel one has been discriminated against.

discriminar [1a] *vt* to discriminate against; to treat unfairly; *dos cosas* to differentiate between.

discriminatoriamente *adv* unfairly, in a biased way.

discriminatorio *adj* discriminatory; unfair, biased.

disculpa *nf* excuse; plea; apology.

disculpable *adj* excusable, pardonable.

disculpar [1a] **1** *vt* (*perdonar*) to excuse, pardon, forgive; to exonerate (*de falta* from blame); **¡disculpa!, ¡discúlpenme!** I'm sorry!; **disculpa el que venga tarde** forgive me for coming late; **le disculpan sus pocos años** his youth is an excuse, his youth provides an excuse; **te ruego ~me con el anfitrión** please make my apologies to the host.

2 disculparse *vr* to excuse o.s. (*de* from); to apologize (*por + infin* for + *ger*); **~ con uno por haber hecho algo** to apologize to sb for having done sth.

disculpativo *adj* apologetic.

discurrideras* *nfpl* wits, brains.

discurrir [3a] **1** *vt* to invent, think up, contrive; **esos chicos no discurren nada bueno** these lads must be cooking up sth nasty, these lads are up to no good.

2 *vi* (**a**) (*recorrer*) to roam, wander (*por* about, along).

(**b**) (*río*) to flow.

(**c**) (*tiempo*) to pass, flow by; (*vida, período, sesión*) to go, pass, be spent; **la sesión discurrió sin novedad** the meeting went off quietly; **el verano discurrió sin grandes calores** the summer passed without great heat.

(**d**) (*meditar*) to think, reason, meditate (*en* about, on); (*hablar*) to speak, discourse (*sobre* about, on); **discurre poco, discurre menos que un mosquito** he just never thinks.

discursear [1a] *vi* to speechify.

discurso *nm* (**a**) (*oración*) speech, address, discourse; **~ de clausura** closing speech; **~ directo** direct speech; **~ indirecto** indirect speech; **~ de informe** (*Jur*) summing-up, address to the jury; **~ programático** ≈ Speech from the Throne, Queen's Speech; **~ referido** reported speech; **pronunciar un ~, dictar un ~** (*LAm*) to make (*o* deliver) a speech.

(**b**) (*tratado*) treatise.

(**c**) (*habla*) speech, faculty of speech.

(**d**) (*mental*) reasoning power, mental powers.

(**e**) (*tiempo*) period; passing, passage; **en el ~ del tiempo** with the passage of time; **en el ~ de 4 generaciones** in the space of 4 generations.

discusión *nf* (*diálogo*) discussion; (*riña*) argument; **~ de grupo, ~ en grupo** group discussion; **eso no admite ~** there can be no argument about that; **estar en ~** to be under discussion; **tener una ~** to have an argument.

discutibilidad *nf* debatable nature.

discutible *adj* debatable; disputed; arguable; **es ~ si ...** it is debatable whether ...; **de mérito algo ~** of somewhat dubious worth.

discutido *adj* much-discussed; controversial; **discutidísimo** highly controversial.

discutidor *adj* argumentative, disputatious.

discutir [3a] **1** *vt* (*debatir*) to discuss, debate, talk over; *precio etc* to argue about; (*contradecir*) to contradict, argue against, object to; **~ a uno lo que uno está diciendo** to contradict what sb is saying.

2 *vi* (*dialogar*) to discuss, talk; (*disputar*) to argue (*de, sobre* about, over); **~ de política** to argue about politics, talk politics; **¡no discutas!** don't argue!

discutón* *adj* argumentative; quarrelsome.

disecar [1g] *vt* (**a**) (*Med y fig*) to dissect. (**b**) (*para museo etc*) *animal* to stuff; *planta* to preserve, mount; *flor etc* to dry, press.

disección *nf* (*V v*) (**a**) dissection. (**b**) stuffing; preservation, mounting.

diseccionar [1a] *vt* (*fig*) to dissect, analyse.

diseminación *nf* dissemination, spread(ing), scattering; **~ nuclear** spread of nuclear weapons.

diseminar [1a] *vt* to disseminate, spread, scatter.

disensión *nf* dissension.

disentería *nf* dysentery.
disentimiento *nm* dissent, disagreement.
disentir [3k] *vi* to dissent (*de* from), disagree (*de* with).
diseñador(a) *nm/f* (*Téc, TV etc*) designer; **~ gráfico** commercial artist; **~ de moda(s)** fashion-designer, dress-designer.
diseñar [1a] *vt* (*Téc etc*) to design; (*Arte*) to draw, sketch; to outline.
diseño *nm* (*Téc etc*) design; (*Arte*) drawing, sketch; (*Cos etc*) pattern, design; (*con palabras*) sketch, outline; **el D~ Divino** the Divine Plan; **~ gráfico** graphic design; **~ industrial** industrial design; **~ asistido por ordenador** computer-assisted design; **camisa de ~** designer shirt.
disertación *nf* dissertation, disquisition, discourse.
disertar [1a] *vi* to speak, discourse; **~ acerca de, ~ sobre** to discourse upon, expound on, speak about; **~ largamente** to speak at length.
disfavor *nm* disfavour.
disforme *adj* (*mal hecho*) ill-proportioned, badly-proportioned; (*monstruoso*) monstrous, huge; (*feo*) ugly.
disforzado* *adj* (*And*) **(a)** (*santurrón*) prim, prudish. **(b)** (*descarado*) cheeky*.
disfraz *nm* **(a)** (*gen*) disguise; (*máscara*) mask; (*traje*) fancy dress; (*fig*) pretext, blind (*de* for); **baile de disfraces** fancy-dress ball; **bajo el ~ de** in the guise of; under the cloak of.
(b) **ser un ~*** to be out of place; to look all wrong.
disfrazado *adj*: **~ de** disguised as; in the guise of; **ir ~ de duque** to be made up like a duke; to masquerade as a duke.
disfrazar [1f] **1** *vt* (*gen*) to disguise; (*ocultar*) to cover up, mask, conceal, cloak; **~ a uno de lavandera** to disguise sb as a washerwoman, make sb up as a washerwoman.
2 disfrazarse *vr*: **~ de** to disguise o.s. as, make o.s. up as.
disfrutar [1a] **1** *vt* to enjoy; to make use of, have the benefit of.
2 *vi* **(a)** (*gozar*) to enjoy o.s., have a good time; **¡cómo disfruto!** I'm enjoying this!, this is the life!; **¡que disfrutes!** have a good time!; **~ como un enano** to have a great time, enjoy o.s. hugely; **~ con algo** to enjoy sth, benefit from sth; **siempre disfruto con los libros así** I always enjoy books of that sort.
(b) **~ de** to enjoy; to have, possess; **~ de buena salud** to enjoy good health; **disfruta de las rentas de su finca** he enjoys (*o* has) the income from his estate.
disfrute *nm* enjoyment; use; possession.
disfuerzo *nm* (*And*) **(a)** (*descaro*) impudence, effrontery. **(b)** (*remilgo*) prudishness. **(c)** **~s** threats, bravado.
disfunción *nf* malfunction, difficulty; defect.
disfuncionalidad *nf* malfunction.
disgregación *nf* disintegration; break(ing)-up; separation; dispersal.
disgregar [1h] **1** *vt* to disintegrate; to break up; to separate (*de* from); to sever (*de* from); *manifestantes* to disperse. **2 disgregarse** *vr* to disintegrate; to break up (*en* into).
disgustar [1a] **1** *vt* (*molestar*) to annoy, upset, displease; (*ofender*) to offend; **es un olor que me disgusta** it's a smell which upsets me; **me disgusta tener que repetirlo** it annoys me to have to repeat it, I don't like having to repeat it; **comprendí que le disgustaba mi presencia** I realized that my presence annoyed him; **estaba muy disgustado con el asunto** he was very upset about the affair.
2 disgustarse *vr* **(a)** (*enfadarse*) to be annoyed, get upset (*con, de* about); (*ofenderse*) to be displeased, be offended, feel hurt (*con, de* about); **~ de algo** to get bored with sth, get fed up with sth.
(b) (*2 personas*) to fall out; **~ con uno** to fall out with sb.
disgusto *nm* **(a)** (*enfado*) annoyance, displeasure; vexation; (*dolor*) grief, chagrin, sorrow; (*repugnancia*) repugnance; (*aburrimiento*) boredom; **a ~** unwillingly, against one's will; **con gran ~ mío** much to my annoyance.
(b) (*un ~*) (*dificultad*) trouble, bother, difficulty; (*percance*) unpleasant experience; (*desgracia*) misfortune; (*golpe*) blow, shock; **reírse de los ~s del prójimo** to laugh at a fellow man's troubles (*o* misfortunes); **me causó un gran ~** it was a great blow to me; it upset me very much; **dar un ~ a uno** to upset sb; **nunca nos dio un ~** he never gave us any trouble; **llevarse un ~** to be upset; **han de sobrevenir ~s** there's trouble ahead; **matar a uno a ~s** to wear sb out with burdens, heap troubles on sb; **sentirse a ~** (*Méx*) to feel (*o* be) ill at ease (*o* uncomfortable).
(c) (*riña*) quarrel, upset; **tener un ~ con uno** to have a quarrel with sb, fall out with sb.
disidencia *nf* dissidence, disagreement; (*Ecl*) dissent.
disidente **1** *adj* dissident; dissenting. **2** *nmf* dissident person (*o* element *etc*); (*Ecl*) dissenter, nonconformist.
disidir [3a] *vi* to dissent.
disílabo **1** *adj* disyllabic. **2** *nm* disyllable.
disímil *adj* not alike, dissimilar.
disimulación *nf* dissimulation; furtiveness; cunning.
disimuladamente *adv* furtively; cunningly, slyly; covertly.
disimulado *adj* (*solapado*) furtive; underhand; (*taimado*) cunning, sly; (*oculto*) covert; **hacerse el ~** to dissemble; to pretend not to notice (*etc*); **hacer la disimulada** to feign ignorance.
disimular [1a] **1** *vt* **(a)** (*ocultar*) to hide; (*fig*) to hide, cloak, disguise; *emoción, intención etc* to conceal.
(b) (*disculpar*) to excuse; (*pasar por alto*) to condone, overlook; (*tolerar*) to tolerate; *ofensa etc* to pass off; *persona etc* to be lenient to, behave tolerantly towards; **te ruego ~ la indiscreción** please pardon the liberty; **disimula mi atrevimiento** forgive me if I have been too bold.
2 *vi* to dissemble, pretend.
disimulo *nm* **(a)** (*fingimiento*) dissimulation; furtiveness; craftiness; **con ~** cunningly, craftily. **(b)** (*tolerancia*) indulgence, tolerance.
disimulón* *adj* furtive, shady.
disipación *nf* dissipation.
disipado *adj* **(a)** (*disoluto*) dissipated; rakish, raffish. **(b)** (*derrochador*) extravagant, spendthrift.
disipador *nm* spendthrift.
disipar [1a] **1** *vt* **(a)** *niebla etc* to drive away, cause to disappear, dispel.
(b) *duda etc* to dispel, remove; *esperanza* to destroy.
(c) *dinero* to squander, fritter away (*en* on).
2 disiparse *vr* **(a)** (*humo etc*) to vanish; to evaporate.
(b) (*duda etc*) to be dispelled, vanish.
disjunto *adj* separate, discrete.
diskette *nm* floppy disk.
dislate *nm* absurdity, silly thing; **~s** nonsense.
dislexia *nf* dyslexia.
disléxico, -a *adj, nm/f* dyslexic.
dislocación *nf* (*gen*) dislocation; (*Med*) dislocation, sprain; (*Geol*) slip, fault.
dislocado *adj* (*fig*) unsettled, restless.
dislocar [1g] *vt* to dislocate; to sprain.
disloque* *nm* **(a)** **es el ~** it's the limit, it's the last straw; **fue el ~** (*hum*) it was the great moment, it was the crowning touch. **(b)** confusion; maladjustment; inappropriateness.
disminución *nf* **(a)** diminution, decrease (*de* of), fall (*de* in); **proceso de ~ de réditos** law of diminishing returns; **continuar sin ~** to continue unchecked, continue unabated; **ir en ~** to diminish, be on the decrease. **(b)** (*Med*) handicap.
disminuido **1** *adj* (*Med*) crippled, handicapped. **2** *nm*, **disminuida** *nf* (*Med*) cripple, handicapped person; **~ físico** physically-handicapped person; **~ psíquico** mentally-handicapped person.
disminuir [3g] *vti* to diminish, decrease, lessen.
Disneylandia *nf* Disneyland (*t fig*).
disociación *nf* dissociation.
disociar [1b] **1** *vt* to dissociate, separate (*de* from). **2 disociarse** *vr* to dissociate o.s. (*de* from).
disoluble *adj* dissoluble, soluble.
disolución *nf* **(a)** (*acto*) dissolution (*t Parl*). **(b)** (*Quím*) solution; **~ de goma** rubber solution. **(c)** (*Com*) liquidation. **(d)** (*moral*) dissoluteness, dissipation.
disoluto *adj* dissolute, dissipated.
disolvente *nm* solvent, thinner.
disolver [2h; *ptp* **disuelto**] **1** *vt* **(a)** (*gen*) to dissolve; (*fundir*) to melt (down).
(b) *contrato, matrimonio* to dissolve; (*Parl*) to dissolve; *manifestación etc* to break up; (*Mil*) to disband.
2 disolverse *vr* **(a)** (*fundirse*) to dissolve, melt.
(b) (*Com*) to be dissolved, go into liquidation; (*Parl*) to dissolve.
disonancia *nf* **(a)** (*Mús*) dissonance. **(b)** (*fig*) discord, disharmony; **hacer ~ con** to be out of harmony with.
disonante *adj* **(a)** (*Mús*) dissonant, discordant. **(b)** (*fig*) discordant.
disonar [1l] *vi* **(a)** (*Mús*) to be discordant, be out of harmony, be out of tune; (*palabra etc*) to sound wrong; **no me disuena** it is not unfamiliar to me.

(**b**) (*fig: no armonizar*) to lack harmony; (*estar en desacuerdo*) to disagree; ~ **con** to be out of keeping with, clash with.

dísono *adj* discordant.

dispar *adj* unlike, different, disparate.

disparada *nf* (*LAm*) sudden flight, stampede, wild rush; **ir a la** ~ to go at full speed; **irse a la** ~ to be off like a shot; **de una** ~ (*Cono Sur*) in a trice, instantly; **tomar la** ~‡ (*Cono Sur*) to beat it*.

disparadero *nm* trigger, trigger mechanism; **poner a uno en el** ~ to drive sb to distraction, make sb resort to violence.

disparado *adj* (**a**) **entrar** ~ to shoot in; **salir** ~ to shoot out, be off like a shot; **ir** ~ to go like mad, go hell for leather.
(**b**) (*Carib*‡) randy*, horny‡.

disparador 1 *adj* (*Méx*) lavish. **2** *nm* (*Mil etc*) trigger; (*Fot, Téc*) release; (*de reloj*) escapement; ~ **de bombas** bomb release.

disparar [1a] **1** *vt* (**a**) *cañon, cohete etc* to shoot, fire (*a, contra* at); *piedra* to throw, hurl, let fly (*contra* at); (*Dep*) *balón* to shoot (*a* at, *en* into).
(**b**) *consumo, precio* to cause to shoot up, increase excessively.
2 *vi* (**a**) (*tirar*) to shoot, fire; **¡disparad!** fire!; ~ **a una distancia de 5 metros** to fire at a range of 5 metres; ~ **a matar** to shoot to kill.
(**b**) = **disparatar.**
(**c**) (*Méx**: *gastar dinero*) to spend lavishly.
3 dispararse *vr* (**a**) (*cañon*) to go off; (*pestillo etc*) to be released.
(**b**) (*persona*) to rush off, dash away; *V* **disparado.**
(**c**) (*caballo etc*) to bolt; (*consumo, precios*) to shoot up.
(**d**) (*enfadarse*) to lose control, blow one's top*; **¡no te dispares!** take it easy!

disparatadamente *adv* absurdly, nonsensically.

disparatado *adj* absurd, crazy, nonsensical.

disparatar [1a] *vi* (*hablar*) to talk nonsense; (*hacer*) to do something silly, blunder.

disparate *nm* (**a**) (*dicho*) foolish remark, (*idea*) silly idea; (*acto*) absurd thing (to do); (*error*) blunder, crass mistake; ~**s** nonsense; **¡no digas ~s!** don't talk nonsense!; **¡qué ~!** what rubbish!, how absurd!; **hiciste un ~ protestando** it was silly of you to complain.
(**b**) **reírse un** ~ to laugh a lot; **costar un** ~ to cost a fortune.
(**c**) (*Arquit*) folly.

disparidad *nf* disparity.

disparo *nm* (**a**) (*tiro*) shot; report; (*de cohete*) firing; (*Dep*) shot; ~**s** shots, shooting, exchange of shots; ~ **de advertencia,** ~ **de amonestación,** ~ **de intimidación** warning shot, (*Náut*) shot across the bows; ~ **inicial** (*de cohete*) blast-off.
(**b**) (*Mec*) release, trip.
(**c**) (*fig*) = **disparate.**

dispendiador *adj* free-spending, big-spending.

dispendio *nm* waste; extravagance.

dispendioso *adj* expensive.

dispensa *nf* exemption, excusal (*de* from); (*Ecl*) dispensation.

dispensabilidad *nf* dispensable nature.

dispensable *adj* dispensable.

dispensación *nf* dispensation.

dispensador *nm* dispenser.

dispensadora *nf*: ~ **de monedas** change machine.

dispensar [1a] **1** *vt* (**a**) (*dar, repartir*) to dispense; to give out, distribute; *honor* to give, grant; *atención* to pay; *ayuda* to give; *acogida etc* to give, accord.
(**b**) (*eximir*) to excuse, exempt (*de* from); *persona, falta etc* to excuse, pardon; **¡Vd dispense!, ¡dispénseme Vd!** I beg your pardon!, do forgive me!; ~ **a uno de una obligación** to excuse sb (from) an obligation; **me dispensaron la multa, me dispensaron del pago de la multa** they excused me (from payment of) the fine; ~ **a uno de** + *infin* to excuse sb from + *ger*, relieve sb of the need to + *infin*; ~ **que uno** + *subj* to excuse sb for + *ger*; **así el cuerpo queda dispensado de ese esfuerzo** thus the body is freed from that effort (*o* relieved of that effort).
2 dispensarse *vr*: **no puedo dispensarme de esa obligación** I cannot escape that duty.

dispensario *nm* dispensary; clinic.

dispepsia *nf* dyspepsia.

dispéptico *adj* dyspeptic.

dispersar [1a] **1** *vt* to disperse, scatter; (*Mil*) to rout; *manifestación etc* to break up, disperse. **2 dispersarse** *vr* to disperse, scatter; to break up.

dispersión *nf* dispersion, dispersal; (*Fís*) dispersion.

disperso *adj* scattered; dispersed; sparse; (*Mil*) separated, straggling.

displicencia *nf* (**a**) (*mal humor*) peevishness, bad temper.
(**b**) (*desgana*) lack of enthusiasm; indifference.

displicente *adj* (**a**) (*malhumorado*) disagreeable, peevish, bad-tempered; fretful. (**b**) (*poco entusiasta*) unenthusiastic, lukewarm; (*indiferente*) indifferent.

disponer [2q] **1** *vt* (**a**) (*arreglar*) to arrange, dispose; to lay out; (*ordenar*) to put in order; (*alinear*) to line up.
(**b**) (*preparar*) to prepare, get ready.
(**c**) (*mandar*) to order, decide; (*Med*) *régimen etc* to order; ~ **que** ... to order that ..., arrange that ..., provide that ...; **la ley dispone que** ... the law provides that ...
2 *vi*: ~ **de** (**a**) (*tener*) to have, own; to have available, have at one's disposal; (*utilizar*) to make use of, avail o.s. of; **dispone de 2 coches** he has 2 cars; **disponemos de poco tiempo** we have very little time (at our disposal).
(**b**) (*utilizar*) to dispose of (as one wishes); **no puede** ~ **de esos bienes** she cannot dispose of those properties.
3 disponerse *vr*: ~ **a** + *infin*, ~ **para** + *infin* to prepare to + *infin*, get ready to + *infin*.

disponibilidad *nf* (**a**) (*gen*) availability; **empleado en** ~ unposted employee, employee available for posting. (**b**) ~**es** resources, means; ~**es líquidas** available liquid assets.

disponible *adj* available; on hand, spare; *renta* disposable.

disposición *nf* (**a**) (*arreglo*) arrangement, disposition; order; layout (*t Arquit, Inform*).
(**b**) (*ley etc*) order; (*cláusula*) provision, disposition; (*condición*) stipulation; **pasar a** ~ **judicial** to be taken into custody; ~ **transitoria** temporary provision; **según las disposiciones del código** according to the provisions of the statute; **última** ~ last will and testament.
(**c**) **disposiciones** (*preparativos*) preparations (*para* for); (*medidas*) steps, measures; **tomar sus disposiciones** to make one's preparations, take steps.
(**d**) (*disponibilidad*) disposal; **a la** ~ **de** at the disposal of; **a la** ~ **de Vd, a su** ~ at your service; **tener algo a su** ~ to have sth at one's disposal, have sth available.
(**e**) (*posición*) position; **estar en** ~ **de** + *infin* to be ready to + *infin*, be in a position to + *infin*.
(**f**) (*temperamento*) disposition, temperament; (*talento*) aptitude (*para* for); turn of mind; ~ **de ánimo** attitude of mind; **no tener** ~ **para** to have no aptitude for.

dispositivo *nm* (**a**) (*Mec*) device, mechanism; appliance; contrivance; gadget; ~ **de alimentación** hopper; storage device; ~ **de arranque** starting mechanism; ~ **intrauterino** intrauterine device; ~ **periférico** peripheral device; ~ **de seguridad** safety catch, safety device; (*fig*) security measure.
(**b**) (*Mil etc*) force, deployment; ~ **de seguridad** security force.

dispuesto *adj y ptp* (**a**) (*arreglado*) arranged, disposed; ~ **según ciertos principios** arranged according to certain principles; **bien** ~ (*Arquit*) well designed, well laid out.
(**b**) (*persona*) **bien** ~ well-disposed (*hacia* towards); **mal** ~ ill-disposed; (*Med*) ill, indisposed.
(**c**) **estar** ~ **a** + *infin* to be prepared to + *infin*; **estar poco** ~ **a** + *infin* to be reluctant to + *infin*.
(**d**) (*listo*) bright, clever, go-ahead.
(**e**) **bien** ~ handsome.

disputa *nf* dispute; argument; controversy; ~ **electoral** electoral contest, election; **los asuntos en** ~ the matters in dispute, the matters at issue; **sin** ~ undoubted(ly), beyond dispute.

disputable *adj* disputable, debatable.

disputado *adj partido* close, tough, hard fought.

disputador 1 *adj* disputatious, argumentative. **2** *nm*, **disputadora** *nf* disputant.

disputar [1a] **1** *vt* (**a**) *asunto* to dispute, question, challenge; to debate.
(**b**) *posesión* to fight for, contend for; *partido* to play.
2 *vi* (**a**) (*discutir*) to debate, argue (*con* with; *de, sobre* about).
(**b**) ~ **con uno por un premio** to contend with sb for a prize.
3 disputarse *vr*: ~ **un premio** to contend for a prize; ~ **la posesión de** to fight over (*o* for) the possession of.

disque‡ *nm*: **darse** ~ (*Cono Sur*) to fancy o.s.*

disquería *nf* (*Carib*) record shop.

disquero *adj* record (*atr*).

disqueta *nf* (*LAm*), **disquete** *nm* (*Inform*) floppy disk, diskette.

disquetera *nf* disk drive.
disquisición *nf* (**a**) (*análisis*) disquisition. (**b**) **disquisiciones** irrelevancies, comments on the side.
Dist. (**a**) *abr de* **distancia** distance, dist. (**b**) *abr de* **Distrito** district, dist.
distancia *nf* (*gen*) distance; (*de tiempo etc*) interval; (*disparidad*) gap, difference, disparity; **~ de despegue** (*Aer*) length of takeoff; **~ focal** focal distance, focal length; **~ de parada** braking distance; **~ de seguridad** (*Aut*) safe distance; **~ del suelo, ~ sobre el suelo** (*Aut etc*) height off the ground, clearance; **a ~** (*adv*) at a distance; (*adj*) remote; **a gran ~, a larga ~** long-distance (*atr*); **ganó X, con Y a 2 golpes de ~** X won, with Y 2 strokes behind; **mantener a uno a ~** to keep sb at a distance; keep sb at arm's length; **mantenerse a ~** to keep one's distance; (*fig*) to hold back, remain aloof; **ganar ~s** to get ahead, make progress; **marcar ~s** to be far ahead; **cada cierta ~** every so often, at intervals; **guardar las ~s** to keep one's distance, maintain proper (social) distinctions; **salvando las ~s** recognizing that the cases are not precisely the same.
distanciado *adj* (**a**) (*remoto*) remote (*de* from); (*aislado*) widely separated, isolated; *carácter* remote, detached.
(**b**) (*fig*) far apart; **estamos algo ~s** we are not particularly close; **ella está distanciada de su familia** she has grown apart from her family, she has no close ties with her family; **estamos muy ~s en ideas** our ideas are poles apart.
distanciador *adj*: **efecto ~** distancing effect.
distanciamiento *nm* (**a**) (*acto*) spacing out. (**b**) (*estado*) remoteness, isolation; (*fig*) distance, lack of close links (*entre* between); **~ generacional** generation gap. (**c**) (*Teat etc*) distancing effect.
distanciar [1b] **1** *vt* (**a**) *objetos* to space out, separate; to put further apart.
(**b**) *rival* to outdistance.
(**c**) *personas* to cause a rift between.
2 distanciarse *vr* (**a**) **~ de un rival** to get ahead of a rival.
(**b**) (*dos personas*) to fall out, become estranged; to become (more) remote from each other.
distante *adj* (**a**) (*lejano*) distant; (*remoto*) far-off, remote; **~ de 10 kms** 10 kms away. (**b**) (*fig*) distant.
distar [1a] *vi* (**a**) **dista 5 kms de aquí** it is 5 kms from here; **dista mucho** it's a long way away; **¿dista mucho?** is it far?, how far is it?
(**b**) **dista mucho de la verdad** it's very far from the truth, it's a long way off the truth; **disto mucho de aprobarlo** I am far from approving of it.
distender [2g] *vt* to distend; to stretch.
distendido *adj* distended; relaxed; **ambiente ~** relaxed atmosphere.
distensión *nf* distension; stretching; relaxation; (*Pol*) détente; (*Med*) strain; **~ muscular** muscular strain.
distensivo *adj* conciliatory.
dístico *nm* distich.
distinción *nf* (**a**) (*diferencia*) distinction, difference; differentness; **a ~ de** unlike, in contrast to; **sin ~** indiscriminately; all together, mixed; **obrar sin ~** to act arbitrarily, act blindly; **sin ~ de personas** without respect to persons, without regard for the differences (of rank *etc*) between people; **sin ~ de edades** irrespective of differences of age; **sin ~ de raza** without distinction of race; **hacer una ~ entre** to make a distinction between, differentiate between; **hacer ~ con uno** to show sb special consideration.
(**b**) (*honor*) distinction, honour; **~ honorífica** honour.
(**c**) (*elegancia*) elegance, refinement.
distingo *nm* (*salvedad*) reservation; (*distinción*) subtle distinction; (*objeción*) (petty) objection; **aquí hago un ~** here I must make a reservation.
distinguible *adj* distinguishable.
distinguido *adj* (**a**) (*gen*) distinguished; (*conocido*) prominent, well-known. (**b**) (*elegante*) elegant, refined; (*culto*) gentlemanly, ladylike, cultured. (**c**) **'D~ Señor'** (*LAm*) 'Dear Sir'.
distinguir [3d] **1** *vt* (**a**) (*lograr ver*) to distinguish, discern, make out; (*reconocer*) to recognize.
(**b**) (*diferenciar*) to distinguish (*de* from, *entre* between), tell (*de* from); **no distingo cuál es el mío** I can't tell which is mine; **lo sabría ~ entre cien iguales** I would know it anywhere.
(**c**) (*separar*) to distinguish, separate, single out; **aquí distingo dos aspectos** here I distinguish two aspects.
(**d**) (*señalar*) to mark, stamp, distinguish; **lo distinguen con una señal especial** they mark it with a special sign.
(**e**) (*señalar*: *fig*) to single out, mark out (for special treatment); (*honrar*) to honour, bestow an honour on; *amigo etc* to have a special regard for; **me distingue con su amistad** he honours me with his friendship.
2 *vi*: **no ~** to have no critical sense, be undiscriminating; **es un hombre que sabe ~** he is a discerning (*o* discriminating) person.
3 distinguirse *vr* (**a**) (*diferenciarse*) to be distinguished (*de* from), differ (*de* from); to stand out (*de* from); **~ por su calidad** to stand out by reason of its quality.
(**b**) (*destacar*) to distinguish o.s.
distintivo 1 *adj* distinctive; *señal etc* distinguishing. **2** *nm* badge, emblem; (*fig*) distinguishing mark, characteristic, typical feature.
distinto *adj* (**a**) (*claro*) clear, distinct, plain; (*definido*) well-defined.
(**b**) (*diferente*) different, distinct (*a, de* from); **son muy ~s** they are very different.
(**c**) **~s** several, various; **hay distintas opiniones sobre eso** there are various opinions about that.
distorsión *nf* (**a**) (*Anat*) sprain. (**b**) (*Rad etc*) distortion.
distorsionador *adj*, **distorsionante** *adj* distorting.
distorsionar [1a] *vt* to distort.
distracción *nf* (**a**) (*recreo*) distraction; amusement, relaxation; (*pasatiempo*) hobby, pastime; **es mi ~ favorita** it's my favourite amusement; **lo hace como ~ nada más** he only does it as a hobby.
(**b**) (*despiste*) absence of mind, forgetfulness; (*falta de atención*) heedlessness; **por ~** through sheer forgetfulness, absent-mindedly.
(**c**) (*error, olvido*) slip, blunder, oversight; **fue una ~ mía** it was an oversight on my part.
(**d**) (*moral*) loose living, dissipation.
distraer [2o] **1** *vt* (**a**) *atención etc* to distract, divert, lead away (*de* from); (*moralmente*) to lead astray; **~ a uno para robarle algo** to distract sb's attention so as to steal sth from him; **~ a uno de su dolor** to take sb's mind off his grief; **~ a uno de su razonamiento** to divert sb from his train of thought.
(**b**) (*entretener*) to amuse, relax, entertain; **la música me distrae** music relaxes me, I find music relaxing.
(**c**) (*Fin*) to embezzle, divert to one's own use.
2 *vi* to be relaxing; **el pescar distrae** fishing is a relaxation.
3 distraerse *vr* (**a**) (*entretenerse*) to amuse o.s., entertain o.s.; to relax; **me distraigo pescando** I relax when I fish, I find fishing relaxing; **no me opongo a que se distraiga honestamente** I don't mind her having a little innocent amusement.
(**b**) (*despistarse*) to be (*o* get) absent-minded; to cease to pay attention; **me distraje un momento** I allowed my attention to wander for a moment; **~ de** to forget about, be inattentive to.
distraídamente *adv* (*V adj*) (**a**) absent-mindedly; unobservantly; (*pey*) inattentively; slackly. (**b**) idly, casually.
distraído 1 *adj* (**a**) *persona* (*despistado*) absent-minded; (*poco práctico*) vague, dreamy, unpractical; (*que no se fija*) unobservant; (*pey*) inattentive; slack, lackadaisical; **iba yo algo ~** I was rather absorbed in other things, I was not taking much notice.
(**b**) *aire, mirada etc* absent-minded; idle, casual; **con aire ~** idly, casually, in a casual manner; **me miró distraída** she gave me a casual glance.
(**c**) *divertido etc* amusing, entertaining.
(**d**) *vida* dissolute.
(**e**) (*Cono Sur, Méx*) (*desaliñado*) slovenly, untidy, shabby.
(**f**) (*Méx**: *chiflado*) crazy.
2 *nm*: **hacerse el ~** (*fingir no ver*) to pretend not to notice; (*fingir no tener interés*) to pretend not to be interested.
distribución *nf* (**a**) (*acto*) distribution; giving-out; sending out; (*Correos*) sorting; delivery; **~ de premios** prize giving.
(**b**) (*Estadística etc*) distribution; incidence; **la ~ de los impuestos** the incidence of taxes.
(**c**) (*estado*) distribution, arrangement; (*Arquit*) layout, ground plan.
(**d**) (*Mec*) timing gears.
distribuido *adj*: **una casa bien distribuida** a well-designed house.
distribuidor 1 *nm* (**a**) (*persona*) distributor; (*Com*) dealer, agent, stockist; **~ automático** (*Com*) (automatic) vending

machine, slot machine.

(**b**) (*Aut*) distributor.

(**c**) (*LAm Aut*) motorway exit.

2 *nm*, **distribuidora**[1] *nf* (*persona*) distributor; (*Com*) dealer, agent, stockist.

distribuidora[2] *nf* (*Agr*) spreader.

distribuir [3g] *vt* (**a**) (*gen*) to distribute; *prospectos etc* to hand out; to give out; (*circular*) to send out, send round; *cartas* (*clasificar*) to sort; *cartas* (*entregar*), *leche* to deliver; *tareas etc* to allocate; *premios* to give out, award; (*Téc*) to spread; *carga etc* to stow, arrange; *peso* to distribute (equally *etc*).

(**b**) (*Arquit*) to design, plan, lay out.

distributivo *adj* distributive.

distrito *nm* (*gen*) district, region, zone; (*Pol*) administrative area; (*Jur*) circuit; ~ **electoral** constituency, ward, electoral area; precinct (*US*); ~ **postal** postal district.

distrofia *nf*: ~ **muscular** (progressive) muscular dystrophy.

disturbio *nm* (**a**) (*gen*) disturbance; (*desorden*) riot, commotion; **los ~s** the disturbances, the troubles. (**b**) (*Téc*) disturbance; ~ **aerodinámico** (*Aer*) wash, slipstream.

disuadir [3a] *vt* to dissuade, deter, discourage (*de* from); ~ **a uno de** + *infin* to dissuade sb from + *ger*.

disuasión *nf* dissuasion; (*Mil etc*) deterrent force; deterrent action; ~ **nuclear** nuclear deterrent; *V* **fuerza**.

disuasivo *adj* discouraging; dissuasive; (*Mil*) deterrent.

disuasorio *adj* (*Mil*) deterrent; *V* **fuerza.**

disyuntiva *nf* (**a**) (*opción*) alternative, choice. (**b**) (*apuro*) dilemma; crisis.

disyuntivo *adj* disjunctive.

disyuntor *nm* (*Elec*) circuit breaker.

dita[1] *nf* (**a**) (*garantía*) surety; (*fianza*) security, bond. (**b**) (*And*: *empréstito*) loan at a high rate of interest; (*LAm*: *deuda*) small debt.

dita[2] *nf* (*Carib*) dish, cup, pot.

ditirambo *nm* dithyramb.

DIU ['diu] *nm abr de* **dispositivo intrauterino** intrauterine device, IUD.

diurético *adj, nm* diuretic.

diurno *adj* diurnal, day (*atr*), daytime (*atr*).

diva *nf* prima donna, diva.

divagación *nf* digression; **divagaciones** wanderings, ramblings.

divagador *adj* rambling, discursive.

divagar [1h] *vi* to digress; to wander, ramble; **¡no ~!** get on with it!, come to the point!

divagatorio *adj* digressive.

diván *nm* divan, sofa; (*de psiquiatra*) couch.

diver* *adj* = **divertido.**

divergencia *nf* divergence.

divergente *adj* divergent; contrary, opposite.

divergir [3c] *vi* (**a**) (*líneas*) to diverge. (**b**) (*opiniones etc*) to differ, be opposed, clash; (*dos personas*) to differ, disagree.

diversidad *nf* diversity, variety.

diversificación *nf* diversification.

diversificado *adj* diversified; **ciclo** ~ (*Venezuela Educ*) upper secondary education.

diversificar [1g] **1** *vt* to diversify. **2 diversificarse** *vr* to diversify.

diversión *nf* (**a**) (*recreo*) amusement, entertainment; recreation; (*pasatiempo*) hobby, pastime; **diversiones de salón** parlour games, indoor games. (**b**) (*Mil*) diversion.

diverso *adj* **1** (**a**) (*variado*) diverse.

(**b**) (*distinto*) different (*de* from); other; **se trata de ~ asunto** it's about a different (*o* another) matter.

(**c**) **~s** several, various; some; sundry; **está en ~s libros** it figures in several books.

2 ~s *nmpl* (*Com*) sundries, miscellaneous (items).

divertido *adj* (**a**) *libro etc* entertaining, amusing; funny; enjoyable; *fiesta etc* gay, merry; *chiste* funny; *persona* funny, amusing, witty.

(**b**) (*iró*) **¡estoy ~!** you kill me!*; **¡estamos ~s!** how terribly amusing! (I don't think).

(**c**) **estar** ~ (*LAm**) to be tight*.

divertimento *nm* divertimento.

divertimiento *nm* (**a**) amusement, entertainment. (**b**) diversion (*t Mil*).

divertir [3i] **1** *vt* (**a**) (*entretener*) to amuse, entertain.

(**b**) *atención* to divert, distract (the attention of).

2 divertirse *vr* to amuse o.s.; to have a good time; **la juventud moderna no quiere más que** ~ all modern youth wants to do is have a good time; ~ **haciendo algo** to amuse o.s. doing sth; ~ **con el amor de uno** to toy with sb's affections; **¡que os divirtáis!** have a good time!

dividendo *nm* dividend; **~s por acción** earnings per share; ~ **a cuenta** interim dividend; ~ **final** final dividend.

dividir [3a] **1** *vt* (*gen*) to divide (up); to split (up), separate; (*repartir*) to share out, distribute; (*Mat*) to divide; ~ **12 entre 4** to divide 12 among 4; ~ **12 por 4** to divide 12 by 4; ~ **algo en 5 partes** to divide sth into 5 parts; ~ **algo por la mitad** to divide sth into two, halve sth; ~ **algo por la mitad** to divide sth down the middle; **divide y vencerás** divide and rule. **2 dividirse** *vr* (*persona*: *fig*) to be in two places at the same time.

divierta* *nf* (*CAm*) village dance, hop*.

divieso *nm* (*Med*) boil.

divinamente *adv* divinely (*t fig*); **lo pasamos** ~ we had a wonderful time.

divinidad *nf* (**a**) (*esencia divina*) divinity.

(**b**) (*una* ~) divinity; godhead; deity; ~ **marina** sea god; ~ **pagana** pagan god(dess), pagan divinity; **la D~** the Deity.

(**c**) (*fig*: *mujer*) goddess, beauty, beautiful woman; (*objeto*) precious thing, lovely object.

divinizar [1f] *vt* to deify; (*fig*) to exalt, extol.

divino 1 *adj* (**a**) divine. (**b**) (*fig*) divine, wonderful; (*) great*, brill*. **3** *adv* **pasarlo ~*** to have a smashing time*.

divisa *nf* (**a**) (*distintivo*) emblem, badge; (*Her*) device, motto. (**b**) **~s** (*Fin*) foreign exchange; **~s fuertes** hard currency; **control de ~s** exchange control.

divisar [1a] *vt* to make out, spy, descry.

divisible *adj* divisible.

división *nf* (**a**) (*Dep, Mat, Mil etc*) division; **primera ~, ~ de honor** first division. (**b**) (*acto*) division; (*Pol: de partido*) split; (*de país*) partition: (*en familia, entre amigos*) split; discord, strife.

divisional *adj* divisional.

divisionismo *nm* divisiveness.

divisionista *adj* divisive.

divisivo *adj* divisive.

divismo *nm* (**a**) (*sistema*) star system. (**b**) (*temperamento*) artistic temperament, star temperament.

divisor *nm* (*Mat*) divisor; **máximo común** ~ highest common factor.

divisoria *nf* dividing line; (*Geog*) divide; ~ **de aguas** watershed; ~ **continental** continental divide.

divisorio *adj* dividing; divisive; **línea divisoria de las aguas** watershed.

divo* *nm* (*pey*) movie star.

divorciado 1 *adj* (**a**) divorced. (**b**) **las opiniones están divorciadas** (*fig*) opinions are divided. **2** *nm*, **divorciada** *nf* divorcee.

divorciar [1b] **1** *vt* (**a**) to divorce. (**b**) (*fig*) to divorce, separate (*de* from). **2 divorciarse** to get divorced, get a divorce (*de* from).

divorcio *nm* (**a**) (*gen*) divorce. (**b**) (*fig*) separation; division, split; **existe un ~ entre A y B** there is a great discrepancy between A and B.

divorcista *nmf* pro-divorce campaigner.

divulgación *nf* spreading, circulation; dissemination; popularizing; (*pey*) disclosure.

divulgar [1h] **1** *vt* to spread, circulate, publish; to disseminate; to popularize; (*pey*) to divulge, disclose, let out.

2 divulgarse *vr* (*secreto*) to leak out; (*rumor etc*) to get about, become known.

divulgativo *adj*, **divulgatorio** *adj* popularizing; informative.

diz (†† *forma de* **dice**; *LAm*): ~ **que** ... they say that ..., it is said that ...; apparently ...; supposedly ...

D.J.C. = **d. de J.C.**

dl. *abr de* **decilitro** decilitre, dl.

DM *abr de* **Deutschmark, marco alemán** Deutschmark, DM.

Dm. (**a**) *abr de* **decámetro** decametre. (**b**) *abr de* **decimal** decimal.

dm. *abr de* **decímetro** decimetre, dm.

D.m. *abr de* **Dios mediante** Deo volente, DV.

D.N. *nf abr de* **Delegación Nacional.**

DNI *nm abr de* **documento nacional de identidad.**

Dña. = **Dª.**

D.O. *abr de* **denominación de origen** denomination of origin.

do *nm* (*Mús*) do, C; ~ **mayor** C major; ~ **de pecho** high C; **dar el ~ de pecho** to give one's all, do one's very best.

dóberman *nm* Doberman.

dobladillar [1a] *vt* to hem.

dobladillo *nm* (*de vestido*) hem; (*de pantalón*) turn-up(s), cuff(s) (*US*).

doblado *adj* (**a**) (*Cos etc*) double; doubled over, folded. (**b**)

(*Anat*) stocky, thickset. (**c**) *terreno* rough. (**d**) (*fig*) sly, deceitful.

doblador*[1] *nm* (*CAm*) roll-your-own*, hand-rolled cigarette.

doblador[2], -a *nm/f* (*Cine*) dubber.

dobladura *nf* fold, crease.

doblaje *nm* (*Cine*) dubbing.

doblamiento *nm* folding, creasing.

doblar [1a] **1** *vt* (**a**) (*gen*) to double; **~ el sueldo a uno** to double sb's salary; **te doblo en edad, te doblo la edad** I'm twice your age.

(**b**) *tela, papel etc* to fold (up, over), crease; *dobladillo* to turn up; *página* to turn down; *cabeza, rodilla etc* to bend; (*Méx: abalear*) to shoot down; **~ a uno a palos** to give sb a beating.

(**c**) *esquina* to turn, round, go round; *cabo* (*Náut*) to round; (*Aut*) to overtake; (*en carrera*) to lap.

(**d**) *película* to dub.

(**e**) **~ dos papeles** (*Teat*) to take two parts.

(**f**) (*Bridge*) to double; *apuesta etc* to double.

(**g**) (*Dep: marcar*) to mark.

2 *vi* (**a**) (*torcer*) to turn (*a la izquierda* to the left).

(**b**) (*campana*) to toll (*a muerto, por uno* for a death).

(**c**) (‡) to peg out‡, die.

3 doblarse *vr* (**a**) (*cantidad etc*) to double.

(**b**) (*plegarse*) to fold (up), crease; to bend, buckle.

(**c**) (*fig*) to give in, yield (*a* to).

doble 1 *adj* (**a**) double; *flor, puerta, sentido etc* double; *control, nacionalidad etc* dual; *fondo* false; *tela* double, extra thick; *cuerda* thick, stout; **~ o nada** double or quits; **~ agente** double agent; **~ cara** (*adj*) double-sided; **~ densidad** (*adj*) double-density; **~ espacio** double spacing; **calle de ~ sentido** (*Aut*) two-way road.

(**b**) (*fig*) insincere; two-faced, deceitful.

2 *nm* (**a**) (*cantidad*) double (quantity); **el ~** twice the quantity, twice the amount; twice as much; **apostar ~ contra sencillo** to bet two to one; **hoy gana el ~** today he earns double, today he earns twice as much; **su sueldo es el ~ del mío** his salary is twice mine; **un ~ de whiskey** a double whisky; **un ~ de cerveza** a big glass of beer.

(**b**) (*Cos etc*) fold, crease.

(**c**) (*de campana*) toll, tolling; knell.

(**d**) (*Tenis etc*) **~s** doubles; **~s (de) damas** ladies' doubles; **~s de caballeros, ~s masculinos** men's doubles; **~s mixtos** mixed doubles.

(**e**) (*Bridge*) double; **~ de castigo** penalty double; **~ de llamada** asking double.

(**f**) (‡: *de cárcel*) prison governor.

3 *nmf* (*Cine*) double, stand-in; **ser el ~ de uno** (*fig*) to be sb's double.

doblegar [1h] **1** *vt* (**a**) (*doblar*) to fold, crease; to bend.

(**b**) *arma* to brandish.

(**c**) (*fig*) to persuade, sway; **~ a uno** to force sb to abandon his course (*o* change his ways *etc*), make sb give in.

2 doblegarse *vr* (*fig*) to yield, give in.

doblemente *adv* (**a**) (*gen*) doubly. (**b**) (*fig*) insincerely; deceitfully.

doblete *nm* (*Ling*) doublet.

doblez 1 *nm* (*pliegue*) fold, crease; (*dobladillo: de vestido*) hem; (*de pantalón*) turn-up(s), cuff(s) (*US*). **2** *nf* insincerity; double-dealing, deceitfulness, duplicity.

doblista *nmf* doubles player.

doblón *nm* (*Hist*) doubloon; **~ de a ocho** piece of eight.

doc. (**a**) *abr de* **docena** dozen, doz. (**b**) *abr de* **documento** document, doc.

doce 1 *adj* twelve; (*fecha*) twelfth; **las ~** twelve o'clock; **los ~** the Twelve (member-countries of EC). **2** *nm* twelve.

doceavo 1 *adj* twelfth. **2** *nm* twelfth; **en ~** (*Tip*) in duodecimo.

docena *nf* dozen; **~ del fraile** baker's dozen; **a ~s** by the dozen, in great numbers; **por ~(s)** by the dozen, in dozens.

docencia *nf* teaching.

doceno *adj* twelfth.

docente 1 *adj* educational; teaching (*atr*); **centro ~** teaching institution; **personal ~** teaching staff, academic staff; **personal no ~** non-academic staff. **2** *nmf* teacher.

dócil *adj* docile; obedient; gentle, mild.

docilidad *nf* docility; obedience; gentleness; mildness.

dócilmente *adv* in a docile way; obediently; gently, mildly.

doctamente *adv* learnedly.

docto 1 *adj* learned, erudite; scholarly. **2** *nm*, **docta** *nf* scholar; learned person.

doctor *nm* (*Med, Univ*) doctor; (*Ecl*) father, saint; **~ en derecho** doctor of laws; **~es tiene la Iglesia** there are plenty of people well able to pass an opinion (on that).

doctora *nf* (*Med*) (woman) doctor; (*Univ*) doctor; (*) bluestocking.

doctorado *nm* doctorate; **estudiante de ~** research student.

doctoral *adj* (**a**) doctoral. (**b**) (*hum*) learned, pompous.

doctorar [1a] **1** *vt* to confer a doctor's degree on. **2 doctorarse** *vr* to take one's doctor's degree (*o* doctorate).

doctrina *nf* (*gen*) doctrine; (*erudición*) learning; (*enseñanza*) teaching; (*en escuela*) catechism, religious instruction.

doctrinal *adj* doctrinal.

doctrinar [1a] *vt* to teach.

doctrinario, -a *adj, nm/f* doctrinaire.

doctrinero *nm* (*LAm*) parish priest (*among Indians*).

docudrama *nm* docudrama, dramatized documentary.

documentación *nf* (**a**) (*gen*) documentation. (**b**) (*papeles*) papers, documents; **~ del barco** ship's papers; **la ~, por favor** your papers, please. (**c**) (*Prensa*) reference section.

documentadamente *adv* in a well-informed way; citing documents in evidence.

documental *adj, nm* documentary.

documentar [1a] **1** *vt* to document, establish with documentary evidence. **2 documentarse** *vr* to get the necessary information, do one's homework.

documento *nm* document (*t Inform*); paper; record; certificate; (*Jur*) exhibit; **~s del coche** papers relating to one's car; **~s de envío** dispatch documents; **~ justificativo** voucher, certificate; supporting document; **~ nacional de identidad** identity card; **~ secretísimo** top-secret document; **~ de trabajo** working paper; **los ~s, por favor** your papers, please.

dodecafónico *adj* dodecaphonic.

dodecafonismo *nm* twelve-note system.

dodo *nm*, **dodó** *nm* dodo.

dodotis *nm invar* nappy, diaper (*US*).

dogal *nm* (*de animal*) halter; (*de verdugo*) hangman's noose; **estar con el ~ al cuello** (*o* **a la garganta**) to be in an awful jam*.

dogma *nm* dogma.

dogmáticamente *adv* dogmatically.

dogmático *adj* dogmatic.

dogmatismo *nm* dogmatism.

dogmatizador(a) *nm/f* dogmatist.

dogmatizar [1f] *vi* to dogmatize.

dogo *nm* (*t* **perro ~**) bulldog; **~ alemán** Great Dane.

dola* *nf* = **pídola**.

dolamas *nfpl*, **dolames** *nfpl* (*Vet*) hidden defects (*of a horse*); (*LAm* ††) chronic illness.

dólar *nm* dollar; **gente montada en el ~*** filthy rich people*.

dolencia *nf* (*achaque*) ailment, complaint, affliction; (*dolor*) ache; (*fig*) ailment, ill; **la ~ de la economía** the ills of the economy.

doler [2i] **1** *vti* (**a**) (*Med*) to hurt, pain; to ache; **me duele el brazo** my arm hurts, my arm aches; **me duele el estómago** I have a pain in my stomach, my stomach aches, I've got stomachache; **¿dónde te duele?** where does it hurt (you)?; **¿duele mucho?** does it hurt much?; **no me ha dolido nada** it didn't hurt at all.

(**b**) (*fig*) to grieve, distress; **le duele aún la pérdida** the loss still grieves him, he still feels the loss; **no me duele el dinero** I don't mind about the money, the money doesn't bother me; **a cualquiera le dolería verlo** it would grieve anyone to see it; **¡ahí (le) duele!** that's the whole point!, you've put your finger on it!

2 dolerse *vr* (**a**) (*afligirse*) to grieve (*de* about, for), feel sorry (*de* about, for); **~ de** to regret; to repent (of); *persona* to feel sorry for, pity; **¡duélete de mí!** pity me!; show some sympathy for me!; **se duele de que no le visitéis** he complains that you don't go to see him; **~ de los pecados** to repent (of) one's sins.

(**b**) (*quejarse*) to complain; to moan, groan; **lo sufre todo sin ~** he puts up with everything without complaining.

dolido *adj*: **estar ~** (*fig*) to be distressed, be upset.

doliente 1 *adj* (**a**) (*Med*) suffering, ill; aching.

(**b**) (*triste*) sad, sorrowful; (*por una muerte*) grieving, mourning; **la familia ~** the bereaved family, the sorrowing relatives.

2 *nmf* (**a**) (*Med*) sufferer, sick person; patient.
(**b**) bereaved person; (*en entierro*) mourner.

dolo *nm* fraud, deceit; **sin ~** openly, honestly.

dolomía *nf* **dolomita** *nf* dolomite.

dolor *nm* (**a**) (*Med*) pain; ache; pang; **~ de cabeza** headache; **con ~ de mi corazón** with an ache in my heart; **~ de espalda, ~ lumbar** backache; **~ de estómago** stomachache; **~ de muelas** toothache; **~ de oídos** earache; **~es del parto** labour pains; **~es de posparto** afterpains; **~ sordo** dull ache; **estar con mucho ~, tener mucho ~** to be in great pain; **estar con ~es** (*mujer*) to feel the labour pains beginning.
(**b**) (*fig*) grief, sorrow; affliction, distress; regret; **le causa mucho ~** it causes him great distress, it is a great grief to him; **con ~ te lo digo** it grieves me to say it to you; **es un ~** it's a shame, it's a pity.

dolorido *adj* (**a**) (*Med*) sore, tender, aching; **la parte dolorida** the part which hurts, the part where the pain is.
(**b**) (*fig*) *persona* distressed; grieving, grief-stricken.
(**c**) *tono* plaintive, sad, pained.

Dolorosa *nf*: **la ~** the Madonna, Our Lady of Sorrow.

dolorosa *nf* (*hum*) bill, check (*US*) (*in a restaurant*).

dolorosamente *adv* (**a**) (*Med*) painfully. (**b**) (*fig*) painfully, grievously, distressingly.

doloroso *adj* (**a**) (*Med*) painful. (**b**) (*fig*) painful, grievous, distressing.

doloso *adj* fraudulent, deceitful.

doma *nf* (**a**) (*de animal*) taming; (*adiestramiento*) training; (*de caballo*) breaking-in. (**b**) (*fig*) mastering, controlling.

domable *adj* tamable; controllable.

domador(a) *nm/f* trainer; tamer; **~ de caballos** horse-breaker.

domadura *nf* = **doma.**

domar [1a] *vt* (**a**) (*amansar*) to tame; (*adiestrar*) to train; *caballo etc* to break in. (**b**) (*fig*) to master, control; (*reprimir*) to repress.

domeñar [1a] *vt* = **domar.**

domesticación *nf* domestication; taming.

domesticado *adj* tame; pet; **un tejón ~** a tame badger, a pet badger.

domesticar [1g] **1** *vt* to tame, domesticate; to make a pet of. **2 domesticarse** *vr* to become tame, become domesticated.

domesticidad *nf* (**a**) (*cualidad*) domesticity, homeliness; (*ambiente*) homely atmosphere.
(**b**) (*de animal*) (state of being in) captivity; **el lobo no vive bien en ~** the wolf does not live happily in captivity, the wolf does not take to captivity.

doméstico 1 *adj* (**a**) *vida etc* domestic; home (*atr*), family (*atr*); **economía doméstica** home economy, housekeeping, home economics (*US*); **gastos ~s** household expenses, housekeeping expenditure; **faenas domésticas** housework.
(**b**) *animal* tame, pet.
2 *nm,* **doméstica** *nf* servant, domestic.

Domiciano *nm* Domitian.

domiciliación *nf* (*Fin*) automatic payment (through a bank), direct debiting.

domiciliar [1b] **1** *vt* (**a**) (*dar un domicilio a*) to domicile, establish; to house. (**b**) (*Méx*) *carta* to address. (**c**) (*Com*) *activo* to place. (**d**) **~ su cuenta** (*o* **cobro, nómina, pago**) to give the number of one's account (for automatic payment), authorize direct debiting of one's account. **2 domiciliarse** *vr* to establish o.s., take up (one's) residence.

domiciliario *adj* domiciliary; home (*atr*); house (*atr*); **arresto ~** house arrest; **asistencia domiciliaria** home help.

domicilio *nm* home; (*en lenguaje oficial*) domicile, residence, abode; (*en formulario*) home address; **~ particular** private residence; **~ social** (*Com*) registered office, head office; **a ~** (*Dep*) at home; **servicio a ~** delivery service; **ventas a ~** door-to-door selling; **trabajar a ~** to work at home, do outwork; **sin ~ fijo** of no fixed abode.

dominación *nf* (**a**) (*gen*) domination; dominance; rule, sway. (**b**) (*Mil*) high ground, commanding position.

dominador *adj* (**a**) *papel etc* dominating, controlling. (**b**) *carácter* domineering.

dominante *adj* (**a**) (*gen*) dominant (*t Mús*), predominant; **la tendencia ~** the dominant tendency, the ruling tendency; **el viento ~** the prevailing wind; **la consideración ~** the overriding consideration.
(**b**) *carácter* domineering; masterful; *amor etc* possessive.

dominar [1a] **1** *vt* (**a**) (*gen*) to dominate; to rule (over), hold sway over; *adversario* to overpower; *barca, caballo, nervios etc* to control, bring under control; *epidemia, incendio* to check, bring under control; *rebelión* to put down, suppress, subdue; *pasión* to control, master; *dolor etc* to get over; **le domina la envidia** he is ruled by envy, his ruling passion is envy.
(**b**) *materia* to have a good grasp of; *lengua* to know well, be fluent in, have a good command of; **domina 7 idiomas** he knows 7 languages well.
(**c**) (*edificio etc*) to dominate, tower above (*o* over), look down on.
2 *vi* (*edificio etc*) to dominate; (*color, rasgo etc*) to stand out; (*opinión, viento, tendencia etc*) to predominate, prevail.
3 dominarse *vr* to control o.s.

dómine *nm* (*Hist*) schoolmaster; (*hum*) pedant.

domingas⁑ *nfpl* boobs⁑.

domingo *nm* Sunday; **D~ de Cuasimodo** Low Sunday; **D~ de Ramos** Palm Sunday; **D~ de la Pasión** Passion Sunday; **D~ de Resurrección** Easter Sunday; **hacer ~** to take a day off, make a day into a holiday.

Domingo *nm* Dominic.

dominguejo *nm* (*And, Cono Sur*: *espantapájaros*) scarecrow.

dominguero 1 *adj* Sunday (*atr*); **pintor ~** Sunday painter; **traje ~** Sunday clothes, Sunday suit.
2 *nm* **dominguera** *nf* Sunday excursionist; Sunday visitor; (*Aut*) Sunday driver; (*) rotten driver*.

Dominica *nf* Dominica.

dominical 1 *adj* Sunday (*atr*); **periódico ~** Sunday newspaper. **2** *nm* Sunday supplement.

dominicanismo *nm* word (*o* phrase *etc*) peculiar to the Dominican Republic.

dominicano 1 *adj* (*Ecl y Pol*) Dominican. **2** *nm* (*Ecl*) Dominican. **3** *nm,* **dominicana** *nf* (*Pol*) Dominican.

dominico *nm* (*Ecl*), **domínico** *nm* (*LAm*) Dominican.

dominio *nm* (**a**) (*gen*) dominion; (*autoridad*) power, sway, authority (*sobre* over); (*supremacía*) ascendancy, supremacy; (*control*) hold, grip (*de* on); (*de lengua*) command (*de* of), fluency (*de* in); **~ público** public property, national property; **la noticia es del ~ público** the news is widely known, the news is common knowledge; **~ de** (*o* **sobre**) **sí mismo** self-control; **¡qué ~ tiene!** isn't he good (at it)?; **tiene el ~ de la situación** he is in control of the situation.
(**b**) (*tierra*) domain; (*Pol*) dominion.
(**c**) (*fig*) subject, discipline; field (of study), domain.

dominó *nm* (**a**) domino; **un ~** a domino; a set of dominoes; **juego de ~** dominoes. (**b**) (⁑) French letter.

dom.º *abr de* **domingo** Sunday, Sun.

don¹ *nm en sobre* ≃ Esquire; *en otros casos no se traduce directamente, p.ej.* **soy alumno de ~ Ramón** I am one of Menéndez Pidal's students; **el rey ~ Pedro** King Peter; *V t* **Juan, Señor.**

don² *nm* (**a**) (*regalo*) gift; present.
(**b**) (*fig*: *talento*) gift; knack; aptitude, talent (*de* for); **tiene un ~ especial** he has a special gift; **~ de acierto** happy knack (of doing things well); intuition; **~ de gentes** personal charm, human touch; **tener ~ de gentes** to have a way with people, have the human touch, know how to handle people; **~ de lenguas** gift for languages; **~ de mando** (qualities of) leadership, (*Mil*) generalship; **~ de palabra** gift of oratory, fluency.

dona *nf* (*Cono Sur*) gift; legacy; **~s** (*Méx*) trousseau.

donación *nf* donation; (*Jur*) gift; **~ de sangre** donation of blood.

donada *nf* lay sister.

donado *nm* lay brother.

donador(a) *nm/f* donor.

donaire *nm* (**a**) (*ingenio*) charm, wit, cleverness. (**b**) (*elegancia*) grace(fulness). (**c**) (*un ~*) witticism; **dice muchos ~s** he's terribly witty.

donante *nmf* donor; **~ de sangre** blood-donor.

donar [1a] *vt* to donate; to grant, bestow.

donativo *nm* donation, contribution.

doncel *nm* (*Hist*) page; young nobleman, young squire.

doncella *nf* (**a**) (*criada*) maid, lady's maid, maidservant.
(**b**) (*virgen*) virgin; (*Hist y liter*) maid, maiden.

doncellez *nf* (**a**) (*estado*) virginity, maidenhood. (**b**) (*Anat*) maidenhead.

donde 1 *rel adv* (**a**) (*gen*) where; (*fig*) wherein; in which; **el sitio ~ lo encontré** the place where I found it; **a ~** to where, to which; **fue a ~ estaban** he went to (the place) where they were; **es a ~ vamos nosotros** that's where we're going; **de ~** from where; from which, out of which; **el país de ~ vienen** the country they come from; **la caja de ~ lo sacó** the box from which he took it, the box he took it out of; **en** ~ where; in which; **por** ~ through which; (*fig*) whereby; **no hay por** ~ **cogerle** there's no way to catch him.

(**b**) (*Cono Sur: ya que*) as, since.

2 *prep* (**a**) **es allí** ~ **el farol** it's where the lamp-post is, it's over there by the lamp-post.

(**b**) (*LAm: en casa de*) at the house (*etc*) of; **están cenando** ~ **mi mamá** they are dining at my mother's (house); **está** ~ **el médico** she's at the doctor's.

dónde *interrog adv* (**a**) where?; **¿~ lo dejaste?** where did you leave it?; **¿a ~ vas?** where are you going (to)?; **¿de ~ vienes?** where have you come from?; **¿en ~?** where?; **¿por ~?** where?, whereabouts?; which way?; why?, for what reason?; **¿por ~ se va al estadio?** which way to the stadium?, how do I get to the stadium?

(**b**) (*indirecto*) where; **no sé ~ lo puse** I don't know where I put it.

(**c**) (*LAm: ¿cómo?*) how?

dondequiera 1 *adv* anywhere; **por** ~ everywhere, all over the place. **2** *conj* anywhere, wherever; ~ **que lo busques** wherever you look for it.

donjuan *nm* wolf*, womanizer.

donjuanismo *nm* wolfishness*, womanizing.

donosamente *adv* (*liter*) wittily, amusingly.

donoso *adj* (*liter*) witty, amusing; (*iró*) fine; **¡donosa idea!** (*iró*) highly amusing I'm sure!

Donosti(a) *nf* San Sebastián.

donostiarra 1 *adj* of San Sebastián. **2** *nmf* native (*o* inhabitant) of San Sebastián; **los ~s** the people of San Sebastián.

Don Quijote *nm* Don Quixote.

donus *nm invar*, **donut** *nm, pl* **donuts** doughnut, donut (*US*).

doña *nf antepuesto al nombre de pila no se traduce;* ~ **Victoria Benito** Mrs Victoria Benito.

dopado 1 *adj* doped, doped-up*. **2** *nm* (*t* **dopaje** *nm*) doping, drugging.

dopar [1a] **1** *vt* to dope, drug. **2 doparse** *vr* to take drugs.

dóping ['dopin] *nm* doping, drugging; administering (*o* use) of a drug.

dopingar [1h] *vt* to dope, drug.

doquier *adv* (†† *o liter*) = **dondequiera**; **por** ~ all over, everywhere; all over the place.

doradito *adj* (*Culin*) light brown.

dorado 1 *adj* golden; (*Téc*) gilt, gilded; gold-plated; **los ~s 60** the golden sixties. **2** *nm* (**a**) (*Téc*) gilding, gilt. (**b**) (*Pez*) dorado.

doradura *nf* gilding.

dorar [1a] *vt* (**a**) (*Téc*) to gild; (*Culin*) to brown, cook lightly. (**b**) (*fig*) to gild; to palliate, make more palatable, put a gloss on; ~ **la píldora** to sweeten the pill.

dorífora *nf* Colorado beetle.

dormida *nf* (*LAm*) nap; **echarse una** ~ to have a nap.

dormidera *nf* (**a**) (*Bot*) (opium) poppy. (**b**) **tener buenas ~s** to get off to sleep easily.

dormidero *nm* (*de ganado*) sleeping place; (*de gallinas*) roost.

dormilón 1 *adj* sleepy; much given to sleeping. **2** *nm,* **dormilona**[1] *nf* sleepyhead; (*pey*) sleepy sort, lazy sort, lie-a-bed. **3 dormilona**[2] *nf* (**a**) (*silla*) reclining chair. (**b**) (*Carib: camisón*) nightdress, nightgown.

dormir [3j] **1** *vt* (**a**) ~ **la siesta** to have one's afternoon nap, have a doze, have a siesta.

(**b**) **~la*** to sleep it off; ~ **la mona*** to sleep off a hangover*.

(**c**) ~ **a uno** to send sb to sleep, make sb go to sleep; (*anestesiar*) to put sb to sleep; **Delius me duerme de maravilla** Delius is marvellous for sending me to sleep.

2 *vi* (*gen*) to sleep; (*pasar la noche*) to stay overnight, spend the night; ~ **como un lirón** (*o* **tronco, poste** etc) to sleep like a log; ~ **como un santo** (*o* **bendito**) to sleep peacefully, be fast asleep; ~ **a pierna suelta** (*o* **tendida**) to sleep soundly, sleep the sleep of the just; ~ **con uno** to sleep with sb; **quedarse dormido** to go to sleep, drop off; **durmiendo se me pasó la hora** the time went by while I slept, I overslept.

3 dormirse *vr* (**a**) (*persona*) to go to sleep, fall asleep.

(**b**) (*pierna etc*) to go to sleep, get numb.

dormirela* *nf* nap, snooze.

dormirlas *nm* hide-and-seek.

dormitar [1a] *vi* to doze, snooze*.

dormitorio 1 *nm* (**a**) (*alcoba*) bedroom; (*de colegio etc*) dormitory. (**b**) (*muebles*) bedroom suite. (**c**) (*Méx Ferro*) couchette. **2** *atr V* **barrio, ciudad**.

dornillo *nm* wooden bowl; (*Agr*) small trough.

Dorotea *nf* Dorothy.

dorsal 1 *adj* dorsal; back (*atr*). **2** *nm* (*Dep*) number (worn on player's back). **3** *nf* ridge.

dorsalmente *adv* dorsally; *flotar* on one's back.

dorso *nm* back (*t fig*); **escribir algo al** ~ to write sth on the back; **'véase al ~'** 'see other side'; 'please turn over' (*PTO*).

dos 1 *adj* (**a**) (*gen*) two; (*fecha*) second; **las** ~ two o'clock; ~ **a** ~ two against two; ~ **por** ~ **son 4** two times two makes 4; **a cada** ~ **por tres** in rapid succession, continually; intermittently; **de** ~ **en** ~ in twos, two by two; **cortar algo en** ~ to cut sth in (to) two; **como ése no hay** ~ they don't come any better than that.

(**b**) **los** ~ the two of them, both (of them); (***) the balls***; **es para los** ~ it's for both of you; **para entre los** ~ (strictly) between you and me.

2 *nm* two; **en un** ~ **por tres** in no time at all; **coger el** ~*** to beat it*.

dos-caballos *nm invar* (*Aut*) deux-chevaux, 2 CV.

doscientos *adj* two hundred.

dosel *nm* canopy.

doselera *nf* valance.

dos(s)ier *nm, pl* **dos(s)iers** [dosi'er] dossier.

dosificación *nf* dosage.

dosificador *nm* dispenser.

dosificar [1g] *vt medicina* to measure out, put up in doses; *ingredientes* to measure out, mix in proportion.

dosis *nf invar* (**a**) (*Med*) dose; dosage, amount, quantity.

(**b**) (*fig*) dose; admixture; **con buena** ~ **de vanidad** with a good proportion of vanity.

dos piezas *nm invar* two-piece.

dotación *nf* (**a**) (*acto, dinero*) endowment; ~ **del premio** amount of the prize.

(**b**) (*plantilla*) staff, establishment, personnel; (*Náut*) crew, complement; (*de coche-patrulla etc*) crew, occupants; **una** ~ **del parque de bomberos** a squad of firemen; **la** ~ **es insuficiente** the staff is inadequate, we are under-staffed.

dotado *adj* (**a**) *persona* gifted; **los niños excepcionalmente ~s** exceptionally gifted children; **bien** ~ highly talented, well-equipped for life. (**b**) ~ **de** *persona* endowed with; *máquina etc* equipped with, fitted with, possessing.

dotar [1a] *vt* (**a**) *mujer* to endow (*con* with), give a dowry to; **la dotó muy bien** he gave her a good dowry; **la dotó con** (*o* **en**) **un millón** he gave her a million as a dowry.

(**b**) (*fig*) to endow (*con, de* with); **la naturaleza le dotó de buenas cualidades** nature endowed him with good qualities.

(**c**) (*destinar bienes a*) to endow; (*destinar fondos a*) to provide funds for, assign money to; (*fijar el sueldo de*) to fix a salary for; (*asignar personas a*) to provide staff (*etc*) for; **son necesarias X pesetas para** ~ **estos puestos de enseñanza** X pesetas are needed to pay for these teaching posts; **la Academia ha dotado 2 premios** the Academy has established (*o* set aside funds for) 2 prizes.

(**d**) (*Mec etc*) to supply, fit, provide (*de* with); ~ **un avión de todos los adelantos modernos** to equip a plane with all the latest devices.

(**e**) *barco etc* to man (*de* with); *laboratorio, oficina etc* to staff (*de* with).

dote *gen nf* (**a**) (*de mujer*) dowry, marriage portion; **con un millón de** ~ with a dowry of a million.

(**b**) (*fig*) **~s** gifts, talents, aptitude; **tiene excelentes ~s** she has great gifts; **~s de adherencia** (*Aut*) road-holding qualities; **~s de mando** (qualities of) leadership.

dovela *nf* keystone, voussoir.

doy *V* **dar**.

dozavo = **doceavo**.

Dpto. *abr de* **Departamento** department, dept.

Dr. *abr de* **doctor** Doctor, Dr.

Dra. *abr de* **doctora** Doctor, Dr.

dracma *nf* (**a**) (*Farm*) drachm, dram. (**b**) (*Fin*) drachma.

draconiano *adj* draconian.

DRAE *nm abr de* **Diccionario de la Real Academia Española**.

draga *nf* dredge; (*barco*) dredger.

dragado *nm* dredging.

dragaminas *nm invar* minesweeper.

dragar [1h] *vt* to dredge; *minas* to sweep.

drago *nm* dragon tree.

dragomán *nm* dragoman.

dragón *nm* (**a**) (*Zool*) dragon. (**b**) (*Mil*) dragoon. (**c**) (*Bot*) snapdragon.

dragona *nf* (**a**) (*Mil*) shoulder knot, epaulette. (**b**) (*And,*

Cono Sur, Méx: *de espada*) guard. (**c**) (*Méx*: *capa*) hooded cloak.

dragoncillo *nm* (*Bot*) tarragon.

dragonear [1a] **1** *vt* (*Cono Sur*: †: *cortejar*) to court, woo. **2** *vi* (*LAm*: *jactarse*) to boast, brag; ~ **de** to boast of being; (*Cono Sur*: *fingir ser*) to pretend to be, pass o.s. off as.

drama *nm* drama (*t fig*).

dramática *nf* drama, dramatic art.

dramáticamente *adv* dramatically.

dramaticidad *nf* dramatic quality.

dramático *adj* **1** dramatic (*t fig*). **2** *nm* dramatist; (tragic) actor.

dramatismo *nm* drama, dramatic quality.

dramatizar [1f] *vt* to dramatize.

dramaturgia *nf* drama, theatre art; play-writing.

dramaturgo *nmf* (*t* **dramaturga** *nf*) dramatist, playwright.

dramón* *nm* (*hum*) strong drama, melodrama; **¡qué ~!** what a scene!

Draque *nm* Drake.

drásticamente *adv* drastically.

drástico *adj* drastic.

drenaje *nm* (*esp Agr, Med*) drainage.

drenar [1a] *vt* to drain; (*Fin*) to remove, syphon off.

Dresde *nm* Dresden.

driblar [1a] *vti* (*Dep*) to dribble; ~ **a uno** to dribble past sb.

drible *nm* (*Dep*) dribble; dribbling.

dril *nm* duck, drill.

drive *nm* (*Golf*) drive.

driza *nf* halyard.

droga *nf* (**a**) (*Med, Farm*) drug; medicine; (*pey*) drug; (*en carreras de caballos etc*) dope; **la** ~ (*como problema*) drugs; ~ **blanda** soft drug; ~ **dura** hard drug; ~ **milagrosa** wonder drug; **el peligro de las ~s** the drug menace.

(**b**) (*) (*engaño*) trick, hoax; (*truco*) stratagem; (*mentira*) fib.

(**c**) (*) (*molestia*) nuisance; **es (mucha)** ~ it's a dreadful nuisance.

(**d**) (*And, Cono Sur, Méx**: *deuda*) debt; bad debt; **hacer** ~ (*endeudarse*) to get into debt; (*no pagar*) to refuse to pay up, duck a bill.

(**e**) (*Com*) drug on the market, unsaleable article.

(**f**) **mandar a uno a la** ~ (*CAm, Carib**) to tell sb to go to hell.

drogadicción *nf* drug addiction.

drogadicto, -a *nm/f* drug addict.

drogado *nm* drugging; drug taking; (*de caballo*) doping.

drogar [1h] **1** *vt* to drug; *caballo* to dope. **2 drogarse** *vr* to drug o.s., take drugs.

drogata‡ *nmf* druggy‡.

drogodelincuencia *nf* drug-related crime.

drogodependencia *nf* dependence on drugs, drug addiction.

drogodependiente *nmf* person dependent on drugs, drug addict.

drogota‡ *nmf* druggy‡.

droguería *nf* store where cleaning materials are sold.

droguero *nm* (**a**) (*tendero*) druggist; owner of a 'droguería'; (* *pey*) drug pusher. (**b**) (*: *estafador*) cheat, crook*. (**c**) (*And, Cono Sur, Méx*: *moroso*) slow payer, defaulter.

droguista *nm* = **droguero.**

drogui* *nm* (*Cono Sur*) (**a**) (*bebida*) liquor, alcohol. (**b**) (*borracho*) drunkard.

dromedario *nm* (**a**) (*Zool*) dromedary. (**b**) (*Méx**) tailor.

dromeo *nm* emu.

dropar [1a] *vt* (*Golf*) to drop.

druida *nm* druid.

drupa *nf* drupe.

DSE *nf abr de* **Dirección de la Seguridad del Estado.**

Dto., D.to *abr de* **descuento** discount.

Dtor. *abr de* **Director** Director, Dir.

Dtora. *abr de* **Directora** Director, Dir.

dual *adj* dual (*t Gram*).

dualidad *nf* (**a**) (*gen*) duality. (**b**) (*Cono Sur Pol*) tied vote, indecisive election.

dualismo *nm* dualism.

dubitativamente *adv* doubtfully, hesitantly.

dubitativo *adj* doubtful; uncertain, hesitant.

Dublín *nm* Dublin.

dublinés 1 *adj* Dublin (*atr*) **2** *nm*, **dublinesa** *nf* Dubliner.

ducado *nm* (**a**) (*territorio*) duchy, dukedom. (**b**) (*Fin*) ducat.

ducal *adj* ducal.

ducentésimo *adj* two hundredth.

duco *nm* thick paint, lacquer; **pintar al** ~ to lacquer, spray (with paint).

dúctil *adj* (**a**) (*lit*) ductile. (**b**) (*fig*) flexible, yielding; easy to handle.

ductilidad *nf* ductility.

ducha *nf* shower, shower bath; (*Med*) douche; ~ **escocesa** alternately hot and cold shower; **tomarse una** ~ to have a shower, shower o.s.; **dar una ~ de agua fría a un proyecto** (*fig*) to pour cold water on a plan.

duchar [1a] **1** *vt* (*Med*) to douche. **2 ducharse** *vr* to have a shower, shower o.s.

ducho *adj* expert, skilled; ~ **en** well versed in, experienced in; skilled at, adept at.

duda *nf* (*gen*) doubt; (*recelo*) misgiving; (*indecisión*) indecision; (*suspense*) suspense; **fuera de toda** ~ beyond all doubt; **sin** ~ undoubtedly, certainly; **¡sin ~!** of course!; **sin ~ alguna** without a shadow of a doubt; **le acometieron ~s** he was assailed by doubts, he began to have doubts; **ello constituye una ~ importante** this is a big question mark, it's a big if; **no cabe** ~ there is no doubt about it; **no cabe ~ de que ...** there can be no doubt that ...; **¿qué ~ cabe (o coge)?** is sth bothering you?; **no te quepa** ~ make no mistake about it, get this straight; **para desvanecer toda** ~ in order to dispel all uncertainty; **queda la ~ en pie** the doubt remains; **surge una** ~ a question arises; **estar en** ~ to be in doubt; **poner algo en** ~ to cast doubt on sth, call sth in question; **sacar a uno de ~s** to settle sb's doubts.

dudar [1a] **1** *vt* to doubt; **no lo dudo** I don't doubt it; **a no ~lo** undoubtedly.

2 *vi* (**a**) (*gen*) to doubt, be in doubt; ~ **acerca de** to be uncertain about; ~ **de** to doubt; to question; to mistrust; **no dudo de su talento** I don't question his talent; ~ **entre A y B** to hesitate between A and B; ~ **que ...**, ~ **si ...** to doubt whether; **dudo que sea capaz de hacerlo** I doubt whether he will be capable of doing it.

(**b**) ~ **en** + *infin* to hesitate to + *infin.*

dudosamente *adv* doubtfully, uncertainly; ~ **eficaz** of doubtful efficacy.

dudoso *adj* (**a**) (*incierto*) doubtful, dubious, uncertain; *punto* debatable; *resultado* unclear, indecisive. (**b**) (*vacilante*) hesitant, undecided. (**c**) (*moralmente*) dubious, suspect.

duela *nf* stave.

duelista *nm* duellist.

duelo¹ *nm* (*Mil*) duel; **batirse en** ~ to fight a duel.

duelo² *nm* (**a**) (*dolor*) grief, sorrow; bereavement; **~s** sufferings, hardships; **sin** ~ unrestrainedly; **gastar sin** ~ to spend lavishly; **pegar a uno sin** ~ to beat sb mercilessly.

(**b**) (*luto etc*) mourning; (*personas*) mourners, party of mourners.

duende *nm* (**a**) (*elfo*) imp, goblin, elf; (*fantasma*) ghost; (*niño*) mischievous child; (*bromista*) prankster; ~ **de imprenta** printer's devil. (**b**) **tener** ~ (*tener encanto*) to have charm, have magic, have a special appeal; (*preocuparse*) to be preoccupied. (**c**) (*Inform*) bug.

duendecillo *nm* (*Aer etc*) gremlin, jinx (*US*).

dueña *nf* (**a**) (*de negocio etc*) owner, proprietress; (*de pensión*) landlady; ~ **de la casa** mistress of the house, lady of the house. (**b**) (*Hist: dama*) lady; (*dama vieja*) matron; (*compañera*) duenna, companion. (**c**) (*fig*) mistress; **la marina era ~ de los mares** the navy was mistress of the seas.

dueño *nm* (*propietario*) owner, proprietor; (*de pensión*) landlord; (*amo*) master; (*empresario*) employer; **organismo de los ~s** (*Com etc*) employers' organization; **ser ~ de** to own, be the owner of, possess; **ser ~ de la baila, ser ~ de la situación** to be the master of the situation, have the situation in hand; **ser ~ de sí mismo** to be self-possessed, have self-control; **ser muy ~ de sí** to be very much in control of o.s.; **es Vd muy ~, es Vd ~ de mi casa** you're very welcome; **ser ~ de** + *infin* to be free to + *infin*; **ser muy ~ de** + *infin* to be amply entitled to + *infin;* **cambiar de** ~ to change hands; **hacerse ~ de** to take over, take possession of; to acquire.

duermevela* *nf* nap, snooze*.

Duero *nm* Douro.

dueto *nm* short duet.

dula *nf* common land, common pasture.

dulcamara *nf* nightshade.

dulce 1 *adj* (*gen*) sweet; *agua* fresh; *metal* soft; *sonido, voz* soft; *carácter* gentle, sweet, mild; *clima* mild; **un instrumento ~** a sweet-sounding instrument; a mellow instrument; **con el acento ~ del país** with the soft accent of the region; **más ~ que el almíbar** (*o* **azúcar** *etc*) sweeter than honey.

2 *adv* gently, softly; **habla muy ~** she speaks very softly.

3 *nm* (**a**) (*gen*) sweet, candy (*US*); **~s** sweets; **~ de almíbar** preserved fruit; **melocotón en ~** preserved peaches; **a nadie le amarga un ~** nobody says no to a bit of luck.

(**b**) (*And, CAm, Carib: azúcar*) (brown) sugar.

(**c**) (*And: paleta*) lollipop.

dulcémele *nm* dulcimer.

dulcemente *adv* sweetly; softly; gently, mildly.

dulcería *nf* confectioner's, sweetshop, candy store (*US*).

dulcificante *nm* sweetener.

dulcificar [1g] **1** *vt* (**a**) *comida* to sweeten. (**b**) (*fig*) to soften, make more gentle; to play down; to make more pleasant, make more tolerable. **2 dulcificarse** *vr* to moderate, become milder; (*tiempo*) to turn mild.

dulzarrón *adj*, **dulzón** *adj* (**a**) (*demasiado dulce*) sickly-sweet, too sugary. (**b**) (*fig*) cloying, sickening.

dulzonería *nf* (**a**) sickly-sweetness. (**b**) cloying nature.

dulzura *nf* sweetness; softness; gentleness; mildness; **con ~** sweetly, softly.

dumón*: **vivir a la gran ~** to live the life of Riley.

dúmper ['dumper] *nm, pl* **dúmpers** dumper.

dúmping ['dumpin] *nm* (*Com*) dumping; **hacer ~** to dump goods.

duna *nf* dune.

dundeco* *adj* (*And, CAm*) silly, stupid.

dundera* *nf* (*And, CAm*) silliness, stupidity.

dundo* *adj* (*And, CAm*) = **dundeco**.

Dunquerque *nm* Dunkirk.

dúo *nm* duet, duo.

duodecimal *adj* duodecimal.

duodécimo *adj* twelfth.

duodenal *adj* duodenal.

duodeno *nm* duodenum.

dup., dpdo *abr de* **duplicado** duplicated, bis.

dúplex *nm invar* (**a**) (*piso*) split-level flat, maisonette; (*casa*) semidetached house. (**b**) (*Telec*) link up. (**c**) (*Inform*) duplex; **~ integral** full duplex.

duplicación *nf* duplication.

duplicado 1 *adj* duplicate; **número 14 ~** (*abr* **dpdo**) No. 14A. **2** *nm* duplicate; **por ~** in duplicate.

duplicar [1g] **1** *vt* (*copiar*) to duplicate; (*repetir*) to repeat; *cantidad, cifra* to double; **las pérdidas duplican las de 1995** the losses are twice (*o* double) what they were in 1995. **2 duplicarse** *vr* to double.

duplicidad *nf* duplicity, deceitfulness.

duplo *adj* double; **12 es ~ de 6** 12 is twice 6.

duque *nm* (**a**) duke. (**b**) (*Orn*) **gran ~** eagle owl.

duquesa *nf* duchess.

durabilidad *nf* durability.

durable *adj* durable, lasting.

duración *nf* duration; period, length of time; (*Aut, Mec etc*) life; **~ media de la vida** average life span; **de larga ~** *enfermedad etc* long-lasting, lengthy; *desempleo etc* long-term; *disco* long-playing.

duradero *adj* (**a**) *ropa, tela etc* hard-wearing, tough, durable. (**b**) *paz, efecto etc* lasting, permanent.

duramente *adv* (*fig*) harshly; cruelly, callously.

durante *prep* during; **~ todo el reinado** during the whole reign, right through the reign; **~ muchos años** for many years; **habló ~ una hora** he spoke for an hour.

durar [1a] *vi* (*período etc*) to last, go on, continue; (*efecto, memoria etc*) to survive, endure, remain; (*ropa etc*) to last, wear (well); **duró 5 años** it lasted 5 years, it went on for 5 years; **no va a ~ mucho más** it won't go on much longer, it'll soon be over.

duraznero *nm* peach-tree.

durazno *nm* (*fruta*) peach; (*árbol*) peach-tree.

Durero *nm* Dürer.

durex ® *nm* (**a**) (*Méx: cinta*) Sellotape ®, sticky tape. (**b**) (*LAm: preservativo*) Durex ®, sheath, condom.

dureza *nf* (**a**) (*gen*) hardness, toughness; (*rigidez*) stiffness; (*Dep*) rough play.

(**b**) (*aspereza*) harshness; callousness; roughness.

(**c**) **~ de oído** hardness of hearing; **~ de vientre** constipation.

(**d**) (*Med*) hard patch, callosity.

durmiente 1 *adj* sleeping. **2** *nmf* (**a**) (*gen*) sleeper; **La bella ~ (del bosque)** Sleeping Beauty. (**b**) (*Pol*) covert supporter. **3** *nm* (*Ferro*) sleeper, tie (*US*).

duro 1 *adj* (**a**) (*gen*) hard; tough; *pan* stale, old; *carne, legumbres etc* tough; *cuello* stiff; *puerta, articulación, mecanismo* stiff; *golpe* hard, heavy; *viento* strong; *luz, agua, sonido,* hard; **más ~ que una piedra** (*etc*) as hard as nails; **más ~ que un mendrugo** as tough as old boots; **tomar las duras con las maduras** to take the rough with the smooth.

(**b**) *carácter, clima, prueba etc* tough; *actitud, política* tough, harsh, hard; (*cruel*) cruel, callous; *juego* hard, rough, physical; (*Pol*) hawkish; *estilo etc* harsh; **ser ~ con uno** to be tough with (*o* on) sb, adopt a tough attitude to sb.

(**c**) **~ de mollera** (*lerdo*) dense, dim; (*terco*) pigheaded; **~ de oído** hard of hearing, (*Mús*) tone deaf; **es muy ~ de pelar** (*o* **roer**) it's a tough job, it's a hard nut to crack.

(**d**) **estar ~** (*: *Méx, Cono Sur*) to be drunk.

2 *adv* hard; **trabajar ~** to work hard; **pega ~** he's got a fierce punch.

3 *nm* (*moneda*) 5-peseta coin; **¡y que te den dos ~s!**‡ and you can get knotted!‡; **estar sin un ~*** to be broke*; **¡lo que faltaba para el ~!*** it's the last straw!; **allí venden ~s a tres pesetas** they're giving it away there.

4 *nm,* **dura** *nf* (*Pol*) hard-liner; hawk.

dux *nm* doge.

DYA *nf abr de* **Detente y Ayuda** *Spanish highway assistance organization.*

E

E, e [e] *nf* (*letra*) E, e.
E *abr de* **este** east, E.
e/ (*Com*) *abr de* **envío** shipment, shpt.
e *conj* (*delante de* **i~** *e* **hi~**, *pero no* **hie~**) and; *V t* **y**.
-e *V* **Aspects of Word Formation in Spanish 2**.
EA *nm* (*Esp Mil*) *abr de* **Ejército del Aire.**
ea *interj* hey!; come on!; **¡~ pues!** well then!; let's see!; **¡~, andamos!** come on, let's go!
EAU *nmpl abr de* **Emiratos Árabes Unidos** United Arab Emirates, UAE.
ebanista *nm* cabinetmaker, carpenter.
ebanistería *nf* (**a**) (*oficio*) cabinetmaking; woodwork, carpentry. (**b**) (*taller*) cabinetmaker's (shop), carpenter's (shop).
ébano *nm* ebony.
ebonita *nf* ebonite.
ebriedad *nf* intoxication.
ebrio *adj* (**a**) intoxicated, drunk. (**b**) (*fig*) blind (*de* with); **~ de alegría** drunk with happiness, beside o.s. with joy.
ebullición *nf* (**a**) boiling; **punto de ~** boiling point; **entrar en ~** to begin to boil, come to the boil.
(**b**) (*fig*: *movimiento*) movement, activity; (*estado cambiante*) state of flux; (*agitación*) ferment; **la juventud está en ~** young people are in a state of ferment; **llevar un asunto a ~** to bring a matter to the boil.
ebúrneo *adj* (*liter*) ivory, like ivory.
eccehomo *nm* poor wretch; **estar hecho un ~** to be in a sorry state.
eccema *nm* eczema.
ECG *nm abr de* **electrocardiograma** electrocardiogram, ECG.
eclecticismo *nm* eclecticism.
ecléctico, -a *adj, nm/f* eclectic.
eclesial *adj* ecclesiastic(al), church (*atr*).
eclesiástico 1 *adj* ecclesiastic(al), church (*atr*). **2** *nm* clergyman, priest, ecclesiastic.
eclipsamiento *nm* eclipse.
eclipsar [1a] *vt* to eclipse; (*fig*) to eclipse, outshine, overshadow.
eclipse *nm* eclipse (*t fig*); **~ lunar** eclipse of the moon; **~ solar** eclipse of the sun.
eclisa *nf* (*Ferro*) fishplate.
eclosión *nf* (**a**) bloom, blooming; **hacer ~** (*fig*) to bloom, blossom (forth). (**b**) (*Ent*) hatching, emerging; **hacer ~** to hatch, emerge.
eclosionar [1a] *vi* (*Ent*) to hatch, emerge.
eco *nm* (**a**) (*gen*) echo; **hacer ~** to echo, awaken an echo.
(**b**) (*fig*) echo; response; **despertar un ~, encontrar un ~** to produce a response (*en* from), awaken an echo (*en* in); **la llamada no encontró ~** the call produced no response, the call had no effect; **hacer ~** to fit, correspond; to make an impression; **hacerse ~ de una opinión** to echo an opinion; **tener ~** to catch on, arouse interest.
eco... *pref* eco...
ecoclimático *adj* ecoclimatic.
ecoequilibrio *nm* ecobalance.
ecología *nf* ecology.
ecológicamente *adv* ecologically.
ecológico *adj* ecological; *producto etc* environment-friendly; *cultivo* organic, organically-grown.
ecologismo *nm* conservation(ism); environmentalism.
ecologista 1 *adj* conservation (*atr*); environmental. **2** *nmf* conservationist; environmentalist.
ecólogo, -a *nm/f* ecologist.
ecómetro *nm* echo-sounder.
economato *nm* cooperative store; cut-price store; company store; (*Mil*) ≈ NAAFI shop, PX (*US*).
econometría *nf* econometrics.
econométrico *adj* econometric.
economía *nf* (**a**) (*gen*) economy; **~ dirigida** planned economy; **~ doméstica** home economy, housekeeping, home economics (*US*); **~ de pleno empleo, ~ de empleo completo** full-employment economy; **~ de guerra** war economy; **~ de libre empresa, ~ de libre mercado** free-market economy; **~ de mercado** market economy; **~ mixta** mixed economy; **~ negra** black economy; **~ oculta, ~ subterránea, ~ sumergida** underground economy, black economy; **~ política** political economy; **~ de subsistencia** subsistence economy.
(**b**) (*ahorro*) economy, saving; **~ de escala** economy of scale; **hacer ~s** to make economies, economize, save.
(**c**) (*cualidad*) economy, thrift, thriftiness.
(**d**) (*estudio*) economics.
(**e**) (**Ministerio de**) **E~** (**y Hacienda**) Ministry of Trade.
económicamente *adv* economically; **los ~ débiles** (*euf*) the poor; **los ~ fuertes** (*euf*) the well-off, the wealthy.
economicidad *nf* (**a**) (*gen*) economic nature (*o* working *etc*). (**b**) (*rentabilidad*) economic viability, profitability.
económico *adj* (**a**) (*gen*) economic; *año etc* fiscal, financial.
(**b**) *persona* economical, thrifty; (*pey*) miserly.
(**c**) (*Com, Fin*) economical, inexpensive; cheap; **edición económica** cheap edition, popular edition.
(**d**) (*rentable*) economic; profitable.
economista *nmf* economist; (*de banco etc*) accountant.
economizar [1f] **1** *vt* to economize (on), save; **~ tiempo** to save time. **2** *vi* to economize, save; to save up; (*pey*) to be miserly, skimp, pinch.
ecónomo, -a *nm/f* trustee, guardian; (*Ecl*) ecclesiastical administrator.
ecosensible *adj* ecosensitive.
ecosistema *nm* ecosystem.
ecosond(e)ador *nm* echo-sounder.
ecotipo *nm* ecotype.
ectópico *adj* ectopic.
ectoplasma *nm* ectoplasm.
ecu *nm* ecu.
ecuación *nf* equation; **~ cuadrática, ~ de segundo grado** quadratic equation; **~ diferencial** differential equation.
ecuador *nm* equator.
Ecuador *nm*: **el ~** Ecuador.
ecualizador *nm* equalizer.
ecualizar [1f] *vt* to equalize.
ecuánime *adj carácter* level-headed, equable; *humor, estado* calm, composed; *juicio etc* impartial.
ecuanimidad *nf* equanimity, level-headedness; calmness, composure; impartiality.
ecuatoreñismo *nm*, **ecuatorianismo** *nm*, word (*o* phrase *etc*) peculiar to Ecuador.
ecuatorial *adj* equatorial.
ecuatoriano, -a *adj, nmf* Ecuador(i)an.
ecuestre *adj* equestrian.
ecuménico *adj* ecumenical.
ecumenismo *nm* ecumenicism.
eczema *nm* = **eccema.**
echacuervos *nm invar* (**a**) (*chulo*) pimp. (**b**) (*tramposo*) cheat, impostor.
echada *nf* (**a**) throw, cast; pitch, shy; (*de moneda etc*) toss. (**b**) (*Méx*) boast; bluff.
echadizo 1 *adj* (**a**) *persona* spying, sent to spy.
(**b**) *propaganda* secretly spread; *carta* circulated in a clandestine way.
(**c**) *material* waste.
2 *nm*, **echadiza** *nf* spy.
echado *adj y ptp* (**a**) **estar ~** to lie, be lying (down).
(**b**) (*CAm, Carib*: *económicamente*) well-placed, in a good position.

(**c**) (*CAm**: *perezoso*) lazy.
(**d**) (*And**: *engreído*) stuck-up*, toffee-nosed*; **está ~ pa'lante*** (= **para adelante**) he's very pushy*; he's got a nerve*; **está ~ p'atrás** (= **para atrás**) he's very shy.

echador 1 *adj* boastful, bragging. **2** *nm* (**a**) (*presumido*) boaster, braggart. (**b**) (*forzudo*) bouncer*.

echadora *nf*: **~ de cartas** fortune-teller.

echamiento *nm* throwing *etc*; *V* **echada**.

echao‡ *adj* = **echado** (**d**).

echar [1a] **1** *vt* (**a**) (*gen*) to throw; to cast, fling, pitch, toss; *áncora, anzuelo* to cast; *moneda* to toss; *mirada* to cast, give; *suertes* to cast, draw; *dados* to throw.
(**b**) (*Culin etc*) to put in, add; **~ un poco de azúcar al líquido** add a little sugar to the liquid; **~ carbón a la lumbre** to put coal on the fire.
(**c**) (*servir*) *vino etc* to pour out; *comida* to serve (out); **échame agua** give me some water, pour me some water.
(**d**) (*despedir*) to emit, send forth, discharge; *gas* to give off, give out; *sangre* to lose, shed; *cartas* to deal; *maldiciones* to mutter.
(**e**) (*expulsar*) *persona* to eject, throw out, chuck out; to turn out; *empleado* to dismiss, fire*; (*de club etc*) to expel; *basura* to throw away, throw out; (*Náut*) to jettison; *piel* to slough; **~ algo de sí** to throw sth off, get rid of sth; **cuando protesté me echaron** when I protested they threw me out; **¡que le echen fuera!** chuck him out!
(**f**) *pelo etc* to grow, begin to grow, begin to have; *dientes* to cut; (*Bot*) *hojas etc* to put forth, sprout.
(**g**) *llave* to turn; *cerrojo* to shoot; *pestillo* to slide, work.
(**h**) (*empujar*) to move, push; **~ a uno a un lado** to push sb aside; **~ atrás a la multitud** to push the crowd back; **~ el cuerpo atrás** to lean suddenly backwards.
(**i**) **~ abajo** to demolish, pull down; (*fig*) to overthrow.
(**j**) *discurso* to give, make, deliver; *reprimenda* to give; *decreto* to issue.
(**k**) *carta* to post, put in the post, mail.
(**l**) *impuesto* to lay, impose (*a* on).
(**m**) (*achacar*) to attribute, ascribe (*a* to); (*pey*) to impute (*a* to); *culpa* to lay (*a* on).
(**n**) (*Carib, Cono Sur*) *animal* to urge on.
(**o**) (*otras locuciones*) *cuenta* to make up, balance; *freno* to apply, put on; *cigarrillo* to have, smoke; *fortuna* to tell; *cimientos* to lay; *raíz* to strike; *partida* to have, play; (*) *obra, película* to put on; **¿qué echan?** what's showing?, what's on?
(**p**) **~la de** to pose as, give o.s. the airs of, claim to be.
(**q**) **~las** (*Cono Sur**) to run away, scarper‡; *para muchas locuciones, V el sustantivo*.
(**r**) **~ a uno por delante** (*CAm**: *culpar*) to put the blame on sb.
2 *vi* (**a**) **~ por una dirección** to go in a direction, turn in a direction; **~ por una calle** to go down a street; **echemos por aquí** let's go this way; **¡echa para adelante!** lead on!; **es un olor que echa para atrás*** it's a smell that knocks you back*.
(**b**) **~ a** + *infin* to begin to + *infin*, start + *ger*; **~ a reír** to start laughing, burst out laughing; **~ a correr** to start to run, break into a run; to run off; *V* **ver** *etc*.
(**c**) **~ a faltar** (*Méx*) to miss.
3 echarse *vr* (**a**) **~ un pitillo** to have a smoke; **~ una novia** to get o.s. a girlfriend; **~ una siestecita** to have a doze; **~ un trago** to have a drink.
(**b**) (*lanzarse*) to throw o.s., fling o.s.; **~ atrás** to throw o.s. back(wards); **~ en brazos de uno** to throw o.s. into sb's arms; **~ por un precipicio** to throw o.s. over a cliff; **~ sobre uno** to hurl o.s. at sb, rush at sb; to fall on sb.
(**c**) (*tumbarse*) to lie down; to stretch out; **se echó en el suelo** he lay down on the floor.
(**d**) (*viento*) to slacken, drop.
(**e**) **~ a** + *infin* = **2** (**b**).
(**f**) **echárselas de** (*jactarse*) to brag of, boast of; (*fingir*) to pose as.
(**g**) (*Méx*) **~ encima algo** (*asumir*) to take responsibility for sth; **~ encima a uno** to alienate sb, turn sb against one.
(**h**) (*Méx*‡: *matar*) **~ a** to bump off‡.

echarpe *nm* scarf, shawl.

echazón *nf* (**a**) (*acto*) throwing. (**b**) (*Náut*) jettison, jetsam.

echón, -ona[1]* *nm/f* (*Carib, Méx*) braggart, swank*; poseur; **¡qué ~!** isn't he full of himself!*

echona[2] *nf* (*Cono Sur*) small sickle, reaping hook.

ed. *abr de* **edición** edition, ed.

edad *nf* (**a**) (*de persona*) age; **¿qué ~ tiene?** what age is he?, how old is he?; **a la ~ de 8 años, en ~ de 8 años** at the age of 8; **de ~** elderly; **de corta ~** young, of tender years; **de ~ madura, de mediana ~** middle-aged; **avanzado de ~, de ~ avanzada** advanced in years; **a una ~ avanzada** at an advanced age, late in life; **mayor ~** majority; **ser mayor de ~** to be of age, be adult; **llegar a mayor ~, cumplir la mayoría de ~** to come of age; **menor ~** minority; **ser menor de ~** to be under age; **el instrumento es como una guitarra menor de ~** the instrument is like a young (*o* undersized, underdeveloped) guitar; **~ adulta** adult age; manhood, womanhood; **llegar a la ~ adulta** to reach manhood (*etc*); **~ crítica** change of life; **~ escolar** school age; **~ escolar obligatoria** compulsory school attendance age; **la ~ ingrata** the awkward age (*13-16*); **~ de jubilación** retirement age; **~ límite** age-limit; **~ mental** mental age; **la ~ del pato, la ~ del pavo, la ~ del chivateo** (*LAm*) the tender years, the green years; the awkward age; **~ penal** age of legal responsibility; **tercera ~** third age; **persona de la tercera ~** senior citizen; **~ tierna** tender years; **~ viril** manhood; prime of life; **ella no aparenta la ~ que tiene** she doesn't look her age; **¿qué ~ le das?** how old do you think she is?; **A le saca mucha ~ a B** A is much older than B.
(**b**) (*Hist*) age, period; **por aquella ~** at that time; **~ de oro** golden age; **~ moderna** modern period, modern times; **E~ de(l) Bronce** Bronze Age; **E~ de(l) Hierro** Iron Age; **E~ Media** Middle Ages; **E~ de (la) Piedra** Stone Age.

edafología *nf* pedology, study of soils.

edecán *nm* aide-de-camp.

edema *nm* oedema.

Edén *nm* Eden, Paradise; **es un ~** it's a garden of Eden, it's an earthly paradise.

edible *adj* (*LAm*) edible.

edición *nf* (**a**) (*acto*) publication, issue; (*industria*) publishing; (*Inform*) editing; **~ en pantalla** on-line editing; **~ de sobremesa** desktop publishing; **el mundo de la ~** the publishing world.
(**b**) (*libro etc*: *nueva version*) edition; (*reimpresión*) reprint; **~ aérea** airmail edition; **~ de bolsillo** pocket edition; **~ económica** cheap edition, popular edition; **~ extraordinaria** special edition; late-night final; **~ de la mañana** morning edition; **~ numerada** numbered edition; **~ príncipe** first edition; **~ semanal** weekly edition; **~ viva** edition in print, available edition; **en ~ de** edited by; **'al cerrar la ~'** 'stop-press'; **ser la segunda ~ de uno** to be the very image of sb.
(**c**) **Ediciones Ramírez** (*Com*) Ramírez Publications.
(**d**) (*fig*) event, occasion; **es la tercera ~ de este festival** this is the third occasion on which this festival has been held.

edicto *nm* edict, proclamation.

edificabilidad *nf* suitability for building; development potential.

edificable *adj*: **terreno ~** building land, land available for building.

edificación *nf* (**a**) (*Arquit*) construction, building. (**b**) (*fig*) edification.

edificante *adj* edifying; improving; uplifting, ennobling; **una escena poco ~** an unedifying spectacle.

edificar [1g] *vt* (**a**) (*Arquit*) to build, construct. (**b**) (*fig*) to edify; to improve; to uplift, ennoble.

edificio *nm* building; edifice; (*fig*) edifice, structure; **~ de apartamentos** block of flats; **~ de oficinas** office block.

edil *nmf* (*España*: *alcalde*) mayor; (*concejal*) town councillor; (*dignatario*) civic dignitary; (*Hist*) aedile.

Edimburgo *nm* Edinburgh.

Edipo *nm* Oedipus.

editaje *nm* editing.

editar [1a] *vt* (**a**) (*publicar*) to publish. (**b**) (*corregir*) to edit, correct. (**c**) *texto* to edit (*t Inform*).

editor 1 *adj* publishing (*atr*); **casa ~a** publishing house. **2** *nm*, **editora** *nf* (**a**) (*de libros, periódicos etc*) publisher. (**b**) (*redactor*) editor, compiler; (*TV*) editor. (**c**) (*LAm*: *de periódico*) newspaper editor. **3** *nm* (*Inform*): **~ de pantalla** screen editor; **~ de texto** text editor.

editorial 1 *adj* (**a**) publishing (*atr*); **casa ~** publishing house. (**b**) *función, política etc* editorial. **2** *nm* leading article, editorial. **3** *nf* publishing house.

editorialista *nmf* leader-writer.

editorializar [1f] *vi* to write editorials; **el periódico editorializa contra ...** the paper argues editorially against ...; **el diario editorializa ...** the paper says in its editorial ...

edredón *nm* eiderdown; feather pillow; duvet.

Eduardo *nm* Edward.

educabilidad *nf* educability.
educable *adj* educable, teachable.
educación *nf* (**a**) (*gen*) education; training; upbringing; ~ **compensatoria** remedial teaching; ~ **especial** special education; ~ **física** physical education; ~ **preescolar** pre-school education, nursery education; ~ **sanitaria** health education; ~ **sexual** sex education; ~ **de la voz** elocution lessons, voice training.
(**b**) (*modales*) (good) manners, (good) breeding; (*cortesía*) politeness, civility; **falta de ~, mala ~** bad manners, incivility; **es de mala ~ escupir** it's bad manners to spit, it's ill-mannered to spit; **es de mala ~ comportarse así** it's rude to behave like that; **es una persona sin ~** he's a badly-bred person, he's an ill-mannered individual; **¡qué falta de ~!** how rude!; **¡habla con más ~!** don't be so rude!, be more civil!; **no tener ~** to lack breeding, lack good manners.
(**c**) (**Ministerio de**) **E~** (**y Ciencia**) Ministry of Education (and Science).
educacional *adj* educational.
educacionista *nmf* education(al)ist.
educado *adj* (*de buenos modales*) well-mannered, polite; nicely behaved; (*culto*) cultivated, cultured; **mal ~** ill-mannered, unmannerly; rude.
educador(a) *nm/f* educator, teacher.
educando, -a *nm/f* pupil.
educar [1g] *vt* (*gen*) to educate; (*entrenar*) to train; (*hijos*) to raise, bring up; *voz* to train.
educativo *adj* educative; educational; **política educativa** education(al) policy.
edulcoración *nf* (*Farm*) sweetening.
edulcorante *nm* sweetener.
edulcorar [1a] *vt* (*Farm*) to sweeten.
EE.UU. *nmpl abr de* **Estados Unidos** *mpl* United States, US, USA.
efectismo *nm* straining after effect; sensationalism.
efectista 1 *adj* strained; sensational. **2** *nmf* strainer after effect; sensationalist.
efectivamente *adv* really; in fact; (*como respuesta*) exactly, precisely, just so; sure enough.
efectividad *nf* effectiveness.
efectivo 1 *adj* (**a**) (*eficaz*) effective; **hacer algo ~** to make sth effective, carry sth out; to put sth into effect; **hacer ~ un cheque** to cash a cheque.
(**b**) (*verdadero*) actual, real; **el poder ~ está en manos de X** the real power is in X's hands.
(**c**) *empleo* regular, permanent, established.
2 *nm* (**a**) cash; specie; **con 50 libras en ~** with £50 in cash; **y 3 premios en ~** and 3 cash prizes; **~ en caja, ~ en existencia** cash in hand.
(**b**) **~s** (*Mil etc*) forces, troops; establishment.
efecto *nm* (**a**) (*consecuencia*) effect; **~ bumerán** boomerang effect; **~ dominó** domino effect; **~ embudo** funnel effect; **~s especiales** special effects; **~ (de) invernadero** greenhouse effect; **~ secundario** side effect; **~s sonoros** sound effects; **~ útil** (*Mec*) efficiency, output; **~ visuales** (*TV*) visual effects; **hacer ~** (*medicina*) to take effect; **hacer ~, surtir ~** to have the desired effect; to work; to tell (*en* on); (*idea etc*) to get across, have an impact; **llevar a ~, poner en ~** to put into effect, carry out; **tener ~** (*entrar en vigor*) to take effect; (*suceso etc*) to take place; **en ~** in effect; in fact, really; (*como respuesta*) yes indeed, precisely.
(**b**) (*resultado*) result; **tener por ~** to have as a result (*o* consequence).
(**c**) (*finalidad*) purpose, end; **a este ~, a estos ~s, a tal ~** to this end; **a cuyo ~** to which end; **a mis ~s** for my purposes; **a ~s fiscales** for tax purposes; **a ~s policiales** so far as the police are concerned; **a ~s de máxima seguridad** in order to ensure the tightest security; **al ~ de que** + *subj* in order that ...; **a ~s de** + *infin* with a view to + *ger*, with the object of + *ger*; **construido al ~** (specially) built for the purpose.
(**d**) (*impresión*) effect, impression, impact; **hacer ~** to make an impression; **me hace el ~ de que ...** it gives me the impression that ...
(**e**) (*de pelota*) spin; **dar ~ a una pelota** to put some spin on a ball; **lanzar una pelota con ~** to throw a ball so that it spins (*o* swerves).
(**f**) **~s** bills, securities; **~s bancarios** bankable bills; **~s a cobrar** bills receivable; **~s descontados** bills discounted; **~s a pagar** bills payable.
(**g**) (*bienes*) **~s** effects, goods; things; (*Fin*) assets; (*Com*) goods, articles, merchandise; **~s de consumo** consumer goods; **~s de escritorio** writing materials; **~s personales** personal effects.
efectuación *nf* accomplishment; bringing about.
efectuar [1e] *vt* to effect, carry out, bring about; *plan, reparación* to carry out; *mejoría, parada, visita, gira, baza etc* to make; *censo* to take.
efeméride *nf* event (remembered on its anniversary); **~s** (*en periódico*) list of the day's anniversaries; (*título*) *equivalente a* '50 years (*etc*) ago today'.
efervescencia *nf* (**a**) effervescence; fizziness; **entrar en ~, estar en ~** to effervesce. (**b**) (*fig*) (*alboroto*) commotion, agitation; (*alegría*) high spirits, effervescence.
efervescente *adj* (**a**) (*gen*) effervescent; (*gaseoso*) fizzy, bubbly. (**b**) (*fig*) effervescent; high-spirited, bubbling.
eficacia *nf* (**a**) (*fuerza*) efficacy, effectiveness. (**b**) (*eficiencia*) efficiency.
eficaz *adj* (**a**) (*efectivo*) efficacious, effective; telling. (**b**) (*eficiente*) efficient.
eficazmente *adv* (**a**) (*con efecto*) efficaciously, effectively; tellingly. (**b**) (*eficientemente*) efficiently.
eficiencia *nf* efficiency.
eficiente *adj* efficient.
eficientemente *adv* efficiently.
efigie *nf* effigy.
efímera *nf* mayfly.
efímero *adj* ephemeral, fleeting, short-lived.
eflorescente *adj* efflorescent.
efluvio *nm* (*emanación*) outpour, outflow; **tiene un ~ de simpatía** (*fig*) there's something nice about him.
efugio *nm* subterfuge, evasion.
efusión *nf* (**a**) (*derramamiento*) outpouring; shedding; **~ de sangre** bloodshed, shedding of blood.
(**b**) (*fig*) (*acto*) effusion, outpouring; (*cualidad*) warmth, effusiveness; (*pey*) gush, gushing manner; **con ~** effusively; **efusiones amorosas** amorous excesses.
efusividad *nf* effusiveness.
efusivo *adj* effusive; *gracias* effusive, warm; *manera* effusive, (*pey*) gushing; **mis más efusivas gracias** my warmest thanks.
EGB *nf abr de* **Educación General Básica** (*from age 6 to 14*).
Egeo *nm*: **el (Mar) ~** the Aegean Sea.
égida *nf* aegis, protection; **bajo la ~ de** under the aegis of.
egipcio, -a *adj, nm/f* Egyptian.
Egipto *nm* Egypt.
egiptología *nf* Egyptology.
eglantina *nf* eglantine.
eglefino *nm* haddock.
égloga *nf* eclogue.
ego *nm* ego.
egocéntrico *adj* egocentric, self-centred.
egocentrista *nmf* egocentric, self-centred person.
egoísmo *nm* egoism; selfishness.
egoísta 1 *adj* egoistical; selfish. **2** *nmf* egoist, selfish person.
egoístamente *adv* egoistically; selfishly.
egoistón* *adj* rather selfish.
egolatría *nf* self-worship.
egotismo *nm* egotism.
egotista 1 *adj* egotistic(al). **2** *nmf* egotist.
egregio *adj* eminent, distinguished.
egresado, -a *nm/f* (*LAm*) graduate.
egresar [1a] *vi* (*LAm*) (**a**) (*irse*) to go out, go away, leave; **~ de** to go away from, leave; to emerge from. (**b**) (*Univ*) to graduate, take one's degree.
egreso *nm* (*LAm*) (**a**) (*acto*) departure, leaving, going away. (**b**) (*salida*) exit. (**c**) (*Univ*) graduation. (**d**) (*Fin*) outgoings, expenditure.
eh *interj* hey!, hi!; I say!
eider *nm* eider, eider duck.
Eire *nm* Eire.
ej. *abr de* **ejemplo** example, ex.
eje *nm* (**a**) (*Geog, Mat*) axis; **partir a uno por el ~*** to muck up sb's plans*; to cause a lot of trouble for sb; to do sb a mischief.
(**b**) (*Mec: de rueda*) axle; **~ delantero** front axle; **~ trasero** rear axle.
(**c**) (*Mec: de máquina*) shaft, spindle; **~ de balancín** rocker shaft; **~ del cigüeñal** crankshaft; **~ de la hélice** propeller shaft; **~ de impulsión, ~ motor** drive shaft.
(**d**) (*Pol*) axis; **las fuerzas del E~** the Axis forces.
(**e**) (*fig*) (*centro*) hinge, hub; (*núcleo*) essential part, crux, core; (*idea*) central idea, main idea.
(**f**) **~ vial** (*Méx Aut*) urban motorway.
ejecución *nf* (**a**) (*gen*) execution, performance, carrying

out; fulfilment; enforcement; **poner en ~** to carry out, carry into effect.
(**b**) (*Jur*) attachment, distraint.
(**c**) (*Mús*) performance, rendition.
(**d**) (*muerte*) execution; **~ sumaria** summary execution.
ejecutable *adj* feasible, practicable; **legalmente ~** legally enforceable.
ejecutante 1 *nmf* (*Mús*) performer. **2** *nm* (*Jur*) distrainer.
ejecutar [1a] *vt* (**a**) *orden etc* to execute, carry out; *deseos* to perform, fulfil; *hecho* to execute.
(**b**) (*Jur*) to attach, distrain on.
(**c**) (*Mús*) to perform, render, play.
(**d**) (*matar*) to execute.
(**e**) (*Inform*) to run.
ejecutiva[1] *nf* (*Pol etc*) executive (body); executive committee.
ejecutivo 1 *adj* (**a**) *función, poder* executive.
(**b**) *demanda etc* pressing, insistent; *negocio* urgent, immediate.
2 *nm*, **ejecutiva[2]** *nf* (*Com*) executive; **~ de cuentas** account executive; **~ de ventas** sales executive.
3 *nm* (*Pol*) **el E~** the Executive.
ejecutor *nm* (*t* **~ testamentario**) executor.
ejecutoria *nf* (**a**) (*diploma*) letters patent of nobility; (*fig*) pedigree. (**b**) (*Jur*) final judgement.
ejem *interj* hem! (*cough*).
ejemplar 1 *adj* exemplary; model.
2 *nm* (**a**) (*ejemplo*) example; (*Zool etc*) specimen, example; (*de libro*) copy; (*de revista*) number, issue; **~ de firma** specimen signature; **~ gratuito** free copy; **~ obsequio, ~ de regalo** complimentary copy.
(**b**) (*precedente*) example, model, precedent; **sin ~** unprecedented.
ejemplaridad *nf* exemplariness.
ejemplarizador *adj*, **ejemplarizante** *adj* exemplary; warning, intended to serve as a warning.
ejemplarizar [1f] *vt* (*esp LAm*) to set an example to; to exemplify, demonstrate by example, set an example of.
ejemplificar [1g] *vt* to exemplify, illustrate, be illustrative of.
ejemplo *nm* (*gen*) example, instance; (*lección*) object lesson; (*precedente*) precedent, parallel; **por ~** for example, for instance; **sin ~** unprecedented, unparalleled; **dar ~** to set an example; **tomar algo por ~** to take sth as an example.
ejercer [2b] **1** *vt* (*gen*) to exercise; *influencia* to exert, use, bring to bear; *poder* to exercise, wield; *profesión* to practise; *negocio etc* to manage, conduct, run; *función* to perform.
2 *vi* to practise (*de* as); to be in office, hold office.
ejercicio *nm* (**a**) (*gen*) exercise; (*práctica*) practice; drill; (*Mil*) exercise, drill, training; (*Escol*) exercise, test; **~ acrobático** (*Aer*) stunt; **~ antiaéreo** air-raid drill; **~ de calentamiento** warm-up exercise; **~ de castigo** (*Escol*) imposition; **~ de comprensión lectora** reading comprehension test; **~ de defensa contra incendios** fire-drill; **~s espirituales** (*Rel*) retreat; **~s gimnásticos** gymnastic exercises; **~ práctico** (*examen*) practical; **~ de tiro** target practice; **hacer ~s** to do exercises; to take exercise; (*Mil*) to drill, train.
(**b**) (*de cargo*) tenure; **abogado en ~** practising lawyer.
(**c**) (*Com, Fin*) fiscal year; financial year; business year; **~ fiscal** tax year; **durante el ~ actual** during the current financial year.
ejerciente *adj* practising.
ejercitar [1a] **1** *vt* to exercise; *profesión* to practise; *tropas* to drill, train. **2 ejercitarse** *vr* to exercise; to practise; (*Mil*) to drill, train.
ejército *nm* army; **miembros de los 3 ~s** members of the forces (*o* Services); **~ de ocupación** army of occupation; **~ permanente** standing army; **E~ de Salvación** Salvation Army; **estar en el ~** to be in the army.
ejidatario, -a *nm/f* (*Méx*) holder of a share in communal lands.
ejido *nm* ≈ common, communal land.
-ejo, -eja *V* **Aspects of Word Formation in Spanish 2.**
ejote *nm* (*CAm, Méx*) string bean.
el[1] *art def m*, **la** *f* the; *no se traduce en los casos siguientes* **La India** India; **en el México de hoy** in present-day Mexico; **me gusta el fútbol** I like football; **está en la cárcel** he's in jail; **el General Prim** General Prim; **¿qué manda la señora?** what would madam like?; **a las ocho** at eight o'clock; **a los quince días** after a fortnight; **el tío ese** that chap; **el hacerlo fue un error** doing it was a mistake, it was a mistake to do it.
el[2] *pron dem* **mi libro y ~ de Vd** my book and yours; **este jugador y ~ de la camisa azul** this player and the one in the blue shirt; **~ de Pepe es mejor** Joe's is better; **y ~ de todos los demás** and that of everybody else, and everybody else's.
el[3]: **~ que** *pron rel* (*t* **la que, los que, las que**) he who, whoever; the one(s) that; **el que quiera, que lo haga** whoever wants to can get on with it; **los que hacen eso son tontos** those who do so are foolish; **el que compramos no vale** the one we bought is no good; **a los que mencionamos añádase éste** add this one to those we mentioned.
él *pron pers m* (**a**) (*sujeto: persona*) he; (*cosa*) it.
(**b**) (*tras prep: persona*) him; (*cosa*) it; **esto es para ~** this is for him; **vamos sin ~** let's go without him.
(**c**) (*tras* **de**: *persona*) his; (*cosa*) its; **mis libros y los de ~** my books and his; **todo eso es de ~** all that is his, all that belongs to him.
elaboración *nf* elaboration; manufacture, production; working; working-out; **~ de presupuestos** (*Com*) budgeting.
elaborar [1a] *vt materia prima* to elaborate; *producto* to make, manufacture, produce; to prepare; *metal, madera etc* to work; *plan etc* to work on, work out.
elación *nf* (**a**) (*orgullo*) haughtiness, pride. (**b**) (*generosidad*) generosity. (**c**) (*de estilo*) pomposity. (**d**) (*LAm: alegría*) elation.
elasticidad *nf* (**a**) (*gen*) elasticity; spring, sponginess; give. (**b**) (*fig*) elasticity; (*moral*) resilience.
elástico 1 *adj* (**a**) (*gen*) elastic; flexible; *superficie etc* springy. (**b**) (*fig*) elastic; (*moralmente*) resilient. **2** *nm* elastic.
ELE, E/LE ['ele] *nm abr de* **español como lengua extranjera** Spanish as a foreign language.
elección *nf* (**a**) (*selección*) choice, selection; (*opción*) option; **una ~ acertada** a sensible choice; **su patria de ~** his chosen country; **no queda otra ~** there is no alternative.
(**b**) (*Pol etc*) election (*a* for); **elecciones autonómicas** regional election; **~ complementaria, elecciones parciales** by-election; **elecciones generales** general election; **elecciones legislativas** parliamentary election; **elecciones municipales** council elections; **elecciones primarias** primary election.
eleccionario *adj* (*LAm*) electoral, election (*atr*).
electivo *adj* elective.
electo *adj* elect; **el presidente ~** the president-elect.
elector(a) *nm/f* elector; voter.
electorado *nm* electorate; voters.
electoral *adj* electoral; **potencia ~** voting power, power in terms of votes.
electoralismo *nm* electioneering; vote-catching.
electoralista *adj* electioneering (*atr*); vote-catching (*atr*).
electoralmente *adv* electorally; in terms of winning votes.
electorista *adj* election (*atr*).
eléctrica[1] *nf* electricity company.
electricidad *nf* electricity; **~ estática** static electricity.
electricista *nmf* electrician.
eléctrico 1 *adj* electric(al). **2** *nm*, **eléctrica[2]** *nf* electrician.
electrificación *nf* electrification.
electrificar [1g] *vt* to electrify.
electrizante *adj* electrifying (*t fig*).
electrizar [1f] *vt* to electrify (*t fig*); **su discurso electrizó al público** his speech electrified his listeners.
electro... *pref* electro...
electrocardiograma *nm* electrocardiogram.
electroconvulsivo *adj* electroconvulsive.
electrocución *nf* electrocution.
electrocutar [1a] *vt* to electrocute.
electrochapado *adj* electroplated.
electrochoque *nm* electroshock.
electrodinámica *nf* electrodynamics.
electrodo *nm*, **eléctrodo** *nm* electrode.
electrodoméstico 1 *adj*: **aparato ~** = 2. **2** *nm* (home electrical) appliance; **~s de línea blanca** white goods.
electroencefalograma *nm* electroencephalogram.
electroimán *nm* electromagnet.
electrólisis *nf* electrolysis.
electromagnético *adj* electromagnetic.
electromagnetismo *nm* electromagnetism.
electromotor *nm* electric motor.
electrón *nm* electron.
electrónica *nf* electronics; **~ de consumo** consumer electronics; **~ de precisión** precision electronics.

electrónico *adj* electronic; *microscopio* electron (*atr*).
electronuclear *adj*: **central ~** nuclear power station; **programa ~** nuclear power programme.
electrotecnia *nf* electrical engineering.
electrotermo *nm* immersion heater.
electrotren *nm* express electric train.
elefante *nm*, **elefanta** *nf* elephant; **~ blanco** white elephant; **como un ~ en una cacharrería** like a bull in a china shop.
elefantino *adj* elephantine.
elegancia *nf* elegance; gracefulness; stylishness, smartness; tastefulness; polish.
elegante *adj* (*gen*) elegant; graceful; *vestido, fiesta, tienda etc* stylish, fashionable, smart; *sociedad* fashionable, elegant; *decoración etc* tasteful; *frase etc* elegant, well-turned, polished; **no es ~ gritar** it's rude to shout, it's not dignified to shout.
elegantemente *adv* elegantly; gracefully; stylishly, fashionably, smartly; tastefully; in a polished way.
elegantoso *adj* (*LAm*) = **elegante.**
elegía *nf* elegy.
elegiaco *adj*, **elegíaco** *adj* elegiac.
elegibilidad *nf* eligibility.
elegible *adj* eligible.
elegido *adj* (**a**) (*selecto*) chosen, selected. (**b**) (*Pol etc*) elect, elected.
elegir [3c *y* 3k] *vt* (**a**) (*escoger*) to choose, select; to opt for; **café con bizcochos a ~** coffee with a choice of cakes; **a ~ entre 5 tipos** there are 5 sorts to choose from; **hablará en francés o italiano, a ~** he will talk in French or Italian, as you (*etc*) prefer; **te toca a ti ~** the choice is yours, it's up to you to choose.
(**b**) (*Pol etc*) to elect.
elementado *adj* (*And, Cono Sur*: *aturdido*) bewildered; (*bobo*) silly, stupid.
elemental *adj* elementary; elemental, fundamental; **eso es ~** that's elementary.
elementarse [1a] *vr* (*Cono Sur*) to get bewildered.
elemento *nm* (**a**) (*gen*) element; **los cuatro ~s** the four elements; **estar en su ~** to be in one's element.
(**b**) (*Quím etc*) element; (*fig*) ingredient, constituent (part); (*de situación*) element, factor; **~s** material, ingredients; **~s de juicio** data, facts (on which to base a judgement).
(**c**) (*Elec*) element; (*de pila*) cell.
(**d**) (*persona*) person, individual; (*LAm**: *tipo*) chap*, guy* (*US*); **vino a verle un ~** someone came to see you; **dos ~s distinguidos** two distinguished individuals.
(**e**) (*And, Carib, Cono Sur*: *imbécil*) dimwit*, ass*.
(**f**) (*Carib*: *tipo raro*) odd person, eccentric.
(**g**) (*Esp pey*) undesirable (person), suspicious individual.
(**h**) **~s** (*de una materia*) elements, rudiments, first principles.
Elena *nf* Helen.
elenco *nm* (*lista*) catalogue, list; (*And, Cono Sur*: *personal*) staff, team; (*esp LAm Cine, Teat*) cast.
elepé *nm* long-playing record.
elevación *nf* (**a**) (*acto*) elevation (*a* to), raising, lifting; (*Ecl*) elevation; (*de precio, tipo etc*) rise.
(**b**) (*Geog etc*) elevation, height, altitude.
(**c**) (*de estilo, mente etc*) elevation; (*de persona*) exaltation, loftiness; (*pey*) conceit, pride.
(**d**) (*éxtasis*) rapture.
elevadamente *adv* loftily, sublimely.
elevado 1 *adj* (**a**) (*alto*) elevated, raised; high, lofty; *edificio* high, tall; *precio, tipo etc* high; *puesto* exalted, high; **a precios elevadísimos** at terribly high prices.
(**b**) *estilo, pensamiento etc* elevated, lofty, noble; grand, sublime; **de pensamientos ~s** of noble thoughts, high-minded.
2 *nm* (*Carib Ferro*) overhead railway; (*Carib Aut*) flyover.
elevador *nm* elevator, hoist; (*LAm*: *ascensor*) lift, elevator (*US*); **~ de granos** (grain) elevator; **~ de tensión, ~ de voltaje** (*Elec*) booster.
elevadorista *nmf* (*Méx*) lift operator.
elevalunas *nm invar* (*Aut*) electric windows.
elevar [1a] **1** *vt* (**a**) (*alzar*) to raise, lift (up), elevate; *precio, tipo* to raise, put up; *producción* to step up; (*Elec*) to boost; (*Mat*) to raise (*a una potencia* to a power); *persona* to promote; to exalt; *estilo* to raise the tone of; **~ los pensamientos a Dios** to raise one's thoughts to God.
(**b**) *informe etc* to present, submit (*a* to); **el comité elevará un informe al ministro** the committee will report to the minister.
2 elevarse *vr* (**a**) (*alzarse*) to rise, go up; (*edificio etc*) to rise, soar, tower; **la cantidad se eleva a ...** the quantity amounts to ...; **los precios se han elevado mucho** prices have risen a lot.
(**b**) (*extasiarse*) to be transported, go into a rapture.
(**c**) (*pey*) to get conceited, become overbearing.
Elías *nm* Elijah.
elidir [3a] **1** *vt* to elide. **2 elidirse** *vr* to elide, be elided.
eliminable *adj* dispensable.
eliminación *nf* elimination; removal; (*Dep*: *t* **~ progresiva**) knockout.
eliminar [1a] **1** *vt* (*gen*) to eliminate; to remove; *necesidad etc* to remove, obviate; *residuos* to get rid of; (*Dep*) to eliminate, knock out; (*matar*) to eliminate, do away with.
2 eliminarse *vr* (**a**) (*Dep*) to play an eliminating round. (**b**) (*Méx*) to go away.
eliminatoria *nf* (*Dep*: *vuelta*) heat, preliminary round, qualifying round; (*competición*) knockout competition.
elipse *nf* (*Mat*) ellipse.
elipsis *nf invar* (*Ling*) ellipsis.
elíptico *adj* elliptic(al).
Elíseo[1] *nm* (*Biblia*) Elishah.
Elíseo[2] *nm* (*clásico*) Elysium.
elisión *nf* elision.
elite [e'lite] *nf*, **élite** ['elite] *nf* élite.
elitismo *nm* elitism.
elitista *adj, nmf* elitist.
elixir *nm* elixir; **~ de la (eterna) juventud** elixir of life.
elocución *nf* elocution.
elocuencia *nf* eloquence.
elocuente *adj* eloquent; (*fig*) telling; significant; **un dato ~** a significant fact, a fact which speaks for itself.
elocuentemente *adv* eloquently.
elogiable *adj* praiseworthy.
elogiar [1b] *vt* to praise, eulogize (*liter*).
elogio *nm* praise, eulogy; tribute; **queda por encima de todo ~** it's beyond praise; **hacer ~ de** to praise, extol; to pay (a) tribute to; **hizo un caluroso ~ del héroe** he paid a warm tribute to the hero, he was warm in his praise of the hero.
elogiosamente *adv* eulogistically; very favourably, with warm approval; **comentó ~ sus cualidades** he spoke very favourably of his qualities.
elogioso *adj* eulogistic; highly favourable, warmly approving; **en términos ~s** in highly favourable terms.
elotada *nf* (*CAm, Méx*) (*Agr*) ears of maize (*collectively*).
elote *nm* (*CAm, Méx*) (*mazorca*) corncob; (*maíz*) maize, corn (*US*), sweet corn; **coger a uno asando ~s** to catch sb red-handed; **pagar los ~s*** to carry the can*.
elotear [1a] *vi* (*CAm, Méx*: *maíz*) to come into ear.
El Salvador *nm* El Salvador.
elucidación *nf* elucidation.
elucidar [1a] *vt* to elucidate.
elucubración *nf* lucubration.
elucubrar [1a] *vi* to lucubrate.
eludible *adj* avoidable.
eludir [3a] *vt* to elude, evade, avoid, escape.
elusivo *adj* (*LAm*) evasive, tricky.
ella *pron pers f* (**a**) (*sujeto*: *persona*) she; (*cosa*) it.
(**b**) (*tras prep*: *persona*) her; (*cosa*) it; **estuve con ~** I was with her; **no podemos sin ~** without her we can't.
(**c**) (*tras* **de**: *persona*) hers; (*cosa*) its; **mi sombrero y el de ~** my hat and hers; **nada de esto es de ~** none of this is hers, none of this belongs to her.
ellas *V* **ellos.**
ello *pron 'neutro'* (**a**) (*gen*) it; this business, that whole affair; **~ es difícil** it's awkward; **~ no me gusta** I don't like it; **todo ~ se acabó** the whole thing is over and done with; **no tiene fuerzas para ~** he is not strong enough for it.
(**b**) (*locuciones*) **~ es que** ... the fact is that ...; **por ~ no quiero** that's why I don't want to; **es por ~ que** ... (*LAm*) that is why ...; **luego será ~** there'll be trouble later; **~ dirá** the event will show; **¡a por ~!** here goes!; **¡aquí fue ~!** and then it started, and that was it.
(**c**) (*Psic*) id.
ellos *pron pers mpl*, **ellas** *pron pers fpl* (**a**) (*sujeto*) they. (**b**) (*tras prep*) them. (**c**) (*tras* **de**) theirs; *V* **él, ella.**
E.M. *abr de* **Estado Mayor** General Staff, GS.
Em.ª *abr de* **Eminencia** Eminence.
emanación *nf* emanation; (*olor*) smell.
emanar [1a] *vi*: **~ de** to emanate from, come from, origi-

nate in.
emancipación *nf* emancipation; freeing.
emancipado *adj* emancipated; independent, free.
emancipar [1a] **1** *vt* to emancipate; to free.
2 emanciparse *vr* to become emancipated (*de* from); to become independent (*de* of); to free o.s. (*de* from).
emascular [1a] *vt* to castrate, emasculate.
embadurnar [1a] *vt* to daub, bedaub, smear (*de* with).
embaidor *nm* cheat, swindler.
embaimiento *nm* imposture, trick, swindle; deceit.
embaír [3a: *defectivo*] *vt* to swindle, cheat.
embajada *nf* (**a**) (*edificio*) embassy. (**b**) (*cargo*) ambassadorship. (**c**) (*fig*) errand, message. (**d**) (*pey*) unwelcome proposal, silly suggestion.
embajador *nm* ambassador (*en* in, *cerca de* to); **~ itinerante, ~ volante** roving ambassador, ambassador at large; **~ político** politically-appointed ambassador.
embajadora *nf* (*oficial*) (woman) ambassador; (*esposa*) ambassador's wife.
embajatorio *adj* ambassadorial.
embalado 1 *adj* (‡) (**a**) (*sexualmente*) randy*. (**b**) (*Carib**: *drogado*) high‡. **2** *nm* packing, packaging.
embalador(a) *nm/f* packer.
embaladura *nf* (*LAm*), **embalaje** *nm* packing.
embalar [1a] **1** *vt* to pack, parcel up, wrap; *mercancías pesadas* to crate, bale.
2 *vi* (**a**) (*Dep*) to sprint, make a dash; (*Aut*) to step on it*.
(**b**) (*Carib*: *huir*) to run off, escape.
3 embalarse *vr* (**a**) (*correr*) to rush off; to go hell for leather; (*Aut*) to race along; (*hablar*) to talk nineteen to the dozen; **el orador estaba embalándose** the speaker was in full flow. (**b**) (*: *ponerse cachondo*) to get randy*.
embaldosado *nm* tiled floor, tiling.
embaldosar [1a] *vt* to tile, pave with tiles.
embalsadero *nm* boggy place.
embalsado *nm* (*Cono Sur*) mass of floating water weeds.
embalsamar [1a] *vt* to embalm.
embalsar [1a] **1** *vt* (**a**) *agua* to dam, dam up; to retain, collect; **este mes se han embalsado X m^3** this month reservoir stocks have gone up by X cubic metres.
(**b**) (*Náut*) to sling, hoist.
2 *vi* (*And*: *cruzar*) to cross a river (*etc*).
embalse *nm* (**a**) (*acto*) damming. (**b**) (*presa*) dam; (*lago*) reservoir.
embanastar [1a] *vt* to put into a basket; (*fig*) to jam in, overcrowd.
embancarse [1g] *vr* (*And, Cono Sur*) to silt up, become blocked by silt.
embanderar [1a] *vt* to deck with flags; **embanderado** beflagged, decked with flags.
embanquetado *nm* (*LAm*) pavement(s), sidewalk(s) (*US*).
embanquetar [1a] *vt* (*LAm*) to provide with pavements *o* sidewalks (*US*).
embarazada 1 *adj* pregnant; **dejar ~ a una** to get a girl pregnant, put a girl in the family way; **estar ~ de 4 meses** to be 4 months pregnant. **2** *nf* pregnant woman, expectant mother.
embarazar [1f] *vt* (**a**) (*estorbar*) to obstruct, hamper, hinder. (**b**) *mujer* to make pregnant, put in the family way.
embarazo *nm* (**a**) (*estorbo*) obstacle, obstruction, hindrance. (**b**) (*de mujer*) pregnancy; **~ no deseado, ~ involuntario** unwanted pregnancy; **~ nervioso** phantom pregnancy; **durante el ~** during pregnancy; **interrumpir el ~** to terminate a pregnancy.
embarazosamente *adv* awkwardly, inconveniently; embarrassingly.
embarazoso *adj* (*molesto*) awkward, inconvenient, troublesome; (*violento*) embarrassing.
embarcación *nf* (**a**) (*barco*) boat, craft, (small) vessel; **~ de arrastre** trawler; **~ auxiliar** tender; **~ de cabotaje** coasting vessel; **~ fueraborda** motorboat; **~ pesquera** fishing boat; **~ de recreo** pleasure boat; **~ de vela** sailing boat.
(**b**) (*acto*) embarkation.
embarcadero *nm* (**a**) pier, landing stage, jetty. (**b**) (*LAm Ferro*) goods station; (*andén*) platform; (*corral*) cattle pen (attached to a railway station).
embarcar [1g] **1** *vt* (**a**) *personas* to embark, put on board; *carga* to ship, get on board, stow.
(**b**) **~ a uno en una empresa** to involve sb in an enterprise.
(**c**) (*LAm**) **~ a uno** to set sb up*.
(**d**) (*Carib**: *engañar*) to con*.
2 embarcarse *vr* (**a**) (*pasajero*) to embark, go on board; (*marinero*) to sign on, join a ship; **~ para** to sail for.
(**b**) (*LAm Ferro etc*) to get on, get in; **se embarcó en el autobús** he got on the bus, he boarded the bus.
(**c**) **~ en un asunto** to get involved in a matter.
embarco *nm* embarcation.
embargar [1h] *vt* (**a**) (*estorbar*) to impede, hinder; (*frenar*) to restrain, put a check on.
(**b**) *sentidos* to blunt, confuse, paralyse, overpower.
(**c**) (*Jur*) to seize, impound, distrain upon.
embargo *nm* (**a**) (*Jur*) seizure, distraint; (*Com etc*) embargo; **sin ~** still, however, none the less; **sin ~ de** despite the fact that.
(**b**) (*Med*) indigestion.
embarnizar [1f] *vt* to varnish.
embarque *nm* (**a**) embarkation; shipment, loading. (**b**) (*Carib**) melodrama; emotional affair.
embarrada* *nf* (*LAm*) blunder.
embarrado *adj calle etc* muddy.
embarradura *nf* smear, daub.
embarrancamiento *nm* running aground; beaching, stranding.
embarrancar [1g] **1** *vti* (**a**) (*Náut*) to run aground.
(**b**) (*Aut etc*) to run into a ditch.
2 embarrancarse *vr* (**a**) (*Náut*) to run aground; **quedar embarrancado** (*ballena etc*) to be beached, be stranded.
(**b**) (*Aut etc*) to run into a ditch; to get stuck; (*fig*) to get bogged down.
embarrar [1a] **1** *vt* (**a**) (*manchar*) to smear, bedaub (*de* with); (*enfangar*) to splash with mud.
(**b**) (*LAm*) *pared* to cover with mud; to plaster.
(**c**) **~ a uno** (*CAm, Méx**) to set sb up*.
(**d**) **~ a uno** (*Carib, Cono Sur*) to smear sb, damage sb's standing.
2 *vi* (*Cono Sur*) to make a mess of things.
3 embarrarse *vr* (*Carib*: *niño*) to dirty o.s.
embarrialarse [1a] *vr* (**a**) (*CAm*: *enfangarse*) to get covered with mud. (**b**) (*CAm Aut*) to get stuck. (**c**) (*CAm, Carib**: *enredarse*) to get o.s. in a mess.
embarullador *adj* bungling.
embarullar [1a] *vt* to bungle, mess up.
embastar [1a] *vt* to baste, stitch, tack.
embaste *nm* basting, stitching, tacking.
embate *nm* (**a**) (*Mil etc*) sudden attack; brunt of the attack. (**b**) (*de olas*) dashing, breaking, beating; violence. (**c**) **~s de la fortuna** (*fig*) blows of fate.
embaucador(a) *nm/f* (*estafador*) trickster, swindler; (*impostor*) impostor; (*farsante*) humbug.
embaucamiento *nm* swindle, swindling; humbug.
embaucar [1g] *vt* to trick, swindle; to fool, lead up the garden path.
embaular *vt* (**a**) to pack (into a trunk). (**b**) (*) *comida* to tuck away*, stuff o.s. with, guzzle; *bebida* to sink*, knock back*. (**c**) (*Carib*) to clean out.
embazar [1f] **1** *vt* (**a**) (*teñir*) to dye brown.
(**b**) (*fig*: *pasmar*) to astound, amaze.
(**c**) (*fig*: *estorbar*) to hinder.
2 *vi* to be dumbfounded, stand amazed.
3 embazarse *vr* to get tired, get bored; to have had enough.
embebecer [2d] **1** *vt* to fascinate. **2 embebecerse** *vr* to be fascinated, be lost in wonder; to be dumbfounded.
embebecimiento *nm* (**a**) (*fascinación*) absorption, fascination; (*encanto*) enchantment. (**b**) (*asombro*) astonishment, wonderment.
embeber [2a] **1** *vt* (**a**) (*absorber*) to absorb, soak up; (*saturar*) to saturate, soak.
(**b**) (*Cos*) to take in, gather in.
(**c**) (*fig*) (*absorber*) to imbibe; (*meter*) to insert, introduce (*en* into); (*abarcar*) to contain, incorporate, comprise.
2 *vi* (*tela*) to shrink.
3 embeberse *vr* (**a**) *lectura, tema etc* to be absorbed, become engrossed (*en* in); to be enraptured, be enchanted (*en* with).
(**b**) **~ de** to imbibe, soak o.s. in, become well versed in.
embelecar [1g] *vt* to deceive, cheat.
embeleco *nm*, **embelequería** *nf* (*And, Carib, Cono Sur*) deceit, fraud.
embelequero *adj* (**a**) (*LAm*: *aspaventero*) given to making a great fuss, highly emotional. (**b**) (*And, Carib*: *tramposo*)

shifty. (**c**) (*Carib*: *frívolo*) frivolous, silly.
embelesado *adj* spellbound, enraptured.
embelesador *adj* enchanting, entrancing.
embelesar [1a] **1** *vt* to enchant, entrance, enrapture. **2** **embelesarse** *vr* to be enchanted, be enraptured.
embeleso *nm* (**a**) (*encanto*) enchantment, rapture, delight. (**b**) (*en oración directa*) sweetheart, my love.
embellecedor *nm* (*Aut*: *tapacubos*) hubcap; (: *adorno*) trim; **~es laterales** 'go-faster' stripes.
embellecer [2d] *vt* to embellish, beautify.
embellecimiento *nm* embellishment.
embestida *nf* (**a**) (*ataque*) assault, onrush, onslaught; (*de toro etc*) charge, rush. (**b**) (*fig*) importunate demand.
embestir [3k] **1** *vt* (**a**) (*agredir*) to assault, attack, assail; (*lanzarse sobre*) to rush at (*o* upon); (*toro etc*) to charge; (*Aut*) to hit, collide with, crash into.
(**b**) **~ a uno** (*fig*) to pester sb for a loan.
2 *vi* to attack; to rush, charge; **~ con, ~ contra** to rush upon; (*toro etc*) to charge down on.
embetunar [1a] *vt superficie* to tar (over), pitch; *zapatos* to black.
embicar [1g] *vt* (**a**) (*Cono Sur*) *barco* to head straight for land. (**b**) (*Carib*) to insert. (**c**) (*Méx*) to turn upside down, upturn.
embicharse [1a] *vr* (*Cono Sur*) to become wormy, get maggoty.
embiste *nm* (*Carib*) = **embestida**.
emblandecer [2d] **1** *vt* to soften; (*fig*) to mollify. **2** **emblandecerse** *vr* to soften, get soft; (*fig*) to relent.
emblanquecer [2d] **1** *vt* to whiten; to bleach. **2** **emblanquecerse** *vr* to whiten, turn white; to bleach.
emblema *nm* emblem.
emblemático *adj* emblematic.
embobamiento *nm* amazement; fascination.
embobar [1a] **1** *vt* (*asombrar*) to amaze; (*fascinar*) to fascinate; **esa niña me emboba*** that girl is driving me crazy.
2 **embobarse** *vr* to be amazed, stand agape (*con, de, en* at); to be fascinated (*con, de, en* by); **reírse embobado** to laugh like mad.
embobecer [2d] **1** *vt* to make silly.
2 **embobecerse** *vr* to get silly.
embocadura *nf* (**a**) narrow entrance; (*de río*) mouth; (*Náut*) passage, narrows.
(**b**) (*Mús*) mouthpiece; (*de cigarrillo etc*) tip; (*de freno*) bit.
(**c**) (*de vino*) taste, flavour.
(**d**) (*Teat*) proscenium arch.
embocar [1g] **1** *vt* (**a**) **~ algo** to put sth into sb's mouth; **~ una cosa en un agujero** to insert sth into a hole; **~ la comida** to cram one's food, wolf one's food; **~ la pelota** (*Golf*) to hole the ball; (*Billar etc*) to pocket the ball, pot the ball.
(**b**) **~ un negocio** to undertake a piece of business.
(**c**) **~ algo a uno** (*fig*) to put one over on sb, hoax sb with sth; **le embocaron la especie** they got him to swallow the tale.
2 *vi* (*Golf*) to hole out.
embochinchar [1a] *vt* (*LAm*) to throw into confusion, create chaos in.
emboinado *adj* wearing a beret.
embolado *nm* (**a**) bull with wooden balls on its horns. (**b**) (*Teat*) bit part, minor role. (**c**) (*: *truco*)) trick. (**d**) (*: *aprieto*) jam*, difficulty; **meter a uno en un ~** to put sb in a difficult position, put sb in a tight spot.
embolador(a) *nm/f* (*And*) bootblack.
embolar [1a] *vt* (**a**) *cuernos* to tip with wooden balls. (**b**) (*And*) *zapatos* to black, shine. (**c**) (*CAm, Méx*: *emborrachar*) to make drunk.
embolia *nf* (*Med*) clot; embolism; **~ cerebral** clot on the brain.
embolismar* [1a] *vt* to gossip about; to make mischief for.
embolismo *nm* (**a**) (*lío*) muddle, mess, confusion. (**b**) (*chismes*) gossip, backbiting. (**c**) (*engaño*) hoax, trick.
émbolo *nm* plunger; (*Mec*) piston.
embolsar [1a] *vt*, **embolsicar** (*LAm*) [1g] *vt* to pocket, put into one's pocket; *dinero, recaudación etc* to pocket, collect, take in; (*Billar*) to pot.
embolsillar [1a] *vt*: **~ las manos** to put one's hands in one's pockets.
embonar [1a] *vt* (**a**) (*Carib, Cono Sur, Méx*) *tierra* to manure.
(**b**) (*fig*) to improve.
(**c**) (*Náut*) to sheathe; (*And, Méx*) *cuerda* to join (the ends of).
(**d**) **le embona el sombrero** (*And, Carib, Méx*) the hat suits him, the hat looks well on him.
emboque *nm* (**a**) tight passage, squeezing through. (**b**) (*) trick, hoax.
emboquillado *adj cigarrillo* tipped.
emboquillar [1a] *vt* (**a**) *cigarrillo* to tip. (**b**) (*Cono Sur Arquit*) to point, repoint.
emborrachar [1a] **1** *vt* to intoxicate, make drunk; to get drunk. **2** **emborracharse** *vr* to get drunk (*con, de* on).
emborrar [1a] *vt* (**a**) (*rellenar*) to stuff, pad, wad (*de* with). (**b**) (*) *comida* to cram, wolf.
emborrascarse [1g] *vr* (**a**) (*Met*) to get stormy. (**b**) (*fig*) to get cross, get worked up. (**c**) (*Com*: *negocio*) to fail, do badly. (**d**) (*CAm, Cono Sur, Méx*: *vena*) to peter out.
emborronar [1a] **1** *vt* (*manchar*) to blot, make blots on; (*escribir*) to scribble on. **2** *vi* to make blots; to scribble.
emboscada *nf* ambush; **tender una ~ a** to lay an ambush for.
emboscarse [1g] *vr* to lie in ambush; to hide away (in the woods); **estaban emboscados cerca del camino** they were in ambush near the road.
embotado *adj* dull, blunt (*t fig*).
embotamiento *nm* (**a**) (*acto*) dulling, blunting (*t fig*). (**b**) (*estado*) dullness, bluntness (*t fig*).
embotar [1a] *vt* (**a**) *objeto* to dull, blunt. (**b**) (*fig*) *sentidos* to dull, blunt; (*debilitar*) to weaken, enervate.
embotellado **1** *adj* bottled; *discurso etc* prepared (beforehand). **2** *nm* bottling.
embotellador(a) *nm/f* bottler.
embotellamiento *nm* (**a**) (*Aut*) traffic jam. (**b**) (*lugar*) bottleneck (*t fig*).
embotellar [1a] **1** *vt* (**a**) (*gen*) to bottle.
(**b**) (*Mil etc*) to bottle up.
(**c**) (*Escol etc**) to mug up*, swot up*.
(**d**) (*Carib*) *discurso* to prepare beforehand, memorize.
2 **embotellarse** *vr* (**a**) (*Aut*) to get into a jam, get jammed.
(**b**) (*Carib*) to learn a speech off by heart.
emboticarse [1g] *vr* (*Cono Sur, Méx*) to stuff o.s. with medicines.
embotijar [1a] **1** *vt* to put into jars; to keep in jars. **2** **embotijarse** *vr* (**a**) (*hincharse*) to swell up. (**b**) (*fig**: *encolerizarse*) to fly into a passion.
embovedar [1a] *vt* to arch, vault.
embozadamente *adv* covertly, stealthily.
embozado *adj* (**a**) (*cubierto*) muffled up (to the eyes). (**b**) (*fig*) covert, stealthy.
embozalar [1a] *vt* (*Cono Sur*) to muzzle.
embozar [1f] **1** *vt* (**a**) (*de ropa*) to muffle (up), wrap (up). (**b**) (*fig*) to cloak, disguise, conceal. **2** **embozarse** *vr* to muffle o.s. up (*con, de* in).
embozo *nm* (**a**) (*de la cara*) muffler; top (*o* fold) of the cape; mask, covering of the face; **quitarse el ~** (*fig*) to drop the mask, end the play-acting.
(**b**) (*de sábana*) turndown.
(**c**) (*fig*) (*astucia*) cunning; (*encubrimiento*) concealment; **sin ~** frankly, openly.
embragar [1h] **1** *vt* (*Aut, Mec*) to engage; *piezas* to connect, couple; (*Náut*) to sling. **2** *vi* (*Aut etc*) to put the clutch in.
embrague *nm* (*Aut, Mec*) clutch; **le patina el ~*** he's not right up top*.
embravecer [2d] **1** *vt* to enrage, infuriate.
2 *vi* (*Bot*) to flourish, grow strongly.
3 **embravecerse** *vr* (**a**) (*mar*) to get rough.
(**b**) (*persona*) to get furious.
embravecido *adj* (**a**) *mar* rough; *viento etc* wild. (**b**) *persona* furious, enraged.
embravecimiento *nm* rage, fury.
embrear [1a] *vt* to tar, cover with tar; to cover with pitch.
embretar [1a] **1** *vt* (*LAm*) *ganado* to pen, corral. **2** *vi* (*Cono Sur*) (*asfixiarse*) to suffocate; (*ahogarse*) to drown.
embriagador *adj olor* intoxicating; *vino etc* heady, strong.
embriagar [1h] **1** *vt* (**a**) (*emborrachar*) to make drunk, intoxicate; to get drunk. (**b**) (*fig*) to enrapture, delight, intoxicate. **2** **embriagarse** *vr* to get drunk.
embriaguez *nf* (**a**) (*gen*) drunkenness, intoxication. (**b**) (*fig*) rapture, delight, intoxication.
embridar [1a] *vt* (**a**) *caballo* to bridle, put a bridle on. (**b**) (*fig*) to check, restrain.
embriología *nf* embryology.
embriólogo, -a *nm/f* embryologist.
embrión *nm* embryo; **en ~** in embryo.
embrionario *adj* embryonic.
embrocación *nf* embrocation.

embrocar [1g] **1** *vt* (**a**) (*Cos*) *hilo* to wind (on to a bobbin); *zapatos* to tack.
(**b**) *líquido* to pour from one container into another.
(**c**) (*volcar*) to turn upside down, invert.
2 embrocarse *vr*: ~ **un vestido** (*Méx*) to put a dress on over one's head.
embrollante *adj* muddling, confusing.
embrollar [1a] **1** *vt asunto* to muddle, confuse, complicate; to mess up; *personas* to involve, embroil (*en* in).
2 embrollarse *vr* to get into a muddle, get into a mess; ~ **en un asunto** to get involved in a matter.
embrollista *nm* (*And, CAm, Cono Sur*) = **embrollón.**
embrollo *nm* (*confusión*) muddle, tangle, confusion; (*aprieto*) fix, jam, entanglement; (*fraude*) fraud, trick.
embrollón, -ona *nm/f* troublemaker, mischief-maker.
embromado *adj* (*LAm*) (**a**) annoying; difficult. (**b**) **estar ~** to be in a fix; to be having a tough time; (*Med*) to be in a bad way; (*Fin*) to be in financial trouble; (*con prisa*) to be in a hurry.
embromar [1a] **1** *vt* (**a**) (*tomar el pelo a*) to tease, make fun of, rag.
(**b**) (*engatusar*) to wheedle, cajole.
(**c**) (*engañar*) to hoodwink.
(**d**) (*LAm: molestar*) to annoy, vex; (*perjudicar*) to harm, set back; (*salud etc*) to affect badly.
2 embromarse *vr* (*LAm*) (*enojarse*) to get cross; (*aburrirse*) to get bored.
embroncarse [1g] *vr* (*Cono Sur*) to get angry.
embrujado *adj persona* bewitched; *casa, lugar* haunted; **una casa embrujada** a haunted house.
embrujar [1a] *vt persona* to bewitch, put a spell on; *casa, lugar* to haunt; **la casa está embrujada** the house is haunted.
embrujo *nm* (**a**) (*acto*) bewitching. (**b**) (*maldición*) curse. (**c**) (*ensalmo*) spell, charm; **el ~ de la Alhambra** the enchantment (*o* magic) of the Alhambra.
embrutecer [2d] **1** *vt* to brutalize, deprave; to coarsen. **2 embrutecerse** *vr* to become brutalized, get depraved; to coarsen.
embuchacarse [1g] *vr*: ~ **algo** (*CAm, Méx*) to pocket sth; (*) to pocket sth, pinch sth*.
embuchado *nm* (**a**) (*Culin*) sausage. (**b**) (*: *pretexto*) pretext, blind; (*Pol*) electoral fraud; (*Teat*) gag.
embuchar [1a] *vt* (**a**) (*Culin*) to stuff with minced meat. (**b**) (*) *comida* to wolf, bolt.
embudar [1a] *vt* (**a**) (*Téc*) to fit with a funnel, put a funnel into. (**b**) (*fig*) to trick.
embudo *nm* (**a**) (*para líquidos*) funnel; (*And, Méx: tolva*) hopper. (**b**) (*fig: fraude*) trick, fraud; *V* **ley.** (**c**) (*fig: Aut etc*) bottleneck.
embullar [1a] (*And, CAm, Carib*) **1** *vt* (**a**) (*excitar*) to excite, disturb.
(**b**) *enemigo* to put to flight.
2 embullarse *vr* (**a**) (*excitarse*) to get excited, get worked up; to become tense.
(**b**) (*divertirse*) to revel, have a good time.
embullo *nm* (*CAm, Carib*) (*ruido*) noise, excitement, bustle; (*juerga*) revelry.
emburujar [1a] **1** *vt* (**a**) (*mezclar*) to jumble together, jumble up; (*amontonar*) to pile up; *hilo etc* to tangle up.
(**b**) (*And: desconcertar*) to bewilder.
2 emburujarse *vr* (*And, Carib, Méx*) to wrap o.s. up.
emburujo *nm* (*Carib*) ruse, trick.
embuste *nm* (**a**) (*trampa*) trick, fraud, imposture; (*mentira*) lie, (*hum*) fib, story. (**b**) **~s** trinkets.
embustería *nf* trickery, deceit; lying.
embustero 1 *adj* (**a**) (*engañador*) deceitful, rascally.
(**b**) **persona embustera** (*Cono Sur*) person who cannot spell properly.
(**c**) (*CAm: altanero*) haughty.
2 *nm*, **embustera** *nf* (*estafador*) cheat; (*impostor*) impostor; (*mentiroso*) liar, (*hum*) fibber, storyteller; (*hipócrita*) hypocrite; ¡~! (*hum*) you rascal!
embute[1]* *nm*: **de ~** smashing*, brilliant*.
embute[2]* *nm* (*Méx*) bribe*.
embutido *nm* (**a**) (*Culin*) sausage. (**b**) (*Téc*) inlay, inlaid work, marquetry. (**c**) (*Carib, Cono Sur, Méx: encaje*) strip of lace.
embutir [3a] **1** *vt* (**a**) (*meter*) to insert (*en* into); (*atiborrar*) to pack tight, stuff, cram (*de* with, *en* into); (*) *comida* to cram, scoff*; ~ **algo a uno** to make sb swallow sth; **estar embutido*** to be safely tucked away*, be in hiding; **ella estuvo embutida en un vestido apretadísimo** she had been poured into a terribly close-fitting dress.
(**b**) (*Téc*) to inlay; *metal* to hammer, work.
2 embutirse* *vr* to stuff o.s. (*de* with)*.
eme* *nf* (*euf*) = **mierda.**
emergencia *nf* (**a**) (*acto*) emergence; appearance. (**b**) (*urgencia*) emergency; **de ~** emergency (*atr*).
emergente *adj* (**a**) (*consiguiente*) resultant, consequent. (**b**) *nación* emergent.
emerger [2c] *vi* to emerge; to appear; (*submarino*) to surface.
emeritense 1 *adj* of Mérida. **2** *nmf* native (*o* inhabitant) of Mérida; **los ~s** the people of Mérida.
emérito *adj* emeritus.
emético *adj, nm* emetic.
emigración *nf* emigration; migration.
emigrado, -a *nm/f* emigrant; (*Pol etc*) emigré(e).
emigrante *adj, nmf* emigrant.
emigrar [1a] *vi* to emigrate; to migrate.
Emilia *nf* Emily.
emilianense *adj* of San Millán de la Cogolla.
eminencia *nf* (**a**) (*Geog*) (*altura*) height, eminence; (*lo alto*) loftiness. (**b**) (*fig*) eminence; prominence. (**c**) (*títulos*) **Su E~** His Eminence; **Vuestra E~** Your Eminence.
eminente *adj* (**a**) (*alto*) high, lofty. (**b**) (*fig*) eminent, distinguished; prominent.
eminentemente *adv* eminently, especially.
emir *nm* emir.
emirato *nm* emirate.
emisario *nm* emissary.
emisión *nf* (**a**) (*gen*) emission; (*Fin etc*) issue; (*Inform*) output; **~ de valores** (*Bolsa*) flotation.
(**b**) (*Rad, TV: acto*) broadcasting; (*programa*) broadcast, programme; **~ deportiva** sports programme; **~ publicitaria** commercial, advertising spot.
emisor 1 *adj*: **banco ~** issuing bank. **2** *nm* (**a**) (*Rad, TV*) transmitter. (**b**) (*Fin*) issuing company.
emisora *nf* radio station; broadcasting station; **~ comercial** commercial radio station; **~ de onda corta** shortwave radio station; **~ pirata** pirate radio station.
emisor-receptor *nm* (*portátil*) walkie-talkie, transmitting and receiving set, transceiver.
emitir [3a] *vt* (**a**) *gas, sonido etc* to emit, give off, give out.
(**b**) *bonos, dinero, sellos etc* to issue; *dinero falso* to put into circulation, utter; *préstamo* to float, launch.
(**c**) *opinión* to express; *veredicto* to return, issue, give; *voto* to give, cast.
(**d**) (*Rad, TV*) to broadcast; *señal* to send out.
emoción *nf* (**a**) (*gen*) emotion; (*sentimiento*) feeling; **sentir una honda ~** to feel a deep emotion; **nos comunica una ~ de nostalgia** it gives us a nostalgic feeling.
(**b**) (*excitación*) excitement; thrill; (*tensión*) tension, suspense; **¡qué ~!** how exciting!; **al abrirlo sentí gran ~** I felt very excited on opening it; **la ~ de la película no disminuye** the excitement (*o* tension) of the film does not flag.
emocionado *adj* deeply moved, deeply stirred.
emocional *adj* emotional.
emocionante *adj* exciting, thrilling; touching, moving; stirring.
emocionar [1a] **1** *vt* (*excitar*) to excite, thrill; (*conmover*) to touch, move; to stir.
2 emocionarse *vr* to get excited, be thrilled; to be moved; to be stirred; **¡no te emociones tanto!** don't get so excited!, don't get so worked up!
emoliente *adj, nm* emollient.
emolumento *nm* emolument.
emotividad *nf* emotive nature.
emotivo *adj* emotive.
empacada *nf* (*LAm*) (**a**) (*de caballo*) balk, shy. (**b**) (*fig*) obstinacy.
empacadora *nf* (**a**) (*Agr*) baler, baling machine. (**b**) **~ de carne** (*Méx*) meat-packing factory.
empacar [1g] **1** *vt* (*gen*) to bale, crate, pack up; (*Agr*) to bale; (*LAm*) to pack; (*And, Méx*) to package.
2 *vi* (*Méx: hacer las maletas*) to pack.
3 empacarse *vr* (**a**) (*confundirse*) to get rattled, get confused.
(**b**) (*LAm: caballo*) to balk, shy; (*fig*) to be obstinate, get stubborn.
empachado *adj* (**a**) clogged; (*Náut*) overloaded; *estómago* upset, uncomfortable. (**b**) (*avergonzado*) embarrassed. (**c**) (*torpe*) awkward, clumsy.
empachar [1a] **1** *vt* (**a**) (*obstruir*) to stop up, clog; (*Náut*) to overload; (*Med*) *estómago* to upset, make uncomfortable; *persona* to give indigestion to.

(**b**) (*estorbar*) to impede, hinder; (*incomodar*) to embarrass.

2 empacharse *vr* (**a**) to get stopped up, get clogged; (*Med*) to get indigestion, have indigestion.

(**b**) (*avergonzarse*) to get embarrassed, feel awkward; to become bashful.

empacho *nm* (**a**) (*estorbo*) hindrance, obstacle.

(**b**) (*Med*) surfeited feeling, indigestion.

(**c**) (*fig*) embarrassment; awkwardness, awkward feeling; bashfulness; **sin ~** without ceremony; unconcernedly; **no tener ~ en** + *infin* to have no objection to + *ger*.

empachoso *adj* (**a**) *comida* cloying, indigestible. (**b**) (*fig*) embarrassing. (**c**) *niños* tiresome.

empadronamiento *nm* (**a**) (*censo*) census; register. (**b**) (*acto*) census-taking; registration.

empadronar [1a] **1** *vt población* to take a census of; *votante* to register, enter on a register. **2 empadronarse** *vr* to register (for electoral purposes).

empajar [1a] *vt* to cover (*o* fill *etc*) with straw; (*And, Cono Sur*) to thatch.

empalagar [1h] **1** *vt* (**a**) (*suj*: *comida*) to pall on. (**b**) (*fig*) to pall on, bore; to sicken. **2** *vi* to pall. **3 empalagarse** *vr* to get surfeited (*de* with).

empalago *nm* (**a**) (*empacho*) cloying, palling. (**b**) (*aburrimiento*) boredom; (*asco*) disgust.

empalagoso *adj* (**a**) (*empachoso*) cloying; *comida* sickeningly sweet, over-rich. (**b**) (*fig*) boring, wearisome; trying.

empalar [1a] **1** *vt* to impale. **2 empalarse** *vr* (*And, Cono Sur*) to dig one's heels in.

empalidecer [2d] *vi* = **palidecer**.

empalizada *nf* fence; (*Mil etc*) palisade, stockade.

empalmar [1a] **1** *vt* (**a**) (*juntar*) to join, connect; *cuerdas* to splice. (**b**) (*fig*) to combine, put together.

2 *vi* (*Ferro etc*: *líneas*) to join, meet, come together; (*trenes*) to connect (*con* with).

3 empalmarse* *vr* to get randy*.

empalme *nm* (**a**) (*Téc*) joint, connection, union; splice; (*Elec*) junction-box. (**b**) (*combinación*) combination. (**c**) (*de carreteras, líneas*) junction; (*de trenes*) connection. (**d**) (⁑) hard-on⁑, erection.

empamparse [1a] *vr* (*LAm*) (**a**) (*desorientarse*) to get lost on the pampas; to get disorientated, lose one's way. (**b**) (*fig*) to be amazed, stand agape.

empanada *nf* (**a**) (*Culin*) ≃ (meat) pie, patty. (**b**) (*: *timo*) fraud, piece of shady business*. (**c**) **~ mental*** confusion.

empanadilla *nf* patty, small pie.

empanado *adj* (*Culin*) done (*o* rolled *etc*) in breadcrumbs, breaded.

empanar [1a] *vt* (**a**) (*Culin*) to do (*o* roll *etc*) in breadcrumbs; to roll in pastry. (**b**) (*Agr*) to sow with wheat.

empantanado *adj* flooded, swampy.

empantanar [1a] **1** *vt* (**a**) (*inundar*) to flood, swamp.

(**b**) (*fig*) to obstruct; to bog down.

2 empantanarse *vr* (**a**) (*inundarse*) to be flooded, get swamped.

(**b**) (*fig*) to be obstructed, be held up; **~ en un asunto** to get bogged down in a matter.

empañado *adj ventana etc* misty, steamy, steamed-up; *contorno* dim, blurred; *superficie* tarnished; *voz* faint, unsteady; *honor* tarnished.

empañar [1a] **1** *vt* (**a**) *bebé* to put a nappy *o* diaper (*US*) on.

(**b**) *ventana etc* to mist, steam up; *contorno* to dim, blur; *superficie, honor* to tarnish.

2 empañarse *vr* (**a**) (*gafas etc*) to film over, get misty; to cloud over; (*voz*) to falter.

(**b**) (*fig*) to become sad, get gloomy.

empañetar [1a] *vt* (*LAm*) to plaster; to whitewash.

empapar [1a] **1** *vt* (**a**) (*mojar*) to soak, saturate, drench; to steep (*t fig*; *de, en* in).

(**b**) (*absorber*) to soak up, absorb.

2 empaparse *vr* (**a**) to soak.

(**b**) **~ de** to soak up, soak in.

(**c**) **~ de, ~ en** (*fig*) to steep o.s. in; to become imbued with.

empapelado *nm* papering, paperhanging.

empapelador(a) *nm/f* paperhanger.

empapelar [1a] *vt* (**a**) *objeto* to wrap in paper; *caja* to paper, line with paper; *cuarto, pared* to paper. (**b**) **~ a uno** (*Jur*) to lay a charge against sb; (*) to do sb*, (*fig*) to throw the book at sb.

empapuzar [1f] *vt* to stuff with food.

empaque *nm* (**a**) (*acto*) packing. (**b**) (*: *aspecto*) look, appearance; (*aire*) manner. (**c**) (*fig*) solemnness, pomposity. (**d**) (*LAm**: *descaro*) nerve*, cheek*. (**e**) (*Méx*) washer, gasket.

empaquetador(a) *nm/f* packer.

empaquetadura *nf* packing; filling; (*Mec*) gasket.

empaquetar [1a] *vt* (**a**) to pack; to pack up, parcel up; (*Com*) to package. (**b**) (*conservar*) *buque etc* to mothball. (**c**) (*Mil*⁑) to punish.

emparamarse [1a] *vr* (*And, Carib*) (*mojarse*) to get soaked; (*entumecerse*) to get numb with cold; (*morir*) to die of cold, freeze to death.

emparar* [1a] (*And*) **1** *vt* to catch. **2 empararse** *vr* (**a**) (*sonrojarse*) to blush. (**b**) **~ de** to mock.

emparedado *nm* sandwich.

emparedar [1a] *vt* to immure, confine.

emparejamiento *nm* (*Biol*) pairing, mating; (*Psiq*) pair-bonding.

emparejar [1a] **1** *vt* (**a**) *dos casas* to pair, match. (**b**) (*nivelar*) to level, make level; to make flush; (*igualar*) to even up. **2** *vi* (**a**) (*llegar a la altura de*) to catch up (*con* with), come abreast (*con* of). (**b**) (*ser igual*) to be even (*con* with). **3 emparejarse** *vr* to pair off.

emparentado *adj* related (by marriage) (*con* to).

emparentar [1j] *vi* to become related by marriage (*con* to); **~ con una familia** to marry into a family.

emparrado *nm* trained vine; vine arbour.

emparrandarse* [1a] *vr* (*LAm*) to go on a binge*.

empastado *adj* (**a**) (*Tip*) clothbound, bound. (**b**) *diente* filled.

empastar [1a] **1** *vt* (**a**) (*engomar*) to paste.

(**b**) (*Tip*) to bind in boards, bind in stiff covers, bind in cloth.

(**c**) *diente* to fill, stop.

(**d**) (*LAm Agr*) to convert into pasture land.

2 empastarse *vr* (*Cono Sur*: *ganado*) to get bloated.

empaste *nm* (**a**) (*de diente*) filling. (**b**) (*Tip*) binding.

empatar [1a] **1** *vt* (**a**) (*LAm*: *juntar*) to join, connect, tie firmly together.

(**b**) (*Carib*: *acosar*) to bother, harass.

(**c**) (*Cono Sur*) *tiempo* to waste.

2 *vi* (*juego*) to draw, tie; (*carrera*) to tie, have a dead heat; (*en voto*) to tie; **los equipos empataron** (*o* **quedaban empatados**) **a 2** the teams drew 2-all; **los tres equipos quedan empatados a puntos** the three teams are level on points (in the league table).

empate *nm* (**a**) (*Dep*) draw, tie; dead heat; **un ~ a 0** a 0-0 draw, a goalless draw. (**b**) (*LAm*: *junta*) joint, connection.

empatía *nf* empathy.

empatizar [1f] *vi* (*t* **empatizarse**) to empathize (*con* with).

empavado* *adj* (*Carib*) unlucky, jinxed*.

empavar* [1a] *vt* (*Carib*) to put a jinx on*, bring bad luck to.

empavesado *nm* bunting.

empavesar [1a] *vt* to deck, adorn; *barco* to dress.

empavonar [1a] **1** *vt* (**a**) (*Téc*) *acero* to blue. (**b**) (*LAm Mec*) to grease, cover with grease. **2 empavonarse** *vr* (*CAm*) to dress up.

empecatado *adj* (**a**) (*incorregible*) incorrigible; (*astuto*) wily, fiendish. (**b**) (*malhadado*) ill-fated. (**c**) (*maldito*) damned, cursed.

empecinadamente *adv* stubbornly, pigheadedly.

empecinado *adj* stubborn, pigheaded.

empecinamiento *nm* stubbornness, pigheadedness.

empecinarse [1a] *vr* to be stubborn, dig one's heels in; **~ en algo** to be stubborn (*o* dig one's heels in) about sth; **~ en** + *infin* to persist in, insist on + *ger*.

empedarse* [1a] *vr* (*Cono Sur, Méx*) to get drunk, get sloshed*.

empedernido *adj* (**a**) *persona* heartless; obdurate; *corazón* flinty, stony.

(**b**) (*en un vicio*) hardened, inveterate; **un fumador ~** a strongly addicted smoker, a smoker firmly set in the habit; **un pecador ~** an unregenerate sinner.

empedernir [3a: *defectivo*] **1** *vt* to harden. **2 empedernirse** *vr* (**a**) to harden; to petrify. (**b**) (*fig*) to harden one's heart, resolve to be tough.

empedrado 1 *adj superficie* paved; (*fig*) pitted (*de* with); *cara* pockmarked; *color* dappled, flecked; *cielo* cloud-flecked. **2** *nm* (*pavimento*) paving; (*CAm*: *calle*) cobbled street.

empedrar [1j] *vt* to pave.

empegado *nm* tarpaulin.

empeine *nm* (**a**) (*Anat*) groin; (*de pie, zapato*) instep. (**b**) (*Bot*) cotton flower. (**c**) **~s** (*Med*) ringworm.
empelotado *adj* (**a**) (*And, Carib, Cono Sur, Méx: desnudo*) naked, stripped. (**b**) (*Méx: enamorado*) in love.
empelotar [1a] **1** *vt* (**a**) (*desnudar*) to undress, strip to the skin.
(**b**) (*LAm Mec*) to strip down, dismantle, take to pieces.
2 empelotarse* *vr* (**a**) (*aturdirse*) to get muddled.
(**b**) (**: meterse en un lío*) to get into a row.
(**c**) (**: desnudarse*) to strip naked, strip off.
(**d**) (*Carib, Méx: enamorarse*) to fall head over heels in love (*con* with).
empelucado *adj* bewigged.
empella *nf* (**a**) (*de zapatero*) vamp; (*de zapato*) uppers. (**b**) (*LAm: manteca de cerdo*) lard.
empellar [1a] *vt* to push, shove, jostle.
empellón *nm* push, shove; **mover a empellones** to shove, move by pushing; **abrirse paso a empellones** to get through by shoving, push one's way rudely through, push roughly past; **dar empellones** to shove, jostle.
empenachado *adj* plumed; (*fig*) pretentious, extravagant; baroque.
empenachar [1a] *vt* to adorn with plumes.
empeñado *adj* (**a**) *objeto* pawned.
(**b**) **estar ~ hasta los ojos** to be deeply in debt.
(**c**) *persona* determined; **estar ~ en** + *infin* to be determined to + *infin*, be completely set on + *ger*.
(**d**) *discusión* bitter, heated.
empeñar [1a] **1** *vt* (**a**) *objeto* to pawn, pledge.
(**b**) *palabra* to pledge, give; *persona* to engage, compel.
(**c**) *batalla* to join; *riña* to start, engage in.
2 empeñarse *vr* (**a**) (*prometer*) to bind o.s., pledge o.s.
(**b**) (*endeudarse*) to get into debt.
(**c**) **~ en algo** to insist on sth; to persist in sth; **~ en** + *infin* to be determined to + *infin*, be set on + *ger*; to insist on + *ger*; **se empeña en que es así** he insists that it is so.
(**d**) **~ en una lucha** to engage in a fight; **~ en una discusión** to get involved in a heated argument.
(**e**) **~ por uno** to intercede for sb, intervene on sb's behalf.
empeñero, -a *nm/f* (*Méx*) pawnbroker, moneylender.
empeño *nm* (**a**) (*objeto*) pledge.
(**b**) (*promesa*) obligation, undertaking.
(**c**) (*resolución*) determination; (*insistencia*) insistence; **su ~ en hacerlo** his determination to do it; his insistence on doing it; **con ~** with determination; insistently; eagerly, keenly; **tener ~ en** + *infin* to be bent on + *ger*, be eager to + *infin*.
(**d**) (*tienda*) pawnshop; moneylender's.
empeñoso *adj* (*LAm*) persevering, diligent.
empeoramiento *nm* deterioration, worsening.
empeorar [1a] **1** *vt* to make worse, worsen; to impair. **2** *vi y* **empeorarse** *vr* to get worse, worsen, deteriorate.
empequeñecer [2d] *vt* (**a**) (*disminuir*) to dwarf, make (seem) smaller. (**b**) (*fig*) to minimize; to belittle.
emperador *nm* (**a**) emperor. (**b**) (*Carib: pez*) swordfish.
emperatriz *nf* empress.
emperejilarse [1a] *vr* to dress up, doll o.s. up*.
empericarse* [1g] *vr* (**a**) (*And: emborracharse*) to get drunk. (**b**) (*Carib, Méx: ruborizarse*) to blush.
emperifollar [1a] **1** *vt* to adorn, deck; *persona* to doll up. **2 emperifollarse** *vr* to dress up, doll o.s. up*.
empernar [1j] *vt* to bolt, secure with a bolt; to fit a bolt to.
empero *conj* (†† *y liter*) but; yet, however; **estaba muy cansado, no se sentó ~** he was very tired, nonetheless he didn't sit down.
emperramiento *nm* stubbornness.
emperrarse [1a] *vr* to get stubborn, be obstinate; **~ en algo** to be stubborn about sth; to persist in sth.
emperro *nm* (*prov, And*) (*terquedad*) stubbornness; (*rabieta*) fit of temper.
empertigar [1h] *vt* (*Cono Sur*) *caballo* to hitch up.
empezar [1f *y* 1j] *vti* to begin, start; **~ a** + *infin* to start to + *infin*; **~ por** + *infin*, **~** + *ger* to begin by + *ger*, start by + *ger*; **empezó diciendo que ...** he began by saying that ...; **bueno, para ~** well, to start with; **¡no empieces!** don't start on that (all over again)!
empicotar [1a] *vt* to pillory.
empiezo *nm* (*And, CAm, Cono Sur*) = **comienzo.**
empilchar [1a] **1** *vt* (*Cono Sur*) *caballo* to saddle; (*) *persona* to keep in clothes. **2 empilcharse*** *vr* (*Cono Sur*) to dress up, get dolled up*.
empilonar [1a] *vt* (*And, Carib*) to pile up.
empinada *nf* (*Aer*) steep climb, zoom upward.
empinado *adj* (**a**) *cuesta* steep; *edificio* high, lofty. (**b**) (*fig*) proud; stiff.
empinar [1a] **1** *vt* (**a**) (*alzar*) to raise, lift; (*botella*) to tip up; *V* **codo.**
(**b**) (*enderezar*) to straighten.
2 *vi* (**: beber*) to drink, booze*.
3 empinarse *vr* (**a**) (*persona*) to stand on tiptoe; (*caballo*) to rear up; (*edificio*) to tower, soar; (*Aer*) to climb steeply, zoom upwards.
(**b**) (*And, Cono Sur: comer en exceso*) to overeat.
empingoratado* *adj* stuck-up*.
empipada* *nf* (*And, Cono Sur*) blow-out*.
empiparse [1a] *vr*: **~ algo** (*And, Cono Sur*) (*comer*) to stuff o.s. with sth, (*beber*) drink sth down.
empírico 1 *adj* empiric(al). **2** *nm*, **empírica** *nf* empiricist.
empirismo *nm* empiricism.
empitonar [1a] *vt* (*Taur*) to gore, impale (on the horns of the bull).
empizarrado *nm* slate roof.
empizarrar [1a] *vt* to roof with slates, slate.
emplantillar [1a] *vt* (**a**) (*And, Carib, Cono Sur*) *zapatos* to put insoles into. (**b**) (*And, Cono Sur*) *pared* to fill with rubble.
emplastar [1a] *vt* (**a**) (*Med*) to put a plaster on, poultice. (**b**) *cara* to make up, paint. (**c**) *trato* to block.
emplasto *nm* (**a**) (*Med*) plaster, poultice. (**b**) (*fig: expediente*) makeshift arrangement. (**c**) (*débil*) weakling; (*inadaptado*) misfit, useless individual. (**d**) (**: pesado*) bore, tedious person, wet*.
emplazamiento *nm* (**a**) (*Jur*) summons; summoning. (**b**) (*sitio*) site, location; (*Mil*) (gun) emplacement.
emplazar [1f] *vt* (**a**) (*llamar*) to summon, convene; (*Jur*) to summons; to subpoena; **~ a uno para el jueves** to give sb an appointment for Thursday. (**b**) (*ubicar*) to site, locate, place; *misil* to site, station; *estatua etc* to set up, erect. (**c**) **~ a uno a hacer algo** to call on sb to do sth.
empleado, -a *nm/f* employee; (*esp*) clerk, office worker, clerical worker; (*LAm*) domestic servant; **~ bancario, ~ de banco** bank clerk; **~ de confianza** confidential clerk; **~ de correos** post-office worker; **~ de cuello y corbata** (*Cono Sur*) white-collar worker; **~ de finca urbana** porter, concierge; **empleada de hogar** servant, maid; **~ de pompas fúnebres** undertaker's assistant, mortician's assistant (*US*); **~ público** civil servant; **~ de ventanilla** booking office clerk, counter clerk.
emplear [1a] **1** *vt herramienta, palabra etc* to use, employ; *persona* to employ; to give a job to, engage, hire; *tiempo* to occupy, spend; to put in; *dinero* to invest; **~ mal** to misuse; **~ mal el tiempo** to waste time; **¡le está bien empleado!** it serves him right!
2 emplearse *vr* to be used, be employed; **~ haciendo algo** to occupy o.s. doing sth; **~ a fondo** to make a great effort, do one's utmost; **¡bien se te emplea!** it serves you right!
empleo *nm* (**a**) (*gen*) use, employment; occupation, spending; (*Com*) investment; **'modo de ~'** (*en etiqueta*) 'instructions for use'; **el ~ de esa palabra es censurable** the use of that word is to be condemned.
(**b**) (*trabajo*) employment, work; **~ comunitario** community work; **~ juvenil** youth employment; **pleno ~** full employment.
(**c**) (*puesto*) job, employment, post; **buscar un ~** to look for a job; **estar sin ~** to be unemployed, be out of a job; **'solicitan ~'** (*encabezamiento*) 'situations wanted'; **suspender a uno de ~ y sueldo** to suspend sb without pay.
emplomadura *nf* leading; lead covering, lead lining; (*Cono Sur: de diente*) filling.
emplomar [1a] *vt vidriera etc* to lead; (*revestir etc*) to cover (*o* line, weight *etc*) with lead; (*precintar*) to seal with lead; (*Cono Sur*) *diente* to fill.
emplumar [1a] **1** *vt* (**a**) (*gen*) to adorn with feathers; (*castigo*) to tar and feather; **¡que me emplumen si ...!** I'll eat my hat if ...!
(**b**) (**‡**: *estafar*) to swindle, con*.
(**c**) (**‡**: *detener*) to nick‡, arrest.
(**d**) **~ algo a uno*** to spring sth on sb.
(**e**) (*CAm*: zurrar*) to beat up*, thrash.
(**f**) (*Carib*) empleado* to fire*.
(**g**) **~las** (*And, Cono Sur**) to run away.
2 *vi* (**a**) (*ave*) to grow feathers.
(**b**) (*LAm*: huir*) to run away, take to one's heels.
3 emplumarse *vr*: **emplumárselas** (*And, Cono Sur*: huir*) to run away.
emplumecer [2d] *vi* to grow feathers.

empobrecer [2d] **1** *vt* to impoverish. **2 empobrecerse** *vr* to become poor, become impoverished.
empobrecimiento *nm* impoverishment.
empolvado *adj sustancia* powdery; *superficie* dusty.
empolvar [1a] **1** *vt cara* to powder; *superficie* to cover with dust, make dusty.
2 empolvarse *vr* (**a**) (*persona*) to powder o.s., powder one's face, put powder on; (*superficie*) to get dusty, gather dust.
(**b**) (*Méx*: *perder la práctica*) to get rusty, get out of practice.
(**c**) (*Carib*: *huir*) to run away.
empollar [1a] **1** *vt* (**a**) *huevos* to incubate, sit on; to hatch.
(**b**) (*Univ etc**) *asignatura* to swot up*.
2 *vi* (**a**) (*gallina*) to sit, brood.
(**b**) (*insectos*) to breed.
(**c**) (*Univ etc**) to swot*, cram.
empolle* *nm* swotting*, cramming; **¡tiene un ~!** he's been working really hard, he really knows his stuff*.
empollón*, -ona *nm/f* (*Univ etc*) swot*, bookworm.
emponchado *adj* (**a**) (*LAm*: *vestido de poncho*) wearing a poncho, covered with a poncho. (**b**) (*And, Cono Sur*) (*sospechoso*) suspicious; (*taimado*) crafty, sharp.
emponcharse [1a] *vr* to put on one's poncho, wrap o.s. up in one's poncho.
emponzoñamiento *nm* poisoning.
emponzoñar [1a] *vt* to poison; (*fig*) to poison; to taint, corrupt.
emporcar [1g *y* 1l] *vt* to soil, dirty, foul.
emporio *nm* emporium, mart, trading centre; (*LAm*) department store.
emporrado‡ *adj*: **estar ~** to be high (on drugs)‡.
emporroso *adj* (*CAm, Carib*) annoying, irritating.
empotrable 1 *adj* fitted, built-in. **2** *nm* fitted unit, built-in unit.
empotrado *adj armario etc* built-in; (*Mec*) fixed, integral.
empotrar [1a] **1** *vt* to embed, fix; *armario etc* to build in.
2 empotrarse *vr*: **el coche se empotró en la tienda** the car embedded itself in the shop; **los vagones se empotraron uno en otro** the carriages telescoped together.
empotrerar [1a] *vt* (**a**) (*LAm*) *ganado* to pasture, put out to pasture. (**b**) (*Carib, Cono Sur*) *tierra* to convert into fenced pasture, enclose.
empozarse [1f] *vr* (*And, Cono Sur*) to form pools.
emprendedor 1 *adj* enterprising; go-ahead, pushy, aggressive. **2** *nm* (*Fin*) entrepreneur.
emprender [2a] *vt* (**a**) *trabajo etc* to undertake; *problema etc* to take on, tackle; *viaje* to begin on, embark on; **~ marcha a** to set out for; **~ el regreso** to go back, return; to begin the homeward journey; **~ la retirada** to begin to retreat.
(**b**) **~la** to start, set out; **~la con uno** to tackle sb about a matter, have it out with sb; to attack sb; to have a row with sb; **la emprendieron con el árbitro a botellazos** they attacked the referee by throwing bottles at him.
empreñador* *adj* irksome, vexatious.
empreñar [1a] **1** *vt* (**a**) *mujer* to make pregnant; *animal* to impregnate, mate with. (**b**) (*: *fastidiar*) to rile*, irk, vex.
2 empreñarse *vr* to become pregnant.
empresa *nf* (**a**) (*espíritu etc*) enterprise; **~ libre, libre ~** free enterprise; **~ privada** private enterprise.
(**b**) (*Com, Fin*) enterprise, undertaking, venture; company, concern; (*patrón*) employer; **~ colectiva** joint venture; **~ fantasma** dummy company; **~ filial** affiliated company; **~ fletadora** shipping company; **~ funeraria** undertaker's; **~ matriz** parent company; **~ particular** private company; **pequeñas y medianas ~s** small and medium-sized companies; **~ pública** public sector company; **~ de seguridad** security company; **~ de servicios públicos** public utility company.
(**c**) (*esp Teat*) management; **la ~ lamenta que ...** the management regrets that ...
empresariado *nm* business (world); managers (*collectively*), management.
empresarial *adj* owners', managers'; *función, clase etc* managerial; **estudios ~es** business studies, management studies; **sector ~** business sector.
empresario *nm* (*Fin*) businessman; (*patrón*) employer; (*Téc*) manager; (*Mús, de ópera etc*) impresario; (*Boxeo*) promoter; (*Com*) contractor; **~ de pompas fúnebres** undertaker, mortician (*US*); **~ de transporte** (*Cono Sur*) shipping agent; **pequeño ~** small businessman.
empresología *nf* business consultancy.
empresólogo, -a *nm/f* business consultant.
emprestar* [1a] *vt* to borrow; (*prestar*) to lend.
empréstito *nm* (public) loan; **~ de guerra** war loan.
empufado* *adj*: **estar ~** to be in debt, be in the red.
empujada *nf* (*And, CAm*) push, shove.
empujadora *nf*: **~ frontal, ~ niveladora** bulldozer.
empujar [1a] **1** *vt* (**a**) (*gen*) to push, shove; to push, thrust (*en* into); (*Mec*) to drive, move, propel; *bicicleta* to push, wheel; *botón* to press; **'empujad'** (*en puerta etc*) 'push'; **~ el botón a fondo** to press the button down hard; **¡no empujen!** stop pushing!, don't shove.
(**b**) (*) *persona* to sack*, give the push to*.
2 *vi* (*fig*) to intrigue, work behind the scenes (*para + infin* to + *infin*).
empujaterrones *nm invar* bulldozer.
empujatierra *nf* bulldozer.
empuje *nm* (**a**) (*gen*) pressure; (*Mec, Fís*) thrust.
(**b**) (*un ~*) push, shove.
(**c**) (*fig*) push, drive; **le falta ~** he hasn't got any go to him, he lacks drive; **en un espíritu de ~** in a thrustful spirit.
empujón *nm* push, shove; dig, poke, jab; **abrirse paso a empujones** to shove (*o* elbow) one's way through, get through by pushing; **avanzar a empujones** to go forward by fits and starts, jerk forward; **trabajar a empujones** to work intermittently.
empulgueras *nfpl* thumbscrew.
empuntar [1a] **1** *vt* (**a**) to put a point on. (**b**) **~las** (*And*) to run away. **2 empuntarse** *vr* (*Carib*) (*empecinarse*) to dig one's heels in; (*caminar*) to walk on tiptoe.
empuñadura *nf* (**a**) (*de espada*) hilt; (*de herramienta*) grip, handle. (**b**) (*de cuento*) start, traditional opening.
empuñar [1a] *vt* (**a**) (*coger*) to grasp, clutch, grip, take (firm) hold of; (*Cono Sur*) *puño* to clench. (**b**) (*fig*) **~ las armas** to take up arms; **~ el bastón** (*fig*) to take command. (**c**) (*And*: *dar un puñetazo a*) to punch, hit with one's fist.
empupar [1a] *vi* (*LAm*) to pupate.
empurar‡ [1a] *vt* (*Mil*) to punish.
empurrarse* [1a] *vr* (*CAm*) (*enojarse*) to get angry; (*hacer pucheros*) to pout.
E.M.T. *nf* (*Esp*) *abr de* **Empresa Municipal de Transportes.**
emú *nm* emu.
emulación *nf* (*gen, Inform*) emulation.
emulador 1 *adj* emulous (*de* of). **2** *nm*, **emuladora** *nf* rival.
emular [1a] **1** *vt* to emulate, rival. **2** *vi*: **~ con** = *vt*.
emulgente *nm* emulsifier.
émulo 1 *adj* emulous. **2** *nm*, **émula** *nf* rival, competitor.
emulsión *nf* emulsion.
emulsionante *nm* emulsifier.
emulsionar [1a] *vt* to emulsify.
EN *nf* (*Esp*) *abr de* **Editora Nacional.**
en *prep* (**a**) (*lugar*) in; into; on, upon; at; **está ~ el cajón** it's in the drawer; **meter algo ~ el bolsillo** to put sth in (*o* into) one's pocket; **no entra ~ el agujero** it won't go into the hole; **está ~ el suelo** it's on the floor; **está ~ Argentina** he's in Argentina; **está ~ Santiago** he's in Santiago; **está ~ algún lugar de la Mancha** he's at some place in la Mancha; **~ casa** at home; **te esperé ~ la estación** I waited for you at the station; **sentarse ~ la mesa** to sit down at table; **trabaja ~ la tienda** she works in the shop; **ir de puerta ~ puerta** to go from door to door; **'curvas peligrosas ~ 2 kilómetros'** 'Dangerous bends 2 kilometres ahead'.
(**b**) (*tiempo*) in; on; **~ 1605** in 1605; **~ el siglo X** in the 10th century; **~ la mañana** (*LAm*) in the morning; **~ la mañana del desastre** (*LAm*) on the morning of the disaster; **~ aquella ocasión** on that occasion; **lo terminaron ~ 3 semanas** they finished it in 3 weeks.
(**c**) (*precio*) at, for; **lo vendió ~ 5 dólares** he sold it at (*o* for) 5 dollars; **vendió la casa ~ 11 millones** she sold the house for 11 millions.
(**d**) (*proporción*) by; **reducir algo ~ una tercera parte** to reduce sth by a third; **ha aumentado ~ un 20 por cien** it has increased by 20%.
(**e**) (*medio*) **le conocí ~ el andar** I recognized him by his walk; **ir ~ avión** to go by plane, go by air; **vine ~ el autobús** I came by bus, I came in the bus.
(**f**) **Hugo ~ Segismundo** (*Cine, Teat*) Hugo as (*o* in the role of) Segismundo.
(**g**) (*con ger*: ††, *prov*) **~ viéndole se lo dije** the moment I saw him I told him; **~ viéndole se lo diré** the moment I see him I'll tell him, as soon as I see him I'll tell him.
(**h**) (*con infin*) **fue el último ~ hacerlo** he was the last to do it.

enaceitar [1a] *vt* (*Cono Sur*) to oil.

ENAGAS, Enagas [ena'ɣas] *nf abr de* **Empresa Nacional del Gas.**

enagua *nf, gen* **~s** *pl* petticoat; underskirt.

enaguazar [1f] *vt* to flood.

enajenación *nf,* **enajenamiento** *nm* (**a**) (*Jur etc*) alienation; transfer; **enajenación forzosa** expropriation.
(**b**) (*entre amigos*) estrangement.
(**c**) (*despiste*) absentmindedness; (*éxtasis*) rapture, trance; (*Psic*) alienation; **~ mental** mental derangement.

enajenar [1a] **1** *vt* (**a**) (*Jur*) *bienes* to alienate, transfer; *derechos* to dispose of.
(**b**) *persona* to alienate, estrange.
(**c**) (*fig: extasiar*) to enrapture, carry away; (*volver loco*) to drive mad.
2 enajenarse *vr* (**a**) **~ algo** to deprive o.s. of sth; **~ las simpatías** to alienate people, make o.s. disliked.
(**b**) (*amigos*) to become estranged.
(**c**) (*extasiarse*) to be enraptured, get carried away.

enaltecer [2d] *vt* to exalt; to praise, extol.

enamoradizo *adj* (*gen*) amorous, that falls in love easily.

enamorado 1 *adj* (**a**) (*gen*) in love, lovesick. (**b**) **estar ~** to be in love (*de* with). (**c**) (*Carib, Cono Sur*) = **enamoradizo. 2** *nm,* **enamorada** *nf* lover.

enamoramiento *nm* falling in love.

enamorar [1a] **1** *vt* to inspire love in, win the love of; **por fin la enamoró** eventually he got her to fall in love with him.
2 enamorarse *vr* to fall in love (*de* with).

enamoricarse [1g] *vr,* **enamoriscarse** [1g] *vr* to be just a bit in love (*de* with).

enancar [1g] **1** *vt*: **~ a uno** (*LAm*) to put sb on the crupper (of one's horse).
2 *vi* (*Cono Sur: seguir*) to follow, be a consequence (*a* of).
3 enancarse *vr* (**a**) (*LAm*) to get up on the crupper, ride behind.
(**b**) (*Méx: caballo*) to rear up.

enanez *nf* dwarfishness; (*fig*) stunted nature.

enangostar [1a] **1** *vt* to narrow. **2 enangostarse** *vr* to narrow, get narrower.

enanito, -a *nm/f* dwarf.

enano 1 *adj* dwarf, small, tiny; stunted. **2** *nm* dwarf; midget; (*pey*) runt.

enantes *adv* (*And*) = **denante(s).**

enarbolar [1a] **1** *vt bandera etc* to hoist, raise; *pancarta etc* to hang up, hang out; *espada etc* to flourish.
2 enarbolarse *vr* (**a**) (*persona*) to get angry.
(**b**) (*caballo*) to rear up.

enarcar [1g] *vt* (**a**) *tonel* to hoop, put a hoop on.
(**b**) to arch; *cejas* to raise, arch; *lomo* to arch; *pecho* to throw out.

enardecer [2d] **1** *vt* to fire, inflame; to fill with enthusiasm. **2 enardecerse** *vr* (**a**) (*Med*) to become inflamed. (**b**) (*fig*) to get excited, get enthusiastic (*por* about); to blaze, be afire (*de* with).

enarenar [1a] **1** *vt* to sand, cover with sand. **2 enarenarse** *vr* (*Náut*) to run aground.

enastado *adj* horned; antlered, with antlers.

encabalgamiento *nm* (*Liter*) enjambement.

encabestrar [1a] **1** *vt* (**a**) *caballo* to put a halter on; to lead by a halter. (**b**) (*fig*) to induce, persuade; to dominate. **2 encabestrarse** *vr* (*LAm*) to dig one's heels in.

encabezado 1 *adj vino* fortified. **2** *nm* (**a**) (*Méx Prensa, Tip*) heading; headline. (**b**) (*Carib: capataz*) foreman.

encabezamiento *nm* (**a**) (*de apartado*) heading; (*de periódico*) headline; rubric; (*preámbulo*) opening words, preamble; (*Com*) bill head, letterhead. (**b**) (*registro*) roll, register.

encabezar [1f] *vt* (**a**) *movimiento, revolución etc* to lead, head.
(**b**) *liga, lista etc* to head, be at the top of, come first in.
(**c**) *papel, documento* to put a heading to; *artículo, dibujo* to head, entitle.
(**d**) *población etc* to register (for tax purposes *etc*).
(**e**) *vino* to fortify.

encabrestarse *vr* (*LAm*) = **emperrarse.**

encabritamiento* *nm* fit of bad temper; anger.

encabritar [1a] **1** *vt* (*) to rile*, upset. **2 encabritarse** *vr* (**a**) (*caballo*) to rear up. (**b**) (*: *enfadarse*) to get riled*, get cross.

encabronar* [1a] **1** *vt* to rile*, upset. **2 encabronarse** *vr* to get riled*, get cross.

encabuyar [1a] *vt* (*And, Carib*) to tie up.

encachado *adj* (*Cono Sur*) appealing, attractive.

encachar [1a] **1** *vt* (*Cono Sur*) *cabeza* to lower. **2** *vi* (*Méx*) to make a conquest.

encachilarse [1a] *vr* (*Cono Sur*) to get furious.

encachimbado* *adj*: **está ~** (*CAm*) he's livid, he's hopping mad*.

encachimbarse* [1a] *vr* (*CAm*) to fly off the handle*, lose one's temper.

encachorrarse* [1a] *vr* (*And*) (*enojarse*) to get angry, fly off the handle*; (*Carib, Cono Sur*) (*empecinarse*) to turn obstinate.

encadenación *nf,* **encadenamiento** *nm* (**a**) chaining (together). (**b**) (*fig*) linking, connection, concatenation.

encadenado *nm* (*Cine*) fade, dissolve.

encadenar [1a] **1** *vt* (**a**) (*atar*) to chain (together); *prisionero etc* to put chains on, fetter, shackle. (**b**) (*fig: inmovilizar*) to shackle, paralyze, immobilize; **los negocios le encadenan al escritorio** business ties him to his desk. (**c**) (*fig: unir*) to connect, link.
2 *vi* (*Cine*) to fade in; **~ a** to fade to.

encajable *adj* (*fig*) feasible; manageable.

encajadura *nf* (**a**) (*acto*) insertion, filling. (**b**) (*hueco*) socket; (*ranura*) groove; (*armazón*) frame.

encajar [1a] **1** *vt* (**a**) (*ajustar*) to insert, fit (*en* into); (*meter*) to push in, thrust in, force in; *máquina etc* to house, encase; *piezas* to join, fit together, fit into each other; (*Dep*) *gol* to net, score; to let in, concede.
(**b**) *comentario, cuenta etc* to get in, put in, intrude; *insinuación* to drop.
(**c**) **~ algo a uno** to palm sth off on sb, foist sth off on sb; **~ una historia a uno** to force sb to listen to a (disagreeable) story.
(**d**) (*) *golpe* to give, deal, fetch (*a* to).
(**e**) (*: *lanzar*) to chuck (*a* at); *insultos* to hurl.
(**f**) (*aguantar*) to put up with, not flinch under, resist; **sabe ~ los golpes** he can take the punches, (*fig*) he can take a lot of stick; **sabes ~ una broma** you know how to take a joke.
2 *vi* (**a**) to fit; to fit well (*o* properly).
(**b**) (*fig*) to fit, match, correspond; to be appropriate; **esto no encaja con lo que dijo antes** this does not square with what he said before.
3 encajarse *vr* (**a**) (*: *meterse con dificultad*) to squeeze (o.s.) in; (*fig*) to intrude, gatecrash; **~ en una reunión** to intrude upon a meeting; **~ en una fiesta** to crash a party*.
(**b**) (*: *interrumpir*) to butt in.
(**c**) **~ una chaqueta** to put on a jacket.
(**d**) (*LAm Aut*) to get stuck.

encaje *nm* (**a**) (*acto*) insertion, fitting; fitting together, joining.
(**b**) (*hueco*) socket, cavity; (*ranura*) groove; (*armazón*) frame; (*Mec*) housing; **aquí la violencia no tiene ~** there is no place for violence here.
(**c**) (*taracea*) inlay, inlaid work, mosaic; (*Cos*) lace; **~ de aplicación** appliqué (work); **~ de bolillos** (*lit*) handmade lace; (*fig*) juggling act, delicate manoeuvre.
(**d**) (*Fin*) reserve, stock; **~ de oro** gold reserve.

encajera *nf* lacemaker.

encajetillar [1a] *vt* (*Méx*) to pack in boxes, box.

encajonado *nm* cofferdam.

encajonar [1a] **1** *vt* (**a**) (*poner en caja*) to box (up), put in a box, crate, pack (in a box); (*Mec*) to box in, encase.
(**b**) *río* to confine (between banks), canalize.
(**c**) (*meter con dificultad*) to squeeze in, squeeze through.
2 encajonarse *vr* (*río*) to run through a narrow place, narrow.

encajoso‡ *nm* (*LAm*) creep‡, toady.

encalabrinar [1a] **1** *vt* (*Med*) to make dizzy, make giddy.
(**b**) **~ a uno** to get sb worked up; to fluster sb.
(**c**) **~ a una*** to attract a girl, click with a girl*, get a girl to show an interest.
2 encalabrinarse* *vr* (**a**) (*empeñarse*) to get an obsession, get the bit between one's teeth; to dig one's heels in.
(**b**) **~ de una** to get infatuated with a girl; **X anda encalabrinado con Z** X is mad keen on Z*.

encaladura *nf* (**a**) (*blanqueo*) whitewash(ing). (**b**) (*Agr*) liming.

encalambrarse [1a] *vr* (*LAm*) to get cramp; (*del frío*) to get stiff with cold.

encalamocar [1g] **1** *vt* (*And, Carib*) (**a**) (*emborrachar*) to make drunk.
(**b**) (*aturdir*) to confuse, bewilder.
2 encalamocarse *vr* (*And, Carib*) (**a**) to get drunk.

(**b**) to get confused, get bewildered.
encalar [1a] *vt* (**a**) *pared* to whitewash. (**b**) (*Agr*) to lime.
encalatarse [1a] *vr* (*And*) (**a**) (*desnudarse*) to strip naked. (**b**) (*fig*) to be ruined.
encalmada *nf* period of calm.
encalmado *adj* (**a**) (*Náut*) becalmed. (**b**) (*Com, Fin*) quiet, slack, dull.
encalmarse [1a] *vr* to be becalmed.
encalomarse‡ [1a] *vr* to hide.
encalvecer [2d] *vi* to go bald.
encalladero *nm* shoal, sandbank.
encalladura *nf* stranding, running aground.
encallar [1a] *vi* (**a**) (*Náut*) to run aground, run ashore, get stranded (*en* on). (**b**) (*fig*) to fail; (*en negociación etc*) to get stuck, get bogged down. (**c**) (*mecanismo*) to jam, stick, get stuck.
encallecer [2d] *vi y* **encallecerse** *vr* to harden, form corns.
encallecido *adj* hardened.
encamar [1a] **1** *vt* (**a**) (*CAm, Méx*: *hospitalizar*) to take to hospital, hospitalize.
(**b**) (*Carib*) *animal* to litter, bed down; (*Méx*) *niño etc* to put to bed.
2 encamarse *vr* (**a**) (*persona*) to take to one's bed; ~ **con una** (*And, Cono Sur*) to go to bed with sb, sleep with sb; **estar encamado** to be confined to bed.
(**b**) (*cosecha etc*) to be laid, be flattened.
(**c**) (*animal*) to crouch, hide.
encamburarse [1a] *vr* (*Carib*) to make good, (*esp*) achieve public office.
encame *nm* den, lair; hiding-place.
encamillado, -a *nm/f* (*CAm, Méx*) stretcher case.
encaminamiento *nm* (*Inform*) routing.
encaminar [1a] **1** *vt* (**a**) *persona* to guide, direct, set on the right road (*a* to); **pude ~le** I was able to tell him the way to go.
(**b**) *vehículo, expedición etc* to route (*por* via); (*Inform*) to route.
(**c**) *atención, energía etc* to direct (*a* towards); **medidas encaminadas a corregir esto** measures designed to correct this; **el proyecto está encaminado a** + *infin* the plan is directed towards + *ger*, the plan is designed to + *infin*.
2 encaminarse *vr* (**a**) ~ **a** (*lit*) to set out for, make for, take the road to.
(**b**) ~ **a** (*fig*) to be directed towards, be intended for.
encamotado *adj*: **estar** ~ (*LAm*) to be in love (*de* with).
encamotarse* [1a] *vr* (*LAm*) to fall madly in love (*de* with).
encampanado *adj* bell-shaped.
encampanar [1a] **1** *vt* (**a**) (*And, Carib*: *encumbrar*) to raise, raise on high.
(**b**) (*And, Carib, Méx**: *abandonar*) to leave in the lurch, leave in a jam.
(**c**) ~ **a uno a** (*Carib*) to send sb to.
(**d**) (*Méx*: *agitar*) to excite, agitate.
2 encampanarse *vr* (**a**) (*LAm*: *jactarse*) to boast, brag.
(**b**) (*And**: *enamorarse*) to fall in love.
(**c**) (*Méx**: *meterse en un lío*) to get into a jam*.
(**d**) (*Carib*) to go off to a remote spot.
(**e**) (*And**: *complicarse*) to become difficult, get complicated.
encanado*, -a *nm/f* (*And*) prisoner.
encanalar [1a] *vt*, **encanalizar** [1f] *vt* to pipe; to channel, canalize.
encanallarse [1a] *vr* to degrade o.s.; to become coarse, acquire coarse habits.
encanar‡ [1a] *vt* (*And, Cono Sur*) to throw into jail.
encandecer [2d] *vt* to make white-hot.
encandelar [1a] *vt* (*Carib*) to annoy, irritate.
encandelillar [1a] *vt* (*LAm*) to dazzle; to bewilder.
encandellar [1a] *vt* (*And*) *fuego* to fan.
encandiladera *nf* procuress; madame.
encandilado *adj* high, erect.
encandiladora *nf* procuress; madame.
encandilar [1a] **1** *vt* (**a**) (*deslumbrar*) to dazzle.
(**b**) *lumbre* to stir, poke.
(**c**) (*fig*: *aturdir*) to daze, bewilder.
(**d**) (*fig*) *emoción* to kindle, stimulate, excite; *deseo* to arouse, stir; ~ **a una** to arouse a woman, make a woman feel randy*.
(**e**) (*And, Carib*: *privar de sueño*) to deprive of sleep.
2 encandilarse *vr* (**a**) (*ojos*) to glitter, sparkle, look unnaturally bright.
(**b**) (*persona*) to get excited, become emotional; (*sexualmente*) to become aroused, feel randy*.
(**c**) (*And, Carib*) (*asustarse*) to get scared; (*Carib, Méx*) (*enfadarse*) to get angry.
encanecer [2d] *vi y* **encanecerse** *vr* (**a**) (*pelo*) to go grey; (*persona*) to go grey, look old. (**b**) (*fig*) to go mouldy.
encanijado *adj* weak, puny.
encanijarse [1a] *vr* to grow weak, become emaciated, begin to look ill.
encanillar [1a] *vt* to wind (on to a spool).
encantado *adj* (**a**) (*hechizado*) bewitched; haunted; *sitio* romantic, bewitching; (*fig*) *casa* rambling.
(**b**) (*contento*) delighted, pleased, charmed; **¡~!** (*presentación*) how do you do!, pleased to meet you; **estoy ~ de conocerle** I'm delighted to meet you; **yo, ~** it's all right with me.
(**c**) (*distraído*) absent-minded, daydreaming; **parecer estar ~** to seem to be in a trance.
encantador 1 *adj* charming, delightful, lovely, enchanting. **2** *nm*, **encantadora** *nf* magician, enchanter; ~ **de serpientes** snake-charmer.
encantadoramente *adv* charmingly, delightfully.
encantamiento *nm* enchantment.
encantar [1a] *vt* (**a**) (*hechizar*) to bewitch, cast a spell on (*o* over).
(**b**) (*gustar*) to charm, delight, enchant, captivate, fascinate; **nos encanta la casa** we are delighted with the house, we are charmed with the house; **pero pronto dejó de ~nos** but we soon stopped liking it.
encanto *nm* (**a**) charm, spell, enchantment; **como por ~** as if by magic; (*fig*) in a flash, instantly.
(**b**) (*fig*) charm; enchantment, delight; **la playa es un ~** the beach is delightful, the beach is marvellous; **el niño es un ~** the child is a little treasure; **¡qué ~ de jardín!** what a lovely garden!
(**c**) (*palabra cariñosa*) sweetheart, my love; **¡oye, ~!*** (*piropo*) hullo gorgeous!* .
encañada *nf* ravine.
encañado *nm* conduit, pipe.
encañar [1a] **1** *vt* (**a**) *agua* to pipe. (**b**) *planta* to stake, prop up. (**c**) *terreno* to drain. (**d**) *seda* to wind (on to a spool). **2** *vi* (*planta*) to form a stalk.
encañonar [1a] **1** *vt* (**a**) *agua* to pipe. (**b**) (‡: *atracar*) to stick up‡, hold up; to cover (with a gun). **2** *vi* (*ave*) to grow feathers.
encapado *adj* cloaked, wearing a cloak.
encapotado *adj* (**a**) (*vestido de capa*) cloaked, wearing a cloak. (**b**) *cielo* cloudy, overcast.
encapotar [1a] **1** *vt* to cover with a cloak.
2 encapotarse *vr* (**a**) (*ponerse la capa*) to put on one's cloak; to wrap up.
(**b**) (*fig*) to frown.
(**c**) (*Met*) to become cloudy, cloud over, become overcast.
encapricharse [1a] *vr* to persist in one's foolishness; to dig one's heels in, insist on having one's way; ~ **con** to take a fancy to, get infatuated with.
encapuchado *adj* hooded.
encapuchar [1a] *vt*: ~ **un pozo de petróleo** to cap an oil-well.
encarado *adj*: **bien ~** good-looking, with nice features; **mal ~** ill-favoured, plain; (*LAm*) wicked-looking, with criminal features.
encaramar [1a] **1** *vt* (**a**) (*alzar*) to raise, lift up.
(**b**) (*alabar*) to praise, extol.
(**c**) (*And, CAm*: *avergonzar*) to embarrass, cause to blush.
2 encaramarse *vr* (**a**) (*ponerse arriba*) to perch, sit up high; (*en carrera*) to rise high; ~ **a** to climb (up, on to), get to the top of.
(**b**) (*And, CAm*) to get embarrassed, blush.
encarapitarse [1a] *vr* (*And, Carib*) = **encaramarse (a)**.
encarar [1a] **1** *vt* (**a**) *arma* to aim, point.
(**b**) *problema etc* to face (up to), confront.
(**c**) *dos cosas* to bring face to face.
2 *vi* (*Cono Sur*) to fall sick.
3 encararse *vr*: ~ **a,** ~ **con** to face, confront, come face to face with; **tendrá que ~ con los electores** he will have to face the electorate; **se encaró en seguida con el problema** he immediately faced up to the problem.
encarcelación *nf*, **encarcelamiento** *nm* imprisonment.
encarcelar [1a] *vt* to imprison, jail.
encarecer [2d] **1** *vt* (**a**) (*Com*) to put up the price of, make more expensive.

(**b**) (*alabar*) to praise, extol; *persona* to recommend; *política etc* to recommend (*a* to), urge (*a* on); *dificultad etc* to stress, emphasize; to exaggerate; **le encarezco que ...** I urge you to + *infin*.

2 *vi y* **encarecerse** *vr* (*Com*) to get dearer, rise in price.

encarecidamente *adv* insistently, earnestly, strongly.

encarecimiento *nm* (**a**) (*Com*) rise in price, price increase.

(**b**) (*elogio*) extolling; stressing, emphasizing; exaggeration, overrating; **con ~** insistently, earnestly, strongly.

encargado 1 *adj*: **el empleado ~ de estos géneros** the employee in charge of these stocks.

2 *nm*, **encargada** *nf* (*agente*) agent, representative; (*responsable*) person in charge; **~ de campo** groundsman; **~ de curso** lecturer in charge; **~ de mostrador** counter clerk; **~ de negocios** (*Pol*) chargé d'affaires; (*And, Méx*) agent; **~ de obra** foreman, site manager; **~ de prensa** press officer; **~ de la recepción** receptionist; **~ de relaciones públicas** public relations officer; **~ de seguridad** security officer; **encargada de vestuario** (*Teat*) wardrobe mistress; **~ de vestuario** (*Cine, TV*) costume designer.

encargar [1h] **1** *vt* (*confiar*) to entrust; (*ordenar*) to charge, commission; (*aconsejar*) to urge, recommend, advise; (*pedir*) to ask for; (*Com*) to order; **~ algo a uno** to entrust sth to sb; to put sb in charge of sth; **~ un deber a uno** to charge sb with a duty.

2 encargarse *vr*: **~ de algo** to take charge of sth; to take sth over; to look after sth, see about sth, attend to sth; **no había queso, pues las ratas se habían encargado de ello** there was no cheese, the rats had seen to that (*o* had made sure of that); **~ de** + *infin* to see about + *ger*, attend to the matter of + *ger*; to undertake to + *infin*.

encargo *nm* (**a**) (*cometido*) assignment, job; (*puesto*) post; (*orden*) charge, commission; (*responsabilidad*) responsibility; **hacer ~s** to run errands; **tener ~ de** + *infin* to have the job of + *ger*, have the responsibility of + *ger*.

(**b**) (*petición*) order, request; (*Com*) order (*de* for); **cancelar el ~ de** to cancel the order for, stop the delivery of; **el cuadro fue de ~** the picture was commissioned.

(**c**) **estar de ~** (*Carib, Cono Sur*) to be in the family way.

(**d**) **traer a uno de ~** (*Méx**) to pester sb.

encargue *nm* (*Cono Sur*) = **encargo.**

encariñado *adj*: **estar ~ con** to be fond of, be attached to.

encariñarse [1a] *vr*: **~ con** to grow fond of, get attached to.

Encarna *nf forma familiar de* **Encarnación**.

encarnación *nf* incarnation; embodiment.

encarnado *adj* (**a**) *diablo* incarnate. (**b**) *color* red, blood-red; flesh-coloured; *tez* ruddy, (*pey*) florid; **ponerse ~** to blush red.

encarnar [1a] **1** *vt* (**a**) (*personificar*) to embody, personify; (*Teat*) to embody, represent; **lago encarna el odio** Iago is hatred personified.

(**b**) *anzuelo* to bait.

2 *vi* (**a**) to take on bodily form; (*Rel etc*) to become incarnate.

(**b**) (*Med*) to heal (over).

(**c**) (*arma*) to enter the flesh, penetrate the body.

encarnecer [2d] *vi* to put on flesh.

encarnizadamente *adv* (*fig*) bloodily, bitterly, fiercely.

encarnizado *adj* (**a**) *herida etc* red, inflamed; *ojo* bloodshot. (**b**) *lucha* bloody; bitter, fierce.

encarnizamiento *nm* rage, fury; bitterness, ferocity.

encarnizar [1f] **1** *vt* (*fig*) to enrage, infuriate; to make cruel.

2 encarnizarse *vr* (**a**) **~ en** to gorge on; to become greedy for.

(**b**) (*fig*) to get furious; to fight fiercely; **~ con, ~ en** to be cruel to, treat cruelly.

encaro *nm* (**a**) (*mirada*) stare, staring, gaze. (**b**) (*puntería*) aim(ing). (**c**) (*Hist*) blunderbuss.

encarpetar [1a] *vt* to file away; to pigeonhole; (*LAm*) *plan etc* to shelve, bury.

encarrilamiento *nm* (*fig*) rectification; correction; direction, guiding.

encarrilar [1a] *vt* (**a**) *tren* to put back on the rails.

(**b**) (*fig*) to put on the right track, start off again on the right lines; (*corregir*) to correct; (*dirigir*) to direct, guide.

(**c**) **ir encarrilado** to be on the right lines, be doing nicely; (*pey*) to be in a rut.

encarrujar [1a] *vt* (*Cono Sur Cos*) to ruffle, frill.

encartado, -a *nm/f* (*Jur*) accused, defendant.

encartar [1a] *vt* (**a**) (*gen*) to enroll, register, enter (on a list); (*Jur*) to summon. (**b**) *criminal* to outlaw.

encarte *nm* (*Tip*) insert, inset.

encartonar [1a] *vt* to cover with cardboard; (*Tip*) to bind in boards.

encartuchar [1a] *vt* (*LAm*) *papel* to make a cone of, roll up into a cone.

encasar [1a] *vt hueso* to set.

encasillado 1 *adj actor* type-cast. **2** *nm* (set of) pigeonholes.

encasillamiento *nm* (**a**) piegonholing; sorting, classification. (**b**) (*Teat etc*) type-casting.

encasillar [1a] *vt* (**a**) (*poner en casillas*) to pigeonhole; (*clasificar*) to sort out, classify; (*archivar*) to file. (**b**) (*Teat etc*) to type-cast.

encasquetar [1a] *vt* (**a**) *sombrero* to pull on, pull down tight, jam on. (**b**) **~ una idea a uno** to get an idea firmly fixed in sb's mind. (**c**) (*Teat*) to typecast. (**d**) **~ algo a uno*** to foist sth on sb.

encasquillador *nm* (*LAm*) blacksmith.

encasquillar [1a] **1** *vt* (**a**) (*poner casquillos a*) to put a tip on.

(**b**) (*LAm*) *caballo* to shoe.

(**c**) (*: *incriminar*) to frame*.

2 encasquillarse *vr* (**a**) (*bala, revólver*) to jam.

(**b**) (*And: en discurso etc*) to get stuck, dry up*.

(**c**) (*Carib: asustarse*) to get scared.

(**d**) (*Carib*: vacilar*) to waver.

encastillado *adj* (**a**) (*Arquit*) castellated. (**b**) (*fig*) haughty; stubborn.

encastillar [1a] **1** *vt* to fortify, defend with castles. **2 encastillarse** *vr* (**a**) (*Mil*) to take to the hills; (*Hist*) to shut o.s. up in a castle. (**b**) (*fig*) to refuse to yield; **~ en un principio** to stick to a principle, refuse to give up a principle.

encatrado *nm* (*Cono Sur*) hurdle.

encatrinarse [1a] *vr* (*Méx*) to dress up.

encauchado *nm* (*And, Carib*) (*tela*) rubberized cloth; (*capa*) waterproof cape.

encauchar [1a] *vt* to rubberize, waterproof.

encausado, -a *nm/f* (*Jur*) accused, defendant.

encausar [1a] *vt* to prosecute, sue; to put on trial.

encauzar [1f] *vt* (**a**) *agua* to channel.

(**b**) (*fig*) to channel, direct, guide; **las protestas se pueden ~ a fines buenos** the protests can be directed towards good objectives, the protests can be guided into useful channels.

encefalitis *nf* encephalitis; **~ (letárgica)** sleeping sickness.

encefalograma *nm* encephalogram.

encefalomielitis *nf*: **~ miálgica** myalgic encephalomyelitis.

encefalopatía *nf*: **~ espongiforme bovina** bovine spongiform encephalopathy.

enceguecer [2d] (*LAm*) **1** *vt* to blind. **2** *vi y* **enceguecerse** *vr* to go blind.

encelar [1a] **1** *vt* to make jealous. **2 encelarse** *vr* (**a**) (*persona*) to become jealous. (**b**) (*Zool*) to rut, be on heat.

encenagado *adj* (**a**) (*enfangado*) muddy, mud-stained. (**b**) (*fig*) sunk in vice, depraved.

encenagarse [1h] *vr* (**a**) to get muddy. (**b**) (*fig*) to wallow in vice, get depraved.

encendedor *nm* (**a**) (*mechero*) lighter; **~ (de cigarrillos)** cigarette lighter; **~ de cocina, ~ de(l) gas** gas lighter. (**b**) (*persona*) lamplighter.

encender [2g] **1** *vt* (**a**) (*gen*) to light; (*pegar fuego a*) to set fire to, ignite; to kindle; *fósforo* to strike, light; *luz, radio* to turn on, switch on, put on; *gas* to light, turn on; (*Inform*) to switch on.

(**b**) (*fig*) to kindle, inflame; to stir up, provoke.

(**c**) (*Carib*) (*azotar*) to beat; (*castigar*) to punish.

2 encenderse *vr* (**a**) (*fuego*) to catch, catch fire, ignite; (*llama*) to burn up, flare up; **¿cuándo se encienden las luces?** when is lighting-up time?

(**b**) (*fig: persona*) to get excited; to flare up.

(**c**) (*fig: cara*) to blush, get red.

encendida* *nf* (*Carib*) (*paliza*) beating; (*reprimenda*) telling-off*.

encendidamente *adv* passionately, ardently.

encendido 1 *adj* (**a**) **estar ~** to be alight, be on fire, be burning; (*luz*) to be on.

(**b**) *color* glowing (*de* with); fiery.

(**c**) *cara* red (*de* with); inflamed (*de* with).

2 *nm* (*Aut*) ignition; (*de la luz*) switching on.

encendimiento *nm* (**a**) burning; kindling. (**b**) (*fig: pasión*) passion, ardour; (*ansia*) eagerness; (*intensidad*) intensity.

encenizar [1f] *vt* to cover with ashes.
encentar [1j] *vt* to begin to use; *pan etc* to cut the first slice from.
encerado 1 *adj* waxed; waxy, wax-coloured. **2** *nm* oilcloth; (*Náut*) tarpaulin. (**c**) (*Escol etc*) blackboard.
encerador(a) *nm/f* polisher, polishing machine; **~ de piso** floor polisher.
encerar [1a] *vt* to wax; *piso* to wax, polish.
encercamiento *nm* (*LAm*) encirclement.
encercar [1g] *vt* (*LAm*) = **cercar**.
encerotar [1a] *vt hilo* to wax.
encerradero *nm* fold, pen.
encerrar [1j] **1** *vt* (**a**) (*gen*) to shut in, shut up; (*con llave*) to lock in, lock up; (*cercar*) to enclose; (*confinar*) to confine, hem in.
(**b**) (*abarcar*) to include, contain, comprise; **el libro encierra profundas verdades** the book contains deep truths.
(**c**) (*implicar*) to involve, imply.
2 encerrarse *vr* (**a**) to shut o.s. up, lock o.s. in; to go into seclusion; **se encerró en su cuarto** she shut herself in her room; **~ en el silencio** to maintain a total silence.
(**b**) (*Méx**: *ser hosco*) to be stand-offish.
encerrona* *nf* (*Escol*) detention; (*protesta*) sit-in; **preparar a uno una ~** (*fig*) to put sb in a tight spot.
encespedar [1a] *vt* to turf.
encestar [1a] *vi* (*Dep*) to score (a basket).
enceste *nm* (*Dep*) basket.
encía *nf* (*Anat*) gum.
encíclica *nf* encyclical.
enciclopedia *nf* encyclopaedia.
enciclopédico *adj* encyclopaedic.
encielar [1a] *vt* (*CAm, Cono Sur*) to roof, put a roof on.
encierra *nf* (*Cono Sur*) (**a**) (*acto*) penning (of cattle, for slaughter). (**b**) (*pasto*) winter pasture.
encierre *nm* (*Carib*) penning (of cattle, for slaughter).
encierro *nm* (**a**) (*acto*) shutting-in, shutting-up, locking, closing; confinement; (*de manifestantes*) sit-in; (*en fábrica*) work-in; sit-down strike.
(**b**) (*cercado*) enclosure; (*cárcel*) prison, lock-up; (*Agr*) pen; (*Taur*) bull-pen.
(**c**) (*Taur*) penning (of bulls), corralling.
encima 1 *adv* (**a**) (*lugar*) above, over; overhead; at the top; on top; **por ~** over, overhead; **muy por ~** (*fig*) very superficially, very hastily; **ponlo ~ y no debajo** put it over and not under, put it on top and not underneath; **el avión pasó ~** the plane passed over.
(**b**) (*fig*) **echarse algo ~** to take sth upon o.s.; **quitarse algo de ~** to get rid of sth; to cast sth off, shake sth off; **se me vino ~** it fell on top of me; **la guerra está ~** war is upon us, war is imminent; **no llevo tabaco ~** I haven't any tobacco on me, I don't carry tobacco; **¿tienes un duro ~?** do you have a *duro* about you?; **¿tienes cambio ~?** have you any change on you?; **tienes bastante ~** you've got enough to worry about.
(**c**) (*fig*: *además*) besides; **y otras muchas cosas ~** and a lot else besides, and much else in addition; **de ~** (*LAm*) into the bargain; **y ~ no me dio las gracias** and on top of all that he didn't even thank me; **no viniste y ~ no me llamaste** you didn't come and on top of that you didn't ring me.
(**d**) (*Cono Sur*) **~ nuestro** (*etc*) above us (*etc*).
2 ~ de *prep* (**a**) (*lugar*) above, over; on; on top of; **por ~ de** over; **pasó ~ de nuestras cabezas** it passed over our heads.
(**b**) (*fig*) besides, in addition to; over and above, in preference to; **y luego ~ de todo eso** and then in addition to all that, and then on top of all that; **han preferido la cantidad por ~ de la calidad** they have preferred quantity to quality.
encimar [1a] (*And, Cono Sur*) **1** *vt* (**a**) (*****: *añadir*) to throw in, add on; **le encimaron el sueldo** they gave him a bonus on top of his wages. (**b**) (*Dep*) to mark. **2** *vi* (*Naipes*) to add a new stake.
encime *nm* (*And*) bonus, extra.
encimera *nf* worktop; top, surface.
encimero *adj* top, upper.
encina *nf* ilex, holm oak, evergreen oak.
encinar *nm* holm-oak wood.
encinta *adj* pregnant; (*Zool*) with young; **mujer ~** pregnant woman, expectant mother; **dejar a una ~** to make a woman pregnant.
encintado *nm* kerb.
encizañar [1a] **1** *vt* to sow discord among, create trouble among. **2** *vi* to sow discord, cause trouble.
enclaustrar [1a] *vt* to cloister; (*fig*) to hide away.
enclavar [1a] **1** *vt* (**a**) (*clavar*) to nail; (*traspasar*) to pierce, transfix.
(**b**) (*empotrar*) to embed, set; *edificio etc* to set, place; **las ruinas están enclavadas en un valle** the ruins are set in a valley, the ruins have a valley as their setting.
(**c**) (*****: *estafar*) to swindle.
2 enclavarse *vr* to interlock.
enclave *nm* enclave; **~ regional de gobierno** regional seat of government.
enclavijar [1a] *vt* to peg, pin; to join.
enclencle *adj* (*LAm*) terribly thin.
enclenco *adj* (*And, Carib*), **enclenque** *adj* weak, weakly, sickly.
enclítica *nf* enclitic.
enclítico *adj* enclitic.
enclocar [1g *y* 1l] *vi*, **encloquecer** [2d] *vi* to go broody.
encobar [1a] *vi y* **encobarse** *vr* (*gallina*) to sit, brood.
encocorante* *adj* annoying, maddening.
encocorar* [1a] **1** *vt* to annoy, enrage, madden. **2 encocorarse** *vr* (**a**) (*enojarse*) to get cross, get mad. (**b**) (*Carib*: *sospechar*) to get suspicious. (**c**) (*Cono Sur**) to put on airs.
encofrado *nm* (*Téc*) form, plank mould.
encofrar [1a] *vt* to plank, timber.
encoger [2c] **1** *vt* (**a**) (*contraer*) to shrink, contract, shorten.
(**b**) (*fig*) to intimidate, scare, discourage.
2 encogerse *vr* (**a**) (*contraerse*) to shrink, contract; to shrivel up.
(**b**) **~ de hombros** to shrug one's shoulders.
(**c**) (*fig*: *acobardarse*) to cringe; (*desalentarse*) to get discouraged, get disheartened; (*ser tímido*) to be shy, be timid.
encogidamente *adv* (*fig*) shyly, timidly, bashfully.
encogido *adj* (**a**) (*contraído*) shrunken; shrivelled. (**b**) (*fig*) shy, timid, bashful.
encogimiento *nm* (**a**) (*contracción*) shrinking, contraction; shrinkage. (**b**) **~ de hombros** shrug (of the shoulders). (**c**) (*fig*) shyness, timidity, bashfulness.
encogollado* *adj* (*Cono Sur*) stuck-up*, snobbish.
encogollarse [1a] *vr* (*Cono Sur*) to get conceited, be haughty.
encohetarse* [1a] *vr* (*And, CAm*) to get furious.
encojar [1a] **1** *vt* to lame, cripple. **2 encojarse** *vr* to go lame; (*****) to pretend to be ill.
encojonarse** [1a] *vr* (*CAm*) to fly off the handle*, explode.
encolar [1a] *vt* (*engomar*) to glue, gum, paste; (*aprestar*) to size; (*pegar*) to stick down, stick together.
encolerizar [1f] **1** *vt* to anger, provoke. **2 encolerizarse** *vr* to get angry.
encomendar [1j] **1** *vt* to entrust, commend (*a* to, to the charge of). **2 encomendarse** *vr*: **~ a** to entrust o.s. to, put one's trust in.
encomendería *nf* (*And*) grocer's, grocery store.
encomendero *nm* (**a**) (*And*) grocer; (*Carib*) wholesale meat supplier. (**b**) (*LAm Hist*) *holder of an encomienda*.
encomiable *adj* laudable, praiseworthy.
encomiar [1b] *vt* to praise, extol, pay tribute to.
encomienda *nf* (**a**) (*Hist Mil*) command (of a military order); (*en LAm*) *encomienda* (*land and inhabitants granted to a conquistador*).
(**b**) (*encargo*) charge, commission.
(**c**) (*protección*) protection; patronage.
(**d**) (*elogio*) praise, tribute, commendation.
(**e**) (*LAm Correos*) parcel; parcel post; **~ contra reembolso** parcel sent cash on delivery.
(**f**) **~s** regards, respects.
encomio *nm* praise, eulogy, tribute.
encomioso *adj* (*LAm*) laudatory, eulogistic.
enconadamente *adv* (*fig*) angrily, bitterly.
enconado *adj* (**a**) (*Med*) inflamed, angry; sore. (**b**) (*fig*: *airado*) angry, bitter. (**c**) (*fig*: *fervoroso*) ardent, fervent.
enconar [1a] **1** *vt* (**a**) (*Med*) to inflame; to make sore.
(**b**) (*fig*) to anger, irritate, provoke.
(**c**) (*Carib, Méx**: *ratear*) to pilfer.
2 enconarse *vr* (**a**) (*Med*) to become inflamed; to fester.
(**b**) (*fig*: *persona*) to get angry, get irritated; (*agravio*) to fester, rankle.
enconcharse [1a] *vr* (*LAm*) (*psicológicamente*) to go into one's shell; (*físicamente*) to retire into seclusion.
encono *nm* (**a**) (*rencor*) rancour, spite(fulness); ill-feeling,

bad blood. (**b**) (*And, Cono Sur*: *Med*) inflammation, soreness.
enconoso *adj* (**a**) (*Med*) inflamed, sore. (**b**) (*fig*) resentful, rancorous, malevolent. (**c**) (*LAm*) *planta* noxious, poisonous.
encontradizo *adj* met by chance; **hacerse el ~** to contrive an apparently chance meeting, manage to bump into sb.
encontrado *adj* contrary, conflicting, hostile; opposed; **las posiciones siguen encontradas** their positions are still poles apart.
encontrar [1l] **1** *vt* (**a**) (*hallar*) to find; **lo encontró bastante fácil** he found it pretty easy; **¿qué tal lo encuentras?** how do you find it?; **no lo encuentro en ninguna parte** I can't find it anywhere; **no sé lo que le encuentran** I don't know what they see in her.
(**b**) (*topar*) to meet, encounter, run into; **~ dificultades** to encounter difficulties, run into trouble.
2 encontrarse *vr* (**a**) (*personas*) to meet, meet each other; **~ con uno** to meet sb, run across sb, encounter sb; **~ con un obstáculo** to run into an obstacle, encounter an obstacle; **me encontré con que no tenía gasolina** I found I was out of petrol; I was faced with the fact that I had no petrol.
(**b**) (*vehículos etc*) to crash, collide; (*opiniones etc*) to clash, conflict, come into collision.
(**c**) (*estar*) to be, be situated, be located, stand; **se encuentra en la plaza principal** it is in the main square; **¿dónde se encuentra el cine?** where is the cinema?
(**d**) (*hallarse*) to find o.s., be; **se encuentra enferma** she is ill; **¿cómo te encuentras ahora?** how are you now?, how do you feel now?, how do you find yourself now?; **me encontré sin coche** I found myself without a car; **en este momento no se encuentra** she's not in at the moment.
encontrón *nm*, **encontronazo** *nm* collision, crash, smash.
encoñamiento‡ *nm* infatuation; whim.
encoñar‡ [1a] **1** *vt* (**a**) (*alentar*) to lead on, draw on, raise (false) hopes in. (**b**) (*enojar*) to upset. **2 encoñarse** *vr*: **~ de** to fall madly in love with, take a great fancy to.
encopetado *adj* (**a**) (*noble*) of noble birth; blue-blooded. (**b**) (*fig*) (*altanero*) haughty, high and mighty; (*presumido*) conceited; (*de buen tono*) posh*, grand.
encopetarse [1a] *vr* to get conceited, give o.s. airs.
encorajar [1a] **1** *vt* (**a**) (*animar*) to encourage, put heart into. (**b**) (*inflamar*) to inflame. **2 encorajarse** *vr* to fly into a rage.
encorajinar [1a] **1** *vt* (**a**) (*LAm*) = **encorajar.** (**b**) (*Méx*: *enfadar*) to anger, irritate. **2 encorajinarse** *vr* (*Cono Sur*: *trato*) to fail, go awry.
encorar [1l] *vt* to cover with leather.
encorbatado *adj* wearing a tie.
encorchado *nm* (**a**) corking. (**b**) hiving.
encorchar [1a] *vt* (**a**) *botella* to cork. (**b**) *abejas* to hive.
encordado *nm* (**a**) (*Cono Sur Mús*) (*cuerdas*) strings; (*guitarra*) guitar. (**b**) (*Boxeo*) ring.
encordar [1l] **1** *vt* (**a**) (*Mús etc*) to string, fit strings to. (**b**) (*atar*) to bind, tie, lash (with ropes); to rope together. (**c**) *espacio, zona* to rope off. **2 encordarse** *vr* (*alpinistas*) to rope themselves together, rope up.
encordelar [1a] *vt* to tie (with string).
encornado *adj*: **un toro bien ~** a bull with good horns.
encornadura *nf* horns.
encornar [1l] *vt* to gore.
encornudar [1a] *vt* to cuckold.
encorralar [1a] *vt* to pen, corral.
encorsetar [1a] *vt* (*fig*) to confine, put into a straitjacket.
encorvada *nf* stoop, bend; **hacer la ~*** to malinger, pretend to be ill.
encorvado *adj* curved, bent; stooping; crooked.
encorvadura *nf* curve, curving, curvature; bend; crookedness.
encorvar [1a] **1** *vt* (*doblar*) to bend, curve; (*hacia abajo*) to bend (down, over); (*en forma de gancho*) to hook; (*torcer*) to make crooked.
2 encorvarse *vr* (**a**) (*inclinarse*) to bend (down, over), stoop.
(**b**) (*combarse*) to sag, warp; (*torcerse*) to buckle.
encrespado *adj pelo* curly; *mar* choppy.
encrespador *nm* curling tongs.
encrespar [1a] **1** *vt* (**a**) *pelo* to curl, frizzle; *plumas* to ruffle; *mar* to make rough, produce waves on.
(**b**) (*fig*) to anger, irritate.
2 encresparse *vr* (**a**) to curl; to ripple; to get rough.
(**b**) (*fig*) to get cross, get irritated.
encrestado *adj* haughty.
encrucijada *nf* crossroads; intersection, junction; **estamos en la ~** (*fig*) we are at the crossroads; we are at the parting of the ways; **poner a uno en la ~** (*fig*) to put sb on the spot.
encuadernación *nf* (**a**) binding; **~ en cuero, ~ en piel** leather binding; **~ en pasta** hardback (binding); **~ en rústica** paperback (binding); **~ en tela** cloth binding. (**b**) (*taller*) bindery, binder's.
encuadernador(a) *nm/f* bookbinder.
encuadernar [1a] *vt* to bind (*en* in); to cover; **libro sin ~** unbound book.
encuadrable *adj*: **~ en** that can be placed in, that can be included in.
encuadramiento *nm* (*acto*) framing; (*fig*) frame, framework.
encuadrar [1a] **1** *vt* (**a**) (*poner cuadro a*) to frame, put in a frame, make a frame for.
(**b**) (*encajar*) to fit, insert (*en* into).
(**c**) (*fig*) to contain, comprise.
(**d**) (*LAm*: *resumir*) to summarize, give a synthesis of.
2 *vi* (*Cono Sur*) to fit, square (*con* with).
encuadre *nm* (*Fot etc*) setting, background, frame; (*fig*) setting.
encuartar [1a] (*Méx*) **1** *vt ganado* to tie up, rope.
2 encuartarse *vr* (**a**) (*animal*) to shy, balk; to get caught in its straps (*etc*).
(**b**) (*fig*) to get involved, get bogged down (*en* in).
(**c**) (*interrumpir*) to butt in.
encuartelar [1a] *vt* (*LAm*) to billet, put in barracks.
encubierta *nf* fraud.
encubierto *adj* (*oculto*) hidden, concealed; (*turbio*) underhand; (*secreto*) undercover; *crítica* veiled.
encubridor 1 *adj* concealing. **2** *nm*, **encubridora** *nf* harbourer; receiver of stolen goods; (*Jur*) accessory after the fact, abettor.
encubrimiento *nm* concealment, hiding; receiving of stolen goods; (*Jur*) complicity, abetment; **se le acusó de ~** he was charged with being an accessory after the fact.
encubrir [3a; *ptp* **encubierto**] *vt* (*ocultar*) to conceal, hide, cover (up), cloak; *criminal, sospechoso* to harbour, shelter; *crimen* to conceal; (*ayudar*) to abet, be an accomplice in.
encucurucharse* [1a] *vr* (*And, CAm*) to get up on top, reach the top.
encuentro *nm* (**a**) meeting; encounter; **~ de escritores** (small) congress of writers; **~ de inteligencias** meeting of minds; **un ~ fortuito** a chance meeting; **su primer ~ con la policía** his first encounter with the police; **ir** (*o* **salir**) **al ~ de uno** to go to meet sb; **ir al ~ de lo desconocido** to go out to face the unknown.
(**b**) (*Mil*) encounter; skirmish, action, fight.
(**c**) (*Dep*) meeting, match, game; **~ de ida** away game; **~ de vuelta** return match.
(**d**) (*Aut etc*) collision, smash, crash; (*de opiniones etc*) clash; **llevarse a uno de ~** (*Carib, Méx**) (*derrotar*) to crush sb; (*arruinar*) to drag sb down to disaster; **llevarse todo de ~** (*Carib**) to ride roughshod over everyone.
encuerada *nf* (*Carib, Méx*) = **encuerista.**
encuerado *adj* (*Carib, Méx*) (*harapiento*) ragged; (*desnudo*) nude, naked.
encuerar [1a] **1** *vt* (*Carib, Cono Sur, Méx*) (**a**) (*desnudar*) to strip (naked).
(**b**) (*fig**) to skin, fleece.
2 encuerarse *vr* (**a**) (*Carib, Cono Sur, Méx*: *desnudarse*) to strip off, get undressed.
(**b**) (*Carib*: *vivir juntos*) to live together.
encueratriz* *nf* (*Méx*) = **encuerista.**
encuerista* *nf* (*Carib, Méx*) striptease artiste, stripper.
encuesta *nf* (**a**) (*Jur*) inquiry, investigation; probe (*de* into); inquest (*fig*); **~ judicial** post-mortem, coroner's inquest.
(**b**) (*sondeo*) public-opinion poll; survey, inquiry; quiz; **E~ Gallup** Gallup Poll; **~ por teléfono** telephone poll.
encuestador(a) *nm/f* pollster.
encuestar [1a] *vt* to poll, take a poll of; **el 69 por 100 de los encuestados** 69% of those polled.
encuetarse‡ [1a] *vr* (*CAm*) to fly off the handle*, lose one's temper.
encuitarse [1a] *vr* (**a**) (*afligirse*) to grieve. (**b**) (*And*: *endeudarse*) to get into debt.
encujado *nm* (*Carib*) framework, lattice.
enculebrarse‡ [1a] *vr* (*CAm*) to fly off the handle*, lose one's temper.
enculecarse [1g] *vr* (*LAm*) to go broody.

encumbrado *adj* (**a**) *torre etc* lofty, towering, high. (**b**) *persona* exalted, eminent. (**c**) (*pey*) high and mighty, haughty.

encumbramiento *nm* (**a**) (*acto*) raising, elevation. (**b**) (*altura*) height, loftiness; (*fig*) exaltation, eminence. (**c**) (*fig*) haughtiness.

encumbrar [1a] **1** *vt* (**a**) (*alzar*) to raise, elevate.

(**b**) *persona* to elevate, exalt (*a* to); (*fig*) to extol.

2 encumbrarse *vr* (**a**) (*torre etc*) to rise, soar, tower.

(**b**) ~ **sobre** (*fig*) to tower over, be far superior to.

(**c**) (*fig: pey*) to be proud, be haughty.

encurdelarse⁑ [1a] *vr* (*Cono Sur*) to get sloshed*.

encurrucarse* [1g] *vr* (*LAm*) (*de cuclillas*) to squat, crouch; (*ovillarse*) to curl up (in a ball).

encurtidos *nmpl* pickles; appetizers, savouries.

encurtir [3a] *vt* to pickle.

enchalecar [1g] *vt* (*fig*) to place in a strait-jacket.

enchapado *nm* plating; veneer.

enchapar [1a] *vt* (**a**) (*con metal*) to plate, overlay (with metal); (*con madera*) to veneer. (**b**) (*Méx*) *puerta* to fit locks to.

enchaquetarse [1a] *vr* (**a**) (*And, Carib: ponerse la chaqueta*) to put one's jacket on. (**b**) (*And: vestirse de etiqueta*) to dress up.

encharcada *nf* pool, puddle.

encharcado *adj* still, stagnant.

encharcar [1g] **1** *vt* to swamp, flood; to cover with puddles, turn into pools.

2 encharcarse *vr* (**a**) (*tierra*) to swamp, get flooded, get covered with puddles.

(**b**) (*agua*) to form puddles, form a pool; to become stagnant.

(**c**) (*LAm: enfangarse*) to get muddy.

(**d**) (*Cono Sur: atascarse*) to get stuck in a puddle.

(**e**) ~ **en los vicios** (*fig*) to wallow in vice.

encharralarse [1a] *vr* (*CAm*) to make an ambush, lie in ambush.

enchastrar⁑ [1a] *vt* (*Cono Sur*) to dirty, cover in muck.

enchauchado* *adj* (*Cono Sur*) well-heeled.

enchicharse* [1a] *vr* (**a**) (*LAm: emborracharse*) to get drunk. (**b**) (*And, CAm: enfadarse*) to get angry, lose control.

enchilada *nf* (*CAm, Méx*) stuffed tortilla.

enchilado 1 *adj* (**a**) (*CAm, Méx Culin*) seasoned with chili; (*picante*) spicy, hot. (**b**) (*Méx: color*) bright red. **2** *nm* (*Carib, Méx*) stew with chili sauce.

enchilar [1a] **1** *vt* (**a**) (*CAm, Méx Culin*) to season with chili. (**b**) (*fig*) (*CAm, Méx: molestar*) to annoy, vex; (*CAm: decepcionar*) to disappoint. **2** *vi* (*CAm, Méx*) to sting, burn. **3 enchilarse** *vr* (*Méx*) to go red in the face; (*fig*) to fly into a rage.

enchiloso *adj* (*CAm, Méx*) *sabor* hot.

enchilotarse* [1a] *vr* (*Cono Sur*) to get cross.

enchinar [1a] **1** *vt* (*Méx*) *pelo* to curl, perm. **2 enchinarse** *vr*: ~ **el cuerpo** to get gooseflesh; to get scared.

enchinchar [1a] **1** *vt* (**a**) (*CAm, Carib, Méx: molestar*) to put out, bother. (**b**) (*Méx: persona*) to cause to waste time; *asunto* to delay. (**c**) (*Cono Sur, Méx*: enojar*) to rile*, annoy. **2 enchincharse** *vr* (**a**) (*And, CAm, Carib, Méx: infestarse*) to get infested with bugs. (**b**) (*Cono Sur*: enfadarse*) to get bad-tempered.

enchiquerar [1a] *vt* (*LAm*) to pen, corral.

enchironar⁑ [1a] *vt* to jug⁑, jail.

enchisparse* [1a] *vr* (*LAm*) to get tight*.

enchisterado *adj* top-hatted, with a top hat on.

enchivarse* [1a] *vr* (*And*) to fly into a rage.

enchufable *adj* which plugs in, plug-in (*atr*).

enchufado, -a* *nm/f* (*influyente*) well-connected person, person with pull; (*cobista*) creep⁑; (*en escuela*) teacher's pet.

enchufar [1a] **1** *vt* (**a**) (*Téc etc*) to join, connect, fit together, fit in; to telescope together; (*Elec*) to plug in. (**b**) (*Com, Fin*) to merge. (**c**) (*) = **2**. **2 enchufarse*** *vr* (*puesto*) to wangle o.s. a job (*etc*)*, get a cushy job⁑; (*relacionarse bien*) to get in with the right people*.

enchufe *nm* (**a**) (*Téc etc: unión*) joint, connection; (*manguito*) sleeve; (*encaje*) socket.

(**b**) (*Elec*) (*clavija*) plug; (*toma*) point, socket; ~ **múltiple** adaptor.

(**c**) (*: *influencia*) connection, useful contact; **tiene un ~ en el ministerio** he's got a contact in the ministry, he can pull wires at the ministry; **hay que tener ~s** you've got to have contacts; **lo hizo por ~** he pulled strings to do it.

(**d**) (*: *puesto*) soft job*, cushy job⁑.

enchufismo* *nm* (system of getting things done by) wire-pulling*, use of contacts to obtain favours; old-boy network.

enchufista* *nm* wirepuller*, contact man, person who uses the old-boy network.

ende *adv* (†† *o liter*): **por ~** hence, therefore.

endeble *adj* (*Med*) feeble, weak, frail; (*fig*) feeble, flimsy.

endeblez *nf* feebleness, weakness, frailty; flimsiness.

endecasílabo 1 *adj* hendecasyllabic. **2** *nm* hendecasyllable.

endecha *nf* lament, dirge.

endecharse [1a] *vr* to grieve, mourn.

endémico *adj* endemic; (*fig*) rife, chronic.

endemoniado *adj* (**a**) (*poseído*) possessed of the devil. (**b**) (*fig: endiablado*) devilish, fiendish; (*perverso*) perverse; (*furioso*) furious, wild.

endemoniar [1b] **1** *vt* (**a**) (*endiablar*) to bedevil. (**b**) (*: *provocar*) to rile*, anger. **2 endemoniarse** *vr* to get riled*.

endenantes* *adv* (*LAm*) a short time back; earlier, before.

endentar [1j] *vti* (*Mec*) to engage, mesh (*con* with).

endentecer [2d] *vi* to teethe, cut one's teeth.

enderezado *adj* appropriate; favourable, opportune.

enderezar [1f] **1** *vt* (**a**) (*poner derecho*) to straighten, straighten out (*o* up); (*destorcer*) to unbend.

(**b**) (*poner vertical*) to set upright, stand vertically; (*Náut*) to right; *vehículo etc* to stand the right way up, put back on its wheels (*etc*), straighten up.

(**c**) (*fig: arreglar*) to put in order, set to rights.

(**d**) (*fig*) (*dirigir*) to direct; to manage; (*dedicar*) to address, dedicate (*a* to); **las medidas están enderezadas a** (*o* **para**) **corregirlo** the measures are designed to correct it.

2 enderezarse *vr* (**a**) (*ponerse recto*) to straighten up, stand up straight, draw o.s. up; (*Náut*) to right itself; (*Aer*) to flatten out.

(**b**) ~ **a un lugar** to set out for a place.

(**c**) ~ **a** + *infin* to take steps to + *infin*, prepare to + *infin*; (*medida etc*) to be designed to + *infin*.

ENDESA, Endesa [en'desa] *nf abr de* **Empresa Nacional de Electricidad, Sociedad Anónima**.

endespués *adv* (*And, Carib*) = **después**.

endeudamiento *nm* indebtedness, (extent of) debt.

endeudarse [1a] *vr* to get into debt (*con* with); ~ **con uno** (*fig*) to become indebted to sb.

endeveras *adv* (*LAm*) = **de veras**.

endiabladamente* *adv*: ~ **difícil** devilish(ly) difficult.

endiablado *adj* (**a**) (*diabólico*) devilish, diabolical, fiendish.

(**b**) (*hum*) impish, mischievous, wicked.

(**c**) (*feo*) ugly.

(**d**) (*enojado*) furious, angry.

(**e**) (*LAm*) *camino etc* difficult, dangerous; *asunto* complicated, tricky.

endiablar [1a] **1** *vt* (**a**) (*endemoniar*) to bedevil, bewitch. (**b**) (*: *corromper*) to pervert, corrupt. **2 endiablarse** *vr* to get furious.

endibia *nf* endive.

endija *nf* (*LAm*) = **rendija**.

endilgar* [1h] *vr* (**a**) (*enviar*) to send, direct; (*encaminar*) to guide.

(**b**) *golpe* to fetch.

(**c**) ~ **algo a uno** to spring sth on sb; to unload sth on to sb; ~ **un sermón a uno** to give sb a lecture, ram a sermon down sb's throat; **le han endilgado el mote de enchufado** they've labelled him a creep⁑.

endiñar [1a] *vt* (**a**) (*) *golpe* to fetch. (**b**) ~**la**⁂ to put it in⁂.

endiosado *adj* stuck-up*, conceited; high and mighty.

endiosamiento *nm* (**a**) (*engreimiento*) vanity, conceit; haughtiness. (**b**) (*ensimismamiento*) absorption.

endiosar [1a] **1** *vt* to deify; (*fig*) to make a god out of.

2 endiosarse *vr* (**a**) (*engreírse*) to get conceited, give o.s. airs; to be high and mighty.

(**b**) ~ **en algo** to be(come) absorbed in sth.

enditarse [1a] *vr* (*And, CAm*) to get into debt.

endocrina *nf* endocrine.

endocrino *adj* endocrine.

endodoncia *nf* endodontics.

endogamia *nf* inbreeding; **engendrado por ~** inbred.

endógeno *adj* endogenous.

endomingado *adj* all dressed up, in one's Sunday best.

endomingarse [1h] *vr* to dress up, put on one's Sunday best.

endomorfo *nm* endomorph.

endorsar [1a] *vt* (**a**) (*CAm, Carib*) = **endosar.** (**b**) (*fig*) to endorse, support, back; to confirm.
endosante *nmf* endorser.
endosar [1a] *vt* (**a**) *cheque etc* to endorse.
(**b**) ~ **algo a uno*** to lumber sb with sth*, make sb put up with sth; to unload sth on to sb.
endosatario, -a *nm/f* endorsee.
endoso *nm* endorsement; **sin** ~ unendorsed.
endriago *nm* fabulous monster, dragon.
endrina *nf* sloe.
endrino *nm* blackthorn, sloe.
endrogarse* [1h] *vr* (*And, Méx*) to get into debt.
endulzante *nm* sweetening, sweetener.
endulzar [1f] *vt* (**a**) to sweeten. (**b**) (*fig*) to sweeten; to soften, mitigate.
endurecer [2d] **1** *vt* (**a**) to harden, make hard; to toughen; to stiffen; *lodo etc* to harden, cake, set.
(**b**) (*fig*) to toughen, inure; *ley etc* to toughen up, make tougher; ~ **a uno a los peligros** to inure sb to dangers.
2 endurecerse *vr* (**a**) to harden, get hard; to stiffen; (*lodo etc*) to cake, set, set firm; (*Fin: precio*) to harden.
(**b**) (*fig*) to become cruel, become hard-hearted.
(**c**) ~ **a los peligros** to become inured to danger, inure o.s. to danger.
endurecido *adj* (**a**) (*duro*) hard; (*fuerte*) tough; (*rígido*) stiff; *lodo etc* hardened, caked, set.
(**b**) (*fig*) hardy, tough; ~ **a** inured to, used to.
(**c**) (*fig: pey*) cruel, callous, hard-hearted; obdurate.
endurecimiento *nm* (**a**) (*acto*) hardening; stiffening; setting; ~ **de las arterias** hardening of the arteries.
(**b**) (*estado*) hardness; toughness; stiffness; firmness.
(**c**) (*fig*) cruelty, callousness, hard-heartedness; obduracy.
ene *nf* the (name of the) letter *n*; **supongamos que hay** ~ **objetos** let us suppose there are X objects.
ENE *abr de* **estenordeste** east-north-east, ENE.
ene. *abr de* **enero** January, Jan.
enea *nf* = **anea.**
Eneas *nm* Aeneas.
enebro *nm* juniper.
Eneida *nf* Aeneid.
enema *nf* enema.
enemiga[1] *nf* enmity, hostility; ill-will.
enemigo 1 *adj* enemy, hostile; unfriendly; **ser** ~ **de** (*fig*) to dislike, be hostile to; (*tendencia etc*) to be inimical to; **una actitud enemiga de todo progreso** an attitude inimical to all progress.
2 *nm*, **enemiga**[2] *nf* enemy; foe, adversary, opponent; **el E~, el** ~ **malo** the devil; ~ **infiltrado,** ~ **interior** enemy within; **pasarse al** ~ to go over to the enemy.
enemistad *nf* enmity.
enemistar [1a] **1** *vt* to make enemies of, cause a rift between, set at odds.
2 enemistarse *vr* to become enemies; ~ **con uno** to become an enemy of sb; to fall out with sb, become estranged from sb.
energético *adj* (**a**) (*Tec*) energy (*atr*), fuel (*atr*), power (*atr*); **la crisis energética** the energy crisis. (**b**) (*LAm*) = **enérgico.**
energía *nf* (**a**) (*gen*) energy; (*vigor*) vigour, drive; (*empuje*) push, go; **obrar con** ~ to act energetically; **reaccionar con** ~ to react vigorously.
(**b**) (*Téc*) power; energy; (*Elec*) power, energy, current; ~(**s**) **alternativa**(**s**) alternative energy; ~ **atómica** atomic energy; ~ **eólica** wind power; ~ **hidráulica** water power; ~ **nuclear** nuclear power; ~ **renovable** renewable energy; ~ **solar** solar energy.
enérgicamente *adv* energetically; vigorously; forcefully; emphatically; strenuously; boldly.
enérgico *adj* energetic; *persona* energetic, vigorous; *manera* forceful, forthright; vital; pushful; *ademán, habla, tono* emphatic, forceful; *esfuerzo* determined, vigorous; *ejercicio* strenuous; *campaña* vigorous, forceful, high-pressure; *golpe* bold; *medida* bold; *ataque* vigorous, strong; **ponerse** ~ **con uno** to get tough with sb.
energizar [1f] *vt* to energize.
energúmeno, -a *nm/f* person possessed of the devil; (*fig*) (*demonio*) demon; (*loco*) wild person, madman; (*gritón*) loud and irascible person; (*Pol etc*) fanatic, extremist; **ponerse como un** ~ to get mad.
enero *nm* January.
enervador *adj*, **enervante** *adj* enervating.
enervar [1a] **1** *vt* (**a**) (*debilitar*) to enervate. (**b**) (*provocar*) to anger, upset. **2 enervarse** *vr* to get cross, get upset.
enésimo *adj* (**a**) (*Mat*) n^{th}; **elevado a la enésima potencia** raised to the nth power, (*fig*) to the nth degree. (**b**) (*fig*) umpteenth*; **por enésima vez** for the umpteenth time*.
enfadadizo *adj* irritable, crotchety.
enfadar [1a] **1** *vt* (**a**) (*enojar*) to anger, irritate, annoy; (*ofender*) to offend.
(**b**) (*LAm: aburrir*) to bore.
2 enfadarse *vr* (**a**) (*enojarse*) to get angry, get cross, get annoyed (*con* with, *de* about, at); **no te enfades** don't be cross; don't be offended; **de nada sirve enfadarte** it's no good getting cross.
(**b**) (*LAm: aburrirse*) to be bored, get bored.
enfado *nm* (**a**) (*enojo*) annoyance, irritation, anger. (**b**) (*molestia*) trouble, bother.
enfadoso *adj* annoying, vexatious; irksome, tedious.
enfajillar [1a] *vt* (*CAm, Méx Correos*) to put a wrapper on.
enfangar [1h] **1** *vt* to cover with mud.
2 enfangarse *vr* (**a**) (*enlodarse*) to get muddy, get covered in mud; to sink into the mud.
(**b**) (*fig*) to dirty one's hands, get involved in dirty work; ~ **en los vicios** to wallow in vice.
enfardado *nm* baling.
enfardadora *nf* (*Agr etc*) baler, baling machine.
enfardar [1a] *vt* to bale.
énfasis *nm invar* (**a**) emphasis; stress; **hablar con** ~ to speak emphatically; to speak ponderously.
(**b**) (*fig*) emphasis; **poner el** ~ **en** to put the emphasis on, stress.
enfático *adj* emphatic; positive; *discurso* heavy, pompous, ponderous; **dijo** ~ he said emphatically.
enfatizar [1f] **1** *vt* to emphasize, stress. **2** *vi*: ~ **en** = *vt.*
enfebrecidamente *adv* feverishly.
enfebrecido *adj* feverish.
enfermar [1a] **1** *vt* to make ill, cause illness in. **2** *vi* to fall ill, be taken ill (*de* with); ~ **del corazón** to develop heart trouble. **3 enfermarse** *vr* (*LAm*) = *vi.*
enfermedad *nf* (**a**) (*indisposición*) illness; sickness; **durante esta** ~ during this illness; **ausentarse por** ~ to be away ill, be away sick.
(**b**) (*una* ~) illness, disease; complaint; (*fig*) disease, malady, ill; **una** ~ **muy peligrosa** a very dangerous disease; ~ **de Alzheimer** Alzheimer's disease; ~ **contagiosa** contagious disease; ~ **de declaración obligatoria** notifiable disease; ~ **degenerativa** degenerative disease; ~ **de la descompresión** decompression sickness; ~ **hereditaria** hereditary disease; ~ **holandesa del olmo** Dutch elm disease; ~ **del legionario** legionnaire's disease; ~ **de la piel** skin disease, skin infection; ~ **profesional** occupational disease; ~ **del sueño** sleeping sickness; ~ **terminal** terminal illness; ~ **transmisible** contagious disease; ~ **de transmisión sexual** sexually transmitted disease; ~ **venérea** venereal disease; ~ **por virus** virus disease; **contagiar a uno con una** ~, **pegar una** ~ **a uno** to give sb a disease.
enfermera *nf* nurse; ~ **ambulante** visiting nurse; ~ **jefa** matron.
enfermería *nf* infirmary; sanatorium; (*de colegio etc*) sick-bay; (*Taur*) hospital, medical section.
enfermero *nm* male nurse; (*Mil*) medical orderly.
enfermizo *adj* sickly, weak, unhealthy; infirm; *mente* morbid, unhealthy.
enfermo 1 *adj* (**a**) ill, sick, unwell; sickly; ~ **de amor** love-sick; ~ **del chape,** ~ **del mate** (*Cono Sur*) crazy; **caer** ~, **ponerse** ~ to fall ill (*de* with); **estar** ~ **de gravedad, estar** ~ **de peligro** to be seriously ill, be dangerously ill.
(**b**) **estar** ~ (*Cono Sur*‡) to be in jug‡, be in jail.
(**c**) (*Cono Sur**) **es** ~ **de malo** it's terribly bad; **es** ~ **de loca** she's clean crazy*.
2 *nm*, **enferma** *nf* patient; invalid, sick person; ~ **terminal** terminal patient, terminally ill person.
enfermoso *adj* (*LAm*) = **enfermizo.**
enfervorizar [1f] *vt* to arouse, arouse fervour in.
enfeudar [1a] *vt* (*Hist*) to enfief; ~ **a uno de una propiedad** to grant sb (the freehold of) a property.
enfiestarse* [1a] *vr* (*LAm*) to have a good time, enjoy o.s.
enfilada *nf* enfilade.
enfilar [1a] *vt* (**a**) (*Mil*) to enfilade.
(**b**) (*alinear*) to line up, put in a row; *cuentas* to thread.
(**c**) *rumbo* to direct, bear.
(**d**) *calle etc* to go straight along (*o* down *etc*); **el piloto trató de** ~ **la pista** the pilot tried to line the aircraft up with the runway.
enfisema *nm* emphysema.
enflaquecer [2d] **1** *vt* to make thin; to weaken, sap the strength of.

2 *vi y* **enflaquecerse** *vr* (**a**) (*adelgazarse*) to get thin, lose weight.

(**b**) (*fig*: *esfuerzo etc*) to flag, weaken; (*persona*) to lose heart.

enflaquecido *adj* thin, extenuated.

enflaquecimiento *nm* (**a**) (*adelgazamiento*) loss of weight; emaciation. (**b**) (*fig*) weakening.

enflatarse* [1a] *vr* (**a**) (*CAm, Carib*: *entristecerse*) to sulk, be grumpy*. (**b**) (*Carib, Méx*: *enfadarse*) to fly off the handle*.

enflautada* *nf* (*And, CAm*) blunder.

enflautado *adj* pompous.

enflautar [1a] *vt*: **~ algo a uno** (*And, CAm, Méx*) to unload sth on to sb.

enfocar [1g] **1** *vt* (**a**) (*Fot etc*) to focus (*a, sobre* on).

(**b**) *problema etc* to approach, consider, look at; to size up; **podemos ~ este problema de tres maneras** we can approach this problem in three ways; **no me gusta su modo de ~ la cuestión** I do not like his approach to the question.

2 *vi y* **enfocarse** *vr* to focus (*a, sobre* on).

enfollonado* *adj* muddled, confused.

enfollonarse* [1a] *vr* to get muddled, get all mixed up.

enfoque *nm* (**a**) (*Fot etc*) focus; focusing. (**b**) (*fig*) grasp; approach.

enfoscar [1g] **1** *vt* to fill with mortar.

2 enfoscarse *vr* (**a**) (*estar de mal humor*) to sulk, be sullen.

(**b**) **~ en** to get absorbed in, get up to the eyes in.

(**c**) (*cielo*) to cloud over.

enfrascar [1g] **1** *vt* to bottle.

2 enfrascarse *vr*: **~ en un libro** to bury o.s. in a book, become absorbed in a book; **~ en su laboratorio** to bury (*o* hide) o.s. away in one's laboratory; **~ en un problema** get deeply involved in a problem.

enfrenar [1a] *vt* (**a**) *caballo* to bridle; (*Mec*) to brake, slow, halt. (**b**) (*fig*) to curb, restrain.

enfrentamiento *nm* clash, confrontation.

enfrentar [1a] **1** *vt* (**a**) (*carear*) to put face to face.

(**b**) *problema etc* to face, confront.

2 *vi* to face.

3 enfrentarse *vr*: **~ con** to face, face up to, confront; to stand up to; (*Dep*) to meet, play against; **hay que ~ con el peligro** one must face up to the danger, one must face the danger squarely.

enfrente 1 *adv* (**a**) opposite; in front, facing; (*fig*) in opposition; **la casa de ~** the house opposite, the house across the street; **sus amigos estaban ~** (*fig*) his friends were against it.

(**b**) (*Cono Sur*) **~ mío** (*etc*) opposite me (*etc*), in front of me (*etc*).

2 ~ de *prep* opposite (to), facing; (*fig*) opposed to, against.

enfriadera *nf* cooling jar; bottle cooler.

enfriadero *nm* cold storage, cold room.

enfriado *nm* cooling, chilling.

enfriador *nm* cooler, cooling plant.

enfriamiento *nm* (**a**) (*acción*) cooling; (*Econ etc*) cooling-down; (*refrigeración*) refrigeration. (**b**) (*Med*) cold, chill.

enfriar [1c] **1** *vt* (**a**) (*helar*) to cool, chill; (*fig*) to cool down, take the heat out of; (*Econ etc*) to cool down.

(**b**) (*LAm*‡: *matar*) to bump off‡.

2 enfriarse *vr* (**a**) (*gen*) to cool, cool down, cool off; **déjelo hasta que se enfríe** leave it till it gets cool, leave it to cool down.

(**b**) (*fig*) to cool off, grow cold.

enfrijolarse [1a] *vr* (*Méx*) to get messed up.

enfullinarse [1a] *vr* (*Cono Sur*) to get angry.

enfundar [1a] *vt* (**a**) *espada* to sheathe; *instrumento etc* to put away, put in its case; **una señora enfundada en visón** a lady swathed in mink. (**b**) (*llenar*) to fill, stuff (*de* with). (**c**) (*) *comida* to scoff*.

enfurecer [2d] **1** *vt* to enrage, madden. **2 enfurecerse** *vr* (**a**) to get furious, fly into a rage. (**b**) (*mar*) to get rough.

enfurruñarse* [1a] *vr* (**a**) to sulk, get sulky. (**b**) (*cielo*) to cloud over.

engaitar* [1a] *vt*: **~ a uno** to wheedle sb, talk sb round.

engajado *adj* (*And*) curly.

engalanar [1a] **1** *vt* to adorn, deck (*de* with). **2 engalanarse** *vr* to adorn o.s.; to dress up, deck o.s. out.

engallado *adj* (*arrogante*) arrogant, haughty; (*confiado*) confident; (*jactancioso*) boastful.

engallinar [1a] *vt* (*LAm*) to cow, intimidate.

enganchado, -a* *nm/f* drug-addict.

enganchar [1a] **1** *vt* (**a**) (*con gancho*) to hook; to hitch; to hang up; *caballo* to harness; *caballa, carro* to hitch up; (*Mec*) to couple, connect; (*Ferro*) to couple (up); **~la‡** to get canned‡.

(**b**) (*fig*: *atraer*) to inveigle, ensnare; to rope in; *marido** to hook, land; (*cautivar*) to hook; **los programas que más enganchan** the programmes which get most people hooked.

(**c**) (*Mil*) to recruit; to persuade to join up, lure into military service; (*Méx*) *trabajadores* to contract.

2 engancharse *vr* (**a**) (*prenderse*) to get hooked up, catch (*en* on); (*Mec*) to engage (*en* with).

(**b**) (*Mil*) to enlist, join up, sign on.

(**c**) **~ a drogas*** to get hooked on drugs*, become addicted to drugs; **estar enganchado*** to be hooked on drugs.

enganche *nm* (**a**) (*acto*) hooking (up); hitching; coupling, connection; (*Telec*) connection.

(**b**) (*gancho*) hook, hooking device; (*Mec*) coupling, connection; (*Ferro*) coupling.

(**c**) (*Mil*) recruitment, enlistment; (*pago*) bounty.

(**d**) (*Méx*: *fianza*) deposit, down payment.

(**e**) (*Carib*: *trabajo*) job; engagement.

(**f**) (*Telec*) connection charge.

enganchón *nm* tear.

engañabobos *nm invar* (**a**) (*persona*) trickster. (**b**) (*trampa*) trick, trap.

engañadizo *adj* gullible.

engañador 1 *adj* deceiving, cheating; deceptive. **2** *nm*, **engañadora** *nf* cheat, deceiver, impostor.

engañapichanga *nf* (*And, Cono Sur*) trick, fraud, hoax.

engañar [1a] **1** *vt* (*embaucar*) to deceive; to cheat, trick, swindle, fool; (*despistar*) to mislead; (*con esperanzas etc*) to beguile, delude; *hambre* to stay; *tiempo* to kill, while away; **a mí no me engaña nadie** you can't fool me; **logró ~ al inspector** he managed to trick the inspector; **engaña a su marido** she's unfaithful to her husband.

2 *vi* to be deceptive; **las apariencias engañan** appearances are deceptive.

3 engañarse *vr* to deceive o.s.; to be wrong, be mistaken; to delude o.s.; **en eso te engañas** you're wrong there; **se engaña con falsas esperanzas** she deludes herself with false hopes; **no te engañes, no te dejes ~** don't go deceiving yourself.

engañifa* *nf* trick, swindle.

engañito *nm* (*Cono Sur*) small gift, token.

engaño *nm* (**a**) (*cualidad*) deceit; (*trampa*) deception; fraud, trick, swindle; (*cosa fingida*) sham; (*decepción*) delusion; (*de pesca*) lure; **todo es ~** it's all a sham; **aquí no hay ~** there is no attempt to deceive anybody here, it's all on the level*; **llamar a ~** to protest that one has been cheated; **que nadie llame a ~** let nobody say he wasn't warned.

(**b**) (*malentendido*) mistake, misunderstanding; **no haya ~** let there be no mistake about it; **padecer ~** to labour under a misunderstanding.

(**c**) **~s** wiles, tricks.

(**d**) (*Cono Sur*: *regalo*) small gift, token.

engañosamente *adv* deceitfully, dishonestly; deceptively; misleadingly, wrongly.

engañoso *adj persona etc* deceitful, dishonest; *apariencia* deceptive; *consejo etc* misleading, wrong.

engarabitarse [1a] *vr* (**a**) (*subir*) to climb, shin up. (**b**) (*padecer frío*) to get stiff with cold. (**c**) (*And*) to grow weak, get thin.

engaratusar [1a] *vt* (*And, CAm, Méx*) = **engatusar.**

engarce *nm* (**a**) (*de joya*) setting, mount. (**b**) (*fig*) linking, connection. (**c**) (*And**: *jaleo*) row, shindy*.

engaripolarse* [1a] *vr* (*Carib*) to doll o.s. up*.

engarrotarse [1a] *vr* (*LAm*) to get stiff, go numb.

engarruñarse* [1a] *vr* (*And, CAm, Méx*) = **engurruñarse.**

engarzar [1f] **1** *vt* (**a**) *joya* to set, mount; *cuentas* to thread; *pelo* to curl.

(**b**) (*fig*) to link, connect.

(**c**) (*And*: *enganchar*) to hook (up).

2 engarzarse *vr* (*Cono Sur*) to get tangled, get stuck.

engastar [1a] *vt* to set, mount.

engaste *nm* setting, mount.

engatado *adj* thievish.

engatusar* [1a] *vt* to coax, wheedle, soft-soap*; **~ a uno para que haga algo** to coax sb into doing sth.

engendrar [1a] *vt* (**a**) (*Bio*) to beget, breed; to have as offspring. (**b**) (*Mat*) to generate. (**c**) (*fig*) to breed, cause, engender.

engendro *nm* (**a**) (*Bio*) foetus; (*pey*) malformed creature, abortion; freak.
(**b**) (*fig*) abortion, monstrosity; (*chapuza*) bungled job; (*proyecto*) idiotic scheme, impossible plan; (*idea*) brain-child; **el proyecto es el ~ del ministro** the plan is some brain-child of the minister.
(**c**) (*****: *feo*) terribly ugly person.
(**d**) **mal ~, ~ del diablo*** bad lot, no-good lout* (*US*).
engerido* *adj* (*And*: *alicaído*) down, glum.
engerirse* [3k] *vr* (*And*) to grow sad.
engestarse [1a] *vr* (*Méx*) to make a wry face.
englobar [1a] *vt* (**a**) (*abarcar*) to include, comprise. (**b**) (*unir*) to lump together, put all together. (**c**) (*****) **estar englobado** to be tight*.
engodo *nm* (*Carib*) bait.
engolado *adj* (*fig*) haughty.
engolfarse [1a] *vr* (**a**) (*Náut*) to sail out to sea, lose sight of land.
(**b**) **~ en** (*fig*) to get deeply involved in; to plunge into, become deeply absorbed in; to launch out into.
engolondrinarse [1a] *vr* (**a**) (*envanecerse*) to get conceited. (**b**) (*amorosamente*) to have a flirtation.
engolosinar [1a] **1** *vt* to tempt, entice. **2 engolosinarse** *vr*: **~ con** to grow fond of.
engolletarse [1a] *vr* to give o.s. airs.
engomado *adj* gummed.
engomar [1a] *vt* to gum, glue, stick.
engominar [1a] *vt pelo* to put hair-cream on; **iba todo engominado** his hair was all smarmed down.
engorda *nf* (**a**) (*And, Cono Sur*: *Agr*: *acto*) fattening (up). (**b**) (*Cono Sur*: *ganado*) fattened animals (*collectively*).
engordante *adj* fattening.
engordar [1a] **1** *vt* (**a**) to fatten (up). (**b**) (*fig*) *número* to swell, increase. **2** *vi* (**a**) (*ponerse gordo*) to get fat; to fill out, put on weight; (*Agr*) to fatten. (**b**) (*****: *enriquecerse*) to get rich.
engorde *nm* fattening (up).
engorrar [1a] *vt* (*Méx, Carib*) to annoy.
engorro *nm* bother, nuisance.
engorroso *adj* bothersome, vexatious, trying; cumbersome, awkward.
engrampador *nm* (*LAm*) stapler.
engrampar [1a] *vt* (*LAm*) to clip together, staple.
engranaje *nm* (*un* ~) gear; (*conjunto*) gears, gearing; (*engrane*) mesh; (*dientes*) gear teeth; **~ de distribución** timing gear.
engranar [1a] **1** *vt* to gear; to put into gear; **~ con** to gear into, engage.
2 *vi* to interlock; (*Mec*) to engage (*con una rueda* a wheel), mesh (*con* with); **A engrana con B** A is in gear with B; **A y B están engranados** A and B are in mesh.
3 engranarse *vr* (*Cono Sur, Méx Mec*) to seize up, get locked, jam.
engrandecer [2d] *vt* (**a**) to enlarge, magnify. (**b**) (*fig*) (*ensalzar*) to extol, magnify; to exalt; (*exagerar*) to exaggerate.
engrandecimiento *nm* (**a**) enlargement. (**b**) exaltation; aggrandizement; exaggeration.
engrane *nm* (**a**) mesh, meshing. (**b**) (*Cono Sur, Méx Mec*) seizing, jamming.
engrasación *nf* greasing, lubrication.
engrasado *nm* greasing, lubrication.
engrasador *nm* (*aceitera*) greaser, lubricator; (*punto*) grease point; (*Aut*) grease nipple; (*recipiente*) grease cup; **~ de compresión, ~ de pistón** grease gun.
engrasamiento *nm* greasing, lubrication.
engrasar [1a] *vt* (**a**) (*Mec*) to grease, lubricate, oil. (**b**) (*manchar*) to make greasy, stain with grease. (**c**) (*Agr*) to manure. (**d**) (*****: *sobornar*) to bribe.
engrase *nm* (**a**) greasing, lubrication. (**b**) (*****) bribe.
engreído *adj* (**a**) vain, conceited, stuck-up*. (**b**) (*LAm*: *afectuoso*) affectionate; (*mimado*) spoiled.
engreimiento *nm* vanity, conceit.
engreír [3k] **1** *vt* (**a**) (*envanecer*) to make vain, make conceited.
(**b**) (*****: *dar coba a*) to butter up*, flatter.
(**c**) (*LAm*) *niño* to spoil, pamper.
2 engreírse *vr* (**a**) to get conceited.
(**b**) (*LAm*) to get spoiled, be pampered.
(**c**) (*LAm*) **~ a, ~ con** to grow fond of.
engrifarse [1a] *vr* (**a**) (*And*) to get haughty. (**b**) (*Méx*) to get cross. (**c**) (‡) to get high on drugs‡.
engrillar [1a] **1** *vt* (**a**) to shackle; to handcuff.
(**b**) (*And, Carib*) to trick.
2 engrillarse *vr* (**a**) (*Carib*: *caballo*) to lower its head.
(**b**) (*Carib*: *engreírse*) to get conceited.
(**c**) (*And, CAm*) to get into debt.
engringolarse [1a] *vr (Carib)* to doll o.s. up.
engriparse [1a] *vr* to catch the flu.
engrosar [1l] **1** *vt* to enlarge; *cantidad* to increase, swell; to thicken. **2** *vi* to get fat. **3 engrosarse** *vr* to increase, swell, expand.
engrudar [1a] *vt* to paste.
engrudo *nm* paste.
engrupido* *adj* (*Cono Sur*) (**a**) (*engreído*) stuck-up*, conceited. (**b**) (*de mucha labia*) smooth-talking.
engrupidor* *nm* (*Cono Sur*) smooth talker; con man*.
engrupir* [3a] (*Cono Sur*) **1** *vt* (*engañar*) to con*. **2** *vi* to blarney one's way in. **3 engrupirse** *vr* to be conned*; (*engreírse*) to get conceited, put on airs.
enguacharse [1a] *vr* (*And*) to coarsen, get coarse.
enguadar [1a] *vt* (*Carib*) = **engatusar**.
engualichar [1a] *vt* (*Cono Sur*) (**a**) (*embrujar*) to bewitch (with a potion). (**b**) *amante* to rule, tyrannize.
enguandos* *nmpl* (*And*) knick-knacks.
enguantado *adj* gloved, wearing a glove.
enguantarse [1a] *vr* to put one's gloves on.
enguaracarse [1g] *vr* (*CAm*) to hide o.s. away.
enguaraparse [1a] *vr* (*CAm*) to ferment.
enguasimar [1a] *vt* (*Carib*) to hang.
enguayabado* *adj*: **está ~** (*And, Carib*) he's got a hang-over*, he's hung over*.
enguijarrado *nm* cobbles.
enguijarrar [1a] *vt* to cobble.
enguirnaldar [1a] *vt* to garland, wreathe (*de, con* with); (*fig*) to wreathe.
engullir [3a *y* 3h] *vt* to gobble, bolt, gulp (down); to devour.
engurrioso* *adj* jealous, envious.
engurruñarse [1a] *vr* to get sad, grow gloomy.
enharinar [1a] *vt* (*Culin*) to flour.
enhebrado *nm* threading.
enhebrar [1a] *vt* to thread.
enhestar [1j] **1** *vt* (**a**) (*erigir*) to erect; (*poner vertical*) to set upright.
(**b**) (*alzar*) to hoist (up), raise (on high).
2 enhestarse *vr* (**a**) to straighten up, stand up straight.
(**b**) to rise high.
enhiesto *adj* (**a**) (*derecho*) erect, straight, upright. (**b**) *bandera etc* raised; (*alto*) lofty, towering.
enhilar [1a] *vt* (**a**) *aguja* to thread. (**b**) (*fig*) to arrange, put in order.
enhorabuena 1 *nf* congratulations; **¡~!** congratulations!, and the best of luck!; **dar la ~ a uno** to congratulate sb, wish sb well; **estar de ~** to be in luck, be on to a good thing.
2 *adv*: **¡~!** all right!; well and good; **~ que ...** thank heavens that ...
enhoramala *interj*: **¡~!** good riddance!; **¡vete ~!** go to the devil!
enhorquetarse [1a] *vr* (*Carib, Cono Sur, Méx*) to sit astride.
enhuerar [1a] *vt* to addle.
enigma *nm* enigma; puzzle; mystery.
enigmáticamente *adv* enigmatically.
enigmático *adj* enigmatic; puzzling; mysterious.
enjabonar [1a] *vt* (**a**) to soap; to lather. (**b**) (*****: *dar coba a*) to soap up*, soft-soap*. (**c**) (*****: *reprender*) to tick off*.
enjaezar [1f] *vt* to harness, saddle up.
enjalbegado *nm*, **enjalbegadura** *nf* whitewashing.
enjalbegar [1h] *vt pared* to whitewash; *cara* to paint, make up.
enjambrar [1a] **1** *vt* to hive. **2** *vi* to swarm.
enjambre *nm* swarm (*t fig*).
enjaranarse [1a] *vr* (*CAm*) to get into debt.
enjarciar [1b] *vt* (*Náut*) to rig.
enjaretado *nm* grating, grille.
enjaretar [1a] **1** *vt* (**a**) (*****: *recitar*) to reel off, spout. (**b**) (*****) **me enjaretó la tarea de ...** he lumbered me with the task of ...* (**c**) (*hacer de prisa*) to rush, rush through. (**d**) (*Cono Sur, Méx*) to slip in. **2 enjaretarse** *vr*: **~ la carrera** to shape one's career, mould one's career.
enjaular [1a] *vt* to cage, put in a cage; to coop up, pen in; (*****) to jail, lock up.
enjertar [1a] *vt* = **injertar**.
enjetado‡ *adj* (*Cono Sur, Méx*) cross-looking, scowling.
enjetarse‡ [1a] *vr* (*Cono Sur, Méx*) (*enojarse*) to get cross; (*hacer muecas*) to scowl.
enjoyado *adj* bejewelled, set with jewels.

enjoyar [1a] *vt* to adorn with jewels, set with precious stones; to set precious stones in; (*fig*) to bejewel, adorn, embellish.
enjuagadientes *nm invar* mouthwash.
enjuagado *nm* rinsing.
enjuagar [1h] *vt* to rinse, rinse out; to wash out, swill out.
enjuague *nm* (**a**) (*líquido*) mouthwash. (**b**) (*acto*) rinse, rinsing; washing, swilling. (**c**) (*fig*) scheme, intrigue.
enjugamanos *nm invar* (*LAm*) towel.
enjugar [1h] *vt* (**a**) to wipe (off), wipe the moisture from; to dry; **~se la frente** to wipe one's brow, mop one's brow. (**b**) *déficit, deuda* to wipe out.
enjuiciamiento *nm* (**a**) (*acto*) judgement. (**b**) (*Jur*) **~ civil** lawsuit, civil suit; **~ criminal** trial, criminal prosecution.
enjuiciar [1b] *vt* (**a**) (*juzgar*) to judge, pass judgement on; (*examinar*) to examine. (**b**) (*Jur*: *acusar*) to indict; (*procesar*) to prosecute, try; (*sentenciar*) to sentence.
enjundia *nf* (**a**) animal fat, grease. (**b**) (*fig*) substance; strength, drive, vigour; essence, character.
enjundioso *adj* (**a**) fat. (**b**) (*fig*) substantial, solid, meaty.
enjuto *adj* (**a**) (*seco*) dry; dried; *V* **pie.** (**b**) (*marchito*) shrivelled up; wizened. (**c**) (*flaco*) lean, skinny, spare; *economía etc* lean (and fit).
enlabiar* [1b] *vt* to blarney, bamboozle*, take in.
enlabio *nm* blarney, honeyed words, plausible talk.
enlace *nm* (**a**) (*vinculación*) link, tie-up, connection; (*vínculo*) bond; (*relación*) relationship; (*Quím, Elec*) linkage; (*Mil etc*) liaison; (*Ferro*) connection; (*matrimonio*) marriage, union; (*encuentro*) meeting, rendezvous; **~ fijo** fixed link; **el ~ de A con B** the marriage of A and B; **~ de datos** (*Inform*) data line; **el ~ de las dos familias** the linking of the two families by marriage; **los buques no lograron efectuar el ~ en el punto indicado** the ships did not manage to rendezvous at the spot indicated; **~ telefónico** telephone link-up.
(**b**) (*persona*) link, go-between; **~ sindical** shop steward.
enladrillado *nm* brick paving.
enladrillar [1a] *vt* to pave with bricks.
enlardar [1a] *vt* (*Culin*) to baste.
enlatado **1** *adj* canned, tinned; (*Mús*) canned. **2** *nm* canning, tinning.
enlatar [1a] *vt* (**a**) to can, tin. (**b**) (*grabar*) to record; (*TV*) to pre-record.
enlazar [1f] **1** *vt* (**a**) to link, connect; to tie (together), bind (together); to knit together.
(**b**) (*LAm*) to lasso.
2 *vi* (*Ferro etc*) to connect (*con* with).
3 enlazarse *vr* to link (up), be linked; to be connected; to join; to interlock; to entwine; (*novios*) to marry, get married; (*familias*) to become linked by marriage (*con* to).
enlentecimiento *nm* slowing-down.
enlistar [1a] *vt* (*CAm, Carib, Méx*) = **alistar.**
enlodar [1a], **enlodazar** [1f] **1** *vt* (**a**) to muddy, cover in mud. (**b**) (*fig*) to besmirch, stain; to smear, defame. **2 enlodarse** *vr*, **enlodazarse** *vr* to get muddy.
enloquecedor *adj* maddening; *dolor de cabeza* splitting; *dolor* excruciating.
enloquecedoramente *adv* maddeningly; excruciatingly.
enloquecer [2d] **1** *vt* to drive mad; (*fig*) to madden, drive crazy. **2** *vi y* **enloquecerse** *vr* to go mad, go out of one's mind.
enloquecimiento *nm* madness.
enlosado *nm* flagstone pavement, tiled pavement.
enlosar [1a] *vt* to pave (with flagstones *o* tiles).
enlozado *adj* (*LAm*) enamelled, glazed.
enlozar [1f] *vt* (*LAm*) to enamel, glaze.
enlucido *nm* plaster.
enlucidor *nm* plasterer.
enlucir [3f] *vt pared* to plaster; *metal* to polish.
enlutado *adj persona* in mourning, wearing mourning; *ciudad etc* stricken.
enlutar [1a] **1** *vt* (**a**) *persona* to put into mourning; to dress in mourning.
(**b**) *vestido etc* to put crêpe on; to put a symbol of mourning on.
(**c**) *ciudad, país etc* to plunge into mourning; (*fig*) to sadden, grieve; **el accidente enlutó a la ciudad entera** the accident plunged the whole town into mourning.
(**d**) (*fig*) to darken.
2 enlutarse *vr* to go into mourning, dress in mourning.
enllavar [1a] *vt* (*CAm*) to lock up.
enmacetar [1a] *vt planta* to pot (up), put in a pot.
enmaderado *adj* timbered; boarded.
enmaderamiento *nm* timbering; boarding.
enmaderar [1a] *vt* to timber; to board (up).
enmadrado* *adj*: **está ~** he's a mummy's boy*, he's tied to his mother's apron strings.
enmalezarse [1f] *vr* (*And, Carib, Cono Sur*) to get overgrown, get covered in scrub.
enmaniguarse [1i] *vr* (*Carib*) (**a**) (*tierra*) to get overgrown with trees, turn into jungle. (**b**) (*: *persona*) to go native.
enmantecar [1g] *vt* (*Culin*) to grease, butter.
enmarañar [1a] **1** *vt* (**a**) to tangle (up), entangle.
(**b**) (*fig*: *asunto*) to complicate, make more involved; *tarea* to make a mess of; *persona* to confuse, perplex; **sólo logró ~ más el asunto** he only managed to make a still worse mess of the matter, he only succeeded in complicating things further.
2 enmarañarse *vr* (**a**) to get tangled (up), become entangled.
(**b**) (*fig*) to get more involved; to get into a mess; to get confused; **~ en un asunto** to get entangled in an affair.
(**c**) (*cielo*) to darken, cloud over.
enmarcado *nm* (*marco*) frame; (*acto*) framing.
enmarcar [1g] **1** *vt* (**a**) *cuadro* to frame. (**b**) (*fig*) to fit into a framework, set in a framework; to provide the setting for, act as a background to. **2 enmarcarse** *vr*: **~ en** to place o.s. in (the context of).
enmarillecerse [2d] *vr* to turn yellow; to turn pale.
enmascarada *nf* masked woman.
enmascarado *nm* masked man.
enmascarar [1a] **1** *vt* (**a**) to mask (*t Inform*). (**b**) (*fig*) to mask, disguise. **2 enmascararse** *vr* (**a**) to put on a mask. (**b**) **~ de** (*fig*) to masquerade as.
enmedallado *adj* bemedalled.
enmendación *nf* emendation, correction.
enmendar [1j] **1** *vt* (**a**) *texto* to emend, correct; *ley, constitución etc* to amend.
(**b**) (*moralmente*) to reform.
(**c**) *pérdida* to make good, compensate for.
2 enmendarse *vr* to reform, mend one's ways.
enmicado *nm* (*Méx*) plastic cover(ing).
enmicar [1g] *vt* (*Méx*) *documento* to cover in plastic, seal in plastic.
enmienda *nf* (**a**) emendation; correction; (*Jur, Pol etc*) amendment; **~ a la totalidad** motion for the rejection of a bill. (**b**) reform. (**c**) compensation, indemnity.
enmohecer [2d] **1** *vt* (**a**) *metal* to rust. (**b**) (*Bot etc*) to make mouldy. **2 enmohecerse** *vr* (**a**) to rust, get rusty. (**b**) (*Bot etc*) to get mouldy.
enmohecido *adj* (**a**) rusty, rust-covered. (**b**) mouldy, mildewed.
enmonarse‡ [1a] *vr* (**a**) (*droga*) to get cold turkey‡, suffer withdrawal symptoms. (**b**) (*LAm*) to get tight*.
enmontarse [1a] *vr* (*And, CAm, Carib*) to get overgrown, revert to scrub.
enmoquetado *adj* carpeted.
enmoquetador *nm* carpet-layer.
enmoquetar [1a] *vt* to carpet.
enmudecer [2d] **1** *vt* to silence. **2 enmudecerse** *vr* (*callarse*) to be silent; to remain silent, say nothing; (*hacerse mudo*) to become dumb; (*no poder hablar*) to lose one's voice.
enmugrar [1a] *vt* (*And, Cono Sur, Méx*), **enmugrecer** [2d] *vt*, **enmugrentar** [1a] *vt* (*Cono Sur*) to soil, dirty.
ennegrecer [2d] **1** *vt* (*poner negro*) to blacken; (*teñir*) to dye black; (*oscurecer*) to darken, obscure. **2** *vi y* **ennegrecerse** *vr* to turn black; to get dark, darken.
ennoblecer [2d] *vt* (**a**) to ennoble. (**b**) (*fig*) to embellish, adorn; to dignify.
ennoblecimiento *nm* ennoblement.
ennoviarse* [1b] *vr* to get engaged.
en.º *abr de* **enero** January, Jan.
enofilia *nf* oenophilia, liking for wines; expertness in wines.
enófilo, -a *nm/f* oenophile, lover of wines; wine expert.
enojada *nf* (*Carib, Méx*) (fit of) anger.
enojadizo *adj* irritable, peevish, short-tempered.
enojado *adj* angry, cross; **dijo ~** he said angrily.
enojar [1a] **1** *vt* to anger; to upset, annoy, vex.
2 enojarse *vr* to get angry, lose one's temper; to get annoyed, get cross (*con, contra* with; *de* at, about); **¡no te enojes!** (*preocuparse*) don't bother!, don't trouble yourself!; (*enfadarse*) don't be (*o* get) angry.
enojo *nm* (**a**) (*ira*) anger; (*irritación*) annoyance, vexation; **decir con ~** to say angrily.
(**b**) **de prontos ~s, de repentinos ~s** quick-tempered;

tener prontos (*o* **repentinos**) ~**s** to be quick to anger, be easily upset.

(**c**) ~**s** troubles, trials.

enojón *adj* (*And, Cono Sur, Méx*) = **enojadizo**.

enojoso *adj* irritating, annoying.

enología *nf* oenology, science of wine(-making).

enólogo, -a *nm/f* oenologist, wine expert; wine-grower.

enorgullecer [2d] **1** *vt* to fill with pride. **2 enorgullecerse** *vr* to be proud, swell with pride; ~ **de** to be proud of, pride o.s. on.

enorme *adj* (**a**) enormous, huge, vast; tremendous. (**b**) (*fig*) heinous, monstrous. (**c**) (*) killing, marvellous; **cuando remeda al profe es** ~ when he takes off the teacher he's killing.

enormemente *adv* enormously, vastly; tremendously.

enormidad *nf* (**a**) (*inmensidad*) enormousness; hugeness.

(**b**) (*fig: de crimen etc*) heinousness, monstrousness, enormity.

(**c**) (*acto etc*) wicked thing, monstrous thing.

(**d**) (*) **me gustó una** ~ I liked it enormously.

enoteca *nf* wine-cellar, collection of wines.

ENP *nf*, **ENPETROL** [enpe'trol] *nf abr de* **Empresa Nacional del Petróleo.**

enqué* *nm*: **lo traeré si encuentro** ~ (*And*) I'll bring it if I can find something to put it in (*o* a bag for it).

enquistamiento *nm* (*fig*) sealing off, shutting off, enclosure.

enquistar [1a] **1** *vt* (*fig*) to seal off, shut off, enclose. **2 enquistarse** *vr* (*Med*) to develop a cyst.

enrabiar [1b] **1** *vt* to enrage. **2 enrabiarse** *vr* to get enraged.

enrabietarse [1a] *vr* to throw a tantrum, get very cross.

enrachado *adj* lucky; enjoying a run of luck.

enraizar [1f] *vi* to take root.

enramada *nf* (**a**) arbour, bower. (**b**) (*Cono Sur: cobertizo*) cover (*etc*) made of branches.

enramar [1a] **1** *vt* to cover with branches. **2** *vi* (*Cono Sur*) to come into leaf.

enranciarse [1b] *vr* to go rancid, get stale.

enrarecer [2d] **1** *vt* (**a**) *aire etc* to rarefy. (**b**) (*hacer que escasee*) to make scarce, cause to become rare.

2 enrarecerse *vr* (**a**) (*aire*) to become rarefied, get thin.

(**b**) (*escasear*) to become scarce, grow rare.

(**c**) (*relaciones*) to deteriorate, become tense.

enrarecido *adj* (**a**) rarefied. (**b**) *relaciones* tense, difficult.

enrarecimiento *nm* (**a**) rarefaction; thinness. (**b**) scarceness, rareness. (**c**) deterioration; tension.

enrastrojarse [1a] *vr* (*LAm*) to get covered in scrub.

enrazado *adj* (*And*) *persona* half-breed; *animal* crossbred.

enrazar [1f] *vt* (*And*) to mix (racially); *animales* to crossbreed.

enredadera *nf* (*Bot*) climbing plant, creeper; ~ (**de campo**) bindweed.

enredador 1 *adj* trouble-making, mischief-making; *niño* naughty. **2** *nm*, **enredadora** *nf* (*chismoso*) gossip; (*entrometido*) busybody, meddler; (*subversivo*) troublemaker, mischief-maker.

enredar [1a] **1** *vt* (**a**) *animal etc* to net, catch in a net.

(**b**) *trampa* to set.

(**c**) (*entrelazar*) to intertwine, interweave; (*pey*) to entangle, tangle (up).

(**d**) *asunto* to confuse, complicate; *tarea* to make a mess of.

(**e**) (*comprometer*) *persona* to embroil, involve, implicate (*en* in).

(**f**) *dos personas* to sow discord among (*o* between); ~ **a A con B** to sow discord between A and B, embroil A with B.

(**g**) (*engañar*) *persona* to deceive.

2 *vi* (*niño etc*) to get up to mischief, cause trouble; ~ **con** to mess about with.

3 enredarse *vr* (**a**) (*enmarañarse*) to get entangled, get tangled (*up*); ~ **en** (*cuerda etc*) to catch on, (*Náut*) foul.

(**b**) (*asunto*) to get complicated; to get into a mess.

(**c**) (*persona*) to get entangled (*con* with), get involved (*con* with); **no te enredes** don't you get mixed up in this, keep out of this mess; **se enredó con una estudiante** he got involved with a student, he had an affair with a student; ~ **de** (*o* **en**) **palabras** to get involved in an argument.

enredista (*LAm*) = **enredador.**

enredo *nm* (**a**) (*de lana etc*) tangle.

(**b**) (*fig: lío*) tangle, entanglement; (*amorío*) love affair; (*confusión*) mess, confusion, mix-up; (*de detalles etc*) maze, tangle.

(**c**) (*apuro*) jam, difficult situation.

(**d**) (*envolvimiento*) embroilment, involvement.

(**e**) (*Teat*) plot.

(**f**) ~**s** (*intrigas*) intrigues; (*mentiras*) mischief, mischievous lies; **comedia de** ~(**s**) comedy of intrigue.

enredoso *adj* (**a**) tangled, complicated; tricky. (**b**) (*Méx*) = **enredador 1.**

enrejado *nm* (*reja*) grating, grille; (*de ventana*) lattice; (*de jardín*) trellis; (*Cos*) openwork; (*verja*) fence, railings; (*de jaula*) bars; ~ **de alambre** wire netting (fence).

enrejar [1a] *vt* (**a**) to fix a grating to, put a grating on; to fence, put railings round.

(**b**) (*LAm*) *caballo* to put a halter on.

(**c**) (*Méx: zurcir*) to darn, patch.

enrejillado *nm* small-mesh grille.

ENRESA, Enresa [en'resa] *nf abr de* **Empresa Nacional de Residuos Nucleares.**

enrevesado *adj* complicated, intricate.

enrielar [1a] *vt* (**a**) (*Téc*) to make into ingots.

(**b**) (*LAm: poner rieles en*) to lay rails on.

(**c**) (*LAm*) *tren* to put on the tracks, set on the rails; (*fig*) to put on the right track.

Enrique *nm* Henry.

enriquecer [2d] **1** *vt* to make rich, enrich.

2 enriquecerse *vr* to get rich; to prosper; (*pey*) to enrich o.s.; ~ **a costa ajena** to do well at other people's expense.

enriquecido *adj producto* enriched.

enriquecimiento *nm* enrichment.

enriscado *adj* craggy, rocky.

enristrar [1a] *vt* (**a**) *ajos* to string, make a string of, put on a string. (**b**) (*fig*) *dificultad* to straighten out, iron out. (**c**) *lugar* to go straight to.

enrizar [1f] **1** *vt* to curl. **2 enrizarse** *vr* to curl.

enrocar [1g] *vi* (*Ajedrez*) to castle.

enrojecer [2d] **1** *vt* (*volver rojo*) to redden, turn red; *persona* to make blush; *metal* to make red-hot.

2 *vi y* **enrojecerse** *vr* to blush, redden; to go red (with anger); to get red-hot.

enrojecimiento *nm* reddening; blushing, blush.

enrolar [1a] (*LAm*) **1** *vt* to enrol, sign on, sign up; (*Mil*) to enlist. **2 enrolarse** *vr* to enrol, sign on; (*Mil*) to enlist, join up; (*Dep*) to enter (*en* for).

enrollable *adj* that rolls up, roll-up (*atr*); **persiana** ~ slatted shutter.

enrollado* 1 *adj*: **un tío muy** ~ a thoroughly turned-on guy*. **2** *nm*, **enrollada** *nf* fan, enthusiast.

enrollamiento *nm* (**a**) rolling up; (*Elec*) coiling. (**b**) (*) event, happening; festival.

enrollante* *adj* smashing*, super*; fascinating.

enrollar [1a] **1** *vt* (**a**) to roll (up), wind (up); *cuerda* to coil. (**b**) (*: *atraer*) to turn on*; **a mí no me enrolla eso** that doesn't turn me on*, I don't dig that*. **2 enrollarse** *vr* (**a**) (*al explicarse*) to go on a long time, jabber on, explain (*etc*) at great length; **cuando se enrolla no hay quien lo pare** when he gets going there's no stopping him. (**b**) **se enrollaron*** they paired off, they started going around together; ~ **con uno** to get involved with sb; (*como amante*) to get off with sb*, make it with sb‡; ~ **bien con uno** to get on well with sb, hit it off with sb; ~ **en** to get involved in. (**c**) (*) to get with it*, get turned on*, get into the swing of things.

enrolle* *nm* boring event, bad scene*, pain*.

enronquecer [2d] **1** *vt* to make hoarse. **2** *vi y* **enronquecerse** *vr* to get hoarse, grow hoarse.

enronquecido *adj* hoarse.

enroque *nm* (*Ajedrez*) castling.

enroscado *adj* (**a**) coiled; twisted; kinky. (**b**) (*And*) angry.

enroscadura *nf* coil; twist; kink.

enroscar [1g] **1** *vt* (**a**) (*arrollar*) to coil (round), wind; (*torcer*) to twist, twine; (*en espiral*) to curl (up).

(**b**) *tornillo* to screw in.

(**c**) (*rodear*) to wreathe (*de* in).

2 enroscarse *vr* to coil, wind; to twist, twine; to curl (up); ~ **alrededor de un árbol** to twine round a tree.

enrostrar [1a] *vt* (*LAm*) to reproach.

enrulado *adj* (*Cono Sur*) curly.

enrular [1a] *vt* (*And, Cono Sur*) to curl.

enrumbar* *vi* (*LAm*) to go, set off.

ensacar [1g] *vt* to sack, bag, put into bags.

ensalada *nf* (**a**) (*Culin*) salad; ~ **de col** coleslaw; ~ **de frutas** fruit salad; ~ **de patatas** potato salad. (**b**) (*fig*) hotchpotch, unholy mixture; mix-up; medley; (*Aut*) traffic

jam; ~ **de tiros*** shoot-out, shooting.
ensaladera *nf* salad-bowl, salad-dish.
ensaladilla *nf* (**a**) ≈ Russian salad. (**b**) (*And, Carib*††: *sátira*) lampoon, satirical verse.
ensalmado *adj* (*LAm*) magic.
ensalmador *nm* quack, bonesetter.
ensalmar [1a] *vt hueso* to set; *enfermedad* to cure by spells, treat by quack remedies.
ensalme *nm* (*And*) spell, incantation.
ensalmo *nm* spell, charm, incantation; (*Med*) quack remedy, quack treatment (using spells); (**como**) **por** ~ as if by magic.
ensalzable *adj* praiseworthy, meritorious.
ensalzamiento *nm* exaltation; extolling.
ensalzar [1f] *vt* to exalt; to praise, extol.
ensamblado *nm* (*Aut etc*) assembly.
ensamblador(a) **1** *nm/f* (**a**) joiner; fitter. **2** *nm* (*Inform*) assembler.
ensambladura *nf* (**a**) (*gen*) joinery; assembling. (**b**) (*Téc*) joint; ~ **de inglete** mitre joint.
ensamblaje *nm* (**a**) (*Téc*) assembly; docking, link-up; **planta de** ~ assembly plant. (**b**) (*Inform*) assembly language.
ensamblar [1a] *vt* (*Téc*) to join; to assemble; *astronaves* to dock, link up.
ensanchar [1a] **1** *vt* to enlarge, widen, extend; to stretch; to expand; (*Cos*) to enlarge, let out.
2 ensancharse *vr* (**a**) to get wider, spread, expand; to stretch.
(**b**) (*fig*) to give o.s. airs.
ensanche *nm* enlargement, widening, extension; expansion; stretch(ing); (*de ciudad*) extension, new suburb, suburban development; (*Cos*) extra piece, room to let out.
ensangrentado *adj* bloodstained; bloody, gory.
ensangrentar [1j] **1** *vt* to stain with blood, cover in blood.
2 ensangrentarse *vr* (*fig*) to get angry; ~ **con,** ~ **contra** to be cruel to, treat cruelly, be vindictive towards.
ensañado *adj* furious; cruel, merciless.
ensañamiento *nm* rage; fury; cruelty, barbarity.
ensañar [1a] **1** *vt* to enrage. **2 ensañarse** *vr*: ~ **con,** ~ **en** to vent one's anger on; to delight in tormenting, take a sadistic pleasure in the sufferings of.
ensarnarse [1a] *vr* (*CAm, Cono Sur, Méx*) to get mangy.
ensartada* *nf*: **pegarse una** ~ (*And*) to be very disappointed, feel let down.
ensartador *nm* (*Cono Sur*) roasting spit.
ensartar [1a] **1** *vt* (**a**) *cuentas etc* to string; *aguja* to thread; *carne* to spit.
(**b**) (*fig*) to string together; to link; *disculpas etc* to reel off, trot out, rattle off.
2 ensartarse* *vr* (**a**) (*And, Carib*) to get into a jam*.
(**b**) (*Cono Sur*: *salir mal*) to mess things up.
ensarte* *nm* (*And*) disappointment, let-down.
ensayar [1a] **1** *vt* (**a**) (*probar*) to test, try, try out.
(**b**) *metal* to assay.
(**c**) (*Mús, Teat*) to rehearse.
2 ensayarse *vr* to practise; to rehearse; ~ **a** + *infin* to practise + *ger*.
ensaye *nm* assay.
ensayista *nmf* essayist.
ensayística *nf* essays, essay-writing; genre of the essay.
ensayístico *adj* essay (*atr*); **obra ensayística** essays, work in essay form.
ensayo *nm* (**a**) (*prueba*) test, trial; (*experimento*) experiment; (*intento*) attempt; (*ejercicio*) practice, exercise; ~ **clínico** clinical trial; ~ **nuclear** nuclear test; **de** ~ tentative; practice (*atr*); experimental; **pedido de** ~ (*Com*) trial order; **viaje de** ~ trial run; **vuelo de** ~ test flight; **hacer algo a modo de** ~ to do sth as an experiment, do sth to try it out; **hacer** ~**s** to practise (*en* on), train.
(**b**) (*de metal*) assay.
(**c**) (*Liter, Escol etc*) essay.
(**d**) (*Mús, Teat*) rehearsal; ~ **general** dress rehearsal.
(**e**) (*Rugby*) try.
ensebado *adj* greased, greasy.
enseguida *adv V* **seguida (b)**.
enselvado *adj* wooded.
ensenada *nf* (**a**) inlet, cove; creek. (**b**) (*Cono Sur*) small fenced pasture.
enseña *nf* ensign, standard.
enseñado *adj* trained; informed; educated; **bien** ~ *perro* house-trained.
enseñante **1** *adj* teaching. **2** *nmf* teacher.
enseñanza *nf* (**a**) (*gen*: *acto*) education; (*acto, profesión*) teaching; instruction, training; schooling; tuition; **primera** ~, ~ **primaria** elementary education; **segunda** ~, ~ **secundaria** secondary education; ~ **superior** higher education; ~ **universitaria** university education; ~ **de los niños atrasados** remedial teaching, teaching of backward children; ~ **para ambos sexos** coeducation; ~ **a distancia** distance learning; ~ **asistida por ordenador** computer-assisted learning; ~ **general básica** education course in Spain from 6 to 14; ~ **programada** programmed learning.
(**b**) (*doctrina*) teaching, doctrine; **la** ~ **de la Iglesia** the teaching of the Church.
enseñar [1a] **1** *vt* (**a**) *persona* to teach, instruct, train; to educate; *asignatura* to teach; ~ **a uno a hacer algo** to teach sb (how) to do sth, train sb to do sth; to show sb how to do sth.
(**b**) (*mostrar*) to show; (*señalar*) to point out; **nos enseñó el museo** he showed us (over) the museum; **te enseñaré mis aguafuertes** I'll show you my etchings; **esto nos enseña las dificultades** this reveals the difficulties to us.
2 enseñarse *vr* (**a**) (*LAm*) to learn; ~ **a hacer algo** to learn (how) to do sth.
(**b**) (*esp LAm*) to accustom o.s., become inured (*a* to); **no me enseño aquí** I can't get used to it here, I can't settle down here.
enseñorearse [1a] *vr*: ~ **de** to take possession of, take over; (*fig*) to overlook, dominate.
enseres *nmpl* (*efectos personales*) goods and chattels; (*avíos*) things, gear, tackle, equipment; ~ **domésticos** household goods; ~ **eléctricos** electrical applicances.
enseriarse [1b] *vr* (*And, CAm, Carib*) to look serious.
ENSIDESA, Ensidesa *nf* (*Esp Com*) *abr de* **Empresa Nacional Siderúrgica, Sociedad Anónima.**
ensilado *nm* ensilage; ~ **de patatas** potato clamp.
ensiladora *nf* silo.
ensilar [1a] *vt* to store in a silo.
ensillar [1a] *vt* to saddle (up), put a saddle on.
ensimismamiento *nm* (**a**) absorption; reverie. (**b**) (*LAm*) conceit.
ensimismarse [1a] *vr* (**a**) to be(come) lost in thought, go into a reverie. (**b**) (*LAm**: *engreírse*) to get conceited.
ensoberbecer [2d] **1** *vt* to make proud. **2 ensoberbecerse** *vr* (**a**) to become proud, become arrogant. (**b**) (*mar*) to get rough.
ensombrecer [2d] **1** *vt* (**a**) to darken, cast a shadow over.
(**b**) (*fig*) to overshadow, put in the shade.
2 ensombrecerse *vr* (**a**) to darken, get dark.
(**b**) (*fig*) to get gloomy.
ensombrerado *adj* with a hat, wearing a hat.
ensoñación *nf* fantasy, fancy, dream; **¡ni por** ~**!** not a bit of it!, never!
ensoñador **1** *adj* dreamy. **2** *nm,* **ensoñadora** *nf* dreamer.
ensopar [1a] **1** *vt galleta etc* to dip, dunk; (*LAm*) to soak, drench; to saturate. **2 ensoparse** *vr* (*LAm*) to get soaked.
ensordecedor *adj* deafening.
ensordecer [2d] **1** *vt persona* to deafen; *ruido* to muffle. **2** *vi* to go deaf; (*fig*) to pretend not to hear, pretend to be deaf.
ensortijar [1a] **1** *vt* (**a**) *pelo* to curl, put curls into. (**b**) *nariz* to ring, fix a ring in. **2 ensortijarse** *vr* to curl.
ensuciamiento *nm* soiling, dirtying.
ensuciar [1b] **1** *vt* (**a**) to soil, dirty; to foul; to mess up, make a mess of.
(**b**) (*fig*) to defile, pollute.
2 ensuciarse *vr* to get dirty; (*niño*) to soil o.s.
ensueño *nm* (**a**) dream, fantasy, illusion; reverie; **de** ~ dream-like; other-wordly; **una cocina de** ~ a dream kitchen, a kitchen of one's dreams; **mundo de** ~ dream world, world of fantasy; **¡ni por** ~**!** not a bit of it!, never!
(**b**) ~**s** visions, fantasies.
entabicar [1g] *vt* (*LAm*) to partition off.
entablado *nm* boarding, planking; wooden flooring.
entabladura *nf* boarding, planking.
entablar [1a] **1** *vt* (**a**) *suelo etc* to board (in, up), plank, cover with boards.
(**b**) (*Ajedrez*) *trebejos* to set up.
(**c**) (*Med*) to splint, put in a splint.
(**d**) *conversación etc* to start, strike up; *contrato* to enter into; *proceso* to begin, file, bring; *reclamación* to file, put in.
2 *vi* (**a**) (*LAm Ajedrez*) to draw.
(**b**) (*And* †: *fanfarronear*) to boast.

3 entablarse *vr* (**a**) (*viento*) to settle. (**b**) (*Méx*) to take place.

entable *nm* (**a**) (*tablas*) boarding, planking.
(**b**) (*Ajedrez*) position.
(**c**) (*LAm: organización*) order, arrangement, disposition.
(**d**) (*And: empresa nueva*) new business; (*And: de terrenos vírgenes*) breaking, opening up.

entablillar [1a] *vt* (*Med*) to splint, put in a splint; **con el brazo entablillado** with his arm in a splint.

entalegar [1h] *vt* (**a**) to bag, put in a bag. (**b**) (*fig*) to hoard, stash away. (**c**) (‡) to jug‡, jail.

entallado *adj* (*Cos*) waisted, with a waist.

entallador(a) *nm/f* sculptor; engraver.

entalladura *nf* (**a**) (*arte, objeto*) sculpture, carving; engraving. (**b**) (*corte*) slot, notch, cut, groove.

entallar [1a] **1** *vt* (**a**) (*esculpir*) to sculpt, carve; (*grabar*) to engrave; ~ **el nombre en un árbol** to carve one's name on a tree.
(**b**) (*hacer un corte en*) to notch, cut a slot in, cut a groove in.
(**c**) (*Cos*) to cut, tailor.
2 *vi* to fit (well); **traje que entalla bien** a suit that fits well, a well-cut suit.

entallecer [2d] *vi y* **entallecerse** *vr* to shoot, sprout.

entapizado 1 *adj* (**a**) upholstered (*de* with); hung (*de* with); covered (*de* with).
(**b**) (*Bot*) overgrown (*de* with).
2 *nm* (*Méx*) wall-coverings, tapestries.

entapizar [1f] *vt* (**a**) *mueble* to upholster (*de* with, in); *pared* to hang with tapestries; *butaca etc* to cover with fabric; (*Cono Sur*) *suelo* to carpet.
(**b**) (*Bot*) to grow over, cover, spread over.

entarascar [1g] **1** *vt* to dress up, doll up. **2 entarascarse** *vr* to dress up, doll up.

entarimado *nm* (**a**) (*tablas*) floorboarding, roof boarding; (*taracea*) inlaid floor; ~ (**de hojas quebradas** *o* **de maderas finas**) parquet. (**b**) (*estrado*) dais, stage, platform.

entarimar [1a] *vt* to board, plank; to put an inlaid floor on (*o* over).

entarugado *nm* block flooring, block paving.

ente *nm* (**a**) entity, being; (*Pol etc*) body, organization; **la E~** (*esp*) the Spanish state TV and radio; ~ **moral** (*Méx*) non-profit-making organization; ~ **gubernamental,** ~ **oficial** official entity, official body; ~ **público** public body, public corporation. (**b**) (*) fellow, chap*; odd sort.

entecarse [1g] *vr* (*Cono Sur*) to be stubborn.

enteco *adj* weak, sickly, frail.

entechar [1a] *vt* (*LAm*) to roof.

entediarse [1b] *vr* to get bored.

entejar [1a] *vt* (*LAm*) to tile.

enteje *nm* (*LAm*) tiling.

Entel *nf abr de* **Empresa Nacional de Telecomunicaciones**.

entelar [1a] *vt pared* to cover with hangings.

entelequia *nf* (*Fil*) entelechy; (*fig: plan etc*) pipe-dream, pie in the sky.

entelerido *adj* (**a**) (*frío*) shivering with cold; (*atemorizado*) shaking with fright. (**b**) (*LAm: débil*) weak, sickly, frail. (**c**) (*LAm: acongojado*) distressed, upset.

entenada *nf* stepdaughter.

entenado *nm* stepson; stepchild.

entendederas* *nfpl* brains; **ser corto de ~, tener malas ~** to be pretty dim, be slow on the uptake; **sus ~ no llegan a más*** he has a brain the size of a pea*, he's bird-brained*.

entendedor(a) *nm/f* understanding person; **al buen ~, pocas palabras (le bastan)** a word to the wise is sufficient; enough said!

entender [2g] **1** *vti* (**a**) (*comprender*) to understand; (*darse cuenta*) to realize, grasp; to comprehend; **¿entiendes?** (do you) understand?, do you get me?; **no le entiendo** I don't understand you; **lo que es ~, entiendo** I understand it as far as anybody can understand it; **no entiendo palabra** it's Greek to me; **no entendió jota** (*o* **una patata** *etc*) he didn't understand a word of it; **a mi ~** to my way of thinking, in my opinion; ~ **mal** to misunderstand; **dar a ~ que ...** to give to understand that ..., imply that ...; **según él da a ~** according to what he says, as he implies; **hacer ~ algo a uno** to make sb understand sth, put sth across to sb; **hacerse ~** to make o.s. understood, get across (*por* to); **lograr ~** to manage to grasp; to get the hang of.
(**b**) (*querer decir*) to intend, mean; **¿qué entiendes con eso?** what do you mean by that?
(**c**) (*creer*) to think, believe; to infer; **entiendo que es ilegal** I feel it is illegal, to my mind it's illegal; **¿debo ~ que lo niegas?** am I to understand that you deny it?
(**d**) (*oír*) to hear.
2 *vi* (**a**) ~ **de** to be an expert on, be good at, know all about; ~ **de carpintería** to know all about carpentry, be an expert carpenter; **yo no entiendo de vinos** I'm no judge of wines; **ella no entiende de coches** she's hopeless with cars.
(**b**) ~ **en** to deal with, be concerned with, have to do with; to be familiar with; ~ **en un asunto** (*juez etc*) to have the authority to handle a matter, be in charge of an affair.
(**c**) ~ **por** (*perro*) to answer to the name of.
3 entenderse *vr* (**a**) (*comprenderse*) to be understood; to be meant; **¿qué se entiende por estas palabras?** what is meant by these words?; **¿cómo se entiende que ...?** how can one understand that ...?, how can one grasp that ...?; **se entiende que ...** it is understood that ...; **eso se entiende** that is understood.
(**b**) (*tener razones*) to know what one is about; **yo me entiendo** I know what I'm up to; I have my reasons; ~ **con algo** to know how to deal with sth.
(**c**) (*2 personas*) to understand each other; to get along (well) together; to have a (secret) understanding; **digamos, para entendernos, que ...** let us say, so that there should be no misunderstanding, that ...; ~ **con uno** to come to an arrangement with sb, fix things with sb; ~ **con una mujer** to have an affair with a woman; **entendérselas con uno** to face up to sb; to have it out with sb.
(**d**) **en caso de duda ~ con el cajero** in case of doubt see the cashier; **eso no se entiende conmigo** that doesn't concern me, that has nothing to do with me.

entendido 1 *adj* (**a**) understood; agreed; **¡~!** agreed!; **bien ~ que ...** on the understanding that ...; **no darse por ~** to pretend not to understand; **tenemos ~ que ...** we understand that ...; **según tenemos ~** as far as we can gather.
(**b**) *persona* (*experto*) expert; (*perito*) skilled, trained; (*sabio*) wise; knowing; (*informado*) well-informed; **ser ~ en** to be versed in, be skilled at.
2 *nm*, **entendida** *nf* knowledgeable person; expert; connoisseur; **según el juicio de los ~s** in the opinion of those who know, according to the experts; **el whisk(e)y de los ~s** the connoisseur's whisky.

entendimiento *nm* (**a**) (*comprensión*) understanding; grasp, comprehension.
(**b**) (*inteligencia*) mind, intellect, understanding; **de poco lucido** of limited understanding.
(**c**) (*juicio*) judgement.

entenebrecer [2d] **1** *vt* (**a**) to darken, obscure.
(**b**) (*fig*) to fog, cloud, obscure; **esto entenebrece más el asunto** this fogs the issue still more.
2 entenebrecerse *vr* to get dark.

entente *nf* (*a veces m*) entente.

enteradillo, -a* *nm/f* little know-all, smarty*.

enterado 1 *adj* (**a**) knowledgeable; well-informed; **estar ~** to be informed, be in the know; **estar ~ de** to know about, be aware of; **estar ~ de que ...** to know that ..., be aware that ...; **no darse por ~** to pretend not to understand, not take the hint; (*declaración*) **quedo ~ de que ...** I understand that ...
(**b**) (*Cono Sur**) conceited, stuck-up*.
2 *nm*, **enterada*** *nf* know-all.

enteramente *adv* entirely, completely; quite.

enterar [1a] **1** *vt* (**a**) to inform (*de* about, of), acquaint (*de* with), tell (*de* about).
(**b**) (*LAm*) *dinero* to pay, hand over; *deuda* to pay off; (*And, Cono Sur, Méx*) *cantidad* to make up, complete, round off.
2 *vi* (**a**) (*LAm: reponerse*) to get better, get well.
(**b**) (*Cono Sur*) to let the days go by.
3 enterarse *vr* (**a**) to find out, get to know; ~ **de** to find out about, learn of, hear of, get to know about; **¿te enteras?** do you hear?; do you understand?, do you get it?; **¡entérate!, ¡entérese!** listen!, get this!*; **¡estás que no te enteras!** you just don't pay attention!; **seguir sin ~** to remain ignorant, remain in the dark; **para que te enteres ...** I'd have you know ...; **ya me voy enterando** I'm beginning to understand; **es así pero no se han enterado** it is so, but they haven't realized it yet.
(**b**) (*LAm: recobrar lo perdido*) to recoup one's losses.

entercado* *adj*: ~ **en hacer algo** (*LAm*) determined to do sth, dead set on doing sth.

entereza *nf* (**a**) entirety; completeness; perfection.
(**b**) (*fig*) integrity; decency, honesty; strength of mind; fortitude; firmness.
(**c**) (*fig*) strictness, severity.

entérico *adj* enteric.
enteritis *nf* enteritis.
enterizo *adj* in one piece.
enternecedor *adj* affecting, touching, moving.
enternecer [2d] **1** *vt* to soften; to affect, touch, move (to pity). **2 enternecerse** *vr* to relent; to be affected, be touched, be moved (to pity); to feel tender.
entero 1 *adj* (**a**) (*gen*) entire, complete; whole; **la cantidad entera** the whole sum, the complete sum; **por el mundo ~** over the whole world; **con entera satisfacción** with complete satisfaction; **por ~** wholly, completely, fully; **el reloj da las enteras** the clock strikes the hours.
(**b**) (*Mat*) whole, integral.
(**c**) (*Bio*) not castrated.
(**d**) (*fig*: *honrado*) upright, honest; (*firme*) resolute, firm.
(**e**) (*fig*: *fuerte*) sound; robust; *tela etc* strong, thick.
(**f**) (*And, CAm, Carib**: *idéntico*) identical, similar; **está ~ a su papá** he's just like his dad*, he's the spitting image of his dad*.
2 *nm* (**a**) (*Mat*) integer, whole number.
(**b**) (*Com, Fin*) point; **las acciones han subido dos ~s** the shares have gone up two points.
(**c**) (*LAm*: *pago*) payment.
(**d**) (*Cono Sur*: *Fin*) balance.
enteropostal *nm* pre-stamped postcard, letter-card.
enterradero *nm* (*Cono Sur*) burial ground.
enterrado *adj* buried; *uña* ingrowing.
enterrador *nm* gravedigger.
enterramiento *nm* burial, interment.
enterrar [1a] *vt* (**a**) to bury, inter. (**b**) (*LAm*) *navaja etc* to bury (*en* in), thrust (*en* into). (**c**) (*fig*: *en olvido*) to bury, forget.
enterratorio *nm* (*Cono Sur*) (*cementerio*) Indian burial ground; (*restos*) archaeological remains, site of archaeological interest.
entesar [1j] *vt* to stretch, tauten.
entibiar [1b] **1** *vt* (**a**) to cool; to take the chill off. (**b**) (*fig*) to cool (down). **2 entibiarse** *vr* (**a**) to become lukewarm, cool down. (**b**) (*fig*) to cool off.
entibo *nm* (*Arquit*) buttress; (*Min*) prop.
entidad *nf* (**a**) entity; (*Pol etc*) body, organization; (*Com, Fin*) firm, concern, company; **~ bancaria** bank; **~ crediticia** credit company; **~ financiera** financial institution. (**b**) importance; solidity, solid reputation; **de ~** of importance, of consequence; **de menor ~** less important, not so large; **el equipo tiene mucha ~** the team has a very solid reputation.
entierro *nm* (**a**) (*acto*) burial, interment. (**b**) (*funeral*) funeral; **asistir al ~** to go to the funeral. (**c**) (*tumba*) grave. (**d**) (*LAm Arqueol*) (buried) treasure; treasure-trove.
entintar [1a] *vt tampón* to ink; *blanco* to ink in; (*manchar*) to stain with ink.
entizar [1f] *vt* (*LAm Billar*) *taco* to chalk.
entoldado *nm* awning(s).
entoldar [1a] **1** *vt* (**a**) (*cubrir con toldo*) to put an awning over, fit with an awning.
(**b**) (*decorar*) to decorate (with hangings).
2 entoldarse *vr* (**a**) (*Met*) to cloud over, become overcast.
(**b**) (*emoción, alegría*) to be dimmed.
(**c**) (*persona*) to give o.s. airs.
entomología *nf* entomology.
entomólogo, -a *nm/f* entomologist.
entonación *nf* (**a**) (*Ling*) intonation. (**b**) (*fig*) conceit.
entonado *adj* (**a**) (*Mús*) toned; harmonious; in tune. (**b**) (*fig*: *engreído*) conceited; (*orgulloso*) haughty, arrogant, stiff. (**c**) (*fig*: *en forma*) lively, in good form.
entonar [1a] **1** *vt* (**a**) (*Mús*) *canción etc* to intone; *voz* to modulate; to sing in tune; *nota* to give, pitch, set; *órgano* to blow.
(**b**) (*fig*) *alabanzas* to sound.
(**c**) (*Arte, Fot*) to tone.
(**d**) (*Med*) to tone up.
(**e**) (*fig*: *vigorizar*) to liven up, enliven, invigorate.
2 *vi* (**a**) (*Mús*) to intone; to be in tune (*con* with).
(**b**) (*fig*) to be in tune (*con* with), harmonize (*con* with).
3 entonarse *vr* to give o.s. airs.
entonces *adv* (**a**) (*tiempo*) then; at that time; **desde ~** since then; **en aquel ~** at that time; **hasta ~** up till then; **las costumbres de ~** the customs of the time; **el ~ embajador de Eslobodia** the Slobodian ambassador at the time; **fue ~ que ...** it was then that ... that was when ...
(**b**) (*concesivo*) and so; then; **pues ~** well then; **¿~ cómo no viniste?** then why didn't you come?; **¡y ~!** (*Carib, Cono Sur*) why of course!
entonelar [1a] *vt* to put into barrels (*o* casks).
entongado* *adj* (*And*) cross, riled*.
entongar [1h] *vt* (**a**) to pile up, pile in layers. (**b**) (*And*: *enojar*) to anger.
entono *nm* (**a**) (*Mús*) intonation, intoning; being in tune, singing in tune. (**b**) (*fig*) conceit; haughtiness.
entontecedor *adj* stupefying.
entontecer [2d] **1** *vt* to make silly. **2** *vi y* **entontecerse** *vr* to get silly.
entorchado *nm* (**a**) gold braid, silver braid. (**b**) (*Mús*) bass string.
entorchar [1a] *vt* (**a**) to twist (up). (**b**) to braid.
entornacional *adj* environmental.
entornado *adj* half-closed; ajar.
entornar [1a] *vt* (**a**) *ojos* to half-close; to screw up; *puerta* to half-close, leave ajar. (**b**) (*volcar*) to upset, tip over.
entorno *nm* (**a**) setting, milieu, ambience; environment; climate; scene; **el ~ cultural** the cultural scene; **~ natural** natural environment; **~ social** social setting. (**b**) (*Inform*) environment; **~ gráfico** graphics environment; **~ de programación** programming environment; **~ de red(es)** network environment; **~ de trabajo** work(ing) environment.
entorpecer [2d] *vt* (**a**) (*entendimiento*) to dull, benumb, stupefy; (*aletargar*) to make torpid, make lethargic.
(**b**) (*estorbar*) to obstruct, hinder; *planes etc* to set back; *movimiento, tráfico* to slow down, slow up; *trabajo* to hinder, delay.
entorpecimiento *nm* (**a**) stupefaction; numbness; torpor, lethargy.
(**b**) obstruction; obstacle, drawback; delay, slowing-up.
entrabar [1a] *vt* (*And*) = **trabar.**
entrada *nf* (**a**) (*lugar*) entrance (*de* to), way in (*de* to); (*puerta*) gate, gateway; (*acceso*) access; (*Min*) entrance, adit; (*pórtico*) porch, doorway; (*hall*) entrance hall; (*de cueva, túnel*) mouth; (*de pelo*) place where the hair is thinning; **tiene ~s** he's got a receding hairline, he's losing his hair.
(**b**) (*Mec*) inlet, intake; **~ de aire** air intake.
(**c**) (*acto*) entry, entrance (*en* into); admission (*en* into); right of entry; **la ~ de las tropas en 1940** the entry of the troops in 1940; **la ~ de turistas este año** this year's influx of tourists; **~ en bolsa** launch(ing) on the stock exchange; **~ en escena** (*Teat*) entrance; **~ en vigor** coming into effect; **~ en una casa** entrée to a house, privilege of entry to a house; **~ a viva fuerza** forced entry; **'~ gratis'** 'admission free'; **'prohibida la ~'** 'no entry', 'no admission', 'keep out'; **su ~ en la Academia** his admission to the Academy; **la ~ de la palabra en el diccionario** the admission of the word into the dictionary, the acceptance of the word for the dictionary; **dar ~ a** to admit; **hacer su ~** to make one's entry, make a formal entry.
(**d**) (*Teat etc*: *billete*) ticket; **~ de favor, ~ de regalo** complimentary ticket.
(**e**) (*Teat etc*: *público*) house, audience; (*Dep*) gate, crowd; **~ floja** thin audience; **gran ~, ~ llena** full house; **hubo poca ~** there was a small audience.
(**f**) (*Teat, Fin*) receipts, takings; (*Dep*) gate money.
(**g**) (*principio*: *de discurso, libro etc*) beginning; (*Prensa*) lead-in, opening paragraph; **la ~ de la primavera** the start of spring; **de ~** right away, from the start; as a start, for a start; **de primera ~** at first sight; **~ en materia** introduction.
(**h**) (*Culin*) entrée; (*LAm*) first course.
(**i**) (*Béisbol*) innings, inning (*US*).
(**j**) (*Com*) entry; (*de catálogo etc*) entry: (*de diccionario*) entry, headword.
(**k**) (*Carib, Méx*: *ataque*) attack, onslaught; assault.
(**l**) (*Carib, Méx*: *paliza*) beating.
(**m**) (*Fin*: *desembolso inicial*) down payment, deposit; (*de club*) entrance fee; (*al alquilar piso*) deposit, key money; **'sin ~'** 'no down payment'.
(**n**) (*Cono Sur Fin*) income; **~s** receipts, takings; income; **~s brutas** gross receipts; **~s familiares** family income; **~s y salidas** income and expenditure.
(**o**) (*Inform*) input; **~ de datos** data entry, data input; **~ inmediata** immediate access; **~ de trabajos a distancia** remote job entry.
(**p**) (*Ftbl*) tackle (*a* on); **~ violenta** hard tackle.
entradilla *nf* (*Prensa*) lead-in, opening paragraph.
entrado *adj* (**a**) **~ en años** elderly, advanced in years.
(**b**) **hasta muy entrada la noche** until late at night; on into the small hours; **hasta bien ~ mayo** until well on into

May.

(**c**) (*Cono Sur*) meddling, officious.

entrador *adj* (**a**) (*LAm: valiente*) brave; spirited; (*enérgico*) energetic; (*emprendedor*) enterprising.

(**b**) (*Cono Sur: entrometido*) meddling, officious.

(**c**) (*LAm: simpático*) charming, likeable, attractive.

(**d**) (*And, Carib, Méx: mujeriego*) amorously inclined.

(**e**) (*CAm: coqueta*) flirtatious.

entramado *nm* (*Arquit*) truss; timber framework; (*de puente*) framework; span; (*fig*) network.

entrambos *adj pl* (*liter*) both.

entrampar [1a] **1** *vt* (**a**) to trap, catch, snare; (*fig*) to snare, trick.

(**b**) (*fig*) to mess up, make a mess of.

(**c**) (*Com*) to burden with debts.

2 entramparse *vr* (*fig*) (**a**) to get into a mess, get tangled up.

(**b**) (*Com*) to get into debt.

entrante 1 *adj* (**a**) next, coming; **la semana** ~ next week.

(**b**) *persona* new, incoming.

2 *nm* (**a**) (*Geog*) inlet.

(**b**) **~s y salientes** people coming to and leaving a house (*etc*).

(**c**) (*Culin*) starter.

entraña *nf* (**a**) (*fig*) core, root, essential part; **esto es la ~ del problema** this is the real core of the problem.

(**b**) **de mala** ~ malicious; evil-minded.

(**c**) **~s** (*Anat*) entrails; insides; bowels; (*fig: lo esencial*) core, innermost parts; (*fig: sentimientos*) heart, feelings; (*temperamento*) disposition; **en las ~s de la tierra** in the bowels of the earth; **¡hijo de mis ~s!** my precious child!; **arrancar las ~s a uno** (*fig*) to break sb's heart; **dar hasta las ~s** to give one's all; (*fig*) to put all one has into it, make a great effort; **echar las ~s** (*fig*) to throw up*; **no tener ~s** (*fig*) to be heartless, lack all feelings.

entrañabilidad *nf* (**a**) closeness, intimacy. (**b**) beloved quality. (**c**) charm, winning nature.

entrañable *adj* (**a**) *amigo* close, intimate; *paisaje etc* beloved, dearly loved. (**b**) (*afectuoso*) affectionate; (*simpático*) charming, winning. (**c**) *afecto, amistad* deep.

entrañablemente *adv amar etc* dearly, deeply.

entrañar [1a] **1** *vt* (**a**) to bury deep.

(**b**) (*fig: contener*) to contain, carry within; (*acarrear*) to entail, mean.

2 entrañarse *vr* (**a**) to become deeply attached (*con* to).

(**b**) ~ **en** to reach to the bottom of, reach to the very heart of.

entrañudo *adj* (*Cono Sur*) (**a**) (*valiente*) brave, daring. (**b**) (*cruel*) cruel, heartless.

entrar [1a] **1** *vt* (**a**) *objeto* to introduce; *persona* to bring in, show in; (*Inform*) to access, enter; **mañana van a ~ el carbón** they'll bring the coal in tomorrow; **no sabe ~ el coche en el garaje** she can't get the car into the garage.

(**b**) (*abordar*) to get at, approach; (*Dep*) to tackle; **sabe ~ a la gente** he knows how to approach (*o* tackle) people.

(**c**) (*Mil*) to attack; to invade; to capture, enter.

2 *vi* (**a**) to go in, come in, enter; **Juan entró tercero** (*Dep*) John came in third; ~ **a** (*LAm*), ~ **en** to go into, come into, enter; (*fig*) to enter into; ~ **bien** to be fitting, be appropriate; to be relevant; ~ **a puerto** to enter port, put into port; **el enchufe entra en esa toma** the plug goes into (*o* fits into) that point; **el paquete no entra en el saco** the parcel won't go into the bag; ~ **en una profesión** to adopt a profession, take up a profession; ~ **en una sociedad** to join a society, become a member of a society, be admitted to a society; **el río entra en el lago** the river flows into the lake; ~ **en el número de** to be one of, count among, be reckoned among; ~ **en detalles** to go into details; **eso no entra en nuestros planes** that does not enter into our plans; **no ~ ni salir en un asunto** to play no part in a matter; **eso entra de lleno en ...** that comes right into the category of ...; **estar entrada en copas** to be in one's cups; **entra por una sexta parte** he gets a sixth, his share is one sixth; **le entraron deseos de** + *infin* he felt a sudden urge to + *infin*.

(**b**) (*año etc*) to begin; (*marea, viento*) to rise; **el año que entra** next year.

(**c**) (*ropa*) to fit, be big enough for; **estos zapatos no me entran** those shoes don't fit.

(**d**) **ese tío no me entra** I can't bear that fellow, I can't get on with that chap; **no me entra la lógica** I can't get the hang of logic; **no le entra a la gente que ...** people can't get it into their heads that ...

(**e**) ~ **a** + *infin* to begin to + *infin*.

entrazado* *adj* (*Cono Sur*) (**a**) *persona* (*vestido*) **mal** ~ shabby, ragged; **bien** ~ well-dressed, natty*. (**b**) *persona* (*expresión*) **mal** ~ nasty-looking; **bien** ~ pleasant-looking.

entre (**a**) *prep* (*dos cosas*) between; (*más de dos cosas*) among, amongst; (*en medio de*) in the midst of; (*dentro de*) within, inside; ~ **tú y yo** between the two of us; ~ **esto y lo otro** what with this and that; ~ **azul y verde** midway between blue and green, of some colour between blue and green; **había ~ todos 12 personas** there were 12 people in all (*o* all told); ~ **los que conozco es el mejor** it's the best of those that I know; **de** ~ out of, from among; **por** ~ through; between; **decir ~ sí** to say to o.s.

(**b**) (*LAm*) ~ **más tiene más quiere** the more he gets the more he wants.

entre... *pref* inter...

entreabierto *adj* half-open; ajar.

entreabrir [3a; *ptp* **entreabierto**] *vt* to half-open, open halfway; to leave ajar.

entreacto *nm* interval, entr'acte.

entreayudarse [1a] *vr* to help one another, be of mutual assistance.

entrecano *adj* greyish, greying.

entrecejo *nm* space between the eyebrows; frown; **arrugar el ~, fruncir el** ~ to frown, wrinkle one's brow.

entrecerrar [1j] *vt* (*CAm, Méx*) to half-close, close halfway; *puerta* to leave ajar.

entrecó *nm* sirloin steak.

entrecoger [2c] *vt* (**a**) to catch, intercept; to seize. (**b**) (*fig*) to press, compel; to corner.

entrecomillado 1 *adj* in inverted commas, in quotes. **2** *nm* inverted commas, quotes.

entrecomillar [1a] *vt* to place in inverted commas, put inverted commas round.

entrecoro *nm* chancel.

entrecortadamente *adv* in a laboured way; falteringly, hesitatingly.

entrecortado *adj respiración* laboured; *habla* faltering, hesitant, confused; **en voz entrecortada** in a faltering voice, in a voice choked with emotion.

entrecortar [1a] *vt* (**a**) (*cortar*) to cut into, partially cut, cut halfway through.

(**b**) (*interrumpir*) to cut off, interrupt (from time to time); *voz* to cause to falter, choke from time to time.

entrecot *nm* sirloin steak.

entrecruzar [1f] **1** *vt* (**a**) to interlace, interweave. (**b**) (*Bio*) to cross, interbreed. **2 entrecruzarse** *vr* (*Bio*) to interbreed.

entrecubierta *nf* (*t* **~s**) between-decks.

entrechocar [1g] **1** *vi* (*dientes*) to chatter. **2 entrechocarse** *vr* to collide, crash; to clash.

entredicho *nm* (**a**) prohibition, ban, interdict; (*Jur*) injunction; **estar en** ~ (*prohibido*) to be under a ban, be banned; (*discutible*) to be questionable, be debatable; **levantar el ~ a** to raise the ban on; **poner algo en** ~ (*prohibir*) to place a ban on sth; (*dudar*) to call sth into question, query sth, cast doubt on sth; (*comprometer*) to jeopardize sth, endanger sth.

(**b**) (*Cono Sur: ruptura*) break-up, split.

(**c**) (*And*) alarm bell.

entredós *nm* (**a**) (*Cos*) insertion, panel. (**b**) (*mueble*) cabinet, dresser.

entrefino *adj* medium, medium-quality.

entrefuerte *adj* (*LAm*) *tabaco* medium strong.

entrega *nf* (**a**) (*acto*) delivery; handing over, surrender; (*Correos*) post, delivery; (*Dep*) pass; **'~ a domicilio'** 'we deliver'; ~ **contra pago,** ~ **contra reembolso** cash on delivery, COD; ~ **en fecha futura** forward delivery; **pagadero a la** ~ payable on delivery; **hacer ~ de** to hand over (formally), present.

(**b**) (*de novela etc*) part, instalment; (*de revista etc*) part, number, fascicule.

(**c**) (*cualidad*) commitment; dedication; enthusiasm.

entregado *adj* committed, devoted; ~ **a** absorbed in; ~ **en** committed to.

entregar [1h] **1** *vt* to deliver; (*dar*) to hand, give; *carta, pedido* to hand over, hand in; (*rendir*) to surrender; (*ceder*) to give up, part with; ~ **algo a un abogado** to refer sth to a lawyer, place a matter in a lawyer's hands; **~la‡** to kick the bucket‡; **no quiso entregármelo** he refused to hand it over to me.

2 entregarse *vr* (**a**) (*Mil etc*) to surrender, give in, submit; **se entregó a la policía** he gave himself up to the police.

(**b**) ~ **a** (*dedicarse*) *carrera etc* to devote o.s. to; (*pey*) to give o.s. up to, abandon o.s. to, indulge in; ~ **a estudiar** to devote o.s. to studying.

(**c**) ~ **de** to take possession of.

entreguerras: **el período de** ~ the inter-war period, the period between the wars (*ie 1918-39*).

entreguismo *nm* (*apaciguamiento*) (policy of) appeasement; (*derrotismo*) defeatism; (*oportunismo*) opportunism; (*traición*) betrayal, selling-out.

entrelazado *adj* entwined, interlaced; criss-crossed (*de* with); interlocking.

entrelazar [1f] **1** *vt* to entwine, interlace, interweave; to interlock. **2 entrelazarse** *vr* to entwine, interlace; to interlock.

entrelistado *adj* striped.

entrelucir [3f] *vi* (**a**) (*verse*) to show through. (**b**) (*relucir*) to gleam, shine dimly.

entremás 1 *adv* (*And, Méx*: *además*) moreover; (*en especial*) especially. **2** *conj*: ~ **lo pienso, más convencido estoy** the more I think about it the more convinced (*o* the surer) I am.

entremedias 1 *adv* in between, halfway; in the meantime. **2** ~ **de** *prep* between; among.

entremedio *nm* (*LAm*) interval, intermission.

entremés *nm* (**a**) (*Teat Hist*) interlude, short farce. (**b**) (*Culin*) side dish; ~ **salado** savoury; **entremeses** hors d'oeuvres.

entremesera *nf* tray for hors d'oeuvres.

entremeter [2a] *vt* to insert, put in; to put between.

entremeterse *etc* = **entrometerse** *etc*.

entremezclar [1a] **1** *vt* to intermingle; **entremezclado de** interspersed with. **2 entremezclarse** *vr* to intermingle.

entrenador 1 *nm* (*Aer*) trainer, training plane. **2** *nm*, **entrenadora** *nf* (*Dep*) trainer, coach.

entrenamiento *nm* training, coaching.

entrenar [1a] **1** *vt* (*Dep*) to train, coach; *caballo* to exercise; **estar entrenado** (*futbolista etc*) to be in training, be fit. **2 entrenarse** *vr* to train.

entreno *nm* (*acto*) training; (*período*) training session.

entreoír [3q] *vt* to half-hear, hear indistinctly.

entrepágina *nf* centrefold.

entrepaño *nm* (**a**) (*muro*) (stretch of) wall. (**b**) (*panel*) door panel; (*anaquel*) shelf.

entrepierna *nf* (*t* ~**s**) crotch, crutch; **pasar algo por la** ~‡ to reject sth totally; to feel utter contempt for sth.

entrepuente *nm* between-decks; steerage.

entrerrejado *adj* interwoven, criss-crossed.

entrerrenglonar [1a] *vt* to interline, write between the lines of.

entresacar [1g] *vt* (*seleccionar*) to pick out, select; (*cribar*) to sift; *pelo, plantas etc* to thin out.

entresemana *nf* (*LAm*) midweek; working days of the week; **de** ~ midweek (*atr*); **cualquier día de** ~ any day midweek (*o* in the middle of the week).

entresijo *nm* (**a**) (*Anat*) mesentery.

(**b**) (*fig*: *secreto*) secret, mystery; (*parte oculta*) hidden aspect; (*pega*) difficulty, snag; **esto tiene muchos** ~**s** this is very complicated, this has its ins and outs; **él tiene sus** ~**s** he's a deep one.

entresuelo *nm* mezzanine, entresol; (*Teat*) dress circle.

entretanto 1 *adj* meanwhile, meantime. **2** *nm* meantime; **en el** ~ in the meantime. **3** *como conj*: ~ **esto se produce** until this happens.

entretecho *nm* (*Cono Sur*) attic, garret.

entretejer [2a] *vt* to interweave; to intertwine, entwine; (*fig*) to interweave, insert, put in.

entretejido *nm* interweaving.

entretela *nf* (**a**) (*Cos*) interlining. (**b**) ~**s** inmost being; heartstrings.

entretelar [1a] *vt* to interline.

entretelón *nm* thick curtain, heavy curtain.

entretención *nf* (*Méx*) entertainment, amusement.

entretener [2l] **1** *vt* (**a**) (*divertir*) to entertain, amuse; (*distraer*) to distract.

(**b**) (*demorar*) to delay; (*detener*) to hold up, detain, keep waiting; to keep occupied; (*tener suspenso*) to keep in suspense; **nos entretuvo en conversación** he engaged us in conversation; he kept us talking; ~ **a los acreedores** to keep one's creditors at bay, hold off one's creditors; **pues no te entretengo más** then I won't keep you any longer.

(**c**) *hambre* to kill, stave off; *dolor* to allay; *tiempo* to while away.

(**d**) (*Mec etc*) to maintain.

2 entretenerse *vr* (**a**) (*divertirse*) to amuse o.s.; (*pasar el rato*) to while away the time.

(**b**) (*tardar*) to delay; to loiter (on the way); **¡no te entretengas!** don't hang about!, don't loiter on the way!

entretenida *nf* (**a**) mistress; kept woman.

(**b**) **dar** (**con**) **la** ~ **a uno** to hold sb off with vague promises, hedge with sb, stall sb; to keep sb talking.

entretenido 1 *adj* entertaining, amusing. **2** *nm* (*) gigolo, toyboy*.

entretenimiento *nm* (**a**) entertainment, amusement; diversion, distraction; recreation; **es un** ~ **nada más** it's just an amusement.

(**b**) (*Mec etc*) upkeep, maintenance; **sólo necesita un** ~ **mínimo** it only needs minimum maintenance.

entretiempo *nm* period between seasons; (*primavera*) spring; (*otoño*) autumn.

entrever [2u] *vt* (**a**) to glimpse, catch a glimpse of; to see indistinctly, make out sth of. (**b**) (*fig*) to guess, suspect (sth of).

entreverado *adj* mixed; patchy; *tocino* streaky.

entreverar [1a] **1** *vt* to mix, intermingle; to mix up.

2 entreverarse *vr* (**a**) to intermix, be intermingled.

(**b**) (*Cono Sur*) to mingle; to get tangled, get mixed up.

entrevero *nm* (**a**) (*LAm*) mix-up; jumble. (**b**) (*And, Cono Sur*) (*desorden*) confusion, disorder; (*riña*) brawl; (*Mil*) confused cavalry skirmish.

entrevía *nf* (*Ferro*) gauge; ~ **angosta** narrow gauge; **de** ~ **angosta** narrow-gauge (*atr*); ~ **normal** standard gauge.

entrevista *nf* interview; meeting; **celebrar** (*o* **tener**) **una** ~ **con** to have an interview with, hold a meeting with; **hacer una** ~ **a** to interview.

entrevistado, -a *nm/f* interviewee, person being interviewed.

entrevistador(a) *nm/f* interviewer.

entrevistar [1a] **1** *vt* to interview.

2 entrevistarse *vr* to have an interview, meet; ~ **con** to interview, meet, have an interview with; **el ministro se entrevistó con la reina ayer** the minister saw the queen yesterday.

entripado *nm* (*secreto*) ghastly secret; (*ira*) concealed anger, suppressed rage.

entripar [1a] **1** *vt* (**a**) (*And**: *enfurecer*) to enrage, madden.

(**b**) (*Carib, Méx*: *mojar*) to soak.

(**c**) (*Méx*‡: *embarazar*) to put in the family way, put in the club.

2 entriparse *vr* (**a**) (*And*) to get cross, get upset.

(**b**) (*Carib, Méx*) to get soaked.

entristecer [2d] **1** *vt* to sadden, grieve. **2 entristecerse** *vr* to grow sad, grieve.

entrometerse [2a] *vr* to meddle, interfere (*en* in, with), intrude.

entrometido 1 *adj* meddlesome, interfering. **2** *nm*, **entrometida** *nf* busybody, meddler; intruder.

entromparse [1a] *vr* (**a**) (*: *emborracharse*) to get very drunk, get tight*. (**b**) (*LAm**: *enojarse*) to fly off the handle*.

entrón *adj* (**a**) (*And*) meddlesome. (**b**) (*Méx*) spirited, daring. (**c**) (*Méx*: *coqueta*) flirtatious.

entroncar [1g] **1** *vt* to connect, establish a relationship between. **2** *vi* (**a**) (*tener parentesco*) to be related, be connected (*con* to, with). (**b**) (*Ferro*) to connect (*con* with).

entronización *nf* (**a**) enthronement. (**b**) (*fig*) exaltation.

entronizar [1f] *vt* (**a**) to enthrone. (**b**) (*fig*) to exalt.

entronque *nm* (**a**) relationship, connection, link. (**b**) (*Aut, Ferro*) junction.

entropía *nf* entropy.

entruchada *nf* (**a**) (*: *trampa*) trap, trick. (**b**) (*Cono Sur**) (*discusión*) slanging match*; (*conversación*) intimate conversation.

entruchar [1a] **1** *vt* (*) to lure, decoy, lead by the nose. **2 entrucharse** *vr* (*Méx*) to stick one's nose into other people's affairs.

entuerto *nm* (**a**) wrong, injustice. (**b**) ~**s** (*Med*) afterpains.

entumecer [2d] **1** *vt* to numb, benumb. **2 entumecerse** *vr* (**a**) (*miembro*) to get numb, go to sleep. (**b**) (*río*) to swell, rise; (*mar*) to surge.

entumecido *adj* numb, stiff.

entumecimiento *nm* numbness, stiffness.

entumido *adj* (**a**) (*LAm*) numb, stiff. (**b**) (*And, Méx*: *tímido*) timid.

enturbiar [1b] **1** *vt* (**a**) *agua* to muddy; to disturb, make cloudy.

(**b**) (*fig*) *asunto* to fog, confuse; *mente, persona* to derange, unhinge.

2 enturbiarse *vr* (**a**) to get muddy; to become cloudy.

(**b**) (*fig*) to get confused, become obscured; to become deranged.

enturcado‡ *adj* (*CAm*) *persona* hopping mad*, livid; **un problema ~** a knotty problem.

entusiasmante *adv* thrilling, exciting.

entusiasmar [1a] **1** *vt* (*gen*) to fill with enthusiasm; to fire, excite; (*encantar*) to delight, please a great deal; **no me entusiasma mucho la idea** I'm not very keen on the idea.

2 entusiasmarse *vr* to get enthusiastic, get excited (*con, por* about); **~ con, ~ por** to be keen on, rave about, be delighted with; **se ha quedado entusiasmada con el vestido** she was delighted with the dress, she raved about the dress.

entusiasmo *nm* enthusiasm (*por* for); **con ~** enthusiastically; keenly.

entusiasta 1 *adj* enthusiastic; keen (*de* on); zealous (*de* for). **2** *nmf* enthusiast; fan, follower, supporter; admirer.

entusiástico *adj* enthusiastic.

enumeración *nf* enumeration; count, reckoning.

enumerar [1a] *vt* (*nombrar*) to enumerate; (*contar*) to count, reckon up.

enunciación *nf* enunciation; statement, declaration.

enunciado *nm* (**a**) (*principio*) principle. (**b**) (*Prensa*) heading.

enunciar [1b] *vt* to enunciate; to state, declare.

enuresis *nf* enuresis, bedwetting.

envagonar *vt* (*LAm*) *mercancías* to load into a railway truck.

envainar [1a] **1** *vt* (**a**) to sheathe, put in a sheath; **¡enváinala!**‡ shut your trap!‡. (**b**) (*And*: *molestar*) to vex, annoy. **2** *vi* (*And*) to succumb. **3 envainarse** *vr* (**a**) (*And, Carib**) to get into trouble; **estar envainado** to be in a jam*. (**b**) **envainársela*** to take back what one has said, back down.

envalentonamiento *nm* boldness; (*pey*) Dutch courage; bravado.

envalentonar [1a] **1** *vt* to embolden; (*pey*) to fill with Dutch courage.

2 envalentonarse *vr* to take courage, become bolder; (*pey*) to strut, brag; to put on a bold front.

envanecer [2d] **1** *vt* to make conceited. **2 envanecerse** *vr* to grow vain, get conceited, give o.s. airs; to swell with pride (*con, de* at).

envanecido *adj* conceited, stuck-up*.

envanecimiento *nm* conceit, vanity.

envaramiento *nm* (*Méx*) numbness, stiffness.

envarar [1a] **1** *vt* (*And*: *Agr*) to stake. **2 envararse** *vr* (*Méx*) to be numb, become stiff.

envasado *nm* packing, packaging.

envasador(a) *nm/f* packer.

envasar [1a] **1** *vt* (**a**) (*en paquete*) to pack, wrap; to package; (*en botella*) to bottle; (*en lata*) to can, tin; (*en tonel*) to barrel; (*en saco*) to sack, bag.

(**b**) (*) *vino* to knock back*, put away*.

(**c**) (*esp LAm*) **~ un puñal en uno** to plunge a dagger into sb, bury a dagger in sb.

2 *vi* (*) to tipple, knock it back*.

envase *nm* (**a**) (*acto*) packing, wrapping; packaging; bottling; canning.

(**b**) (*recipiente*) container; (*papel*) package, wrapping; (*botella*) bottle; (*botella vacía*) empty; (*lata*) can, tin; (*tonel*) barrel; (*saco*) bag; **~ de hojalata** tin can; **~ de vidrio** glass container; **precio con ~** price including packing; **géneros sin ~** unpackaged goods; **~s a devolver** returnable empties.

envasijar [1a] *vt* (*LAm*) = **envasar**.

envedijarse [1a] *vr* (**a**) to get tangled (up). (**b**) (*personas*) to come to blows.

envegarse [1h] *vr* (*Cono Sur*) to get swampy, turn into a swamp.

envejecer [2d] **1** *vt* to age, make (seem) old.

2 *vi y* **envejecerse** *vr* (**a**) (*persona*) to age, get old, grow old; to look old; **en 2 años ha envejecido mucho** he's got very old these last two years.

(**b**) (*objeto*) to become old-fashioned, become antiquated, get out-of-date.

envejecido *adj* old, aged; old-looking; **está muy ~** he looks terribly old.

envejecimiento *nm* ageing.

envelar [1a] *vi* (*Cono Sur Náut*) to hoist the sails; (*t* **~las**) to run away.

envenenador(a) *nm/f* poisoner.

envenenamiento *nm* poisoning.

envenenar [1a] **1** *vt* to poison; (*fig*) to poison, embitter. **2 envenenarse** *vr* to poison o.s., take poison.

enverdecer [2r] *vi* to turn green.

enveredar [1a] *vi*: **~ hacia** to head for, make a beeline for.

envergadura *nf* (**a**) expanse, spread, extent; (*Náut*) breadth, beam; (*Aer*: *t* **~ de alas**) wingspan; (*Ent, Orn*) span, wingspan; (*de boxeador*) reach.

(**b**) (*fig*) scope, compass; magnitude; **un programa de gran ~** a programme of considerable scope, a far-reaching programme; **una operación de cierta ~** an operation of some magnitude; an operation of some size; **la obra es de ~** the plan is ambitious.

envés *nm* (*de tela*) back, wrong side; (*de espada*) back, flat; (*Anat**) back.

enviado, -a *nm/f* envoy; **~ especial** (*Periodismo*) special correspondent.

enviar [1c] *vt* to send; **~ a uno a hacer algo** to send sb to do sth; **~ a uno a una misión** to send sb on a mission; **~ por el médico** to send for the doctor, fetch the doctor.

enviciador(a) *nm/f* (*LAm*) drug-pusher.

enviciar [1b] **1** *vt* to corrupt; (*fig*) to vitiate. **2 enviciarse** *vr* to get corrupted; **~ con, ~ en** to become addicted to.

envidar [1a] *vti* (*Naipes*) to bid; **~ en falso** to bluff.

envidia *nf* envy, jealousy; desire; bad feeling; **es pura ~** it's sheer envy; **tener ~ a** to envy.

envidiable *adj* enviable.

envidiar [1b] *vt* to envy; to desire, covet; **~ algo a uno** to envy sb sth, begrudge sb sth; **A no tiene nada que ~ a B** A is at least as good as B, A is quite up to the standard of B.

envidioso *adj* envious, jealous; covetous.

envilecer [2d] **1** *vt* to debase, degrade. **2 envilecerse** *vr* to degrade o.s., lower o.s.; to grovel, crawl.

envilecimiento *nm* degradation, debasement.

envinado *adj* (*Cono Sur*) drunk.

envío *nm* (**a**) (*acto*) sending, dispatch; (*en barco*) shipment; **gastos de ~** (cost of) postage and packing, transport charges; **~ de segundo curso** second-class mail; **~ de datos** data transmission; **~ a domicilio** home delivery (service); **~ contra reembolso** cash on delivery, COD.

(**b**) (*mercancías*) consignment, lot, (*Náut*) shipment; (*dinero*) remittance.

envión *nm* push, shove.

envite *nm* (**a**) (*apuesta*) stake; side bet. (**b**) (*oferta*) offer, bid; invitation. (**c**) (*empuje*) push, shove; **al primer ~** right away, from the very start.

enviudar [1a] *vi* to become a widow(er), be widowed; **~ de su primera mujer** to lose one's first wife; **enviudó 3 veces** she lost three husbands.

envoltijo *nm*, **envoltorio** *nm* bundle, package; *V* **envoltura**.

envoltura *nf* (*gen*) cover; (*papel*) wrapper, wrapping; (*Mec etc*) case, casing; sheath; (*Aer, Bot etc*) envelope; **~s** baby-clothes.

envolvedero *nm*, **envolvedor** *nm* cover; wrapper, wrapping; envelope.

envolvente *adj* (**a**) (*que rodea*) surrounding; (*Mil*) *movimiento* encircling, enveloping; **asiento ~** bucket seat. (**b**) (*fig*) comprehensive. (**c**) (*Carib, Cono Sur*) fascinating, intriguing.

envolver [2h; *ptp* **envuelto**] **1** *vt* (**a**) (*con papel etc*) to wrap (up), pack (up), tie up, do up; (*con ropa*) to wrap, swathe, cover; to envelop, enfold; to muffle (up); **envuelto en una capa** wrapped in a cloak, muffled up in a cloak; **dos paquetes envueltos en papel** two parcels wrapped in paper; **¿quiere que se lo envuelva?** shall I wrap it (up) for you?

(**b**) (*Mil*) to encircle, surround.

(**c**) (*fig*) to imply, involve; *persona* to involve, implicate (*en* in); **son elogios que envuelven una censura** it is praise which implies blame.

2 envolverse *vr* (**a**) to wrap o.s. up (*en* in).

(**b**) (*fig*) to become involved (*en* in).

envolvimiento *nm* (**a**) wrapping; envelopment. (**b**) (*Mil*) encirclement. (**c**) (*fig*) involvement.

enyerbar [1a] **1** *vt* (*And, Cono Sur, Méx*: *hechizar*) to bewitch.

2 enyerbarse *vr* (**a**) (*LAm*: *campo etc*) to get covered with grass.

(**b**) (*Carib*: *trato*) to fail.

(**c**) (*CAm, Méx*: *envenenarse*) to poison o.s.

(**d**) (*Méx*: *enamorarse*) to fall madly in love.

(**e**) (*Carib**: *complicarse*) to get complicated.

enyesado *nm*, **enyesadura** *nf* plastering; (*Med*) plaster cast.

enyesar [1a] *vt* (**a**) to plaster. (**b**) (*Med*) to put in a plaster cast.
enyeyado* *adj* (*Carib*) gloomy, depressed.
enyugar [1h] *vt* to yoke.
enyuntar [1a] *vt* (*LAm*) to put together, join.
enzacatarse [1a] *vr* (*CAm, Méx*) to get covered with grass.
enzarzar [1f] **1** *vt* (*fig*) to involve (in a dispute), entangle, embroil.
2 enzarzarse *vr* to get involved in a dispute; to get o.s. into trouble; ~ **a golpes** to come to blows; ~ **en una discusión** to get involved in an argument.
enzima *nf* enzyme.
enzocar [1g] *vt* (*Cono Sur*) to insert, put in, fit in.
-eo *V* **Aspects of Word Formation in Spanish 2.**
EOI *nf abr de* **Escuela Oficial de Idiomas.**
eólico *adj* wind (*atr*); **energía eólica** wind power.
eón *nm* aeon.
epa*, épale* *interj* (*LAm*) hey!; wow!*
epatante* *adj* amazing, astonishing; startling, dazzling.
epatar* [1a] *vt* (*asombrar*) to amaze, astonish; (*deslumbrar*) to startle, dazzle.
epazote *nm* (*Méx*) herb tea.
E.P.D. *abr de* **en paz descanse** may he rest in peace, R.I.P.
epi... *pref* epi...
épica *nf* epic.
epiceno *adj* (*Ling*) epicene.
epicentro *nm* epicentre.
épico *adj* epic.
epicúreo, -a *adj, nm/f* epicurean.
epicureísmo *nm*, **epicurismo** *nm* epicureanism.
epidemia *nf* epidemic.
epidémico *adj* epidemic.
epidérmico *adj* skin (*atr*); (*fig*) superficial, skin-deep.
epidermis *nf* epidermis.
Epifanía *nf* Epiphany.
epiglotis *nf* epiglottis.
epígrafe *nm* epigraph; (*inscripción*) inscription; (*encabezamiento*) title, headline; (*pie*) caption; (*lema*) motto.
epigrafía *nf* epigraphy.
epigrama *nm* epigram.
epigramático *adj* epigrammatic(al).
epilepsia *nf* epilepsy.
epiléptico, -a *adj, nm/f* epileptic.
epilogar [1h] *vt* to sum up; to round off, provide a conclusion to.
epílogo *nm* epilogue.
episcopado *nm* (**a**) (*oficio*) bishopric. (**b**) (*período*) episcopate. (**c**) (*obispos*) bishops (*collectively*), episcopacy.
episcopal *adj* episcopal.
episcopalista *adj, nmf* Episcopalian.
episódico *adj* episodic.
episodio *nm* episode; incident; (*entrega etc*) episode, instalment, part.
epistemología *nf* epistemology.
epístola *nf* epistle.
epistolar *adj* epistolary.
epistolario *nm* collected letters.
epitafio *nm* epitaph.
epíteto *nm* epithet.
epitomar [1a] *vt* to condense, abridge; to summarize.
epítome *nm* epitome, summary, abstract, résumé; compendium.
época *nf* (**a**) (*gen*) period, time; age, epoch; spell; **la ~ de Carlos III** the age of Charles III; **en la ~ de Carlos III** in Charles III's time; **en aquella ~** at that time, in that period; ~ **dorada** golden age; ~ **glacial** ice-age; ~ **de la serpiente de mar** (*hum*) silly season; **muebles de ~** period furniture; **coche de ~** vintage car; **drama de ~** costume drama; **un Picasso de primera ~** an early (period) Picasso; **la ~ azul del pintor** the painter's blue period; **con decoraciones de ~** with period set; **anticiparse** (*o* **adelantarse**) **a su ~** to be ahead of one's time; **formar ~, hacer ~** to be epoch-making, be a landmark; **el invento hace ~** it's an epoch-making discovery; **eso hizo ~ en nuestra historia** that was a landmark in our history; **todos tenemos ~s así** we all go through spells like that.
(**b**) (*del año*) season; time; ~ **del año** season of the year, time of year; ~ **de celo** mating season; ~ **de lluvias** rainy season; ~ **monzónica** monsoon season; ~ **de (la) sequía** dry season.
epopeya *nf* epic (*t fig*).
equi... *pref* equi...
equidad *nf* equity; justice, fairness, impartiality; (*de precio etc*) reasonableness.
equidistante *adj* equidistant.
equilátero *adj* equilateral.
equilibradamente *adv* in a balanced way.
equilibrado 1 *adj* balanced. **2** *nm*: ~ **de ruedas** wheel-balancing.
equilibrar [1a] **1** *vt* (**a**) to balance; to poise. (**b**) (*fig*) to balance; to adjust, redress; *presupuesto* to balance.
2 equilibrarse *vr* to balance (o.s.; *en* on).
equilibrio *nm* (**a**) balance, equilibrium; **perder el ~** to lose one's balance. (**b**) (*fig*) balance; (*social etc*) poise; ~ **de fuerzas,** ~ **de poderes,** ~ **político** balance of power; ~ **del terror** balance of terror.
equilibrista *nmf* (**a**) tightrope walker; acrobat. (**b**) (*LAm*) politician of shifting allegiance.
equino 1 *adj* equine, horse (*atr*). **2** *nm* (**a**) (*caballo*) horse; (**carne** *f* **de**) ~ horsemeat. (**b**) (*de mar*) sea urchin.
equinoccial *adj* equinoctial.
equinoccio *nm* equinox; ~ **otoñal** autumnal equinox; ~ **vernal** vernal equinox.
equipaje *nm* (**a**) (*el* ~) luggage, baggage (*US*); (*un* ~) piece of luggage, piece of baggage (*US*); (*avíos*) equipment, outfit, kit; ~ **de mano** hand-luggage; **facturar el ~** to register one's luggage; **hacer el ~** to pack, do the packing.
(**b**) (*Náut*) crew.
equipal *nm* (*Méx*) leather chair.
equipamiento *nm* equipment.
equipar [1a] *vt* to equip, furnish, fit up (*con, de* with); (*Náut*) to fit out.
equiparable *adj* comparable (*con* to, with); applicable (*con* to).
equiparación *nf* comparison.
equiparar [1a] **1** *vt* (*igualar*) to put on the same level, consider equal; (*comparar*) to compare (*con* with).
2 equipararse *vr*: ~ **con** to be on a level with, rank equally with.
equipazo* *nm* crack team.
equipo *nm* (**a**) (*conjunto de cosas*) equipment; outfit, kit; (*avíos*) gear, tackle; (*industrial*) plant; (*de turbinas etc*) set; **el ~ de la fábrica está bastante anticuado** the factory plant is pretty antiquated; ~ **de alpinismo** climbing kit; ~ **de boda** wedding outfit; ~ **de caza** hunting gear; ~ **cinematográfico móvil** mobile film unit; ~ **de conversión** conversion kit; ~ **físico** hardware; ~ **de fumador** smoker's outfit, smoker's accessories; ~ **lógico** software; ~ **luminoso** lighting; ~ **de novia** trousseau; ~ **de oficina** office furniture; ~ **de primeros auxilios** first-aid kit; ~ **de reparaciones** repair kit; ~ **rodante** rolling stock; ~ **de sonido** sound system; public-address system.
(**b**) (*personas*) team; gang; (*tanda*) shift; ~ **de cámara** camera crew; ~ **de desactivación de explosivos** bomb-disposal unit; ~ **de día** day shift; ~ **médico** medical team, medical unit; ~ **de rescate,** ~ **de socorro** rescue team.
(**c**) (*Dep*) team; side; ~ **de casa** home team; ~ **de fuera** away team; ~ **de fútbol** football team; ~ **de relevos** relay team; ~ **titular** first team, A team; ~ **visitante** visiting team; **los ~s formaron así ...** the teams lined up as follows ...
equis *nf* (**a**) the (name of the) letter *x*; **pongamos que cuesta ~ dólares** let us suppose it costs X dollars; **averiguar la ~** to find the value of X; **tenía que hacer ~ cosas*** I had to do any amount of things.
(**b**) (*And, CAm**) **estar en la ~** (*flaco*) to be all skin and bones; (*sin dinero*) to be broke*.
equitación *nf* (**a**) (*acto*) riding; **escuela de ~** riding school. (**b**) (*arte*) horsemanship.
equitativamente *adv* equitably, fairly; reasonably.
equitativo *adj* equitable, fair; reasonable; **trato ~** fair deal, square deal.
equivalencia *nf* equivalence.
equivalente 1 *adj* equivalent (*a* to). **2** *nm* equivalent.
equivaler [2q] *vi* to be equivalent, be equal; ~ **a** to be equivalent to, be equal to; to rank as, rank with, be on a level with.
equivocación *nf* (*error*) mistake, error; (*olvido*) oversight; (*malentendido*) misunderstanding; **por ~** by mistake, in error; mistakenly; **ha sido por ~** it was a mistake.
equivocado *adj* wrong, mistaken; *afecto, confianza etc* misplaced; **estás ~** you are mistaken.
equivocar [1g] **1** *vt* to mistake; ~ **A con B** to mistake A for B; ~ **el camino** to take the wrong road, go the wrong way; ~ **el golpe,** ~ **el tiro** to miss.
2 equivocarse *vr* to be wrong, be mistaken; to make a mistake; **pero se equivocó** but he was wrong; **A puede ~ con B** A can be mistaken for B; ~ **de casa** to go to the

wrong house; ~ **de camino** to take the wrong road; ~ **en una elección** to make a wrong choice, choose wrongly.
equívoco 1 *adj* (**a**) equivocal, ambiguous. (**b**) (*LAm*) mistaken. **2** *nm* (**a**) (*ambigüedad*) equivocation, ambiguity; quibble. (**b**) (*juego de palabras*) pun, wordplay, play on words; (*doble sentido*) double meaning. (**c**) (*LAm*) mistake.
equivoquista *nmf* quibbler; punster.
era[1] *etc V* **ser**.
era[2] *nf* era, age; ~ **atómica** atomic age; ~ **cristiana**, ~ **de Cristo** Christian era; ~ **espacial** space age; ~ **española**, ~ **hispánica** Spanish Era (*from 38 B.C.*); ~ **glacial** ice-age.
era[3] *nf* (*Agr*) threshing floor; (*Hort*) bed, plot, patch.
erario *nm* exchequer, treasury; public funds, public finance.
-eras *V* **Aspects of Word Formation in Spanish 2**.
erasmismo *nm* Erasmism.
erasmista *adj, nmf* Erasmist.
Erasmo *nm* Erasmus.
erección *nf* (*acto*) erection, raising; (*fig*) establishment, foundation; (*Anat*) erection.
ereccionarse [1a] *vr* to become erect.
eremita *nm* hermit; recluse.
eremitismo *nm* living like a hermit, hermit's way of life.
ergio *nm* erg.
ergonomía *nf* ergonomics.
ergonómico *adj* ergonomic.
erguido *adj* (**a**) erect, straight. (**b**) (*fig*) proud.
erguir [3m] **1** *vt* (**a**) (*alzar*) to raise, lift; ~ **la cabeza** (*fig*) to hold one's head high.
(**b**) (*enderezar*) to straighten.
2 erguirse *vr* (**a**) to straighten up, stand up straight, sit up straight.
(**b**) (*fig*) to swell with pride.
-ería *V* **Aspects of Word Formation in Spanish 2**.
erial 1 *adj* uncultivated, untilled. **2** *nm* uncultivated land; piece of waste ground.
erigir [3c] **1** *vt* (**a**) to erect, raise, build.
(**b**) (*fig*) to establish, found.
(**c**) ~ **a uno en algo** to set sb up as sth.
2 erigirse *vr*: ~ **en algo** to set o.s. up as sth.
erisipela *nf* erysipelas.
erizado *adj* (**a**) bristly; ~ **de espinas** covered with thorns, with prickles all over. (**b**) ~ **de problemas** bristling with problems.
erizar [1f] **1** *vt* (**a**) **el gato erizó el pelo** the cat bristled, the cat's hair stood on end. (**b**) *asunto* to complicate, surround with difficulties. **2 erizarse** *vr* (*pelo*) to bristle, stand on end.
erizo *nm* (**a**) (*Zool*) hedgehog; ~ **de mar**, ~ **marino** sea urchin. (**b**) (*Bot*) burr; prickly husk. (**c**) (*) surly individual, grumpy sort*; prickly person.
ermita *nf* hermitage.
ermitaño *nm* (**a**) hermit. (**b**) (*Zool*) hermit crab.
Ernesto *nm* Ernest.
-ero *V* **Aspects of Word Formation in Spanish 2**.
erogación *nf* (**a**) distribution. (**b**) (*Cono Sur, Méx*: *gastos*) expenditure; outlay; (*And, Carib*: *contribución*) contribution.
erogar [1h] *vt* (**a**) *bienes* to distribute. (**b**) (*Cono Sur*) to pay; *deuda* to settle; (*And, Cono Sur*: *contribuir*) to contribute; (*Méx*: *gastar*) to spend, lay out.
erógeno *adj* erogenous.
Eros *nm* Eros.
erosión *nf* (*Geol etc*) erosion; (*Med*) graze; **causar** ~ **en** to erode.
erosionable *adj* subject to erosion; **un suelo fácilmente** ~ a soil which is easily eroded.
erosionante *adj* erosive.
erosionar [1a] **1** *vt* to erode. **2 erosionarse** *vr* to erode, be eroded.
erosivo *adj* erosive.
erótico *adj* erotic; *poesía etc* love (*atr*); **el género** ~ the genre of love poetry.
erotismo *nm* eroticism.
erotizar [1a] **1** *vt* to eroticize; to stimulate. **2 erotizarse** *vr* to be (sexually) stimulated.
erotomanía *nf* (pathological) eroticism.
erotómano *adj* (pathologically) erotic.
errabundear [1a] *vi* to wander, rove.
errabundeo *nm* wanderings.
errabundo *adj* wandering, roving.
erradamente *adj* mistakenly.
erradicación *nf* eradication.
erradicar [1g] *vt* to eradicate.
erradizo *adj* wandering, roving.
errado *adj* mistaken, wrong; wide of the mark; unwise.
errante *adj* (**a**) wandering, roving; itinerant; nomadic; *animal* lost, stray. (**b**) (*fig*) errant; **el marido** ~ the errant husband.
errar [1k] **1** *vt tiro* to miss with, aim badly; *blanco* to miss; *vocación etc* to miss, mistake; ~ **el camino** to lose one's way.
2 *vi* (**a**) (*vagar*) to wander, rove; to roam about.
(**b**) = *vr*.
3 errarse *vr* (*equivocarse*) to err, go astray, be mistaken; ~ **es humano, de los hombres es** ~ to err is human.
errata *nf* misprint, erratum, printer's error; **es** ~ **por 'poder'** it's a misprint for 'poder'.
errático *adj* erratic.
erratismo *nm* wandering tendencies, tendency to wander; erratic movement.
erre *nf* the (name of the) letter *r*, *rr*; ~ **que** ~ stubbornly, pigheadedly.
erróneamente *adv* mistakenly, erroneously; falsely.
erróneo *adj* mistaken, erroneous; false, untrue.
error *nm* (*gen*) error, mistake; (*defecto*) fault; (*de teoría etc*) fallacy; (*Inform*) bug; ~ **de copia** clerical error; ~ **de escritura** (*Inform*) write error; ~ **freudiano** Freudian slip; ~ **de imprenta**, ~ **tipográfico** misprint, printer's error; ~ **judicial** miscarriage of justice; ~ **de lectura** (*Inform*) read error; ~ **de máquina** typing error; ~ **de pluma** clerical error; **por** ~ by mistake, in error; **caer en un** ~ to fall into error; **salvo** ~ **u omisión** errors and omissions excepted.
ERT (**a**) *nmpl* (*Esp*) *abr de* **Explosivos Río Tinto**. (**b**) *nm* (*Argentina*) *abr de* **Ente de Radiotelevisión**.
ertzaina [er'tʃaina] **1** *nmf* member of the Basque police force, policeman, policewoman. **2** *nf*: **E**~ Basque police force.
Ertzaintza [er'tʃaintʃa] *nf* Basque police force.
eructación *nf* belch.
eructar [1a] *vi* to belch.
eructo *nm* belch.
erudición *nf* erudition, learning, scholarship.
eruditamente *adv* learnedly.
erudito 1 *adj* erudite, learned, scholarly.
2 *nm*, **erudita** *nf* scholar; savant; learned person; **los** ~**s en esta materia** those who are expert in this subject, those who really know about this subject; ~ **a la violeta** pundit, pseudo-intellectual, soi-disant expert.
erupción *nf* (**a**) (*Geol*) eruption; ~ **solar** solar flare; **estar en** ~ to be erupting; **entrar en** ~ to (begin to) erupt.
(**b**) (*Med*: *t* ~ **cutánea**) rash, eruption.
(**c**) (*fig*) eruption; outbreak, explosion; outburst.
eruptivo *adj* eruptive.
esa, ésa *etc V* **ese, ése**.
Esaú *nm* Esau.
esbeltez *nf* slimness, slenderness; litheness; gracefulness.
esbelto *adj* slim, slender; lithe, willowy; graceful.
esbirro *nm* (**a**) (*ayudante*) henchman, minion; (*sicario*) killer; (*Carib*‡: *soplón*) grass‡, informer. (**b**) (*Hist*) bailiff, constable.
esbozar [1f] *vt* to sketch, outline; ~ **una sonrisa** to smile wanly, force a smile.
esbozo *nm* sketch, outline.
escabechado *nm* pickling, marinating.
escabechar [1a] *vt* (**a**) (*Culin*) to pickle, souse, marinate. (**b**) *pelo* to dye. (**c**) (‡) to do in‡, carve up*. (**d**) (*Univ**) to plough*.
escabeche *nm* (**a**) (*de escabechar*) (liquid) pickle, brine, (*salsa*) sauce of vinegar, oil, garlic etc. (**b**) (*pescado*) soused fish.
escabechina *nf* slaughter; (*fig*) destruction, slaughter; ravages; **hacer una** ~* to wreak havoc.
escabel *nm* low stool, footstool.
escabinado *nm* jury of lay people and judges.
escabiosa *nf* scabious.
escabioso *adj* scabby; mangy.
escabro *nm* (*Vet*) sheep scab, scabs; (*Bot*) scab.
escabrosamente *adv* (*fig*) riskily, salaciously.
escabrosidad *nf* (*V adj*) (**a**) roughness, ruggedness; unevenness. (**b**) harshness. (**c**) toughness, difficulty. (**d**) riskiness, salaciousness.
escabroso *adj* (**a**) *terreno* rough, rugged; *superficie* uneven. (**b**) (*fig*) *sonido etc* harsh. (**c**) *problema etc* tough, difficult, thorny. (**d**) *chiste etc* risky, risqué, blue.
escabuche *nm* weeding hoe.
escabullarse [1a] *vr* (*LAm*), **escabullirse** [3h] *vr* to slip

away, slip off, clear out; to make o.s. scarce; ~ **por** to slip through.
escachalandrado* *adj* (*And, CAm*) slovenly.
escachifollarse* [1a] *vr* to break, smash, come to bits.
escafandra *nf* diving suit; ~ **autónoma** scuba suit; ~ **espacial** spacesuit.
escafandrismo *nm* underwater fishing; deep-sea diving.
escafandrista *nmf* underwater fisherman; deep-sea diver.
escala *nf* (**a**) ladder; ~ **de cuerda,** ~ **de viento** (*Náut*) rope ladder.
(**b**) (*Mat, Mús y fig*) scale; (*de colores, velocidades etc*) range; ~ (**de**) **Beaufort** Beaufort scale; ~ **móvil** sliding scale; (*salarial*) index-linked automatic wage review; ~ **de la popularidad** popularity chart, (*Mús*) hit parade; ~ (**de**) **Richter** Richter scale; ~ **de sueldos** salary scale; **modelo a** ~ scale model; **el dibujo no está a** ~ the drawing is not to scale; **a** (*o* **en**) **pequeña** ~ on a small scale; **a** (*o* **en**) ~ **nacional** on a national scale; **una investigación a** ~ **nacional** a nation-wide inquiry, a countrywide investigation; **en gran(de)** ~ on a large scale, in a big way; **un plan en gran** ~ a large-scale plan; **reproducir según** ~ to reproduce to scale.
(**c**) (*parada*) stopping place; (*Náut*) port of call; intermediate stop, stopover; ~ **técnica** (*Aer*) refuelling stop; **vuelo sin** ~**s** non-stop flight; **hacer** ~ **en** to stop at, make an intermediate stop at, (*Náut*) to call at, put in at.
escalada *nf* (**a**) (*Alpinismo etc*) climb; climbing, scaling; ~ **en rocas** rock-climbing. (**b**) (*Mil, Pol*) escalation; boom, increase.
escalador(a) *nm/f* (**a**) (*alpinista*) climber; mountaineer; ~ **en rocas** rock climber. (**b**) (*ladrón*) burglar, housebreaker.
escalafón *nm* (**a**) (*de personas*) roll, list, register; (*plantilla*) list of officials, establishment; (*de promoción*) promotion ladder; **seguir el** ~ to work one's way up.
(**b**) (*de sueldos*) salary scale, wage scale.
(**c**) (*fig*) table, chart; **en esta industria España ocupa el tercer lugar en el** ~ **mundial** Spain occupies third place in the world table for this industry.
escalamiento *nm* (**a**) = **escalada.** (**b**) (*Méx Jur*) burglary, housebreaking.
escálamo *nm* thole, tholepin.
escalante *adj* escalating; **la crisis** ~ the escalating crisis.
escalar [1a] **1** *vt* (**a**) *montaña etc* to climb, scale; ~ **puestos** (*fig*) to move up.
(**b**) *casa* to burgle, burglarize (*US*), break into, force an entry into.
(**c**) (*Inform: reducir*) to scale down; (*aumentar*) to scale up.
2 *vi* (**a**) to climb; (*fig*) to climb the social ladder, rise, get on.
(**b**) (*Náut*) to call, put in (*en* at).
(**c**) (*Mil, Pol*) to escalate.
Escalda *nm* Scheldt.
escaldado *adj* (**a**) wary, fly, cautious. (**b**) *mujer* loose.
escaldadura *nf* (**a**) scald, scalding. (**b**) chafing.
escaldar [1a] **1** *vt* (**a**) (*quemar*) to scald. (**b**) (*rozar*) to chafe, rub. (**c**) *metal* to make red-hot. **2 escaldarse** *vr* (**a**) to get scalded, scald o.s. (**b**) to chafe.
escalera *nf* (**a**) (*de casa*) stairs, staircase, stairway; (*escala*) ladder; (*escalinata*) steps, flight of steps; (*de camión, carro*) tailboard; ~ **de caracol** spiral staircase, winding staircase; ~ **de cuerda,** ~ **de nudos** rope ladder; ~ **doble,** ~ **de mano,** ~ **de pintor,** ~ **de tijera** steps, stepladder; ~ **de incendios** fire-escape; ~ **mecánica,** ~ **móvil,** ~ **rodante** escalator, moving staircase; ~ **de servicio** service stairs, backstairs.
(**b**) (*Naipes*) run, sequence.
escalerilla *nf* small ladder; low step; (*Náut*) gangway, companionway; (*Aer*) steps.
escalfador *nm* chafing dish.
escalfar [1a] *vt* (**a**) *huevo* to poach. (**b**) (*Méx: desfalcar*) to embezzle.
escalilla *nf* (**a**) (*Téc*) calibrated scale. (**b**) (*de ascenso*) promotion ladder.
escalinata *nf* steps, flight of steps; outside staircase.
escalofriado *adj*: **estar** ~ to feel chilly, feel shivery, feel hot-and-cold.
escalofriante *adj* bloodcurdling, hair-raising; chilling, frightening.
escalofriarse [1c] *vr* (**a**) to feel chilly, get the shivers, feel hot-and-cold by turns. (**b**) to shiver with fright, get a cold shiver of fright.
escalofrío *nm* (**a**) (*Med*) chill, feverish chill. (**b**) ~**s** (*fig*) shivers; shivery fright.
escalón *nm* (**a**) (*peldaño*) step, stair; (*de escalera de mano*) rung; tread; (*de cohete*) stage; ~ **de hielo** ice step.
(**b**) (*fig*) stage, grade; (*hacia el éxito etc*) ladder; rung, stepping stone.
(**c**) (*Mil*) echelon.
escalonadamente *adv* step by step, in a series of steps.
escalonar [1a] *vt* to spread out at intervals; (*Mil etc*) to echelon; *tierra* to terrace, cut in a series of steps; *horas, producción etc* to stagger; (*Med*) *dosis* to regulate; *novedad* to phase in.
escalope *nm* escalope; ~ **de ternera** escalope of veal.
escalopín *nm* fillet.
escalpar [1a] *vt* to scalp.
escalpelo *nm* scalpel.
escama *nf* (**a**) (*Bot, Pez etc*) scale; (*de jabón etc*) flake; (*de pintura*) flake; ~**s de jabón, jabón en** ~**s** soapflakes. (**b**) (*fig*) resentment, grudge; suspicion. (**c**) (*Méx**) cocaine.
escamado *adj* (**a**) wary, cautious. (**b**) (*Cono Sur: harto*) wearied, cloyed.
escamar [1a] **1** *vt* (**a**) to scale, remove the scales from.
(**b**) (*fig*) to make wary, create distrust in, shake the confidence of; **eso me escama** that makes me suspicious, that sounds ominous to me.
2 escamarse *vr* (**a**) to scale (off), flake off.
(**b**) (*fig*) to get wary, become suspicious; to smell a rat; **y luego se escamó** and after that he was on his guard.
escamocha* *nf* (*Méx*) left-overs.
escamón *adj* wary, distrustful; apprehensive.
escamondar [1a] *vt* to prune; (*fig*) to prune, trim.
escamoso *adj pez* scaly; *sustancia* flaky.
escamoteable *adj* retractable.
escamoteador(a) *nm/f* (**a**) conjurer, juggler. (**b**) (*pey*) swindler.
escamotear [1a] *vt* (**a**) (*hacer desaparecer*) to whisk away, whisk out of sight, snatch away, make vanish; *naipe* to palm; (*Téc*) to retract.
(**b**) (*) to lift*.
(**c**) (*fig*) *dificultad etc* to shirk, disregard.
escamoteo *nm* (**a**) (*destreza*) sleight of hand; (*ilusionismo*) conjuring; (*de naipe*) palming.
(**b**) (*un* ~) conjuring trick.
(**c**) (*) lifting*; swindling; (*un* ~) swindle.
(**d**) shirking.
escampar [1a] **1** *vt* to clear out.
2 *vi* (**a**) (*cielo*) to clear; (*lluvia*) to stop; (*tiempo*) to clear up, stop raining.
(**b**) (*Carib, Méx: de la lluvia*) to shelter from the rain.
(**c**) (*LAm**) to clear off*.
escampavía *nf* revenue cutter.
escanciador *nm* wine waiter; (*Hist*) cupbearer.
escanciar [1b] **1** *vt* (*liter*) *vino* to pour (out), serve; *vaso* to drain. **2** *vi* to drink a lot of wine, make merry on wine.
escandalizante *adj* scandalous, shocking.
escandalizar [1f] **1** *vt* to scandalize, shock.
2 *vi* to make a fuss, kick up a row.
3 escandalizarse *vr* to be shocked (*de* at, by), be scandalized; to be offended (*de* at, by); **se escandalizó ante la pintura** he threw up his hands in horror at the picture.
escándalo *nm* (**a**) (*gen*) scandal; outrage; **un resultado de** ~ a scandalous result, (*fig*) a great result, an outstanding result; **¡qué** ~**!** what a scandal!
(**b**) (*alboroto*) row, uproar, commotion, fuss; **armar un** ~ to make a scene, cause an uproar.
(**c**) (*asombro*) sense of shock; astonishment; **llamar a** ~ to cause astonishment, be a shock.
escandalosa *nf* (**a**) (*Náut*) topsail. (**b**) (*And: tulipán*) tulip. (**c**) **echar la** ~ to fly off the handle, curse and swear.
escandalosamente *adv* scandalously, shockingly, outrageously; flagrantly; licentiously.
escandaloso *adj* (*gen*) scandalous, shocking, outrageous; *crimen etc* flagrant; *vida* scandalous; disorderly, licentious; *risa* uproarious, hearty; *niño* noisy; uncontrollable, undisciplined; *color* (*And*) loud.
escandallo *nm* (**a**) (*Náut*) lead. (**b**) (*Com: etiqueta*) price tag; (*acto*) pricing. (**c**) (*Com: prueba*) sampling.
Escandinavia *nf* Scandinavia.
escandinavo, -a *adj, nm/f* Scandinavian.
escandir [3a] *vt versos* to scan.
escáner *nm* (*Inform, Med*) scanner.
escansión *nf* scansion.
escantillón *nm* pattern, template.
escaño *nm* bench; settle; (*Parl*) seat.
escapada *nf* (**a**) (*huida*) escape, flight; **en una** ~ in a jiffy;

haré la comida en una ~ I'll get the meal right away; **¿puedes comprarme tabaco en una ~?** can you slip out and get me some cigarettes?

(**b**) (*Dep*) breakaway.

(**c**) (*viaje*) flying visit, quick trip; **hice una ~ a la capital** I made a flying visit to the capital.

(**d**) (*pey*) escapade.

escapado *adj, adv* at top speed, in a rush; **irse** ~ to rush off, be off like a shot; **se volvió** ~ he rushed back; **tengo que volverme ~ a la tienda** I must get back double-quick to the shop; **lo harán ~s** they'll do it like a shot.

escapar [1a] **1** *vt caballo* to ride hard, drive hard.

2 *vi* (**a**) to escape, flee, run away; **~ a uno** to escape from sb; **~ de la cárcel** to escape from prison; **escapó de mis manos** it escaped from my hands, it eluded my grasp.

(**b**) (*Dep*) to break away.

(**c**) **no escapa a los estudiantes que tienen que aplicarse más** the students are well aware that they need to buckle down more.

3 escaparse *vr* (**a**) (*persona*) to escape, flee, run away, get away; **~ con algo** to make off with sth; **~ de morir** to miss death narrowly; **~ por un pelo, ~ en una tabla** to have a narrow escape, have a close shave.

(**b**) (*gas etc*) to leak, leak out, escape.

(**c**) (*detalle, noticia etc*) **se me escapa** it eludes me, it escapes me; **se me escapa su nombre** his name escapes me; **se le escapó la fecha de la reunión** he let the date of the meeting slip out, he unintentionally revealed the date of the meeting; **ese detalle se me había escapado** that detail had escaped my notice; **no se me escapa que ...** I am perfectly aware that ...

escaparate *nm* (**a**) (*de tienda*) shop window; (*vitrina*) showcase, display case; (*fig*) showcase; **ir de ~s, mirar ~s** to go window-shopping. (**b**) (*LAm*: *armario*) wardrobe. (**c**) (‡) tits‡, bosom.

escaparatismo *nm* window-dressing.

escaparatista *nmf* window dresser.

escapatoria *nf* (**a**) escape, flight; getaway; (*) secret trip; **~ del trabajo** escape from work. (**b**) (*fig*) let-out, way out, loophole; excuse, pretext.

escape *nm* (**a**) (*huida*) escape, flight, getaway; **a ~** at full speed; in a great hurry; **salir a ~** to rush out.

(**b**) (*de gas etc*) leak, leakage, escape.

(**c**) (*Téc*) exhaust; **gases de ~** exhaust (fumes); **tubo de ~** exhaust (pipe).

(**d**) (*Mec*) escapement.

escapismo *nm* escapism.

escapista *adj, nmf* escapist.

escápula *nf* scapula, shoulder blade.

escapulario *nm* scapular(y).

escaque *nm* (*de tablero*) square; **~s** (*Hist*) chess.

escaqueado *adj* checked, chequered.

escaquearse* [1a] *vr* (*rajarse*) to duck out; (*gandulear*) to shirk, skive‡; (*negar la responsabilidad*) to pass the buck*; (*irse*) to slope off*.

escara *nf* (*Med*) crust, slough.

escarabajas *nfpl* firewood, kindling.

escarabajear [1a] **1** *vt* (*) to bother, worry. **2** *vi* (**a**) (*arrastrarse*) to crawl; (*agitarse*) to wriggle, squirm. (**b**) (*garabatear*) to scrawl, scribble.

escarabajo *nm* (**a**) (*Ent*) beetle; **~ de Colorado, ~ de la patata** Colorado beetle. (**b**) (*Téc*) flaw. (**c**) (*: *persona*) dwarf, runt. (**d**) **~s** (*: *garabatos*) scrawl, scribble. (**e**) (*Aut*) Beetle.

escaramujo *nm* (**a**) (*Bot*) wild rose, dog rose, briar; (*fruto*) hip. (**b**) (*Zool*) goose barnacle. (**c**) (*Carib*: *mal de ojo*) spell, curse.

escaramuza *nf* (**a**) (*Mil*) skirmish, brush. (**b**) (*fig*) brush; squabble.

escaramuzar [1f] *vi* to skirmish.

escarapela nf (**a**) cockade, rosette. (**b**) (*) brawl, shindy*.

escarapelar [1a] **1** *vt* (**a**) (*LAm*: *descascarar*) to scrape off, scale off, chip off.

(**b**) (*And*: *arrugar*) to crumple, rumple, muss.

2 *vi* (**a**) (*reñir*) to wrangle, quarrel.

(**b**) = *vr*.

3 escarapelarse *vr* (**a**) (*LAm*: *descascararse*) to peel off, flake off.

(**b**) (*And, Méx*: *temblar*) to go weak at the knees, tremble all over.

escarbadientes *nm invar* toothpick.

escarbador *nm* scraper.

escarbar [1a] **1** *vt* (**a**) *tierra* to scratch; *fuego* to poke; *dientes, oreja* to pick, clean.

(**b**) (*fig*) to inquire into, investigate, delve into; (*pey*) to pry into; to rake around in (*o* among).

2 *vi* (**a**) to scratch.

(**b**) **~ en = 1** (**b**).

escarcear [1a] *vi* (*Carib, Cono Sur*) to prance.

escarcela *nf* (*Caza*) pouch, bag.

escarceos *nmpl* (**a**) (*de caballo*) nervous movement; prance; (*fig*) amateur effort.

(**b**) (*olas*) small waves.

(**c**) **~ amorosos** amorous posturings, amorous attitudinizing; love affairs.

escarcha *nf* frost, hoarfrost.

escarchado *adj* (**a**) covered in hoarfrost, frosted. (**b**) *fruta* crystallized.

escarchar [1a] **1** *vt* (**a**) to frost, cover in hoarfrost.

(**b**) (*Culin*) *tarta* to ice; *fruta* to crystallize (in liqueur).

(**c**) (*Cos*) to embroider with silver (*o* gold).

2 *vi*: **escarcha** there is a frost, it's frosty, it's freezing.

escarchilla *nf* (*And, Carib*) hail.

escarcho *nm* (red) gurnard.

escarda *nf* (**a**) (*acto*) weeding, hoeing; (*fig*) weeding out. (**b**) (*herramiento*) weeding hoe.

escardador *nm* weeding hoe.

escardadura *nf* weeding, hoeing.

escardar [1a] *vt* (**a**) to weed, weed out. (**b**) (*fig*) to weed out.

escardillo *nm* weeding hoe.

escariador *nm* reamer.

escariar [1b] *vt* to ream.

escarificación *nf* (*Agr, Med*) scarification.

escarificador *nm* scarifier.

escarificar [1g] *vt* to scarify.

escarlata 1 *adj invar* scarlet. **2** *nf* (**a**) (*color*) scarlet. (**b**) (*tela*) scarlet cloth. (**c**) (*Med*) scarlet fever.

escarlatina *nf* scarlet fever.

escarmenar [1a] *vt* (**a**) *lana* to comb. (**b**) (*fig*) to punish; **~ algo a uno*** to swindle sb out of sth.

escarmentado *adj* wary, cautious.

escarmentar [1j] **1** *vt* to punish severely, teach a lesson to.

2 *vi* to learn one's lesson; **yo escarmenté y no lo volví a hacer** I learned my lesson and never did it again; **¡para que escarmientes!** that'll teach you!; **~ en cabeza ajena** to learn by someone else's mistakes.

escarmiento *nm* (*castigo*) punishment; (*aviso*) lesson, warning, example; **para ~ de los malhechores** as a lesson to wrongdoers; **que esto te sirva de ~** let this be a lesson (*o* warning) to you.

escarnecedor 1 *adj* mocking. **2** *nm*, **escarnecedora** *nf* scoffer, mocker.

escarnecer [2d] *vt* to scoff at, mock, ridicule.

escarnio *nm* jibe, taunt; derision, ridicule.

escarola *nf* (**a**) (*Bot*) endive. (**b**) (*Méx Cos*) ruff, flounce.

escarolar [1a] *vt* (*Cos*) to frill, flounce; to curl.

escarpa *nf* (**a**) slope; (*Geog, Mil*) scarp, escarpment. (**b**) (*Méx*) pavement.

escarpado *adj* steep, sheer; craggy.

escarpadura *nf* = **escarpa** (**a**).

escarpar [1a] *vt* (**a**) (*Geog etc*) to escarp. (**b**) (*Téc*) to rasp.

escarpia *nf* spike; meat hook; (*Téc*) tenterhook.

escarpín *nm* (*zapatilla*) pump, slipper; (*calcetín*) extra sock, outer sock; (*de niña*) ankle sock.

escarrancharse* [1a] *vr* to do the splits.

escasamente *adv* (**a**) scantily, sparingly; meagrely. (**b**) (*apenas*) scarcely, hardly, barely.

escasear [1a] **1** *vt* to be sparing with, give out in small amounts, skimp. **2** *vi* to be scarce, get scarce; to be in short supply; to fall short; to diminish.

escasez *nf* (**a**) (*falta*) scarcity, shortage, lack; (*pobreza*) poverty, want; **~ de dinero** lack of money, shortage of funds; **vivir con ~** to live in poverty. (**b**) (*tacañería*) meanness, stinginess.

escaso *adj* (**a**) (*gen*) scarce; scant, scanty; limited; slight; *ración* meagre, skimpy; *cosecha, público* thin, sparse; *posibilidad* slim, slender, small; *recursos* slender; *dinero* scarce, tight; *provisión* small, short, insufficient; *visibilidad* poor; **~ de población** thinly populated; **~ de recursos naturales** poor in natural resources; **andar ~ de dinero** to be short of money, be in need of money; **estar ~ de víveres** to be short of food supplies; **con escasa compasión** with scant pity; **su inteligencia es escasa** his intelligence is slight, his intelligence is limited.

(**b**) (*muy justo*) bare; **hay 2 toneladas escasas** there are barely 2 tons; **tiene 15 años ~s** he's barely 15, he's hardly 15; **ganar por una cabeza escasa** to win by a short head.

(**c**) (*tacaño*) mean, stingy; sparing.

escatimar [1a] *vt* (*reducir*) to curtail, cut down; (*dar poco de*) to give grudgingly, skimp, stint; to be sparing of; **no ~ esfuerzo para** + *infin* to spare no effort to + *infin*; **no escatimaba sus alabanzas de ...** he was unstinting in his praise of ..., he did not stint his praise of ...

escatimoso *adj* (**a**) (*tacaño*) sparing, scrimpy, mean. (**b**) (*taimado*) sly.

escatología¹ *nf* (*Rel*) eschatology.

escatología² *nf* scatology.

escatológico¹ *adj* (*Rel*) eschatological.

escatológico² *adj* scatological.

escay *nm* imitation leather.

escayola *nf* (*Med etc*) plaster.

escayolado *nm* plastering.

escayolar [1a] *vt* to put in plaster; **con la pierna escayolada** with his leg in plaster; **tener el cuello escayolado** to have one's neck in plaster.

escena *nf* (**a**) (*gen*) scene; **una ~ conmovedora** a touching scene; **con ~s de la revolución** with scenes from the revolution; **~ muda** by-play; **~ retrospectiva** (*Cine*) flashback.

(**b**) (*Teat*: *escenario*) stage; **entrar en ~** to enter, come on; **poner en ~** to stage, put on, perform.

escenario *nm* (**a**) (*Teat*) stage; setting; scenery; **en el ~** on (the) stage.

(**b**) (*Cine*) scenario; continuity.

(**c**) (*fig*) scene, scenario; setting; **el ~ del crimen** the scene of the crime; **fue ~ de un motín** it was the scene of a riot; **desapareció del ~ político** he disappeared from the political scene; **la ceremonia tuvo por ~ X** the ceremony was set in X, the ceremony had X as its setting.

escénico *adj* scenic.

escenificación *nf* staging; dramatization.

escenificar [1g] *vt comedia* to stage; *novela etc* to dramatize, make a stage version of; *suceso histórico* to re-enact, reproduce.

escenografía *nf* scenography; stage design.

escenógrafo, -a *nm/f* theatrical designer, designer of sets; scene painter.

escenotecnia *nf* staging, stagecraft.

escepticismo *nm* scepticism.

escéptico 1 *adj* sceptical. **2** *nm*, **escéptica** *nf* sceptic; doubter.

Escila *nf* Scylla; **~ y Caribdis** Scylla and Charybdis.

escindible *adj* fissionable.

escindir [3a] **1** *vt* to split; **el partido está escindido** the party is split. **2 escindirse** *vr* (*partido etc*) to split (*en* into); (*facción*) to split off.

Escipión *nm* Scipio.

escisión *nf* (**a**) scission; fission; split; (*Med*) excision; **~ nuclear** nuclear fission. (**b**) (*fig*) split, divison.

escisionismo *nm* (*Pol*) tendency to split into factions.

escisionista *adj*: **tendencia ~** breakaway tendency, tendency to split (off).

esclarecedor *adj explicación* illuminating.

esclarecer [2d] **1** *vt* (**a**) to light up, illuminate. (**b**) (*fig*: *explicar*) to explain, elucidate, shed light on; *crimen* to clear up. (**c**) (*fig*: *instruir*) to enlighten. (**d**) (*fig*: *ennoblecer*) to ennoble. **2** *vi* to dawn.

esclarecido *adj* illustrious, distinguished.

esclarecimiento *nm* (**a**) illumination. (**b**) explanation, elucidation, clarification. (**c**) enlightenment. (**d**) ennoblement.

esclava *nf* (**a**) slave; (*fig*) slave, drudge; **~ blanca** white slave. (**b**) (*pulsera*) slave bangle, bracelet.

esclavatura *nf* (*LAm Hist*) (**a**) (*personas*) slaves (*collectively*). (**b**) (*período*) period of slavery. (**c**) (*esclavitud*) slavery.

esclavina *nf* short cloak, cape, tippet.

esclavismo *nm* = **esclavitud**.

esclavitud *nf* slavery, servitude, bondage.

esclavizar [1f] *vt* to enslave.

esclavo *nm* slave; **ser ~ del tabaco** to be a slave to tobacco; **vender a uno como ~** to sell sb into slavery.

esclerosis *nf* (**a**) sclerosis; **~ múltiple** multiple sclerosis. (**b**) (*fig*) fossilization, stagnation.

esclerotizado *adj* (*fig*) fossilized, stagnant.

esclusa *nf* lock, sluice; floodgate; **~ de aire** airlock.

esclusero *nm* lock keeper.

-esco *V* **Aspects of Word Formation in Spanish 2**.

escoba 1 *nf* (**a**) broom; brush; **~ mecánica** carpet-sweeper; **esto no vende una ~** this is a dead loss. (**b**) (*Bot*) broom. **2** *nm* (*Dep*) sweeper.

escobada *nf* brush, sweep.

escobar [1a] *vt* to sweep, sweep out.

escobazo *nm* (**a**) (*golpe*) blow with a broom. (**b**) (*barrido*) quick sweep; **dar un ~** to have a quick sweep-up; **echar a uno a ~s** to kick sb out.

escobilla *nf* (**a**) small broom, brush; whisk; (*Aut*) windscreen wiper; **~ de dientes** (*And*) toothbrush. (**b**) (*Aut, Elec*) brush. (**c**) (*Bot*) teasel.

escobillar [1a] **1** *vi* (*LAm*) to tap one's feet on the floor. **2** *vt* (*And*) (*cepillar*) to brush; (*restregar*) to scrub.

escobillón *nm* swab.

escobón *nm* (*escoba*) large broom, long-handled broom; (*bruza*) scrubbing brush; (*algodón etc*) swab.

escocedor *adj* painful, hurtful.

escocedura *nf* = **escozor**.

escocer [2b *y* 2h] **1** *vt* to annoy, hurt.

2 *vi* to smart, sting; to feel a burning pain; **esto escuece en la lengua, esto me escuece la lengua** it makes my tongue smart.

3 escocerse *vr* to chafe, get chafed.

escocés 1 *adj* Scotch, Scots, Scottish; *dibujo* tartan (*atr*). **2** *nm* (**a**) (*persona*) Scot, Scotsman. (**b**) (*whisky*) Scotch; **~ de malta** malt whisky. **3** *nm* (*Ling*) Scots.

escocesa *nf* Scot, Scotswoman.

Escocia *nf* Scotland.

escoda *nf* stonecutter's hammer.

escofina *nf* rasp, file.

escofinar [1a] *vt* to rasp, file.

escogedor *nm* (*Agr etc*) riddle.

escogencia *nf* (*And, Carib*) choice.

escoger [2c] *vti* to choose (*entre* between), select, pick (out); (*por voto*) to elect; **puestos a ~, ellos ...** faced with the choice, they ...

escogido *adj* (**a**) chosen, selected; (*en calidad*) choice, select; *obras* selected. (**b**) **ser muy ~** to be choosy; fussy (*para, con* about).

escogimiento *nm* choice, selection.

escolar 1 *adj* scholastic; school (*atr*); **año ~** school year. **2** *nm* schoolboy, pupil. **3** *nf* schoolgirl, pupil.

escolaridad *nf* schooling; **~ obligatoria** compulsory schooling, compulsory attendance at school; **el porcentaje de ~ es elevado** the school population is high, the proportion of those in school is high.

escolarización *nf* schooling; school attendance; enrolment in school.

escolarizar [1f] *vt* to enrol in school, send to school; to provide with schooling; **niños sin ~** children not in school, children receiving no schooling.

escolástica *nf*, **escolasticismo** *nm* scholasticism.

escolástico 1 *adj* scholastic. **2** *nm* scholastic, schoolman.

escoleta *nf* (*Méx*) (**a**) (*banda*) amateur band. (**b**) (*ensayo*) rehearsal, practice (of an amateur band). (**c**) (*lección de baile*) dancing lesson.

escolopendra *nf* (*Zool*) centipede.

escolta 1 *nf* escort; **dar ~ a** to escort, accompany. **2** *nmf* (*persona*) escort; (*guardaespaldas*) bodyguard; (*de ministro etc*) minder*.

escoltar [1a] *vt* (*gen*) to escort; (*proteger*) to guard, protect; (*acompañar*) to attend, accompany; (*Náut*) to escort, convoy.

escollar [1a] *vi* (**a**) (*And, Cono Sur Náut*) to hit a reef, strike a rock. (**b**) (*Cono Sur*: *empresa*) to fail, come unstuck.

escollera *nf* breakwater, jetty.

escollo *nm* (**a**) reef, rock. (**b**) (*fig*: *problema etc*) pitfall; (*obstáculo*) stumbling block; (*peligro oculto*) hidden danger; **los muchos ~s del inglés** the many pitfalls of English.

escombrar [1a] *vt* to clear out, clean out, clear of rubbish.

escombrera *nf* tip, dump, rubbish heap; (*Min*) slag heap.

escombro¹ *nm* (*Pez*) mackerel.

escombro² *nm* (*frec* **~s** *pl*) rubbish; debris, wreckage, rubble; (*Min*) waste, slag.

escondedero *nm* hiding place.

escondeloro *nm* (*CAm*) hide-and-seek.

esconder [2a] **1** *vt* to hide, conceal (*de* from). **2 esconderse** *vr* to hide (*de* from); to hide o.s., conceal o.s.; to be hidden; to lurk.

escondida(s) *nf(pl)* (**a**) **hacer algo a ~s** to do sth secretly, do sth by stealth; **hacer algo a ~s de uno** to do sth behind sb's back.

(**b**) (*LAm*) hide-and-seek; **jugar a (las) ~** to play hide-and-seek.

escondite *nm* (**a**) (*escondrijo*) hiding place; (*Caza, Orn*) hide. (**b**) (*juego*) hide-and-seek; **jugar al ~ con** (*fig*) to play hide-and-seek with.

escondido(s) *nm(pl)* (*LAm*) hide-and-seek.
escondrijo *nm* hiding place, hideout; (*fig*) nook.
escoñado⁑ *nm* has-been.
escoñar⁑ [1a] **1** *vt* (*dañar*) to smash up, break, shatter; (*matar*) to do in⁑; (*arruinar*) to smash, ruin, destroy. **2 escoñarse** *vr* (**a**) (*persona*) to hurt o.s.; **estoy escoñado** I'm knackered*; ~ **de risa** to laugh o.s. silly*. (**b**) (*Mec*) to break, get broken; to have a breakdown. (**c**) (*proyecto etc*) to fail.
escopeta *nf* (**a**) shotgun; ~ **de aire comprimido** airgun; ~ **de cañones recortados,** ~ **recortada** sawn-off shotgun; ~ **paralela,** ~ **de dos cañones,** ~ **de tiro doble** double-barrelled gun; ~ **de perdigones,** ~ **de postas** shotgun; ~ **de viento** airgun. (**b**) (⁑) prick⁑.
escopetazo *nm* (**a**) (*disparo*) gunshot; (*herida*) gunshot wound. (**b**) (*fig*) bad news; blow; bombshell. (**c**) **dar un** ~⁑ to have a screw⁑.
escopeteado *adj*: **salir** ~ to be off like a shot; **voy** ~ I'm in a terrible rush; **ella hablaba escopeteada** her words came in a torrent, her words came pouring out.
escopetear [1a] **1** *vt* (**a**) to shoot at (with a shotgun).
(**b**) (*Méx**) to get at, have a dig at*.
2 *vi* (*Carib*) to answer irritably.
3 escopetearse *vr*: **se escopetearon en el bosque** they shot at each other in the wood; **se escopetean a injurias** they shower one another with insults, they heap insults upon each other.
escopeteo *nm* (**a**) (*disparos*) shooting, volley of shots. (**b**) (*de injurias, cumplimientos etc*) shower, lively exchange.
escopetero *nm* gunsmith; (*Mil*) rifleman.
escoplear [1a] *vt* to chisel.
escoplo *nm* chisel.
escor *nm* (*LAm*) score.
escora *nf* (*Náut*) (**a**) (*línea*) level line, load line. (**b**) (*apoyo*) prop, shore. (**c**) (*inclinación*) list; **con una** ~ **de 30 grados** with a thirty-degree list.
escoración *nf*, **escorada** *nf* (**a**) (*Náut*) list (*a, hacia* to). (**b**) (*fig*) leaning, inclination.
escorar [1a] (*Náut*) **1** *vt* to shore up. **2** *vi* (**a**) (*Náut*) to list, heel (over); ~ **a babor** to list to port. (**b**) (*fig*) ~ **a,** ~ **hacia** to lean towards, be inclined towards.
escorbútico *adj* scorbutic.
escorbuto *nm* scurvy.
escorchar [1a] *vt* (**a**) to flay, skin. (**b**) (*Cono Sur*: *fastidiar*) to bother, annoy.
escoria *nf* (**a**) (*Metal*) slag, dross; ~ **básica** basic slag. (**b**) (*fig*) scum, dregs; **la** ~ **de la humanidad** the scum of humanity.
escorial *nm* (*industrial*) dump, slag heap, tip; (*Geol*) bed of lava, deposit of volcanic ash.
escorpena *nf*, **escorpina** *nf* scorpion fish.
escorpión *nm* scorpion; **E~** (*Zodíaco*) Scorpio.
escorrentía *nf* (*Agr*) run-off (*of chemicals etc*); (*torrente*) rush, torrent; (*derrame*) overflow; ~ **superficial** surface run-off.
escorzar [1f] *vt* to foreshorten.
escorzo *nm* foreshortening.
escota *nf* (*Náut*: *cabo*) sheet.
escotado 1 *adj vestido* low-cut, low-necked, cut low, décolleté. **2** *nm* = **escotadura.**
escotadura *nf* (**a**) (*Cos*) low neck(line). (**b**) (*Teat*) large trap door. (**c**) (*hueco*) recess; (*corte*) notch.
escotar [1a] **1** *vt* (**a**) (*Cos*) to cut out, cut to fit; to cut low in front. (**b**) *río etc* to draw water from. **2** *vi* to pay one's share.
escote *nm* (**a**) (*Cos*) low neck; décolletage; cleavage; ~ **en pico,** ~ **en V** V-neck; ~ **profundo** plunging neckline. (**b**) (*Fin*) share; **ir a** ~, **pagar a** ~ to share the expenses, go fifty-fifty, (*pareja*) to go Dutch.
escotilla *nf* (*Náut etc*) hatch, hatchway; (*fig*) floodgates; **atrancar las** ~**s** (*fig*) to batten down the hatches.
escotillón *nm* trap door.
escotch *nm* (*LAm*) sticky tape.
escozor *nm* (**a**) smart, sting; burning pain. (**b**) (*fig*) grief, heartache.
escriba *nm* scribe.
escribanía *nf* (**a**) (*mueble*) writing desk; writing case. (**b**) (*enseres*) writing materials; inkstand. (**c**) (*Jur*: *cargo*) clerkship; (*oficina*) clerk's office, (*Hist*) notary's office.
escribano *nm* (**a**) court clerk; lawyer's clerk; (*Hist*) notary; ~ **municipal** town clerk. (**b**) (*Orn*) bunting; ~ **cerillo** yellowhammer.
escribiente *nm* copyist, amanuensis; clerk.
escribir [3a; *ptp* **escrito**] **1** *vti* (**a**) to write; ~ **a mano** to write in longhand; to write out; ~ **a máquina** to type; **el que esto escribe** the present writer; (*Prensa etc*) this correspondent.
(**b**) (*ortografiar*) to spell; **'voy' se escribe con 'v'** 'voy' is spelled with a 'v'; **¿cómo se escribe eso?** how is that spelled?, how do you spell that?
2 escribirse *vr* (**a**) to write to each other.
(**b**) ~ **con** to correspond with, write to.
escrito 1 *ptp de* **escribir.**
2 *adj* (*en forma escrita*) written; (*dicho*) said, stated; **lo arriba** ~ what has been said above.
3 *nm* writing, document; text; manuscript; (*Jur*) brief; ~**s** (*Liter etc*) writings, works; **por** ~ in writing; in black and white; **acuerdo por** ~ written agreement, agreement in writing; **poner algo por** ~ to commit sth to paper; to write sth down, get sth down in writing; **tomar algo por** ~ to write sth down, take sth down in writing.
escritor(a) *nm/f* writer; ~ **de material publicitario** copywriter; ~ **satírico** satirist, satirical writer.
escritorio *nm* (**a**) (*mueble*) desk, bureau; writing case; **de** ~ (*frec*) desktop (*atr*). (**b**) (*despacho*) office.
escritorzuelo, -a *nm/f* hack (writer), scribbler.
escritura *nf* (**a**) (*acto, arte*) writing.
(**b**) (*de nación*) writing, script; alphabet; (*de persona*) writing, handwriting; **tiene malísima** ~ her writing is terrible; **no acierto a leer su** ~ I can't read his writing; ~ **aérea** skywriting; ~ **automática** automatic writing; ~ **corrida,** ~ **normal** longhand; ~ **china** Chinese writing, Chinese script; ~ **fonética** phonetic script; ~ **a máquina** typing.
(**c**) **Sagrada E~** (Holy) Scripture.
(**d**) (*Jur*) deed; document, instrument; ~ **de aprendizaje** indenture; ~ **de propiedad** title deed; ~ **de seguro** insurance certificate; ~ **de traspaso** conveyance, deed of transfer.
escriturado *adj capital etc* registered.
escriturar [1a] *vt* (**a**) (*Jur*) *documentos* to execute by deed, formalize legally; *aprendiz* to indenture. (**b**) (*Teat etc*) to book, engage, sign up.
escriturario *adj*, **escriturístico** *adj* scriptural.
escrófula *nf* scrofula.
escrofuloso *adj* scrofulous.
escroto *nm* scrotum.
escrupulizar [1f] *vt* to scruple, hesitate; **no** ~ **en** + *infin* not to scruple to + *infin.*
escrúpulo *nm* (**a**) (*duda*) scruple; doubt, hesitation; **falta de** ~**s** unscrupulousness; **sin** ~ unscrupulous; **no hizo** ~ **de** + *infin* he did not scruple to + *infin,* he did not hesitate to + *infin.*
(**b**) (*cualidad*) scrupulousness.
(**c**) (*Farm*) scruple.
escrupulosamente *adv* scrupulously; exactly, precisely.
escrupulosidad *nf* scrupulousness; exactness, preciseness.
escrupuloso *adj* scrupulous; exact, particular, precise.
escrutador 1 *adj mirada etc* searching, penetrating. **2** *nm*, **escrutadora** *nf* (*Pol*) returning officer, scrutineer; inspector of election returns; (*Parl*) teller.
escrutar [1a] *vt* (**a**) (*examinar*) to scrutinize, examine. (**b**) *votos* to count.
escrutinio *nm* (**a**) scrutiny, examination, inspection. (**b**) (*Pol*: *cuenta*) count, counting (of votes); (*votación*) voting, ballot.
escuadra *nf* (**a**) (*Téc*) carpenter's square, draughtsman's square; bracket, angle iron; ~ **de delineante** set square; **a** ~ square, at right angles; **fuera de** ~ out of true.
(**b**) (*Mil*) squad; (*Náut*) squadron; (*de coches etc*) fleet; ~ **de demolición** demolition squad; ~ **de fusilamiento** firing squad.
(**c**) (*And*: *pistola*) pistol.
(**d**) (*LAm Dep*) team.
escuadrar [1a] *vt* (*Téc*) to square.
escuadrilla *nf* (*Aer*) squadron.
escuadrón *nm* (*Aer*) squadron; (*Mil*) squadron, troop; ~ **de la muerte** death squad, murder squad; ~ **volante** flying squad.
escualidez *nf* (**a**) paleness, weakness, emaciation; skinniness, scragginess. (**b**) squalor, filth.
escuálido *adj* (**a**) (*débil*) pale, weak, emaciated; (*flaco*) skinny, scraggy. (**b**) (*sucio*) squalid, filthy.
escualo *nm* dogfish.
escucha 1 *nf* (**a**) (*acto*) listening; listening-in; (*Rad*) monitoring; ~**s telefónicas** telephone tapping; **estar a la** ~ to listen in; **estar de** ~ to spy, eavesdrop.
(**b**) (*Ecl*) chaperon.

2 *nm* (*Mil*) scout; (*Rad*) monitor (*person*); listener.
escuchar [1a] **1** *vt* to listen to; (*LAm*) to hear; *consejo etc* to listen to, heed, pay attention to; *aplausos, avisos etc* to receive. **2** *vi* to listen. **3 escucharse** *vr* to hear; **le gusta ~** he likes the sound of his own voice.
escucho *nm* (*And*) whispered secret.
escuchón *adj* (*And*) prying, inquisitive.
escudar [1a] **1** *vt* to shield; (*fig*) to shield, protect, defend. **2 escudarse** *vr* to shield o.s., protect o.s.
escudería *nf* motor-racing team.
escudero *nm* (*Hist*) squire; page.
escudete *nm* (**a**) (*Her, Hist*) escutcheon. (**b**) (*Cos*) gusset. (**c**) (*Bot*) white water lily.
escudilla *nf* bowl, basin.
escudo *nm* shield (*t fig*); **~ de armas** (*Her*) coat of arms; **~ humano** human shield; **~ térmico** heat shield.
escudriñar [1a] *vt* (*investigar*) to inquire into, investigate; (*examinar*) to examine, scan, scrutinize.
escuela *nf* (**a**) school; **~ de artes y oficios** technical school, trade school; **~ automovilista** driving school; **~ de baile** school of dancing; ballet school; **~ de cine** film school; **~ de comercio** business school, school of business studies; **~ elemental, ~ primaria, ~ de primera enseñanza** primary school; **~ de enfermería** nursing college; **~ de equitación, ~ hípica** riding school; **~ de formación profesional** polytechnic; **~ de hogar** domestic science college; **~ infantil** primary school; **~ laboral** technical school; trade school; **~ naval** naval academy; **~ nocturna** night school; **~ normal** training college, college of education; **~ de pago** fee-paying school; **~ particular, ~ privada** private school; **~ de párvulos** infant(s') school, kindergarten; **~ pública** state school; **~ unitaria** school having one teacher; **~ de verano** summer school; **abandonar la ~** to drop out of school; **estar en la ~** to be at school; **ir a la ~** to go to school; **soplarse la ~** to play truant.
(**b**) (*Arte, de pensamiento etc*) school; **la ~ catalana** the Catalan school; **gente de la vieja ~** people of the old school; **formarse en una ~ dura** to learn in a tough school.
escuelante *nmf* (**a**) (*Méx*) country schoolteacher. (**b**) (*And: alumno*) schoolboy, schoolgirl.
escuelero 1 *adj* (*LAm*) school (*atr*). **2** *nm* (*And, Carib, Cono Sur: pey: maestro*) schoolmaster. **3** *nm*, **escuelera** *nf* (*And*) (*alumno*) schoolboy, schoolgirl; (*: *estudioso*) swot*.
escuerzo *nm* (**a**) (*Zool*) toad. (**b**) (*fig*) wretched creature, runt; pitiful object, scarecrow.
escuetamente *adv* plainly; baldly, without frills.
escueto *adj* plain, unadorned, bare; bald; *mensaje etc* short, abrupt, succinct.
escuincle* *nm* (*Méx*) (*chico*) kid*; (*animal*) runt.
esculcar [1g] *vt* (*LAm*) to search.
esculpir [3a] *vt* to sculpt, sculpture; to carve, engrave; *inscripción* to cut.
esculque *nm* (*LAm*) body search.
escultismo *nm* = **escutismo.**
escultor *nm* sculptor.
escultora *nf* sculptress.
escultórico *adj* sculptural.
escultura *nf* sculpture, carving; **~ en madera** wood carving.
escultural *adj* sculptural; (*fig*) *talla etc* statuesque.
escupe* *nm* (*Prensa*) scoop.
escupidera *nf* (**a**) spittoon, cuspidor (*US*). (**b**) (*LAm: euf*) chamberpot; **pedir la ~** to get scared; to give in, give o.s. up.
escupidor *nm* (**a**) (*persona*) spitter. (**b**) (*And, Carib: recipiente*) spittoon. (**c**) (*And: estera*) round mat, doormat.
escupir [3a] *vti* (**a**) *sangre* to spit; *comida etc* to spit out; **~ a uno** to spit at sb; **~ a la cara a uno** to spit in sb's face; **~ en el suelo** to spit on the ground; **ser de medio ~*** to be as common as dirt.
(**b**) (*fig*) *palabra* to spit, spit out, fling (*a* at); *llamas etc* to spit, belch, give out; to throw off, fling off, cast aside; **~ a** to scoff at.
(**c**) (‡: *confesar*) to cough‡, sing‡.
(**d**) (‡: *pagar*) to cough up*.
escupitajo* *nm* spit.
escurana *nf* (*LAm*) darkness; (*cielo*) overcast sky, threatening sky.
escurialense *adj* of (*o* from) El Escorial.
escurreplatos *nm invar* plate rack.
escurribanda *nf* (**a**) (*Med: de vientre*) looseness, diarrhoea. (**b**) (*Med: de úlcera*) running. (**c**) (*fuga*) escape; (*fig*) loophole, way out. (**d**) (*paliza*) thrashing.
escurrideras *nfpl* (*Méx, CAm*) = **escurriduras.**
escurridero *nm* draining board, drainboard (*US*).
escurridizo *adj* (**a**) *superficie* slippery; *objeto* difficult to hold; *nudo* running; *idea* elusive; **hacerse ~** to slip away, vanish. (**b**) *carácter* slippery.
escurrido *adj* (**a**) (*delgado*) *mujer* narrow-hipped, slightly built; wearing a tight-fitting skirt. (**b**) (*And, Carib, Méx*) (*avergonzado*) abashed, ashamed; (*tímido*) shy.
escurridor *nm* (*de ropa*) wringer; **~ (de loza)** plate rack; (*Culin*) colander, strainer; (*Fot*) drying rack.
escurriduras *nfpl* (*heces*) dregs; (*gotas*) drops.
escurrir [3a] **1** *vt ropa* to wring (out); *platos, líquido* to drain; *sustancia* to press dry, squeeze dry; *V* **bulto.**
2 *vi* (**a**) (*líquido*) to drip, trickle; to ooze; (*objeto*) to slip, slide.
(**b**) (*superficie*) to be slippery.
3 escurrirse *vr* (**a**) (*líquido*) to drip, trickle; to ooze; (*objeto*) to slip, slide; **se me escurrió de entre las manos** it slipped out of my hands.
(**b**) (*platos*) to drain; (*Culin*) to drain, strain; **'se escurre bien'** (*receta*) 'drain well'.
(**c**) (*observación etc*) to slip out.
(**d**) (*persona etc*) to slip away, sneak off; to glide away.
(**e**) (*excederse*) to go too far; **se escurrió en la reprimenda** she laid it on with a very heavy hand; **se escurrió en la propina** his tip was much too generous.
(**f**) (⁑) to come⁑.
escúter *nm* (motor) scooter.
escutismo *nm* scouting (movement), boy scouts.
esdrújulo 1 *adj* having dactylic stress, accented on the antepenult.
2 *nm* word having dactylic stress, word accented on the antepenult (*p.ej.* **mísero**).
ESE *abr de* **estesudeste** east-south-east, ESE.
ese[1] *nf* (**a**) the (name of the) letter *s*. (**b**) (*pieza etc*) S-shaped part (*o* link *etc*); **hacer ~s** (*camino*) to zigzag, twist and turn; (*borracho*) to reel about, stagger along.
ese[2] *adj dem m*, **esa** *f* that; **esos** *adj dem mpl*, **esas** *fpl* those.
ése *pron dem m*, **ésa** *f* that; that one; the former; **ésos** *pron dem mpl*, **ésas** *fpl* those; the former; **en ésa** in your town; **... y cosas de ésas** ... and suchlike; **ni por ésas** on no account, under no circumstances; **¡no me salgas ahora con ésas!** don't bring all that up again!; **no es una chica de ésas** she's not one of those, she's not that kind of a girl.
esencia *nf* essence; (*de problema etc*) heart, core; **quinta ~** quintessence; **en ~** in essence.
esencial *adj* essential; chief, main; **lo ~** the essential thing, the main thing; **cosa no ~** non-essential thing, inessential.
esfagno *nm* sphagnum.
esfera *nf* (**a**) (*Geog, Mat etc*) sphere; globe; **~ celeste** celestial sphere; **~ impresora** (*Tip*) golfball; **en forma de ~** spherical, globular.
(**b**) (*Téc*) dial; (*de reloj*) face, dial.
(**c**) (*fig*) sphere; plane, field; **~ de acción** scope; field of action; range; **~ de actividad** sphere of activity; **~ de influencia** sphere of influence.
esférico 1 *adj* spherical. **2** *nm* (*Dep*) ball, football.
esferográfica *nf* (*Carib*) ballpoint pen.
esferoide *nm* spheroid.
esfinge *nf* (**a**) sphinx; **ser como una ~** to be expressionless; to have one's lips sealed. (**b**) (*Ent*) hawk moth.
esfínter *nm* sphincter.
esforzadamente *adv* vigorously, energetically; enterprisingly; bravely.
esforzado *adj* (*fuerte*) vigorous, energetic, strong; (*duro*) tough; (*emprendedor*) enterprising; (*valiente*) brave, valiant.
esforzar [1f *y* 1m] **1** *vt* (**a**) (*fortalecer*) to strengthen; to invigorate.
(**b**) (*animar*) to encourage, raise the spirits of.
2 esforzarse *vr* to exert o.s., make an effort; to strain; **hay que ~ más** you must try harder, you must put more effort into it; **~ en** + *infin*, **~ por** + *infin* to struggle to + *infin*, strive to + *infin*.
esfuerzo *nm* (**a**) (*gen*) effort, endeavour; exertion; (*imaginación*) effort, stretch; **sin ~** effortlessly, without strain; **no perdonar ~s para** + *infin* to spare no effort to + *infin*; **bien vale el ~** it's well worth the effort.
(**b**) (*Mec*) stress.
(**c**) (*valentía*) courage, spirit; (*vigor*) vigour; **con ~** with spirit.
esfumar [1a] **1** *vt* (*Arte*) to shade (in); to tone down, sof-

ten.

2 esfumarse *vr* (**a**) (*esperanzas etc*) to fade away, melt away.

(**b**) (*persona*) to vanish, make o.s. scarce; **¡esfúmate!‡** get lost!‡

esfumino *nm* (*Arte*) stump.

esgrima *nf* (*Dep*: *como arte*) fencing; (*Mil*: *arte*) swordsmanship.

esgrimidor 1 *nm* (*Mil*) swordsman. **2** *nm*, **esgrimidora** *nf* (*Dep*) fencer.

esgrimir [3a] **1** *vt espada* to wield; to brandish; (*fig*) *argumento etc* to use; to brandish, flourish, fling about; **~ que ...** to argue that ..., maintain that ... **2** *vi* to fence.

esgrimista *nmf* (*LAm*) fencer.

esguazar [1f] *vt* to ford.

esguince *nm* (**a**) (*movimiento*) swerve, dodge, avoiding action; **dar un ~** to swerve, duck, dodge.

(**b**) (*Med*) sprain.

(**c**) (*ceño*) scowl, frown; (*mirada*) scornful look.

(**d**) (*fig*: *de intriga etc*) twist; **un ~ ingenioso** an ingenious twist.

eslabón *nm* (*de cadena*) link (*t fig*); (*chaira*) steel; (*Náut, Téc*) shackle; **~ giratorio** swivel; **~ perdido** missing link.

eslabonar [1a] *vt* to link (together, up), join; (*fig*) to link, interlink, connect, knit together.

eslálom *nm*, **eslalon** *nm* = **slalom.**

eslavo 1 *adj* Slav, Slavonic. **2** *nm*, **eslava** *nf* Slav. **3** *nm* (*Ling*) Slavonic.

eslinga *nf* (*Náut*) sling.

eslingar [1h] *vt* (*Náut*) to sling.

eslip *nm*, *pl* **eslips** = **slip.**

eslogan *nm* = **slogan.**

eslomar [1a] *vt* = **deslomar.**

eslora *nf* (*Náut*) length; **tiene 250 m de ~** she is 250 m in length.

eslovaco 1 *adj* Slovak(ian). **2** *nm*, **eslovaca** *nf* Slovak.

Eslovaquia *nf* Slovakia.

Eslovenia *nf* Slovenia.

esloveno, -a *adj, nm/f* Slovene.

esmaltar [1a] *vt* (**a**) *metal* to enamel; *uñas* to varnish, paint. (**b**) (*fig*) to embellish, beautify, adorn (with a variety of colours).

esmalte *nm* (**a**) (*Anat, Téc*) enamel; enamelwork, smalt; **~ de uñas** nail-varnish, nail-polish. (**b**) (*fig*) lustre.

esmeradamente *adv* carefully, neatly; elegantly.

esmerado *adj* (**a**) *trabajo* careful, neat; polished, elegant. (**b**) *persona* careful, painstaking, conscientious.

esmeralda *nf* emerald.

esmerar [1a] **1** *vt* to polish, brighten up.

2 esmerarse *vr* to take great pains (*en* over), exercise great care (*en* in), do one's best; to shine, do well; **~ en** + *infin* to take great pains to + *infin*, go to great trouble to + *infin*.

esmerejón *nm* merlin.

esmeril *nm* emery.

esmerilar [1a] *vt* to polish with emery.

esmero *nm* care, carefulness; neatness; polish, elegance; refinement; **con el mayor ~** with the greatest care; **poner ~ en algo** to take great care over sth.

Esmirna *n* Smyrna.

esmirriado *adj* = **desmirriado.**

esmoladera *nf* grindstone.

esmoquin *nm* dinner-jacket, tuxedo (*US*).

esnifada* *nf* sniff; snort‡.

esnifar‡ [1a] *vt colas etc* to sniff; *cocaína* to snort‡.

esnife‡ *nm* sniff.

esnob 1 *adj* (*) *invar persona* snobbish; *coche, restaurante etc* posh*, de luxe, swish*. **2** *nmf*, *pl* **esnobs** [ez'noß] snob.

esnobear* [1a] *vt* to snub, cold-shoulder.

esnobismo *nm* snobbery, snobbishness.

esnobista *adj* snobbish.

eso *pron dem 'neutro'* that; that thing, that affair, that matter; **~ no me gusta** I don't like that; **¿qué es ~?** what's that?; **~ de su coche** that business about his car; **~ de no tener dinero el colegio** that story about the college having no money; **~ de que los cerdos volarán algún día** the idea that pigs will fly one day; **¿qué es ~ de que ...?** what's all this about ...?; **¡~!** that's right!; **¡~ a ellos!** that's their look-out!; **~ es** that's it, that's right; that's just it; **no es ~** that's not the reason; **¡no es ~!** hardly!; **nada de ~** nothing of the kind, far from it; **¡nada de ~!** not a bit of it!; **¿no es ~?** isn't that so?; **¿y ~?** why? how so?*; **~ sí** yes; naturally, of course; **~ digo yo** I quite agree; (*respondiendo a pregunta*) that's what I'd like to know; **el coche es viejo, ~ sí** the car is certainly old, to be sure the car is old; **a ~ de las 2** at about 2 o'clock, round about 2; **antes de ~** before that; **después de ~** after that; **en ~** thereupon, at that point; **por ~** therefore, and so; **por ~ no vine** that's why I didn't come; **es por ~ que no vino** that's why she didn't come; **y ~ que llovía** in spite of the fact that it was raining; bearing in mind that it was raining.

esófago *nm* oesophagus, gullet.

Esopo *nm* Aesop.

esotérico *adj* esoteric.

esoterismo *nm* (*culto*) cult of the esoteric; (*como género*) esoterics; (*carácter*) esoteric nature.

esp. *abr de* **español** Spanish, Sp., Span.

espabilada* *nf* (*And*) blink; **en una ~** in a jiffy*.

espabilar [1a] **1** *vt* (**a**) *vela* to snuff; *V* **despabilar.**

(**b**) (‡: *robar*) to nick‡.

(**c**) (‡: *matar*) to do in‡.

2 *vi* (*And*) to blink.

3 espabilarse *vr* to wake up; (*fig*) to look lively, get a move on; to pull one's socks up; **¡espabílate!** get a move on!; jump to it!; **¡espabilado!** (*iró*) wake up!, you're a bright one!

espaciadamente *adv*: **la revista saldrá más ~** the journal will come out less frequently (*o* at longer intervals).

espaciado *nm* (*Tip, Inform*) spacing.

espaciador *nm* spacing key, spacing bar.

espacial *adj* (**a**) (*Mat etc*) spatial. (**b**) (*atr*) space; **programa ~** space programme; **viajes ~es** space travel.

espaciar [1b] **1** *vt* (*t Tip*) to space (out); to spread, expand; *noticia* to spread; *pago* to spread out, stagger.

2 espaciarse *vr* (**a**) (*hablando*) to expatiate, spread o.s.; **~ en un tema** to enlarge on a subject, expatiate on a subject.

(**b**) (*esparcirse*) to relax, take one's ease; (*estar de juerga*) to make merry.

espacio *nm* (**a**) (*gen*) space; room; distance; period, interval; **~ aéreo** air space; **~ amortiguador** buffer zone; **~ libre** room, clear space; **~ de maniobra** room for manoeuvre; **~ muerto** clearance; **~ natural** open space; **~ vital** living space, (*Pol*) lebensraum; **en el ~ de una hora** in the space of one hour; **en el ~ de 3 generaciones** in the space of 3 generations, over 3 generations; **por ~ de** during, for; **por ~ de 3 años** over 3 years; **ocupa mucho ~** it takes up a lot of room.

(**b**) (*Aer, Geog*) space; **exploración del ~** space exploration; **~ estelar, ~ exterior, ~ extraterrestre** outer space.

(**c**) (*tardanza*) delay, slowness.

(**d**) (*Tip, Inform*) space; spacing; **a un ~** single-spaced; **a dos ~s, a doble ~** double-spaced.

(**e**) (*Mús*) interval.

(**f**) (*Rad, TV*) short programme, item; spot, slot; **~ informativo** newscast; **~ publicitario** advertising spot, commercial.

espacioso *adj* (**a**) *cuarto etc* spacious, roomy, big; capacious. (**b**) *movimiento* slow, deliberate.

espaciotemporal *adj* spatio-temporal.

espachurrar [1a] *vt* to squash, flatten.

espada 1 *nf* (**a**) (*arma*) sword; (‡) picklock; **estar entre la ~ y la pared** to be between the devil and the deep blue sea; **estar hecho una ~** to be as thin as a rake; **poner a ~** to put to the sword.

(**b**) **~s** (*Naipes*) spades.

(**c**) (*persona*) swordsman.

2 *nm* (*Taur*) matador.

espadachín *nm* skilled swordsman; (*pey*) bully, thug.

espadaña *nf* (**a**) (*Bot*) bullrush. (**b**) (*Arquit*) steeple, belfry.

espadarte *nm* swordfish.

espadazo *nm* sword thrust, slash with a sword.

espadero *nm* swordsmith.

espadín *nm* (**a**) (*espada*) dress sword, ceremonial sword. (**b**) (*de espadista*) picklock. (**c**) (*Pez*: *t* **espadines**) whitebait.

espadista‡ *nm* burglar, lock-picker.

espadón *nm* (**a**) broadsword. (**b**) (*hum**) big shot*, top person; (*Mil*) brass hat*.

espaguetis *nmpl* spaghetti.

espalda *nf* (**a**) (*t* **~s**) back, shoulder(s); **a ~s de uno** behind sb's back; **a ~s (vueltas)** treacherously; **eso ha quedado ya a la ~** that's all behind us now; **atar las manos a la ~** to tie sb's hands behind his back; **echar algo a las ~s** to forget about sth; **tiene 40 años de eso a las ~s** he has 40 years of that behind him; **~ con ~** back to back;

de ~s from behind; **dar de ~s** to fall on one's back; **estar de ~s** to be on one's back; **estar de ~s a** (*fig*) to ignore, pay no heed to; **de ~s a la marcha** facing backwards, with one's back to the engine (*etc*); **volverse de ~s a** to turn one's back on (*t fig*); **fue muerto por la ~** he was killed from behind; **cubrir las ~s** (*fig*) to cover o.s., protect o.s.; **dar la ~ a la pared** to have one's back to the wall; **echar algo sobre las ~s** to take sth on, take charge of sth; **tener guardadas las ~s** to have influential friends; **volver la ~** to turn away; (*pey*) to turn tail; **volver las ~s a uno** to give sb the cold shoulder, cold-shoulder sb.

(**b**) (*Natación*) backstroke.

(**c**) (*And*: *destino*) fate, destiny; star.

(**d**) **~ mojada** (*Méx**) wetback.

espaldar *nm* (**a**) (*de silla*) back. (**b**) (*Hort*) trellis, espalier. (**c**) **~es** wall hangings.

espaldarazo *nm* slap on the back; pat on the back; (*Hist*) accolade.

espaldera *nf* trellis, espalier.

espaldero *nm* (*Carib*) bodyguard, henchman.

espaldilla *nf* (*Anat*) shoulder blade; (*Méx Culin*) shoulder of pork.

espantá* *nf* = **espantada**.

espantable *adj* = **espantoso**.

espantada *nf* (**a**) (*miedo*) sudden scare, sudden fear; **dar la ~** to bolt. (**b**) (*huida*) stampede, panic.

espantadizo *adj* shy, timid, easily scared (off).

espantado *adj* frightened, scared, terrified; (*LAm*) sick with fear.

espantador *adj* (**a**) (*espantoso*) frightening. (**b**) (*And, CAm, Cono Sur*) = **espantadizo**.

espantajo *nm* (**a**) (*lit*) scarecrow. (**b**) (*fig*) scarecrow; sight, fright; bogey, bogeyman.

espantamoscas *nm invar* fly-swat.

espantapájaros *nm invar* scarecrow.

espantar [1a] **1** *vt* (*asustar*) to frighten, scare; (*ahuyentar*) to frighten off, scare away; (*horrorizar*) to appal, horrify.

2 espantarse *vr* (**a**) (*asustarse*) to get frightened, get scared (*de* at, of); to be appalled; (*asombrarse*) to be amazed, be astonished (*de* at).

(**b**) (*Carib*: *sospechar*) to get suspicious.

espanto *nm* (**a**) (*miedo*) fright, terror; (*consternación*) consternation, dismay; (*asombro*) amazement, astonishment.

(**b**) (*amenaza*) threat, menace.

(**c**) (*LAm*: *fantasma*) ghost.

(**d**) (*) **¡qué ~!** how awful!; goodness!; **es un coche de ~** it's a smashing car*, it's a tremendous car*; **hace un frío de ~** it's terribly cold.

espantosamente *adv* frightfully; terrifyingly; shockingly; amazingly.

espantosidad *nf* (*And*) terror, fear.

espantoso *adj* frightful, dreadful; terrifying; shocking; appalling; amazing.

España *nf* Spain; **las ~s** (*hum**) Spain; **Nueva ~** (*Hist*) New Spain (*ie* Mexico); **la ~ de pandereta** (*pey*) touristy Spain, pseudo-romantic Spain, picturesque Spain.

español 1 *adj* Spanish.

2 *nm*, **española**[1] *nf* Spaniard; **los ~es** the Spaniards, the Spanish.

3 *nm* (*Ling*) Spanish; **~ antiguo** Old Spanish; **~ medieval** Medieval Spanish; **~ moderno** Modern Spanish.

española[2] *nf* (*Méx*) spanner.

españolada *nf* typically Spanish product (*o* feature *etc*) (*t pey*).

españolidad *nf* (*carácter español*) Spanishness; (*patriotismo*) Spanish patriotism; (*sentimientos nacionales*) Spanish national feelings.

españolísimo *adj superl* typically Spanish, unmistakably Spanish, Spanish to the core; terribly Spanish.

españolismo *nm* (**a**) (*amor a lo español*) love of Spain, love of things Spanish; (*tendencia a españolizarse*) tendency to adopt Spanish ways (*etc*).

(**b**) (*carácter*) Spanishness; Spanish nature, essentially Spanish character.

(**c**) (*Ling*) hispanicism, word (*o* phrase *etc*) borrowed from Spanish.

españolista 1 *adj* centralist, unionist (as opposed to regionalist). **2** *nmf* member (*o* supporter) of a Madrid-based party.

españolito* *nm* ordinary Spaniard, man in the Spanish street; **algún ~** some poor little Spaniard; **cada ~ de a pie** each poor little Spaniard that there is.

españolizar [1f] **1** *vt* to make Spanish, hispanicize; to give a Spanish flavour (*o* colouring *etc*) to.

2 españolizarse *vr* to adopt Spanish ways (*etc*); to acquire a Spanish flavour (*etc*); (*pey*) to affect Spanish ways; **se españolizó por completo** he became completely Spanish.

esparadrapo *nm* sticking plaster; adhesive tape.

esparaván *nm* (**a**) (*Orn*) sparrowhawk. (**b**) (*Vet*) spavin.

esparavel *nm* (casting) net.

esparceta *nf* sainfoin.

esparcido *adj* (**a**) (*desparramado*) scattered; (*extendido*) widespread. (**b**) (*fig*: *alegre*) merry, jolly, cheerful; (*franco*) open, frank.

esparcimiento *nm* (**a**) (*gen*) spreading, scattering. (**b**) (*fig*: *descanso*) relaxation; (*recreo*) amusement, diversion; recreation. (**c**) (*fig*) (*alegría*) cheerfulness; (*franqueza*) openness, frankness.

esparcir [3b] **1** *vt* (**a**) (*desparramar*) to spread, scatter; (*sembrar*) to sow; (*divulgar*) to disseminate.

(**b**) (*fig*) to amuse, divert.

2 esparcirse *vr* (**a**) (*desparramarse*) to spread (out), scatter, be scattered.

(**b**) (*fig*) (*relajarse*) to relax; (*distraerse*) to amuse o.s.

espárrago *nm* asparagus; **~ triguero** wild asparagus; **estar hecho un ~** to be as thin as a rake; **¡ve a freír ~s!*** go to hell!; **mandar a uno a freír ~s*** to tell sb to go to hell.

esparrancado *adj* (with legs) wide apart, (with legs) spread far apart.

esparrancarse [1g] *vr* to spread one's legs (wide apart); to do the splits; **~ sobre algo** to straddle sth.

Esparta *n* Sparta.

espartal *nm* esparto field.

espartano, -a *adj, nm/f* Spartan.

esparteña *nf* = **alpargata**.

espartillo *nm* (*LAm*) esparto (grass).

espartizal *nm* esparto field.

esparto *nm* esparto (grass); **estar como el ~** to be all dried up.

Espasa *nm*: **ser el ~*** to be a walking encyclopedia.

espasmo *nm* spasm.

espasmódicamente *adv* spasmodically.

espasmódico *adj* spasmodic.

espasticidad *nf* spasticity.

espástico, -a *adj, nm/f* spastic.

espatarrarse* [1a] *vr* = **esparrancarse**.

espato *nm* (*Geol*) spar; **~ de Islandia** Iceland spar.

espátula *nf* (**a**) (*Med*) spatula; (*Arte*) palette knife; (*Arquit*) putty knife; **estar hecho una ~** to be as thin as a rake. (**b**) (*Orn*) spoonbill.

especia *nf* spice.

especiado *adj* spiced, spicy.

especial 1 *adj* (**a**) special, especial; **en ~** especially, particularly. (**b**) *persona* particular, fussy (*en* about). **2** *nf* (*Méx Com*) special offer. **3** *nm* (*Méx Teat*) show.

especialidad *nf* speciality, specialty; special branch, special field (of study *etc*), line; **no es de mi ~** it's not in my line.

especialista *nmf* (**a**) (*gen*) specialist. (**b**) (*Cine etc*) stuntman, stuntwoman.

especializado *adj* specialized; *obrero* skilled, trained; **mano de obra especializada** skilled labour.

especializarse [1f] *vr* to specialize (*en* in).

especialmente *adv* (e)specially, particularly.

especiar [1b] *vt* to spice.

especie *nf* (**a**) (*Bio*) species; **~ amenazada, ~ en peligro** endangered species; **~ protegida** protected species.

(**b**) (*clase*) kind, sort; **de otra ~** of another kind.

(**c**) (*asunto*) matter; (*idea*) idea, notion; (*noticia*) rumour piece of false news; (*observación*) remark; (*pretexto*) pretext; **con la ~ de que ...** on the pretext that ...; **corre la ~ de que ...** there is a rumour about that ...; **soltar una ~** to fly a kite.

(**d**) **en ~** in kind; **pagar en ~** to pay in kind.

especificación *nf* specification.

específicamente *adv* specifically.

especificar [1g] *vt* to specify; to particularize; to list, itemize.

específico 1 *adj* specific. **2** *nm* (*Med*) specific; patent medicine.

especifidad *nf* specific nature, specificity.

espécimen *nm, pl* **especímenes** specimen.

especioso *adj* specious, plausible; deceitful.

espectacular *adj* spectacular.

espectacularidad *nf* spectacular nature; showiness.

espectacularmente *adv* spectacularly, in spectacular fashion.

espectáculo 1 *nm* spectacle; sight; (*Teat etc*) show; function, performance; ~ **de variedades** variety show; ~ **de luz y sonido** son et lumière show; **dar un** ~ to make a scene; to create a stir. **2** *atr*: **atletismo** ~ athletics on the grand scale; **cine** ~ epic films; **fútbol** ~ soccer presented as show-biz; **programa** ~ TV variety show; **restaurante** ~ restaurant with a floor-show.
espectador(a) *nm/f* spectator; onlooker, looker-on; **los ~es** the spectators; (*Teat etc*) the audience.
espectral *adj* (**a**) (*Fís*) spectral;. (**b**) (*fig*) ghostly; unearthly.
espectro *nm* (**a**) (*Fís*) spectrum (*t fig*); **de amplio** ~ wide-ranging, covering a broad spectrum. (**b**) (*fantasma*) spectre, ghost; (*fig*) spectre; **el** ~ **del hambre** the spectre of famine.
espectrógrafo *nm* spectrograph.
espectrograma *nm* spectrogram.
espectrometría *nf* spectrometry.
espectrómetro *nm* spectrometer.
espectroscopia *nf* spectroscopy.
espectroscopio *nm* spectroscope.
especulación *nf* (**a**) (*gen*) speculation; (*meditación*) contemplation, meditation. (**b**) (*Com, Fin*) speculation; venture; ~ **bursátil** speculation on the stock exchange; ~ **inmobiliaria** property speculation.
especulador(a) *nm/f* speculator.
especular¹ [1a] **1** *vt* (*examinar*) to examine, inspect; (*meditar sobre*) to speculate about, reflect on, contemplate.
2 *vi* (**a**) to speculate, meditate.
(**b**) (*Com, Fin*) to speculate (*en, sobre* in, on).
especular² [1a] *vt* (*LAm*) to ruffle the hair of.
especulativo *adj* speculative.
espéculo *nm* (*Med*) speculum.
espejado *adj* glossy, bright, shining, mirror-like.
espejeante *adj* gleaming, glistening.
espejear [1a] *vi* to shine (like a mirror), gleam, glimmer, glint.
espejeras *nfpl* (*Carib*) chafing, chafed patch.
espejismo *nm* (**a**) (*gen*) mirage. (**b**) (*fig*) mirage, illusion; (piece of) wishful thinking, (piece of) wish fulfilment.
espejito *nm* small mirror; handbag mirror.
espejo *nm* (**a**) (*gen*) mirror, looking-glass; ~ **de cortesía** courtesy mirror; ~ **de cuerpo entero** full-length mirror, pier glass; ~ **retrovisor,** ~ **de retrovisión** driving mirror, rear-view mirror; **mirarse al** (*o* **en el**) ~ to look at o.s. in the mirror.
(**b**) (*Zool*) white patch.
(**c**) (*fig*) mirror, reflection; model; **un** ~ **de caballería** a model of chivalry.
espejoso *adj* = **espejado.**
espejuelo *nm* small looking-glass; **~s** lenses, spectacles.
espeleoarqueología *nf* cave archaeology.
espeleobuceo *nm* cave diving.
espeleología *nf* speleology, potholing, caving.
espeleólogo, -a *nm/f* speleologist, potholer, caver.
espelta *nf* (*Bot*) spelt.
espelunca *nf* (*liter*) cave.
espeluznante *adj* hair-raising, horrifying, bloodcurdling; lurid.
espeluzno *nm* (*Méx*) = **escalofrío.**
espera *nf* (**a**) (*período*) wait, period of waiting; waiting; delay; **en** ~ **de** waiting for; expecting; **en** ~ **de su contestación** awaiting your reply; **estar a la** ~ **de una carta** to be expecting a letter; **la cosa no tiene** ~ the matter brooks no delay, the affair is most urgent.
(**b**) (*Jur*) stay, respite.
(**c**) (*cualidad*) patience.
esperable *adj* to be hoped for; to be expected.
esperantista *nmf* Esperantist.
esperanto *nm* Esperanto.
esperanza *nf* hope; expectation; prospect; **un jugador de ~s** a promising player, a player of promise; (**gran**) ~ **blanca** great white hope; ~ **de vida** life expectancy; **¡qué ~!** (*LAm*) some hope!; not on your life!; **con la** ~ **de que** ... in the hope that ...; **hay pocas ~s de que venga** there is little prospect of his coming; **no daba ~s de permitirlo** he held out no prospect of allowing it, he gave no hope of allowing it; **tener ~s de** to have hopes of; **tener la** ~ **puesta en** to pin one's faith to; to set one's heart on.
esperanzador *adj* hopeful, encouraging; promising.
esperanzadoramente *adv* encouragingly; promisingly.
esperanzar [1f] *vt* to give hope to, buoy up with hope.
esperar [1a] **1** *vt* (**a**) (*tener esperanza de*) to hope for; to expect (*de* of); **no esperaba yo menos, no se podía** ~ **menos** it was the least that could be expected; **no esperaba menos de Vd** I expected nothing less of you, I hoped for nothing less from you; ~ **que** + *subj* to hope that ...; **espero que sea así** I hope it is so, I hope it will be so; **espero que te haya gustado** I hope you liked it; **espero que vengas** I hope you'll come.
(**b**) (*aguardar*) to wait for, await; *bebé, visita etc* to expect; ~ **el avión** to wait for the plane; **espero la llamada en cualquier momento** I expect his call at any moment; **ir a** ~ **a uno** to go and meet sb; **no me esperes después de las 7** don't wait for me after 7; ~ **algo como el agua de mayo** to await sth with eager anticipation; **un lío de aquí te espero*** a tremendous row*, the father and mother of a row*.
2 *vi* (**a**) (*tener esperanza*) to hope; to expect; ~ + *infin* to hope to + *infin*; ~ **a que** + *subj* to expect that ..., anticipate that ...; ~ **en uno** to put one's hopes (*o* trust) in sb; ~ **en Dios** to trust in God; ~ **desesperando** to hope against hope.
(**b**) (*aguardar*) to wait; to stay; **esperaré aquí** I'll wait here; **¡espera un momento!** wait a moment!, just a minute!; ~ **que salga uno** to wait for sb to come out; ~ **a** (*o* **hasta**) **que uno haga algo** to wait for sb to do sth, wait until sb does sth; **hacer** ~ **a uno** to make sb wait, keep sb waiting; **espera y verás** wait and see.
3 esperarse *vr*: **como podía** ~ as might have been expected, as was to be expected; **no fue tan bueno como se esperaba** it was not so good as was hoped, it did not come up to expectations; **se espera que todo esté listo** it is hoped that all will be ready.
esperma *nf* (**a**) (*Bio*) sperm; ~ **de ballena** spermaceti. (**b**) (*LAm: vela*) candle.
espermatozoo *nm* spermatozoon.
espermicida *nm* spermicide.
espermio *nm* sperm.
espernancarse [1g] *vr* (*LAm*) = **esparrancarse.**
esperón *nm* (*Carib*) long wait.
esperpéntico *adj* (**a**) (*absurdo*) absurd, nonsensical. (**b**) (*grotesco*) grotesque, exaggerated; caricaturesque; macabre.
esperpentización *nf* presentation in an absurd (*o* grotesque *etc*) manner; caricaturing.
esperpentizar [1f] *vt* to present in an absurd (*o* grotesque *etc*) way; to caricature.
esperpento *nm* (**a**) (*persona*) fright, sight; scarecrow. (**b**) (*disparate*) absurdity, (piece of) nonsense. (**c**) (*cuento*) macabre story, grotesque tale. (**d**) (*Teat*) *play which focuses on the grotesque.*
espesamente *adv* thickly; densely.
espesante *nm* thickener, thickening agent.
espesar [1a] **1** *vt* (**a**) *líquido etc* to thicken; to make dense(r).
(**b**) *tejido* to weave tighter; to knit tighter.
2 espesarse *vr* to thicken, get thicker, get denser; to coagulate, solidify.
espeso *adj* (**a**) (*gen*) thick; *bosque* dense; *nieve* deep; *pasta etc* stiff; *líquido* thick, heavy. (**b**) (*sucio*) dirty, untidy.
espesor *nm* thickness; density; (*de nieve*) depth; **tiene medio metro de** ~ it is half a metre thick.
espesura *nf* (**a**) (*espesor*) thickness; density; **en la** ~ **de la selva** in the depths of the jungle.
(**b**) (*Bot*) thicket, overgrown place; **se refugiaron en las ~s serranas** they took refuge in the mountain fastnesses.
(**c**) (*suciedad*) dirtiness, untidiness.
espeta‡ *nm* cop*.
espetar [1a] **1** *vt* (**a**) (*atravesar*) to transfix, pierce, run through; *carne* to skewer, spit; *persona* to run through.
(**b**) (*fig*) *orden* to rap out; *lección, sermón* to read; *pregunta* to fire; ~ **algo a uno** to broach a subject (unexpectedly) with sb, spring sth on sb.
2 espetarse *vr* (**a**) (*ponerse cómodo*) to steady o.s., settle o.s.
(**b**) (*envanecerse*) to get on one's high horse.
espetera‡ *nf* tits‡, bosom.
espetón *nm* (**a**) (*broqueta*) skewer, spit; (*clavija*) large pin, iron pin; (*atizador*) poker. (**b**) (*pinchazo*) jab, poke.
espía 1 *nmf* spy. **2** *atr*: **avión** ~ spy plane; **buque** ~ spy ship; **satélite** ~ spy satellite.
espiantar* [1a] **1** *vt* (*Cono Sur: robar*) to pinch*. **2** *vi y* **espiantarse** *vr* (*Cono Sur*) to scram*, beat it*.
espiar [1c] **1** *vt* (**a**) (*vigilar*) to spy on; to keep (a) watch on. (**b**) (*CAm, Cono Sur: mirar*) to look at, see, watch. **2** *vi* to spy.
espicha *nf* (*Asturias*) cider party.

espichar[1] [1a] **1** *vt* (**a**) (*pinchar*) to prick.
(**b**) (*Cono Sur**: *entregar*) to hand over reluctantly, relinquish.
(**c**) (*And, Cono Sur Téc*) to put a tap on.
(**d**) **~la(s)**‡ = **2**.
2 *vi* (‡) to peg out‡.
3 espicharse *vr* (**a**) (*And*: *neumático*) to go flat.
(**b**) (*Carib, Méx*: *enflaquecerse*) to get thin.
(**c**) (*CAm*: *asustarse*) to get scared.
espichar[2] [1a] *vi* (*LAm*: *pronunciar un discurso*) to make a speech; to speechify.
espiche[1] *nm* spike; peg.
espiche[2] *nm* (*LAm*) speech.
espidómetro *nm* (*LAm*) speedometer.
espiedo *nm* (*Cono Sur Culin*) spit.
espiga *nf* (**a**) (*Bot*) (*de trigo*) ear; (*de flores*) spike.
(**b**) (*Téc*) spigot; (*clavija*) tenon, dowel, peg; (*de pestillo etc*) shaft; (*de cuchillo, herramienta*) tang.
(**c**) (*badajo*) clapper.
(**d**) (*Mil*) fuse.
(**e**) (*Náut*) masthead.
espigadera *nf* gleaner.
espigado *adj* (**a**) (*Bot*) ripe; ready to seed. (**b**) *persona* tall, tall and slim, lanky; **¡tan ~!** how he's shot up!
espigador(a) *nm/f* gleaner.
espigar [1h] **1** *vt* (**a**) (*Agr*) to glean (*t fig*); (*fig*) *fruta etc* to look closely at, scrutinize; *libro etc* to consult.
(**b**) (*Téc*) to pin, peg, dowel.
2 *vi* (**a**) (*trigo*) to form ears, come into ear; (*flor*) to run to seed.
(**b**) = **3**.
3 espigarse *vr* to get very tall, shoot up.
espigón *nm* (**a**) (*Bot*) ear; spike. (**b**) (*Zool*) sting. (**c**) (*de herramienta*) sharp point, spike. (**d**) (*Náut*) breakwater, groyne.
espigueo *nm* gleaning.
espiguero *nm* (*Méx*) granary.
espiguilla *nf* herring-bone pattern.
espín *nm* porcupine.
espina *nf* (**a**) (*Bot*) thorn, prickle; (*astilla*) splinter; **mala ~** spite, resentment, ill-will; **estar en ~s** to be on tenterhooks, be all on edge; **me da mala ~** it worries me, it makes me suspicious; it gives me a bad impression; **sacarse la ~** (*fig*) to pay off an old score, get even; **sacarse la ~ de una dificultad** to master a problem, overcome a longstanding difficulty.
(**b**) (*de pez*) bone.
(**c**) (*Anat*: *t* **~ dorsal**) spine; **~ bífida** spina bifida; **doblar la ~** to bend over.
(**d**) (*fig*) doubt, worry, suspicion.
espinaca *nf* spinach.
espinal *adj* spinal.
espinaquer *nm* spinnaker.
espinar 1 [1a] *vt* (**a**) (*punzar*) to prick. (**b**) (*fig*) to sting, hurt, nettle. **2 espinarse** *vr* to prick o.s. **3** *nm* (**a**) (*Bot*) thicket, thornbrake, thorny place. (**b**) (*fig*) difficulty.
espinazo *nm* spine, backbone; **doblar el ~** (*fig*) to knuckle under.
espineta *nf* (*Mús*) spinet.
espingarda *nf* (**a**) (*Hist*) (kind of) cannon; Moorish musket. (**b**) (*: *chica*) lanky girl.
espinglés *nm* (*hum*) Spanglish.
espinilla *nf* (**a**) (*Anat*) shin, shinbone. (**b**) (*Med*) blackhead.
espinillera *nf* shinpad, shin guard (*US*).
espinita *nf* (*fig*) irritation.
espino *nm* (*t* **~ albar, ~ blanco**) hawthorn; **~ cerval** buckthorn; **~ negro** blackthorn, sloe.
espinoso 1 *adj* (**a**) *planta* thorny, prickly; *pez* bony, spiny. (**b**) (*fig*) thorny, knotty, difficult. **2** *nm* stickleback.
espinudo *adj* (*LAm*) = **espinoso 1**.
espión *nm* spy.
espionaje *nm* spying, espionage; **~ industrial** industrial espionage; **novela de ~** spy story.
espíquer *nm* (*Téc*) speaker.
espira *nf* (*Mat etc*) spiral; (*Zool*) whorl, ring; (*de espiral, hélice*) turn.
espiráculo *nm* blow-hole; spiracle.
espiral 1 *adj* spiral; winding; (*Téc*) helical; corkscrew (*atr*), corkscrew-shaped.
2 *nf* spiral; corkscrew (shape); (*anticonceptiva*) intra-uterine coil; (*Téc*) whorl; (*de reloj*) hairspring; (*de humo etc*) spiral, wreath; (*Dep*) corkscrew dive; **la ~ inflacionista** the inflationary spiral; **dar vueltas en ~** to spiral (up *etc*); **el humo subía en ~** the smoke went spiralling up.
espiralado *adj* spiral.
espirar [1a] **1** *vt aire etc* to breathe out, exhale; *olor* to give off, give out. **2** *vi* to breathe; to breathe out, exhale.
espirea *nf* spiraea.
espiritado *adj* (*fig*) like a wraith, ghost-like.
espiritismo *nm* spiritualism.
espiritista 1 *adj* spiritualist(ic). **2** *nmf* spiritualist.
espiritoso *adj* (**a**) *licor* spirituous. (**b**) *persona* spirited, lively.
espíritu *nm* (**a**) (*gen*) spirit; **~ de cuerpo** esprit de corps; **~ de equipo** team spirit; **~ guerrero, ~ de lucha** fighting spirit; **en la letra y en el ~** in the letter and in the spirit; **pobre de ~** poor in spirit; **levantar el ~ de uno** to raise sb's spirits.
(**b**) (*mente*) mind; (*inteligencia*) intelligence; (*talento*) turn of mind; **con ~ amplio** with an open mind; in a generous spirit; **de ~ crítico** of a critical turn of mind.
(**c**) (*Rel*) spirit, soul; **E~ Santo** Holy Ghost; **dar el ~, rendir el ~** to give up the ghost.
(**d**) (*fantasma*) spirit, ghost; **~ maligno** evil spirit.
(**e**) (*alcohol*) spirits, liquor; **~ de vino** spirits of wine.
espiritual 1 *adj* (**a**) (*Rel etc*) spiritual. (**b**) (*fantasmal*) unworldly; ghostly. (**c**) (*And, Cono Sur*: *gracioso*) gay, witty.
2 *nm* (Negro) spiritual.
espiritualidad *nf* spirituality.
espiritualizar [1f] *vt* to spiritualize.
espiritualmente *adv* spiritually.
espirituoso *adj* = **espiritoso**.
espita *nf* (**a**) tap, faucet (*US*), cock, spigot; **~ de entrada del gas** gas-tap; **abrir la ~ de las lágrimas** (*hum*) to weep buckets*. (**b**) (*) drunkard, soak‡. (**c**) (**) prick**.
espitar [1a] *vt* to tap, broach.
espléndidamente *adv* (*V adj*) (**a**) splendidly, magnificently, grandly. (**b**) lavishly; generously; **'gratificaré ~'** 'there will be a generous reward'.
esplendidez *nf* (*V adj*) (**a**) splendour; magnificence, grandeur; pomp. (**b**) lavishness; generosity.
espléndido *adj* (**a**) (*magnífico*) splendid; magnificent, grand. (**b**) (*generoso*) lavish; liberal, generous.
esplendor *nm* splendour; magnificence, grandeur; brilliance.
esplendoroso *adj* magnificent; brilliant, radiant.
esplénico *adj* splenetic.
espliego *nm* lavender.
esplín *nm* melancholy, depression, the blues.
espolada *nf* (**a**) (*espolazo*) prick with a spur. (**b**) **~ de vino*** swig of wine*.
espolazo *nm* prick with a spur.
espolear [1a] *vt* (**a**) *caballo* to spur (on). (**b**) (*fig*) to spur on, stimulate; to stir up, enliven.
espoleta *nf* (**a**) (*Mil*) fuse; **~ de tiempo** time-fuse. (**b**) (*Anat*) wishbone.
espolón 1 *nm* (**a**) (*Zool*: *de gallo*) spur; (*de caballo*) fetlock.
(**b**) (*Geog*) spur (of a mountain range).
(**c**) (*Náut*: *proa*) stem; (*para atacar*) ram.
(**d**) (*Náut*: *malecón*) sea wall, dike; jetty; (*de puente*) cutwater; (*Arquit*) buttress.
(**e**) (*paseo*) promenade.
(**f**) (*Med**) chilblain.
2 *adj* (*And**) sharp, astute.
espolvoreador *nm* (*Culin*) dredge.
espolvorear [1a] *vt* to dust, sprinkle (*de* with); **espolvoree X sobre la superficie** dust X on the surface, dust the surface with X.
espondeo *nm* spondee.
esponja *nf* (**a**) (*gen*) sponge; **~ de baño** bath sponge; **arrojar la ~** (*fig*) to throw in the towel; **beber como una ~** to drink like a fish; **pasemos la ~ por todo aquello** let's forget all about it.
(**b**) (*: *gorrón*) sponger*.
(**c**) (*Cono Sur, Méx*‡) old soak‡, boozer*, lush‡ (*US*).
esponjado *adj* (**a**) (*lit*) spongy; fluffy. (**b**) (*fig*) puffed up, pompous.
esponjar [1a] **1** *vt* to make spongy; *lana etc* to fluff up, make fluffy.
2 esponjarse *vr* (**a**) (*lit*) to become spongy; to fluff up, become fluffy.
(**b**) (*fig*: *rebosar salud*) to glow with health; (*tener aspecto próspero*) to look prosperous.
(**c**) (*fig*: *engreírse*) to be puffed up, swell with conceit.
esponjera *nf* sponge bag, make-up bag.

esponjosidad *nf* sponginess; sogginess.
esponjoso *adj materia* spongy; porous; *tierra* soggy, waterlogged.
esponsales *nmpl* betrothal.
esponsor *nm*, **espónsor** *nm* (*Com, Dep etc*) sponsor.
esponsorizar [1f] *vt* to sponsor.
espontáneamente *adv* spontaneously.
espontanearse [1a] *vr* (*confesar*) to own up; (*hablar francamente*) to speak frankly; (*abrir su pecho*) to unbosom o.s. (*con* to).
espontaneidad *nf* spontaneity.
espontaneísmo *nm* amateurish enthusiasm, enthusiasm without experience.
espontáneo 1 *adj* spontaneous; impromptu, unprepared. **2** *nm* (*Taur*) intruder, spectator who rushes into the ring and attempts to take part; (*bombero*) volunteer fireman.
espora *nf* spore.
esporádicamente *adv* sporadically; in a desultory way.
esporádico *adj* sporadic; desultory.
esportillo *nm* basket, pannier.
esportivo *adj* (*LAm*) sporty.
esportón *nm* large basket; **a esportones** in vast quantities, by the ton.
esposa *nf* (**a**) (*mujer*) wife. (**b**) **~s** handcuffs; manacles; **poner las ~s a uno** to handcuff sb.
esposar [1a] *vt* to handcuff.
esposo *nm* husband; **los ~s** husband and wife, the couple.
espray *nm* = **spray**.
esprín *nm* (*CAm*) interior sprung mattress.
esprint *nm etc* = **sprint** *etc*.
espuela *nf* (**a**) (*t fig*) spur; **~ de caballero** (*Bot*) larkspur.
(**b**) (*And*: *de mujer*) feminine charm; coquettishness.
(**c**) (*And Com*) skill in business, acumen.
(**d**) (*: *bebida*) last drink, one for the road*.
espueleado *adj* (*And, Carib*) tested, tried.
espuelear [1a] *vt* (**a**) (*LAm*: *espolear*) to spur, spur on. (**b**) (*And, Carib*: *probar*) to test, try out.
espuelón *adj* (*And*) sharp, astute.
espuerta *nf* basket, pannier; **a ~s** in vast quantities, by the ton.
espulgar [1h] *vt* (**a**) (*quitar las pulgas a*) to delouse, rid of fleas, get the lice (*o* fleas) out of. (**b**) (*fig*) to go through with a fine tooth comb.
espuma *nf* (*sobre agua*) foam, spray; (*sobre olas*) surf; (*sobre cerveza*) froth, head; (*de jabón*) lather; (*residuos*) floating waste, surface scum; **~ de baño** bubble-bath; **~ de caucho, ~ de látex** foam rubber; **~ de mar** (*fig*) meerschaum; **crecer como la ~** to flourish like the green bay tree; **echar ~** to foam, froth.
espumadera *nf*, **espumador** *nm* (*Culin*) whisk; (*LAm Culin etc*) skimmer, skimming ladle; (*de atomizador*) nozzle.
espumajear [1a] *vi* to foam at the mouth.
espumajo *nm* froth, foam (*at the mouth*).
espumajoso *adj* frothy, foamy.
espumar [1a] **1** *vt* to skim off. **2** *vi* to froth, foam; (*vino*) to sparkle.
espumarajo *nm* froth, foam (*at the mouth*); **echar ~s (de rabia)** to foam with rage, splutter with rage.
espumear [1a] *vi* to foam.
espumilla *nf* (*And, CAm*) meringue.
espumoso *adj* frothy, foamy; foaming; *vino* sparkling.
espúreo *adj*, **espurio** *adj* spurious; adulterated; *niño* illegitimate, bastard.
esputar [1a] *vti* to spit (out), hawk (up).
esputo *nm* spit, spittle, (*Med*) sputum.
esqueje *nm* (*Hort*) slip, cutting.
esquela *nf* (**a**) (*nota*) note; short letter; **~ amorosa** love letter, billet doux. (**b**) (*anuncio*) notice, announcement; **~ (de defunción)**, **~ (mortuoria)** death notice, announcement of death.
esquelético *adj* skeletal; (*) thin, skinny.
esqueleto *nm* (**a**) (*Anat*) skeleton; **menear el ~*** to shake a hoof*, dance; **tumbar el ~** to hit the hay*, go to bed.
(**b**) (*fig*) skeleton; bare bones (of a matter); framework; (*LAm*: *borrador*) rough draft, outline, preliminary plan; **en ~** unfinished, incomplete.
(**c**) (*And, CAm, Méx*: *formulario*) blank, form.
esquema *nm* (**a**) (*diagrama*) diagram, plan; (*proyecto*) scheme; (*esbozo*) sketch, outline. (**b**) (*Filos*) schema.
esquemático *adj* schematic; diagrammatic.
esquí *nm, pl* **~s** (**a**) (*objeto*) ski. (**b**) (*Dep*) skiing; **~ acuático, ~ náutico** water-skiing; surfriding; **~ alpino** alpine skiing; **~ de fondo, ~ de travesía** cross-country skiing; **hacer ~** to go skiing.
esquiable *adj*: **pista ~** slope suitable for skiing, slope that can be skiied on.
esquiador(a) *nm/f* skier; **~ acuático, ~ náutico** water-skier; surfrider.
esquiar [1c] *vi* to ski.
esquife *nm* skiff.
esquila¹ *nf* (*campanilla*) small bell, handbell; cowbell.
esquila² *nf*, **esquilado** *nm* (*Agr*) shearing.
esquilador *nm* shearer.
esquilar [1a] *vt* to shear; to clip, crop.
esquileo *nm* shearing.
esquilimoso *adj* fastidious, finicky.
esquilmar [1a] *vt* (**a**) *cosecha* to harvest. (**b**) *tierra* (*t fig*) to exhaust, impoverish.
esquilmo *nm* harvest, crop; yield.
Esquilo *nm* Aeschylus.
esquimal 1 *adj, nm/f* Eskimo. **2** *nm* (*Ling*) Eskimo.
esquina *nf* (**a**) (*gen*) corner (*t Dep*); **doblar la ~** to turn the corner; (*Cono Sur**: *morir*) to die; **sacar de ~** to take a corner-kick; **la tienda de la ~** the corner shop. (**b**) (*LAm*: *tienda*) corner shop, village store. (**c**) (*) **la ~** the game*, prostitution.
esquinado *adj* (**a**) (*que tiene esquinas*) having corners; sharp-cornered. (**b**) (*LAm*) *mueble* standing in a corner, corner (*atr*). (**c**) *pelota* swerving, with a spin on it; **tiro ~** low shot into the corner of the net. (**d**) (*fig*) *persona* (*antipático*) unpleasant; (*difícil*) awkward, prickly; (*malévolo*) malicious; *noticia etc* malicious, ill-intentioned, designed to cause trouble.
esquinar [1a] **1** *vt* (**a**) (*hacer esquina*) to form a corner with; to be on the corner of.
(**b**) *madera etc* to square (off).
(**c**) (*LAm*: *meter*) to put in a corner.
(**d**) *pelota* to swerve, slice.
(**e**) *personas* to set at odds.
2 *vi*: **~ con** to form a corner with; to be on the corner of.
3 esquinarse *vr* (**a**) (*pelearse*) to quarrel (*con* with), fall out (*con* with).
(**b**) (*estar resentido*) to get a chip on one's shoulder.
esquinazo *nm* (**a**) (*: *esquina*) corner. (**b**) (*Cono Sur*: *serenata*) serenade. (**c**) **dar ~ a uno** to dodge sb, give sb the slip, shake sb off.
esquinera *nf* (**a**) (*) whore. (**b**) (*LAm*) corner cupboard.
esquinero 1 *adj* corner (*atr*); **farol ~** corner lamppost, lamppost on the corner; **café ~** corner café. **2** *nm* (*) idler, layabout.
esquirla *nf* splinter.
esquirol *nm* blackleg, scab*, strikebreaker, fink (*US*‡).
esquirolada *nf* strike-breaking action, work of a scab.
esquirolaje *nm*, **esquirolismo** *nm* blacklegging, strikebreaking.
esquisto *nm* schist.
esquites *nmpl* (*CAm, Méx*) popcorn.
esquivada *nf* (*LAm*) dodge, evasion.
esquivar [1a] **1** *vt* to avoid, shun; to elude, dodge, sidestep; **~ el contacto con uno** to avoid meeting sb; **~ un golpe** to dodge a blow; **~ +** *infin* to avoid + *ger*, be chary of + *ger*, be shy of + *ger*.
2 esquivarse *vr* to withdraw, stand back, shy away; to dodge.
esquivez *nf* shyness, reserve, aloofness; unsociability; elusiveness; evasiveness.
esquivo *adj* (*tímido*) shy, reserved, aloof; (*hurano*) unsociable; (*difícil de encontrar*) elusive; (*evasivo*) evasive.
esquizo* *adj, nm* schizo*.
esquizofrenia *nf* schizophrenia.
esquizofrénico, -a *adj, nm/f* schizophrenic.
esquizoide *adj, nm/f* schizoid.
esta, ésta *etc V* **este, éste**.
estabilidad *nf* stability.
estabilización *nf* stabilization.
estabilizador *nm* stabilizer; (*Aut*) anti-roll bar; **~ de cola** tailplane, rudder.
estabilizante 1 *adj* stabilizing. **2** *nm* stabilizer.
estabilizar [1f] **1** *vt* to stabilize; to make stable, steady; *precios* to stabilize, peg. **2 estabilizarse** *vr* to become stable, become stabilized; (*en la vida*) to settle down.
estable *adj* (*firme*) stable, steady; firm; (*habitual*) regular.
establecer [2d] **1** *vt* (*gen*) to establish; (*fundar*) to set up, found, institute; *colonos* to settle; *alegato* to justify, substantiate; *récord* to set (up); *domicilio* to take up, establish; **la ley establece que ...** the law provides that ...

2 establecerse *vr* to establish o.s., settle; (*Com*) to set up in business, start a business; to open an office, open a branch.
establecimiento *nm* (**a**) (*acto*) establishment, setting-up, founding; institution; settlement.
(**b**) (*local*) establishment; (*Cono Sur*) plant, works; **~ central** head office; **~ comercial** commercial establishment, business house; (*bar*) bar; (*tienda*) shop.
(**c**) (*Jur*) statute, ordinance.
establero *nm* stableboy, groom.
establo *nm* (**a**) cowshed, stall; (*esp LAm*: *granero*) barn; **~s de Augias** Augean stables. (**b**) (*Carib*: *garaje*) garage.
estaca *nf* (**a**) (*poste*) stake, post, paling; (*de tienda etc*) peg; (*palo*) cudgel, stick; **plantar la ~**** to have a crap**.
(**b**) (*Agr*) cutting.
(**c**) (*And, Cono Sur*: *espuela*) spur.
(**d**) (*And, Cono Sur*: *Min*) mining claim, mining property.
(**e**) **arrancar la ~** (*Méx*) to champ at the bit, strain at the leash.
(**f**) (*Carib*) (*indirecta*) hint; (*pulla*) taunt.
estacada *nf* (**a**) (*cerca*) fence, fencing; (*Mil*) palisade, stockade; (*LAm*: *malecón*) dike; **dejar a uno en la ~** (*fig*) to leave sb in the lurch; **estar** (*o* **quedar**) **en la ~** (*fig*) to be in a jam, be left in the lurch; to fail disastrously.
(**b**) (*LAm*: *herida*) jab, prick.
estacar [1g] **1** *vt* (**a**) *tierra, propiedad etc* to stake (out, off), mark with stakes; to fence with stakes; (*LAm*) to stretch by fastening to stakes.
(**b**) *animal* to tie to a post.
(**c**) (*Carib*: *herir*) to wound, prick.
(**d**) (*And, Carib*: *engañar*) to deceive.
2 estacarse *vr* (**a**) (*quedarse inmóvil*) to stand rooted to the spot, stand stiff as a pole.
(**b**) **~ un pie** (*And, CAm, Carib*) to prick o.s. in the foot, hurt one's foot.
estación *nf* (**a**) (*gen*) station; (*de vacaciones*) (holiday) resort; **~ balnearia** spa; **~ ballenera** whaling station; **~ biológica** biological research station; **~ de bombeo** pumping-station; **~ cabecera, ~ de cabeza** terminus; **~ carbonera** coaling station; **~ clasificadora** marshalling yard; **~ de contenedores** container terminal; **~ cósmica, ~ espacial** space-station; **~ depuradora** water purifying plant; **~ emisora** broadcasting station; **~ de empalme, ~ de enlace** junction; **~ de escucha** listening-post; **~ de esquí** ski resort; **~ de ferrocarril** railway station; **~ de fuerza** power station; **~ de gasolina** petrol station; **~ invernal, ~ de invierno** winter sports resort; **~ marítima** ferry terminal; **~ de mercancías** goods station; **~ meteorológica** weather station; **~ orbital** orbiting space-station; **~ de peaje** line of toll booths, toll plaza (*US*); **~ purificadora de aguas residuales** sewage works, sewage farm; **~ de rastreo, ~ de seguimiento** tracking station; **~ de servicio** service station; **~ de televisión** television station; **~ termal** spa; **~ terminal** terminus; **~ de trabajo** (*Inform*) workstation; **~ transformadora** substation; **~ transmisora** transmitter; **~ de trasbordo** junction; **~ veraniega** summer resort.
(**b**) **Estaciones de la vía Crucis** (*Ecl*) Stations of the Cross; Maundy Thursday devotions; **correr las estaciones*** to go on a pub-crawl*.
(**c**) (*temporada*) season; **~ de** (**las**) **lluvias** rainy reason; **~ muerta** off season, dead season; **~ de plantar** planting season.
estacional *adj* seasonal.
estacionalidad *nf* seasonal nature; seasonal variation.
estacionalmente *adv* seasonally; according to the season.
estacionamiento *nm* (**a**) stationing, placing. (**b**) (*Aut*) (*acto*) parking; (*sitio*) car-park; **~ limitado** restricted parking.
estacionar [1a] **1** *vt* to station, place; (*Aut*) to park. **2 estacionarse** *vr* to station o.s.; (*Aut*) to park; to remain stationary, be parked.
estacionario *adj* stationary; motionless; (*Med*) stable; (*Com, Fin*) slack.
estacionómetro *nm* (*Méx*) parking meter.
estacón *nm* (*LAm*) prick, jab.
estacha *nf* (*Náut*) line, mooring rope.
estada *nf* (*LAm*) stay.
estadía *nf* (**a**) (*Com*) demurrage. (**b**) (*Náut*) stay in port. (**c**) (*LAm*) (*estancia*) stay; (*duración*) length of stay.
estadillo *nm* count, survey; inventory.
estadio *nm* (**a**) (*fase*) stage, phase. (**b**) (*Mat*) furlong. (**c**) (*Dep*) stadium.
estadista *nm* (**a**) (*Pol*) statesman. (**b**) (*Mat*) statistician.
estadística[1] *nf* (**a**) (*gen*) statistics; official return(s). (**b**) (*una* ~) figure, statistic.
estadísticamente *adv* statistically.
estadístico 1 *adj* statistical. **2** *nm*, **estadística**[2] *nf* statistician.
estadizo *adj comida* not quite fresh, stale, off.
estado *nm* (**a**) (*gen*) state, condition; **~ de alarma, ~ de alerta, ~ de atención** state of alert; **~ de ánimo** state of mind; **~ de emergencia, ~ de excepción** state of emergency; **~ de gracia** (*fig*) honeymoon period; **~ de guerra** state of war; **~ de sitio** state of siege; **~ sólido** solid state; **estar en ~** (**interesante**), **estar en ~ de buena esperanza** to be pregnant, be expecting, be in the family way; **estar en buen ~** to be in good condition; to be in good order, be in working order; **estar en malísimo ~** to be in a terrible condition; **quedar en ~** to become pregnant.
(**b**) (*status*) status; rank, class; **~ civil** marital status; **el ~ matrimonial** the married state.
(**c**) (*Pol Hist*) estate; **~ llano** third estate, commoners; **tercer ~** third estate.
(**d**) (*Mil*) **~ mayor** staff; **~ mayor general** general staff.
(**e**) (*Pol*) state; **las fuerzas del E~** the forces of the state; **~ asistencial, ~ benefactor, ~ de(l) bienestar, ~ de previsión** welfare state; **~ colchón, ~ tapón** buffer state; **~ de derecho** state ruled by law, constitutional state; **~ policíaco, ~ policial** police state; **hombre de ~** statesman.
(**f**) (*lista*) list (of employees).
(**g**) (*Com, Fin*) (*resumen*) summary; (*informe*) report, statement; **~ de contabilidad** (*Méx*) balance-sheet; **~ de cuenta**(**s**) statement of account, bank statement; **~ financiero** financial statement; **~ de pérdidas y ganancias** profit and loss account; **~ de reconciliación** reconciliation statement.
estado-ciudad *nm, pl* **estados-ciudad** city-state.
estado-nación *nm, pl* **estados-nación** nation-state.
Estados Unidos *nmpl* United States (of America).
estadounidense 1 *adj* United States (*atr*), American. **2** *nmf* United States citizen (*etc*), American.
estafa *nf* swindle, trick; (*Com, Fin*) racket, ramp*, fraud.
estafador(a) *nm/f* swindler, trickster; (*Com, Fin*) swindler; racketeer.
estafar [1a] *vt* to swindle, defraud, twist*; **~ algo a uno** to swindle sth out of sb, defraud sb of sth.
estafermo *nm* (**a**) (*Hist*) quintain, dummy target. (**b**) (*: *idiota*) twit*, idiot.
estafeta *nf* (**a**) (*Correos*) post; **~ diplomática** diplomatic post. (**b**) (*oficina*) (sub) post-office. (**c**) (*persona*) courier (*t nm*); (*LAm*) drug courier.
estafetero *nm* postmaster, post-office clerk.
estafilococo *nm* staphylococcus.
estagnación *nf* (*CAm, Carib*) = **estancamiento.**
estaje *nm* (*CAm*) piecework.
estajear [1a] *vt* (*CAm*) to do as piecework; to discuss rates and conditions for.
estajero, -a *nm/f* (*CAm*) pieceworker.
estalactita *nf* stalactite.
estalagmita *nf* stalagmite.
estaliniano *adj* Stalinist.
estalinismo *nm* Stalinism.
estalinista *adj, nmf* Stalinist.
estallar [1a] *vi* (*bomba etc*) to burst, explode, go off; (*volcán*) to erupt; (*neumático*) to burst; (*vidrio etc*) to shatter; (*látigo*) to crack; (*epidemia*) to break out; (*motín*) to break out, flare up; **~ en llanto** to burst into tears; **el parabrisas estalló en pedazos** the windscreen shattered; **cuando estalló la guerra** when the war broke out; **hacer ~** to set off; (*fig*) to spark off, start.
estallido *nm* explosion, report; crash, crack; (*fig*) outbreak; **el gran ~** the big bang.
estambre *nm* (**a**) (*tela*) worsted, woollen yarn. (**b**) (*Bot*) stamen.
Estambul *nm* Istanbul.
estamento *nm* (*Pol*) estate; (*cuerpo*) body; (*estrato*) stratum, layer, level; (*clase*) class.
estameña *nf* serge.
estampa *nf* (**a**) (*huella*) imprint; footprint, track.
(**b**) (*Tip*: *imagen*) print, engraving; (*en libro*) picture; (*fig*) vignette.
(**c**) (*fig*: *aspecto*) stamp; appearance, aspect; **de buena ~** decent-looking; **de ~ poco agradable** of disagreeable appearance, unpleasant-looking; **ser la propia ~ de uno** to be the very image of sb.
(**d**) (*imprenta*: *arte*) printing; (*máquina*) printing press;

dar un libro a la ~ to publish a book.
estampación *nf* (*acto*) printing; engraving; (*fileteado*) tooling.
estampado 1 *adj tela* printed; *vestido* print. **2** *nm* (**a**) (*impresión*) printing; stamping. (**b**) (*vestido*) print (dress), cotton print.
estampar [1a] *vt* (*imprimir*) to print; (*marcar*) to stamp; (*grabar*) to engrave; (*filetear*) to tool; *beso* to plant, place (*en* on); (*fig*) to stamp, imprint (*en* on); **quedaba estampado en la memoria** it was stamped on one's memory.
estampía: **de ~** *adv* suddenly, without warning, unexpectedly.
estampida *nf* (**a**) (*Agr, Zool*: *esp LAm*) stampede. (**b**) **de ~** *V* **estampía.** (**c**) = **estampido.**
estampido *nm* report; detonation; bang, boom, crash; **~ sónico** sonic boom.
estampilla *nf* (**a**) (*sello*) stamp, seal; rubber stamp. (**b**) (*LAm Correos*) stamp.
estampillado *nm* (*LAm*) stamp duty.
estampillar [1a] *vt* to rubber-stamp.
estampita *nf* (**a**) (*Rel*) small religious picture. (**b**) (*) con trick*.
estancado *adj* (**a**) *agua* stagnant. (**b**) (*fig*) static; **estar ~** to be held up, be blocked, be at a standstill; to be deadlocked.
estancamiento *nm* (**a**) (*de agua*) stagnancy, stagnation. (**b**) (*fig*) stagnation; blockage, stoppage, suspension; deadlock.
estancar [1g] **1** *vt* (**a**) *agua* to hold up, hold back, stem.

(**b**) (*fig*) *progreso* to stem, block, check, hold up; *negocio* to stop, suspend; *negociación* to bring to a standstill; to deadlock; (*Com*) to monopolize, establish a monopoly in; (*pey*) to corner.

2 estancarse *vr* (**a**) (*agua*) to stagnate, become stagnant; to be held back.

(**b**) (*fig*) to stagnate.
estancia *nf* (**a**) (*permanencia*) stay. (**b**) (*domicilio*) dwelling, abode; (*cuarto*) living room. (**c**) (*LAm*: *de ganado*) farm, cattle ranch; country estate; (*Carib*: *quinta pequeña*) small farm, smallholding. (**d**) (*Poét*) stanza.
estanciera *nf* (*Cono Sur*) station wagon.
estanciero *nm* (*LAm*) farmer, rancher.
estanco 1 *adj* watertight; **~ al aire** airtight.

2 *nm* state monopoly; government store where monopoly goods are sold, (*esp*) tobacconist's (shop), cigar store (*US*); (*And*: *bodega*) liquor store.
estand *nm* = **stand.**
estándar *adj, nm* standard.
estandar(d)ización *nf* standardization.
estandar(d)izado *adj* standardized.
estandar(d)izar [1f] *vt* to standardize.
estandarte *nm* banner, standard; **~ real** royal standard.
estanflación *nf* stagflation.
estánnico *adj* stannic.
estanque *nm* (**a**) pool, pond, small lake; (*Agr etc*) tank, reservoir; **~ de juegos, ~ para chapotear** paddling-pool. (**b**) (*Cono Sur*) (petrol)-tank.
estanqueidad *nf* (*al agua*) watertightness; (*al aire*) air tightness.
estanquero, -a *nm/f* tobaconnist.
estanquillo *nm* (**a**) (*Méx*) booth, kiosk, stall. (**b**) = **estanco.**
estante *nm* (**a**) (*mueble*) rack, stand; piece of furniture with shelves; **~ (para libros)** bookcase. (**b**) (*LAm*: *soporte*) prop.
estantería *nf* shelving, shelves.
estantigua *nf* apparition; (*) fright, sight, scarecrow.
estantillo *nm* (*And, Carib*) prop, support.
estañar [1a] *vt* (*Téc*) to tin; to solder.
estaño *nm* tin; **~ para soldar** solder.
estaquear [1a] *vt* (*LAm*) *pieles* to stretch on stakes.
estaquilla *nf* (*de madera*) peg; pin; (*clavo*) spike, long nail; (*de tienda*) tent peg.
estaquillar [1a] *vt* to pin, peg (down, out), fasten with pegs.
estar [1o] **1** *vi* (**a**) (*gen*) to be; (*hallarse*) to stand, be found; (*estar en casa*) to be in, be at home; (*permanecer*) to stay, remain, keep; (*asistir*) to be present (*en* at); **el monumento está en el mercado** the monument is (*o* stands) in the market; **¿está?** is he in?; **la señora no está** madam is not in, madam is not at home; **está fuera** she's away; she's out of town, she's on a trip; **para eso estamos** that's why we're here, that's why we've come; (*respondiendo a gracias*) it's the least we can do; **¿cómo está?** how is he?; **está mucho mejor** he's much better; **¿cómo estamos?** how do we stand?; (*Dep*) what's the score?; **aquí no se puede ~** it's intolerable here; it's too hot (*o* cold *o* dangerous *etc*) here; **el día que estuve a verlo** the day I went to see it.

(**b**) (+ *adj*) to be; **está enfermo** he is ill; **ahora está vacío** now it's empty; **¡qué elegante estás!** how smart you're looking!; **está más viejo** he looks older, he seems older.

(**c**) (*comprensión*) **¿está Vd?** do you get it?, understand?; (*acuerdo*) **¿estamos?** are we agreed?, right?, OK?*

(**d**) (*estar listo*) to be ready; **en seguida está** it'll be ready in a moment; **dos vueltas más y ya está** two more turns and that's it, two more turns and it's done; **ya estoy** I'm ready; I'm all done, I'm finished; **¡ya estamos!** that's it!; (*enfadado*) that's enough!, I'll not listen to any more!

(**e**) (+ *ger*) to be; **estaba corriendo** he was running; **me está molestando** he's annoying me; **está siendo preparado** it is being prepared; **nos estamos engañando** we are deceiving ourselves.

(**f**) (+ *ptp*) to be; **está envuelto en papel** it is wrapped in paper; **para las 5 estará terminado** it will be finished for 5 o'clock.

(**g**) (*fecha*) **estamos a 5 de mayo** it is the 5th of May, today is the 5th of May; **¿a cuántos estamos?** what's the date?

(**h**) (*precio etc*) **~ a** to be, sell at, stand at; (*récord*) to stand at; **las uvas están a 50 pesetas** grapes are at 50 pesetas; **el récord anterior estaba a** (*o* **en**) **33 minutos** the previous record stood at 33 minutes.

(**i**) **~ a lo que resulte** to stand by the result.

(**j**) **~ con la gripe** to have flu, be down with flu; **estuvo con la enfermedad durante 2 años** she suffered from the disease for 2 years.

(**k**) **~ de vacaciones** to be (away) on holiday; **~ de paseo** to be out for a walk; **~ de uniforme** to be in uniform; **~ de viaje** to be travelling, be on a trip.

(**l**) **está de jefe** he is acting as head, he is the acting head; **está de camarero** he's working as a waiter.

(**m**) **estoy así de nervioso** I'm so nervous, I'm that nervous.

(**n**) **~ en** (*causar*) to be the cause of; **en eso está** that's the reason, that must be the motive.

(**o**) **~ en algo** (*involucrado*) to be involved in sth, be mixed up in sth; **en ello estamos** we're doing all we can.

(**p**) **no está en él hacerlo** it is not in his power to do it; **no está en sí** she's not in her right mind.

(**q**) **~ en que ...** (*persona*) to believe that ..., understand that ...; to be sure that ...; **el problema está en que ...** the problem lies in the fact that ...

(**r**) **~ para** + *infin* to be about to + *infin*, be on the point of + *ger*.

(**s**) **~ para** + *n* to be in the mood for + *n*.

(**t**) **~ por** *política* to be in favour of; *persona* to back, support, side with.

(**u**) **~ por** + *infin* to be half inclined to + *infin*, have half a mind to + *infin*; **yo estoy por dejarlo** I vote (*o* say) we leave it; **está por llover** (*LAm*) it's about to rain.

(**v**) **está todavía por hacer** it remains to be done, it is still to be done; **la historia de aquello está por escribir** the history of that is still to be written.

(**w**) **está que rabia** he's hopping mad, he's furious.

(**x**) **están sin vender** they remain unsold, they have not been sold.

(**y**) **~ sobre sí** to have o.s. under control; to be puffed up with conceit; *V* **bien 1** (**a**), **mal 1** (**a**), **más 1** (**e**) *y muchos sustantivos.*

2 estarse *vr* (**a**) *refuerza el sentido del vi*: **se estaba muriendo** he was (gradually, at that moment) dying.

(**b**) (*quedarse*) to stay, remain; **~ tranquilamente en casa** to stay quietly at home.

(**c**) **¡estáte quieto!** keep still!, stop fidgeting!; behave yourself!

(**d**) **se está bien aquí** it's nice here.
estarcido *nm* stencil, stencilled sketch.
estarcir [3b] *vt* to stencil.
estaribel‡ *nm* nick‡, prison.
estárter *nm* = **stárter.**
estatal *adj* state (*atr*); (*Esp frec*) national, nationwide.
estatalismo *nm* state ownership.
estatalista 1 *adj* (*Esp*) national, nationwide. **2** *nmf* member of a nationwide party.
estatalización *nf* nationalization, taking into public ownership.

estatalizar [1f] *vt* to nationalize; take into public ownership.
estática *nf* statics.
estático *adj* (**a**) static. (**b**) = **extático.**
estatificación *nf* nationalization, taking into public ownership.
estatificado *adj* nationalized, publicly-owned.
estatificar [1g] *vt* to nationalize, take into public ownership.
estatismo *nm* (**a**) stillness, motionlessness. (**b**) (*Pol*) state control.
estatización *nf* nationalization, taking into public ownership.
estatizar [1f] *vt* to nationalize, take into public ownership.
estator *nm* (*Elec, Mat*) stator.
estatua *nf* statue.
estatuaria *nf* statuary (*art*).
estatuario *adj* statuesque.
estatuilla *nf* statuette, figure, figurine.
estatuir [3g] *vt* (**a**) (*ordenar*) to establish, enact, ordain. (**b**) (*probar*) to prove.
estatura *nf* stature, height; **de regular** ~ of average height; **un hombre de 1,80m de** ~ a man 1.80m in height.
estatus *nm invar* status.
estatutario *adj* statutory.
estatuto *nm* (*Jur*) statute; (*de ciudad etc*) by-law; (*de comité etc*) rule, standing rule; **E~ de Autonomía** (*Esp Pol*) statute of autonomy.
estay *nm* (*Náut*) stay.
este[1] (*Geog*) **1** *adj parte* east, eastern; *dirección* easterly; *viento* east, easterly.
2 *nm* (**a**) (*Geog*) east; **los países del E~** the countries of the East (of Europe); **en la parte del** ~ in the eastern part; **al** ~ **de Toledo** to the east of Toledo, on the east side of Toledo; **eso cae más hacia el** ~ that lies further (to the) east.
(**b**) (*viento*) east wind.
este[2] *adj dem m,* **esta** *f* this; **estos** *adj dem mpl,* **estas** *fpl* these.
éste *pron dem m,* **ésta** *f* (**a**) this; this one; the latter; **éstos** *pron dem mpl,* **éstas** *fpl* these; the latter; **en ésta** in this town (from where I am writing); **jurar por éstas** to swear by all that is holy. (**b**) (*LAm**) **este ...*** er ...*, um ...*
estearina *nf* (**a**) (*Quím*) stearin. (**b**) (*LAm*: *vela*) candle.
esteatita *nf* soapstone.
Esteban *nm* Stephen.
estela *nf* (**a**) (*Náut*) wake; (*Aer*) trail; ~ **de condensación,** ~ **de humo** vapour trail.
(**b**) (*fig*) trail; **el discurso dejó larga** ~ **de comentarios** the speech caused a great deal of comment.
(**c**) (*Arquit*) stele, stela.
estelar *adj* (**a**) (*Astron*) stellar, sidereal. (**b**) (*Teat etc*) star (*atr*); **cargo** ~ star role; **combate** ~ (*Boxeo*) star bout, star contest; **función** ~ all-star show.
estemple *nm* pit prop.
esténcil *nm* (*LAm*) stencil.
estenografía *nf* shorthand, stenography.
estenografiar [1c] *vt* to take down in shorthand.
estenográfico *adj* shorthand (*atr*).
estenógrafo, -a *nm/f* shorthand writer, stenographer.
estenotipia *nf* shorthand typing.
estenotipista *nmf* shorthand typist.
estentóreamente *adv* in a stentorian voice.
estentóreo *adj voz* stentorian, booming; *sonido* strident.
estepa *nf* (**a**) (*Geog*) steppe. (**b**) (*Bot*) rockrose.
estera *nf* mat, matting; ~ **de baño** bathmat.
esteral *nm* (*Cono Sur*) swamp, marsh.
esterar [1a] **1** *vt* to cover with a mat, put a mat on (*o* over). **2** *vi* (*) to put on one's winter clothes (ahead of time).
estecolado *nm,* **estercoladura** *nf,* **estercolamiento** *nm* manuring; muck-spreading.
estercolar [1a] *vt* to manure.
estercolero *nm* manure heap, dunghill.
estéreo *nm* stereo.
estéreo... *pref* stereo...
estereofonía *nf* stereophony.
estereofónico *adj* stereophonic, stereo.
estereoscópico *adj* stereoscopic.
estereoscopio *nm* stereoscope.
estereotipación *nf* stereotyping.
estereotipado *adj* stereotyped.
estereotipar [1a] *vt* to stereotype.
estereotipo *nm* stereotype.
esterero *nm*: **quedar en el** ~ (*Carib**) to be on one's uppers*.
estéril *adj* (**a**) *terreno* sterile, barren. (**b**) (*fig*) *esfuerzo etc* vain, futile, unproductive.
esterilidad *nf* (**a**) (*de terreno*) sterility, barrenness. (**b**) (*fig*) futility, uselessness.
esterilización *nf* sterilization.
esterilizar [1f] *vt* to sterilize.
estérilmente *adv* (*fig*) vainly, uselessly, fruitlessly.
esterilla *nf* (**a**) (*alfombrilla*) small mat; straw mat.
(**b**) (*materia*) matting; (*LAm*) wickerwork, rush matting; **silla de** ~ rush chair, wicker chair; ~ **de alambre** wire mesh.
(**c**) (*Cos*) gold (*o* silver) braid.
esterlina *adj*: **libra** ~ pound sterling.
esternón *nm* breastbone, sternum.
estero[1] *nm* matting.
estero[2] *nm* (**a**) (*estuario*) estuary; tideland; inlet. (**b**) (*Cono Sur*: *pantano*) swamp, marsh. (**c**) (*Cono Sur, And*: *arroyo*) brook. (**d**) **estar en el** ~ (*Carib**) to be in a fix*.
esteroide *nm* steroid; ~ **anabólico,** ~ **anabolizante** anabolic steroid.
estertor *nm* death rattle.
estertoroso *adj* stertorous.
esteta *nmf* aesthete.
estética *nf* aesthetics; aesthetic doctrine, aesthetic outlook.
esteticién *nf* beautician, beauty specialist.
esteticismo *nm* aestheticism.
esteticista *nmf* beauty consultant, beauty specialist.
estético *adj* aesthetic.
estetoscopio *nm* stethoscope.
esteva *nf* plough handle.
estevado *adj* bow-legged, bandy-legged.
estiaje *nm* low water.
estiba *nf* (**a**) (*Mil Hist*) rammer. (**b**) (*Náut*) stowage; **mudar la** ~ to shift the cargo about. (**c**) (*Náut*: *acto*) loading. (**d**) (‡) beating up*, bashing*.
estibado *nm* stowage.
estibador 1 *adj*: **empresa estibadora** shipping company. **2** *nm* stevedore.
estibar [1a] *vt* (**a**) (*Náut*: *meter*) to stow, put; (*cargar*) to load; (*almacenar*) to house, store. (**b**) *lana etc* to pack tight, compress.
estiércol *nm* dung, manure; ~ **de caballo** horse manure; ~ **líquido** liquid manure.
Estigio *nm* Styx.
estigio *adj* Stygian.
estigma *m* (**a**) (*lit, fig*) stigma; (*marca*) mark, brand; (*marca de nacimiento*) birthmark; (*Rel*: *t* **~s** *pl*) stigmata. (**b**) (*Bot*) stigma.
estigmatizar [1f] *vt* to stigmatize.
estilar [1a] **1** *vt* (**a**) *documento* to draw up (in due form).
(**b**) (*usar*) to use, be in the habit of using; to wear, adopt.
2 *vi* **estilarse** *vr* to be in fashion, be used, be worn; **ya no se estila la chistera** top hats aren't in fashion any more; ~ + *infin* to be customary to + *infin.*
estilete *nm* (*arma*) stiletto; (*de tocadiscos*) stylus.
estilismo *nm* fashion design(ing).
estilista *nmf* (*Liter etc*) stylist; (*Téc*) designer; (*de vestidos*) dress stylist, fashion designer.
estilística *nf* stylistics.
estilístico *adj* stylistic.
estilización *nf* (*Téc*) styling.
estilizado *adj* stylized.
estilizar [1f] **1** *vt* to stylize; (*Téc*) to design, style. **2** *vi* to cut a dash, show off.
estilo *nm* (**a**) (*gen*) style; manner; fashion; **el** ~ **oscuro del escritor** the writer's obscure style; ~ **directo** (*Ling*) direct speech; ~ **indirecto libre** free indirect style; ~ **de vida** lifestyle; way of life; **el** ~ **de vida británico** the British way of life; **un comedor** ~ **Luis XV** a dining-room suite in Louis XV style; **un andar** ~ **oso** a gait like a bear's; **una casa** ~ **Tudor** a Tudor-style house; **al** ~ **de** in the style of; after the manner of; **al** ~ **antiguo** in the old style; **algo por el** ~ something of the sort, that sort of thing; something along these lines; **los dictadores y otros por el** ~ dictators and others of that sort, dictators and suchlike; **no tenemos nada por ese** ~ we have nothing in that line.
(**b**) (*Natación*) stroke; ~ (**libre**) freestyle; ~ (**de**) **pecho** breast-stroke.
(**c**) (*pluma*: *Téc*) stylus; (*de reloj de sol*) gnomon, needle.
(**d**) (*Bot*) style.

estilográfica *nf* fountain-pen.
estiloso *adj* stylish.
estima *nf* (**a**) (*aprecio*) esteem, respect; **tener a uno en gran ~** to hold sb in high esteem. (**b**) (*Náut*) dead reckoning; **a ~** by dead reckoning.
estimable *adj* (**a**) (*gen*) estimable, esteemed; reputable; **su ~ carta** (*Com*) your esteemed letter. (**b**) *cantidad etc* considerable.
estimación *nf* (**a**) (*acto*) estimation; (*evaluación*) valuation; (*pronóstico*) forecast. (**b**) estimate, estimation; valuation. (**c**) (*aprecio*) esteem, regard; **~ propia** self-esteem.
estimado *adj* esteemed, respected; **'E~ Señor ...'** 'Dear Sir ...'.
estimar [1a] **1** *vt* (**a**) (*evaluar*) to estimate; to appraise; (*calibrar*) to gauge; (*calcular*) reckon, compute; **~ algo en mil pesetas** to value sth at a thousand pesetas.
(**b**) **~ que** ... to think that ..., reckon that ...
(**c**) (*apreciar*) to esteem, respect; **~ a uno en mucho** to have a high regard for sb; **~ a uno en poco** to have a low opinion of sb; **se lo estimo mucho** I am much indebted to you for it.
2 estimarse *vr* (**a**) (*evaluarse*) to be estimated (*en* at), be valued (*en* at).
(**b**) **¡se estima!** thanks very much!, I appreciate it!
(**c**) (*uno mismo*) to have a good opinion of o.s.; **si se estima no hará tal cosa** if he has any self-respect he'll do nothing of the sort.
estimativamente *adv* roughly, by guesswork.
estimativo *adj* rough, approximate.
estimulante 1 *adj* stimulating. **2** *nm* stimulant.
estimular [1a] *vt* (*gen*) to stimulate; to encourage, excite, incite, prompt; *apetito* to stimulate; *debate etc* to promote; *esfuerzo, industria* to encourage, boost.
estímulo *nm* stimulus, stimulation; encouragement; inducement, incentive.
estío *nm* summer.
estipendiar [1b] *vt* to pay a stipend to.
estipendiario *adj, nm* stipendiary.
estipendio *nm* (*sueldo*) stipend; salary; (*derechos*) fee.
estíptico 1 *adj* (**a**) (*Med*) styptic. (**b**) (*estreñido*) constipated. (**c**) (*fig*) mean, miserly. **2** *nm* styptic.
estipulación *nf* stipulation, condition, proviso.
estipular [1a] *vt* to stipulate.
estirada *nf* (*Dep*) dive, stretch.
estirado 1 *adj* (**a**) stretched, extended; stretched tight; (*alambre*) drawn. (**b**) (*fig*) (*tieso*) stiff, starchy; (*pomposo*) pompous; (*Cono Sur: engreído*) vain, stuck-up*. (**c**) (*fig: tacaño*) tight-fisted. **2** *nm* (*de vidrio*) drawing; (*de pelo*) straightening; **~ de (la) piel** face-lift, cosmetic surgery.
estirador *nm* (*Téc*) stretcher.
estirajar* [1a] = **estirar**.
estiraje *nm* stretching.
estiramiento *nm*: **~ facial** face-lift.
estirar [1a] **1** *vt* (**a**) (*extender*) to stretch, pull out, draw out; to extend; (*Téc*) *alambre etc* to draw; *oído* to prick up; *cuello* to stretch, crane; *ropa* to iron lightly, run the iron over.
(**b**) (*demasiado*) to overstretch, strain.
(**c**) (*fig*) *discurso etc* to spin out, stretch out; *dinero* to eke out.
(**d**) (*And**: *matar*) to kill, shoot.
(**e**) (*And* ††: *azotar*) to flog.
(**f**) (*Cono Sur, Méx: tirar*) to pull, tug at.
2 estirarse *vr* (**a**) (*alargarse*) to stretch. (**b**) (*Dep*) **el equipo se estiró** the team moved upfield; **el jugador se estiró por la banda** the player ran up the touchline.
estirón *nm* (**a**) (*tirón*) pull, tug, jerk. (**b**) (*crecimiento*) spurt, sudden growth; **dar un ~** to shoot up.
estironear [1a] *vt* (*Cono Sur*) to pull hard at, tug sharply at.
estirpe *nf* stock, lineage; race; **de la ~ regia** of royal stock, of the blood royal.
estítico = **estíptico**.
estitiquez *nf* (*LAm*) constipation.
estival *adj* summer (*atr*); summery.
esto *pron dem 'neutro'* this; this thing, this affair, this matter; **~ es difícil** this is difficult; **todo ~ es inútil** all this is useless; **~ es, ...** that is (to say), ...; **~ de la boda** this business about the wedding; **antes de ~** before this; **con ~** herewith; whereupon; **durante ~** in the meantime, while this was going on; **en ~** at this point; **por ~** for this reason; **¿qué es ~?** what's all this?; **y esto ¿qué es?** whatever is this?; **~ ...** (*vacilando*) er ..., um ...
estocada *nf* (**a**) (*golpe*) stab, thrust; lunge; (*herida*) stab wound; (*Taur etc*) death blow, (final) thrust. (**b**) (*fig*) sharp retort.
Estocolmo *nm* Stockholm.
estofa *nf* (**a**) (*tela*) quilting, quilted material. (**b**) (*fig*) quality, class; **de baja ~** poor-quality, *persona* low-class.
estofado 1 *adj* (**a**) (*Culin*) stewed. (**b**) (*Cos*) quilted. **2** *nm* stew, hotpot.
estofar [1a] *vt* (**a**) (*Culin*) to stew. (**b**) (*Cos*) to quilt.
estoicidad *nf* stoicism.
estoicismo *nm* stoicism.
estoico 1 *adj* stoic(al). **2** *nm* stoic.
estola *nf* stole; **~ de visón** mink cape.
estolidez *nf* stupidity.
estólido *adj* stupid.
estomacal 1 *adj* stomachic; stomach (*atr*); **trastorno ~** stomach upset. **2** *nm* stomachic.
estomagante *adj* (**a**) *comida* indigestible. (**b**) (*: *molesto*) upsetting, annoying; revolting.
estomagar [1h] *vt* (**a**) (*Med*) to give indigestion to, upset. (**b**) (*fig*) to upset, annoy.
estómago *nm* stomach; **dolor de ~** stomach ache; **revolver el ~ a uno** to revolt sb, make sb's stomach turn over; (*fig*) to upset sb, annoy sb; **tener buen ~** (*fig*) to be thick-skinned; to have an elastic conscience, be none too scrupulous.
estomatólogo, -a *nm/f* dentist.
Estonia *nf* Esthonia.
estonio, -a 1 *adj, nm/f* Esthonian. **2** *nm* (*Ling*) Esthonian.
estopa *nf* (**a**) (*del cáñamo*) tow; (*harpillera*) burlap; (*Náut*) oakum; (*Carib*) cotton waste. (**b**) **largar** (*etc*) **~ a**‡ to bash*, hit.
estopero *nm* (*Méx Aut*) oil seal.
estoperol *nm* (**a**) (*mecha*) tow, wick. (**b**) (*And: tachuela*) brass tack. (**c**) (*And: sartén*) frying pan.
estopilla *nf* cheesecloth.
estoque *nm* (**a**) (*espada*) rapier, sword; **estar hecho un ~** to be as thin as a rake. (**b**) (*Bot*) gladiolus.
estoquear [1a] *vt* to stab, run through.
estorbar [1a] **1** *vt* (*obstaculizar*) to hinder, obstruct, impede, be (*o* get) in the way of; (*dificultar*) to interfere with; (*molestar*) to bother, disturb, upset. **2** *vi* to be in the way.
estorbo *nm* hindrance, obstruction, impediment, obstacle; drag; nuisance; **no hay ~ para que se haga** there is no obstacle (*o* bar, impediment) to its being done; **el mayor ~ es el director** the biggest obstacle is the headmaster.
estornino *nm* starling.
estornudar [1a] *vi* to sneeze.
estornudo *nm* sneeze.
estoy *etc V* **estar**.
estrábico *adj persona* wall-eyed; *ojo* squinting, strabismic.
estrabismo *nm* squint, strabismus.
Estrabón *nm* Strabo.
estrada *nf* (**a**) (*carretera*) road, highway; **batir la ~** (*Mil*) to reconnoitre. (**b**) (*And: Agr*) section of a rubber plantation (*150 trees*).
estrado *nm* stage, platform; dais; (*Mús*) bandstand; (*Hist*) drawing room; **~s** law courts; **~ del testigo** witness stand; **citar a uno para ~s** to subpoena sb.
estrafalario *adj* (**a**) (*excéntrico*) odd, outlandish, eccentric. (**b**) *ropa* slovenly, sloppy.
estragado *adj* (*arruinado*) ruined; (*corrumpido*) corrupted, spoiled, perverted; (*depravado*) depraved; (*descuidado*) slovenly, careless, disorderly.
estragante *adj* damaging, destructive.
estragar [1h] *vt* to ruin; *gusto etc* to corrupt, spoil, pervert; to deprave.
estrago *nm* ruin, destruction; corruption, perversion; **~s** havoc, destruction, ravages; **~s** (*Jur*) criminal damage; **los ~s del tiempo** the ravages of time; **hacer ~s en** (*o* **entre**) to play havoc with, wreak havoc among.
estragón *nm* (*Bot, Culin*) tarragon.
estramador *nm* (*Méx*) comb.
estrambólico *adj* (*LAm*), **estrambótico** *adj* odd, outlandish, eccentric.
estrambote *nm* (*Poét*) extra lines, extra verses, addition.
estrangis* *adv*: **de ~** secretly, on the quiet.
estrangul *nm* (*Mús*) mouthpiece.
estrangulación *nf* strangulation.
estrangulado *adj* (*Med*) strangulated.
estrangulador *nm* (**a**) (*persona*) strangler. (**b**) (*Mec*) throttle; (*Aut etc*) choke.
estrangulamiento *nm* (*Aut*) narrow stretch of road, bottleneck.

estrangular [1a] *vt* (**a**) *persona* to strangle. (**b**) (*Med*) to strangulate. (**c**) (*Mec*) to throttle; to choke.
estranji *adv* = **estrangis.**
estranqui* *nmf* = **extranjero.**
estraperlear* [1a] *vi* to deal in black-market goods.
estraperlista 1 *adj* black-market (*atr*). **2** *nmf* blackmarketeer.
estraperlo *nm* black market; **comprar algo en el ~, comprar algo de ~** to buy sth on the black market.
estrapontín *nm* (*Aut*) back seat; side seat, extra seat.
Estrasburgo *nm* Strasbourg.
estratagema *nf* stratagem.
estratega *nmf* strategist; *V t* **gabinete.**
estrategia *nf* strategy; generalship; **~ de la tensión** destabilizing campaign.
estratégico *adj* strategic(al).
estratificación *nf* stratification.
estratificado *adj* stratified; *madera* laminated.
estratificar [1g] **1** *vt* to stratify. **2 estratificarse** *vr* to stratify, be stratified.
estratigrafía *nf* stratigraphy.
estratigráfico *adj* stratigraphic.
estrato *nm* (**a**) (*gen*) stratum, layer. (**b**) (*nube*) stratus.
estratocúmulo *nm* stratocumulus.
estratosfera *nf* stratosphere.
estratosférico *adj* stratospheric.
estraza *nf* rag; **papel de ~** brown paper, wrapping paper.
estrechamente *adv* (**a**) (*apretadamente*) narrowly; tightly. (**b**) (*austeramente*) austerely. (**c**) (*íntimamente*) closely, intimately. (**d**) (*severamente*) strictly, rigidly; meanly; narrow-mindedly.
estrechar [1a] **1** *vt* (**a**) (*hacer estrecho*) to narrow; *ropa* to make smaller, reduce, take in; *amistad etc* to draw tighter.
(**b**) (*apretar*) to squeeze; *persona* to hug, embrace, enfold in one's arms; *mano* to grasp, clasp; to shake.
(**c**) (*fig*) *enemigo* to press hard.
(**d**) (*fig: presionar*) to compel, constrain, bring pressure to bear on.
2 estrecharse *vr* (**a**) (*encogerse*) to narrow, get narrow; to tighten, get tighter; **~ en** to squeeze into.
(**b**) (*dos personas*) to embrace (one another), hug.
(**c**) **se estrecharon la mano** they shook hands.
(**d**) (*amistad etc*) to become closer, become more intimate; **~ con uno** to get very friendly with sb.
(**e**) **~ (en los gastos)** (*Fin*) to stint o.s., economize, cut down on expenditure.
estrechez *nf* (**a**) (*angostura*) narrowness, tightness; (*falta de espacio*) cramped nature, smallness, lack of room.
(**b**) (*Fin*) want; financial stringency; **~ del dinero** tightness of money, shortage of money; **estrecheces** financial difficulties, financial straits; **vivir con ~** to live in straitened circumstances.
(**c**) (*de amistad*) closeness, intimacy.
(**d**) (*rigidez*) strictness, rigidity; (*austeridad*) austerity; **~ de conciencia** small-mindedness; **~ de miras** narrow-mindedness.
estrecho 1 *adj* (**a**) (*angosto*) narrow; tight; *cuarto* cramped, small; *falda etc* tight; *pantalón* tight, narrow, close-fitting; **estos zapatos me están muy ~s** these shoes are too small for me, these shoes pinch my feet.
(**b**) *dinero etc* tight, short; *vida* austere.
(**c**) *relación etc* close, intimate; *amistad* close.
(**d**) *actitud, prohibición* strict, rigid; *carácter* austere; (*pey*) mean, mean-spirited; (*t* **~ de conciencia**) small-minded; (*t* **~ de miras**) narrow-minded; insular, parochial; **es muy estrecha** she's very strait-laced; **hacerse el ~ con uno** to be mean to sb, be difficult with sb; **¡no te hagas la estrecha!** don't be so coy!
2 *nm* (**a**) (*Geog*) strait(s); narrows, channel; **E~ de Gibraltar** Straits of Gibraltar.
(**b**) (*: *aprieto*) fix*, jam*, predicament; **al ~** by force, under compulsion; **poner a uno en el ~ de +** *infin* to force sb into a position of having to + *infin.*
estrechura *nf* (**a**) = **estrechez.** (**b**) = **estrecho 2.**
estregadera *nf* (**a**) (*bruza*) scrubbing brush; (*fregasuelos*) floor mop. (**b**) (*de puerta*) door scraper, boot scraper.
estregar [1h *y* 1j] *vt* (*frotar*) to rub; (*rasear*) to scrape; (*con cepillo*) to scrub, scour.
estrella 1 *nf* (**a**) (*Astron y fig*) star; **~ de Belén** star of Bethlehem; **~ de David** Star of David; **~ fija** fixed star; **~ fugaz** shooting star; **~ de guía** guiding star; **~ de mar** starfish; **~ de neutrones, ~ neutrónica** neutron star; **~ del norte** north star; **~ polar** polar star; **~ de rabo** comet; **~ vespertina** evening star; **creer en su buena ~** to believe in one's lucky star; **nacer con ~** to be born under a lucky star, be born lucky; **poner a uno sobre las ~s** to praise sb to the skies; **tener (buena) ~** to be lucky; **tener mala ~** to be unlucky; **ver las ~s** (*fig*) to see stars.
(**b**) (*Tip*) asterisk, star; **un hotel (de) cinco ~s** a five-star hotel.
(**c**) (*Zool*) blaze, white patch.
(**d**) (*Mil*) star, pip.
(**e**) (*Cine, Teat etc*) star; **~ del cine** movie star, film star; **ser la ~** to star, be the star.
2 *atr* star (*atr*); **atracción ~** star attraction.
estrelladera *nf* (*Culin etc*) slice.
estrellado *adj* (**a**) (*con estrellas*) starred; (*de forma de estrella*) star-shaped; *cielo* starry, full of stars; *vestido* spangled. (**b**) (*roto*) smashed, shattered. (**c**) (*Culin*) *huevo* fried.
estrellamar *nf* starfish.
estrellar [1a] **1** *vt* (**a**) (*decorar*) to star, spangle, cover with stars.
(**b**) (*romper*) to smash, shatter; to dash to pieces, smash to pieces; **lo estrelló contra la pared** he smashed it against the wall; **estrelló el balón en el poste** he crashed the ball into the goal-post; **la corriente amenazaba con ~ el barco contra las rocas** the current threatened to dash the boat on to the rocks.
(**c**) *huevo* to fry.
2 estrellarse *vr* to smash, shatter, crash (*contra* against); to be dashed to pieces; **~ contra** to crash into; **~ con una dificultad** to come right up against a difficulty.
estrellato *nm* stardom.
estrellón *nm* (**a**) (*fig*) (*estrella*) star, large star; (*fuegos artificiales*) star firework. (**b**) (*esp LAm*) (*Aer*) crash; (*Aut*) crash, smash, collision.
estremecedor *adj* alarming, disturbing, shattering.
estremecer [2d] **1** *vt* (*t fig*) to shake.
2 estremecerse *vr* (*edificio etc*) to shake, vibrate, tremble; (*persona: miedo*) to tremble (*ante* at, *de* with); (*horror*) to shiver, shudder (*de* with); (*emoción*) to tingle, tremble, thrill (*de* with); (*frío*) to shiver (*de* with).
estremecido *adj* shaking, trembling (*de* with).
estremecimiento *nm*, **estremezón** *nm* (**a**) (*V vr*) (*And, Carib*) tremor, vibration; shiver, shudder; shaking, trembling; tingling.
(**b**) (*And, Carib: de tierra*) tremor.
estrena *nf* (**a**) (*regalo*) good-luck gift, token; **~s** (*de Navidad*) Christmas presents. (**b**) = **estreno.**
estrenar [1a] **1** *vt* (**a**) to use for the first time; *ropa* to wear (*o* put on *etc*) for the first time, show off for the first time.
(**b**) (*Cine*) to give its première, show for the first time; to release, put on release; (*Teat*) to perform for the first time, give a first performance to.
2 *vi* (**a**) (*Teat*) **aquí estrenan mucho** they stage a lot of premières here, they put on a lot of new plays here.
(**b**) (*Carib Com*) to make a down payment.
3 estrenarse *vr* (**a**) (*persona*) to make one's début, appear for the first time; (*) to start to do some work; **no se estrena** he hasn't done a hand's turn.
(**b**) (*Cine*) to have its première, be shown for the first time; (*Teat*) to open, have its first night; to be performed for the first time.
(**c**) (*Com*) to make the first sale of the day.
(**d**) (*) to cough up*, pay up.
estrenista *nmf* (*Teat*) first-nighter.
estreno *nm* (**a**) first use; first appearance; **fue cuando el ~ del coche nuevo** it was when we went out in the new car for the first time.
(**b**) (*de persona*) début, first appearance; **¡mal ~!** what a wretched start!
(**c**) (*Cine*) première; release; (*Teat*) first night, first performance; **~ general** general release; **riguroso ~** world première.
(**d**) (*Carib*) down payment, deposit.
estrenque *nm* stout esparto rope.
estrenuo *adj* vigorous, energetic; enterprising.
estreñido *adj* constipated, costive.
estreñimiento *nm* constipation.
estreñir [3h *y* 3k] **1** *vt* to constipate, bind. **2 estreñirse** *vr* to get constipated.
estrepitarse [1a] *vr* (*Carib*) to kick up a fuss, make a scene.
estrépito *nm* noise, racket, row; tremendous din; fuss; **reírse con ~** to laugh uproariously.
estrepitosamente *adv* noisily; loudly, deafeningly;

rowdily, boisterously.

estrepitoso *adj* noisy; loud, deafening; *fiesta, persona etc* rowdy, boisterous; **con aplausos ~s** with loud applause.

estreptococo *nm* streptococcus.

estreptomicina *nf* streptomycin.

estrés *nm* stress.

estresante *adj* stressful.

estresar [1a] *vt* to cause stress to, put stress on.

estría *nf* groove; (*Arquit*) flute, fluting; (*Anat*) stretch-mark; (*Bio, Geol etc*) striation.

estriado 1 *adj* grooved; (*Arquit*) fluted; (*Bio, Geol etc*) striate, striated. **2** *nm* grooving; fluting; striation.

estriar [1c] *vt* to groove, make a groove in; to flute; to striate.

estribación *nf* (*Geog etc*) spur; **estribaciones** spurs, foot-hills.

estribar [1a] *vi*: **~ en** to rest on, be supported by; (*fig*) to rest on, be based on; **la dificultad estriba en el texto** the difficulty lies in the text, the difficulty stems from the text; **su prosperidad estriba en esta industria** their prosperity is based on (*o* derives from) this industry.

estribera *nf* (**a**) (*estribo*) stirrup; (*de moto*) footrest. (**b**) (*LAm*: *cincha*) girth, saddle strap.

estriberón *nm* stepping stone.

estribillo *nm* (*Liter*) refrain; (*Mús*) chorus; (*fig*) pet word, pet phrase; **¡siempre (con) el mismo ~!** the same old story!

estribo *nm* (**a**) (*de jinete*) stirrup; (*Aut etc*) running board, step, footboard; (*apoyapié*) footrest; **perder los ~s** (*fig*) to fly off the handle*, lose one's temper; to get hot under the collar; to lose one's head; **tomar algo para el ~, tomar la del ~** (*And, Cono Sur*) (*jinete*) to drink a stirrup cup; (*gen*) to have one for the road*.

(**b**) (*Téc*) brace, bracket, stay.

(**c**) (*Arquit*) buttress; (*de puente*) pier, support.

(**d**) (*Geog*) spur.

(**e**) (*fig*) basis, foundation.

estribor *nm* starboard.

estricnina *nf* strychnine.

estricote *nm*: **andar al ~** (*Carib**) to live a wild life.

estrictamente *adv* strictly; severely.

estrictez *nf* (*LAm*) strictness; severity.

estricto *adj* strict; severe.

estridencia *nf* stridency; raucousness; **llevaba ropa cara pero sin ~s** she was expensively but not loudly dressed.

estridente *adj ruido* strident, raucous, unpleasant-sounding; jangling; *color* loud.

estridentemente *adv* stridently, raucously; loudly.

estridor *nm* stridency; raucousness; screech.

estrillar [1a] *vi* (*And, Cono Sur*) to get cross.

estrillo *nm* (*And, Cono Sur*) bad temper, annoyance.

estriptís* *nm*, **estriptise*** *nm* (*And*) striptease.

estriptisero*, -a *nm/f* (*And*) stripper*, striptease artist.

estriptista* *nf* stripper*.

estro *nm* (**a**) (*inspiración*) inspiration. (**b**) (*Med, Vet*) oestrus.

estrofa *nf* verse, stanza, strophe.

estrófico *adj* strophic; composed in stanzas.

estrógeno *nm* oestrogen.

estroncio *nm* strontium; **~ 90** strontium 90.

estropajo *nm* (**a**) (*de fregar*) scourer, scouring pad, scrubber; (*trapo*) dishcloth; (*fregasuelos*) swab, mop; **~ de acero** steel wool; **poner a uno como un ~** to shower insults on sb; to make sb feel a heel; **servir de ~** to be exploited, be used to do the dirty work.

(**b**) (*basura*) dirt, rubbish; (*objeto inútil*) worthless object; (*persona*) dead loss.

estropajoso *adj* (**a**) *carne etc* tough, leathery, gristly. (**b**) *habla* stammering; indistinct. (**c**) *persona* (*desaseado*) slovenly; scruffy; (*vil*) mean, despicable. (**d**) *pelo* straw-like.

estropeado *adj* damaged, spoiled; ruined; crumpled, torn; *persona* maimed, crippled; **está muy estropeada** she looks older than she is.

estropear [1a] **1** *vt comida, cosecha* to damage, spoil; to ruin; *proyecto, vida* to mess up, make a mess of; *tela* to crumple, tear; *persona* to maim, cripple, hurt; *texto etc* to mangle; *sentido* to pervert, distort.

2 estropearse *vr* to get damaged; to spoil, go bad; to deteriorate; (*plan etc*) to fail.

estropicio* *nm* (**a**) (*rotura*) breakage, smashing, smash-up.

(**b**) (*efectos*) harmful effects, damaging results; **ese alimento es responsable de muchos ~s** that foodstuff can have very harmful effects.

(**c**) (*fig*) rumpus*, row, fuss; turmoil.

estructura *nf* (*gen*) structure; (*armazón*) frame, framework; (*orden*) arrangement; (*liter*) structure; plot; **~ atómica** atomic structure; **~ del poder** power structure; **~ profunda** deep structure; **~ salarial** pay structure.

estructuración *nf* structure; structuring.

estructural *adj* structural.

estructuralismo *nm* structuralism.

estructuralista *adj, nmf* structuralist.

estructuralmente *adv* structurally.

estructurar [1a] *vt* to construct; to arrange, organize.

estruendo *nm* (**a**) (*ruido*) noise, clamour, din; crash, clatter, racket; thunder. (**b**) (*fig*: *alboroto*) uproar, turmoil, confusion. (**c**) (*fig*: *pompa*) pomp, ostentation.

estruendosamente *adv* noisily, uproariously; loudly, obstreperously.

estruendoso *adj* noisy; uproarious; *persona* loud, obstreperous.

estrujado *nm* (*de uvas*) pressing.

estrujadura *nf* squeeze, press(ing).

estrujar [1a] **1** *vt* (*exprimir*) to squeeze; (*apretar*) to press, crush; (*machacar*) to bruise, mash; (*fig*) to drain, bleed white.

2 estrujarse *vr*: **~ la mollera*** to rack one's brains.

estrujón *nm* squeeze, press; pressing, crushing; (*Agr*) final pressing of grapes; (*) crush, jam.

Estuardo *nm* Stuart.

estuario *nm* estuary.

estucado 1 *adj* (**a**) *papel* coated. (**b**) *pared* plastered, stuccoed. **2** *nm* stucco, stucco work.

estucar [1g] *vt* to stucco, plaster.

estuco *nm* stucco, plaster.

estuche *nm* (**a**) (*caja*) box, case, container; (*vaina*) sheath; **~ de afeites** vanity case; **~ de aseo** toilet case; **~ de cigarros** cigar-case; **~ de costura** sewing basket; **~ de cubiertos** canteen of cutlery; **~ de herramientas** toolbox; **~ de joyas** jewel-box.

(**b**) **ser un ~*** to be a handyman, be a useful chap*.

estuchero* *nm* (*Méx*) safebreaker.

estudiado *adj* (*fig*) studied, elaborate; (*pey*) *persona* affected; *estilo* recherché.

estudiantado *nm* students (*collectively*), student body.

estudiante *nmf* (*t* **estudianta*** *nf*) student; **~ de derecho** law student; **~ de medicina** medical student; **~ de ruso** student of Russian.

estudiantil *adj* student (*atr*); **vida ~** student life; **los problemas ~es** student problems, problems of students, problems relating to students.

estudiantina *nf* student music group, student band.

estudiantino *adj* student (*atr*); **a la estudiantina** like a student, in the manner of students.

estudiar [1b] **1** *vti* to study; to work; to think about, think over, ponder; **~ para abogado** to study to become a lawyer, study law; **tengo que ir a ~** I must go and work; **estudia todo el día en la biblioteca** he works all day in the library; **lo estudiaré** I'll think about it. **2 estudiarse** *vr*: **se está estudiando** it is under consideration.

estudio *nm* (**a**) (*gen*) study; (*encuesta*) research; survey; (*investigación*) investigation; (*proyecto*) plan, design (*de* for); (*planificación*) planning; **~s** (*educación*) schooling, education; (*investigaciones*) work, studies, researches; **le pagaron los ~s** they paid for his schooling, they paid for his education; **hizo sus ~s en París** he studied in Paris; **se fue a Suiza para completar sus ~s** she went to Switzerland to finish her education; **los ~s de Menéndez Pidal sobre la épica española** Menéndez Pidal's work on Spanish epic; **los últimos ~s de lingüística** the latest work in linguistics, recent research in linguistics; **publicó un ~ sobre Bécquer** he published a study of Bécquer; **~ de campo** field study; **~s empresariales** business studies; **~s del mercado, ~ de mercados** market research; **~ de las posibilidades, ~ de viabilidad** feasibility study; **~s de tiempo y movimiento** time and motion study; **estar en ~** to be under consideration.

(**b**) (*cuarto en casa*) study; (*piso*) bedsitter, one-room flat; studio flat.

(**c**) (*Arte, Cine, Rad etc*: *sala*) studio; **~ de cine, ~ cinematográfico** film studio; **~ de diseños** design studio; **~ de grabación** recording studio; **~ radiofónico** broadcasting studio; **~ de registro de sonidos** sound-recording studio; **~ de televisión** television studio.

(**d**) (*Arte*: *cuadro etc*) study.

(**e**) (*Mús*: *composición*) study, étude.

(**f**) (*Cono Sur*: *de abogado etc*) office.
(**g**) (*erudición*) learning; **un hombre de mucho ~** a man of great learning.

estudiosamente *adv* studiously.

estudioso 1 *adj* studious; bookish. **2** *nm*, **estudiosa** *nf* student, scholar.

estufa *nf* (**a**) (*calentador*) stove, heater; (*LAm*) cooker; **~ eléctrica** electric fire; **~ de gas** gas fire; **~ de petróleo** oil stove. (**b**) (*Agr*) hothouse; **criar a uno en ~** (*fig*: *horno*) to pamper sb.

estufilla *nf* (**a**) (*brasero*) small stove, brazier. (**b**) (*manguito*) muff.

estulticia *nf* (*liter*) stupidity, foolishness.

estultificar [1g] *vt* (*CAm*): **~ a uno** to make sb look stupid, make sb out to be a fool.

estulto *adj* (*liter*) stupid, foolish.

estupa* 1 *nf* drug squad. **2** *nm* member of the drug squad.

estupefacción *nf* stupefaction.

estupefaciente 1 *adj* stupifying; narcotic; **sustancia ~** = 2. **2** *nm* narcotic, drug.

estupefacto *adj* astonished, speechless, thunderstruck; **me miró ~** he looked at me in amazement; **dejar a uno ~** to leave sb speechless.

estupendamente *adv* stupendously; (*) marvellously, wonderfully, terrifically*; **estoy ~** (*salud*) I feel great; **le salió ~** he did it very well.

estupendo *adj* stupendous; (*) marvellous, wonderful, terrific*, great*; ¡~! that's great!*, splendid!; **tiene un coche ~** he's got a marvellous car; **hay chicas estupendas** there are some smashing girls*; **es ~ para tocar la trompeta** he's great on the trumpet*.

estúpidamente *adv* stupidly.

estupidez *nf* (**a**) (*cualidad*) stupidity, silliness. (**b**) (*acto*) stupid thing, piece of stupidity; **fue una ~ mía** it was a silly mistake of mine; **cometer una ~** to do something silly.

estupidizador *adj* stupefying.

estúpido *adj* stupid, silly.

estupor *nm* (**a**) (*Med etc*) stupor. (**b**) (*fig*) astonishment, amazement.

estuprar [1a] *vt* to rape.

estupro *nm* rape.

estuque *nm* stucco.

estuquería *nf* stuccoing, stucco work.

esturión *nm* sturgeon.

estuve *etc V* **estar**.

ET *nm* (*Esp Mil*) *abr de* **Ejército de Tierra**.

ETA ['eta] *nf* (*Esp Pol*) *abr de* **Euskadi Ta Askatasuna = Patria Vasca y Libertad**; **~ p-m** *abr de* **ETA político-militar**.

-eta *V* **Aspects of Word Formation in Spanish 2**.

etanol *nm* ethanol.

etapa *nf* (**a**) (*de viaje etc*) stage; (*Dep*) stage, leg; lap; (*Mil*) stopping place; **a cortas ~s, a pequeñas ~s** in easy stages; **hacer ~ en** to break one's journey at; **quemar ~s** to make rapid progress.
(**b**) (*de cohete*) stage; **cohete de 3 ~s** 3-stage rocket.
(**c**) (*Mil*) food ration (*for stage of a march*).
(**d**) (*fig*) stage, phase; **en la segunda ~ del plan** in the second phase of the plan; **una adquisición proyectada por ~s** a phased takeover; **desarrollo por ~s** phased development, development in stages; **lo haremos por ~s** we'll do it in stages, we'll do it gradually.

etano *nm* (*Quím*) ethane.

etario *adj* age (*atr*); **grupo ~** age group.

etarra 1 *adj* of ETA. **2** *nmf* member of ETA; *V* **ETA**.

etc. *abr de* **etcétera**.

etcétera *adv* etcetera, *etc*; **gatos y perros ~, ~** cats and dogs and so on, cats and dogs and what have you; **y un largo ~** and a lot more besides, and much much more; **y un largo ~ de autores** and many more authors besides.

-ete *V* **Aspects of Word Formation in Spanish 2**.

éter *nm* ether.

etéreo *adj* ethereal (*t fig*).

eternamente *adv* eternally, everlastingly.

eternidad *nf* eternity.

eternizar [1f] **1** *vt* to etern(al)ize, perpetuate; to make everlasting; (*pey*) to drag out, prolong endlessly. **2 eternizarse** *vr* (*pey*) to be interminable; **~ en** to take hours over, take all day over; to dwell endlessly on; **~ haciendo algo** to be very slow doing sth.

eterno *adj* eternal, everlasting.

ethos ['etos] *nm* ethos.

ética *nf* ethics; **~ profesional** professional ethics.

ético[1] *adj* ethical.

ético[2] *adj* (*Med*: = **héctico, hético**) consumptive; (*fig*) frail.

eticoso* *adj* (*And*) fussy, finicky.

etileno *nm* (*Quím*) ethylene.

etilo *nm* ethyl.

étimo *nm* etymon.

etimología *nf* etymology.

etimológico *adj* etymological.

etíope, etiope *adj, nmf* Ethiopian.

Etiopía *nf* Ethiopia.

etiquencia *nf* (*Carib, Méx Med*) consumption.

etiqueta *nf* (**a**) (*formalismo*) etiquette; formality; **de ~** formal, full-dress (*atr*); **baile de ~** ball, dress ball, formal dance; **ir de ~** to wear evening dress; (*invitación*) **'vestir de ~'** 'dress: formal'.
(**b**) (*rótulo*) ticket, label, tag; **~ del precio** price-tag.

etiquetación *nf*, **etiquetado** *nm*, **etiquetaje** *nm* labelling.

etiquetar [1a] *vt* to label.

etiquetero *adj* formal, ceremonious, punctilious; stiff, prim.

etnia *nf* ethnic group; race.

étnico *adj* ethnic.

etnocéntrico *adj* ethnocentric.

etnocentrismo *nm* ethnocentrism.

etnografía *nf* ethnography.

etnográfico *adj* ethnographic.

etnología *nf* ethnology.

etnológico *adj* ethnological.

etnomusicología *nf* ethnomusicology.

etrusco, -a 1 *adj, nm/f* Etruscan. **2** *nm* (*Ling*) Etruscan.

ETS (**a**) *nf* (*Med*) *abr de* **enfermedad de transmisión sexual** sexually transmitted disease, STD.
(**b**) (*Esp*) *abr de* **Escuelas Técnicas Superiores**.

EUA *nmpl* (*LAm*) *abr de* **Estados Unidos de América** United States of America, USA.

eucaliptal *nm*, **eucaliptar** *nm* eucalyptus plantation.

eucalipto *nm* eucalyptus, gum-tree.

Eucaristía *nf* Eucharist.

eucarístico *adj* eucharistic.

Euclides *nm* Euclid.

euclidiano *adj* Euclidean.

eufemismo *nm* euphemism.

eufemístico *adj* euphemistic.

eufonía *nf* euphony.

eufónico *adj* euphonic, euphonious.

euforia *nf* euphoria; exuberance, elation.

eufórico *adj* euphoric; exuberant.

euforizante *adj*: **droga ~** drug that produces euphoria.

euforizar [1f] **1** *vt* to produce euphoria in, exhilarate. **2 euforizarse** *vr* to become exhilarated.

Eufrates *nm* Euphrates.

eugenesia *nf* eugenics.

eugenésico *adj* eugenic.

Eugenio *nm* Eugene.

eugenismo *nm* eugenics.

eunuco *nm* eunuch.

eurasiático, -a *adj, nm/f* Eurasian.

eureka *excl* eureka!

Eurídice *nf* Eurydice.

Eurípedes *nm* Euripides.

eurítmica *nf* eurhythmics.

euro *nm* (*liter*) east wind.

euro... *pref* Euro...

eurobonos *nmpl* Eurobonds.

eurocomisario, -a *nm/f* Euro-commissioner.

eurocomunismo *nm* Eurocommunism.

eurocomunista *adj, nmf* Eurocommunist.

eurócrata *nmf* Eurocrat.

Eurocrédito *nm* Eurocredit.

eurocheque *nm* Eurocheque.

eurodiputado, -a *nm/f* Euro MP, member of the European Parliament.

eurodivisa *nf* Eurocurrency.

eurodólar *nm* Eurodollar.

eurófilo, -a *adj, nm/f* Europhile.

eurófobo, -a *adj, nm/f* Europhobe.

euromercado *nm* Euromarket.

euromisil *nm* short-range nuclear missile.

Europa *nf* Europe.

europarlamentario, -a *nm/f* member of the European Parliament.

europarlamento *nm* European Parliament.

europeidad *nf* Europeanness; Europe-mindedness; European character.

europeísmo *nm* Europeanism.
europeísta 1 *adj* pro-European; European-minded. **2** *nmf* pro-European; European-minded person.
europeización *nf* Europeanization.
europeizante *adj (LAm)* = **europeísta.**
europeizar [1f] **1** *vt* to Europeanize. **2 europeizarse** *vr* to become Europeanized.
europeo, -a *adj, nm/f* European.
Eurovisión *nf* Eurovision.
éuscaro *adj, nm* = **euskera** *etc.*
Euskadi *nm* Basque Country; ~ **norte** Pays Basque *(France)*.
euskaldún 1 *adj* Basque; *(Ling)* Basque-speaking. **2** *nm,* **euskalduna** *nf* Basque speaker.
euskaldunización *nf* conversion to Basque norms; *(Ling)* conversion to Basque, process of making people *(etc)* Basque-speaking.
euskaldunizar [1f] *vt* to convert to Basque norms; *(Ling)* to convert to Basque, make Basque-speaking.
euskera, eusquera, éusquero 1 *adj* Basque. **2** *nm (Ling)* Basque; ~ **batua** standard Basque.
eutanasia *nf* euthanasia, mercy killing.
Eva *nf* Eve.
evacuación *nf* **(a)** *(acto)* evacuation. **(b)** *(Téc)* waste; exhaust. **(c)** *(Med)* evacuation, bowel movement.
evacuado, -a *nm/f* evacuee.
evacuar [1d] *vt* **(a)** *(gen)* to evacuate; to move out of, leave empty, vacate; *ciudad, población* to evacuate; *recipiente* to empty; *(Med) llaga* to drain.
(b) ~ **el vientre** to have a movement of the bowels.
(c) *deber* to fulfil; *consulta* to carry out, undertake; *negocio* to transact; *trato* to conclude.
(d) *(Jur) dictamen* to issue.
evacuatorio *nm* public lavatory.
evadido, -a *nm/f* fugitive, escaped prisoner.
evadir [3a] **1** *vt* **(a)** to evade, avoid. **(b)** *dinero etc* to pass, get away with. **2 evadirse** *vr* **(a)** to escape; to break out, slip away. **(b)** *(LAm*‡*)* to trip‡.
evaluación *nf* **(a)** *(gen)* evaluation; assessment; appraisal; refereeing. **(b)** *(Escol)* report, assessment; ~ **continua** continuous assessment; ~ **por pares** peer review.
evaluador(a) *nm/f* assessor; appraiser; referee.
evaluar [1e] *vt* to evaluate, assess; *personal* to appraise; *artículo* to referee.
evaluativo *adj* evaluative.
evanescente *adj* evanescent.
evangélico *adj* evangelic(al).
evangelio *nm* gospel; **el E~ según San Juan** the Gospel according to St John; **se aceptan sus ideas como el** ~ his ideas are accepted as gospel truth; **dice como el** ~ he speaks the gospel truth.
evangelismo *nm* evangelism; revivalism.
Evangelista *adj*: **San Juan** ~ St John the Evangelist.
evangelista *nmf* **(a)** *(Rel)* gospeller; revivalist; member of an Evangelical church; **los cuatro ~s** the four evangelists. **(b)** *(Méx)* scribe.
evangelizador(a) *nm/f* evangelist.
evangelizar [1f] *vt* to evangelize.
evaporación *nf* evaporation.
evaporar [1a] **1** *vt* to evaporate. **2 evaporarse** *vr* to evaporate; *(fig)* to vanish.
evaporizar [1f] **1** *vt* to vaporize. **2 evaporizarse** *vr* to vaporize.
evasión *nf* escape, flight; *(fig)* evasion, escapism; **lectura de** ~ light reading, escapist literature; ~ **de capitales** flight of capital; ~ **fiscal,** ~ **de impuestos,** ~ **tributaria** tax evasion.
evasionario *adj (Liter)* escapist.
evasionismo *nm* escapism.
evasiva *nf* evasion; *(escapatoria)* loophole, way out; *(pretexto)* excuse; **viene con sus ~s** he avoids a straight answer.
evasivo *adj* evasive, non-committal, ambiguous.
evento *nm* **(a)** *(incidente)* unforeseen happening; contingency; eventuality; **a todo** ~ whatever happens, in any event.
(b) *(acontecimiento)* event; *(Dep)* sporting fixture; *(fiesta etc)* social event.
eventual 1 *adj* **(a)** *(casual)* fortuitous; *(posible)* possible; conditional upon circumstances. **(b)** *obrero, trabajo* temporary, casual; *oficial etc* acting; *solución* stopgap, temporary. **(c)** *(LAm)* eventual. **2** *nmf* temporary worker.
eventualidad *nf* **(a)** *(casualidad)* eventuality; contingency; **en esa** ~ in that eventuality. **(b)** *(trabajo)* casual employment.
eventualmente *adv* **(a)** *(accidentalmente)* by chance, fortuitously. **(b)** *(posiblemente)* possibly, depending upon circumstances; **algún número de la revista se publicará** ~ special issues of the journal will be published from time to time. **(c)** *(LAm: por fin)* eventually.
evidencia *nf* **(a)** *(pruebas)* evidence, proof; **poner en** ~ *(hacer claro)* to make clear; *(demostrar)* to show, demonstrate; *(fig)* to make a fool of, make a laughing stock of; **ponerse en** ~ to put o.s. forward; **dejar** *(o* **poner)** **a uno en** ~ to put sb in an embarrassing position, show sb up in a bad light. **(b)** *(cualidad)* obviousness.
evidencial *adj* tangible, visible.
evidenciar [1b] *vt* to prove, show, demonstrate; to make evident; ~ **de modo inconfundible** to give clear proof of, prove unmistakably.
evidente *adj* obvious, clear, evident; **¡~!** naturally!, obviously!
evidentemente *adv* obviously, clearly, evidently.
evitable *adj* avoidable, preventable; **un accidente fácilmente** ~ an accident which could easily be avoided.
evitación *nf* avoidance, prevention; ~ **de accidentes** accident prevention.
evitar [1a] *vt (gen)* to avoid; *(precaver)* to prevent; *peligro etc* to avoid, escape; *molestia* to save, spare; *tentación etc* to shun; **para** ~ **tales dificultades** in order to avoid such difficulties; **para ~se trabajo** in order to save o.s. trouble; **no lo lograrán si puedo ~lo** they won't get away with that if I can help it; ~ **hacer algo** to avoid doing sth; to be chary of doing sth.
evocación *nf* evocation; invocation.
evocador *adj* evocative; reminiscent *(de* of).
evocar [1g] *vt* to evoke, call forth, conjure up; *espíritu etc* to invoke, call up.
evocativo *adj (LAm)* evocative.
evolución *nf* **(a)** *(Bio)* evolution. **(b)** *(fig)* evolution, change, development; *(Med)* progress. **(c)** *(Mil etc)* manoeuvre; *(movimiento)* movement.
evolucionar [1a] *vi* **(a)** *(Bio)* to evolve. **(b)** *(fig)* to evolve, change, develop; *(Med etc)* to progress. **(c)** *(Mil)* to manoeuvre, wheel; *(Aer)* to manoeuvre, circle, wheel.
evolutivo *adj* evolutionary.
ex 1 *pref* ex-; former, late; ~ **secretario** ex-secretary, former secretary; **la** ~ **querida de** the former mistress of, the ex-mistress of, the one-time mistress of. **2** *nmf*: **mi ~*** my ex* (husband *o* wife); **un** ~ **del equipo** an ex-member of the team, a former member of the team.
exabrupto *nm (hum: ataque)* broadside; sudden attack; *(interjección)* interjection; *(observación)* sharp remark.
exacción *nf* **(a)** *(acto)* exaction, extortion. **(b)** *(suma etc)* demand; levy.
exacerbante *adj (LAm)* irritating, provoking; *(fig)* aggravating.
exacerbar [1a] *vt* to irritate, provoke; *(fig)* to aggravate, exacerbate.
exactamente *adv* exactly; accurately; precisely; punctually; correctly.
exactitud *nf* exactness; accuracy; precision; punctuality; correctness.
exacto *adj (gen)* exact; *(acertado)* accurate; *(preciso)* precise; *(puntual)* punctual; *(correcto)* right, correct; **¡~!** exactly!, quite right!; that's just what I say!; **eso no es del todo** ~ that's not quite right.
exageración *nf* exaggeration.
exageradamente *adv* in an exaggerated way; excessively, exorbitantly; over-demonstratively, theatrically; intensely; fulsomely; oddly.
exagerado *adj pretensión etc* exaggerated; *relato* highly-coloured; *precio etc* excessive, exorbitant, steep; *persona* over-demonstrative, theatrical, given to extravagant gestures; *(de fuertes emociones)* intense; *elogio* fulsome; *(en vestir)* over-dressed, dressy; *(raro)* peculiar, odd.
exageradura *nf (Carib)* exaggeration.
exagerar [1a] **1** *vt (gen)* to exaggerate; to overdo, overstate, make too much of; *(aumentar)* to enlarge upon. **2** *vi* to exaggerate; *(pey)* to overdo it, overdo things; **creo que eso sería** ~ I think that would be going a bit far.
exaltación *nf* **(a)** *(ensalzamiento)* exaltation. **(b)** *(sobreexcitación)* overexcitement; elation; excitability, intenseness; hotheadedness; passion, impassioned nature. **(c)** *(Pol)* extremism.
exaltado 1 *adj* **(a)** *(elevado)* exalted.
(b) *estado, humor* over-excited, worked up; elated; *carácter* excitable, intense; *(fanático)* hot-headed; *discurso*

etc impassioned.

(**c**) (*Pol*) extreme, far out.

2 *nm,* **exaltada** *nf* (*fanático*) hothead; (*Pol*) extremist, far-out person; (*loco*) mad person, deranged person.

exaltante *adj* exciting; uplifting.

exaltar [1a] **1** *vt* (**a**) (*elevar*) to exalt; to elevate, raise (*a* to).

(**b**) (*fig*: *elogiar*) to extol, praise.

(**c**) (*emocionar*) *persona* to excite, carry away, work up; *emoción* to intensify; *imaginación* to fire.

2 exaltarse *vr* (*persona*) to get excited, get worked up; to get carried away (*con* by); (*en discusión*) to get heated; (*emoción*) to run high, become very intense; **¡no te exaltes!** don't get so worked up!

exalumno, -a *nm/f* (*LAm*: *Univ*) graduate; former student; alumnus, alumna (*US*).

examen *nm* (*gen*) examination; exam; (*encuesta*) inquiry (*de* into); (*inspección*) inspection; ~ **de acceso,** ~ **de admisión,** ~ **de ingreso** entrance examination; ~ **de conductor** driving test; ~ **de consecución** achievement test; ~ **eliminatorio** qualifying examination; ~ **de fin de curso** final examination, finals; ~ **ocular** visual inspection; ~ **oral** oral examination; ~ **de suficiencia** proficiency test; ~ **tipo test** multiple-choice test; **presentarse a un** ~ to enter (*o* go in for, sit) an examination.

examinado, -a *nm/f* examinee, candidate.

examinador(a) *nm/f* examiner.

examinando, -a *nm/f* examinee, candidate.

examinar [1a] **1** *vt* (*gen*) (*t Med, Escol, Univ etc*) to examine; (*poner a prueba*) to test; (*inspeccionar*) to inspect, look through, go over; (*indagar*) to inquire into, investigate, look into; *problema* to examine, consider.

2 examinarse *vr* to take an examination, be examined (*en* in; *de* for the degree of); ~ **de doctor** to take one's doctoral examination.

exangüe *adj* bloodless; anaemic; (*fig*) weak.

exánime *adj* lifeless; (*fig*) weak, exhausted, lifeless; **caer** ~ to fall in a faint.

exasperación *nf* exasperation.

exasperador *adj,* **exasperante** *adj* exasperating, infuriating.

exasperar [1a] **1** *vt* to exasperate, infuriate. **2 exasperarse** *vr* to get exasperated, lose patience.

Exc.ª *abr de* **Excelencia** Excellency.

excarcelación *nf* release (from prison).

excarcelado, -a *nm/f* ex-prisoner, former prisoner.

excarcelar [1a] *vt* to release (from prison).

excavación *nf* excavation.

excavador(a)[1] *nm/f* (*persona*) excavator, digger.

excavadora[2] *nf* (*Mec*) digger, power shovel.

excavar [1a] *vt* to excavate, dig (out); to hollow out.

excedencia *nf* leave of absence, leave without pay; ~ **por maternidad** maternity leave; ~ **primada** voluntary severance; ~ **voluntaria** voluntary retirement; **pedir la** ~ to ask for leave of absence.

excedentario *adj* surplus.

excedente 1 *adj* excess, surplus; excessive; *trabajador* redundant. **2** *nm* excess, surplus; ~ **empresarial** profit margin; ~ **laboral** surplus (of) labour, overmanning. **3** *nmf* person on leave of absence; ~ **forzoso** person on compulsory leave of absence.

exceder [2a] **1** *vt* (*superar*) to exceed, surpass; (*sobrepasar*) to pass, outdo, excel; (*en importancia etc*) to transcend.

2 *vi*: ~ **de** to exceed, surpass.

3 excederse *vr* (**a**) (*gen*) to excel o.s.

(**b**) (*pey*) to overreach o.s.; to go too far, go to extremes; ~ **en sus funciones** to exceed one's duty.

(**c**) ~ **de** to exceed, surpass; **no** ~ **de lo corriente** to be no more than average.

excelencia *nf* (**a**) excellence; superiority, superior quality; **por** ~ par excellence. (**b**) **su E~** his Excellency; **sí, E~** yes, your Excellency.

excelente *adj* excellent; superior.

excelentemente *adv* excellently.

excelso *adj* lofty, exalted, sublime.

excentricidad *nf* eccentricity.

excéntrico, -a *adj, nm/f* eccentric.

excepción *nf* exception; ~ **de la regla** exception to the rule; **la** ~ **confirma la regla** the exception proves the rule; **un libro de** ~ an exceptional book; **a** ~ **de,** ~ **hecha de** with the exception of, except for; **hacer una** ~ to make an exception; *V* **estado.**

excepcional *adj* exceptional.

excepcionalidad *nf* exceptional nature.

excepcionalmente *adv* exceptionally; as an exception.

excepto *prep* except (for), excepting.

exceptuar [1e] *vt* to except, exclude, leave out of account; (*Jur etc*) to exempt.

excesivamente *adv* excessively; unreasonably, unduly.

excesivo *adj* (*gen*) excessive; (*indebido*) unreasonable, undue; over-, *p.ej.* **con generosidad excesiva** over-generously, with excessive generosity.

exceso *nm* (**a**) (*gen*) excess; (*de comida*) surfeit; (*Com, Fin*) surplus; ~ **de equipaje** excess luggage, excess baggage (*US*); ~ **de mano de obra,** ~ **de plantillas** overmanning, overstaffing; ~ **de peso** excess weight; **debido al** ~ **de peso** because of the extra weight; **me detuvieron por** ~ **de velocidad** they arrested me for speeding, they booked me for exceeding the speed limit; **en** ~**, por** ~ excessively, to excess; **cuidadoso en** ~ excessively careful, too careful; **una cantidad en** ~ **de X toneladas** a quantity in excess of (*o* over) X tons; **generoso hasta el** ~ generous to a fault; **beber en** ~ to drink to excess; **llevar algo al** ~ to carry sth to excess, overdo sth.

(**b**) (*fig*) excess; **los** ~**s de la revolución** the excesses of the revolution.

excisión *nf* (*Med*) excision.

excitabilidad *nf* excitability.

excitable *adj* excitable; highly-strung, high-strung (*US*), nervy; temperamental.

excitación *nf* (**a**) (*acto*) exciting, inciting; (*estado*) excitement. (**b**) (*Elec*) excitation.

excitante 1 *adj* (**a**) (*emocionante*) exciting. (**b**) (*Med*) stimulating. **2** *nm* stimulant.

excitar [1a] **1** *vt* (**a**) (*gen*) to excite; *emoción* to excite, arouse, stir up; *duda, esperanza* to raise.

(**b**) (*incitar*) to incite, urge on; ~ **al pueblo a la rebelión** to incite the populace to rebellion; ~ **a uno a hacer algo** to urge sb to do sth.

(**c**) (*Elec*) to excite, energize.

2 excitarse *vr* to get excited, get worked up.

exclamación *nf* exclamation; cry.

exclamar [1a] **1** *vi* to exclaim; to cry out. **2 exclamarse** *vr* to complain (*contra* about), protest (*contra* against).

exclamativo *adj* (**a**) exclamatory. (**b**) *ropa* loud.

exclamatorio *adj* exclamatory.

exclaustración *nf* (*Ecl*) secularization; expulsion (*of monks or nuns*).

exclaustrada *nf* secularized nun; expelled nun; ex-nun.

exclaustrado (*Ecl*) **1** *adj* secularized; expelled (from the order). **2** *nm* secularized monk; expelled monk; ex-monk.

excluir [3g] *vt* to exclude (*from* de); to shut out; *solución* to reject; *posibilidad etc* to exclude, rule out, preclude.

exclusión *nf* exclusion; **con** ~ **de** excluding, to the exclusion of.

exclusiva *nf* (**a**) (*Com*) sole right, sole agency; **tener la** ~ **de un producto** to have the sole right to sell a product, be the sole agents for a product.

(**b**) (*Periodismo*) exclusive interview (*o* story *etc*); exclusive news release; (*pisotón*) scoop.

(**c**) (*negativa*) rejection (*for a post etc*).

(**d**) **trabajar en** ~ **para** to work exclusively for.

exclusivamente *adv* exclusively.

exclusive *adv* exclusively; exclusive of, not counting; **hasta el primero de enero** ~ till the first of January exclusive.

exclusividad *nf* (**a**) (*cualidad*) exclusiveness; clannishness; snobbery. (**b**) (*Com*) = **exclusiva (a).**

exclusivista *adj club etc* exclusive, select; *grupo* clannish; *actitud* snobbish.

exclusivo *adj* exclusive; sole; (*horas de trabajo*) full-time.

excluyente *adj* (*LAm*) *clase, club etc* exclusive.

excluyentemente *adv* exclusively.

Excma., Excmo. *abr de* **Excelentísima, Excelentísimo** (*courtesy title*).

excombatiente *nm* exserviceman, veteran (*US*).

excomulgado 1 *adj* (**a**) (*Ecl*) excommunicated. (**b**) (**: maldito*) blessed*, cursed. **2** *nm,* **excomulgada** *nf* excommunicated person.

excomulgar [1h] *vt* (**a**) (*Ecl*) to excommunicate. (**b**) (*fig*) to ban, banish; (**: maldecir*) to curse.

excomunión *nf* excommunication.

excoriación *nf* graze; chafing.

excoriar [1b] **1** *vt* (*despellejar*) to skin, flay; (*raspar*) to graze, take the skin off; (*rozar*) to chafe. **2 excoriarse** *vr* to graze o.s., skin o.s.

excrecencia *nf* excrescence.

excreción *nf* excretion.

excremento *nm* excrement, excreta.

excretar [1a] *vt* to excrete.
exculpación *nf* exoneration; (*Jur*) acquittal.
exculpar [1a] **1** *vt* to exonerate, exculpate; (*Jur*) to acquit (*de* of). **2 exculparse** *vr* to exonerate o.s.
exculpatorio *adj*: **declaración exculpatoria** statement of innocence.
excursión *nf* excursion, outing, trip; (*Mil*) raid, incursion; ~ **campestre** picnic; ~ **de caza** hunting trip; ~ **a pie** walk, hike, ramble; **ir de** ~ to go (off) on a trip, go on an outing.
excursionar [1a] *vi* to go on a trip, have an outing.
excursionismo *nm* going on trips; sightseeing; walking, hiking, rambling.
excursionista *nmf* (*turista*) tourist; sightseer; (*en excursión de un solo día*) day-tripper; (*por campo, montaña*) hiker, rambler.
excurso *nm*, **excursus** *nm invar* excursus.
excusa *nf* excuse; apology; **buscar** ~ to look for an excuse; **presentar sus ~s** to make one's excuses, excuse o.s.; **presentar ~s de su país** to make excuses for one's country.
excusabaraja *nf* hamper, basket with a lid.
excusable *adj* excusable, pardonable.
excusado 1 *adj* (**a**) (*inútil*) unnecessary, superfluous; ~ **es decir que** ... needless to say ..., I (*etc*) need scarcely say that ...; **pensar en lo** ~ to think of something which is quite out of the question.
(**b**) **estar** ~ **de** to be exempt from.
(**c**) (*privado*) reserved, private; *entrada* concealed.
2 *nm* lavatory, toilet.
excusar [1a] **1** *vt* (**a**) (*disculpar*) to excuse; ~ **a A con B** to tell B that A begs to be excused, to present A's apologies to B.
(**b**) (*eximir*) to exempt (*de* from).
(**c**) (*evitar*) to avoid, prevent; **así excusamos disgustos** this way we avoid difficulties; **podemos** ~ **lo otro** we can forget about the rest of it, we don't have to bother with the rest.
(**d**) ~ + *infin* not to have to + *infin*; to save the trouble of + *ger*; **excusamos decirle que** ... we don't have to tell you that ...; **por eso excuso escribirte más largo** so I can save myself the trouble of writing at greater length.
2 excusarse *vr* to excuse o.s.; to apologize (*de* for); ~ **de** + *infin* to decline to + *infin*; to apologize for not being able to + *infin*; ~ **de haber hecho algo** to apologize for having done sth.
execrable *adj* execrable.
execración *nf* execration.
execrar [1a] *vt* to execrate, loathe, abominate.
exégesis *nf* exegesis.
exención *nf* exemption (*de* from); immunity, freedom (*de* from); ~ **contributiva,** ~ **de impuestos** tax exemption, tax allowance.
exencionar [1a] *vt* = **exentar**.
exentar [1a] *vt* to exempt (*de* from); to excuse (*de* from).
exento *adj* (**a**) (*libre*) exempt (*de* from); free (*de* from, of); ~ **de alquileres** rent-free; ~ **de derechos** duty-free; ~ **de impuestos** tax-free, tax-exempt (*US*), free of tax; **un libro** ~ **de interés** a book devoid of interest; **estar** ~ **de cuidados** to be free of worries; **una expedición no exenta de peligros** an expedition not without (its) dangers.
(**b**) *lugar etc* unobstructed, open.
(**c**) (*Arquit*) free-standing.
exequias *nfpl* funeral rites, obsequies.
exfoliador *nm* (*Cono Sur*) tear-off pad, loose-leaf notebook.
exhalación *nf* (**a**) (*acto*) exhalation; (*vapor*) fumes, vapour. (**b**) (*Astron*) shooting star; **como una** ~ at top speed, like lightning.
exhalar [1a] **1** *vt aire etc* to exhale, breathe out; *gas etc* to emit, give off, give out; *suspiro* to breathe, heave; *gemido* to utter.
2 exhalarse *vr* (*jadear*) to breathe hard; (*darse prisa*) to hurry, run.
exhaustivamente *adv* exhaustively; thoroughly; comprehensively.
exhaustividad *nf* exhaustiveness; thoroughness.
exhaustivo *adj* exhaustive; thorough; comprehensive.
exhausto *adj* exhausted.
exheredar [1a] *vt* to disinherit.
exhibición *nf* exhibition, display, show; (*Cine*) showing; ~ **aérea** flying display; ~ **de escaparate** window display; ~ **folklórica** folk festival, display of folk-dancing (*etc*); **la pobre** ~ **del equipo** the team's poor showing; **una impresionante** ~ **de fuerza** an impressive show of strength.
exhibicionismo *nm* (**a**) exhibitionism. (**b**) (*sexual*) indecent exposure, flashing*.
exhibicionista 1 *adj* exhibitionist. **2** *nmf* (**a**) exhibitionist. (**b**) (*sexual*: *m*) flasher‡.
exhibidor *nm* display case.
exhibir [3a] **1** *vt* (**a**) to exhibit, display, show; *pasaporte* to show; *película* to show, screen; (*mostrar con orgullo*) to show off. (**b**) (*Méx*) to pay in cash. **2 exhibirse** *vr* (**a**) to show o.s. (**b**) (*sexualmente*) to expose o.s., flash*.
exhortación *nf* exhortation.
exhortar [1a] *vt* to exhort (*a* + *infin* to + *infin*).
exhumación *nf* exhumation, disinterment.
exhumar [1a] *vt* to exhume, disinter.
exigencia *nf* (**a**) (*requerimiento*) demand, requirement; exigency; **según las ~s de la situación** as the situation requires; **tener muchas ~s** to be very demanding.
(**b**) (*Carib*: *petición*) request.
(**c**) (*CAm*: *escasez*) need, lack.
exigente *adj* demanding, exacting, exigent; particular; *profesor* strict; **ser** ~ **con uno** to be hard on sb; **es muy** ~ **en la limpieza** she is very particular about cleanliness.
exigir [3c] *vt* (**a**) *contribución etc* to exact, levy (*a* from).
(**b**) (*requerir*) to demand, require (*a* of, from); to call for, ask for (*a* from); to insist on; ~ **el pago** to demand payment; **esto exige mucho cuidado** this needs a lot of care; **exigirá mucho dinero** it will require (*o* need, take) a lot of money; **ello no exige comentario** it does not call for any comment, comment on it would be superfluous; **exija recibo** insist on getting a receipt; **exige mucho** he's very demanding.
(**c**) (*Carib*) *cosa* to ask for, request; *persona* to beg, plead with, entreat.
exiguo *adj* meagre, small, scanty, exiguous.
exilado 1 *adj* exiled, in exile. **2** *nm*, **exilada** *nf* exile.
exilar [1a] **1** *vt* to exile. **2 exilarse** *vr* to go into exile; to exile o.s.
exiliado = **exilado**.
exiliar *vt* = **exilar**.
exilio *nm* exile; **estar en el** ~, **vivir en el** ~ to be in exile; **gobierno en el** ~ government in exile.
eximente *nm* excuse; justification; reason for being exempt.
eximio *adj persona* distinguished, eminent.
eximir [3a] **1** *vt* to exempt (*de* from); to free, excuse (*de* from); **esto me exime de toda obligación con él** this frees me from any obligation to him.
2 eximirse *vr*: ~ **de** + *infin* to excuse o.s. from + *ger*; to free o.s. from having to + *infin*.
existencia *nf* (**a**) (*vida*) existence; being; life; **lucha por la** ~ struggle for survival; **amargar la** ~ **a uno** to make sb's life a misery; **quitarse la** ~ (*euf*) to do away with o.s., commit suicide.
(**b**) (*t ~s*: *Com*) stock; goods; **nuestras ~s de carbón** our coal stocks, our stock(s) of coal; **estar en** ~ to be in stock; **liquidar ~s** to clear stock; **tener en** ~ to have in stock.
existencial *adj* existential.
existencialismo *nm* existentialism.
existencialista *adj*, *nmf* existentialist.
existente *adj* (**a**) existing; in being, in existence; actual; *texto etc* extant; surviving; **la situación** ~ the existing (*o* present) situation. (**b**) (*Com*) in stock.
existir [3a] *vi* to exist, be; **dejar de** ~ to pass out of existence, come to an end; (*morir*: *euf*) to pass away; **esta sociedad existe desde hace 90 años** the company has been in existence for 90 years, the company was founded 90 years ago; **no existe tal cosa** there's no such thing.
exitazo *nm* great success; (*Mús, Teat etc*) smash hit.
éxito *nm* (**a**) (*resultado*) result, outcome; **buen** ~ happy outcome, success; **con buen** ~ successfully; **tener buen** ~ to succeed, be successful; **tener mal** ~ to have an unfortunate outcome, fail, be unsuccessful.
(**b**) (*logro*) success; **con** ~ successfully; **tener** ~ **en** to be successful in; to make a success of; **el hombre de** ~ the successful man; **es una chica de mucho** ~ she's a girl who has lots of success (with the men).
(**c**) (*Mús, Teat, t fig*) success, hit; ~ **editorial,** ~ **de librería** best-seller; ~ **de taquilla** box-office success, successful play; ~ **de venta(s)** best-seller; ~ **clamoroso,** ~ **fulminante,** ~ **rotundo** huge success, overwhelming success; (*Mús etc*) hit song, smash hit; **los mejores ~s de** ... the greatest hits of ...
exitosamente *adv* successfully.
exitoso *adj* successful.
éxodo *nm* exodus; **el** ~ **rural** the depopulation of the coun-

tryside, the drift from the land.

exoneración *nf* (**a**) exoneration; freeing, relief. (**b**) dismissal.

exonerar [1a] *vt* (**a**) (*de culpa etc*) to exonerate; to exempt (*de un impuesto* from a tax); **~ a uno de un deber** to free sb from a duty, relieve sb of a duty; **le exoneraron de sus condecoraciones** they stripped him of his decorations.

(**b**) *empleado* to dismiss.

(**c**) **~ el vientre** to have a movement of the bowels.

exorbitancia *nf* exorbitance.

exorbitante *adj* exorbitant.

exorcismo *nm* exorcism.

exorcista 1 *adj*: **prácticas ~s** rites designed to secure exorcism. **2** *nmf* exorcist.

exorcizar [1f] *vt* to exorcise.

exordio *nm* exordium; preface, preamble, introduction.

exornar [1a] *vt* to adorn, embellish (*de* with).

exosto *nm* (*LAm Aut*) exhaust.

exótica* *nf* (*Méx*) stripper*, striptease artist.

exótico *adj* exotic.

exotismo *nm* exoticism; taste for the exotic.

expandible *adj* expansible.

expandir [3a] **1** *vt* (*gen*) to expand; *ropa* to spread out; (*Com etc*) to expand, enlarge; (*fig*) to expand, extend, spread; *noticia* to spread; **~ el mercado de un producto** to expand the market for a product; **~ la afición a la lectura** to spread a love of reading; **en caracteres expandidos** (*Tip, Inform*) double width.

2 expandirse *vr* to expand; to extend, spread.

expansible *adj* expansible; that can be expanded (*o* extended *etc*).

expansión *nf* (**a**) (*gen*) expansion; enlargement; extension, spread(ing); **la ~ económica** economic growth; **la ~ industrial** industrial expansion.

(**b**) (*fig*: *relajación*) relaxation; pleasure.

(**c**) (*fig*: *efusión*) expansiveness.

expansionar [1a] **1** *vt mercado etc* to expand.

2 expansionarse *vr* (**a**) to expand.

(**b**) (*fig*: *relajarse*) to relax.

(**c**) (*fig*: *desahogarse*) to unbosom o.s., open one's heart (*con* to).

expansionismo *nm* (*Pol etc*) expansionism.

expansionista *adj* (*Pol etc*) expansionist.

expansividad *nf* expansiveness.

expansivo *adj* (**a**) (*gen*) expansive. (**b**) (*fig*) expansive, affable; communicative.

expatriación *nf* expatriation; exile.

expatriado, -a *nm/f* expatriate; exile.

expatriarse [1b *o* 1c] *vr* to emigrate, leave one's country; (*Pol etc*) to go into exile.

expectación *nf* (*esperanza*) expectation, expectancy, anticipation; (*ansia*) eagerness; (*ilusión*) excitement; **la ~ crece de un momento a otro** the excitement is growing every moment.

expectante *adj* expectant; eager; excited.

expectativa *nf* expectation; hope, prospect; **~ de vida** life expectancy; **estar a la ~** to wait and see (what will happen); **estar a la ~ de algo** to look out for sth, be on the watch for sth.

expectorar [1a] *vti* to expectorate.

expedición *nf* (**a**) (*t Geog, Mil etc*) expedition; (*Dep*) away fixture; **~ de salvamento** rescue expedition; **~ militar** military expedition.

(**b**) (*Com etc*) shipment, shipping; **gastos de ~** shipping charges.

(**c**) (*prontitud*) speed, dispatch.

expedicionario *adj* expeditionary.

expedidor *nm* shipper, shipping agent.

expedientar [1a] *vt* (*investigar*) to make a file on, draw up a dossier on; (*censurar*) to censure, reprimand; (*expulsar*) to expel; *médico etc* to strike off the register; (*despedir*) to dismiss.

expediente *nm* (**a**) (*medio*) expedient; means; device, make-shift; **recurrir al ~ de** + *infin* to resort to the device of + *ger*.

(**b**) (*Jur*) action, proceedings; records of a case; **~ disciplinario** disciplinary proceedings; **~ judicial** legal proceedings; **~ de regulación de empleo** procedure for issuing notices of dismissal; **abrir ~, incoar ~** to start proceedings; **instruir un ~** to collect all the documents.

(**c**) (*historial*) record; (*dossier*) dossier; (*ficha*) file; **~ académico** student's record, pupil's record card, transcript (*US*); **~ personal** personal file; **~ policíaco** police dossier.

(**d**) (*despido*) dismissal.

(**e**) **cubrir el ~** to do just enough to keep out of trouble.

expedienteo *nm* bureaucracy, red tape.

expedir [3k] *vt mercancías etc* to send, ship off, forward; *documento* to draw up; to make out, issue; *orden, pasaporte, billete etc* to issue; *negocio* to deal with, dispatch.

expeditar [1a] *vt* (*LAm*) to expedite, hurry along; (*concluir*) to conclude.

expeditivo *adj* expeditious; prompt, efficient.

expedito *adj* (**a**) (*pronto*) expeditious, prompt, speedy. (**b**) *camino* clear, unobstructed, free; **dejar ~ el camino para** to clear the way for. (**c**) (*LAm*: *fácil*) easy.

expeler [2a] *vt* to expel, eject.

expendedor 1 *nm*, **expendedora** *nf* (*persona*: *al detalle*) dealer, retailer; (*agente*) agent; (*de tabaco*) tobacconist; (*Teat*) ticket agent; **~ de billetes** ticket clerk, booking clerk; **~ de moneda falsa** distributor of counterfeit money.

2 *nm* ticket machine; **~ automático** vending machine; **~ automático de bebidas** drink vending machine.

expendeduría *nf* retail shop, (*esp*) tobacconist's (shop), cigar store (*US*).

expender [2a] *vt* (**a**) *dinero* to expend, spend.

(**b**) *moneda falsa* to utter; to pass, circulate.

(**c**) *mercancías* to sell (retail); to be an agent for, sell on commission; to deal in.

(**d**) (*Jur*) **~ de moneda falsa** issuing false coin, passing false coin.

expendio *nm* (**a**) (*gasto*) expense, outlay.

(**b**) (*LAm*: *tienda*) small shop; **~ de boletos** (*Méx*) ticket office.

(**c**) (*acto*: *And, Cono Sur, Méx*) retailing, retail selling.

(**d**) (*Jur*) **~ de moneda falsa** issuing false coin, passing false coin.

expensar [1a] *vt* (*LAm*) to defray the costs of.

expensas *nfpl* expenses; (*Jur*) costs; **a ~ de** at the expense of (*t fig*); at the mercy of, subject to; **a mis ~** at my expense.

experiencia *nf* (**a**) experience; **~ laboral** work experience; **una triste ~** a sad experience; **aprender por la ~** to learn by experience; **intercambiar ~s** to swap stories; **saber algo por ~** to know sth from experience.

(**b**) (*experimento etc*) experiment (*en* on); **~ clínica** clinical trial; **~ piloto** pilot scheme.

experienciar [1b] *vt* = **experimentar.**

experimentación *nf* experimentation.

experimentado *adj* experienced.

experimental *adj* experimental.

experimentalmente *adv* experimentally.

experimentar [1a] **1** *vt* (**a**) (*Téc etc*) to test, try out; to experiment with; **el nuevo fármaco está siendo experimentado** the new drug is being tested, experiments with the new drug are going on; **están experimentando un nuevo helicóptero** they are testing a new helicopter.

(**b**) (*sufrir*) *cambio etc* to experience, undergo, go through; *deterioro, pérdida* to suffer; *aumento* to show; *emoción* to feel; **las cifras han experimentado un aumento de un 5 por 100** the figures show an increase of 5%; **no experimenté ninguna sensación nueva** I felt no new sensation.

2 *vi* to experiment (*con* with, *en* on).

experimento *nm* experiment (*con* with, *en* on); **como ~** as an experiment, by way of experiment; **hacer ~s** to experiment (*con* with, *en* on).

experticia *nf* (*LAm*) expertise.

expertización *nf* expert assessment.

expertizar [1f] *vt* to appraise as an expert, give an expert assessment of.

experto 1 *adj* expert; skilled, experienced; seasoned; knowledgeable. **2** *nm*, **experta** *nf* expert.

expiación *nf* expiation, atonement.

expiar [1c] *vt* to expiate, atone for.

expiatorio *adj* expiatory.

expiración *nf* expiration.

expirar [1a] *vi* to expire.

explanación *nf* (**a**) (*Téc*) levelling. (**b**) (*fig*) explanation, elucidation.

explanada *nf* (*plataforma*) raised area, terrace, platform; (*zona nivelada*) levelled area; (*paseo*) esplanade; (*Mil*) glacis; **~ de ensillado** saddling enclosure.

explanar [1a] *vt* (**a**) (*Ferro, Téc etc*) to level, grade. (**b**) (*fig*) to unfold; to explain, elucidate.

explayar [1a] **1** *vt* to extend, expand, enlarge.

2 explayarse *vr* (**a**) (*extender*) to extend, spread; to open out, unfold.

(**b**) (*fig: relajarse*) to relax, take it easy; to take an outing.

(**c**) (*fig: en discurso etc*) to speak at length; to spread o.s.; ~ **a su gusto** to talk one's head off, talk to one's heart's content; ~ **con uno** to unbosom o.s. to sb, confide in sb.

explicable *adj* explicable, explainable, that can be explained; **cosas no fácilmente ~s** things not easily explained, things not easy to explain.

explicación *nf* (**a**) explanation; reason (*de* for); **sin dar explicaciones** without giving any reason. (**b**) (*Univ etc*) lecture, class.

explicaderas *nfpl*: **tener buenas ~** to be good at explaining things (away); (*pey*) to be plausible.

explicar [1g] **1** *vt* (*gen*) to explain; *teoría etc* to expound; *curso* to lecture on, teach; *materia* to lecture in; *clase* to give, deliver.

2 explicarse *vr* (**a**) to explain (o.s.); **se explica con claridad** he states things clearly; **¡explíquese Vd!** explain yourself!; **explíquese con la mayor brevedad** please be as brief as possible; **se explica de acuerdo con las nuevas teorías** he follows the latest theories.

(**b**) ~ **algo** to understand sth; **no me lo explico** I can't understand it, I can't make it out.

(**c**) (*ser explicable*) to be explained; **esto no se explica fácilmente** this cannot be explained (away) easily.

(**d**) (*: *pagar*) to cough up*, pay.

explicativo *adj*, **explicatorio** *adj* explanatory.

explícitamente *adv* explicitly.

explicitar [1a] *vt* (*declarar*) to state, assert, make explicit; (*aclarar*) to clarify; ~ **que** ... to make clear that ...

explícito *adj* explicit.

exploración *nf* exploration; (*Mil*) reconnaissance, scouting; (*Radar etc*) scanning; ~ **física** (*Med*) physical examination; ~ **submarina** underwater exploration; (*como deporte*) skin-diving.

explorador *nm* (**a**) (*Geog etc*) explorer; pioneer; (*Mil*) scout; (**niño**) ~ (boy) scout. (**b**) (*Med*) probe; (*Radar etc*) scanner; ~ **láser** laser scanner.

exploradora *nf* girl guide, girl scout (*US*).

explorar [1a] **1** *vt* (*Geog etc*) to explore; to pioneer, open up; (*Med*) to probe; (*Radar etc*) to scan. **2** *vi* to explore; (*Mil*) to scout, reconnoitre.

exploratorio *adj* exploratory.

explosión *nf* (**a**) explosion; blast; ~ **controlada** controlled explosion; ~ **por simpatía** secondary explosion; **motor de** ~ internal combustion engine; **teoría de la gran** ~ big bang theory; **hacer** ~ to explode.

(**b**) (*fig*) explosion, outburst; **una ~ de cólera** an explosion of anger; ~ **demográfica** population explosion.

explosionar [1a] *vti* to explode, blow up.

explosiva *nf* (*Ling*) plosive (consonant).

explosivo 1 *adj* (**a**) (*gen, t fig*) explosive. (**b**) (*Ling*) plosive. **2** *nm* explosive; **alto ~, ~ detonante, ~ de gran potencia** high explosive; ~ **plástico** plastic explosive; ~ **de ruido** stun grenade.

explotable *adj* exploitable, that can be exploited.

explotación *nf* exploitation; running, operation; (*Min etc*) working; ~ **agrícola** farm; ~ **a cielo abierto** opencast working, opencast mining; ~ **forestal** forestry; **en** ~ in operation; **gastos de** ~ operating costs, operating expenses.

explotador 1 *adj* exploitative. **2** *nm*, **explotadora** *nf* exploiter.

explotar [1a] **1** *vt* (**a**) (*gen*) to exploit; *fábrica etc* to run, operate; *mina, veta* to work; *recursos* to exploit, tap; to harness.

(**b**) (*pey*) *obreros* to exploit; *situación* to exploit, make capital out of.

(**c**) (*Mil etc*) to explode.

2 *vi* (*Mil etc*) to explode; to go off; **explotaron 2 bombas** 2 bombs exploded; **cayó sin** ~ it fell but did not go off, it landed without going off.

expoliación *nf* pillaging, sacking.

expoliar [1b] *vt* (**a**) to pillage, sack. (**b**) (*desposeer*) to dispossess.

expolio *nm* (**a**) pillaging, sacking. (**b**) **armar un** ~ to cause a hullaballoo*.

exponencial *adj* exponential.

exponente 1 *nmf* (*persona*) exponent.

2 *nm* (**a**) (*Mat*) index, exponent.

(**b**) (*LAm: ejemplo*) model, (prime) example; **el tabaco cubano es ~ de calidad** Cuban tobacco is the best of its kind.

exponer [2q] **1** *vt* (**a**) (*gen, Ecl, Fot*) to expose; *cuadro etc* to show, exhibit, put on show; *cartel* to display, put up.

(**b**) *vida* to risk.

(**c**) *niño* to abandon.

(**d**) *argumento* to expound; *idea* to explain, unfold; *hechos* to set out, set forth, state; (*Jur*) *acusación* to bring.

2 *vi* (*pintor*) to exhibit, hold an exhibition.

3 exponerse *vr*: ~ **a** to expose o.s. to, lay o.s. open to; ~ **a** + *infin* to run the risk of + *ger*.

exportable *adj* exportable.

exportación *nf* (**a**) (*acto*) export, exportation; ~ **en pie** live export.

(**b**) (*artículo*) export, exported article; (*mercancías*) exports; **géneros de** ~ exports, exported goods; **comercio de** ~ export trade.

exportador(a) *nm/f* exporter; shipper.

exportar [1a] *vt* to export.

exposición *nf* (**a**) (*acto*) exposing, exposure; display; (*Fot*) exposure; (*de cuadro etc*) showing.

(**b**) (*de hechos etc*) statement, exposition; (*petición*) petition, claim; ~ **de motivos** (*Jur*) explanatory preamble.

(**c**) (*Arte etc*) show, exhibition; (*Com*) show, fair; ~ **canina** dog show; ~ **itinerante** travelling show; ~ **de modas** fashion show; ~ **universal** world fair.

exposímetro *nm* (*Fot*) exposure meter.

expósito 1 *adj*: **niño** ~ = **2**. **2** *nm*, **expósita** *nf* foundling.

expositor(a) 1 *nm/f* (*persona*: *Arte etc*) exhibitor; (*de teoría*) exponent. **2** *nm* (*vitrina*) showcase, display case; (*puesto*) sales stand.

exprés *nm* (**a**) (*LAm*) express train. (**b**) (*Méx*) black coffee.

expresado *adj* above-mentioned; **según las cifras expresadas** according to these figures, according to the figures I (*etc*) have already quoted, according to the figures given earlier.

expresamente *adv* expressly; on purpose, deliberately; clearly, plainly; **no lo dijo** ~ he didn't say so in so many words.

expresar [1a] **1** *vt* (*gen*) to express; to voice; (*redactar*) to word, phrase, put; (*declarar*) to state, set forth; (*citar*) to quote; **expresa las opiniones de todos** he is voicing the opinions of us all; **estaba expresado de otro modo** it was worded differently; **el papel no lo expresa** the paper doesn't say so; **Vd deberá ~ el número del giro postal** you should quote (*o* give, state) the number of the postal order.

2 expresarse *vr* (**a**) (*persona*) to express o.s.; **no se expresa bien** he doesn't express himself well.

(**b**) (*cifra, dato*) to be stated; **el número no se expresa** the number is not given, the number is not stated; **como abajo se expresa** as is stated below.

expresión *nf* (**a**) (*acto*) expression; ~ **corporal** self-expression through movement; **esta ~ de nuestro agradecimiento** this expression of our gratitude.

(**b**) (*Ling*) expression; ~ **familiar** colloquialism, conversational expression; **la ~ es poco clara** the expression is not very clear.

(**c**) **expresiones** (††) greetings, regards.

expresionismo *nm* expressionism.

expresionista *adj, nmf* expressionist.

expresivamente *adv* (**a**) (*gen*) expressively. (**b**) (*cariñosamente*) tenderly, affectionately, warmly.

expresividad *nf* expressiveness.

expresivo *adj* (**a**) (*gen*) expressive. (**b**) (*afectuoso*) tender, affectionate, warm.

expreso 1 *adj* (**a**) (*explícito*) express; (*exacto*) specific, clear, exact.

(**b**) *tren etc* fast; **carta (por) ~** special delivery letter.

2 *nm* (**a**) (*persona*) special messenger; **mandar algo por** ~ to send sth by express (delivery).

(**b**) (*Ferro etc*) fast train.

(**c**) (*Carib: autobús*) long-distance coach.

exprimelimones *nm invar* lemon-squeezer.

exprimidera *nf* squeezer.

exprimidor *nm* squeezer; ~ **de limones** lemon-squeezer.

exprimir [3a] *vt* (**a**) *fruta etc* to squeeze; *zumo* to squeeze out, press out, express; *ropa* to wring out, squeeze dry; *limón etc* to squeeze.

(**b**) ~ **a uno** to exploit sb.

ex profeso *adv* on purpose.

expropiación *nf* expropriation; commandeering; ~ **forzosa** compulsory purchase; **orden de** ~ compulsory purchase order.

expropiar [1b] *vt* to expropriate; to commandeer.

expuesto 1 *ptp de* **exponer**; **según lo arriba ~** according to what has been stated (*o* set out, said) above.

2 *adj* (**a**) *sitio etc* exposed; dangerous.

(**b**) *cuadro etc* on show, on display, on view; **los artículos ~s en el escaparate** the goods displayed in the window.

(**c**) **estar ~ a** to be exposed to, be open to; to be liable to.

expugnar [1a] *vt* to take by storm.

expulsar [1a] *vt* to expel (*de* from), eject (*de* from), turn out (*de* of); *jugador* to send off; **~ a uno a puntapiés** to kick sb out.

expulsión *nf* expulsion, ejection; (*Dep*) sending-off; (*Econ*) crowding out effect.

expulsor 1 *adj*: **asiento ~** (*Aer*) ejector seat. **2** *nm* (*Téc*) ejector.

expurgar [1h] *vt* to expurgate.

expurgatorio *adj* expurgatory; **índice ~** (*Ecl*) Index.

exquisitamente *adv* (*V adj*) (**a**) exquisitely; deliciously, delightfully; excellently. (**b**) (*pey*) affectedly.

exquisitez *nf* (**a**) exquisiteness; excellence. (**b**) (*pey*) affectation.

exquisito *adj* (**a**) (*excelente*) exquisite; delicious, delightful; excellent. (**b**) *persona* (*afectado*) affected; (*melindroso*) choosy*, finicky.

Ext. (**a**) *abr de* **Exterior** external, ext. (**b**) *abr de* **Extensión** extension, ext.

extasiar [1c] **1** *vt* to entrance, enrapture, captivate. **2 extasiarse** *vr* to become entranced; to go into ecstasies, rhapsodize (*ante* over, about).

éxtasis *nm invar* ecstasy; rapture; (*de médium etc*) trance; **estar en el ~** to be in ecstasy.

extático *adj* ecstatic, rapturous; **lo miró ~** he looked at it ecstatically.

extemporal *adj*, **extemporáneo** *adj lluvia etc* unseasonable; *viaje* untimely.

extender [2g] **1** *vt* (**a**) (*gen*) to extend; (*ampliar*) to enlarge, make bigger; to prolong; to stretch (out), expand; *mapa, tela etc* to spread (out), open (out); to lay out; *cartas* to lay down; *crema de belleza, mantequilla* to spread; *pila* to spread out; *guerra* to extend, widen, escalate; *conocimiento* to extend, spread (*a* to); *brazo, mano* to stretch out.

(**b**) *documento* to draw up; to write out; *cheque* to draw, make out; *recibo* to make out; *certificado* to issue.

2 extenderse *vr* (**a**) (*en el espacio*) to extend; to stretch (out); to spread (out); to be, lie; **delante de nosotros se extendía la mar** before us the sea stretched away, the sea lay spread out before us; **sus terrenos se extienden sobre muchos kilómetros** his lands spread over many miles; **no se extiende más al oeste** it does not go any further west.

(**b**) (*espacio: fig*) to range, extend; **las posibilidades se extienden de A a Z** the possibilities range from A to Z.

(**c**) (*en el tiempo*) to extend, last (*a* to, till; *de* from).

(**d**) (*fig: conocimiento, costumbre*) to spread, extend; (*guerra*) to escalate, widen, broaden; **su venganza se extendió hasta matar a las mujeres** in his vengeance he even killed the women; **la epidemia se extendió rápidamente** the epidemic spread rapidly.

(**e**) (*cantidad*) **~ a** to amount to, reach, go as high as; (*tamaño*) to run to; **el libro se extiende a 400 páginas** the book runs to 400 pages.

(**f**) (*fig: en discurso*) to spread o.s.; **~ sobre un tema** to enlarge on a subject.

extendido *adj* (**a**) *tela etc* spread out, open; extended; *brazos* outstretched, spread wide.

(**b**) *costumbre etc* widespread; prevalent, (*pey*) rife, rampant; *conocimiento* widespread.

extensamente *adv* (**a**) *viajar, leer* extensively, widely. (**b**) *tratar* fully, in full, with full details.

extensible *adj* extending, extensible, extendable; **un período ~ a 3 meses** a period which can be extended to three months.

extensión *nf* (**a**) (*acto*) extension; stretching; spreading; **~ de plazo** (*Com*) extension; **por ~** by extension.

(**b**) (*dimensiones*) extent, size; spaciousness; **un solar de mayor ~** a site of greater size, a site of larger area.

(**c**) (*de mar, tierra*) expanse, stretch; **por toda la ~ del paisaje** over the whole (expanse) of the countryside.

(**d**) (*de tiempo*) length, duration; span.

(**e**) (*Mús*) range, compass.

(**f**) (*fig: de conocimientos etc*) extent, range; (*de sentidos*) range; (*de plan, programa*) scope.

(**g**) (*Telec*) extension.

(**h**) **~ de cable** (*Elec*) extension lead.

(**i**) **E~ Agraria** agricultural advisory service; **E~ Universitaria** extramural studies.

extensivo *adj* extensive; **hacer ~ a** to extend to, apply to, make applicable to; **la crítica se hizo extensiva a toda la ciudad** the criticism applied to the whole city.

extenso *adj* (**a**) (*grande*) extensive; vast; *cuarto etc* big, broad, spacious; *imperio* far-flung.

(**b**) *conocimiento etc* widespread; *informe, narración* full; **en ~, por ~** in full, with full particulars, at length.

extensor *nm* chest expander.

extenuación *nf* emaciation, weakness; exhaustion.

extenuado *adj* emaciated, wasted, weak; exhausted.

extenuar [1e] **1** *vt* to emaciate, weaken; to exhaust. **2 extenuarse** *vr* to become emaciated, waste away; to get weak.

exterior 1 *adj* (**a**) (*gen*) exterior, external; outer; *aspecto* outward; *cuarto* outside, outward-facing.

(**b**) *deuda, relaciones* foreign; **asuntos ~es** foreign affairs; **comercio ~** foreign trade, overseas trade.

2 *nm* (**a**) (*parte, de casa etc*) exterior, outside; (*aspecto*) outward appearance; **al ~, por el ~** on the outside; outwardly; (*carreras*) **avanzar por el ~** to come up on the outside; **de ~ poco agradable** of unprepossessing appearance; **con el ~ pintado de azul** with the outside painted blue; **rodar en ~es** to film on location.

(**b**) (*países extranjeros*) foreign parts; **así aquí como en el ~** both here and abroad; **noticias del ~** foreign news, overseas news, news from abroad; **comercio con el ~** foreign trade, overseas trade.

(**c**) (*Dep*) wing, wing-forward, winger; **~ derecho** outside-right; **~ izquierdo** outside-left.

(**d**) **E~es** (*Pol*) (Ministry of) Foreign Affairs.

exterioridad *nf* (**a**) (*apariencia*) outward appearance, externals. (**b**) **~es** (*fig*) pomp, show; formalities.

exteriorizar [1f] *vt* (*expresar*) to express outwardly; (*mostrar*) to show, reveal.

exteriormente *adv* outwardly.

exterminar [1a] *vt* to exterminate.

exterminio *nm* extermination.

externamente *adv* externally; outwardly.

externo 1 *adj* external, outside; outward. **2** *nm*, **externa** *nf* day pupil.

extinción *nf* extinction.

extinguido *adj* (**a**) **estar ~** (*incendio*) to be out, be extinguished. (**b**) *animal, volcán* extinct.

extinguir [3d] **1** *vt* (**a**) *incendio etc* to extinguish, put out; *sublevación* to put down.

(**b**) (*Bio*) to exterminate, wipe out.

(**c**) *deuda etc* to wipe out.

(**d**) **~ una sentencia** (*Jur*) to serve a sentence.

2 extinguirse *vr* (**a**) (*fuego*) to go out.

(**b**) (*Bio*) to die out, become extinct.

extinto *adj* (**a**) extinct. (**b**) (*Cono Sur, Méx: euf*) dead, deceased.

extintor *nm* (*t* **~ de incendios**) fire extinguisher; **~ de espuma** foam extinguisher.

extirpación *nf* (**a**) extirpation, eradication. (**b**) (*Med*) removal.

extirpar [1a] *vt* (**a**) to extirpate, eradicate, root out.

(**b**) (*Med*) to remove (surgically), take out.

extorno *nm* (*Com*) rebate.

extorsión *nf* (**a**) (*Fin etc*) extortion, exaction; (*chantaje*) blackmail. (**b**) (*molestia*) inconvenience.

extorsionador(a) *nm/f* extortioner; (*chantajista*) blackmailer.

extorsionar [1a] *vt* (**a**) (*usurpar*) to extort, extract (*de* from). (**b**) (*fig*) to pester, bother.

extorsionista *nmf* (*Méx*) extortionist, blackmailer.

extra[1] **1** *adj invar* extra; **vino ~** high-quality wine; **gasolina ~** high-octane petrol; **~ de** in addition to, on top of. **2** *nm* (**a**) (*de menú, cuenta*) extra; (*de pago*) bonus. (**b**) (*Tip*) extra, special edition, special supplement. **3** *nmf* (*Cine*) extra.

extra[2]**...** *pref* extra...

extraacadémico *adj* non-university (*atr*), (taking place) outside the university.

extracción *nf* extraction; (*de lotería*) draw.

extracomunitario *adj*: **países ~s** countries outside the European Community.

extraconstitucional *adj* unconstitutional.

extraconyugal *adj* extramarital, adulterous.

extracorto *adj onda* ultra-short.

extractar [1a] *vt* (**a**) to make extracts from. (**b**) (*resumir*) to abridge, summarize.

extracto *nm* (**a**) (*Quím etc*) extract. (**b**) (*Liter*) abstract, summary. (**c**) ~ **de cuentas** (*LAm Fin*) statement (of account), bank statement.

extractor *nm* extractor; ~ **de humos** extractor fan.

extracurricular *adj* extracurricular, outside the curriculum.

extradeportivo *adj* unrelated to sport; (*antideportivo*) unsporting.

extradición *nf* extradition; **crimen sujeto a** ~ extraditable offence.

extradicionar [1a] *vt* to extradite.

extradir [3a] *vt* to extradite.

extraditable 1 *adj* subject to extradition. **2** *nmf* person subject to extradition.

extraditar [1a] *vt* to extradite.

extraer [2o] *vt* to extract (*t Mat, Med, Min*), take out, pull out.

extraescolar *adj*: **actividad** ~ out-of-school activity.

extrafino *adj* superfine.

extraíble *adj* removable, detachable.

extrajudicial *adj* extrajudicial, out of court.

extrajurídico *adj* outside the law.

extralimitación *nf* abuse (of authority).

extralimitarse [1a] *vr* to go too far, exceed (*o* abuse) one's authority; to go beyond what is proper, overstep the mark.

extramarital *adj* extramarital.

extramuros 1 *adv* outside the city; (*liter*) without (*liter*). **2** *prep*: ~ **de** outside.

extranjería *nf* alien status, status of foreigners; **ley de** ~ law on aliens.

extranjerismo *nm* foreign word (*o* phrase *etc*).

extranjerizante *adj* tending to favour foreign ways (*etc*); *palabra* foreign-looking, foreign-sounding.

extranjero 1 *adj* foreign; alien.

2 *nm*, **extranjera** *nf* foreigner; alien.

3 *nm* foreign country; foreign lands; **cosas del** ~ things from abroad; foreign things; **estar en el** ~ to be abroad, be overseas, be in foreign parts; **ir al** ~ to go abroad; **pasó 6 años en el** ~ he spent 6 years abroad; **no me siento a gusto en el** ~ I don't feel at ease abroad.

extranjis*: **de** ~ *adv* (**a**) (*súbitamente*) unexpectedly. (**b**) (*secretamente*) secretly, on the sly.

extrañamente *adv* strangely, oddly.

extrañamiento *nm* (**a**) (*enajenación*) estrangement (*de* from). (**b**) = **extrañeza.** (**c**) (*Jur* ††) banishment.

extrañar [1a] **1** *vt* (**a**) (*asombrar*) to find strange, find odd, wonder at; **extrañaba la falta de autobuses** she found the absence of buses strange; **me extrañaba que no hubieras venido** I was surprised that you had not come; **apenas es de** ~ **que** ... it is hardly surprising that ...; **eso me extraña** that surprises me, that puzzles me, I find that odd; **me extraña su conducta** I am surprised at your behaviour.

(**b**) (*LAm*: *echar de menos*) to miss; to feel the lack of, regret the absence of; to yearn for.

(**c**) (*Jur*) to deport, send away; (††) to banish.

2 extrañarse *vr* (**a**) (*asombrarse*) to be amazed, be surprised (*de* at); (*maravillarse*) to marvel (*de* at); ~ **de que** ... to be surprised that ...; to marvel that ...

(**b**) (*negarse*) to refuse.

(**c**) (*amigos*) to become estranged, grow apart.

extrañeza *nf* (**a**) (*rareza*) strangeness, oddness, oddity.

(**b**) (*asombro*) surprise, amazement; (*inquietud*) uneasiness; **me miró con** ~ he looked at me in surprise.

(**c**) (*de amigos*) estrangement, alienation.

extraño 1 *adj* (**a**) (*raro*) strange, odd, queer; singular; **es muy** ~ it's very odd; **¡cosa extraña!** how strange!, how odd!; **parece** ~ **que** ... it seems strange that ...

(**b**) (*ajeno*) extraneous (*a* to); **cosas extrañas a las que tratamos** things unconnected with those we handle.

(**c**) (*extranjero*) foreign.

2 *nm*, **extraña** *nf* foreigner.

extrañoso *adj* (*And*) surprised.

extraoficial *adj* unofficial; informal.

extraoficialmente *adv* unofficially; informally.

extraordinariamente *adv* extraordinarily.

extraordinario 1 *adj* (*gen*) extraordinary; (*insólito*) unusual; (*destacado*) outstanding; *descuento, edición, número etc* special; *cobro* extra, supplementary; **por sus servicios** ~**s** for his outstanding services; **no tiene nada de** ~ there's nothing special about it.

2 *nm* (**a**) (*de menú*) special dish, extra dish.

(**b**) (*de periódico*) special issue.

extraparlamentario *adj* (taking place) outside parliament.

extrapeninsular *adj* outside Iberia, relating to areas outside the Peninsula.

extraplano *adj* super-slim.

extraplomado *adj* overhanging.

extraplomo *nm* overhang.

extrapolable *adj* comparable.

extrapolación *nf* extrapolation.

extrapolar [1a] *vt* to extrapolate.

extrarradio *nm* (*de ciudad*) outer parts, outlying area.

extrasensorial *adj* extrasensory.

extratasa *nf* surcharge, extra charge.

extraterrenal *adj* (*LAm*), **extraterreno** *adj* (*LAm*) extraterrestrial, from another planet.

extraterrestre 1 *adj* extraterrestrial. **2** *nmf* extraterrestrial being.

extraterritorial *adj* extraterritorial.

extravagancia *nf* (**a**) (*cualidad*) extravagance; outlandishness; oddness, strangeness. (**b**) (*una* ~) (*capricho*) whim; (*rareza*) vagary, peculiarity; ~**s** nonsense; **tiene sus** ~**s** he has his oddities.

extravagante *adj* extravagant; (*estrafalario*) outlandish, eccentric; (*raro*) odd, strange, nonsensical.

extravagantemente *adv* extravagantly; eccentrically; oddly, strangely; nonsensically.

extravasarse [1a] *vr* to leak out, flow out; (*sangre*) to ooze out.

extravertido = **extrovertido.**

extraviado *adj* lost; missing; *animal* lost, stray.

extraviar [1c] **1** *vt* (**a**) *persona* to mislead, misdirect; to lead astray.

(**b**) *objeto* to lose, mislay, misplace.

(**c**) *dinero* (*pey*) to embezzle.

2 extraviarse *vr* (**a**) (*persona*) to lose one's way, get lost; (*animal*) to stray, wander; (*carta*) to go astray, get lost in the post, miscarry.

(**b**) (*moralmente*) to go astray, err, fall into evil ways.

extravío *nm* (**a**) (*pérdida*) loss, misplacement, mislaying; straying; wandering; (*fig*) deviation (*from* de). (**b**) (*fig*: *moral*) misconduct, erring, evil ways.

extremadamente *adv* extremely, exceedingly; extraordinarily.

extremado *adj* (*gen*) extreme; excessive; (*intenso*) intense; (*muy bueno*) extremely good; (*muy malo*) extremely bad; **frío** ~ extreme cold; **con extremada delicadeza** with extraordinary delicacy.

Extremadura *nf* Estremadura.

extremar [1a] **1** *vt* to carry to extremes; to force the sense of, stretch the application of; to overdo; **sin** ~ **el sentimentalismo** without overdoing the sentimentality; **el dictador extrema sus incendiarios discursos** the dictator is making even more inflammatory speeches, the dictator is being still more outrageous in his inflammatory speeches.

2 extremarse *vr* to do one's utmost, exert o.s. to the full, make every effort (*en* + *infin* to + *infin*).

extremaunción *nf* extreme unction.

extremeño, -a *adj, nm/f* Extremaduran.

extremidad *nf* (**a**) (*punta*) end, tip, extremity; (*borde*) edge, outermost part. (**b**) ~**es** (*Anat*) extremities.

extremismo *nm* extremism.

extremista *adj, nmf* extremist.

extremo 1 *adj* (**a**) (*lugar*) extreme, last; end (*atr*); (*más remoto*) far, furthest, outer, outermost.

(**b**) (*en orden*) last.

(**c**) (*fig*) extreme; utmost; critical, desperate; **en caso** ~ as a last resort, in an extreme case.

2 *nm* (**a**) (*cabo, límite*) end; extremity; ~ **muerto** dead end; **pasar de un** ~ **a otro** to go from one end to the other, (*fig*) go from one extreme to the other.

(**b**) (*fig*: *punto más alto*) highest point, highest degree; (*punto más bajo*) lowest point; (*punto más remoto*) extreme; **al** ~ **de, hasta el** ~ **de** to the point of; **con** ~, **en** ~ in the extreme; **en último** ~ as a last resort; in the final analysis; **por** ~ extremely; **hacer** ~**s** to gush, behave effusively; **quedó reducido al** ~ **de ir a pie** he was reduced to (the extreme of) going on foot; **los** ~**s se tocan** extremes meet.

(**c**) (*fig*: *asunto*) point, matter, question; **los** ~**s de la declaración** the detailed content of the statement; **ese** ~ **no se tocó en la discusión** that point was not dealt with in the discussion.

(**d**) (*fig*: *cuidado*) great care.

(**e**) (*Dep*) wing; (*persona*) wing-forward, winger; ~ **derecho** outside-right; ~ **izquierdo** outside-left.

Extremo Oriente *nm* Far East.
extremoso *adj* (*persona*) gushing, effusive; (*vehemente*) vehement, extreme in his (*etc*) attitudes (*o* reactions).
extrínseco *adj* extrinsic.
extrovertido **1** *adj* extrovert; outgoing. **2** *nm*, **extrovertida** *nf* extrovert.
exuberancia *nf* (**a**) (*gen*) exuberance. (**b**) (*Bot*) luxuriance, lushness. (**c**) (*de tipo*) fullness, buxomness.
exuberante *adj* (**a**) (*gen*) exuberant. (**b**) (*Bot*) luxuriant, lush. (**c**) *tipo etc* full, buxom, well-covered.
exudación *nf* exudation.
exudar [1a] **1** *vt* to exude, ooze (*de* from). **2** *vi* to exude, ooze out.
exultación *nf* exultation.
exultar [1a] *vi* to exult.
exvoto *nm* votive offering.
eyaculación *nf* (*Med*) ejaculation; ~ **precoz** premature ejaculation.
eyacular [1a] *vti* (*Med*) to ejaculate.
eyectable *adj*: **asiento** ~ ejector seat.
eyectarse [1a] *vr* (*Aer*) to eject.
eyector *nm* (*Téc*) ejector.
-ez *V* **Aspects of Word Formation in Spanish 2.**
Ezequiel *nm* Ezekiel.

F

F, f [efe] *nf* (*letra*) F, f.

F (**a**) *abr de* **fuerza** force; **un viento F8** a force 8 wind. (**b**) *abr de* **febrero** February, Feb.; **el 23-F** the 23rd February (*date of the Tejero coup, 1981*).

f.ª (*Com*) *abr de* **factura** Invoice, Inv.

fa *nm* (*Mús*) F; **~ mayor** F major.

f.a.b. *abr de* **franco a bordo** free on board, f.o.b.

fabada *nf* (*Asturias*) *rich stew of beans, pork etc.*

fabe *nf* broad bean.

fabla *nf* (**a**) (*Hist*) pseudo-archaic style. (**b**) **~ aragonesa** Aragonese dialect.

fábrica *nf* (**a**) (*Téc*) factory; works, plant; mill; (*And: alambique*) still, distillery; **~ de armas** arms factory, ordnance factory; **~ de cerveza** brewery; **~ de conservas** canning plant; **~ experimental** pilot plant; **~ de gas** gasworks; **~ de moneda** mint; **~ de papel** paper-mill; **~ de vidrio** glassworks; **marca de ~** trademark; **precio en ~** price ex-factory, price ex-works.

(**b**) (*acto*) manufacture, making.

(**c**) (*origen*) make; **de ~ alemana** of German make, German-made.

(**d**) (*Arquit*) building, structure; fabric; masonry.

fabricación *nf* manufacture, making, production; make; **~ asistida por ordenador** computer-assisted manufacturing; **~ de coches** car manufacture; **~ de tejas** tile making; **de ~ casera** home-made; **de ~ nacional** made in Spain (*o* Britain *etc*); **de ~ propia** made on the premises, our own make; **~ en serie** mass production; **estar en ~** to be in production.

fabricante *nmf* manufacturer; maker; (*industrial*) factory owner, mill owner.

fabricar [1g] *vt* (**a**) (*producir*) to manufacture, make; to put together; (*Arquit*) to build, construct; **~ en serie** to mass-produce.

(**b**) (*fig: pey*) to fabricate, invent; *documento* to fabricate, falsify; *mentira* to concoct.

fabril *adj* manufacturing, industrial.

fabriquero *nm* (**a**) = **fabricante.** (**b**) (*Ecl*) churchwarden. (**c**) (*Méx: destilador*) distillery operator (in a sugar mill).

fábula *nf* (**a**) (*Liter etc*) fable; myth; tale.

(**b**) (*Liter: argumento*) story, plot, action.

(**c**) (*rumor*) rumour; (*chisme*) piece of gossip; (*mentira*) fib.

(**d**) (*persona*) talk of the town; laughing-stock.

(**e**) (*****) **un negocio de ~** a splendid piece of business; **es una cosa de ~** it's fabulous*.

fabulario *nm* collection of fables.

fabulista *nmf* writer of fables.

fabulosamente *adv* fabulously.

fabuloso *adj* (**a**) (*gen*) fabulous; (*mítico*) mythical; imaginary, fictitious. (**b**) (*****: *estupendo*) fabulous*, fantastic*; **es francamente ~** it's just fabulous*.

FACA ['faka] *nm* (*Esp*) *abr de* **Futuro avión de combate y ataque.**

facción *nf* (**a**) (*Pol*) faction; (*pey*) breakaway group; hostile group, group of troublemakers.

(**b**) (*Anat*) feature; **de facciones irregulares** with irregular features.

(**c**) (*Mil*) routine duty; **estar de ~** to be on duty.

faccioso 1 *adj* factious; hostile; rebellious, seditious. **2** *nm*, **facciosa** *nf* rebel; hostile person, troublemaker.

faceta *nf* facet (*t fig*).

faceto* *adj* (*Méx*) cocksure, arrogant.

facial 1 *adj* facial; **valor ~** face value. **2** *nm* facial.

fácil 1 *adj* (**a**) (*gen*) easy; (*sencillo*) simple, straightforward; **~ para el usuario, ~ de usar** easy to use, (*Inform*) user-friendly; **es ~ ver que ...** it is easy to see that ...; **~ de hacer** easy to do.

(**b**) *estilo etc* easy, fluent; ready; (*pey*) facile, too easy; glib.

(**c**) *persona* docile, compliant; *mujer* easy, loose.

(**d**) **es ~ que venga** he may well come; **no veo muy ~ que ...** I don't think it is at all likely that ...; **es ~ que proteste** she is liable to protest.

2 *adv* (*****) = **fácilmente.**

facilidad *nf* (**a**) (*gen*) ease, easiness, facility; simplicity, straightforwardness; **con la mayor ~** with the greatest ease.

(**b**) (*Ling*) fluency; **~ de palabra** fluency in speech, readiness with which one talks.

(**c**) (*docilidad*) docility, compliant nature.

(**d**) **~es** facilities; **~es de crédito** credit facilities; **'~es de pago'** 'easy payment terms'; **las ~es del puerto** the port facilities; **me dieron todas las ~es** they gave me every facility.

facilitar [1a] *vt* (**a**) (*hacer fácil*) to facilitate, make easy; (*agilizar*) to expedite.

(**b**) (*proporcionar*) to provide, furnish, supply; *documento* to issue; **¿quién facilitó el dinero?** who provided the money?; **me facilitó un coche** he supplied me with a car, he provided a car.

(**c**) **~ algo** (*Cono Sur*) to make sth out to be easier than it really is, play down the difficulty of sth.

fácilmente *adv* easily; readily; simply, straightforwardly.

facilón *adj* very easy.

facilonería *nf* taking the easy way out, recourse to simple solutions.

facilongo* *adj*: **es ~** (*And*) it's a piece of cake*.

facineroso 1 *adj* criminal; wicked, villainous. **2** *nm*, **facinerosa** *nf* criminal; wicked person.

facistol 1 *adj* (**a**) (*And, Carib: descarado*) insolent.

(**b**) **es tan ~** (*Carib*) he's full of tricks, he loves playing jokes on people.

(**c**) (*Carib: pedante*) pedantic.

2 *nm* (**a**) (*Ecl*) lectern.

(**b**) (*And, Carib*) (*descarado*) insolent person; (*jactancioso*) braggart.

facistolería *nf* (*And, Carib, Méx*) insolence; boastfulness, conceit.

facochero *nm* warthog.

facón *nm* (*Cono Sur*) long knife, gaucho knife.

facsímil(e) *adj, nm* facsimile.

factibilidad *nf* feasibility; practicality; **estudio de ~** feasibility study.

factible *adj* feasible; workable, practical; **es ~ que lo haga** she might do it.

fácticamente *adv* really, actually, in fact.

facticio *adj* artificial, factitious.

fáctico *adj* real, actual; **los poderes ~s** the powers that be.

factor *nm* (**a**) (*Mat*) factor.

(**b**) (*elemento*) factor, element; **~ determinante** determining factor; **~ humano** human factor; **~ Rh** rhesus factor; **~ de seguridad** safety factor; **~ sorpresa** element of surprise; **el ~ suerte** the luck factor, the element of chance; **~ tiempo** time factor; **es un nuevo ~ de la situación** it is a new factor in the situation.

(**c**) (*Com*: *t* **factora** *nf*) agent, factor; commission merchant.

(**d**) (*Ferro*: *t* **factora** *nf*) freight clerk.

factoría *nf* (**a**) (*Com*) trading post; agency. (**b**) (*LAm: fábrica*) factory; (*And: fundición*) foundry.

factorización *nf* factoring.

factótum *nm* (**a**) (*empleado*) factotum; jack-of-all-trades. (**b**) (*pey*) busybody.

factual *adj* factual; based on fact(s), consisting of facts.

factura *nf* (**a**) (*Com*) bill, invoice; **~ proforma, ~ simulada**

pro forma (invoice); **según ~** as per invoice; **pasar ~, presentar ~** to send an invoice, send the bill (*t fig*); (*) to cash in. (**b**) (*Cono Sur*) bun, cake.

facturación *nf* (**a**) (*Com: acto*) invoicing. (**b**) (*Com: ventas*) sales (collectively), turnover. (**c**) (*Aer*) check(ing)-in; (*Ferro*) registration.

facturar [1a] *vt* (**a**) (*Com*) *géneros* to invoice; *persona* to bill. (**b**) (*Com*) **la compañía facturó X pesetas en 1995** the company turned over (*o* had a turnover of) X pesetas in 1995. (**c**) (*Ferro*) *equipaje* to register, check (*US*); (*Aer*) to check in.

facultad *nf* (**a**) (*gen*) faculty.
(**b**) (*autoridad*) power, authority; (*permiso*) permission; **tener la ~ de** + *infin* to have the power to + *infin*; **tener ~(es) para** + *infin* to be authorized to + *infin*.
(**c**) (*de mente*) **~es** faculties, powers; **~es del alma, ~es mentales** mental powers.
(**d**) (*Univ*) faculty, school; **F~ de Filosofía y Letras** Faculty of Arts; **F~ de Derecho** Faculty of Law; **está en la ~** he's at the university; **quedarse a comer en la ~** to lunch at the university.

facultar [1a] *vt* to authorize, empower; **~ a uno para hacer algo** to empower sb to do sth.

facultativo 1 *adj* (**a**) (*de opción*) optional.
(**b**) (*Univ*) faculty (*atr*).
(**c**) (*profesional*) professional; (*Med*) *dictamen etc* medical.
2 *nm*, **facultativa** *nf* doctor, practitioner.

facundia *nf* eloquence.

facundo *adj* eloquent.

facha[1] **1** *nf* (**a**) (*) (*aspecto*) look, appearance; (*cara*) face; (*persona*) sight, object; **~ a ~** face to face; **estar hecho una ~** to look a sight, look terrible; **tiene ~ de poli** he looks like a copper*; **tiene ~ de buena gente** he looks OK*. (**b**) **ponerse en ~** (*Náut*) to lie to. **2** *nmf* (*) posh person*. **3** *adj invar* (*) posh*, classy*.

facha[2]* *nmf* (*fascista*) reactionary, fascist.

fachada *nf* (**a**) (*Arquit*) façade, front; (*medida etc*) frontage; **con ~ al parque** looking towards the park, overlooking the park; **con 15 metros de ~** with a frontage of 15 metres.
(**b**) (*Tip*) title page.
(**c**) (*fig*) façade, outward show; **no tiene más que ~** it's all just show with him; **tener mucha ~** to be all show and no substance.
(**d**) (⁑: *cara*) mug⁑, face.

fachado* *adj*: **bien ~** good-looking; **mal ~** ugly, plain.

fachenda* **1** *nf* swank*, conceit. **2** *nm* swank*, show-off*.

fachendear* [1a] *vi* to swank*, show off.

fachendista*, fachendón*, fachendoso*, fachento* (*CAm*) **1** *adj* swanky*, conceited; snooty*. **2** *nm* swank*, show-off*.

fachinal *nm* (*Cono Sur*), swamp, swampy place.

fachoso *adj* (**a**) (*LAm*) = **fachendista.** (**b**) (*raro*) ridiculous, odd-looking. (**c**) (*And, Cono Sur*: elegante*) elegant, natty*.

faena *nf* (**a**) (*trabajo*) task, job, piece of work; duty; (*) tough job, sweat*, fag*; (*Mil*) fatigue; (*LAm*) obligatory work, compulsory labour; (*CAm, Carib, Mex: horas extraordinarias*) extra work, overtime; **~ doméstica** housework; **~s** (*de casa*) chores; **esto es una ~** this is a tough one, this is a real sweat*; **estar de ~** to be at work; **estar en plena ~** to be hard at work; **tener mucha ~** to be terribly busy.
(**b**) (*: *t* **mala ~**) dirty trick; **hacer una ~ a uno** to play a dirty trick on sb; **¡menuda ~ la que me hizo!** a fine thing he did to me!
(**c**) (*Taur*) play with the cape; performance; **hizo una ~ maravillosa** he gave a splendid performance (with the cape).
(**d**) (*Cono Sur*) (*obreros*) gang of workers; (*local*) working place.

faenar [1a] **1** *vt* (**a**) *ganado* to slaughter. (**b**) (*Cono Sur*) *madera* to cut, work. **2** *vi* (**a**) (*Cono Sur: trabajar*) to work, labour. (**b**) (*pescador*) to fish, work.

faenero *nm* (*Cono Sur*) farmhand, farm worker.

fafarechero (*LAm**) **1** *adj* swanky*, conceited. **2** *nm* swank*, show-off*.

fagocitar [1a] *vt* (*fig*) to absorb, gobble up.

fagocito *nm* phagocyte.

fagot 1 *nm* (*instrumento*) bassoon. **2** *nmf* bassoonist.

failear [1a] *vt* (*CAm, Cono Sur*) to file.

fain *adj* (*CAm*) fine.

fainada *nf* (*Carib*), **fainera** *nf* (*CAm*) silly thing, foolish act.

faíno *adj* (*Carib*) rude; coarse, rough.

faisán *nm* pheasant.

faisanaje *nm* hanging (of game).

faite (*LAm*) **1** *adj* tough, strong. **2** *nm* (**a**) (*luchador*) tough man, good fighter. (**b**) (*pey*) quarrelsome sort, brawler.

faitear* [1a] *vi* (*LAm*) to brawl.

faja *nf* (**a**) (*tira de tela*) strip, band; (*prenda*) sash, belt; (*de mujer*) girdle, corset; (*Mil*) sash; (*Med*) bandage, support; (*And Aut*) fanbelt; **~ pantalón** panty girdle.
(**b**) (*Correos*) wrapper (*t* **~ postal**).
(**c**) (*Geog*) strip, belt, zone; **una estrecha ~ de terreno** a narrow strip of land.
(**d**) (*Aut*) lane.
(**e**) (*Rad, TV*) channel.
(**f**) (*Arquit*) band, fascia.
(**g**) (*Méx Tip*) label, title (on spine of book).

fajada *nf* (**a**) (*Carib: ataque*) attack, rush. (**b**) (*Cono Sur*: paliza*) beating. (**c**) (*Carib: decepción*) disappointment.

fajador(a)* *nm/f* grafter*, hard worker.

fajar [1a] **1** *vt* (**a**) (*envolver*) to wrap; to swathe; (*vendar*) to bandage; (*Correos*) to wrap up, put a wrapper on.
(**b**) (*LAm: atacar*) to attack, lay into*; (*golpear*) to bash*, beat; to thrash; *mujer* to try to seduce.
(**c**) **¡que lo fajen!** (*Cono Sur, Méx*⁑) tell him to wrap up!*
2 *vi*: **~ con uno*** to go for sb, lay into sb*.
3 fajarse *vr* (**a**) (*ponerse una faja*) to put on one's belt (*o* sash *etc*).
(**b**) (*LAm: pelear*) to come to blows; to fight, bash each other*; **los boxeadores se fajaron duro** the boxers really laid into each other*.
(**c**) **~ a una**⁑ to fuck sb⁑.

fajilla *nf* (*de periódicos, revistas, impresos*) seal, address label; (*Cono Sur Correos*) wrapper.

fajín *nm* (*Mil*) sash.

fajina *nf* (**a**) (*Agr*) shock, pile, rick.
(**b**) (*leña*) kindling, brushwood, faggots.
(**c**) (*Mil*) bugle call, (*esp*) call to mess.
(**d**) (*Cono Sur: trabajo*) task, job (to be done quickly); hard work; **tenemos mucha ~** we've a lot to do, we've a tough job on here.
(**e**) (*Carib: horas extraordinarias*) extra work, overtime.
(**f**) (*Cono Sur*) **ropa de ~** working clothes; **uniforme de ~** ordinary uniform.

fajo *nm* (**a**) (*papeles*) bundle, sheaf; (*billetes*) roll, wad. (**b**) (*de bebé*) **~s** baby clothes. (**c**) (*Méx: golpe*) blow. (**d**) (*LAm*: trago*) swig (of liquor)*. (**e**) (*Méx: cinturón*) belt.

falacia *nf* (**a**) (*engaño*) deceit, fraud; (*error*) fallacy, error.
(**b**) (*cualidad*) deceitfulness.

falange *nf* (**a**) (*Mil*) phalanx; **la F~** (*Pol*) the Falange. (**b**) (*Anat*) phalange.

falangista *adj, nmf* Falangist.

falaz *adj persona* deceitful; treacherous; *doctrina etc* fallacious; *aspecto etc* deceptive, misleading.

falca *nf* (**a**) (*And, Carib, Méx: transbordador*) river ferry-boat. (**b**) (*And: alambique*) small still.

falciforme *adj* sickle-shaped.

falda *nf* (**a**) (*prenda*) skirt; (*Cos*) flap, fold; **~ escocesa** kilt; **~ pantalón** culotte, divided skirt; **~ de tablas, ~ tableada** pleated skirt; **estar cosido a las ~s de su madre** to be tied to mother's apron strings; **estar cosido a las ~s de su mujer** to be dominated by one's wife; **haberse criado bajo las ~s de mamá** to have led a very sheltered life.
(**b**) (*Anat*) lap; **sentarse en la ~ de una** to sit on sb's lap.
(**c**) (*: *mujer*) bird⁑, dame*; **ser muy aficionado a ~s** to be fond of the ladies; **es asunto de ~s** there's a woman in it somewhere.
(**d**) (*Geog*) slope, hillside; foot, bottom (of a slope); **a la ~ de la montaña** at the foot of the mountain.
(**e**) (*de sombrero*) brim.
(**f**) (*Culin*) brisket.
(**g**) (*de camilla*) table cover.

faldear [1a] *vt montaña* to skirt.

faldilla *nf* (*Aut*) apron, skirt; flap.

faldellín *nm* (**a**) (*falda*) short skirt; (*enagua*) underskirt. (**b**) (*Carib: de bautizo*) christening robe.

faldero *adj*: **perro ~** lap-dog; **hombre ~** ladies' man; **es muy ~** he's a great one for the ladies.

faldicorto *adj* short-skirted.

faldillas *nfpl* coat-tails.

faldón *nm* (**a**) (*de vestido*) tail, skirt; coat-tails; (*Cos*) flap; (*de bebé*) long dress. (**b**) (*Arquit*) gable. (**c**) (*Aut*) apron, skirt.

falena *nf* moth.

falencia *nf* (**a**) (*error*) error, misstatement. (**b**) (*LAm: bancarrota*) bankruptcy.
falibilidad *nf* fallibility.
falible *adj* fallible.
fálico *adj* phallic.
falo *nm* phallus.
falocracia* *nf* male domination, male chauvinism.
falócrata *nm* male chauvinist pig.
falocrático *adj* male chauvinist (*atr*); **actitud falocrática** male chauvinist attitude.
falopa‡ *nf* (*Cono Sur*) hard drugs.
falopearse‡ [1a] *vr* (*Cono Sur*) to take drugs, be a junkie‡.
falopero, -a‡ *nm/f* (*Cono Sur*) junkie‡.
falsamente *adv* falsely; unsoundly, mistakenly; insincerely, dishonestly.
falsario, -a *nm/f* (**a**) (*mentiroso*) falsifier; liar. (**b**) (*falseador*) forger, counterfeiter.
falseable *adj*: **fácilmente ~** easy to forge, readily forged.
falseador(a) *nm/f* forger, counterfeiter.
falsear [1a] **1** *vt* (*falsificar*) to falsify; *firma etc* to forge, counterfeit, fake; *moneda* to counterfeit; *cifras, voto* to fiddle (with), juggle with; *cerradura* to pick; (*Téc*) to bevel. **2** *vi* (**a**) (*ceder*) to buckle, sag, give way; (*fig*) to flag, slacken. (**b**) (*Mús*) to be out of tune.
falsedad *nf* (**a**) (*gen*) falseness; falsity; unsoundness; hollowness, insincerity; dishonesty; treachery, deceit. (**b**) (*una* ~) falsehood.
falsete *nm* (**a**) (*Téc*) plug, bung. (**b**) (*Mús*) falsetto. (**c**) (*And**) hypocrite.
falsía *nf* falseness, duplicity.
falsificación *nf* (**a**) (*acto*) falsification, forging. (**b**) (*objeto*) forgery; fabrication.
falsificador(a) *nm/f* forger, counterfeiter.
falsificar [1g] *vt* (*gen*) to falsify; *moneda* to counterfeit; *cuadro, sello etc* to forge, fake; *elección etc* to rig, fiddle (with), juggle with.
falsilla *nf* guide (*in copying*).
falso 1 *adj* (**a**) false; *moneda* false, counterfeit, bad, dud*; *cuadro, sello etc* forged, fake; bogus, sham; *joya* imitation (*atr*); *caballo, mula* vicious; *declaración* false; *opinión, teoría* unsound; mistaken; *testimonio* false, untrue; perjured; *persona* hollow, insincere; dishonest; *amigo* false, treacherous.
(**b**) **en ~** falsely; without proper support; **coger a uno en ~** to catch sb in a lie; **jurar en ~** to commit perjury; **dar un paso en ~** to step on something that is not there, trip; (*fig*) to take a false step.
2 *nm* (*CAm, Méx*) false evidence.
falta *nf* (**a**) (*carencia*) lack, want, need; (*ausencia*) absence; (*escasez*) shortage; (*Jur*) default; non-, *p.j.* **~ de asistencia** non-attendance; **~ de pago** non-payment; **a ~ de** (*prep*) failing; **a ~ de, por ~ de** for want of, for lack of; **~ de dinero** shortage of money; **~ de peso** short weight; **~ de respeto** lack of respect, disrespect; **~ de seriedad** frivolity; irresponsibility; **echar algo en ~** to miss sth; **hacer ~** to be lacking, be wanting; to be missed; **el hombre que hace ~** the right man, the man we (*etc*) want; **eso me hace (mucha) ~** I need it (badly); **me hizo Vd mucha ~** I missed you a lot; **aquí no haces ~** you are not needed here; **¡~ hacía!** and about time too!; **hacer ~** + *infin* to be necessary to + *infin*; **hace ~ pintarlo** sb ought to paint it, it needs painting; **poner ~ a uno** (*Escol*) to mark sb absent, put sb down as absent.
(**b**) (*fallo*) failure, shortcoming; (*culpa*) fault; (*error*) mistake; (*fechoría*) misdeed; (*de fabricación etc*) flaw, defect, fault; (*Mec*) trouble; **~ de ortografía** spelling mistake; **~ garrafal** stupid mistake; gross blunder; **sin ~** without fail; **sacar ~s a uno** to point out sb's defects.
(**c**) (*Jur*) misdemeanour; (*Dep*) foul, infringement; (*Tenis*) fault; **cometer una ~ contra uno** to commit a foul on sb, foul sb.
faltar [1a] **1** *vt* (*Carib, Cono Sur, Méx*: *al respeto*) to be rude to, show disrespect for.
2 *vi* (**a**) (*ser necesario*) to be lacking, be wanting; **le falta dinero** he lacks money, he needs money; **no le faltan buenas cualidades** he is not lacking in good qualities; **nos falta tiempo para hacerlo** we lack the time to do it, we are short of time to do it, we haven't the time to do it; **lo que falta son libros** what is lacking is books.
(**b**) (*estar ausente*) to be absent, be missing (*de* from); **faltaron 3 de la reunión** there were 3 missing (*o* absent) from the meeting; **~ a clase** to miss class, not go to class; **~ a una cita** to miss an appointment, break an appointment, not turn up for a date; **~ al trabajo** to stay away from work; **¿falta algo?** is anything missing?; **faltan 9** there are 9 missing, we are 9 short; **no falta quien opina que ...** there are some who think that ...; **en 8 años no he faltado ni una sola vez** I've not missed once in 8 years.
(**c**) (*Mec etc*: *fallar*) to fail, go wrong, break down.
(**d**) (*ser infiel a*) **~ a** *principio* to be false to; *persona* to fail; to offend; **~ a la decencia** to offend against decency; **~ a una promesa** to break a promise, go back on one's word; **~ al respeto** to be disrespectful (*a* to); **~ a la verdad** to lie, be untruthful; **~ en los pagos** to default on one's payments.
(**e**) **~ en hacer algo** to fail to do sth; **no faltaré en comunicárselo** I shall not fail to tell him.
(**f**) (*cantidad, tiempo etc*) **faltan pocos minutos para el comienzo** it's only a few minutes to go to the start; **faltan 3 semanas para las elecciones** there are 3 weeks to go to the election, the election is 3 weeks off; **falta poco para las 8** it's nearly 8 o'clock, it's getting on for 8 o'clock; **faltan 5 para las 8** (*LAm*) it's five to eight; **falta mucho todavía** there's plenty of time yet; **¿falta mucho?** is there long to go?; **falta poco para terminar** it's almost over; it's almost finished; **le faltaba poco para decírselo** she was about to tell him; **falta todavía por hacer** it remains to be done, it is still to be done.
(**g**) (*locuciones*) **¡no faltaba más!** (*no hay de qué*) don't mention it!; (*naturalmente*) of course, naturally; (*¡ni hablar!*) certainly not!, no way!*; (*¡es el colmo!*) it's the limit!, it's the last straw!; **¡lo que faltaba!, ¡es lo único que faltaba!** that's the very end!, it's all I *etc* needed!; **¡no faltaría más!** (*naturalmente*) of course, naturally; (*¡es el colmo!*) it's the limit!, it's the last straw!
(**h**) (*esp LAm*: *ser grosero*) to be rude, be disrespectful.
falto *adj* (**a**) (*deficiente*) short, deficient, lacking; **estar ~ de** to be short of; *cualidad etc* to be wanting in, be lacking in; **estar ~ de personal** to be short-handed.
(**b**) (*moralmente*) poor, wretched, mean.
(**c**) (*And*: *fatuo*) fatuous, vain.
faltón *adj* (**a**) (*negligente*) remiss, neglectful, unreliable; (*LAm*: *vago*) slack (about work), work-shy. (**b**) (*Andalucía, Carib*: *irrespetuoso*) disrespectful, rude.
faltoso *adj* (**a**) (*CAm, Méx*) = **faltón** (**a**). (**b**) (*CAm, Méx*: *irrespetuoso*) disrespectful. (**c**) (*And*: *discutidor*) quarrelsome.
faltriquera *nf* (*bolsillo*) pocket, pouch; (*de reloj*) fob, watch pocket; (*bolso*) handbag; **rascarse la ~** (*fig*) to dig into one's pocket.
falúa *nf* launch; tender.
falla *nf* (**a**) (*fallo*) fault, defect, failure; (*LAm*: *escasez*) lack, shortage; (*LAm*: *error*) error, oversight; (*LAm*: *defecto moral*) failure to keep one's promises; **~ en caja** cash shortage; **géneros que tienen ~s** (*Com*) defective goods, seconds.
(**b**) (*Geol*) fault.
(**c**) (*Mec*) failure, breakdown; **~ de encendido** (*Aut*) ignition fault; **~ de tiro** (*Mil*) misfire.
(**d**) (*And Naipes*) void.
fallada *nf* (*Naipes*) ruff, trumping.
fallar [1a] **1** *vt* (**a**) (*Naipes*) to ruff, trump.
(**b**) (*Jur*) to pronounce sentence on; *premio* to award, decide (on).
(**c**) (*errar*) to miss; **~ el blanco** to miss the target.
2 *vi* (**a**) (*cosecha, freno, memoria etc*) to fail; (*plan*) to go wrong, miscarry; (*tiro*) to miss, go astray; (*apoyo, cuerda etc*) to break, snap, give way; (*piernas*) to give way; (*fusil*) to misfire, fail to go off; (*motor*) to miss; **~ a uno** to fail sb, let sb down; **algo le falla a X** there's sth up with X; **algo falló en sus planes** sth went wrong with his plans; **le falló el corazón** his heart failed; **no falla nunca** it never fails.
(**b**) (*faltar*) to be missing, be lacking.
(**c**) (*Jur*) to pronounce sentence, pass judgement.
(**d**) (*Naipes*) to ruff, trump (in).
Fallas *nfpl* (*Valencia*) celebration of the feast of St Joseph.
falleba *nf* door (*o* window) catch, espagnolette.
fallecer [2d] *vi* (**a**) (*morir*) to pass away, die. (**b**) (*caducar*) to end, run out, expire.
fallecido 1 *adj* late. **2** *nm*, **fallecida** *nf* deceased, person who has lately died.
fallecimiento *nm* decease, demise, passing.
fallero *adj* (*Cono Sur*) slack (about work), work-shy.
fallido 1 *adj* (**a**) *esfuerzo etc* unsuccessful; *esperanza* disappointed; (*Mec, Mil etc*) dud; *deuda* bad, uncollectable.
(**b**) (*Com*) bankrupt.
2 *nm*, **fallida** *nf* bankrupt.

fallir [3a] *vi* (**a**) (*fallar*) to fail. (**b**) (*caducar*) to end, run out, expire. (**c**) (*Carib*: *quebrar*) to go bankrupt.

fallo 1 *adj* (**a**) (*Naipes*) **estar ~** to be out of a suit; **estar ~ de** (*Naipes*) to be out of, have a void in; (*Méx*) to lack, be without.

(**b**) (*Cono Sur*: *fatuo*) fatuous; stupid.

2 *nm* (**a**) (*defecto*) shortcoming, defect; (*Mec*) failure, trouble, breakdown; (*Inform*) bug; (*Med*) failure; (*Dep*) mistake, tactical error, mix-up; **debido a un ~ de los frenos** because of a brake failure; **~ cardíaco, ~ de corazón** heart failure; **~ de diseño** design fault; **~ humano** human error.

(**b**) (*Naipes*) void; **tener un ~ a corazones** to have a void in hearts.

(**c**) (*Jur etc*) sentence, verdict; decision, ruling; findings; **recurrir el ~** to appeal against the verdict.

fallón* *adj* unreliable, given to making mistakes; shaky; bungling.

fallutería *nf* (*Cono Sur*) (**a**) untrustworthiness. (**b**) hypocrisy.

falluto* *adj* (*Cono Sur*) (**a**) (*fracasado*) unsuccessful, failed. (**b**) (*poco fiable*) untrustworthy. (**c**) (*hipócrita*) two-faced, hypocritical.

fama *nf* (**a**) (*renombre*) fame; (*reputación*) reputation, repute; **mala ~** bad reputation; notoriety; **de mala ~** of ill fame; **el libro que le dio ~** the book which made him famous, the book which made his name; **tener ~ de gran cazador** to have the reputation of being a great hunter, be known as a great hunter; **tiene ~ de poco escrupuloso** he is thought to be unscrupulous.

(**b**) (*rumor*) report, rumour; **corre la ~ de que ...** it is rumoured that ...

famélico *adj* starving, famished; **los ~s** the starving.

familia *nf* (**a**) family; (*los que viven en una misma casa*) household; **~ nuclear** nuclear family; **~ numerosa** large family; **~ política** relatives by marriage, in-laws; **de buena ~** of good family; **tener mucha ~** to have lots of children; **ser como de la ~** to be one of the family; **eso viene de ~** that runs in the family; **acordarse de la ~ de uno*** to insult sb at length; **sentirse como en ~** to feel thoroughly at home.

(**b**) (*And, Carib, Méx*: *pariente*) relative; **él es ~** he's family, he's a relative.

(**c**) (*Tip*) fount.

familiar 1 *adj* (**a**) (*de la familia*) family (*atr*); **los lazos ~es** the family bond, the ties of blood; **subsidio ~** family allowance; **dioses ~es** household gods.

(**b**) (*conocido*) familiar (*a* to).

(**c**) (*fig*) (*casero*) homely, domestic; (*sin ceremonia*) informal; (*llano*) plain, ordinary; (*Ling*) colloquial, familiar; *estilo* familiar.

2 *nmf* (*pariente*) relative, relation; (*de casa*) member of the household; (*amigo*) intimate friend, close acquaintance.

familiaridad *nf* familiarity (*con* with); homeliness; informality; **~es** familiarities.

familiarizar [1f] **1** *vt* to familiarize, acquaint (*con* with). **2 familiarizarse** *vr*: **~ con** to familiarize o.s. with, make o.s. familiar with, get to know.

famosillo 1 *adj* well-known in limited circles. **2** *nm*, **famosilla** *nf* minor celebrity.

famoso 1 *adj* (**a**) famous (*por* for). (**b**) (*: *estupendo*) famous, great*, splendid. **2** *nm*, **famosa** *nf* famous person, celebrity; **los ~s** the famous.

fan *nmf*, *pl* **fans** (*Cine*, *Mús etc*) fan.

fanal *nm* (**a**) (*faro*) lighthouse; (harbour) beacon; (*linterna*) lantern; (*Aut*) headlight. (**b**) (*campana*) bell glass; (*pantalla*) (glass) lampshade.

fanaticada *nf* (*Carib*) fans.

fanático 1 *adj* fanatical.

2 *nm*, **fanática** *nf* fanatic; bigot; (*Cine*, *Dep etc*) fan, supporter, admirer; **es un ~ del aeromodelismo** he's mad about model aeroplanes; **los ~s de la estrella** the star's fans, the star's admirers.

fanatismo *nm* fanaticism; bigotry; enthusiasm.

fanatizar [1f] *vt* to arouse fanaticism in.

fancine *nm* = **fanzine**.

fandango *nm* (**a**) (*Mús*) fandango. (**b**) (*: *jaleo*) row, shindy*; **se armó un ~** there was a great row. (**c**) (*LAm**: *fiesta*) rowdy party, booze-up*.

fandanguear [1a] *vi* (*Cono Sur*) to live it up*.

fané *adj* (*LAm*) (*arrugado*) messed-up, crumpled, rumpled; (*cursi*) vulgar; **estar ~** (*persona*) to be in a terrible state.

faneca *nf* (*Pez*) *a species of flatfish.*

fanega *nf* (**a**) *grain measure* (= *Spain 1.58 bushels*, *Méx 2.57 bushels*, *Cono Sur 3.89 bushels*). (**b**) *land measure* (= *Spain 1.59 acres*, *Carib 1.73 acres*).

fanfarrear [1a] *vi* = **fanfarronear**.

fanfarria *nf* (**a**) (*jactancia*) bluster, bravado, bragging. (**b**) (*Mús*) fanfare.

fanfarrón 1 *adj* blustering, boastful; flashy. **2** *nm* blusterer, braggart; bully; flashy type.

fanfarronada *nf* bluster, bravado, swagger; bluff.

fanfarronear [1a] *vi* to bluster, boast, swagger; to rant; to talk big*, bluff.

fanfarronería *nf* blustering, boasting, bragging; ranting; big talk, bluffing.

fangal *nm* bog; quagmire, muddy place.

fango *nm* mud, mire; slush; (*fig*) mire, dirt.

fangoso *adj* muddy, miry; slushy.

fanguero 1 *adj* (*Cono Sur*) *animal*, *jugador* suited to heavy going. **2** *nm* (*Carib*, *Méx*) = **fango, fangal**.

fantasear [1a] *vi* to fantasize, daydream, let one's imagination run free.

fantaseo *nm* fantasizing, dreaming, imagining.

fantasía *nf* (**a**) (*facultad*) fantasy, imagination, fancy; **es obra de la ~** it is a work of the imagination; **dejar correr la ~** to let one's imagination roam.

(**b**) (*Arte*, *Liter etc*) fantasy; fantastic tale; work of the imagination; (*Mús*) fantasia.

(**c**) (*capricho*) whim, fancy.

(**d**) (*afectación*) conceit, vanity, airs.

(**e**) (*Com*) **de ~** fancy; **joyas de ~** imitation jewellery.

fantasioso* *adj* (**a**) (*engreído*) vain, conceited, stuck-up*; **¡fantasiosa!** you vain thing! (**b**) (*soñador*) dreamy.

fantasma 1 *nm* (**a**) (*lit*) ghost, phantom, apparition. (**b**) (*: *presumido*) show-off*, stuck-up person*; (*: *fanfarrón*) boaster, braggart; **¡no seas ~!** stop showing off! (**c**) (*TV*) ghost image. (**d**) (*Esp* Fin*) 5000 pesetas. **2** *atr* ghost, phantom (*atr*); **buque ~** ghost ship; **ciudad ~** ghost city; **compañía ~** dummy company; **un lugar ~** an imaginary place.

fantasmada* *nf* bluster, bravado; empty show.

fantasmagoría *nf* phantasmagoria.

fantasmagórico *adj* phantasmagoric.

fantasmal *adj* ghostly; phantom (*atr*).

fantasmear* [1a] *vi* to show off, put on a display.

fantasmón* 1 *adj* bigheaded*, stuck up*. **2** *nm*, **fantasmona** *nf* bighead*, swank*.

fantásticamente *adv* fantastically; weirdly; fancifully.

fantástico 1 *adj* (**a**) (*gen*) fantastic; (*extraño*) weird, unreal; (*caprichoso*) fanciful, whimsical. (**b**) (*vanidoso*) vain. (**c**) (*: *estupendo*) fantastic. (**d**) (*Cono Sur*: *jactancioso*) bragging, swaggering.

2 *excl* fantastic!*, great!*, terrific!*

fantoche 1 *nm* (**a**) (*muñeco*) puppet, marionette. (**b**) (*: *persona*) (*mediocre*) mediocrity, nonentity; (*presumido*) braggart, loud-mouth*. **2** *atr* puppet (*atr*); **régimen ~** puppet régime.

fantochesco *adj* puppet-like.

fantomático *adj* shadowy, mysterious, imaginary.

fanzine *nm* fanzine.

FAO ['faw] *nf* (**a**) *abr de* **Organización de las Naciones Unidas para la Agricultura y la Alimentación** Food and Agriculture Organization of the United Nations, FAO. (**b**) *abr de* **fabricación asistida por ordenador** computer-assisted manufacture, CAM.

faquín *nm* porter, errand-boy.

faquir *nm* fakir.

farabute* *nm* (*Cono Sur*) (*pícaro*) rogue; (*poco cumplidor*) untrustworthy person; (*pobre diablo*) poor wretch.

faralá *nm* flounce, frill; **~s** (*pey*) frills, buttons and bows.

farallón *nm* (*Geog*) steep rock, cliff; headland; bluff; (*Geol*) outcrop; (*Cono Sur*) rocky peak.

faramalla* *nf* (**a**) (*labia*) blarney, humbug, claptrap*; (*Com etc*) patter, spiel.

(**b**) (*impostura*) empty show, sham.

(**c**) (*Cono Sur*: *jactancia*) bragging, boasting.

faramallear [1a] *vi* (*Cono Sur*, *Méx*) to brag, boast.

faramallero *adj* (*Cono Sur*) bragging, boastful.

farándula *nf* (**a**) (*Teat*: *Hist*) troupe of strolling players; **el mundo de la ~** the theatre world.

(**b**) (*) (*labia*) humbug, claptrap*; (*mentiras*) pack of lies; (*trampa*) confidence trick, confidence game (*US*), swindle; (*chisme*) wicked gossip.

faranduleo *nm* trickery.

farandulero 1 *adj* (*LAm*) = **farolero**.

2 *nm*, **farandulera** *nf* (**a**) (*Teat*: *Hist*) strolling player.

(**b**) (*timador*) confidence trickster, con man, swindler, rogue.
Faraón *nm* Pharaoh.
faraónico *adj* Pharaonic.
faraute *nm* (**a**) (††) herald. (**b**) (*: *entrometido*) busybody.
fardada* *nf* show, display; piece of showmanship; **ese cuadro es una ~** that picture is something to really boast about; **¡vaya ~!** that's really great!*; **pegarse una ~** to swank*, show off.
fardar* [1a] *vi* (**a**) (*objeto*) to be classy*; **es un coche que farda mucho** it's a car with a lot of class. (**b**) (*persona*) to show off, put on a display; **~ bien** to dress nattily*. (**c**) (*jactarse*) to boast, shoot a line*; **fardaba de sus amigas** he boasted about his girlfriends.
farde* *nm* (**a**) tone, class. (**b**) showing-off, display. (**c**) boasting, swanking*.
fardel *nm* (**a**) (*talega*) bag, knapsack; ragbag. (**b**) (*bulto*) bundle.
fardo *nm* bundle; bale, pack; (*fig*) burden.
fardón* **1** *adj* (**a**) (*precioso*) nice, lovely, great*. (**b**) (*de clase*) classy*, posh*. (**c**) (*elegante*) natty*, nattily dressed*. (**d**) (*vanidoso*) stuck-up*, swanky*. **2** *nm* swank*, show-off*.
farero *nm* lighthouse-keeper.
farfulla* **1** *nf* (**a**) (*tartamudez*) splutter(ing); jabber(ing). (**b**) (*LAm: jactancia*) bragging, boasting. **2** *nmf* jabberer, gabbler.
farfullador *adj* spluttering; jabbering; gabbling.
farfullar [1a] **1** *vt* to do hastily, botch, scamp. **2** *vi* to splutter; to jabber, gabble.
farfulleo *nm* spluttering; jabbering, gabbling.
farfullero* *adj* (**a**) = **farfullador**. (**b**) (*LAm*) = **fanfarrón**.
farináceo *adj* starchy, farinaceous.
faringe *nf* pharynx.
faringitis *nf* pharyngitis.
fariña *nf* (*And, Cono Sur*) coarse manioc flour.
fario *nm*: **mal ~** bad luck.
farisaico *adj* Pharisaic(al), hypocritical; smug.
fariseo *nm* Pharisee, hypocrite; smug sort.
farmacéutico **1** *adj* pharmaceutical. **2** *nm*, **farmacéutica** *nf* chemist, pharmacist.
farmacia *nf* (**a**) (*ciencia*) pharmacy. (**b**) (*tienda*) chemist's (shop), drugstore (*US*); **~ de guardia** all-night chemist's.
fármaco *nm* medicament, medicine.
farmacodependencia *nf* dependence on drugs.
farmacológico *adj* pharmacological.
farmacología *nf* pharmacology.
farmacólogo, -a *nm/f* pharmacologist.
farmacopea *nf* pharmacopoeia.
faro **1** *nm* (**a**) (*Náut*) (*torre*) lighthouse; (*señal*) beacon; **~ aéreo** air beacon.
(**b**) (*Náut: luz*) light, lantern; (*Aut*) headlamp, headlight; **~ antiniebla** foglamp; **~ lateral** sidelight; **~ piloto, ~ trasero** rear light, tail light; **~ de marcha atrás** reversing light; *V t* **luz** (**d**). (**c**) **~s**⁑ peepers⁑, eyes.
2 (*) *como adj*: **idea ~** bright idea, brilliant idea.
farol *nm* (**a**) (*linterna*) lantern, lamp; (*Ferro*) headlamp; **~ de calle, ~ público** street lamp; **~ de viento** hurricane lamp; **¡adelante con los ~es!** press on regardless!; (*LAm*) if they don't like it they can lump it!*
(**b**) (*farola*) lamppost; (*Gimnasia*) handstand.
(**c**) (*envase*) wrapping of tobacco packet.
(**d**) **~es** (*LAm**) eyes.
(**e**) (*And, Cono Sur: ventana*) bay window, glassed-in balcony.
(**f**) (*: *ostentación*) swank*; **echarse un ~, marcarse un ~** to shoot a line*, swank*, brag; **tiene mucho ~** he's terribly swanky*.
(**g**) (*) (*mentira*) lie, fib; (*Naipes etc*) bluff, piece of bluff; **echarse un ~, tirarse un ~** to tell a fib, (*Naipes etc*) to bluff.
(**h**) **hacer de ~*** to play gooseberry.
farola *nf* street lamp; lamppost.
faroladas* *nfpl* showing-off, boasting.
farolazo* *nm* (*CAm, Méx*) swig of liquor*.
farolear* [1a] *vi* to swank*, strut around; to brag.
farolero **1** **adj* vain, stuck-up*. **2** *nm* (**a**) lamp-maker; lamplighter. (**b**) (*) braggart, loud-mouth*.
farolillo *nm* (**a**) (*Elec*) fairy-light, Chinese lantern; **~ rojo** (*fig*) back marker, team (*etc*) in last place. (**b**) (*Bot*) Canterbury bell.
farra[1] *nf* (*pez*) salmon trout.
farra[2] *nf* (**a**) (*juerga*) spree, party, carousal; **ir de ~** to go on a spree. (**b**) (*mofa*) mockery, teasing; **tomar a uno para la ~** to pull sb's leg.
fárrago *nm* medley, hotchpotch.
farragoso *adj* cumbersome; *discurso etc* involved, dense.
farrear [1a] **1** *vi* to make merry. **2** **farrearse** *vr* (**a**) **~ de uno** to tease sb. (**b**) **~ el dinero** to spend one's money on drink.
farrero **1** *adj* (*And, Cono Sur*) merry; fun-loving. **2** *nm*, **farrera** *nf* reveller.
farrista *adj* (*Cono Sur*) (*borracho*) dissipated, hard-drinking; (*juerguista*) boisterous, rowdy.
farruco* *adj* pig-headed; **estar** (*o* **ponerse**) **~** to get aggressive.
farruto *adj* (*And*) sickly, weak.
farsa[1] *nf* (**a**) (*Teat*) farce; (*pey*) bad play, crude play. (**b**) (*fig*) humbug, sham, masquerade.
farsa[2] *nf* (*Culin*) stuffing.
farsante* *nm* humbug, fraud, pseud*.
farsear [1a] *vi* (*CAm*) to joke.
farsesco *adj* farcical.
fas: **por ~ o por nefas** by hook or by crook, rightly or wrongly; at any cost.
FAS *nfpl abr de* **Fuerzas Armadas** armed forces.
fascículo *nm* fascicule, part, instalment.
fascinación *nf* fascination.
fascinador *adj* fascinating.
fascinar [1a] *vti* (*gen*) to fascinate; to captivate; (*hechizar*) to bewitch; (*aojar*) cast the evil eye on.
fascismo *nm* fascism.
fascista *adj, nmf* fascist.
fase *nf* (**a**) phase, stage; (*Dep*) half; **~ terminal** terminal phase; **estar en ~ ascendente** to be on one's way up; to be on a winning run; **estar fuera de ~** to be out of phase. (**b**) (*Astron, Bio, Elec*) phase. (**c**) (*de cohete*) stage.
faso* *nm* (*Cono Sur*) cigarette, fag⁑.
fastidiar [1b] **1** *vt* (**a**) (*molestar*) to annoy, bother, vex; (*aburrir*) to bore; (*dar asco a*) to upset, disgust, sicken, irk; **eso me fastidia terriblemente** it annoys me no end; it upsets me terribly; **¡no fastidies!** you can't mean it!, you're kidding!; **¡no me fastidies!** stop bothering me!
(**b**) (*dañar*) to harm, damage.
2 fastidiarse *vr* (**a**) (*enojarse*) to get cross; (*aburrirse*) to get bored; **¡a ~!*, ¡fastídiate!*** get lost!⁑; **¡que se fastidie!*** tell him to go to blazes!; that's his funeral!*; **¡para que te fastidies!*** so there!*
(**b**) (*hacerse daño*) to harm o.s., do o.s. an injury.
(**c**) (*aguantarse*) to put up with it.
fastidio *nm* (**a**) (*molestia*) annoyance, bother, nuisance; **¡qué ~!** what a nuisance! (**b**) (*aburrimiento*) boredom. (**c**) (*asco*) disgust, repugnance.
fastidioso *adj* (**a**) (*molesto*) annoying, bothersome, vexing; (*aburrido*) tedious, tiresome, boring; irksome; (*asqueroso*) sickening. (**b**) (*LAm: quisquilloso*) fastidious.
fasto *nm* (**a**) (*pompa*) pomp, pageantry. (**b**) **~s** (*Liter*) annals.
fastuosamente *adv* magnificently, splendidly; lavishly; pompously.
fastuoso *adj* magnificent, splendid; lavish; pompous.
fatal **1** *adj* (**a**) (*mortal*) fatal; (*malhadado*) ill-fated, disastrous.
(**b**) (*irrevocable*) irrevocable; (*inevitable*) unavoidable, fated.
(**c**) (*: *horrible*) awful, ghastly*, rotten*; **tiene un inglés ~** he speaks awful English; **la obra estuvo ~*** the play was rotten*.
2 *adv* (*) awfully, terribly (badly); **lo pasaron ~** they had a terrible time (of it); **canta ~** she sings terribly*.
fatalidad *nf* (**a**) (*destino*) fate; fatality. (**b**) (*desdicha*) mischance, misfortune, ill-luck.
fatalismo *nm* fatalism.
fatalista **1** *adj* fatalistic. **2** *nmf* fatalist.
fatalizarse [1f] *vr* (**a**) (*And: cometer un delito*) to commit a grave crime.
(**b**) (*Cono Sur: sufrir herida*) to be seriously wounded; (*And: sufrir desgracia*) to suffer a series of misfortunes (as a punishment for a wrong committed).
fatalmente *adv* (*V adj*) (**a**) fatally; disastrously. (**b**) unavoidably, irremediably.
fatídicamente *adv* (*V adj*) (**a**) prophetically. (**b**) fatefully, ominously.
fatídico *adj* (**a**) (*profético*) prophetic. (**b**) (*de mal agüero*) fateful, ominous.
fatiga *nf* (**a**) (*cansancio*) fatigue, weariness; **~ cerebral** mental fatigue. (**b**) (*Téc*) fatigue; **~ del metal** metal fatigue. (**c**) **~s** hardships, troubles, toils.

fatigabilidad *nf* tendency to tire easily.
fatigadamente *adv* with difficulty, wearily.
fatigar [1h] **1** *vt* (**a**) (*cansar*) to tire, weary, fatigue. (**b**) (*molestar*) to annoy. **2 fatigarse** *vr* to tire, get tired, grow weary; ~ **de andar** to wear o.s. out walking.
fatigosamente *adv* painfully, with difficulty.
fatigoso *adj* (**a**) (*que cansa*) tiring, exhausting, fatiguing. (**b**) (*Med*) laboured, difficult; **respiración fatigosa** laboured breathing. (**c**) (*molesto*) trying, tiresome.
fato* *nm* (*Cono Sur*) (**a**) (*negocio*) shady deal. (**b**) (*amorío*) love affair.
fatuidad *nf* (*V adj*) (**a**) fatuity, foolishness, inanity. (**b**) conceit.
fatuo *adj* (**a**) (*necio*) fatuous, foolish, inane. (**b**) (*vanidoso*) conceited; *V* **fuego.**
fauces *nfpl* (*Anat*) fauces, gullet; (*LAm*: *colmillos*) tusks, teeth; (*fig*: *boca*) jaws, maw.
faul *nm* (*Méx*: *Dep*) foul.
faulear [1a] *vt* (*Méx*: *Dep*) to foul.
fauna *nf* fauna.
faunístico *adj* faunal; **riqueza faunística** wealth of the fauna.
fauno *nm* faun.
Fausto *nm* Faust.
fausto 1 *adj* lucky, fortunate; auspicious. **2** *nm* splendour, pomp, magnificence.
fautor(a) *nm/f* accomplice, helper; instigator.
favor *nm* (**a**) (*ayuda, servicio*) favour, service, good turn, kindness; ~**es** (*de mujer*) favours; **entrada de** ~ complimentary ticket; **es de** ~ it's complimentary, it's free; **por** ~ please; **no es** ~**, no hay** ~ (*contestando a 'por favor'*) think nothing of it, it's no trouble; **haga el** ~ **de esperar** please wait, kindly wait; **haga el** ~ **de no fumar** please be so good as to refrain from smoking; **¿me haces el** ~ **de pasar la sal?** would you please pass the salt?, would you be so kind as to pass the salt?; ~ **que me haces** you're very kind, it's good of you; **si hace** ~ (*LAm*) if you don't mind; **¡está para hacerle un** ~**!*** she's really something!*; ~ **de venir puntualmente** (*LAm*) please be punctual.
(**b**) (*gracia*) favour, good graces; **estar en** ~ to be in favour; **gozar de** ~ **cerca de uno** to be in favour with sb.
(**c**) (*apoyo*) protection, support; **gracias al** ~ **del rey** thanks to the king's protection.
(**d**) (*símbolo*) favour; token; (*regalo*) gift.
(**e**) **a** ~ **de** in favour of; on behalf of; (*Com*) to the order of; **a** ~ **de la marea** helped by the tide, taking advantage of the tide; **a** ~ **de la noche** under the cover of night, helped by the darkness.
favorable *adj* favourable; auspicious; advantageous.
favorablemente *adv* favourably; auspiciously; advantageously.
favorecedor *adj vestido etc* becoming; *relato, retrato* flattering.
favorecer [2d] *vt* (**a**) (*gen*) to favour; (*amparar*) to help, protect; (*tratar bien*) to treat favourably; (*fortuna*) to favour, smile on. (**b**) (*vestido*) to become, flatter, look well on; (*relato, retrato*) to flatter.
favorecido *adj* favoured; **trato de nación más favorecida** most-favoured nation treatment.
favoritismo *nm* favouritism.
favorito, -a *adj, nm/f* favourite (*t Dep*).
fax *nm* fax, fax machine.
faxear [1a] *vt* to fax, send by fax.
fayuca *nf* (*Méx*) smuggling.
fayuquear [1a] *vt* (*Méx*) to smuggle.
fayuquero, -a *nm/f* (*Cono Sur*) travelling salesman, travelling saleswoman; (*Méx*) seller of smuggled goods.
fayuto *adj* (*Cono Sur*) = **falluto.**
faz *nf* (**a**) (*liter, fig*) face; front; aspect; ~ **a** ~ face to face; ~ **de la tierra** face of the earth. (**b**) (*de moneda*) obverse.
FC, f.c. *abr de* **ferrocarril** railway, Rly.
Fco. *abr de* **Francisco.**
Fdez *abr de* **Fernández.**
FE *nf* (*Hist*) *abr de* **Falange Española.**
fe *nf* (**a**) (*Rel*) faith (*en* in); **la** ~ **católica** the Catholic faith.
(**b**) (*confianza*) faith, belief; reliance; **de buena** ~ in good faith; (*Jur*) bona fide; **obrar de buena** ~ to act in good faith; **mala** ~ bad faith; **a** ~ **mía, por mi** ~ (††) by my faith, upon my honour; **dar** ~ **a, prestar** ~ **a** to believe, credit, place reliance on; **tener** ~ **en** to have faith in, believe in.
(**c**) (*palabra*) assurance; **a** ~ in truth; **en** ~ **de lo cual** in witness whereof; **dar** ~ **de** to testify to, bear witness to; **de eso doy** ~ I'll swear to that.
(**d**) (*lealtad*) fidelity, loyalty.
(**e**) (*certificado*) certificate; ~ **de bautismo** certificate of baptism; ~ **de erratas** errata; ~ **de vida** document proving that a person is still alive.
FEA *nf* (**a**) (*Aut*) *abr de* **Federación Española de Automovilismo.**
(**b**) (*Dep*) *abr de* **Federación Española de Atletismo.**
(**c**) (*Hist*) *abr de* **Falange Española Auténtica.**
fea *nf* ugly woman, plain girl; **ser la** ~ **del baile** to be a wallflower; **me tocó la** ~ **del baile** (*fig*) I got the short straw.
fealdad *nf* ugliness, hideousness.
feamente *adj* hideously.
feb., feb.º *abr de* **febrero** February, Feb.
feble *adj* feeble, weak.
Febo *nm* Phoebus.
febrero *nm* February.
febril *adj* (**a**) (*Med*) fevered, feverish. (**b**) (*fig*) feverish, hectic.
febrilmente *adv* (*fig*) feverishly, hectically.
fecal *adj* faecal; **aguas** ~**es** sewage.
FECOM *nm abr de* **Fondo Europeo de Cooperación Monetaria** European Monetary Cooperation Fund, EMCF.
fécula *nf* starch; ~ **de papa** (*LAm*) potato flour.
feculento *adj* starchy.
fecundación *nf* fertilization; ~ **artificial** artificial insemination; ~ **in vitro** in vitro fertilization.
fecundar [1a] *vt* to fertilize; ~ **por fertilización cruzada** to cross-fertilize.
fecundidad *nf* (**a**) (*gen*) fertility; fecundity. (**b**) (*fig*) fruitfulness, productiveness.
fecundizar [1f] *vt* to fertilize.
fecundo *adj* (**a**) (*Bio etc*) fertile; fecund; prolific.
(**b**) (*fig*) fruitful; (*copioso*) copious, abundant; (*productivo*) productive; ~ **de palabras** fluent, eloquent; ~ **en** fruitful of, productive of; **una época muy fecunda en buenos poetas** a period abounding in good poets, a period in which good poets abounded; **un libro** ~ **en ideas** a book full of ideas.
fecha *nf* (**a**) date; ~ **de caducidad** (*de billete etc*) expiry date; ~ **de caducidad,** ~ **de consumo preferente** sell-by date; ~ **de emisión** date of issue; ~ **de entrega** delivery date; ~ **límite** deadline; ~ **de nacimiento** date of birth; ~ **tope** closing date, last date; **a la** ~ to date; at that time; **de larga** ~ (*Fin*) long-dated; **a partir de esta** ~ from today, starting from today; **a 30 días** ~ (*Com*) at 30 days' sight; **con** ~ **del 15 de agosto** dated the 15th of August; **con** ~ **adelantada** *cheque* post-dated; **en alguna** ~ **futura** at some future date; **en** ~ **próxima** soon, at an early date; **hasta la** ~ to date, so far; **manuscrito sin** ~ undated manuscript; **pasarse de** ~ (*Com*) to pass the sell-by date.
(**b**) (*: *día*) **unas** ~**s de descanso** a few days' rest; **dentro de breves** ~**s** soon; **hace unas** ~**s** a few days ago; **para estas** ~**s** by this time; **por estas** ~**s** now, about now; at this time of year.
fechable *adj* datable (*en* to).
fechado *nm* dating.
fechador *nm* date-stamp.
fechar [1a] *vt* to date.
fechoría *nf* misdeed, villainy.
FED *nm abr de* **Fondo Europeo de Desarrollo** European Development Fund, EDF.
FEDER *nm abr de* **Fondo Europeo de Desarrollo Regional** European Regional Development Fund, ERDF.
federación *nf* federation.
federal *adj* federal.
federalismo *nm* federalism.
federalista *nmf* federalist.
federalizar [1f] *vt* to federate, federalize.
federar [1a] **1** *vt* to federate. **2 federarse** *vr* (**a**) (*Pol*) to federate. (**b**) (*hacerse socio*) to become a member.
federativo *adj* federative.
Federico *nm* Frederick.
feérico *adj* fairy (*atr*).
féferes *nmpl* (*LAm*) junk, lumber; things (in general), thingummyjigs*.
fehaciente *adj* reliable, authentic; irrefutable.
fehacientemente *adv* reliably; irrefutably.
feíllo* *adj* a bit plain, rather unattractive.
FE-JONS [fe'xons] *nf* (*Hist*) *abr de* **Falange Española de las Juntas de Ofensiva Nacional Sindicalista.**
felación *nf* fellatio.

feldespato nm felspar.
feliciano** nm: echar un ~ to have a screw**.
felicidad nf (a) (alegría) happiness.
(b) viajamos con toda ~ all went well on the journey.
(c) ~es best wishes, congratulations; os deseo toda clase de ~es I wish you every kind of happiness; ¡~es! best wishes!; happy birthday! (etc); ¡mis ~es! congratulations!
felicitación nf congratulation; (Mil) commendation; ~ de Navidad Christmas greetings, (tarjeta) Christmas card.
felicitar [1a] vt to congratulate (a uno por algo sb on sth); ¡te felicito! congratulations!; ~ la Navidad (etc) a uno to wish sb a happy Christmas (etc).
feligrés nm, **feligresa** nf parishioner.
feligresía nf parish; parishioners (collectively).
felino adj feline, catlike.
Felipe nm Philip.
felipismo nm policies of Felipe González (Spanish prime minister from 1982).
felipista 1 adj characteristic of Felipe González; la mayoría ~ the pro-Felipe González majority. 2 nmf supporter of Felipe González.
feliz adj (a) (gen) happy; ¡~ año nuevo! happy new year!; ¡~ viaje! bon voyage!; y vivieron felices, fueron felices y comieron perdices and they lived happily ever after.
(b) frase etc felicitous, happy, exactly right.
(c) (afortunado) lucky, fortunate; successful; la cosa tuvo un fin ~ the affair had a successful outcome, the affair turned out well; no ha sido ~ con sus biógrafos she has not been lucky with her biographers.
felizmente adv (V adj) (a) happily. (b) felicitously. (c) luckily, fortunately; successfully.
felón 1 adj wicked, treacherous. 2 nm, **felona** nf wicked person, villain.
felonía nf (LAm) felony, crime.
felpa nf (a) plush. (b) (*: tunda) hiding*; (reprimenda) dressing-down*.
felpar [1a] vt to cover with plush; (fig) to carpet (de with).
felpeada* nf (Cono Sur, Méx) dressing-down*.
felpear* [1a] vt (Cono Sur, Méx) (regañar) to dress down*; (azotar) to beat, thrash.
felpilla nf chenille, candlewick.
felpudo 1 adj plush, plushy. 2 nm doormat.
femenil adj (a) feminine, womanly. (b) (CAm, Méx) women's (atr); equipo ~ women's team.
femenino 1 adj feminine; sexo female; deporte ~ sport for women; equipo ~ women's team; del género ~ of the feminine gender. 2 nm (Ling) feminine.
fémina nf (hum o pey) woman, female.
feminidad nf femininity.
feminismo nm feminism.
feminista nmf feminist.
FEMP nf abr de Federación Española de Municipios y Provincias.
fémur nm femur.
fenecer [2d] 1 vt to finish, conclude, close. 2 vi (a) (terminar) to come to an end, cease. (b) (euf) to pass away, die; to perish.
fenecimiento nm (a) (fin) end, conclusion, close. (b) (euf) passing, demise.
Fenicia nf Phoenicia.
fenicio, -a adj, nm/f Phoenician.
fénico adj carbolic.
fénix nm phoenix; (fig) marvel; el F~ de los ingenios the Prince of Wits, the genius of our times (Lope de Vega).
fenol nm phenol, carbolic acid.
fenomenal adj (a) phenomenal. (b) (*: estupendo) tremendous*, terrific*.
fenomenalmente* adv terrifically (well)*.
fenómeno 1 nm (a) phenomenon; (fig) freak, accident. (b) Pedro es un ~ Peter is a genius, Peter is altogether exceptional.
2 adj (*) great*, marvellous; una chica fenómena a smashing girl*; ¡él estuvo ~! he was great!*; he was the tops!*
3 adv (*) lo hemos pasado ~ we had a terrific time; le va ~ he's getting on tremendously well*.
feo 1 adj (a) aspecto ugly; hideous, unsightly; más ~ que Picio, más ~ que un grajo (etc) as ugly as sin; me tocó bailar con la más fea (fig) I got the short straw.
(b) (desagradable) olor etc bad, nasty; jugada dirty, foul; tiempo nasty, awful, foul; situación nasty; ugly; es una costumbre fea it's a nasty habit; eso es muy ~ that's nasty, that's not nice; él me puso el problema ~ he made me see the difficulties of the problem; esto se está poniendo ~ this is beginning to look bad, I don't like the look of this; hace ~ comerse las uñas en público it's not done (o it's bad-mannered) to bite your nails in public.
(c) (LAm) (asqueroso) disgusting, foul; (de olor) foul-smelling; (de sabor) foul-tasting.
2 nm insult, slight; hacer un ~ a uno to insult sb, offend sb; ¿me vas a hacer ese ~? but you can't refuse!
3 adv (LAm*) bad, badly; oler ~ to smell bad, have a nasty smell; cantar ~ to sing terribly.
FEOGA nm abr de Fondo Europeo de Orientación y de Garantía Agrícola European Agricultural Guidance and Guarantee Fund, EAGGF.
feón* adj (LAm) ugly; medio ~ rather ugly.
feote* adj terribly ugly.
feracidad nf fertility, productivity.
feralla nf scrap metal.
feraz adj fertile, productive.
féretro nm coffin, casket (US); bier.
feri nm (LAm) = ferryboat.
feria nf (a) (Com etc) fair, market; (Agr) agricultural show; (carnaval) carnival; (LAm: mercado) village market, weekly market; la F~ de Sevilla the Seville Fair, the Seville Carnival; ~ agrícola agricultural show; ~ de ganado cattle-show; ~ de libros book-fair; ~ de muestras trade show, trade exhibition; ~ de vanidades empty show, inane spectacle; irle a uno como en ~ (Méx*) to go very badly.
(b) (descanso) holiday; rest, rest day.
(c) (Méx Fin) change; (CAm: propina) tip.
feriado 1 adj: día ~ holiday, day off; día medio ~ half-holiday, half-day off.
2 nm (LAm) bank holiday (Brit), public holiday.
ferial 1 adj fair (atr), fairground (atr); recinto ~ fairground; exhibition area. 2 nm fair, market; fairground.
feriante nmf (a) (vendedor) stallholder, trader; (de espectáculos) showman. (b) fair-goer.
feriar [1b] 1 vt (a) (comerciar) to buy, sell (in a market, at a fair); to trade, exchange; (Méx) dinero to change. (b) (And: vender barato) to sell cheap. 2 vi to take time off, take a break.
ferino adj savage, wild; tos ferina whooping cough.
fermata nf (Mús) run.
fermentación nf fermentation.
fermentado 1 adj fermented. 2 nm fermentation.
fermentar [1a] vi to ferment; hacer ~ to ferment, cause fermentation in.
fermento nm (a) (acto) ferment. (b) (sustancia) leaven, leavening.
fermio nm (Quím) fermium.
Fernán nm, **Fernando** nm Ferdinand; te lo han puesto como a ~ VII they've given it to you on a plate.
ferocidad nf fierceness, ferocity, savageness; cruelty.
Feroe nf: Islas fpl ~ Faroe Islands, the Faroes.
feromona nf pheromone.
feroz adj (a) fierce, ferocious, savage; cruel. (b) (LAm: feo) ugly.
ferozmente adv fiercely, ferociously, savagely; cruelly.
férreo adj (a) (gen) iron; (Quím) ferrous; metal no ~ non-ferrous metal. (b) (Ferro) rail (atr); vía férrea railway. (c) (fig) iron; hard, rigid, tough; con voluntad férrea with an iron will, with a will of iron.
ferrería nf ironworks, foundry.
ferretería nf (a) (objetos) ironmongery, hardware. (b) (tienda) ironmonger's (shop), hardware store. (c) = ferrería.
ferretero, -a nm/f ironmonger, hardware dealer.
férrico adj ferric.
ferroaleación nf ferro-alloy.
ferrobús nm (Ferro) diesel car.
ferrocarril nm railway, railroad (US); ~ de cercanías suburban rail network; ~ de cremallera rack railway; ~ elevado elevated railway, overhead railway; ~ funicular funicular (railway); ~ subterráneo underground railway; ~ de vía estrecha narrow-gauge railway; ~ de vía única single-track railway; por ~ by rail, by train; de ~ railway (atr), railroad (atr: US), rail (atr).
ferrocarrilero (LAm) 1 adj railway (atr), railroad (atr: US), rail (atr). 2 nm railway, railroad (US). 3 nm, **ferrocarrilera** nf (LAm: trabajador) railway worker.
ferroprusiato nm (Arquit, Téc) blueprint.
ferroso adj ferrous; metal no ~ non-ferrous metal.
ferrotipo nm (Fot) tintype.
ferroviario 1 adj railway (atr), railroad (atr: US), rail

(*atr*). **2** *nm* railwayman.
ferry ['feri] *nm* ferry.
ferry boat [feri'βot] *nm* (*LAm*) ferryboat, railway ferry, train-ferry.
fértil *adj* fertile, fruitful, productive; rich (*en* in); *imaginación etc* fertile.
fertilidad *nf* fertility; fruitfulness; richness.
fertilización *nf* fertilization; ~ **cruzada** cross-fertilization.
fertilizante *nm* fertilizer.
fertilizar [1f] *vt* to fertilize; to make fruitful; to enrich.
férula *nf* (**a**) (*vara*) ferule, birch, rod.
(**b**) (*Med*) splint.
(**c**) (*fig*) rule, domination; **vivir bajo la ~ de un tirano** to live under the harsh rule (*o* jackboot) of a tyrant.
férvido *adj* fervid, ardent.
ferviente *adj* fervent.
fervor *nm* fervour, ardour, passion.
fervorosamente *adv* fervently, ardently, passionately.
fervoroso *adj* fervent, ardent, passionate.
festejar [1a] *vt* (**a**) *persona* to feast, wine and dine; to throw a party for; to entertain; to fête.
(**b**) *aniversario, ocasión etc* to celebrate.
(**c**) *mujer* to woo, court.
(**d**) (*LAm*: *azotar*) to thrash.
festejo *nm* (**a**) (*fiesta*) feast; entertainment; (*And*) revelry; ~ **nupcial** wedding reception. (**b**) (*celebración*) celebration; **~s** public festivities, rejoicings; **hacer ~s a uno** to make a great fuss of sb. (**c**) (*cortejo*) wooing, courtship.
festín *nm* feast, banquet.
festinar [1a] *vt* (**a**) (*CAm*) (*agasajar*) to feast, wine and dine; (*entretener*) to entertain. (**b**) (*LAm*: *arruinar*) to mess up, ruin (by being overhasty). (**c**) (*LAm*: *acelerar*) to hurry along, speed up.
festival *nm* festival.
festivalero 1 *adj* festival (*atr*). **2** *nm*, **festivalera** *nf* festival-goer.
festivamente *adj* wittily, facetiously, humorously; jovially.
festividad *nf* (**a**) (*actos*) festivity, merrymaking. (**b**) (*Ecl*) feast, festivity; holiday. (**c**) (*gracia*) wit, humour; (*alegría*) joviality.
festivo *adj* (**a**) (*alegre*) festive, merry, gay. (**b**) **día ~** holiday. (**c**) (*gracioso*) witty, facetious, humorous; jovial; (*Liter etc*) humorous, comic, burlesque.
festón *nm* (*Cos*) festoon, scallop; (*de flores*) garland.
festonear [1a] *vt* to festoon, scallop; to garland.
FET [fet] *nf* (**a**) (*Dep*) *abr de* **Federación Española de Tenis**.
(**b**) (*Hist*) *abr de* **Falange Española Tradicionalista**.
fetal *adj* foetal.
fetén* **1** *adj invar* (**a**) (*auténtico*) real, authentic.
(**b**) (*estupendo*) smashing*, super*; **una chica ~** a smashing girl*.
2 *adv* splendidly, marvellously.
3 *nf* (**a**) **de ~** (*estupendo*) smashing*, super*; **ser la ~ (y la chipén)** to be smashing*.
(**b**) (*verdad*) truth; **ser la ~** to be gospel truth.
fetiche *nm* fetish; (*fig*) mumbo-jumbo, rigmarole.
fetichismo *nm* fetishism.
fetichista 1 *adj* fetishistic. **2** *nmf* fetishist.
fetidez *nf* smelliness, rankness.
fétido *adj* foul-smelling, stinking, rank.
feto *nm* (**a**) (*Bio*) foetus. (**b**) (*: *monstruo*) abortion, monster; (*chica*) plain girl, ugly girl.
feúcho* *adj* plain, homely (*US*).
feudal *adj* feudal.
feudalismo *nm* feudalism.
feudo *nm* (**a**) (*Hist*) fief; manor. (**b**) **~ franco** (*Jur*) freehold.
feúra *nf* (*LAm*) (**a**) (*gen*) ugliness. (**b**) (*una ~*) ugly person, ugly thing.
FEVE ['feβe] *nf abr de* **Ferrocarriles Españoles de Vía Estrecha**.
fez *nm* fez.
FF, f.f. *abr de* **franco (en) fábrica**; **precio ~** price ex-factory.
FFAA *abr de* **Fuerzas Armadas** armed forces.
FFCC *abr de* **Ferrocarriles**.
FGD *nm abr de* **Fondo de Garantía de Depósitos**.
fha. *abr de* **fecha** date, *d.*
fiabilidad *nf* reliability, trustworthiness; credibility.
fiable *adj* reliable, trustworthy; credible.
fiaca‡ *nf* (*Cono Sur*) laziness, apathy.
fiado *nm* (**a**) **al ~** on trust, (*Com*) on credit. (**b**) **en ~** (*Jur*) on bail.
fiador 1 *nm*, **fiadora** *nf* (*Jur*: *persona*) surety, guarantor; (*Com*) sponsor, backer; **salir ~ por uno** to go bail for sb, stand security for sb.
2 *nm* (**a**) (*Mec*) catch, fastener, pawl, trigger; (*de revólver*) safety catch; (*de cerradura*) tumbler; (*de ventana*) fastener, bolt.
(**b**) (*: *trasero*) bottom, backside.
(**c**) (*And, Cono Sur*: *de perro*) muzzle; (*And, Cono Sur*: *de casco*) chinstrap.
fiambre 1 *adj* (**a**) (*Culin*) cold, served cold.
(**b**) (*) *noticia etc* old, stale.
2 *nm* (**a**) (*Culin*) cold meat, cold food; cold lunch, buffet lunch; **~s** cold meats, cold cuts (*US*).
(**b**) (*Méx Culin*) *pork, avocado and chili dish.*
(**c**) (*: *cadáver*) corpse, stiff‡; **el pobre está ~** the poor chap is stone dead, the poor fellow is cold meat now*.
(**d**) (*: *noticia*) (piece of) stale news.
(**e**) (*: *chiste*) corny joke*, chestnut*.
(**f**) (*Cono Sur*: *fiesta*) lifeless party, cold affair.
fiambrera *nf* (**a**) (*canasto*) lunch basket, dinner pail (*US*).
(**b**) (*Cono Sur*: *fresquera*) meat safe; icebox.
fiambrería *nf* (*LAm*) delicatessen.
fianza *nf* (**a**) (*garantía*) surety, security, bond; (*señal*) deposit; **bajo ~** (*Jur*) on bail; **~ de aduana** customs bond; **~ de averías** average bond; **~ carcelera** bail. (**b**) (*persona*) surety, guarantor.
fiar [1c] **1** *vt* (**a**) (*gen*) to entrust, confide (*a* to).
(**b**) (*Fin etc*) to guarantee, vouch for; to stand security for; (*Jur*) to go bail for.
(**c**) (*Com*: *a crédito*) to sell on credit; (*LAm*) to buy on credit.
2 *vi* to trust (*en* in); **ser de ~** to be reliable, be trustworthy.
3 fiarse *vr*: **~ de uno** to trust sb; to rely on sb, depend on sb; to confide in sb; **me fié completamente de ti** I trusted in you completely; **no me fío de él** I don't trust him; **nos fiamos de Vd para conseguirlo** we rely on you to get it; (*en tienda*) **'no se fía'** 'no credit given'.
fiasco *nm* fiasco.
fíat *nm*, *pl* **fíats** official sanction, fiat; consent, blessing.
fibra *nf* (**a**) (*gen*) fibre; **~ acrílica** acrylic fibre; **~ de amianto** asbestos fibre; **~ artificial** man-made fibre; **~ de carbono** carbon fibre; **~ dietética** dietary fibre; **~ ocular** ocular fibre; **~ sintética** synthetic fibre; **~ de vidrio** fibre-glass.
(**b**) (*en madera*) grain; (*Min*) vein.
(**c**) (*fig*) vigour, toughness; sinews; **~s del corazón** heartstrings; **despertar la ~ sensible** to strike a sympathetic cord, awaken a sympathetic response.
fibravidrio *nm* fibre-glass.
fibrina *nf* fibrin.
fibroóptica *nf* fibre optics.
fibrosis *nf* fibrosis; **~ cística** cystic fibrosis.
fibrositis *nf* fibrositis.
fibroso *adj* fibrous.
fíbula *nf* (*Hist*) fibula, brooch.
ficción 1 *nf* (**a**) fiction; (*pey*) invention, fabrication. (**b**) (*Liter*) fiction; **~ científica** science-fiction; **obras de no ~** non-fiction books. **2** *atr* fictitious, make-believe; mock; **historia ~** (piece of) historical fiction, fictionalized history; **reportaje ~** dramatized documentary.
ficcioso (*Cono Sur*) **1** *adj* bluffing; false, double-dealing. **2** *nm* bluffer; double-dealer.
ficticio *adj* fictitious; imaginary; (*pey*) fabricated.
ficus *nm invar* (*Bot*) rubber plant.
ficha *nf* (**a**) (*Telec etc*) token; (*en juegos*) token, counter, marker; (*póquer*) chip; (*Com, Fin*) token, tally; **~ del dominó** domino; **~ de silicio** silicon chip.
(**b**) (*tarjeta*) card; index card, record-card, catalogue card; (*en hotel*) registration form; **~ antropométrica** card recording personal particulars; **~ perforada** punched card; **~ policíaca** police record, police dossier; **~ técnica** (*TV etc*) (list of) credits.
(**c**) (*CAm, Carib, Cono Sur* ††) 5-cent piece; (*CAm**: *moneda*) coin.
(**d**) (*Méx*: *de botella*) flat bottle cap.
(**e**) (*And, Carib*: *t* **mala ~**) rogue, villain.
(**f**) (*Dep*) signing-on fee.
fichaje *nm* (**a**) (*Dep*) signing (up); (*Fin*) signing-on fee. (**b**) **nuevos ~s** (*Pol*) new members, new supporters.
fichar [1a] **1** *vt* (**a**) *ficha* to file, index.
(**b**) *persona* to file the personal particulars of; *dato* to record, enter (on a card *etc*); **está fichado** he's got a (police) record; **le tenemos fichado** we have his record, (*fig*) we've got him taped*, we know all about him.
(**c**) *dominó* to play.

(**d**) (*Dep etc*) to sign up, sign on (*en un club* for a club, with a team).
(**e**) (*Carib*: *engañar*) to swindle.
2 *vi* (**a**) (*Dep etc*) to sign up, sign on; (*en fábrica etc*) to clock in.
(**b**) (*And*: *morir*) to die.
fichero *nm* card-index; filing-cabinet; (*Inform*) file; ~ **de datos** datafile; ~ **fotográfico de delincuentes** photographic records of criminals, rogues' gallery; ~ **indexado** index file; ~ **informático** computer file.
FIDA *nm abr de* **Fondo Internacional de Desarrollo Agrícola** International Fund for Agricultural Development, IFAD.
fidedigno *adj* reliable, trustworthy.
fideería *nf* (*LAm*) pasta factory.
fideicomisario 1 *adj* trust (*atr*); **banco** ~ trust company. **2** *nm*, **fideicomisaria** *nf* trustee. **3** *nm* trust.
fideicomiso *nm* trust.
fidelería *nf* (*LAm*) pasta factory.
fidelidad *nf* (**a**) (*lealtad*) fidelity, loyalty (*a* to).
(**b**) (*exactitud*) accuracy.
(**c**) **alta** ~ (*Rad*) high fidelity; **de alta** ~ high-fidelity (*atr*), hi-fi.
fideo *nm* (**a**) ~**s** (*Culin*) noodles, spaghetti. (**b**) (*: *persona*) beanpole*.
fiduciario 1 *adj* fiduciary. **2** *nm*, **fiduciaria** *nf* fiduciary, trustee.
fiebre *nf* (**a**) (*Med*) fever; ~ **aftosa** foot-and-mouth disease; ~ **amarilla** yellow fever; ~ **entérica** enteric fever; ~ **glandular** glandular fever; ~ **del heno** hay fever; ~ **palúdica** malaria; ~ **porcina** swine fever; ~ **reumática** rheumatic fever; ~ **tifoidea** typhoid; **tener** ~ to have a (high) temperature, be feverish; to have fever, be in a fever.
(**b**) (*fig*) fever; feverish excitement, fevered atmosphere; **la** ~ **del juego** the gambling fever; ~ **del oro** gold fever; gold-rush.
(**c**) (*Cono Sur**: *taimado*) slippery customer*.
fiel 1 *adj* (**a**) (*gen*) faithful, loyal; (*fiable*) honest, reliable, trustworthy; **seguir siendo** ~ **a** to remain loyal to, remain true to.
(**b**) *relación, traducción etc* accurate, exact, faithful.
2 los ~**es** (*Ecl*) *nmpl* the faithful.
3 *nm* (**a**) (*persona*) inspector of weights and measures.
(**b**) (*Téc*) needle, pointer.
fielmente *adv* (**a**) (*gen*) faithfully, loyally; reliably. (**b**) (*exactamente*) accurately, exactly.
fieltro *nm* (**a**) (*tela*) felt. (**b**) (*objeto*) felt, piece of felt; felt rug; felt hat.
fiera 1 *nf* (**a**) wild beast, wild animal; (*Taur*) bull.
(**b**) ~ **sarda** (*And*) expert, top man.
2 *nmf* (*fig*) fiend; virago, dragon; (*en buen sentido*) ball of fire, highly energetic person; **como una** ~ **enjaulada** like a caged tiger; **es un** ~ **para el trabajo** he's a demon for work; **es una** ~ **para el deporte** he's a fiend for sport, he's a sports fiend; **estar hecho una** ~ to be wild, be furious; **ella entró hecha una** ~ she came in absolutely furious.
fierecilla *nf* (*fig*) shrew.
fiereza *nf* (**a**) (*ferocidad*) fierceness; ferocity; cruelty; frightfulness. (**b**) (*fealdad*) ugly deformity.
fiero 1 *adj* (**a**) (*feroz*) fierce, ferocious; (*Zool*) wild, fierce; (*cruel*) cruel; (*horroroso*) frightful. (**b**) (*: *feo*) ugly. **2** ~**s** *nmpl* threats, boasts; **echar** ~**s, hacer** ~**s** to utter threats, bluster, brag.
fierro *nm* (**a**) (*LAm*: *gen*) iron; (*Agr*) marking-iron, brand; (*Cono Sur*: *cuchillo*) knife; (*Cono Sur*: *Aut*) accelerator; (*Cono Sur**: *arma*) gun, weapon. (**b**) ~**s** (*Méx*: *fig*) money; (*LAm*: *resortes*) springs.
fiesta *nf* (**a**) (*en casa etc*) party, entertainment; social gathering; celebration; (*de ciudad etc*) festival, fête; ~**s** public festivities, public rejoicings; ~ **de armas** (*Hist*) tournament; **la** ~ **brava, la** ~ **nacional** (*Taur*) bullfighting; ~ **de disfraces** fancy-dress party; **organizar una** ~ **en honor de uno** to give a party in sb's honour; **¡se acabó la** ~**!** (*fig*) drop it!, that's enough of that!, joke over!; **aguar la** ~ to spoil the fun, be a spoilsport; to spoil the party; **la noticia del accidente nos aguó la** ~ **a todos** news of the accident put a real dampener on us all; **estar en** ~**s** to be en fête; **para coronar la** ~**, por fin de** ~ to round it all off, as a finishing touch; **no sabe de qué va la** ~ he hasn't a clue; **¡tengamos la** ~ **en paz!** none of that!; cut it out!
(**b**) (*Ecl*) feast, feast day; holiday; ~**s** holidays; ~**s*** (*esp*) Christmas festivities, Christmas season; ~ **de la banderita** flag day; ~ **cívica,** ~ **laboral** public holiday; ~ **fija,** ~ **inmoble** immovable feast; ~ **de guardar,** ~ **de precepto** day of obligation, holiday; **F**~ **de la Hispanidad, F**~ **de la Raza** Columbus Day; ~ **movible,** ~ **móvil** movable feast; ~ **nacional** public holiday, bank holiday; **F**~ **del Trabajo** Labour Day; **mañana es** ~ it's a holiday tomorrow; **la** ~ **del santo** the saint's feast, the saint's day; **celebrar la** ~**, guardar la** ~ to observe the feast (*de* of); **hacer** ~ to take a day off.
(**c**) (*juerga*) merrymaking, festivities, fun and games; **la** ~ **continuó hasta muy tarde** the festivities went on very late; **estar de** ~**s** to be in high good humour; **¡estás de** ~**!** you're joking!; **no estoy para** ~**s** I'm in no mood for jokes.
(**d**) ~**s** (*palabras*) endearments; soothing words, flattering words; (*caricias*) caresses; **hacer** ~**s a** to caress, fondle; (*perro*) to fawn on; (*fig*) to make a great fuss of.
fiestero *adj* gay; fun-loving, pleasure-seeking; fond of parties.
fiestorro* *nm* (*hum*) grand party, big party.
fifí † *nm* (*LAm*) playboy, young man about town.
fifiriche *adj* (*CAm, Méx*) weak, sickly.
figón *nm* cheap restaurant.
figulino *adj* clay (*atr*); **arcilla figulina** potter's clay.
figura 1 *nf* (**a**) (*gen, Arte etc*) figure; shape, form; image; **de** ~ **entera** full-length; ~ **de nieve** snowman.
(**b**) (*persona*) figure; **una** ~ **destacada** an outstanding figure; ~ **del partido** man of the match; ~ **de culto** cult figure; **las principales** ~**s del partido** the chief figures in the party; **cuando uno es** ~ when one is a famous person; **hacer** ~ to cut a figure.
(**c**) (††) countenance; **hacer** ~**s** to make faces.
(**d**) (*Mat etc, Tip*) figure, drawing, diagram; ~ **celeste** horoscope.
(**e**) (*Ling*) figure; ~ **retórica** rhetorical figure, figure of speech.
(**f**) (*Teat*: *personaje*) character, role; **en la** ~ **de** in the role of.
(**g**) (*Teat*: *títere*) marionette.
(**h**) (*Naipes*) picture card, court card; (*Ajedrez*) piece, man.
(**i**) (*Baile, Patinaje*) figure.
(**j**) (*Mús*) note.
2 *nm*: **ser un** ~ to be a big name, be somebody.
figuración *nf* (*Cine*) extras.
figuradamente *adv* figuratively.
figurado *adj* figurative.
figurante *nm*, **figuranta** *nf* (**a**) (*Teat*) extra, walker-on, super(numerary). (**b**) (*fig*) figurehead.
figurar [1a] **1** *vt* to figure, shape, form; to represent.
2 *vi* (**a**) (*incluirse*) to figure (*como* as, *entre* among), appear; **los nombres no figuran aquí** the names do not appear here.
(**b**) (*fig*) to show off, cut a dash; **todo se debe al afán de** ~ it's all due to the urge to cut a dash, it's the urge to be somebody that causes it all.
3 figurarse *vr* to suppose; to expect; to imagine, fancy; to figure (*US*); **¡figúrate!, ¡figúrese!** just think!, just imagine!; **¡figúrate lo que sería con dos!** imagine what it would be like with two of them!; **ya me lo figuraba** I thought as much; **me figuro que es caro** I fancy it's dear, I imagine it's dear; **¿qué te figuras que me preguntó ayer?** what do you think he asked me yesterday?; **no te vayas a figurar que ...** don't go thinking that ...
figurativismo *nm* representational art.
figurativo *adj* figurative; *arte* representational.
figurilla *nf* figurine.
figurín *nm* fashion plate; model; dummy; (*Teat*) design for a costume.
figurinismo *nm* (*Teat*) costume design.
figurinista *nmf* (*Teat*) costume designer.
figurón *nm* (**a**) (*gen*) grotesque figure, huge figure; ~ **de proa** figurehead. (**b**) (*: *presumido*) pretentious nobody; pompous ass*.
figuroso *adj* (*Cono Sur, Méx*) showy, loud.
fija *nf* (**a**) (*Téc*) hinge; (*Arquit*) trowel.
(**b**) (*And, Cono Sur*: *Carreras*) favourite; **es una** ~ (*Cono Sur*) it's a cert*; **ésa es la** ~ that's for sure; **ésta es la** ~ it's a sure thing.
fijación *nf* (**a**) (*acto*) fixing; securing; fastening; sticking (on); posting; establishing. (**b**) (*Med*) fixation. (**c**) (*de esquí*) binding, harness.
fijador *nm* (**a**) (*Fot*) fixer; fixing bath. (**b**) ~ **para el pelo** hair lotion, haircream.
fijamente *adv* firmly, steadily, securely; fixedly; **mirar** ~ **a uno** to stare at sb, look hard at sb.
fijapelo *nm* hair lotion, haircream.

fijar [1a] **1** *vt* (**a**) (*gen*) to fix; (*clavar*) to secure, fasten (on, down *etc*); *sello etc* to affix, stick (on), paste on, glue on; *cartel* to post, stick, put up; *pelo* to set; (*Fot*) to fix; *residencia* to take up, establish; *ojos* to fix (*en* on); *atención* to focus, fix (*en* on).
(**b**) (*fig: determinar*) to settle (on), decide, determine; *fecha, hora, precio etc* to fix, set; **la fecha no se puede ~ con precisión** the date cannot exactly be determined; **hemos fijado una hora** we have fixed a time, we have agreed on a time.
(**c**) (*) *persona* to catch (the attention of), draw, pull.
2 fijarse *vr* (**a**) (*establecerse*) to become fixed, get set; to settle, lodge; to establish o.s.; **el dolor se ha fijado en la pierna** the pain has settled in the leg.
(**b**) (*prestar atención*) to notice, pay attention; **lo malo es que no se fija** the trouble is he doesn't pay attention; **el debería fijarse más en lo que dice** he ought to be more careful about what he says; **no me había fijado** I hadn't noticed; **fíjese bien** pay close attention, watch this carefully; **¡fíjate!** fancy that!, just imagine!; **¿te fijas?** (*: *esp LAm*) see what I mean?*
(**c**) **~ en algo** to notice sth, observe sth, pay attention to sth; (*mirar*) to stare at sth; **~ en un detalle** to seize upon a detail; **¡fíjense en los precios!** just look at these prices!; **se fijó en mí en seguida** he fixed on me at once; **~ en** + *infin* to be intent on + *ger*.
fijasellos *nm invar* stamp hinge.
fijativo *nm* fixative.
fijeza *nf* firmness, stability; constancy; fixity; **mirar con ~ a uno** to stare at sb, look hard at sb.
fijo 1 *adj* (**a**) (*gen*) fixed; (*firme*) firm, steady, stable, secure; *estrella, fecha, precio etc* fixed; *mirada* fixed, steady; *color* fast; *cliente* regular; **de ~** certainly, for sure.
(**b**) *propósito etc* fixed, firm.
(**c**) *plantilla* permanent, established; *novio* regular, steady.
2 *excl*: **¡~!** quite right!
fil *nm*: **~ derecho** leapfrog.
fila *nm* (**a**) (*gen*) row, line; (*en marcha*) file; (*Dep, Teat etc*) row, tier (of seats); (*cola*) queue; **una ~ de coches** a line of cars; **~ cero** row of seats for VIPs; **~ india** single file, Indian file; **una chaqueta de dos ~s** a double-breasted jacket; **en ~** in a row; in a line; **en ~ de a uno, en ~ india** in single file; **aparcar en doble ~** to double-park; **ponerse en ~** to line up, get into line; (*fig*) **salir de la ~** to step out of line.
(**b**) (*Mil*) rank; (*fig*) **las ~s** the ranks; **los eslobodios de ~s** the rank-and-file Slobodians; **¡en ~s!** fall in!; (*fig*) **apretar las ~s** to close ranks; **cerrar ~s** to close ranks (*t fig*); **estar en ~s** to be with the colours, be on active service; **formar ~s** to form up, fall in; **llamar a uno a ~s** to call sb up, call sb to the colours; **romper ~s** to fall out, dismiss; **¡rompan ~s!** dismiss!; **romper las ~s** to break ranks.
(**c**) (*: *antipatía*) dislike, antipathy; **el jefe le tiene ~** the boss has it in for him*.
(**d**) (*CAm*: *cumbre*) peak, summit.
filacteria *nf* phylactery.
Filadelfia *n* Philadelphia.
filamento *nm* filament.
filamentoso *adj* filamentous; sinewy.
filantropía *nf* philanthropy.
filantrópico *adj* philanthropic.
filantropismo *nm* philanthropy.
filántropo *nm*, **filántropa** *nf* philanthropist.
filar* [1a] *vt* (**a**) (*calar*) to size up, rumble*. (**b**) (*observar*) to notice, spot, take note of.
filarmónico *adj* philharmonic.
filatelia *nf* (**a**) (*gen*) philately, stamp collecting. (**b**) (*tienda*) stamp shop, stamp dealer's.
filatélico 1 *adj* philatelic; stamp (*atr*). **2** *nm*, **filatélica** *nf* stamp dealer.
filatelista *nmf* philatelist, stamp collector.
filático *adj* (*And*) *caballo* vicious; *persona* (*travieso*) mischievous; (*taimado*) crafty; (*grosero*) rude.
filete *nm* (**a**) (*Arquit*) fillet.
(**b**) (*Mec*: *de tornillo*) thread, worm; (*de brida*) snaffle (-bit).
(**c**) (*Culin*: *carne*) fillet, tenderloin, steak; (*pescado*) fillet; **darse el ~*** to neck*, pet*; **darse el ~ con*** to feel*, touch up‡.
(**d**) (*Cos*) narrow hem.
(**e**) (*Tip*) fillet.
filetear [1a] *vt* to fillet; to cut into strips.
filetón *nm* fillet steak.
filfa* *nf* (**a**) (*fraude*) fraud, hoax; piece of humbug. (**b**) (*falsificación*) fake. (**c**) (*rumor*) rumour, canard.
fili‡ *nm* pocket; **~ de la buena** breast pocket (of a jacket).
filiación *nf* (**a**) (*relación*) filiation; (*de ideas etc*) connection, relationship. (**b**) (*señas*) personal description; characteristics, particulars. (**c**) (*Pol*) affiliation.
filial 1 *adj* filial; (*Com*) subsidiary, affiliated; (*Dep*) sister (*atr*). **2** *nf* (*Com*) subsidiary, affiliated company. **3** *nm* (*Dep*) sister club.
filibusterismo *nm* (*piratería*) buccaneering; (*Parl*) filibustering.
filibustero *nm* (**a**) (*bucanero*) buccaneer, freebooter. (**b**) (*fig*) rogue.
filiforme *adj* thread-like; *persona* (*hum*) skinny.
filigrana *nf* (**a**) (*Téc*) filigree; filigree work; (*Tip*) watermark. (**b**) (*Dep etc*) delicate move, clever piece of play; **~s** (*fig*) elegant play, fancy footwork.
filípica *nf* harangue, tirade, philippic.
Filipinas *nfpl*: **las (Islas) ~** the Philippines.
filipino 1 *adj* Philippine. **2** *nm*, **filipina** *nf* Philippine, Filipino.
filisteísmo *nm* Philistinism.
filisteo 1 *adj* Philistine. **2** *nm* (**a**) (*Hist, fig*) Philistine. (**b**) (*fig*) big man, giant.
film *nm, pl* **films** [film] film; picture, movie (*US*).
filmación *nf* (**a**) (*acto*) filming, shooting. (**b**) **filmaciones** footage.
filmador *nm* film-maker.
filmadora *nf* (*estudio*) film studio; (*aparato*) film camera.
filmar [1a] *vt* to film, shoot.
filme *nm* = **film.**
fílmico *adj* film (*atr*), movie (*atr*: *US*); screen (*atr*); **su carrera fílmica** her film career, her career in films; **obras teatrales y fílmicas** theatrical and screen works, works for stage and screen.
filmina *nf* (*Fot*: *diapositiva*) slide, transparency; (*película*) filmstrip, short film; (*de microscopio*) slide.
filmografía *nf* (**a**) (*estudio*) study of the film; **la ~ de la estrella** the star's film history, the star's screen history. (**b**) (*filmes*) films (*collectively*); **la ~ del Oeste** the history of the Western, films (*collectively*) about the West, the West on the screen.
filmología *nf* science of film-making, art of film-making.
filmoteca *nf* film library, film archive.
filo¹ *nm* (**a**) (*de herramienta etc*) edge; cutting edge, blade; (*línea*) dividing-line; (*cresta*) ridge; **~ de la navaja** (*fig*) razor's edge; **~ del viento** (*Náut*) direction of the wind; **de doble ~, de dos ~s** double-edged (*t fig*); **al ~ de las 12** at 12 precisely; **por ~** exactly; **de ~** (*And*) resolutely; **dar (un) ~ a, sacar el ~ a** to sharpen, put an edge on; **dar ~ a** (*fig*: *And*) to tell off, (*Carib*) to wound with a knife; **herir a uno por los mismos ~s** to pay sb back in his own coin; **pasar al ~ de la espada** to put to the sword.
(**b**) (*CAm, Méx*: *hambre*) hunger; **tener ~*** to be starving, be ravenous.
(**c**) (*Cono Sur**: *cuento*) tale, tall story.
(**d**) (*Cono Sur**: *pretendiente*) suitor; (*novia*) girlfriend; (*cortejo*) courtship.
filo² *nm* (*Bio*) phylum.
filo³‡ *nm* con-man's accomplice*.
-filo *suf* -phile, *p.ej.* **francófilo** *nm*, **francófila** *nf* francophile.
filo... *pref* philo..., pro..., *p.ej.* **filosoviético** pro-Soviet; **filoterrorista** sympathetic to terrorism.
filocomunismo *nm* pro-communist feeling(s); fellow-travelling.
filocomunista 1 *adj* pro-communist; with communist leanings, fellow-travelling. **2** *nmf* pro-communist; fellow traveller.
filología *nf* philology.
filológico *adj* philological.
filólogo, -a *nm/f* philologist.
filomela *nf*, **filomena** *nf* (*poét*) nightingale.
filón *nm* (*Min*) seam, vein, lode; (*fig*) rich seam, gold-mine.
filongo *nm* (*Cono Sur*) girlfriend (of inferior social status).
filosa‡ *nf* (**a**) (*navaja*) chiv‡, knife. (**b**) (*cera*) mug‡, face.
filoso *adj* (**a**) (*CAm, Cono Sur, Méx*) sharp. (**b**) (*Cono Sur**) **él es ~** he's sharp, he's really on the ball; **estar ~ en algo** to be well up on sth. (**c**) (*CAm*) hungry.
filosofal *adj*: **piedra ~** philosopher's stone.
filosofar [1a] *vi* to philosophize.
filosofía *nf* philosophy; **~ de la ciencia** philosophy of science; **~ moral** moral philosophy; **~ natural** natural

philosophy; ~ **de la vida** philosophy of life.
filosófico *adj* philosophic(al).
filósofo, -a *nm/f* philosopher.
filosoviético *adj* pro-Soviet.
filote *nm* (*And*) ear of green maize; maize silk; **estar en ~** (*niño*) to begin to grow hair.
filotear [1a] *vi* (*And: maíz*) to come into ear, begin to ripen; (*niño*) to grow hair.
filoxera *nf* phylloxera.
filtración *nf* (**a**) (*Téc*) filtration; seepage, leakage, loss. (**b**) (*información*) leak(age), leaking.
filtrado 1 *adj* (**a**) *información* leaked. (**b**) (*) **estoy ~** (*Cono Sur*) I'm whacked*. **2** *nm* filtering; screening.
filtrador 1 *adj* filtering. **2** *nm* filter.
filtraje *nm* filtering; screening.
filtrar [1a] **1** *vt* (**a**) (*Téc*) to filter; (*fig*) to screen.
(**b**) *información etc* to leak (*a* to).
2 *vi y* **filtrarse** *vr* (**a**) (*gen*) to filter; **~ por** to filter through; to percolate (through); to seep through, leak through.
(**b**) (*fig: dinero etc*) to dwindle, disappear bit by bit.
filtro *nm* (**a**) (*Téc*) filter; screen; (*en carretera, de policía*) checkpoint, roadblock; **~ de aceite** oil-filter; **~ de aire** air-filter; **cigarrillo con ~** filter-tipped cigarette.
(**b**) (*Hist*) love-potion, philtre.
filudo *adj* (*LAm*) sharp.
filván *nm* feather-edge; (*de papel*) deckle edge; (*de cuchillo*) burr.
fimbria *nf* (*Cos*) border, hem.
fin *nm* (**a**) (*final*) end; ending; conclusion; **'~ de la cita'** 'end of quote', 'unquote'; **función de ~ de curso** end-of-year party; **~ de fichero** end-of-file; **~ de fiesta** (*Teat*) grand finale; **~ de semana** weekend; **a ~es del mes** at (*o* about) the end of the month; **hacia ~es del siglo** towards the end of the century; **al ~** finally, in the end; **al ~ y al cabo** at long last; in the end; after all, when all is said and done; **en ~, por ~** finally, at last; in short; **en ~** (*fig*) well, well then; **¡en ~!** so that's that!, what next?; **pero en ~, ...** but still, ...; **en ~ de cuentas** in the last analysis; **sin ~** (*adv*) endlessly; (*adj*: *t Téc*) endless; **correa sin ~** endless belt; **un sin ~** *V* **sinfín**; **dar ~ a un discurso** to end a speech, close a speech; **llegar a ~ de mes** (*fig*) to make ends meet; to hold out; **llevar algo a buen ~** to carry sth through to a successful conclusion; **poner ~ a** to stop, put a stop to.
(**b**) (*objetivo*) aim, purpose, objective; scope; **los ~es de este estudio** the aims of this study; the scope of this study; **a ~ de** + *infin* in order to + *infin*, so as to + *infin*; **a ~ de que** ... in order that ..., so that ...; **a tal ~** with this aim in view; **con el ~ de** + *infin* with the purpose of + *ger*; **con ~es deshonestos** with an immoral purpose.
Fina *nf forma familiar de* **Josefina**.
finado 1 *adj* late, deceased; **el ~ presidente** the late president. **2** *nm*, **finada** *nf* deceased. **3** *nm* (*Téc*) finishing.
final 1 *adj* final, last; ultimate; eventual. **2** *nm* end; conclusion; (*Liter etc*) ending; (*Mús*) finale; **~ feliz** happy ending; **al ~ de la calle** at the end of the street; **por ~** finally. **3** *nf* (*Dep etc*) final; **~ de consolación** play-off among losers (for third place *etc*).
finalidad *nf* (**a**) (*propósito*) object, purpose, intention; **la ~ de este libro** the aim of this book; **¿qué ~ tendrá todo esto?** what can be the purpose of all this?; **perseguir algo como ~** to set sth as one's goal.
(**b**) (*Filos etc*) finality.
finalista *nmf* finalist.
finalización *nf* ending, conclusion.
finalizar [1f] **1** *vt* (*gen*) to end, finish; **dar algo por finalizado** to consider sth finished; **~ la sesión** (*Inform*) to log out (*o* log off).
2 *vi y* **finalizarse** *vr* to end, finish, conclude.
finalmente *adv* finally, lastly.
finamente *adv* politely; elegantly; acutely, shrewdly; subtly; delicately.
finamiento *nm* decease, demise, passing.
financiador(a) *nm/f* financial backer.
financiamiento *nm*, **financiación** *nf* financing.
financiar [1b] *vt* to finance.
financiero 1 *adj* financial; **los medios ~s** the financial means; **el mundo ~** the financial world, the world of finance. **2** *nm*, **financiera** *nf* (*banquero*) financier. **3** *nf* (*empresa*) finance company, finance house.
financista 1 *adj* financial. **2** *nmf* (*LAm*) (*patrocinador*) financier; (*experto*) financial expert.
finanzas *nfpl* finances.
finar [1a] **1** *vi* to pass away, die. **2** **finarse** *vr* to long, yearn (*por* for).
finca *nf* (**a**) (*propiedad etc*) property; land, real estate; **~ raíz** (*And*) real estate; **~ urbana** town property.
(**b**) (*casa etc*) country estate, country house; (*LAm*) farm; (*minifundio*) small rural holding; (*de ganado*) ranch; **~ azucarera** sugar plantation; **~ cafetera** coffee plantation; **~ de experimentación** experimental farm; **cazar en ~ ajena** to poach (on sb else's property); **penetrar en ~ ajena** to trespass (on sb else's property); **tienen una ~ en Guadalajara** they have a country house (*o* property, estate) in Guadalajara; **pasan un mes en su ~** they're spending a month at their country place.
fincar [1g] **1** *vt* (*Carib*) to till, cultivate. **2** *vi*: **~ en** (*And, Méx*) to consist of, comprise.
finchado* *adj* stuck-up*, conceited.
fincharse* [1a] *vr* to get conceited.
finde* *nm* weekend.
finés = **finlandés.**
fineza *nf* (**a**) (*calidad*) fineness, excellence; purity; select quality.
(**b**) (*de modales*) refinement; elegance.
(**c**) (*acto*) kindness, favour; courtesy, nice thing (to say *o* do *etc*); (*cumplido*) compliment; (*regalo*) small gift, token.
fingar⁑ [1h] *vt* to nick⁑, swipe⁑.
fingidamente *adv* feignedly; in a sham way; as a piece of make-believe.
fingido *adj* feigned, false; fake, sham; mock; make-believe; **nombre ~** false name, assumed name.
fingimiento *nm* pretence; simulation, feigning.
fingir [3c] **1** *vt* to sham, fake; to invent; to simulate; **~ desinterés** to feign disinterest, pretend not to be interested; **~ mucha humildad** to pretend to be very humble; **lo habrán fingido** I expect they invented it, I expect they faked it up.
2 *vi* to pretend, feign; **~ dormir** to pretend to be asleep, to feign sleep.
3 fingirse *vr*: **~ un sabio** to pretend to be an expert; **~ dormido** to pretend to be asleep.
finiquitar [1a] *vt cuenta* to settle and close, balance up; (*) *asunto* to conclude, finish off, wind up.
finiquito *nm* (*Com, Fin*) settlement.
finisecular *adj* fin-de-siècle (*atr*).
finito *adj* finite.
finlandés 1 *adj* Finnish. **2** *nm*, **finlandesa** *nf* Finn. **3** *nm* (*Ling*) Finnish.
Finlandia *nf* Finland.
finlandización *nf* neutralization and subordination (of one country to another).
finlandizar [1f] *vt país* to neutralize and subordinate.
fino 1 *adj* (**a**) (*de buena calidad*) fine, excellent; pure; *fruta, vino etc* choice, quality (*atr*); *tabaco etc* select; *jerez* fino, dry; (*Min*) refined; **oro ~** pure gold, refined gold.
(**b**) (*delgado*) thin; *persona* slender, slight; *tela* thin, delicate, sheer; *capa etc* thin.
(**c**) *punta* sharp.
(**d**) (*cortés*) *persona* polite, well-bred, refined; *modales* refined, cultured; *cumplido etc* elegant, well-turned; **ponerse ~** to turn on the charm.
(**e**) *inteligencia* shrewd, acute, penetrating; *gusto* fine, discriminating; *oído* sharp, acute.
(**f**) (*sutil*) *distinción etc* fine, subtle, delicate; *ironía* subtle.
2 *nm* dry sherry, fino sherry.
finolis *adj invar* affected.
finta *nf* feint; **hacer ~s** to feint, spar.
fintar [1a] *vi*, **fintear** [1a] *vi* to feint, spar.
finura *nf* (**a**) (*calidad de fino*) fineness, excellence; purity; choiceness, high quality.
(**b**) (*cortesía*) politeness, courtesy, refinement; elegance; **¡qué ~!** what refinement!, how charming!
(**c**) (*astucia*) shrewdness, acuteness.
(**d**) (*sutileza*) subtlety, delicacy.
fiñe *adj* (*Carib*) small, weak, sickly.
fiordo *nm* fiord.
FIP [fip] *nf* (*Esp*) *abr de* **Formación Intensiva Profesional.**
fique *nm* (*And, Méx, Carib*) (*fibra*) henequen; fibre; (*cuerda*) rope, cord.
F.I.R. [fir] *nm* (*Esp*) *abr de* **farmacéutico interno residente.**
firma *nf* (**a**) (*gen*) signature; (*acto*) signing; **es de mi ~** I signed that; **6 novelas de su ~** 6 novels of his, 6 novels which he has written; **~ de libros** book-signing session.
(**b**) (*Com, Fin*) firm, company, concern.

firmamento *nm* firmament.

firmante 1 *adj* signatory (*de* to). **2** *nmf* signatory; **el abajo ~** the undersigned; **el último ~** the last person signing (*o* to sign).

firmar [1a] *vti* to sign; **firmado y lacrado, firmado y sellado** signed and sealed.

firme 1 *adj* (**a**) (*gen*) firm; (*estable*) steady, secure, stable; (*duro*) hard; (*sólido*) solid, compact; *color* fast; *resistencia etc* firm; resolute; **estar en lo ~** to be in the right; to be positive; **mantenerse ~** to hold one's ground, not give way.

(**b**) (*Com, Fin*) *mercado* steady; *precio* firm, stable.

(**c**) *persona* staunch, steadfast, resolute.

(**d**) (*Mil*) **¡~s!** attention!; **estar en posición de ~s** to stand at attention; **poner ~s a un pelotón** to bring a squad to attention; **ponerse ~(s)** to come to attention.

(**e**) **de ~** firmly, strongly; steadily; **batir de ~** to strike hard; **resistir de ~** to resist strongly; **trabajar de ~** to work hard, work solidly.

(**f**) (*Com*) **oferta en ~** firm offer; **pedido en ~** firm order.

2 *adv* hard; **pegar ~** to hit hard; **trabajar ~** to work hard.

3 *nm* roadbed, road foundation layer; road surface; '**~ ondulado**' 'uneven surface'; '**~ provisional**' 'temporary surface'.

firmemente *adv* (**a**) firmly; securely, solidly. (**b**) (*lealmente*) staunchly, steadfastly.

firmeza *nf* (**a**) firmness; steadiness, stability; solidity, compactness. (**b**) (*Com, Fin*) steadiness. (**c**) (*moral*) firmness; steadfastness, resolution.

firmita* *nf* (mere) signature; **echar una ~** to sign on the dotted line (*t fig*); **¿me echas una ~?** would you sign here, please?

firuletes* *nmpl* (*LAm*) (*objetos*) knick-knacks; (*al bailar*) gyrations, contortions.

fiscal 1 *adj* (*económico*) fiscal, financial; (*relativo a impuestos*) tax (*atr*); **año ~** fiscal year, financial year.

2 *nmf* (*t* **fiscala** *nf*) (**a**) (*Jur*) public prosecutor, district attorney (*US*); **~ general de Estado** attorney-general.

(**b**) (*: *entrometido*) busybody, meddler.

fiscalía *nf* office of the public prosecutor.

fiscalidad *nf* taxation; tax system, tax regulations.

fiscalista *adj*: **abogado ~** lawyer specializing in tax affairs.

fiscalizar [1f] *vt* (**a**) (*controlar*) to control, oversee, inspect (officially). (**b**) (*fig*) to criticize, find fault with. (**c**) (*: *entrometerse*) to pry into, meddle with.

fiscalmente *adv* fiscally; from a tax point of view, taxation-wise.

fisco *nm* treasury, exchequer; **declarar algo al ~** to declare sth for tax purposes.

fisga *nf* (**a**) (*de pesca*) fish spear; (*CAm*: *Taur*) banderilla. (**b**) (*fig*) banter, chaff; **hacer ~ a uno** to tease sb, banter sb.

fisgar [1h] **1** *vt* (**a**) *pez* to spear, harpoon. (**b**) (*fig*) to pry into, spy on. **2** *vi* (**a**) (*fisgonear*) to pry, snoop*, spy. (**b**) (*mofarse*) to mock, scoff, jeer.

fisgón 1 *adj* (**a**) (*curioso*) snooping*, prying, nosey*. (**b**) (*guasón*) bantering, teasing; (*mofador*) mocking. **2** *nm*, **fisgona** *nf* (**a**) snooper*, nosey-parker*. (**b**) banterer, tease; mocker.

fisgonear* [1a] *vt* to be always prying into, spy continually on.

fisgoneo* *nm* constant prying; chronic nosiness.

física[1] *nf* physics; **~ de alta(s) energía(s)** high-energy physics; **~ cuántica** quantum physics; **~ del estado sólido** solid-state physics; **~ nuclear** nuclear physics; **~ de partículas** particle physics.

físicamente *adv* physically.

físico 1 *adj* (**a**) physical.

(**b**) (*Carib, Méx*) (*melindroso*) finicky; (*afectado*) affected.

2 *nm*, **física**[2] *nf* physicist; (*Med*: ††) physician; **~ nuclear** nuclear physicist.

3 *nm* (*Anat*) physique; (*aspecto*) appearance, looks; **de ~ regular** ordinary-looking.

físil *adj* fissile.

fisiología *nf* physiology.

fisiológico *adj* physiological.

fisiólogo *nm*, **fisióloga** *nf* physiologist.

fisión *nf* fission; **~ nuclear** nuclear fission.

fisionable *adj* fissionable.

fisionarse [1a] *vr* to undergo fission, split.

fisioterapeuta *nmf* physiotherapist.

fisioterapia *nf* physiotherapy.

fisioterapista *nmf* physiotherapist.

fiso‡ *nm* (*LAm*: *cara*) mug‡, dial‡.

fisonomía *nf* (**a**) (*cara*) physiognomy, face; features. (**b**) **la ~ de la ciudad** the appearance of the city.

fisonomista *nmf*: **ser buen ~** to have a good memory for faces.

fístula *nf* fistule.

fisura *nf* fissure; crack; (*Med*) fissure, hairline fracture.

fitobiología *nf* phytobiology, plant breeding.

fitocultura *nf* plant breeding.

fitófago 1 *adj* plant-eating. **2** *nm*, **fitófaga** *nf* plant-eater.

fitopatología *nf* phytopathology, plant pathology.

FIV *nf abr de* **fecundación in vitro** in vitro fertilization, IVF.

flac(c)idez *nf* flaccidity; softness, flabbiness.

flác(c)ido *adj* flaccid; soft, flabby.

flaco 1 *adj* (**a**) (*Anat*) thin, skinny, lean; (*And*) slim; **ponerse ~** to get thin. (**b**) (*fig*) weak, feeble; *memoria* bad, short; *lado, punto* weak; *año* lean; (*LAm*) *tierra* barren. **2** *nm* weakness, weak spot, failing. **3** *nf*: **la F~** (*Méx*) Death; **acompañar a la ~** to pass away.

flacón *adj* (*Carib, Cono Sur*) very thin.

flacuchento *adj* (*LAm*) very thin.

flacura *nf* (**a**) (*delgadez*) thinness, skinniness. (**b**) (*debilidad*) weakness, feebleness.

flagelación *nf* flagellation, whipping.

flagelar [1a] *vt* (**a**) (*azotar*) to flagellate, whip, scourge. (**b**) (*fig*) to flay, criticize severely.

flagelo *nm* (**a**) (*azote*) whip, scourge. (**b**) (*fig*) scourge, calamity.

flagrante *adj* flagrant; **en ~** in the act, red-handed.

flamante *adj* (**a**) (*lit*) brilliant, flaming. (**b**) (*fig*: *nuevo*) brand-new; (*lujoso*) luxurious, high-class; (*estupendo*) superb.

flam(b)eado *adj* flambé.

flamear [1a] **1** *vi* (**a**) to flame, blaze (up). (**b**) (*Náut*: *vela*) to flap; (*bandera*) to flutter. **2** *vt* (*Culin*) to flambé.

flamenco[1] *nm* (*Orn*) flamingo.

flamenco[2] **1** *adj* (**a**) (*Geog*) Flemish.

(**b**) (*Mús etc*) Andalusian gipsy (*atr*); **cante ~** flamenco (*Andalusian gipsy singing*).

(**c**) (*pey*) flashy, vulgar, gaudy.

(**d**) **ponerse ~*** (*engreído*) to get cocky*; (*satisfecho*) to get on one's high horse; (*chulo*) to become obstreperous, turn nasty.

(**e**) (*CAm, Carib, Méx*) = **flaco**.

2 *nm*, **flamenca** *nf* Fleming; **los ~s** the Flemings, the Flemish.

3 *nm* (**a**) flamenco (*Andalusian gipsy singing and dancing*).

(**b**) (*Ling*) Flemish.

flamencología *nf* study of flamenco music and dance.

flamencólogo, -a *nm/f* student of flamenco music and dance.

flamenquilla *nf* marigold.

flamígero *adj*: **estilo gótico ~** flamboyant Gothic style.

flámula *nf* streamer.

flan *nm* caramel cream; **estar hecho** (*o* **estar como**) **un ~** to shake like a jelly.

flanco *nm* (**a**) (*Anat*) side, flank. (**b**) (*Mil*) flank; **coger a uno por el ~** to catch sb off guard.

Flandes *nm* Flanders.

flanear* [1a] *vi* to stroll, saunter.

flanecito *nm* dumpling.

flanín *nm* caramel cream.

flanquear [1a] *vt* (**a**) (*gen*) to flank. (**b**) (*Mil*) to outflank.

flaquear [1a] *vi* to weaken, grow weak; (*esfuerzo*) to slacken, flag; (*madera etc*) to give way; (*salud*) to decline, get worse; (*moralmente*) to lose heart, become dispirited.

flaquencia *nf* (*LAm*) = **flacura**.

flaqueza *nf* (**a**) (*cualidad*) thinness, leanness; weakness; feebleness, frailty; **la ~ de su memoria** his poor memory; **la ~ humana** human frailty.

(**b**) (*una ~*) failing, weakness; **las ~s de la carne** the frailties to which the flesh is heir.

flash [flas] *nm, pl* **flashes** *o* **flashs** [flas] (**a**) (*noticia*) newsflash. (**b**) (*Fot*) flash, flashlight; **con ~** by flashlight. (**c**) (*) surprise, strong impression, shattering experience; **¡qué ~!** how awful (for you)!

flato *nm* (**a**) (*Med*) flatulence, wind; stitch. (**b**) (*LAm*: *depresión*) gloom, depression; (*And, Carib, CAm*: *temor*) fear, apprehension.

flatoso *adj* (**a**) (*Med*) flatulent, windy. (**b**) (*Carib*: *deprimido*) gloomy, depressed; (*CAm, Carib*: *aprensivo*) apprehensive.

flatulencia *nf* flatulence.

flatulento *adj* flatulent.
flatuoso *adj* flatulent, windy.
flauta 1 *nf* (a) (*instrumento*) flute; ~ **dulce** recorder; **estar hecho una** ~ to be as thin as a rake; **por fortuna sonó la** ~* it was a lucky coincidence.
(b) (*LAm*) **de la gran** ~* terrific*, tremendous*; **hijo de la gran** ~‡ son of a bitch‡, bastard‡.
2 *nmf* (*persona*) flautist, flute player.
3 (*) *interj* (*And, Cono Sur*) ¡~ **la** ~! gosh!*; **¡la gran** ~! my God!; **¡por la** ~! (*Cono Sur*) oh dear!
flautín 1 *nm* (*instrumento*) piccolo. **2** *nmf* (*persona*) piccolo player.
flautista *nmf* flautist, flute player; **el** ~ **de Hamelin** the Pied Piper of Hamelin.
flavina *nf* flavin.
flebitis *nf* phlebitis.
fleco *nm* (*pelo*) fringe, fringe curls; (*Cos*) tassel; ~(**s**) frayed edge (of cloth); ~**s** (*fig*) loose ends.
flecha 1 *nf* (a) arrow; dart; (*And*) sling; (*Méx Aut*) axle; (*de billar*) cue rest; ~ **de mar** squid; ~ **de dirección** (*Aut*) trafficator; **como una** ~ like an arrow, like a shot; **con alas en** ~ swept-wing, with swept-back wings; **subida en** ~ sharp rise; **subir en** ~ to rise sharply.
(b) (*Cono Sur**: *coqueta*) flirt.
2 *nm* (*: *Hist*) member of the Falangist youth movement.
flechar [1a] *vt* (a) *arco* to draw, stretch.
(b) (*herir etc*) to wound (*o* kill) with an arrow, shoot (with an arrow).
(c) (*) *mujer* to make a hit with, sweep off her feet.
(d) (*Cono Sur*: *picar*) to prick (*esp* with a goad); (*sol*) to burn, scorch.
flechazo *nm* (a) (*acto*) arrow shot, bowshot; (*herida*) arrow wound; (*And*) slingshot.
(b) (*: *amor*) love at first sight; **con nosotros fue el** ~ with us it was love at first sight.
(c) (*: *revelación*) sudden illumination, revelation; **aquello fue el** ~ then it hit me, that was the moment of illumination.
flechero *nm* archer, bowman; arrow maker.
fleje *nm* iron hoop, metal band.
flema *nf* (a) (*Med*) phlegm. (b) (*fig*) imperturbability; impassiveness; sangfroid.
flemático *adj* phlegmatic, matter-of-fact, unruffled.
flemón *nm* gumboil.
flemudo *adj* slow, sluggish.
flequetería *nf* (*And*) cheating, swindling.
flequetero *adj* (*And*) tricky, dishonest.
flequillo *nm* fringe.
Flesinga *nm* Flushing.
fleta *nf* (*And, Carib*) (a) (*fricción*) rub, rubbing. (b) (*paliza*) thrashing.
fletado* *adj* (a) (*CAm*) sharp, clever. (b) (*Carib, Méx**) **salir** ~* to be off like a shot.
fletador 1 *adj* shipping (*atr*), freighting (*atr*). **2** *nm* shipper, freighter.
fletamento *nm*, **fletamiento** *nm* (*Méx*) charter, chartering; **contrato de** ~ chartering agreement.
fletar [1a] **1** *vt* (a) *avión, barco* to charter; to load, freight.
(b) (*LAm*) *vehículo etc* to hire.
(c) (*And, Cono Sur*) *insultos* to let fly, utter; *golpe* to deal.
(d) (*Cono Sur**) (*despedir*) to fire*, sack*; (*expulsar*) to chuck out, remove by force.
2 fletarse *vr* (a) (*) (*And, Carib, Méx*: *largarse*) to get out, beat it*; to slip away, get away unseen; (*Cono Sur*: *colarse*) to gatecrash.
(b) (*CAm**: *enojarse*) to be annoyed, get cross.
(c) (*Cono Sur*) **'se fleta'** (*letrero*) 'to let'.
flete *nm* (a) (*alquiler*) charter; **vuelo** ~ charter flight.
(b) (*carga*) freight, cargo; **salir sin** ~**s** (*And, Carib*) to leave in a hurry, be off like a shot.
(c) (*gastos*) freightage; (*LAm*: *de transporte*) transport charges, carriage; (*LAm*: *gen*) hire, hire charge, hiring fee; ~ **por cobrar** freight forward; ~ **pagado** advance freight.
(d) (*And, Cono Sur*) (*caballo*) fast horse; (*de carreras*) racehorse; (*Cono Sur*: *rocín*) old nag.
(e) (*And*: *amante*) lover, companion.
(f) (‡: *prostitución*) prostitution, the game*.
(g) **echarse un** ~ ** to have a screw**.
fletera *nf* (*Carib*) prostitute.
fletero 1 *adj* (a) (*LAm*: *chárter*) charter (*atr*); freight (*atr*); **avión** ~ charter plane.
(b) (*LAm*: *de alquiler*) hired, for hire; **camión** ~ lorry for hire.
2 *nm* (a) (*LAm*) (*transportista*) owner of vehicles for hire; owner of a transport business; (*recaudador*) collector of transport charges.
(b) (*And, Guat*: *mozo*) porter.
flexibilidad *nf* flexibility; suppleness, pliability; compliant nature; ~ **laboral,** ~ **de plantillas** (*euf*) ability to redeploy the workforce, freedom to hire and fire.
flexibilizar [1f] *vt* to make (more) flexible; to adjust, adapt; *plantilla* to redeploy.
flexible 1 *adj* flexible; soft, supple, pliable; *sombrero* soft; *persona* open-minded, open to argument; (*pey*) compliant.
2 *nm* (a) (*sombrero*) soft hat. (b) (*Elec*) flex, cord, wire.
flexión *nf* (a) (*gen*) flexion; (*ejercicio*) press-up. (b) (*Ling*) inflexion.
flexional *adj* flexional, inflected.
flexionar [1a] *vt* to bend; *músculo* to flex.
flexo *nm* adjustable table-lamp.
flipado‡, -a *nm/f* drop-out.
flipante‡ *adj* (a) cool‡; great*, smashing*. (b) (*pasmoso*) amazing.
flipar‡ [1a] **1** *vt* (a) (*gustar*) to turn on*, send*; **esto me flipa** this really sends me, I just adore this.
(b) (*pasmar*) to amaze, knock sideways.
2 *vi* (a) (*desmadrarse*) to freak out‡; (*volverse loco*) to go round the twist*; (*drogarse, emborracharse*) to get stoned‡.
(b) (*pasarlo bien*) to have a great time*; ~ **con algo** (*disfrutar*) to enjoy sth, rave about sth*; (*pasmarse*) to be amazed at sth; ~ **por algo** to be mad keen on (*o* to get *etc*) sth; to be dying for sth.
(c) (*ser atractivo*) to be very attractive, be really gorgeous.
3 fliparse *vr* to get excited, get carried away (*con, por* by); *V t* **2**.
flipe‡ *nm* (a) (*experiencia*) amazing experience, startling revelation.
(b) (*droga*) high‡; trip‡.
flipper ['fliper] *nm* pinball machine; **jugar a** ~ to play pinball.
flirt*, *pl* **flirts** [flir] *nm* (a) (*persona*) sweetheart; boyfriend, girlfriend; **la estrella vino con su** ~ **del momento** the star came with her current boyfriend.
(b) (*amorío*) flirtation, (light-hearted) affair; **A tuvo un** ~ **con B** A had a brief affair with B.
flirteador(a) *nm/f* flirt.
flirtear* [1a] *vi* to flirt (*con* with), have a light-hearted affair (*con* with).
flirteo* *nm* (a) (*gen*) flirting. (b) (*un* ~) flirtation, (light-hearted) affair.
flojamente *adv* (a) (*sueltamente*) loosely, slackly; limply.
(b) (*débilmente*) weakly, feebly; (*ligeramente*) lightly.
flojear [1a] *vi* to weaken; to slacken, ease up.
flojedad *nf* (*V adj*) (a) looseness, slackness; limpness.
(b) weakness, feebleness; lightness.
(c) limpness, flaccidity.
(d) poor quality.
(e) slackness, laxity, negligence.
flojel *nm* (*de tela*) nap; (*Orn*) down.
flojera *nf* (a) (*) = **flojedad.** (b) (*LAm*: *pereza*) laziness; **me da** ~ (**hacerlo**) I can't be bothered (doing it).
flojito *adj* (*gen*) = **flojo;** *viento* very light, slack.
flojo *adj* (a) *cuerda etc* loose, slack; limp; *tuerca etc* loose; **me la trae floja‡** it leaves me stone-cold; **la tengo floja‡** I'm not bothered; **a mí me la trae floja la política** I don't give a damn about politics.
(b) *esfuerzo* weak, feeble; *viento* light.
(c) *carne etc* soft, limp, flaccid.
(d) *té, vino etc* weak; *obra literaria etc* poor, thin, weak, feeble.
(e) *estudiante etc* poor, weak; *actitud* slack, lax.
(f) *precio* low, weak; *mercado* slack, dull.
(g) (*LAm*) (*vago*) lazy; (*tímido*) timid, cowardly.
floppy ['flopi] *nm, pl* **floppys** floppy disk.
flor 1 *nf* (a) (*Bot*) flower, blossom, bloom; ~ **de mano** artificial flower; ~ **de nieve** snowdrop; ~ **de** (**la**) **Pascua** poinsettia; ~ **del sol** sunflower; ~ **somnífera** (*LAm*) opium poppy; **en** ~ in flower, in bloom; **en plena** ~ in full bloom; **hijos como una** ~ lovely children; **de** ~ (*Carib*) very good, splendid; **no es** ~ **de un día** this is no mere flash in the pan; **ser una** ~ **de estufa** to be very delicate; **¡ni ~es!*** no way!*
(b) (*de ciruela etc*) bloom.

(**c**) (*de cuero*) grain.

(**d**) (*fig*) flower, best part, cream; ~ **de azúcar** icing-sugar; ~ **de harina** finest flour; **la ~ y nata de la sociedad** the cream of society, the pick of society; **es la ~ de la canela** it's the very best; **en la ~ de la edad** in the flower of one's youth; **en la ~ de la vida** in the prime of life.

(**e**) (*Téc*) surface; **a ~ de** level with, on a level with; flush with; on the surface of; **a ~ del agua** at water level, close to the surface of the water; (*barca*) awash; **a ~ de cuño** in mint condition; **tiene el humorismo a ~ de piel** his humour is always ready to break out, his wit is never far below the surface; **los odios salen a ~ de piel** hatred comes out into the open, hatred comes to the surface; **ajustado a ~** flush.

(**f**) (*piropo*) compliment, nice thing (to say); **decir** (*o* **echar**) **~es a una** to pay pretty compliments to a girl, flirt with a girl.

(**g**) **~es** (*Cono Sur*) popcorn.

(**h**) (*LAm*) *p.ej.* ~ **de caballo** splendid horse, great horse; ~ **de alegre** very cheerful.

2 *adj* (*LAm*) splendid, excellent.

flora *nf* flora.

floración *nf* flowering; bloom.

floral *adj* floral.

florar [1a] *vi* to flower, bloom.

florcita *nf* (*LAm*) little flower.

floreado *adj* (**a**) *tela* flowery, flowered. (**b**) *pan* of the finest flour, top-quality. (**c**) (*Mús*) elaborate, with flourishes.

florear [1a] **1** *vt* (**a**) *tela etc* to adorn with flowers, add a flowery design to.

(**b**) *harina* to sift.

(**c**) *naipes* to stack.

(**d**) (*fig*: *adular*) to flatter.

2 *vi* (**a**) (*LAm Bot*) to flower, bloom.

(**b**) (*Mús*) to play a flourish, play elaborate variations; (*Esgrima*) to flourish.

(**c**) (*piropear*) to indulge in flowery compliments, flatter.

3 florearse *vr* (*LAm*) to show off; to perform brilliantly.

florecer [2d] *vi* (**a**) (*Bot*) to flower, bloom. (**b**) (*fig*) to flourish, thrive; to flower.

floreciente *adj* (**a**) (*Bot*) in flower, flowering, blooming. (**b**) (*fig*) flourishing, thriving.

florecimiento *nm* (**a**) (*Bot*) flowering, blooming. (**b**) (*fig*) flourishing, thriving; flowering.

Florencia *nf* Florence.

florentino 1 *adj* Florentine, of Florence. **2** *nm*, **florentina** *nf* Florentine.

floreo *nm* (**a**) (*Esgrima, Mús*) flourish. (**b**) (*gracia*) witty but insubstantial talk; (*cumplido*) compliment, nicely-turned phrase; **andarse con ~s** to beat about the bush.

florería *nf* (*LAm*) florist's (shop).

florero 1 *nm*, **florera** *nf* florist; (street) flower-seller. **2** *nm* (**a**) (*recipiente*) vase; (*fig*) ornament. (**b**) (*Arte*) flower painting. (**c**) (*persona*) flatterer; specialist in elegant compliments.

florescencia *nf* florescence.

floresta *nf* (**a**) (*bosque*) wood, grove; (*claro*) glade; (*lugar atractivo*) beauty spot; (*escena rural*) charming rural scene; (*And*: *bosque*) forest, jungle. (**b**) (*Liter*) anthology.

florete *nm* (*Esgrima*) foil.

floretear [1a] *vt* to decorate with flowers.

floretista *nmf* (*LAm*) fencer.

florícola *adj*: **el sector** ~ the flower-growing sector.

floricultor(a) *nm/f* flower-grower.

floricultura *nf* flower-growing.

florido *adj* (**a**) *campo etc* flowery, full of flowers; *árbol etc* in bloom, in flower. (**b**) (*fig*) choice, select. (**c**) *estilo* flowery, florid.

florilegio *nm* anthology.

florín *nm* florin; (*holandés*) guilder.

florión *nm*, **floriona** *nf* (*And*) = **fanfarrón**.

floripón *nm* (*LAm*), **floripondio** *nm* (*LAm*) (**a**) (*Cos etc*) big flower. (**b**) (*Liter*) rhetorical flourish, extravagant figure. (**c**) (‡) effeminate person, pansy‡. (**d**) (*And Bot*) lily of the valley.

florista *nmf* florist.

floristería *nf* florist's (shop).

florístico *adj* botanical; floral.

florón *nm* (**a**) (*Bot*) big flower. (**b**) (*Arquit*) fleuron, rosette. (**c**) (*Tip*) fleuron.

flota *nf* (**a**) (*Náut*) fleet; shipping; ~ **de altura** deep-sea fishing fleet; ~ **de bajura** inshore fishing fleet; ~ **mercante** merchant marine; **la ~ española** the Spanish fleet.

(**b**) (*Aer, Aut*) fleet.

(**c**) (*And etc*: *autobús*) long-distance bus, inter-city bus.

(**d**) (*LAm*: *muchedumbre*) lot, crowd, heap; **una ~ de** a lot of, a crowd of.

(**e**) (*And, CAm*: *jactancia*) boasting, bluster; **echar ~s** (*And, CAm, Carib*) to brag.

flotación *nf* floating, flotation; *V* **línea**.

flotador *nm* (*gen*) float; (*de cisterna*) ballcock; (*de niño*) rubber ring, float.

flotante 1 *adj* (*gen*) floating; *pieza* loose, hanging loose; **de coma ~** (*Inform*) floating point. **2** *nm* (*And*) braggart.

flotar [1a] *vi* (**a**) (*gen*) to float. (**b**) (*pieza etc*) to hang, hang loose; (*bandera etc*) to flutter; ~ **en el aire** to float in the air; to hover; (*pelo etc*) ~ **al viento** to stream in the wind. (**c**) (*Fin*) to float.

flote *nm*: **estar a ~** to be afloat; **poner a ~** to float, set afloat; (*t* **sacar a ~**) to refloat, raise; (*fig*: *revelar*) to bring into the open; (*fig*: *Econ etc*) to make viable, restore to profitability; **ponerse a ~** (*fig*) to get back on one's feet, get out of a jam; **sostenerse a ~** to keep afloat.

flotilla *nf* flotilla, fleet of small ships; line of vessels being towed, string of barges; (*de taxis, camiones etc*) fleet.

flou [flo] *nm* soft focus (effect).

flox [flos] *nm* phlox.

fluctuación *nf* (**a**) (*gen*) fluctuation; **las fluctuaciones de la moda** the fluctuations of fashion, the ups and downs of fashion. (**b**) (*indecisión*) uncertainty, hesitation.

fluctuante *adj* fluctuating; *población* floating.

fluctuar [1e] *vi* (**a**) (*gen*) to fluctuate. (**b**) (*vacilar*) to waver, hesitate.

fluente *adj* fluid, flowing.

fluidez *nf* (**a**) (*gen*) fluidity. (**b**) (*fig*) fluency, smoothness.

fluido, flúido 1 *adj* (**a**) (*Téc*) fluid; **la circulación es bastante fluida** traffic is moving quite freely. (**b**) (*fig*) *lenguaje* fluent; *estilo* smooth, free-flowing. **2** *nm* (**a**) (*líquido*) fluid; **~s del cuerpo** body fluids. (**b**) (*Elec*) current, power; **cortar el ~** to cut off the electricity.

fluir [3g] *vi* to flow, run.

flujo *nm* (**a**) (*gen*) flow; stream; flux; (*Náut*) flow, rising tide, incoming tide; (*de votantes*) swing; ~ **de caja, ~ de fondos** cash-flow; ~ **de consciencia** stream of consciousness; ~ **y reflujo** ebb and flood, (*fig*) ebb and flow.

(**b**) (*Med*) ~ **de sangre** flow of blood, loss of blood, haemorrhage; ~ **de vientre** diarrhoea.

flujograma *nm* flow chart.

fluminense (*LAm*) **1** *adj* of Río de Janeiro. **2** *nmf* native (*o* inhabitant) of Río de Janeiro; **los ~s** the people of Río de Janeiro.

fluor *nm* fluoride.

fluoración *nf* fluoridation.

fluorescencia *nf* fluorescence.

fluorescente *adj* fluorescent.

fluorización *nf* fluoridation.

fluorizar [1f] *vt* to fluoridate.

fluoruro *nm* fluoride.

flus *nm* (*And, Carib*) suit of clothes.

flute *nf* champagne glass.

fluvial *adj* fluvial, river (*atr*); *pez* river (*atr*), freshwater (*atr*).

flux [flus] *nm invar* (**a**) (*Naipes*) flush; ~ **real** royal flush.

(**b**) (*CAm**: *suerte*) stroke of luck.

(**c**) (*And, Carib*: *traje*) suit of clothes.

(**d**) (*Méx**) **estar a ~, quedarse a ~** not to have a bean*; **hacer ~** to blow all one's money*.

FM *nf abr de* **Frecuencia Modulada** frequency modulation, FM.

FMI *nm abr de* **Fondo Monetario Internacional** International Monetary Fund, IMF.

FNAS *nm* (*Esp*) *abr de* **Fondo Nacional de Asistencia Social.**

FNMT *nf* (*Esp*) *abr de* **Fábrica Nacional de Moneda y Timbre.**

FNPT *nm* (*Esp*) *abr de* **Fondo Nacional de Protección del Trabajo.**

f.º, fol. *abr de* **folio** folio, fo., fol.

fobia *nf* phobia.

-fobia *suf* -phobia, *p.ej.* **agorafobia** *nf* agoraphobia.

fóbico *adj* phobic.

-fobo *suf* -phobe, *p.ej.* **francófobo, -a** *nm/f* francophobe.

foca *nf* (**a**) (*Zool*) seal; ~ **de trompa** sea elephant. (**b**) (*: *persona fea*) ugly lump*. (**c**) (*: *dormilón*) lie-abed, lazy individual.

focal *adj* focal.

focalizar [1f] *vt objeto* to focus on, get into focus; *atención etc* to focus.

foco *nm* (**a**) (*Mat, Med, Fís etc*) focus; (*centro*) focal point,

centre; (de calor, luz) source; (de incendio) seat; estar fuera de ~ to be out of focus.
(b) (Elec) floodlight; (Aut) headlight; (Teat etc: t ~ direccional) spotlight; (LAm: de lámpara etc) electric light bulb; (LAm: de calle) street light.
(c) (fig) centre, focal point.

focha nf coot.
foche* adj smelly, pongy‡.
fodolí adj meddlesome.
fodongo* adj (Méx) (sucio) filthy; (vago) lazy, bone-idle.
foete nm = fuete.
fofadal nm (Cono Sur) bog, quagmire.
fofera nf, fofez nf flabbiness.
fofo adj (a) (esponjoso) soft, spongy; porous; fluffy; carnes flabby. (b) (*: rechoncho) fat, plump.
fofoscientos* adj umpteen; fofoscientas mil pesetas umpteen thousand pesetas.
fogaje nm (a) (LAm) (calor) scorching heat; (bochorno) sultry weather. (b) (Carib, Méx) (sarpullido) heat rash; (rubor) blush; (fig) fluster. (c) (And: fuego) fire, blaze.
fogarada nf, fogarata nf (Cono Sur), fogata nf blaze, bonfire.
fogón nm (a) (Culin) stove, kitchen range; (Ferro) firebox; (Náut) galley. (b) (de cañón, máquina) vent. (c) (CAm, Cono Sur) (fuego) fire, bonfire; (hogar) hearth.
fogonazo nm (a) (estallido) flash, explosion. (b) (Méx: carajillo) coffee with spirits added.
fogonero nm (a) (Náut) stoker. (b) (Ferro) fireman, stoker. (c) (And: chófer) chauffeur.
fogosidad nf spirit, mettle; fire, dash, verve; fieriness, friskiness.
fogoso adj spirited, mettlesome; fiery, ardent; caballo fiery, frisky.
fogueado adj (a) (LAm: perito) expert, experienced. (b) (And: cansado) weary.
foguear [1a] (LAm) 1 vt to fire on. 2 foguearse vr to have one's baptism of fire; to gain experience, become hardened.
fogueo nm: bala de ~ blank cartridge.
foguerear [1a] vt (Carib, Cono Sur) maleza to burn off; fogata to set light to.
foguista nm (Cono Sur) = fogonero.
foja¹ nm coot.
foja² nf (LAm) = hoja; ~ de servicios record.
foil nm (Méx Culin) foil.
fol. abr de folio folio, fol.
folclore etc = folklore.
folgo nm foot muff.
foliación nf (a) (Bot) foliation. (b) (Tip) foliation, page numbering.
foliar [1b] vt to foliate, number the pages of; páginas sin ~ unnumbered pages.
folio nm (a) (gen) folio; (hoja) leaf, sheet; (Tip) running title, page heading; al primer ~ (fig) from the very start, at a glance; en ~ in folio; libro en ~ folio (book). (b) (tamaño de papel) A4-size (paper); doble ~ A3-size (paper). (c) (And) (dádiva) tip; (de bautismo) money given as christening present.
folklore nm (a) folklore. (b) (*) row, shindy*; se armó un ~ there was a row.
folklórico 1 adj (a) folklore (atr); folk (atr), popular, traditional; es muy ~ it's very quaint, it's full of local colour; it is rich in historical interest. (b) (pey) frivolous, unserious; overblown; laughable. 2 nm, folklórica nf (a) (Mus) folk singer. (b) (pey) clown, figure of fun.
folklorista 1 adj folklore (atr). 2 nmf folklorist, specialist in folklore, student of folklore.
folklorizar [1f] 1 vt to give a popular (o folksy) character to. 2 folklorizarse vr to acquire popular (o folksy) features.
follá‡ nf: tener mala ~ to be thoroughly nasty.
follada** nf fuck**.
follado nm (And) petticoat.
follador** 1 adj fond of screwing**. 2 nm fornicator.
follaje¹ nm (a) (Bot) foliage, leaves; (Arte) leaf motif. (b) (fig) excessive ornamentation; bombast, verbiage, waffle*.
follaje²** nm fucking**, screwing**.
follar [1m] 1 vt (a) (Téc) to blow (on) with bellows. (b) (**) to fuck**. (c) (‡) to bother, annoy; to harm. 2 vi (**) to fuck**. 3 follarse vr (a) (**: echar un pedo) to fart silently**. (b) (**: joder) to fuck**; se la folló he screwed her**. (c) me lo voy a follar vivo‡ I'll have his guts for garters‡.
folletería nf leaflets.
folletín nm newspaper serial; (TV) soap-opera, TV serial.
folletinesco adj make-believe, romantic, improbable.
folletista nmf pamphleteer.
folleto nm pamphlet; folder, brochure, leaflet; ~ informativo information leaflet.
follín* nm (Cono Sur) bad-tempered individual.
follisca nf (And) (lío) confusion, shindy; (riña) brawl.
follón 1 adj (a) (perezoso) lazy, slack.
(b) (arrogante) arrogant, puffed-up; (fanfarrón) blustering.
(c) (cobarde) cowardly.
(d) (CAm) vestido roomy, loose.
2 nm (a) (Bot) sucker.
(b) (persona) good-for-nothing, layabout; conceited person.
(c) (cohete) noiseless rocket; (**) silent fart**.
(d) (*: jaleo) rumpus*, row, shindy*; (lío) mess, trouble; fuss; armar un ~ to make a row, kick up a fuss.
(e) (And: prenda) petticoat.
(f) (Carib: juerga de borrachera) drinking bout.
follonarse** [1a] vr (Cono Sur, Méx) to fart silently**.
follonero* 1 adj conducta outrageous; provoking; persona rowdy, trouble-making, boisterous; rebellious. 2 nm rowdy element, troublemaker; rebel.
fome* adj (Cono Sur) boring, dull.
fomentación nf (Med) fomentation, poultice.
fomentar [1a] vt (a) (Med) to foment; to warm.
(b) (fig) to promote, foster, encourage, foment; odio, rebelión to foment, stir up; producción etc to boost.
(c) (Carib) negocio to found, promote.
fomento nm (a) (Med) fomentation.
(b) (fig) promotion, fostering, encouragement, fomentation; Ministerio de F~ (Hist) ministry responsible for public works, buildings etc.
fonda nf (Hist) inn, tavern; (restaurante) small restaurant; (pensión) boarding-house; (Ferro) buffet; (Cono Sur) refreshment stall; (LAm pey) cheap restaurant.
fondeadero nm anchorage; berth.
fondeado adj (a) estar ~ (Náut) to be anchored, be at anchor. (b) (LAm*) estar ~ to be in the money, be well heeled*; quedar ~ (Cono Sur*) to be broke*.
fondear [1a] 1 vt (a) (Náut) profundidad to sound; barco (anclar) to anchor; (registrar) to search; (fig) to examine thoroughly.
(b) (Carib: violar) to rape.
(c) (CAm: financiar) to provide with money, finance.
(d) (Cono Sur) to throw into the sea.
2 vi to anchor, drop anchor.
3 fondearse vr (a) (LAm*: enriquecerse) to get rich; (ahorrar) to save for the future.
(b) (LAm*: emborracharse) to get drunk.
fondero, -a nm/f (LAm) innkeeper; restaurant owner.
fondillos nmpl (a) (del pantalón) seat (of trousers). (b) (LAm: Anat) seat, bottom.
fondilludo, -a* nm/f (LAm): es un ~ he's got a big backside.
fondista nmf (a) (de fonda) innkeeper; restaurant owner. (b) (Dep) long-distance runner.
fondo nm (a) (de caja, mar etc) bottom; (de sala etc) back, far end; (en medidas) depth; doble ~, ~ falso false bottom; ~ del mar bottom of the sea, sea bed, sea floor; a ~ (adj) thorough; (adv) thoroughly; una investigación a ~ a thorough investigation; conocer algo a ~ to know sth thoroughly; emplearse a ~ to do one's utmost, go all out; al ~ (de sala etc) at the back, at the rear; al ~ de at the bottom of; at the back of; de ~ (Dep) long-distance (atr), endurance (atr); corredor de medio ~ middle-distance runner; pruebas de medio ~ middle-distance events; cuestión de ~ basic question; el problema de ~ the fundamental problem, the underlying problem; de bajo ~ shallow; flat; en el ~ (fig) at bottom; basically; at heart; really; en el ~ del corazón deep down in one's heart; sin ~ bottomless; dar ~ to anchor; echar un buque al ~ to sink a ship; to scuttle a ship; irse al ~ to sink, founder, go to the bottom; llegar al ~ de un misterio to get to the bottom of a mystery; tener poco ~ (Med) to be short-winded, quickly get out of breath; tocar ~ to touch bottom (t fig).
(b) (Arte) background, ground; (Cos) ground; se ve una casa en el ~ there is a house in the background.
(c) bajos ~s sociales dregs of society, underworld.
(d) (Com, Fin) fund; ~s funds; money; finance; resources; ~ de amortización sinking fund; ~s bloqueados frozen assets; ~ de comercio goodwill; ~ de compensación

compensation fund; ~ **consolidado** consolidated fund; ~ **de empréstitos** loan fund; ~ **de huelga** strike fund; ~ **para imprevistos** contingency fund; ~ **mutualista** mutual fund; ~ **de previsión** provident fund; **cheque sin ~s** bad cheque; **estar sin ~s** to have no money, be broke*; **a ~ perdido** (*adv*) without security, (*adj*) unsecured, non-repayable; **subvención a ~ perdido** capital grant; **invertir a ~ perdido** to invest without hope of recovering one's money; **reunir ~s** to get money together, raise funds.

(**e**) (*fig: reservas*) fund, supply, reservoir; **tiene un ~ de alegría** he has a fund of cheerfulness; **tiene un ~ de energías** he has reserves of energy.

(**f**) (*fig: carácter*) nature, disposition; **de ~ jovial** of cheery disposition; **tener buen ~** to be good at heart.

(**g**) (*And: finca*) country estate.

(**h**) (*LAm: prenda*) petticoat; **medio ~** slip.

fondón* *adj* big-bottomed*, broad in the beam*; weighty, fat.

fondongo *nm* (*Carib Anat*) bottom.

fonducha *nf* (*And*) = **fonducho**.

fonducho *nm* cheap restaurant.

fonema *nm* phoneme.

fonémico *adj* phonemic.

fonética *nf* phonetics.

fonético *adj* phonetic.

fonetista *nmf* phonetician.

foniatra *nmf* speech therapist.

foniatría *nf* speech therapy.

fónico *adj* phonic.

fono *nm* (**a**) (*Cono Sur Telec*) (*auricular*) earpiece; (*número*) telephone number. (**b**) (*Ling*) phone.

fonocaptor *nm* (*de tocadiscos*) pick-up.

fonógrafo *nm* gramophone, phonograph (*US*).

fonología *nf* phonology.

fonológico *adj* phonological.

fonoteca *nf* record library, sound archive.

fonta* *nm* (*Pol*) = **fontanero**.

fontanal *nm*, **fontanar** *nm* spring.

fontanería *nf* (**a**) (*arte*) plumbing. (**b**) (*tienda*) plumber's shop.

fontanero *nm* plumber; (* *Pol*) back-room boy; investigator of leaks.

footing ['futin] *nm* jogging; **hacer ~** to jog, go jogging.

F.O.P. [fop] *nfpl* (*Esp*) *abr de* **Fuerzas del Orden Público** forces of law and order, security forces.

foque *nm* jib.

foquismo *nm* (*LAm Pol*) theory of guerrilla war advocated by Che Guevara.

foquillos *nmpl* fairy-lights.

forajido *nm* outlaw, bandit; desperado.

foral *adj* relative to the *fueros*, pertaining to the privileges of a town (*o* region); statutory.

foramen *nm* (*Méx*) hole.

foráneo *adj* foreign; (from) outside.

forasta* *nmf* = **forastero**.

forastero 1 *adj* alien, strange; (from) outside; exotic. **2** *nm*, **forastera** *nf* stranger; outsider; visitor; person from another part.

forcej(e)ar [1a] *vi* to struggle, wrestle; to make violent efforts; to flounder about.

forcej(e)o *nm* struggle; violent efforts; floundering.

forcejudo *adv* tough, strong, powerful.

fórceps *nm invar* forceps.

forcito *nm* (*LAm*) little Ford (*vehicle*).

forense 1 *adj* forensic, legal; *V* **médico**. **2** *nmf* pathologist.

forestación *nf* afforestation.

forestal *adj* forest (*atr*); woodland (*atr*), tree (*atr*); **cubierta ~** tree cover; *V* **repoblación** *etc*.

forestalista *nmf* owner of a woodland.

forestar [1a] *vt* (*LAm*) to afforest.

forfait [for'fe] *nm* (**a**) (*ausencia*) absence, non-appearance; (*retirada*) withdrawal, scratching; **declararse ~** to withdraw; **ganar por ~** to win by default; **hacer ~** to fail to show up.

(**b**) (*precio*) flat rate, fixed price; (*Esquí etc*) all-in charge.

fori‡ *nm* hankie*, handkerchief.

forito *nm* (*LAm*) = **fotingo**.

forja *nf* (**a**) (*fragua*) forge; (*fundición*) foundry. (**b**) (*acto*) forging.

forjado *adj hierro* wrought.

forjar [1a] *vt* (**a**) *hierro etc* to forge, shape, beat (into shape).

(**b**) (*formar*) to forge, shape, make; **~ un plan** to make a plan, hammer out a plan; **tratamos de ~ un estado moderno** we are trying to build a modern state.

(**c**) (*pey*) to invent, think up, concoct; to forge.

forma *nf* (**a**) (*gen*) form, shape; **de ~ triangular** of triangular shape, triangular in shape; **en ~ de U** U-shaped, shaped like a U.

(**b**) (*Téc*) mould; block, pattern; (*de sombrero*) hatter's block; (*de zapatero*) last.

(**c**) (*Dep etc*) form; (*Med*) fitness; **estar en ~** to be in (good) form; to be fit; (*) to be in the mood (for sex); **estar en baja ~** to be off form; to be going through a bad spell; **estar en plena ~** to be on top form, be on the top of one's form; **mantenerse en ~** to keep fit; **ponerse en ~** to get fit.

(**d**) (*modo*) way, means, method; **la única ~ de hacerlo es** ... the only way to do it is ...; **no hubo ~ de convencerle** there was no means of persuading him, it was impossible to persuade him; **~ de pago** (*Com*) manner of payment, method of payment; **~ de ser** character, temperament; **de esta ~** in this way; **de (tal) ~ que ...** so that ...; in such a way that ...; so much so that ...; **de todas ~s** at any rate, in any case, anyway; **en debida ~** duly, in due form; **ver la ~ de** + *infin* to see one's way to + *infin o ger*.

(**e**) **~s** social forms, conventions; **buenas ~s** good manners; **por la(s) ~(s)** for form's sake, as a matter of form; **cubrir las ~s, guardar las ~s** to keep up appearances.

(**f**) (*fórmula*) formula; **es pura ~** it's just for form's sake, it's a mere formality.

(**g**) (*Tip*) forme, form (*US*).

formación *nf* (**a**) (*gen*) formation. (**b**) (*Geol*) formation. (**c**) (*educación*) training, education; **~ laboral, ~ ocupacional** occupational training; **~ profesional** vocational training; **~ sexual** sex education; **sin la debida ~ en la investigación** without the proper research training.

formado *adj* formed; grown; **bien ~** nicely-shaped, well-formed; **hombre (ya) ~** grown man.

formal *adj* (**a**) (*rel a la forma*) formal.

(**b**) (*serio*) serious; official; *declaración, promesa etc* formal, express, definite; *aire* serious, earnest, inspiring confidence; *persona* (*de fiar*) reliable, dependable; businesslike; steady, stable; (*grave*) dignified; (*puntual*) punctual; (*en edad*) adult, grown-up; *niño* well-behaved; **es una persona muy ~** he is a perfectly reliable sort; **¿has sido ~?** (*a niño*) did you behave yourself?; **¡estáte ~!** behave yourself!; **siempre estuvo muy ~ conmigo** he was always very correct towards me, he always treated me very properly.

(**c**) (*And: afable*) affable, pleasant.

(**d**) *vestido etc* formal.

formaldehido *nm* formaldehyde.

formaleta *nf* (*And, CAm, Méx*) bird trap.

formalidad *nf* (**a**) (*requisito*) form, formality; established practice; **son las ~es de costumbre** these are the usual formalities; **es pura ~** it's a pure formality, it's just a matter of form; **hay muchas ~es** there are a lot of formalities, there's a lot of red tape.

(**b**) (*seriedad*) seriousness; formal nature, express character; earnestness; reliability, dependable nature; steadiness, stability; (*de niño*) good behaviour; **hablar con ~** to speak in earnest; **¡niños, ~!** kids, behave yourselves!*; **¡señores, un poco de ~!** gentlemen, let's be serious!

formalina *nf* formalin(e).

formalismo *nm* (**a**) (*Liter*) formalism. (**b**) (*pey*) conventionalism; (*burocrático etc*) red tape, useless formalities.

formalista 1 *adj* (**a**) (*Liter*) formalist. (**b**) (*pey*) conventional, rigid. **2** *nmf* (**a**) (*Liter*) formalist. (**b**) (*pey*) stickler for the regulations.

formalito* *adj* prim and proper.

formalizar [1f] **1** *vt* to formalize; to formulate, draw up; to put in order, give proper form to, regularize; **~ el noviazgo, ~ sus relaciones** to become formally engaged.

2 formalizarse *vr* (**a**) (*relación*) to acquire a proper form, get on to a proper footing; (*situación*) to be regularized.

(**b**) (*ponerse serio*) to grow serious.

(**c**) (*ofenderse*) to take offence.

formalote* *adj* stiff, serious.

formar [1a] **1** *vt* (**a**) (*gen*) to form, shape, fashion, make; *plan etc* to make, lay; *existenciar, reserva* to build up.

(**b**) (*integrar*) to form, make up, constitute; **está formado por** it is formed by, it is made up of.

(**c**) (*educar*) to train, educate.

(**d**) (*Mil*) to form up, parade.

2 *vi* (*Mil*) to form up, fall in; (*Dep*) to line up; **¡a ~!** (*Mil*) fall in!; **los equipos formaron así:** ... the line-up of the teams was: ...

3 formarse *vr* (**a**) (*gen*) to form; to take form, begin to form; (*desarrollarse*) to shape, develop.

(**b**) (*educarse*) to be trained, be educated; **se formó en la escuela de Praga** he was trained in the Prague school.

(**c**) (*Mil*) to form up, fall in, get into line; (*Dep*) to line up; **¡fórmense!** fall in line!; **el equipo se formó sin González** the team lined up without Gonzalez; the team left out Gonzalez at the start.

(**d**) **~ una opinión** to form an opinion; **¿qué impresión se ha formado?** what impression have you formed?

formateado *nm* formatting.

formatear [1a] *vt* to format.

formateo *nm* formatting.

formativo *adj* formative.

formato *nm* (*Inform, Tip*) format; (*tamaño de papel*) size; **papel (de) ~ holandesa** (*aprox*) foolscap; **periódico de ~ reducido** tabloid newspaper; **~ fijo** fixed format; **~ libre** free format; **~ de registro** record format; **¿de qué ~ lo quiere?** what size do you want?

formica *nf* Formica ®.

fórmico *adj*: **ácido ~** formic acid.

formidable *adj* (**a**) (*terrible*) formidable, redoubtable; (*enorme*) huge; forbidding. (**b**) (*: *estupendo*) terrific*, tremendous*; **¡~!** that's great!*, splendid!

formón *nm* chisel.

Formosa *nf*: **(la Isla de) ~** (*Hist*) Formosa.

fórmula *nf* (*Quím, Mat, fig*) formula; (*Med etc*) prescription; **~ mágica** magic formula; **una ~ para conseguir el éxito** a formula to ensure success; **por pura ~** just for form's sake, purely as a matter of form.

formulación *nf* formulation; **~ de datos** data capture.

formulaico *adj* formulaic.

formular [1a] *vt* to formulate; to draw up, make out; *pregunta* to frame, pose; *protesta* to make, lodge; *reivindicación* to file, put in.

formulario 1 *adj* routine, ritual; formulaic. **2** *nm* (**a**) (*fórmulas*) (*t Farm*) formulary, collection of formulae. (**b**) (*hoja*) form, blank; **~ de inscripción, ~ de solicitud** application form; registration form; **~ de pedido** order blank, order form; **llenar un ~** to fill in a form.

formulismo *nm* red tape; useless formalities.

fornicación *nf* fornication.

fornicador, fornicario 1 *adj* fornicating. **2** *nm* fornicator; adulterer.

fornicar [1g] *vi* to fornicate.

fornicio *nm* fornication.

fornido *adj* well-built, strapping, hefty.

fornitura *nf* (*CAm, Carib*) furniture.

foro *nm* (**a**) (*reunión*) forum, (open) meeting; (*Hist*) forum. (**b**) (*Jur*) court of justice; (*fig*) bar, legal profession; **el F~** (*Esp*) Madrid. (**c**) (*Teat*) back of the stage, upstage area.

forofada* *nf* fans, supporters (*collectively*).

forofismo *nm* (volume of) support.

forofo, -a* *nm/f* fan, supporter.

FORPPA *nm abr de* **Fondo de Ordenación y Regulación de Precios y Productos Agrarios.**

forrado *adj* (**a**) (*Cos etc*) lined; **~ de nilón** lined with nylon; **un libro ~ de pergamino** a book bound in parchment; **un coche ~ de ...** a car upholstered in ...

(**b**) (*: *rico*) well heeled*, moneyed.

forraje *nm* (**a**) (*pienso*) forage, fodder. (**b**) (*acto*) foraging. (**c**) (*: *mezcolanza*) hotchpotch, mixture.

forrajear [1a] *vi* to forage.

forrapelotas‡ *nmf invar* (**a**) (*caradura*) rotter*, berk‡. (**b**) (*tonto*) idiot.

forrar [1a] **1** *vt* (*Cos etc*) to line (*de* with); to pad; *libro* to cover (*de* with); *coche* to upholster; (*Téc*) to line, face, cover; *cisterna, tubo* to lag.

2 forrarse *vr* (**a**) (*: *enriquecerse*) to line one's pockets; to make one's pile*.

(**b**) (*: *de comida*) to stuff o.s. (*de* with)*.

(**c**) (*CAm, Méx*: *proveerse*) to stock up (*de* with).

forro *nm* (**a**) (*Cos*) lining; padding; (*Tip*) cover, dust-cover, jacket; (*Náut*) sheathing; (*Téc*) lining; facing, sheathing; (*Aut*) upholstery; (*Cono Sur Aut*) tyre; **con ~ de piel** with a fur lining, fur-lined; **~ de freno** brake lining; **ni por el ~** not in the slightest; **limpiar el ~ a uno** (*LAm‡*) to bump sb off‡.

(**b**) (*Cono Sur**: *preservativo*) rubber‡, sheath.

(**c**) (*Carib*: *timo*) swindle, fraud.

(**d**) (*Cono Sur*: *talento*) aptitude.

forsitia *nf* forsythia.

fortacho *nm* (*Cono Sur*) strongly-built car, good car; (*pey*) old car, old crock.

fortachón* *adj* strong, tough.

fortalecer [2d] **1** *vt* (**a**) (*gen*) to strengthen; (*Mil*) to fortify.

(**b**) (*moralmente*) to encourage; *moral* to stiffen; **~ a uno en una opinión** to encourage sb in a belief.

2 fortalecerse *vr* (**a**) (*gen*) to fortify o.s. (*con* with).

(**b**) (*opinión etc*) to become stronger.

fortalecimiento *nm* (**a**) (*gen*) strengthening; fortification, fortifying. (**b**) (*fig*) encouragement; stiffening.

fortaleza *nf* (**a**) (*Mil*) fortress, stronghold. (**b**) (*cualidad*) strength, toughness, vigour; (*moral*) fortitude, resolution. (**c**) (*Cono Sur, Méx‡*: *olor*) stench, pong‡.

fortificación *nf* fortification.

fortificar [1g] *vi* to fortify; (*fig*) to strengthen.

fortín *nm* (small) fort; pillbox, bunker, blockhouse.

fortísimo *adj superl de* **fuerte**; (*Mús*) fortissimo.

fortuitamente *adv* fortuitously; accidentally; by chance, by coincidence.

fortuito *adj* fortuitous; accidental; chance (*atr*).

fortuna *nf* (**a**) (*gen*) fortune; chance; (*suerte*) (good) luck; **mala ~** misfortune; **por ~** luckily, fortunately; **pista de ~** emergency airstrip, improvised airstrip; **hacer ~** to be a success, make a hit; **tener la ~ de** + *infin* to have the good fortune to + *infin*; **probar ~** to try one's luck, have a shot.

(**b**) (*Náut*) storm; **correr ~** to go through a storm, experience a storm.

(**c**) (*Fin*) fortune; wealth.

fortunón* *nm* vast fortune, pile*.

fórum *nm* = **foro.**

forúnculo *nm* boil.

forzadamente *adv* forcibly, by force; **sonreír ~** to force a smile; **reírse ~** to laugh in a forced way.

forzado *adj* forced; compulsory; **sonrisa forzada** forced smile; *V* **trabajo.**

forzar [1f *y* 1m] *vt* (**a**) (*obligar*) to force, compel, make; **~ a uno a hacer algo** to force sb to do sth, make sb do sth.

(**b**) *puerta etc* to force, break down, break open; *cerradura* to force, pick; *casa* to break into, enter by force, force a way into; *bloqueo* to run; (*Mil*) to storm, take; to force a passage through; *mujer* to ravish, rape.

(**c**) *ojos etc* to strain.

forzosamente *adv* necessarily; inescapably; compulsorily; **tiene ~ que ser así** it must necessarily be so; **tuvieron ~ que venderlo** they had no choice but to sell it.

forzoso *adj* (*necesario*) necessary; (*inevitable*) inescapable, unavoidable; (*obligatorio*) compulsory; *aterrizaje etc* forced; **es ~ que** ... it is inevitable that ...; **le fue ~ hacerlo** he was forced to do it, he had no choice but to do it.

forzudo 1 *adj* strong, tough, brawny. **2** *nm* (*de circo*) strong man; (*pey*) thug, tough*; tough guy.

fosa *nf* (**a**) (*gen*) pit; (*sepultura*) grave; **~ atlántica** Atlantic trench; **~ común** common grave; **~ fecal, ~ séptica** septic tank; **~ marina, ~ oceánica** deep trough in the ocean bed.

(**b**) (*Anat*) fossa, fosse; cavity; **~s nasales** nasal cavities.

(**c**) (*fig*) chasm, wide gap.

fosar [1a] *vt* to dig a ditch (*o* trench *etc*) round.

fosco *adj* (**a**) *pelo* wild, disordered. (**b**) = **hosco.**

fosfato *nm* phosphate.

fosforecer [2d] *vi* to phosphoresce, glow.

fosforera *nf* (**a**) (*cajita*) matchbox. (**b**) (*fábrica*) match factory.

fosforescencia *nf* phosphorescence.

fosforescente *adj* phosphorescent.

fosfórico *adj* phosphoric.

fósforo *nm* (**a**) (*Quím*) phosphorus.

(**b**) (*cerilla*) match; (*And*: *cápsula fulminante*) percussion cap.

(**c**) (*Méx*: *carajillo*) coffee laced with brandy.

(**d**) **tener ~** (*Cono Sur**) to be shrewd, be sharp.

(**e**) (*CAm*: *exaltado*) hothead.

(**f**) (*CAm**: *pelirrojo*) redhead.

fosforoso *adj* phosphorous.

fosgeno *nm* phosgene.

fósil 1 *adj* fossil, fossilized. **2** *nm* (**a**) (*Geol*) fossil. (**b**) (*) (*chocho*) old crock, old dodderer; (*carroza*) old square*.

fosilizado *adj* fossilized.

fosilizarse [1f] *vr* to fossilize, become fossilized.

foso *nm* pit, hole; ditch, trench; (*Teat*) pit (*below stage*); (*Mil*) moat, fosse; entrenchment, defensive ditch; **~ de**

agua (*Dep*) water jump; ~ **generacional** generation gap; ~ **de reconocimiento** (*Aut*) inspection pit; **irse al ~, venirse al ~** (*Teat*) to flop*, fail.

fotingo *nm* (*LAm*) old car, old crock.

foto *nf* photo; snap, snapshot; ~ **aérea** aerial photograph; ~ **de carnet** passport(-size) photograph; ~ **de conjunto** group photo; ~ **fija** still, still photograph; ~ **robot** quick photo; booth for quick photography; **sacar una ~, tomar una ~** to take a photo (*de* of); **ella saca buena ~** she photographs well.

foto... *pref* photo...

fotocalco *nm* photoprint.

fotocomponedora *nf* photocomposer.

fotocomposición *nf* filmsetting, photosetting (*US*), photocomposition.

fotocompositora *nf* filmsetting machine, photosetting machine (*US*).

fotocontrol *nm* photocontrol; **resultado comprobado por ~** photo-finish.

fotocopia *nf* (**a**) (*una* ~) photocopy, print. (**b**) (*acto*) photocopying.

fotocopiadora *nf* photocopier.

fotocopiar [1b] *vt* to photocopy.

fotocromía *nf* colour photography.

fotoeléctrico *adj* photoelectric.

fotogenia *nf* photogenic qualities; **es de una ~ maravillosa** she's wonderfully photogenic.

fotogénico *adj* photogenic.

fotograbado *nm* photogravure, photoengraving.

fotografía *nf* (**a**) (*gen*) photography; ~ **aérea** aerial photography; ~ **en colores** colour photography.
(**b**) (*una* ~) photograph; ~ **en colores** colour photograph; ~ **al flash,** ~ **al magnesio** flashlight photograph; ~ **instantánea** snapshot; '~ **de X'** (*pie de foto*) 'photographed by X'; **hacer una ~ de** to take a photograph of, photograph; *V t* **foto.**

fotografiar [1c] **1** *vt* to photograph. **2** *vi* to come out well in photographs.

fotográficamente *adv* photographically; **le reconocieron ~** they recognized him through photographs.

fotográfico *adj* photographic.

fotógrafo, -a *nm/f* photographer; ~ **aficionado** amateur photographer; ~ **ambulante,** ~ **callejero** street photographer; ~ **de estudio** portrait photographer; ~ **de prensa** press photographer.

fotograma *nm* (*Cine*) shot, still.

fotogrametría *nf*: ~ **aérea** aerial photography, mapmaking from the air.

fotomatón *nm* (**a**) (*quiosco*) photograph booth. (**b**) (*: *foto*) passport-type photo.

fotómetro *nm* exposure meter, light meter, photometer.

fotomodelo *nf* photographic model.

fotomontaje *nm* photomontage.

fotón *nm* photon.

fotonoticia *nf* photographic reportage.

fotonovela *nf* romance (*o* crime story *etc*) illustrated with photos.

fotoperiodismo *nm* photojournalism.

fotoperiodista *nmf* photojournalist.

fotoquímico *adj* photochemical.

fotosensible *adj* photosensitive.

fotosíntesis *nf* photosynthesis.

fotostatar [1a] *vt* to photostat.

fotostato *nm* photostat.

fototeca *nf* collection of photographs, photographic library.

fototopografía *nf* = **fotogrametría.**

fototropismo *nm* phototropism.

fotovoltaico *adj* photovoltaic.

fotuto *nm* (*LAm Aut*) horn.

foul [faul] **1** *interj* (*Dep*) foul! **2** *nm* (*LAm*) foul.

foulard [fu'lar] *nm* (*de mujer*) (head)scarf; (*de hombre*) cravate.

fox [fos] *nm, pl* **fox** [fos] foxtrot.

FP (**a**) *nf* (*Esp Escol, Com*) *abr de* **Formación Profesional** technical education. (**b**) *nm* (*Pol*) *abr de* **Frente Popular** Popular Front.

FPA *nf* (*Argentina, Esp*: *Escol, Com*) *abr de* **Formación Profesional Acelerada.**

Fr. *abr de* **Fray** Friar, Fr.

frac *nm, pl* **~s** *o* **fraques** dress coat, tails.

fracasado 1 *adj* failed; unsuccessful. **2** *nm,* **fracasada** *nf* failure, person who is a failure.

fracasar [1a] **1** *vt* (*LAm*) to mess up, make a mess of. **2** *vi* to fail, be unsuccessful; (*plan etc*) to fail, come to grief, fall through.

fracaso *nm* failure; fiasco; collapse, breakdown; ~ **escolar** school drop-out; failure in end-of-year exams; ~ **sentimental** disappointment in love, disastrous love affair; **el ~ de las negociaciones** the failure of the negotiations, the breakdown of the talks; **es un ~ total** it's a complete disaster; **ir a un ~** to court disaster.

fracción *nf* (**a**) (*Mat*) fraction; ~ **decimal** fraction.
(**b**) (*parte*) fraction, part, fragment.
(**c**) (*Pol etc*) faction, splinter group.
(**d**) (*acto*) division, breaking-up (*en* into).

fraccionado *adj*: **pago ~** payment by instalments.

fraccionalismo *nm* (*Pol*) tendency to form splinter-groups.

fraccionamiento *nm* (**a**) (*gen*) division; breaking-up (*en* into). (**b**) (*Méx Constr*) ≈ housing estate.

fraccionar [1a] *vt* to divide, break up, split up (*en* into).

fraccionario *adj* fractional; *dinero* small, in small units; **'Se ruega moneda fraccionaria'** 'Please tender exact fare'.

fractura *nf* fracture, break (*t Med*); ~ **complicada** compound fracture.

fracturar [1a] **1** *vt* to fracture, break. **2 fracturarse** *vr* to fracture, break.

fragancia *nf* fragrance, sweet smell, perfume.

fragante *adj* (**a**) (*gen*) fragrant, sweet-smelling, scented. (**b**) = **flagrante.**

fragata *nf* frigate.

frágil *adj* fragile, frail; (*Com*) breakable; (*fig*) frail, delicate.

fragilidad *nf* fragility, frailty; (*fig*) frailty, delicacy.

fragmentación *nf* fragmentation.

fragmentadamente *adv*: **pagar ~** to pay in instalments.

fragmentado *adj* fragmented.

fragmentariedad *nf* fragmentary nature.

fragmentario *adj* fragmentary.

fragmento *nm* fragment; piece, bit.

fragor *nm* din, clamour, noise; uproar; crash, clash; (*de máquina, río*) roar.

fragoroso *adj* deafening, thunderous.

fragosidad *nf* (**a**) (*cualidad*) roughness, unevenness; difficult nature; denseness. (**b**) (*una* ~) rough spot; rough road.

fragoso *adj* rough, uneven; *terreno* difficult; *bosque* dense, overgrown.

fragua *nf* forge.

fraguado *nm* (**a**) (*de metal*) forging. (**b**) (*de hormigón etc*) hardening, setting.

fraguar [1i] **1** *vt* (**a**) *hierro etc* to forge. (**b**) (*fig*) to hatch, concoct; to plot. **2** *vi* (*hormigón etc*) to harden, set. **3 fraguarse** *vr* (*tormenta*) to blow up; (*fig*) to blow up, be brewing, be in the offing.

fraile *nm* (**a**) (*Rel*) friar; monk; (*pey*) (any) priest; ~ **descalzo** discalced friar; ~ **mendicante** mendicant friar (*gen* Franciscan); ~ **de misa y olla** ignorant friar, simple-minded friar; ~ **predicador** friar preacher.
(**b**) (*Carib*: *bagazo*) bagasse, residue of sugar cane.

frailecillo *nm* (*Orn*) puffin.

frailería *nf* friars (*collectively*); monks (*collectively*); (*pey*) priests.

frailesco *adj,* **frailuno** *adj* (*pey*) monkish.

frambuesa *nf* raspberry.

frambuesero *nm,* **frambueso** *nm* raspberry cane.

francachela* *nf* (*comida*) spread*, big feed*; (*juerga*) spree, binge*.

francachón *adj* (*LAm*: *pey*) too direct, too outspoken.

francamente *adv* (**a**) (*hablar etc*) frankly, openly, forthrightly.
(**b**) (*realmente*) frankly; really, definitely; ~ **no lo sé** frankly I don't know, I really don't know; **eso está ~ mal** that is definitely wrong; **es una obra ~ divertida** it's a really funny play.

francés 1 *adj* French; **a la francesa** in the French manner (*o* style *etc*); **despedirse a la francesa** to take French leave.
2 *nm* (**a**) (*persona*) Frenchman. (**b**) (*Ling*) French. (**c**) (******) blow job******.

francesa *nf* Frenchwoman.

francesilla *nf* (**a**) (*Bot*) buttercup. (**b**) (*Culin*) roll.

Francia *nf* France.

fráncico 1 *adj* Frankish. **2** *nm* (*Ling*) Frankish.

francio *nm* (*Quím*) francium.

Francisca *nf* Frances.

franciscano *adj, nm* Franciscan.

Francisco *nm* Francis.

francmasón *nm* (free)mason.

francmasonería *nf* (free)masonry.

franco¹ (*Hist*) **1** *adj* Frankish. **2** *nm* Frank.
franco² *nm* (*Fin*) franc.
franco³ *adj* **(a)** (*directo*) frank, open, forthright, candid; (*familiar*) familiar; free; intimate; (*patente*) clear, evident; **si he de ser** ~ frankly, to tell the truth; **seré** ~ **contigo** I will be frank with you, I will be plain with you; **son francas imposibilidades** they are plain impossibilities, they are downright impossible; **estar en franca rebeldía** to be in open rebellion; **estar en franca decadencia** to be in full decline.
(b) (*Com etc*) free, gratis; exempt; *camino etc* free, open; *puerto etc* free; ~ **a bordo** free on board; ~ **de derechos** duty-free; **precio** ~ **(en) fábrica** price ex-factory, price ex-works; ~ **de porte** (*Com*) carriage-free, (*Correos*) post-free; ~ **sobre vagón** free on rail; **mantener mesa franca** to keep open house.
(c) ~ **de servicio** (*Mil*) off-duty; **estar de** ~ (*Cono Sur*) to be off duty, be on leave.
franco... *pref* franco...
francocanadiense *adj, nmf* French-Canadian.
francófilo, -a *nm/f* francophile.
francófobo 1 *adj* francophobe, francophobic. **2** *nm,* **francófoba** *nf* francophobe.
francófono 1 *adj* French-speaking. **2** *nm,* **francófona** *nf* French speaker.
franco-hispano *adj* Franco-Spanish.
francote *adj* outspoken, blunt, bluff.
francotirador *nm* **(a)** (*Mil*) sniper, sharpshooter. **(b)** (*periodista etc*) freelance.
franchute *nm,* **franchuta** *nf* (*pey*) Frenchy*, Frog‡.
franela *nf* **(a)** (*tela*) flannel. **(b)** (*LAm*: *ropa interior*) vest, undershirt (*US*); (*camiseta*) T-shirt.
franelear‡ [1a] *vi* to pet*.
frangollar [1a] **1** *vt* **(a)** (*chapucear*) to bungle, botch, rush. **(b)** (*Cono Sur*) *granos* to grind. **2** *vi* (*And*) to dissemble.
frangollero *adj* (*And, Cono Sur*) bungling.
frangollo *nm* **(a)** (*Culin*) crushed and boiled corn, wheat porridge; (*Carib*: *dulce*) sweet made from mashed bananas; (*Cono Sur*: *locro*) meat and maize stew.
(b) (*LAm Orn*) birdseed.
(c) (*Méx*) (*lío*) muddle, mess; (*mezcla*) mixture.
frangollón (*LAm*) **1** *adj* bungling. **2** *nm,* **frangollona** *nf* bungler.
franja *nf* **(a)** (*Cos*) fringe, border, trimming; braid.
(b) (*zona*) fringe, strip, band; ~ **de tierra** strip of land; **la F~ de Gaza** the Gaza Strip.
franj(e)ar [1a] *vt* to fringe, trim (*de* with).
franqueadora *nf* (*Correos*: *t* **máquina** ~) franking machine.
franquear [1a] **1** *vt* **(a)** *esclavo* to free, liberate; *contribuyente etc* to free, exempt (*de* from).
(b) *derecho etc* to grant, allow, concede (*a* to); ~ **la entrada a** to give free entry to.
(c) *camino etc* to clear, open.
(d) *río etc* to cross; *obstáculo* to negotiate, overcome, get round.
(e) (*Correos*) to frank, stamp; to pay postage on; **una carta franqueada** a post-paid letter, a letter with the postage paid on it; **una carta insuficientemente franqueada** a letter with insufficient postage.
2 franquearse *vr*: ~ **a uno,** ~ **con uno** to unbosom o.s. to sb, have a heart-to-heart talk with sb.
franqueo *nm* postage; franking; **con** ~ **insuficiente** with insufficient postage, with postage underpaid.
franqueza *nf* frankness, openness, forthrightness, candidness; familiarity; freedom, intimacy; **con** ~ frankly; **lo digo con toda** ~ I say so quite frankly; **tengo suficiente** ~ **con él para discrepar** I am on close enough terms with him to disagree.
franquía *nf* (*Náut*) searoom, room to manoeuvre.
franquicia *nf* **(a)** (*exención*) exemption (*de* from); ~ **aduanera,** ~ **arancelaria** exemption from customs duties; ~ **de equipaje** (*Aer*) free baggage allowance; ~ **postal** privilege of franking letters. **(b)** (*Com*) franchise.
franquiciado, -a *nm/f* franchise-holder, franchisee.
franquiciador(a) *nm/f* franchisor.
franquiciamiento *nm* franchising.
franquismo *nm*: **el** ~ (*período*) the Franco years, the Franco period; (*política*) the Franco system, the Franco policy, the Franco outlook; **bajo el** ~ under Franco; **luchó contra el** ~ he fought against Franco.
franquista 1 *adj* pro-Franco; **tendencia** ~ tendency to support Franco, pro-Franco tendency; **una familia muy** ~ a strongly pro-Franco family, a family which strongly supported Franco.
2 *nmf* supporter of Franco.
frasca *nf* **(a)** dry leaves, small twigs. **(b)** (*CAm, Méx*: *fiesta*) riotous party. **(c) pegarle a la** ~* to hit the bottle*.
frasco *nm* **(a)** flask, bottle; ~ **de bolsillo** hip flask; ~ **de campaña** (*LAm*) water bottle; ~ **de perfume** scent bottle; ~ **al vacío** vacuum flask; **¡chupa del** ~**!‡**, **¡toma del** ~, **(Carrrasco)!‡** stone the crows!‡
(b) (*medida*) *liquid measure* (*Carib* = *2.44 litres, Cono Sur* = *21.37 litres*).
frase *nf* **(a)** (*oración*) sentence; ~ **compleja** complex sentence. **(b)** (*locución*) phrase, expression; (*cita*) quotation; ~ **hecha** saying, proverb; idiom; (*pey*) cliché, stock phrase; ~ **lapidaria** axiom; **diccionario de** ~**s** dictionary of quotations.
fraseo *nm* (*Mús*) phrasing.
fraseología *nf* **(a)** phraseology. **(b)** (*pey*) verbosity, verbiage.
Frasquita *nf forma familiar de* **Francisca.**
Frasquito *nm forma familiar de* **Francisco.**
fratás *nm* (plastering) trowel.
fraterna* *nf* ticking-off*.
fraternal *adj* brotherly, fraternal.
fraternidad *nf* brotherhood, fraternity; (*CAm, Carib*: *Univ*) fraternity.
fraternización *nf* fraternization.
fraternizar [1f] *vi* to fraternize.
fraterno *adj* brotherly, fraternal.
fratricida 1 *adj* fratricidal. **2** *nmf* fratricide (*person*).
fratricidio *nm* fratricide (*act*).
fraude *nm* **(a)** (*cualidad*) dishonesty, fraudulence. **(b)** (*acto*) fraud, swindle; deception; ~ **fiscal** tax fraud; **por** ~ by fraud, by false pretences.
fraudulencia *nf* fraudulence.
fraudulentamente *adv* fraudulently, by fraud; dishonestly.
fraudulento *adj* fraudulent; dishonest, deceitful.
fray *nm* (*Ecl*) brother, friar.
frazada *nf* (*esp LAm*) blanket.
freático *adj V* **capa.**
frecuencia *nf* **(a)** frequency; **con** ~ frequently, often. **(b)** (*Elec, Inform, Rad*) frequency; **alta** ~ high frequency; **de alta** ~ high-frequency (*atr*); ~ **modulada** frequency modulation; ~ **de red** mains frequency; ~ **del reloj** clock speed.
frecuentador(a) *nm/f* frequenter.
frecuentar [1a] *vt* to frequent; to haunt.
frecuente *adj* **(a)** frequent; common; *costumbre etc* common, usual, prevalent. **(b)** (*Méx*: *familiar*) familiar, over-familiar; **andarse** ~ **con** to be on close terms with.
frecuentemente *adv* frequently, often.
fregada* *nf* (*CAm, Méx*) (*embrollo*) mess, muck-up*; (*problema*) snag; (*molestia*) nuisance, drag; **¡la** ~**!‡** you don't say!, never!; **¡me lleva la** ~**!‡** well, I'm blowed!*
fregadera* *nm* (*LAm*) nuisance, annoyance.
fregadero *nm* **(a)** (*recipiente*) (kitchen) sink. **(b)** (*pieza*) scullery. **(c)** (*CAm, Méx**: *molestia*) pain in the neck*.
fregado 1 *adj* (*) **(a)** (*LAm*: *molesto*) tiresome, annoying; (‡: *puñetero*) bloody‡, lousy‡; (*Cono Sur*: *difícil*) difficult, problematic.
(b) (*LAm*) *asunto* nasty, messy, dishonest.
(c) (*LAm*: *tonto*) silly, stupid.
(d) (*And, CAm, Méx*: *astuto*) cunning, sly.
(e) (*And, CAm, Carib*) (*testarudo*) pigheaded; (*tenaz*) persistent.
(f) (*Carib*: *fresco*) cheeky*, fresh*.
(g) (*Méx**: *pobre*) poor.
2 *nm* **(a)** (*acto*) rubbing, scrubbing, scouring; (*de platos*) washing-up; **hacer el** ~ to do the washing-up, wash up.
(b) (*: *lío*) mess, messy affair; (*: *asunto turbio*) nasty affair, dishonest deal.
(c) (*LAm**: *riña*) row, tiff; **tener un** ~ **con uno** to have a row with sb.
(d) dar un ~ **a uno*** to give sb a dressing-down*.
(e) es un ~ (*And, Cono Sur**) he's a dead loss.
fregador *nm* **(a)** (*fregadero*) sink. **(b)** (*trapo*) dishcloth; scourer; mop.
fregadura *nf* = **fregado 2 (a).**
fregancia *nf* (*And*) = **fregada.**
fregandera *nf* (*Méx*) charwoman, cleaner.
fregantina *nf* (*And, Cono Sur*) = **fregada.**
fregar [1h *y* 1k] **1** *vt* **(a)** (*estregar*) to rub, scrub; to scour; *suelo* to mop, scrub; *platos* to wash (up).
(b) (*LAm**) (*fastidiar*) to bother, annoy; (*acosar*) to worry, harass; (*arruinar*) to mess up, make a mess of;

¡no me friegues! stop bothering me!, leave me alone!
(c) (Carib*) (pegar) to thrash; (Dep) to beat, thrash.
(d) (Cono Sur**) to screw**.
2 fregarse vr (CAm, Méx*: malograrse) to break down, go wrong.

fregasuelos nm invar mop.

fregazón* nm (Cono Sur) = fregada.

fregón* adj (a) (And, CAm, Méx*: molesto) trying, tiresome, annoying. (b) (LAm: tonto) silly, stupid. (c) (And, Carib: fresco) brazen, fresh.

fregona nf (a) (persona) kitchen maid, dishwasher; (pey) skivvy; (Carib: sinvergüenza) shameless hussy. (b) (*: utensilio) mop.

fregota‡ nm waiter.

freidera nf (Carib) frying-pan.

freidora nf frying-pan.

freiduría nf (t ~ de pescado) fried-fish shop.

freír [3m; ptp frito] 1 vt (a) (Culin) to fry; (fig: sol) to burn, fry; al ~ será el reír the proof of the pudding is in the eating.
(b) (fig) (molestar) to annoy; (atormentar) to torment; (acosar) to harass; (aburrir) to bore; ~le a uno a preguntas to bombard sb with questions.
(c) (‡: matar) to do in‡.
2 freírse vr (a) (Culin) to fry, be frying; ~ de calor to fry in the heat, be roasted.
(b) ~la a uno* to have sb on.

fréjol nm = fríjol.

frenada nf, frenaje nm (Aut) braking.

frenar [1a] vt (a) (Aut, Mec) to brake; to put the brake on, apply the brake to. (b) (fig) to check, curb, restrain.

frenazo nm (acto) sudden braking; (parada) sudden halt; (ruido) squeal of brakes; dar un ~ to brake suddenly, brake hard.

frenesí nm frenzy.

frenéticamente adv frantically, frenziedly; furiously, wildly.

frenético adj frantic, frenzied; furious, wild.

frenillo nm: tener ~ (fig) to have a speech defect.

freno nm (a) (Aut, Mec etc) brake; ~ de aire airbrake; ~s de disco disc brakes; ~ hidráulico hydraulic brake; ~ de mano handbrake; ~ de pedal footbrake; ~ de tambor drum brake; poner el ~, echar los ~s to put the brake(s) on, apply the brake(s); ¡echa el ~, Madaleno!‡ put a sock in it!*; soltar el ~ to release the brake.
(b) (de caballo) bit; bridle; morder (o tascar) el ~ (fig) to restrain o.s., hold back.
(c) (fig) check, curb, restraint; ~s y contrapesos, ~s y equilibrios (Pol) checks and balances; poner ~ a to curb, check; poner ~ a las malas lenguas to stop the gossip.
(d) (Cono Sur: hambre) hunger.

frenología nf phrenology.

frenólogo, -a nm/f phrenologist.

frentazo* nm (Cono Sur, Méx) rebuff, disappointment; pegarse un ~ to come a cropper*.

frente 1 nm (a) (parte delantera) front, front part; face; (Arquit) front, face, façade; ~ de arranque, ~ de trabajo (Min) working face; al ~ in front (de of); al ~ de (fig) in charge of, at the head of; ¡de ~ (mar)! forward march!, by the right quick march!; ir de ~ to go forward; to face forwards; chocar de ~ to crash head-on; atacar de ~ to make a frontal attack; mirar de ~ to look (straight) ahead; viajar de ~ a la marcha (Ferro) to travel facing the engine; marchar 6 de ~ to march 6 abreast; en ~ opposite; in front; la casa de en ~ the house opposite; estar ~ por ~ de to be directly opposite; hacer ~ a to resist, stand up to, face; hacer ~ a unos grandes gastos to (have to) meet considerable expenses; hacer ~ a un temporal (Náut) to ride out a storm.
(b) (Mil) front; ~ de batalla battle front, firing-line; ~ del oeste western front; cambiar de ~ to wheel.
(c) (Pol) front; ~ popular popular front; hacer ~ común con uno to make common cause with sb.
(d) (Met) front; ~ cálido warm front; ~ frío cold front.
2 nf forehead, brow; face; ~ a ~ face to face; adornar la ~ a uno* to cuckold sb; arrugar la ~ to knit one's brow, frown; llevarlo escrito en la ~ to make no effort to hide one's feelings.
3 prep: ~ a opposite (to), facing; in front of; (fig) as opposed to, as contrasted with.
4 adv (Cono Sur): ~ mío (etc) opposite me (etc), in front of me (etc).

freo nm channel, strait.

fresa 1 nf (a) (Bot) (fruta) strawberry (esp wild); (planta) strawberry plant. (b) (Téc) milling cutter; (dentist's) drill. 2 adj: la gente ~ (Méx*) the in crowd.

fresado nm (Mec) milling.

fresadora nm (Mec) milling machine; ~ de roscar thread cutter.

fresal nm strawberry bed.

fresar [1a] vt (Mec) to mill.

fresca nf (a) (aire) fresh air, cool air; (período) cool part of the day; tomar la ~ to get some fresh air, go out for a breath of air.
(b) decir cuatro ~s a uno* to give sb a piece of one's mind.
(c) (*) (descarada) shameless woman, brazen woman; (puta) whore; ¡es una ~! she's a hussy!, she's quite brazen!

frescachón adj (a) (robusto) glowing with health, ruddy; robust. (b) niño bouncing, healthy. (c) mujer buxom. (d) (Náut) viento fresh, stiff.

frescales nm invar cheeky rascal, rogue.

fresco 1 adj (a) (gen) fresh; (nuevo) new, recent; pan new; huevo new-laid; cosas todavía frescas en la memoria things still fresh in the memory.
(b) (algo frío) cool; agua fresca cold water; bebida fresca cool drink, cooling drink, cold drink; hacer ~ (Met) to be cool, be fresh.
(c) viento fresh.
(d) tela, vestido light, thin.
(e) tez fresh, ruddy, healthy.
(f) (sereno) cool, calm, unabashed; tan ~ quite unabashed, quite unconcerned; me lo dijo tan ~ he said it to me as cool as you please; estar más ~ que una lechuga to be as cool as a cucumber.
(g) (*: descarado) cool, fresh*; cheeky*, saucy; bad-mannered; ¡qué ~! what cheek!*, what a nerve!*; ponerse ~ con una to get fresh with a girl*.
(h) dejar ~ a uno to disappoint sb; quedarse ~ to be disappointed, feel cheated.
2 nm (a) (aire) fresh air, cool air; al ~ in the open air, out of doors; tomar el ~ to get some fresh air, go for a stroll in the open; ¡vete a tomar el ~!* get lost!‡; me trae al ~ it leaves me cold.
(b) (Arquit, Arte) fresco; pintar al ~ to paint in fresco.
(c) (*: sinvergüenza) fresh guy* (US), shameless individual; bad-mannered person; ¡Vd es un ~! you've got a nerve!*; mind your manners!
(d) echar ~ a uno (LAm) to tell sb a few home truths.
(e) (CAm: jugo) fruit juice, fruit drink.

frescor nm freshness; coolness; gozar del ~ nocturno to enjoy the cool night air.

frescote adj blooming; buxom.

frescura nf (a) (gen) freshness; (frío) coolness; (de tez) freshness.
(b) (serenidad) coolness, calmness, unconcern; con la mayor ~ with the greatest unconcern, completely unconcerned.
(c) (*: descaro) cheek*, sauce*, nerve*; ¡qué ~! what a nerve!*; tiene la mar de ~ he's got the cheek of the devil*.
(d) (*: impertinencia) impudent remark, cheeky thing (to say)*; me dijo unas ~s he said some cheeky things to me*.

fresia nf freesia.

fresnada nf ash grove.

fresno nm ash, ash tree.

fresón nm (fruta) strawberry (esp cultivated); (planta) strawberry plant.

fresquera nf meat safe; icebox.

fresquería nf (LAm) refreshment stall.

fresquito adj viento rather fresh; V fresco.

freudiano, -a adj, nm/f Freudian.

freza nf (a) (huevos) spawn; (acto, estación) spawning. (b) (Zool) dung, droppings.

frezadero nm spawning ground.

frezar [1f] vi to spawn.

friable adj friable.

frialdad nf (a) (gen) coldness, cold, chilliness. (b) (fig) coldness, coolness; indifference, unconcern. (c) (Méx) (impotencia) impotence; (esterilidad) sterility.

fríamente adv (fig) coldly.

frica nf (Cono Sur) beating.

fricandó nm, fricasé nm fricassee.

fricativa nf fricative.

fricativo adj fricative.

fricción nf rub, rubbing; (Med) massage; (Mec) friction;

(*fig*: *Pol etc*) friction, trouble.
friccionar [1a] *vt* to rub; (*Med*) to rub, massage.
friega *nf* (**a**) (*gen*) rub, rubbing; (*Med*) massage.
(**b**) (*LAm**: *molestia*) nuisance, annoyance; bother; (*lío*) fuss.
(**c**) (*LAm**: *idiotez*) silliness, stupidity.
(**d**) (*And, Carib, Cono Sur**: *paliza*) thrashing.
(**e**) (*And, Méx**: *reprimenda*) ticking-off*.
friegaplatos *nm invar* (**a**) (*aparato*) dishwasher. (**b**) (*persona*) dishwasher, washer-up.
friegasuelos *nm invar* floor mop.
frígano *nm* caddis fly.
frigidaire *nm of* (*LAm*) refrigerator.
frigidez *nf* frigidity (*t Med*).
frígido *adj* frigid (*t Med*).
frigo* *nm* fridge, refrigerator.
frigorífico 1 *adj* refrigerating, cold-storage (*atr*); **camión ~** refrigerator lorry, refrigerator truck (*US*); **instalación frigorífica** cold-storage plant.
2 *nm* refrigerator; (*Cono Sur*) cold-storage plant, meat-packing depot; (*Náut*) refrigerator ship.
frigorífico-congelador *nm, pl* **frigoríficos-congeladores** fridge-freezer.
frigorista *nmf* refrigeration engineer.
frijar⁑ [1a] *vi* to have a screw⁑.
fríjol *nm*, **frijol** *nm* (**a**) (*Bot*) kidney bean, French bean; **~ de café** coffee-bean; **~ de soja** soya bean.
(**b**) **~es** (*LAm*: *comida*) food (*in general*).
(**c**) (*Méx**: *mofa*) taunt; **echar ~es** to blow one's own trumpet.
(**d**) **¡~es!** (*Carib*) certainly not!, not on your life!.
(**e**) (*And, Méx*: *cobarde*) coward; **ser como los ~es que al primer hervor se arrugan** to run at the first sign of trouble.
(**f**) (*Fin⁑*) dough⁑, money.
fringolear [1a] *vt* (*Cono Sur*) to thrash, beat.
frío 1 *adj* (**a**) (*gen*) cold; chilly; **más ~ que el hielo, ~ como un mármol** as cold as ice; **quedarse ~*** to peg out⁑.
(**b**) *bala* spent.
(**c**) (*fig*) cold, unconcerned, unmoved, indifferent; *acogida* cool; **¡me deja Vd ~!** you amaze me!; **eso me deja ~** that leaves me cold.
2 *nm* (**a**) cold; coldness; **¡qué ~!** isn't it cold!, how cold it is!; **hace ~** it's cold; **hace mucho ~** it's very cold; **coger ~** to catch cold; **pasar ~** to be cold, suffer cold; **tener ~** to be cold, feel cold; **no me da ni ~ ni calor** it's all the same to me; it leaves me cold; *V* **helador** *etc.*
(**b**) (*fig*) coldness, indifference.
(**c**) **~s** (*And, CAm, Méx*) (*fiebre*) intermittent fever; (*paludismo*) malaria.
friolento *adj* = **friolero**.
friolera *nf* trifle, mere nothing.
friolero *adj persona* chilly, sensitive to cold, shivery.
friorizado *adj* deep-frozen.
frisa *nf* (**a**) (*tela*) frieze.
(**b**) (*And, Cono Sur Cos*) nap (on cloth); (*Cono Sur*: *pelusa*) fluff; (*Carib*: *manta*) blanket; **sacar a uno la ~*** (*Cono Sur*) to tan sb's hide*; **sacar la ~ a algo*** (*Cono Sur*) to make the most of sth.
frisar [1a] **1** *vt tela* to frizz, rub. **2** *vi*: **~ en** to border on, be close to; **frisa en los 50** she's close on 50, she's getting on for 50.
Frisia *nf* Friesland.
friso *nm* frieze; wainscot, dado.
fritada *nf* fry, fried dish.
fritanga *nf* (**a**) (*And, CAm*: *guiso*) ≈ hotpot, stew; (*Cono Sur, CAm*: *pey*) greasy food. (**b**) (*CAm*: *restaurante*) cheap restaurant. (**c**) (*Cono Sur**: *molestia*) nuisance, pain in the neck*.
fritar [1a] *vt* (*LAm*) to fry.
frito 1 *adj* (**a**) (*Culin*) fried.
(**b**) (*) **tener ~ a uno, traer ~ a uno** (*acosar*) to worry sb to death; (*vencer*) to defeat sb; (*enojar*) to make sb cross; **ese hombre me trae ~** that chap bothers me all day long*, that chap makes me really cross*; **las matemáticas me traen ~** maths is getting me down, maths just defeats me.
(**c**) *pelo* frizzy.
(**d**) **dejar a uno ~⁑** (*matar*) to do sb in⁑; **estar ~⁑** (*dormido*) to be kipping⁑; (*muerto*) to be a goner⁑; (*excitado*) to be really worked up; (*Carib, Cono Sur*) to be finished, be done for; **quedarse ~⁑** (*dormirse*) to go out like a light; (*morir*) to snuff it⁑.
2 *nm* (**a**) (*plato*) fry, fried dish; **~s variados** mixed fry.
(**b**) **a esa mujer le gusta el ~** (*Cono Sur⁑*) she looks like hot stuff*.
(**c**) (*en disco*) hiss, crackling sound.
fritura *nf* (**a**) (*plato frito*) fry, fried dish. (**b**) (*buñuelo*) fritter. (**c**) (*Telec*) interference, crackling.
frívolamente *adv* frivolously.
frivolidad *nf* frivolity, frivolousness.
frivolité *nm* (*Cos*) tatting.
frivolizar [1f] *vt* to trivialize; to play down.
frívolo *adj* frivolous.
frivolón *adj* superficial, frothy, lightweight.
frízer *nm* (*Cono Sur*) freezer.
fronda *nf* frond; **~s** fronds; foliage, leaves.
frondís *adj* (*And*) dirty.
frondosidad *nf* leafiness; luxuriance.
frondoso *adj* leafy; luxuriant.
frontal 1 *adj* (**a**) frontal; *parte, posición* front; (*Inform*) front-end; **choque ~** head-on collision. (**b**) *rechazo etc* outright, forthright, total. **2** *nm* front, front part.
frontalmente *adv* frontally; **chocar ~** to collide head-on; **está situado ~** it is placed on the front; **se oponen ~** they are directly opposed.
frontera *nf* (**a**) frontier, border; (*zona*) frontier area, borderland (*t fig*). (**b**) (*Arquit*) façade.
fronterizo *adj* (**a**) frontier (*atr*); border (*atr*). (**b**) (*enfrente*) opposite, facing; **las casas fronterizas** the houses opposite; **el puente ~ con Eslobodia** the bridge bordering Slobodia.
frontero *adj* opposite, facing.
frontis *nm* (*Arquit*) façade.
frontispicio *nm* (**a**) (*Arquit*) façade; (*Tip*) frontispiece. (**b**) (⁑: *cara*) clock⁑, face.
frontón *nm* (**a**) (*Arquit*) pediment. (**b**) (*Dep*) pelota court; (main) wall of a pelota court.
frotación *nf*, **frotadura** *nf*, **frotamiento** *nm* rub, rubbing; (*Mec*) friction.
frotar [1a] **1** *vt* to rub; *cerilla* to strike; **quitar algo frotando** to rub sth off. **2 frotarse** *vr* to rub, chafe; **~ las manos** to rub one's hands; **frotársela⁑** to wank⁑.
frote *nm* rub.
frotis *nm*: **~ cervical** cervical smear; **~ vaginal** vaginal smear.
fr(s). *abr de* **franco(s)** franc(s), fr.
fructífero *adj* (**a**) (*Bot etc*) productive, fruit-bearing. (**b**) (*fig*) fruitful.
fructificación *nf* (*fig*) fruition.
fructificar [1g] *vi* (**a**) (*Bot*) to produce, yield a crop, bear fruit. (**b**) (*fig*) to yield a profit; to bear fruit; to come to fruition.
fructuosamente *adv* fruitfully.
fructuoso *adj* fruitful.
frugal *adj* frugal; thrifty; parsimonious.
frugalidad *nf* frugality; thrift, thriftiness; parsimony.
frugalmente *adv* frugally; thriftily; parsimoniously.
fruición *nf* enjoyment; satisfaction, delight; **~ maliciosa** malicious pleasure.
frunce *nm* pleat, tuck, gather, shirr.
fruncido 1 *adj* (**a**) (*gen*) contracted; (*Cos*) pleated, gathered; *frente* wrinkled, furrowed; *cara* frowning.
(**b**) (*Cono Sur**) (*remilgado*) prudish, demure; (*afectado*) affected.
2 *nm* = **frunce**.
fruncimiento *nm* = **frunce**.
fruncir [3b] *vt* to contract, pucker; to ruffle; (*Cos*) to pleat, gather, shirr, put a tuck in; *frente* to wrinkle, knit; *labios* to purse; *V* **ceño** *etc.*
fruslería *nf* trifle, trinket; (*fig*) trifle, small thing, triviality.
frustración *nf* frustration.
frustrante *adj* frustrating.
frustrar [1a] **1** *vt* to frustrate, thwart. **2 frustrarse** *vr* to be frustrated; (*plan etc*) to fail, miscarry.
frustre* *nm* = **frustración**.
fruta *nf* (**a**) fruit; **~s** (*Culin*) fruit; **~s confitadas** candied fruits; **~ de la pasión** passionfruit; **~ prohibida** forbidden fruit; **~ de sartén** fritter; **~ seca** dried fruit; **~ del tiempo** (*Culin*) seasonal fruit. (**b**) (*fig*) fruit, consequence.
frutal 1 *adj* fruit-bearing, fruit (*atr*); **árbol ~** = **2**. **2** *nm* fruit-tree.
frutar [1a] *vi* to fruit, bear fruit.
frutera *nf* fruit-dish, fruit-bowl.
frutería *nf* fruiterer's (shop), fruit shop.
frutero 1 *adj* fruit (*atr*); **plato ~** fruit-dish. **2** *nm* (**a**) (*persona*) fruiterer. (**b**) (*recipiente*) fruit-dish, fruit-bowl; basket of fruit.

fruticultor(a) *nm/f* fruit-farmer, fruit-grower.
fruticultura *nf* fruit-growing, fruit-farming.
frutilla *nf* (*LAm*) strawberry.
fruto *nm* (**a**) (*Bot*) fruit; ~ **del árbol del pan** breadfruit; **~s del país** (*Cono Sur*) agricultural products; **dar** ~ to fruit, bear fruit.
(**b**) (*fig*) fruits; (*resultado*) result, consequence; (*beneficio*) profit, benefit; (*hijo etc*) offspring, child; ~ **de bendición** legitimate offspring; **el ~ de esta unión** the offspring of this marriage; **dar** ~ to bear fruit; **sacar ~ de** to profit from, derive benefit from.
frutosidad *nf* fruitiness, fruity flavour.
FSE *nm abr de* **Fondo Social Europeo** European Social Fund, ESF.
FSM *nf abr de* **Federación Sindical Mundial** World Federation of Trade Unions, WFTU.
fu[1] *interj* ugh!
fu[2]: **ni ~ ni fa** neither one thing nor the other.
fuácata* *nf*: **estar en la** ~ (*Carib, Méx*) to be broke*.
fucilazo *nm* (flash of) sheet lightning.
fuco *nm* (*Bot*) wrack.
fucsia *nf* fuchsia.
fudiño *adj* (*Carib*) weak, sickly.
fudre‡ *nm* drunk*, old soak‡.
fuego *nm* (**a**) (*gen*) fire; conflagration; **~s artificiales** fireworks; ~ **fatuo** will-o'-the-wisp; **apagar el** ~ to put out the fire; **atizar el** ~ to poke the fire; **encender un** ~ to light a fire; **se declaró el** ~ fire broke out; **echar ~ por los ojos** to glare, look daggers; **jugar con** ~ (*fig*) to play with fire; **matar a uno a ~ lento** to worry sb to death; **pegar** (*o* **prender**) ~ **a** to set fire to, set on fire; **poner un pueblo a ~ y sangre** to lay a village waste.
(**b**) (*Culin: de gas*) burner, ring; (*Elec*) plate, hot plate; **una cocina a gas de 4 ~s** a gas cooker with 4 burners.
(**c**) (*Culin: calor*) flame, heat; **a ~ suave, sobre un ~ bajo** on a low flame, on a low gas; **a ~ vivo** on a high flame, on a high gas; **hervir a ~ lento** to simmer.
(**d**) (*Náut etc*) beacon, signal fire.
(**e**) (*para cigarro*) light; **¿tienes ~?** have you got a light?; **le pedí** ~ I asked him for a light.
(**f**) (*Mil*) fire; firing; **¡~!** fire!; **¡alto el ~!** cease fire!; ~ **de andanada** (*Náut*) broadside; ~ **cruzado** crossfire; ~ **graneado,** ~ **nutrido** heavy fire; **disparos con ~ real** shooting with live bullets; **abrir** ~ to open fire; **hacer** ~ to fire (*sobre* at, on); **romper el** ~ to open fire.
(**g**) (*Med*) rash, skin eruption; (*Méx: bucal*) mouth ulcer; ~ **pérsico** shingles.
(**h**) (*hogar*) hearth, home; **un pueblo de 50 ~s** a village of 50 houses (*o* families).
(**i**) (*fig*) fire, ardour, passion; **apagar los ~s de uno** to damp down sb's ardour; **atizar el** ~ to add fuel to the flames, stir things up.
fueguear [1a] *vt* (*CAm*) to set fire to.
fueguino (*Cono Sur*) **1** *adj* of Tierra del Fuego. **2** *nm*, **fueguina** *nf* native (*o* inhabitant) of Tierra del Fuego; **los ~s** the people of Tierra del Fuego.
fuel [fuel] *nm*, **fuel-oil** [fuel'oil] *nm* paraffin, kerosene.
fuelle *nm* (**a**) (*de soplar*) bellows; blower; (*Mús: de gaita*) bag; ~ **de pie** footpump; **tener el ~ flojo**‡‡ to fart‡‡.
(**b**) (*Aut etc*) folding hood, folding top (*US*); (*Fot*) bellows; ~ **quitasol** (*Fot*) hood.
(**c**) (*: *soplón*) telltale.
(**d**) (*fig*) vigour, force; inspiration.
fuente *nf* (**a**) (*manantial*) fountain, spring; ~ **de beber** drinking fountain; ~ **de río** source of a river; ~ **de soda** (*LAm*) soda fountain, café; ~ **termal** hot spring; **abrir la ~ de las lágrimas** (*hum*) to weep buckets.
(**b**) (*Culin*) (large) serving dish, platter; ~ **de horno** oven dish.
(**c**) (*fig*) source; origin; ~ **de alimentación** (*Elec*) power supply; **de ~ desconocida** from an unknown source; **de ~ fidedigna** from a reliable source; ~ **de ingresos** source of income; ~ **de suministro** source of supply.
(**d**) ~ **de soda** (*Cono Sur*) snack bar, soda fountain (*US*).
fuer *nm* (*liter*): **a ~ de caballero** as a gentleman; **a ~ de hombre honrado** as an honest man.
fuera 1 *adv* (**a**) (*situación*) outside; (*dirección*) out; **¡~!** get out!, off with you!; chuck him out!; **¡segundos ~!** (*Boxeo*) seconds out!; **'¡ruritanos ~!'** 'Ruritanians go home!'; **ir** ~ to go out, go away, go outside; **con la camisa** ~ with his shirt hanging out; **esta camisa se lleva** ~ this shirt is worn outside, this shirt is not tucked in; **el perro tenía la lengua** ~ the dog had his tongue hanging out; **la parte de** ~ the outside part, the outer part; **desde** ~ from outside; **por** ~ (on the) outside; **los de** ~ those from outside; strangers, newcomers.
(**b**) (*fuera del país*) abroad; **estar** ~ (*persona*) to be out of town, be on a trip; to be away; to be abroad; **estuvo ~ 8 semanas** he was away for 8 weeks; **salir** ~ to go abroad; **trabajar** ~ to work away (from home).
(**c**) (*Dep: ~ de juego*) **estar** ~ to be out, be in touch; **poner** ~ to put into touch; **tirar** ~ to shoot wide.
(**d**) (*Dep: ~ de casa*) away; **los de ~, el equipo de ~** the away team; **jugar** ~ to play away.
2 ~ de (*prep*) (**a**) (*lugar*) outside (of); out of; **estaba ~ de su jaula** it was outside (*o* out of) its cage; **esperamos ~ de la puerta** we waited outside the door; ~ **de alcance** out of reach, beyond one's reach; ~ **de moda** out of fashion; **estar ~ de sí** to be beside o.s.; *V* **combate** *etc*.
(**b**) (*fig*) in addition to, besides, beyond; **pero ~ de eso** but in addition to that; but aside from that; **todo ~ de eso** anything short of that.
3 ~ de serie *nmf* exceptional person.
fuera-borda *nm invar*, **fuerabordo** *nm invar* outboard engine, outboard motor; dinghy with an outboard engine.
fuereño, -a *nm/f* (*Méx*) outsider, incomer.
fuerino, -a *nm/f* (*Cono Sur*) stranger, non-resident.
fuero *nm* (**a**) (*carta municipal*) municipal charter; (*de región etc*) local (*o* regional *etc*) law-code; (*de grupo*) privilege, exemption; **a** ~ according to law; **¿con qué ~?** by what right?; **de** ~ de jure, in law.
(**b**) (*autoridad*) jurisdiction, authority; **el ~ no alcanza a tanto** his authority does not extend that far.
(**c**) **en nuestro ~ interno** inwardly, in our hearts.
fuerte 1 *adj* (*gen*) strong; tough, sturdy; robust; vigorous; solid; *argumento, defensa, fe, objeción etc* strong; *terreno* rough, difficult; *golpe* hard, heavy; *ruido* loud; *gastos, lluvia* heavy; *comida* heavy, big; *plato* main; rich; *curva* sharp; *sabor, té, vino etc* strong; *calor, dolor etc* intense, great, considerable; *crisis* grave; *ejercicio* strenuous; *rigor etc* excessive, extreme; **¡qué ~!*** (*estupendo*) that's great!*; (*qué sorpresa*) well!, extraordinary!; ~ **como un león** (*o* **roble** *etc*) as strong as a horse; **¡eso es un poco ~!** that's a bit much!; **eso es muy** ~ that's a very serious thing to say; **hacerse ~ en una colina** to entrench o.s. on a hill, make a fortified position on a hill; **se hicieron ~s en la casa** they prepared to defend the house; they barricaded themselves in the house; they made a stand in the house; **ser ~ en filosofía** to be strong in (*o* on) philosophy, be well up in philosophy.
2 *adv* strongly; *golpear* hard; *hablar, tocar* loud, loudly; **pegar ~ al enemigo** to hit the enemy hard; **toca muy** ~ she plays very loud; **¡más ~!** (*a orador*) speak up!; **poner la radio más** ~ to turn the radio up; **comer** ~ to eat a big meal, eat too much.
3 *nm* (**a**) (*Mil*) fort, strongpoint.
(**b**) (*Mús*) forte.
(**c**) (*fig*) forte, strong point; **el canto no es mi** ~ singing is not my strong point.
fuertemente *adv* strongly; loudly; intensely.
fuerza *nf* (**a**) (*gen*) strength; toughness, sturdiness; vigour; solidity; power; intensity; **~s** (*de persona*) strength; (*de argumento*) force, strength, effect; **un viento de ~ 6** a force 6 wind; ~ **de voluntad** willpower; **a ~ de** by dint of, by force of; **a viva** ~ by sheer strength, by main force; **entrada a viva** ~ forced entry, **cobrar ~s** to recover one's strength; to gather strength; **hacer ~ de vela** to crowd on sail; **írsele a uno la ~ por la boca*** to be all talk and no action, be all mouth*; **restar ~s a** to weaken; **sacar ~s de flaqueza** to make a supreme effort; to screw up one's courage; **no me siento con ~s para eso** I don't feel up to it; **tener ~s para** + *infin* to have the strength to + *infin*, be strong enough to + *infin*.
(**b**) (*Mec, Fís*) force; power; ~ **de arrastre** pulling power; ~ **ascensional** (*Aer*) buoyancy; ~ **de brazos** manpower; ~ **centrífuga** centrifugal force; ~ **centrípeta** centripetal force; ~ **de gravedad** force of gravity; ~ **hidráulica** water power, hydraulic power; **~s del mercado** market forces; ~ **motriz** motive power; (*fig*) driving force; ~ **de sustentación** (*Aer*) lift.
(**c**) (*Elec*) power, current, energy; **han cortado la** ~ they've cut off the power.
(**d**) (*obligación*) force, compulsion; (*presión*) pressure; ~ **mayor** force majeure; act of God; **es una cosa de ~ mayor** it's a question of dire necessity; **a la ~, por** ~ by force; willy-nilly, against one's will; under pressure, compulsively; perforce, of necessity; **por la ~ de la costumbre** (*fig*) out of habit; **en ~ de** by virtue of; **es** ~

reconocer que ... we must needs recognize that ..., it must be admitted that ...

(**e**) (*violencia*) force, violence; ~ **bruta** brute force; **hacer ~ a una mujer** to rape a woman; **recurrir a la ~** to resort to force, use violence; **rendirse a la ~** to yield to superior force; **sin usar ~** without using force, without using violence.

(**f**) (*Mil etc*) force, forces; **~s aéreas** air force; **~s aliadas** allied forces; **~ de apoyo** back-up force; **~s armadas** armed forces; **~ de choque** storm-troops; (*fig*) spearhead; **~ de disuasión, ~ disuasoria, ~ disuasiva** deterrent; **~ expedicionaria** expeditionary force, task force; **~s de mar y de tierra** land and sea forces; **~s del orden** (**público**) forces of law and order; **~ de pacificación** peace-keeping force; **~ pública** police (force); **~s de seguridad** security forces; **~s terrestres** land forces; **~ de trabajo** workforce; **~ de ventas** sales force.

fuetazo *nm* (*LAm*) lash.

fuete *nm* (*LAm*) whip; **dar ~ a** to whip.

fuetear [1a] *vt* (*LAm*) to whip.

fuga[1] *nf* (**a**) (*huida*) flight, escape; (*de amantes*) elopement; **~ hacia adelante** desperate fling, crazy attempt; **~ de capitales** flight of capital abroad; **~ de la cárcel** escape from prison, jailbreak; **le aplicaron la ley de ~** (*LAm*) he was shot while trying to escape; **apelar a la ~, darse a la ~, ponerse en ~** to flee, take to flight; **poner al enemigo en ~** to put the enemy to flight. (**b**) (*de gas etc*) leak, escape; **~ de cerebros** brain-drain. (**c**) (*fig*) ardour, impetuosity.

fuga[2] *nf* (*Mús*) fugue.

fugacidad *nf* fleetingness, transitory nature, brevity.

fugado *nm* escapee.

fugar [1h] *vi* (*LAm*) *y* **fugarse** *vr* (**a**) (*huir*) to flee, escape (*a* to); to run away (*con* with); (*amantes*) to elope (*con* with); **~ de la ley** to abscond from justice.

(**b**) (*gas etc*) to leak out, escape.

fugaz *adj* (**a**) *momento etc* fleeting, short-lived, transitory, brief. (**b**) (*esquivo*) elusive. (**c**) **estrella ~** shooting star.

fugazmente *adv* fleetingly, briefly.

fugitivo 1 *adj* (**a**) (*que huye*) fugitive, fleeing. (**b**) = **fugaz. 2** *nm*, **fugitiva** *nf* fugitive.

fuguista *nmf* escaper, jailbreaker.

fui, fuimos *etc V* **ser**; *V* **ir.**

fuina *nf* marten.

ful[1] **1** *adj* (*And*) full, full up. **2** *nm* (*And*) **marchar a todo ~** to work at full capacity.

ful[2]‡ *adj* = **fulastre.**

ful[3]‡ *nf* (*droga*) hash*.

fulana *nf* (**a**) **Doña F~** Mrs So-and-so, Mrs Blank. (**b**) (*: *puta*) tart‡, whore.

fulaneo* *nm* whoring.

fulano *nm* so-and-so, what's-his-name; (*) bloke‡, guy*; **~ de tal, Don F~** Mr So-and-so, Mr Blank; Joe Soap, John Doe (*US*); **~, zutano y mengano** Tom, Dick and Harry; **me lo dijo ~** somebody told me; old what's-his-name told me; **no te vas a casar con un ~** you're not going to marry just anybody; **nombramos a ~ y ya está** we nominate some chap and that's that.

fular *nm* = **foulard.**

fulastre‡ *adj* (*falso*) false, sham; (*malo*) bad, rotten*.

fulbito *nm* five-a-side football.

fulcro *nm* fulcrum.

fulero *adj* (**a**) (*inútil*) useless; (*falso*) sham, bogus; (*pobremente hecho*) poor-quality, poorly made; nasty. (**b**) (*taimado*) tricky, sly. (**c**) (*torpe*) blundering, incompetent.

fulgente *adj*, **fúlgido** *adj* dazzling, bright, brilliant, radiant.

fulgir [3c] *vi* to glow, shine; to glitter.

fulgor *nm* brilliance, radiance, glow; (*fig*) splendour.

fulgurante *adj* (**a**) (*brillante*) bright, shining. (**b**) (*fig*) shattering, stunning.

fulgurar [1a] *vi* to shine, gleam, glow; to flash.

fulguroso *adj* bright, shining, gleaming; flashing.

fúlica *nf* coot.

fulmicotón *nm* gun-cotton.

fulminación *nf* fulmination.

fulminador 1 *adj* = **fulminante. 2** *nm*, **fulminadora** *nf* fulminator (*de* against), thunderer (*de* against).

fulminante 1 *adj* (**a**) *polvo* fulminating; **cápsula ~** percussion cap.

(**b**) (*Med*) fulminant; sudden; *V* **ataque** (**b**).

(**c**) (*) *éxito etc* terrific*, tremendous*; **golpe ~** terrific blow*, smash hit; **tiro ~** (*Dep*) sizzling shot.

2 *nm* (*LAm*: *cápsula fulminante*) percussion cap.

fulminantemente *adv* without warning; **despedir ~ a uno** to fire sb on the spot*.

fulminar [1a] **1** *vt* (**a**) (*gen*) to fulminate; *amenazas* to utter, thunder (*contra* against); **~ a uno con la mirada** to look daggers at sb.

(**b**) (*con rayo*) to strike with lightning; **murió fulminado** he was killed by lightning.

2 *vi* to fulminate, explode.

fulo *adj* (**a**) (*CAm*: *rubio*) blond(e), fair. (**b**) (*Cono Sur**: *furioso*) furious, hopping mad*.

fullerear* [1a] *vi* (*And*) to swank*.

fullería *nf* (**a**) (*Naipes etc*: *acto*) cheating, cardsharping; (*cualidad*) guile, low cunning. (**b**) (*trampas*) trickery. (**c**) (*And**: *ostentación*) swankiness*, conceit.

fullero *nm* (**a**) (*Naipes etc*) cheat, card-sharper; (*criminal*) crook*; (*tramposo*) tricky individual. (**b**) (*And**: *fachendón*) swank*, show-off*.

fullingue *adj* (*Cono Sur*) (**a**) *tabaco* inferior, poor-quality. (**b**) *niño* small, sickly.

fumada *nf* whiff of smoke, puff of smoke; (*LAm*) puff, pull.

fumadero *nm* smoking room; **~ de opio** opium den.

fumado‡ *adj*: **estar ~** to be stoned‡.

fumador(a) *nm/f* smoker; **gran ~** heavy smoker; **~ pasivo** passive smoker; **~ de pipa** pipe-smoker.

fumar [1a] **1** *vti* to smoke; **'prohibido ~'** 'no smoking'; **zona de no ~** no-smoking area; **~ como una chimenea** to smoke like a chimney; **él fuma en pipa** he smokes a pipe; **está fumando su pipa** he is smoking his pipe; **¿puedo ~?, ¿se permite ~?** may I smoke?

2 fumarse *vr* (**a**) (*) *dinero* to dissipate, squander; *clase* to cut, miss. (**b**) (*Méx**: *escaparse*) to vanish, slope off*.

(**c**) **fumárselo a uno** (*LAm**) to outdo sb; **~ de uno** to trick sb, swindle sb.

(**d**) **~ a una**‡ to screw sb‡.

fumarada *nf* (**a**) (*fumada*) puff of smoke. (**b**) (*en pipa*) pipeful.

fumata 1 *nf* (**a**) (‡) smoking session (of drugs). (**b**) (*Rel*) **~ blanca** white smoke; (*fig*) indication of success. **2** *nmf* (‡: *persona*) pot-smoker‡. **3** *nm* (‡: *cigarrillo*) fag‡, gasper‡.

fumeta‡ *nmf* pot-smoker‡.

fumeteo‡ *nm* pot-smoking‡.

fumigación *nf* fumigation: **~ aérea** crop-dusting, crop-spraying.

fumigar [1h] *vt* to fumigate; *cosecha* to dust, spray.

fumista *nm* (**a**) (*gandul*) idler, shirker. (**b**) (*Cono Sur*: *bromista*) joker, tease.

fumo *nm* (*Carib*) puff of smoke.

fumosidad *nf* smokiness.

fumoso *adj* smoky.

funambulesco *adj* grotesque, wildly extravagant.

funambulista *nmf*, **funámbulo, -a** *nm/f* tightrope walker.

funcia *nf* (*And, CAm, Cono Sur*: *hum*) = **función.**

función *nf* (**a**) (*gen*) function; (*de máquina*) functioning, operation; **en ~ de** according to, depending on.

(**b**) (*de puesto*) duties; **presidente en funciones** acting president; **entrar en funciones** to take up one's duties; **excederse en sus funciones** to exceed one's duty.

(**c**) (*Teat etc*) show, performance; entertainment; spectacle; **~ benéfica** charity performance; **~ de despedida** farewell performance; **~ de la tarde** matinée; **~ de títeres** puppet show; **~ taquillera** box-office success, big draw; **mañana no hay ~** there will be no performance tomorrow.

(**d**) **~ pública** civil service, civil servants (*collectively*).

funcional *adj* functional.

funcionalidad *nf* functional character; functionality, functioning.

funcionalismo *nm* functionalism.

funcionamiento *nm* (**a**) (*gen*) functioning, operation; (*Mec, Téc*) operation, working, running; performance; behaviour; **máquina en ~** machine in working order; **sociedad en ~** going concern; **entrar en ~** to come into operation; **poner en ~** to bring into operation, bring into service. (**b**) **cursillo en ~** in-service course; **formación en ~** in-service training.

funcionar [1a] *vi* (*gen*) to function; (*Mec, Téc*) to go, work, run; (*Aut etc*) to perform; to behave; (*idea, película etc*) to work, be a success; **'funcionando'** (*en anuncio etc*) 'in working order', 'in running order'; **'no funciona'** (*aviso*) 'out of order'; **hacer ~ una máquina** to operate a machine.

funcionariado *nm* civil service, bureaucracy.

funcionarial *adj* administrative; (*pey*) bureaucratic.

funcionario, -a *nm/f* official, functionary; employee; civil servant; (*de banco etc*) clerk; ~ **aduanero** customs official; ~ **penitenciario** prison official; ~ **público** civil servant, official; clerk; (*de cárcel*) prison officer.

funda *nf* (**a**) (*gen*) case, cover, sheath; (*de disco*) sleeve, jacket; (*) French letter; ~ **de almohada** pillowcase, pillowslip; ~ **de pistola** holster; ~ **protectora del disco** (*Inform*) disk-jacket; ~ **sobaquera** shoulder holster. (**b**) (*bolsa*) small bag, holdall. (**c**) (*And: falda*) skirt.

fundación *nf* foundation.

fundadamente *adv* with good reason, on good grounds.

fundado *adj* firm, well-founded, justified; **una pretensión mal fundada** an ill-founded claim.

fundador(a) *nm/f* founder.

fundamental *adj* fundamental, basic; essential.

fundamentalismo *nm* fundamentalism.

fundamentalista *adj, nmf* fundamentalist.

fundamentalmente *adv* fundamentally, basically; essentially.

fundamentar [1a] **1** *vt* (**a**) (*sentar los bases de*) to lay the foundations of. (**b**) (*fig*) *argumento etc* to base, found (*en* on). **2 fundamentarse** *vr*: ~ **en** to base o.s. on; to be based on.

fundamento *nm* (**a**) (*Arquit etc*) foundation(s).

(**b**) (*fig: base*) foundation, basis; groundwork; grounds, reason; **eso carece de** ~ that is groundless, that is completely unjustified; **creencia sin** ~ groundless belief, unfounded belief; **¿qué** ~ **tiene esta teoría?** what is the basis of this theory?, what is the basic justification for this theory.

(**c**) (*fig: moral*) reliability, trustworthiness.

(**d**) (*Téc*) weft, woof.

(**e**) ~**s** (*fig*) fundamentals; basic essentials.

fundar [1a] **1** *vt* (**a**) (*gen*) to found; (*crear*) to institute, set up, establish; (*erigir*) to raise, erect; (*dotar*) to endow.

(**b**) *teoría etc* to base, found (*en* on).

2 fundarse *vr* (**a**) (*gen*) to be founded, be established.

(**b**) ~ **en** to be founded on, be based on; to base o.s. on; **me fundo en los siguientes hechos** I base myself on the following facts.

fundente 1 *adj* melting. **2** *nm* (*Quím*) dissolvent; flux.

fundería *nf* foundry; ~ **de hierro** iron foundry.

fundición *nf* (**a**) (*acto*) fusing, fusion; (*Téc*) smelting, founding; melting.

(**b**) (*fábrica*) foundry, forge, smelting plant; ~ **de hierro** iron foundry.

(**c**) (*objeto*) cast-iron; casting; ~ **de acero** steel casting.

(**d**) (*Tip*) fount, font (*esp US*).

fundido 1 *adj* (*LAm Com*) ruined, bankrupt. **2** *nm* (**a**) (*Cine*) dissolve, fading; ~ (**de cierre**) fade-out. (**b**) ~ **nuclear** (*Téc*) nuclear melt-down.

fundidor *nm* smelter, founder.

fundillo(s) *nm(pl)* (*LAm: de pantalón*) seat; (*: *trasero*) seat*, bottom.

fundir [3a] **1** *vt* (**a**) (*fusionar*) to fuse (together); (*unir*) to join, unite.

(**b**) (*Téc*) to melt (down), smelt; *nieve etc* to melt; (*Elec*) to fuse; *pieza* to found, cast; (*Com*) to merge.

(**c**) (*: *arruinar*) to spoil, upset, ruin; (*LAm*) to ruin, bankrupt.

(**d**) (‡) *dinero* to throw away, chuck around.

2 *vi* (*Cine*) to fade (*a* to).

3 fundirse *vr* (**a**) (*gen*) to fuse (together); to join, unite; (*colores, efectos etc*) to merge, blend (together).

(**b**) (*derretirse*) to melt (*t fig*); (*Elec: fusible, lámpara*) to blow, burn out.

(**c**) (*LAm: arruinarse*) to ruin oneself; to be ruined.

fundo *nm* (*LAm*) country property, estate; farm.

fundón *nm* (*And, Carib*) riding-habit.

fúnebre *adj* (**a**) *pompa etc* funeral (*atr*). (**b**) (*fig*) funereal; *sonido etc* mournful, lugubrious.

funeral 1 *adj* funeral (*atr*). **2** *nm* funeral; ~**es** funeral, obsequies.

funerala *nf*: **marchar a la** ~ to march with reversed arms; **ojo a la** ~ black eye.

funeraria *nf* undertaker's, undertaker's establishment, funeral parlor (*US*); **director de** ~ undertaker, funeral director, mortician (*US*).

funerario *adj*, **funéreo** *adj* funeral (*atr*); funereal.

funestamente *adv* banefully; fatally, disastrously.

funestidad *nf* (*Méx*) calamity.

funesto *adj* ill-fated, unfortunate; baneful; fatal, disastrous (*para* for).

fungible *adj* (*Jur*) **bienes ~s** perishable goods.

fungicida *nm* fungicide.

fungiforme *adj* mushroom-shaped.

fungir [3c] *vi* (*CAm, Méx*) to act (*de* as); (*Carib*) to substitute, stand in (*a* for).

fungoideo *adj* fungoid.

fungoso *adj* fungous.

funguelar‡ [1a] *vi* to pong‡.

funicular *nm* funicular (railway).

fuñido *adj* (**a**) (*Carib*) (*pendenciero*) quarrelsome; (*insociable*) unsociable. (**b**) (*Carib: enfermizo*) weak, sickly, feeble.

fuñingue *adj* (*Cono Sur*) weak.

fuñir‡ [3h] *vt*: **~la** to make a real mess of things, mess things up.

furcia* *nf* tart‡, whore; ¡~! you slut!

furgón *nm* wagon, van, truck; (*Ferro*) van; ~ **blindado** armoured van; ~ **celular** police van, prison van; ~ **de cola** guard's-van; caboose (*US*); ~ **de equipajes** luggage-van, baggage car (*US*); ~ **funerario** hearse; ~ **de mudanzas** removal van.

furgonada *nf* wagonload, vanload.

furgonero *nm* carter, vanman.

furgoneta *nf* (*Com*) van; transit van, pick-up truck (*US*); (*coche particular*) estate car; ~ **de reparto** delivery van.

furia *nf* fury; rage, violence; **a la** ~ (*Cono Sur*) at top speed; **ella salió como una ~, ella salió hecha una** ~ she went out furiously (angry); **trabajar a toda** ~ to work like fury.

furibundo *adj* furious; frenzied.

furiosamente *adv* furiously; violently; frantically.

furioso *adj* furious; violent; frantic, raging; **estar** ~ to be furious; **ponerse** ~ to get furious.

furor *nm* (**a**) (*ira*) fury, rage; (*pasión*) frenzy; passion; ~ **uterino** nymphomania; **dijo con** ~ he said furiously.

(**b**) (*fig*) rage, craze, furore; **hacer** ~ to be all the rage; **tener** ~ **por** (*LAm*) to have a passion for.

furquina *nf* (*And*) short skirt.

furriel *nm*, **furrier** *nm* quartermaster.

furrús* *nm* switch, swap, change.

furrusca* *nf* (*And*) row, brawl.

furtivamente *adv* furtively; in a clandestine way; slyly, stealthily.

furtivismo *nm* poaching, illegal hunting (*o* fishing).

furtivo *adj* furtive; clandestine; sly, stealthy; *edición* pirated; *V* **cazador.**

furuminga *nf* (*Cono Sur*) intrigue, scheme, plot.

furúnculo *nm* (*Med*) boil.

fusa *nf* demisemiquaver, thirty-second note (*US*).

fusca‡ *nf*, **fusco‡** *nm* rod‡, gun.

fuselado *adj* streamlined.

fuselaje *nm* fuselage; **de ~ ancho** wide-bodied.

fusible *nm* fuse.

fusil *nm* rifle, gun; ~ **de asalto** assault rifle; ~ **de juguete** popgun, toy gun.

fusilamiento *nm* (**a**) shooting, execution. (**b**) (*) pinching*, plagiarism; (*de producto*) piracy, illegal copying.

fusilar [1a] *vt* (**a**) (*ejecutar*) to shoot, execute; (*Carib: matar*) to kill; (*Dep*) *gol* to shoot. (**b**) (*: *plagiar*) to pinch*, plagiarize; *producto* to pirate, copy illegally.

fusilazo *nm* rifle-shot.

fusilería *nf* gunfire, rifle-fire.

fusilero *nm* rifleman, fusilier.

fusión *nf* (*Fís etc*) fusion; (*unión*) joining, uniting; (*Inform*) merge; (*de metal etc*) melting; (*Com*) merger, amalgamation; ~ **nuclear** nuclear fusion.

fusionamiento *nm* (*Com*) merger, amalgamation.

fusionar [1a] **1** *vt* to fuse (together); (*Inform*) to merge; (*Com*) to merge, amalgamate. **2 fusionarse** *vr* to fuse; (*Com*) to merge, amalgamate.

fusta *nf* (**a**) (*látigo*) long whip; riding whip. (**b**) (*leña*) brushwood, twigs.

fustán *nm* (**a**) (*tela*) fustian. (**b**) (*LAm: enaguas*) petticoat, underskirt; (*And: falda*) skirt.

fuste *nm* (**a**) (*madera*) wood, timber; **de** ~ wooden.

(**b**) (*de arma*) shaft; (*de columna, chimenea*) shaft; **de** ~ (*fig*) important, of some consequence; **de poco** ~ (*fig*) unimportant.

(**c**) (*silla*) saddle tree.

(**d**) (*CAm* Anat*) bottom.

fustigar [1h] *vt* (**a**) (*lit*) to whip, lash. (**b**) (*fig*) to upbraid, lash (with one's tongue).

futbito *nm* five-a-side football.

fútbol (*frec* **futbol** *en LAm*) *nm* football; ~ **americano** American football; ~ **asociación** association football, soccer.

futbolero 1 *adj* football (*atr*); footballing (*atr*). **2** *nm*, **futbolera** *nf* soccer supporter.
futbolín *nm* table football, bar football.
futbolista *nmf* footballer, football player.
futbolístico *adj* football (*atr*).
fútbol-rugby *nm* rugby (*Brit*), American football (*US*).
fútbol-sala *nm* indoor football, seven-a-side football.
futearse [1a] *vr* (*And*: *fruta etc*) to go bad, rot.
futesa *nf* trifle, mere nothing; **~s** small talk, trivialities.
fútil *adj* trifling, trivial.
futileza *nf* (*Cono Sur*) trifle, bagatelle.
futilidad *nf* (**a**) (*gen*) triviality, trifling nature, unimportance. (**b**) (*una ~*) trifle.
futing ['futin] *nm* = **footing.**
futre *nm* (*LAm*) dandy, toff*, dude* (*US*).
futrería *nf* (*And, Cono Sur*) (**a**) (*conducta*) affected behaviour.
(**b**) (*grupo*) group of dandies, group of dudes* (*US*).
(**c**) (*querencia*) dude's hang-out* (*US*).
futura *nf* (**a**) (*Jur*) reversion. (**b**) (*: *novia*) fiancée.
futurible 1 *adj* (*venidero*) forthcoming; (*potencial*) potential; (*probable*) likely; (*especulativo*) speculative; (*digno de ascenso*) promotion-worthy. **2** *nmf* (*Pol*) potential minister; potential leader. **3** *nm* hot tip, good bet; **es un ~ Olímpico** he's a good prospect for the Olympics.
futurismo *nm* futurism.
futurista *adj*, **futurístico** *adj* futuristic.
futuro 1 *adj* future; **futura madre** mother-to-be; **los equipos más ~s son A y B** the teams with the best prospects are A and B.
2 *nm* (**a**) future; **en el ~** in (the) future; **en un ~** some time in the future; **en un ~ próximo** in the very near future, very soon; **el ~ se presenta muy oscuro** the future looks bleak.
(**b**) (*Ling*) future, future tense.
(**c**) (*: *novio*) fiancé.
(**d**) **~s** (*Com*) futures.
futurología *nf* futurology.
futurólogo, -a *nm/f* futurologist.

G

G, g [xe] *nf* (*letra*) G, g.
g/ *abr de* **giro** draft, money order.
gaba *nmf* (*Tejas*: *pey*) white American, Yankee.
gabacho 1 *adj* (**a**) (*Geog*) Pyrenean.
(**b**) (*afrancesado*) frenchified.
(**c**) **le salió gabacha la cosa** (*And*, *Méx**) it came to nothing, the affair was a failure.
2 *nm*, **gabacha**[1] *nf* (**a**) (*Geog*) Pyrenean villager.
(**b**) (*****) (*pey*) Frenchy*, Froggy*; frenchified Spaniard; (*Tejas*) white American, Yankee; (*Méx*) (*any*) foreigner, outsider.
3 gabacha[2] *nf* (*CAm*) overall.
gabán *nm* overcoat, topcoat; (*Carib*) jacket.
gabanear [1a] **1** *vt* (*CAm*) to steal. **2** *vi* (*Méx*) to flee.
gabanero *nm* hall wardrobe.
gabarda *nf* wild rose.
gabardina[1] *nf* (*tela*) gabardine; (*prenda*) raincoat, mackintosh; **en ~** coated in batter.
gabardino, -a[2] *nm/f* (*Tejas*: *pey*) white American, Yankee.
gabarra *nf* barge, lighter, flatboat; **botar la ~*** to push the boat out*.
gabarrero *nm* bargee, bargeman, lighterman.
gabarro *nm* (**a**) (*de tela*) flaw, defect. (**b**) (*Vet*) (*de caballo*) tumour; (*de gallina*) pip. (**c**) (*fig*) (*error*) error, slip, miscalculation; (*pega*) snag; (*molestia*) annoyance.
gabear [1a] *vt* (*Carib*) to climb.
gabela *nf* (**a**) (*Hist*) tax, duty; (*fig*) burden. (**b**) (*And*: *ventaja*) advantage, profit.
gabinete *nm* (**a**) (*estudio*) study, library; (*cuarto de estar*) private sitting room; (*tocador*) boudoir; (*Jur*, *Med*) office; (*laboratorio*) laboratory; (*museo*) museum; (*Arte*) studio; (*And*) enclosed balcony; **~ de consulta** consulting-room; **~ de estrategia** (*Pol etc*) think-tank; **~ fiscal** tax advisory office; **~ de imagen** public relations office; **~ de lectura** reading room; **~ de prensa** press office; **~ de teléfono** (*Méx*) telephone booth; **estratega de ~** armchair strategist.
(**b**) (*Pol*) cabinet; **~ fantasma, ~ en la sombra** shadow cabinet.
(**c**) (*muebles*) suite of office furniture.
gablete *nm* gable.
Gabriel *nm* Gabriel.
gacel *nm*, **gacela** *nf* gazelle.
gaceta *nf* (**a**) (*boletín*) gazette, official journal; (*LAm*: *diario*) newspaper. (**b**) (*Carib**) (*chismoso*) gossip; (*soplón*) telltale.
gacetero, -a *nm/f* (**a**) (*periodista*) newswriter, journalist. (**b**) (*vendedor*) newspaper seller.
gacetilla *nf* (**a**) (*notas de sociedad*) gossip column; (*noticias*) section of local news, section of miscellaneous news items; **'G~'** (*título*) 'News in Brief'.
(**b**) (*****) gossip, scandalmonger; **ella es una ~ andando** (*o* **con dos patas**) she's a dreadful gossip.
gacetillero, -a *nm/f* newspaper reporter; gossip columnist; (*pey*) hack.
gacetista *nmf* gossip, scandalmonger.
gacilla *nf* (*CAm Cos*) clasp, hook and eye.
gacha *nf* (**a**) thin paste; watery mass, mush; **~s** (*Culin*) pap; porridge; **~s de avena** oatmeal porridge; **se ha hecho unas ~s** it's got mushy, it's got soggy, (*fig*) she's turned all sentimental.
(**b**) (*And*, *Carib*: *cerámica*) earthenware bowl.
gachí‡ *nf*, *pl* **gachís** *o* **gachises** (**a**) (*mujer*) bird‡, dame* (*US*). (**b**) **ser del ~** to be one of the people, be common, be very ordinary.
gacho *adj* (**a**) bent down, turned downward; *cuerno* downcurved; *vaca* with down-curved horns; *sombrero* with down-turned brim; *orejas etc* drooping, floppy; **sombrero ~** slouch hat.
(**b**) (*Méx*) (*desagradable*) unpleasant, disagreeable; (*sin suerte*) unlucky.
(**c**) **ir a gachas** to go on all fours.
(**d**) **a cabeza gacha** (*Cono Sur*) obediently.
gachó‡ *nm*, *pl* **gachós** chap*, bloke‡; **¡~!** brother!*
gachón* *adj* (*encantador*) nice, charming, sweet; *niño* spoilt; (**‡**) *mujer* sexy.
gachumbo *nm* (*LAm*) hollowed-out shell.
gachupín *nm* (*LAm*), **gachuzo** *nm* (*Méx*) (*pey*) (*any*) Spaniard.
gaditano 1 *adj* of Cadiz. **2** *nm*, **gaditana** *nf* native (*o* inhabitant) of Cadiz; **los ~s** the people of Cadiz.
GAE *nm* (*Esp Mil*) *abr de* **Grupo Aéreo Embarcado**.
gaélico 1 *adj* Gaelic. **2** *nm*, **gaélica** *nf* Gael. **3** *nm* (*Ling*) Gaelic.
gafa[1] *nf* (*grapa*) grapple; (*abrazadera*) clamp; **~s** glasses, spectacles; (*Aut etc*) goggles; **~s ahumadas** smoked glasses; **~s de aro** John Lennon glasses; **~s sin aros** rimless glasses; **~s de baño, ~s de bucear** diving goggles; **~s bifocales, ~s graduadas** bifocals; **~s de cerca, ~s de leer** reading glasses; **~s de esquiar** skiing goggles; **~s de media luna** half-moon glasses; **~s de motorista** motorcyclist's goggles; **~s negras** dark glasses; **~s protectoras** protective goggles; **~s de sol, ~s para sol** sunglasses; **~s submarinas** underwater goggles.
gafancia* *nf* propensity to attract bad luck; accident-proneness.
gafar [1a] *vt* (**a**) (*agarrar*) to hook, claw, latch on to. (**b**) (*****: *traer mala suerte a*) to bring bad luck to, put a jinx on*; (*estropear*) to spoil, mess up; **la máquina parece gafada*** the machine is jinxed*, the machine seems to have a jinx on it*.
gafe* 1 *adj*: **ser ~** to have constant bad luck; to have a jinx*, be jinxed*. **2** *nm* (*****) bad luck; jinx*.
gafete *nm* clasp, hook and eye.
gafitas *nfpl* granny glasses.
gafo 1 *adj* (**a**) (*LAm*) footsore, dog-tired; (*Méx**) numb; **estar ~** (*CAm**) to be broke*.
(**b**) (*Carib*) (*****: *no confiable*) unreliable, erratic; (**‡**: *bruto*) thick*.
2 *nm*, **gafa**[2] *nf* (*Carib*) idiot.
gafudo *adj* that wears glasses, with glasses.
gag [gax] *nm*, *pl* **gags** [gax] (*Teat etc*) gag.
gagá* 1 *adj*: **estar ~** to be gaga*. **2** *nmf* old dodderer.
gago (*LAm**) **1** *adj* stammering, stuttering. **2** *nm*, **gaga** *nf* stammerer, stutterer.
gagoso *adj* (*And**) stammering, stuttering.
gaguear [1a] *vi* (*LAm**) to stammer, stutter.
gagueo *nm* (*LAm**) stammer(ing), stutter(ing).
gaguera *nf* (*LAm*) stammer, stutter, speech defect.
gaita 1 *nf* (**a**) (*Mús*) (*flauta*) flute, flageolet; (*organillo*) hurdy-gurdy; **~** (**gallega**) bagpipe; **ser como una ~** to be dissatisfied, be very demanding; **estar de ~** to be merry; **templar ~s** to calm sb down, smooth things out.
(**b**) (*****: *cuello*) neck; **estirar la ~** to crane one's neck.
(**c**) (*molestia*) bother, nuisance; (*trabajo*) tough job; **y toda esa ~*** and all that jazz*.
(**d**) (*Venezuela*) folk music.
(**e**) (*****: *persona*) cheat, trickster.
2 *nmf* (*LAm*: *hum*) Galician, (*any*) Spaniard.
gaitero 1 *adj* (**a**) (*llamativo*) gaudy, flashy. (**b**) *persona* buffoonish. **2** *nm*, **gaitera** *nf* (bag)piper.
gaje *nm* (**a**) (*t* **~s** *pl*) emoluments; perquisite; (*fig*) reward, bonus; **~ del oficio** (*hum*) occupational hazards, occupational risks. (**b**) **en ~ de** (*LAm*) as a token of, as a sign of.
gajo *nm* (**a**) (*rama*) (torn-off) branch, bough; (*de uvas etc*) small cluster, bunch. (**b**) (*de naranja etc*) slice, segment,

quarter. (**c**) (*de tenedor*) point, prong; (*Geog*) spur. (**d**) (*And*) curl, ringlet.

GAL [gal] *nmpl* (*Esp*) *abr de* **Grupos Antiterroristas de Liberación** *anti-ETA terrorist group*.

gal *nmf* member of GAL.

gala *nf* (**a**) (*traje de etiqueta*) full dress; best dress; court dress; **de ~** state (*atr*), dress (*atr*), full-dress (*atr*); gala (*atr*); **estar de ~** to be in full dress; to be in one's best dress, be all dressed up; (*ciudad etc*) to be bedecked, be in festive mood.
(**b**) (*lujos*) **~s** finery, trappings; jewels, adornments; regalia; fine things; **~s de novia** bridal attire.
(**c**) (*fig*) (*elegancia*) elegance, gracefulness; (*pompa*) pomp, display; **hacer ~ de** to display, show off; to boast of, glory in; **tener algo a ~** to be proud of sth; **tener a ~** + *infin* to be proud to + *infin*.
(**d**) (*fig*) (*lo más selecto*) cream, flower; (*orgullo*) pride, chief ornament; **es la ~ de la ciudad** it is the pride of the city.
(**e**) (*fig*: *especialidad*) speciality, special accomplishment.
(**f**) (*LAm*) (*regalo*) gift; (*propina*) tip.
(**g**) (*Mús*) gig, show, concert.
(**h**) (*espectáculo etc*) show; **~ benéfica** charity event.

galáctico *adj* galactic.

galafate *nm* expert thief, sly thief.

galaico *adj* Galician.

galán 1 *nm* (**a**) (*joven*) handsome fellow, attractive young man; (*Don Juan*) ladies' man; (*Hist*) young gentleman, courtier.
(**b**) (*novio*) gallant, beau; (*pretendiente*) suitor.
(**c**) (*Teat*) male lead, chief male part; hero; **~ de cine** matinée idol; **joven ~** juvenile lead; **primer ~** leading man.
(**d**) (*mueble*) clothes-rack.
(**e**) (*CAm Bot*) night-flowering cactus.
2 *adv* (*LAm**) = **bien.**

galanamente *adv* (*V adj* (**a**)) smartly, sprucely; elegantly, tastefully.

galanas *nfpl* (*CAm*): **echar ~** to boast, brag; **hacer ~** to do naughty things, be wicked.

galancete *nm* handsome young man; (*hum*) dapper little man; (*Teat*) male juvenile lead.

galancito *nm* juvenile lead.

galano *adj* (**a**) (*pulcro*) smart, spruce; (*elegante*) elegant, tasteful; (*gallardo*) gaily dressed. (**b**) (*Carib*) *vaca* mottled (*with red and white patches*).

galante *adj* (**a**) *hombre* gallant; (*atento*) charming, attentive (to women); (*cortés*) polite, urbane. (**b**) *mujer* flirtatious; (*pey*) wanton, free, licentious.

galantear [1a] *vt* (*cortejar*) to court, woo; (*coquetear con*) to flirt with.

galantemente *adj* (*V adj*) gallantly; charmingly, attentively; politely.

galanteo *nm* courting, courtship, wooing; flirting.

galantería *nf* (**a**) (*gen*) gallantry; attentiveness (to women); politeness, urbanity. (**b**) (*cumplido*) compliment; (*piropo*) charming thing (to say), gallantry.

galanto *nm* (*Bot*) snowdrop.

galanura *nf* prettiness; charm; elegance, tastefulness.

galápago *nm* (**a**) (*Zool*) tortoise. (**b**) (*Agr*) mouldboard. (**c**) (*Téc*) ingot, pig. (**d**) (*silla de montar*) light saddle; (*LAm*) sidesaddle.

Galápagos: Islas *nfpl* **~** Galapagos Islands.

galardón *nm* (*liter*) reward, prize; award.

galardonado, -a *nm/f* prize-winner, award-winner.

galardonar [1a] *vt* (*liter*) to reward, recompense (*de* with); (*Liter*) *obra* to give a prize to; **obra galardonada por la Academia** work which won an Academy prize.

galaxia *nf* galaxy.

galbana* *nf* sloth, laziness; shiftlessness.

galbanoso* *adj* slothful, lazy; shiftless.

galdosiano *adj* relating to Benito Pérez Galdós; **estudios ~s** Galdós studies.

galdufo *nm* swine‡, villain.

galembo *nm* (*And, Carib*) turkey buzzard.

Galeno *nm* Galen; **g~** (*LAm*: *médico*) doctor.

galeón *nm* galleon.

galeote *nm* galley slave.

galera *nf* (**a**) (*Náut*) galley.
(**b**) (*carro*) (covered) wagon.
(**c**) (*Med*) hospital ward; (*Hist*) women's prison; (*CAm, Méx*: *cobertizo*) open shed; (*CAm*) slaughterhouse.
(**d**) (*LAm*) (*chistera*) top hat; (*fieltro*) felt hat; (*hongo*) bowler hat.
(**e**) (*Tip*) galley.

galerada *nf* (**a**) (*carga*) wagonload. (**b**) (*Tip*) galley proof.

galería *nf* (*gen*) gallery; (*pasillo*) passage, corridor; (*Min*) gallery; (*balcón*) veranda(h); (*Arte*) gallery; (*And, Carib*) store; **~ de alimentación** food hall; **~ de arte** art gallery; **~ de columnas** colonnade; **~ de la muerte** death row; **~ de popa** (*Náut*) stern gallery; **~ secreta** secret passage; **~ de tiro** shooting gallery; **~ de viento** (*Aer*) wind-tunnel.

galerista *nmf* owner (*o* director) of an art gallery.

galerita *nf* crested lark.

galerna *nf*, **galerno** *nm* violent north-west wind (*on N coast of Spain*).

galerón *nm* (**a**) (*CAm*) shed; shed roof; (*Méx*) hall, large room. (**b**) (*Carib*) folk dance.

Gales *nm* Wales.

galés 1 *adj* Welsh. **2** *nm*, **galesa** *nf* Welshman, Welshwoman. **3** *nm* (*Ling*) Welsh.

galfaro *nm* (*Carib*) little rascal.

galga *nf* (**a**) (*Zool*) greyhound (bitch). (**b**) (*Geol*) boulder, rolling stone; (*Téc*) millstone (of an oil press). (**c**) (*Agr*) hub brake (on a cart). (**d**) (*Mec*) gauge.

galgo[1] *nm* greyhound; **~ afgano** Afghan; **~ ruso** borzoi, Russian wolfhound; **¡échale un ~!*** not a hope!, no way!*; **¡vaya Vd a espulgar un ~!*** go to blazes!*

galgo[2]* *adj* (*And*) sweet-toothed, fond of sweets.

galgón* *adj* (*And*) = **galgo[2]**.

galguear* [1a] *vi* (*CAm, Cono Sur*) to be starving, be ravenous; to wander about looking for food.

Galia *nf* Gaul.

gálibo *nm* (*Téc*) gauge; (*luz*) warning light, flashing light.

galicano *adj* Gallic; (*Rel*) Gallican.

galiciano, -a *adj, nm/f* Galician.

galicismo *nm* gallicism.

gálico 1 *adj* Gallic. **2** *nm* syphilis.

galicoso, -a *adj, nm/f* syphilitic.

Galilea *nf* Galilee.

galillo *nm* (*Anat*) uvula.

galimatías *nm invar* rigmarole; gibberish, nonsense.

galo 1 *adj* Gallic; (*moderno*) French. **2** *nm*, **gala** *nf* Gaul; (*moderno*) Frenchman, Frenchwoman.

galocha *nf* clog, patten.

galón[1] *nm* (*Cos*) braid; (*Mil*) stripe, chevron; **quitar los galones a uno** to take his stripes away from sb, demote sb; **la acción le valió 2 galones** the action got him a couple of stripes.

galón[2] *nm* (*medida*) gallon.

galonear [1a] *vt* to trim with braid.

galopada *nf* gallop.

galopante *adj* galloping (*t Med y fig*).

galopar [1a] *vi* to gallop; **echar a ~** to break into a gallop.

galope *nm* gallop; **a ~, al ~** (*LAm*), **de ~** at a gallop, (*fig*) in great haste, in a rush; **a ~ tendido** at full gallop; **alejarse a ~** to gallop off; **desfilar a ~** to gallop past; **llegar a ~** to gallop up; **medio ~** canter.

galopín *nm* (*pícaro*) ragamuffin, urchin; (*bribón*) scoundrel, rogue; (*sabelotodo*) smart Aleck*, clever Dick*; (*Náut*) cabin boy.

galpón *nm* (**a**) (*LAm*) (*cobertizo*) (large) shed, storehouse; (*Hist*: *para esclavos*) slaves' quarters; (*Aut*) garage. (**b**) (*And*: *tejar*) tileworks, pottery.

galucha *nf* (*LAm*) short gallop; (*Carib*) start of a gallop.

galuchar [1a] *vi* (*LAm*) to gallop.

galvánico *adj* galvanic.

galvanismo *nm* galvanism.

galvanizado *adj* galvanized.

galvanizar [1f] *vt* (*lit*) to galvanize, electroplate; (*fig*) to galvanize.

galvano *nm* (*Cono Sur*: *placa*) commemorative plaque.

galla‡ *nf* (*Cono Sur*) bird‡, girl.

gallada *nf* (**a**) (*And, Cono Sur*: *baladronada*) boast. (**b**) **la ~** (*Cono Sur**: *chicos*) the lads, the boys; (*gente*) people.

gallardamente *adv* (*V adj*) gracefully, elegantly; splendidly; bravely; gallantly, dashingly; nobly.

gallardear [1a] *vi* (*comportarse con elegancia*) to be elegant, be graceful, act with ease and grace; (*tener buen porte*) to bear o.s. well; (*pavonearse*) to strut.

gallardete *nm* pennant, streamer.

gallardía *nf* (*V adj*) gracefulness, elegance; fineness, splendidness; bravery; gallantry, dash; nobleness.

gallardo *adj* (*elegante*) graceful, elegant; (*magnífica*) fine, splendid; (*valiente*) brave; (*bizarro*) gallant, dashing; (*noble*) noble.

gallareta *nf* (*LAm*) South American coot; *V* **pato.**

gallear [1a] **1** *vt* (*gallo*) to tread.
2 *vi* (**a**) (*destacar*) to excel, stand out.
(**b**) (*descollar*) to put on airs, strut; (*envalentonarse*) to bully, chuck one's weight about; (*jactarse*) to brag; (*gritar*) to bluster, bawl.

gallego 1 *adj* (**a**) Galician.
(**b**) (*LAm*: *pey*) Spanish (*gen used of immigrants*).
(**c**) (*) yellow, cowardly.
2 *nm*, **gallega** *nf* (**a**) Galician.
(**b**) (*LAm*: *pey*) (any immigrant) Spaniard.
(**c**) (‡) free-loader*, sponger*.
(**d**) (*viento*) north-west wind.
3 *nm* (*Ling*) Galician.

galleguismo *nm* (**a**) (*Ling*) galleguism, word (*o* phrase *etc*) peculiar to Galicia.
(**b**) sense of the differentness of Galicia; (*Pol*) doctrine of (*o* belief in) Galician autonomy.

galleguista 1 *adj* that supports (*etc*) Galician autonomy; **el movimiento** ~ the movement for Galician autonomy; **la familia es muy** ~ the family strongly supports Galician autonomy. **2** *nmf* supporter (*etc*) of Galician autonomy.

gallera *nf* (*LAm*: *palenque*) cockpit; (*And, CAm*: *gallinero*) coop (for gamecocks).

gallería *nf* (*Carib*) (**a**) (*palenque*) cockpit. (**b**) (*fig*) egotism, selfishness.

gallero 1 *adj* (*LAm*) fond of cockfighting. **2** *nm* (**a**) (*LAm*) (*responsable*) man in charge of gamecocks (*o* cockfighting); (*aficionado*) cockfighting enthusiast. (**b**) (*Cono Sur Ferro*) pilferer.

galleta *nf* (**a**) biscuit; cracker; cookie (*US*); wafer; (*Náut*) ship's biscuit, hardtack; (*Cono Sur*) coarse bread; ~ **de perro** dog biscuit; **ir a toda** ~* to go full-speed.
(**b**) (*puñetazo*) bash*, punch, slap.
(**c**) (*Andes, Cono Sur*) gourd for drinking maté.
(**d**) (*Cono Sur**: *bronca*) ticking-off*.
(**e**) (*Cono Sur**) **colgar la** ~ **a uno, dar la** ~ **a uno** (*despedir*) to sack sb*, to give sb the boot*; (*rechazar*) to give sb the brush-off*; (*no hacer caso a*) to give sb the cold shoulder; **le dieron una buena** ~ they gave him a good ticking-off*; **hacerse una** ~ to get in a mess.
(**f**) ~ **del tráfico** (*Carib*) (*embotellamiento*) traffic jam; (*burla*) practical joke.
(**g**) **tener mucha** ~ (*Méx*) to be very strong.

galletear* [1a] *vt* (*Cono Sur*) (**a**) (*despedir*) to sack*, fire*; (*reñir*) to tick off*. (**b**) (*golpear*) to bash*, belt*.

galletero *nm* (**a**) (*recipiente*) biscuit barrel, biscuit tin. (**b**) (*Cono Sur*: *persona*) quick-tempered person; argumentative sort, brawler.

gallina 1 *nf* (**a**) hen, fowl; ~ **de agua** coot; ~ **de bantam** bantam; ~ **clueca** broody hen; ~ **de Guinea** guinea fowl; ~ **ponedora** laying hen, hen in lay; **acostarse con las ~s** to go to bed early; **andar como ~ clueca** (*Méx*) to be as pleased as Punch; **estar como ~ con huevos** to be very distrustful; **estar como ~ en corral ajeno** to have no freedom of movement; to be like a fish out of water; to be timid, be shy; **¡hasta que meen las ~s!*** pigs might fly!*; **la ~ de arriba ensucia a la de abajo** (*LAm*) the underdog always suffers; **matar la ~ de los huevos de oro** to kill the goose that lays the golden eggs.
(**b**) ~ **ciega** (*juego*) blind man's buff.
(**c**) ~ **de mar** gurnard.
(**d**) ~ **ciega** (*CAm, Carib*: *gusano*) white worm.
2 *nmf* (**a**) (*) coward.
(**b**) (*And*: *pey*) Peruvian.

gallinacera *nf* (*And*) bunch of Negroes.

gallinaza *nf* hen droppings.

gallinazo *nm* (*LAm*) turkey buzzard.

gallinería *nf* (**a**) (*gallinas*) flock of hens. (**b**) (*Com*) (*tienda*) poultry shop; (*mercado*) chicken market. (**c**) (*fig*) cowardice.

gallinero *nm* (**a**) (*criadero*) henhouse, coop; (*cesta*) poultry basket.
(**b**) (*persona*) chicken farmer; poulterer, poultry dealer.
(**c**) (*Teat*) gods, top gallery.
(**d**) (*confusión*) babel, hubbub; (*griterío*) noisy gathering; madhouse, bedlam.

gallineta *nf* (*Orn*) woodcock; coot; (*LAm*) guinea-fowl.

gallinilla *nf*: ~ **de bantam** bantam.

gallipavo *nm* (**a**) (*Orn*) turkey. (**b**) (*Mús*) false note, squeak, squawk.

gallito 1 *adj* (*) cocky*, cocksure. **2** *nm* (**a**) (*Orn*) small cock. (**b**) (*fig*) rowdy, tough*, troublemaker; **el** ~ (**del mundo**) the cock-o'-the walk, the top dog. (**c**) (*And*) small arrow, dart.

gallo *nm* (**a**) (*Orn*) cock, cockerel, rooster; ~ **lira** black grouse; ~ **montés**, ~ **silvestre** capercaillie; ~ **de combate**, ~ **de pelea**, ~ **de riña** gamecock, fighting cock; **al primer** ~ (*Méx*) at midnight; **estar como ~ en gallinero** to be much esteemed, be well thought of; **en menos que canta un** ~ in an instant; **otro ~ me cantara** that would be quite a different matter; **comer** ~ (*And, CAm**) to suffer a setback; **ha comido** ~ (*Méx*) he's in a fighting mood; **dormírsele a uno el** ~ (*CAm**) to let an opportunity slip; **hay ~ tapado** (*LAm*) I smell a rat; **no me va nada en el** ~ (*Méx**) it doesn't matter to me, it's no skin off my nose‡; **levantar el** ~ (*Carib, Méx**) to throw in the towel; **matar a uno el ~ en la mano** to floor sb (in an argument), shut sb up*; **pelar** ~ (*Méx**) to make tracks*.
(**b**) (*: *jefe*) boss; (*LAm*) expert, master; **yo he sido ~ para eso** I was a great one at that.
(**c**) **alzar el** ~, **levantar el** ~ (*fig*) to put on airs, brag; to bawl, behave noisily; **tener mucho** ~ to be cocky.
(**d**) (*Pesca*) cork float.
(**e**) (*Mús*) false note, squeak, squawk; **soltó un** ~ his voice cracked.
(**f**) (*LAm*‡) (*flema*) phlegm, spit, spittle; (*escupitajo*) gob‡ of spit.
(**g**) (*And*: *flecha*) small arrow, dart.
(**h**) (*And, Cono Sur*: *de bomberos*) fire-engine, hose truck.
(**i**) (*Méx Mús*) street serenade.
(**j**) **vestirse de** ~ (*Méx*) to wear old clothes.
(**k**) (*Cono Sur**) bloke‡, guy*.
(**l**) (*Pez*) john dory.
(**m**) ~ **pinto** (*CAm Culin*) rice and beans.
(**n**) (*LAm Dep*) shuttlecock.
(**o**) (*Boxeo*) bantamweight.

gallofero 1 *adj* idle, loafing; vagabond. **2** *nm* idler, loafer; tramp; beggar.

gallón* 1 *adj* (*Méx*) cocky*. **2** *nm* local boss.

gallote* 1 *adj* (*CAm, Méx*) cocky*. **2** *nm* (*CAm*) cop*.

gallumbos‡ *nmpl* (*pantalones*) pants, trousers; (*calzoncillos*) underpants.

gama[1] *nf* (*Mús*) scale; (*fig*) range, scale, gamut; **una extensa ~ de colores** an extensive range of colours; ~ **de frecuencias** frequency range; ~ **de ondas** wave range; ~ **sonora** sound range; **alto de** ~, **de ~ alta** in the top part of the range; **bajo de** ~, **de ~ baja** in the lower part of the range.

gama[2] *nf* (*letra*) gamma.

gama[3] *nf* (*Zool*) doe (of fallow deer); **sentársele a uno la** ~ (*Cono Sur*) to get discouraged.

gamarra *nf* (*CAm*) halter; **llevar a uno de la** ~* to lead sb by the nose.

gamba *nf* (**a**) (*Zool*) prawn. (**b**) (‡) 100 pesetas; **media** ~ 50 pesetas. (**c**) (‡: *pierna*) leg; **meter la** ~ to put one's foot in it.

gambado *adj* (*Carib*) knock-kneed.

gamberrada *nf* (*pey*) piece of hooliganism, loutish thing (to do); (*inocente*) lark*, rag*, piece of horseplay; **hacer ~s** = **gamberrear**.

gamberrear [1a] *vi* (*pey*) to go around causing trouble, act like a hooligan; to be a lout; (*gandulear*) to loaf; (*tontear*) to lark about*, horse around*.

gamberrismo *nm* hooliganism; loutishness.

gamberrístico *adj* loutish, ill-bred.

gamberro 1 *adj* (*pey*) ill-bred, loutish, rough; (*inocente*) boisterous, high-spirited. **2** *nm* (*pey*) lout, hooligan, troublemaker; roughneck*; boisterous youth, high-spirited lad; **hacer el** ~* to act like a hooligan; = **gamberrear**.

gambeta *nf* (**a**) (*de caballo*) prance, caper. (**b**) (*And, Cono Sur*: *esguince*) dodge, avoiding action; (*) dodge, pretext.

gambito *nm* gambit.

gambuza *nf* (*Náut*) store, storeroom.

gamella *nf* trough; washtub.

gamín* *nm* (*And*) street urchin.

gamo *nm* buck (of fallow deer).

gamonal *nm* (*And, CAm*) = **cacique**.

gamonalismo *nm* (*And, CAm*) = **caciquismo**.

gamulán *nm* (*Cono Sur*) sheepskin.

gamuza *nf* (**a**) (*Zool*) chamois. (**b**) (*piel*) chamois leather, wash leather; (*sacudidor*) duster.

gana *nf* (*deseo*) desire, wish (*de* for); (*apetito*) appetite (*de* for); (*afán*) inclination, longing (*de* for); **¡las ~s!** you'll wish you had (agreed)!; **son ~s de joder*‡** (*o* **molestar** *etc*) they're just trying to be awkward; **es** ~ (*And, Carib, Méx*) it's a waste of time, there's no point; ~ **tiene de coles quien besa al hortelano** it's just cupboard love; **donde hay ~ hay maña** where there's a will there's a way; **con**

~s (*CAm, Carib*: *de veras*) really, truly; **con ~(s)** (*LAm**) with a will; **comer con ~** to eat heartily; **ser malo con ~** (*CAm, Carib*) to be thoroughly nasty; **hacer algo con ~s** to do sth willingly (*o* enthusiastically); **hacer algo sin ~s** to do sth reluctantly (*o* unwillingly); **de ~** (*And**) (*sin querer*) unintentionally; (*en broma*) as a joke, in fun; **de buena ~** willingly, readily; **¡de buena ~!** gladly!; **de mala ~** unwillingly, reluctantly, grudgingly; **hasta las ~s** (*Méx*) right up to the end; **me da la ~ de** + *infin* I feel like + *ger*, I want to + *infin*, I have an inclination to + *infin*; **esto da ~s de comerlo** it makes you want to eat it; **porque no me da la** (**real** *o* **realísima**) **~** because I don't (damned well) want to; **como te dé la ~** just as you wish; **le entran ~s de** + *infin* he begins to want to + *infin*, he feels the urge to + *infin*; **siempre hace su regalada ~** (*Méx**) he always goes his own sweet way; **pagar hasta las ~s*** to pay over the odds; **no me pega la ~** (*Méx**) I don't feel like it; **quedarse con las ~s** to fail, be disappointed; to have one's hopes dashed; **quitársele a uno las ~s de** to spoil one's appetite for; **tener ~*** to be in the mood; **tener ~s de** + *infin* to feel like + *ger*, have a mind to + *infin*; **tengo pocas ~s de** + *infin* I don't much feel like + *ger;* **tengo ~s de verte** I'm longing to see you.

ganadería *nf* (**a**) (*crianza*) cattle raising, stockbreeding; ranching. (**b**) (*estancia*) stock farm; (*rancho*) cattle ranch. (**c**) (*ganado*) cattle, livestock; (*raza*) strain, breed, race (of cattle).

ganadero 1 *adj animal* cattle (*atr*), stock (*atr*); cattle-raising (*atr*). **2** *nm* (*persona*) stockbreeder, rancher (*US*); cattle dealer.

ganado *nm* (**a**) (*gen*) stock, livestock; (*esp LAm*) cattle; (*un ~*) herd, flock; **~ asnal, ~ asnar** donkeys; **~ caballar** horses; **~ cabrío** goats; **~ lanar, ~ ovejuno** sheep; **~ mayor** cattle, horses and mules; **~ menor** sheep, goats and pigs; **~ porcino** pigs; **~ vacuno** cattle.
(**b**) **un ~ de** (*LAm*: *fig*) a crowd of, a mob of.

ganador 1 *adj* winning, victorious; **el equipo ~** the winning team; **apostar a ~ y colocado** to back (a horse) each way, back for a win and a place.
2 *nm*, **ganadora** *nf* winner; (*Fin*) earner; (*fig*) gainer, one who gains.

ganancia *nf* (**a**) (*beneficio*) gain; (*aumento*) increase; (*Com, Fin*) profit; **~s** earnings; profits, winnings; **~s y pérdidas** profit and loss; **~ bruta** gross profit; **~ líquida** net profit; **no le arriendo la ~** I don't envy him; **sacar ~ de** to draw profit from. (**b**) (*LAm*: *propina*) extra, bonus.

ganancial *adj* profit (*atr*).

ganancioso 1 *adj* (**a**) (*lucrativo*) gainful; profitable, lucrative. (**b**) (*triunfador*) winning; **salir ~** to be the winner. **2** *nm*, **gananciosa** *nf*: **en esto el ~ es él** he'll come out of this better off.

ganapán *nm* (**a**) (*recadero*) messenger, porter. (**b**) (*temporero*) casual labourer; odd-job man. (**c**) (*patán*) lout, rough individual.

ganar [1a] **1** *vt* (**a**) (*adquirir*) to gain; (*lograr*) to get, acquire, obtain; (*Com, Fin*) to earn; *interés* to earn; to draw; *dinero* to earn, make; *premio* to win; **gana un sueldo** he earns a salary; **¿cuánto ganas al mes?** how much do you earn (*o* make) a month?; **ha ganado mucho dinero** she has made a great deal of money; **tierras ganadas al mar** land reclaimed from the sea, land won from the sea.
(**b**) (*Dep etc*) *carrera, partido*, to win; *punto* to score, win; *contrario* to beat; *rival* to outstrip, surpass, leave behind; **~ unas oposiciones para un puesto** to win a post by public competition; **A le ganó a B esta vez** A beat B this time; **no hay quien le gane** there's nobody who can beat him; **A le gana a B en pericia** A has more expert knowledge than B; **A le gana a B trabajando** A is a better worker than B; **A le ganó 5 duros a B** A won 5 duros from (*o* off) B.
(**c**) (*Mil*) *ciudad etc* to take, capture.
(**d**) (*alcanzar*) to reach; **~ la orilla** to reach the shore; **~ la orilla nadando** to swim to the shore.
(**e**) (*fig*: *conquistar*) to win over; *apoyo, partidarios* to win, get; **dejarse ~ por** to allow o.s. to be won over by; **no se deja ~ en ningún momento por la desesperación** he never gives way to despair.
2 *vi* (**a**) (*Dep etc*) to win; to gain.
(**b**) (*fig*) to thrive, improve; (*prosperar*) to do well; **ha ganado mucho en salud** he has much improved in health; **saldrás ganando** you'll do well out of it.
(**c**) (*t* **ganarse**; *LAm*) to go off; to escape, take refuge; **~ a la cama** to go off to bed; **~ hasta la casa** to get to the house; **se ganó en la iglesia** he took refuge in the church; **el caballo ganó para el bosque** the horse moved off towards the wood, the horse made for the wood.
3 ganarse *vr*: **~ la confianza de uno** to win sb's trust; **~ las antipatías de uno** to attract sb's dislike.

gancha‡ *nf* hash*, pot‡.

ganchera *nf* (*Cono Sur*) matchmaker.

ganchero *nm* (*Cono Sur*) (*ayudante*) helper, assistant; (*factótum*) odd-job man.

ganchete *nm*: **mirar al ~** (*Carib**) to look out of the corner of one's eye (at); **ir de ~** (*LAm*) to go arm-in-arm.

ganchillo *nm* (**a**) small hook; (*Cos*) crochet hook. (**b**) (*labor*) crochet, crochet work; **hacer ~** to crochet.

gancho *nm* (**a**) (*gen*) hook; (*colgador*) hanger; (*de árbol*) stump; (*Agr*) shepherd's crook; (*LAm*: *horquilla*) hairpin; (*CAm*: *imperdible*) safety pin; (*Boxeo*) hook; **~ a la cara** uppercut; **~ de carnicero** butcher's hook; **echar el ~ a** (*fig*) to hook, land, capture; **estar en ~s** (*LAm*‡) to be hooked on drugs*.
(**b**) (*persona*) (*coime*) pimp, procurer; (*agente*) tout; (*cómplice*) mate, partner.
(**c**) (*: *atractivo*) appeal, attraction; drawing power; (*de slogan etc*) bite, pull; (*de mujer*) charm, attractiveness; **tiene muchísimo ~** she's very charming.
(**d**) (*And*) lady's saddle.
(**e**) (*LAm**) (*ayuda*) help; (*protección*) protection; **hacer ~** (*CAm, Cono Sur*) to lend a hand.

ganchoso *adj*, **ganchudo** *adj* hooked, curved.

gandalla‡ *nmf* (*Méx*) (*vagabundo*) tramp, bum (*US*); (*arribista*) upstart.

gandido *adj* (*And*) greedy.

gandinga *nf* (*Carib*) (**a**) (*Culin*) thick stew. (**b**) (*: *apatía*) sloth, apathy; **tener poca ~** to have no sense of shame.

gandola *nf* (*LAm*) articulated truck.

gandul 1 *adj* idle, lazy, slack; good-for-nothing. **2** *nm*, **gandula**[1] *nf* idler, slacker; good-for-nothing.

gandula[2]* *nf* (*Jur*) law on vagrancy.

gandulear [1a] *vi* to idle, loaf, slack.

gandulería *nf* idleness, loafing, slackness.

gandulitis *nf* (*hum*) congenital laziness.

gane *nm* (*CAm Dep*) win, victory; **llevarse el ~, lograr el ~** to win.

ganga *nf* (**a**) (*Com*) bargain; **¡una verdadera ~!** a genuine bargain!; **precio de ~** bargain price, give away price. (**b**) (*fig*) (*extra*) extra, bonus; cheap acquisition; (*suerte*) windfall; (*cosa fácil*) cinch‡, gift; **esto es una ~** this is a cinch‡. (**c**) (*Méx**: *sarcasmo*) taunt, jeer.

Ganges *nm*: **el** (**Río**) **~** the Ganges.

ganglio *nm* ganglion; swelling; **~s**‡ tits‡.

gangosear [1a] *vi* (*And, Cono Sur*) (**a**) (*pey**) to talk through one's nose, whine. (**b**) = **ganguear.**

gangoseo *nm* (*And, Cono Sur*) = **gangueo.**

gangoso *adj acento* nasal, twanging.

gangrena *nf* gangrene.

gangrenar [1a] **1** *vt* (**a**) (*Med*) to make gangrenous, cause gangrene in. (**b**) (*fig*) to infect, destroy. **2 gangrenarse** *vr* to become gangrenous.

gangrenoso *adj* gangrenous.

gán(g)ster ['ganster] *nm*, *pl* **gán(g)sters** ['ganster] gangster, gunman.

gan(g)sterismo [ganste'rizmo] *nm* gangsterism.

ganguear [1a] *vi* to talk with a nasal accent, speak with a twang.

gangueo *nm* nasal accent, twang.

ganoso *adj* (**a**) (*afanoso*) anxious, keen; **~ de** + *infin* anxious to + *infin*, keen to + *infin*. (**b**) (*Cono Sur*) *caballo* spirited, fiery.

gansa *nf* (**a**) (*Orn*) goose. (**b**) (*) goose, silly girl.

gansada *nf* daft thing to do; lark*, caper.

ganso 1 *nm* (**a**) (*Orn*) goose, gander; **~ salvaje** wild goose. (**b**) (*) idiot, dimwit*, dolt; country bumpkin; **¡no seas ~!** don't be an idiot!; **hacer el ~** to play the fool. **2** *adj* (*) (*grande*) huge, hefty; (*atractivo*) hunky*, dishy*.

gánster *nm* gangster.

Gante *nm* Ghent.

ganzúa 1 *nf* picklock, skeleton key. **2** *nmf* (*ladrón*) burglar, thief; (*curioso*) inquisitive person, smeller out of secrets.

gañán *nm* farmhand, labourer.

gañido *nm* (*V v*) yelp, howl; croak; wheeze.

gañir [3h] *vi* (*perro*) to yelp, howl; (*pájaro*) to croak; (*persona*) to wheeze, talk hoarsely, croak.

gañón* *nm*, **gañote*** *nm* throat, gullet.

gapo‡ *nm*: **echar un ~** to gob‡, spit.

GAR *nm abr de* **Grupo Antiterrorista Rural.**

garabatear [1a] **1** *vt* to scribble, scrawl. **2** *vi* (**a**) (*Mec*) to use a hook. (**b**) (*escribiendo*) to scribble, scrawl. (**c**) (*andar con rodeos*) to beat about the bush.

garabato *nm* (**a**) (*gancho*) hook; grapple, grapnel; (*Carib*) long forked pole; (*Náut*) grappling iron.
(**b**) (*en ejercicio de escritura*) pothook; **~s** scribble, scrawl.
(**c**) (*Carib**: *flaco*) beanpole*.
(**d**) (*Cono Sur*: *palabrota*) swearword; **echar ~s** to swear.
(**e**) = **gancho** (**c**).

garabina *nf* (**a**) (*And*: *bagatela*) trifle, bagatelle; cheap finery. (**b**) (*Carib*: *crisálida*) chrysalis.

garabito *nm* (**a**) (*de mercado*) market stall. (**b**) (*Cono Sur*) tramp, hobo (*US*).

garabullo‡ *nm* 5 pesetas.

garaje *nm* garage; **el ~ La Estrella** (*hum*) the street.

garajista *nm* (*dueño*) garage owner; (*trabajador*) garage man, garage attendant.

garambaina *nf* (**a**) (*adornos*) cheap finery, tawdry finery.
(**b**) (*carácter chillón*) gaudiness.
(**c**) **~s** (*muecas*) (affected) grimaces; (*ademanes*) absurd mannerisms; **¡déjate de ~s!** stop that silly simpering!
(**d**) **~s** (*garabatos*) scribble, scrawl.

garambetas *nfpl* (*Carib**) (**a**) = **garambaina** (**a**) *y* (**c**). (**b**) **hacer ~** to pull faces.

garandumba *nf* (*Cono Sur*) (**a**) (*Náut*) flatboat, flat river boat. (**b**) (*hum*) big woman.

garante 1 *adj* (*responsable*) guaranteeing, responsible. **2** *nmf* (*Fin*) guarantor, surety.

garantía *nf* (*gen*) guarantee; (*seguridad*) pledge, security; (*compromiso*) undertaking; (*Jur*) warranty; **bajo ~** under guarantee; **~s constitucionales** constitutional safeguards; **~ en efectivo** cash guarantee, surety; **~ escrita** express warranty; **~ implícita** implied warranty; **de máxima ~** absolutely guaranteed.

garantir [3a; *defectivo*] *vt* (**a**) to guarantee. (**b**) (*And, Carib, Cono Sur*: *asegurar*) to guarantee, assure; **le garanto** I assure you, I warrant you.

garantizadamente *adv* genuinely, authentically.

garantizado *adj* guaranteed; (*fig*) genuine, authentic.

garantizar [1f] *vt* to guarantee, warrant; to vouch for.

garañón *nm* (**a**) (*asno*) stud jackass; (*LAm*: *semental*) stallion. (**b**) (*Cono Sur*) brothel keeper.

garapiña *nf* (**a**) (*Culin*) sugar icing, sugar coating. (**b**) (*LAm*: *bebida*) iced pineapple drink. (**c**) (*Méx*: *robo*) theft.

garapiñada *nf* sugar and almond sweet.

garapiñados *nmpl* sugared almonds.

garapiñar [1a] *vt helado etc* to freeze; *nata* to clot; *pastel* to ice, coat with sugar; *fruta* to candy.

garapiñera *nf* ice-cream freezer.

garapullo *nm* (*rehilete*) dart; (*Taur*) banderilla.

garata *nf* (*Carib**) fight, brawl.

garatusas *nfpl*: **hacer ~ a uno** to coax sb, wheedle sb.

garba *nf* (*Agr*) sheaf.

garbanzo *nm* (**a**) (*Bot*) chickpea; **ser el ~ negro** to be the black sheep of the family; **ganarse los ~s** to earn one's living.
(**b**) **de ~** ordinary, unpretentious, common; **gente de ~** humble folk, ordinary people.

garbear [1a] **1** *vt* (*: *robar*) to pinch*, swipe‡. **2** *vi* (**a**) (*afectar garbo*) to affect elegance, make a show, show o.s. off. (**b**) (*robar*) to steal (for a living). (**c**) = **3. 3 garbearse** *vr* to get along, rub along.

garbeo *nm* affected elegance, show; **darse un ~*, pegarse un ~*** to go for a walk.

garbera *nf* (*Agr*) stook, shock.

garbí *nm* south-west wind (*Catalonia*).

garbillar [1a] *vt* (*Agr*) to sift, sieve; (*Min*) to sift, screen, riddle.

garbillo *nm* sieve; screen, riddle.

garbo *nm* (**a**) (*elegancia*) grace, elegance; (*porte*) graceful bearing, fine carriage; (*aire*) jauntiness, jaunty bearing; (*de mujer*) glamour, allure, attractiveness; (*de escrito etc*) style, stylishness; **andar con ~** to walk gracefully, carry o.s. well; **hacer algo con ~** to do sth with grace and ease (*o* with style); **¡qué ~!** isn't she lovely?
(**b**) (*largueza*) magnanimity, generosity.

garbosamente *adv* (*V adj*) (**a**) gracefully, elegantly; jauntily; stylishly. (**b**) generously.

garboso *adj* (**a**) (*elegante*) graceful, elegant; *andar* jaunty; *escrito* stylish. (**b**) (*generoso*) magnanimous, generous.

garceta *nf* egret.

garcilla *nf*: **~ bueyera** cattle egret.

garçon: **con pelo a lo ~** with bobbed hair, with hair in a boyish style.

gardenia *nf* gardenia.

garduña¹ *nf* (*Zool*) marten.

garduño, -a² *nm/f* sneak thief.

garete *nm*: **estar al ~, ir al ~** to be adrift; (*fig*) to be all at sea.

garfa *nf* claw.

garfada *nf* clawing, scratching.

garfil* *nm* (*Méx*) cop*.

garfio *nm* hook; gaff; (*Téc*) grapple, grappling iron, claw; (*Alpinismo*) climbing iron.

gargá‡ *nf* = **garganta**.

gargajear [1a] *vi* to spit phlegm, hawk.

gargajo *nm* phlegm, sputum.

garganta *nf* (**a**) (*Anat*) throat, gullet; neck; **mojar la ~*** to wet one's whistle*; **le tengo atravesado en la ~** he sticks in my gullet; **tener el agua a la ~** to be in great danger.
(**b**) (*Anat*: *de pie*) instep.
(**c**) (*Mús*) singing voice; **tener buena ~** to have a good singing voice.
(**d**) (*de botella*) neck.
(**e**) (*Geog*) gorge, ravine; narrow pass.
(**f**) (*Arquit*: *de columna etc*) shaft.

gargantear [1a] *vi* (*Mús*) to warble, quaver, trill.

garganteo *nm* warble, quaver, trill.

gargantilla *nf* necklace.

gargantuesco *adj* gargantuan.

gárgara *nf* (*t* **~s** *pl*) gargle, gargling; **hacer ~** to gargle; **¡vaya Vd a hacer ~!** go to blazes!*; **mandar a uno a hacer ~*** to tell sb to go to hell.

gargarear [1a] *vi* (*And, CAm, Cono Sur*) to gargle.

gargarismo *nm* (**a**) (*líquido*) gargle, gargling solution. (**b**) (*acto*) gargle, gargling.

gargarizar [1f] *vi* to gargle.

gárgol *nm* (*Téc*: *ranura*) groove.

gárgola *nf* gargoyle.

garguero *nm* gullet; windpipe.

garifo *adj* (**a**) (*elegante*) spruce, elegant, natty*. (**b**) (*Cono Sur*: *astuto*) sharp. (**c**) (*And**: *engreído*) stuck-up*. (**d**) (*CAm, And*: *hambriento*) hungry. (**e**) **estar ~** (*And*) to be broke*.

gariga *nf* (*Méx*) drizzle.

garita *nf* (*caseta*) cabin, hut, box; (*Mil*) sentry box; (*de camión etc*) cab; (*conserjería*) porter's lodge; (*de vigilancia*) look-out post; (*: *WC*) water closet; (*LAm*: *de policía de tráfico*) stand, box; **~ de control** checkpoint; **~ de señales** signal-box.

garitea *nf* (*And*) river flatboat.

garitero, -a *nm/f* (*dueño*) keeper of a gaming house; (*jugador*) gambler.

garito *nm* (**a**) (*club*) nightclub, night spot; (*de juego*) gaming house, gambling-den. (**b**) (*ganancias*) winnings.

garla *nf* talk, chatter.

garlador 1 *adj* garrulous. **2** *nm*, **garladora** *nf* chatterer, great talker.

garlito *nm* fish trap; (*fig*) snare, trap; **caer en el ~** to fall into the trap; **coger a uno en el ~** to catch sb in the act.

garlopa *nf* jack plane.

garnacha *nf* (**a**) (*Jur*: *Hist*) gown, robe. (**b**) (*persona*) judge. (**c**) (*Méx Culin*) *tortilla with filling.* (**d**) **a la ~** (*CAm**) violently; **¡ni de ~!** (*Carib**) not on your life! (**e**) (*vino*) garnacha (*a sweet wine made from purple grapes*).

garnachear [1a] *vt* (*Cono Sur*: *llevar ventaja a*) to have the edge over.

garnucho *nm* (*Méx*) tap, rap on the nose.

Garona *nm* Garonne.

garpar‡ [1a] *vt* (*Cono Sur*) to pay, fork out*.

garra *nf* (**a**) (*Zool*) claw; talon; (*mano*: *pey*) paw; (*Méx**) muscular strength; **echar la ~ a uno** to arrest sb, seize sb; **estar como una ~** (*And, Cono Sur*) to be as thin as a rake*.
(**b**) **~s** (*Zool*) claws, talons; (*fig*) clutches; **caer en las ~s de uno** to fall into sb's clutches.
(**c**) (*Téc*) claw, tooth, hook; (*Mec*) clutch; **~ de seguridad** safety clutch.
(**d**) (*) (*fig*) bite, penetration; (*Dep*) sharpness, edge; **esa canción no tiene ~** that song has no bite to it.
(**e**) (*LAm*) piece of old leather; **~s** (*Méx**) bits, pieces, scraps; **no hay cuero sin ~s** (*Méx**) you can't make an omelette without breaking eggs.
(**f**) (*And*: *bolsa*) leather bag.

garrafa *nf* (*de vino, licor*) carafe; (*LAm*: *bombona*) cylinder.

garrafal *adj* enormous, terrific; *error etc* monumental, terrible.

garrafón *nm* demijohn.

garrancha* *nf* (*espada*) sword; (*And*: *gancho*) hook.

garrapata *nf* (**a**) (*Zool*) tick. (**b**) (*Mil*: *hum*) disabled horse, useless horse.

garrapatear [1a] *vi* to scribble, scrawl.

garrapatero *nm* (*Orn*) cowbird, buffalo bird; (*LAm*) tick-eater.

garrapato *nm* pothook; **~s** (*fig*) scribble, scrawl.

garrapaticida *nm* (*LAm*) insecticide, tick-killing agent.

garrear [1a] (*Cono Sur*) **1** *vt* (**a**) *animal* to skin the feet of. (**b**) (*: *robar*) to pinch*. **2** *vi* to sponge, live off other people.

garreo* *nm*: **es de puro ~** (*Cono Sur*) it's a piece of cake*.

garrete *nm* (*And, CAm, Cono Sur*) (*de caballo*) hock; (*de persona*) back of the knee.

garrido *adj* (**a**) (*elegante*) neat, elegant, smart. (**b**) (††: *bien parecido*) handsome; pretty.

garroba *nf* carob bean.

garrobo *nm* (*CAm*) (*iguana*) iguana; (*caimán*) small alligator.

garrocha *nf* (*Agr*) goad; (*Taur*) spear; (*LAm Dep*) vaulting pole.

garrón *nm* (*Orn*) spur; talon; (*Zool*) paw; heel; (*de carne*) shank; (*Cono Sur*: *de caballo*) hock; (*Bot*) snag, spur; **vivir de ~** (*Cono Sur*) = **garronear**.

garronear [1a] *vi* (*Cono Sur*: *vivir de gorra*) to sponge*, live off other people.

garrotazo *nm* blow with a stick (*o* club *etc*).

garrote *nm* (**a**) (*bastón*) stick, club, cudgel; **política del ~ y la zanahoria** the carrot-and-stick approach; **usar el gran ~** (*fig*) to use the big stick.

(**b**) (*Med*) tourniquet; (*Jur*) garrotte; **dar ~ a uno** to garrotte sb.

(**c**) (*Méx*) (*Aut*) brake; **darse ~*** to check o.s., hold o.s. back.

garrotero 1 *adj* (*Carib, Cono Sur**) stingy. **2** *nm* (**a**) (*Méx*) brakeman. (**b**) (*And, Cono Sur*) (*matón*) bully, tough*; (*pendenciero*) brawler, troublemaker. (**c**) (*Carib*: *prestamista*) moneylender.

garrotillo *nm* (**a**) (*Med*) croup. (**b**) (*Cono Sur*: *granizada*) summer hail.

garrucha *nf* pulley.

garrudo *adj* (**a**) (*Méx*) tough, muscular. (**b**) (*And*) *vaca* terribly thin.

garrulería *nf* chatter.

garrulidad *nf* garrulousness, talkativeness.

gárrulo *adj persona* garrulous, chattering, talkative; *pájaro* twittering; *agua* babbling, murmuring; *viento* noisy.

garúa *nf* (**a**) (*LAm*: *lloviznar*) drizzle. (**b**) (*Carib*: *alboroto*) row, din.

garuar [1e] *vi* (*LAm*: *lloviznar*) to drizzle; **¡qué le garúe fino!** I wish you luck!, I hope it keeps fine for you!

garubar [1a] *vi* (*Cono Sur*) = **garuar**.

garufa* *nf*: **ir de ~** (*Cono Sur*) to go on a spree.

garuga *nf* (*CAm, Cono Sur, Méx*) = **garúa**.

garugar [1h] *vi* (*Cono Sur*) = **garuar**.

garulla 1 *nf* (**a**) (*uvas*) loose grapes. (**b**) (*: *gentío*) mob, rabble. **2** *nmf* (*) urchin, rascal.

garullada* *nf* mob, rabble.

garza[1] *nf* (*t* **~ real**) heron; **~ imperial** purple heron.

garza[2] *nf* (*Cono Sur*) beer glass.

garzo *adj* (*liter*) *ojos* blue, bluish; *persona* blue-eyed.

garzón *nm* (*Cono Sur*) waiter.

garzona *nf* (*Cono Sur*) waitress.

gas *nm* (**a**) gas; (*vapores*) fumes; **~ del alumbrado** coalgas; **~ asfixiante, ~ tóxico** poison gas; **~ butano** butane; **~es de escape** exhaust (fumes); **~ hilarante** laughing-gas; **~ inerte** inert gas; **~ invernadero** greenhouse gas; **~ lacrimógeno** teargas; **~ licuado** (*Cono Sur*) Calor gas ®; **~ mostaza** mustard-gas; **~ natural** natural gas; **~ nervioso** nerve-gas; **~ de los pantanos** marsh gas; **~ pobre** producer gas; **asfixiar con ~** to gas; **estar ~** (*CAm*: *hum*) to be head over heels in love.

(**b**) (*gasolina*) petrol, gas (*US*); **darle ~** to step on the gas*; **ir a todo ~** (*Aut, t fig*) to go flat out; **perder ~** (*fig*) to slow down, lose impetus.

gasa *nf* gauze; (*Med*) lint; (*luto*) crêpe; (*de pañal*) nappy-liner; **~ higiénica** sanitary towel.

Gascuña *nf* Gascony.

gaseado *adj* carbonated, aerated.

gasear [1a] *vt* to gas, kill with gas.

gaseosa *nf* mineral water; (*frec*) pop*, fizz, fizzy drink; **~ de limón** fizzy lemonade.

gaseoso *adj* gaseous; aerated, carbonated; gassy; *bebida* fizzy.

gásfiter *nm*, *pl* **gásfiters** (*Cono Sur*) plumber.

gasfitería *nf* (*And, Cono Sur*) plumber's (shop).

gasfitero, -a *nm/f* (*And, Cono Sur*) plumber.

gasificación *nf* (**a**) (*Quím*) gasification. (**b**) (*de ciudad*) supply of piped gas (*de* to).

gasista 1 *adj* gas (*atr*); **industria ~** gas industry. **2** *nm* gas fitter, gasman.

gasístico *adj* gas (*atr*).

gasoducto *nm* gas pipeline.

gas-oil [ga'soil] *nm* diesel oil.

gasóleo *nm* diesel oil; **~ B** red diesel.

gasolero *nm* diesel-powered car.

gasolina *nf* (**a**) (*Aut*) petrol, motor spirit, gasoline (*US*), gas (*US*); **~ de aviación** aviation spirit; **~ normal** two-star petrol; **~ súper** three-star petrol; **~ extra** four-star petrol; **~ sin plomo** unleaded petrol; **~ de alto octanaje** high-octane petrol; **echar ~⁑** to take a leak⁑; **repostar ~⁑** to have a drink.

(**b**) (*Carib*: *gasolinera*) petrol-station, gas station (*US*).

gasolinera *nf* (**a**) (*Náut*) motorboat. (**b**) (*Aut*) petrol-station, gas station (*US*).

gasolinero *nm* (*dueño*) owner of a filling-station; (*empleado*) petrol-pump attendant.

gasómetro *nm* gasometer.

gásquet *nm*, *pl* **gásquets** (*LAm*) gasket.

gastable *adj* expendable; dispensable.

gastado *adj* (**a**) (*usado*) spent; used up. (**b**) (*decaído*) worn out; *ropa* shabby, threadbare. (**c**) (*trillado*) hackneyed, trite; *chiste* old, corny*.

gastador 1 *adj* (*extravagante*) extravagant, lavish; (*disipador*) wasteful. **2** *nm*, **gastadora** *nf* (*derrochador*) spender; (*pey*) spendthrift. **3** (*Mil*: *Hist*) sapper, pioneer.

gastar [1a] **1** *vt* (**a**) *dinero, esfuerzo, tiempo* to spend; *dinero* to expend, lay out; **han gastado un dineral** they've spent a fortune.

(**b**) (*consumir*) to use up, consume.

(**c**) (*pey*) to waste; **~ palabras** to waste words, waste one's breath.

(**d**) (*Mec etc*) to wear away, wear down; *ropa, zapatos* to wear out; to spoil.

(**e**) (*vestir*) to have, wear, sport; (*usar*) to use; *coche etc* to have, own, run; **~ barba** to have a beard, wear a beard, sport a beard; **antes no gastaba gafas** he used not to wear glasses; **¿qué número (de zapatos) gasta Vd?** (*Esp*) what size (of shoes) do you take?

(**f**) *broma* to crack; *burla* to play (*a* on).

(**g**) **~las*** to act, behave; **todos sabemos cómo las gasta Juan** we all know how John carries on*.

2 *vi* to spend, spend money.

3 gastarse *vr* to become exhausted; to run out; to wear out; to waste, go to waste, spoil.

Gasteiz *nm* Vitoria.

gasto *nm* (**a**) (*acto*) spending, expenditure.

(**b**) (*cantidad*) amount spent, expenditure, expense; **supone un gran ~ para él** it means a considerable expense for him.

(**c**) (*consumo*) consumption, use.

(**d**) (*Mec etc*) wear.

(**e**) (*pey*) waste.

(**f**) (*de gas etc*) flow, rate of flow.

(**g**) (*Com, Fin*) **~s** expenses; charge(s), cost(s), rate(s); **~s de acarreo** transport charges, haulage; **~s de administración, ~s administrativos** administrative costs, overheads; **~s bancarios** bank charges; **~s comerciales** business expenses; **~s de comunidad, ~s de escalera** service charge; **~s de conservación, ~s de mantenimiento** upkeep costs, maintenance costs; **~s de correo** postal charges; **~s corrientes** running costs; **~s de defensa** (*Mil*) defence costs; **~s de desplazamiento** (*al mudarse*) removal expenses; (*de viaje*) travelling expenses; **~s de entrega** (*t* **~s de envío**) delivery charge; **~s de envío** charge for post and packing; **~s de explotación** operating costs, operating expenses; **~s fijos** fixed charges; **~s de flete** freight charges; **~s generales** overheads; **~s menores (de caja)** petty cash; **~s del negocio** business expenses; **~ público** public expenditure; **~ de representación** entertainment allowance; **~s de servicio** service charge; **~s de viaje** travelling expenses; **cubrir ~s** to cover expenses; **meterse en ~s** to go to expense, incur expense; **pagar los ~s** to pay the expenses, foot the bill; **con todos los ~s pagados** with all expenses paid.

gastón[1]⁑ *nm* (*CAm*: *diarrea*) the runs⁑.

gastón[2]* *adj* free-spending.

gastoso *adj* extravagant, wasteful.
gástrico *adj* gastric.
gastritis *nf* gastritis.
gastroenteritis *nf* gastroenteritis.
gastronomía *nf* gastronomy.
gastronómico *adj* gastronomic.
gastrónomo, -a *nm/f* gastronome, gourmet.
gastrópodo *nm* gastropod.
gata *nf* (**a**) (*Zool*) cat, she-cat.
(**b**) (*: *madrileña*) Madrid woman; (*Méx*) servant, maid; ~ **de callejón** (*fig*) alley cat.
(**c**) (*Met*) hill cloud.
(**d**) (*And, Cono Sur*) crank, handle; (*Aut*) car jack.
(**e**) **a ~s** (*lit*) on all fours; (*And, Cono Sur**) barely, by the skin of one's teeth; **andar a ~s** to go on all fours; to creep, crawl; (*niño*) to crawl.
(**f**) (*) **echar la ~** (*CAm*), **soltar la ~** (*And*) to lift*, steal.
(**g**) **tener ~** (*agujetas*) to ache all over.
gatada *nf* (**a**) (*movimiento etc*) movement (*o act etc*) typical of a cat. (**b**) (*arañazos*) scratch, clawing. (**c**) (*trampa*) artful dodge, sly trick.
gatazo *nm*: **dar el ~** (*LAm**) to look younger than one is, not to show one's age.
gateado 1 *adj* (**a**) (*gatuno*) catlike, feline.
(**b**) *mármol* striped, veined.
2 *nm* (**a**) (*movimiento: gatear*) crawl, crawling; (*subir*) climb, climbing.
(**b**) (*arañazos*) scratch, clawing.
(**c**) (*Carib*) hard veined wood (used in cabinet-making).
gateamiento *nm* = **gateado 2** (**a**) *y* (**b**).
gatear [1a] **1** *vt* (**a**) (*arañar*) to scratch, claw.
(**b**) (*) to pinch*, steal.
(**c**) (*CAm, Méx: seducir*) to seduce.
2 *vi* (**a**) (*trepar*) to climb, clamber (*por* up); (*andar a gatas*) to creep, crawl, go on all fours.
(**b**) (*LAm*) to be on the prowl.
gatera 1 *nf* (**a**) (*aficionada a gatos*) cat-lover. (**b**) (*apertura: Náut*) cat hole; (*de gato*) catflap. (**c**) (*And*) market woman, stallholder. **2** *nm* (*) sneak thief.
gatería *nf* (**a**) (*gatos*) cats, collection of cats. (**b**) (*pandilla*) gang of louts. (**c**) (*cualidad*) false modesty.
gatero 1 *adj* fond of cats. **2** *nm* cat-lover; *V t* **gatera 1** (**a**).
gatillar [1a] *vt* to cock.
gatillero *nm* gunman, hitman.
gatillo *nm* (**a**) (*Mil*) trigger; (*Med*) dental forceps; (*Téc*) clamp. (**b**) (*Zool*) nape (of the neck). (**c**) (*) young thief, young pickpocket.
gatito, -a *nm/f* kitten; puss, pussy.
gato[1] *nm* (**a**) (*Zool*) cat, tomcat; **~ de algalia** civet cat; **~ de Angora** Angora cat; **~ callejero** alley cat, stray cat; **~ montés** wild cat; **~ romano** tabby cat; **~ siamés** Siamese cat; **'El ~ con botas'** 'Puss in Boots'; **¡es pa'l ~!*** it's rubbish!; **no había más que cuatro ~s** there was hardly a soul; **de noche todos los ~s son pardos** at night all cats are grey; **dar a uno ~ por liebre** to take sb in*, pull the wool over sb's eyes, swindle sb; **el ~ escaldado del agua fría huye** once bitten twice shy; **aquí hay ~ encerrado** I smell a rat, there's sth fishy here*; **jugar al ~ y ratón con uno** to play a cat-and-mouse game with sb; **llevar el ~ al agua** to pull off sth difficult; **a ver quién se lleva el ~ al agua** let's see who can manage to come out on top; **pasar sobre algo como ~ sobre ascuas** to tread carefully round sth, pass gingerly over sth; **ser ~ viejo** to be an old hand.
(**b**) (*Téc, Aut etc*) jack; (*torno*) clamp, vice; (*grapa*) grab; (*Méx: de arma*) trigger **~ de tornillo** screw jack.
(**c**) (*Fin*) money-bag.
(**d**) (*) (*ladrón*) sneak thief, cat burglar; (*taimado*) slyboots*.
(**e**) (*: *madrileño*) native of Madrid.
(**f**) (*Méx: criado*) servant.
(**g**) (*CAm: músculo*) muscle.
(**h**) (*Méx: propina*) tip.
(**i**) (*Cono Sur: bolsa de agua*) hot-water bottle.
(**j**) (*Cono Sur: baile*) *Argentine folk dance*.
gato[2] *nm* (*And*) open-air market, market place.
gatopardo *nm* ocelot.
gatuno *adj* catlike, feline.
gatuperio *nm* (**a**) (*mezcla*) hotchpotch. (**b**) (*fraude*) fraud, piece of underhand dealing.
gaucano* *nm* (*Carib*) rum-based cocktail.
gaucha *nf* (*Cono Sur*: †: *marimacho*) mannish woman.
gauchada *nf* (*Cono Sur*) (**a**) (*personas*) gauchos (*collectively*). (**b**) (*acto*) gaucho exploit, (*pey*) typical gaucho trick. (**c**) (*favor*) favour; good turn; helping hand; **hacer una ~ a uno*** to do sb a favour.
gauchaje *nm* (*Cono Sur*) gauchos (*collectively*); gathering of gauchos; (* *pey*) riffraff, rabble.
gauchear [1a] *vi* (*Cono Sur: vivir de gaucho*) to live as a gaucho.
gauchesco *adj* (*Cono Sur*) gaucho (*atr*); like a gaucho; of the gauchos; **vida gauchesca** gaucho life.
gaucho 1 *nm* (**a**) (*LAm*) gaucho, cowboy.
(**b**) (*Cono Sur: jinete*) good rider, expert horseman.
(**c**) (*And: sombrero*) wide-brimmed straw hat.
2 *adj* (**a**) gaucho (*atr*); of the gauchos.
(**b**) (*LAm: pey*) coarse, rough; sly, tricky.
gaudeamus* *nm* (*hum*) party, beano*.
gaulista *adj, nmf* Gaullist.
gavera *nf* (*LAm*) crate.
gaveta *nf* drawer, till; locker.
gavia *nf* (**a**) (*Náut*) (main) topsail. (**b**) (*Orn*) seagull. (**c**) (*Agr*) ditch.
gavilán *nm* (**a**) (*Orn*) sparrowhawk. (**b**) (*de plumilla*) nib. (**c**) (*de espada*) quillon. (**d**) (*CAm, Carib*) ingrowing nail.
gavilla *nf* (**a**) (*Agr*) sheaf. (**b**) (*) gang, band.
gavillero *nm* (*LAm*) gunman, trigger-man.
gaviota *nf* (**a**) (*Orn*) seagull, gull; **~ argéntea** herring-gull.
(**b**) (*Méx*: hum*) flier.
gavota *nf* gavotte.
gay [gai] **1** *adj invar* gay. **2** *nm, pl* **gays** gay man, gay; **los ~s** the gays.
gaya *nf* (**a**) (*Orn*) magpie. (**b**) (*en tela*) coloured stripe.
gayo *adj* (**a**) (*alegre*) merry, gay; **gaya ciencia** art of poetry, art of the troubadours. (**b**) (*vistoso*) bright, showy.
gayola *nf* (*jaula*) cage; (*: *cárcel*) jail.
gaza *nf* loop; (*Náut*) bend, bight.
gazafatón* *nm* = **gazapatón**.
gazapa* *nf* fib, lie.
gazapatón* *nm* (*error*) blunder, slip; (*disparate*) piece of nonsense.
gazapera *nf* (**a**) (*conejera*) rabbit hole, warren. (**b**) (* *fig*) den of thieves. (**c**) (*riña*) brawl, shindy*.
gazapo *nm* (**a**) (*Zool*) young rabbit. (**b**) (*taimado*) sly fellow; (*: *ladrón*) cat burglar; (*LAm: mentiroso*) liar. (**c**) (*disparate*) blunder, bloomer*; (*mentira*) lie; (*Tip*) misprint; **cazar un ~** to spot a mistake. (**d**) (*Carib: estafa*) trick.
gazmoñada *nf*, **gazmoñería** *nf* (*V adj*) (**a**) hypocrisy, cant. (**b**) prudery, priggishness; sanctimoniousness.
gazmoñero *adj*, **gazmoño 1** *adj* (**a**) (*hipócrita*) hypocritical, canting.
(**b**) (*remilgado*) prudish, priggish; strait-laced; (*beato*) sanctimonious.
2 *nm*, **gazmoñera** *nf*, **gazmoña** *nf* (**a**) hypocrite.
(**b**) prude, prig; sanctimonious person.
gaznápiro, -a *nm/f* dolt, simpleton.
gaznatada‡ *nf* (*CAm, Carib, Méx*) smack, slap.
gaznate *nm* (**a**) gullet; windpipe, throttle; **remojar el ~*** to have a drink. (**b**) (*Méx*) (fruit) fritter.
gaznetón 1 *adj* (*And, Méx*) loud-mouthed. **2** *nm*, **gaznetona** *nf* loudmouth*.
gazpacho *nm* (**a**) gazpacho (*Andalusian cold soup*); **de ~ no hay empacho** one can never have too much of a good thing. (**b**) (*CAm*) (*bebida*) dregs; (*comida*) left-overs.
gazuza *nf* (**a**) (*) ravenous hunger. (**b**) (*CAm: alboroto*) din, row. (**c**) (*CAm‡: chusma*)) common people. (**d**) **es una ~** (*CAm**) she's a wily old bird.
GC *nf abr de* **Guardia Civil**.
geco *nm* gecko.
géiser *nm* (*Geog*) geyser.
geisha ['geiʃa] *nf* geisha (girl).
gel *nm, pl* **gels** [gel] *o* **geles** gel.
gelatina *nf* gelatin(e), jelly; **~ explosiva** gelignite.
gelatinoso *adj* (**a**) gelatinous. (**b**) (*And*) lazy, stolid.
gelidez *nf* chill, iciness.
gélido *adj* chill, icy.
gelificarse [1g] *vr* to gel, coagulate.
gelignita *nf* gelignite.
gema *nf* (**a**) (*joya*) gem, jewel. (**b**) (*Bot*) bud.
gemelo 1 *adj* twin; **buque ~** sister ship; **hermanas gemelas** twin sisters.
2 *nm* (*Náut*) sister ship.
3 *nm*, **gemela** *nf* twin; **G~s** (*Zodíaco*) Gemini; **~s idénticos** identical twins.
4 *nmpl* (**a**) (*Cos*) cufflinks.
(**b**) **~s de campo** field glasses, binoculars; **~s de teatro** opera glasses.

gemido *nm* groan, moan; wail, howl.
gemidor *adj* groaning, moaning; wailing, howling.
Géminis *nmpl* (*Zodíaco*) Gemini.
gemiquear [1a] *vi* (*Cono Sur*) to whine.
gemiqueo *nm* (*Cono Sur*) whining.
gemir [31] *vi* (*quejarse*) to groan, moan; (*lamentarse*) to wail, howl; (*animal*) to whine; (*viento etc*) to moan, howl; (*fig*) to moan, lament; (*en cárcel*) to languish, rot; **'Sí' dijo gimiendo** 'Yes' he groaned.
gen. (*Ling*) (**a**) *abr de* **género** gender, gen. (**b**) *abr de* **genitivo** genitive, gen.
gen *nm* gene.
genciana *nf* gentian.
gendarme *nm* policeman, gendarme.
gendarmería *nf* police, gendarmerie.
gene *nm* gene.
genealogía *nf* (*ascendientes*) genealogy; (*árbol*) family tree; (*raza*) pedigree.
genealógico *adj* genealogical.
genealogista *nmf* genealogist.
generación *nf* (**a**) (*acto*) generation.
(**b**) (*grupo*) generation; **la ~ del '98** the 1898 generation; **las nuevas generaciones** the rising generation; **la quinta ~ de ordenadores** the fifth generation of computers.
(**c**) (*descendencia*) progeny, offspring; (*sucesión*) succession; (*cría*) brood.
generacional *adj* generation (*atr*).
generacionalmente *adv* in terms of generation(s).
generador 1 *adj* generating. **2** *nm* generator.
general 1 *adj* general; (*amplio*) wide; (*común*) common, prevailing, (*pey*) rife; (*frecuente*) usual; **es ~ por toda España** it is common throughout Spain, it exists in the whole of Spain; **de distribución ~** of general distribution, generally distributed; **en ~, por lo ~** generally, as a general rule, in general; for the most part; **el mundo en ~** the world in general, the world at large.
2 *nm* (**a**) (*Mil*) general; **~ de brigada** brigadier-general; **~ de división** major-general.
(**b**) (*Teat*) stalls.
3 *nf* (*Aut*) main road.
4 *nfpl*: **~es de la ley** prescribed personal questions.
generala *nf* (**a**) (*persona*) (woman) general; (*Hist*) general's wife. (**b**) (*llamamiento*) call to arms, general alert.
generalato *nm* (**a**) (*arte, puesto*) generalship. (**b**) (*personas*) generals (*collectively*). (**c**) (*Méx**: *madama*) madame, brothel keeper.
generalidad *nf* (**a**) generality; mass, majority; **la ~ de los hombres** the mass of ordinary people, the common run of men.
(**b**) (*vaguedad*) vague answer, generalization, general statement.
(**c**) **la G~** (*Pol*) *Catalan autonomous government*.
generalísimo *nm* generalissimo, supreme commander; **el G~ Franco** General Franco.
generalista *nmf* general practitioner.
Generalitat *nf* = **generalidad** (**c**).
generalización *nf* (**a**) (*acto*) generalization. (**b**) (*de conflicto*) widening, escalation.
generalizar [1f] **1** *vt* (**a**) to generalize; to make more widely known, bring into general use.
(**b**) (*Mil*: *ampliar*) to widen, escalate, scale up.
2 *vi* to generalize.
3 generalizarse *vr* (**a**) to become general, become universal; to become widely known (*o* used *etc*).
(**b**) (*Mil*) to widen, escalate.
generalmente *adv* generally.
generar [1a] *vt* to generate.
generativo *adj* generative.
genérico *adj* generic.
género *nm* (**a**) (*clase*) class, kind, type, sort; **~ humano** human race, mankind; **te deseo todo ~ de felicidades** I wish you all the happiness in the world.
(**b**) (*Bio*) genus.
(**c**) (*Arte, Liter*) genre; type; **~ chico** (genre of) comic one-act pieces; (*sainetes*) short farces; (*zarzuela*) *zarzuela*, Spanish operetta; **~ novelístico** novel genre, fiction; **pintor de ~** genre painter; **es todo un ~ de literatura** it is a whole type of literature.
(**d**) (*Ling*) gender.
(**e**) (*Com*) cloth, stuff, material; **~s** (*productos*) goods, merchandise; commodities; **~s de lino** linen goods; **~s de punto** knitwear, knitted goods; **le conozco el ~** I know his sort; I know all about him, I recognize the type.
generosamente *adv* (*V adj*) generously; nobly, magnanimously.
generosidad *nf* (**a**) (*largueza*) generosity; nobility, magnanimity. (**b**) (*liter*) nobility; valour.
generoso *adj* (**a**) (*liberal*) generous (*con, para* to); (*noble*) noble, magnanimous.
(**b**) (*liter*) noble, highborn; gentlemanly; brave, valiant; **de sangre generosa** of noble blood; **en pecho ~** in a noble heart.
(**c**) *vino* rich, full-bodied.
genésico *adj* genetic.
génesis *nf* genesis.
Génesis *nm* (*Bíb*) Genesis.
genética *nf* genetics.
genéticamente *adv* genetically.
geneticista *nmf* geneticist.
genético *adj* genetic.
genetista *nmf* geneticist.
genial *adj* (**a**) (*brillante*) inspired, brilliant, of genius; **escritor ~** writer of genius; **fue una idea ~** it was a brilliant idea; **¡eso fue ~!** it was marvellous!, it was wonderful!
(**b**) (*agradable*) pleasant, cheerful, genial; (*afable*) cordial, affable; (*divertido*) witty.
(**c**) (*propio*) in character, characteristic; (*singular*) individual; (*típico*) typical.
genialidad *nf* (**a**) (*genio*) genius. (**b**) (*una ~*) stroke of genius, brilliant idea; (*obra*) brilliant work; **eso fue una ~** that was a stroke of genius. (**c**) (*acción extravagante*) eccentricity.
genialmente *adv* (**a**) (*con genio*) in an inspired way, brilliantly, with genius. (**b**) (*alegremente*) pleasantly, cheerfully.
genio *nm* (**a**) (*temperamento*) disposition, nature, character; **~ alegre** cheerful nature; **buen ~** good nature; **~ y figura (hasta la sepultura)** the leopard cannot change its spots; **de ~ franco** of an open nature; **mal ~** bad temper; evil disposition; **de mal ~** bad-tempered; ill-disposed; **estar de mal ~** to be in a bad temper; **~ vivo** quick temper, hot temper; **corto de ~** spiritless, timid; **llevar el ~ a uno** to humour sb; not to dare to contradict sb.
(**b**) (*mal carácter*) bad temper; **es una mujer de mucho ~** she's a quick-tempered woman; **tiene ~** he's temperamental; he has an uncertain temper, he's bad-tempered.
(**c**) (*talento*) genius; **¡eres un ~!** you're a genius!
(**d**) (*peculiaridad*) genius, special nature, peculiarities; **esto va en contra del ~ de la lengua** this goes against the genius of the language.
(**e**) (*Mit, Rel*) spirit; genie; **~ del mal** evil spirit; **~ tutelar** guardian spirit.
genioso *adj* (*CAm*) bad-tempered.
genista *nf* broom, genista.
genital 1 *adj* genital. **2 ~es** *nmpl* genitals, genital organs.
genitalidad *nf* sexual activity.
genitivo 1 *adj* generative, reproductive. **2** *nm* (*Ling*) genitive.
genocida *nmf* person accused (*o* guilty) of genocide.
genocidio *nm* genocide.
Génova *nf* Genoa.
genovés, -esa *adj, nm/f* Genoese.
genoveva *nf* vintage car, classic car.
gental *nm* (*And*) lot, mass; **un ~ de gente** a mass of people.
gente *nf* (**a**) (*gen*) people, folk; (*nación*) race, nation; (*Mil*) men, troops, (*séquito*) followers, retinue; (*****: *parientes*) relatives, folks, people; **el rey y su ~** the king and his retinue; **mi ~** my people, my folks; **son ~ inculta** they're rough people; **no me gusta esa ~** I don't like those people; **hay muy poca ~** there are very few people; **~ baja** lower classes, low-class people; **~ bien** upper-class people; nice people, respectable people; (*pey*) posh people*; smart set; **~ de bien** honest folk, decent people; **~ de capa parda** country folk; **~ de color** coloured people; **~ de la cuchilla** butchers; **~ gorda = ~ bien; ~ guapa** beautiful people; **~ de mar** seafaring men; **~ menuda** (*humildes*) small fry; humble folk; (*niños*) children, kids*, little people; **~ natural** (*CAm*) Indians, natives; **~ de paz** peace-loving people; **¡~ de paz!** (*Mil*) friend!; **~ de pelo** well-to-do people; **~ de medio pelo** people of limited means; **~ perdida** bad people; criminals; idlers, loafers; **~ de pluma** clerks, penpushers; **~ principal** nobility, gentry; **~ de tomuza** (*Carib*‡) Negroes, black people; **~ de trato** tradespeople; **de ~ en ~** from generation to generation; **hacer ~** to make a crowd.
(**b**) (*esp LAm*) upper-class people; nice people, respectable people; **ser ~** to be somebody, have social

importance.

(**c**) (*LAm*) person; **había dos ~s** there were two people; **Carlos es buena ~** (*LAm**) *o* **muy ~** (*Cono Sur**) Carlos is a good sort.

gentecilla *nf* unimportant people; (*pey*) rabble, riffraff.

genterío *nm* (*CAm*) = **gentío**.

gentil 1 *adj* (**a**) (*elegante*) elegant, graceful, attractive; (*encantador*) charming; (*fino*) courteous; (*Méx*) kind, helpful.

(**b**) (*iró*) pretty, fine; **¡~ cumplido!** a fine compliment!

(**c**) (*Rel*) pagan, heathen; gentile.

2 *nmf* pagan, heathen; gentile.

gentileza *nf* (**a**) (*elegancia*) elegance, gracefulness; (*encanto*) charm; (*finura*) courtesy; **'por ~ de X'** 'by courtesy of X'. (**b**) (*boato*) show, splendour, ostentation. (**c**) (*bizarría*) dash, gallantry.

gentilhombre *nm* (*Hist*: *corte*) gentleman; **~ de cámara** gentleman-in-waiting.

gentilicio 1 *adj*: **nombre ~** = **2**. **2** *nm* name of the inhabitants of a country (*o* region *etc*).

gentilidad *nf*, **gentilismo** *nm* the pagan world; heathenism, paganism.

gentilmente *adv* (**a**) (*con elegancia*) elegantly, gracefully, attractively; (*con encanto*) charmingly; (*con gracia*) prettily; (*cortésmente*) courteously. (**b**) (*iró*) prettily.

gentío *nm* crowd, throng; **había un ~** there were lots of people.

gentualla *nf*, **gentuza** *nf* rabble, mob; riffraff; **¡qué ~!** what a shower!‡

genuflexión *nf* genuflexion.

genuflexo *adj* (*Cono Sur*) servile, slavish.

genuinamente *adv* genuinely; really, truly.

genuino *adj* (**a**) genuine; real, pure, true. (**b**) (*And**) smashing*, super*.

GEO ['xeo] *nmpl* (*Esp*) *abr de* **Grupo Especial de Operaciones** *special police unit*.

geo *nmf* member of GEO.

geo... *pref* geo...

geodesía *nf* geodesy.

geodésico *adj* geodesic.

geoestrategia *nf* geostrategy.

geoestratégico *adj* geostrategic.

geofísica[1] *nf* geophysics.

geofísico 1 *adj* geophysical. **2** *nm*, **geofísica**[2] *nf* geophysicist.

Geofredo *nm* Geoffrey.

geografía *nf* (**a**) geography; **~ física** physical geography; **~ humana** human geography; **~ política** political geography. (**b**) (*país*) territory; country; **en toda la ~ nacional** all over the country; **recorrer la ~ nacional** to travel all over the country.

geográfico *adj* geographical.

geógrafo, -a *nm/f* geographer.

geología *nf* geology.

geológico *adj* geological.

geólogo, -a *nm/f* geologist.

geomagnético *adj* geomagnetic.

geometría *nf* geometry; **~ del espacio** solid geometry; **de ~ variable** (*Aer*) variable-geometry (*atr*).

geométrico *adj* geometric(al).

geomorfología *nf* geomorphology.

geopolítica *nf* geopolitics.

geopolítico *adj* geopolitical.

Georgia del Sur *nf* South Georgia.

georgiano *adj* Georgian.

geostacionario *adj* geostationary.

geranio *nm* geranium.

Gerardo *nm* Gerald, Gerard.

gerencia *nf* (**a**) (*dirección*) management. (**b**) (*cargo*) managership, post of manager. (**c**) (*oficina*) manager's office. (**d**) (*personas*) management, managers (*collectively*); **~ intermedia** middle management.

gerencial *adj* managerial.

gerenciar [1b] *vt* to manage.

gerente *nmf* manager, director; executive; **~ de fábrica** works manager.

geriatra *nmf* geriatrician.

geriatría *nf* geriatrics.

geriátrico, -a *adj, nm/f* geriatric.

gerifalte *nm* (**a**) (*Orn*) gerfalcon. (**b**) (*fig*) important person; **estar** (*o* **vivir**) **como un ~** to live like a king.

germanesco *adj*: **palabra germanesca** a word from thieves' slang, cant word.

germanía *nf* thieves' slang.

germánico *adj* Germanic.

germanio *nm* germanium.

germanística *nf* German studies.

germano 1 *adj* Germanic; German. **2** *nm*, **germana** *nf* German.

germanófilo, -a *nm/f* germanophile.

germanófobo 1 *adj* germanophobe, germanophobic. **2** *nm*, **germanófoba** *nf* germanophobe.

germanófono 1 *adj* German-speaking. **2** *nm*, **germanófona** *nf* German speaker.

germanooccidental *adj, nmf* (*Hist*) West German.

germanooriental *adj, nmf* (*Hist*) East German.

germen *nm* (**a**) (*Bio, Med*) germ; **~ plasma** germ plasma; **~ de trigo** wheat germ. (**b**) (*fig*) germ, seed; source, origin; **el ~ de una idea** the germ of an idea.

germicida 1 *adj* germicidal. **2** *nm* germicide, germ killer.

germinación *nf* germination.

germinar [1a] *vi* to germinate; to sprout, shoot.

Gerona *nf* Gerona.

gerontocracia *nf* gerontocracy.

gerontología *nf* gerontology.

gerontólogo, -a *nm/f* gerontologist.

Gertrudis *nf* Gertrude.

gerundense 1 *adj* of Gerona. **2** *nmf* native (*o* inhabitant) of Gerona; **los ~s** the people of Gerona.

gerundiano *adj* bombastic.

gerundino *nm* gerundive (*Latin*).

gerundio *nm* gerund; **bebiendo, que es ~** drinking, and I do mean drinking; **andando, que es ~** get a move on — now!

gervasio *nm* (*And*) fellow, guy*; shrewd fellow.

gesta *nf* (**a**) (*hazaña*) heroic deed, epic achievement. (**b**) (*Liter*: *Hist*) epic, epic poem; *V t* **cantar**.

gestación *nf* gestation; **~ de alquiler** surrogate motherhood.

gestante *adj*: **mujer ~** pregnant woman, expectant mother.

Gestapo *nf* Gestapo.

gestar [1a] **1** *vt* (*Bio*) to gestate; (*fig*) to prepare, hatch. **2 gestarse** *vr* (*Bio*) to gestate; (*fig*) to be in preparation, be brewing.

gestear [1a] *vi* (*hacer ademanes*) to gesture; (*hacer muecas*) to grimace.

gesticulación *nf* (**a**) (*ademán*) gesticulation. (**b**) (*mueca*) grimace, (wry) face.

gesticular [1a] *vi* (**a**) (*hacer ademanes*) to gesticulate, gesture. (**b**) (*hacer muecas*) to grimace, make a face.

gestión *nf* (**a**) (*Com etc*) management, conduct; **~ de datos** data management; **~ forestal** woodland management.

(**b**) (*negociación*) negotiation.

(**c**) (*medida*) measure, step; (*acción*) action; (*esfuerzo*) effort; (*operación*) operation; **gestiones** measures, steps; **hacer las gestiones necesarias para** + *infin* to take the necessary steps to + *infin*; **hacer las gestiones preliminares** to do the groundwork, make the first steps; **donde él tenía que realizar unas gestiones** where he had some business to transact; **el gobierno tendrá que hacer las primeras gestiones** the government will have to make the first move.

gestionable *adj* manageable; **difícilmente ~** difficult to manage.

gestionar [1a] *vt* (**a**) (*conducir*) to manage, conduct. (**b**) (*negociar*) to negotiate (for). (**c**) (*procurar*) to try to arrange, strive to bring about, work towards.

gesto *nm* (**a**) (*cara*) face; (*semblante*) expression on one's face; **estar de buen ~** to be in a good mood; **estar de mal ~** to be in a bad mood; **poner mal ~, torcer el ~** to make a (wry) face; to scowl, look cross.

(**b**) (*mueca*) grimace, (wry) face; scowl; **hacer ~s** to make faces (*a* at); **hacer un ~** to make a face; **hizo un ~ de asco** he looked disgusted; **hizo un ~ de extrañeza** he looked surprised.

(**c**) (*ademán*) gesture (*t fig*); (*señal*) sign; **hacer ~s** to make gestures (*a* to); **con un ~ de cansancio** with a weary gesture; **con un ~ generoso remitió la deuda** in a generous gesture he let him off the debt.

gestología *nf* study of body-language.

gestor 1 *adj* managing. **2** *nm*, **gestora**[1] *nf* manager; promoter; business agent, representative; **~ de carteras** portfolio management.

gestora[2] *nf* committee of management.

gestoría *nf* agency (*for undertaking business with government departments, insurance companies, etc*).

gestual *adj* gestural; **lenguaje ~** body-language.

gestualidad *nf* body-language.

Getsemaní *nm* Gethsemane.
geyser *nm* geyser.
Ghana *nf* Ghana.
ghanés, -esa *adj, nm/f* Ghanaian.
ghetto *nm* ghetto.
giba *nf* (**a**) (*lit*) hump; hunchback. (**b**) (*) nuisance, bother.
gibado *adj* with a hump, hunchbacked.
gibar* [1a] **1** *vt* (**a**) (*molestar*) to bother, annoy. (**b**) (*embaucar*) to put one over on*; (*tomar la revancha*) to get one's own back on; to do down*. **2 gibarse** *vr* to put up with it; **se van a ~** they'll have to lump it.
gibón *nm* gibbon.
giboso *adj* with a hump, hunchbacked.
Gibraltar *nm* Gibraltar.
gibraltareño 1 *adj* of Gibraltar, Gibraltarian. **2** *nm*, **gibraltareña** *nf* Gibraltarian, native (*o* inhabitant) of Gibraltar; **los ~s** the Gibraltarians, the people of Gibraltar.
gigabyte *nm* gigabyte.
giganta *nf* (**a**) giantess. (**b**) (*Bot*) sunflower.
gigante 1 *adj* giant, gigantic. **2** *nm* giant.
gigantesco *adj* gigantic, giant.
gigantez *nf* gigantic stature, vast size.
gigantismo *nm* (*Med*) gigantism, giantism.
gigantón, -ona 1 *nm/f* giant carnival figure. **2** *nf* (*CAm*: *baile*) *folk dance with giant masks.*
gigoló *nm* gigolo.
Gijón *nm* Gijón.
gijonés 1 *adj* of Gijón. **2** *nm*, **gijonesa** *f* native (*o* inhabitant) of Gijón; **los gijoneses** the people of Gijón.
Gil *nm* Giles.
gil‡ (*Cono Sur*) **1** *adj* stupid, silly. **2** *nmf* berk‡, twit*.
gilar‡ [1a] *vt* to watch, keep tabs on.
gilda *nf* lollipop.
gilí* 1 *adj* (**a**) (*tonto*) stupid, silly. (**b**) (*vanidoso*) stuck-up*; (*presumido*) presumptuous. **2** *nmf* (**a**) (*tonto*) twit*, idiot. (**b**) (*vanidoso*) conceited individual, pompous ass.
gilipollada‡ *nf* silly thing.
gilipollas‡ *nmf invar* = **gilí 2.**
gilipollear‡ [1a] *vi* to do silly things, play the fool.
gilipollesco‡ *adj* stupid, idiotic.
gilipollez‡ *nf* (**a**) (*idiotez*) idiocy, silliness; **es una ~** that's nonsense, that's silly. (**b**) (*vanidad*) conceit, presumption. (**c**) **decir gilipolleces** to talk rubbish.
gilipuertas* *nmf invar* (*euf*) = **gilí 2.**
gillet(t)e [xi'lete] *nf* (*hoja*) (*any*) razorblade; (*maquinilla*) safety razor.
gimnasia *nf* gymnastics; physical training; **~ aeróbica** aerobics; **~ deportiva** competitive gymnastics; **~ de mantenimiento** keep-fit exercises; **~ respiratoria** deep breathing; **~ rítmica** eurhythmics; **hacer ~** to do gymnastics, do physical training.
gimnasio *nm* gymnasium, gym; **~ múltiple** multigym.
gimnasta *nmf* gymnast.
gimnástica *nf* gymnastics.
gimnástico *adj* gymnastic.
gimotear [1a] *vi* (*gemir*) to whine, whimper; (*lamentar*) to wail; (*niño*: *lloriquear*) to snivel, grizzle.
gimoteo *nm* (*gemido*) whine, whining; whimpering; (*lamento*) wailing; (*lloriqueo*) snivelling, grizzling.
gincana *nf* gymkhana.
Ginebra¹ *nf* (*Geog*) Geneva.
Ginebra² *nf* (*Hist*) Guinevere.
ginebra¹ *nf* gin.
ginebra²* *nf* bedlam, uproar, confusion.
ginecología *nf* gynaecology.
ginecólogo, -a *nm/f* gynaecologist.
ginesta *nf* (*Bot*) broom.
gineta *nf* genet.
giña‡ *nf* (*Carib*) hatred.
Gioconda *nf*: **la ~** (the) Mona Lisa.
gira *nf* (*Mús, Teat etc*) tour; trip; **estar en ~** to be on tour; *V t* **jira.**
giradiscos *nm invar* record turntable.
girado, -a *nm/f* (*Com*) drawee.
girador(a) *nm/f* (*Com*) drawer.
giralda *nf*, **giraldilla** *nf* weathercock.
girante *adj* revolving, rotating.
girar [1a] **1** *vt* (**a**) (*dar vuelta a*) to turn, turn round, rotate; (*torcer*) to twist; (*revolver*) to spin; **~ la manivela 2 veces** turn the crank twice.
(**b**) (*volver*) to swing, swivel; **~ la vista** to look round.
(**c**) (*Com*) to draw (*a cargo de, contra* on), issue.
2 *vi* (**a**) (*voltearse*) to turn, turn round, go round; (*dar vueltas*) to rotate, revolve; (*Mec*) to spin, gyrate; (*rodar*) to wheel; (*Dep*: *pelota*) to spin; **~ hacia la derecha** to turn (to the) right, swing right; **gira a 1600 rpm** it rotates at 1600 rpm; **el satélite gira alrededor del mundo** the satellite circles the earth, the satellite revolves round the earth; **la conversación giraba en torno de las elecciones** the conversation turned on (*o* centred on) the election; **el número de asistentes giraba alrededor de 500 personas** there were about 500 people in the audience.
(**b**) (*balancear*) to swing (from side to side), swivel; (*sobre gozne*) to hinge; (*en equilibrio*) to pivot; **la puerta giró sobre sus goznes** the door swung on its hinges.
(**c**) (*Com, Fin*) to operate, do business; **la compañía gira bajo la razón social de X** the company operates under the name of X.
(**d**) (*Com*) to draw; **~ en descubierto** to overdraw.
(**e**) (*Mús, Teat etc*) to go on tour.
girasol *nm* sunflower.
giratorio *adj* (*gen*) revolving, rotatory; gyratory; *escena, puerta etc* revolving; *puente* swing (*atr*), swivel (*atr*); *silla* swivel (*atr*).
girl* *nf* (*Teat*) showgirl, chorus-girl; (*Dep*) junior player.
giro¹ *nm* (**a**) (*vuelta*) turn; (*revolución*) revolution, rotation; gyration; **hacer un ~** to turn, make a turn; **el coche dio un ~ brusco** the car swung away suddenly.
(**b**) (*fig*: *de sucesos etc*) (*tendencia*) trend, tendency, course; (*cambio*) switch, change, turn; **~ de 180 grados, ~ copernicano** U-turn, complete turnabout; **la cosa ha tomado un ~ favorable** the affair has taken a turn for the better; **la intriga tiene un ~ inesperado** the plot has an unexpected twist in it.
(**c**) (*Ling*) turn of phrase, expression.
(**d**) (*Com*) draft; bill of exchange; **~ bancario** bank giro, bank draft; **~ en descubierto** overdraft; **~ postal** money order, postal order; **~ postal internacional** international money order; **~ a la vista** sight draft.
giro² *adj* (**a**) (*LAm*) *gallo* with some yellow colouring. (**b**) (*Carib*: *atolondrado*) scatterbrained, thoughtless. (**c**) (*CAm**: *ebrio*) drunk. (**d**) (*Méx**: *confiado*) cocky, confident.
girocompás *nm* gyrocompass.
girola *nf* ambulatory.
Gironda *nm* Gironde.
giroscópico *adj* gyroscopic.
giroscopio *nm*, **giróscopo** *nm* gyroscope.
gis *nm* (**a**) (*LAm*: *tiza*) chalk; (*And*: *lápiz de pizarra*) slate pencil. (**b**) (*Méx*) *pulque,* (*any*) colourless drink.
gitana *nf* gipsy; (*de feria etc*) fortuneteller.
gitanada *nf* (**a**) (*acto*) gipsy trick, mean trick. (**b**) (*gen*) wheedling, cajolery; humbug.
gitanear [1a] *vt* to wheedle, cajole.
gitanería *nf* (**a**) (*gitanos*) band of gipsies; gathering of gipsies. (**b**) (*vida*) gipsy (way of) life. (**c**) (*dicho*) gipsy saying. (**d**) (*fig*: *gitanada*)) wheedling, cajolery.
gitanesco *adj* (**a**) gipsy (*atr*); gipsy-like. (**b**) (*pey*) wily, tricky.
gitano 1 *adj* (**a**) gipsy (*atr*). (**b**) (*fig*: *halagüeño*) wheedling, cajoling; (*zalamero*) smooth, flattering. (**c**) (*fig*: *taimado*) wily, tricky, sly. (**d**) (*: *sucio*) dirty. **2** *nm* gipsy; **vivir como ~s** to live from hand to mouth; **volvió hecho un ~** he came back dirty all over.
glabro *adj* hairless.
glaciación *nf* glaciation.
glacial *adj* (**a**) glacial; *viento etc* icy, bitter, freezing. (**b**) (*fig*) icy, cold, stony.
glaciar *nm* glacier.
gladiador *nm* gladiator.
gladio *nm*, **gladiolo** *nm*, **gladíolo** *nm* gladiolus.
glamour [gla'mur] *nm* glamour.
glamo(u)roso *adj* glamorous.
glándula *nf* gland; **~ cerrada, ~ de secreción interna** ductless gland; **~ endocrina** endocrine gland; **~ pituitaria** pituitary (gland); **~ prostática** prostate (gland); **~ tiroides** thyroid (gland).
glandular *adj* glandular.
glas *adj*: **azúcar ~** icing-sugar.
glaseado *adj* glazed, glossy; (*Culin*) glacé, glazed.
glasear [1a] *vt papel etc* to glaze; (*Culin*) to glacé, glaze.
glauco *adj* (*liter*) glaucous, light green; (*esp LAm*) green.
glaucoma *nm* glaucoma.
gleba *nf* (**a**) clod. (**b**) (*Hist*) glebe.
glicerina *nf* glycerin(e).
glicina *nf* (*Bot*) wisteria.
global *adj* (*en conjunto*) global; (*completo*) total, complete,

overall; *informe, investigación etc* full, searching, comprehensive; *suma* total, aggregate.
globalidad *nf* totality; **la ~ del problema** the problem as a whole; the problem in its widest sense; **en su ~** as a whole.
globalización *nf* making universal, world-wide extension.
globalizador *adj* comprehensive.
globalizante *adj* universalizing, world-wide.
globalizar [1f] *vt* (**a**) (*abarcar*) to encompass, include. (**b**) (*extender*) to make universal, extend world-wide.
globalmente *adv considerar, examinar* as a whole; (*en total*) all in all.
globo *nm* (**a**) globe, sphere; **~s‡** boobs‡; **~ de luz** spherical lamp; **~ del ojo, ~ ocular** eyeball; **~ terráqueo** globe, schoolroom globe.
(**b**) (*Aer*) **~** (**aerostático**) balloon; **~ de aire caliente** hot-air balloon; **~ de barrera** barrage-balloon; **~ cautivo** captive balloon; **~ dirigible** dirigible; **~ meteorológico** weather ballon; **~ de protección** barrage-balloon.
(**c**) (‡: *preservativo*) French letter.
(**d**) **en ~** as a whole, all in all; (*Com*) in bulk; (*fig*) in broad outline only.
(**e**) (‡) **tener un ~** to be stoned‡.
(**f**) (*Tenis*) lob.
globoso *adj*, **globular** *adj* globular, spherical.
glóbulo *nm* (**a**) globule. (**b**) (*Anat*) corpuscle; **~ blanco** white corpuscle; **~ rojo** red corpuscle; **~ sanguíneo** blood cell.
gloria *nf* (**a**) (*fama*) glory; (*Rel*) eternal glory, heaven; (*fig*) glory; (*delicia*) delight; (*éxtasis*) bliss; **una vieja ~** a has-been, a great figure (*etc*) from the past; **el día es pura ~** it's a wonderful day; **¡sí, ~!** yes, my love!; **¡por la ~ de mi madre!** by all that's holy!; **estar en su(s) ~(s)** to be in one's element, be in one's glory; **ganarse la ~** to go to heaven; **oler a ~** to smell divine; **saber a ~** to taste heavenly; **que santa ~ haya, Dios le tenga en su santa ~** God rest his soul.
(**b**) (‡: *droga*) hash*, pot‡.
gloriado *nm* (*And*) hot toddy.
gloriarse [1c] *vr*: **~ de algo** to boast of sth, be proud of sth; **~ en algo** to glory in sth, rejoice in sth.
glorieta *nf* (**a**) (*pérgola*) bower, arbour; (*cenador*) summerhouse. (**b**) (*Aut*) roundabout, traffic circle (*US*); (*plaza redonda*) circus; (*cruce*) junction, intersection.
glorificación *nf* glorification.
glorificar [1g] **1** *vt* to glorify, extol, praise.
2 glorificarse *vr*: **~ de, ~ en** to boast of, be proud of, glory in.
gloriosamente *adv* gloriously.
glorioso *adj* (**a**) glorious; (*Ecl*) *Santo* blessed, in glory; *memoria* blessed; **la Gloriosa** (*Ecl*) the Blessed Virgin; (*Hist*) *the 1868 revolution* (*in Spain*). (**b**) (*pey*) proud, boastful.
glosa *nf* gloss; comment, note, annotation; (*And*) telling off.
glosar [1a] *vt* to gloss; to comment on, annotate; (*fig*) to put an unfavourable interpretation on, criticize.
glosario *nm* glossary.
glosopeda *nf* foot-and-mouth disease.
glotal *adj*, **glótico** *adj* glottal.
glotis *nf invar* glottis.
glotón 1 *adj* gluttonous, greedy. **2** *nm*, **glotona** *nf* glutton. **3** *nm* (*Zool*) wolverine.
glotonear [1a] *vi* to be greedy, be gluttonous.
glotonería *nf* gluttony, greediness.
glub *interj* gulp!
glucosa *nf* glucose.
gluglú *nm* (**a**) (*de agua*) gurgle, gurgling; glug-glug; **hacer ~** to gurgle. (**b**) (*de pavo*) gobble, gobbling; **hacer ~** to gobble.
gluglutear [1a] *vi* (*pavo*) to gobble.
gluten *nm* gluten.
glutinoso *adj* glutinous.
gneis [neis] *nm* gneiss.
gnomo ['nomo] *nm* gnome.
gobelino *nm* Gobelin tapestry.
gobernable *adj* (**a**) (*Pol*) governable; **un pueblo difícilmente ~** a people hard to govern, an unruly people. (**b**) (*Náut*) navigable, steerable.
gobernación *nf* (**a**) (*acto*) governing, government; **Ministerio de la G~** Ministry of the Interior, ≈ Home Office (*Brit*), Department of the Interior (*US*); **Ministro de la G~** (*Esp*) Minister of the Interior.
(**b**) (*residencia*) governor's residence; (*oficina*) governor's office; (*Méx Pol*) Ministry of the Interior.
gobernador 1 *adj* governing, ruling. **2** *nm*, **gobernadora** *nf* governor, ruler; **~ civil** civil governor; **~ general** governor-general; **~ militar** military governor.
gobernalle *nm* rudder, helm.
gobernanta *nf* (*niñera*) governess; (*de hotel*) staff manageress, housekeeper.
gobernante 1 *adj* (*que gobierna*) ruling, governing. **2** *nmf* (*líder*) ruler, governor; (*político*) politician; (*en el poder*) person in power; (*fig*) self-appointed boss (*o* leader *etc*).
gobernar [1j] **1** *vt* (**a**) (*Pol*) to govern, rule.
(**b**) (*en general*) to govern; (*dirigir*) to guide, direct; (*controlar*) to control, manage, run; (*manejar*) to handle.
(**c**) (*Náut*) to steer, sail.
2 *vi* (**a**) (*Pol*) to govern, rule; **~ mal** to misgovern.
(**b**) (*Náut*) to handle, steer.
gobi‡ *nf* nick‡, jail.
gobierno *nm* (**a**) (*Pol*) government; **~ autonómico, ~ autónomo** autonomous government; **~ central** central government; **~ de coalición** coalition government; **~ de concentración** government of national unity; **~ directo** direct rule; **~ fantasma** shadow cabinet; **~ en funciones, ~ de gestión, ~ interino, ~ de transición** caretaker government; **~ militar** military government.
(**b**) (*en general*) guidance, direction; control, management, running; handling; **~ doméstico, ~ de la casa** housekeeping, running of the household; **para su ~** for your guidance, for your information; **servir de ~ a** to act as a guide to, serve as a norm for.
(**c**) (*puesto*) governorship.
(**d**) (*Náut*) steering; helm; **buen ~** navigability, good steering qualities; **de buen ~** navigable, easily steerable.
(**e**) **mirar contra el ~** (*Cono Sur‡*) to squint, be boss-eyed*.
gobio *nm* gudgeon.
gob.no *abr de* **gobierno** government, govt.
goce *nm* enjoyment; possession.
gocho* *nm* pig.
godo 1 *adj* Gothic.
2 *nm*, **goda** *nf* (**a**) (*Hist*) Goth.
(**b**) (*LAm pey*: *español*) Spaniard; (*Hist*: *primera parte del s. XIX*) loyalist; (*Pol moderna*) conservative, reactionary.
(**c**) (*Canarias*) (peninsular) Spaniard.
Godofredo *nm* Godfrey.
gofio *nm* (*Canarias, LAm*) *roasted maize meal* (*often stirred into coffee*).
gofre *nm* waffle.
gogó 1 *nf* go-go girl, go-go dancer. **2 a ~** *adv* in plenty, by the bucketful.
gol *nm* goal; **¡~!** goal!; **~ del empate** equalizer; **~ del honor** consolation goal; **meter un ~ a uno** (*fig*) to score a point against sb, outsmart sb, put one over on sb*.
gola *nf* (**a**) (*Anat*) throat, gullet. (**b**) (*Mil*: *Hist*) gorget; (*Cos*: *Hist*) ruff; (*Ecl*) clerical collar, dog-collar. (**c**) (*Arquit*) cyma, ogee.
golaverage *nm* goal-average.
golazo* *nm* great goal.
goleada *nf* quantity of goals, high score; **ganar por ~** to win by a lot of goals, thrash the opponents.
goleador 1 *adj* (**a**) **el equipo más ~** the team which has scored most goals. (**b**) **deseos ~es** goal-scoring intentions; **aumentó su cuenta goleadora** he improved his goal-scoring record. **2** *nm*, **goleadora** *nf* (goal) scorer; **el máximo ~ de la liga** the top goal scorer in the league.
golear [1a] **1** *vt* to score a goal against; **Eslobodia goleó a Ruritania por 13 a 0** Slobodia overwhelmed Ruritania by 13-0; **A fue goleado por B** A had a lot of goals scored against it by B; **el portero menos goleado** the keeper who has let in fewest goals; **el equipo más goleado** the team against which most goals have been scored.
2 *vi* to score (a goal).
goleta *nf* schooner.
golf *nm* (*juego*) golf; (*pista*) golf-course; (*club*) golf-club; (*chalet*) clubhouse; **~ miniatura** miniature golf(-course).
golfa* *nf* tart‡, whore.
golfada *nf* mischief, piece of hooliganism.
golfán *nm* water-lily.
golfante 1 *adj* loutish; delinquent, criminal. **2** *nm* oaf, lout; rascal.
golfear [1a] *vi* to loaf, idle; to live like a street urchin.
golferas* *nm invar* = **golfo2**.
golfería *nf* (**a**) (*golfos*) loafers (*collectively*); street urchins (*collectively*). (**b**) (*acto*) loafing, idling; (*estilo de vida*) life

of idleness; life in the gutter. (**c**) (*trampa*) dirty trick.
golfillo *nm* urchin, street urchin.
golfismo *nm* golfing.
golfista *nmf* golfer.
golfístico *adj* golf (*atr*), golfing (*atr*).
golfo[1] *nm* (*Geog*) (**a**) (*bahía*) gulf, bay; **G~ de Méjico** Gulf of Mexico; **G~ Pérsico** Persian Gulf; **~ de Vizcaya** Bay of Biscay. (**b**) (*mar*) open sea.
golfo[2] *nm* urchin, street urchin; tramp; oaf, lout; loafer.
Gólgota *nm* Golgotha.
Goliat *nm* Goliath.
golilla *nf* (**a**) (*Cos: Hist*) ruff, gorget; magistrate's collar; (*And, Cono Sur*) neckcloth, neckerchief; **alzar ~** (*Méx*) to puff out one's chest; **andar de ~** (*And, Cono Sur**) to be dressed up to the nines.
(**b**) (*LAm Orn*) collar, ruff.
(**c**) (*Téc*) flange (of a pipe).
(**d**) (*Carib: deuda*) debt.
(**e**) (*Carib: trampa*) trick, ruse.
(**f**) **de ~** (*CAm: gratis*) free, for nothing; (*Carib*: por casualidad*) by chance, accidentally.
golondrina *nf* (**a**) (*Orn*) swallow; **~ de mar** tern; **una ~ no hace verano** one swallow does not make a summer. (**b**) (*lancha*) motor-launch. (**c**) (*Cono Sur*) migrant worker. (**d**) (*Cono Sur Aut*) furniture van.
golondrino *nm* (**a**) (*vagabundo*) rolling stone, drifter; (*Mil*) deserter. (**b**) (*Med*) tumour under the armpit.
golondro* *nm* fancy, yen*, longing; **andar en ~s** to cherish foolish hopes; **campar de ~** to sponge*, live on other people.
golosina *nf* (**a**) (*manjar*) titbit, delicacy, dainty; (*dulce*) sweet.
(**b**) (*bagatela*) bauble, knick-knack.
(**c**) (*deseo*) desire, longing; (*antojo*) fancy.
(**d**) (*gula*) sweet tooth, liking for sweet things; (*glotonería*) greed.
goloso *adj* (**a**) (*de lo dulce*) sweet-toothed, fond of dainties. (**b**) (*pey*) greedy. (**c**) (*apetitoso*) appetising, attractive.
golpe *nm* (**a**) (*gen*) (*impacto*) blow; hit, punch, knock; (*manotazo*) smack; (*encuentro*) bump; (*de remo etc*) stroke; (*de corazón*) beat, throb; (*de reloj etc*) tick; **se dio un ~ en la cabeza** he got a bump on his head, he banged his head; **A le dio a B un ~ en el pecho** A punched B on the chest; **A dio a B un ~ con un palo** A gave B a blow with his stick, A hit B with his stick; **~ aplastante** crushing blow, knockout blow; **~ bien dado** hit, well-aimed blow; **~ de gracia** (*t fig*); coup de grâce; **~ mortal** death blow; **arma de primer ~** first-strike weapon; **dar ~s en la puerta** to thump the door, pound (at, on) the door; **descargar ~s sobre uno** to rain blows on sb; **darse ~s de pecho** to beat one's breast; **no dar ~*** not to do a stroke, be bone-idle; **a ~ dado no hay quite** (*CAm**) what's done cannot be undone.
(**b**) (*Téc*) stroke; **~ de émbolo** piston stroke.
(**c**) (*Dep*) (*Boxeo*) blow, punch; (*Ftbl etc*) kick; (*Béisbol, Golf, Tenis etc*) hit, stroke, shot; **con un total de 280 ~s** (*Golf*) with a total of 280 strokes; **~ de acercamiento** (*Golf*) approach shot; **~ bajo** low blow, punch below the belt; (*fig*) dirty trick; **~ de castigo** (*Ftbl etc*) penalty kick; **~ franco, ~ libre** (*Ftbl*) free kick; **~ libre indirecto** indirect free kick; **~ de martillo** (*Tenis*) smash; **~ de penalidad** (*Golf*) penalty stroke; **~ de salida** (*Golf*) tee shot; **preparar el ~** (*Golf*) to address the ball.
(**d**) (*fig: desgracia etc*) blow, (hard) knock, misfortune; (*Med*) bruise; **ha sufrido un ~ duro** it was a hard knock for him.
(**e**) (*fig: choque*) shock, clash.
(**f**) (*fig: sorpresa*)) surprise, astonishment.
(**g**) (*: *criminal*) job*; attack, holdup; **preparaba su primer ~** he was planning his first job*; **dieron un ~ en un banco** they did a bank job*.
(**h**) (*salida*) witticism, sally; **¡qué ~!** how very clever!, what a good one!
(**i**) (*Pol*) coup; **~ de estado** coup d'état; **~ de mano** rising; sudden attack; **~ de palacio** palace coup.
(**j**) (*fig*); **~ de agua** heavy fall of rain; **~ de calor** heatstroke; **~ de efecto** coup de théâtre; **~ de fortuna** stroke of luck; **~ maestro** master stroke, stroke of genius; **~ de mar** heavy sea, surge; **~ de sol** sunstroke; **~ de suerte** stroke of luck; **~ de teatro** coup de théâtre; **~ de teléfono** telephone call; **~ de timón** change of direction; **~ de tos** fit of coughing; **~ de viento** gust of wind; **~ de vista** look, glance; **dar el ~** to come up with a telling phrase.
(**k**) (*locuciones con prep*) **a ~ seguro** with an assurance of success, without any risk; **ir a ~ de calcetín** (*o* **alpargata** *etc*)* to go on Shanks' pony; **a ~ de** by means of; **al ~** (*Carib*) instantly; **de ~** (**y porrazo**) suddenly, unexpectedly; **de un ~** at one stroke, in one go; outright; at a stretch; **abrir una puerta de ~** to fling open a door; **la puerta se abrió de ~** the door flew open; **cerrar una puerta de ~** to slam a door.
(**l**) (*fig*) (*multitud*) crowd, mass; (*abundancia*) abundance; **~ de gente** crowd of people.
(**m**) (*Mec*) spring lock; **de ~** spring (*atr*), *p.ej.* **pestillo de ~** spring bolt.
(**n**) (*Cos*) pocket flap; (*And*) facing.
(**o**) (*Méx*) sledgehammer.
(**p**) (*Carib**) swig*, slug* (of liquor).
golpeador *nm* (*CAm*) door knocker.
golpeadura *nf* = **golpeo.**
golpear [1a] **1** *vt* (*gen*) to strike, knock, hit; *superficie* to beat, pound (on, at); (*a puñetazos*) to punch; *mesa etc* to thump, bang; *alfombra etc* to beat; *puerta* to bang; (*suj: desastre natural*) to hit, strike; *abuso etc* to strike a blow against; (*suavemente*) to tap; **ha sido golpeado por la vida** life has treated him badly.
2 *vi* (*latir*) to throb, tick; (*Aut, Mec*) to knock; **el ~ de las olas** the buffeting of the waves, the pounding of the sea.
golpecito *nm* (light) blow, tap, rap; **dar ~s en** to tap (on), rap (on).
golpeo *nm* (*V v*) striking, knocking, hitting; beating, pounding; punching; thumping, banging; tapping; (*Aut, Mec*) knock, knocking.
golpetear [1a] *vti* to beat (repeatedly); (*martillar*) to knock, hammer, drum, tap; (*traquetear*) to rattle.
golpeteo *nm* (*V v*) beating; knocking, hammering, drumming, tapping; rattling.
golpismo *nm* tendency to military coups; coup d'état mentality; government by a clique installed by a military coup.
golpista 1 *adj tendencia etc*: *V* **golpismo. 2** *nmf* participant in a coup d'état.
golpiza *nf* bash*, bashing*, beating-up*; **dar una ~ a uno** to bash sb*, beat sb up*.
gollería *nf* (**a**) (*Culin: golosina*) dainty, titbit, delicacy; **pedir ~s** to ask too much. (**b**) (*) extra, special treat; (*Com etc*) perk*; **un empleo con muchas ~s** a job with lots of perks*.
golleroso *adj* affected; pernickety.
gollete *nm* (*Anat: garganta*) throat, neck; (*de botella*) neck; **estar hasta el ~*** to be fed up*; **beber a ~** to drink straight from the bottle.
golletero* *nm* (*LAm*) scrounger*.
goma *nf* (**a**) (*gen*) gum; rubber; (*Cos*) elastic; **~ arábiga** gum arabic; **~ espumosa** foam rubber; **~ de mascar** chewing gum; **~ de pegar** gum, glue.
(**b**) (*una ~*) (*gomita*) rubber band, elastic band; length of elastic, piece of elastic; (*Aut*) tyre; (*: *preservativo*) French letter; (*LAm*) rubber overshoe; **~ de borrar** rubber, eraser; **~ de borrar de máquina** typewriter rubber.
(**c**) **~ 2** plastic explosive.
(**d**) (‡: *droga*) hash*, pot‡; (*LAm*) opium den.
(**e**) (‡: *de policía*) truncheon.
(**f**) **estar de ~** (*CAm**) to have a hangover*.
gomaespuma *nf* foam rubber.
gomal *nm* (*And*) rubber plantation.
Gomera *nf*: **la ~** Gomera.
gomero 1 *adj* gum (*atr*); rubber (*atr*). **2** *nm* (**a**) (*Bot: árbol*) gum-tree; rubber tree. (**b**) (*persona*) (*dueño*) rubber planter, rubber producer; (*obrero*) rubber-plantation worker.
gomina *nf* (*para hombres*) haircream; (*fijador*) (hair) gel.
gominola *nf* winegum.
gomita *nf* rubber band, elastic band.
Gomorra *nm* Gomorrah.
gomosidad *nf* gumminess, stickiness.
gomoso 1 *adj* gummy, sticky.
2 *nm* (†: *petimetre*) dandy.
gónada *nf* gonad.
góndola *nf* (*Náut*) gondola; (*Ferro*) goods wagon, freight truck (*US*); (*Com*) gondola; (*And, Cono Sur*) bus; **~ de cable** cable-car; ski-lift; **~ del motor** (*Aer*) engine casing.
gondolero *nm* gondolier.
gong [gon] *nm, pl* **gongs** [gon], **gongo** *nm* gong.
gongorino *adj* relating to Luis de Góngora; **estilo ~** Gongorine style; **estudios ~s** Góngora studies.
gonorrea *nf* gonorrhoea.

gorda* *nf* (**a**) (*mujer*) fat woman; (*Cono Sur, Méx*: *en oración directa*) darling.

(**b**) (*Fin**) = **perra gorda; ni ~** absolutely nothing; **no tener ni ~** to be broke*; **no entiende ni ~** he doesn't understand a blind thing*.

(**c**) **la G~** *the 1868 revolution* (*in Spain*); **se armó la ~*** there was a hell of a row, there was a tremendous fuss; **aquí se va a armar la ~*** there's going to be trouble; **ahora nos va a tocar la ~*** now we're for it.

(**d**) (*Méx Culin*) thick tortilla.

gordal 1 *adj* fat, big, thick. **2** *nm kind of large olive.*

gordiflón* *adj*, **gordinflón*** *adj* podgy, chubby; **¡~!** fatty!*

gordito 1 *adj* chubby, plump. **2** *nm*, **gordita** *nf* chubby person, plump person.

gordo 1 *adj* (**a**) *persona* fat; stout, plump; *objeto* big; *hilo, tela etc* thick, coarse, rough; *hecho, suceso* important, big; *premio* first, big, main; **está más ~ que nunca** he's fatter than ever; **en mi vida las he visto más gordas** (*fig*) I've never been in a tougher spot; **fue el desastre más ~ de su historia** it was the biggest (*o* worst) disaster in their history; **hacer de lo ~**⁂ to have a crap⁂.

(**b**) *comida, sustancia* fatty, greasy, oily.

(**c**) *agua* hard.

(**d**) (*) unpleasant; **ese tipo me cae ~** that chap gets on my nerves, I can't bear that fellow; **eso me cae ~** (*Méx*‡) it gets right up my nose‡; **lo más ~ fue ...** the most outrageous part was ...

2 *adv*: **hablar ~*** to talk big*.

3 *nm* (**a**) (*persona*) fat man; **¡~!** fatty!*; (*Cono Sur, Méx*: *en oración directa*) darling.

(**b**) (*Culin*) fat, suet.

(**c**) (*: *premio*) first prize, big prize; jackpot; **ganar el ~** to win the big prize; **sacarse el ~** (*fig*) to bring home the bacon*.

gordolobo *nm* mullein.

gordura *nf* (**a**) (*obesidad*) fat, fatness; (*corpulencia*) corpulence, stoutness. (**b**) (*Culin*: *grasa*) grease, fat. (**c**) (*Carib, Cono Sur**: *crema*) cream.

gorgojo *nm* (**a**) (*Ent*) grub; weevil. (**b**) (*fig*) dwarf, runt.

gorgón *nm* (*And*) concrete.

gorgoritear [1a] *vi* to trill, warble.

gorgorito *nm* trill, warble.

gorgorizar [1f] *vi* to trill, warble.

górgoro *nm* (*Méx*) bubble.

gorgotear [1a] *vi* to gurgle.

gorgoteo *nm* gurgle.

gorguera *nf* ruff; (*Mil Hist*) gorget.

gori* *nm*: **armar el ~** to make a row, kick up a fuss.

gorigori* *nm* wailing, keening.

gorila *nm* (**a**) (*Zool*) gorilla. (**b**) (*) (*matón*) tough, bruiser, thug; (*de club*) bouncer*; (*guardaespaldas*) henchman, minder*, bodyguard; strong-arm man. (**c**) (*LAm Pol*) reactionary; (*Mil*) senior officer.

gorilismo *nm* thuggery.

goriloide *nm* (*fig*) brute, thug.

gorja *nf* throat, gorge; **estar de ~*** to be very cheerful.

gorjear [1a] **1** *vi* to chirp, twitter, trill. **2 gorjearse** *vr* (*niño*) to crow, gurgle, burble.

gorjeo *nm* (*V v*) chirping, twittering, trilling; crowing, gurgling, burbling.

gorobeto *adj* (*And*) twisted, bent, warped.

gorra 1 *nf* (peaked) cap; (*de bebé*) bonnet; (*Mil*) bearskin, busby; (*Univ*) cap; **~ de montar** riding cap; **~ de paño** cloth cap; **~ de punto** knitted cap; **~ de visera** peaked cap; **~ de yate** yachting cap; **pasar la ~** to pass the hat round; **pegar la ~*** to be unfaithful.

2 *nmf* (*) cadger, sponger*, parasite; **andar** (*o* **ir, vivir**) **de ~** to cadge, sponge*, scrounge*, live at sb else's expense; **colarse de ~** to gatecrash; **comer de ~** to scrounge a meal*; **entrar de ~** to get in free; **sacar algo de ~** to scrounge sth*; **me** *etc* **vino de ~** (*CAm**: *por suerte*) it was a stroke of luck, it came out of the blue.

gorrazo *nm*: **correr a uno a ~s** to run sb out of town.

gorrear [1a] **1** *vt* (*Cono Sur*‡) to cuckold. **2** *vi* (*LAm*) to sponge*, live off others.

gorrero, -a *nm/f* (**a**) cap maker. (**b**) *nm* (*) = **gorra 2**.

gorrinada *nf* (**a**) (*cerdos*) (number of) pigs. (**b**) (*fig*: *mala pasada*) dirty trick.

gorrinera *nf* pigsty.

gorrinería *nf* (**a**) dirt. (**b**) (*fig*: *mala pasada*) dirty trick.

gorrino *nm*, **gorrina** *nf* (**a**) (*cochinito*) small pig, sucking-pig; (*cerdo*) hog; (*cerda*) sow. (**b**) (*fig*) dirty individual.

gorrión *nm* sparrow; **de ~** (*Carib*) = **de gorra**.

gorrista* *nmf* = **gorra 2**.

gorro *nm* cap; (*de mujer, niño*) bonnet; **~ de baño** bathing cap; **~ de caña** pith helmet; **~ de dormir** nightcap; **~ frigio** Phrygian cap, revolutionary cap; **~ de montaña** Balaclava (helmet); **~ de papel** paper hat; **~ de piel** fur hat; **estar hasta el ~ de*** to be fed up with*; **me hincha el ~**‡ he gets on my wick‡; **poner el ~ a uno** to embarrass sb; (*Cono Sur, Méx*‡) to be unfaithful to sb.

gorrón¹ *nm* (**a**) (*guijarro*) pebble; cobblestone. (**b**) (*Mec*) pivot, journal, gudgeon.

gorrón²* *nm* = **gorra 2**.

gorrona* *nf* tart‡, whore.

gorronear* [1a] **1** *vt* to scrounge*; **~ algo a uno** to scrounge sth from sb*; **le gorronean los amigos** his friends scrounge off him*. **2** *vi* (*) to cadge, sponge*, scrounge*, live at sb else's expense.

gorroneo* *nm* cadging, scrounging*.

gorronería* *nf* (**a**) (*el sablear*) cadging, sponging. (**b**) (*And*: *avaricia*) avarice, greed.

gospel *nm* gospel music.

gota *nf* (**a**) (*gen*) drop; (*de sudor*) bead; (*de pintura*) blob; (*Med*) (saline *etc*) drip; **~s amargas** bitters; **~ a ~** drop by drop; (*fig*) in dribs and drabs; (*nm*: *Med*) drip, drip-feed; (*Agr*) trickle irrigation; **¡ni ~!** not a bit!; **caer a ~s** to drip; **parecerse como dos ~s de agua** to be as like as two peas; **unas ~s de coñac** a few drops of brandy; **la ~ que colma el vaso** the straw that breaks the camel's back, the last straw; **sudar la ~ gorda** to sweat blood; **no ver ~** not to see a thing.

(**b**) (*Med*) gout; **~ caduca, ~ coral** epilepsy.

(**c**) (*Met*) **~ fría** cold front.

(**d**) **~s de leche** (*LAm*: *fig*) child welfare clinic, welfare food centre.

goteado *adj* speckled, spotted.

gotear [1a] *vi* (*destilar*) to drip, dribble; (*escurrir*) to trickle; (*salirse*) to leak; (*vela*) to gutter; (*Met*) to spit, rain lightly.

goteo *nm* (*V v*) dripping, dribbling; trickle, trickling; leak; (*Med*) drip.

gotera *nf* (**a**) (*gotas*) drip; trickle; (*agujero*) leak.

(**b**) (*mancha*) mark left by dripping water, stain.

(**c**) (*de colgadura*) valance.

(**d**) (*Med*) chronic ailment; **estar lleno de ~s** to be full of aches and pains, feel a wreck.

(**e**) **~s** (*LAm*: *afueras*) outskirts, environs.

gotero *nm* (*Med*) drip, drip-feed; (*LAm Med*) dropper.

goterón *nm* big raindrop.

gótico 1 *adj* Gothic; (*fig*) noble, illustrious. **2** *nm* (*Ling*) Gothic.

gotita *nf* droplet; **¡una ~ nada más!** (*al servir bebida*) just a drop!; **hubo dos ~s de lluvia** it rained a drop or two.

gotoso *adj* gouty.

gourmet [gur'me] *nm*, *pl* **gourmets** [gur'me] gourmet, connoisseur (of food).

goyesco *adj* (**a**) (*de Goya*) of Goya, pertaining to Goya. (**b**) *estilo artístico* Goy(a)esque, in the style of Goya, after the manner of Goya.

gozada* *nf* (great) pleasure, delight; **es una ~** it's a real joy.

gozar [1f] **1** *vt* (**a**) (*disfrutar*) to enjoy; (*poseer*) to have, possess.

(**b**) (††) *mujer* to have, enjoy, seduce.

2 *vi* (**a**) (*divertirse*) to enjoy o.s., have a good time; **~ de** to enjoy; to have, possess; **~ de buena salud** to enjoy good health.

(**b**) (⁂) to come⁂.

3 gozarse *vr* to enjoy o.s.; to rejoice; **~ en** + *infin* to enjoy + *ger*, take pleasure in + *ger*.

gozne *nm* hinge.

gozo *nm* (**a**) (*placer*) enjoyment, pleasure; (*complacencia*) delight; (*alegría*) joy, gladness, rejoicing; **es un ~ para los ojos** it's a joy to see, it's a sight for sore eyes; **¡mi ~ en el pozo!** I'm sunk!, it's all ruined!; **no caber** (**en sí**) **de ~** to be beside o.s. with joy, be overjoyed; **da ~ escucharle** it's a pleasure to listen to him.

(**b**) **~s** (*Liter, Mús*) verses in honour of the Virgin.

gozosamente *adv* joyfully, delightedly.

gozoso *adj* glad, joyful, delighted (*con, de* about).

gozque *nm* small yapping dog; (*cachorro*) puppy.

g.p. *nm abr de* **giro postal** postal order, p.o., money order, m.o. (*US*).

gr. *abr de* **gramos** grams, grammes, gr.

grabación *nf* recording; **~ en cinta, ~ magnetofónica** tape-recording; **~ digital** digital recording.

grabado 1 *adj música etc* recorded; (*en cinta*) on tape.
2 *nm* engraving, print; (*en libro*) illustration, picture, print; (*Inform*) writing; **~ al agua fuerte** etching; **~ al agua tinta** aquatint; **~ en cobre** *o* **en dulce** copperplate; **~ en madera** woodcut.

grabador 1 *nm* (*Elec*) tape-recorder. **2** *nm*, **grabadora**[1] *nf* (*persona*) engraver.

grabadora[2] *nf* (**a**) (*Téc*) graver, cutting tool. (**b**) (*Elec etc*) recorder; **~ de cassette, ~ de cinta** (*LAm*) tape-recorder. (**c**) (*Com*) recording company.

grabadura *nf* (act of) engraving.

grabar [1a] *vt* (**a**) (*Arte*) to engrave; **~ al agua fuerte** to etch.
(**b**) (*en cinta, disco*) to record.
(**c**) (*fig*) to engrave, impress; **~ algo en el ánimo de uno** to impress sth on sb's mind; **la escena está grabada en mi memoria** the scene is engraved on my memory.

gracejada *nf* (*CAm, Méx*) stupid joke.

gracejo *nm* (**a**) (*chispa*) wit; (*encanto*) charm, gracefulness. (**b**) (*CAm, Méx: payaso*) clown.

gracia *nf* (**a**) (*garbo*) grace, gracefulness; (*atractivo*) attractiveness; **sin ~** graceless, unattractive.
(**b**) (*favor*) favour, kindness; **de ~** free, gratis; **hacer a uno ~ de algo** to excuse sb sth, spare sb sth; **te hago ~ de los detalles** I'll spare you the details; **¡vaya ~ que me ha hecho!** (*iró*) some favour he's done me!
(**c**) (*benevolencia*) graciousness.
(**d**) (*agrado*) grace, good graces, favour; **caer de la ~ de uno** to lose sb's favour; **me cayó en ~** I took (a liking) to him.
(**e**) (*Jur*) pardon, mercy.
(**f**) (*chiste*) joke, witticism.
(**g**) (*humor*) humour, funniness; (*ingenio*) wit; (*sentido*) point (of a joke); **por ~** in fun, as a joke; **¡qué ~!** how funny!, (*iró*) what a nerve!*, the very idea!; **coger** (*o* **pescar**) **la ~** to see the point (of a joke); **ha dado en la ~ de decir que ...** he's taken to saying ..., he's taken it into his head to say ...; **ahí está la ~** that's what's so funny about it; **hacer ~ a uno** to amuse sb, strike sb as funny; **no nos hace ~** we are not amused; **no me hace ~ la idea** I'm not keen on the idea; **tener ~** to be funny, be amusing; **el tío tiene mucha ~ hablando*** the chap talks very amusingly*, the fellow is an amusing talker; **si lo haces se va la ~** if you do it it breaks the spell.
(**h**) (*) first name; **¿cómo es su ~, señorita?** what's your (first) name, miss?
(**i**) (*Rel*) grace; **~ de Dios** (*fig*) sunshine, fresh air; **por la G~ de Dios** (*en moneda etc*) by the grace of God; **estar en ~ (de Dios)** to be in a state of grace.
(**j**) **en ~ a** for the sake of; on account of, because of; **en ~ a la brevedad** for brevity's sake, to be brief.
(**k**) **~s** thanks; **¡~s!** (*aceptando*) thanks!, thank you!; (*negando*) no thanks!, thank you but no; **¡muchas ~s!, ¡muchísimas ~s!** many thanks!, thanks very much!; **~s a Dios** thank heaven; **~s a la ayuda de otros** thanks to the help of others; **y ~s si no llegó a más** and we *etc* were lucky to get off so lightly; **~s a que ...** thanks to the fact that ..., because of the fact that ...; **toma eso, ¡y ~s!** take that and be thankful!; **con anticipadas ~s** thanking you in advance; **con repetidas ~s** thanking you again; **dar las ~s a uno por algo** to thank sb for sth.
(**l**) **las G~s** (*Mit*) the Three Graces.

graciable *adj* (**a**) (*benévolo*) gracious; (*afable*) affable. (**b**) *concesión etc* easily granted. (**c**) *pago* discretionary.

graciablemente *adv* (**a**) graciously; affably. (**b**) *pagar* on a discretionary basis.

grácil *adj* (*garboso*) graceful; (*esbelto*) slender; (*fino*) small, delicate.

graciosamente *adv* (*V adj*) (**a**) gracefully; pleasingly, elegantly. (**b**) funnily, amusingly; wittily; comically.

graciosidad *nf* (*V adj*) (**a**) grace, gracefulness; elegance; beauty. (**b**) funniness, amusing qualities; wittiness.

gracioso 1 *adj* (**a**) (*garboso*) graceful; (*atractivo*) pleasing, elegant.
(**b**) (*chistoso*) funny, amusing; (*ingenioso*) witty; **una situación muy graciosa** a very amusing situation; **¡qué ~!** how funny!; **es un tío de lo más ~** he's a most amusing chap; **lo ~ del caso es que ...** the funny thing about it is that ...
(**c**) (*gratuito*) free.
2 *nm* (*Teat: Hist*) comic character, fool, funny man; **¡no se haga el ~!** don't try to be funny!

grada *nf* (**a**) (*peldaño*) step, stair; (*Ecl*) altar step; **~s** (flight of) steps.
(**b**) (*Dep, Teat etc*) tier, row (of seats).
(**c**) **~s** (*Náut*) slips, slipway; **~s de construcción** shipyard, shipbuilding yard; **~ de lanzamiento** slipway.
(**d**) (*Agr*) harrow; **~ de disco** disk harrow; **~ de mano** hoe, cultivator.
(**e**) **~s** (*And, Cono Sur*) paved terrace (in front of a building).

gradación *nf* (**a**) (*progresión*) gradation; (*serie*) graded series. (**b**) (*Retórica*) climax; (*Ling*) comparison.

gradar [1a] *vt* (*Agr*) to harrow; to hoe.

gradería *nf*, **graderío** *nm* (**a**) (*escalón*) (flight of) steps. (**b**) (*Dep*) terrace, tiers; (*Teat*), rows (of seats); **~ cubierta** covered stand, grandstand.

grado *nm* (**a**) (*peldaño*) step.
(**b**) (*punto*) degree; (*etapa*) stage, step; (*medida*) measure; (*nivel*) rate; **quemaduras de primer ~** first-degree burns; **el ~ que ahora hemos alcanzado** the stage we have now reached; **está en el segundo ~ de elaboración** it is now in the second stage of production; **~ de velocidad** (rate of) speed; **es lo mismo pero en mayor ~** it's the same only more so; **de ~ en ~, por ~s** by degrees, gradually, step by step; **en sumo ~, en ~ superlativo** in the highest degree; in the extreme; vastly.
(**c**) (*calidad*) grade, quality; (*Mil*) rank; **de ~ superior** of superior quality.
(**d**) (*Escol*) class, year, grade (*US*).
(**e**) (*Univ*) degree; **~ universitario** university degree.
(**f**) (*Fís, Geog, Mat*) degree; **~ cero** zero; **~ de latitud** degree of latitude; **en un ángulo de 45 ~s** at an angle of 45 degrees; **la temperatura es de 40 ~s** the temperature is 40 degrees; **este vino es de 12 ~** this wine is 12 degrees proof.
(**g**) (*Ling*) degree (of comparison).
(**h**) (*de parentesco*) degree; **dentro de los ~s prohibidos** within the prohibited degrees.
(**i**) (*gana*) willingness; **de ~, de buen ~** willingly; **de mal ~, mal de mi ~** unwillingly; **de ~ o por fuerza** willy-nilly.
(**j**) **~s** (*Ecl*) minor orders.

graduable *adj* adjustable, that can be adjusted.

graduación *nf* (**a**) (*acto*) gradation, grading; (*Univ*) graduation.
(**b**) (*clasificación*) rating, grading; (*de bebida*) alcoholic strength, proof grading; **~ octánica** octane rating.
(**c**) (*Mil*) rank; **de alta ~** of high rank, high-ranking.

graduado, -a *nm/f* graduate; **~ escolar** certificate of success in EGB course (*age 14*), school-leaving certificate.

gradual *adj* gradual.

gradualidad *nf* gradualness.

gradualismo *nm* (*esp Pol*) gradualism.

gradualista *adj, nmf* gradualist.

gradualmente *adv* gradually.

graduar [1e] **1** *vt* (**a**) (*clasificar*) to grade, classify (*de, por* as); (*evaluar*) to appraise; (*medir*) to gauge, measure; (*Téc*) to calibrate; *vista* to test; *termómetro etc* to graduate.
(**b**) (*Univ*) to confer a degree on.
(**c**) (*Mil*) to confer a rank on, commission; **~ a uno de capitán** to confer the rank of captain on sb.
2 graduarse *vr* (**a**) (*Univ*) to graduate, take one's degree; **~ de** to take the degree of.
(**b**) (*Mil*) to take a commission (*de* as).

GRAE *nf abr de* **Gramática de la Real Academia Española.**

grafía *nf* (*Ling*) graph, signs representing the sound of a word; (*ortografía*) (way of) spelling; **se inclina por la ~ 'jira'** he prefers the spelling 'jira'.

gráfica *nf* (*Mat*) graph; (*diagrama*) diagram; **~ de fiebre, ~ de temperatura** (*Med*) temperature chart.

graficación *nf* (**a**) (*Inform*) graphics. (**b**) (*Mat*) representation on a graph.

gráficamente *adv* graphically.

gráfico 1 *adj* (**a**) graphic; *revista etc* pictorial, illustrated. (**b**) (*fig*) graphic, vivid, lively. **2** *nm* (*t* **gráfica** *nf*) (*Mat etc*) graph; diagram; chart; (*Ferro etc*) timetable; **~s** (*Inform*) graphics; **~ de barras** bar graph; **~ de porción de pastel** pie-chart.

grafiosis *nf* Dutch elm disease.

grafismo *nm* (*Inform*) computer graphics; (*logotipo*) logo; (*escritura*) graphology; (*Arte*) graphic art.

grafista *nmf* (*Arte*) graphic artist; (*TV*) graphic designer.

grafiti *nmpl* graffiti.

grafito *nm* graphite, black lead.

grafología *nf* graphology.

grafólogo, -a *nm/f* graphologist.

gragea *nf* small coloured sweets; (*Med*) pill.
graja *nf* rook.
grajea *nf* (*And*) fine shot, birdshot.
grajear [1a] *vi* (*Orn*) to caw; (*bebé*) to gurgle.
grajiento *adj* (*LAm*) sweaty, smelly.
grajilla *nf* jackdaw.
grajo *nm* (**a**) (*Orn*) rook. (**b**) (*LAm*) body odour, smell of sweat; underarm odour.
Gral. *abr de* **General** General, Gen.
grama *nf* (*esp LAm*) grass; (*Carib**: *césped*) lawn.
gramaje *nm* weight (*of paper etc*).
gramática¹ *nf* (**a**) grammar; ~ **generativa** generative grammar; ~ **profunda** deep grammar; ~ **transformacional** transformational grammar. (**b**) ~ **parda** native wit, horse-sense; **andar a la** ~ to look out for o.s.
gramatical *adj* grammatical.
gramático 1 *adj* grammatical. **2** *nm*, **gramática²** *nf* grammarian.
gramil *nm* (*Téc*) gauge.
gramilla *nf* (*LAm*: *césped*) grass, lawn; turf.
gramillar *nm* (*Cono Sur*) meadow, grassland.
gramínea *nf* grass; (*LAm*) pulse.
gramo *nm* gramme, gram (*US*).
gramófono *nm* gramophone, phonograph (*US*).
gramola *nf* gramophone, phonograph (*US*); (*en café etc*) jukebox.
grampa *nf* (*LAm*) = **grapa**.
gran *adj V* **grande**.
grana¹ *nf* (*Bot*) (**a**) (*semilla*) small seed; **dar en** ~ to go to seed, run to seed. (**b**) (*acto*) seeding; (*estación*) seeding time. (**c**) (*LAm*: *pasto*) grass; (*CAm, Méx*: *Dep*) turf.
grana² *nf* (*Zool etc*) cochineal; (*tinte*) kermes; (*color*) scarlet; (*tela*) scarlet cloth; **de** ~ scarlet, bright red; **ponerse como la** ~ to turn scarlet.
Granada *nf* (*Caribe*) Grenada.
granada *nf* (**a**) (*Bot*: *fruta*) pomegranate. (**b**) (*Mil*) shell; grenade; ~ **anticarro** anti-tank grenade; ~ **detonadora** stun grenade; ~ **fallida** dud shell; ~ **de fragmentación** fragmentation grenade; ~ **de humo** smoke-bomb; ~ **lacrimógena** teargas grenade; ~ **de mano** hand-grenade; ~ **de metralla** shrapnel shell; **a prueba de** ~ shellproof.
granadero *nm* (*Mil*) grenadier; ~**s** (*Méx*: *policía*) riot police.
granadilla *nf* (*flor*) passionflower; (*fruta*) passion fruit.
granadino 1 *adj* of Granada. **2** *nm*, **granadina** *nf* native (*o* inhabitant) of Granada; **los** ~**s** the people of Granada.
granado¹ *nm* (*Bot*) pomegranate tree.
granado² *adj* (**a**) (*selecto*) fine, choice, select; (*maduro*) mature; (*notable*) distinguished, illustrious; **lo más** ~ **de** the cream of, the pick of. (**b**) (*alto*) tall, full-grown.
granangular *adj*: **objetivo** ~ wide-angle lens.
granar [1a] *vi* to seed, run to seed.
granate 1 *nm* garnet. **2** *adj invar* deep red, dark crimson.
granazón *nf* seeding.
Gran Bretaña *nf* Great Britain.
grancanario 1 *adj* of Grand Canary. **2** *nm*, **grancanaria** *nf* native (*o* inhabitant) of Grand Canary; **los** ~**s** the people of Grand Canary.
grande 1 *adj* (**gran** *delante de nmf sing*) (**a**) (*de tamaño*) big, large; (*de estatura*) big, tall; *número, velocidad etc* high, great; (*LAm*: *mayor*) *persona* old, elderly; **el gran Buenos Aires** greater Buenos Aires; ~ **como una montaña** as big as a house; **en cantidades más** ~**s** in larger quantities; **hay una diferencia no muy** ~ there is not a very big difference; **los zapatos le están (muy)** ~**s** the shoes are too big for her; **con gran placer** with great pleasure; **¿cómo es de** ~**?** how big is it?, what size is it?; **lo hace por lo** ~ he does it in style.
(**b**) (*moralmente etc*) great; **un gran hombre** a great man; **fue una gran hazaña** it was a great achievement.
(**c**) (*impresionante*) grand, grandiose, impressive.
(**d**) **en** ~ (*en conjunto*) as a whole; (*en gran escala*) on a large scale, on a grand scale, in a big way; **estar en** ~ to be going strong; **pasarlo en** ~* to have a tremendous time*; **hacer algo en** ~* to do sth in style, make a splash doing sth*; **vivir en** ~* to live in style.
(**e**) **¡qué** ~**!** (*Cono Sur**) how funny!
2 *adv* (*Cono Sur**) much, a lot.
3 *nm* (**a**) **los** ~**s** the great; **los** ~**s de la industria** the major companies in the industry; **uno de los** ~**s de la pantalla** one of the screen greats; **los siete** ~**s (bancos)** the Big Seven.
(**b**) ~ **(de España)** grandee.
(**c**) (‡) 1000-peseta note; **3 de los** ~**s*** 3000 pesetas.
4 *nf* (**a**) (*Cono Sur*) first prize, big prize (*in the lottery*).
(**b**) (*And, Cono Sur*) naughty thing, misdeed.
(**c**) (*And*‡) clink‡, jail.
5 *nmf* (*LAm*: *adulto*) adult.
grandemente *adv* greatly, extremely; ~ **equivocado** greatly mistaken.
grandeza *nf* (**a**) (*gran tamaño*) bigness; size, magnitude.
(**b**) (*moral*) greatness.
(**c**) (*lo impresionante etc*) grandness, grandiose quality, impressiveness; grandeur, magnificence.
(**d**) (*rango*) status of grandee.
(**e**) (*personas*) grandees (*collectively*), nobility.
grandilocuencia *nf* grandiloquence.
grandilocuente *adj* (*LAm*) boastful, arrogant.
grandílocuo *adj* grandiloquent.
grandiosidad *nf* = **grandeza (c)**.
grandioso *adj* grand, impressive, magnificent; (*pey*) grandiose.
grandísimo *adj superl de* **grande** (*hum, iró*) great big, huge; **un coche** ~ a whacking great car*, a car and a half*; **¡**~ **tunante!** you old crook!
grandón *adj* solidly-built.
grandor *nm* size.
grandote *adj* great big, huge.
grandulón *adj* (*And*) = **grandullón**.
grandullón* *adj* overgrown, oversized.
grandura *nf* (*Cono Sur*) = **grandeza (b)** *y* **(c)**.
granear [1a] *vt* (**a**) *semilla* to sow. (**b**) (*Arte*) to grain, stipple.
granel *nm* (*montón*) heap of corn; (*Com*) bulk commodity, commodity in bulk; **a** ~ (*en abundancia*) in abundance; (*a montones*) by the score, by the ton; (*con profusión*) lavishly; (*al azar*) at random; (*Com*) in bulk, loose; in quantity; **vino a** ~ wine in bulk, wine in the barrel.
granelero *nm* (*Náut*) bulk-carrier.
granero *nm* granary, barn; (*fig*) granary, corn-producing area.
granete *nm* (*Téc*) punch.
granguiñolesco *adj* melodramatic, exaggerated.
granilla *nf* grain (in cloth).
granítico *adj* granitic, granite (*atr*).
granito¹ *nm* (*Geol*) granite.
granito² *nm* (*Agr etc*) small grain; granule; (*Med*) pimple.
granizada *nf* (**a**) (*Met*) hail, hailstorm. (**b**) (*fig*) hail; shower, volley; vast number; **una** ~ **de balas** a hail of bullets. (**c**) (*And, Cono Sur*: *bebida*) iced drink.
granizado *nm* iced drink; ~ **de café** iced coffee.
granizal *nm* (*LAm*) hailstorm.
granizar [1f] *vi* to hail; (*fig*) to rain, shower.
granizo *nm* hail.
granja *nf* (*gen*) farm; (*cortijo*) farmhouse; (*lechería*) dairy; ~ **avícola** chicken farm, poultry farm; ~ **colectiva** collective farm; ~ **escuela** educational farm; ~ **marina** fish-farm.
granjear [1a] **1** *vt* to gain, earn; to win; (*And, Cono Sur*: *robar*) to steal. **2 granjearse** *vr afecto, antipatía etc* to win for o.s., gain for o.s.
granjería *nf* (**a**) (*Com, Fin*) profits, earnings; (*Agr*) farm earnings. (**b**) (*Agr*) farming, husbandry.
granjero *nm* farmer.
grano *nm* (**a**) (*Agr, Bot*) grain; (*semilla*) seed; (*baya*) berry; ~**s** grain, corn, cereals; ~ **de arroz** grain of rice; ~ **de cacao** cocoa bean; ~ **de café** coffee-bean; ~ **de polen** pollen grain; ~ **de sésamo** sesame seed; ~ **de trigo** grain of wheat; ~**s panificables** bread grains; **no es** ~ **de anís*** it isn't peanuts*, it's no small matter; **tomarlo con un** ~ **de sal** to take it with a pinch of salt; **ir al** ~ to get to the point, get down to brass tacks; **¡vamos al** ~**!** let's get on with it!
(**b**) (*partícula*) particle, grain; (*punto*) speck; ~ **de arena** grain of sand; **no es** ~ **de anís (***o* **arena)** it's not just a small thing, you can't laugh this one off; **poner su** ~ **de arena** (*fig*) to make one's contribution.
(**c**) (*en madera, piedra etc*) grain; **de** ~ **fino** fine-grained; **de** ~ **gordo** coarse-grained.
(**d**) (*Med*) pimple, spot.
(**e**) (*Farm*) grain.
(**f**) (‡: *droga*) fix‡, shot*.
granoso *adj* granular; granulated; grainy.
granuja 1 *nf* loose grapes; grape seed. **2** *nm* urchin, ragamuffin; rogue.
granujería *nf* urchins (*collectively*), rogues (*collectively*).
granujiento *adj*, **granujoso** *adj* pimply, spotty.
granulación *nf* granulation.

granular[1] *adj* granular.
granular[2] [1a] **1** *vt* to granulate. **2 granularse** *vr* (**a**) to granulate, become granulated. (**b**) (*Med*) to break out in pimples, become spotty.
gránulo *nm* granule.
granuloso *adj* granular.
grapa[1] *nf* (*para papeles*) staple; clip, fastener; (*Mec*) dog, clamp; (*Arquit*) cramp.
grapa[2] *nf* (*Cono Sur*) grape liquor, grappa.
grapadora *nf* stapler, stapling machine.
grapar [1a] *vt papeles* to staple.
GRAPO ['grapo] *nmpl* (*Esp Pol*) *abr de* **Grupos de Resistencia Antifascista Primero de Octubre.**
grapo *nmf* member of GRAPO.
grasa 1 *nf* (**a**) (*gen*) grease; (*Culin*) fat; (*sebo*) suet; **~ de ballena** blubber; **~ de pescado** fish oil; **~ saturada** saturated fat; **~ vegetal** vegetable fat; **alimentos bajos en ~s** low-fat foods.
(**b**) (*Aut, Mec*) oil; grease; **~ para ejes** axle grease.
(**c**) (*Anat*) fat, fattiness; **tener mucha ~** to be very fat.
(**d**) (*Méx*) shoe polish.
(**e**) (*pey*) grease, greasy dirt, filth.
(**f**) **~s** (*Min*) slag.
2 *adj* (*Cono Sur*: pey*) common.
3 *nm*: **es un ~** (*Cono Sur**) he's common.
grasiento *adj* (*grasoso*) greasy, oily; (*resbaladizo*) greasy, slippery; (*pey*) filthy.
graso 1 *adj* fatty; greasy; *comida* oily. **2** *nm* fattiness; greasiness; oiliness.
grasoso *adj* (*graso*) fatty; (*grasiento*) greasy.
grata *nf* (*Com*): **su ~ del 8** your letter of the 8th.
gratamente *adv* pleasingly, pleasantly, agreeably; gratifyingly.
gratificación *nf* (**a**) (*Fin etc*) (*recompensa*) reward, recompense; (*propina*) tip; gratuity; (*de sueldo*) bonus (on wages); bounty. (**b**) (*esp LAm*) gratification, pleasure, satisfaction.
gratificador *adj* (*LAm*) gratifying; pleasurable, satisfying.
gratificante *adj* gratifying.
gratificar [1g] *vt* (**a**) (*Fin etc*) to reward, recompense; to tip, give a gratuity to; to give a bonus to, pay extra to; **'se gratificará'** 'a reward is offered'.
(**b**) (*satisfacer*) to gratify; (*contentar*) to give pleasure to, satisfy; *anhelo* to gratify, indulge.
gratinado 1 *adj* au gratin. **2** *nm* dish cooked au gratin.
gratinador *nm* overhead grill.
gratis *adv* gratis, free, for nothing; **'entrada ~'** 'admission free'; **de ~** (*LAm*) gratis.
gratitud *nf* gratitude.
grato *adj* (**a**) (*placentero*) pleasing, pleasant; (*agradable*) agreeable; (*satisfactorio*) welcome, gratifying; **una decisión muy grata para todos** a very welcome decision for everybody; **recibir una impresión grata** to get a pleasing impression; **nos es ~ informarle que ...** we are pleased to inform you that ...
(**b**) (*And, Cono Sur*: *agradecido*) grateful; **le estoy ~** (*frm*) I am most grateful to you.
gratuidad *nf* cost-free status.
gratuitamente *adv* (**a**) (*gratis*) free, for nothing. (**b**) *comentar* gratuitously; *acusar* unfoundedly.
gratuito *adj* (**a**) (*gratis*) free, free of charge. (**b**) *observación etc* gratuitous, uncalled-for; *acusación* unfounded, unjustified.
gratulatorio *adj* congratulatory.
grava *nf* (*guijos*) gravel; (*piedra molida*) crushed stone; (*de carretera*) road metal.
gravable *adj* taxable, subject to tax.
gravamen *nm* (*carga*) burden, obligation; (*Jur*) lien, encumbrance; (*Fin*) tax, impost; **libre de ~** unencumbered, free from encumbrances; **~ bancario** banker's lien; **~ general** general lien; **~ del vendedor** vendor's lien.
gravar [1a] **1** *vt* (*cargar*) to burden, encumber (*de* with); (*Jur*) *propiedad* to place a lien upon; (*Fin*) to assess for tax; **~ con impuestos** to burden with taxes; **~ un producto con un impuesto** to place a tax on a product; **los impuestos que gravan esta vivienda** the taxes to which this dwelling is subject; **el préstamo y el interés que se le grava** the loan and the interest charged upon it.
2 gravarse *vr* (*LAm*) to get worse, become more serious.
gravativo *adj* burdensome.
grave *adj* (**a**) (*pesado*) heavy, weighty.
(**b**) (*fig*) (*serio*) grave, serious; (*espinoso*) critical; (*importante*) important, momentous; *pérdida etc* grave, severe, grievous; **un deber muy ~** a very grave duty; **la situación es ~** the situation is grave (*o* critical); **me es muy ~ tener que** + *infin* it is a very serious matter for me to + *infin*.
(**c**) (*de carácter*) serious, sedate, dignified; **y otros hombres ~s** and other worthy men.
(**d**) (*Med*) *enfermedad, estado*, grave serious; *herida* severe; **estar ~** to be seriously ill, be critically ill.
(**e**) (*Mús*) *nota, tono*, low, deep; *voz* deep.
(**f**) (*Ling*) *acento* grave; *palabra* paroxytone, stressed on the penultimate syllable (*p.ej. padre, romance*).
gravedad *nf* (**a**) (*Fís*) gravity; **~ nula** zero gravity.
(**b**) (*fig*) gravity, seriousness; (*grandeza*) importance; (*severidad*) severity, grievousness.
(**c**) (*dignidad*) seriousness, dignity.
(**d**) (*Med*) gravity; **estar de ~** to be seriously ill, be dangerously ill; **estar herido de ~** to be severely injured (*o* wounded); **tiene heridas de ~** he has serious injuries; **parece que la lesión es sin ~** it seems that the injury is not serious.
(**e**) (*Mús*) depth.
gravemente *adv* gravely, seriously; critically; severely, grievously; **habló ~** he spoke gravely; **estar ~ enfermo** to be critically ill.
gravera *nf* gravel bed, gravel pit.
grávido *adj* (**a**) (*embarazado*) pregnant; (*Zool*) with young, carrying young.
(**b**) (*fig*) full (*de* of), heavy (*de* with); **me sentí ~ de emociones** I was heavy with emotions, I was weighed down with emotions.
gravilla *nf* gravel.
gravitación *nf* gravitation.
gravitacional *adj* gravitational.
gravitante *adj* (*fig*) menacing.
gravitar [1a] *vi* (**a**) (*Fís*) to gravitate (*hacia* towards). (**b**) **~ sobre** to rest on; (*caer sobre*) to bear down on, weigh down on; (*fig*: *pesar sobre*) to be a burden to; to encumber.
gravitatorio *adj* gravitational.
gravoso *adj* (**a**) (*molesto*) burdensome, oppressive, onerous; **ser ~ a** to be a burden to, weigh on.
(**b**) (*Fin*) costly, expensive; burdensome; *precio* extortionate.
(**c**) (*insufrible*) tiresome, vexatious.
graznar [1a] *vi* (*gen*) to squawk; (*cuervo*) to caw, croak; (*ganso*) to cackle; (*pato*) to quack; (*cantante*: *hum*) to croak.
graznido *nm* squawk; caw, croak; cackle; quack.
grébano *nm* (*Cono Sur*: *pey*) Italian, wop‡.
Grecia *nf* Greece.
greca *nf* (*franja, orla*) border.
greco (*liter*) = **griego.**
grecochipriota *adj, nmf* Greek-Cypriot.
greda *nf* (*Geol*) clay; (*Téc*) fuller's earth.
gredal *nm* claypit.
gredoso *adj* clayey.
green [grin] *nm, pl* **greens** [grin] (*Golf*) green.
gregario 1 *adj* (**a**) gregarious; **instinto ~** herd instinct. (**b**) (*fig*) servile, slavish. **2** *nm* (*Dep*) domestic.
gregarismo *nm* gregariousness.
gregoriano *adj* Gregorian; **canto ~** Gregorian chant.
Gregorio *nm* Gregory.
greguería *nf* (**a**) hubbub, uproar, hullabaloo. (**b**) (*Liter*) *brief, humorous and often mildly poetic comment or aphorism about life.*
grelos *nmpl* parsnip tops, turnip tops.
gremial 1 *adj* (**a**) (*Hist*) guild (*atr*). (**b**) (*Pol*: *sindical*) trade-union (*atr*), trades-union (*atr*); (*LAm*) trade (*atr*). **2** *nmf* (*miembro*) union member.
gremialista *nmf* trade unionist.
gremio *nm* (**a**) (*Hist*) guild, corporation, company. (**b**) (*Pol*: *sindicato*) union; **~ obrero, ~ de obreros** trade union, trades union. (**c**) **ella es del ~*** she's on the game*.
greña *nf* (**a**) (*t* **~s**) (*cabellos revueltos*) shock of hair, mat (*o* mop) of hair, matted hair.
(**b**) (*fig*) tangle, entanglement; **andar a la ~** to bicker, squabble; **estar a la ~ con uno** to be at daggers drawn with sb.
(**c**) **en ~** (*Méx*) *seda* raw; *plata* unpolished; *azúcar* unrefined.
greñudo *adj pelo* tangled, matted; *persona* dishevelled.
gres *nm* (**a**) (*Geol*) potter's clay. (**b**) (*alfarería*) earthenware, stoneware.
gresca *nf* uproar, hubbub; row, shindy*; **andar a la ~** to

row, brawl.
grey *nf* (*Ecl*) flock, congregation.
Grial *nm*: **Santo** ~ Holy Grail.
griego 1 *adj* Greek, Grecian.
2 *nm*, **griega** *nf* (**a**) Greek.
(**b**) (*) cheat.
3 *nm* (*Ling*) (**a**) Greek; ~ **antiguo** ancient Greek.
(**b**) (* *fig*) gibberish, double Dutch*; **para mí es** ~ it's Greek to me; **hablar en** ~* to talk double Dutch*.
(**c**) (‡) anal intercourse.
grieta *nf* fissure, crack; chink; crevice; chasm; (*de piel*) chap, crack; (*Pol etc*) rift.
grietarse [1a] *vr* = **agrietarse**.
grifa‡ 1 *nf* hash*, pot‡, (*esp*) Moroccan marijuana. **2** *nmf* (*Méx**) drug addict.
grifear‡ [1a] *vi* to smoke pot‡.
grifería[1] *nf* plumbing, fixtures, taps (*collectively*), faucets (*collectively*: *US*).
grifería[2] *nf* (*Carib*‡) Negroes (*collectively*).
grifero *nm* (*And*) petrol-pump attendant.
grifo[1] *nm* (**a**) tap, faucet (*US*); cock; (*Cono Sur*) fire hydrant; **cerveza (servida) al** ~ draught beer, beer on draught; **cerrar el** ~ (*fig*) to turn off the tap, cut off the funds. (**b**) (*LAm*: *surtidor de gasolina*) petrol-pump; (*And*: *gasolinera*) petrol-station, gas station (*US*); (*bar*) dive‡; drink shop.
grifo[2]**‡ 1** *adj* (**a**) (*Méx*) (*borracho*) drunk, plastered‡; (*drogado*) high‡, doped up; (*loco*) nuts‡, crazy.
(**b**) (*And*: *engreído*) snobbish, stuck-up*.
2 *nm* (**a**) (*droga*) pot‡, hash*.
(**b**) (*drogado*) marijuana addict, pot smoker‡.
(**c**) (*borracho*) drunkard.
grifo[3] (*Carib*) **1** *adj* (**a**) *pelo* curly, kinky. (**b**) *persona* (*euf*) coloured, black. **2** *nm* (**a**) kinky hair. (**b**) (*euf*) Negro, coloured person.
grifo[4] *nm* (*Mit*) griffin.
grifón *nm* (*perro*) griffon; (*mítico*) gryphon.
grifota‡ *nmf* pot-smoker‡.
grigallo *nm* blackcock.
grilo‡ *nm* (**a**) (*cárcel*) nick‡, jail. (**b**) (*bolsillo*) pocket; ~ **bueno** right-hand pocket.
grill [gril] *nm* (*aparato*) grill; (*local*) grillroom; **asar al** ~ to grill.
grilla *nf* (**a**) (*Ent*) female cricket; **¡ésa es ~ (y no canta)!*** that's a likely story!; **dice la ~ que ...** (*Méx*) there's word going round that ... (**b**) (*And*: *pleito*) row, quarrel.
grillado‡ *adj* barmy‡.
grilladura‡ *nf* barminess‡.
grillera *nf* (**a**) (*jaula*) cage for crickets; (*nido*) cricket hole. (**b**) (*fig*) madhouse, bedlam. (**c**) (‡) police wagon.
grillete *nm* fetter, shackle.
grillo *nm* (**a**) (*Ent*) cricket; ~ **cebollero,** ~ **real** mole cricket. (**b**) (*Bot*) shoot, sprout. (**c**) ~**s** (*grilletes*) fetters, shackles, irons; (*: *esposas*) handcuffs; (*fig*) shackles.
grima *nf* (**a**) (*asco*), loathing, disgust; (*aversión*) aversion, reluctance; (*inquietud*) uneasiness; (*molestia*) annoyance, irritation, displeasure; **un dato de** ~ a really shattering piece of information; **me da** ~ it gets on my nerves, it gives me the shivers; it sickens me.
(**b**) **una ~ de licor** (*Cono Sur*) just a drop (of spirits).
(**c**) **en** ~ (*And*) alone.
grimillón *nm* (*Cono Sur*) lot, heap.
grímpola *nf* pennant.
gringada‡ *nf*, **gringaje‡** *nm* (*Cono Sur*) dirty foreigners; (*grupo*) group of dirty foreigners.
gringo 1 *adj* (**a**) (*LAm*) foreign (*V* **2**).
(**b**) (*LAm*) *lenguaje* foreign, unintelligible.
(**c**) (*And, Cono Sur*) blond(e), fair.
2 *nm*, **gringa** *nf* (**a**) (*LAm*) (*extranjero*) dirty foreigner; (†: *británico*) Briton, Anglo-Saxon; (*norteamericano*) North American, Yankee; (*Cono Sur*: *italiano*) Italian, wop‡.
(**b**) (*And, Cono Sur*: *rubio*) blond(e), fair-haired person.
3 *nm* (*LAm**: *Ling*) gibberish, unintelligible speech; **hablar en** ~ to talk double Dutch*.
gringuería *nf* (*LAm*) group of gringos.
gripa *nf* (*Méx*) = **gripe**.
gripaje *nm* (*Mec*) seize-up.
gripal *adj* flu (*atr*).
gripar* [1a] *vi* to seize up.
gripazo *nm* attack of flu.
gripe* *nf* influenza, flu; ~ **asiática** Asian flu; ~ **del cerdo** swine fever.
griposo *adj*: **estar** ~ to have flu.
gris 1 *adj* grey; *día, tiempo* grey, dull; ~ **carbón** charcoal grey; ~ **ceniza** ash-grey; ~ **marengo** (*tela*) dark grey; ~ **perla** pearl-grey. **2** *nm* (**a**) grey; **hace un** ~ there's a cold wind. (**b**) (‡) cop*; **los ~es** the fuzz‡.
grisáceo *adj* greyish.
grisalla *nf* (*Méx*) rubbish; scrap metal.
grisma *nf* (*Cono Sur*) strand, shred, bit.
grisoso *adj* (*LAm*) greyish.
gristapo‡ *nf* (*hum*) police.
grisú *nm* firedamp.
grisura *nf* greyness; dullness.
grita *nf* uproar, hubbub; shouting; (*Teat*) catcalls, booing; **dar ~ a** to boo, hoot (at).
gritadera *nf* (*LAm*) loud shouting, clamour.
gritar [1a] *vti* to shout, yell; to scream, shriek, cry out; (*Teat etc*) to hoot, boo; **¡no grites!** stop shouting!
gritería *nf* (**a**) = **griterío**. (**b**) (*CAm Rel*) festival of the Virgin.
griterío *nm* shouting, uproar, clamour.
grito *nm* (**a**) shout, yell; scream, shriek, cry; (*Teat etc*) hoot, boo; (*Zool*) cry, sound; (*Orn*) call, cry; **a ~s, a ~ herido, a ~ pelado, a voz en** ~ at the top of one's voice; **dar ~s** to shout out, cry out; **llorar a ~s** to weep and wail; **poner el ~ en el cielo** to make a great fuss, scream blue murder*; **es el último** ~* it's the very latest; **es el último ~ del lujo** it's the last word in luxury.
(**b**) (*LAm*) proclamation; ~ **de independencia** proclamation of independence; **el ~ de Dolores** *the proclamation of Mexican independence* (*1810*).
gritón *adj* loud-mouthed; screaming, shouting.
gro *nm* grosgrain.
groenlandés 1 *adj* Greenland (*atr*). **2** *nm*, **groenlandesa** *nf* Greenlander.
Groenlandia *nf* Greenland.
groggy ['grogi] *adj*, **grogui** *adj* (*Boxeo etc*) groggy; (*fig*) shattered, shocked, in a state of shock.
groncho‡ *nm* (*Cono Sur*: *pey*) worker.
grosella *nf* (red)currant; ~ **espinosa** gooseberry; ~ **negra** blackcurrant; ~ **colorada,** ~ **roja** redcurrant.
grosellero *nm* currant bush; ~ **espinoso** gooseberry bush.
groseramente *adv* (*descortésmente*) rudely, discourteously; (*ordinariamente*) coarsely, crudely, vulgarly, indelicately; (*toscamente*) roughly, loutishly; grossly, stupidly.
grosería *nf* (**a**) (*gen*) rudeness, discourtesy; (*ordinariez*) coarseness, crudeness, vulgarity; (*tosquedad*) roughness; (*estupidez*) stupidity.
(**b**) (*observación etc*) rude thing, coarse thing, vulgar remark (*etc*); (*palabrota*) swearword.
grosero *adj* (*descortés*) rude, discourteous; (*ordinario*) coarse, crude, vulgar; (*indecente*) indelicate; (*maleducado*) rough, loutish; *error etc* gross, stupid.
grosor *nm* thickness.
grosura *nf* fat, suet.
grotesca *nf* (*Tip*) sans serif.
grotescamente *adv* grotesquely, bizarrely, absurdly.
grotesco *adj* grotesque; bizarre, absurd.
grúa *nf* (*Téc*) crane; derrick; (*Aut*) tow-truck, towing vehicle; breakdown truck; ~ **corredera,** ~ **corrediza,** ~ **móvil** travelling crane; ~ **de pescante** jib crane; ~ **(de) puente** gantry crane, overhead crane; ~ **de torre** tower crane.
gruesa *nf* gross, twelve dozen.
grueso 1 *adj* (**a**) (*espeso*) thick; (*voluminoso*) bulky, stout, massive, solid; (*grande, pesado*) big, heavy; *persona* stout, thickset; *artillería, mar*, heavy; *intestino* large; *tronco etc* thick, massive.
(**b**) *tela etc* coarse.
2 *nm* (**a**) (*calidad*) thickness; (*tamaño*) bulkiness, bulk, size; (*densidad*) density.
(**b**) (*parte principal*) thick part; main part, major portion; (*de multitud, tropas etc*) main body, mass; **el ~ del pelotón** (*Dep*) the ruck of the runners; **va mezclado con el ~ del pasaje** he is mingling with the mass of the passengers.
(**c**) **en** ~ (*Com*) in bulk.
grulla[1] *nf* (*Orn*: *t* ~ **común**) crane.
grullo 1 *adj* (**a**) (*) uncouth, rough.
(**b**) (*Méx*) sponging*, cadging.
(**c**) (*CAm, Méx*) *caballo, mula* grey.
2 *nm*, **grulla**[2] *nf* bumpkin, yokel.
3 *nm* (*Méx*) grey (horse); (*Cono Sur*) big colt, large stallion.
grumete *nm* cabin boy, ship's boy.
grumo *nm* (**a**) (*coágulo*) clot, lump; (*masa*) dollop; (*de san-*

gre) clot; ~ **de leche** curd. (**b**) (*de uvas etc*) bunch, cluster.

grumoso *adj* clotted; lumpy.

gruñido *nm* grunt, growl; snarl; (*fig*) grouse*, grumble; **dar ~s** = **gruñir**.

gruñidor 1 *adj* grunting, growling; snarling; (*fig*) grumbling. **2** *nm*, **gruñidora** *nf* (*fig*) grumbler.

gruñir [3h] *vi* to grunt, growl; to snarl; (*fig*) to grouse*, grumble; (*puerta etc*) to creak.

gruñón 1 *adj* grumpy, grumbling. **2** *nm*, **gruñona** *nf* grumbler.

grupa *nf* hindquarters, rump (of horse).

grupal *adj* group (*atr*).

grupalmente *adv* in groups.

grupera *nf* (*de caballo*) pillion (seat); **ir en la ~** to sit behind the rider, be carried on the horse's rump.

grupi‡ *nf* groupie*.

grupín* *nm* (*Cono Sur*) crook*; embezzler; (*en subasta*) false bidder.

grupo *nm* (**a**) (*gen*) group; (*de árboles etc*) cluster, clump; (*Pol*) group; ~ **avanzado** advance party; ~ **(de) control** control group; ~ **del dólar** dollar block; ~ **de encuentro** encounter group; ~ **de estafas** fraud squad; ~ **de estupefacientes** drug squad; ~ **de homicidios** murder squad; ~ **de presión** pressure group; ~ **de riesgo** high-risk group; ~ **sanguíneo** blood-group; ~ **testigo** control group; ~ **de trabajo** working party; **discusión en ~** group discussion; **reunirse en ~s** to gather in groups; **reunirse en ~ en torno a** to gather round, cluster round.

(**b**) (*Elec, Téc etc*) unit, set, plant; assembly; ~ **compresor** compressor unit; ~ **dental** dentist's operating equipment; ~ **electrógeno**, ~ **generador** generating set, power plant.

(**c**) (‡: *trampista*) con man's accomplice*; (*Cono Sur*: *trampa*) trick, con*.

grupúsculo *nm* (*Pol*) small group, splinter group.

gruta *nf* cavern, grotto.

Gta. (*Aut*) *abr de* **glorieta** roundabout, traffic circle (*US*).

gua *interj* (*LAm*: *inquietud*) oh dear!; (*sorpresa*) well!; (*desdén*) get away!*.

gua...: *para diversas palabras escritas así en LAm, V t* **hua...**

guabiroba *nf* (*Cono Sur*) dugout canoe.

guaca *nf* (**a**) (*LAm*: *tumba*) (Indian) tomb, funeral mound; (*tesoro*) buried treasure; (*riqueza*) wealth, money; (*de armas, droga*) cache; (*And, CAm, Carib, Méx*: *alcancía*) moneybox; **hacer ~** (*And, Carib, Méx‡*) to make money, make one's pile*; **hacer su ~** (*Carib, Cono Sur*) to make hay while the sun shines.

(**b**) (*Carib**: *reprimenda*) ticking-off*.

(**c**) (*Méx*: *escopeta*) double-barrelled shotgun.

(**d**) (*Carib Med*) large sore.

guacal *nm* (*LAm*) (*cajón*) wooden crate; (*calabaza*) gourd, vessel.

guacamarón *nm* (*Carib*) brave man.

guacamayo 1 *adj* (*Cono Sur**: †) dressed garishly. **2** *nm* (**a**) (*Orn*) macaw. (**b**) (*Carib*: *pey*) Spaniard.

guacamole *nm* (*Méx*) guacamole, avocado sauce.

guacamote *nm* (*Méx Bot*) yucca plant.

guacarnaco *adj* (**a**) (*And, Carib, Cono Sur*) silly, stupid. (**b**) (*Cono Sur*) long-legged.

guachada *nf* (*LAm*) dirty trick.

guachafita *nf* (*Carib*) (**a**) (*ruido*) hubbub, din; (*desorden*) disorder. (**b**) (*garito*) gambling joint‡. (**c**) (*mofa*) mockery, jeering.

guachaje *nm* (*Cono Sur*) orphaned animal; group of calves separated from their mothers.

guachalomo *nm* (*Cono Sur*) sirloin steak.

guachapear [1a] **1** *vt* (**a**) *agua* to dabble in, splash about in.

(**b**) (*estropear*) to botch, mess up, bungle.

(**c**) (*Cono Sur**) to pinch*, borrow.

(**d**) (*And*) *maleza* to clear, cut.

2 *vi* to rattle, clatter, bang about.

guachar [1a] *vt* (*Méx*) to watch.

guáchara* *nf* (*Carib*) lie.

guácharo *nm* (*CAm Orn*) nightingale.

guache*[1] *nm* (*And, Carib*: *persona rural*) rustic, peasant; (*pey*) layabout, loafer.

guache[2] *nm* (*Arte*) gouache.

guachicar(ro) *nm* (*Méx*) parking attendant.

guachimán *nm* (*LAm*) watchman.

guachinanga *nf* (*Carib*) wooden bar (on door *etc*).

guachinango 1 *adj* (**a**) (*And**: *zalamero*) smooth; slimy. (**b**) (*Carib**) sharp, clever; smooth-tongued. **2** *nm* (**a**) (*Carib*: *pey*) Mexican. (**b**) (*Carib*: *persona astuta*) clever person. (**c**) (*Ling*) Latin-American colloquial Spanish.

guacho 1 *adj* (*esp And, Cono Sur*) (**a**) *persona* (*sin casa*) homeless; *niño* abandoned; *animal* motherless.

(**b**) *zapato etc* odd.

(**c**) (*Méx‡*: *capitalino*) of Mexico City.

2 *nm* (**a**) (*Orn*) baby bird, chick.

(**b**) (*And, Cono Sur*) (*niño abandonado*) homeless child, abandoned child; (*huérfano*) orphan, foundling; (*bastardo*) illegitimate child, (*pey*) bastard; (*Agr*) motherless animal.

(**c**) (*Cono Sur, And*: *objeto*) odd one (of a pair).

(**d**) (*Méx‡*: *capitalino*) person from Mexico City.

guadal *nm* (*And, Cono Sur*) sandy bog.

guadalajareño 1 *adj* of Guadalajara. **2** *nm*, **guadalajarense** *nf*, **guadalajereña** *nf* native (*o* inhabitant) of Guadalajara; **los ~s** the people of Guadalajara.

guadaloso *adj* (*Cono Sur*) boggy.

Guadalquivir *nm*: **el (Río) ~** the Guadalquivir.

guadamecí *nm* embossed leather.

guadaña *nf* scythe.

guadañadora *nf* mowing machine.

guadañar [1a] *vt* to scythe, mow.

guadañero *nm* mower.

guadaño *nm* (*Carib, Méx*) lighter, small harbour boat.

Guadiana *nm*: **el (Río) ~** the Guadiana; **aparece y desaparece como el ~** it keeps coming and going; now you see it now you don't.

guadianesco *adj* sporadic, intermittent; will-o'-the-wisp-like.

guágara* *nf*: **echar ~** (*Méx*) to gossip, chew the fat.

guagua[1] *nf* (*Carib, Canarias*) bus.

guagua[2] **1** *adj* (*And*) small, little. **2** *nf* (*a veces t nm*) (**a**) (*LAm*: *bebé*) baby. (**b**) (*bagatela*) trifle, small thing; **de ~** (*Carib, Méx*) free, for nothing.

guaguarear* [1a] *vi* (*CAm, Méx*) to babble, chatter.

guaguatear [1a] *vt* (*CAm, Cono Sur*) to carry in one's arms.

guaguatera *nf* (*Cono Sur*) nurse.

guagüero (*Carib*) **1** *adj* (**a**) sponging*, parasitical. (**b**) bus (*atr*). **2** *nm*, **guagüera** *nf* (**a**) bus-driver. (**b**) (*pey*) scrounger*, sponger*.

guai* *adj* = **guay**.

guaica *nf* (*Cono Sur*: *cuenta*) rosary bead; (*And*: *collar*) bead necklace.

guaico *nm* (*And*) (*hondonada*) hollow, dip; (*hoyo*) ravine; (*barranco*) hole, pit; (*avalancha*) avalanche; (*estercolero*) dung heap; (*basurero*) rubbish tip, garbage tip (*US*).

guaina 1 *nf* (*Cono Sur*) girl, young woman. **2** *nm* (*And*) youth, young man.

guaino *nm* (*And, Cono Sur*: *Dep*) jockey.

guaipe *nm* (*LAm*) wiper, cloth, cotton waste.

guáiper *nm* (*CAm*) windscreen wiper, windshield wiper (*US*).

guaira *nf* (**a**) (*CAm Mús*) Indian flute. (**b**) (*And, Cono Sur*) earthenware smelting furnace (*for silver ore*).

guairana *nf* (**a**) (*And*: *de cal*) limekiln. (**b**) = **guaira**.

guairuro *nm* (*And, CAm*) dried seed.

guajada *nf* (*Méx*) stupid thing.

guajalote (*Carib, Méx*) = **guajolote**.

guaje[1] **1** *adj* (*CAm, Méx*) silly, stupid; **hacer ~ a uno** to fool sb, take sb in*.

2 *nm* (**a**) (*CAm, Méx Bot*) gourd, calabash, squash (*US*).

(**b**) (*CAm**: *trasto*) old thing, piece of junk.

3 *nmf* (*CAm**: *tonto*) fool, idiot.

guaje[2], **-a** *nm/f* (**a**) (*) child. (**b**) (*Min*) mining apprentice.

guajear [1a] *vi* (*Méx*) to play the fool, be silly.

guajería *nf* (*Méx*) (**a**) (*estupidez*) idiocy, foolishness. (**b**) (*acto*) stupid thing, foolish act.

guajero, -a *nm/f*, **guajiro**[1], **-a** *nm/f* (*Carib*) (white) peasant; (*CAm*) countryman; outsider.

guajiro[2] *nm* (*Cuba*) peasant.

guajolote (*Méx*) **1** *adj* silly, stupid. **2** *nm* (**a**) (*Orn*) turkey. (**b**) (*) fool, idiot, turkey (*US*).

gualda *nf* dyer's greenweed, reseda.

gualdo *adj* yellow, golden; *V* **bandera**.

gualdrapa *nf* (**a**) (*de caballo*) trappings. (**b**) (*) tatter, ragged end. (**c**) (*CAm‡*) down-and-out, bum (*US*).

gualdrapear [1a] *vi* (**a**) (*Náut*: *vela*) to flap. (**b**) (*Carib*: *caballo*) to walk.

gualicho *nm* (**a**) (*And, Cono Sur*: ††: *diablo*) devil, evil spirit; (††: *maleficio*) evil spell. (**b**) (*Cono Sur*: *talismán*) talisman, good-luck charm.

Gualterio *nm* Walter.

guallipén *nm* (*Cono Sur*) fool, idiot.

guama *nf* (**a**) (*And, CAm, mentira*) lie. (**b**) (*And*) (*pie*) big foot; (*mano*) big hand. (**c**) (*And, Carib: desastre*) calamity, disaster.

guambito *nm* (*And*) kid*, boy.

guambra *nmf* (*And*) (**a**) young Indian. (**b**) child, baby; (*: *amor*) sweetheart.

guamiza* *nf* (*Méx*) beating-up*.

guampa *nf* (*Carib, Cono Sur*) horn.

guampara *nf* (*Carib*) machete.

guámparo *nm* (*Cono Sur*) horn; drinking vessel.

guanábana *nm* (**a**) (*Bot*) custard apple. (**b**) (*And*) fool.

guanacada *nmf* (*LAm*) simpleton, dimwit*; rustic.

guanaco 1 *adj* (*LAm*) (*tonto*) simple, silly; (*lento*) slow.
2 *nm* (**a**) (*Zool*) guanaco.
(**b**) (*LAm*: tonto*) simpleton, dimwit* (*CAm**) bumpkin, country cousin.
(**c**) (*CAm*: pey: salvadoreño*) Salvadorean.
(**d**) (*Cono Sur*) water-cannon.

guanajada* *nf* (*Carib*) silly thing, foolish act.

guanajo, -a *nm/f* (*Carib*) (**a**) (*Orn*) turkey. (**b**) (*) fool, idiot.

guanay *nm* (*Cono Sur*) oarsman; longshoreman; (*fig*) tough man.

guanayerías* *nfpl* (*Carib*) silly actions.

guanche 1 *adj* Guanche. **2** *nmf* Guanche (*original inhabitant of Canary Islands*).

guanear [1a] **1** *vt* (**a**) (*And*) to fertilize with guano. (**b**) (*And*) to dirty, soil. **2** *vi* (*LAm: animales*) to defecate.

guanera *nf* guano deposit.

guanero *adj* guano (*atr*), pertaining to guano.

guango* *adj* (*LAm*) *andar* loose, floppy.

guanín *nm* (*And, Carib, Cono Sur: Hist*) base gold.

guano[1] *nm* (**a**) guano; artificial manure; (*And, Cono Sur*) dung, manure. (**b**) (*Carib: hum*) money, brass; **meter ~** (*Carib*: fig*) to put one's back into it.

guano[2] *nm* (*Carib*) (*árbol*) palm tree; (*penca*) palm leaf.

guantada *nf*, **guantazo** *nm* slap.

guante *nm* (**a**) glove; **~ de boxeo** boxing-glove; **~ de cabritilla** kid glove; **~ de goma** rubber glove; **~s de terciopelo** (*fig*) kid gloves; **~ con puño** gauntlet; **tratamiento de ~ blanco** gentlemanly treatment; **crimen de ~ blanco** white-collar crime; **se ajusta como un ~** it fits like a glove; **me conviene como un ~** it suits me down to the ground; **ser como un ~** (*fig*) to be very meek and mild, be submissive; **arrojar el ~** to throw down the gauntlet; **echar un ~** to take a collection (*a beneficio de* for, on behalf of); **echar el ~ a uno** to catch hold of sb, seize sb; (*fig*) to catch sb out, come down on sb; **hacer ~s** to take up boxing; **recoger el ~** to take up the challenge.
(**b**) (*Cono Sur*) whip, cat-o'nine-tails.
(**c**) **~s** (*gratificación*) tip, commission.

guantear [1a] *vt* (*Cono Sur*) to slap, smack.

guantelete *nm* gauntlet.

guantera *nf* (*Aut*) glove compartment.

guantería *nf* (**a**) (*tienda*) glove shop; (*fábrica*) glove factory. (**b**) (*fabricación*) glove making.

guantero, -a *nm/f* glover.

guantón *nm* (*LAm*) slap, hit, blow.

guañusco* *adj* (*Cono Sur*) (**a**) (*marchito*) withered, faded. (**b**) (*quemado*) burned, burned up.

guapear* [1a] **1** *vi* (**a**) (*ostentarse*) to cut a dash, dress flashily. (**b**) (*fanfarronear*) to bluster, swagger. **2** *vt* (*And*) to urge on.

guaperas* *invar* **1** *adj* excessively good-looking. **2** *nm* excessively good-looking youth; (*iró*) heart-throb*, dreamboy*.

guapetón 1 *adj* (**a**) good-looking, handsome; dashing; **guapetona** good-looking in a mature way, full-figured and very attractive. (**b**) (*pey*) flashy. **2** *nm* bully, roughneck‡.

guapeza *nf* (**a**) (*atractivo*) good looks; prettiness, attractiveness. (**b**) (*elegancia*) smartness, elegance; (*pey: ostentación*) flashiness. (**c**) boldness, dash; (*pey: bravata*) bravado.

guapo 1 *adj* (**a**) (*atractivo*) good-looking; *chica* pretty, attractive; *hombre* handsome; **¡oye, guapa!** hey, beautiful!*
(**b**) (*elegante*) smart, elegant, well-dressed; (*pey*) flashy, overdressed; **¡hombre, qué ~ estás!** how smart you're looking!; **va de ~ por la vida** he goes through life with every confidence in his good looks.
(**c**) (*valiente*) bold, dashing; (*Carib*) brave; (*Cono Sur: duro*) tough; (*Cono Sur: sin escrúpulos*) unscrupulous.
(**d**) (‡: *increíble*) incredible; (*interesante*) interesting; (*encantador*) nice; (*guay*) ace*, brill‡.
2 *nm* (**a**) (*amante*) lover, boyfriend.
(**b**) (*currutaco*) dandy; (*LAm: pey*) bully, tough guy* (*US*); (*fanfarrón*) braggart.
(**c**) (*CAm Cine*) male lead.

guaposo *adj* (*Carib*) bold, dashing.

guapucha* *nf* (*And*) cheating.

guaquear [1a] *vt* (*And, CAm*) *tumba* to rob, sack (*in search of archaeological valuables*).

guaqueo *nm* (*And, CAm*) graverobbing.

guaquero, -a *nm/f* (*And, CAm*) graverobber.

guara *nf* (**a**) (*And*) lot, heap. (**b**) **~s** (*Cono Sur*) tricks, wiles.

guaraca *nf* (*And*) (*honda*) catapult, slingshot (*US*); (*cordel*) cord, string; (*para trompo*) whip.

guaracha *nf* (**a**) (*Carib*) (*canción*) popular song; (*baile*) folk dance.
(**b**) (*Carib**) (*alboroto*) din, racket; (*riña*) quarrel; (*juerga*) party, shindig*.
(**c**) (*Carib: banda*) street band.
(**d**) (*Carib*) joke.
(**e**) (*And*) litter, rough bed.
(**f**) **~s** (*CAm*) old shoes.
(**g**) (*CAm*) = **guarache.**

guarache *nm* (*Méx*) (**a**) (*chancleta*) sandal. (**b**) (*Aut*) patch.

guarachear* [1a] *vi* (*Carib*) to revel; (*fig*) to let one's hair down.

guaragua *nf* (**a**) **~s** (*And*) adornments, finery.
(**b**) (*CAm*: mentira*) lie.
(**c**) (*CAm*) liar, taleteller.
(**d**) (*And, Cono Sur*) rhythmical movement (*of the body in dancing*).

guaral *nm* (*And, Carib*) (*cuerda*) rope, cord; (*de trompo*) whip.

guarangada *nf* (*LAm*) rude remark.

guarango *adj* (**a**) (*And, Cono Sur*: grosero*) *acto etc* rude; *persona* uncouth. (**b**) (*And*) (*sucio*) dirty; (*harapiento*) ragged.

guaranguear* [1a] *vi* (*And, Cono Sur*) to be rude, be badmannered.

guaranguería* *nf* (*Cono Sur*) rudeness, uncouthness.

guaraní 1 *adj, nmf* Guaraní. **2** *nm* (*Ling*) Guaraní.

guaranismo *nm* word (*o expression etc*) from Guaraní.

guarapazo *nm* (*And*) (**a**) (*de bebida*) shot*, slug*. (**b**) (*golpe*) blow, knock; (*caída*) hard fall.

guarapear [1a] *vi y* **guarapearse** *vr* (*And*) to drink sugar-cane liquor; (*Carib*: emborracharse*) to get tight*.

guarapo *nm* (*LAm*) sugar-cane liquor; palm wine; (*Carib*) watered-down drink; (*Carib*) fermented pineapple juice; **menear el ~** (*Carib*) to get a move on; **se le enfrió el ~** (*Carib**: †) he lost the urge; **volver ~ algo** to tear sth up.

guarapón *nm* (*And, Cono Sur*) broad-brimmed hat.

guarda 1 *nmf* (*persona: gen*) guard; (*cuidador*) keeper, custodian; (*Cono Sur Ferro*) ticket collector; **~ de coto, ~ forestal** forest ranger, gamekeeper, game warden; **~ fluvial, ~ de pesca** water bailiff; **~ jurado** (*de empresa etc*) security guard; (*caza*) gamekeeper, game warden; **~ de dique** lock-keeper; **~ nocturno** night watchman.
2 *nf* (**a**) (*acto*) guard, guarding; safekeeping; custody.
(**b**) (*de ley*) observance.
(**c**) (*de cerradura*) ward; (*de espada, máquina*) guard; (*Tip*) flyleaf, endpaper.
(**d**) (*Cono Sur: adorno*) trimming.

guarda(a)gujas *nm invar* (*Ferro*) pointsman, switchman (*US*).

guard(a)almacén *nmf* storekeeper.

guardabarrera 1 *nmf* (*Ferro: persona*) crossing keeper. **2** *nf* (*paso*) level-crossing gate(s), grade-crossing gate(s) (*US*).

guardabarros *nm invar* mudguard, fender (*US*).

guardabosque(s) *nm* gamekeeper, game warden; ranger, forester.

guardabrisa *nf* (*Aut*) windscreen, windshield (*US*); (*de vela*) shade; (*Méx*) screen.

guardacabo *nm* (*Náut*) thimble.

guardacabras *nmf invar* goatherd.

guardacalor *nm* (tea) cosy, cover.

guardacamisa *nf* (*Carib*) vest, undershirt (*US*).

guardacantón *nm* roadside post, corner post.

guardacoches *nmf invar* parking attendant.

guardacostas *nm invar* coastguard vessel, revenue cutter.

guardador 1 *adj* (**a**) (*protector*) protective.
(**b**) (*de ley etc*) observant; scrupulous.
(**c**) (*pey*) mean, stingy.

2 *nm*, **guardadora** *nf* (**a**) (*cuidador etc*) keeper; guardian; protector.

(**b**) (*de ley etc*) observer.

(**c**) (*pey*) mean person.

guardaespaldas *nm invar* bodyguard, henchman; minder*.

guardaesquinas* *nmf invar* layabout.

guardafango *nm* mudguard, fender (*US*).

guardafrenos *nm invar* guard, brakeman.

guardagujas *nm invar* (*Ferro*) pointsman, switchman (*US*).

guardajoyas *nm invar* jewel case.

guardajurado, -a *nm/f* security guard.

guardalado *nm* railing, parapet.

guardalmacén *nmf* storekeeper.

guardalodos *nm invar* mudguard, fender (*US*).

guardamano *nm* guard (*of a sword*).

guardamechones *nm invar* locket.

guardameta *nm* goalkeeper.

guardamuebles *nm invar* furniture repository.

guardapapeles *nm invar* filing cabinet.

guardapelo *nm* locket.

guardapolvo *nm* (**a**) (*cubierta*) dust-cover, dust-sheet. (**b**) (*ropa*) dustcoat; (*mono*) overalls; (*abrigo*) outdoor coat. (**c**) (*de reloj*) inner lid.

guardapolvos** *nm invar* (**a**) (*Anat*) cunt**. (**b**) (*goma*) rubber*.

guardapuerta *nf* (*puerta*) outer door, storm door; (*cortina*) door curtain, draught excluder.

guardapuntas *nm invar* top (*of pencil etc*).

guardar [1a] **1** *vt* (**a**) (*cuidar*) to guard; (*proteger*) to watch over, protect, take care of, keep safe; (*preservar*) to maintain, preserve; *rebaño etc* to watch over, tend; **¡Dios guarde a la Reina!** God save the Queen!; **Dios os guarde** (††) may God be with you.

(**b**) (*retener*) to keep, hold, hold on to, retain; (*Inform*) to save; (*conservar*) to put away, put by, lay by, store away; (*ahorrar*) to save; ~ **algo para sí** to keep sth for o.s.; **lo guardó en el bolsillo** he put it away in his pocket; **te lo puedes** ~ you keep it, you can keep it; **guardo los sellos para mi hermano** I save the stamps for my brother; **guardo los mejores recuerdos** I have the nicest memories; **guárdame un asiento** save me a seat.

(**c**) *promesa, secreto* to keep.

(**d**) *mandamiento etc* to keep; *ley* to observe, respect.

(**e**) *respeto etc* to have, show (*a* for); *rencor etc* to bear, have (*a* for, towards); *V* **cama, silencio** *etc*.

2 guardarse *vr* (**a**) (*precaverse*) to be on one's guard, look out for o.s.

(**b**) ~ **de algo** (*evitar*) to avoid sth; (*cuidarse*) to look out for sth; (*abstenerse*) to refrain from sth; (*protegerse*) (*abstenerse*) to protect o.s. against sth; ~ **de** + *infin* to be careful not to + *infin*; to refrain from + *ger*; to avoid + *ger*; to guard against + *ger*; **guárdate de no ofenderle** take care not to upset him; **¡ya te guardarás de hacerlo!** I bet you won't!; you wouldn't dare!

(**c**) ~**la a uno** to have it in for sb, bear a grudge against sb.

guardarraya *nf* (*And, CAm, Carib*) boundary.

guardarropa 1 *nm* (**a**) (*cuarto*) cloakroom, checkroom (*US*). (**b**) (*ropero*) wardrobe. **2** *nmf* cloakroom attendant.

guardarropía *nf* (*Teat*) wardrobe; (*accesorios*) properties, props*; **de** ~ make-believe, (*pey*) sham, fake.

guardatiempo(s) *nm* timekeeper.

guardatrén *nm* (*Cono Sur Ferro*) guard, brakeman.

guardavalla(s) *nm* (*LAm*) goalkeeper.

guardavía *nm* (*Ferro*) linesman.

guardavidas *nm invar* (*Cono Sur*: *de playa*) lifeguard.

guardavista *nm* visor, sunshade.

guardería *nf*: ~ **infantil** crèche, day nursery, day-care centre.

guardés, -esa *nm/f* guard; (*de puerta*) doorman; (*de casa de campo*) gatekeeper.

guardia 1 *nf* (**a**) (*gen*) custody, care; (*defensa*) defence, protection; (*Mil etc*) guarding; (*turno*) shift, spell of duty; **farmacia de** ~ all-night chemist's; **médico de** ~ doctor on call; **estar de** ~ to be on guard, be on duty; to keep watch; **estar en** ~ **contra** to be on one's guard against; **hacer** ~, **montar** (**la**) ~ to mount guard; **poner a uno en** ~ to put sb on his guard.

(**b**) (*hombres*) guard; (*Mil*) guard; (*policía*) police; (*Náut*) watch; ~ **de asalto** riot police; **G~ Civil** Civil Guard; ~ **de corps** bodyguard; ~ **de honor** guard of honour; ~**s montadas** horse guards; ~ **municipal,** ~ **urbana** municipal police; ~ **real** household troops; **vieja** ~ old guard; **relevar la** ~ to change guard.

(**c**) (*Esgrima*: *posición*) guard; **aflojar** (*o* **bajar**) la ~ to lower one's guard (*t fig*); **estar en** ~ to be on guard.

2 *nmf* (*policía*) (*hombre*) policeman; (*mujer*) policewoman; (*Mil*) guard, guardsman; ~**s de asalto** riot police, (*Mil*) shock troops; ~ **de la circulación,** ~ **de tráfico** traffic policeman; ~ **civil** civil guard; ~ **forestal** game warden, ranger; ~ **jurado** security guard; ~ **marina** midshipman; ~ **municipal,** ~ **urbano** municipal policeman; ~ **nocturno** night watchman.

guardián, -ana *nm/f* guardian, custodian, keeper; warden; watchman; (*Zool*) keeper; ~ **de parque** park keeper.

guardiero *nm* (*Carib*) watchman (*on an estate*).

guardilla *nf* attic, garret; attic room.

guardiola* *nf* piggy-bank, moneybox.

guardoso *adj* careful, thrifty; (*pey*) mean.

guare *nm* (*And*) punt pole.

guarearse* [1a] *vr* (*CAm*) to get tight*.

guarecer [2d] **1** *vt* to protect, give shelter to, take in; to preserve. **2 guarecerse** *vr* to shelter, take refuge (*de* from).

guargüero *nm* (*LAm*) throat, throttle.

guari *nm* (*Cono Sur*) throat, throttle.

guaricha* *nf* (*And, CAm, Carib*) (*mujer*) woman; (*vieja*) old bag*.

guariche *nm* (*And*) = **guaricha.**

guaricho *nm* (*Carib*: †) young farm labourer.

guarida *nf* (*Zool*) den, lair, hideout; (*fig*) refuge, shelter; cover; (*de persona*) haunt, hideout.

guarismo *nm* figure, numeral.

guarnecer [2d] *vt* (**a**) (*proveer*) to equip, provide (*de* with); (*adornar*) to adorn, embellish, garnish (*de* with); (*Cos*) to trim, edge (*de* with); *frenos* to line; *pared* to plaster, stucco; *joya* to set, mount; *caballo* to harness; (*Téc*) to cover, protect, reinforce (*de* with).

(**b**) (*Mil*) to man, garrison; to be stationed in.

guarnecido *nm* (*de pared*) plaster, plastering; (*Aut*) upholstery.

guarnés *nm* (*Méx*: *para arneses*) harness room.

guarnición *nf* (**a**) (*acto*) equipment, provision; fitting; adorning, embellishing; (*Culin*) garnishing.

(**b**) (*adorno*) adornment; (*Cos*) trimming, edging, binding; (*de freno*) lining; (*de pared*) plastering; (*de joya*) setting, mount; (*de espada*) guard; (*Mec*) packing; (*Culin*) garnish(ing).

(**c**) **guarniciones** (*de caballo*) harness; (*equipo*) gear; (*de casa*) fittings, fixtures; **guarniciones del alumbrado** light fittings.

(**d**) (*Mil*) garrison.

guarnicionar [1a] *vt* to garrison, man; to be stationed in.

guarnicionero *nm* harness maker; leather worker, craftsman in leather.

guaro *nm* (**a**) (*CAm**: *licor*) liquor, spirits. (**b**) (*Orn*) small parrot.

guarola* *nf* (*CAm*: *coche*) old crock, old banger‡.

guarolo *adj* (*Carib*) stubborn.

guarra *nf* (**a**) (*Zool*) sow; (*fig*) slut. (**b**) (‡) punch, bash*.

guarrada *nf*, **guarrería** *nf* (*trampa*) dirty trick; (*dicho*) rotten thing (to say); (*indecencia*) indecent act, vulgar thing (to do).

guarrear [1a] *vt* to dirty, mess up.

guarreta* *nf* slut.

guarro 1 *adj* dirty, filthy. **2** *nm* pig, hog; (*fig*) dirty person, slovenly person.

guarrusca *nf* (*And*) machete, big knife.

guarte *interj* (††) look out!, take care!

guarura* *nm* (*Méx*) (*policía*) cop*; (*guardaespaldas*) bodyguard, minder*.

guasa[1] *nf* (**a**) (*broma*) joke; (*chanza*) joking, teasing, kidding*; **con** ~, **de** ~ jokingly, in fun.

(**b**) (*sosería*) dullness, insipidness.

(**c**) (*Cono Sur*) peasant woman.

(**d**) (*CAm*: *suerte*) luck.

guasábara *nf* (*And, Carib*) (*Hist*: *de esclavos*) uprising; (††: *clamor*) clamour, uproar.

guasada‡ *nf* (*Cono Sur*: *expresión*) obscenity.

guasamaco *adj* (*Cono Sur*) rough, coarse.

guasanga *nf* (**a**) (*And, Carib*) = **guasábara**; (*CAm*: *bulla*) uproar. (**b**) (*CAm*: *chiste*) joke.

guasca[1] *nf* (**a**) (*LAm*) leather strap, rawhide thong; (*And*) riding-whip, crop; **dar** ~ **a** (*LAm*) to whip, flog; (*Cono Sur*) to insist stubbornly on; (*And*) to wind up; **¡déle** ~ **no más!** (*Cono Sur*) keep at it!; **pisarse la** ~ (*And, Cono Sur‡*) to fall into the trap; **volverse** ~ (*And*) to be full of longing.

(**b**) (*Cono Sur*⁂) prick⁂.

guasca[2] *nf* (*And*) mountain peak.

guascaro *adj* (*And*) impulsive.

guascazo *nm* (*LAm*) lash; blow, punch.

guasearse [1a] *vr* to joke, tease, kid*, rag.

guasería* *nf* (*And, Cono Sur*) obscenity.

guaserío *nm* (*Cono Sur*) rabble.

guaso **1** *adj* (*And, Carib, Cono Sur**: *grosero*) coarse, crude, rough; (*Cono Sur*) (*tímido*) shy; (*sencillo*) simple, unsophisticated. **2** *nm*, **guasa**[2] *nf* (*And, Cono Sur*: *campesino*) peasant, countryman, countrywoman; (*vaquero*) cowboy; (*Cono Sur**: *grosero*) uncouth person. **3** *nm* (*Carib**: *parranda*) merrymaking, revelry.

guasón **1** *adj* (**a**) (*gracioso*) witty, humorous; (*burlón*) joking; **dijo ~** he said jokingly, he said teasingly.
(**b**) (*soso*) dull, insipid; (*aburrido*) boring.
2 *nm*, **guasona** *nf* (**a**) wag, wit; joker, tease.
(**b**) tedious person, bore.

guasqueada *nf* (*Cono Sur*) lash; whipping, flogging.

guasquear [1a] *vt* (*Cono Sur**) to whip, flog.

guata[1] *nf* (**a**) (*And, Cono Sur**: *barriga*) paunch, belly; (*Cono Sur Culin*) tripe; **echar ~** (*Cono Sur**) to get fat. (**b**) (*Cono Sur*) warping, bulging.

guata[2] *nf* (**a**) (*algodón*) raw cotton; (*relleno*) padding; (*And*) twine, cord.
(**b**) (*Carib**) lie, fib.
(**c**) (*And**) inseparable friend, bosom buddy.

guata[3] *nmf* (*And*) inhabitant of the interior.

guataca (*Carib*) **1** *nf* (**a**) (*Agr*) small hoe; wooden shovel. (**b**) (*Anat*) big ear. **2** *nmf* creep⁑, bootlicker*.

guataco *adj* (**a**) (*And*) Indian, native. (**b**) (*CAm, Méx**) chubby, plump.

guatal *nm* (*CAm*) hillock.

guate *nm* (**a**) (*CAm Agr*) maize plantation.
(**b**) (*: *serrano*) highlander; (*Carib**: *colombiano*) Colombian.
(**c**) (*And**) bosom buddy.

guatearse [1a] *vr* (*Cono Sur*) to warp, bulge.

Guatemala *nf* (**a**) Guatemala. (**b**) **salir de ~ y entrar en Guatepeor** to jump out of the frying pan into the fire.

guatemalteco **1** *adj* Guatemalan, of Guatemala. **2** *nm*, **guatemalteca** *nf* Guatemalan.

guatemaltequismo *nm* word (*o* phrase *etc*) peculiar to Guatemala.

guateque *nm* party, celebration, binge*.

guatero *nm* (*Cono Sur*) hot-water bottle.

guatitas *nfpl* (*And, Cono Sur Culin*) tripe.

guato⁑ *nm* (*LAm*) joint⁑, reefer⁑.

guatón *adj* (*Cono Sur**: *barrigón*) paunchy, pot-bellied; (*regordete*) plump; **sí, ~*** yes darling.

guatuso *adj* (*CAm*) blond(e), fair.

guau[1] **1** *interj etc* bow-wow! **2** *nm* bark.

guau[2] *excl* wow!*

guay* *adj* super*, great*, smashing*.

guaya *nf* (*Carib*) wire.

guayaba *nf* (**a**) (*Bot*) guava; (*jalea*) guava jelly. (**b**) (*fig y hum*: *LAm*) fib, lie; (*LAm*: *tobillo*) ankle; (*CAm*: *beso*) kiss; (*CAm*⁑: *boca*) gob⁑; **la ~** (*CAm Pol*) power.

guayabal *nm* grove of guava trees.

guayabear⁑ [1a] **1** *vt* (*CAm*) to kiss. **2** *vi* (*Carib, Cono Sur*) to lie, tell fibs.

guayabera *nf* (*LAm*) *loose shirt with large pockets*; lightweight jacket.

guayabero⁑ *adj* (*Carib, Cono Sur*) lying, deceitful.

guayabo *nm* (**a**) (*Bot*) guava tree. (**b**) (*And*) (*pena*) grief, sorrow; (*murria*) nostalgia; (*And, Cono Sur**: *resaca*) hangover*. (**c**) (*: *guapa*) pretty girl, smasher⁑; **está hecha un ~** (*atractiva*) she looks marvellous; (*joven*) she looks very young. (**d**) (*Méx*⁂) cunt⁂.

guayaca **1** *adj* (*Cono Sur*) slow, dull; simple-minded. **2** *nf* (*LAm*) bag, purse.

guayacán *nm* lignum vitae.

Guayana *nf* Guyana; (*Hist*) Guiana; **~ Británica** British Guiana; **~ Francesa** French Guiana; **~ Holandesa** Dutch Guiana.

guayanés, -esa *adj, nm/f* Guyanese.

guayar [1a] *vt* (*Carib Culin*) to grate.

guayo *nm* (*Carib*) (*Culin*) grater; (*Mús**) bad street band.

guayuco* *nm* (*And, Carib*) loincloth.

guayunga *nf* (*And*) lot, heap.

gubernamental **1** *adj* government (*atr*), governmental; (*de facción*) loyalist. **2** *nmf* loyalist, government supporter; (*Mil*) government soldier.

gubernamentalización *nf* (increase in) government intervention (*o* control).

gubernativo *adj* governmental.

gubia *nf* gouge.

guedeja *nf* long hair, lock; (*de león*) mane.

güe... (*prov, LAm*) *a veces se escriben así diversas palabras que empiezan* **hue...**; *p.ej. para* **güevón** *V* **huevón**.

güegüecho **1** *adj* (**a**) (*And**) silly, stupid.
(**b**) (*CAm, Méx Med*) suffering from goitre.
2 *nm* (**a**) (*LAm Med*) goitre.
(**b**) (*CAm Orn*) turkey.
(**c**) (*CAm**: *bohío*) hovel.

güeñi *nm* (*Cono Sur*) (*chico*) boy; (*criado*) servant.

guepardo *nm* cheetah.

güerequeque *nm* (*And Orn*) plover.

Guernesey *nm* Guernsey.

güero *adj* (*CAm, Méx*) *pelo, persona* blond(e), fair; *persona* (*de tez*) fair, light-skinned.

guerra *nf* (**a**) war; warfare; struggle, fight, conflict; **~ de agotamiento**, **~ de desgaste** war of attrition; **~ atómica** atomic war(fare); **~ bacteriana**, **~ bacteriológica** germ warfare; **~ biológica** biological warfare; **~ caliente** hot war, shooting war; **~ del catorce** Great War, First World War; **~ civil** civil war; **~ comercial** trade war; **~ convencional** conventional warfare; **~ fría** cold war; **~ de las galaxias** Star Wars; **~ de guerrillas** guerrilla warfare; **~ a muerte** war to the knife, war to the bitter end; **~ mundial** world war; **~ de nervios** war of nerves; **~ nuclear** nuclear war(fare); **~ de precios** price war; **~ psicológica** psychological warfare; **~ química** chemical warfare; **~ relámpago** blitzkrieg; **~ santa** holy war, crusade; **~ sucia** dirty war; **~ a tiros** shooting war, hot war; **~ de trincheras** trench warfare; **G~ de los Cien Años** Hundred Years' War; **G~ de los Treinta Años** Thirty Years' War; **G~ de la Independencia** (*LAm*) War of Independence; (*Esp*) Peninsular War; **G~ de Sucesión** War of Spanish Succession; **G~ del Transvaal** Boer War; **Primera G~ Mundial** First World War; **Segunda G~ Mundial** Second World War; **de ~** military; war (*atr*); **Ministerio de G~** Ministry of War, War Office (*Brit*), War Department (*US*); **estar en ~** to be at war (*con* with); **dar ~** to be annoying (*a* to), be a nuisance (*a* to), make trouble (*a* for); (*niño*) to carry on, make a great fuss; **dar ~ a uno** to rag sb; **declarar la ~** to declare war (*a* on); **hacer la ~** to wage war, make war (*a* on); **pedir** (*o* **querer**) **~** (*: *sexualmente*) to feel randy*.
(**b**) (*juego*) (kind of) billiards.

guerrear [1a] *vi* to wage war, fight; (*fig*) to put up a fight, resist.

guerrera[1] *nf* trench coat; combat jacket; (*Mil*) military jacket.

guerrero **1** *adj* (**a**) (*belicoso*) fighting (*atr*); war (*atr*); **espíritu ~** fighting spirit.
(**b**) (*contrario*) warring.
(**c**) *carácter* warlike, martial; **un pueblo ~** a warlike people.
2 *nm*, **guerrera**[2] *nf* warrior, soldier, fighter.
3 *nm* (*Carib**) rum and vodka-based cocktail.

guerrilla *nf* (**a**) (*grupo*) guerrilla band; group of partisans; (*fuerzas*) guerrilla forces. (**b**) (*lucha*) guerrilla warfare.

guerrillear [1a] *vi* to wage guerrilla warfare; to fight as a guerrilla band.

guerrillero, -a *nm/f* guerrilla (fighter); partisan; irregular; **~ urbano** urban guerrilla.

guerrista *adj* combative, fighting.

güesear⁑ [1a] *vt* (*CAm*) to wash.

gueto *nm* ghetto.

güevo *nm*: **a ~, de ~** (*Méx*) by hook or by crook.

güevón (*LAm*) = **huevón**.

güi... *para diversas palabras escritas así en LAm, V t* **hui...**

guía **1** *nf* (**a**) (*acto*) guidance, guiding; **~ vocacional** vocational guidance; **para que te sirva de ~** for your guidance.
(**b**) (*Tip*) guide, guidebook (*de* to); (*manual*) handbook; (*Telec etc*) directory; (*Inform*) prompt; **~ de campo** (*Bio*) field guide; **~ de carga** (*Ferro*) waybill; **~ de datos** data directory; **~ del ocio** 'what's on' booklet; **~ oficial de ferrocarriles** official railway guide, official timetable; **~ telefónica, ~ de teléfonos** telephone directory; **~ del turista** tourist's guide; **~ del viajero** traveller's guide.
(**c**) (*Mec*) guide; (*de bicicleta*) handlebars; (*caballo*) leader, front horse; **~s** reins; **~ sonora** (*Cine*) soundtrack.
2 *nmf* (*persona*) guide; leader; adviser; (*de grupo de viajeros*) courier, guide.
3 *atr* guide (*atr*), guiding; **manual ~** guidebook; **cable ~** guiding wire, guiderope.

guiado *nm* guiding, guidance; (*de misil*) guiding, steering.

guiar [1c] **1** *vt* (**a**) (*gen*) to guide; (*dirigir*) to lead, direct; (*controlar*) to manage; (*orientar*) to advise.
(**b**) (*Aut etc*) to drive; (*Náut*) to steer; (*Aer*) to pilot.
(**c**) (*Bot*) to train.
2 guiarse *vr*: ~ **por** to be guided by, be ruled by, go by.

güicoy *nm* (*CAm Bot*) courgette.

Guido *nm* Guy.

guija¹ *nf* (*piedra*) pebble; (*de camino*) cobble, cobblestone.

guija² *nf* (*Bot*) vetch.

guijarral *nm* stony place; (*en playa*) shingle, pebbles, pebbly part.

guijarro *nm* pebble; (*de camino*) cobble, cobblestone.

guijarroso *adj terreno* stony; *camino* cobbled; *playa* pebbly, shingly.

guijo *nm* (**a**) (*grava*) gravel; (*en playa*) shingle. (**b**) (*Carib, Méx*) shaft.

guil‡ *nm* 5-peseta coin.

güila¹ *nf* (**a**) (*Méx: puta*) whore. (**b**) (*CAm: trompito*) small spinning top.

güila²* *nmf* (*CAm*) kid*.

guili* *nm* bobby*, cop*.

güiliento *adj* (*Cono Sur*) ragged, tattered.

güilo *adj* (*Méx*) maimed, crippled.

guillame *nm* (*Téc*) rabbet plane.

guillarse [1a] *vr* (**a**) (*: *chiflarse*) to go round the twist*. (**b**) (‡) (*t* **guillárselas**: *irse*) to beat it*. (**c**) **guillárselas‡** (*morir*) to kick the bucket‡.

Guillermo *nm* William.

guillotina *nf* guillotine; paper-cutter; **ventana de** ~ sash window.

guillotinar [1a] *vt* to guillotine.

güincha *nf* (*And, Cono Sur*) (**a**) (*ribete*) narrow strip of cloth; (*cinta*) ribbon; (*para pelo*) hair ribbon. (**b**) (*Dep*) (*meta*) tape, finishing-line; (*salida*) starting-line. (**c**) **¡las ~s!** rubbish!, forget it!

güinche *nm* (*LAm*) winch, hoist; crane.

güinchero *nm* (*LAm*) winch operator; crane operator.

guinda *nf* (**a**) (*Bot*) mazzard cherry, morello cherry; **poner la ~ a la oferta** (*fig*) to top off the offer, add a final attraction to the offer; **poner ~s a la tarta** (*fig*) to put the icing on the cake; **ponerse como una** ~ to turn scarlet.
(**b**) (*Náut*) height of masts.
(**c**) (*Carib*) guttering, spout.
(**d**) **eso es una** ~ (*Cono Sur‡*) that's simple, it's a cinch‡.
(**e**) **~s** (*Cono Sur***) balls**, bollocks**.

guindalejo *nm* (*And, Carib*) (*ropa vieja*) old clothes; (*trastos*) junk, lumber.

guindaleza *nf* hawser.

guindar [1a] **1** *vt* (**a**) to hoist, hang up (high); (*Carib: colgar*) to hang (up); (*: *ahorcar*) *criminal* to hang, string up*.
(**b**) (‡) to win (against competition), land; (*robar*) to nick‡.
2 guindarse* *vr* to hang o.s.

guindaste *nm* (*CAm*) jib crane.

guinde‡ *nm* nicking‡, thieving; **un** ~ a job*.

guindilla 1 *nf* (*Bot, Culin*) hot pepper, red chili pepper. **2** *nm* (*) bobby*, copper*.

guindo¹ *nm* mazzard (*o* morello) cherry-tree; **caer del ~*** to twig*, cotton on*.

guindo² *nm* (*CAm*) ravine.

guindola *nf* lifebuoy.

guindón‡ *nm* thief.

Guinea *nf* Guinea; ~ **Española** Spanish Guinea.

guinea¹ *nf* (*moneda*) guinea.

guineo¹ 1 *adj* Guinea(n), of Guinea. **2** *nm*, **guinea²** *nf* Guinean.

guineo² *nm* (*LAm Bot*) banana.

guiña *nf* (*And, Carib*) bad luck; (*And*) witchcraft.

guiñada *nf* (**a**) wink; blink. (**b**) (*Aer, Náut*) yaw.

guiñapo *nm* (**a**) (*andrajo*) rag, tatter; **poner a uno como un** ~ to shower insults on sb. (**b**) (*persona*) slovenly person; ragamuffin; rogue, reprobate.

guiñar [1a] **1** *vt* (*parpadear*) to wink; (*pestañear*) to blink. **2** *vi* (**a**) to wink; to blink. (**b**) (*Aer, Náut*) to yaw.

guiño *nm* (**a**) (*parpadeo*) wink; (*mueca*) grimace, wry face; **hacer ~s a** to wink at, (*amantes*) to make eyes at. (**b**) (*Aer, Náut*) yaw.

guiñol *nm* art of the puppeteer, puppet theatre, Punch-and-Judy show.

guiñolista *nmf* puppeteer.

guión *nm* (**a**) (*Orn, persona*) leader.
(**b**) (*Tip*) hyphen, dash.
(**c**) (*Liter*) summary, outline; handout; explanatory text; (*Cine: texto*) script; (*Cine: traducción*) subtitle.
(**d**) (*bandera*) royal standard; (*Ecl*) processional cross, processional banner.
(**e**) ~ **de codornices** (*Orn*) corncrake.

guionista *nmf* (*Cine*) scriptwriter; writer of subtitles.

guionizar [1f] *vt* to script, write the script for.

guipar‡ [1a] *vt* (**a**) (*ver*) to see. (**b**) (*observar*) to spot; (*entender*) to cotton on to*, catch on to.

Guipúzcoa *nf* Guipúzcoa.

guipuzcoano 1 *adj* of Guipúzcoa. **2** *nm*, **guipuzcoana** *nf* native (*o* inhabitant) of Guipúzcoa; **los ~s** the people of Guipúzcoa.

guiri 1 *nm* (*Hist*) Carlist soldier; (*) policeman; civil guard. **2** *nmf* (‡) (*extranjero*) foreigner; (*turista*) tourist. **3** *nm*: **en el ~‡** abroad, in foreign parts.

guirigay *nm* (**a**) (*Ling*) gibberish, jargon. (**b**) (*gritería*) hubbub, uproar; (*confusión*) chaos, confusion; **¡esto es un ~!** the place is like a bear garden!

guirizapa *nf* (*Carib*) quarrel, squabble.

guirlache *nm* (*turrón*) *type of nougat.*

guirnalda *nf* garland; (*de funeral*) wreath; (*Arte*) garland, floral motif.

güiro *nm* (**a**) (*LAm Bot*) bottle gourd.
(**b**) (*Carib Mús*) *musical instrument made of a gourd.*
(**c**) (*Carib*: cabeza*) head, nut‡.
(**d**) (*CAm: bebé*) small baby.
(**e**) (*Carib: mujerzuela*) loose woman.
(**f**) (*And: brote de maíz*) maize shoot.

güirro 1 *adj* (*LAm*) weak, sickly. **2** *nm* (*CAm*) small baby.

guisa *nf*: **a ~ de** as, like, in the manner of; **de tal** ~ in such a way (*que* that).

guisado *nm* stew.

guisador(a) *nm/f*, **guisandero, -a** *nm/f* cook.

guisante *nm* pea; ~ **de olor** sweet pea.

guisar [1a] *vt* (**a**) to prepare; to arrange. (**b**) (*Culin*) to cook; to stew.

güisingue *nm* (*And*) whip.

güisinguear [1a] *vt* (*And*) to whip.

guiso *nm* (**a**) cooked dish; (*esp LAm: guisado*) stew. (**b**) (*aliño*) seasoning.

guisote *nm* (*pey*) hash, poor-quality stew; (*mezcla*) concoction; (*comida*) grub‡.

güisquería *nf* night-club.

güisqui *nm* whisky.

guita *nm* (**a**) twine; packthread. (**b**) (‡: *esp Cono Sur*) dough‡.

güita *nf* (*Méx‡*) dough‡.

guitarra 1 *nf* (*instrumento*) guitar; ~ **baja** bass guitar; ~ **clásica** classical guitar; ~ **eléctrica** electrical guitar; **ser como ~ en un entierro** to be quite out of place, strike the wrong note; **chafar la ~ a uno** to queer sb's pitch. **2** *nmf* (*person*) guitarist.

guitarrear [1a] *vi* to play the guitar, strum a guitar.

guitarrero, -a *nm/f* (electric) guitarist.

guitarrista *nmf* guitarist.

guitarrón *nm* (**a**) (*Méx Mús*) large guitar. (**b**) (*CAm: abeja*) bee.

güitos** *nmpl* balls**.

güizcal *nm* (*CAm Bot*) chayote.

gula *nf* greed, gluttony.

guloso *adj* greedy, gluttonous.

gulusmear [1a] *vi* to nibble titbits; to sniff the cooking; to snoop.

guma‡ *nf* hen.

gumarra* *nm* (*Méx*) cop*.

gurguciar [1b] **1** *vt* (*CAm*) to sniff at, sniff out. **2** *vi* (*Méx*: gruñir*) to grunt, snort.

guri‡ *nm* (*policía*) copper*, bobby*; (*Mil*) soldier.

gurí *nm*, *pl* **gurís, guríes,** *o* **gurises** (*Cono Sur*) (†: *mestizo*) mestizo, Indian child, child of mixed race; (*: *muchacho*) boy, lad.

guripa‡ *nm* (*Mil*) soldier; (*policía*) cop*; (*pillo*) rascal, rogue; (*tonto*) berk‡; (*sujeto*) bloke‡, guy*.

gurisa *nf* (*Cono Sur*) (†: *mestiza*) Indian child, child of mixed race; (*: *chica*) girl, lass; (*: *esposa*) young wife.

gurrí *nm* (*LAm*) wild duck.

gurrumino 1 *adj* (**a**) (*débil*) weak, sickly; (*pequeño*) small, puny.
(**b**) *marido* complaisant, indulgent.
(**c**) (*And*) cowardly.
(**d**) (*CAm: listo*) clever, sharp.

2 *nm* cuckold; complaisant husband, indulgent husband.
3 *nm*, **gurrumina** *nf* (**a**) (*Méx*: *niño*) child.
(**b**) (*LAm**: *persona astuta*) sharp customer*.
4 *nf* (*And**: *molestia*) bother, nuisance.

gur(r)upié *nm* (**a**) (*LAm*: *de garito*) croupier. (**b**) (*Carib*, *And*: *en subasta*) false bidder. (**c**) (*Carib**: *amigo*) buddy (*esp US*), pal*.

gurú *nm*, **guru** *nm*, *pl* **gurús** guru.

gus *nm* (*And*) turkey buzzard.

gusa* *nm* (*a veces f*) (= **gusanillo**) hunger; **me anda el ~** I'm hungry; **tener ~** to be hungry.

gusanera *nf* (**a**) nest of maggots; breeding ground for maggots. (**b**) (*fig*) bunch, lot, crowd; **una ~ de chiquillos** a bunch of kids.

gusaniento *adj* maggoty, worm-eaten, grub-infested.

gusanillo *nm* (**a**) small maggot, small worm; **~ de la conciencia** (*fig*) prickings of conscience; **me anda el ~** I feel peckish*; **matar el ~** to have a snack, take the edge off one's appetite; to have a nip of liquor first thing in the morning.
(**b**) (*: *manía*) craze, obsession; **le entró el ~ de las motos** he was bitten by the motorbike craze.

gusano *nm* (**a**) maggot, grub, worm; (*de mariposa, polilla*) caterpillar; (*de tierra*) earthworm; **~ de luz** glow-worm; **~ de seda** silkworm; **criar ~s*** to be pushing up the daisies*; **matar el ~*** (*beber*) to have a drink, (*comer*) to have a bite to eat.
(**b**) (*fig*) worm, contemptible person; meek creature.
(**c**) (*Inform*) virus, worm.
(**d**) (*Cuba**: *Pol*) traitor (*Cuban in self-imposed exile*).

gusanoso *adj* = **gusaniento.**

gusgo *adj* (*Méx*) sweet-toothed.

gustación *nf* tasting, sampling.

gustado *adj* (*LAm*) esteemed, well-liked, popular.

gustar [1a] **1** *vt* (**a**) to taste, try, sample. (**b**) (*Méx**) **gusto un café** I'd like a coffee.
2 *vi* (**a**) to please, be pleasing; **es una película que siempre gusta** it's a film which always pleases (*o* gives pleasure); **la comedia no gustó** the play was not a success, the play was not much liked; **mi número ya no gusta** my act isn't popular any more.
(**b**) (*con complemento personal*) **me gusta el té** I like tea; **¿te gusta Méjico?** do you like Mexico?; **no le gusta que le llamen Pepe** he doesn't like to be called Joe; **no me gusta mucho** I don't like it much, I'm not very struck (on it); **me gusta como anda** I like the way she walks.
(**c**) (*fórmulas*) **¿gusta Vd?** would you like some?, may I offer you some?; **si Vd gusta** if you please, if you don't mind; **como Vd guste** as you wish.
(**d**) **~ de algo** to like sth, enjoy sth; **~ de** + *infin* to like to + *infin*, be fond of + *ger*, enjoy + *ger*.

gustazo* *nm* great pleasure; (*malsano*) unhealthy pleasure, nasty pleasure.

gustillo *nm* suggestion, touch, tang; aftertaste.

gustito *nm* sheer pleasure, honest enjoyment.

gusto *nm* (**a**) (*sentido*) taste; **agregue azúcar al ~** add sugar to taste.
(**b**) (*sabor*) taste, flavour; **tiene un ~ amargo** it has a bitter taste, it tastes bitter.
(**c**) (*Arte etc*) taste; (*estilo*) style, fashion; **buen ~** good taste; **mal ~** bad taste; **de buen ~** in good taste; **es de un mal ~ extraordinario** it is in extraordinarily bad taste; **para mi ~** to my taste; **al ~ de hoy, según el ~ de hoy** in the taste of today; **ser persona de ~** to be a person of taste; **sobre ~s no hay disputa, de ~s no hay nada escrito** there's no accounting for tastes; **tiene ~ para vestir** she dresses elegantly, she has taste in dresses.
(**d**) (*placer*) pleasure; **con mucho ~** with pleasure; (*con voluntad*) gladly, willingly; **con sumo ~** with the very greatest pleasure; **por ~ de** for the sake of; **comer con ~** to eat heartily; **da ~ hacerlo** it's nice to do it; **dar ~ a uno** to gratify sb's wishes, do as sb wishes; **estar a ~** to be at ease, feel comfortable; to feel at home; **aquí me encuentro a ~** I like it here, I feel at home here; **acomodarse a su ~** to make o.s. comfortable, make o.s. at home; **es por ~ que siga allí** (*LAm*) you'll wait there in vain; **sentirse mal a ~** to feel ill at ease; **tengo los pies a ~ y calientes** my feet are nice and warm; **tener el ~ de** + *ger* to have the pleasure of + *ger*; **tener ~ en** + *infin* to be glad to + *infin;* **tomar el ~ a** to take a liking to.
(**e**) (*presentaciones*) **¡mucho ~!, ¡tanto ~!** how do you do?; pleased to meet you; **el ~ es mío** how do you do?; the pleasure is mine; **tengo mucho ~ en presentar al Sr X** allow me to introduce Mr X; **tengo mucho ~ en conocerle** I'm very pleased to meet you.
(**f**) (*agrado*) liking (*por* for); **al ~ de** to the liking of; **ser del ~ de uno** to be to sb's liking; **tener ~ por** to have a liking for, have an eye for; **tomar ~ a** to take a liking to.
(**g**) (*antojo*) whim, fancy; **a ~** at will, according to one's fancy.
(**h**) (*Cono Sur Com*) style, design, colour; range, assortment.

gustosamente *adv* gladly, with pleasure.

gustoso *adj* (**a**) (*sabroso*) tasty, savoury, nice.
(**b**) (*agradable*) pleasant.
(**c**) (*con placer*) willing, glad; **lo hizo ~** he did it gladly, he did it with pleasure; **le ofrezco ~ una habitación de matrimonio** I am glad to be able to offer you a double room.

gutapercha *nf* gutta-percha.

gutifarra *nf* (*LAm*) = **butifarra.**

gutural *adj* guttural (*t Ling*); throaty.

Guyana *nf* Guyana.

guyanés, -esa *adj*, *nm/f* Guyanese.

H

H, h ['atʃe] *nf* (*letra*) H, h.
h. (**a**) *abr de* **hacia** circa, about, c. (**b**) *abr de* **hora(s)** hour(s), h, hr. (**c**) *abr de* **habitantes** population, pop.
H. (**a**) (*Fin*) *abr de* **haber** credit, Cr. (**b**) *abr de* **hectárea(s)** hectare(s). (**c**) (*Rel*) *abr de* **Hermano** Brother, Br. (**d**) (*Quím*) *abr de* **hidrógeno** hydrogen, H.
ha[1] *V* **haber.**
ha[2] *interj* oh!
Ha. *abr de* **hectárea** *nf*, **hectáreas** *nfpl* hectare, hectares.
haba *nf* (**a**) (*Bot*) (broad) bean; (*de café etc*) bean; **~ de las Indias** sweet pea; **~ de soja** soya bean; **son ~s contadas** we know all about that; it's a sure thing, it's a certainty; **en todas partes cuecen ~s** it's the same the whole world over.
(**b**) (*Vet*) tumour.
(**c**) (**) prick**.
Habana *nf*: **La ~** Havana.
habanera[1] *nf* (*Mús*) habanera.
habanero 1 *adj* of Havana. **2** *nm*, **habanera**[2] *nf* native (*o* inhabitant) of Havana; **los ~s** the people of Havana.
habano 1 *adj y n* = **habanero. 2** *nm* (*puro*) Havana cigar.
hábeas corpus *nm* habeas corpus.
haber [2j] **1** *vt* (**a**) (††: *tener*) to have, possess.
(**b**) (*liter*: *obtener*) to get; to catch, lay hands on; **lee cuantos libros puede ~** he reads all the books he can lay his hands on.
(**c**) (*Rel*: *fórmula*) **bien haya ...** blessed be ...; **X, que Dios haya** X, God rest his soul.
(**d**) (*Jur*: *fórmula*) **todos los inventos habidos y por ~** all inventions present and future, the present inventions and any others that may be made; **las bajas habidas y por ~** casualties suffered and still to be suffered.
(**e**) (*liter, periodismo*) **en el encuentro habido ayer** in the fight which occurred yesterday; **la baja de temperatura habida ayer** the fall in temperature recorded yesterday; **la lista de los caídos habidos** the list of casualties suffered.
2 *v aux* (**a**) (*en tiempos compuestos*) to have; **he comido** I have eaten; **lo hubiéramos hecho** we would have done it; **antes de ~lo visto** before seeing him, before having seen him; **de ~lo sabido** if I had known it.
(**b**) **~ de** + *infin*; **he de hacerlo** I have to do it, I am to do it, I must do it; **¿qué he de hacer?** what am I to do?; **¿qué ha de tenerlo?** why should he have it?, how could he possibly have it?; **ha de llegar hoy** he is due to arrive today; **ha de haberse perdido** it must have got lost; **han de ser las 9** it must be about 9 o'clock; **has de estar equivocado** (*LAm*) you must be mistaken; **los has de ver** (*LAm*) you'll see them.
3 *v impers* (**a**) (*gen*) **hay** there is, there are; **hay calefacción** there is heating; **hay tanto que hacer** there is so much to be done; **no hay plátanos** there are no bananas, we have no bananas; **no lo hay** there isn't any; **no hubo discusión** there was no discussion; **'mejores no hay'** (*Com*: *slogan*) 'none better!'; **¡hay gaseosa!** (*Com*: *pregón*) soft drinks!; **buen chico si los hay** a good lad if ever there was one; **¿habrá tiempo?** will there be time?; **¿hay puros?** have you any cigars?; **tomará lo que haya** he'll take whatever there is, he'll take whatever is going; **lo que hay es que ...** what's happening is that ..., it's like this ...; **hay sol** the sun is shining, it is sunny; **¿qué hay?** what's up?, what's the matter?, what goes on?; **¡no hay de qué!** don't mention it!, not at all!; **¿cuánto hay de aquí a Cuzco?** how far is it from here to Cuzco?; **¿qué hubo?** (*Méx*) hi!, how are you?
(**b**) **hay que** + *infin* it is necessary to + *infin*, one must + *infin*; **hay que trabajar** one has to work, everyone must work; **hay que trabajar más** (*to individual*) you must work harder; **hay que hacerlo** it has to be done; **¡había que verlo!** you should have seen it!; **hay que ser fuertes** we must be strong; **no hay que tomarlo a mal** there's no cause to take it badly, you mustn't get upset about it; **y no hay más que conformarse** there's nothing one can do but fall into line.
(**c**) (*tiempo*) **3 años ha** 3 years ago; **poco tiempo ha** a short time ago.
4 haberse *vr* (**a**) (††) to behave, comport o.s.; **se ha habido con honradez** he has behaved honourably.
(**b**) **habérselas con uno** to be up against sb, have to do with sb, have to contend with sb; **tenemos que habérnoslas con un enemigo despiadado** we are up against a ruthless enemy; **¡allá te las hayas!** that's your affair!
5 *nm* (*ingresos*) income, salary; (*sueldo*) pay, wages; (*Com*) assets; (*en balance*) credit side; **~es** assets, property, goods; **asentar algo al ~ de uno, pasar algo al ~ de uno** to credit sth to sb; **¿cuánto tenemos en el ~?** how much have we on the credit side? (*t fig*); **la autora tiene 6 libros en el ~** the author has 6 books behind her (*o* to her credit).
habichuela *nf* kidney bean; **ganarse las ~s** to earn one's living.
hábil *adj* (**a**) (*listo*) clever; (*diestro*) skilful; (*capaz*) able, capable, proficient; (*experto*) good, expert (*en* at); (*pey*) cunning, smart.
(**b**) **~ para** fit for.
(**c**) **día ~** working day.
(**d**) (*Jur*) competent.
habilidad *nf* (**a**) (*gen*) cleverness; skill; (*capacidad*) ability, proficiency; (*destreza*) expertness, expertise; (*pey*) cunning, smartness; **hombre de gran ~ política** a man of great political skill; **tener ~ manual** to be clever with one's hands.
(**b**) fitness (*para* for).
(**c**) (*Jur*) competence.
habilidoso *adj* capable, handy; (*esp pey*) clever, smart.
habilitación *nf* (**a**) (*título*) qualification, entitlement.
(**b**) (*de casa etc*) equipment, fitting out.
(**c**) (*Fin*) financing; (*Cono Sur Agr*) credit in kind; (*CAm, Méx**: *anticipo*) advance, sub*.
(**d**) (*Cono Sur*: *sociedad*) offer of a partnership to an employee.
(**e**) (*oficina*) paymaster's office.
habilitado *nm* paymaster.
habilitar [1a] *vt* (**a**) (*gen*) to qualify, entitle (*para que haga* to do); (*permitir*) to enable (*para que haga* to do); (*autorizar*) to empower, authorize (*para que haga* to do).
(**b**) *casa etc* to equip, fit out, set up; **las aulas están habilitadas con TV** the rooms are equipped with TV.
(**c**) (*Fin*) to finance; **~ a uno** (*Cono Sur Agr*) to make sb a loan in kind (with the next crop as security), give sb credit facilities; (*CAm, Méx**) to give sb an advance, sub* sb.
(**d**) (*Cono Sur Com*) to take into partnership.
(**e**) (*CAm Agr*) to cover, serve.
(**f**) (*Carib*) to annoy, bother.
hábilmente *adv* cleverly; skilfully; ably, proficiently, expertly; (*pey*) cunningly, smartly.
habiloso *adj* (*Cono Sur*) = **habilidoso.**
habitabilidad *nf* habitability; (*de casa*) quality, condition.
habitable *adj* inhabitable, that can be lived in.
habitación *nf* (**a**) (*vivienda*) habitation; dwelling, abode; (*alquilado*) lodging(s), apartment; (*Bio*) habitat.
(**b**) (*cuarto*) room; **habitaciones (particulares)** rooms, suite; **~ de dos camas, ~ doble, ~ de matrimonio** double room; **~ individual** single room; **~ para invitado** guest-room.
habitáculo *nm* living space; (*Aut*) inside, interior.

habitado *adj* inhabited; lived-in; *satélite etc* manned, carrying a crew.
habitante 1 *nmf* (*gen*) inhabitant; (*vecino*) resident; (*inquilino*) occupant, tenant; **una ciudad de 10.000 ~s** a town of 10,000 inhabitants (*o* people), a town with a population of 10,000. **2** *nm* (*hum*: *piojo*) louse; **tener ~s** to be lousy.
habitar [1a] **1** *vt* to inhabit, live in, dwell in; *casa etc* to occupy, be the occupant of. **2** *vi* to live.
hábitat *nm, pl* **hábitats** habitat.
hábito *nm* (**a**) habit, custom; **una droga que conduce al ~ morboso** a habit-forming drug; **tener el ~ de** + *infin* to be in the habit of + *ger*.
(**b**) (*Ecl*) habit; **~ monástico** monastic habit; **ahorcar** (*o* **colgar**) **los ~s** to leave the priesthood; **tomar el ~** (*hombre*) to take holy orders, become a monk, (*mujer*) to take the veil, become a nun.
habituado, -a *nm/f* habitué(e).
habitual 1 *adj* habitual, customary, usual; *cliente, lector etc* regular; *criminal* hardened; *mentiroso* incorrigible; *pecado* besetting; **su restaurante ~** one's usual restaurant; **como lector ~ de esa revista** as a regular reader of your journal.
2 *nmf* (*de bar etc*) habitué(e); (*de tienda*) regular customer.
habituar [1e] **1** *vt* to accustom (*a* to). **2 habituarse** *vr*: **~ a** to become accustomed to, get used to.
habla *nf* (**a**) (*facultad*) speech; **estar sin ~** to be speechless; **perder el ~** to become speechless.
(**b**) (*nacional etc*) language; (*regional*) dialect, speech; (*de clase, profesión etc*) talk, speech; (*Liter*) language, style; **de ~ francesa** French-speaking.
(**c**) (*acto*) talk; **¡García al ~!** (*Telec*) García speaking!; **estar al ~** to be in contact, be in touch; (*Náut*) to be within hailing distance; (*Telec*) to be on the line, be speaking (*con* to); **negar** (*o* **quitar**) **el ~ a uno** to stop speaking to sb, not be on speaking terms with sb; **ponerse al ~ con uno** to get into touch with sb.
hablachento *adj* (*Carib*) talkative.
hablada *nf* (**a**) (*Cono Sur*) speech.
(**b**) (*Méx*: *t* **~s**: *fanfarronada*) boast.
(**c**) (*And**) scolding, telling-off*.
(**d**) (*CAm, Cono Sur, Méx*) (*indirecta*) hint, innuendo; (*chisme*) rumour, piece of gossip; **echar ~s** to drop hints, make innuendoes.
habladera *nf* (**a**) (*LAm*) talking, noise of talking. (**b**) (*Cono Sur, Méx*) = **habladuría**.
habladero *nm* (*Carib**) piece of gossip.
hablado 1 *ptp de* **hablar** spoken; **el lenguage ~** the spoken language.
2 *adj*: **bien ~** nicely-spoken, well-spoken; **mal ~** coarse, rude; foul-mouthed.
hablador 1 *adj* (**a**) (*parlanchín*) talkative; chatty; voluble.
(**b**) (*chismoso*) gossipy, given to gossip.
(**c**) (*Méx*) (*jactancioso*) boastful; (*amenazador*) bullying.
(**d**) (*Carib, Méx**) (*mentiroso*) lying; (*gritón*) loud-mouthed.
2 *nm*, **habladora** *nf* (**a**) talkative person, great talker, chatterbox.
(**b**) gossip.
habladuría *nf* (*rumor*) rumour; (*injuria*) nasty remark, sarcastic remark; (*chisme*) idle chatter, piece of gossip; **~s** gossip, scandal.
hablanchín *adj* talkative, garrulous.
hablante 1 *adj* speaking. **2** *nmf* speaker.
-hablante *en palabras compuestas, p.ej.* **castellanohablante** (*adj*) Castilian-speaking, (*nmf*) Castilian speaker.
hablantín *adj* = **hablanchín**.
hablantina *nf* (*And*: *sin sentido*) gibberish, meaningless torrent; (*And, Carib*: *cháchara*) empty talk, idle chatter; (*Carib*: *algarabia*) hubbub, din.
hablantino(so) *adj* (*And, Carib*) = **hablador** (**a**) *y* (**b**).
hablar [1a] **1** *vt lengua* to speak, talk; *tonterías etc* to talk; **habla bien el portugués** he speaks good Portuguese, he speaks Portuguese well; **~lo todo** to talk too much, give the game away; **y no hay más que ~** so there's no more to be said about it; **eso habrá que ~lo con X** you'll have to discuss that with X.
2 *vi* to speak, talk (*a, con* to; *de* about, of); **que hable él** let him speak, let him have his say; **¡hable!, ¡puede ~!** (*Telec*) you're through!; **¿quién habla?** (*Telec*) who is it?, who's calling?; **¡quién fue a ~!** look who's talking!; **¡ni ~!** nonsense!; no fear!, not likely!; not a bit of it!; **de eso ni ~** that's out of the question, that's not on; **~ alto** to speak loudly, (*fig*) to speak out (frankly); **~ bajo** to talk quietly, speak in a low voice; **~ claro** (*fig*) to speak plainly, speak bluntly; **¡para que luego hablen de coches!** as if cars came into it!; **~ por ~** to talk just for talking's sake; **habla por sí mismo** it speaks for itself; **los datos hablan por sí solos** the facts speak for themselves; **el retrato está hablando** the portrait is a speaking likeness; **dar que ~ a la gente** to make people talk, cause people to gossip; **hacer ~ a uno** (*fig*) to make sb talk; **el vino hace ~** wine loosens people's tongues.
3 hablarse *vr*: **'se habla inglés'** 'English spoken here'; **en el Brasil se habla portugués** Portuguese is spoken in Brazil; **se habla de que van a comprarlo** there is talk of their buying it; **no se hablan** they are not on speaking terms, they don't speak; **¡no se hable más!** enough said!; that's settled!, there's an end to it!
hablilla *nf* rumour, story; (piece of) gossip, tittle-tattle.
hablista *nmf* good speaker, elegant user of language; linguistically-conscious person.
habloteo *nm* incomprehensible talk.
Habsburgo *nm* Hapsburg.
hacedero *adj* practicable, feasible.
hacedor(a) *nm/f* maker; **el** (**Supremo**) **H~** the Maker.
hacendado 1 *adj* landed, property-owning. **2** *nm* landowner; gentleman farmer; (*LAm*: *de ganado*) rancher; (*Carib*: *de ingenio*) sugar-plantation owner.
hacendario *adj* (*Méx*) treasury *atr*, budgetary.
hacendista *nmf* economist, financial expert.
hacendoso *adj* (*trabajador*) industrious, hard-working; (*ocupado*) busy, bustling.
hacer [2r] **1** *vt* (**a**) (*gen*) to make, create; (*Téc*) to make, manufacture; (*construir*) to build, construct; *vestido etc* to make; *obra de arte* to make; to fashion; (*Liter, Mús*) to compose; *dinero* to make, earn; *humo etc* to make, give off, emit, produce; *guerra* to fight, wage; **~ ~ algo** to have sth made; **~lo** (*euf*) to have sex, do it; **lo harán en la tele*** they'll show it on the telly*.
(**b**) (*preparar*) to make, prepare; *cama* to make; *comida* to make, prepare, get, cook; *maleta* to pack; *corbata* to tie; (*Com*) *balance* to strike; *apuesta* to lay; *objeción* to make, raise; *pregunta* to put, ask; *orden* to give; *discurso* to make, deliver; *visita* to pay; **~ la barba a uno** to shave sb (*V t* **barba**[1]); **~ el pelo a una** to do sb's hair; **~ un recado** to run a message, go on an errand.
(**c**) (*causar*) to cause, make; *sombra* to cast; **el árbol hace sombra** the tree gives shade, the tree casts a shadow.
(**d**) (*dedicarse a*) **~ cine** to make films, be engaged in film work, be working for the cinema; **este año hace turismo en África** this year he's gone touring (*o* as a tourist) in Africa.
(**e**) (*efectuar etc*) to do; (*realizar*) to execute, perform, put into practice; (*Teat*) to do, perform; *milagro etc* to do, work, perform; **no sé qué ~** I don't know what to do; **haga lo que quiera** do as you please; **¿qué haces ahí?** what are you doing?, what are you up to?; **¿qué le vamos a ~?** what can we do about it?; isn't he awful?; **~ por ~** to do sth for the sake of doing it, do sth even though it is not necessary; **la ha hecho buena** (*iró*) a fine mess he's made of it; *V* **bien, mal** *etc*.
(**f**) (*sustituye a otro verbo*) to do; **él protestó y yo hice lo mismo** he protested and I did the same; **no viene como lo solía ~** he doesn't come as he used to (do).
(**g**) **~ algo pedazos** (*etc*): V **pedazo** *etc*.
(**h**) **~ el malo** (*Teat*) to play the (part of the) villain, act the villain.
(**i**) (*pensar*) to imagine, think, assume; **yo le hacía más viejo** I thought he was older; **te hacíamos en el Perú** we thought you were in Peru, we assumed you were in Peru.
(**j**) **me hizo con dinero** (*proveer*) he provided me with money.
(**k**) (*acostumbrar*) to accustom, inure; **~ el cuerpo al frío** to inure the body to cold, get the body used to cold.
(**l**) (+ *infin etc*) to make, force, oblige, compel; **les hice venir** I made them come; **nos hizo que fuésemos** he made us go; **yo haré que vengan** I'll see to it that they come; **hágale entrar** show him in, have him come in; **me lo hizo saber** he told me it, he informed me of it; **~ construir una casa** to have a house built, get a house built; **hago lavar la ropa a una vecina** I have a neighbour (to) wash my clothes.
(**m**) (*Mat*) to make (up), amount to; **6 y 3 hacen 9** 6 and 3 make 9; **éste hace 100** this one makes 100.
(**n**) (*volver*) to make, turn, render, send; **el vino lo hizo borracho** the wine made him drunk; **la tinta lo hizo azul** the ink made (*o* turned) it blue; **esto lo hará más difícil**

this will make (*o* render) it more difficult.

2 *vi* (**a**) (*comportarse*) to act, behave; (*fingir*) to pretend; ~ **como que ...**, ~ **como si ...** to act as if ...; ~ **uno como que no quiere** to be reluctant, seem not to want to; ~ **de** to act as, (*Teat*) to act, play the part of; ~ **el muerto** to pretend to be dead (*V t* **muerto**); ~ **el tonto** to act the fool, play the fool; **¡no le hagas!** (*Méx**) don't give me that!*

(**b**) **dar que** ~ to cause trouble; to make work; **daban que** ~ **a la policía** they gave the police trouble, they caused trouble to the police.

(**c**) ~ **para** + *infin*, ~ **por** + *infin* to try to + *infin*, make an effort to + *infin*.

(**d**) (*importar*) to be important, matter; **no le hace** (*LAm*) it doesn't matter, never mind; **¿te hace que vayamos a tomar unas copas?** how about a drink?, what say we go for a drink?

(**e**) (*convenir*) to be suitable, be fitting; **hace a todo** he's good for anything; **¿hace?** will it do?, is it all right?; OK?*; is it a deal?; **la llave hace a todas las puertas** the key fits (*o* does for) all the doors.

(**f**) ~ **bueno** (*Méx*) *persona* to make good.

3 *v impers* (**a**) (*Met*) to be; *V* **calor, frío, tiempo** *etc*.

(**b**) (*LAm*) **hace sed** I'm thirsty; **hace sueño** I'm sleepy.

(**c**) (*tiempo*) ago; **hace 3 años** 3 years ago; **hace 2 años que se fue** he left 2 years ago, it's 2 years since he left; **desde hace 4 años** for (the last) 4 years; **está perdido desde hace 15 días** it's been lost for a fortnight; **hace poco** a short while back, a short time ago; **no hace mucho** not long ago; **hace de esto varios años** this has been going on for some years; **X, conocido hace mucho por sus cuadros** X, long known for his pictures; *V* **tiempo** *etc*.

4 hacerse *vr* (*efectuarse etc*) (**a**) to be made, be done *etc*; **se hará de ladrillos** it will be built of brick; **todavía no se ha hecho** it still has not been done; **¡eso no se hace!** that's not done!; **la respuesta no se hizo esperar** the answer was not slow in coming.

(**b**) ~ **cortesías** (*mutuamente*) to exchange courtesies.

(**c**) (*personal*) **se hizo cortar el pelo** she had her hair cut; **me hago confeccionar un traje** I'm having a suit made; ~ **un retrato**, ~ **retratar** to have one's portrait painted; ~ **afeitar** to have a shave, have o.s. shaved.

(**d**) (*llegar a ser*) to become; **se hicieron amigos** they became friends; ~ **enfermera** to become a nurse, take up nursing, go into nursing.

(**e**) (*fingirse*) to pretend; ~ **el sordo** to pretend not to hear, turn a deaf ear; ~ **el sueco** to pretend not to hear (*o* understand); to act dumb*, not let on*; ~ **el tonto** to act the fool, play the fool.

(**f**) (*volverse*) to become, grow, get; to turn (into), come to be; **esto se hace pesado** this is becoming tedious; **si las cosas se hacen difíciles** if things get difficult, if things turn awkward; ~ **grande** to grow tall, get tall; ~ **viejo** to grow old, get old; ~ **cristiano** to turn Christian, become a Christian, be converted to Christianity; **se me hace imposible trabajar** it's becoming impossible for me to work, I'm finding it impossible to work.

(**g**) ~ **a** + *infin* to get used to + *ger*, become accustomed to + *ger*; ~ **a una idea** to get used to an idea.

(**h**) **se me hace que ...** (*esp LAm*) I think that ..., it seems to me that ..., I get the impression that ...

(**i**) ~ **con algo** to get hold of sth; to take sth, appropriate sth; to confiscate sth; **logró** ~ **con una copia** he managed to get hold of a copy.

(**j**) ~ **de algo** (*Méx*: *obtener*) to get (hold of) sth.

(**k**) ~ **a un lado** to stand aside (*t fig*), move over; ~ **atrás** to move back, fall back; *para muchas locuciones, V el adj o n.*

hacia *prep* (**a**) (*lugar*) towards, in the direction of; (*cerca*) about, near; ~ **abajo** down, downwards; ~ **arriba** up, upwards; **ir** ~ **las montañas** to go towards the mountains; **eso está más** ~ **el este** that's further over to the east, that is more in an easterly direction; **vamos** ~ **allá** let's go in that direction, let's go over that way; **¿~ dónde vamos?** where are we going?

(**b**) (*tiempo*) about; ~ **mediodía** about noon, towards noon.

(**c**) (*actitud*) towards; **su hostilidad** ~ **la idea** his hostility towards the idea.

hacienda *nf* (**a**) (*finca*) property; country estate, large farm; (*LAm*: *de ganado*)) (cattle) ranch; (*Carib*: *ingenio*) sugar plantation.

(**b**) (*Cono Sur*) cattle, livestock.

(**c**) ~ **pública** public finance; (**Ministerio de**) **H~** Treasury, Exchequer, Ministry of Finance.

(**d**) ~**s** household chores.

hacina *nf* pile, heap; (*Agr*) stack, rick.

hacinado *adj* crowded; **la gente estaba hacinada** people were crowded (*o* packed) together; **viven ~s** they live in overcrowded conditions.

hacinamiento *nm* heaping (up); (*Agr*) stacking; (*fig*) crowding, overcrowding; accumulation.

hacinar [1a] **1** *vt* (*amontonar*) to pile (up), heap (up); (*Agr*) to stack, put into a stack (*o* rick); (*fig*) to crowd, overcrowd; (*acumular*) to accumulate, amass; (*ahorrar*) to hoard.

2 hacinarse *vr*: ~ **en** (*fig*: *gente*) to be packed into.

hacha[1] *nf* (**a**) axe; chopper; hatchet; ~ **de armas** battle-axe.

(**b**) (*nmf*) (*) genius; **¡eres un ~!** you're a genius!; **es un** ~ **para el bridge** he's a genius at bridge, he's a brilliant bridge-player.

(**c**) (*locuciones*) **de** ~ **y tiza** (*Cono Sur**) tough, virile; (*pey*) brawling; **de** ~ (*Cono Sur*: *adv*) unexpectedly, without warning; **dar con el** ~ **a uno** (*Cono Sur**) to tear a strip off sb*; **ser** ~ **para la ropa** (*Méx*) to be hard on one's clothes; **estar** ~ (*Méx*) to be ready; **estar con el** ~ (*Cono Sur**) to have a hangover*.

hacha[2] *nf* (*tea*) torch, firebrand; (*vela*) large candle; **como** ~ **de muerto** *luz* dim, weak.

hachador *nm* (*CAm*) woodman, lumberjack.

hachar [1a] *vt* (*LAm*) = **hachear**.

hachazo *nm* (**a**) (*golpe*) axe blow, stroke with an axe; hack, cut.

(**b**) (*LAm*) gash, open wound.

(**c**) (*And*: *de caballo*) bolt, dash.

hache *nf* the (name of the) letter *h*; **por** ~ **o por be** for one reason or another; **llámele Vd** ~ call it what you will; **volverse ~s y erres** (*And*), **volverse ~s y cúes** (*Cono Sur*) to come to nothing, fall through.

hachear [1a] **1** *vt* to hew, cut (down *etc*). **2** *vi* to wield an axe.

hachero[1] *nm* woodman, lumberjack; (*Mil*) sapper.

hachero[2] *nm* torch stand, sconce.

hacheta *nf* adze; small axe, hatchet.

hachich *nm*, **hachís**[1] *nm* hashish.

hachís[2] *interj* atishoo!

hacho *nm* (*fuego*) beacon; (*colina etc*) beacon hill.

hachón *nm* (large) torch, firebrand.

hachuela *nf* = **hacheta**.

hada *nf* fairy; ~ **buena** good fairy; ~ **madrina** fairy godmother; **cuento de ~s** fairy tale.

hado *nm* fate, destiny.

haga, hago *etc*: *V* **hacer**.

hágalo Vd mismo *nm* do-it-yourself.

hagiografía *nf* hagiography.

hagiógrafo, -a *nm/f* hagiographer.

haiga* *nm* big car, posh car*.

Haití *nm* Haiti.

haitiano, -a *adj, nm/f* Haitian.

hala *interj* (**a**) (*oye*) hi!, hoy! (**b**) (*vamos*) come on!, let's go! (**c**) (*anda*) get on with it!, hurry up! (**d**) (*Náut*) heave!; *V t* **jalar**. (**e**) **no quiero, ¡~!** I don't want to, so there! (**f**) (*sorpresa, admiración*) good heavens!

halaco *nm* (*CAm*) piece of junk, useless object.

halagar [1h] *vt* (**a**) (*mostrar afecto*) to show affection to, make up to.

(**b**) (*agradar*) to please, gratify; (*atraer*) to allure, attract; **es una perspectiva que me halaga** it's a possibility which pleases me.

(**c**) (*lisonjear*) to flatter; to cajole.

halago *nm* (**a**) (*t ~s*: *V vt* (**b**)) pleasure, delight; gratification; allurement, attraction; **los ~s de la vida de campo** the attractions of country life, the blandishments of country life. (**b**) (*t ~s*: *lisonjas*) flattery; (*pey*) cajolery.

halagüeño *adj* (*agradable*) pleasing, gratifying; (*atraente*) alluring, attractive; *opinión, observación* flattering (*para* to); *perspectiva* promising, hopeful.

halar [1a] *vt y vi* = **jalar**.

halcón *nm* (**a**) falcon, hawk; ~ **común**, ~ **peregrino** peregrine; ~ **abejero** honey buzzard. (**b**) (*fig*) hawk, hardliner; **los halcones y las palomas** the hawks and the doves. (**c**) (*Méx**) young thug of the ruling party.

halconería *nf* falconry, hawking.

halconero *nm* falconer.

halda *nf* (**a**) (*falda*) skirt; **de ~s o de mangas** at all costs, by hook or by crook. (**b**) (*arpillera*) sackcloth, coarse wrapping material.

haleche *nm* anchovy.
halibut [ali'ßu] *nm, pl* **halibuts** [ali'ßu] halibut.
hálito *nm* (*aliento*) breath; (*vapor*) vapour, exhalation; (*poét*) gentle breeze.
halitosis *nf* halitosis, bad breath.
halo *nm* halo, aura.
halógeno 1 *adj* halogenous, halogen (*atr*); **lámpara halógena** halogen lamp. **2** *nm* halogen.
halón *nm* (*LAm*) = **jalón (c)**.
haltera 1 *nf* dumb-bell; bar-bell; ~**s** weights. **2** *nmf* weight-lifter.
halterofilia *nf* weight-lifting.
halterófilo, -a *nm/f* weight-lifter.
hall [xol] *nm, pl* **halls** [xol] hall; (*Teat*) foyer; (*de hotel*) lounge, foyer.
hallaca *nf* (*Carib*) tamale.
hallador(a) *nm/f* finder.
hallar [1a] **1** *vt* (*gen*) to find; (*descubrir*) to discover; (*localizar*) to locate; (*averiguar*) to find out; *oposición etc* to meet with, run up against.
2 hallarse *vr* to be; to find o.s.; **se hallaba fuera** he was away at the time; **¿dónde se halla la catedral?** where is the cathedral?; **se halla sin dinero** he has no money, he finds himself out of money; ~ **enfermo** to be ill; ~ **mejor** to be better; **aquí me hallo a gusto** I'm all right here, I'm comfortable here; **no se hallaba a gusto en la fiesta** she felt out of place at the party; **no se halla bien con el nuevo jefe** he doesn't get on with the new boss; ~ **con un obstáculo** to encounter an obstacle, be up against an obstacle; **se halla en todo** he's mixed up in everything.
hallazgo *nm* (**a**) (*acto*) finding, discovery.
(**b**) (*objeto*) find, thing found; **un** ~ **interesantísimo** a most interesting find.
(**c**) (*premio*) finder's reward; **'500 pesos de** ~**'** '500 pesos reward'.
hamaca *nf* (**a**) hammock. (**b**) (*Cono Sur*) (*columpio*) swing; (*mecedora*) rocking chair; ~ **plegable** deckchair.
hamacar [1g], **hamaquear** [1a] (*LAm*) **1** *vt* (**a**) to rock, swing. (**b**) ~ **a uno** (*Méx**) to keep sb on tenterhooks. (**c**) (*Carib*) to beat, ill-treat. **2 hamacarse, hamaquearse** *vr* to rock (o.s.), swing.
hambre *nf* (**a**) (*gen*) hunger; (*de población entera*) famine; (*mortal*) starvation; ~ **canina,** ~ **feroz,** ~ **de lobo** ravenous hunger; **estar con** ~, **padecer** ~, **pasar** ~ to be hungry, go hungry, starve; **entretener el** ~ to stave off hunger; **matar el** ~ to satisfy one's hunger; **morir de** ~ to die of (*o* from) starvation, starve to death; **hacer morir de** ~ to starve to death; **tener** ~ to be hungry; **tener mucha** ~ to be very hungry; **vengo con mucha** ~ I'm terribly hungry, I've got a vast appetite.
(**b**) (*fig*) hunger, keen desire, longing (*de* for); **tener** ~ **de** to hunger for, be hungry for.
(**c**) (‡: *sexual*) randiness*; **pasar** ~, **tener** ~ to want it*.
hambreado *adj* (*LAm*) = **hambriento.**
hambreador *nm* (*And, Cono Sur*) monopolist; exploiter.
hambrear [1a] **1** *vt* to starve; (*fig*: *LAm*) to exploit. **2** *vi* to starve, be hungry, be famished.
hambriento 1 *adj* (**a**) starving, hungry, famished.
(**b**) ~ **de** (*fig*) starved of, hungry for, longing for.
(**c**) (‡: *sexual*) randy*.
2 *nm,* **hambrienta** *nf* starving person; **los** ~**s** the hungry, the starving.
hambruna *nf* (*And, Cono Sur*), **hambrusia** *nf* (*Carib*) ravenous hunger; **tener** ~ to be ravenously hungry, be starving.
Hamburgo *nm* Hamburg.
hamburguesa *nf* hamburger.
hamburguesería *nf* hamburger restaurant.
hamo *nm* fish-hook.
hampa *nf* underworld, low life, criminal classes; (*Hist*) rogue's life, vagrancy; **gente del** ~ people of the underworld, criminals, riffraff.
hampesco *adj* underworld (*atr*), criminal.
hampón *nm* tough, rowdy, thug.
hámster *nm, pl* **hámsters** hamster.
han *V* **haber.**
hand [xan] *nm* (*CAm Dep*) handball.
handicap ['xandikap] *nm, pl* **handicaps** handicap.
handicapar [xandika'par] [1a] *vt* to handicap.
hándling ['xanlin] *n* (*Aer*) handling (of baggage *etc*).
hangar *nm* (*Aer*) hangar.
Hanovre *nm* Hanover.
hápax *nm invar* hapax, nonce-word.
haragán 1 *adj* idle, lazy, good-for-nothing. **2** *nm,* **haragana** *nf* idler, layabout, good-for-nothing. **3** *nm* (*Carib*: *limpiapisos*) mop. **4** *nf* (*CAm**) reclining chair.
haraganear [1a] *vi* to idle, waste one's time; to lounge about, loaf around.
haraganería *nf* idleness, laziness.
harapiento *adj* ragged, tattered, in rags.
harapo *nm* rag, tatter; ~**s** (*Méx*‡) clothes, clobber‡; **estar hecho un** ~ to go about in rags.
haraposo *adj* = **harapiento.**
haraquiri *nm* hara-kiri; **hacerse el** ~ to commit hara-kiri.
hard [xar] *nm* hardware.
hardware ['xarwer] *nm* hardware.
harén *nm* harem.
harina *nf* (**a**) flour; meal; powder; ~ **de arroz** ground rice; ~ **de avena** oatmeal; ~ **de fuerza,** ~ **para levadura** self-raising flour; ~ **de huesos** bonemeal; ~ **lacteada** malted milk; ~ **de maíz** cornflour, corn meal; ~ **de patata** potato flour; ~ **de pescado** fish-meal; ~ **de soja** soya flour; ~ **de trigo** wheat flour; **eso es** ~ **de otro costal** that's another story, that's a horse of a different colour; **el coche se hizo** ~ the car was smashed up; **meterse en** ~ (*fig*) to get involved; **estar en** ~**s** (*And**) to be broke*.
(**b**) (*And*) small piece; **una** ~ **de pan** a bit of bread.
(**c**) (*Carib*‡) money, dough‡.
harinear [1a] *vi* (*Carib*) to drizzle.
harineo *nm* (*Carib*) drizzle.
harinero 1 *adj* flour (*atr*). **2** *nm* (**a**) (*persona*) flour merchant. (**b**) (*recipiente*) flour bin.
harinoso *adj* floury.
harnear [1a] *vt* (*And, Cono Sur, Méx*) to sieve, sift.
harnero *nm* sieve.
harpagón‡ *adj* (*And*) very thin, skinny.
harpillera *nf* sacking, sackcloth.
hartar [1a] **1** *vt* (**a**) to satiate, surfeit, glut, more than satisfy (*con, de* with).
(**b**) (*fig*) to weary, tire.
(**c**) ~ **a uno de algo** (*fig*) to overwhelm sb with sth; ~ **a uno de palos** to rain blows on sb.
(**d**) (*CAm*: *maldecir de*) to malign, slander.
2 hartarse *vr* (**a**) to eat one's fill (*con* of), gorge (*con* on), be satiated; **comer hasta** ~ to eat to repletion; ~ **de uvas** to stuff o.s. with grapes, eat too many grapes.
(**b**) (*fig*) to weary, get weary (*de* of); to get fed up (*de* with); ~ **de reír** to laugh fit to burst; **no se hartaron de reír** they couldn't stop laughing.
hartazgo *nm* surfeit, satiety; repletion; glut; bellyful; **darse un** ~ to eat to repletion, overeat; **darse un** ~ **de** to eat one's fill of; (*fig*) to give o.s. a bellyful of, have too much of.
harto 1 *adj* (**a**) full (*de* of), satiated; glutted (*de* with).
(**b**) (*fig*) **estar** ~ **de** to be fed up with*, be tired of; **¡estamos** ~**s ya!** we're fed up!*, enough is enough!; **¡estoy** ~ **de decírtelo!** I'm fed up with telling you so!*
(**c**) (*LAm*) a lot of; much, many.
2 *adv* (*liter en España, normal en LAm*) amply; very, quite; **una tarea** ~ **difícil** a very difficult task, a difficult enough task; **lo sé** ~ **bien** I know (it) all too well; **ha habido** ~ **accidentes** (*LAm*) there were a lot of accidents.
hartón 1 *adj* (**a**) (*CAm, Méx*: *glotón*) greedy, gluttonous. (**b**) (*Méx**) (*estúpido*) stupid; (*molesto*) annoying. **2** *nm* (*And, Carib, Méx*) large banana.
hartura *nf* (**a**) surfeit; glut; (*abundancia*) abundance, plenty; **con** ~ in abundance, in plenty. (**b**) (*de deseo*) full satisfaction, fulfilment.
has *V* **haber.**
has. *abr de* **hectáreas** *nfpl* hectares.
hasta 1 *adv* even; **y** ~ **la pegó** and he even hit her; ~ **en Valencia hiela a veces** even in Valencia it freezes sometimes.
2 *prep* (**a**) (*lugar*) as far as; up to, down to; **lo llevó** ~ **la iglesia** he carried it as far as the church; **los árboles crecen** ~ **los 4.000 metros** the trees grow up to 4,000 metres.
(**b**) (*tiempo*) till, until; as late as; up to; **se quedará** ~ **el martes** she will stay till Tuesday; **siguió en pie** ~ **el siglo pasado** it stood until (*o* up to, as late as) the last century; **no me levanto** ~ **las 9** I don't get up until (*o* before) 9 o'clock; **no iré** ~ **después de la reunión** I shan't go till after the meeting; *V* **luego, vista** *etc.*
(**c**) (*CAm, Méx*) not until; ~ **mañana viene** he's not coming till tomorrow; ~ **hoy lo conocí** I didn't meet him till today, I met him only today.
3 *conj*: ~ **que** till, until; ~ **que me lo des** until you give it to me.

hastiador *adj* = **hastiante**.

hastial *nm* (**a**) (*Arquit*) gable end. (**b**) [*gen* xas'tjal] (‡) roughneck*, lout.

hastiante *adj* wearisome, boring; sickening.

hastiar [1c] **1** *vt* (*fastidiar*) to weary, bore; (*asquear*) to sicken, disgust. **2 hastiarse** *vr*; ~ **de** to tire of, get fed up with*.

hastío *nm* weariness; boredom; disgust, loathing.

hatajo *nm* lot, collection; **un ~ de pícaros** a bunch of rogues.

hatillo *nm* = **hato**.

hato *nm* (**a**) (*ropa*) clothes, set of clothing; (*enseres*) personal effects, possessions; **~ y garabato** (*And, Carib**) all that one has; **coger el ~, echar el ~ a cuestas, liar el ~** to pack up; to clear out; **menear el ~ a uno** to beat sb up*; **revolver el ~** to stir up trouble.

(**b**) (*víveres*) provisions.

(**c**) (*choza*) shepherd's hut; (*parada*) stopping place (of migratory flocks *etc*).

(**d**) (*Agr*: *animales*) flock, herd; (*gente*) group, crowd, collection; (*pey*) bunch, band, gang; (*de objetos, observaciones etc*) lot, collection.

(**e**) (*And, Carib*) cattle ranch.

Hawai *nm* (*t* **Islas ~**) Hawaii.

hawaiano, -a 1 *adj, nm/f* Hawaian. **2** *nf* (*Cono Sur*: *chancleta*) flip-flop.

hay, haya *etc*: *V* **haber**.

Haya *nf*: **La ~** The Hague.

haya *nf* beech, beech tree.

hayaca *nf* (*And*) tamale; (*Carib*) *stuffed cornmeal pasty*.

hayal *nm*, **hayedo** *nm* beechwood.

hayo *nm* (*Bot*) coca; coca leaves.

hayuco *nm* beechnut; (*t* **~s**) beechnuts, beechmast.

haz[1] *nm* (**a**) (*lío*) bundle, bunch; (*Agr*: *de trigo*) sheaf; (*de paja*) truss; **haces** (*Hist Pol*) fasces.

(**b**) (*rayo, TV etc*) beam; **~ de electrones** electron beam; **~ láser** laser beam; **~ de luz** beam of light, pencil of light; **~ de partículas** particle beam.

haz[2] *nf* (*Anat*: *liter*) face; (*fig*) face, surface; (*de tela*) right side; **~ de la tierra** face of the earth; **de dos haces** two-faced.

haz[3] *V* **hacer**.

haza *nf* small field, plot of arable land.

hazaña *nf* feat, exploit, deed, achievement; **las ~s del héroe** the hero's exploits, the hero's great deeds; **sería una ~** it would be a great thing to do, it would be a great achievement.

hazañería *nf* fuss, exaggerated show; histrionics.

hazañero *adj persona* dramatic, histrionic, given to making a great fuss; *acción* histrionic, exaggerated.

hazañoso *adj persona* heroic, gallant, dauntless; *acción* heroic, doughty.

hazmerreír *nm* laughing stock, joke.

HB *nm* (*Esp Pol*) *abr de* **Herri Batasuna** *Basque political party*.

he[1] *V* **haber**.

he[2] *adv* (*liter*): **~ aquí** here is, here are; this is, these are; (*más dramático*) behold; **¡heme aquí!, ¡héteme aquí!** here I am!; **¡helo aquí!** here it is!; **¡helos allí!** there they are!; **~ aquí la razón de que ..., ~ aquí por qué ...** that is why ...; **~ aquí los resultados** these are the results, here you have the results.

hebdomadario *adj, nm* weekly.

hebilla *nf* buckle, clasp.

hebra *nf* (*Cos*) thread; piece of thread, length of thread; (*Bot etc*) fibre; strand; (*de gusano de seda*) thread; (*de madera*) grain; (*de metal*) vein, streak; (*fig*) thread (of the conversation); **~s** (*poét*) hair; **ni ~** (*And**) nothing; **tabaco de ~** loose tobacco; **de una ~** (*Cono Sur, Méx**) in one go; **pegar la ~** to start a conversation; to chatter, talk nineteen to the dozen; **no quedó ni ~ de comida** (*And**) there wasn't a scrap of food left; **se rompió la ~ entre los dos amigos** (*Méx**) the two friends fell out.

hebraico *adj* Hebraic.

hebraísta *nmf* Hebraist.

hebreo 1 *adj* (*Hist*) Hebrew; (*moderno*) Israeli. **2** *nm*, **hebrea** *nf* (*Hist*) Hebrew; (*moderno*) Israeli; (*pey**) usurer, extortioner; pawnbroker. **3** *nm* (*Ling*) Hebrew; **jurar en ~*** to blow one's top*.

Hébridas *nfpl* Hebrides.

hebroso *adj* fibrous; *carne* stringy.

hecatombe *nf* hecatomb; (*fig*) slaughter, butchery; **¡aquello fue la ~!** what a disaster that was!, you should have seen it!

heces *nfpl V* **hez**.

hectárea *nf* hectare (= *2.471 acres*).

héctico *adj* consumptive.

hectogramo *nm* hectogramme, hectogram (*US*).

hectolitro *nm* hectolitre, hectoliter (*US*).

Héctor *nm* Hector.

hechicera *nf* sorceress, enchantress, witch.

hechicería *nf* (**a**) (*gen*) sorcery, witchcraft. (**b**) (*una ~*) spell. (**c**) (*fig*) spell, enchantment, charm.

hechicero 1 *adj* magic(al); bewitching, enchanting. **2** *nm* wizard, sorcerer, enchanter; (*en África etc*) witch doctor.

hechizante *adj* enchanting, bewitching.

hechizar [1f] *vt* (**a**) to bewitch, cast a spell on. (**b**) (*fig*) to charm, enchant, fascinate; (*pey*) to bedevil.

hechizo 1 *adj* (**a**) (*falso*) artificial, false, fake.

(**b**) (*separable*) detachable, removable.

(**c**) (*Téc*) manufactured.

(**d**) (*And, Cono Sur, Méx*) home-made; (*Méx, And*: *pey*) home-made, rough and ready.

2 *nm* (**a**) (*gen*) magic, witchcraft; (*un ~*) magic spell, charm.

(**b**) (*fig*) magic, spell, enchantment; glamour; fascination; **~s** (*de mujer etc*) charms.

hecho 1 (*ptp de* **hacer**) done; **¡~!** agreed!, it's a deal!; **a lo ~ pecho** we must make the best of it now; **lo ~ ~ está** what's done cannot be undone; **bien ~** well done; well made; *persona* well-proportioned; **¡bien ~!** well done!; **mal ~** badly done; poorly made; *persona* ill-proportioned; **él, ~ un ...** he, like a ...; **ella, hecha una furia, se lanzó ...** she hurled herself furiously ..., she threw herself in a fury ...; **estar ~ a** to be used to, be inured to; *V* **basilisco, fiera** *etc*.

2 *adj* (**a**) (*acabado*) complete, finished; *hombre, queso, vino etc* mature; perfect; (*Cos*) ready-made, ready-to-wear; made-up; **~ y derecho** complete, right and true, as it should be in every way; **un hombre ~ y derecho** a real man, every inch a man; *V* **frase**.

(**b**) (*Culin*) **muy ~** overdone, well-cooked; **no muy ~, poco ~** underdone, undercooked.

3 *nm* (**a**) (*acto*) deed, act, action; **~ de armas** feat of arms; **H~s de los Apóstoles** Acts of the Apostles; **~s que no palabras** deeds not words.

(**b**) (*realidad*) fact; (*factor*) factor; (*asunto*) matter; (*suceso*) event; **~ consumado** fait accompli; **esto es un ~** this is a fact; **el ~ es que ...** the fact is that ..., the position is that ...; **volvamos al ~** let's get back to the facts; **de ~** in fact, as a matter of fact; (*Pol etc*: *adj y adv*) de facto; **de ~ y de derecho** de facto and de jure; **en ~ de verdad** as a matter of solid fact.

hechor *nm* (**a**) (*LAm*) stud donkey. (**b**) (*Cono Sur*) = **malhechor**.

hechura *nf* (**a**) (*acto*) making, creation; **no tiene ~** it can't be done.

(**b**) (*objeto etc*) creation, product; **somos ~ de Dios** we are God's handiwork.

(**c**) (*forma*) form, shape; (*de persona*) build; (*de traje*) cut; **a ~ de** like, after the manner of; **tener ~s de algo** to show an aptitude for sth; **no tener uno ~** (*Cono Sur, Méx*) to be a dead loss.

(**d**) (*Cos*) making-up, confection; **~s** cost of making up; **de ~ sastre** tailor-made.

(**e**) (*Téc*) craftsmanship, workmanship; **de exquisita ~** of exquisite workmanship.

(**f**) (*fig*) creature, puppet; **él es una ~ del ministro** he is a creature of the minister.

heder [2g] *vi* (**a**) to stink, smell, reek (*a* of). (**b**) (*fig*) to annoy, be unbearable.

hediondez *nf* (**a**) (*olor*) stink, stench. (**b**) (*cosa*) stinking thing.

hediondo *adj* (**a**) (*maloliente*) stinking, foul-smelling, smelly. (**b**) (*sucio*) filthy; (*repugnante*) repulsive; (*obsceno*) obscene. (**c**) (*fig*: *inaguantable*) annoying, unbearable.

hedonismo *nm* hedonism.

hedonista 1 *adj* hedonistic. **2** *nmf* hedonist.

hedor *nm* stink, stench, smell (*a* of).

hegemonía *nf* hegemony.

hégira *nf* hegira.

helada *nf* frost; freeze, freeze-up; **~ blanca** hoarfrost; **~ de madrugada** early-morning frost.

heladamente *adv* (*fig*) icily.

heladera *nf* (*Cono Sur*) refrigerator, icebox (*US*).

heladería *nf* ice-cream stall, ice-cream parlour.

heladero 1 *adj* ice-cream (*atr*). **2** *nm* (*And, Cono Sur*) ice-cream man.

helado 1 *adj* (**a**) frozen; freezing, icy; icebound.

(**b**) (*fig*) chilly, icy, cold, disdainful.

(**c**) **dejar ~ a uno** to dumbfound sb, shatter sb; **¡me dejas ~!** you amaze me!; **quedarse ~** to be scared stiff.

(**d**) (*Carib Culin*) iced, frosted.

2 *nm* ice cream.

helador *adj viento etc* icy, freezing; **hace un frío ~** it's icy cold, it's perishing cold.

heladora *nf* (*de nevera*) freezing unit, freezer; (*LAm*) refrigerator, icebox (*US*).

helaje *nm* (*And*) (*frío intenso*) intense cold; (*sensación*) chill.

helar [1j] **1** *vt* (**a**) (*Met*) to freeze; to ice (up); *líquido* to congeal, harden; *bebida etc* to ice, chill.

(**b**) (*fig*) (*pasmar*) to dumbfound, shatter, amaze; (*desalentar*) to discourage; (*aterrar*) to scare to death.

2 *vi* to freeze.

3 helarse *vr* (*Met*) to freeze; to be frozen; (*Aer, Ferro etc*) to ice (up), freeze up: (*líquido*) to congeal, harden, set.

helecho *nm* bracken, fern.

Helena *nf* Helen.

helénico *adj* Hellenic, Greek.

heleno *nm*, **helena** *nf* Hellene, Greek.

Helesponto *nm* Hellespont.

hélice *nf* (**a**) spiral; (*Anat, Elec, Mat*) helix; **~ doble** double helix. (**b**) (*Aer*) propeller, airscrew; (*Náut*) propeller, screw.

helicoidal *adj* spiral, helicoidal, helical.

helicóptero *nm* helicopter; **~ artillado, ~ de ataque, ~ de combate** helicopter gunship; **~ fumigador** crop-spraying helicopter.

helio *nm* helium.

heliógrafo *nm* heliograph.

helioterapia *nf* heliotherapy, sunray treatment.

heliotropo *nm* heliotrope.

helipuerto *nm* heliport.

helitransportar [1a] *vt* to transport by helicopter; (*Mil etc*) to helicopter (in).

helmántico *adj* (*Esp*) of Salamanca.

helvético, -a *adj, nm/f* Swiss.

hematología *nf* haematology.

hematoma *nm* bruise.

hembra *nf* (**a**) (*Bot, Zool*) female; (*humana*) woman; (*pey*) female; **el armiño ~** the female stoat, the she-stoat; **el pájaro ~** the female bird, the hen bird; **una real ~** a fine figure of a woman; **5 hijos, esto es 2 varones y 3 ~s** 5 children, that is 2 boys and 3 girls.

(**b**) (*Mec*) nut; **~ de terraja** die.

(**c**) (*Cos*) eye.

hembraje *nm* (*LAm*) female flock, female herd; (*hum*) womenfolk.

hembrería* *nf* (*Carib, Méx*), **hembrerío*** *nm* gaggle of women, crowd of women.

hembrilla *nf* (*Mec*) nut; eyebolt.

hembrista *nmf* (*hum*) feminist.

hemerográfico *adj* newspaper (*atr*).

hemeroteca *nf* newspaper archive.

hemiciclo *nm* semicircular theatre; (*Parl*) chamber; floor.

hemiplejía *nf* hemiplegia; stroke.

hemisferio *nm* hemisphere.

hemistiquio *nm* hemistich.

hemodonación *nf* donation of blood.

hemofilia *nf* haemophilia.

hemofílico, -a *adj, nm/f* haemophiliac.

hemoglobina *nf* haemoglobin.

hemorragia *nf* (*Med*) haemorrhage; bleeding, loss of blood; (*fig*) drain, loss; **~ cerebral** cerebral haemorrhage; **~ nasal** nosebleed; **morir por ~** to bleed to death.

hemorroides *nfpl* haemorrhoids, piles.

henal *nm* hayloft.

henar *nm* meadow, hayfield.

henchir [3h] **1** *vt* to fill (up), stuff, cram (*de* with). **2 henchirse** *vr* (**a**) to swell; (*persona*) to stuff o.s. (with food). (**b**) **~ de orgullo** to swell with pride.

Hendaya *nf* Hendaye.

hendedura *nf* crack, fissure, crevice; cleft, split, slit; (*Geol*) rift, fissure.

hender [2g] *vt* (*gen*) to crack; (*cortar*) to cleave, split, slit; *olas* to cleave, breast; (*abrirse paso*) to make one's way through; (*fig*) to split.

hendidura *nf* = **hendedura**.

hendija *nf* (*LAm*) crack, crevice.

hendir [3i] *vt* (*LAm*) = **hender**.

henequén *nm* (*LAm*) (*planta*) agave, henequen; (*fibra*) agave fibre, henequen.

henificación *nf* haymaking; tedding.

henificar [1g] *vt* to ted.

henil *nm* hayloft.

heniquén *nm* (*Carib, Méx*) = **henequén**.

heno *nm* hay.

heñir [3h *y* 3k] *vt* to knead.

hepático *adj* hepatic, liver (*atr*); **trasplante ~** liver transplant.

hepatitis *nf* hepatitis.

heptagonal *adj* heptagonal.

heptágono *nm* heptagon.

heptámetro *nm* heptameter.

heptatlón *nm* heptathlon.

heráldica *nf* heraldry.

heráldico *adj* heraldic.

heraldo *nm* herald.

herales‡ *nmpl* pants, trousers.

herbáceo *adj* herbaceous.

herbaje *nm* (**a**) herbage; grass, pasture. (**b**) (*Náut*) coarse woollen cloth.

herbaj(e)ar [1a] **1** *vt* to graze, put out to pasture. **2** *vi* to graze.

herbario 1 *adj* herbal. **2** *nm* (**a**) (*colección*) herbarium, plant collection. (**b**) (*persona*) herbalist; (*botánico*) botanist.

herbazal *nm* grassland, pasture.

herbicida *nm* weed-killer; **~ selectivo** selective weed-killer.

herbívoro 1 *adj* herbivorous. **2** *nm* herbivore.

herbolario 1 *adj* (*fig*) crazy, cracked. **2** *nm*, **herbolaria** *nf* (*persona*) herbalist. **3** *nm* (*tienda*) herbalist's (shop), health food shop.

herborizar [1f] *vi* to gather herbs, pick herbs; (*como coleccionista*) to botanize, collect plants.

herboso *adj* grassy.

hercio *nm* hertz.

hercúleo *adj* Herculean.

Hércules *nm* Hercules; **h~** (*de circo*) strong man; **es un ~** (*fig*) he's awfully strong.

heredabilidad *nf* inheritability.

heredable *adj* inheritable, that can be inherited.

heredad *nf* landed property; country estate, farm.

heredar [1a] *vt* (**a**) *propiedad* to inherit (*de* from); to be heir to. (**b**) *persona* to name as one's heir. (**c**) (*LAm*) to leave, bequeath (*a* to).

heredera *nf* heiress.

heredero *nm* heir (*de* to); inheritor (*de* of); **~ forzoso** heir apparent; **~ presunto** heir presumptive; sole heir, sole beneficiary; **príncipe ~** crown prince; **~ del trono** heir to the throne.

hereditario *adj* hereditary.

hereje 1 *adj* (**a**) (*Cono Sur**: *irrespetuoso*) disrespectful. (**b**) (*And, Carib*: *excesivo*) excessive; **un trabajo ~*** a heavy task. **2** *nmf* heretic; **¡~!*** you brute!

herejía *nf* (**a**) (*Rel y fig*) heresy. (**b**) (*fig*: *trampa*) dirty trick, low deed; (*injuria*) insult. (**c**) (*And, Méx*) silly remark, gaffe.

herencia *nf* (**a**) inheritance, estate, legacy; (*fig*) heritage. (**b**) (*Bio*) heredity.

hereque *nm* (*Carib Med*) skin disease; (*Bot*) *a disease of coffee*.

heresiarca *nmf* heresiarch, arch-heretic.

herético *adj* heretical.

herida *nf* (**a**) wound, injury. (**b**) (*fig*) wound, insult, outrage; **hurgar en la ~** (*fig*) to reopen an old wound; **lamer las ~s** to lick one's wounds.

herido 1 *adj* (**a**) injured; hurt; (*Mil etc*) wounded.

(**b**) (*fig*) wounded, offended.

2 *nm* (**a**) injured man; (*Mil*) wounded man; **los ~s** (*Mil*) the wounded; **el número de los ~s en el accidente** the number of people hurt in the accident, the number of casualties in the accident.

(**b**) (*Cono Sur*) ditch, channel.

herir [3i] *vt* (**a**) (*dañar*) to injure, hurt; (*Mil etc*) to wound; **~ a uno en el brazo** to wound sb in the arm.

(**b**) (*golpear*) to beat, strike, hit; (*Mús*) to pluck, strike, play; (*sol*) to strike on; to beat down on; **un sonido me hirió el oído** a sound reached (*o* struck *o* offended) my ear; **es un color que hiere la vista** it's a colour which offends the eye.

(**c**) (*fig*) *corazón etc* to touch, move, sway.

(**d**) (*fig*: *ofender*) to offend, hurt.

hermafrodita *adj, nm* hermaphrodite.

hermana *nf* (**a**) sister; **media ~** half-sister; **prima ~** first

cousin; ~ **gemela** twin sister; ~ **mayor** elder sister; ~ **política** sister-in-law.
(**b**) (*Ecl*) sister; ~ **lega** lay sister.
(**c**) (*una de par*) twin; other half (*of pair*), corresponding part.
hermanable *adj* (**a**) (*de hermano*) fraternal. (**b**) (*compatible*) compatible. (**c**) (*a tono etc*) matching, that can be matched.
hermanamiento *nm*: ~ **de ciudades** town-twinning.
hermanar [1a] *vt* (*para formar par*) to match, put together; (*unir*) to join; *ciudades* to twin; (*relacionar*) to relate; (*armonizar*) to harmonize, bring into harmony; (*Cono Sur*: *hacer pares*) to pair.
hermanastra *nf* stepsister.
hermanastro *nm* stepbrother.
hermandad *nf* (**a**) (*relación*) brotherhood; close relationship, intimacy. (**b**) (*grupo etc*) brotherhood, fraternity; sisterhood; **Santa H~** (*Hist*) rural police (*15th to 19th centuries*).
hermanita *nf* little sister; **~s de la caridad** Little Sisters of Charity.
hermanito *nm* little brother.
hermano 1 *adj* similar; matched, matching; *barco* sister; **ciudades hermanas** twin towns.
2 *nm* (**a**) brother; (*Bio*) sibling; **medio** ~ half-brother; **primo** ~ first cousin; ~ **carnal** full brother; ~ **gemelo** twin brother; ~ **de leche** foster-brother; ~ **mayor** elder brother, big brother; ~ **político** brother-in-law; **mis ~s** my brothers, my brothers and sisters; **el Gran H~ te vigila** Big Brother is watching you; **su ~ pequeño**⁑ his willy⁑.
(**b**) (*Ecl*) brother; **~s** brothers, brethren.
(**c**) (*uno de par*) twin; other half (*of pair*), corresponding part.
(**d**) (*LAm*: *espectro*) ghost.
herméticamente *adv* hermetically.
hermeticidad *nf* hermetic nature, hermeticism.
hermético *adj* hermetic; airtight, watertight; (*fig*) self-contained; *persona* reserved, secretive; *teoría* watertight; *misterio* impenetrable.
hermetismo *nm* (*fig*) tight secrecy, close secrecy; silence, reserve; hermeticism.
hermetizar [1f] *vt* (*fig*) to seal off, close off.
hermosamente *adv* beautifully; handsomely.
hermosear [1a] *vt* to beautify, embellish, adorn.
hermoso *adj* (**a**) (*bello*) beautiful, lovely; (*espléndido*) fine, splendid; (*abundante*) abundant, lavish; *hombre* handsome; **un día** ~ a fine day, a lovely day; **¡qué escena más hermosa!** what a lovely scene!; **seis ~s toros** six magnificent bulls.
(**b**) (*LAm*) large, robust; *persona* large, impressive, stout.
hermosura *nf* (**a**) (*gen*) beauty, loveliness; splendour; lavishness; handsomeness. (**b**) (*persona*) beauty, belle; (*en oración directa*) darling.
hernia *nf* rupture, hernia; ~ **discal** slipped disc; ~ **estrangulada** strangulated hernia.
herniarse [1b] *vr* to rupture o.s.
Herodes *nm* Herod; **hacer lo de ~*** to put up with it; **ir de ~ a Pilatos** to be driven from pillar to post.
héroe *nm* hero.
heroicamente *adv* heroically.
heroicidad *nf* (**a**) (*cualidad*) heroism. (**b**) (*una* ~) heroic deed.
heroico *adj* heroic.
heroicocómico *adj* mock-heroic.
heroína[1] *nf* heroine.
heroína[2] *nf* (*Farm*) heroin.
heroinomanía *nf* heroin addiction.
heroinómano, -a *nm/f* heroin addict.
heroísmo *nm* heroism.
herpes *nm o nfpl* (*Med*) herpes, shingles; ~ **genital** genital herpes.
herrada *nf* (**a**) bucket. (**b**) (*And Agr*) branding.
herrador *nm* farrier, blacksmith.
herradura *nf* horseshoe; **camino de** ~ bridle path; **curva en** ~ (*Aut*) hairpin bend; **mostrar las ~s** (*fig*) to bolt, show a clean pair of heels.
herraje *nm* (**a**) ironwork, iron fittings. (**b**) (*Cono Sur*) horseshoe. (**c**) (*Méx*) silver harness fittings.
herramental *nm* toolkit, toolbag.
herramienta *nf* (**a**) (*gen*) tool; implement, appliance; (*equipo*) set of tools; (⁑) tool⁑; ~ **de filo** edge tool; ~ **de mano** hand tool; ~ **mecánica** power tool. (**b**) (*de toro*) horns; (*dientes*) teeth.
herranza *nf* (*And*) branding.
herrar [1j] *vt* (*Agr*) *caballo* to shoe; *ganado* to brand; (*Téc*) to bind with iron, trim with ironwork.
herrería *nf* (**a**) (*taller*) smithy, forge, blacksmith's (shop). (**b**) (*fábrica*) ironworks. (**c**) (*oficio*) blacksmith's trade, craft of the smith. (**d**) (*fig*) uproar, tumult.
herrerillo *nm* (*Orn*) tit.
herrero *nm* blacksmith, smith; ~ **de grueso** foundry worker.
herrete *nm* metal tip, ferrule, tag; (*LAm*) branding-iron, brand.
herrumbre *nf* (**a**) rust. (**b**) (*Bot*) rust. (**c**) (*fig*) iron taste, taste of iron.
herrumbroso *adj* rusty.
hervederas* *nfpl* (*Carib*) heartburn, indigestion.
hervidero *nm* (**a**) (*acto*) boiling; bubbling, seething.
(**b**) (*manantial*) hot spring; bubbling spring.
(**c**) (*fig*) swarm, throng, crowd; **un ~ de gente** a swarm of people; **un ~ de disturbios** a hotbed of unrest.
hervido 1 *ptp y adj* boiled. **2** *nm* (**a**) (*acto*) boiling. (**b**) (*LAm*: *guiso*) stew.
hervidor *nm* kettle; boiler.
hervidora *nf*: ~ **de agua** water heater.
hervir [3i] **1** *vt* (*esp LAm*) to boil; to cook.
2 *vi* (**a**) (*gen*) to boil; (*burbujear*) to bubble, seethe; (*mar etc*) to seethe, surge; ~ **a fuego lento** to simmer; **dejar de** ~ to stop boiling, go off the boil; **empezar a** ~ to begin to boil, come to the boil.
(**b**) (*fig*) ~ **de,** ~ **en** to swarm with, seethe with, teem with; **la cama hervía de pulgas** the bed was swarming with fleas.
hervor *nm* (**a**) (*acto*) boiling; seething; **alzar el ~, levantar el** ~ to come to the boil. (**b**) (*fig*) fire, fervour (of youth); passion; restlessness.
hervoroso *adj* (**a**) boiling, seething; *sol* burning. (**b**) (*fig*) = **fervoroso.**
heteo, -a *adj, nm/f* Hittite.
hetero* *adj* = **heterosexual.**
heterodoxo *adj* heterodox, unorthodox.
heterogéneo *adj* heterogeneous.
heterosexual *adj, nmf* heterosexual.
heterosexualidad *nf* heterosexuality.
heticarse [1g] *vr* (*Carib*) to contract tuberculosis.
hético *adj* consumptive.
hetiquencia *nf* (*Carib*) tuberculosis.
heurístico *adj* heuristic.
hexadecimal *adj* hexadecimal.
hexagonal *adj* hexagonal.
hexágono *nm* hexagon; **el** ~ (*Geog*) France.
hexámetro *nm* hexameter.
hez *nf* (*esp* **heces** *pl*) sediment, dregs; slops; (*Med*) faeces; (*de vino*) lees; (*fig*) dregs, scum; **la ~ de la sociedad** the scum of society.
hg. *abr de* **hectogramos** hectogram(me)s, hg.
hiato *nm* (*Ling*) hiatus.
hibernación *nf* hibernation; **estar en** ~ (*fig*) to be dormant.
hibernal *adj* wintry, winter (*atr*).
hibernar [1a] *vi* to hibernate.
hibridación *nf*, **hibridaje** *nm* hybridization.
hibridar [1a] *vti* to hybridize.
hibridismo *nm* hybridism.
hibridizar [1f] *vt* (*Bio*) to hybridize; (*fig*) to lend a mixed appearance to, produce a hybrid appearance in.
híbrido, -a *adj, nm/f* hybrid.
hice *etc V* **hacer.**
hidalga *nf* noblewoman.
hidalgo 1 *adj* noble; illustrious; (*fig*) gentlemanly, honourable; generous. **2** *nm* (**a**) nobleman, hidalgo. (**b**) (*Méx Hist*) 10-peso gold coin.
hidalguía *nf* nobility; (*fig*) nobility, gentlemanliness, honourableness; generosity.
hidra *nf* hydra; **H~** (*Mit*) Hydra.
hidratante 1 *adj crema* moisturizing. **2** *nf* moisturizing cream.
hidratar [1a] *vt* to hydrate; to moisturize.
hidrato *nm* hydrate; ~ **de carbono** carbohydrate.
hidráulica *nf* hydraulics.
hidráulico *adj* hydraulic, water (*atr*); **fuerza hidráulica** water power, hydraulic power.
hídrico *adj* water (*atr*).
hidro... *pref* hydro..., water-...
hidroala *nf* hydrofoil.
hidroavión *nm* seaplane, flying boat.
hidrocarburo *nm* hydrocarbon.

hidrocefalía *nf* (*Med*) hydrocephalus, water on the brain.
hidrodeslizador *nm* hovercraft.
hidrodinámica *nf* hydrodynamics.
hidroeléctrico *adj* hydroelectric.
hidrófilo *adj* absorbent.
hidrofobia *nf* hydrophobia; rabies.
hidrofóbico *adj*, **hidrófobo** *adj* hydrophobic.
hidrofuerza *nf* hydropower.
hidrófugo *adj* damp-proof, damp-resistant, water-repellent.
hidrógeno *nm* hydrogen.
hidrografía *nf* hydrography.
hidrólisis *nf* hydrolysis.
hidrolizar [1f] **1** *vt* to hydrolyze. **2 hidrolizarse** *vr* to hydrolyze.
hidropesía *nf* dropsy.
hidrópico *adj* dropsical.
hidroplano *nm* hydroplane.
hidroponia *nf* hydroponics, aquiculture.
hidropónico *adj* hydroponic.
hidrosoluble *adj* soluble in water, water-soluble.
hidroterapia *nf* hydrotherapy.
hidróxido *nm* hydroxide; ~ **amónico** ammonium hydroxide.
hiedra *nf* ivy.
hiel *nf* (**a**) (*Anat*) gall, bile; **echar la** ~* to overwork, sweat one's guts out*.
(**b**) (*fig*) gall, bitterness; **no tener** ~ to be very sweet-tempered.
(**c**) ~**es** (*fig*) troubles, upsets.
hielera *nf* ice tray; (*CAm, Méx*) refrigerator.
hielo *nm* (**a**) ice; frost; ~ **a la deriva,** ~ **flotante,** ~ **movedizo** drift ice; ~ **picado** crushed ice; ~ **seco** dry ice; **con** ~ (*bebida*) with ice, on the rocks*; **romper el** ~ (*fig*) to break the ice. (**b**) (*fig*) coldness, indifference; **ser más frío que el** ~ to be as cold as ice.
hiena *nf* hyena; **hecho una** ~ furious; **ponerse como una** ~ to get furious.
hieratismo *nm* hieratic attitude; solemnity, stateliness.
hierba *nf* grass; small plant; (*Med*) herb, medicinal plant; (‡) pot‡, hash*; ~**s** grass, pasture; **mala** ~ weed, (*fig*) evil influence; ~ **artificial** artificial playing surface; ~ **cana** groundsel; ~ **gatera** catmint; ~ **lombriguera** ragwort; ~ **mate** maté; ~ **mora** nightshade; ~ **rastrera** cotton grass; ~ **de San Juan** St John's-wort; **y otras** ~**s** (*fig*) and so forth, and suchlike; **a las finas** ~**s** cooked with herbs; **oír** (*o* **sentir, ver**) **crecer la** ~ to be pretty smart; **pisar mala** ~ to have bad luck.
hierbabuena *nf* mint.
hierbajo *nm* weed.
hierbajoso *adj* weedy, weed-infested.
hierbaluisa *nf* lemon verbena, aloysia.
hierra *nf* (*LAm*) branding.
hierro *nm* (**a**) (*metal*) iron; ~ **acanalado** corrugated iron; ~ **batido** wrought iron; ~ **bruto** crude iron, pig iron; ~ **colado** cast iron; ~ **forjado** wrought iron; ~ **de fundición,** ~ **fundido** cast iron; ~ **en lingotes** pig iron; ~ **ondulado** corrugated iron; ~ **viejo** scrap iron, old iron; **a** ~ **candente batir de repente** strike while the iron is hot; **como el** ~ like iron, tough, strong; **de** ~ iron (*atr*); **llevar** ~ **a Vizcaya** to carry coals to Newcastle; **machacar en** ~ **frío** to beat one's head against a wall, flog a dead horse; **el que a** ~ **mata, a** ~ **muere** those that live by the sword die by the sword; **quitar** ~ to minimize an issue, cut things down to their proper size.
(**b**) (*objeto*) iron object; (*herramienta*) tool; (*de flecha etc*) head; (*Agr*) brand, branding-iron; (*Golf*) iron; (**) rod**; (*pistola*) gun; ~**s** irons.
hi-fi [i'fi] *nm, pl* **hi-fis** hi-fi.
higa *nf* rude sign, obscene gesture (*with fist and thumb*); (*fig*) scorn, derision; **no da una** ~* he doesn't give a damn; **dar** ~ **a** to jeer at, mock.
hígado *nm* (**a**) (*Anat*) liver; **castigar el** ~* to drink a lot; **echar los** ~**s*** to sweat one's guts out*; **tener** ~ **de indio** (*CAm, Méx*) to be a disagreeable sort.
(**b**) ~**s** (*fig**) guts, pluck.
(**c**) **ser un** ~ (*CAm, Méx*‡) to be a pain in the neck*.
higadoso *adj*: **ser** ~ (*CAm, Méx*‡) to be a pain in the neck*.
higiene *nf* hygiene.
higiénico *adj* hygienic; sanitary.
higienización *nf* cleaning, cleansing.
higienizar [1f] **1** *vt* to clean up, cleanse. **2 higienizarse** *vr* (*Cono Sur*) to wash, bath.
higo *nm* (**a**) (*Bot*) fig, green fig; ~ **chumbo,** ~ **de tuna** prickly pear; ~ **paso,** ~ **seco** dried fig; **de** ~**s a brevas** once in a blue moon; **ser un** ~ **mustio** to be weakly; to be off-colour; *V* **importar** *etc.*
(**b**) (*Vet*) thrush.
(**c**) (**) cunt**.
higuera *nf* fig tree; ~ **chumba,** ~ **de tuna** prickly pear (cactus), Indian fig tree; ~ **del infierno,** ~ **infernal** castor-oil plant; **caer de la** ~ to come down to earth with a bump; **estar en la** ~ to be naïve; to be at a loss, not know what to do; to be day-dreaming.
higuerilla *nf* (*Méx*) castor-oil plant.
hija *nf* daughter; child; (*en oración directa, frec no se traduce, p.ej.*) ~ **no te lo puedo decir** I can't tell you; ~ **política** daughter-in-law; *V t* **hijo.**
hijastra *nf* stepdaughter.
hijastro *nm* stepson.
hijo *nm* (**a**) son; child; ~**s** (*frec*) children; sons and daughters; offspring, descendants; **sin** ~**s** childless, without children; **¿cuántos** ~**s tiene?** how many children has she?; **Pitt** ~ Pitt the Younger, the younger Pitt; **Juan Pérez,** ~ Juan Pérez Junior; ~ **de bendición** legitimate child; ~ **de la cuna** foundling; ~ **de la chingada** (*Méx*‡) bastard‡, son of a bitch‡; ~ **de leche** foster child; ~ **natural** illegitimate child; ~ **político** son-in-law; **nombrar a uno** ~ **predilecto de la ciudad** to name sb a favourite son of the city; ~ **pródigo** prodigal son; **el** ~ **de mi madre*** I (myself), yours truly*; **cada** ~ **de vecino** everyone, every mother's son; **como cada** ~ **de vecino** like everyone else, like the next man; ~ **de puta**‡ bastard‡, son of a bitch‡; **ser** ~ **de sus obras** to be a self-made man; **ser (muy)** ~ **de papá** to be daddy's boy, be a spoiled child; to have led a very sheltered life; **entró en el negocio como** ~ **de papá** he just followed his father in the business (so it was easy for him); **hacer a una un** ~ to get a girl pregnant; **hacer a uno un** ~ **macho** (*LAm*) to do sb harm.
(**b**) (*en oración directa: a chico*) son, sonny*, my boy; (*a adulto*) man, old chap* (*pero frec no se traduce*); **¡**~ **de mi alma!, ¡**~ **de mis entrañas!** my precious child!; **¡híjo(le)!** (*Méx**) good God!
hijodeputa‡ *nm*, **hijoputa**‡ *nm* bastard‡, son of a bitch‡.
hijoputada‡ *nf* dirty trick.
hijoputesco‡ *adj* rotten*, dirty.
hijoputez *nf* dirty trick.
hijuela *nf* (**a**) (*niña*) little girl; (*hijita*) small daughter.
(**b**) (*filial*) offshoot, branch, dependency.
(**c**) (*Jur*) estate of a deceased person; share, portion, inheritance; list of bequests.
(**d**) (*And, Cono Sur*) plot of land.
(**e**) (*Cos*) piece of material (*for widening a garment*).
(**f**) (*Agr*) small irrigation channel.
(**g**) (*Méx Min*) seam of ore.
hijuelo *nm* (**a**) (*niño*) little boy; (*hijito*) small son; ~**s** small children, (*Zool*) young. (**b**) (*Bot*) shoot. (**c**) (*And: camino*) side road, minor road.
hijuemadre** *excl*: **¡**~**!** (*CAm*) bloody hell!**, Jesus Christ!**
hijueputa** *excl*: **¡**~**!** (*CAm*) bloody hell!**, Jesus Christ!**
hijuna‡ (*LAm*) *interj* you bastard!‡
hila *nf* (**a**) (*fila*) row, line; **a la** ~ in a row, in single file. (**b**) (*cuerda*) thin gut; ~**s** (*Med*) lint.
hilacha *nf* (*hilo*) loose thread, hanging thread; shred; fibre, filament; ~ **de vidrio** spun glass; ~**s** (*Med*) lint; **mostrar la** ~ (*Cono Sur**) to show (o.s. in) one's true colours.
hilachento *adj* (*LAm*) ragged, tattered; frayed; shabby.
hilacho *nm* (**a**) = **hilacha.** (**b**) ~**s** (*Méx*) rags, tatters. (**c**) **dar vuelo al** ~ (*Méx**) to have a wild time.
hilachudo *adj* (*Méx*) = **hilachento.**
hilada *nf* row, line; (*Arquit*) course.
hilado 1 *adj y ptp* spun; **seda hilada** spun silk. **2** *nm* (**a**) (*acto*) spinning. (**b**) (*hilo*) thread, yarn.
hilador *nm* spinner.
hiladora *nf* (**a**) (*persona*) spinner. (**b**) (*Téc*) spinning jenny.
hilandería *nf* (**a**) (*arte*) spinning. (**b**) (*fábrica*) spinning mill; ~ **de algodón** cotton mill.
hilandero *nm*, **hilandera** *nf* spinner.
hilangos *nmpl* (*And*) rags, tatters.
hilar [1a] *vt* (**a**) to spin (*t Zool*). (**b**) (*fig*) to reason, infer; ~ **(muy) delgado,** ~ **fino** to be very particular (*o* meticulous, demanding); (*pey*) to split hairs; ~ **delgado** (*Cono Sur: morir*) to be dying.
hilaracha *nf* = **hilacha.**
hilarante *adj* hilarious; merry, mirthful; **gas** ~ laughing gas.

hilaridad *nf* hilarity; merriment, mirth.
hilatura *nf* spinning.
hilaza *nf* yarn, coarse thread; **descubrir la ~** to show (o.s. in) one's true colours.
hilazón *nf* connection.
hilera *nf* (**a**) row, line; string; (*Mil etc*) rank, file; (*Arquit*) course; (*Agr*) row, drill. (**b**) (*Cos*) fine thread.
hilo *nm* (**a**) (*Cos etc*) thread, yarn; (*Bot etc*) fibre, filament; **~ bramante** twine; **~ de Escocia** lisle, strong cotton; **~ de perlas** string of pearls; **~ de zurcir** darning wool; **a ~** uninterruptedly, continuously; **coser al ~** to sew on the straight, sew with the weave; **dar mucho ~ que torcer** to cause a lot of trouble; **escapar con el ~ en una pata** (*Carib, Cono Sur**) to get out of a corner, wriggle out of a jam*; **colgar** (*o* **pender**) **de un ~** to hang by a thread; **contar algo del ~ al ovillo** to tell sth without omitting a single detail; **estar al ~** to be watchful, be on the look-out; **estar hecho un ~** to be as thin as a rake; **tela de ~** (*And, Carib*) linen cloth.
(**b**) (*de metal*) thin wire; (*Elec*) wire; flex; (*Telec*) line; **~ directo** direct line, hot line; **~ de tierra** earth wire, ground wire (*US*).
(**c**) (*de líquido etc*) thin line, thin stream, trickle; (*de gente*) thin line; **~ dental** dental floss; **~ de humo** thin line of smoke, plume of smoke; **~ de música, ~ musical** piped music, muzak; **decir algo con un ~ de la voz** to say sth in a whisper; **irse tras el ~ de la gente** to follow the crowd.
(**d**) (*tela*) linen; **traje de ~** linen dress.
(**e**) (*fig: de conversación, discurso*) thread, theme; (*de vida*) course; (*de pensamiento*) train; **~ conductor** connecting theme, principal theme; **coger el ~** to pick up the thread; (*en carrera etc*) to catch up; **perder el ~** to lose the thread; **seguir el ~** (*de razonamiento*) to follow, understand.
hilván *nm* tacking, basting; (*Cono Sur: hilo*) basting thread; (*Carib: dobladillo*) hem.
hilvanar [1a] *vt* (**a**) (*Cos*) to tack, baste. (**b**) (*fig*) *trabajo* to do hurriedly; *construcción* to throw together, knock up hurriedly; **bien hilvanado** well done, well constructed.
Himalaya *nm*: **el ~, los montes ~** the Himalayas.
himen *nm* hymen, maidenhead.
himeneo *nm* (**a**) (*liter*) nuptials (*liter*), wedding. (**b**) (*Poét*) epithalamium.
himnario *nm* hymnal, hymnbook.
himno *nm* hymn; **~ nacional** national anthem.
hincada *nf* (**a**) (*Carib: hincadura*) thrust. (**b**) (*Cono Sur: cortesía*) genuflection. (**c**) (*Carib: dolor*) sharp pain, stabbing pain.
hincadura *nf* thrust, thrusting, driving.
hincapié *nm*: **hacer ~** to make a stand, take a firm stand; **hacer ~ en** to insist on; to dwell on, emphasize, make a special point of.
hincapilotes *nm invar* (*Cono Sur*) pile-driver.
hincar [1g] **1** *vt* (*meter*) to thrust (in), drive (in), push (in); *diente* to sink (*en* into); *pie etc* to set (firmly) (*en* on); **~la*** to slog, work; **hincó la mirada en ella** he fixed his gaze on her, he stared at her fixedly; **hincó el bastón en el suelo** he stuck his stick in the ground, he thrust his stick into the ground; *V* **diente, rodilla.**
2 hincarse *vr*: **~ de rodillas** to kneel (down).
hinco *nm* (*Cono Sur*) post, stake.
hincha 1 *nf* (**a**) ill will, animosity, bad blood; grudge; **uno de mis ~s** one of my pet hates*; **tener ~ a uno** to have a grudge against sb; **tomar ~ a uno** to take a dislike to sb.
(**b**) **¡qué ~!** (*Cono Sur**) what a bore!
2 *nmf* (**a**) (*Dep etc*) fan, supporter, rooter (*US**); **los ~s del Madrid** the Madrid supporters.
(**b**) (*And**) pal*, chum*.
hinchable *adj* inflatable.
hinchabolas‡ *nmf invar* (*Cono Sur*) = **hinchapelotas.**
hinchada *nf* supporters, fans.
hinchado *adj* (**a**) swollen. (**b**) (‡) **hinchada** pregnant; **dejar a una hinchada** to get a girl pregnant. (**c**) (*fig*) *persona* arrogant, vain; *estilo etc* pompous, high-flown, windy.
hinchador *nm* (**a**) **~ de ruedas** tyre inflator. (**b**) (*Cono Sur*‡) pest, bloody nuisance‡.
hinchante‡ *adj* (**a**) (*molesto*) annoying, tiresome. (**b**) (*gracioso*) funny.
hinchapelotas‡ *nmf invar*: **es un ~** (*Cono Sur*) (*molesto*) he's a real pain in the neck*; (*aburrido*) he's a crashing bore.
hinchar [1a] **1** *vt* (**a**) to swell; to distend, enlarge; *neumático etc* to blow up, inflate, pump up; **~ a una**‡ to get a girl pregnant.
(**b**) (*fig: exagerar*)) to exaggerate.
(**c**) (*Cono Sur*‡: *molestar*) to annoy, upset; **me hincha todo el tiempo** he keeps on at me all the time.
2 hincharse *vr* (**a**) to swell (up); to get distended; to stuff o.s. (*de* with).
(**b**) (*fig: engreírse*) to get conceited, become vain.
(**c**) (*: *enriquecerse*) to make a pile*.
(**d**) **~ a correr** (*etc*) to run (*etc*) hard, run (*etc*) about a lot; **~ a reír** to laugh a lot, have a good laugh.
hinchazón *nf* (**a**) (*Med etc*) swelling; bump, lump.
(**b**) (*fig*) arrogance, vanity, conceit; (*de estilo etc*) pomposity, windiness.
hindi *nm* Hindi.
hindú, -a *adj, nm/f* Hindu.
hinduismo *nm* Hinduism.
hiniesta *nf* (*Bot*) broom.
hinojo[1] *nm* (*Bot, Culin*) fennel.
hinojo[2] *nm* (*Anat*: ††) knee; **de ~s** on bended knee; **ponerse de ~s** to kneel (down), go down on one's knees.
hipar [1a] **1** *vi* (**a**) to hiccup, hiccough.
(**b**) (*perro*) to pant; **~ por algo** to long for sth, yearn for sth; **~ por** + *infin* to long to + *infin*, yearn to + *infin*.
(**c**) (*fig*) to be worn out, be exhausted.
2 *vi* [xi'par] to whine, whimper.
hipato* *adj* (*And: repleto*) full, swollen; (*And, Carib: pálido*) pale, anaemic; (*soso*) tasteless.
hipear [1a] *vi* (*Méx*) = **hipar.**
hiper* *nm invar* hypermarket.
hiper... *pref* hyper...; (*) *p.ej.* **una cosa hipercara** a dreadfully expensive thing; **estoy hiperocupado** I'm up to my ears.
hiperacidez *nf* hyperacidity.
hiperactividad *nf* hyperactivity.
hiperactivo *adj* hyperactive.
hiperagudo *adj* abnormally acute.
hipérbaton *nm, pl* **hipérbatos** hyperbaton.
hipérbola *nf* hyperbola.
hipérbole *nf* hyperbole.
hiperbólico *adj* hyperbolic(al), exaggerated.
hipercorrección *nf* hypercorrection.
hipercrítico *adj* hypercritical; carping, censorious.
hiperinflación *nf* runaway inflation, hyperinflation.
hipermercado *nm* hypermarket.
hipermetropía *nf*, **hiperopía** *nf* long-sight, long-sightedness; **tener ~** to be long-sighted.
hipernervioso *adj* excessively nervous, highly strung.
hipersensibilidad *nf* hypersensitivity; over-sensitiveness, touchiness.
hipersensible *adj* hypersensitive; over-sensitive, touchy.
hipersónico *adj* supersonic.
hipertensión *nf* hypertension; **~ arterial** high blood-pressure.
hipertrofia *nf* hypertrophy.
hipiar [1b] *vi* (*Méx*) = **hipar.**
hípico *adj* horse (*atr*); equine.
hipido *nm* whine, whimper.
hipismo *nm* horse-racing.
hipnosis *nf* hypnosis.
hipnótico, -a *adj, nm/f* hypnotic.
hipnotismo *nm* hypnotism.
hipnotista *nmf* hypnotist.
hipnotizable *adj* susceptible to hypnosis.
hipnotizador *adj* hypnotizing.
hipnotizante *nmf* hypnotist.
hipnotizar [1f] *vt* to hypnotize, mesmerize.
hipo *nm* (**a**) hiccup(s), hiccough(s); **quitar el ~ a uno** to cure sb's hiccups, (*fig*) to take sb's breath away, be a shock to sb; **tener ~** to have hiccups.
(**b**) (*fig: deseo*) longing, yearning; **tener ~ por** to long for, crave.
(**c**) (*fig*) (*asco*) disgust; (*rencor*) grudge, ill will; **tener ~ con uno** to have a grudge against sb, have it in for sb.
hipo... *pref* hypo...
hipocampo *nm* sea horse.
hipocondria *nf* hypochondria.
hipocondriaco, hipocondríaco 1 *adj* hypochondriac(al). **2** *nm*, **hipocondriaca, hipocondríaca** *nf* hypochondriac.
hipocorístico *adj*: **nombre ~** pet name, affectionate form of a name (*p.ej.* **Merche = Mercedes, Jim = James**).
Hipócrates *nm* Hippocrates.
hipocrático *adj*: **juramento ~** Hippocratic oath.
hipocresía *nf* hypocrisy.
hipócrita 1 *adj* hypocritical. **2** *nmf* hypocrite.

hipócritamente *adv* hypocritically.
hipodérmico *adj* hypodermic.
hipódromo *nm* racetrack, racecourse; (*Hist*) hippodrome.
hipopótamo *nm* hippopotamus.
hiposulfito *nm*: ~ **sódico** (*Fot*) hypo, sodium thiosulphate.
hipoteca *nf* mortgage; ~ **dotal** endowment mortgage; **levantar una** ~ to raise a mortgage; **redimir una** ~ to pay off a mortgage.
hipotecar [1g] **1** *vt* to mortgage. **2 hipotecarse** *vr* (*fig*) to commit o.s.
hipotecario *adj* mortgage (*atr*).
hipotenusa *nf* hypotenuse.
hipotermia *nf* hypothermia.
hipótesis *nf invar* hypothesis; supposition; theory, idea, notion.
hipotéticamente *adv* hypothetically.
hipotético *adj* hypothetic(al).
hiriente *adj observación, tono* wounding, cutting.
hirsutez *nf* hairiness.
hirsuto *adj* (**a**) hairy, hirsute; bristly. (**b**) (*fig*: *brusco*) brusque, gruff, rough.
hirvición* *nf* (*And*) abundance, multitude.
hirviendo (*como adj*) boiling.
hirviente *adj* boiling, seething.
hisca *nf* birdlime.
hisopear [1a] *vt* (*Ecl*) to sprinkle with holy water, asperse.
hisopo *nm* (**a**) (*Ecl*) sprinkler, aspergillum. (**b**) (*Bot*) hyssop. (**c**) (*LAm*: *brocha*) paintbrush; (*Cono Sur*: *trapo*)) dishcloth; (*Cono Sur*: *de algodón*) cotton bud.
hispalense *adj, nmf* Sevillian.
Híspalis *n* (*liter*) Seville.
Hispania *nf* (*Hist*) Hispania, Roman Spain.
hispánico *adj* Hispanic, Spanish.
hispanidad *nf* (**a**) (*cualidad*) Spanishness; Spanish quality, Spanish characteristics. (**b**) (*Pol*) Spanish world, Hispanic world; **Día de la H~** Columbus Day (*12 October*).
hispanismo *nm* (**a**) word (*o* phrase *etc*) peculiar to Spain; word (*etc*) borrowed from Spanish, hispanicism.
(**b**) (*Univ etc*) Hispanism, Hispanic studies; **el h~ holandés** Hispanic studies in Holland.
hispanista *nmf (Univ etc)* hispanist, Spanish scholar, student of Spain and Latin America.
hispanística *nf* Hispanic studies.
hispanizar [1f] *vt* to hispanicize.
hispano 1 *adj* Spanish, Hispanic; (*en EE. UU.*) Hispanic. **2** *nm,* **hispana** *nf* Spaniard; (*en EE. UU.*) Hispanic.
hispano-... *pref* Hispano-..., Spanish-...; **pacto ~ruritano** Hispano-Ruritanian pact.
Hispanoamérica *nf* Spanish America, Latin America.
hispanoamericano 1 *adj* Spanish American, Latin American. **2** *nm,* **hispanoamericana** *nf* Spanish American, Latin American.
hispanófilo *nm,* **hispanófila** *nf* hispanophile.
hispanófobo *nm,* **hispanófoba** *nf* hispanophobe.
hispanohablante 1 *adj* Spanish-speaking. **2** *nmf* Spanish speaker.
hispanomarroquí *adj* Spanish-Moroccan.
hispanoparlante = **hispanohablante.**
hispinglés *nm* (*hum*) Spanglish.
histerectomía *nf* hysterectomy.
histeria *nf* hysteria.
histéricamente *adv* hysterically.
histérico *adj* (**a**) hysterical; **paroxismo** ~ hysterics. (**b**) (*Cono Sur*‡) queer‡.
histerismo *nm* hysteria; hysterics.
histograma *nm* histogram.
histología *nf* histology.
historia *nf* (**a**) (*narración*) story; (*cuento*) tale; **~s** (*pey*) tales, gossip; (*Cono Sur*: *fig*) mix-up, messy business; **la ~ es larga de contar** it's a long story; **dejarse de ~s** to come to the point, stop beating about the bush; **tener ~*** to be a long story; **no me vengas con ~s** don't give me that (one)*.
(**b**) (~ *humana etc*) history; **en toda la ~ humana** in the whole of human history; ~ **antigua** ancient history; ~ **del arte** history of art, art history; ~ **clínica** case-history; ~ **natural** natural history; **H~ Sacra, H~ Sagrada** Biblical history, (*en escuela*) Scripture; ~ **universal** world history; **es una mujer que tiene** ~ she's a woman with a past; **ser de** ~ to be famous, (*pey*) to be notorious; **pasar a la** ~ to go down in (*o* to) history (*como* as); **picar en** ~ to be a serious matter.
historiador(a) *nm/f* historian; chronicler, recorder.
historial 1 *adj* historical. **2** *nm* record; dossier; (*Med*: *t* ~ **clínico**) case-history; **el brillante ~ del club** the club's brilliant record.
historiar [1b] *vt* (**a**) to tell the story of; to write the history of; to record, chronicle, write up. (**b**) (*Arte etc*) to paint, depict.
historicismo *nm* historicism.
historicista *adj* historicist.
histórico 1 *adj* (**a**) historical; (*esp fig*) historic. (**b**) *miembro etc* long-serving, original; long-established. **2** *nm,* **histórica** *nf* long-serving member, original member.
historiero *adj* (*Cono Sur*) gossipy.
historieta *nf* short story, tale; anecdote; (*Tip*) strip cartoon, comic strip.
historietista *nmf* strip cartoonist.
historiografía *nf* historiography, writing of history.
historiógrafo, -a *nm/f* historiographer.
histrión *nm* (*liter*) actor, player; (*pey*) playactor; buffoon.
histriónico *adj* histrionic.
histrionismo *nm* (**a**) (*Teat*) acting, art of acting. (**b**) (*fig*) histrionics. (**c**) (*actores*) actors (*collectively*), theatre people.
hita *nf* (**a**) (*Téc*) brad, headless nail. (**b**) = **hito.**
hitita 1 *adj, nmf* Hittite. **2** *nm* (*Ling*) Hittite.
hitleriano *adj* Hitlerian.
hito *nm* (**a**) boundary post, boundary mark; milestone; ~ **kilométrico** kilometre stone.
(**b**) (*fig*) landmark, milestone; **es un ~ en nuestra historia** it is a landmark in our history; **esto marca un ~ histórico** this marks a historical milestone.
(**c**) (*Dep*) quoits.
(**d**) (*Mil*) target; (*fig*) aim, goal; **a** ~ fixedly; **dar en el** ~ to hit the nail on the head; **mudar de** ~ to change one's tactics.
(**e**) **mirar a uno de ~ en ~** to stare at sb.
hizo *V* **hacer.**
hm. *abr de* **hectómetro(s)** hectometre(s), hm.
Hna(s) *abr de* **Hermana(s)** Sister(s), Sr(s).
Hno(s) *abr de* **Hermano(s)** Brother, Bro(s).
hobby ['xobi] *nm, pl* **hobbys** ['xobis] hobby.
hocicada* *nf*: **darse una ~ en el suelo** to fall flat on one's face; **darse una ~ con la puerta** to bash one's face against the door*.
hocicar [1g] **1** *vt* (*cerdo*) to root among; (*persona etc*) to nuzzle.
2 *vi* (**a**) (*cerdo*) to root; (*persona*) to nuzzle; (*amantes*) to pet; ~ **con,** ~ **en** to put one's nose against (*o* into *etc*).
(**b**) (*Náut*) to pitch.
(**c**) (*caer*) to fall on one's face.
(**d**) (*fig*) to run into trouble, come up against it.
hocico *nm* (**a**) (*Zool*) snout, muzzle, nose; (*de persona**: *nariz*) snout; (*cara*) face, mug‡; **caer** (*o* **dar**) **de ~s** to fall on one's face; **dar de ~s contra algo** to bump into sth, go slap into sth; **cerrar el ~‡** to shut one's trap‡; **estar de** ~ to be in a bad mood; **meter el** ~ to meddle, shove one's nose in.
(**b**) (*fig*) angry face, grimace; **poner** ~ to show one's anger (*o* resentment) in one's expression; **torcer el** ~ to make a (wry) face; to scowl, look cross.
hocicón *adj* (*And*) angry, cross.
hocicudo* *adj* (*And, Carib*) (*con mala cara*) scowling; (*de mal humor*) grumpy*.
hociquear [1a] *vti* = **hocicar.**
hociquera *nf* (*And, Carib*) muzzle.
hockey ['oki *o* 'xoki] *nm* hockey (*t* ~ **sobre césped,** ~ **sobre hierba**); ~ **sobre hielo** ice-hockey.
hodierno *adj* daily; (*fig*) frequent.
hogaño *adv* (†† *o liter*) this year; these days, nowadays.
hogar *nm* (**a**) fireplace, hearth; fireside; (*Téc*) furnace; (*Ferro*) firebox.
(**b**) (*fig*) home, house; (*vida familiar*) home life, family life; (*personas*) household; **artículos de ~** domestic goods; ~ **de ancianos,** ~ **de jubilados,** ~ **de pensionistas** old folk's (*o* people's) home; ~ **nacional judío** Jewish national home; ~ **protegido** sheltered housing; **los (que han quedado) sin** ~ the homeless, those left homeless; **no tienen** ~ they have no home.
hogareño *adj* home (*atr*), family (*atr*); fireside (*atr*); *persona* home-loving, stay-at-home.
hogaza *nf* large loaf, cottage loaf.
hoguera *nf* (**a**) bonfire; blaze; **la casa estaba hecha una ~** the house was ablaze, the house was an inferno. (**b**) (*Hist*) stake; **morir en la** ~ to die at the stake.
hoja *nf* (**a**) (*Bot*) leaf; petal; (*de hierba*) blade; **la** ~ (*LAm*‡) pot‡, hash*; ~ **de parra** (*fig*) figleaf; **de ~ ancha**

broad-leaved; **de ~ caduca** deciduous; **de ~ perenne** evergreen.

(**b**) (*de papel*) leaf, sheet; (*Tip*) leaf, page; (*formulario etc*) sheet, form, document; **~ de cálculo, ~ electrónica** spreadsheet; **~ de cumplido** compliments slip; **~ de embalaje** packing-slip; **~ de guarda** flyleaf; **~ de inscripción** registration form; **~ de pedido** order form; **~ parroquial** parish magazine; **~ de reclamación** complaint form, form on which to make a complaint; **~ de ruta** waybill; **~ de servicio** record (of service); **~s sueltas** loose sheets, loose-leaf paper; **~ de trabajo** worksheet; **~ volandera, ~ volante** leaflet, handbill, pamphlet; **~ de vida** (*And*) curriculum vitae, CV; **doblar la ~** (*fig*) to change the subject; **volver la ~** to turn the page; (*fig*: *cambiar de tema*) to change the subject; (*fig*) to turn over a new leaf.

(**c**) (*de metal*) sheet; thin plate; (*de puerta*) leaf; (*de espada, patín*) blade; (*de vidrio*) sheet, pane; **~ de afeitar** razor blade; **~ de estaño** tinfoil; **~ de lata** tin, tinplate; **~ plegadiza** flap (*of table etc*); **~ de tocino** side of bacon, flitch.

hojalata *nf* tin, tinplate; (*Lam*) corrugated iron.

hojalatería *nf* (**a**) (*obra*) tinwork; sheet-metal work. (**b**) (*tienda*) tinsmith's (shop). (**c**) (*LAm*: *objetos*) tinware.

hojalaterío *nm* (*And, CAm, Méx*) tinware.

hojalatero *nm* tinsmith.

hojalda *nf* (*LAm*), **hojaldra** *nf* (*LAm*), **hojaldre** *gen nm* puff-pastry.

hojarasca *nf* (**a**) dead leaves, fallen leaves. (**b**) (*fig*: *basura*) rubbish, trash, worthless stuff; (*palabras*) empty verbiage, waffle.

hojear [1a] **1** *vt* to turn the pages of, leaf through; to skim through, glance through.

2 *vi* (**a**) (*Méx Bot*) to put out leaves.

(**b**) (*CAm, Méx*: *Agr*) to eat leaves.

(**c**) (*superficie*) to scale off, flake off.

hojerío *nm* (*CAm*) leaves, foliage.

hojoso *adj* leafy.

hojuela *nf* (**a**) (*Bot*) leaflet, little leaf.

(**b**) (*hoja delgada*) flake; (*de metal*) foil, thin sheet; **~ de estaño** tinfoil.

(**c**) (*Culin*) pancake; (*LAm*) ordinary fare, daily food; (*Carib, Méx*: *Culin*) puff pastry.

hola *interj* (*saludo*) hullo!; (*sorpresa*) hullo!, hey!, I say!; (*Cono Sur Telec*) hullo?

holán *nm* (**a**) cambric, fine linen. (**b**) (*Méx*) flounce, frill.

Holanda *nf* Holland.

holandés 1 *adj* Dutch. **2** *nm* Dutchman; **el ~ errante** the Flying Dutchman; **los holandeses** the Dutch. **3** *nm* (*Ling*) Dutch.

holandesa *nf* (**a**) Dutchwoman. (**b**) (*Tip*) quarto sheet

holding ['xoldin] *nm, pl* **holdings** ['xoldin] holding company.

holgadamente *adv* (**a**) loosely, comfortably; **caben ~** they fit in easily, they go in with room to spare.

(**b**) idly; in leisurely fashion.

(**c**) **vivir ~** to live comfortably, live in luxury, be well off.

holgado *adj* (**a**) *ropa etc* loose, full, comfortable; roomy; baggy; *tipo* full; **demasiado ~** too big.

(**b**) (*sin trabajo*) idle, unoccupied, free; leisured.

(**c**) (*Fin*) comfortably off, well-to-do; **vida holgada** comfortable life, life of luxury.

holganza *nf* (**a**) idleness; (*descanso*) rest; (*ocio*) leisure, ease. (**b**) (*diversión*) amusement, enjoyment.

holgar [1h *y* 1l] **1** *vi* (**a**) (*descansar*) to rest, take one's ease, be at leisure; (*obrero etc*) to be idle, be out of work; (*objeto*) to lie unused.

(**b**) (*sobrar*) to be unnecessary, be superfluous; **huelga toda protesta** no protest is necessary, it is not necessary to protest; **huelga decir que ...** it goes without saying that ..., needless to say, ...

(**c**) = **2**; **huelgo de saberlo** I'm delighted to hear it.

2 holgarse *vr* to amuse o.s., enjoy o.s., have a good time; **~ con algo** to take pleasure in sth; **~ con una noticia** to be pleased about a piece of news; **~ de que ...** to be pleased that ..., be glad that ...

holgazán 1 *adj* idle, lazy, slack. **2** *nm*, **holgazana** *nf* idler, slacker, loafer; ne'er-do-well.

holgazanear [1a] *vi* to laze around, be idle, slack, loaf.

holgazanería *nf* idleness, laziness, slackness.

holgazanitis *nf* (*hum*) congenital laziness, work-shyness.

holgorio *nm* = **jolgorio**.

holgura *nf* (**a**) (*Cos etc*) looseness, fullness; roominess, bagginess; (*Mec*) play, free movement.

(**b**) (*ocio*) freedom, leisure; (*confort*) ease, comfort.

(**c**) (*goce*) enjoyment; (*alegría*) merriment, merrymaking.

(**d**) (*lujo*) comfortable living, luxury; **vivir con ~** to live well, live comfortably, live in luxury.

holocausto *nm* (*Rel*: *Hist*) holocaust, burnt offering; (*fig*) sacrifice; (*fig*: *desastre*) holocaust; **el H~** the Holocaust; **~ nuclear** nuclear holocaust.

holograma *nm* hologram.

hollar [1l] *vt* (**a**) to tread, tread on; to trample down, trample underfoot. (**b**) (*fig*) to trample underfoot; to humiliate, humble.

hollejo *nm* (*Bot*) skin, peel.

hollín *nm* soot.

holliniento *adj*, **hollinoso** *adj* sooty, covered in soot.

hombracho *nm*, **hombrachón** *nm* hulking great brute, big tough fellow.

hombrada *nf* manly deed, brave act.

hombradía *nf* manliness; courage, guts.

hombre 1 *nm* (*un ~*) man; (*gen*) man, mankind; **su ~*** her man, her husband; **es otro ~** he's a changed man; **pobre ~** poor devil, (*pey*) poor fish, weak man; slow-witted chap; **es un pobre ~** he's a poor fish*; **está hecho un pobre ~** he's now a man to be pitied, he's a shadow of his former self; **una charla de ~ a ~** a man-to-man talk; **el ~ propone, pero Dios dispone** man proposes, God disposes; **ser muy ~** to be a real man, be pretty tough; **no me fastidien, pues sé ser muy ~** don't provoke me, because I can get tough; **desde que el ~ es ~** always, since the year dot; **si lo compras, me haces un ~*** if you buy it, you'll be doing me a big favour; **¡~ al agua!, ¡~ al mar!** man overboard!; **~ de armas** man-at-arms; **~ de bien** honest man, good man; **~ blanco** white man; paleface; **~ bueno** (*Jur*) arbiter; **el ~ de** (*o* **en**) **la calle** the man in the street; **~ de las cavernas** caveman; **~ de confianza** right-hand man; **~ del día** man of the moment; **~ de empresa** businessman; **~ de estado** statesman; **el ~ fuerte de Ruritania** the strong man of Ruritania; **~ hecho** grown man; **~ de letras** man of letters; **~ de mar** seafaring man, seaman; **el ~ masa, el ~ medio, el ~ del montón** the average man, the ordinary man, the man in the street; **~ mundano** man-about-town; **~ de mundo** man of the world; **~ de negocios** businessman; **el abominable ~ de las nieves** the abominable snowman; **~ orquesta** one-man band; **~ de paja** stooge*, man of straw; **~ de pro, ~ de provecho** worthy man, honest man; **~ del tiempo** weatherman.

2 *nm* (*elemento con guión*) *p.ej.*: **~-gol** striker who can score goals; **~-milagro** miracle-man; **~-mito** man who is a myth in his own lifetime; **~-mosca** trapeze artist; *V* **~-rana** *etc.*

3 *interj* (**a**) (*en oración directa*) old chap*, my boy, man (*pero frec no se traduce*); **sí ~** yes, yes of course.

(**b**) (*sorpresa*) well!, good heavens!, you don't say!

(**c**) (*compasión*) dear me!; yes I know!

(**d**) (*protesta*) come now!, but my dear fellow!, heavens man!

hombre-anuncio *nm, pl* **hombres-anuncio** sandwich man.

hombrear[1] [1a] *vi* (*joven*) to play the man, act grown-up; (*hombre*) to act tough, try to be somebody.

hombrear[2] [1a] **1** *vt* (**a**) to shoulder; to push with one's shoulder, put one's shoulder to.

(**b**) (*And, Cono Sur, Méx*) to help, lend a hand to.

2 *vi*: **~ con uno** to try to keep up with sb, strive to equal sb.

3 hombrearse *vr* = **2**.

hombrecillo *nm* (**a**) little man, little fellow. (**b**) (*Bot*) hop.

hombre-lobo *nm, pl* **hombres-lobo** werewolf.

hombre-masa *nm invar* ordinary man, man in the street.

hombre-mono *nm, pl* **hombres-mono** apeman.

hombrera *nf* (*tirante*) shoulder strap; (*almohadilla*) shoulder pad; (*Mil*) epaulette.

hombre-rana *nm, pl* **hombres-rana** frogman.

hombría *nf* manliness; **~ de bien** honesty, uprightness, worthiness.

hombrillo *nm* (*Carib Aut*) hard shoulder.

hombro *nm* shoulder; **~ a ~, ~ con ~** shoulder to shoulder; **¡armas al ~!, ¡sobre el ~ armas!** shoulder arms!; **arrimar el ~** to put one's shoulder to the wheel, lend a hand; **cargar algo sobre los ~s** to shoulder sth; **echar algo al ~** (*fig*) to shoulder sth, take sth upon o.s.; **encogerse de ~s** to shrug one's shoulders; **enderezar los ~s** to square one's shoulders, straighten up; **mirar a uno por encima del ~** to look down on sb; **poner el ~** (*Cono Sur fig*) to put one's shoulder to the wheel; **sacar a uno en ~s** to carry sb out on (their) shoulders; **el vencedor salió en ~s** the victor was carried out shoulder-high.

hombruno *adj* mannish, manlike.

homenaje 1 *nm* (**a**) (*Hist, Jur etc*) homage; allegiance; **rendir ~ a** to do (*o* pay, render) homage to, swear allegiance to.

(**b**) (*fig*) tribute, testimonial; **en ~ a** in honour of; in recognition of; **rendir ~ a, tributar ~ a** to pay a tribute to; **rendir el último ~** to pay one's last respects; **una cena (de) ~ para don XY** a dinner in honour of don XY.

(**c**) (*LAm*) celebration; gathering (*in honour of sb*).

(**d**) (*LAm*: *regalo*) gift, favour.

2 *atr*: **una cena-~ para don XY** a dinner in honour of don XY; **un concierto-~ para el compositor** a concert in honour of the composer; **libro-~** homage volume; **partido-~** benefit match, testimonial game.

homenajeado, -a *nm/f*: **el ~** the person being honoured, the guest of honour.

homenajear [1a] *vt* to honour, pay tribute to.

homeópata *nmf* homeopath.

homeopatía *nf* homeopathy.

homeopático *adj* homeopathic.

homérico *adj* Homeric.

Homero *nm* Homer.

homicida 1 *adj* murderous, homicidal; **el arma ~** the murder weapon. **2** *nm* murderer. **3** *nf* murderess.

homicidio *nm* murder, homicide; manslaughter; **~ frustrado** attempted murder.

homilía *nf* homily.

homínido *nm* hominid.

homofobia *nf* homophobia.

homofóbico *adj* homophobic.

homogeneidad *nf* homogeneity.

homogeneización *nf* levelling (down), equalization, unification.

homogéneo *adj* homogeneous.

homogen(e)izar [1f] *vt* to homogenize; to level (down), equalize, unify.

homógrafo *nm* homonym, homograph.

homologable *adj* equivalent, comparable (*a, con* to).

homologación *nf* official approval, authorization, sanction(ing); (*de sueldos*) parity.

homologado *adj* officially approved, authorized.

homologar [1h] *vt* (**a**) (*coordinar*) to coordinate; (*estandarizar*) to bring into line, standardize. (**b**) (*comparar*) to compare. (**c**) (*aprobar*) to check and approve; to approve officially, authorize, sanction; *récord* to accept.

homólogo 1 *adj* equivalent (*de* to). **2** *nm*, **homóloga** *nf* counterpart, equivalent, opposite number.

homónimo 1 *adj* homonymous. **2** *nm* homonym; (*persona*) namesake.

homosexual *adj, nmf* homosexual.

homosexualidad *nf*, **homosexualismo** *nm* homosexuality.

honda *nf* sling; (*LAm*) catapult.

hondear[1] [1a] *vt* (*Náut*) (**a**) (*sondear*) to sound. (**b**) (*descargar*) to unload.

hondear[2] [1a] *vt* (*LAm*) to hit with a slingshot, kill with a sling; to hit with a catapult.

hondo 1 *adj* (**a**) (*gen*) deep; (*bajo*) low.

(**b**) (*Carib*) *río etc* swollen, high.

(**c**) (*fig*) profound, deep, heartfelt; **con ~ pesar** with deep regret, with profound sorrow.

2 *adv*: **respirar ~** to breathe deeply.

3 *nm* depth(s); bottom.

hondón *nm* (**a**) (*de taza, valle etc*) bottom; (*de espuela*) footrest. (**b**) (*de aguja*) eye.

hondonada *nf* (**a**) (*vallecito*) hollow, coombe; (*hoyo*) dip, depression; (*barranco*) gully, ravine. (**b**) (*llano*) lowland.

hondura *nf* (**a**) (*medida*) depth; profundity. (**b**) (*lugar*) depth; deep place; **meterse en ~s** to get out of one's depth, get into deep water (*t fig*).

Honduras *nf* Honduras; **~ Británica** (*Hist*) British Honduras.

hondureñismo *nm* word (*o* phrase *etc*) peculiar to Honduras.

hondureño, -a *adj, nm/f* Honduran.

honestamente *adv* (**a**) decently, properly, decorously. (**b**) modestly; purely. (**c**) fairly, justly, reasonably. (**d**) honourably; honestly, really, frankly.

honestidad *nf* (**a**) decency, decorum. (**b**) modesty; purity, chastity. (**c**) fairness, justice. (**d**) honourableness; honesty.

honesto *adj* (**a**) (*decente*) decent, proper, decorous. (**b**) (*modesto*) modest; (*casto*) pure, chaste. (**c**) (*justo*) fair, just, reasonable. (**d**) (*honrado*) honourable, honest.

hong kongés 1 *adj* Hong Kong (*atr*), of Hong Kong. **2** *nm*, **hong kongesa** *nf* native (*o* inhabitant) of Hong Kong; **los hong kongeses** the people of Hong Kong.

hongo *nm* (**a**) (*Bot*) fungus; (*comestible*) mushroom; (*tóxico*) toadstool; **un enorme ~ de humo** an enormous mushroom of smoke; **crecen** (*o* **proliferan**) **como ~s** they grow like mushrooms. (**b**) (*sombrero*) bowler, bowler hat, derby (*US*).

Honolulú *nm* Honolulu.

honor *nm* honour; (*de mujer*) honour, virtue, good name; (*fig*) glory; **~es** (*Mil etc*) honours, honorary status (*o* rank); **~ profesional** professional etiquette; **en ~ a la verdad** to be fair, for the sake of truth; **en ~ de uno** in sb's honour; **13 puntos de ~es** (*Naipes*) 13 honours points; **hacer ~ a un compromiso** to honour a pledge; **hacer ~ a su firma** to honour one's signature; **hacer los ~es de la casa** to do the honours (of the house); **hacer los debidos ~es a una comida** to do full justice to a meal; **sepultar a uno con todos los ~es militares** to bury sb with full military honours; **tener el ~ de +** *infin* to have the honour to + *infin*, to be proud to + *infin*; **el poeta X, ~ de esta ciudad** the poet X in whom this city glories, the poet X who is this city's claim to fame.

honorabilidad *nf* (**a**) (*cualidad*) honourableness, honour; worthiness. (**b**) (*persona*) distinguished person.

honorable *adj* honourable, worthy.

honorario 1 *adj* honorary, honorific. **2** *nm* honorarium; **~s** (professional) fees, charges.

honorífico *adj* honourable; honorific; **mención honorífica** honourable mention.

honra *nf* self-esteem, sense of personal honour, dignity; (*de mujer*) honour, virtue, good name; **~s fúnebres** last honours, funeral rites; **¡a mucha ~!** I'm honoured!, delighted!; **puritano, sí, y a bastante ~** I'm a puritan, certainly, and proud of it; **tener algo a mucha ~** to be proud of sth, consider sth an honour; **tener a mucha ~ +** *infin* to be proud to + *infin*, deem it an honour to + *infin; V* **atentado.**

honradamente *adv* honestly; honourably, uprightly.

honradez *nf* honesty; honourableness, uprightness, integrity.

honrado *adj* honest; honourable, upright; **hombre ~** honest man, decent man, honourable man.

honrar [1a] **1** *vt* (**a**) to honour, revere, respect; to do honour to.

(**b**) (*Com etc*) to honour.

2 honrarse *vr*: **me honro con su amistad** I am honoured by his friendship; **~ de +** *infin* to be honoured to + *infin*, deem it an honour to + *infin*.

honrilla *nf*: **por la negra ~** out of concern for what people will say, out of a sense of shame; for the sake of appearances.

honrosamente *adv* honourably.

honroso *adj* honourable; respectable, reputable; **es una profesión honrosa** it is an honourable profession, it is a respectable profession.

hontanar *nm* spring, group of springs.

hopa[1] *nf* cassock.

hopa[2] *interj* (**a**) (*Cono Sur*: *¡deja!*) stop it!, that hurts! (**b**) (*And, CAm, Méx*: *saludo*) hullo!

hopo[1] ['xopo] *nm* (fox's) brush, tail.

hopo[2] *interj* out!, get out!

hora *nf* (**a**) hour; (*tiempo*) time; **media ~** half an hour; **durante 2 ~s** for 2 hours; **esperamos ~s y ~s** we waited hours and hours; **en la ~ de su muerte** at the moment of his death, at the time of his death; **¿a qué ~?** at what time?; **¿qué ~ es?** what is the time?, what time is it?; **¡la ~!, ¡es la ~!** time's up!; **es ~ de +** *infin* it is time to + *infin*; **es ~ de irnos** it's time we went, it's time for us to go; **¡ya es** (*o* **va siendo**) **~ de que ...!** it is high time that ...!; **¡ya era ~!** and about time too!; **no comer entre ~s** not to eat between meals.

(**b**) (*con adj o prep*) **a altas ~s, en las altas ~s** in the small hours, late at night; **~ de apertura** opening time; **a una ~ avanzada** at a late hour; **a buena ~** opportunely; **¡a buena ~, mangas verdes!** a fine time you choose to tell me that!, it's too late now!; **en buena ~** fortunately; safely; **~ cero** zero hour; **desde las cero ~s** from the start of the day, from midnight; **~ del cierre** closing time; **~ de comer** mealtime; **a la ~ de comer** at lunchtime; **~s de comercio, ~s comerciales** business hours; **~s de consulta** consulting hours; **~s extra, ~s extraordinarias** overtime; **~ H** zero hour; **¡~ inglesa!*** on the dot; **~s de insolación** hours of sunshine; **~ insular** time in the Canary Islands; **~s lectivas** working time (in school); **~ legal** official time, standard time; **~s libres** free time, spare time; **~ local** local time; **en mala ~** unluckily; **~ media de Greenwich** Greenwich mean time; **~s muertas** dead period; **~ oficial** official time, standard time; **~s de oficina** business hours, office hours; **~ peninsular** time in mainland Spain; **a primera ~** first thing in the morning; **~ pico** (*LAm*), **~ punta** peak hour, rush hour; **~s punta** peak hours, rush hours; **~ de recreo** playtime; **dos ~s de reloj** two hours exactly; **~s suplementarias** overtime; **~ suprema** one's last hour, hour of death; **~s de trabajo** working hours; working day; **'última ~'** (*Prensa*) 'stop-press'; **a última ~** at the last moment; in the nick of time; at the eleventh hour; last thing at night; **noticias de última ~** last-minute news; **dejar las cosas hasta última ~** to leave things until the last moment; **~s valle** off-peak times; **~ de verano** summer time; **~s de vuelo** (*Aer*) flying time; (*experiencia*) experience; (*antigüedad*) seniority; **a la ~** punctually, on the dot; **a la ~ justa** on the stroke of time; **a estas ~s** now, at this time; **a la ~ de pagar** when it comes to paying; **antes de ~** too early; **fuera de ~s** out of hours, out of working hours; **por ~s** by the hour; **sueldo por ~** hourly wage; **trabajar por ~s** to be paid by the hour; to work part-time.

(**c**) (*con verbo*) **dar ~** to fix a time, offer an appointment; **dar la ~** to strike (the hour); **estar en sus ~s más bajas** to be at an all-time low, be at its (*o* one's) lowest ebb; **hacer ~s** (**extra**) to work overtime; **se le ha llegado la ~** her time has come; **poner el reloj en ~** to set one's watch, put one's watch right; **tener ~** to have an appointment; **no ver la ~ de algo** to be scarcely able to wait for sth, look forward impatiently to sth.

(**d**) (*Ecl*) **~s** book of hours; **~s canónicas** canonical hours.

horaciano *adj* Horatian.

Horacio *nm* Horace.

horadar [1a] *vt* to bore (through), pierce, drill, perforate; to tunnel (into).

hora-hombre *nf, pl* **horas-hombre** man-hour.

horario 1 *adj* hourly; hour (*atr*), time (*atr*).

2 *nm* (*de reloj*) hour hand; (*Aer, Ferro etc*; *t LAm*: *escuela*) timetable; **llegar a ~** (*LAm*) to arrive on time, be on schedule; **~ comercial** business hours; **~ flexible** flexitime; **puesto de ~ partido** job involving a split day; **~ de visitas** (*de hospital etc*) visiting hours, (*de médico*) doctor's surgery hours.

horca *nf* (**a**) (*de ejecución*) gallows, gibbet; **condenar a uno a la ~** to condemn sb to the gallows.

(**b**) (*Agr*) pitchfork; hayfork; manure fork.

(**c**) (*de ajos etc*) string.

(**d**) (*Carib*: *regalo*) birthday present, present given on one's saint's day.

horcadura *nf* fork (of a tree).

horcajadas: **a ~** *adv* astride.

horcajadura *nf* (*Anat*) crotch.

horcajo *nm* (**a**) (*Agr*) yoke. (**b**) (*de árbol, río*) fork.

horcar [1g] *vt* (*LAm*) = **ahorcar.**

horcón *nm* (**a**) (*Agr*: *horca*)) pitchfork. (**b**) (*Agr*: *para frutales*) forked prop; (*LAm*: *para techo*) prop, support.

horchata *nf* tiger nut milk.

horchatería *nf* refreshment stall.

horda *nf* horde; (*fig*) gang.

hordiate *nm* barley water.

horero *nm* (*And, Méx*) hour hand.

horita *adv* (*LAm*) = **ahorita.**

horizontal 1 *adj* horizontal. **2** *nf* (**a**) horizontal position; **tomar la ~** to stand upright. (**b**) (**‡**: *prostituta*) prostitute.

horizontalmente *adv* horizontally.

horizonte *nm* horizon (*t fig*); (*t* **línea del ~**) skyline.

horma *nf* (**a**) (*Téc*) form, mould; **~ de sombrero** hat block; **~ (de calzado)** last, boot tree; **encontrar(se con) la ~ de su zapato** to meet one's match; to find just what one wanted, find the very thing. (**b**) (*muro*) dry-stone wall.

hormadoras *nfpl* (*And*) petticoat.

hormiga *nf* (**a**) (*Ent*) ant; **~ blanca** white ant; **~ león** ant lion; **~ obrera** worker ant; **~ roja** red ant.

(**b**) **~s** (*Med*) itch; pins and needles.

(**c**) **ser una ~** (*Cono Sur**) (*trabajador*) to be hardworking; (*ahorrativo*) to be thrifty.

hormigón *nm* concrete; **~ armado** reinforced concrete; **~ pretensado** pre-stressed concrete.

hormigonera *nf* concrete mixer.

hormigonero *adj* concrete (*atr*).

hormiguear [1a] *vi* (**a**) (*piel etc*) to itch; to have pins and needles; to have a feeling as though insects were crawling over one. (**b**) (*insectos*) to swarm, teem.

hormigueo *nm* (**a**) itch, itching; tingling, prickly feeling, pins and needles. (**b**) (*fig*) anxiety, uneasiness. (**c**) swarming.

hormiguero 1 *adj* ant-eating; **oso ~** anteater. **2** *nm* (**a**) (*Ent*) ants' nest, ant hill. (**b**) (*fig*) ant hill; swarm of people, place swarming with people.

hormiguillo *nm* = **hormigueo** (**a**).

hormona *nf* hormone; **~ de(l) crecimiento** growth hormone.

hormonal *adj* hormonal.

hormonarse [1a] *vr* to have hormone treatment.

hornacina *nf* (vaulted) niche.

hornada *nf* (**a**) batch (of loaves *etc*), baking. (**b**) (*fig*) batch, collection, crop.

hornalla *nf* (*Cono Sur*: *horno*) oven; (*de estufa*) hotplate, ring.

hornazo *nm* (**a**) batch (of cakes *etc*), baking. (**b**) (*pastel*) Easter cake.

horneado *nm* cooking (time), baking (time).

hornear [1a] **1** *vt* to cook, bake. **2** *vi* to bake, be a baker.

hornero, -a *nm/f* baker.

hornillo *nm* (**a**) (*Téc*) small furnace; (*Culin*) cooker, stove; portable stove; (*de pipa*) bowl; **~ eléctrico** hotplate; **~ de gas** gas ring. (**b**) (*Mil Hist*) mine.

horno *nm* (*Culin*) oven; (*Téc*) furnace; (*de alfarero*) kiln; (*de pipa*) bowl; **alto ~** blast furnace; **~ de cal** lime kiln; **~ crematorio** crematorium; **~ de fundición** smelting furnace; **~ de ladrillos** brick kiln; **~ (de) microondas** microwave oven; **resistente al ~** ovenproof; **asar al ~** to bake; **el ~ no está para bollos** this is the wrong moment, this is a bad time to ask; **meter un plato al ~ fuerte** to put a dish into a high oven.

horóscopo *nm* horoscope.

horqueta *nf* (*Agr*) pitchfork; (*Bot*) fork of a tree); (*LAm*) bend in the road.

horquetear [1a] **1** *vt* (**a**) (*Cono Sur*) *oído* to prick up; *persona* to listen suspiciously to. (**b**) (*Méx*) to sit astride, straddle. **2** *vi* (*LAm*) to grow branches, put out branches.

horquilla *nf* (*del pelo*) hairpin, hairclip; (*Agr*) pitchfork; (*de bicicleta*) fork; (*Mec*) yoke; (*Telec*) rest, cradle; (*de zanco*) footrest; **~ (de cavar)** garden fork; **~ de salarios** (*fig*) wage levels.

horrarse [1a] *vr* (*LAm Agr*) to abort.

horrendo *adj* horrible; hideous; dire, frightful.

hórreo *nm* (*prov*) (raised) granary.

horrible *adj* (**a**) horrible, dreadful, ghastly. (**b**) (*fig*) dreadful, nasty, terrible; **¡qué persona más ~!** what a dreadful man!; **la película es ~** the film is dreadful.

horriblemente *adv* (**a**) horribly, dreadfully. (**b**) (*fig*) dreadfully, terribly.

horripilante *adj* hair-raising, horrifying; harrowing; grisly; creepy.

horripilar [1a] **1** *vt*: **~ a uno** to make sb's hair stand on end, horrify sb, give sb the creeps. **2 horripilarse** *vr* to be horrified, be terrified; **era para ~** it was enough to make your hair stand on end.

horro *adj* (**a**) (*exento*) free, exempt, enfranchised; **~ de** bereft of, devoid of. (**b**) (*Bio*) sterile.

horror *nm* (**a**) (*gen*) horror, dread, terror (*a* of); abhorrence (*a* of); enormity; frightfulness; **¡qué ~!** how ghastly!*; isn't it dreadful?; well!, goodness!; **la fiesta ... ¡un ~!** the party was ghastly!*; **se dicen ~es de la cocina inglesa** awful things are said about English cooking; **tener ~ a algo** to have a horror of sth; **tener algo en ~** to detest sth, loathe sth.

(**b**) (*acto*) atrocity, terrible thing.

(**c**) (*: *como adv*) **me gusta ~es** *o* **un ~** I like it awfully; **hoy he trabajado un ~** today I worked awfully hard; **se divirtieron ~es** they had a tremendous time*; **me duele ~es** it's frightfully painful, it hurts a lot; **ella sabe ~es** she knows a hell of a lot; **había ~es de gente** there were masses of people.

horrorizar [1f] **1** *vt* to horrify; to terrify, frighten. **2 horrorizarse** *vr* to be horrified, be aghast.

horrorosamente *adv* (**a**) horrifyingly; horribly, frightfully. (**b**) (*fig*) dreadfully, awfully.

horroroso *adj* (**a**) horrifying, terrifying; horrible, frightful. (**b**) (*fig*) ghastly*, dreadful, awful; (*feo*) hideous, ugly.

horrura *nf* filth, dirt; rubbish.

hortaliza *nf* (**a**) vegetable; **~s** vegetables, garden produce. (**b**) (*Méx*) vegetable garden.

hortelano *nm* gardener; market gardener, truck farmer

(*US*).

hortensia *nf* hydrangea.

hortera 1 *nf* wooden bowl. **2** *nm* (**a**) shop-assistant, grocer's boy (**b**) (*fig*) (*inculto*) rough type, coarse person; (*ostentoso*) flashy type; (*palurdo*) bumpkin; (*fingido*) fraud, sham. **3** *adj invar* (*ordinario*) common, vulgar; crude, tasteless; (*ostentoso*) flashy.

horterada *nf* crude thing; coarse remark; vulgarity; **ese vestido es una ~** that dress is a disgrace; **los celos son una ~** it's vulgar to be jealous.

horterez *nf* coarseness, vulgarity.

horterismo *nm* fraud, sham, pretence.

horterizar [1f] *vt* to coarsen, cheapen, make vulgar.

hortícola 1 *adj* horticultural; garden (*atr*). **2** *nmf* = **horticultor(a)**.

horticultor(a) *nm/f* horticulturist; gardener; nurseryman.

horticultura *nf* horticulture; gardening.

hortofrutícola *adj* fruit and vegetable (*atr*).

hortofruticultura *nf* fruit and vegetable growing.

hosco *adj* (**a**) (*oscuro*) dark; (*lúgubre*) gloomy. (**b**) *persona* sullen; morose; grim.

hospedador *nm* (*Bio*) host.

hospedaje *nm* lodging; (cost of) board and lodging.

hospedar [1a] **1** *vt* to put up, lodge, give a room (*etc*) to; to receive as a guest, entertain. **2 hospedarse** *vr* to stay, stop, put up, lodge (*con* with, *en* at).

hospedera *nf* hostess; innkeeper's wife.

hospedería *nf* (**a**) (*fonda*) hostelry, inn. (**b**) (*habitación*) guest room. (**c**) (*Ecl*) hospice, guest quarters.

hospedero *nm* host; innkeeper, landlord.

hospiciano, -a *nm/f*, **hospiciante** *nmf* (*LAm*) inmate of an orphanage, orphan.

hospicio *nm* poorhouse; orphanage; (*Cono Sur*) old people's home; (*Ecl*) hospice.

hospital *nm* hospital; infirmary; **~ de aislamiento, ~ de contagiosos** isolation hospital; **~ de campaña** field hospital; **~ de día** day hospital; **~ de (primera) sangre** field dressing station.

hospitalariamente *adv*: **fue atendido ~** he was treated in hospital.

hospitalario *adj* (**a**) hospitable. (**b**) (*Med*) hospital (*atr*); **estancia hospitalaria** stay in hospital.

hospitalidad *nf* hospitality.

hospitalización *nf* hospitalization.

hospitalizar [1f] **1** *vt* to send (*o* take) to hospital, hospitalize; **quedó hospitalizado durante 3 meses** he spent 3 months in hospital. **2 hospitalizarse** *vr* (*LAm*) to go into hospital.

hosquedad *nf* sullenness; moroseness; grimness.

hostal *nm* boarding house, cheap hotel.

hostelería *nf* hotel trade, hotel business; **empresa de ~** catering company.

hostelero *nm* innkeeper, landlord.

hostería *nf* inn, hostelry; (*Cono Sur*) tourist hotel.

hostia *nf* (**a**) (*Ecl*) host, consecrated wafer.

(**b**) (*) (*golpe*) punch, bash*; (*choque*) bang, bash*, smash; **liarse a ~s** to get involved in a punch-up*; **le pegaron un par de ~s** they hit him twice.

(**c**) (‡: *lo mejor*) **es la ~** she's the tops*; she's incredible; **eso no quiere decir que yo sea la ~** that doesn't mean I'm anything special.

(**d**) (‡) **¡~!, ¡~s!, ¡qué ~s!** (*sorpresa*) Christ almighty!‡; (*fastidio*) damn it all!; (*negación*) get away!, never!; not a bit of it!; (*rechazo*) balls!*‡; **¿qué ~s quieres?** what the hell do you want?; **¡qué libros ni qué ~s!** books, nothing!*

(**e**) (‡: *locuciones*) **y toda la ~** and all the rest; **ese inspector de la ~** that bloody inspector‡; **había un tráfico de la ~** the traffic was appalling; **una tormenta de la ~** a storm and a half*; **echar ~s** to shout blue murder*; to go up the wall*; **no entiendo ni ~** I don't understand a word of it; **estar de mala ~** to be in a bad mood; **hacer un par como unas ~s** to muck it all up*; **ir a toda ~** to go like the clappers*; **salió cagando ~s** he shot out like a bat out of hell; **tener mala ~** (*carácter*) to have a nasty streak; (*suerte*) to have rotten luck*; **no tiene media ~** he's no use at all.

hostiar [1b] *vt* (‡) to bash*, sock*.

hostiazo‡ *nm* bash*, sock*.

hostigamiento *nm* (*fig*) harassment.

hostigar [1h] *vt* (**a**) to lash, whip, scourge. (**b**) (*fig*) to harass, plague, pester; to bore. (**c**) (*LAm*: *comida*) to surfeit, cloy.

hostigoso *adj* (*And, Cono Sur*) *comida* sickly, cloying; *persona* annoying, tedious.

hostil *adj* hostile.

hostilidad *nf* (**a**) (*gen*) hostility. (**b**) (*acto*) hostile act; **romper las ~es** to start hostilities.

hostilizar [1f] *vt* (*Mil*) to harry, harass, worry.

hostión‡ *nm* bash*, sock*.

hotel *nm* (**a**) (*Com*) hotel. (**b**) (*casa*) detached house, suburban house, villa. (**c**) (‡: *cárcel*; *t* **~ del Estado, ~ rejas**) nick‡; (*Mil*) glasshouse‡. (**d**) **~ garaje** (*Méx*), **~ alojamiento** (*Cono Sur*) *hotel where one pays by the hour.*

hotelería *nf* (**a**) (*hoteles*) hotels (*collectively*). (**b**) (*negocio*) hotel trade. (**c**) (*gerencia*) hotel management.

hotelero 1 *adj* hotel (*atr*); **la industria hotelera** the hotel trade. **2** *nm*, **hotelera** *nf* hotelkeeper, hotel manager, hotelier.

hotelito *nm* small house, (*esp*) cottage, vacation retreat, second home.

hoy *adv* today; now, nowadays; **la juventud de ~** the youth of today; **en el correo de ~** in today's post; **~ día, ~ en día** nowadays; in this day and age; **~ por ~** at the present time, right now, as things stand (at present); **de ~ en ocho días, de ~ en una semana** today week, a week today; **de ~ en quince (días)** today fortnight, a fortnight today; **de ~ a mañana** any time now; **está para llegar de ~ a mañana** it might happen any day now; **de ~ en adelante** from now on, henceforward; **de ~ no pasa que le escriba** I'll write to him this very day; **desde ~** from now on, starting from now; **¡y hasta ~!** and I've heard no more about it!, and that was the last I heard!; **por ~** for the present.

hoya *nf* (**a**) (*agujero*) pit, hole; (*tumba*) grave; **~ de arena** bunker. (**b**) (*Geog*) wide valley, plain (among hills); (*LAm*) riverbed, river basin. (**c**) (*Agr*) seedbed.

hoyada *nf* hollow, depression.

hoyador *nm* (*And, Carib*) dibber, seed drill.

hoyanco *nm* (*Carib, Méx*: *bache*) pothole, hole in the road.

hoyar [1a] *vt* (*CAm, Carib, Méx*) to make holes (*for sowing seeds*).

hoyito *nm* (*LAm*) dimple.

hoyo *nm* (**a**) (*agujero*) hole, pit; (*hueco*) hollow, cavity; (*tumba*) grave; **irse al ~*** (*Cono Sur*) to get into an awful jam*; to face ruin; **se cree el ~ del queque*** (*Cono Sur*) he thinks he's the cat's pyjamas. (**b**) (*Golf*) hole; **en el ~ 18** at the 18th hole. (**c**) (*Med*) pockmark.

hoyuelo *nm* dimple.

hoz *nf* (**a**) (*Agr*) sickle; **~ y martillo** hammer and sickle. (**b**) (*Geog*) defile, narrow pass, gorge. (**c**) **de ~ y coz** wildly, recklessly.

hozar [1f] *vt* (*suj*: *cerdo*) to root in, root among.

hua...: *para diversas palabras escritas así en LAm, V t* **gua...**; *p.ej., para* **huaico** *V* **guaico**.

huaca *nf etc* = **guaca** *etc*.

huacalón *adj* (*Méx*: *de voz áspera*) gravel-voiced.

huacarear‡ [1a] *vi* (*LAm*) to throw up.

huaco 1 *adj* (*LAm*: *sin dientes*) toothless. **2** *nm* (*And Hist*) *ancient Peruvian pottery artefact.*

huacha *nf* (*And*) washer.

huachafería *nf* (*And*) (**a**) (*gente*) middle-class snobs, social climbers. (**b**) (*actitud*) snobbery, airs and graces.

huachafo (*And*) **1** *adj* = **cursi**. **2** *nm*, **huachafa** *nf* middle-class snob, social climber. **3** *nm* (*Carib*) funny man, comic.

huacho 1 *nm* (**a**) (*And*) section of a lottery ticket. (**b**) (*Méx**) common soldier.

2 *adj* (*Méx*) = **guacho**.

huahua *nf* (*And, Méx*) = **guagua**.

huaica *nf* (*And*) bargain sale.

huaico *nm* (*And*) alluvium.

huáncar *nm*, **huáncara** *nf* (*And*) Indian drum.

huaquero, -a *nm/f* (*And*) = **guaquero**.

huaraca *nf* (*And*) = **guaraca**.

huarache *nm* (*Méx*) = **guarache**.

huasicama *nmf* (*And*) Indian servant.

huasteca *nf*: **la H~** *the region round the Gulf of Mexico.*

huave *nmf* (*Méx*) Huave Indian.

huayco‡ *nm* (*And*) paid thug.

huayno *nm* (*And*) (*ritmo*) *traditional folk tune;* (*canción*) *traditional ballad.*

hube *etc V* **haber**.

hucha *nf* (**a**) (*arca*) chest, bin; (*alcancía*) moneybox; **~ petitoria** charity collecting box. (**b**) (*fig*: *ahorros*) savings; **tener una buena ~** to have money laid by, have a good nest-egg.

hueca‡ *nf* pansy‡, queer‡.

hueco 1 *adj* (**a**) (*gen*) hollow; (*vacío*) empty.

(**b**) (*blando*) soft, spongy.
(**c**) *sonido, voz* resonant, resounding, booming.
(**d**) *persona* conceited; *estilo* pompous, affected.
2 *nm* (**a**) (*vacío*) hollow, cavity; (*agujero*) hole; (*brecha*) gap, opening; (*espacio*) empty space; (*en formulario*) blank; (*Arquit*) recess, window space; (*de escalera*) well; (*de ascensor*) shaft; (*: *vacante*) vacancy; ~ **de la mano** hollow of the hand; **deja un ~ que será difícil llenar** he leaves a gap which it will be hard to fill.
(**b**) (*Méx*‡) queer‡, faggot‡ (*US*).

huecograbado *nm* (*Tip*) photogravure.

huelán (*Cono Sur*) *adj* (**a**) (*inmaduro*) immature, not fully developed; *madera* unseasoned; *hierba* withered; *trigo* unripe. (**b**) **una persona huelana** a person who has come down in the world.

huelebraguetas* *nm invar* private eye*.

hueleguisos* *nm invar* (*And*) sponger*, scrounger*.

huelehuele* *nmf* (*Carib*) idiot.

huelga *nf* (**a**) (*descanso*) rest, repose; (*ocio*) leisure; idleness; (*recreo*) recreation.
(**b**) (*Pol etc*) strike; stoppage, walkout; ~ **de brazos caídos** sit-down strike; ~ **de celo** work-to-rule, go-slow; ~ **general** general strike; ~ **de hambre** hunger strike; ~ **de hostigamiento** guerrilla strike; ~ **patronal** lock out; ~ **de reglamento** work-to-rule, go-slow; ~ **relámpago** lightning strike; ~ **salvaje** (*o* **descabellada**) wildcat strike; ~ **por solidaridad** sympathy strike; **los obreros en ~** the workers on strike, the striking workers; **estar en ~** to be on strike; **declarar la ~, declararse en ~, ir a la ~, ponerse en ~** to come out on strike, go on strike; to walk out.
(**c**) (*Mec*) play, free movement.

huelgo *nm* (**a**) (*aliento*) breath; **tomar ~** to take breath, pause. (**b**) (*espacio*) room, space; **entra con ~** it goes in easily, it goes in with room to spare. (**c**) (*Mec*) play, free movement.

huelguear [1a] *vi* (*And*) to strike, be on strike.

huelguismo *nm* strike mentality, readiness to strike.

huelguista *nmf* striker.

huelguístico *adj* strike (*atr*); **movimiento ~** wave of strikes; **el panorama ~** the strike scene.

Huelva *nf* Huelva.

huella *nf* (**a**) (*acto*) tread, treading.
(**b**) (*rastro*) trace, mark, sign, imprint; (*de pie*) footprint; footstep; (*de animal, coche etc*) track; ~ **dactilar,** ~ **digital** fingerprint; **sin dejar ~** without leaving a trace, leaving no sign; **seguir las ~s de uno** to follow in sb's footsteps.
(**c**) (*de escalera*) tread.

huellear [1a] *vt* (*And*) to track, follow the trail of.

huellero *adj*: **perro ~** (*And*) tracking dog.

huello *nm* condition of the ground *etc* (for walking); **camino de buen ~** good road for walking; **camino de mal ~** bad road for walking, badly-surfaced road.

huérfano 1 *adj* (**a**) orphan, orphaned; (*fig*) unprotected, defenceless, uncared-for; **una niña huérfana de madre** a motherless child, a child that has lost her mother.
(**b**) **~ de** (*fig*) bereft of, short of, without.
2 *nm*, **huérfana** *nf* orphan.

huero *adj* (**a**) *huevo* addled, rotten. (**b**) (*fig*) empty; (*estéril*) sterile; (*podrido*) rotten; dud; **un discurso ~** an empty speech. (**c**) (*CAm, Méx*) = **güero**.

huerta *nf* (**a**) vegetable garden, kitchen garden; (large) market garden, truck farm (*US*).
(**b**) (*esp Murcia, Valencia*) irrigated region, fertile irrigated area.
(**c**) (*And*: *de cacao*) cocoa plantation.

huertano 1 *adj* of the 'huerta'. **2** *nm*, **huertana** *nf* inhabitant of the 'huerta'; market gardener, farmer (of the 'huerta').

huertero, -a *nm/f* (*Cono Sur*) market gardener.

huerto *nm* (*de verduras*) kitchen garden; (*Com*) (small) market garden, truck garden (*US*); (*de frutales*) orchard; (*de casa pequeña*) back garden; **le llevaron al ~*** they put one over on him*, they led him up the garden path.

huesa *nf* grave.

huesear‡ [1a] *vi* (*LAm*) to beg.

huesecillo *nm* small bone.

hueserío *nm* (*And*) unsaleable merchandise.

huesillo *nm* (*And, Cono Sur*) sun-dried peach.

huesista* *nmf* (*Méx*) person with a soft job.

hueso *nm* (**a**) (*Anat*) bone; ~ **de la alegría** funny bone; **un ~ duro de roer** a hard nut to crack, a tough assignment; ~ **de la suerte** wishbone; **sin ~** boneless; **la sin ~*** the tongue; **darle a la sin ~*** to talk a lot; **irse de la sin ~, soltar la sin ~*** to shoot one's mouth off*; to let the cat out of the bag; **dar con sus ~s en la cárcel** to land (*o* end up) in jail; **no dejar ~ sano a uno** to pull sb to pieces; **estar en los ~s** to be nothing but skin and bone; **tener los ~s molidos** to be shattered, ache all over.
(**b**) (*Bot*) stone, pit (*US*); core.
(**c**) (*And*) unsaleable article.
(**d**) (*fig*) (*trabajo*) hard work, drudgery; (*obstáculo*) stumbling block.
(**e**) (*CAm, Méx Pol*: *sinecura*) government job, sinecure; (*puesto cómodo*) soft job.
(**f**) (*: *persona*) very strict person; **su profesor es un ~** her teacher is terribly strict.
(**g**) (*And*) mule; **ser ~** (*fig*) to be stingy.
(**h**) **~ colorado** (*Méx*) strong northerly wind.

huesoso *adj* bony; bone (*atr*).

huésped 1 *nm* (**a**) (*invitado*) guest; (*en pensión etc*) lodger, boarder, resident. (**b**) (*anfitrión*) host. (**c**) (*Hist*) innkeeper, landlord. **2** *atr*: **ordenador ~** host computer; **hembra ~** host female.

huéspeda *nf* (**a**) (*invitada*) guest; (*en pensión etc*) lodger, boarder, resident. (**b**) (*anfitriona*) hostess. (**c**) (*Hist*) innkeeper's wife; **no contar con la ~** to reckon without one's host.

hueste *nf* (**a**) (††) host, army. (**b**) (*muchedumbre*) crowd, mass; (*partidarios*) followers.

huesudo *adj* bony; big-boned, raw-boned.

hueva *nf* (**a**) (*de pez*) (hard) roe; **~s** eggs, spawn; ~ **de lisa** (*Méx*) cod roe. (**b**) **~s** (*Cono Sur***) balls**.

huevada *nf* (**a**) (*LAm*) nest of eggs, clutch of eggs; number of eggs. (**b**) (*And, Cono Sur**) (*comentario*) (piece of) nonsense; (*acto*) stupid thing (to do); (*idea*) crazy idea; **~s** (*tonterías*) nonsense, rubbish. (**c**) **~s** (**) balls**.
(**d**) (*: *como adv*) **una ~** a hell of a lot; **se divirtió una ~** he had a tremendous time*.

huevera *nf* (**a**) eggcup. (**b**) (‡: *suspensorio*) jockstrap.

huevero *adj* egg (*atr*); **industria huevera** egg industry.

huevo *nm* (**a**) egg; ~ **amelcochado** (*CAm*) (soft-)boiled egg; ~ **en cáscara** (soft-)boiled egg; ~ **a la copa** (*And, Cono Sur*) boiled egg; **~s de corral** free-range eggs; ~ **crudo** raw egg; ~ **duro** hard-boiled egg; ~ **escalfado** poached egg; ~ **a la escocesa** Scotch egg; ~ **estrellado,** ~ **frito,** ~ **al plato** fried egg; ~ **fresco** new-laid egg; ~ **de gallina de pasto libre** free-range egg; ~ **moreno** brown egg; ~ **pasado por agua,** ~ **tibio** (*And, CAm, Méx*) (soft-)boiled egg; ~ **de Pascua** Easter egg; ~ **de Paslama** (*CAm*) turtle's egg; **~s pericos** (*And*), ~ **revueltos** scrambled eggs; **andar sobre ~s** to go very gingerly; **ser como el ~ de Colón** to be simple, be easy; **¡que te frían un ~!**‡ get knotted!‡; **hacerle ~ a algo** (*CAm*‡) to face up to sth; **pensar en los ~s del gallo** (*And, CAm*) to be in a daydream; **a ~** cheap; easy; **nos lo han puesto a ~** they've made it easy for us; **lo tenemos a ~** we've got it made, we've got it taped*.
(**b**) (**) ball**, testicle; **¡un ~!** bollocks!**, no way!*; **me costó un ~** (*precio*) it cost me an arm and a leg, it cost me a bomb*; **nos costó un ~ terminarlo** it was one hell of a job to finish it; we sweated blood to finish it; **tener ~s** to have guts, be tough; *para muchas locuciones, V* **cojón**.
(**c**) **un ~*** (*como adv*): **sufrí un ~** I suffered a lot; **le queremos un ~** we like him a lot; **sabe un ~ de vinos** he knows a lot about wine.
(**d**) (*CAm*) courage, guts, toughness.
(**e**) (*LAm*) (*vago*) idler, loafer; (*imbécil*) idiot; (*cobarde*) coward.

huevón‡ (*LAm*) **1** *adj* (**a**) (*vago*) idle, lazy; (*tonto*) dim*, thick*; (*lento*) slow; (*cobarde*) chicken-livered, yellow.
(**b**) (*valiente*) brave, gutsy*.
2 *nm* (*flojera*) laziness, idleness; (*torpeza*) slowness, dullness; (*cobardía*) cowardice.
3 *nm*, **huevona** *nf* (*vago*) lazy sod**, skiver‡; (*imbécil*) idiot, berk‡.

Hugo *nm* Hugh, Hugo.

hugonote, -a *adj, nm/f* Huguenot.

hui...: *para palabras que en LAm se escriben así V t* **gui..., güi...** *p.ej.* **huinche** *V* **güinche**.

huida[1] *nf* (**a**) flight, escape; ~ **hacia adelante** relentless pursuit of the unattainable; ~ **de capitales** flight of capital. (**b**) (*de caballo*) shy(ing), bolt(ing).

huidizo *adj* (**a**) *persona etc* shy; elusive. (**b**) *impresión etc* fleeting. (**c**) *frente* receding.

huido 1 *adj* (**a**) (*que ha huido*) fugitive, on the run; **un esclavo ~** a runaway slave. (**b**) (*tímido*) very shy, easily scared. **2** *nm*, **huida**[2] *nf* fugitive.

huile *nm* (*Méx*) roasting grill.
huilón *adj* (*And*) elusive.
huincha *nf* (*Cono Sur*) = **güincha.**
huipil *nm* (*CAm, Méx*) embroidered smock.
huir [3g] **1** *vt* to run away from, flee (from), escape (from); to avoid, shun. **2** *vi y* **huirse** *vr* to run away, flee, escape; (*tiempo*) to fly; (*LAm*) to elope.
huira *nf* (*And, Cono Sur*) (*cuerda*) rope; (*cabestro*) halter, tether; **dar ~ a uno*** to thrash sb; **sacar las ~s a uno*** to beat sb up*.
huiro *nm* (*Cono Sur*) seaweed.
huisache 1 *nmf* (*CAm, Méx*: *leguleyo*) shyster lawyer. **2** *nm* (*LAm*: *árbol*) acacia.
huisachear [1a] *vi* (*CAm, Méx*) (**a**) (*litigar*) to go to law, engage in litigation. (**b**) (*: *ejercer sin título*) to practise law without a qualification.
huisachería *nf* (*CAm, Méx*) (**a**) lawyer's tricks, legal intricacies. (**b**) practice of law without a qualification.
huisachero *nm* (*CAm, Méx*) (**a**) (*leguleyo*) shyster lawyer, unqualified lawyer. (**b**) (*Méx*: *plumífero*) scribbler, penpusher.
huitlacoche *nm* (*Méx Bot*) type of edible fungus.
huizache *etc* (*Méx*) = **huisache** *etc.*
hulado *nm* (*CAm*) (*tela*) oilskin, rubberized cloth; (*capa*) oilskin.
hular *nm* (*Méx*) rubber plantation.
hule[1] *nm* (**a**) (*goma*) rubber. (**b**) (*tela*) oilskin, oilcloth. (**c**) (*CAm, Méx*: *Bot*) rubber tree. (**d**) (*Méx**: *preservativo*) condom, sheath.
hule[2] *nm* (*Taur*) goring; row; **habrá ~** there's going to be trouble.
hulear [1a] *vi* (*CAm*) to extract rubber.
hulero 1 *adj* (*CAm*) rubber (*atr*). **2** *nm*, **hulera** *nf* rubber tapper.
huloso *adj* (*CAm*) rubbery, elastic.
hulla *nf* coal, soft coal.
hullera *nf* colliery, coalmine.
hullero *adj* coal (*atr*).
humanamente *adv* (**a**) (*en términos humanos*) humanly; in human terms. (**b**) (*con humanidad*) humanely.
humanar [1a] **1** *vt* to humanize.
2 humanarse *vr* (**a**) to become more human; **~ a** + *infin* (*LAm*) to condescend to + *infin.*
(**b**) (*Rel*: *Cristo*) to become man.
humanidad *nf* (**a**) (*género humano*) humanity, mankind. (**b**) (*cualidad*) humanity, humaneness. (**c**) (*: *gordura*) corpulence. (**d**) **las ~es** the humanities.
humanismo *nm* humanism.
humanista *nmf* humanist.
humanístico *adj* humanistic.
humanitario 1 *adj* humanitarian; humane. **2** *nm*, **humanitaria** *nf* humanitarian.
humanitarismo *nm* humanitarianism.
humanización *nf* humanization.
humanizador *adj* humanizing.
humanizar [1f] **1** *vt* to humanize, make more human. **2 humanizarse** *vr* to become more human.
humano 1 *adj* (**a**) (*relativo al humano*) human. (**b**) (*benévolo*) humane. (**c**) **ciencias humanas** humane learning, humanistic learning, humanities. **2** *nm* human (being).
humanoide *adj, nmf* humanoid.
humarasca *nf* (*CAm*), **humareda** *nf* cloud of smoke.
humazo *nm* dense smoke, cloud of smoke; **dar ~ a uno** to get rid of sb.
humeante *adj* smoking, smoky; steaming.
humear [1a] **1** *vt* (**a**) (*And, Carib, Méx*: *fumigar*) to fumigate.
(**b**) (*Méx**: *golpear*) to beat, thrash.
2 *vi* (**a**) (*humo*) to smoke, give out smoke; (*vapor*) to fume, steam, give off fumes.
(**b**) (*fig*: *memoria, rencor etc*) to be still alive, linger on.
(**c**) (*fig*: *presumir*) to give o.s. airs, be conceited.
humectador *nm* humidifier; humidor.
humectante *adj* moisturizing.
humectar [1a] *vt* = **humedecer.**
húmeda* *nf*: **la ~** the tongue.
humedad *nf* humidity; damp, dampness; moisture; **a prueba de ~** damp-proof; **sentir la ~** (*And, Carib**) to have to answer for one's actions.
humedal *nm* wetland.
humedecedor *nm* humidifier.
humedecer [2d] **1** *vt* to dampen, wet, moisten; to humidify. **2 humedecerse** *vr* to get damp, get wet; **se le humedecieron los ojos** his eyes filled with tears, tears came into his eyes.
húmedo *adj* humid; damp, wet; moist.
humera *nf* (**a**) (*Carib*) cloud of smoke. (**b**) = **jumera.**
humero *nm* (**a**) chimney, smokestack; flue. (**b**) (*And*) cloud of smoke.
húmero *nm* humerus.
humidificar [1g] *vt* to wet; to dampen, moisten.
humildad *nf* (**a**) humbleness, humility; meekness. (**b**) humbleness; lowliness.
humilde *adj* (**a**) *carácter etc* humble; meek; *voz* small. (**b**) *clase etc* low, modest; lowly, lowborn, humble; **son gente ~** they are humble people, they are poor people.
humildemente *adv* humbly; meekly.
humillación *nf* humiliation; humbling.
humillante *adj* humiliating; humbling; degrading.
humillar [1a] **1** *vt* to humiliate; to humble; *cabeza* to bow, bend; *enemigos, rebeldes etc* to crush.
2 humillarse *vr* to humble o.s.; **~ a** to bow to, bow down before; to grovel to.
humita *nf* (*And, Cono Sur*) (*tamal*) tamale; (*maíz molido*) ground maize, ground corn (*US*); **~s** *snack of meat and cornflour wrapped in a leaf.*
humo *nm* (**a**) (*gen*) smoke; (*gases*) fumes; (*vapor*) vapour, steam; **a ~ de pajas** thoughtlessly, heedlessly; **ni hablaba a ~ de pajas** nor was he talking idly; **quedó en ~ de pajas** it all came to nothing; **hacer ~, echar ~** to smoke; **lo que hace ~ es porque está ardiendo, donde se hace ~ es porque hay fuego** there's no smoke without fire; **hacerse ~, irse todo en ~** to go up in smoke; (*fig*) to disappear completely, vanish without trace; **írsele al ~ a uno** (*Cono Sur, Méx**) to jump sb*; **tomar la del ~‡** to beat it*.
(**b**) **~s** (*fig*: *hogares*) homes, hearths.
(**c**) **~s** (*fig*: *presunción*) conceit, airs; **bajar los ~s a uno** to take sb down a peg; **darse ~s** to brag, swank*; **tener muchos ~s** to be terribly vain, have a big head; **tener ~s para** + *infin* to have the nerve to* + *infin*; **vender ~s** to brag, talk big*.
humor *nm* (**a**) mood, humour; temper, disposition; (*Med*) humour; **buen ~** good humour, good mood, high spirits; **estar de buen ~** to be in a good mood; **mal ~** bad mood, bad temper; **en un tono de mal ~** in an ill-tempered tone; **seguir el ~ a uno** to humour sb, go along with sb's mood.
(**b**) (*gracia*) humour; humorousness; **~ negro** black humour.
humorada *nf* (**a**) (*chiste*) joke, witticism, pleasantry. (**b**) (*capricho*) caprice, whim.
humorado *adj*: **bien ~** good-humoured, good-tempered; **mal ~** bad-tempered, cross, peevish.
humorismo *nm* humour; humorousness.
humorista *nmf* humorist.
humorísticamente *adv* humorously, facetiously.
humorístico *adj* humorous, funny, facetious.
humoso *adj* smoky.
humus *nm* humus.
hundible *adj* sinkable.
hundido *adj* sunken; *ojos* deep-set, hollow.
hundimiento *nm* (**a**) (*gen*) sinking. (**b**) (*de edificio*) collapse, fall, ruin, destruction; (*de tierra*) cave-in, subsidence.
hundir [3a] **1** *vt* (**a**) (*gen*) to sink; (*sumergir*) to submerge, engulf.
(**b**) *edificio etc* to ruin, destroy, cause the collapse of; *plan etc* to sink, ruin; (*en debate*) to confound.
2 hundirse *vr* (**a**) (*Náut*) to sink; (*en arena, lodo etc*) to sink; (*nadador etc*) to plunge, go down.
(**b**) (*edificio etc*) to collapse, tumble (down), fall (down); (*tierra*) to cave in, subside.
(**c**) (*fig*) to be destroyed, be ruined; (*persona*) to collapse, break down; to disappear, vanish; **se hundió la economía** the economy collapsed; **se hundieron los precios** prices slumped; **se hundió en el estudio de la historia** he plunged into the study of history, he became absorbed in the study of history; **se hundió en la meditación** he became lost in meditation.
húngaro, -a 1 *adj, nm/f* Hungarian. **2** *nm* (*Ling*) Hungarian.
Hungría *nf* Hungary.
huno *nm* Hun.
huracán *nm* hurricane.
huracanado *adj*: **viento ~** hurricane wind, violent wind.
huraco *nm* (*LAm*) hole.
hurañía *nf* (*timidez*) shyness; (*insociabilidad*) unsociableness; (*esquivez*) elusiveness.
huraño *adj* (*tímido*) shy; (*poco sociable*) unsociable; *animal*

shy, elusive; (*salvaje*) wild.
hure *nm* (*And*) large pot.
hureque *nm* (*And*) = **huraco**.
hurgar [1h] **1** *vt* (**a**) to poke, jab; to stir (up); *fuego* to poke, rake.
(**b**) (*LAm*) = **hurguetear**.
(**c**) (*fig*) to stir up, excite, provoke.
2 *vi*: ~ **en el bolsillo** to feel in one's pocket, rummage in one's pocket.
3 hurgarse *vr* (*t* ~ **las narices**) to pick one's nose.
hurgón *nm* (**a**) (*de fuego*) poker, fire rake. (**b**) (*con arma*) thrust, stab.
hurgonada *nf*, **hurgonazo** *nm* poke, jab; poking, raking.
hurgonear [1a] *vt fuego* to poke, rake (out); *adversario etc* to thrust at, jab (at).
hurgonero *nm* poker, fire rake.
hurguete *nm* (*Cono Sur**) busybody, nosey-parker*.
hurguetear [1a] *vt* (*LAm*: *remover*) to finger, turn over, rummage (inquisitively) among; (*fisgonear*) to shove one's nose into*, pry into.
hurí *nf* houri.
hurón 1 *adj* (**a**) shy, unsociable.
(**b**) (*Cono Sur**: *glotón*) greedy.
2 *nm* (**a**) (*Zool*) ferret.
(**b**) (*fig*) shy person, unsociable person.
(**c**) (*fig*: *pey*) busybody, nosey-parker*, snooper.
huronear [1a] *vt* (*fig*) to ferret out; to pry into, shove one's nose into*.
huronera *nf* ferret hole; (*fig*) den, lair; hiding place.
hurra *interj* hurray!, hurrah!
hurtadillas: **a** ~ *adv* stealthily, by stealth, on the sly.
hurtar [1a] **1** *vt* (**a**) (*robar*) to steal; (*Liter etc*) to plagiarize, pinch*, lift*; **con esta maniobra pretenden ~ al país las elecciones** they are trying with this manoeuvre to deprive the country of (the chance of holding) elections.
(**b**) (*mar etc*) to eat away, erode, encroach on.
(**c**) ~ **el cuerpo** to dodge, move (one's body) out of the way.
2 hurtarse *vr* (*retirarse*) to withdraw; (*irse*) to make off; (*no tomar parte*) to keep out of the way.
hurto *nm* (**a**) (*acto*) theft, robbery; (*gen*) thieving, robbery; (*Jur*) larceny; **a** ~ stealthily, by stealth, on the sly. (**b**) (*cosa robada*) thing stolen, (piece of) stolen property, loot.
húsar *nm* hussar.
husillo *nm* (**a**) (*Mec*) spindle, shaft; (*de prensa etc*) screw, worm. (**b**) (*conducto*) drain.
husma *nf* snooping*; prying; **andar a la** ~ to go snooping around*, go prying (*de* after, for).
husmear [1a] **1** *vt* (**a**) to scent, get wind of, sniff out. (**b**) (*fig*) to smell out; to nose into, pry into. **2** *vi* (*carne*) to (begin to) smell high, be smelly.
husmeo *nm* (**a**) scenting. (**b**) (*fig*) smelling-out; prying, snooping*.
husmo *nm* high smell, strong smell, gaminess; **estar al** ~ to watch one's chance.
huso *nm* (**a**) (*Tec*) spindle; bobbin; (*de torno etc*) drum. (**b**) (*Cono Sur*) kneecap. (**c**) ~ **horario** (*Geog*) time zone.
huy *interj* (*dolor*) ow!, ouch!; (*sorpresa*) well!; (*alivio*) phew!
huyente *adj frente* receding.
huyón (*LAm*) **1** *adj* (*cobarde*) cowardly; (*huraño*) shy, unsociable. **2** *nm*, **huyona** *nf* coward; shy person, unsociable person.

I

I, i [i] *nf* (*letra*) I, i; ~ **griega** Y, y.

IA *nf abr de* **inteligencia artificial** artificial intelligence, AI.

IAC *nf abr de* **ingeniería asistida por computadora** computer-assisted engineering, CAE.

-iano *V* **Aspects of Word Formation in Spanish 2.**

IAO *nf abr de* **instrucción asistida por ordenador** computer-assisted instruction, CAI.

IB *n* (*Aer*) *abr de* **Iberia, Líneas Aéreas de España, Sociedad Anónima.**

iba *etc V* **ir.**

Iberia *nf* Iberia.

ibérico *adj* Iberian; **la Península Ibérica** the Iberian Peninsula.

ibero, -a, íbero, -a *adj, nm/f* Iberian.

Iberoamérica *nf* Latin America.

iberoamericano, -a *adj, nm/f* Latin-American.

íbice *nm* ibex.

ibicenco 1 *adj* of Ibiza. **2** *nm*, **ibicenca** *nf* native (*o* inhabitant) of Ibiza; **los ~s** the people of Ibiza.

-ibilidad *V* **Aspects of Word Formation in Spanish 2.**

ibis *nf invar* ibis.

Ibiza *nf* Ibiza.

-ible *V* **Aspects of Word Formation in Spanish 2.**

ibón *nm* Pyrenean lake, tarn.

ícaro *nm* (*LAm Dep*) hang-glider.

ICE [ˈiθe] *nm* (**a**) (*Esp Escol*) *abr de* **Instituto de Ciencias de la Educación.** (**b**) (*Esp Com*) *abr de* **Instituto de Ciencias Económicas.**

iceberg *nm* [ˈiθeβer], *pl* **icebergs** [ˈiθeβer] iceberg.

ICEX [ˈiθeks] *nm abr de* **Instituto de Comercio Exterior.**

ICH *nm* (*Esp*) *abr de* **Instituto de Cultura Hispánica.**

ICI [ˈiθi] *nm* (*Esp*) *abr de* **Instituto de Cooperación Iberoamericana.**

ICO *nm* (*Esp*) *abr de* **Instituto de Crédito Oficial.**

-ico, -ica *V* **Aspects of Word Formation in Spanish 2.**

ICONA, Icona [iˈkona] *nm* (*Esp*) *abr de* **Instituto para la Conservación de la Naturaleza.**

icono *nm* ikon, icon.

iconoclasta 1 *adj* iconoclastic. **2** *nmf* iconoclast.

iconoclas(t)ia *nf* iconoclasm.

iconografía *nf* iconography.

iconográfico *adj* iconographic.

ictericia *nf* jaundice.

ictiofauna *nf* fish, fishes.

ICYT [ˈɪθit] *nm abr de* **Instituto de Información y Documentación sobre Ciencia y Tecnología.**

id[1] *nm* id.

id[2] *V* **ir.**

íd. *abr de* **ídem** ditto, do.

ida *nf* (**a**) (*partida*) going, departure; **~s y venidas** comings and goings; **en dos ~s y venidas** in an instant; **dejar las ~s por las venidas** to miss the boat; (**viaje de**) ~ outward journey, trip out; **~ y vuelta** round trip; **partido de ~** away game (in two-match contest).

(**b**) (*Caza*) track, trail.

(**c**) (*fig*) rash act; rashness, hastiness.

IDCA [ˈiðka] *nm abr de* **Instituto de Desarrollo Cooperativo en América.**

iddish [ˈidiʃ] *nm* Yiddish.

IDE *nf abr de* **Iniciativa de Defensa Estratégica** Strategic Defence Initiative, SDI.

idea *nf* (**a**) (*noción*) idea, notion; **~ faro*, ~ genial, ~ luminosa** bright idea, brilliant idea; **~ fija** fixed idea, obsession, idée fixe; **~ fuerza** key idea, central idea; **~ monstruo*** fantastic idea; **una persona de mala ~** a malicious person, an evil-minded person; **¡ni ~!** I haven't a clue!, search me!*; **meterse una ~ en la cabeza** to get an idea into one's head; **no tengo la menor ~, no tengo la más remota ~** I haven't the faintest (*o* foggiest) idea; **no tenía la menor ~ de que ...** I had no idea that ...; **tiene ~s de bombero** he's all at sea, he hasn't a clue.

(**b**) (*impresión*) idea, opinion, estimate; **¿qué ~ tienes de él?** what impression do you have of him?; **darse una ~ de, hacerse una ~ de** to get an idea of, form an impression of.

(**c**) (*propósito*) idea, intention; **con la ~ de** + *infin* with the idea of + *ger*; **cambiar de ~, mudar de ~** to change one's mind; **hace falta que cambie de ~** he'll have to alter his outlook; he'll have to buck his ideas up*; **llevar ~ de** + *infin* to have the idea of + *ger*, intend to + *infin*.

(**d**) (*inventiva*) ingenuity, inventiveness.

ideación *nf* conception, thinking-out.

ideal *adj, nm* ideal.

idealismo *nm* idealism.

idealista 1 *adj* idealistic. **2** *nmf* idealist.

idealización *nf* idealization.

idealizar [1f] *vt* to idealize.

idealmente *adv* ideally.

idear [1a] *vt* to think up; to contrive, invent, devise; to plan, design.

ideario *nm* set of ideas; ideology; ideological formation.

ideático *adj* (**a**) (*LAm*: *excéntrico*) eccentric, odd. (**b**) (*CAm*: *inventivo*) ingenious, full of ideas.

IDEM [ˈiðem] *nm* (*Esp*) *abr de* **Instituto de los Derechos de la Mujer.**

ídem 1 *pron* ditto, the same, idem. **2** *nm*: **ser un ~ de lienzo** to be another of the same sort, be tarred with the same brush; **y ella, ~ de lienzo** and she (did) the same.

idénticamente *adv* identically.

idéntico *adj* identical; the same, the very same.

identidad *nf* identity; sameness, similarity; **~ corporativa** corporate identity.

identificable *adj* identifiable.

identificación *nf* identification; **~ errónea** mistaken identity.

identificador 1 *adj* identifying. **2** *nm* identifier.

identificar [1g] **1** *vt* to identify; to recognize, spot, pick out; **víctima sin ~** unidentified victim. **2 identificarse** *vr*: **~ con** to identify (o.s.) with.

identificatorio *adj* identifying.

ideograma *nm* ideogram.

ideología *nf* ideology.

ideológicamente *adv* ideologically.

ideológico *adj* ideological.

ideólogo, -a *nm/f* ideologue, ideologist.

ideoso *adj* (*Méx*) (*maniático*) obsessive; (*caprichoso*) wilful.

idílico *adj* idyllic.

idilio *nm* idyll; (*amor*) romance, love-affair.

idiolecto *nm* idiolect.

idioma *nm* language; **los ~s de trabajo de la CE** the working languages of the European Community.

idiomático *adj* language (*atr*), linguistic; idiomatic.

idiosincrasia *nf* idiosyncrasy.

idiosincrásico *adj* idiosyncratic.

idiota 1 *adj* idiotic, stupid. **2** *nmf* idiot; **¡~!** you idiot!

idiotez *nf* idiocy; **hablar idioteces** to talk rubbish.

idiotismo *nm* (**a**) (*Ling*) idiom, idiomatic expression. (**b**) (*ignorancia*) ignorance.

idiotizar [1f] *vt* (**a**) to reduce to a state of idiocy, make an idiot of; (*fig*) to stupefy. (**b**) **~ a uno** (*LAm**) to drive sb crazy.

IDO [ˈiðo] *nm* (*Esp*) *abr de* **Instituto de Denominaciones de Origen.**

ido 1 *adj* (**a**) (*LAm**: *despistado*) absent-minded.

(**b**) (*LAm**: *chiflado*) crazy; **estar ~** (**de la cabeza**) to be crazy.

(**c**) **estar ~** (*CAm, Méx**) to be drunk.

2 *nmpl*: **los ~s** the dead, the departed.
idólatra 1 *adj* idolatrous. **2** *nmf* idolater, idolatress.
idolatrar [1a] *vt* to worship, adore; (*fig*) to idolize.
idolatría *nf* idolatry.
idolátrico *adj* idolatrous.
ídolo *nm* idol.
idoneidad *nf* suitability, fitness; (*capacidad*) aptitude, ability.
idoneizar [1f] *vt* to make suitable.
idóneo *adj* (*apropiado*) suitable, fit, fitting; (*Méx: genuino*) genuine.
idus *nmpl* ides.
IEE *nm* (**a**) (*Admin*) *abr de* **Instituto Español de Emigración.** (**b**) (*Esp Com*) *abr de* **Instituto de Estudios Económicos.**
IEI *nm* (*Esp*) *abr de* **Instituto de Educación e Investigación.**
IEM *nm* (*Esp*) *abr de* **Instituto de Enseñanza Media.**
iglesia *nf* church; **I~ Anglicana** Church of England, Anglican Church; **~ catedral** cathedral; **I~ Católica** Catholic Church; **~ colegial** collegiate church; **~ parroquial** parish church; **casarse por la ~** to get married in church, have a church wedding; **casarse por detrás de la ~** to set up house together; **cumplir con la ~** to fulfil one's religious obligations; **llevar a una a la ~** to lead sb to the altar; **¡con la ~ hemos topado!** now we're really up against it!
iglesiero* *adj* (*LAm*) churchy*, church-going.
iglú *nm* igloo.
IGN *nm* (*Esp, Honduras*) *abr de* **Instituto Geográfico Nacional.**
Ignacio *nm* Ignatius.
ignaro *adj* ignorant.
ígneo *adj* igneous.
ignición *nf* ignition.
ignífugo *adj* fireproof, fire-resistant.
igniscible *adj* flammable, easy to ignite.
ignominia *nf* (**a**) (*gen*) ignominy, shame, disgrace. (**b**) (*acto*) disgraceful act.
ignominiosamente *adv* ignominiously, shamefully.
ignominioso *adj* ignominious, shameful, disgraceful.
ignorado *adj* unknown; obscure, little-known.
ignorancia *nf* ignorance; **por ~** through ignorance.
ignorante 1 *adj* ignorant; uninformed. **2** *nmf* ignoramus.
ignorar [1a] *vt* (**a**) (*desconocer*) not to know, be ignorant of, be unaware of; **lo ignoro en absoluto** (*o* **por completo**) I don't know at all, I've no idea; **ignoramos su paradero** we don't know his whereabouts; **no ignoro que** ... I am fully aware that ..., of course I know that ...
(**b**) (*no hacer caso a*) to ignore.
ignoto *adj* unknown; undiscovered.
igual 1 *adj* (**a**) (*gen*) equal (*a* to); (the) same; (*semejante*) alike, similar; **no vi nunca cosa ~** I never saw the like; **1 kilómetro es ~ a 1.000 metros** a kilometre is equal to 1,000 metres, a kilometre equals 1,000 metres; **A es ~ a B** A is like B, A is the same as B; **es ~** it makes no difference, it's all the same; **me es ~** it's all the same to me, I don't mind.
(**b**) (*llano*) even, level; (*constante*) uniform, constant, unvarying, unchanging; (*liso*) smooth; *temperatura* even; *clima* equable; **ir ~es** (*en carrera*) to be level, be even.
(**c**) **~ que** (*como prep*) like, the same as; **A, ~ que B, no sabe** A, like B, doesn't know.
(**d**) **al ~ que** (*como prep o conj*) like, just like; while, whereas; **Chile, al ~ que Argentina, estima que** ... Chile, (just) like Argentina, thinks that ...
2 *adv* (**a**) **~ no sabe*** he may not know, maybe he doesn't know.
(**b**) (*LAm*) all the same, in spite of everything.
3 *nmf* equal; **al ~, por ~** equally, on an equal basis; **sin ~** without equal, matchless; **ser el ~ de** to be the equal of, be a match for; **no tener ~** to be unrivalled, have no equal; **alternar de ~ a ~** to be on an equal footing; **tratar a uno de ~ a ~** to treat sb as an equal.
4 *nm* (**a**) (*Mat*) equals sign, sign of equality.
(**b**) **~es** (*Guardia Civil*‡) Civil Guard.
iguala *nf* (**a**) equalization. (**b**) (*Com*) agreement; agreed fee.
igualación *nf* equalization; evening up, levelling; (*Mat*) equating.
igualada *nf* (*Dep: tanto*) equalizer, equalizing goal (*etc*); (*igualdad de puntos*) level score.
igualado *adj* (*CAm, Méx*) (*irrespetuoso*) cheeky; (*astuto*) sly.
igualar [1a] **1** *vt* (**a**) (*hacer igual*) to equalize, make equal; (*Mat*) to equate (*a* to); (*fig*) to compare, match (*a* with).
(**b**) (*allanar*) to level, level off, level up; to even, even out; (*alisar*) to smooth; (*fig*) to even out, adjust.
(**c**) (*Com*) to agree upon.
2 *vi e* **igualarse** *vr* (**a**) to be equal; **~ a, ~ con** to equal, be equal to, be the equal of.
(**b**) (*Dep*) to equalize, score the equalizer; to tie.
(**c**) (*Com*) to come to an agreement.
(**d**) (*CAm, Méx**) to be too familiar, be cheeky*.
igualatorio *nm* (*Med*) insurance group.
igualdad *nf* (**a**) (*gen*) equality; (*semejanza*) sameness; (*Mat*) equality; **~ de oportunidades** equality of opportunity; **~ de retribución** equal pay; **en ~ de condiciones** on the same conditions, on an equal basis, on a level footing.
(**b**) (*de superficie etc*) evenness, levelness; uniformity; smoothness; **~ de ánimo** equanimity.
igualitario *adj* egalitarian.
igualitarismo *nm* egalitarianism.
igualito *adj* (*diminutivo de* **igual**) (*esp LAm*) exactly the same, identical; **los dos están ~s** they're the spitting image of each other.
igualización *nf* equalization.
igualmente *adv* (**a**) (*gen*) equally. (**b**) (*de modo uniforme*) evenly; uniformly. (**c**) (*también*) likewise, also. (**d**) (*respuesta a saludo etc*) the same to you.
iguana *nf* iguana.
IHS *abr de* **Jesús** Jesus, IHS.
III *nm* (*Méx*) *abr de* **Instituto Indigenista Interamericano.**
ijada *nf* (**a**) (*Anat*) flank, side, loin. (**b**) (*Med: dolor*) stitch, pain in the side; **esto tiene su ~** this has its weak side.
ijadear [1a] *vi* (*Zool*) to pant.
ijar *nm* flank, side.
ikastola *nf* Basque language school.
ikurriña *nf* Basque national flag.
-il *V* **Aspects of Word Formation in Spanish 2.**
ilación *nf* inference; connection, relationship.
ILARI [i'lari] *nm abr de* **Instituto Latinoamericano de Relaciones Internacionales.**
ilativo *adj* inferential; (*Ling*) illative.
ilegal *adj* illegal, unlawful.
ilegalidad *nf* illegality, unlawfulness.
ilegalización *nf* outlawing, banning.
ilegalizar [1f] *vt* to outlaw, declare illegal, ban.
ilegalmente *adv* illegally, unlawfully.
ilegible *adj* illegible, unreadable.
ilegítimamente *adv* illegitimately.
ilegitimar [1a] *vt* to make illegal.
ilegitimidad *nf* illegitimacy.
ilegítimo *adj* (**a**) (*gen*) illegitimate; (*ilegal*) unlawful. (**b**) (*falso*) false, spurious.
ilerdense 1 *adj* of Lérida. **2** *nmf* native (*o* inhabitant) of Lérida; **los ~s** the people of Lérida.
ileso *adj* unhurt, unharmed; untouched; **salió ~ del accidente** he came out of the accident unharmed, he got out of the accident unscathed; **los pasajeros resultaron ~s** the passengers were unhurt.
iletrado *adj* uncultured, illiterate.
Ilíada *nf* Iliad.
iliberal *adj* illiberal.
ilícitamente *adv* illicitly, illegally, unlawfully.
ilicitano 1 *adj* of Elche. **2** *nm,* **ilicitana** *nf* native (*o* inhabitant) of Elche; **los ~s** the people of Elche.
ilícito *adj* illicit, illegal, unlawful.
ilimitado *adj* unlimited, limitless, unbounded.
iliterato *adj* illiterate.
Ilma., Ilmo. *abr de* **Ilustrísima, Ilustrísimo** (*courtesy title*).
ilocalizable *adj* that cannot be found; unavailable; **ayer X seguía ~** X could still not be found yesterday; X was still unavailable yesterday.
ilógicamente *adv* illogically.
ilógico *adj* illogical.
ILPES ['ilpes] *nm abr de* **Instituto Latinoamericano de Planificación Económica y Social.**
ilu* *nf* = **ilusión**; **¡qué ~!** how thrilling!, how exciting!
iluminación *nf* (**a**) (*gen*) illumination, lighting; floodlighting; **~ indirecta** indirect lighting. (**b**) (*fig*) enlightenment.
iluminado 1 *adj* (**a**) illuminated, lighted, lit; (*fig*) enlightened.
(**b**) **estar ~**‡ (*borracho*) to be lit up‡; (*drogado*) to be high (on drugs)‡.
2 *nm,* **iluminada** *nf* visionary; illuminist; **los I~s** the Illuminati.
iluminador 1 *adj* illuminating. **2** *nm,* **iluminadora** *nf* illuminator.
iluminar [1a] *vt* (**a**) (*alumbrar*) to illuminate, light, light up; *edificio etc* to floodlight. (**b**) (*fig*) to enlighten.
iluminista *nmf* (*Cine, TV*) electrician, lighting engineer.

ilusión *nf* (**a**) (*noción falsa*) illusion; delusion; ~ **óptica** optical illusion; **todo es** ~ it's all an illusion.

(**b**) (*esperanza, sueño*) (unfounded) hope, dream; piece of wishful thinking; hopefulness; **con** ~ hopefully; **el hombre de sus ilusiones** the man of her dreams; **su** ~ **era comprarlo** her dream was to buy it, she dreamed of buying it; **forjarse ilusiones, hacerse ilusiones** to build up (false) hopes, deceive o.s. with false hopes, indulge in wishful thinking; **no te hagas ilusiones** don't get any false ideas, don't kid yourself*; **se hace la** ~ **de que** ... she fondly imagines that ...; **no me hago muchas ilusiones de que** ... I am not very hopeful that ...; **poner su** ~ **en algo** to pin one's hopes on sth; **tendió la mano con** ~ she put her hand out hopefully.

(**c**) (*emoción*) excitement, thrill; (*entusiasmo*) eagerness; (*expectación*) hopeful anticipation; **¡qué** ~**!** how thrilling!, how exciting!; **comer con** ~ to eat eagerly; **trabajar con** ~ to work with a will; **el viaje me hace mucha** ~ I am so looking forward to the trip, I am getting very excited about the trip; **tu carta me hizo mucha** ~ I was thrilled to get your letter; **me hace una gran** ~ **que** ... it gives me a thrill that ...; **tener** ~ **por** to look forward to.

ilusionadamente *adv* with high hopes; excitedly.

ilusionado 1 *adj* hopeful; excited, eager; **el viaje me trae muy** ~ I am so looking forward to the trip, I am getting very excited about the trip. **2** *nm*, **ilusionada** *nf* hopeful; **joven** ~ young hopeful.

ilusionante *adj* exciting.

ilusionar [1a] **1** *vt* (*: *engañar*) to deceive; (*alentar*) to give false hopes to, encourage falsely.

2 ilusionarse *vr* to have unfounded hopes, indulge in wishful thinking; **no te ilusiones** don't get any false ideas.

ilusionismo *nm* conjuring, illusionism.

ilusionista *nmf* conjurer, illusionist.

iluso 1 *adj* easily deceived; deluded. **2** *nm*, **ilusa** *nf* dreamer, visionary; **¡**~**!** you're hopeful!

ilusorio *adj* illusory, deceptive, unreal; empty, ineffectual.

ilustración *nf* (**a**) (*gen*) illustration. (**b**) (*Tip*) illustration, picture, drawing. (**c**) (*erudición*) learning, erudition; enlightenment; **la I**~ the Enlightenment, the Age of Enlightenment.

ilustrado *adj* (**a**) illustrated. (**b**) learned, erudite; enlightened.

ilustrador 1 *adj* illustrative; enlightening. **2** *nm*, **ilustradora** *nf* illustrator.

ilustrar [1a] **1** *vt* (**a**) (*gen*) to illustrate.

(**b**) (*aclarar*) to explain, elucidate, make clear.

(**c**) (*instruir*) to instruct, enlighten.

(**d**) (*hacer famoso*) to make famous, make illustrious.

2 ilustrarse *vr* (**a**) (*instruirse*) to acquire knowledge, become enlightened.

(**b**) (*hacerse famoso*) to become famous.

ilustrativo *adj* illustrative.

ilustre *adj* illustrious, famous.

ilustrísimo *adj* most illustrious; **Su Ilustrísima** His Grace; His Lordship; **Vuestra Ilustrísima** Your Grace; Your Lordship.

illanco *nm* (*And*) slow stream, quiet-flowing stream.

-illo, -illa *V* **Aspects of Word Formation in Spanish 2.**

IM *nm abr de* **Instituto de la Mujer.**

IMAC [ɪ'mak] *nm abr de* **Instituto de Mediación, Arbitraje y Conciliación** ≃ Advisory, Conciliation and Arbitration Service, ACAS.

imagen *nf* (**a**) (*gen*) image; (*idea*) (mental) picture; (*semejanza*) likeness; ~ **de marca** brand image; ~ **pública** public image, public face; **cultivar la** ~ to cultivate one's image; **ser la viva** ~ **de** to be the living image of; **hacer a uno a su** ~ to make sb in one's own image.

(**b**) (*Ecl*) image, statue; **quedar para vestir imágenes** to be an old maid.

(**c**) (*Prensa, TV*) picture; ~ **fantasma** ghost image; ~ **fija** still (picture).

(**d**) (*Liter*) image; **imágenes** (*en conjunto*) imagery.

imaginable *adj* imaginable, conceivable.

imaginación *nf* imagination; fancy; **ni por** ~ on no account; **no se me pasó por la** ~ **que** ... it never even occurred to me that ...; **ella se deja llevar por la** ~ she lets her imagination run away with her.

imaginar [1a] **1** *vt* (*gen*) to imagine; (*visualizar*) to visualize; (*idear*) to think up, invent; **cosas que nadie imagina** things that no-one imagines; **¿quién imaginó esto?** who thought this one up?

2 *vi e* **imaginarse** *vr* to imagine, fancy, suppose; to picture (to o.s.); **¡imagínate!** just imagine!, just fancy!; **imagínese que** ... suppose that ..., imagine that ...; **me imagino que** ... I suppose that ...; **me imagino que sí** I suppose so; **sí, me imagino** yes, I can imagine.

imaginaria *nf* (*Mil*) reserve guard, night guard.

imaginario *adj* imaginary.

imaginativa *nf* imagination, imaginativeness.

imaginativo *adj* imaginative.

imaginería *nf* (**a**) (*Ecl*) images, statues. (**b**) (*Liter*) imagery.

imaginero, -a *nm/f* maker (*o* painter) of religious images.

imam *nm*, **imán**[1] *nm* (*Rel*) imam.

imán[2] *nm* (*Téc*) magnet (*t fig*); ~ **de herradura** horseshoe magnet.

iman(t)ación *nf* magnetization.

iman(t)ar [1a] *vt* to magnetize.

imbatibilidad *nf* unbeatable character; (*Dep*) unbeaten record.

imbatible *adj* unbeatable.

imbatido *adj* unbeaten.

imbebible *adj* undrinkable.

imbécil 1 *adj* (**a**) (*Med*) imbecile, feeble-minded. (**b**) (*fig*) silly, stupid. **2** *nmf* (**a**) (*Med*) imbecile. (**b**) (*fig*) imbecile, idiot; **¡**~**!** you idiot!

imbecilidad *nf* (**a**) (*Med*) imbecility, feeble-mindedness. (**b**) (*fig*) silliness, stupidity, idiocy; **decir** ~**es** to say silly things.

imbecilizar [1f] *vt* to reduce to a state of idiocy; (*fig*) to stupefy.

imberbe *adj* beardless.

imbíbito *adj* (*CAm, Méx*) included (in the bill).

imbombera *nf* (*Carib*) pernicious anaemia.

imbombo *adj* (*Carib*) anaemic.

imbornal *nm* scupper; **irse por los** ~**es** (*LAm**) to go off at a tangent.

imborrable *adj* ineffaceable, indelible; *recuerdo etc* unforgettable.

imbricación *nf* overlapping; interweaving, interdependence.

imbricado *adj* (*LAm*) (*sobrepuesto*) overlapping; *asunto etc* involved.

imbricar [1g] **1** *vt* to overlap; to interweave; ~ **a uno*** to involve sb. **2 imbricarse** *vr* to overlap; to be interwoven.

imbuir [3g] *vt* to imbue, infuse (*de, en* with); **imbuido de la cultura de** imbued with the culture of, full of the culture of.

imbunchar [1a] *vt* (*Cono Sur*) (**a**) (*hechizar*) to bewitch. (**b**) (*estafar*) to swindle, cheat.

imbunche *nm* (*Cono Sur*) (**a**) (*hechizo*) spell, piece of witchcraft; (*brujo*) sorcerer, wizard. (**b**) (*confusión*) mess; (*lío*) fuss, row.

IMCE ['imse] *nm abr de* **Instituto Mejicano de Comercio Exterior.**

IMEC [ɪ'mek] *nf abr de* **Instrucción Militar de la Escala de Complemento.**

imitable *adj* imitable; to be imitated, worthy of imitation.

imitación *nf* (**a**) (*gen*) imitation; (*parodia*) mimicry; **a** ~ **de** in imitation of; **desconfíe de las imitaciones** beware of imitations.

(**b**) **de** ~ imitation (*atr*); **joyas de** ~ imitation jewellery.

(**c**) (*Teat*) imitation, impersonation.

imitador 1 *adj* imitative. **2** *nm*, **imitadora** *nf* imitator; follower; (*Teat*) imitator, impersonator; impressionist.

imitar [1a] *vt* (**a**) (*gen*) to imitate; (*parodiar*) to mimic, ape; (*copiar*) to follow. (**b**) (*falsificar*) to counterfeit.

imitativo *adj* imitative.

impaciencia *nf* impatience.

impacientar [1a] **1** *vt* to make impatient; to irritate, exasperate.

2 impacientarse *vr* to get impatient (*ante, por* about, at; *con* with), lose patience, get worked up; to fret; ~ **por** + *infin* to be impatient to + *infin*.

impaciente *adj* impatient; anxious; fretful; ~ **por empezar** impatient to start, keen to get going; **¡estoy** ~**!** I can't wait! (*por* + *infin* to + *infin*).

impacientemente *adv* impatiently; anxiously; fretfully.

impactante *adj* (*impresionante*) striking, impressive; (*contundente*) shattering; (*abrumador*) crushing, overwhelming.

impactar [1a] **1** *vt* (*impresionar*) to impress, have an impact on; (*gustar*) to please, delight, be a hit with. **2** *vi* to hit, strike; ~ **en** to affect, have an effect on, influence.

3 impactarse *vr*: ~ **ante,** ~ **por** to be overawed by.

impacto *nm* (**a**) impact; (*repercusión*) incidence; (*Mil*) hit; (*LAm Boxeo*) punch, blow; ~ **directo** direct hit; ~ **político**

political impact. (**b**) (*esp LAm: fig*) impression; shock.
impagable *adj* unpayable; (*fig*) priceless, inestimable.
impagado *adj* unpaid, still to be paid.
impagador(a) *nm/f* defaulter, non-payer.
impago (*LAm*) **1** *adj* unpaid, still to be paid. **2** *nm* non-payment, failure to pay.
impajaritable *adj* (*Cono Sur*) necessary, imperative.
impalpable *adj* impalpable.
impar 1 *adj* (**a**) (*Mat*) odd; **los números ~es** the odd numbers. (**b**) (*fig*) unique, exceptional. **2** *nm* odd number.
imparable *adj* (*Dep*) unstoppable.
imparablemente *adv* unstoppably.
imparcial *adj* impartial, unbiassed, fair.
imparcialidad *nf* impartiality, lack of bias, fairness.
imparcialmente *adv* impartially, fairly.
impartible *adj* indivisible, that cannot be shared out.
impartición *nf* teaching.
impartir [3a] *vt instrucción etc* to impart, give, convey; *orden* to give.
impase [im'pas] *nm o nf* (**a**) (*atascamiento*) impasse. (**b**) (*Bridge*) finesse; **hacer el ~ a uno** to finesse against sb.
impasible *adj* impassive, unmoved.
impávidamente *adv* (*V adj*) (**a**) intrepidly; dauntlessly. (**b**) (*LAm*) cheekily.
impavidez *nf* (*V adj*) (**a**) intrepidity; dauntlessness. (**b**) (*LAm*) cheek, cheekiness.
impávido *adj* (**a**) (*valiente*) intrepid; (*impasible*) dauntless, undaunted. (**b**) (*LAm: insolente*) cheeky.
IMPE ['impe] *nm* (*Esp*) *abr de* **Instituto de la Mediana y Pequeña Empresa.**
impecable *adj* impeccable, faultless.
impecablemente *adv* impeccably, faultlessly.
impedido 1 *adj* crippled, disabled, handicapped; **estar ~ para algo** to be unfit for sth. **2** *nm*, **impedida** *nf* cripple, handicapped person.
impedimenta *nf* (*Mil*) impedimenta (*pl*).
impedimento *nm* (**a**) (*obstáculo*) impediment (*t Jur*), obstacle, hindrance. (**b**) (*Med*) disability, handicap; **~ del habla** speech impediment.
impedir [3k] *vt* (**a**) (*dificultar*) to impede, obstruct, hinder, hamper; (*disuadir*) to deter; **~ el tráfico** to block the traffic, obstruct the traffic.
(**b**) (*prohibir*) to stop, prevent; (*frustrar*) to thwart; **~ algo a uno** to keep sb from doing sth, to make sth impossible for sb; **~ a uno hacer algo, ~ que uno haga algo** to stop sb doing sth, prevent sb (from) doing sth; **me veo impedido para ayudar** I find it impossible for me to help; **esto no impide que ...** this does not alter the fact that ...; **lo que no se puede ~** what cannot be prevented.
impeditivo *adj* preventive.
impeler [2a] *vt* (**a**) (*Mec*) to drive, propel. (**b**) (*fig*) to drive, impel; to urge; **~ a uno a hacer algo** to drive sb to do sth; to urge sb to do sth; **impelido por la necesidad** impelled by necessity.
impenetrabilidad *nf* impenetrability.
impenetrable *adj* impenetrable (*t fig*); impervious; (*fig*) obscure, incomprehensible.
impenitencia *nf* impenitence.
impenitente *adj* impenitent, unrepentant.
impensable *adj* unthinkable.
impensadamente *adv* (**a**) unexpectedly. (**b**) at random, by chance. (**c**) (*sin querer*) inadvertently; unintentionally.
impensado *adj* (**a**) (*imprevisto*) unexpected, unforeseen. (**b**) (*casual*) random, chance (*atr*).
impepinable* *adj* certain, inevitable, undeniable.
impepinablemente* *adv* inevitably; **~ se le olvida** he's sure to forget, he always forgets.
imperante *adj* ruling (*t Com*), prevailing.
imperar [1a] *vi* (**a**) (*reinar*) to rule, reign; (*mandar*) to be in command. (**b**) (*fig*) (*prevalecer*) to reign, prevail; (*precio etc*) to be in force, be current.
imperativamente *adv* (**a**) imperatively. (**b**) *decir etc* imperiously, in a commanding tone.
imperatividad *nf* imperative nature; compulsory character.
imperativo 1 *adj* (**a**) (*gen*) imperative (*t Ling*). (**b**) *tono etc* imperious, commanding. **2** *nm* (**a**) (*necesidad etc*) imperative; need; essential task; **~ categórico** moral imperative. (**b**) (*Ling*) imperative (mood).
imperceptibilidad *nf* imperceptibility.
imperceptible *adj* imperceptible, undiscernible.
imperceptiblemente *adv* imperceptibly.
imperdible *nm* safety pin.
imperdonable *adj* unpardonable, unforgivable, inexcusable.
imperdonablemente *adv* unpardonably, inexcusably.
imperecedero *adj* imperishable, undying; (*fig*) immortal.
imperfección *nf* imperfection; flaw, fault, blemish.
imperfeccionar *vt* (*Cono Sur*) to spoil.
imperfectamente *adv* imperfectly.
imperfecto 1 *adj* (**a**) *objeto etc* imperfect, faulty. (**b**) *tarea* unfinished, incomplete. (**c**) (*Ling*) imperfect. **2** *nm* (*Ling*) imperfect (tense).
imperial 1 *adj* imperial. **2** *nf* (*de autobús*) top, upper deck.
imperialismo *nm* imperialism.
imperialista 1 *adj* imperialist(ic). **2** *nmf* imperialist.
imperialmente *adv* imperially.
impericia *nf* unskilfulness; lack of experience, inexperience; **a prueba de ~** foolproof.
imperio *nm* (**a**) empire; **I~ Español** Spanish Empire; **vale un ~, vale siete ~s** it's worth a fortune. (**b**) (*autoridad*) rule, authority; sway; **el ~ de la ley** the rule of law. (**c**) (*fig*) haughtiness, pride.
imperiosamente *adv* (*V adj*) (**a**) imperiously. (**b**) urgently; imperatively, overridingly.
imperiosidad *nf* pressing necessity, overriding need.
imperioso *adj* (**a**) *porte, tono etc* imperious; lordly. (**b**) (*urgente*) urgent; imperative, overriding; **necesidad imperiosa** absolute necessity, pressing need.
imperito *adj* (*inhábil*) inexpert, unskilled; (*inexperto*) inexperienced; (*torpe*) clumsy.
impermanente *adv* impermanent.
impermeabilidad *nf* impermeability, imperviousness.
impermeabilización *nf* waterproofing; (*Aut*) undersealing.
impermeabilizar [1f] *vt* to waterproof, make waterproof; (*Aut*) to underseal; *frontera etc* to seal off.
impermeable 1 *adj* impermeable, impervious (*a* to); waterproof. **2** *nm* (**a**) (*prenda de vestir*) raincoat, mackintosh, mac. (**b**) (*‡: preservativo*) French letter.
impersonal *adj* impersonal.
impersonalidad *nf* impersonality.
impersonalismo *nm* impersonality; (*LAm*) disinterestedness.
impersonalmente *adv* impersonally.
impertérrito *adj* unafraid, unshaken, undaunted, fearless.
impertinencia *nf* (**a**) (*irrelevancia*) irrelevance. (**b**) (*insistencia*) fussiness; peevishness. (**c**) (*insolencia*) impertinence; intrusion.
impertinente 1 *adj* (**a**) (*irrelevante*) irrelevant, not pertinent; (*fuera de lugar*) uncalled for. (**b**) (*quisquilloso*) touchy, fussy; (*malhumorado*) peevish. (**c**) (*insolente*) impertinent; (*intruso*) intrusive. **2 ~s** *nmpl* lorgnette.
impertinentemente *adv* (*V adj* (**a**), (**c**)) (**a**) irrelevantly. (**b**) impertinently.
imperturbable *adj* imperturbable; (*sereno*) unruffled, unflappable; (*impasible*) impassive.
imperturbablemente *adv* imperturbably; impassively.
imperturbado *adj* unperturbed.
impétigo *nm* impetigo.
impetrar [1a] *vt* (**a**) (*rogar*) to beg for, beseech. (**b**) (*obtener*) to obtain, win.
ímpetu *nm* (**a**) (*gen*) impetus, impulse; (*Mec*) momentum. (**b**) (*acometida*) rush, onrush. (**c**) (*prisa*) haste; (*violencia*) violence; (*impetuosidad*) impetuosity.
impetuosamente *adv* impetuously, impulsively; violently; hastily.
impetuosidad *nf* impetuousness, impulsiveness; violence; haste, hastiness.
impetuoso *adj persona* impetuous, impulsive; headstrong; *torrente etc* rushing, violent; *acto* hasty, impetuous.
impiadoso *adj* (*LAm*) impious.
impiedad *nf* impiety, ungodliness.
impío *adj* impious, ungodly.
implacable *adj* implacable, relentless, inexorable.
implacablemente *adv* implacably, relentlessly, inexorably.
implantable *adj* that can be implanted.
implantación *nf* implantation; introduction.
implantar [1a] *vt* to implant; *costumbre etc* to introduce.
implante *nm* implant.
implementar [1a] (*LAm*) **1** *vt* to implement. **2** *vi* to help, give aid.
implemento *nm* (*LAm*) means; tool, implement; (*Agr: esp LAm*) implement.
implicación *nf* (**a**) (*contradicción*) contradiction (in terms). (**b**) (*complicidad*) involvement, implication, complicity. (**c**) (*significado*) implication.
implicancia *nf* (*LAm*) implication.

implicar [1g] *vt* (**a**) (*involucrar*) to implicate, involve; **las partes implicadas** the parties concerned. (**b**) (*significar*) to imply; **esto no implica que** ... this does not imply that ..., this does not mean that ...
implícitamente *adv* implicitly.
implícito *adj* implicit, implied.
imploración *nf* supplication, entreaty.
implorar [1a] *vt* to implore, beg, beseech.
implosionar [1a] *vi* to implode.
implotar [1a] *vi* to implode.
implume *adj* featherless; unfledged.
impolítico *adj* (**a**) (*imprudente*) impolitic, imprudent, tactless, undiplomatic. (**b**) (*descortés*) impolite.
impoluto *adj* unpolluted, pure.
imponderable 1 *adj* imponderable; (*fig*) priceless. **2 ~s** *nmpl* imponderables.
imponencia *nf* (*LAm*) imposing character, impressiveness; stateliness, grandness.
imponente 1 *adj* (**a**) imposing, impressive; stately, grand. (**b**) (*) terrific*, tremendous*, smashing*. **2** *nmf* (*Fin*) depositor.
imponer [2q] **1** *vt* (**a**) (*gen*) to impose; (*Tip*) to impose; *obligación, pena, silencio etc* to impose (*a* on); *carga* to lay, thrust (*a* upon); *tarea* to set; *impuesto* to put, impose (*a, sobre* on); (*Ecl*) *manos* to lay.
(**b**) *obediencia etc* to exact (*a* from), demand (*a* from), respeto (*a* upon); *respeto* to command (*a* from); *miedo etc* to inspire (*a* in).
(**c**) (*achacar*) to impute falsely (*a* to).
(**d**) (*instruir*) to inform, instruct (*en* in).
(**e**) (*Fin*) deposit.
2 imponerse *vr* (**a**) **~ un deber** to assume a duty, take on a duty.
(**b**) (*hacerse obedecer*) to assert o.s., get one's way; **~ a** to dominate, impose one's authority on, exact obedience from.
(**c**) (*prevalecer*) to prevail (*a* over); (*costumbre*) to grow up; **~ a** (*Dep*) to get the better of; **se impondrá el buen sentido** good sense will prevail.
(**d**) (*ser inevitable*) to be necessary, to impose itself; **la conclusión se impone** the conclusion is inescapable.
(**e**) **~ de** (*instruirse*) to acquaint o.s. with, inform o.s. about.
(**f**) (*Méx**: *acostumbrarse*) to get accustomed (*a* + *infin* to + *infin*).
imponible *adj* (*Fin*) taxable, subject to tax; *importación* dutiable, subject to duty; **no ~** free of tax, tax-free, tax-exempt (*US*).
impopular *adj* unpopular.
impopularidad *nf* unpopularity.
importación *nf* (**a**) (*acto*) importation, importing; **artículo de ~** imported article; **comercio de ~** import trade. (**b**) (*artículo*) import; imports.
importador(a) *nm/f* importer.
importancia *nf* importance; significance, weight; size, magnitude; **de cierta ~** of some importance; **sin ~** unimportant, insignificant, minor; **carecer de ~** to be unimportant; **conceder** (*o* **dar**) **mucha ~ a** to attach great importance to, make much of, put the emphasis on; **no dar ~ a** to consider unimportant; to make light of; **darse ~** to give o.s. airs; **restar ~ a** to diminish the importance of; to play down, make light of; **no tiene ~** it's nothing, it's not important.
importante *adj* (**a**) (*gen*) important; significant, weighty, momentous; **lo ~ es ..., lo más ~ es** ... the main thing is ...; **poco ~** unimportant.
(**b**) *cantidad, pérdida* considerable, sizeable; *sala etc* magnificent, imposing; *capa* thick; *retraso* serious.
importantizarse* [1f] *vr* (*Carib*) to give o.s. airs.
importar[1] [1a] *vt* (*Com*) to import (*a, en* into; *de* from).
importar[2] [1a] **1** *vt* (**a**) (*Fin*) to amount to; to cost, be worth; **la cuenta importa 500 pesos** the bill amounts to 500 pesos; **el libro importa 50 dólares** the book costs 50 dollars.
(**b**) (*implicar*) to involve, imply, carry with it.
2 *vi* to be important, be of consequence, matter; **~ a** to concern; **esto importa mucho** this is very important; **no importa** it doesn't matter; **¡no importa!** never mind!; **¿qué importa?** what does it matter?, what difference does it make?; who cares?; **y a ti ¿qué te importa?** and what business is it of yours?; **¡a ti no te importa!** it's nothing to do with you!; **no le importa** he doesn't care, it doesn't bother him; **(no) me importa un bledo** (*o* **higo** *etc*) I don't care two hoots (*de* about); **¿te importa prestármelo?** would you mind lending it to me?; **no le importa conducir todo el día** he doesn't mind driving all day; **'no importa precio'** 'cost no object'; **lo comprará a no importa que precio** he'll buy it at any price, he'll buy it regardless of the price; **iremos no importa el tiempo que haga** we'll go whatever the weather.
importe *nm* amount; (*coste*) value, cost; (*total*) total; **~ total** final total, grand total; **hasta el ~ de** up to the amount of; **por ~ de** to the value of; **el ~ de esta factura** the amount of this bill.
importunación *nf* pestering; **~ sexual** sexual harassment.
importunar [1a] *vt* to importune, bother, pester.
importunidad *nf* (**a**) (*acto*) importunity, pestering. (**b**) (*efecto*) annoyance, nuisance.
importuno *adj* (**a**) (*molesto*) importunate, troublesome, annoying. (**b**) (*inoportuno*) inopportune, ill-timed.
imposibilidad *nf* (**a**) impossibility. (**b**) **mi ~ para** + *infin* my inability to + *infin*.
imposibilitado *adj* (**a**) (*Med*) disabled, crippled; (*Fin*) helpless, without means. (**b**) **estar ~ para** + *infin*, **verse ~ para** *o* **de** + *infin* to be unable to + *infin*, be prevented from + *ger*.
imposibilitar [1a] *vt* (**a**) (*Med*) to disable; (*incapacitar*) to make unfit, incapacitate (*para* for).
(**b**) (*impedir*) to make impossible, preclude, prevent; **esto me imposibilita hacerlo** this makes it impossible for me to do it, this prevents me from doing it.
imposible 1 *adj* (**a**) (*gen*) impossible; (*inaguantable*) intolerable, unbearable; **es ~** it's impossible, it's out of the question; **es ~ de predecir** it's impossible to forecast; **hacer lo ~** to do one's utmost (*para* + *infin* to + *infin*); **¡parece ~!** I don't believe it!
(**b**) *persona* difficult, awkward, impossible.
(**c**) (*LAm*) (*descuidado*) slovenly, dirty; (*repugnante*) repulsive.
2 *nm* the impossible; impossible thing.
imposición *nf* (**a**) (*gen*) imposition.
(**b**) (*Com, Fin*) tax, impost, imposition; **~ directa** direct taxation.
(**c**) (*Tip*) imposition.
(**d**) (*Fin*) deposit; **~ a plazo (fijo)** fixed-term deposit; **efectuar una ~** to make a deposit; to deposit money.
(**e**) **~ de manos** (*Ecl*) laying-on of hands.
impositiva *nf* (*LAm*) tax office.
impositivamente *adv* for tax purposes, with regard to taxation.
impositivo *adj* (**a**) (*Fin*) tax (*atr*); **sistema ~** taxation, tax system. (**b**) (*And, Cono Sur*) (*autoritario*) authoritative, domineering; (*imperativo*) imperative.
impostergable *adj* that cannot be delayed; ineluctable; **una cita ~** an appointment that cannot be put off.
impostor(a) *nm/f* (**a**) (*charlatán*) impostor, fraud. (**b**) (*calumniador*) slanderer.
impostura *nf* (**a**) (*fraude*) imposture, fraud; sham. (**b**) (*calumnia*) aspersion, slur, slander.
impotable *adj* undrinkable.
impotencia *nf* (**a**) (*gen*) impotence, powerlessness, helplessness. (**b**) (*Med*) impotence.
impotente (**a**) (*gen*) impotent, powerless, helpless. (**b**) (*Med*) impotent.
impracticabilidad *nf* impracticability.
impracticable *adj* (**a**) (*gen*) impracticable, unworkable. (**b**) *carretera* impassable, unusable.
imprecación *nf* imprecation, curse.
imprecar [1g] *vt* to curse.
imprecisable *adj* indeterminable.
imprecisión *nf* lack of precision, vagueness.
impreciso *adj* imprecise, vague.
impredecibilidad *nf* unpredictability.
impredecible *adj* unpredictable.
impregnación *nf* impregnation.
impregnar [1a] *vt* to impregnate (*de* with); to saturate (*de* with); (*fig*) to pervade.
impremeditado *adj* unpremeditated.
imprenta *nf* (**a**) (*arte*) printing, art of printing. (**b**) (*aparato*) press; (*taller*) printer's, printing house, printing office. (**c**) (*letra*) print; letterpress. (**d**) (*impresos*) printed matter.
imprentar [1a] *vt* (**a**) (*Cono Sur Cos*) to put a permanent crease into. (**b**) (*LAm*) to mark.
impreparado *adj* unprepared.
imprescindible *adj* essential, indispensable, vital; **cosas ~s** essential things, things one cannot do without; **es ~ que** ... it is essential that ..., it is imperative that ...
impresentable *adj* unpresentable; *acto* disgraceful; *per-*

sona disreputable; **Juan es ~** you can't take John anywhere.

impresión *nf* (**a**) (*gen*) impression; (*huella*) imprint; **~ dactilar, ~ digital** fingerprint.

(**b**) (*Tip*: *gen*) printing; (*letra*) print; (*tirada*) edition, impression, issue; **quinta ~** fifth impression; **una ~ de 5.000 ejemplares** an edition of 5,000 copies; **~ en color(es)** colour printing.

(**c**) (*Fot*) print.

(**d**) (*Inform*) printout.

(**e**) (*fig*) impression; (*desagradable*) shock; **cambiar impresiones** to exchange impressions, compare notes; **da la ~ de** + *infin* it gives the impression of + *ger*; **formarse una ~ de** to get an idea of; **hacer buena ~** to make a good impression, impress; **no me hizo buena ~** I was not impressed (with it); **su muerte me causó una gran ~** her death was a great shock to me; **¿qué ~ te produjo?** how did it impress you?, what impression did it make on you?; **tener la ~ de que** ... to have the impression that ...; **¡estabas de ~!*** you were great!*; **esto le caerá de ~*** this will surely impress you.

(**f**) (*Bio, Psic*) imprinting.

impresionable *adj* impressionable.

impresionado *adj* (**a**) (*gen*) impressed. (**b**) (*Fot*) exposed; **excesivamente ~** overexposed.

impresionante *adj* (*gen*) impressive; (*espectacular*) striking; (*conmovedor*) moving, affecting; (*espantoso*) awesome, frightening.

impresionar [1a] **1** *vt* (**a**) *disco* to cut; (*Fot*) to expose; **película sin ~** unexposed film.

(**b**) (*fig*) to impress, strike; to move, affect; to shock; **me impresionó mucho** it greatly impressed me; **no se deja fácilmente ~** he is not easily impressed.

2 *vi* to impress, make an impression; **lo hace sólo para ~** he just does it to impress.

3 impresionarse *vr* to be impressed; to be moved, be affected.

impresionismo *nm* impressionism.

impresionista 1 *adj* impressionist(ic). **2** *nm* impressionist.

impreso 1 *adj* printed. **2** *nm* (**a**) (*artículo*) printed paper; (*libro*) printed book (*etc*). (**b**) (*formulario*) form; **~ de afiliación, ~ de solicitud** application form. (**c**) **~s** printed matter.

impresor *nm* printer.

impresora *nf* (*Inform*) printer; **~ (de) calidad carta** letter-quality printer; **~ de chorro de tinta** ink-jet printer; **~ de impacto** impact printer; **~ de no impacto** non-impact printer; **~ (por) láser** laser printer; **~ de línea** line-printer; **~ de margarita** daisy-wheel printer; **~ matricial, ~ de matriz de puntos** dot-matrix printer; **~ en paralelo** parallel printer.

imprevisibilidad *nf* unpredictability.

imprevisible *adj* unforeseeable.

imprevisión *nf* improvidence; lack of foresight; thoughtlessness.

imprevisor *adj* improvident; lacking foresight; thoughtless, happy-go-lucky.

imprevisto 1 *adj* unforeseen, unexpected. **2** *nm* (*t* **~s**) incidentals, unforeseen expense; contingencies; **si no surgen ~s** (*o* **un ~**) if nothing unexpected occurs.

imprimar [1a] *vt* (*Arte*) to prime.

imprimátur *nm* imprimatur.

imprimible *adj* printable.

imprimir [3a; *ptp* **impreso**] *vt* (**a**) (*gen*) to imprint, impress, stamp (*a, en* on; *t fig*). (**b**) (*Tip*) to print. (**c**) (*Bio, Psic*) to imprint (*a* on).

improbabilidad *nf* improbability, unlikelihood.

improbable *adj* improbable, unlikely.

improbar [1b] *vt* (*Carib*) to fail to approve, not approve.

improbidad *nf* dishonesty.

ímprobo *adj* (**a**) (*poco honrado*) dishonest, corrupt. (**b**) *tarea* arduous, thankless, tough; *esfuerzo etc* tremendous, awful, strenuous.

improcedencia *nf* (*V adj*) (**a**) wrongness; inappropriateness, inapplicability; irrelevancy. (**b**) (*Jur*) inadmissibility.

improcedente *adj* (**a**) (*incorrecto*) wrong, not right; (*inadecuado*) inappropriate, inapplicable; irrelevant. (**b**) (*Jur*) unfounded, inadmissible; out of order; **despido ~** unfair dismissal.

improductividad *nf* unproductiveness.

improductivo *adj* unproductive; non-productive.

impronta *nf* stamp, impress, impression; (*fig*) stamp, mark.

impronunciable *adj* unpronounceable.

improperio *nm* insult, taunt.

impropiamente *adv* improperly; inappropriately, unsuitably.

impropicio *adj* inauspicious, unpropitious.

impropiedad *nf* (**a**) (*gen*) inappropriateness, unsuitability. (**b**) (*Ling*) impropriety, infelicity (of language).

impropio *adj* improper (*t Mat, Ling*); inappropriate, unsuitable; **~ de, ~ para** inappropriate for; unbecoming to; foreign to.

improrrogable *adj fecha* that cannot be extended.

impróvidamente *adv* improvidently.

impróvido *adj* improvident.

improvisación *nf* improvisation; extemporization; (*Mús*) impromptu; (*Teat*) ad-lib.

improvisado *adj* improvised; *reparación* makeshift; (*Mús etc*) extempore, impromptu.

improvisamente *adv* unexpectedly, suddenly.

improvisar [1a] *vti* to improvise; to extemporize; (*Mús*) to extemporize; (*Teat*) to ad-lib; **~ una comida** to rustle up a meal*.

improviso *adj* (**a**) (*imprevisto*) unexpected, unforeseen. (**b**) **al ~, de ~** unexpectedly, suddenly; on the spur of the moment; **en un ~** (*And**: *de golpe*) suddenly, without warning; **hablar de ~** to speak extempore, speak unprepared; **tocar de ~** to play impromptu.

improvisto *adj* unexpected, unforeseen; **de ~** unexpectedly, suddenly.

imprudencia (*V adj*) *nf* imprudence; rashness; indiscretion; carelessness; **~ temeraria** criminal negligence; **ser acusado de conducir con ~ temeraria** to be charged with dangerous driving.

imprudente *adj* (*precipitado*) unwise, imprudent, rash; (*indiscreto*) indiscreet; (*descuidado*) careless.

imprudentemente *adv* unwisely, imprudently; rashly; carelessly.

Impte *abr de* **Importe** amount, amt.

impúber *adj* not having reached puberty, immature.

impublicable *adj* unprintable.

impudencia *nf* shamelessness, brazenness.

impudente *adj* shameless, brazen.

impúdicamente *adv* immodestly, shamelessly; (*obscenamente*) lewdly; lecherously.

impudicia *nf* immodesty, shamelessness; (*obscenidad*) lewdness; lechery.

impúdico *adj* immodest, shameless; (*obsceno*) lewd; lecherous.

impudor *nm* = **impudicia**.

impuesto 1 *ptp de* **imponer**; **estar ~ de, quedar ~ de** to be informed about; **estar ~ en** to be well versed in. **2** *nm* tax; duty, levy (*sobre* on); **~s** taxes, (*como sistema*) taxation; **libre de ~s** tax-free; duty-free; **sujeto a ~** taxable, dutiable; **~ sobre apuestas** betting tax; **~ sobre los bienes heredados, ~ sobre herencias, ~ sobre las sucesiones** estate duty; **~ sobre el capital** capital levy; **~ directo** direct tax; **~ sobre espectáculos** entertainments tax; **~ de plusvalía** capital gains tax; **~ sobre la propiedad** property tax; **~ de radicación** property tax; **~ sobre la renta** income tax; **~ revolucionario** protection money paid to terrorists; **~ sobre la riqueza** wealth tax; **~ sobre sociedades** corporation tax; **~ del timbre** stamp duty; **~ sobre el valor añadido (IVA)** value-added tax (VAT); **~ de venta** sales tax, purchase tax.

impugnar [1a] *vt* to oppose, contest, challenge; *teoría etc* to impugn, refute.

impulsador *nm* (*Aer*) booster.

impulsar [1a] *vt* to stimulate, promote; to drive; *V* **impeler**.

impulsión *nf* (**a**) (*gen*) impulsion; (*Mec*) propulsion, drive; **~ por correa** belt drive. (**b**) (*fig*) impulse.

impulsividad *nf* impulsiveness.

impulsivo *adj* impulsive; **compra impulsiva** impulse buying.

impulso *nm* (**a**) (*gen*) impulse; (*Mec*) drive, thrust; (*empuje*) impetus, momentum.

(**b**) (*fig*) impulse; stimulus, urge; **los ~s del corazón** the promptings of the heart; **~ sexual** sexual urge, sex drive; **a ~s del miedo** driven on by fear; **no resisto al ~ de decir que** ... I can't resist saying that ...

impulsor 1 *adj* drive (*atr*), driving. **2** *nm* (*Mec*) drive; (*Aer*) booster. **3** *nm*, **impulsora** *nf* (*persona*) promoter, instigator.

impune *adj* unpunished.

impunemente *adv* with impunity.

impunidad *nf* impunity.

impuntual *adj* unpunctual.

impuntualidad *nf* unpunctuality.
impureza *nf* (**a**) (*gen*) impurity. (**b**) (*fig*) unchastity, lewdness.
impurificar [1g] *vt* (**a**) (*adulterar*) to adulterate, make impure. (**b**) (*fig*: *corromper*) to corrupt, defile.
impuro *adj* (**a**) (*gen*) impure. (**b**) (*fig*) impure, unchaste, lewd.
imputable *adj*: **fracasos que son ~s a** failures which can be attributed to, failures which are attributable to.
imputación *nf* imputation, charge.
imputar [1a] *vt*: **~ a** to impute to, attribute to, charge with; **los hechos que se les imputan** the acts with which they are charged.
imputrescible *adj* rot-proof; (*pey*) non-biodegradable.
in* *adj invar* in*; fashionable, up-to-date, state-of-the-art; **es el estilo más ~** this is the really in style*; **lo ~ es hablar de** ... the in thing is to talk about ...; **lo que llevan los más ~** what people who are really with it are wearing*.
-ín, -ina *V* **Aspects of Word Formation in Spanish 2.**
inabarcable *adj* vast, extensive.
inabordable *adj* unapproachable.
inacabable *adj* endless, interminable.
inacabablemente *adv* endlessly, interminably.
inacabado *adj* unfinished; *problema* unresolved.
inaccesibilidad *nf* inaccessibility.
inaccesible *adj* inaccessible.
inacción *nf* inaction; inactivity, idleness; drift.
inacentuado *adj* unaccented, unstressed.
inaceptabilidad *nf* unacceptability.
inaceptable *adj* unacceptable.
inactividad *nf* inactivity; laziness, idleness; (*Com, Fin*) dullness.
inactivo *adj* inactive; lazy, idle; (*Com, Fin*) dull.
inactual *adj* lacking present validity, no longer applicable; old-fashioned, out-of-date.
inadaptable *adj* unadaptable.
inadaptación *nf* maladjustment; failure of adjustment, failure to adjust (*a* to).
inadaptado 1 *adj* maladjusted, who fails to adjust (*a* to). **2** *nm*, **inadaptada** *nf* misfit; person who fails to adjust.
inadecuación *nf* inadequacy; unsuitability, inappropriateness.
inadecuado *adj* inadequate; unsuitable, inappropriate.
inadmisibilidad *nf* inadmissibility, unacceptable nature.
inadmisible *adj* inadmissible, unacceptable.
inadvertencia *nf* (**a**) (*gen*) inadvertence; **por ~** inadvertently, through inadvertence. (**b**) (*una ~*) oversight, slip.
inadvertidamente *adv* inadvertently.
inadvertido *adj* (**a**) (*despistado*) unobservant, inattentive; (*descuidado*) careless. (**b**) (*no visto*) unnoticed, unobserved; **pasar ~** to escape notice, slip by.
inafectado *adj* unaffected.
inagotabilidad *nf* inexhaustability; tireless nature.
inagotable *adj* inexhaustible, tireless.
inaguantable *adj* intolerable, unbearable.
inaguantablemente *adv* intolerably, unbearably.
inajenable *adj* inalienable; not transferable.
inalámbrico *adj* wireless; (*Telec*) cordless.
in albis *adv*: **quedarse ~** (*no saber*) not to know a thing; to be left in the dark; (*fracasar*) to get nothing for one's trouble, achieve nothing.
inalcanzable *adj* unattainable.
inalienable *adj* inalienable; not transferable.
inalterabilidad *nf* inalterability, unchangingness; immutability.
inalterable *adj* unalterable, unchanging; immutable; *cara* impassive; *color* fast; *lustre etc* permanent.
inalterado *adj* unchanged, unaltered.
inamistoso *adj* unfriendly.
inamovible *adj* fixed, immovable; undetachable.
inanición *nf* starvation, (*Med*) inanition; **morir de ~** to die of starvation.
inanidad *nf* inanity.
inanimado *adj* inanimate.
inánime *adj* lifeless.
INAP [i'nap] *nm* (*Esp*) *abr de* **Instituto Nacional de la Administración Pública.**
inapagable *adj* unquenchable; inextinguishable.
inapeable *adj* (**a**) (*oscuro*) incomprehensible. (**b**) (*terco*) obstinate, stubborn.
inapelabilidad *nf* finality, unappealable nature.
inapelable *adj* (*Jur*) unappealable, not open to appeal; (*fig*) inevitable, irremediable; **las decisiones de los jueces serán ~s** the judges' decisions will be final.
inapercibido *adj* unperceived.
inapetencia *nf* lack of appetite, loss of appetite.
inapetente *adj*: **estar ~** to be suffering from loss of appetite.
inaplazable *adj* which cannot be postponed, pressing, urgent.
inaplicable *adj* inapplicable, not applicable.
inaplicado *adj* slack, lazy.
inapreciable *adj* (**a**) *diferencia etc* imperceptible. (**b**) (*de valor*) invaluable, inestimable.
inaprensible *adj* indefinite, hard to pin down; hard to grasp.
inaptitud *nf* unsuitability.
inapto *adj* unsuited (*para* to).
inarmónico *adj* unharmonious, unmusical.
inarrugable *adj* crease-resistant, which does not crease.
inarticulado *adj* inarticulate.
inasequible *adj* unattainable, out of reach; unobtainable.
inasistencia *nf* absence, failure to attend.
inastillable *adj cristal* shatterproof.
inasumible *adj* unacceptable.
inatacable *adj* unassailable.
inatención *nf* inattention, lack of attention (*a* to).
inatento *adj* inattentive.
inaudible *adj* inaudible.
inaudito *adj* unheard-of; unprecedented; outrageous.
inauguración *nf* inauguration; opening; unveiling; (*Com*) setting up; (*fig*: *fiesta*) house-warming party; **~ privada** (*Arte*) private viewing.
inaugural *adj* inaugural; opening; *viaje etc* maiden.
inaugurar [1a] *vt* to inaugurate; *canal, puente, exposición etc* to open (formally); *estatua etc* to unveil.
inautenticidad *nf* lack of authenticity.
inauténtico *adj* not genuine, false.
INB *nm* (*Esp Escol*) *abr de* **Instituto Nacional de Bachillerato.**
INBAD [im'bað] *nm* (*Esp*) *abr de* **Instituto Nacional de Bachillerato a Distancia.**
INC *nm* (**a**) (*Esp*) *abr de* **Instituto Nacional de Colonización** (*land settlement institute*). (**b**) (*Esp Com*) *abr de* **Instituto Nacional de Consumo.**
inca *nmf* Inca.
incachable* *adj* (*LAm*) useless.
incaico *adj* Inca (*atr*).
incalculable *adj* incalculable.
incalificable *adj* indescribable, unspeakable.
incalificablemente *adv* indescribably, unspeakably.
incanato *nm* (*And Hist*) (*época*) Inca period; (*reinado*) reign of an Inca.
incandescencia *nf* incandescence; white heat; glow.
incandescente *adj* (**a**) incandescent; white hot; glowing. (**b**) *mirada* burning, passionate.
incansable *adj* tireless, untiring, unflagging.
incansablemente *adv* tirelessly, untiringly.
incapacidad *nf* incapacity; unfitness (*para* por); inadequacy, incompetence; **~ laboral** sick-leave; **~ laboral transitoria** short sick-leave; **su ~ para** + *infin* his inability to + *infin*.
incapacitación *nf*: **proceso de ~ presidencial** impeachment of a president.
incapacitado *adj* (**a**) incapacitated; unfitted (*para* for). (**b**) (*Méx*: *minusválido*) disabled, handicapped.
incapacitante *adj* incapacitating.
incapacitar [1a] *vt* to incapacitate, render unfit, handicap (*para* for); (*Jur etc*) to disqualify (*para* for).
incapaz *adj* (**a**) (*gen*) incapable (*de* of); (*no apto*) unfit; (*inadecuado*) inadequate, incompetent; (*Jur*) incompetent; **~ de** + *infin* unable to + *infin*. (**b**) (*CAm, Méx*) *niño* trying, difficult.
incapturable *adj* unattainable.
incardinar [1a] *vt* to include (as an integral part).
incario *nm* (*And*) Inca period.
incasable *adj* unmarriageable.
incásico *adj* (*LAm*) Inca (*atr*).
incatalogable *adj* indefinable; off-beat; **persona ~** person who refuses to be pigeon-holed.
incautación *nf* seizure, confiscation.
incautamente *adv* unwarily, incautiously.
incautarse [1a] *vr*: **~ de** to seize, confiscate, impound; to take possession of.
incauto *adj* unwary, incautious; gullible.
incendiar [1b] **1** *vt* to set on fire, set fire to, set alight; (*fig*) to kindle, inflame. **2 incendiarse** *vr* to catch fire.
incendiario 1 *adj* (**a**) incendiary. (**b**) (*fig*) inflammatory. **2** *nm*, **incendiaria** *nf* fire-raiser, pyromaniac; incendiary; ~

de la guerra warmonger.
incendiarismo *nm* pyromania.
incendio *nm* fire; conflagration; ~ **forestal** forest fire; ~ **intencionado,** ~ **malicioso,** ~ **provocado** arson, fire-raising; **echar** (*o* **hablar**) ~**s de uno** (*And, Cono Sur*) to sling mud at sb.
incensar [1j] *vt* (*Ecl*) to cense, incense; (*fig*) to flatter.
incensario *nm* censer.
incentivación *nf* (**a**) motivation. (**b**) (*Fin*) incentive scheme; productivity bonus.
incentivar [1a] *vt* to encourage, stimulate, provide incentives for; **baja incentivada** voluntary severance.
incentivo *nm* incentive; ~ **fiscal** tax incentive; **baja por** ~ voluntary severance.
incertidumbre *nf* uncertainty, doubt.
incesable *adj*, **incesante** *adj* incessant, unceasing.
incesantemente *adv* incessantly, unceasingly.
incesto *nm* incest.
incestuoso *adj* incestuous.
incidencia *nf* (**a**) (*Mat etc*) incidence. (**b**) (*suceso*) incident. (**c**) (*impacto*) effect, impact; **la huelga tuvo escasa** ~ the strike was not widely supported, the strike had little impact.
incidentado *adj* unruly, riotous, turbulent.
incidental *adj* incidental.
incidente 1 *adj* incidental. **2** *nm* incident.
incidentemente *adv* incidentally.
incidir [3a] **1** *vt* (*Med*) to incise, cut.
2 *vi* (**a**) ~ **en** (*cargar en*) to fall upon; (*afectar*) to influence, affect, impinge on; ~ **en un error** to fall into error; **el impuesto incide más en ellos** the tax falls most heavily on them, the tax affects them worst; **la familia ha incidido fuertemente en la historia** the family has influenced history a lot, the family has made itself strongly felt in history.
(**b**) ~ **en un tema** to touch upon a subject.
incienso *nm* (*Ecl*) incense; (*Bíb*) frankincense; (*fig*) flattery.
inciertamente *adv* uncertainly.
incierto *adj* uncertain, doubtful; inconstant.
incineración *nf* incineration; ~ **(de cadáveres)** cremation.
incinerador *nm*, **incineradora** *nf* incinerator.
incinerar [1a] *vt* to incinerate, burn; *cadáver* to cremate.
incipiente *adj* incipient.
incircunciso *adj* uncircumcised.
incisión *nf* incision.
incisividad *nf* incisiveness.
incisivo 1 *adj* sharp, cutting; (*fig*) incisive. **2** *nm* incisor.
inciso *nm* (**a**) (*Ling*) clause, sentence; comma. (**b**) (*Tip*) subsection. (**c**) (*observación*) parenthetical comment, aside. (**d**) (*conversación*) interjection, interruption.
incitación *nf* incitement; provocation.
incitante *adj* provoking, provocative, inviting.
incitar [1a] *vt* to incite, rouse, spur on; ~ **a uno a hacer algo** to urge sb to do sth; ~ **a uno contra otro** to incite sb against another person.
incívico 1 *adj* antisocial. **2** *nm*, **incívica** *nf* antisocial person.
incivil *adj* uncivil, rude.
incivilidad *nf* incivility, rudeness; **una** ~ an incivility, a piece of rudeness.
incivilizado *adj* uncivilized.
incivismo *nm* antisocial behaviour (*o* outlook *etc*).
inclasificable *adj* unclassifiable, nondescript.
inclemencia *nf* harshness, severity, inclemency; **la** ~ **del tiempo** the inclemency of the weather; **dejar algo a la** ~ to leave sth exposed to wind and weather.
inclemente *adj* harsh, severe, inclement.
inclinación *nf* (**a**) (*gen*) inclination; (*pendiente*) slope, incline; (*Náut*) pitch, tilt; (*de cuerpo*) stoop; ~ **lateral** (*Aer*) bank; **a una** ~ **de 45 grados** at an inclination of 45 degrees.
(**b**) (*reverencia*) bow; (*de cabeza*) nod.
(**c**) (*fig*) inclination, leaning, propensity; **de malas inclinaciones** evilly inclined; **tener** ~ **hacia la poesía** to have a penchant for poetry.
inclinado *adj* (**a**) (*en ángulo*) inclined, sloping, leaning, slanting; *plano* inclined.
(**b**) **estar** ~ **a** + *infin* (*esp LAm*: *fig*) to be inclined to + *infin*.
inclinar [1a] **1** *vt* (**a**) (*gen*) to incline; (*sesgar*) to slope, slant, tilt; (*cabeza*: *afirmando*) to incline, bend, nod; (*bajar*) to bow.
(**b**) ~ **a uno a hacer algo** (*fig*) to induce sb to do sth; to persuade sb to do sth.
2 *vi*: ~ **a uno** to take after sb, resemble sb.
3 inclinarse *vr* (**a**) (*estar inclinado*) to incline; to slope, slant, tilt, be inclined.
(**b**) (*encorvarse*) to stoop, bend; (*hacer reverencia*) to bow; ~ **a favor de** to be in favour of, support; ~ **ante** (*fig*) to bow to, bow down before.
(**c**) ~ **a uno** (*parecerse*) to take after sb, resemble sb.
(**d**) ~ **a hacer algo** to be inclined to do sth, tend to do sth; **me inclino a decir que** ... I am inclined to say that ...
ínclito *adj* illustrious, renowned.
incluir [3g] *vt* to include; to comprise, contain; to incorporate; (*en carta*) to enclose; **todo incluido** (*Com*) inclusive terms; all found, all-in.
inclusa *nf* foundling hospital.
inclusero, -a *nm/f* foundling.
inclusión *nf* inclusion; **con** ~ **de** including.
inclusivamente *adv* inclusive, inclusively.
inclusive *adv* inclusive, inclusively; **hasta el próximo domingo** ~ up to and including next Sunday.
inclusivo *adj* inclusive.
incluso 1 *adj* included; enclosed. **2** *adv* even, actually; ~ **la pegó** he even hit her, he actually hit her. **3** *prep* including.
incoación *nf* inception.
incoar [1a] *vt* to start, initiate.
incobrable *adj* irrecoverable; *deuda* bad.
incógnita *nf* (*Mat*) unknown quantity; (*fig*) unknown quantity; unknown factor; hidden motive; mystery; **queda en pie la** ~ **sobre su influencia** there is still a question-mark over his influence.
incógnito 1 *adj* unknown. **2** *nm* incognito; **viajar de** ~ to travel incognito.
incognoscible *adj* unknowable.
incoherencia *nf* incoherence; disconnectedness.
incoherente *adj* incoherent; disconnected.
incoloro *adj* colourless; *barniz etc* clear.
incólume *adj* safe; unhurt, unharmed, unscathed; **salir** ~ **del accidente** to emerge unscathed from the accident.
incombustible *adj* incombustible, fire-resisting; fireproof.
incomible *adj* uneatable, inedible.
incómodamente *adv* inconveniently; uncomfortably.
incomodar [1a] **1** *vt* to inconvenience, trouble, put out.
2 incomodarse *vr* (**a**) (*tomarse molestia*) to put o.s. out, take trouble; **¡no se incomode!** don't bother!, don't trouble yourself!
(**b**) (*enfadarse*) to get cross, get annoyed (*con* with); ~ **con** to fall out with; **estar incomodado con** to be cross with; to be at odds with.
incomodidad *nf* (**a**) (*inoportunidad*) inconvenience; (*falta de comodidad*) discomfort, uncomfortableness. (**b**) (*fastidio*) annoyance, irritation.
incomodo *nm* = **incomodidad (b)**.
incómodo 1 *adj* (*inoportuno*) inconvenient; (*nada comodo*) uncomfortable; (*molesto*) tiresome, annoying; **un bulto** ~ an awkward package, a cumbersome package; **una casa incómoda** an inconvenient house; **sentirse** ~ to feel uncomfortable, feel ill-at-ease; **estar** ~ **con uno** (*Cono Sur*) to be fed up with sb*, be cross with sb.
2 *nm* (*LAm*) = **incomodidad (b)**.
incomparable *adj* incomparable, matchless.
incomparablemente *adv* incomparably.
incomparecencia *nf* failure to appear (in court *etc*), non-appearance.
incomparecimiento *nm*: **pleito perdido por** ~ suit lost by default (*o* failure to appear); undefended suit.
incompasivo *adj* unsympathetic; pitiless.
incompatibilidad *nf* incompatibility; ~ **de intereses** conflict of interests; **ley de** ~**es** law against the holding of multiple posts.
incompatible *adj* incompatible.
incompetencia *nf* incompetence.
incompetente *adj* incompetent.
incompletamente *adv* incompletely.
incompleto *adj* incomplete, unfinished.
incomprendido 1 *adj persona* misunderstood; not appreciated. **2** *nm*, **incomprendida** *nf* misunderstood person; person who is not appreciated.
incomprensibilidad *nf* incomprehensibility.
incomprensible *adj* incomprehensible.
incomprensión *nf* incomprehension, lack of understanding; lack of appreciation.
incomprobable *adj* unprovable.
incomunicación *nf* isolation; lack of communication;

(*Jur*) solitary confinement; **ello permite la ~ de los detenidos** it allows those detained to be held incommunicado.

incomunicado *adj* isolated, cut off; (*Jur*) in solitary confinement, incommunicado.

incomunicar [1g] **1** *vt* to cut off the communications of, leave without communications; to cut off, isolate; (*Jur*) to put into solitary confinement; **~ un detenido** to refuse a prisoner access to a lawyer.

2 incomunicarse *vr* to isolate o.s., withdraw from society.

inconcebible *adj* inconceivable, unthinkable.

inconcebiblemente *adv* inconceivably.

inconciliable *adj* irreconcilable.

inconcluso *adj* unfinished, incomplete.

inconcluyente *adj* inconclusive.

inconcuso *adj* indisputable, undeniable, incontroverible.

inconcreción *nf* vagueness.

inconcreto *adj* vague.

incondicional 1 *adj* (**a**) (*gen*) unconditional; *fe* implicit, complete, unquestioning; *apoyo* wholehearted; *afirmación* unqualified; *amigo, partidario etc* staunch, stalwart.

(**b**) (*LAm*: pey*) servile, fawning.

2 *nmf* (**a**) (*partidario*) stalwart, staunch supporter (*etc*); (*pey*) diehard, hardliner.

(**b**) (*LAm*: pey*) toady, yes-man*.

incondicionalidad *nf* unconditional support; unquestioning loyalty.

incondicionalismo *nm* (*LAm*) toadyism, servility.

incondicionalmente *adv* unconditionally, unreservedly; implicitly, unquestioningly; wholeheartedly; staunchly.

inconexión *nf* disconnectedness; incongruity.

inconexo *adj* unconnected; (*desarticulado*) disconnected, disjointed; (*no relacionado*) unrelated; (*incongruo*) incongruous.

inconfesable *adj* which cannot be told (*o* confessed); shameful, disgraceful.

inconfeso *adj reo* who does not confess; **homosexual ~** closet homosexual.

inconforme *adj* nonconformist; **estar** (*o* **mostrarse**) **~ con algo** (*CAm*) to disagree with sth.

inconformismo *nm* nonconformism.

inconformista *adj, nmf* nonconformist.

inconfundible *adj* unmistakable.

inconfundiblemente *adv* unmistakably.

incongruencia *nf* incongruity.

incongruente *adj*, **incongruo** *adj* incongruous.

inconmensurable *adj* immeasurable, vast; incommensurate; fantastic.

inconmovible *adj* unshakeable.

inconmutable *adj* immutable.

inconocible *adj* unknowable; (*LAm**: *irreconocible*) unrecognizable; **lo ~** the unknowable.

inconquistable *adj* unconquerable; (*fig*) inconquerable, unyielding.

inconsciencia *nf* (**a**) (*Med*) unconsciousness. (**b**) (*fig*: *ignorancia*) unawareness. (**c**) (*fig*: *irreflexión*) thoughtlessness; recklessness.

inconsciente 1 *adj* (**a**) (*Med*) unconscious; **lo ~** the unconscious; **le encontraron ~** they found him unconscious.

(**b**) (*fig*: *ignorante*) unconscious, unaware (*de* of); oblivious (*de* to); (*sin saber*) unwitting.

(**c**) (*fig*: *irreflexivo*) thoughtless, reckless, carefree; **es más ~ que malo** he's thoughtless rather than wicked; **son gente ~** they're thoughtless people.

2 *nm* unconscious; **el ~ colectivo** the collective unconscious.

inconscientemente *adv* (**a**) (*sin saber*) unconsciously; unawares, unwittingly. (**b**) (*sin pensar*) thoughtlessly; recklessly; in a carefree manner.

inconsecuencia *nf* inconsistency; inconsequence.

inconsecuente *adj* inconsistent; inconsequent, inconsequential.

inconsideración *nf* inconsiderateness, thoughtlessness; rashness, haste.

inconsideradamente *adv* inconsiderately, thoughtlessly; rashly, hastily.

inconsiderado *adj* inconsiderate, thoughtless; rash, hasty.

inconsistencia *nf* lack of firmness; unevenness; weakness; looseness; flimsiness.

inconsistente *adj* (*poco sólido*) lacking firmness, not solid; (*irregular*) uneven; *argumento* weak; *tierra etc* loose; *tela* flimsy, thin; (*Culin*) lumpy.

inconsolable *adj* inconsolable.

inconstancia *nf* inconstancy; unsteadiness; fickleness.

inconstante *adj* (*gen*) inconstant, changeable; (*poco firme*) unsteady; (*caprichoso*) fickle.

inconstantemente *adv* inconstantly; unsteadily; in a fickle way.

inconstitucional *adj* unconstitutional.

inconstitucionalidad *nf* unconstitutional nature.

inconstitucionalmente *adv* unconstitutionally.

inconsumible *adj* unfit for consumption.

incontable *adj* countless, innumerable.

incontaminante *adj* non-polluting.

incontenible *adj* uncontrollable, unstoppable, uncontainable.

incontestable *adj* unanswerable; undeniable, unchallengeable, indisputable.

incontestablemente *adv* unanswerably; undeniably, indisputably.

incontestado *adj* unanswered; unchallenged, unquestioned; undisputed.

incontinencia *nf* incontinence (*t Med*).

incontinente 1 *adj* incontinent (*t Med*). **2** *adv* = **incontinenti.**

incontinenti *adv* at once, instantly, forthwith.

incontrastable *adj dificultad* insuperable; *argumento* unanswerable; *persona* unshakeable, unyielding.

incontrolable *adj* uncontrollable.

incontrolablemente *adv* uncontrollably.

incontrolado 1 *adj* uncontrolled; unauthorized; violent, wild. **2** *nm*, **incontrolada** *nf* violent person; (*esp*) policeman (*etc*) who acts outside the law; (*Pol*) strong-arm man, bully-boy.

incontrovertible *adj* incontrovertible, indisputable.

incontrovertido *adj* undisputed.

inconveniencia *nf* (**a**) (*gen*) unsuitability, inappropriateness; inadvisability; inconvenience. (**b**) (*descortesía*) impoliteness. (**c**) (*incorrección*) impropriety, wrongness. (**d**) (*disparate*) silly remark, tactless remark; (*acto*) improper thing to do (*etc*), wrong thing to do (*etc*).

inconveniente 1 *adj* (**a**) (*impropio*) unsuitable, inappropriate; (*no aconsejable*) inadvisable; (*inoportuno*) inconvenient.

(**b**) (*descortés*) impolite.

(**c**) (*incorrecto*) improper, wrong.

2 *nm* (*dificultad*) obstacle, difficulty; (*desventaja*) disadvantage, drawback; (*objeción*) objection; **el ~ es que ...** the trouble is that ..., the difficulty is that ...; **no hay ~ en** + *infin*, **no hay ~ para** + *infin* there is no objection to + *ger*; there will be no diffculty about + *ger*; **poner un ~** to raise an objection; **no tengo ~** I have no objection, I don't mind; **¿tienes algún ~ en venir?** do you mind coming?; **no veo ~** I see no objection, I see no difficulty.

inconvertibilidad *nf* inconvertibility.

inconvertible *adj* inconvertible.

incordiante* 1 *adj* annoying, bothersome, irksome. **2** *nmf* troublemaker.

incordiar* [1b] *vt* to bother, annoy; **¡déjate de ~!** stop bothering me!; **¡no incordies!** stop it!, behave yourself!

incordio* *nm* nuisance.

incorporación *nf* incorporation, embodiment; inclusion; involvement; (*a filas*) enlisting, enlistment.

incorporado *adj* (*Téc*) built-in; **con antena incorporada** with built-in aerial.

incorporal *adj* = **incorpóreo.**

incorporar [1a] **1** *vt* (**a**) (*gen*) to incorporate (*a, con, en* into, in); to embody (*a, con, en* in); (*incluir*) to include (*a* in); (*involucrar*) to involve (*a* in, with); (*Culin*) to mix (in) (*a* with), add (*a* to); **X incorpora al personaje de Z** (*Teat etc*) X plays the part of Z; **~ a filas** (*Mil*) to call up, enlist.

(**b**) **~ a uno** to make sb sit up (in bed), help sb to sit up.

2 incorporarse *vr* (**a**) (*cuando se está acostado*) to sit up, raise o.s.; **~ en la cama** to sit up in bed.

(**b**) **~ a** *regimiento, sociedad etc* to join; **~ a filas** (*Mil*) to join up, enlist; **~ al trabajo** to go to work, report for work.

incorpóreo *adj* incorporeal, bodiless; intangible.

incorrección *nf* (**a**) (*de datos*) incorrectness, inaccuracy.

(**b**) (*irregularidad*) irregularity.

(**c**) (*descortesía*) discourtesy; piece of bad manners, gaffe; impropriety; **cometer una ~** to commit a faux pas.

(**d**) (*Ling*) mistake.

incorrectamente *adv* (*V adj* (**a**), (**c**)) (**a**) incorrectly, inaccurately, wrongly. (**b**) discourteously; improperly.

incorrecto *adj* (**a**) *cálculo, dato etc* incorrect, inaccurate, wrong.

(**b**) *facciones* irregular, odd.
(**c**) *conducta* discourteous, bad-mannered; improper; **ser ~ con una** to take liberties with sb.
incorregible *adj* incorrigible.
incorrosible *adj* rustproof.
incorruptible *adj* incorruptible.
incorrupto *adj* (**a**) *cuerpo* incorrupt; uncorrupted. (**b**) (*fig*) pure, chaste, undefiled.
incredibilidad *nf* incredibility.
incredulidad *nf* incredulity, unbelief.
incrédulo 1 *adj* incredulous, unbelieving, sceptical. **2** *nm*, **incrédula** *nf* unbeliever, sceptic.
increíble *adj* incredible, unbelievable; **es ~ que ...** it is unbelievable that ...
increíblemente *adv* incredibly, unbelievably.
incremental *adj* incremental.
incrementar [1a] **1** *vt* to increase; to promote. **2 incrementarse** *vr* to increase.
incremento *nm* increment; increase, rise, addition; growth; **~ salarial** pay increase, rise in wages; **~ de temperatura** rise in temperature; **tomar ~** to increase.
increpación *nf* severe reprimand, upbraiding.
increpar [1a] *vt* to reprimand severely, upbraid.
in crescendo 1 *adv*: **ir ~** to increase, intensify, spiral upwards. **2** *nm* increase, upward spiral.
incriminación *nf* accusation.
incriminar [1a] *vt* (**a**) (*Jur*) *persona* to accuse; *actividad* to make a crime of, consider criminal. (**b**) *falta etc* to magnify. (**c**) *artículos etc* to obtain illegally.
incruento *adj* bloodless.
incrúspido* *adj* (*LAm*) clumsy; ham-fisted.
incrustación *nf* (**a**) (*gen*) incrustation; (*fig*) grafting. (**b**) (*Arte*) inlay, inlaid work.
incrustar [1a] **1** *vt* to incrust (*de* with); (*de joyas etc*) to inlay (*de* with); (*fig*) to graft (*en* on to), introduce (*en* into); **una espada incrustada de joyas** a sword encrusted with jewels.
2 incrustarse *vr*: **~ en** (*bomba etc*) to lodge in, embed itself in; **se le ha incrustado esta idea en la mente** he's got this idea firmly fixed in his head.
incubación *nf* incubation.
incubadora *nf* incubator.
incubar [1a] **1** *vt* to incubate; to hatch (*t fig*). **2 incubarse** *vr* to incubate.
íncubo *nm* incubus; nightmare.
incuestionable *adj* unquestionable, unchallengeable.
incuestionablemente *adv* unquestionably.
inculcar [1g] **1** *vt* to instil, inculcate (*en* in, into). **2 inculcarse** *vr* to be obstinate.
inculpable *adj* blameless, guiltless.
inculpación *nf* charge, accusation.
inculpado, -a *nm/f* accused person; **el ~** the accused, the defendant.
inculpar [1a] *vt* to charge (*de* with), accuse (*de* of); to blame (*de* for); **los crímenes que se le inculpan** the crimes with which he is charged.
incultamente *adv* in an uncultured way; uncouthly.
incultivable *adj* uncultivable, unworkable.
inculto *adj* (**a**) (*Agr*) uncultivated, unworked, untilled; **dejar un terreno ~** to leave land uncultivated. (**b**) (*fig*) uncultured; uncivilized; uncouth.
incultura *nf* lack of culture; uncouthness.
incumbencia *nf* obligation, duty, concern; **no es de mi ~** it is not my job, it's not my province.
incumbir [3a] *vi*: **~ a** to be incumbent upon; **no me incumbe a mí** it's not my job, it is no concern of mine; **le incumbe hacerlo** it is his business to do it; it behoves him to do it, it's his duty to do it.
incumplible *adj* unattainable.
incumplido *adj* unfulfilled.
incumplimiento *nm* non-fulfilment; non-completion; **~ de contrato** breach of contract; **~ de promesa matrimonial** breach of promise; **por ~** by default.
incumplir [3a] *vt regla* to break, disobey, fail to observe; *promesa* to break, fail to keep.
incunable *nm* incunable, incunabulum; **~s** incunabula.
incurable 1 *adj* (*Med*) incurable; (*fig*) hopeless, irremediable. **2** *nmf* incurable.
incuria *nf* negligence; carelessness, shiftlessness; **por ~** through negligence.
incurrir [3a] *vi*: **~ en** *error* to fall into; *crimen etc* to commit; *deuda, ira, odio etc* to incur; *desastre etc* to bring on o.s., become a victim of.
incursión *nf* raid, incursion, attack; **~ aérea** air-raid.
incursionar [1a] **1** *vt* = **2**. **2** *vi*: **~ en** to make a raid into, penetrate into; **~ en un tema** to tackle a subject, broach a subject.
indagación *nf* investigation, inquiry.
indagador(a) *nm/f* investigator (*de* into, of), inquirer (*de* into).
indagar [1h] *vt* (*examinar*) to investigate, inquire into; (*averiguar*) to find out, ascertain.
indagatorio 1 *adj* investigatory. **2 indagatoria** *nf* (*Méx*) investigation, inquiry.
indebidamente *adv* unduly; improperly; illegally, wrongfully.
indebido *adj* undue; improper; illegal, wrongful.
indecencia *nf* (**a**) (*gen*) indecency; (*obscenidad*) obscenity. (**b**) (*porquería*) filth; wretchedness. (**c**) (*acto*) indecent act; (*palabra*) indecent thing.
indecente *adj* (**a**) (*gen*) indecent, improper; (*obsceno*) obscene; **¡~!** you brute!
(**b**) (*asqueroso*) filthy; (*despreciable*) miserable, wretched; (*vil*) low, mean; **algún empleadillo ~** some wretched clerk; **un cuchitril ~** a miserable pigsty of a place; **la calle está ~ de lodo*** the street is terribly muddy; **es una persona ~** he's a low sort, he's a mean character.
indecentemente *adv* (**a**) indecently; obscenely. (**b**) miserably, wretchedly.
indecible *adj* unspeakable, unutterable; indescribable; **sufrir lo ~** to suffer terribly.
indeciblemente *adv* unspeakably, unutterably; indescribably.
indecisión *nf* indecision, hesitation; indecisiveness.
indeciso 1 *adj* (**a**) *persona* undecided; hesitant, irresolute; vague. (**b**) *resultado etc* indecisive. **2** *nm*, **indecisa** *nf* (*Pol*) undecided voter; (*en encuesta*) don't-know.
indeclarable *adj* undeclarable.
indeclinable *adj* (**a**) (*Ling*) indeclinable. (**b**) (*inevitable*) unavoidable.
indecoro *nm* unseemliness, indecorum; indelicacy.
indecorosamente *adv* indecorously, unbecomingly; indelicately.
indecoroso *adj* unseemly, indecorous, unbecoming; indelicate.
indefectible *adj* unfailing, infallible.
indefectiblemente *adv* unfailingly, infallibly.
indefendible *adj* indefensible.
indefensión *nf* defencelessness.
indefenso *adj* defenceless, helpless.
indefinible *adj* indefinable; inexpressible.
indefinición *nf* lack of definition; absence of clarity, vagueness.
indefinidamente *adv* indefinitely.
indefinido *adj* indefinite; undefined, vague; (*Ling*) indefinite; **por tiempo ~** for an indefinite time, indefinitely.
indeformable *adj* rigid, crush-proof; that keeps its shape.
indeleble *adj* indelible.
indelicadeza *nf* indelicacy.
indelicado *adj* indelicate, unscrupulous.
indemne *adj* undamaged; *persona* unharmed, unhurt.
indemnidad *nf* immunity, indemnity.
indemnizable *adj* that can be indemnified, recoverable.
indemnización *nf* (**a**) (*acto*) indemnification.
(**b**) (*pago*) indemnity, compensation; **indemnizaciones** (*p.ej. 1918*) reparations; **~ de despido** severance pay; **~ por enfermedad** sick pay; **pagó un dólar de ~** he paid a dollar in damages (*o* in compensation).
indemnizar [1f] *vt* to indemnify (*de* against, for), compensate (*de* for).
indemnizatorio *adj* compensatory.
independencia *nf* independence; **con ~ de** independent of (*que* whether), irrespective of (*que* whether).
independentista *adj, nmf* = **independista**.
independiente 1 *adj* independent; self-sufficient, self-contained; (*Inform*) stand-alone; **hacerse ~** to become independent. **2** *nmf* independent.
independientemente *adv* independently; **~ de que vengan más personas** irrespective (*o* regardless) of whether more people come.
independista 1 *adj* independence (*atr*). **2** *nmf* supporter of a movement for independence.
independizar [1f] **1** *vt* to emancipate, free; to make independent, grant independence to.
2 independizarse *vr* to become free, become independent (*de* of).
indesarraigable *adj* ineradicable.
indescifrable *adj* undecipherable, indecipherable; *misterio*

impenetrable.

indescriptible *adj* indescribable.

indescriptiblemente *adv* indescribably.

indeseable 1 *adj* undesirable. **2** *nmf* undesirable (person); **es un ~** he's an unsavoury sort, he's beyond the pale.

indeseado *adj* unwanted.

indesligable *adj* inseparable (*de* from).

indesmallable *adj media etc* ladderproof, which does not ladder, runproof.

indesmayable *adj* unfaltering.

indesmentible *adj* undeniable.

indespegable *adj* that will not come unstuck.

indestructible *adj* indestructible.

indetectable *adj* undetectable.

indeterminado *adj* (**a**) (*gen*) indeterminate; *resultado* inconclusive; (*incierto*) vague; (*Ling*) indefinite. (**b**) *persona* irresolute.

indexación *nf* indexation; (*Fin*) index-linking; (*Inform*) indexing.

indexado *adj* (*Fin*) index-linked.

indexar [1a] *vt* (*Fin*) to index-link.

India *nf*: **la ~** India; **las ~s** the Indies; **~s Occidentales** West Indies; **~s Orientales** East Indies.

indiada *nf* (**a**) (*LAm*: *reunión etc*) group of Indians, crowd of Indians; (*Cono Sur*: *pey*) mob. (**b**) (*LAm*: *acto etc*) typically Indian thing to do (*o* say *etc*).

indiana *nf* printed calico.

indiano 1 *adj* (Spanish-)American. **2** *nm* (*Hist*) *Spaniard returning rich from America, equivalent to* nabob; **~ de hilo negro** miser.

indicación *nf* (**a**) (*señal*) indication, sign; (*Med*: *síntoma*) sign, symptom.

(**b**) (*sugerencia*) hint, suggestion; **por ~ de** at the suggestion of; **aprovechó la ~** he took the hint; **seguiré sus indicaciones** I will follow your suggestion, I will do what you say.

(**c**) (*dato*) piece of information; (*Téc*: *de termómetro etc*) reading.

(**d**) **indicaciones** (*Com*) instructions, directions; **indicaciones para el empleo** instructions for use.

indicado *adj* right, suitable, proper; obvious; likely; **el sitio más ~** the most obvious place; **una elección indicada** an obvious choice; **es el más ~ para el puesto** he is the most suitable man for the job, he is the best man for the job; **eso es lo más ~** that's the best thing; **tú eres el menos ~ para hacerlo** you're the last person to do it, you're the least suitable person to do it.

indicador *nm* (*gen*) indicator; (*Téc*) gauge, meter, dial; (*aguja*) hand, pointer; **~ de carretera** roadsign; **~ de dirección** (*Aut*) indicator, trafficator; **~ económico** economic indicator; **~ de encendido** (*Inform*) power-on indicator; **~ de velocidades** speedometer.

indicar [1g] *vt* (**a**) (*Téc etc*) to indicate, show; to register, record; (*termómetro etc*) to read.

(**b**) (*señalar*) to indicate, point out, point to; (*mostrar*) to show; (*sugerir*) to suggest, hint, intimate; **me indicó que ...** he told me that ..., he suggested to me that ...

indicativo 1 *adj* indicative (*t Ling*). **2** *nm* (**a**) (*Ling*) indicative. (**b**) (*Rad*) call sign; **~ de nacionalidad** (*Aut*) national identification plate.

índice *nm* (**a**) (*Tip etc*) index; (*catálogo*) (library) catalogue; **~ de materias** table of contents.

(**b**) (*Mat etc*) index; ratio, rate; **~ de audiencia** (*TV*) audience ratings; **~ de compresión** (*Mec*) compression ratio; **~ del coste de (la) vida** cost-of-living index; **~ de deuda** debt ratio; **~ Dow Jones** Dow Jones index; **~ expurgatorio** (*Ecl*) Index; **~ de mortalidad** death rate; **~ de natalidad** birth-rate; **~ de ocupación** occupancy rate (of hotel rooms *etc*); **~ de participación** (*Pol*) electoral turnout; **~ de precios al consumo** retail price index; **~ de vida** expectation of life, life expectancy.

(**c**) (*Téc*: *aguja*) pointer, needle, hand; (*de reloj*) hand.

(**d**) (*Anat*) index finger, forefinger.

indiciación *nf* indexing; (*Fin*) index-linking.

indiciario *adj*: **prueba indiciaria** circumstantial proof.

indicio *nm* (**a**) (*gen*) indication, sign; token; (*Jur etc*) piece of evidence, clue (*de* to); (*vestigio*) trace, vestige; **es ~ de** it is an indication of, it is a sign of; **no hay el menor ~ de él** there isn't the faintest sign of him, there isn't the least trace of him; **dar ~s de sorpresa** to show surprise, evince surprise.

(**b**) **~s** (*Jur*) circumstantial evidence.

indiferencia *nf* indifference; apathy, lack of interest.

indiferente *adj* (**a**) (*gen*) indifferent (*a* to), unconcerned (*a* about); (*apático*) apathetic, uninterested.

(**b**) (*fig*) indifferent, immaterial; **me es ~** it is immaterial to me, it makes no difference to me.

indiferentemente *adv* indifferently.

indiferentismo *nm* indifference; apathy; (*Rel*) scepticism, indifferentism.

indígena 1 *adj* indigenous (*de* to), native (*de* to); (*LAm*) Indian. **2** *nmf* native; (*LAm*) Indian.

indigencia *nf* poverty, destitution, indigence.

indigenismo *nm* (**a**) (*Ling*) word (*o* phrase *etc*) borrowed from a native language. (**b**) (*LAm Pol*) indigenism, pro-Indian political movement.

indigenista 1 *adj*: **propaganda ~** pro-Indian propaganda, propaganda for the Indian cause. **2** *nmf* supporter of the Indian cause.

indigente 1 *adj* destitute, poverty-stricken, indigent. **2** *nmf* poor person.

indigerible *adj* undigestible.

indigestar [1a] **1** *vt* to cause indigestion to.

2 indigestarse *vr* (**a**) (*persona*) to get indigestion, have indigestion.

(**b**) (*comida*) to cause indigestion, be indigestible; **esa carne se me indigestó** that meat gave me indigestion, I couldn't digest that meat.

(**c**) (*fig*) to be insufferable; **se me indigesta ese tío** I can't stand that fellow.

(**d**) (*LAm*: *inquietarse*) to get worried, get alarmed.

indigestible *adj* indigestible.

indigestión *nf* indigestion.

indigesto *adj* undigested; indigestible, hard to digest; (*fig*) muddled, turgid, badly thought-out.

indignación *nf* indignation, anger; **descargar la ~ sobre** to vent one's spleen on, take out one's anger on.

indignado *adj* indignant, angry (*con, contra* with; *por* at, about).

indignamente *adv* (**a**) (*no merecedor*) unworthily. (**b**) (*merecedor de desprecio*) contemptibly, meanly.

indignante *adj* outrageous, infuriating, unworthy, humiliating.

indignar [1a] **1** *vt* to anger, make indignant; to provoke, stir up.

2 indignarse *vr* to get angry, get indignant; **~ con uno** to get indignant with sb; **¡es para ~!** it's infuriating!; **~ por algo** to get indignant about sth, get angry about sth.

indignidad *nf* (**a**) (*cualidad*) unworthiness. (**b**) (*acto*) unworthy act; (*ofensa*) indignity, insult; **sufrir la ~ de** + *infin* to suffer the indignity of + *ger*.

indigno *adj* (**a**) (*sin mérito*) unworthy (*de* of). (**b**) (*vil*) contemptible, mean, low.

índigo *nm* indigo.

indino* *adj* (**a**) (*insolente*) cheeky*. (**b**) (*And, Carib**: *tacaño*) mean, stingy.

indio 1 *adj* (**a**) *persona* Indian.

(**b**) (*azul*) blue.

2 *nm*, **india** *nf* (**a**) Indian (*of India, of West Indies, of America*).

(**b**) **hacer el ~** to play the fool; to make a silly mistake; **le salió el ~** (*CAm, Cono Sur**) he behaved like a boor; **se le subió el ~** (*Cono Sur**) he flew off the handle*; **ser el ~ gorrón*** to live by scrounging*.

(**c**) **~ viejo** (*CAm, Méx Culin*) stewed meat with maize and herbs.

indirecta *nf* hint; insinuation, innuendo; **~ del padre Cobos** broad hint; **soltar una ~** to drop a hint, make an insinuation.

indirectamente *adv* indirectly.

indirecto *adj* indirect; roundabout.

indiscernible *adj* indiscernible.

indisciplina *nf* indiscipline, lack of discipline; insubordination.

indisciplinado *adj* undisciplined; lax.

indisciplinarse [1a] *vr* to get out of control.

indiscreción *nf* (*gen*) indiscretion; (*falta social*) tactless thing (to do), tactless remark (*etc*), gaffe; **..., si no es ~** ..., if you don't mind my saying ...; **cometió la ~ de** + *infin* he committed the indiscretion of + *ger*, he was so tactless as to + *infin*.

indiscretamente *adv* indiscreetly; tactlessly.

indiscreto *adj* indiscreet; tactless.

indiscriminadamente *adv* indiscriminately.

indiscriminado *adj* indiscriminate.

indisculpable *adj* inexcusable, unforgivable.

indiscutible *adj* indisputable, unquestionable.

indiscutiblemente *adv* indisputably, unquestionably.

indisimulable *adj* that cannot be disguised.
indisimulado *adj* undisguised.
indisociable *adj* inseparable (*de* from).
indisolubilidad *nf* indissolubility.
indisoluble *adj* indissoluble; inseparable.
indisolublemente *adv* indissolubly; inseparably.
indispensable *adj* indispensable, essential.
indisponer [2q] **1** *vt* (**a**) *plan etc* to spoil, upset.
(**b**) (*Med*) to upset, make ill, make unfit.
(**c**) ~ **a uno con otro** to set sb against another person, prejudice sb against another person.
2 indisponerse *vr* (**a**) (*Med*) to become ill, fall ill.
(**b**) ~ **con uno** to fall out with sb.
indisponible *adj* not available, unavailable.
indisposición *nf* (**a**) (*Med*) indisposition, slight illness. (**b**) (*desgana*) disinclination, unwillingness.
indispuesto *adj* (**a**) (*Med*) indisposed, unwell, slightly ill; **sentirse** ~ to feel slightly ill, feel queer. (**b**) (*sin ganas*) disinclined, unwilling.
indisputable *adj* indisputable, unquestioned; unchallenged.
indistinción *nf* (**a**) (*gen*) indistinctness; vagueness. (**b**) (*falta de discriminación*) lack of discrimination. (**c**) (*igualdad*) lack of distinction, sameness, identity.
indistinguible *adj* indistinguishable (*de* from).
indistintamente *adv* (*V adj*) (**a**) indistinctly; vaguely. (**b**) without distinction, indiscriminately. (**c**) **pueden firmar** ~ either (joint holder of the account *etc*) may sign.
indistinto *adj* (**a**) (*poco claro*) indistinct; vague; (*borroso*) faint, dim. (**b**) (*indiscriminado*) indiscriminate.
individua* *nf* (*pey*) woman, female.
individual 1 *adj* (**a**) (*gen*) individual; (*particular*) peculiar, special; *cama, habitación* single.
(**b**) (*And, Cono Sur**: *idéntico*) identical; **A es ~ a B** A is the spitting image of B.
2 *nm* (*Dep*) singles, singles match; ~ **femenino** women's singles; ~ **masculino** men's singles.
individualidad *nf* individuality.
individualismo *nm* individualism.
individualista 1 *adj* individualistic. **2** *nmf* individualist.
individualizar [1f] *vt* to individualize.
individualmente *adv* individually.
individuar [1e] *vt* to individualize.
individuo 1 *adj* individual. **2** *nm* (**a**) individual; (*pey*) individual, chap, fellow; **el ~ en cuestión** the person in question; **él cuida bien de su ~*** he knows how to look after Number One. (**b**) (*de sociedad*) member, fellow.
indivisibilidad *nf* indivisibility.
indivisible *adj* indivisible.
indiviso *adj* undivided.
indización *nf* indexation; (*Fin*) index-linking; (*Inform*) indexing.
indizado *adj* (*Fin*) index-linked.
indizar [1f] *vt* to index; (*Fin*) to index-link.
INDO *nm* (*Com*) *abr de* **Instituto Nacional de Denominaciones de Origen (de los Vinos Españoles)**.
Indo *nm* (*Geog*) Indus.
indo, -a *adj, nm/f* Indian, Hindu.
indo... *pref* Indo...
indócil *adj* unmanageable, headstrong; disobedient.
indocilidad *nf* unmanageableness, headstrong character; disobedience.
indocto *adj* ignorant, unlearned.
indoctrinar [1a] *vt* (*LAm*) to indoctrinate.
indocumentado 1 *adj* without identifying documents, who carries no identity papers. **2** *nm*, **indocumentada** *nf* person who carries no identity papers; (*Méx etc*) illegal immigrant; (*hum*) ignoramus.
Indochina *nf*: **la** ~ Indochina.
indoeuropeo, -a 1 *adj, nm/f* Indo-European. **2** *nm* (*Ling*) Indo-European.
índole *nf* (**a**) (*naturaleza*) nature; character, disposition. (**b**) (*clase*) class, kind, sort; **cosas de esta** ~ things of this kind.
indolencia *nf* indolence, laziness; listlessness.
indolente *adj* indolent, lazy; listless.
indoloro *adj* painless.
indomable *adj espíritu etc* indomitable; *animal* untameable; (*fig*) unmanageable, uncontrollable.
indomado *adj* wild, untamed.
indomesticable *adj* untameable.
indómito *adj* = **indomable**.
Indonesia *nf* Indonesia.
indonesio, -a *adj, nm/f* Indonesian.
indormia* *nf* (*And, Carib*) trick, wangle*, wheeze*.
Indostán *nm* Hindustan.
indostanés, -esa *adj, nm/f* Hindustani.
indostaní *nm* (*Ling*) Hindustani.
indostánico 1 *adj* Hindustani. **2** *nm* (*Ling*) Hindustani.
indotado *adj* without a dowry.
indte. *abr de* **indistintamente**.
Indubán [indu'ban] *nm* (*Esp Fin*) *abr de* **Banco de Financiación Industrial**.
indubitable *adj* indubitable, undoubted, certain.
indubitablemente *adv* indubitably, undoubtedly.
inducción *nf* (**a**) (*Elec, Filos*) induction; **por** ~ by induction, inductively. (**b**) (*persuasión*) inducement, persuasion.
inducido *nm* (*Elec*) armature.
inducir [3n] *vt* (**a**) (*Elec*) to induce; (*Filos*) to infer.
(**b**) (*persuadir*) to induce, persuade; ~ **a uno a hacer algo** to induce sb to do sth; ~ **a uno en el** (*o* **al**) **error** to lead sb into error.
inductivo *adj* inductive; **pregunta inductiva** leading question.
indudable *adj* undoubted, indubitable; unquestionable; **es ~ que** ... there is no doubt that ...
indudablemente *adv* undoubtedly, doubtless; unquestionably.
indulgencia *nf* (**a**) (*gen*) indulgence; forbearance; **proceder sin ~ contra** to proceed ruthlessly against.
(**b**) (*Ecl*) indulgence; ~ **plenaria** plenary indulgence.
indulgente *adj* indulgent, lenient (*con* towards).
indulgentemente *adv* indulgently, leniently.
indultar [1a] **1** *vt* (**a**) (*Jur*) to pardon, reprieve (*de* from).
(**b**) (*eximir*) to exempt, excuse (*de* from).
2 indultarse *vr* (**a**) (*And*: *entrometerse*) to meddle, pry.
(**b**) (*Carib**) to get o.s. out of a jam*.
indulto *nm* (**a**) (*Jur*) pardon, reprieve. (**b**) (*exención*) exemption, excusal.
indumentaria *nf* (**a**) (*ropa*) clothing, apparel, dress. (**b**) (*estudio*) (history of) costume.
indumentario *adj* clothing (*atr*); **elegancia indumentaria** elegance of dress, sartorial elegance.
indumento *nm* clothing, apparel, dress.
industria *nf* (**a**) (*Com etc*) industry; ~ **algodonera** cotton industry; ~ **artesanal** *o* **doméstica** cottage industry; ~ **del automóvil** car industry, automobile industry (*US*); ~ **básica** basic industry; ~ **casera** cottage industry; **~s con chimeneas** smokestack industries; ~ **ligera** light industry; ~ **militar** weapons industry, defence industry; ~ **pesada** heavy industry; ~ **primaria** extractive industry; ~ **secundaria** manufacturing industry; ~ **siderúrgica** iron and steel industry; ~ **terciaria** service industry.
(**b**) (*dedicación*) industry, industriousness.
(**c**) (*maña*) ingenuity, skill, expertise; **de** ~ on purpose.
industrial 1 *adj* (**a**) (*de la industria*) industrial. (**b**) (*no casero*) factory-made, industrially produced; (*fig*) large, massive; large-scale. **2** *nmf* industrialist, manufacturer.
industrialismo *nm* industrialism.
industrialista *nm/f* (*LAm*) industrialist.
industrialización *nf* industrialization.
industrializar [1f] **1** *vt* to industrialize. **2 industrializarse** *vr* to become industrialized.
industriarse [1b] *vr* to manage, find a way; ~ **para** + *infin* to manage to + *infin*, contrive to + *infin*.
industriosamente *adv* (**a**) industriously. (**b**) skilfully, resourcefully.
industrioso *adj* (**a**) (*trabajador*) industrious. (**b**) (*mañoso*) skilful, resourceful, versatile, handy.
INE ['ine] *nm* (*Esp*) *abr de* **Instituto Nacional de Estadística**.
inédito *adj* (**a**) (*Liter*) unpublished; **un texto rigurosamente ~** a text never published previously in any form.
(**b**) (*fig*) new; not known hitherto, hitherto unheard-of; **una experiencia inédita** a completely new experience.
ineducable *adj* ineducable.
ineducado *adj* (**a**) (*sin instrucción*) uneducated. (**b**) (*maleducado*) ill-bred, bad-mannered, uncouth.
INEF [ɪ'nef] *nm abr de* **Instituto Nacional de Educación Física**.
inefable *adj* indescribable, inexpressible, ineffable.
inefectivo *adj* (*LAm*) ineffective.
ineficacia *nf* (**a**) (*de medida*) ineffectiveness. (**b**) (*de proceso*) inefficiency.
ineficaz *adj* (*V n*) (**a**) ineffective, ineffectual. (**b**) inefficient.
ineficazmente *adv* (*V n*) (**a**) ineffectively, ineffectually. (**b**) inefficiently.
ineficiencia *nf* inefficiency.
ineficiente *adj* inefficient.
inelástico *adj* inelastic.

inelegancia *nf* inelegance, lack of elegance.
inelegante *adj* inelegant.
inelegantemente *adv* inelegantly.
inelegibilidad *nf* ineligibility.
inelegible *adj* ineligible.
ineluctable *adj*, **ineludible** *adj* unavoidable, inescapable; **elemento** ~ essential element.
INEM [i'nem] *nm* (**a**) (*Esp*) *abr de* **Instituto Nacional de Empleo.** (**b**) (*Esp*) *abr de* **Instituto Nacional de Enseñanza Media.**
INEN [i'nen] *nm* (*Méx*) *abr de* **Instituto Nacional de Energía Nuclear.**
inenarrable *adj* inexpressible.
inencogible *adj* unshrinkable, non-shrink, which will not shrink.
inencontrolable *adj* that cannot be found, impossible to find; extremely scarce.
inepcia *nf* (**a**) (*gen*) ineptitude, incompetence; stupidity. (**b**) (*impropiedad*) unsuitability. (**c**) (*necedad*) silly thing (to say *etc*); **decir ~s** to talk rubbish.
ineptitud *nf* (*V* **inepcia**) (**a**) ineptitude, incompetence. (**b**) unsuitability.
inepto *adj* (**a**) (*incompetente*) inept, incompetent; stupid; ~ **de toda ineptitud** utterly incompetent. (**b**) (*no apto*) unsuited (*para* to), unsuitable (*para* for).
inequívoco *adj* unequivocal, unambiguous; unmistakable.
inercia *nf* (**a**) (*Fís*) inertia. (**b**) (*fig*) passivity; sluggishness, slowness.
inerme *adj* unarmed; defenceless, unprotected.
inerte *adj* (**a**) (*Fís*) inert. (**b**) (*fig*) passive, inactive; sluggish, slow.
Inés *nf* Agnes.
inescamoteable *adj* that cannot be got rid of, unavoidable.
inescrupuloso *adj* unscrupulous.
inescrutabilidad *nf* inscrutability.
inescrutable *adj* inscrutable.
inespecífico *adj* unspecific, non-specific.
inesperadamente *adv* unexpectedly; without warning, suddenly.
inesperado *adj* unexpected, unforeseen; sudden.
inesquivable *adj* unavoidable.
inestabilidad *nf* instability, unsteadiness.
inestabilizar [1f] **1** *vt* to destabilize. **2 inestabilizarse** *vr* to become unstable.
inestable *adj* unstable, unsteady.
inestimable *adj* inestimable, invaluable.
inevitabilidad *nf* inevitability.
inevitable *adj* inevitable, unavoidable.
inevitablemente *adv* inevitably, unavoidably.
inexactitud *nf* inaccuracy; incorrectness.
inexacto *adj* inaccurate; incorrect, untrue; **esto es** ~ this is not so, this is incorrect.
inexcusable *adj* (**a**) (*imperdonable*) inexcusable, unforgivable. (**b**) (*inevitable*) necessary, unavoidable, inevitable; **una visita** ~ a trip which must not be missed, an absolutely essential visit.
inexcusablemente *adv* inexcusably, unforgivably; **el depósito será devuelto ~ si ...** the deposit will be returned as a matter of obligation if ...
inexhausto *adj* inexhaustible, unending.
inexistencia *nf* non-existence.
inexistente *adj* non-existent; which no longer exists, defunct.
inexorable *adj* inexorable.
inexorablemente *adv* inexorably.
inexperiencia *nf* inexperience; unskilfulness, lack of skill.
inexperimentado *adj* inexperienced.
inexperto *adj* inexperienced; unskilled, inexpert.
inexplicable *adj* inexplicable, unaccountable.
inexplicablemente *adv* inexplicably, unaccountably.
inexplicado *adj* unexplained.
inexplorado *adj* unexplored; *mar etc* uncharted.
inexplotado *adj* unexploited, unused.
inexportable *adj* that cannot be exported.
inexpresable *adj* inexpressible.
inexpresividad *nf* inexpressiveness; flatness, woodenness.
inexpresivo *adj* inexpressive; dull, flat, wooden.
inexpuesto *adj* (*Fot*) unexposed.
inexpugnabilidad *nf* impregnability.
inexpugnable *adj* (**a**) (*Mil*) impregnable. (**b**) (*fig*) firm, unyielding, unshakeable.
inextinguible *adj* inextinguishable, unquenchable.
inextirpable *adj* ineradicable.
in extremis *adv*: **estar** ~ to be at death's door, be at one's last gasp.
inextricable *adj* inextricable; *bosque etc* impenetrable.
infalibilidad *nf* infallibility; certainty ~ **pontificia** papal infallibility.
infalible *adj* infallible; certain, sure; foolproof; *puntería* unerring.
infaliblemente *adv* infallibly; surely; unerringly.
infaltable *adj* (*LAm*) not to be missed.
infamación *nf* defamation.
infamador 1 *adj* defamatory, slanderous. **2** *nm*, **infamadora** *nf* slanderer.
infamante *adj* (*injurioso*) offensive, rude; (*difamatorio*) slanderous; *pena etc* shameful, degrading.
infamar [1a] *vt* to dishonour, discredit; to defame, slander.
infamatorio *adj* defamatory, slanderous.
infame 1 *adj* infamous, odious, vile; *tarea* terrible, thankless; **esto es** ~ this is montrous, this is infamous. **2** *nmf* vile person, villain.
infamia *nf* infamy; disgrace.
infancia *nf* (**a**) (*edad*) infancy, childhood; (*fig*) infancy. (**b**) (*niños*) children.
infanta *nf* (**a**) (*niña*) infant. (**b**) (*princesa*) infanta, princess.
infante *nm* (**a**) (*niño*) infant. (**b**) (*príncipe*) infante, prince; (*Mil*: *Hist*) infantryman; ~ **de marina** marine.
infantería *nf* infantry; ~ **de marina** marines.
infanticida *nmf* infanticide (*person*), child-killer.
infanticidio *nm* infanticide (*act*); (*) liking for young girls.
infantil *adj* (**a**) (*de niño*) infant; child's, children's; **libros ~es** children's books; (**de**) **tamaño** ~ child's size; **para el uso** ~ for children (to use). (**b**) (*inocente*) childlike, innocent; (*pey*) infantile, childish.
infantilismo *nm* infantilism.
infantiloide *adj* childish, puerile.
infanzón *nm*, **infanzona** *nf* (*Hist*) *member of the lowest rank of the nobility*.
infarto *nm*: ~ (**de miocardio**) heart attack; (*Med*) coronary thrombosis.
infatigable *adj* tireless, untiring.
infatigablemente *adv* tirelessly, untiringly.
infatuación *nf* vanity, conceit.
infatuar [1d] **1** *vt* to make conceited. **2 infatuarse** *vr* to get conceited (*con* about).
infausto *adj* unlucky; ill-starred, ill-fated.
INFE ['ɪnfe] *nm abr de* **Instituto de Fomento de las Exportaciones.**
infección *nf* infection.
infecciosidad *nf* infectiousness.
infeccioso *adj*, **infectante** *adj* infectious.
infectar [1a] **1** *vt* (**a**) (*gen*) to infect. (**b**) (*contaminar*) to contaminate, corrupt; (*pervertir*) to pervert. **2 infectarse** *vr* to become infected (*de* with; *t fig*).
infecto *adj* infected (*de* with); foul; corrupt, tainted.
infecundidad *nf* infertility; sterility, barrenness.
infecundo *adj* infertile; sterile, barren; **la época infecunda de la mujer** the woman's infertile period.
infelicidad *nf* unhappiness; misfortune.
infeliz 1 *adj* (**a**) (*desgraciado*) unhappy; (*desdichado*) unfortunate, miserable, wretched; *tentativa etc* unsuccessful.
(**b**) (*bonachón*) simple, kind-hearted, good-natured; (*pey*) gullible.
(**c**) (*Cono Sur, Méx**: *nimio*) trifling, insignificant.
2 *nmf* (**a**) (*desgraciado*) wretch, poor devil.
(**b**) (*inocentón*) simpleton.
infelizmente *adv* unhappily.
infelizón* *nm*, **infelizote*** *nm* = **infeliz 2** (**a**).
inferencia *nf* inference; **por** ~ by inference.
inferior 1 *adj* (**a**) (*situación*) lower (*a* than); **la parte** ~ the lower part; **el lado** ~ the underside, the side underneath; **el Egipto** ~ lower Egypt.
(**b**) (*calidad, rango*) inferior (*a* to), lower (*a* than); **de calidad** ~ of inferior quality; **no ser ~ a nadie** to be inferior to none; **le es ~ en talento** he is inferior to him in talent.
(**c**) (*Mat*) lower; **cualquier número ~ a 9** any number under 9, any number below 9, any number less than 9; **una cantidad** ~ a lesser quantity.
2 *nmf* inferior, subordinate; (*pey*) underling.
inferioridad *nf* inferiority; **en ~ de condiciones** on less good conditions.
inferir [3i] *vt* (**a**) (*deducir*) to infer, deduce; **~ una cosa de** (*o* **por**) **otra** to infer one thing from another.

(**b**) *herida* to inflict (*a, en* on); *daños* to cause; *insulto* to offer (*a* to).
infernáculo *nm* hopscotch.
infernal *adj* infernal; (*fig*) infernal, hellish, devilish.
infernillo *nm* (*t* ~ **de alcohol**) spirit lamp, spirit stove; ~ **campestre** camp stove; ~ **de gasolina** petrol stove.
infértil *adj* infertile.
infestación *nf* infestation.
infestante *adj* invasive, pervasive.
infestar [1a] *vt* (**a**) (*infectar*) to infect; (*insectos etc*) to infest; (*invadir*) to overrun, invade. (**b**) (*fig*) to harass, beset.
inficionar [1a] *vt* = **infectar**.
infidelidad *nf* (**a**) (*adulterio*) infidelity, unfaithfulness; ~ **conyugal** marital infidelity. (**b**) (*Ecl*) unbelief, lack of faith. (**c**) (*Ecl: personas*) unbelievers, infidels.
infidencia *nf* (**a**) (*cualidad*) disloyalty, faithlessness; treason. (**b**) (*acto*) disloyal act; breach of trust.
infiel 1 *adj* (**a**) (*desleal*) unfaithful, disloyal (*a, con, para* to); **fue ~ a su mujer** he was unfaithful to his wife.
(**b**) (*Ecl*) unbelieving, infidel.
(**c**) *informe etc* inaccurate; **la memoria le fue ~** his memory failed him.
2 *nmf* (*Ecl*) unbeliever, infidel.
infielmente *adv* (*V adj*) (**a**) unfaithfully, disloyally. (**b**) inaccurately.
infierno *nm* (**a**) hell.
(**b**) (*fig y en locuciones*) hell, inferno; hades; **¡anda al ~!** go to hell!; **está en el quinto ~** it's at the back of beyond, it's right off the map; **mandar a uno al quinto ~** (*o* **a los quintos ~s**) to tell sb to go to hell.
infijo *nm* infix.
infiltración *nf* infiltration.
infiltrado, -a *nm/f* infiltrator.
infiltrar [1a] **1** *vt* to infiltrate (*en* into); (*fig*) to inculcate (*en* in). **2 infiltrarse** *vr* to infiltrate (*t fig; en* into), filter (*en* in, through); to percolate.
ínfimo *adj* lowest; (*fig*) very poor, of very poor quality; vile, mean; least; **a precios ~s** at very low prices, at ridiculously low prices.
infinidad *nf* (**a**) (*Mat etc*) infinity.
(**b**) (*fig*) great quantity, enormous number; **~ de** an infinity of, vast numbers of; **durante una ~ de días** for days on end; **~ de veces** countless times; **hay ~ de personas que ...** there are great numbers of people who ...
infinitamente *adj* infinitely.
infinitesimal *adj* infinitesimal.
infinitivo 1 *adj* infinitive. **2** *nm* infinitive (mood).
infinito 1 *adj* (**a**) (*Mat etc*) infinite.
(**b**) (*fig*) infinite; boundless, limitless, endless; **hasta lo ~** ad infinitum.
2 *adv* infinitely, immensely; **se lo agradezco ~** I'm enormously grateful to you (for it).
3 *nm* (*Mat*) infinity; **el ~** (*Filos etc*) the infinite.
infinitud *nf* infinitude.
inflable *adj* inflatable.
inflación *nf* (**a**) (*gen, t Econ*) inflation; (*hinchazón*) swelling. (**b**) (*fig*) pride, conceit.
inflacionario *adj* inflationary.
inflacionismo *nm* (*Econ*) inflation, inflationism.
inflacionista *adj* inflationary.
inflado *nm* inflating, pumping up.
inflador *nm* (*LAm*) bicycle pump.
inflagaitas* *nmf invar* twit*.
inflamabilidad *nf* inflammability.
inflamable *adj* inflammable, flammable.
inflamación *nf* (**a**) (*combustión*) ignition, combustion. (**b**) (*Med*) inflammation.
inflamar [1a] **1** *vt* (**a**) (*lit*) to set on fire, ignite.
(**b**) (*Med*) to inflame.
(**c**) (*fig*) to inflame, excite, arouse.
2 inflamarse *vr* (**a**) to catch fire, flame up, ignite; **se inflama fácilmente** it is highly inflammable.
(**b**) (*Med*) to become inflamed.
(**c**) (*fig*) to become inflamed (*de, en* with), get excited.
inflamatorio *adj* inflammatory.
inflapollas‡ *nm invar* berk‡, wimp‡.
inflar [1a] **1** *vt* (**a**) (*hinchar*) to inflate, blow up, pump air into.
(**b**) (*fig*) to inflate, exaggerate; to make conceited.
(**c**) (*Cono Sur*) to heed, pay attention to.
(**d**) (*Econ*) to reinflate.
2 *vi* (*Méx**) to booze*, drink.
3 inflarse *vr* (**a**) to swell.
(**b**) (*fig*) to get conceited, get puffed up.
inflatorio *adj* inflationary.
inflexibilidad *nf* inflexibility; unyielding nature.
inflexible *adj* inflexible; unbending, unyielding; **~ a los ruegos** unmoved by appeals, unresponsive to appeals; **regla ~** strict rule, hard-and-fast rule.
inflexión *nf* inflexion.
infligir [3c] *vt* to inflict (*a* on).
influencia *nf* influence (*sobre* on); **bajo la ~ de** under the influence of.
influenciable *adj* impressionable, easily influenced.
influenciar [1b] *vt* to influence.
influenza *nf* influenza.
influir [3g] **1** *vt* to influence; **A, influido por B ...** A, influenced by B ...
2 *vi* (**a**) to have influence, carry weight, have pull (*con* with); **es hombre que influye** he's a man of influence, he's a man who carries weight.
(**b**) **~ en, ~ sobre** to influence, affect, have an influence on; to have a hand in.
influjo *nm* influence (*sobre* on).
influyente *adj* influential.
información *nf* (**a**) (*gen*) information; (*noticias*) news; (*Mil*) intelligence; (*Inform*) data; **una ~** a piece of information, a piece of news; **~ caliente** hot tip; **~ secreta** secret information, classified information.
(**b**) (*informe*) report, account; (*referencia*) reference, testimonial; (*apartado de periódico*) section; **~ de crédito** credit report; **~ deportiva** sports section, sporting page; **~ extranjera** news from abroad, foreign news; **~ periodística** newspaper report.
(**c**) (*Jur*) legal proceedings; judicial inquiry, investigation; **abrir una ~** to begin proceedings.
informado *adj* informed.
informador(a) *nm/f* (*gen*) informant; **~ (de policía)** informer; **~ gráfico** reporter, pressman; photojournalist; **~ turístico** tourist guide; **los ~es (de la Prensa** *etc*) (the representatives of) the media.
informal *adj* (**a**) (*pey: incorrecto*) irregular, incorrect; *conducta etc* bad, unmannerly; (*poco usual*) unconventional.
(**b**) (*pey*) *persona* (*poco fiable*) unreliable, untrustworthy; shifty; (*incapaz*) unbusinesslike, disorganized; (*maleducado*) offhand, bad-mannered; (*frívolo*) frivolous.
(**c**) (*no oficial*) informal; **conversación ~** informal talk; **lenguaje ~** informal language, non-official language.
informalidad *nf* (*V adj*) (**a**) irregularity, incorrectness; unmannerliness; unconventionality.
(**b**) unreliability, untrustworthiness, shiftiness; unbusinesslike nature; offhandedness, bad manners; frivolity, levity.
(**c**) informality, non-official nature.
informalmente *adv* (*V adj*) (**a**) irregularly; badly; unconventionally. (**b**) unreliably; shiftily; in an unbusinesslike way; offhandedly; frivolously. (**c**) informally, unofficially.
informante *nmf* informant.
informar [1a] **1** *vt* (**a**) (*enterar*) to inform, tell (*de* of, *sobre* about); to announce (*que* that); **quedo informado de que ...** I understand that ....
(**b**) (*dar forma a*) to form, shape.
2 *vi* (**a**) (*gen*) to report (*acerca de, de* on); **el profesor informará de su descubrimiento** the professor will report on his discovery.
(**b**) (*Jur: abogado*) to plead.
(**c**) (*Jur: delator*) to inform (*contra* against), lay information (*contra* against).
3 informarse *vr* to find out, inform o.s.; **~ de** to find out about, acquaint o.s. with, inquire into; **~ sobre algo** to gather information about sth.
informática[1] *nf* information science, computer science, informatics, computing; **~ gráfica** computer graphics.
informático 1 *adj* computer (*atr*); **centro ~** computer centre; **servicios ~s** computer services.
2 *nm*, **informática**[2] *nf* computer scientist; computer programmer.
informatividad *nf* informativity, informative nature.
informativo 1 *adj* (**a**) (*gen*) informative; news (*atr*); **un folleto ~** a booklet of information, an explanatory booklet; **programa ~** (*TV etc*) news programme. (**b**) *comité etc* consultative, advisory. **2** *nm* (*Rad, TV*) news programme.
informatización *nf* computerization.
informatizar [1f] *vt* to computerize.
informe[1] *adj* shapeless.

informe² *nm* (**a**) (*declaración*) report, statement; announcement; (*Parl*) report, white paper; ~ **forense** coroner's report; ~ **de prensa** press release; **el** ~ **del ministro** the minister's statement.

(**b**) (*dato*) piece of information; **~s** information; data, particulars, references; **según mis ~s** according to my information; **dar ~s sobre** to give information about; **pedir ~s** to ask for information, make inquiries (*a* of, *sobre* about); **tomar ~s** to gather information.

(**c**) (*Jur*) plea; ~ **forense,** ~ **jurídico** pleading.

infortunado *adj* unfortunate, unlucky.

infortunio *nm* misfortune, ill luck; mishap.

infra... *pref* infra..., under...

infraalimentación *nf* undernourishment.

infra(a)limentado *adj* underfed, undernourished.

infracción *nf* infraction, infringement (*de* of); breach (*de* of); (*Aut etc*) offence (*de* against); ~ **de contrato** breach of contract.

infractor(a) *nm/f* offender (*de* against).

infradesarrollado *adj* under-developed.

infradesarrollo *nm* under-development.

infradotado 1 *adj* short of resources, insufficiently supplied; understaffed. **2** *nm,* **infradotada** *nf* subnormal person.

infra(e)scrito 1 *adj* undersigned; undermentioned. **2** *nm,* **infra(e)scrita** *nf*: **el** ~ the undersigned; (*LAm*: *hum*) the present speaker, I myself.

infraestimación *nf* underestimate.

infraestimar [1a] *vt* to underestimate.

infra(e)structura *nf* infrastructure.

in fraganti *adv*: **coger a uno** ~ to catch sb red-handed.

infrahumano *adj* subhuman.

infraliteratura *nf* pulp fiction.

inframundo *nm* underworld.

infrangible *adj* unbreakable.

infranqueable *adj* impassable; (*fig*) unsurmountable.

infrarrojo *adj* infrared.

infrautilización *nf* under-use.

infrautilizar [1f] *vt* to under-use.

infravaloración *nf* undervaluing; underestimate.

infravalorar [1a] *vt* to undervalue; to underestimate.

infravaluar [1e] *vt* to underestimate; to play down.

infraviviendas *nfpl* sub-standard housing.

infrecuencia *nf* infrequency.

infrecuente *adj* infrequent.

infringir [3c] *vt* to infringe, break, contravene.

infructuosamente *adv* fruitlessly, unsuccessfully; unprofitably.

infructuoso *adj* fruitless, unsuccessful; unprofitable.

ínfulas *nfpl* (*vanidad*) conceit; (*disparates*) pretentious nonsense; **darse** ~ to put on airs, get on one's high horse; **tener** (**muchas**) ~ **de** to fancy o.s. as.

infumable *adj* (**a**) (*gen*) unsmokable. (**b**) (*fig*: *insoportable*) unbearable, intolerable.

infundado *adj* unfounded, baseless, groundless.

infundia* *nf* (*LAm*) fat.

infundio* *nm* fairy tale, lie; malicious story.

infundir [3a] *vt* (**a**) (*gen*) to infuse (*a, en* into).

(**b**) (*fig*) to instil (*a, en* into); ~ **ánimo a uno** to encourage sb; ~ **miedo a uno** to scare sb, frighten sb, fill sb with fear; ~ **un espíritu nuevo a un club** to inject new life into a club, put new life into a club.

infusión *nf* infusion; ~ **de hierbas** herbal tea.

Ing. *abr de* **ingeniero, ingeniera** engineer.

ingeniar [1a] **1** *vt* to devise, think up, contrive.

2 ingeniarse *vr* to manage, find a way, get along; ~ **con algo** to manage with sth, make do with sth; ~ (*o* **ingeniárselas**) para + *infin* to manage to + *infin*, contrive to + *infin*.

ingeniería *nf* engineering; ~ **civil** civil engineering; ~ **de control** control engineering; ~ **eléctrica** electrical engineering; ~ **genética** genetic engineering; ~ **química** chemical engineering; ~ **de sistemas** systems engineering; ~ **social** social engineering.

ingeniero, -a *nm/f* (**a**) engineer (*t Mil, Náut*); ~ **agrónomo** agronomist, agricultural expert; ~ **de caminos, canales y puertos** civil engineer; ~ **forestal,** ~ **de montes** forestry expert; ~ **de mantenimiento** maintenance engineer; ~ **de minas** mining engineer; ~ **naval** shipbuilder, naval architect; ~ **pecuario** veterinary surgeon; ~ **químico** chemical engineer; ~ **de sonido** sound engineer; ~ **de vuelo** flight engineer.

(**b**) (*LAm Univ, frec*) graduate; **el I~ Pérez** Dr Pérez.

ingenio *nm* (**a**) (*inventiva*) ingenuity, inventiveness; (*talento*) talent; creativeness; (*agudeza*) wit, wits; **aguzar el** ~ to sharpen one's wits.

(**b**) (*persona*) clever person, talented person; (*Hist*) wit.

(**c**) (*Mec*) apparatus, engine, machine, device; (*Mil*) device; ~ **nuclear** nuclear device.

(**d**) (*Téc*) mill, plant; (*And*: *de acero*) foundry, steel works; ~ (**de azúcar**), ~ **azucarero** sugar mill, sugar refinery.

ingeniosamente *adv* (**a**) ingeniously, cleverly. (**b**) wittily.

ingeniosidad *nf* (**a**) (*maña*) ingenuity, ingeniousness, cleverness, resourcefulness. (**b**) (*una* ~) clever idea. (**c**) (*agudeza*) wittiness.

ingenioso *adj* (**a**) (*mañoso*) ingenious, clever, resourceful. (**b**) (*agudo*) witty.

ingénito *adj* innate, inborn.

ingente *adj* huge, enormous.

ingenuamente *adv* ingenuously, naïvely; with candour; simply, unaffectedly.

ingenuidad *nf* ingenuousness, naïveté; candour; simplicity.

ingenuo *adj* ingenuous, candid; simple, unaffected.

ingerido* *adj* (*Méx*) (*enfermo*) ill, under the weather; (*abatido*) downcast.

ingerir [3i] *vt* to swallow; to ingest, consume, take in; **el automovilista había ingerido 3 litros de alcohol** the motorist had drunk 3 litres of alcohol.

ingesta *nf* ingestion, intake.

ingestión *nf* swallowing; ingestion.

Inglaterra *nf* England; (*en sentido no estricto frec*) Great Britain, United Kingdom; **la batalla de** ~ the Battle of Britain (*1940*).

ingle *nf* groin.

inglés 1 *adj* English; (*en sentido no estricto frec*) British. **2** *nm* Englishman; Briton, Britisher (*US*); **los ingleses** the English, the British. **3** *nm* (*Ling*) English.

inglesa *nf* Englishwoman; Briton, Britisher (*US*); **montar a la** ~ to ride sidesaddle.

inglesismo *nm* anglicism.

inglete *nm* angle of 45°; (*ensambladura*) mitre joint.

ingobernabilidad *nf* uncontrollable nature; (*Pol*) ungovernable nature.

ingobernable *adj* uncontrollable, unmanageable; (*Pol*) ungovernable.

ingratitud *nf* ingratitude.

ingrato *adj* (**a**) *persona* ungrateful; **¡~!** you wretch! (**b**) *sabor* unpleasant, disagreeable; *tarea etc* thankless, unrewarding.

ingravidez *nf* weightlessness.

ingrávido *adj* weightless; very light.

ingrediente *nm* ingredient; **~s** (*Cono Sur*) hors d'oeuvres (*on the bar counter*).

ingresado, -a *nm/f* (*Univ etc*) entrant, new student.

ingresar [1a] **1** *vt* (**a**) *dinero* to deposit, pay in; *ganancias* to receive, take in; ~ **dinero en una cuenta** to pay money into an account.

(**b**) ~ **al hijo en un colegio** to get one's son into a school; **la cárcel donde X está ingresado** the prison in which X is being held.

(**c**) ~ **a uno** (*Med*) to admit sb (as a patient); **X continúa ingresado en el hospital** X is still in hospital.

2 *vi* to come in, enter; ~ **en** (*LAm*: **a**) **una sociedad** to join a club, become a member of a club, be admitted to a society; ~ **en la Academia** to be admitted to the Academy, be received into the Academy; ~ **en el ejército** to join the army, join up; ~ **en el hospital** to be admitted to hospital; **pero ingresó cadáver** but he was dead on arrival (at hospital).

3 ingresarse *vr* (*Méx*) to join, become a member; (*Méx*: *Mil*) to join up.

ingreso *nm* (**a**) (*acto*) entry (*en* into), joining; admission (*en* to); **su** ~ **en la Academia** his admission to the Academy; **examen de** ~ entrance examination.

(**b**) (*Com*) entry; deposit; sum received; ~ **gravable** taxable income.

(**c**) **~s** (*Fin*: *renta*) income; revenue; receipts, takings; **~s accesorios** additional earnings, earnings on the side; fringe benefits; **~s anuales** annual income; **~s brutos** gross receipts; **~s devengados** earned income; **~s ocasionales** casual earnings; **vivir con arreglo a los ~s** to live within one's income.

íngrimo *adj* (*LAm*) all alone.

inguandia *nf* (*And*) fib, tale.

INH *nm abr de* **Instituto Nacional de Hidrocarburos.**

inhábil *adj* (**a**) (*torpe*) unskilful, inexpert, clumsy;

(*incompetente*) incompetent. (**b**) (*no apto*) unfit (*para* for, *para + infin* to + *infin*). (**c**) **día** ~ non-working day.

inhabilidad *nf* (*V adj*) (**a**) unskilfulness; clumsiness; incompetence. (**b**) unfitness (*para* for).

inhabilitación *nf* (**a**) (*Pol Jur*) disqualification; *V* **nota**. (**b**) (*Med*) disablement.

inhabilitar [1a] *vt* (**a**) (*Pol Jur*) to disqualify (*para + infin* from + *ger*); to remove (from office). (**b**) (*Med*) to disable; to render unfit (*para* for).

inhabitable *adj* uninhabitable.

inhabitado *adj* uninhabited.

inhabituado *adj* unaccustomed (*a* to).

inhabitual *adj* unusual, out of the ordinary, exceptional.

inhalación *nf* inhalation; ~ **de colas** glue-sniffing.

inhalador *nm* (*Med*) inhaler.

inhalante *nm* inhalant.

inhalar [1a] *vt* to inhale; *colas* to sniff.

inherente *adj* inherent (*a* in); **la función ~ a un oficio** the function pertaining to a post, the duties attached to an office.

inhibición *nf* inhibition.

inhibidor 1 *adj* inhibiting. **2** *nm* inhibitor; ~ **del apetito** appetite depressant; ~ **del crecimiento** growth inhibitor.

inhibir [3a] **1** *vt* to inhibit; (*Jur*) to restrain, stay. **2 inhibirse** *vr* to keep out (*de* of), to stay away (*de* from); to refrain (*de* from).

inhibitorio *adj* inhibitory.

inhospitalario *adj* inhospitable; (*fig*) bleak, cheerless, uninviting.

inhospitalidad *nf* inhospitality.

inhóspito *adj* inhospitable.

inhumación *nf* burial, inhumation.

inhumanamente *adv* inhumanly.

inhumanidad *nf* inhumanity.

inhumano *adj* inhuman; (*Cono Sur*) dirty, disgusting.

inhumar [1a] *vt* to bury, inter.

INI ['ini] *nm* (**a**) (*Esp Com*) *abr de* **Instituto Nacional de Industria.** (**b**) (*Chile*) *abr de* **Instituto Nacional de Investigaciones.**

INIA *nm* (**a**) (*Esp Agr*) *abr de* **Instituto Nacional de Investigación Agraria.** (**b**) (*Méx*) *abr de* **Instituto Nacional de Investigaciones Agrícolas.**

iniciación *nf* initiation; beginning.

iniciado 1 *adj* initiate(d). **2** *nm*, **iniciada** *nf* initiate.

iniciador(a) 1 *nm/f* initiator, starter; pioneer. **2** *nm* (*de bomba*) primer, priming device.

inicial 1 *adj* initial. **2** *nf* (**a**) initial. (**b**) (*Carib*) deposit, down payment.

inicializar [1f] *vt* to initialize.

iniciar [1b] *vt* (**a**) (*gen*) to initiate (*en* into); ~ **a uno en un secreto** to let sb into a secret. (**b**) (*comenzar*) to begin, start, initiate; (*originar*) to originate, set on foot; (*fundar*) to pioneer; ~ **la sesión** (*Inform*) to log in (*o* on).

iniciático *adj* (**a**) initial. (**b**) **ritos ~s** initiation rites.

iniciativa *nf* initiative, enterprise; (*liderazgo*) lead, leadership; **~s** initiatives; (*propósitos*) plans, intentions; ~ **de paz** peace initiative; ~ **privada** private enterprise; **bajo su** ~ on his initiative; **por ~ propia** on one's own initiative; **carecer de** ~ to lack initiative; **tomar la** ~ to take the initiative.

inicio *nm* start, beginning.

inicuamente *adv* wickedly, iniquitously.

inicuo *adj* wicked, iniquitous.

inidentificable *adj* unidentifiable.

inidentificado *adj* unidentified.

inigualable *adj* unsurpassable.

inigualado *adj* unequalled.

inimaginable *adj* unimaginable, inconceivable, incredible.

inimitable *adj* inimitable.

ininflamable *adj* non-flammable, fire-resistant.

ininteligente *adj* unintelligent.

ininteligibilidad *nf* unintelligibility.

ininteligible *adj* unintelligible.

ininterrumpidamente *adv* uninterruptedly; continuously, without a break; steadily.

ininterrumpido *adj* uninterrupted; continuous, without a break; steady; prolonged, sustained.

iniquidad *nf* wickedness, iniquity; injustice.

in itinere *adv*: **siniestros** ~ accidents which happen on one's way to or from work.

injerencia *nf* interference, meddling (*en* in).

injerir [3i] **1** *vt* to insert, introduce (*en* into); (*Agr*) to graft (*en* on, on to). **2 injerirse** *vr* to interfere, meddle (*en* in).

injertar [1a] *vt* (*Agr, Med*) to graft (*en* on, on to); (*fig*) to graft.

injerto *nm* (**a**) (*acto*) grafting. (**b**) (*Agr, Med*) graft; ~ **de piel** skin graft.

injuria *nf* (**a**) (*insulto*) insult, offence, affront (*para* to); (*injusticia*) outrage, injustice; **~s** insults, abuse; **llenar a uno de ~s** to heap abuse on sb. (**b**) (*liter*) damage; **las ~s del tiempo**†† the ravages of time.

injuriar [1b] *vt* (**a**) (*gen*) to insult, abuse, revile; to wrong. (**b**) (*liter*: *dañar*) to injure, damage, harm.

injuriosamente *adv* (*V adj*) (**a**) insultingly, offensively; outrageously. (**b**) harmfully.

injurioso *adj* (**a**) (*ofensivo*) insulting, offensive; outrageous. (**b**) (*dañoso*) harmful, damaging.

injustamente *adv* unjustly, unfairly; wrongfully.

injusticia *nf* injustice; unfairness; **una gran** ~ a terrible injustice; **con** ~ unjustly.

injustificable *adj* unjustifiable.

injustificadamente *adv* unjustifiably.

injustificado *adj* unjustified, unwarranted.

injusto *adj* unjust, unfair; wrong, wrongful; **ser ~ con uno** to be unjust to sb.

INLE ['inle] *nm abr de* **Instituto Nacional del Libro Español.**

inllevable *adj* unbearable, intolerable.

inmaculado *adj* immaculate.

inmadurez *nf* immaturity.

inmaduro *adj individuo* immature; *fruta* unripe.

inmancable *adj* (*And, Carib*) unfailing, infallible.

inmanejable *adj* unmanageable.

inmanente *adj* immanent; inherent (*a* in).

inmarcesible *adj*, **inmarchitable** *adj* imperishable, undying, unfading.

inmaterial *adj* immaterial.

INME ['inme] *nm abr de* **Instituto Nacional de Moneda Extranjera.**

inmediaciones *nfpl* neighbourhood, surroundings, environs; immediate area; **en las ~ de** in the neighbourhood of.

inmediata* *nf*: **la** ~ the natural thing, the first thing.

inmediatamente 1 *adv* immediately, at once. **2** *prep*: ~ **de recibido** on being received.

inmediatez *nf* immediacy.

inmediato *adj* (**a**) (*tiempo*) immediate; prompt; **de** ~ immediately, promptly; **en lo** ~ in the near future. (**b**) (*lugar*) immediate, next; adjoining; ~ **a** close to, next to.

inmejorable *adj* unsurpassable; that cannot be bettered; **~s recomendaciones** excellent references; **precios ~s** unbeatable prices; **de calidad** ~ of the very best quality.

inmejorablemente *adv* in a way that could not be bettered; **portarse** ~ to behave perfectly.

inmemorable *adj*, **inmemorial** *adj* immemorial.

inmensamente *adv* immensely, vastly.

inmensidad *nf* immensity, hugeness, vastness.

inmenso *adj* immense, huge, vast; **sentir una tristeza inmensa** to be terribly sad.

inmensurable *adj* immeasurable.

inmerecidamente *adv* undeservedly.

inmerecido *adj*, **inmérito** *adj* undeserved; uncalled-for.

inmergir [3c] *vt* to immerse.

inmersión *nf* immersion; (*de buzo etc*) dive, plunge; (*pesca submarina*) skin-diving, underwater fishing.

inmigración *nf* immigration.

inmigrado, -a *nm/f* immigrant.

inmigrante *adj, nmf* immigrant.

inmigrar [1a] *vi* to immigrate.

inminencia *nf* imminence.

inminente *adj* imminent, impending.

inmiscuirse [3g] *vr* to interfere, meddle (*en* in).

inmisericorde *adj* insensitive, hard-hearted, pitiless.

inmisericordioso *adj* merciless.

inmobiliaria[1] *nf* construction company, builder(s); property company.

inmobiliario 1 *adj* real-estate (*atr*), property (*atr*); **venta inmobiliaria** property sale. **2** *nm*, **inmobiliaria**[2] *nf* property developer.

inmoble *adj* (**a**) (*inmóvil*) immovable; motionless. (**b**) (*fig*) unmoved, unshaken.

inmoderación *nf* (*Cono Sur*) excess.

inmoderadamente *adv* immoderately, excessively.

inmoderado *adj* immoderate, excessive.

inmodestamente *adv* immodestly.

inmodestia *nf* immodesty.

inmodesto *adj* immodest.

inmodificable *adj* that cannot be modified.

inmolar [1a] *vt* to immolate.

inmoral *adj* immoral; unethical.

inmoralidad *nf* immorality; unethical nature.
inmortal *adj, nmf* immortal.
inmortalidad *nf* immortality.
inmortalizar [1f] *vt* to immortalize.
inmotivación *nf* lack of motivation.
inmotivado *adj* motiveless, unmotivated, without motive.
inmoto *adj* unmoved.
inmovible *adj* immovable.
inmóvil *adj* (**a**) (*inamovible*) immovable; immobile; (*sin mover*) motionless, still; **quedar ~** to remain (*o* be, stand *etc*) motionless; (*vehículo etc*) to remain stationary. (**b**) (*fig*) steadfast, unshaken.
inmovilidad *nf* immovability; immobility; stillness.
inmovilismo *nm* (*fig*) stagnation; resistance to change; do-nothing policy; idleness, lack of activity; (*Pol*) ultra-conservatism.
inmovilista *adj* stagnant; resistant to change; idle, inactive; (*Pol*) ultraconservative.
inmovilización *nf* immobilization; stopping, paralysing; **~ de coches** (*Méx*) traffic-jam.
inmovilizado *nm* capital assets, fixed assets.
inmovilizar [1f] *vr* to immobilize; to stop, paralyse, bring to a standstill; (*Fin*) *capital* to tie up, lock up.
inmueble 1 *adj*: **bienes ~s** real estate, landed property. **2** *nm* property; building; **~s** real estate, landed property.
inmundicia *nf* filth, dirt; nastiness; **~s** filth, rubbish; **esto es una ~** this is absolutely disgraceful.
inmundo *adj* filthy, dirty; foul, nasty.
inmune *adj* (**a**) (*Med*) immune (*contra* against, to). (**b**) (*fig*) exempt, free (*de* from).
inmunidad *nf* (**a**) (*gen, Med*) immunity; **~ diplomática** diplomatic immunity; **~ parlamentaria** parliamentary immunity. (**b**) (*fisco*) exemption.
inmunitario *adj*: **sistema ~** immune system.
inmunizar [1f] *vt* to immunize.
inmunodeficiencia *nf* immunodeficiency.
inmunología *nf* immunology.
inmunológico *adj* immune (*atr*); **sistema ~** immune system.
inmunólogo, -a *nm/f* immunologist.
inmunosupresor 1 *adj* immunosuppressive. **2** *nm* immunosuppressant.
inmunoterapia *nf* immunotherapy.
inmutabilidad *nf* immutability.
inmutable *adj* immutable, changeless.
inmutarse [1a] *vr* to change countenance, turn pale, lose one's self-possession; **se inmutó** his face fell, he seemed disappointed; **no ~** to keep a stiff upper lip, not turn a hair; **siguió sin ~** he carried on unperturbed, he showed no sign of what he was feeling.
innato *adj* innate, inborn; inbred.
innatural *adj* unnatural.
innavegable *adj río etc* unnavigable; *barco* unseaworthy.
innecesariamente *adv* unnecessarily.
innecesario *adj* unnecessary.
innegable *adj* undeniable.
innegociable *adj* non-negotiable.
innoble *adj* ignoble.
innocuo *adj* innocuous, harmless.
innominado *adj* nameless, unnamed.
innovación *nf* (*acto*) innovation; (*novedad*) innovation, novelty, new thing.
innovador 1 *adj* innovative, innovatory. **2** *nm*, **innovadora** *nf* innovator.
innovar [1a] **1** *vt* to introduce. **2** *vi* to innovate, introduce something new.
innovativo *adj* innovative, innovatory.
innumerable *adj*, **innúmero** *adj* innumerable, countless.
inobediencia *nf* disobedience.
inobediente *adj* disobedient.
inobjetable *adj* unobjectionable; (*inatacable*) unassailable, unimpeachable; impeccable.
inobservado *adj* unobserved.
inobservancia *nf* non-observance (*de* of); disregard (*de* for); neglect; (*de ley*) violation, breaking (*de* of).
inocencia *nf* innocence.
Inocencio *nm* (*papa*) Innocent.
inocentada *nf* (**a**) (*dicho*) naïve remark, simple-minded thing; (*error*) blunder. (**b**) (*trastada*) practical joke, April Fool joke; hoax.
inocente[1] **1** *adj* (**a**) (*sin culpa*) innocent (*de* of); (*sin malicia*) harmless.
(**b**) (*ingenuo*) simple, naïve.
2 *nmf* (**a**) (*gen*) innocent, innocent person.
(**b**) (*bobo*) simple soul, naïve person.
inocente[2] *nm* (**a**) (*And, Cono Sur*) avocado pear. (**b**) (*And*) masquerade.
inocentemente *adv* innocently.
inocentón 1 *adj* simple, naïve, gullible. **2** *nm*, **inocentona** *nf* simple soul, naïve person.
inocuidad *nf* innocuousness, harmlessness.
inoculación *nf* inoculation.
inocular [1a] *vt* (**a**) (*Med*) to inoculate (*contra* against, *de* with). (**b**) (*fig*) to corrupt, contaminate (*de* with).
inocuo *adj* = **innocuo**.
inodoro 1 *adj* odourless, having no smell. **2** *nm* lavatory, toilet; **~ químico** chemical closet.
inofensivo *adj* inoffensive, harmless.
inoficioso* *adj* (*LAm*) useless.
inolvidable *adj* unforgettable.
inolvidablemente *adv* unforgettably.
inope *adj* impecunious, indigent.
inoperable *adj* (*CAm, Cono Sur, Méx Med*) inoperable.
inoperancia *nf* (*V adj*) (**a**) inoperative character; unworkable nature; ineffectiveness, impotence. (**b**) (*LAm*) uselessness, fruitlessness.
inoperante *adj* (**a**) *plan* inoperative; unworkable; ineffective, impotent. (**b**) (*LAm*) (*inútil*) useless, fruitless, unproductive; (*inactivo*) inactive, out of use.
inopia *nf* indigence, poverty; **estar en la ~** (*fig: no saber*) to be in the dark, have no idea; (*estar despistado*) to be dreaming, be far away.
inopinadamente *adv* unexpectedly.
inopinado *adj* unexpected.
inoportunamente *adv* (*V adj*) (**a**) inopportunely, at the wrong time. (**b**) inconveniently; inappropriately.
inoportunidad *nf* (*V adj*) (**a**) inopportuneness, untimeliness. (**b**) inconvenience; inexpediency; inappropriateness.
inoportuno *adj* (**a**) (*intempestivo*) inopportune, untimely, ill-timed. (**b**) (*molesto*) inconvenient; (*imprudente*) inexpedient; (*no apto*) inappropriate.
inorgánico *adj* inorganic.
inoxidable *adj* rustless, rustproof; *acero* stainless.
inquebrantable *adj* (**a**) unbreakable. (**b**) (*fig*) unshakeable, unyielding, unswerving.
inquietador *adj* = **inquietante**.
inquietamente *adv* (**a**) (*con ansiedad*) anxiously, uneasily. (**b**) (*agitadamente*) restlessly.
inquietante *adj* worrying, disturbing.
inquietar [1a] **1** *vt* to worry, disturb, trouble, upset; to torment. **2 inquietarse** *vr* to worry, get worried, upset o.s.; **¡no te inquietes!** don't worry!
inquieto *adj* (**a**) (*preocupado*) anxious, worried, uneasy; **estar ~ por** to be anxious about, be worried about. (**b**) (*agitado*) restless, unsettled.
inquietud *nf* (*V adj*) (**a**) anxiety, worry, uneasiness, disquiet. (**b**) restlessness.
inquilinaje *nm* (**a**) (*Cono Sur*) = **inquilinato**. (**b**) (*Méx*) tenants.
inquilinato *nm* (**a**) (*gen*) tenancy; (*Jur*) lease, leasehold. (**b**) (*alquiler*) rent; (**impuesto de**) **~** rates. (**c**) (*Cono Sur*) tenement house, slum.
inquilino, -a *nm/f* (*arrendatario*) tenant; lessee; (*Cono Sur Agr*) tenant farmer.
inquina *nf* dislike, aversion; ill will, spite; **tener ~ a uno** to have a grudge against sb, have one's knife in sb.
inquiridor 1 *adj* inquiring. **2** *nm*, **inquiridora** *nf* inquirer; investigator.
inquiriente *nmf* inquirer.
inquirir [3i] **1** *vt* to enquire into, investigate, look into. **2** *vt* to inquire.
inquisición *nf* inquiry, investigation; **la I~** the Inquisition.
inquisidor *nm* inquisitor.
inquisitivo *adj* inquisitive, curious; *mirada* prying.
inquisitorial *adj* inquisitorial.
inrayable *adj* scratch-proof.
inri *nm* shame; (mental) suffering; **para más** (*o* **mayor**) **~** to make matters worse; to drive the point home; **hacer el ~** to do something ridiculous, make oneself look silly.
insaciable *adj* insatiable.
insaciablemente *adv* insatiably.
insalubre *adj* unhealthy, insalubrious; insanitary.
insalubridad *nf* unhealthiness.
INSALUD, Insalud ['insa'luð] *nm* (*Esp*) *abr de* **Instituto Nacional de la Salud.**
insalvable *adj obstáculo* insuperable.
insanable *adj* incurable.
insania *nf* insanity.

insano *adj* (**a**) (*loco*) insane, mad. (**b**) (*malsano*) unhealthy.
insatisfacción *nf* dissatisfaction.
insatisfactorio *adj* unsatisfactory.
insatisfecho *adj* unsatisfied; dissatisfied.
insaturado *adj* unsaturated.
inscribir [3a; *ptp* **inscrito**] **1** *vt* (*grabar*) to inscribe (*t Mat*); (*poner en lista*) to list, enter (on a list); (*matricular*) to enrol; (*registrar*) to register, record. **2 inscribirse** *vr* to enrol, register.
inscripción *nf* (**a**) (*acto*) inscription; enrolment; registering, recording. (**b**) (*texto*) inscription; lettering.
insecticida *nm* insecticide.
insectívoro *adj* insectivorous.
insecto *nm* insect.
inseguridad *nf* unsafeness; insecurity; unsteadiness; uncertainty; ~ **ciudadana** lack of safety in the streets, decline in law and order.
inseguro *adj* (*peligroso*) unsafe; insecure; *paso etc* unsteady; (*incierto*) uncertain.
inseminación *nf* insemination; ~ **artificial** artificial insemination.
inseminar [1a] *vt* to inseminate, fertilize.
insensatez *nf* folly, foolishness, stupidity.
insensato *adj* senseless, foolish, stupid.
insensibilidad *nf* (**a**) (*gen*) insensitivity; lack of feeling; (*indiferencia*) callousness. (**b**) (*Med*) insensibility, unconsciousness; numbness.
insensibilizar [1f] *vt* to render insensitive, make callous; (*Téc*) to desensitize.
insensible *adj* (**a**) *persona* insensitive (*a* to); unfeeling; callous. (**b**) (*imperceptible*) imperceptible. (**c**) (*Med*) insensible, unconscious; *miembro* numb, without feeling.
insensiblemente *adv* (*V adj*) (**a**) insensitively; unfeelingly. (**b**) imperceptibly.
inseparable *adj* inseparable.
inseparablemente *adv* inseparably.
insepulto *adj* unburied; without burial.
inserción *nf* insertion.
INSERSO, Inserso ['in'serso] *nm* (*Esp*) *abr de* **Instituto Nacional de Servicios Sociales.**
insertar [1a] *vt* to insert.
inserto 1 *adj*: **problemas en los que está ~ el gobierno** problems with which the government finds itself involved. **2** *nm* insert.
inservible *adj* useless; unusable.
insidia *nf* (**a**) (*trampa*) snare, trap. (**b**) (*acto*) malicious act. (**c**) (*cualidad*) maliciousness.
insidiosamente *adv* insidiously; treacherously.
insidioso *adj* insidious; treacherous.
insigne *adj* distinguished; notable, famous.
insignia *nf* (**a**) (*señal*) badge, device, emblem; decoration. (**b**) (*bandera*) flag, banner; (*Náut*) pennant. (**c**) **~s** insignia.
insignificancia *nf* insignificance, trifle.
insignificante *adj* insignificant; trivial, tiny, petty.
insinceridad *nf* insincerity.
insincero *adj* insincere.
insinuación *nf* insinuation.
insinuador *adj* insinuating.
insinuante *adj* (**a**) (*que insinúa*) insinuating; (*atrevido*) forward, suggestive. (**b**) (*zalamero*) ingratiating. (**c**) (*taimado*) cunning, crafty.
insinuar [1e] **1** *vt* (**a**) to insinuate, hint at, imply; **~ que ...** to hint that ..., imply that ...

(**b**) **~ una observación** to slip in a comment.

2 insinuarse *vr* (**a**) **~ con uno** to ingratiate o.s. with sb.

(**b**) **~ en** to worm one's way into, creep into, slip into; **~ en el ánimo de uno** to work one's way gradually into sb's mind.

(**c**) (*atreverse*) to drop (suggestive) hints, make (suggestive) advances; **~ a una mujer** to make advances to a woman.
insipidez *nf* insipidness, tastelessness; (*fig*) dullness, flatness.
insípido *adj* insipid, tasteless; (*fig*) dull, flat, tedious.
insistencia *nf* insistence (*en* on); persistence; **a ~ de** at the insistence of; **con ~ machacona** with wearisome insistence.
insistente *adj* insistent; persistent.
insistentemente *adv* insistently; persistently.
insistir [3a] *vi* to insist; to persist; **~ en algo** to insist on sth; to stress sth, emphasize sth; **~ en una idea** to press an idea; **~ en hacer algo** to insist on doing sth; **~ en que se haga algo** to insist that sth should be done; **~ en que algo es así** to insist that sth is so.
in situ *adv* in situ; on the spot.
insobornable *adj* incorruptible.
insociabilidad *nf* unsociability.
insociable *adj* unsociable.
insolación *nf* (**a**) (*Met*) sunshine; **horas de ~** hours of sunshine; **la ~ media diaria es de ...** the daily sunshine average is ...

(**b**) (*pey*) exposure (to the sun); (*Med*) sunstroke; **darse** (*o* **coger**) **una ~** to get sunstroke.
insolar [1a] **1** *vt* to expose to the sun, put in the sun. **2 insolarse** *vr* (*Med*) to get sunstroke.
insoldable *adj* (*Esp*: *fig*) irremediable; unmendable.
insolencia *nf* (**a**) (*descaro*) insolence, effrontery. (**b**) (*acto*) piece of rudeness, rude thing.
insolentarse [1a] *vr* to be insolent (*con* to), become insolent.
insolente *adj* (**a**) (*descarado*) insolent, rude; unblushing. (**b**) (*altivo*) haughty, contemptuous.
insolentemente *adv* (*V adj*) (**a**) insolently, rudely; unblushingly. (**b**) haughtily, contemptuously.
insolidaridad *nf* lack of solidarity; lack of brotherly feelings.
insolidario *adj* unsupportive, uncooperative; self-interested; **hacerse ~ de** to dissociate o.s. from, declare o.s. out of sympathy with.
insolidarizarse [1f] *vr*: **~ con** to dissociate oneself from.
insólitamente *adv* unusually, unwontedly.
insólito *adj* unusual, unwonted.
insolubilidad *nf* insolubility.
insoluble *adj* insoluble.
insolvencia *nf* insolvency, bankruptcy.
insolvente *adj* insolvent, bankrupt.
insomne 1 *adj* sleepless. **2** *nmf* insomniac.
insomnio *nm* sleeplessness, insomnia.
insondable *adj* bottomless; (*fig*) unfathomable, impenetrable, inscrutable.
insonorización *nf* soundproofing.
insonorizado *adj* soundproof; **estar ~** to be soundproofed.
insonorizar [1f] *vt* to soundproof.
insonoro *adj* noiseless, soundless.
insoportable *adj* unbearable, intolerable.
insoportablemente *adv* unbearably, intolerably.
insoria *nf* (*Carib*) insignificant thing; **una ~** a minimal amount.
insoslayable *adj* *problema etc* unavoidable, which cannot be got round.
insoslayablemente *adv* unavoidably.
insospechable *adj* beyond suspicion.
insospechado *adj* unsuspected.
insostenible *adj* untenable.
inspección *nf* inspection, examination; check; survey; **~ ocular** visual examination; **~ técnica de vehículos** ≈ MOT test.
inspeccionar [1a] *vt* (*examinar*) to inspect, examine; (*controlar*) to check; to survey; (*supervisar*) to supervise.
inspector(a) *nm/f* inspector; superintendent, supervisor; (*Cono Sur*: *de bus*) conductor; **~ de aduanas** customs officer; **~ de enseñanza** school inspector; **~ de Hacienda** tax inspector.
inspectorado *nm* inspectorate.
inspiración *nf* (**a**) (*gen*) inspiration. (**b**) (*Med*) inhalation.
inspirador 1 *adj* inspiring; inspirational. **2** *nm*, **inspiradora** *nf* inspirer; creator, originator.
inspirar [1a] **1** *vt* (**a**) (*gen*) to inspire; **~ algo a uno** to inspire sb with sth; to inspire sth in sb.

(**b**) (*Med*) to inhale, breathe in.

2 inspirarse *vr*: **~ en** to be inspired by, find inspiration in, draw inspiration from.
inspirativo *adj* inspiring; inspirational.
INSS *nm* (*Esp*) *abr de* **Instituto Nacional de Seguridad Social.**
instable *adj* = **inestable.**
instalación *nf* (**a**) (*acto*) installation, instalment. (**b**) (*equipo*) installation; fittings, equipment; (*Téc*) plant; **~ de fuerza** power plant; **instalaciones deportivas** sports facilities; **instalaciones portuarias** harbour installations; **instalaciones recreativas** recreational facilities; **~ sanitaria** sanitation, plumbing.
instalador *nm* installer; fitter; **~ eléctrico** electrician.
instalar [1a] **1** *vt* to install; to set up, erect, fit up, lay on. **2 instalarse** *vr* to install o.s., establish o.s., settle (down).
instancia *nf* (**a**) (*solicitud*) request; application; (*Jur*) peti-

tion; **a ~(s) de** at the request of; **pedir algo con ~** to demand sth insistently, demand sth urgently. (**b**) (*formulario*) application form. (**c**) **en última ~** in the last analysis, **de prima ~** first of all. (**d**) (*Pol etc*) authority; agency; **~s del poder** (*fig*) corridors of power.

instantánea *nf* (**a**) (*Fot*) snap, snapshot. (**b**) (‡) tart‡, whore.

instantáneamente *adv* instantaneously, instantly.

instantáneo *adj* instantaneous, instant; **café ~** instant coffee.

instante *nm* instant, moment; **al ~** instantly, at once; (**a**) **cada ~** every single moment, all the time; **en un ~** in a flash; **por ~s** incessantly, all the time; **hace un ~** a moment ago.

instantemente *adv* insistently, urgently.

instar [1a] **1** *vt* to urge, press; **~ a uno a hacer algo, ~ a uno para que haga algo** to urge sb to do sth. **2** *vi* to be urgent, be pressing.

instauración *nf* (*V v*) (**a**) restoration, renewal. (**b**) establishment, setting-up.

instaurar [1a] *vt* (**a**) (*renovar*) to restore, renew. (**b**) (*fundar*) to establish, set up (again).

instigación *nf* instigation; **a ~ de** at the instigation of.

instigador(a) *nm/f* instigator; **~ de un delito** instigator of a crime, (*Jur*) accessory before the fact.

instigar [1h] *vt* to instigate; to abet; **~ a uno a hacer algo** to incite sb to do sth, urge sb to do sth, induce sb to do sth.

instilar [1a] *vt* to instil (*a, en* into).

instintivamente *adv* instinctively.

instintivo *adj* instinctive.

instinto *nm* instinct; impulse, urge; **~ asesino, ~ de matar** killer instinct; **~ sexual** sexual urge, sexual desire; **~ de supervivencia** instinct for survival, survival instinct; **por ~** by instinct, instinctively.

institución *nf* (**a**) (*acto*) institution, establishment. (**b**) (*organismo*) institution; establishment; **~ benéfica, ~ de beneficencia** charitable organization, charitable foundation; **~ pública** public institution, public body. (**c**) **instituciones** (*bases*) principles.

institucional *adj* institutional.

institucionalizado *adj* institutionalized.

instituir [3g] *vt* to institute, establish; to found, set up.

instituto *nm* (**a**) (*gen*) institute, institution; **los ~s armados** the army, the military; **~ de belleza** (*Esp*) beauty parlour; **el benemérito ~** the Civil Guard; **~ financiero** financial institution; **~ laboral** technical school; **~ (de segunda enseñanza)** secondary school, grammar school, high school (*US*). (**b**) (*regla*) principle, rule; (*Ecl*) rule.

institutriz *nf* governess.

instrucción *nf* (**a**) (*gen*) instruction; education, teaching; (*Mil etc*) training, drill; (*Dep*) coaching, training; **~ primaria** primary education; **~ programada** programmed teaching; **~ pública** state education.

(**b**) (*conocimientos*) knowledge, learning, instruction; **tener poca ~ en** to have little knowledge of, know little about.

(**c**) (*Jur*) (institution of) proceedings.

(**d**) (*Inform*) statement; instruction, command.

(**e**) **instrucciones** (*órdenes*) instructions, orders, direction; **de acuerdo con sus instrucciones** in accordance with your instructions; **instrucciones para el uso** directions for use; **instrucciones de funcionamiento** operating instructions.

instructivo *adj* instructive; illuminating, enlightening; *película etc* educational.

instructor(a) *nm/f* (**a**) instructor, teacher; (*Dep*) coach, trainer; **~ de vuelo** flight instructor. (**b**) **~ de diligencias** (*Jur*) judge appointed to look into a case.

instruido *adj* well-educated; well-informed.

instruir [3g] **1** *vt* (**a**) to instruct, teach (*de, en, sobre* in, about); to educate; (*Mil etc*) to train, drill; (*Dep*) to coach, train. (**b**) (*Jur*) *proceso* to prepare, draw up; to investigate. **2 instruirse** *vr* to learn, teach o.s. (*de, en, sobre* about).

instrumentación *nf* orchestration, scoring.

instrumental 1 *adj* instrumental. **2** *nm* instruments, set of instruments.

instrumentalizar [1f] *vt* (**a**) (*llevar a cabo*) to carry out. (**b**) **~ a uno** to use sb as a tool, make cynical use of sb; to exploit sb, manipulate sb.

instrumentar [1a] *vt* (**a**) (*Mús*) to score, orchestrate; **está instrumentado para ...** it is scored for ... (**b**) (*fig*) *campaña* to orchestrate. (**c**) (*fig*: *manipular*) to manipulate.

instrumentista *nmf* (**a**) (*Mús*) instrumentalist; (*fabricante*) instrument maker; **~ de cuerda** string player. (**b**) (*Med*) theatre nurse. (**c**) (*Mec*) machinist.

instrumento *nm* (**a**) (*gen*) instrument; (*herramienta*) tool, implement; (‡‡) tool‡‡; **~ auditivo** listening device; **~s científicos** scientific instruments; **~s de mando** (*Aer etc*) controls; **~ de precisión** precision instrument; **~s quirúrgicos** surgical instruments; **~s topográficos** surveying instruments; **volar por ~s** to fly on instruments.

(**b**) (*Mús*) instrument; **~ de batería, ~ de percusión** percussion instrument; **~ de cuerda** stringed instrument; **~ musical, ~ músico** musical instrument; **~ de tecla** keyboard instrument; **~ de viento** wind instrument.

(**c**) (*fig*) instrument, tool; **fue solamente el ~ del dictador** he was merely the dictator's tool, he was just a tool in the dictator's hands.

(**d**) (*Jur*) deed, legal document, instrument; **~ de venta** bill of sale.

insubordinación *nf* insubordination; turbulence, unruliness.

insubordinado *adj* insubordinate; turbulent, rebellious, unruly.

insubordinar [1a] **1** *vt* to stir up, rouse to rebellion. **2 insubordinarse** *vr* to become unruly; to rebel.

insubsanable *adj problema* insoluble.

insubstituible *adj* = **insustituible.**

insudar [1a] *vi* (*liter*) to toil away.

insuficiencia *nf* (**a**) insufficiency, inadequacy; lack, shortage; **~ de franqueo** underpaid postage; **debido a la ~ de personal** through shortage of staff.

(**b**) incompetence.

(**c**) (*Med*) **~ cardíaca** heart failure, **~ renal** kidney failure.

insuficiente *adj* (**a**) (*inadecuado*) insufficient, inadequate. (**b**) *persona* incompetent.

insuficientemente *adv* insufficiently, inadequately.

insuflar [1a] *vt* to breathe into, introduce by blowing.

insufrible *adj* unbearable, insufferable.

insufriblemente *adv* unbearably, insufferably.

insular *adj* insular.

insularidad *nf* insularity.

insulina *nf* insulin.

insulsez *nf* (**a**) (*insipidez*) tastelessness, insipidity. (**b**) (*fig*) flatness, dullness.

insulso *adj* (**a**) (*insípido*) tasteless, insipid. (**b**) (*fig*) flat, dull.

insultante *adj* insulting; abusive.

insultar [1a] *vt* to insult.

insulto *nm* (**a**) (*ofensa*) insult (*para* to). (**b**) (*Méx**: *indigestión*) bellyache, stomach-ache.

insumergible *adj* unsinkable.

insumisión *nf* rebelliousness; (*esp*) refusal to do military service.

insumiso 1 *adj* unsubmissive, rebellious. **2** *nm* (*esp*) man who refuses to do military service.

insumo *nm* (**a**) (*LAm*) consumption. (**b**) (*Cono Sur*) ingredient, component. (**c**) **~s** (*Econ*) input, materials.

insuperable *adj* insuperable, unsurmountable; *calidad* unsurpassable.

insuperado *adj* unsurpassed.

insurgencia *nf* (**a**) (*acto*) rebellion, uprising. (**b**) (*fuerzas*) insurgent forces.

insurgente *adj, nmf* insurgent.

insurrección *nf* revolt, insurrection.

insurreccional *adj* insurrectionary.

insurreccionar [1a] **1** *vt* to rouse to revolt, incite to rebel. **2 insurreccionarse** *vr* to rebel, rise in revolt.

insurrecto, -a *adj, nm/f* rebel, insurgent.

insustancial *adj* unsubstantial.

insustituible *adj* irreplaceable.

INTA *nm* (**a**) (*Esp Aer*) *abr de* **Instituto Nacional de Técnica Aerospacial.** (**b**) (*Argentina Agr*) *abr de* **Instituto Nacional de Tecnología Agropecuaria.** (**c**) (*Guatemala*) *abr de* **Instituto Nacional de Transformación Agraria.**

intacto *adj* untouched; whole, intact, undamaged; pure.

intachable *adj* irreproachable; faultless, perfect.

intangible *adj* intangible, impalpable.

integérrimo *adj superl de* **íntegro.**

integración *nf* integration; **~ a muy gran escala** very large-scale integration; **~ racial** racial integration.

integrado *adj* (**a**) (*entero*) integrated; in one piece, all of a piece; *sociedad* integrated. (**b**) **un grupo ~ por** a group made up of, a group consisting of.

integral 1 *adj* (**a**) integral; (*Mec etc*) built-in; (*Mat*) inte-

gral; *cereal* wholegrain; *pan* wholemeal. (**b**) (*) total, complete; **un idiota** ~ an utter fool. **2** *nf* (*Mat*) integral; integral sign.
íntegramente *adv* (**a**) wholly, entirely, completely. (**b**) (*fig*) uprightly, with integrity.
integrante 1 *adj* integral; **una parte** ~ **de** an integral part of. **2** *nmf* member; **los ~s del conjunto** the members of the group.
integrar [1a] *vt* (**a**) (*formar*) to make up, compose, form; **y los que integran el otro grupo** and those who make up the other group.
(**b**) (*Mat y fig*) to integrate.
(**c**) (*Fin*) to repay, reimburse; (*And, Cono Sur, Méx: pagar*) to hand over, pay up.
integridad *nf* (**a**) (*entereza*) wholeness, completeness; ~ **física** physical wellbeing; **en su** ~ in its entirety. (**b**) (*fig: honradez*) uprightness, integrity. (**c**) (*Jur*) **delito contra la** ~ **de la persona** crime against the person; **peligró su** ~ **física** he was nearly hurt, he came close to suffering personal injury. (**d**) (*fig: virginidad*) virginity.
integrismo *nm* reaction; entrenched traditionalism; fundamentalism.
integrista 1 *adj* reactionary; traditionalist; fundamentalist. **2** *nmf* reactionary; traditionalist; fundamentalist.
íntegro *adj* (**a**) whole, entire, complete; integral; **la cantidad íntegra** the whole sum, the sum in full; **versión íntegra** (*Liter*) unabridged version; **en versión íntegra de Pérez** in Pérez's edition of the complete text.
(**b**) (*fig*) honest, upright.
integumento *nm* integument.
intelectiva *nf* intellect, mental faculty.
intelecto *nm* intellect; understanding; brains.
intelectual *adj, nmf* intellectual.
intelectuala* *nf* (*hum*) bluestocking.
intelectualidad *nf* (**a**) (*cualidad*) intellectuality; intellectual character. (**b**) (*personas*) intelligentsia, intellectual people, intellectuals.
intelectualmente *adv* intellectually.
intelectualoide *adj, nmf* pseudo-intellectual.
inteligencia *nf* (**a**) (*intelecto etc*) intelligence; mind, wits, understanding; ability; (*Inform*) intelligence; ~ **artificial** artificial intelligence; ~ **máquina** machine intelligence; **de mediocre** ~ of mediocre intelligence; **una persona de fina** ~ a person with a sharp mind.
(**b**) (*comprensión*) understanding; **la buena** ~ **entre los pueblos** good understanding between peoples.
(**c**) (*Mil etc*) intelligence.
(**d**) (*pey*) secret agreement, collusion.
(**e**) (*personas*) intelligentsia.
inteligente *adj* (**a**) (*gen*) intelligent; (*listo*) clever, brainy, talented. (**b**) (*hábil*) skilful; (*experto*) skilled, trained (*en* in). (**c**) (*Inform*) intelligent; *misil* smart.
inteligentemente *adv* intelligently.
inteligibilidad *nf* intelligibility.
inteligible *adj* intelligible.
inteligiblemente *adv* intelligibly.
intemperancia *nf* intemperance, excess.
intemperante *adj* intemperate, excessive.
intemperie *nf* inclemency (of the weather); bad weather, rough weather; **estar a la** ~ to be out in the open, be exposed to wind and weather, be at the mercy of the elements; **aguantar la** ~ to put up with wind and weather; **una cara curtida a la** ~ a face tanned by wind and weather.
intempestivamente *adv* in an untimely way, at a bad time; unseasonably.
intempestivo *adj* untimely, ill-timed; unseasonable.
intención *nf* intention; purpose; plan; **mis intenciones** my intentions, my plans; ~ **delictiva** criminal intent; **intenciones delictivas** criminal intentions; **segunda** ~ duplicity, underhandedness; ulterior motive; ~ **de voto** voting intention; **con** ~ deliberately; **con (segunda)** ~ meaningfully; with a second meaning, implying sth else; (*pey*) nastily; **dicho con** ~ said deliberately, said provocatively; **con la** ~ **de** + *infin* with the idea of + *ger*, intending to + *infin*; **de** ~ on purpose; **aceptar las intenciones de uno** to accept sb's advances, respond to sb's advances; **curar a uno de primera** ~ to give sb first aid; **sin hacer la menor** ~ **de** + *infin* without making the least move to + *infin*; **tener la** ~ **de** + *infin* to intend to + *infin*, mean to + *infin*.
intencionadamente *adv* (*V adj*) (**a**) meaningfully; nastily. (**b**) deliberately.
intencionado *adj* (**a**) (*significativo*) meaningful. (**b**) (*deliberado*) deliberate. (**c**) **bien** ~ well-meaning; **mal** ~ ill-disposed, hostile, unkind; malicious.
intencional *adj* intentional, deliberate.
intencionalidad *nf* (**a**) (*propósito*) purpose, intention; motivation; **la** ~ **del incendio** the fact that the fire was deliberately started. (**b**) **una pregunta cargada de** ~ a loaded question, a question full of implications.
intencionalmente *adv* intentionally.
intendencia *nf* (**a**) (*dirección*) management, administration.
(**b**) (*oficina*) manager's office.
(**c**) (*Mil: t* **cuerpo de** ~) ≃ service corps, quartermaster corps (*US*).
(**d**) (*Cono Sur*) (*alcaldía*) mayoralty; (*cargo de gobernador*) governorship.
intendente *nm* (**a**) (*gerente*) manager. (**b**) ~ **de ejército** quartermaster-general. (**c**) (*Cono Sur*) (*alcalde*) mayor; (*gobernador*) governor; (*Méx*) police inspector.
intensamente *adv* intensely; powerfully, strongly; vividly, profoundly.
intensar [1a] **1** *vt* to intensify. **2 intensarse** *vr* to intensify.
intensidad *nf* intensity; power, strength; vividness; deepness; (*Elec, Téc*) strength.
intensificación *nf* intensification.
intensificar [1g] *vt* to intensify.
intensión *nf* intensity, intenseness.
intensivamente *adv* intensively.
intensivo *adj* intensive.
intenso *adj* (*gen*) intense; *emoción, sentimiento* intense, powerful, strong; *impresión* vivid, profound; *bronceado* deep; *color* deep, intense; (*Elec etc*) strong.
intentar [1a] *vt* (**a**) (*probar*) to try, attempt; ~ **algo** to have a go at sth, try sth; ~ + *infin* to try to + *infin*, attempt to + *infin*, endeavour to + *infin*.
(**b**) (*proponerse*) to mean, intend (*con* by); ~ + *infin* to mean to + *infin*.
intento *nm* (**a**) (*propósito*) intention, intent, purpose; **al** ~ **de** + *infin* (*Cono Sur*) with the aim of + *ger*; **de** ~ on purpose.
(**b**) (*tentativa*) attempt; ~ **fracasado** failed attempt, unsuccessful attempt; ~ **de suicidio** attempted suicide; **acusado de** ~ **de violación** charged with attempted rape.
intentona *nf* foolhardy attempt, wild attempt; (*Pol*) putsch, rising.
inter... *pref* inter...
ínter *nm* (*And, Cono Sur Rel*) curate.
interacción *nf* interaction, interplay.
interaccionar [1a] *vi* to interact (*con* with; *t Inform*).
interactivo *adj* interactive.
interactuación *nf* interaction.
interactuar [1e] *vi* to interact (*con* with; *t Inform*).
interamericano *adj* inter-American.
interandino *adj* inter-Andean, concerning areas on both sides of the Andes.
interanual *adj*: **promedio** ~ year-on-year average; **variación** ~ variation from year to year.
interbancario *adj* inter-bank (*atr*).
interbibliotecario *adj* inter-library (*atr*); **préstamo** ~ inter-library loan.
intercalación *nf* intercalation, insertion; (*Inform*) merging.
intercalar [1a] *vt* to intercalate, insert; (*Inform*) to merge.
intercambiable *adj* interchangeable.
intercambiar [1b] *vt* to change over, interchange; *prisioneros, revistas etc* to exchange; *sellos etc* to exchange, swap.
intercambio *nm* interchange; exchange; swap, swapping.
interceder [2a] *vi* to intercede; ~ **con A por B** to intercede with A on B's behalf, to plead with A for B.
interceptación *nf* interception; stoppage, holdup.
interceptar [1a] *vt* to intercept, cut off; *tráfico* to stop, hold up.
interceptor *nm* (**a**) interceptor. (**b**) (*Mec*) trap; separator.
intercesión *nf* intercession; mediation.
interclasista *adj* inter-class, which crosses class barriers; classless.
inter-club *adj partido* inter-club, between two clubs.
intercomunicación *nf* intercommunication.
intercomunicador *nm* intercom.
intercomunicar [1g] *vt* to link.
intercomunión *nf* intercommunion.
interconectar [1a] *vt* to interconnect.
interconexión *nf* interconnection.
interconfesional *adj* interdenominational.
intercontinental *adj* intercontinental.
interdecir [3o] *vt* to forbid, prohibit.

interdependencia *nf* interdependence.
interdependiente *adj* interdependent.
interdicción *nf* prohibition, interdiction.
interdicto *nm* prohibition, ban, interdict.
interdisciplinar(io) *adj* interdisciplinary.
interdisciplinariedad *nf* interdisciplinary nature.
interés *nm* (**a**) (*gen*) interest; concern; **con gran ~** with great interest; **de gran ~** of great interest, very interesting; **su ~ en, su ~ por** his interest in; his concern for; **poner ~ en** to take an interest in; **sentir ~ por** to be interested in, feel an interest in; **no tiene ~** it has no interest.
(**b**) (*participación*) interest, share, part; **intereses** interests, affairs; **~ controlador** controlling interest; **los intereses españoles en Africa** Spanish interests in Africa; **intereses creados** vested interests; **en ~ de** in the interest of; **en ~ de la higiene** in the interest of hygiene, for the sake of cleanliness; **fomentar los intereses de uno** to promote sb's interests.
(**c**) (*pey*) self-interest; selfishness, egotism; **todo es cuestión de ~** it's all a matter of self-interest.
(**d**) (*Com, Fin*) interest; **con ~ de 9 por cien, con un ~ del 9 por cien** at an interest of 9%; **~ compuesto** compound interest; **~ devengado** accrued interest, earned interest; **~ simple** simple interest; **dar a ~** to lend at interest; **devengar intereses** to bear interest; **intereses por cobrar** interest receivable; **intereses por pagar** interest payable; **poner a ~** to put out at interest, invest.
interesadamente *adv* (*V adj*) in a biassed way; selfishly.
interesado 1 *adj* (**a**) (*gen*) interested; concerned; **estar ~ en** to be interested in, have an interest in; **la compañía está interesada en comprarlo** the company is interested in buying it.
(**b**) (*parcial*) biassed, prejudiced; **actuar de una manera interesada** to act in a biassed way.
(**c**) (*egoísta*) selfish, self-seeking; having an ulterior motive; mercenary.
2 *nm*, **interesada** *nf* (**a**) person concerned, interested party; **los ~s** those interested, those concerned.
(**b**) (*firmante*) the undersigned, the applicant.
interesante *adj* (*de interés*) interesting; (*útil*) useful, convenient; (*provechoso*) profitable, valuable; *precio, sueldo etc* attractive; **hacerse el** (*o* **la**) **~** to try to attract attention.
interesar [1a] **1** *vt* (**a**) (*tener interés en*) to interest, be of interest to; to appeal to; **¿te interesa el fútbol?** are you interested in football?; **no me interesan los toros** I'm not interested in bullfighting, bullfighting does not appeal to me; **la propuesta no nos interesa** the proposal is of no interest to us.
(**b**) (*captar el interés de*) to interest (*in* en); **logré ~le en mi idea** I succeeded in interesting him in my idea.
(**c**) (*afectar*) to concern, involve; **el asunto interesa a todos** the matter concerns everybody; **a quien interese, a quien pueda ~** to whom it may concern.
(**d**) (*Med*) to affect, involve; **la lesión interesa la región lumbar** the injury affects the lumbar region.
(**e**) **el portador interesa 100 pesetas en ...** the bearer has a stake of 100 pesetas in ... (*lottery ticket*).
2 *vi* to be of interest; to be important; **la idea no interesó** the idea was of no interest, the idea did not interest anybody.
3 interesarse *vr* to be interested, take an interest (*en, por* in); **~ en una empresa** to participate in an enterprise, concern o.s. with an enterprise; **~ por** to ask after, inquire about.
interestatal *adj* inter-state.
interestelar *adj* interstellar.
interface *nm* (*a veces f*), **interfase** *nf* interface; **~ de serie** serial interface.
interfaz *nf* interface.
interfecto 1 *adj* killed, murdered. **2** *nm*, **interfecta** *nf* (**a**) murdered person, murder victim. (**b**) (*) person in question, punter*.
interferencia *nf* (**a**) (*Fís, Rad*) interference, (*con intención*) jamming; (*Inform*) glitch. (**b**) (*injerencia*) interference (*en* in); **no ~** non-interference.
interferir [3i] **1** *vt* (**a**) (*Fís, Rad*) to interfere with, (*con intención*) jam.
(**b**) (*injerirse en*) to interfere with, upset, affect; **su acción ha interferido nuestras operaciones** his action has interfered with our operations.
2 *vi* to interfere (*en* in, with).
3 interferirse *vr* to interfere (*en* in, with); **no está en posición de ~ en el conflicto** he is in no position to interfere in the conflict.
interferón *nm* interferon.
interfijo *nm* infix.
interfono *nm* intercom, interphone.
intergubernamental *adj* inter-governmental, between governments.
ínterin 1 *adv* meanwhile. **2** *conj* while; until. **3** *nm* (*pl* **intérines**) (**a**) (*tiempo*) interim; **en el ~** in the interim, in the meantime. (**b**) (*en un puesto*) temporary incumbency.
interinamente *adv* (**a**) (*entretanto*) in the interim, meanwhile. (**b**) (*temporalmente*) temporarily, as a temporary holder of the post (*etc*), as a stopgap.
interinar [1a] *vt puesto* to occupy temporarily, occupy in an acting capacity.
interinato *nm* (**a**) (*Cono Sur*: *temporaneidad*) temporary nature.
(**b**) (*Cono Sur*: *período*) period of temporary occupation of a post.
(**c**) (*CAm Med*) residence, internship (*US*).
interinidad *nf* temporary nature; provisional status; **una situación de ~** a temporary state.
interino 1 *adj* (**a**) provisional, temporary, interim; **informe ~** interim report, progress report. (**b**) *persona* acting. **2** *nm*, **interina** *nf* temporary holder of a post, acting official (*etc*); stopgap, stand-in; (*Ecl, Med*) locum, locum tenens. **3** *nf* (*criada*) non-resident maid.
interior 1 *adj* (*gen*) interior, inner, inside; *pensamiento etc* inward, inner; *comercio, política* domestic, internal; (*Geog*) inland, inner; **habitación ~** room without a view; **en la parte ~** inside, on the inside; **pista ~** (*Dep*) inside track; *V* **ropa** *etc.*
2 *nm* (**a**) (*gen*) interior, inside; (*parte*) inner part; (*Cine*) interior.
(**b**) (*fig*) mind, soul; **en su ~** in one's heart, deep inside one; **dije para mi ~** I said to myself.
(**c**) (*Geog*) interior; **Ministerio del I~** Ministry of the Interior, Home Office (*Brit*), Department of the Interior (*US*).
(**d**) (*Dep*) inside-forward; **~ derecho** inside-right; **~ izquierdo** inside-left.
(**e**) **~es** (*Anat*) insides.
(**f**) (*LAm*: *prenda*) underpants.
interioridad *nf* (**a**) inwardness; (*fig*) inner being; (*pensamientos*) innermost thoughts; **en su ~, sabe que ...** (*CAm*) in his heart he knows that ..., deep down he knows that ...
(**b**) **~es** family secrets, private affairs; inner history, secret goings-on; ins and outs; **explicó las ~es de la lucha** he explained the inner history of the struggle; **desconocen las ~es del mercado** they don't know all the ins and outs of the market.
interiorismo *nm* interior decoration, interior design.
interiorista *nmf* interior decorator, interior designer.
interiorizar [1f] **1** *vt* (**a**) (*Psic*) to internalize. (**b**) (*LAm*) to look into, investigate closely. **2 interiorizarse** *vr*: **~ algo** to familiarize o.s. with sth.
interiormente *adv* internally, inwardly; **lo que pasa ~** what goes on inside.
interjección *nf* interjection.
interlínea *nf* (*Inform*) line feed.
interlineado *nm* space (*o* writing) between the lines.
interlineal *adj* interlinear.
interlinear [1a] *vt* (**a**) (*gen*) to interline, write (*o* print *etc*) between the lines. (**b**) (*Tip*) to space, lead.
interlocutor(a) *nm/f* speaker, interlocutor; **mi ~** the person I was speaking to, the person who spoke to me; **~ válido** official negotiator; official spokesman.
intérlope 1 *adj* (*Méx*: *fraudulento*) fraudulent. **2** *nm* (*Com*) interloper, unauthorized trader.
interludio *nm* interlude.
intermediación *nf* mediation; (*Fin*) brokerage.
intermediario 1 *adj* (**a**) (*gen*) intermediary. (**b**) (*mediador*) mediating. **2** *nm*, **intermediaria** *nf* (**a**) (*gen*) intermediary, go-between; negotiator; (*Com*) middleman. (**b**) (*árbitro*) mediator.
intermedio 1 *adj* (**a**) *etapa* intermediate, halfway (*entre* between).
(**b**) *tiempo* intervening; **el período ~** the intervening period, the period between.
2 *nm* (**a**) interval (*t Teat*); (*Parl*) recess.
(**b**) **por ~ de** (*LAm*) through, by means of.
intermezzo [inter'metso] *nm* intermezzo.
interminable *adj* endless, interminable.
interminablemente *adv* endlessly, interminably.
intermisión *nf* intermission.
intermitente 1 *adj* intermittent. **2** *nm* (*Aut*) directional

light, flashing light, indicator; (*Inform*) indicator light.

internación *nf* internment.

internacional 1 *adj* international. **2** *nf*: **I~** Internationale.

internacionalidad *nf* international nature; international standing.

internacionalismo *nm* internationalism.

internacionalizar [1f] *vt* to internationalize.

internacionalmente *adv* internationally.

internada[1] *nf* (*Dep*) run towards goal.

internado, -a[2] **1** *nm/f* (*Mil etc*) internee. **2** *nm* (**a**) (*colegio*) boarding-school; (*acto*) boarding. (**b**) (*alumnos*) boarders.

internamiento *nm* (**a**) (*Pol*) internment. (**b**) (*Med*) admission (to hospital).

internar [1a] **1** *vt* (**a**) (*Mil*) to intern; (*Med*) to admit (*en* to); **~ a uno en un manicomio** to put sb into a psychiatric hospital, commit sb to a psychiatric hospital.

(**b**) (*enviar tierra adentro*) to send inland.

2 internarse *vr* (**a**) (*avanzar*) to advance (deeply); to penetrate; **el jugador se interna** the player goes deep into the opponent's half.

(**b**) (*avanzar*) **~ en** to go into, go deeply into, penetrate into; **se internó en el edificio** he went into the building, he disappeared into the building; **~ en un país** to go into the interior of a country.

(**c**) **~ en un estudio** to go deeply into a subject, study a subject in depth.

interno 1 *adj* internal, interior; inside; **criada interna** live-in servant, servant who lives in; **la política interna** internal politics, domestic politics; **por vía interna** (*Med*) internally. **2** *nm*, **interna** *nf* (**a**) (*alumno*) boarder. (**b**) (*preso*) inmate, prisoner, convict. **3** *nm* (*Cono Sur Telec*) extension.

interpelación *nf* appeal, plea, interpellation.

interpelante *nmf* (*Parl etc*) questioner.

interpelar [1a] *vt* (**a**) (*impetrar*) to implore, beseech; to interpellate; to beg for the aid of. (**b**) (*dirigirse a*) to address, speak to; (*Parl etc*) to ask for explanations, question formally.

interpersonal *adj* interpersonal.

interplanetario *adj* interplanetary.

Interpol *nf* Interpol.

interpolación *nf* interpolation.

interpolar [1a] *vt* (**a**) to interpolate. (**b**) to interrupt briefly.

interponer [2q] **1** *vt* (**a**) (*insertar*) to interpose, put in, insert. (**b**) (*Jur*) *apelación* to lodge, put in. (**c**) (*en discurso*) to interpose, interject. **2 interponerse** *vr* to intervene.

interposición *nf* (**a**) (*inserción*) insertion. (**b**) (*Jur*) lodging, formulation. (**c**) (*en discurso*) interjection.

interpretable *adj* interpretable.

interpretación *nf* (**a**) (*gen*) interpretation; **mala ~** misinterpretation, misunderstanding.

(**b**) (*traducción*) interpretation, translation; **~ simultánea** simultaneous translation.

(**c**) (*Mús*) rendition, performance; interpretation; **~ en directo** live performance.

(**d**) (*Teat*) performance; playing.

interpretar [1a] *vt* (**a**) (*gen*) to interpret; **~ mal** to misinterpret, misunderstand, misconstrue.

(**b**) (*Ling*) to interpret, translate; **~ del chino al ruso** to translate (*o* interpret) from Chinese into Russian.

(**c**) (*Mús*) to render, perform; to interpret; (*Teat*) *obra* to perform; *papel* to play.

interpretativo *adj* interpretative.

intérprete *nmf* (**a**) (*Ling*) interpreter, translator. (**b**) (*Mús*) performer; exponent; artist(e). (**c**) (*Inform*) interpreter.

interprovincial *nm* (*And*) long-distance bus, coach.

interracial *adj* interracial.

interregno *nm* interregnum; (*LAm*) interval, intervening period; **en el ~** in the meantime.

interrelación *nf* interrelation.

interrelacionado *adj* interrelated.

interrelacionar [1a] *vt* to interrelate.

interrogación *nf* (**a**) (*de policía etc*) interrogation. (**b**) (*pregunta*) question; (*Inform*) inquiry. (**c**) (*signo*) question-mark.

interrogador(a) *nm/f* interrogator; questioner.

interrogante 1 *adj* questioning. **2** *nmf* (*persona*) interrogator; questioner. **3** *nf* (*a veces nm*; *signo*) question-mark; (*fig*) question-mark, query; (*pregunta*) question, query.

interrogar [1h] *vt* to question, interrogate; (*Jur*) to examine.

interrogativo *adj, nm* interrogative.

interrogatorio *nm* (**a**) (*gen*) questioning; (*Mil*) debriefing; (*Jur*) examination. (**b**) (*cuestionario*) questionnaire.

interrumpir [3a] *vt* (*gen*) to interrupt; *vacaciones etc* to interrupt, cut short; *electricidad, servicio* to cut off; *tráfico etc* to block, hold up; (*Elec*: *apagar*) to switch off; (*Inform*) to abort; *embarazo* to terminate.

interrupción *nf* interruption; break; stoppage, holdup; disturbance; (*de embarazo*) termination.

interruptor *nm* (*Elec*) switch; **~ de dos direcciones** two-way switch; **~ con regulador de intensidad** dimmer switch; **~ de seguridad** safety switch.

intersecarse [1g] *vr* to intersect.

intersección *nf* intersection; (*Aut*) intersection, crossing, junction.

intersticio *nm* (*gen*) interstice; (*grieta*) crack; (*intervalo*) interval, gap; (*Mec*) clearance.

intertanto (*LAm*) **1** *adv* meanwhile. **2** *conj*: **~ que él llegue** until he comes, while we wait for him to come. **3** *nm*: **en el ~** in the meantime.

intertítulo *nm* caption, subtitle.

interurbano 1 *adj* inter-city; (*Telec*) long-distance, trunk (*atr*). **2** *nm* (*CAm*: *colectivo*) inter-city taxi.

intervalo *nm*, **intérvalo** *nm* (*tiempo*) interval; break; (*Mús*) interval; (*espacio*) gap; **a ~s** at intervals; intermittently; every now and then.

intervención *nf* (**a**) (*control*) supervision, control; (*LAm*: *de sindicato*) government takeover.

(**b**) (*Com*) audit, auditing.

(**c**) (*Med*) operation; **~ quirúrgica** surgical operation.

(**d**) (*Telec*) tapping.

(**e**) (*participación*) intervention (*en* in); participation (*en* in), contribution (*en* to); **su ~ en la discusión** his contribution to the discussion; **la política de no ~** the policy of non-intervention, the non-intervention policy.

intervenir [3r] **1** *vt* (**a**) (*controlar*) to supervise, control; (*LAm*) *sindicato* to instal government appointees in, take over the control of.

(**b**) (*Com*) to audit.

(**c**) (*Med*) to operate on.

(**d**) (*Telec*) to tap, bug*.

(**e**) (*Jur*) to confiscate, seize.

2 *vi* (**a**) (*tomar parte*) to intervene (*en* in); to take part, participate (*en* in); to contribute (*en* to); **no intervino en el debate** he did not take part in the debate, he did not contribute to the debate; **él no intervino en la decisión** he did not have a hand in the decision; **una reyerta en la que intervino X** a brawl in which X was involved.

(**b**) (*interceder*) to intercede; (*mediar*) to mediate; **~ por uno** to intercede for sb.

interventor(a) *nm/f* inspector, supervisor; (*Com*: *t* **~ de cuentas**) auditor.

interviniente *nmf* participant.

interviú *nf* (*a veces nm*), **interview** *nf* interview; **hacer una ~ a uno** to interview sb.

interviu(v)ador(a) *nm/f* interviewer.

interviu(v)ar [1a] *vt* to interview, have an interview with.

intestado *adj* intestate.

intestinal *adj* intestinal.

intestino 1 *adj* internal; domestic, civil. **2** *nm* intestine; gut; **~ ciego** caecum; **~ delgado** small intestine; **~ grueso** large intestine.

inti *nm* (*And Fin*) Peruvian national currency.

intimación *nf* intimation, announcement, notification.

íntimamente *adv* intimately.

intimar [1a] **1** *vt* (*notificar*) to intimate, announce, notify (*a* to); (*ordenar*) to order, require (*que* that).

2 *vi y* **intimarse** *vr* to become intimate, become friendly (*con* with); **ahora intiman mucho** they're very friendly now.

intimidación *nf* intimidation; *V* **disparo.**

intimidad *nf* (**a**) (*amistad etc*) intimacy, familiarity; **disfrutar de la ~ de uno** to be on close terms with sb, enjoy sb's confidence; **entrar en ~ con uno** to become friendly with sb.

(**b**) (*vida privada*) privacy, private life; **conocido en la ~ como X** known in private life as X; **la ceremonia se celebró en la ~** the wedding took place privately, it was a quiet wedding.

(**c**) **~es** *pl* (*Anat*) private parts.

intimidador *adj* intimidating.

intimidar [1a] **1** *vt* to intimidate, overawe; to bully, scare. **2 intimidarse** *vr* to be intimidated, be overawed; to get scared.

intimidatorio *adj* intimidating.

intimista *adj* intimate, private.

íntimo *adj* intimate; *relación* intimate, close; *pensamientos* inner, innermost; *vida etc* private; **una boda íntima** a quiet wedding, a private wedding; **es ~ amigo mío** he is a close friend of mine; **en lo más ~ de su corazón** in one's heart of hearts.
intitular [1a] *vt* to entitle, call.
intocable 1 *adj* untouchable; (*fig*) sacrosanct. **2** *nmf* untouchable.
intolerable *adj* intolerable, unbearable.
intolerancia *nf* intolerance; narrow-mindedness, bigotry.
intolerante *adj* intolerant (*con, para* of); narrow-minded, bigoted (*en* about).
intonso *adj* (**a**) *persona* with long hair, unshorn, shaggy. (**b**) *libro* (with edges) untrimmed. (**c**) (*grosero*) boorish.
intoxicación *nf* (**a**) poisoning; **~ alimenticia** food poisoning; **~ etílica** alcohol poisoning, (*euf*) drunken state. (**b**) (*Pol*) disinformation, black propaganda.
intoxicador 1 *adj* (**a**) intoxicating. (**b**) (*Pol*) misleading, deceptive. **2** *nm*, **intoxicadora** *nf* spreader of disinformation, black propagandist.
intoxicar [1g] *vt* (**a**) to poison. (**b**) (*Pol*) to mislead, disinform.
intra... *pref* intra...
intracomunitario *adj* within the European Community.
intraducible *adj* untranslatable.
intragable *adj* unpalatable; (*fig*) unpalatable; intolerable, unacceptable.
intramatrimonial *adj*: **agresión ~** violence within a marriage, violence between husband and wife.
intramuros *adv* within the city, within the walls.
intranquilidad *nf* worry, uneasiness, disquiet, anxiety.
intranquilizar [1f] **1** *vt* to worry, disquiet, make uneasy. **2 intranquilizarse** *vr* to get worried, feel uneasy, be anxious.
intranquilo *adj* worried, uneasy, anxious; restless.
intra(n)scendencia *nf* unimportance, insignificance.
intra(n)scendente *adj* unimportant, insignificant.
intranscribible *adj* unprintable.
intransferible *adj* untransferable, not transferable.
intransigencia *nf* intransigence; uncompromising attitude, intolerance.
intransigente *adj* intransigent; uncompromising, intolerant; unyielding; diehard.
intransitable *adj* impassable.
intransitivo *adj* intransitive.
intratable *adj* *problema* intractable; awkward, tough; *persona* unsociable; difficult, impossible; **¡son ~s!** they're impossible!
intrauterino *adj* intrauterine.
intravenoso *adj* intravenous.
intrépidamente *adv* intrepidly, dauntlessly, fearlessly.
intrepidez *nf* intrepidity, fearlessness.
intrépido *adj* intrepid, dauntless, fearless.
intriga *nf* intrigue; plot, scheme; (*Teat*) plot; **~ secundaria** subplot.
intrigante 1 *adj* (**a**) (*pey*) intriguing, scheming. (**b**) (*interesante*) intriguing, interesting, puzzling. **2** *nmf* intriguer.
intrigar [1h] **1** *vt* (**a**) to intrigue, interest, puzzle.
(**b**) (*LAm*) *asunto* to conduct in a surprising way.
2 *vi* to intrigue, scheme, plot.
3 intrigarse *vr* (*LAm*) to be intrigued, be puzzled.
intrincadamente *adv* (*V adj*) (**a**) densely, impenetrably. (**b**) (*fig*) intricately.
intrincado *adj* (**a**) (*impenetrable*) dense, impenetrable; tangled. (**b**) (*fig*: *complicado*) intricate; involved, complicated.
intrincar [1g] *vt* to entangle; to confuse, complicate.
intríngulis* *nm invar* (*motivo*) ulterior motive; (*pega*) hidden snag, catch; (*misterio*) puzzle, mystery.
intrínsecamente *adv* intrinsically; inherently.
intrínseco *adj* intrinsic; inherent.
intro... *pref* intro...
introducción *nf* introduction; insertion; creation; (*libro*) foreword; (*Inform*) input.
introducir [3n] **1** *vt* (*gen*) to introduce; *visita etc* to bring in, show in; *objeto* to insert, introduce, put in; *discordia etc* to create, sow, cause; (*Inform*) to input, enter.
2 introducirse *vr* (**a**) (*meterse*) to get in, slip in, gain access (*en* to); (*fig*) to insinuate o.s., worm one's way (*en* into).
(**b**) (*fig*: *entrometerse*) to interfere, meddle.
introductor *adj* introductory.
introductorio *adj* introductory.
introito *nm* (*Teat*) prologue; (*Ecl*) introit.
intromisión *nf* (**a**) (*inserción*) introduction, insertion. (**b**) (*pey*) interference, meddling.
introspección *nf* introspection.
introspectivo *adj* introspective.
introversión *nf* introversion.
introvertido 1 *adj* introvert, introverted; inward-looking. **2** *nm*, **introvertida** *nf* introvert.
intrusión *nf* intrusion; (*Jur*) trespass; **~ informática** hacking, computer piracy.
intrusismo *nm* infiltration.
intruso 1 *adj* intrusive. **2** *nm*, **intrusa** *nf* (*gen*) intruder, interloper; (*forastero*) outsider; (*en fiesta etc*) gatecrasher; (*Jur*) trespasser; (*Mil, Pol*) infiltrator; **~ informático** hacker, computer pirate.
intuible *adj* that can be intuited.
intuición *nf* intuition; **por ~** by intuition, intuitively.
intuir [3g] **1** *vt* to know by intuition; to intuit; to sense, feel, have an intuition of.
2 intuirse *vr*: **eso se intuye** that can be guessed; **se intuye que ...** one can tell intuitively that ..., one can guess that ...; you can feel that ...; **el hombre se intuye observado** the man realizes he is under observation.
intuitivamente *adv* intuitively.
intuitivo *adj* intuitive.
intumescencia *nf* swelling.
intumescente *adj* intumescent, swollen.
inundación *nf* flood, flooding.
inundadizo *adj* (*LAm*) liable to flooding.
inundar [1a] *vt* to flood, inundate, swamp (*t fig*; *de, en* with); **~ el mercado de un producto** to flood the market with a product; **quedamos inundados de ofertas** we are swamped with offers; **la lluvia inundó la campiña** the rain flooded the countryside, the rain left the countryside under water.
inusitado *adj* unusual, unwonted, rare.
inusual *adj* unusual.
inusualmente *adv* unusually.
inútil *adj* (*gen*) useless; *tentativa etc* vain, fruitless; *esfuerzo* vain; **todo es ~** nothing is any use; **es ~ que Vd proteste** it is useless for you to protest, it's no good your protesting.
inutilidad *nf* uselessness.
inutilizable *adj* unusable, unfit for use.
inutilización *nf* disablement; spoiling; cancellation.
inutilizar [1f] **1** *vt* (*gen*) to make useless, render useless; *barco etc* to disable, put out of action; (*estropear*) to spoil, ruin; *esfuerzo etc* to nullify; *sello* to cancel.
2 inutilizarse *vr* to become useless; to be disabled; to be spoiled.
inútilmente *adv* uselessly; vainly, fruitlessly.
INV *nm* (*Esp*) *abr de* **Instituto Nacional de la Vivienda**.
invadeable *adj* unfordable; (*fig*) impassable; (*fig*) unsurmountable.
invadir [3a] *vt* (**a**) (*Mil etc*) to invade; to overrun; **la turba invadió las calles** the mob poured out on to the streets. (**b**) (*fig*) *derechos etc* to encroach upon.
invalidante *adj* disabling, incapacitating.
invalidar [1a] *vt* to invalidate, nullify.
invalidez *nf* (**a**) (*Med*) disablement; unfitness; disability; **~ permanente** permanent disability. (**b**) (*Jur*) invalidity, nullity.
inválido 1 *adj* (**a**) (*Med*) invalid, disabled; unfit.
(**b**) (*Jur etc*) invalid, null and void; **declarar inválida una elección** to declare an election invalid.
2 *nm*, **inválida** *nf* (*Med*) invalid.
3 *nm* (*Mil*: *Med*) disabled soldier, wounded soldier; pensioner.
invaluable *adj* (*LAm*) invaluable.
invariable *adj* invariable.
invariablemente *adv* invariably.
invariancia *nf* invariability, lack of variation.
invasión *nf* (**a**) (*gen*) invasion (*t Med*); attack. (**b**) (*fig*) encroachment (*de* on); inroad (*de* into).
invasor 1 *adj* invading. **2** *nm*, **invasora** *nf* invader, attacker.
invectiva *nf* invective; **una ~** a piece of invective, a tirade.
invectivar [1a] *vt* to inveigh against; to heap abuse upon.
invencibilidad *nf* invincibility.
invencible *adj* invincible; *obstáculo* unsurmountable, insuperable; **La I~** the Armada (*1588*).
invenciblemente *adv* invincibly; insuperably.
invención *nf* (*invento*) invention; (*descubrimiento*) discovery, finding; (*pey*) fabrication; (*Poét etc*) fiction, tale, fable.

invendible *adj* unsaleable, unmarketable.
invendido 1 *adj* unsold. **2** *nm* unsold item.
inventar [1a] *vt* to invent; (*idear*) to devise; (*pey*) to make up, fabricate, concoct.
inventariado *nm* detailed account.
inventariar [1b] *vt* to inventory, make an inventory of.
inventario *nm* inventory; stocktaking; ~ **continuo** continuous inventory; **hacer ~ de** to make an inventory of, take stock of.
inventiva *nf* inventiveness; ingenuity, resourcefulness.
inventivo *adj* inventive; ingenious, resourceful.
invento *nm* invention; ~ **del tebeo*** silly idea.
inventor(a) *nm/f* inventor.
inverificable *adj* unverifiable.
invernáculo *nm* = **invernadero** (**a**).
invernada *nf* (**a**) (*estación*) winter season.
(**b**) (*etapa invernal*) wintering; (*hibernación*) hibernation.
(**c**) (*And, Cono Sur*: *pasto*) winter pasture.
(**d**) (*Carib*: *tempestad*) heavy rainstorm.
invernadero *nm* (**a**) greenhouse, hothouse; conservatory. (**b**) (*LAm*) winter pasture.
invernal *adj* wintry, winter (*atr*).
invernante 1 *adj* over-wintering. **2** *nm* (*Orn*) over-wintering species, winter visitor.
invernar [1j] *vi* to winter, spend the winter; (*Zool*) to hibernate.
invernazo* *nm* (*Carib*) rainy season (*July to September*).
inverne *nm* (*LAm*) winter pasturing; winter fattening.
invernizo *adj* wintry, winter (*atr*).
inverosímil *adj* unlikely, improbable; implausible.
inverosimilitud *nf* unlikeliness, improbability; implausibility.
inversamente *adv* inversely; **e ~** and vice versa.
inversión *nf* (**a**) (*gen*) inversion; reversal; (*Aut, Mec*) reversing; ~ **de marcha** reversing, backing; ~ **sexual** homosexuality; ~ **térmica** temperature inversion.
(**b**) (*Com, Fin*) investment (*en* in); ~ **de capital(es)** capital investment.
inversionista *nmf* (*Com, Fin*) investor.
inverso *adj* inverse, inverted; reverse, contrary; *cara* reverse; **a la inversa** inversely, the other way round; (*fig*) vice versa; on the contrary.
inversor 1 *adj* investment (*atr*). **2** *nm*, **inversora** *nf* investor; ~ **financiero** investments manager; ~ **inmobiliario** property investor; ~ **institucional** institutional investor.
invertebrado *adj, nm* invertebrate.
invertido 1 *adj* (**a**) (*volcado*) inverted; (*al revés*) reversed; **escritura invertida** mirror writing. (**b**) (*Bio*) homosexual. **2** *nm*, **invertida** *nf* homosexual.
invertir [3i] *vt* (**a**) (*volcar*) to invert, turn upside down; (*poner al revés*) to reverse, put the other way round; (*cambiar el orden de*) to change over, change the order of; (*Aut, Mec*) to reverse; (*Mat*) to invert.
(**b**) *esfuerzo, tiempo* to spend, put in (*en* on); **invirtieron 5 días en el viaje** they spent 5 days on the journey.
(**c**) (*Com, Fin*) to invest (*en* in).
investidura *nf* investiture; (*Parl*) vote of confidence (in the prime minister).
investigación *nf* (**a**) (*indagación*) investigation; inquiry (*de* into); ~ **policíaca** police investigation. (**b**) (*Univ etc*) research, research work (*de* in, into); ~ **básica** basic research; ~ **y desarrollo** research and development; ~ **operativa** operational research.
investigador 1 *adj* investigative; research (*atr*); **capacidad ~a** research ability, ability in research. **2** *nm*, **investigadora** *nf* (**a**) investigator; ~ **privado** private detective. (**b**) (*Univ etc*) research worker, researcher; (*de doctorado*) research student.
investigar [1h] *vt* (**a**) (*indagar*) to investigate; to inquire into, look into. (**b**) (*Univ etc*) to do research into, do research work on.
investir [3k] *vt*: ~ **a uno con el título de doctor** to confer the title of doctor on sb.
inveterado *adj* inveterate; *criminal* confirmed, hardened; *hábito* deep-seated, well-established.
inviabilidad *nf* impossibility, non-viability; invalidity.
inviable *adj* impossible, non-viable; *reclamación* invalid.
invicto *adj* unconquered, unbeaten.
invidencia *nf* sightlessness.
invidente 1 *adj* sightless, blind. **2** *nmf* sightless person, blind person.
invierno *nm* (**a**) winter, wintertime; ~ **nuclear** nuclear winter. (**b**) (*And, CAm, Carib*: *meses de lluvia*) rainy season. (**c**) (*Carib*: *aguacero*) heavy shower.
inviolabilidad *nf* inviolability; ~ **parlamentaria** parliamentary immunity.
inviolable *adj* inviolable.
inviolado *adj* inviolate.
invisibilidad *nf* invisibility.
invisible 1 *adj* invisible. **2** *nm* (*And, Cono Sur*) hairpin.
invitación *nf* invitation (*a* to); **a ~ de** at the invitation of.
invitado, -a *adj, nm/f* guest; ~ **de honor** guest of honour; **estrella invitada** guest star.
invitar [1a] *vt* to invite; ~ **a uno a hacer algo** to invite sb to do sth; to call on sb to do sth; **invito yo** it's on me, be my guest; **hoy invito a café** today I'll buy the coffee, today I'll stand coffees all round; **nos invitó a cenar fuera** she took us out for a meal; **dio las gracias a los que le habían invitado** he thanked his hosts.
invocación *nf* invocation.
invocar [1g] *vt* (**a**) (*llamar en ayuda*) to invoke, call on; ~ **la ley** to invoke the law. (**b**) (*rogar*) to beg for, implore; ~ **la ayuda de** to beg for the help of. (**c**) (*Inform*) to call.
involución *nf* (*Pol*) regression, reaction, turning back.
involucionismo *nm* (*Pol*) reaction; reactionary forces.
involucionista (*Pol*) **1** *adj* regressive, reactionary. **2** *nmf* reactionary.
involucrar [1a] **1** *vt* (**a**) (*implicar*) to involve; ~ **a uno en algo** to involve sb in sth; **andar involucrado en** to be mixed up in.
(**b**) (*mezclar*) to jumble up, mix up; **lo tiene todo involucrado** he's got it all mixed up.
2 involucrarse *vr* to meddle, interfere (*en* in); to get involved (*en* in); **las personas involucradas en el caso** the people involved in the affair, the persons concerned in the matter.
involuntariamente *adv* involuntarily; unintentionally.
involuntario *adj* involuntary; *ofensa etc* unintentional.
involutivo *adj* (*Pol*) reactionary.
invulnerabilidad *nf* invulnerability.
invulnerable *adj* invulnerable.
inyectable *nm* serum, vaccine; injection.
inyección *nf* injection, shot*, jab*; (*Fin, Mec*) injection; **hacerse** (*o* **ponerse**) **una ~** to give o.s. an injection.
inyectado *adj*: **ojos ~s** (**en sangre**) bloodshot eyes.
inyectar [1a] **1** *vt* to inject (*en* into); ~ **algo en uno** to inject sb with sth. **2 inyectarse** *vr* to give oneself an injection, shoot up‡.
inyector *nm* injector; (*Téc*) nozzle.
ion *nm* ion.
iónico *adj* (*Quím*) ionic.
ionizar [1f] *vt* to ionize.
ionosfera *nf* ionosphere.
IORTV *nm abr de* **Instituto Oficial de Radiodifusión y Televisión**.
iota *nf* iota.
IPC *nm abr de* **índice de precios al consumidor** (*o* **consumo**) retail price index, RPI.
ipecacuana *nf* ipecacuanha.
ipomea *nf* (*Bot*) morning glory.
IPPV *nm abr de* **Instituto para la Promoción Pública de la Vivienda**.
ir [3s] **1** *vi* (**a**) (*gen*) to go; to move; to travel; (*en pie*) to go, walk; (*en coche etc*) to go, drive; (*en bicicleta, caballo etc*) to go, ride; ~ **a Quito** to go to Quito; **este camino va a Huesca** this road goes to Huesca, this is the road to Huesca; ~ **hacia Sevilla** to go towards Seville, go in the direction of Seville; ~ **hasta León** to go as far as León; **fui en coche** I went by car, I drove; **fui en tren** I went by train, I went by rail; ~ **despacio** to go slow(ly); ~ **con tiento** to go carefully, go cautiously; **vaya donde vaya, encontrará ...** wherever you go, you will find ...; **ya ha ido*** you've had it*; **¡voy!** I'm coming!, I'll be with you in a moment!; **¡ahora voy!** I'll be right there!; **¡vamos!** let's go! (*V t* (**k**)); **¿quién va?** (*Mil etc*) who goes there?; ~ **por leña** to fetch wood, go and fetch wood, go for wood; **voy por el médico** I'll (go and) fetch the doctor, I'll call the doctor; ~ **tras una chica** to chase (after) a girl.
(**b**) (*locuciones*) ~ **con uno** to agree with sb; ~ **de mal en peor** to go from bad to worse, get worse; **esto va de veras** this is serious; I'm in earnest; **es el no va más*** it's the very last word, it's the latest thing; **en lo que va de año** so far this year; **a eso voy** I'm coming to that; **a lo que iba** as I was saying; **si vamos a eso** for that matter, as for that; ~ **a lo suyo** to go one's own way; (*pey*) to act selfishly, think only of o.s.; **va para 5 años que entré en la Universidad** it's getting on for five years since I started University; **va para los 40** he's going on for 40, he's knock-

ing on 40; **va para viejo** he's getting old; **con éste van 30** that makes 30; ~ **y marcharse**: **fue y se marchó** (*Méx**) he just upped and left*; **¡que le vaya bien!** (*LAm*) goodbye!; **le va al Cruz Azul** (*Méx Dep*) he supports Cruz Azul.

(c) (*progresar*) to go; (*Med*) to be, go, get along; **¿cómo va eso?** how are things going?; **¿cómo te va?** how goes it?; **¿cómo va el ensayo?** how are you getting on with the essay?; **no me va bien el inglés** I'm not doing very well with English; **el enfermo va mejor** the patient is better, the patient is getting along nicely.

(d) (*diferencia*) **va mucho de A a B** there's a lot of difference between A and B, A is very different from B; **¡lo que va del padre al hijo!** what a difference there is between father and son!; **de 7 a 9 van 2** 7 from 9 leaves 2.

(e) **eso no va por ti** (*intención*) I wasn't referring to you, that wasn't meant for you; it's not your fault.

(f) (*importar*) **va mucho en esto** a lot depends on it; **¿qué te va en ello?** what does it matter to you?; **no le va la vida en esto** it's not as though his life depends on it; **ni le va ni le viene** it's nothing to do with him, he's not concerned, he doesn't care.

(g) (*apuestas*) **van 5 dólares a que no lo haces** I bet 5 dollars that you won't do it; **¿cuánto va?** how much do you bet?

(h) **va para ingeniero** (*carrera etc*) he's going to become an engineer, he's going into engineering.

(i) (*Naipes*) to lead; to go.

(j) (*ropa*) to suit, become; **¿me va bien esto?** does this suit me?; **no le va bien el sombrero** the hat doesn't suit her.

(k) (*interj etc*) **¡vaya!** (*sorpresa*) well!, there!, I say!; (*enfado*) damn!; **¡vaya coche!** what a car!, there's a car for you!, that's some car!; **¡vaya susto que me pegué!** what a fright I got!; **¡vaya, vaya!** well I'm blowed!*; come now!; **¡vamos!** well!; **vamos, no es difícil** come now, it's not difficult; **una chica, vamos, una mujer** a girl, well ... a woman; **¡qué va!** rubbish!; nonsense!; **es molesto, pero ¡vamos!** it's a nuisance, but there it is; **¡vaya por Pepe!** (*Esp*) here's to Joe!

(l) (*en tiempos continuos*) **iba anocheciendo** it was getting dark; **iban fumando** they were smoking; **voy comprendiendo que** ... I am beginning to see that ..., I am in the process of learning that ...

(m) (*con ptp*) **iba cansado** he was tired; **van escritas 3 cartas** that's 3 letters I've written; **va vendido todo** everything has been sold.

(n) (~ **a** + *infin*) **voy a hacerlo** I'm going to do it; **vamos a hacerlo** we are going to do it; let's do it; **fui a verle** I went to see him, I went and saw him; **¿no irá a soplar?**‡ I hope he's not going to split on us*; **no vaya a ser que** + *subj* lest he should + *infin*, in case he should + *infin*; **¿cómo lo iba a tener?** how could he have had it?; **¡no lo va a saber!** of course he knows!; *V* **hacer.**

(o) (~ **de** + *n*): **el país va de democracia** the country is in a democratic mood; **Pérez va de presidente** Pérez is all set for the presidency; **sabe de qué va 'el rollo'** she knows what 'el rollo' is; **¿de qué vas?** what are you on about?*; **la película va de sexo** the film is all sex; **la que va de negro** the girl in black; *para locuciones de* ~ **de** + *sustantivo V el sustantivo, p.ej.* **campo, etiqueta.**

2 irse *vr* **(a)** **por aquí se va a Jaca** this is the way to Jaca; **¿por dónde se va al aeropuerto?** which way to the airport?

(b) (*marcharse*) to go away, leave, depart; **se fueron** they went, they went off, they left; **es hora de irnos** it's time we went, it's time for us to go; **¡vete!** go away!, get out!; **¡vete ya!** off with you!; **¡no te vayas!** don't go!; **¡vámonos!** let's go!, (*Ferro etc*) all aboard!; ~ **de algo** to discard sth; **me voy de con Vd** (*CAm*) I'm leaving you.

(c) (*resbalar*) to slip, lose one's balance; (*muro etc*) to give way; *V* **mano, pie** *etc.*

(d) (*recipiente*) to leak; to overflow; (*contenido*) to leak out, overflow, ooze out; to evaporate; **se fue el vino** the wine was lost; **el neumático se va** the tyre is losing air.

(e) (*morir*: *euf*) to be dying; to die; **se nos va el amo** the master is dying; **se nos fue hace 3 años** he departed from us 3 years ago, he passed away 3 years ago.

(f) (**‡**: *echar un pedo*) to fart**‡**.

(g) (**‡**: *eyacular*) to come**‡**.

ira *nf* (*lit*) anger, rage, wrath (*liter*); (*de viento etc*) fury, violence.

iracundia *nf* ire; irascibility.

iracundo *adj* irate; irascible.

Irak *nm* Iraq.

irakí = **iraquí.**

Irán *nm*: **(el)** ~ Iran.

iranés = **iraní.**

iraní 1 *adj, nmf* Iranian, Persian. **2** *nm* (*Ling*) Iranian, Persian, Farsi.

iranio (*Hist*) = **iraní.**

Iraq *nm* Iraq.

iraquí *adj, nmf* Iraqui.

irascibilidad *nf* irascibility.

irascible *adj* irascible.

iridiscente *adj* iridescent.

iris *nm* (*Met*) rainbow; (*Anat*) iris; **hacer un** ~ (*LAm**) to wink.

irisación *nf* iridescence.

irisado *adj* iridescent.

irisar [1a] *vi* to be iridescent, iridesce.

Irlanda *nf* Ireland; ~ **del Norte** Northern Ireland, Ulster.

irlandés 1 *adj* Irish. **2** *nm* Irishman; **los irlandeses** the Irish. **3** *nm* (*Ling*) Irish.

irlandesa *nf* Irishwoman.

ironía *nf* irony; **con** ~ ironically.

irónicamente *adv* ironically.

irónico *adj* ironical.

ironizar [1f] **1** *vt* to ridicule. **2** *vi* to speak ironically; **"~", ironizó Z** "~", said Z ironically.

IRPF *nm* (*Esp*) *abr de* **impuesto sobre la renta de las personas físicas** (personal income-tax).

irracional 1 *adj* irrational; unreasoning; **ser** ~ brute, brute creature. **2** *nm* brute, brute creature.

irracionalidad *nf* irrationality; unreasonableness.

irracionalmente *adv* irrationally; unreasonably, unreasoningly.

irradiación *nf* irradiation.

irradiar [1b] *vt* to irradiate, radiate.

irrayable *adj* scratch-proof.

irrazonable *adj* unreasonable.

irreal *adj* unreal.

irrealidad *nf* unreality.

irrealista *adj* unrealistic.

irrealizable *adj* unrealizable; *plan* unworkable; impossible to carry out; *meta etc* unattainable.

irrebatible *adj* unanswerable, irrefutable, unassailable.

irrecomendable *adj* inadvisable.

irreconciliable *adj* irreconcilable; inconsistent, incompatible.

irreconocible *adj* unrecognizable.

irrecuperable *adj* irrecoverable, irretrievable.

irrecurrible *adj*: **la decisión es** ~ there is no appeal against this decision.

irrecusable *adj* unimpeachable.

irrechazable *adj* irresistible.

irredimible *adj* irredeemable.

irreducible *adj* **(a)** *mínimo* irreducible. **(b)** *diferencias* irreconcilable, incompatible.

irreductible *adj defensor etc* uncompromising, unyielding; (*pey*) hidebound, bigoted.

irreembolsable *adj depósito* non-returnable.

irreemplazable *adj* irreplaceable.

irreflexión *nf* thoughtlessness; rashness, impetuosity.

irreflexivamente *adv* thoughtlessly, unthinkingly; rashly.

irreflexivo *adj* thoughtless, unthinking; rash, impetuous; *acto* rash, ill-considered.

irrefrenable *adj violencia etc* unrestrained, unbridled, uncontrollable; *persona* irrepressible; unmanageable; *deseo, fuerza* unstoppable.

irrefutable *adj* irrefutable, unanswerable.

irregular *adj* irregular; abnormal.

irregularidad *nf* irregularity; abnormality.

irregularmente *adv* irregularly; abnormally.

irrelevante *adj* irrelevant.

irreligioso *adj* irreligious; ungodly.

irrellenable *adj botella, encendedor* disposable.

irremediable *adj* irremediable; incurable; hopeless.

irremediablemente *adv* irremediably; incurably; hopelessly.

irremisible *adj falta* unpardonable; *pérdida* irretrievable.

irremisiblemente *adv* unpardonably; ~ **perdido** irretrievably lost, lost beyond hope of recovery.

irremontable *adj barrera* insurmountable.

irremunerado *adj* unremunerated.

irrentable *adj* unprofitable.

irrenunciable *adj*: **una aspiración** ~ an aspiration which can never be given up.

irreparable *adj* irreparable.

irreparablemente *adv* irreparably.
irrepetible *adj* one-and-only, unique.
irreprensible *adj* irreproachable.
irreprimible *adj* irrepressible.
irreprochable *adj* irreproachable.
irreproducible *adj* that cannot be reproduced, unrepeatable.
irresistible *adj* irresistible; (*pey*) unbearable, insufferable; (*demasiado fuerte*) impossibly strong.
irresistiblemente *adv* irresistibly.
irresoluble *adj* unsolvable; unresolved.
irresolución *nf* irresolution, hesitation, undecidedness.
irresoluto *adj* (**a**) *carácter* irresolute, hesitant, undecided. (**b**) *problema* unresolved.
irrespetuosamente *adv* disrespectfully.
irrespetuoso *adj* disrespectful.
irrespirable *adj* unbreathable.
irresponsabilidad *nf* irresponsibility.
irresponsable *adj* irresponsible.
irrestricto *adj* (*LAm*) *apoyo etc* unconditional.
irresuelto *adj* = **irresoluto** (**a**).
irreverencia *nf* irreverence; disrespect.
irreverente *adj* irreverent; disrespectful.
irreversible *adj* irreversible.
irrevocable *adj* irrevocable, irreversible.
irrevocablemente *adv* irrevocably.
irrigación *nf* irrigation.
irrigador *nm* sprinkler.
irrigar [1h] *vt* to irrigate.
irrisible *adj* laughable, absurd; *precio* absurdly low, bargain (*atr*).
irrisión *nf* (**a**) (*mofa*) derision, ridicule. (**b**) (*persona*) laughing stock.
irrisorio *adj* derisory, ridiculous, absurd; *precio* absurdly low, bargain (*atr*).
irritabilidad *nf* irritability.
irritable *adj* irritable.
irritación *nf* irritation.
irritador *adj* irritating.
irritante 1 *adj* irritating. **2** *nm* irritant.
irritar [1a] **1** *vt* (**a**) (*gen*) to irritate, anger, exasperate. (**b**) (*fig*) to stir up, inflame. (**c**) (*Med*) to irritate, inflame. **2 irritarse** *vr* to get angry, lose one's temper (*de* about, at, with).
irrompible *adj* unbreakable.
irrumpir [3a] *vi*: ~ **en** to burst into, rush into; to invade.
irrupción *nf* irruption; inrush; invasion.
IRTP *nm* (*Esp*) *abr de* **impuesto sobre el rendimiento del trabajo personal** ≃ pay-as-you-earn, PAYE.
IRYDA [ɪ'riða] *nm abr de* **Instituto para la Reforma y el Desarrollo Agrario.**
Isaac *nm* Isaac.
Isabel *nf* Isabel, Elizabeth; (*reinas de Inglaterra*) Elizabeth.
isabelino *adj*: **la España isabelina** Isabelline Spain, the Spain of Isabel (II); **la Inglaterra isabelina** Elizabethan England, the England of Elizabeth.
Isabelita *nf* Betty; Bess, Bessie; Liz.
Isaías *nm* Isaiah.
iscocoro‡ *nm* (*CAm pey*) Indian.
ISDE *nm* (*Esp Com*) *abr de* **Instituto Superior de Dirección de Empresas.**
Iseo *nf* Iseult, Isolde.
Isías *nm* Isaiah.
isidrada *nf*, **isidros** *nmpl* celebration of St Isidore (*patron saint of Madrid*).
-ísimo *V* **Aspects of Word Formation in Spanish 2.**
Isla *nf*: **~s Británicas** British Isles; **~ de Francia** Mauritius; *para otros nombres, V el segundo elemento.*
isla *nf* (**a**) (*Geog*) island; isle. (**b**) (*Arquit*) block; (*Aut*) traffic island. (**c**) (*Méx*: *árboles*) isolated clump of trees. (**d**) (*Méx*: *istmo*) spit of land.
Islam *nm* Islam.
islámico *adj* Islamic.
islamización *nf* Islamization.
islamizar [1f] *vt* to Islamize, convert to Islam.
islandés 1 *adj* Icelandic. **2** *nm*, **islandesa** *nf* Icelander. **3** *nm* (*Ling*) Icelandic.
Islandia *nf* Iceland.
islándico *adj* Icelandic.
isleño 1 *adj* island (*atr*). **2** *nm*, **isleña** *nf* islander.
isleta *nf* islet.
islote *nm* small island, rocky isle.
ismo *nm* ism.
-ismo *V* **Aspects of Word Formation in Spanish 2.**
iso... *pref* iso...
isobara, isóbara *nf* isobar.
isoca *nf* (*Cono Sur*) caterpillar.
isohispa *nf* contour line.
Isolde *nf* Iseult, Isolde.
isométrica *nf* isometrics, isometric exercises.
isométrico *adj* isometric.
isósceles *adj*: **triángulo** ~ isosceles triangle.
isoterma *nf* isotherm.
isotérmico *adj* insulated; isothermal.
isótopo *nm* isotope.
Israel *nm* Israel.
israelí *adj, nmf* Israeli.
israelita *adj, nmf* Israelite.
-ista *V* **Aspects of Word Formation in Spanish 2.**
istmeño 1 *adj* of the Isthmus, (*frec*) Panamanian. **2** *nm*, **istmeña** *nf* native (*o* inhabitant) of the Isthmus, (*frec*) Panamanian.
istmo *nm* isthmus; neck; **~ de Panamá** Isthmus of Panama; **el I~** (*Méx*) the isthmus of Tehuantepec.
itacate *nm* (*Méx*) food, provisions.
Italia *nf* Italy.
italianismo *nm* italianism, word (*o* phrase *etc*) borrowed from Italian.
italiano, -a 1 *adj, nm/f* Italian. **2** *nm* (*Ling*) Italian.
itálica *nf*: **en** ~ in italics.
ITE ['ite] *nm* (*Esp Hist*) *abr de* **impuesto de tráfico de empresas.**
ítem 1 *nm* item. **2** *adv* also, moreover.
itemizar [1f] *vt* (*LAm*) to itemize, specify; to divide into sections.
iterar [1a] *vt* to repeat.
iterativo *adj* iterative.
itinerante *adj* itinerant, roving, travelling; *embajador* roving, at large.
itinerario *nm* itinerary, route; (*Méx Ferro*) timetable.
-itis *V* **Aspects of Word Formation in Spanish 2.**
-ito, -ita *V* **Aspects of Word Formation in Spanish 2.**
ITV *nf* (*Esp*) *abr de* **Inspección Técnica de Vehículos** ≃ Ministry of Transport Test Certificate, MOT.
IVA ['iβa] *nm* (*Esp*) *abr de* **impuesto sobre el valor añadido** value-added tax, VAT.
Ivan *nm* Ivan; **~ el Terrible** Ivan the Terrible.
IVP *nm abr de* **Instituto Venezolano de Petroquímica.**
ixtle *nm* (*Méx*) fibre.
I. y D. *nf abr de* **Investigación y Desarrollo** Research and Development, R and D.
iza‡ *nf* whore.
izada *nf* (*LAm*) raising, lifting.
izado *nm*: **~ de la bandera** raising the flag.
-izante *V* **Aspects of Word Formation in Spanish 2.**
izar [1f] *vt* (*Náut*) to hoist, haul up; *bandera* to raise, hoist, run up; **la bandera está izada** the flag is flying.
izcuinche *nm* (*Méx*) (**a**) (*perro*) mangy dog, mongrel. (**b**) (*niño*) ragged child, urchin.
izda, izq.ª *abr de* **izquierda.**
izdo, izq, izq.º *abr de* **izquierdo.**
-izo *V* **Aspects of Word Formation in Spanish 2.**
izquierda *nf* (**a**) (*mano*) left hand; (*lado*) left side, left-hand side; **estar a la ~ de** to be on the left of; **torcer a la ~** to turn (to the) left; **conducción por la ~** (*Aut*) left-hand drive; **el árbol de la ~** the tree on the left; **seguir por la ~** to keep (to the) left. (**b**) (*Pol*) left.
izquierdismo *nm* left-wing outlook (*o* tendencies *etc*), leftism.
izquierdista 1 *adj* leftist, left-wing. **2** *nmf* leftist, left-winger.
izquierdo *adj* (**a**) (*gen*) left; left-hand. (**b**) (*zurdo*) left-handed. (**c**) (*fig*) crooked, twisted.
izquierdoso* (*pey*) **1** *adj* leftish. **2** *nm*, **izquierdosa** *nf* lefty*.

J

J, j ['xota] *nf* (*letra*) J, j.
ja[1] *interj* ha!
ja[2]⁑ *nf* (*mujer*) wife; (*amante*) bird⁑.
jaba *nf* **(a)** (*LAm*: *cesto*) straw basket; (*caja*) crate.
(b) (*Carib*) beggar's bag; (*) poverty; **llevar** (*o* **tener**) **algo en** ~ (*fig**) to have sth up one's sleeve; **no poder ver a otro con** ~ **grande*** to envy sb; **soltar la** ~ to go up in the world, acquire polish; **tomar la** ~ to be reduced to begging.
(c) (*LAm Bot*) = **haba.**
jabado *adj* **(a)** (*Carib, Méx*) white with brown patches. **(b)** (*indeciso*) hesitant, undecided.
jabalí *nm* wild boar; ~ **verrugoso** warthog.
jabalina *nf* **(a)** (*Zool*) wild sow, female wild boar. **(b)** (*Dep*) javelin.
jabato 1 *adj* **(a)** (*valiente*) brave, bold. **(b)** (*Carib, Méx*) (*grosero*) rude, gruff; (*malhumorado*) ill-tempered. **2** *nm* **(a)** young wild boar; **portarse como un** ~ to be very brave. **(b)** (*) tough guy*.
jábega *nf* **(a)** (*red*) dragnet. **(b)** (*barco*) fishing smack.
jabón *nm* **(a)** soap; (*un* ~) piece of soap, bar of soap; ~ **de afeitar** shaving soap; ~ **en escama** soapflakes; ~ **líquido** liquid soap; ~ **de olor,** ~ **de tocador** toilet soap; ~ **en polvo** soap powder; ~ **de sastre** French chalk; **no es lo mismo** ~ **que hilo negro** (*And, Carib*) they're as different as chalk from cheese.
(b) (*: *adulación*) soft soap*, flattery; **dar** ~ **a uno** to soft-soap sb*.
(c) **dar un** ~ **a uno** (⁑: *reprimenda*) to tell sb off*.
(d) **hacer** ~ to laze around.
(e) (*Carib, Cono Sur, Méx*: *susto*) fright, scare; **agarrarse un** ~ to get a fright.
jabonada *nf* (*LAm*) = **jabonadura.**
jabonado *nm* **(a)** (*acto*) soaping. **(b)** (*ropa*) wash, laundry. **(c)** (*: *bronca*) ticking-off*.
jabonadura *nf* **(a)** (*acto*) soaping. **(b)** **~s** (*espuma*) lather, soapsuds. **(c)** (*) telling-off*; **dar una** ~ **a uno** to tell sb off*.
jabonar [1a] *vt* **(a)** (*gen*) to soap; *ropa* to wash; *barba* to soap, lather. **(b)** (*) to tell off*, dress down*.
jaboncillo *nm* (piece of) toilet soap; ~ **de sastre** French chalk.
jabonera *nf* soapdish.
jabonería *nf* soap factory.
jabonete *nm* piece of toilet soap.
jabonoso *adj* soapy.
jabuco *nm* (*Carib*) (*caja*) large basket, big crate; (*bolsa*) bag; **dar** ~ **a uno** to snub sb, give sb the cold shoulder.
jaca *nf* **(a)** pony, cob, small horse; (*yegua*) mare; (*Carib*) gelding. **(b)** (⁑) bird⁑, dame*.
jacal *nm* (*CAm, Carib, Méx*) shack, hut; **al** ~ **viejo no le faltan goteras** old age is bound to have its problems; **no tiene** ~ **donde meterse** he's without a roof over his head.
jacalear* [1a] *vi* (*Méx*) to wander about gossiping.
jacalón *nm* (*Méx*) (*cobertizo*) shed; (*casucha*) shack, hovel; (*Teat**) fleapit*.
jácara *nf* **(a)** (*Liter*: *Hist*) comic ballad of low life; (*Mús*: *Hist*) *a merry dance*; (*personas*) band of night revellers; **estar de** ~ to be very merry.
(b) (*: *cuento*) fib, story; hoax.
(c) (*: *molestia*) annoyance.
jacarandá *nm o f* jacaranda.
jacarandoso *adj* (*alegre*) merry, jolly; lively; (*airoso*) spirited, stylish.
jacaré *nm* (*LAm*) alligator.
jacarear [1a] *vi* **(a)** (*cantar por la calle*) to sing in the streets at nights, (*dar serenata*) to go serenading. **(b)** (*fig*) (*armar un lío*) to cause a commotion; (*insultar*) to be rude, make offensive remarks.
jacarero 1 *adj* merry, fun-loving. **2** *nm* amusing person, wag.
jácena *nf* (*Téc*) summer.
jacinto *nm* (*Bot*) hyacinth; (*Min*) hyacinth, jacinth.
jaco *nm* **(a)** small horse, young horse; (*pey*) nag, hack. **(b)** (⁑) horse⁑, heroin.
jacobeo *adj* **(a)** (*Ecl*) of St James; **la devoción jacobea** the devotion to St James, the cult of St James. **(b)** (*Geog*) of Santiago de Compostela; **la ruta jacobea** the pilgrims' road to Santiago.
jacobino, -a *adj, nm/f* Jacobin.
Jacobo *nm* Jacob.
jactancia *nf* boasting, bragging; boastfulness.
jactanciosamente *adv* boastfully.
jactancioso *adj* boastful.
jactarse [1a] *vr* to boast, brag; ~ **de** to boast about, boast of; ~ **de** + *infin* to boast of + *ger*.
jachís *nm* = **hachís.**
jachudo *adj* (*And*) strong, tough; obstinate.
jade *nm* (*Min*) jade.
jadeante *adj* panting, gasping, breathless.
jadear [1a] *vi* to pant, gasp for breath, puff and blow.
jadeo *nm* panting, gasping, puffing and blowing.
jaez *nm* **(a)** harness, piece of harness; **jaeces** trappings. **(b)** (*fig*) kind, sort; **y gente de ese** ~ and people of that sort.
jaguar *nm* jaguar.
jagüel *nm*, **jagüey** *nm* (*LAm*) pool; (*pozo*) well, cistern.
jai⁑ *nf* bird⁑, dame*.
jaiba 1 *nf* **(a)** (*LAm*: *cangrejo*) crab.
(b) (*And*: *boca*) mouth; **abrir la** ~ to show o.s. greedy for money.
2 *nmf* (*Carib, Méx**) sharp customer*.
jáibol *nm* (*LAm*) highball (*US*).
jaibón* *adj* (*CAm*) stuck-up*, pretentious, snobbish.
jáilaif (*LAm*) **1** *adj* high-life (*atr*).
2 *nf* high life.
jailoso *adj* (*And*) well-bred; (*pey*) stuck-up*, pretentious, snobbish.
Jaime *nm* James; **hacer el Jaimito*** to horse around*.
jalada *nf* (*Méx*) **(a)** (*tirón*) pull, tug, heave. **(b)** (*reprimenda*) ticking-off*. **(c)** (*And* Univ*) failure.
jaladera *nf* (*Méx*) handle.
jalador *nm* (*LAm*) door-handle.
jalamecate* *nm* (*LAm*) toady, creep⁑.
jalapeño *nm* (*Méx*) (kind of) chili.
jalar [1a] **1** *vt* **(a)** (*LAm*: *tirar de*) to pull, haul; (*Náut*) to heave; (*LAm Pol*) to draw, attract, win.
(b) (*LAm*: *trabajar mucho*) to work hard at.
(c) (*And, Carib**: *hacer*) to make, do, perform.
(d) (*) to guzzle.
(e) (*Méx**: *dar aventón a*) to pick up, give a lift to.
(f) (*LAm**: *conquistar*) to pull.
(g) **eso le jala** (*Méx**) she's big on that*, she's a fan of that.
2 *vi* **(a)** (*LAm*: *tirar*) to pull; ~ **de** to pull at, tug at.
(b) (*LAm*: *trabajar*) to work hard.
(c) (*LAm*: *irse*) to go, go off, clear out*; ~ **para su casa** to clear off home.
(d) (*And⁑ Univ*) to flunk⁑, fail.
(e) (*CAm, Méx**: *amantes*) to be courting.
(f) (*Méx*: *exagerar*) to exaggerate.
(g) (⁑: *correr*) to run.
(h) (*Méx*: *tener influencia*) to have pull.
(i) (*And⁑*: *fumar marijuana*) to smoke dope⁑.
3 jalarse *vr* **(a)** (*CAm**: *amantes*) to be courting.
(b) (*LAm*: *emborracharse*) to get drunk.
(c) = *vi* **(c)**.

(**d**) (**: *masturbarse*) to wank**.

jalbegar [1h] *vt* to whitewash; *cara* (*) to make up, paint.

jalbegue *nm* whitewash; whitewashing; (*) make-up, paint.

jalde *adj*, **jaldo** *adj* bright yellow.

jalea *nf* jelly; ~ **de guayaba** guava jelly; ~ **real** royal jelly; **hacerse una** ~** to be madly in love; (*pey*) to be a creep**.

jalear [1a] **1** *vt* (**a**) *perro* to urge on; *bailarina* to encourage (by shouting and clapping). (**b**) (*Méx*: *burlarse*) to jeer at. **2** *vi* (*Méx*) to have a high old time*.

jaleo *nm* (**a**) (*juerga*) spree, binge*; **estar de** ~ to make merry, have a good time.

(**b**) (*ruido*) row, racket, uproar; (*confusión*) hassle, fuss; **armar un** ~ to kick up a row; **se armó un tremendo** ~ there was a hell of a row; **¡qué** ~! what a mess!, what a hassle!*

(**c**) (*Caza*) hallooing.

(**d**) (*Mús*) shouting and clapping (*to encourage dancers*).

jaleoso *adj* noisy, rowdy, boisterous.

jalisco[1]** *adj* (*CAm, Méx*) plastered**.

jalisco[2] *nm* (*CAm, Méx*) straw hat.

jalón *nm* (**a**) (*poste*) stake, pole; (*de agrimensor*) surveying rod.

(**b**) (*fig*) (*etapa*) stage; (*hito*) landmark, milestone; **esto marca un** ~ **en** ... this is a milestone in ...

(**c**) (*LAm*) pull, tug; (**: *robo*) snatch*; **hacer algo de un** ~ (*Méx*) to do sth in one go.

(**d**) (*LAm*: *distancia*) distance, stretch; **hay un buen** ~ it's a good way.

(**e**) (*CAm, Méx**: *trago*) swig*, drink.

(**f**) (*CAm*: *amante*) lover, sweetheart; (*pretendiente*) suitor.

jalona *nf* (*CAm*) flirt, flighty girl.

jalonamiento *nm* staking out, marking out.

jalonar [1a] *vt* to stake out, mark out; (*fig*) to mark; **el camino está jalonado por plazas fuertes** the route is marked out by a series of strongholds, a line of strongholds marks the route.

jalonazo *nm* (*CAm, Méx*) pull, tug.

jalonear [1a] **1** *vt* (*Méx*) to pull at, yank out. **2** *vi* (**a**) (*CAm, Méx*: *tirar*) to pull, tug. (**b**) (*CAm, Méx**: *regatear*) to haggle.

jalonero** *nm* bag-snatcher.

jalufa** *nf* hunger; **pasar** ~, **tener** ~ to be hungry.

jallo *adj* (*Méx*) (*ostentoso*) showy, flashy; (*quisquilloso*) touchy.

Jamaica *nf* Jamaica.

jamaica[1] *nf* (*CAm, Méx*) jumble sale, charity sale (*US*).

jamaica[2] *nf* (*Carib, Méx Bot*) hibiscus.

jamaicano, -a, jamaiquino, -a (*LAm*) *adj, nm/f* Jamaican.

jamancia** *nf* (**a**) (*comida*) grub**. (**b**) (*hambre*) hunger; **pasar** ~, **tener** ~ to be hungry.

jamar** [1a] **1** *vi* to eat, stuff oneself. **2 jamarse** *vr*: **se lo jamó todo** he scoffed the lot*.

jamás *adv* never; (not) ever; **¿se vio** ~ **tal cosa?** did you ever see such a thing?; **¡**~! never!; **¡**~ **de los jamases!** never in your life!; *V* **nunca** *etc*.

jamba[1] *nf* jamb; ~ **de puerta** jamb, door post.

jamba[2]** *nf* bird**, dame*.

jambado* *adj* (*Méx*) greedy, gluttonous; **estar** ~ to be feeling over-full.

jambarse* [1a] *vr* (*CAm, Méx*) to stuff o.s.

jambo** *nm* bloke**, geezer**.

jamelgo *nm* wretched horse, nag, jade.

jamón 1 *nm* (**a**) (*gen*) ham; ~ **(en) dulce,** ~ **(de) York** boiled ham; ~ **serrano** cured ham; **¡y un** ~ **(con chorreras)!*** get away!*, my foot!*; you're hopeful!, you want jam on it!*

(**b**) (*Carib*: *ganga*) bargain.

(**c**) (*Carib*: *conflicto*) difficulty.

2 *adj* (*) *persona* dishy*, attractive; **un plato que está** ~ a delicious meal.

jamona *nf* buxom (middle-aged) woman.

jampa *nf* (*And, Méx*: *umbral*) threshold; (*puerta*) doorway.

jámparo *nm* (*And*) canoe, small boat.

jamurar* [1a] *vt* (*And*) to rinse.

jan *nm* (*Carib Agr*) seed drill; **ensartarse en los** ~**es** to get involved in an unprofitable piece of business.

jandinga** *nf* (*Carib*) grub**.

janearse [1a] *vr* (*Carib*) (**a**) to leap into the saddle. (**b**) (*: *pararse*) to come to a complete stop.

jangada[1] *nf* (*Náut*) raft.

jangada[2] *nf* (*disparate*) stupid remark; (*trampa*) dirty trick.

Jano *nm* Janus.

janpa *nf* = **jampa**.

Japón *nm*: **el** ~ Japan.

japonés, -esa 1 *adj, nm/f* Japanese. **2** *nm* (*Ling*) Japanese.

jaque *nm* (**a**) (*Ajedrez*) check; **¡**~ **(al rey)!** check!; ~ **continuo** continuous check; ~ **mate** checkmate; **¡**~ **de aquí!** get out of here!; **dar** ~ **a** to check; **dar** ~ **mate a** to checkmate, mate; **tener en** ~ to check; (*fig*: *amenazar*) to hold a threat over; (*fig*: *mantener a raya*) to keep in check, hold at bay; (*fig*: *acosar*) to harass, worry.

(**b**) (*: *matón*) bully, braggart.

jaquear [1a] *vt* (*Ajedrez*) to check; (*Mil y fig*) to harass; **quedar jaqueado** to be rendered powerless.

jaqueca *nf* (severe) headache, migraine; (*Cono Sur*: *resaca*) hangover; **dar** ~ **a** (*fig*: *aburrir*) to bore; (*fig*: *acosar*) to bother, pester.

jaquetón* *nm* bully, braggart.

jáquima *nf* (**a**) (*LAm*: *de caballo*) headstall. (**b**) (*CAm, Méx**) drunkenness, drunken state.

jaquimón *nm* (*LAm*) headstall, halter.

jara[1] *nf* (**a**) (*Bot*) rock rose, cistus; (*mata*) clump, thicket. (**b**) (*dardo*) dart, arrow. (**c**) **la** ~ (*Méx**) the cops*.

jara[2] *nf* (*And*) halt, rest.

jarabe *nm* (**a**) syrup; sweet drink; ~ **de arce** maple syrup; ~ **de palo*** beating; ~ **de pico** (*fig*) mere words, blarney; ~ **para** (*o* **contra**) **la tos** cough syrup, cough mixture; **dar** ~ **a uno*** to butter sb up.

(**b**) (*Méx*) *a popular dance*.

jaral *nm* (**a**) (*maleza*) ground covered with *jaras*, scrub; thicket. (**b**) (*fig*) difficult affair, thorny question.

jaramago *nm* hedge mustard.

jarana *nf* (**a**) (*juerga*) spree, binge*; (*lío*) rumpus, row; **andar de** ~ to carouse; to lark about, have a high old time; **ir de** ~ to go on the spree.

(**b**) (*trampa*) trick, deceit; (*LAm*) joke, practical joke, hoax; (*And*) fib; **la** ~ **sale a la cara** (*CAm*) a hoax can have a boomerang effect.

(**c**) (*And, Carib, Méx*: *baile*) folk dance; (*Carib*: *banda*) dance band.

(**d**) (*Mús Méx*) small guitar.

(**e**) (*Fin CAm*) debt.

jaranear [1a] **1** *vt* (*And, CAm*) to cheat, swindle. **2** *vi* (**a**) (*divertirse*) to lark about, have a high old time. (**b**) (*CAm*: *endeudarse*) to get into debt.

jaranero *adj* (**a**) (*de juerguista*) merry, roistering, rowdy. (**b**) (*CAm*: *tramposo*) deceitful, tricky.

jaranista *adj* (*LAm*) = **jaranero (a)**.

jarano *nm* (*Méx*) broad hat, sombrero.

jarcia *nf* (**a**) (*de pesca*) tackle, fishing tackle; (*Náut*: *t* ~**s**) ropes, rigging; (*Carib, Méx*: *cuerda*) rope (*made from agave fibre*).

(**b**) (*CAm, Méx Bot*) agave.

(**c**) (*montón*) heap, mess.

jarcha *nf* kharja.

jardín *nm* garden, flower garden; ~ **alpestre,** ~ **rocoso** rock garden; ~ **botánico** botanical garden; ~ **de (la) infancia,** ~ **de infantes** (*LAm*) kindergarten, nursery school; ~ **de rosas** (*fig*) bed of roses; ~ **zoológico** zoo.

jardinaje *nm* (*LAm*) gardening.

jardinera *nf* (**a**) (*persona*) (woman) gardener.

(**b**) (*de balcón*) window box.

(**c**) (*Cono Sur*: *carrito*) handcart, barrow.

(**d**) (*And*: *saco*) jacket; (*Cono Sur*: *mono*) overalls.

jardinería *nf* gardening.

jardinero *nm* (**a**) (*gen*) gardener. (**b**) (*Cono Sur*: *de niño*) rompers.

jarea *nf* (*Méx*) hunger, keen appetite.

jarear [1a] *vi* (*And*) to halt, stop for a rest.

jarearse [1a] *vr* (*Méx*) (**a**) (*hambrear*) to be dying of hunger. (**b**) (*huir*) to flee.

jareta *nf* (**a**) (*Cos*) casing; (*red*) netting; (*Náut*) cable, rope. (**b**) (*CAm, Cono Sur*: *de pantalón*) trouser flies. (**c**) (*Carib*: *contratiempo*) snag, setback.

jarete *nm* (*Carib*) paddle.

jari* *nm* row, racket.

jarifo *adj* (*liter*) elegant, showy, spruce.

jaripeo* *nm* (*Méx*) horse show.

jaro *nm* arum lily.

jarope *nm* syrup; (*) brew, concoction, nasty drink; **resultó un** ~ **poco agradable** it was a bitter pill to swallow.

jarra *nf* jar, pitcher; (*para leche*) churn; (*para cerveza*) mug, tankard; **de** ~**s, en** ~**s** with arms akimbo.

jarrada *nf* (*LAm*) jarful, jugful.
jarrete *nm* (*Anat*) back of the knee; (*de caballo*) hock; (*And*) heel.
jarro *nm* jug, pitcher; **echar un ~ de agua fría a una idea** to pour cold water on an idea; **caer como un ~ de agua fría** to come as a complete shock.
jarrón *nm* vase; (*Arquit*) urn.
jartón* *adj* (*CAm, Méx*) greedy, gluttonous.
Jartum *nm*, **Jartún** *nm* Khartoum.
jaspe *nm* jasper.
jaspeado *adj* mottled, speckled, marbled; streaked.
jaspear [1a] **1** *vt* to speckle, marble; to streak. **2 jaspearse*** *vr* (*Carib*) to get cross.
jato *nm* (**a**) (*ternero*) calf.
(**b**) (*Carib*: *perro*) stray dog, mongrel.
(**c**) (*Méx*: *carga*) load.
(**d**) (*And*: *silla de montar*) saddle.
(**e**) (*LAm*) = **hato.**
jauja *nf* (**a**) (*t* **J~**) promised land, earthly paradise; **¡esto es ~!** this is the life!; **¿estamos aquí o en ~?** where do you think you are?; **vivir en ~** to live in luxury, have a marvellous life.
(**b**) (*Cono Sur**: *chisme*) rumour, tale.
jaula *nf* (*gen*) cage; (*Min*) cage; (*de embalaje etc*) crate; (*de loco*) cell; (*: *tienda*) lock-up; (*Aut*) lock-up garage; (*Méx** *Ferro*) cattle-truck; (*Carib*) Black Maria, police wagon (*US*); **hacer ~** (*Méx*) to dig one's heels in.
jauría *nf* pack of hounds.
java* *nf* (*Carib*) trick.
Java *nf* Java.
Javier *nm* Xavier.
jay‡ *nf* = **jai.**
jayán *nm* (**a**) big strong man; (*pey*) hulking great brute, tough guy*.
(**b**) (*CAm‡*: *grosero*) foul-mouthed person.
jayares‡ *nmpl* bread‡, money.
jáyaro* *adj* (*And*) rough, uncouth.
jazmín *nm* jasmine; **~ del Cabo, ~ de la India** gardenia.
jazz [jaθ *o* jas] *nm* jazz.
jazzista 1 *adj* jazz (*atr*); jazzy. **2** *nmf* jazz player.
jazzístico *adj* jazz (*atr*).
J.C. *abr de* **Jesu Cristo** Jesus Christ, J.C.
jebe *nm* (**a**) (*LAm*) (*Bot*) rubber plant; (*goma*) rubber; (*elástico*) elastic. (**b**) (*porra*) club, cudgel; **llevar ~** to suffer a lot. (**c**) (**‡*: *trasero*) arse*‡*. (**d**) (*And‡*: *preservativo*) French letter.
jebero *nm* (*LAm*) rubber-plantation worker.
jeep [jip] *nm* jeep.
jefa *nf* (**a**) (woman) head, (woman) boss; manager(ess); (*líder*) leader; **~ de sastrería** (*Teat*) wardrobe mistress. (**b**) (*: *mujer mandona*) bossy woman.
jefatura *nf* (**a**) (*liderato*) leadership; chieftainship; **bajo la ~ de** under the leadership of; **dimitir la ~ del partido** to resign the party leadership.
(**b**) (*sede*) headquarters; central office; **~ de policía** police headquarters.
(**c**) (*Carib*: *registro*) registry office.
jefazo* *nm* big shot*, big noise*.
jefe *nmf* (*V t* **jefa**) (**a**) (*gen*) chief, head, boss; (*líder*) leader; (*gerente*) manager; (*Mil*) field officer, officer in command; **~ de almacén** warehouse manager; **~ de bomberos** fire officer; **~ de cabina** (*Aer*) chief steward; **~ de camareros** head waiter; **~ civil** (*Carib*) registrar; **~ de cocina** chef; **~ de estación** station master; **~ de estado** head of state, chief of state; **~ de estado mayor** chief of staff; **~ de estudios** (*Escol*) deputy head; **~ de filas** (*Pol*) party leader; **~ de máquinas** (*Náut*) chief engineer; **~ de márketing** marketing manager; **~ de los mozos** head groom; **~ de obras** project manager; site manager; **~ de personal** personnel manager; **~ de pista** ringmaster; **~ de plató** (*Cine, TV*) floor-manager; **~ político** (*LAm Pol*) *second-in-command to local politician*; **~ de protocolo** chief of protocol; **~ de realización** (*Cine, TV*) production manager; **~ de redacción** editor-in-chief; **~ supremo** commander-in-chief; **~ de taller** foreman; **~ de tren** guard, conductor (*US*); **~ de ventas** sales manager; **comandante en ~** commander-in-chief; **¡oiga ~!** hey, mate!*; **¡sí, (mi) ~!** (*esp LAm*) yes, sir!, yes, boss! (*US*); **ser el ~** (*fig*) to be the boss.
(**b**) (*de tribu*) chief.
Jehová *nm* Jehovah.
jején *nm* (**a**) (*Zool*) mosquito; gnat; **sabe donde el ~ puso el huevo** (*Carib*) he's pretty smart.
(**b**) (*And, Méx**: *montón*) heaps*, masses; **un ~ de cosas** a lot of things.
(**c**) (*Méx**: *multitud*) mob.
jelenque* *nm* (*Méx*) din, racket.
jemeres *nmpl*: **los ~ rojos** the Khmer Rouge.
jemiquear [1a] *vi* (*Cono Sur*) = **jeremiquear.**
JEN [xen] *nf* (*Esp*) *abr de* **Junta de Energía Nuclear** Nuclear Energy Authority.
jengibre *nm* ginger.
jenízaro 1 *adj* mixed, hybrid. **2** *nm* (*Hist*) janissary.
Jenofonte *nm* Xenophon.
jeque *nm* sheik(h).
jerarca *nm* chief, leader; important person; (*pey*) big shot*.
jerarquía *nf* hierarchy; (high) rank; **una persona de ~** a high-ranking person.
jerárquico *adj* hierarchic(al).
jerarquización *nf* hierarchical structuring; arranging in order (of importance).
jerarquizado *adj* hierarchical.
jerarquizar [1f] *vt organismo* to give a hierarchical structure to; *elementos* to arrange in order (of importance).
jeremiada *nf* jeremiad.
Jeremías *nm* Jeremy; (*Bib*) Jeremiah.
jeremiquear [1a] *vi* (*LAm*) (*lloriquear*) to snivel, whimper; (*regañar*) to nag.
jerez *nm* sherry.
Jerez *nf*: **~ de la Frontera** Jerez.
jerezano 1 *adj* of Jerez. **2** *nm*, **jerezana** *nf* native (*o* inhabitant) of Jerez; **los ~s** the people of Jerez.
jerga[1] *nf* coarse cloth, sackcloth; (*LAm*: *manta de caballo*) horse blanket; (*And*) coarse cloak; (*Méx*) floor cloth.
jerga[2] *nf* jargon; slang, cant; gibberish; **~ de germanía** thieves' cant; **~ informática** computer jargon; **~ publicitaria** sales talk, salesman's patter.
jergal *adj* jargon (*atr*); slang (*atr*), cant (*atr*).
jergón *nm* (**a**) palliasse, straw mattress. (**b**) (*: *vestido*) ill-fitting garment. (**c**) (*: *persona*) awkward-looking person, oaf.
jeribeque *nm*: **hacer ~s** to make faces, grimace.
Jericó *nm* Jericho.
jerigonza *nf* (**a**) = **jerga**[2]. (**b**) (*estupidez*) silly thing, piece of folly.
jeringa *nf* (**a**) (*gen*) syringe; **~ de engrase** grease-gun; **~ de un solo uso** throw-away syringe. (**b**) (*LAm**: *persona*) pest, nuisance.
jeringador *adj* (*LAm*) annoying, bothersome.
jeringar [1h] **1** *vt* (**a**) to syringe; to inject; to squirt. (**b**) (‡: *molestar*) to annoy, bother, plague; **¡no jeringues!** stop mucking about!; **¡nos ha jeringado!** he's done it on us!*
2 jeringarse* *vr* to put up with it; **¡que se jeringue!** he can lump it!*
jeringazo *nm* syringing; injection; squirt.
jeringón* 1 *adj* (*LAm*) = **jeringador. 2** *nm*, **jeringona** *nf* (*LAm*) pest, nuisance.
jeringuear [1a] *vt* (*LAm*) = **jeringar** (**b**).
jeringuilla[1] *nf* mock orange, syringa.
jeringuilla[2] *nf*: **~ hipodérmica** (*Med*) syringe.
Jerjes *nm* Xerxes.
jeró‡ *nm* clock‡, mug‡.
jeroglífico 1 *adj* hieroglyphic. **2** *nm* hieroglyph(ic); (*fig*) puzzle.
Jerónimo *nm* Jerome.
jerónimo[1] *adj, nm* (*Ecl*) Hieronymite.
jerónimo[2] *nm*: **sin ~ de duda** (*LAm*: *hum*) without a shadow of doubt.
jersé *nm*, **jersei** *nm*, **jersey** [xer'sei] *nm*, *pl* **jerseis, jerseys** [xer'seis] jersey, sweater, pullover; jumper; (*LAm*: *tela*) jersey.
Jerusalén *nm* Jerusalem.
jeruza‡ *nf* (*CAm*) clink‡, jail.
Jesucristo *nm* Jesus Christ.
jesuita 1 *adj* (*Ecl*) Jesuit; (*fig*) Jesuitic(al). **2** *nm* (*Ecl*) Jesuit; (*fig*) hypocrite, sly person.
jesuítico *adj* Jesuitic(al).
Jesús *nm* Jesus; **¡~!** good heavens!; (*al estornudar*) bless you!; **en un (decir) ~** in an instant, before one can say Jack Robinson; **morir sin decir ~** to die very suddenly.
jet [jet], *pl* **jets** [jet] **1** *nm* (*Aer*) jet, jet plane. **2** *nf* jet-set.
jeta 1 *nf* (**a**) (*Anat*) thick lips.
(**b**) (*Zool*) snout; (*: *cara*) mug‡, dial‡; **estirar la ~** (*Cono Sur‡*) to kick the bucket‡; **te romperé la ~** I'll smash your mug in‡.
(**c**) (*: *ceño*) frown, scowl, disagreeable expression;

poner ~ to frown, scowl.

(**d**) (*: *descaro*) cheek*, nerve*; **¡qué ~ tiene!** he's got a nerve!; **lo hace por la ~** he gets away with it by sheer cheek.

2 *nm* (*) swine, bastard‡.

jetazo* *nm* bash*, punch.

jetear [1a] *vi* (*Cono Sur*) to eat at someone else's expense.

jetón *adj*, **jetudo** *adj* (**a**) thick-lipped. (**b**) (*Cono Sur*) stupid.

Jezabel *nf* Jezebel.

JHS *abr de* **Jesús** Jesus, IHS.

ji *interj*: ¡~, ~, ~! ha ha!; (*iró*) tee hee!

jibarear [1a] *vi* (*Carib*) to flirt.

jíbaro 1 *adj* (*Carib, Méx*) (*rústico*) country (*atr*), rustic; (*huraño*) sullen.

2 *nm*, **jíbara** *nf* (*Carib, Méx*) peasant.

3 *nm* (**a**) (*CAm*‡: *traficante*) (drug) dealer.

(**b**) (*Carib*: *animal*) wild animal.

jibia 1 *nf* (*Zool*) cuttlefish. **2** *nm* (‡) queer‡, poof‡.

jícama *nf* (*CAm, Méx*) edible tuber.

jícara *nf* (**a**) (*tacita*) small cup (for drinking-chocolate *etc*).

(**b**) (*CAm, Méx*) (*calabaza, vasija*) gourd, calabash; (*Méx**: *calva*) pate; **bailar la ~ a uno*** to soft-soap sb*; **sacar la ~ a uno** to shower sb with attentions.

jicarazo *nm* (cup of) poison, poisonous drink; (*CAm, Méx*) cupful.

jícaro *nm* (*CAm, Méx*) (**a**) (*Bot*) calabash tree. (**b**) (*plato*) bowl.

jicarón *adj* (*CAm*) big-headed.

jicarudo *adj* (*Méx**) broad-faced, broad-browed.

jicote *nm* (*CAm, Méx*) wasp.

jicotera *nf* (*CAm, Méx*) (*nido*) wasps' nest; (*zumbido*) buzzing of wasps; **armar una ~** to kick up a row.

jiche *nm* (*CAm, Méx*) tendon, sinew.

jiennense 1 *adj* of Jaén. **2** *nmf* native (*o* inhabitant) of Jaén; **los ~s** the people of Jaén.

jifero 1 *adj* (*) filthy. **2** *nm* (**a**) (*matarife*) slaughterer, butcher. (**b**) (*cuchillo*) butcher's knife.

jijona *nm* soft nougat (*made in Jijona*).

jilguero *nm* goldfinch; **¡mi ~!*** my angel!

jilibioso* *adj* (*Cono Sur*) (*lloroso*) weepy, tearful; (*delicado*) finicky, hard to please; *caballo* nervous.

jilote *nm* (*CAm, Méx*) (*elote*) green ear of maize; (*maíz verde*) young maize, young corn (*US*).

jilotear [1a] *vi* (*CAm, Méx*) to come into ear.

jimagua (*Carib*) **1** *adj* twin; identical. **2** *nmf* twin.

jimba *nf* (**a**) (*And*: *trenza*) pigtail, plait; (*Méx*: *bambú*) bamboo. (**b**) (*Méx**: *borrachera*) drunkenness.

jimbal *nm* (*Méx*) bamboo thicket.

jimbito *nm* (*CAm*) (*avispa*) small wasp; (*nido*) wasps' nest.

jimbo *adj* (*Méx*) drunk.

jimeno‡ *nm* (*Méx*) cop*.

jimio *nm* = **simio**.

jinaiste* *nm* (*Méx*) bunch of kids.

jincar* [1g] *vt* (*CAm*) to spike.

jindama* *nf* fear, funk*.

jindarse [1a] *vr*: **se lo jindó todo** he scoffed the lot*.

jineta¹ *nf* (**a**) (*esp LAm*) horsewoman, rider. (**b**) **a la ~** with short stirrups.

jineta² *nf* (*Zool*) genet.

jinete *nm* horseman, rider; (*Mil*) cavalryman.

jinetear [1a] **1** *vt* (**a**) (*LAm*) (*domar*) to break in; (*montar*) to ride; **~ la burra** (*CAm*) to go the whole hog, stake everything.

(**b**) (*Méx**) *fondos* to misappropriate.

2 *vi* to ride around, show off one's horsemanship.

3 jinetearse *vr* (**a**) (*And, Méx*) (*no caer*) to stay in the saddle; (*) to hang on, keep going.

(**b**) (*And*: *ser presumido*) to be vain.

jingoísmo *nm* jingoism.

jingoísta 1 *adj* jingoistic. **2** *nmf* jingoist, jingo.

jiote *nm* (*CAm, Méx*: *Med*) impetigo.

jipa *nf* (*And*) straw hat.

jipar* [1a] *vt*: **le tengo jipado** I've got him taped*, I've got him all sized up.

jipatera *nf* (*And, Carib, Méx*), **jipatez** *nf* (*Carib, Méx*) paleness, wanness.

jipato *adj* (*LAm*) (*pálido*) pale, wan; (*enclenque*) sickly, frail; (*soso*) tasteless.

jipe *nm* (*And, Méx*), **jipi¹** *nm* straw hat.

jipi² *nmf* hippy.

jipijapa 1 *nf* (*paja*) straw for weaving. **2** *nm* (*sombrero*) straw hat.

jipioso *adj* hippy (*atr*).

jipismo *nm* hippy outlook; hippy culture.

jira¹ *nf* (*de tela*) strip.

jira² *nf* excursion, outing; picnic (*t* **~ campestre**); **ir de ~** to go on an outing, go for a picnic; *V t* **gira**.

jirafa *nf* (**a**) (*Zool*) giraffe. (**b**) (*Téc*) jib, arm, boom.

jiribilla *nf* (*Méx*) spin, turn; **tener ~** (*Carib*) to have its awkward points; (*persona*) to be anxious.

jirimiquear [1a] *vi* (*LAm*) = **jeremiquear**.

jirón *nm* (**a**) (*andrajo*) rag, shred, tatter; **en jirones** in shreds; **hacer algo jirones** to tear sth to shreds.

(**b**) (*fig*) bit, shred.

(**c**) (*And*: *calle*) street.

jit* [xit] *nm*, *pl* **jits** [xit] (*LAm*) hit.

jitazo *nm* (*Méx*) hit, blow; (*Dep*) hit, stroke.

jitomate *nm* (*Méx*) tomato.

jiu-jitsu *nm* jiu-jitsu.

JJ.OO. *nmpl abr de* **Juegos Olímpicos** Olympic Games.

jo* *interj* (**a**) ¡~! (*sorpresa*) well I'm blowed!*; (*alivio*) phew!; (*saludo*) hey*, hi*; ¡~, ~! (*risa*) ha ha!, ho ho! (**b**) (*euf*) = **joder** *etc*.

Job *nm* Job.

jobo *nm* (**a**) (*CAm, Méx*: *Bot*) cedar (tree). (**b**) (*CAm**: *aguardiente*) spirits.

jockey ['joki] *nm*, *pl* **jockeys** ['jokis] jockey; (*LAm*) jockey cap.

joco *adj* (**a**) (*CAm, Méx*: *amargo*) sharp, sour, bitter. (**b**) (*And*: *hueco*) hollow.

jocolote* *nm* (*CAm*) hut, shack.

jocoque *nm* (*Méx*) sour cream.

jocosamente *adv* humorously, comically.

jocoserio *adj* seriocomic.

jocosidad *nf* humour; jokiness; (*una ~*) joke.

jocoso *adj* humorous, comic, jocular, jokey.

joda** *nf* (*LAm*) (**a**) (*molestia*) annoyance; bother; (*daño*) harm; (*dificultad*) trouble. (**b**) (*broma*) joke; **lo dijo en ~** he said it as a joke; **estar de ~** to have a booze-up‡.

jodedera** *nf* screwing**.

joder** [2a] **1** *vt* (**a**) (*Esp*) to fuck**, screw**; ¡~! (*enfado*) damn it!, damnation!; (*sorpresa*) well I'm damned!

(**b**) (‡*fig*) (*fastidiar*) to annoy, upset; (*dañar*) to harm, spoil; to damage; (*acosar*) to pester; (*estropear*) to mess up; **esto me jode** I'm fed up with this*; **esta ciudad está jodida** this town is all screwed up**; **son ganas de ~** they're just trying to be awkward; **¡no me jodas!** (*no fastidies*) stop bothering me!; (*rechazo*) come off it!, tell us another!; (*no te creo*) you're joking!

(**c**) (‡: *robar*) to pinch*, steal; **alguien le jodió el puesto** sb pinched the job from him.

2 *vi* to fuck**, screw**.

3 joderse *vr* (**a**) **¡que te jodas!** get stuffed!**; **¡hay que ~!** this is the end!, to hell with it all!

(**b**) (*fracasar*) to flop; (*estropearse*) to get spoiled, get messed up; **se jodió todo** everything was spoiled; **se ha jodido la función** the show was a failure.

jodido‡ *adj* (**a**) (*difícil*) awkward, difficult, tough; **es un libro ~** it's a very difficult book; ¡~! sod it!**

(**b**) **estoy ~** (*cansado*) I'm worn out, I'm shagged‡.

(**c**) (*condenado*) bloody**; **ni una jodida peseta** not one bloody peseta**.

(**d**) **todo está ~** (*estropeado*) it's all cocked up‡.

(**e**) (*LAm*) *persona* (*egoísta*) selfish; (*malo*) evil, wicked; (*quisquilloso*) awkward, prickly; (*zalamero*) smarmy, oily.

jodienda** *nf* (*Cono Sur, Méx*) fucking nuisance**.

jodón** *adj* (*LAm*) (**a**) (*molesto*) bloody annoying‡; **es tan ~** (*bromista*) he loves arsing about**. (**b**) (*tramposo*) slippery.

jodontón** *adj* randy*, oversexed.

jofaina *nf* washbasin.

jogging ['joɣin] *nm* (**a**) (*Dep*) jogging; **hacer ~** to jog. (**b**) (*Cono Sur*) jogging suit.

jojoto (*Carib*) **1** *adj fruta* (*manchado*) bruised; (*inmaduro*) green, underripe; *maíz* soft, tender. **2** *nm* ear of maize.

jol *nm* hall, lobby.

jolgórico *adj* riotous, hilarious; rowdy.

jolgorio *nm* (**a**) (*juerga*) fun, merriment; high jinks; revelry; rowdiness. (**b**) (*un ~*) spree, binge*; lark*; **ir de ~** to go on a binge*.

jolín*, jolines* *interj* sugar!*

jolinche *adj*, **jolino** *adj* (*Méx*) short-tailed, bob-tailed.

jolón *nm* (*Méx*) (*avispa*) wasp; (*avispero*) wasps' nest.

jolongo *nm* (**a**) (*Carib*) shoulder-bag. (**b**) (*) problem.

jolote *nm* (*CAm, Méx*) turkey.

joma *nf* (*Méx*) hump.

jomb(e)ado *adj* (*Méx*) hunchbacked.

Jonás *nm* Jonah.
Jonatás *nm* Jonathan.
jónico *adj* Ionic.
jonja *nf* (*Cono Sur*) mimicry.
jonjear [1a] *vt* (*Cono Sur*) to tease, make fun of.
jonjolear* [1a] *vt* (*And*) to spoil.
jonrón *nm* (*LAm Dep*) home run.
jonronear [1a] *vi* (*LAm Dep*) to make a home run.
JONS [xons] *nfpl* (*Esp Hist*) *abr de* **Juntas de Ofensiva Nacional Sindicalista.**
jopé‡ *interj* cor!‡
jopo[1] = **hopo**[2].
jopo[2] *nm* = **hopo**[1].
jora *nf* (*LAm*) *maize specially prepared for making high-grade chicha.*
Jordán *nm* Jordan (*river*); **ir al ~** (*fig*) to be rejuvenated.
Jordania *nf* Jordan (*country*).
jordano, -a *adj, nm/f* Jordanian.
jorga* *nf* (*And*) gang.
Jorge *nm* George.
jorguín *nm* sorcerer, wizard.
jorguina *nf* sorceress, witch.
jorguinería *nf* sorcery, witchcraft.
jorgón *nm* (*And*) lot, abundance.
jornada *nf* (**a**) (*viaje*) day's journey; (*etapa*) stage (of a journey); **a largas ~s** (*Mil*) by forced marches; **al fin de la ~** at the end.
(**b**) (*día de trabajo*) working day; (*horas*) hours of work; (*turno*) shift; (*fig*) lifetime, span of life; **~ de 8 horas** 8-hour day; **~ anual** working days in the year; **~ inglesa** five-day week; **~ laboral** (*semana*) working week, (*anual*) working year; **~ legal** maximum legal working hours; **~ de lucha** day of action; **~ partida** split shift; **~ de puertas abiertas** open day; **~ de reflexión** (*Pol*) day before election (*on which campaigning is banned*); **~ semanal** working week; **hay ~ limitada en la industria** there is short-time working in the industry; **trabajar en ~s reducidas** to work short-time.
(**c**) (*Mil*) expedition; **la ~ de Orán** the expedition against Oran.
(**d**) (*Univ etc*) congress, conference; **J~s Cervantinas** Conference on Cervantes, Cervantes Conference.
(**e**) (*Teat Hist*) act.
(**f**) (*Cono Sur: sueldo*) day's wage.
jornadista *nmf* (*Univ etc*) conference member, delegate.
jornal *nm* (*sueldo*) (day's) wage; (*trabajo*) day's work; **~ mínimo** minimum wage; **política de ~es y precios** prices and incomes policy; **trabajar a ~** to work for a day wage, be paid by the day.
jornalero *nm* (day) labourer.
joro *nm* (*Carib*) small basket.
joroba 1 *nf* (**a**) (*Anat*) hump, hunched back. (**b**) (*fig*) nuisance, bother, annoyance. **2** *nmf* hunchback.
jorobado 1 *adj* hunchbacked. **2** *nm*, **jorobada** *nf* hunchback.
jorobar* [1a] **1** *vt* (**a**) (*fastidiar*) to annoy, pester, bother; **esto me joroba** I'm fed up with this*, this gives me the hump*; **¡no me jorobes!** stop bothering me!
(**b**) (*estropear*) to break, smash; to mess up.
2 jorobarse *vr* (**a**) (*enfadarse*) to get cross, get worked up; (*cansarse*) to get fed up*.
(**b**) (*aguantar*) to put up with it; **pues ¡que se jorobe!** well, he can lump it!*
(**c**) (*fracasar*) to fail, go down the drain; to spoil, be spoiled.
(**d**) (*romperse*) to break, smash, be damaged.
(**e**) **¡~!** (*excl*) hell!, well I'm damned!; **¡hay que ~!** to hell with it!
jorobeta *nf* (*Cono Sur*) nuisance.
jorobón *adj* (*LAm*) annoying.
joronche* *nm* (*Méx*) hunchback.
jorongo *nm* (*Méx*) poncho.
joropo *nm* (*Carib*) *a popular dance.*
jorro *nm* (*Carib*) poor-quality cigarette.
jorungo* *adj* (*Carib: molesto*) annoying, irritating.
José *nm* Joseph.
Josefina *nf* Josephine.
Josué *nm* Joshua.
jota[1] *nf* (**a**) (*letra*) the (name of the) letter *j*.
(**b**) (*fig*) jot, iota; **no entendió ni ~** he didn't understand a word of it; **sin faltar una ~** to a T, with complete accuracy, just as it should be; **no sabe ni ~** he hasn't a clue (*de* about).
jota[2] *nf* (*And, Cono Sur Orn*) vulture.
jota[3] *nf Spanish dance and tune* (*esp Aragonese*).
jota[4] *nf* (*Naipes*) knave, jack.
jote *nm* (*Cono Sur*) (**a**) (*Orn*) buzzard; (*cometa*) large kite. (**b**) (*desagradecido*) ungrateful person; (*: *cura*) priest.
joto 1 *adj* (*Méx*) effeminate. **2** *nm* (**a**) (*And*) bundle. (**b**) (*Méx‡*) queer‡.
jovata* *nf* (*Cono Sur*) old woman.
jovato* *nm* (*Cono Sur*) old man.
joven 1 *adj* young; *aspecto etc* youthful.
2 *nm* (**a**) young man, youth; **los jóvenes** young people, youth, the young; **¡eh, ~!** I say, young man!
(**b**) (*Cono Sur*) waiter.
3 *nf* young woman, young lady, girl.
jovencito, -a *nm/f* youngster.
jovial *adj* jolly, cheerful, jovial.
jovialidad *nf* jolliness, cheerfulness, joviality.
jovialmente *adv* in a jolly way, cheerfully, jovially.
joya *nf* (**a**) (*gen*) jewel, gem, piece of jewellery; **~ de familia** heirloom.
(**b**) **~s** jewels, jewellery; (*de novia*) trousseau; **~s de fantasía, ~s de imitación** imitation jewellery.
(**c**) (*fig*) gem, treasure, precious thing; (*persona*) gem, treasure.
joyería *nf* (**a**) (*joyas*) jewellery, jewels. (**b**) (*tienda*) jeweller's (shop).
joyero *nm* (**a**) (*persona*) jeweller. (**b**) (*estuche*) jewel case.
Jruschov *nm* Khrushchev.
juagar [1h] *vt* (*And*) = **enjuagar.**
Juan *nm* John; **don ~** don John, don Juan; (*Mús*) Don Giovanni; **San ~ Bautista** St John the Baptist; **San ~ Evangelista** St John the Evangelist; **San ~ de la Cruz** St John of the Cross; **el Papa ~ Pablo II** Pope John Paul II; **un buen ~** a simple soul, a good-natured fool; **~ Lanas, ~ Vainas** (*CAm: pey*) simpleton; (*marido*) henpecked husband; **~ Palomo** (*solitario*) lone wolf, loner; (*egoísta*) person who looks after Number One; **~ Zoquete** rustic, idiot.
juan *nm* (*And, Méx*) common soldier.
Juana *nf* Joan, Jean, Jane; **~ de Arco** Joan of Arc.
juana *nf* (**a**) (*And: prostituta*) whore. (**b**) (*Méx**) marijuana. (**c**) (*CAm**) cop*.
juancho *nm* (*And*) boyfriend, lover.
juanete *nm* (**a**) (*Med*) bunion; (*pómulo*) prominent cheekbone; (*del pie*) ball of the foot. (**b**) (*Náut*) topgallant sail. (**c**) (*And, CAm: cadera*) hip.
juanillo* *nm* (*And, Cono Sur*) bribe.
juapao *nm* (*Carib*) beating, thrashing.
jubilación *nf* (**a**) (*acto, estado*) retirement; **~ anticipada, ~ prematura** early retirement; **~ forzosa** compulsory retirement; **~ voluntaria** voluntary retirement. (**b**) (*pago*) pension, retirement pension.
jubilado 1 *adj* (**a**) retired. (**b**) (*And, Carib*: sagaz*) wise. (**c**) (*And*: lerdo*) thick*, slow-witted. **2** *nm*, **jubilada** *nf* retired person, pensioner.
jubilar [1a] **1** *vt* (**a**) *persona* to pension off, retire.
(**b**) (*fig*) *persona* to shunt aside, put out to grass; *objeto* to discard, get rid of, cast aside; to banish, relegate.
2 *vi* to rejoice.
3 jubilarse *vr* (**a**) to retire, take one's pension.
(**b**) (*CAm: hacer novillos*) to play truant.
(**c**) (*Carib*: ponerse listo*) to gain experience.
(**d**) (*And**) (*deteriorar*) to deteriorate, go downhill; (*enloquecer*) to lose one's head.
jubileo *nm* (**a**) (*Rel*) jubilee; **por ~** once in a lifetime. (**b**) (*) comings and goings.
júbilo *nm* joy, jubilation, rejoicing; **con ~** joyfully, with jubilation.
jubiloso *adj* jubilant.
jubón *nm* (*de hombre*) doublet, jerkin, close-fitting jacket; (*de mujer*) bodice.
jud *nm* (*CAm Aut*) bonnet, hood (*US*).
Judá *nm* Judah.
judaico *adj* Jewish, Judaic.
judaísmo *nm* Judaism.
judaizante 1 *adj* Judaizing. **2** *nmf* Judaizer.
Judas *nm* Judas; (*fig*) traitor, betrayer.
judas *nm* (**a**) (*LAm: en puerta*) peephole. (**b**) (*Méx: figura de papel*) *figure burnt on Easter bonfires.* (**c**) (*Cono Sur**) snooper*.
Judea *nf* Judea.
judeo-español *adj, nm* Judeo-Spanish.
judería *nf* (**a**) (*barrio*) Jewish quarter, ghetto. (**b**) (*judíos*) Jewry. (**c**) (*CAm, Méx*: travesura*) prank.
judía *nf* (**a**) Jewess, Jewish woman. (**b**) (*Bot*) kidney bean;

~ **blanca** haricot bean; ~ **colorada,** ~ **escarlata,** ~ **de España,** ~ **negra** runner bean; ~ **de Lima,** ~ **de la peladilla** Lima bean; ~ **pinta** pinto bean; ~ **verde** French bean, green bean.

judiada *nf* (**a**) (*acto cruel*) cruel act, cruel thing. (**b**) (*Fin*) extortion.

judicatura *nf* (**a**) (*jueces*) judicature. (**b**) (*cargo*) judgeship, office of judge.

judicial *adj* judicial; **recurrir a la vía** ~ to go to law, have recourse to the law.

judío 1 *adj* Jewish. **2** *nm* Jew.

Judit *nf* Judith.

judo *nm* judo.

juego[1] *etc* (*verbo*) *V* **jugar**.

juego[2] *nm* (**a**) (*gen, acto*) play, playing; (*Dep*) sport; (*diversión*) fun, amusement; **los niños en el** ~ children at play; ~ **doble** double-dealing; ~ **duro** rough play; ~ **limpio** fair play; ~ **de roles** role-playing; ~ **sucio** foul play, dirty play; **el balón está en** ~ the ball is in play; **hay diversos intereses en** ~ there are various interests concerned; **entrar en** ~ (*persona*) to take a hand; (*factor*) to come into play; **poner algo en** ~ to set sth in motion, bring sth into play; **estar fuera de** ~ (*persona*) to be offside; (*balón*) to be out, be out of play; **por** ~ in fun, for fun.

(**b**) (*recreo: un* ~) game, sport; **es solamente un** ~ it's only a game; ~**s atléticos** (athletic) sports; ~ **de azar** game of chance; ~ **de las bochas** bowls; ~ **de (las) bolas** American skittles; ~ **de las bolitas,** ~ **de las canicas** marbles; ~ **de bolos** ninepins, skittles, tenpin bowling; ~ **de cartas** card game; ~ **de la cuna** cat's cradle; ~ **de damas** draughts, checkers (*US*); ~ **de destreza** game of skill; ~ **educativo** educational game; ~**s infantiles** children's games; ~**s malabares** juggling; ~ **de manos** conjuring trick; ~**s de manos** conjuring; ~ **de mesa** table game; ~ **de naipes** card game; **J~s Olímpicos** Olympic Games; **J~s Olímpicos de invierno** Winter Olympics; ~ **de palabras** pun, play on words; ~ **de prendas** (game of) forfeits; ~ **de salón,** ~ **de sociedad** parlour game, party game; ~ **del tejo** hopscotch.

(**c**) (~ *terminado*) (complete *o* finished) game; (*Tenis*) game; (*Bridge*) rubber; ~**, set y partido** game, set and match.

(**d**) (*fig*) game; **le conozco el** ~**, le veo el** ~ I know his little game, I know what he's up to; **seguirle el** ~ **a alguien** to play along with sb.

(**e**) (*con apuestas*) gambling, gaming; **el** ~ **es un vicio** gambling is a vice; **lo perdió todo en el** ~ he lost the lot gambling; **lo que está en** ~ what is at stake; **¡hagan** ~**!** place your bets!

(**f**) (*Mec*) play, movement; **estar en** ~ to be in gear, be in mesh.

(**g**) (*luz etc*) play; **el** ~ **de luces sobre el agua** the play of light on the water; **el** ~ **de los colores** the interplay of the colours.

(**h**) (*pista*) pitch, court; **en el** ~ **de pelota** on the pelota court.

(**i**) (*conjunto*) set; (*vajilla*) set, service; (*muebles*) suite; (*herramientas etc*) set, kit, outfit; (*cartas*) hand; pack; ~ **de bolas** (*Mec*) ball bearing, set of ball bearings; ~ **de café** coffee set; ~ **de campanas** peal of bells; ~ **de caracteres** character set; ~ **de comedor** dining-room suite; ~ **de mesa** dinner service; ~ **de programas** suite of programmes; **una falda a** ~ **con un jersey** a skirt with a jersey to match; a skirt which goes with a jersey; **con falda a** ~ with matching skirt, with skirt to match; **hacen** ~ they match, they go well together.

juepucha‡ *interj* (*Cono Sur*) well I'm damned!

juerga* *nf* binge*, spree, carousal; good time; **correr las grandes** ~**s** to live it up*; **¡vaya** ~ **que nos vamos a correr con ellas!** what a time we'll have with them!; **ir de** ~ to go on a spree, go out for a good time.

juergata‡ *nf* = **juerga**.

juerguearse* [1a] *vr* to live it up*.

juerguista* *nmf* reveller.

jueves *nm invar* Thursday; **J~ Santo** Maundy Thursday; **no es cosa del otro** ~ it's nothing to write home about.

juez *nmf* (*t* **jueza** *nf*) (**a**) (*Jur*) judge (*t fig*); **Jueces** (*Bíb*) Book of Judges; ~ **árbitro** arbitrator, referee; ~ **de diligencias,** ~ **de instrucción,** ~ **instructor** examining magistrate; ~ **municipal** magistrate.

(**b**) (*Dep*) judge; ~ **de banda,** ~ **lateral,** ~ **de línea** (*Fútbol etc*) linesman, (*Rugby*) touch judge; ~ **de llegada,** ~ **de meta,** ~ **de raya** (*Cono Sur*) judge; ~ **de salida** starter; ~ **de silla** (*Tenis*) umpire.

jugable *adj* playable, suitable for playing.

jugada *nf* (**a**) (*gen*) play; playing.

(**b**) (*una* ~) piece of play; (*Ajedrez etc*) move; (*golpe*) stroke, shot; (*echada*) throw; **una bonita** ~ a pretty piece of play, a pretty shot; **con dos** ~**s más** in two more moves; **hacer una** ~ to make a move, make a shot (*etc*); ~ **limpia** fair play; ~ **de pizarra** textbook move.

(**c**) (**mala**) ~ bad turn, dirty trick; **hacer una mala** ~ **a uno** to play sb a dirty trick.

(**d**) (*Méx*) dodge.

jugado *adj* (*And*) expert, skilled.

jugador(a) *nm/f* player; (*de apuestas*) gambler; ~ **de bolsa** speculator, gambler on the stock exchange; ~ **de fútbol** footballer, football player; ~ **de manos** juggler, conjurer; **capitán no** ~ non-playing captain.

jugar [1h *y* 1n] **1** *vt* (**a**) *carta, papel, truco etc* to play; **¡me la han jugado!*** they've done it on me!*

(**b**) (*apostar*) to gamble, stake; ~ **5 dólares a una carta** to stake (*o* put) 5 dollars on a card; **lo jugó todo** he gambled it all away.

(**c**) *arma* to handle, wield.

2 *vi* (**a**) (*gen*) to play (*con* with, *contra* against); ~ **limpio** to play fair, play the game; ~ **sucio** to play unfairly, indulge in dirty play; **yo no juego** I don't play, I can't play; ~ **al tenis** to play tennis; ~ **al ajedrez** to play chess; **la niña juega a ser madre** the little girl plays at being mother; ~ **con** (*pey*) to play about with; (*manosear*) to finger, handle, mess up; (*fig*) to toy with, trifle with; **solamente está jugando contigo** he's just trifling with you, he's just having a game with you; **un coche de** ~ a toy car, a model car; **de a jugando** (*Cono Sur**) two-facedly; **de jugando** (*Carib**) in fun, for fun.

(**b**) (*hacer una jugada*) to play, make a move; **¿quién juega?** whose move is it?, whose turn is it?, who's to play next?

(**c**) (*apostar*) to gamble; (*Fin*) to speculate, gamble; *V* **bolsa** *etc*.

(**d**) (*LAm Mec*) to have room to move about.

(**e**) (*hacer juego*) to match, go together.

3 jugarse *vr* (**a**) to gamble (away), risk; **se jugó 500 dólares** he staked 500 dollars; **esto es** ~ **la vida** this means risking one's life; **jugárselo todo,** ~ **el todo por el todo** to stake one's all, (*fig*) go to extremes, go the whole hog.

(**b**) **jugársela*** to be unfaithful.

(**c**) **el partido se juega hoy** (*Dep*) the match is being played today.

jugarreta *nf* (**a**) (*jugada*) bad move, poor piece of play. (**b**) (*trampa*) dirty trick; **hacer una** ~ **a uno** to play a dirty trick on sb.

juglar *nm* (*Hist*) minstrel, jongleur; juggler, tumbler, entertainer.

juglaresco *adj* (*Hist*) **arte** ~ art of the minstrel(s); **estilo** ~ minstrel style, popular style.

juglaría *nf* (*Hist*) minstrelsy, art of the minstrel(s).

jugo *nm* (**a**) (*Bot etc*) juice; sap; (*de carne*) juice; gravy; ~**s digestivos** digestive juices; ~ **de naranja** orange juice; ~ **de muñeca** elbow grease.

(**b**) (*fig*) essence, substance, pith; **sacar el** ~ **a uno** to get the most out of sb, to pick sb's brains.

jugosidad *nf* (**a**) (*suculencia*) juiciness, succulence. (**b**) (*fig*) substantial nature, pithiness.

jugoso *adj* (**a**) (*suculento*) juicy, succulent.

(**b**) (*fig*) substantial, pithy; meaty, full of good stuff, full of solid sense; (*rentable*) profitable; **un discurso** ~ a solid sort of speech, a speech full of good things.

juguera *nf* (*Cono Sur*) liquidizer, blender.

juguete *nm* (**a**) (*de niño*) toy; ~ **educativo** educational toy; **un cañón de** ~ a toy gun.

(**b**) (*fig*) toy, plaything; **fue el** ~ **de las olas** it was the plaything of the waves.

(**c**) (*chiste*) joke.

(**d**) (*Teat*) skit, sketch.

juguetear [1a] *vi* to play, romp, sport; ~ **con** to play with, sport with.

jugueteo *nm* playing, romping.

juguetería *nf* (**a**) (*negocio*) toy trade, toy business. (**b**) (*tienda*) toyshop.

juguetero *adj* toy (*atr*).

juguetón *adj* playful; frisky, frolicsome.

juicio *nm* (**a**) (*facultad*) judgement, reason.

(**b**) (*razón*) sanity, reason; (*buen sentido*) good sense, prudence, wisdom; **asentar el** ~ to come to one's senses, return to sanity; **lo dejo a su** ~ I leave it to your discretion, I leave it to you to decide; **estar en su (cabal)** ~ to be in one's right mind; **estar fuera de** ~ to be out of one's mind; **perder el** ~ to lose one's reason, go mad; **no tener** ~ to lack common sense; **¿se te ha vuelto el ~?** are you mad?, have you gone out of your mind?

(**c**) (*opinión*) opinion; ~ **de valor** value judgement; **a mi** ~ in my opinion, to my mind.

(**d**) (*Jur*: *proceso*) trial; ~ **con** (*o* **por**) **jurado** trial by jury; ~ **de Dios** trial by ordeal; **pedir a uno en** ~ to sue sb.

(**e**) (*Jur*: *veredicto*) verdict, judgement; **J~ Final** Last Judgement; ~ **en rebeldía** judgement by default.

(**f**) (*Jur*: *pena*) punishment; ~ **público** public punishment, carrying out of a sentence in public.

juicioso *adj* judicious, wise, prudent, sensible.

juilipío *nm* (*And*) sparrow.

juilón‡ *adj* (*Méx*) yellow.

JUJEM [xu'xem] *nf* (*Esp Mil*) *abr de* **Junta de Jefes del Estado Mayor.**

jul. *abr de* **julio** July, Jul.

jula‡ *nm* (**a**) (*marica*) queer‡. (**b**) (*idiota*) twit*, berk‡.

julai‡ *nm* poofter‡.

julandra‡ *nm*, **julandrón‡** *nm* queer‡.

julepe *nm* (**a**) julep.

(**b**) (*: *reprimenda*) telling-off*, dressing-down*.

(**c**) (*LAm**: *susto*) scare, fright; **irse de ~, salir de** ~ (*And*) to run away in terror.

(**d**) (*Carib, Méx**: *trabajo*) bind*.

(**e**) **meter un** ~ (*And*) to hurry on, speed up.

(**f**) (*Naipes*) *a card game.*

julepear* [1a] **1** *vt* (**a**) (*Cono Sur*: *asustar*) to scare, terrify.

(**b**) (*Méx*: *cansar*) to wear out, tire out.

(**c**) (*And*: *apresurar*) to hurry along, speed up.

2 julepearse *vr* (*Cono Sur*) (*asustarse*) to get scared; (*estar atento*) to smell danger.

julia* *nf* (*Méx*) Black Maria, paddy wagon* (*US*).

Julián *nm*, **Juliano** *nm* Julian.

Julieta *nf* Juliet.

Julio *nm* Julius; ~ **César** Julius Caesar.

julio *nm* (**a**) July. (**b**) (†) 100-peseta note.

juma* *nf* (*LAm*) drunkenness, drunken state.

jumadera* *nf* (*Méx*) (**a**) (*borrachera*) drunkenness, drunken state. (**b**) (*humareda*) cloud of smoke.

jumado* *adj* (*LAm*) drunk, tight*.

jumar‡ [1a] *vi* to pong‡, stink.

jumarse* [1a] *vr* (*LAm*) to get drunk.

jumatán* *nm* (*Carib*) drunkard.

jumazo‡ *nm* (*Carib*) fag‡.

jumbo *nm* jumbo, jumbo jet.

jumeado* *adj* (*And*) drunk, tight*.

jumelar‡ [1a] *vi* to pong‡, stink.

jumento *nm* donkey; beast of burden; (*fig*) dolt.

jumo *adj* (*LAm*) drunk.

jun. *abr de* **junio** June, Jun.

junar‡ [1a] **1** *vt* (*ver*) to see; (*mirar*) to watch. **2** *vi* (*Cono Sur*) to keep a look-out.

juncal 1 *adj* (**a**) (*Bot*) rushy, reedy. (**b**) (*fig*) willowy, lissom. **2** *nm* = **juncar.**

juncar *nm* ground covered in rushes; reed bed.

juncia *nf* sedge.

junco¹ *nm* (*Bot*) rush, reed; (*CAm*) rattan; ~ **de Indias** rattan.

junco² *nm* (*Náut*) junk.

juncoso *adj* (**a**) (*Bot*) rushy, reedy, reed-like. (**b**) *lugar* covered in rushes.

jungla *nf* jungle; ~ **de asfalto** concrete jungle.

junio *nm* June.

júnior *nm, pl* **juniores** (**a**) (*Ecl*) novice monk, junior novice. (**b**) (*Cono Sur*) office-boy.

junior *nmf, pl* **juniors** (*Dep*) junior.

Juno *nf* Juno.

junquera *nf* rush; bulrush.

junquillo *nm* (**a**) (*Bot*) jonquil; reed. (**b**) (*bastón*) rattan; (*madera*) strip of light wood. (**c**) (*Carib, Méx*) gold necklace.

junta *nf* (**a**) (*asamblea*) meeting, assembly; (*sesión*) session; ~ **de acreedores** meeting of creditors; ~ **general** general meeting; ~ **general de accionistas** annual general meeting (of shareholders); ~ **general extraordinaria** special general meeting; **celebrar** ~ to hold a meeting; to sit.

(**b**) (*consejo*) board, council, committee; (*Com, Fin*) board; **la ~ de la asociación** the committee of the association; ~ **directiva** board of management; executive committee; ~ **de gobierno** governing body; ~ **de portavoces** (*Parl*) House business committee.

(**c**) (*punto de unión*) junction, (point of) union.

(**d**) (*Téc*) (*acoplamiento*) joint; coupling; ~ **cardán,** ~ **universal** universal joint.

(**e**) (*Téc*: *arandela*) washer, gasket.

(**f**) (*Pol*) junta; ~ **militar** military junta.

juntadero *nm* (*Cono Sur*) meeting place.

juntamente *adv* (**a**) **hacer algo** ~ to do sth together; to do sth at the same time.

(**b**) **A ~ con B** A together with B; **ella y yo** ~ she and I together, she and I jointly.

juntar [1a] **1** *vt* (**a**) (*unir*) to join, unite; (*montar*) to assemble, put together; (*acumular*) to collect, gather (together), amass; *dinero* to collect, raise.

(**b**) *puerta* to pull to, push to.

2 juntarse *vr* (**a**) (*unirse*) to join, come together; (*gente*) to meet, assemble, gather (together); ~ **con uno** to join sb; to meet (up with) sb; to associate with sb; **se juntaron para oírle** they assembled to hear him, they came together to hear him; **se juntó con ellos en la estación** he met them at the station, he joined them at the station.

(**b**) (*Zool*) to mate, copulate.

(**c**) (*personas*: *euf*) to live together.

juntillo *etc V* **pie.**

junto 1 *adj* (**a**) joined, united; together; **fuimos ~s** we went together; **tenía los ojos muy ~s** his eyes were very close together; **vivir ~s** to live together.

(**b**) **~s** (*LAm**: *ambos*) both.

2 *adv* (**a**) near, close; together; (**de**) **por** ~, **en** ~ in all, all together; (*Com*) wholesale; **demasiado** ~ too close; **muy** ~ very close, very near; **ocurrió todo** ~ it happened all at once.

(**b**) (*LAm*) ~ **suyo** (*etc*) with him (*etc*), together with him (*etc*).

3 *prep*: ~ **a** near (to), close to, next to; ~ **con** together with.

juntura *nf* join, junction; (*Anat*) joint; (*Téc*) seam; (*Téc*) joint, coupling.

jupa *nf* (*CAm, Méx*) gourd; (‡) head, nut‡.

jupata‡ *nf* jacket.

jupiarse [1b] *vr* (*CAm*) to get drunk.

Júpiter *nm* Jupiter.

jura¹ *nf* oath, pledge; ~ **de la bandera** (taking the) oath of loyalty (*o* allegiance).

jura²‡ 1 *nm* (*CAm, Carib*) cop*. **2** *nf*: **la** ~ the cops*, the fuzz‡.

juraco* *nm* (*CAm*) hole.

jurado 1 *adj* (*en profesión*) qualified, chartered. **2** *nm* (**a**) (*cuerpo*: *Jur*) jury; (*en concurso, TV etc*) panel (of judges). (**b**) (*persona*: *Jur*) juror, juryman; (*en concurso etc*) member of a panel.

juramentar [1a] **1** *vt* to swear in, administer the oath to. **2 juramentarse** *vr* to be sworn in, take the oath.

juramento *nm* (**a**) (*promesa*) oath; ~ **de fidelidad** oath of loyalty; ~ **hipocrático** Hippocratic oath; **bajo** ~ on oath; **prestar** ~ to take the oath (*sobre* on); **tomar ~ a uno** to swear sb in, administer the oath to sb.

(**b**) (*palabrota*) oath, swearword, curse; **decir ~s a uno** to swear at sb.

jurar [1a] **1** *vti* to swear; ~ **decir la verdad** to swear to tell the truth; **le juro a Vd que ...** I swear to you that ...; **¡no jures!** don't swear!; ~ **como un carretero** to swear like a trooper; ~ **en falso** to commit perjury.

2 jurarse *vr*: **jurárselas a uno** to have it in for sb.

jurdós‡ *nm* bread‡, money.

jurel *nm* (**a**) horse mackerel. (**b**) **coger ~*** to get a fright.

jurero, -a *nm/f* (*And, Cono Sur*) perjurer, false witness.

jurgo *nm*, **jurgonera** *nf* (*And*) = **jorga.**

jurídico *adj* juridical; legal; **departamento** ~ (*Com*) legal department.

jurisdicción *nf* (**a**) (*gen*) jurisdiction. (**b**) (*distrito*) district, administrative area.

jurisdiccional *adj*: **aguas ~es** territorial waters.

jurispericia *nf* jurisprudence.

jurisperito, -a *nm/f* jurist, legal expert.

jurisprudencia *nf* jurisprudence, (study of the) law.

jurista *nmf* jurist, lawyer.

juro *nm* (*derecho*) right of perpetual ownership; (*pago*) annuity, pension; **a** ~ (*And, Carib*), **de** ~ certainly.

justa *nf* (*Hist*) joust, tournament; (*fig*) contest.

justamente *adv* (**a**) (*con justicia*) justly, fairly.

(**b**) (*precisamente*) just, precisely, exactly; **¡~!** precisely!; that's just it!; **de eso se trata** ~ that's just the point, that's exactly the point; **son ~ las que no están en venta** they are precisely the ones which are not for sale.

justar [1a] *vi* to joust, tilt.
justicia *nf* (**a**) (*gen*) justice; (*equidad*) fairness, equity, rightness; (*derecho*) right; ~ **catalana** summary justice; ~ **gratuita** legal aid; ~ **poética** poetic justice; ~ **social** social justice; **de** ~ justly, deservedly; **lo estimo de** ~ I think it right; **es de** ~ **añadir que ...** it is only right to add that ...; **en** ~ by rights; **hacer** ~ **a** to do justice to; **hacerse** ~ **por sí mismo, tomarse la** ~ **por su mano** to take the law into one's own hands.
(**b**) (*persona*) policeman; representative of authority; ~**s y ladrones** cops and robbers*.
justiciable *adj* (**a**) (*procesable*) actionable. (**b**) *decisión* subject to review by a court; subject to arbitration.
justicieramente *adv* justly.
justiciero *adj* (strictly) just, righteous.
justificable *adj* justifiable.
justificación *nf* justification; ~ **automática** (*Inform*) automatic justification.
justificante *nm* voucher; receipt; supporting document, evidence in support.
justificar [1g] *vt* (*gen*) to justify; (*probar*) to verify, substantiate; *sospechoso* to clear (*de* of), vindicate.
justificativo *adj*: **documento** ~ voucher, certificate; supporting document.
justillo *nm* jerkin.
justipreciar [1b] *vt* to evaluate, appraise.
justiprecio *nm* evaluation, appraisal.
justo 1 *adj* (**a**) (*correcto*) just, fair, right; **una decisión justa** a just decision; **los** ~**s** the righteous; **pagan** ~**s por pecadores** the innocent often pay for the guilty; **me parece muy** ~ it seems perfectly fair to me; **más de lo** ~ more than is proper, more than usual.
(**b**) (*exacto*) exact, correct; **el peso** ~ the correct weight; ¡~! that's it!, correct!, right!
(**c**) *ropa* tight; **el traje me viene muy** ~ the suit is rather tight for me, the suit is a very tight fit.
2 *adv* (**a**) (*con justicia*) justly.
(**b**) (*exactamente*) right; **vino** ~ **a tiempo** he came just in time; **llegaste en** ~ you just made it; **llegar con las justas** to arrive just on time.
(**c**) (*con dificultad*) tightly; **tener** ~ **para vivir** to have just enough to live on; **vivir muy** ~ to be hard up*, have only just enough to live on.
jute *nm* (*CAm*) edible snail.
juvenil *adj* youthful; **equipo** ~ (*Dep*) youth team, junior team; **obra** ~ youthful work, early work; **en los años** ~**es** in one's early years, in one's youth; **de aspecto** ~ young-looking, youthful in appearance.
juventud *nf* (**a**) (*época*) youth; early life.
(**b**) (*jóvenes*) young people; **la** ~ **de hoy** young people today, today's youth; **J**~**es Comunistas** (*etc*) Young Communists (*etc*); ~ **no conoce virtud** boys will be boys.
juyungo, -a* *nm/f* (*And*) Negro.
juzgado *nm* court, tribunal; ~ **de primera instancia** court of first instance, low-level court; **esto es (asunto) de** ~ **de guardia** (*fig*) this is an absolute outrage.
juzgar [1h] *vti* to judge; ~ **mal** to misjudge; **júzguelo Vd mismo** see for yourself, form your own judgement; **lo juzgo mi deber** I consider it my duty, I deem it my duty; **juzgue Vd mi sorpresa** imagine my surprise; ~ **de** to judge of, pass judgement on, appraise; **a** ~ **por** to judge by, judging by; **a** ~ **por lo que hemos visto** to judge by (*o* from) what we have seen.
juzgón *adj* (*CAm, Méx*) hypercritical, carping.

K

K, k [ka] *nf* (*letra*) K, k.
K *nm* (**a**) *abr de* **kilobyte** kilobyte, K. (**b**) **vehículo K** unmarked police-car.
kafkiano *adj* Kafkaesque.
kaki *nm* (*LAm*) khaki.
kamikaze *nm* kamikaze.
Kampuchea *nf* Kampuchea.
kampucheano, -a *adj, nm/f* Kampuchean.
kaperuj *nm* (*And*) embroidered shawl.
kaput* [ka'pu] *adj* kaput*; **hacer ~** to go kaput*, go phut*.
kárate *nm*, **karate** *nm* karate.
kárting ['kartin] *nm* go-carting.
Katar *nm* Qatar.
kayac *nm*, **kayak** *nm* kayak.
k/c. *abr de* **kilociclos** kilocycles, klc.
kebab *nm, pl* **kebabs** kebab.
kéfir *nm* (*And*) *type of yoghurt.*
Kenia *nf* Kenya.
keniano, -a *adj, nm/f* Kenyan.
keniata = **keniano.**
kepi(s) *nm* (*LAm*) kepi.
kermes *nm*, **kermesse** *nm* charity fair, bazaar.
kerosén *nm*, **kerosene** *nm*, **kerosín** *nm* (*CAm*), **kerosina** *nf* (*CAm*), kerosene, paraffin.
keynesiano, -a *adj, nm/f* Keynesian.
kg. *abr de* **kilogramo(s)** kilogram(s), kg.
kiki‡ *nm* joint‡, reefer‡.
kilate *nm* = **quilate.**
kilo 1 *nm* (**a**) kilo. (**b**) (‡) one million pesetas. **2** *como adv* (*) a lot, a great deal.
kilobyte ['kiloβait] *nm* kilobyte.
kilociclo *nm* kilocycle.
kilogramo *nm* kilogramme, kilogram (*US*).
kilohercio *nm* kilohertz.
kilolitro *nm* kilolitre, kiloliter (*US*).
kilometraje *nm* (**a**) distance (*o* rate *etc*) in kilometres, mileage. (**b**) (*Fin*) ≃ mileage allowance.
kilometrar [1a] *vt* to measure (in kilometres).
kilométrico 1 *adj* (**a**) (*gen*) kilometric; **billete ~** runabout ticket, mileage book. (**b**) (*) very long; **palabra kilométrica** very long word, multisyllabic word. **2** *nm* = **billete ~.**
kilómetro *nm* kilometre, kilometer (*US*); **~ cero** (*fig*) starting-point; central point.
kiloocteto *nm* kilobyte.
kilotón *nm* kiloton.
kilovatio *nm* kilowatt.
kilovatio-hora *nm, pl* **kilovatios-hora** kilowatt hour.
kimona *nf* (*Carib, Méx*), **kimono** *nm* (*Cono Sur*) kimono.
kínder *nm* (*LAm*), **kindergarten** *nm* (*LAm*) kindergarten.
kión *nm* (*And*) ginger.
kiosco *nm* = **quiosco.**
kiwi *nm* (**a**) (*Orn*) kiwi. (**b**) (*fruta*) kiwi fruit.
klínex *nm inv* tissue, Kleenex ®.
km. *abr de* **kilómetro** kilometre, km.
km/h. *abr de* **kilómetros por hora** kilometres per hour, km/h.
knock-out ['nokau] *nm*, **K.O.** [kaw] *nm* knockout; knockout blow; **dejar a uno ~, poner a uno ~** to knock sb out, give sb a knockout blow; (*fig*) to put sb out of action, leave sb stretched out cold.
kodak [ko'ðak] *nf, pl* **kodaks** [ko'ðak] small camera.
krausismo *nm philosophy and doctrine of K.C.F. Krause.*
krausista 1 *adj* Krausist, of Krause. **2** *nmf* follower of Krause.
Kurdistán *nm* Kurdistan.
kurdo 1 *adj* kurdish. **2** *nm*, **kurda** *nf* Kurd. **3** *nm* (*Ling*) Kurdish.
Kuwait *nm* Kuwait.
kuwaití *adj, nmf* Kuwaiti.
kv. *abr de* **kilovatio, kilovatios** kilowatt, kilowatts, kw.
kv/h. *abr de* **kilovatios-hora** kilowatt hours, kw/h.

L

L, l ['ele] *nf* (*letra*) L, l.
l. (**a**) *abr de* **litro**(**s**) litre(s), l. (**b**) (*Liter*) *abr de* **libro** book, bk. (**c**) (*Jur*) *abr de* **ley** law.
L/ *abr de* **Letra** letter.
l/100 km *abr de* **litros por 100 kilómetros** litres per 100 kilometres; ≈ miles per gallon, mpg.
la[1] *art def f* the (*para ejemplos de uso, V* **el**[1]).
la[2] *pron* (*persona*) her; (*Vd*) you; (*cosa*) it.
la[3] *pron dem*: **mi casa y ~ de Vd** my house and yours; **esta chica y ~ del sombrero verde** this girl and the one in the green hat; **~ de Pedro es mejor** Peter's is better; **y ~ de todos los demás** and that of everybody else; **~ de Rodríguez** Mrs Rodríguez; **¡~ de goles que marcó!** what a lot of goals he scored!; **¡~ de veces que se equivoca!** how often he's wrong!; **ir a ~ de Pepe** to go to Pepe's place.
la[4]: **~ que** *pron rel*: *V* **el**[3] **que.**
la[5] *nm* (*Mús*) A; **~ menor** A minor.
laberintero *adj* (*Méx*) = **laberintoso.**
laberíntico *adj* labyrinthine; *casa etc* rambling.
laberinto *nm* (**a**) labyrinth, maze; (*fig*) maze, tangle. (**b**) (*LAm**: *griterío*) row, racket.
laberintoso *adj* (*Méx*) (*ruidoso*) rowdy, brawling; (*chismoso*) gossipy.
labia *nf* fluency, blarney; (*pey*) glibness; **tener mucha ~** to have the gift of the gab*, be terribly persuasive.
labial *adj, nf* labial.
labihendido *adj* harelipped.
labio *nm* (*Anat*) lip; (*de vasija etc*) lip, edge, rim; (*fig*) tongue; **~s** lips, mouth; **~ inferior** lower lip; **~ superior** upper lip; **~ leporino** harelip; **lamerse los ~s** to lick one's lips; **no morderse los ~s** to be outspoken, pull no punches; **no descoser los ~s** to keep one's mouth shut; **sin despegar los ~s** without uttering a word; **es muy valiente de ~s para afuera** he comes over brave enough, outwardly he seems brave.
labiolectura *nf*, **labiología** *nf* lip-reading.
labiosear* [1a] *vt* (*CAm*) to flatter.
labiosidad* *nf* (*And, CAm*) flattery.
labioso *adj* (*LAm*) (*hablador*) talkative; (*lisonjero*) flattering; (*persuasivo*) persuasive, glib; (*taimado*) sly.
labor *nf* (**a**) (*trabajo*) labour, work; (*una ~*) job, task, piece of work; **'sus ~es'** (*censo etc*) 'housewife'; **~ de chinos** tedious task; **~ de equipo** teamwork.
(**b**) (*Agr*) (*cultivo*) farm work, cultivation; (*arada*) ploughing.
(**c**) (*CAm, Carib*) small farm, smallholding.
(**d**) (*Cos*) needlework, sewing; (*bordado*) embroidery; (*punto*) knitting; **una ~** a piece of needlework (*etc*); **~ de aguja, ~es femeninas** needlework; **~ de ganchillo** crochet, crocheting.
(**e**) **~es** (*Min*) workings.
laborable *adj* workable; arable; *V* **día.**
laboral *adj* labour (*atr*); technical; *V* **escuela** *etc.*
laboralista *adj* labour (*atr*); **abogado ~** labour lawyer.
laboralmente *adv*: **~ productivo** productive in terms of work; **~, estoy en paro** so far as work goes, I'm unemployed.
laboratorio *nm* laboratory; **~ espacial** space laboratory; **~ de idiomas** language laboratory.
laborar [1a] **1** *vt* (*Agr*) to work, till. **2** *vi* (**a**) (*CAm**) to work. (**b**) (*pey*) to scheme, plot.
laborear [1a] *vt* to work (*t Min*); (*Agr*) to work, till.
laboreo *nm* (*Agr*) working, cultivation, tilling; (*Min*) working.
laborero *nm* (*And, Cono Sur*) foreman.
laboriosamente *adv* industriously; painstakingly; with great difficulty.
laboriosidad *nf* (**a**) (*trabajo*) industry; painstaking skill. (**b**) (*pesadez*) laboriousness.
laborioso *adj* (**a**) *persona* hard-working, industrious, painstaking. (**b**) *trabajo* tough, hard, laborious, difficult.
laborismo *nm* (*LAm*) labour movement, workers' movement; (*Brit*) Labour Party, Labour Movement.
laborista **1** *adj* (*Brit*) Labour (*atr*); **Partido L~** Labour Party; **miembro ~** Labour member.
2 *nmf* (**a**) (*CAm*) small farmer, smallholder.
(**b**) (*Brit Pol*) Labour Party member, supporter of the Labour Party; Labour member of parliament.
laborterapia *nf* work-therapy.
labra *nf* carving, working, cutting.
labradío *adj* arable.
labrado **1** *adj* worked; *metal* wrought; *madera etc* carved; *tela* patterned, embroidered.
2 *nm* cultivated field; **~s** cultivated land.
Labrador *nm* (*Geog*) Labrador.
labrador *nm* (**a**) (*granjero*) farmer; (*labriego*) farm labourer; (*arador*) ploughman; (*campesino*) peasant; (*Méx*) lumberjack. (**b**) (*perro*) Labrador.
labradora *nf* peasant (woman).
labrantín *nm* small farmer.
labrantío *adj* arable.
labranza *nf* (**a**) (*cultivo*) farming; cultivation. (**b**) (*granja*) farm; (*tierras*) farmland.
labrar [1a] *vt* to work; to fashion, shape; *metal* to work; *madera etc* to carve; (*CAm, Méx*) *árbol* to fell and smooth; *tierra* to work, farm, till; *tela* to embroider; (*fig*) to cause, bring about.
labriego, -a *nm/f* farmhand, labourer; peasant.
laburante* *nm* (*Cono Sur*) worker.
laburar* [1a] *vi* (*Cono Sur*) to work.
laburno *nm* laburnum.
laburo* *nm* (*Cono Sur*) (*trabajo*) work; (*puesto*) job; **¡qué ~!*** what a job!
laca *nf* (**a**) (*t* **goma ~**) shellac; (*barniz*) lacquer; (*de pelo*) hair-spray; (*color*) lake; **~ de uñas, ~ para uñas** nail polish, nail varnish. (**b**) (*Cono Sur*) = **lacra.**
lacado *nm* lacquer.
lacar [1g] *vt* to lacquer.
lacayo *nm* footman; (*fig*) lackey.
laceada *nf* (*Cono Sur*) whipping.
lacear [1a] *vt* (**a**) (*adornar*) to beribbon, adorn with bows; (*atar*) to tie with a bow; (*CAm, Méx*) *carga* to tie on firmly, strap securely.
(**b**) (*Cono Sur*: *zurrar*) to whip.
(**c**) (*Caza*) (*coger*) to snare, trap; (*ojear*) to beat, drive; (*LAm*) to lasso.
laceración *nf* laceration; (*fig*) damage, spoiling.
lacerante *adj* (*fig*) wounding, hurtful.
lacerar [1a] *vt* to lacerate, tear, mangle; (*fig*) to damage, spoil.
laceria *nf* (*pobreza*) poverty, want; (*sufrimiento*) distress, wretchedness; (*trabajo*) toil.
laciar [1b] *vt* (*LAm*) *pelo rizado* to straighten.
Lacio *nm* Latium.
lacio *adj* (*Bot*) withered, faded; *pelo* lank, straight; *movimiento etc* limp, languid.
lacón *nm* shoulder of pork.
lacónicamente *adv* laconically, tersely.
lacónico *adj* laconic, terse.
laconismo *nm* laconic style (*o* manner *etc*), terseness.
lacra *nf* (**a**) (*Med*) mark, trace, scar; (*LAm*: *llaga*) sore, ulcer.
(**b**) (*fig*) blot, blemish; **la prostitución es una ~ social** prostitution is a blot on society, prostitution is a disgrace to society.
lacrar[1] [1a] **1** *vt* (**a**) (*Med*) to injure the health of; to infect,

strike (with a disease).

(**b**) (*fig*) to injure, harm, cause damage (*o* loss) to.

2 lacrarse *vr*: ~ **con algo** to suffer harm (*o* damage, loss *etc*) from sth; ~ **con el trabajo excesivo** to harm o.s. through overwork.

lacrar[2] [1a] *vt* to seal (*with sealing wax*).

lacre 1 *adj* (*LAm*) bright red. **2** *nm* sealing wax.

lacrimógeno *adj* (**a**) tear-producing; **gas** ~ teargas. (**b**) (*fig*) tearful, highly sentimental; weepy*; **canción lacrimógena, comedia lacrimógena** tear-jerker*.

lacrimoso *adj* tearful, lachrymose.

lacrosse [la'kros] *nf* lacrosse.

lactación *nf*, **lactancia** *nf* lactation; breast-feeding.

lactante *adj*: **mujer** ~ nursing mother.

lactar [1a] **1** *vt* to breast-feed, nurse, to feed on milk. **2** *vi* to suckle; to feed on milk.

lácteo *adj* lacteal, milk (*atr*); *producto* dairy (*atr*); (*fig*) milky, lacteous.

láctico *adj* lactic.

lactosa *nf* lactose.

lacustre *adj* lake (*atr*), lacustrine; (*LAm*) marshy.

lacha‡ *nf* (*honor*) sense of honour; (*vergüenza*) sense of shame; (*valentía*) guts.

lachear* [1a] *vt* (*Cono Sur*) to chat up*.

lacho* *nm* (*Cono Sur*) lover.

ladeado *adj* (**a**) (*inclinado*) tilted, leaning, inclined.

(**b**) (*Cono Sur*: *descuidado*) slovenly.

(**c**) (*Cono Sur*‡: *taimado*) crooked*.

(**d**) (*Cono Sur**) **andar** ~ to be in a bad temper; **andar** ~ **con uno** to be in a huff with sb.

ladear [1a] **1** *vt* (**a**) (*inclinar*) to tilt, tip; to incline (to one side); (*Aer*) to bank, turn; *cabeza* to tilt, put on one side.

(**b**) *montaña etc* to skirt, go round the side of.

2 *vi* (**a**) (*inclinarse*) to tilt, tip, lean.

(**b**) (*apartarse*) to turn aside, turn off.

3 ladearse *vr* (**a**) (*inclinarse*) to lean, incline (*t fig*: *a* towards); (*Aer*) to bank, turn; **se ladea al otro partido** he leans towards the other party.

(**b**) ~ **con** to be equal to, be even with.

(**c**) (*Cono Sur*: *enamorarse*) to fall in love (*con* with).

ladeo *nm* (**a**) (*inclinación*) tilting, inclination, leaning; (*Aer*) banking, turning. (**b**) (*fig*) inclination.

ladera *nf* slope, hillside.

ladero 1 *adj* side (*atr*), lateral. **2** *nm* (*Cono Sur**) backer.

ladilla *nf* crab louse; **¡qué ~!** (*Carib**) what a pain!*

ladillento *adj* (*CAm, Méx*) lousy.

ladillo *nm* (*Prensa*) subhead, subtitle.

ladinazo *adj* (*Cono Sur*) cunning, shrewd.

ladino 1 *adj* (**a**) (*taimado*) cunning, wily; (*astuto*) smart, shrewd.

(**b**) (*LAm*) *indio* Spanish-speaking.

(**c**) (*CAm, Méx*) half-breed, mestizo; (*blanco*) non-Indian, white, of Spanish descent.

(**d**) (*LAm*: *adulador*) smooth-tongued, smarmy*.

(**e**) (*Méx**) *voz* high-pitched, fluty.

2 *nm*, **ladina** *nf* (**a**) (*LAm*) Spanish-speaking Indian.

(**b**) (*CAm, Méx*) half-breed, mestizo; (*blanco*) non-Indian, white.

3 *nm* (*Ling*) Ladin (*Rhaeto-Romance dialect*); (*de sefardíes*) Ladino, Sephardic, Judeo-Spanish.

lado *nm* (**a**) (*gen*) side; ~ **débil** weak spot; ~ **izquierdo** left(-hand) side; **de ~ a ~** side by side; **al** ~ near, at hand; **al ~ de** by the side of, beside; **estuvo a mi** ~ she was at my side, she was beside me; **al otro ~ de la calle** on the other side of the street, across the street; **llevar algo al otro ~ del río** to carry sth across (*o* over) the river; **al ~ de aquello, esto no es nada** beside (*o* in comparison with) that, this is nothing; **la casa de al** ~ the house next door; **viven al ~ de nosotros** they live next door to us; **estar de un ~ para otro** to be up and down; **ir de un ~ a otro** to go to and fro, walk up and down; **poner algo de** ~ to put sth on its side; **por el ~ del mar** towards the sea, on the sea side; **por el ~ de Madrid** in the direction of Madrid; **salieron corriendo cada uno por su** ~ they all ran off in different directions; **por todos ~s** on all sides, all round; **por un ~ ..., por otro ...** on the one hand ..., on the other ...; **dar a uno de** ~ to disregard sb, be unconcerned about sb; **me da de** ~ I don't care; **dejar a un** ~ to skip, omit, pass over; to leave aside; **echar a un** ~ to cast aside; **hacer** ~ to make room (*a* for); **hacerse a un** ~ to stand aside (*t fig*), move over; **mirar de (medio)** ~ to look askance at; to steal a glance at; to look at out of the corner of one's eye; **poner a un** ~ to put aside.

(**b**) (*Mil*) flank.

(**c**) (*Dep*) end; **cambiar de** ~ to change ends.

(**d**) (*genealógico*) side; **por el ~ de la madre** on the mother's side.

(**e**) (*Pol etc*) side; faction; **ponerse al ~ de uno** to side with sb.

(**f**) (*favor*) favour, protection; **tener buenos ~s** to have good connections.

ladrar [1a] *vi* (*perro*) to bark; (*tripas*) to rumble; **está que ladra*** he's hopping mad*; **ladran, luego andamos** you can tell it's having some effect; **esta semana estoy ladrando** (*Carib**) I'm flat broke this week*.

ladrería *nf* (*And, Carib, Méx*), **ladrerío** *nm* (*Méx*) barking.

ladrido *nm* bark, barking; (*fig*) slander, scandal.

ladrillado *nm* (*de ladrillos*) brick floor; (*de azulejos*) tile floor.

ladrillar 1 *nm* brickworks. **2** *vt* to brick, pave with bricks.

ladriller(í)a *nf* (*LAm*) brickworks.

ladrillo *nm* (*gen*) brick; (*azulejo*) tile; (*de chocolate*) block, ~ **de fuego,** ~ **refractario** firebrick; ~ **ventilador** air-brick.

ladrón 1 *adj* thieving. **2** *nm*, **ladrona** *nf* thief; ~ **de corazones** ladykiller; ~ **de guante blanco** white-collar criminal; **¡al ~!** stop thief! **3** *nm* (*Elec*) adaptor, multiple plug.

ladronera *nf* (**a**) (*guarida*) den of thieves. (**b**) (*acto*) robbery, theft.

lagaña *nf* = **legaña.**

lagar *nm* (*de vino*) winepress; (*de aceite*) oil press.

lagarta *nf* (**a**) (*Zool*) lizard. (**b**) (*Ent*) gipsy moth; ~ **falsa** lackey moth. (**c**) (*mujer*) sly woman; **¡~!** you bitch!‡

lagartear [1a] *vt* (**a**) (*Cono Sur**: *inmovilizar*) to pinion, pin down. (**b**) (*And**: *falsear*) to fiddle*, wangle*.

lagartera *nf* lizard hole.

lagartija *nf* (**a**) (*Zool*) (small) lizard, wall lizard. (**b**) (*Méx**: *salvavidas*) lifeguard. (**c**) (*ejercicio*) press-up.

lagarto *nm* (**a**) (*Zool*) lizard; (*LAm*: *t* ~ **de Indias**) alligator; **¡~, ~!** (*toca madera*) touch wood!; (*And, Méx*: *Dios nos libre*) God forbid!

(**b**) (*persona*) sly fellow, fox.

(**c**) (*CAm, Méx**: *codicioso*) get-rich-quick type*; (*And**: *sableador*) scrounger*, sponger*; (*And**: *especulador*) profiteer.

(**d**) (*Méx**: *astuto*) sharp customer, smart operator.

largartón* *adj* (*CAm, Méx*) (*codicioso*) greedy; (*listo*) sharp, shrewd; (*taimado*) sly.

lago *nm* lake; **los Grandes L~s** the Great Lakes.

Lagos *n* Lagos.

lágrima *nf* tear; (*gota*) drop; **~s de cocodrilo** crocodile tears; **~s de don Pedro** (*Cono Sur*) June rains; **beberse las ~s** to hold back one's tears; **derramar una lagrimita** (*iró*) to shed a tear; **deshacerse en ~s** to burst into tears; **llorar a ~ viva** to sob one's heart out, cry uncontrollably; **nadie soltará una ~ por eso** nobody is going to shed a tear over that.

lagrimal *nm* corner of the eye.

lagrimar [1a] *vi* to cry.

lagrimear [1a] *vi* (*persona*) to shed tears easily, be tearful; (*ojos*) to water, fill with tears.

lagrimilla *nf* (*Cono Sur*) unfermented grape juice.

lagrimoso *adj persona* lachrymose, tearful; *ojos* watery.

laguna *nf* (**a**) (*Geog*) pool; (*de atolón*) lagoon. (**b**) (*Liter etc*) gap, lacuna; (*en escritos, conocimientos*) gap, blank; (*en proceso*) hiatus, gap, break.

lagunajo *nm*, **lagunato** *nm* (*Carib*) (*estanco*) pool, pond; (*charco*) puddle.

lagunoso *adj* marshy, swampy.

laicado *nm* laity.

laical *adj* lay.

laicidad *nf* (*LAm*), **laicismo** *nm* laicism (*doctrine of the independence of the state etc from church interference*).

laicizar [1f] *vt* to laicize.

laico 1 *adj* lay. **2** *nm* layman.

laísmo *nm use of* **la** *and* **las** *as indirect objects.*

laísta 1 *adj that uses* **la** *and* **las** *as indirect objects.* **2** *nmf user of* **la** *and* **las** *as indirect objects.*

laja[1] *nf* (**a**) (*CAm, Cono Sur*) (*piedra*) sandstone; (*roca*) rock. (**b**) (*And*) (*lugar*) steep ground.

laja[2] *nf* (*And*) fine rope.

laja[3]‡ *nf* (*chica*) bird‡, dame*.

Lalo *nm* (*LAm*) *forma familiar de* **Eduardo.**

lama[1] *nf* (**a**) mud, slime, ooze. (**b**) (*And, Méx*: *moho*) mould, mildew; (*Méx*: *musgo*) moss.

lama[2] *nm* (*Rel*) lama.

lama[3] *nf* (*de persiana*) slat.

lama[4] *nf* (*tejido*) lamé.

lambarear* [1a] *vi* (*Carib*) to wander aimlessly about.
lambeculo‡ *nmf* (*Cono Sur, Méx*) creep‡.
lambeladrillos* *nm invar* (*And*) hypocrite.
lambeplatos* *nmf invar* (*LAm*) (**a**) (*lameculos*) bootlicker*. (**b**) (*pobre hombre*) poor wretch.
lamber [2a] *vt* (*LAm*) (**a**) = **lamer**. (**b**) (*) to fawn on, toady to, suck up to*.
lambeta‡ *nmf* (*Cono Sur*) creep‡, bootlicker*.
lambetada *nf* (*Carib, Cono Sur, Méx*) (**a**) (*lit*) lick. (**b**) (* *fig*) (*acto*) grovelling; (*adulación*) soft-soaping*.
lambetazo *nm* (*LAm*) (**a**) (*lit*) lick. (**b**) = **lambetada**.
lambetear [1a] *vt* (*LAm*) (**a**) (*lit*) to lick; to lick greedily, lick noisily. (**b**) (*) to suck up to*.
lambiche *adj* (*Méx*) = **lambiscón**.
lambida *nf* (*LAm*) lick.
lambido* *adj* (*LAm*) (*desvergonzado*) cheeky*; (*presumido*) cocky*, cocksure.
lambioche* *adj* (*Méx*) servile, fawning.
lambiscón *adj* (*And, Méx*) (**a**) (*glotón*) greedy, gluttonous. (**b**) = **lambioche**.
lambisconear [1a] (*LAm*) **1** *vt* (**a**) (*lit*) to lick. (**b**) (*) to suck up to*. **2** *vi* (*) to creep*, crawl.
lambisconería *nf* (*LAm*) (**a**) (*: *gula*) greediness, gluttony. (**b**) (‡: *adulación*) fawning, grovelling. (**c**) (‡: *presunción*) cockiness*.
lambisquear [1a] (*And, Méx*) = **lambisconear**.
lambón *adj* (*LAm*) = **lambioche**.
lambraña *nmf* (*And*) wretch.
lambrijo* *adj* (*Méx*) skinny.
lambrusquear [1a] *vt* (*Cono Sur, Méx*) to lick.
lambuzo *adj* (*And, Carib, Méx*) (**a**) (*glotón*) greedy, gluttonous. (**b**) (*desvergonzado*) shameless, brazen.
lamé *nm* lamé.
lameculismo‡ *nm* bootlicking*, toadyism.
lameculos‡ *nmf invar* bootlicker*, toady.
lamedura *nf* lick, licking.
lamentable *adj* regrettable; lamentable; pitiful; **es ~ que** ... it is regrettable that ...
lamentablemente *adv* regrettably; (*LAm*) unfortunately.
lamentación *nf* lamentation; sorrow.
lamentar [1a] **1** *vt* to be sorry about, regret; *pérdida etc* to lament, bemoan, bewail; *muerte* to mourn; **~ que** ... to be sorry that ..., regret that ...; **lamentamos mucho que ...** we very much regret that ...; **lamento lo que pasó** I'm sorry about what happened; **no hay que ~ víctimas** fortunately there were no casualties.
2 lamentarse *vr* to lament, wail, moan (*de, por* about, over); (*por muerte*) to mourn (*de, por* over); (*quejarse*) to complain (*de, por* about).
lamento *nm* lament; moan, wail; **~s** lamentation.
lamentoso *adj* (**a**) = **lamentable**. (**b**) plaintive.
lameplatos *nmf invar* (**a**) (*lit*) person who eats scraps. (**b**) (*Méx**) (*adulón*) toady; (*parásito*) scrounger*; (*inútil*) disaster.
lamer [2a] **1** *vt* to lick; (*olas*) to lap, lap against; (*pasar rozando*) to graze. **2 lamerse‡** *vr*: **un problema** (*etc*) **que no se lame** a bloody great problem‡ (*etc*).
lametada *nf* lick; (*de ola*) lap.
lametazo *nm* lick; (*del sol*) touch, caress.
lamido *adj* (**a**) (*flaco*) very thin, emaciated; (*pálido*) pale. (**b**) (*afectado*) prim, affected.
lámina¹ *nf* (*de metal, vidrio, etc*) sheet; (*Metal, Fot, Tip*) plate; (*Inform*) chip; (*en libro etc*) plate, illustration, picture; (*grabado*) engraving; **~s de acero** steel in sheets, sheet steel; **~ de queso** slice of cheese; **~ de silicio** silicon wafer.
lámina² *nmf* (*And*) rogue, rascal.
laminado *adj* (**a**) (*gen*) laminate(d). (**b**) (*Téc*) sheet (*atr*), rolled; **cobre ~** sheet copper, rolled copper.
laminador *nm* rolling mill.
laminar [1a] *vt* to laminate; (*Téc*) to roll; (*fig*) to smash, destroy.
lamiscar [1g] *vt* to lick greedily, lick noisily.
lampa *nf* (*And*: *de mineros*) pick.
lampacear [1a] *vt* (*CAm*) *piso etc* to mop.
lampalague *nf* (**a**) (*Cono Sur*: *serpiente*) boa constrictor. (**b**) (*Cono Sur*: *fig*) glutton.
lampancia* *nf* ravenous hunger.
lampante* *nmf* beggar.
lámpara 1 *nf* (*gen*) lamp, light; (*bombilla*) bulb; (*Rad*) valve, tube (*US*); **~s** (*LAm*: *ojos*) eyes; **~ de Aladino** Aladdin's lamp; **~ de alcohol** spirit lamp; **~ de arco** arc-lamp; **~ de bolsillo** torch, flashlight; **~ bronceador** sun-lamp; **~ de cuarzo** quartz lamp; **~ de escritorio** desk-lamp; **~ flexo** adjustable table-lamp; **~ de lectura** reading lamp; **~ de mesa** table-lamp; **~ de pared** wall light; **~ de pie** standard lamp; **~ de señales** signalling lamp; **~ de sol artificial, ~ solar ultravioleta** sun-ray lamp; **~ de soldar** blowlamp, blowtorch; **~ de techo** overhead lamp; **atizar la ~*** to fill up the glasses; **quebrar la ~** (*Carib**) to ruin everything, blow it‡.
2 *nmf* (*Carib*) (*ladrón*) thief; (*estafador*) con man*.
lamparazo *nm* flash of light.
lamparilla *nf* (**a**) (*lámpara*) small lamp; nightlight. (**b**) (*Bot*) aspen.
lamparín *nm* (*Cono Sur*: *vela*) candle; (*And*: *quinqué*) paraffin lamp.
lámparo *adj* (*And*) penniless, broke*.
lamparón *nm* (**a**) (*Med*) scrofula. (**b**) (*mancha*) large grease spot.
lampazo¹ *nm* (*Bot*) burdock.
lampazo² *nm* (**a**) (*Náut*) swab; (*LAm*: *estropajo*) floor mop. (**b**) (*And, Carib*: *azotamiento*) whipping.
lampear [1a] *vt* (*And*) (*con pala*) to shovel; (*con azada*) to hoe.
lampiño *adj* hairless; *muchacho* beardless.
lampión *nm* lantern.
lampista *nm* plumber.
lampistería *nf* electrical shop.
lampón¹ *adj* (*And*) starving, hungry.
lampón² *nm* (*And*) (*pala*) spade; (*azada*) hoe.
lamprea *nf* (**a**) (*Pez*) lamprey. (**b**) (*Carib*) sore, ulcer.
lamprear [1a] *vt* (*CAm*) to whip.
lana¹ *nf* (**a**) (*gen*) wool; (*vellón*) fleece; (*tela*) woollen cloth; **~s** (*: *hum*) long hair, locks; **~ de acero** steel wool; **~ para labores** knitting wool; **~ virgen** pure new wool; **de ~, hecho de ~** wool (*atr*), woollen; **ir por ~ y volver trasquilado** to get more than one bargained for.
(**b**) (*And, Méx‡*: *dinero*) dough‡, money.
(**c**) (*CAm**: *estafador*) swindler.
lana² *nf* (*CAm*) = **lama¹** (**b**).
lanar *adj* wool (*atr*), wool-bearing; **ganado ~** sheep.
lance *nm* (**a**) (*de red etc*) throw, cast.
(**b**) (*peces*) catch, quantity of fish caught.
(**c**) (*jugada etc*) stroke, move, piece of play.
(**d**) (*suceso*) incident, event, occurrence; (*episodio*) episode; (*accidente*) chance, accident; **~ de fortuna** stroke of luck; **~ de honor** affair of honour, duel; **el libro tiene pocos ~s emocionantes** the book is dull, not much happens in the book; **tirarse** (**a**) **un ~** (*Cono Sur*) to take a chance.
(**e**) (*momento*) critical moment, difficult moment.
(**f**) (*riña*) row, quarrel.
(**g**) (*Cono Sur*: *agachada*) duck, dodge; **sacar ~** to dodge, duck away.
(**h**) (*Cono Sur Arquit*) section, range; **casa de 3 ~s** house in 3 sections.
(**i**) (*Com*) **de ~** secondhand; cheap; **libros de ~** secondhand books; **comprar algo de ~** to buy sth secondhand, buy sth cheap.
lancear [1a] *vt* to spear.
lancero 1 *nm* (*Mil*) lancer; **~s** (*Mús*) lancers. **2** *nmf* (*Cono Sur**: *soñador*) dreamer, blind optimist.
lanceta *nf* (**a**) (*Med etc*) lancet; **abrir con ~** to lance. (**b**) (*LAm*: *aguijada*) goad; (*de insecto*) sting.
lancinante *adj dolor* piercing.
lancinar [1a] *vt* to lance, pierce.
lancha¹ *nf* (**a**) (*Náut*) launch; (small) boat; lighter, barge; **~ (automóvil)** motor-launch, motorboat; **~ cañonera** gunboat; **~ de carga** lighter, barge; **~ de carreras** speedboat; **~ de desembarco** landing-craft; **~ fuera borda** outboard dinghy; **~ inflable** rubber dinghy; **~ motora** motorboat, speedboat; **~ neumática** rubber dinghy; **~ patrullera** patrol-boat; **~ de pesca** fishing-boat; **~ rápida** speedboat; **~ de salvamento, ~ salvavidas, ~ de socorro** lifeboat; **~ torpedera** torpedo boat.
(**b**) (*Cono Sur**) police car.
lancha² *nf* (*And*) mist, fog; (hoar)frost.
lanchaje *nm* (*Méx*) ferry charges.
lanchar [1a] *vi* († *And*) (*encapotarse*) to become overcast; (*helar*) to freeze.
lanchero *nm* (**a**) boatman; lighterman, bargee. (**b**) (*Carib*) Cuban refugee.
lanchón *nm* lighter, barge; **~ de desembarco** landing-craft.
Landas *nfpl*: **las ~** the Landes.
landó *nm* (**a**) landau. (**b**) (*And Mús*) *Peruvian folk music*.
landre *nf*: **¡mala ~ te coma!** curse you!
lanería *nf* (**a**) (*géneros*) woollen goods. (**b**) (*tienda*) wool shop.

lanero 1 *adj* wool (*atr*); woollen; **la industria lanera** the wool industry. **2** *nm* (**a**) (*persona*) woolman, wool dealer. (**b**) (*almacén*) wool warehouse.
lángara‡ *nmf* (*Méx*) creep‡.
lángaro *adj* (**a**) (*CAm*: *vago*) vagrant, wandering, idle; (*And, Méx*: *hambriento*) starving, poverty-stricken; (*Méx*: *malo*) wicked; (*taimado*) sly, untrustworthy. (**b**) (*CAm*: *larguirucho*) lanky.
langarucho *adj* (*CAm, Méx*), **langarote** *adj* (*And*) lanky.
langosta *nf* (**a**) (*de mar*) lobster; (*de río*) crayfish. (**b**) (*Ent*) locust.
langostera *nf* lobster pot.
langostín *nm*, **langostino** *nm* prawn.
langostinero *adj*: **barco ~** prawn-fishing boat.
languceta *adj* (*Cono Sur*), **languciento** *adj* (*Cono Sur, Méx*), **langucio** *adj* (*Cono Sur*) (*hambriento*) starving; (*enclenque*) sickly.
lánguidamente *adv* languidly; weakly, listlessly.
languidecer [2d] *vi* to languish, pine (away).
languidez *nf* languor, lassitude; listlessness.
lánguido *adj* languid; weak, listless, drooping.
languso *adj* (*Méx*) (**a**) (*taimado*) sly, shrewd. (**b**) (*larguirucho*) lanky.
lanilla *nf* (*flojel*) nap; (*tela*) thin flannel cloth.
lanolina *nf* lanolin(e).
lanoso *adj* woolly, fleecy.
lanudo *adj* (**a**) (*lanoso*) woolly, fleecy. (**b**) (*And, Carib*: *maleducado*) rustic, uncouth. (**c**) (*Carib, Méx**: *rico*) well off.
lanza 1 *nf* (**a**) (*Mil*) lance, spear; **estar ~ en ristre** to be ready for action; **medir ~s** to cross swords; **romper ~s por** to stick up for; **ser una ~** to be pretty sharp; (*Méx*) to be sly, be a rogue.
(**b**) (*de carro*) pole.
(**c**) (*de manguera*) nozzle.
2 *nm* (*LAm**: *estafador*) shark*; (*Cono Sur*: *tironista*) bag-snatcher; (*ratero*) pickpocket.
lanzabengalas *nm invar* flare.
lanzabombas *nm invar* (*Aer*) bomb-release; (*Mil*) trench mortar.
lanzacohetes *nm invar* rocket-launcher; **~ múltiple** multiple rocket-launcher.
lanzada *nf* spear thrust; spear wound.
lanzadera *nf* shuttle; **~ espacial** space-shuttle; **~ de misiles** missile-launcher.
lanzadestellos *nm invar* (*Aut*) flashing light.
lanzado* *adj* (**a**) (*ser*) forward, brazen; impudent; confident with women. (**b**) (*estar*) randy*, in the mood.
lanzador *nm* (**a**) (*t* **lanzadora** *nf*: *gen*) thrower; (*Béisbol*) pitcher; **~ de cuchillos** knife-thrower; **~ de jabalina** javelin-thrower; **~ de martillo** hammer-thrower; **~ de peso** shot-putter. (**b**) (*t* **lanzadora** *nf*: *Com, Fin*) promoter. (**c**) (*Mil*: *de cohetes etc*) launcher; (*Aer*) launch vehicle.
lanzaespumas *nm invar* foam sprayer.
lanzagranadas *nm invar* grenade-launcher, mortar.
lanzallamas *nm invar* flamethrower.
lanzamiento *nm* (**a**) (*acto*) throw, cast; throwing, casting, hurling; (*Aer*) drop (*by parachute*), jump, descent; **~ de disco** discus-throwing, the discus; **~ de martillo** hammer-throwing, the hammer; **~ de pesos** putting the shot, shot-putting.
(**b**) (*Aer, Náut*) launch, launching.
(**c**) (*Com, Fin*) launching; promotion; **~ publicitario** launching of an advertising campaign; **oferta de ~** promotional offer.
(**d**) (*Jur*) dispossession, eviction.
lanzaminas *nm invar* minelayer.
lanzamisiles *nm invar* missile-launcher.
lanzar [1f] **1** *vt* (**a**) (*gen*) to throw, cast; (*con violencia*) fling, hurl; (*Dep*) *pelota* to pitch, bowl (*a* at, to); *pesa* to put; (*Aer*) to drop (*by parachute*); (*Med*) to bring up, throw up, vomit; *desafío* to throw out, throw down; *crítica* to hurl.
(**b**) *grito* to give, utter; *mirada* to give, cast (*a* at).
(**c**) (*Náut*) to launch.
(**d**) (*Bot*) *hojas etc* to put forth.
(**e**) (*Com, Fin*) to launch, promote.
(**f**) (*Jur*) to dispossess, evict.
2 lanzarse *vr* (**a**) (*gen*) to throw o.s., hurl o.s., fling o.s. (*a, en* into; *sobre* on); to rush (*sobre* at, on), fly (*sobre* at); (*Aer*) to jump (*by parachute*), bale out; **se lanzó a la pelea** he rushed into the fray; **se lanzó al río** he jumped into the river, he dived into the river.
(**b**) **~ a** (*fig*) to launch into; to embark upon, undertake.
Lanzarote *nm* (**a**) (*persona*) Lancelot. (**b**) (*isla*) Lanzarote.
lanzaroteño 1 *adj* of Lanzarote. **2** *nm*, **lanzaroteña** *nf* native (*o* inhabitant) of Lanzarote; **los ~s** the people of Lanzarote.
lanzatorpedos *nm invar* torpedo tube.
laña *nf* clamp; rivet.
lañar [1a] *vt* (**a**) (*Téc*) to clamp (together); to rivet. (**b**) (‡: *robar*) to nick‡, steal.
Laos *nm* Laos.
laosiano, -a *adj, nm/f* Laotian.
lapa *nf* (**a**) (*Zool*) limpet. (**b**) (*persona*) nuisance, pest. (**c**) (*And, Cono Sur Bot*) half gourd (*used as bowl etc*). (**d**) (*And*: *sombrero*) large flat-topped hat.
lapalada *nf* (*Méx*) drizzle.
lape *adj* (*Cono Sur*) (**a**) (*enredado*) matted. (**b**) *baile etc* merry, lively.
lapicera *nf* (*Cono Sur*) = **lapicero**.
lapicero *nm* (**a**) (*lápiz*) propelling pencil; **~ hemostático** styptic pencil.
(**b**) (*LAm*) (*plumafuente*) fountain-pen; (*bolígrafo*) ball-point pen, Biro ®.
(**c**) (**) prick**.
lápida *nf* stone, stone tablet, memorial tablet; **~ conmemorativa** commemorative tablet; **~ mortuoria** headstone, gravestone; **~ mural** tablet let into a wall; **~ sepulcral** tombstone.
lapidar [1a] *vt* (**a**) to stone, throw stones at; to stone to death. (**b**) (*And, CAm*) *joya* to cut.
lapidario 1 *adj* lapidary; **frase lapidaria** immortal phrase. **2** *nm*, **lapidaria** *nf* lapidary.
lapislázuli *nm* lapis lazuli.
lápiz *nm* (**a**) (*gen*) pencil; crayon; **~ de carbón** charcoal pencil; **~ de carmín**, **~ labial**, **~ de labios** lipstick; **~ de cejas** eyebrow pencil; **~ electrónico**, **~ de luz**, **~ óptico** light pen; **~ lector** data pen; **~ negro** (*en la censura*) blue pencil; **~ de ojos** eyeliner; **~ a pasta** (*Cono Sur*) ball-point pen; **~ (de) plomo** lead pencil; **escribir algo a** (*o* **con**) **~** to write sth in pencil; **está añadido a ~** it is added in pencil; it is pencilled in; **meter ~ a** to sign.
(**b**) (*Min*) blacklead, graphite.
lapo *nm* (**a**) (*: *golpe*) bash*, swipe; **de un ~** (*And*) at one go. (**b**) (*And, Carib*: *trago*) swig*. (**c**) (*Carib*: *inocente*) simple soul.
lapón, -ona *nm/f* Lapp, Laplander.
Laponia *nf* Lapland.
lapso *nm* lapse; **~ de tiempo** interval of time, passage of time; **en un ~ de 5 días** in (the space of) five days.
lapsus *nm invar* lapse, mistake; **~ calami** slip of the pen; **~ freudiano** Freudian slip; **~ linguae** slip of the tongue; **~ de memoria** lapse of memory.
laqueado *adj* lacquered; varnished.
laquear [1a] *vt* to lacquer; *uñas* to varnish, paint.
LAR [lar] *nf* (*Esp Jur*) *abr de* **Ley de Arrendamientos Rústicos**.
lard(e)ar [1a] *vt* to lard, baste.
lardo *nm* lard, animal fat.
lardoso *adj* lardy, fatty; greasy.
larga *nf* (*Dep*) length; **nadar 20 ~s** to swim 20 lengths (*V t* **largo 1** (**f**)).
largada *nf* (*Dep*) start.
largamente *adv* (**a**) (*de tiempo*) for a long time; *narrar* at length, fully; **conversamos ~** we talked at length, we had a long conversation.
(**b**) *vivir* comfortably, at ease.
(**c**) *compensar, tratar etc* generously.
largar [1h] **1** *vt* (**a**) (*soltar*) to let go, let loose, release; (*aflojar*) to loosen, slacken; *cuerda* to let out, pay out; *bandera, vela* to unfurl; *barca* to launch, put out; *persona* (*despedir*) to sack*, fire*, (*expulsar*) to throw out.
(**b**) *golpe* to give, fetch, deal.
(**c**) *insulto etc* to let fly; *exclamación, suspiro etc* to let out.
(**d**) (*decir*) **nos largó ese rollo de ...** he gave us that spiel* about ...; **le largó una tremenda bronca** she gave him a good ticking-off*; **les largó todo un discurso** he gave them a whole speech.
(**e**) (*And**: *lanzar*) to throw, hurl.
(**f**) (*And**: *entregar*) to hand over.
2 *vi* (‡) to speak, talk; to prattle on.
3 largarse *vr* (**a**) (*) to beat it*, hop it*; to quit; **¡lárgate!** clear off!*.
(**b**) (*Náut*) to set sail, start out.
(**c**) (*LAm*: *empezar*) to start, begin; **~ a** + *infin* to start to + *infin*.
largavistas *nm invar* (*Cono Sur*) binoculars.
largo 1 *adj* (**a**) (*distancia, medida*) long; (*tiempo*) long,

lengthy; (*demasiado* ~) too long; **parece** ~ it looks too long; **de pelo** ~ long-haired; ~ **de uñas** light-fingered, thieving; ~**s años** long years, many years; ~ **y tendido** (*como adv*) at great length; **no es bastante** ~ it's not long enough; **es muy** ~ **de contar** it's a long story.

(**b**) ¡~ (**de aquí**)!*, clear off!*, get out!

(**c**) (*con* de) **estar de** ~ to be in a long dress; **ponerse de** ~ to put on grown-up clothes, dress as an adult (for the first time); (*fig*) to come out (in society); **pasar de** ~ to pass by, go by (without stopping); **dejar pasar a uno de** ~ to give sb a wide berth; **seguir de** ~ (*LAm**) (*no parar*) to keep on going; (*pasar de lado*) to pass by; **este problema viene de** ~ this problem started way back, this problem has been with us a long time.

(**d**) (*con* lo) **a lo más** ~ at the most; **a lo** ~ *poner* lengthways; *contar* at great length, lengthily; *ver etc* in the distance, far off; **a lo** ~ **de** along; alongside; (*tiempo*) all through, throughout; **a lo** ~ **del río** along the river; **a lo** ~ **del túnel** throughout the tunnel; **a lo** ~ **y a lo ancho de** throughout the length and breadth of.

(**e**) (*cantidad*) full, good; **tardó media hora larga** he took a good (*o* full) half-hour; **los aventajó en un minuto** ~ he beat them by a full minute; **le costó 50 dólares** ~**s** it cost him all of 50 dollars, it cost him a good 50 dollars; **una dama sesentañera larga** a lady well on in her sixties.

(**f**) (*larga*) **a la larga** in the long run; eventually, in the end; **a la larga o a la corta** sooner or later; **dar largas a un asunto** to delay a matter, put off making a decision about a matter; **me dio largas con una promesa** she put me off with a promise; **saberla larga** to be shrewd; to know one's way about.

(**g**) (*generoso*) generous; lavish; **tirar de** ~ to spend lavishly.

(**h**) (*copioso*) abundant, copious; *cosecha* heavy.

(**i**) (*astuto*) sharp, shrewd; quick.

(**j**) (*Náut*) *cuerda* loose, slack.

2 *nm* (**a**) (*gen*) length; **el** ~ **de las faldas** the length of skirts; **tiene 9 metros de** ~ it is 9 metres long; **¿cuánto tiene de** ~**?** how long is it?; **he nadado 4** ~**s** I've swum four lengths (of the pool).

(**b**) (*Mús*) largo.

(**c**) (*Cine**) = **largometraje**.

largometraje *nm* full-length film, feature film.

largón⁑ *nm* spy, informer.

largona *nf* (**a**) (*And, Cono Sur*: *demora*) delay. (**b**) **darse una** ~ (*Cono Sur**) to take a rest; **dar** ~**s a algo** (*And**) to keep putting sth off.

largor *nm* length.

largucho *adj* (*LAm*) lanky.

larguero 1 *adj* (**a**) (*Cono Sur**) (*largo*) long, lengthy; *discurso* wordy, long-drawn-out; *persona* slow, slow-working; (*Dep*) trained for long-distance running.

(**b**) (*Cono Sur**) (*generoso*) generous; lavish; (*copioso*) abundant, copious.

2 *nm* (*Arquit*) beam, support; (*de puerta*) jamb; (*Dep*) crossbar; (*de cama*) bolster.

largueza *nf* largesse, generosity.

larguirucho *adj* lanky, gangling.

largura *nf* length.

largurucho *adj* (*LAm*) lanky, gangling.

lárice *nm* larch.

laringe *nf* larynx.

laringitis *nf* laryngitis.

larva *nf* larva; grub, maggot.

larvado *adj* hidden, latent; embryonic; gradually evolving; **permanecer** ~ to be latent, remain dormant.

las *art def fpl etc*: *V* **los**.

lasca *nf* chip, stone chips; (*de comida*) slice.

lascadura *nf* (*Méx*) (*rozadura*) graze, abrasion; (*herida*) injury.

lascar [1g] **1** *vt* (**a**) (*Náut*) to slacken. (**b**) (*Méx*) *piel* to graze, bruise; *piedra* to chip, chip off. **2** *vi* (*Méx*) to chip off, flake off.

lascivamente *adv* lewdly, lasciviously; lustfully; (*fig*) playfully, wantonly.

lascivia *nf* lewdness, lasciviousness; lust, lustfulness; (*fig*) playfulness.

lascivo *adj* lewd, lascivious; lustful; (*fig*) playful, wanton.

láser *nm* laser.

lasérico *adj* laser (*atr*).

laserterapia *nf* laser therapy.

lasitud *nf* lassitude, weariness.

laso *adj* (*liter*: *cansado*) weary; (*débil*) weak; (*lánguido*) limp, slack, languid.

lástima *nf* (**a**) (*sentimiento*) pity; compassion; shame; **¡qué** ~**!** what a pity!, what a shame!, that's too bad!; **¡qué** ~ **de hombre!** isn't he pitiful?; **es una** ~ it's a shame; **es** ~ **que** ... it's a pity that ..., it's too bad that ...; **dar** ~ to be pitiful, rouse to pity; **eso me da mucha** ~ I feel very sorry about that; **es una película que da** ~ it's a pathetic film; (*pey*) it's a pathetically bad film; **todos me dan** ~ I feel sorry for them all.

(**b**) (*objeto*) pitiful object; (*escena*) pitiful sight; **estar hecho una** ~ to be a sorry sight, be in a dreadful state.

(**c**) (*queja*) complaint, tale of woe.

lastimada *nf* (*CAm, Méx*) = **lastimadura.**

lastimador *adj* harmful, injurious.

lastimadura *nf* (*LAm*) (*herida*) wound, injury; (*moretón*) bruise.

lastimar [1a] **1** *vt* (**a**) (*lesionar*) to hurt, harm, injure; (*herir*) to wound; (*magullar*) to bruise.

(**b**) (*ofender*) to offend, distress.

(**c**) (*apiadarse de*) to pity, sympathize with, feel pity for.

(**d**) (*apiadar*) to move to pity.

2 lastimarse *vr* (**a**) to hurt o.s., injure o.s.; **se lastimó el brazo** he hurt his arm.

(**b**) ~ **de** (*quejarse*) to complain about; (*apiadarse*) to feel sorry for, pity.

lastimero *adj* (**a**) (*dañoso*) harmful, injurious. (**b**) = **lastimoso.**

lastimón *nm* (*LAm*) = **lastimadura.**

lastimosamente *adv* pitifully, pathetically.

lastimoso *adj* piteous, pitiful, pathetic.

lastrante *adj* (*fig*) burdensome.

lastrar [1a] *vt* to ballast; (*fig*) to burden, weigh down.

lastre *nm* (**a**) (*Téc*) ballast; **en** ~ (*Náut*) in ballast. (**b**) (*fig*: *carga*) ballast; dead weight, useless load. (**c**) (*juicio*) good sense, steadiness, balance. (**d**) (*Cono Sur*⁑: *comida*) grub⁑.

lata *nf* (**a**) (*metal*) tinplate; (*envase*) tin, can; (*And*: *comida*) food, daily ration; ~ **petitoria** collecting tin (*for charity*); **sardinas en** ~ tinned sardines, canned sardines; **sonar a** ~ (*Mús etc*) to sound tinny.

(**b**) (*) nuisance, drag, bind*; **es una** ~ **tener que** ... it's a nuisance having to ...; **¡vaya una** ~**!, ¡qué** ~**!** what a nuisance!; **dar** ~ (*And, CAm**: *parlotear*) to babble on; (*And**: *insistir*) to nag, go on; **dar** ~ **a** (*Carib*) to condemn, censure; **dar la** ~ to be a nuisance, be annoying, be boring; **dar la** ~ **a uno** to annoy sb.

(**c**) (*madera*) lath.

(**d**) (⁑: *dinero*) dough⁑; **estar sin** ~**s, estar en la**(**s**) ~(**s**) (*And, CAm*) to be penniless, be broke*.

(**e**) (*Aut*⁑) **un cuatro** ~**s** an old banger⁑.

(**f**) (*LAm**: *persona*) drag.

latazo* *nm* nuisance, bore, bind*.

latear* [1a] *vi* (*LAm*) (**a**) (*dar la lata*) to be a nuisance, be annoying. (**b**) (*hablar*) to talk a lot, chatter away pointlessly. (**c**) (*LAm**) to pet*.

lateazo* *nm* (*LAm*) petting*.

latente *adj* (**a**) (*gen*) latent. (**b**) (*LAm*: *vivo*) alive, intense, vigorous; *memoria* fresh, alive.

lateral 1 *adj* lateral, side (*atr*). **2** *nm* (**a**) (*Teat*) wings, side of the stage. (**b**) (*Dep*) wing(er).

lateralmente *adv* laterally; sideways.

latería *nf* (*CAm*) tinplate; (*Carib, Cono Sur*) tinsmith's workshop; tinworks.

laterío *nm* (*Méx*) tinned goods, canned goods.

latero *nm* (*LAm*) (**a**) (*Téc*) tinsmith. (**b**) (*) bore, drag.

látex *nm* latex.

latido *nm* (**a**) (*de corazón*) beat, beating; throb, throbbing; palpitation. (**b**) (*de perro*) bark, yelp.

latifundio *nm* large estate.

latifundista *nmf* (*LAm*) important landowner, owner of a large estate.

latigazo *nm* (**a**) (*golpe*) lash; (*chasquido*) crack (of a whip). (**b**) (*fig*: *reprimenda*) harsh reproof; verbal lashing. (**c**) (*: *trago*) swig*, swallow. (**d**) **dar un** ~⁂ to have a screw⁂.

látigo *nm* (**a**) whip; (*And, CAm*: *latigazo*) crack (of a whip). (**b**) (*Cono Sur*: *Dep*) finishing post, finishing line; **salir al** ~ to complete a task. (**c**) (*And, Cono Sur*: *jinete*) horseman, rider.

latigudo *adj* (*LAm*) leathery.

latigueada *nf* (*And, CAm, Cono Sur*) whipping, thrashing.

latiguear [1a] *vt* (*And, CAm, Cono Sur*) to whip, thrash.

latiguera *nf* (*And*) whipping, thrashing.

latiguillo *nm* cliché, overworked phrase, well-worn maxim.

latín *nm* (**a**) (*Ling*) Latin; **bajo** ~ Low Latin; ~ **clásico**

Classical Latin; ~ **tardío** Late Latin; ~ **vulgar** Vulgar Latin; **saber (mucho) ~*** to be pretty sharp. (**b**) **latines** Latin tags.
latinajo *nm* dog Latin, bad Latin; **~s** Latin tags.
latinidad *nf* latinity.
latinismo *nm* latinism.
latinista *nmf* latinist.
latinización *nf* latinization.
latinizar [1f] *vti* to latinize.
latino 1 *adj* Latin; (*LAm*) Latin-American. **2** *nm*, **latina** *nf* Latin; (*LAm*) Latin-American; **te cantan los cinco ~s‡** your feet smell.
Latinoamérica *nf* Latin America.
latinoamericano, -a *adj, nm/f* Latin-American.
latir [3a] **1** *vt* (*And, Méx**) **me late que todo saldrá bien** something tells me that everything will turn out all right. **2** *vi* (**a**) (*corazón*) to beat, throb, palpitate. (**b**) (*perro*) to bark, yelp.
latitud *nf* (*Geog y fig*) latitude; (*extensión*) breadth; (*área*) area, extent.
latitudinal *adj* latitudinal.
LATN *nf* (*Paraguay Aer*) *abr de* **Líneas Aéreas de Transporte Nacional.**
lato *adj* broad, wide, extensive; *sentido* broad.
latón *nm* (**a**) (*metal*) brass. (**b**) (*Cono Sur*) big tin, large tin container; (*And*: *balde*) tin bucket.
latoso* 1 *adj* annoying, tiresome; boring. **2** *nm*, **latosa** *nf* bore, drag.
latrocinio *nm* robbery, theft.
Latvia *nf* Latvia.
latvio, -a 1 *adj, nm/f* Latvian. **2** *nm* (*Ling*) Latvian, Lettish.
LAU *nf* (**a**) (*Esp Jur*) *abr de* **Ley de Autonomía Universitaria.** (**b**) (*Esp Jur*) *abr de* **Ley de Arrendamientos Urbanos.**
lauca *nf* (*Cono Sur*) baldness, loss of hair.
laucadura *nf* (*Cono Sur*) baldness.
laucar [1g] *vt* (*Cono Sur*) to fleece, shear, remove the hair (*o* wool) from.
lauco *adj* (*Cono Sur*) bald, hairless.
laucha *nf* (**a**) (*Cono Sur*) (*Zool*) mouse; (*: *flacón*) weed*; (‡: *viejo verde*) dirty old man. (**b**) (*And*) expert; **ser una ~, ser una lauchita** (*Cono Sur*) to be very sharp, be quick; **aguaitar la ~, catear la ~** (*Cono Sur**) to bide one's time.
laúd *nm* (*Mús*) lute.
laudable *adj* laudable, praiseworthy.
laudablemente *adv* laudably, in a praiseworthy way.
láudano *nm* laudanum.
laudatorio *adj* laudatory.
laudo *nm* (*Jur*) award, decision, finding; arbitration (award); ~ **de obligado cumplimiento** binding decision.
laureado 1 *adj persona* honoured, distinguished, famous; *obra* prize-winning. **2** *nm*, **laureada** *nf* laureate; (*premiado*) prizewinner.
laurear [1a] *vt* to crown with laurel; (*fig*) to honour, reward.
laurel *nm* laurel; (*fig*) laurels; (*premio*) honour, reward; (**hojas de**) ~ (*Culin*) bay (leaves); ~ **cerezo** cherry-laurel; **descansar** (*o* **dormirse**) **sobre sus ~es** to rest on one's laurels.
laurencio *nm* (*Quím*) lawrencium.
lauréola *nf* (**a**) (*gen*) laurel wreath, crown of laurel; halo. (**b**) (*Bot*) daphne.
lauro *nm* laurel; (*fig*) laurels; glory, fame.
Lausana *nf* Lausanne.
lava¹ *nf* (*Geol*) lava.
lava² *nf* (*Min*) washing; **camisa de ~ y pon** drip-dry shirt.
lavable *adj* washable.
lavabo *nm* (**a**) (*jofaina*) washbasin; washstand. (**b**) (*retrete*) lavatory, toilet (*Brit*), washroom (*US*).
lavacara *nf* (*And*) washbasin.
lavacaras* *nmf invar* toady, creep‡.
lavada *nf* (*LAm*) wash, washing.
lavadero *nm* (**a**) (*lavandería*) laundry, wash-house; (*de río*) washing place; (*Cono Sur*: *de casa*) utility room. (**b**) (*LAm*) gold-bearing sands (*in river*).
lavado *nm* (**a**) (*acto*) wash, washing; ~ **de bonos** bond-washing; ~ **de cabeza** shampoo; ~ **de cara** (*fig*) clean-up; facelift; ~ **de cerebro** brainwashing; **campaña de ~ de imagen** image-saving campaign; ~ **en seco** dry cleaning; **le hicieron un ~ de estómago** he had his stomach pumped. (**b**) (*ropa*) wash, laundry. (**c**) (*Arte*) wash.
lavador *nm* (**a**) (*Cono Sur*: *fregadero*) washbasin. (**b**) (*Cono Sur*: *excusado*) lavatory, toilet (*Brit*), washroom (*US*).
lavadora *nf* (**a**) (*de ropa*) washing machine; ~ **de coches** car-wash; ~ **de platos** dish-washer. (**b**) (*And*: *persona*) laundress, washerwoman.
lavadura *nf* (**a**) (*acto*) washing. (**b**) (*agua*) dirty water.
lavafrutas *nm invar* finger bowl.
lavagallos *nm* (*And, Carib*) firewater.
lavaje *nm* (*Cono Sur*) (**a**) = **lavadura.** (**b**) (*Med*) enema.
lavaluneta *nm* rear window washer.
lavamanos *nm invar* washbasin.
lavanda *nf* (*Bot*) lavender; (*agua*) lavender water.
lavandera *nf* (**a**) laundress, washerwoman. (**b**) (*Orn*) wagtail.
lavandería *nf* laundry; ~ **automática** launderette.
lavandero *nm* launderer, laundryman.
lavandina *nf* (*Cono Sur*) bleach.
lavándula *nf* lavender.
lavaojos *nm invar* eye bath.
lavaplatos *nm invar* (**a**) (*aparato*) dishwasher. (**b**) (*persona*) dishwasher, washer-up. (**c**) (*Cono Sur, Méx*: *fregadero*) sink.
lavar [1a] **1** *vt* (**a**) to wash; (*) *dinero* to launder*; ~ **y marcar** *pelo* to shampoo and set; **tejanos lavados a la piedra** stonewashed jeans; ~ **en seco** to dry-clean; ~ **la cabeza** to wash one's hair.
(**b**) (*fig*) to wipe away; to wipe out.
2 lavarse *vr* to wash, have a wash; ~ **las manos** to wash one's hands; (*fig*) to wash one's hands of it.
lavarropas *nm invar* washing machine.
lavativa *nf* (**a**) (*Med*) enema. (**b**) (*fig*) nuisance, bother, bore.
lavatorio *nm* (**a**) washstand. (**b**) (*LAm*) lavatory, washroom (*US*). (**c**) (*Med*) lotion.
lavavajillas *nm invar* (*aparato*) dishwasher; (*líquido*) washing-up liquid.
lavazas *nfpl* dishwater, dirty water, slops.
lavoteo* *nm* quick wash, cat-lick*.
laxante *adj, nm* laxative.
laxar [1a] *vt* to ease, relax, slacken; *vientre* to loosen.
laxativo *adj* laxative.
laxitud *nf* laxity, slackness.
laxo *adj* lax, slack.
laya *nf* (**a**) (*pala*) spade; ~ **de puntas** (garden) fork. (**b**) (*liter*) kind, sort; **de esta ~** of this kind.
lazada *nf* bow, knot.
lazar [1f] **1** *vt* to lasso, rope. **2** *vi* (*CAm*: *tren*) to connect.
lazareto *nm* (*Hist*) leper hospital, isolation hospital.
lazariento *adj* (*CAm, Cono Sur, Méx*) leprous.
lazarillo *nm* blind man's guide.
lazarino 1 *adj* leprous. **2** *nm*, **lazarina** *nf* leper.
Lázaro *nm* Lazarus.
lazo *nm* (**a**) (*gen*) bow, knot; loop; (*Agr*) lasso, lariat; ~ **corredizo** slipknot; ~ **de zapato** bootlace.
(**b**) (*Caza*) snare, trap (*t fig*); **caer en el ~** to fall into the trap; **tender un ~ a uno** to set a trap for sb.
(**c**) (*Aut*) bend, loop.
(**d**) (*fig*: *vínculo*) link, bond, tie; **los ~s culturales entre A y B** cultural ties between A and B; **los ~s familiares** the family bond, the ties of blood.
LBE *nf* (*Esp Jur*) *abr de* **Ley Básica de Empleo.**
L/C *nf abr de* **Letra de Crédito** bill of exchange, B/E.
Lda., Ldo. *abr de* **Licenciada, Licenciado.**
le *pron pers* (**a**) (*ac*) him; (*Vd*) you; **no le veo** I don't see him; **¿le ayudo?** shall I help you?
(**b**) (*dativo*) (to) him, (to) her, (to) it; (*Vd*) (to) you; **le hablé** I spoke to him, I spoke to her; **quiero darle esto** I want to give you this; **le he comprado esto** I bought this for you; **uno de los mejores papeles que le hayamos visto** one of the best performances we have seen from him; **no se le conoce otra obra** no other work of his is known.
lea‡ *nf* tart‡, whore.
leal *adj* loyal, faithful, trustworthy; *competencia* fair.
lealmente *adv* loyally, faithfully.
lealtad *nf* loyalty, fidelity; trustworthiness; ~ **de marca** brand loyalty, loyalty to a brand.
leandra‡ *nf* one peseta.
Leandro *nm* Leander.
lebrato *nm* leveret.
lebrel *nm* greyhound.
lebrillo *nm* earthenware bowl.
lebrón* *adj* (*Méx*) (**a**) (*listo*) sharp, wide-awake. (**b**) (*arrogante*) boastful, insolent. (**c**) (*taimado*) sly; evil-minded.
LEC [lek] *nf* (*Esp Jur*) *abr de* **Ley de Enjuiciamiento Civil.**
lección *nf* (**a**) lesson (*t Ecl*); (*Escuela*) lesson, class, (*Univ*) lecture, class; (*fig*) warning, example; ~ **magistral** (*Mús*)

master class; ~ **particular** private lesson; ~ **práctica** object-lesson (*de* in); **dar lecciones** to teach, give lessons; **dar una ~ a uno** (*fig*) to teach sb a lesson; **saberse la ~*** to know what the score is*; **¡que te sirva de ~!** let that be a lesson to you!; **tomar ~** to have a lesson.
(**b**) (*Liter*: *de MS etc*) reading.
leco‡ *adj* (*Méx*) nuts‡, round the bend‡.
lectivo *adj* school (*atr*); *V* **año, día** *etc.*
lectoescritura *nf* reading and writing.
lector 1 *adj*: **el público ~** the reading public. **2** *nm*, **lectora** *nf* (**a**) (*lit*) reader; ~ **de cartas** card-reader, fortune-teller. (**b**) (*Colegio, Univ*) conversation assistant. **3** *nm* (*aparato*) reader; ~ **de fichas** card reader; ~ **óptico** optical reader, optical scanner; ~ **de tarjeta magnética** magnetic card reader.
lectorado *nm* (**a**) (*de periódico etc*) readership. (**b**) (*Univ*) post of *lector*.
lectura *nf* reading; reading matter; (*Inform*) read-out; **una persona de mucha ~** a well-read person; ~ **labial** lip-reading; ~ **de marcas** (*Inform*) mark sensing; ~ **del pensamiento** mind-reading; **dar ~ a** to read (publicly), deliver.
lecha *nf* milt, (soft) roe.
lechada *nf* (**a**) (*cal*) whitewash; (*pasta*) paste; grout; (*pulpa*) pulp. (**b**) (*LAm*) milking. (**c**) (**) spunk**, semen.
lechal 1 *adj* sucking; **cordero ~** baby lamb, young lamb. **2** *nm* milk (*fig*), milky juice.
lechar [1a] *vt* (**a**) (*LAm*: *ordeñar*) to milk; (*And, CAm*: *amamantar*) to suckle. (**b**) (*CAm, Méx**: *blanquear*) to whitewash.
lechazo[1] *nm* young lamb.
lechazo[2]**‡** *nm* (*golpe*) bash*, swipe; (*choque*) bash*, bang.
leche *nf* (**a**) (*gen*) milk; ~ **completa,** ~ **entera** unskimmed milk; ~ **condensada** condensed milk; ~ **descremada,** ~ **desnatada** skim(med) milk; ~ **sin desnatar** (*Esp*) whole milk; ~ **de larga duración,** ~ **de larga vida** long-life milk; ~ **evaporada** evaporated milk; ~ **de magnesia** milk of magnesia; ~ **materna** mother's milk; ~ **merengada** milk-shake flavoured with cinnamon; ~ **paste(u)rizada** pasteurized milk; ~ **en polvo** powdered milk; ~ **semidesnatada** semi-skimmed milk; **estar con** (*o* **tener**) **la ~ en los labios** (*fig*) to be young and inexperienced, be wet behind the ears.
(**b**) (*Bot*) milk, milky juice; (*And*) rubber; (*Carib*) rubber tree.
(**c**) (**: *semen*) semen, spunk**; **un tío de mala ~** a nasty sort, an evil person; a disagreeable chap*; **estar de mala ~** to feel pissed off**, be in a foul temper; **poner a uno de mala ~** to annoy sb, make sb cross; **tener mala ~** to be vindictive, be nasty; **hay mucha mala ~ entre ellos** there's a lot of bad blood between them; **aquí hay mucha mala ~** there's a lot of ill-feeling here.
(**d**) (*: *suerte*) good luck; **estar con ~, estar de ~, tener ~** to be lucky; **¡qué ~ tienes!** you lucky devil!
(**e**) (*: *golpe*) bash*, swipe; (*choque*) bash*, bang; **darse una ~** (*fig*) to come a cropper*.
(**f**) (*: *molestia*) bore, pain*; **¡es la ~!** it's such a pain!
(**g**) (‡: *otras locuciones*) **¡~!** hell!, hell's teeth!; **¡~s!** no way!*, get away!; **¿qué ~s quieres?** what the hell do you want?; **muchos vinos** (*etc*) **y mucha ~** lots of wines (*etc*) and all that jazz*; **¡qué coche ni qué ~!** car my foot!*; **no entiende ni ~s** he doesn't understand a bloody thing‡; **echar ~s** to go up the wall*; **salió echando** (*o* **cagando****) **~s** he went like a bat out of hell*; **ir a toda ~** to scorch along*; **cantando es la ~** when she sings she's a bloody marvel‡, (*pey*) when she sings she's bloody awful‡.
lecheada *nf* (*Cono Sur*) = **lechada.**
lechear [1a] *vt* (*LAm*) to milk.
lechecillas *nfpl* sweetbreads.
lechera *nf* (**a**) (*persona*) milkmaid, dairymaid. (**b**) (*recipiente*) milk can, milk churn. (**c**) (*LAm*) cow. (**d**) (*) police-car.
lechería *nf* (**a**) (*edificio*) dairy, creamery; (*And, Cono Sur*) milking parlour. (**b**) (*Cono Sur*: *vacas*) cows, herd. (**c**) (*And, Méx*: *tacañería*) meanness.
lecherita *nf* milk jug.
lechero 1 *adj* (**a**) (*gen*) milk (*atr*); dairy (*atr*); **ganado ~** dairy herd; **producción lechera** milk production; *V* **vaca.**
(**b**) (*LAm*: *con suerte*) lucky.
(**c**) (*Méx**: *tacaño*) mean, stingy.
(**d**) (*Carib*: *codicioso*) greedy, grasping.
2 *nm* (*de granja*) dairyman; (*repartidor*) milkman.
lechigada *nf* litter, brood; (*fig*) gang.
lecho *nm* (**a**) (*cama*) bed; couch; (*Agr*) bedding; ~ **de enfermo** sickbed; ~ **de muerte,** ~ **mortuorio** deathbed; ~ **de rosas** (*fig*) bed of roses. (**b**) (*de río*) bed; bottom, floor; (*Geol*) layer; ~ **del mar,** ~ **marino** sea-bed; ~ **de roca** bed-rock.
lechón *nm* (**a**) (*lit*) piglet, sucking-pig. (**b**) (*fig*) pig, filthy person.
lechona *nf* (**a**) (*lit*) sow. (**b**) (*fig*) pig, sow; slob*.
lechoncillo *nm* piglet, sucking-pig.
lechosa *nf* (*LAm*) papaya (*fruit*).
lechosidad *nf* milkiness.
lechoso *adj* (**a**) *líquido* milky. (**b**) (‡: *suertudo*) jammy‡, lucky.
lechucear [1a] *vi* (*And*) to be on night duty.
lechucero *nm* (*And*) (**a**) (*obrero*) nightshift worker; (*taxista*) night driver. (**b**) (*taxi*) night taxi.
lechudo *adj* (*LAm*) lucky.
lechuga *nf* (**a**) (*Bot*) lettuce; ~ **Cos,** ~ **francesa,** ~ **orejona** (*Méx*) cos lettuce. (**b**) (*Cos*) frill, flounce. (**c**) (*Esp*‡) 1000-peseta note; (*Carib*) banknote. (**d**) (*: *euf*) = **leche** (**c**).
lechuguilla *nf* (*Cos*) frill, flounce, ruff.
lechuguino *nm* (**a**) (*Bot*) young lettuce. (**b**) (‡) toff*, dude (*US*).
lechuza *nf* (**a**) (*Orn*) owl; ~ **común** barn owl. (**b**) (*Cono Sur, Méx*: *albino*) albino, light blond(e). (**c**) (*Carib, Méx*: *puta*) whore.
lechuzo* *nm* (**a**) (*feo*) ugly devil*. (**b**) (*lerdo*) dimwit*.
leer [2e] *vti* to read; ~ **en la boca** to lip-read; ~ **entre líneas** to read between the lines; ~ **la mano a uno** to read sb's palm; **'al que leyere'** 'to the reader'.
lefa** *nf* spunk**, semen.
lega *nf* lay sister.
legación *nf* legation.
legado *nm* (**a**) (*enviado*) legate. (**b**) (*Jur*) legacy, bequest.
legajar *vt* (*And, Cono Sur, Méx*) to file.
legajo *nm* file, bundle (of papers).
legal *adj* (**a**) (*gen*) legal, lawful; *hora* standard. (**b**) *persona* trustworthy, truthful; loyal, reliable; (*Jur*) clean*, with no police record; **tío ~*** good bloke‡. (**c**) (*And**: *excelente*) fine, marvellous.
legalidad *nf* legality, lawfulness.
legalista *adj* legalistic.
legalización *nf* legalization; authentication.
legalizar [1f] *vt* to legalize, make lawful; *documento* to authenticate.
legalmente *adv* legally, lawfully.
légamo *nm* slime, mud, ooze; (*arcilla*) clay.
legamoso *adj* slimy, oozy; clayey.
legaña *nf* rheum, sleep.
legañoso *adj* bleary.
legar [1h] *vt* to bequeath (*t Jur, fig*), leave (*a* to).
legatario, -a *nm/f* legatee.
legendario *adj* legendary.
legía* *nm* legionnaire, member of the Spanish Foreign Legion.
legibilidad *nf* legibility.
legible *adj* legible; ~ **por máquina** machine-readable.
legiblemente *adv* legibly.
legión *nf* legion; **L~ Extranjera** Foreign Legion; **la L~** (*esp*) the Spanish Foreign Legion; **son ~** they are legion; **el autor ~** (*Liter*) the author whose name is legion, the collectivity of anonymous authors (*of ballads etc*).
legionario 1 *adj* legionary. **2** *nm* legionary; legionnaire.
legionella *nf* legionnaire's disease.
legislación *nf* legislation.
legislador(a) *nm/f* legislator, lawmaker.
legislar [1a] *vi* to legislate.
legislativas *nfpl* parliamentary elections.
legislativo *adj* legislative.
legislatura *nf* (*Jur*) term; (*Pol*) session; period of office; **agotar la ~** to serve out one's term of office; (*LAm*: *cuerpo*) legislature, legislative body.
legista 1 *nmf* jurist, legist. **2** *adj* (*LAm*): **médico ~** forensic expert, criminal pathologist.
legítima* *nf*: **la ~** my better half.
legitimación *nf* legitimation.
legítimamente *adv* legitimately, rightfully; justly; genuinely.
legitimar [1a] **1** *vt* to legitimize; to legalize. **2 legitimarse** *vr* to establish one's identity; to establish one's title (*o* claim *etc*); **considerarse legitimado para** + *infin* to consider o.s. entitled to + *infin*.
legitimidad *nf* legitimacy; justice; authenticity.
legitimista *adj, nmf* royalist.
legítimo *adj* (*gen*) legitimate, rightful; just; (*auténtico*)

genuine, authentic, real; (*Aut*) *repuestos* genuine.
lego **1** *adj* (**a**) (*Ecl*) lay; secular. (**b**) (*fig*) ignorant, uninformed. **2** *nm* layman; lay brother; (*fig*) layman; **los ~s** the laity.
legón *nm* hoe.
legua *nf* league; **eso se ve** (*o* **se nota**) **a la ~** you can tell it a mile away.
leguaje *nm* (**a**) (*CAm*: *distancia*) distance in leagues. (**b**) (*And Parl*: *gastos de viaje*) travelling expenses.
leguleyo *nm* pettifogging lawyer.
legumbre *nf* vegetable.
leguminosa *nf* (*Bot*) pulse.
leguminoso *adj* leguminous.
leíble *adj* legible.
Leida, Leide *nm* Leyden.
leída *nf* (*LAm*) reading; **de una ~** in one reading, at one go; **dar una ~ a*** to read over.
leído *adj* (*iró*) *persona* well-read; **muy ~ (y escribido)** pedantic, pretentious.
leísmo *nm use of* **le** *instead of* **lo** *and* **la** (*direct objects*).
leísta **1** *adj that uses* **le** *instead of* **lo** *and* **la** (*direct objects*). **2** *nmf user of* **le** *instead of* **lo** *and* **la.**
lejanía *nf* (*distancia*) distance, remoteness; (*lugar*) remote place.
lejano *adj* distant, remote, far-off.
Lejano Oriente *nm* Far East.
lejas *adj pl*: **de ~ tierras** of (*o* from) some distant land.
lejía[1] *nf* (**a**) (*gen*) bleach; lye. (**b**) (*) dressing-down*.
lejía[2] *nm* = **legía**.
lejos **1** *adv* far, far away, far off; **a lo ~** in the distance, far off; **de ~, desde ~** from afar, from a long way off; **más ~** further (off); **en eso no andaba muy ~** he wasn't far off the mark; **está muy ~** it's a long way (away); **¿está ~?** is it far?; **eso queda demasiado ~** that's too far (away); **ir ~** to go far (*t fig*); **para no ir más ~** (*fig*), **sin ir más ~** to take an obvious example; **eso viene de ~** (*fig*) that's been going on for a long time.
2 ~ de *prep* far from; **estoy muy ~ de pensar que ...** I am very far from thinking that ...
3 *nm* distant view; appearance from a distance; glimpse; (*Arte*) background; **tiene buen ~** it looks all right at a distance.
lejura *nf* (*And*) distance; **~s** (*Cono Sur*) remote place, remote area.
lele *adj* (*CAm, Cono Sur*), **lelo** *adj* silly, stupid; **quedarse ~** to be stunned.
lema *nm* motto, device; theme; (*Pol etc*) slogan, watchword.
lem(m)ing ['lemin] *nm* lemming.
lempira *nm* lempira (*Honduran unit of currency*).
lempo **1** *adj* (*And*) big, large. **2** *nm* (**a**) (*And*) bit, piece. (**b**) **un ~ de caballo** (*And*) a big horse.
lémur *nm* lemur.
lencería *nf* (**a**) (*telas*) linen, drapery; (*ropa interior*) lingerie. (**b**) (*tienda*) draper's (shop). (**c**) (*armario*) linen cupboard.
lencero, -a *nm/f* draper.
lendakari *nm* head of the Basque autonomous government.
lendroso *adj* lousy, infested with lice.
lengón *adj* (*And*) = **lenguón.**
lengua *nf* (**a**) (*Anat y fig*) tongue; **mala ~, ~ larga** (*LAm*), **~ de trapo** (*LAm*), **~ viperina** gossip; **según las malas ~s** ... according to gossip ...; **de ~ en ~** from mouth to mouth; **andar en ~s** to be the talk of the town; **atar la ~ a uno** (*fig*) to silence sb; **beber con la ~** to lap up; **buscar la ~ a uno** to pick a quarrel with sb; **dar a la ~** to chatter, talk too much; **darse la ~*** to kiss passionately; **estar con la ~ fuera*** to be dead beat, be exhausted; **hacerse ~s de** to praise to the skies, rave about; **irse de la ~, írsele a uno la ~** to talk too much; to let the cat out of the bag; **morderse la ~** to hold one's tongue; to keep sth back; **no morderse la ~** not to mince one's words, not to pull one's punches; **nacer con la ~ fuera** to be born idle; **retener la ~** to hold one's tongue; **sacar la ~ a uno** to poke one's tongue out at sb; **soltar la ~*** to spill the beans*; **tener mucha ~*** to be cheeky*; **tirar de la ~ a uno** to draw sb out, make sb talk; to provoke sb; **se le trabó la ~** he began to stammer.
(**b**) (*de campana*) clapper.
(**c**) **~ de tierra** (*Geog*) spit of land, tongue of land.
(**d**) (*Ling*) language, tongue; (*Esp Escol*) Spanish language (as a school subject); **~ franca** lingua franca; **~ madre** parent language; **~ materna** mother tongue; first language; **~ minoritaria** minority language; **~ moderna** modern language; **~ muerta** dead language; **~ viva** living language; **hablar en ~** (*And*) to speak Quichua.
lenguado *nm* sole, dab.
lenguaje *nm* (**a**) (*gen*) language; (faculty of) speech.
(**b**) (*forma de hablar*) idiom, parlance, (mode of) speech; style; **~ comercial** business language; **~ del cuerpo** body-language; **~ de gestos, ~ de las manos** sign language; **~ periodístico** newspaper language, journalese; **~ vulgar** common speech, ordinary speech; **en ~ llano** in plain English (*etc*).
(**c**) (*Liter*) style, diction.
(**d**) (*Inform*) language; **~ de alto nivel** high-level language; **~ de bajo nivel** low-level language; **~ ensamblador** assembly language; **~ fuente** source language; **~ informático, ~ máquina** computer language; **~ objeto** target language; **~ de programación** program(m)ing language.
lenguaraz *adj* talkative; (*pey*) foul-mouthed.
lenguaz *adj* garrulous.
lengüeta *nf* (**a**) (*gen*) tab, small tongue; (*Téc, Mús, de zapato*) tongue; (*Anat*) epiglottis; (*de balanza etc*) needle, pointer; (*de flecha*) barb.
(**b**) (*LAm*) (*hablador*) chatterbox; (*chismoso*) gossip.
(**c**) (*LAm*: *cortapapeles*) paper knife.
(**d**) (*LAm Cos*) fringe of a petticoat.
lengüetada *nf* lick.
lengüetazo *nm* (*LAm*) lick.
lengüetear [1a] **1** *vt* (*LAm*) to lick. **2** *vi* (*LAm*) to stick one's tongue out; (*Carib*) to jabber, chatter.
lengüeterías *nfpl* (*LAm*) gossip, tittle-tattle.
lengüetero *adj* (*Carib*) (*hablador*) garrulous; (*chismoso*) gossiping.
lengüicorto* *adj* shy, timid.
lengüilargo *adj*, **lengüisucio** *adj* (*Carib*) foul-mouthed.
lenguón (*LAm*) **1** *adj* (*hablador*) garrulous; (*franco*) outspoken; (*chismoso*) gossiping. **2** *nm*, **lenguona** *nf* gossip, talebearer.
lenidad *nf* lenience, softness.
Lenin *nm* Lenin.
Leningrado *nm* Leningrad.
leninismo *nm* Leninism.
leninista *adj, nmf* Leninist.
lenitivo **1** *adj* lenitive. **2** *nm* lenitive, palliative.
lenocinio *nm* pandering, procuring; **(casa de) ~** brothel.
lentamente *adv* slowly.
lente *nm o f* lens; eyeglass; **~s** (*Hist, t Carib*) spectacles; **~ de aumento** magnifying glass; **~s de contacto, ~s corneales** contact lenses; **~ de gran ángulo, ~ granangular** wide-angle lens; **~ zoom** zoom-lens.
lenteja *nf* lentil; **ganarse las ~s** to earn one's bread and butter; **~s** lentil soup.
lentejuela *nf* spangle, sequin.
lentificar [1g] **1** *vt* to slow down. **2** **lentificarse** *vr* to slow down.
lentillas *nfpl* contact lenses.
lentitud *nf* slowness; **con ~** slowly.
lento *adj* slow.
lentorro* *adj* sluggish, slow.
leña *nf* (**a**) (*lit*) firewood; sticks, kindling; **~ de oveja** (*Cono Sur*) sheep droppings; **echar ~ al fuego** to add fuel to the flames; **llevar ~ al monte** to carry coals to Newcastle.
(**b**) (*) thrashing; (*fig*) stick, punishment; **cargar de ~, dar ~ a, hartar de ~** to lay it on, thrash; **repartir ~** to dish out the punishment; **trincar ~** to sweat blood.
leñador *nm* woodcutter, woodman.
leñar [1a] *vt* (*Cono Sur, Méx*), **leñatear** [1a] *vt* (*And*) to make into firewood, cut up for firewood.
leñateo *nm* (*And, CAm*) woodpile.
leñatero *nm* (*Cono Sur*) woodcutter, woodman.
leñazo *nm* (*golpe*) bash*; blow with a stick; (*choque*) collision, bash*.
leñe *nm* (*euf*) = **leche** (**c**).
leñera *nf* woodshed.
leñero *nm* (**a**) (*comerciante*) dealer in wood. (**b**) (*depósito*) woodshed.
leño *nm* (**a**) (*tronco*) log; (*madera*) timber, wood, piece of wood; **hacer ~ del árbol caído** to kick sb when he's down. (**b**) (*) blockhead.
leñoso *adj* woody.
Leo *nm* (*Zodíaco*) Leo.
León *nm* (**a**) (*nombre*) Leon, Leo. (**b**) (*Geog*) León.
león *nm* (**a**) (*Zool*) lion (*t fig*); (*LAm*) puma; **L~** (*Zodíaco*) Leo; **~ marino** sea lion; **estar hecho un ~** to be furious; **ponerse como un ~** to get furious. (**b**) **leones** (**‡**: *dados*) loaded dice.

leona *nf* (**a**) (*Zool*) lioness. (**b**) (*Cono Sur*) confusion, mess, mix-up. (**c**) (*: *portera*) porter, concierge. (**d**) (‡: *puta*) tart‡.

leonado *adj* tawny.

leonera *nf* (**a**) (*jaula*) lion's cage; (*cueva etc*) lion's den. (**b**) (*: *de juego*) gambling den, dive‡; (*de niños*) glory hole*; (*para hobby*) hideout, hideaway; (*And, Cono Sur: celda*) communal prison cell; (*And*) noisy gathering.

leonés 1 *adj* Leonese; (*LAm*) from León. **2** *nm*, **leonesa** *nf* Leonese; (*LAm*) native (*o* inhabitant) of León. **3** *nm* (*Ling*) Leonese.

leonino *adj* (**a**) (*Poét*) leonine. (**b**) *contrato* one-sided, unfair.

Leonor *nf* Eleanor.

leontina *nf* watch chain.

leopardo *nm* leopard; ~ **cazador** cheetah.

leotardo *nm* (*t* ~**s**) leotard, tights.

Lepe *n*: **ser más tonto que** ~ to be a complete twit*; **ir donde las** ~ (*Cono Sur*) to make a bloomer* (*in calculating*); **saber más que** ~ to be pretty smart, have lots of savoir-faire.

leperada *nf* (*CAm, Méx*) (*en el habla*) coarse remark; (*acto*) dirty trick, rotten thing (to do)*.

lépero* 1 *adj* (**a**) (*CAm, Méx*) rough, uncouth; rude. (**b**) (*And*) **estar** ~ to be broke*. **2** *nm*, **lépera** *nf* low-class person; guttersnipe.

leperusco *adj* (*Méx*) low-class, plebeian; (*pey*) rotten*, villainous.

lepidopterólogo, -a *nm/f* lepidopterist.

lepidópteros *nmpl* lepidoptera, butterflies and moths.

lepisma *nf* silverfish.

leporino *adj* leporine; hare-like; **labio** ~ harelip.

lepra *nf* leprosy; ~ **de montaña** (*LAm*) mountain leprosy, leishmaniasis.

leprosario *nm* (*Méx*), **leprosería** *nf* leper colony.

leproso 1 *adj* leprous. **2** *nm*, **leprosa** *nf* leper.

lerdear [1a] *vi* (*CAm*) to be slow (about doing things), do things unwillingly.

lerdera *nf* (*CAm*) = **lerdez**.

lerdez* *nf*, **lerdeza** *nf* (*CAm*) slowness; heaviness, dullness; slow-wittedness; clumsiness.

lerdo *adj* (*lento*) slow; (*pesado*) heavy, dull; (*de pocas luces*) slow-witted; (*torpe*) clumsy.

lerdura *nf* (*Cono Sur*) = **lerdez**.

lerén* *nm* (*And*) (*tipo*) bloke‡, guy*; (*de baja estatura*) midget.

leridano 1 *adj* of Lérida. **2** *nm*, **leridana** *nf* native (*o* inhabitant) of Lérida; **los ~s** the people of Lérida.

les *pron pers* (**a**) (*ac*) them; (*Vds*) you. (**b**) (*dativo*) (to) them; (*Vds*) (to) you; *para ejemplos de uso, V* **le**.

lesa *adj*: ~ **majestad** lese majesty; **crimen de** ~ **humanidad** crime against humanity; **acción de** ~ **patria** act of treachery to one's country.

lesbiana *nf* lesbian.

lesbianismo *nm* lesbianism.

lésbico *adj* lesbian.

lesbio *adj* lesbian.

lesera* *nf* (*And, Cono Sur: estupidez*) stupidity; (*tonterías*) nonsense.

lesión *nf* wound, lesion; injury (*t fig*); (*Jur*) **lesiones** assault and battery; ~ **cerebral** brain-damage.

lesionado *adj* hurt, injured; *jugador* injured, unfit.

lesionar [1a] **1** *vt* (*dañar*) to hurt, injure; (*herir*) to wound. **2 lesionarse** *vr* to get hurt.

lesividad *nf* harmfulness.

lesivo *adj* harmful, damaging.

lesna *nf* awl.

leso *adj* (**a**) (*herido*) hurt; (*ofendido*) injured, offended. (**b**) (*And, Cono Sur**) simple, stupid; **no está para** ~ (*Cono Sur*) he's not easily taken in; **hacer** ~ **a uno** (*Cono Sur*) to play a trick on sb; **hacerse el** ~ to pretend not to know (*o* notice).

Lesoto *nm* Lesotho.

lesura *nf* (*Cono Sur*) stupidity.

letal *adj* deadly, lethal.

letalidad *nf* deadliness, lethal nature; **la enfermedad tiene una elevada** ~ there is a high death-rate from this disease.

letanía *nf* (*Ecl*) litany; (*fig*) rigmarole; (*lista*) long list; (*recitado*) tedious recitation.

letárgico *adj* lethargic.

letargo *nm* lethargy.

Lete(o) *nm* Lethe.

letón, -ona 1 *adj, nm/f* Latvian. **2** *nm* (*Ling*) Latvian, Lettish.

Letonia *nf* Latvia.

letra *nf* (**a**) (*Tip etc*) letter; ~ **gótica** Gothic script, black letter; ~ **de imprenta** print; ~ **inicial** initial letter; ~ **mayúscula** capital letter; **la** ~ **menuda, la** ~ **pequeña** the small print; ~ **minúscula** small letter; **en ~s de molde** in print; in block letters; ~ **muerta** dead letter; ~ **negrilla** bold type, heavy type; ~ **versal** capital letter; ~ **versalita** small capital; **decir a una las cuatro ~s*** to call a woman a slut.

(**b**) (*fig*) letter, literal meaning; **a la** ~ to the letter; **atarse a la** ~ to stick to the literal meaning.

(**c**) (*escrito*) **~s** piece of writing; **poner unas** (*o* **dos**) **~s a uno** to drop sb a line.

(**d**) (*escritura*) writing, handwriting; ~ **cursiva** cursive writing; **tiene buena** ~ he writes a good hand; **tiene malísima** ~ his writing is shocking.

(**e**) (*Com*) letter, bill, draft; (*plazo*) hire-purchase instalment; ~ **abierta** letter of credit; ~ **aceptada** accepted letter; ~ **bancaria** banker's draft, bank draft; ~ **de cambio** bill (of exchange), bank draft; ~ **del Tesoro** Treasury bill; ~ **a la vista** sight draft; **pagar a** ~ **vista** to pay on sight.

(**f**) (*Mús*) words, lyric.

(**g**) (*fig*) **~s** letters, learning; (*Univ*) Arts; **bellas ~s** belles lettres, literature; **~s humanas** humanities; **primeras ~s** elementary education, three Rs; **~s sagradas** Scripture.

(**h**) (*: *euf*) = **leche** (**f**).

letrado 1 *adj* learned; (*pey*) pedantic; **derecho a la asistencia letrada** right to have a lawyer present. **2** *nm*, **letrada** *nf* (*t* **la letrado**) counsel, legal representative.

letrero *nm* (*anuncio*) sign, notice; (*cartel*) placard, poster; (*Com*) label; (*inscripción*) inscription; (*escrito*) words, (piece of) writing.

letrina *nf* latrine, privy; (*fig*) sewer, sump, filthy place; **el río es una** ~ the river is an open sewer.

letrista *nmf* (*Mús*) lyricist, songwriter.

leucemia *nf* leukaemia.

leucémico, -a *nm/f* person suffering from leukaemia.

leucocito *nm* (*Med*) leucocyte.

leudar [1a] **1** *vt* to leaven. **2 leudarse** *vr* (*pan etc*) to rise.

leva *nf* (**a**) (*Náut*) weighing anchor.

(**b**) (*Mil*) levy.

(**c**) (*Mec*) lever; cam.

(**d**) (*And, CAm: estafa*) trick, swindle, ruse; **bajar la** ~ **a uno** (*And, Cono Sur*) to do sb a mischief; **caer de** ~ (*CAm*) to play the fool; **echar ~s** (*: *And, Méx: jactarse*) to boast; (*And**: *amenazar*) to bluster, utter threats; **encender la** ~ **a uno** (*Carib**) to give sb a good hiding*.

(**e**) **ponerse la** ~ (*And**) (*Escol*) to play truant; (*del trabajo*) to stay away from work; (*largarse*) to beat it*.

levadizo *adj* that can be raised; **puente** ~ drawbridge.

levado *nm* raising; **sistema de** ~ raising mechanism.

levadura *nf* (**a**) yeast, leaven; ~ **de cerveza** brewer's yeast; ~ **de panadero** baker's yeast; ~ **en polvo** baking powder. (**b**) (*: *euf*) **mala** ~ = **mala leche**.

levantador *nm*: ~ **de pesas** weight-lifter.

levantamiento *nm* (**a**) (*lit*) raising, lifting; elevation; ~ **del cadáver** removal of the body; ~ **cartográfico** topographical survey, mapping; ~ **de pesas** weight-lifting. (**b**) (*Pol*) rising, revolt.

levantamuertos* *nm invar* (*And Culin*) vegetable broth.

levantar [1a] **1** *vt* (**a**) (*gen*) to raise, lift (up); (*elevar*) to elevate; *objeto caído* to raise up, stand up; (*enderezar*) to straighten; (*recoger*) to pick up; (*Dep*) *pesa* to lift; (*Arquit*) to raise, build, erect; (*Med*) *bollo* to raise; *ejército* to raise, recruit; *censo* to take; *polvo* to raise; *caza* to flush, put up; *casa* to move, remove; *plano* to make, draw up; *sesión* to adjourn; *asedio* to raise; *tono, voz* to raise; **levantó la mano** he raised his hand, he put up his hand; ~ **los ojos** to look up, raise one's eyes; **¡no levantes la voz!** keep your voice down!; **fue imposible ~lo** it was impossible to lift it.

(**b**) *mesa, mantel* to clear away; *campamento* to strike; *tienda* to take down.

(**c**) *prohibición* to raise, lift.

(**d**) (*fig*) *persona* to uplift, hearten, cheer up; *ánimos* to raise; (*Pol*) to rouse, stir up.

(**e**) (*) *dinero* to make, earn.

(**f**) (*And*‡) to nick‡, arrest.

(**g**) (*Cono Sur**) *amante* to pick up*.

2 *vi*: **no levanta del suelo más de 1,40 m** she stands only 1.40 metres.

3 levantarse *vr* (**a**) (*gen*) to rise; (*incorporarse*) to get up, stand up, rise to one's feet; to straighten up; ~ (**de la**

cama) to get up, get out of bed; ~ **en el pie izquierdo** (*And**) to get out of bed on the wrong side.
(**b**) (*niebla*) to lift; (*viento etc*) to rise.
(**c**) (*destacarse etc*) to stand up, stick up, stand out; **se levanta por encima de los demás edificios** it stands up higher than the other buildings.
(**d**) (*sesión*) to be adjourned; to conclude, be concluded.
(**e**) ~ **con algo** to make off with sth.
(**f**) (*Pol*) to rise, revolt, rebel.

levantaválvulas *nm invar* valve tappet.
Levante *nm* (**a**) (*gen*) Levant; **el** ~ the Levant, the (Near) East. (**b**) (*España*) east coast, south-east coast.
levante[1] *nm* (*Geog*) (**a**) (*este*) east. (**b**) (*viento*) east wind.
levante[2] *nm* (**a**) (*Carib Pol*) uprising.
(**b**) (*Carib*: *arreo*) driving of cattle.
(**c**) (*And*: *arrogancia*) arrogance, haughtiness.
(**d**) **dar** (*o* **pegar**) **un** ~ **a uno** (*Cono Sur**) to give sb a dressing-down*.
(**e**) (*Cono Sur**: *encuentro*) pick-up*; **hacer un** ~ **a uno** to pick sb up*.
(**f**) **hacer un** ~ (*Carib**) to fall in love.
levantino 1 *adj* (**a**) Levantine.
(**b**) (*de España*) of the eastern coast (*o* provinces *etc*) of Spain.
2 *nm*, **levantina** *nf* (**a**) (*gen*) Levantine.
(**b**) (*de España*) native (*o* inhabitant) of the eastern provinces of Spain; **los ~s** the people of the east of Spain.
levantisco *adj* restless, turbulent.
levar [1a] **1** *vt*: ~ **anclas** to weigh anchor. **2 levarse** *vr* to weigh anchor, set sail.
leve *adj* (*gen*) light; (*mínimo*) slight; (*poco importante*) trivial, small, unimportant; **una herida** ~ a slight wound; **sin el más** ~ **optimismo** without the slightest optimism.
levedad *nf* lightness; (*fig*) levity.
levemente *adv* lightly; slightly.
leviatán *nm* leviathan.
levita[1] *nf* frock coat.
levita[2] *nm* Levite.
levitación *nf* levitation.
levitar [1a] *vi* to levitate.
Levítico *nm* Leviticus.
lexema *nm* lexeme.
lexicalizar [1f] *vt* to lexicalize.
léxico 1 *adj* lexical. **2** *nm* lexicon, dictionary; vocabulary; word list.
lexicografía *nf* lexicography.
lexicográfico *adj* lexicographical.
lexicógrafo, -a *nm/f* lexicographer.
lexicólogo, -a *nm/f* lexicologist.
ley *nf* (**a**) (*gen*) law; (*Parl*) act, bill, measure; (*Dep etc*) rule, law; ~ **de la calle** mob law, lynch law; ~ **cambiaria** currency exchange regulations; ~ **del embudo** unfair law; force majeure; ~ **no escrita** unwritten law; ~ **del más fuerte** (principle of) might is right; **se le aplicó la** ~ **de fugas** he was shot while trying to escape; ~ **fundamental,** ~ **orgánica** constitutional law; ~ **marcial** martial law; ~ **de Moisés** the Law (*Jewish*); ~ **natural** law of nature; ~ **seca** prohibition law; ~ **de la selva** law of the jungle; ~ **de la ventaja** (*Dep*) advantage rule; **a** ~ **de** on the word of; **de acuerdo con la** ~, **según la** ~ in accordance with the law; by law, in law; **con todas las de la** ~ properly; completely; **es la** ~ it's the law; **su palabra es** ~ his word is law; **está fuera de la** ~ he's outside the law; **un fuera de** ~ an outlaw; **está por encima de la** ~ he's above the law; **hecha la** ~ **hecha la trampa** every law has a loophole, laws are made to be broken; **recurrir a la** ~ to go to law.
(**b**) (*fig*) loyalty, devotion; **tener** ~ **a** to be devoted to; to have great respect for.
(**c**) (*Metal*) legal standard of fineness; **oro de** ~ standard gold; **bajo de** ~ base; **de buena** ~ (*fig*) genuine, reliable; **de mala** ~ (*fig*) base, disreputable; **en buena** ~ really; **entonces me toca esperar en buena** ~ then I really do have to wait.
leyenda *nf* (**a**) (*historia*) legend; **la** ~ **negra** the black legend. (**b**) (*Tip*) legend, inscription; key. (**c**) (*eslogan*) heading; footnote; slogan.
leyente *nmf* reader.
leyista *nm* (*Carib*) pettifogging lawyer.
leyoso *adj* (*And*) cunning, sly; sophistical.
lezna *nf* awl.
lía *nf* (*LAm*) plaited esparto grass.
liana *nf* liana.
liante* *nmf* (*revoltoso*) trouble-maker; (*difícil*) problem person; (*timador*) con man*, swindler.
liar [1c] **1** *vt* (**a**) (*atar*) to tie, tie up, do up; to bind; (*envolver*) to wrap up; *cigarrillo* to roll; **estoy muy liado ahora** (*fig*) I'm tied up right now.
(**b**) (**fig*) to confuse, embroil; **~la** to stir up trouble; to make a mess of things; **¡la liamos!*** we've cocked it up!‡, now we've done it!*
(**c**) **~las** (‡: *irse*) to beat it*; (*morir*) to peg out‡.
2 liarse *vr* (**a**) (*gen*) to get tied up; to entwine.
(**b**) (*fig*) to get involved (*con* with), get embroiled (*con* in).
(**c**) (*: *amantes*) to get involved in an affair (*con* with), form a liaison (*con* with); **estar liado con** to live with.
(**d**) ~ **a hostias** (*o* **palos** *etc*) to start fighting, come to blows.
lib. *abr de* **libro** book, bk.
libación *nf* libation; **libaciones** libations, potations.
libanés, -esa *adj, nm/f* Lebanese.
Líbano *nm*: **el** ~ the Lebanon.
libar [1a] **1** *vt* to suck; to sip; to taste. **2** *vi* (*LAm**) to booze*, drink.
libelista *nmf* lampoonist, writer of lampoons.
libelo *nm* (**a**) (*sátira*) lampoon, satire (*contra* of). (**b**) (*Jur*) petition.
libélula *nf* dragonfly.
liberación *nf* liberation; release; ~ **de la mujer** women's liberation.
liberacionista* *nf* women's libber*.
liberada *adj mujer* liberated.
liberado 1 *adj* (**a**) (*Com, Fin*) paid-up, paid-in (*US*). (**b**) (*Pol*) full-time, paid; **miembro** ~ = 2. **2** *nm*, **liberada** *nf* (*Pol*) paid agent, full-time worker (of a trade-union *o* of a terrorist organization).
liberal 1 *adj* (**a**) (*Pol*) liberal. (**b**) *carácter* liberal, generous; lavish. **2** *nmf* liberal.
liberalidad *nf* liberality, generosity, lavishness.
liberalismo *nm* liberalism.
liberalización *nf* liberalization.
liberalizador *adj* liberalizing.
liberalizar [1f] *vt* to liberalize; *mercado etc* to deregulate.
liberalmente *adv* liberally, generously; lavishly.
liberar [1a] *vt* to free, liberate; ~ **a uno de una obligación** to release sb from a duty; ~ **a uno de una contribución** to exempt sb from a tax; **estar liberado de servicios** to be free of duties.
Liberia *nf* Liberia.
liberiano, -a *adj, nm/f* Liberian.
líbero *nm* (*Dep*) sweeper.
libérrimo *adj* entirely free, absolutely free.
libertad *nf* liberty, freedom; (*pey*) licence; (undue) familiarity; '¡~!' (*slogan*) 'freedom!'; ~ **de cátedra** academic freedom, freedom to teach; **~es civiles** civil liberties; ~ **de comercio** free trade; ~ **de conciencia** freedom of thought; ~ **condicional,** ~ **vigilada** (*Jur*) probation; **estar en** ~ **condicional** (*o* **vigilada**) to be on probation; ~ **de cultos** freedom of worship, religious freedom; ~ **de empresa** free enterprise; ~ **bajo fianza** release on bail; ~ **de imprenta** freedom of the press; ~ **bajo palabra,** ~ **a prueba** parole; ~ **de** (**la**) **palabra** (*o* **de expresión**) freedom of speech; ~ **de prensa** freedom of the press; ~ **de voto** (*Parl*) free vote; **estar en** ~ to be free, be at liberty; **poner a uno en** ~ to set sb free, release sb, set sb at liberty; **tomarse una** ~ to take a liberty; **tomarse la** ~ **de** + *infin* to take the liberty of + *ger*, presume to + *infin*.
libertador 1 *adj* liberating. **2** *nm*, **libertadora** *nf* liberator.
libertar [1a] *vt* (*gen*) to set free, liberate, release (*de* from); (*eximir*) to exempt, release (*de* from); (*salvar*) to save, deliver (*de* from); ~ **a uno de la muerte** to save sb from death.
libertario, -a *adj, nm/f* libertarian.
libertinaje *nm* licentiousness; profligacy.
libertino 1 *adj* (**a**) (*vicioso*) loose-living, rakish, profligate. (**b**) (*Rel Hist*) freethinking. **2** *nm* (**a**) (*juerguista*) libertine, rake. (**b**) (*Rel Hist*) freethinker.
Libia *nf* Libya.
libídine *nf* lewdness, lasciviousness; libido.
libidinoso *adj* lustful, libidinous.
libido *nf* libido.
libio, -a *adj, nm/f* Libyan.
liborio* *adj* Cuban.
libra *nf* (**a**) pound; ~ **esterlina** pound sterling. (**b**) (‡) 100 pesetas; **media** ~ 50 pesetas.
Libra *nf* (*Zodíaco*) Libra, the Scales.
libraco *nm* boring book, worthless book; old tome.

librado, -a *nm/f* (*Com*) drawee.
librador(a) *nm/f* (*Com*) drawer.
libramiento *nm* rescue, delivery (*de* from).
librante *nmf* (*Com*) drawer.
libranza *nf* (**a**) (*Com*) draft, bill of exchange; ~ **de correos** (*LAm*), ~ **postal** (*LAm*) money order. (**b**) (*de trabajador*) time off.
librar [1a] **1** *vt* (**a**) (*libertar*) to save, free, rescue, deliver (*de* from); (*Jur*) to exempt, free, release (*de* from); ~ **a uno de una obligación** to free sb from an obligation; **¡Dios me libre!** Heaven forbid!; **¡líbreme Dios de maldecir a nadie!** Heaven forbid that I should curse anyone!
(**b**) *confianza, esperanzas* to place (*en* in).
(**c**) *sentencia* to pass; *edicto etc* to issue; *secreto* to reveal.
(**d**) (*Com*) to draw; *cheque* to make out; ~ **a cargo de** to draw on.
(**e**) *batalla* to fight, wage; to join.
2 *vi* (**a**) to give birth.
(**b**) ~ **bien** to fare well, succeed; ~ **mal** to fare badly, fail.
(**c**) (*tiempo*) **libro a las 3** I'm free at 3, I finish work at 3; **trabaja 6 horas y libra 2** he works 6 hours and has 2 hours off.
3 librarse *vr* to free o.s., escape; ~ **de** to escape from, get out of, get away from; to get rid of; **de buena nos hemos librado** we did well to get out of that, we're well out of that.
libre 1 *adj* (**a**) (*gen*) free (*de* from, of); **¿estás ~?** are you free?; **esa plaza no está** ~ that seat is not free; **cada cual es ~ de hacer lo que quiera** everyone is free to do as he wishes; **por fin estamos ~s de él** at last we're rid of him; **estar ~ de servicio** to be off duty; ~ **de derechos** free of duty, duty-free; **al aire** ~ in the open air; **examinarse por** ~ to take one's exams as an independent candidate; **ahora funciono por** ~ now I'm on my own; **trabajar por** ~ to freelance, work on one's own account, work for o.s.
(**b**) (*pey*) free, outspoken; licentious, loose, immoral; **de vida** ~ loose-living, immoral.
(**c**) (*Dep*) free, free-style; **los 200 metros ~s** the 200 metre free-style race; **golpe** (*etc*) ~ free kick.
(**d**) ~ **a bordo** (*Com*) free on board.
2 *nm* (**a**) (*Dep*: *golpe*) free kick; ~ **directo** direct free kick; ~ **indirecto** indirect free kick.
(**b**) (*Dep*: *persona*) sweeper.
(**c**) (*Méx*) taxi.
librea 1 *nf* livery, uniform. **2** *nm* (*Cono Sur*) footman.
librecambio *nm* free trade.
librecambista 1 *adj* free-trade (*atr*). **2** *nm* free-trader.
librepensador(a) *nm/f* freethinker.
librepensamiento *nm* freethinking.
librera[1] *nf* (*Cono Sur*) bookcase.
librería *nf* (**a**) (*tienda*) bookshop; ~ **anticuaria,** ~ **de antiguo** antiquarian bookshop; ~ **de ocasión,** ~ **de viejo** second-hand bookshop.
(**b**) (*estante*) bookcase; (*biblioteca*) library.
(**c**) (*comercio*) bookselling, book trade, book business.
librero[1], **-a**[2] *nm/f* (*persona*) bookseller; ~ **de viejo** second-hand bookseller.
librero[2] *nm* (*Carib, Cono Sur, Méx*: *estante*) bookcase.
libresco *adj* bookish.
libreta *nf* (**a**) notebook; (*Com*) account-book; (*Cono Sur Aut*) driving licence; ~ **de ahorros,** ~ **de banco,** ~ **de depósitos** bank-book, passbook; ~ **de direcciones** address-book; ~ **militar** (*LAm*) certificate of military service. (**b**) (*pan*) one-pound loaf.
librete *nm* booklet.
libretista *nmf* librettist.
libreto *nm* libretto; (*LAm*) film script.
libro *nm* book; ~ **de actas** minute book; ~ **de apuntes** notebook; ~ **blanco** (*Parl*) white paper; ~ **de bolsillo** paperback; ~ **de cabecera** bedside book; ~ **de caja** cashbook; ~ **de cálculos hechos** ready-reckoner; ~ **de cocina** cookery-book, cookbook (*US*); ~ **de consulta** reference book, work of reference; ~ **de cría** register of pedigrees; ~ **de cuentas,** ~ **de contabilidad** account-book; ~ **de cuentos** storybook; ~ **de cheques** chequebook; ~ **desplegable,** ~ **mágico,** ~ **móvil,** ~ **vivo** pop-up book; ~ **diario** journal; ~ **de direcciones** address-book; ~ **de encargos** order-book; ~ **escolar** (*informe*) school report; (*de texto*) schoolbook; ~ **de estilo** style-book; ~ **de familia** marriage certificate; ~ **genealógico** (*Agr*) herd-book; ~ **de hojas cambiables** loose-leaf book; ~ **de honor** distinguished visitors' book; ~ **de imágenes** picture-book; ~ **de lectura** reader; ~ **mayor** ledger; ~ **de orígenes** register of pedigrees; ~ **parroquial** parish register; ~ **de pedidos** order-book; ~ **de reclamaciones** complaints book; **l~ rojo** (*Parl*) white paper; ~ **en rústica** paperback (book); ~ **talonario** receipt book; book of tickets, book of counterfoils; ~ **de texto** textbook; ~ **verde** (*Parl*) green paper; ~ **de visitas** visitors' book; ~ **de vuelos** (*Aer*) logbook; **ahorcar los ~s, arrimar los ~s, colgar los ~s** (*fig*) to abandon one's studies; **cerrar los ~s** (*Fin*) to close the books; **no estar en el ~, no tener el ~** to be unaware of a matter; to be uninterested in a matter, have no intention of pursuing a matter; **hacer ~ nuevo** to turn over a new leaf; **llevar los ~s** (*Fin*) to keep the books.
librote *nm* big book, tome.
Lic. *abr de* **Licenciado, Licenciada.**
licencia *nf* (**a**) (*permiso*) licence, permission; **sin mi** ~ without my permission; **dar su** ~ to give one's permission, grant permission.
(**b**) (*documento*) licence, permit; ~ **de armas** gun licence; ~ **de caza** game licence, hunting permit; ~ **de conducir,** ~ **de conductor,** ~ **de manejar** (*LAm*) driving licence; ~ **de matrimonio** marriage licence; ~ **de obras** building permit; ~ **de piloto,** ~ **de vuelo** pilot's licence.
(**c**) (*Mil etc*) leave (*of absence*); ~ **por enfermedad** sick leave; ~ **de maternidad** maternity leave; ~ **sin sueldo** leave without pay, unpaid leave; **estar de** ~ to be on leave; **ir de** ~ to go on leave.
(**d**) (*Mil*: *t* ~ **absoluta**) discharge; ~ **honrosa** honourable discharge.
(**e**) (*moral*) licence, licentiousness; ~ **poética** poetic licence.
(**f**) (*Univ Hist*) degree.
licenciado, -a *nm/f* (**a**) (*Univ*) licenciate, bachelor; **L~ en Filosofía y Letras** ≃ Bachelor of Arts. (**b**) (*LAm*: *abogado*) lawyer (*not translated as title before proper name*).
licenciar [1b] **1** *vt* (**a**) (*dar permiso para*) to license, grant a permit (*o* licence) to.
(**b**) (*permitir*) to permit, allow.
(**c**) (*Mil*) to discharge.
(**d**) (*Univ*) to confer a degree on.
2 licenciarse *vr* to graduate, take one's degree; ~ **en Derecho** to take a degree in Law.
licenciatario, -a *nm/f* licensee.
licenciatura *nf* (**a**) (*título*) degree, licentiate. (**b**) (*acto*) graduation. (**c**) (*estudios*) degree course, university degree.
licencioso *adj* licentious.
liceo *nm* lyceum; (*Cono Sur, Méx*) secondary school.
licitación *nf* bidding (*at auction*).
licitador(a) *nm/f* bidder; (*LAm*) auctioneer.
licitar [1a] **1** *vt* (**a**) (*en subasta*: *ofrecer*) to bid for. (**b**) (*LAm*) to sell by auction. **2** *vi* to bid.
lícito *adj* (*gen*) lawful, legal, licit; (*justo*) fair, just; (*permisible*) permissible; **si es ~ preguntarlo** if one may ask.
licitud *nf* legality; fairness, justness; **la controversia sobre la ~ del aborto** the controversy about whether abortion should be permitted.
licor *nm* (**a**) (*gen*) liquid. (**b**) (*alcohol*) (alcoholic) liquor, spirits; (*de frutas etc*) liqueur.
licorería *nf* (*LAm*) distillery.
licorero *nm* (*LAm*) distiller.
licorista *nm* (*fabricante*) distiller; (*comerciante*) dealer in liquor, seller of liquor.
licoroso *adj vino etc* strong, of high alcoholic content.
licuación *nf* liquefaction; melting.
licuado *nm*: ~ **(de frutas)** (*LAm*) milk shake.
licuadora *nf* (*Culin*) blender, liquidizer.
licuar [1d] *vt* to liquefy, turn into liquid; *nieve* to melt.
licuefacción *nf* liquefaction.
licha‡ *nf*, **liche‡** *nf* street.
lichi *nm* lychee.
líchigo *nm* (*And*) provisions, food.
lid *nf* (*combate*) fight, combat; (*disputa*) dispute, controversy; **en buena** ~ in (a) fair fight, (*fig*) by fair means, fairly.
líder 1 *adj* top, leading, foremost; **marca** ~ leading brand, brand leader. **2** *nmf, pl* **liders** *o* **líderes** leader; (*Dep*) leader, league leader, top club (*etc*).
liderar [1a] *vt* to lead; to head.
liderato *nm*, **liderazgo** *nm* leadership; (*Dep*) lead, leadership, top position.
lidia *nf* (**a**) (*Taur*) bullfight; bullfighting; **toro de** ~ fighting bull. (**b**) (*Méx*: *molestia*) trouble, nuisance; **dar** ~ to be trying, be a nuisance.
lidiador *nm* fighter; (*Taur*) bullfighter.

lidiar [1b] **1** *vt toro* to fight. **2** *vi* to fight (*t fig*; *con, contra* against, *por* for).

liebre *nf* (**a**) (*Zool*) hare; (*fig*) coward; **ser ~ corrida** (*Méx**) to be an old hand; **coger una ~*** to come a cropper*; **levantar la ~** to blow the gaff‡. (**b**) (*Dep*) pacemaker. (**c**) (*And, Cono Sur*: *bus*) small bus.

Lieja *nf* Liège.

liencillo *nm* (*LAm*) thick cotton material.

liendre *nf* nit.

lienzo *nm* (**a**) (*tela*) linen; (*Arte*) canvas; (*pañuelo*) handkerchief; **un ~** a piece of linen (*etc*). (**b**) (*Arquit*: *muro*) wall; (*fachada*) face, front; (*LAm*) section (*of fence etc*); (*Méx*) corral, pen.

liftar [1a] *vt pelota* to loft.

lifting ['liftin] *n* facelift (*t fig*); plastic surgery.

liga *nf* (**a**) (*Pol etc*) league.

(**b**) (*Cos*) band; (*prenda*) suspender, garter.

(**c**) (*Metal*) alloy; mixture.

(**d**) (*Bot*) mistletoe.

(**e**) (*trampa viscosa*) birdlime.

(**f**) (*CAm, Carib*) binding; state of being bound.

(**g**) (*And**: *amigo*) bosom friend.

(**h**) (*: *persona*) pick-up‡.

ligado *nm* (*Mús*) slur, tie; legato; (*Tip*) ligature.

ligadura *nf* (*vínculo*) bond, tie; (*Náut*) lashing; (*Med*) ligature; (*Mús*) ligature, legato.

ligamento *nm* ligament.

ligamiento *nm* bond, tie.

ligar [1h] **1** *vt* (**a**) (*gen*) to tie, bind; (*Metal*) to alloy; to mix; (*Med*) to put a ligature on, bind up; (*Mús*) to slur; (*fig*) to join, bind together; *bebidas* to mix; **estar ligado por contrato a** to be bound by contract to.

(**b**) (*) *chica etc* to pick up*, get off with*.

(**c**) (‡: *conseguir*) to get, lay hold of; (*comprar*) to buy; (*robar*) to nick‡; (*detener*) to nick‡.

(**d**) (*Carib Agr*) to contract in advance for.

2 *vi* (**a**) (*ir juntos*) to mix (well), blend, go well together; **ligan A y B** (*And, CAm*) A and B get on well together.

(**b**) (*Carib, Méx**: *tener suerte*) to have a bit of luck, be lucky; **la cosa le ligó** (*And, CAm*) the affair went well for him.

(**c**) (*Carib, Méx*: *mirar*) to look, stare.

(**d**) **le ligó su deseo** (*And, Carib**) her wish came true.

(**e**) **~ con una*** (*flirtear*) to flirt with sb; (*conocer*) to pick a girl up*; **salieron dispuestas a ~** they went out to try to pick up a man*; **han ligado A y Z** A and Z have paired up.

3 ligarse *vr* (**a**) (*unirse*) to unite, band together.

(**b**) (*fig*) to bind o.s., commit o.s.

(**c**) **~ con uno** (*Méx**) to get off with sb*.

ligazón *nf* (**a**) (*Náut*) rib, beam. (**b**) (*fig*) bond, tie, union.

ligeramente *adv* (**a**) lightly. (**b**) *conocer etc* slightly. (**c**) *juzgar etc* hastily.

ligerear [1a] *vi* (*Cono Sur*) to walk fast, move quickly.

ligereza *nf* (*V* **ligero**) (**a**) lightness; thinness.

(**b**) swiftness, quickness, speed.

(**c**) agility, nimbleness.

(**d**) slightness.

(**e**) superficiality, shallowness; flippancy; frivolity; **obrar con ~** to act rashly, act thoughtlessly.

(**f**) **~ de espíritu** light-heartedness, gaiety.

(**g**) (*acto*) indiscretion.

ligero 1 *adj* (**a**) (*de poco peso*) light; *tela* light, lightweight, thin; *comida, sueño* light; *té* weak; **~ de ropa** lightly clad, scantily clad, not wearing much; **más ~ que un corcho** (*o* **una pluma** *etc*) as light as a feather.

(**b**) (*rápido*) swift, quick, rapid; **~ de dedos** light-fingered; **~ de pies** light-footed, quick; **más ~ que una bala** (*o* **el viento** *etc*) as quick as a flash.

(**c**) (*ágil*) agile, quick, nimble.

(**d**) (*modesto*) slight; **un ~ conocimiento** a slight acquaintance, a superficial acquaintance.

(**e**) *carácter* superficial, shallow, flippant; frivolous, flighty; **~ de cascos** scatterbrained, frivolous; **hacer algo a la ligera** to do sth quickly; to do sth without fuss; (*pey*) to do sth perfunctorily; **juzgar a la ligera** to judge hastily, jump to conclusions; **obrar de ~** to act rashly, act thoughtlessly.

2 *adv* lightly; quickly, swiftly; **así andamos más ~** we go quicker like this.

light [laɪt] *adj invar tabaco* low-tar (*atr*); *comida* low in calories; *plan, política* diluted, watered-down, toned-down.

lignito *nm* lignite.

ligón[1] *nm* hoe.

ligón[2]* **1** *adj* (**a**) *persona* flirtatious; **es muy ~** he's a great one for the girls.

(**b**) *prenda* attractive; provocative, sexy.

(**c**) (*distinguido*) posh*, classy*.

2 *nm* womanizer, wolf*.

3 ligona *nf*: **es una ligona** she'll go with anybody, she's an easy lay‡.

ligue* *nm* (**a**) (*acto*: *gen*) **se dedica mucho al ~** he's always after the women, he's always having affairs; **ir de ~** to go looking for partners. (**b**) (*acto*: *un ~*) pick-up*, date; affair. (**c**) (*persona*) pick-up*, date; (*chico*) boyfriend, bloke‡; (*chica*) girlfriend, bird‡.

liguero[1] *nm* suspender belt, garter belt (*US*).

liguero[2] *adj* (*Dep*) league (*atr*); **líder ~** league leader.

liguilla *nf* (*Dep*) section (*of competition*); group of teams which play off to determine promotion; small tournament.

ligur (*Hist*) **1** *adj* Ligurian. **2** *nmf* Ligur, Ligurian.

ligustro *nm* privet.

lija *nf* (**a**) (*Zool*) dogfish. (**b**) (*Téc*: *t* **papel de ~**) sandpaper; **~ esmeril** emery paper. (**c**) **darse ~** (*Carib**) to give o.s. airs.

lijadora *nf* sander, sanding machine.

lijar [1a] *vt* to sand, sandpaper.

lijoso* *adj* (*Carib*) vain, stuck-up*.

Lila *nf* Lille.

lila[1] *nf* (*Bot*) lilac.

lila[2]‡ *nm* twit*, wimp*; sucker‡.

lila[3]‡ *nm* 5,000 pesetas.

lilailas* *nfpl* tricks.

lile* *adj* (*Cono Sur*) weak, sickly.

liliche* *nm* (*CAm*) piece of junk.

liliputiense *adj, nmf* Lilliputian.

liliquear [1a] *vi* (*Cono Sur*) to tremble, shake.

Lima *nf* Lima.

lima[1] *nf* (*Bot*) lime, sweet-lime tree.

lima[2] *nf* (*Téc*) (**a**) (*herramienta*) file; **~ de uñas, ~ para las uñas** nail file. (**b**) (*acto*) filing, polishing. (**c**) (*fig*) polish, finish; **dar la última ~ a una obra** to give a work its final polish.

lima[3]‡ *nf* (*camisa*) shirt.

limadura *nf* (**a**) (*acto*) filing; polishing. (**b**) **~s** filings.

limar [1a] *vt* (*Téc*) to file, file down, file off; to smooth (over); (*fig*: *pulir*) to polish (up), put the final polish on; *diferencias* to smooth over, iron out.

limatón *nm* (*LAm*) crossbeam, roofbeam.

limaza *nf* slug.

limazo *nm* slime, sliminess.

limbo *nm* limbo; **estar en el ~** to be in limbo; (*fig*) to be distracted, be bewildered.

limeño 1 *adj* of Lima. **2** *nm*, **limeña** *nf* native (*o* inhabitant) of Lima; **los ~s** the people of Lima.

limero *nm* lime (tree).

limeta *nf* (*Cono Sur*) (**a**) (*frente*) broad brow, domed forehead; (*calvo*) bald head. (**b**) (*botella*) bottle.

liminar *adj* (*fig*) preliminary, introductory.

limitación *nf* limitation, restriction; **~ de velocidad** speed restriction; **sin ~** unlimited.

limitado *adj* (**a**) (*gen*) limited (*t Com*). (**b**) (*corto de luces*) slow-witted, dim.

limitar [1a] **1** *vt* (*restringir*) to limit, restrict; (*reducir*) to cut down, reduce; **~ a uno a** + *infin* to limit sb to + *ger*, restrict sb to + *infin*.

2 *vi*: **~ con** to border on, be adjacent to, be bounded by.

3 limitarse *vr* to limit o.s., restrict o.s.; **~ a** + *infin* to limit o.s. to + *infin*, confine o.s. to + *infin*.

limitativo *adj*, **limitatorio** *adj* limiting, restrictive.

límite 1 *nm* limit; end; (*Geog, Pol*) boundary, border; **~ de crédito** credit limit; **~ forestal** timber line, tree line; **~ de gastos** spending limit; **~ de velocidad** speed limit; **asciende a 100 como ~** it goes up to 100 at the most; **se celebrará en octubre como ~** it will be held in October at the latest; **sin ~s** limitless; **poner un ~ a** to set a limit to; (*fig*) to draw the line at; **no tener ~s** to have no limits, know no bounds.

2 *atr* extreme, maximum; **caso ~** extreme case; **competición ~** out-and-out contest; **concentración ~** maximum concentration; **jornada ~** maximum possible working week; **sentencia ~** definitive ruling; **situaciones ~** extreme situations; **someter una máquina a pruebas ~** to test a machine to destruction.

limítrofe *adj* bordering, neighbouring.

limo *nm* (**a**) (*barro*) slime, mud. (**b**) (‡: *bolso*) handbag.

limón *nm* (**a**) (*Bot*) lemon; (*Carib*) lime. (**b**) **limones**‡ tits‡.

limonada *nf* lemonade; ~ **natural** lemon juice.
limonado *adj* lemon, lemon-coloured.
limonar *nm* lemon grove.
limonero *nm* lemon-tree.
limosina *nf* limousine.
limosna *nf* alms; charity; **¡una ~, señor!** can't you spare sth, sir?; **pedir** ~ to beg; **vivir de** ~ to live by begging, live on charity.
limosnear [1a] *vi* to beg, ask for alms.
limosnera[1] *nf* collecting tin (*for charity*).
limosnero 1 *adj* charitable. **2** *nm* (**a**) (*Hist*) almoner. **3** *nm*, **limosnera**[2] *nf* (*LAm*) beggar.
limoso *adj* slimy, muddy.
limpia 1 *nf* (**a**) (*acto de limpiar*) cleaning; (*CAm, Méx Agr*) weeding, cleaning, clearing; (*fig Pol etc*) clean-up, purge.
(**b**) (*And, Cono Sur, Méx**: *azotes*) beating.
2 *nm* (*) (**a**) (*persona*) bootblack. (**b**) (*Aut*) windscreen-wiper.
limpiabarros *nm invar* scraper; doormat.
limpiabotas *nm invar* bootblack.
limpiacristales *nm invar* (**a**) (*persona*) window-cleaner. (**b**) (*líquido*) window-cleaning fluid; (*trapo*) cleaning cloth. (**c**) (*Aut*) windscreen-wiper.
limpiachimeneas *nm invar* chimney-sweep.
limpiada *nf* (**a**) (*LAm*) clean, clean-up. (**b**) (*Cono Sur: claro de bosque*) treeless area, bare ground; clearing in a wood.
limpiadientes *nm invar* toothpick.
limpiador(a) *nmf* cleaner.
limpiadura *nf* (**a**) (*acto de limpiar*) cleaning, cleaning-up. (**b**) ~**s** dirt, dust, scourings.
limpiahogares *nm invar* household cleaning fluid.
limpiamanos *nm invar* (*CAm, Méx*) hand towel.
limpiamente *adv* cleanly; neatly; honestly; skilfully.
limpiametales *nm invar* metal-polish.
limpiamuebles *nm invar* furniture polish.
limpiaparabrisas *nm invar* windscreen-wiper, windshield wiper (*US*).
limpiapiés *nm invar* scraper; (*Méx: estera*) doormat.
limpiaplicador *nm* (*Méx*) cotton bud.
limpiaplumas *nm invar* penwiper.
limpiar [1b] **1** *vt* (**a**) (*gen*) to clean; to cleanse; (*enjugar*) to wipe, wipe off, wipe clean; to wipe away; *zapatos* to shine, polish; (*Culin*) *conejo etc* to paunch; *pez* to gut; ~ **en seco** to dry-clean; ~ **las narices a un niño** to wipe a child's nose.
(**b**) (*fig*) to cleanse, purify, clean up; (*Mil etc*) to mop up; (*policía*) to clean up; (*Bot*) to prune, cut back.
(**c**) (*: *en el juego*) to clean out*.
(**d**) (‡: *robar*) to nick‡.
(**e**) (‡: *matar*) to do in‡.
(**f**) (*Méx: pegar*) to hit, bash*, beat.
2 limpiarse *vr* to clean o.s.; to wipe o.s.; ~ **las narices** to wipe one's nose.
limpiaventanas *nm invar* (*líquido*) window-cleaner.
limpiavía *nm* (*LAm Ferro*) cowcatcher.
límpido *adj* limpid.
limpieza *nf* (**a**) (*acto*) clean; cleaning, cleansing; shine, shining, polishing; ~ **en seco** dry-cleaning; **hacer la** ~ to clean (up).
(**b**) (*acto: fig*) cleansing, cleaning-up; (*Mil*) mopping-up; (*de policía*) clean-up.
(**c**) (*estado*) cleanness, cleanliness; ~ **de sangre** purity of blood, racial purity.
(**d**) (*cualidad*) purity; integrity, honesty; (*Dep etc*) fair play.
(**e**) **hace las jugadas con mucha** ~ he makes the moves with great skill (*o* very neatly).
limpio 1 *adj* (**a**) (*gen*) clean; (*ordenado*) neat, tidy; (*sangre*) pure; *agua etc* pure, clean; (*despejado*) clear; ~ **de** free from, clear of; **más ~ que el oro** (*etc*) as clean as can be.
(**b**) (*moralmente*) pure; (*honrado*) honest; *juego* fair, clean.
(**c**) (*Fin*) clear, net; **50 dólares de ganancia limpia** 50 dollars of clear profit.
(**d**) (*solo*) alone; **se defendieron a pedrada limpia** they defended themselves with stones alone; **lo hizo a clavo** ~ he simply nailed it together, he did it just using nails; **luchar a puñetazo** ~ to fight with bare fists.
(**e**) **estar** ~* not to know a single thing; **quedar(se)** ~ to be cleaned out*.
2 *adv jugar* fair, clean.
3 *nm* (**a**) **en** ~ (*como adv*) clearly; (*Fin*) clear, net; **copia en** ~ fair copy; **estar** (*o* **quedar**) **en** ~*, **estar ~ y soplado** (*And**) to be broke*; **poner algo en** ~ to make a fair copy of sth; **poner un texto en** ~ to tidy a text up, produce a final version of a text; **quedó en ~ que** ... it was clear that ...; **sacar algo en** ~ to make sense of sth; **no pude sacar nada en** ~ I couldn't make anything of it.
(**b**) (*Méx: claro de bosque*) treeless area, bare ground; clearing in a wood.
limpión *nm* (**a**) (*acto*) wipe, (quick) clean; **dar un ~ a algo** to give sth a wipe. (**b**) (*trapo*) cleaning rag, cleaning cloth; (*And, CAm, Carib*) dishcloth. (**c**) (*persona*) cleaner. (**d**) (*And**) ticking-off*.
limusina *nf* limousine.
lina *nf* (*Cono Sur*) (**a**) (*lana*) skein of coarse wool. (**b**) (*trenza*) pigtail, long hair.
linaje *nm* (**a**) (*familia*) lineage, family; **de ~ de reyes** descended from royalty, of royal descent; **de ~ honrado** of good parentage.
(**b**) ~**s** (*familias*) (local) nobility, noble families.
(**c**) (*clase*) class, kind; ~ **humano** mankind; **de otro** ~ of another kind.
linajudo *adj* highborn, noble, blue-blooded.
linar *nm* flax field.
linaza *nf* linseed.
lince 1 *nm* (**a**) (*Zool*) lynx; (*CAm, Méx*) wild cat; ~ **ibérico** pardal lynx, Spanish lynx.
(**b**) **ser un** ~ (*fig*) to be very observant, be sharp-eyed; to be shrewd.
(**c**) (*LAm*) sharpness, intelligence.
2 *adj*: **ojos ~s** sharp eyes; **es muy** ~ he's very observant, he's very sharp-eyed; he's pretty shrewd.
linchamiento *nm* lynching.
linchar [1a] *vt* to lynch.
linche *nm* (*And*) knapsack; ~**s** (*Méx*†: *alforjas*) saddlebags.
lindamente *adv* (**a**) (*con elegancia*) prettily; daintily; elegantly. (**b**) (*iró*) well, jolly well*. (**c**) (*esp LAm*) excellently, marvellously, jolly well*.
lindante *adj* bordering (*con* on), adjoining, adjacent (*con* to).
lindar [1a] *vi* to adjoin, be adjacent; ~ **con** to border on, adjoin, be adjacent to; to extend to, be bounded by; (*Arquit*) to abut on.
linde *nm o f* boundary.
lindero 1 *adj* (*t* ~ **con**) adjoining, bordering. **2** *nm* edge, border; boundary.
lindeza *nf* (**a**) (*atractivo*) prettiness; (*finura*) daintiness; (*elegancia*) elegance.
(**b**) (*esp LAm*) (*amabilidad*) niceness; (*excelencia*) excellence, high quality.
(**c**) (*ocurrencia*) witticism.
(**d**) ~**s** pretty things; pretty ways, charming ways.
(**e**) ~**s** (*iró*) insults, abuse.
lindo 1 *adj* (*esp LAm*) (**a**) (*bonito*) pretty; (*exquisito*) exquisite, elegant, delicate; *hombre* good-looking.
(**b**) (*iró*) fine, pretty.
(**c**) (*precioso*) nice, lovely; (*excelente*) fine, excellent, first-rate, marvellous; **un ~ carro** a lovely car, a fine car; **un ~ partido** a first-rate game; **un ~ concierto** a marvellous concert; **de lo** ~ a lot, a great deal; wonderfully, marvellously, jolly well*; **es de** ~ (*LAm*) it's fine, it's marvellous.
2 *adv* (*LAm*) nicely, well, marvellously; **baila** ~ she dances beautifully.
3 *nm* (*Hist*) fop.
lindura *nf* (**a**) (*Cono Sur: cualidad*) prettiness, loveliness; **está hecha una** ~* she looks very pretty.
(**b**) (*Carib, Cono Sur: persona*) ace, champion; expert; **ella es una ~ en el vestir** she's an expert on clothes.
(**c**) (*LAm: objeto*) precious thing, thing of beauty.
línea 1 *nf* (**a**) (*gen*) line; (*Elec*) line, cable; (*Telec etc*) line; (*Com, de géneros*) line; ~**s** (*Mil*) lines; ~ **aérea** (*Aer*) airline; (*Elec*) overhead cable; ~ **de alto el fuego** ceasefire line; ~ **de balón muerto** dead-ball line; ~ **de banda** sideline, touchline; ~ **de base** (*Agrimensura*) base-line; ~ **de batalla** line of battle, battle line; ~ **blanca** white goods; ~ **caliente** hot line; ~ **de cambio de fecha** international dateline; ~ **de medio campo**, ~ **de centro** halfway line; ~ **de carga** load-line; ~ **compartida** shared line; ~ **de conducción eléctrica** power line; ~ **delantera** forward line; ~ **derivada** (*Telec*) extension; ~ **discontinua** broken line; ~ **divisoria** dividing-line; (*Aut*) lane markings; ~ **de estado** (*Inform*) status line; ~ **exterior** (*Telec*) outside line; ~ **férrea** railway; ~ **de flotación** waterline; ~ **de fondo** (*Dep*) by-line; ~ **de fuego** firing-line; ~ **de gol** goal-line; ~ **lateral** sideline, touchline; ~ **de llegada** finishing-line; ~ **de meta** (*Fútbol etc*) goal-line; (*en carrera*) finishing-line; ~ **de**

montaje assembly-line; production line; **primera** ~ front line; ~ **de puerta** goal-line; ~ **de puntos** dotted line; ~ **recta** straight line; ~ **roja** (*Telec*) hot line; ~ **de sangre** blood-line; ~ **de saque** baseline, service line; ~ **de situación** (*Inform*) status line; ~ **de alta tensión** high-tension cable; ~ **de tiro** line of fire; ~ **de toque** touchline; ~ **a trazos** broken line; ~ **de la vida** life line; **autobús de** ~ service bus, regular bus; **explicar algo a grandes ~s, explicar algo en sus ~s generales** to set sth out in broad outline, give the broad outline of sth; **de** ~ (*Mil*) regular, front-line, (*Náut*) of the line; **de primera** ~ first-rate, top-ranking; **en** ~ (*lit*) in (a) line, in a row; (*Inform*) on-line; **en** ~ **recta** in a straight line; **en toda la** ~ all along the line; **cerrar ~s** to close ranks; **leer entre ~s** to read between the lines; **fuera de** ~ (*Inform*) off-line; **poner unas ~s a uno** to drop a line to sb; **tirar una** ~ (*Arte*) to draw a line.

(**b**) (*talle*) figure; (*de barco etc*) lines, outline; **guardar** (*o* **conservar, mantener**) **la** ~ to keep one's figure (trim); **la** ~ **de 1902** the 1902 line, the fashion line of 1902.

(**c**) (*genealogía*) line (*t fig*); **en** ~ **directa** in an unbroken line; **es único en su** ~ it is unique in its line, it is the only one of its kind; **en esa** ~ **no tenemos nada** we have nothing in that line.

(**d**) (*moral, Pol etc*) line; ~ **de conducta** course of action; ~ **dura** (*Pol*) hard line; ~ **de partido** party line; **ser de** (**una** *o* **una sola**) ~ (*Carib, Cono Sur**) to be as straight as a die, be absolutely straight.

(**e**) (‡: *de droga*) dose, shot*; (*de cocaína*) line.

2 *nm* (*Dep*) linesman.

lineal *adj* linear; (*Inform*) on-line; **dibujo** ~ line drawing; **impuesto** ~ flat-rate tax; **aumento** ~ **de sueldos** across-the-board pay increase.

lineamento *nm* lineament.

linear [1a] *vt* (**a**) (*gen*) to line, draw lines on. (**b**) (*Arte*) to sketch, outline.

linense 1 *adj* of La Línea. **2** *nmf* native (*o* inhabitant) of La Línea; **los ~s** the people of La Línea.

linfa *nf* lymph.

linfático *adj* lymphatic.

linfocito *nm* (*Med*) lymphocyte.

lingotazo* *nm* swig*, shot*.

lingote *nm* ingot.

lingüista *nmf* (*especialista en lenguas*) linguist, language specialist; (*en lingüística*) linguistician.

lingüística *nf* linguistics; ~ **computacional** computational linguistics.

lingüístico *adj* linguistic.

linier *nm, pl* **liniers** (*Dep*) linesman.

linimento *nm* liniment.

lino *nm* (**a**) (*Bot*) flax. (**b**) (*Carib, Cono Sur*) linseed. (**c**) (*tela fina*) linen; (*lona*) canvas; **géneros de** ~ linen goods.

linóleo *nm* lino, linoleum.

linón *nm* lawn (*fabric*).

linotipia *nf*, **linotipo** *nm* linotype.

linterna *nf* lantern; lamp; (*And Aut*) headlight; **~s** (*LAm*: *ojos*) eyes; ~ **eléctrica,** ~ **de bolsillo,** ~ **a pila** torch, flashlight; ~ **mágica** magic lantern; ~ **roja** (*fig*) back marker, team (*etc*) in last place.

linyera *nm* (*Cono Sur*) tramp, bum (*US*).

lío *nm* (**a**) (*gen*) bundle; (*paquete*) package, parcel; (*Cono Sur*) truss.

(**b**) (*) (*jaleo*) row, fuss; (*confusión*) mess, mix-up, confusion, muddle; (*aprieto*) jam; **ese** ~ **de los pasaportes** that fuss about the passports; **armar un** ~ to make a fuss, kick up a row; to cause confusion; **se armó un tremendo** ~ there was an almighty row*; **hacerse un** ~ to get all mixed up, get into a muddle; **meterse en un** ~ to get into a jam*; **tener ~s con el profesor** to have problems with the teacher.

(**c**) (*: *amorío*) affair, liaison; **tener un** ~ **con una** to be having an affair with sb.

(**d**) (*chisme*) tale, piece of gossip; **no me venga con ~s** don't come telling tales to me, I don't want to know.

liofilizado *adj* freeze-dried.

Liorna *nf* (†) Leghorn.

lioso *adj* gossipy.

lipa *nf* (*Carib*) belly.

lipe *nm* (*LAm*: *t* **piedra** ~) vitriol; copper sulphate.

lipidia 1 *nf* (*CAm*) poverty. **2** *nmf* (*Carib, Méx*) nuisance, pest.

lipidiar [1b] *vt* (*Carib, Méx*) to annoy, bother, pester.

lipidioso *adj* (*Carib, Méx*) (*impertinente*) cheeky; (*molesto*) annoying.

lipón *adj* (*Carib*) fat, pot-bellied.

lipotimia *nf* faint, black-out.

lique‡ *nm* kick; **dar el** ~ **a uno** to kick sb out; **dar el** ~ to clear out*.

liquen *nm* lichen.

líquida *nf* (*Ling*) liquid.

liquidación *nf* (**a**) (*Quím*) liquefaction.

(**b**) (*Com, Fin*) liquidation; winding-up; (*de cuenta*) settlement; ~ **forzosa,** ~ **obligatoria** compulsory liquidation; **entrar en** ~ to go into liquidation.

(**c**) (*t* **venta de** ~) sale, clearance sale; ~ **por cierre del negocio** closing-down sale; **vender en** ~ to sell up.

(**d**) (*Pol*) liquidation, elimination.

(**e**) (*Méx*) redundancy pay.

(**f**) **oficina** (*o* **sección**) **de** ~ accounts section, payments office.

liquidador(a) *nm/f* liquidator.

liquidar [1a] **1** *vt* (**a**) (*Quím*) to liquefy.

(**b**) (*Com, Fin*) to liquidate; *cuenta* to settle; *negocio* to wind up; *deuda* to settle, pay off, clear; *existencias* to sell off, sell up, clear.

(**c**) (*Pol*) to liquidate, eliminate; (*LAm**: *matar*) to bump off‡.

(**d**) (*LAm*: *destrozar*) to destroy, ruin, render useless.

(**e**) (*Méx*) *obreros* to dismiss, pay off.

2 liquidarse *vr* (*Quím*) to liquefy.

liquidez *nf* liquidity, fluidity; (*Fin*) liquidity.

líquido 1 *adj* (**a**) (*gen*) liquid; fluid.

(**b**) (*Ling*) liquid.

(**c**) (*Com*) net; **ganancia líquida** net profit.

(**d**) (*LAm*) exact; accurate, right, correctly measured; **4 varas líquidas** exactly 4 yards.

2 *nm* (**a**) (*gen*) liquid; fluid; ~ **anticongelante** anti-freeze; ~ **de frenos** brake fluid.

(**b**) (*Fin*: *efectivo*) cash, ready money; (*Com, Fin*) net amount, net profit; ~ **imponible** net taxable income.

liquiliqui *nm* (*Carib*) Venezuelan national dress.

lira *nf* (**a**) (*Mús*) lyre; (*Liter*) *a 5-line stanza popular in the 16th century.* (**b**) (*Fin*) lira.

lírica *nf* lyrical poetry, lyric.

lírico 1 *adj* (**a**) (*Liter*) lyric(al); (*Teat*) musical. (**b**) (*LAm*) *persona* full of idealistic plans; (*Cono Sur*) *plan* Utopian, fantastic. **2** *nm* (*Cono Sur*) dreamer, Utopian.

lirio *nm* iris; ~ **de los valles** lily of the valley.

lirismo *nm* (**a**) lyricism; lyrical feeling, sentimentality, (*pey*) gush, effusiveness. (**b**) (*LAm*: *sueños*) fantasy, dreams, Utopian ideals; (*cualidad*) dreaminess, fancifulness.

lirón *nm* dormouse; (*fig*) sleepyhead; **dormir como un** ~ to sleep like a log.

lirondo *V* **mondo**.

lisamente *adv* smoothly, evenly; **lisa y llanamente** plainly, in plain language.

Lisboa *n* Lisbon.

lisboeta 1 *adj* of Lisbon. **2** *nmf* native (*o* inhabitant) of Lisbon; **los ~s** the people of Lisbon.

lisbonense, lisbonés = **lisboeta.**

lisérgico *adj*: **ácido** ~ lysergic acid.

lisiado 1 *adj* (*gen*) injured, hurt; (*cojo*) lame, crippled. **2** *nm,* **lisiada** *nf* cripple; ~ **de guerra** wounded ex-serviceman.

lisiar [1b] *vt* (*herir*) to injure (permanently), hurt (seriously); (*tullir*) to cripple, maim.

liso 1 *adj* (**a**) (*gen*) smooth, even; *pelo* straight; *mar* calm; *carrera* flat; *neumático* bald; **los 400 metros ~s** the 400-metres flat; ~ **como la palma de la mano** as smooth as glass.

(**b**) (*fig*) plain, unadorned; ~ **y llano** straightforward, simple; **la tiene lisa*** he's got it made*; *V t* **lisamente.**

(**c**) (*And, Méx**) fresh*, cheeky*; rude; **irse** ~ (*Carib**) to leave without a word.

(**d**) (*: *de poco pecho*) flat-chested.

2 *nm* (*Cono Sur*) tall beer glass.

3 lisa *nf* (**a**) (*Carib**: *cerveza*) beer. (**b**) (*And*: *pez*) mullet.

lisol *nm* lysol.

lisonja *nf* flattery.

lisonjear [1a] *vt* (**a**) (*halagar*) to flatter. (**b**) (*agradar*) to please, delight.

lisonjeramente *adv* (*V adj*) (**a**) flatteringly; gratifyingly. (**b**) pleasingly, agreeably.

lisonjero 1 *adj* (**a**) (*halagüeño*) flattering; gratifying. (**b**) (*agradable*) pleasing, agreeable. **2** *nm,* **lisonjera** *nf* flatterer.

lista *nf* (**a**) (*gen*) list; (*catálogo*) catalogue; (*Mil*) roll; roll call; (*en escuela*) roll, register; ~ **de comidas** menu; ~ **de correos** poste restante; ~ **de direcciones** mailing list; ~ **electoral** electoral roll, register of voters; ~ **de encuentros** (*Dep*) fixture-list; ~ **de espera** waiting-list; ~ **de éxitos** (*Mús*) hit parade; ~ **negra** blacklist; ~ **de pagos** payroll; ~ **de platos** menu; ~ **de precios** price-list; ~ **de premios** prize (*o* honours) list; ~ **de raya** (*Méx*) payroll; ~ **de tandas** duty roster, rota; ~ **de vinos** winelist; **pasar** ~ (*Mil*) to call the roll, (*Escol*) to call the register, call the roll.

(**b**) (*de tela*) strip; (*de papel*) slip.

(**c**) (*raya*) stripe; **tela a ~s** striped material.

listadillo *nm* (*And, Carib, Méx*) striped (white and blue) cotton cloth.

listado¹ 1 *adj* striped. **2** *nm* (*And, Carib*) = **listadillo.**

listado² *nm* (**a**) (*Inform*) print-out; listing; ~ **de alternativas** paged listing; ~ **de comprobación** checklist; ~ **paginado** paged listing. (**b**) (*Carib*) list.

listar [1a] *vt* to list, enter on a list.

listeria *nf* listeria.

listero, -a *nm/f* timekeeper, wages clerk.

listillo, -a *nm/f* know-all, smart Aleck*.

listín *nm* (*Telec*) telephone directory; list of numbers; (*Carib*) newspaper.

listo 1 *adj* (**a**) (*gen*) ready, prepared; **una pintura lista para usar** a ready-to-use paint; **un traje** ~ (*Méx*) a ready-made suit; **el avión estará ~ para volar en 6 meses** the plane will be ready to fly in 6 months; **¿estás ~?** are you ready?; **todo está** ~ everything is ready, everything is in order; **¡~ el pollo!** mission accomplished!

(**b**) **¡~!** (*interj*) (*bien*) all right!, O.K.!*; (*estoy dispuesto*) ready!; (*se acabó*) that's the lot!; it's all over!

(**c**) *carácter* clever, smart, sharp, quick; **¡~!** (*iró*) wake up!, you're a bright one!; **es la mar de ~*** he's terribly clever; **ser más ~ que el hambre** to be as smart as they come; **dárselas de** ~ to think o.s. very clever; **pasarse de** ~ to be too clever by half.

(**d**) (*) **estoy** ~ I'm done for, I'm finished; **¡estás ~!** no way!*, not likely!; **¡estamos ~s!** that's done it!*; **están** (*o* **van**) **~s si piensan eso** if they think that they've got another think coming*.

2 *nm* (*) con man*.

listón *nm* (*Cos*) ribbon; (*de madera*) strip, lath; (*Dep*: *en salto de altura*) bar; (*de goma, metal etc*) strip; (*Arquit*) fillet; (*fig*) level, norm, standard; ~ **de la pobreza** poverty line; ~ **de los precios** level of prices; **bajar el** ~ (*fig*) to make things too easy.

lisura *nf* (**a**) *superficie* smoothness, evenness; straightness; calmness.

(**b**) (*sinceridad*) plainness; sincerity; naïvety.

(**c**) (*LAm*: *descaro*) shamelessness, brazenness, impudence.

(**d**) (*LAm**: *dicho*) cheeky remark*, disrespectful thing (to say); (*And*) coarse remark, rude thing (to do *o* say).

lisurero *adj* (*And*), **lisuriento** *adj* (*And*) cheeky*.

litera *nf* (*Hist*) litter; (*cama*) bunk, bunk bed; (*Náut*) bunk, berth; (*Ferro*) couchette.

literal *adj* literal.

literalmente *adv* literally (*t fig*).

literario *adj* literary.

literata *nf* woman writer, literary lady; (*pey*) bluestocking.

literato *nm* man of letters, writer; **~s** (*frec*) literati.

literatura *nf* literature; ~ **comparada** (study of) comparative literature; ~ **de evasión** escapist literature; ~ **gris**, ~ **negra** promotional literature.

litigación *nf* litigation.

litigante *nmf* litigant.

litigar [1h] **1** *vt* to dispute at law; to fight. **2** *vi* (*Jur*) to go to law; to indulge in lawsuits; (*fig*) to argue, dispute.

litigio *nm* litigation; lawsuit; (*fig*) dispute; **en** ~ at stake, in dispute; **el asunto en** ~ the matter under debate.

litigioso *adj* litigious; contentious.

litio *nm* lithium.

litisexpensas *nfpl* (*Jur*) costs.

litografía *nf* (**a**) (*Arte*) lithography. (**b**) (*cuadro*) lithograph.

litografiar [1c] *vt* to lithograph.

litoral 1 *adj* coastal, littoral, seaboard (*atr*). **2** *nm* seaboard, littoral, coast.

litre *nm* (*Cono Sur*) rash.

litri* *adj* affected, dandified.

litro¹ *nm* litre, liter (*US*).

litro² *nm* (*Cono Sur*) coarse woollen cloth.

litrona* *nf* litre bottle (of beer).

Lituania *nf* Lithuania.

lituano, -a 1 *adj, nm/f* Lithuanian. **2** *nm* (*Ling*) Lithuanian.

liturgia *nf* liturgy.

litúrgico *adj* liturgical.

livianamente *adv* (*V adj*) (**a**) in a fickle way; frivolously; in a trivial way. (**b**) lewdly.

liviandad *nf* (*V adj*) (**a**) fickleness; frivolity, triviality. (**b**) lewdness. (**c**) (*LAm*) lightness.

liviano 1 *adj* (**a**) (*inconstante*) fickle; (*frívolo*) frivolous, trivial. (**b**) (*lascivo*) lewd. (**c**) (*LAm*) light. **2 ~s** *nmpl* lights, lungs.

lividez *nf* (**a**) lividness. (**b**) (*LAm*) paleness, pallor.

lívido *adj* (**a**) (*morado*) livid; (*amoratado*) black and blue. (**b**) (*pálido*) pale, pallid.

living ['lißin] *nm, pl* **livings** ['lißin] living-room, lounge.

lixiviar [1b] **1** *vt* to leach. **2 lixiviarse** *vr* to leach.

liza *nf* (*Hist*) lists; (*fig*) contest.

lo¹ *art def 'neutro'* (**a**) ~ **bello** the beautiful, what is beautiful, that which is beautiful; ~ **difícil** what is difficult; ~ **difícil es que ...** the difficult thing about it is that ...; **quiero ~ justo** I want what is just; **defiendo ~ mío** I defend what is mine; **visto ~ ocurrido** in view of what has happened; ~ **insospechado del caso** what was unsuspected about the matter; ~ **totalmente inesperado del descubrimiento** the completely unexpected nature of the discovery; ~ **mejor de la película** the best part of the film, the best thing about the film; **sufre ~ indecible** she suffers terribly.

(**b**) (*estilo*) **construido a ~ campesino** built in peasant style; **viste a ~ americano** he dresses in the American style, he dresses like an American.

(**c**) (*cuán*) **no saben ~ aburrido que es** they don't know how boring it is; **me doy cuenta de ~ amables que ellas son** I realize how kind they are.

lo² *pron* (**a**) (*persona*) him; (*cosa*) it; ~ **tengo aquí** I have it here; ~ **creo** I think so; ~ **veo** I see; ~ **sé** I know; **no ~ hay** there isn't any; **'¿anarquista?' ... 'no ~ soy'** 'an anarchist?' ... 'I'm not'; **'¿estás cansado?' ... '~ estoy'** 'are you tired?' ... 'I am' (*o* 'yes'); **guapa sí que ~ es** she's certainly very pretty, I should jolly well say she's pretty*. (**b**) (*LAm*) = **le.**

lo³ *pron dem*: ~ **de** that matter of, that business about; ~ **de ayer** what happened yesterday; ~ **de Rumasa** the Rumasa affair; ~ **de no traer dinero** that business about not having any money.

lo⁴ *pron rel*: ~ **que** (**a**) what, that which; ~ **que digo es ...** what I say is ...; **toma ~ que quieras** take what(ever) you want; **con ~ que él gana** with what he earns; **¡~ que sufre un hombre honrado!** what an honourable man has to suffer!; ~ **que pasa es que ...**, ~ **que hay es que ...** what's happening is that ..., it's like this ...; **empezó a tocar, ~ que le fastidió** she began to play, which made him cross.

(**b**) (*locuciones*) ~ **que es eso** as for that; **¡~ que has tardado!** you've been a long time!; **¡~ que cuesta vivir!** isn't living expensive!; **¡~ que es saber lenguas!** isn't it wonderful to speak several languages!; ~ **que se dice feo** really ugly; ~ **que se dice un hombre** a real man; **¡~ que he dicho!** I stand by what I said!; **¡~ que ves!** can't you see?, it's there for you to see!

(**c**) **en ~ que ...** *como conj* whilst ...

(**d**) (*LAm*) **a lo que ...** as soon as; **a lo que me vio me saludó** as soon as he saw me he said hullo.

loa *nf* (**a**) (*elogio*) praise. (**b**) (*Teat Hist*) prologue, playlet. (**c**) (*CAm, Méx**: *regañada*) reproof.

loable *adv* praiseworthy, commendable, laudable.

loablemente *adv* commendably.

LOAPA [lo'apa] *nf* (*Esp Jur*) *abr de* **Ley Orgánica de Armonización del Proceso Autonómico.**

loar [1a] *vt* to praise.

lob *nm* lob.

loba *nf* (**a**) (*Zool*) she-wolf. (**b**) (*Agr*) ridge (between furrows). (**c**) (*: *prostituta*) whore. (**d**) (*LAm*) half-breed.

lobanillo *nm* wen, cyst.

lobato *nm* wolf cub.

lobby ['loßi] *nm, pl* **lobbys** ['loßi] lobby, pressure-group; **hacer** ~ to lobby (*a favor de* for).

lobelia *nf* lobelia.

lobezno *nm* wolf cub.

lobito *nm* (*Cono Sur*: *t* ~ **de río**) otter.

lobo 1 *adj* (*Cono Sur**) shy.

2 *nm* (**a**) wolf; ~ **de mar** old salt, sea dog, (*Cono Sur*) seal; ~ **marino** seal; **son ~s de una camada** they're birds of a feather; **arrojar a uno a los ~s** to throw sb to the wolves; **gritar ¡al ~!** to cry wolf; **pillar un ~‡** to get plastered‡.

(**b**) (*Méx**) traffic cop*.

(**c**) (*LAm*) half-breed.

lobotomía *nf* lobotomy.

lóbrego *adj* dark, murky, gloomy.

lobreguez *nf* darkness, murk(iness), gloom(iness).

lóbulo *nm* lobe.

lobuno *adj* wolf (*atr*); wolfish, wolflike.

loca *nf* (**a**) (*gen*) madwoman, lunatic. (**b**) (*Cono Sur‡*) whore. (**c**) **dar** (*o* **venir**) **a uno la ~** (*Cono Sur*) to get cross, get into a temper. (**d**) (‡) queer‡, fairy‡.

local 1 *adj* local; **equipo ~** home team. **2** *nm* (*gen*) place; (*sitio*) site, scene; rooms; (*Com etc*) premises.

localidad *nf* (**a**) (*gen*) locality; location; (*pueblo*) place, town, locality. (**b**) (*Teat*) seat, ticket; **sacar ~es** to get tickets; **'no hay ~es'** 'house full', 'sold out'.

localizable *adj*: **fácilmente ~** easy to find; **difícilmente ~** hard to find; **el director no estaba ~** the director was not available.

localización *nf* location; placing, siting; finding.

localizador *nm* pager, paging device, beeper.

localizar [1f] **1** *vt* (**a**) (*ubicar*) to locate; (*colocar*) to place, site; (*encontrar*) to find, track down; **el sitio donde se va a ~ la nueva industria** the place where the new industry is to be sited.

(**b**) (*Med etc*) to localize.

2 localizarse *vr* (**a**) (*Méx*: *situarse*) to be located.

(**b**) (*Med*: *dolor etc*) to be localized.

locamente *adv* madly; wildly; **~ enamorado** madly in love.

locatario, -a *nm/f* (*LAm*) tenant, lessee.

locatis* *nm invar* madman, crackpot, crazy sort.

locería *nf* (*And*) (*loza fina*) china; (*loza*) pottery; (*Méx*: *vajilla*) crockery.

locero, -a *nm/f* (*And, CAm, Méx*) potter.

loción *nf* lotion; wash; **~ capilar, ~ para el cabello** hair restorer; **~ facial, ~ para después del afeitado** after-shave lotion.

loco[1] 1 *adj* (**a**) (*gen*) mad, crazy; (*fig*) wild, mad; **~ de atar, ~ perdido** *o* **de rematar** *o* **de remate** *o* **rematado** (*LAm*) raving mad, (as) mad as a hatter; **~ de verano** (*Cono Sur*) cracked, crazy; **~ lindo** (*Cono Sur*) mad in a nice sort of way; **más ~ que una cabra** as mad as a hatter; **andar ~ con algo** to be worried to death about sth; **ando ~ con el examen** the exam is driving me crazy; **estar ~ de alegría** to be mad with joy; **estar ~ por** (**una chica**) to be mad about (a girl); **estar ~ por hacer algo** to be mad keen to do sth; **está loca por la música‡** she's an easy lay‡; **esto me tiene** (*o* **trae**) **~** it's driving me crazy; **no lo hago ni ~*** no way will I do that*; **poner ~ a uno*, volver ~ a uno** to drive sb mad; **volverse ~** to go mad; **esto es para volverse ~** it's maddening, it's enough to drive you mad; **estar para volverse ~** to be at one's wit's end.

(**b**) (*Mec*) loose, free.

(**c**) (*: *enorme*) huge, tremendous*; **un éxito ~** a huge success; **estoy con** (*o* **tengo**) **una prisa loca** I'm in a tremendous rush*; **he tenido una suerte loca** I've been fantastically lucky*; **una loquísima bailarina*** a fantastic dancer*.

2 *nm* madman; lunatic, maniac; **correr como un ~** to run like mad; **gritar como un ~** to shout like a madman.

loco[2] *nm* (*Cono Sur Zool*) abalone.

locomoción *nf* (**a**) locomotion. (**b**) (*LAm*) transport; **~ colectiva** public transport.

locomotividad *nf* power of locomotion.

locomotora *nf* (**a**) (*Ferro*) engine, locomotive; **~ de maniobras** shunting engine, switch engine (*US*). (**b**) (*fig*) driving force, engine, powerhouse.

locomóvil *nf* traction engine.

locrear [1a] *vi* (*LAm*) to eat, have a meal.

locro *nm* (*LAm*) meat and vegetable stew.

locuacidad *nf* talkativeness, loquacity.

locuaz *adj* talkative, loquacious, voluble.

locución *nf* (**a**) expression, idiom, phrase. (**b**) **'~'** (*TV*) 'voice', 'reader'.

locuelo* 1 *adj* daft, loony‡. **2** *nm*, **locuela** *nf* loony‡, crackpot.

locumba (*And*) **1** *nf* grape liquor. **2** *adj invar* (*: *loco*) nuts‡, crazy.

locura *nf* (**a**) (*cualidad, estado*) madness, lunacy, insanity; **¡qué ~!** it's madness!, what lunacy!; **me gusta con ~*** I'm crazy about it; **es una casa de ~*** it's a smashing house*.

(**b**) (*acto*) mad thing, crazy thing; **~s** folly; **es capaz de cometer cualquier ~** he is capable of any madness.

(**c**) (*manifestación*) explosion of joy, joyful celebration.

locutor(a) *nm/f* (*Rad*) announcer; (*comentarista*) commentator; (*TV*) newscaster, newsreader; (*de show*) compère; (*de desfile de modelos etc*) presenter; **~ de continuidad** (*TV, Rad*) linkman; **~ deportivo** sports commentator.

locutorio *nm* (*Ecl*) parlour; (*de cárcel*) visiting-room; (*Telec*) telephone box; **~ radiofónico** studio.

locha *nf* loach.

loche *nm* (*And*: *bermejo*) ginger colour.

locho *adj* (*And*: *bermejo*) ginger, reddish.

lodacero *nm* (*And*), **lodazal** *nm* muddy place, mudhole, quagmire.

LODE ['loðe] *nf* (*Esp Escol*) *abr de* **Ley Orgánica Reguladora del Derecho a la Educación.**

lodo *nm* mud, mire; sludge; **~s** (*Med*) mudbath.

lodoso *adj* muddy.

loga *nf* (**a**) (*CAm*) eulogy; (*: *iró*) **echar una ~ a uno** to tell sb off*. (**b**) (*Cono Sur*) ballad, short poem.

logaritmo *nm* logarithm.

logia *nf* (**a**) (*de masones etc*) lodge. (**b**) (*Arquit*) loggia.

lógica[1] *nf* logic; **~ booleana** Boolean logic; **~ simbólica** symbolic logic; **ser de una ~ aplastante** to be as clear as day, be crushingly obvious.

logical *nm* software.

lógicamente *adv* logically.

logicial *nm* software.

lógico 1 *adj* logical; natural, right, reasonable; (*Inform*) logic (*atr*); **¡~!** of course!; **es ~** it's only natural; **lo más ~ sería** + *infin* the most sensible thing would be to + *infin*; **es ~ que** ... it is natural that ..., it stands to reason that ...

2 *nm*, **lógica[2]** *nf* logician.

logística *nf* logistics.

logístico *adj* logistic.

logo *nm* logo.

logopeda *nmf* speech therapist.

logopedia *nf* speech therapy.

logoprocesadora *nf* word processor.

logoterapeuta *nmf* speech therapist.

logoterapia *nf* speech therapy.

logotipo *nm* logo.

logradamente *adv* successfully.

logrado *adj* successful.

lograr [1a] *vt* (**a**) (*conseguir*) to get, obtain; to achieve, attain; **por fin lo logró** eventually he achieved it, eventually he managed it; **logra cuanto quiere** he achieves whatever he wants; **¡no lo lograrán!** they shan't get away with it!

(**b**) **~ hacer algo** to manage to do sth, succeed in doing sth; **~ que uno haga algo** to (manage to) get sb to do sth, persuade sb to do sth.

logrear [1a] *vi* to lend money at interest, be a moneylender.

logrero *nm* (**a**) (*prestamista*) moneylender, (*pey*) profiteer. (**b**) (*LAm*) sponger, parasite.

logro *nm* (**a**) (*éxito*) achievement, attainment; success; **uno de sus mayores ~s** one of his greatest successes (*o* achievements). (**b**) (*Com, Fin*) profit; (*pey*) usury; **a ~** at (a high rate of) interest.

logroñés 1 *adj* of Logroño. **2** *nm*, **logroñesa** *nf* native (*o* inhabitant) of Logroño; **los logroñeses** the people of Logroño.

LOGSE ['loɣse] *nf abr de* **Ley Orgánica de Ordenación General del Sistema Educativo.**

Loira *nm* Loire.

loísmo *nm use of* **lo** *instead of* **le** (*indirect object*).

loísta 1 *adj that uses* **lo** *instead of* **le** (*indirect object*). **2** *nmf user of* **lo** *instead of* **le.**

Lola *nf*, **Lolita** *nf formas familiares de* **María de los Dolores.**

lola* *nf* (*Cono Sur*) girl, young woman.

lolailo*, -a *nm/f* young Andalusian established in Barcelona.

lolo* *nm* (*Cono Sur*) lad, youth, young man.

loma *nf* (**a**) hillock, low ridge. (**b**) (*Cono Sur**) **en la ~ del diablo** (*o* **del quinoto**) at the back of beyond*. (**c**) (‡: *mano*) mitt‡, flipper‡.

lomada *nf* (*LAm*) = **loma.**

lombarda[1] *nf* (*Agr*) red cabbage.

Lombardía *nf* Lombardy.

lombardo, -a[2] *adj, nm/f* Lombard.

lombriciento *adj* (*LAm*) suffering from worms.

lombriz *nf* worm, earthworm; **~ intestinal** (*o* **solitaria**) tapeworm; **~ de mar** lugworm.

lomería *nf*, **lomerío** *nm* (*CAm, Méx*) group of low hills,

series of ridges.
lometón *nm* (*Carib, Méx*) isolated hillock.
lomillería *nf* (*Cono Sur*) (**a**) (*taller*) harness maker's; (*tienda*) harness shop. (**b**) (*equipo*) harness, harness accessories.
lomillero *nm* (*Cono Sur*) harness maker; harness seller.
lomillo *nm* (**a**) (*Cos*) cross-stitch. (**b**) **~s** (*LAm*) pads (of a pack saddle).
lomo *nm* (**a**) (*Anat*) back; (*carne*) loin; **~s** ribs; **iba a ~s de una mula** he was riding a mule, he was mounted on a mule. (**b**) (*Agr*) balk, ridge. (**c**) (*de libro*) spine, back; (*de papel, tela*) fold.
lona¹ *nf* canvas; (*Náut*) sailcloth; (*Cono Sur, Méx*) sackcloth; (*fig*: *Dep*) **la ~** the canvas, the ring; **estar en la ~** (*And, Carib**) to be broke*.
lona²* *adj invar* (*Cono Sur*): **estar ~** to be knackered*, be worn out.
loncha *nf* = **lonja¹**.
lonchar [1a] (*LAm*) **1** *vt* to have for lunch. **2** *vi* to have lunch, lunch.
lonche *nm* (*And*: *merienda*) tea, afternoon snack.
lonchera *nf* (*And*) lunch box.
lonchería *nf* (*LAm*) lunch counter, snack-bar.
loncho *nm* (*And*) bit, piece, slice.
londinense 1 *adj* London (*atr*), of London. **2** *nmf* Londoner; **los ~s** the people of London, (the) Londoners.
Londres *nm* London.
londri *nm* (*LAm*) laundry.
loneta *nf* (*LAm*) canvas.
longa *nf* (*And*) Indian girl.
longanimidad *nf* (*liter*) forbearance.
longánimo *adj* (*liter*) forbearing.
longaniza *nf* (**a**) (*salchicha*) long pork sausage. (**b**) (*Cono Sur*: *serie*) string, series. (**c**) (**) prick**.
longevidad *nf* longevity.
longevo *adj* long-lived; **las mujeres son más longevas que los hombres** women live longer than men.
longitud *nf* (**a**) (*gen*) length; **~ de onda** wavelength. (**b**) (*Geog*) longitude. (**c**) (*Dep*: *salto*) long-jump.
longitudinal *adj* longitudinal.
longitudinalmente *adv* longitudinally; lengthways.
longo *nm* (*And*) Indian youth.
longui(s)* *nm*: **hacerse el ~** to pretend not to know; to pretend not to be interested; to not let on*, keep mum.
lonja¹ *nf* (**a**) slice; (*de tocino*) rasher. (**b**) (*Cono Sur*) strip of leather; **sacar ~s a uno** to give sb a good thrashing.
lonja² *nf* (*Com*) (**a**) market, exchange; **~ de granos** corn exchange; **~ de pescado** fish market; **manipular la ~** to rig the market. (**b**) (*abacería*) grocer's (shop).
lonjear [1a] *vt* (*Cono Sur**) *persona* to give a good thrashing to.
lonjista *nmf* grocer.
lontananza *nf* (*Arte*) background; **en ~** far away, in the distance.
loor *nm* (*liter*) praise.
LOPJ *nf* (*Esp Jur*) *abr de* **Ley Orgánica del Poder Judicial.**
loquear [1a] *vi* to play the fool; to make merry, have a high old time*.
loqueo *nm* (*Cono Sur*) uproar, hullaballoo.
loquera *nf* (**a**) (*manicomio*) madhouse, lunatic asylum. (**b**) (*LAm*: *locura*) madness.
loquería‡ *nf* (*And, Cono Sur*) madhouse, lunatic asylum.
loquero *nm* (**a**) (*persona*) nurse in an asylum. (**b**) **esta oficina es un ~** (*Cono Sur**) this office is a madhouse.
loquina *nf* (*And*) foolish thing, idiocy.
loquincho* *adj* (*Cono Sur*) crazy.
lora *nf* (**a**) (*LAm*: *Orn*) (female) parrot. (**b**) (*Cono Sur**) (*fea*) old boot‡; (*habladora*) chatterbox. (**c**) (*And, Carib*: *herida*) severe wound, open wound.
lord [lor] *nm, pl* **lores** lord.
Lorena *nf* Lorraine.
Lorenzo *nm* Laurence, Lawrence.
lorna‡ *adj invar* (*Cono Sur*) daft, crackpot.
loro *nm* (**a**) (*Orn*) parrot.
(**b**) (*: *arpía*) old bat*, old bag‡.
(**c**) (*Cono Sur*) thieves' lookout man.
(**d**) (*Cono Sur Med*) bedpan.
(**e**) **sacar los ~s** (*Cono Sur**) to pick one's nose.
(**f**) (*Carib*) pointed and curved knife.
(**g**) (*) radio; transistor; radio-cassette; **estar al ~** (*alerta*) to be on the alert; (*informado*) to be on the ball, know the score*; **¡al ~!** watch out!; **está al ~ de lo que dice la gente** he's in touch with what people are saying.
lorquiano *adj* relating to Federico García Lorca; **estudios ~s** Lorca studies; **las influencias lorquianas** Lorca's influences.
los¹ *art def mpl*, **las** *fpl* the; *para ejemplos de uso, V* **el¹**.
los², **las** *pron* them; **¿los hay?** are there any?; **los hay** there are some.
los³, **las** *pron dem*: **mis libros y los de Vd** my books and yours; **nuestros cines y los de París** our cinemas and those of Paris, our cinemas and the Paris ones; **las de Juan son verdes** John's are green; **una inocentada de las de niño pequeño** a practical joke typical of a small child, a practical joke such as a small child might play; **un bombardeo de los de cataclismo** a really shattering bombardment.
los⁴, **las**: **los que, las que** *pron rel*: *V* **el³ que.**
losa *nf* (stone) slab, flagstone; **~ sepulcral** gravestone, tombstone.
losange *nm* diamond (shape); (*Mat*) rhomb; (*Her*) lozenge; (*Dep*) diamond.
loseta *nf* carpet square, carpet tile; floor tile.
lota *nf* burbot.
lote¹ *nm* (**a**) (*porción*) portion, share; (*Com etc*) lot; (*Inform*) batch; (*LAm*: *solar*) building site; (*LAm**) cache (*of drugs*).
(**b**) *medida*: (*Méx*) = *about 100 hectares*; (*Cono Sur*) = *about 400 hectares*.
(**c**) **al ~** (*Cono Sur**) any old how*; casually, carelessly.
(**d**) (‡) affair; **darse** (*o* **pegarse**) **el ~ con una** to make it with a girl‡.
lote²* *nm* (*Cono Sur*) idiot, clot‡.
lotear [1a] *vt* (*Cono Sur*) to divide into lots.
lotería *nf* lottery; **~ primitiva** *weekly state-run lottery*; **le cayó la ~, le tocó la ~, se sacó la ~** (*LAm*) he won a big prize in the lottery; (*fig*) he struck lucky, he struck it rich; **jugar a la ~** to buy lottery tickets.
lotero, -a *nm/f* seller of lottery tickets.
lotificar [1g] *vt* (*CAm, Méx*), **lotizar** [1f] *vt* (*And*) to divide into lots.
loto¹ *nm* lotus.
loto*² *nf* lottery.
Lovaina *nf* Louvain.
loza *nf* crockery; earthenware; **~ fina** china, chinaware.
lozanamente *adv* (*V adj*) (**a**) luxuriantly; rankly; profusely; vigorously; in a lively fashion, in a sprightly way. (**b**) in a self-assured way; arrogantly.
lozanear [1a] *vi* (*Bot*) to flourish, do well, grow strongly; to grow profusely; (*persona*) to be full of life, be vigorous, flourish.
lozanía *nf* (*V adj*) (**a**) lushness, luxuriance; vigour; liveliness, sprightliness. (**b**) self-assurance; arrogance.
lozano *adj* (**a**) (*Bot*) lush, luxuriant; rank; profuse; *persona, animal* vigorous, lusty; lively, sprightly. (**b**) (*seguro de sí*) self-assured; (*arrogante*) arrogant.
LRA *nf abr de* **Ley de Reforma Agraria.**
LRU *nf abr de* **Ley de Reforma Universitaria.**
LSM *adj abr de* **libre del servicio militar.**
lúa‡ *nf* one peseta.
lubina *nf* sea-bass.
lubricación *nf* lubrication.
lubricador 1 *adj* lubricating. **2** *nm* lubricator.
lubricante 1 *adj* (**a**) (*Téc*) lubricant, lubricating. (**b**) (*) *persona* oily. **2** *nm* lubricant.
lubricar [1g] *vt* to lubricate, oil, grease.
lubricidad *nf* (*V adj*) (**a**) slipperiness. (**b**) lewdness, lubricity.
lúbrico *adj* (**a**) (*resbaladizo*) slippery. (**b**) (*fig*) lewd, lubricious.
lubrificar [1f] *vt etc* = **lubricar** *etc.*
Lucano *nm* Lucan.
Lucas *nm* Luke, Lucas; (*Ecl*) Luke.
lucas *adj invar* (*Méx*) crazy, cracked.
lucecitas *nfpl* (*esp*) fairy-lights.
lucense 1 *adj* of Lugo. **2** *nmf* native (*o* inhabitant) of Lugo; **los ~s** the people of Lugo.
lucera *nf* skylight.
Lucerna *nf* Lucerne.
lucerna *nf* chandelier.
lucernario *nm* skylight.
lucero *nm* (**a**) (*Astron*) bright star, (*esp*) Venus; **~ del alba** morning star; **~ de la tarde, ~ vespertino** evening star. (**b**) (*fig*) brilliance, radiance.
Lucía *nf* Lucy.
lucidez *nf* (**a**) (*claridad*) lucidity, clarity. (**b**) (*CAm, Cono Sur*: *brillantez*) brilliance.
lúcido *adj* lucid, clear.

lucido *adj* (**a**) (*brillante*) splendid, brilliant; (*magnífico*) sumptuous, magnificent; (*elegante*) elegant; (*exitoso*) successful; **lucidísimo** brilliant, very clever.

(**b**) (*iró*) **estar ~, quedar(se)** ~ to do splendidly (*iro*), make a mess of things; **¡estamos ~s!** a fine mess we're in!; **~s estaríamos si ...** a fine thing it would be (for us) if ...

luciente *adj* bright, shining, brilliant.

luciérnaga *nf* glow-worm.

Lucifer *nm* Lucifer.

lucimiento *nm* (*gen*) brilliance, lustre, splendour; (*ostentación*) show, ostentation; (*brío*) dash, verve; (*éxito*) success; **hacer algo con** ~ to do sth outstandingly well, do sth very successfully.

lucio[1] *nm* (*Pez*) pike.

lucio[2] *adj* = **lúcido**.

lución *nm* slow-worm.

lucir [3f] **1** *vt* (**a**) (*iluminar*) to illuminate, light up.

(**b**) (*ostentar*) to show off, display; to sport; **~ las habilidades** to show off one's talents; **lucía traje nuevo** he was sporting a new suit.

2 *vi* (**a**) to shine; to sparkle, glitter, gleam.

(**b**) (*fig*) to shine, be brilliant; to be a success; (*con ropa etc*) to look nice, cut a dash; (*hacer ostentación*) to show off; **no lucía en los estudios** he did not shine at his studies.

(**c**) (*LAm*: *parecer*) to look, seem; **(te) luce lindo** it looks nice (on you).

3 lucirse *vr* (**a**) to dress up, dress elegantly.

(**b**) = *vi* (**b**).

(**c**) (*iró*) to make a fool of o.s., make a mess of things; **¡te has lucido!** a fine thing you've done! (*iro*), what a mess you've made!

lucrarse [1a] *vr* to do well out of a deal; (*pey*) to enrich o.s., feather one's nest.

lucrativo *adj* lucrative, profitable, remunerative; **institución no lucrativa** non-profitmaking institution.

Lucrecia *nf* Lucretia.

Lucrecio *nm* Lucretius.

lucro *nm* profit; **~s y daños** (*Fin*) profit and loss; *V* **ánimo**.

luctuoso *adj* mournful, sad, tragic.

lucubración *nf* lucubration.

lúcuma *nf* (**a**) (*Cono Sur*) (*fruta*) *a pear-shaped fruit*; (*berenjena*) aubergine, egg plant. (**b**) (‡: *cabeza*) head, nut‡. (**c**) **coger la** ~ (*Carib**) (*enojarse*) to get mad*; (*afanarse*) to keep at it; **dar la** ~ (*Méx**: *empeñarse*) to keep trying.

Lucha *nf forma familiar de* **Luz, Lucía**.

lucha *nf* (**a**) fight, struggle (*por* for); conflict; contest, dispute; **~ armada** armed struggle; **~ de clases** class war; **~ contra la subversión** struggle against subversive elements.

(**b**) (*Dep*) **~ de la cuerda** tug-of-war; **~ grecorromana, ~ libre** (all-in) wrestling.

luchador(a) *nm/f* fighter; (*Dep*) wrestler; **~ por la libertad** freedom fighter.

luchar [1a] *vi* (**a**) (*gen*) to fight, struggle (*por algo* for sth; *por hacer* to do); **luchaba con los mandos** he was struggling (*o* wrestling) with the controls; **~ con uno, ~ contra uno** to fight (against) sb. (**b**) (*Dep*) to wrestle (*con* with).

luche *nm* (*Cono Sur*) (**a**) (*juego*) hopscotch. (**b**) (*Bot*) *an edible seaweed.*

ludibrio *nm* mockery, derision.

lúdico *adj* (*liter*) ludic, playful.

ludir [3a] *vt* to rub (*con, contra* against).

ludoparque *nm* sports centre, sports complex.

ludoteca *nf* children's play-centre.

luego 1 *adv* (**a**) (*gen*) then, next; (*pronto*) presently, soon; (*más tarde*) later (on), afterwards; (*en seguida*: *t Méx*) at once, instantly, immediately; (*CAm*: *después*) later; (*And, Carib, Cono Sur, Méx*: *de vez en cuando*) sometimes, from time to time; (*Cono Sur*: *ya*) already, earlier, previously; **~, ~** (*Méx**: *en seguida*) straightaway; **¿y ~?** what next?, what happened then?; **desde ~** naturally, of course; **desde ~ que no** of course not; **¡hasta ~!** see you later, so long!*; **¡para ~ es tarde!** (*lit*) later won't do; (*fig*) go on then, prove it!; **~ de eso** immediately after that; **~ de haberlo dicho** immediately after saying it.

(**b**) (*así que*) and so, therefore; consequently; **~ X vale 7** therefore X = 7.

2 *conj*: **~ que** ... (*tan pronto*) as soon as ...; (*LAm*: *después que*) after ...

lueguito *adv* (**a**) (*CAm, Cono Sur, Méx*) at once, immediately. (**b**) (*CAm, Cono Sur, Méx*) nearby; **aquí ~** right here, near here.

lúes *nf* syphilis.

luengo *adj* (††, *liter, t LAm*) long.

lugar *nm* (**a**) (*gen*) place, spot; (*posición*) position; **~ de encuentro(s)** meeting-place; **los Santos L~es** the Holy Places; **~ seguro** safe place; **~ al sol, ~ bajo el sol** (*fig*) place in the sun; **el ~ del crimen** the scene of the crime; **una emisión de algún ~ de Europa** a broadcast from somewhere in Europe; **en ~ de** instead of, in place of; **en primer ~** in the first place, firstly; for one thing ...; **yo en su ~** if I were him; in his place, I ...; **en su ~, ¡descanso!** (*Mil*) stand easy!; **estar fuera de ~** to be out of place (*t fig*); **dejar a uno en mal ~** to let sb down, leave sb in the lurch; **devolver un libro a su ~** to put a book back (in its place); **ocupar el ~ de** to take the place of; **poner las cosas en su ~** (*fig*) to put things straight, put the record straight; **póngase en mi ~** put yourself in my place; **tener ~** to take place, happen, occur.

(**b**) (*espacio*) room, space; **¿hay ~?** is there any room?; **hacer ~ para** to make room for, make way for.

(**c**) (*pueblo*) village, town, place.

(**d**) (*razón*) reason (*para* for), cause; **no hay ~ para preocupaciones** there is no cause for concern, there is no need for worry.

(**e**) (*oportunidad*) opportunity; **si se me da el ~** if I have the chance; **dar ~ a** to give rise to, occasion; **dejar ~ a** to allow, permit of; **a como dé** (*o* **diera**) **~** (*Méx*) somehow or other, whatever way it may be; at any cost, by all possible means.

(**f**) **~ común** commonplace, cliché, platitude.

lugareño 1 *adj* (**a**) village (*atr*). (**b**) (*Méx*) local, regional; native. **2** *nm*, **lugareña** *nf* villager.

lugarteniente *nm* deputy.

lugo *nm* (*And Zool*) ram.

lugre *nm* lugger.

lúgubre *adj* mournful, lugubrious, dismal.

luir [3g] *vt* (*Cono Sur*) (*arrugar*) to rumple, mess up; *cerámica* to polish.

Luis *nm* Louis.

Luisa *nf* Louise.

Luisiana *nf* Louisiana.

lujo *nm* (**a**) (*gen*) luxury; sumptuousness, lavishness; **~ asiático, ~ oriental** greatest possible luxury; **de ~** de luxe, luxury (*atr*); **vivir en el ~** to live in luxury. (**b**) (*fig*) profusion, wealth, abundance; **con ~ de fuerza** with an excessive show of force; **con todo ~ de detalles** with profuse details.

lujosamente *adv* luxuriously; sumptuously, lavishly; ostentatiously; profusely.

lujoso *adj* luxurious; sumptuous, lavish; ostentatious; profuse.

lujuria *nf* lust, lechery; lewdness.

lujuriante *adj* (**a**) (*Bot*) luxuriant, lush. (**b**) (*lascivo*) lustful.

lujuriar [1b] *vi* to lust.

lujurioso *adj* lustful, lecherous; lewd, sensual.

lulo 1 *adj* (*Cono Sur**) (**a**) *persona* lanky. (**b**) (*torpe*) dull, slow. **2** *nm* (**a**) (*Cono Sur*) (*lío*) bundle; (*rizo*) kiss curl. (**b**) **~ del ojo** (*And*) eyeball; **al ~** (*Carib**) one after another.

lulú *nm* (*t* **~ de Pomerania**) Pomeranian, pom.

lullir‡ [3h] *vt* (*And, CAm, Méx*) to rub (*con, contra* against, on).

luma* *nf* (*Cono Sur*: *bastón*) police truncheon; (*reprimenda*) ticking-off*.

lumbago *nm* lumbago.

lumbar *adj* lumbar.

lumbre *nf* (**a**) (*fuego*) fire; **cerca de la ~** near the fire, at the fireside; **echar ~** to be furious.

(**b**) (*para cigarrillo*) light; **¿tienes ~?, ¿me das ~?** have you got a light?

(**c**) (*luz*) light; (*brillo*) brightness, brilliance, splendour; **~ del agua** surface of the water.

(**d**) (*Arquit*) light, opening (in a wall); skylight.

lumbrera *nf* (**a**) luminary; (*Arquit*) skylight.

(**b**) (*Mec*) vent, port; **~ de admisión** inlet; **~ de escape** exhaust vent.

(**c**) (*fig*) luminary, leading light, authority; **estaba rodeado de ~s literarias** he was surrounded by leading literary figures.

(**d**) (*Méx Taur, Teat*) box.

lumi‡ *nf* whore.

luminar *nm* luminary; = **lumbrera** (**c**).

luminaria *nf* sanctuary lamp; **~s** illuminations, lights.

luminescencia *nf* luminescence.

luminescente *adj* luminescent.
lumínico *adj* light (*atr*).
luminosidad *nf* (**a**) (*brillantez*) brightness (*t TV*), luminosity. (**b**) (*fig*) brightness, brilliance.
luminoso 1 *adj* (**a**) (*brillante*) bright, luminous, shining; *letrero* illuminated. (**b**) (*fig*) *idea* bright, brilliant. **2** *nm* (*Com*) neon sign; (*Dep*) electronic scoreboard.
luminotecnia *nf* lighting.
luminotécnico *adj* lighting (*atr*); **efectos ~s** lighting effects.
luna *nf* (**a**) (*lit*) moon; **claro de ~** moonlight; **~ creciente** crescent moon, waxing moon; **~ llena** full moon; **media ~** half-moon, (*fig*) crescent; **~ menguante** waning moon; **~ nueva** new moon; **~ de miel** honeymoon; (*fig, Pol etc*) honeymoon (period); **estar de buena ~** to be in a good mood; **estar de mala ~** to be in a bad mood; **eso es hablar de la ~** that's nonsense; **quedarse a la ~ de Valencia** to be disappointed, be left in the lurch; **quedarse en la ~ de Paita** (*And**) to be struck dumb; **estar en la ~** to have one's head in the clouds; to be woolgathering.
(**b**) (*cristal*) plate glass; (*espejo*) mirror; (*de gafas*) lens; (*Aut etc*) window; pane; **~ térmica** (*Aut*) heated rear window.
lunar 1 *adj* lunar. **2** *nm* (*Anat*) mole, spot; (*fig*) defect, flaw, blemish; (*moral*) stain, blot; black spot; **~ postizo** beauty spot; **hay ~es en la prosperidad general** there are black spots in the general prosperity.
lunarejo *adj* (*LAm*) spotty, spotty-faced.
lunático, –a *adj, nm/f* lunatic.
lunch [lunʃ] *nm, pl* **lunchs** [lunʃ] lunch; midday snack; midday reception, cold buffet.
lunchería *nf* (*LAm*) = **lonchería**.
lunes *nm invar* Monday; **hacer San L~** (*LAm*) to stay away from work on Monday (*while nursing a hangover**); **no ocurre cada ~ y cada martes** it doesn't happen every day of the week.
luneta *nf* (**a**) (*de gafas*) lens, glass (of spectacles); (*Aut etc*) window; **~ trasera** rear window; **~ trasera térmica** heated rear window. (**b**) (*media luna*) half-moon shape, crescent. (**c**) (*Teat: Hist, Méx*) stall.
lunfa* *nm* (*Cono Sur*) thief.
lunfardismo *nm* (*Cono Sur: palabra*) slang word.
lunfardo *nm* (*Cono Sur Ling*) (*criminal*) thieves' slang, language of the underworld; (*argot*) slang (*in general*).
lupa *nf* lens, magnifying glass.
lupanar *nm* brothel.
Lupe *nf forma familiar de* **Guadalupe**.
lupia[1] *nf* (**a**) (*lobanillo*) wen, cyst. (**b**) (*And; t* **~s**) small amount of money; small change.
lupia[2*] *nmf* (*CAm*) quack.
lúpulo *nm* (*Bot*) hop, hops.
luquete *nm* (*Cono Sur*) (*Agr*) unploughed patch of land; (*calva*) bald patch; (*mancha*) grease spot.
lurio* *adj* (*Méx*) (*enamorado*) besotted; (*chiflado*) nutty‡.
lusitano 1 *adj* Portuguese; (*Hist*) Lusitanian. **2** *nm,* **lusitana** *nf* Portuguese; (*Hist*) Lusitanian.
luso *adj* = **lusitano**.
lustrabotas *nm invar* (*LAm*) shoeshine boy.
lustrada *nf* (*LAm*) shoeshine.
lustrador *nm* (**a**) (*Téc*) polisher. (**b**) (*LAm*) shoeshine boy.
lustradora *nf* (**a**) (*Cono Sur Téc*) polisher. (**b**) (*LAm: lustrabotas*) shoeshine girl.
lustrar [1a] *vt* to shine, polish.
lustre *nm* (**a**) (*brillo*) polish, shine, gloss, lustre; **dar ~ a** to polish, put a shine on. (**b**) (*sustancia*) polish; **~ para calzado** shoe polish; **~ para metales** metal polish. (**c**) (*fig*) lustre, glory.
lustrín *nm* (*Cono Sur*) shoeshine parlour.
lustrina *nf* (**a**) (*Cono Sur*) shiny material of alpaca; (*And: tela*) silk cloth. (**b**) (*Cono Sur: betún*) shoe polish.
lustro *nm* lustrum, period of five years.
lustroso *adj* glossy, bright, shining.
lutencio *nm* (*Quím*) lutetium.
luteranismo *nm* Lutheranism.
luterano, –a *adj, nm/f* Lutheran.
Lutero *nm* Luther.
luto *nm* (**a**) (*gen*) mourning; (*duelo*) grief, sorrow; **medio ~** half-mourning; **~ riguroso** deep mourning; **estar de ~, llevar ~** to be in mourning (*por* for); **dejar el ~** to come out of mourning. (**b**) **~s** (*ropa*) mourning (clothes), crêpe.
luxación *nf* (*Med*) dislocation.
luxemburgués 1 *adj* of (*o* from) Luxembourg. **2** *nm,* **luxemburguesa** *nf* native (*o* inhabitant) of Luxembourg.
Luxemburgo *nm* Luxembourg.
luz *nf* (**a**) (*gen*) light; (*de día*) daylight; **~ y sombra** light and shade; **la ~ del día** the light of day; **a la ~ del día** (*fig*) in the cold light of day; **como la ~ del día** as clear as daylight; **~ eléctrica** electric light; **~ de la luna** moonlight; **~ del sol, ~ solar** sunlight; **~ ultravioleta** ultraviolet light; **a la ~ de una vela** by the light of a candle; **a primera ~** at first light; **espectáculo de ~ y sonido** son et lumière show; **entre dos luces** at twilight; (*****: *borracho*) mellow, tipsy; **dar a ~** to give birth; **dar a ~ un niño** to give birth to a child; **dar a ~ un libro** to publish a book; **negar la ~ del día a uno** to concede absolutely nothing to sb; **quitar la ~ a uno** to stand in sb's light; **sacar a ~** to bring to light; *libro* to publish; **salir a ~** to come to light; (*libro*) to appear, come out, be published; **ver la ~ al final del túnel** to see light at the end of the tunnel.
(**b**) (*Elec**) electricity, electric current; **han cortado la ~** they've cut off the juice*.
(**c**) (*fig*) light; **a la ~ de** in the light of; **a la ~ de un nuevo descubrimiento** in the light of a new discovery; **a todas luces** anyway; evidently; by any reckoning; **arrojar ~ sobre** to cast (*o* shed, throw) light on; **dar ~ verde a un proyecto** to give a plan the go-ahead; **estudiar algo a nueva ~** to study sth in a new light; **recibir ~ verde** to get the green light, get the go-ahead; **tuvo una larga experiencia de estar a la ~ de la publicidad** he had long experience of the limelight, he was used to being in the public eye.
(**d**) (*Elec etc*) light, lamp; **~ alta/baja** (*LAm Aut*) full-beam/dipped headlights; **~ antiniebla** foglamp; **luces de aterrizaje** (*Aer*) landing-lights; **~ de balización** (*Aer*) runway lights; **~ de Bengala** (*Mil*) flare, star-shell; (*LAm: fuego de artificio*) sparkler; **luces de carretera** full-beam headlights; **luces cortas** dipped headlights; **~ de cortesía** courtesy light; (*CAm*) sidelight; **~ de costado** sidelight; **luces de cruce** dipped headlights; **~ destelladora** winking light; **luces de detención, luces de freno** brake-lights; **luces de estacionamiento** parking lights; **~ de giro** direction indicator; **~ intermitente** winking light; **luces largas, luces intensas** (*LAm*) full-beam headlights, bright lights (*US*); **~ lateral** sidelight; **luces de navegación** navigation lights; **~ piloto, ~ de situación** sidelight, parking light; **luces de posición** sidelights; **~ relámpago** (*Fot*) flashlight; **~ roja** red light; **luces de tráfico** traffic-lights; **luces traseras** rear lights, tail lamps; **~ verde** green light; **dar ~ verde a** (*fig*) to give the green light to, give the go-ahead to; **~ vuelta** (*Méx*) direction indicator; **apagar la ~** to switch off (*o* put off, turn off) the light; **poner la ~, prender la ~** (*LAm*) to switch on (*o* put on, turn on) the light; **poner una lámpara a media ~** to dim a light; **hacer algo con ~ y taquígrafos** (*fig*) to do sth in the open; **reunirse sin ~ ni taquígrafos** (*fig*) to meet behind closed doors; to do something in a hole-in-the-corner way.
(**e**) (*Arquit etc*) light; window, opening; (*de puente*) space, span; (*Cono Sur: distancia*) distance between two objects; **~ al suelo** clearance (under a vehicle); **dar ~ a uno** (*Cono Sur Dep*) to give sb a start; **te doy 10 metros de ~** I'll give you 10 metres' start.
(**f**) (*fig*) **luces** enlightenment; intelligence; **corto de luces, de pocas luces** dim, stupid; **el siglo de las luces** the Age of Enlightenment (*18th century*).
(**g**) (*And‡*) dough‡, money.
Lyón *nm* Lyons.

LL

Ll, ll ['eʎe] *nf* (*letra*) Ll, ll.
llacsa *nf* (*Cono Sur*) molten metal.
llaga *nf* (**a**) (*herida*) wound; (*úlcera*) ulcer, sore. (**b**) (*fig*) sore, affliction, torment; **las ~s de la guerra** the afflictions of war, the havoc of war; **renovar la ~** to open up an old wound.
llagar [1h] *vt* to wound, injure (*t fig*).
llalla *nf* (*Cono Sur*) = **yaya.**
llama¹ *nf* (*Zool*) llama.
llama² *nf* (**a**) (*gen*) flame; blaze; **~ piloto** pilot light (*on stove*); **~ solar** solar flare; **arder sin ~** to smoulder; **entregar algo a las ~s** to commit sth to the flames; **estallar en ~s** to burst into flames; **salir de las ~s y caer en las brasas** to jump out of the frying pan into the fire.
(**b**) (*fig*) flame; passion, ardour.
llamada *nf* (**a**) (*gen*) call; (*a la puerta*) (*golpe*) knock, (*timbrazo*) ring; (*Telec*) call; (*Mil*) call to arms; **~ de atención** warning; **~ a larga distancia, ~ interurbana** long-distance call, trunk call; **~ internacional** international call; **~ local, ~ urbana** local call; **~ al orden** call to order; **~ a procedimiento** (*Inform*) procedure call.
(**b**) (*ademán*) signal, sign, gesture.
(**c**) (*Tip*) reference mark.
(**d**) (*Méx*: *cobardía*) cowardliness; timidity.
llamado 1 *adj* so-called. **2** *nm* (*LAm*) = **llamada.**
llamador *nm* (**a**) (*persona*) caller. (**b**) (*aldaba*) door-knocker; (*timbre*) bell; (*botón*) push-button.
llamamiento *nm* call; **~ a filas** call-up papers; **hacer un ~ a uno para que** + *subj* to call on sb to + *infin.*
llamar [1a] **1** *vt* (**a**) (*nombrar*) to call, name; **le llamaron el Gordo** they called him Fatty; **¿cómo le van a ~?** what are they going to call him?; **el mal llamado problema** what has erroneously been called a problem.
(**b**) (*hacer una llamada a*) to call; (*convocar*) to summon; (*invocar*) to invoke, call upon; (*con ademán*) to beckon; (*Telec*) to call, ring up, telephone (to); **¿quién me llama?** who's asking for me?; **que me llamen a las 7** please have them call me at 7; **le llamaron a palacio** they called (*o* summoned) him to the palace; **te llaman desde París** they're calling you from Paris; **~ a uno a hacer algo** to call on sb to do sth.
(**c**) (*atraer*) to draw, attract; *atención* to attract.
(**d**) **estar llamado a** + *infin* to be destined to + *infin*; **esto está llamado a ser de gran utilidad** this is destined to be very useful; **estaba llamado a fracasar** it was doomed to failure.
2 *vi* (**a**) (*gen*) to call; **¿quién llama?** (*Telec*) who's calling?, who's that?; **'llama D de Dulcinea'** (*Aer etc*) 'this is D for Dulcinea (calling)'; **~ por ayuda** to call for help.
(**b**) (*a la puerta*) (*golpe*) to knock, (*timbre*) ring; **~ a la puerta** to knock at the door; **¿quién llama?** who's there?
3 llamarse *vr* to be called, be named; **me llamo Mimi** my name is Mimi, they call me Mimi; **¿cómo te llamas?** what's your name?; **¿cómo se llama esto?*** how much is this?, what's the damage?*; **¡eso sí que se llama cantar!** that's what you really call singing!; **¡eso sí que se llama hablar!** now you're talking!, that's more like it!; **¡como me llamo Rodríguez, que lo haré!** as sure as my name's Rodríguez, I'll do it!
llamarada *nf* flare-up, sudden blaze; (*en cara*) sudden flush; (*fig*) flare-up, outburst.
llamarón *nm* (*And, CAm, Cono Sur*) = **llamarada.**
llamativo *adj* gaudy, flashy, showy; *color* loud; **de modo ~** in such a way as to draw attention.
llame *nm* (*Cono Sur*) bird trap.
llameante *adj* blazing.
llamear [1a] *vi* to blaze, flame, flare.
llamón‡ *adj* (*Méx*) whining, whingeing*.
llampo *nm* (*And, Cono Sur*) ore, pulverized ore.
llana *nf* (**a**) (*Geog*) plain; flat ground. (**b**) (*Arquit*) mason's trowel.
llanada *nf* plain; flat ground.
llanamente *adv* (*V adj*) (**a**) smoothly, evenly. (**b**) plainly, simply; clearly, straightforwardly; openly, frankly; *V* **lisamente.**
llanca *nf* (*And*) earthworm.
llanear [1a] *vi* (*Aut*) to cruise, coast along.
llanero *nm*, **llanera** *nf* plainsman, plainswoman; (*Carib*: *vaquero*) cowboy; **~ solitario** lone ranger.
llaneza *nf* (*fig*) plainness, simplicity; clearness, straightforwardness; naturalness; modesty; openness, frankness; informality.
llanito*, -a *nm/f* Gibraltarian.
llano 1 *adj* (**a**) *superficie* level, flat, smooth, even.
(**b**) (*fig*) (*sencillo*) plain, simple, unadorned; (*fácil*) clear, easy, straightforward; (*franco*) open, frank; **en lenguaje ~** in plain language; **a la llana** simply; openly, frankly; **decir algo por lo ~** to put matters bluntly, say things straight out; **de ~** openly.
2 *nm* plain, flat ground.
llanque *nm* (*And*) rustic sandal.
llanta¹ *nf* (*esp LAm*) tyre; (*borde*) rim; (*cámara de aire*) inner tube; (*Carib*: *anillo*) large finger-ring; **~s de aleación** alloy wheels; **~ de oruga** caterpillar track.
llanta² *nf* (*And*) sunshade, awning.
llantén *nm* plantain.
llantería* *nf* (*Cono Sur*) weeping and wailing.
llantina* *nf* sobbing; **¡no empieces con la ~!** cut out the sob stuff!*
llanto *nm* weeping, crying; tears; (*fig*) lamentation; (*Liter*) dirge, funeral lament; **dejar el ~** to stop crying.
llanura *nf* (**a**) *superficie* flatness, smoothness, evenness. (**b**) (*Geog*) plain; prairie.
llapa *nf* = **yapa.**
llapango* *adj* (*And*) barefoot.
llapingacho *nm* (*And*) ≈ cheese omelette.
llaretá *nf* (*And*) dried llama dung.
llauto *nm* (*And*) headband.
llave *nf* (**a**) (*de puerta*) key; (*Téc*) key; **~ de cambio** shift key; **~ de contacto, ~ del contactor** (*Aut*) ignition key; **~s de la ciudad, ~s de oro** (*fig*) freedom of the city; **~ espacial** spacing bar; **~ maestra** skeleton key, master key; **¡por las ~s de San Pedro!** by heaven!; **bajo ~, debajo de ~** under lock and key; **'~ en mano'** 'with vacant possession'; **cerrar una puerta con ~** to lock a door; **echar la ~** (**a**) to lock up; **guardar algo bajo siete ~s** to keep sth under lock and key.
(**b**) (*grifo*) tap, faucet (*US*); (*Elec*) switch; **~ de bola, ~ de flotador** ballcock; **~ de cierre, ~ de paso** stopcock.
(**c**) (*Mec*) spanner; **~ inglesa** adjustable spanner, (monkey-)wrench; **~ de ruedas (en cruz)** wheel brace.
(**d**) (*Mús*) stop, key.
(**e**) (*Tip*) bracket ({).
(**f**) (*lucha libre*) lock; (*de judo*) hold.
(**g**) (*de escopeta*) lock.
(**h**) (*Cono Sur*: *Arquit*) beam, joist.
(**i**) **~s** (*Méx Taur*) horns.
llavero *nm* (**a**) *objeto* key ring. (**b**) (*persona*: *t* **~ de cárcel**) turnkey.
llavín *nm* latchkey.
llegada *nf* arrival, coming.
llegar [1h] **1** *vt* (*acercar*) to bring up, bring over, draw up; (*reunir*) to gather together.
2 *vi* (**a**) (*gen*) to arrive, come; **~ a** to arrive at, reach; **por fin llegamos** we're here at last; **avíseme cuando llegue** tell me when he comes; **hacer ~ una carta a** to send a

letter to; **cuando llegue eso** when that happens; **le llegó el año pasado** (*LAm*) he died last year; **me llega** (*And**) I don't give a damn; ~ **a las manos** (*pelear*) to come to blows.

(**b**) (*fig*) to arrive, get to the top, triumph; to make it*.

(**c**) (*alcanzar*) to reach; (*bastar*) to be enough; (*sumar etc*) to amount to, equal, be equal to; **esta cuerda no llega** this rope won't reach, this rope isn't long enough; **las personas no llegan a 100** the people don't amount to 100, the people are fewer than 100; **el importe llega a 50 pesos** the total is 50 pesos; **con ese dinero no vas a** ~ you won't have enough money; **el pobrecito no llega a Navidades** the poor chap won't last out (*o* live) till Christmas; **hacer** ~ **el dinero** to make one's money last out, eke out one's money; **hacer** ~ **el sueldo** to make both ends meet (on one's salary); **¡hasta allí podíamos** ~**!** that's the limit!, what a nerve!

(**d**) **se nos hizo** ~ **que** ... we were made to realize that ..., it was brought home to us that ...

(**e**) (*con verbo*) ~ **a** + *infin* to reach the point of + *ger*; to manage to + *infin*, succeed in + *ger*; **por fin llegó a hacerlo** he managed to do it eventually; **llegué a creerlo** I even believed it; ~ **a saber algo** to find sth out; to get wind of sth; **si llego a saberlo** if I had known it; ~ **a ser** + *adj o n* to become + *adj o n*; ~ **a ser el jefe** to become the boss; **el país llegará a ser una nulidad** the country will become a nonentity.

3 llegarse *vr* to come near, draw near, approach; **llégate más a mí** come closer to me; **llégate a mi casa mañana** drop round tomorrow.

llenador *adj* (*Cono Sur*) *comida* filling, satisfying.

llenar [1a] **1** *vt* (**a**) (*gen*) to fill (*de* with); *superficie etc* to cover (*de* with); *espacio, tiempo etc* to fill, occupy, take up (*de* with); *formulario* to fill in, fill up, fill out (*US*).

(**b**) (*cumplir*) *deber etc* to fulfil; *deseo* to satisfy; *requisitos* to meet, satisfy.

(**c**) (*fig*) ~ **a uno de elogios** to heap praises on sb; ~ **a uno de insultos** to heap insults on sb, revile sb.

2 llenarse *vr* (**a**) to fill, fill up (*de* with); (*) *comida* to stuff o.s. (*de* with); **la superficie se llenó de polvo** the surface got covered in dust.

(**b**) (*fig*) to get cross, lose patience.

llenazón *nm* (*Méx*) blown-out feeling, indigestion.

lleno 1 *adj* (**a**) full (*de* of), filled (*de* with); full up; ~ **hasta el borde** brimful (*de* of); **estar** ~ **a reventar** to be full to bursting; **estar** ~ **de polvo** to be covered in dust; **estar** ~ **de sí mismo** to be full of o.s., be conceited; **de** ~ fully, entirely; **le dio de** ~ **en la oreja** it hit him right on the ear; **dio de** ~ **consigo contra el muro** he went fair and square into the wall.

(**b**) *vino* strong, heady.

2 *nm* (**a**) (*abundancia*) abundance, plenty; (*perfección*) perfection.

(**b**) (*Teat*) full house, sellout.

(**c**) (*Astron*) full moon.

llevadero *adj* bearable, tolerable.

llevar [1a] **1** *vt* (**a**) (*gen*) to carry, take, transport, convey; **¿me llevas esta carta?** will you take this letter for me?; **yo llevaba la maleta** I was carrying the case; **es muy pesado para** ~**lo los dos** it's too heavy for the two of us to carry; ~ **adelante** *plan etc* to carry forward, go on with; ~ **a uno por delante** (*LAm Aut*) to run sb over; **comida para** ~ food to take away, take-away food.

(**b**) *ropa etc* to wear; *objeto pequeño* to have, wear, carry (on one); *armas, nombre, título* to bear; **llevaba traje azul** he wore a blue suit; **llevaba puesto un sombrero raro** she had an odd hat on, she was wearing an odd hat; **no llevo dinero encima** (*o* **conmigo**) I have no money on me, I have no money about me; **lleva un rótulo que dice** ... it has a label which says ...; **el libro lleva el título de** ... the book has the title of ..., the book is entitled ...; **el tren no lleva coche-comedor** the train has no dining car; **el avión no llevaba paracaídas** the plane had no parachutes, the plane was not carrying parachutes.

(**c**) (*con objeto personal*) to take (*a* to); to lead (*a* to); **este camino nos lleva a Bogotá** this road takes us to Bogotá; **le llevamos al teatro** we took him to the theatre; ~ **a uno de la mano** to lead sb by the hand; **¿adónde me llevan Vds?** where are you taking me?; **me llevaron de suplente** they took me along as a substitute.

(**d**) *ruta* to follow, keep to; **¿qué dirección llevaba?** what direction was he going in?, what route was he following?

(**e**) (*apartar*) to carry off, take away, cut off; **el viento llevó una rama** the wind carried a branch away; **la bala le llevó dos dedos** the shot took off two of his fingers.

(**f**) *premio etc* to win, get, carry off.

(**g**) *precio* to charge; **¿cuánto me van a** ~**?** what are you going to charge me?

(**h**) (*Agr*) to bear, produce; (*Com, Fin*) to bear, carry; **no lleva fruto este año** it has no fruit this year; **los bonos llevan un 8 por cien de interés** the bonds bear interest at 8%.

(**i**) *vida* to lead; ~ **una vida tranquila** to live a quiet life, lead a quiet life.

(**j**) (*soportar*) to bear, stand, put up with; ~ **las desgracias con paciencia** to bear misfortunes patiently.

(**k**) (*tiempo*) to spend; **llevo 3 días aquí** I have been here for 3 days, I have so far spent 3 days here; **¿cuánto tiempo llevas aquí?** how long have you been here?; **el tren lleva una hora de retraso** the train is an hour late.

(**l**) (*como v aux*) **llevo 3 meses buscándolo** I have been looking for it for 3 months; **lleva conseguidas muchas victorias** he has won many victories; **llevo estudiados 3 capítulos** I have studied 3 chapters, I have covered 3 chapters; **llevaba hecha la mitad** he had done half of it.

(**m**) *asunto, negocio etc* to conduct, direct, manage; ~ **una finca** to manage an estate; ~ **los libros** (*Com*) to keep the books; ~ **la casa** to run the house (*V t* **casa**); ~ **una materia** (*Méx*) to study a subject.

(**n**) (*exceder*) to exceed; **ella me lleva 2 años** she's 2 years older than I am; **él me lleva la cabeza** he's taller than me by a head; **les llevamos una gran ventaja** we have a great advantage over them.

(**o**) (*Mat*) to carry.

(**p**) (*inducir*) ~ **a uno a creer que** ... to lead sb to think that ...; **esto me lleva a pensar que** ... this leads me to think that ...

(**q**) (*locuciones*) **la lleva hecha** he's got it all worked out; **lleva las de ganar** he holds all the winning cards, he looks like a winner; **llevar las de perder** to be fighting a losing battle; to look like losing; ~ **lo mejor** to get the best of it; ~ **lo peor** to get the worst of it; **no las lleva todas consigo** he's not at all sure of himself; **¡la que llevaba encima aquella noche!*** how drunk he was that night!

2 *vi* (*camino*) to go, lead; **esta carretera lleva a La Paz** this road goes to La Paz.

3 llevarse *vr* (**a**) *objeto, persona* to carry off, take away, remove; **se lo llevaron al cine** they took him off to the cinema; **se llevó mi máquina** he took my camera, he went off with my camera; **los ladrones se llevaron la caja** the thieves took the safe away; **¡que se lo lleve el diablo!** to hell with it!; **el pistolero se llevó 10.000 libras** the gunman got away with £10,000; **se llevó el primer premio** she carried off the first prize; **¡no lo toques o te la llevas!*** don't touch it or you'll live to regret it!

(**b**) ~ **bien** to get on well (together); **no se lleva bien con el jefe** he doesn't get on (*o* along) with the boss.

(**c**) ~ **a uno por delante** (*LAm*) to offend sb; to ride roughshod over sb.

(**d**) (*: *estar de moda*) to be in fashion, be in*.

llicla *nf* (*And*) woollen shawl.

llicta *nf* (*And*) quinine paste.

llimo *adj* (*Cono Sur*) small-eared; earless.

llocalla *nm* (*And*) boy.

lloquena *nf* (*And*) fish spear, harpoon.

llora *nf* (*Carib*) wake.

llorado *adj*: **el** ~ **rey** the (late) lamented king; **un hombre no** ~ an unlamented man.

llorar [1a] **1** *vt* to weep over, weep for, cry about; to bewail, lament; *muerte, pérdida* to mourn.

2 *vi* (**a**) (*persona*) to cry, weep; **¡no llores!** don't cry!; ~ **a cuajo,** ~ **lágrima viva,** ~ **a moco y baba,** ~ **a moco tendido** to sob one's heart out, cry uncontrollably; ~ **como una fuente** (*o* **criatura** *etc*)* to weep buckets*; **el que no llora no mama** if you don't ask you don't get.

(**b**) (*ojos*) to water; (*grifo etc*) to drip.

(**c**) (*Cono Sur*: *quedar bien*) to suit, be becoming, look nice (*a* on).

(**d**) (*And, Carib, Cono Sur*: *quedar muy mal*) to be very unbecoming.

llorera* *nf* sobbing, fit of crying.

lloretas* *nmf invar* (*And, CAm*) crybaby.

lloricón* *adj persona* weepy*, tearful; *film etc* tear-jerking*.

lloriquear [1a] *vi* to snivel, whimper.

lloriqueo *nm* snivelling, whimpering.

llorisquear [1a] *vi* (*Carib, Cono Sur*) *etc* = **lloriquear** *etc.*

lloro *nm* (**a**) crying, weeping; tears; wailing. (**b**) (*en grabación*) wow.

llorón 1 *adj* weeping, tearful; snivelling, whining; *V* **sauce. 2** *nm*, **llorona¹** *nf* tearful person, weepy sort*; crybaby. **3 llorona²** *nf* hired mourner; (*Méx*) ghost, soul in torment. **4 lloronas** *nfpl* (*And, Cono Sur*) large spurs.

lloroso *adj* weeping, tearful; sad.

llovedera *nf* (*And, CAm, Carib*), **llovedero** *nm* (*Cono Sur*) (period of) continuous rain; (*época*) rainy season; (*tormenta*) rainstorm.

llovedizo *adj* (**a**) *techo* leaky. (**b**) **agua llovediza** rainwater.

llover [2h] *vi* (**a**) (*gen*) to rain; **llueve, está lloviendo** it is raining; **~ a cántaros, ~ a cubos, ~ a chuzos, ~ a mares, ~ a torrentes** to rain cats and dogs, rain in torrents; **como llovido (del cielo)** unexpectedly; **ser una cosa llovida del cielo** to come just right, be a godsend; **está llovido en la milpita*** (*Méx**) we're (*etc*) having a run of bad luck, we're (*etc*) going through a bad patch; **llueva o no** rain or shine, come what may; **mucho** (*o* **ya**) **ha llovido desde entonces** much water has flowed under the bridge since then; **¡como ahora llueve pepinos** (*o* **uvas**)! (*And*) rubbish!; **siempre que llueve escampa** (*Carib*) every cloud has a silver lining; *V* **mojado.**

(**b**) (*fig*) to rain; **le llovieron regalos encima** gifts were rained on him, he was showered with gifts.

llovida *nf* (*LAm*) rain, shower.

llovido *nm* stowaway.

llovizna *nf* drizzle.

lloviznar [1a] *vi* to drizzle.

lloviznoso *adj* drizzly.

llueca *nf* broody hen.

lluqui *adj* (*And*) left-handed.

lluvia *nf* rain; shower; (*cantidad*) rainfall; (*insecticida etc*) spray; (*de balas, misiles*) hail, shower; (*de regadera*) rose; (*Cono Sur*: *ducha*) shower, shower bath; (*fig*) shower, mass, abundance; **día de ~** rainy day; **~ ácida** acid rain; **~ artificial** cloud seeding; **~ menuda** fine rain, drizzle; **~ de meteoros** meteor shower; **~s monzónicas** monsoon rains; **~ de oro** (*Bot*) laburnum; **~ radiactiva** radioactive fallout; **~ torrencial** torrential rain; **una ~ de regalos** a shower of gifts; **la ~ cae sobre los buenos como sobre los malos** it rains on the just as well as on the unjust.

lluvioso *adj* rainy, wet.

M

M, m ['eme] *nf* (*letra*) M, m.
M. (**a**) *abr de* **Madrid**. (**b**) (*Ferro*) *abr de* **Metropolitano** Metro. (**c**) (*Geog*) *abr de* **Meridiano**. (**d**) *abr de* **María**.
m. (**a**) *abr de* **metro**(**s**) metre(s), m. (**b**) *abr de* **minuto**(**s**) minute(s), m, min. (**c**) *abr de* **masculino** masculine, masc., m.
m² *abr de* **metros cuadrados** square metres, sq. m., m².
m³ *abr de* **metros cúbicos** cubic metres, cu. m., m³.
M-19 *nm* (*Colombia Pol*) *abr de* **Movimiento 19 de Abril**.
M.ª *abr de* **María**.
maca¹ *nf* (*defecto*) flaw, defect; spot; (*en fruta*) bruise, blemish, bad patch.
maca² *nf* (*Carib*) parrot.
maca³‡ *nm* = **macarra**.
macabí *nm* (**a**) (*And*) shrewd person. (**b**) (*Carib*) bandit.
macabro *adj* macabre.
macaco 1 *adj* (**a**) (*LAm**: *feo*) ugly. (**b**) (*CAm, Carib**: *tonto*) silly. **2** *nm* (**a**) (*Zool*) macaque. (**b**) (*Cono Sur**: *pey*) Brazilian. (**c**) (*Carib*) big shot*, bigwig. (**d**) (*Méx*) bogey.
macadamizar [1f] *vt* to macadamize.
macadán *nm* macadam.
macagua *nf* (*LAm*) macaw.
macana *nf* (**a**) (*LAm*) (*porra*) club, cudgel; (*de policía*) truncheon.
(**b**) (*And, Cono Sur**) (*disparate*) stupid comment; (*mentira*) lie; **~s** (*Esp*) nonsense, rubbish.
(**c**) (*Cono Sur**: *chapuza*) bad job, mess.
(**d**) (*Cono Sur**: *charla*) long boring conversation; **¡qué ~!** what a bind!*
(**e**) (*Carib*) **de ~** undoubtedly; **es de ~ que** ... of course ...
macanazo *nm* (**a**) (*Carib*) blow (with a club). (**b**) (*Cono Sur*) = **macana** (**b**). (**c**) (*molestia*) nuisance, bore.
macaneador* (*Cono Sur*) **1** *adj* (*mañoso*) deceitful; (*poco fiable*) unreliable. **2** *nm*, **macaneadora** *nf* charlatan.
macanear [1a] **1** *vt* (**a**) (*Carib*: *aporrear*) to beat, hit.
(**b**) (*Carib*) to weed, clear of weeds.
(**c**) (*Carib*) *asunto* to handle.
2 *vi* (**a**) (*And, Cono Sur**) to talk nonsense, talk rubbish; to exaggerate wildly, tell tall stories.
(**b**) (*LAm**: *trabajar*) to work hard, keep one's nose to the grindstone.
macanero* *adj* (*And, Cono Sur*) given to talking nonsense, silly; given to telling tall stories.
macanudo *adj* (**a**) (*****) smashing*, great*. (**b**) (*Cono Sur, Méx*: *abultado*) swollen, overlarge; (*Cono Sur**: *exagerado*) disproportionate. (**c**) (*And*) *persona* strong, tough; *trabajo* tough, difficult.
Macao *nm* Macao.
macaquear [1a] **1** *vt* (*CAm*) to steal. **2** *vi* (*Cono Sur*) to make faces.
macarra‡ 1 *nm* (*Esp*: *marica*) queer‡; (*Esp*: *coime*) pimp; (*bruto*) lout, thug, bully-boy; (*mal vestido*) scruffily-dressed lad. **2** *nf* (**a**) (*acto*) brutal deed, loutish thing (to do). (**b**) (*porquería*) mess, filth; **esa camisa es una ~** that shirt looks a right mess*.
macarrada* *nf* piece of vulgarity; mess; filthy thing.
macarrón¹ *nm* (**a**) (*dulce*) macaroon. (**b**) **macarrones** (*pasta*) macaroni.
macarrón² *nm* (*Náut*) bulwark.
macarrónico *adj* macaronic.
macarse [1g] *vr* (*fruta*) to get bruised, (begin to) rot.
macear [1a] **1** *vt* to hammer, pound. **2** *vi* (**a**) = **machacar 2**. (**b**) (*CAm**) to bet.
macedonia *nf*: **~ de frutas** fruit salad.
maceración *nf* (**a**) (*Culin*) softening, soaking; maceration; **dejar en ~** to leave to soak. (**b**) (*fig*) mortification.
macerar [1a] **1** *vt* to soften, soak, macerate. **2 macerarse** *vr* to soften, soak, macerate; (*fig*) to mortify o.s.
macero *nm* macebearer.
maceta 1 *adj* (**a**) (*And, Cono Sur**) slow, thick*; **ponerse ~** to get old.
(**b**) (*Carib**) miserly.
2 *nf* (**a**) (*tiesto*) flowerpot; pot of flowers; (*Cono Sur*: *ramo*) bouquet, bunch of flowers.
(**b**) (*martillo*) mallet, small hammer; stonecutter's hammer.
(**c**) (*Méx**: *cabeza*) nut‡; **ser duro de ~** (*And, Cono Sur**) to be pretty thick*.
macetero *nm* flowerpot stand (*o* holder); (*And, Carib, Cono Sur*) flowerpot.
macetón *nm* tub (*for plants*).
macia *nf* = **macis**.
macicez *nf* massiveness; solidity; stoutness.
macilento *adj* wan, haggard; gaunt; emaciated.
macillo *nm* (*Mús*) hammer.
macis *nf* mace (*spice*).
maciza *nf* (*LAm*) chipboard.
macizamente *adj* massively; solidly; stoutly.
macizar [1f] *vt* to fill up, fill in, pack solid.
macizo 1 *adj* (**a**) (*grande*) massive; *neumático, oro, puerta etc* solid; (*bien hecho*) solidly made, stoutly made; *persona* solid, stoutly built; **de roble ~** of solid oak; **~ de gente** solid with people. (**b**) (*****) *chica* smashing*.
2 *adv* (*CAm, Méx*) quickly, fast.
3 *nm* (**a**) (*masa*) mass; (*trozo*) lump, chunk, solid piece; (*de plantas*) clump.
(**b**) (*Geog*) massif.
(**c**) (*Hort*) bed, plot.
(**d**) (*Aut*) solid tyre.
(**e**) (*Arquit*) stretch, section (of a wall).
macizorro* *adj hombre* hunky*; *mujer* well-stacked*.
maco‡ *nm* nick‡, prison; (*Mil*) glasshouse.
macollo *nm* bunch, cluster.
macro... *pref* macro...
macró *nm* pimp.
macrobiótico *adj* macrobiotic.
macrocefalía *nf* macrocephaly; (*fig*) top-heaviness.
macrocefálico *adj* macrocephalic; (*fig*) top-heavy.
macrocomando *nm* macro (command).
macrocosmo(s) *nm* macrocosm.
macroeconomía *nf* macroeconomy.
macroeconómica *nf* macroeconomics.
macroeconómico *adj* macroeconomic.
macuache* *adj* (*Méx*) rough, coarse.
macuco 1 *adj* (**a**) (*And, Cono Sur**: *astuto*) crafty, cunning. (**b**) (*And*: *inútil*) old and useless. (**c**) (*And, Cono Sur*) (*grande*) big, great; (*demasiado grande*) overgrown. **2** *nm* (*And, Cono Sur**) overgrown boy, big lad.
macuenco *adj* (**a**) (*Carib**: *débil*) thin, weak, feeble. (**b**) (*Carib*: *inútil*) useless. (**c**) (*And*: *demasiado grande*) big; overgrown, extra large; (*****) splendid, terrific*.
mácula *nf* (**a**) (*gen fig*) stain, spot, blemish; **~ solar** sunspot. (**b**) (*trampa*) trick, fraud.
macular [1a] *vt* to stain, spot.
macundales *nmpl* (*And, Carib*), **macundos** *nmpl* (*Carib*) (*trastos*) things, gear, junk; (*negocios*) affairs, business.
macutazo* *nm* rumour; hoax.
macuto *nm* (**a**) (*mochila*) knapsack; satchel. (**b**) (*Carib*) begging basket.
macha *nf* (*And, Carib*) mannish woman.
machaca 1 *nf* (*aparato*) crusher, pounder. **2** *nmf* (*persona*) pest, bore.
machacadora *nf* crusher, pounder.
machacante 1 *adj* insistent; monotonous. **2** *nm* (*Esp*†) 5 pesetas.

machacar [1g] **1** *vt* (**a**) (*hacer polvo*) to crush, pound; (*moler*) to grind (up); (*aplastar*) to mash.

(**b**) (*fig*) *objeto* to knock to bits; *enemigo* to maul, crush; (*en debate*) to crush, flatten, make mincemeat of; *precio* to slash.

(**c**) (*: *Básquet*) to dunk, slam dunk.

2 *vi* (**a**) (*Esp*: *insistir*) to go on, keep on; to nag; **~ en un asunto** to keep on about a matter, harp on a matter; **¡no machaques!** don't go on so!, stop harping on it!; *V* **hierro.**

(**b**) (*: *Univ etc*) to swot*.

3 machacarse *vr* (**a**) **~ el verano*** to spend the summer swotting*. (**b**) **machacársela** (*Esp*‡‡) to wank‡‡; **¡a mí me la machaco!** (*Esp*‡) get away!, no way!*

machacón 1 *adj* (*pesado*) tiresome, wearisome; (*insistente*) insistent; (*monótono*) monotonous, repetitive; **con insistencia machacona** with wearisome insistence. **2** *nm*, **machacona** *nf* pest, bore.

machaconamente *adv* tiresomely; insistently; monotonously, repetitively.

machaconeo *nm* insistence; monotony, repetitiveness.

machada *nf* (**a**) manly act, act of courage; heroic deed; (*pey*) piece of bravado. (**b**) **~s** nonsense; fooling around.

machado *nm* hatchet.

machamartillo: **a ~** *adv*: **creer a ~** to believe firmly, (*pey*) to believe blindly; **cumplir a ~** to carry out a task to the letter, perform a task down to the last detail; **eran cristianos a ~** they were absolutely convinced Christians.

machango *adj* (*Cono Sur*) tedious.

machaque* *nm* dunk, slam dunk.

machaquear [1a] *vti* (*Méx*) = **machacar.**

machaqueo *nm* crushing, pounding.

machaquería *nf* tiresomeness; insistence, harping (on a subject); monotony.

macharse‡ [1a] *vr* (*Cono Sur*) to get drunk.

machetazo *nm* (*LAm*) (**a**) (*instrumento*) large *machete.* (**b**) (*golpe*) blow (*o* slash) with a *machete.*

machete[1] *nm* (*LAm*) *machete,* cane knife, big knife.

machete[2] *adj* mean, stingy.

machetear [1a] **1** *vt* (**a**) (*LAm*) *caña etc* to cut down with a *machete*; *persona* to slash (*o* wound, stab *etc*) with a *machete.*

(**b**) (*And**: *vender barato*) to sell cheap.

2 *vi* (**a**) (*And, Méx*: *obstinarse*) to dig one's heels in.

(**b**) (*Méx*) (*trabajar*) to hammer away; (*estudiante*) to plod on.

machetero *nm* (**a**) (*LAm Agr*) cane cutter. (**b**) (*Méx*: *cargador*) porter. (**c**) (*Carib*††) revolutionary; **~ de salón** armchair radical. (**d**) (*Méx Univ*) plodder. (**e**) (*Carib**: *soldado*) soldier.

machi *nm*, **machí** *nm* (*LAm*) medicine man.

machiega *nf* (*t* **abeja ~**) queen bee.

machihembrado *nm* (*Téc*) dovetail (joint).

machihembrar [1a] *vt* to dovetail.

machina *nf* (**a**) (*Mec*) crane, derrick; pile driver. (**b**) (*Carib*) merry-go-round.

machirulo (*Esp*) **1** *adj* tomboyish; mannish. **2** *nm* tomboy; mannish woman.

machismo *nm* machismo, masculinity; (*orgullo*) male pride, maleness; (*virilidad*) virility; (*pey*) male chauvinism.

machista 1 *adj* full of machismo, full of male pride, very masculine; (*pey*) male chauvinistic. **2** *nm* (*pey*) male chauvinist.

machito[1] *nm* (*Méx*) fried offal.

machito[2] *nm*: **estar montado** (*o* **subido**) **en el ~** to be well placed, be riding high.

macho 1 *adj* (**a**) (*Bio*) male; **la flor ~** the male flower; **una rata ~** a male rat.

(**b**) (*fig*) macho, masculine; strong, tough; **es muy ~** he's very tough.

(**c**) (*Mec*) male.

(**d**) (*) stupid.

(**e**) (*And**: *fantástico*) splendid, terrific*.

2 *nm* (**a**) (*Bio*) male; (*Zool*) mule; (*: *a persona, en oración directa*) man*, mate*, brother*; **~ cabrío** he-goat, billy-goat; **~ de varas** leading mule; (*fig*) person in charge; **atarse** (*o* **apretarse**) **los ~s** to pull out all the stops, make a great effort.

(**b**) (*Mec*) pin, peg; (*Elec*) pin; plug; (*Cos*) hook.

(**c**) (*Téc*) sledgehammer.

(**d**) (*Arquit*) buttress.

(**e**) (*fig*: *persona*) macho, tough guy (*US**), he-man*; (*pey*) idiot.

(**f**) **parar el ~ a uno** (*LAm*) to take the wind out of sb's sails.

(**g**) (*CAm**: *Mil*) US marine.

(**h**) (*Esp*†‡) 5 pesetas.

machón *nm* buttress.

machona *nf* (*And, Carib, Cono Sur*) (*mujer*) mannish woman; (*niña*) tomboy.

machorra‡ *nf* dyke‡, lesbian.

machota *nf* (**a**) (*mujer*) mannish woman. (**b**) (*Téc*) hammer, mallet; rammer. (**c**) **a la ~** (*And, Carib*) carelessly; (*CAm*) rudely, roughly.

machote *nm* (**a**) (*) tough guy (*US**), he-man*. (**b**) (*LAm*) (*borrador*) rough draft, sketch; (*modelo*) model; (*pauta*) pattern. (**c**) (*Méx*) blank form.

machucar [1g] *vt* (**a**) (*hacer polvo*) to pound, crush; (*golpear*) to beat; (*abollar*) to dent; (*dañar*) to knock about, damage.

(**b**) (*Med*) to bruise.

(**c**) (*And, Carib, Méx*) *caballo* to tire out (*before a race*).

(**d**) (*Carib*) *ropa* to rinse through.

machucón *nm* (*LAm*) bruise.

machucho *adj* (**a**) (*mayor*) elderly, getting on in years. (**b**) (*prudente*) prudent; (*tranquilo*) sedate; (*juicioso*) sensible. (**c**) (*And, Méx**: *taimado*) cunning, sly, shrewd.

Madagascar *nm* Madagascar.

madaleno‡ *nm* secret policeman.

madama *nf* (*And, Cono Sur*), **madame** *nf* madame, brothel-keeper.

madeja 1 *nf* (*de lana*) skein, hank; (*de pelo*) mass, mop; **~ de nervios** bundle of nerves; **se está enredando la ~** the affair is getting complicated, the plot thickens. **2** *nm* (*persona*) layabout, idler.

Madera *nf* Madeira.

madera[1] *nm* Madeira (*wine*).

madera[2] *nf* (**a**) (*gen*) wood; (*Mús*) woodwind section (of the orchestra; *t* **~s**); **~ (de construcción** *etc***)** timber; (*una* **~**) piece of wood; **la ~** (*Dep*) the woodwork; **~ contrachapada, ~ (multi)laminada, ~ terciada** plywood; **~ de deriva** driftwood; **~ dura** hardwood; **~ fósil** lignite; **de ~** wood, wooden; **¡toca ~!** touch wood!, knock on wood! (*US*).

(**b**) (*Zool*) horny part (*of hoof*).

(**c**) (*fig*) nature, temperament; aptitude; **tiene buena ~** there's a lot (of good) in him, he's made of solid stuff; **tiene ~ de futbolista** he'll make a footballer, he's got football in him.

(**d**) (‡) fuzz‡, police.

maderable *adj*: **árbol ~** tree useful for its wood; **bosque ~** wood containing useful timber.

maderaje *nm*, **maderamen** *nm* timber, wood; woodwork, timbering.

maderero 1 *adj* wood (*atr*), timber (*atr*); **industria maderera** timber industry; **productos ~s** wood products. **2** *nm* timber merchant; lumberman.

maderismo *nm* (*Méx Pol*) *reform movement led by Madero.*

maderista *nmf* (*Méx Pol*) supporter of Madero.

madero *nm* (**a**) (*viga*) beam; (*tronco*) log; (*trozo de madera*) (piece of) timber. (**b**) (*fig*: *Náut*) ship, vessel. (**c**) (*: *idiota*) oaf, blockhead. (**d**) (*Esp*‡: *policía*) cop‡.

Madona *nf* Madonna.

madrastra *nf* stepmother; (*fig*) unloving mother.

madrazo* *nm* (*Méx*) hefty blow*.

madre 1 *adj* (**a**) (*lit*) mother; **buque ~** mother ship; **lengua ~** parent language; **acequia ~** main channel; **alcantarilla ~** main sewer, principal sewer.

(**b**) **color ~** dominant colour, theme colour; **la cuestión ~** the chief problem, the central problem.

(**c**) (*LAm**) tremendous*, terrific*; **una regañada ~** one hell of a telling-off*.

2 *nf* (**a**) mother; (*orfanato etc*) matron; **~ adoptiva** foster-mother; **~ alquilada, ~ de alquiler, ~ portadora** surrogate mother; **~ biológica, ~ genética** biological mother, true mother; **~ política** mother-in-law; **~ soltera** single mother; **~ trabajadora** working mother; **M~ de Dios** Mother of God; **¡M~ de Dios!** good heavens!; **futura ~** expectant mother; **su señora ~** your mother; **sin ~** motherless; **¡~ mía!** well!; oh dear!; **¡tu ~!**‡‡ up yours!‡‡, get stuffed!‡‡; **a toda ~** (*LAm*‡), **de la ~** (*LAm*‡) great*, terrific*; **ni ~*** not a thing; **ahí está la ~ del cordero** that's just the trouble; **mentar a la ~ a uno** to swear at sb; **él no tiene ~*** he's a real swine*; **esto no tiene ~*** this is the limit; *V* **ciento.**

(**b**) (*fig*: *de civilización etc*) origin, cradle.

(**c**) **la ~** (*en juegos*) home.

(**d**) (*Anat*) womb.

(**e**) (*de río*) bed; **sacar de ~ a uno** to provoke sb, upset sb; **salirse de ~** (*río*) to overflow, burst its banks; (*persona*) to lose all self-control; (*proceso etc*) to go beyond its normal limits.

(**f**) (*de vino etc*) dregs, lees; sediment.

(**g**) (*Agr*) main channel, main irrigation ditch; (*Téc*) main sewer.

(**h**) (*And*) dead skin, scab.

(**i**) (‡) queer‡.

madrejón *nm* (*Cono Sur Agr*) watercourse.

madreperla *nf* (*ostra*) pearl oyster; (*nácar*) mother-of-pearl; **~ de río** freshwater mussel.

madreselva *nf* honeysuckle; **~ siempreverde** Cape honeysuckle.

Madrid *nm* Madrid.

madrigal *nm* madrigal.

madriguera *nf* (**a**) (*Zool*) den; burrow. (**b**) (*fig*) den.

madrileño 1 *adj* of Madrid; **madrileñísimo** typical of Madrid, full of the character of Madrid; **la madrileñísima Cibeles** Cibeles Square which is so typical of Madrid, Cibeles Square which sums up so much of Madrid.

2 *nm*, **madrileña** *nf* native (*o* inhabitant) of Madrid; **los ~s** the people of Madrid.

Madriles* *nmpl*: **Los ~** Madrid.

madrina *nf* (**a**) (*en bautizo*) godmother; (*de empresa etc*) patron(ess), protectress; **~ de boda** ≈ bridesmaid.

(**b**) (*Arquit etc*) prop, shore; (*Téc*) brace.

(**c**) (*Agr*) lead mare.

(**d**) (*LAm*) tame animal (*used in breaking in or catching others*).

(**e**) (*Méx**) police informer.

madriza‡ *nf* (*Méx*) bashing*, beating-up*.

madroño *nm* strawberry tree, arbutus.

madrugada *nf* early morning; dawn, daybreak; **levantarse de ~** to get up early; **a las 4 de la ~** at 4 o'clock in the morning, at 4 a.m.

madrugador 1 *adj* early rising, who gets up early. **2** *nm*, **madrugadora** *nf* early riser; (*fig*) early bird.

madrugar [1h] **1** *vt*: **~ a uno** (*adelantarse a*) to forestall sb, get in ahead of sb; (*CAm‡*: *matar*) to bump sb off‡.

2 *vi* (**a**) (*levantarse*) to get up early; to be an early riser; **a quien madruga, Dios le ayuda** God helps those who help themselves.

(**b**) (*fig*) to get ahead; to get in first (in replying *etc*); to jump the gun.

madrugón *nm*: **darse** (*o* **pegarse**) **un ~** to get up terribly early.

maduración *nf* ripening; maturing.

madurar [1a] **1** *vt* (**a**) *frutos* to ripen. (**b**) (*fig*) to mature; *plan etc* to think out. **2** *vi* (**a**) (*frutos*) to ripen. (**b**) (*fig*) to mature. **3 madurarse** *vr* to ripen.

madurez *nf* (**a**) (*lit*) ripeness. (**b**) (*fig*) maturity; mellowness; sageness, wisdom.

maduro 1 *adj* (**a**) *fruta* ripe; **poco ~** unripe, underripe.

(**b**) (*fig*) mature; mellow; **de edad madura** of mature years; **la cosa está madura para la reforma** the business is ripe for reform; **el divieso está ~** the boil is about to burst.

2 *nm* (*LAm*) plantain.

MAE *nm* (*Esp Pol*) *abr de* **Ministerio de Asuntos Exteriores.**

maesa *nf* queen bee.

maestra *nf* (**a**) (*Escol*) teacher (*t fig*); **~ de escuela** schoolteacher. (**b**) (*Ent*) queen bee. (**c**) (*Arquit*) guide line.

maestranza *nf* (**a**) (*Mil*) arsenal, armoury; (*Náut*) naval dockyard. (**b**) (*personal*) staff of an arsenal (*o* dockyard). (**c**) (*LAm*) machine shop.

maestrazgo *nm* (*Hist*) office of grand master.

maestre *nm* (*Hist*) grand master (*of a military order*).

maestrear [1a] *vt* (**a**) (*dirigir*) to direct, manage. (**b**) (*Agr*) to prune.

maestría *nf* (**a**) (*dominio*) mastery; (*habilidad*) skill, expertise; **lo hizo con ~** he did it very skilfully, he did it in a masterly fashion. (**b**) (*Univ*) master's degree.

maestro 1 *adj* (**a**) (*genial*) masterly; (*experto*) skilled, expert.

(**b**) (*Téc*) main, principal; master (*atr*); **cloaca maestra** main sewer; **llave maestra** skeleton key, master key; **obra maestra** masterpiece; **viga maestra** main beam.

(**c**) (*Ent*) **abeja maestra** queen bee.

(**d**) *animal* trained; **halcón ~** trained hawk.

2 *nm* (**a**) (*gen*) master; (*profesor*) teacher; (*autoridad*) authority; **~ (de escuela)** schoolteacher; (*Téc*) master craftsman; **el ~ de todos los medievalistas españoles** the greatest authority among the Spanish medievalists; **gran ~** (*Ajedrez*) grand master; **beber en los grandes ~s** to absorb wisdom from the great teachers; **¿por dónde, ~?*** which way, squire?*

(**b**) (*aposición*) master ...; **~ albañil** mason, skilled building craftsman; **~ sastre** master tailor; **'Los ~s cantores'** 'The Mastersingers'.

(**c**) (*Mús*) maestro; **el ~ Falla** the great musician (*o* composer) Falla.

(**d**) **~ de armas, ~ de esgrima** fencing master; **~ de ceremonias** master of ceremonies; **~ de cocina** chef; **~ de coros** choirmaster; **~ de maquillaje** make-up expert; **~ de obras** master builder; foreman, clerk of works.

(**e**) (*LAm*: *artesano*) skilled workman, craftsman; (*Cono Sur*) repairman; **~ de caminos** skilled road-construction man.

mafafa *nf* (*LAm*) marijuana.

mafia *nf* mafia, criminal gang, ring; **la M~** the Mafia.

mafioso *nm* mafioso, (*de la Mafia*) member of the Mafia; (*criminal*: *gen*) hood‡, gangster.

Magallanes *nm* Magellan.

magancear [1a] *vi* (*And, Cono Sur*) to idle, loaf.

maganto *adj* (**a**) (*macilento*) wan, wasted. (**b**) (*preocupado*) worried; (*soso*) lifeless, dull.

maganza* *nf* (*And*) idleness, laziness.

maga(n)zón *nm* (*LAm*) idler, loafer.

maganzonería *nf* (*LAm*) = **maganza**.

Magdalena *nf* Magdalen, Madeleine; **La ~** Mary Magdalene; **m~** penitent woman; **llorar como una ~** to cry one's eyes out.

magenta *nf* magenta.

magia *nf* magic; **~ blanca** white magic; **~ negra** black magic; **por arte de ~** (as if) by magic.

magiar *adj, nmf* Magyar.

mágico 1 *adj* magic, magical. **2** *nm* magician.

magín* *nm* fancy, imagination; mind; **todo eso salió de su ~** it all came out of his own head.

magisterio *nm* (**a**) (*enseñanza*) teaching; (*profesión*) teaching profession; (*formación*) teachers' training; **dedicarse al ~** to go in for teaching; **ejerció el ~ durante 40 años** he taught for 40 years.

(**b**) (*personas*) teachers (*collectively*).

(**c**) (*fig*) pompousness, pedantry.

(**d**) **M~** (*CAm Univ*) Department of Education.

magistrado, -a *nm/f* magistrate; judge; **primer M~** (*LAm*) president, prime minister.

magistral 1 *adj* (**a**) magisterial. (**b**) (*fig*: *genial*) masterly. (**c**) (*pey*) pompous, pedantic. **2** *nm* (**reloj**) **~** master clock.

magistratura *nf* magistracy; judgeship; **alta ~** (*fig*) highest authority; **~ de trabajo** industrial tribunal.

magnánimamente *adv* magnanimously.

magnanimidad *nf* magnanimity.

magnánimo *adj* magnanimous.

magnate *nm* magnate; tycoon; (*Hist*) baron; **los ~s de la industria** the top people in industry, the big industrialists; **~ de la prensa** press baron, press lord.

magnavoz *nm* (*Méx*) loudspeaker.

magnesia *nf* magnesia.

magnesio *nm* (*Quím*) magnesium; (*Fot*) flash, flashlight.

magnéticamente *adv* magnetically.

magnético *adj* magnetic.

magnetismo *nm* magnetism.

magnetizable *adj* magnetizable.

magnetizar [1f] *vt* to magnetize.

magneto *nf* magneto.

magnetofón *nm* (*Esp*), **magnetófono** *nm* (*Esp*) tape-recorder.

magnetofónico *adj* tape (*atr*), recording (*atr*); **cinta magnetofónica** recording tape.

magnetómetro *nm* magnetometer.

magnetoscopio *nm* video recorder.

magnetosfera *nf* magnetosphere.

magnicida *nmf* assassin (of an important person).

magnicidio *nm* assassination (of an important person).

magníficamente *adv* splendidly, wonderfully, superbly, magnificently.

magnificar [1g] *vt* to praise, extol.

magnificencia *nf* (**a**) (*esplendor*) splendour, magnificence. (**b**) (*generosidad*) lavishness, generosity.

magnífico *adj* splendid, wonderful, superb, magnificent; **¡~!** splendid!, that's grand!; **~ rector** (*Esp Univ*) honourable Chancellor; **es un muchacho ~** he's a fine boy; **tenemos un ~ profesor** we have a splendid teacher.

magnitud *nf* magnitude (*t Astron*); **de primera ~** (*Astron*)

of the first magnitude.
magno *adj* (*liter*) great.
magnolia *nf* magnolia.
mago *nm* magician, wizard; *V* **rey**.
magra *nf* (**a**) (*de carne*) lean part (*of meat*). (**b**) (*lonja*) slice; rasher. (**c**) **¡~!‡** rubbish!, not on your nelly!‡ (**d**) (*Esp*‡: *casa*) house.
magrear‡ [1a] *vt* (*Esp*) to feel, touch up‡.
Magreb *nm* Maghrib.
magrebí *adj*, **magrebino** *adj* Maghribian.
magreo‡ *nm* (*Esp*) touching up‡.
magrez *nf* leanness.
magro *adj* (**a**) *persona* thin, lean. (**b**) *carne* lean; *queso* low-fat. (**c**) *tierra* poor, thin.
magrura *nf* leanness.
magua *nf* (*Carib*) disappointment; failure, setback.
maguarse* [1i] *vr* (*Carib*) (**a**) (*fiesta etc*) to be a flop*. (**b**) (*persona*) (*decepcionarse*) to suffer a disappointment; (*deprimirse*) to get depressed.
maguer (††, *liter*) **1** *prep* in spite of, despite. **2** *conj* although.
maguey *nm* (*Bot*) maguey.
maguillo *nm* wild apple tree.
magulladura *nf* bruise.
magullar [1a] *vt* (*amoratar*) to bruise; (*dañar*) to hurt, damage; (*golpear*) to batter, bash*; (*And, Carib*) to crumple, rumple.
magullón *nm* (*LAm*) bruise.
Maguncia *nf* Mainz.
maharajá *nm* maharajah; **vivir como un ~** to live like a prince.
mahdi *nm* Mahdi.
Mahoma *nm* Mahomet, Muhammad.
mahometano, -a *adj, nm/f* Mahommedan.
mahometismo *nm* Mahommedanism.
mahonesa *nf* mayonnaise.
mai‡ *nm* joint‡.
maicena *nf* blancmange; (*LAm*) cornflour, corn starch (*US*).
maicero *adj* maize (*atr*), corn (*atr*: *US*).
maicillo *nm* (*Cono Sur*) gravel.
mailing ['mailin] *nm, pl* **mailings** ['mailin] mailshot.
maitines *nmpl* matins.
maître ['metre] *nm* (*t* **~ d'hôtel**) head waiter.
maíz *nm* (**a**) (*Agr*) maize, corn (*US*), sweet corn, Indian corn; **~ en la mazorca** corn on the cob. (**b**) **coger a uno asando ~** (*Carib*) to catch sb red-handed; **dar a uno ~ tostado** (*And*) to give sb their comeuppance.
maizal *nm* maize field, cornfield (*US*).
maizena *nf* (*LAm*) = **maicena**.
maizudo *adj* (*CAm*) rich, wealthy.
maja *nf* woman (*o* girl) of the people (*esp of Madrid*).
majada *nf* (**a**) (*corral*) sheepfold. (**b**) (*estiércol*) dung. (**c**) (*Cono Sur*) (*de ovejas*) flock of sheep; (*de chivos*) herd of goats.
majaderear [1a] *vt* (*LAm*) to bother, annoy.
majadería *nf* (**a**) (*tontería*) silliness; (*sin sentido*) absurdity. (**b**) (*una ~*) silly thing, absurdity; **~s** nonsense.
majadero 1 *adj* silly, stupid. **2** *nm* (**a**) (*tonto*) idiot, fool; **¡~!** you idiot! (**b**) (*Téc*) pestle. (**c**) (*Cos*) bobbin.
majador *nm* pestle.
majagranzas* *invar* = **majadero**.
majagua *nf* (*Carib*) (**a**) (*Dep*) baseball bat. (**b**) (*: *traje*) suit.
majar [1a] *vt* (**a**) (*aplastar*) to pound, crush, grind; to mash; (*Med*) to bruise. (**b**) (*) to bother, pester.
majara* *adj invar*, **majareta*** *adj invar* cracked, potty*.
maje 1 *adj* (*Méx*‡) gullible; **hacer ~ al marido** to cheat on one's husband. **2** *nmf* (*Méx*‡) sucker‡. **3** *nm* (*CAm**: *tipo*) bloke‡, guy*.
majestad *nf* majesty; stateliness; **Su M~** His (*o* Her) Majesty; **M~, Vuestra M~** Your Majesty.
majestuosamente *adv* majestically.
majestuosidad *nf* majesty, stateliness.
majestuoso *adj* majestic, stately, imposing.
majete* 1 *adj* nice, likeable. **2** *nm* guy*, bloke‡; **¡jo, ~!** hey man!*
majeza *nf* (**a**) (*atractivo*) good looks, attractiveness; loveliness. (**b**) (*elegancia*) smartness, nattiness*; (*pey*) flashiness, gaudiness.
majo 1 *adj* (*Esp*) (**a**) (*agradable*) nice; (*guapa*) pretty, (*guapo*) attractive, handsome; (*precioso*) lovely.
(**b**) (*elegante*) smart, natty*; (*pey*) flashy, gaudy.
2 *nm* (**a**) toff*, masher‡††, sport* (*esp from the lower classes of Madrid, 19th century*); (*pey*) flashy sort; (*) *V* **majete**.
(**b**) (*pey*) lout, bully; **echársela de ~** to brag, give o.s. airs.
majuela *nf* haw, hawthorn berry.
majuelo *nm* (**a**) (*vid*) young vine. (**b**) (*espino*) hawthorn.
mal 1 *adv* (**a**) (*de mala manera*) badly; poorly; (*equivocadamente*) wrongly; (*apenas*) hardly, with difficulty; **¡~!** that's bad!, oh dear!; **lo hace muy ~** he does it very badly; **hace ~ en** + *infin* he is wrong to + *infin*, he is mistaken in + *ger*, it is unwise of him to + *infin*; **oigo ~** I don't hear well, I have difficulty in hearing; **ahora veo bastante ~** my sight is rather weak now; **huele ~** it smells bad; **sabe ~** it tastes nasty; **eso está ~** that's bad; that's wrong; **sentirse ~** to feel ill, feel bad; **está muy ~ escrito** it's very badly written; **lo hice lo menos ~ que pude** I did it as well as I could; **me entendió ~** he misunderstood me; **pero digo ~** but I am wrong to say ...; **~ puedo hablar yo de este asunto** I can hardly talk about this matter, I'm hardly the right person to talk about this.
(**b**) (*locuciones*) **~ que bien** somehow or other, by some means or other; **hacer algo ~ que bien** to do sth somehow; **ir de ~ en peor** to go from bad to worse, get worse; **¡menos ~!** that's a relief!; thank goodness!; I'm glad to hear it; **menos ~ que** ... it's just as well that ..., it's a good job that ...
2 *conj*: **~ que le pese** however much he resents it, even though he hates the idea.
3 *adj V* **malo**.
4 *nm* (**a**) (*gen*) evil, wrong; **el bien y el ~** good and evil, right and wrong; **~ menor** lesser evil; **caer en el ~** to fall into evil ways; **combatir el ~** to fight against evil; **echar algo a ~** to despise sth; to waste sth, squander sth; **el ~ está en que** ... the trouble is ...; **estar a ~ con uno** to be on bad terms with sb; **no hay ~ que por bien no venga** it's an ill wind that blows nobody any good; it may be a blessing in disguise; **parar en ~** to come to a bad end.
(**b**) (*daño*) harm, hurt, damage; (*desgracia*) misfortune; **no le deseo ningún ~** I don't wish him any harm (*o* ill); **hacer ~ a uno** to do sb harm; **el ~ ya está hecho** the harm is done now; **no hay ningún ~** there's no harm done; **¡~ haya quien ...!** a curse on whoever ...!; **decir ~ de uno** to speak ill of sb, slander sb; **llevar** (*o* **tomar**) **algo a ~** to take sth amiss, be offended about sth.
(**c**) (*Med*) disease, illness; (*fig*) suffering; **~es** (*fig*) ills; **~ de altura** altitude sickness; **~ de amores** lovesickness; **~ caduco** epilepsy; **~ francés** (*Hist*) syphilis; **~ de mar** seasickness; **~ de ojo** evil eye; **~ de la tierra** homesickness; **los ~es de la economía** the things that are wrong with the economy; **dar ~ a uno** to make sb suffer; **darse ~** to torment o.s.
(**d**) (*LAm Med*) epileptic fit.
mala[1] *nf* bad luck.
mala[2] *nf* (*saco*) mailbag; (*correo*) mail, post.
malabar *adj*: **juegos ~es** juggling.
malabarismo *nm* (**a**) (*lit*) juggling, conjuring. (**b**) **~s** (*fig*) juggling; balancing act.
malabarista *nmf* juggler, conjurer.
malacate *nm* winch, capstan; (*CAm, Méx*: *huso*) spindle.
malaconsejado *adj* ill-advised.
malaconsejar [1a] *vt* to give bad advice to.
malacostumbrado *adj* (**a**) (*vicioso*) having bad habits, vicious. (**b**) (*mimado*) spoiled, pampered.
malacostumbrar [1a] *vt*: **~ a uno** (*CAm*) to get sb into bad habits.
malacrianza *nf* (*LAm*) = **malcriadez**.
malagradecido *adj* ungrateful.
malagueño 1 *adj* of Málaga. **2** *nm*, **malagueña** *nf* native (*o* inhabitant) of Málaga; **los ~s** the people of Málaga.
Malaisia *nf* Malaysia.
malaje* *nm* (**a**) (*mala sombra*) malign influence; bad vibes*; (*mala suerte*) bad luck. (**b**) (*sosería*) dullness, lifelessness; lack of charm. (**c**) (*persona*: *malévolo*) swine*, rotter*; (*soso*) bore, pain*.
malamente *adv* badly; poorly; wrongly; **estar ~ de dinero** to be badly off for money; **tenemos gasolina ~ para** + *infin* we hardly have enough petrol to + *infin*; **~ puede hacerse si** ... it can scarcely be done if ...
malandante *adj* unfortunate.
malandanza *nf* misfortune.
malandrín, -ina *nm/f* († *o hum*) scoundrel, rogue.
malandro‡ *nm* (*Carib*) scrounger*.
malanga 1 *adj* (*Carib**) thick*. **2** *nf* (*CAm, Carib, Méx*) *tuber resembling a sweet potato.*

malapata* *nmf* pest, nuisance; tedious individual; clumsy sort.
malaria *nf* malaria.
Malasia *nf* Malaysia.
malasio, -a *adj, nm/f* Malaysian.
malasombra* *nmf* = **malapata**.
Malaui, Malawi *nm* Malawi.
malauiano, -a, malawiano, -a *adj, nm/f* Malawian.
malavenido *adj*: **estar ~s** to be in disagreement, be in conflict.
malaventura *nf* misfortune.
malaventurado *adj* unfortunate.
Malaya *nf* Malaya.
malaya *interj* (*LAm*) damn!
malayo 1 *adj* Malay(an). **2** *nm*, **malaya** *nf* Malay. **3** *nm* (*Ling*) Malay.
Malaysia *nf* Malaysia.
malbaratar [1a] *vt* (*Com*) to sell off cheap, sell at a loss; (*fig*) to squander.
malcarado *adj* ugly, repulsive; fierce-looking, cross-looking.
malcasado *adj* (*infeliz*) unhappily married; (*infiel*) errant, unfaithful.
malcasarse [1a] *vr* to make an unhappy marriage.
malcomer [2a] *vi* to have a poor meal, eat badly.
malcontento 1 *adj* discontented. **2** *nm*, **malcontenta** *nf* malcontent.
malcriadez *nf* (*LAm*) bad breeding, lack of breeding.
malcriado *adj* rude, bad-mannered, coarse.
malcriar [1c] *vt niño* to spoil, pamper.
maldad *nf* (**a**) (*gen*) evil, wickedness. (**b**) (*una* ~) wicked thing.
maldecir [*aprox* 3o] **1** *vt* (**a**) (*con maldición*) to curse. (**b**) (*odiar*) to loathe, detest. **2** *vi*: **~ de** (**a**) (*hablar mal de*) to speak ill of; (*difamar*) to slander; (*denigrar*) to disparage, run down. (**b**) (*quejarse*) to curse, complain bitterly of.
maldiciente 1 *adj* (*quejumbroso*) that speaks ill of everything, forever criticizing; (*grosero*) foul-mouthed. **2** *nmf* grumbler, complainer; malcontent; slanderer.
maldición *nf* curse; ¡~! curse it!, damn!; **parece que ha caído una ~ sobre este programa** there seems to be a curse on this programme.
maldispuesto *adj* ill-disposed; (*Med*) ill, indisposed.
maldita *nf* (**a**) (*lengua*) tongue; **soltar la ~** (*hablar mucho*) to talk too much; (*enojarse*) to explode angrily, blow up. (**b**) (*Carib*) (*llaga*) sore, swelling; (*picadura*) insect bite.
malditismo *nm* aura of doom.
maldito 1 *adj* (**a**) (*gen*) damned (*t Ecl*), accursed.
(**b**) (*: *condenado*) damned; **¡~ sea!** damn it!; **ese ~ niño** that wretched child, that blessed child; **ese ~ libro** that damned book; **~ lo que me importa** I don't care a damn; **no le hace ~ el caso** he doesn't take a blind bit of notice*; **no le encuentro maldita la gracia** I don't find it in the least amusing; **no sabe maldita la cosa de ello** he knows damn-all about it‡.
(**c**) (*maligno*) wicked.
(**d**) (*Méx*: *taimado*) crafty.
2 *nm* (**a**) **el ~** the devil.
(**b**) (*Teat*) extra.
maldormir [3j] *vi* to sleep badly, sleep in fits and starts.
maleabilidad *nf* malleability.
maleable *adj* malleable.
maleado *adj* (*LAm*) corrupt.
maleante 1 *adj* wicked; villainous, rascally; unsavoury. **2** *nmf* (*malhechor*) malefactor, unsavoury character, suspicious person; (*vago*) vagrant.
malear [1a] **1** *vt* to damage, spoil, harm; *tierra* to sour; (*fig*) to corrupt, pervert. **2 malearse** *vr* to spoil, be harmed; to be corrupted, get into evil ways, go to the bad.
malecón *nm* pier, jetty, mole.
maledicencia *nf* slander, scandal.
maledicente *adj* slanderous, scandalous.
maleducado *adj* ill-bred, bad-mannered.
maleducar [1g] *vt niños* to spoil.
maleficiar [1b] *vt* (**a**) (*hechizar*) to bewitch, cast an evil spell on. (**b**) (*dañar*) to harm, damage.
maleficio *nm* (*hechizo*) curse, spell; (*brujería*) witchcraft.
maléfico *adj* harmful, damaging, evil.
malejo* *adj* rather bad, pretty bad.
malencarado *adj* sour-faced.
malentendido *nm* misunderstanding.
malestar *nm* (**a**) (*Med*) discomfort; indisposition. (**b**) (*fig*) uneasiness, malaise; (*Pol etc*) unrest.
maleta[1]* *adj* (**a**) (*And, CAm, Carib, Méx*) (*travieso*) naughty; mischievous; (*malo*) wicked. (**b**) (*And, Cono Sur*) (*tonto*) stupid; (*inútil*) useless. (**c**) (*Cono Sur*: *astuto*) sly. (**d**) (*Cono Sur, Méx*: *vago*) lazy. (**e**) (*CAm, Méx*: *torpe*) ham-fisted.
maleta[2] 1 *nf* (**a**) (*gen*) case, suitcase; travelling bag; **hacer la ~, hacer las ~s** to pack (up); **ya puede preparar la ~** he's on his way out, the skids are under him*.
(**b**) (*Aut*) boot, trunk (*US*).
(**c**) (*CAm, Cono Sur*) saddlebag.
(**d**) (*And, CAm, Cono Sur*) bundle of clothes.
(**e**) (*And, Carib*: *joroba*) hump.
2 *nm* (*) bungler, clumsy novice; (*Taur*) clumsy bullfighter; (*Dep*) poor player, rabbit*; (*Teat*) ham*.
maletera *nf* (**a**) (*And, Méx*) saddlebag. (**b**) (*And Aut*) boot, trunk (*US*). (**c**) (*Cono Sur*: *cortabolsas*) pickpocket.
maletero *nm* (**a**) (*Aut*) boot, trunk (*US*). (**b**) (*cargador*) porter. (**c**) (*Cono Sur*: *cortabolsas*) pickpocket.
maletilla *nm* (*Taur*) itinerant aspiring bullfighter.
maletín *nm* small case, bag; briefcase; satchel; **~ de excursiones** picnic case; **~ de grupa** saddlebag.
maletón *adj* (*And*) hunchbacked.
maletudo (*And, Carib*) **1** *adj* hunchbacked. **2** *nm*, **maletuda** *nf* hunchback.
malevolencia *nf* malevolence, malice, spite, ill-will; **por ~** out of spite; **sin ~ para nadie** with malice toward none.
malevolente *adj*, **malévolo** *adj* malevolent, malicious, spiteful.
maleza *nf* (**a**) (*Agr*) weeds. (**b**) (*monte bajo*) scrub; undergrowth; (*broza*) brushwood; (*matorral*) thicket. (**c**) (*Cono Sur Med*) pus. (**d**) (*CAm*: *enfermedad*) sickness, illness.
malezal *nm* (**a**) (*Carib, Cono Sur*) mass of weeds. (**b**) (*Cono Sur Med*) pus.
malfamado *adj* notorious.
malformación *nf* malformation.
malformado *adj* malformed.
Malgache *nm* Malgache, Madagascar.
malgache 1 *adj* of Madagascar. **2** *nmf* native (*o* inhabitant) of Madagascar.
malgastador 1 *adj* spendthrift, thriftless, wasteful. **2** *nm*, **malgastadora** *nf* spendthrift.
malgastar [1a] *vt dinero, recursos* to waste, squander; *esfuerzo, tiempo* to waste; *salud* to ruin.
malgeniado *adj*, **malgenio(so)** *adj* (*LAm*) bad-tempered.
malhabido *adj ganancia* ill-gotten.
malhablado *adj* coarse, rude; foul-mouthed.
malhadado *adj* ill-fated, ill-starred.
malhaya *interj* (*LAm*) damn!; **¡~ sea!** damn him! (*etc*).
malhecho 1 *adj* (*) ugly; misshapen. **2** *nm* misdeed.
malhechor(a) *nm/f* malefactor, criminal, wrongdoer.
malhumorado *adj* bad-tempered, cross, tetchy.
mali‡ *nm* joint‡.
malicia *nf* (**a**) (*maldad*) wickedness.
(**b**) (*intención*) evil intention; spite, malice, maliciousness; **lo dijo sin ~** he said it without any evil intention, he said it in all innocence.
(**c**) (*carácter*) viciousness, vicious nature; mischief, mischievous nature.
(**d**) (*de mirada, chiste etc*) roguishness, naughtiness, provocative nature; **contó un chiste con mucha ~** he told a very naughty story; **el niño tiene demasiada ~ para su edad** the kid is too knowing for his age*.
(**e**) (*astucia*) slyness, guile.
(**f**) **~s** (*sospechas*) suspicions; **tengo mis ~s** I have my suspicions.
maliciarse [1b] *vr* to suspect, have one's suspicions; **ya me lo maliciaba** I thought as much, it's just what I suspected.
maliciosamente *adv* (*V adj*) (**a**) wickedly. (**b**) spitefully, maliciously. (**c**) viciously; mischievously. (**d**) roguishly, naughtily, provocatively. (**e**) slyly.
malicioso *adj* (**a**) (*malo*) wicked, evil.
(**b**) (*malintencionado*) ill-intentioned; (*rencoroso*) spiteful, malicious.
(**c**) (*vicioso*) vicious; (*travieso*) mischievous.
(**d**) (*pícaro*) roguish, naughty, provocative; **una mirada maliciosa** a roguish look, a provocative glance.
(**e**) (*taimado*) sly, crafty.
malignidad *nf* (**a**) (*Med*) malignancy. (**b**) (*maldad*) evil nature, viciousness; (*daño*) harmfulness; (*rencor*) malice.
maligno 1 *adj* (**a**) (*Med*) malignant; pernicious. (**b**) *persona* evil, vicious; *influencia* evil, pernicious, harmful; *actitud, observación* malicious. **2** *nm*: **el ~** the Evil One, the devil.
malinformar [1a] *vt* to misinform.

malintencionado *adj* ill-disposed, hostile, unkind; malicious.

malinterpretar [1a] *vt* to misinterpret, misunderstand.

malísimamente *adv* very badly, dreadfully, appallingly.

malísimo *adj* very bad, dreadful, appalling.

malito *adj*: **estar ~** to be in poor shape, be rather poorly.

malmandado *adj* (*desobediente*) disobedient; (*terco*) obstinate, bloody-minded‡.

malmedido *nm* (*Méx*) civil engineer.

malmirado *adj* (**a**) **estar ~** to be disliked. (**b**) (*desconsiderado*) thoughtless, inconsiderate.

malmodado‡ *adj* (*Carib, Méx*) (*hosco*) heavy-handed, rough; (*insolente*) rude, insolent.

malnacido* *adj* rotten*, awful.

malnutrido *adj* undernourished.

malo 1 *adj* (**mal** *delante de nm sing*) (**a**) (*gen*) bad; poor; wretched, dreadful; *olor etc* bad, nasty, unpleasant; *joya* false; *dedo, diente etc* bad, sore; *niño* bad, naughty, disobedient; **este papel es ~ para escribir** this paper is bad for writing; **ir por mal camino** to be on the wrong road; **¡no seas ~!** don't be naughty!, behave yourself!; that's a wicked thing to say.

(**b**) (*Med*) **estar ~** to be ill; **sentirse ~** to feel ill, feel bad; **me puse ~ de risa** I nearly died laughing.

(**c**) (*difícil*) hard, difficult; **es muy ~ de vencer** he's very hard to beat; **es un animal ~ de domesticar** it's a difficult animal to tame.

(**d**) (*locuciones*) **¡~!** oh dear!, that's bad!; **lo ~ es que ...** the trouble is that ...; **~ sería que no ganáramos** we're certain to win, I'd be surprised if we didn't win; **¿qué tiene de ~?** what's wrong with that?; **¿qué tiene de ~ comer helados en invierno?** what's wrong with eating ice cream in winter?; **a la mala** if the worst comes to the worst; (*And, Carib: a la fuerza*) by force, forcibly; (*Carib, Cono Sur, Méx: con doblez*) treacherously; **andar a malas con uno** to be on bad terms with sb; **los dos se pusieron a malas** the two fell out; **ponerse a malas con uno** to fall foul of sb, get on the wrong side of sb; **estar de malas** to be out of luck; to be in a bad mood; **venir de malas** to have evil intentions; **por las malas** by force, willy-nilly.

2 *nm* (**a**) **el ~** (*Rel*) the Evil One, the devil.

(**b**) (*Teat*) villain; (*Cine*) bad guy, baddie*.

(**c**) (‡) **los ~s** the fuzz‡, the police.

3 *nf* **mala**[3] spell of bad luck.

maloca *nf* (**a**) (*Cono Sur Hist*) Indian raid. (**b**) (*And*) village of uncivilized Indians.

malogrado *adj* (**a**) *plan etc* abortive; ill-fated; *esfuerzo etc* wasted. (**b**) *persona* who died before his time, who died early; **el ~ ministro** the late-lamented minister.

malograr [1a] **1** *vt* (*arruinar*) to spoil, upset, ruin; (*desperdiciar*) to waste.

2 malograrse *vr* (**a**) (*plan etc*) to fail, miscarry, come to grief; (*decepcionar*) to fail to come up to expectations, not fulfil its early promise; (*And Aut, Mec*) to break down.

(**b**) (*persona*) to die before one's time, die early, come to an untimely end.

malogro *nm* (**a**) (*fracaso*) failure; (*desperdicio*) waste. (**b**) (*muerte*) early death, untimely end.

maloliente *adj* stinking, smelly.

malón *nm* (**a**) (*Cono Sur Hist*) Indian raid. (**b**) (*LAm: persona*) tough, thug.

malpagar [1h] *vt* to pay badly, underpay.

malparado *adj*: **salir ~** to come off badly; **salir ~ de** to get the worst of.

malparar [1a] *vt* (*dañar*) to damage; (*estropear*) to harm, impair, wreck; (*maltratar*) to ill-treat.

malparir [3a] *vt* to have a miscarriage, miscarry.

malparto *nm* miscarriage.

malpensado *adj* nasty, evil-minded; **¡no seas ~!** don't be nasty!, don't be so horrid!*

malqueda* *nmf* shifty sort, unreliable type.

malquerencia *nf* dislike.

malquistar [1a] **1** *vt*: **~ a dos personas** to cause a rift between two people, set one person against another; **~ a A con B** to set A against B.

2 malquistarse *vr* (**a**) (*persona*) **~ con uno** to incur the dislike of sb, become estranged from sb.

(**b**) (*2 personas*) to fall out, become estranged.

malquisto *adj*: **estar ~** to be disliked, be unpopular; **los dos están ~s** the two are estranged.

malrotar [1a] *vt* to squander.

malsano *adj* (**a**) *clima, atmósfera etc* unhealthy, bad. (**b**) (*Med*) sickly; *mente* sick, morbid.

malsín *nm* (*difamador*) slanderer; (*soplón*) informer, talebearer.

malsonante *adj palabra* nasty, rude, offensive.

malsufrido *adj* impatient.

Malta *nf* Malta.

malta *nf* malt.

maltés, -esa 1 *adj, nm/f* Maltese. **2** *nm* (*Ling*) Maltese.

maltirar [1a] *vi* to get by with difficulty, scrape a living.

maltón *nm*, **maltoncillo** *nm* (*LAm Zool*) young animal; (*niño*) child.

maltraer [2o] *vt* (**a**) (*injuriar*) to insult, abuse. (**b**) (*maltratar*) to ill-treat.

maltraído* *adj* (*And, Cono Sur*) shabby, untidy.

maltratado *adj bebé, mujer* battered.

maltratamiento *nm* = **maltrato.**

maltratar [1a] *vt* (**a**) *persona* to ill-treat, maltreat; *mujer, hijo* to batter; *objeto* to handle roughly, knock about, damage. (**b**) (*t* **~ de palabra**) to abuse, insult.

maltrato *nm* (**a**) (*de persona*) ill-treatment, maltreatment; (*de objeto*) rough handling, damage; (*de bebé, mujer*) battering; **~ al niño** child abuse. (**b**) (*injurias*) abuse, insults.

maltrecho *adj* battered, damaged; injured; **dejar ~ a uno** to leave sb in a bad way.

malucho* *adj* (*Med*) poorly, under the weather.

malura* *nf* (*Cono Sur*) (*dolor*) pain, discomfort; (*malestar*) sickness, indisposition; **~ de estómago** stomach ache.

malva 1 *adj invar* mauve. **2** *nf* mallow; **~ loca, ~ real, ~ rósea** hollyhock; (**de**) **color de ~** mauve; **criar ~s** (*Esp**) to be pushing up the daisies*; **ser como una ~** to be very meek and mild.

malvado 1 *adj* evil, wicked, villainous. **2** *nm* villain.

malvarrosa *nf* hollyhock.

malvasía *nf* malmsey.

malvavisco *nm* (*Bot*) marshmallow.

malvender [2a] *vt* to sell off cheap, sell at a loss.

malversación *nf* embezzlement, misappropriation.

malversador(a) *nm/f* embezzler.

malversar [1a] *vt* (*Fin*) to embezzle, misappropriate; (*distorsionar*) to distort.

Malvinas: Islas *nfpl* **~** Falkland Isles.

malvinés 1 *adj* of the Falkland Islands. **2** *nm*, **malvinesa** *nf* Falkland islander.

malviviente *nmf* (*Méx*) = **maleante.**

malvivir [3a] *vi* to live badly, live poorly; **malviven de lo que pueden** they get along as best they can.

malvón *nm* (*Cono Sur*) geranium.

malla *nf* (**a**) (*red*) mesh; network; **~ de alambre** wire mesh, wire netting; **hacer ~** to knit. (**b**) **las ~s** (*Dep*) the net. (**c**) (*Hist*) chain mail; (*Cono Sur*) swimsuit. (**d**) **~s** (*Teat etc*) tights.

mallo *nm* mallet.

Mallorca *nf* Majorca.

mallorquín, -ina 1 *adj, nm/f* Majorcan. **2** *nm* (*Ling*) Majorcan.

mama *nf* (*Bio*) mammary gland; (*de mujer*) breast; (*de vaca etc*) udder.

mamá *nf* (**a**) (*) mummy*, mum*, mamma (*US**), mom (*US**). (**b**) (*LAm*) mother; **futura ~** expectant mother, mother-to-be; **~ grande, ~ señora** grandmother.

mamacallos* *nmf invar* (*Esp*) useless person.

mamacona‡ *nf* (*And*) old lady.

mamada *nf* (**a**) (*chupada*) suck; (*leche*) milk; (*hora*) feeding time; (‡) blow job‡. (**b**) (*LAm**) (*cosa fácil*) cinch‡; (*prebenda*) soft job, sinecure; (*ganga*) bargain. (**c**) (*Cono Sur*: borrachera*) drunkenness.

mamadera *nf* (*CAm, Cono Sur: tetilla*) rubber teat; (*LAm: biberón*) feeding-bottle; **~s‡** boobs‡.

mamado‡ *adj* (**a**) (*LAm: borracho*) drunk. (**b**) (*Carib: tonto*) silly, stupid. (**c**) (*: *fácil*) easy; (*sencillo*) dead simple.

mamagrande *nf* (*Cono Sur, Méx*) grandmother.

mamaíta* *nf* = **mamá** (**a**).

mamalón *adj* (*Carib*) idle; sponging.

mamamama* *nf* (*And*) grandma*.

mamandurria* *nf* (*prebenda*) cushy job‡; (*sueldo*) fat salary; (*gajes*) rich pickings.

mamantear [1a] *vt* (*LAm*) (**a**) (*mamar*) to nurse, feed, suckle. (**b**) (*fig*) to spoil, pamper.

mamaón *nm* (*Méx Culin*) tipsy cake.

mamar [1a] **1** *vt* (**a**) *leche, pecho* to suck.

(**b**) (*fig*) to absorb, assimilate; to acquire in infancy; **nació mamando el oficio** he was born to the trade.

(**c**) (*) *comida* to wolf, bolt; *recursos etc* to milk, suck dry; *fondos* to pocket (illegally); (*beber*) to booze*, drink;

¡cómo la mamamos! this is the life!, we never had it so good!

(**d**) (⁂) to suck off⁂.

2 *vi* (**a**) (*lit*) to suck; **dar de ~ a** to feed, suckle.

(**b**) (*: *obtener gratis*) to get something for free*.

(**c**) **¡no mames!** (*Méx*⁑) come off it!*, don't give me that!*

(**d**) (*beber*) to booze*, drink.

3 mamarse* *vr* (**a**) *puesto, ventaja etc* to wangle*, fiddle*; (*conseguir*) to land, manage to get.

(**b**) **~ un susto** to give o.s. a scare.

(**c**) **~ a uno** (*madrugar a*) to get the better of sb; (*And, Cono Sur*: engañar*) to cheat sb; (*CAm*⁑: *matar*) to do sb in⁑.

(**d**) (*: *emborracharse*) to get tight*.

(**e**) (*And*) to go back on one's word.

mamario *adj* mammary.

mamarracha *nf*, **mamarracho** *nm* grotesque object, ridiculous sight; mess, botch; (*persona*) sight, object, scarecrow; (*Arte*) daub; **estaba hecha una ~** he looked a complete mess.

mamá-señora *nf* (*LAm*) grandmother.

mamela* *nf* bribe, backhander*; (*por callar*) hush-money.

mameluca⁑ *nf* (*Cono Sur*) whore.

mameluco *nm* (**a**) (*Hist*) Mameluke. (**b**) (*LAm*) Brazilian mestizo, half-breed. (**c**) (*: *idiota*) chump*, idiot. (**d**) (*LAm*: *t* **~s**) (*de niño*) rompers; (*de trabajo*) overalls.

mamerto, -a *nm/f* twit*, idiot.

mamey *nm* (*LAm*) mamey; **ser ~ colorado** (*Carib**) to be out of this world.

mameyal *nm* (*LAm*) mamey plantation.

mamífero 1 *adj* mammalian, mammal (*atr*). **2** *nm* mammal.

Mammón *nm* (*Bib, fig*) Mammon.

mamografía *nf* mammography.

mamola *nf* chuck under the chin; **dar** (*o* **hacer**) **la ~ a uno** to chuck sb under the chin; (⁑) to make a sucker out of sb⁑.

mamón 1 *adj* (**a**) *niño* small, baby, suckling.

(**b**) (*Méx**) (*bruto*) thick*; (*engreído*) cocky*.

2 *nm* (**a**) (*bebé*) small baby, baby still at the breast.

(**b**) (⁑: *idiota*) berk⁑, idiot.

(**c**) (⁑: *gorrón*) scrounger*; (*indeseable*) rotter*, swine.

(**d**) (*Bot*) sucker, shoot.

(**e**) (*And, Cono Sur*) (*árbol*) papaya tree; (*fruta*) papaya.

(**f**) (*Cono Sur, Méx*) suck.

(**g**) (*CAm*) club, stick.

(**h**) (*Méx Culin*) soft spongecake.

mamonear [1a] *vt* (**a**) (*CAm*) to beat. (**b**) (*Carib*) (*aplazar*) to postpone; *tiempo* to waste.

mamotrético *adj* gigantic; unwieldy.

mamotreto *nm* (**a**) (*libro*) hefty tome, whacking great book*; (*fig*) monstrosity, vast useless object. (**b**) (*LAm**) (*aparato*) contraption; (*bulto*) lump; (*coche viejo*) old crock, jalopy. (**c**) (*Méx*⁑: *inútil*) dead loss.

mampara *nf* screen; partition.

mamparo *nm* (*Náut*) bulkhead.

mamplora⁑ *nm* (*CAm*) queer⁑.

mamporrera* *nf* madame, brothel-keeper.

mamporro* *nm* bash*, punch, clout; (*al caer*) bump; **atizar un ~ a uno** to give sb a swipe; **liarse a ~s con uno** to come to blows with sb.

mampostería *nf* masonry; (*sin labrar*) rubblework.

mampuesto *nm* (**a**) (*piedra*) rough stone. (**b**) (*muro*) wall, parapet. (**c**) (*LAm*) rest. (**d**) **de ~** spare, emergency (*atr*), extra.

mamúa⁑ *nf* (*Cono Sur*) drunkenness.

mamut *nm, pl* **mamuts** mammoth.

mana *nf* (**a**) (*And, CAm*: *fuente*) spring, fountain. (**b**) (*LAm*) = **maná**.

maná *nm* manna.

manada *nf* (**a**) (*Zool*) herd, flock; (*de lobos*) pack; (*de leones*) pride. (**b**) crowd, mob; **a ~s, en ~** in a mob; in crowds.

manadero *nm* shepherd, herdsman, drover.

mánager ['manaʒer] *nm, pl* **mánagers** ['manaʒer] (*Dep, Teat etc*) manager.

managua 1 *adj invar* of Managua. **2** *nmf* native (*o* inhabitant) of Managua; **los ~s** the people of Managua.

manantial 1 *adj*: **agua ~** running water, flowing water. **2** *nm* (**a**) (*manantial*) spring, fountain; **~ termal** hot spring; **agua de ~** spring water. (**b**) (*fig*) source, origin; cause.

manantío *adj* running, flowing.

manar [1a] **1** *vt* to run with, flow with; **~ sangre** to run with blood; **la herida manaba sangre** blood flowed from the wound.

2 *vi* (**a**) (*líquido*) to run, flow (*de* from, *en* with); to pour out, stream, gush forth; to well up.

(**b**) (*fig*) to abound, be plentiful; **~ de** to spring from, flow from; **~ en** to flow with, abound in.

manatí *nm* manatee.

mánayer *nm* (*Dep*) manager.

manaza *nf* (**a**) (*mano*) great big hand; dirty hand. (**b**) **ser** (**un**) **~s** to be clumsy.

manazo *nm* punch, slap.

mancar [1g] **1** *vt* (**a**) (*mutilar*) to maim, cripple. (**b**) (*Cono Sur*) **~ el tiro** to miss. **2** *vi* (*And**) (*Escol*) to fail; (*fracasar*) to blow it⁑.

mancarrón *nm* (**a**) (*Cono Sur*: *caballo*) worn-out horse, nag. (**b**) (*And, Cono Sur*: *obrero*) disabled workman. (**c**) (*And, Cono Sur*: *presa*) small dam.

manceba *nf* lover, mistress; concubine.

mancebía *nf* (††: *burdel*) brothel.

mancebo *nm* (**a**) (*joven*) youth, young man. (**b**) (*soltero*) bachelor. (**c**) (*Com*) clerk; (*Farm*) assistant, dispenser.

mancera *nf* plough handle.

mancilla *nf* stain, blemish; **sin ~** unblemished, (*Rel*) immaculate, pure.

mancillar [1a] *vt honor* to stain, sully.

manco 1 *adj* (**a**) (*de una mano*) one-handed; (*de un brazo*) one-armed; (*sin brazos*) armless; (*tullido*) crippled, maimed, disabled; **~ de la izquierda** with a maimed left hand, lacking a left hand.

(**b**) (*fig*) defective, faulty.

(**c**) **no ser ~** (*útil*) to be useful, be active; (*: *largo de uñas*) to be light-fingered; (*sin escrúpulos*) to be quite unscrupulous; **A, jugador que tampoco es ~** A, who is a pretty useful player; **no ser ~ en** not to be backward in, not be lacking in skill (*etc*) in.

2 *nm*, **manca** *nf* (**a**) (*tullido*) cripple, disabled person; (*de un brazo*) one-armed person; (*de una mano*) one-handed person.

(**b**) (*Cono Sur*: *caballo*) old horse, nag.

mancomún: de ~ *adv, t* **mancomunadamente** *adv* (*junto*) jointly, conjointly, together; (*de común acuerdo*) by common consent; **obrar de mancomún con uno** to act jointly with sb.

mancomunado *adj* joint, jointly held.

mancomunar [1a] **1** *vt personas* to unite, associate, bring together; *intereses* to combine; *recursos* to pool; (*Jur*) to make jointly responsible. **2 mancomunarse** *vr* to unite, merge, combine, join together.

mancomunidad *nf* union, association; pool; community; (*Pol*) commonwealth; (*Jur*) joint responsibility; **la M~ Británica** the British Commonwealth.

mancornar [1l] *vt* (**a**) *toro* to seize by the horns; to hobble. (**b**) (*fig*) to join, couple.

mancornas *nfpl* (*LAm*), **mancuernas** *nfpl* (*Méx*), **mancuernillas** *nfpl* (*CAm, Méx*) cufflinks.

mancha *nf* (**a**) (*Zool etc*) spot, mark; speckle; (*en diseño*) spot, fleck; (*de suciedad*) spot, stain, mark; (*de tinta etc*) blot, smudge; (*Med*) spot; bruise, mark; (*vegetación etc*) patch, small area; (*Arte*) shading, shaded area; **~ de petróleo** oil slick; **~ solar** sunspot; **~s del sarampión** measles spots; **propagarse como una ~ de aceite** to spread like wildfire.

(**b**) (*fig*) stain, stigma; blemish, blot; **sin ~** unblemished.

(**c**) (*And, Carib*) cloud, swarm (*of locusts etc*); (*de gente*) swarm.

manchado *adj piel* spotty; *animal* spotted; dappled; *ave* speckled; pied; *papel etc* smudged, smudgy, covered with smudges (*etc*); **un abrigo ~ de barro** a coat stained (*o* bespattered) with mud.

manchar [1a] **1** *vt* (**a**) (*marcar*) to spot, mark; (*ensuciar*) to soil, dirty, stain; *tinta* to smudge.

(**b**) (*fig*) *honor etc* to stain, sully; *persona* to soil; **~ a otro** to smear sb else's reputation.

2 mancharse *vr* (**a**) (*ensuciarse*) to get dirty.

(**b**) (*fig*) to stain one's reputation; to dirty one's hands, soil o.s.

manchego 1 *adj* of La Mancha. **2** *nm*, **manchega** *nf* native (*o* inhabitant) of La Mancha; **los ~s** the people of La Mancha.

mancheta *nf* (*de libro*) blurb; (*de periódico*) masthead.

manchón¹ *nm* large stain, big spot (*etc*), patch; (*Bot*) patch of dense vegetation.

manchón² *nm* (*Cono Sur*) muff.

Manchuria *nf* Manchuria.
manchuriano, -a *adj, nm/f* Manchurian.
manda *nf* (**a**) (*legado*) bequest. (**b**) (*LAm*) religious vow.
mandadero *nm* messenger; errand boy, office boy.
mandado *nm* (**a**) (*orden*) order; (*recado*) commission, errand, job; **muchacho de ~s** errand boy, office boy; **hacer los ~s, ir a los ~s** to run errands. (**b**) (‡: *golpe*) bash*, sock*.
mandamás* *nm invar* big shot*.
mandamiento *nm* (**a**) (*orden*) order, command. (**b**) (*Jur*) writ; warrant; **~ de entrada y registro** search warrant; **~ judicial** warrant; **~ de venir** summons. (**c**) (*Ecl*) commandment; **los diez ~s** the Ten Commandments.
mandanga *nf* (**a**) (*: *cualidad*) calmness, self-possession. (**b**) (*: *cuento*) tale, story; excuse; **¡no me vengas con ~s!*** who are you trying to kid?* (**c**) (‡: *golpe*) bash*. (**d**) (‡: *droga*) pot‡, hash*.
mandanguero, -a‡ *nm/f* pot-smoker‡; dealer in pot‡.
mandar [1a] **1** *vt* (**a**) (*ordenar*) to order; **~ que ...** to order that ..., give orders that ...; **~ a uno hacer algo** to order sb to do sth; **~ hacer un traje** to order a suit, have a suit made; **~ reparar el coche** to get (*o* have) the car repaired; **~ llamar a uno** to send for sb; **~ salir a uno** to order sb out; **mándele sentarse** please ask him to take a seat.
(**b**) (*Com*) to order, ask for; **¿qué manda Vd?** what can I do for you?; **¿manda Vd algo más?** is there anything else?
(**c**) (*Mil etc*) to lead, command; *grupo* to be in charge of, lead, be the leader of.
(**d**) (*enviar*) to send; **le manda muchos recuerdos** he sends you warmest regards; **se lo mandaremos por correo** we'll send it to you by post, we'll post it to you.
(**e**) (*legar*) to bequeath.
(**f**) (*LAm*) (*echar*) to throw, hurl; (*tirar*) to throw away.
(**g**) (*LAm*) *golpe* to give, strike, fetch; *persona* to hit, punch.
(**h**) (*LAm: caballo*) to break in.
(**i**) (*Cono Sur Dep*) to start.
2 *vi* (**a**) (*ser el jefe*) to be in charge, be in command; to be in control; **¿quién manda aquí?** who's in charge here?; **aquí mando yo** I give the orders here, I'm the boss.
(**b**) (*dar órdenes*) to give the orders; **¡mande Vd!** at your service!; **¿mande?** pardon?, what did you say?; (*Méx*) yes sir? (*etc*), what can I do for you?; (*LAm: en restaurante*) what will you have?; **¡mande!** (*And, Méx*) I beg your pardon!; **~ por uno** to send for sb, fetch sb.
(**c**) (*pey*) to be bossy, boss people about.
3 mandarse *vr* (**a**) (*Med*) to get about by o.s., manage unaided.
(**b**) (*Arquit: cuartos*) to communicate (*con* with).
(**c**) (*Carib, Cono Sur*) (*irse*) to go away, slip away; (*desaparecer*) to disappear secretly.
(**d**) **~ algo** (*LAm**) (*comerse*) to scoff sth*; (*beberse*) to knock sth back*.
(**e**) **~ una sinfonía** (*Cono Sur: Mús*) to play (*o* perform) a symphony.
(**f**) (*LAm*) **mándese entrar** (*o* **pasar**) please come in; **~ cambiar, ~ mudar** to go away, leave; (‡) to get out; **~ con uno** to be rude to sb, be bossy to sb.
mandarín *nm* (*lit*) mandarin; (*pey*) petty bureaucrat, jack-in-office; (*LAm*) little Hitler.
mandarina *nf* (**a**) (*Bot*) tangerine, mandarin (orange); **¡chúpate esa ~!** (*Esp*‡) get that!*, hark at him! (*etc*). (**b**) (*Ling*) Mandarin.
mandarino *nm* mandarin (orange) tree.
mandatario *nm* (**a**) (*Jur*) agent, attorney. (**b**) (*Pol*) leader; political figure; **primer ~** head of state.
mandato *nm* (**a**) (*orden*) order; (*Jur*) writ, warrant; (*Inform*) command; **~ judicial** (search) warrant; **~ de prisión** warrant of arrest.
(**b**) (*Jur: poder*) power of attorney.
(**c**) (*Pol: gobierno*) mandate; **territorio bajo ~** mandated territory.
(**d**) (*Pol: período*) term (of office); period of rule; **durante su ~** during his term of office.
(**e**) (*Ecl*) maundy.
(**f**) **~ internacional** (*Correo*) international money order.
(**g**) (*de comisión*) terms of reference, brief; **pero eso no forma parte de mi ~** but that is not in my brief.
mandíbula *nf* jaw (*t Téc*), mandible; **reírse a ~ batiente** to laugh one's head off.
mandil *nm* (*de albañil*) (leather) apron; (*de mujer*) pinafore dress; (*Cono Sur*) horse-blanket.
mandilón *nm* (**a**) (*babi*) smock, pinafore dress. (**b**) (*overol*) overalls. (**c**) (*) coward.
mandinga 1 *adj* (**a**) (*CAm, Cono Sur*: afeminado*) effeminate. (**b**) (*Carib, Cono Sur: travieso*) impish, mischievous. **2** *nm* (**a**) (*LAm*) (*diablo*) devil; (*duende*) goblin; evil spirit. (**b**) (*And, Carib: negro*) Black.
mandioca *nf* cassava, tapioca, manioc.
mandiocal *nm* (*LAm*) cassava plot.
mando *nm* (**a**) (*Mil etc*) command; (*de país etc*) rule; control; authority; (*liderazgo*) leadership; **alto ~** high command; **~ supremo** commander-in-chief; **un oficial al ~ de un pelotón** an officer in command of a squad; **un pelotón al ~ de un oficial** a squad under the command of (*o* led by) an officer; **ejercer el ~, estar al ~, tener el ~** to be in command, be in control; **entregar el ~** to hand over command (*o* control).
(**b**) (*en carrera*) lead; **tomar el ~** to take the lead.
(**c**) **~s** (*personas*) leaders, leadership, top people.
(**d**) (*Mec*) drive; **~ a la izquierda** left-hand drive.
(**e**) (*Mec*) control; **~ a distancia, ~ remoto** remote control; **con ~ a distancia** remote-controlled; **~ por botón, ~ de teclado** push-button control; **palanca de ~** control lever, (*Aer*) joystick; **retrovisor de ~ interior** wing-mirror controlled from inside the car; **~ selector** control knob.
(**f**) **~s** (*Rad, Téc etc*) controls.
(**g**) (*Pol etc*) term of office.
mandoble *nm* (**a**) (*golpe*) two-handed blow, powerful blow (with a sword). (**b**) (*espada*) large sword, broadsword. (**c**) (*) ticking-off*.
mandolina *nf* mandolin(e).
mandón 1 *adj* bossy, domineering. **2** *nm* (*Cono Sur*) mine foreman; (*Dep*) starter.
mandrágora *nf* mandrake.
mandria 1 *adj* worthless. **2** *nm* useless individual, weakling.
mandril[1] *nm* (*Zool*) mandrill.
mandril[2] *nm* (*Téc*) mandrel.
manduca‡ *nf* grub‡.
manducar* [1g] *vt* to scoff*, stuff oneself with.
manducatoria‡ *nf* grub‡.
manea *nf* hobble.
maneador *nm* (*Cono Sur, Méx*) hobble; (*Cono Sur*) whip; (*Méx*) halter.
manear [1a] **1** *vt* to hobble. **2 manearse** *vr* (*And, Méx*) to trip over one's own feet.
manecilla *nf* (**a**) (*Téc*) pointer, hand; (*de reloj*) hand; **~ grande** minute hand; **~ pequeña** hour hand. (**b**) (*de libro*) clasp.
maneco *adj* (*Carib, Cono Sur, Méx*) (*tullido*) maimed; (*de manos*) with deformed hands; (*de pies*) with deformed feet; (*patizambo*) knock-kneed.
manejabilidad *nf* manageability; handiness; manoeuvrability.
manejable *adj* manageable; *herramienta etc* handy, easy to use; (*Aer etc*) manoeuvrable.
manejador(a) *nm/f* (*Méx Aut*) driver, motorist.
manejar [1a] **1** *vt* (**a**) *caballo, herramienta, lengua etc* to handle; *máquina* to run, work, operate; *casa, empresa etc* to run, manage.
(**b**) *persona* to manage; to push around; **ella maneja a su marido** she manages her husband, she bosses her husband about.
(**c**) (*LAm Aut*) to drive.
2 *vi* (**a**) **'~ con cuidado'** 'handle with care'.
(**b**) (*LAm*) to drive.
3 manejarse *vr* (**a**) (*comportarse*) to act, behave.
(**b**) (*Esp: arreglárselas*) to manage; **se maneja bien con los chiquillos** she manages all right with the kids; **¿cómo te manejas para hacer eso?** how do you manage to do that?, how do you set about doing that?; **ya se manejarán** they'll manage, they'll find a way.
(**c**) (*Med*) to get about unaided.
manejo *nm* (**a**) (*acto*) handling; running, working, operation; management; (*de lengua*) command; **~ de crisis** crisis management; **~ a distancia** remote control; **~ doméstico, ~ de la casa** housekeeping, running the house; **una casa de fácil ~** an easily-run house, a house which is easy to run; **llevar todo el ~ de** to be in sole charge of; **tiene un buen ~ del alemán** she has a good command of German.
(**b**) (*seguridad*) confidence, ease of manner; (*perspicacia*) savoir-faire, shrewdness; **no tiene bastante ~** he's not sufficiently wide-awake.
(**c**) (*prontitud*) address, quickness, speed of action; **hay que ver el ~ que tiene la chica** you should see how quick the girl is.

(**d**) (*pey*) intrigue; stratagem; (*de cifras etc*) fiddling*; (*negocio turbio*) shady deal; **~s turbios** intrigues, underhand dealing.
(**e**) (*LAm Aut*) driving.

manera *nf* (**a**) (*modo*) way, manner, fashion; **~ de obrar** way of going about things; conduct; **~ de ser** way of life; behaviour, manner (*of person*); **es su ~ de ser** that's the way she is; **no me gusta su ~ de ser** I don't like his way of doing things; **hay varias ~s de hacerlo** there are various ways of doing it; **no hay ~** there's no solution, there's nothing one can do; **no hay ~ con él** he's hopeless; **no hay ~ de** + *infin* there's no way of + *ger*; **no había ~ de persuadirle** there was no convincing him; **¡qué ~ de** + *infin*!, **¡vaya una ~ de** + *infin*! what a way to + *infin*!
(**b**) (*locuciones con prep*) **a la ~ de** in the manner of, after the fashion of; **siguen arando a la ~ de los abuelos** they still plough as their grandfathers did; **a mi ~ de ver** in my view, as I see it; **de esta ~** (in) this way, like this; **¡llovía de una ~!** it was just pouring!, you should have seen how it rained!; **de la ~ que sea** in whatever way you (*etc*) like; however he (*etc*) does it; **la pegó de mala ~** he hit her really hard; **le han estafado de mala ~** they really have cheated him, they've properly done him down; **de la misma ~** in the same way; **de otra ~** otherwise, if not; **de alguna ~** somehow; in a way; **de ninguna ~** by no means; **¡de ninguna ~!** certainly not!, never!; **de tal ~ que ...** in such a way that ...; to such a degree that ...; **de ~ que ...** so that ...; **¿de ~ que esto no le gusta?** so you don't like it?; **de todas ~s** at any rate; **en cierta ~** up to a point, to some degree; **en gran ~** in great measure; greatly, extremely; **sobre ~** exceedingly; *para otras locuciones V* **modo** (**a**) *y* (**b**).
(**c**) (*liter*) kind, sort; **es otra ~ de afirmación** it is another kind of affirmation; it is another method of saying yes; **que es otra ~ de valentía** which is another kind of courage.
(**d**) (*Arte, Liter etc*) manner, style; **la segunda ~ de Picasso** Picasso's second manner; **las dos ~s de Góngora** the two styles of Góngora.
(**e**) (*modales*) **~s** manners; **buenas ~s** good manners; **de ~s muy groseras** with very bad manners; **se lo dije con buenas ~s** I told him politely; **tener ~s** (*LAm*) to have good manners, be well-mannered.

maneta *nf* lever.

maneto *adj* (*And, CAm, Carib*) = **maneco**.

manflor(ita)⁑ *nm* (*LAm*) pansy⁑, queer⁑.

manga *nf* (**a**) (*Cos*) sleeve; **~ de camisa** shirtsleeve; **estar en ~s de camisa** to be in one's shirtsleeves; **sin ~s** sleeveless; **bajo ~*** under the counter; **estar de ~** to be in league; **~ ancha** tolerance, tolerant attitude; lenience; broad-mindedness; **ser de ~ ancha, tener ~ ancha** to be easy-going, be overindulgent, be too lenient; to be broad-minded; (*pey*) to be not overscrupulous; **andar ~ por hombro** to be a mess, be all over the place; **hacer ~s y capirotes de uno** to ignore sb completely; **pegar las ~s⁑** to kick the bucket⁑; **traer algo por la ~** to have something up one's sleeve.
(**b**) (*t* **~ de riego**) hose, hosepipe; **~ de incendios** fire hose.
(**c**) (*Culin*) cloth strainer.
(**d**) (*Aer*) windsock, windgauge; **~ de mariposas** butterfly-net.
(**e**) (*bolso*) travelling bag.
(**f**) (*Met*) cloudburst; **~ marina** waterspout; **~ de viento** whirlwind.
(**g**) (*Náut*) beam, breadth.
(**h**) (*Dep*) leg, round; (*de competición*) section; (*Tenis*) set; (*Bridge*) game; **~ clasificatoria** qualifying round; **~ de consolación** play-off among runners-up.
(**i**) (*LAm*: *multitud*) crowd, mob, swarm.
(**j**) (*LAm Agr*) corral entrance.
(**k**) (*CAm*) poncho, coarse blanket; **~ de agua** rain cape.
(**l**) (*And*) pasture.
(**m**) (*Méx⁑*: *preservativo*) condom, sheath.

mangal *nm* (*LAm*) (**a**) = **manglar**. (**b**) (*Méx**: *trampa*) dirty trick. (**c**) (*And*: *plantío*) mango plantation.

mangana *nf* lasso, lariat.

mangancia* *nf* (**a**) (*timo*) swindle, racket; (*ratería*) shoplifting; (*gorronería*) scrounging*. (**b**) (*cuento*) story, fib.

manganear [1a] **1** *vt* (*coger con lazo*) to lasso; (*CAm, Cono Sur*) (*saquear*) to pillage, plunder; (*: *robar*) to pinch*, lift*. **2** *vi* (*Carib*) to loaf, hang about.

manganeso *nm* manganese.

manganeta *nf* (*LAm*), **manganilla** *nf* (*Méx*) disappearing trick; (*fig*) swindle, dodge, racket.

mangante* **1** *adj* brazen. **2** *nm* (*mendigo*) beggar; (*gorrón*) scrounger*, freeloader*; (*ladrón*) thief; (*ratero*) shoplifter; (*vago*) loafer, layabout; (*caradura*) rotter*, villain.

mangar* [1h] **1** *vt* (**a**) (*robar*) to pinch*, lift*. (**b**) (*mendigar*) to beg (for), scrounge*. **2** *vi* (*robar*) to pilfer; to shoplift; (*Cono Sur*) to scrounge*.

mangazón* *adj* (*LAm*) lazy.

manglar *nm* mangrove swamp.

mangle *nm* mangrove.

mango[1] *nm* (**a**) (*Bot*) mango. (**b**) (*Cono Sur⁑*) dough⁑. (**c**) (*Méx**) good-looking lad.

mango[2] *nm* handle, haft; **~ de escoba** broomstick, (*Aer*) joystick; **~ de pluma** penholder.

mangón *nm* (*And*) (*prado*) pasture; (*estancia*) cattle ranch.

mangoneador* *nm* (**a**) (*entrometido*) meddler, interfering sort; (*mandón*) bossy individual. (**b**) (*LAm*) corrupt official, grafter.

mangonear* [1a] **1** *vt* (**a**) *persona* to manage, boss about.
(**b**) (*robar*) to pinch*, lift*.
(**c**) (*LAm*: *saquear*) to pillage, plunder.
2 *vi* (**a**) (*entrometerse*) to meddle, interfere (*en* in); (*interesarse*) to dabble (*en* in).
(**b**) (*ser mandón*) to boss people about; to run everything, take charge and insist on doing everything oneself.
(**c**) (*LAm*) to graft*, be on the fiddle*; (*Pol*) to fix things, fiddle the results*.

mangoneo* *nm* (**a**) (*entrometimiento*) meddling, interference. (**b**) (*con personas*) bossing people about; personal dominance; brazenness. (**c**) (*LAm*) graft*, fiddling*; (*Pol*) fixing, fiddling of results*.

mangoneón*, mangonero* **1** *adj* meddlesome, interfering; bossy; brazen. **2** *nm* busybody; bossy individual; brazen sort.

mangosta *nf* mongoose.

manguear [1a] **1** *vt* (*Cono Sur, Méx*) *ganado* to drive; *caza* to beat, put up.
2 *vi* (**a**) (*And, Carib**: *gandulear*) to skive⁑.
(**b**) (*Cono Sur**: *sablear*) to scrounge money*.

mangueo* *nm* thieving; scrounging*.

manguera *nf* (**a**) (*de riego*) hose, hosepipe; (*tubo*) pipe, tube; **~ antidisturbios** water-cannon; **~ de aspiración** suction pump; **~ de incendios** fire hose.
(**b**) (*And*) bicycle tyre, inner tube.
(**c**) (*Met*) waterspout.
(**d**) (*Cono Sur*) corral, yard.

mangui* *nm* (*ladrón*) thief; small-time crook*; (*canalla*) villain, rotter*.

manguillo *nm* (*Méx*) penholder.

manguito *nm* (**a**) (*lit*) muff. (**b**) (*Téc*) sleeve; coupling; **~ incandescente** gas mantle.

mangurrina* *nf* bash*, wallop*.

mangurrino* *adj* rotten*, worthless.

manguta* *nm* (*ladrón*) small-time thief; (*indeseable*) good-for-nothing.

mani* *nf* demo*.

maní *nm, pl* **maníes** *o* **manises** (**a**) (*esp LAm*) peanut; groundnut plant. (**b**) (*Carib⁑*) dough⁑, money. (**c**) **¡~!** (*Cono Sur*) never!

manía *nf* (**a**) (*Med*) mania; **~ de grandezas** megalomania; **~ persecutoria** persecution mania.
(**b**) (*fig*) mania; (*moda*) rage, craze (*de* for); (*capricho*) whim, fad; (*peculiaridad*) peculiarity, oddity; **la ~ del fútbol** the soccer craze; **la ~ de la minifalda** the craze for miniskirts; **tiene ~s** he's rather odd, he has his little ways; **tiene la ~ de las motos** he's obsessed with motorbikes, he's bike-crazy*; **tiene la ~ de** + *infin* he has the (odd) habit of + *ger*; **ha dado en la ~ de salir sin abrigo** he's taken to going out without a coat.
(**c**) (*pey*) dislike; spite, ill will; **tener ~ a uno** to dislike sb; **el maestro me tiene ~** the teacher's got it in for me; **tiene ~ a los eslobodos** he can't stand the Slobodians.

maniabierto *adj* (*Carib*) lavish, generous.

maniaco, maníaco **1** *adj* maniac(al). **2** *nm,* **maniaca** *nf,* **maníaca** *nf* maniac; **~ sexual** sex maniac.

maniacodepresivo **1** *adj* manic-depressive. **2** *nm,* **maniacodepresiva** *nf* manic-depressive.

maniatar [1a] *vt persona* to tie the hands of; to handcuff; *animal* to hobble.

maniático **1** *adj* (**a**) (*lit*) maniacal; (*hum*) fanatical.
(**b**) (*fig*) (*chiflado*) crazy; (*excéntrico*) odd, eccentric, peculiar; cranky*; (*delicado*) fussy.
(**c**) (*terco*) stubborn.

2 *nm,* **maniática** *nf* (**a**) (*lit*) maniac; (*hum*) fanatic; ~ **de la ecología** ecology fanatic.

(**b**) (*fig*) maniac; odd individual, eccentric, crank*.

manicero, -a *nm/f* (*LAm*) peanut seller.

manicomio *nm* lunatic asylum, mental hospital.

manicura *nf* manicure.

manicuro, -a *nm/f* manicurist.

manida *nf* lair, den.

manido *adj* (**a**) *carne* high, gamy; smelly. (**b**) *tema etc* trite, stale.

manierismo *nm* (*Arte, Liter*) mannerism.

manierista *adj, nmf* mannerist.

manifestación *nf* (**a**) (*de emoción etc*) manifestation; show; sign; **una gran ~ de entusiasmo** a great show of enthusiasm.

(**b**) (*declaración*) statement, declaration.

(**c**) (*Pol*) demonstration; mass meeting; rally.

(**d**) **~ de impuesto** (*Méx*) tax return.

manifestante *nmf* demonstrator.

manifestar [1j] **1** *vt* (**a**) *emoción etc* to show, manifest, demonstrate, reveal.

(**b**) *política etc* to state, declare; to express.

2 manifestarse *vr* (**a**) (*emoción etc*) to show, be manifest; to become apparent; **~ en** to be evident in (*o* from), be revealed by, be shown by.

(**b**) (*Pol*) to demonstrate; to hold a mass meeting, hold a rally.

manifiesto 1 *adj* (*claro*) clear, manifest; (*patente*) evident, obvious; *error* glaring, obvious; *verdad* manifest; **poner algo de ~** to make sth clear; to disclose sth, reveal sth; **quiero poner de ~ que ...** I wish to state that ...; **quedar ~** to be plain, be clear.

2 *nm* (**a**) (*Náut*) manifest.

(**b**) (*Pol*) manifesto.

manigua *nf* (*Carib, Méx*) (**a**) (*ciénaga*) swamp; (*maleza*) scrubland; (*selva*) jungle; (*fig*) countryside; **irse a la ~** (††) to take to the hills (in revolt). (**b**) **agarrar ~** (*Carib**) to get flustered.

manigual *nm* (*Carib*) = **manigua.**

manigueta *nf* (**a**) (*mango*) handle, haft; (*manivela*) crank; (*Cono Sur Aut*) starting handle. (**b**) (*maniota*) hobble.

manija *nf* (**a**) (*gen*) handle; (*And, Méx*: *de puerta*) door handle. (**b**) (*Mec*) clamp, collar; (*Ferro*) coupling. (**c**) (*Agr*) hobble. (**d**) (*Cono Sur*: *vaso*) mug, tankard. (**e**) (*Cono Sur Aut*) starting handle; **dar ~ a uno** to egg sb on.

Manila *nf* Manila.

manilargo *adj* (**a**) (*generoso*) open-handed. (**b**) (*LAm**) light-fingered, thievish.

manilense 1 *adj* of Manila. **2** *nmf* native (*o* inhabitant) of Manila; **los ~s** the people of Manila.

manileño = **manilense.**

manilla *nf* (**a**) (*pulsera*) bracelet; **~s (de hierro)** handcuffs, manacles. (**b**) (*de reloj*) hand. (**c**) (*And, Méx*) door handle. (**d**) (*de tabaco etc*) bundle.

manillar *nm* handlebar(s).

maniobra *nf* (**a**) (*acto*) handling; manoeuvring; operation, control; (*Ferro*) shunting; **hacer ~s** to manoeuvre; (*Ferro*) to shunt.

(**b**) (*Náut*: *arte*) seamanship, (art of) navigation; handling.

(**c**) (*Náut*: *aparejo*) gear, rigging.

(**d**) **~s** (*Mil*) manoeuvres.

(**e**) (*fig*) manoeuvre, move; (*pey*) trick, stratagem; **~ dilatoria** delaying tactic; **mediante una hábil ~** by a clever move; **es una ~ para expulsar al jefe** it's a manoeuvre to get rid of the chief.

maniobrabilidad *nf* manoeuvrability; handling qualities.

maniobrable *adj* manoeuvrable; easy to handle.

maniobrar [1a] **1** *vt* to handle, operate; to manoeuvre; (*Ferro*) to shunt. **2** *vi* to manoeuvre (*t fig*).

maniota *nf* hobble.

manipulable *adj* (**a**) (*Téc*) operable, that can be operated. (**b**) *persona* easily influenced, readily manipulated.

manipulación *nf* manipulation.

manipulado *nm* handling.

manipulador(a) 1 *nm/f* manipulator; handler. **2** *nm* (*Elec, Telec*) key, tapper.

manipular [1a] **1** *vt* to manipulate; to handle; (*pey*) to interfere with. **2** *vi*: **~ con, ~ en** to manipulate.

manipulativo *adj* manipulative.

maniqueísmo *nm* (*Hist*) Manicheanism; (*fig*) tendency to see things in black and white; **discutir sin ~s** to discuss without taking up extreme positions.

maniqueo 1 *adj* Manichean. **2** *nm,* **maniquea** *nf* (*Hist*) Manichean; (*fig*) extremist; person who tends to see things in terms of black and white.

maniquí 1 *nm* (**a**) (*de sastre*) dummy, manikin; (*Esgrima etc*) dummy figure. (**b**) (*fig*) puppet. **2** *nf* mannequin, model. **3** *nmf* (*) poser*.

manir [3a] **1** *vt carne* to hang. **2 manirse** *vr* (*CAm*) to go off.

manirroto 1 *adj* lavish, extravagant, prodigal. **2** *nm* spendthrift.

manisero *nm* (*LAm*) = **manicero.**

manisuelto 1 *adj* extravagant, spendthrift. **2** *nm,* **manisuelta** *nf* spendthrift.

manita *nf* little hand; **~s de cerdo** (*etc*) trotters; **~s de plata** (*o* **de oro**) delicate hands, artistic hands, talented hands; **echar una ~ a uno** to lend sb a hand; **hacer ~s** (*amantes*) to hold hands (*con* with); **ser ~s** to be handy, be clever with one's hands.

manito[1] *nm* (*LAm*) pal*, buddy*; (*en oración directa*) mate*, chum*.

manito[2]* *nm* (*LAm*) = **manita.**

manivacío *adj* empty-handed.

manivela *nf* crank; **~ de arranque** starting handle.

manjar *nm* (**a**) (tasty) dish, special dish; **~ blanco** blancmange; **~ delicado, ~ exquisito** tasty morsel; **~ dulce** (*And*) fudge; **~ espiritual** food for the mind, spiritual sustenance. (**b**) (*CAm, Méx*) suit.

mano[1] *nf* (**a**) (*Anat*) hand; (*Zool*) foot, forefoot, paw; (*de elefante*) trunk; (*de ave*) foot, (*de halcón*) claws, talons; **~s de cerdo** pig's trotters.

(**b**) (*en locuciones, fig, gen*) hand; **~ derecha** (*fig*) right-hand man; **~ dura** harsh treatment, (*Pol*) tough policy; **Señor M~s Limpias** Mr Clean; (*Jur*) **~s muertas** mortmain; **~ de santo** sure remedy; **última ~** final touch, finishing touch; **~s de mantequilla, ~s de trapo** (*fig*) butterfingers; **¡~s a la obra!** to work!, let's get on with it!; **¡~s quietas!** hands off!, keep your hands to yourself!; **¡qué ~!** (*LAm*: *suerte*) what a stroke of luck!; **fue ~ de santo** it came just right, it was just what the doctor ordered; **¡~s fuera de Eslobodia!** (*slogan*) Hands off Slobodia!

(**c**) (*locuciones con prep*) **a ~** by hand; **bordado a ~** hand-embroidered; **hecho a ~** handmade; **escribir a ~** to write in longhand, write out; **girar una manivela a ~** to turn a crank by hand; **mandar algo a ~** to send sth by hand; **estar a (la) ~** to be at hand, be on hand, be handy; to be within one's grasp; **¡eso está a la ~!** that's obvious!; **a ~ airada** violently; **robo a ~ armada** armed robbery; **a ~ salva** without risk; **estar** (*o* **quedar**) **a ~** (*LAm*) to be quits, be even; **a ~s llenas** lavishly, generously; **morir a ~s de** to die at the hands of; **llegó a mis ~s** it reached me, it came into my hands; **irse a las ~s** (*LAm*), **llegar a las ~s** to come to blows; **si a ~ viene** should the occasion arise; **votar a ~ alzada** to vote by a show of hands; **¡arriba las ~s!** hands up!; **bajo ~** in secret, behind the scenes; in an underhand way; **estar con una ~ adelante y otra atrás** to be broke; **coger a uno con las ~s en la masa** to catch sb red-handed, catch sb in the act; **de ~** hand (*atr*), *p.ej.* **equipaje de ~** hand-luggage; **los dos iban de la ~** the two were walking hand-in-hand; **llevar a uno de la ~** to lead sb by the hand; **de buena ~** on good authority; **de primera ~** (at) first-hand; **de segunda ~** (at) secondhand; **de ~s de** at the hands of; **recibir algo de ~s de uno** to receive sth from sb; **de ~s a boca** unexpectedly, suddenly; **vivir de la ~ a la boca** to live from hand to mouth; **dar de ~** to knock off*, stop working; **darse de ~s con uno** to come across sb; **dejar a uno de la ~** to abandon sb; **no pude dejar el libro de la ~** I couldn't put the book down; **ponerse de ~s** (*caballo*) to rear (up); **en ~s de** in the hands of, into the hands of; **carta en ~** letter delivered by hand; **ha hecho cuanto ha estado en su ~** he has done all in his power (*para + infin* to + *infin*); **traer un asunto entre ~s** to have a matter in hand; to have a matter on one's hands; **¡fuera las ~s!** hands off!, keep your hands to yourself!; **ganar por la ~ a uno** to beat sb to it; **tomarse la justicia por su ~** to take justice into one's own hands; **estar ~ sobre ~** to sit twiddling one's thumbs.

(**d**) (*locuciones con verbo*) **alzar la ~ a** (*o* **contra**) to raise one's hand against; **cargar la ~** to overdo it; to press too hard, be too exacting; (*Com*) to overcharge; (*Culin*) to put too much spice (*etc*) in; **dar una ~** (*LAm*) to lend a hand; **darse las ~s** to join hands; to shake hands on it; **echar una ~** to lend a hand (*a* to); **echar ~ a** to lay hands on; **echar ~ de** to make use of; to resort to; **estrechar la ~ a uno** to shake sb's hand; **se le fue la ~** his hand slipped (*t fig*); (*exagerar*) he overdid it; **llevarse las ~s a la cabeza** to throw one's hands in the air; **meter ~ a uno** to bring sb to book; **meter ~ a una*** (*hablando*) to make a pass at a girl*; (*tocando*) to (try to) touch up a girl‡; **no hay quien le meta ~** there's nobody to touch him; **meterle ~ a una cuestión** to take up a matter; to get a grasp on a problem; **pasar la ~ a uno** (*CAm*) to flatter sb, suck up to sb*; **pasar la ~ por la pared** (*Esp*‡) to have a feel‡; **sentar la ~ a uno** to beat sb; (*fig*) to bring sb to heel; (*Com*) to overcharge sb; **tener buena ~** to be lucky; to have the knack; **tener mala ~** to be clumsy, be awkward; **tener** (**mucha**) **~ con** to have a way with; **tiene ~ izquierda con las mujeres** he's got a way with women; he knows what's what where women are concerned; **tener ~ para** to be clever at; **tener las ~s largas** to be light-fingered; **untar la ~ a uno** to grease sb's palm; **¡venga esa ~!** shake!, put it there!

(**e**) (*Dep*) handling, handball; ¡~! handball!

(**f**) (*de reloj*) hand.

(**g**) (*de pintura*) coat; (*de jabón*) wash, soaping; **dar una ~ de jabón a la ropa** to give the clothes a soaping.

(**h**) (*Naipes etc*) hand; round; game; **echar una ~ de mus** to have a game (*o* hand) of *mus*; **ser ~, tener la ~** to lead; **soy ~** it's my lead.

(**i**) (*Mús*) scale.

(**j**) **~ de almirez, ~ de mortero** pestle.

(**k**) (*grupo*) lot, series; (*And, CAm, Cono Sur, Méx*) group of 5 (*o* 4, 6) things of the same kind; (*de plátanos*) bunch, hand; **una ~ de bofetadas** a series of punches; **una ~ de papel** a quire of paper.

(**l**) **~ de obra** labour, manpower; labour force; **~ de obra especializada** skilled labour.

(**m**) (*destreza*) skill, dexterity.

(**n**) (*personas*) **~s** hands, workmen; **contratar ~s** to sign up workmen.

(**o**) (*LAm*) (*desgracia*) misfortune, mishap; (*suceso imprevisto*) unexpected event.

(**p**) (*LAm Aut*) direction; **~ única** one-way street.

(**q**) **~ a ~** *nm* contest, struggle.

(**r**) **función ~s libres** hands-free function.

mano[2]* *nm* (*LAm*: *hermano*) pal*, buddy, chum*; (*en oración directa*) mate*, chum*.

manoizquierdoso *adj* knowing, cunning; sophisticated.

manojo *nm* handful, bunch; (*) bunch; (*Carib*) bundle of raw tobacco (*about 2 lbs*); **~ de hierba** tuft of grass; **~ de llaves** bunch of keys; **~ de pillos** bunch of rogues.

manola‡ *nf* needle, syringe.

manoletina *nf* (*Taur*) *a kind of pass with the cape.*

Manolo *m forma familiar de* **Manuel**.

manolo *nm* toff*, masher* (*esp Madrid*: *equivalent of cockney*).

manómetro *nm* pressure-gauge, manometer.

manopla *nf* (**a**) (*paño*) flannel, face-flannel. (**b**) (*guante*) mitten; (*Hist, Téc etc*) gauntlet; (*Culin*) oven-glove. (**c**) (*Carib, Cono Sur*: *puño de hierro*) knuckleduster. (**d**) (*Cono Sur*: *llave inglesa*) spanner.

manoseado *adj* (*fig*) hackneyed, well-worn.

manosear [1a] *vt* (**a**) (*tocar*) to handle, finger, touch; (*ajar*) to rumple, mess up; to paw*; (*jugar con*) to fiddle with, mess about with; (*LAm**) to feel up‡, touch up‡. (**b**) *tema etc* to overwork, repeat.

manoseo *nm* (*V vt*) (**a**) handling, fingering, touching; rumpling; pawing*; (*LAm**) feeling up‡, touching up‡. (**b**) overworking, repetition.

manotada *nf* (**a**) (*golpe*) slap, smack. (**b**) (*And, Cono Sur, Méx*) handful, fistful.

manotazo *nm* slap, smack.

manoteador *nm* (*Cono Sur, Méx*) (**a**) (*ladrón*) thief; (*bolsista*) bag-snatcher; (*estafador*) fiddler*. (**b**) (*que hace ademanes*) gesticulator.

manotear [1a] **1** *vt* to slap, smack, cuff. **2** *vi* to gesticulate, move (*o* use) one's hands.

manoteo *nm* (**a**) (*gestos*) gesticulation. (**b**) (*Méx**) (*robo*) theft, robbery; (*estafa*) fiddling*.

manque* *conj* (*esp LAm*) = **aunque**.

manquear [1a] *vi* to be maimed, be crippled; to pretend to be crippled; (*Cono Sur, Méx*) to limp.

manquedad *nf*, **manquera** *nf* (**a**) (*incapacidad*) disablement, crippled state, bodily incapacity. (**b**) (*fig*) defect.

mansalino *adj* (*Cono Sur*) huge; extraordinary; excellent.

mansalva: **a ~** *adv* (*sin riesgo*) without risk, without any danger; (*a granel*) in abundance; (*en gran escala*) on a large scale; **le dispararon a ~** they shot at him with complete certainty of hitting him; **estar a ~ de** to be safe from.

mansamente *adv* gently, mildly, meekly.

mansarda *nf* attic.

mansedumbre *nf* (**a**) (*de persona*) gentleness, meekness. (**b**) (*de animal*) tameness.

mansión *nf* (*esp LAm*) mansion.

manso 1 *adj* (**a**) *persona* gentle, mild, meek. (**b**) *animal* tame. (**c**) (*Cono Sur**) great, extraordinary. **2** *nm* (*Esp*‡) mattress.

manta[1] *nf* (**a**) (*de cama*) blanket; (*chal*) shawl; **~ eléctrica** electric blanket; **~ de viaje** travelling rug; **a ~** (**de Dios**) plentifully, abundantly; **a ~s** by the ton; **liarse la ~ a la cabeza** to decide to go the whole hog; to press on regardless; **tirar de la ~** to let the cat out of the bag, give the game away.

(**b**) (*And, Carib, Méx*) (*tela*) calico; (*poncho*) poncho.

(**c**) (*) hiding*.

manta[2]* (*Esp*) **1** *adj* bone-idle. **2** *nmf* idler, slacker. **3** *nf* idleness.

mantadril *nm* (*CAm*) denim.

mantear [1a] *vt* (**a**) (*lit*) to toss in a blanket. (**b**) (*Carib*) to ill-treat, abuse. (**c**) (*Carib*) to set on, beat up*.

manteca *nf* (**a**) (animal) fat; (*Cono Sur*) butter; **~ de cacahuete** peanut butter; **~ de cacao** cocoa butter; **~ de cerdo** lard; **~ de vaca** butter; **~ vegetal** vegetable fat.

(**b**) (‡) (*dinero*) dough‡, money; (*géneros*) goods.

(**c**) (*LAm*‡) hash*, marijuana.

(**d**) (*And*) servant, girl.

mantecada *nf* small cake, iced bun.

mantecado *nm* (*aprox*: *helado*) ice cream; (*pastel*) lardy cake.

mantecón* *nm* milksop, mollycoddle.

mantecoso 1 *adj* fat, greasy; lardy; buttery. **2** *nm* (*Cono Sur*) cheese.

mantel *nm* tablecloth; (*Ecl*) altar cloth; **~ individual** place-mat; **una cena de ~ largo** (*Cono Sur**) a formal dinner; **levantar los ~es** to clear the table; **poner los ~es** to lay the table.

mantelería *nf* table linen.

mantelillo *nm* table runner.

mantelito *nm* doily.

mantención *nf* (*LAm*) = **manutención**.

mantenedor *nm* (*de certamen*) chairman, president; **~ de la familia** breadwinner.

mantener [2k] **1** *vt* (**a**) (*Arquit, Téc etc*) to hold up, support; **~ algo en equilibrio** to keep sth balanced.

(**b**) *idea, opinión* to support, defend, maintain; *persona* to sustain, support; **mantenella y no emendalla** firm defence of a decision (*etc*).

(**c**) *fuego etc* to keep in, keep going; (*alimentar*) to sustain; **le mantiene la esperanza** he is sustained by hope, hope keeps him going.

(**d**) (*Fin*) to maintain, support.

(**e**) (*Mec etc*) to maintain, service.

(**f**) *costumbre, disciplina, relaciones etc* to keep up, maintain.

(**g**) **~** + *adj* to keep + *adj*; **~ la comida caliente** to keep the food hot; **'Mantenga limpia España'** 'Keep Spain clean'; **'mantenga su derecha'** (*Aut*) 'keep to the right'.

2 mantenerse *vr* (**a**) **se mantiene todavía en pie** it is still standing.

(**b**) **~ firme** to hold one's ground, not give way; **~ en vigor** to stand, remain in force; **~ en un puesto** to stay in one's job, keep one's post; **~ en contacto con** to keep up one's contacts with.

(**c**) (*alimentarse*) to sustain o.s., subsist, keep going (*con, de* on); **se mantiene con leche** she keeps going on milk.

mantenibilidad *nf* ease of maintenance.

mantenido *nm* (*CAm, Méx*) (*chulo*) pimp; (*amante*) kept man, gigolo; (*gorrón*) sponger*, parasite.

mantenimiento *nm* maintenance (*t Aut, Mec*); (*Aut etc*) service, servicing; upkeep; support, sustenance; **clase de ~** keep-fit class.

manteo *nm* (*de hombre*) long cloak; (*de mujer*) full skirt.

mantequera *nf* (**a**) (*para batir*) churn. (**b**) (*de mesa*) butter dish.

mantequería *nf* (*lechería*) dairy, creamery; (*ultramarinos*) grocer's (shop).

mantequilla *nf* butter.

mantequillera *nf* butter-dish.

mantilla *nf* (**a**) (*de mujer*) mantilla; **~ de blonda, ~ de encajes** lace mantilla.

(**b**) (*de bebé*) **~s** baby clothes; **estar en ~s** (*persona*) to be terribly innocent; (*plan*) to be in the very early stages, be in its infancy; **dejar a uno en ~s** to leave sb in the dark.

mantillo *nm* humus, mould; mulch.

mantillón *nm* (**a**) (*CAm, Méx*) horse-blanket. (**b**) (*Méx**) (*amante: hombre*) kept man, (*mujer*) kept woman, mistress; (*parásito*) sponger.

mantis *nf invar* mantis; **~ religiosa** praying mantis.

manto *nm* (**a**) (*capa*) cloak; (*Ecl, Jur etc*) robe, gown.
(**b**) (*Zool*) mantle.
(**c**) (*Arquit: t* **~ de chimenea**) mantel.
(**d**) (*Min*) layer, stratum.
(**e**) (*fig*) cloak, mantle.

mantón *nm* shawl.

mantra *nm* mantra.

mantudo *adj* (**a**) *ave* with drooping wings. (**b**) (*CAm: disfrazado*) masked, in disguise.

manuable *adj* handy, easy to handle.

manual 1 *adj* (**a**) (*lit*) manual, hand (*atr*); **habilidad ~** manual skill; **tener habilidad ~** to be clever with one's hands; **obrero ~** manual worker, worker who uses his hands; **trabajo ~** manual labour.
(**b**) = **manuable.**
2 *nm* manual, handbook, guide; **~ de estilo** stylebook; **~ de operación** instruction manual.

manualidad *nf* (**a**) (*arte*) manual craft; **~es** (*Escol*) handicraft. (**b**) (*objeto*) craft product.

manualmente *adv* manually, by hand.

manubrio *nm* (**a**) (*manivela*) handle, crank; (*torno*) winch. (**b**) (*de bicicleta*) handlebar(s); (*LAm Aut*) steering-wheel. (**c**) (*Mús*) barrel-organ.

manudo *adj* (*LAm*) with big hands.

Manuel *nm* Emmanuel.

manuelita *nf* (*Carib*) rolled pancake.

manufactura *nf* (**a**) (*acto, producto*) manufacture. (**b**) (*fábrica*) factory.

manufacturar [1a] *vt* to manufacture.

manufacturero 1 *adj* manufacturing. **2** *nm* (*LAm*) manufacturer. **3** *nm*, **manufacturera** *nf* manufacturing company.

manumitir [3a] *vt* to manumit.

manú(s)‡ *nm* (*Esp*) bloke‡.

manuscrito 1 *adj* handwritten, manuscript. **2** *nm* manuscript; **~s del Mar Muerto** Dead Sea scrolls.

manutención *nf* (**a**) (*gen*) maintenance; (*sustento*) support; (*pensión*) keep, board. (**b**) (*Mec etc*) maintenance.

manyar‡ [1a] *vti* (*Carib, Cono Sur*) to eat.

manzana *nf* (**a**) apple; **~ ácida** cooking apple; **~ de la discordia** apple of discord, bone of contention; **~ de mesa** eating apple; **~ de sidra** cider apple; **~ silvestre** wild apple, crabapple.
(**b**) **~ de Adán** (*LAm Anat*) Adam's apple.
(**c**) (*Arquit: esp LAm*) block.
(**d**) (*Cono Sur*) *land measure, = 2.5 acres*; (*CAm*) *land measure, = 1.75 acres.*

manzanal *nm* (**a**) (*huerto*) apple orchard. (**b**) (*manzano*) apple tree.

manzanar *nm* apple orchard.

manzanilla *nf* (**a**) (*Bot*) camomile; camomile tea. (**b**) *a variety of small olive.* (**c**) (*jerez*) manzanilla, manzanilla sherry.

manzano *nm* apple tree.

maña *nf* (**a**) (*gen*) skill, dexterity; ingenuity; (*pey*) craft, guile; **con ~** craftily, slyly; **darse ~ para** + *infin* to contrive to + *infin*.
(**b**) (*una ~*) trick, knack; (**malas**) **~s** evil ways, bad habits, vices; (*de niño etc*) naughty ways; **tiene ~ para hacerlo** he's got the knack of doing it; **es una ~ para conseguir algo** it's a trick (*o* ruse) to get sth.
(**c**) (*And*) idleness; **hacer ~** to kill time.

mañana 1 *adv* tomorrow; **~ por la ~** tomorrow morning; **¡hasta ~!** see you tomorrow!; **pasado ~** the day after tomorrow; **~ temprano** early tomorrow.
2 *nm* future; **el ~ es incierto** the future is uncertain; **el día de ~** at some future time, in the future.
3 *nf* (**a**) (*lit*) morning; tomorrow; **primera ~** period from 7 to 9 a.m.; **a la ~** in the morning; **a la ~ siguiente** (on) the following morning, the morning after; **a las 7 de la ~** at 7 o'clock, at 7 a.m.; **de ~, por la ~** in the morning; **muy de ~** very early in the morning; **en la ~ de hoy** this morning; **en la ~ de ayer** yesterday morning; **~ es otro día** there's a new day tomorrow.
(**b**) **tomar** (*LAm*: **hacer**) **la ~*** to take a shot of liquor before breakfast.

mañanero 1 *adj* early-rising, who gets up early. **2** *nm*, **mañanera** *nf* early riser.

mañanita *nf* (**a**) (*madrugada*) early morning; **de ~** very early in the morning, at the crack of dawn. (**b**) (*chal*) bed jacket. (**c**) **~s** (*Méx*) serenade.

mañear [1a] **1** *vt* to manage cleverly, contrive skilfully. **2** *vi* to act shrewdly, go about things cunningly; (*pey*) to get up to one's tricks.

mañero *adj* (**a**) = **mañoso** (**a**). (**b**) (*Cono Sur*) *animal* vicious; obstinate; shy, nervous.

maño, -a *adj, nm/f* Aragonese.

mañosamente *adv* cleverly, ingeniously, skilfully; (*pey*) craftily.

mañosear [1a] *vi* (**a**) (*And, Carib, Cono Sur*) = **mañear 2.** (**b**) (*And, Cono Sur, Méx: niño*) to be difficult, be finicky (*esp* about food).

mañoso 1 *adj* (**a**) (*hábil*) clever, ingenious, skilful; (*pey*) sharp, crafty, wily.
(**b**) (*And: perezoso*) lazy, indolent.
(**c**) (*And, CAm, Cono Sur, Méx*) *animal* vicious; (*terco*) obstinate; (*tímido*) shy, nervous; (*And, Cono Sur, Méx*) difficult (*esp* about food).
2 *nm*, **mañosa** *nf* (*CAm: ladrón*) thief.

maoísmo *nm* Maoism.

maoísta *adj, nmf* Maoist.

Mao Zedong *nm* Mao Tse-tung.

MAPA ['mapa] *nm abr de* **Ministerio de Agricultura, Pesca y Alimentación.**

mapa *nm* map; **~ de carreteras** roadmap; **~ geológico** geological map; **~ hipsométrico** contour map; **~ meteorológico, ~ del tiempo** weather map; **~ mural** wall map; **~ en relieve** relief map; **el ~ político** the political scene; the political spectrum; **desaparecer del ~** to vanish off the face of the earth.

mapache *nm* rac(c)oon.

mapamundi *nm* (**a**) (*lit*) globe; world map. (**b**) (*: *trasero*) bottom.

mapeango *adj*, **mapiango** *adj* (*Carib, Méx*) useless, incompetent.

mapear [1a] *vt* (*Inform etc*) to map.

mapuche 1 *adj* Araucanian. **2** *nmf* Araucanian (Indian).

mapurito *nm* (*CAm*) skunk.

maque *nm* lacquer.

maquear [1a] **1** *vt* to lacquer; **ir** (**bien**) **maqueado*** to be all dressed up. **2 maquearse** *vr* (*) to get ready (to go out), get dressed.

maqueta *nf* (**a**) model; (*a escala: Arquit*) scale model; (*Mús*) demo(nstration) tape. (**b**) (*libro*) dummy.

maquetación *nf* (*Prensa*) layout, design.

maquetear [1a] *vt* to lay out, design.

maquetista *nmf* model-maker.

maqueto *nm* (*pey*) immigrant worker (*in the Basque Country*).

maquiavélico *adj* Machiavellian.

Maquiavelo *nm* Machiavelli.

maquiladora *nf* (*Méx*) assembly plant.

maquilar [1a] *vt* (*Méx*) to assemble.

maquillador(a) *nm/f* (*Teat etc*) make-up artist.

maquillaje *nm* (*pintura*) make-up; (*acto*) making-up; **~ base, ~ de fondo** foundation make-up.

maquillar [1a] **1** *vt* (**a**) to make up. (**b**) (*) *cifras, cuentas* to massage*. **2 maquillarse** *vr* to make up.

máquina *nf* (**a**) (*gen*) machine; (*Ferro*) engine, locomotive; (*Fot*) camera; (*: *bicicleta*) bike; (*moto*) motorbike; (*Carib: coche*) car; taxi; (*de bar*) fruit-machine; **~ de afeitar** (safety) razor; **~ de afeitar eléctrica** electric razor, shaver; **~ de azar** gaming machine; **~ de calcular, ~ computadora** computer; **~ de contabilidad, ~ de sumar** adding-machine; **~ copiadora** copier, copying machine; **~ de coser** sewing machine; **~ de discos** jukebox; **~ electrónica, ~ tragaperras** fruit-machine, one-armed bandit; (*Com*) slot-machine; (*Mús*) jukebox; **~ de escribir** typewriter; **~ excavadora** mechanical digger; **~ expendedora** vending machine; **~ fotográfica** camera; **~ franqueadora, ~ de franquear** franking machine; **~ de lavar** washing machine; **~ ordeñadora** milking-machine; **~ para hacer punto, ~ de tricotar** knitting-machine; **~ picadora** mincer; **~ quitanieves** snowplough; **~ recreativa** game machine; **~ registradora** (*LAm*) cash-register; **~ tejedora** knitting-machine; **~ de vapor** steam engine; **a toda ~** full-speed, all-out; **hecho a ~** machine-made; *escrito* typed; **acabar a ~, coser** (*etc*) **a ~** to machine; **escribir a ~** to type; **entrar en ~** to go to press.
(**b**) (*Arquit*) imposing building; edifice; structure.
(**c**) (*fig*) (*maquinaria*) machinery, workings; scheme of

things.
(**d**) (*fig*: *proyecto*) plan, project.
maquinación *nf* machination, scheme, plot.
maquinador(a) *nm/f* schemer, plotter.
máquina-herramienta *nf*, *pl* **máquinas-herramientas** machine-tool.
maquinal *adj* (*fig*) mechanical, automatic.
maquinalmente *adv* (*fig*) mechanically, automatically.
maquinar [1a] *vti* to plot, machinate.
maquinaria *nf* (**a**) (*gen*) machinery; (*equipo*) plant; **~ agrícola** agricultural machinery, farm implements. (**b**) (*de reloj etc*) mechanism, works. (**c**) (*Pol*) machine.
maquinilla *nf* (*máquina pequeña*) small machine; (*torno*) winch; (*tijeras*) clippers; **~ de afeitar** (safety) razor; **~ eléctrica** electric razor, shaver; **~ para liar cigarrillos** cigarette(-rolling) machine.
maquinista *nm* (*Ferro*) engine-driver, engineer (*US*); (*Náut etc*) engineer; (*Téc*) operator, machinist; (*Teat*) scene-shifter.
maquis *nm invar* resistance movement.
mar. *abr de* **marzo** March, Mar.
mar[1] *nm y f* (**a**) (*gen*) sea; (*océano*) ocean; (*marea*) tide; **~ arbolada** heavy sea; **~ de fondo** groundswell; **~ gruesa** heavy sea; **~ llena** high tide; **~ rizada** choppy sea; **~ adentro, ~ afuera** out at sea, out to sea; **caer al ~** to fall into the sea, (*desde barco*) to fall overboard; **de alta ~** *barco* seagoing, ocean-going; *pesca* deepwater (*atr*); **en alta ~** on the high seas; **por ~** by sea, by boat; **arar en el ~** to labour in vain; **echar a la ~** to launch; **es hablar de la ~** it's all very vague; it's just a dream; **hacer un ~ con un vaso de agua** to make a mountain out of a molehill; **hacerse a la ~** to put to sea; to stand out to sea.
(**b**) **M~ Adriático** Adriatic Sea; **M~ de las Antillas, M~ Caribe** Caribbean Sea; **M~ Báltico** Baltic Sea; **M~ Caspio** Caspian Sea; **M~ Mediterráneo** Mediterranean Sea; **M~ Muerto** Dead Sea; **M~ Negro** Black Sea; **M~ del Norte** North Sea; **M~ Rojo** Red Sea.
(**c**) (*fig*) **un ~ de confusiones** a sea of confusion, a welter of confusion; **hay un ~ de diferencia** there's a world of difference.
(**d**) (*fig*) **estar hecho un ~ de lágrimas, llorar a ~es** to weep floods; **llover a ~es** to rain cats and dogs, rain in torrents.
(**e**) (*) **la ~** (*como adv*) a lot; **la ~ de cosas** lots of things, no end of things, ever so many things; **es la ~ de tonto** he's no end of a fool; **es la ~ de guapa** she's awfully pretty; **está la ~ de contento** he's terribly happy.
mar[2] *nf euf de* **madre** (*in obscene expressions*).
mar[3] *interj* (*Mil*) march!; *V* **frente** *etc.*
mara‡ *nf* group of people, mob.
marabunta *nf* (**a**) (*de hormigas*) plague of ants. (**b**) (*fig*) (*daños*) havoc, ravages; (*multitud*) crowd.
maraca *nf* (**a**) (*Mús*) maraca, rattle. (**b**) (*Cono Sur*: *prostituta*) whore. (**c**) (*And, Carib*: *inútil*) dead loss.
maraco* *nm* (*Carib*) youngest child, baby of the family.
maracucho 1 *adj* of Maracaibo. **2** *nm*, **maracucha** *nf* native (*o* inhabitant) of Maracaibo.
maracuyá *nm* passionfruit.
marajá *nm* = **maharajá**.
maraña *nf* (**a**) (*Bot*) thicket; tangle of plants. (**b**) (*de hilos etc*) tangle. (**c**) (*fig*) mess, tangle; jungle; puzzle. (**d**) (*: *trampa*) trick, ruse. (**e**) (*And*) small tip.
marañero 1 *adj* scheming. **2** *nm*, **marañera** *nf* schemer.
marañón *nm* (*Bot*) cashew.
maraquear* [1a] *vt* (*LAm*) to shake, rattle.
maraquero *nm* (*And, Carib*) maraca player.
marar‡ [1a] *vt* (**a**) (*matar*) to do in‡. (**b**) (*pegar*) to bash*; to beat up*.
marasmo *nm* (**a**) (*Med*) wasting; atrophy. (**b**) (*fig*) paralysis, stagnation.
maratón *nm* (*a veces f*) marathon.
maratoniano 1 *adj* marathon. **2** *nm*, **maratoniana** *nf* (*t* **maratonista** *mf*) marathon runner.
maravedí *nm*, *pl* **maravedís** *o* **maravedises** *old Spanish coin.*
maravilla *nf* (**a**) (*objeto, asunto*) marvel, wonder; (*sentimiento*) wonderment; **las siete ~s del mundo** the seven wonders of the world; **hacer ~s** to work wonders; **ir a ~, ir a las mil ~s** to go wonderfully well, go extremely well; to go swimmingly; **lo hace a ~** he does it perfectly, he does it splendidly; **de ~** marvellous, wonderful; **por ~** for a wonder; by chance; very seldom.
(**b**) (*Bot*) marigold.
maravillar [1a] **1** *vt* to astonish, amaze. **2 maravillarse** *vr* to be astonished, be amazed (*con, de* at); **~ con, ~ de** to wonder at, marvel at.
maravillosamente *adv* wonderfully, marvellously.
maravilloso *adj* wonderful, marvellous.
marbellí 1 *adj* of Marbella. **2** *nmf* native (*o* inhabitant) of Marbella; **los ~es** the people of Marbella.
marbete *nm* (**a**) (*etiqueta*) label; tag, ticket, docket; **~ engomado** sticker. (**b**) (*Cos*) edge, border.
marca *nf* (**a**) (*gen*) mark; stamp; (*de nombre*) name tab; (*huella*) footprint, footmark; (*en papel*) watermark; (*Com*) trademark; (*Com*) make, brand; **~ de agua, ~ transparente** watermark; **~ comercial, ~ de fábrica** trademark; **~ de ley** hallmark; **~ de nacimiento** birthmark; **~ registrada** registered trademark; **de ~** excellent, outstanding; **de ~ mayor** absolutely outstanding; really big; **coches de 3 ~s distintas** cars of 3 different makes; **productos de varias ~s** various brands of products.
(**b**) (*Náut*) seamark; marker, buoy; landmark.
(**c**) (*Dep*) record; **batir la ~, mejorar la ~** to break the record; **establecer una ~** to set up a record.
(**d**) (*Naipes*) bid.
(**e**) (*herramienta*) stamp.
(**f**) (*Hist*) march, frontier area; **la M~ Hispánica** the Spanish March (*Catalonia*).
marcable *adj* (*Naipes*) biddable.
marcación *nf* (**a**) (*Náut*) bearing. (**b**) (*Telec*) dialling; **~ automática** autodial.
marcadamente *adv* markedly.
marcado 1 *adj* marked, strong, pronounced; distinct; **con ~ acento argentino** with a marked Argentinian accent. **2** *nm* (**a**) (*de pelo*) set. (**b**) (*Agr*) branding. (**c**) (*pluma*) marker pen.
marcador *nm* (**a**) marker (*t Billar*); (*de libro*) bookmark; (*para escribir*) highlighter; **~ de caminos** roadsign. (**b**) (*Dep*) scoreboard; (*persona*) scorer; **~ electrónico** electronic scoreboard; **abrir el ~, inaugurar el ~** to open the scoring. (**c**) (*Telec*) dial.
marcaje *nm* (**a**) (*Dep*) marking; (*entrada*) tackle, tackling. (**b**) (*de criminal etc*) shadowing, following; **hacer ~ a uno** to shadow sb, tail sb.
marcapasos *nm invar* (*Med*) pacemaker.
marcar [1g] **1** *vt* (**a**) (*gen*) to mark (*de* with); *ganado etc* to brand, stamp (*de* with); *tierra etc* to mark off, mark out; *ropa* to put one's name on, embroider a name on.
(**b**) (*fig*) (*indicar*) to mark, indicate, point to; (*cuadrante, termómetro etc*) to show, register, record, read, say; **las agujas marcan las 2** the hands point to 2 o'clock; **el tanteador marca 3 goles** the scoreboard shows 3 goals; **mi reloj marca la hora exacta** my watch is showing the exact time.
(**c**) *números etc* to keep a tally (*o* score) of, record; (*Dep*) *tanteo* to keep.
(**d**) (*Mús etc*) *paso* to mark; *compás* to beat, keep.
(**e**) (*Telec*) to dial.
(**f**) (*Naipes*) to bid.
(**g**) (*Dep*) *gol, tanto* to score (*t fig*); **~ un tanto en la discusión** to score a point in the argument.
(**h**) (*Dep*) *jugador contrario* to mark; (*Méx*) to tackle; *sospechoso* to shadow, tail.
(**i**) *tarea* to assign, set; *política* to lay down.
(**j**) (*Com*) to put a price on.
(**k**) (*Esp*) *pelo* to set, style.
2 *vi* (**a**) (*Dep*) to score.
(**b**) (*Telec*) to dial.
(**c**) (*: *jactarse*) to shoot a line*.
3 marcarse *vr* (**a**) (*Náut*) to take one's bearings.
(**b**) (*Dep*) to score.
(**c**) (*) to make one's mark, stand out; **~ con relieve** to stand out in relief.
(**d**) **~ un rollo** (*etc*)* to go on at great length.
(**e**) (*pelo*) to have one's hair set (*o* styled).
Marcial *nm* Martial.
marcial *adj ley etc* martial; *poste, disciplina* military.
marcianitos *nmpl* (*juego*) space-invaders.
marciano, -a *adj, nm/f* Martian.
marco 1 *nm* (**a**) (*Arquit, Arte, de espejo etc*) frame; **~ de chimenea** mantelpiece; **~ para cuadro** picture-frame; **~ de ventana** window-frame; **poner ~ a un cuadro** to frame a picture.
(**b**) (*Dep*) goalposts, goal.
(**c**) (*fig*) setting; **el paisaje ofreció un bello ~ para la fiesta** the countryside made a splendid setting for the festivity.
(**d**) (*fig*: *de plan etc*) framework.

(**e**) (*Fin*) mark.
(**f**) (*de pesos etc*) standard.
2 *atr*: **acuerdo ~** general framework of agreement; set of agreed guidelines; **ley ~** framework law; **plan ~** overall plan; **programa ~** overall programme.

márcola *nf* (*prov*) pruning hook.

Marcos *nm* Mark.

marcha *nf* (**a**) (*Mil etc*) march; (*Pol etc*) (protest) march; **~ forzada** forced march; **~ del hambre** hunger march; **larga ~** (*Pol, fig*) long march; **a largas ~s** speedily; **a ~s forzadas** (*fig*) with all speed, as a matter of great urgency; **abrir la ~** to come first, be at the head of the procession (*etc*); **cerrar la ~** to come last, bring up the rear; **¡en ~!** (*Mil*) forward march!; (*fig*) let's go!, (*a otra persona*) get going!, get moving!; (*fig*) here goes!; **España es país en ~** Spain is a country on the move; **estar en ~** to be in motion, be going; (*Náut*) to be under way; (*fig*) to be on the move; **poner en ~** to start; (*fig*) to get going, set in motion, set on foot; **ponerse en ~** to start, get going; **comer sobre la ~** to eat as one goes along, eat along the way.
(**b**) (*Dep*) walk; (*excursión*) walk, hike; **~ atlética**, **~ de competición** walk, walking race.
(**c**) (*velocidad*) speed; **'~ moderada'** (*Aut*) 'drive slowly'; **moderar la ~ de un coche** to slow a car down, reduce the speed of a car; **a toda ~** at full speed, at top speed; (*fig*) at full blast, full-blast.
(**d**) (*Mec*) running, working, functioning, operation; **apearse en ~** to get off while the bus (*etc*) is moving; (⁑) to withdraw; **estar en ~** to be working; to be in working order.
(**e**) (*Aut, Mec*) gear; speed; **~ adelante** forward gear; **~ atrás** reverse gear; **~ corta** low gear; **~ directa** top gear; **~ larga** high gear; **primera ~** first gear; **dar ~ atrás, poner en ~ atrás, invertir la ~** to reverse, put into reverse; **el coche tiene cinco ~s** the car has five gears.
(**f**) (*Mús*) march; **~ fúnebre** funeral march, dead march; **~ lenta** slow march; **~ nupcial** wedding march; **M~ Real** national anthem; **tiene mucha ~** it's got a good beat.
(**g**) (*fig*) (*progreso*) progress; (*avance*) march; (*rumbo*) trend, course; (*de huracán*) path, track; **la ~ de los acontecimientos** the march of events, the course of events; **coger la ~ de algo** to get into the way (*o* habit) of sth, get the hang of sth; **dar ~ atrás** to back down, back off; (⁑) to withdraw, practise coitus interruptus.
(**h**) (*: *rollo*) **la ~** the scene, the action*; **me va la ~** I'm having a great time*; **no le va la ~** he's not with it*; **pedir ~** to be looking for the action; **la ciudad tiene mucha ~** it's a very lively town, the town has a lot going on.
(**i**) (*) (*duende*) charm, magic, appeal; charisma; (*misterio*) mystery; (*inspiración*) inspiration; (*estilo*) style.
(**j**) (*Carib: de caballo*) slow trot.
(**k**) (*Méx Aut*) self-starter.

marchador(a) *nm/f* (*Dep*) walker.

marchamo *nm* label, tag; (*de aduana*) customs mark; (*fig*) stamp.

marchantaje *nm* (*LAm*) clients, clientèle.

marchante, -a *nm/f* (**a**) (*tratante*) dealer, merchant; (*LAm: ambulante*) pedlar. (**b**) (*LAm*: cliente*) client, customer. (**c**) (*Carib*) trickster.

marchantía* *nf* (*CAm, Carib*) clients, clientèle.

marchar [1a] **1** *vi* (**a**) (*ir*) to go; (*viajar*) to move, travel; (*Mil*) to march.
(**b**) = **marcharse; ¡marchando!** get moving!, on your way!
(**c**) (*Mec etc*) to go; to run, function, work; (*tren etc*) to run; **el motor no marcha** the engine isn't working, the engine won't work; **el motor marcha mal** the engine is running badly; **~ en vacío** to tick over; **el reloj marcha atrasado** the watch is slow.
(**d**) (*fig*) to go, proceed; **todo marcha bien** everything is going well; **el proyecto marcha bien** the plan is coming along nicely; **el negocio no marcha** the business is getting nowhere, the deal is making no progress.
(**e**) (*Carib, Cono Sur: caballo*) to trot.
(**f**) (*Méx Mil**) to do military service.
2 marcharse *vr* to go (away), leave; **~ a otro sitio** to go somewhere else, leave for another place; **~ de la capital** to leave the capital; **¿os marcháis?** are you leaving?, must you go?; **con permiso me marcho** if you don't mind I must go.

marchista *nmf* (protest) marcher.

marchitar [1a] **1** *vt* to wither, fade, shrivel, dry up. **2 marchitarse** *vr* (**a**) (*Bot*) to wither, fade, shrivel up. (**b**) (*fig*) to languish, fade away; to go into a decline.

marchitez *nf* withered state, faded condition.

marchito *adj* (**a**) (*lit*) withered, faded. (**b**) (*fig*) faded; in decline.

marchoso* 1 *adj* (**a**) (*moderno*) ultramodern; trendy, hip*. (**b**) (*animado*) lively, fast-living, turned-on*. (**c**) (*amigo de placeres*) fun-loving. **2** *nmf* go-getter.

marduga* *nmf* (*CAm*) tramp.

marea *nf* (**a**) (*lit*) tide; **~ alta** high tide, high water; **~ baja** low tide, low water; **~ creciente** rising tide; **~ menguante** ebb tide; **~ muerta** neap tide; **~ negra** oil spill, large oil slick; **~ viva** spring tide.
(**b**) (*fig*) tide; **la ~ de la rebelión** the tide of revolt.
(**c**) (*brisa*) light sea breeze.
(**d**) (*llovizna*) drizzle; (*Cono Sur*) sea mist.
(**e**) (*período*) spell of duty at sea.

mareado *adj*: **estar ~** (**a**) (*nauseado*) to feel sick; (*aturdido*) to feel dizzy; (*Náut*) to be (*o* feel) seasick. (**b**) (*: *bebido*) to be a bit drunk.

mareaje *nm* (**a**) (*marinería*) navigation, seamanship. (**b**) (*rumbo*) ship's course.

marear [1a] **1** *vt* (**a**) (*Náut*) to sail, navigate.
(**b**) (*Med*) **~ a uno** (*causar náuseas a*) to make sb feel sick; (*en mar*) to make sb seasick; (*aturdir*) to make sb feel dizzy.
(**c**) (*fig*) (*irritar*) to annoy, upset, disturb; (*cargar*) to burden with (useless) things to do.
(**d**) (*Carib, Méx*) to cheat.
2 marearse *vr* (**a**) (*Med*) to feel sick; to be (*o* get, feel) seasick; to feel dizzy, feel giddy; to feel faint.
(**b**) **no te marees con esto** don't bother your head about this.
(**c**) (⁑) to get a bit drunk; to be high⁑.
(**d**) (*Carib, Cono Sur: paño*) to fade.

marejada *nf* (**a**) (*Náut*) swell, heavy sea; surge. (**b**) (*fig*) undercurrent (of unrest *etc*); wave, upsurge.

marejadilla *nf* slight swell.

maremagno *nm*, **mare mágnum** *nm* (*fig*) ocean, abundance; (*fig*) noisy confusion.

maremoto *nm* tidal wave.

mareo *nm* (**a**) (*Med*) (*náuseas*) sick feeling; (*en viaje*) travel sickness, (*en mar*) seasickness; (*aturdimiento*) dizziness, giddiness.
(**b**) (*fig*) (*irritación*) irritation; (*confusión*) confusion; (*nervios*) nervy state; (*aburrimiento*) boredom.
(**c**) (*lata*) nuisance, bore; **es un ~ tener que ...** it is a nuisance having to ...; **¡qué ~ de hombre!** what a bore that man is!

marfil *nm* (**a**) ivory. (**b**) (*LAm*) fine-toothed comb.

marfileño *adj* ivory, like ivory.

marga *nf* marl, loam.

margal *nm* marly patch; marlpit.

margarina *nf* margarine.

Margarita *nf* Margaret.

margarita *nf* (**a**) (*Zool: perla*) pearl; **echar ~s a los puercos** to cast pearls before swine.
(**b**) (*Zool: concha*) winkle.
(**c**) (*Bot*) daisy; **criar ~s*** to be pushing up the daisies*; **deshojar la ~** (*vacilar*) to vacillate; (*juego*) to play 'she loves me, she loves me not'; **ir a coger ~s⁑** to (go to) spend a penny⁑.
(**d**) (*Tip*) daisy-wheel.
(**e**) (*cóctel*) cocktail of tequila and fruit juice.

margen 1 *nm* (**a**) (*borde*) border, edge, fringe; (*de papel, Tip*) margin; **al ~** in the margin.
(**b**) (*Liter*) marginal note.
(**c**) (*fig*) margin; (*intervalo*) gap, space; (*libertad de acción*) leeway; **~ de beneficio, ~ de ganancia** profit margin; **~ bruto** gross margin; **~ comercial** mark-up; **~ de credibilidad** credibility gap; **~ de error** margin of (*o* for) error; **~ de seguridad** safety margin; **hay un ~ de aproximación de 8 días** we allow a week each way; **le digo el número con un ~ de unos 20** I'm telling you the number, give or take about 20.
(**d**) (*fig*) **al ~ de** outside; apart from; **al ~ de lo que digas** despite what you may say; **dejar a uno al ~** to leave sb out (in the cold); **mantenerse al ~** to keep out, stand aside.
(**e**) (*fig*) occasion, opportunity; **dar ~ para** to give an opportunity for, give scope for.
2 *nf* (*de río etc*) bank.

marginación *nf* (**a**) (*acto*) exclusion, rejection. (**b**) (*estado*) isolation.

marginado 1 *adj*: **estar ~, quedar ~** to be excluded, be left out; to be neglected; to be pushed aside; **sentirse ~** to feel rejected. **2** *nm*, **marginada** *nf* outsider; outcast; drop-out; underprivileged person, poor person.

marginal *adj* marginal; (*fig*) *grupo etc* marginalized.

marginalidad *nf* state of being excluded (*o* rejected); state of being isolated.

marginar [1a] **1** *vt* (**a**) *persona* to exclude, leave out, push aside; to reject; to isolate. (**b**) *página* to leave margins on. (**c**) *texto* to add marginal notes to, write marginal notes against. **2 marginarse** *vr* to exclude oneself, isolate oneself.

margoso *adj* marly, loamy.

margullo *nm* (*Carib*) shoot, runner.

Mari *nf forma familiar de* **María.**

María *nf* Mary; **~ Antonieta** Marie Antoinette; **~ Estuardo** Mary Stuart; **~ Magdalena** Mary Magdalene; **las tres ~s*** (*Colegio: Hist*) *religious, patriotic and physical training.*

maría¹‡ *nf* (*Esp: droga*) pot‡, hash*.

maría²‡ *nf* (*caja de caudales*) peter‡, safe.

maría³* *nf* (*Escol*) unimportant subject; easy subject; (*fig*) soft option.

maría⁴* *nf* (*Méx*) migrant from the country into Mexico City.

mariachi (*Méx*) **1** *nm* (*música*) mariachi music; (*conjunto*) mariachi band. **2** *nmf* mariachi musician.

marial *adj*, **mariano** *adj* Marian.

maribén‡ *nf* (*Esp*) death.

marica 1 *nf* (*Orn*) magpie. **2** *nm* (**a**) (*) weak character; milksop, sissy*, mollycoddle. (**b**) (‡) = **maricón.**

Maricastaña *n*: **en los días de ~, en tiempos de ~** (*Esp*) way back, long ago; in the good old days.

maricón‡ *nm* queer‡, pansy‡; **¡~ el último!** the last one's a sissy!*

mariconada‡ *nf* dirty trick.

mariconear‡ [1a] *vi* to act like a pansy‡.

mariconeo‡ *nm* homosexual activities.

mariconera‡ *nf* (man's) handbag.

maridaje *nm* (**a**) (*vida*) conjugal life; (*unión*) marriage ties. (**b**) (*fig*) marriage, close association, intimate connection. (**c**) (*pey*) cohabitation; (*Pol etc*) unholy alliance.

marido *nm* husband.

marielito* *nm* (*Carib*) Cuban exile.

marijuana *nf* (*t* **mariguana, marihuana**) marijuana, cannabis, Indian hemp.

marijuanero 1 *adj* marijuana (*atr*), cannabis (*atr*). **2** *nm* (*cultivador*) cannabis grower; (*fumador*) marijuana smoker.

marimacha *nf* (*And*) = **marimacho.**

marimacho 1 *adj* butch‡, mannish. **2** *nf* butch type‡, mannish woman.

marimandón* 1 *adj* nagging; overbearing, bossy. **2** *nm*, **marimandona** *nf* bossy-boots.

marimba 1 *nf* (**a**) (*Mús*) kind of drum; (*LAm*) marimba; (*Carib, Cono Sur*) out-of-tune instrument. (**b**) (*Cono Sur: paliza*) beating. (**c**) (*And Med*) large goitre. **2** *adj* (*CAm, Carib*) cowardly.

marimoña *nf* buttercup.

marimorena *nf* (*Esp*) fuss, row, shindy*; **armar una ~** to kick up a row.

marina *nf* (**a**) (*Geog*) coast, coastal area.

(**b**) (*marinería*) seamanship; navigation; **término de ~** term from navigation, nautical term.

(**c**) (*barcos*) ships; **~ (de guerra)** navy; **la ~ española** the Spanish navy, the Spanish fleet; **~ mercante** merchant navy; **servir en la ~** to serve in the navy.

(**d**) (*Arte*) sea-piece, seascape.

(**e**) (*de yates*) marina, yachting harbour.

marinar [1a] *vt* (*Culin*) to marinade, marinate.

marinería *nf* (**a**) (*arte*) seamanship. (**b**) (*tripulación*) ship's crew; seamen, sailors (*collectively*).

marinero 1 *adj* (**a**) = **marino.**

(**b**) *gente* sea (*atr*), seafaring.

(**c**) *barco* seaworthy.

(**d**) **a la marinera, a lo ~** in a seamanlike way; sailor-fashion.

2 *nm* sailor, seaman; mariner, seafarer; **~ de agua dulce** landlubber; **~ de cubierta** deckhand; **~ de primera** able seaman.

3 marinera *nf* (*And*) (*baile*) *Peruvian folkdance*; (*música*) *Peruvian folkmusic.*

marinesco *adj* seamanly; **a la marinesca** in a seamanlike way; sailor-fashion.

marino 1 *adj* sea (*atr*), marine; **pez ~** sea fish; **fauna marina** marine life, sea creatures. **2** *nm* sailor, seaman; (*oficial*) Navy officer.

mariolatría *nf* mariolatry.

marioneta *nf* marionette, puppet; (*fig*) puppet; **régimen ~** puppet régime.

marionetista *nmf* puppeteer.

mariposa *nf* (**a**) (*Ent*) butterfly; **~ (nocturna)** moth; **~ de la col** cabbage-white (butterfly); **~ cabeza de muerte, ~ de calavera** death's-head moth.

(**b**) (*Natación*) butterfly stroke; **100 metros ~** 100 metres butterfly.

(**c**) (*And, CAm: juguete*) toy windmill.

(**d**) (*And*) blind-man's buff.

(**e**) (‡: *gay*) pansy‡, fairy‡.

mariposear [1a] *vi* (**a**) (*revolotear*) to flutter about, flit to and fro. (**b**) (*fig*) (*ser inconstante*) to be fickle, act capriciously; (*coquetear*) to flirt; **~ alrededor de uno** to dance attendance on sb, be constantly fluttering round sb.

mariposilla *nf* small moth, (*esp*) clothes-moth.

mariposo‡ *nm* gay, homosexual.

mariposón *nm* (**a**) (*: *coqueto*) flirt, wolf*. (**b**) (‡: *gay*) queer‡, pansy‡.

Mariquita *nf forma familiar de* **María.**

mariquita 1 *nf* (**a**) (*Ent*) ladybird. (**b**) (*Orn*) parakeet. (**c**) (*Méx*‡) hash*, pot‡. **2** *nm* (*) = **marica 2.**

marisabidilla *nf* know-all.

mariscada *nf* seafood dish.

mariscador(a) *nm/f* gatherer of shellfish.

mariscal *nm* (*Hist*) blacksmith, farrier; (*Hist: Mil*) major-general; **~ de campo** field-marshal.

mariscala *nf* (woman) marshal; (*Hist*) marshal's wife.

mariscar [1g] **1** *vt* (‡) to nick‡, swipe‡. **2** *vi* to gather shellfish.

mariscos *nmpl* shellfish, seafood.

marisma *nf* marsh, swamp; mudflats.

marisqueo *nm* gathering shellfish, shellfishing.

marisquería *nf* shellfish bar, seafood restaurant.

marisquero *adj* shellfish (*atr*), seafood (*atr*); **barco ~** shellfishing boat.

marital *adj* marital.

maritatas *nfpl* (*Andalusia, LAm*), **maritates** *nmpl* (*CAm, Méx*) gear, tackle, tools; (*pey*) things, junk.

marítimo *adj* maritime; marine, sea (*atr*); *agente etc* shipping (*atr*); **ciudad marítima** seaside town, coastal town; **ruta marítima** ocean route, seaway, route by sea; **seguro ~** marine insurance.

maritornes *nf invar* (*criada*) sluttish servant; (*putilla*) wench, tart*.

marjal *nm* marsh, fen, bog.

márketing ['marketin] *nm* marketing; marketing technique(s); marketing campaign.

marmaja‡ *nf* (*Méx*) dough‡, money.

marmellas‡ *nfpl* (*Esp*) tits‡, breasts.

marmita *nf* (**a**) (*Culin*) pot; (*Mil*) mess tin; (*Méx*) kettle. (**b**) **~ de gigante** (*Geol*) pothole.

marmitón *nm* kitchen boy, scullion.

mármol *nm* marble; (*de cocina*) worktop; (*Culin*) chopping-block.

marmolejo *nm* small marble column.

marmolería *nf*: **~ funeraria** monumental masonry.

marmolista *nmf* monumental mason.

marmóreo *adj* marble; marmoreal.

marmosete *nm* (*Tip*) tailpiece, vignette.

marmota *nf* (**a**) (*Zool*) marmot; **~ de Alemania** hamster; **~ de América** woodchuck; **dormir como una ~** to sleep like a log. (**b**) (*fig*) sleepyhead. (**c**) (*: *criada*) maid, servant.

maroma *nf* (**a**) (*cuerda*) rope. (**b**) (*LAm*) (*cuerda floja*) tightrope; (*actuación*) acrobatic performance; (*Carib*) circus. (**c**) (*LAm*) **~s** acrobatics, acrobatic stunts; **hacer ~s = maromear.**

maromear [1a] *vi* (*LAm*) (**a**) (*en cuerda floja*) to walk (on) a tightrope; to do acrobatic stunts.

(**b**) (*fig: política*) to change one's political allegiance, climb on the bandwaggon; to keep in with all parties, do a political balancing act.

maromero *nm* (*LAm*) (**a**) (*acróbata*) tightrope walker, acrobat. (**b**) (*fig: político*) clever politician, politician who manages to be on good terms with all parties.

maromo‡ *nm* (*Esp*) bloke‡.

marona* *nf*: **tiene 60 años y ~** (*Carib*) he's well over sixty.

marqués *nm* marquis.

marquesa *nf* marchioness.

marquesina *nf* (*cobertizo*) glass canopy, porch; (*techo*) glass roof, cantilever roof; (*Ferro*) roof, cab (*of* *locomotive*); (*de tienda de campaña*) flysheet; (*de parada*) bus-shelter.

marquetería *nf* marquetry, inlaid work.

márquetin *nm* marketing.

marquezote *nm* (*CAm*) sweet bread.

marquito *nm* slide mounting.

marrajo 1 *adj toro* vicious, dangerous; *persona* sly. **2** *nm* (**a**) (*Zool*) shark. (**b**) (*Méx*: *tacaño*) skinflint. (**c**) (*: *candado*) padlock.

marramizar [1f] *vi* (*gato*) to howl, caterwaul.

marrana *nf* (**a**) (*Zool*) sow. (**b**) (*) slut.

marranada *nf*, **marranería** *nf* (**a**) (*gen*) filthiness. (**b**) (*acto*) filthy act; dirty trick, vile deed.

marrano 1 *adj* filthy, dirty. **2** *nm* (**a**) (*Zool*) pig, boar. (**b**) (*) swine*; dirty pig. (**c**) (*Hist*) Jew, converted Jew.

Marraquech *nm*, **Marraqués** *nm* Marrakesh.

marrar [1a] **1** *vt*: ~ **el tiro** to miss; ~ **el golpe** to miss (with a blow). **2** *vi* (**a**) (*gen*) to miss; (*fig*) to miss the mark. (**b**) (*fig*: *fallar*) to fail, miscarry, go astray; **no me marra una** everything's going well for me.

marras *adv* (**a**) **de** ~ old; long-standing; well-known, that you (*etc*) know all about; in question, aforementioned; **es el problema de** ~ it's the same old problem; **volver a lo de** ~ to go back over the same old stuff.

(**b**) **hace** ~ **que no le veo** (*And**) it's ages since I saw him.

marrazo *nm* (*pico*) mattock; (*cuchillo*) short *machete*; (*Méx*) bayonet.

marrocata‡ *nf* Moroccan hashish.

marrón 1 *adj* chestnut, brown; *zapatos* brown.

2 *nm* (**a**) chestnut (colour); brown.

(**b**) (*Culin*) marron glacé.

(**c**) (*LAm Hist*) maroon.

(**d**) (*And*) curlpaper.

(**e**) (*Carib*) coffee with milk.

(**f**) (*Fin‡*) 100-peseta note.

(**g**) (*Jur**) (*acusación*) charge; (*condena*) sentence; **comerse un** ~ to cough‡, own up; **le pillaron de** ~ they caught him red-handed; **le dieron 5 años de** ~ they gave him 5 years' bird‡.

(**h**) (‡: *policía*) cop*.

marroncito *nm* (*Carib*) coffee with milk.

marroquí 1 *adj*, *nmf* Moroccan. **2** *nm* (*Téc*) morocco (leather).

marrubio *nm* (*Bot*) horehound.

marrueco = **marroquí 1**.

Marruecos *nm* Morocco; **el** ~ **Español** (*Hist*) Spanish Morocco.

marrullería *nf* (**a**) (*cualidad*) smoothness, glibness, plausibility. (**b**) (*una* ~) plausible excuse; **~s** smooth approach, cajolery, wheedling.

marrullero 1 *adj* smooth, glib, plausible; cajoling, wheedling. **2** *nm* smooth type, plausible individual.

Marsella *nf* Marseilles.

Marsellesa *nf* Marseillaise.

marsopa *nf* porpoise.

marsupial *adj*, *nm* marsupial.

marta *nf* (*Zool*) (pine) marten; (*piel*) sable; ~ **cebellina** sable.

martajar [1a] *vt* (*CAm*, *Méx*) (**a**) *maíz* to pound, grind. (**b**) ~ **el español** to speak broken Spanish.

Marte *nm* Mars.

martellina *nf* sledgehammer.

martes *nm invar* Tuesday; ~ **de carnaval**, ~ **de carnestolendas** Shrove Tuesday; ~ **y trece** = Friday 13th.

martillada *nf* hammer blow, blow with a hammer.

martillar [1a] *vt* (**a**) (*golpear con martillo*) to hammer; (*machacar*) to pound. (**b**) (*fig*) to worry, torment.

martillazo *nm* (heavy) blow with a hammer; **a ~s** by hammering; **formar algo a ~s** to hammer sth out (*o* into shape); **lograr algo a ~s** (*fig*) to succeed in doing sth by sheer force (*o* the hard way).

martilleante *adj* insistent, repetitious.

martillear [1a] **1** *vt* = **martillar**. **2** *vi* (*motor*) to knock.

martilleo *nm* hammering; pounding.

martillero, -a *nm/f* (*And*, *Carib*) auctioneer.

martillo *nm* (**a**) hammer (*t Dep*); (*de presidente etc*) gavel; ~ **de hielo** ice-pick; ~ **de madera** mallet; ~ **mecánico** power hammer; ~ **neumático** pneumatic drill, jackhammer (*US*); ~ **de orejas**, ~ **sacaclavos** claw-hammer; ~ **picador** pneumatic drill; ~ **pilón** steam hammer.

(**b**) (*Com*) auction-room.

(**c**) (*Arquit*) projecting part, house (*etc*) that sticks out from the row; (*LAm*) wing (of a building).

(**d**) (*fig*: *persona*) hammer, scourge.

Martín *nm* Martin; **San** ~ St Martin, (*fiesta*) Martinmas, (*Agr*) season for slaughtering pigs; **a cada puerco le llega su San** ~ (††) everyone comes to his day of reckoning; *V* **veranillo**.

martín *nm*: ~ **pescador** kingfisher.

martinete *nm* drop hammer; pile driver; (*Mús*) hammer.

martingala* *nf* knack, trick; (*pey*: *LAm*) trick, fiddle*.

Martinica *nf* Martinique.

mártir *nmf* martyr.

martirio *nm* (**a**) (*Ecl*) martyrdom. (**b**) (*fig*) torture, torment.

martirizador *adj* (*fig*) agonizing, excruciating.

martirizar [1f] *vt* (**a**) (*Ecl*) to martyr. (**b**) (*fig*) to torture, torment.

martirologio *nm* martyrology.

Marucha *nf*, **Maruja** *nf formas familiares de* **María**.

marucha *nf* (*And*) rump steak.

marula *nf* (*Méx*) teat.

marusa *nf* (*Carib*) shoulder bag.

maruto *nm* (*Carib*) (**a**) (*Anat*) navel. (**b**) (*Med*) wart; bruise, welt.

marxismo *nm* Marxism.

marxista *adj*, *nmf* Marxist.

marzal *adj* March (*atr*), of March.

marzo *nm* March.

más 1 *adv y adj* (**a**) (*comparaciones básicas*) (*comp*) more, (*superl*) most; **A es** ~ **difícil que B** A is more difficult than B, A is harder than B; **ella es la** ~ **guapa de todas** she is the prettiest of all; **él es el** ~ **inteligente** he is the most intelligent (one); **es el que sabe** ~ he's the one who knows most; **tiene** ~ **dinero que yo** he has more money than I (do); **un libro de lo** ~ **divertido** a most amusing book, a highly amusing book; **es de lo** ~ **verde** it's as dirty as can be, it's as dirty as they come; **un hombre de lo** ~ **desaprensivo** a completely unscrupulous man.

(**b**) (*ejemplos de uso con ciertos verbos*) **correr** ~ to run faster; **durar** ~ to last longer; **trabajar** ~ to work harder; **ha viajado** ~ he has travelled more (widely); ~ **quiero** + *infin* I would rather + *infin*, I would prefer to + *infin*.

(**c**) (*uso coloquial con adjs*) **¡qué perro** ~ **feo!** what an ugly dog!; **¡ya verán qué cena** ~ **rica!** you wait and see what a splendid supper it will be!; **¡es** ~ **bueno!** he's so kind!, he's ever so kind!

(**d**) (*comparaciones de calidad y cantidad*) ~ **de**, ~ **de lo que**, ~ **que** more than; ~ **de 10** more than 10; **con** ~ **dinero de lo que creíamos** with more money than we thought; **no veo** ~ **solución que de ...** I see no other solution than to ... (*o* but to); **se trata de voluntad** ~ **que de fuerza** it's more a question of will power than of strength, it's a matter of will power rather than of strength; **se estima en** ~ **de mil** it is reckoned at more than a thousand; **no** ~ **que ayer** only yesterday; **hace no** ~ **que 3 semanas** only 3 weeks ago, no longer than 3 weeks ago; **nadie lo sabe** ~ **que yo** nobody knows it better than I do.

(**e**) (*otros usos, y locuciones con prep*) ~ **y** ~ more and more; ~ **o menos** more or less; **el que** ~ **y el que menos** every single one; the whole lot; **2** ~ **2 menos** give or take a couple; **los** ~ most people; **los** ~ **de** most of, the majority of; **es** ~ ... furthermore ..., moreover ...; **a** ~ in addition, besides; **y a** ~ and moreover, and what is more; **a** ~ **de** in addition to, besides; **a lo** ~ at most, at the most; **a las 8 a** ~ **tardar** at 8 o'clock at the latest; **está nevando a** ~ **y mejor** it really is snowing, it's snowing harder than ever; **la cosa no fue a** ~ things did not get out of hand; **como el que** ~ as well as anyone, as well as the next man; **llevaba 3 de** ~ he was carrying 3 too many; **trae una manta de** ~ bring an extra blanket; **estar de** ~ to be unnecessary, be superfluous; **aquí yo estoy de** ~ I'm not needed here, I'm de trop here, I'm in the way here; **unas copas no estarían de** ~ a few drinks wouldn't do any harm; **está de** ~ **decir que ...** it is unnecessary to say that ...; **no estará por de** ~ **preguntar** there's no harm in asking; **de** ~ **en** ~ more and more; **hasta no** ~ to the utmost, to the limit; **nada** ~ nothing else; **¡nada** ~**!** that's all!, that's the lot!; **¿nada** ~**?** anything else?; **ocurrió nada** ~ **iniciado el partido** it happened when the game had scarcely begun; **aparecen nada** ~ **terminado el invierno** they come when the winter is hardly over; **nada** ~ **llegar te llamo** I'll call you as soon as I arrive; **son 10 pesos nada** ~ (*And*, *Méx*) it's only 10 pesos; **nada** ~ **que estoy muy cansado** (*And*, *Méx*) it's just that I'm very tired; **nadie** ~ **que tú** only you, nobody but you; **ni** ~ **ni menos** neither more nor less; just; **es un genio ni ~ ni menos** he's nothing more nor less than a genius, he's a real genius; **no ~** no more; **habían llegado no ~** they had just arrived; **no ~ llegué me echaron** (*LAm*) no sooner had I arrived than they threw me out; **vengo no ~ a verlo** I've come just to see it; **así no ~** (*LAm*) just like that; **entre** *o* **pase no ~** please go in; **siéntese no ~** (*LAm*) do sit down; **sírvase no ~** (*LAm*) please help yourself; **pruébelo no ~** (*LAm*) just try it; **ayer no ~** (*LAm*) only yesterday; **¡espera no ~!** (*LAm*) just you wait!; **no trabaja ~** he no longer works, he doesn't work any more; **por ~ que se esfuerce** however much (*o* hard) he tries, no matter how (hard) he tries; **por ~ que quisiera ayudar** much as I should like to help; **¿qué ~?** what else?; what next?; **¿qué ~ da?** what difference does it make?; **sin ~ (ni ~)** without more ado; **todo lo ~** at most, at the most; *V* **allá, bien, cuento, nunca** *etc.*

2 *conj* and, plus; **2 ~ 3 son 5** 2 and 3 are 5, 2 plus 3 are 5; **con éstos ~ los que había antes** with these and (*o* together with) what there were before; **España ~ Portugal** Spain together with Portugal.

3 *nm* **(a)** (*Mat*) plus, plus sign.

(b) tiene sus ~ y sus menos it has its good and bad points, there are things to be said on both sides.

mas *conj* (*liter*) but.

masa[1] *nf* **(a)** (*Culin*) dough. **(b)** (*Cono Sur*: *pastelito*) small bun, teacake; (*And, Cono Sur*) puff-pastry; **~ quebrada** short pastry. **(c)** (*Arquit*) mortar, plaster.

masa[2] *nf* **(a)** (*Fís etc*) mass; (*fig*) mass; bulk; volume, quantity; **las ~s** the masses; **~ coral** choir; **~ crítica** critical mass; (*fig*) requisite number; **~ monetaria** money supply; **~ polar** polar icecap; **~ salarial** total wages bill; **en ~** (*gente*) en masse, in a body, all together; (*And, Cono Sur*: *en conjunto*) as a whole, altogether; **reunir(se) en ~** to mass; **llevar algo en la ~ de la sangre** to have sth in one's blood, have a natural inclination towards sth.

(b) (*Elec*) earth, ground (*US*); **conectar un aparato con ~** to earth a piece of apparatus, ground a piece of apparatus (*US*).

masacrar [1a] *vt* to massacre.

masacre *nf* (*a veces m*) massacre.

masacrear‡ [1a] *vt* (*Carib*) to touch up‡.

masada *nf* farm.

masadero *nm* farmer.

masaje *nm* massage; **dar ~ a** to massage; **hacerse dar ~s** to have o.s. massaged.

masajear [1a] *vt* to massage.

masajista 1 *nm* masseur. **2** *nf* masseuse.

masar* [1a] *vt* (*Dep*) to massage.

masato *nm* (*And, CAm*) *drink made from fermented maize or rice*; (*And*: *dulce de coco*) *coconut sweet*; (*And*: *de plátanos*) *banana custard.*

mascada *nf* **(a)** (*LAm*: *tabaco*) plug of chewing tobacco.

(b) (*And, CAm*) (*tesoro*) buried treasure; (*ahorros*) store of money, nest-egg; (*Cono Sur*: *ganancias*) illicit gains; (*: *tajada*) rake-off*, cut.

(c) (*CAm*: *reprimenda*) rebuke.

(d) (*CAm, Méx*: *pañuelo*) silk handkerchief.

mascado* *adj* (*CAm*) creased, rumpled.

mascadura *nf* chewing.

mascar [1g] **1** *vt* **(a)** *comida* to chew. **(b)** (*) *palabras* to mumble, mutter. **(c) ~ un asunto, dar mascado un asunto*** to explain a matter in very simple terms. **2** *vi* to chew; (*esp LAm*) to chew tobacco.

máscara 1 *nf* **(a)** (*lit*) mask; **~ antigás** gasmask; **~ para esgrima** fencing mask; **~ de oxígeno** (*Med*) oxygen mask; (*Aer etc*) breathing apparatus.

(b) ~s (*Teat*) masque, masquerade.

(c) (*fig*) mask; disguise; **quitar la ~ a uno** to unmask sb; **quitarse la ~** to reveal o.s.

(d) (*rimel*) mascara.

2 *nmf* masked person.

mascarada *nf* **(a)** (*lit*) masque, masquerade. **(b)** (*fig*) masquerade; farce, charade.

mascarilla *nf* mask (*t Med*); (*vaciado*) plaster cast (of the face); (*maquillaje*) facepack; **~ de arcilla** mudpack; **~ mortuoria** death mask; **~ con oxígeno** oxygen mask.

mascarón *nm* large mask; **~ de proa** figurehead.

mascota *nf* mascot.

masculinidad *nf* masculinity, manliness.

masculino 1 *adj* masculine, manly; (*Bio*) male; (*Ling*) masculine; **ropa masculina** men's clothing. **2** *nm* (*Ling*) masculine.

mascullar [1a] *vt* to mumble, mutter.

masera *nf* kneading trough.

masía *nf* (*Aragón, Catalonia*) farm.

masificación *nf* growth, extension; overcrowding; excessive quantity.

masificado *adj* overcrowded; overfull; overgrown, overextended.

masificarse [1g] *vr* to get too big, become over-extended; to get overcrowded.

masilla *nf* (*para ventanas*) putty; (*para agujeros*) filler.

masillo *nm* (*Carib*) plaster.

masita *nf* (*LAm*) small bun, teacake, pastry.

masitero *nm* (*And, Carib, Cono Sur*) pastrycook, confectioner.

masivamente *adv* massively; en masse, on a large scale.

masivo *adj ataque, dosis etc* massive; *evacuación etc* en masse, large-scale, general; *ejecución* mass (*atr*), wholesale; **reunión masiva** mass meeting.

masmediático *adj* mass-media (*atr*); **mucha atención masmediática** a lot of attention from the mass media.

masoca* 1 *adj* masochistic. **2** *nmf* masochist.

masocotudo *adj* (*And, Cono Sur*) = **amazacotado.**

masón *nm* (free)mason.

masonería *nf* (free)masonry.

masónico *adj* masonic.

masoquismo *nm* masochism.

masoquista 1 *adj* masochistic. **2** *nmf* masochist.

mastate *nm* (*CAm, Méx*) loincloth.

mastectomia *nf* mastectomy.

mastelero *nm* topmast.

master 1 *adj copia* master. **2** *nm, pl* **masters (a)** (*Univ*) master's degree (*en* in). **(b)** (*Cine, Mús*) master copy. **(c)** (*Dep*) masters' competition.

masticación *nf* mastication.

masticar [1g] *vt* to masticate, chew.

mástil *nm* **(a)** (*palo*) pole, post; (*sostén*) support; (*de bandera*) flagpole; (*Náut*) mast; (*Arquit*) upright; **~ de tienda** tent pole. **(b)** (*de guitarra*) neck. **(c)** (*de pluma*) shaft.

mastín *nm* mastiff; **~ danés** Great Dane; **~ del Pirineo** Pyrenean mountain dog.

mastique *nm* plaster; cement; putty.

mastitis *nf* mastitis.

masto *nm* (*Agr, Hort*) stock (*for grafting*).

mastodonte *nm* mastodon; (*) elephantine person (*u* object *etc*).

mastodóntico *adj* (*fig*) colossal, huge.

mastoides *adj, nf* mastoid.

mastuerzo *nm* **(a)** (*Bot*) cress; **~ (de agua)** watercress. **(b)** (*) dolt.

masturbación *nf* masturbation.

masturbarse [1a] *vr* to masturbate.

masturbatorio *adj* masturbatory.

Mat. *abr de* **Matemáticas** mathematics, maths*.

mata *nf* **(a)** (*arbusto*) bush, shrub; (*esp LAm*: *cualquier planta*) plant; **~ de coco** (*Carib*) coconut palm; **~ de plátano** (*Carib*) banana tree; **~ rubia** kermes oak.

(b) (*ramita*) sprig; tuft, blade; (*raíz*) clump, root; (*ramo*) bunch.

(c) ~s thicket, bushes; scrub.

(d) (*Agr*) field, plot; **~ de olivos** field of olive trees, olive grove.

(e) (*LAm*: *arboleda*) clump, group (of trees), grove; (*And*: *huerto*) orchard; (*Méx*: *matorral*) scrub; **~ de bananos** clump of banana trees, banana plantation.

(f) ~ de pelo head of hair; mop of hair.

mataburros *nm invar* (*Carib, Cono Sur*: *hum*) dictionary.

matacaballo *adv*: **a ~** at breakneck speed.

matacán *nm* **(a)** (*And, Carib*) fawn, young deer. **(b)** (*CAm*) calf.

matachín *nm* bully.

matadero *nm* **(a)** (*lit*) slaughterhouse, abattoir. **(b)** (*fig*) drudgery. **(c)** (*Méx, Cono Sur*‡) brothel.

matador 1 *adj* **(a)** (*lit*) killing. **(b)** (*: *ridículo*) ridiculous; absurd; **el vestido le está ~** the dress looks absurd on her. **2** *nm,* **matadora** *nf* killer. **3** *nm* (*Taur*) matador, bullfighter.

matadura *nf* (*Vet*) sore.

matafuego *nm* fire extinguisher.

matagigantes *nm invar* giant-killer.

matalahúga *nf,* **matalahúva** *nf* aniseed.

mátalas callando* *nm* smooth type, sly sort.

matalobos *nm invar* aconite, wolf's-bane.

matalón 1 *adj caballo* old, broken-down. **2** *nm* broken-down old horse, nag.

matalotaje *nm* **(a)** (*Náut*) ship's stores. **(b)** (*) jumble, mess.

matambre *nm* cold meat brawn.

matamoros *nm invar* swashbuckler, braggart.

matamoscas *nm invar* fly-swat; flypaper; flyspray.

matanza *nf* (**a**) (*lit*) slaughter, killing; (*Agr*) slaughtering, (*esp*) pig-killing; (*temporada*) slaughtering season; ~ **sistemática** culling; (*fig*) slaughter, massacre, butchery.
(**b**) (*Carib*: *matadero*) slaughterhouse; (*And*: *tienda*) butcher's (shop); (*CAm*: *mercado*) meat market.

mataperrada* *nf* (*And, Cono Sur*) prank; (*pey*) piece of hooliganism.

mataperrear* [1a] *vi* (*And, Cono Sur*) to wander the streets.

mataperros* *nm invar* urchin, hooligan.

matar [1a] **1** *vt* (**a**) *persona* to kill; to slay; *animal* to slaughter; ~ **a uno a disgustos** to make sb's life a misery; **así me maten** ... for the life of me ...; **que me maten si** ... I'll eat my hat if ...; believe me, I never ...; ~**las callando** to do o.s. a lot of good on the quiet, go about things slyly; **se llevan a** ~ they're at daggers drawn.
(**b**) (*fig*) *tiempo* to kill; *hambre* to stay; *polvo* to lay; *cal* to slake; *sello* to postmark, cancel; *ángulo, borde etc* to file down, smooth, round off; *color* to tone down; *violencia etc* to diminish, reduce.
(**c**) (*: *fastidiar*) to upset, annoy.
(**d**) (*: *aturdir*) to amaze, astound.
2 *vi* (**a**) (*gen*) to kill; **no matarás** thou shalt not kill; **estar a** ~ **con uno** to be at daggers drawn with sb.
(**b**) (*Ajedrez*) to mate.
3 matarse *vr* (**a**) (*suicidarse*) to kill o.s., commit suicide; (*en accidente*) to be killed, get killed.
(**b**) (*fig*) to wear o.s. out, kill o.s.; ~ **a trabajar** to kill o.s. with work, overwork; ~ **por** + *infin* to struggle to + *infin*, make a great effort to + *infin*.

matarife *nm* butcher, slaughterman; ~ **de caballos** knacker.

matarratas *nm invar* rat poison; (*fig*) hooch*, bad liquor.

matasanos *nm invar* quack (doctor).

matasellado *nm* cancellation, postmark.

matasellar [1a] *vt* to cancel, postmark.

matasellos *nm invar* cancellation, postmark.

matasiete *nm* braggart, bully.

matasuegras *nm invar* streamer, blower (*toy*).

matasuelo *nm*: **darse un** ~ (*And**) to come a cropper*.

matate *nm* (*CAm*) canvas bag.

matazón *nm* (*And, CAm, Carib*) = **matanza**.

match [maʃ] *nm, pl* **matchs** [maʃ] (*Dep*) match.

mate[1] *adj* dull, matt, unpolished.

mate[2] *nm* (*Ajedrez*) mate, checkmate; **dar** ~ **a** to mate, checkmate.

mate[3] *nm* (*LAm*) (**a**) (*bebida*) maté, Paraguayan tea (*herb and drink similar to tea*). (**b**) (*vasija*) gourd, drinking vessel; maté pot; **pegar** ~ (*CAm*) to go crazy; **tener mucho** ~ (*CAm*) to be sharp. (**c**) (*Cono Sur*‡) head, nut‡.

mate[4] *nm* (*Tenis*) smash.

matear[1] [1a] **1** *vt* (*Agr*) to plant at regular intervals, sow in groups. **2** *vi* (**a**) (*Bot*) to sprout (thickly). (**b**) (*Caza*: *perro*) to hunt among the bushes.

matear[2] [1a] *vi* (*LAm*) to drink maté.

matear[3] [1a] *vt* (*Cono Sur*) (**a**) (*Ajedrez*) to checkmate. (**b**) (*mezclar*) to mix.

matemáticamente *adv* mathematically.

matemáticas *nfpl* mathematics; ~ **aplicadas** applied mathematics; ~ **puras** pure mathematics.

matemático 1 *adj* mathematical; *cálculo* precise. **2** *nm*, **matemática** *nf* mathematician.

Mateo *nm* Matthew.

materia *nf* (**a**) (*lit*) matter (*t Med, Fís*); material; stuff; ~ **colorante** dyestuff; ~ **gris** grey matter; ~ **fecal** faeces; ~ **prima** raw material; ~ **vegetal** vegetable matter.
(**b**) (*Liter etc*) matter, subject matter; (*Univ etc*) subject; **índice de** ~**s** table of contents; **en** ~ **de** in the matter of, on the subject of; as regards; **entrar en** ~ to begin on one's subject (after a preamble), get to the point; **será** ~ **de muchas discusiones** it will be the subject of a lot of argument, it will give rise to a lot of argument.

material 1 *adj* (**a**) (*gen*) material.
(**b**) (*físico*) physical; **la presencia** ~ **de uno** sb's physical (*o* bodily) presence; **dolor** ~ physical pain; **daños** ~**es** physical damage; damage to property.
(**c**) (*real*) real, true; (*literal*) literal; physical; **la imposibilidad** ~ **de** ... the physical impossibility of ...; **el autor** ~ **del hecho** the actual perpetrator of the deed.
2 *nm* (**a**) (*gen*) material; **hecho de mal** ~ made of bad material(s); ~ **bélico**, ~ **de guerra** war material; ~ **de construcción** building material; ~**es de derribo** rubble; ~ **de desecho** waste material; ~**es plásticos** plastics, plastic materials.
(**b**) (*Téc*) equipment, plant; materials; ~**es didácticos**, ~ **escolar** teaching materials, school equipment; ~ **de envasado** packaging material; ~ **fotográfico** photographic equipment; ~ **informático** hardware; ~ **de limpieza** cleaning materials; ~ **móvil**, ~ **rodante** rolling-stock; ~ **de oficina** stationery; office supplies; **el nuevo** ~ **de la fábrica** the new factory plant.
(**c**) (*Tip*) copy.
(**d**) (*: *de zapatos*) leather.
(**e**) **de** ~ (*LAm*) made of bricks, brick-built.

materialidad *nf* material nature; outward appearance; literalness; substance; **percibe solamente la** ~ **del asunto** he sees only the superficial aspects; **es menos la** ~ **del insulto que** ... it's not so much the insult itself as ...

materialismo *nm* materialism.

materialista 1 *adj* materialist(ic). **2** *nmf* materialist. **3** *nm* (**a**) (*Méx*: *camionero*) lorry driver, truckdriver (*US*). (**b**) (*Méx*: *contratista*) building contractor.

materializable *adj* realizable, attainable.

materializar [1f] **1** *vt* to materialize. **2 materializarse** *vr* to materialize.

materialmente *adv* (**a**) (*gen*) materially; physically, in the physical sense.
(**b**) (*absolutamente*) absolutely; (*textualmente*) literally; **nos es** ~ **imposible** it is quite (*o* absolutely) impossible for us; **estaba** ~ **mojado** he was completely soaked.

maternal 1 *adj* motherly; maternal. **2** *nm* (*Carib*) nursery.

maternidad *nf* (**a**) (*lit*) motherhood, maternity. (**b**) (*t* **casa de** ~) maternity hospital.

materno *adj* (**a**) *lengua etc* mother (*atr*); *casa etc* mother's; **leche materna** mother's milk. (**b**) *parentesco* maternal; **abuelo** ~ maternal grandfather, grandfather on the mother's side.

matero *adj* (*Cono Sur*) (**a**) (*de mate*) of maté, relating to maté. (**b**) *persona* fond of drinking maté.

mates* *nfpl* maths*, math* (*US*).

matete* *nm* (*Cono Sur*) (**a**) (*revoltijo*) mess, hash. (**b**) (*fig*: *riña*) quarrel, brawl. (**c**) (*fig*: *confusión*) confusion.

Matilde *nf* Mat(h)ilda.

matinal *adj* morning (*atr*).

matinée *nm* (**a**) (*Teat*) matinée. (**b**) (*And*: *fiesta infantil*) children's party.

matiz *nm* (**a**) (*de color*) shade, hue, tint. (**b**) (*de significado*) shade, nuance; (*de ironía etc*) touch.

matización *nf* (**a**) (*Arte*) blending. (**b**) (*teñido*) tinging, tinting; (*fig*) variation; toning down; refinement, fine-tuning; clarification.

matizado *adj*: ~ **de**, ~ **en** tinged with, touched with (*t fig*).

matizar [1f] *vt* (**a**) (*Arte*) to blend.
(**b**) *color* to tinge, tint (*de* with; *t fig*); *tono etc* to vary, introduce some variety into; *contraste, intensidad* to tone down; (*aclarar*) to make more precise, add precision to, fine-tune; to clarify; (*sutilizar*) to go into fine detail over, introduce subtle distinctions into; ~ **que** ... to explain that ...; **se matizarán los cursos con deportes** classes will be interspersed with sports, there will be sports in addition to classes; ~ **un discurso de ironía** to introduce ironical notes into a speech, give a speech an ironical slant.

matojal *nm* (*Carib*), **matojo** *nm* (*And, Carib, Méx*) = **matorral**.

matón *nm* bully, lout, thug.

matonismo *nm* bullying, loutishness; racketeering.

matonista *nm* bully, thug; (*en cárcel*) racketeer.

matorral *nm* thicket; brushwood, scrub.

matorro *nm* (*And*) = **matorral**.

matra *nf* (*Cono Sur*) horseblanket.

matraca 1 *nf* (**a**) (*objeto*) rattle.
(**b**) (*) (*lata*) nuisance, bore; (*guasa*) chaff, banter; **dar** ~ **a uno** to pester sb, keep bothering sb; to banter sb.
(**c**) (*And*‡) hash*, pot‡.
(**d**) ~**s** (*Escol*‡) maths*.
(**e**) (*Méx**: *metralleta*) machine-gun.
2 *nmf* (*) nuisance, bore.

matraquear [1a] *vt* (**a**) (*hacer sonar*) to rattle. (**b**) (*) = **dar matraca a**.

matraz *nm* (*Quím*) flask.

matreraje *nm* (*Cono Sur*) banditry, brigandage.

matrero 1 *adj* (**a**) (*astuto*) cunning, sly, knowing. (**b**) (*LAm*) suspicious, distrustful. **2** *nm* (*LAm*) (*bandido*) bandit, brigand; (*fugitivo*) fugitive from justice; (*tramposo*) trickster.

matriarca *nf* matriarch.
matriarcado *nm* matriarchy.
matriarcal *adj* matriarchal.
matricería *nf* die-stamping.
matricida *nmf* matricide (*person*).
matricidio *nm* matricide (*act*).
matrícula *nf* (**a**) (*registro*) register, list, roll; (*Náut*) register.
(**b**) (*acto*) (*Náut*) registration; (*Univ*) registration, matriculation; **un buque de ~ extranjera** a foreign ship, a ship with foreign registration; **un barco con ~ de Bilbao** a boat registered in Bilbao; **~ de honor** first class with distinction (and remission of registration fee).
(**c**) (*licencia*) licence; (*Aut*) registration number; (*placa*) number-plate, licence plate; **~ de encargo** personalized number-plate.
matriculación *nf* registration; enrolment; licensing.
matricular [1a] **1** *vt* to register; to enrol; to license. **2 matricularse** *vr* to register; to enrol, sign on; **~ en el curso de ...** to sign on for the course in ...
matrimonial *adj* matrimonial; **enlace ~** link by marriage; **capitulaciones ~es** marriage settlement; **vida ~** married life, conjugal life.
matrimonialista *adj*: **abogado ~** lawyer specializing in matrimonial cases.
matrimoniar [1b] *vi* to marry, get married.
matrimonio *nm* (**a**) (*gen*) marriage, matrimony; married state; (*acto*) marriage; **~ abierto** open marriage; **~ canónico** canonical marriage; church wedding; **~ civil** civil marriage; **~ clandestino** secret marriage; **~ consensual** common-law marriage; **~ de conveniencia, ~ de interés** marriage of convenience; **~ por la iglesia** church wedding; **contraer ~ (con)** to marry; **hacer uso del ~** (*hum*) to make love; **hacer vida de ~** to live together.
(**b**) (*personas*) couple, married couple; **el ~ García** the Garcías, Mr and Mrs García; **de ~** *cama etc* double.
matritense = **madrileño.**
matriz 1 *nf* (**a**) (*Anat*) womb, uterus.
(**b**) (*Téc*) mould, die; (*Tip*) matrix; (*LAm*) stencil.
(**c**) (*Mat*) matrix; (*Inform*) array.
(**d**) (*de talonario etc*) stub, counterfoil.
(**e**) (*Jur*) original, master copy.
2 *atr*: **casa ~** (*Com etc*) head office; parent company; **convento ~** (*Ecl*) parent house.
matrona *nf* (**a**) (*lit*) matron. (**b**) (*Esp Med*) midwife.
matronal *adj* matronly.
matungo‡ (*Carib, Cono Sur*) **1** *adj* old, worn-out. **2** *nm* (*caballo*) old horse, nag; (*persona*) beanpole*.
maturrango 1 *adj* (*Cono Sur*) clumsy, awkward; (*And, Cono Sur*) *jinete* poor, incompetent. **2** *nm* (*And, Cono Sur*) poor rider, incompetent horseman.
Matusalén *nm* Methuselah.
matute *nm* (**a**) (*acto*) smuggling, contraband; **de ~** (*Com*) smuggled, contraband; (*como adv*) secretly, stealthily; **introducir una idea de ~** to bring in a (dangerous) notion from outside.
(**b**) (*géneros*) smuggled goods, contraband.
(**c**) (*casa de juego*) gambling den.
matuteo *nm* smuggling.
matutero *nm* smuggler.
matutino 1 *adj* morning (*atr*). **2** *nm* newspaper (published in the morning).
maula 1 *adj* (*LAm*) *animal* useless, vicious, lazy; (*Cono Sur, Méx*) *persona* good-for-nothing, unreliable; (*Cono Sur*) yellow.
2 *nf* (**a**) (*Cos*) remnant.
(**b**) (*objeto*) piece of junk, useless object; white elephant.
(**c**) (*: *persona*) useless individual, dead loss.
(**d**) (*: *trampa*) dirty trick, fraud.
3 *nmf* (**a**) (*vago*) idler, slacker.
(**b**) (*tramposo*) cheat, trickster; tricky individual; (*Fin*) bad payer.
maulería *nf* cunning, trickiness.
maulero *nm* (**a**) (*tramposo*) cheat, trickster; (*engañador*) smooth and deceitful type. (**b**) (*ilusionista*) conjurer.
maullar [1a] *vi* to mew, miaow.
maullido *nm* mew, miaow.
Mauricio[1] *nm* Maurice.
Mauricio[2] *nm* (*Geog*) Mauritius.
Mauritania *nf* Mauritania.
mauritano, -a *adj, nm/f* Mauritanian.
maurofilia *nf* (*Hist*) liking for Moors; liking for Moorish things.
maurofobia *nf* (*Hist*) dislike of Moors; dislike of Moorish things.
mausoleo *nm* mausoleum.
maxi... *pref* maxi...
maxifalda *nf* maxiskirt.
maxilar 1 *adj* maxillary. **2** *nm* jaw, jawbone.
máxima *nf* maxim.
maximalismo *nm* going all out; (*Pol*) extremism, advocacy of extreme solutions.
maximalista 1 *adj* far-out, extreme. **2** *nmf* person who goes all out; (*Pol*) extremist, advocate of extreme solutions.
máxime *adv* especially; principally; all the more so.
maximización *nf* maximization.
maximizar [1f] *vt* to maximize.
máximo 1 *adj* maximum; top; highest, greatest; **el ~ dirigente** the top leader; **el ~ premio** the highest award, the top prize; **su ~ esfuerzo** their greatest effort; **llegar al punto ~** to reach the highest point; **es lo ~ en la moda juvenil**‡ it's the most in young people's fashions‡.
2 *nm* maximum; **como ~** at most, at the outside; **al ~** to the maximum, to the utmost.
máximum *nm* maximum.
maxisencillo *nm*, **maxisingle** *nm* maxisingle, twelve-incher.
maxtate *nm* (*Méx*) straw basket.
maya[1] *nf* (**a**) (*Bot*) daisy. (**b**) (*persona*) May Queen, Queen of the May.
maya[2] (*Hist*) **1** *adj* Mayan. **2** *nmf* Maya, Mayan.
mayal *nm* flail.
mayestático *adj* majestic; royal, regal; **el plural ~** the royal 'we'.
mayo *nm* (**a**) (*mes*) May. (**b**) (*palo*) maypole.
mayólica *nf* (*And*) wall tile.
mayonesa *nf* mayonnaise.
mayor 1 *adj* (**a**) *parte etc* main, major, larger; **y otros animales ~es** and other larger animals.
(**b**) *altar, calle, misa etc* high; *plaza* main, principal; *mástil* main; *V* **colegio, libro** *etc.*
(**c**) (*Mús*) major.
(**d**) *persona* (*adulto*) grown up, adult; (*de edad*) of age; (*anciano*) elderly; **ser ~ de edad** to be of age, be adult; **hacerse ~** to grow up.
(**e**) (*en rango etc*) head, chief; **montero ~** head huntsman.
2 *adj comp* (**a**) (*en tamaño*) bigger, larger, greater (*que* than).
(**b**) (*en edad*) older (*que* than), elder; (*en rango*) senior (*que* to).
3 *adj superl* (**a**) (*en tamaño*) biggest, largest, greatest (*t fig*); **su ~ cuidado** his biggest worry; **su ~ enemigo** his greatest enemy; **hacer algo con el ~ cuidado** to do sth with the greatest care; **viven en la ~ miseria** they live in the greatest poverty.
(**b**) (*en edad*) oldest, eldest; (*en rango*) most senior.
4 *nmf* (**a**) (*en rango*) chief, boss, superior; (*en oficina*) chief clerk; (*LAm Mil*) major.
(**b**) (*adulto*) **~ de edad** adult, person legally of age; **~es** grown-ups, adults; elders (and betters); **eso es sólo para ~es** that's only for grown-ups; **¡más respeto con los ~es!** be more respectful to your elders (and betters)!
(**c**) (*antepasados*) **~es** ancestors, forefathers.
(**d**) (*situación*) **llegar a ~es** to get out of hand, get out of control.
5 *nm*: **al por ~** wholesale (*t fig*); **vender al por ~** to sell wholesale; **repartir golpes al por ~** to deal out punches wholesale, throw punches left and right.
mayoral *nm* (*Téc etc*) foreman, overseer, gaffer; (*Agr*) (*pastor*) head shepherd; (*mayordomo*) steward; farm manager; (*Hist*) coachman.
mayorazgo *nm* (**a**) (*institución*) primogeniture. (**b**) (*tierras*) entailed estate. (**c**) (*hijo*) eldest son, first-born.
mayorcito *adj* rather older, a bit more grown-up; **eres ~ ya** you're grown up, you're a big boy now; **ya eres un poco ~ para hacer eso** you're too old now to be doing that.
mayordomo *nm* (*de casa*) steward, butler; (*Náut*) steward; (*de hacienda*) steward; (*Cono Sur: capataz*) foreman; (*And: criado*) servant; (*LAm Rel*) patron (saint).
mayorear* [1a] *vi* (*CAm*) to be in charge, be the boss.
mayoreo *nm* (*Cono Sur, Méx*) wholesale (trade).
mayorete *nf* majorette.
mayoría *nf* (**a**) (*gen*) majority, greater part, larger part; **la ~ de los españoles** the majority of Spaniards, most Spaniards; **en la ~ de los casos** in most cases; **en su ~** in

the main; ~ **absoluta** absolute majority; **la abrumadora** ~, **la inmensa** ~ the overwhelming majority, the vast majority; **por una** ~ **arrolladora** by an overwhelming majority; ~ **silenciosa** silent majority; ~ **simple** simple majority.

(**b**) (*Pol etc*) majority; **una** ~ **de las cuatro quintas partes** a four-fifths majority; **gobierno de la** ~ majority rule, majority government.

(**c**) ~ **de edad** majority, adult age; **cumplir** (*o* **llegar a**) **la** ~ **de edad** to come of age.

mayorista *nmf* wholesaler.

mayoritariamente *adv* preponderantly, for the most part; (*al votar*) by a majority; **gente** ~ **joven** young people for the most part; **votar** ~ **por** to vote by a majority for.

mayoritario *adj* majority (*atr*); **gobierno** ~ majority government.

mayormente *adv* (*principalmente*) chiefly, mainly; (*especialmente*) especially; (*tanto más*) all the more so; **no me interesa** ~ I'm not particularly interested.

mayúscula *nf* capital (letter); (*Tip*) upper case letter.

mayúsculo *adj* (**a**) *letra* capital. (**b**) (*fig*) big, tremendous; **un susto** ~ a big scare; **un error** ~ a tremendous mistake.

maza *nf* (**a**) (*Hist*) mace; war club; (*Dep*) bat; (*de polo*) stick, mallet; (*Mús*) drumstick; (*de taco de billar etc*) thick end; (*de cáñamo, lino*) brake; ~ **de fraga** drop hammer; ~ **de gimnasia** Indian club.

(**b**) (*) pest, bore.

(**c**) (*LAm*: *de rueda*) hub.

(**d**) (*And, Carib*: *de ingenio*) drum (of a sugar mill).

mazacote *nm* (**a**) (*gen*) hard mass; (*Culin*) dry doughy food; (*Arquit*) concrete; **el arroz se ha hecho un** ~ the rice has gone lumpy, the rice has set like concrete.

(**b**) (*Arte, Liter etc*) crude piece of work; mess, hotchpotch.

(**c**) (*: *lata*) bore.

(**d**) (*Carib***) arse**.

mazacotudo *adj* = **amazacotado**.

mazada *nf* (**a**) (*golpe*) bash*, blow (with a club); **dar** ~ **a** (*fig*) to hurt, injure. (**b**) (*fig*) blow; **fue una** ~ **para él** it came as a blow to him.

mazamorra *nf* (**a**) (*LAm Culin*) maize, porridge; (*pey*) mush. (**b**) (*LAm*: *ampolla*) blister.

mazamorrero* (*And*) **1** *adj* of Lima. **2** *nm*, **mazamorrera** *nf* native (*o* inhabitant) of Lima; **los** ~**s** the people of Lima.

mazapán *nm* marzipan.

mazazo *nm* heavy blow.

mazmorra *nf* dungeon.

mazo *nm* (**a**) (*porra*) club; (*martillo*) mallet; (*de mortero*) pestle; (*Dep*) club, bat, (*de croquet*) mallet; (*Aragón*: *de campana*) clapper.

(**b**) (*manojo*) bunch, handful; (*lío*) bundle, packet; ~ **de papeles** sheaf of papers, bundle of papers; ~ **de naipes** pack of cards; ~ **de billetes** wad of notes (*o* bills: *US*).

(**c**) (*: *lata*) bore.

mazorca *nf* (**a**) (*Bot*) spike; (*de maíz*) cob, ear; ~ **de maíz** corncob; **maíz en la** ~ corn on the cob.

(**b**) (*Téc*) spindle.

(**c**) (*Cono Sur Hist*) (*gobierno*) despotic government; (*banda*) political gang, terrorist band.

mazota *nf* (*And, Méx*) = **mazorca** (**a**).

mazote *nm* (*And, Méx*: *manotada*) handful; **de a** ~ free.

Mb *nm abr de* **megabyte** megabyte, Mb.

Mbytes *nmpl abr de* **megabytes** megabytes, Mbytes.

M.C. *nm abr de* **Mercado Común** Common Market, C.M.

MCCA *nm abr de* **Mercado Común Centroamericano** Central American Common Market, CACM.

MCE *nm* (*Com*) *abr de* **Mercado Común Europeo.**

MCI *nm abr de* **Mercado Común Iberoamericano.**

me *pron pers* (**a**) (*ac*) me.

(**b**) (*dativo*) (to) me; **¡dámelo!** give it to me!; ~ **lo compró** he bought it from me; he bought it for me; ~ **rompí el brazo** I broke my arm.

(**c**) (*reflexivo*) (to) myself; ~ **lavé** I washed, I washed myself; ~ **retiro** I withdraw.

meada *nf* (**a**) (**‡: *orina*) piss**‡. (**b**) (*mancha*) mark (*o* stain *etc*) of urine. (**c**) (‡: *dicho etc*) put-down*.

meadero‡ *nm* bog‡, jakes‡.

meado‡ *adj* (**a**) **esto está** ~ it's a cinch‡, it's dead easy. (**b**) (*Cono Sur*) **estar** ~ to be canned‡.

meados‡** *nmpl* piss**‡.

meaja *nf* crumb.

meandro *nm* meander.

meapilas‡ **1** *adj* sanctimonious, holier-than-thou. **2** *nmf invar* sanctimonious person; goody-goody*.

mear‡** [1a] **1** *vt* (**a**) (*lit*) to piss on**‡. (**b**) (*Dep*) to beat easily, walk all over. (**c**) (*humillar*) to walk all over. **2** *vi* to piss**‡, have a piss**‡. **3 mearse** *vr* to wet o.s.; ~ (**de risa**) to piss o.s. laughing**‡.

MEC [mek] *nm* (*Esp*) *abr de* **Ministerio de Educación y Ciencia.**

Meca *nf*: **La** ~ Mecca.

meca *nf* (*And**) prostitute; **ser la** ~ to be an ace.

mecachis *interj* (*Esp*: *euf de* **¡me cago!**) *V* **cagar.**

mecánica[1] *nf* (**a**) (*gen*) mechanics; ~ **de precisión** precision engineering. (**b**) (*mecanismo*) mechanism, works.

mecánicamente *adv* mechanically.

mecánico **1** *adj* (**a**) (*gen*) mechanical; (*con motor*) power-driven, power-operated; (*de máquina*) machine (*atr*).

(**b**) *oficio etc* manual.

2 *nm*, **mecánica[2]** *nf* mechanic; (*operario*) machinist; (*ajustador*) fitter, repairman; (*Aut*) driver, chauffeur; (*Aer*) rigger, fitter; ~ **de vuelo** flight engineer.

mecanismo *nm* (**a**) (*gen*) mechanism; works, machinery; gear; ~ **de destrucción** destruct mechanism; ~ **de dirección** steering gear; **lubricar el** ~ (*fig*) to oil the wheels.

(**b**) (*movimiento*) action, movement.

(**c**) (*fig*) mechanism; machinery, structure; process; ~ **de defensa** defence mechanism.

mecanización *nf* mechanization.

mecanizado *adj* mechanized.

mecanizar [1f] *vt* to mechanize.

mecanografía *nf* typing, typewriting; ~ **al tacto** touch-typing.

mecanografiado **1** *adj* typewritten, typescript. **2** *nm* typescript; typing.

mecanografiar [1c] *vt* to type.

mecanógrafo, -a *nm/f* typist.

mecapal *nm* (*CAm, Méx*) *headband used for attaching loads carried on one's back.*

mecapalero *nm* (*CAm, Méx*) porter.

mecatazo *nm* (*CAm*) (**a**) (*golpe*) lash, slash. (**b**) (*: *trago*) swig of liquor*.

mecate *nm* (*LAm*) (**a**) (*fibra*) strip of pita fibre; (*cuerda*) rope, string, cord; (*tosco*) twine; **¡es todo** ~! (*Méx**) it's terrific!*; **jalear el** ~ **a uno*** to suck up to sb*. (**b**) (*persona*) boor; (*: *pesado*) oaf.

mecateada *nf* (*CAm, Méx*) lashing, beating.

mecatear[1] [1a] **1** *vt* (**a**) (*CAm, Méx*) (*atar*) to tie up; (*azotar*) to lash, whip. (**b**) (*LAm**) to suck up to*. **2** **mecatearse‡** *vr*: ~, **mecateárselas** (*Méx‡*) to run away, beat it*.

mecatear[2] [1a] *vi* (*And*) to eat cakes.

mecatero‡ *nm* (*LAm*) creep‡, toady.

mecato *nm* (*And*) cakes, pastries.

mecedor **1** *adj* rocking; swinging. **2** *nm* (**a**) (*columpio*) swing. (**b**) (*CAm, Carib, Méx*: *asiento*) rocking-chair. (**c**) (*Carib*: *cuchara*) stirrer, spoon.

mecedora *nf* rocking-chair.

Mecenas *nm* Maecenas; **m**~ (*fig*) patron.

mecenazgo *nm* patronage.

mecer [2b] **1** *vt* (**a**) *columpio* to swing; *cuna etc* to rock; *niño* to rock (to and fro), dandle; *rama etc* to sway, move to and fro.

(**b**) *líquido, recipiente* to stir, shake (up).

2 mecerse *vr* to swing; to rock (to and fro); to sway, move to and fro.

meción *nm* (*CAm, Carib*) jerk, jolt.

meco‡ *adj* (*CAm, Méx*) (*salvaje*) uncivilized, wild; (*bruto*) thick*; (*ordinario*) crude.

mecha *nf* (**a**) (*de vela*) wick; (*Mil etc*) fuse; ~ **lenta** slow fuse; ~ **tardía** time fuse; **aguantar** (**la**) ~ (*fig*) to grin and bear it; **a toda** ~ at full speed; **encender la** ~ to stir up trouble; **tener mucha** ~ **para algo** to be good at sth, have a knack for sth.

(**b**) (*Esp Culin*) slice of bacon (*for larding*).

(**c**) (*pelo etc*) = **mechón.**

(**d**) (*And, Cono Sur*: *Téc*) bit (*of brace*).

(**e**) (*And, Carib**: *broma*) joke.

(**f**) (*Méx**: *miedo*) fear.

(**g**) (*: *ratería*) shoplifting.

(**h**) (*And*: *baratija*) trinket.

mechar [1a] *vt* (*Culin*) to lard; to stuff.

mechero **1** *nm* (**a**) (*encendedor*) cigarette lighter; (*de cocina*) burner; jet; (*And, Cono Sur*) oil lamp; ~ **Bunsen** Bunsen burner; ~ **encendedor,** ~ **piloto** pilot light; ~ **de gas** gas burner, gas jet, gas lighter.

(**b**) (*CAm, Méx*) mop of hair.

(**c**) (*Carib**: *bromista*) joker.
(**d**) (**) prick**.
2 *nm,* **mechera** *nf* (*: *persona*) shoplifter.
mechificar* [1g] *vt* (*And, Carib*) (*engañar*) to trick, deceive; (*mofarse de*) to mock.
mecho *nm* (*And, CAm*) (*vela*) candle; (*cabo*) candle end; (*candelero*) candlestick.
mechón *nm* (*de pelo*) tuft, lock; (*de hilos*) bundle.
mechudo *adj* (*CAm, Cono Sur*) tousled, unkempt.
medalla *nf* medal.
medallero, -a *nm/f* (*Dep*) medallist; ~ **de bronce** bronze medallist; ~ **de oro** gold medallist; ~ **de plata** silver medallist.
medallista *nmf* medal designer; (*Dep*) = **medallero**.
medallón *nm* (**a**) (*medalla*) medallion. (**b**) (*relicario*) locket. (**c**) (*Culin*) round, slice.
médano *nm,* **medaño** *nm* sand dune; sandbank.
media *nf* (**a**) (*gen*) stocking; (*LAm*: *de hombre*) sock; ~ **de malla** net stocking; ~ **de nylon** nylon stocking; ~ **pantalón,** ~ **panti** panty-hose, tights; **~s de red, ~s de rejilla** fishnet stockings.
(**b**) **de** ~ knitting (*atr*); *punto* plain; **hacer** ~ to knit.
(**c**) (*Dep*) half-back line.
(**d**) (*Mat*) mean; ~ **aritmética** arithmetic mean; ~ **ponderada** weighted average; **100 de** ~ **al día** 100 as a daily average, 100 each day on the average.
(**e**) ~ **de cerveza** ⅓ litre bottle of beer.
mediación *nf* (**a**) (*intercesión*) mediation; intercession. (**b**) **por** ~ **de** (*mediante*) through.
mediado *adj* (**a**) (*medio lleno*) half full; *proceso, trabajo* halfway through, half completed; **el local estaba** ~ the place was half full; **mediada la tarde** halfway through the afternoon; **llevo** ~ **el trabajo** I am halfway through the job, I have completed half the work.
(**b**) (*de tiempo*) **a ~s de marzo** in the middle of March, halfway through March; **hacia ~s del siglo pasado** about the middle of last century.
mediador(a) *nm/f* mediator.
mediagua *nf* (*Cono Sur*) hut, shack.
medial *adj* medial.
medialuna *nf* croissant, breakfast roll.
mediana *nf* (*Aut*) central reservation, median (*US*).
medianamente *adv* moderately, fairly; moderately well; **un trabajo** ~ **bueno** a moderately good piece of work; **quedó** ~ **en los exámenes** he did moderately well in the exams.
medianera *nf* (*And, Cono Sur*) party wall, dividing wall.
medianería *nf* (**a**) (*pared*) party wall. (**b**) (*Carib, Méx Com*) partnership; (*Agr*) share-cropping.
medianero 1 *adj* (**a**) *pared* party (*atr*), dividing; *valla* boundary (*atr*). (**b**) (*contiguo*) adjacent, next. **2** *nm* (**a**) (*de casa*) owner of the adjoining house (*o* property *etc*). (**b**) (*Carib, Méx Com*) partner; (*Agr*) share-cropper.
medianía *nf* (**a**) (*promedio*) average; (*punto medio*) halfway point; middling position; (*Econ*) moderate means, modest circumstances; (*en sociedad*) undistinguished social position.
(**b**) (*persona*) ordinary sort, mediocrity; **no pasa de ser una** ~ he's no better than average, he's rather a mediocrity.
(**c**) (*Com*) middleman.
mediano *adj* (*regular*) middling, medium, average; *empresa etc* medium-sized; (*indiferente*) indifferent, undistinguished; (*euf*) mediocre, rather poor; **de tamaño** ~ medium-sized; **de mediana edad** middle-aged; **es** ~ **de talento** he has average talent.
medianoche *nf* midnight.
mediante *prep* by means of, through, by; with the help of.
mediar [1b] *vi* (**a**) (*estar en medio*) to be in the middle; (*llegar a la mitad*) to get to the middle, get halfway; **entre A y B median 30 kms** it is 30 kms from A to B; **entre estas 2 casas median otras 3** there are 3 other houses between those 2; **media un abismo entre los dos gobiernos** there is a wide gap between the two governments; **entre los dos sucesos mediaron varios años** several years elapsed between the two events, there were some years between the two events; **mediaba el otoño** autumn was half over; **mediaba el mes de julio** it was halfway through July; **sin** ~ **palabra** directly.
(**b**) (*suceder*) to come up, happen; (*intervenir*) to intervene; (*existir*) to exist; **pero medió la muerte de su madre** but his mother's death intervened; **media el hecho de que** ... there is the fact that ... to be considered; there is an obstacle in the fact that ...; **median relaciones cordiales entre los dos** cordial relations exist between the two.
(**c**) (*interceder*) to mediate (*en* in, *entre* between), intervene; ~ **con uno** to intercede with sb.
mediatizar [1f] *vt* (**a**) (*estorbar*) to interfere with, obstruct; to affect adversely, influence for the worse. (**b**) (*Pol*) to annexe, take control of.
medible *adj* measurable; detectable, appreciable.
médica *nf* (woman) doctor.
medicación *nf* medication, treatment.
médicamente *adv* medically.
medicamento *nm* medicine, drug; ~ **de patente** patent medicine.
medicastro *nm* (*pey*) quack (doctor).
medicina *nf* medicine; ~ **alternativa** alternative (*o* complementary) medicine; ~ **forense,** ~ **legal** forensic medicine; ~ **general** general practice; ~ **preventiva** preventive medicine; **estudiante de** ~ medical student.
medicinal *adj* medicinal.
medicinar [1a] **1** *vt* to treat, prescribe for. **2 medicinarse** *vr*: ~ **algo** to dose o.s. with sth.
medición *nf* measurement, measuring; **hacer mediciones** to take measurements.
médico 1 *adj* medical.
2 *nmf* doctor; medical practitioner, physician; ~ **de cabecera** family doctor; ~ **dentista** dental surgeon; ~ **forense** forensic surgeon, expert in forensic medicine; (*Jur*) coroner; ~ **general** general practitioner; ~ **interno,** ~ **residente** house physician, houseman, intern (*US*); ~ **partero** obstetrician; ~ **pediatra,** ~ **puericultor** paediatrician.
medida *nf* (**a**) (*Mat*) measurement; (*acto*) measuring, measurement; **a la** ~ in proportion; suitable; **el precio es a la** ~ **del tamaño** the price depends on the size; **hay uno a la** ~ **de sus necesidades** there is one to suit your needs; **no tenemos un sombrero a su** ~ we don't have a hat in your size (*o* to fit you); **una caja a la** ~ a specially made box, a box made for the purpose; **un traje a la** ~**, un traje hecho a la** ~ a made-to-measure suit; **tiene una novia a la** ~ he has a girl who is just right for him; **es una solución a la** ~ it's a perfect solution; **a la** ~ **de mi deseo** just as I would have wished, exactly as I wanted (it); **a** ~ **de** in proportion to, in keeping with; **a** ~ **que** ... as ...; **a** ~ **que vaya bajando el agua** as the water goes down; **en cierta** ~ up to a point, in a way; **en buena** ~**, en gran** ~ to a great extent; **en la** ~ **de lo posible** as far as possible; **en la** ~ **en que esto sea verdad** insofar as this is true; **en no pequeña** ~ in no small measure; **~s vitales** vital statistics; **tomar las ~s a uno** to measure sb, take sb's measurements; (*fig*) to size sb up; **tomar sus ~s** to size a situation up.
(**b**) (*sistema, recipiente etc*) measure; **pesas y ~s** weights and measures; ~ **agraria** land measure; ~ **para áridos** dry measure; ~ **para líquidos** liquid measure; **esto colma la** ~ (*fig*) this is the last straw; **con esto se colmó la** ~ **de la paciencia de su padre** this finally exhausted her father's patience.
(**c**) (*de camisa, zapato etc*) size, fitting; **ropa a sobre** ~ (*Méx*) outsize clothing; **¿cuál es su** ~**?** (*LAm*) what size do you take?
(**d**) (*Liter*) (correct) scansion.
(**e**) (*fig*: *disposición*) measure, step, move; ~ **cautelar** precautionary measure; ~ **preventiva** preventive measure; ~ **represiva** deterrent, check (*contra* to); **tomar ~s** to take steps (*para que* to ensure that).
(**f**) (*fig*: *moderación*) moderation, prudence; restraint; **sin** ~ immoderately, in an unrestrained fashion.
medidor *nm* (*LAm*) meter; gauge; ~ **de lluvia** rain gauge.
mediero, -a *nm/f* (*LAm*) share-cropper.
medieval *adj* medieval.
medievalismo *nm* medievalism.
medievalista *nmf* medievalist.
medio 1 *adj* (**a**) (*mitad*) half (a).
(**b**) **media naranja** half an orange, a half orange; **media hora** half an hour; **nos queda media botella** we've half a bottle left; **media luna** half-moon, (*fig*) crescent; ~ **luto** half-mourning; **media luz** half-light; **acudió media provincia** half the province turned up.
(**c**) *punto etc* mid, midway, middle; **clase media** middle class(es); **dedo** ~ middle finger; **a media tarde** halfway through the afternoon.
(**d**) (*Mat*) mean, average; (*fig*) average; **el hombre** ~ the average man, the ordinary man, the man in the street; *V* **término** *etc.*
(**e**) (*LAm*: *grande*) big, huge.
(**f**) **a medias** half; by halves; **está escrito a medias** it's

half-written; **lo dejó hecho a medias** he left it half-done; **estoy satisfecho sólo a medias** I am only partly satisfied; **ir a medias** to go fifty-fifty (*con* with), divide the costs (*etc*) equally; **lo pagamos a medias** we share the cost; **verdad a medias** half-truth.

2 *adv* (**a**) (*a medias*) half; ~ **dormido** half asleep; **estar ~ borracho** to be half drunk; **está ~ escrito, está a ~ escribir** it is half-written; **eso no está ni ~ bien** that isn't at all right; **A ~ se ennovió con Z** A became half-engaged to Z.

(**b**) (*LAm: bastante*) quite, rather; ~ **tonto** a bit of a fool; **fue ~ difícil** it was pretty hard; ~ **se sonrió** she gave a half-smile.

3 *nm* (**a**) (*centro*) middle, centre; (*término medio*) half-way point (*etc*); (*Mat*) mean; ~ **aritmético** arithmetical mean; **justo ~** happy medium, golden mean; fair compromise; **equivocarse de ~ a ~** to be completely wrong; **en ~** in the middle; in between; **en ~ de la plaza** in the middle of the square; **en ~ de tanta confusión** in the midst of such confusion; **la casa de en ~** the middle house; the house in between; **quitar algo de en ~** to remove sth; to get rid of sth, get sth out of the way; **quitarse de en ~** to get out of the way; to duck, dodge; to remove o.s.; **pasar por ~ de** to go through (the middle of); **tomar algo por el ~** to grasp sth round the middle; **de por ~** in between; **hay dificultades de por ~** there are snags in the way; **habrá una falda de por ~** a woman probably comes into it somewhere; **meterse de por ~** to intervene; **día (de) por ~** (*LAm*) every other day.

(**b**) (*Dep*) half-back; ~ **centro** centre-half; ~ **de melé** (*Rugby*) scrum-half.

(**c**) (*Espiritismo*) medium.

(**d**) (*método*) means, way, method; medium; (*medida*) measure, expedient; **los ~s de comunicación, los ~s de difusión** the media; **~s de comunicación de masas** mass media; **~s informativos** news media; **~s de transporte** means of transport; **por ~ de** by means of, by, through; **por todos los ~s** by all possible means, in every possible way; **no hay ~ de conseguirlo** there is no way of getting it; **poner todos los ~s para** + *infin*, **no regatear ~ para** + *infin* to spare no effort to + *infin*.

(**e**) **~s** (*Econ, Fin*) means, resources.

(**f**) (*ambiente*) atmosphere; (*contorno*) milieu, ambience; environment; (*círculo*) circle; (*Bio*: *t* **~ ambiente**) environment; **~ de cultivo** culture medium; **en los ~s financieros** in financial circles; **encontrarse en su ~** to be in one's element.

medioambiental *adj* environmental.

medioambientalista *nmf* environmentalist.

mediocampista *nmf* midfield player.

mediocampo *nm* midfield.

mediocre *adj* middling, average; (*pey*) mediocre, rather poor.

mediocridad *nf* middling quality; (*pey*) mediocrity; **es una ~** he's a nonentity, he's a dead loss.

mediodía *nm* (**a**) (*gen*) midday, noon; **a ~** at noon. (**b**) (*Geog*) south.

medioevo *nm* Middle Ages.

mediofondista *nmf* (*Dep*) middle-distance runner.

mediofondo *nm* (*Carib*) petticoat.

mediogrande *adj* medium large.

mediometraje *nm* medium-length film.

mediooeste *nm* Midwest.

mediooriental *adj* Middle East(ern).

Medio Oriente *nm* Middle East.

mediopequeño *adj* medium small.

mediquillo *nm* (*pey*) quack (doctor).

medir [3k] **1** *vt* (**a**) (*gen*) to measure; *tierra* to survey, plot; **~ a millas, ~ por millas** to measure in miles; **~ a uno (con la vista**: *fig*) to size sb up.

(**b**) *posibilidad, proyecto etc* to weigh up.

(**c**) (*Liter*) *verso* to scan (properly).

2 *vi* (**a**) *objeto, persona* to measure, be; **la tela mide 90 cms** the cloth measures 90 cms; **el papel mide 20 cms de ancho** the paper is 20 cms wide; **ella mide 1,50 m** she is 1.50 m tall; **mide 88 cms de pecho** she is 88 cms round the chest, her bust measurement is 88 cms.

(**b**) (*Liter*) to scan (properly).

3 medirse *vr* (**a**) **~ con uno** to measure up to sb; to test o.s. against sb.

(**b**) (*fig*) to be moderate, act with restraint; (*Méx**: *no perder la calma*) to keep one's head.

(**c**) (*LAm*) (*Dep*) to play each other, meet; (*reñir*) to quarrel, come to blows.

(**d**) (*LAm*) *ropa* to try on.

meditabundo *adj* pensive, thoughtful.

meditación *nf* meditation; pondering; **~ trascendental** transcendental meditation; **meditaciones** meditations (*sobre* on).

meditar [1a] **1** *vt* to ponder, think over, meditate (on); *plan etc* to think out, work out, plan. **2** *vi* to ponder, think, meditate; to muse.

Mediterráneo *nm* Mediterranean; **descubrir el ~*** to re-invent the wheel, state the obvious.

mediterráneo *adj* Mediterranean; (*gen*) land-locked.

médium *nmf, pl* **médiums** medium.

mediúmnico *adj*: **sesión mediúmnica** session with a medium; **revelaciones mediúmnicas** revelations from a medium.

medo *nm*: **los ~s y los persas** the Medes and the Persians.

medra *nf* increase, growth; improvement; (*Econ etc*) prosperity.

medrar [1a] *vi* (*aumentarse*) to increase, grow; (*mejorar*) to improve, do well, do better; (*Econ etc*) to prosper, thrive, do well; (*animal, planta*) to grow, thrive; **¡medrados estamos!** (*iró*) a fine thing you've done!

medro *nm* = **medra.**

medroso *adj* fearful, timid, fainthearted.

medula *nf*, **médula** *nf* (**a**) (*Anat*) marrow; medulla; **~ espinal** spinal cord; **~ ósea** bone-marrow; **hasta la ~** (*fig*) to the core; through and through; **estoy convencido hasta la ~** I am profoundly convinced.

(**b**) (*Bot*) pith.

(**c**) (*fig*) essence; substance; pith.

medular *adj* (*fig*) central, fundamental, essential.

medusa *nf* jellyfish.

Mefistófeles *nm* Mephistopheles.

mefítico *adj* (*venenoso*) poisonous; (*hediondo*) foul-smelling.

mefitismo *nm* foul air; foul smells.

mega... *pref* mega...

megabyte ['megabait] *nm* megabyte.

megaciclo *nm* megacycle.

megafonía *nf* public address system.

megáfono *nm* megaphone.

megalítico *adj* megalithic.

megalito *nm* megalith.

megalomanía *nf* megalomania.

megalómano, -a *nm/f* megalomaniac.

megalópolis *nm* (*hum*) super-city.

megaocteto *nm* megabyte.

megatón *nm* megaton.

megavatio *nm* megawatt.

megavoltio *nm* megavolt.

meiga *nf* (*Galicia*) wise woman.

mejicanismo *nm* mexicanism, word (*o* phrase *etc*) peculiar to Mexico.

mejicano, -a *adj, nm/f* Mexican.

Méjico *nm* Mexico.

mejido *adj huevo* beaten.

mejilla *nf* cheek.

mejillón *nm* mussel.

mejillonera *nf* mussel-bed.

mejillonero *adj* mussel (*atr*); **industria mejillonera** mussel industry.

mejor 1 *adj* (**a**) (*comp*) better (*que* than).

(**b**) (*superl*) best; *oferta, postor* highest; **es el ~ de todos** he's the best of all; **lo ~** the best thing, the best part (*etc*); **lo ~ de la novela** the best part of the novel, the best thing about the novel; **lo ~ de la vida** the prime of life; **hice lo ~ que pude** I did the best I could, I did my best; **llevar lo ~** to get the best of it; **a lo ~, a la ~** (*LAm*) probably, maybe; with any luck; suddenly, when least expected; **'¿crees que lo hará?' ... 'a lo ~'** 'do you think he'll do it?' ... 'he may do', *o* 'maybe'.

2 *adv* (**a**) (*comp*) better; **A canta ~ que B** A sings better than B; **~ quisiera** + *infin* I would rather + *infin*; **¡~!** good!, that's fine!; **~ que ~** better and better, all the better; **tanto ~** all the better, so much the better (*para* for); **está mucho ~** he's much better.

(**b**) (*superl*) best.

3 *como conj* (*esp LAm**) **~ me voy, ~ me vaya** I'd better go; **~ te vayas, ~ vete** you'd better go.

mejora *nf* (**a**) (*gen*) improvement; **~s** (*de casa etc*) improvements; alterations, repairs. (**b**) (*en subasta*) higher bid. (**c**) (*Méx Agr*) weeding.

mejorable *adj* improvable.

mejoramiento *nm* improvement.

mejorana *nf* marjoram.

mejorar [1a] **1** *vt* (**a**) (*gen*) to improve, make better, ameliorate; (*Inform etc*) to upgrade; (*realzar*) to enhance; *postura* to raise; *oferta* to improve, increase; *récord* to break.

(**b**) ~ **a** to be better than, be superior to.

2 *vi y* **mejorarse** *vr* (**a**) (*situación*) to improve, get better; (*Med*) to get better; (*Met*) to improve, clear up; (*Fin etc*) to do well, prosper; **los negocios mejoran** business is improving, business is picking up; **¡que se mejore!** get well soon!

(**b**) (*en subasta*) to raise one's bid.

mejorcito *adj* choice, select; **lo ~ del programa** the very best (item) in the programme; **lo ~ de la clientela** la crème de la crème among the customers.

mejoría *nf* improvement; recovery; **¡que siga la ~!** I hope the improvement continues.

mejunje *nm* (**a**) (*mezcla*) brew, mixture, concoction. (**b**) (*: *fraude*) fraud. (**c**) (*LAm*‡: *lío*) mess, mix-up.

melado 1 *adj* honey-coloured. **2** *nm* treacle, syrup; (*LAm: de caña*) cane syrup.

meladura *nf* (*Carib, Méx*) cane syrup.

melancolía *nf* melancholy, gloom(iness), sadness; (*Med*) melancholia.

melancólicamente *adv* gloomily, sadly, in a melancholy way; wistfully.

melancólico *adj* (*triste*) melancholy, gloomy, sad; (*soñador*) dreamy, wistful.

melanismo *nm* melanism.

melanoma *nm* melanoma.

melarchía *nf* (*CAm*) = **melancolía**.

melaza *nf* (*t* ~**s**) molasses; treacle.

melcocha *nf* (*melaza*) molasses; treacle; (*azúcar de cande*) candy, molasses toffee.

melcochado *adj fruta etc* candied; (*de color*) golden, honey-coloured.

melcocharse [1a] *vr* to thicken (*in boiling*).

mele* *nm* bash*, punch.

melé *nf*, **mêlée** [me'le] *nf* (*Rugby*) scrum; (*fig*) confusion, confused scene, imbroglio.

melena *nf* (*de hombre*) long hair; (*de mujer*) loose hair, flowing hair; (*pey*) mop of hair, bushy hair; (*cola de caballo*) ponytail; (*Zool*) mane; **andar a la ~** to pull one another's hair, (*fig*) to quarrel; **estar en ~** to have one's hair down.

melenas‡ *nm invar*, **melenero*** *nm* long-haired yob‡.

melenudo *adj* long-haired.

melga *nf* (*Cono Sur, Méx*) plot of land prepared for sowing.

melifluo *adj* mellifluous, sweet.

melillense 1 *adj* of Melilla. **2** *nmf* native (*o* inhabitant) of Melilla; **los ~s** the people of Melilla.

melindre *nm* (**a**) (*Culin*) (*bollo*) sweet cake, iced bun; (*buñuelo*) honey fritter.

(**b**) ~**s** (*delicadeza*) daintiness, dainty ways; (*pey*) (*afectación*) affectation, affected ways; squeamishness; (*mojigatería*) prudery, prudishness; **gastar ~s** = **melindrear**.

melindrear [1a] *vi* to be affected, indulge in affectation; to be squeamish; to be prudish; to be excessively finicky, be terribly fussy.

melindroso *adj* affected; squeamish; prudish; finicky, fussy.

meliorativo *adj* ameliorative.

melisca *nf* (*Cono Sur*) gleaning.

melo* *nm* = **melodrama.**

melocotón *nm* (*fruto*) peach; (*árbol*) peach-tree.

melocotonero *nm* peach-tree.

melodía *nf* (**a**) (*una* ~) melody; tune, air. (**b**) (*cualidad*) melodiousness.

melódico *adj* melodic.

melodiosamente *adv* melodiously, tunefully.

melodioso *adj* melodious, tuneful.

melodrama *nm* melodrama.

melodramáticamente *adv* melodramatically.

melodramático *adj* melodramatic.

melómano, -a *nm/f* music-lover.

melón[1] *nm* (**a**) (*Bot*) melon; **los melones, a cata** the proof of the pudding is in the eating. (**b**) (‡: *cabeza*) head, nut‡; **estrujarse el ~** to rack one's brains. (**c**) (‡: *idiota*) idiot, nutter‡.

melón[2] *nm* (*Zool*) = **meloncillo.**

melonada *nf* silly thing, idiotic remark (*etc*).

melonar *nm* bed of melons, melon plot.

meloncillo *nm* (*Zool*) ichneumon, (kind of) mongoose.

melopea‡ *nf* spree, binge*; **coger** (*etc*) **una ~** to get canned‡.

melosidad *nf* (**a**) (*lit*) sweetness; (*pey*) cloying sweetness. (**b**) (*fig*) sweetness; gentleness; (*pey*) smoothness.

meloso *adj* (**a**) (*dulce*) honeyed, sweet; (*pey*) cloying. (**b**) (*fig*) *voz etc* sweet, musical; gentle; (*pey*) smooth, soapy*.

mella *nf* (**a**) (*rotura*) nick, dent, notch; (*en dientes etc*) gap; **hacer ~** (*fig*) to make an impression, sink in, strike home; **hacer ~ en** (*o* **a**) to make an impression on, tell on.

(**b**) (*fig: daño*) harm, damage; **hacer ~ en** to do damage to, harm.

mellado *adj borde* jagged, nicked, ragged; *persona* gap-toothed; (*Cono Sur*) hare-lipped.

mellar [1a] *vt* (**a**) (*hacer muescas en*) to nick, dent, notch; to take a chip out of. (**b**) (*fig: dañar*) to damage, harm.

mellizo, -a *adj, nm/f* twin.

membrana *nf* (**a**) (*piel*) membrane; (*Orn*) membrane, web; **~ mucosa** mucous membrane; **~ virginal** hymen. (**b**) (*Cono Sur Med*) diphtheria.

membranoso *adj* membranous.

membresía *nf* (*Méx*) membership.

membretado *adj*: **papel ~** headed notepaper.

membrete *nm* letterhead, heading.

membrillero *nm* quince tree.

membrillo *nm* (**a**) (*fruto*) quince; (*árbol*) quince tree; (**carne de**) ~ quince jelly. (**b**) (*: *cobarde*) softie*, coward. (**c**) (‡: *chivato*) nark‡, informer.

membrudo *adj* burly, brawny, tough.

memela *nf* (*CAm, Méx*) (*tortilla*) maize tortilla; (*rellena*) *fried tortilla filled with beans.*

memez *nf* silly thing; farce, absurdity.

memo[1] 1 *adj* silly, stupid. **2** *nm* idiot.

memo[2]* *nm* memo*, memorandum.

memorable *adj* memorable.

memorablemente *adv* memorably.

memorando *nm*, **memorándum** *nm, pl* **memorándums** (**a**) (*libreta*) notebook. (**b**) (*Pol etc*) memorandum.

memoria *nf* (**a**) (*gen*) memory; **de buena ~, de feliz ~** of happy memory; **digno de ~** memorable; **falta de ~** forgetfulness; **flaco de ~** forgetful; **aprender algo de ~** to learn sth by heart; to memorize sth, commit sth to memory; **hablar de ~** to speak from memory; **guardar la ~ de** to retain the memory of; **se le fue de la ~** he forgot it, it slipped his mind; **en ~ de** in memory of; **la peor tormenta de que hay ~** the worst storm in living memory; the worst storm on record; **hacer ~** to try to remember; **deben hacer ~** they should search their memories; **hacer ~ de algo** to recall sth, bring sth to mind; **no queda ~ de eso** there is no memory (*o* record) of that; **saber de ~** to know by heart; **tener mala ~** to have a bad memory; **si tengo buena ~** if my memory serves me; **traer algo a la ~** to recall sth; **no me viene a la ~** I can't remember.

(**b**) (*informe*) note, report, statement; (*relación*) record; (*memorándum*) aide-mémoire, memorandum; (*petición*) petition; (*artículo*) (learned) paper; (*Univ*) thesis, dissertation; **~ anual** annual report; **~s** (*personales*) memoirs, (*de sociedad*) transactions.

(**c**) **~s** (†: *saludo*) regards, remembrances.

(**d**) (*Inform*) memory; **~ de acceso aleatorio** random access memory, RAM; **~ auxiliar** backing storage; **~ burbuja** bubble memory; **~ caché** storage memory, cache memory; **~ central, ~ principal** main memory; **~ externa** external storage; **~ intermedia** buffer; **~ interna** internal storage, main memory; **~ muerta** read-only memory, ROM; **~ de núcleos** core memory; **~ programable** programmable read-only memory; **~ de sólo lectura** = **~ muerta**; **~ del teclado** keyboard memory; **~ virtual** virtual memory.

memorial *nm* memorial, petition; (*Jur*) brief.

memorialista *nm* amanuensis.

memorión 1 *adj*: **es muy ~** he has a wonderful memory. **2** *nm* good memory, amazing memory.

memorioso *adj* (*LAm*) having a retentive memory; that remembers everything.

memorista *adj* (*LAm*) having a retentive memory; **es ~** (*pey*) he just memorizes things.

memorístico *adj* memory (*atr*); **enseñanza memorística** learning by rote.

memorización *nf* memorizing.

memorizar [1f] *vt* to memorize.

mena *nf* ore.

menaje *nm* (**a**) (*familia*) family, household; **~ de tres** ménage à trois; **vida de ~** (*LAm*) family life, domestic life.

(**b**) (*economía doméstica*) housekeeping; (*quehaceres*) housework, upkeep of the house.

(**c**) (*Com etc*) household equipment, furnishings; (*de colegio*) school equipment; **sección de ~** (*en almacenes*) hardware and kitchen department.
mención *nf* mention; **~ honorífica** honourable mention; **hacer ~ de** to mention.
mencionado *adj* aforementioned.
mencionar [1a] *vt* to mention, refer to; to name; **sin ~ ...** let alone ...; **dejar de ~** to fail to mention, leave unmentioned.
Menchu *nf forma familiar de* **Carmen**.
menda* *pron* (*t* **~s**) *p.ej.* **lo hizo este ~ (lerenda)** yours truly did it*, I did it.
mendacidad *nf* (**a**) (*gen*) mendacity, untruthfulness. (**b**) (*una ~*) untruth, gross lie.
mendaz *adj* mendacious; lying, untruthful.
mendeliano *adj* Mendelian.
mendelismo *nm* Mendelism, Mendelianism.
mendicante *adj, nmf* mendicant.
mendicidad *nf* begging; mendicity.
mendigar [1h] **1** *vt* to beg (for). **2** *vi* to beg (for alms).
mendigo 1 *nm,* **mendiga** *nf* beggar. **2** *adj* (*Méx**: *cobarde*) yellow, yellow-bellied‡.
mendrugo *nm* (**a**) (hard) crust. (**b**) (*: *tonto*) dolt, blockhead.
meneado *adj* (*Carib*) drunk.
menear [1a] **1** *vt* (**a**) (*gen*) to move, shift; *cabeza etc* to shake, toss; *cola* to wag; *caderas* to sway, swing, waggle; **sin ~ el dedo** without lifting a finger; **peor es ~lo** it's best to leave that alone; don't go stirring all that up; **¡me la menean!‡** they leave me cold!
(**b**) **~ cálamo** to wield a pen.
(**c**) *asunto* to get on with, get moving; *negocio etc* to handle, conduct.
2 menearse *vr* (**a**) (*gen*) to move; (*agitarse*) to shake; (*cola*) to wag; (*caderas*) to sway, swing, waggle; **~‡‡, meneársela** to wank‡‡; **un vapuleo de no te menees** a terrific beating-up*.
(**b**) (*apurarse*) to hustle, bestir o.s., get a move on; **¡~!** get going!, jump to it!
Menelao *nm* Menelaus.
meneo *nm* (**a**) (*movimiento*) movement; shake, toss; wag; sway(ing), swing(ing); waggle; jerk, jolt; **dar un ~ a** to jerk, jolt, move suddenly. (**b**) (*) (*paliza*) hiding*; (*bronca*) dressing-down*. (**c**) (*: *actividad etc*) = **movida**.
menequear [1a] *vt,* **menequetear** [1a] *vt* (*Cono Sur, Méx*) to shake, wag.
meneque(te)o *nm* (*Cono Sur, Méx*) shaking, wagging.
menester *nm* (**a**) **ser ~** to be necessary; **cuando sea ~** when it is necessary; **es ~ +** *infin* it is necessary to + *infin*, we (*etc*) must + *infin*; **todo es ~** everything is welcome.
(**b**) (*trabajo*) job, piece of business; (*recado*) errand; **~es** (*deberes*) duties, jobs, business; (*ocupación*) occupation; (*función*) function; **salir para un ~** to go out on an errand; **hacer sus ~es** (*euf*) to do one's business (*euf*).
(**c**) **~es** (*Téc*) gear, tackle, tools.
menesteroso *adj* needy.
menestra *nf* (**a**) (*Culin*: *potaje*) vegetable soup, stew. (**b**) **~s** dried vegetables.
menestral *nmf* (*t* **menestrala** *nf*) skilled worker, artisan.
menestrón *nm* (*And*) = minestrone soup.
mengano, -a *nm/f* Mr (*o* Mrs *etc*) So-and-so; *V* **fulano**.
mengua *nf* (**a**) (*disminución*) decrease, diminishment; dwindling; (*decadencia*) decay, decline; **ir en ~ de** to contribute to the lessening of, assist the decrease (*o* restriction *etc*) of; **sin ~** complete, whole; untouched.
(**b**) (*falta*) lack, want; (*pérdida*) loss.
(**c**) (*pobreza*) poverty.
(**d**) (*persona*: *debilidad*) spinelessness, weakness of character.
(**e**) (*descrédito*) discredit; **ir en ~ de uno** to be to sb's discredit.
menguadamente *adv* (**a**) (*fig*) wretchedly; weakly, spinelessly. (**b**) (*con tacañería*) meanly. (**c**) (*estúpidamente*) foolishly.
menguado 1 *adj* (**a**) (*disminuido*) decreased, diminished.
(**b**) (*fig*) (*despreciable*) wretched, miserable; (*débil*) weak, spineless, weak in character; (*cobarde*) cowardly.
(**c**) (*aciago*) unlucky; **en hora menguada** at an unlucky moment.
(**d**) (*tacaño*) mean.
(**e**) (*tonto*) foolish.
(**f**) **medias menguadas** fully-fashioned stockings.
2 *nm* (*en punto*) decrease.
menguante 1 *adj* (*que disminuye*) decreasing, diminishing; dwindling; (*decadente*) decaying; *luna* waning; *marea* ebb (*atr*).
2 *nf* (**a**) (*Náut*) ebb tide, low water.
(**b**) (*de luna*) waning; *V* **cuarto 2**.
(**c**) (*fig*) decay, decline; **estar en ~** to be in decline.
menguar [1i] **1** *vt* (**a**) (*disminuir*) to lessen, diminish, reduce; (*labor de punto*) to decrease (by).
(**b**) (*fig*) to discredit.
2 *vi* (**a**) (*disminuir*) to diminish, get less, dwindle, decrease; (*marea, número etc*) to go down; (*luna*) to wane.
(**b**) (*fig*) to wane, decay, decline.
mengue* *nm* the devil; **¡malos ~s te lleven!** go to hell!
meninges‡ *nfpl*: **estrujarse las ~** to rack one's brains.
meningitis *nf* meningitis.
menisco *nm* meniscus.
menjunje *nm,* **menjurje** *nm* = **mejunje**.
menopausia *nf* menopause.
menopáusico *adj* menopausal.
menor 1 *adj* (*Ecl*) *orden* minor; (*Mús*) minor.
2 *adj comp* (**a**) (*en tamaño*) smaller (*que* than); less, lesser; **en ~ número** in smaller numbers; **celidonia ~** lesser celandine.
(**b**) (*en edad*) younger (*que* than); junior (*que* to); **el hermano ~** the younger brother; **Juanito es ~ que Pepe** Johnnie is younger than Joe; *V* **edad**.
3 *adj superl* (**a**) (*en tamaño*) smallest; least; **éste es el ~ de todos** this is the smallest of the lot; **no le doy la ~ importancia** I don't attach the least (*o* slightest) importance to it.
(**b**) (*en edad*) youngest; most junior; **ella es la ~ de todas** she is the youngest of all.
4 *nmf* young person, juvenile; (*Jur*) minor; **un ~ de 14** an under-14; **los ~es de edad** those who are under age, the juveniles; **apto para ~es** (*Cine*) for all ages; **no apto para ~es** (*Cine*) not suitable for juveniles, 'Adults Only'.
5 *nm* (**a**) **al por ~** (*Com*) retail; **vender un género al por ~** to sell goods retail.
(**b**) **contar algo por ~** to recount sth in detail.
Menorca *nf* Minorca.
menoría *nf* (**a**) (*Jur*) minority. (**b**) (*inferioridad*) inferiority; (*subordinación*) subordination.
menorista (*And, Cono Sur*) **1** *adj* retail (*atr*). **2** *nmf* retailer.
menorquín, -ina *adj, nm/f* Minorcan.
menos 1 *adj* (**a**) (*Mat*) *signo* minus.
(**b**) (*comp*) less; fewer; **con ~ ruido** with less noise; **con ~ hombres** with fewer men; **A tiene ~ ventajas que B** A has fewer advantages than B; **A tiene ~ años que B** A is younger than B; **éste es ~ coche que el anterior*** this is not such a good car as the old one.
(**c**) (*superl*) least; fewest; **es el que ~ culpa tiene** least blame attaches to him, he is least to blame.
2 *adv* (**a**) (*comp*) less, (*superl*) least; **hoy se va ~** people don't go so much nowadays, nowadays people go less; **es el ~ inteligente de los 4** he is the least intelligent of the 4; **no quiero alquilarlo ni ~ comprarlo** I don't want to rent it and still less to buy it; **¿qué ~?*** what else did you expect?, it's the least one would expect; **~ de, ~ de lo que, ~ que** less than; **~ de lo que piensas** less than you think; **fue nada ~ que un rey** he was nothing less than a king, he was a king no less; **hay 7 de ~** we're 7 short, there are 7 missing; **me dieron un paquete con medio kilo de ~** they gave me a packet which was half a kilo short (*o* under weight); **me han pagado 2 libras de ~** they have underpaid me by £2.
(**b**) (*locuciones con lo*) **lo ~ 10** 10 at least; **lo ~ posible** as little as possible; **eso es lo de ~** that's the least of it; **es lo ~ que se puede esperar** it's the least one can expect; **al ~, a lo ~, por lo ~** at least.
(**c**) (*modismos*) **a ~ de** without; **tener a ~ +** *infin* to consider it beneath o.s. to + *infin*; **ir a ~, venir a ~** to come down in the world; to decline, decay; to run to seed; **darse de ~** to underestimate o.s., hide one's light under a bushel; **echar a uno de ~** to miss sb; **hacer de ~ a uno** to be unfaithful to sb; **hacer a uno de ~** to despise sb; to belittle sb; **no se quedó en ~** he was not to be outdone; **en ~ que se santigua un cura loco*** in no time at all; **no es para ~** it's worth all that and more; quite right too; *V* **cuando, mucho, poder**.
3 *prep* (**a**) (*excepto*) except; **todos ~ él** everybody except him; **¡todo ~ eso!** anything but that!
(**b**) (*Mat*) minus, less; **7 ~ 2 son 5** 2 from 7 leaves 5, 7 take away 2 leaves 5; **las 7 ~ 20** (*hora*) 20 to 7.

4 *conj*: **a ~ que** ... unless ...
5 *nm* (**a**) (*Mat*) minus sign (-).
(**b**) *V* **más.**

menoscabar [1a] *vt* (**a**) (*disminuir*) to lessen, reduce, diminish; (*dañar*) to damage, harm, impair. (**b**) (*desacreditar*) to discredit.

menoscabo *nm* lessening, reduction; damage, harm; loss; **con ~ de, en ~ de** to the detriment of; **sin ~** unimpaired; **sufrir ~** to suffer damage, suffer loss.

menospreciable *adj* contemptible.

menospreciador *adj* scornful.

menospreciar [1b] *vt* (**a**) (*despreciar*) to scorn, despise. (**b**) (*ofender*) to slight. (**c**) (*subestimar*) to underrate, undervalue.

menospreciativo *adj* scornful, contemptuous; slighting.

menosprecio *nm* (**a**) (*desdén*) scorn, contempt. (**b**) (*subestimación*) underrating, undervaluation. (**c**) (*falta de respeto*) disrespect; **con ~ del sexo de la víctima** without regard for the sex of the victim.

mensáfono *nm* bleeper, pager.

mensaje *nm* message; **~ de buenos augurios** goodwill message; **~ de la corona** (*Parl*) speech from the throne; **~ de error** (*Inform*) error message.

mensajero, -a *nm/f* messenger; courier.

menso* *adj* (*Méx*) stupid.

menstruación *nf* menstruation.

menstrual *adj* menstrual.

menstruar [1e] *vi* to menstruate.

menstruo *nm* (**a**) (*acción*) menstruation. (**b**) (*producto*) menses.

mensual *adj* monthly; **50 dólares ~es** 50 dollars a month.

mensualidad *nf* monthly payment (*o* salary, instalment *etc*).

mensualmente *adv* monthly.

mensuario *nm* (*LAm*) monthly journal.

ménsula *nf* bracket; (*Arquit*) corbel.

mensura *nf* measurement.

mensurable *adj* measurable.

mensuración *nf* mensuration.

menta *nf* mint; **~ romana, ~ verde** spearmint.

mentada[1] *nf*: **hacer a uno una ~** (*LAm*) = **mentar la madre**; *V* **madre.**

mentada[2] *nf* (*Méx*) insult.

mentado *adj* (**a**) (*mencionado*) aforementioned. (**b**) (*famoso*) well-known, famous.

mental *adj* mental; *capacidad, trabajo etc* intellectual.

mentalidad *nf* mentality, mind.

mentalización *nf* (mental) preparation; conditioning; sensitization; persuasion; inspiration; (*pey*) brainwashing.

mentalizar [1f] **1** *vt* to prepare (mentally), condition; to sensitize, make aware; (*convencer*) to persuade, convince; (*inspirar*) to inspire; (*pey*) to brainwash.
2 mentalizarse *vr* to prepare o.s. (mentally); to make o.s. aware; to get used to an idea.

mentalmente *adv* mentally.

mentar [1j] *vt* to mention, name.

mentas* *nfpl* (*And, Cono Sur*) (**a**) (*reputación*) good name, reputation; **una persona de buenas ~** a highly-regarded (*o* well-respected) person. (**b**) (*chismes*) rumours, gossip.

mente *nf* mind; intelligence, understanding; **~ consciente** conscious mind; **~ subconsciente** subconscious mind; **cambiar de ~** to change one's mind; **no está en mi ~** + *infin*, **no tengo en ~** + *infin* it is not in my mind to + *infin*, it is not my intention to + *infin*; **no lo tenía en ~** it slipped his mind; **se le fue completamente de la ~** it completely slipped his mind.

mentecatería *nf*, **mentecatez** *nf* stupidity, foolishness.

mentecato 1 *adj* silly, stupid. **2** *nm*, **mentecata** *nf* idiot, fool.

mentidero *nm* place where people gossip, gossip shop*.

mentir [3i] **1** *vt* (*liter*) to feign, pretend; to suggest (falsely) to; **la sed me mintió un arroyo cercano** my thirst led me to suppose there was a stream nearby.
2 *vi* (*gen*) to lie, tell a lie, tell lies; (*engañar*) to be deceptive; **¡miento!** sorry, I'm wrong!, my mistake!; **¡esta carta no me dejará ~!** this letter will bear me out!, this letter will confirm what I say!

mentira *nf* (**a**) (*una ~*) lie, falsehood; (*gen*) lying, untruthfulness, deceitfulness; (*Liter*) fiction, invention; **¡~!** it's a lie!; **una ~ como una casa*** (*o* **catedral**) a whopping great lie*; **~ caritativa, ~ oficiosa, ~ piadosa, ~ reverenda** (*Cono Sur*) white lie; **¡parece ~!** well (I never)!; you don't say so!; **aunque parezca ~** however incredible it seems, strange though it may seem; **parece ~ que** ... it seems impossible that ...; **parece ~ que no te acuerdas** I'm surprised you don't remember it; **no hay ~ que no salga** truth will out; **coger a uno en una ~** to catch sb in a lie.
(**b**) (*señal*) white mark (*on fingernail*).
(**c**) **sacar ~s** (*And, Cono Sur*) to crack one's knuckles.
(**d**) **de ~** (*LAm**: *artificial*) pretend, sham.

mentirijillas *nfpl*: **es de ~, va de ~** it's only a joke; (*a niño*) just pretend, it's just make-believe; **jugar de ~** to play for fun (*ie not for money*).

mentirilla *nf* fib; white lie.

mentirosillo, -a *nm/f* fibber.

mentiroso 1 *adj* (**a**) (*que miente*) lying, deceitful, untruthful; (*falso*) deceptive, false. (**b**) *texto* full of errors, full of misprints. **2** *nm*, **mentirosa** *nf* liar; deceiver.

mentís *nm invar* denial; **dar el ~ a** to refute, deny, give the lie to.

mentol *nm* menthol.

mentolado *adj* mentholated.

mentolatum* *nm*: **ser un ~** (*Cono Sur*) to be a jack of all trades.

mentón *nm* chin.

mentor *nm* mentor.

menú *nm* (**a**) (*lista*) menu; (*menú del día*) table d'hôte, set meal. (**b**) (*Inform*) menu.

menudear [1a] **1** *vt* (**a**) (*repetir*) to repeat frequently, do repeatedly; *narración etc* to tell in great detail.
(**b**) (*LAm*: *vender*) to sell retail.
2 *vi* (**a**) (*ser frecuente*) to be frequent, happen frequently; (*misiles etc*) to rain, come thick and fast; to come in abundance.
(**b**) (*al explicarse*) to go into great detail.
(**c**) (*Cono Sur, Méx*) (*abundar*) to abound; (*proliferar*) to increase, grow in number.

menudencia *nf* (**a**) (*bagatela*) trifle, small thing; **~s** little things, odds and ends. (**b**) (*minuciosidad*) minuteness; exactness; meticulousness. (**c**) **~s** (*Culin*) (*de cerdo*) pork products; (*menudillos*) offal.

menudeo *nm* (*Com*) retail trade; **vender al ~** to sell retail.

menudez *nf* smallness, minuteness.

menudillos *nmpl* giblets.

menudo 1 *adj* (**a**) (*pequeño*) small, tiny, minute; (*fig*) slight, petty, insignificant; **moneda menuda** small change, coins of low denomination.
(**b**) *persona* exact, meticulous.
(**c**) (*iró**) fine, some; **¡~ negocio!** some deal!; **¡menuda plancha!** what a bloomer!*; **¡menuda vidorra nos vamos a dar!** we won't half live it up!*; **¡menuda me la han hecho!** they've done it on me!*
(**d**) (*con prep*) **a ~** frequently, often; **a la menuda, por la menuda** (*Com*) retail; **contar algo por ~** to tell sth in detail.
2 *nm* (**a**) (*Fin*) small change.
(**b**) **~s** (*Culin*) offal; giblets; (*Méx*: *guisado*) tripe stew.

meñique 1 *adj* tiny, very small; **dedo ~** = **2. 2** *nm* little finger.

meódromo** *nm* bog**, loo*.

meollo *nm* (**a**) (*Anat*) marrow, brains. (**b**) (*de pan*) soft part, inside, crumb. (**c**) (*fig*: *de persona*) brains. (**d**) (*fig*: *de asunto etc*) gist, essence, core; solid substance, solid part, meat.

meón* 1 *adj niño* that constantly wets itself. **2** *nm*, **meona** *nf* baby (boy, girl).

meos*** *nmpl* piss***.

meque* *nm* (*Carib*) rap.

mequetrefe *nm* (*vago*) good-for-nothing, whippersnapper; (*curiosón*) busybody.

meramente *adv* merely, only, solely.

merca 1 *nm* food market; shopping centre. **2** *nf* (*Méx*) shopping, purchases; (*Cono Sur*) contraband goods.

mercachifle *nm* (**a**) (*comerciante*) small-time trader, dealer; (*vendedor ambulante*) hawker, huckster. (**b**) (*fig*) moneygrubber.

mercadear [1a] **1** *vt* (*vender*) to market; (*regatear*) to haggle over. **2** *vi* to deal, trade.

mercadeo *nm* marketing.

mercader *nm* (*esp Hist*) merchant.

mercadería *nf* commodity; **~s** goods, merchandise.

mercadillo *nm* street market; (*benéfico*) (charity) bazaar.

mercado *nm* market; **~ cambiario, ~ de divisas** foreign exchange market; **~ cautivo** captive market; **M~ Común** Common Market; **~ de demanda** seller's market; **~ de dinero** money market; **~ exterior** overseas market; **~ de futuros** futures market; **~ inmobiliario** property market; **~ interior, ~ nacional** home market; **~ libre** free market (*de* in); ~ **mundial** world market; ~ **negro** black market; ~ **de oferta** buyer's market; ~ **persa** (*Cono Sur*) cut-price store; ~ **de trabajo** labour market; ~ **único** single market; ~ **de valores** stock market; ~ **de viejo** flea-market; ~ **de la vivienda** housing market; ~ **de signo favorable al comprador,** ~ **de compradores** buyer's market; ~ **de signo favorable al vendedor,** ~ **de vendedores** seller's market; **inundar el** ~ **de** to flood the market with; **salir al** ~ to come on to the market.

mercadológico *adj* market (*atr*), marketing (*atr*).

mercadotecnia *nf* marketing; **estudios de** ~ market research.

mercadotécnico *adj* marketing (*atr*).

mercancía 1 *nf* commodity; **~s** goods, merchandise; **~s de general** (*Náut*) general cargo; **~s perecederas** perishable goods. **2** *nm*: **~s** goods train, freight train (*US*).

mercante 1 *adj* merchant (*atr*), trading, commercial; **buque** ~ = **2**. **2** *nm* merchantman, merchant ship.

mercantil *adj* mercantile, trading, commercial; *derecho* commercial.

mercantilismo *nm* mercantilism.

mercantilización *nf* commercialism; commercialization.

mercantilizar [1f] *vt* to commercialize.

mercar [1g] *vt* to buy.

merced *nf* (**a**) (†) (*favor*) favour; (*premio*) benefit, reward; (*placer*) pleasure, will; **hacer la** ~ **de** + *infin* to do sb the favour of + *ger*; **tenga la** ~ **de** + *infin* please be so good as to + *infin*.

(**b**) ~ **a** thanks to.

(**c**) (††) **vuestra** ~ your honour, your worship, sir.

(**d**) **estar a la** ~ **de** to be at the mercy of.

mercedario, -a *adj, nm/f* Mercedarian.

mercenario 1 *adj* mercenary. **2** *nm* (*Mil*) mercenary; (*Agr*) day labourer; (*fig*) hack, hireling.

mercería *nf* (**a**) (*géneros*) haberdashery, notions (*US*). (**b**) (*tienda*) haberdasher's (shop), notions store (*US*); (*And, Carib, Méx*) draper's (shop), dry-goods store (*US*); (*Cono Sur*) ironmonger's, hardware store.

mercero, -a *nm/f* haberdasher; (*And, Carib, Méx*) draper.

mercurial *adj* mercurial.

Mercurio *nm* Mercury.

mercurio *nm* mercury.

Merche *nf forma familiar de* **Mercedes.**

merchero* *nm* petty criminal, delinquent.

merdoso** *adj* filthy.

merecedor *adj* deserving, worthy (*de* of); ~ **de crédito** solvent; ~ **de confianza** trustworthy; **ser** ~ **de** to deserve, be deserving of.

merecer [2d] **1** *vt* (**a**) (*gen*) to deserve, be worthy of, merit; ~ + *infin* to deserve to + *infin*; **merece que se le dé el premio** he deserves to receive the prize; **el trato que él nos merece** the treatment he deserves from us; **te lo tienes merecido** it serves you right.

(**b**) (*And*) (*atrapar*) to catch; (*robar*) to snatch, pinch*; (*encontrar*) to find.

2 *vi* to be deserving, be worthy; ~ **mucho** to be very deserving; ~ **bien de la patria** to deserve well of one's country, deserve one's country's gratitude.

merecidamente *adv* deservedly.

merecido 1 *adj* well deserved, fully deserved; **bien** ~ **lo tiene** it serves him right. **2** *nm* (just) deserts; **llevar su** ~ to get one's deserts.

merecimiento *nm* (**a**) (*lo merecido*) deserts. (**b**) (*cualidad*) merit, worthiness.

merendar [1j] **1** *vt* (**a**) (*lit*) to have as an afternoon snack.

(**b**) ~ **lo que escribe otro** to look at what sb else is writing; ~ **las cartas de otro** to peep at sb else's cards, take a sly look at an opponent's cards.

2 *vi* to have an afternoon snack, (*aprox*) to have tea; (*en el campo*) to picnic, take tea out.

3 merendarse* *vr* (**a**) ~ **algo** to wangle sth*, get sth by a fiddle*.

(**b**) ~ **una fortuna** to squander a fortune.

(**c**) ~ **a uno*** (*fig*) to gobble sb up, make short work of sb; (*And*) to beat sb; (*And, Cono Sur, Méx*: *matar*) to bump sb off‡; (*Cono Sur*: *estafar*) to fleece sb.

merendero *nm* open-air café, snack bar; (*en el campo*) picnic spot; (*Méx*: *restaurán*) café, lunch counter.

merengar‡ [1h] *vt* to upset, annoy.

merengue 1 *adj* (of) Real Madrid F.C. **2** *nm* (**a**) (*Culin*) meringue. (**b**) (*And, Carib, Cono Sur**: *enclenque*) sickly person, invalid. (**c**) (*Cono Sur**: *alboroto*) row, fuss. (**d**) (*And, Carib*) *a popular dance*. **3** *nmpl* Real Madrid F.C.

meretriz *nf* prostitute.

mergo *nm* cormorant.

meridiana *nf* (**a**) (*diván*) divan, couch; (†) chaise longue; (*cama*) day bed. (**b**) **a la** ~ at noon.

meridianamente *adv* (*fig*) clearly, with complete clarity; **eso queda** ~ **claro** that is crystal-clear.

meridiano 1 *adj* (**a**) (*calor, hora etc*) midday (*atr*). (**b**) (*fig*) *luz* very bright; *hecho etc* clear as day, crystal-clear. **2** *nm* (*Astron, Geog*) meridian.

meridional 1 *adj* southern. **2** *nmf* southerner.

merienda *nf* tea; afternoon snack; (*para viaje*) packed meal; (*en el campo*: *t* ~ **campestre**) picnic; (*And*) supper; ~ **de negros*** (*confusión*) bedlam; (*trato sucio*) crooked deal*, dishonest share-out; **ir de** ~ to go for a picnic; **juntar ~s** (*fig*) to join forces, pool one's resources.

merino 1 *adj* merino. **2** *nm* merino (sheep); merino wool.

mérito *nm* (*valor*) merit; worth, value; (*excelencia*) excellence; (*ventaja*) advantage; **de** ~ worthy, of merit; **~s de guerra** *corresponde a* mention in dispatches; **hacer** ~ **de** to mention; **hacer ~s** to strive to be deserving; to strive for recognition; **restar** ~ **de** to detract from; **alega los siguientes ~s** he quotes the following facts in support (*o* in his favour); **'serán ~s los idiomas'** (*anuncio*) 'languages an advantage'.

meritocracia *nf* meritocracy.

meritócrata *nmf* meritocrat.

meritoriaje *nm* actor's apprenticeship.

meritorio 1 *adj* meritorious, worthy, deserving; praiseworthy. **2** *nm* unpaid employee, apprentice, unpaid trainee.

merla *nf* = **mirlo.**

merlan *nm* whiting.

merlango *nm* haddock.

Merlín *nm* Merlin; **saber más que** ~ to know the lot.

merlo[1] *nm* (*Pez*) black wrasse.

merlo[2]* *nm* (*LAm*) idiot.

merluza *nf* (**a**) (*Pez*) hake. (**b**) (*) **coger una** ~ to get tight*; **estar ~*, estar con la ~*** to get boozed up*.

merluzo‡ *adj* silly, stupid.

merma *nf* (*disminución*) decrease; shrinkage; (*pérdida*) wastage, loss.

mermar [1a] **1** *vt* to reduce, lessen; to deplete; *pago, raciones etc* to cut down. **2** *vi y* **mermarse** *vr* to decrease, dwindle; to be depleted; (*líquido*) to go down; (*fig*) to waste away.

mermelada *nf* jam; ~ **de albaricoques** apricot jam; ~ **de naranjas amargas** marmalade.

mero[1] 1 *adj* (**a**) mere, pure, simple; **el** ~ **hecho de** ... the mere (*o* simple) fact of ...

(**b**) (*Méx*: *preciso*) precise, exact; **a la mera hora** (*lit*) right on time; (*fig**) when it comes right down to it*.

(**c**) (*Méx*: *justo*) right; **en el momento** ~ at the right moment (*o* time).

(**d**) (*Méx*: *mismo*) **el** ~ **centro** the very centre; **la mera verdad** the plain truth; **el** ~ **Pedro** Pedro himself; **en la mera calle** right there on the street; **tu** ~ **papá** your own father.

2 *nm*: **el** ~**, el** ~ ~ (*Méx**) the big boss, the top dog.

3 *adv* (**a**) (*And*: *sólo*) only.

(**b**) (*CAm, Méx*: *pronto*) soon; **ya** ~ **llega** he'll be here any minute now; **ahora** ~ in a moment.

(**c**) (*CAm*: *de verdad*) really, truly.

(**d**) (*Méx*: *muy*) very.

(**e**) (*Méx*) (*hace poco*) just; (*precisamente*) exactly, precisely; **ahora** ~ right now; **ahora** ~ **llegó** he's just got here; **aquí** ~ right here; **¡ya ~!*** just coming!; **él va** ~ **adelante** he's just ahead; **¡eso ~!** right!, you've got it!

mero[2] *nm* (*Pez*) grouper.

merodeador 1 *adj* marauding; prowling. **2** *nm* (*Mil etc*) marauder; raider; (*de noche*) prowler.

merodear [1a] *vi* (**a**) (*Mil etc*) to maraud; (*de noche*) to prowl (about), rove about. (**b**) (*Méx*) to make money by illicit means.

merodeo *nm* marauding; prowling, roving.

merolico *nm* (*Méx*) quack, medicine man.

merovingio, -a *adj, nm/f* Merovingian.

mersa*, merza* (*Cono Sur*) **1** *adj* (*de mal gusto*) naff‡; (*ostentoso*) flashy. **2** *nmf* parvenu. **3** *nf* (*hampa*) mob, gang.

mes *nm* (**a**) (*lit*) month; **50 dólares al** ~ 50 dollars a month; ~ **lunar** lunar month; **el** ~ **corriente** the current month, this month; **el** ~ **que viene, el** ~ **próximo** next month.

(**b**) (*Fin*) (*sueldo*) month's pay; (*pago*) monthly payment; **el treceavo** ~ the annual bonus.

(**c**) (*Med*) menses; **estar con el ~, tener el ~** to be having one's period.

mesa *nf* (**a**) (*gen*) table; (*t* **~ de trabajo**) desk; (*Com*) counter; **~ de alas abatibles** gate-leg(ged) table, table with flaps; **~ auxiliar** side-table; **~ de billar** billiard-table; **~ de café, ~ de centro** coffee-table; café table; **~ de comedor** dining-table; **~ de despacho** office desk; **~ digitalizadora** graph pad; **~ de negociación** negotiating table; **~ de noche** bedside table; **~ de operaciones, ~ operatoria** operating table; **~ ratona** (*Cono Sur*) coffee-table; **~ redonda** (*restaurante*) general table; (*Hist*) Round Table; (*Pol*) round table; (*conferencia*) round-table conference; **~ de tijera** folding table; **~ de trabajo** desk; **dinero sobre la ~** (offer of) money on the table; **alzar la ~, levantar la ~, quitar la ~** to clear away, clear the table; **bendecir la ~** to say grace; **poner la ~** to lay the table; **ponerlos sobre la ~‡** to lay down the law; **sentarse a la ~** to sit down to table; **¡a la ~!** dinner's ready!; **servir a la ~** to wait at table; **vino de ~** table wine.

(**b**) (*pensión*) board; **~ y cama** bed and board; **tener a uno a ~ y mantel** to give sb free board.

(**c**) (*Geog*) meseta, tableland, plateau.

(**d**) (*Arquit*) landing.

(**e**) (*de herramienta*) side, flat.

(**f**) (*personas*) presiding committee, board; **~ electoral** officials in charge of a polling-station.

(**g**) (*negociación*) discussion, negotiating session.

mesada *nf* monthly payment.

mesana *nf* mizzen.

mesarse [1a] *vr* (**a**) (*2 personas*) to pull each other's hair. (**b**) **~ el pelo** (*o* **los cabellos**) to tear one's hair.

mescalina *nf* mescaline.

mescolanza *nf* = **mezcolanza.**

mesenterio *nm* mesentery.

mesera *nf* (*And, Méx*) waitress.

mesero *nm* (*And, Méx*) waiter.

meseta *nf* (**a**) (*Geog*) meseta, tableland, plateau. (**b**) (*Arquit*) landing.

mesetario *adj* of the Castilian meseta; (*fig*) Castilian.

mesiánico *adj* messianic.

Mesías *nm* Messiah.

mesilla *nf* (**a**) (*gen*) small table, side table, occasional table; **~ de chimenea** mantelpiece; **~ de noche** bedside table; **~ plegable** folding table; **~ de ruedas** trolley. (**b**) (*Carib*) market stall.

mesmeriano *adj* mesmeric.

mesmerismo *nm* mesmerism.

mesmerizar [1f] *vt* to mesmerize.

mesnada *nf* armed retinue; (*fig*) troop, band.

mesoamericano, -a *adj, nm/f* Indo-American.

mesolítico *adj* mesolithic; **el M~** the Mesolithic.

mesolito *nm* mesolith.

mesomorfo *nm* mesomorph.

mesón¹ *nm* (*Fís*) meson.

mesón² *nm* (**a**) (††: *hostería*) inn; (*moderno*) hotel with period décor, olde-worlde pub. (**b**) (*CAm*) lodging-house, rooming house (*US*). (**c**) (*Cono Sur*) large table; counter.

mesonera *nf* (††) innkeeper; (*dueña*) landlady; (*Carib*) waitress.

mesonero *nm* (††) innkeeper; (*dueño*) landlord; (*Carib*) waiter.

mesteño (*Méx*) **1** *adj caballo* wild, untamed. **2** *nm* mustang.

mestizaje *nm* (**a**) (*acto*) crossbreeding; miscegenation. (**b**) (*personas*) half-castes (*collectively*).

mestizar [1f] *vt* to crossbreed; *raza* to adulterate by crossbreeding.

mestizo 1 *adj persona* half-caste, half-breed, mixed-race; (*Zool*) crossbred; hybrid; mongrel. **2** *nm,* **mestiza** *nf* mestizo, half-caste, half-breed; (*Zool*) crossbred animal; hybrid; mongrel.

mesura *nf* (**a**) (*gravedad*) gravity, dignity, calm. (**b**) (*moderación*) moderation, restraint. (**c**) (*cortesía*) courtesy.

mesurado *adj* (**a**) (*grave*) grave, dignified, calm. (**b**) (*moderado*) moderate, restrained. (**c**) (*cortés*) courteous.

mesurar [1a] **1** *vt* (**a**) (*contener*) to restrain, temper. (**b**) (*LAm*) to measure. **2 mesurarse** *vr* to restrain o.s., act with restraint.

meta 1 *nf* (**a**) (*Dep*) goal; (*de carrera*) winning post, finishing-line; **~ volante** (*ciclismo*) sprint; **entrar en ~** to finish, reach the finishing-line. (**b**) (*fig*) goal, aim, objective. **2** *nm* (*Dep*) goalkeeper.

meta... *pref* meta...

metabólico *adj* metabolic.

metabolismo *nm* metabolism.

metabolizar [1f] *vt* to metabolize.

metacarpiano *nm* metacarpal.

metadona *nf* methadone.

metafísica¹ *nf* metaphysics.

metafísico 1 *adj* metaphysical. **2** *nm,* **metafísica²** *nf* metaphysician.

metáfora *nf* metaphor.

metafórico *adj* metaphoric(al).

metal *nm* (**a**) (*gen*) metal; (*Mús*) brass; (*Méx*) ore; **~ en láminas, ~ laminado** sheet metal; **~ pesado** heavy metal; **el vil ~** filthy lucre. (**b**) (*de voz*) timbre; (*fig*) quality.

metalenguaje *nm* metalanguage.

metalero *adj* (*And, Cono Sur*) metal (*atr*).

metálico 1 *adj* metallic; metal (*atr*). **2** *nm* (*en barras*) specie, bullion; (*moneda*) coin; (*contante*) cash; **pagar en ~** to pay (in) cash; **premio en ~** cash prize.

metalista *nmf* metalworker.

metalistería *nf* metalwork.

metalizado *adj* (**a**) *pintura* metallic. (**b**) (*fig*) mercenary, dedicated to making money; who sees everything in terms of money.

metalizarse [1f] *vr* (*fig*) to become mercenary.

metalmecánico *adj*: **industria metalmecánica** (*Cono Sur*) metallurgical industry.

metalurgia *nf* metallurgy.

metalúrgico 1 *adj* metallurgic(al). **2** *nm,* **metalúrgica** *nf* metallurgist.

metamórfico *adj* metamorphic.

metamorfosear [1a] **1** *vt* to metamorphose, transform (*en* into). **2 metamorfosearse** *vr* to be metamorphosed, be transformed, change.

metamorfosis *nf invar* metamorphosis, transformation, change.

metano *nm* methane.

metatarsiano *nm* metatarsal.

metate *nm* (*CAm, Méx*) flat stone for grinding.

metátesis *nf invar* metathesis.

metedor(a) *nm/f* smuggler.

metedura *nf* (**a**) (*acto de meter*) putting, placing; insertion. (**b**) **~ de pata*** bloomer*, clanger‡.

meteduría *nf* smuggling.

metejón* *nm* (**a**) (*Cono Sur*) violent love. (**b**) (*And*: *enredo*) mess.

metelón* *adj* (*Méx*) meddling.

metempsicosis *nf invar* metempsychosis.

meteórico *adj* meteoric (*t fig*).

meteorito *nm* meteor, meteorite.

meteoro *nm* (*esp fig*) meteor.

meteoroide *nm* meteoroid.

meteorología *nf* meteorology.

meteorológico *adj* meteorological, weather (*atr*).

meteorologista *nmf,* **meteorólogo, -a** *nm/f* meteorologist.

metepatas* *nmf invar* person who is always putting his (*o* her) foot in it.

meter [2a] **1** *vt* (**a**) (*gen*) to put, place; to insert, introduce (*en* in, into); to fit in; to squeeze in; (*Culin*) *ingrediente* to add (*en* to), put (*en* in); *herramienta* to use, ply; **a todo ~*** full-speed; **le están poniendo inyecciones a todo ~** they're pumping injections into him as fast as they can; **¡métetelo donde te quepa!‡** you can stuff it!‡

(**b**) (*Dep*) *tanto* to score (*a* against).

(**c**) (*Com*: *t* **~ de contrabando**) *géneros* to smuggle in.

(**d**) (*causar*) to make, cause; **~ ruido** to cause a stir (*y V* **ruido**); **~ un lío** to make a fuss, stir up trouble; **~ miedo a uno** to scare sb, frighten sb; **~ un susto a uno** to put the wind up sb; **~ prisa a uno** to make sb get a move on.

(**e**) (*apostar*) *dinero* to stake, wager (*en* on); (*Fin*) to invest (*en* in).

(**f**) **no hay quien le meta aquello** nobody seems able to make him understand that, nobody is able to get that idea into his head.

(**g**) *persona* to involve (*en* in); **tú me metiste en este lío** you got me into this mess; **A le metió a B en muchos disgustos** A let B in for a lot of trouble; **¿quién le mete en esto?** who told you to interfere?

(**h**) **~ a uno a trabajar** to put sb to work; **~ a uno a un oficio** to put sb to a trade; **~ a un chico de panadero** to apprentice a lad to a baker, put a lad to the baking trade.

(**i**) (*Cos*) *vestido* to take in, take up, gather.

(**j**) (*) *golpe* to give, deal.

(**k**) (*: *encajar*) **~ algo a uno** to palm sth off on sb; to force sb to accept sth; **nos metió un largo discurso** he gave us a terribly long speech; **le metieron 5 años de cárcel** they put him away for 5 years; **nos van a ~ más trabajo** they're going to lumber us with more work; **no me meta esas peras** don't try to foist those pears off on me.

(**l**) **~las** (*And*‡) to beat it*.

2 meterse *vr* (**a**) (*introducirse*) ~ **en** to go into, get into, enter; ~ **en un agujero** to get into a hole, squeeze into a hole; **se metió en la cama** she got into bed; **se metió en la tienda** he went into the shop; ~ **en un negocio turbio** to take part in a shady deal, get involved in a shady deal; ~ **en peligro** to get into danger; ~ **en sí mismo** to withdraw into one's shell; **¿dónde se habrá metido el lápiz?** where can the pencil have got to?

(**b**) (*Geog*) to extend, project; **el cabo se mete en el mar** the cape extends (*o* goes out) into the sea; **el río se mete en el mar** the river flows into the sea.

(**c**) (*fig*) ~ **en** to interfere in, meddle in; **¡no se meta en lo que no le importa!, ¡no se meta donde no le llaman!** mind your own business!

(**d**) ~ **con uno** (*provocar*) to provoke sb, pick a quarrel with sb; (*abordar*) to accost sb, molest sb; (*mofarse*) to tease sb, have a go at sb.

(**e**) **se ha metido con las tijeras** she has taken the scissors to it.

(**f**) ~ **monja** to become a nun; ~ **a escritor** to become a writer, (*pey*) set o.s. up as a writer; ~ **de aprendiz en un oficio** to go into a trade as an apprentice.

(**g**) ~ **a** + *infin* to start (without due preparation) to + *infin*; to take it upon o.s. to + *infin*.

meterete* *nm*, **metereta*** *nf* (*Cono Sur*), **metete*** *nm* (*And, CAm, Cono Sur*) busybody, meddler.

meticón* *nm* = **metijón.**

meticulosamente *adv* meticulously, scrupulously, thoroughly.

meticulosidad *nf* meticulousness, scrupulousness, thoroughness.

meticuloso *adj* meticulous, scrupulous, thorough; (*esp LAm*: *pey*) fussy, petty, small-minded.

metiche *adj* (*And, Méx**) meddling, meddlesome.

metida* *nf* = **metedura.**

metido 1 *adj* (**a**) ~ **en sí**, ~ **para adentro** introspective.

(**b**) **estar muy ~ en un asunto** to be deeply involved in a matter.

(**c**) ~ **en años** elderly, advanced in years; **está algo metidita en años** she must be getting on a bit now; ~ **en carnes** (*Esp*) plump.

(**d**) **estar muy ~ con uno** to be well in with sb.

(**e**) (*LAm*: *entrometido*) meddling, meddlesome.

(**f**) (*Carib, Cono Sur**: *bebido*) half tight*.

2 *nm* (**a**) (*: *reprimenda*) ticking-off*; **dar** (*o* **pegar**) **un ~ a uno** to give sb a dressing-down*.

(**b**) (‡: *sablazo*) touch*; **pegar un ~ a uno** to touch sb for money*.

(**c**) (*: *golpe*) bash*; shove; **pegar un buen ~ a una tarta** to take a good chunk out of a cake.

metijón* *nm* busybody, meddler.

metilado *adj*: **alcohol** ~ methylated spirit.

metilo *nm* methyl.

metimiento *nm* (**a**) (*inserción*) insertion. (**b**) (*) influence, pull.

metódicamente *adv* methodically.

metódico *adj* methodical.

metodismo *nm* Methodism.

metodista *adj, nmf* Methodist.

método *nm* method.

metodología *nf* methodology.

metodológico *adj* methodological.

metomentodo 1 *adj invar* meddling, interfering. **2** *nm* meddler, busybody.

metraje *nm* length; (*Dep*) distance; (*Cine*) length; **cinta de largo** ~ full-length film; **un discurso de largo** ~ (*fig*) a long-winded speech; *V* **cortometraje, mediometraje.**

metralla *nf* (**a**) (*Mil*) shrapnel. (**b**) (*) coppers, small change.

metralleta *nf* submachine gun, tommy gun.

métrica *nf* metrics.

métrico *adj* metric(al).

metro[1] *nm* (**a**) (*Mat*: *medida*) metre, meter (*US*); ~ **cuadrado** square metre; ~ **cúbico** cubic metre. (**b**) (*Mat*: *instrumento*) rule, ruler (*t* ~ **plegable**); ~ **de cinta** tape measure.

metro[2] *nm* (*Ferro*: *sistema*) underground, tube, subway (*US*); (*estación*) tube station.

metrobús *nm* combined bus and underground railway ticket.

metrónomo *nm* metronome.

metrópoli *nf* metropolis; (*de imperio*) mother country.

metropolitano 1 *adj* metropolitan. **2** *nm* (**a**) (*Ecl*) metropolitan. (**b**) (*Ferro*) = **metro**[2].

mexicano (*LAm*) = **mejicano.**

México *nm* (*LAm*) Mexico.

mezcal *nm* (*Méx*) mezcal.

mezcla *nf* (**a**) (*acto*) mixing.

(**b**) (*sustancia*) mixture; (*fig*) blend, combination; medley; (*Cos*) mixture; mixed cloth; **sin ~** pure, unadulterated; *bebida* neat; ~ **explosiva** explosive mixture; (*) unholy mixture.

(**c**) (*Arquit*) mortar.

mezclado *nm* mixing.

mezclador 1 *nm* mixing bowl. **2** *nm*, **mezcladora**[1] *nf* (**a**) (*TV*) ~ **de imágenes** vision mixer; ~ **de sonido** dubbing mixer. (**b**) (*Telec*) scrambler.

mezcladora[2] *nf* (*Culin*) mixer; ~ **de hormigón** concrete mixer.

mezclar [1a] **1** *vt* (**a**) (*gen*) to mix, mix up (together); (*armonizar*) to blend; (*combinar*) to merge, combine; *cartas* to shuffle.

(**b**) (*fig*) ~ **a A con B** to involve A with B, get A into trouble with B; ~ **a la Iglesia en el debate** to drag the Church into the debate.

2 mezclarse *vr* (**a**) (*gen*) to mix, mingle (*con* with); to blend (*con* with).

(**b**) (*alternar*) ~ **con cierta gente** to mix with certain people; **hizo mal en ~ con esa familia** she did wrong to marry (beneath herself) into that family.

(**c**) ~ **en** (*entrometerse*) to get mixed up in, get involved in; to meddle in.

mezclillo *nm* (*Cono Sur*) denim.

mezcolanza *nf* hotchpotch, jumble.

mezquinar [1a] **1** *vt* (**a**) (*LAm*) to be stingy with, give sparingly.

(**b**) (*Cono Sur*) ~ **el cuerpo** to dodge, swerve; ~ **el saludo*** to ignore somebody.

(**c**) (*And*) ~ **a uno** to defend sb; ~ **a un niño** to let a child off a punishment.

2 *vi* (*LAm*) to be mean, be stingy.

mezquindad *nf* (**a**) (*cualidad*) meanness, stinginess; poor spirit; pettiness; ignoble nature; paltriness, wretchedness. (**b**) (*acto*) mean action, petty deed.

mezquino 1 *adj* (**a**) (*tacaño*) mean, stingy.

(**b**) (*de miras estrechas*) poor-spirited; small-minded, petty; (*vil*) ignoble; (*interesado*) materialistic, lacking the finer sentiments.

(**c**) *cualidad etc* miserable, paltry, tiny; *pago etc* wretched, wretchedly small.

2 *nm* (**a**) (*avaro*) mean person, miser; (*miserable*) petty individual, wretch.

(**b**) (*And, CAm, Méx*: *verruga*) wart.

mezquita *nf* mosque.

mezzanine [metsa'nine] *nm* (*And Teat*) circle.

mezzosoprano ['metso-] *nf* mezzo-soprano.

M.F. *nf abr de* **modulación de frecuencia** frequency modulation, FM.

mg. *abr de* **miligramo** milligram(me), mg.

mi[1] *adj pos* my.

mi[2] *nm* (*Mús*) E; ~ **mayor** E major.

mí *pron* (*tras prep*) me; myself; **¡a ~!** (*Esp*) help!; **¡a ~ con ésas!** come off it!*, tell me another!; **¿y a ~ qué?** so what?, what has that got to do with me?; **para ~ no hay duda** so far as I'm concerned there's no doubt, I don't believe there can be any doubt; **por ~, puede ir** so far as I'm concerned she can go; **por ~ mismo** by myself; on my own account.

miaja *nf* (**a**) (*gen*) crumb. (**b**) (*fig*) bit, tiny portion; **ni** (**una**) ~ **de** not the least little bit of. (**c**) (*como adv*) a bit; **me quiere una ~** she likes me a bit.

mialgia *nf* myalgia.

miasma *nm* miasma.

miasmático *adj* miasmic.

miau *nm* mew, miaow.

Mibor *nm abr de* **Madrid inter-bank offered rate.**

mica[1] *nf* (**a**) (*Min*) mica. (**b**) (*Carib Aut*) sidelight.

mica[2] *nf* (*And*) chamberpot.

mica[3]* *nf* (*CAm*) drunkenness; **ponerse una ~** to get drunk.

micada *nf* (*CAm, Méx*) flourish.

mico *nm*, **mica**[4] *nf* (**a**) (*Zool*) monkey, (*esp*) long-tailed monkey.

(**b**) (*) (*feo*) ugly devil; (*engreído*) conceited person, swank*; (*mariposón*) flirt; (*cachondo*) randy man*, old goat*; **¡~!** (*a niño*) you little monkey!
(**c**) **dar ~, hacer ~** to miss a date, stand sb up*; **dar el ~** (*estafar*) to cheat; (*decepcionar*) to disappoint, behave differently from what had been hoped; **volverse ~ para hacer algo** to be at one's wits' end to know how to do sth.
(**d**) (*CAm***) cunt**.
micoleón *nm* (*CAm*) kincajou.
micología *nf* mycology.
micrero *nm* (*Cono Sur*) minibus driver.
micro[1]* *nm* (*Rad*) mike*, microphone.
micro[2] *nm* (*a veces nf*) (*And, Cono Sur: corta distancia*) minibus, bus; (*Cono Sur: larga distancia*) coach.
micro[3] *nm* (*Inform*) micro, microcomputer.
micro... *pref* micro...; mini...
microbiano *adj* microbial.
microbio *nm* (**a**) microbe. (**b**) (‡) sprog‡, small child.
microbiología *nf* microbiology.
microbiológico *adj* microbiological.
microbiólogo, -a *nm/f* microbiologist.
microbús *nm* minibus.
microcircuitería *nf* microcircuitry.
microcircuito *nm* microcircuit.
microcirugía *nf* microsurgery.
microclima *nm* microclimate.
microcomputador *nm*, **microcomputadora** *nf* micro(computer).
microcosmo(s) *nm* microcosm.
microchip *nm, pl* **microchips** microchip.
microeconomía *nf* microeconomy.
microeconómica *nf* microeconomics.
microeconómico *adj* microeconomic.
microelectrónica *nf* microelectronics.
microelectrónico *adj* microelectronic.
microespaciado *nm* microspacing.
microficha *nf* microfiche.
microfilm *nm, pl* **microfilms, microfilmes** *nm* microfilm.
microfilmar [1a] *vt* to microfilm.
micrófono *nm* microphone; (*Telec*) mouthpiece; **~ sin hilos, ~ inalámbrico** cordless microphone.
microforma *nf* microform.
microfundio *nm* smallholding, small farm.
microinformática *nf* microcomputing.
microlentillas *nfpl* (*Esp*) contact lenses.
micrómetro *nm* micrometer.
microonda *nf* microwave; **~s** (*m*), **horno** (**de**) **~s** microwave oven.
microordenador *nm* micro(computer).
microorganismo *nm* microorganism.
microplaquita *nf*: **~ de silicio** silicon chip.
microprocesador *nm* microcomputer.
micropunto *nm* microdot.
microscopía *nf* microscopy.
microscópico *adj* microscopic.
microscopio *nm* microscope; **~ electrónico** electron microscope.
microsegundo *nm* microsecond.
microsurco *nm* microgroove; **disco** (**de**) **~** long-playing record (*LP*).
microtaxi *nm* minicab.
microtecnia *nf*, **microtecnología** *nf* microtechnology.
microtenis *nm* (*LAm*) table-tennis.
microtransmisor *nm* micro-transmitter.
miche *nm* (**a**) (*Méx: gato*) cat. (**b**) (*Carib: licor*) liquor, spirits. (**c**) (*Cono Sur: juego*) game of marbles. (**d**) (*CAm: pelea*) fight, brawl.
michelín* *nm* spare tyre, roll of fat.
michi *nm* (*And*) noughts and crosses.
michino, -a *nm/f*, **micho, -a*** *nm/f* puss, pussy cat.
Midas *nm* Midas.
midi *nm*, **midifalda** *nf* midiskirt.
MIE *nm* (*Esp*) *abr de* **Ministerio de Industria y Energía**.
miedica(s)* *nmf* coward.
mieditis* *nf* funk*; jitters*.
miedo *nm* (**a**) (*gen*) fear, dread (*a, de* of); apprehension, nervousness; **~ cerval, ~ espantoso** great fear; (*Teat etc*) **~ al público** stage fright; **por ~ a, por ~ de** for fear of; **por ~ de que ...** for fear that ...; **dar ~ a, infundir ~ a, meter ~ a** to scare, frighten, fill with fear; **me da ~** he scares me, he makes me nervous; **le daba ~ hacerlo** he was nervous about doing it; **en este punto siempre me entra un ~ terrible** I always get terribly nervous at this point; **tener ~** to be afraid (*a* of); **no tengas ~** don't worry; **tener ~ de** + *infin* to be afraid to + *infin*, be afraid (*o* nervous) of + *ger*.
(**b**) (*) **¡qué ~!** how awful!; **de ~** (*adj*) wonderful, smashing*, marvellous; (*pey*) awful, ghastly*; (*adv*) wonderfully, marvellously; (*pey*) awfully; **es un coche de ~** it's a smashing car*; **eso fue de ~** it was tremendous*, (*pey*) it was ghastly*; **hace un frío de ~** it's terribly cold.
miedoso *adj* fearful, fainthearted; timid, nervous, shy.
miel *nf* (**a**) (*lit*) honey.
(**b**) (*melaza: t* **~ de caña, ~ negra**) molasses.
(**c**) (*locuciones*) **las ~es del triunfo** the sweets of success; **es ~ sobre hojuelas** it's marvellous, it's even better than I (*etc*) expected; **no hay ~ sin hiel** nothing is ever entirely perfect; **dejar a uno con la ~ en los labios** to snatch sth away from sb, spoil sb's fun; **quedarse con la ~ en los labios** to get a taste but no more, remain unsatisfied; to come close to success without attaining it; **hacerse de ~** to be excessively kind, be almost too sweet; **hazte de ~ y te comerán las moscas** if you are too nice people will take advantage of you.
mielero *nm* honeypot.
mielga *nf* lucerne, alfalfa.
miembro 1 *nm* (**a**) (*Anat*) limb, member; **~** (**viril**) (male) member, penis.
(**b**) (*Ling, Mat etc*) member.
2 *nmf* (*persona*) member; fellow, associate; **no ~** non-member; **hacerse ~ de** to become a member of.
3 *como adj* member; **los países ~s** the member countries.
mientes *nfpl*: **¡ni por ~!** never!, not on your life!; **parar ~ en** to reflect on, consider carefully; **traer a las ~** to recall; **se le vino a las ~** it occurred to him, it came to his mind.
mientras 1 *conj* (**a**) (*gen*) while; as long as; **~ duraba la guerra** while the war lasted, as long as the war lasted; **~ él estaba fuera** while he was abroad; **~ no venga** until he comes.
(**b**) **~** (**que**) whereas; **~ más tienen más quieren** the more they have the more they want.
(**c**) (*LAm*) **~ más lo repetía, menos lo creía** the more he repeated it, the less I believed him.
2 *adv* meanwhile, meantime (*t* **y ~, ~ tanto**); all the while.
mierc. *abr de* **miércoles** Wednesday, Weds., Wed.
miércoles *nm invar* (**a**) Wednesday; **~ de ceniza** Ash Wednesday. (**b**) (*: *euf*) **¡~!** sugar!*
mierda** *nf* (**a**) (*lit*) shit**; (*fig*) filth, dirt; **¡~!** shit!**
(**b**) (*fig*) **es un**(**a**) **~** he's a shit**; **es un don M~** he's a nobody; **el libro es una ~** the book is crap**; **¡50 dólares, una ~!** 50 dollars, nearly nothing!; **es una ~ de coche** it's a bloody awful car‡; **una película de ~** a crappy film**; **esos políticos de ~** those lousy politicians‡; **marcó un gol de pura ~** he scored a goal by an almighty fluke*; **¿qué ~s ocurre?** what the hell is going on?; **coger** (*o* **pillar**) **una ~** (*Esp*) to get sozzled‡; **¡vaya Vd a la ~!** go to hell!, piss off!**
(**c**) (*droga*) hash*.
mierdear‡ [1a] *vt* to upset, bother, mess around.
mierdoso‡ *adj* filthy.
mies *nf* (**a**) (*granos*) (ripe) corn, wheat, grain. (**b**) (*temporada*) harvest time. (**c**) (*campos*) **~es** cornfields.
miga *nf* (**a**) (*gen*) crumb; (*fig*) bit; **~s** (*Culin*) fried breadcrumbs.
(**b**) (*fig*) core, substance, essence; **esto tiene su ~** there's sth in this; there's more in this than meets the eye.
(**c**) **hacer algo ~s** to break sth up, smash sth into little pieces; **hacer ~s a uno** to leave sb in a sorry state; **tener los pies hechos ~s** to be footsore; **hacer buenas ~s** to get on well, hit it off (*con* with).
migajas *nfpl* crumbs; bits; (*fig*) leavings, scraps.
migar [1h] *vt* to crumble, break up.
migra* *nf* (*LAm*) corps of immigration police, immigration authorities.
migración *nf* migration.
migraña *nf* migraine.
migrar [1a] *vi* to migrate.
migratorio *adj* migratory.
Miguel *nm* Michael; **~ Ángel** Michelangelo.
mijo *nm* millet.
mil *adj y nm* thousand; **tres ~ coches** three thousand cars; **~ doscientos dólares** one thousand two hundred dollars; **lo ha hecho ~ veces** he's done it hundreds of times; **~es y ~es** thousands and thousands; **a las ~*** at some ungodly

hour*, terribly late.
miladi *nf* milady.
milagro 1 *nm* miracle; (*fig*) miracle, wonder, marvel; ~ **económico** economic miracle; **¡ni de ~!** not a bit of it!; **es un ~ que** ... it is a miracle (*o* wonder) that ...; ~ **(sería) que** ... it would be a miracle if ...; **salvarse de ~** to escape miraculously, have a miraculous escape; **vivir de ~** to have a hard time of it, keep going somehow; to manage to stay alive; **hacer ~s** (*fig*) to work wonders. **2** *atr* miracle (*atr*), miraculous, wonder-working; **cura ~** miracle cure; **entrenador ~** wonder-working coach.
milagrosa* *nf* police badge.
milagrosamente *adv* miraculously.
milagroso *adj* miraculous.
Milán *nm* Milan.
milano *nm* (*Orn*) kite.
mildeu (*t* **mildiu, mildiú**) *nm* mildew.
mildo *adj* (*Cono Sur*) timid, shy.
milenariamente *adv*: **un pueblo ~ libre** a people which has been free for a thousand years.
milenario 1 *adj* millennial; (*fig*) very ancient, age-old. **2** *nm* millennium.
milenio *nm* millennium.
milenrama *nf* yarrow.
milésima *nf* thousandth.
milésimo *adj, nm* thousandth; **hasta el ~** to three places of decimals.
mili* *nf* (*Esp*) military service; **estar en la ~, hacer la ~** to do one's military service.
miliar *adj*: **piedra ~** milestone.
milibar *nm* millibar.
milicia *nf* (**a**) (*cuerpo, servicio*) militia; (*soldados*) military, soldiery. (**b**) (*arte*) art of war; science of warfare; (*profesión*) soldiering, military profession. (**c**) (*período*) (period of) military service.
miliciano *nm* (*And, Cono Sur*) (*soldado*) militiaman; (*conscripto*) conscript.
milico *nm* (**a**) (*And*) = **miliciano.** (**b**) (*And, Cono Sur**: *pey*) soldier; policeman; (*soldado raso*) squaddie*; **los ~s** the military.
miligramo *nm* milligram.
mililitro *nm* millilitre, milliliter (*US*).
milimetrado *adj* (*fig*) minutely calculated; **papel ~** graph paper.
milimétricamente *adv* (*fig*) *calcular etc* precisely, minutely, down to the last detail.
milimétrico *adj* (*fig*) precise, minute; **con precisión milimétrica** with pinpoint accuracy.
milímetro *nm* millimetre, millimeter (*US*); **lo calculó hasta el ~** (*fig*) he calculated it very precisely; **nos siguió al ~** he stuck very close to us.
milisegundo *nm* millisecond.
militancia *nf* (**a**) (*cualidad*) militancy. (**b**) (*Pol: personas*) (active) membership; **~ de base** rank-and-file members; ordinary supporters; **¿cuál es su ~ política?** what is his political affiliation?
militante 1 *adj* militant. **2** *nmf* militant; (*Pol*) (active) member; **~ de base** rank-and-file member.
militantismo *nm* militancy.
militar 1 *adj* military; *espíritu etc* warlike; **ciencia ~** art of war.
2 *nm* (*soldado*) soldier, military man; serviceman; **~ de carrera** professional soldier; career officer.
3 [1a] *vi* (**a**) (*Mil*) to serve (in the army); to soldier.
(**b**) **~ en un partido** (*fig*) to belong to a party, be an active member of a party.
(**c**) (*fig*) **~ contra** to militate against; **~ en defensa de, ~ en favor de** to speak for, argue in favour of, lend weight to.
militarada *nf* military rising, putsch.
militarismo *nm* militarism.
militarista 1 *adj* militaristic. **2** *nmf* militarist.
militarizar [1f] *vt* to militarize; (*disciplinar*) to put under military discipline.
militarote *nm* (*LAm: pey*) rough soldier; blustering soldier.
milonga *nf* (**a**) (*: *mentirilla*) fib, tale. (**b**) (*And, Cono Sur*) (*baile*) *kind of dance rhythm*; (*canción*) *type of song*; (*cabaret*) cabaret; (*: *fiesta*) party. (**c**) (*And, Cono Sur: chismes*) gossip.
milonguero, -a *nm/f* (**a**) (*Mús*) singer of *milongas.* (**b**) (*And: fiestero*) partylover.
milor *nm*, **milord** [mi'lor] *nm* milord; **vive como un ~** he lives like a lord.

milpa *nf* (*CAm, Méx*) (*plantación*) maize field, cornfield (*US*); (*planta*) maize, Indian corn.
milpear [1a] **1** *vt* (*CAm, Méx*) to prepare for the sowing of maize. **2** *vi* (**a**) (*CAm, Méx*) to sow a field with maize. (**b**) (*Méx: maíz*) to sprout.
milpero *nm* (*CAm, Méx*) maize grower.
milpiés *nm invar* millipede.
milla *nf* mile; **~ marina** nautical mile.
millar *nm* thousand; **a ~es** in thousands, by the thousand; **los había a ~es** they were there in thousands.
millarada *nf* (about a) thousand.
millas-pasajero *nfpl* passenger miles.
millo *nm*, **millón¹** *nm* (*CAm, Méx*) (*variety of*) millet.
millón² *nm* million; **un ~ de sellos** a million stamps; **3 millones de niños** 3 million children; **¡un ~ de gracias!** a thousand thanks!
millonada* *nf* million, vast number; **lo vendió por una ~** he sold it for a cool million.
millonario, -a *nm/f* millionaire.
millonésimo *adj, nm* millionth.
mimado *adj* spoiled.
mimar [1a] *vt niño etc* to spoil, pamper, indulge.
mimbre *nm o f* (**a**) (*Bot*) osier, willow. (**b**) (*materia*) wicker; **de ~** wicker, wickerwork.
mimbrearse [1a] *vr* to sway.
mimbrera *nf* osier.
mimbreral *nm* osier bed.
mimeografiar [1c] *vt* to mimeograph.
mimeógrafo *nm* mimeograph.
miméticamente *adv* mimetically, by way of imitation.
mimético *adj* mimetic, imitation (*atr*).
mimetismo *nm* mimetism; imitation; (*Zool etc*) mimicry.
mimetización *nf* copying, mimicry, imitation; camouflage.
mimetizarse [1f] *vr* to change colour, camouflage o.s.
mímica *nf* (**a**) (*señas*) sign language; (*ademanes*) gesticulation. (**b**) (*imitación*) mimicry; (*una ~*) mime.
mímico *adj* mimic; imitative; **lenguaje ~** sign language.
mimo *nm* (**a**) (*Teat: Hist*) mime; **hacer ~ de** to mime, mimic.
(**b**) (*caricia*) affectionate caress; (*piropo*) nice remark (*etc*); (*gen*) pampering, indulgence; **dar ~s a un niño** to spoil a child; **hacer ~s a uno** to make a great fuss of sb, fuss over sb.
mimosa *nf* mimosa.
mimoso *adj* (**a**) (*mimado*) spoilt, pampered; (*blandengue*) soft; (*delicado*) fussy, finicky. (**b**) (*con relación al otro sexo*) arch, coy, provocative; kittenish.
mina¹ *nf* (**a**) (*Min*) mine; **~ a cielo abierto** opencast mine; **~ de carbón, ~ hullera** coalmine.
(**b**) (*galería*) underground passage; gallery; (*pozo*) shaft.
(**c**) (*Mil, Náut*) mine.
(**d**) (*de lapicero*) lead; refill.
(**e**) (*fig*) mine, storehouse; gold-mine; **~ de información** mine of information.
mina²⁑ *nf* (*Cono Sur*) bird⁑, girl.
minada *nf* (*Mil*) mining.
minador *nm* (**a**) (*Mil*) sapper; (*Min*) mining engineer. (**b**) (*Náut*: *t* **buque ~**) minelayer.
minar [1a] *vt* (**a**) (*Min*) to mine. (**b**) (*Mil, Náut*) to mine. (**c**) (*fig*) to undermine, sap, wear away.
minarete *nm* minaret.
mineral 1 *adj* mineral. **2** *nm* (*Geol*) mineral; (*Min*) ore; **~ de hierro** iron ore.
mineralero *nm* ore-carrier.
mineralogía *nf* mineralogy.
mineralogista *nmf* mineralogist.
minería *nf* mining.
minero 1 *adj* mining. **2** *nm*, **minera** *nf* miner; **~ de carbón** coalminer; **~ de interior** underground worker.
Minerva *nf* Minerva.
minestrone *nf* minestrone.
minga¹⁑ *nf* (*Esp*) prick⁑.
minga² *nf* (*LAm*) (**a**) (*trabajo*) voluntary communal labour, cooperative work. (**b**) (*equipo*) crew, team, gang (of cooperative workers).
mingaco *nm* (*And, Cono Sur*) = **minga² (a)**.
mingar [1h] *vt* (**a**) (*And, Cono Sur*) *proyecto, tarea* to work communally on, contribute cooperatively to. (**b**) (*And, Cono Sur*) *obreros* to call together for a communal task. (**c**) (*And: atacar*) to set on, attack.
mingitorio* *nm* urinal.
Mingo *nm forma familiar de* **Domingo.**
mini *nm* (*falda*) mini, miniskirt; (*Aut*) Mini; (*Inform*)

microcomputer.
mini... *pref* mini...; (*como pref hum*) **minibikini** microscopic bikini; **mininovillo** (*Taur*) baby bull, tiny bull.
miniar [1b] *vt manuscrito* to illuminate.
miniatura 1 *adj invar* miniature; *perro etc* toy; **golf ~** miniature golf(course); **relojes ~** miniature watches. **2** *nf* miniature; **en ~** in miniature.
miniaturista *nmf* miniaturist.
miniaturización *nf* miniaturization.
miniaturizar [1f] *vt* to miniaturize.
minibar *nm* minibar.
minicalculadora *nf* pocket calculator.
minicasino *nm* small gambling club.
minicoche *nm* (*Esp*) minicar.
minidisco *nm* (*Inform*) diskette.
miniestadio *nm* small sports arena.
minifalda *nf* miniskirt.
minifaldero *adj* short-skirted, miniskirted.
minifundio *nm* smallholding, small farm.
minifundismo *nm* (*fig*) tendency to fragment, fragmentation.
minifundista *nmf* smallholder.
minigira *nf* short tour.
minigolf *nm* putting (green), miniature golf(-course).
minihorno *nm* small oven.
minimalista *adj, nmf* minimalist.
mínimamente *adv* minimally.
minimizar [1f] *vt* to minimize.
mínimo 1 *adj* (*gen*) minimum; (*insignificante*) minimal; (*más pequeño*) smallest, slightest, least; **cifra mínima** minimum number, smallest figure; **sin el más ~ esfuerzo** without the slightest effort; **no contribuye en lo más ~** it doesn't help at all, it doesn't help in the least; **no me importa en lo más ~** it doesn't matter to me in the least.
2 *nm* (**a**) minimum; **como ~** as a minimum, at the very least; **~ de presión** (*Met*) low-pressure area, trough; **estar bajo ~s** to be at a low ebb.
(**b**) (*Carib*: *Aut*) choke.
mínimum *nm* minimum.
minina[1]**‡** *nf* (*Esp*) willie‡.
minino, -a[2] *nm/f* puss, pussy-cat.
minio *nm* red lead, minium.
miniordenador *nm* microcomputer.
minipíldora *nf* minipill.
Minipimer ® *nm* electric mixer.
miniserie *nf* miniseries.
ministerial *adj* ministerial; governmental.
ministerio *nm* ministry; *V* **asunto, gobernación** *etc*.
ministrable *nmf* candidate for minister; possible minister, potential minister.
ministro, -a *nm/f* minister; **primer ~, primera ministra** prime minister; **~ portavoz** government spokesperson; **~ sin cartera** minister without portfolio; **~ en la sombra** shadow minister.
minivestido *nm* minidress.
minoración *nf* reduction, diminution.
minorar [1a] *vt* to reduce, diminish.
minoría *nf* minority; **~ de edad** minority.
minoridad *nf* minority (*of age*).
minorista *nm* (*Carib, Cono Sur*) retailer, retail trader.
minoritario *adj* minority (*atr*); **gobierno ~** minority government.
Minotauro *nm* Minotaur.
minucia *nf* (*detalle*) trifle, insignificant detail; (*bagatela*) mere nothing; (*pedazo*) morsel, tiny bit; **~s** petty details, minutiae.
minuciosamente *adv* thoroughly, meticulously; in a very detailed way; minutely.
minuciosidad *nf* thoroughness, meticulousness; detailed nature; minuteness.
minucioso *adj* (*meticuloso*) thorough, meticulous; (*detallado*) very detailed; (*pequeño*) minute.
minué *nm* minuet.
minúscula *nf* small letter; (*Tip*) lower case letter.
minúsculo *adj* tiny, minute, minuscule; (*Tip*) small.
minusvalía *nf* (**a**) (physical) handicap. (**b**) (*Com*) depreciation, capital loss.
minusvalidez *nf* state of being (physically) handicapped, disablement, disability.
minusválido 1 *adj* (physically) handicapped, disabled. **2** *nm*, **minusválida** *nf* handicapped person, disabled person; **los ~s** the handicapped; **~ físico** physically handicapped person; **~ psíquico** mentally handicapped person.
minusvalorar [1a] *vt* to undervalue; to underestimate.
minuta *nf* (**a**) (*borrador*) rough draft, first draft; (*copia*) carbon copy.
(**b**) (*apunte*) note, memorandum; (*Jur*) lawyer's bill.
(**c**) (*lista*) list, roll.
(**d**) (*Culin*) menu; **a la ~** (*Carib, Cono Sur*) rolled in breadcrumbs.
(**e**) (*Cono Sur*) (*basura*) junk, trash; (*tienda*) junk shop.
(**f**) (*CAm*: *bebida*) flavoured ice drink.
minutado *nm*, **minutaje** *nm* timing, running time; timing schedule.
minutar [1a] *vt* (**a**) *contrato* to draft. (**b**) *cliente* to bill.
minutario *nm* minute book.
minutero *nm* (*manecilla*) minute-hand; (*reloj*) timer.
minutisa *nf* sweet william.
minuto *nm* minute.
miñango* *nm* (*And, Cono Sur*) bit, small piece; **hecho ~s** smashed to pieces, in smithereens.
miñoco *nm* (*And*) grimace.
miñón *adj* (*LAm*) sweet, cute.
mío *adj y pron* mine, of mine; **es ~, es el ~** it is mine; **lo ~** (what is) mine, what belongs to me; **no es amigo ~** he's no friend of mine; **¡hijo ~!** my dear boy!; **los ~s** my people, my relations, my family.
miope 1 *adj* short-sighted, myopic. **2** *nmf* short-sighted person.
miopía *nf* short-sightedness, myopia.
MIPS *nmpl abr de* **millones de instrucciones por segundo** millions of instructions per second, MIPS.
MIR [mir] *nm* (*Esp Med*) *abr de* **Médico interno y residente**.
mira *nf* (**a**) **estar a la ~** to be on the look-out, keep watch (*de* for).
(**b**) (*Mil, Téc etc*) sight(s); **~ de bombardeo** bombsight; **~ telescópica** telescopic sight; **con la ~ puesta en** (*fig*) with one's sights set on.
(**c**) (*Mil*) watchtower, look-out post.
(**d**) (*fig*) aim, intention; **con la ~ de** + *infin* with the aim of + *ger*; **con ~s a** with a view to; **llevar una ~ interesada** to have a selfish end in view; **poner la ~ en** to aim at, aspire to; **tener ~s sobre** to have designs on.
(**e**) (*fig*) **de amplias ~s** broad in outlook; tolerant, broad-minded; **de ~s estrechas** narrow-minded; insular, parochial.
mirada *nf* (**a**) (*gen*) look, glance; gaze; **~ fija** stare; hard look; **~ de soslayo** sidelong glance; **~ perdida, ~ vaga** vague look, distant look; **aguantar la ~ de uno** to stare sb out; **apartar la ~** to look away (*de* from); **apuñalar** (*o* **fulminar**) **a uno con la ~** to look daggers at sb; **clavar la ~ en** to fix one's eyes on; **echar una ~ a** to glance at; to keep an eye on; **huir de las ~s de uno** to avoid looking sb in the eye; **lanzar una ~ a** to glance at, cast a glance at; **levantar la ~** to raise one's eyes; **no levanta la ~ del libro** he never takes his eyes off the book; **resistir la ~ de uno** to stare back at sb, stare sb out.
(**b**) (*expresión*) look, expression; **con una ~ triste** with a sad look.
miradero *nm* (**a**) (*atalaya*) look-out, vantage point. (**b**) (*atracción*) cynosure (of every eye), person (*etc*) that attracts every eye.
mirado *adj* (**a**) (*estimado*) **bien ~** well thought of, well liked, highly regarded; **no está bien ~ que ...** it is not thought proper that ...; **mal ~** disliked (*V t* **malmirado**).
(**b**) (*juicioso*) sensible; (*educado*) well-behaved; (*considerado*) considerate, thoughtful; (*cauto*) cautious; **ser ~ en los gastos** to be sensible about what one spends, be a careful spender.
(**c**) (*pey*) finicky, fussy.
(**d**) **bien ~** (*como adv*) by rights, in justice, if everything is weighed up.
mirador *nm* (**a**) (*Arquit*) (*ventana*) bay window; (*balcón*) (enclosed) balcony; **~ de popa** (*Náut*) stern gallery. (**b**) (*atalaya*) viewpoint, vantage point.
miramiento *nm* (**a**) (*consideración*) considerateness; (*cortesía*) courtesy; **sin ~** without consideration, discourteously.
(**b**) (*circunspección*) caution, circumspection, care; (*pey*) timidity, excessive caution.
(**c**) **~s** (*cortesías*) courtesies, attentions; **sin ~s** unceremoniously; high-handed(ly); **sin ~s de** regardless of; **andar con ~s** to tread carefully; **tratar sin ~s a uno** to treat sb without consideration, ride roughshod over sb.
miranda* *nf*: **estar de ~** (*gandulear*) to be idle, loaf around; (*mirar*) to look on, be an onlooker.
mirar [1a] **1** *vt* (**a**) (*gen*) to look at; to gaze at; (*observar*) to watch; **miraba la foto** she was looking at the photo;

miraba los barcos she was watching the boats; **la miré subir la escalera** I watched her go (*o* going) upstairs; **le miraron la cartera** they looked at his wallet; **~ fijamente a uno** to stare at sb, look hard at sb; **~ algo por encima** to glance over sth, glance cursorily at sth.

(**b**) (*fig: pensar*) to consider, think over, think carefully about; **lo hago mirando el porvenir** I do it bearing the future in mind; **no mira las dificultades** he doesn't take account of the difficulties; **mirándolo bien** all in all; by rights; on second thoughts; **¡mira lo que haces!** just think what you're doing!; **¡mira con quien hablas!** just remember who you're talking to!

(**c**) **~ a uno como** (*fig: considerar*) to look on sb as, consider sb to be.

(**d**) (*fig: vigilar*) to watch, keep an eye on, be careful about; **conviene ~ el bolso** it's best to keep an eye on your handbag.

(**e**) (*fig: estimar*) to value, think highly of; **~ bien** to like; **~ mal** to dislike.

(**f**) (*LAm*) to see.

2 *vi* (**a**) (*gen*) to look; to glance; **no habla pero mira mucho** he never speaks but he keeps on looking; **¡mira!, ¡mire!** look!; (*protesta*) look here!; **¡pero mire!** now look here!; **¡mira que no tenemos dinero!** remember that we haven't any money!; **¡mira lo que tenemos que aguantar!** look at what we have to put up with!; **¡mira que si es mentira!** just suppose it isn't true!, what if it's not true?; **mira si ha venido el taxi** look and see if the taxi has come; **¡(pues) mira por donde ...!** just imagine ...!; surprise, surprise!; **~ alrededor** to look around; **~ atrás** to look back (*fig*), think about the past; **~ hacia otro lado** to look the other way; **~ por la ventana** to look out of the window; **~ por un agujero** to look through a hole; **~ de través** to squint (*V t* **través 2**).

(**b**) (*Arquit*) to face; to look on to, open on to; **la casa mira al sur** the house faces south.

(**c**) **~ a** (*fig*) to aim at, have in mind.

(**d**) **por lo que mira a** as for, as regards.

(**e**) (*fig*) **~ por** to look after, take care of; **~ por sí** to look out for o.s., consider one's own safety.

3 mirarse *vr* (**a**) (*gen*) to look at o.s.; **~ al espejo** to look at o.s. in the mirror.

(**b**) (*2 personas*) to look at one another; **nos miramos asombrados** we looked at each other in amazement; **~ a los ojos** to look into each other's eyes.

(**c**) **se mire como se mire** whichever way one looks at it; **~ muy bien de hacer algo** to think twice about doing sth; to think carefully before doing sth; **~ en ello** to watch one's step.

mirasol *nm* sunflower.

miríada *nf* myriad; **~(s) de moscas** a myriad flies.

mirilla *nf* peephole, spyhole; (*Fot*) viewer.

miriñaque *nm* (**a**) (*Hist*) crinoline, hoop skirt. (**b**) (*Cono Sur Ferro*) cowcatcher. (**c**) (*Carib, Méx*) thin cotton cloth.

miriópodo *nm* millipede; myriapod.

miristiquívoro *adj* myristicivorous.

mirlarse [1a] *vr* to put on airs, act important.

mirlo *nm* (**a**) (*Orn*) blackbird.

(**b**) **~ blanco** (*fig*) exceptional thing, highly unusual thing; one in a million; impossible dream.

(**c**) (*fig*) self-important air, pompousness.

(**d**) (‡: *lengua*) tongue; **achantar el ~** to shut one's trap‡.

mirobrigense 1 *adj* of Ciudad Rodrigo. **2** *nmf* native (*o* inhabitant) of Ciudad Rodrigo; **los ~s** the people of Ciudad Rodrigo.

mirón 1 *adj* inquisitive, curious.

2 *nm*, **mirona** *nf* (*espectador*) onlooker, watcher, observer; (*pey*) nosey-parker*; (*voyer*) voyeur; (*Naipes*) kibitzer; **los mirones son de piedra** those watching the game are not allowed to speak; **estar de ~** to look on (without doing anything); to stand by (doing nothing); **ir de ~** to go along just to see.

mironismo *nm* voyeurism.

mirra *nf* (**a**) myrrh. (**b**) (*Carib: trocito*) small piece.

mirtilo *nm* bilberry, whortleberry.

mirto *nm* myrtle.

mis *nf* = **miss.**

misa *nf* mass; **~ del alba** early morning mass; **~ del gallo** midnight mass (on Christmas Eve); **~ mayor, ~ solemne** high mass; **~ negra** black mass; **~ rezada** low mass; **como en ~** in dead silence; **celebrar** (*o* **decir**) **~** to celebrate mass; **ir a ~** to go to mass, go to church; **oír ~** to go to mass, attend mass; **ser como ~ de pobre** to last all too short a time; **no saben de la ~ la media** they don't know the half of it; **eso va a ~** (*fig*) that's the honest truth; **estos datos van a ~** (*fig*) these facts are utterly trustworthy.

misacantano *nm* priest saying his first mass; ordained priest.

misal *nm* missal.

misantropía *nf* misanthropy.

misantrópico *adj* misanthropic.

misántropo, -a *nm/f* misanthrope, misanthropist.

misario *nm* acolyte, altar boy.

miscelánea *nf* (**a**) (*lit*) miscellany. (**b**) (*Méx*) corner shop.

misceláneo *adj* miscellaneous.

misera *nf* lobster.

miserable 1 *adj* (**a**) *persona* mean, stingy; miserly; *suma etc* miserable, paltry, pitifully small.

(**b**) (*moralmente*) rotten*, vile, contemptible, despicable; **¡~!** you rotter!*, you wretch!

(**c**) *cuarto, lugar etc* squalid, sordid.

2 *nmf* wretch; rotter*, cad; **¡eres un ~!** you're a rotter!*

miserando *adj* (*esp LAm*) pitiful.

miseria *nf* (**a**) (*pobreza*) poverty, destitution; (*carencia*) want; **caer en la ~** to fall into abject poverty; **vivir en la ~** to live in poverty.

(**b**) (*condiciones*) squalor, squalid conditions.

(**c**) (*piojos*) fleas, lice; **estar lleno de ~** to be covered with vermin.

(**d**) **una ~** (*Fin*) a tiny sum, a mere pittance; a tiny amount.

(**e**) (*tacañería*) meanness, stinginess.

misericordia *nf* (**a**) (*compasión*) pity, compassion. (**b**) (*perdón*) forgiveness; mercy.

misericordioso *adj* (*V nf*) (**a**) compassionate. (**b**) forgiving; merciful.

misero* *adj* churchy, fond of going to church.

mísero *adj* (**a**) (*desgraciado*) wretched. (**b**) = **miserable.**

misérrimo *adj* utterly wretched.

misil *nm* missile; **~ de alcance medio** medium-range missile; **~ antimisil** antimissile missile; **~ autodirigido** guided missile; **~ balístico** ballistic missile; **~ buscador del calor** heat-seeking missile; **~ (de) crucero** cruise missile; **~ tierra-aire** ground-to-air missile.

misilístico *adj* missile (*atr*).

misión *nf* mission; job, task; **misiones** missions, missionary work (*Ecl*); **~ investigadora** fact-finding mission; **~ de buena voluntad** goodwill mission.

misional *adj* missionary.

misionero, -a *nm/f* missionary.

Misisipí *nm* Mississippi.

misiva *nf* missive.

miskito *nm* Miskito.

mismamente* *adv* (*sólo*) only, just; (*literalmente*) literally; (*hasta*) even; (*en realidad*) really, actually; **ayer ~ vino** it was only yesterday he came.

mismísimo *adj superl* selfsame, very same; **por mis ~s ojos** with my very own eyes; **es Vd el ~ diablo** you're the very devil in person; **estuvo el ~ obispo** the bishop himself was there; **es el ~ que yo perdí** it's the very (same) one I lost; **estoy hasta los ~s*** I'm utterly fed up*.

mismo 1 *adj* (**a**) (*lit*) same (*que* as, that); **el ~ coche** the same car; **viven en la misma calle** they live in the same street; **es el ~ que vi ayer** it's the same (one) as I saw yesterday; **el policía y el ladrón son el ~** the policeman and the thief are one and the same; **quedar en las mismas** to be no further forward, show no progress.

(**b**) (*con* **lo**) **lo ~** the same, the same thing; **es lo ~** it's the same thing, it comes to the same thing; **no es lo ~** it's not the same (at all); **él diría lo ~** he would say the same; **por lo ~** for the same reason; **lo ~ A que B** both A and B; **o lo que es lo ~** or what amounts to the same thing; **lo ~ si viene que si no viene** whether he comes or not; **lo ~ no vienen** they may (equally well) not come; *V* **dar.**

(**c**) (*con pron pers*) -self; **yo ~** I myself; **yo ~ lo vi** I saw it myself; **lo hizo por sí ~** he did it by himself; **perjudicarse a sí ~** to harm one's own interests.

(**d**) (*enfático*) very; selfsame; **en ese ~ momento** at that very moment; **en Argentina misma, en la misma Argentina** in Argentina itself; **hoy ~** this very day; **ayer ~** only yesterday; **estuvo el ~ ministro** the (very) minister himself was there; **ella es la misma caridad** she is charity itself; **eso ~ digo yo** that's just what I say.

(**e**) (*Méx: relativo*) **~ que** who; which.

2 *adv* right; **aquí ~** right here, on this very spot; **ayer ~**

only yesterday; **delante ~ de la casa** right in front of the house.

3 *como conj*: **lo ~ que** just like, just as (if); **lo ~ que Vd es médico yo soy ingeniero** just as you are a doctor I am an engineer; **nos divertimos lo ~ que si hubiéramos ido al baile** we had just as good a time as if we had gone to the dance; **lo ~ que me levanto a las 6 me levantaría a las 5** just as I get up at 6 so I would gladly get up at 5.

misogamia *nf* misogamy.
misógamo, -a *nm/f* misogamist.
misoginia *nf* misogyny.
misógino *nm* misogynist.
miss [mis] *nf* beauty queen; **M~ España** Miss Spain.
míster *nm* (**a**) (*hum*) (any) Briton. (**b**) (*Dep*) trainer, coach.
misterio *nm* (**a**) (*gen*) mystery; **no hay ~** there's no mystery about it. (**b**) (*lo secreto*) secrecy; **obrar con ~** to go about sth secretly, go to work in secrecy. (**c**) (*Teat: Hist*) mystery play.
misteriosamente *adv* mysteriously; puzzlingly.
misterioso *adj* mysterious; mystifying, puzzling.
mística[1] *nf*, **misticismo** *nm* mysticism.
místico 1 *adj* mystic(al). **2** *nm*, **mística**[2] *nf* mystic.
mistificación *nf* (**a**) (*broma*) hoax, practical joke; (*jerga etc*) hocus-pocus. (**b**) **sin mistificaciones** plain, without frills, with no nonsense about it; **una persona no dada a mistificaciones** a no-nonsense person.
mistificar [1g] *vt* (**a**) (*embromar*) to hoax, play a practical joke on; (*engañar*) to hoodwink, take in. (**b**) (*confundir*) to mix up, make a mess of. (**c**) (*falsificar*) to falsify.
mistongo* *adj* (*Cono Sur*) wretched, miserable.
Misurí *nm* Missouri.
mitad *nf* (**a**) (*gen*) half; **~ y ~** half-and-half; (*fig*) so-so, yes and no; **es ~ blanco y ~ rojo** it's half white and half red; **mi otra ~, mi cara ~** my better half; **me queda la ~** I have half left; **a ~ de precio** half-price, at half the cost; **reducir en una ~** to cut by half, halve.

(**b**) (*centro*) middle; **a ~ de, en ~ de** halfway along (*o* through *etc*); **a ~ de la distancia entre A y Z** halfway between A and Z; **está a la ~** it's half empty, it's half gone (*etc*); **estar a ~ de camino** to be halfway there; **atravesar de ~ a ~** to pierce right through; **hacia la ~ de la película** halfway through the film; **cortar por la ~** to cut down the middle; **partir a uno por la ~** (*fig*) to upset sb's plans, queer sb's pitch; *V* **dividir**.

(**c**) (*Dep*) half; **la primera ~** the first half.

mítico *adj* mythical.
mitificar [1g] *vt* to mythologize, convert into a myth.
mitigación *nf* mitigation; relief; quenching; appeasement; tempering; reduction.
mitigar [1h] *vt* (*gen*) to mitigate, allay; *dolor* to relieve; *sed* to quench; *ira* to appease, mollify; *dureza etc* to temper, mitigate; *inquietud* to allay; *calor* to reduce; *soledad* to alleviate, relieve.
mitin *nm* (**a**) (*esp Pol: reunión*) meeting; **~ popular** mass meeting, rally. (**b**) (*discurso*) political speech; (*pey*) rabble-rousing speech; **dar un ~** to make a speech. (**c**) (*) rumpus*, riot, rough-house*; **dar el** (*o* **un**) **~*** to kick up a fuss.
mitinear [1a] *vi* to make a (political) speech; (*pey*) to make a rabble-rousing speech.
mitinero 1 *adj* demagogic, rabble-rousing. **2** *nm*, **mitinera** *nf* demagogue, rabble-rouser.
mitinesco *adj* rabble-rousing; (*fig*) rowdy, rough.
mito *nm* myth.
mitología *nf* mythology.
mitológico *adj* mythological.
mitómano, -a *nm/f* myth-maker, person who exaggerates; (*pey*) liar.
mitón *nm* mitten.
mitote *nm* (*Méx*) (*Hist*) *Aztec ritual dance*; (*: *pelea*) brawl; (*: *jaleo*) uproar; (*: *charla*) gossip, chat; **estar en el ~** to have a chat.
Mitra *nm* Mithras.
mitra *nf* mitre.
mitrado *nm* bishop, prelate.
mitraico *adj* Mithraic.
mitraísmo *nm* Mithraism.
mítulo *nm* mussel.
mixomatosis *nf* myxomatosis.
Mixteca *nf* (*Méx*) southern Mexico.
mixteco *nm*: **el ~** (*Méx Hist*) (*pueblo*) the Mixtecs; (*civilización*) Mixtec civilization.
mixtificar [1g] *vt* = **mistificar**.
mixtión *nf* mixture.
mixto 1 *adj* mixed. **2** *nm* (**a**) (*fósforo*) match; (*Mil*) explosive compound. (**b**) (*Ferro*) passenger and goods train.
mixtolobo *nm* Alsatian (dog).
mixtura *nf* mixture (*t Farm*).
mixturar [1a] *vt* to mix.
ml. *abr de* **mililitro** millilitre, ml.
mm. *abr de* **milímetro** millimetre, mm.
m/n (*Fin*) *abr de* **moneda nacional**.
mnemónica *nf*, **mnemotécnica** *nf* mnemonics.
mnemotécnico *adj* mnemonic.
M.º (**a**) (*Pol*) *abr de* **Ministerio** Ministry, Min. (**b**) (*Escol*) *abr de* **Maestro** Master.
M.O. *abr de* **mano de obra** manpower.
m/o (*Com*) *abr de* **mi orden** my order.
moaré *nm* moiré.
mobiliario *nm* (*muebles*) furniture; (*artículos domésticos*) household goods; (*juego*) suite (of furniture); **~ y enseres** furnishings and fittings; **~ sanitario** bathroom furnishings.
moblaje *nm* = **mobiliario**.
moca[1] *nm* mocha.
moca[2] *nf* quagmire, muddy place.
moca[3] *nf* (*Méx*) coffee-flavoured cake (*o* biscuit).
mocarro *nm* mucus, snot*.
mocasín *nm* moccasin.
mocear [1a] *vi* to play around, live a bit wildly, sow one's wild oats.
mocedad *nf* (**a**) (*juventud*) youth; **en mis ~es** in my young days. (**b**) **~es** (*bromas*) youthful pranks; (*vida desordenada*) wild living; **pasar las ~es** to sow one's wild oats.
moceril *adj* youthful; typical of youth.
mocerío *nm* young people, lads and lasses (*collectively*).
mocero *adj* rakish, loose-living; fond of the girls.
mocetón *nm* strapping youth.
mocetona *nf* big girl, hefty wench.
moción *nf* (**a**) (*movimiento*) motion, movement. (**b**) (*Parl etc*) motion; **~ de censura** motion of censure, censure motion; **~ de confianza** vote of confidence; **hacer** (*o* **presentar** *o* **plantar**) **una ~** to propose a motion.
mocionante *nmf* (*LAm*) proposer (of a motion).
mocionar [1a] *vti* (*LAm*) to move, propose.
mocito 1 *adj* very young. **2** *nm*, **mocita** *nf* youngster.
moco *nm* (**a**) (*gen*) mucus; snot*; **limpiarse los ~s** to blow one's nose; **llorar a ~ y baba, llorar a ~ tendido** to sob one's heart out, cry uncontrollably; **soltar el ~** to burst into tears; **tirarse el ~*** (*vacilar*) to hesitate; (*mentir*) to lie; (*exagerar*) to exaggerate, shoot a line*.

(**b**) (*Orn*) crest; **no es ~ de pavo** it's not just a small thing; you can't laugh this one off.

(**c**) (*mecha*) snuff, burnt wick; (*gotas*) candle grease, candle drippings; **a ~ de candil** by candlelight.

(**d**) (*Téc*) slag.

(**e**) (*: *farol*) brag, boast; tall story.

mocoso 1 *adj* (*lloroso*) snivelling; (*fig*) ill-bred, rude. **2** *nm*, **mocosa*** *nf* brat; (*LAm*) child.
mocha‡ *nf* (*Esp*) nut‡, head.
mochales‡ *adj*: **estar ~** (*Esp*) to be round the bend‡.
mochar [1a] *vt* (**a**) = **desmochar**. (**b**) (*And, Carib*) (*cortar*) to chop off, hack off (clumsily); (*Med*) to amputate. (**c**) (*Cono Sur*: robar*) to pinch*. (**d**) (*And*: despedir*) to fire*, sack*.
mochila *nf* rucksack, knapsack, back-pack (*US*); (*Mil*) pack; (*de bicicleta*) bag, basket; (*Cono Sur*) school satchel; **~ portabebés** baby-carrier; **tener algo casi en la ~*** to have sth almost in the bag*.
mochilero, -a *nm/f* back-packer.
mocho 1 *adj* (**a**) (*truncado*) cut off, short, truncated; *muñón* stubby; *herramienta etc* blunt, short; *árbol* lopped, pollarded; *vaca* hornless, polled; *torre* flat-topped; (*) *persona* shorn; (*LAm*) mutilated; (*Carib*) one-armed.

(**b**) (*And: grande*) big, huge.

(**c**) (*CAm, Méx*) (*reaccionario*) reactionary; (*beato*) sanctimonious.

2 *nm* (**a**) (*de cigarrillo*) butt; (*de utensilio*) blunt end, thick end.

(**b**) (*: *tarea*) burden, chore, bind*; **cargar con el ~** to get landed with it; to carry the can*; **colgar** (*o* **echar**) **el ~ a uno** to lumber sb with the job*, (*culpa*) to make sb carry the can*, (*crimen*) to frame sb.

(**c**) (*And, Carib*: caballo*) nag.

3 *nm*, **mocha** *nf* (**a**) (*CAm*: huérfano*) orphan.

(**b**) (*Méx*) (*reaccionario*) reactionary; (*beato*) bigot.

mochuelo *nm* (**a**) (*Orn*: *t* **~ común**) little owl; **cada ~ a su**

sitio everything in its place. (**b**) (*) = **mocho** (**b**). (**c**) (**) cunt**.

moda *nf* fashion; style; **a la ~** (*adj*) in fashion, fashionable; (*adv*) fashionably; **un sombrero a la ~** a fashionable hat; **a la ~ de** after the fashion of; **estar a la ~** to be in fashion, be fashionable; **ponerse a la ~** to smarten up, get some new clothes; (*) to get with it*; **de ~** in fashion, fashionable; **fuera de ~** out of fashion; **pasado de ~** old-fashioned, out-dated; **pasarse de ~** to go out of fashion; **ponerse de ~** to become fashionable; **estar muy de ~** to be highly fashionable; **ha entrado la ~ de las medias amarillas** yellow stockings have come in, yellow stockings are in*.

modal 1 *adj* modal.

2 ~es *nmpl* manners.

modalidad *nf* (*clase*) form, kind, variety; (*moda*) fashion; (*manera*) way; **una nueva ~ teatral** a new dramatic form; a new fashion in the theatre; **~ de pago** (*Com*) method of payment; **~ de texto** (*Inform*) text mode; **hay varias ~es del juego** there are various forms of the game, there are several ways of playing the game.

modelado *nm* modelling.

modelador(a) *nm/f* modeller.

modelaje *nm* modelling.

modelar [1a] **1** *vt* (**a**) (*lit*) to model (*sobre, según* on). (**b**) (*formar*) to fashion, shape, form. **2 modelarse** *vr*: **~ sobre** to model o.s. on.

modélicamente *adv* in a model way, in an exemplary fashion.

modélico *adj* model, ideal, exemplary.

modelismo *nm* modelling, model-making.

modelista *nmf* model-maker.

modelización *nf* modelling, creation of models; **~ cognoscitiva** cognitive modelling.

modelizar [1f] *vt* to model, create a model of.

modelo 1 *nm* (**a**) (*gen*) model; (*patrón*) pattern; (*norma*) standard; (*para hacer punto*) pattern; **~ a escala** scale model; **~ de maridos** model husband; **~ de vida** lifestyle, way of life; **presentar algo como un ~** to hold sth up as a model; **servir de ~** to serve as a model; **tomar por ~** to take as a model.

(**b**) (*Méx: forma*) blank form.

2 *nmf* (*Alta Costura, Arte, Fot*) model; **~ de portada** cover-girl; **servir de ~ a un pintor** to sit for a painter, pose for a painter.

3 *atr* model; ideal, exemplary; **cárcel ~** model prison; **empresa ~** model company; pilot plant; **marido ~** model husband; **un coche último ~** a latest-model car.

módem *nm* modem.

moderación *nf* moderation; **~ salarial** wage restraint; **con ~** in moderation.

moderadamente *adv* moderately.

moderado *adj* moderate.

moderador(a) *nm/f* (*TV etc*) presenter.

moderar [1a] **1** *vt* to moderate; *violencia* to restrain, control; *velocidad* to reduce. **2 moderarse** *vr* (*fig*) to restrain o.s., control o.s.; to calm down.

modernamente *adv* nowadays, in modern times; (*recientemente*) recently.

modernez *nf* (**a**) (*calidad*) modernity. (**b**) (*truco*) gimmick.

modernidad *nf* modernity.

modernismo *nm* modernism.

modernista 1 *adj* modernist(ic). **2** *nmf* modernist.

modernización *nf* modernization.

modernizador 1 *adj* modernizing. **2** *nm*, **modernizadora** *nf* modernizer.

modernizar [1f] **1** *vt* to modernize. **2 modernizarse** *vr* to modernize (o.s.); to catch up, get up to date.

moderno 1 *adj* modern; present-day; up-to-date; **a la moderna** in the modern way; modern. **2** *nm*, **moderna** *nf* trendy.

modestamente *adv* modestly.

modestia *nf* modesty.

modesto *adj* modest.

modex *nm* (*Carib*) press-on sanitary towel.

modicidad *nf* reasonableness, moderateness.

módico *adj* reasonable, moderate; **la módica suma de ...** the modest sum of ...

modificable *adj* modifiable, that can be modified; **los precios son ~s** the prices are subject to change.

modificación *nf* modification; **~ de (la) conducta** change of behaviour.

modificar [1g] *vt* to modify.

modismo *nm* idiom.

modista *nf* dressmaker, modiste; **~ de sombreros** milliner.

modistilla *nf* seamstress.

modisto *nmf* fashion designer, couturier/couturière.

modo *nm* (**a**) (*manera*) way, manner; (*estilo*) fashion; (*método*) mode, method; **'~ de empleo'** (*en etiqueta*) 'instructions for use'; **~ de gobierno** form of government; **~ de pensar** way of thinking; **según mi ~ de pensar** according to my way of thinking; **~ de ser** = **manera de ser; a mi ~ de ver** in my view; as I see it; **¡ni ~!** (*Méx*) but what can you do!

(**b**) (*locuciones con prep*) **a mi ~** in my (own) way; **a ~ de** like; **uno a ~ de saco** a sort of bag, some kind of bag; **al ~ inglés** in the English way (*o* style); **de este ~** (in) this way, like this; **de ese ~** (*fig*) at that rate; **del mismo ~ (que)**, **de igual ~ (que)** in the same way (as), just (as); **del mismo ~ otros dicen que no** similarly, others say no; **de igual ~, ...** in the same way, ...; **¡de ~ que sí fuiste tú!** so it was you after all!; **de diversos ~s** in various ways; **declaraba su edad de diversos ~s** she gave her several different versions of her age; **de un ~ o de otro** (in) one way or another; by some means or other; *para otras locuciones, V* **manera** (**a**), (**b**).

(**c**) (*modales*) **~s** manners; **buenos ~s** good manners; **contestar con buenos ~s** to answer courteously; **contestar con malos ~s** to answer rudely.

(**d**) (*Inform, Mús*) mode.

(**e**) (*Ling*) mood; **~ imperativo** imperative mood; **~ indicativo** indicative mood; **~ subjuntivo** subjunctive mood.

(**f**) (*fig*) moderation; **beber con ~** to drink in moderation.

modorra *nf* (**a**) (*sueño*) drowsiness, heaviness. (**b**) (*Vet*) staggers.

modorro *adj* (**a**) (*soñoliento*) drowsy, heavy. (**b**) *fruta* soft, sleepy. (**c**) (*: *tonto*) dull, stupid.

modoso *adj* quiet, well-mannered, nicely-behaved; *muchacha* demure.

modulación *nf* modulation; **~ de frecuencia** frequency modulation.

modulado *adj* modulated.

modulador *nm* modulator.

modulador-demodulador *nm* (*Inform*) modem.

modular [1a] **1** *adj* modular. **2** *vt* to modulate. **3** *nm* (*Cono Sur*) shelf unit.

modularidad *nf* modularity.

módulo *nm* module; (*And*) platform; **~ lunar** lunar module; **~ de mando** command module.

moer *nm* moiré.

mofa *nf* (**a**) (*gen*) mockery, ridicule, derision; **exponer a uno a la ~ pública** to hold sb up to public ridicule; **hacer ~ de** to scoff at, jeer at. (**b**) (*una ~*) jibe, taunt, sneer.

mofador 1 *adj* mocking, scoffing, sneering. **2** *nm*, **mofadora** *nf* mocker, scoffer.

mofar [1a] **1** *vi* to mock, scoff, sneer. **2 mofarse** *vr*: **~ de** to mock, scoff at, sneer at.

mofeta *nf* (**a**) (*Zool*) skunk. (**b**) (*Min*) firedamp, mephitis. (**c**) (**) fart**.

mofinco* *nm* (*Carib*) firewater*, gut-rot*.

mofle *nm* (*Méx Aut*) silencer.

moflete *nm* (**a**) (*mejilla*) fat cheek. (**b**) **~s** (*fig*) chubbiness.

mofletudo *adj* fat-cheeked, chubby.

mogol: = **mongol; el Gran M~** the Great Mogul.

Mogolia *nf* = **Mongolia.**

mogolla *nf* (*And, Cono Sur*) bargain.

mogollón* 1 *nm* (**a**) (*t* **mogollona** *nf*) (*gorrón*) sponger*, hanger-on; spiv*; (*en fiesta etc*) gatecrasher; **colarse de ~ en un sitio** to get into a place without paying; **comer de ~** to scrounge a meal*; **lograr un puesto de ~** to wangle a job*.

(**b**) (*lío*) fuss, row.

(**c**) (*cantidad*) large amount, mass; **gente a ~, un ~ de gente** a mass of people, loads of people; **tengo un ~ de discos*** I've got loads of records.

2 *adv V* **cantidad 2.**

mogollónico* *adj* huge, colossal.

mogote *nm* (*otero*) flat-topped hillock; (*pila*) heap, pile; (*de gavillas etc*) stack, rick.

mohair [mo'xair, mo'air] *nm* mohair.

mohín *nm* (wry) face, grimace; pout; **hacer un ~** to make a face; **con un leve ~ de chanza** with a faintly humorous expression.

mohína *nf* (**a**) (*enfado*) annoyance, displeasure; (*rencor*) resentment. (**b**) (*una ~*) grudge. (**c**) (*mal humor*) the sulks, sulkiness; **ser fácil a las ~s** to be easily depressed.

mohíno *adj* (*triste*) gloomy, depressed; (*malhumorado*) sulky, sullen; (*rencoroso*) resentful; (*displicente*) peevish.

moho *nm* (**a**) (*en metal*) rust.

(**b**) (*Bot*) mould, mildew; **cubierto de ~** mouldy, mildewed.

(**c**) (*pereza*) lazy feeling; workshyness; **no cría ~** he doesn't let the grass grow under his feet, he's always on the go; **no dejar criar ~ a uno** to keep sb on the go.

mohoso *adj* (**a**) (*metal*) rusty. (**b**) (*Bot*) mouldy, mildewed; musty. (**c**) (*fig*) *chiste etc* stale.

Moisés *nm* Moses.

moisés *nm* Moses basket, cradle; carrycot.

moja‡ *nf* stab, thrust; stab wound.

mojada 1 *nf* (**a**) (*al mojarse*) wetting, soaking. (**b**) (*herida*) stab (wound).

mojado 1 *adj* wet; damp, moist; drenched, soaked; **llover sobre ~** to be quite unnecessary, be entirely superfluous; **luego llovió sobre ~** then on top of all that sth else happened; **llueve sobre ~** it never rains but it pours. **2** *nm* (*Méx*) wetback (*US*), illegal immigrant.

mojadura *nf* wetting, soaking.

mojama *nf* salted tuna.

mojar [1a] **1** *vt* (**a**) (*gen*) to wet; (*humedecer*) to damp(en), moisten; (*empapar*) to drench, soak; **~la**** to have a screw**; **la lluvia mojó a todos** the rain soaked everybody; **moje ligeramente el sello** moisten the stamp a little; **~ la ropa en un líquido** to soak (*o* steep) clothes in a liquid.

(**b**) **~ la pluma en la tinta** to dip one's pen into the ink; **~ el pan en el café** to dip one's bread into one's coffee.

(**c**) (*Ling*) to palatalize.

(**d**) (*apuñalar*) to stab.

(**e**) (*) *triunfo etc* to celebrate (with a drink).

(**f**) (*Carib*) to tip; (*Carib**: *sobornar*) to bribe.

2 *vi* (**a**) (**) to have a screw**. (**b**) **~ en** (*fig*) to dabble in; to meddle in, get involved in.

3 mojarse *vr* (**a**) to get wet; to get drenched, get soaked; **~ las orejas** (*Cono Sur fig*) to give way, back down. (**b**) (*) **no se mojó** he kept out of it, he didn't get involved.

mojarra *nf* (**a**) (‡: *lengua*) tongue. (**b**) (*LAm*) short broad knife.

mojera *nf* whitebeam.

mojicón *nm* (**a**) (*Culin*) sponge cake; bun. (**b**) (*: *bofetada*) punch in the face, biff*, slap.

mojiganga *nf* (*Hist*) masquerade, mummery; (*farsa*) farce, piece of clowning.

mojigatería *nf* hypocrisy; sanctimoniousness, affected piety; prudery, prudishness.

mojigato 1 *adj* (*hipócrita*) hypocritical; (*santurrón*) sanctimonious, affectedly pious; (*gazmoño*) prudish, strait-laced. **2** *nm*, **mojigata** *nf* hypocrite; sanctimonious person; prude.

mojinete *nm* (*de techo*) ridge; (*de muro*) tiling, coping.

mojito *nm* (*Cuba*) long drink with a base of rum.

mojo *nm* (*Méx*) garlic sauce.

mojón 1 *nm* (**a**) (*hito*) landmark; (*piedra*) boundary stone; (*t* **~ kilométrico**) milestone; (*señal*) signpost; (*montón*) heap, pile.

(**b**) (*And***) shit**; crap**.

2 *nm*, **mojona** *nf* (*Carib*‡) (*bruto*) idiot, thickhead*; (*chaparro*) shortie*.

mol. (*Fís*) *abr de* **molécula** molecule, mol.

mola *nf* rounded mountain.

molar[1] *nm* molar.

molar[2]* [1a] **1** *vt* (*gustar*) to please; to suit; **lo que más me mola es ...** what I'm really into is ...*; **lo que mola mil** (*Esp*) what gets people really going; **tía, me molas mucho** (*Esp*) I'm crazy about you, baby*; **¿te mola un pitillo?** would you like a smoke?; **no me mola** I don't go for that*, I don't fancy that.

2 *vi* (**a**) (*estar de moda*) to be in*, be fashionable; **eso mola mucho ahora** that's very in now*, it's all the rage now.

(**b**) (*dar tono*) to be classy*, be real posh*.

(**c**) (*darse tono*) to swank*.

(**d**) (*valer*) to be OK*; **por partes iguales, ¿mola?** equal shares then, OK?*

(**e**) **la cosa no mola** (*marchar*) it's not going well at all.

molcajete *nm* (*Méx*) mortar.

molde *nm* (**a**) (*Téc*) mould; (*Culin*) mould, shape; (*vaciado etc*) cast; (*Tip*) forme; **romper ~s** (*fig*) to break the mould.

(**b**) (*Cos*) (*patrón*) pattern; (*aguja*) knitting needle.

(**c**) (*fig*) model.

(**d**) **de ~** perfect, just right; **el vestido le está de ~** the dress suits her perfectly, the dress is just right for (*o* on) her; **venir de ~** to come just right; *V* **letra**.

moldear [1a] *vt* (**a**) (*gen*) to mould, shape; (*en yeso etc*) to cast. (**b**) (*fig*) to mould, shape, form.

moldeo *nm* moulding.

moldura *nf* moulding; **~ lateral** (*Aut*) side stripe.

mole[1] *nf* (*masa*) mass, bulk; (*de edificio*) pile; **se sentó con toda su ~** he sat down with his full weight; **la enorme ~ del buque** the vast mass of the ship; **esa mujer es una ~** that woman is massive.

mole[2] *nm* (*Méx*) black chili sauce; **~ de olla** meat stew; **ser el ~ de uno*** to be sb's favourite thing.

molécula *nf* molecule.

molecular *adj* molecular.

moledor 1 *adj* (**a**) (*que muele*) grinding, crushing. (**b**) (*) boring. **2** *nm* (**a**) (*Téc*) grinder, crusher; roller. (**b**) (*) bore.

moledora *nf* (*Téc*) grinder, crusher; mill.

moler [2h] *vt* (**a**) *café etc* to grind; (*machacar*) to crush; (*pulverizar*) to pound; *trigo* to mill; (*) to chew (up); **~ a uno a palos** to beat sb up*.

(**b**) (*fig*) (*cansar*) to tire out, weary, exhaust; **estoy molida de tanto trabajar** all that work has left me exhausted.

(**c**) (*fig*) (*fastidiar*) to annoy; (*aburrir*) to bore.

molestar [1a] **1** *vt* (*fastidiar*) to annoy; (*incomodar*) to bother, inconvenience, put out; (*incordiar*) to upset; (*dolor*) to trouble, bother, hurt; **me molesta ese ruido** that noise upsets me, that noise gets on my nerves; **¿te molesta el ruido?** do you mind (*o* object to) the noise?, does the noise bother you?; **los críos me molestan para estudiar*** the kids disturb my work*, the kids stop me working*; **me molesta tener que repetirlo** I hate having to repeat it; **¿te molesta que abra la ventana?** do you mind if I open the window?; **¿te molesta que fume?** will it bother you if I smoke?

2 *vi* (*fastidiar*) to be a nuisance; (*estorbar*) to get in the way, be awkward; **no quiero ~** I don't want to intrude, I don't want to be in the way, I don't wish to cause any trouble.

3 molestarse *vr* (**a**) (*darse trabajo*) to bother (*con* about); (*incomodarse*) to go to trouble, put o.s. out; **~ en** + *infin* to bother to + *infin*; **¡no se moleste!** don't bother!, don't trouble yourself!

(**b**) (*enfadarse*) to get cross; (*ofenderse*) to take offence, get upset; **se molesta por nada** he gets annoyed at the slightest thing.

molestia *nf* bother, trouble, nuisance; inconvenience; (*Med*) discomfort; **es una ~** it's a nuisance; **no es ~** it's no trouble; **ahorrarse ~s** to save o.s. trouble, spare o.s. effort; **darse la ~ de** + *infin*, **tomarse la ~ de** + *infin* to take the trouble to + *infin*, go out of one's way to + *infin*.

molesto *adj* (**a**) (*que fastidia*) troublesome, annoying; (*pesado*) trying, tiresome; (*incómodo*) inconvenient; *tarea* irksome; *olor, sabor* nasty; **es muy ~ para mí** it's very inconvenient for me; **si no es ~ para Vd** if it's no trouble to you; **es una persona muy molesta** she's a very trying person.

(**b**) (*descontento*) discontented; (*inquieto*) restless; (*incómodo*) ill-at-ease; uncomfortable; (*ofendido*) upset, offended; (*azorado*) embarrassed; **estar ~** (*Med*) to be in some discomfort; **estar ~ con uno** to be cross with sb; **me sentí ~** I felt uncomfortable, I felt embarrassed.

molestoso *adj* (*And, Carib, Cono Sur*) annoying.

molibdeno *nm* molybdenum.

molicie *nf* (**a**) (*blandura*) softness. (**b**) (*fig*) soft living, luxurious living; effeminacy.

molido *adj* (**a**) (*machacado*) ground, crushed; (*pulverizado*) powdered. (**b**) **estar ~** (*fig*) to be exhausted, be dead beat; **estoy ~ de tanto viajar** I'm exhausted with all this travelling.

molienda *nf* (**a**) (*acto*) grinding; milling. (**b**) (*trigo*) quantity of corn (*etc*) to be ground. (**c**) (*molino*) mill. (**d**) (*: *cansancio*) weariness. (**e**) (*: *molestia*) nuisance.

molinero *nm* miller.

molinete *nm* (toy) windmill.

molinillo *nm* (**a**) (*gen*) hand mill; **~ de aceite** olive press; **~ de café** coffee-mill, coffee grinder; **~ de carne** mincer. (**b**) (*juguete*) (toy) windmill.

molino *nm* (**a**) (*gen*) mill; (*trituradora*) grinder; **~ de agua** water mill; **~ de cubo** water-wheel; **~ de viento** windmill. (**b**) (*) (*inquieto*) restless person; (*pesado*) bore, tedious individual.

molo *nm* (*Cono Sur*) breakwater, seawall.

molón* *adj* (**a**) (*bueno*) super*, smashing*. (**b**) (*Esp: elegante*) posh*, classy*. (**c**) (*Esp: engreído*) swanky*, stuck-up*. (**d**) (*CAm, Méx*) tiresome.
molondra‡ *nf* bonce‡, head.
molote *nm* (**a**) (*Méx: ovillo*) ball of wool (*etc*). (**b**) (*Méx Culin*) fried maize pancake. (**c**) (*And, Méx*) dirty trick. (**d**) (*CAm, Carib, Méx*) riot, commotion.
molotov *nm*: **cóctel** (*o* **bomba**) ~ Molotov cocktail.
molturar [1a] *vt* to grind, mill.
molusco *nm* mollusc.
mollar *adj* (**a**) *fruta* soft, tender; easily shelled. (**b**) *carne* boned, boneless. (**c**) (*: *crédulo*) gullible. (**d** (*) *trabajo etc* cushy‡, easy. (**e**) (*: *bueno*) super*, brilliant*; *mujer* smashing*.
mollate *nm* plonk*.
molledo *nm* (**a**) (*Anat*) fleshy part (*of a limb*). (**b**) (*de pan*) crumb.
molleja *nf* gizzard; **~s** sweetbreads.
mollejón* *nm* softie*; (*pey*) fat slob*.
mollera *nf* (*Anat*) crown of the head; (*) brains, sense; **cerrado de ~, duro de ~** (*estúpido*) dense, dim; (*terco*) pigheaded; **no les cabe en la ~** they just can't believe it; **secar la ~ a uno** to drive sb crazy; **tener buena ~** to have brains, be brainy.
mollete *nm* (**a**) (*Culin*) muffin. (**b**) (*Anat*) (*brazo*) fleshy part of the arm; (*mejilla*) fat cheek.
momentáneamente *adv* momentarily.
momentáneo *adj* momentary.
momento *nm* (**a**) (*gen*) moment; (*instante*) instant; (*tiempo*) time; **¡momentito!** (*esp LAm*) just a moment!; **~s después** a few moments later; **al ~** at once; **a cada ~** every instant, all the time; **de ~** at the moment, for the moment; **continúa de ~ en el puesto** he stays in the job for the time being; **no los vi de ~** I didn't see them at first; **de un ~ a otro** at any moment; **en el ~ actual** at the present time; **en el ~ bueno** at the right moment, at the proper time; **en este ~** at this moment; right now; **en su ~** (*pasado*) in its time, (*futuro*) in due time, in due course, when the time is right; **hace un ~** not a moment ago; **por el ~** for the moment; **está cambiando por ~s** it is changing all the time; **atravesamos un ~ difícil** we are going through a difficult time; **ha llegado el ~ de** + *infin* the time has come to + *infin*.
(**b**) (*Mec*) momentum; moment.
(**c**) (*fig*) consequence, importance; **de poco ~** unimportant.
momería *nf* mummery, clowning.
momia *nf* mummy.
momificación *nf* mummification.
momificar [1g] **1** *vt* to mummify. **2 momificarse** *vr* to mummify, become mummified.
momio 1 *adj carne* lean. **2** *nm* (**a**) (*ganga*) bargain; (*extra*) extra; (*prebenda*) cushy job‡; (*trato*) profitable deal; **de ~** free, gratis. (**b**) (*Cono Sur*) square*, fuddy-duddy*; (*Pol*) reactionary.
momo *nm* (**a**) (*cara*) funny face. (**b**) (*payasadas*) clowning, buffoonery.
mona *nf* (**a**) (*Zool*) female monkey; (*especie*) Barbary ape; **estar hecho una ~** to be embarrassed, be quite put out; **mandar a uno a freír ~s‡** to tell sb to go to blazes*.
(**b**) (*: *imitador*) ape, copycat*.
(**c**) (*) (*borrachera*) drunk*; (*resaca*) hangover*; **coger** (*o* **pillar**) **una ~** to get tight*; **dormir la ~** to sleep off a hangover*.
(**d**) (*And: rubio*) blonde.
(**e**) (*LAm**) Colombian golden marijuana.
(**f**) **andar** (*o* **estar**) **como la ~** (*Cono Sur*) to be broke; to feel wretched.
monacal *adj* monastic.
monacato *nm* monasticism; monastic life, monk's way of life.
monacillo *nm* acolyte, altar boy.
Mónaco *nm* Monaco.
monada *nf* (*esp Esp*) (**a**) (*acto*) (*mueca*) monkey face; *comportamiento* monkeyish way (*o* movement *etc*); *hábito* silly habit; *tontería* silly thing (to say *etc*).
(**b**) (*de niño*) charming habit, sweet little way.
(**c**) (*cualidad*) silliness, childishness.
(**d**) (*) (*objeto precioso*) lovely thing; beauty, cute little thing; (*chica*) pretty girl; **la casa es una ~** the house is lovely, the house is a gem; **¡qué ~!** isn't it cute?, isn't it lovely?; **¡hola, ~!** hullo, beautiful!*
(**e**) **~s** (*: *halagos*) flattery.
mónada *nf* monad.
monago *nm*, **monaguillo** *nm* acolyte, altar-boy.
monarca *nmf* monarch, ruler.
monarquía *nf* monarchy.
monárquico 1 *adj* monarchic(al); (*Pol*) royalist, monarchist. **2** *nm*, **monárquica** *nf* royalist, monarchist.
monarquismo *nm* monarchism.
monasterio *nm* (*de hombres*) monastery; (*de mujeres*) convent.
monástico *adj* monastic.
Moncloa: **la ~** *nf official residence of the Spanish prime minister* (*Madrid*).
monclovita *adj* of the Moncloa palace; (*frec*) of the prime minister, prime ministerial.
Moncho *nm forma familiar de* **Ramón**.
monda[1] *nf* (**a**) (*acto*) pruning, lopping, trimming; peeling. (**b**) (*temporada*) pruning season. (**c**) (*piel*) peel, peelings, skin. (**d**) (*And, Carib, Méx*) beating.
monda[2]* *nf*: **¡es la ~!** (**a**) (*fantástico*) it's great!*; (*pey: el colmo*) it's the limit, it's the end; it's sheer hell; **este nuevo baile es la ~** this new dance is the greatest*, (*pey*) this new dance is awful; **fue la ~** (*para reírse*) it was a scream*.
(**b**) (*persona*) he's great*, he's a knockout*; (*pey*) he's a shocker*, he's a terror.
mondadientes *nm invar* toothpick.
mondador *nm* (*Méx*) shredder.
mondadura *nf* (**a**) = **monda[1]** (**a**); (*limpieza*) cleaning, cleansing. (**b**) **~s** = **monda[1]** (**c**).
mondar [1a] **1** *vt* (**a**) *árbol* to prune, lop, trim.
(**b**) *fruta* to peel, skin; *patata* to peel; *guisante, nuez* to shell; *palo* to peel, pare, remove the bark from; **~ a uno** to cut sb's hair.
(**c**) (*limpiar*) to clean, cleanse; *canal etc* to clean out.
(**d**) (*: *pelar*) to fleece, strip bare, clean out*.
(**e**) **¡que te monden!*** get away!*, rubbish!
(**f**) (*And, Carib: dar una paliza a*) to beat, thrash; (*Carib Dep etc*) to wipe the floor with*.
2 mondarse *vr* (**a**) **~ los dientes** to pick one's teeth.
(**b**) **~ (de risa)*** to die laughing*.
mondo *adj* (**a**) (*limpio*) clean; (*puro*) pure; (*sencillo*) plain; neat; *cabeza* completely shorn.
(**b**) (*fig*) bare, plain, without addition; **el asunto ~ es esto** the plain fact of the matter is; **tiene su sueldo ~ y nada más** he has his bare salary and nothing more; **me he quedado ~*** I'm cleaned out‡, I haven't a cent; **~ y lirondo*** plain, pure and simple.
mondongo *nm* (*: *entrañas*) guts, insides; (*Culin*) tripe.
mondongudo *adj* (*esp Cono Sur*) paunchy, potbellied.
monear [1a] *vi* (**a**) (*comportarse*) to act like a monkey; (*hacer muecas*) to make monkey faces. (**b**) (*Cono Sur, Méx*: jactarse*) to boast, swank*.
moneda *nf* (**a**) (*gen*) currency, money, coinage; **~ blanda, ~ débil** soft currency; **~ convertible** convertible currency; **~ de curso legal** legal tender; **~ decimal** decimal currency; **~ dura, ~ fuerte** hard currency; **~ fraccionaria** money in small units; **~ menuda, ~ suelta** small change, coins of low denomination; **~ nacional** national currency; **en ~ española** in Spanish money; **pagar a uno con** (*o* **en**) **la misma ~** to pay sb back in his own coin.
(**b**) (*una ~*) coin, piece; **~ falsa** false coin, dud coin; **una ~ de 5 dólares** a 5-dollar piece; **es tan probable como que ahora lluevan ~s de 5 duros** it's about as likely as my becoming pope.
moned(e)ar [1a] *vt* to coin, mint.
monedero *nm* (**a**) **~ falso** counterfeiter. (**b**) (*portamonedas*) purse.
monegasco 1 *adj* of Monaco. **2** *nm*, **monegasca** *nf* native (*o* inhabitant) of Monaco; **los ~s** the people of Monaco.
monería *nf* (**a**) (*mueca*) funny face, monkey face; (*imitación*) mimicry. (**b**) (*payasada*) antic, prank, caper, playful trick. (**c**) (*pey*) trifle, triviality.
monetario *adj* monetary, financial.
monetarismo *nm* monetarism.
monetarista *adj, nmf* monetarist.
mongol, -ola 1 *adj, nm/f* Mongol, Mongolian. **2** *nm* (*Ling*) Mongolian.
Mongolia *nf* Mongolia.
mongólico, -a *adj, nm/f* (*Med*) Mongol.
mongolismo *nm* mongolism, Down's syndrome.
moni* *nf* (*LAm*) money.
monicaco*, -a *nm/f* chump*, twit*.
monicongo *nm* (*LAm*) cartoon film.
monigote *nm* (**a**) (*muñeca*) rag doll; (*títere*) puppet;

(*figura ridícula*) grotesque figure; ~ **de nieve** snowman.
(**b**) (*fig*) colourless individual, weak character, little man; ¡~! (*a niño*) you chump!*
(**c**) (*Arte*) humorous sketch, cartoon; (*pey*) bad painting (*o* statue), daub; doodle.
monises‡ *nmpl* brass*, dough‡.
monitor 1 *nm* monitor (*t Inform, Téc*); ~ **en color** colour monitor; ~ **fósfor verde** green screen. **2** *nm*, **monitora** *nf* (*persona*: *Escol*) monitor; (*Dep etc*) instructor, coach; (*de gira etc*) group leader; ~ **de campamento** camp leader; ~ **de esquí** ski instructor.
monitoreado *nm* monitoring.
monitorear [1a] *vt* to monitor.
monitorio *adj* admonitory.
monitorización *nf* monitoring.
monitorizar [1f] *vt* to monitor.
monja *nf* nun; sister.
monje *nm* (**a**) (*Rel*) monk. (**b**) (*Carib*) five-peso note.
monjil 1 *adj* nun's, of (*o* like) a nun; (*fig*) excessively demure. **2** *nm* (*hábito*) nun's habit.
mono¹ *nm* (**a**) (*Zool*) monkey, ape; ¡~! (*a niño*) you little monkey!
(**b**) (*fig*: *imitador*) ape, mimic; ~ **de imitación** (*niño etc*) copycat*; **ser un** ~ **de repetición** to repeat things like a parrot; to talk endlessly.
(**c**) (*: *engreído*) cocky youngster*, show-off*.
(**d**) (*Arte*) = **monigote** (**c**); ~**s** (*Cono Sur*) doodles, rough drawings; ~**s animados** (*Cono Sur*) cartoon(s).
(**e**) (*Naipes*) joker.
(**f**) (*: *feo*) ugly devil, ugly monkey.
(**g**) (‡: *maricón*) pansy‡, queer‡.
(**h**) (‡: *policía*) copper*.
(**i**) (*Med**) withdrawal symptoms (following deprivation of drugs), cold turkey; **estar con el** ~ to be suffering withdrawal symptoms.
(**j**) (*Carib**: *deuda*) debt.
(**k**) (*: *seña*) sign (*between lovers etc*); **hacerse** ~**s** to make eyes at each other, make little signs to each other.
(**l**) (*locuciones*) **no lo aguantaría ni que fuera yo un** ~ I wouldn't put up with it at any price; **no me mirarían más ni que tuviera** ~**s en la cara** they couldn't have stared at me more if I had come from the moon; **es el último** ~ he's a nobody; **estar de** ~**s** to be at daggers drawn; **meter los** ~**s a uno** (*And, Carib**) to put the wind up sb*.
mono² *adj* pretty, lovely, attractive; nice, charming, cute; **una chica muy mona** a very attractive girl, a very nice girl; **¡qué sombrero más** ~! what a cute little hat!
mono³ *nm* (*de obrero*) overalls; boilersuit; (*de niño*) rompers; (*de mujer*) jumpsuit; ~ **de esquí** ski suit.
mono⁴ 1 *adj* (*And*: *rubio*) blond, reddish blond. **2** *nm* (*Cono Sur*) (*de fruta*: *montón*) pile; (*de sandía*) slice.
mono⁵* *adj* = **monofónico**.
mono... *pref* mono...
monocarril *nm* monorail.
monocasco *nm* monohull.
monocolor *adj* one-colour, of a single colour; **gobierno** ~ one-party government.
monocorde *adj* (**a**) (*Mús*) single-stringed. (**b**) (*fig*) monotonous, unvaried.
monocromo 1 *adj* monochrome; (*TV*) black-and-white. **2** *nm* monochrome.
monóculo *nm* monocle.
monocultivo *nm* monoculture, single crop; one-crop farming; **el** ~ **es un peligro para muchos países** in many countries dependence upon a single crop is dangerous.
monofónico *adj* monophonic.
monogamia *nf* monogamy.
monógamo *adj* monogamous.
monografía *nf* monograph; occasional paper.
monográfico *adj*: **estudio** ~ monograph; **número** ~ **de la revista** an issue of the journal devoted to a single subject; **programa** ~ programme devoted to a single subject.
monograma *nm* monogram.
monokini *nm* topless swimsuit, monokini.
monolingüe 1 *adj* monolingual, monoglot. **2** *nmf* monoglot.
monolingüismo *nm* monolingualism.
monolítico *adj* monolithic.
monolitismo *nm* (*Pol etc*) monolithic nature; monolithic system.
monolito *nm* monolith.
monologar [1h] *vi* to soliloquize.
monólogo *nm* monologue; ~ **interior** stream of consciousness.
monomando *nm* mixer tap.
monomanía *nf* monomania; mania, obsession.
monomaniaco, -a, monomaníaco, -a *adj, nm/f* monomaniac.
monomio *nm* monomial.
monomotor *adj* single-engined.
monono* *adj* (*Cono Sur*) pretty, attractive; dressed up.
mononucleosis *nf*: ~ **infecciosa** glandular fever.
monoparental *adj*: **familia** ~ single-parent family.
monoparentalidad *nf* single parenthood.
monopartidismo *nm* single-party system.
monopatín *nm* skateboard.
monopatinaje *nm* skateboarding.
monoplano *nm* monoplane.
monoplaza *nm* single-seater.
monopolio *nm* monopoly.
monopolístico *adj* monopolistic.
monopolización *nf* monopolization.
monopolizar [1f] *vt* to monopolize.
monopsonio *nm* monopsony.
monoquini *nm* = **monokini**.
mono(r)rail *nm* monorail.
monorrimo *adj estrofa etc* having the same rhyme throughout.
monosabio *nm* (**a**) (*Zool*) trained monkey. (**b**) (*Taur*) *picador's assistant*; *employee who leads the horse team dragging the dead bull*.
monosilábico *adj* monosyllabic.
monosílabo 1 *adj* monosyllabic. **2** *nm* monosyllable.
monoteísmo *nm* monotheism.
monoteísta 1 *adj* monotheistic. **2** *nmf* monotheist.
monotemático *adj* having a single theme.
monotonía *nf* (*sonido*) monotone; (*fig*) monotony; sameness, dreariness.
monótono *adj* on one note; (*fig*) monotonous; humdrum, dreary.
monousuario *adj* single-user (*atr*).
mono-usuario *adj invar* (*Inform*) single-user.
monóxido *nm* monoxide; ~ **de carbono** carbon monoxide; ~ **de cloro** chlorine monoxide.
Mons. *abr de* **Monseñor** Monsignor, Mgr, Mons.
monseñor *nm* monsignor.
monserga *nf* (**a**) (*jerigonza*) gibberish, jargon. (**b**) (*disparates*) drivel, tedious talk; **dar la** ~ to get on sb's nerves, be a bore; **¡no me vengas con** ~**s!** give my head peace!
monstruo 1 *nm* (**a**) (*gen*: *t fig*) monster; giant; (*del mundo pop*) idol, wonder boy; (*Mús, Teat etc*) great figure, all-time great*; (*Cine*) superstar, megastar; **ese niño es un monstruito** that child is the very devil; ~ **sagrado** megastar; **Lope,** ~ **de la naturaleza** Lope, a marvel of nature.
(**b**) (*Bio*) freak, monster; ~ **de circo** circus freak.
2 *atr** (**a**) (*grande*) huge, monster; **mitín** ~ huge meeting. (**b**) (*maravilloso*) fantastic*, fabulous*; **idea** ~ fantastic idea*; **es un plan** ~ it's a fabulous scheme*.
monstruosidad *nf* monstrosity; (*Bio*) freak.
monstruoso *adj* monstrous, huge, monster (*atr*); (*Bio*) freakish, freak (*atr*); (*fig*) monstrous, hideous; **es** ~ **que** ... it is monstrous that ...
monta *nf* (**a**) (*acto*) mounting. (**b**) (*Mat*) total, sum. (**c**) (*fig*) value; **de poca** ~ of small account, unimportant. (**d**) (*Agr*) (*caballeriza*) stud; (*temporada*) mating season (*of horses*); (*acto*) mating.
montacargas *nm invar* service lift, hoist, freight elevator (*US*).
montadito *nm* titbit, dainty item.
montado 1 *adj* (**a**) (*a caballo*) mounted; **artillería montada** horse artillery; **guardias montadas** horse guards; **estar** ~‡ (*con dinero*) to be flush‡; (*boyante*) to be sitting pretty.
(**b**) (*Téc*) built-in.
2 montada *nf*: **la** ~ (*CAm*) the mounted rural police.
montador *nm* (**a**) (*objeto*) mounting block. (**b**) (*persona*) fitter; ~ **de escena** (*Cine*) (*diseñador*) set designer; (*que hace el montaje*) film editor.
montadura *nf* (**a**) (*acto*) mounting. (**b**) = **montura**.
montaje *nm* (**a**) (*Mec etc*) assembly; fitting-up; (*Arquit*) erection; (*: *arreglado de antemano*) set-up, put-up job*, frame-up*; (*: *estafa*) fiddle*, plot; (*apariencia*) (outward) show; ~ **publicitario** advertising stunt, publicity stunt. (**b**) (*Rad*) hook-up. (**c**) (*Arte, Cine, Fot*) montage; (*Teat*) stage design, décor.
montante *nm* (**a**) (*Hist*) broadsword. (**b**) (*Téc*) (*poste*) upright, post; (*soporte*) stanchion; (*Arquit*) (*de puerta*) transom; (*de ventana*) mullion. (**c**) (*Arquit*) small window over a door. (**d**) (*suma*) total, amount; ~ **compensatorio**

monetario monetary compensation amount.

montaña 1 *nf* (**a**) (*gen*) mountain; mountains, mountainous area; ~ **de mantequilla** butter mountain; ~ **rusa** switchback, big dipper. (**b**) (*And, Carib*) forest; (*CAm*) virgin jungle. **2** *nmf*: ~ **del Pirineo** Pyrenean mountain dog.

montañero 1 *adj* mountain (*atr*). **2** *nm*, **montañera** *nf* mountaineer, climber.

montañés 1 *adj* (**a**) (*gen*) mountain (*atr*); hill (*atr*); highland (*atr*). (**b**) (*de Santander*) of (*o* from) the Santander region. **2** *nm*, **montañesa** *nf* (**a**) (*gen*) highlander. (**b**) (*de Santander*) native (*o* inhabitant) of the Santander region.

montañismo *nm* mountaineering, climbing.

montañoso *adj* mountainous.

montaplatos *nm invar* service-lift, dumbwaiter (*US*).

montar [1a] **1** *vt* (**a**) *bicicleta, caballo etc* to mount, get on; to ride; **hoy ella monta mi caballo** she's riding my horse today.

(**b**) ~ **a uno sobre un tronco** to lift sb on to a log; **montó al niño en el burro** he lifted the child on to the donkey, he put the child up on the donkey, he sat the child on the donkey.

(**c**) (*Bio*) to cover, mate with; (**‡**) *mujer* to screw**‡**.

(**d**) (*traslapar*) to overlap; ~ **un color sobre otro** to overlap one colour with another, to cover one colour partially with another.

(**e**) (*Mec*) to assemble, fit (up), put together, set up; (*Arquit*) to erect, put up; *joya* to set, mount; *pistola* to cock; *reloj, resorte* to wind (up); (*Cos*) *puntos* to cast on; *guardia* to mount; (*Cine*) *película* to edit; (*Teat*) *obra* to stage, put on; ~ **una casa** to set up house, furnish a house; ~ **una tienda** to open a shop; ~ **un negocio** to start a business, found a business; **tiene una clínica ya montada** she has a fully-equipped clinic.

(**f**) (*Culin*) *huevo* to beat, whip; *helado* to whip.

(**g**) (*) ~**la** to kick up a fuss.

2 *vi* (**a**) to mount (*a un caballo, en un caballo* a horse), get up (*a, en* on); to get on; to ride; ~ **a caballo** to ride; ~ **en bicicleta** to ride a bicycle, cycle; **me ayudó a** ~ he helped me up; he helped me to mount; **montó en la bicicleta y desapareció** he got on his bicycle and disappeared; **mi hermana monta a diario** my sister rides every day; ~ **para una cuadra de carreras** to ride for a racing stable.

(**b**) (*traslaparse*) to overlap; **el mapa monta sobre el texto** the map overlaps the text, the map covers part of the text.

(**c**) ~ **en cólera**, ~ **en indignación** to get angry.

(**d**) ~ **a** (*Fin*) to amount to, come to, add up to.

(**e**) **tanto monta** it makes no odds; it's all the same, it doesn't matter either way; **tanto monta que vengas o no** it's all the same whether you come or not.

3 montarse *vr* = **2** (**a**), (**b**) *y* (**c**); (*) **montárselo** to set oneself up, get things going; to do one's thing*; **él se lo monta mejor** he does things better, he gets himself better organized; **él se lo ha montado realmente bien** he's got a nice little thing going for him*; **se lo monta muy mal** he's no idea how to manage things, he's just not with it*; ~ **en el dólar*** to make a mint.

montaraz 1 *adj* (**a**) (*de montaña*) mountain (*atr*), highland (*atr*). (**b**) (*salvaje*) wild, untamed; (*pey*) rough, coarse, uncivilized; (*huraño*) unsociable. **2** *nm* (*guardabosque*) gamekeeper, game warden.

montarrón *nm* (*And*) forest.

monte *nm* (**a**) (*montaña*) mountain; **M~s Apalaches** Appalachians; **M~s Cárpatos** Carpathians; **M~ de la Mesa** Table Mountain; **los M~s Pirineos** the Pyrenees; **echarse al** ~ to take to the hills.

(**b**) (*bosque*) woodland; (*despoblado*) wilds, wild country; ~ **alto** forest; ~ **bajo** scrub; **un conejo de** ~ a wild rabbit; **batir el** ~ to beat for game, go hunting; **creer que todo el ~ es orégano** to think everything in the garden is lovely; to think everything is plain sailing; **no todo el ~ es orégano** all that glitters is not gold.

(**c**) ~ **de piedad** (state-owned) pawnshop.

(**d**) (*CAm, Carib*: *alrededores*) outskirts, surrounding country.

(**e**) (*Méx*: *pasto*) grass, fallow pasture.

(**f**) (*LAm**: *droga*) hash*, pot**‡**.

(**g**) (*Naipes*: *baraja*) pile; (*banca*) bank; (*juego*) *a card game*.

(**h**) (*: *obstáculo*) obstacle, snag; **todo se le hace un** ~ he sees difficulties everywhere, he makes a mountain out of every molehill.

montear [1a] *vt* to hunt.

montecillo *nm* mound, hummock, hump.

montepío *nm* (**a**) (*sociedad*) charitable fund for dependants, friendly society. (**b**) (*LAm*) pawnshop. (**c**) (*And, Cono Sur* = *viudedad*) widow's pension.

montera *nf* (**a**) (*sombrero*) cloth cap; (*Taur*) bullfighter's hat; **ponerse algo por** ~ to laugh at sth; **ponerse el mundo por** ~ not to care what anybody thinks. (**b**) (*Téc*) rise. (**c**) (*Arquit*) skylight.

montería *nf* (**a**) (*arte*) (art of) hunting; (*cacería*) hunt, chase.

(**b**) (*Arte*) hunting scene.

(**c**) (*personas*) hunting party.

(**d**) (*LAm*) (*animales*) animals, game; (*lugar*) hunting ground.

(**e**) (*And*: *canoa*) canoe.

(**f**) (*CAm*: *concesión*) concession.

(**g**) (*CAm, Méx*: *maderería*) timber camp.

montero *nm* huntsman, hunter; beater.

montés *adj gato etc* wild.

montevideano, -a *adj, nm/f* Montevidean.

montículo *nm* = **montecillo**.

monto *nm* total, amount.

montón *nm* (**a**) (*gen*) heap, pile; (*de nieve*) drift.

(**b**) (*fig*) **del** ~ ordinary, average, commonplace; **un hombre del** ~ an ordinary chap; **salirse del** ~ to be exceptional, stand out from the crowd.

(**c**) (*) stack*, heap*, lot; (*de gente*) crowd, mass; **un ~ de gente** a crowd, a mass of people, masses of people; **tengo un ~ de cosas que decirte** I have lots (*o* heaps*, stacks*) of things to tell you; **tenemos montones** we have heaps* (*o* tons*, loads); **a** ~ together, all lumped together; **a montones** in great abundance, by the score (*etc*), galore.

montonera *nf* (**a**) (*LAm*: *guerrilla*) band of guerrilla fighters. (**b**) (*Carib*: *montón*) pile, heap; (*And*: *almiar*) haystack, strawstack.

montonero 1 *adj* (*Méx*) *persona* overbearing. **2** *nm* (*LAm*) guerrilla fighter.

montuno *adj* (**a**) (*de montaña*) mountain (*atr*); forest (*atr*). (**b**) (*LAm*) (*salvaje*) wild, untamed; (*rústico*) rustic.

montuosidad *nf* hilliness, mountainous nature.

montuoso *adj* hilly, mountainous.

montura *nf* (**a**) (*cabalgadura*) mount. (**b**) (*silla*) saddle; (*arreos*) harness, trappings; **cabalgar sin** ~ to ride bareback. (**c**) (*de joya etc*) mount, mounting, setting; (*de gafas etc*) frame.

monumental *adj* (**a**) (*enorme*) monumental. (**b**) (*: *excelente*) tremendous*, terrific*.

monumentalidad *nf* monumental character.

monumentalismo *nm* tendency to construct vast buildings (*o* monuments).

monumento 1 *nm* (**a**) (*lit*: *t fig*) monument; memorial; ~ **a los caídos** war memorial; ~ **histórico-artístico** ≃ conservation area; listed building; ~ **al soldado desconocido** tomb of the unknown soldier; **~s prehistóricos** prehistoric remains; **visitar los ~s de una ciudad** to see the sights of a town, visit the places of interest in a city.

(**b**) ~**s** (*documentos*) documents, source material.

(**c**) (*: *chica*) pretty girl.

2 *atr*: **un éxito** ~ a tremendous success*, a huge success.

monzón *nm o f* monsoon.

monzónico *adj* monsoon (*atr*); **lluvias monzónicas** monsoon rains.

moña *nf* (**a**) (*cinta*) hair ribbon, bow; (*Taur*) bullfighter's ribbon; (*de premio*) sash, prize ribbon. (**b**) (*: *muñeca*) doll. (**c**) **estar con la ~*** to be tight*. (**d**) (*Cono Sur*) bar. (**e**) (**‡**: *gay*) queer**‡**.

moño *nm* (**a**) (*de pelo*) bun, chignon; topknot; (*Cono Sur*) (*cabello*) man's hair; (*de caballo*) horse's forelock; **agarrarse del** ~ to tear each other's hair; **estar con el ~ torcido** (*Carib, Méx*) to be in a bad mood; **estar hasta el ~*** to be fed up to the back teeth*; **ponerse ~s*** to give o.s. airs, put it on.

(**b**) (*Orn*) crest.

(**c**) = **moña** (**a**).

(**d**) ~**s** (*fig*) frippery, buttons and bows.

(**e**) (*LAm*: *altivez*) pride, haughtiness; **agachar el** ~ (*Cono Sur**) to give in; **bajar el ~ a uno** to take sb down a peg*.

(**f**) (*Cono Sur*) bar.

MOPU ['mopu] *nm* (*Esp*) *abr de* **Ministerio de Obras Públicas y Urbanismo**.

moquear [1a] *vi* to have a runny nose.
moqueo *nm* runny nose.
moquero *nm* handkerchief.
moqueta *nf* moquette; (fitted) carpet.
moquete *nm* punch on the nose.
moquillo *nm* (*Vet*) distemper; pip.
mor: **por ~ de** *prep* because of, on account of; for the sake of; **por ~ de la amistad** for friendship's sake.
mora[1] *nf* (**a**) (*Bot*) (*del moral*) mulberry; (*de zarzamora*) blackberry. (**b**) (*And*) bullet. (**c**) (*Méx**) pot‡, hash*.
mora[2] *nf* (*Jur*) delay; **ponerse en ~** to default, get into arrears.
mora[3] *nf* (*Cono Sur*) blood sausage, black pudding.
morada *nf* (**a**) (*casa*) dwelling, abode, home; **la eterna ~** the great beyond; **última ~** (last) resting-place; **no tener ~ fija** to be of no fixed abode. (**b**) (*estancia*) stay, period of residence.
morado 1 *adj* purple, violet; **ojo ~** black eye; **pasarlas moradas** to have a tough time of it; **ponerse ~*** to do o.s. well, gorge o.s. **2** *nm* (**a**) bruise. (**b**) (*Cono Sur*) coward.
morador(a) *nm/f* inhabitant.
moradura *nf* bruise.
moral[1] *nm* (*Bot*) mulberry tree.
moral[2] 1 *adj* moral. **2** *nf* (**a**) (*moralidad*) morals, morality; (*como estudio*) ethics; **tiene más ~ que el alcoyano** he has the patience of Job, he keeps going against all the odds. (**b**) (*de ejército etc*) morale.
moraleja *nf* moral.
moralidad *nf* (**a**) (*moral*) morals, morality, ethics. (**b**) (*moraleja etc*) moral; **me tocó la ~*** it quite upset me; **sus críticas me tocan la ~** his criticisms get me down.
moralina *nf* moral.
moralista *nmf* moralist.
moralizador 1 *adj* moralizing; moralistic. **2** *nm*, **moralizadora** *nf* moralist.
moralizante *adj* moralizing; moralistic.
moralizar [1f] *vt* to moralize; to improve ethical standards in.
moralmente *adv* morally.
morapio* *nm* (cheap) red wine, plonk*.
morar [1a] *vi* to live, dwell; to stay.
moratón *nm* bruise.
moratoria *nf* moratorium.
morbidez *nf* (*Arte etc*) softness, delicacy.
morbididad *nf* = **morbilidad**.
mórbido *adj* (**a**) (*enfermo*) morbid; diseased. (**b**) (*Arte etc*) soft, delicate.
morbilidad *nf* morbidity, sickness rate.
morbo *nm* (**a**) (*Med*) disease, illness. (**b**) (*fig*) unhealthy curiosity; ghoulish delight, morbid pleasure.
morbosidad *nf* (**a**) (*enfermedad*) morbidity, morbidness; unhealthiness. (**b**) (*estadística*) sick rate, morbidity.
morboso *adj* (**a**) (*enfermo*) morbid; (*malsano*) unhealthy, likely to cause disease(s). (**b**) (*fig*) diseased, morbid.
morcilla *nf* (**a**) (*Culin*) blood sausage, black pudding; (*Méx*: *callos*) tripe; **dar ~ a‡** (*matar*) to bump off‡, kill; (*dañar*) to hurt, harm; **¡vete a tomar ~!****, **¡que te den ~!**** get stuffed!**.
(**b**) (*Teat*) gag, unscripted lines, improvised part.
(**c**) (**) prick**.
(**d**) (*Carib*: *mentira*) lie.
morcillo *adj caballo* black with reddish hairs.
morcón *nm* (**a**) (*Culin*) big blood sausage. (**b**) (*: *rechoncho*) stocky person. (**c**) (*: *descuidado*) sloppy individual, shabby sort.
mordacidad *nf* sharpness, pungency; bite.
mordaga‡ *nf*, **mordaguera‡** *nf* drunkenness; **coger** (*o* **pillar**) **una ~** to get plastered‡.
mordaz *adj crítica etc* biting, scathing, pungent.
mordaza *nf* (**a**) (*de boca*) gag. (**b**) (*Téc*) clamp, jaw.
mordazmente *adv* bitingly, scathingly.
mordedura *nf* bite.
mordelón 1 *adj* (**a**) (*CAm, Méx*: *sobornable*) given to taking bribes. (**b**) (*And, Carib*) *perro* snappy. **2** *nm* (*Méx‡*) traffic cop*.
morder [2h] **1** *vt* (**a**) (*gen*) to bite; (*pinchar*) to nip; (*mordisquear*) to nibble (at).
(**b**) (*Quím*) to corrode, eat away, eat into; *recursos etc* to eat into.
(**c**) (*Mec*) to catch; to clutch, seize.
(**d**) (*: *denigrar*) to gossip about, run down.
(**e**) (*Méx*: *estafar*) to cheat; (*CAm, Méx*: *exigir soborno*) to exact a bribe from.
(**f**) (‡: *reconocer*) to recognize.
2 *vi* to bite (*t fig*); **estoy que muerdo** I'm simply furious; **está que muerde** he's hopping mad; **~ sobre** (*fig*) to bite into.
mordicar [1g] *vi* to smart, sting.
mordida *nf* (**a**) (*LAm*) bite. (**b**) (*) (*soborno*) bribe; (*tajada*) rake-off*, kickback*.
mordiscar [1g] **1** *vt* (*gen*) to nibble at; (*con fuerza*) to gnaw at; (*pinchar*) to nip; (*caballo*) to champ. **2** *vi* to nibble; to champ.
mordisco *nm* (**a**) (*acto*) bite, nip; nibble; (*fig*) attack, onslaught; **deshacer algo a ~s** to bite sth to pieces.
(**b**) (*trozo*) bite, piece bitten off.
(**c**) (‡: *beso*) love-bite.
mordisquear [1a] = **mordiscar**.
morena[1] *nf* (*Geol*) moraine.
morena[2] *nf* (*Pez*) moray.
morena[3] *nf* dark girl, brunette.
morenal *nm* (*CAm*) shanty town.
morenear [1a] **1** *vt* to tan, brown. **2 morenearse** *vr* to tan, brown.
morenez *nf* suntan, brownness.
moreno *adj* (dark) brown; *huevo* brown; *persona* dark; swarthy; dark-haired; (*bronceado*) brown, tanned; *pelo* dark, black; (*euf*) coloured (*euf*), Negro; (*And, Carib*) mulatto; **ponerse ~** to get brown, acquire a suntan.
morera *nf* mulberry tree.
morería *nf* (*Hist*) Moorish lands, Moorish territory; (*barrio*) Moorish quarter.
moretón *nm* (*esp LAm*) bruise.
morfa* *nf* = **morfina**.
morfar‡ [1a] (*Cono Sur*) **1** *vt* to eat; (*con gula*) to gobble up, put away*. **2** *vi* to nosh‡, scoff*.
morfema *nm* morpheme.
morfémico *adj* morphemic.
morfi‡ *nm* (*Cono Sur*) grub‡ nosh*, food.
morfina *nf* morphia, morphine.
morfinomanía *nf* morphine addiction, opium addiction.
morfinómano 1 *adj* addicted to morphine, addicted to opium. **2** *nm*, **morfinómana** *nf* morphine addict, opium addict.
morfología *nf* morphology.
morfológico *adj* morphological.
morfón‡ *adj* (*Cono Sur*) piggish, greedy.
morganático *adj* morganatic.
morgue *nf* morgue.
moribundo 1 *adj* dying; (*esp fig*) moribund. **2** *nm*, **moribunda** *nf* dying person.
moricho *nm* (*Carib*) hammock.
morigeración *nf* good behaviour.
morigerado *adj* well-behaved, law-abiding.
morigerar [1a] *vt* to restrain, moderate.
morillo *nm* firedog.
morir [3j; *ptp* **muerto**] **1** *vt* (*sólo ptp y perfecto*) to kill; **le han muerto** they have killed him; **fue muerto en un accidente** he was killed in an accident; **fue muerto a tiros** he was shot (dead).
2 *vi* (**a**) (*gen*: *t fig*) to die; **~ del corazón** to die of a heart-attack; **~ de difteria** to die of diphtheria; **~ joven** to die young; **~ de vejez** to die of old age; **~ ahogado** to drown; **~ ahorcado** to be hanged, die by hanging; **~ de frío** to die of cold, freeze to death; **~ fusilado** to be shot; **~ de hambre** to die of (*o* from) starvation, starve to death; **~ sin decir Jesús** to die very suddenly; **¡muera!** kill him!; **¡muera el tirano!** down with the tyrant!; **¡así se muera!** (*fig*) God rot him!; **y allí muere** (*LAm*) and that's all there is to it.
(**b**) (*irse apagando*) (*fuego*) to die down, burn low; to go out; (*luz*) to get dim, go out; **moría el día** the day was almost over, night was falling.
(**c**) (*Ferro etc*: *línea*) to end (*en* at); (*calle*) to come out (*en* at).
3 morirse *vr* (**a**) (*gen*) to die; **se le murió el tío** an uncle of his died; **se nos va a ~ el burro** the donkey is going to die on us; **~ de hambre** = **morir de hambre**; **¡me muero de hambre!** (*fig*) I'm starving!; **no es cosa de ~** it's not as bad as all that.
(**b**) (*fig*) to be dying; **me moría de vergüenza** I nearly died of shame; **se moría de envidia** he was green with envy; **me moría de miedo** I was half-dead with fright; **se van a ~ de risa** they'll die of laughing.
(**c**) **~ por algo** to be dying for sth; **~ por uno** to be crazy about sb; **se muere por el fútbol** he's mad keen on football; **~ por** + *infin* to be dying to + *infin*.
(**d**) (*miembro*) to go to sleep, go numb.

morisco 1 *adj* Moorish; (*Arquit*) Mauresque, in the Moorish style.

2 *nm*, **morisca** *nf* (**a**) (*Hist*) Moslem convert to Christianity, subject Moslem (*of 15th and 16th centuries*).

(**b**) (*Méx*: ††) quadroon.

morisma *nf* Moors (*collectively*).

morisqueta *nf* fraud, dirty trick.

mormón, -ona *nm/f* Mormon.

mormónico *adj* Mormon.

mormonismo *nm* Mormonism.

moro 1 *adj* (**a**) (*lit*) Moorish.

(**b**) *caballo* dappled, piebald.

2 *nm*, **mora**[4] *nf* (**a**) (*lit*) Moor; ~ **de paz** peaceful person; **¡hay ~s en la costa!** watch out!; **dar a ~ muerto gran lanzada** to kick a man when he's down.

(**b**) (*LAm*: *caballo*) piebald horse.

3 *nm* (**a**) (*: *marido*) domineering husband.

(**b**) (‡: *vendedor de droga*) drug pusher.

(**c**) **~s y cristianos** (*Carib* *Culin*) rice with black beans.

(**d**) (*por extensión*) Morocco; **bajar al ~** to go to Morocco.

(**e**) (*Mús**) false note.

morocha *nf* (*Carib*) double-barrelled gun.

morocho 1 *adj* (**a**) (*LAm*: *moreno*) dark, swarthy; brunette.

(**b**) (*And, Carib, Cono Sur*) (*fuerte*) strong, tough; (*fornido*) well-built.

(**c**) (*Carib*: *gemelo*) twin.

2 *nm* (**a**) (*LAm*: *maíz*) hard maize, corn (*US*).

(**b**) (*And, Carib, Cono Sur*: *duro*) *persona* tough person, hard guy*.

(**c**) (*Carib*: *gemelo*) twin.

morón *nm* hillock.

morondanga *nf* hotchpotch.

morondo *adj* (**a**) (*calvo*) bald; (*sin hojas*) leafless, bare. (**b**) (*fig*) bare, plain.

moronga *nf* (*CAm, Méx*) blood sausage, black pudding.

morosidad *nf* (**a**) (*lentitud*) slowness, sluggishness; dilatoriness; (*apatía*) apathy. (**b**) (*Fin*) slowness in paying up; (*atrasos*) arrears (of payment).

moroso 1 *adj* (**a**) (*lento*) slow, sluggish; dilatory; (*Com, Fin*) slow to pay up; **deudor ~** slow payer, defaulter; **una película de acción morosa** a film with slow action, a slow-moving film.

(**b**) **delectación morosa** lingering enjoyment, (*pey*) morbid enjoyment, unhealthy enjoyment.

2 *nm*, **morosa** *nf* (*Com, Fin*) slow payer, bad debtor, defaulter.

morra *nf* top of the head; **andar a la ~** to exchange blows.

morrada *nf* (*cabezazo*) butt; bang on the head; (*golpe*) bash*, punch; **darse una ~** to fall flat on one's face.

morral *nm* (**a**) (*mochila*) haversack, knapsack; (*Caza*) pouch, gamebag; (*de caballo*) nosebag. (**b**) (*: *matón*) lout, rough type.

morralla *nf* (**a**) (*peces*) small fry, little fish. (**b**) (*basura*) rubbish. (**c**) (*personas*) rabble, common sort. (**d**) (*fig*) trinket. (**e**) (*Méx*) small change.

morrear‡ [1a] *vti* to kiss.

morrena *nf* moraine.

morreo‡ *nm* kiss; kissing.

morrera‡ *nf* (*labios*) lips; (*boca*) kisser‡.

morrillo *nm* (*Zool*) fleshy part of the neck; neck, back of the neck.

morriña *nf* (*Esp*) depression, depressed state, blues; **~ de la tierra** homesickness.

morriñoso *adj* homesick.

morrión *nm* (*Mil*) helmet, shako.

morro *nm* (**a**) (*Zool*) snout, nose; (*) lip, thick lip; **andar de ~ con uno** to be at odds with sb; **beber a ~** (*Esp*) to drink from the bottle; **dar a uno en los ~s*** to bash sb*; (*fig*) to get one's own back on sb; **estar de ~s** to be in a bad mood; **estar de ~(s) con uno** to be cross with sb; **¡cierra los ~s!‡** shut your trap!‡; **partir los ~s a uno*** to bash sb's face in*; **poner ~, torcer el ~** (*ofenderse*) to look cross, (*hacer una mueca*) to turn up one's nose; **poner morritos** to look sullen; **tiene un ~ que te lo pisas*** he's got a real brass neck*; **¡qué ~ tienes!*** you've got a nerve!*

(**b**) (*Aer, Aut etc*) nose; **caer de ~** to nose-dive (into the ground).

(**c**) (*Geog*) headland, promontory.

(**d**) (*guijarro*) pebble.

(**e**) (*cerro*) small rounded hill, rounded rock.

morrocotudo* *adj* (**a**) (*muy bueno*) smashing*, terrific*, splendid; *golpe, riña etc* tremendous*.

(**b**) (*fuerte*) strong; (*pesado*) heavy; (*Cono Sur*) clumsy, awkward.

(**c**) *asunto* (*difícil*) sticky, awkward; (*de peso*) important, weighty.

(**d**) (*Cono Sur, Méx*: *grande*) big.

(**e**) (*And*: *rico*) rich.

morrocoy *nm* (*CAm*) = **morrocoyo** (**a**).

morrocoyo *nm* (*Carib*) (**a**) (*Zool*) turtle. (**b**) (‡) (*gordo*) fat person; (*tullido*) deformed person.

morrón *nm* (*LAm*) sweet pepper.

morrongo, -a *nm/f* cat.

morronguero* *adj* (*Carib*) (*tacaño*) stingy; (*cobarde*) yellow*.

morroña* *nf* (*CAm*) idleness, laziness.

morroñoso *adj* (**a**) (*CAm*) rough. (**b**) (*And*) (*pequeño*) small; (*endeble*) feeble; (*miserable*) wretched, poverty-stricken.

morrudo *adj* (**a**) thick-lipped, blubber-lipped. (**b**) (*Cono Sur*) tough, brawny.

morsa *nf* walrus.

morse *nm* morse.

mortadela *nf* bologna sausage.

mortaja *nf* (**a**) (*de muerto*) shroud. (**b**) (*Téc*) mortise. (**c**) (*LAm**) cigarette-paper.

mortal 1 *adj* (**a**) (*que muere*) mortal.

(**b**) *herida etc* mortal, fatal; *golpe* deadly.

(**c**) (*) *distancia, espera etc* deadly, unending.

(**d**) **quedarse*** ~ to be thunderstruck.

(**e**) **las señas son ~es** the signs are very clear.

2 *nmf* mortal.

mortalidad *nf* (**a**) (*condición de mortal*) mortality. (**b**) (*cantidad de muertos*) mortality; loss of life, toll, number of victims; (*mortandad*) death rate; **~ infantil** (rate of) infant mortality.

mortalmente *adv* (*V adj*) (**a**) mortally. (**b**) fatally.

mortandad *nf* toll, loss of life, number of victims; (*Mil*) slaughter, carnage.

mortecino *adj* (**a**) (*débil*) weak, failing; **hacer la mortecina** to pretend to be dead. (**b**) *luz* dim, fading, failing; *color* dull, faded.

morterada* *nf*: **gana una ~** he earns a small fortune, he earns a tidy bit*.

mortero *nm* mortar.

mortífero *adj* deadly, lethal.

mortificación *nf* mortification; humiliation.

mortificar [1g] **1** *vt* (**a**) (*Med*) to damage, affect seriously.

(**b**) *carne* to mortify; (*insecto, zapato etc*) to torment, plague; **me han mortificado toda la noche los mosquitos** the mosquitos tormented me all night; **estos zapatos me mortifican** these shoes are killing me.

(**c**) (*fig*) to mortify, humiliate; to spite.

2 mortificarse *vr* (*Méx*) (*avergonzarse*) to feel ashamed; (*ser tímido*) to be embarrassed, feel bashful.

mortuorio *adj* mortuary, death (*atr*); **casa mortuoria** house of mourning, home of the deceased.

morueco *nm* (*Zool*) ram.

moruno *adj* (*pey*) Moorish.

morza *nf* (*Cono Sur*) carpenter's vice.

Mosa *nm* Meuse.

mosaico[1] *adj* Mosaic, of Moses.

mosaico[2] *nm* mosaic; tessellated pavement; **~ de madera** marquetry.

mosca 1 *nf* (**a**) (*Ent*) fly; **~ blanca** whitefly; **~ de burro** horsefly; **~ de la carne** meatfly; **~ doméstica** housefly; **~ de España** Spanish fly, cantharides; **~ de la fruta** fruitfly; **~ muerta** (*fig*) hypocrite, slyboots; **~ tsetsé** tsetse fly; **por si las ~s** just in case; **se asaban las ~s*** it was darned hot*; **mandar a uno a capar ~s‡** to tell sb to go to blazes*; **no se oía ni una ~** you could have heard a pin drop; **papar ~s*** to gape, gawp*; **pescar a ~** to fish with a fly; **le picó la ~** (*fig*) he suddenly got worried; **¿que ~ te picó?** what's eating you?; **tener la ~ en** (*o* **detrás de**) **la oreja** to be wary, be suspicious.

(**b**) (‡: *dinero*) dough‡; **aflojar la ~, soltar la ~** to fork out*, stump up.

(**c**) (*: *persona*) pest, bore.

(**d**) (*pelo*) tuft of hair, small growth of hair; (*barba*) small goatee beard.

(**e**) **~s** (*centellas*) sparks; **~s volantes** spots before the eyes.

(**f**) (*Méx**) sponger*.

2 *adj invar* (*Esp**) **estar ~** (*recelar*) to smell a rat, be suspicious, be distrustful; (*harto*) to be utterly fed up*; **estar ~ con uno** to be cross with sb.

moscarda *nf* blowfly, bluebottle.
moscardón *nm* (**a**) (*Ent*) (*moscarda*) botfly, blowfly; (*abejón*) hornet. (**b**) (*) pest, bore, nuisance.
moscatel[1] *adj, nm* muscatel.
moscatel[2] *nm* (**a**) (*pesado*) bore, pest. (**b**) (*mocetón*) big lad, overgrown lad.
moscón *nm* (**a**) (*Ent*) = **moscarda**. (**b**) (*Bot*) maple. (**c**) (*: *pesado*) pest, nuisance.
moscovita *adj, nmf* Muscovite.
Moscú *nm* Moscow.
Mosela *nm* Moselle.
mosqueado *adj* (**a**) (*moteado*) spotted. (**b**) (*enfadado*) angry, resentful.
mosqueador *nm* fly-whisk; (*: *cola*) tail.
mosqueante *adj* (**a**) (*modesto*) annoying, irritating. (**b**) (*sospechoso*) suspicious, fishy*.
mosquearse [1a] *vr* (*recelar*) to smell a rat, get suspicious; (*ofenderse*) to get cross, take offence; (*: *hartarse*) to get fed up (*de* with)*.
mosqueo *nm* (**a**) (*enfado*) annoyance, anger, resentment; **se llevó un** ~ he got angry. (**b**) (*lío*) hassle, fuss.
mosquete *nm* musket.
mosquetero *nm* (*Hist*: *Mil*) musketeer; (*Teat*) groundling.
mosquita *nf*: ~ **muerta** (*fig*) hypocrite, slyboots; **hacerse la** ~ **muerta** to look as if butter would not melt in one's mouth.
mosquitero *nm* mosquito net.
mosquito *nm* mosquito; gnat.
mostacera *nf*, **mostacero** *nm* mustard pot.
mostacilla *nf* (*And*) bead necklace.
mostacho *nm* moustache.
mostachón *nm* macaroon.
mostaza *nf* (**a**) (*lit*) mustard; **un vestido** ~ a mustard-yellow dress. (**b**) (*And, Méx*‡) pot‡, hash*.
mostela *nf* sheaf.
mosto *nm* must, unfermented grape juice.
mostrador *nm* (**a**) (*de tienda*) counter; (*de café etc*) bar; ~ **de caja** cashdesk; ~ **de facturación** check-in desk; ~ **de tránsito** transit desk. (**b**) (*de reloj*) face, dial. (**c**) (‡: *pecho*) bosom, tits‡.
mostrar [1l] **1** *vt* (*gen*) to show; (*exponer*) to display, exhibit; (*señalar*) to point out; (*explicar*) to explain; (*demostrar*) to demonstrate; ~ **en pantalla** (*Inform*) to display.
2 mostrarse *vr* (**a**) (*gen*) to show o.s.; to appear.
(**b**) (*con adj*) to appear, show o.s. to be; **se mostró muy amable** he was very kind, he proved to be very kind; **se mostró ofendido** he appeared (to be) cross; **no se muestra muy imaginativa** she does not seem to be very imaginative.
mostrenco *adj* (**a**) (*sin dueño*) ownerless, unclaimed; *título* in abeyance; *animal* stray; *persona* homeless, rootless. (**b**) (*) (*lento*) dense, slow; (*gordo*) fat. (**c**) (*) *objeto* crude, roughly made.
mostro* *adj* (*And*) great*, superb.
mota[1] *nf* (**a**) (*partícula*) speck, tiny piece; (*pelusa*) piece of fluff; ~ **de carbonilla** smut, speck of coaldust; ~ **de polvo** speck of dust; **ver la** ~ **en el ojo ajeno** to see the mote in sb else's eye.
(**b**) (*dibujo*) dot; **diseño a** ~**s** design with (*o* of) dots.
(**c**) (*nudillo en paño*) burl, kink; (*fig*) fault, blemish, defect.
(**d**) **no** ... ~ nothing, no, *p.ej.* **no hace** ~ **de aire** there isn't a breath of air.
(**e**) (*Geog*) hillock.
(**f**) (*Agr*: *mojón*) ridge, boundary mark.
(**g**) (*Agr*: *césped*) turf, clod (*used to block off irrigation channel*).
(**h**) (*LAm*: *pelo*) lock of wavy hair.
(**i**) (*And, Carib, Méx*: *borla*) powder puff.
(**j**) (*Méx*) (*Bot*) marijuana plant; (*: *droga*) grass‡, dope‡.
mote[1] *nm* (**a**) (*Hist*) motto, device. (**b**) (*apodo*) nickname, by-name.
mote[2] *nm* (**a**) (*LAm*) (*trigo*) boiled wheat; (*maíz*) boiled maize, boiled corn (*US*). (**b**) (*Cono Sur*) **pelar** ~ to gossip; **como** ~ in large numbers.
moteado *adj piel* speckled, mottled, dappled (*de* with); *tela etc* flecked, dotted, with a design of dots.
motear [1a] *vt* to speck (*de* with); to speckle, dapple.
motejar [1a] *vt* to nickname; ~ **a uno de** to brand sb as, accuse sb of being.
motel *nm* motel.
motero*, -a *nm/f* biker*, motorcyclist.
motete *nm* motet; anthem.
motín *nm* (*rebelión*) revolt, rising; (*disturbio*) riot, disturbance; ~ **carcelario** prison riot.
motivación *nf* motivation.
motivacional *adj* motivational.
motivar [1a] *vt* (**a**) (*causar*) to cause, motivate, give rise to. (**b**) (*explicar*) to explain, justify (*con, en* by, by reference to).
motivo 1 *adj* motive.
2 *nm* (**a**) (*gen*) motive, reason (*de* for), cause (*de* of); ~**s de divorcio** grounds for divorce; ~ **oculto** ulterior motive; (*en formulario*) '~ **del viaje**' 'purpose of visit'; **con** ~ **de** because of, owing to; on the occasion of; in connection with; for the purpose of; **fue allí con** ~ **de la boda de su hija** he went there for his daughter's wedding; **con este** ~ for this reason, because of this; **por cuyo** ~ for which reason, on account of which; **por** ~**s de salud** for reasons of health; **sin** ~ for no reason at all, without good reason; ~ **más que sobrado para** ... all the more reason to ...; **un crimen sin** ~ a crime without a motive, a pointless crime; **tengo mis** ~**s** I have my reasons.
(**b**) (*Arte, Mús*) motif; ~ **principal** leitmotif; (*de musical etc*) theme song.
moto[1]* *nf* (*motocicleta*) motorbike*; (*escúter*) (motor) scooter.
moto[2] **1** *adj* (**a**) (*CAm*) orphaned, abandoned. (**b**) (*And*) tailless. **2** *nm*, **mota**[2] *nf* (*CAm*) orphan.
motobomba *nf* fire engine.
motocarro *nm* three-wheeler, light delivery van.
motocicleta *nf* motorcycle; ~ **con sidecar** motorcycle combination.
motociclismo *nm* motorcycling.
motociclista *nmf* motorcyclist; ~ **de escolta** outrider.
moto-cross *nm* moto-cross.
motocultor *nm* cultivator.
motón *nm* (*Náut*) pulley.
motonáutica *nf* speedboat racing.
motonave *nf* motor ship, motor vessel.
motoneta *nf* (*LAm*) motor scooter.
motonieve *nf* snowmobile.
motoniveladora *nf* bulldozer.
motor 1 *adj* (**a**) (*Téc*) motive; **potencia** ~**a** motive power.
(**b**) (*Anat*) motor.
2 *nm* motor, engine; **con 6** ~**es** 6-engined; **aviación con** ~ powered flight; ~ **de arranque,** ~ **de puesta en marcha** starter, starting motor; ~ **de aviación** aircraft engine; ~ **de combustión interna,** ~ **de explosión** internal combustion engine; ~ **a chorro** jet engine; ~ **delantero** front-mounted engine; ~ **diesel** diesel engine; ~ **(de) fuera (de) borda** outboard motor; ~ **de** (*o* **a**) **inyección** fuel-injection engine; ~ **de pistón** piston engine; ~ **radial** radial engine; ~ **de** (*o* **a**) **reacción** jet engine; ~ **refrigerado por aire** air-cooled engine; ~ **trasero** rear-mounted engine; **calentar** ~**es** to warm up; **cargar** ~**es** (*fig*) to prepare oneself, get ready; to get charged up.
motora *nf*, **motorbote** *nm* motorboat, speedboat.
motorismo *nm* motorcycling.
motorista *nmf* (**a**) (*motociclista*) motorcyclist. (**b**) (*LAm*) driver.
motorístico *adj* motor-racing (*atr*).
motorización *nf* (**a**) (*acto*) motorization; mechanization. (**b**) (*capacidad*) engine size.
motorizado *adj* motorized; *tropas* mechanized; **patrulla motorizada** motorized patrol, mobile unit; **personas no motorizadas** people who do not own a car, people who do not have their own transport.
motorizar [1f] **1** *vt* to motorize; to mechanize. **2 motorizarse** *vr* (*hum*) to become mobile, get a car.
motosierra *nf* mechanical saw, power saw.
motoso *adj* (*And, Cono Sur*) *pelo* kinky.
motricidad *nf* mobility.
motriz *adj* (*f irreg*: *de* **motor**) motive, driving; *V* **fuerza**.
motudo *adj* (*Cono Sur*) *pelo* kinky.
mousse [mu:s] *nf* (*Culin*) mousse; (*de pelo*) hair-conditioner; (*de afeitar*) shaving foam.
movedizo *adj* (**a**) (*movible*) easily moved, movable; (*suelto*) loose; (*poco seguro*) unsteady, shaky; *arenas* shifting. (**b**) (*cambiadizo*) *persona* fickle; *situación etc* shifting, unsettled, changeable; troubled.
mover [2h] **1** *vt* (**a**) (*gen*) *objeto etc* to move; (*cambiar de sitio*) to shift; to move about, move along; *cabeza* (*negando*) to shake; (*asintiendo*) to nod; *cola* to wag; (*Ajedrez etc*) to move; (*LAm**) *droga* to push; **'no nos moverán'**

(*eslogan*) 'we shall not be moved'.

(**b**) (*Mec*) to drive, power, work; to pull; **el agua mueve la rueda** the water turns (*o* drives) the wheel; **la máquina mueve 14 coches** the engine pulls 14 coaches; **el vapor mueve el émbolo** the steam drives (*o* works) the piston.

(**c**) (*fig*) to cause, provoke, induce; *descontento etc* to stir up; **~ un jaleo** to cause a row, make a fuss; **~ guerra a uno** to wage war on sb; **~ pleito a uno** to take proceedings against sb; **~ a uno a piedad** to move sb to pity, arouse compassion in sb; **~ a uno a risa** to make sb laugh; **~ a uno a hacer algo** to move (*o* prompt, lead) sb to do sth.

(**d**) **la empresa mueve X pesetas al año** the firm has an annual turnover of X pesetas.

2 *vi* (*Bot*) to bud, sprout.

3 moverse *vr* (**a**) (*gen*) to move; to stir (*de* from); (*hacer lugar*) to move over (*o* along, up *etc*); **no se ha movido de su asiento** he has not stirred from his place; **¡deja de moverte!** stop fidgeting!

(**b**) (*mar*) to get rough; (*viento*) to rise.

(**c**) (*fig*) (*apurarse*) to move o.s., get a move on; (*evolucionar*) to be on the move; **¡muévete!** hurry up!; **hay que ~** (*darse prisa*) we must get a move on; (*estar alerta*) you have to keep on your toes; **si no te mueves lo perderás** if you don't hustle (*o* unless you do sth) it will be lost; **la moda masculina se mueve** men's fashions are changing, men's fashions are on the move.

movible *adj* (**a**) (*no fijo*) movable; (*móvil*) mobile. (**b**) (*fig*) changeable; fickle.

movida *nf* (**a**) (*Ajedrez etc*) move; **~ clave** key-move.

(**b**) (*Pol etc*) movement.

(**c**) (*) (*asunto*) thing, affair, business; (*concentración*) gathering; (*acontecimiento*) happening; (*pelea*) scrap*, set-to*; **la ~ cultural** the cultural scene; **la ~ madrileña** the Madrid scene*, swinging Madrid*, where the action is in Madrid*.

movido *adj* (**a**) (*Fot*) blurred (*by camera shake etc*).

(**b**) *persona* (*activo*) active; (*inquieto*) restless, always on the go; *reunión etc* lively; turbulent; **unos días moviditos** several furiously busy days; **la acción era muy movidita** the action was pretty lively.

(**c**) (*And, CAm, Cono Sur*) *huevo* soft-shelled.

(**d**) (*And, CAm, Cono Sur*: *débil*) weak, feeble; (*CAm, Méx*) (*lento*) slow, sluggish; (*indeciso*) irresolute.

movidón* *nm* rave-up*, wild party.

móvil 1 *adj* = **movible** (**a**) *y* (**b**); *V* **material** *etc.* **2** *nm* (**a**) motive (*de* for); incentive. (**b**) (*Arte*) mobile.

movilidad *nf* mobility; **~ ascendente** upward mobility; **~ social** social mobility.

movilización *nf* mobilization; **~ de capital** raising of capital; **~ de los trabajadores** (call for) industrial action.

movilizar [1f] *vt* (**a**) (*organizar*) to mobilize. (**b**) (*Cono Sur*) to unblock, free.

movimiento *nm* (**a**) (*gen*) movement; (*Mec, Fís*) motion; (*estadística etc*) movement; (*de cabeza*) (*negando*) shake; (*asintiendo*) nod; **~ ascensional de los precios** upward trend (*o* movement) of prices; **~ ascendente de las líneas** upward sweep of the lines; **~ continuo, ~ perpetuo** perpetual motion; **~ de efectivo** cash flow; **~ de mercancías** turnover, volume of business; **~ de pinza** pincer movement; **~ de los precios** changes in prices; **~ sísmico** earth tremor; **estar en ~** to be in motion, be moving; to be on the move; **mantener algo en ~** to keep sth moving; **mantener en ~ la circulación** to keep the traffic on the move; **poner algo en ~** to set sth in motion, start sth, get sth going.

(**b**) (*actividad etc*) movement; activity; (*bullicio*) bustle, stir; (*Aut*) traffic; **una tienda de mucho ~** a busy shop, a much-frequented shop; **~ máximo** (*Aut*) peak traffic; **había mucho ~ en el tribunal** there was great activity in the court.

(**c**) (*Liter, Teat etc*) action; **el libro no tiene bastante ~** the book does not have enough action, not enough happens in the book.

(**d**) (*Mús*) (*compás*) tempo; (*tiempo*) movement.

(**e**) (*de emociones*) *cambio* change, alteration; (*arranque*) fit, outburst; **~ de ánimo** perturbation; **en un ~ de celos** in a rush of jealousy; **obró en un ~ de pasión** he acted in a surge of passion.

(**f**) (*Arte, Liter, Pol etc*) movement; **~ de liberación de la mujer** women's liberation movement; **el ~ revolucionario** the revolutionary movement; **el ~ iniciado por Picasso** the movement started by Picasso; **el M~** (*Esp, 1936 etc*) the Falangist Movement.

(**g**) **~ de bloques** (*Inform*) block move.

moviolas *nfpl* magic-lantern (show); (*Cine*) hand viewer for film editing.

moza *nf* (*muchacha*) girl; (*criada*) servant; (*pey*) wench; **buena ~, real ~** handsome girl, good-looking girl; **~ de partido** prostitute; **~ de servicio** (*Esp* †) domestic servant; **~ de taberna** (*Esp* †) barmaid.

mozalbete *nm* lad.

Mozambique *nm* Mozambique.

mozambiqueño, -a *adj, nm/f* Mozambican.

mozárabe 1 *adj* Mozarabic. **2** *nmf* Mozarab. **3** *nm* (*Ling*) Mozarabic.

mozarrón *nm* big lad, strapping young fellow.

mozo 1 *adj* (**a**) (*joven*) young; **en sus años ~s** in his youth, in his young days.

(**b**) (*soltero*) single, unmarried.

2 *nm* youth, young fellow, lad; servant; (*en café*) waiter; (*Ferro etc*) porter; **buen ~** handsome lad; well set-up young man; **~ de caballos** groom; **~ de café** waiter; **~ de cámara** cabin boy; **~ de cuadra** stableboy; **~ de cuerda, ~ de estación, ~ de equipajes** porter; **~ de hotel** page, buttons, bellhop (*US*); **~ de laboratorio** laboratory assistant; **~ de panadería** baker's boy.

mozuela *nf* girl; wench.

mozuelo *nm* (young) lad.

MTC *nm* (*Esp*) *abr de* **Ministerio de Transportes y Comunicaciones.**

mu‡: **¡achanta la ~!** (*Méx*) shut your face!‡; **no pasó ni ~** nothing at all happened; **no dijo ni ~** she didn't say a word.

muaré *nm* moiré.

mucama *nf* (*Cono Sur y LAm* ††) maid, servant.

mucamo *nm* (*Cono Sur*) servant.

muceta *nf* (*Univ*) cape.

mucilaginoso *adj* mucilaginous.

mucílago *nm* mucilage.

mucosa *nf* mucous membrane; mucus.

mucosidad *nf* mucus.

mucoso *adj* mucous.

múcura *nf* (*And, Carib*) earthenware jug.

muchá *nmf* (*LAm*) = **muchacho, muchacha.**

muchacha *nf* (**a**) (*chica*) girl. (**b**) (*criada*: *t* **~ de servicio**) maid, servant.

muchachada *nf* (**a**) (*travesura*) childish prank. (**b**) (*esp LAm*: *grupo*) group of youths, bunch of youngsters.

muchacha-guía *nf, pl* **muchachas-guías** girl guide, girl scout (*US*).

muchachería *nf* = **muchachada** (**a**) *y* (**b**).

muchachil *adj* boyish, girlish.

muchacho *nm* (**a**) (*chico*) boy, lad; (*criado*) servant. (**b**) (*LAm*: *abrazadera*) clamp, holdfast; (*Cono Sur*: *de zapato*) shoehorn; (*And*) (*lámpara*) miner's lamp; (*sostén*) prop.

muchedumbre *nf* crowd, mass, throng; (*pey*) mob, herd; **una ~ de** a great crowd of, a great number of.

muchísimo *adj, adv superl de* **mucho**; very much, a very great deal (*etc*).

mucho 1 *adj* (**a**) (*sing*) a lot of; much, great; (*demasiado*) too much; **~ tiempo** a long time (*y V* **tiempo**); **~ dinero** a lot of money; **con ~ valor** with much courage, with great courage; **hace ~ calor** it's very hot; **es ~ dinero para un niño** it's too much money for a child; **con mucha menor frecuencia** much less often, with much less frequency.

(**b**) (*sing, colectivo*) **había ~ borracho** there were a lot of drunks*; **aquí hay ~ maricón**‡ there are lots of queers here‡.

(**c**) (*sing**) **es ~ jugador** he's a great player; **es mucha mujer** what a woman she is!, there's a woman for you!; **ésta es mucha casa para nosotros** this house is far too big for us.

(**d**) (*pl*) **~s** many, lots of; many a; (*demasiados*) too many; **hay ~s conejos** there are lots of rabbits; **~s de los ausentes** many of those absent; **somos ~s** there are a lot of us; **se me hacen ~s** I think there are too many; **son ~s los que no quieren** there are many who don't want to.

2 *pron*: **tengo ~ que hacer** I have a lot to do; **~s dicen que** ... a lot of people say that ...; **el plan tiene ~ de positivo** there's a lot about the plan which is positive.

3 *adv* (**a**) (*gen*) a lot, a great deal, much; **~ más** much more, a lot more; **~ menos** much less; **10 cuando ~** 10 at the outside; **~ peor** much worse; **toca ~** she plays a lot, she plays a great deal; **me alegro ~** I'm very glad; **correr ~** to run fast; **trabajar ~** to work hard; **viene ~** he comes a lot, he comes often; **es ~** it's a lot, it's too much; **si no es ~ pedir** if that's not asking too much; **se guardará muy**

~ **de hacerlo*** he'll jolly well be careful not to do it*; *V* **antes** *etc.*

(**b**) (*tiempo*) long; **¿te vas a quedar ~?** are you staying long?

(**c**) (*como respuesta*) very; **¿estás cansado? - ¡~!** are you tired? - very (*o* I certainly am, yes indeed).

(**d**) (*locuciones*) **¡~ que sí!** I should jolly well think so!*, of course!; **¡~ lo sientes tú!** a fat lot you care!*; **con ~** by far, far and away, easily; **con ~ el mejor** far and away the best; **ni con ~** not nearly, nothing like; not by a long chalk; **ni ~ menos** far from it; **no es ~ que** ... it is no wonder that ...; **¡qué ~ si se odian?** is it any surprise if they loathe each other?; **no es para ~** it's not up to much; **tener a uno en ~** to think highly of sb, have a high opinion of sb.

(**e**) (*Méx*) **es ~ muy difícil** it's jolly difficult; **es ~ muy bueno** it's very good, it's excellent.

muda *nf* (**a**) (*ropa*) change of clothing. (**b**) (*Orn, Zool*) moult; (*de serpiente*) slough. (**c**) (*temporada*) moulting season. (**d**) **está de ~** (*chico*) his voice is breaking.

mudable *adj*, **mudadizo** *adj* changeable, variable; shifting; *carácter etc* fickle.

mudanza *nf* (**a**) (*gen*) change; **sufrir ~** to undergo a change. (**b**) (*de casa*) move, removal; **camión de ~s** removal van; **estar de ~** to be moving. (**c**) (*Baile*) figure. (**d**) **~s** (*fig*) fickleness; moodiness, uncertainty of mood.

mudar [1a] **1** *vt* (**a**) (*cambiar*) to change, alter; **~ en** to change into, transform into; **me van a ~ la pluma** they're going to change the pen for me; **le han mudado a otra oficina** they've moved (*o* switched) him to another office; **esto mudó la tristeza en alegría** this changed (*o* turned, transformed) the sadness into joy; **le mudan las sábanas todos los días** they change his sheets every day.

(**b**) (*Orn, Zool*) to shed, moult; *piel* to slough.

2 *vi* to change; **~ de ropa** to change one's clothes; **~ de color** to change colour; **he mudado de parecer** I've changed my mind; **mandarse ~** (*esp LAm**) to clear off*, leave.

3 mudarse *vr* (**a**) = *vi.*

(**b**) (*t* **~ de casa**) to move, move house.

(**c**) (*voz*) to break.

mudéjar 1 *adj* Mudejar. **2** *nmf* (*Hist*) Mudejar (*Moslem permitted to live under Christian rule*).

mudejarismo *nm* (*Arte etc*) Mudejar character (*o* style *etc*).

mudenco *adj* (*CAm*) (*tartamudo*) stuttering; (*tonto*) stupid.

mudengo *adj* (*And*) silly.

mudez *nf* dumbness.

mudo *adj* (**a**) (*sin facultad de hablar*) dumb; (*callado*) silent, mute; **quedarse ~ de** (*fig*) to be dumb with; **quedarse ~ de asombro** to be dumbfounded, be speechless; **se quedó ~ durante 3 horas** he remained silent for 3 hours, he did not speak for 3 hours; **quedarse ~ de envidia** (*Esp*) to be green with envy.

(**b**) (*Ling*) *letra* mute, silent.

(**c**) *película* silent; **papel ~** (*Teat*) walk-on part.

(**d**) (*And, CAm**) foolish, silly.

mueblaje *nm* = **mobiliario.**

mueble 1 *adj* movable.

2 *nm* (**a**) piece of furniture; **~s** furniture; (*de tienda etc*) fittings; **con ~s** furnished; **sin ~s** unfurnished; **~ combinado, ~ de elementos adicionables** piece of unit furniture; **~s y enseres** furniture and fittings; **~s de época** period furniture; **~ librería** bookcase unit; **~s de oficina** office furniture.

(**b**) (*Méx**: *coche*) car.

mueblé* *nm* brothel.

mueble-bar *nm* cocktail cabinet.

mueblería *nf* (*fábrica*) furniture factory; (*tienda*) furniture shop.

mueca *nf* (wry) face, grimace; **hacer ~s a** to make faces at.

muela *nf* (**a**) (*Anat*) tooth, (*estrictamente*) molar, back tooth; **~ del juicio** wisdom tooth; **dolor de ~s** toothache; **está que echa las ~s** he's hopping mad; **hacer la ~** (*Carib*‡) to skive‡.

(**b**) (*Téc*) (*de molino*) millstone; (*de afilar*) grindstone.

(**c**) (*Geog*) mound, hillock.

(**d**) (*And*) gluttony.

(**e**) (*Carib*) trickery.

muellaje *nm* wharfage.

muelle[1] **1** *adj* (**a**) (*blando*) soft; (*delicado*) delicate; (*elástico*) springy, bouncy. (**b**) (*fig*) *vida* soft, easy, luxurious. **2** *nm* spring; **~ real** mainspring; **colchón de ~s** spring mattress, interior sprung mattress.

muelle[2] *nm* (**a**) (*Náut*) wharf, quay; pier; **~ de atraque** (*Náut*) mooring quay, (*Aer*) docking bay. (**b**) (*Ferro etc*: *t* **~ de carga**) loading bay.

muenda *nf* (*And*) thrashing.

muérdago *nm* mistletoe.

muerdo‡ *nm* bite.

muérgano *nm* (**a**) (*And, Carib*: *cacharro*) useless object, piece of junk. (**b**) (*And*: *desharrapado*) shabby person; (*And*: *maleducado*) ill-bred person, lout. (**c**) (*And*: *caballo*) vicious horse.

muermo* 1 *adj* (*Esp*) (*pesado*) boring; (*débil*) wet*, indecisive; (*lento*) slow, slow-witted.

2 *nm*, **muerma** *nf* (*Esp*) (*pesado*) crashing bore; (*débil*) drip, wet fish*; (*tonto*) dolt, idiot; **¡no seas ~!** don't be an idiot!

3 *nm* (**a**) (*aburrimiento*) boredom; (*depresión*) blues.

(**b**) (*asunto etc*) bore, pain*.

(**c**) (*droga*) bad trip*.

muerte 1 *nf* (**a**) (*lit*: *t fig*) death; (*homicidio*) murder; **~ civil** loss of civil rights; **~ a mano airada, ~ violenta** violent death; **~ cerebral** brain death; **~ natural** natural death; **~ repentina** sudden death; **~ súbita** (*Dep*) sudden death (play-off); (*Tenis*) tiebreak; **causar la ~ a, producir la ~ a** to kill (*in an accident*), cause the death of, bring about the death of; **dar ~ a** to kill; **me da ~*** I can't be bothered; **encontrar la ~** to meet one's death; **estar a la ~** to be at death's door.

(**b**) (*locuciones fig*) **guerra a ~** war to the knife, war to the bitter end; **luchar a ~** to fight to the death; **un susto de ~** a terrible fright; **odiar a uno a ~** to loathe sb; **aburrirse de ~** to be bored to death; **un empleo de mala ~*** an awful job, a lousy job‡; **un pueblo de mala ~*** an awful dump (of a town)*; **es la ~*** it's deadly (boring).

2 *adj* (*Cono Sur**) super*, brilliant*.

muerto 1 *adj* (**a**) (*gen, fig*) dead; lifeless; **~ en acción, ~ en campaña** killed in action; **nacido ~** stillborn; **más ~ que vivo** half-dead, more dead than alive; (*fig*: *aterrado*) frightened to death; **más ~ que mi abuela, más ~ que una piedra** as dead as a doornail, stone-dead; **dar por ~ a uno** to give sb up for dead; **no tener donde caerse ~** to be utterly destitute, not have a thing; **resultó ~ en el acto** he died instantly.

(**b**) (*fig*) **estar ~ de cansancio** to be dead tired, be dog-tired; **estar ~ de hambre** to be dying of hunger; **estar ~ de miedo** to be half-dead with fear, be panic-stricken; **estar ~ de risa** to be helpless with laughter.

(**c**) *color* dull.

(**d**) *lengua* dead; *V* **marea, naturaleza** *etc.*

(**e**) *cal* slaked.

2 *nm*, **muerta** *nf* (**a**) (*gen*) dead man, dead woman; (*difunto*) deceased; (*cadáver*) corpse; **los ~s** the dead; **callarse como un ~** to keep absolutely quiet; **cargar con el ~*** to carry the can*; **doblar a ~, tocar a ~** to toll (for a death); **echar el ~ a uno** to put the blame on sb else; **no hablan los ~s** dead men tell no tales; **hacer el ~** (*nadador*) to float; **hacerse el ~** to pretend to be dead; **poner los ~s** to provide cannon-fodder.

(**b**) (*) (*lento*) slowcoach*; (*pesado*) bore, tedious sort.

3 *nm* (**a**) (*Naipes*) dummy.

(**b**) (*: *trabajo*) drag, slog.

muesca *nf* (*corte*) notch, nick; (*ranura*) groove, slot.

muesli *nm* muesli.

muestra *nf* (**a**) (*señal*) indication, sign; (*ejemplo*) example; (*demostración*) demonstration; (*prueba*) proof; (*testimonio*) token; (*Com*: *exposición*) trade fair; **es ~ de cariño** it is a token of affection; **el no hacerlo es ~ de desprecio** not doing it is an indication of contempt; **quieren hacer una ~ de su poder** they want to give a demonstration of their power; **da ~s de deterioro** it's showing signs of wear.

(**b**) (*Com etc*) sample; specimen; **~ gratuita** free sample.

(**c**) (*estadística*) sample; **~ aleatoria, ~ al azar** random sample; **~ representativa** cross-section sample.

(**d**) (*pauta*) model, pattern, guide; (*Cos*) pattern; **es ~ de cómo debe hacerse** it is a model of how it should be done.

(**e**) (*de reloj*) face.

(**f**) (*de tienda etc*) sign, signboard.

muestral *adj* sample (*atr*).

muestrario *nm* collection of samples (*o* specimens); pattern book.

muestrear [1a] *vt* to sample.

muestreo *nm* sampling; survey.

mufa* *nf* (*Cono Sur*) (*mala suerte*) bad luck, misfortune;

(*mal humor*) bad mood; (*aburrimiento*) boredom, tedium.
mufado* *adj* (*Cono Sur*): **estar ~** to be in a bad mood; to feel blue*.
mugido *nm* moo, lowing; bellow; roar, howl.
mugir [3c] *vi* (*vaca*) to moo, low; (*toro*) to bellow; (*con dolor*) to roar, howl; (*mar etc*) to roar.
mugre *nf* dirt, filth; grease, grime; **sacarse la ~*** (*Cono Sur: trabajar*) to work hard; (*sufrir un percance*) to have a nasty accident.
mugriento *adj* dirty, filthy; greasy, grimy.
mugrón *nm* (*de vid*) sucker, layer; (*vástago*) shoot, sprout.
mugroso *adj* = **mugriento**.
muguete *nm* lily of the valley.
mui‡ *nf* = **muy 2**.
muina* *nf* (*Méx*): **me da la ~** it gets on my nerves, it upsets me.
mujahedín, mujahidín, mujaidín *nm* mujaheddin.
mujer *nf* (**a**) (*gen*) woman; **~ alegre, ~ de vida alegre, ~ de la vida, ~ de mala vida, ~ pública** prostitute; **~ empresaria, ~ de negocios** businesswoman; **~ fatal** femme fatale; **~ de la limpieza** cleaning lady, cleaner; **~ piloto** (woman) pilot; **~ policía** policewoman; **~ sacerdote** woman priest; **ser muy ~** to be very feminine; **ser muy ~ de su casa** to be a good housewife; to be very houseproud.
(**b**) (*esposa*) wife; **mi ~** my wife; **~ golpeada, ~ maltratada** battered wife; **tomar ~** to take a wife, marry.
(**c**) **¡~!**: *en oración directa no se traduce*; **¡déjalo, ~!** leave it alone!
mujeraza *nf* shrew, bitch, horrid woman*.
mujercita *nf* little woman, little lady.
mujerengo *adj* (*CAm, Cono Sur*) (**a**) (*afeminado*) effeminate. (**b**) (*mujeriego*) fond of women.
mujerero *adj* (*LAm*) fond of women.
mujeriego 1 *adj* (**a**) fond of women, given to chasing the girls, wolfish. (**b**) **cabalgar a mujeriegas** to ride sidesaddle. **2** *nm* womanizer, wolf*.
mujeril *adj* womanly.
mujerío *nm* (*Esp*): **ir de ~** to go whoring; to go looking for a woman.
mujer-objeto *nf, pl* **mujeres-objeto** woman treated as an object, sex object.
mujerzuela *nf* whore.
mújol *nm* grey mullet.
mula *nf* (**a**) (*Zool*) mule.
(**b**) (*Méx: trastos*) trash, junk, unsaleable goods.
(**c**) (*CAm: vergüenza*) shame.
(**d**) (*And: pipa*) pipe.
(**e**) (*And: idiota*) idiot.
(**f**) (*Méx: duro*) tough guy (*US**).
(**g**) (*Cono Sur**) (*mentira*) lie; (*engaño*) trick; **meter la ~** to tell lies; **meter la ~ a uno** to trick sb.
mulada *nf* drove of mules.
muladar *nm* dungheap, dunghill, midden.
mulato, -a *adj, nm/f* mulatto.
mulé‡ *nm*: **dar ~ a** to bump off‡.
mulero 1 *nm* (*lit*) muleteer. **2** *nm*, **mulera** *nf* (*Cono Sur**: *mentiroso*) liar.
muleta *nf* (**a**) (*para andar*) crutch. (**b**) (*Taur*) *matador's stick with red cloth attached.* (**c**) (*fig*) prop, support.
muletilla *nf* (**a**) (*bastón*) cross-handled cane; (*Téc: botón*) wooden toggle; large wooden button; (*Taur*) = **muleta** (**b**).
(**b**) (*fig*) (*palabra*) pet word, tag, cliché; (*de cómico etc*) catch-phrase.
muletón *nm* flanelette.
mulo *nm* mule.
mulón *adj* (*And, Cono Sur*) (*tartamudo*) stammering; *niño* slow in learning to talk, backward.
multa *nf* fine; (*Dep etc*) penalty; **echar una ~ a, (im)poner una ~ a** to impose a fine (*o* penalty) on.
multar [1a] *vt* to fine; (*Dep etc*) to penalize; **~ a uno en 100 dólares** to fine sb 100 dollars.
multi... *pref* multi...
multicanal *adj* (*TV*) multichannel.
multicapa *adj invar* multilayer(ed).
multicine *nm* multiscreen cinema, multiplex.
multicolor *adj* multicoloured, many-coloured; motley, variegated.
multiconfesional *adj* of (*o* for *etc*) several different faiths.
multicopista *nm* duplicator.
multidimensional *adj* multidimensional.
multidireccional *adj* multidirectional.
multidisciplinar(io) *adj*: **estudio ~** cross-disciplinary study, study involving a variety of disciplines.
multifacético *adj* many-sided.
multifamiliar *adj*: **edificio ~** block of flats, block of tenements.
multiforme *adj* manifold, multifarious; multiform; having different forms.
multifuncional *adj* multifunctional.
multigrado *adj aceite etc* multigrade.
multilaminar *nm* (*t* **madera ~**) plywood.
multilateral *adj*, **multilátero** *adj* multilateral, many-sided.
multilingüe *adj* multilingual.
multimedia *adj invar* multimedia (*atr*).
multimillonario, -a *nm/f* multimillionaire.
multinacional 1 *adj* multinational. **2** *nf* multinational (company).
multipartidismo *nm* multi-party system.
multipartidista *adj* multi-party (*atr*).
múltiple *adj* (**a**) (*Mat*) multiple; (*fig*) many-sided. (**b**) (*fig*) **~s** (*muchos*) many, numerous; (*variados*) manifold, multifarious; **tiene ~s actividades** he has multifarious activities, he has very numerous activities.
multiplexor *nm* multiplexor.
multiplicación *nf* multiplication.
multiplicado *nm* multiplicand.
multiplicar [1g] **1** *vt* (*Mat y fig*) to multiply (*por* by); *posibilidades etc* to increase; (*Mec*) to gear up.
2 multiplicarse *vr* (**a**) (*Mat, Bio etc*) to multiply; to increase.
(**b**) (*fig*) to be everywhere at once; to attend to a lot of things all at once; **no puedo multiplicarme** I can't be in half-a-dozen places at once.
multiplicidad *nf* multiplicity.
múltiplo 1 *adj* multiple. **2** *nm* multiple; **mínimo común ~** lowest common multiple.
multiprocesador *nm* multiprocessor.
multiprocesamiento *nm*, **multiproceso** *nm* multiprocessing.
multirracial *adj* multiracial.
multirregulable *adj* adjustable (to a variety of positions).
multirreincidencia *nf* persistent offending.
multirreincidente *nmf* persistent offender.
multirriesgo *atr*: **póliza ~** fully comprehensive policy.
multisecular *adj* age-old, centuries-old, very ancient.
multitarea 1 *adj invar* multitasking. **2** *nf* multitask.
multitud *nf* multitude; (*de gente*) crowd; **la ~** (*pey*) the multitude, the masses; **~ de*** lots of, heaps of*; **tengo ~ de cosas que hacer** I have loads of things to do.
multitudinario *adj* massive, mass (*atr*); *reunión etc* big, attended by large numbers; *manifestación* mass (*atr*); *recepción* tumultuous, exuberant.
multiuso *adj invar* for many uses, multipurpose.
multiusuario *adj invar* multiuser.
multiviaje *adj invar*: **billete ~** season ticket.
mullido 1 *adj* (**a**) *cama etc* soft, sprung; fluffy; *hierba etc* soft, springy. (**b**) **dejar a uno ~*** to leave sb all in, wear sb out. **2** *nm* (*relleno*) stuffing, filling.
mullir [3a] *vt* (**a**) *almohada, lana etc* to make fluffy, fluff up; (*ablandar*) to soften; *cama* to shake up; *tierra* to hoe, loosen. (**b**) *plantas* to hoe round, loosen the earth round.
mullo *nm* (red) mullet.
mun. *abr de* **municipio** town.
mundanal *adj* (*liter*) worldly, of the world.
mundanalidad *nf* (*liter*) worldliness.
mundanería *nf* worldliness.
mundano 1 *adj* (**a**) (*del mundo*) worldly, of the world.
(**b**) (*de alta sociedad*) society (*atr*); fashionable; social; **son gente muy mundana** they're great society people; **una reunión mundana** a fashionable gathering, a gathering of society people.
2 *nm*, **mundana** *nf* society person, socialite.
mundial 1 *adj* world-wide, universal; *distribución, guerra, marca etc* world (*atr*); **las comunicaciones ~es** world communications; **un invento de aplicación ~** an invention of world-wide application; **otra guerra ~** another world war.
2 *nm* world championship, (*esp*) **el M~** the World Cup (*soccer*).
mundialización *nf* extension world-wide; internationalization.
mundialmente *adv* throughout the world; universally; **~ famoso** world-famous; **hacer algo ~ popular** to make sth popular throughout the world.
mundillo *nm* (**a**) (*gen*) world, circle; **en el ~ teatral** in the theatre world, in theatrical circles. (**b**) (*Bot*) viburnum.
mundo *nm* world; (*fig*) world, people; society; (*Ecl*)

world, secular life; ~ **antiguo** ancient world; ~ **feliz** brave new world; **Nuevo M~** New World; **Tercer M~** Third World; **Viejo M~** Old World; **el ~ hispánico** the Hispanic world; **el gran ~** high life, high society; **el ~ del espectáculo** show business; **este pícaro ~** this wicked world; **en el ~ de las ideas** in the world of ideas, in the realm of ideas; **medio ~** almost everybody, a huge number; **estaba medio ~** there were hordes of people; **el otro ~** the other world, the next world; **no es nada del otro ~** it's nothing extraordinary; **hacer algo del otro ~** to do sth quite extraordinary; **todo el ~** everybody; **en todo el ~** everywhere; throughout the world; **es lo que más desea en el ~** it's what she wants most in the world; **por esos ~s (de Dios)** there; all over, here there and everywhere; **el ~ es un pañuelo** it's a small world; **desde que el ~ es ~** since time began; **se le cae el ~ encima** he gets disheartened; **echar al ~** to bring into the world; **echarse al ~** to take to prostitution; **aunque se hunda el ~** come what may; **no por eso se hundirá el ~** it won't be the end of the world; **irse al otro ~** to pass away; **así va el ~** that's the way it is; **ponerse el ~ por montera** to care nothing for public opinion; **tener (mucho) ~** to be experienced, be sophisticated, know one's way around; **tener poco ~** to be inexperienced; **como Dios lo trajo al ~, tal como vino al ~** stark naked; **ver ~** to see life, see the world; **ha visto mucho ~** he's knocked around a lot.

mundología *nf* worldly-wisdom, experience of the world, savoir-faire.

mundonuevo *nm* peep show.

munición *nf* (**a**) (*t* **municiones**) (*balas etc*) ammunition; munitions; (*provisiones*) stores, supplies; **municiones de boca** provisions, rations. (**b**) **de ~** army (*atr*), service (*atr*); **botas de ~** army boots. (**c**) (*CAm*) uniform.

municionera *nf* (*Carib*) ammunition pouch.

municipal 1 *adj* municipal; *cocejo etc* town (*atr*); *piscina* public. **2** *nm* (*guardia*) (city) policeman.

municipalidad *nf* municipality.

municipio *nm* (**a**) (*distrito*) municipality; town, township. (**b**) (*ayuntamiento*) corporation; town council. (**c**) (*edificio*) town hall.

munificencia *nf* munificence.

munífico *adj* munificent.

muniqués 1 *adj* of Munich. **2** *nm*, **muniquesa** *nf* native (*o* inhabitant) of Munich; **los muniqueses** the people of Munich.

muñeca *nf* (**a**) (*Anat*) wrist. (**b**) (*de niño*) doll; (*de sastre*) dummy; (⁑: *chica*) doll⁑; ~ **de trapo** rag doll. (**c**) (*trapos*) bunch of rags, cleaning (*o* polishing) pad. (**d**) (*Cono Sur**) pull, influence.

muñeco *nm* (**a**) (*figura*) figure; (*juguete*) (boy) doll; (*espantapájaros*) guy, scarecrow; (*títere*) puppet, marionette; (*de sastre*) dummy; ~ **de nieve** snowman.

(**b**) (*fig*: *instrumento*) puppet, pawn.

(**c**) (*: *niño*) pretty little boy, little angel; (*pey*) sissy*.

(**d**) (*: *lío*) row, shindy*.

(**e**) **entrarle los ~s a uno** (*And**) to have butterflies in one's stomach.

muñeira *nf a popular Galician dance.*

muñequado* *adj* (*And*) jumpy, nervous.

muñequera[1] *nf* wristband.

muñequero, -a[2] *nm/f* puppeteer.

muñir [3h] *vt* (**a**) (*convocar*) to summon, convoke, call. (**b**) (*pey*) to rig, fix, arrange in a fraudulent fashion.

muñón *nm* (**a**) (*Anat*) stump. (**b**) (*Mec*) trunnion; pivot, journal.

mural 1 *adj* mural, wall (*atr*); **mapa ~** wall map. **2** *nm* mural.

muralla *nf* (city) wall, walls; rampart; (*LAm*) (*any*) wall; **la Gran M~ china** the Great Wall of China.

murar [1a] *vt* to wall.

Murcia *nf* Murcia.

murciano, -a *adj, nm/f* Murcian.

murciélago *nm* bat.

murga *nf* (**a**) (*banda*) street band. (**b**) (*: *lata*) bore, nuisance, bind*; **dar la ~** to be a pain*, be a pest.

murguista *nm* (**a**) (*músico*) street musician; (*hum**) bad musician, poor player. (**b**) (*: *pesado*) bore.

múrido *nm* rodent.

murmullo *nm* (**a**) (*susurro*) murmur(ing); whisper(ing); mutter(ing). (**b**) (*de agua*) murmur, rippling; (*de hojas, viento*) rustle, rustling; (*ruido confuso*) hum(ming).

murmuración *nf* gossip; slanderous talk, backbiting; constant complaining.

murmurador 1 *adj* (*chismoso*) gossip; (*criticón*) backbiting; critical; complaining, grumbling. **2** *nm*, **murmuradora** *nf* (*chismoso*) gossip; (*criticón*) backbiter; critic; complainer, grumbler.

murmurar [1a] *vi* (**a**) (*persona*) (*susurrar*) to murmur, whisper; (*quejarse*) to mutter.

(**b**) (*agua*) to murmur, ripple; (*hojas, viento etc*) to rustle; (*abejas, multitud etc*) to hum.

(**c**) (*fig*) (*cotillear*) to gossip (*de* about); (*criticar*) to criticize (*de uno* sb); (*quejarse*) to grumble (*de* about), mutter (*de* about); **siempre están murmurando del jefe** they're always grumbling about the boss, they're always criticizing the boss.

muro *nm* wall; ~ **de Berlín** Berlin Wall; ~ **de contención** containing wall; **M~ de las Lamentaciones** Wailing Wall.

murria *nf* (*Esp*) depression, blues; sulks; **tener ~** to feel blue, be down in the dumps*; to feel sulky.

murrio *adj* depressed, dejected; sulky, sullen.

murruco* *adj* (*CAm*) curly-haired.

mus[1] *nm a card game.*

mus[2] = **chus**; **sin decir ni ~** without saying a word.

musa *nf* muse; **las M~s** the Muses.

musaraña *nf* (**a**) (*Zool*) shrew; (*any*) small creature, bug, creepy-crawly*. (**b**) (*mota*) speck floating in the eye; **mirar a las ~s** to stare vacantly; **pensar en las ~s** to go woolgathering.

musculación *nf* muscle-building.

muscular *adj* muscular.

musculatura *nf* muscles, musculature; (*fig*) muscle; **doblar** (*o* **estirar**) **su ~** to flex one's muscles (*t fig*).

músculo *nm* muscle.

musculoso *adj* muscular; tough, brawny.

museística *nf* museum studies.

museístico *adj* museum (*atr*).

muselina *nf* muslin.

museo *nm* museum; gallery; ~ **de arte**, ~ **de pintura** art gallery; ~ **de cera** waxworks.

musgaño *nm* shrew.

musgo *nm* moss.

musgoso *adj* mossy, moss-covered.

música *nf* (**a**) (*gen*) music; ~ **ambiental** piped music; background music; ~ **de cámara** chamber music; ~ **celestial*** fine talk, empty promises, hot air*; ~ **concreta** concrete music; ~ **coreada** choral music; ~ **enlatada*** canned music; ~ **de fondo** background music; ~ **ligera** light music; ~ **mundana**, ~ **de las esferas**, ~ **de los planetas** music of the spheres; ~ **sagrada** sacred music; **poner ~ a** to set to music; **irse con la ~ a otra parte** to take one's troubles elsewhere; to go away, go somewhere else; **me suena a ~ de caballitos** it sounds all too familiar; **¡con la ~ a otra parte!** off with you!, get out!

(**b**) (*banda*) band.

(**c**) (*: *tonterías*) **~s** drivel; **no estoy para ~s** I'm not in the mood to listen to such drivel.

(**d**) (*Esp*⁑: *cartera*) wallet.

(**e**) (⁑: *dinero*) bread⁑, money.

musical *adj, nm* musical.

musicalidad *nf* musicality, musical quality.

musicalizar [1f] *vt* to set to music.

musicar [1g] *vt* to set to music.

músico 1 *adj* musical. **2** *nmf* (**a**) (*Mús*) musician, player; ~ **callejero** street musician; ~ **mayor** bandmaster. (**b**) (*) pickpocket.

musicología *nf* musicology.

musicólogo *nm*, **musicóloga** *nf* musicologist.

musiqueo *nm* monotonous sound.

musiquilla *nf* tune; piece of light music.

musitar [1a] *vti* to mumble, mutter.

muslada⁑ *nf*, **muslamen**⁑ *nm* thighs.

muslime *adj, nmf* Moslem.

muslímico *adj* Moslem.

muslo *nm* thigh.

mustango *nm* mustang.

mustela *nf* weasel.

mustiarse [1b] *vr* to wither, wilt.

mustio *adj* (**a**) (*Bot*) withered, faded. (**b**) (*poco tieso*) soft, slack. (**c**) (*triste*) depressed, gloomy. (**d**) (*Méx*) hypocritical.

musulmán, -ana *adj, nm/f* Moslem.

mutabilidad *nf* mutability; changeableness.

mutación *nf* (**a**) (*cambio*) (sudden) change. (**b**) (*Bio*) mutation. (**c**) (*Ling*) mutation. (**d**) (*Teat*) change of scene.

mutagene *nm* mutagen.

mutante *adj, nmf* mutant.

mutil *nm* (*Hist*) Carlist soldier.

mutilación *nf* mutilation.

mutilado 1 *adj* crippled, disabled. **2** *nm,* **mutilada** *nf* cripple, disabled person; ~ **de guerra** war cripple.

mutilar [1a] *vt* (**a**) (*gen*) to mutilate; (*lisiar*) to cripple, maim, disable. (**b**) (*fig*) *texto etc* to mutilate, hack about, spoil; *cuento* to garble; *objeto* to deface.

mutis *nm invar* (*Teat*) exit; ¡~! sh!; **hacer** ~ (*Teat*) to exit, go off; (*fig*) to say nothing, keep quiet; **hacer ~ por el foro** (*fig*) to make oneself scarce.

mutismo *nm* dumbness; (*fig*) silence, uncommunicativeness.

mutual *nf* (*And, Cono Sur*) friendly society.

mutualidad *nf* (**a**) (*reciprocidad*) mutuality, mutual character. (**b**) (*ayuda*) mutual aid, reciprocal aid. (**c**) (*sociedad*) friendly society, mutual benefit society.

mutuamente *adv* mutually, reciprocally.

mutuo *adj* mutual, reciprocal; joint.

muy 1 *adv* very; greatly, highly; (*demasiado*) too; ~ **bueno** very good; ~ **lentamente** very slowly; ~ **buscado** very much sought-after, highly prized; ~ **de noche** very late at night; **tener ~ en cuenta** to bear very much in mind; **venir ~ tarde** to come very late; **es ~ de sentir** it is much to be regretted; **eso es ~ español** that's very Spanish, that's typically Spanish; **eso es ~ de él** that's just like him; **es ~ hombre** he's a real man, he's pretty tough; **es ~ mujer** she's very feminine; as a woman she's terribly attractive; **el ~ bestia de Pedro** that great idiot Peter; **¡el ~ bandido!** the rat!*

2 *nf* (‡) (*lengua*) tongue; (*boca*) trap‡, mouth; **achantar la ~** to shut one's trap‡; **irse de la ~** to spill the beans*; **largar por la ~** to speak, tell.

N

N, n ['ene] *nf* (*letra*) N, n.

n. (**a**) *abr de* **nuestro** *o* **nuestra** our. (**b**) *abr de* **nacido** born, b. (**c**) *abr de* **número** number, No.

N (**a**) (*Geog*) *abr de* **norte** *adj y nm* north, N. (**b**) (*Aut*) *abr de* **nacional** main road. (**c**) *abr de* **noviembre** November, Nov.

na*, ná* *pron etc* = **nada.**

naba *nf* (*Bot*) swede.

nabab *nm* nabob.

nabina *nf* rapeseed.

nabiza *nf* (*Esp*) turnip greens.

nabo *nm* (**a**) (*Bot*) turnip; (*any*) root vegetable, thick root; ~ **gallego,** ~ **sueco** swede.

(**b**) (*Anat*) root of the tail.

(**c**) (*Arquit*) newel, stair post.

(**d**) (*Náut*) mast.

(**e**) (**) prick**.

Nabucodonosor *nm* Nebuchadnezzar.

nácar *nm* mother-of-pearl, nacre.

nacarado *adj*, **nacarino** *adj* mother-of-pearl (*atr*), pearly, nacreous.

nacatamal *nm* (*CAm, Méx*) *maize, meat and rice wrapped in banana leaf.*

nacatete *nm* (*Méx*), **nacatón** *nm*, **nacatona** *nf* (*CAm, Méx*) unfledged chick.

nacedera *nf* (*CAm*: *t* **cerca** ~) hedge.

nacencia *nf* (*LAm*) = **nacimiento.**

nacer [2d] **1** *vi* (**a**) (*gen*) to be born; (*de huevo*) to hatch; **nací en Cuba** I was born in Cuba; **cuando nazca el niño** when the baby is born; ~ **al amor** to awaken to love; **con esa exposición nació a la vida artística** that exhibition saw the beginning of his artistic career; ~ **parado** (*And**) to be born with a silver spoon in one's mouth; ~ **de pie** to be born lucky; **no nació para sufrir** she was not born to suffer; **nació para poeta** he was born to be a poet; **nadie nace enseñado** we all have to learn.

(**b**) (*Bot*) to sprout, bud; to come up; (*estrella etc*) to rise; (*río*) to rise; (*agua*) to spring up, appear, begin to flow; (*camino*) to begin, start (*de* from, *en* in); **le nacieron alas** it grew wings; **le nació mucho pelo** it sprouted a lot of hair.

(**c**) (*fig*: *idea etc*) to be born; to begin, originate, have its origin (*en* in); **nació una sospecha en su mente** a suspicion formed in her mind; **el error nace del hecho de que ...** the error springs (*o* stems) from the fact that ...; **entre ellos ha nacido una fuerte simpatía** a strong friendship has sprung up between them; **¿de dónde nace la idea?** where does the idea come from?

2 nacerse *vr* (**a**) (*Bot*) to bud, sprout.

(**b**) (*Cos*) to split.

nacido 1 *adj* born; ~ **a la libertad** born free; ~ **para el amor** born to love; ~ **de padres ricos** born of wealthy parents; **bien** ~ of noble birth; well-bred; **mal** ~ mean, base, wicked; ill-bred (*V t* **malnacido**); **recién** ~ newborn.

2 *nm* (**a**) (*ser*) human being; **todos los** ~**s** everybody, all mankind; **ningún** ~ nobody.

(**b**) (*Med*) tumour, growth; boil.

(**c**) (*Cos*) split.

naciente 1 *adj* (*que nace*) nascent; (*nuevo*) new, recent; (*creciente*) growing; *sol* rising; **el** ~ **interés por ...** the newfound interest in ..., the growing interest in ...

2 *nm* (**a**) (*este*) east.

(**b**) (*Cono Sur*: *t* ~**s**) spring, source.

nacimiento *nm* (**a**) (*gen*) birth; (*Orn etc*) hatching; ~ **sin violencia** natural childbirth; **ciego de** ~ blind from birth; **un tonto de** ~ a born fool; **este defecto lo tiene de** ~ he has had this defect since birth, he was born with this defect.

(**b**) (*fig*: *estirpe*) descent, family; **de** ~ **noble** of noble birth, of noble family.

(**c**) (*de agua, río*) source.

(**d**) (*fig*) birth; (*origen*) origin, beginning, start; **dar** ~ **a** to give rise to; **el partido tuvo su** ~ **en ...** the party had its origins in ...

(**e**) (*Arte, Ecl*) nativity (scene).

nación 1 *nf* nation; people; **Naciones Unidas** United Nations; **trato de** ~ **más favorecida** most favoured nation treatment; **ruritano de** ~ Ruritanian by birth, of Ruritanian nationality. **2** *nmf* (*Cono Sur*) foreigner.

nacional 1 *adj* national; *industria, producto etc* home (*atr*), local; home-produced; indigenous; **páginas de** ~ (*Prensa*) home news pages; (*anuncio*) **'vuelos** ~**es'** 'domestic flights'. **2** *nmf* national; **los** ~**es** (*España, 1936 etc*) the Franco forces.

nacionalcatolicismo *nm* Spanish Catholicism considered as an ally of Franco.

nacionalidad *nf* (**a**) nationality; **de** ~ **argentina** Argentine by birth, of Argentine nationality; ~ **doble** dual nationality. (**b**) ((*Esp Pol*) autonomous region, regional government.

nacionalismo *nm* nationalism.

nacionalista 1 *adj* nationalist(ic). **2** *nmf* nationalist.

nacionalización *nf* (**a**) (*de inmigrante*) naturalization. (**b**) (*Econ*) nationalization.

nacionalizar [1f] **1** *vt* (**a**) *persona* to naturalize. (**b**) *industria* to nationalize. **2 nacionalizarse** *vr* to become naturalized; to be nationalized.

nacionalsocialismo *nm* national socialism.

naco* 1 *adj* (*Méx*) (*bobo*) stupid; (*cobarde*) yellow.

2 *nm* (**a**) (*CAm*: *cobarde*) coward; (*endeble*) weakling, milksop.

(**b**) (*And, Cono Sur*: *tabaco*) plug of tobacco.

(**c**) (*And*) *maize kernels cooked with salt*; mashed potatoes.

(**d**) (*Cono Sur*: *susto*) fright, scare.

(**e**) ~**s** (*Cono Sur*) roll of banknotes.

Nacho *nm forma familiar de* Ignacio.

nada 1 *pron* nothing; **no dijo** ~ she said nothing, she didn't say anything; **¡~, ~!** not a bit of it!; ~ **de** ~ absolutely nothing, nothing at all; ~ **de eso** nothing of the kind, far from it; **¡~ de eso!** not a bit of it!; **¡~ de excusas!** no excuses!; **¡~ de marcharse!** forget about leaving!; **¡de eso ~, monada!*** no way!*; **esto y ~, es lo mismo** it all boils down to nothing; **no tiene ~ de particular** there's nothing special about it; **no le conozco de ~** I don't know him from Adam; ~ **entre dos platos** a lot of fuss, much ado about nothing; *V* **más; a cada (de)** ~ (*LAm*) all the time, at every step; **antes de** ~ very soon, right away; **antes de ~ tengo que ...** before I do anything else I must ...; **a cada ~*** (*LAm*) constantly; **casi** ~ next to nothing; **¡casi ~!** a mere bagatelle!, just peanuts!*; **como si** ~ as if it didn't matter, as if it were only a small thing; **¡de ~!** not at all!, don't mention it!; **estuvo en ~ que lo perdiesen** they very nearly lost it; **quedar(se) en** ~ to come to nothing; **no reparar en** ~ to stop at nothing; **en ~ de tiempo** in no time at all; **hace** ~ just a moment ago; **no quiere comer ni** ~ he won't eat or anything; **¡ni curas ni ~!*** blow the priests!*; I don't want to hear about the priests!; **no los mencionó para** ~ he never mentioned them at all; **no servir para** ~ to be no use at all, be utterly useless; **¡por ~!** (*Cono Sur*) not at all!, don't mention it! **llorar por** ~ to cry for no reason at all; **por ~ del mundo** not for anything in the world; **por menos de** ~ for two pins; **no lo hago por ~ ni por nadie** I won't do it and that's that; **no por ~ le llaman 'tufos'** he's not called 'stinker' for nothing; **no por ~ decidimos comprar** we had good reason to buy; **¡pues ~!** not to worry!;

no ha sido ~ it's nothing; **y** ~ and that was that, so there it was.

2 *adv* not at all, by no means; **no es** ~ **fácil** it's not at all easy, it's far from easy.

3 *nf* nothingness; **la** ~ the void; **el avión parecía salir de la** ~ the aircraft seemed to come from nowhere.

nadaderas *nfpl* water wings.

nadador(a) *nm/f* swimmer.

nadar [1a] *vi* (**a**) (*gen*) to swim; (*corcho etc*) to float; (*And*) to take a bath; **querer** ~ **y guardar la ropa** to want to have it both ways, want to have one's cake and eat it.

(**b**) (*Cos*) **estos pantalones le quedan nadando** he's lost inside these trousers, these trousers are much too big for him.

(**c**) ~ **en** (*fig*) *dinero etc* to wallow in, be rolling in.

nadería *nf* small thing, mere trifle.

nadie *pron* (**a**) (*gen*) nobody, no-one; ~ **lo tiene, no lo tiene** ~ nobody has it; **no he visto a** ~ I haven't seen anybody; **apenas** ~ hardly anybody; **lo hace como** ~ she does it jolly well.

(**b**) **no es** ~ he's nobody (that matters); **es un don** ~ he's a nobody.

nadir *nm* nadir.

nadita (*LAm*) = **nada.**

nado 1 *adv*: **cruzar** (*o* **pasar**) **a** ~ to swim, swim across. **2** *nm* (*) swimming stroke, swimming style.

nafta *nf* naphtha; (*Cono Sur*) petrol, gasoline (*US*).

naftaleno *nm*, **naftalina** *nf* naphthalene.

nagual *nm* (**a**) (*CAm, Méx*: *brujo*) sorcerer, wizard. (**b**) (*CAm*: *compañero*) inseparable companion. (**c**) (*Méx*: *mentira*) lie.

nagualear‡ [1a] *vi* (*Méx*) (**a**) (*mentir*) to lie. (**b**) (*robar*) to nick things‡. (**c**) (*jaranear*) to paint the town red.

naguas *nfpl* petticoat.

nagüeta *nf* (*CAm*) overskirt.

nahual *nm* (*CAm, Méx*) (*Mit*) spirit, phantom; (*doble*) double; (*: *ladrón*) cat burglar.

nahuatl *nm* (*Ling*) Nahuatl.

naide* *pron* (*hum*) = **nadie.**

nailon *nm* nylon.

naipe *nm* playing card; ~ **de figura** court card, picture; ~**s** cards.

naipeador *adj* (*Cono Sur*) fond of cards.

naipear [1a] *vi* (*Cono Sur*) to play cards.

naja‡: **de** ~(**s**) at full speed, like the clappers*; **darse de** ~, **salir de** ~ to get out, beat it*.

najarse‡ [1a] *vr* to beat it*.

najencia‡ *interj* scram!‡

nal. *abr de* **nacional** national, nat.

nalga *nf* buttock; ~**s** buttocks, backside, rump; **dar de** ~**s** to fall on one's bottom.

nalgada *nf* (**a**) (*Culin*) ham. (**b**) (*azote*) smack on the bottom; ~**s** spanking.

nalguiento *adj* (*And*), **nalgón** *adj* (*And*), **nalgudo** *adj* big-bottomed, broad in the beam*.

Namibia *nf* Namibia.

namibio, -a *adj, nm/f* Namibian.

nana[1] *nf* (**a**) (*abuela*) grandma*, granny*; *V* **año.** (**b**) (*Mús*) lullaby, cradlesong. (**c**) (*pelele*) baby's sleeping bag. (**d**) (*CAm, Méx*) (*nodriza*) wet-nurse; (*niñera*) nursemaid. (**e**) (*CAm*: *mamá*) mum*, mummy*.

nana[2]* *nf* (*Cono Sur*: *dolor*) pain.

nanai*, nanay* *interj* no way!*, not on your life!; **me hizo ver que** ~ **de la China** he made me see there was nothing doing, he showed me it just wasn't on*.

nano, -a[3]‡ *nm/f* kid.

nao *nf* (*Hist*) ship..

napa *nf* imitation leather.

napalm *nm* napalm.

napia‡ *nf* (*t* ~**s** *pl*) snout*, nose.

napo‡ *nm* 1000-peseta note.

Napoleón *nm* Napoleon.

napoleón *nm* (*Cono Sur*) pliers, wire-cutters.

napoleónico *adj* Napoleonic.

Nápoles *nm* Naples.

napolitano, -a *adj, nm/f* Neapolitan.

narajái‡ *nm* (*Esp*) priest.

naranja 1 *nf* (**a**) (*gen*) orange; ~ **cajel,** ~ **zajarí** Seville orange; ~ **sanguina** blood orange.

(**b**) (*) **¡~s!, ¡~s chinas!, ¡~s de la China!** nonsense!, rubbish!

(**c**) (*Esp*: *pareja*) **la media** ~ one's better half; **esperar la media** ~ to wait for Mr Right; **encontrar su media** ~ to find one's life partner; **¡sí, naranjita!** yes darling!

(**d**) (*Carib*) bitter orange.

2 *adj invar* orange.

naranjada *nf* orangeade.

naranjado *adj* orange, orange-coloured.

naranjal *nm* orange grove.

naranjo *nm* orange tree.

Narbona *nf* Narbonne.

narcisismo *nm* narcissism.

narcisista *adj* narcissistic.

Narciso *nm* Narcissus.

narciso *nm* (**a**) (*Bot*) narcissus; ~ **atrompetado,** ~ **trompón** daffodil. (**b**) (*fig*) dandy, fop.

narco* *nm* = **narcotraficante;** = **narcotráfico.**

narco... *pref* narco...; drug(s) ... (*atr*).

narcosis *nf* narcosis.

narcoterrorismo *nm* drug-related terrorism.

narcótico 1 *adj* narcotic. **2** *nm* narcotic; (*somnífero*) sleeping pill; ~**s** (*en sentido lato*) drugs, dope.

narcotismo *nm* narcosis, narcotism.

narcotizar [1f] *vt* to narcotize; (*en sentido lato*) to drug, dope.

narcotraficante *nmf* drug dealer.

narcotráfico *nm* drugs traffic, traffic in drugs.

nardo *nm* nard; spikenard.

narguile *nm* hookah.

naricear* [1a] *vt* (*And*) to smell (out); (*fig*) to poke one's nose into.

narigada *nf* (*LAm*) snuff.

narigón 1 *adj* big-nosed. **2** *nm* (*Carib, Méx*) nose ring.

narigudo *adj* big-nosed.

narigueta *adj* (*Cono Sur*) big-nosed.

nariz *nf* (**a**) (*Anat*) nose; nostril.

(**b**) (*Anat*) **narices** *pl* nostrils; (*) nose; **¡narices!*** rubbish!, nonsense!; **un rapapolvo de narices*** a real good telling-off*; **era guapa de narices*** she was pretty and then some*; **me encuentro de narices*** I'm on top of the world; **he dormido de narices*** I slept jolly well*; **cerrar la puerta en las narices de uno, dar con la puerta en las narices de uno** to shut the door in sb's face; **dar de narices** to fall flat on one's face; **dar de narices contra la puerta** to bang one's face on the door; **en mis propias narices** under my very nose; **estar hasta las narices*** to be completely fed up (*de* with)*; **hablar por las narices** to talk through one's nose, speak with a nasal twang; **lo hará por narices*** she'll do it because she wants to; **para el lunes por narices*** by Monday without fail; **se le hincharon las narices** he got very cross; **ese tío me hincha las narices*** that chap gets on my nerves; **meter las narices en algo** to poke one's nose into sth; **eso me lo paso por las narices*** I don't care tuppence about that*; **hazlo o te rompo las narices*** do it or I'll smash your face in*; **¡tiene narices la cosa!*** well I'm damned!; **tocarse las narices*** to slack, be idle; to stand idly by; to let one's attention wander.

(**c**) (*olfato*) sense of smell.

(**d**) (*de vino*) bouquet, nose.

narizota *nf* big nose; **¡~s!*** (*Esp*) (*canalla*) you villain!; (*idiota*) you idiot!

narizudo *adj* (*LAm*) big-nosed.

narpias‡ *nfpl* = **napia.**

narración *nf* narration, account.

narrador(a) *nm/f* narrator.

narrar [1a] *vt* to tell, narrate, recount.

narrativa *nf* (**a**) (*narración*) narrative, story. (**b**) (*arte*) narrative skill, skill in storytelling. (**c**) (*género*) fiction.

narrativo *adj* narrative.

narval *nm* narwhal.

nasa *nf* (*de pan*) bread bin, flour bin; (*cesta*) basket, creel; (*trampa*) fish trap.

nasal *adj, nf* nasal.

nasalidad *nf* nasality.

nasalización *nf* nasalization.

nasalizar [1f] *vt* to nasalize.

nasalmente *adv* nasally.

naso‡ *nm* (*Cono Sur*) nose, conk‡.

N.ª S.ra *abr* de **Nuestra Señora** Our Lady, the Virgin.

nasti‡ 1 *interj* no way!*

2 *adv*: **de eso** ~, (**monasti**)! no way!*, get away!*

nata *nf* (**a**) (*Esp*) (*gen*) cream; (*en leche hervida etc*) skin; ~ **batida** whipped cream; ~ **líquida** cream. (**b**) (*fig*) cream, choicest part, best part; *V* **flor.**

natación *nf* (**a**) (*gen*) swimming.

(**b**) (*estilo*) style (of swimming), stroke; ~ **a braza,** ~ **de pecho** breast-stroke; ~ **de costado,** ~ **en cuchillo** side-stroke; ~ **de espalda** backstroke; ~ **sincronizada**

synchronized swimming; ~ **submarina** underwater swimming; skin diving.
natal *adj* natal; *suelo etc* native; *pueblo etc* home (*atr*).
natalicio 1 *adj* birthday (*atr*). **2** *nm* birthday.
natalidad *nf* birth rate.
natillas *nfpl* (*Esp*) custard; ~ **de huevo** egg custard.
natividad *nf* nativity.
nativo 1 *adj* (**a**) (*gen*) native; *país etc* native, home (*atr*); **lengua nativa** native language, mother tongue.
(**b**) (*natural*) natural, innate.
(**c**) (*Min*) native.
2 *nm*, **nativa** *nf* native.
nato *adj* (**a**) (*gen*) born; **un actor** ~ a born actor; **un criminal** ~ a hardened criminal, an incorrigible criminal; **es un pintor** ~ he's a natural painter.
(**b**) (*por derecho*) ex officio; **el secretario es miembro** ~ **de** ... the secretary is ex officio a member of ...
natura *nf* (*Anat*) genitals.
naturaca‡ *interj* naturally!, natch‡.
natural 1 *adj* (**a**) (*gen*) natural; **es** ~ **que** ... it is natural that ...
(**b**) *fruta* fresh, raw; *agua* plain; *flor* real.
(**c**) (*Mús*) natural.
2 *nmf* native, inhabitant; **fue** ~ **de Sigüenza** he was a native of Sigüenza; **trató sin miramientos a los ~es** he treated the inhabitants unceremoniously; **¿de dónde es Vd ~?** where are you from?, where were you born?
3 *nm* (**a**) (*temperamento*) nature, disposition, temperament; **buen** ~ good nature.
(**b**) **fruta al** ~ fruit in its own juice; **se sirve al** ~ it is served at room temperature; **una descripción al** ~ a true-to-life description, a realistic description; **vivir al** ~ to live according to nature; **está muy guapa al** ~ she is very pretty just as she is (without make-up *etc*); **pintar del** ~ to paint from life, paint from nature; **clase de dibujo del** ~ life-class.
(**c**) (*Taur*) natural, *a kind of pass with the cape.*
naturaleza *nf* (**a**) (*gen*) nature; ~ **humana** human nature.
(**b**) ~ **muerta** (*Arte*) still life.
(**c**) (*Pol*) nationality; **el joven es suizo de** ~ the young man is Swiss by nationality.
(**d**) (*Pol*) citizenship (*granted to a foreigner*); **carta de** ~ naturalization papers.
(**e**) **romper la** ~ to reach puberty, start to menstruate.
naturalidad *nf* naturalness; **con la mayor** ~ (**del mundo**) as if nothing had happened; as if it were the most natural thing in the world; **lo dijo con la mayor** ~ he said it in a perfectly ordinary tone; **allí le pegan un tiro con la mayor** ~ they'll shoot you there and think nothing of it.
naturalismo *nm* (**a**) (*Arte etc*) naturalism; realism. (**b**) (*nudismo*) naturism.
naturalista 1 *adj* naturalistic; realistic. **2** *nmf* (**a**) (*Arte etc*) naturalist. (**b**) (*nudista*) naturist.
naturalización *nf* naturalization.
naturalizar [1f] **1** *vt* to naturalize. **2 naturalizarse** *vr* to become naturalized.
naturalmente *adv* (**a**) (*de modo natural*) naturally; in a natural way. (**b**) ¡~! naturally!, of course!; you bet!
naturismo *nm* naturism; naturopathy.
naturista *nmf* naturist, naturopath.
naturópata *nmf* naturopath.
naturopatía *nf* naturopathy.
naufragar [1h] *vi* (**a**) (*barco*) to be wrecked, sink; (*persona*) to be shipwrecked. (**b**) (*fig*) to fail, miscarry, suffer a disaster.
naufragio *nm* (**a**) (*lit*) shipwreck. (**b**) (*fig*) failure, disaster, ruin.
náufrago 1 *adj* shipwrecked. **2** *nm*, **náufraga** *nf* shipwrecked sailor, shipwrecked person; castaway.
náusea *nf* nausea, sick feeling; (*fig*) disgust, repulsion; **dar ~s a** to nauseate, sicken, disgust; **tener ~s** to feel nauseated, feel sick; (*fig*) to be nauseated, be sickened.
nauseabundo *adj* nauseating, sickening.
náutica *nf* navigation, seamanship.
náutico *adj* nautical.
nautilo *nm* nautilus.
navaja *nf* (**a**) (*cuchillo*) clasp knife, jack-knife; ~ (**de afeitar**) razor; ~ **automática,** ~ **de muelle,** ~ **de resorte** flick knife; ~ **barbera** cutthroat razor; ~ **multiuso**(**s**) Swiss army knife. (**b**) (*Zool*) (*colmillo*) tusk; (*molusco*) razor shell; (*Ent*) sting. (**c**) (*fig*) sharp tongue, evil tongue.
navajada *nf*, **navajazo** *nm* slash, gash, razor wound.
navajeo *nm* knifing, stabbing; (*fig*) infighting; backstabbing, stabbing in the back.
navajero *nm* criminal who carries a knife.
naval *adj* naval; ship (*atr*), sea (*atr*).
Navarra *nf* Navarre.
navarrica* *adj y nmf* = **navarro.**
navarro, -a 1 *adj, nm/f* Navarrese. **2** *nm* (*Ling*) Navarrese.
nave *nf* (**a**) (*Náut*) ship, vessel; **quemar las ~s** to burn one's boats; ~ **insignia** flagship; **la N~ de San Pedro** (*Ecl*) the Roman Catholic Church.
(**b**) ~ **espacial** spaceship, spacecraft.
(**c**) (*Arquit*) (*de iglesia*) nave; (*de fábrica etc*) bay; ~ **lateral** aisle.
(**d**) (*Téc*) large building, large shed; factory, mill, plant; ~ **industrial** factory premises; ~ **de laminación** rolling mill.
(**e**) (*Méx**: *coche*) car.
navegabilidad *nf* navigability; seaworthiness.
navegable *adj río etc* navigable; *barco* seaworthy.
navegación *nf* (**a**) (*gen*: *arte*) navigation; ~ **a vela** sailing.
(**b**) (*viaje*) sea voyage; ~ **costanera** coasting, coastal traffic; ~ **fluvial** river sailing, river navigation.
(**c**) (*barcos*) ships, shipping; **cerrado a la** ~ closed to shipping.
navegador *nm*, **navegante** *nm* navigator; ~ **a vela** yachtsman.
navegar [1h] **1** *vt barco* to sail; to navigate; *avión* to fly; ~ **los mares** to sail the seas. **2** *vi* to sail; ~ **a 15 nudos** to sail at 15 knots, go at 15 knots; ~ **a (la) vela** to sail, go sailing.
Navidad *nf* Christmas; (**día de**) ~ Christmas Day; **~es** Christmas time; **por ~es** at Christmas (time); **¡feliz ~!** happy Christmas!
navideño *adj* Christmas (*atr*).
naviera *nf* shipping company.
naviero 1 *adj* shipping (*atr*). **2** *nm* shipowner.
navío *nm* ship; ~ **de alto bordo,** ~ **de línea** (*Hist*) ship of the line.
náyade *nf* naiad.
naylón *nm* nylon.
nazarenas *nfpl* (*And, Cono Sur*) large *gaucho* spurs.
nazareno, -a 1 *adj* Nazarene. **2** *nm/f* (**a**) (*Hist*) Nazarene. (**b**) (*Rel*) penitent in a Holy Week procession. **3** *nm* (*) (**a**) (*fraude*) con trick*. (**b**) (*persona*) con man*.
Nazaret *nm* Nazareth.
nazi *adj, nmf* Nazi.
nazismo *nm* Nazism.
nazista *adj* Nazi.
N. de la R. *abr de* **nota de la redacción** editor's note.
N. de la T, N. del T *abr de* **Nota de la Traductora, Nota del Traductor** translator's note.
NE *abr de* **nor(d)este** north-east, NE.
neblina *nf* mist; mistiness; (*fig*) fog.
neblinoso *adj* misty.
nebulosa *nf* nebula.
nebulosidad *nf* (**a**) (*lit*) nebulosity; cloudiness; mistiness; gloominess. (**b**) (*fig*) vagueness; obscurity.
nebuloso *adj* (**a**) (*Astron*) nebular, nebulous; *cielo* cloudy; *aire* misty, foggy; (*tétrico*) dark, gloomy. (**b**) (*fig*) nebulous, vague; obscure.
necedad *nf* (**a**) (*cualidad*) foolishness, silliness. (**b**) (*una* ~) silly thing; **~es** nonsense.
necesariamente *adv* necessarily.
necesario *adj* necessary; **es** ~ **que lo hagas** it is necessary that you should do it, it is necessary for you to do it; **todo es** ~ it all helps, every little helps; **si es ~, de ser** ~ if need(s) be.
neceser *nm* toilet case, dressing case; holdall; ~ **de belleza** vanity case; ~ **de costura** workbox; ~ **de fin de semana** weekend bag, weekend case.
necesidad *nf* (**a**) (*gen*) necessity; need (*de* for); ~ **imperiosa,** ~ **primordial** absolute necessity, pressing need; **de ~, por** ~ of necessity; **esto es de primera** ~ this is absolutely essential; **no hay** ~ **de** + *infin* there is no need to + *infin*; **satisfacer las ~es de uno** to satisfy sb's needs.
(**b**) (*apuro*) necessity; tight spot, awkward situation; **en caso de** ~ in case of need; **encontrarse en una** ~ to be in a difficult situation.
(**c**) (*miseria*) need, necessity, want; (*pobreza*) poverty; **están en la mayor** ~ they are in great need.
(**d**) **~es** hardships; **pasar ~es** to suffer hardships.
(**e**) (*euf*) business; **hacer sus ~es** to do one's business, relieve o.s.; **sentir una gran** ~ to be dying to relieve o.s.
necesitado 1 *adj* (**a**) ~ **de** in need of; **estamos ~s de mano de obra** we need workers, we are in need of labour. (**b**) (*pobre*) needy. **2** *nmpl*: **los ~s** the needy, those in need.

necesitar [1a] **1** *vt* to need, want; to necessitate, require; **necesitamos 2 más** we need 2 more; **necesita un poco de cuidado** it needs (*o* requires, takes) a little care; ~ + *infin* to need to + *infin*, must + *infin*; **no necesitas hacerlo** you don't need to do it, you don't have to do it.

2 *vi*: ~ **de** to need.

3 necesitarse *vr* to be needed, be wanted; **'necesítase coche'** (*anuncio*) 'car wanted'.

neciamente *adv* foolishly, stupidly.

necio 1 *adj* (**a**) (*tonto*) silly, stupid.

(**b**) (*And etc*: *displicente*) peevish.

(**c**) (*And, Carib, Cono Sur*: *quisquilloso*) touchy, hypersensitive.

(**d**) (*CAm*) *enfermedad* stubborn, long-lasting.

(**e**) (*Méx*: *testarudo*) stubborn, pig-headed.

2 *nm*, **necia** *nf* fool.

nécora *nf* small crab.

necrófago *nm* ghoul.

necrofilia *nf* necrophilia.

necrófilo, -a *adj, nm/f* necrophiliac.

necrología *nf*, **necrológica** *nf* obituary (notice), necrology.

necrológico *adj* necrological, obituary (*atr*).

necromancia *nf*, **necromancía** *nf* necromancy.

necrópolis *nf invar* necropolis.

necropsia *nf* autopsy.

néctar *nm* nectar (*t fig*); (*Culin*) fruit essence.

nectarina *nf* nectarine.

neerlandés 1 *adj* Dutch, Netherlands (*atr*). **2** *nm*, **neerlandesa** *nf* Dutchman, Dutchwoman, Netherlander. **3** *nm* (*Ling*) Dutch.

nefando *adj* unspeakable, abominable.

nefario *adj* nefarious.

nefasto *adj influencia* pernicious; harmful; *viaje* unlucky, ill-fated; (*LAm*: *atroz*) dreadful, terrible.

nefato* *adj* (*Carib*) stupid, dim*.

nefrítico *adj* nephritic.

nefritis *nf* nephritis.

negación *nf* (**a**) (*gen*) negation; (*negativa*) refusal, denial. (**b**) (*Ling*) negation; negative.

negado 1 *adj* (**a**) (*tonto*) dull, stupid. (**b**) ~ **para** inept at, unfitted for. **2** *nm*, **negada** *nf* useless person.

negar [1h *y* 1j] **1** *vt* (**a**) *hecho, verdad etc* to deny; *acusación* to deny, reject, refute; ~ **que algo sea así** to deny that sth is so.

(**b**) *permiso etc* to deny, refuse (*a* to); to withhold (*a* from); ~ **la mano a uno** to refuse to shake hands with sb; ~ **el saludo a uno** to cut sb; **le negaron el paso por la frontera** they refused to let him cross the frontier; **pasé por la casa pero me la negaron** I called at the house but they refused to let me see her.

(**c**) *relación, responsabilidad etc* to disclaim, disown.

2 *vi*: ~ **con la cabeza** to shake one's head.

3 negarse *vr* (**a**) ~ **a** + *infin* to refuse to + *infin*.

(**b**) ~ **a una visita** to refuse to see a visitor, not be at home to a caller.

negativa *nf* negative; denial, refusal; ~ **rotunda** flat refusal; **la ~ a comer es peligrosa** the refusal to eat is dangerous.

negativamente *adv* negatively; **contestar** ~ to answer in the negative; **valorar algo** ~ to take a hostile (*o* critical) view of sth.

negatividad *nf*, **negativismo** *nm* negative attitude.

negativizar [1f] *vt* to neutralize.

negativo 1 *adj* (**a**) (*gen*) negative; **voto** ~ vote against, contrary vote, no vote. (**b**) (*Mat*) minus. (**c**) (*Fot*) negative. **2** *nm* (*Fot*) negative.

negligencia *nf* negligence; neglect, slackness, carelessness; nonchalance.

negligente *adj* (*gen*) negligent; neglectful, slack, careless; *postura etc* careless, nonchalant.

negligentemente *adv* negligently; slackly, carelessly; nonchalantly.

negociable *adj* negotiable.

negociación *nf* negotiation; deal, transaction; (*de cheque*) clearance; ~ **colectiva (de salarios)** collective bargaining; **entrar en negociaciones con** to enter into negotiations with.

negociadamente *adv*: **resolver un problema** ~ to settle a problem by negotiation.

negociado *nm* (**a**) (*sección*) department, section. (**b**) (*Cono Sur*) shop, store. (**c**) (*And, Cono Sur*: *turbio*) illegal transaction, shady deal.

negociador 1 *adj* negotiating; **comisión ~a** negotiating committee. **2** *nm*, **negociadora** *nf* negotiator.

negociante *nmf* (*t* **negocianta** *nf*) businessman, businesswoman; merchant, dealer.

negociar [1b] **1** *vt* to negotiate. **2** *vi* (**a**) (*Pol etc*) to negotiate. (**b**) ~ **en** (*Com*) to deal in, trade in.

negocio *nm* (**a**) (*asunto*) affair; **mal** ~ bad business; **¡mal ~!** it looks bad!; **eso es ~ tuyo** that's your affair.

(**b**) (*Com, Fin*: *empresa*) business; **el ~ del libro** the book trade, the book business; **el ~ del espectáculo** show business; **montar un ~ de frutas** to start a fruit business; **traspasar un** ~ to transfer a business, sell a business.

(**c**) (*Com, Fin*: *trato*) deal, transaction, piece of business; (*iró*) bargain; **buen** ~ profitable deal, (good) bargain; ~ **sucio,** ~ **turbio** shady deal; **el ~ es el** ~ business is business; **hacer un buen** ~ to pull off a profitable deal; **¡hiciste un buen ~!** (*iró*) that was a fine deal you did!; **hacer su propio** ~ to look after one's own interests.

(**d**) (*Com, Fin*: *gen*) **~s** business; trade; **hombre de ~s** businessman; **el mundo de los ~s** the business world; **a malos ~s sombrero de copa** one must accept losses with dignity, one must make the best of a bad job; **estar de ~s** to be (away) on business; **retirarse de los ~s** to retire from business.

(**e**) (*And, Cono Sur*) (*firma*) firm, company; (*casa*) place of business.

(**f**) (*And, Carib**) **el** ~ the fact, the truth; **pero el ~ es que ...** but the fact is that ...

(**g**) (*And*) tale, piece of gossip.

negocioso *adj* industrious; businesslike.

negra[1] *nf* (**a**) (*persona*) Negress*, black woman.

(**b**) (*Mús*) crotchet.

(**c**) (*Ajedrez*) black piece.

(**d**) (*CAm*: *fig*) black mark.

(**e**) (*mala suerte*) bad luck; **tener la** ~ to be out of luck, have a run of bad luck; **le tocó la** ~ he had bad luck; **ése me trae la** ~ he brings me bad luck; he mucks things up for me.

negrada *nf* (*LAm*) (**a**) (*grupo*) group of Negroes; Negroes (*collectively*). (**b**) (*dicho etc*) remark (*o* act *etc*) typical of a Negro; (*fraude*) cheat, fraud.

negrear [1a] *vi* (**a**) (*volverse negro*) to go black, turn black. (**b**) (*tirar a negro*) to be blackish; (*mostrarse negro*) to show black, look black.

negrería *nf* (*LAm*), **negrerío** *nm* (*LAm*) = **negrada** (**a**).

negrero *nm* (*lit*) slave trader; (*fig*) slave driver.

negrilla *nf* (**a**) (*Tip*) = **negrita** (**a**). (**b**) (*Bot*) elm.

negrita *nf* (**a**) (*Tip*) bold face; **en** ~ in bold type, in heavy type. (**b**) (*CAm*: *fig*) black mark.

negrito *nm* (*Carib*) black coffee.

negritud *nf* negritude.

negro 1 *adj* (**a**) (*gen*) black; (*oscuro*) dark; *persona* black, Negro†; (*moreno*) dark, swarthy; ~ **azabache** pitch-black; ~ **como boca de lobo,** ~ **como un pozo** as black as pitch, pitch-dark; **más ~ que el azabache** (*etc*) as black as ink, coal-black.

(**b**) (*fig*) *estado, humor etc* sad; black, gloomy; *suerte* awful*, atrocious; **pasarlas negras** to have a tough time of it; **la cosa se pone negra** it's not going well, it looks bad; **ve muy ~ el porvenir** he's very gloomy about the future; **lo ve todo** ~ he's terribly pessimistic about everything; **vérselas negras** to find o.s. in trouble; **verse ~ para** + *infin* to have one's work cut out to + *infin*; **nos veíamos ~s para salir del apuro** we had a tough time getting out of it.

(**c**) (*: *enfadado*) cross, peeved*; **estoy ~ con esto** I'm getting desperate about it; **poner ~ a uno** to make sb cross, upset sb; **ponerse** ~ to get cross, cut up rough.

(**d**) (*ilegal*) black; **economía negra** black economy; **dinero** ~ hot money, money not declared for tax.

(**e**) (*Pol*) fascist; **terrorismo** ~ fascist terrorism.

2 *nm* (**a**) (*color*) black; **en** ~ (*Fot*) in black and white; ~ **de humo** lampblack.

(**b**) (*persona*) Negro†, black, coloured person†; **¡no somos ~s!** we won't stand for it!, you can't do that to us!; **sacar lo que el ~ del sermón** to understand nothing of what has been said.

(**c**) (*: *escritor*) ghost writer.

(**d**) (*Carib*) black coffee.

3 *nm*, **negra**[2] *nf* (*LAm*: *en oración directa*) dear, honey (*US*).

negroide *adj* negroid.

negrura *nf* blackness.

negruzco *adj* blackish.

nel‡ *excl* (*Méx*) yep*.

neli‡ *adv* = **nada**.

nema *nf* (*Méx Admin*) seal.

neme *nm* (*And*) asphalt.
nemotécnica *nf etc* = **mnemoténica** *etc.*
nene *nm*, **nena** *nf* baby, small child; **¡sí, nena!** (*a mujer*) yes dear!, yes darling!
nenúfar *nm* water lily.
neo *nm* neon.
neo... *pref* neo...
neoclasicismo *nm* neoclassicism.
neoclásico *adj* neoclassical.
neocolonialismo *nm* neocolonialism.
neofascismo *nm* neofascism.
neofascista *adj, nmf* neofascist.
neófito, -a *nm/f* neophyte.
neogótico *adj* neogothic.
neolatino *adj*: **lenguas neolatinas** Romance languages.
neolengua *nf* newspeak.
neolítico *adj* neolithic.
neologismo *nm* neologism.
neón *nm* neon; neon light.
neonatal *adj asistencia etc* postnatal, neonatal.
neonatólogo, -a *nm/f* neonatologist.
neonazi *adj, nmf* neonazi.
neonazista *adj* neonazi.
neoplatónico *adj* neoplatonic.
neoplatonismo *nm* neoplatonism.
neoplatonista *nmf* neoplatonist.
neoyorquino 1 *adj* New York (*atr*), of New York. **2** *nm*, **neoyorquina** *nf* New Yorker.
neozelandés 1 *adj* New Zealand (*atr*), of New Zealand. **2** *nm*, **neozelandesa** *nf* New Zealander.
Nepal *nm* Nepal.
nepalés, -esa *adj, nm/f*, **nepalí** *adj, nmf* Nepalese.
nepotismo *nm* nepotism.
Neptuno *nm* Neptune.
nereida *nf* nereid.
Nerón *nm* Nero.
nervadura *nf* (*Arquit*) ribs; (*Bot, Ent*) nervure, vein.
nervio *nm* (**a**) (*Anat*: *gen*) nerve; **crispar los ~s a uno, poner los ~s en punta a uno** to get on sb's nerves; to jar on sb, grate on sb; **perder los ~s** to lose one's temper; **tener los ~s en punta** to be all keyed up, have one's nerves on edge; **tener los ~s a flor de piel** to be ready to explode; **tener los ~s como las cuerdas de un violín** to be as jumpy as a cat; **tener ~ de acero** to have nerves of steel.
(**b**) (*Anat*: *tendón*) tendon, sinew; (*de carne*) sinew, tough part.
(**c**) (*Arquit, Bot*) rib; (*Ent*) vein; (*de libro*) rib; (*Mús*) string.
(**d**) (*fig*) (*vigor*) vigour, strength; fibre; (*resistencia*) stamina, toughness; (*moral*) moral fibre, moral strength; **un hombre sin ~** a weak man, a spineless man; **tener ~** to have character.
(**e**) (*fig*: *persona*) soul, leading light, guiding spirit; **él es el ~ de la sociedad** he is the guiding spirit of the club.
(**f**) (*fig*: *fondo*) core, crux.
nerviosamente *adv* nervously.
nerviosera *nf* attack of nerves.
nerviosidad *nf*, **nerviosismo** *nm* nervousness; nervous anticipation, nerves; agitation, restlessness, impatience.
nervioso *adj* (**a**) (*Anat*) nerve (*atr*), nervous; **ataque ~** (attack of) hysterics; **centro ~** nerve centre; **crisis nerviosa, depresión nerviosa** nervous breakdown; **sistema ~** nervous system.
(**b**) (*Anat*) *mano etc* sinewy, wiry.
(**c**) *persona* (*de temperamento*) nervy, highly-strung, excitable; (*estado temporal*) nervous, nervy; (*impaciente*) restless, impatient; (*sobreexcitado*) overwrought; (*inquieto*) upset, agitated; **poner ~ a uno** to make sb nervous, get on sb's nerves; to get sb worked up; to make sb cross; **ponerse ~** to get nervous; to get worked up; to get upset, get cross; to get rattled*; **¡no te pongas ~!** take it easy!, calm down!
(**d**) *estilo etc* vigorous, forceful.
nervoso *adj* (**a**) *persona* = **nervioso** (**c**). (**b**) *carne* sinewy, tough.
nervudo *adj* (**a**) (*fuerte*) tough, strong. (**b**) *mano etc* sinewy, wiry.
nesga *nf* (*Cos*) flare, gore.
nesgado *adj falda etc* flared.
nesgar [1h] *vt* (*Cos*) to flare, gore.
netamente *adv* clearly; purely; genuinely; **una construcción ~ española** a purely Spanish construction, a genuinely Spanish construction.
neto *adj* (**a**) (*gen*) clear; (*puro*) clean, pure; neat; *verdad etc* pure, simple; **tiene su sueldo ~** he has (just) his bare salary.
(**b**) (*Com, Fin*) net; **peso ~** net weight; **sueldo ~** net salary, salary after deductions.
neumático 1 *adj* pneumatic; air (*atr*). **2** *nm* (*Aut*) tyre; **~ balón** balloon tyre; **~ sin cámara** tubeless tyre; **~ radial** radial tyre; **~ de recambio, ~ de repuesto** spare tyre.
neumoconiosis *nf* pneumoconiosis.
neumonía *nf* pneumonia.
neura* *nf* (**a**) (*manía*) mania; obsession; crazy idea, strange notion. (**b**) (*depre*) depression; bad mood.
neural *adj* neural.
neuralgia *nf* neuralgia.
neurálgico *adj* neuralgic, nerve (*atr*); (*fig*) crucial, vital; most important.
neurastenia *nf* (**a**) (*Med*) neurasthenia; nervous exhaustion. (**b**) (*fig*) excitability, highly-strung nature, nerviness.
neurasténico *adj* (**a**) (*Med*) neurasthenic. (**b**) (*fig*) excitable, highly-strung, nervy, neurotic.
neuritis *nf* neuritis.
neuro... *pref* neuro...
neurobiología *nf* neurobiology.
neurocirugía *nf* neurosurgery.
neurología *nf* neurology.
neurólogo, -a *nm/f* neurologist.
neurona *nf* neuron, nerve cell.
neurópata *nmf* neuropath.
neuropsicología *nf* neuropsychology.
neurosis *nf invar* neurosis; **~ de guerra** shellshock.
neurótico, -a *adj, nm/f* neurotic.
neurotizar [1f] **1** *vt* to make neurotic. **2 neurotizarse** *vr* to become neurotic.
neutral *adj, nmf* neutral.
neutralidad *nf* neutrality.
neutralismo *nm* neutralism.
neutralista *adj, nmf* neutralist.
neutralización *nf* neutralization.
neutralizar [1f] **1** *vt* to neutralize; *tendencia etc* to counteract. **2 neutralizarse** *vr* to neutralize each other; to cancel (each other) out.
neutro *adj* (**a**) (*gen*) neutral. (**b**) (*Bio*) neuter, sexless, without sex; **abeja neutra** worker bee. (**c**) (*Ling*) neuter; **género ~** neuter; **verbo ~** intransitive verb.
neutrón *nm* neutron.
nevada *nf* snowstorm; snowfall.
nevado 1 *adj* (**a**) (*cubierto de nieve*) snow-covered; *montaña* snowcapped. (**b**) (*fig*) snowy, snow-white. **2** *nm* (*And, Cono Sur*) snow-capped mountain.
nevar [1j] **1** *vt* to cover with snow; (*fig*) to whiten. **2** *vi* to snow.
nevasca *nf* snowstorm.
nevazón *nf* (*And, Cono Sur*) snowstorm.
nevera *nf* refrigerator, icebox; (*fig*) icebox.
nevera-congelador *nf* fridge-freezer.
nevero *nm* snowfield, icefield, place of perpetual snow.
nevisca *nf* light snowfall, flurry of snow.
neviscar [1g] *vi* to snow lightly.
nevoso *adj* snowy.
newtoniano *adj* Newtonian.
newtonio *nm* newton.
nexo *nm* link, connection; nexus.
n/f. *abr de* **nuestro favor** our favour.
n/g. *abr de* **nuestro giro** our money order.
ni *conj* (**a**) (*gen*) nor, neither; **no bebe ~ fuma** he doesn't smoke or drink, he neither smokes nor drinks; **~ el uno ~ el otro** neither one nor the other; **~ vino ~ llamó por teléfono** he neither came nor rang up; **no quiere ~ sal ~ mostaza** he doesn't want either salt or mustard; **sin temor ~ favor** without fear or favour; **sin padre ~ madre** without father or mother; **~ yo** nor me; *V* **siquiera**.
(**b**) not ... even; **~ uno** not even one; **~ se sabe** even that is unknown; God knows!; **no lo sabrán ~ por fuerza** they won't find it out even by force; **~ a ti te lo dirá** he won't tell even you.
(**c**) **~ que** ... not even if ...; **~ que fueses su mujer** not even if you were his wife; **~ que fuera de plomo pesaría tanto** it wouldn't weigh so much even if it were lead; **¡~ que fueras su madre!** anyone would think you were his mother!
Niágara *nm* Niagara.
niara *nf* (*Agr*) stack, rick.
nica* *adj, nmf* (*CAm*) Nicaraguan.
nicabar‡ [1a] *vt* to rip off‡, nick‡.

Nicaragua *nf* Nicaragua.
nicaragüense *adj, nmf* Nicaraguan.
nicaragüismo *nm* word (*o* phrase *etc*) peculiar to Nicaragua.
Nico *nm forma familiar de* **Nicolás.**
nicotiana *nf* nicotiana, tobacco plant.
Nicolás *nm* Nicholas.
nicotina *nf* nicotine.
nicotínico *adj* nicotinic, nicotine (*atr*).
nicho *nm* niche (*t fig*); recess; hollow; ~ **ecológico** ecological niche.
nidada *nf* (*huevos*) sitting, clutch; (*pajarillos*) brood.
nidal *nm* (**a**) (*Orn*) nest; (*nido artificial*) nesting box. (**b**) (*dinero*) nest egg. (**c**) (*) (*guarida*) haunt, hang-out*; (*escondite*) hiding-place.
nidificación *nf* nesting; nest-building.
nidificante *adj*: **ave** ~ nesting bird.
nidificar [1g] *vi* to nest.
nido *nm* (**a**) (*lit, fig*) nest; ~ **de abeja** (*tela etc*) honeycomb pattern; ~ **de amor** love-nest; **caer del** ~ (*fig*) to come down to earth with a bump; **se ha caído de un** ~ he's dreadfully innocent, he's a bit wet behind the ears*; **manchar el propio** ~ to foul one's own nest.
(**b**) (*fig: guarida*) nest, haunt, abode, den; ~ **de ladrones** nest of thieves, den of thieves; ~ **de víboras** nest of vipers.
(**c**) (*fig*) (*escondite*) hiding-place; (*depósito*) secret store.
(**d**) (*fig: criadero*) centre, hotbed; **el reparto de premios fue un** ~ **de polémicas** the prize giving was a centre of controversy, the prize giving gave rise to heated arguments.
(**e**) (*Escol*) nursery-school.
(**f**) (*camita*) cot; (*corralito*) play-pen.
NIE *nm abr de* **número de identificación de extranjero.**
niebla *nf* (**a**) (*lit*) fog, mist; ~ **artificial** smoke screen; ~ **de humo** smog; **un día de** ~ a foggy day; **hay** ~ it is foggy.
(**b**) (*fig*) fog, confusion.
(**c**) (*Bot*) mildew.
nieta *nf* granddaughter.
nietísimo, -a *nm/f* (*hum*) extra-special grandchild (*esp with reference to Franco's grandchildren*).
nieto *nm* (**a**) (*lit*) grandson; **~s** grandchildren. (**b**) (*fig*) descendant.
nieve *nf* (**a**) snow; **las primeras ~s** the first snows, the first snowfall; ~ **abundante, copiosa** ~ heavy snow; ~ **artificial** artificial snow; **~s perpetuas** permanent snow; ~ **(en) polvo** powdery snow. (**b**) (*LAm*) (*helado*) ice-cream; (*sorbete*) sorbet, water-ice. (**c**) (‡: *cocaína*) snow‡, cocaine. (**d**) (*TV*) snow.
NIF [nif] *nm abr de* **número de identificación fiscal.**
nifear‡ [1a] *vt*: ~ **a uno** to muck sb about (bureaucratically), tie sb up in red tape.
Nigeria *nf* Nigeria.
nigeriano, -a *adj, nm/f* Nigerian.
night* [naɪt] *nm* nightclub.
nigromancia *nf*, **nigromancía** *nf* necromancy, black magic.
nigromante *nm* necromancer.
nigua *nf* (*And*) chigoe, jigger flea.
nihilismo *nm* nihilism.
nihilista *adj, nmf* nihilist.
niki *nm* (*Esp*) T-shirt.
Nilo *nm* Nile.
nilón [ni'lon, 'nailon] *nm* nylon.
nimbo *nm* (*Arte, Astron, Ecl*) halo; (*Met*) nimbus.
nimbostrato *nm* nimbostratus.
nimiamente *adv* (*V adj*) (**a**) trivially; with a host of petty details. (**b**) fussily; small-mindedly; long-windedly. (**c**) excessively.
nimiedad *nf* (**a**) (*cualidad*) triviality; fussiness; small-mindedness; long-windedness; excess; **tratar un asunto con** ~ to discuss a subject in great detail, treat a theme exhaustively; (*pey*) to discuss a subject in excessive detail.
(**b**) (*una* ~) very small thing, tiny detail; **riñeron por una** ~ they quarrelled over some triviality.
nimiez *nf* bagatelle, trifle.
nimio *adj* (**a**) (*pequeño*) insignificant, trivial, tiny; **un sinfín de detalles ~s** a host of petty details.
(**b**) *persona* (*exigente*) fussy (about details), too meticulous; (*de miras estrechas*) small-minded; (*prolijo*) long-winded.
(**c**) (*excesivo*) excessive (*en* in).
ninchi‡ *nm* (**a**) (*imbécil*) berk‡, twit*. (**b**) (*niño*) kid*, child. (**c**) (*amigo*) pal*, buddy.
ninfa *nf* (**a**) (*lit*) nymph. (**b**) (*Esp‡*: *chica*) bird‡, girl.
ninfeta *nf*, **ninfilla** *nf*, **ninfita** *nf* nymphet.
ninfómana *nf* nymphomaniac.
ninfomanía *nf* nymphomania.
ninfómano *adj* nymphomaniac.
nínfula *nf* nymphet.
ningún *adj V* **ninguno.**
ningunear [1a] *vt* to scorn; ~ **a uno** (*despreciar*) to look down one's nose at sb; (*hacer el vacío a*) to cold-shoulder sb, pay no attention to sb; (*empequeñecer*) to make sb feel small; (*tratar mal*) to treat sb badly.
ninguno 1 *adj* (**ningún** *delante de nm sing*) no; **ningún hombre** no man; **ninguna belleza** no beauty; **no hay ningún libro que valga más** there is no book that is worth more; **no voy a ninguna parte** I'm not going anywhere; **sin ningún sentimiento** without any regret, without regret of any kind; **no es ningún tonto** he's no fool, he's no sort of fool.
2 *pron* nobody, no-one; none; neither; **no lo sabe** ~ nobody knows; ~ **de ellos** none of them; **lo hace como** ~ he does it like nobody else; ~ **de los dos** neither of them; **¿cuál prefieres? —** ~ which do you prefer? — neither (of them).
niña *nf* (**a**) girl, little girl, child (*V t* **niño 2 (a)**); ~ **exploradora** girl guide, girl scout (*US*); ~ **bonita*** pride and joy, special treasure; (*15*) number fifteen.
(**b**) (*: *prostituta*) tart‡, whore.
(**c**) (*LAm: en oración directa*) miss, mistress; **la** ~ the mistress of the house.
(**d**) (*Anat*) pupil; **ser las ~s de los ojos de uno** to be the apple of sb's eye.
niñada *nf* = **niñería.**
niñato* *nm* (*pey*) kid*, youth; (*adulto*) playboy.
niñear [1a] *vi* to act childishly.
niñera *nf* nursemaid, nanny.
niñería *nf* (**a**) (*cualidad*) childishness. (**b**) (*acto*) childish thing; silly thing, triviality; **llora por cualquier** ~ she cries about any triviality.
niñero *adj* fond of children.
niñez *nf* childhood; infancy (*t fig*).
niño 1 *adj* (**a**) (*gen*) young; (*sin experiencia*) immature, inexperienced; (*pey*) childish; **es muy** ~ **todavía** he's still very young (*o* small).
(**b**) (*And*) *fruta* green, unripe.
2 *nm* (**a**) boy, little boy, child; (*gen*) child; (*no nacido, recién nacido*) baby; (*en oración directa*) my boy, my lad; **¡~!*** look out!, be careful!; **los ~s** the children; **el N~ Jesús** the Christ-child, (*con menos formalidad*) Baby Jesus; ~ **azul** blue baby; ~ **bien,** ~ **bonito,** ~ **gótico** playboy; **el N~ de la bola** the infant Jesus; (*fig*) fortune's favourite; **el** ~ **bonito del toreo** the golden boy of bullfighting; ~ **de coro** choirboy; ~ **explorador** boy scout; ~ **expósito** foundling; ~ **maltratado** battered baby; ~ **de pecho** small baby, babe-in-arms; ~ **pera*,** ~ **pijo*** pampered child; daddy's boy; ~ **probeta** test-tube baby; ~ **prodigio** child prodigy; ~ **terrible** enfant terrible; **de** ~ as a child; when a child; **desde** ~ since childhood, since I (*etc*) was a child; **¡no seas** ~**!** don't be such a baby!; **ser el** ~ **mimado de uno** to be sb's pet, be sb's white-haired boy; **¡qué coche ni qué** ~ **muerto!*** all this nonsense about a car!, car my foot!*; **hacer un** ~ **a una** to get a girl in the family way; **va a tener un** ~ she's going to have a baby; **cuando nazca el** ~ when the baby (*o* child) is born.
(**b**) (*LAm: en oración directa*) master, sir; **el** ~ the (young) master.
(**c**) (*Cono Sur*) undesirable.
nipón, -ona *adj, nm/f* Japanese.
nipos‡ *nmpl* dough‡, money.
níquel *nm* (**a**) (*gen*) nickel; (*Téc*) nickel-plating. (**b**) (*LAm*) small coin, nickel (*US*); **~es** (*esp Cono Sur, Méx*) dough‡.
niquelado *adj* nickel-plated.
niquelar [1a] **1** *vt* to nickel-plate. **2** *vi* (*Esp‡*) to shoot a line*.
niquelera *nf* (*And*) purse.
niqui *nm* T-shirt.
nirvana *nm* Nirvana.
níspero *nm*, **níspola** *nf* medlar.
nítidamente *adv* brightly, cleanly; spotlessly; clearly, sharply.
nitidez *nf* (**a**) (*gen*) brightness; (*limpieza*) spotlessness; (*Fot etc*) clarity, sharpness. (**b**) (*fig*) unblemished nature.
nítido *adj* (**a**) (*gen*) bright, clean; (*limpio*) spotless; *contorno* (*t Fot*) clear, sharp. (**b**) (*fig*) pure, unblemished.
nitral *nm* nitrate deposit, saltpetre bed.
nitrato *nm* nitrate; ~ **de cloro** chlorine nitrate; ~ **potásico**

potassium nitrate.
nitrera *nf* (*Cono Sur*) nitrate deposit.
nítrico *adj* nitric.
nitro *nm* nitre, saltpetre.
nitrobenceno *nm* nitrobenzene.
nitrogenado *adj* nitrogenous.
nitrógeno *nm* nitrogen.
nitroglicerina *nf* nitroglycerin(e).
nitroso *adj* nitrous.
nivel *nm* (**a**) (*Geog etc*) level, height; ~ **de(l) aceite** (*Aut etc*) oil level; ~ **del agua** water level; ~ **freático** water-table; ~ **del mar** sea level; **a los 900 m sobre el ~ del mar** at 900 m above sea level; **la nieve alcanzó un ~ de 1,5 m** the snow reached a depth of 1.5 m; **a ~** level; true; flush; horizontal; **al ~ de** on the same level as, on a level with, at the same height as.
(**b**) (*fig*) level, standard; **el ~ cultural del país** the cultural standard of the country; ~ **de vida** standard of living; **alto ~ de trabajo** high level of employment; **conferencia al más alto ~, conferencia de alto ~** high-level conference, top-level conference; **a ~ internacional** on the international level; **estar al ~ de** to be on a level with, be equal to; **no está al ~ de los demás** he is not up to the standard of the others; **estar al ~ de las circunstancias** to rise to the occasion; **de primer ~** top-level; **dar el ~** to come up to scratch.
(**c**) **a ~ de** *prep* (*en cuanto a*) as for, as regards; (*como*) as; (*a tono con*) in keeping with; **a ~ de ministro es un desastre** as a minister he's a disaster; **a ~ de viajes** so far as travel is concerned, regarding travel.
(**d**) ~ **de aire,** ~ **de burbuja** (*Téc*) spirit level.
nivelación *nf* levelling; levelling-up, levelling-out, equalization.
nivelado 1 *adj* level, flat; flush. **2** *nm* levelling.
niveladora *nf* bulldozer.
nivelar [1a] *vt* (**a**) (*gen*) to level (out); (*Ferro etc*) to grade. (**b**) (*fig*) to level (up), equalize, even (out, up), make even; (*Fin etc*) to balance (*con* against), adjust (*con* to); *déficit* to cover, deal with.
níveo *adj* (*liter*) snowy, snow-white.
nivosidad *nf* snowfall, (depth of) snow.
Niza *nf* Nice.
n/l. *abr de* **nuestra letra** our letter.
NN *abr de* **ningún nombre** no name (*mark on grave of unknown person*).
NNE *abr de* **nornordeste** north-north-east, NNE.
NNO *abr de* **nornoroeste** north-north-west, NNW.
NN.UU. *abr de* **Naciones Unidas** United Nations, UN.
NO *abr de* **noroeste** north-west, NW.
n/o. *abr de* **nuestra orden** our order.
no *adv* (**a**) (*en respuestas*) no; (*en frases sin verbo*) not; (*con verbo*) not; **un 'no' contundente** a resounding 'no', a firm 'no;' **¡no!** no!; **¡yo no!** not I!; **¡rey no!** we don't want a king!; **¡Paco no, Pepe sí!** Paco out, Pepe in!; **no sé** I do not know, I don't know; **me rogó no hacerlo** he asked me not to do it; **¿vives aquí, no?** *V* **¿no es verdad?** (*en* **verdad**); **decir que no** to say no; **creo que no** I don't think so; **¡que no!** I tell you it isn't! (*o* doesn't *etc*); **¡a que no!** I bet you can't!, I bet you it isn't! (*etc*); **¿oh no?, ¿a que no?** oh no?; do you dare me to?, do you think I can't?; **¡a que no lo sabes!** I bet you don't know!; **de no, ...** (*LAm*) if not, ...; **está de que no** he is in a mood to refuse, I guess he'll say no; **no sea que ...** lest ...; **si no** if not, otherwise; unless you (*etc*) do; **todavía no** not yet; *V* **más 1 (e), sino** *etc.*
(**b**) (*en doble negación*) **no tengo nada** I have nothing, I don't have anything; *V* **nada, nunca** *etc.*
(**c**) (*palabras compuestas*) *p.ej.* **el no conformismo** non-conformism, non-conformity; **país no alineado** non-aligned country; **pacto de no agresión** non-aggression pact; **la política de no intervención** the policy of non-intervention, the non-intervention policy; **cosa no esencial** non-essential thing, inessential; **la no necesidad del latín en partes de la misa** the fact that Latin is not to be insisted upon in parts of the mass; *para otros casos, V el n o adj.*
n.º *abr de* **número** number, No.
Nobel *nm* (**a**) (*t* **Premio ~**) Nobel Prize. (**b**) (*persona*) Nobel prizewinner.
nobiliario *adj* (**a**) *título etc* noble. (**b**) *libro etc* genealogical.
nobilizar [1f] *vt* to enhance, dignify, ennoble.
noble 1 *adj* (**a**) (*gen*) noble; (*honrado*) honest, upright. (**b**) *madera* fine. **2** *nm* noble, nobleman; **los ~s** the nobles, the nobility.
noblemente *adv* nobly; honestly, uprightly.
nobleza *nf* (**a**) (*cualidad*) nobility; honesty, uprightness; ~ **obliga** noblesse oblige. (**b**) (*personas*) nobility, aristocracy.
nocaut *nm*, **nocáut** *nm* (*LAm*) knockout.
nocautear [1a] *vt* to knock out, K.O*.
nocdáun *nm* knockdown.
noción *nf* (**a**) (*gen*) notion, idea; **no tener la menor ~ de algo** to have not the faintest idea about sth. (**b**) **nociones** elements, rudiments; smattering; **tiene algunas nociones de árabe** he has a smattering of Arabic.
nocional *adj* notional.
nocividad *nf* harmfulness.
nocivo *adj* harmful, injurious (*para* to).
noctambulear [1a] *vi* to wander about at night.
noctambulismo *nm* sleepwalking.
noctámbulo 1 *adj* active at night. **2** *nm*, **noctámbula** *nf* (*sonámbulo*) sleepwalker; (*nocherniego*) night-bird, person who goes around at night; (*jaranero*) roisterer.
noctiluca *nf* (*Ent*) glow-worm.
noctívago = **noctámbulo.**
nocturnidad *nf* evening hours, night hours; **obrar con ~** to operate under cover of darkness; **con la agravante de la ~** made more serious by the fact that it was done at night.
nocturno 1 *adj* night (*atr*); evening (*atr*); (*Zool etc*) nocturnal; **clase nocturna** evening class; **vida nocturna** night life. **2** *nm* (**a**) (*Mús*) nocturne. (**b**) (*Escol*) evening class.
noche *nf* night; night-time; (late) evening; dark, darkness (*fig*); **ayer ~** last night; **esta ~** tonight; **¡buenas ~s!** good evening!, (*de despedida o al acostarse uno*) good night!; **Las mil y una ~s** The Arabian Nights; ~ **de bodas** wedding-night; ~ **de los cuchillos largos** night of the long knives; ~ **de estreno** (*Teat*) first night; ~ **toledana** sleepless night; ~ **vieja** New Year's Eve; **a primera ~** shortly after dark; **a la ~** at nightfall; **de ~** (*adv*) at night, by night, in the night-time; **de ~** (*adj*) late-night (*atr*), evening (*atr*), *p.ej.* **función de ~** late-night show, evening performance, **traje de ~** evening dress; **de la ~ a la mañana** (*t fig*) overnight; **en la ~ de ayer** last night; **en la ~ de hoy** tonight; **hasta muy entrada la ~, hasta muy por la ~** until late at night; on into the small hours; **¡está para una ~!‡, ¡qué ~ tiene!‡** she's a bit of all right!‡; **por la ~** at night, during the night; **ha cerrado la ~** the darkness has come down, night has closed in; **hacer ~ en un sitio** to spend the night in a place; **se hace de ~** it's getting dark, night is falling; **pasar la ~ en blanco, pasar la ~ de claro en claro** to have a sleepless night.
Nochebuena *nf* Christmas Eve.
nochecita *nf* (*LAm*) dusk, nightfall.
nocherniego 1 *adj* nocturnal, that goes out (*etc*) at night, given to wandering about at night. **2** *nm* night-bird (*fig*).
nochero 1 *adj* (*LAm*) = **nocherniego. 2** *nm* (**a**) (*And, Cono Sur: guardia*) night watchman. (**b**) (*CAm: mesilla*) bedside table. **3** *nm*, **nochera** *nf* (*CAm*) night worker.
nodo¹ *nm* node.
nodo², No-do *nm* (*Cine Hist*) newsreel.
nodriza *nf* wet-nurse; **barco ~** supply ship.
nodular *adj* nodular.
nódulo *nm* nodule.
Noé *nm* Noah.
nogal *nm* (*madera*) walnut; (*árbol*) walnut tree.
noguera *nf* walnut tree.
noluntad *nf* unwillingness, reluctance, refusal.
nómada 1 *adj* nomadic. **2** *nmf* nomad.
nomadear [1a] *vi* to wander.
nomadeo *nm* wanderings.
nomadismo *nm* nomadism.
nomás *adv* (*LAm*) just; only; *y V* **más.**
nombradía *nf* fame, renown.
nombrado *adj* (**a**) (*susodicho*) aforementioned. (**b**) (*fig*) famous, renowned.
nombramiento *nm* (**a**) (*denominación*) naming; designation. (**b**) (*mención*) mention. (**c**) (*para un puesto etc*) nomination; appointment; (*Mil*) commission.
nombrar [1a] *vt* (**a**) (*dar nombre a*) to name; to designate.
(**b**) (*mencionar*) to mention.
(**c**) (*para un puesto etc*) to nominate; to appoint; (*Mil*) to commission; ~ **a uno embajador** to nominate sb as ambassador, appoint sb ambassador.
nombre *nm* (**a**) name; **mal ~** nickname; **Bradomín, por mal ~ Tufo** Bradomín, nicknamed Stinker; **un sobre a mi ~** an envelope addressed to me; ~ **y apellidos** name in full, full name; ~ **artístico** (*Liter*) pen-name; (*Teat*) stage-name; ~ **de bautismo** given name; ~ **comercial** trade name; ~ **de familia,** ~ **gentilicio** family name; *V* **hipocorístico;** ~ **de lugar** place-name; ~ **de pila** first name, Christian name; ~

propietario proprietary name; ~ **propio** proper name; ~ **de religión** name in religion; ~ **social** corporate name; **no hay nadie a ~ de María** there's no one by the name of María; **bajo el ~ de** under the name of; **de ~** by name, *p.ej.* **de ~ García** García by name; **conocer a uno de ~** to know sb by name; **era rey tan sólo de ~, de rey no tenía más que el ~** he was king in name only; **no existe sino de ~** it exists in name only; **en ~ de** in the name of, on behalf of; **en ~ de la libertad** in the name of liberty; **¡abran en ~ de la ley!** open up, in the name of the law!; **por ~ de** by the name of, called; **sin ~** nameless; **poner ~ a** to call, name; **¿qué ~ le van a poner?** what are they going to call him?, what name are they giving him?; **le pusieron el ~ de su abuelo** they named him after his grandfather; **su conducta no tiene ~** his conduct is unspeakable.

(**b**) (*Ling*) noun; ~ **abstracto** abstract noun; ~ **colectivo** collective noun; ~ **común** common noun; ~ **concreto** concrete noun.

(**c**) (*fig*) name, reputation; **un médico de ~** a famous doctor; **tiene ~ en el mundo entero** it has a world-wide reputation.

nomenclador *nm*, **nomenclátor** *nm* catalogue of names.

nomenclatura *nf* nomenclature.

nomeolvides *nf invar* (**a**) (*Bot*) forget-me-not. (**b**) (*pulsera*) bracelet (with lover's name *etc*).

nómina *nf* list, roll; (*Com, Fin*) payroll; **tiene una ~ de 500 personas** he has 500 on his payroll.

nominación *nf* nomination.

nominal *adj* (**a**) *jefe, rey etc* nominal, titular, in name only. (**b**) *valor* face (*atr*), nominal; *sueldo etc* nominal. (**c**) (*Ling*) noun (*atr*), substantival.

nominalismo *nm* nominalism.

nominalmente *adv* nominally, in name; **al menos ~** at least in name.

nominar [1a] *vt* to nominate.

nominativo 1 *adj* (**a**) (*Ling*) nominative. (**b**) (*Com, Fin*) bearing a person's name, made out to an individual; **el cheque será ~ a favor** (*o* **nombre**) **de X** the cheque should be made out to X. **2** *nm* (*Ling*) nominative.

non 1 *adj número* odd, uneven.

2 *nm* odd number; **pares y ~es** odds and evens; **los ~es** the odd ones; **un zapato de ~** an odd shoe; **queda uno de ~** there's an odd one, there's one left over; **estar de ~** (*persona*) to be odd man out, (*fig*) be useless; **andar de ~es** to have nothing to do.

nona* *nf* (*Cono Sur*) grandma*, granny*.

nonada *nf* trifle, mere nothing.

nonagenario 1 *adj* nonagenarian, ninety-year old. **2** *nm*, **nonagenaria** *nf* nonagenarian, person in his (*o* her) nineties.

nonagésimo *adj* ninetieth.

nonato *adj* not born naturally; unborn.

noneco *adj* **nonejo** *adj* (*CAm*) thick.

nones* *adv* no; **¡~! no way!***; **decir que ~** to say flatly no.

nono[1] *adj* ninth.

nono[2]* *nm* (*Cono Sur*) granddad*.

nopal *nm* prickly pear.

nopalera *nf* patch of prickly pears, area where prickly pears grow.

noqueada *nf* (*esp LAm*) (*acto*) knockout; (*golpe*) knockout blow.

noqueado* *adj* (*LAm*: *cansado*) shattered*, knackered*.

noquear [1a] *vt* to knock out, K.O.

noratlántico *adj* north-Atlantic.

noray *nm* bollard.

norcoreano, -a *adj, nm/f* North Korean.

nordeste 1 *adj parte* north-east, north-eastern; *dirección* north-easterly; *viento* north-east, north-easterly.

2 *nm* (**a**) (*región*) north-east.

(**b**) (*viento*) north-east wind.

nordestino *adj* north-eastern.

nórdico 1 *adj* (**a**) (*gen*) northern, northerly; **es la ciudad más nórdica de Europa** it is the most northerly city in Europe.

(**b**) (*Hist*) Nordic, Norse.

2 *nm*, **nórdica** *nf* (**a**) (*gen*) northerner.

(**b**) (*Hist*) Northman.

3 *nm* (*Ling*) Norse.

noreste = **nordeste**.

noria *nf* (**a**) (*Agr*) waterwheel, chain pump. (**b**) (*de feria*) big wheel, Ferris wheel (*US*).

norirlandés 1 *adj* Northern Irish. **2** *nm*, **norirlandesa** *nf* Northern Irishman, Northern Irishwoman.

norma *nf* (**a**) (*gen*) standard, norm, rule; (*pauta*) pattern; (*método*) method; ~ **de comprobación** (*Fís etc*) control; **~s de conducta** (*de periódico etc*) policy; **~s de seguridad** safety regulations; ~ **de vida** principle, guiding principle; **está sujeto a ciertas ~s** it is subject to certain rules.

(**b**) (*Arquit, Téc*) square.

normal 1 *adj* normal; regular, usual, natural; (*Téc etc*) standard; **es perfectamente ~** it's perfectly normal, it's completely usual. **2** *nf* (**a**) (*Aut*) 3-star petrol. (**b**) (*LAm Educ*) teacher(s') training college (*primary*).

normalidad *nf* normality, normalcy; (*Pol*) calm, normal conditions; **la situación ha vuelto a la ~** the situation has returned to normal; **la vuelta a la ~ es completa en la provincia** calm has been completely restored in the province.

normalillo, normalito *adj* quite ordinary; run-of-the-mill.

normalista *nmf* (*LAm*) student teacher; schoolteacher.

normalización *nf* normalization.

normalizado *adj* standard(ized).

normalizar [1f] **1** *vt* to normalize, restore to normal; (*Téc*) to standardize. **2 normalizarse** *vr* to return to normal, settle down.

normalmente *adv* normally; usually.

Normandía *nf* Normandy.

normando 1 *adj* Norman; **Islas Normandas** Channel Isles. **2** *nm*, **normanda** *nf* Norman; Northman, Norseman.

normar [1a] *vt* (*LAm*) to lay down rules for, establish norms for.

normativa *nf* (set of) rules, regulations; guideline(s); **según la ~ vigente** according to current guidelines.

normativo *adj* (**a**) (*prescrito*) normative, preceptive.

(**b**) (*regular*) regular, standard; **español ~** standard Spanish, received Spanish; **es ~ en todos los coches nuevos** it is standard in all new cars, it is the norm in all new cars.

noroccidental *adj* north-western.

noroeste 1 *adj parte* north-west, north-western; *dirección* north-westerly; *viento* north-west, north-westerly. **2** *nm* (**a**) (*región*) north-west. (**b**) (*viento*) north-west wind.

nororiental *adj* north-eastern.

norsa *nf* (*LAm*) (*enfermera*) nurse; (*institutriz*) governess; (*niñera*) nursemaid.

nortada *nf* (steady) northerly wind.

norte 1 *adj parte* north, northern; *dirección* northerly; *viento* north, northerly.

2 *nm* (**a**) (*región*) north; **en la parte del ~** in the northern part; **al ~ de Segovia** to the north of Segovia, on the north side of Segovia; **eso cae más hacia el ~** that lies further (to the) north.

(**b**) (*viento*) north wind.

(**c**) (*fig*) (*guía*) guide; (*meta*) aim, objective; (*estrella*) lodestar; **pregunta sin ~** aimless question; **perder el ~** to lose one's way, go astray.

(**d**) (*Carib*: *se refiere vagamente a*) United States.

(**e**) (*Carib*: *llovizna*) drizzle.

norteafricano, -a *adj, nm/f* North African.

Norteamérica *nf* North America.

norteamericano, -a *adj, nm/f* North American, American.

nortear [1a] *vi*: **nortea** (*And, CAm, Carib*) the north wind is blowing.

norteño 1 *adj* northern. **2** *nm*, **norteña** *nf* northerner.

nortino = **norteño**.

Noruega *nf* Norway.

noruego, -a 1 *adj, nm/f* Norwegian. **2** *nm* (*Ling*) Norwegian.

norvietnamés, -esa *adj, nm/f* (*LAm*) North Vietnamese.

norvietnamita *adj, nmf* North Vietnamese.

nos *pron pers pl* (**a**) (*ac*) us.

(**b**) (*dativo*) (to) us; **~ lo dará** he will give it to us; **~ lo compró** he bought it from us; he bought it for us; **~ cortamos el pelo** we had our hair cut.

(**c**) (*reflexivo*) (to) ourselves; (*recíproco*) (to) each other; **~ lavamos** we washed; **no ~ hablamos** we don't speak to each other; **~ levantamos a las 7** we get up at 7.

nosocomio *nm* (*Méx*) hospital.

nosotros, nosotras *pron pers pl* (**a**) (*sujeto*) we. (**b**) (*tras prep*) us; ourselves; **entre ~** between you and me; between ourselves; **no irán sin ~** they won't go without us; **no pedimos nada para ~** we ask nothing for ourselves.

nostalgia *nf* nostalgia, homesickness; longing.

nostálgico *adj* nostalgic, homesick; longing.

nostalgioso *adj* (*Cono Sur*) = **nostálgico**.

nota 1 *nf* (**a**) (*gen*) note; memorandum; (*Liter*) footnote, marginal note; (*Com*) account; (*recibo*) receipt; (*en periódico*) note; (*LAm*: *pagaré*) IOU, promissory note; (*Méx*:

cuenta) bill; ~ **de cargo** debit note; ~ **de entrega** delivery note; ~ **de gastos** expense account; ~ **informativa** press release; ~ **de inhabilitación** (*Aut*) endorsement (*in licence*); ~ **a pie de página** footnote; ~ **de prensa** press release; ~ **de la redacción** editor's note; ~ **de sociedad** gossip column, column of society news; **texto con ~s de ...** text edited with notes by ..., text annotated by ...; **pagar la ~** (*fig*) to carry the can*; **tomar ~s** to take notes.

(**b**) (*Escol etc*) grade, mark, class; (*t* ~ **escolar**) (terminal) report; **obtener buenas ~s** to get good marks; **ir para ~*** to overdo it, put too much into it.

(**c**) (*Mús y fig*) note; ~ **de adorno** grace note; **una ~ de buen gusto** a tasteful note; **como ~ de color** as a colourful note; as a bit of local colour; ~ **dominante** dominant feature; **dar la ~** (*fig: dar el tono*) to set the tone; (*armar un lío*) to cause trouble; (*destacar*) to get oneself noticed, act up; **entonar la ~** to pitch a note, give the note (*for singers to start*).

(**d**) (*fig: reputación*) reputation; **de ~** of note, famous; **de mala ~** notorious; of ill fame; **tiene ~ de tacaño** he has a reputation for meanness.

(**e**) **digno de ~** notable, worthy of note; **tomar ~** to take note.

(**f**) **quedarse ~‡** (*invar*) to be amazed.

(**g**) (*LAm‡*) effects of drugs.

2 *nm* (**a**) (‡) bloke‡. (**b**) **es un ~s*** he's an oddball*; his face doesn't fit.

notabilidad *nf* (**a**) (*cualidad*) noteworthiness, notability. (**b**) (*persona*) notable, worthy.

notable 1 *adj* (**a**) (*gen*) noteworthy, notable; remarkable. (**b**) (*Escol*) outstanding. (**c**) (*Univ etc*) creditable, of the second class. **2** *nmf* (*gen*) notable, worthy. **3** *nm* (*Univ etc*) credit (mark), second class (mark).

notablemente *adv* notably; remarkably, outstandingly.

notación *nf* notation; ~ **binaria** binary notation; ~ **hexadecimal** hexadecimal notation.

notar [1a] **1** *vt* (**a**) (*observar*) to note, notice; (*percibir*) to feel, perceive; (*ver*) to see; **no noto frío alguno** I don't feel cold at all; **no lo había notado** I hadn't noticed it; **te noto muy cambiado** I find you very changed; **hacer ~ que ...** to note that ..., observe that ...; **hacerse ~** to stand out, catch the eye, draw attention to o.s.

(**b**) (*apuntar*) to note down.

(**c**) (*marcar*) to mark, indicate.

(**d**) (*criticar*) to criticize; (*desacreditar*) to discredit; ~ **a uno de oscuro** to brand sb as obscure, criticize sb for being obscure.

2 notarse *vr* to show, be apparent, be obvious; **se nota que ...** one observes that ..., one notes that ...; **la combinación no se le nota** your slip doesn't show; **no se nota en absoluto su origen extranjero** his foreign origin is not in the least obvious, you can't tell at all that he is foreign.

notaría *nf* (**a**) (*profesión*) profession of notary; **gastos de ~** legal fees, lawyer's fees. (**b**) (*despacho*) notary's office.

notarial *adj* notarial; *estilo etc* legal, lawyer's.

notarialmente *adv* by legal process; **recurrir ~ a uno** to bring a legal action against sb; **tiene que certificarse ~** it must be legally certified, it must be certified before a commissioner for oaths.

notario, -a *nm/f* notary, notary public; (*en ciertos aspectos, equivale a*) solicitor.

noticia *nf* (**a**) (*gen*) piece of news; (*en periódico, TV etc*) news item; **~s** news; information; ~ **necrológica** notice of a death, obituary notice; **según nuestras ~s** according to our information; **eso no es ~** that's not news; **estar atrasado de ~s** to be behind the times, lack up-to-date information; **tener ~s de uno** to have news of sb, hear from sb; **hace tiempo que no tenemos ~s suyas** we haven't heard from her for a long time.

(**b**) (*conocimientos*) knowledge; notion; **no tener la menor ~ de algo** to know nothing at all about a matter, be completely ignorant of sth.

noticiable *adj* newsworthy.

noticiar [1b] *vt* to notify.

noticiario *nm* (*Rad*) news bulletin; (*Cine*) newsreel.

noticiero 1 *adj* (**a**) (*relativo a noticias*) news (*atr*). (**b**) (*que da noticias*) news-bearing, news-giving. (**c**) (*ávido de noticias*) fond of receiving news. **2** *nm* (**a**) (*periódico*) newspaper, gazette. (**b**) (*Carib*) newsreel; (*LAm TV*) news bulletin, newcast.

notición *nm* bombshell.

noticioso 1 *adj* (**a**) *fuente etc* well-informed; *reportaje* news (*atr*); *suceso* newsworthy; **texto ~** news report. (**b**) **~ de que Vd quería verme ...** hearing that (*o* on being informed that) you wished to see me ... **2** *nm* (*LAm*) news bulletin, newscast.

notificación *nf* notification.

notificar [1g] *vt* to notify, inform.

notoriamente *adv* obviously; glaringly, blatantly, flagrantly; **una sentencia ~ injusta** a glaringly unjust sentence.

notoriedad *nf* fame, renown; wide knowledge; **hechos de amplia ~** widely-known facts.

notorio *adj* (**a**) (*conocido*) well-known, publicly known; (*famoso*) famous; **un hecho ~** a well-known fact; **es ~ que ...** it is well-known that ... (**b**) (*obvio*) obvious; *error etc* glaring, blatant, flagrant.

nov. *abr de* **noviembre** November, Nov.

novador 1 *adj* innovating, revolutionary. **2** *nm*, **novadora** *nf* innovator.

noval *adj tierra* newly-broken.

novatada *nf* (**a**) (*broma*) rag, ragging, hazing (*US*) (*of new member etc*). (**b**) (*error*) beginner's mistake, elementary blunder; **pagar la ~** to learn the hard way.

novato 1 *adj* (*inexperto*) raw, green, new. **2** *nm* (*principiante*) beginner, tyro.

novecientos *adj* nine hundred; **en el ~** in the twentieth century.

novedad *nf* (**a**) (*cualidad*) newness, novelty; (*extrañeza*) strangeness.

(**b**) (*objecto etc*) novelty; surprise; **~es** (*noticias*) latest news; **~es, últimas ~es** (*Com*) novelties, latest fashions, latest models.

(**c**) (*innovación*) new feature, new development; (*cambio*) change; **sin ~ en el frente** all quiet on the front; **no hay ~es** there's nothing to report; **llegar sin ~** to arrive without mishap, arrive safely; **la jornada ha sido sin ~** it has been a quiet (*o* normal) day, it has been a day without incident; **el enfermo sigue sin ~** the patient's condition is unchanged.

novedoso *adj* (**a**) *idea, método etc* novel; new; full of novelties. (**b**) (*Cono Sur, Méx*) = **novelesco.**

novel 1 *adj* (*nuevo*) new; inexperienced; **una escritora ~** a new writer. **2** *nm* (*principiante*) beginner.

novela *nf* novel; ~ **de amor** love story, romance; ~ **de aprendizaje,** ~ **iniciática** Bildungsroman; **~s científicas** science fiction; ~ **por entregas** serial; ~ **epistolar** epistolary novel; ~ **gótica** Gothic novel; ~ **histórica** historical novel; ~ **de misterio** mystery story; ~ **negra** thriller; ~ **policíaca** detective story, whodunit*; ~ **radiofónica** radio serial; ~ **río** saga; ~ **rosa** romantic novel; **la ~ española en el siglo XX** the 20th century Spanish novel.

novelación *nf* fictionalization.

novelado *adj* fictionalized.

novelar [1a] **1** *vt* to make a novel out of; to tell in novel form; to fictionalize. **2** *vi* to write novels.

novelero 1 *adj* (**a**) (*lleno de imaginación*) highly imaginative; (*romántico*) dreamy, romantic.

(**b**) (*aficionado a novedades*) fond of novelty.

(**c**) (*aficionado a novelas*) fond of novels.

(**d**) *cuento etc* romantic, novelettish.

(**e**) (*chismoso*) gossipy, fond of gossiping.

2 *nm*, **novelera** *nf* novel reader.

novelesco *adj* (**a**) (*Liter*) fictional; **el género ~** fiction, the novel. (**b**) (*romántico*) romantic, fantastic, novelettish; *aventura etc* storybook (*atr*).

novelista *nmf* novelist.

novelística *nf*: **la ~** fiction, the novel.

novelón *nm* big novel, three-decker novel; (*pey*) pulp novel.

novelucha *nf* (*pey*) cheap novel, yellowback; pulp novel.

novena *nf* (*Ecl*) novena.

noveno *adj, nm* ninth.

noventa *adj* ninety; ninetieth; **los (años) ~** the nineties; **los escritores del ~ y ocho** the writers of the 1898 Generation.

noventayochista *adj*: *p.ej.* **un escritor ~** a writer of the 1898 Generation.

noventón 1 *adj* ninety-year-old, ninetyish. **2** *nm*, **noventona** *nf* person of about ninety.

novia *nf* (**a**) (*amiga*) sweetheart; (*prometida*) fiancée; (*en boda*) bride; (*recién casada*) newly-married girl; **echarse una ~** to get o.s. a girl; **Juan y su ~** John and his fiancée; **traje de ~** bridal gown, wedding dress.

(**b**) (*Mil‡*) rifle, gun.

noviar [1b] *vi*: ~ **con** (*Cono Sur*) to court, go out with, date.

noviazgo *nm* engagement.

noviciado *nm* apprenticeship, training; (*Ecl*) novitiate.

novicio, -a *nm/f* beginner, novice; apprentice; (*Ecl*) novice.
noviembre *nm* November.
noviero* *adj*: **es muy ~** he has had lots of girlfriends; he's always falling in love.
novilunio *nm* (*Astron*) new moon.
novilla *nf* heifer.
novillada *nf* (*Taur*) novillada, *bullfight with young bulls (and novice bullfighters)*.
novillero *nm* (**a**) (*Taur*) novice, young bullfighter. (**b**) (*Escol**) truant.
novillo *nm* (**a**) (*Zool*) young bull, bullock, steer; **~s** = **novillada.** (**b**) (*) cuckold. (**c**) **hacer ~s** to stay away, not turn up; (*Escol*) to play truant.
novio *nm* (*amigo*) sweetheart; (*prometido*) fiancé; (*en boda*) bridegroom, (*recién casado*) newly-married man; **los ~s** (*prometidos*) the engaged couple; (*en boda*) the bride and groom; (*recién casados*) the newly-weds; **ser ~s formales** to be formally engaged; **Maruja y su ~** Mary and her young man, Mary and her fiancée; **viaje de ~s** honeymoon.
novísimo *adj* newest, latest, most recent; brand-new.
NPI‡ (*Esp*) *abr de* **ni puta** (*o* **puñetera**) **idea** no bloody idea‡, not the faintest*.
nra., nro. *abr de* **nuestra, nuestro** our.
N.S. *abr de* **Nuestro Señor** Our Lord.
ns *abr de* **no sabe(n)** don't know(s) (*in opinion poll*).
ns/nc *abr de* **no sabe(n)/no contesta(n)** don't know(s)/non-respondents (*in opinion poll*).
N.T. (**a**) (*Rel*) *abr de* **Nuevo Testamento** New Testament, NT. (**b**) (*Téc*) *abr de* **nuevas tecnologías** new technology.
nubada *nf*, **nubarrada** *nf* (**a**) (*chaparrón*) downpour, sudden shower. (**b**) (*fig*) shower; abundance; mass.
nubarrón *nm* storm cloud.
nube *nf* (**a**) (*gen*) cloud; **~ de lluvia** raincloud; **~ de tormenta** storm cloud.
(**b**) (*fig: de humo, insectos etc*) cloud; crowd, mass, multitude; **una ~ de pordioseros** a swarm of beggars; **una ~ de críticas** a storm of criticism.
(**c**) (*Med: en ojo*) cloud, film.
(**d**) **los precios están por las ~s** prices are sky-high; **poner a uno en** (*o* **por, sobre**) **las ~s** to praise sb to the skies; **ponerse por las ~s*** (*persona*) to go up the wall*; (*precio*) to rocket, soar; **andar por las ~s, estar en las ~s** to have one's head in the clouds, be daydreaming, be remote from it all.
núbil *adj* marriageable, nubile.
nublado 1 *adj* cloudy, overcast.
2 *nm* (**a**) (*nube*) storm cloud, black cloud.
(**b**) (*fig*) (*amenaza*) threat; (*peligro*) impending danger.
(**c**) (*fig: multitud*) swarm, crowd, multitude; **un ~ de** a swarm of, a host of.
(**d**) (*fig: enfado*) anger, black mood.
nublar [1a] **1** *vt* (**a**) (*gen*) to darken, obscure. (**b**) (*fig*) *vista* to cloud, disturb; *razón* to affect; *felicidad etc* to cloud, destroy. **2 nublarse** *vr* to become cloudy, cloud over.
nublazón *nm* (*LAm*) = **nublado.**
nublo *adj* (*LAm*) cloudy.
nubloso *adj* (**a**) (*lit*) cloudy. (**b**) (*fig*) unlucky, unfortunate; gloomy.
nubosidad *nf* cloudiness, clouds; **~ de desarrollo, ~ de evolución** developing clouds.
nuboso *adj* cloudy.
nuca *nf* nape (of the neck), back of the neck.
nuclear 1 *adj* nuclear. **2** [1a] *vt* (**a**) (*reunir*) to bring together; (*combinar*) to combine; (*concentrar*) to concentrate; *miembros etc* to provide a focus for, act as a forum for. (**b**) (*liderar*) to lead. **3** *nf* nuclear power station.
nuclearización *nf* introduction of nuclear energy (*de* to); conversion to nuclear energy.
nuclearizarse [1f] *vr* (*Elec*) to build nuclear power stations, go nuclear; (*Mil*) to make (*o* acquire) nuclear weapons; **países nuclearizados** countries possessing nuclear weapons.
nucleizar [1f] *vt* = **nuclear 2.**
núcleo *nm* nucleus; (*Elec*) core; (*Bot*) kernel, stone; (*fig*) core, essence; **~ duro** hard core; **~ rural** (new) village, village settlement; **~ urbano** city centre.
nudillo *nm* knuckle.
nudismo *nm* nudism.
nudista *nmf* nudist.
nudo[1] *adj*: **nuda propiedad** bare ownership, bare title to property.
nudo[2] *nm* (**a**) (*gen*) knot; **~ corredizo** slipknot; **~ gordiano** Gordian knot; **~ llano, ~ de rizos** reef knot.
(**b**) (*Náut*) knot.
(**c**) (*Bot*) knot; node.
(**d**) (*parte gruesa*) thick part, thickening, lump; **con un ~ en la garganta** with a lump in one's throat; **se me hizo un ~ en la garganta** I got a lump in my throat.
(**e**) (*de comunicaciones etc*) centre; (*de carreteras*) cloverleaf, system of flyovers, motorway interchange; (*Ferro*) junction.
(**f**) (*fig: vínculo*) bond, tie, link.
(**g**) (*fig: de problema*) knotty point; core, crux; (*de drama etc*) crisis, point of greatest complexity.
nudoso *adj madera etc* knotty, full of knots; *tronco* gnarled; *bastón* knobbly.
nuégado *nm* nougat.
nuera *nf* daughter-in-law.
nuestro 1 *adj pos* our; (*tras n*) of ours, *p.ej.* **un barco ~** a boat of ours, one of our boats; **no es amigo ~** he's not a friend of ours; **lo ~** (what is) ours, what belongs to us.
2 *pron pos* ours, of ours; **es el ~** it is ours; **los ~s** (*parientes*) our people, our relations, our family; (*Dep, Mil etc*) our men, our side.
nueva *nf* piece of news; **~s** news; **me cogió de ~s** it was news to me, it took me by surprise; **hacerse de ~s** to pretend not to have heard a piece of news before, pretend to be surprised.
Nueva Caledonia *nf* New Caledonia.
Nueva Delhi *nf* New Delhi.
Nueva Escocia *nf* Nova Scotia.
Nueva Gales *nf* **del Sur** New South Wales.
Nueva Guinea *nf* New Guinea.
Nueva Inglaterra *nf* New England.
nuevamente *adv* again; anew.
neuvaolero *adj* new-wave (*atr*).
Nueva Orleáns *nf* New Orleans.
Nueva York *nf* New York.
Nueva Zelanda *nf*, **Nueva Zelandia** *nf* (*LAm*) New Zealand.
nueve 1 *adj* nine; (*fecha*) ninth; **las ~** nine o'clock. **2** *nm* nine.
neuvecito *adj* brand-new.
nuevo *adj* (*gen*) new; fresh; novel; (*adicional*) further, additional; *sello* mint, unused; **de ~** again; **es ~ en la ciudad** he's new to the town; **es ~ en el oficio** he's new to the trade; **somos ~s aquí** we're new here; **no hay nada ~** there's nothing fresh; **no hay nada ~ bajo las estrellas** there's nothing new under the sun; **es más ~ que yo** he is junior to me; **con ~s argumentos** with new arguments, with further arguments; **la casa es nueva** the house is new; **la casa está nueva** the house is as good as new; **¿qué hay de ~?*** what's new?*, what's the news?
nuevomejicano, -a *adj, nm/f* New Mexican.
Nuevo Méjico *nm* New Mexico.
nuez *nf* (**a**) nut, (*esp*) walnut; (*Méx*) pecan nut; **~ del Brasil, ~ de Pará** Brazil nut; **~ moscada** nutmeg; **~ nogal** (*o* **de Castilla**) (*Méx*) walnut; **~ de la garganta** Adam's apple. (**b**) (*fig*) core, heart of the matter.
nulidad *nf* (**a**) (*Jur*) nullity. (**b**) (*incapacidad*) incompetence, incapacity. (**c**) (*persona*) nonentity; **es una ~** he's a dead loss, he's useless.
nulo 1 *adj* (**a**) (*Jur*) void, null and void; invalid, without force; **~ y sin efecto** null and void.
(**b**) *persona* useless; **es ~ para la música** he's useless at music, he's no good at music, he's a dead loss as a musician.
(**c**) *partido* drawn, tied.
2 *nmpl*: **~s** (*Naipes*) misère; **bridge con ~s** bridge with the misère variation.
núm. *abr de* **número** number, No.
Numancia *nf* Numantia; (*fig*) *symbol of heroic* (*o last-ditch*) *resistance.*
numantino 1 *adj* Numantine, of Numantia; (*fig*) *resistencia* heroic, last-ditch, (*pey*) diehard, stubborn. **2** *nmpl*: **los ~s** the Numantines, the people of Numantia.
numen *nm* inspiration; talent, inventiveness; **~ poético** poetic inspiration; **de propio ~** out of one's head.
numeración *nf* (**a**) (*acto*) numeration, numbering. (**b**) (*números*) numbers, numerals; **~ arábiga** Arabic numerals; **~ romana** Roman numerals.
numerador *nm* numerator.
numeral 1 *adj* numeral, number (*atr*). **2** *nm* numeral.
numerar [1a] **1** *vt* to number; **páginas sin ~** unnumbered pages. **2 numerarse** *vr* (*Mil etc*) to number off.
numerario 1 *adj claustral, miembro etc* full; *profesor* tenured, with tenure, permanent; **no ~** without tenure, not

permanent. **2** *nm* (*Fin*) cash, hard cash.
numerero* *adj* far-out*, over-the-top, outrageous.
numéricamente *adv* numerically.
numérico *adj* numerical; (*Inform*) numeric.
numerito *nm* (*Teat*) short act; fill-in act.
número *nm* (**a**) (*gen*) number **~ arábigo** Arabic numeral; **~ binario** binary number; **~ cardinal** cardinal number; **~ entero** whole number; **~ fraccionario** (*o* **quebrado**) fraction; **~ impar** odd number; **~ de matrícula** (*Aut etc*) registration number; **~ ordinal** ordinal number; **~ par** even number; **~ primo** prime number; **~ redondo** round number; **en ~s redondos** in round numbers, in round figures; **~ de referencia** reference number; **~ romano** Roman numeral; **~ de serie** serial number; **N~ Uno** (*criminal*) Mr Big; **el jugador ~ uno de su país** the number one player of his country; **el ~ dos del grupo** the second in command (*o* number two) of the group; **en ~ de** to the number of; **miembro de ~** full member; **sin ~** (*fig*) numberless, unnumbered; countless; **estar en** (*o* **tener**) **~s rojos** to be in the red; **tomar el ~ cambiado*** (*engañar*) to try to put one over*; (*excederse*) to go too far; **volver a ~s negros** to get back into the black, return to profitability.

(**b**) (*de zapato etc*) size.

(**c**) (*de periódico etc*) number, issue; **~ atrasado** back number; **~ cero** (*Prensa*) dummy number, dummy run; **~ extraordinario** special edition, special issue; **~ suelto** single issue.

(**d**) (*de programa*) item, number; (*Teat etc*) turn, act, number; sketch; **hacer el ~*, montar el ~*** to do something pretty far-out*, go over the top; to make a scene; **¡ya empiezas con tus ~s!** there you go with your old tricks again!

(**e**) **de ~** (*Cono Sur*) first-class.

(**f**) **¡vaya ~!*** what a character!

(**g**) **profesor de ~** tenured teacher, teacher with tenure, teacher with a permanent post.

(**h**) (*Mil etc*) man; (*soldado raso*) private; (*policía*) policeman; **un sargento y 4 ~s** a sergeant and 4 men.

(**i**) (*: *billete de lotería*) ticket.

numerología *nf* numerology.
numeroso *adj* numerous; **familia numerosa** large family.
numerus clausus *nm* system of restricted (*o* selective) entry (to university *etc*), quota system.
numísmata *nmf* numismatist.
numismática[1] *nf* numismatics.
numismático 1 *adj* numismatic. **2** *nm*, **numismática**[2] *nf* numismatist.
nunca *adv* never; ever; **no viene ~, ~ viene** he never comes, he doesn't ever come; **¡~!** never!; **casi ~** almost never, hardly ever; **¡hasta ~!** I don't care if I never see you again!; **más que ~** more than ever; **~ jamás, ~ más** never again, nevermore; **¿has visto ~ cosa igual?** have you ever seen anything like this?
nunciatura *nf* nunciature.
nuncio *nm* (**a**) (*Ecl*) nuncio; **~ apostólico, ~ pontificio** papal nuncio; **¡cuéntaselo al ~!** tell that to the marines!; **¡que lo haga el ~!** get sb else to do it! (**b**) (*mensajero*) messenger; (*fig*) herald, harbinger; **~ de la primavera** harbinger of spring.
nunquita *adv* (*LAm*) = **nunca**.
nupcial *adj* wedding (*atr*), nuptial.
nupcialidad *nf* rate of marriage, marriage statistics.
nupcias *nfpl* wedding, nuptials; **casarse en segundas ~, contraer nuevas ~** to marry again, get married a second time; **A, que se casó en segundas ~ con B** A, who made a second marriage to B.
nurse ['nurse] *nf* (*enfermera*) nurse; (*institutriz*) governess; (*niñera*) nursemaid.
nursería *nf* nursing mothers' room, mother-and-baby room.
nutria *nf* otter.
nutrición *nf* nutrition.
nutricional *adj* nutritional.
nutricionista *nmf* dietician, nutritionist.
nutrido *adj* (**a**) (*alimentado*) **bien ~** well-nourished; **mal ~** undernourished.

(**b**) (*fig*) (*grande*) large, considerable; (*numeroso*) numerous; (*abundante*) abundant; **~ de** full of, abounding in; **una nutrida concurrencia** a large attendance; **~s aplausos** loud applause; **fuego ~** (*Mil*) heavy fire.

nutriente *nm* nutrient.
nutrimento *nm* nutriment, nourishment.
nutrir [3a] *vt* (**a**) (*lit*) to feed, nourish. (**b**) (*fig*) to feed, strengthen; to support, foment, encourage.
nutritivo *adj* nourishing, nutritious; **valor ~** nutritional value, food value.
nylon [ni'lon, 'nailon] *nm* nylon.

Ñ

Ñ, ñ ['eɲe] *nf* (*letra*) Ñ, ñ.
ña *nf* (*LAm*) = **doña, señora.**
ñácara *nf* (*CAm*) ulcer, sore.
ñaco *nm* (*Méx*) popcorn.
ñafiar *vt* (*Carib*) to pilfer.
ñaka *interj* quick as a flash.
ñam* *interj*: **¡~, ~, ~!** yum, yum!*
ñame *nm* yam.
ñandú *nm* (*Cono Sur*) rhea, South American ostrich.
ñanga *nf* (**a**) (*CAm*: *pantano*) marsh, swampy ground. (**b**) (*And*: *trozo*) bit, small portion.
ñangada *nf* (*CAm*) (**a**) (*mordedura*) nip, bite. (**b**) **¡qué ~ hiciste!*** that was a stupid thing to do!
ñangado *adj* (*Carib*) (*patizambo*) knock-kneed; (*estevado*) bow-legged.
ñangara *nmf* (*Carib Pol*) guerrilla.
ñangué: **en los tiempos de ~** (*And**) way back, in the dim and distant past.
ñango* *adj* (**a**) (*Cono Sur*: *patoso*) awkward, clumsy. (**b**) (*Cono Sur*: *de piernas cortas*) short-legged, waddling. (**c**) (*Méx*: *débil*) weak, feeble. (**d**) (*Carib*) = **ñangado.**
ñangotarse* [1a] *vr* (*And, Carib*) (**a**) (*agacharse*) to squat, crouch down. (**b**) (*desanimarse*) to lose heart.
ñaña *nf* (**a**) (*Cono Sur**: *hermana*) elder sister; (*Carib, Cono Sur**: *nodriza*) nursemaid, wet-nurse. (**b**) (*CAm‡*) crap**.
ñaño 1 *adj* (**a**) (*And, CAm, Cono Sur*) *amigo* close; (*And, CAm*: *mimado*) spoiled, pampered; **estar ~s** to be on very close terms.
(**b**) (*Cono Sur*: *tonto*) silly.
2 *nm* (*And, CAm, Cono Sur*: *amigo*) close friend, chum; (*And, Cono Sur**: *hermano*) elder brother; (*And*: *niño*) baby, child.
ñapa *nf* (*LAm*) extra, bonus; tip; **de ~** (*And, Carib*) as an extra, in addition.
ñapango *nm* (*And*) mulatto, mestizo, half-breed.
ñaque *nm* junk, worthless stuff; odds and ends.
ñata *nf* (**a**) (*LAm*: *nariz*) nose. (**b**) (*And*: *muerte*) death.
ñato 1 *adj* (**a**) (*LAm*: *de nariz*) flat-nosed, snub-nosed. (**b**) (*And*: *nasal*) nasal, twangy. (**c**) (*Cono Sur*) (*feo*) ugly; (*deforme*) bent, deformed. (**d**) (*CAm*: *afeminado*) effeminate. **2** *nm* (*Cono Sur**) chap*, guy*.
ñau *excl* (*LAm*) mew, miaow; **hacer ~ ~** (*lit*) to miaow; (*arañar*) to scratch.
ñauar [1a] *vi* (*LAm*) to miaow.
ñeque* 1 *adj* (*And, CAm, Cono Sur*) (*fuerte*) strong; (*vigoroso*) vigorous; (*listo*) clever, capable; (*CAm, Carib*: *valiente*) brave.
2 *nm* (**a**) (*LAm*) (*fuerza*) strength; (*vigor*) energy, vigour; (*valor*) courage.
(**b**) (*CAm, Méx*: *golpe*) blow, punch.
(**c**) **~s** (*And*) fists.
ñique* *nm* (*CAm, Cono Sur*: *cabezazo*) butt with the head; (*CAm*: *puñetazo*) punch.
ñiquiñaque *nm* (**a**) (*trastos*) trash, junk, rubbish. (**b**) (*persona*) worthless individual.
ñisca *nf* (**a**) (*And, CAm, Cono Sur*: *pedazo*) bit, small piece. (**b**) (*And, CAm‡*: *excremento*) crap**.
ñoca *nf* (*And*) crack, fissure.
ñoco 1 *adj* (*And, Carib*) (*sin dedo*) lacking a finger; (*sin mano*) one-handed. **2** *nm* (*Cono Sur*: *puñetazo*) straight punch.
ñola *nf* (**a**) (*And, CAm‡*: *excremento*) crap**. (**b**) (*CAm**: *úlcera*) ulcer, sore.
ñongarse [1h] *vr* (*And*) (**a**) (*agacharse*) to squat, crouch down. (**b**) **~ el pie** to twist one's foot.
ñongo *adj* (**a**) (*Carib, Cono Sur, Méx**: *estúpido*) stupid; (*Cono Sur*) (*lento*) slow, lazy; (*perdido*) good-for-nothing; (*humilde*) creepy.
(**b**) (*And, Carib*: *lisiado*) crippled.
(**c**) (*Carib*) (*tramposo*) tricky, deceitful; (*feo*) unsightly; (*infausto*) of ill omen; (*quisquilloso*) touchy.
ñoñería *nf*, **ñoñez** *nf* (**a**) (*sosería*) insipidness; (*falta de carácter*) spinelessness; (*timidez*) shyness, bashfulness; (*melindrería*) fussiness.
(**b**) (*Cono Sur*: *vejez*) senility; dotage.
(**c**) (*Carib*: *estupidez*) inanity, stupid thing.
(**d**) (*Carib*) (*nombre cariñoso*) endearment; (*halagos*) flattery.
ñoño 1 *adj* (**a**) (*soso*) characterless, insipid; (*insustancial*) insubstantial; *persona* spineless.
(**b**) (*tímido*) shy, bashful.
(**c**) (*quisquilloso*) fussy, finicky.
(**d**) (*LAm**: *viejo*) senile, decrepit.
(**e**) (*And, Carib*: *vanidoso*) vain, that likes to be flattered.
(**f**) (*Méx**: *bruto*) thick*.
2 *nm*, **ñoña** *nf* spineless person, drip‡.
ñoqui *nm* (**a**) **~s** (*Culin*) gnocchi. (**b**) (*Cono Sur**: *golpe*) thump.
ñorba *nf* (*And*), **ñorbo** *nm* (*And*) passionflower.
ñorda** *nf* turd**, shit**; **¡una ~!** get away!*; **ser una ~** to be a shit**.
ñu *nm* gnu, wildebeest.
ñuco *adj* (*And*) *animal* dehorned; (*) *persona* limbless.
ñudo: **al ~** *adv* (*LAm*) in vain; for nothing.
ñudoso *adj* = **nudoso.**
ñufla* 1 *nf* (*Cono Sur*) piece of junk. **2** *adj* worthless.
ñuño* *nf* (*And*) wet-nurse.
ñusca‡ *nf* (*And*) crap**.
ñusta *nf* (*And Hist*) princess of royal blood.
ñutir [3a] *vi* (*And*) to grunt.
ñuto* *adj* (*And*) crushed, ground.

O

O, o [o] *nf* (*letra*) O, o.
O (**a**) (*Geog*) *abr de* **oeste** west, W. (**b**) *abr de* **octubre** October, Oct.
o (*Com*) *abr de* **orden** order, o.
o *conj* or; ~ ... ~ either ... or.
ó *conj* (*en números para evitar confusión*) or; **5 ó 6** 5 or 6.
OAA *nf abr de* **Organización de las Naciones Unidas para la Alimentación y la Agricultura** Food and Agriculture Organization, FAO.
OACI *nf abr de* **Organización de la Aviación Civil Internacional** International Civil Aviation Organization, ICAO.
oasis *nm invar* oasis.
obcecación *nf* blindness, blind obstinacy; mental blockage, disturbance; **en un momento de ~** when the balance of his (*etc*) mind was disturbed.
obcecadamente *adv* blindly; stubbornly, obdurately; in a disturbed state.
obcecado *adj* (*ciego*) blind; mentally blinded; (*terco*) stubborn, obdurate; (*trastornado*) disturbed.
obcecar [1g] *vt* to blind (mentally), disturb the mind of; **el amor le ha obcecado** love has blinded him (to all else).
obedecer [2d] *vti* (**a**) (*gen*) to obey.
(**b**) **~ a** (*Med*) to yield to, respond to (treatment by).
(**c**) **~ a, ~ al hecho de que ...** to be due to ..., arise from ...; **su viaje obedece a dos motivos** his journey has two reasons.
obediencia *nf* obedience.
obediente *adj* obedient.
obelisco *nm* obelisk; (*Tip*) dagger.
obenques *nmpl* (*Náut*) shrouds.
oberol *nm* overalls.
obertura *nf* overture.
obesidad *nf* obesity.
obeso *adj* obese.
óbice *nm* obstacle, impediment; **eso no es ~ para que lo haga** that is not an obstacle to my doing it.
obispado *nm* bishopric.
obispo *nm* bishop.
óbito *nm* (*liter*) decease, demise.
obituario *nm* (*LAm*) (**a**) (*muerte*) decease, demise. (**b**) (*necrología*) obituary; (*sección de periódico*) obituary section.
objeción *nf* objection; **~ de conciencia** conscientious objection; **hacer objeciones** to raise objections; **no hacen ninguna ~** they make (*o* raise) no objection.
objetable *adj* objectionable, open to objection.
objetante *nmf* objector; (*en mitin*) heckler, protester.
objetar [1a] *vti* (*gen*) to object; *objeción* to make, offer, raise; *argumento* to present, put forward; **le objeté que no había dinero para ello** I pointed out to him (*o* I protested to him) that there was no money for it.
objetivamente *adv* objectively; clearly, obviously.
objetivar [1a] *vt*, **objetivizar** [1f] *vt* to objectify; to put in objective terms.
objetividad *nf* objectivity.
objetivo 1 *adj* (**a**) (*no subjetivo*) objective. (**b**) (*claro*) clear, obvious. **2** *nm* (**a**) (*meta*) objective, aim, end. (**b**) (*Mil*) objective, target. (**c**) (*Fot*) lens; object lens; **~ zoom** zoom lens.
objeto *nm* (**a**) (*artículo*) object, thing; **~ de arte** objet d'art; **~ contundente** blunt instrument; **~s de escritorio** writing materials; **'~s perdidos'** (*letrero*) 'lost property'; **~ de recuerdo** souvenir; **~ sexual** sex object; **~s de tocador** toilet articles.
(**b**) (*meta*) object, aim, end, purpose; **al ~ de** + *infin*, **con ~ de** + *infin* with the object of + *ger*, with the aim of + *ger*; **esta carta tiene por ~** + *infin* this letter has the aim of + *ger*, this letter aims to + *infin;* **fue el ~ de un asalto** she was the target of an attack, she suffered an attack.
(**c**) (*tema etc*) theme, subject matter.
(**d**) (*Ling*) object.
objetor *nm* objector; **~ de conciencia** conscientious objector.
oblación *nf* oblation, offering.
oblar [1a] *vt* (*Cono Sur*) *deuda* to pay in cash.
oblata *nf* oblation, offering.
oblea *nf* (**a**) (*Ecl y fig*) wafer; very thin slice; **quedar como una ~** to be as thin as a rake. (**b**) (*Cono Sur Correos*) stamp.
oblicuamente *adv* obliquely.
oblicuar [1d] **1** *vt* to slant, place obliquely, cant, tilt. **2** *vi* to deviate from the perpendicular.
oblicuidad *nf* obliquity, oblique angle (*o* position *etc*).
oblicuo *adj* oblique; slanting; *mirada* sidelong.
obligación *nf* (**a**) (*gen*) obligation; duty; responsibility; **obligaciones** (*esp*) family responsibilities; **cumplir con una ~** to fulfil a duty; **faltar a sus obligaciones** to fail in one's duty, fail to carry out one's obligations; **tener ~ de** + *infin* to have a duty to + *infin*, be under an obligation to + *infin*; **primero es la ~ que la devoción** business before pleasure.
(**b**) (*Com, Fin*) bond; debenture; **obligaciones** bonds, securities; **~ de banco** bank bill; **~ convertible** convertible debenture; **~ tributaria** (*Méx*) tax liability.
obligacional *adj* compulsory; binding.
obligacionista *nmf* bondholder.
obligado *adj* obligatory, unavoidable.
obligar [1h] **1** *vt* (**a**) (*gen*) to force, compel, oblige; **~ a uno a hacer algo** to force (*o* compel) sb to do sth; **verse obligado a** + *infin* to be obliged to + *infin*, find o.s. compelled to + *infin*; **estar** (*o* **quedar**) **obligado a uno** to be obliged to sb, be in sb's debt.
(**b**) *zapatos etc* to force, stretch; (*empujar*) to push; **el libro sólo entra allí obligándolo** the book goes in there but only with a hard push (*o* but only by forcing it).
2 obligarse *vr* to put o.s. under an obligation; **~ a** + *infin* to bind o.s. to + *infin.*
obligatoriamente *adv* compulsorily; of necessity.
obligatoriedad *nf* obligatory nature; **de ~ jurídica** legally binding.
obligatorio *adj* obligatory, compulsory; binding; **es ~** + *infin* it is obligatory to + *infin*; **escolaridad obligatoria** compulsory schooling, compulsory attendance at school.
obliteración *nf* (*Med*) obliteration.
obliterar [1a] *vt* (**a**) (*Med*) to obliterate. (**b**) (*LAm*) to obliterate, efface, destroy; (*Med*) *herida* to staunch.
oblongo *adj* oblong.
obnubilación *nf* = **ofuscación.**
obnubilado *adj* (*furioso*) furious, hopping mad; (*ofuscado*) flustered.
obnubilar [1a] *vt* = **ofuscar.**
oboe 1 *nm* (*instrumento*) oboe. **2** *nmf* (*persona*) oboist, oboe player.
óbolo *nm* (*fig*) mite, small contribution; **~ de San Pedro** Peter's pence.
ob.po *abr de* **obispo** Bishop, Bp.
obra *nf* (**a**) (*gen*) work; (*una ~*) piece of work; **~ de arte** work of art; **~ benéfica, ~ de misericordia, ~ piadosa** charity; **buenas ~s, ~s de caridad** good works; **~s de carretera** roadworks; **~ de construcción** building site; **~ maestra** masterpiece; **~ pía** religious foundation; **~s públicas** public works; **Ministerio de O~s Públicas** Ministry of Works; **es ~ de benedictinos** it's a long job, it will take great patience; **es ~ de romanos** it's a huge task, it's a labour of Hercules; **¡manos a la ~!** to work!, let's get on with it!; **por ~** (**y gracia**) **de** thanks to, thanks to the efforts of; **poner algo por ~** to put sth in hand; **~s son**

amores que no buenas razones actions speak louder than words.

(**b**) (*Arte*) work; (*Liter*) work, book; (*Teat*) play; ~ **de consulta** reference book, work of reference; ~ **de encargo** commission, commissioned work; ~ **literaria** literary work; ~ **de vulgarización** popular work; ~**s completas** complete works, collected works; **las ~s de Cervantes** the works of Cervantes.

(**c**) (*Teat*: ~ **dramática,** ~ **de teatro**) play.

(**d**) (*Mús*) work, opus, composition.

(**e**) (*Arquit*: *t* ~**s**) work; construction, building; (*LAm*: *solar, edificio en construcción*) building site; ~ **de hierro** ironwork; ~**s** (*frec*) repairs, alterations; **'cerrado por ~s'** 'closed for repairs (*o* alterations)'; **estamos en ~s** there are building repairs going on; we have the workmen in; **la autopista está en ~s entre A y B** there are roadworks on the motorway between A and B; **se han comenzado las ~s del nuevo embalse** work has been begun on the new dam.

(**f**) (*hechura*) workmanship, craftsmanship; handiwork; **la ~ es buena pero con malos materiales** the workmanship is good but the materials were bad.

(**g**) (*Cono Sur*) brickworks.

(**h**) ~ **de** about; **en ~ de 8 semanas** in about 8 weeks, in a matter of 8 weeks.

(**i**) (*Rel*) **la O~** (*Esp*) Opus Dei.

obradera* *nf* (*And, CAm euf*) diarrhoea.

obrador *nm* workroom, workshop.

obraje *nm* (**a**) (*And, Cono Sur*: *aserradero*) sawmill, timber-yard. (**b**) (*Méx*: *carnicería*) butcher's (shop). (**c**) (*And*: *textil*) textile plant.

obrajero *nm* (**a**) (*capataz*) foreman, overseer. (**b**) (*Cono Sur*: *maderero*) lumberman. (**c**) (*And*: *artesano*) craftsman, skilled worker. (**d**) (*Méx*) pork butcher.

obrar [1a] **1** *vt* (**a**) *madera etc* to work.

(**b**) (*Med*) to work on, have an effect on.

(**c**) (*Cono Sur*: *construir*) to build.

(**d**) *milagro etc* to work, bring about.

2 *vi* (**a**) (*actuar*) to act, behave; to proceed; ~ **de acuerdo con** to proceed in accordance with; ~ **con precaución** to act cautiously, proceed warily.

(**b**) (*medicina*) to work, have an effect.

(**c**) **su carta obra en mi poder** (*Com*) I have received your letter, your letter is to hand; **el expediente obra en manos del juez** (*Jur*) the file is in the judge's hands.

(**d**) (*) to relieve nature.

obr. cit. *nf abr de* **obra citada** opere citato, op. cit.

obrerado *nm* work force.

obrerismo *nm* working-class movement.

obrero 1 *adj clase* working; *sindicato etc* labour (*atr*); **el movimiento ~** the working-class movement.

2 *nm* worker (*t Pol*), workman; man, hand; labourer; ~ **autónomo** self-employed worker; ~ **cualificado,** ~ **especializado** skilled worker; ~ **escenógrafo** stagehand; ~ **portuario** dock worker.

3 obrera *nf* worker, woman worker.

obsecuente *adj* humble, obsequious.

obscenamente *adv* obscenely.

obscenidad *nf* obscenity.

obsceno *adj* obscene.

obseder [2a] *vt* (*LAm*) to obsess.

obsequiar [1b] *vt* (**a**) (*gen*) to lavish attentions on, make a fuss of; **le obsequiaron con un reloj** they presented him with a clock, they gave him a clock; **le van a ~ con un banquete** (*Esp*) they are going to hold a dinner for him, they are going to honour him with a dinner.

(**b**) **le obsequiaron un reloj** (*LAm*) they presented him with a watch.

obsequio *nm* (**a**) (*regalo*) present, gift; (*de jubilación etc*) presentation; (*Com*) free gift; **ejemplar de ~, ~ del autor** complimentary copy, presentation copy.

(**b**) (*atenciones*) attention, kindness, courtesy; **en ~ de** in honour of; **hágame el ~ de** + *infin* please + *infin*.

obsequiosamente *adv* obligingly, helpfully.

obsequioso *adj* (**a**) (*servicial*) obliging, helpful, attentive. (**b**) (*Méx*) fond of giving presents.

observable *adj* observable.

observación *nf* (**a**) (*acto*) observation; (*de ley etc*) observance; ~ **de aves** bird-watching; ~ **postal** interception of mail; ~ **telefónica** telephone tap; **estar en ~** to be under observation.

(**b**) (*comentario*) observation, remark, comment; (*objeción*) objection; **hacer una ~** to make a remark, comment, observe; **hacer una ~ a** (*objetar*) to raise an objection to.

observador 1 *adj* observant. **2** *nm,* **observadora** *nf* observer; ~ **extranjero** foreign observer.

observancia *nf* observance.

observar [1a] *vt* (**a**) (*mirar*) to observe, watch; (*notar*) to see, notice, spot; (*Astron*) to observe; ~ **que** ... to observe that ..., notice that ...

(**b**) *ley etc* to observe, respect; to keep; *regla* to abide by, adhere to; ~ **buena conducta** (*And*) to behave o.s.

(**c**) ~ **algo a uno** (*LAm*) to point sth out to sb, draw sb's attention to sth.

(**d**) (*mostrar*) to show, give signs of; **el paciente observa una mejoría** the patient shows some improvement.

observatorio *nm* observatory.

obsesión *nf* obsession.

obsesionante *adj* haunting; obsessive.

obsesionar [1a] *vt* to obsess, haunt; **estar obsesionado con** (*o* **por**) **algo** to be obsessed by sth; to have sth on the brain.

obsesivo *adj* obsessive; obsessional.

obseso *adj* obsessed, haunted.

obsidiana *nf* obsidian.

obsoleto *adj* obsolete.

obstaculización *nf* hindering, hampering.

obstaculizar [1f] *vt* to hinder, hamper, hold up; to prevent, stand in the way of.

obstáculo *nm* obstacle; hindrance; handicap, drawback; (*Mil, Dep etc*) obstacle; ~**s** (*carrera*) steeplechase; **no es ~ para que yo** + *subj* it is no obstacle to my + *ger*.

obstante: **no ~ 1** *adv* nevertheless, however; all the same. **2** *prep* in spite of.

obstar [1a] *vi*: ~ **a,** ~ **para** to hinder; to prevent; **eso no obsta para que lo haga** that is no obstacle to his doing it, that does not prevent him from doing it.

obstetra *nmf* obstetrician.

obstetricia *nf* obstetrics.

obstétrico 1 *adj* obstetric(al). **2** *nm,* **obstétrica** *nf* obstetrician.

obstinación *nf* obstinacy, stubbornness.

obstinadamente *adv* obstinately, stubbornly.

obstinado *adj* obstinate, stubborn.

obstinarse [1a] *vr* to be obstinate; to dig one's heels in; ~ **en** + *infin* to persist in + *ger,* continue obstinately to + *infin.*

obstrucción *nf* obstruction (*t Parl*).

obstruccionar [1a] *vt* (*LAm*) to obstruct.

obstruccionismo *nm* obstructionism.

obstruccionista 1 *adj* obstructionist, obstructive.

2 *nmf* obstructionist.

obstructivismo *nm* obstructiveness.

obstructivo *adj,* **obstructor** *adj* obstructive.

obstruir [3g] *vt* (*gen*) to obstruct; (*bloquear*) to block; (*atascar*) to bung up, clog; (*estorbar*) to hinder, impede; (*dificultar*) to interfere with.

obtención *nf* obtaining, securing.

obtener [2k] *vt* to get, obtain, secure; *meta* to achieve.

obtenible *adj* obtainable, accessible; achievable.

obturación *nf* plugging, stopping; sealing off; filling; **velocidad de ~** (*Fot*) shutter speed.

obturador *nm* plug, stopper; (*Mec*) choke; (*Fot*) shutter.

obturar [1a] *vt* to plug, stop (up); to seal off; *diente* to fill.

obtuso *adj* (**a**) *filo etc* blunt, dull. (**b**) (*Mat y fig*) obtuse.

obús *nm* (**a**) (*Mil*) (*cañón*) howitzer; (*proyectil*) shell. (**b**) (*Aut*) core valve.

obvención *nf* bonus, perquisite.

obvencional *adj* bonus, extra; incidental.

obviamente *adv* obviously.

obviar [1c] **1** *vt* (*evitar*) to obviate, remove. **2** *vi* (*estorbar*) to stand in the way.

obviedad *nf* (**a**) (*gen*) obvious nature, obviousness. (**b**) (*una* ~) obvious remark (*etc*); **la respuesta parece ser una ~** the reply seems to be an obvious one.

obvio *adj* obvious.

OC *nf abr de* **onda corta** short wave, SW.

oca *nf* (**a**) goose; **¡es la ~!‡** it's the tops!*. (**b**) (*And*) root vegetable.

ocasión *nf* (**a**) (*vez*) occasion, time; **con ~ de** on the occasion of; **en algunas ocasiones** sometimes; **en aquella ~** on that occasion, at that time, then; **venir en una mala ~** to come at a bad moment.

(**b**) (*oportunidad*) chance, opportunity, occasion; **aprovechar la ~** to take one's chance, seize one's opportunity; **dar a uno la ~ de** + *infin* to give sb a chance (*o* opportunity) to + *infin;* **a la ~ la pintan calva** it's an offer one can't refuse.

(**c**) (*motivo*) cause, motive; **no hay ~ para quejarse** there is no cause to complain.

(**d**) **de** ~ (*Com*) secondhand; old, used; **librería de** ~ secondhand bookshop.

(**e**) (*LAm*: *ganga*) bargain; **precio de** ~ bargain price, reduced price.

ocasional *adj* (**a**) (*fortuito*) chance, accidental; incidental. (**b**) *composición etc* occasional. (**c**) *persona* part-time. (**d**) (*que ocurre a veces*) occasional.

ocasionalmente *adv* by chance, accidentally; incidentally.

ocasionar [1a] *vt* to cause, produce, occasion.

ocaso *nm* (**a**) (*Astron*) sunset; (*de astro*) setting. (**b**) (*Geog*) west. (**c**) (*fig*) decline, end, fall.

occidental 1 *adj* western. **2** *nmf* westerner.

occidentalidad *nf* (*Pol*) allegiance to the western bloc.

occidentalista *adj* (*Pol*) western; western bloc (*atr*).

occidentalizado *adj* westernized.

occidentalizar [1f] *vt* to westernize.

occidente *nm* west; **el O~** the West.

occipucio *nm* occiput.

occiso, -a *nm/f* murdered person, murder victim.

Occitania *nf* Occitania.

OCDE *nf abr de* **Organización para la Cooperación y el Desarrollo Económico** Organization for Economic Cooperation and Development, OECD.

oceanario *nm* oceanarium.

Oceanía *nf* Oceania.

oceánico *adj* oceanic.

océano *nm* ocean; **O~ Atlántico** Atlantic Ocean; **O~ Glacial Ártico** Arctic Ocean; **O~ Índico** Indian Ocean; **O~ Pacífico** Pacific Ocean.

oceanografía *nf* oceanography.

oceanográfico *adj* oceanographic.

ocelote *nm* ocelot.

ocio *nm* (**a**) (*tiempo libre*) leisure, idleness; (*pey*) idleness; **~s, ratos de ~** leisure, spare time, free time; **entretener los ~s de uno** to occupy sb's spare time.

(**b**) **~s** (*pasatiempo*) pastime, diversion.

ociosamente *adv* idly.

ociosear* [1a] *vi* (*Cono Sur*) to be at leisure; (*pey*) to idle, loaf about.

ociosidad *nf* idleness; **la ~ es madre de todos los vicios** the devil finds work for idle hands.

ocioso *adj* (**a**) (*inactivo*) idle; at leisure; inactive; **estar ~** to be idle.

(**b**) *acto, palabras etc* useless, pointless, idle; **dinero ~** money lying idle; **es ~ especular** it is idle to speculate.

oclusión *nf* (**a**) (*Ling etc*) occlusion; **~ glotal** glottal stop. (**b**) (*Met*) occluded front.

oclusiva *nf* (*Ling*) occlusive, plosive.

oclusivo *adj* (*Ling*) occlusive, plosive.

ocote *nm* (*CAm, Méx*) (*tea*) torch; (*Bot*) ocote pine; **echar ~** to make trouble.

-ocracia *V* **Aspects of Word Formation in Spanish 2.**

ocre *nm* ochre; **~ amarillo** yellow ochre; **~ rojo** red ochre.

OCSHA *nf* (*Rel*) *abr de* **Obra de la Cooperación Sacerdotal Hispanoamericana.**

oct. *nm abr de* **octubre** October, Oct.

octaedro *nm* octahedron.

octagonal *adj* octagonal.

octágono *nm* octagon.

octanaje *nm* octane number; **de alto ~** high-octane.

octano *nm* octane.

octava *nf* (*Mús, Poét*) octave.

octavilla *nf* pamphlet, leaflet.

octavín *nm* piccolo.

Octavio *nm* Octavian.

octavo 1 *adj* eighth. **2** *nm* (**a**) eighth. (**b**) (*Tip*) **libro en ~** octavo. (**c**) **~s de final** (*Dep*) quarter-finals. (**d**) (**‡**: *droga*) small dose, small shot*.

octeto *nm* (*Mús*) octet(te); (*Inform*) byte.

octogenario 1 *adj* octogenarian, eighty-year-old.

2 *nm*, **octogenaria** *nf* octogenarian, person in his (*o* her) eighties.

octogésimo *adj* eightieth.

octosílabo 1 *adj* octosyllabic. **2** *nm* octosyllable.

octubre *nm* October.

OCU ['oku] *nf* (*Esp*) *abr de* **Organización de Consumidores y Usuarios** ≈ Consumers' Association, CA.

ocular 1 *adj* ocular; eye (*atr*); **mediante examen ~** by visual inspection, with the eye; **testigo ~** eyewitness. **2** *nm* eyepiece.

oculista *nmf* oculist.

ocultación *nf*, **ocultamiento** *nm* hiding, concealment.

ocultamente *adv* secretly; mysteriously; stealthily.

ocultar [1a] **1** *vt* (*esconder*) to hide, conceal (*a, de* from); (*disfrazar*) to screen, mask.

2 ocultarse *vr* to hide (o.s.); **~ a la vista** to keep out of sight; **~ con, ~ tras** to hide behind; **se me oculta la razón** I do not know the reason, the reason is a mystery to me; **no se me oculta que ...** I am fully aware that ...

ocultismo *nm* occultism.

ocultista *nmf* occultist.

oculto *adj* (**a**) (*escondido*) hidden, concealed; **permanecer ~** to stay hidden, remain in hiding.

(**b**) (*fig*) secret; mysterious; *ciencia* occult; *pensamiento* secret, inner; *motivo* ulterior.

ocupación *nf* occupation; **fuerzas de ~** forces of occupation, occupying forces.

ocupacional *adj* occupational.

ocupado *adj* (**a**) *plaza etc* occupied, taken; **¿está ocupada la silla?** is that seat taken?

(**b**) **la línea está ocupada** (*Telec*) the line is engaged, the line is busy (*US*); **señal de ~** engaged tone, busy signal (*US*).

(**c**) *persona* (*atareado*) busy; **estoy muy ~** I'm very busy (*en* with).

(**d**) *persona* (*que tiene trabajo*) in work, working; **la población ocupada** the working population; **el porcentaje de ~s** the percentage of people in work.

(**e**) **estar ocupada** (*Esp*: *mujer*) to be pregnant.

ocupante *nmf* occupant; **~ de casa, ~ de vivienda** squatter.

ocupar [1a] **1** *vt* (**a**) *espacio, silla etc* to occupy, fill, take up; *habitación* to occupy, live in, inhabit; *atmósfera* to fill, pervade; (*Mil*) *ciudad, país* to occupy; to take over, take control of.

(**b**) *puesto* to occupy, fill.

(**c**) *persona* to occupy, engage; to keep busy; *obreros* to employ, provide work for; **las obras ocupan más de 1000 hombres** the work keeps more than 1000 men busy, the work employs more than 1000 men.

(**d**) *tiempo* to occupy, fill up, take up; **ocupa sus ratos libres pintando** he uses his spare time to paint, he paints in his spare time.

(**e**) *confiscar* to seize, confiscate; **la policía le ocupó la navaja con que hirió a su mujer** the police impounded the razor with which he wounded his wife; **les ocuparon todo el contrabando** they seized all the contraband from them.

(**f**) (*Méx*: *emplear*) to use; **¿está ocupando la pluma?** are you using the pen?

2 ocuparse *vr*: **~ con, ~ de, ~ en** to concern o.s. with; to pay attention to; to busy o.s. with; to take care of, look after; **los críticos no se ocuparon del libro** the critics paid no attention to the book, the critics did not take note of the book; **me ocuparé de ello mañana** I will deal with it tomorrow; I will look into it tomorrow; **en esta sección el autor se ocupa de los peces** in this section the author deals with fish; **conviene ~ de lo suyo** it's best to mind one's own business; **¡ocúpate de lo tuyo!*** mind your own business!

ocurrencia *nf* (**a**) (*suceso*) occurrence; incident, event.

(**b**) (*idea*) idea, bright idea; **me dio la ~ de** + *infin* it occurred to me to + *infin*, I had the idea of + *ger*; **¡qué ~!** (*iró*) what a bright idea.

(**c**) (*chiste*) witty remark, witticism.

ocurrente *adj* (*chistoso*) witty; (*listo*) bright, clever; (*gracioso*) entertaining, amusing.

ocurrido *adj* (**a**) **lo ~** what has happened. (**b**) (*And*: *gracioso*) witty, funny.

ocurrir [3a] **1** *vi* to happen, occur; **¿qué ocurre?** what's going on?; **por lo que pudiera ~** because of what might happen; **ocurre que ...** it (so) happens that ...; **lo que ocurre es que ...** the thing is ...

2 ocurrirse *vr*: **se le ocurre** + *infin* it occurs to him to + *infin*; **si se le ocurre huir** if he takes it into his head to escape; **se me ocurre que ...** it occurs to me that ...; **no se me ocurriría nunca** I wouldn't dream of it; **nunca se me había ocurrido** it had never crossed my mind.

ochar* [1a] (*Cono Sur*) **1** *vt* (**a**) *perro* to urge on, provoke to attack. (**b**) (*espiar*) to spy on. **2** *vi* (*ladrar*) to bark.

ochavado *adj* eight-sided, octagonal.

ochavo *nm* (†: *moneda*) ochavo; **no tener ni un ~*** to be broke*.

ochenta *adj* eighty; eightieth; **los (años) ~** the eighties.

ochentón 1 *adj* eighty-year-old, eightyish. **2** *nm*, **ochentona** *nf* person of about eighty.

ocho 1 *adj* eight; (*fecha*) eighth; **las ~** eight o'clock. **2** *nm* (**a**) eight. (**b**) (*Cos*) **~s** cable-stitch. (**c**) (*Dep*) eight.

ochocentista *adj* nineteenth-century (*atr*).

ochocientos *adj* eight hundred; **en el ~** in the eighteenth century.
ochote *nm* choir of eight voices.
oda *nf* ode.
odalisca *nf* odalisque.
ODECA [o'ðeka] *nf abr de* **Organización de los Estados Centroamericanos.**
ODEPA [o'ðepa] *nf abr de* **Organización Deportiva Panamericana.**
odiar [1b] *vt* (**a**) to hate. (**b**) (*Cono Sur*) (*fastidiar*) to irk, annoy; (*aburrir*) to bore.
odio *nm* (**a**) (*gen*) hatred; (*rencor*) ill will; (*antipatía*) dislike; **~ de clases** class hatred; **~ de sangre** feud, vendetta; **almacenar ~** to store up hatred; **tener ~ a** to hate.
(**b**) (*Cono Sur*) (*molestia*) annoyance, bother; (*tedio*) boredom, tedium.
odiosear* [1a] *vt* (*And, Cono Sur*) to pester, annoy.
odiosidad *nf* (*V adj*) (**a**) odiousness, hatefulness; nastiness. (**b**) (*And, Carib, Cono Sur*) irksomeness, annoyance.
odioso *adj* (**a**) (*gen*) odious, hateful, detestable; nasty, unpleasant; **hacerse ~ a uno** to incur sb's dislike.
(**b**) (*And, Cono Sur*) (*molesto*) irksome, annoying; (*presumido*) stuck-up*, snobbish.
odisea *nf* (*fig*) odyssey, epic journey.
Odisea *nf* Odyssey; **o~** odyssey.
Odiseo *nm* Odysseus.
odómetro *nm* milometer.
odontología *nf* dentistry, dental surgery, odontology.
odontólogo, -a *nm/f* dentist, dental surgeon, odontologist.
odorífero *adj*, **odorífico** *adj* sweet-smelling, odoriferous.
odre *nm* (**a**) (*liter*) wineskin. (**b**) (*****: *borracho*) toper, old soak‡.
OEA *nf abr de* **Organización de Estados Americanos** Organization of American States, OAS.
OECE *nf abr de* **Organización Europea de Cooperación Económica** Organization for European Economic Cooperation, OEEC.
oeste 1 *adj parte* west, western; *dirección* westerly; *viento* west, westerly.
2 *nm* (**a**) (*región*) west; **en la parte del ~** in the western part; **al ~ de Bilbao** to the west of Bilbao, on the west side of Bilbao; **eso cae más hacia el ~** that lies further (to the) west; **una película del O~** a western, a film of the Wild West.
(**b**) (*viento*) west wind.
Ofelia *nf* Ophelia.
ofender [2a] **1** *vt* (**a**) (*gen*) to offend; (*insultar*) to slight, insult; (*hacer injusticia a*) to wrong; **por temor a ~le** for fear of offending him.
(**b**) *sentido* to offend, be offensive to; **~ a la vista** to offend one's sight.
(**c**) (*Méx*‡) *mujer* to touch up‡, feel‡.
2 ofenderse *vr* to take offence (*de, por* at).
ofendido *adj* offended; **darse por ~** to take offence.
ofensa *nf* offence; slight; wrong.
ofensiva *nf* offensive; **~ de paz** peace offensive; **tomar la ~** to take the offensive.
ofensivo *adj* (**a**) (*Mil*) offensive. (**b**) (*gen*) offensive; (*grosero*) rude, insulting; (*asqueroso*) nasty, disgusting.
ofensor 1 *adj* offending. **2** *nm*, **ofensora** *nf* offender.
oferta *nf* (**a**) (*gen*) offer; (*propuesta*) proposal, proposition.
(**b**) (*Com*) offer; (*para contrato*) tender; (*en subasta*) bid; (*ganga*) special offer; **~ cerrada** sealed bid; **~ condicional** conditional offer; **~ y demanda** supply and demand; **~ monetaria** money supply; **~ pública de adquisición (de acciones)** takeover bid; **la ~ es superior a la demanda** (the) supply exceeds (the) demand; **estar en** (*o* **de**) **~** to be on offer.
(**c**) (*regalo*) gift, present.
ofertante *nmf* (*Com*) bidder.
ofertar [1a] *vt* (**a**) *suma de dinero, producto* to offer. (**b**) (*Com*) to tender; to bid. (**c**) (*ofrecer barato*) to sell on special offer; to offer cheap, sell cheaply.
ofertorio *nm* offertory.
off [of] *nm*: **voz en ~** voice off; **ruido en ~** background noise; **pasa algo en ~** (*Cine*) something happens offscreen; **hay una discusión en ~** there is an argument offstage, there is an argument spoken by unseen actors; **poner un aparato en ~** to switch a machine off.
office ['ofis] *nm* (*Esp*) (*despensa*) pantry; (*trascocina*) scullery; utility room; (*cocina pequeña*) kitchenette; (*Aer*) galley.
offset ['ofset] *nm* (*Tip*) offset.
offside [or'sai] *nm* (*Dep*) offside; **¡~!** offside!; **estar en ~** to be offside; (*****) to be out of touch, be out of date; to be daydreaming.
oficial 1 *adj* official.
2 *nmf* official, officer; (*Mil*) officer; (*Téc*) skilled workman; (*artesano*) craftsman; journeyman; (*de oficina*) clerk; **primer ~** (*Náut*) first officer, first mate; **~ del día** orderly officer; **~ ejecutivo** executive officer; **~ de enlace** liaison officer; **~ de guardia** (*Náut*) officer of the watch; **~ mayor** chief clerk; **~ médico** medical officer; **~ pagador** paymaster.
oficiala *nf* skilled woman worker; clerk.
oficialada *nf* (*Cono Sur, Méx*) = **oficialidad.**
oficialidad *nf* (*Mil*) officers (*collectively*).
oficialismo *nm* government party; pro-government political forces; (*LAm*) government, authorities.
oficialista 1 *adj* governmental; of the party in power. **2** *nmf* member (*o* supporter) of the governing party; (*LAm*) governmental.
oficializar [1f] *vt* to make official, give official status to.
oficialmente *adv* officially.
oficiante *nm* (*Ecl*) officiant, celebrant.
oficiar [1b] **1** *vt* (**a**) (*informar*) to inform officially. (**b**) *misa* to celebrate; *funeral etc* to conduct, officiate at. **2** *vi* (**a**) (*Ecl*) to officiate. (**b**) **~ de** to officiate as, act as.
oficina *nf* office; (*Farm*) laboratory; (*Téc*) workshop; (*Cono Sur*) nitrate works; **horas de ~** business hours, office hours; **~ de colocación, ~ de empleo** job centre, labour exchange, employment agency; **~ de información** information bureau; **~ meteorológica** weather bureau; **~ paisaje** open-plan office; **~ de objetos perdidos** lost property office, lost-and-found department (*US*); **~ de prensa** press office.
Ofines [o'fines] *nf abr de* **Oficina Internacional de Información y Observación del Español.**
oficinesco *adj* office (*atr*); clerical, white-collar (*atr*); (*pey*) bureaucratic.
oficinista *nmf* office worker, clerk; white-collar worker.
oficio *nm* (**a**) (*profesión*) job, profession, occupation; (*Téc*) craft, trade; **es del ~** (*experto*) he's an old hand; (*****: *prostituta*) she's on the game*; **un profesional con mucho ~** a seasoned professional; **sabe su ~** he knows his job; **aprender un ~** to learn a trade; **mi ~ es enseñar** my job is to teach; my profession is teaching; **tiene mucho ~** he is very experienced; **no tener ni ~ ni beneficio** to be out of work, be idle.
(**b**) (*puesto*) job, role, post; office; (*Mec etc*) function; **los deberes del ~** the duties of the post; **el ~ de esta pieza es de ...** the function (*o* job) of this part is to ...
(**c**) **buenos ~s** good offices; **ofrecer sus buenos ~s** to offer one's good offices.
(**d**) **Santo O~** (*Hist*) Holy Office, Inquisition.
(**e**) (*comunicado*) official letter.
(**f**) (*Ecl*) service; mass (*t* **~s** *pl*); **~ de difuntos** office for the dead, funeral service; **~ divino** (divine) office.
(**g**) (*Arquit*) scullery.
(**h**) **de ~**: **4 matones de ~** 4 professional thugs, 4 hired toughs*; **fue enterrado de ~** he was buried at the State's expense; **le informaremos de ~** we will inform you officially.
oficiosamente *adv* (*V adj*) (**a**) semiofficially; informally. (**b**) helpfully. (**c**) (*pey*) officiously.
oficiosidad *nf* (**a**) (*amabilidad*) helpfulness. (**b**) (*pey*) officiousness, meddlesomeness.
oficioso *adj* (**a**) (*no oficial*) semiofficial; unofficial, informal; **de fuente oficiosa** from a semiofficial source.
(**b**) (*amable*) kind, helpful, obliging.
(**c**) (*pey*) officious, meddlesome, interfering.
(**d**) *V* **mentira.**
-ófilo *sufijo*: *V p.ej.* **anglófilo.**
ofimática *nf* office automation, office computerization (*o* computing).
ofimático *adj*: **sistema ~** office computer system; **gestión ofimática integrada** integrated computer system for office management.
-ófobo *sufijo*: *V p.ej.* **anglófobo.**
-ófono *sufijo*: *V p.ej.* **anglófono.**
ofrecer [2d] **1** *vt* (*gen, t Com*) to offer; (*presentar*) to present; *gracias* to give, offer; *respetos* to pay; *bienvenida* to extend; **'ofrecen trabajo'** 'situations vacant'; **~ a uno hacer algo** to offer to do sth for sb; **me ha ofrecido no fumar más** he has promised me that he won't smoke any more.
2 ofrecerse *vr* (**a**) (*persona*) to offer o.s., volunteer; **~ a +** *infin* to offer to + *infin*, volunteer to + *infin*; **me ofrezco de guía** I offer myself as a guide.
(**b**) (*oportunidad, vista etc*) to offer itself, present itself.

(**c**) (*suceder*) to occur; **¿qué se ofrece?** what's going on?, what's happening?; **se me ofrece una duda** a doubt occurs to me.

(**d**) **¿se le ofrece algo?** do you want anything?; is there anything I can get you?; **no se me ofrece nada por ahora** I don't want anything for the moment.

ofrecimiento *nm* offer, offering; ~ **de paz** peace offer.

ofrenda *nf* offering, gift; (*Ecl*) offering; (*fig*) tribute.

ofrendar [1a] *vt* to offer, give as an offering.

oftalmía *nf* ophthalmia.

oftálmico *adj* ophthalmic.

oftalmología *nf* ophthalmology.

oftalmólogo, -a *nm/f* ophthalmologist.

ofuscación *nf*, **ofuscamiento** *nm* (*fig*) dazzled state; blindness; bewilderment, confusion, mystification.

ofuscar [1g] *vt* (**a**) (*luz*) to dazzle.

(**b**) (*fig*) (*deslumbrar*) to dazzle; (*confundir*) to bewilder, confuse, mystify.

(**c**) (*fig: cegar*) to blind; **estar ofuscado por la cólera** to be blinded by anger.

Ogino, ogino *nm*: **método** ~ rhythm method (of birth-control).

ogro *nm* ogre.

oh *interj* oh!

ohmio *nm* ohm.

oíble *adj* audible.

OIC *nf* (**a**) (*Com*) *abr de* **Organización Internacional del Comercio.** (**b**) (*Com*) *abr de* **Organización Interamericana del Café.**

OICE [o'ise] *nf abr de* **Organización Interamericana de Cooperación Económica.**

OICI [o'isi] *nf abr de* **Organización Interamericana de Cooperación Intermunicipal** Inter-American Municipal Organization, IAMO.

OID *nf abr de* **Oficina de Información Diplomática.**

oída *nf* hearing; **de ~s, por ~s** by hearsay.

-oide *V* **Aspects of Word Formation in Spanish 2.**

oído *nm* (**a**) (*sentido*) (sense of) hearing; **duro de ~, mal del** ~ hard of hearing.

(**b**) (*Anat*) ear; ~ **interno** inner ear; **¡~ a la caja!, ¡~ al parche!** pay attention!; **aguzar los ~s** to prick up one's ears; **aplicar el** ~ to listen carefully; **dar ~s a** to listen to, give ear to; **apenas pude dar crédito a mis ~s** I could scarcely believe my ears; **decir algo al ~ de uno** to whisper sth to sb, whisper sth in sb's ear; **entra por un ~ y sale por otro** it goes in one ear and out (of) the other; **hacer ~s a** to pay attention to, take heed of; **hacer ~s sordos a** to turn a deaf ear to; **es una canción que se pega al ~** it's a catchy song; **prestar ~(s) a** to give ear to; **ser todo ~s** to be all ears; **le estarán zumbando los ~s** his ears must be burning.

(**c**) (*Mús*) ear; **de ~** by ear; **tener (buen) ~** to have a good ear.

oidor *nm* (*Hist*) judge.

OIEA *nm abr de* **Organismo Internacional de Energía Atómica** International Atomic Energy Agency, IAEA.

oigo *etc V* **oír.**

OIN *nf abr de* **Organización Internacional de Normalización** International Standards Organization, ISO.

OIP [o'ip] *nf* (**a**) *abr de* **Organización Internacional de Periodistas.** (**b**) (*Aer*) *abr de* **Organización Iberoamericana de Pilotos.**

OIR [o'ir] *nf* (**a**) *abr de* **Organización Internacional para los Refugiados** International Refuge Organization, IRO. (**b**) *abr de* **Organización Internacional de Radiodifusión.**

oír [3p] **1** *vti* (**a**) (*gen*) to hear; to listen (to); *confesión* to hear; *misa* to go to, attend, hear; *consejo* to hear, pay attention to, heed; ~ **decir que ...** to hear it said that ..., hear that ...; ~ **hablar de** to hear about, hear of; ~ **de** (*LAm*) to hear from; **le oí abrir la puerta** I heard him open (*o* opening) the door; **como lo oyes, lo que oyes** it really is so, just like I'm telling you; **lo oyó como quien oye llover** she paid no attention, she turned a deaf ear to it.

(**b**) (*interj etc*) **¡oye!, ¡oiga!** listen!, listen to this!; (*llamando atención*) hi!, hey!; I say!; (*protesta*) now look here!; (*sorpresa*) I say!, say! (*US*); (*con permiso*) excuse me!; (*en tienda*) shop!; (*Telec*) **¡oiga!** hullo?

(**c**) *súplica* to hear, heed, answer; **Dios oyó mi ruego** God answered my prayer; **¡Dios te oiga!** I just hope you're right!

(**d**) (*Jur*) *causa* to hear.

2 oírse *vr*: **le gusta** ~ he likes the sound of his own voice.

OIT *nf abr de* **Oficina** (*u* **Organización**) **Internacional del Trabajo** International Labour Organization, ILO.

ojada *nf* (*And*) skylight.

ojal *nm* buttonhole.

ojalá 1 *interj* (*empleado sólo*) if only it were so!, if only it would! (*etc*); let's hope so!, I do hope you're right!; no such luck!, some hope!; **'mañana puede que haga sol' ... '¡~!'** 'it may be fine tomorrow' ... 'I hope it will be!', (*pesimista*) 'some hope!'.

2 *conj* (*t* ~ **que**) (**a**) (*gen*) I wish ...!, if only ...!, (*en tono retórico*) would that ...!; **¡~ venga pronto!** I hope he comes soon!, I wish he'd come!; **¡~ pudiera!** I wish I could!, if only I could!

(**b**) (*LAm*) even though; **no lo haré, ~ me maten** I won't do it even if they kill me.

ojazos *nmpl* big eyes, wide eyes; (*atractivos*) lovely big eyes; **echar los ~ a uno** to make eyes at sb.

OJD *nf abr de* **Oficina de Justificación de la Difusión** *office which keeps statistics of newspaper circulations.*

OJE ['oxe] *nf* (†) *abr de* **Organización Juvenil Española.**

ojeada *nf* glance; **echar una ~ a** to glance at, take a quick look at.

ojeador *nm* (*Caza*) beater; (*Dep etc*) talent scout, talent spotter.

ojear[1] [1a] *vt* (*mirar*) to eye; to stare at; **voy a ~ cómo va el trabajo** I'm going to see how the work is getting on.

ojear[2] [1a] *vt* (**a**) (*ahuyentar*) to drive away, drive off, shoo. (**b**) (*Caza*) to beat, put up, drive. (**c**) (*Cono Sur*: *hechizar*) to put the evil eye on.

ojén *nm* anisette.

ojeo *nm* (*Caza*) beating.

ojera *nf* (**a**) (*sombra*) ring under the eye; **tener ~s** to have rings (*o* circles) under the eyes. (**b**) (*Med*) eyebath.

ojeriza *nf* spite, ill will; **tener ~ a** to have a grudge against, have it in for*.

ojeroso *adj* with rings under the eyes; tired, haggard.

ojete *nm* (**a**) (*Cos*) eyelet. (**b**) (*LAm***) arsehole**.

ojiabierto *adj* wide-eyed.

ojillos *nmpl* bright eyes; lovely eyes; roguish eyes; **¡tiene unos ~!** you should see what eyes she's got!

ojímetro *nm*: **a ~** roughly, at a rough guess.

ojinegro *adj* black-eyed.

ojituerto *adj* cross-eyed.

ojiva *nf* (*Arquit*) ogive, pointed arch; (*Mil*) warhead.

ojival *adj* ogival, pointed.

ojo *nm* (**a**) (*Anat*) eye; **~s de almendra** almond eyes; **~ de cristal** glass eye; **~ a la funerala, ~ amoratado, ~ a la pava, ~ a la virulé, ~ morado** black eye; **~ del huracán** eye of the hurricane; **~ mágico** magic eye, photocell; **~ de pez** (*Fot*) wide-angle lens; **~s saltones** bulging eyes, goggle eyes; **~s que hablan** expressive eyes; **a los ~s de** in the eyes of; **a ~ (de buen cubero)** by guesswork; roughly, at a rough guess; **a ~s cerrados** blindly; on trust; **dependiente a ~s cerrados en** blindly dependent on; **a ~ vistas** publicly, openly; *crecer etc* before one's (very) eyes; *suceder etc* right under one's nose; *disminuir* visibly; **con buenos ~s** kindly, favourably; **delante de mis propios ~s** before my very eyes; **estar hasta los ~s de trabajo** to be up to one's eyes in work; **~ por ~** an eye for an eye; tit for tat; **abrir el ~, abrir los ~s** to keep one's eyes open; to be careful; **abrir los ~s a uno** to open sb's eyes to sth; **en un abrir y cerrar de ~s** in the twinkling of an eye; **avivar el ~** to be on the alert; **cerrar los ~s a algo** to shut one's eyes to sth; **clavar los ~s en** to fix one's eyes on, stare at; **costar un ~ de la cara** to cost a small fortune; **dar en los ~s** to be conspicuous; to be self-evident; **dejar a uno con los ~s fuera de órbita** to make sb's eyes pop; **echar el ~ a** to have one's eye on, covet; **guiñar el ~** to wink (*a* at); to turn a blind eye (*a* on); **hacer del ~** to wink; **se le fueron los ~s tras la chica** he couldn't keep his eyes off the girl; **pasar los ~s por algo** to look sth over; **no pegué ~ en toda la noche** I didn't get a wink of sleep all night; **poner ~s (*u* ojitos) a una joven** to look longingly at a girl; **en mi vida le puse los ~s encima** I never set eyes on him in my life; **recrear los ~s en** to feast one's eyes on; **salir de ~** to be obvious, leap to the eye; **saltar a los ~s** to be blindingly obvious; **ser el ~ derecho de uno** to be the apple of sb's eye; **ser todo ~s** to be all eyes; **¡no es nada lo del ~!** there's a lot more to it than that!; there's more to it than meets the eye; **tener ~ clínico** to have good intuition; **tener a uno entre ~s** to loathe sb; **tener los ~s puestos en** (*fig*) to have set one's heart on; **torcer los ~s** to squint; **ver con malos ~s** to look unfavourably upon; **~s que no ven, corazón que no siente** out of sight, out of mind; *V* **alerta, avizor, besugo, blanco** *etc.*

(**b**) (*de aguja etc*) eye; (*en queso etc*) hole; ~ **de la llave** keyhole.

(**c**) (*de puente*) span; space underneath the span; **un puente de 4 ~s** a bridge with 4 arches (*o* spans).

(**d**) ~ **de agua** (*LAm*) spring.

(**e**) ~ **del culo**‡ arse‡.

(**f**) (*Arquit*) ~ **de buey** bull's-eye window, (*Náut*) porthole.

(**g**) ~ **de gallo,** ~ **de pollo** (*LAm*) corn, callus; ~ **de pescado** (*Carib*) callus (on the hand).

(**h**) (*fig*) (*perspicacia*) perspicacity; (*juicio*) judgement; (*agudeza*) sharpness; **tener ~ para conocer algo** to have the perspicacity to recognize sth.

(**i**) (*fig: cuidado*) care, caution; **¡~!** careful!, look out!; (*nota marginal*) N.B.; **hay que tener mucho ~ con los carteristas** one must be very careful of pickpockets, one must beware of pickpockets; ~ **con creer que ...** let us beware of thinking that ...

ojón *adj* (*LAm*) big-eyed, having big eyes.

ojota *nf* (**a**) (*LAm: sandalia*) sandal. (**b**) (*And, Cono Sur: piel de llama*) tanned llama leather.

ojotes* *nmpl* (*And, CAm*) (*pey*) bulging eyes, goggle eyes; (*bellos*) lovely big eyes.

ojuelos *nmpl* = **ojillos.**

okapi *nm* okapi.

okupa* *nmf* squatter.

OL *nf abr de* **onda larga** long wage, LW.

ola *nf* wave (*t fig*); ~ **de calor** heat wave; ~ **delictiva** crime wave; ~ **de frío** cold wave; ~ **de marea,** ~ **sísmica** tidal wave; **la nueva** ~ the latest fashion, the current trend, the most modern style; (*personas*) the new generation; (*Cine*) the new wave, the Nouvelle Vague; **batir las ~s** (*fig*) to ply the seas; **hacer ~s** (*fig*) to make waves; to rock the boat.

OLADE [o'laðe] *nf abr de* **Organización Latinoamericana de Energía.**

OLAVU [o'laβu] *nf abr de* **Organización Latinoamericana del Vino y de la Uva.**

olé *interj* bravo!; well done!, jolly good!*; **¡y ~ morena!*** wow!*

oleada *nf* (**a**) (*Náut*) big wave; surge, swell.

(**b**) (*fig*) wave; surge; **una gran ~ de gente** a great surge of people; **la primera ~ del ataque** the first wave of the attack; **esta última ~ de huelgas** this latest wave of strikes.

(**c**) (*Méx*) run of luck.

oleaginosa *nf* oil product.

oleaginoso *adj* oily, oleaginous.

oleaje *nm* swell, surge; surf.

olear[1] [1a] *vi* to wave, flutter.

olear[2] [1a] *vt* to shout 'olé' to, cheer, encourage.

oleícola *adj* oil (*atr*); olive-oil (*atr*).

oleicultor(a) *nm/f* olive-grower.

oleicultura *nf* olive-growing.

oleo... *pref* oleo..., oil ...

óleo *nm* (**a**) (*Ecl*) oil; (*Arte*) oil; **santo(s) ~(s)** holy oil(s); **pintar al** ~ to paint in oils. (**b**) (*Arte: cuadro*) oil painting. (**c**) (*LAm: fig*) baptism.

oleoducto *nm* (oil) pipeline.

oleoso *adj* oily.

oler [2i] **1** *vt* (**a**) (*gen*) to smell; (‡) *cocaína* to snort‡.

(**b**) (*fig: inquirir*) to pry into, poke one's nose into.

(**c**) (*fig: descubrir*) to smell out, sniff out, uncover.

2 *vi* (*t fig*) to smell (*a* of, like); **huele mal** it smells bad.

oletear [1a] *vt* (*And*) to pry into.

oletón *adj* (*And*) prying.

olfa* *nmf* (*Cono Sur*) (*lameculos*) creep‡, bootlicker*; (*admirador*) admirer, follower.

olfatear [1a] *vt* (**a**) (*gen*) to smell, sniff (*t fig*); (*perro*) to smell out, scent out, nose out (*t fig*).

(**b**) (*fig*) to pry into, poke one's nose into.

olfativo *adj* olfactory.

olfato *nm* (**a**) (sense of) smell. (**b**) (*fig*) good nose; instinct, intuition.

olfatorio *adj* olfactory.

oligarquía *nf* oligarchy.

oligárquico *adj* oligarchic(al).

oligo... *pref* oligo...

oligofrénico 1 *adj* mentally retarded. **2** *nm,* **oligofrénica** *nf* mentally retarded person.

oligopolio *nm* oligopoly.

oligopolístico *adj* oligopolistic.

oligopsonio *nm* oligopsony.

olimpiada *nf,* **olimpíada** *nf* Olympiad; **las O~s** the Olympics; **O~ de Invierno** Winter Olympics.

olímpico 1 *adj* Olympian; *juegos* Olympic. **2** *nm,* **olímpica** *nf* Olympic athlete.

olimpismo *nm* Olympic movement; Olympic Games.

Olimpo *nm* Olympus.

oliscar [1g] **1** *vt* (**a**) (*gen*) to smell, sniff (gently). (**b**) (*fig*) to investigate, look into. **2** *vi* to smell (bad).

olisco *adj* (*Cono Sur*), **oliscón** *adj* (*And*), **oliscoso** *adj* (*And, Carib*) smelly.

olisquear [1a] = **oliscar.**

oliva 1 *nf* (**a**) (*aceituna*) olive; (*árbol*) olive tree. (**b**) (*Orn*) = **lechuza. 2** *adj invar* olive.

oliváceo *adj* olive, olive-green.

olivar *nm* olive grove.

olivarero 1 *adj* olive (*atr*). **2** *nm,* **olivarera** *nf* olive-producer, olive-oil producer.

Oliverio *nm* Oliver.

olivero *adj* olive (*atr*), olive-growing (*atr*); **región olivera** olive-growing region.

olivo *nm* olive tree; **tomar el ~**‡ to beat it*.

olmeca 1 *adj* Olmec. **2** *nmf* Olmec; **los ~s** the Olmecs.

olmeda *nf,* **olmedo** *nm* elm grove.

olmo *nm* elm, elm tree; ~ **campestre** common elm; ~ **de montaña** wych-elm.

ológrafo *adj, nm* holograph.

olor *nm* (**a**) (*gen*) smell; (*aroma*) odour, scent; **buen** ~ nice smell, pleasant smell; **mal** ~ bad smell, nasty smell, stink; **tiene mal** ~ it smells bad; ~ **corporal** body odour; ~ **de santidad** odour of sanctity.

(**b**) (*fig*) smell; suspicion; **acudir al ~ del dinero** to come to where the money is, get wind of the money.

(**c**) **~es** (*Cono Sur, Méx Culin*) spices.

olorcillo *nm* faint smell; delicate aroma; (*fig, pey*) whiff (a *of*).

oloroso 1 *adj* sweet-smelling, scented, fragrant. **2** *nm* oloroso (sherry).

olote *nm* (*CAm, Méx*) (**a**) (*Agr*) corncob; maize stalk. (**b**) **un ~** (*fig*) a nobody, a nonentity.

olotear [1a] *vi* (*CAm, Méx*) to gather (*o* harvest) maize (*o* corn: *US*).

olotera *nf* (*CAm, Méx*) (**a**) (*montón*) heap of corncobs. (**b**) (*máquina*) maize thresher.

OLP *nf abr de* **Organización para la Liberación de Palestina** Palestine Liberation Organization, PLO.

olvidadizo *adj* forgetful; absent-minded.

olvidado *adj* (**a**) (*gen*) forgotten.

(**b**) *persona* forgetful; ~ **de** forgetful of, oblivious to.

(**c**) (*fig: ingrato*) ungrateful.

(**d**) (*And, Cono Sur*) = **olvidadizo.**

olvidar [1a] **1** *vt* to forget; to leave behind; to leave out, omit; **¡olvídame!*** get lost!‡; ~ **hacer algo** to forget to do sth.

2 olvidarse *vr* (**a**) **se me olvidó** I forgot; **se me olvidó el paraguas** I forgot my umbrella; **se me olvida la fecha** I forget the date, the date escapes me, I can't think of the date; ~ **de hacer algo** to forget to do sth, neglect to do sth.

(**b**) (*fig*) to be forgetful of self; (*pey*) to forget o.s.

olvido *nm* (**a**) (*estado*) oblivion; **caer en el** ~ to fall into oblivion; **echar al** ~ to forget; **enterrar** (*o* **hundir**) **en el** ~ to forget (deliberately), cast into oblivion; **rescatar del** ~ to save from oblivion.

(**b**) (*cualidad*) forgetfulness; (*acto*) omission, oversight; slip; **ha sido por** ~ it was an oversight.

olvidón *adj* (*And*) forgetful.

olla *nf* (**a**) (*recipiente*) pot, pan; (*para hervir agua*) kettle; ~ **eléctrica** electric kettle; ~ **exprés,** ~ **de** (*o* **a**) **presión** pressure cooker.

(**b**) (*Culin*) stew; ~ **podrida** Spanish stew; (*fig*) hotchpotch.

(**c**) (*de río*) pool; eddy, whirlpool.

(**d**) (*Alpinismo*) chimney.

(**e**) ~ **común** soup-kitchen (*t* ~ **popular**); (*Cono Sur*) canteen.

ollar *nm* (horse's) nose; **~es** (horse's) nostrils.

ollero, -a *nm/f* maker of (*o* dealer in) pots and pans.

OM (**a**) (*Pol*) *nf abr de* **Orden Ministerial** ministerial decree. (**b**) (*Rad*) *nf abr de* **onda media** medium wave, MW. (**c**) (*Geog*) *nm abr de* **Oriente Medio** Middle East.

Omán *nm* Oman.

ombligo *nm* navel; **arrugársele el ~ a uno*, encogérsele el ~ a uno*** to get the wind up*, get cold feet; **meter a uno el ~ para dentro*** to put the wind up sb*; **mirarse el** ~ to contemplate one's navel.

ombliguera *nf* (*And*) striptease artiste.

ombudsman *nm* ombudsman.

omega *nf* omega.
OMI *nf abr de* **Organización Marítima Internacional** International Maritime Organization, IMO.
OMIC *nf abr de* **Oficina Municipal de Información al Consumidor.**
ominoso *adj* (**a**) (*pasmoso*) awful, dreadful. (**b**) (*de mal agüero*) ominous.
omisión *nf* (**a**) (*gen*) omission; oversight; ~ **de auxilio** (*Jur*) failure to give assistance, failure to go to somebody's aid; **su ~ de** + *infin* his failure to + *infin*, the fact that he omits to + *infin*. (**b**) (*cualidad*) neglect.
omiso *adj V* **caso.**
omitir [3a] *vt* (**a**) (*gen*) to leave out, miss out, omit. (**b**) ~ **hacer algo** to omit to do sth, fail to do sth.
OMM *nf abr de* **Organización Meteorológica Mundial** World Meteorological Organization, WMO.
omni... *pref* omni...; all-...
ómnibus 1 *adj V* **tren. 2** *nm* omnibus; (*And*) (municipal) bus.
omnibús *nm* (*Cono Sur*) bus.
omnicomprensivo *adj* all-inclusive.
omnidireccional *adj* omnidirectional.
omnímodo *adj* all-embracing; *poder* absolute.
omnipotencia *nf* omnipotence.
omnipotente *adv* omnipotent, all-powerful.
omnipresencia *nf* omnipresence.
omnipresente *adj* omnipresent.
omnisapiente *adj* omniscient, all-knowing.
omnisciencia *nf* omniscience.
omnisciente *adj*, **omniscio** *adj* omniscient, all-knowing.
omnívoro *adj* omnivorous.
omoplato *nm*, **omóplato** *nm* shoulder-blade.
OMS *nf abr de* **Organización Mundial de la Salud** World Health Organization, WHO.
OMT *nf* (*Esp*) *abr de* **Oficina Municipal de Transportes.**
-ón -ona *V* **Aspects of Word Formation in Spanish 2.**
onanismo *nm* onanism.
once 1 *adj* eleven; (*fecha*) eleventh; **las ~** eleven o'clock; **las ~*** elevenses*; (*de mañana*) mid-morning snack; (*And, Cono Sur: merienda*) tea, afternoon snack.
2 *nm* eleven.
ONCE ['onθe] *nf abr de* **Organización Nacional de Ciegos Españoles.**
oncear [1a] *vi* (*And*) to have an afternoon snack.
onceavo *adj, nm* eleventh.
onceno *adj* eleventh.
oncólogo, -a *nm/f* cancer specialist.
onda *nf* (**a**) (*gen*) wave; (*Cos*) scallop; ~ **corta** short wave; **de ~ corta** shortwave (*atr*); ~ **de choque,** ~ **expansiva,** ~ **sísmica** shock wave; ~ **explosiva,** ~ **expansiva** blast, shock wave; ~ **extracorta** ultra-short wave; ~ **larga** long wave; ~ **luminosa** light wave; ~ **media** medium wave; ~ **de radio** radio wave; ~ **sonora** sound wave; **tratamiento de ~ ultravioleta** ultra-violet treatment.
(**b**) (*fig*) **buena ~*** good vibes*; **de ~*** in fashion, hip*, trendy; **coger** (*LAm*: **agarrar**) **la ~*** (*entender*) to get it*, get the point*; (*coger el tino*) to be get the hang of it; **estar en ~‡** (*drogado*) to be high‡ (on drugs); **estar en la ~*** (*moda*) to be in*; *persona* (*a la moda*) to be hip*; (*al tanto*) to be on the ball, be up to date; **estar en ~ gay** to be of the gay persuasion, be into the gay thing*; **se merece un regalo en su ~*** he deserves a present suited to his needs; **perder la ~*** to lose one's touch; **¿qué ~?** (*LAm**) what gives?*
ondeante *adj* = **ondulante.**
ondear [1a] **1** *vt bandera* to wave; *pelo* to wave; (*Cos*) to pink, scallop.
2 *vi* to wave (up and down), undulate; to be wavy; to fluctuate; (*agua*) to ripple; (*bandera etc*) to fly, flutter, wave; (*pelo*) to flow, fall; (*flotar al viento*) to stream; **la bandera ondea en lo alto del edificio** the flag flies (*o* flutters) from the top of the building; **la bandera ondea a media asta** the flag is flying at half mast.
3 ondearse *vr* to swing, sway.
ondia* *interj* (*euf*) = **hostia.**
ondímetro *nm* wavemeter.
ondulación *nf* undulation; wavy motion; (*en agua*) wave, ripple; (*en pelo*) wave; **ondulaciones** (*de superficie*) undulations, ups and downs; unevenness; ~ **permanente** permanent wave.
ondulado 1 *adj pelo etc* wavy; *superficie* undulating, uneven; *camino* uneven, rough; *terreno* undulating, rolling; *hierro, papel etc* corrugated.
2 *nm* (*en pelo*) wave.
ondulante *adj* (**a**) *movimiento* undulating; from side to side, (gently) swaying; *sonido* rising and falling. (**b**) = **ondulado.**
ondular [1a] **1** *vt pelo* to wave; **hacerse ~ el pelo** to have one's hair waved. **2** *vi, y* **ondularse** *vr* to undulate; to sway; to wriggle.
ondulatorio *adj* undulatory, wavy.
oneroso *adj* (**a**) (*pesado*) onerous, burdensome. (**b**) **comprar algo a título ~** to purchase sth compulsorily.
ONG *nf abr de* **organización no gubernamental.**
ónice *nm*, **ónix** *nm* onyx.
onírico *adj* oneiric, dream (*atr*).
ONO *abr de* **oesnoroeste** west-north-west, WNW.
onomástica *nf* (**a**) personal names, proper names; onomastics, study of personal names. (**b**) (*t* **fiesta ~**) name day.
onomástico 1 *adj* onomastic, name (*atr*), of names; **índice ~** index of names; **lista onomástica** list of names; **fiesta onomástica** = **2. 2** *nm* one's saint's day, one's name day (*celebrated in Spain and Latin America as equivalent to one's birthday*).
onomatopeya *nf* onomatopoeia.
onomatopéyico *adj* onomatopoeic.
ontología *nf* ontology.
ontológico *adj* ontological.
ONU *nf abr de* **Organización de las Naciones Unidas** United Nations Organization, UNO.
onubense 1 *adj* of Huelva. **2** *nmf* native (*o* inhabitant) of Huelva; **los ~s** the people of Huelva.
ONUDI [o'nuði] *nf abr de* **Organización de las Naciones Unidas para el Desarrollo Industrial** United Nations Industrial Development Organization, UNIDO.
onusiano *adj* United Nations (*atr*).
onza[1] *nf* ounce.
onza[2] *nf* (*LAm Zool*) snow leopard.
oolítico *adj* oolitic.
oolito *nm* oolite.
O.P. (**a**) *abr de* **Obras Publicas** public works. (**b**) (*Ecl*) *abr de* **Orden de Predicadores** Order of St Dominic, O.S.D.
OPA ['opa] *nf abr de* **oferta pública de adquisición.**
opa[1] *adj* (*And, Cono Sur*) (**a**) deaf and dumb; mentally retarded. (**b**) (*) stupid.
opa[2] *interj* (*LAm*) = **hola**; (*Cono Sur*) stop it!
opacar [1g] **1** *vt* (*LAm*) (**a**) (*hacer opaco*) to make opaque; (*oscurecer*) to darken; (*empañar*) to mist up; (*deslustrar*) to dull, tarnish.
(**b**) (*persona*) to outshine, overshadow.
2 opacarse *vr* (**a**) (*LAm*: *V vt* (**a**)) to become opaque; to darken; to mist up; to lose its shine, become tarnished.
(**b**) (*And, CAm Met*) to cloud over.
opacidad *nf* (**a**) (*gen*) opacity, opaqueness. (**b**) (*fig: oscuridad*) dullness, lifelessness. (**c**) (*fig: melancolía*) gloominess.
opaco *adj* (**a**) (*gen*) opaque; dark; **una pantalla opaca a los rayos X** a screen which does not let X-rays through, a screen resistant to X-rays.
(**b**) (*fig: oscuro*) dull, lustreless, lifeless.
(**c**) (*fig: lúgubre*) gloomy, sad.
opado *adj* (*And, Carib*) pale.
opalescencia *nf* opalescence.
opalescente *adj* opalescent.
ópalo *nm* opal.
opaparado *adj* (*And*) bewildered.
opar [1a] *vti* to put in a takeover bid (for) (*V* **OPA**).
opción *nf* (**a**) (*elección*) option, choice; **opciones por defecto** default options; **no hay ~** there is no choice, you (*etc*) do not have the option.
(**b**) (*derecho*) right; **tiene ~ a viajar gratis** he has the right to travel free.
(**c**) (*Com*) option (*a* on); ~ **de adquisición** option to purchase; **con ~ a 8 más, con ~ para 8 más** with an option on 8 more; **este dispositivo es de ~** this gadget is optional; **suscribir una ~ para la compra de** to take out an option on.
(**d**) (*posibilidad*) chance, likelihood; **no tiene ~ real al triunfo** she has no real chance of winning.
opcional *adj* optional.
opcionalmente *adv* optionally.
Op.D. *nm* (*Rel*) *abr de* **Opus Dei.**
opear* [1a] *vi* (*And, Cono Sur*) to act the fool, fool about.
OPEP ['opep] *nf abr de* **Organización de Países Exportadores del Petróleo** Organization of Petroleum Exporting Countries, OPEC.
ópera *nf* opera; ~ **bufa** comic opera; **gran ~** grand opera.
operación *nf* (**a**) (*Med*) operation; ~ **cesárea** Caesarean

operation; ~ **a corazón abierto** open-heart surgery; ~ **de estómago** stomach operation, operation on the stomach.

(**b**) (*Mil etc*) operation; ~ **de ablandamiento** softening-up operation; **operaciones conjuntas** joint operations; ~ **encubierta** under-cover operation; ~ **de limpia,** ~ **de limpieza** mopping-up operation; **operaciones de rescate, operaciones de salvamento** rescue operations; ~ **retorno** effort to control traffic returning to Madrid (*etc*) after a major holiday.

(**c**) (*Com*) transaction, deal; operation; ~ **a plazo** forward transaction; **operaciones de bolsa, operaciones bursátiles** stock-exchange transactions; ~ **'llave en mano'** turnkey operation; ~ **mercantil** business deal.

(**d**) (*Mat*) operation.

(**e**) (*LAm*) (*Min*) operation, working, exploitation; (*Com*) management.

(**f**) **operaciones accesorias** (*Inform*) housekeeping.

operacional *adj* operational.

operador(a) *nm/f* (*gen*) operator; (*Med*) operating surgeon; (*Cine*: *rodaje*) cameraman, film cameraman; (*t* ~ **de cabina**) projectionist, operator; ~ **del telégrafo** (*LAm*) telegraph operator; ~ **de télex** telex operator; ~ **turístico** tour operator.

operante *adj* (**a**) (*gen*) operating. (**b**) (*fig*) effective, active; **el motivo** ~ the real reason, the actual motive.

operar [1a] **1** *vt* (**a**) *cambio, cura etc* to produce, bring about, effect; *milagro* to work.

(**b**) (*Med*) to operate on; ~ **a uno de apendicitis** to operate on sb for appendicitis.

(**c**) (*LAm*) *máquina* to use, operate; *negocio* to manage, run; (*Min*) to work, exploit.

2 *vi* (**a**) to operate (*t Mat*).

(**b**) (*Com*) to operate; to deal, do business; **hoy no se ha operado en la bolsa** there has been no dealing on the stock exchange today.

3 operarse *vr* (**a**) (*ocurrir*) to occur, come about; **se han operado grandes cambios** great changes have come about, there have been great changes.

(**b**) (*Med*) to have an operation (*de* for).

operario, -a *nm/f* operative; (*unskilled*) worker, hand; ~ **de máquina** machinist.

ópera-rock *nf, pl* **óperas-rock** rock opera.

operatividad *nf* (**a**) (*acto*) functioning, working; action. (**b**) (*eficacia*) effectiveness, efficiency.

operativizar [1f] *vt* to put into operation, make operative.

operativo 1 *adj* operative. **2** *nm* (*LAm*) operation; ~ **policial** police operation.

opereta *nf* operetta, light opera.

opería *nf* (*And, Cono Sur*) stupidity.

operista *nmf* opera singer.

operístico *adj* operatic, opera (*atr*).

operófilo, -a *nm/f* opera-lover.

operoso* *adj* (*Carib*) irritable.

opiáceo *nm* opiate.

opiarse* [1b] *vr* (*Cono Sur*) to get bored, get fed up*.

opiata *nf* opiate.

opimo *adj* plentiful, abundant, rich.

opinable *adj* debatable, open to a variety of opinions.

opinar [1a] *vi* (**a**) (*pensar*) to think; ~ **que ...** to think that ..., be of the opinion that ...

(**b**) ~ **bien de** to think well of, have a good opinion of.

(**c**) (*dar su opinión*) to give one's opinion; **fueron opinando uno tras otro** they gave their opinions in turn; **hubo un 7 por 100 que no quisieron** ~, **no opinaron el 7 por 100** (*sondeo*) there were 7% 'don't knows'.

opinión *nf* opinion, view; ~ **pública** public opinion; **en mi** ~ in my opinion; **abundar en** (*o* **compartir**) **la** ~ **de uno** to share sb's opinion (*o* view); **cambiar** (*o* **mudar**) **de** ~ to change one's mind; **formarse una** ~ to form an opinion; **ser de** ~ **que ...** to be of the opinion that ..., take the view that ...

opio *nm* opium; **dar el** ~ **a uno*** to enchant sb, captivate sb; **ella le dio el** ~* she knocked him all of a heap; **la película es un** ~ (*Cono Sur**) the film is a drag.

opiómano, -a *nm/f* opium addict.

opíparo *adj comida* sumptuous.

oponente 1 *adj* opposing, contrary. **2** *nmf* opponent.

oponer [2q] **1** *vt* (**a**) ~ **A a B** to pit A against B, set up A in opposition to B; to play off A against B; ~ **dos opiniones** to contrast two views.

(**b**) *objeción* to raise (*a* to); *resistencia* to put up, offer (*a* to); *arma* to use (*a* against); ~ **la razón a la pasión** to use reason against passion, rely on reason and not passion; ~ **un dique al mar** to set up defences against the sea.

2 oponerse *vr* to be opposed; (*2 personas*) to oppose each other, be in opposition; **yo no me opongo** I don't oppose it, I don't object; ~ **a** to oppose, be opposed to, be against; to object to; to defy, resist; **se opone a hacerlo** he resists the idea of doing it, he is unwilling to do it, he objects to doing it; **se opone rotundamente a ello** he is flatly opposed to it.

Oporto *nm* Oporto.

oportunamente *adv* opportunely, in a timely way; at the proper time; appropriately, suitably; conveniently; expediently.

oportunidad *nf* (**a**) (*cualidad*) opportuneness; timeliness; appropriateness; expediency.

(**b**) (*una* ~) opportunity, chance; **'~es'** (*en tienda*) 'bargains'; **igualdad de ~es** equality of opportunity; **en la primera** ~ at the first opportunity; **tener la** ~ **de** + *infin* to have the chance of + *ger*, have a chance to + *infin*.

(**c**) (*vez*) time, occasion; **en dos ~es** on two occasions.

oportunismo *nm* opportunism.

oportunista 1 *adj* opportunist; opportunistic. **2** *nmf* opportunist.

oportuno *adj* (**a**) (*en buena hora*) opportune, timely; (*apropiado*) appropriate, suitable; (*adecuado*) convenient; (*aconsejable*) expedient; **una respuesta oportuna** a suitable reply; **en el momento** ~ at the right moment; at a convenient time; **las medidas que se estimen oportunas** the measures which may be considered appropriate; **sería** ~ **hacerlo en seguida** it would be best to do it at once.

(**b**) *persona* witty, quick.

oposición *nf* (**a**) (*gen*) opposition.

(**b**) (*Esp*) **oposiciones** public competition (for a post), public entrance (*o* promotion) examination; **hacer oposiciones a, presentarse a unas oposiciones a** to be a candidate for, go in for; **hacer oposiciones para una cátedra** (*etc*) to compete for a chair (*etc*); **ganar unas oposiciones** to be successful in a public competition.

oposicional *adj* (*Pol*) opposition (*atr*).

oposicionista 1 *adj* opposition (*atr*). **2** *nmf* member of the opposition.

opositar [1a] *vi* (*Esp*) to go in for a public competition (for a post), sit for a public entrance (*o* promotion) examination.

opositor 1 *adj* (*contrario*) opposing; (*Pol*) opposition (*atr*), of the opposition; **el líder** ~ the leader of the opposition, the opposing leader. **2** *nm,* **opositora** *nf* (**a**) (*Univ etc*) competitor, candidate (*a* for). (**b**) (*Pol*) opponent.

opresión *nf* (**a**) (*gen*) oppression; oppressiveness. (**b**) (*Med*) difficulty in breathing, tightness of the chest; **sentir** ~ to find it difficult to breathe.

opresivo *adj* oppressive.

opresor 1 *adj* oppressive, tyrannical. **2** *nm,* **opresora** *nf* oppressor.

oprimente *adj* oppressive.

oprimir [3a] *vt* (**a**) (*presionar*) to squeeze, press, exert pressure on; *mango etc* to grasp, clutch; *botón etc* to press; *gas* to compress; (*ropa*) to be too tight for, constrict; to strangle.

(**b**) (*fig*) to oppress; to burden, weigh down, bear down on; to crush.

oprobio *nm* shame, ignominy, opprobrium.

oprobioso *adj* shameful, ignominious, opprobrious.

optar [1a] *vi* (**a**) (*gen*) to choose, decide; ~ **entre** to choose between; ~ **por** to choose, decide on, opt for; ~ **por** + *infin* to choose to + *infin*.

(**b**) ~ **a** to compete for, challenge for, fight for; ~ **a un premio** to compete for a prize; **poder** ~ **a** to (have the right to) apply for, go in for; **ésos no pueden** ~ **a las becas** those do not have the right to apply for the scholarships.

optativamente *adv* optionally.

optativo 1 *adj* (**a**) (*opcional*) optional. (**b**) (*Ling*) optative. **2** *nm* (*Ling*) optative.

óptica[1] *nf* (**a**) (*ciencia*) optics. (**b**) (*tienda*) optician's (shop). (**c**) (*fig*) point of view, viewpoint; outlook; **bajo** (*o* **desde**) **esta** ~ from this point of view.

óptico 1 *adj* optic(al). **2** *nm,* **óptica**[2] *nf* optician.

óptico-cinético *nm* light show.

optimación *nf* optimization.

óptimamente *adv* ideally; in ideal conditions.

optimar [1a] *vt* to optimize.

optimismo *nm* optimism; ~ **cauto,** ~ **matizado** cautious optimism.

optimista 1 *adj* optimistic, hopeful. **2** *nmf* optimist.

optimización *nf* optimization; improvement, perfection.

optimizar [1f] *vt* to optimize; to improve, perfect.

óptimo *adj* very good, very best; *condiciones etc* optimal, optimum.
optometrista *nmf* optometrist.
opuesto *adj* (**a**) *ángulo, lado etc* opposite; **en dirección opuesta** in the opposite direction. (**b**) *opinión etc* contrary, opposing, opposite.
opugnar [1a] *vt* to attack.
opulencia *nf* opulence; luxury; affluence; **sociedad de la ~** affluent society; **vivir en la ~** to live in luxury, live in affluence.
opulento *adj* opulent, rich; luxurious; affluent.
opuncia *nf* (*Méx*) prickly pear.
opúsculo *nm* booklet; short work, tract, brief treatise.
opusdeísta *nmf* member of Opus Dei.
oquedad *nf* hollow, cavity; (*fig*) void; hollowness, emptiness.
oquedal *nm* wood of grown timber, plantation.
ORA ['ora] *nf abr de* **Operación de Regulación de Aparcamientos.**
ora *adv* (*liter*): **~ A, ~ B** now A, now B; sometimes A, at other times B.
oración *nf* (**a**) (*discurso*) oration, speech; **~ fúnebre** funeral oration; **pronunciar una ~** to make a speech.
(**b**) (*Ecl*) prayer; **oraciones por la paz** prayers for peace; **estar en ~** to be at prayer.
(**c**) (*LAm*) pagan invocation, magic charm.
(**d**) (*Ling*) sentence; clause; **~ compuesta** complex sentence; **~ directa** direct speech; **~ indirecta** to indirect speech, reported speech; **~ subordinada** subordinate clause; **partes de la ~** parts of speech.
oráculo *nm* oracle.
orador(a) *nm/f* speaker, orator.
oral *adj* oral.
orangután *nm* orang-outang.
orante 1 *adj*: **actitud ~** kneeling position, posture of prayer. **2** *nmf* (*persona*) worshipper, person at prayer.
orar [1a] *vi* (**a**) (*Ecl*) to pray (*a* to, *por* for). (**b**) (*disertar*) to speak, make a speech.
orate *nmf* lunatic.
orático *adj* (*CAm*) crazy, lunatic.
oratoria *nf* oratory.
oratorio 1 *adj* oratorical. **2** *nm* (**a**) (*Mús*) oratorio. (**b**) (*Ecl*) oratory, chapel.
orbe *nm* (**a**) (*gen*) orb, sphere. (**b**) (*fig*) world; **en todo el ~** throughout the world.
órbita *nf* (**a**) (*gen*) orbit (*t fig*); **estar en ~** to be in orbit; **entrar en ~ alrededor de la luna** to go into orbit round the moon; **poner en ~** to place in orbit. (**b**) (*Méx*) socket (of the eye).
orbital *adj* orbital.
orbitar [1a] *vti* to orbit.
orca *nf* grampus, killer whale.
Orcadas *nfpl* Orkneys, Orkney Islands.
órdago*: **de ~** *adj* first-class, super*, swell* (*US*); (*pey*) awful, tremendous*.
ordalías *nfpl* (*Hist*) ordeal, trial by ordeal.
orden 1 *nm* (**a**) (*gen*) order; arrangement; **~ del día** agenda; **de primer ~** first-rate, of the first order; **en ~** in order; **en ~ a** (*con miras a*) with a view to; (*en cuanto a*) with regard to; **en ~ a** + *infin* in order to + *infin;* **en ~ de batalla** in battle order; **en ~ de marchar** in marching order; **'en otro ~ de cosas ...'** (*en discurso*) 'passing now to other matters ...'; **hacemos progresos en todos los órdenes** we are making progress on all fronts; **fuera de ~** out of order; out of turn; **por (su) ~** in order; **por ~ de antigüedad** in order of seniority; **por ~ cronológico** in chronological order; **poner en ~** to put in order, arrange (properly); to tidy up.
(**b**) (*Jur etc*) order; **~ público** public order, law and order; **alterar el ~ público** to disturb the peace; **las fuerzas del ~** the forces of law and order; **llamar al ~** to take to task, reprimand; to call to order; **mantener el ~** to keep order.
(**c**) **una cifra del ~ de 600** a figure of the order of 600.
(**d**) (*Arquit*) order; **~ dórico** Doric order.
2 *nf* (**a**) (*mandamiento*) order; (*Jur*) order, warrant, writ; (*Méx: pedido*) order; **~ de allanamiento** (*Méx*) search warrant; **~ de búsqueda y captura, ~ de detención** arrest warrant; **~ de citación** (*Méx*), **~ de comparación** (*Méx*) summons, subpoena; **~ del día** (*Mil*) order of the day; **~ judicial** court order; **O~ Real** Order in Council; **a la ~** (*Com*) to order; **¡a la ~!** (*LAm*) (*en tienda etc*) what can I get you?; (*no hay de qué*) you're welcome, don't mention it!; **a la ~ de Vd, a sus órdenes** at your service; **cheques a la ~ de Suárez** cheques to be made out to Suárez; **eso ahora está a la ~ del día** that is now the order of the day; **¡a las órdenes!** (*Mil*) yes sir?; **hasta nueva ~** until further notice, till further orders; **por ~ de** on the orders of, by order of; **¡es una ~!** that's an order!; **dar una ~** to give an order; **dar la ~ de** + *infin* to give the order to + *infin.*
(**b**) (*Ecl*) order; **órdenes menores** minor orders; **~ monástica** monastic order; **~ religiosa** religious order; **órdenes sagradas** holy orders; **O~ de San Benito** Benedictine Order.
(**c**) (*Hist, Mil*) **~ de caballería** order of knighthood; **~ militar** military order; **O~ de Calatrava** Order of Caltrava.
(**d**) (*Com, Fin*) order; **~ bancaria** banker's order; **~ de compra** purchase order.
(**e**) (*Méx: porción*) portion, helping (of food).
ordenación *nf* (**a**) (*estado*) order; arrangement; (*acto*) ordering, arranging; (*Inform*) sorting; **~ territorial** town and country planning. (**b**) (*Ecl*) ordination.
ordenada *nf* ordinate.
ordenadamente *adv* in an orderly way; tidily; methodically.
ordenado *adj* (**a**) (*en orden*) (*estado*) orderly; tidy; well arranged. (**b**) *persona* methodical; tidy. (**c**) (*Ecl*) in holy orders.
ordenador *nm* computer; **~ analógico** analog(ue) computer; **~ central** mainframe computer; **~ doméstico** home computer; **~ de gestión** business computer; **~ personal** personal computer; **~ portátil, ~ transportable** portable computer; **~ de (sobre)mesa** desktop computer.
ordenamiento *nm* (**a**) ordering, arranging. (**b**) (*Jur*) **~ jurídico** (piece of) legislation; **~ constitutional** statute.
ordenancista *nmf* disciplinarian, martinet.
ordenando *nm* (*Ecl*) ordinand.
ordenanza 1 *nf* (*decreto*) ordinance, decree; **~s municipales** by-laws; **ser de ~** to be the rule.
2 *nm* (*Com etc*) office boy, messenger; errand boy; (*Mil*) orderly, batman.
ordenar [1a] **1** *vt* (**a**) (*poner en orden*) to arrange, put in order; to marshal; to draw up; (*Inform*) to sort; **~ sus asuntos** to put one's affairs in order; **~ su vida** to arrange one's life.
(**b**) (*mandar*) to order; **~ a uno hacer algo** to order sb to do sth; **tono de ordeno y mando** dictatorial tone.
(**c**) (*Ecl*) to ordain.
2 ordenarse *vr* (*Ecl*) to take holy orders, be ordained (*de* as).
ordeña *nf* (*Cono Sur, Méx*) milking.
ordeñadero *nm* milking pail.
ordeñadora *nf* milking machine.
ordeñar [1a] *vt* to milk.
ordeñe *nm* (*Carib*), **ordeño** *nm* milking.
órdiga‡ *nf* = **¡(anda) la ~!** (*Esp*) bloody hell!‡
ordinal *adj, nm* ordinal.
ordinariamente *adv* ordinarily, usually.
ordinariez *nf* (**a**) (*cualidad*) commonness, coarseness, vulgarity. (**b**) (*una ~*) coarse remark (*o* joke etc), piece of vulgarity.
ordinario 1 *adj* (**a**) (*normal*) ordinary; usual; (*corriente*) current; *gastos* daily; **de ~** usually, ordinarily.
(**b**) (*vulgar*) common, coarse, vulgar; (*grosero*) rude; *chiste* coarse, crude; **son gente muy ordinaria** they're very common people.
2 *nm* (**a**) (*gastos*) daily household expenses.
(**b**) (*recadero*) carrier, delivery man.
ordinograma *nm* organization chart; flowchart.
orear [1a] **1** *vt* to air. **2 orearse** *vr* (**a**) (*ropa*) to air. (**b**) (*persona*) to get some fresh air, take a breather.
orégano *nm* marjoram; (*Méx‡*) grass‡.
oreja 1 *nf* (**a**) (*Anat*) ear; **con las ~s gachas** (*fig*) ashamed; embarrassed; **aguzar las ~s** to prick up one's ears; **asomar** (*o* **descubrir, enseñar**) **la ~** (*traicionarse*) to give o.s. away, reveal one's true nature; (*aparecer*) to show o.s., show up; **calentar las ~s a uno** (*golpear*) to box sb's ears; (*irritar*) to get on sb's nerves; (*despachar*) to send sb away with a flea in his ear; **chafar la ~‡** to kip‡, sleep; **estar hasta las ~s*** to be utterly fed up*; **hacer ~s de mercader** to turn a deaf ear; **planchar ~‡** to kip‡, sleep; **se la ve la ~*** you can see his little game; **verle las ~s al lobo** to escape from great danger.
(**b**) (*de zapato etc*) tab; tag; (*de jarra*) lug, handle; (*Mec*) lug, flange; (*de sillón*) wing; (*de libro*) flap; (‡) tit‡.
(**c**) (*LAm*) (*curiosidad*) curiosity; (*escucha*) eavesdropping; (*prudencia*) caution.
2 *nmf* (‡: *soplón*) grass‡, informer.

orejano 1 *adj* (**a**) (*LAm*) *animal* unbranded, ownerless.
(**b**) (*LAm*) (*tímido*) shy, easily scared; (*huraño*) unsociable.
(**c**) (*Carib*: *cauteloso*) cautious.
2 *nm* (*CAm, Carib*) peasant, countryman.
orejear* [1a] *vi* (**a**) (*LAm*: *escuchar*) to eavesdrop.
(**b**) (*And, Carib, Cono Sur*: *recelar*) to suspect, be distrustful.
(**c**) (*Cono Sur Naipes*) to uncover one's cards one by one.
orejera *nf* earflap.
orejero* 1 *adj* (**a**) (*LAm**) (*receloso*) suspicious; (*prudente*) cautious. (**b**) (*Cono Sur**: *chismoso*) telltale. (**c**) (*And**: *rencoroso*) malicious. **2** *nm* (**a**) wing chair. (**b**) (*Cono Sur**) boss's right-hand man.
orejeta *nf* (*Téc*) lug.
orejón 1 *adj* (**a**) (*LAm*) = **orejudo.**
(**b**) (*And*: *distraído*) absent-minded.
(**c**) (*And, CAm, Méx*: *tosco*) rough, coarse.
2 *nm* (**a**) (*tiró*) pull on the ear, tug at one's ear.
(**b**) (*fruta*) strip of dried peach (*o* apricot).
(**c**) (*And Med*) goitre.
(**d**) (*And*) (*vaquero*) herdsman; (*llanero*) plainsman.
(**e**) (*Méx*‡: *marido*) cuckold.
(**f**) (*And Hist*) Inca nobleman.
orejonas *nfpl* (*And, Carib*) big spurs.
orejudo *adj* big-eared, with big ears.
orensano 1 *adj* of Orense. **2** *nmf* native (*o* inhabitant) of Orense; **los ~s** the people of Orense.
orfanato *nm*, **orfanatorio** *nm* (*LAm*) orphanage.
orfandad *nf* (**a**) (*lit*) orphanhood. (**b**) (*fig*: *abandono*) neglect, abandonment. (**c**) (*fig*: *escasez*) dearth, scarcity, paucity.
orfebre *nm* goldsmith, silversmith.
orfebrería *nf* gold work, silver work, craftsmanship in precious metals.
orfelinato *nm* orphanage.
Orfeo *nm* Orpheus.
orfeón *nm* glee club, choral society.
organdí *nm* organdie.
orgánicamente *adv* organically.
orgánico *adj* organic; *V* **ley.**
organigrama *nm* flow chart; organization chart.
organillero *nm* organ-grinder.
organillo *nm* barrel organ, hurdy-gurdy.
organismo *nm* (**a**) (*Bio*) organism.
(**b**) (*Pol etc*) organization; body, institution; **~s de gobierno** organs of government, state bodies; **~ rector** governing body; **~ de sondaje** public-opinion poll, institute of public opinion.
organista *nmf* organist.
organito *nm* (*Cono Sur*) = **organillo.**
organización *nf* organization; **O~ de Estados Americanos** Organization of American States; **O~ de las Naciones Unidas** United Nations Organization.
organizadamente *adv* in an organized way.
organizador(a) 1 *nm/f* organizer. **2** *nm*: **~ personal** personal organizer
organizar [1f] **1** *vt* to organize. **2 organizarse** *vr* to manage one's affairs, organize one's life; to get one's priorities right.
organizativo *adj* organizational.
órgano *nm* (**a**) (*Anat, Mec etc*) organ; **~ del habla** speech organ. (**b**) (*Mús*) organ; **~ eléctrico** electric organ. (**c**) (*fig*) organ, means, medium; **~ de enlace** means of communication.
orgásmico *adj* orgasmic.
orgasmo *nm* orgasm.
orgía *nf* orgy.
orgiástico *adj* orgiastic.
orgullo *nm* pride; (*pey*) pride, haughtiness, arrogance.
orgullosamente *adv* proudly; haughtily.
orgulloso *adj* proud; haughty; **estar ~ de algo** to be proud of sth; **estar ~ de** + *infin* to be proud to + *infin.*
oricio *nm* sea-urchin.
orientable *adj* adjustable.
orientación *nf* (**a**) (*gen*) orientation, position(ing); (*dirección*) direction, course; (*Arquit*) aspect, prospect; **~ sexual** sexual orientation; **la ~ actual del partido** the party's present course (*o* position); **una casa con ~ sur** a house with a southerly aspect, a house facing south.
(**b**) (*guía*) guidance; (*formación*) training; **~ profesional, ~ vocacional** vocational guidance; **me ayudó en la ~ bibliográfica** he helped me with bibliographical information; **importa mucho en la ~ de los maestros** it is very important in the training of teachers; **lo hizo para mi ~** he did it for my guidance.
(**c**) (*Dep*) orienteering.
orientador(a) *nm/f* careers adviser.
oriental 1 *adj* (**a**) oriental; eastern. (**b**) (*Cono Sur*) Uruguayan; (*Cuba*) of (*o* from) Oriente province. **2** *nmf* (**a**) oriental. (**b**) (*Cono Sur*) Uruguayan; (*Cuba*) native (*o* inhabitant) of Oriente province.
orientalismo *nm* orientalism.
orientalista *adj, nmf* orientalist.
orientar [1a] **1** *vt* (**a**) (*gen*) to orientate, position; (*dirigir*) to point (*hacia* towards); to give a direction to, direct; (*Náut*) *vela* to trim; **la casa está orientada hacia el suroeste** the house faces (*o* looks) south-west; **hay que ~ las investigaciones en otro sentido** you will have to change the direction of your inquiries, you will have to pursue your researches in another direction.
(**b**) *persona* (*guiar*) to guide, direct; (*formar*) to train; **me ha orientado en la materia** he has guided me through the subject, he has given me guidance about the subject.
2 orientarse *vr* (**a**) (*objeto etc*) to point, face (*hacia* towards).
(**b**) (*persona*) to get one's bearings, orient o.s., get orientated; (*fig*) to get one's bearings; to establish o.s.; to decide on a course of conduct (*etc*); **es difícil ~ en este terreno** it's hard to get one's bearings (*o* find one's way about) in this country.
orientativamente *adv* by way of guidance.
orientativo *adj* guiding, illustrative; **los pesos reseñados son puramente ~s** the weights shown are for guidance only.
oriente *nm* (**a**) (*este*) east.
(**b**) **el O~** the Orient, the East; **Cercano O~, Próximo O~** Near East; **Extremo O~, Lejano O~** Far East; **O~ Medio** Middle East.
(**c**) (*viento*) east wind.
(**d**) (*de masones*) masonic lodge.
orificación *nf* gold filling.
orificar [1g] *vt muela* to fill with gold.
orificio *nm* orifice, hole; vent.
origen *nm* origin; source; **los orígenes de la guerra** the origins of the war, the causes of the war; **país de ~** country of origin; **de ~ argentino** of Argentinian origin; **dar ~ a** to cause, give rise to.
original 1 *adj* (**a**) (*gen*) original.
(**b**) (*fig*: *nuevo*) original; novel; (*raro*) odd, eccentric, strange.
(**c**) = **originario** (**b**).
2 *nm* (**a**) (*gen*) original; **el ~ es mejor que la copia** the original is better than the copy.
(**b**) (*Tip*) manuscript, original; copy; **tenemos exceso de ~** we have too much copy.
(**c**) (*persona*) character, eccentric, original type.
originalidad *nf* (*V adj* **a, b**) (**a**) originality. (**b**) eccentricity, oddness.
originar [1a] **1** *vt* to originate; to start, cause, give rise to. **2 originarse** *vr* to originate (*de* from, *en* in); to be started, be caused.
originariamente *adv* originally.
originario *adj* (**a**) (*original*) original; **en su forma originaria** in its original form.
(**b**) **ser ~ de** to originate from, be a native of; **una familia originaria de Sicilia** a family originating from Sicily.
(**c**) **país ~** country of origin, native country.
(**d**) **una decisión originaria de disgustos** a decision which gave rise to trouble, a decision which was a source of trouble.
orilla *nf* (**a**) (*gen*) edge, border; (*de río*) bank; (*de lago*) side, shore; (*de mar*) shore; (*de mesa etc*) edge; (*de taza etc*) rim, lip; **~ del mar** seashore; **a ~s de** on the banks of; **vive ~ de mi casa*** he lives next door to me.
(**b**) (*Cos*) edge, border, trimming; hem.
(**c**) **de ~** (*Carib*) trivial, of no account; worthless.
(**d**) (*LAm*: *acera*) pavement, sidewalk (*US*).
(**e**) **~s** (*LAm*) (*arrabales*) outlying districts; (*pey*) poor quarter; (*Méx*) shanty town.
orillar [1a] *vt* (**a**) (*Cos*) to edge, trim (*de* with).
(**b**) *bosque, lago etc* to skirt, go round; to pass along the edge of.
(**c**) *tema* to touch briefly on.
(**d**) *asuntos* to put in order, tidy up; (*concluir*) to wind up.
(**e**) *dificultad, obstáculo* to get round.
(**f**) **~ a uno a hacer algo** (*Méx*) to lead sb to do sth.

orillero *adj* (*LAm*) = **arrabalero.**
orillo *nm* selvage.
orín *nm* rust; **tomarse de** ~ to get rusty.
orina *nf* urine.
orinal *nm* (**a**) (*gen*) chamberpot; ~ **de cama** bedpan. (**b**) (*Mil**) tin hat*, helmet.
orinar [1a] **1** *vti* to urinate. **2 orinarse** *vr* to urinate (involuntarily); to wet o.s.; ~ **en la cama** to wet one's bed.
orines *nmpl* urine.
Orinoco *nm*: **el río** ~ the Orinoco (River).
oriundo 1 *adj*: ~ **de** native to; **ser** ~ **de** to be a native of, come from, hail from. **2** *nm*, **oriunda** *nf* (*nativo*) native, inhabitant.
orla *nf*, **orladura** *nf* (**a**) border; fringe; trimming; ~ **litoral** coastal strip. (**b**) (*Escol*) class graduation photograph.
orlar [1a] *vt* to border, edge, trim (*de* with).
ornamentación *nf* ornamentation, adornment.
ornamental *adj* ornamental.
ornamentar [1a] *vt* to adorn (*de* with).
ornamento *nm* (**a**) (*gen*) ornament, adornment; ~**s** (*Ecl*) ornaments, vestments. (**b**) ~**s** (*fig*) good qualities, moral qualities.
ornar [1a] *vt* to adorn (*de* with).
ornato *nm* adornment, decoration.
ornitofauna *nf* birds, bird population.
ornitología *nf* ornithology.
ornitológico *adj* ornithological.
ornitólogo, -a *nm/f* ornithologist.
ornitorrinco *nm* platypus.
oro *nm* (**a**) gold; ~ **en barras** gold bars, bullion; ~ **batido** gold leaf; ~ **laminado** rolled gold; ~ **molido** ormolu; ~ **negro** black gold, oil; ~ **en polvo** gold dust; **de** ~ gold, golden; **como un** ~ like new; spick and span; **no es** ~ **todo lo que reluce** all that glitters is not gold; **es de** ~ (*fig*) he's a treasure; he's a marvel; **tiene una voz de** ~ she has a marvellous voice; **apalear** ~ to be rolling in money; **guardar algo como** ~ **en paño** to treasure sth; **hacerse de** ~ to make a fortune; **poner a uno de** ~ **y azul** to lay into sb (verbally)*, heap insults on sb; **prometer el** ~ **y el moro** to promise the moon.
(**b**) ~**s** (*Naipes*) diamonds.
orografía *nf* orography.
orográfico *adj* orographical.
orondo *adj* (**a**) *vasija etc* big, big-bellied, rounded; *persona* fat, potbellied.
(**b**) (*satisfecho*) smug, self-satisfied; (*pomposo*) pompous.
(**c**) (*LAm*) calm, serene.
oropel *nm* tinsel; **de** ~ flashy, bright but tawdry; unsubstantial; **tener mucho** ~ to be all show, (*esp*) make a pretence of being wealthy.
oropéndola *nf* golden oriole.
oroya *nf* (*And*) *basket of a rope bridge;* (*And Ferro*) funicular railway.
orozuz *nm* liquorice.
orquesta *nf* orchestra; ~ **de baile** dance band; ~ **de cámara** chamber orchestra; ~ **de jazz** jazz band; ~ **sinfónica** symphony orchestra.
orquestación *nf* orchestration (*t fig*).
orquestal *adj* orchestral.
orquestar [1a] *vt* to orchestrate (*t fig*).
orquídea *nf* orchid, orchis.
orsay *nm* = **offside.**
ortiga *nf* nettle, stinging nettle.
orto... *pref* ortho...
orto¹ *nm* sunrise.
orto²** *nm* (*Cono Sur*) (*culo*) arse**; (*ano*) arsehole**.
ortodoncia *nf* orthodontics.
ortodoncista *nmf* orthodontist.
ortodoxia *nf* orthodoxy.
ortodoxo *adj* orthodox.
ortofonista *nmf* speech therapist.
ortografía *nf* spelling; orthography.
ortográfico *adj* spelling (*atr*); orthographic(al); **reforma ortográfica** spelling reform.
ortopeda *nmf* orthopaedist.
ortopedia *nf* orthopaedics.
ortopédico *adj* orthopaedic.
ortopedista *nmf* orthopaedist.
oruga *nf* (**a**) (*Ent*) caterpillar. (**b**) (*Bot*) rocket. (**c**) (*Téc*) caterpillar, caterpillar track; (*Mil*) tracked personnel carrier; **tractor de** ~ caterpillar tractor.
orujo *nm refuse of grapes* (*u olives*) *after pressing;* (*bebida*) *liquor distilled from grape refuse.*
orza¹ *nf* (*jarra*) glazed earthenware jar.
orza² *nf* (*Náut*) luff, luffing; **ir de** ~ (*fig*) to be on the wrong track.
orzar [1f] *vi* (*Náut*) to luff.
orzuelo *nm* (*Med*) stye.
os¹ *pron pers pl* (**a**) (*ac*) you.
(**b**) (*dativo*) (to) you; ~ **lo di** I gave it to you; ~ **lo compré** I bought it from you; I bought it for you; ~ **quitáis el abrigo** you take off your coats.
(**c**) (*reflexivo*) (to) yourselves; (*recíproco*) (to) each other; **vosotros** ~ **laváis** you wash yourselves; **cuando** ~ **marchéis** when you leave.
os² *interj* shoo!
osa *nf* she-bear; **O~ Mayor** Ursa Major, Great Bear; **O~ Menor** Ursa Minor, Little Bear; **¡la ~!*** gosh!*; **¡anda la ~!*** what a carry-on!*
osadamente *adv* daringly, boldly.
osadía *nf* daring, boldness.
osado *adj* daring, bold.
osamenta *nf* bones; skeleton.
osar [1a] *vi* to dare; ~ **hacer algo** to dare to do sth.
osario *nm* ossuary, charnel house.
Oscar, óscar *nm* Oscar.
oscarizado 1 *adj film* Oscar-winning. **2** *nm*, **oscarizada** *nf* Oscar winner.
oscense 1 *adj* of Huesca. **2** *nmf* native (*o* inhabitant) of Huesca; **los** ~**s** the people of Huesca.
oscilación *nf* (**a**) (*gen*) oscillation; (*vaivén*) swing, sway, to and fro movement; rocking; (*luz*) winking, blinking. (**b**) (*de precios*) fluctuation. (**c**) (*fig*) hesitation, wavering.
oscilador 1 *adj* oscillating. **2** *nm* oscillator.
oscilante *adj* oscillating; swinging.
oscilar [1a] *vi* (**a**) (*gen*) to oscillate; (*péndulo etc*) to swing, sway, move to and fro; (*mecerse*) to rock; (*luz*) to wink, blink.
(**b**) (*fig*) to fluctuate (*entre* between); to vary (*entre* between); to range (*entre* between); **la distancia oscila entre los 100 y 500 m** the distance ranges between 100 and 500 m; **los precios oscilan mucho** prices are fluctuating a lot.
(**c**) (*persona*) to hesitate; to waver (*entre* between); **oscila entre la alegría y el pesimismo** he passes from cheerfulness to pessimism.
oscilatorio *adj* oscillatory.
osciloscopio *nm* oscilloscope.
oscular [1a] *vt* (*liter*) to osculate, kiss.
ósculo *nm* (*liter*) osculation, kiss; ~ **de paz** kiss of peace.
oscuramente *adv* obscurely; in an obscure way.
oscurana *nf* (*CAm: de polvo*) cloud of volcanic dust; (*And**, *Méx: oscuridad*) darkness.
oscurantismo *nm* obscurantism.
oscurantista *adj, nmf* obscurantist.
oscurear [1a] (*Méx*) = **oscurecer.**
oscurecer [2d] **1** *vt* (**a**) (*gen*) to obscure, darken; to dim; to black out.
(**b**) (*fig*) *asunto* to confuse, cloud, fog; *rival* to overshadow, put in the shade; *fama* to dim, tarnish.
(**c**) (*Arte*) to shade.
2 *vi*, **oscurecerse** *vr* to grow dark, get dark.
oscuridad *nf* (**a**) (*gen*) darkness, obscurity; gloom, gloominess. (**b**) (*fig*) obscurity.
oscuro *adj* (**a**) (*gen*) dark; dim, gloomy, obscure; *contorno* confused, indistinct; **a oscuras** in the dark (*t fig*), in darkness; **quedarse a oscuras** to be left in the dark.
(**b**) *color* dark, deep; **un hermoso azul** ~ a beautiful dark blue.
(**c**) (*Met*) overcast, cloudy.
(**d**) (*fig*) obscure; confused; *futuro etc* uncertain; *asunto* shady; **de origen** ~ of obscure origin(s).
óseo *adj* bony, osseous.
osezno *nm* bear cub.
osificación *nf* ossification.
osificar [1g] **1** *vt* to ossify. **2 osificarse** *vr* to ossify, become ossified.
-osis *V* **Aspects of Word Formation in Spanish 2.**
osito *nm* (*juguete*) toy bear; (*Cono Sur: de bebé*) all-in-one suit; ~ **de felpa,** ~ **de peluche** teddy bear; ~ **panda** panda.
osmosis *nf*, **ósmosis** *nf* osmosis.
osmótico *adj* osmotic.
OSO *abr de* **oessudoeste** west-south-west, WSW.
oso *nm* (**a**) bear; ~ **blanco** polar bear; ~ **colmenero** (*LAm*) anteater; ~ **de las cavernas** cave bear; ~ **gris** grizzly (bear); ~ **hormiguero** anteater; ~ **marsupial** koala bear; ~ **pardo** brown bear; ~ **de peluche** teddy bear; **ser un** ~ to be a prickly sort; **hacer el** ~ to play the fool; to play the

sentimental lover.
(**b**) (*Carib*) braggart; bully.

Ostende *nm* Ostend.

ostensible *adj* obvious, evident; **hacer algo ~** to reveal sth, make sth clear; (*LAm*) to express sth, register sth; **procurar no hacerse ~** to keep out of the way, lie low.

ostensiblemente *adv* obviously, evidently; openly; perceptibly, visibly; **se mostró ~ conmovido** he was visibly affected.

ostensorio *nm* monstrance.

ostenta *nf* (*And, Cono Sur*) = **ostentación**.

ostentación *nf* (**a**) (*gen*) ostentation, display; pomp. (**b**) (*acto*) show, display; **hacer ~ de** to show off, display, parade.

ostentar [1a] *vt* (**a**) (*mostrar*) to show; (*pey*) to show off, display, make a parade of, flaunt.
(**b**) (*tener*) to have, carry, show; **ostenta todavía las cicatrices** he still has (*o* carries) the scars.
(**c**) *poderes legales etc* to have, possess; *honor, título etc* to have, hold; **~ el título mundial en el deporte** to hold the world title in the sport, be the world record holder.

ostentativo *adj* ostentatious.

ostentosamente *adv* ostentatiously.

ostentoso *adj* ostentatious.

osteo... *pref* osteo...

osteoartritis *nf* osteoarthritis.

osteópata *nmf* osteopath.

osteopatía *nf* osteopathy.

osti⁑ *interj* = **hostia**.

ostión *nm* large oyster.

ostionería *nf* (*LAm*) oyster bar.

ostra *nf* (**a**) (*Zool*) oyster.
(**b**) (*fig*: *pesado*) dull person; (*huraño*) retiring individual; (*permanente*) regular; **las ~s del café** the café regulars, the café habitués; **es una ~** he's a fixture here.
(**c**) **¡~s!** (*Esp**) hell!

ostracismo *nm* ostracism.

ostral *nm* oyster bed.

ostrería *nf* oyster bar.

ostrero *nm* (**a**) (*lugar*) oyster bed. (**b**) (*Orn*) oystercatcher.

osuno *adj* bear-like.

OTAN ['otan] *nf abr de* **Organización del Tratado del Atlántico Norte** North Atlantic Treaty Organization, NATO.

otánico *adj* NATO (*atr*).

otanista *nmf* supporter of NATO.

otario* **1** *adj* (*Cono Sur*) simple, gullible. **2** *nm* sucker⁑.

OTASE [o'tase] *nf abr de* **Organización del Tratado del Sudeste Asiático** South-East Asia Treaty Organization, SEATO.

otate *nm* (*Méx*) cane, stick; reed, rush.

-ote, -ota *V* **Aspects of Word Formation in Spanish 2**.

oteadero *nm* look-out post.

otear [1a] *vt* (**a**) (*alcanzar a ver*) to descry, make out, glimpse; (*mirar desde arriba*) to look down on, look over; (*espiar*) to watch (from above), spy on; *horizonte* to scan.
(**b**) (*fig*) to examine, look into.

Otelo *nm* Othello.

otero *nm* low hill, hillock, knoll.

OTI ['oti] *nf* (*TV*) *abr de* **Organización de la Televisión Iberoamericana**.

otitis *nf* earache.

otomana *nf* ottoman.

otomano, -a *adj, nm/f* Ottoman.

otomía *nf* (*Méx*) atrocity; **hacer ~s*** to get up to no good, misbehave.

Otón *nm* Otto.

otoñada *nf* autumn, fall (*US*).

otoñal *adj* autumnal, autumn (*atr*), fall (*atr*: *US*).

otoño *nm* autumn, fall (*US*); (*fig*: *edad*) maturity.

otorgamiento *nm* (**a**) (*acto*) granting, conferring; consent; (*Jur*) execution. (**b**) (*documento*) legal document, deed.

otorgar [1h] *vt* (**a**) (*dar*) to grant, give (*a* to); *poderes etc* to confer (*a* on); *esfuerzo, tiempo* to devote (*a* to); *premio etc* to award (*a* to); *privilegio etc* to grant; (*Jur*) *instrumento etc* to execute; *testamento* to make.
(**b**) (*consentir en*) to consent, agree to.

otoronco *nm* (*And Zool*) mountain bear.

otorrino(laringólogo) *nmf* (*Med*) ear, nose and throat specialist.

otramente *adv* in a different way.

otredad *nf* otherness.

otro 1 *adj* (*sing*) another, (*pl*) other; (*en serie*: *anterior*) last, previous; (*posterior*) next, following; **a la otra semana** the following week; **otra taza de café** another cup of coffee; **con ~s trajes** with other dresses; with different dresses; **con otras 8 personas** with another 8 people, with 8 other people; **¡otra!** (*Teat*) encore!; **otra cosa** sth else; **tropezamos con otra nueva dificultad** we run up against yet another (*o* a further) difficulty; **va a ser ~ Manolete** he's going to be another (*o* a second) Manolete; **~ que** other than; different from; **fue no ~ que el obispo** it was none other than the bishop, it was no lesser person than the bishop; **ser muy ~** to be very different; **los tiempos son ~s** times have changed.
2 *pron* (*sing*) another one, (*pl*) others; **el ~** the other one; **lo ~** the rest (of it); **los ~s** the others; the rest; **¿~?** another one?; **lo ~ es más triste** the rest of it is sadder; **lo ~ no importa** the rest isn't important; **tomar el sombrero de ~** to take somebody else's hat; **conformarse con las costumbres de los ~s** to adapt o.s. to other people's habits; **algún ~** somebody else; **que lo haga ~** let somebody else do it; **~ dijo que ...** somebody else said ...; **como dijo el ~** as the saying goes; **¡~ que tal!** here we go again!, we've heard all that before!; *V* **alguno, parte, tanto** *etc.*

otrora *adv* (††, *liter*) (**a**) (*antiguamente*) formerly, in olden times. (**b**) (*como adj invar*) one-time, former; **el ~ señor del país** the one-time ruler of the country.

otrosí *adv* furthermore.

OUA *nf abr de* **Organización de la Unidad Africana** Organization of African Unity, OAU.

OUAA *nf abr de* **Organización de la Unidad Afro-americana**.

output ['autpu] *nm, pl* **outputs** ['autpu] (*Inform*) printout.

ovación *nf* ovation.

ovacionar [1a] *vt* to acclaim, cheer to the echo.

oval *adj*, **ovalado** *adj* oval.

óvalo *nm* oval; (*Méx Med*) pessary.

ovario *nm* ovary.

ovas *nfpl* fish eggs, roe.

oveja *nf* (**a**) sheep, ewe; **~ negra** (*fig*) black sheep (of the family); **cada ~ con su pareja** it's best to stick to people like o.s.; birds of a feather flock together; **apartar las ~s de los cabritos** (*fig*) to separate the sheep from the goats; **cargar con la ~ muerta** to be left holding the baby.
(**b**) (*Cono Sur*) whore.

ovejera *nf* (*Méx*) sheepfold.

ovejería *nf* (*Cono Sur*) sheep farm; sheep farming.

ovejero *nm* sheepdog; **~ alemán** German shepherd (dog), Alsatian.

ovejo *nm*, **ovejón** *nm* (*LAm*) ram.

ovejuno *adj* sheep (*atr*).

overear [1a] *vt* (*And, Cono Sur Culin*) to cook to a golden colour, brown.

overol *nm* (*LAm*) overalls.

ovetense 1 *adj* of Oviedo. **2** *nmf* native (*o* inhabitant) of Oviedo; **los ~s** the people of Oviedo.

Ovidio *nm* Ovid.

oviducto *nm* oviduct.

oviforme *adj* egg-shaped, oviform.

ovillar [1a] **1** *vt lana etc* to wind, wind into a ball. **2 ovillarse** *vr* to curl up into a ball.

ovillo *nm* (*de lana etc*) ball; (*fig*) tangle; **hacerse un ~** (*descansando etc*) to curl up into a ball; (*con miedo*) to crouch, cower; (*en discurso etc*) to get tied up in knots.

ovino 1 *adj* ovine; sheep (*atr*); **ganado ~** sheep. **2** *nm* (*animales*) sheep; **carne de ~** sheep meat; mutton, lamb.

ovíparo *adj* oviparous.

OVNI, ovni ['oβni] *nm abr de* **objeto volante** (*o* **volador**) **no identificado** unidentified flying object, UFO.

ovoide 1 *adj* ovoid, egg-shaped. **2** *nm* ovoid; (*LAm Dep*) rugby ball.

ovulación *nf* ovulation.

ovular [1a] *vi* to ovulate.

óvulo *nm* ovule, ovum.

ox [os] *interj* shoo!

oxálico *adj* oxalic.

oxear [1a] *vt* to shoo (away).

oxiacanta *nf* hawthorn.

oxiacetilénico *adj* oxyacetylene (*atr*).

oxidación *nf* rusting; (*Quím*) oxidation.

oxidado *adj* rusty; (*Quím*) oxidized.

oxidar [1a] **1** *vt* (*gen*) to rust; (*Quím*) to oxidize. **2 oxidarse** *vr* to rust, go rusty, get rusty; (*Quím*) to oxidize.

óxido *nm* rust; (*Quím*) oxide; **~ de hierro** iron oxide; **~ nitroso** nitrous oxide.

oxigenación *nf* oxygenation.

oxigenado 1 *adj* (**a**) (*Quím*) oxygenated.
(**b**) *pelo* peroxided, bleached; **una rubia oxigenada** a peroxide blonde.
2 *nm* peroxide (*for hair*).
oxigenar [1a] **1** *vt* to oxygenate. **2 oxigenarse** *vr* (**a**) (*lit*) to become oxygenated. (**b**) (*fig*) to get some fresh air.
oxígeno *nm* oxygen.
oxte *interj* shoo!; get out!, hop it!*; **sin decir ~ ni moxte** without a word.
oye, oyendo *etc V* **oír.**
oyente *nmf* (**a**) (*gen*) listener, hearer; (*Rad*) **'queridos ~s ...'** 'dear listeners ...'.
(**b**) (*Univ*) unregistered student, occasional student, auditor (*US*).
ozono *nm* ozone.
ozonosfera *nf* ozonosphere, ozone layer.

P

P, p [pe] *nf* (*letra*) P, p.

P (**a**) (*Ecl*) *abr de* **Padre** Father, F., Fr. (**b**) *abr de* **Papa** pope. (**c**) *abr de* **pregunta** question, Q.

p. (**a**) (*Tip*) *abr de* **página** page, p. (**b**) (*Cos*) *abr de* **punto** stitch.

pa‡ *prep pronunciación vulgar o jocosa de* **para**; *p.ej.* **es pal gato**; *V* **gato.**

p.a. (**a**) *abr de* **por autorización.** (**b**) *abr de* **por ausencia.**

p.ª *abr de* **para.**

PAAU *nfpl abr de* **Pruebas para el Acceso a la Universidad.**

pabellón *nm* (**a**) (*tienda*) bell tent.

(**b**) (*de cama*) canopy, hangings.

(**c**) (*Arquit*) pavilion; (*en jardín*) summerhouse, hut; (*de hospital etc*) block, section; ~ **de aduanas** customs house; ~ **de caza** shooting box; ~ **de conciertos,** ~ **de música** bandstand; ~ **(poli)deportivo** sports hall; ~ **de hidroterapia** pumproom.

(**d**) (*de trompeta etc*) mouth; ~ **de la oreja** outer ear.

(**e**) (*Mil*) stack.

(**f**) (*bandera*) flag; ~ **de conveniencia** flag of convenience; ~ **nacional** national flag; **un buque de ~ panameño** a ship with Panamanian registration, a ship flying the Panamanian flag.

pabilo *nm*, **pábilo** *nm* wick; snuff (*of candle*).

Pablo *nm* Paul.

pábulo *nm* (**a**) (*gen*) food.

(**b**) (*fig*) food, fuel; encouragement; **dar ~ a** to feed, encourage; **dar ~ a las llamas** to add fuel to the flames; **dar ~ a los rumores** to encourage rumours.

PAC *nf abr de* **Política Agraria Común** Common Agricultural Policy, CAP.

Paca *nf forma familiar de* **Francisca.**

paca[1] *nf* bale.

paca[2] *nf* (*LAm*: *Zool*) paca, spotted cavy.

pacapaca *nf* (*And*) owl; **le vino la ~*** it all went wrong for him.

pacatería *nf* (*véase adj*) (**a**) timidity. (**b**) excessive modesty, prudishness.

pacato *adj* (**a**) (*tímido*) timid, quiet. (**b**) (*modesto*) excessively modest, prudish.

pacense 1 *adj* of Badajoz. **2** *nmf* native (*o* inhabitant) of Badajoz; **los ~s** the people of Badajoz.

paceño 1 *adj* of La Paz. **2** *nm*, **paceña** *nf* native (*o* inhabitant) of La Paz; **los ~s** the people of La Paz.

pacer [2d] **1** *vt* (**a**) *hierba etc* to eat, graze. (**b**) *ganado* to graze, pasture. **2** *vi* to graze.

paciencia *nf* patience; forbearance; **¡~!** be patient!; (*Cono Sur*) that's just too bad!; **¡~ y barajar!** keep trying!, don't give up! **se me acaba** (*o* **agota**) **la ~, no tengo más ~** my patience is running out, I'm at the end of my tether; **armarse** (*o* **cargarse, revestirse**) **de ~** to arm o.s. with patience, resolve to be patient; **perder la ~** to lose one's temper.

pacienciosо *adj* (*And, Cono Sur*) long-suffering.

paciente *adj, nmf* patient.

pacientemente *adv* patiently.

pacienzudo *adj* very patient, long-suffering.

pacificación *nf* pacification.

pacificador 1 *adj* pacifying, peace-making. **2** *nm*, **pacificadora** *nf* peace-maker.

pacíficamente *adv* pacifically, peaceably.

pacificar [1g] **1** *vt* (*Mil*) to pacify; (*calmar*) to calm; (*apaciguar*) to appease. **2 pacificarse** *vr* (*calmarse*) to calm down.

Pacífico *nm* (*t* **Océano ~**) Pacific (Ocean).

pacífico *adj* pacific, peaceable; peace-loving.

pacifismo *nm* pacifism.

pacifista *adj, nmf* pacifist.

Paco *nm forma familiar de* **Francisco**; **ya vendrá el tío ~ con la rebaja** it won't be as bad as you think.

paco[1] *nm* (*Mil*) sniper, sharpshooter.

paco[2]‡ *nm* (*LAm*) cop‡, policeman.

paco[3] 1 *adj* (*And, Cono Sur*) reddish. **2** *nm* (*And, Cono Sur*) alpaca.

pacota* *nf* (*Méx*) (*trasto*) piece of junk; (*persona*) layabout*.

pacotada* *nf* (*And*) blunder, gaffe.

pacotilla *nf* (**a**) (*gen*) trash, junk, inferior stuff; **de ~** trashy, shoddy; **hacer su ~** to be doing nicely, make a nice profit.

(**b**) (*And, CAm, Cono Sur*) rabble, crowd, mob.

pacotillero 1 *adj* (*And*) rude, uncouth. **2** *nm* (*And, Carib, Cono Sur*) pedlar, peddler (*US*), hawker.

pactable *adj* negotiable.

pactar [1a] **1** *vt* to agree to, agree on; to stipulate, contract for. **2** *vi* to come to an agreement; to compromise.

pacto *nm* pact; agreement, covenant; **P~ Andino** Andean Pact; ~ **de no agresión** non-aggression pact; ~ **de** (*o* **entre**) **caballeros** gentlemen's agreement; ~ **de recompra,** ~ **de retro** (*Com*) repurchase agreement; ~ **social** social contract; wages agreement; **P~ de Varsovia** Warsaw Pact.

pacha *nf* (*CAm*) baby's bottle.

pachá *nm* pasha; **vivir como un ~** to live like a prince.

pachaco* *adj* (*CAm*) weak, feeble.

pachacho *adj* (*Cono Sur*) (*rechoncho*) chubby; (*bajetón*) squat.

pachamama *nf* (*And, Cono Sur*) the good earth, Mother Earth.

pachamanca *nf* (*And*) barbecue; (*fig*) feast.

pachanga *nf* (**a**) (: *fiesta*) party; (*juerga*) binge*, booze-up‡. (**b**) (*Carib**: *lío*) mix-up. (**c**) (*Mús*) a Cuban dance.

pachanguear* [1a] *vi* to go on a spree.

panchanguero* *adj* (**a**) noisy, rowdy. (**b**) (*Méx*) (*alegre*) merry; (*chistoso*) witty; (*campechano*) expansive.

pacharán *nm* sloe brandy.

pacho* *adj* (**a**) (*CAm, Cono Sur**) *persona* (*rechoncho*) chubby; (*achaparrado*) squat; (*CAm*) *objeto* flat, flattened; *sombrero* flat-brimmed. (**b**) (*Carib*) slow, phlegmatic.

pachocha *nf* (*LAm*) = **pachorra.**

pachol *nm* (*Méx*) mat of hair.

pachón 1 *adj* (**a**) (*CAm, Cono Sur**: *peludo*) shaggy, hairy; (*CAm, Méx**: *lanudo*) woolly.

(**b**) (*And*: *gordito*) plump.

(**c**) (*And**: *lerdo*) dim*, dense*.

2 *nm* (**a**) (*persona*) dull person, slow sort.

(**b**) (*t* **perro ~**) beagle.

pachorra *nf* slowness, sluggishness; phlegm, phlegmatic nature; **Juan, con su santa ~** ... John, as slow as ever ...

pachorrada* *nf* (*Carib, Cono Sur*) blunder, gaffe.

pachorrear [1a] *vi* (*CAm*) to be slow, be sluggish.

pachorriento *adj* (*And, Cono Sur*), **pachorro** *adj* (*And, Carib*), **pachorrudo** *adj* slow, sluggish; phlegmatic.

pachotada *nf* (*And, Méx*) = **patochada.**

pachuco* 1 *adj* (*Méx*: *majo*) flashy, flashily dressed. **2** *nm* (*bien vestido*) sharp dresser, snappy dresser; (*pey*) Chicano.

pachucho *adj fruta* overripe; *persona* (*enfermo*) off-colour, poorly.

pachulí *nm* (**a**) (*Bot, perfume*) patchouli. (**b**) (*Esp*‡: *tío*) bloke‡, guy*.

padecer [2d] **1** *vt* (*gen*) to suffer (from); (*aguantar*) to endure, put up with; *error etc* to labour under, be a victim of.

2 *vi* ~ **de** to suffer from; **padece del corazón** he suffers with his heart, he has heart trouble; **padece en su amor propio** his self-respect suffers; **ella padece por todos** she suffers on everybody's account; **se embala bien para que no padezca en el viaje** it is well packed so that it will not get damaged on the journey.

padecimiento *nm* suffering; (*Med*) ailment.

padrastro *nm* (**a**) (*gen*) stepfather; (*fig*) harsh father, cruel parent. (**b**) (*fig*: *dificultad*) obstacle, difficulty. (**c**) (*Anat*) hangnail.

padrazo *nm* indulgent father.

padre 1 *nm* (**a**) father; (*Zool*) father, sire; **~s** father and mother, parents; (*antepasados*) ancestors; **García ~** García senior, the elder García; **~ de familia** father of a family, man with family responsibilities; (*en censo etc*) head of a household; **~ de pila** godfather; **~ político** father-in-law; **~ soltero** single father; **su señor ~** your father; **es el ~ de estos estudios** he is the father of this discipline; **¡eres mi ~!*** you're a marvel!; **¡mi ~!*, ¡su ~!*** hell's bells!*; **¡tu ~!**‡** up yours!**‡

(**b**) (*Ecl*) father, priest; **el P~ Las Casas** Father Las Casas; **~ espiritual** confessor; **P~ Nuestro** Lord's Prayer, Our Father; **P~ Santo** Holy Father, Pope.

(**c**) **una paliza de ~ y muy señor mío*** a terrific bashing*, a beating and a half, the father and mother of a thrashing*.

2 *adj* (*: *enorme*) huge, tremendous*; **un éxito ~** a terrific success*; **un lío ~** an almighty row*; **un susto ~** an awful fright.

padrejón *nm* (*Cono Sur*) stallion.

padrenuestro *nm* Lord's Prayer, paternoster; **en menos que se reza un ~** in no time at all.

padrillo *nm* (*And, Cono Sur*) stallion.

padrinazgo *nm* being a godfather; (*fig*) sponsorship, patronage; protection.

padrino *nm* (**a**) (*Ecl*) godfather; (*t* **~ de boda**) best man; (*en duelo*) second; (*de mafia*) godfather; (*fig*) sponsor, patron; **~s** godparents. (**b**) (‡: *víctima*) sucker‡, victim.

padrón *nm* (**a**) (*lista de habitantes*) list of inhabitants, roll; (*censo*) census; (*de miembros etc*) register; (*Pol*) electoral register.

(**b**) (*Téc*) pattern.

(**c**) (*Arquit*) inscribed column, commemorative column.

(**d**) (*fig*: *t* **~ de ignominia**) stain, blot; **el trabajo es un ~ para su autor** the work is a disgrace to its author; **será un ~ para todos nosotros** it will be a stain on all of us.

(**e**) (*: *padrazo*) indulgent father.

(**f**) (*LAm*: *caballo*) stallion; (*And*: *toro*) breeding bull.

padrote *nm* (**a**) (*LAm*) (*caballo*) stallion; (*toro*) breeding bull. (**b**) (*Méx**: *chulo*) pimp.

pae‡, pai‡: **¿qué ~?** = **¿qué pasa?** (*V* **pasar**).

paella *nf* paella.

paellada *nf* paella party.

paellera¹ *nf* (*Culin*) paella dish; (*hum*) dish aerial, TV satellite dish.

paellero 1 *adj* paella (*atr*). **2** *nm*, **paellera²** *nf* paella cook.

paf *interj* bang!; plop!, splash!

pág. *abr de* **página** page, p.

paga *nf* (**a**) (*acto*) payment; **entrega contra ~** cash on delivery. (**b**) (*sueldo*) pay, wages; (*pensión*) allowance; (*honorarios*) fee; **~ extra** salary bonus (*paid in July and December*). (**c**) **mala ~*** bad payer.

pagadero *adj* payable, due; **~ a la entrega** payable on delivery; **~ a plazos** payable in instalments; **~ al portador** payable to bearer.

pagado *adj* (*fig*) pleased; **~ de sí mismo** self-satisfied, smug; **quedamos ~s** we're quits.

pagador(a) *nm/f* (**a**) (*que paga*) payer; **mal ~** bad payer. (**b**) (*de banco*) teller, cashier; (*Mil*: *t* **oficial ~**) paymaster.

pagaduría *nf* pay office, cashier's office; (*Mil*) paymaster's office.

paganini* *nm*: **ser el ~** to be the one who pays.

paganismo *nm* paganism, heathenism.

pagano¹, -a *adj, nm/f* pagan, heathen.

pagano², -a* *nm/f* person who pays for others; scapegoat, dupe, victim.

pagar [1h] **1** *vti* (**a**) (*gen*) to pay; *deuda* to pay, pay off, repay; *compras* to pay for; *póliza* to pay out on; **su tío le paga los estudios** his uncle is paying for his education; **no lo podemos ~** we can't afford it; **paga 20 dólares de habitación** he pays 20 dollars for his room; **a ~** (*Correos*) postage due; **cuenta a ~, cuenta por ~** unpaid bill, outstanding account; **~ por adelantado** to pay in advance; **~ al contado** to pay cash.

(**b**) (*fig*) *favor* to repay; *amor* to return, requite; *visita* to return; *crimen, ofensa* to pay for, atone for; **lo pagó con la vida** he paid for it with his life; **¡me las pagarás!** I'll pay you out for this!, I'll get you for this!; **el que la hace la paga** one must face the consequences; **¡las vas a ~!** you'll catch it!*, you've got it coming to you!

2 *vi* (**a**) (*LAm*) to pay; **el negocio no paga** the business doesn't pay.

(**b**) (*Cono Sur*: *tomar apuestas*) to take bets, make a book.

3 pagarse *vr* (**a**) **~ con algo** to be content with sth.

(**b**) **~ de algo** to be pleased with sth; to take a liking to sth; (*pey*) to boast of sth; **~ de sí mismo** to be conceited, be smug; to be very full of o.s.; **se paga mucho de su pelo** she's terribly vain about her hair.

pagaré *nm* promissory note, IOU; **~ del Tesoro** Treasury bill, Treasury bond.

página *nf* page; **~s amarillas** yellow pages; **es primera ~** it's front-page news; **anuncio a toda ~, anuncio a ~ entera** full-page advertisement; **currarse la ~‡** to pretend, try it on*.

paginación *nf* pagination.

paginar [1a] *vt* to paginate, number the pages of; **con 6 hojas sin ~** with 6 unnumbered pages.

pago¹ 1 *nm* (**a**) (*Fin*) payment; (*devolución*) repayment; **~ anticipado** advance payment; **~ al contado** cash payment; **~ a cuenta** payment on account; **~ a la entrega, ~ contra recepción** cash on delivery; **~ en especie** payment in kind; **~ fraccionado** instalment, part-payment; **~ inicial** first payment, down payment, deposit; **~ íntegro** gross payment; **~ a la orden** direct debit; **~ a plazos** payment by instalments, deferred payments; **~ a la presentación de factura** payment on invoice; **~ por resultados** payment by results; **~ simbólico** token payment; **'nada de ~'** (*en aduana*) 'nothing to declare'; **colegio de ~** fee-paying school; **huésped de ~** paying guest; **atrasarse en los ~s** to be in arrears; **efectuar un ~** to make a payment; **faltar en los ~s** to default on one's payments; **suspender los ~s** to stop payments.

(**b**) (*fig*) return, reward; **en ~ de** in return for; as a reward for.

2 *adj* paid; **estar ~** to be paid; (*fig*) to be even, be quits.

pago² *nm* (*distrito*) district; (*finca*) estate, property (*esp planted with vines or olives*); (*Cono Sur*) region, area; home area, native part; **en estos ~s** hereabouts, round here, in this neck of the woods.

pagoda *nf* pagoda.

pagote* *nm* scapegoat.

pagua *nf* (**a**) (*Cono Sur*) (*hernia*) hernia; (*hinchazón*) large swelling. (**b**) (*Méx*) large avocado pear.

paguacha *nf* (*Cono Sur*) (**a**) = **pagua** (**a**). (**b**) (*melón*) large melon. (**c**) (‡: *cabeza*) nut‡, bonce‡.

paguala *nf* (*Carib*) swordfish.

pai *nm* (*LAm*) pie.

paiche *nm* (*And*) dried salted fish.

paila *nf* (**a**) large pan; (*sartén*) frying-pan. (**b**) (*Cono Sur*) meal of fried food.

pailero *nm* (**a**) (*And, Méx**: *italiano*) immigrant Italian, Wop‡. (**b**) (*CAm, Carib, Méx*) (*cobrero*) coppersmith; (*calderero*) tinker.

pailón *nm* (**a**) (*And, Carib*) pot, pan. (**b**) (*And, CAm Geog*) bowl. (**c**) (*Carib*) whirlpool.

paíño *nm* petrel.

pairo *nm*: **estar al ~** (*Náut*) to lie to; **quedarse al ~** (*fig*) to sit back and do nothing.

país *nm* (**a**) (*nación*) country; (*tierra*) land, region, area; (*paisaje*) landscape; **~ cliente** client state; **~ en (vías de) desarrollo** developing country; **~ deudor** debtor nation; **~ de las maravillas** wonderland; **~ natal** native land; **~ de nunca jamás** never-never land; **~ satélite** satellite country; **los ~es miembros, los ~es participantes** the member countries; **vino del ~** local wine; **así se cuece en mi ~** that's how it's cooked in my part of the country; **vivir sobre el ~** to live off the country.

(**b**) **P~es Bajos** Low Countries; **P~ Vasco** Basque Country.

paisa* *nmf* (*LAm*) = **paisano 2** (**c**).

paisaje *nm* landscape, countryside, scenery; **~ interior** state of mind.

paisajismo *nm* (*de jardines*) landscaping, landscape gardening; (*Arte*) landscape painting.

paisajista *nmf* landscape gardener; (*Arte*) landscape painter.

paisajístico *adj* landscape (*atr*), scenic.

paisanada *nf* (*Cono Sur*) group of peasants, peasants (*collectively*).

paisanaje *nm* (**a**) (*gen*) civil population. (**b**) (*Cono Sur*) = **paisanada.**

paisano 1 *adj* of the same country.

2 *nm,* **paisana** *nf* (**a**) (*Mil*) civilian; **vestir de ~** (*soldado*) to be in mufti, be in civvies*, (*policía*) be in plain clothes.

(**b**) (*compatriota*) compatriot, fellow countryman, fellow countrywoman; **es ~ mío** he's a fellow countryman (of mine).

(**c**) (*Cono Sur: extranjero*) foreigner; (*Cono Sur: árabe*) Arab; (*Méx*) Spaniard; (*And, Cono Sur*) Chinaman, Chinese woman.

paja *nf* (**a**) (*Agr*) straw; (*LAm: de beber*) straw; (*LAm: leña*) dried brushwood; **hombre de ~*** stooge*; **techo de ~** thatched roof.

(**b**) **hacerse una** (*o* **la**) **~**** to wank**, jerk off**; **riñeron por un quítame allá esas ~s** they fell out over some tiny thing, they quarrelled over some trifle; **lo hizo en un quitarme las ~s*** she did it in a jiffy*; **ver la ~ en el ojo ajeno y no la viga en el propio** to see the mote in sb else's eye and not the beam in one's own; **volarse la ~** (*CAm***) to wank**, jerk off**.

(**c**) (*fig*) trash, rubbish; (*lit*) padding, waffle*; **hinchar un libro con mucha ~** to pad a book out; **meter ~** to pad.

(**d**) (*And, CAm: t* **~ de agua**) (*grifo*) tap, faucet (*US*); (*canal*) canal.

(**e**) (*Cono Sur‡: droga*) dope‡.

(**f**) (*CAm‡: mentira*) lie.

pajar *nm* straw loft; straw rick.

pájara *nf* (**a**) (*Orn*) hen, hen bird; (*esp*) hen partridge.

(**b**) (*cometa*) kite; (*pájaro de papel*) paper bird.

(**c**) (*putilla*) loose woman; (*ladrona*) thieving woman.

(**d**) **~ pinta** (game of) forfeits.

(**e**) (*Dep*) wall, collapse.

(**f**) **dar ~ a uno** (*And, CAm*) to swindle sb.

pajarada *nf* (*And*) flock of birds.

pajarear [1a] **1** *vt* (**a**) (*LAm*) *pájaros* to scare, keep off.

(**b**) (*And: observar*) to watch intently.

(**c**) (*And: matar*) to murder.

2 *vi* (**a**) (*holgazanear*) to loaf; to loiter.

(**b**) (*LAm: caballo*) to shy.

(**c**) (*Cono Sur*: estar distraído*) to have one's head in the clouds.

(**d**) (*Méx*: escuchar*) to keep an ear open.

pajarera *nf* aviary.

pajarería *nf* (**a**) (*tienda*) pet shop. (**b**) (*pájaros*) large flock of birds. (**c**) (*Carib**) vanity.

pajarero 1 *adj* (**a**) (*Orn*) bird (*atr*).

(**b**) *persona* (*alegre*) fun-loving; (*chistoso*) facetious, waggish.

(**c**) *ropa etc* gaudy, flashy, loud.

(**d**) (*LAm*) *caballo* nervous; (*And, Carib, Méx*) *caballo* spirited.

(**e**) (*Carib*: entrometido*) meddlesome.

2 *nm* (*cazador*) bird catcher; (*criador*) bird fancier, breeder of birds; (*Com*) bird dealer; (*And, CAm*) bird-scarer.

pajarilla *nf* paper kite; **se le alegraron las ~s*** he was tickled pink*.

pajarita *nf* (**a**) **~ de las nieves** white wagtail. (**b**) (*cometa*) paper kite; (*pájaro de papel*) paper bird. (**c**) (**corbata de**) **~** bow tie; *V* **cuello** (**b**).

pajarito *nm* (**a**) (*Orn*) baby bird, fledgling; (*hum*) birdie; (*fig*) very small person; **me lo dijo un ~** a little bird told me; **quedarse como un ~** to die peacefully, fade away.

(**b**) (*Carib: bichito*) bug, insect.

pájaro 1 *nm* (**a**) (*Orn*) bird; **~ de mal agüero** bird of ill omen; **~ azul** bluebird; **~ bobo** penguin; **~ cantor, ~ cantarín** songbird; **~ carpintero** woodpecker; **~ mosca** (*Esp*) hummingbird; **matar dos ~s de un tiro** to kill two birds with one stone; **quedarse como un ~** to die peacefully; **más vale ~ en mano que ciento volando** a bird in the hand is worth two in the bush; **tener ~s en la cabeza, tener la cabeza a ~s** (*o* **llena de ~s**) to be featherbrained.

(**b**) (*: *persona; t* **~ de cuenta**) (*taimado*) wily bird, nasty type; (*de cuidado*) dangerous person; (*importante*) big noise*, big shot*; **~ bravo** (*Carib*) smart Alec*.

(**c**) (**) prick**.

(**d**) (*Carib‡: homosexual*) queer‡, poof‡.

2 *adj* (**a**) (*Cono Sur*) (*atolondrado*) scatty, featherbrained; (*sospechoso*) shady, dubious; (*chillón*) loud, flashy.

(**b**) (*Carib‡: afeminado*) poofy‡, queer‡.

(**c**) (*Cono Sur*) vague, distracted.

pajarón (*Cono Sur*) **1** *adj* vague, ineffectual, stupid.

2 *nm,* **pajarona** *nf* (**a**) (*poco fiable*) untrustworthy sort; (*ineficaz*) unbusinesslike person.

(**b**) (*charro*) flashily dressed person.

pajarota* *nf* (*Esp*) false rumour, canard.

pajarraca* *nf* to-do*, fuss.

pajarraco *nm* (**a**) (*Orn*) big ugly bird. (**b**) (*) slyboots*.

paje *nm* page; (*Náut*) cabin boy.

pajel *nm* sea-bream.

pajero 1 *adj* (*CAm**) lying.

2 *nm,* **pajera** *nf* (**a**) (*CAm**) liar. (**b**) (*CAm: fontanero*) plumber. (**c**) (**) tosser**, wanker**.

3 *nf* (*Agr*) straw loft.

pajilla *nf* (*CAm, Carib, Méx*) straw hat; (*LAm*) *type of cigarette made from rolled maize.*

pajita *nf* (drinking) straw; **quedarse mascando ~*** (*Carib*) to be left feeling foolish.

pajizo *adj* (**a**) (*de paja*) straw, made of straw; *techo* thatched. (**b**) (*color*) straw-coloured.

pajolero* *adj* (**a**) (*condenado*) blessed, wretched. (**b**) (*tonto*) stupid. (**c**) (*travieso*) naughty, mischievous; (*molesto*) irritating.

pajón* *adj* (*Méx*) *pelo* (*lacio*) lank; (*crespo*) curly.

pajonal *nm* (*LAm*) scrubland.

pajoso *adj* (**a**) *grano* full of chaff. (**b**) (*color*) straw-coloured; (*como paja*) like straw.

pajuela *nf* spill; (*And*) match; (*And, Cono Sur, Méx*) toothpick; (*Carib Mús*) plectrum; **el tiempo de la ~** olden days, bygone times.

pajúo* *adj* (*Carib*) daft, stupid.

Pakistán *nm* Pakistan.

pakistaní *adj, nmf* Pakistani.

pala *nf* (**a**) (*gen*) shovel, spade; scoop; **~ cargadora** mechanical loader; **~ excavadora** digger; **~ mecánica** power shovel; **~ de patatas** potato fork; **~ quitanieves** snowplough; **~ topadora** (*Cono Sur*) power shovel.

(**b**) (*Culin*) slice; **~ para el pescado** fish slice.

(**c**) (*Dep*) bat; racquet; **jugar a ~** to play beach-tennis.

(**d**) (*de hélice, remo*) blade.

(**e**) **~ matamoscas** fly swat.

(**f**) (*de zapato*) vamp.

(**g**) (‡: *mano*) mitt‡, hand; **¡choca la ~!** shake on it!*

(**h**) (*fig*) cunning, wiliness.

palabra *nf* (**a**) (*vocablo*) word; **~ clave** keyword; **~s cruzadas** crossword (puzzle); **~s gruesas, ~s mayores** strong words, abuse; **dos ~s, cuatro ~s** a couple of words; **medias ~s** hints, insinuations; **¡ni una ~ más!** not another word!; **de ~** by word of mouth; **en una ~** in a word; **~ por ~** word for word; verbatim; **a ~s necias, oídos sordos** it's best not to listen to such nonsense; **ser la última ~ en lujo** to be the last word in luxury; **cambiar unas ~s con uno** to have a few words with sb; **coger a uno la ~** to take sb at his word; to keep sb to his word; to call sb's bluff; **comerse las ~s** to mumble; **no cruzar** (**una**) **~ con uno** not to say a word to sb; **sin chistar ~** without a word; **dejar a uno con la ~ en la boca** to interrupt sb, leave sb in mid-sentence; **no encuentro ~s para expresarme** words fail me; **no entiendo ~** it's Greek to me; **gastar ~s** to waste words, waste one's breath; **medir las ~s** to choose one's words carefully; **negar la ~ de Dios a uno** to concede absolutely nothing to sb; **tuvo ~s de elogio para el ministro** he paid tribute to the minister; **trabarse de ~s** to get involved in an argument; to wrangle, squabble.

(**b**) (*facultad*) speech, power of speech, faculty of speech; **de ~ fácil** fluent; **perder la ~** to lose one's power of speech.

(**c**) (*Parl*) right to speak; **ceder la ~ a uno** to call on sb to speak; **dirigir la ~ a uno** to address sb; **hacer uso de la ~, tomar la ~** to speak; **pedir la ~** to ask to be allowed to speak; **tener la ~** to have the floor; **Vd tiene la ~** the floor is yours; **yo no tengo la ~** it's not for me to say; **tomar la ~** (*en un mitin*) to take the floor, begin one's speech.

(**d**) (*promesa*) word, promise; **¡~!** honest!, really!; **~ de casamiento, ~ de matrimonio** promise to marry; **~ de honor** word of honour; **bajo ~** (*Mil*) on parole; **es hombre de ~** he is a man of his word; **cumplir la ~** to keep one's word; **dar su ~, empeñar su ~** to give one's word, give a pledge; **faltar a su ~** to go back on one's word.

palabrear [1a] *vt* (**a**) (*And, Cono Sur*) to agree verbally to; **~ a una** to promise to marry sb. (**b**) (*Cono Sur: insultar*) to abuse.

palabreja *nf* strange word; nasty-sounding word.

palabrería *nf,* **palabrerío** *nm* (*CAm, Cono Sur*) wordiness; verbiage, hot air.

palabrero 1 *adj* wordy, windy. **2** *nm*, **palabrera** *nf* windbag.
palabro* *nm* (*palabrota*) rude word; (*palabra rara*) odd word; pretentious term; (*barbarismo*) barbarism.
palabrota *nf* rude word, swearword.
palabrudo* *adj* (*Cono Sur*) foulmouthed.
palacete *nm* small palace.
palacial *adj* (*LAm*) palatial.
palaciego 1 *adj* palace (*atr*), court (*atr*). **2** *nm* (*persona*) courtier.
palacio *nm* (*de rey*) palace; (*casa grande*) mansion, large house; **~ de congresos** conference centre, conference hall; **P~ de las Comunicaciones** (*Madrid*) General Post Office; **~ de (los) deportes** sports centre; **~ episcopal** bishop's palace; **~ de justicia** courthouse; **~ municipal** city hall; **P~ Nacional** (*p.ej. Guatemala*) Parliament Building; **~ real** royal palace; **el ~ de los Marqueses de Tal** the house of the Marquis of Tal; **ir a ~** to go to court; **tener un puesto en ~** to have a post at court.
palada *nf* (**a**) (*gen*) shovelful, spadeful. (**b**) (*de remo*) stroke.
paladar *nm* (hard) palate, roof of the mouth; (*fig*) palate, taste; **tener un ~ delicado** to have a delicate palate.
paladear [1a] *vt* to taste; to relish, savour; **beber algo paladeándolo** to sip a drink (to see what it tastes like).
paladeo *nm* tasting; relishing, savouring; sipping.
paladín *nm* (*Hist*) paladin; (*fig*) champion.
paladinamente *adv* openly, publicly; clearly.
paladino *adj* open, public; clear; **más ~ no puede ser** it couldn't be clearer.
palafrén *nm* palfrey.
palafrenero *nm* groom.
palana *nf* (*And*) (*pala*) shovel, spade; (*azadón*) hoe.
palanca *nf* (**a**) (*gen*) lever; crowbar; (*Mec*) lever; **~ de arranque** kick-starter; **~ de cambio(s)** gear-lever, gearshift (*US*); **~ de freno** brake lever; **~ de mando** control lever; (*Inform*) joystick.
(**b**) (*fig*) lever; pull, influence; **~s del poder** levers of power; **tener ~*** to have pull, to know people in the right places.
(**c**) (*And, Méx: de barca*) punting pole.
palangana 1 *nf* (**a**) (*gen*) washbasin.
(**b**) (*And, CAm*) platter, serving dish.
2 *nmf* (*: *t* **~s**) (*Cono Sur: intruso*) intruder; (*LAm: frívolo*) shallow person; (*charlatán*) charlatan; (*jactancioso*) braggart.
palanganear* [1a] *vi* (*LAm*) to brag; to show off*.
palanganero *nm* washstand.
palangre *nm* fishing line (with multiple hooks).
palanquear [1a] **1** *vt* (**a**) (*And, CAm*) to lever (along), move with a lever; (*And, Carib, Méx*) *barca* to punt, pole along.
(**b**) (*fig*) **¿quién te palanqueó?** who got you fixed up?
2 *vi* (*And, Carib, Cono Sur**) to pull strings.
palanquera *nf* stockade.
palanquero *nm* (*And, Cono Sur Ferro*) brakeman; (*And*) lumberman; (*Cono Sur*: ladrón*) burglar, housebreaker.
palanqueta *nf* small lever; (*de ladrón*) jemmy; (*Cono Sur, Méx: peso*) weight; (*Pesas*) bar.
palanquetazo* *nm* break-in, burglary.
palanquista* *nm* burglar.
p'alante‡ *adv* = **para adelante**.
palatal *adj, nf* palatal.
palatalizar [1f] **1** *vt* to palatalize. **2 palatalizarse** *vr* to palatalize.
palatinado *nm* palatinate.
palatino *adj* (**a**) (*Pol*) palace (*atr*), court (*atr*), palatine. (**b**) (*Anat*) palatal.
palatosquisis *nf* cleft palate.
palca *nf* (*And*) crossroads.
palco *nm* (**a**) (*Teat etc*) box; (*Fút*) director's box; **~ de autoridades, ~ de honor** royal box; box for distinguished persons; **~ de la presidencia** (*Taur*) president's box; **~ de proscenio** stage box. (**b**) (*) balcony.
palde *nm* (*Cono Sur*) pointed digging tool; (*puñal*) dagger.
palé *nm board game similar to Monopoly*.
palear [1a] **1** *vt* (**a**) (*LAm*) *barca* to punt, pole. (**b**) (*LAm*) *tierra* to shovel; *zanja* to dig. (**c**) (*Cono Sur*) to thresh. **2** *vi* (*piragüista*) to paddle.
palenque *nm* (**a**) (*estacada*) fence, stockade, palisade.
(**b**) (*recinto*) arena, ring, enclosure; (*de gallos*) pit.
(**c**) (*And, Cono Sur: de caballos*) tethering-post, rail.
(**d**) (*Cono Sur*: alboroto*) din, racket.
palenquear [1a] *vt* (*Cono Sur*) to hitch, tether.
palentino 1 *adj* of Palencia.
2 *nm*, **palentina** *nf* native (*o* inhabitant) of Palencia; **los ~s** the people of Palencia.
paleo... *pref* pal(a)eo...
paleografía *nf* paleography.
paleógrafo, -a *nm/f* paleographer.
paleolítico *adj* paleolithic.
paleontología *nf* paleontology.
paleontólogo, -a *nm/f* paleontologist.
palero* 1 *adj* (*And*) big-headed*. **2** *nm* (*Méx*) front man*.
Palestina *nf* Palestine.
palestino, -a *adj, nm/f* Palestinian.
palestra *nf* arena; (*fig*) lists; **salir** (*o* **saltar**) **a la ~** (*fig*) to take the field, take the floor.
paleta 1 *nf* (**a**) (*pala*) small shovel, small spade; scoop (*t Culin*); fire shovel; (*Arquit*) trowel.
(**b**) (*Arte*) palette.
(**c**) (*Tec: de turbina etc*) blade; vane; (*de noria*) paddle; (*de rueda*) bucket; (*plataforma*) pallet, platform (*for lifting and stacking goods*).
(**d**) (*Anat*) shoulder-blade.
(**e**) (*LAm: pala*) wooden paddle for beating clothes.
(**f**) (*LAm: pirulí*) lollipop.
(**g**) (*LAm Culin*) topside of beef.
2 *nm* (*) building worker, brickie*.
paletada *nf* shovelful, spadeful.
paletear [1a] **1** *vt* (*Cono Sur*) *caballo* to pat; (*fig*) to flatter. **2** *vi* (*Cono Sur*) to be out of work.
paletería[1] *nf* (*Culin*) palate, sense of taste.
paletería[2]* *nf* collection of yokels, shower‡.
paletero *nm* (*And*) tuberculosis.
paletilla *nf* shoulder blade.
paleto 1 *adj* boorish, stupid. **2** *nm* (**a**) (*Zool*) fallow deer. (**b**) (*) yokel, country bumpkin.
palia *nf* altar cloth, pall.
paliacate *nm* (*Méx*) scarf, kerchief.
paliar [1b] *vt* (**a**) (*gen*) to palliate, mitigate, alleviate; *dolor* to relieve; *efecto* to lessen, cushion; *importancia* to diminish.
(**b**) *defecto* to conceal, gloss over.
(**c**) *ofensa etc* to mitigate, excuse.
paliativo 1 *adj* palliative; mitigating; concealing. **2** *nm* palliative.
palidecer [2d] *vi* to pale, turn pale.
palidez *nf* paleness, pallor; wanness; sickliness.
pálido *adj* pale, pallid (*t fig*); wan; (*enfermizo*) sickly.
palidoso *adj* (*And*) = **pálido**.
palier *nm* (*Mec*) bearing; (*plataforma*) pallet.
palillo *nm* (**a**) (*gen*) small stick; (*mondadientes*) toothpick; (*Mús*) drumstick; (*Taur**) banderilla; (*Cono Sur*) knitting-needle; (*CAm, Méx*) penholder; **~s** (*Mús*) castanets; **~s chinos** chopsticks; **unas piernas como ~s de dientes** legs like matchsticks.
(**b**) (*hum*) very thin person; **estar hecho un ~** to be as thin as a rake.
palimpsesto *nm* palimpsest.
palindroma *nm*, **palindromo** *nm* palindrome.
palinodia *nf* recantation; **cantar la ~** to recant.
palio *nm* (*manto*) cloak; (*dosel*) canopy; (*Ecl*) pallium.
palique* *nm* chat; small talk, chitchat; **darle al ~, estar de ~** to be chatting, have a chat.
palista *nmf* (*Dep*) canoeist.
palitroque *nm* (**a**) (*Taur**) banderilla. (**b**) (*Cono Sur*) (*juego*) skittles, bowling (*US*); (*local*) skittle alley, bowling alley (*US*).
paliza 1 *nf* (**a**) (*lit*) beating, thrashing; beating-up*; **dar una ~ a uno** to give sb a beating, beat sb up*; **dar la ~*** (*travesear*) to play up*, make trouble; (*ponerse pesado*) to lay down the law; **darse la ~** to flog o.s., slog.
(**b**) (*fig: Dep etc*) beating, drubbing; **¡qué ~ aquélla!** what a beating that was!; **el viaje fue una ~** the journey was ghastly*; **le espera una ~ en la oficina** he'll get a dressing-down at the office*, he's got it coming to him at the office; **los críticos le dieron una ~ a la novela** the critics panned the novel*, the novel took a beating from the critics.
2 *nmf invar* (*: *pesado*) bore, pain*.
palizada *nf* (**a**) (*valla*) fence, stockade, palisade. (**b**) (*recinto*) fenced enclosure.
palizas* *nmf invar* bore, pain*.
Palma *nf*: **Isla de la ~** (*Canarias*) Island of Palma; **~ de Mallorca** Palma; **Las ~s** (*ciudad, provincia*) Las Palmas.
palma *nf* (**a**) (*Anat*) palm; **batir ~s, dar ~s** to clap hands, applaud; (*Mús*) to clap hands; **como la ~ de la mano**

(llano) as flat as the palm of one's hand; (fácil) very easy, straightforward; conocer como la ~ de la mano to know like the back of one's hand.

(b) ~s (fig) clapping, applause; ~s de tango slow handclap.

(c) (Bot) (árbol) palm, palm tree; (hoja) palm leaf; ganar la ~, llevarse la ~ to carry off the palm, triumph, win.

palmada nf (a) (gen) slap, pat (on the shoulder etc); darse una ~ en la frente to clap one's hand to one's brow.

(b) ~s clapping, applause; dar ~s to clap, applaud.

palmadita nf pat, light tap.

palmado⁑ adj (CAm) skint⁑, flat broke*.

palmar[1] nm (Bot) palm grove, cluster of palms.

palmar[2]⁑ [1a] 1 vi (a) (morir) to peg out⁑, die. (b) (en juego) to lose.

2 vt: ~la = 1 (a).

palmar[3] adj, **palmario** adj clear, obvious, self-evident.

palmarés nm (Dep) list of victories; list of winners; (Mil etc) service record.

palmarote⁑ nm (Carib) yokel.

palmatoria nf (a) (de vela) candlestick. (b) (de castigo) cane.

palmazón* nm: estar en el ~ (CAm) to be broke*.

palmeado adj pata webbed.

palmear [1a] vi to clap.

palmense 1 adj of Las Palmas. 2 nmf native (o inhabitant) of Las Palmas; los ~s the people of Las Palmas.

palmera[1] nf, **palmero[1]** nm (And, Cono Sur, Méx) palm, palm tree; ~ datilera date-palm; estar en la ~* to be broke*.

palmero[2] 1 adj of the Island of Palma.

2 nm, **palmera[2]** nf native (o inhabitant) of the Island of Palma.

palmeta nf (palo) cane; (acto) caning, swish with a cane; ~ matamoscas fly swat.

palmetazo nm caning, swish with a cane; (fig) blow, slap in the face; light slap (of admonition).

palmillas nfpl: llevar a uno en ~ to treat sb with great consideration.

palmípedo adj web-footed.

palmista nmf (LAm) palmist.

palmiste nm palm kernel; palm oil.

palmita nf: tener (o llevar, traer) a uno en ~s (mimar) to spoil sb; (tratar con cuidado) to handle sb with kid gloves.

palmito nm (LAm) palm heart.

palmo nm (a) span; (fig) few inches, small amount; ~ a ~ inch by inch; con un ~ de lengua fuera with his tongue hanging out; avanzar ~ a ~ to go forward inch by inch; conocer el terreno ~ a ~ (o a ~s), tener medido el terreno a ~s to know every inch of the ground; crecer a ~s to shoot up; dejar a uno con un ~ de narices to disappoint sb greatly, leave sb very crestfallen; no hay un ~ de A a B there's hardly any distance (o difference) between A and B, there's nothing to choose between A and B; no levantaba un ~ del suelo cuando ... he was knee-high to a grasshopper when ...

(b) (CAm⁑) cunt⁑.

palmotear [1a] vi to clap, applaud.

palmoteo nm clapping, applause.

palo nm (a) (gen) stick; (Telec etc) post, pole; (porra) club; (de herramienta etc) handle, haft, shaft; (Taur*: banderilla) banderilla; (*: garrocha) spear; (Dep: de portería) post; (Dep Golf) club; (⁑) prick⁑; ~ ensebado greasy pole; ~ de escoba broomstick; ~ de golf golf club; ~ de tienda tent pole; de tal ~ tal astilla like father like son; ¡~ y tentetieso!* be tough with him (etc)!; la política del ~ y la zanahoria the policy of the stick and the carrot; estar hecho un ~ to be as thin as a rake; meter ~s en las ruedas (fig) to put a spanner in the works*.

(b) (Náut) mast; spar; ~ mayor mainmast; ~ de mesana mizzenmast; ~ de trinquete foremast; que cada ~ aguante su vela everyone must take what's coming to him.

(c) (Bot) stalk (of grape etc).

(d) (madera) wood; cuchara de ~ wooden spoon.

(e) (árbol: esp LAm) tree; ~ dulce liquorice root; ~ de hule (CAm) rubber tree; ~ de mango mango tree; ~ rosa (CAm) rosewood; ~ santo lignum vitae.

(f) (Tip: de letra) ascender, descender.

(g) (golpe) blow, hit (with a stick); andar a ~s to be always squabbling; dar un ~ a uno (fig) to criticize sb severely, take sb to task; los críticos le dieron un ~ a la obra the critics panned (o slated) the play; dar de ~s a uno, doblar (o matar) (o moler) a uno a ~s to give sb a beating; dar ~s de ciego to lash out wildly; es un ~ it's a blow, it's come as a shock.

(h) (Naipes) suit; ~ de(l) triunfo trump suit, trumps; asistir al ~, seguir el ~, servir del ~ to follow suit; cambiar de ~ (fig) to change tack.

(i) (LAm*) swig*, draught of liquor; a medio ~ (borracho) half-drunk; darse al ~ to take to drink; pegarse unos ~s to have a few drinks.

(j) a ~ seco bare; by itself, pure, with nothing else; vermut a ~ seco straight vermouth; beber a ~ seco to drink without having anything to eat; tiene el sueldo a ~ seco he has just his salary, he has his bare salary and nothing else.

(k) (⁑) dar un ~, pegar un ~ (robo) to do a job*; (mala pasada) to play a dirty trick.

(l) echar el (o un) ~⁑, ir de ~⁑ to have a screw⁑.

(m) (LAm) un ~ de casa a splendid house, a marvellous house; es un ~ de hombre he's a great guy; ~ de agua cloudburst, sudden downpour; cayó un ~ de agua there was a tremendous lot of rain*.

(n) ~ grueso (And*) big shot*; tirar el ~* to brag.

paloma nf (a) (Orn) dove, pigeon; ~ buscadora de blancos homing pigeon; ~ mensajera carrier pigeon; ~ torcaz wood-pigeon, ringdove; ¡palomita! darling!

(b) (Pol) dove; ~ sin hiel pet, lamb.

(c) (ejercicio) handstand.

(d) (CAm, Carib, Méx: cometa) kite.

(e) ~s (Náut) white caps (of waves), white horses.

palomar nm dovecot(e), pigeon loft.

palomear [1a] vt (a) (Carib) to swindle. (b) (And) enemigos to hunt down one by one; (tirar a matar) to shoot to kill, shoot dead; (matar a traición) to shoot down in cold blood.

palomilla nf (a) (Ent) moth; (esp) grain moth; (crisálida) nymph, chrysalis.

(b) (Téc: tuerca) wing nut.

(c) (Téc: escuadra) wall bracket, angle iron.

(d) (de caballo) back, backbone.

(e) (And, Cono Sur*: travieso) urchin, ragamuffin; (CAm, Cono Sur, Méx*: de niños) mob of kids*; (*: pandilla) crowd of layabouts, band of hooligans.

palomino 1 adj (And, Cono Sur, Méx) caballo palomino; (blanco) white. 2 nm (a) (Orn) young pigeon. (b) (And, Cono Sur, Méx) palomino (horse); (blanco) white horse. (c) (excremento) pigeon droppings.

palomita nf (a) (Dep) full-length dive.

(b) (Méx) tick.

palomitas nfpl popcorn.

palomo 1 adj (And, Cono Sur, Méx) = palomino. 2 nm (cock) pigeon; ~ de arcilla clay pigeon.

palotada nf: no dar ~ (no trabajar) not to do a stroke of work; (no hacer nada) to do nothing; (hacerlo mal) to get nothing right.

palote nm (a) (Mús) drumstick. (b) (en escritura) downstroke; pothook. (c) (Carib, Cono Sur Culin) rolling-pin; (Cono Sur*: persona) beanpole*.

palotear [1a] vi to bicker, wrangle.

paloteo nm bickering, wrangling.

palpable adj palpable; (fig) tangible, palpable; concrete.

palpamiento nm (LAm) frisking, body-search.

palpar [1a] 1 vt (a) (gen) to touch, feel; (amorosamente) to feel, caress, fondle; (esp LAm) sospechoso to frisk, search for weapons; muro etc to feel one's way along, grope one's way past.

(b) (fig) to feel; to appreciate, understand; ahora palpa las consecuencias now he's really feeling the consequences; ya palparás lo que es esto one day you'll really understand all this.

2 palparse vr (fig) to be felt; se palpaba el descontento you could feel the restlessness; hay una enemistad que se palpa you can feel the hostility, there is a tangible hostility.

palpitación nf palpitation, throb(bing), beat(ing); quiver(ing); flutter(ing).

palpitante adj (a) (gen) palpitating, (corazón) throbbing. (b) (fig) interés, cuestión burning.

palpitar [1a] vi (a) (gen) to palpitate; (corazón) to throb, beat; (nerviosamente) to quiver; to flutter.

(b) (fig) to throb; en la poesía palpita la emoción the poem throbs with emotion.

(c) (And, Cono Sur) me palpita I have a hunch; ya me palpitaba el fracaso I had a hunch it would be a failure.

palpite nm, **pálpito** nm hunch, presentiment; (Esp) me da el ~ de que ..., tengo el ~ de que ... I have a hunch that ...

palquista‡ *nm* cat burglar.
palta *nf* (*Cono Sur*) avocado pear.
palto *nm* (*Sono Sur*) avocado tree.
paltó *nm* (*And, CAm, Carib*) jacket.
palúdico *adj* marshy; (*Med*) malarial.
paludismo *nm* malaria.
palurdo 1 *adj* rustic; coarse, uncouth. **2** *nm* rustic, yokel, hick (*US*); (*pey*) lout.
palustre1 *nm* (*Téc*) trowel.
palustre2 *adj* marsh (*atr*); marshy.
palla *nf* (*And Hist*) Inca princess.
pallador *nm* (*LAm*) *etc* = **payador** *etc*.
pallar1 [1a] *vt* (*Min*) to extract; (*Agr*) to glean.
pallar2 *nm* (*And, Cono Sur*) Lima bean.
pallasca *nf* (*And, Cono Sur*), **pallaso** *nm* (*And, Cono Sur*) mattress.
pamela *nf* picture hat, sun hat.
pamema *nf* (**a**) (*dicho etc*) silly thing, stupid remark (*etc*); **~s** nonsense, humbug; **¡déjate de ~s!** stop your nonsense.
(**b**) (*bagatela*) triviality, trifle.
(**c**) **~s** (*halagos*) flattery; coaxing, wheedling.
(**d**) **~s** (*quejas etc*) fuss; **¡déjate de ~s!** stop your fussing! that's enough of that!
pampa1 *nf* (**a**) (*Geog*) pampa(s), prairie; **la P~** the Pampas.
(**b**) (*Cono Sur*) (*Min*) region of nitrate deposits; (*descampado*) open area on the outskirts of a town.
(**c**) (*And*: *en la sierra*) high grassy plateau.
(**d**) **a** (*o* **en**) **la ~** (*LAm**: *al aire libre*) in the open; **en ~** (*LAm**: *desnudo*) in the nude, with nothing on; **estar en ~ y la vía** (*Cono Sur**) to be flat broke*; **quedarse en ~** (*Cono Sur**) to come to nothing, fall through.
pampa2 1 *adj* (**a**) (*And, Cono Sur**) *negocio* shady, dishonest.
(**b**) (*And*: *endeble*) weak, feeble.
2 *nmf* (*Cono Sur*) pampean Indian.
3 *nm* (*Ling*) language of the pampean Indians.
pámpana *nf* vine leaf; **zurrar la ~ a uno** (*Esp**) to give sb a hiding*.
pámpano *nm* vine shoot, vine tendril.
pampeano *adj* of (*o* from) the pampas.
pampear1 [1a] *vi* (*Cono Sur*) to travel over the pampas.
pampear2 [1a] *vt* (*And*) (**a**) (*tocar*) to tap, pat (on the shoulder). (**b**) *masa* to roll out.
pampero (*LAm*) **1** *adj* of (*o* from) the pampas. **2** *nm* (**a**) (*persona*) inhabitant of the pampas, plainsman. (**b**) (*viento*) strong wind (*blowing over the pampas from the Andes*).
pampinflar‡ [1a] *vt*: **¡me la pampinflas!** you stupid git!‡
pampino 1 *adj* (*LAm*) of (*o* from) the pampas. **2** *nm*, **pampina** *nf* (*Cono Sur*) inhabitant of the Chilean pampas.
pamplina *nf* (**a**) (*Bot*) chickweed.
(**b**) (*: *tontería*) silly remark; **~s** (*disparates*) nonsense; (*lío*) fuss; (*: *jabón*) soft soap*; **¡~s!** rubbish!; **sin más ~s** without any more beating about the bush; **esas son ~s** that's a load of rubbish*; **no me venga Vd con ~s** don't come to me with that soft soap*.
pamplinero *adj* (**a**) (*tonto*) silly, nonsensical. (**b**) (*aspaventero*) fussy, emotional, given to making a great fuss. (**c**) (*engreído*) vain.
pamplonada *nf* (*LAm*) triviality; silly thing, piece of nonsense.
pamplonés *adj y nm*, **pamplonesa** *nf* = **pamplonica**.
pamplonica 1 *adj* of Pamplona. **2** *nmf* native (*o* inhabitant) of Pamplona; **los ~s** the people of Pamplona.
pampon *nm* (*And*) open space, open ground.
pamporcino *nm* cyclamen.
pan *nm* (**a**) (*gen*) bread; (*un ~*) loaf; (*fig*) bread; **~ blanco, ~ candeal, ~ de flor** white bread; **~ casero** home-made bread; **~ cenceño** unleavened bread; **~ de centeno** rye bread; **~ integral** wholemeal bread; **~ de molde** standard loaf; **~ moreno** brown bread; **el ~ nuestro de cada día** our daily bread; **es el ~ nuestro de cada día** (*fig*) it's a daily event, it happens every day; it's commonplace; **estar a ~ y agua** to be on (*o* condemned to a diet of) bread and water; **ganarse el ~** to earn one's living.
(**b**) (*Bot*) wheat; **~es** (*fig*) crops, harvest; **año de mucho ~** good year for wheat, year of a heavy wheat crop; **tierras de ~ llevar** arable land, wheat-growing land.
(**c**) **~ de azúcar** sugar loaf; **~ de hierba** turf, sod; **~ de higos** block of dried figs; **~ de jabón** bar of soap, cake of soap.
(**d**) (*Téc*) gold leaf, silver leaf.
(**e**) (*locuciones*) **eso es ~ comido** it's dead easy; **contigo ~ y cebolla** (with you I'd gladly have) love in a cottage; **con su ~ se lo coma** that's his look-out, it's his funeral*, let him get on with it; **echar ~es** (*And, Cono Sur*) to boast, brag; **llamar al ~ ~ y al vino vino** to call a spade a spade; **venderse como ~ bendito** to sell like hot cakes.
pan... *pref* pan..., *p.ej.* **panasiático** pan-Asiatic.
pana1 *nf* (*paño*) velveteen, corduroy.
pana2 *nf* (*And Aut*) breakdown; **tener una ~** to break down.
pana3 *nf* (*Cono Sur*) liver; (*) guts, courage; **helársele a uno la ~** (*Cono Sur*) to lose one's nerve; **tirar ~s** (*And**) to put on airs.
pana4 *nmf* (*Carib*) pal*, buddy.
panacea *nf* panacea, cure-all.
panaché *nm* mixed salad.
panadería *nf* (*tahona*) bakery, bakehouse; (*tienda*) baker's (shop).
panadero *nm* baker.
panadizo *nm* (*Med*) whitlow.
panal *nm* honeycomb.
Panamá *nm* Panama.
panamá *nm* panama hat.
panameñismo *nm* word (*o* phrase *etc*) peculiar to Panama.
panameño, -a *adj, nm/f* Panamanian.
panamericanismo *nm* Pan-Americanism.
panamericano 1 *adj* Pan-American. **2** *nf*: **la Panamericana** the Pan-American highway.
panamitos *nmpl*, **panamos** *nmpl* (*And*) beans; (*fig*) food, daily bread.
panca *nf* (*And*) dry leaf of maize.
pancarta *nf* placard, banner.
pancista 1 *adj* unprincipled. **2** *nmf* trimmer, opportunist.
pancita *nf* (*Méx Culin*) tripe.
pancito *nm* (*Méx*) lump of sugar.
páncreas *nm* pancreas.
pancreático *adj* pancreatic.
pancromático *adj* panchromatic.
pancha* *nf* = **panza**.
pancho1 1 *adj* (**a**) (*Cono Sur*) brown, tan. (**b**) (*And, Carib*) broad and flat; squat; **ni tan ~ ni tan ancho** (*Carib‡*) neither one thing nor the other. **2** *nm* (*Cono Sur Culin*) hot dog.
pancho2 *adj* calm, unruffled; **estar tan ~** (*Cono Sur, Esp*) to remain perfectly calm, not turn a hair.
pancho3 *nm* (*pez*) young sea-bream.
Pancho *nm forma familiar de* **Francisco**.
panda1 *nmf* (*Zool*) panda.
panda2 *nf* (*Carib*) = **pandeo**.
panda3* *nf* = **pandilla**.
pandear [1a] *vi y* **pandearse** *vr* to bend, warp; to sag; to bulge.
pandemonio *nm*, **pandemónium** *nm* pandemonium; **fue el ~*** all hell broke loose, there was pandemonium.
pandeo *nm* bend; sag(ging); bulge, bulging.
pandereta *nf* tambourine; **zumbar la ~ a uno** (*Esp**) to tan sb's hide*.
panderetear [1a] *vi* to play the tambourine.
pandero *nm* (**a**) (*Mús*) tambourine. (**b**) (*cometa*) kite. (**c**) (*: *tonto*) idiot. (**d**) (*: *culo*) backside.
pandibó‡ *nm* slammer‡, prison.
pandilla *nf* set, group; (*pey*) clique, coterie, set; bunch, load; (*criminal etc*) gang.
pandillero *nm* member of a clique (*etc*); (*LAm*) gangster.
pando *adj* (**a**) *viga etc* sagging; *muro* bulging; *madera* warped. (**b**) *plato* shallow; flat. (**c**) *río, persona* slow. (**d**) (*CAm*) (*oprimido*) oppressed; (*: *saciado*) full (up). (**e**) (*CAm, Méx*: *de hombros*) round-shouldered.
Pandora *nf*: **la caja de ~** Pandora's box.
pandorga *nf* (**a**) (*gorda*) fat woman. (**b**) (*cometa*) kite. (**c**) (*And**) (*molestia*) bother, nuisance; (*mentira*) lie. (**d**) (*Méx**) (*broma*) practical joke; (*estudiantil*) student prank.
pandorgo *adj* (**a**) (*Méx*) dim, stupid. (**b**) (*Carib*) fat and slow-moving.
pane *nm* (*And Aut*) breakdown.
panear *vi* (*And, Cono Sur*) to boast, show off.
panecillo *nm* roll.
panegírico *nm* panegyric.
panel *nm* (**a**) (*madera etc*) panel; **~es** (*Arquit*) panelling; **~ explicativo** display panel; **~ de información de vuelos** flight information board; **~ solar** solar panel. (**b**) **~ de instrumentos** (*Aut etc*) dashboard; **~ de mandos** (*Aer etc*) controls. (**c**) (*jurado*) panel; **~ de audiencia** TV viewers' panel.
panela *nf* (**a**) (*LAm Culin*) brown sugar, coarse sugar;

sugar loaf.
(**b**) (*Méx*: *sombrero*) straw hat.
(**c**) (*And, Méx**) (*pesado*) bore, drag; (*zalamero*) creep⁑.

panelería *nf* panelling.
panera *nf* bread basket.
pánfilo *adj* (**a**) (*tonto*) simple, gullible; stupid. (**b**) (*And*) pale, discoloured.
panfletario *adj estilo* violent, highly-coloured; *propaganda* cheap, demagogic.
panfletista *nmf* pamphleteer; satirist, lampoonist.
panfleto *nm* pamphlet; (*pey*) satire, lampoon, scandal sheet.
panga *nf* (*CAm, Méx*: *lancha*) barge, lighter; (*transbordador*) ferry(boat).
pangolín *nm* scaly anteater.
paniaguado *nm* (*Pol etc*) henchman; protégé.
paniaguarse [1i] *vr* (*Méx*) to become friends, pal up*.
pánico 1 *adj* panic. **2** *nm* (**a**) panic, fear; **el ~ comprador** panic buying; **yo le tengo un ~ tremendo*** I'm scared stiff of him. (**b**) **de ~* = de miedo.**
paniego *adj*: **tierra paniega** cornland.
panificable *adj*: **granos ~s** bread grains.
panificadora *nf* bakery.
panil *nm* (*Cono Sur*) celery.
panizo *nm* (**a**) (*Bot*) millet; maize. (**b**) (*Cono Sur*) mineral deposit; (*fig*) treasure, gem, valuable object; (*Com*) profitable deal, gold mine.
panocha *nf*, **panoja** *nf* (**a**) (*Bot*) corncob, ear of maize; ear of wheat (*etc*).
(**b**) (*Méx*) (*azúcar*) unrefined brown sugar; (*dulce*) brown sugar candy.
(**c**) (*And, CAm, Cono Sur*) large pancake of maize and cheese.
(**d**) (*: *dinero*) brass*, money.
(**e**) (*Méx*⁑) cunt⁑.
panocho 1 *adj* Murcian, of Murcia. **2** *nm*, **panocha** *nf* Murcian. **3** *nm* (*Ling*) Murcian dialect.
panoli(s)* *nmf, pl* **panolis** (*Esp*) chump*, idiot.
panoplia *nf* panoply; collection of arms.
panorama *nm* panorama (*t fig*); vista, view, scene; (*perspectiva*) outlook, prospect; (*Arte, Fot*) view; **el ~ actual político** the present political scene.
panorámica *nf* general view, survey.
panorámico *adj* panoramic; **punto ~** viewpoint, vantage point.
panoramizar [1f] *vti* (*Cine*) to pan.
panqué *nm* (*CAm, Carib*), **panqueque** *nm* (*LAm*) pancake.
panquequera *nf* pancake iron.
panquequería *nf* (*LAm*) pancake house.
pantaleta *nf* (*LAm*) bloomers, drawers; panties.
pantalón *nm*, **pantalones** *nmpl* (**a**) (*de hombre*) trousers, pants (*US*); (*de mujer*: *exterior*) slacks, trousers, (*interior*) knickers; **pantalones cortos** shorts; **pantalones de esquí** ski pants; **~ de montar** riding breeches; **~ pitillo** drainpipe trousers; **pantalones tejanos, pantalones vaqueros** jeans; **bajarse los pantalones** (*Esp*⁑) to throw in the sponge; **no caber en los pantalones** to get too big for one's boots; **es ella la que lleva los pantalones*** she's the one who wears the trousers; **llevar los pantalones bien puestos** (*Carib**) to have guts.
(**b**) (*And*) man, male.
(**c**) (*Carib*) guts, courage.
pantalla *nf* (**a**) (*biombo*) screen; (*de lámpara*) shade, lampshade.
(**b**) (*Cine etc*) screen; **~ acústica** loudspeaker; **~ grande** big screen; **~ plana** flat screen; **~ de radar** radar screen; **~ de rayos** (*en aeropuerto*) X-ray security apparatus; **~ de televisión** television screen; **~ de vídeo** video screen; **los personajes de la ~** screen personalities; **la pequeña ~** the small screen, the TV screen; **llevar una historia a la ~** to film a story.
(**c**) (*Inform*) screen, display; **~ de ayuda** help screen; **~ de cristal líquido** liquid crystal display; **~ de plasma** plasma panel; **~ táctil** touch-sensitive screen.
(**d**) (*Cono Sur*: *abanico*) fan.
(**e**) (*fig*) blind, pretext; decoy; **hacer la ~** (*Dep*) to form the wall; **servir de ~ a** to be a blind for.
(**f**) (*LAm*: *esbirro*) henchman, bodyguard.
(**g**) (*CAm*) large mirror.
pantanal *nm* marshland.
pantano *nm* (**a**) (*natural*) marsh, swamp, bog; wetland; (*artificial*) reservoir, dam.
(**b**) (*) jam*, fix*, difficulty; **salir de un ~** to get out of a jam*.
pantanoso *adj* (**a**) (*lit*) marshy, swampy, boggy. (**b**) (*fig*) difficult, problematic.
panteísmo *nm* pantheism.
panteísta 1 *adj* pantheistic. **2** *nmf* pantheist.
panteón *nm* (**a**) (*gen*) pantheon; **~ familiar** family vault; **el ~ de los reyes** the burial place of the royal family, the pantheon of the kings.
(**b**) (*Andalucía, LAm*: *cementerio*) cemetery.
(**c**) (*Cono Sur*) ore, mineral.
panteonero *nm* (*LAm*) gravedigger.
pantera *nf* (**a**) (*Zool*) panther; (*Carib*) jaguar, ocelot. (**b**) (*Méx*) (*matón*) heavy*; (*atrevido*) risk taker.
pantimedias *nfpl* (*Méx*) panty-hose.
pantis *nmpl* tights, panty-hose.
pantógrafo *nm* pantograph.
pantomima *nf* pantomime, dumb show.
pantoque *nm* (*Náut*) bilge; **agua de ~** bilge water.
pantorra* *nf* (*Anat*) (fat) calf.
pantorrilla *nf* (**a**) (*Anat*) calf (of the leg). (**b**) (*And*) vanity.
pantorrilludo *adj* (**a**) (*de piernas gordas*) fat in the leg, thick-calved.
(**b**) (*And**: *vanidoso*) vain.
pantufla *nf*, **pantuflo** *nm* slipper.
panty *nm, pl* **pantys, panties** (*Esp*: *medias*) tights, panty-hose; (*LAm*: *bragas*) panties.
panucho *nm* (*Méx*) stuffed tortilla.
panudo* (*And*) **1** *adj* boastful, bragging. **2** *nm*, **panuda** *nf* loudmouth*.
panul *nm* (*Cono Sur*) celery.
panza *nf* belly; (*abultado*) belly, paunch; **~ de burro** (*Alpinismo*) overhang; **~ mojada** (*Méx*) wetback (*US*); **estrellarse de ~** to do a belly-flop, make a pancake landing.
panzada* *nf* (**a**) (*hartazgo*) bellyful; **una ~ de** (*fig*) a lot of, a bellyful of; **darse una ~⁑, darse las grandes ~s⁑** to have a blow-out⁑.
(**b**) (*golpe*) blow in the belly.
panzazo *nm* (**a**) (*And, Cono Sur*) blow in the belly.
(**b**) (*Méx*) = **panzada** (**a**).
(**c**) **pasar de ~** (*LAm*⁑) to get through by the skin of one's teeth.
panzón *adj*, **panzudo** *adj* paunchy, fat, potbellied.
pañal *nm* (**a**) (*de bebé*) nappy, diaper (*US*); (*de camisa*) shirttail; **~ desechable** disposable nappy.
(**b**) **~es** baby clothes; (*fig*) early stages, infancy; **de humildes ~es** of humble origins; **criarse en buenos ~es** to be born with a silver spoon in one's mouth; **esto ha dejado en ~es a los rivales** this has left the competition way behind; **estar todavía en ~es** (*persona*) to be very innocent still; (*ciencia, técnica*) to be in its infancy; **yo de informática estoy en ~es** I'm completely in the dark about computing, I know nothing about computing.
pañería *nf* (*géneros*) drapery; (*tienda*) draper's (shop), dry-goods store (*US*), clothier's (shop).
pañero, -a *nm/f* draper, dry-goods dealer (*US*), clothier.
pañete *nm* (**a**) (*tela*) light cloth. (**b**) **~s** shorts, trunks. (**c**) (*And*) coat of fine plaster. (**d**) (*Cono Sur*) horse blanket.
pañí[1] *nm* (*Cono Sur*) sun trap.
pañí[2]⁑ *nf*: **dar la ~** to give a tip-off, tip the wink*.
pañito *nm* (*Esp*) table runner; traycloth.
paño *nm* (**a**) (*gen*) cloth; stuff, material; **el buen ~ en el arca se vende** good wine needs no bush; **le conozco el ~** I know his sort, I know all about him, I recognize the type.
(**b**) (*un ~*) (piece of) cloth; (*trapo*) duster, rag, cleaning cloth; **~ de altar** altar cloth; **~s calientes, ~s tibios** (*LAm fig*) half-measures, ineffective remedies; **no andarse con ~s calientes** to pull no punches, not go in for half-measures; **~ de cocina** dishcloth; **~ higiénico** (*Esp*) sanitary towel, sanitary napkin (*US*); **~ de lágrimas** (*fig*) standby, consolation; **~ de manos** towel; **~ mortuorio** pall; **~ de los platos, ~ de secar** tea towel; **jugar a dos ~s** to play a double game.
(**c**) (*Cos*) piece of cloth, width; panel.
(**d**) **~s** (*ropa*) clothes; (*Arte*) drapes; **~s menores** underclothes, undies*.
(**e**) **al ~** (*Teat*) offstage.
(**f**) (*Arquit*) stretch, length (*of wall*).
(**g**) (*en cristal etc*) mist, cloud, cloudiness; (*en diamante*) flaw.
(**h**) (*Carib*: *red*) fishing net.
(**i**) (*And*: *tierra*) plot of land.
pañol *nm* (*Náut*) store, storeroom; **~ del agua** water store; **~ del carbón** coal bunker.

pañoleta *nf* fichu.

pañolón *nm* shawl.

pañuelo *nm* **(a)** (*gen*) handkerchief; (*de cabeza*) scarf, headscarf, shawl; ~ **de cuello** cravate; ~ **de papel** paper handkerchief. **(b)** (‡†: *billete*) 100-peseta note.

papa¹ *nm* (*Ecl*) pope; ~ **negro** black pope (*General of the Jesuits*).

papa² *nf* **(a)** (*esp LAm*) potato; **~s colchas** (*CAm*) crisps; **echar las ~s** (*Esp**) to be sick; **cuando las ~s queman** (*Cono Sur*) when things hot up.

(b) (*) **ni ~** not a blind thing*; **no entiendo ni ~** I don't understand a word; **no oyó ni ~** she didn't hear a thing.

(c) (*Cono Sur**) bash*, blow.

(d) (*Carib**) soft job*, plum.

(e) (*Méx*: *sopa*) porridge, gruel; (*Cono Sur*) baby food.

(f) (*Méx**: *mentira*) lie, fib; (*fraude*) hoax.

papa³ *adj invar* (*Cono Sur**) jolly good*, first-rate.

papá *nm* **(a)** (*) dad*, daddy*, papa, pop* (*US*); **P~ Noel** Father Christmas.

(b) (*LAm*) father; **~s** mother and father, parents.

(c) ~ **grande** (*LAm**) grandfather, grandpa*.

papacote (*CAm*) **1** *nm* (*cometa*) kite. **2** *nmf* (*fig*) bigwig, big shot*.

papachar* [1a] *vt* (*Méx*) (*sobar*) to stroke; (*mimar*) to spoil.

papachos *nmpl* (*Méx*) cuddles; caresses.

papada *nf* (*de persona*) double chin; (*de animal*) dewlap.

papadeno‡ *nm* (*Carib*) Jehovah's Witness.

papadilla *nf* dewlap.

papado *nm* papacy.

papagayo *nm* **(a)** (*Orn*) parrot.

(b) (*fig*) parrot; chatterbox; person who repeats parrot fashion.

(c) (*Carib, Méx*: *cometa*) large kite.

(d) (*And*: *bacinilla*) bedpan.

papal¹ *adj* (*Ecl*) papal.

papal² *nm* (*LAm*) potato field.

papalina *nf* **(a)** (*gorra*) cap with earflaps; bonnet; mobcap. **(b)** (*: *juerga*) binge*; **coger una ~** to get tight*. **(c)** (*CAm Culin*) crisps (*Brit*), potato chips (*US*).

papalón* *nm* (*Méx*) rat*, swine*.

papalote *nm* (*LAm*) (*cometa*) kite; (*molino: de niño*) windmill.

papalotear [1a] *vi* (*CAm, Méx**: *vagabundear*) to wander about; (*Méx**: *agonizar*) to give one's last gasp.

papamoscas *nm invar* **(a)** (*Orn*) flycatcher. **(b)** = **papanatas.**

papamóvil *nm* popemobile.

papanatas* *nm invar* simpleton, sucker‡.

papanatería *nf*, **papanatismo** *nm* gullibility, simple-mindedness.

papandujo *adj* (*Esp*) soft, overripe.

papapa *nf* (*CAm*) stupidity.

papar [1a] **1** *vt* (*tragar*) to swallow, gulp (down).

2 paparse* *vr* **(a)** ~ **algo** to eat sth up, scoff sth*; **se lo papó todo** he scoffed the lot*; **¡pápate ésa!** (*Esp*) put that in your pipe and smoke it!*

(b) (‡: *recibir un golpe*) to get a sudden knock, be hit real hard*.

paparazzo *nm, pl* **paparazzi** intrusive news photographer.

paparrucha *nf* **(a)** (*disparate*) piece of nonsense, silly thing. **(b)** (*chapuza*) botch, worthless object. **(c)** (*truco*) hoax.

paparruta *nmf* (*Cono Sur*) humbug.

paparulo* *nm* (*Cono Sur*) sucker‡.

papas *nfpl* pap, mushy food; (‡) grub‡.

papaya *nf* **(a)** (*LAm Bot*) papaya, pawpaw. **(b)** (*Carib**‡) cunt*‡.

papayo *nm* (*LAm*) papaya (tree), pawpaw (tree).

papear‡ [1a] *vi* to eat, scoff*.

papel *nm* **(a)** (*gen*) paper; ~ **(de) aluminio** tinfoil, (*Culin*) aluminium foil; ~ **de arroz** rice paper; ~ **atrapamoscas** flypaper; ~ **biblia,** ~ **de China** India paper; ~ **de calcar,** ~ **de calco** tracing-paper; ~ **carbón** carbon paper, carbon; ~ **de cartas** notepaper, stationery; ~ **cel(l)o** adhesive tape; ~ **craft** (*CAm, Méx*) waxed paper; ~ **cuadriculado** squared paper; ~ **charol** shiny wrapping paper; ~ **de desecho** waste paper; ~ **de embalar,** ~ **de envolver** brown paper, wrapping paper; ~ **de empapelar** wallpaper; ~ **encerado** wax(ed) paper; ~ **engomado** gummed paper; ~ **de estaño** tinfoil; ~ **de estraza** brown paper, wrapping paper; ~ **estucado** art paper; ~ **de excusado** toilet-paper; ~ **de filtro** filter paper; ~ **de fumar** cigarette-paper; **entre A y B no cabía un ~ de fumar** (*Esp*) you couldn't have got a razor's edge between them; **yo no me lo cojo con ~ de fumar** (*Esp*) I wouldn't touch it with a bargepole; ~ **de grasa** greaseproof paper; ~ **higiénico** toilet-paper; ~ **de lija** sandpaper; ~ **madera** (*Cono Sur*) cardboard; ~ **de mano** handmade paper; ~ **para máquinas de escribir** typing paper; ~ **matamoscas** flypaper; ~ **mojado** (*fig*) scrap of paper, worthless bit of paper; ~ **de oficio** (*LAm*) official foolscap paper; ~ **ondulado** corrugated paper; ~ **de paja de arroz** rice paper; ~ **de paredes,** ~ **pintado** wallpaper; ~ **pautado** ruled paper; ~ **de plata** silver paper; ~ **prensa** newsprint; ~ **reciclado** recycled paper; ~ **de regalo** gift-wrap paper; ~ **sanitario** (*CAm*) toilet-paper; ~ **secante** blotting-paper; blotter; ~ **(de) seda** tissue paper; ~ **sellado** stamped paper; ~ **de tina** handmade paper; ~ **(de) tornasol** litmus paper; ~ **transparente** tracing-paper; ~ **vitela** vellum paper; **sobre el ~** (*fig*) on paper, in theory.

(b) (*un ~*) piece of paper, sheet (of paper); **~es** papers; **los ~es** (*prensa*) the papers, the newspapers; ~ **usado, ~es usados, ~es viejos** waste paper.

(c) (*oficial*) **~es** papers, documents; identification papers; **los ~es, por favor** your papers, please; **tiene los ~es en regla** his papers are in order.

(d) (*Fin*: *billetes*) ~ **moneda** paper money, banknotes; **mil dólares en ~** a thousand dollars in notes.

(e) (*Fin*: *valores*) stocks and shares; ~ **del Estado** government bonds.

(f) (*Fin, Teat etc*: *recaudación*) takings, receipts.

(g) (*Fin*‡) 1000-peseta note; (*And*) one-peso note.

(h) (*LAm*) bag.

(i) (*Cine, Teat etc*) part, role; ~ **estelar** star part; **desempeñar un ~** (*fig*), **hacer un ~** to play a part; **el ~ del gobierno en este asunto** the government's role in this matter; **hacer buen** (*o* **mal**) **~** to make a good (*o* bad) impression; **hizo el ~ de Cleopatra** she played the part of Cleopatra; **el equipo hizo un buen ~ en el torneo** the team did well in the tournament, the team put up a good show in the tournament; **hacer el ~ de** (*fig*) to act as, undertake the job of; **tuvo que desempeñar un ~ secundario** he had to play second fiddle, he had to take a minor role.

papela *nf* **(a)** (*Esp**) paper, document; identity card, ID. **(b)** (‡: *droga*) = **papelina.**

papelada *nf* (*CAm*) farce, pretence, charade.

papelamen* *nm* papers, masses of paper.

papelear [1a] *vi* **(a)** (*revolver papeles*) to rummage through papers. **(b)** (*atraer la atención*) to make a splash, draw attention to o.s.

papeleo *nm* (*trámites*) paperwork; (*pey*) red tape.

papelera *nf* **(a)** (*para basura*) litter bin; wastepaper basket. **(b)** (*mesa*) desk. **(c)** (*fábrica*) paper-mill.

papelería *nf* **(a)** (*papel etc para correspondencia*) stationery. **(b)** (*tienda*) stationer's (shop). **(c)** (*montón*) mass of papers, heap of papers; (*lío*) sheaf of papers.

papelerío *nm* (*LAm*) = **papelería (c).**

papelero 1 *adj* (*LAm*) paper (*atr*). **2** *nm* **(a)** (*vendedor*) stationer; (*fabricante*) paper manufacturer. **(b)** (*Méx*) paper-boy. **(c)** (*Cono Sur*) ridiculous person.

papeleta *nf* **(a)** (*trozo de papel*) slip of paper, bit of paper; (*ficha*) card, index card, file card; (*Pol*) voting paper, ballot paper; (*CAm*) visiting card, calling card (*US*); ~ **de empeño** pawn ticket; ~ **de examen** (*Escol*) (examination) report; **¡vaya ~!** this is a tough one! **(b)** (*LAm*) bag. **(c)** (*And**: *multa*) fine.

papelillo *nm* cigarette; **~s** confetti.

papelina *nf* fold of paper (*containing drug*).

papelista *nmf* (*Carib, Cono Sur*) = **picapleitos.**

papelito *nm* **(a)** (*trozo de papel*) slip of paper, bit of paper. **(b)** (*Teat etc*) minor role, bit part.

papelón *nm* **(a)** (*papel usado*) (piece of) wastepaper; (*cartulina*) pasteboard.

(b) (*impostor*) impostor; (*engreído*) bluffer, show-off*.

(c) (*Teat etc*) leading role, big part; **hacer un ~** to do something ridiculous, make oneself a laughing-stock.

(d) (*And, Carib*) sugar loaf.

papelonero *adj* (*Cono Sur*) ridiculous.

papelote *nm*, **papelucho** *nm* useless bit of paper; worthless document; (*Liter*) trashy piece of writing.

papeo‡ *nm* (*comida*) grub‡, food; (*el comer*) eating.

papera *nf* goitre; (*t* **~s**) mumps.

papero 1 *adj* **(a)** (*LAm*) potato (*atr*). **(b)** (*Méx*) lying, deceitful. **2** *nm* (*Agr*) potato grower; (*Com*) potato dealer.

papi* *nm* dad*, daddy*.

papilla *nf* **(a)** (*de bebé*) baby food. **(b)** (*fig*) guile, deceit. **(c)** **estar hecho ~** (*roto*) to be smashed to pieces (*o* to pulp); (*cansado*) to be dog-tired.

papillote *nm* buttered paper, greased paper.
papira‡ *nf* letter.
papiro *nm* papyrus.
pápiro* *nm* (big) banknote; **~s** (*fig*) brass*, cash; **tener afán de ~s** to be greedy for money.
papiroflexia *nf* origami.
papirotazo *nm*, **papirote** *nm* flick.
papismo *nm* (*pey*) papism (*pey*), popery (*pey*).
papista 1 *adj* papist, popish (*pey*); **es más ~ que el papa** he's more Catholic than the pope. **2** *nmf* papist.
papo *nm* (**a**) (*Orn*) crop; (*Zool*) dewlap; (*de persona*) jowl, double chin; **estar de ~ de mona** (*Esp**) to be first-rate; **pasarlo de ~ de mona** (*Esp**) to have a super time*. (**b**) (*Med*) goitre. (**c**) (*Esp***) cunt**.
paprika *nf* paprika.
papudo *adj persona* with a heavy jowl, double-chinned; (*Zool*) dewlapped.
papujado *adj* swollen, puffed up.
papujo *adj* (**a**) (*Méx*: *hinchado*) swollen, puffed up; (*And*) fat-cheeked. (**b**) (*Méx*: *enfermizo*) wan, sickly, anaemic.
paquebote *nm* packet boat, packet.
paquero *nm* (*Méx*) swindler, crook.
paquete 1 *nm* (**a**) (*Correos*) packet, parcel, package; **~ de cigarrillos** (*Esp*) packet (*o* pack *US*) of cigarettes; **en un ~ discreto** under plain cover; **~ de flores** bunch of flowers; **~ de muestra** sample pack; **~s postales** (*como servicio*) parcel post; **dejar a una con el ~*** to put a girl in the family way; **ir** (*o* **viajar**) **de ~*** (*en moto*) to ride pillion; (*fig, con amantes*) to play gooseberry; **soltar el ~*** to give birth.
(**b**) (*fig*) package; **~ de acciones, ~ accionarial** holding of shares; **~ de beneficios** benefits package; **~ de medidas económicas** package of financial measures.
(**c**) (*: *majo*) dandy; **estar hecho un ~** to be all dressed up, be dressed in style.
(**d**) **meter un ~ a uno** (*Mil**) to put sb on a charge.
(**e**) (*Inform*) package; **~ de aplicaciones** application package; **~ estadístico** statistical package; **~ integrado** integrated package.
(**f**) (‡) equipment‡, naughty bits‡; **marcar ~** to wear very tight trousers.
(**g**) (*Med‡*) dose (of VD)‡.
(**h**) (*LAm*: *cosa pesada*) nuisance, bore; **¡menudo ~!, ¡vaya ~!** what a bore!
(**i**) **darse ~** (*CAm, Méx*) to give o.s. airs.
(**j**) (*Méx*: *asunto*) tough job, hard one.
(**k**) (*Cono Sur‡*) queer‡, poof‡.
(**l**) (*LAm*: *vacaciones*) package holiday.
(**m**) (*Náut*) packet boat, packet.
2 *adj invar* (*LAm*) chic, elegant, spruce; **estar de a ~** to look chic.
paquetear [1a] *vi* (*LAm*) to be very smart.
paquete-bomba *nm*, *pl* **paquetes-bomba** parcel-bomb.
paquetería *nf* (**a**) (*Cono Sur**) **¡qué ~!** how elegant!; **se puso toda su ~** she put on her Sunday best; **¡vaya ~ que lleva!*** she's wearing everything but the kitchen sink*! (**b**) (*LAm Com*) parcels; **servicio de ~** parcel service.
paquetero* *nm* card sharper.
paquetudo* *adj* (*LAm*) (**a**) = **paquete 2**. (**b**) (*orgulloso*) stuck-up*.
paquidermo *nm* pachyderm.
paquistaní = **pakistaní**.
Paquita *nf forma familiar de* **Francisca**.
Paquito *nm forma familiar de* **Francisco**.
par 1 *adj* like, equal; *número* even.
2 *nm* (**a**) (*dos*) pair; couple; **un ~ de guantes** a pair of gloves; **por un ~ de dólares** for a couple of dollars; **solamente un ~ de veces** only a couple of times; **a ~es** in pairs, in twos; **un discurso a tres ~es*** a very lengthy speech.
(**b**) (*igual*) equal; **al ~** equally; together, jointly; **es útil a ~ que** (*o* **y al ~**) **divertido** it is both useful and amusing, it is useful and amusing at the same time; **está al ~ de los mejores** it is on a level with the best, it's up to the standard of the best; **caminar al ~ de** to walk abreast of; **sin ~** matchless, peerless; unparalleled; **no tener ~** to have no parallel, be unique.
(**c**) (*Mat*) even number; **~es o nones** odds or evens.
(**d**) (*Golf*) par; **~ de(l) campo** par for the course; **lo hizo con 4 por debajo del ~** he did it in 4 under par.
(**e**) (*Mec*) **~ de fuerzas** couple; **~ de torsión** torque.
(**f**) **estar abierto de ~ en ~** to be wide open.
(**g**) (*persona*) peer; **los doce ~es** the twelve peers.
3 *nf* (**a**) (*esp Com, Fin*) par; **a la ~** at par; (*fig*) = **al par**; **estar a la ~** to be at par; **estar por encima de la ~** to be above (*o* over) par; **estar por debajo de la ~** to be under (*o* below) par.
(**b**) **a la ~ que ...** while ..., at the same time as ...
para[1] *prep* (**a**) (*destino, finalidad, uso etc*) for; intended for; **un regalo ~ ti** a present for you; **lo traje ~ ti** I brought it for you; **~ mí que ...** in my opinion ..., if you ask me ...; **no tengo ~ el viaje** I haven't the money for the trip; **un hotel ~ turistas** a hotel (intended) for tourists, a tourist hotel; **una taza ~ café** a coffee cup, a cup for coffee; **no es ~ comer** it's not for eating, it's not to be eaten; **nació ~ poeta** he was born to be a poet; **ir ~ casa** to go home, head for home; **salir ~ Panamá** to leave for Panama; **decir ~ sí** to say to o.s.; **léelo ~ ti** read it to yourself; **~ esto, podíamos habernos quedado en casa** if this is all it is we might as well have stayed at home; **psicológicamente no estoy ~ ello** I'm not up to it psychologically.
(**b**) **¿~ qué?** why?, for what purpose?, what's the use?; **¿~ qué lo quieres?** why do you want it?
(**c**) **~** + *infin* (*finalidad*) to + *infin*, in order to + *infin*; **lo hizo ~ salvarse** he did it (in order) to save himself; **~ comprarlo necesitas 5 dólares más** to buy it you need another 5 dollars; **el rey visitará A ~ volar después a B** the king will visit A and then fly on to B.
(**d**) (*bastante, demasiado, muy*: **~** + *infin*) **tengo bastante ~ vivir** I have enough to live on; **es demasiado cara ~ nuestros recursos** it's too dear for us, it's beyond our means; **tiene demasiada inteligencia ~ pensar así** he's too intelligent to think that.
(**e**) **~ que** *conj* in order that, so that; **lo traje ~ que lo veas** I brought it so that you could see it, I brought it for you to see; **~ que eso fuera posible habría que trabajar mucho** you would have to work hard for that to be possible (*o* to bring that about).
(**f**) **~** + *infin* (*resultado*) only to + *infin*; **se casaron ~ separarse en seguida** they married only to separate at once.
(**g**) (*tiempo*) **~ mañana** for tomorrow; by tomorrow; **lo dejamos ~ mañana** we left it till tomorrow; **lo tendré listo ~ fin de mes** I'll have it ready by (*o* for) the end of the month; **~ las 2 estaba lloviendo** by 2 o'clock it was raining; **ahora ~ la feria de agosto hará un año** it'll be a year ago this (*o* come the) August holiday; **10 ~ las 8** (*LAm*) 10 to 8; *V* **ir** *etc*.
(**h**) (*relación, trato*: *t* **~ con**) to, towards; **tan amable ~ todos** so kind to everybody; **no hay hombre grande ~ su ayuda de cámara** no man is a hero to (*o* in the eyes of) his valet.
(**i**) (*contrastes*) **~ profesor habla muy mal** he talks very badly for a professor; **~ niño lo hace muy bien** he does it very well for a child; **~ ruidosos, los españoles** for noisy people, there's nobody like the Spaniards; **~ locos, los nuestros** if it's madmen you want we've got plenty right here at home; **es mucho ~ lo que suele dar** this is a lot in comparison with what he usually gives; **¿quién es Vd ~ gritar así?** who are you to shout like that?
(**j**) *V* **estar 1** (**r**) *y* (**s**); *V* **ir 1** (**b**) *etc*.
para[2]* *nm* paratrooper, para*.
para... *pref* para...
parabién *nm* congratulations; **dar el ~ a uno to** congratulate sb (*por* on).
parábola *nf* (**a**) (*Mat*) parabola. (**b**) (*Liter*) parable.
parabólica *nf* satellite dish.
parabólico *adj* parabolic.
parabrisas *nm invar* windscreen, windshield (*US*).
paraca[1]* *nm* paratrooper, para*.
paraca[2] *nf* (*And*) strong wind from the sea.
paracaídas *nm invar* parachute; **lanzar algo en ~** to send sth down by parachute; **lanzarse en ~** to parachute (down); (*en emergencia*) to bale out.
paracaidismo *nm* (**a**) parachuting; **~ acrobático** skydiving. (**b**) (*Méx*) squatting.
paracaidista *nmf* (**a**) parachutist; (*Mil*) paratrooper; **acrobático** skydiver. (**b**) (*Méx**) (*colado*) gatecrasher; (*ocupante*) squatter.
parachispas *nm* fireguard, firescreen.
parachoques *nm invar* (*Aut*) bumper, fender (*US*); (*Ferro*) buffer(s).
parada *nf* (**a**) (*acto de parar*) stop; stopping; (*Dep*) save, stop; (*sitio*) stopping place; (*de industria etc*) shutdown, stoppage; standstill; (*de pagos*) suspension; **~ de autobús** bus-stop; **~ cardíaca** cardiac arrest; **~ discrecional** request stop; **~ en seco** sudden stop; **~ de taxis** taxi stand, cabrank; **correr en ~** to run on the spot, run in place (*US*).

(**b**) (*equipo de caballos*) relay, team.
(**c**) (*apuesta*) bet, stake.
(**d**) (*presa*) dam.
(**e**) (*Esgrima*) parry.
(**f**) (*caballeriza*) stud, breeding establishment.
(**g**) (*Mil etc*) parade; (*LAm*) civic procession; ~ **nupcial** (*Orn*) courtship display; **formar en** ~ to parade.
(**h**) (*CAm, Méx*: *cartuchos*) clip of cartridges.
(**i**) (*LAm*) (*vanidad*) vanity, pride, presumption; (*jactancia*) boastfulness; **meter** ~ to boast, be proud.
(**j**) (*And*) crafty trick.
(**k**) (*And*) farmer's market (*US*), open market.
(**l**) **hacer** ~ **a uno** (*Cono Sur, Méx*: *desafiar*) to challenge sb.

paradear* [1a] *vi* (*Cono Sur*) to brag; to swank, show off; ~ **con algo** to brag about sth, show sth off.

paradero *nm* (**a**) (*gen*) whereabouts; **no sabemos su** ~ we do not know where it is; **averiguar el** ~ **de** to ascertain the whereabouts of, locate; **X, ahora en** ~ **desconocido** X, whose whereabouts are unknown.
(**b**) (*parada*) stopping place; (*alojamiento*) lodging; (*LAm Ferro*) wayside halt; (*And*: *de bus*)-bus stop.
(**c**) (*fin*) end; **seguramente tendrá mal** ~ he's sure to come to a bad end.

paradigma *nm* paradigm.

paradigmático *adj* paradigmatic.

paradisiaco *adj*, **paradisíaco** *adj* heavenly.

parado 1 *adj* (**a**) **estar** ~ *persona* to be motionless, be standing still; *fábrica* to be closed, be at a standstill; *coche etc* to be stopped, be standing; **salida parada** (*Dep*) standing start.
(**b**) **estar** ~ (*Esp*) *obrero* to be unemployed, be idle; **los ~s** the unemployed.
(**c**) **estar** ~ (*LAm*) to be standing (up); to be on one's feet; **estuve** ~ **durante 2 horas** I was standing for 2 hours, I stood for 2 hours.
(**d**) **dejar a uno** ~ (*fig*) to amaze sb; to bewilder sb, leave sb confused; to leave sb in doubt; **¡me deja Vd ~!** you amaze me!; **me quedé** ~ I was completely confused, I was at a loss.
(**e**) **salir bien** ~ to come off well, come out of it well; **salió mejor** ~ **de lo que cabía esperar** he came out of it better than could be expected; **estar bien** ~ (*LAm*) (*estar bien colocado*) to be well placed; (*tener influencia*) to have influence; (*And, Carib*: *tener suerte*) to be lucky; **estar mal** ~ (*And, Carib*) to be unlucky; **caer** ~ (**como los gatos**) (*LAm*) to land on one's feet, be lucky.
(**f**) **ser** ~ (*Esp*) *persona* to be slow, be dull, be inactive; (*soso*) to lack character, be weak.
(**g**) (*LAm*) *pelo* stiff, straight; *poste etc* upright.
(**h**) (*Carib, Cono Sur**: *vanidoso*) vain, cocky*.
2 *nm* (**a**) unemployed person; **los ~s** the unemployed; **los ~s de larga duración** the long-term unemployed. (**b**) (*Méx*) air, look, resemblance; **tener** ~ **de** to look like.

paradoja *nf* paradox.

paradójicamente *adv* paradoxically.

paradójico *adj* paradoxical.

paradón* *nm* (*Dep*) great save, fantastic stop*.

parador *nm* (**a**) (*Esp*) (*Hist*) inn; (*moderno*) parador, state-owned hotel. (**b**) (*jugador*) (heavy) gambler.

paraestatal *adj* semi-official, public.

parafernalia *nf* paraphernalia.

parafina *nf* paraffin wax; (*Cono Sur*) paraffin; ~ **líquida** liquid paraffin.

parafinado *adj* waxed, waterproofed.

parafrasear [1a] *vt* to paraphrase.

paráfrasis *nf invar* paraphrase.

paragolpes *nm invar* (*Cono Sur*) = **parachoques.**

parágrafo *nm* (*Carib*) paragraph.

paraguas *nm invar* (**a**) umbrella (*t fig*); ~ **nuclear** nuclear umbrella; ~ **protector** protective umbrella. (**b**) (*And, Carib, Méx*) (*seta comestible*) mushroom; (*no comestible*) toadstool; (*moho*) fungus. (**c**) (‡) French letter.

Paraguay *nm*: **el** ~ Paraguay.

paraguayismo *nm* word (*o* phrase *etc*) peculiar to Paraguay.

paraguayo 1 *adj* Paraguayan. **2** *nm*, **paraguaya** *nf* Paraguayan. **3** *nm* (**a**) (*And*) whip. (**b**) (*Carib*) long straight knife.

paragüero 1 *nm* umbrella stand. **2** *nm*, **paragüera** *nf* (*hum*) native (*o* inhabitant) of Orense; **los ~s** the people of Orense.

paraíso *nm* (**a**) (*Rel*) paradise, heaven; ~ **fiscal** tax haven; ~ **terrenal** earthly paradise. (**b**) (*Teat*) upper gallery, gods.

paraje *nm* place, spot.

paral *nm* (*Méx*) shore, prop; post.

paralela *nf* parallel (line); **~s** parallel bars.

paralelamente *adv* parallel; (*fig*) in a parallel way, comparably.

paralelismo *nm* parallelism.

paralelo 1 *adj* (**a**) (*Mat etc*) parallel (*t fig*: *a* to). (**b**) (*fig*) unofficial; irregular; (*pey*) illegal; **medicina paralela** alternative medicine; **importaciones paralelas** unauthorized imports, illegal imports. **2** *nm* parallel; **en** ~ (*Elec*) in parallel; **en** ~ **con** (*fig*) in parallel with; **circular en** ~ to cycle (*etc*) two abreast.

paralelogramo *nm* parallelogram.

parálisis *nf* paralysis; ~ **cerebral** cerebral palsy; ~ **infantil** infantile paralysis; ~ **progresiva** creeping paralysis.

paralítico, -a *adj, nm/f* paralytic.

paralización *nf* paralysis; (*Com*) stagnation.

paralizar [1f] **1** *vt* to paralyze (*t fig*); *tráfico etc* to stop, block; **estar paralizado de un brazo** to be paralyzed in one arm; **estar paralizado de miedo** to be paralyzed with fright.
2 paralizarse *vr* to become paralyzed; (*fig*) to be paralyzed, come to a standstill; (*Com etc*) to stagnate.

paramar *nm* (*And*) season of wind and snow.

param(e)ar [1a] *vi* (*And, Carib*) to drizzle.

paramédico *adj* paramedical.

paramento *nm* (**a**) (*adorno*) ornament, ornamental cover; (*colgadura*) hangings; (*de caballo*) trappings; **~s sacerdotales** liturgical vestments. (**b**) (*de pared, piedra*) face.

paramera[1] *nf* (**a**) (*Geog*) high moorland. (**b**) (*Carib*) mountain sickness.

paramero 1 *adj* (*And, Carib*) upland, highland. **2** *nm*, **paramera**[2] *nf* highlander.

parámetro *nm* parameter.

paramilitar *adj* paramilitary.

páramo *nm* (**a**) (*brezal*) bleak plateau, high moor. (**b**) (*descampado*) waste land. (**c**) (*And*) (*llovizna*) drizzle; (*tormenta*) storm of wind and snow. (**d**) (*Carib*) mountain heights.

paramoso *adj* (*And*) drizzly.

paramuno *adj* (*And*) upland, highland.

paranera *nf* (*LAm*) grassland.

parangón *nm* comparison; **sin** ~ incomparable, matchless; **no tiene** ~ **en otro país** there is nothing comparable (*o* equivalent) in any other country.

parangonable *adj* comparable (*con* to).

parangonar [1a] *vt* to compare (*con* to).

paraninfo *nm* (*Univ*) central hall; auditorium.

paranoia *nf* paranoia.

paranoico *nm* paranoic.

paranoide *adj* paranoid.

paranormal *adj* paranormal.

paranza *nf* (*Caza*) hide.

parapetarse [1a] *vr* (**a**) (*gen*) to protect o.s., shelter (*tras* behind). (**b**) ~ **tras media docena de excusas** (*fig*) to take refuge in half-a-dozen excuses.

parapeto *nm* parapet, breastwork; defence, barricade.

paraplejía *nf* paraplegia.

parapléjico, -a *adj, nm/f* paraplegic.

parapsicología *nf* parapsychology.

parar [1a] **1** *vt* (**a**) (*gen*) to stop; *coche, motor, respiración etc* to stop; *progresos* to stop, check, halt.
(**b**) *amenaza, golpe* to ward off; (*Esgrima*) to parry; (*Dep*) *pase* to intercept, cut off; *tiro* to stop, save.
(**c**) *atención* to fix (*en* on) *V* **mientes.**
(**d**) (*fig*) to lead; **ahí le paró esa manera de vida** that's where that way of life led him.
(**e**) (*Naipes etc*) to bet, lay, stake.
(**f**) (*arreglar*) to prepare, arrange.
(**g**) (*LAm*) to raise; to stand upright, cause to stand (up).
(**h**) **~la con uno** (*And**) to take it out on sb.
2 *vi* (**a**) (*gen*) to stop; to come to rest; to come to an end; (*en el trabajo*) to stop work, strike; **¡pare!** stop!; **el coche ha parado** the car has stopped; **el autobús para enfrente** the bus stops opposite; **sin** ~ without stopping; without a break; ~ **en seco** to stop dead, stop suddenly; **no parará hasta conseguirlo** he won't give up until he gets it; **¡y no para!** (*orador*) he just goes on and on!, there's no stopping him!; **vino a** ~ **a mis pies** it came to rest at my feet; **¿adónde vamos a ~?** (*fig*) where's it all going to end?

(**b**) ~ **de** + *infin* to stop + *ger*; **ha parado de llover** it has stopped raining; **no para de quejarse** he never stops complaining, he complains all the time; ... **y pare Vd de contar** ... and that's the lot, ... and that's it.

(**c**) ~ **con uno** (*And**) to hang about with sb.

(**d**) ~ **en** (*proyecto etc*) to end up as, result in, come down to; (*persona*) to end up at; **no sabemos en qué va a ~ todo esto** we don't know where all this is going to end; **el edificio paró en hotel** the building ended up as a hotel; **fueron a ~ en la comisaría** they finished (*o* ended) up at the police station; **irá a ~ (en) mal** he'll come to a bad end.

(**e**) (*hospedarse*) to stay, put up, lodge (*en* at); **siempre paro en este hotel** I always stay at this hotel.

(**f**) (*Caza*: *perro*) to point.

3 pararse *vr* (**a**) (*persona etc*) to stop; (*coche etc*) to stop, pull up, draw up; (*proceso*) to come to a halt; (*trabajo etc*) to stop, come to a standstill, cease; ~ **a** + *infin* to stop to + *infin*, pause to + *infin;* ~ **en** (*Ferro*) to stop at, call at.

(**b**) ~ **en algo** to pay attention to sth, notice sth.

(**c**) (*LAm*) (*levantarse*) to stand (up), get up; (*enderezarse*) to straighten up, sit (*etc*) erect; (*de la cama*) to get up; (*pelo*) to stand on end.

(**d**) (*Tip*) to set.

(**e**) (*LAm**) to make one's pile*, get rich.

pararrayos *nm invar* lightning conductor.

parasitar [1a] **1** *vt* to parasitize. **2** *vi*: ~ **en** to parasitize.

parasitario *adj*, **parasítico** *adj* parasitic(al).

parasitismo *nm* parasitism.

parásito 1 *adj* parasitic (*de* on). **2** *nm* (**a**) (*gen*) parasite (*t fig*). (**b**) ~**s** (*Rad*) atmospherics, statics, interference. (**c**) (*CAm*) squatter.

parasitología *nf* parasitology.

parasitosis *nf* parasitism.

parasol *nm* parasol, sunshade.

parateatral *adj* theatre-related; quasi-dramatic.

paratifoidea *nf* paratyphoid.

Parcas *nfpl*: **las** ~ the Parcae, the Fates.

parcela *nf* (**a**) (*solar*) plot, piece of ground; (*Agr*) smallholding. (**b**) (*fig*) part, portion; area; ~ **de poder** power domain; sphere of influence.

parcelar [1a] *vt* to divide into plots; *finca* to break up, parcel out.

parcelario *adj*: **tierra parcelaria** land divided into plots.

parcelero, -a *nm/f*, **parcelista** *nmf* owner of a plot, smallholder.

parcial 1 *adj* (**a**) (*incompleto*) partial; part-; **examen** ~ class examination. (**b**) *opinión etc* partial, prejudiced, biassed; (*partidista*) partisan. **2 parciales** *nfpl* by-election.

parcialidad *nf* (**a**) (*cualidad*) partiality, prejudice, bias; partisanship. (**b**) (*grupo*) party, faction, group, (*esp*) rebel group.

parcidad *nf* = **parquedad.**

parcamente *adv* frugally, sparingly; parsimoniously; moderately.

parco *adj* frugal, sparing; parsimonious; moderate, temperate; **muy ~ en comer** very frugal in one's eating habits; ~ **en elogios** sparing in one's praises.

parcómetro *nm* parking meter.

parchar [1a] *vt* (*LAm*) to patch, put a patch on.

parche *nm* (**a**) (*Med*) sticking plaster; (*de ojo*) eye patch; (*en neumático*) patch; (*fig*) patch, mend, botch; temporary remedy, stopgap solution; **poner ~s a** to apply temporary remedies to.

(**b**) (*Mús*) drumhead; drum; (*fig*) busking; **dar el** ~ to busk.

(**c**) **pegar un ~ a uno*** to put one over on sb*.

parchear[1] [1a] *vt* to patch (up).

parchear[2]‡ [1a] *vt* to feel‡, touch up‡.

parcheo *nm* (*fig*) temporary remedies, stopgap solutions.

parchís *nm a board game.*

parchita *nf* (*Carib*) passion fruit.

parcho *nm* (*Carib*) = **parche.**

pardal *nm* (**a**) (*Orn*) sparrow; linnet. (**b**) (*Bot*) aconite. (**c**) (*: *pillo*) sly fellow, rogue; ¡~! (*a niño*) you rascal!

pardiez *interj* (*Esp*††) by gad!

pardillo *nm* (**a**) (*paño*) brown cloth; **gente del** ~ country folk. (**b**) (*persona*: *rústico*) yokel, rustic. (**c**) (*: *principiante*) beginner, novice. (**d**) (*Orn*: *t* ~ **común**) linnet.

pardo 1 *adj* (**a**) *color* dun; drab, dark grey; (*descolorado*) discoloured; *cerveza, nube* black, dark; *cielo* overcast. (**b**) *voz* flat, dull. **2** *nm* (*Carib, Cono Sur*) mulatto, half-breed; (*Méx*‡) poor devil.

pardusco *adj* = **pardo.**

pareado *nm* (*Liter*) couplet; (*slogan*) jingle.

parear [1a] **1** *vt* (**a**) (*formar pares de*) to match, put together; to form pairs of. (**b**) (*Bio*) to mate, pair. **2** *vi* (*Carib*‡) to skive‡. **3 parearse** *vr* to pair off.

parecer [2d] **1** *nm* (**a**) (*opinión*) opinion, view; **a mi** ~ in my opinion; **al** ~ apparently, seemingly; **por el bien** (*o* **buen**) ~ for form's sake, as a matter of courtesy; in order not to seem rude; **mudar de** ~ to change one's mind.

(**b**) (*aspecto*) looks; **de buen** ~ good-looking, nice-looking, handsome; **de mal** ~ plain, ugly.

2 *vi* (**a**) (*gen*) to seem; to look; **parece muy difícil** it seems very difficult, it looks very difficult; **parecía volar** it seemed to fly; **así parece** so it seems; **a lo que parece, según parece** to all appearances; seemingly, apparently; **aunque no lo parezca** surprising though it may seem, incredible though it is; **parece como si quisieras** ... it looks as if you wanted to ...; **parece que va a llover** it looks as though it's going to rain, it seems that it's going to rain.

(**b**) (*: *comparaciones*: *hum*) **parece un alfeñique** he's terribly thin; **parece una ballena** she's as fat as a cow*; **parece un juez** he looks terribly serious.

(**c**) (*con pron pers*) **me parece que** ... I think (that) ..., it seems to me that ...; **como te parece, si a Vd le parece** as you wish; if you think so, if you want to; **¿te parece?** OK?*, all right?, does that suit you?; **¿qué te parece?** what do you think (of it)?; **vamos a la piscina, ¿te parece?** do you fancy the swimming pool?, what about going to the swimming pool?; **me parece bien que vayas** I think you should go, it seems to me proper you should go; **si a Vd le parece mal** if you don't like it; **le parece mal que no vayas** she takes a poor view of your not going, she doesn't like the idea of your not going; **¡me parece muy mal!** I think it's shocking!

(**d**) (*semejar*) to look like, seem like, resemble; **una casa que parece un palacio** a house that looks like a palace; **¡pareces una reina!** you look like a queen!

(**e**) (*aparecer*) to appear, show; (*persona*) to turn up, show up, appear; (*objeto perdido*) to turn up, reappear; **pareció el sol entre las nubes** the sun showed (*o* shone) through the clouds; **cuando la luna parezca** when the moon comes up; **ya parecieron los guantes** the gloves have turned up; **¡ya pareció aquello!** so that was it!

3 parecerse *vr* (**a**) (*2 cosas etc*) to look alike, resemble each other; **se parecen mucho** they look very much alike, they resemble each other closely; **ni cosa que se parezca** nor anything of the sort; far from it.

(**b**) ~ **a** to look like, resemble; **se parece al abuelo** he takes after his grandfather, he has his grandfather's looks; **el retrato no se le parece (en nada)** the picture isn't a bit like him.

parecidamente *adv* similarly, equally.

parecido 1 *adj* (**a**) (*semejante*) similar (*de, en* in, in respect of); ~ **a** like, similar to; **son muy ~s** they are very similar, they are very much alike.

(**b**) **bien** ~ good-looking, nice-looking, handsome; **no es mal parecido** he's not bad-looking.

2 *nm* (*semejanza*) similarity, likeness, resemblance (*a* to, *entre* between); **tienen mucho** ~ they are very alike.

3 *nm*, **parecida** *nf* (*persona*) look-alike.

parecimiento *nm* (**a**) (*Cono Sur, Méx*) = **parecido 2.** (**b**) (*Cono Sur*) (*comparecencia*) appearance; (*aparición*) apparition.

pared *nf* (**a**) wall; (*Alpinismo*) face, wall; ~ **arterial** wall of the artery; ~ **celular** cell wall; ~ **medianera** party wall; ~ **por medio** next door; **estar cara a la** ~ (*Escol*) to be stood in the corner; **ni que hablara uno a la** ~ I might as well talk to a brick wall; **ponerse blanco como la** ~ to go as white as a sheet; **subirse por las ~es*** to go up the wall*; **me hace subirme por las ~es*** it drives me up the wall*.

paredeño *adj* adjoining, next-door (*con* to).

paredón *nm* (**a**) (*muro*) thick wall; (*de ruina*) standing wall.

(**b**) (*de roca*) wall of rock, rock face.

(**c**) **llevar a uno al** ~ to put sb up against a wall, shoot sb; **¡al ~!** shoot him!

pareja *nf* (**a**) (*par*) pair, couple; (*policías*) pair of Civil Guards; (*esposos etc*) couple; (*Naipes*) pair; ~ **abierta,** ~ **libre** open marriage; ~ **reproductora** (*Orn*) breeding pair.

(**b**) (*otro*) other one (of a pair); ~ **de baile** dancing partner; **no encuentro la ~ de este guante** I can't find the glove that goes with this one, I can't find my other glove; **correr ~s** to be on a par, go together, keep pace (*con* with).

(**c**) (*amigo*) boyfriend, (*amiga*) girlfriend; (*amante*) lover; (*cónyuge*) other half, better half; **hogar sin ~** one-parent family; **madre sin ~, padre sin ~** single parent; **la vida en ~** living as a couple, life together; **nuestra vida como ~** our life together; **llevamos una relación de ~** we're an item*, we live together.

(**d**) (*LAm*) (*caballos*) pair of horses; (*de tiro*) team of draught animals; (*de bueyes*) yoke of oxen.

parejamente *adv* equally.

parejería *nf* (*Carib*) vanity, conceit.

parejero 1 *adj* (*Carib**) (*demasiado confiado*) cheeky; (*presumido*) cocky, over-confident.

2 *nm* (**a**) (*LAm*) racehorse.

(**b**) (*Carib**) hanger-on.

parejita* *nf* pigeon pair (*son and daughter*).

parejo 1 *adj* (**a**) (*igual*) equal; (*semejante*) similar, alike; **6 todos ~s** 6 all the same; **por ~** on a par; **ir ~s** to be neck and neck; **ir ~ con** to be on a par with, be paralleled by.

(**b**) (*Téc*) smooth, even, flush; (*LAm*) flat, level.

2 *adv* (*LAm*) at the same time, together.

3 *nm* (*CAm, Carib*) dancing partner, escort.

paremiología *nf* study of proverbs.

parentela *nf* relations.

parenteral *adj* parenteral; **inyección ~** intravenous injection.

parentesco *nm* relationship, kinship.

paréntesis *nm invar* (**a**) (*Ling*) parenthesis; digression; aside.

(**b**) (*Tip*) parenthesis, bracket; **~ cuadrados** square brackets; **entre ~** (*adj*) parenthetical, incidental; (*adv*) parenthetically, incidentally; **y, entre ~ ...** and, by the way ..., and, I may add in passing ...

(**c**) (*fig*) interruption, interval, break; gap; lull; **el ~ vacacional** the break for the holidays, the holiday interruption; **hacer ~** to digress.

pareo¹ *nm* pareo; (*de playa*) beach wrap; (*taparrabos*) loincloth; (*chal*) rectangular shawl.

pareo² *nm* (*unión*) pairing off; matching; (*Zool*) mating.

paria *nmf* pariah.

parián *nm* (*Méx*) market.

parida *nf* (**a**) (*mujer*) woman who has recently given birth. (**b**) (*: *dicho etc*) silly thing, stupid remark (*etc*); **~s** nonsense; **salir con alguna ~** to come out with some silly remark.

paridad *nf* (**a**) (*igualdad*) parity, equality; (*semejanza*) similarity. (**b**) (*comparación*) comparison.

parido* *adj* successful.

paridora *adj f* fertile, productive.

parienta *nf* (**a**) (*gen*) relative, relation; **~ pobre** poor relation. (**b**) **la ~*** the wife*, the missus*.

pariente *nm* (**a**) (*gen*) relative, relation; **~ político** relative by marriage; **los ~s políticos** the in-laws; **medio ~** distant relative. (**b**) **el ~*** the old man*, my (*etc*) hubby*.

parietal *adj* parietal.

parihuela *nf* (*gen* **parihuelas** *pl*) stretcher; **~ de mariscos** (*LAm*) seafood platter.

paripé* *nm*: **hacer** (*o* **montar**) **el ~** to put on a show, keep up the show.

parir [3a] **1** *vt* (**a**) (*Bio*) to give birth to, bear. (**b**) **~la⁑** to drop a clanger⁑.

2 *vi* (*mujer*) to give birth, have a baby; to be delivered; (*vaca*) to calve (*y hay verbos parecidos para otras especies*); **ha parido 4 veces** she has had 4 children, she has given birth 4 times; **poner a ~ a uno*** to run sb down*, criticize sb behind his back.

París *nm* Paris.

parisién *adj*, **parisino** *adj* Parisian.

parisiense *adj, nmf* Parisian.

paritario *adj* peer (*atr*); **grupo ~** peer group.

paritorio *nm* maternity ward.

parking ['parkin] *nm* car-park, parking lot; parking space.

parla *nf* chatter, gossip.

parlador *adj* talkative.

parlamentar [1a] *vi* to converse, talk; (*enemigos*) to parley.

parlamentario 1 *adj* parliamentary. **2** *nm*, **parlamentaria** *nf* parliamentarian; member of parliament; **~ autónomo** member of a regional parliament.

parlamento *nm* (**a**) (*Pol*) parliament; **~ autónomo** regional parliament; **P~ Europeo** European Parliament. (**b**) (*entre enemigos*) parley. (**c**) (*Jur, Teat*) speech.

parlana *nf* (*CAm Zool*) turtle.

parlanchín 1 *adj* loose-tongued, indiscreet. **2** *nm*, **parlanchina** *nf* (**a**) (*parlador*) chatterbox, great talker. (**b**) (*indiscreto*) indiscreet person.

parlante 1 *adj máquina etc* talking. **2** *nm* (*LAm*) loudspeaker.

-parlante *suf en palabras compuestas, p.ej.* **castellanoparlante** (*adj*) Castilian-speaking, (*nmf*) Castilian speaker.

parlar [1a] *vi* to chatter (away), talk (a lot), gossip; (*loro*) to talk.

parlero *adj* (**a**) (*hablador*) talkative, garrulous; (*cotilla*) gossipy. (**b**) *pájaro* talking; singing, song (*atr*); *arroyo* musical; *ojos* expressive.

parleta *nf* chat, small talk.

parlotear [1a] *vi* to chatter, prattle.

parloteo *nm* chatter, prattle.

Parnaso *nm* Parnassus.

parné⁑ *nm* dough⁑, money.

paro¹ *nm* (*Orn*) tit.

paro² *nm* (**a**) (*parada*) stoppage (of work); standstill; (*LAm*: *huelga*) strike; **~ cardíaco** cardiac arrest; **hay ~ en la industria** work in the industry is at a standstill.

(**b**) (*desempleo*: *t* **~ forzoso, ~ obrero**) unemployment; **~ encubierto** hidden unemployment; **~ estacional** (*Esp*) seasonal unemployment; **enviar al ~** to put out of a job, make unemployed; **estar en ~** to be unemployed, be on the dole.

(**c**) (*pago*) unemployment benefit; **cobrar el ~** to receive unemployment benefit, (*frec*) be on the dole.

(**d**) (*And, Carib*: *dados*) throw.

(**e**) **en ~** (*And*) all at once, in one go.

parodia *nf* parody, travesty, takeoff; (*fig*) travesty.

parodiar [1b] *vt* to parody, travesty, take off.

paródico *adj* parodic.

parodista *nmf* parodist, writer of parodies.

parola *nf* (**a**) (*soltura*) fluency; (*verborrea*) verbosity; (*labia*) gift of the gab*. (**b**) (*charla*) chitchat; wearisome talk; **son ~s** (*Cono Sur**) it's all hot air*.

parón *nm* sudden halt, complete stop; general stoppage, shutdown.

paroxismo *nm* paroxysm; **~ histérico** hysterics; **~ de risa** convulsions of laughter; **en un ~ de celos** in a fit of jealousy, in a paroxysm of jealousy.

parpadear [1a] *vi* (*ojo*) to blink, wink; (*luz*) to blink, flicker; (*estrella*) to twinkle.

parpadeo *nm* blinking, winking; flickering; twinkling.

párpado *nm* eyelid; **restregarse los ~s** to rub one's eyes.

parpichuela⁑ *nf*: **hacerse una ~** to wank⁑.

parque *nm* (**a**) (*gen*) park; **~ acuático** waterpark; **~ de atracciones** funfair, fairground; **~ de automóviles, ~ de estacionamiento** car-park, parking lot (*US*); **~ central** (*Méx*) town square; **~ cerrado** (*Aut*) pit, pits; **~ de chatarra** scrapyard; **~ eólico** windfarm; **~ infantil** playpark; **~ nacional** national park; **~ natural** nature reserve; **~ tecnológico** technology park; **~ zoológico** zoo.

(**b**) (*Mil etc*) depot; **~ de artillería** artillery depot, artillery stores; **~ de bomberos** fire-station.

(**c**) (*Aut etc*) fleet; **~ móvil** official cars; **el ~ nacional de automóviles** the total number of cars in the country; **el ~ provincial de tractores** the number of tractors in use in the province.

(**d**) **~ (de jugar)** playpen.

(**e**) (*LAm Mil*) (*equipo*) equipment; (*munición*) ammunition; (*depósito*) ammunition dump.

parqué *nm*, **parquet** [par'ke] *nm*, *pl* **parquets** [par'ke] parquet; (*Fin*) **el ~** the Floor (of the stock exchange), (*fig*) the stock market.

parqueadero *nm* (*LAm*) (*local*) car-park, parking lot (*US*); (*espacio individual*) parking-place.

parquear [1a] *vti* (*LAm*) to park.

parquedad *nf* frugality, sparingness; parsimony; moderation.

parqueo *nm* (*LAm*) (*acto*) parking; (*local*) car-park, parking lot (*US*); (*espacio individual*) parking-place.

parquímetro *nm* parking meter.

parra *nf* grapevine; climbing vine, trained vine; **subirse a la ~*** to blow one's top*.

parrafada* *nf* (*esp LAm*) chat, talk; **echar la ~** to have a chat; **soltar la ~, tirarse la ~** to give a lengthy spiel*.

párrafo *nm* paragraph; **echar un ~*** to have a chat (*con* with); **hacer ~ aparte** to start a new paragraph; (*fig*) to change the subject.

parral *nm* vine arbour.

parranda *nf* (**a**) (*: *juerga*) spree, party; **andar** (*o* **ir** *etc*) **de ~** to go on a binge*. (**b**) (*And, Cono Sur, Méx*) lot, group, heap; **una ~ de** a lot of.

parricida *nmf* (*persona*) parricide.

parricidio *nm* (*act*) parricide.

parrilla *nf* (**a**) (*objeto*) grating, gridiron, grille; (*de nevera*) shelf; (*Culin*) grill; **carne a la ~** grilled meat.

(**b**) (*restaurante*) grillroom, steak restaurant.

(**c**) (*Aut*) (*de radiador*) radiator grille; (*Cono Sur*) roof-rack; **~ de salida** (*Aut*) starting grid; (*de caballos*) starting gate, starting stalls.

(**d**) (*de bicicleta*) carrier.

parrillada *nf* (**a**) grill; barbecue. (**b**) (*restaurante*) steak house.

párroco *nm* parish priest.

parroquia *nf* (**a**) (*Ecl*) (*zona*) parish; (*iglesia*) parish church.

(**b**) (*Com*) clientèle, customers; **hoy hay poca ~** there are few customers today; **una tienda con mucha ~** a shop with a large clientèle, a well-patronized shop.

parroquial *adj* parochial, parish (*atr*).

parroquiano, -a *nm/f* (**a**) (*Ecl*) parishioner.

(**b**) (*Com*) client, customer, patron; **ser ~ de** to be a regular client of, shop regularly at, patronize.

parsi *nmf* Parsee.

parsimonia *nf* (**a**) (*prudencia*) carefulness (about money *etc*); (*frugalidad*) sparingness.

(**b**) (*calma*) deliberateness, calmness; (*flema*) phlegmatic nature; **con ~** deliberately, calmly, unhurriedly.

parsimonioso *adj* (**a**) (*prudente*) sensible, careful (about money *etc*); economical; (*frugal*) sparing. (**b**) (*tranquilo*) slow, deliberate, calm, unhurried; phlegmatic.

parte[1] *nm* (*Telec*) message; (*informe*) report; (*Mil*) dispatch, communiqué; (*Rad*†) news bulletin; (*Cono Sur*: *de boda*) wedding invitation; (*Cono Sur Aut*) ticket for speeding; **~ de baja** sick note; **~ de clase** school report; **~ de defunción** death certificate; **~ facultativo** medical bulletin; **~ de guerra** military communiqué, war report; **~ matrimonial** wedding announcement; **~ médico** medical report, medical bulletin; **~ meteorológico** weather report, weather forecast; **~ de nacimiento** birth announcement; **dar ~ a uno** to report to sb, inform sb.

parte[2] *nf* (**a**) (*gen*) part; (*sección*) portion, section; **cuarta ~** quarter, fourth part; **tercera ~** third; **reducir algo en una tercera ~** to reduce sth by a third; **primera ~** (*Dep*) first half; **la mayor ~ de** most of; the greater part of, the great majority of; **la mayor ~ de los argentinos** most Argentinians, most of the Argentinians; **~ del mundo** part of the world; **en las cinco ~s del mundo** (*Esp*) in the four corners of the earth; **~ de la oración** part of speech; **ser ~ esencial** (*o* **integral, integrante**) **de** to be an essential part of; **de algún tiempo a esta ~** for some time past; **como ~ del pago** in part payment; in part exchange; **de una ~ a otra** back and forth, to and fro; **de ~ a ~** through and through, right through; **de ~ de** from, on behalf of; in the name of; **¿de ~ de quién?** (*Telec*) who's calling?, who is that talking?, who shall I say (is calling)?; **de ~ de todos nosotros** on behalf of us all; **salúdale de mi ~** give him regards from me, give him my regards; **en ~** in part, partly; **en gran ~** to a large extent, in large measure; **por ~ de** on the part of; **con concesiones por ambas ~s** with concessions on both sides; **por ~s** bit by bit; stage by stage, systematically; **por otra ~** (or) again, on the other hand; moreover; **por una ~ ... por otra** (~) on the one hand, ... on the other; **yo por mi ~** I for my part; **por la mayor ~** mostly, for the most part; **echar algo a mala ~** to look on sth with disapproval, be offended about sth; **echar una palabra a mala ~** to take offence at a remark; (**entrar a**) **formar ~ de** to form a part of, be a part of; (*persona*) to be a member of; **no formaba ~ del equipo** he was not in the team; **tomar algo en buena ~** to take sth in good part.

(**b**) (*participación, porción*) share; **la ~ del león** the lion's share; **a ~s iguales** in equal shares; **ir a la ~** to go shares; **llevar la mejor ~** to have the advantage, be on the way to winning; **llevarse la mejor ~** to come off best, get the best of it; **tener ~ en** to share in; **tomar ~** to take part (*en* in).

(**c**) (*región, Geog etc*) part; **en alguna ~** somewhere; **en alguna ~ de Europa** somewhere in Europe; **en cualquier ~** anywhere; **por ahí no se va a ninguna ~** that leads nowhere, (*fig*) this is getting us nowhere; **en ninguna ~ del país** in no part of the country, nowhere in the country; **no esperes ayuda de ninguna ~** don't expect help from any quarter; **ir a otra ~** to go somewhere else; **mirar a otra ~** to look the other way, look in another direction; **ha de estar en otra ~** it must be somewhere else; **¿en qué ~ del país?** in which part of the country? **¿en qué ~ lo dejaste?** whereabouts did you leave it?; **en todas ~s** everywhere; **en todas ~s de España** in all parts of Spain, everywhere in Spain, all over Spain; **por todas ~s se va a Roma** all roads lead to Rome.

(**d**) (*lado*) side; **por cualquier ~ que lo mires** from whichever side you look at it.

(**e**) (*Mús, Teat*) part.

(**f**) (*de parentesco*) side; **por ~ de madre** on the mother's side.

(**g**) (*persona*) contender; (*Jur*) party, side; **~ actora** prosecution; plaintiff; **las ~s contratantes** the contracting parties; **~ contraria** opposing party, other side; **tercera ~** third party; **ponerse de ~ de** to take the side of, side with.

(**h**) (*cualidades*) **~s** parts, qualities, talents; **buenas ~s** good parts.

(**i**) (*Anat*) **~s** parts; **~s íntimas, ~s pudendas** pudenda, private parts; **la ~ donde la espalda pierde su honesto nombre** (*hum*) one's anatomy; **le dio en salva sea la ~** (*Esp euf*) it hit her on a part of her anatomy.

(**j**) (*Méx Mec*) spare part.

parteaguas *nm invar* divide, ridge; watershed; **~ continental** continental divide.

partear [1a] *vt mujer* to deliver.

parteluz *nm* mullion.

partenogénesis *nf* parthenogenesis.

Partenón *nm* Parthenon.

partenueces *nm invar* nutcracker.

partera *nf* midwife.

partero *nm* (*Méx*) gynaecologist.

parterre *nf* (**a**) (*de flores*) flower bed. (**b**) (*Teat etc*) stalls.

partición *nf* division, sharing-out; (*Pol etc*) partition.

participación *nf* (**a**) (*acto*) participation, taking part.

(**b**) (*interés, parte*) share; (*Fin*) share, stock (*US*), investment; interest, holding; **~ accionarial** holding, shareholding; **~ en los beneficios** profit-sharing; **~ electoral** turnout (of voters); **~ del mercado** market share, share in the market; **la ~ de la compañía A en la compañía B** company A's holding in company B; **su ~ en estos asuntos** his share (*o* part) in these matters.

(**c**) (*Dep*) entry; **hubo una nutrida ~** there was a big entry, there were numerous entrants.

(**d**) (*de lotería*) (part of a) lottery ticket.

(**e**) (*aviso*) notice, notification; **~ de boda** notice of a forthcoming wedding; **dar ~ a uno de algo** to inform sb of sth.

participante *nmf* participant; (*Dep*) entrant, entry; **los países ~s** the participating countries.

participar [1a] **1** *vt* (*informar*) to notify, inform; **~ algo a uno** to notify sb of sth; **le participo que ...** I have to tell you that ...; I warn you that ...

2 *vi* (**a**) (*tomar parte*) to take part, participate (*en* in); **~ en una carrera** to enter for a race, run in a race, take part in a race.

(**b**) **~ de** (*o* **en**) **una herencia** to share in an estate; **~ en una empresa** (*Fin*) to invest in an enterprise.

(**c**) **~ de una cualidad** to share a quality, partake of a quality, have a quality in common.

participativo *adj* participatory, participating.

partícipe *nmf* participant; **hacer ~ a uno de algo** to share sth with sb, inform sb of sth.

participial *adj* participial.

participio *nm* participle; **~ de pasado, ~ pasivo, ~ de pretérito** past participle; **~ activo, ~ de presente** present participle.

partícula *nf* particle; **~ alfa** alpha particle; **~ atómica** atomic particle; **~ elemental** fundamental particle.

particular 1 *adj* (**a**) (*especial*) particular, special; (*propio*) peculiar (*a* to); **nada de ~** nothing special; **lo que tiene de ~ es que ...** what's remarkable about it is that ...; **en ~** in particular; **en este caso ~** in this particular case; **tiene un sabor ~** it has a special flavour, it has a flavour of its own.

(**b**) (*personal*) private, personal; **tiene coche ~** he has a car of his own, he has a car to himself; **clase ~** private lesson; **secretario ~** private secretary; **en ~** in private.

2 *nm* (**a**) (*asunto*) particular, point, matter; **no dijo mucho sobre el ~** he didn't say much about the matter.

(**b**) (*persona*) individual, private individual; **iba vestido de ~** he was in civilian clothes; **no comerciamos con ~es** we don't do business with individuals.

particularidad *nf* (**a**) (*propiedad*) particularity, peculiarity; (*rasgo distintivo*) special feature, characteristic; **tiene la ~ de que ...** one of its special features is ..., it has the characteristic that ...

(**b**) (*amistad*) friendship, intimacy.

particularizar [1f] **1** *vt* (**a**) (*distinguir*) to distinguish, characterize, mark out.

(**b**) (*especificar*) to particularize, specify.

(**c**) (*distinguir con la amistad*) to show special friendship to.

(**d**) (*dar detalles*) to give details about.

2 particularizarse *vr* (**a**) (*distinguirse*) to distinguish itself, stand out, mark itself out; (*persona*) to make one's mark, do sth outstanding.

(**b**) ~ **con uno** to single sb out (for special treatment *etc*).

particularmente *adv* (**a**) particularly, specially. (**b**) privately, personally.

partida *nf* (**a**) (*salida*) departure.

(**b**) (*registro*) register; (*documento*) certificate; (*entrada*) entry (in a register *etc*); ~ **bautismal,** ~ **de bautismo** certificate of baptism; ~ **de defunción** death certificate; ~ **de matrimonio** marriage certificate; ~ **de nacimiento** birth certificate.

(**c**) (*Com, Fin*) (*entrada*) entry, item; (*de presupuesto etc*) item, section, heading; ~ **doble** double entry; ~ **simple** single entry.

(**d**) (*Com: envío*) consignment, shipment; (*LAm*) consignment of drugs.

(**e**) (*Naipes*) game, hand; (*Ajedrez etc*) game; ~ **de dobles** doubles match; ~ **de individuales,** ~ **de simples** singles match; **echar una** ~ to have a game.

(**f**) (*apuesta*) stake, wager, bet.

(**g**) (*personas*) party; (*Mil etc*) band, group; faction; ~ **de caza** hunting party; ~ **de campo** picnic (party); ~ **de excursión** group of trippers.

(**h**) (**mala**) ~, ~ **serrana** dirty trick.

partidario 1 *adj* partisan; **soy muy** ~ **de** ... I'm very fond of ..., I'm very partial to ...

2 *nm*, **partidaria** *nf* (**a**) (*gen*) supporter, follower (*de* of); partisan; **soy** ~ **de** + *infin* I'm in favour of + *ger*. (**b**) (*And, Carib*) sharecropper.

partidillo *nm* (*Dep*) practice game.

partidismo *nm* partisanship, bias; partisan spirit; (*Pol, pey*: *t* ~**s**) party feeling, party politics.

partidista 1 *adj* partisan; party (*atr*). **2** *nmf* partisan.

partido *nm* (**a**) (*Pol etc*) party; ~ **político** political party; ~ **de la oposición** opposition party; ~ **de la reforma** reforming party; ~ **republicano** republican party; **sistema de** ~ **único** one-party system, single-party system; **P~ Verde** Green Party.

(**b**) (*Dep etc: encuentro*) game, match; fixture; ~ **amistoso** friendly game; ~ **de casa** home game; ~ **de desempate** replay; ~ **de exhibición** exhibition match; ~ **de fútbol** football match; ~ (**de**) **homenaje** benefit match; ~ **de ida** away game; ~ **internacional** international match; ~ **de vuelta** return match.

(**c**) (*Dep etc: equipo*) team, side.

(**d**) (*distrito*: *t* ~ **judicial**) district, administrative area.

(**e**) **darse a** ~, **venir**(**se**) **a** ~ to give way; **tomar** ~ to decide, make up one's mind; to take sides.

(**f**) (*provecho*) advantage, profit; **sacar** ~ **de** to profit from, benefit from; to put to use.

(**g**) (*apoyo*) support; **tiene** ~ **en todas las clases** he has support among all classes.

(**h**) **es un** (**buen**) ~, **es de** ~ he's a good catch*, he's very eligible.

(**i**) (*Cono Sur Naipes*) hand.

(**j**) (*Méx: aparcía*) crop share.

(**k**) (*And, Carib*:*) **a** ~, **al** ~ share and share alike, in equal shares.

partija *nf* (**a**) (*partición*) partition, division. (**b**) (*pey*) = **parte**[2].

partiota *nf* (*Carib*) dollar bill.

partir [3a] **1** *vt* (**a**) (*dividir*) to split (up, into two *etc*), divide (up); *nuez etc* to crack; (*abrir*) to break open; (*romper*) to split open; ~ **la cabeza a uno** to split (*o* crack) sb's head open.

(**b**) (*repartir*) to share (out), distribute, divide (up); ~ **algo con otros** to share sth with others.

(**c**) *cartas* to cut.

2 *vi* (**a**) (*ponerse en camino*) to start, set off, set out, depart (*de* from, *para* for, *con rumbo a* for, in the direction of).

(**b**) (*comenzar*) to start (*de* from); **a** ~ **del lunes** from Monday, starting on (*o* from) Monday; **es el tercero a** ~ **de la esquina** it's the third one counting from the corner; **a** ~ **de estos datos** starting from these data; **hemos partido de un supuesto falso** we have started from a false assumption.

3 partirse *vr* to crack, split, break (in two *etc*); ~ **de risa** to split one's sides laughing.

partisano, -a *adj, nm/f* partisan.

partitivo *adj* partitive.

partitura *nf* (*Mús*) score.

parto *nm* (**a**) (*Med*) birth, childbirth; delivery; labour; ~ **sin dolor,** ~ **sin violencia** painless childbirth; ~ **múltiple** multiple birth; ~ **natural** natural childbirth; ~ **de los montes** anticlimax, bathos; **estar de** ~ to be in labour; **tener un** ~ **difícil** to have a difficult labour.

(**b**) (*fig*) product, creation; ~ **del ingenio** brain child; **el ensayo ha sido un** ~ **difícil** I sweated blood over the essay.

parturición *nf* parturition.

parturienta *nf* woman in labour; woman who has just given birth.

party *nm o f, pl* **partys** party; (*cóctel*) cocktail party, reception.

parva *nf* (heap of) unthreshed corn; (*fig*) heap, pile.

parvada *nf* (*LAm*) flock.

parvedad *nf* littleness, smallness; fewness; ~ **de recursos** limited resources, scant resources.

parvulario *nm* (*Esp*) nursery school, kindergarten, crèche.

parvulista *nmf* nursery teacher.

párvulo, -a *nm/f* child, infant; (*Escol*) infant.

pasa *nf* (**a**) raisin; ~ **de Corinto** (*Esp*) currant; ~ **de Esmirna** (*Esp*) sultana. (**b**) **está hecho una** ~ (* *fig*) he's as shrivelled as a prune.

pasable *adj* (**a**) (*tolerable*) passable, tolerable. (**b**) (*LAm*) *arroyo etc* fordable, that can be forded. (**c**) (*Cono Sur*) saleable.

pasablemente *adv* passably, tolerably (well).

pasabocas *nm invar* (*And*) snack, appetizer.

pasacalles *nm invar* street band; informal theatre troupe.

pasacintas *nm invar* suspender-belt.

pasada *nf* (**a**) (*acto*) passing, passage; (*con trapo etc*) rub, clean, polish; ~ **de pintura** coat of paint; **dar dos** ~**s de jabón a la ropa** to soap the clothes twice; **dar una** ~ **con la plancha a** to run the iron over.

(**b**) **de** ~ in passing, incidentally.

(**c**) (*Cos*) (*línea*) row of stitches; (*hilvanado*) tacking stitch; ~**s** patch, mend.

(**d**) **mala** ~ dirty trick.

(**e**) **una** ~ **de*** a lot of, a whole heap of.

(**f**) (*ultraje*) outrage, excess; **esto fue una** ~ **suya** in this he went too far, with this he overstepped the bounds.

(**g**) (*CAm, Cono Sur**) telling-off*.

(**h**) (*And*) shame, embarrassment.

pasadera *nf* stepping stone.

pasadero 1 *adj* (*tolerable*) passable, tolerable. **2** *nm* (*piedra*) stepping stone.

pasadizo *nm* (*Arquit*) passage, corridor; (*callejón*) passageway, alley; (*con tiendas*) arcade; (*pasarela*) gangway; catwalk.

pasado 1 *adj* (**a**) (*gen*) past; **lo** ~ the past; **lo** ~, ~ let bygones be bygones; **el mes** (**próximo**) ~ last month; ~ **mañana** the day after tomorrow; ~**s dos días** after two days.

(**b**) *comida* stale, bad; *fruta* overripe; *caza* (*en buen sentido*) high; (*muy hecho*) overdone; *cuento, noticia* stale; *idea* antiquated, out of date; *ropa etc* old, worn, threadbare; *belleza* faded; **la carne está pasada** the meat is off (*o* bad); **ella está un poco pasada** she's a little past her best.

2 *nm* (**a**) (*tiempo*) past.

(**b**) (*Ling*) past (tense).

(**c**) ~**s** ancestors.

pasador *nm* (**a**) (*pestillo etc*) bolt, fastener; (*de corbata*) (tie) pin; (*de pelo*) hairclip; (*Téc*) bolt; split pin.

(**b**) (*Culin*) colander; (*de té*) strainer; (*Téc*) filter.

(**c**) ~**es** (*gemelos*) cufflinks; (*And*) shoelaces.

(**d**) (*persona*) smuggler; (*LAm*) drug courier.

pasaje *nm* (**a**) (*acto*) passage, passing; (*Náut*) voyage, crossing.

(**b**) (*tarifa*) fare; **cobrar el** ~ to collect fares.

(**c**) (*viajeros*) passengers (*collectively*).

(**d**) (*callejón*) passageway, alleyway; (*con tiendas*) arcade; (*Carib, Cono Sur, Méx*) cul-de-sac.

(**e**) (*Liter, Mús*) passage.

(**f**) (*And, Carib: cuento*) story, anecdote.

(**g**) (*And: pisos*) tenement building.

pasajeramente *adv* fleetingly.

pasajero 1 *adj* (**a**) *momento etc* passing, fleeting, transient.

(**b**) **pájaro** ~ bird of passage, migratory bird.

(**c**) *calle etc* busy.

2 *nm*, **pasajera** *nf* passenger; traveller.
3 *nm* (*Méx*) ferryman.

pasamano(s) *nm* (**a**) (*barra*) rail, handrail; (*de escalera*) banisters. (**b**) (*Cos*) braid. (**c**) (*Cono Sur*) strap (*for standing passenger*). (**d**) (*Cono Sur*: *propina*) tip.

pasandito* *adv* (*CAm, Méx*) on tiptoe.

pasamontañas *nm invar* Balaclava (helmet), ski mask (*US*).

pasante *nm* (*gen*) assistant; (*Escol*) assistant teacher; tutor; (*Jur*) articled clerk.

pasapalos *nm invar* (*Carib*) snack, appetizer.

pasapasa *nm* sleight of hand.

pasaporte *nm* passport; **dar el ~ a uno*** (*despedir*) to boot sb out; (*matar*) to bump sb off‡.

pasaport(e)ar‡ [1a] *vt* to bump off‡.

pasapuré(s) *nm invar* mixer, blender.

pasar [1a] **1** *vt* (**a**) (*gen*) to pass; *objeto* to hand, give, pass (*a* to); *noticia, recado* to give, pass on; *cuenta* to send; *propiedad* to transfer; *persona* to take, lead, conduct (*a* to, into); *página* to turn; **¿me pasas la sal, por favor?** would you please pass the salt?; **nos hicieron pasar a otra habitación** they showed us into another room; **nos pasaron a ver al director** they took us to see the director; *V* **lista, revista** *etc*.

(**b**) *enfermedad* to give, infect with; **me has pasado tu tos** you've given me that cough.

(**c**) *visita etc* to make, carry out; **el médico pasará visita** the doctor will call.

(**d**) *calle, río* to cross, go over.

(**e**) *armadura etc* to pierce, penetrate, go through; *barrera* to pass through (*o* across, over), go through; *frontera, límite etc* to cross, go beyond; **el túnel pasa la montaña** the tunnel goes right through the mountain; **esto pasa los límites de lo razonable** this goes beyond anything that is reasonable.

(**f**) (*introducir*) to insert, put in; (*colar*) to put through; **~ el café por el colador** to put the coffee through a filter, strain the coffee.

(**g**) (*tragar*) to swallow; (*LAm*) to bear, stand, put up with; **no puedo ~ este vino** I can't get this wine down; **no puedo ~ a ese hombre** I can't bear that chap*.

(**h**) *examen etc* to pass.

(**i**) *falta etc* to overlook, tolerate; *persona* to forgive, indulge, be soft on; **no te voy a ~ más** I'm not going to indulge you any more.

(**j**) *moneda falsa* to pass (off); *contrabanda* to smuggle (in, out); **a ése se le puede ~ cualquier cosa** you can get anything past him.

(**k**) (*superar*) to surpass, excel; *rival* to do better than, beat, outdistance; (*Aut*) to pass, overtake; **él me pasa ya 3 cms** he's already 3 cms taller than I am.

(**l**) *fecha, suceso etc* to pass, go past; *enfermedad* to get over; **hemos pasado el aniversario** we are past the anniversary, the anniversary is behind us.

(**m**) (*omitir*) to omit, leave out, pass over; to skip; to overlook; *V* **alto 3** (**f**).

(**n**) *tiempo* to spend, pass; **~ las vacaciones** to spend one's holidays; **fuimos a ~ el día en la playa** we went to the seaside for a day; **~lo bien** to have a good time; **¡que lo pases bien!** have a good time!, enjoy yourself!; **lo pasaremos tan ricamente** we'll have such a good time; **~lo mal** to have a bad time (of it); **~las moradas** *o* **negras** (*etc*) to have a tough time of it.

(**o**) *penas* to suffer, endure, go through.

(**p**) **~ la mano por algo** to pass (*o* run) one's hand over sth; to stroke sth; **~ el rosario** to tell one's beads; **~ el cepillo por el pelo** to run a brush through (*o* over) one's hair.

(**q**) *película, programa* to screen, show.

(**r**) (*Cono Sur**) to cheat, swindle.

2 *vi* (**a**) (*gen*) to pass, go; **pasó de mis manos a las suyas** it passed from my hands into his; **la cuerda pasa de un lado a otro de la calle** the rope goes from one side of the street to the other; **el hilo pasa por el agujero** the thread goes through the hole; **el río pasa por la ciudad** the river flows (*o* goes, runs) through the city; **el autobús pasa delante de nuestra casa** the bus goes past our house.

(**b**) (*gen*: *persona*) to pass, go; to move; to come in, go in; **¡pase Vd!** come in!; after you!; **~ a un cuarto contiguo** to go into an adjoining room, move into an adjoining room; **no se puede ~** you can't go in; you can't go through; **pasamos directamente a ver al jefe** we went straight in to see the boss; **nos hicieron ~** they showed us in (*a* to), they ushered us in; **~ a decir algo** to go on to say sth; **y luego pasaron a otra cosa** and then they went on to sth else; **los moros pasaron a España** the Moors crossed into (*o* over to) Spain; **~ adelante** to go on, continue, proceed; **~ de Inglaterra al Canadá** to move (*o* go, migrate) from England to Canada; **~ de teniente a general** to go from lieutenant to general; **~ por una crisis** to go through a crisis; **pasaré por tu casa** I'll call on you (at home), I'll drop in.

(**c**) (*ser aceptado*) (*propuesta*) to pass, get through, be approved; (*disculpa*) to be accepted; **puede ~** it's passable, it's O.K.*; **esta moneda no pasa** this coin is a dud*, this coin is no good; **que me llames carroza, pase, pero fascista, no** you can call me an old square if you like, but not a fascist.

(**d**) **~ de** (*exceder*) to go beyond; to exceed; **~ de los límites** to exceed the limits; **pasa ya de los 70** he's over 70; **esto pasa de ser una broma** this goes beyond a joke; **no pasa de ser una mediocridad** he's no more than a mediocrity; **no pasan de 60 los que lo tienen** those who have it do not number more than 60; **de ésta no pasa** this is the very last time; **de hoy no pasa que le escriba** I'll write to him this very day; **yo de ahí no paso** that's as far as I can go; I draw the line at that; there I stick.

(**e**) (*Naipes*) to pass; **paso** I pass, no bid.

(**f**) **Juan pasa por francés** John could be taken for a Frenchman; **pasa por buen pintor** he is considered to be a good painter; **pasa por sabio** he has a reputation for learning; **se hace ~ por médico** he passes himself off as a doctor, he poses as a doctor.

(**g**) (*depender de*) **el futuro de la empresa pasa por este acuerdo** the company's future depends on this agreement (*o* requires this agreement as a condition).

(**h**) **ir pasando** (*fig*) to get by, manage (somehow); **~ con poco** to get along with very little; **tendrá que ~ sin coche** he'll have to get along without a car; **pasa por todo con tal que no le hagan trabajar** he'll put up with anything as long as they don't make him work.

(**i**) (*Esp**: *como pasota*) to be indifferent, to stand back, stand aside, not take part; to drop out; **~ de** to do without, get by without; to have no interest in, have no concern for; (*desatender*) to ignore; **yo pas(s)o de política** I'm not into politics*, politics is not for me; **siguen pasando de este problema** they go on ignoring this problem.

(**j**) (*tiempo*) to pass, go by, elapse; **han pasado 4 años** 4 years have gone by; **¡cómo pasa el tiempo!** how time passes!

(**k**) (*condición*) to be over; to pass away; (*efecto*) to pass off, wear off; **ha pasado la crisis** the crisis is over; **ya pasó aquello** that's all over (and done with) now.

(**l**) (*suceder*) to happen; **aquí pasa algo misterioso** sth odd is going on here; **¿pasa algo?** is anything up?, is anything wrong?; **¿qué pasa?** what's happening?, what's going on?, what's up?; **¿qué le pasa a ése?** what's the matter with him?; **¿qué ha pasado con ella?** what's become of her?; **¿qué pasa que no entra?** why on earth doesn't she come in?; **algo le pasa al motor** sth's the matter with the engine; **lo que pasa es que ..., pasa una cosa y es que ...** what's happening is that ..., what you find is that ..., it's like this ...; **como si no hubiese pasado nada** as if nothing (unusual) had happened; **pase lo que pase** whatever happens, come what may; **no me ha pasado otra (igual) en la vida** nothing like it has ever happened to me before; **siempre pasa igual** it's always the same; **siempre me pasa lo mismo** I'm always having the same trouble; **¿(qué) pas(s)a contigo?*** what gives?*, how are you?

3 pasarse *vr* (**a**) (*efecto etc*) to pass, pass off; **ya se te pasará** you'll get over it.

(**b**) (*perderse*) **se me pasó el turno** I missed my turn; **no se te pase la oportunidad** don't miss the chance this time.

(**c**) (*trasladarse etc*) = **1** (**a**); **~ al enemigo** to go over to the enemy.

(**d**) (*belleza, flor etc*) to fade; (*fruta*) to go soft, get overripe; (*comida*) to go bad, go off, get stale; (*té*) to stew; (*tela*) to wear, show signs of wear, get threadbare; (*mujer*) to lose her charms; **no se pasará si se tapa la botella** it will keep if you put the cap on the bottle.

(**e**) (*excederse*) to go too far, go over the line (*etc*); (*fig*) to overdo it; to say too much, go too far; **se pasa en mostrar agradecimiento** he overdoes the gratitude; **¡te has pas(s)ado, tío!*** bravo, friend!; well done, man!*

(**f**) (*tiempo*) = **1** (**n**); **se ha pasado todo el día leyendo** he has spent the whole day reading.

(**g**) **~ con, ~ sin**; *V* **2** (**g**).

(**h**) **no se le pasa nada** nothing escapes him, nothing

gets past him, he misses nothing; **se me pasó** it slipped my mind, I forgot; **se me pasó llamarle** I forgot to ring him.

(**i**) ~ **de** + *adj* to be too + *adj*, be excessively + *adj*; **se pasa de generoso** he's too generous; *V* **listo**.

4 *nm*: **un modesto** ~ a modest competence; **tener un buen** ~ to be well off.

pasarela *nf* (*puente*) footbridge; (*Teat etc*) walkway, catwalk; (*Náut*) gangway, gangplank; ~ **telescópica** airport walkway.

pasarrato *nm* (*Carib, Méx*) = **pasatiempo**.

pasatiempo *nm* pastime, (leisure) pursuit; hobby; amusement.

pascana *nf* (**a**) (*And, Cono Sur*: *fonda*) wayside inn. (**b**) (*And, Cono Sur*: *etapa*) stage, part (of a journey). (**c**) (*And*) part of a journey done without stopping.

Pascua *nf*, **pascua** *nf* (**a**) ~ **florida,** ~ **de Resurrección** Easter; ~ **de Navidad** Christmas; ~ **de Pentecostés** Whitsun, Whitsuntide; ~**s** Christmas holiday, Christmas time (*strictly, Christmas Day to Twelfth Night*); **¡felices** ~**s!** merry Christmas!; **cumplir con P**~ to do one's Easter duty.

(**b**) ~ **de los hebreos,** ~ **de los judíos** Passover.

(**c**) (*locuciones*) ... **y santas** ~**s** ... and that's that, ... and that's the lot; ... and there's nothing one can do about it; **de** ~**s a Ramos** once in a blue moon; **estar como unas** ~**s** to be as happy as a sandboy (*o* lark (*US*)); **hacer la** ~ **a uno*** to do the dirty on sb; to bug sb*; **¡que se hagan la** ~**!** (*Esp**) and they can lump it!

pascual *adj* paschal; **cordero** ~ (older) lamb.

pase *nm* (**a**) (*documento*) pass; (*Com*) permit; ~ **de embarque** (*Aer*) boarding-pass; ~ **de favor** (*Pol etc*) safe-conduct; (*Com*) complementary ticket; ~ **de lista** (*Mil*) rollcall.

(**b**) (*Dep*) pass; ~ **atrás** back pass.

(**c**) (*Cine*) showing; ~ **de modas,** ~ **de modelos** fashion show.

(**d**) (‡: *contrabando*) drug smuggling; (*LAm*‡) dose (of a drug), fix‡.

paseandero *adj* (*Cono Sur*) fond of strolling.

paseante *nmf* (**a**) (*que pasea*) walker, stroller; (*transeúnte*) passer-by; (*pey*: *t* ~ **en corte**) loafer, idler. (**b**) (*pretendiente*) suitor.

pasear [1a] **1** *vt* (**a**) *perro, niño etc* to take for a walk, walk.

(**b**) *pancarta etc* to parade, show off, exhibit; to walk about (the streets) with.

(**c**) ~ **la calle a una muchacha** (*Esp*) to walk up and down the street where a girl lives.

(**d**) (*CAm*) *dinero* to squander.

(**e**) (*Esp* Hist*) = **dar el paseo a** (*V* **paseo** (**e**)).

2 *vi y* **pasearse** *vr* (**a**) (*gen*) to walk, go for a walk, stroll; to walk about, walk up and down; ~ **en bicicleta** to go for a ride, go cycling; ~ **en coche** to go for a drive, go driving, go for a run; ~ **a caballo** to ride, go riding; ~ **en bote** (*etc*) to go sailing, go on a trip.

(**b**) ~ (*Esp fig*) to idle, loaf about.

(**c**) **pasearse por un tema** (*Esp*) to deal superficially with a subject.

(**d**) ~ (*Méx*) to take a day off.

paseíllo *nm* (*Taur*) inaugural procession (*o* ceremonial entry) of bullfighters.

paseo *nm* (**a**) (*acto*) stroll, walk; (*excursión*) outing; ~ **en bicicleta,** ~ **a caballo** ride; ~ **en coche** drive, run, ride, outing; ~ **espacial** walk in space; ~ **por la naturaleza** nature trail; ~ **de vigilancia** round, tour of inspection; **no va a ser un** ~ (*Esp*) it's not going to be easy, it won't be a walk-over; **dar un** ~ to go for a walk, take a walk (*o* stroll); to go for a ride (*etc*); **estar de** ~ to be out for a walk; **enviar** (*o* **mandar**) **a uno a** ~‡ to tell sb to go to blazes*, to chuck sb out, send sb packing; **¡vete a** ~**!**‡ get lost!‡; **llevar** (*o* **sacar**) **a un niño de** ~ to take a child out for a walk.

(**b**) (*avenida*) parade, avenue; ~ **marítimo** promenade, esplanade.

(**c**) (*distancia*) short walk; **entre las dos casas no hay más que un** ~ it's only a short walk between the two houses.

(**d**) ~ **cívico** (*LAm*) civic procession.

(**e**) (*Esp* Hist*) (journey leading to the) summary execution of a political opponent; **dar el** ~ **a uno** to execute sb summarily; (*moderno*) to bump sb off‡.

pasero *nm* (*And*) ferryman.

pashá *nm* = **pachá**.

pasible *adj* (*liter*) able to endure, long-suffering.

paseíto *nm* little walk, gentle stroll.

pasillear [1a] *vi* (*Parl*) to engage in lobby discussions, lobby.

pasilleo *nm* lobby discussions, lobbying.

pasillo *nm* (**a**) (*Arquit*) passage, corridor; (*Parl*: *fig*) lobby; (*Náut*) gangway; ~ **aéreo** air corridor, airlane; ~ **móvil,** ~ **rodante** travelator. (**b**) (*Teat*) short piece, sketch.

pasión *nf* (**a**) passion; **la P**~ (*Rel*) the Passion; **tener** ~ **por** to be passionately fond of, have a passion for. (**b**) (*pey*) bias, prejudice, partiality.

pasional *adj* (**a**) *persona etc* passionate; **crimen** ~ crime of passion. (**b**) (*caprichoso*) temperamental.

pasionaria *nf* passionflower.

pasito *adv* gently, softly.

pasivamente *adv* passively.

pasividad *nf* passiveness, passivity.

pasivo 1 *adj* (**a**) (*gen*) passive; (*Econ*) inactive. (**b**) (*Ling*) passive. **2** *nm* (**a**) (*Com, Fin*) liabilities, debts; (*de cuenta*) debit side; ~ **circulante,** ~ **corriente** current liabilities; ~ **diferido** deferred liabilities. (**b**) (*Ling*) passive (voice).

pasma‡ **1** *nm* cop*. **2** *nf* (*Esp*) cops*, fuzz‡.

pasmado *adj* (**a**) (*asombrado*) astonished, amazed; **dejar** ~ **a uno** to amaze sb; **estar** (*o* **quedar**) ~ **de** to be amazed at, be astonished at; **mirar con cara de** ~ to look in astonishment (at).

(**b**) (*atontado*) bewildered; **estar** (*o* **quedar**) ~ to stand gaping, be flabbergasted, be bewildered, look silly; **se quedó ahí** ~ he just stood there gaping; **¡oye,** ~**!*** hey, you dope!*

(**c**) (*LAm*) *herida* infected, unhealthy; *persona* unhealthy-looking, ill-looking.

(**d**) (*CAm, Méx*) (*tonto*) thick; stupid; (*torpe*) clumsy.

(**e**) (*LAm*) *fruta* overripe.

pasmar [1a] **1** *vt* (**a**) (*asombrar*) to amaze, astonish, astound; to flabbergast; (*atontar*) to stun, dumbfound.

(**b**) (*enfriar*) to chill (to the bone); *planta* to nip, cut.

2 pasmarse *vr* (**a**) (*asombrarse*) to be amazed (*etc; de* at); to be dumbfounded; to marvel, wonder (*de* at).

(**b**) (*estar helado*) to be chilled to the bone; (*resfriarse*) to catch a chill.

(**c**) (*LAm*) (*infectarse*) to become infected; (*enfermar*) to fall ill; (*con fiebre*) to catch a fever; (*con trismo*) to get lockjaw.

(**d**) (*Carib, Méx*: *fruta*) to dry up, wither.

(**e**) (*color*) to fade.

pasmarota *nf*, **pasmarotada** *nf* display of shocked surprise, exaggerated reaction.

pasmazón *nm* (*CAm, Carib, Méx*) = **pasmo**.

pasmo *nm* (**a**) (*asombro*) amazement, astonishment; awe; (*fig*) wonder, marvel, prodigy; **es el** ~ **de cuantos lo ven** it is a marvel (*o* a source of wonder) to all who see it.

(**b**) (*Med*: *trismo*) lockjaw, tetanus.

(**c**) (*Med*: *enfriamiento*) chill.

(**d**) (*LAm*: *fiebre*) fever.

pasmosamente *adv* amazingly; awesomely; wonderfully.

pasmoso *adj* amazing, astonishing; awesome, breathtaking; wonderful.

paso[1] *adj fruta* dried.

paso[2] **1** *nm* (**a**) (*acto*) passing, passage; crossing; (*Aut*) overtaking, passing; (*Orn, Zool*) migration, passage; (*fig*) transition; progress; **el** ~ **del tiempo** the passage of time; **lo recogeré al** (*o* **de**) ~ I'll pick it up when I'm passing; **salir al** ~ **a** (*o* **de**) to waylay; to confront; (*fig*) to nip in the bud; to strangle at birth; *rumor* to refute, deny, contradict; **de** ~ (*al mismo tiempo*) in passing; (*a propósito*) by the way, incidentally; **estar de** ~ to be passing through; **entrar de** ~ to drop in, call in (for a moment).

(**b**) (*camino*) way through, passage; (*Arquit*) passage; **¡**~**!** make way!, gangway!; ~ **de cebra** (*Esp*) zebra crossing; ~ **elevado,** ~ **a desnivel,** ~ **a distinto nivel** (*Aut*) flyover; ~ **franco,** ~ **libre** free passage, free access; clear way through; ~ **inferior** underpass; ~ **a nivel** level-crossing, grade crossing (*US*); ~ **a nivel sin barrera** unguarded level-crossing; ~ **de** (*o* **para**) **peatones** pedestrian crossing; ~ **salmonero** salmon ladder; ~ **subterráneo** subway, underpass (*US*); ~ **superior** (*Aut*) overpass, flyover; **'**~ **prohibido', 'prohibido el** ~**'** 'no throughfare', 'no entry'; **abrir** ~ **para** to make way for; **abrirse** ~ to make one's way (*entre, por* through), force a way through; **abrirse** ~ **luchando** to fight one's way through; **abrirse** ~ **a tiros** to shoot one's way through; **ceder el** ~ to make way; (*Aut*) to give way, yield (*US*); **'ceda el** ~**'** (*Aut*) 'give way'; **ceder el** ~ **a** (*fig*), **dar** ~ **a** to give way to, give place to; **cerrar el** ~**, impedir el** ~ to block the way; **dejar** ~ **a** to open the way for, leave the way clear for; **dejarle** ~ **a uno** to let sb by.

(c) (*Geog*) pass; (*Náut*) strait.

(d) (*de pie*: *acto*) step, pace; (*huella*) footprint; (*sonido*) footstep, footfall; (*distancia*) pace; ~ **atrás** step backwards, (*fig*) backward step; ~ **de baile** dance step; ~ **a dos** pas de deux; ~ **en falso** false step; ~ **a** ~ step by step; **a cada** ~ at every step, at every turn; **a grandes ~s, a ~s agigantados** (*fig*) by leaps and bounds; **a dos ~s de aquí** two steps from here, very near here; **estar a un ~ mínimo de** to border on, verge closely on; **por sus ~s contados** step by step, systematically; **coger el** ~ (*lit, fig*) to fall into step (*con* with); **dar un** ~ to take a step; **dar un ~ en falso** to stumble; (*fig*) to take a false step; **no da un ~ sin hacer alguna barbaridad** he can't take a step without doing something awful; **llevar el** ~ to keep in step, keep time; **marcar el** ~ (*LAm*) (*lit*) to keep time, (*fig*) to mark time; **seguir los ~s a uno** to tail sb, shadow sb; **seguir los ~s de uno** to follow in sb's footsteps; **volver sobre los ~s** to retrace one's steps; (*fig*) to retract.

(e) (*modo de andar*) walk, gait; (*ritmo*) speed, pace, rate; (*de caballo*) gait; ~ **de andadura** amble; ~ **de ganso** (*LAm*), ~ **de (la) oca** goose step; **buen** ~ quick step, good pace; **a buen** ~ quickly; (*fig*) at a good rate; **a ~ lento** at a slow pace, slowly; **a ~ ligero** (*Mil*), **a ~ redoblado** (*LAm*) at the double; **a ~ de tortuga** at a snail's pace; **a ese** ~ (*fig*) at that rate; **al** ~ slowly; **al ~ que vamos** at the rate we're going; **al ~ que ...** (*como conj*) at the same time as ...; while ..., whereas ...; **acelerar** (*o* **apretar, avivar** *etc*) **el** ~ to go faster, quicken one's pace; **aflojar el** ~ to slow down, slacken one's pace; **establecer el** ~ to make the pace, set the pace; **romper el** ~ to break step.

(f) (*de baile*) step; ~ **a dos** pas de deux; ~ **de vals** waltz step.

(g) (*fig*) step, move; measure; (*Inform*) step; ~ **adelante** step forward, advance; **es un ~ hacia nuestro objetivo** it's a step towards our objective; **andar en malos ~s** to be mixed up in shady affairs; **dar un mal** ~ to take a false step, make a false move; to get in the family way; **dar los primeros ~s** to make the first moves; *V t sentidos figurados en* (**d**).

(h) (*episodio*) episode, incident, event.

(i) (*Teat Hist*) sketch, interlude; (*Ecl*) *float* (*o series of sculptures etc*) *representing part of the Easter story, carried in procession.*

(j) (*Elec, Téc*) pitch.

(k) ~ **de armas** (*Mil Hist*) passage of arms.

(l) (*apuro*) difficulty, awkward situation, crisis; **salir del** ~ to get out of a jam*, get out of trouble.

(m) (*LAm*: *vado*) ford.

(n) (*Telec*) metered unit.

2 *adv* softly, gently; **¡~!** not so fast!, easy there!

pasoso *adj* (**a**) (*LAm*) (*poroso*) porous, permeable; (*absorbente*) absorbent. (**b**) (*Cono Sur*: *sudoroso*) perspiring, sweaty. (**c**) (*And Med*) contagious.

pasota* **1** *adj invar* (**a**) (*Esp*) **filosofía** ~ hippy (*o* drop-out) outlook (*o* mentality); **vida** ~ hippy (*o* drop-out) life style.

(**b**) (*Méx*: *pasado de moda*) passé, out of fashion.

2 *nmf* hippy, drop-out; non-conformist.

pasote* *nm* outrage; exaggeration.

pasotismo *nm* (*Esp*) hippy (*o* drop-out) mentality; hippy life-style.

paspa *nf* (*And*), **paspadura** *nf* (*Cono Sur*) chapped skin, cracked skin.

pasparse [1a] *vr* (*LAm*: *piel*) to chap, crack.

paspartú *nm* passe-partout.

pasquín *nm* (*Liter*) skit, satire, lampoon; (*Pol etc*) wall poster.

passar* [1a] *vi* (*hum*) *pronunciación de* **pasar** (*esp sentidos* **2** (**i**) *y* (**l**), **3** (**e**).

passim *adv* passim.

pasta *nf* (**a**) (*gen*) paste; ~ **de carne** meat paste; ~ **de coca** cocaine paste; ~ **de dientes,** ~ **dentífrica** toothpaste; ~ **de madera** wood pulp.

(**b**) (*de muelas*) filling; (*de lapicero*) lead.

(**c**) (*cartón*) cardboard; papier-mâché; (*Tip*) boards; ~ **española** marbled leather binding; **media** ~ half-binding; **libro en** ~ book in boards.

(**d**) (*Culin*: *masa*) dough; (*para pastel*) pastry (mixture); **~s** (*pasteles*) pastries, cakes; (*fideos*) noodles, spaghetti.

(**e**) (*) dough‡, money; **una** ~ a lot of money; ~ **gansa** big money; **soltar la** ~ to cough up*.

(**f**) **de buena** ~ (*Esp*) equable; kindly, good-natured.

(**g**) (*LAm*) drug tablet.

pastaje *nm* (*And, CAm, Cono Sur*), **pastal** *nm* (*LAm*) (*pastizal*) pasture, grazing land; (*pasto*) grass, pasture.

pastaplumón *nm* felt-tip pen.

pastar [1a] *vti* to graze.

pastear [1a] *vt* to graze.

pastejón *nm* solid mass, lump.

pastel 1 *nm* (**a**) (*Culin*) (*de frutas etc*) cake; (*de carne etc*) pie; **~es** pastry, confectionery; **repartirse el** ~ (*fig*) to divide up the cake (*o* pie (*US*)).

(**b**) (*Arte*) pastel; pastel drawing (*t* **pintura al** ~).

(**c**) (*Naipes*) sharp practice; (*fig*) plot; undercover agreement, cynical compromise, deal; **descubrir el** ~ to give the game away; **se le descubrió el** ~ his little game was found out.

(**d**) (*: *chapuza*) botch, mess.

2 *atr*: **tono** ~ pastel shade.

pastelado *nm* (*Carib*) choc-ice.

pastelear [1a] *vi* (**a**) (*trampear*) to go in for sharp practice; to plot; to make cynical compromises. (**b**) (*temporizar*) to stall, spin it out to gain time. (**c**) (*: *adular*) to creep*, be a bootlicker*.

pastelería *nf* (**a**) (*arte*) (art of) confectionery, pastry-making. (**b**) (*pasteles*) pastry, pastries (*collectively*). (**c**) (*tienda*) confectioner's, pastry shop, cake shop.

pastelero 1 *adj* (**a**) (*Culin*) **masa pastelera** dough; cake-mix; **rodillo** ~ rolling-pin. (**b**) **no tengo ni pastelera idea*** (*euf*) I haven't a clue*. (**c**) (*Cono Sur*) meddlesome, intriguing. **2** *nm*, **pastelera** *nf* (**a**) (*Culin*) pastrycook; confectioner. (**b**) (*LAm Pol*) turncoat. (**c**) (*And*‡: *traficante*) drug dealer, drug trafficker.

pastelillo *nm* small cake; ~ **de mantequilla** (*Esp*) pat of butter; ~ **de hígado de ganso** (*Esp*) pâté de foie gras.

pastelón *nm* (*Cono Sur*) large paving stone.

pasterizar [1f] *vt etc* = **pasteurizar** *etc.*

pasteurización *nf* pasteurization.

pasteurizado *adj* pasteurized.

pasteurizar [1f] *vt* to pasteurize.

pastiche *nm* pastiche.

pastilla 1 *nf* (*Med*) tablet, pastille; (*de jabón etc*) cake, bar; (*de chocolate*) bar, piece; (*Inform*) chip; **la** ~ (*esp Med*) the pill; ~ **de caldo** stock cube; ~ **de freno**(**s**) (*Aut*) brake-lining; ~ **de silicío** silicon chip; ~ **para la tos** cough-drop, throat lozenge; **ir a toda** ~ (*Esp**) to go full-belt*. **2** *adj invar* (*Esp*‡) boring.

pastillero *nm* pillbox.

pastinaca *nf* parsnip.

pastizal *nm* pasture.

pastizara‡ *nf* bread‡, money; **una** ~ a whole heap of money.

pasto *nm* (**a**) (*hierba*) grass, herbage, fodder; grazing; (*Méx*‡) grass‡, pot‡; ~ **seco** fodder; **un sitio abundante en ~s** a place with rich grazing.

(**b**) (*comida*) (*any*) food, feed (*for cattle*).

(**c**) (*campo*) pasture, field; (*LAm*) grass, lawn; **echar el ganado al** ~ to put animals out to pasture.

(**d**) (*fig*) food, nourishment; fuel; **fue ~ del fuego, fue ~ de las llamas** it was fuel to the flames, the flames devoured it; **es ~ de la murmuración** it is a subject for gossip, gossip thrives on it; **fue ~ de los mirones** the onlookers lapped it up; **es ~ de la actualidad** it's headline material, it's highly newsworthy; ~ **espiritual** spiritual nourishment.

(**e**) **a** ~ abundantly; **había fruta a** ~ there was fruit in unlimited quantities; **beber a todo** ~ to drink for all one is worth, drink to excess; **correr a todo** ~ to run like hell*; **cita refranes a todo** ~ he quotes vast quantities of proverbs, he greatly overdoes the proverbs.

(**f**) **vino de** ~ ordinary wine.

pastón‡ *nm*: **un** ~ a whole heap of money*.

pastor *nm* (**a**) (*Agr*) (*de ovejas*) shepherd; (*de ganado*) herdsman; (*de cabras*) goatherd; (*de vacas*) cowman (*etc*); **el Buen P~** the Good Shepherd.

(**b**) (*Ecl*) (Protestant) minister, clergyman, pastor.

(**c**) ~ **alemán** Alsatian (dog); **viejo ~ inglés** old English sheepdog.

pastora *nf* (**a**) (*Agr*) shepherdess. (**b**) (*Ecl*) (woman) minister, (woman) pastor.

pastorada *nf* Nativity procession, moving tableau of the Nativity.

pastoral 1 *adj* pastoral. **2** *nf* (**a**) (*Liter etc*) pastoral, idyll. (**b**) (*Ecl*) pastoral letter.

pastorear [1a] *vt* (**a**) *rebaño* to pasture, graze, shepherd; to look after; (*Ecl*) to guide, lead.

(**b**) (*CAm, Cono Sur*: *acechar*) to lie in wait for.

(**c**) (*CAm*: *mimar*) to spoil, pamper.

pastorela *nf* (*Liter*) pastourelle.

pastoreo *nm* grazing.

pastoril *adj* (*Liter*) pastoral.

pastoso *adj* (**a**) *material* doughy; soft; pasty. (**b**) *voz* rich, mellow, pleasant; *vino* mellow, rich. (**c**) (*Cono Sur*: *con hierba*) grassy. (**d**) (*And**: *vago*) lazy.

pastura *nf* (**a**) (*campo*) pasture. (**b**) (*comida*) food, fodder, feed.

pasturaje *nm* common pasture.

pasudo *adj* (*Méx*) *pelo* kinky.

pat *nm, pl* **pats** [pat] putt.

pat. *abr de* **patente** patent, pat.

pata 1 *nf* (**a**) (*Zool*) foot, leg; paw; (*Orn*) foot; (*de persona, hum*) foot; (*de mueble etc*) leg; (*Cono Sur*: *fig*) stage, leg; **~ de cabra** (*Téc*) crowbar; **~ de gallina** (*And, Carib*) crow's-feet (*wrinkles*); **~ de gallo** crow's-feet; (*: *disparate*) silly remark, piece of nonsense; (*: *plancha*) bloomer*; **~ hendida** cloven hoof; **andar a la ~ coja, andar a la ~ sola** (*And*) to play hopscotch; **eso lo sé hacer a la ~ coja** I can do that blindfold; **~s arriba** on one's back, upside down; (*fig*) upside down, topsy-turvy; **poner a uno ~s arriba*** to dumbfound sb; **a ~** on foot; **a cuatro ~s** on all fours; **a la ~ la llana** plainly, simply, directly; bluntly; **andar a ~s** (*niño*) to crawl, go on all fours; **andar a ~ renca** (*LAm*) to limp; **enseñar la ~, sacar la ~** to give oneself away; **estirar la ~*** to peg out‡; **hacer la ~ a uno** (*Cono Sur**) to soft-soap sb*; **meter ~** (*Cono Sur* Aut*) to step on the gas*; **meter la ~*** to put one's foot in it, make a blunder; to blot one's copybook; to butt in; **ser ~(s)** to be even, tie; **es un diccionario con dos ~s** he's a walking dictionary; **es la virtud con dos ~s** she is virtue personified; **tener ~s*** (*Cono Sur*) to be brash; be cheeky*; **tener buena ~** to be lucky; **tener mala ~** (*suerte*) to be unlucky; (*torpe*) to be clumsy; **ser de mala ~** to be unlucky, bring bad luck; **ser ~ de perro** (*Cono Sur*) to be footloose, be fond of travelling.

(**b**) (*Zool*) (female) duck.

(**c**) **P~s*** Old Nick; **~s cortas*** shorty*, little man.

2 *nmf* (*And*) (*amigo*) pal*, mate*, buddy (*US*); (*tipo*) bloke‡, bird‡.

pataca *nf* Jerusalem artichoke.

patacón *nm* (**a**) (*And Culin*) slice of fried banana. (**b**) (*Cono Sur*: *moretón*) bruise, welt.

patache *nm* (**a**) (*barca*) flat-bottomed boat. (**b**) (*And*) (*sopa*) soup; (‡: *comida*) food, grub‡.

patacho *nm* (**a**) (*Cono Sur*: *lancha*) flat-bottomed boat. (**b**) (*CAm, Méx*: *recua*) train of mules.

patada *nf* (**a**) (*coz*) kick; (*en el suelo*) stamp; **~ hacia arriba*** kick upstairs; **a ~s** in abundance, galore; (*tratar etc*) roughly, inconsiderately; **en dos ~s*** (*sin esfuerzo*) with no trouble at all; (*en seguida*) in a jiffy*, right away; **esto lo termino en dos ~s** I'll finish (*o* be through with) this in no time at all, it won't take me any time to finish this; **dar ~s** to kick; to stamp; **dar ~s para conseguir algo** to take steps to obtain sth; **dar la ~ a uno*** to give sb the boot*; **dar a uno una ~ en el culo** (*Esp**) to kick sb up the backside; **me da cien ~s*** (*objeto*) it gets on my nerves; (*persona*) he gives me a pain in the neck*, I can't stand him; **echar a uno a ~s** to kick sb out; **me sentó como una ~ en el estómago*** (*o* **en los cojones****) it was like a kick in the teeth*; **tratar a uno a ~s** to kick sb around.

(**b**) **me** *etc* **fue de la ~** (*CAm, Méx**) it was a disaster, it all went wrong.

patadón *nm* big kick; (*Dep*) long kick, long ball; long clearance.

patagón, -ona *adj, nm/f* Patagonian.

patagónico *adj* Patagonian.

patalear [1a] *vi* (**a**) (*en el suelo*) to stamp (angrily).

(**b**) (*fig*) to protest; to make a fuss; **por mí, que patalee** so far as I'm concerned he can make all the fuss he likes.

(**c**) (*bebé etc*) to kick out, kick about.

pataleo *nm* (**a**) (*en el suelo*) stamping; (*en el aire*) kicking. (**b**) (*fig*) protest; (*lío*) scene, fuss; **derecho al ~** right to protest, right to make a fuss; **tener derecho al ~** (*fig*) to have the right to complain.

pataleta *nf* (*rabieta*) tantrum; (*Med*) fit, convulsion; **¡qué ~!** what a fuss!; **dar ~s** (*LAm*: *niño*) to stamp one's feet.

patán *nm* rustic, yokel; (*pey*) lout.

pataplaf, pataplás, pataplún (*LAm*) *interj* bang!, crash!

patarata *nf* (**a**) (*afectación*) gush, affectation; (*aspaviento*) emotional fuss; excessive show of feeling. (**b**) (*disparate*) silly thing; (*bagatela*) triviality; **~s** nonsense, tomfoolery.

pataratero *adj* (**a**) (*afectado*) gushing, affected. (**b**) (*tonto*) silly.

pataruco *adj* (*Carib*) (**a**) (*tosco*) coarse, rough. (**b**) (*cobarde*) cowardly.

patasca *nf* (*And Culin*) pork stew with corn; **armar una ~*** to kick up a racket.

patata *nf* (*Esp*) (**a**) potato; **~s bravas** fried potatoes with spicy tomato sauce; **~ caliente** (*fig*) hot potato, hot issue; **~s deshechas** mashed potatoes; **~s enteras, ~s con su piel** jacket potatoes, potatoes in their jackets; **~s fritas** chips, French fries (*US*); **~ fritas** (**a la inglesa**) crisps, potato chips (*US*); **~s nuevas** new potatoes; **~ de siembra** seed potato; **~ temprana** early potato.

(**b**) (*: *locuciones*) **ni ~** not a thing; **no se me da una ~,** (**no**) **me importa una ~** I don't care two hoots (*de* about); **no entendió una ~** he didn't understand a word of it; **pasar la ~ caliente*** to pass the buck*.

(**c**) (**) cunt**.

patatal *nm*, **patatar** *nm* potato field, potato patch.

patatera *nf* potato plant.

patatero* *adj*: **oficial ~** ranker.

patatín*: **y ~ patatán** and so on; **que** (**si**) **~, que** (**si**) **patatán** this, that and the other; **en el año ~** in such-and-such a year.

patato* *adj* (*Carib*), **patatuco*** *adj* (*Carib*) short.

patatús *nm* dizzy spell, queer turn.

pateada *nf* (**a**) (*Cono Sur*) long tiring walk. (**b**) = **pateadura**.

pateador *nm* (*Dep*) kicker.

pateadura *nf*, **pateamiento** *nm* (**a**) (*acto*) stamping, kicking. (**b**) (*fig*: *en discusión*) flat denial; violent interjection; (*Teat*) noisy protest, catcalls.

patear[1] [1a] **1** *vt* (**a**) (*pisotear*) to stamp on, trample (on); (*dar patadas a*) to kick, boot; (*Dep*) *pelota* to kick.

(**b**) (*Esp**: *andar por*) to tramp round, cover, go over; **tuve que ~ toda la ciudad** I had to tramp round the whole town; **~ el mercado** to put in some legwork (and go looking for business).

(**c**) (*fig*) to trample on, treat roughly, treat inconsiderately.

(**d**) (*Carib*) to abuse.

(**e**) **la comida me ha pateado** (*Cono Sur**) the meal has upset my stomach.

2 *vi* (**a**) (*patalear*) to stamp (with rage), stamp one's foot; (*Teat etc*) to stamp.

(**b**) (*LAm*: *animal, arma*) to kick.

(**c**) (*: *ir a pata*) to walk (it); (*Cono Sur*) to go long distances on foot.

(**d**) (*: *ir y venir*) to be always on the go, bustle about.

3 patearse* *vr* (**a**) **nos hemos pateado Madrid** we explored (*o* did*) Madrid on foot. (**b**) **~ el dinero** to blow one's money*.

patear[2] [1a] *vi* to putt.

patena *nf* paten.

patentado *adj* patent; proprietary.

patentar [1a] *vt* to patent.

patente 1 *adj* (**a**) (*gen*) patent, obvious, evident; **hacer ~** to show clearly, establish.

(**b**) (*Com etc*) patent.

(**c**) (*Cono Sur**: *excelente*) superb, great.

2 *nf* (**a**) (*Jur etc*) grant; warrant; (*Com*) patent; **~ de corso** licence to do whatever one pleases; **~ de invención** patent; **~ de navegación** ship's certificate of registration; **~ de privilegio** letters patent; **~ de sanidad** bill of health; **de ~** patent; (*Cono Sur*) first-rate.

(**b**) (*LAm Aut*) (*placa*) number-plate; (*carnet*) driving licence.

3 *nm* (*Carib*) patent medicine.

patentizar [1f] **1** *vt* to show, reveal, make evident. **2 patentizarse** *vr* to show plainly, become obvious.

pateo *nm* stamping; (*Teat*) stamping, noisy protest.

páter* *nm* (*Mil*) padre*.

paternal *adj* fatherly, paternal.

paternalismo *nm* paternalism; (*pey*) patronizing attitude.

paternalista 1 *adj* paternalistic; (*pey*) patronizing. **2** *nm* paternalist; (*pey*) patronizing person.

paternalmente *adv* paternally, in a fatherly fashion.

paternidad *nf* (**a**) (*gen*) fatherhood, parenthood. (**b**) (*de hijo*) paternity; **~ literaria** authorship.

paterno *adj* paternal; **abuelo ~** paternal grandfather, grandfather on the father's side.

patero* *adj* (**a**) (*Cono Sur*: *adulador*) fawning. (**b**) (*And*: *embustero*) slippery, wily.

patéticamente *adv* pathetically, movingly, poignantly.

patético *adj* (**a**) (*gen*) pathetic, moving, poignant. (**b**)

(*Cono Sur*) clear, evident. (**c**) **es muy** ~ (*And**: *andador*) he loves walking.

patetismo *nm* pathos, poignancy.

patiabierto *adj* bow-legged.

patibulario *adj* (**a**) (*horroroso*) horrifying, harrowing. (**b**) *persona* sinister.

patíbulo *nm* scaffold; gallows, gibbet.

paticorto *adj* short-legged.

patidifuso* *adj* aghast, shattered; openmouthed; nonplussed; **dejar a uno** ~ to shatter sb; to nonplus sb.

patiestevado *adj* bandy-legged.

patihendido *adj* cloven-hoofed.

patilargo *adj* long-legged.

patilla 1 *nf* (**a**) (*Cono Sur*) bench.

(**b**) (*And, Carib*: *sandía*) water-melon.

(**c**) (*Cono Sur Bot*) layer.

(**d**) (*de gafas*) sidepiece, temple (*US*); (*de vestido*) pocket flap.

(**e**) (*Inform*) pin.

(**f**) ~**s** (*esp Esp*) (*de hombre*) sideburns; (*de mujer*) kiss curl.

2 ~**s** *nm*: **P~s*** Old Nick; **ser un ~s** (*Esp**) to be a weak character, be a poor fish.

patimocho *adj* (*LAm*: *cojo*) lame.

patín *nm* (**a**) (*Dep*) skate; (*de trineo*) runner; (*Aer*) skid; **patines** (*Cono Sur*) soft over-slippers; ~ **de cola** (*Aer*) tailskid; ~ **de cuchilla,** ~ **de hielo** ice-skate; ~ **de ruedas** roller-skate. (**b**) (*Náut*: *t* ~ **a pedal,** ~ **playero**) pedalo, pedal-boat; (*de niño*) scooter; (*Aut**) banger‡, old car.

pátina *nf* patina.

patinadero *nm* skating rink.

patinado *adj* shiny, glossy.

patinador(a) *nm/f* skater.

patinadura *nf* (*Carib*) skid, skidding.

patinaje *nm* skating; ~ **artístico,** ~ **de figuras** figure-skating; ~ **sobre hielo** ice-skating; ~ **sobre ruedas** roller-skating; ~ **de velocidad** speed skating.

patinar [1a] *vi* (**a**) (*persona*) to skate. (**b**) (*Aut etc*) to skid, slip. (**c**) (*: *meter la pata*) to boob*, make a blunder. (**d**) (*Cono Sur*) to fail.

patinazo *nm* (**a**) (*Aut*) skid. (**b**) (*: *error*) boob*, blunder; **dar un ~, pegar un** ~ to make a boob*, blunder.

patinete *nm,* **patineta** *nf* scooter.

patio *nm* (*Arquit*) court, courtyard, patio; (*Teat*) pit; (*de garaje*) forecourt; (*Méx Ferro*) shunting yard; ~ **de armas** parade-ground; ~ **de luces** well (of a building); ~ **de operaciones** floor (of the stock exchange); ~ **de recreo** playground; **¡cómo está el ~!*** what a to-do!; **llevar el** ~ to rule the roost.

patiquín *nm* (*Carib*) fop, dandy.

patita *nf*: *V* **calle** (**a**).

patitieso *adj* (**a**) (*paralizado*) paralyzed with cold (*o* fright *etc*). (**b**) (*fig*) = **patidifuso.** (**c**) (*fig*: *engreído*) conceited, stuck-up*.

patito *nm* duckling; ~ **feo** ugly duckling (*also fig*); **los dos ~s*** number twenty-two.

patituerto *adj* bandy-legged.

patizambo *adj* knock-kneed.

pato *nm* (**a**) (*Orn*) duck; ~ (**macho**) drake; ~ **real,** ~ **silvestre** mallard, wild duck; ~ **de reclamo** decoy duck; **pagar el ~*** to foot the bill; to take the blame, carry the can*; **ser el ~ de la boda** (*o* **fiesta**) (*LAm*) to be a laughing stock; **salga ~ o gallareta** (*LAm*) whatever the results.

(**b**) (*Esp**: *pesado*) bore, dull person; **estar hecho un** ~ to be terribly dull.

(**c**) (*: *aburrimiento*) boredom; (*período aburrido*) boring time; (*fiesta etc sosa*) boring party (*etc*).

(**d**) **ser un** ~ (*torpe*) to be clumsy.

(**e**) (*And**: *gorrón*) sponger*; **viajar de** ~ to stow away.

(**f**) (*And**: *inocentón*) sucker‡.

(**g**) **hacer el ~, hacerse** ~ (*Méx*) to act the fool.

(**h**) (*Cono Sur**) **ser un ~, estar** ~ to be broke*; **pasarse de ~ a ganso** to go too far.

(**i**) (*LAm Med*) bedpan.

patochada *nf* blunder, bloomer*.

patógeno *nm* pathogen.

patojo* 1 *adj* (*LAm*) lame. **2** *nm,* **patoja** *nf* (*And, CAm*) (*niño*) child; (*novio*) sweetheart, boyfriend/girlfriend; (*pey*) urchin, ragamuffin. **3** *nm* (*CAm*) (*niño*) kid*; (*muchacho*) lad, boy.

patología *nf* pathology.

patológico *adj* pathological.

patólogo, -a *nm/f* pathologist.

patomachera* *nf* (*Carib*) slanging match*.

patoso* 1 *adj* (**a**) (*aburrido*) boring, tedious.

(**b**) (*sabihondo*) would-be clever.

(**c**) (*molesto*) troublesome; **ponerse** ~ to get stroppy*, get awkward; to make trouble.

(**d**) (*torpe*) clumsy, heavy-footed.

2 *nm* (**a**) (*pelmazo*) bore.

(**b**) (*sabihondo*) clever Dick*, smart Aleck*.

(**c**) (*agitador*) trouble-maker.

patota* *nf* (*Cono Sur*: *pandilla*) street gang, mob of young thugs, (*grupo*) large group; (*Carib, Cono Sur*: *amigos*) mob, crowd (of friends).

patotear* [1a] *vt* (*Cono Sur*) to beat up*.

patotero* *nm* (*Cono Sur*) rowdy, young thug.

patraña* *nf* (*cuento*) story, fib; (*mistificación*) hoax; (*narración confusa*) rigmarole, long involved story.

patraquear [1a] *vt* (*Cono Sur*) *objeto* to steal; *persona* to hold up, mug*.

patraquero *nm* (*Cono Sur*) thief; holdup man, mugger*.

patria *nf* native land, mother country; fatherland; ~ **adoptiva** country of adoption; ~ **chica** home town, home area; **madre** ~ mother country; **hacer** ~ to fly the flag*; **luchar por la** ~ to fight for one's country; *V* **merecer.**

patriada *nf* (*Cono Sur Hist*) rising, revolt.

patriarca *nm* patriarch.

patriarcado *nm* patriarchy.

patriarcal *adj* patriarchal.

Patricia *nf* Patricia.

Patricio *nm* Patrick.

patricio, -a *adj, nm/f* patrician.

patrimonial *adj* hereditary.

patrimonio *nm* (**a**) (*Jur*) inheritance.

(**b**) (*fig*) heritage; birthright; **el ~ artístico de la nación** our national art heritage, the national art treasures; **nuestro ~ forestal** our national stock of trees, the forestry resources we have inherited; ~ **nacional** national wealth, national resources.

(**c**) (*Com*) net worth, capital resources.

patrio *adj* (**a**) (*Pol*) native, home (*atr*); **amor** ~ love of one's country, patriotism; **el suelo** ~ one's native land, one's native soil. (**b**) (*Jur*) *poder etc* paternal.

patrocinado, -a *nm/f* (*Jur*) client.

patriota 1 *nmf* patriot. **2** *nm* (*CAm*) banana.

patriotería *nf* ostentatious patriotism, flag-waving; chauvinism; jingoism.

patrioterismo *nm* flag-waving, chauvinism, jingoism.

patriotero 1 *adj* ostentatiously patriotic; chauvinistic; jingoistic. **2** *nm,* **patriotera** *nf* flag-waver; chauvinist; jingoist.

patrióticamente *adv* patriotically.

patriótico *adj* patriotic.

patriotismo *nm* patriotism.

patrocinador(a) 1 *adj*: **empresa patrocinadora** sponsoring company. **2** *nm/f* sponsor; patron(ess); promoter.

patrocinar [1a] *vt* to sponsor, act as patron to; to back, support; (*Dep*) to sponsor; **un movimiento patrocinado por ...** a movement under the auspices of (*o* under the patronage of) ...

patrocinazgo *nm* sponsorship; patronage.

patrocinio *nm* sponsorship, patronage; backing, support; (*Dep*) sponsorship.

patrón 1 *nm* (**a**) (*protector*) patron; (*Ecl*: *t* **santo** ~) patron saint; (*de esclavo*) master; (*fig*: *jefe*) master, boss, chief; (*Náut*) skipper; (*de pensión etc*) landlord.

(**b**) (*Cos, Téc*) pattern; (*de medida etc*) standard; ~ **de distribución** distribution pattern; ~ **oro** gold standard; ~ **picado** stencilled pattern.

(**c**) (*Agr*: *puntal*) prop, shore.

(**d**) (*Agr*: *de árbol*) stock (*for grafting*).

2 *atr* standard, regular; master (*atr*); sample (*atr*).

patrona *nf* patron(ess); (*Ecl*) patron saint; (*dueña*) employer, owner; (*de pensión etc*) landlady.

patronaje *nm* pattern-making; designing.

patronal 1 *adj* (**a**) **organización** ~ employers' organization, owners' organization; **la clase** ~ management, the managerial class; **cerrado por acto** ~ closed by the employers, closed by the owners (*o* management); **cierre** ~ lockout.

(**b**) (*Ecl*) of a patron saint.

2 *nf* employers' organization; management.

patronato *nm* (**a**) (*acto*) patronage; sponsorship; **bajo el ~ de** under the auspices of, under the patronage of.

(**b**) (*Com, Fin*) employers' association, owners' organization; (*Pol*) the owners (*as a class*), management; **el ~ francés** French industrialists.

(**c**) (*junta*) board of trustees, board of management; **el ~ de turismo** the tourist board, the tourist organization.

(**d**) (*fundación*) trust, foundation.

patronear [1a] *vt barco* to skipper.

patronímico *adj, nm* patronymic.

patronista *nmf* pattern-maker; designer.

patronizar [1f] *vt* to patronize.

patrono *nm* patron; sponsor; protector, supporter; (*Ecl*) patron saint; (*Com, Fin*) owner, employer.

patrulla *nf* patrol.

patrullaje *nm* patrolling; **bajo un fuerte ~ policial** under heavy police patrol.

patrullar [1a] **1** *vt* to patrol, police. **2** *vi* to patrol.

patrullera *nf* patrol-boat.

patrullero *nm* (**a**) (*Aut*) patrol-car. (**b**) (*Náut*) patrol-boat. (**c**) (*Méx*) patrolman, policeman.

patucos *nmpl* (*de bebé*) bootees; (*****) shoes.

patucho *adj* (*And*) short, squat.

patudo 1 *adj* (*Cono Sur*) rough, brash. **2** *nm* (*And*): **el ~** the devil.

patueco *adj* (*CAm*) = **patojo.**

patulea* *nf* mob, rabble.

patuleco *adj* (*LAm*), **patulejo** *adj* (*Cono Sur*), **patuleque** *adj* (*Carib*) = **patojo, patituerto.**

patulenco* *adj* (*CAm*) clumsy, awkward.

patullar [1a] *vi* (**a**) (*pisar*) to trample about, stamp around. (**b**) (*trajinar*) to bustle about. (**c**) (*charlar*) to chat; (*hacer ruido*) to talk noisily, make a lot of noise.

paturro *adj* (*And, Cono Sur*) chubby, plump; squat.

paúl *nm* marsh.

paular *nm* marshy ground.

paulatinamente *adv* gradually, slowly.

paulatino *adj* gradual, slow.

paulina* *nf* (**a**) (*reprimenda*) telling-off*. (**b**) (*carta*) poison-pen letter.

Paulo *nm* Paul.

pauperismo *nm* pauperism.

paupérrimo *adj* very poor, terribly poor.

pausa *nf* (**a**) (*gen*) pause; break, respite; interruption; (*Mús*) rest. (**b**) **con ~** slowly, deliberately.

pausadamente *adv* slowly, deliberately.

pausado *adj* slow, deliberate.

pausar [1a] **1** *vt* to slow down; to interrupt. **2** *vi* to go slow.

pauta *nf* (**a**) (*línea*) line, guideline.

(**b**) (*regla*) ruler.

(**c**) (*fig*) guide, guidelines, model; standard, norm; outline, plan, key; (*Med*) **~ del sueño** sleep pattern; **dar** (*o* **marcar**) **la ~** to set a standard, lay down a norm; **servir de ~ a** to act as a model for.

pautado 1 *adj*: **papel ~** ruled paper. **2** *nm* (*Mús*) stave.

pautar [1a] *vt* (**a**) *papel* to rule. (**b**) (*fig: esp CAm*) to mark, characterize; to establish a norm for, lay down a pattern for, give directions for.

pava *nf* (**a**) (*Orn*) turkey (hen); **~ real** peahen; **pelar la ~** (*Esp**) to talk, court (*esp* at a balcony).

(**b**) (*LAm*) (*para hervir*) kettle; (*tetera*) teapot; (*para maté*) pot for making maté.

(**c**) (*And, Carib: sombrero*) broad-brimmed straw hat.

(**d**) (*And, CAm: fleco*) fringe.

(**e**) (*Cono Sur, Méx: orinal*) chamber-pot.

(**f**) (*And, Cono Sur*) (*guasa*) coarse banter; (*chiste*) tasteless joke; **hacer la ~ a uno*** to make sb look stupid.

(**g**) (*And, CAm*: colilla*) cigarette-end, fag-end‡.

(**h**) (‡: *chica*) bird‡, girl.

(**i**) **es una ~** (*Esp**) she's a dull person.

(**j**) (‡) **echar la ~** to be sick, throw up.

pavada *nf* (**a**) (*esp Cono Sur*) (*disparate*) silly thing; (*tontería*) silliness, stupidity; **no digas ~s** don't talk rubbish. (**b**) *Cono Sur*: *bagatela*) triviality; very small amount; **cuesta una ~** it costs next to nothing. (**c**) (*Carib: mala suerte*) bit of bad luck.

pavear [1a] **1** *vt* (**a**) (*And*) to kill treacherously.

(**b**) (*And, Cono Sur*) to play a joke on.

2 *vi* (**a**) (*Cono Sur*: hacer el tonto*) to play the fool, mess about.

(**b**) (*Cono Sur*: enamorados*) to whisper sweet nothings.

(**c**) (*And*: hacer novillos*) to play truant.

pavería *nf* (*Cono Sur*) silliness, stupidity.

pavero, -a *nm/f* (*And, Cono Sur*) practical joker.

pavimentar [1a] *vt* to pave; to floor.

pavimento *nm* (*de losas*) pavement, paving; (*de interior*) flooring; (*firme*) roadway, road surface.

pavipollo *nm* (**a**) (*Orn*) young turkey. (**b**) (*****) twit*, idiot.

pavisoso* *adj* dull, graceless.

pavitonto* *adj* silly.

pavo 1 *nm* (**a**) (*Orn*) turkey (cock); **~ real** peacock; **estar en la edad del ~** to be going through the awkward stage (of adolescence).

(**b**) **comer ~*** to be a wallflower (*at a dance*); (*LAm*) to be disappointed.

(**c**) (*****) (*necio*) idiot; (*víctima*) sucker‡; **¡no seas ~!** (*Esp*) don't be silly!

(**d**) (*Fin*‡) 5 pesetas, one *duro*.

(**e**) **ponerse hecho un ~, subirse a uno el ~** to blush like a lobster; **tener mucho ~** to blush a lot.

(**f**) (*And: cometa*) large kite.

(**g**) (*And**) (*espadón*) big shot*; (*sospechoso*) evil-looking person.

(**h**) **ir de ~** (*LAm**) to travel free, get a free ride.

(**i**) (*Carib*: reprimenda*) telling-off*.

(**j**) (‡: *hombre*) bloke‡; (*Carib*‡: *joven*) youngster, kid*.

(**k**) (‡: *drogas*) cold turkey*.

2 *nm* idiot, fool.

3 *adj* (*LAm**) stupid, idiotic.

pavón *nm* (**a**) (*Orn*) peacock. (**b**) (*Téc*) bluing, bronzing.

pavonearse [1a] *vr* to swagger, strut (about); to swank*, show off.

pavoneo *nm* swagger(ing), strutting; swanking*, showing-off.

pavor *nm* dread, terror.

pavorosamente *adv* frighteningly, terrifyingly.

pavoroso *adj* dreadful, frightening, terrifying.

pavoso *adj* (*Carib*) unlucky; that brings bad luck.

paya *nf* (*Cono Sur*) improvised ballad.

payacate *nm* (*Méx*) (*de bolsillo*) handkerchief; (*prenda*) scarf, kerchief.

payada *nf* (*Cono Sur*) *improvised gaucho folksong*; **~ de contrapunto** contest between two *payadores.*

payador *nm* (*Cono Sur*) *gaucho minstrel.*

payar [1a] *vi* (*Cono Sur*) to improvise songs to a guitar accompaniment; (*fig**) to talk big*, shoot a line*.

payasada *nf* clownish trick, stunt; (*pey*) ridiculous thing (to do); **~s** clowning, tomfoolery; (*Teat etc*) slapstick, knockabout humour.

payasear [1a] *vi* (*LAm*) to clown around.

payaso, -a *nm/f* clown (*t fig*).

payés *nm* (*Cataluña, Islas Baleares*) peasant farmer.

payo 1 *adj* (**a**) (*Cono Sur*) albino. (**b**) (*Méx: simple*) rustic, simple. (**c**) (*Méx*) *ropa etc* loud, flashy, tasteless. **2** *nm* (*entre gitanos*) non-gipsy.

payuelas *nfpl* chickenpox.

paz *nf* (**a**) (*gen*) peace; peacefulness, tranquility; **¡a la ~ de Dios!** God be with you!; **en ~ y en guerra** in peace and war, in peacetime and wartime; **no dar ~ a** to give no rest (*o* respite to); **no dar ~ a la lengua** to keep on and on; **dejar a uno en ~** to leave sb alone, leave sb in peace; **¡déjame en ~!** leave me alone!; **descansar en ~** to rest in peace; **su madre, que en ~ descanse, lo decía** her mother (God rest her soul) used to say so; **estar en ~** to be at peace; (*fig*) to be even, be quits, be all square (*con* with); (*Méx*‡) to be high‡ (on drugs); **¡haya ~!** stop it!, that's enough!; **mantener la ~** to keep the peace; **perturbar la ~** to disturb the peace; **¡... y en ~!, ¡aquí ~ y después gloria!** and that's that!, and Bob's your uncle!*

(**b**) (*tratado*) peace, peace treaty; **la ~ de los Pirineos** the Peace of the Pyrenees (*1659*); **hacer las paces** to make peace, (*fig*) to make it up.

(**c**) (*Ecl*) kiss of peace, sign of peace.

pazo *nm* (*Galicia*) country house.

pazguato *adj* (**a**) (*necio*) simple, stupid. (**b**) (*remilgado*) prudish.

PC *nm abr de* **Partido Comunista** *p.ej.* **PCCH** *abr de* **Partido Comunista Chileno; PCE** *abr de* **Partido Comunista de España.**

p.c. *nm abr de* **por cien**(**to**) per cent, %.

PCB *nm abr de* **policlorobifenilo** polychlorinated biphenyl, PCB.

P.D *abr de* **posdata** postscript, P.S.

pe *nf* the (name of the) letter *p*; **de ~ a pa** from A to Z, from beginning to end.

P.e *abr de* **Padre** Father, F., Fr.

peaje *nm* toll.

peajista *nmf* collector of tolls.

peal *nm* (*LAm*) lasso.

pealar [1a] *vt* (*LAm*) to lasso.

peana *nf* stand, pedestal, base; (*Golf*) tee; (*****) foot.

peatón *nm* pedestrian, person on foot; walker.

peatonal *adj* pedestrian (*atr*); **calle ~** pedestrian precinct.

peaton(al)ización *nf* pedestrianization.
peaton(al)izar [1f] *vt* to pedestrianize.
pebete 1 *nm* (a) (*incienso*) joss stick. (b) (*de cohete*) fuse. (c) (*olor*) stink. (d) (*Cono Sur*: *panecillo*) roll. **2** *nm*, **pebeta** *nf* (*Cono Sur*) (*niño*) kid*, child; (*persona baja*) short person.
peca *nf* freckle.
pecado *nm* sin; ~ capital capital sin; ~ grave, ~ mortal mortal sin; ~ de comisión sin of commission; ~ nefando sodomy; ~ original original sin; ~ venial venial sin; por mis ~s for my sins; sería un ~ no aprovecharlo it would be a crime (*o* sin, pity) not to make use of it.
pecador 1 *adj* sinful, sinning. **2** *nm*, **pecadora** *nf* sinner.
pecaminosidad *nf* sinfulness.
pecaminoso *adj* sinful.
pecar [1g] *vi* (a) (*Ecl*) to sin; (*fig*) to err, go astray; si he pecado en esto, ha sido por ... if I have been at fault in this, it is because ...; si me lo pones delante, acabaré pecando if you put temptation in front of me, I shall fall.
(b) (*fig*) ~ de + *adj* to be too + *adj*; peca de generoso he is too generous, he is generous to a fault; nunca se peca por demasiado cuidado one can't be too careful; peca por exceso de confianza he is too confident, he errs on the side of over-confidence.
pecari *nm* (*LAm*), **pecarí** *nm* (*LAm*) peccary.
pecé* 1 *nm* (*Esp*: *partido*) Communist Party. **2** *nmf* (*persona*) Communist.
pececillos *nmpl* (*Pez*) fry.
pecera[1] *nf* fishbowl, fishtank.
pecero,* -a[2] *nm/f* (*Pol*) member of the Communist Party.
pecio *nm* wrecked ship, shipwreck; ~s flotsam, wreckage.
pécora *nf* (*esp* mala ~) (*lagarta*) bitch; (*arpía*) harpy; (*puta*) loose woman, whore.
pecoso *adj* freckled.
pecotra *nf* (*Cono Sur*) (*Anat*) bump, swelling; (*en madera*) knot.
pectina *nf* pectin.
pectoral 1 *adj* pectoral. **2** *nm* (a) (*Ecl*) pectoral cross. (b) ~es *pl* (*Anat*) pectorals.
pecuaca *nf* (*And, Carib*) = pecueca.
pecuario *adj* cattle (*atr*).
pecueca *nf* (*And, Carib*) (*pezuña*) hoof; (*hum*) smell of feet.
peculado *nm* peculation.
peculiar *adj* special, peculiar; typical, characteristic.
peculiaridad *nf* peculiarity; special feature, characteristic.
peculio *nm* one's own money; modest savings; de su ~ out of one's own pocket.
pecunia* *nf* brass*; (*Carib*: *moneda*) coin.
pecuniario *adj* pecuniary, money (*atr*).
pecha *nf* (*Cono Sur*), push, shove.
pechada* *nf* (a) una ~ de a lot of, an excess of; llevamos una ~ de andar that's more than enough walking (for one day). (b) (*LAm*) push, shove; (*) scrounging*.
pechador* *adj* (*Cono Sur*) demanding.
pechar[1] [1a] *vti* to pay (as a tax).
pechar[2] [1a] **1** *vt* (a) (*LAm*: *empujar*) to push, shove. (b) ~ a uno (*LAm**) to touch sb for a loan*. (c) (*Cono Sur**) to collar*, grab. **2** *vi*: ~ con* (a) (*a desgana*) to get stuck with, get landed with; siempre tengo que ~ con la más fea I always get stuck with the plainest one. (b) *cometido etc* to shoulder, take on; *problema* to face up to.
pechazo *nm* (*LAm*) push, shove; (*) touch (for a loan)*.
pechblenda *nf* pitchblende.
peche** (*CAm*) **1** *adj* skinny, weak. **2** *nm* child.
pechera *nf* (a) (*Cos*: *de camisa*) shirt front; (*de vestido*) front, bosom; (*Mil etc*) chest protector; ~ postiza dicky. (b) (*Anat*: *hum*) (big) bosom. (c) (*Cono Sur Téc*) apron.
pechero[1] *nm* (*Hist*) commoner, plebeian.
pechero[2] *nm* (*Cos*) front (*of dress*); (*babero*) bib.
pechicato *adj* (*Carib*) = pichicato.
pechina *nf* scallop.
pecho[1] *nm* (a) (*Anat*) chest; de ~ plano flat-chested; a ~ descubierto unarmed, defenceless; (*fig*) openly, frankly; dar el ~ to face things squarely; estar de ~s sobre una barandilla to be leaning on a railing; gritar a todo ~ (*And, Carib*) to shout at the top of one's voice; quedarse con algo entre ~ y espalda to keep sth back; to have sth on one's mind; sacar el ~ to thrust one's chest out, draw o.s. up.
(b) (*de mujer*) breast; los ~s the breasts, the bosom, the bust; dar el ~ a to feed, suckle, nurse.
(c) (*fig*) heart, breast; abrir (*o* descubrir) su ~ a uno to unbosom o.s. to sb; no le cabía en el ~ de alegría he was bursting with happiness; tomar algo a ~ to take sth to heart.
(d) (*fig*: *valor*) courage, spirit; ¡~ al agua! courage!; a lo hecho ~; *V* hecho.
(e) (*Geog*) slope, gradient.
pecho[2] *nm* (*Hist*) tax, tribute.
pechoño *adj* (*And, Cono Sur*) sanctimonious.
pechuga *nf* (a) (*de pollo etc*) breast; (*hum*: *de mujer*) bosom; cleavage.
(b) (*Geog*) slope, hill.
(c) (*LAm*: *pey*) nerve*, gall, cheek.
(d) (*And, CAm**: *abuso de confianza*) abuse of trust.
(e) (*CAm*: *molestia*) trouble, annoyance.
pechugón* 1 *adj* (a) (*de mucho pecho*) busty*, big-bosomed.
(b) (*LAm*) (*descarado*) forward; (*franco*) outspoken; sponging, parasitical; (*egoísta*) egoistical, selfish.
(c) (*Cono Sur*: *resuelto*) bold, single-minded.
(d) (*: *atractivo*) dishy*.
2 *nm* (*LAm*) (*descarado*) shameless individual, impudent person; (*gorrón*) sponger*, parasite.
pechuguera *nf* (*And, Méx*) (*ronquera*) hoarseness; (*resfriado*) chest cold.
pedagogía *nf* pedagogy.
pedagógico *adj* pedagogic(al).
pedagogo, -a *nm/f* teacher; educator; (*pey*) pedagogue.
pedal *nm* (a) (*gen*) pedal; ~ de acelerador accelerator (pedal); ~ de embrague clutch (pedal); ~ de freno footbrake, brake (pedal); ~ dulce, ~ piano, ~ suave (*Mús*) soft pedal; ~ fuerte (*Mús*) loud pedal. (b) coger (*o* tener) un ~** to get canned**.
pedalear [1a] *vi* to pedal; ~ en agua to tread water.
pédalo *nm* pedal boat.
pedáneo *adj*: alcalde ~ mayor of a small town; juez ~ local magistrate.
pedanía *nf* district.
pedante 1 *adj* pedantic; pompous, conceited. **2** *nmf* pedant.
pedantería *nf* pedantry; pompousness, conceit.
pedantescamente *adv* pedantically.
pedantesco *adj* pedantic.
pedazo *nm* (a) piece, bit; scrap; morsel; un ~ de papel a piece of paper; un ~ de pan a bit of bread, a scrap of bread; es un ~ de pan (*Esp fig*) he's a terribly nice person; trabaja por un ~ de pan he works for a mere pittance; hacer algo a ~s to do sth in pieces, do sth piecemeal; hacer ~s to break to pieces, tear (*o* pull) to pieces; to shatter, smash; se hizo ~s it fell to pieces, it came apart; it broke up; it shattered, it smashed (itself); estoy hecho ~s I'm worn out.
(b) (*fig*) ~ del alma, ~ de las entrañas, ~ del corazón one's darling, the apple of one's eye; (*en oración directa*) my darling; ~ de animal*, ~ de atún* blockhead; ¡~ de animal!*, ¡~ de bruto!* you idiot!; you beast!
pederasta *nm* pederast.
pederastia *nf* pederasty.
pedernal *nm* flint; como un ~ (*fig*) of flint, flinty.
pederse** [2a] *vr* to fart**.
pedestal *nm* pedestal, stand, base.
pedestre *adj* (a) *viajero etc* on foot; walking. (b) (*fig*) pedestrian.
pedestrismo *nm* race walking.
pediatra *nmf*, **pedíatra** *nmf* paediatrician.
pediatría *nf* paediatrics.
pediátrico *adj* paediatric.
pedicura *nf* chiropody.
pedicuro *nmf* chiropodist.
pedida *nf*: ~ de mano engagement; *V* pulsera.
pedidera *nf* (*And, CAm, Carib*) = petición.
pedido *nm* (*Com*) order; ~ al contado cash order; ~ de ensayo trial order; ~s pendientes backlog; ~ de repetición repeat order; a ~ on request; a ~ de at the request of; hacer algo bajo (*o* sobre) ~ to make sth to order.
pedigree [pedi'gri] *nm*, **pedigrí** *nm* pedigree.
pedigüeño *adj* insistent, importunate; demanding.
pedilón 1 *adj* (*LAm*) = pedigüeño. **2** *nm* (*LAm*) pest, nuisance.
pedimento *nm* petition; (*Jur*) claim, bill; (*Méx Com*) licence, permit.
pedir [3k] **1** *vt* (a) (*gen*) to ask for, request; *comida etc* to order; (*Com*) to order (*a* from); ~ algo a uno to ask sb for sth; ~ la paz to sue for peace; ~ que ... to ask that ...; me pidió que cerrara la puerta he asked me to shut the door; pidió que se volviera a estudiar la cuestión he asked that the matter should be studied afresh; el pescado es tal que no hay más que ~ the fish is as good as it could

possibly be.

(**b**) (*Com*) *precio* to ask; **¿cuánto piden por él?** how much are they asking for it?

(**c**) ~ **a una joven** to ask for a girl's hand in marriage; **fue anoche a ~la a su padre** he went last night to ask for permission to marry her.

(**d**) (*Jur*) to file a claim against; ~ **a uno en justicia** to sue sb.

(**e**) (*fig*) to need, demand, require; to cry out for; **la casa está pidiendo una mano de pintura** the house is crying out for a dab of paint; **ese color pide una cortina azul** that colour needs a blue curtain to go with it; **el triunfo pide que bebamos algo** the victory demands to be celebrated with a drink.

2 *vi* (**a**) to ask; **por ~ que no quede** it does no harm to ask, one might as well ask.

(**b**) (*t* ~ **por Dios**) to beg.

(**c**) *V* **boca** (**a**).

pedo 1 *nm* (**a**) (**) fart**; **tirarse un** ~ to let off a fart**.

(**b**) ~ **de lobo** (*Bot*) puffball.

(**c**) ~ **de monja** (*Culin*) very light pastry.

(**d**) (‡) **agarrarse un** ~ to get sloshed‡; **estar en** ~ to be sloshed‡; **¡estás en ~!** (*al hablar*) you must be kidding!; **no me gusta trabajar al** ~ I don't like working for the sake of it.

(**e**) (‡: *drogas*) high‡.

2 *adj invar* (‡): **andar ~, estar** ~ (*borracho*) to be sloshed‡, (*drogado*) be high‡; **ponerse** ~ (*borracho*) to get sloshed‡; (*drogado*) to get high‡.

pedofilia *nf* paedophilia.

pedófilo *nm* paedophile.

pedología *nf* pedology, study of soils.

pedorrero** *adj* given to farting**, windy.

pedrada *nf* (**a**) (*acto*) throw of a stone; (*golpe*) hit (*o* blow) from a stone; **matar a uno a ~s** to stone sb to death; **pegar una ~ a uno** to throw a stone at sb.

(**b**) (*fig*) wounding remark, snide remark, dig.

(**c**) **la cosa le sentó como una** ~ he took it very ill, the affair went down very badly with him; **me sienta como una ~ tener que irme** I don't in the least want to go; **venir como ~ en ojo de boticario** to come just right, be just what the doctor ordered.

pedrea *nf* (**a**) (*combate*) stone-throwing, fight with stones. (**b**) (*Met*) hailstorm. (**c**) (*: *premios*) small prizes in the lottery.

pedregal *nm* stony place, rocky ground; (*Méx*) lava field.

pedregón *nm* (*LAm*) rock, boulder.

pedregoso *adj* stony, rocky.

pedregullo *nm* (*Cono Sur*) crushed stone, grit.

pedrejón *nm* big stone, rock, boulder.

pedrera *nf* stone quarry.

pedrería *nf* precious stones, jewels.

pedrero *nm* (**a**) (*persona*) quarryman, stone cutter. (**b**) (*And, CAm, Cono Sur*) = **pedregal.**

pedrisco *nm* (**a**) (*lluvia de piedras*) shower of stones; (*Met*) hailstorm. (**b**) (*montón*) heap of stones.

Pedro *nm* Peter; **entrar como ~ por su casa** to come in as if one owned the place.

pedrusco *nm* (**a**) rough stone; piece of stone, lump of stone. (**b**) (*LAm*) = **pedregal.**

pedúnculo *nm* stem, stalk.

peerse** [2a] *vr* = **pederse****.

pega 1 *nf* (**a**) (*acto*) sticking.

(**b**) (*paliza*) beating; beating-up*.

(**c**) (*chasco*) practical joke; (*truco*) hoax, trick.

(**d**) (*dificultad*) snag, difficulty; **todo son ~s** there's nothing but problems; **poner ~s** to raise objections; to make trouble.

(**e**) (*pregunta*) searching question; catch question, trick question.

(**f**) **de ~*** false, dud*; fake, sham, bogus; **un billete (de banco) de** ~ a dud banknote*.

(**g**) (*Carib, Cono Sur, Méx*: trabajo*) job, work.

(**h**) (*Carib*: *liga*) birdlime.

(**i**) (*Cono Sur*: *de enfermedad*) infectious period.

(**j**) **estar en la** ~ (*Cono Sur*) to be at one's best.

(**k**) **jugar a la** ~ (*And*) to play tag.

2 *nm*: **ser el ~*** to be the one who always sees problems.

pegachento *adj* sticky, (*esp*) that sticks to one's teeth.

pegada[1] *nf* (*Cono Sur*) (**a**) (*mentira*) fib, lie. (**b**) (*suerte*) piece of luck. (**c**) (‡: *atractivo*) charm, appeal; **tiene** ~ she's got plenty of it*.

pegada[2] *nf* (*Boxeo*) exchange of punches.

pegadillo *nm* (*And*) lace.

pegadizo 1 *adj* (**a**) (*pegajoso*) sticky.

(**b**) (*Med*) infectious, catching.

(**c**) (*Mús*) *melodía* catchy.

(**d**) (*postizo*) sham, imitation.

(**e**) *persona* parasitic, sponging*.

2 *nm* sponger*, hanger-on.

pegado 1 *adj* (*fig*): **dejar a uno** ~ to leave sb nonplussed; **estar** ~ to have no idea, be stuck; **quedarse** ~ to be bewildered, be nonplussed.

2 *nm* patch, sticking plaster.

pegadura *nf* (*And*) practical joke.

pegajoso *adj* (**a**) (*gen*) sticky, adhesive; viscous.

(**b**) (*Med*) infectious, catching; (*fig*) contagious; tempting.

(**c**) *persona* over-sweet; sloppy, cloying; clinging.

pegamento *nm* glue, adhesive; (*droga*) glue; ~ **de caucho** (*Aut etc*) rubber solution.

pegar [1h] **1** *vt* (**a**) (*gen*) to stick (on, together, up); (*con cola*) to glue, gum, paste; *cartel* to post, stick up; (*Cos*) to sew (on), fasten (on); *piezas* to join, fix together; ~ **un sello** to stick a stamp on; ~ **una estantería a una pared** to put a set of shelves against a wall; ~ **una silla a una pared** to move a chair up against a wall.

(**b**) (*Med*) *enfermedad* to give, infect with; *idea etc* to give, communicate (*a* to).

(**c**) *golpe* to give, hit, deal; *pelota* to hit; *persona* to hit, strike; to smack, slap; **dicen que pega a su mujer** they say he knocks his wife about; **es un crimen ~ a los niños** it's a crime to hit (*o* smack) children; **'pegad fuerte a Eslobodia'** (*eslogan*) 'hit Slobodia hard'; **hazlo o te pego** do it or I'll bash you*.

(**d**) (*) ~ **un grito** to let out a yell; ~ **un puntapié a uno** to give sb a kick; ~ **un salto** to jump (with fright *etc*); *V* **susto, fuego** *etc*.

(**e**) **~la** (*LAm*) (*tener suerte*) to be lucky; (*lograrlo*) to manage it, get what one wants; (*caer en gracia*) to make a hit (*con* with).

(**f**) (*Méx*) to tie, fasten (down); *caballo etc* to hitch up.

(**g**) (*Carib*) *trabajo* to start.

2 *vi* (**a**) (*adherir*) to stick, adhere; *V* **cola.**

(**b**) ~ **en** to touch; **el piano pega en la pared** the piano is touching the wall.

(**c**) (*Bot*) to take root; (*remedio*) to take; (*fuego*) to catch.

(**d**) ~ **con uno** to run into sb.

(**e**) (*ser apropiado etc*) (*colores*) to match, go together; **no pega** (*fig*) it doesn't add up; **es una cosa que no pega** (*Culin*) it's a thing which does not go well with other dishes; **la cita no pega** the quotation is quite out of place, the quotation is most unsuitable; ~ **con** to match, go with; **ese sombrero no pega con el abrigo** that hat doesn't go with the coat.

(**f**) (*dar golpes*) to hit; to beat; ~ **en** to hit, strike (against); **la flecha pegó en el blanco** the arrow hit the target; **pegaba con un palo en la puerta** he was hitting (*o* pounding on) the door with a stick; **las ramas pegan en los cristales** the branches beat against the windows.

(**g**) (*sol*) to strike hot; **a estas horas el sol pega fuerte** the sun strikes very hot at this time; **esta canción está pegando muy fuerte** this song is rocketing up the charts; **este vino pega** this wine goes to your head; **el sol pega en esta ventana** the sun comes (*o* shines) in through this window.

(**h**) (*Carib, Méx*: trabajar duro*) to work hard.

3 pegarse *vr* (**a**) (*adherirse*) to stick.

(**b**) (*darse golpes*) to hit each other, fight.

(**c**) ~ **a uno** to stick to sb, attach o.s. to sb; ~ **a uno como una lapa** (*Esp*) to stick to sb like a limpet; ~ **a una reunión** to gatecrash a meeting.

(**d**) (*Med*) to be catching.

(**e**) (*Culin*) to burn, stick to the pot.

(**f**) (*) (*fracasar*) to fail, come a cropper*; **pegársela** (*con objeto*) to trick; to double-cross, do down*; *marido* to deceive, cuckold; **ella se la pega a su marido** she's deceiving her husband, she's unfaithful to her husband.

(**g**) ~ **un tiro** to shoot o.s.; **¡es para ~ un tiro!** it's enough to make you scream!; **se pega una vida de millonario*** he lives the life of Riley, he has a whale of a time* (*V t* **vida**).

Pegaso *nm* Pegasus.

pegata* *nf*, **pegatín** *nm*, **pegatina** *nf* sticker; badge.

pegativo *adj* (*CAm, Cono Sur*) sticky.

pego* *nm* (*Esp*) (**a**) **da el** ~ it looks great*, that looks just right. (**b**) **me ha dado el** ~ he's done me down.

pegón* *adj* (**a**) *persona* tough, hard, given to violence. (**b**) *vino* strong.

pegoste *nm* (**a**) (*LAm*) (*esparadrapo*) sticking plaster. (**b**) (*Carib**: *colado*) gatecrasher; (*CAm*‡: *parásito*) scrounger*.

pegote *nm* (**a**) (*Med*) sticking plaster; (*fig*) patch, ugly mend, botch.
(**b**) (*Culin**) sticky mess, sticky lump.
(**c**) (*: *chapuza*) botch, clumsy job.
(**d**) (*: *gorrón*) sponger*, hanger-on.
(**e**) **echarse un** ~*, **tirarse el** ~* to show off.

pegotear* [1a] *vi* to sponge*, cadge.

pegujal *nm* (**a**) (*Fin*) wealth, money; estate. (**b**) (*Agr*) small plot; small private plot, smallholding.

PEIN *nm abr de* **Plan Electrónico e Informático Nacional.**

peina *nf* back comb, ornamental comb.

peinada *nf* combing; **darse una** ~ to comb one's hair.

peinado 1 *adj* (**a**) **bien** ~ *pelo* well-combed; *persona* neat, well-groomed.
(**b**) (*fig*) foppish, over elegant, overdressed; *estilo, ingenio* affected, overdone.
2 *nm* (**a**) (*de pelo*) hairdo; coiffure, hair style; ~ **de paje** pageboy hair style.
(**b**) (*: *investigación*) check, investigation; (*redada*) sweep, raid; house-to-house search.

peinador *nm* (**a**) (*persona*) hairdresser. (**b**) (*bata*) peignoir, dressing gown. (**c**) (*LAm*: *tocador*) dressing table.

peinadora *nf* hairdresser.

peinadura *nf* (**a**) combing. (**b**) ~**s** combings.

peinar [1a] **1** *vt* (**a**) *pelo* to comb; to do, arrange, style; *caballo* to comb, curry.
(**b**) *zona* to comb, search thoroughly.
(**c**) (*LAm*) *roca* to cut.
(**d**) (*Cono Sur*) to flatter.
(**e**) (*Dep**) *balón* to head.
2 peinarse *vr* to comb one's hair, do one's hair; ~ **a la griega** to do one's hair in the Greek style.

peine *nm* comb; **¡ya pareció el** ~! (*Esp*) so that was it!; **¡se va a enterar de lo que vale un** ~! (*Esp*) now he'll find out what's what!

peinecillo *nm* small back comb.

peineta *nf* back comb, ornamental comb.

peinilla *nf* (*And, Carib*) large machete.

p.ej. *abr de* **por ejemplo** *exempli gratia*, for example, *e.g.*

peje 1 *adj* (*Méx*) stupid. **2** *nm* (**a**) (*Zool*) fish; ~ **araña** weever; ~ **sapo** monkfish. (**b**) (*: *listillo*) sly fellow, twister.

pejiguera* *nf* bother, nuisance.

Pekín *nm* Pekin(g).

pela *nf* (**a**) (*Culin*) peeling. (**b**) (‡) one peseta; (*gen*) money; **mucha** ~, ~ **larga** lots of dough‡; **cambiar** (*o* **echar**) **la** ~ to throw up; **mirar la** ~ to be concerned only about money. (**c**) (*LAm*: *zurra*) beating. (**d**) (*Méx*: *trabajo*) slog, hard work; (*CAm*: *fatiga*) exhaustion.

pelada *nf* (**a**) (*LAm*: *corte de pelo*) haircut.
(**b**) (*Cono Sur*) (*calva*) bald head; head of close-cropped hair.
(**c**) (*And, CAm, Carib*: *error*) blunder.
(**d**) **la P**~ (*And, Carib, Cono Sur*) death.

peladar *nm* (*Cono Sur*) arid plain.

peladera *nf* (*CAm, Méx*) (**a**) (*chismes*) gossip, backbiting. (**b**) = **peladar.**

peladero *nm* (*LAm*) = **pelador.**

peladez *nf* (**a**) (*And*: *pobreza*) poverty. (**b**) (*Méx*: *vulgaridad*) vulgarity; (*palabrota*) rude word, obscenity.

peladilla *nf* (*Esp*) sugared almond, coated almond.

pelado 1 *adj* (**a**) *cabeza etc* shorn; hairless; *tronco etc* bare, smooth; *hueso* clean; *manzana* peeled; *campo etc* treeless, bare; *paisaje* bare.
(**b**) (*fig*) bare; **cobra el sueldo** ~ he gets just the bare salary; **el cinco mil** ~ exactly five thousand; five thousand as a round number.
(**c**) (*LAm**: *sin dinero*) broke*, penniless, down and out.
(**d**) (*Méx**: *grosero*) coarse, crude.
(**e**) (*CAm, Carib*: *descarado*) impudent; barefaced.
2 *nm* (**a**) (*calva etc*) bare patch.
(**b**) (*pobre*) poor man, member of the lowest class; (*fig*) poor devil, wretch.
(**c**) (*: *joven* ~) skinhead.
(**d**) (*And, CAm**: *bebé*) baby.

pelador *nm* (*Culin*) peeler.

peladura *nf* (**a**) (*acción*) peeling. (**b**) (*calva etc*) bare patch. (**c**) ~**s** peel, peelings.

pelafustán *nm*, **pelafustana** *nf* layabout, good-for-nothing.

pelagallos *nm invar* = **pelagatos.**

pelagatos *nm invar* nobody; poor devil, wretch.

pelágico *adj* pelagic.

pelaje *nm* (**a**) (*Zool*) fur, coat. (**b**) = **pelambre** (**a**). (**c**) (*fig*) appearance; quality; **y otros de ese** ~ and others like him, and others of that ilk; **de todo** ~ of every kind.

pelambre *nm* (**a**) (*de persona*) thick hair, long hair, mop of hair; unkempt hair. (**b**) (*Zool*) fur, fleece (*cut from animal*). (**c**) (*calva*) bare patch. (**d**) (*Cono Sur*: *murmullos*) gossip, slander.

pelambrera *nf* = **pelambre** (**a**).

pelanas *nm invar* = **pelado 2** (**b**).

pelandusca* *nf* (*Esp*) tart‡, slut.

pelar [1a] **1** *vt* (**a**) *animal* to cut the hair of, shear; *animal muerto* to flay, skin; *pollo* to pluck; *fruta* to peel, skin, take the skin off; *patatas etc* to peel; *guisantes etc* to shell.
(**b**) (*: *calumniar*) to blacken, slander, speak ill of; to criticize.
(**c**) (*: *Naipes etc*) to fleece, clean out*.
(**d**) (‡: *matar*) to do in‡, bump off‡.
(**e**) (*LAm*) to beat up*.
(**f**) ~**la** (*And**: *morir*) to die, kick the bucket‡.
2 *vi* (**a**) (*Cono Sur*) to gossip. (**b**) **hace un frío que pela** (*Esp*) it's bitterly cold.
3 pelarse *vr* (**a**) (*piel etc*) to peel off.
(**b**) (*persona*) to lose one's hair; **voy a pelarme** I'm going to get my hair cut.
(**c**) **pelárselas por algo*** to crave (for) sth; **pelárselas por** + *infin* to crave to + *infin*, long to + *infin*.
(**d**) **corre que se las pela*** he runs like nobody's business*.
(**e**) **pelársela** (**‡) to toss off**‡.
(**f**) (*Méx*‡) to peg out‡.

pelazón *nf* (*CAm, Méx*) (**a**) (*chismes*) gossip, backbiting. (**b**) (*pobreza*) chronic poverty.

peldaño *nm* step, stair; (*de escalera portátil*) rung.

pelea *nf* (**a**) (*gen*) fight, tussle, scuffle; (*riña*) quarrel, row; **armar una** ~ to kick up a row, start a fight. (**b**) ~ **de gallos** cockfight; **gallo de** ~ gamecock, fighting cock.

peleador *adj* brawling; combative, quarrelsome.

pelear [1a] **1** *vi* (*gen*) to fight; to scuffle, brawl; (*fig*) to fight, struggle (*por* for); (*reñir*) to quarrel; (*competir*) to vie.
2 pelearse *vr* (**a**) (*gen*) to fight; to scuffle, brawl; to come to blows; ~ **con uno** to fight sb (*por* for).
(**b**) (*fig*) to fall out, quarrel (*con* with; *por* about, over); **estamos peleados** we're not on speaking terms, we've fallen out.

pelechar [1a] *vi* (**a**) (*Zool*) to moult, shed its hair; to get new hair.
(**b**) (*persona*: *de salud*) to be on the mend; (*negocio*) to be turning the corner; (*Cono Sur*: *enriquecerse*) to improve one's position, prosper.

pelecho *nm* (*Cono Sur, Méx*) (**a**) (*pelo*) moulted fur; (*piel*) sloughed skin. (**b**) (*ropa*) old clothing.

pelele *nm* (**a**) (*figura*) guy, dummy, figure of straw; (*fig*) tool, cat's-paw, puppet. (**b**) (*de niño*: *traje*) rompers, creepers (*US*); (*de dormir*) baby's sleeping-bag.

pelendengue *nm* = **perendengue.**

peleón *adj* (**a**) *persona* pugnacious, aggressive; quarrelsome; argumentative. (**b**) *vino* cheap, ordinary; strong.

peleona* *nf* row, set-to*; brawl.

peleonero *adj* (*Lam*) = **peleón.**

pelero *nm* (**a**) (*CAm, Cono Sur*) horse blanket. (**b**) (*Carib*) = **pelambre.**

pelés‡ *nmpl* (*Esp*) balls‡; **estar en** ~ to be stark naked.

pelete *nm* = **pelado 2** (**b**); **en** ~ stark naked.

peletería *nf* furrier's, fur shop; (*Carib*) shoe shop.

peletero *nm* furrier.

peli* *nf* = **película** (**b**).

peliagudo *adj tema* tricky, ticklish.

pelicano¹ *adj* grey-haired.

pelicano² *nm*, **pelícano** *nm* pelican.

pelicorto *adj* short-haired.

película *nf* (**a**) (*Téc*) film; thin covering; ~ **autoadheribie** (*Méx*) Clingfilm ®.
(**b**) (*Cine*) film, movie (*US*), motion picture (*US*); ~ **de animación** cartoon film; ~ **en colores** colour film; ~ **de dibujos** (**animados**) cartoon film; ~ **estereofónica** stereophonic film; ~ **muda** silent film; ~ **del Oeste** western; ~ **S** porn film; ~ **de la serie B** B film; ~ **sonora** talkie; ~ **de terror** horror film; ~ **vídeo** video film; **una cosa de** ~ (*fig*)

like something in the movies; an astonishing thing, something out of this world; **fue de ~** it was an incredible scene; **¡allí ~s!*** it's nothing to do with me!
(**c**) (*Fot*) film; roll of film, reel of film; **~ virgen** unexposed film.
(**d**) (*fig*) story, catalogue (of events); (*: *cuento*) tall story, tale; **¡cuánta ~!** what a load of rubbish!*
(**e**) (*Carib*: *disparate*) silly remark; (*lío*) row, rumpus.

peliculero 1 *adj* (**a**) film (*atr*), cine (*atr*), movie (*US atr*). (**b**) (*aficionado*) fond of films, fond of the cinema. **2** *nm* film-maker; scenario writer; film-actor.

peligrar [1a] *vi* to be in danger; **~ de** + *infin* to be in danger of + *ger*.

peligro *nm* (*gen*) danger, peril; (*riesgo*) risk; (*amenaza*) menace, threat; **~ amarillo** yellow peril; **'~ (de muerte)'** (*aviso*) 'danger'; **con ~ de la vida** at the risk of one's life; **estar en ~** to be in danger; to be at stake; **estar fuera de ~** to be out of danger; **correr ~** to be in danger; to run a risk; **correr ~ de** + *infin* to run the risk of + *ger*; **poner algo en ~** to endanger sth; **estar enfermo de ~** to be seriously ill, be dangerously ill.

peligrosamente *adv* dangerously; riskily.

peligrosidad *nf* danger; riskiness.

peligroso *adj* dangerous; risky; *herida etc* ugly, nasty.

pelillo *nm* slight annoyance; triviality; **echar ~s a la mar** to make it up, bury the hatchet; **¡~s a la mar!** (*Esp*) let bygones be bygones!; **no se para en ~s** he doesn't stick at trifles, he won't let a little thing like that deter him.

pelín* 1 *nm* bit, small amount; **un ~ de música** a bit of music. **2** *adv* a bit, just a bit; **es un ~ tacaño** he's just a bit mean; **te pasaste un ~** you went a bit too far.

pelinegro *adj* black-haired.

pelirrojo *adj* red-haired, ginger; **la pequeña pelirroja** the little redhead.

pelirrubio *adj* fair-haired.

pelma 1 *nmf* (*) bore; **¡no seas ~!** don't be such a bore!, don't go on about it! **2** *nm* lump, solid mass.

pelmazamente* *adv* boringly.

pelmazo* 1 *adj* boring, tedious. **2** *nm* = **pelma.**

pelo *nm* (**a**) (*gen*) hair; (*de barba, bigote*) whisker; (*de animal*) hair, fur, coat; (*de cebada etc*) beard; (*de ave, de fruta*) down; (*de alfombra, tela*) nap, pile; (*Téc*) fibre, filament, strand; (*en joya*) flaw; (*de reloj*) hairspring; **un ~ rubio** a blonde hair; **tiene ~ rubio** she has blonde hair; **~ de camello** camel-hair, camel's hair (*US*); **dos caballos del mismo ~** two horses of the same colour; **cortarse el ~** to have one's hair cut; **hacer el ~ a una** to do sb's hair.
(**b**) (*locuciones*) **a ~** (*sin sombrero*) bareheaded, hatless; (*desnudo*) in the buff*; (*cabalgar*) bareback; **a medios ~s*** half-seas over; **al ~*** just right; **ha quedado al ~** it fits like a glove; **venir** (*o* **ir**) **al ~** to come just right, be exactly what one needs; **con es(t)os ~s*** unprepared, in a right state; **con (sus) ~s y señales** with full details, with chapter and verse; **de medio ~** *persona* of no social standing, socially unimportant; *cosa* mediocre; **hombre de ~ en pecho** brave man; real man, he-man*, tough guy*; (*pey*) hard-hearted man; **en ~*** naked; **por los ~s** by the skin of one's teeth; **escaparse por un ~** to have a narrow escape, have a close shave; **pasó el examen por los ~s** he scraped through the exam; **no afloja un ~** (*Cono Sur*) he won't give an inch; **agarrarse** (*o* **asirse**) **a un ~** to clutch at any opportunity; **¡se te va a caer el ~!** (*Esp**) you're for it now!, now you've really done it!; **no se cortó un ~** he didn't bat an eyelid; **cortar un ~ en el aire** (*fig*) to be pretty smart; **así nos crece** (*o* **luce**) **el ~*** and that's the awful state we're in, that's why we're so badly off; **dar a uno para el ~*** to knock sb silly*; (*en discusión*) to flatten sb; (*regañar*) to dress sb down*; **echar el ~** (*Cono Sur*) to waste time, idle; **estuvo en un ~ que lo perdiéramos** we came within an inch of losing it, we very nearly lost it; **no se mueve un ~ de aire** (*o* **viento**) there isn't a breath of air stirring; **se me pusieron los ~s de punta, se me paró el ~** (*LAm*) my hair stood on end; **ser de dos ~s** (*Cono Sur*) to be two-faced; **soltarse el ~** to burst out, drop all restraint; to show one's true colours; **tener el ~ de la dehesa** to betray one's rustic (*o* humble) origins; **no tiene ~ de tonto** he's no fool; **no tener ~s en la lengua** to be outspoken, not mince words; **no tocar un ~ (de la ropa) a uno** not to lay a finger on sb; **tomar el ~ a uno*** to pull sb's leg*; to rag sb; **parece traído por los ~s** it seems far-fetched.
(**c**) (*Téc*: *grieta*) hairline, fine crack.
(**d**) (*Téc*: *sierra*) fine saw.

pelón 1 *adj* (**a**) (*calvo*) hairless, bald; (*rapado*) close-cropped, with a crew cut.
(**b**) (*) (*pobre*) poor; (*sin recursos*) broke*, penniless.
(**c**) (*And*) hairy, long-haired.
2 *nm* (**a**) (*) = **pelado 2** (**b**).
(**b**) (*LAm*: *niño*) child, baby.
(**c**) (*Cono Sur*: *melocotón*) nectarine.
(**d**) (*Carib** : *error*) blunder, boob*.

pelona *nf* (**a**) (*calvicie*) baldness. (**b**) **la P~*** death.

peloso *adj* hairy.

pelota 1 *nf* (**a**) (*Dep etc*) ball; (‡) nut‡, head; **~ base** baseball; **~ de goma** (*Mil*) rubber bullet; **~ vasca** pelota; **devolver la ~ a uno** (*fig*) to turn the tables on sb; **echar ~s** (*fig*) to give it a go, let rip; **hacer la ~ a uno** (*Esp**) to suck up to sb*; **lanzar ~s fuera** (*fig*) to dodge the issue; **pasarse la ~** (*fig*) to pass the buck*; **la ~ sigue en el tejado** (*fig*) the situation is still unresolved.
(**b**) **~s** (**‡) balls**‡, bollocks**‡; **¡las ~!** (*Cono Sur*) don't give me that!*
(**c**) **en ~*** stark naked; **coger** (*o* **pillar**) **a uno en ~s** to catch sb on the hop; **dejar a uno en ~** to strip sb of all that he has; (*en el juego*) to clean sb out*; **estar en ~s** (*sin dinero*) to be broke*.
(**d**) (*LAm*‡: *de amigos*) bunch, gang.
(**e**) (*CAm, Carib, Méx*: *pasión*) passion; **tener ~ por** to have a passion for; to be madly in love with.
(**f**) (*CAm, Carib, Méx*: *amante*) girlfriend, mistress.
(**g**) (‡: *en cárcel*) **estar en la ~** to be in solitary*.
2 *nmf* (*) = **pelotillero.**

pelotari *nm* pelota player.

pelotazo *nm* (**a**) (*Dep*) (*fuerte*) fierce shot; (*largo*) long ball. (**b**) (*Esp*‡) drink; **pegarse un ~** to have a drink.

pelote‡ *nm* 5 pesetas.

pelotear [1a] **1** *vt* (**a**) *cuenta* to audit.
(**b**) **~ un asunto** (*And**) to turn sth over in one's mind.
(**c**) (*LAm**: *captar*) to catch, pick up.
2 *vi* (**a**) (*Dep*) to knock (*o* kick) a ball about; (*Tenis*) to knock up (*before a game*).
(**b**) (*discutir*) to bicker, argue.

peloteo *nm* (*Tenis*) knock-up (*before a game*); rally, long exchange of shots; (*de notas etc*) exchange, sending back and forth; **hubo mucho ~ diplomático** there was a lot of diplomatic to-ing and fro-ing.

pelotera* *nf* row, scrap*, set-to*.

pelotero 1 *adj* (*) = **pelotillero. 2** *nm* (**a**) (*LAm*) ball player, sportsman, (*esp*) footballer, baseball player. (**b**) (*: *lameculos*) creep‡, toady.

pelotilla* *nf*: **hacer la ~ a** to suck up to*, ingratiate o.s. with.

pelotilleo* *nm* boot-licking; favouritism.

pelotillero* 1 *adj* creeping, soapy*. **2** *nm* toady, creep‡, crawler; yes-man*, stooge*.

pelotón *nm* (**a**) (*pelota*) big ball.
(**b**) (*de hilos etc*) mass, tangle, mat.
(**c**) (*de personas*) knot, crowd; (*de atletas etc*) group, bunch; **~ de cabeza** leading group (of runners *etc*).
(**d**) (*Mil*) squad, party, detachment; **~ de abordaje** boarding party; **~ de demolición** demolition squad; **~ de ejecución, ~ de fusilamiento** firing-squad.

pelotudo *adj* (**a**) (‡: *valiente*) tough, full of guts. (**b**) (*LAm*‡) *persona* (*inútil*) useless; (*tonto*) daft; (*descuidado*) slack, sloppy. (**c**) (*CAm**) *salsa* lumpy.

pelpa‡ *nf* (*LAm*) joint‡, reefer‡.

peltre *nm* pewter.

peluca *nf* (**a**) wig. (**b**) (*) dressing-down*.

peluco‡ *nm* clock, watch.

pelucón 1 *adj* (*And*) long-haired. **2** *nm* (*Cono Sur*: †) conservative; (*And*) bigwig, big shot*.

peluche *nm* felt; plush; *V* **oso.**

peluchento *adj* silky, smooth.

peludo 1 *adj* (**a**) (*gen*) hairy, shaggy; *animal* long-haired, shaggy; furry; *barba etc* bushy.
(**b**) (*CAm**: *difícil*) hard, sticky*.
2 *nm* (**a**) (*felpudo*) round mat.
(**b**) (*Cono Sur Zool*) (species of) armadillo.
(**c**) **agarrarse un ~** (*Cono Sur*‡) to get sloshed‡.

peluquearse [1a] *vr* (*LAm*) to have a haircut.

peluquería *nf* hairdresser's, barber's (shop), barber-shop (*US*).

peluquero *nm* (*de mujeres*) hairdresser; (*de hombres*) barber.

peluquín *nm* hairpiece, toupée; **ni hablar del ~** it's out of the question.

pelusa *nf* (**a**) (*Bot*) down; (*en cara*) down, fuzz; (*de paño*) fluff; (*bajo mueble etc*) fluff, dust. (**b**) (*: *entre niños*) envy, jealousy.

pelusiento *adj* (*And, Carib*) hairy, shaggy.
peluso‡ *nm* (*Mil*) squaddie*, recruit.
pélvico *adj* pelvic.
pelvis *nf* pelvis.
pella *nf* (**a**) (*gen*) ball, pellet, round mass; roll; dollop; (*Culin*) lump of lard. (**b**) (*Bot*: *de coliflor etc*) head. (**c**) (*) sum of money. (**d**) **hacer ~s*** to play truant.
pelleja *nf* (**a**) (*piel*) skin, hide. (**b**) (*: *puta*) whore. (**c**) (*: *persona delgada*) thin person. (**d**) (*Esp‡*: *cartera*) wallet.
pellejería *nf* (**a**) (*pieles*) skins, hides. (**b**) (*curtidería*) tannery. (**c**) **~s** (*Cono Sur*) difficulty, jam.
pellejero‡ *nm* pickpocket.
pellejo *nm* (**a**) (*de animal*) skin, hide, pelt; (*de persona*, *esp LAm*) skin; (*Bot*) skin, peel, rind.
(**b**) (*odre*) wineskin; (*borracho*) drunk*, toper.
(**c**) (*) (*puta*) whore; (*mujeriego*) rake, womanizer.
(**d**) (*fig*) skin, hide; **arriesgarse el ~, jugarse el ~** to risk one's neck; **perder el ~** to lose one's life; **no quisiera estar en su ~** I wouldn't like to be in his shoes; **quitar el ~ a uno** to flay sb, criticize sb harshly; **salvar el ~** to save one's skin; **no tener más que el ~** to be all skin and bones.
pellet *nm, pl* **pellets** pellet.
pellingajo *nm* (*And, Cono Sur*) (**a**) (*trapo*) dishcloth. (**b**) (*objeto*) piece of junk.
pelliza *nf* fur jacket.
pellizcar [1g] *vt* (**a**) to pinch, nip; *comida etc* to take a small bit of. (**b**) (*fig**) to attract, tickle sb's fancy.
pellizco *nm* (**a**) (*gen*) pinch, nip. (**b**) (*Culin etc*) small bit; **un ~ de sal** a pinch of salt; **un buen ~*** a tidy sum*. (**c**) (*de sombrero*) pinch, dent.
pellón *nm* (*LAm*) sheepskin saddle blanket.
peme* *nm* military policeman.
PEMEX ['pemeks] *nm abr de* **Petróleos Mejicanos.**
PEN ['pen] *nm* (**a**) (*Esp*) *abr de* **Plan Energético Nacional.** (**b**) (*Argentina*) *abr de* **Poder Ejecutivo Nacional.**
pena *nf* (**a**) (*tristeza*) grief, sadness, sorrow; (*congoja*) distress; (*malestar*) anxiety; (*sentimiento*) regret; **¡allá ~s!** I don't care!, that's not my worry!; **un partido sin ~ ni gloria** an ordinary sort of game; **pasó sin ~ ni gloria** it happened unnoticed, it happened but left no impression; **¡qué ~!** what a shame!; **es una ~** it's a shame, it's a pity (*que* that); **me dan ~** I'm sorry for them; **da ~ verlos así** it grieves me to see them like that; **da ~ que no vengan más** it's a pity they don't come more often; **me da (mucha) ~** (*Méx*) I'm (very) sorry; **merecer la ~, valer la ~** to be worth while; **no merece la ~** it's not worth the trouble; **merece la ~ (de) ir a verlo** it's worth taking the trouble to go and see it, it's worth seeing; **morir de ~** to die of a broken heart.
(**b**) (*: *dolor*) pain; **tener una ~** to have a pain.
(**c**) (*dificultad*) trouble; **~s** hardships; toil; **alma en ~** soul in torment; **a duras ~s** (*con dificultad*) with great difficulty; (*apenas*) hardly, scarcely; **ahorrarse la ~** to save o.s. the trouble; **pasar las ~s del purgatorio** (*fig*) to go through hell; **con muchas ~s llegamos a la cumbre** after much toil we reached the top.
(**d**) (*Jur*) punishment, penalty; (*Com*) penalty; **~ capital** capital punishment; **~ de muerte** death penalty; **~ pecuniaria** fine; **bajo ~ de, so ~ de** on pain of, on penalty of.
(**e**) (*LAm*) (*timidez*) bashfulness, shyness, timidity; (*vergüenza*) embarrassment; **sentir** (*o* **tener**) **~** (*tímido*) to be bashful, be shy; (*vergüenza*) to be ashamed; (*incómodo*) to be embarrassed, be ill at ease.
(**f**) (*And*) ghost.
penable *adj* punishable (by law).
penacho *nm* (**a**) (*Orn*) tuft, crest; (*en casco*) plume. (**b**) (*de humo etc*) plume; wreath. (**c**) (*fig*) pride, arrogance.
penado 1 *adj* = **penoso. 2** *nm* convict.
penal 1 *adj* penal; criminal. **2** *nm* (**a**) (*prisión*) prison. (**b**) (*LAm Dep*) foul (in the penalty area); penalty (kick).
penales* *nm invar* police record.
penalidad *nf* (**a**) (*trabajos*) trouble, hardship. (**b**) (*Jur*) penalty, punishment.
penalista *nmf* penologist, expert in criminal law.
penalización *nf* (**a**) penalty; penalization; **recorrido sin penalizaciones** (*Dep*) clear round. (**b**) criminalization.
penalizar [1f] *vt* (**a**) (*penar*) to penalize. (**b**) (*hacer criminal*) to criminalize.
penalti *nm, pl* **~s, penálty** *nm, pl* **penálty(e)s, penalties** (*etc*) penalty (kick); **casarse de ~*** to have a shotgun wedding; **marcar de ~** to score from a penalty; **pitar ~, señalar ~** to award a penalty; **transformar un ~** to convert a penalty.
penar [1a] **1** *vt* to penalize; to punish.
2 *vi* (**a**) (*gen*) to suffer; (*alma*) to be in torment; **~ de amores** to be unhappy in love, go through the pains of love; **ella pena por todos** she takes everybody's sufferings upon herself.
(**b**) **~ por** to pine for, long for.
(**c**) (*And*: *ver fantasmas*) to see ghosts.
3 penarse *vr* to grieve, mourn.
penca *nf* (**a**) (*Bot*: *hoja*) fleshy leaf; main rib of a leaf; (*LAm*) palm leaf; (*chumbera*) prickly pear; (*Carib*) fan; (*Méx*: *de cuchillo*) blade.
(**b**) **hacerse de ~s** to have to be coaxed into doing something.
(**c**) (*And*) **~ de hombre/mujer** a fine-looking man/woman; **una ~ de casa** a great big house.
(**d**) **agarrar una ~** (*LAm**) to get drunk.
(**e**) (*LAm**‡*) prick**‡*.
pencar‡ [1g] *vi* to slog away, work hard.
pencazo* *nm* (*CAm*) (*golpe*) smack; **cayó un ~ de agua** it pelted down, the skies opened.
penco 1 *adj* (*CAm**: *trabajador*) hard-working. **2** *nm* (**a**) (*CAm, Méx*: *caballo*) horse. (**b**) (*And*) **un ~ de hombre** a fine-looking man. (**c**) (*Carib‡*) poof‡, queer‡.
pendango *adj* (*Carib*) effeminate; cowardly.
pendejada *nf* (*LAm*) (**a**) (*acto*) (*disparate*) foolish act; (*cobardía*) cowardly act. (**b**) (*molestia*) curse, nuisance. (**c**) (*cualidad*) (*necedad*) foolishness, stupidity; (*cobardía*) cowardliness.
pendejear [1a] *vi* (*And, Méx*) to act the fool; to act irresponsibly.
pendejeta *nmf* (*And*) idiot.
pendejo 1 *adj* (**a**) (*LAm*) (*necio*) silly, stupid; (*irresponsable*) irresponsible; (*despreciable*) contemptible; (*cobarde*) cowardly, yellow.
(**b**) (*And**) (*listo*) smart; (*taimado*) cunning.
(**c**) (*Carib, Méx ‡*: *torpe*) ham-fisted.
2 *nm* (**a**) (*Cono Sur**) (*muchacho*) kid*, lad; (*sabelotodo*) know-all.
(**b**) (*LAm**: *del pubis*) pubic hair.
(**c**) (*LAm**) (*imbécil*) berk‡, idiot; (*cobarde*) wet*, coward.
pendencia *nf* quarrel; fight, brawl; **armar ~** to fight, brawl; to stir up trouble.
pendenciero 1 *adj* quarrelsome, argumentative; brawling, given to fighting. **2** *nm* rowdy, lout, tough*.
pender [2a] *vi* (**a**) (*gen*) to hang (*de, en* from; *sobre* over); to hang down, dangle; to droop.
(**b**) (*Jur*) to be pending.
(**c**) **~ sobre** (*fig*: *amenaza etc*) to hang over.
pendiente 1 *adj* (**a**) (*colgado*) hanging; **estar ~** to be hanging; to hang, dangle.
(**b**) (*fig*) *asunto* pending, unsettled; *cuenta* outstanding, unpaid; (*Univ*) *asignatura* to be retaken; **tener una asignatura ~** to have to resit a subject.
(**c**) (*fig*) **estar ~ de un cabello** to hang by a thread; **estar ~ de los labios de uno** to hang on sb's lips (*o* words); **estamos ~s de lo que él decida** we are dependent on what he may decide, everything hangs for us on his decision; **quedamos ~s de sus órdenes** we await your instructions.
(**d**) **estar ~ de un problema** (*LAm*) to be worried by a problem.
2 *nm* (*joya*) earring; pendant.
3 *nf* (*Geog*) slope, incline; (*Aut etc*) hill, slope; (*Arquit*) pitch; **estar en la ~ vital** to be over the hill.
pendil *nm* (woman's) cloak; **tomar el ~*** to pack up*, clear out*.
péndola *nf* (**a**) (*pluma*) pen, quill. (**b**) (*de puente etc*) suspension cable.
pendolear [1a] *vi* (**a**) (*LAm*: *escribir mucho*) to write a lot; (*Cono Sur*: *tener buena letra*) to write neatly. (**b**) (*Méx*) to be good in difficult situations, know how to manage people sensibly.
pendolista *nmf* penman, calligrapher.
pendón *nm* (**a**) (*estandarte*) banner, standard; pennant. (**b**) (*: *persona*) tall shabby person. (**c**) (*) (*vaga*) lazy woman; (*marrana*) worthless woman, trollop, slut; (*puta*) whore. (**d**) **ser un ~*** to be an awkward customer*.
pendona* *nf* whore.
pendonear* [1a] *vi* to loaf around the streets.
péndulo *nm* pendulum.
pene *nm* penis.
Penélope *nf* Penelope.
penene *nmf V* **PNN.**
peneque 1 *adj*: **estar ~‡** to be pickled‡. **2** *nm* (*Méx Culin*)

stuffed tortilla.

penetrable *adj* penetrable.

penetración *nf* (**a**) (*acto*) penetration. (**b**) (*cualidad*) penetration, sharpness, acuteness; insight.

penetrador *adj* = **penetrante** (**c**).

penetrante *adj* (**a**) *herida* deep.

(**b**) *arma* sharp; *frío, viento* biting; *sonido* penetrating, piercing; *mirada* searching; sharp, penetrating; *vista* acute; *aroma* strong; *ironía etc* biting.

(**c**) *mente, persona* sharp, acute, keen.

penetrar [1a] **1** *vt* (**a**) *defensa, metal, roca etc* to penetrate, pierce; to permeate.

(**b**) *misterio etc* to fathom, grasp, see the explanation of; *secreto* to lay bare, understand; *intención* to see through, grasp; *significado* to grasp.

2 *vi* (**a**) (*gen*) to penetrate; to go in; (*líquido etc*) to sink in, soak in; ~ **en,** ~ **entre,** ~ **por** to penetrate; **el cuchillo penetró en la carne** the knife went into (*ó* entered, penetrated) the flesh; **penetramos poco en el mar** we did not go far out to sea; **el frío penetra en los huesos** the cold gets right into one's bones.

(**b**) (*persona*) to enter, go in; ~ **en** (*LAm*: **a**) **un cuarto** to go into a room.

(**c**) (*emoción etc*) to pierce; **la ingratitud penetró hondamente en su corazón** the ingratitude pierced him to the heart (*o* wounded him deeply).

3 penetrarse *vr*: ~ **de** (**a**) (*absorber*) to become imbued with.

(**b**) (*Esp*: *comprender*) to understand fully, become fully aware of (the significance of).

peneuvista (*Esp*) **1** *adj*: **política** ~ policy of the PNV, PNV policy; *V* **PNV. 2** *nmf* member of the PNV.

penga *nf* (*And*) bunch of bananas.

penicilina *nf* penicillin.

penín* *nf*: **la** ~ Spain.

península *nf* peninsula; **P~ Ibérica** Iberian Peninsula.

peninsular 1 *adj* peninsular. **2** *nmf*: **los ~es** the people(s) of the (Iberian) Peninsula.

penique *nm* penny.

penitencia *nf* (**a**) (*condición*) penitence.

(**b**) (*acto, castigo*) penance; **en** ~ as a penance; **imponer una** ~ **a uno** to give sb a penance; **hacer** ~ to do penance (*por* for); to do sth unpleasant; **ven a hacer** ~ **conmigo mañana*** come and eat with me tomorrow, but you'll have to take potluck.

penitenciado *nm* (*LAm*) convict.

penitencial *adj* penitential.

penitenciar [1b] *vt* to impose a penance on.

penitenciaría *nf* prison, penitentiary (*esp US*).

penitenciario 1 *adj* penitentiary, prison (*atr*). **2** *nm* (*Ecl*) confessor.

penitente 1 *adj* (**a**) (*Ecl*) penitent. (**b**) (*And*) silly. **2** *nmf* (*Ecl*) penitent. **3** *nm* (*Cono Sur*: *pico*) rock pinnacle, isolated cone of rock; (*figura de nieve*) snowman.

penol *nm* yardarm.

penosamente *adv* (**a**) (*dolorosamente*) painfully, distressingly. (**b**) (*con dificultad*) laboriously, with difficulty.

penoso *adj* (**a**) (*doloroso*) painful, distressing. (**b**) (*difícil*) arduous, laborious, difficult. (**c**) (*And, Carib, Méx*: *tímido*) bashful, timid, shy.

penquista (*Chile*) **1** *adj* of Concepción. **2** *nmf* native (*o* inhabitant) of Concepión; **los ~s** the people of Concepción.

pensado *adj* (**a**) **un proyecto poco** ~ a badly thought-out scheme; **lo tengo bien** ~ I have thought it over (*o* out) carefully; **tengo** ~ **hacerlo mañana** I have it in mind to do it tomorrow.

(**b**) **bien** ~ well-intentioned; **mal** ~ = **malpensado.**

(**c**) **en el momento menos** ~ when least expected; much sooner than one thinks.

pensador(a) *nm/f* thinker.

pensamiento *nm* (**a**) (*facultad*) thought; **como el** ~ (*fig*) in a flash.

(**b**) (*mente*) mind; **acudir** (*o* **venir**) **al** ~ to come to sb's mind; **envenenar el** ~ **de uno** to poison sb's mind (*contra* against); **ni por** ~ I wouldn't dream of it; **no le pasó por el** ~ it never occurred to him.

(**c**) (*un* ~) thought; ~ **desiderativo** wishful thinking; **mal** ~ nasty thought, wicked thought; **el** ~ **de Quevedo** Quevedo's thought; **nuestro** ~ **sobre este tema** our thinking on this subject; **adivinar los** ~**s de uno** to read sb's thoughts.

(**d**) (*propósito*) idea, intention; **mi** ~ **es** + *infin* my idea is to + *infin.*

(**e**) (*Bot*) pansy.

pensante *adj* thinking.

pensar [1j] **1** *vt* (**a**) (*gen*) *etc* to think; ~ **que** ... to think that ...; **cuando menos lo pensamos** when we least expect it; **¿qué piensas de ella?** what do you think of her?, what is your opinion of her?; **lo pensó mejor** she thought better of it; ~ **con los pies** to talk through one's hat; **dar que** ~ **a uno** to give sb food for thought; to give sb pause; **dar que** ~ **a la gente** to arouse suspicions, set people thinking; **¡ni ~lo!** not a bit of it!, forget it!

(**b**) *problema etc* to think over, think out; **lo pensaré** I'll think about it; **esto es para ~lo** this needs thinking about; **pensándolo bien** on reflection, after mature consideration.

(**c**) ~ **que ...** (*concluir*) to decide that ..., come to the conclusion that ...

(**d**) ~ + *infin* to intend to + *infin,* plan to + *infin,* propose to + *infin.*

(**e**) (*ideas*) *etc* to think up, invent; **¿quién pensó este plan?** who thought this one up?

2 *vi* (**a**) (*gen*) to think; ~ **en** to think of, think about; **¿en qué piensas?** what are you thinking about?; ~ **entre sí,** ~ **para sí** to think to o.s.; ~ **sobre** to think about, think over; **sin** ~ (*sin reflexionar*) without thinking; (*imprudentemente*) rashly; (*sin querer*) involuntarily; (*de repente*) unexpectedly.

(**b**) ~ **en** to aim at, aspire to; **piensa en una cátedra** he's aiming at a chair.

pensativamente *adv* thoughtfully, pensively.

pensativo *adj* thoughtful, pensive.

penseque* *nm* careless mistake, thoughtless error.

Pensilvania *nf* Pennsylvania.

pensión *nf* (**a**) (*Fin*) pension; allowance; ~ **alimenticia** alimony, maintenance; ~ **asistencial** state pension; ~ **contributiva** contributory pension; ~ **de invalidez** disability allowance; ~ **de retiro** retirement pension; ~ **vitalicia** annuity; ~ **de viudedad** widow's pension.

(**b**) (*Univ etc*) scholarship, fellowship; travel grant.

(**c**) (*casa de huéspedes*) boarding house, guest house, lodging house; (*para estudiantes etc*) lodgings; (*And*) bar, café.

(**d**) (*precio*) board and lodging; ~ **completa** full board, room and all meals; **media** ~ half board.

(**e**) (*fig*) drawback, snag.

(**f**) (*And, Cono Sur*) (*preocupación*) worry, anxiety; (*remordimiento*) regret.

pensionado 1 *nm* boarding school. **2** *nm,* **pensionada** *nf* pensioner.

pensionar [1a] *vt* (**a**) (*gen*) to pension, give a pension to; *estudiante* to give a grant to. (**b**) (*And, Cono Sur*) (*molestar*) to bother; (*preocupar*) to worry.

pensionista *nmf* (**a**) (*jubilado*) pensioner, old-age pensioner. (**b**) (*huésped*) lodger, paying guest. (**c**) (*interno*) boarder; boarding-school pupil. (**d**) (*LAm*) subscriber.

pentagonal *adj* pentagonal.

pentágono *nm* pentagon; **el P~** the Pentagon.

pentagrama *nm* (*Mús*) stave, staff.

pentámetro *nm* pentameter.

Pentateuco *nm* Pentateuch.

pentatlón *nm* pentathlon.

pentatónico *adj* pentatonic.

Pentecostés *nm* (*a veces f*) (**a**) (*cristiano*) Whitsun, Whitsuntide; **domingo de** ~ Whit Sunday. (**b**) (*judío*) Pentecost.

penúltima *nf* (**a**) (*Ling*) penult. (**b**) **la ~*** one for the road.

penúltimo *adj* penultimate, last but one, next to last.

penumbra *nf* penumbra; half-light, semi-darkness; shadows; **sentado en la** ~ seated in the shadows.

penuria *nf* (*escasez*) shortage, dearth; (*pobreza*) poverty, penury.

peña *nf* (**a**) (*Geog*) cliff, crag; ~ **viva** bare rock, living rock.

(**b**) (*grupo*) group, circle; (*pey*) coterie, clique; (*LAm*) (*club*) folk club; (*fiesta*) party; ~ **deportiva** supporters' club; ~ **taurina** club of bullfighting enthusiasts; **forma parte de la** ~ he's a member of the circle; **hay** ~ **en el café los domingos** the group meets in the café on Sundays.

(**c**) (*And, CAm, Carib*) *V* **sordo 1** (**a**).

(**d**) (*Cono Sur*: *montepío*) pawnshop.

peñascal *nm* rocky place; rocky hill.

peñasco *nm* (**a**) (*piedra*) large rock, boulder. (**b**) (*risco*) rock, crag; (*pico*) pinnacle of rock; **no se me pasó por el ~*** it never occurred to me.

peñascoso *adj* rocky, craggy.

peñista *nmf* (*Dep*) member of a supporters' club, fan, supporter.

peñón *nm* mass of rock; wall of rock, crag; **el P~** the Rock (of Gibraltar).

peños‡ *nmpl* ivories*, teeth.

peñusco* *nm* (*Carib, Cono Sur*) crowd.

peo‡ *nm*: **¡vete al ~!** go to hell!

peón *nm* (**a**) (*Téc: persona*) unskilled workman; (*Taur*) assistant; (*Agr, esp LAm*) labourer, farmhand; (*Méx: aprendiz*) apprentice; (*ayudante*) assistant; **~ de albañil** building labourer, bricklayer's mate; **~ caminero** navvy, roadman, roadmender.
(**b**) (*Mil Hist*) infantryman, foot-soldier.
(**c**) (*Ajedrez*) pawn.
(**d**) (*peonza*) spinning top.
(**e**) (*Mec*) spindle, shaft, axle.

peonada *nf* (**a**) (*Agr*) day's stint; period of time spent at work. (**b**) (*personas*) gang of workmen, gang of labourers.

peonaje *nm* labourers (*collectively*), group of labourers; (*Taur*) assistants.

peonar [1a] *vi* (*Cono Sur*) to work as a labourer.

peonía *nf* peony.

peonza *nf* (**a**) spinning top, whipping top. (**b**) (*: *persona*) busy little person; **ser un ~** (*fig*) to be always on the go. (**c**) **ir a ~‡** to go on foot, hoof it*.

peor *adj y adv* (*comp*) worse; (*superl*) worst; **~ que ~** worse and worse; **A es ~ que B** A is worse than B; **Z es el ~ de todos** Z is the worst of all; **lo ~ es que ...** the worst of it is that ...; **tendencia a ~** tendency to worsen; **cambiar para ~** to change for the worse; **llevar lo ~** to get the worst of it; **o si no, será ~ para ti** or if you don't, it will be the worse for you; **~ es nada** (*LAm*) it's better than nothing; *V* **mal, tanto** *etc*.

peoría *nf* worsening, deterioration.

Pepa *nf forma familiar de* **Josefa**; **¡viva la ~!** as if he (*etc*) cared!, and to blazes with everybody else!*; jolly good!*

pepa *nf* (**a**) (*LAm Bot*) seed, pip, stone; **aflojar la ~*** to spill the beans*. (**b**) (*LAm: canica*) marble. (**c**) (*And*: mentira*) lie. (**d**) (*And*: pillo*) rogue.

pepazo *nm* (**a**) (*LAm*) shot, hit, throw; accurate shot. (**b**) (*And*) = **pepa** (**c**).

Pepe *nm forma familiar de* **José**; **ponerse como un ~*** to have a great time*.

pepe *nm* (**a**) (*And, Carib *: currutaco*) dandy. (**b**) (*CAm*) feeding-bottle.

pepena *nf* (*Méx*) rubbish collection.

pepenado, -a *nm/f* (*CAm, Méx*) orphan; foundling.

pepenador(a) *nm/f* (*Méx*) rubbish collector, dustman; scavenger (*on rubbish tip*).

pepenar [1a] **1** *vt* (**a**) (*And, CAm, Méx*) (*recoger*) to pick up; (*buscar*) to search out; *basura* to search through; (*escoger*) to choose; (*obtener*) to get, obtain.
(**b**) (*Méx*) (*agarrar*) to grab hold of; (*registrar*) to pick through, poke about in; (*robar*) to steal; *huérfano* to take in, bring up.
2 *vi* (*LAm*) to scour the rubbish.

pepián *nm* (*And, CAm, Méx*) = **pipián**.

pepinillo *nm* gherkin.

pepino *nm* (**a**) (*Bot*) cucumber; **no se me da un ~, (no) me importa un ~** I don't care two hoots (*de* about). (**b**) (‡: *cabeza*) bean‡, head. (**c**) (**) prick**.

Pepita *nf forma familiar de* **Josefa**.

pepita *nf* (**a**) (*Vet*) pip; **no tener ~ en la lengua** to be outspoken, not mince words; to talk nineteen to the dozen.
(**b**) (*Bot*) pip.
(**c**) (*Min*) nugget.

Pepito *nm forma familiar de* **José**.

pepito *nm* (**a**) (*Culin*) meat sandwich. (**b**) (*And, CAm, Carib**) dandy.

pepitoria *nf* (**a**) **pollo en ~** (*Esp Culin*) fricassée of chicken. (**b**) (*fig*) hotchpotch, mixture. (**c**) (*CAm: semillas*) dried pumpkin seeds.

pepón‡ *adj* (*And*) good-looking, dishy*.

pepsina *nf* pepsin.

péptico *adj* peptic.

peptona *nf* peptone.

peque* *nmf* kid*, child.

pequeñez *nf* (**a**) (*tamaño*) smallness, littleness, small size; shortness; (*infancia*) infancy.
(**b**) (*estrechez de miras*) pettiness, small-mindedness.
(**c**) (*bagatela*) trifle, triviality; **preocuparse por pequeñeces** to worry about trifles.

pequeño *adj* (*gen*) small, little; *cifra* small, low; *estatura* short; **los ~s** the children, the little ones; **un castillo en ~** a miniature castle; **un negocio en ~** a small-scale business.

pequeñoburgués 1 *adj* petit bourgeois. **2** *nm*, **pequeñoburguesa** *nf* petit(e) bourgeois(e).

pequero *nm* (*Cono Sur*) cardsharper.

pequinés¹, -esa *adj, nm/f* Pekinese.

pequinés² *nm* (*perro*) Pekinese.

pera¹ *nf* (**a**) (*Bot*) pear; (‡) nut‡, head; **esperar a ver de qué lado caen las ~s** to wait and see which way the cat will jump; **partir ~s con uno** to fall out with sb; **eso es pedir ~s al olmo** that's asking the impossible; **poner a uno las ~s a cuarto** to tell sb a few home truths.
(**b**) (*barba*) goatee; (*Cono Sur: barbilla*) chin.
(**c**) (*de atomizador, bocina etc*) bulb.
(**d**) (*Elec*) (*bombilla*) bulb; (*interruptor*) switch.
(**e**) **hacerse una ~**** to wank**; **tocarse la ~‡** to sit on one's backside (doing nothing).
(**f**) (*: *empleo*) cushy job‡.
(**g**) (*LAm Dep*) punchball.
(**h**) **tirarse la ~** (*And**) to play truant.

pera²* 1 *adj invar* elegant; classy*, posh*; **niño ~** spoiled upper-class child; (*Com, Fin*) yuppie; **es un pollo ~** (*Esp*) he's a real toff*; **fuimos a un restaurante muy ~** (*Esp*) we went to a really swish restaurant*. **2** *nf*: **son la ~ de buenos** they're mighty good*, they're real good*; **esto nos viene de ~** this suits us fine.

pera³‡ *nm* fence*, receiver (of stolen goods).

peral *nm* pear-tree.

peraltado 1 *adj* canted, sloping; banked, cambered. **2** *nm* = **peralte**.

peralte *nm* (*Arquit*) cant, slope; (*de carretera*) banking, camber.

perca *nf* (*Pez*) perch.

percal *nm*, **percala** *nf* (*And, Méx*) (**a**) percale; **conocer el ~*** to know what the score is*. (**b**) (‡: *dinero*) bread‡, money.

percán *nm* (*Cono Sur*) mould.

percance *nm* (**a**) (*gen*) misfortune, mishap; accident; (*de plan etc*) setback, hitch; **sufrir un ~, tener un ~** to have a mishap. (**b**) (*Fin*) perquisite.

percanque *nm* (*Cono Sur*) mould.

per cápita *adv* per capita.

percatarse [1a] *vr*: **~ de** (*observar*) to notice, take note of; (*hacer caso de*) to heed; (*guardarse de*) to guard against; (*comprender*) to realize, come to understand.

percebe *nm* (**a**) (*Zool*) barnacle. (**b**) (*) idiot, twit*.

percentil *nm* percentile.

percepción *nf* (**a**) (*gen*) perception; **~ extrasensorial** extrasensory perception. (**b**) (*idea*) notion, idea. (**c**) (*Com, Fin*) collection; receipt.

perceptible *adj* (**a**) (*visible*) perceptible, noticeable, detectable. (**b**) (*Com, Fin*) payable, receivable.

perceptiblemente *adv* perceptibly, noticeably.

perceptivo *adj* perceptive.

perceptor(a) *nm/f* recipient; (*de impuestos etc*) receiver; **~ de subsidio de desempleo** person who draws unemployment benefit.

percibir [3a] *vt* (**a**) (*notar*) to perceive, notice, detect; (*ver*) to see, observe; *peligro etc* to sense, scent; **~ que ...** to perceive that ..., observe that ...
(**b**) (*Com, Fin*) *sueldo* to earn, receive, get.

percollar [1a] *vt* (*And*) to monopolize.

percuchante *nm* (*And*) fool.

percudir [3a] *vt* (*deslustrar*) to tarnish, dull; *ropa etc* to dirty, mess up; *cutis* to spoil.

percusión *nf* percussion; **instrumento de ~** percussion instrument.

percusionar [1a] *vt* to hit, strike.

percusionista *nmf* percussionist, drummer.

percusor *nm*, **percutor** *nm* (*Téc*) striker, hammer.

percutir [3a] *vt* to strike, tap.

percha *nf* (**a**) (*palo*) pole, support; (*perchero*) rack; coatstand, hallstand; (*colgador*) coat-hanger; (*Orn*) perch; **vestido de ~** ready-made dress, dress off the peg; **~ de herramientas** toolrack.
(**b**) (*And: ostentación*) showiness; **tener ~** (*Cono Sur*) to be smart.
(**c**) (*fig*) clothes, wardrobe; (*And: ropa*) new clothes, smart clothing; (*Carib*) (*chaqueta*) jacket; (*traje*) suit.
(**d**) (*Cono Sur: montón*) pile.
(**e**) (*Méx*: grupo*) gang.
(**f**) (*: *tipo*) build, physique; (*de mujer*) figure.

perchero *nm* clothes rack, hallstand.

perchudo *adj* (*And*) smart, elegant.

perdedor 1 *adj* (**a**) *baza, equipo etc* losing.

(**b**) (*olvidadizo*) forgetful, given to losing things.

2 *nm*, **perdedora** *nf* loser; **buen** ~ good loser, good sport.

perder [2g] **1** *vt* (**a**) (*gen*) to lose; **¿dónde lo perdió?** where did you lose it?; **he perdido 5 kilos** I've lost 5 kilos; **he perdido la costumbre** I have got out of the habit (*y V* **costumbre**).

(**b**) *esfuerzo, tiempo etc* to waste; *oportunidad* to miss, lose, waste; *tren etc* to miss; (*Jur*) to lose, forfeit, give up; **no pierde nada** he doesn't miss a thing; **sin** ~ **un momento** without wasting a moment; **te he perdido*** I've lost you, I don't follow, I'm not with you*.

(**c**) (*arruinar*) to ruin, spoil; **ese vicio le perderá** that vice will be his ruin, that vice will destroy him; **ese error le perdió** that mistake was his undoing; **lo que le pierde es ...** where he comes unstuck is ...

(**d**) (*Univ*) *asignatura* to fail.

2 *vi* (**a**) (*gen*) to lose; **el equipo perdió por 2-5** the team lost 2-5; **salir perdiendo** to lose, be the loser; to lose on a deal; **saber** ~, **tener buen** ~ to be a good loser; **tienen todas las de** ~ they're on a hiding to nothing.

(**b**) (*decaer*) to decline, deteriorate, go down(hill); (*perder influencia*) to lose influence; **ha perdido mucho en mi estimación** he has gone down a lot in my estimation; **era guapísimo, pero ha perdido bastante** he used to be very good-looking, but he's deteriorated quite a bit.

(**c**) (*tela*) to fade, discolour.

(**d**) **echar a** ~ *comida etc* to spoil, ruin; *oportunidad* to waste; **echarse a** ~ to be spoiled, be ruined; to go downhill.

3 perderse *vr* (**a**) (*errar el camino*) to get lost (*t fig*), lose o.s.; to stray; to lose one's way; **¡piérdete!*** get lost!‡; **se perdieron en el bosque** they got lost in the wood; **se perdió en un mar de contradicciones** he got lost in a mass of contradictions; **¿qué se les ha perdido en Eslobodia?*** what business have they (to be) in Slobodia?

(**b**) (*desaparecer*) to disappear, be lost (to view); **el tren se perdió en la niebla** the train disappeared into the fog, the train was lost to sight in the fog; **el arroyo se pierde en la roca** the stream disappears into the rock.

(**c**) (*desperdiciarse*) to be wasted; to go (*o* run) to waste; **nada se pierde con intentar** there's no harm in trying.

(**d**) (*arruinarse*) to be ruined, get spoiled; **con la lluvia se ha perdido la mitad de la cosecha** with so much rain half the crop has been ruined (*o* lost).

(**e**) (*Náut*) to sink, be wrecked.

(**f**) (*persona*) to be ruined; **se perdió por el juego** he was ruined through gambling.

(**g**) ~ **por** to be mad about, long for; ~ **por** + *infin* to be mad keen to + *infin*, long to + *infin*.

(**h**) (*LAm**: *prostituirse*) to go on the streets.

(**i**) **¡no te lo pierdas!** don't miss it!; **no se pierde ni una** she doesn't miss out on anything.

perdición *nf* perdition (*t Rel*), undoing, ruin; **fue su** ~ it was his undoing; **será mi** ~ it will be the ruin of me.

pérdida *nf* (*gen*) loss; (*de tiempo etc*) waste; (*Jur*) forfeiture, loss; (*de líquido etc*) wastage; ~**s** (*Fin, Mil etc*) losses; ~ **de conocimiento** loss of consciousness; ~ **contable** book loss; ~ **efectiva** actual loss; **a** ~ **de vista** as far as the eye can see; **entrar en** ~ (*Aer*) to stall; **¡no tiene** ~**!** you can't miss!, you can't go wrong!; **vender algo con** ~ to sell sth at a loss.

perdidamente *adv*: ~ **enamorado** passionately in love, hopelessly in love.

perdidizo *adj*: **hacer algo** ~ to hide sth away, deliberately lose sth; **hacerse el** ~ (*en juego*) to lose deliberately; (*irse*) to make o.s. scarce, slip away.

perdido 1 *adj* (**a**) (*gen*) lost; *bala* stray; *momentos* idle; spare; **dar algo por** ~ to give sth up for lost; **darse por** ~ to give o.s. up for lost.

(**b**) (*vicioso*) vicious; incorrigible; *borracho etc* inveterate, hardened; (*Med*) terminally ill; **es un loco** ~ he's a raving lunatic; **es un caso** ~ he (*etc*) is a hopeless case; **de** ~**s, al río** in for a penny, in for a pound.

(**c**) **estar** ~ **por** to be mad about, be crazy about.

(**d**) **ponerse** ~ **de barro** to get covered in mud, be mud all over; **puso** ~ **su pantalón** he ruined his trousers.

(**e**) (*LAm*) (*vago*) idle; (*pobre*) down and out.

2 *nm* (**a**) **hacerse el** ~ to make o.s. scarce, slip away.

(**b**) (*libertino*) rake, libertine, profligate.

perdidoso *adj* (**a**) (*que pierde etc*) losing. (**b**) (*que se pierde fácilmente*) easily lost, easily mislaid.

perdigar [1h] *vt* to half-cook, brown.

perdigón *nm* (**a**) (*Orn*) young partridge. (**b**) (*balita*) pellet; ~ **zorrero** buckshot; **perdigones** shot, pellets.

perdis* *nm* rake.

perdiz *nf* partridge; ~ **blanca,** ~ **nival** ptarmigan.

perdón *nm* (*gen*) pardon (*t Jur*), forgiveness; (*indulto*) mercy; (*de pecado etc*) remission; **¡**~**!** sorry!, I beg your pardon!; **¡le pido** ~**!** I am so sorry!, do forgive me!; **pedir** ~ **a uno** to ask sb's forgiveness, apologize to sb; **con** ~ if I may, if you don't mind, by your leave; excuse me; **con** ~ **de los presentes** present company excepted; **hablando con** ~ if I may say so, if you'll pardon the expression; **no cabe** ~ it's inexcusable.

perdonable *adj* pardonable, excusable.

perdonador *adj* forgiving.

perdonar [1a] *vti* (**a**) *ofensa etc, persona* to pardon (*t Jur*), forgive, excuse; **¡perdone (Vd)!** sorry!, I beg your pardon!; **perdone, pero me parece que ...** excuse me, but I think ...; **perdónanos nuestras deudas** forgive us our trespasses; **Dios le haya perdonado** may God have mercy on him; **no perdona nada** he is wholly unforgiving; he doesn't miss a trick.

(**b**) ~ **la vida a uno** to spare sb's life.

(**c**) (*de obligación etc*) to exempt, excuse; **les he perdonado las clases** I have excused them from classes.

(**d**) **no** ~ **esfuerzo** to spare no effort; **no** ~ **ocasión** to miss no chance (*de* + *infin* to + *infin*); **no** ~ **medio para** + *infin* to use all possible means to + *infin*; **sin** ~ **detalle** without omitting a single detail.

perdonavidas *nm invar* (*matón*) bully, tough, thug; (*suficiente*) superior person, condescending type.

perdulario 1 *adj* (**a**) (*olvidadizo*) forgetful, given to losing things. (**b**) (*descuidado*) careless, sloppy, inefficient. (**c**) (*vicioso*) vicious, dissolute. **2** *nm* rake.

perdurable *adj* lasting, abiding; everlasting.

perdurar [1a] *vi* to last, endure, survive; to stand, still exist.

perecedero *adj* (*Com etc*) perishable; *vida etc* transitory, which must come to an end; *persona* mortal; **géneros no** ~**s** non-perishable goods.

perecer [2d] **1** *vi* to perish, die; (*objeto*) to shatter; ~ **ahogado** to drown; to suffocate.

2 perecerse *vr* (**a**) ~ **de risa** to die (of) laughing; ~ **de envidia** to be dying of jealousy.

(**b**) ~ **por algo** to long for, be dying for, crave; ~ **por una mujer** to be crazy about a woman; **se perece por los calamares** he's passionately fond of squid; ~ **por** + *infin* to long to + *infin*, be dying to + *infin*.

peregrinación *nf* (**a**) (*viajes*) long tour, travels; (*hum*) peregrination.

(**b**) (*Ecl*) pilgrimage; **ir en** ~ to go on a pilgrimage, make a pilgrimage (*a* to).

peregrinar [1a] *vi* (**a**) (*ir*) to go to and fro; (*viajar*) to travel extensively (abroad). (**b**) (*Ecl*) to go on a pilgrimage (*a* to).

peregrino 1 *adj* (**a**) *persona* wandering; travelling; *ave* migratory.

(**b**) *costumbre, planta etc* alien, newly introduced; adventitious.

(**c**) (*fig*: *raro*) odd, strange, surprising.

(**d**) (*fig*: *excepcional*) fine, extraordinary, rare; (*exótico*) exotic.

2 *nm*, **peregrina** *nf* pilgrim.

perejil *nm* (**a**) (*Bot*) parsley.

(**b**) ~**es** (*Cos** *etc*) buttons and bows, trimmings, fripperies.

(**c**) ~**es** (*: *títulos*) extra titles, handles (to one's name)*.

(**d**) **andar como** ~ (*Cono Sur*) to be shabbily dressed.

perendengue *nm* (**a**) (*adorno*) trinket, cheap ornament; silly adornment.

(**b**) (‡) ~**s** (*pegas*) snags, problems; **el problema tiene sus** ~**s** the question has its tricky points; **un proyecto de muchos** ~**s** a plan with a lot of snags.

(**c**) ~**s** (*: *categoría*) (high) standing, importance.

(**d**) ~**s** (*: *valor*) bravery; spirit, guts.

perenne *adj* everlasting, constant, perennial; (*Bot*) perennial; **de hoja** ~ evergreen.

perennemente *adv* everlastingly, constantly, perennially.

perennidad *nf* perennial nature; perpetuity.

perentoriamente *adv* urgently, peremptorily.

perentorio *adj* (**a**) *orden etc* urgent, peremptory. (**b**) *plazo* set, fixed.

pereque* *nm* (*LAm*) nuisance, bore.

pereza *nf* (**a**) (*gen*) sloth, laziness; slowness; idleness. (**b**)

¡qué ~!* (*And*) what a drag!
perezosa *nf* (*And, Cono Sur*) deckchair.
perezosamente *adv* lazily; slowly; sluggishly.
perezoso 1 *adj* slothful, lazy; slow, sluggish, idle. **2** *nm* (**a**) (*Zool*) sloth. (**b**) (*Carib, Méx*) safety-pin.
perfección *nf* (**a**) perfection; **a la ~** to perfection. (**b**) (*acto*) completion.
perfeccionamiento *nm* perfection; improvement.
perfeccionar [1a] *vt* (**a**) (*hacer perfecto*) to perfect; (*mejorar*) to improve. (**b**) *proceso etc* to complete, finish.
perfeccionismo *nm* perfectionism.
perfeccionista *adj, nmf* perfectionist.
perfectamente *adv* perfectly; **¡~!** precisely!, just so!; of course!
perfectibilidad *nf* perfectibility.
perfectible *adj* perfectible, capable of being perfected; with scope for improvement.
perfecto 1 *adj* (**a**) (*gen*) perfect; **¡~!** fine!; **me parece ~ que lo hagan** I think it right that they should. (**b**) (*completo*) complete, finished; perfected. **2** *nm* (*Ling*) perfect (tense).
pérfidamente *adv* perfidiously, treacherously.
perfidia *nf* perfidy, treachery.
pérfido *adj* perfidious, treacherous.
perfil *nm* (**a**) (*gen*) profile (*t fig*); (*contorno*) silhouette, outline; (*Arquit, Geol etc*) section, cross section, sectional view; (*Fot*) side view; **~ aerodinámico** streamlining; **en ~** in profile, from the side.
(**b**) **~es** (*rasgos*) features, characteristics.
(**c**) **~es** (*cortesías*) social courtesies; (*retoques*) finishing touches.
perfilado *adj* well-shaped, well-finished; *rostro* long and thin; *nariz* well-formed, shapely; (*Aer*) streamlined.
perfilador *nm* lip pencil.
perfilar [1a] **1** *vt* (**a**) (*gen*) to outline; (*fig*) to shape, give character to; **son los lectores los que perfilan los periódicos** it is the readers who shape their newspapers.
(**b**) (*Aer etc*) to streamline.
(**c**) (*fig*: *rematar*) to put the finishing touches to; to round off, perfect.
2 perfilarse *vr* (**a**) (*persona*) to show one's profile, give a side view; (*Taur*) to draw o.s. up (and prepare for the kill); (*edificio etc*) to show in outline, appear in silhouette (*en* against).
(**b**) (*fig*) to take shape; to become more definite; **el proyecto se va perfilando** the plan is taking shape.
(**c**) (*LAm*) to slim, get slim.
(**d**) (*Cono Sur Dep*) to dribble and shoot.
perforación *nf* (**a**) (*gen*) perforation; (*proceso*) piercing; drilling, boring; punching. (**b**) (*Min*) drilling; drill, bore.
perforadora *nf* punch; drill; **~ neumática** pneumatic drill; **~ de tarjetas** card punch.
perforar [1a] **1** *vt* (*gen*) to perforate; to pierce; (*pinchar*) to puncture (*t Med*); *agujero* to make, drill, bore; *pozo* to sink; *tarjeta etc* to punch, punch a hole in; *ficha* to punch.
2 *vi* (*Min*) to drill, bore.
perforista *nmf* (*Inform*) card puncher.
performance [per'formans] *nm o f* (*Aut, Mec*) performance.
perfumado *adj* scented; sweet-smelling.
perfumar [1a] *vt* to scent, perfume.
perfume *nm* scent, perfume.
perfumería *nf* perfume shop; perfumery.
pergamino *nm* parchment; **una familia de muchos ~s** a very blue-blooded family, a very ancient family.
pergenio* *nm* (*Cono Sur*: *hum*) bright boy, clever kid*.
pergeñar [1a] *vt* (**a**) (*gen*) to sketch; to do roughly, do in rough; *texto etc* to do a draft of, prepare. (**b**) (*: *arreglar*) *cita etc* to fix up, arrange. (**c**) (*Cono Sur**) *persona* to eye from head to toe.
pergeño *nm* aspect, appearance.
pérgola *nf* pergola.
peri... *pref* peri...
perica *nf* (**a**) (*And, CAm*) (*navaja*) razor, knife; (*machete*) machete; (*espada*) short sword. (**b**) **agarrar una ~** (*And, CAm**) to get sloshed*. (**c**) (⁑) (*chica*) bird⁑; (*puta*) whore. (**d**) (⁑: *droga*) cocaine, snow⁑.
pericia *nf* skill, skilfulness; expertness, expertise.
pericial *adj* expert; **tasación ~** expert valuation; **testigo ~** expert witness.
periclitar [1a] *vi* (*liter*) (**a**) (*peligrar*) to be in danger. (**b**) (*declinar*) to decay, decline; (*quedar anticuado*) to become outmoded; **ésos quedan ya periclitados** those are out of date now.
Perico *nm forma familiar de* **Pedro**; **~ el de los palotes** (*Esp*) anybody, somebody; so-and-so; any Tom, Dick or Harry; **ser p~ entre ellas** to be a ladies' man.
perico *nm* (**a**) (*Orn*) parakeet.
(**b**) (*peluca*) wig, toupé.
(**c**) (*: *orinal*) chamberpot.
(**d**) (⁑: *puta*) whore, slut.
(**e**) (⁑: *droga*) snow⁑, cocaine.
(**f**) (*And*) coffee with a dash of milk.
(**g**) (**huevos**) **~s** (*And, Carib*) scrambled eggs with fried onions.
pericote *nm* (**a**) (*And, Cono Sur*: *ratón*) large rat. (**b**) (*And, Cono Sur**: *niño*) kid*, nipper*.
periferia *nf* (**a**) (*gen*) periphery; (*de ciudad*) outskirts. (**b**) **los que viven en la ~ social** those who live on the fringes of society. (**c**) (*Inform*) peripherals.
periférico 1 *adj* peripheral; marginal; *barrio etc* outlying, on the outskirts; **carretera periférica** ring-road. **2** *nm* (**a**) (*Méx Aut*) ring-road. (**b**) **~s** (*Inform*) peripherals.
perifollo *nm* (**a**) (*Bot*) chervil. (**b**) **~s** (*adornos*) buttons and bows, trimmings, fripperies.
perífrasis *nf invar* periphrasis.
perifrástico *adj* periphrastic.
perilla *nf* (*joya*) pear-shaped ornament, drop; (*Elec*) switch; (*Méx*: *manija*) handle; (*tirador*) doorknob; (*barba*) goatee; **~ de la oreja** lobe of the ear; **~ del timbre** bell-push; **venir de ~(s)** to come just right, be very welcome, be perfect.
perillán* *nm* rogue, rascal; **¡~!** (*a niño*) you rascal!
perimetral *adj* perimeter (*atr*); **vallado ~** perimeter fence.
perímetro *nm* perimeter.
perinatal *adj* perinatal.
perinola 1 *nf* teetotum. **2** *adv*: **de ~** (*Carib*) utterly, absolutely.
periódicamente *adv* periodically.
periodicidad *nf* periodicity; regular recurrence, regular nature; (*Prensa*) frequency (of publication); **una revista de ~ mensual** a monthly review, a review which comes out monthly.
periódico 1 *adj* periodic(al); (*Mat*) recurrent. **2** *nm* newspaper; periodical; **~ del domingo** Sunday newspaper; **~ mural** wall newspaper; **~ de la tarde** evening newspaper.
periodicucho* *nm* rag*.
periodismo *nm* journalism; **~ deportivo** sports journalism; **~ gráfico** photoreportage; **~ de investigación, ~ investigativo** investigative journalism.
periodista *nmf* journalist; (*m*) pressman, newsman, newspaperman; **deportivo** sports writer; **~ de televisión** television journalist.
periodístico *adj* journalistic; newspaper (*atr*); **estilo ~** journalistic style, journalese; **de interés ~** newsworthy.
periodización *nf* periodization.
periodo *nm*, **período** *nm* (**a**) (*gen*) period (*t Med*). (**b**) (*Ling*) sentence, period.
peripatético *adj* peripatetic.
peripecia *nf* vicissitude; sudden change, unforeseen change; **~s** vicissitudes, ups and downs; adventures, incidents.
periplo *nm* (long) journey, tour; (*Náut*) (long) voyage; (*errabundeo*) wanderings; (*hum*) peregrination; (*Hist*) periplus.
peripuesto* *adj* dressed up, smart; overdressed, dressy; **tan ~** all dressed up (to the nines).
periquear* [1a] *vi* (*And*: *t* **~se** *vr*) to get dressed up, get dolled up*.
periquete* *nm*: **en un ~** in a tick.
periquito *nm* (**a**) (*Orn*) parakeet. (**b**) (⁑: *droga*) snow⁑, cocaine.
periscopio *nm* periscope.
perista* *nm* fence*, receiver (of stolen goods).
peristilo *nm* peristyle.
perita¹* *adj* = **pera²**.
perita² *n*: **~ en dulce** dainty.
peritaje *nm* (**a**) (*trabajo*) expert work; (*pericia*) expertise; (*informe*) report of an expert; specialist's report. (**b**) (*honorarios*) expert's fee. (**c**) (*formación*) professional training.
peritar [1a] *vt* to judge expertly, give an expert opinion on.
perito 1 *adj* skilled, skilful; expert; experienced, seasoned; **~ en** skilled in, expert at.
2 *nm*, **perita³** *nf* expert; skilled person, qualified person; technician; **~ agrónomo** agronomist; **~ electricista** qualified electrician; **~ forense** legal expert; **~ en metales** metal expert, specialist in metals; **~ testigo** (*Méx*) expert

witness.

peritoneo *nm* peritoneum.

peritonitis *nf* peritonitis.

perjudicar [1g] *vt* (**a**) (*dañar*) to damage, harm, impair; *posibilidades etc* to damage, prejudice; **me perjudica que digan eso** for them to say that lowers me in the eyes of others.

(**b**) (*desfavorecer*) to be unbecoming to; **ese sombrero le perjudica** that hat does not become her, she doesn't look good in that hat.

(**c**) (*LAm*) to malign, slander.

perjudicial 1 *adj* harmful, injurious, damaging (*a, para* to); detrimental, prejudicial (*a, para* to). **2** *nm* (*Méx*‡) secret policeman.

perjuicio *nm* damage, harm; (*Fin*) financial loss; **en ~ de** to the detriment of; **redundar en ~ de** to be detrimental to, harm; **sin ~ de** without prejudice to; without detriment to; **sin ~ de que pueda ocurrir** even though it might happen, in spite of the fact that it might happen; **sufrir grandes ~s** to suffer great damage.

perjurar [1a] **1** *vi* (**a**) (*Jur*) to perjure o.s., commit perjury. (**b**) (*jurar*) to swear a lot. **2 perjurarse** *vr* to perjure o.s.

perjurio *nm* perjury.

perjuro 1 *adj* perjured. **2** *nm*, **perjura** *nf* perjurer.

perla *nf* (**a**) pearl; **~ cultivada** cultivated pearl, cultured pearl; **~s de imitación** imitation pearls.

(**b**) (*fig*) pearl (*de* of, among), gem; **me está de ~s, me viene de ~s** it comes just right; it suits me perfectly; **me parece de ~s** it all seems splendid to me; **ser una ~** to be a treasure.

perlático *adj* paralytic, palsied.

perlesía *nf* paralysis, palsy.

perlífero *adj* pearl-bearing; **ostra perlífera** pearl oyster.

perlino *adj* pearly.

permagel *nm* permafrost.

permanecer [2d] *vi* (**a**) (*gen*) to stay, remain; **¿cuánto tiempo vas a ~?** how long are you staying?

(**b**) **~** + *adj* to go on being + *adj*, remain + *adj*; **~ indeciso** to remain undecided, be still undecided; **~ dormido** to go on sleeping.

permanencia *nf* (**a**) (*cualidad*) permanence. (**b**) (*estancia*) stay; **~ en filas** (period of) military service. (**c**) **~s** (*Escol: de profesores*) *obligatory administrative duties.*

permanente 1 *adj* permanent; constant; *color* fast; *comisión, ejército etc* standing.

2 *nf* permanent wave, perm; **hacerse una ~** to have one's hair permed.

permanentemente *adv* permanently; constantly.

permanganato *nm* permanganate.

permeabilidad *nf* permeability, pervious nature.

permeable *adj* permeable, pervious (*a* to).

permisible *adj* allowable, permissible.

permisionario, -a *nm/f* (*LAm*) official agent, official agency, concessionaire.

permisividad *nf* permissiveness; (*Fin*) liberal policies.

permisivo *adj* permissive.

permiso *nm* (**a**) (*gen*) permission; **con (su) ~** (*pidiendo ver algo etc*) if I may; (*queriendo entrar, pasar*) excuse me; **con ~ de Vds me voy** excuse me but I must go, if you don't mind I must go; **¡permisito!** (*LAm: para pasar*) excuse me! **dar su ~** to give one's permission; **tener ~ para** + *infin* to have permission to + *infin.*

(**b**) (*documento*) permit, licence; **~ de armas** gun licence, firearms certificate; **~ de conducción, ~ de conducir, ~ de conductor, ~ de manejo** (*LAm*) driving licence; **~ de entrada** entry permit; **~ de exportación** export permit; **~ de importación** import permit; **~ de residencia** residence permit; **~ de salida** exit permit; **~ de trabajo** work permit.

(**c**) (*Mil etc*) leave; **~ de convalecencia** sick leave; **~ de** (*o* **por**) **maternidad, ~ por parto** maternity leave; **estar de ~** to be on leave.

permisología *nf* (*LAm: hum*) science of keeping on good terms with bureaucracy; craft of obtaining permits.

permitir [3a] **1** *vt* to permit, allow; to allow of; **~ a uno hacer algo** to allow sb to do sth; **¿me permite?** (*¿le importa?*) may I?, do you mind?; (*al pasar*) excuse me!; **¿me permite ver?** may I see (it)?, would you mind showing it to me? **permítame que le diga que ...** permit me to tell you that ...; **si el tiempo lo permite** weather permitting; **la fábrica permitirá una producción anual de ...** the factory will provide an annual production of ..., the factory will make possible an annual production of ...; **este método permite construir más casas** this method allows more houses to be built.

2 permitirse *vr* (**a**) (*gen*) to be permitted, be allowed; **eso no se permite** that is not allowed; **si se me permite la expresión** if you'll pardon the expression; so to speak; **no se permite fumar** no smoking, you can't smoke here; **¿se permite fumar?** may I smoke?

(**b**) **~ algo** to permit o.s. sth; to (be able to) afford sth; **me permito 2 cigarrillos al día** I allow myself two cigarettes a day; **me permito recordarle que ...** may I remind you that ...

permuta *nf* barter, exchange; interchange.

permutación *nf* (**a**) (*Mat etc*) permutation. (**b**) = **permuta.**

permutar [1a] **1** *vt* (**a**) (*Mat etc*) to permute.

(**b**) (*cambiar*) to exchange (*con* with, *por* for); to interchange (*con* with); **~ algo con uno** to exchange sth with sb; **~ destinos con uno** to exchange jobs with sb.

2 *vi*: **~ con uno** to exchange (jobs) with sb, swap with sb.

pernada *nf* (**a**) (*coz*) kick; wild movement of the leg(s); **dar ~s** to kick out, lash out with the leg(s).

(**b**) (*Hist*) droit de seigneur.

pernear [1a] *vi* (**a**) (*agitar las piernas*) to shake one's legs; to kick one's legs. (**b**) (*patear*) to stamp one's foot (with rage). (**c**) (*: *darse prisa*) to hustle, get cracking*.

pernera *nf* trouser leg.

perneta *nf*: **en ~s** bare-legged, with bare legs.

perniabierto *adj* bow-legged.

pernicioso *adj* pernicious (*t Med*); *persona* wicked, evil; *insecto etc* injurious (*para* to).

pernicorto *adj* short-legged.

perniche* *nm* blanket.

pernigordo *adj* fat-legged.

pernil *nm* (**a**) (*Zool*) upper leg, haunch; (*Culin*) leg; (*Carib*) leg of pork, pork. (**b**) (*Cos*) trouser leg.

pernio *nm* hinge.

perno *nm* bolt; **estar hasta el ~** (*And**) to be at the end of one's tether; to be at one's wits' end.

pernoctación *nf* overnight stay; **con 3 pernoctaciones en hotel** with 3 nights in a hotel.

pernoctar [1a] *vi* to spend the night, stay for the night.

pero[1] 1 *conj* (**a**) (*gen*) but; (*sin embargo*) yet.

(**b**) (*) **una chica guapa, ~ muy guapa** what you really call a pretty girl, a pretty girl and no mistake; **hizo muy mal, ~ muy mal** he was wrong, a thousand times wrong; I should jolly well say he was wrong*; **~ vamos a ver** well let's see; **¡~ que muy bien!** jolly good!*; **¡estoy ~ que muy harto!** I'm damn well fed up!*; **no había nadie, ~ que nadie** there was nobody, and I do mean nobody; **¡~ si no tiene coche!** I tell you he hasn't got a car!

2 *nm* (**a**) (*defecto*) flaw, defect; snag; **el plan no tiene ~** there's nothing wrong with the plan, the plan hasn't any snags; **he encontrado un ~** I've found a snag.

(**b**) (*objeción*) objection; **poner ~s a** to raise objections to, find fault with; **el programa tiene dos ~s** the programme is open to two objections; **¡no hay ~ que valga!** there are no buts about it!

pero[2] *nm* (*And, Cono Sur*) pear tree.

perogrullada *nf* platitude, truism.

perogrullesco *adj* platitudinous.

Perogrullo *nm*, **Pero Grullo** *nm*: **verdad de ~** platitude, truism.

perol *nm* pan; (*Carib: cacerola*) saucepan; (*Cono Sur, Méx: para poner al horno*) metal casserole dish; (*Carib: útil*) kitchen utensil; (*Carib: fig*) piece of junk, worthless object.

perola *nf* saucepan.

perolero *nm* (**a**) (*Carib: hojalatero*) tinsmith. (**b**) (*objetos*) pile of junk; collection of odds and ends.

peronacho* *nm* (*Cono Sur: pey*) Peronist.

peroné *nm* fibula.

peronismo *nm* Peronism.

peronista *adj, nmf* Peronist.

peroración *nf* (**a**) (*discurso*) peroration, speech; long speech. (**b**) (*conclusión*) conclusion of a speech.

perorar [1a] *vi* to make a speech; (*hum*) to orate, spout.

perorata *nf* long-winded speech; violent speech, harangue.

peróxido *nm* peroxide; **~ de hidrógeno** hydrogen peroxide.

perpendicular 1 *adj* (**a**) perpendicular (*a* to).

(**b**) (*en ángulo recto*) at right angles (*a* to); **el camino es ~ al río** the road is at right angles to the river.

2 *nf* perpendicular; vertical; **salir de la ~** to be out of the perpendicular (*o* vertical).

perpendicularmente *adv* perpendicularly; vertically.

perpetración *nf* perpetration.

perpetrador(a) *nm/f* perpetrator.
perpetrar [1a] *vt* to perpetrate.
perpetuación *nf* perpetuation.
perpetuamente *adv* perpetually; everlastingly, ceaselessly.
perpetuar [1e] *vt* to perpetuate.
perpetuidad *nf* perpetuity; **a ~** in perpetuity, for ever; **condena a ~** life sentence, sentence of life imprisonment; **le condenaron a prisión a ~** he was sentenced to life imprisonment.
perpetuo *adj* perpetual; everlasting; ceaseless; *condena, exilio etc* life (*atr*); (*Bot*) everlasting.
Perpiñán *nm* Perpignan.
perplejamente *adv* perplexedly; in a puzzled way; in perplexity.
perplejidad *nf* (**a**) (*gen*) perplexity; bewilderment; puzzlement; hesitation. (**b**) (*situación*) perplexing situation; dilemma.
perplejo *adj* perplexed; bewildered; puzzled; **me miró ~** he looked at me in perplexity, he looked at me in a puzzled way; **dejar a uno ~** to perplex sb, puzzle sb; **se quedó ~ un momento** he looked perplexed for a moment, he hesitated a moment.
perra *nf* (**a**) (*Zool*) bitch; female dog, lady dog (*euf*); **~ salida** bitch on heat.
(**b**) (*Esp* Fin*) **~ chica** 5-céntimo coin; **~ gorda** 10-céntimo coin; **~s** small change; **costó unas ~s** it cost a few coppers; **no tener una ~** to be flat broke*.
(**c**) (*: *rabieta*) tantrum, pet; **el niño cogió una ~** the child had a tantrum, the child began to cry violently.
(**d**) (*: *manía*) mania, crazy idea; **está con la ~ de un abrigo de pieles** she's got the crazy idea that she must have a fur coat; **le cogió la ~ de ir a Eslobodia** he got an obsession (*o* thing*) about going to Slobodia.
(**e**) (*Cono Sur*) (*sombrero*) old hat; (*cantimplora*) leather water bottle.
perrada *nf* (**a**) (*perros*) pack of dogs. (**b**) (*: *acción*) dirty trick.
perraje *nm* (*And*) pack of dogs; (*) people of humble origins; lower orders, lower ranks.
perramus *nm* (*And, Cono Sur*) raincoat.
perrera *nf* (**a**) (*para perros*) kennel; kennels; (*hum*) remand centre.
(**b**) (*carro*) cart in which stray dogs are picked up.
(**c**) (*trabajo*) badly-paid job; drudgery, grind.
(**d**) (*: *rabieta*) = **perra** (**c**).
(**e**) (*Carib*) row, shindy.
perrería *nf* (**a**) (*perros*) pack of dogs; (*fig*) gang of villains.
(**b**) (*palabra*) harsh word, angry word; **decir ~s de uno** to say harsh things about sb.
(**c**) (*: *trampa*) dirty trick.
perrillo *nm* (**a**) (*perro joven*) puppy; (*raza pequeña*) small (breed of) dog; miniature dog; (*diminutivo sentimental*) doggie. (**b**) (*Mil*) trigger.
perrito, -a 1 *nm/f* puppy. **2** *nm*: **~ caliente** hot dog.
perro 1 *nm* (**a**) (*Zool*) dog; **'~ peligroso'** 'beware of the dog'; **~ afgano** Afghan hound; **~ de agua** (*CAm*) coypu; **~ de aguas** spaniel; **~ antiexplosivos** sniffer dog; **~ buscadrogas** sniffer dog; **~ callejero** mongrel; **~ de caza** hunting dog; **~ de ciego, ~ de guía, ~ lazarillo** guide-dog; **~ cobrador** retriever; **~ dálmata** dalmatian; **~ danés** Great Dane; **~ dogo** bulldog; **~ esquimal** husky; **~ faldero** lapdog; **~ guardián** watchdog; **~ del hortelano** dog in the manger; **~ de lanas** poodle; **~ lebrel** whippet; **~ lobo** alsatian; wolfhound; **~ marino** dogfish; **~ de muestra** pointer, setter; **~ pastor** sheepdog; **~ pequinés** Pekinese; **~ policía** police dog; **~ de presa** bulldog; **~ raposero** fox-hound; fox-terrier; **~ rastreador, ~ rastrero** tracker dog; **~ salchicha*** sausage dog; **~ (de) San Bernardo** St Bernard; **~ tejonero** dachshund; **~ de Terranova** Newfoundland dog; **~ de trineo** husky; **~ vagabundo** stray (dog); **~ zorrero** foxhound; fox-terrier.
(**b**) (*locuciones*) **ser ~ viejo** to be an old hand; to be an old fox; **tiempo de ~s** dirty weather, awful weather; **¡a otro ~ con ese hueso!** tell that to the marines!; **atar ~s con longaniza** to court disaster; **darse a ~s** to get wild; **echar los ~s a uno*** to come down on sb like a ton of bricks; **echar a uno los ~s encima** to persecute sb, keep after sb; **echar una hora a ~s** to waste a whole hour, get absolutely nothing done in an hour; **hacer ~ muerto** (*And*) to avoid paying; **heder a ~ muerto** to stink to high heaven; **se llevan como ~s y gatos** they're always squabbling; **meter los ~s en danza** to set the cat among the pigeons; **¿qué ~ te mordió?** (*Carib**) what's up with you?*; what's got into you?; **~ que ladra no muerde, ~ ladrador, poco mordedor** his bark is worse than his bite; **ser como ~ en misa** to be wholly out of place; **a ~ flaco no le faltan pulgas** it never rains but it pours; **tratar a alguien como a un perro** to treat sb like dirt.
(**c**) (*pey*) dog, swine, hound.
(**d**) (*And*) drowsiness.
(**e**) (*Cono Sur*) clothes-peg.
(**f**) (*Culin*) **~ caliente** hot dog.
2 *adj* (*) awful, wretched; **esta perra vida** this wretched life; **he pasado una temporada perra** I've had a ghastly time*.
perro-guía *nm, pl* **perros-guía** guide-dog.
perrona *nf* (†: *moneda*) 10 céntimos; **de (a) ~*** cheapo*, cheap.
perronero* *adj* cheapo*, cheap.
perrucho *nm* (*pey*) hound, cur.
perruna *nf* dog biscuit.
perruno *adj* canine, dog (*atr*); *devoción etc* doglike.
persa 1 *adj, nmf* Persian. **2** *nm* (*Ling*) Persian. **3** *nf* (*Cono Sur*) cut-price store.
persecución *nf* (**a**) (*acoso*) pursuit, hunt, chase; **~ individual** (*Ciclismo*) individual pursuit; **~ sexual** sexual harrassment; **estar en plena ~** to be in full cry. (**b**) (*Ecl, Pol etc*) persecution.
persecutorio *adj*: **manía persecutoria** persecution mania; **trato ~** cruel treatment.
perseguible *adj* (**a**) (*Jur*) *delito* indictable; *persona* liable to prosecution; **~ a instancia de parte** liable to private prosecution; **~ de oficio** liable to prosecution by the state.
perseguidor(a) *nm/f* (**a**) (*gen*) pursuer. (**b**) (*Ecl, Pol etc*) persecutor.
perseguimiento *nm* pursuit, hunt, chase; **en ~ de** in pursuit of.
perseguir [3d *y* 3k] *vt* (**a**) *caza, fugitivo* to pursue, hunt, chase; to hunt out, hunt down.
(**b**) (*fig*) *chica, empleo etc* to chase after, go after; *propósito* to pursue; **la persiguió durante 2 años** he was after her for 2 years, he pursued her for 2 years.
(**c**) (*Ecl, Pol etc*) to persecute; (*fig*) to persecute, harass; to pester, annoy; **me persiguieron hasta que dije que sí** they pestered me until I said yes; **le persiguen los remordimientos** he is gnawed by remorse, his conscience pricks him constantly; **le persigue la mala suerte** he is dogged by ill luck.
perseverancia *nf* perseverance, persistence.
perseverante *adj* persevering, persistent.
perseverantemente *adv* perseveringly.
perseverar [1a] *vi* to persevere, keep on, persist; **~ en** to persevere in, persist with.
Persia *nf* Persia.
persiana *nf* (Venetian) blind; slatted shutter (*t* **~ enrollable**).
persignarse [1a] *vr* to cross o.s.
persistencia *nf* persistence.
persistente *adj* persistent.
persistentemente *adv* persistently.
persistir [3a] *vi* to persist (*en* in; *en* + *infin* in + *ger*).
persoga *nf* (*CAm, Méx*) halter (of plaited vegetable fibre).
persona *nf* person; **20 ~s** 20 people; **aquellas ~s que lo deseen** those who wish; **es para animales y no para ~s** it's for animals not people; **es buena ~** he's a good sort, he's a decent chap*; **tercera ~** third party; (*Ling*) third person; **un pronombre de primera ~** a first person pronoun; **~ física** (*Jur*) natural person; **~ no grata** persona non grata; **~ de historia** person with a past, dubious individual; **~ jurídica** legal entity; **~s reales** royalty, king and queen; **en ~** in person; in the flesh; **en la ~ de** in the person of; **3 caramelos por ~** 3 sweets per person, 3 sweets each; **pagaron 2 dólares por ~** they paid 2 dollars a head (*o* each).
personaje *nm* (**a**) (*sujeto notable*) personage, important person; celebrity; **ser un ~** to be somebody, be important.
(**b**) (*Liter, Teat etc*) character.
personajillo *nm* insignificant person; minor character; (*hum*) minor celebrity.
personal 1 *adj* (**a**) (*gen*) personal.
(**b**) *habitación, asiento etc* single, for one person.
2 *nm* (**a**) (*plantilla*) personnel, staff; (*total*) establishment; (*esp Mil*) force; (*Náut*) crew, complement; **~ de cabina** cabin staff; **~ de exterior** surface workers; **~ de interior** underground workers; **~ de servicios** maintenance staff; **~ de tierra** (*Aer*) ground-crew, groundstaff; **estar falto de ~** to be short-handed; **quedarse con el ~*** to make

a hit with people.

(**b**) (*) **el** ~ people; the public; **había exceso de ~ en el cine** there were too many people in the cinema.

3 *nf* (*Dep*) foul.

personalidad *nf* (**a**) (*gen*) personality; ~ **desdoblada** split personality. (**b**) (*Jur*) legal entity.

personalísimo *adj* intensely personal, highly individualistic.

personalismo *nm* (**a**) (*observación*) personal reference; **tenemos que proceder sin ~s** we must proceed without indulging in personalities (*o* personal attacks).

(**b**) (*egoísmo*) selfishness, egoism.

(**c**) (*parcialidad*) personal preference, partiality; **obrar sin ~s** to act with partiality towards none, act fairly with regard to the persons involved.

personalizar [1f] **1** *vt* to personalize; *virtud etc* to embody, personify. **2** *vi* to make a personal reference. **3 personalizarse** *vr* to become personal.

personalmente *adv* personally.

personarse [1a] *vr* to appear in person; ~ **en** to present o.s. at; to report to; ~ **en forma** (*Jur*) to be officially represented; **el juez se personó en el lugar del accidente** the judge made an official visit to the scene of the accident.

personería *nf* (**a**) (*Cono Sur*) (*personalidad*) personality; (*talento*) aptitude, talent. (**b**) (*LAm Jur*) proxy.

personero, -a *nm/f* (*LAm*) spokesperson; representative; (*Jur*) proxy.

personificación *nf* personification; embodiment.

personificar [1g] *vt* (**a**) (*encarnar*) to personify; to embody, be the embodiment of.

(**b**) **en esta mujer el autor personifica la maldad** the author makes this woman a symbol of wickedness.

(**c**) (*en discurso etc*) to single out for special mention.

perspectiva *nf* (**a**) (*Arte y fig*) perspective; **en ~** in perspective; **le falta ~** he lacks a sense of perspective.

(**b**) (*vista*) view, scene, panorama.

(**c**) (*porvenir etc*) outlook, prospect; future development; **'buenas ~s de mejora'** (*anuncio*) 'good prospects'; **las ~s de la cosecha son favorables** the harvest outlook is good; **es una ~ nada halagüeña** it's a most unwelcome prospect; **se alegró con la ~ de pasar un día en el campo** he cheered up with the prospect of spending a day in the country; **encontrarse ante la ~ de** + *infin* to be faced with the prospect of + *ger*; **tener algo en ~** to have sth in view, have a prospect of sth; **hay ocupaciones en ~** there's a busy time ahead.

perspicacia *nf* (**a**) (*agudeza de vista*) keen-sightedness. (**b**) (*fig*) perspicacity, shrewdness, discernment.

perspicaz *adj* (**a**) *vista* keen; *persona* keen-sighted. (**b**) (*fig*) perspicacious, shrewd, discerning.

perspicuidad *nf* perspicuity, clarity.

perspicuo *adj* clear, intelligible.

persuadir [3a] **1** *vt* to persuade; to convince, prevail upon; ~ **a uno a hacer algo** to persuade sb to do sth; **dejarse ~** to allow o.s. to be persuaded.

2 persuadirse *vr* to be persuaded, become convinced.

persuasión *nf* (**a**) (*acto*) persuasion. (**b**) (*estado*) conviction; **tener la ~ de que ...** to have the conviction that ..., be convinced that ...

persuasiva *nf* persuasiveness, power of persuasion.

persuasivo *adj* persuasive; convincing.

pertenecer [2d] *vi* (**a**) (*gen*) to belong (*a* to). (**b**) (*fig*) ~ **a** to concern; to apply to, pertain to; **le pertenece a él hacerlo** it's his job to do it.

perteneciente *adj* (**a**) **los países ~s** the member countries, the countries which belong; **las personas ~s al organismo** persons who are members of the organization. (**b**) (*relacionado*) ~ **a** pertaining to, relevant to.

pertenencia *nf* (**a**) (*gen*) ownership; **las cosas de su ~** the things which belong to him, his possessions, his property.

(**b**) **~s** possessions, property; estate; (*de finca etc*) appurtenances, accessories.

pértica *nf land measure = 2.70 metres.*

pértiga *nf* pole; (*salto con ~*) pole-vault; ~ **de trole** trolley pole.

pertiguero *nm* verger.

pertiguista *nmf* pole-vaulter.

pertinacia *nf* (**a**) (*persistencia*) persistence; prolonged nature. (**b**) (*obstinación*) pertinacity, obstinacy.

pertinaz *adj* (**a**) *tos etc* persistent; *sequía* persistent, long-lasting, prolonged. (**b**) *persona* pertinacious, obstinate.

pertinencia *nf* relevance, pertinence; appropriateness.

pertinente *adj* (**a**) (*gen*) relevant, pertinent; appropriate; **no es ~ hacerlo ahora** this is not the appropriate time to do it.

(**b**) ~ **a** concerning, relevant to; **en lo ~ a libros** as regards books, as far as books are concerned.

pertinentemente *adv* relevantly, pertinently; appropriately.

pertrechar [1a] **1** *vt* to supply (*con, de* with); to equip (*con, de* with); (*Mil*) to supply with ammunition and stores, equip.

2 pertrecharse *vr*: ~ **de algo** to provide o.s. with sth.

pertrechos *nmpl* implements, equipment; gear; (*Mil*) supplies and stores, provisions; (*Mil*) munitions; ~ **de pesca** fishing tackle.

perturbación *nf* (**a**) (*Met, Pol etc*) disturbance; ~ **del orden público** breach of the peace.

(**b**) (*Med*) upset, disturbance; (*mental*) perturbation, (*grave*) mental disorder, alienation.

perturbado 1 *adj* mentally unbalanced. **2** *nm*, **perturbada** *nf* mentally unbalanced person.

perturbador 1 *adj* (**a**) *noticia etc* perturbing, disturbing.

(**b**) *conducta* unruly, disorderly; *movimiento* subversive.

2 *nm*, **perturbadora** *nf* disturber (of the peace); (*Pol*) disorderly element, unruly person; subversive.

perturbadoramente *adv* disturbingly.

perturbar [1a] *vt* (**a**) *orden etc* to disturb; *calma* to disturb, ruffle, upset.

(**b**) (*Med*) to upset, disturb; (*mentalmente*) to perturb; to cause mental disorder in.

Perú *nm*: **el ~** Peru.

peruanismo *nm* word (*o* phrase *etc*) peculiar to Peru.

peruano, -a *adj, nm/f* Peruvian.

Perucho* *nm*: **viven en plan de ~** (*Carib**) they get on like a house on fire.

peruétano* **1** *adj* (*And, Carib, Méx*) boring, tedious; stupid. **2** *nm* (*And, Carib, Méx*) (*pelma*) bore; (*necio*) dolt; **ese muchacho es un ~** (*Cono Sur: metido*) that lad is always sticking his nose where it doesn't belong.

perversamente *adv* perversely; wickedly.

perversidad *nf* (**a**) (*cualidad*) perversity; depravity; wickedness. (**b**) (*una ~*) evil deed, wrongdoing.

perversión *nf* (**a**) (*gen*) perversion; deviance; ~ **sexual** sexual perversion. (**b**) (*maldad*) wickedness; (*corrupción*) corruption.

perverso *adj* perverse; depraved; wicked.

pervertido 1 *adj* perverted, deviant. **2** *nm*, **pervertida** *nf* pervert; deviant.

pervertimiento *nm* perversion, corruption.

pervertir [3i] **1** *vt* to pervert, corrupt; *texto etc* to distort, corrupt; *gusto* to corrupt. **2 pervertirse** *vr* to become perverted.

pervinca *nf* (*Bot*) periwinkle.

pervivir [3a] *vi* to survive.

pesa *nf* (**a**) (*gen*) weight; (*Dep*) weight, shot; dumbbell; **~s y medidas** weights and measures; **hacer ~s** to do weight training. (**b**) **~s**** balls**. (**c**) (*And, CAm, Carib: carnicería*) butcher's shop.

pesadamente *adv* (**a**) (*gen*) heavily; **caer ~** to fall heavily. (**b**) (*lentamente*) slowly, ponderously; sluggishly; stiffly. (**c**) (*de manera aburrida*) boringly, tediously.

pesadez *nf* (**a**) (*peso*) heaviness; weight.

(**b**) (*lentitud*) slowness, ponderousness; sluggishness.

(**c**) (*Med*) drowsiness; dull feeling, heavy feeling.

(**d**) (*fatiga*) tediousness, boring nature; (*molestia*) annoyance; **es una ~ tener que ...** it's a bore having to ...; **¡qué ~!** what a bore!

pesadilla *nf* (**a**) (*gen*) nightmare, bad dream; **una experiencia de ~** a nightmarish experience.

(**b**) (*fig*) worry, obsession, nightmare; bogey; (*persona*) pet aversion; bogeyman; **ese equipo es nuestra ~** that is our bogey team; **ha sido la ~ de todos** it has been a nightmare for everybody.

pesado 1 *adj* (**a**) (*gen*) heavy (*t fig*), weighty.

(**b**) (*tardo*) *persona etc* slow, slow-moving, ponderous; sluggish; *trabajo etc* slow; *mecanismo* stiff.

(**c**) (*Met*) heavy, sultry.

(**d**) *sueño* deep, heavy.

(**e**) **tengo la cabeza pesada** my head feels heavy, I can hardly keep my head up, my head feels like lead; **tener el estómago ~** to feel full up.

(**f**) *tarea etc* (*difícil*) tough, hard; (*aburrido*) tedious; boring; *lectura etc* boring, stodgy; *persona* tedious, boring; annoying; **esto se hace ~** this is becoming tedious; **la lectura del libro resultó pesada** the book was heavy going, I got bored with the book; **es una persona de lo más ~** he's a terribly dull sort, he's a person of the most boring kind;

ése me cae ~ (*Carib, Méx**) that chap gets on my nerves*; **es** ~ **tener que ...** it's such a bore having to ..., it's tough having to ...; **¡no seas** ~! come off it!; don't be so difficult!

(**g**) (*And*) very good, excellent.

2 *nm*, **pesada** *nf* (**a**) (*aburrido*) boring person, bore; (*fanfarrón*) loudmouth*; **es un** ~ he's such a bore.

(**b**) (*Carib**) big shot*.

3 *nm* (*acto*) weighing.

pesador *nm* (*And, CAm, Carib*) butcher.

pesadumbre *nf* grief, sorrow, affliction.

pesaje *nm* weighing; (*Dep*) weigh-in.

pésame *nm* expression of condolence, message of sympathy; **dar el** ~ to express one's condolences, send one's sympathy (*por* for, on).

pesantez *nf* weight, heaviness; (*Fís*) gravity.

pesar [1a] **1** *vt* (**a**) (*averiguar el peso de*) to weigh.

(**b**) (*resultar pesado para*) to weigh down, be heavy for; **me pesa el abrigo** the coat weighs me down.

(**c**) (*fig: resultar difícil para*) to weigh heavily on; **le pesa tanta responsabilidad** so much responsibility bears heavily on him (*o* is a burden to him).

(**d**) (*fig*) (*examinar*) to weigh; (*valorar*) to appraise, value; (*estimar*) to reckon up; ~ **las posibilidades** to weigh up one's chances; ~ **las palabras** to weigh one's words.

(**e**) (*fig: afligir*) to grieve, afflict, distress; **me pesa mucho** it grieves me, I am very sorry about it (*o* to hear it *etc*); **no me pesa haberlo hecho** I'm not sorry I did it; **le pesa que no le hayan nombrado** it grieves him that he has not been appointed; **¡ya le pesará!** you'll be sorry!; **pese a las dificultades** in spite of the difficulties; **pese a quien pese** regardless of the consequences; in spite of everything; come what may; *V* **mal**.

2 *vi* (**a**) (*tener peso*) to weigh; (*Fís*) to have weight; **pesa 5 kilos** it weighs 5 kilos.

(**b**) (*pesar mucho*) to weigh a lot, be heavy; (*tiempo*) to drag, hang heavy; **ese paquete no pesa** that parcel isn't heavy, that parcel hardly weighs anything; **¿pesa mucho?** is it heavy?; ~ **como una losa** to weigh like a millstone round one's neck.

(**c**) (*fig: resultar pesado*) to weigh heavily; **sobre ella pesan muchas obligaciones** many obligations bear heavily on her; **la hipoteca que pesa sobre la finca** the mortgage with which the estate is burdened.

(**d**) (*fig: opinión etc*) to carry weight, count for a lot; **esa consideración no ha pesado conmigo** that consideration has not weighed with me (*o* influenced me).

(**e**) (*And, CAm*) to sell meat.

3 *nm* (**a**) (*arrepentimiento*) regret; (*tristeza*) grief, sorrow; **a mi** ~ to my regret; **a** ~ **suyo** (*LAm*) in spite of himself; **con gran** ~ **mío** much to my sorrow; **causar** ~ **a uno** to grieve sb, cause grief to sb; **sentir** (*o* **tener**) ~ **por no haber ...** to regret not having ...

(**b**) **a** ~ **de** in spite of, despite; **a** ~ **de eso** in spite of that, notwithstanding that; **a** ~ **de que no tiene dinero** in spite of the fact that he has no money; **a** ~ **de los** ~**es*** in spite of everything.

pesario *nm* pessary.

pesaroso *adj* sorrowful, regretful, sad.

pesca *nf* (**a**) (*acto*) fishing; ~ **de altura** deep-sea fishing; ~ **en bajura** shallow water fishing, coastal fishing; ~ **de la ballena** whaling; ~ **a caña** angling; ~ **a mosca** fly-fishing; ~ **de perlas** pearl fishing; ~ **submarina** underwater fishing; skin diving; **allí la** ~ **es muy buena** the fishing is very good there; **ir de** ~ to go fishing; **andar a la** ~ **de** (*fig*) to fish for, angle for.

(**b**) (*peces*) catch, quantity (of fish) caught; **la** ~ **ha sido mala** it's been a poor catch; **... y toda la** ~* and all the rest, and whatnot*.

pescada *nf* hake.

pescadería *nf* (*mercado*) fish-market; (*tienda*) fish-shop.

pescadero, -a *nm/f* fishmonger.

pescadilla *nf* whiting; small hake.

pescado *nm* (**a**) fish; ~ **azul** blue fish. (**b**) (*And, Cono Sur**) secret police.

pescador(a) *nm/f* fisherman, fisherwoman; ~ **de caña** angler, fisherman; ~ **a mosca** fly-fisherman.

pescante *nm* (**a**) (*de carruaje*) coachman's seat, driver's seat. (**b**) (*Teat*) wire. (**c**) (*Téc*) jib; (*Náut*) davit.

pescar [1g] **1** *vt* (**a**) (*coger*) to catch; to land.

(**b**) (*intentar coger*) to fish for, try to catch; **¿qué pescáis aquí?** what are you fishing for here?, what fish are you after here?

(**c**) (*) (*lograr*) to catch, get hold of, land; *puesto etc* to land, manage to get; *enfermedad* to catch; *significación* to grasp; *hechos etc* to dredge up; (*detener*) to arrest; **viene a** ~ **un marido** she's come to get herself a husband; **logró** ~ **unos cuantos datos** he managed to bring up a few facts, he was able to find a few facts.

(**d**) (*) *persona* to catch (out), catch in a lie; to catch unawares; **¡ya te pesqué!** now I've found you out!

2 *vi* (**a**) (*gen*) to fish; to go fishing; ~ **a mosca** to fish with a fly; ~ **al arrastre,** ~ **a la rastra** to trawl.

(**b**) (*) **la chica viene a ver si pesca** the girl is coming to see if she can get hitched‡.

(**c**) (*And, Cono Sur*) to nod, doze.

3 pescarse* *vr*: **no sabe lo que se pesca** he hasn't a clue*, he has no idea.

pescata *nf* catch, haul.

pescocear [1a] *vt* (*LAm*) to grab by the scruff of the neck.

pescozón *nm* blow on the neck.

pescozudo *adj* thick-necked, fat in the neck.

pescuezo *nm* (**a**) (*Zool*) neck; (*: *de persona*) scruff of the neck; **retorcer el** ~ **a una gallina** to wring a chicken's neck; **¡calla, o te retuerzo el** ~! shut up, or I'll wring your neck!

(**b**) (*fig*) vanity; haughtiness, pride.

pescuezón *adj* (*LAm*) (**a**) = **pescozudo.** (**b**) (*de cuello largo*) long-necked.

pese: ~ **a** *prep* despite, in spite of.

pesebre *nm* (**a**) (*Agr*) manger; stall. (**b**) (*esp LAm*) Nativity scene, crib.

pesebrera *nf* (*Cono Sur, Méx*) = **pesebre** (**b**).

pesera *nf* (*Méx*) = **pesero** (**b**).

pesero *nm* (**a**) (*And, CAm, Carib*) butcher; slaughterman. (**b**) (*Méx*) taxi bus.

peseta 1 *nf* peseta; **cambiar la** ~* to throw up. **2** *nm* (‡) taxi driver.

pesetada *nf* (*LAm*) joke, trick.

pesetera *nf* (*CAm, Méx*) prostitute.

pesetero *adj* (**a**) (*avaro*) money-grubbing, mercenary. (**b**) (*Méx*) *comerciante* small-time. (**c**) (*Carib: tacaño*) mean. (**d**) (*And, CAm, Carib: gorrón*) sponging*, parasitic.

pésimamente *adv* abominably, wretchedly.

pesimismo *nm* pessimism.

pesimista 1 *adj* pessimistic. **2** *nmf* pessimist.

pésimo 1 *adj* abominable, wretched, vile. **2** *adv*: **lo hiciste** ~ (*Méx**) you did it terribly.

peso *nm* (**a**) (*gen*) weight; weightiness, heaviness; (*Fís*) gravity; ~**s y medidas** weights and measures; ~ **atómico** atomic weight; ~ **bruto** gross weight; ~ **específico** specific gravity; (*fig*) influence; muscle, clout*; ~ **muerto** dead weight; ~ **neto** net weight; ~ **en vivo** live weight; **comprar algo a** ~ **de oro** to buy sth at a very high price; **vender al** ~ to sell by weight; **de poco** ~ light, lightweight; **de mucho** ~ (very) heavy; **eso cae de su** ~ that goes without saying, that's obvious; **coger** ~ to put on weight; **no da el** ~ (*fig*) he doesn't make the grade; **echar a uno en** ~ **por una ventana** to throw sb bodily through a window; **sostener algo en** ~ to support the full weight of sth; **lleva toda la dirección en** ~ he carries all the burden of the management; **llevar el** ~ **de un ataque** to bear the brunt of an attack.

(**b**) (*objeto*) weight, weighty object; (*carga*) burden, load; (*Dep*) weight; shot; (*prueba*) shot-putting, putting the shot; **lanzar el** ~ to put the shot; **levantamiento de** ~**s** weightlifting.

(**c**) (*Boxeo*) weight; ~ **bantam** bantam-weight; ~ **completo** (*CAm, Méx*), ~ **fuerte** heavyweight (*t fig*); ~ **gallo** bantam-weight; ~ **ligero** lightweight; ~ **medio** middleweight; ~ **medio fuerte** light heavyweight, cruiser-weight; ~ **mosca** flyweight; ~ **pesado** heavyweight; ~ **pluma** featherweight; ~ **welter** welterweight.

(**d**) (*modorra*) heavy feeling, dull feeling (*in head etc*).

(**e**) (*fig*) weight; **el** ~ **de los años** the weight of the years, the burden of age; **argumento de** ~ weighty argument; **razones de** ~ good reasons, sound reasons.

(**f**) (*balanza*) scales, balance, weighing machine; ~ **de baño** bathroom scales; ~ **de muelle** spring balance.

(**g**) (*Fin*) *unit of currency of certain LAm countries.*

pesor *nm* (*CAm, Carib*) weight, heaviness.

pespunt(e)ar [1a] *vti* to backstitch.

pespunte *nm* backstitch(ing).

pesquera *nf* (**a**) (*zona*) fishing-ground, fishery. (**b**) (*presa*) weir.

pesquería *nf* fishing-ground, fishery.

pesquero 1 *adj* fishing (*atr*). **2** *nm* fishing-boat.

pesquis* *nm* nous*; know-how; **tener el** ~ **para** + *infin* to have the nous to + *infin**.

pesquisa 1 *nf* (*indagación*) investigation, inquiry; (*registro*) search. **2** *nm* (*And, Cono Sur**) (*policía*) secret police; (*detective*) detective.

pesquisador(a) *nm/f* investigator, inquirer; (*And, Cono Sur**) (*policía*) member of the secret police; (*detective*) detective.

pesquisar [1a] *vt* to investigate, inquire into.

pesquisidor *nm* investigator, inquirer.

pestaña 1 *nf* (**a**) (*Anat: de ojo*) eyelash; (*Anat, Bot etc: de pelo*) fringe; **no pegué ~*** I didn't get a wink of sleep; **quemarse las ~s** (*fig*) (*excederse*) to go too far, burn one's fingers; (*estudiar*) to burn the midnight oil; **tener ~** to be pretty smart. (**b**) (*Téc*) flange; (*de neumático*) rim. **2** *nm* (*Esp*‡) (*policía*) cop*; (*policías*) cops*, fuzz‡.

pestañar [1a] *vi* (*LAm*), **pestañear** [1a] *vi* to blink, wink; **sin ~** without batting an eyelid.

pestañeo *nm* blink(ing), wink(ing).

pestazo* *nm* stink, stench.

peste *nf* (**a**) (*Med*) plague, epidemic; (*And, Carib*) bubonic plague; (*Cono Sur: viruela*) smallpox; (*And: resfrío*) cold; (*Cono Sur: enfermedad*) (*any*) infectious disease; **~ aviar** fowl pest; **~ bubónica** bubonic plague; **~ negra** Black Death; **~ porcina** swine fever.

(**b**) (*fig: plaga*) plague; evil menace; nuisance; **una ~ de ratones** a plague of mice; **los chiquillos son una ~** the kids are a pest, the kids are a nuisance.

(**c**) (*hedor*) stink, stench, foul smell; **¡qué ~ hay aquí!** what a stink!

(**d**) **echar ~s de** to swear about, fume at, utter bitter words about; **se hablan ~s de la cocina inglesa** awful things are said about English cooking.

pesticida *nm* pesticide.

pestífero *adj* (*dañino*) pestiferous; *olor* foul; *influencia etc* noxious, harmful.

pestilencia *nf* (**a**) (*plaga*) pestilence, plague. (**b**) (*hedor*) stink, stench.

pestilencial *adj* pestilential.

pestilente *adj* (**a**) (*dañino*) pestilent. (**b**) (*que huele*) smelly, foul.

pestillo *nm* bolt, latch; catch, fastener; (*Cono Sur: de puerta*) door handle.

pestiño* *nm* (*Esp*) (**a**) (*lata*) bore, drag; **fue un ~** it was a real drag. (**b**) (*chica*) plain girl.

pestozos‡ *nmpl* socks.

peta[1]‡ *nf* (*Esp*) peseta.

peta[2]‡ *nm* (**a**) (*droga*) joint‡, reefer‡.

(**b**) (*nombre*) name; **~ chungo** false name.

(**c**) (*documentación*) papers.

petaca 1 *nf* (**a**) (*de cigarrillos*) cigarette-case; (*de puros*) cigar-case; (*de pipa*) tobacco pouch; **hacerle la ~ a uno** to make an apple-pie bed for sb.

(**b**) (*cesto*) wicker basket; hamper; (*LAm*) leather-covered chest; (*Méx**) (*maleta*) suitcase; (*baúl*) trunk; (*equipaje*) luggage.

(**c**) (*CAm, Méx*: Anat*) hump; **~s** (*Carib, Méx*‡) (*nalgas*) buttocks; (*pechos*) big breasts.

2 *nmf* (*LAm*: rechoncho*) (**a**) short squat person.

(**b**) (*vago*) lazy person.

(**c**) **írsele las ~s a uno** to lose one's patience.

3 *adj invar* (**a**) (*LAm*: vago*) lazy, idle; (*Cono Sur*: torpe*) slow.

(**b**) (*Carib*: grosero*) coarse.

petacón* *adj* (*And, Cono Sur: gordito*) plump, chubby; (*And: barrigón*) potbellied, paunchy; **es petacona** (*CAm, Carib, Méx*) she's rather broad in the beam*.

petacudo* *adj* (**a**) (*And*) stout, fat; (*CAm*) hunchbacked; (*Méx*) broad in the beam*. (**b**) (*lento*) slow, ponderous, sluggish.

petacho *nm* patch, mend.

pétalo *nm* petal.

petanca *nf* pétanque.

petardazo *nm* (**a**) (*fuegos artificiales*) firework display.

(**b**) (*sonido*) crack, bang.

(**c**) (*sorpresa*) shock result, upset.

petardear [1a] **1** *vt* (*) to cheat, swindle. **2** *vi* (*Aut*) to backfire.

petardista* *nm* cheat, swindler; (*Méx*) crooked politician*.

petardo *nm* (**a**) (*gen*) firework, firecracker; (small) explosive device, incendiary device; (*Mil*) petard. (**b**) (*estafa*) fraud, swindle; **pegar un ~** to practise a fraud, pull a fast one (*a* on); **ser un ~*** to be dead boring*. (**c**) (‡: *droga*) joint‡. (**d**) (‡: *mujer*) old bag‡.

petate *nm* (**a**) (*estera*) grass mat; (*LAm*) palm matting; (*de dormir*) sleeping mat.

(**b**) (*lío de cama*) bedroll; (*equipaje*) baggage; **liar el ~*** to pack up; (*irse*) to pack up and go, clear out*; (*morir*) to peg out‡.

(**c**) (*: *estafador*) cheat, trickster.

(**d**) (*: *pobre hombre*) poor devil.

(**e**) **se descubrió el ~*** the fraud was discovered.

petatearse‡ [1a] *vr* (*Méx*) to peg out‡, kick the bucket‡.

peteneras *nfpl*: **salir por ~** (*Esp*) to butt in with some silly remark, say (*o* do) something quite inappropriate.

petición *nf* request, plea; petition; (*Jur*) plea; claim; **a ~** by request; **a ~ de** at the request of; **programa a ~ de radioyentes** listeners' request programme; **aborto a ~** abortion on demand; **~ de aumento de salarios** demand for higher wages, wage demand, wage claim; **~ de divorcio** petition for divorce; **~ de extradición** request for extradition; **cometer ~ de principio** to beg the question.

peticionar [1a] *vt* (*LAm*) to petition.

peticionario, -a *nm/f* petitioner, applicant.

petimetre 1 *adj* foppish. **2** *nm* fop, dandy.

petirrojo *nm* robin.

petiso (*And, Cono Sur*), **petizo** (*And, Cono Sur*) **1** *adj* (*bajo*) small, short; (*rechoncho*) stocky; chubby. **2** *nm* small horse. **3** *nm*, **petisa** *nf*, **petiza** *nf* short person.

petisú *nm* cream puff.

petitorio *adj*: **mesa petitoria** stall (*for charity collection*).

petizón *adj* (*And, Cono Sur*) = **petiso 1, petizo 1.**

peto *nm* (*corpiño*) bodice; (*babero*) bib; (*Mil*) breastplate; (*Taur*) *protective covering of picador's horse.*

petral *nm* breast-strap (*of harness*).

Petrarca *nm* Petrarch.

petrarquismo *nm* Petrarchism.

petrarquista *adj* Petrarchan.

petrel *nm* petrel.

pétreo *adj* stony; rocky.

petrificación *nf* petrifaction.

petrificado *adj* petrified.

petrificar [1g] **1** *vt* to petrify (*t fig*), turn to stone. **2 petrificarse** *vr* to petrify, become petrified (*t fig*), turn to stone.

petrodólar *nm* petrodollar.

petróleo *nm* (*Min*) oil, petroleum; (*LAm: kerosene*) paraffin; **~ de alumbrado** paraffin (oil); **~ combustible** fuel oil; **~ crudo** crude oil.

petrolero 1 *adj* oil (*atr*), petroleum (*atr*); **flota petrolera** tanker fleet; **industria petrolera** oil industry; **sindicato ~** oil workers' union. **2** *nm* (**a**) (*Com*) oil man; (*obrero*) oil worker; (*criminal*) arsonist. (**b**) (*Náut*) tanker.

petrolífero *adj* (**a**) (*Min*) petroliferous, oil-bearing. (**b**) (*Com*) oil (*atr*); **compañía petrolífera** oil company.

petrología *nf* petrology.

petroquímica *nf* (*ciencia*) petrochemistry; (*Com*) petrochemical company; (*fábrica*) petrochemical factory.

petroquímico *adj* petrochemical.

petulancia *nf* vanity, self-satisfaction, opinionated nature.

petulante *adj* vain, self-satisfied, opinionated.

petunia *nf* petunia.

peuquino *adj* (*Cono Sur*) greyish.

peyorativo *adj* pejorative.

peyote *nm* (*LAm*) peyote cactus.

pez[1] **1** *nm* (**a**) fish; **~ de colores** goldfish; **~ espada** swordfish; **~ mujer** manatee; **~ sierra** sawfish; **~ volante** flying fish; **estar como el ~ en el agua** to feel completely at home, be in one's element; **¡me río de los peces de colores!*** I couldn't care less!

(**b**) **~ gordo*** big shot*, fat cat*.

(**c**) **buen ~*** rogue, rascal.

2 *adj* (*) **estar ~ de** (*o* **en**) **algo** to be completely ignorant of sth, know nothing at all about sth; **están algo peces en idiomas** they're rather backward at languages.

pez[2] *nf* pitch, tar.

pezón *nm* (**a**) (*Anat*) teat, nipple. (**b**) (*Bot*) stalk. (**c**) (*Mec*) **~ de engrase** nipple, lubrication point.

pezonera *nf* (*Cono Sur*) feeding bottle.

pezuña *nf* (**a**) (*Zool*) hoof; (*: *de persona*) hoof*, foot. (**b**) (*And, Méx*) dirt hardened on the feet.

piada *nf* (**a**) (*Orn*) cheep, cheeping. (**b**) (*fig*) borrowed phrase.

piadosamente *adv* (*V adj*) (**a**) piously, devoutly. (**b**) kindly, mercifully.

piadoso *adj* (**a**) (*Rel*) pious, devout. (**b**) (*amable*) kind, merciful (*para, con* to); *V* **mentira**.

piafar [1a] *vi* (*caballo*) to paw the ground, stamp.

pial *nm* lasso.

pialar [1a] *vt* to lasso.
Piamonte *nm* Piedmont.
piamontés, -esa *adj, nm/f* Piedmontese.
pianista *nmf* pianist.
pianístico *adj* piano (*atr*).
piano *nm* piano; ~ **de cola** grand piano; ~ **de media cola** baby grand; ~ **mecánico** pianola; ~ **recto,** ~ **vertical** upright piano; **como un** ~ (*Esp**) real big*; **tocar el** ~ to play the piano, (*: *lavar platos*) do the washing-up; (‡: *huella dactilar*) to have one's fingerprints taken, be fingerprinted; **tocar** ~ (*LAm**) to rob, steal.
piantado‡ (*Cono Sur*) **1** *adj* nuts‡, crazy. **2** *nm* madman, nutcase‡.
piantarse‡ [1a] *vr* (*Cono Sur*) to escape, get out.
piante* *nmf*: **es un** ~ he's a pain*.
piar [1c] *vi* (**a**) (*Orn*) to cheep; (*: *hablar*) to talk, chatter. (**b**) ~ **por*** to cry for, be dying for. (**c**) (*: *quejarse*) to whine, snivel, grouse*; ~**las*** to be forever grousing*. (**d**) (*: *soplar*) to spill the beans*; **¡no la píes!** don't let on!*
piara *nf* herd; drove.
piastra *nf* piastre.
PIB *nm abr de* **producto interior bruto** gross national product, GNP.
piba‡ *nf* whore.
pibe, -a* *nm/f* (*niño*) kid*, child; (*muchacho*) boy; (*muchacha*) girl; (*amiguito*) boyfriend; (*amiguita*) girlfriend.
pibil *nm* (*Méx*) chili sauce.
pica[1] *nf* (*Orn*) magpie.
pica[2] *nf* (*Mil*) pike; (*Taur*) goad; (**) prick**; **poner una** ~ **en Flandes** to bring off something difficult, achieve a signal success.
pica[3] *nf* (*And Agr*) tapping (*of rubber trees*).
pica[4] *nf* (*And*: *resentimiento*) pique, resentment; (*Cono Sur*: *mal humor*) annoyance, irritation; **sacar** ~ to cause annoyance; to arouse envy.
pica[5] *nf* (*And, CAm, Carib*: *camino*) forest trail, narrow path.
pica[6] *nf*: ~**s** (*Naipes*) spades.
pica[7]* *nm* (*de autobús etc*) inspector.
picacera* *nf* (*And, Cono Sur*) irritation.
picacho *nm* peak, summit.
picada[1] *nf* (**a**) (*gen*) prick; (*de insecto etc*) sting; bite; (*de ave*) peck. (**b**) (*Cono Sur*: *mal humor*) bad temper, anger. (**c**) **ir en** ~ (*LAm*) to nose-dive; (*fig*) to plummet, take a nose-dive. (**d**) (*Culin*) spicy sauce.
picada[2] *nf* (*LAm*) forest trail, narrow path; (*And*) ford.
picada[3] *nf* (*Cono Sur*) small restaurant.
picadero *nm* (**a**) (*escuela*) riding-school. (**b**) (‡: *habitación*) pad‡, flat; (*pey*) apartment used for sexual encounters. (**c**) (*LAm‡*) shooting gallery‡ (*for drug taking*). (**d**) (*And*: *matadero*) slaughterhouse.
picadillo *nm* mince, minced meat; **ser como el** ~ (*Carib**) to be boring.
picado 1 *adj* (**a**) *material* pricked, perforated; with a row of holes; *superficie* pitted; ~ **de viruelas** pockmarked.
(**b**) *carne etc* minced; *tabaco* cut; *mar* choppy.
(**c**) *vino* pricked, slightly sour.
(**d**) **estar** ~ (*enojado*) to be offended, be cross; (*borracho*) to be tipsy; **están picados desde hace muchos años** they fell out years ago.
(**e**) **estar** ~ **por algo** to go for sth in a big way.*
(**f**) **quedarse** ~ to be frustrated.
2 *nm* (**a**) (*Aer, Orn*) dive; **caer en** ~ (*fig*) to take a dive, go downhill fast, slump.
(**b**) (*Mús*) pizzicato, staccato.
(**c**) (*de vino*) souring.
picador *nm* (**a**) (*gen*) horse-trainer, horse-breaker. (**b**) (*Taur*) picador, bullfighter's assistant (*mounted, with a pike*). (**c**) (*Min*) faceworker.
picadora *nf*: ~ **de carne** mincer, mincing machine.
picadura *nf* (**a**) (*gen*) prick; (*pinchazo*) puncture; (*de insecto etc*) sting, bite. (**b**) (*tabaco*) cut tobacco.
picaflor *nm* (*LAm*) (**a**) (*Orn*) humming-bird. (**b**) (*) (*tenorio*) ladykiller; (*mariposón*) flirt; (*amante*) lover, boyfriend.
picafuego *nm* poker.
picajón* *adj*, **picajoso*** *adj* touchy.
picamaderos *nm invar* woodpecker.
picana *nf* (*LAm*) cattle prod, goad; ~ **eléctrica** electric prod (*for torture*).
picanear [1a] *vt* (*LAm*) to spur on, goad on; *preso* to torture with electric shocks.
picante 1 *adj* (**a**) *comida, sabor* hot; peppery; spicy.
(**b**) (*fig*) *comentario* sharp, stinging, cutting; *chiste etc* racy, spicy; *situación, contraste* piquant.
2 *nm* (**a**) (*sabor*) hot taste.
(**b**) (*fig*) sharpness, pungency; raciness, spiciness; piquancy.
(**c**) (*And, Cono Sur*: *salsa*) chili sauce; (*And*: *guisado*) meat stew with chili sauce; (*LAm*: *chile*) chili.
(**d**) ~**s‡** socks.
picantería *nf* (*And, Cono Sur*) restaurant specializing in spicy dishes.
picantón *nm* spicy sauce.
picapedrero *nm* stonecutter, quarryman.
picapica *nf* (**a**) (*And*: *serpentina*) streamer. (**b**) *V* **polvos.**
picapleitos *nm invar* (*pey*) lawyer; litigious person.
picaporte *nm* (*tirador*) door-handle; (*pestillo*) latch; (*aldaba*) door-knocker; (*llave*) latchkey.
picar [1g] **1** *vt* (**a**) (*perforar*) to prick, puncture; *papel etc* to prick (a line of) holes in, pierce with holes, perforate; *superficie* to pit, pock; (*Arte*) to stipple; (*Cos*) to pink; *ticket* to punch, clip.
(**b**) (*insecto*) to sting; to bite; (*culebra*) to bite; (*espina*) to prick.
(**c**) (*ave*) to peck; to peck at; (*persona*) *comida* to nibble (at), pick at; (*pez*) to bite.
(**d**) *caballo* to put spurs to, spur on; *toro* to stick, prick (with the goad); (*fig*) to incite, goad, stimulate; (*fig*) (*herir*) to wound; (*ofender*) to pique; (*molestar*) to annoy, bother; **le pican los celos** he is feeling pangs of jealousy.
(**e**) (*Mús*) to play staccato; (*: *escribir a máquina*) to type.
(**f**) *piedra* to chip, chip pieces off; *piedra de molino* to sharpen; *piedra* (*pulverizar*) to grind (up); (*Culin*) to mince, chop (up); *tabaco* to cut.
(**g**) *lengua* to burn, sting.
(**h**) (*Mil*) to harass.
(**i**) (‡: *matar*) to bump off‡.
(**j**) (**) to screw**.
2 *vi* (**a**) (*espina*) to prick; (*insecto*) to sting, bite; **no es de los que pican** it's not the kind that stings.
(**b**) (*ave*) ~ **en** to peck at; (*persona etc*) to nibble at, pick at; (*fig*) to dabble in, study superficially; **ha picado en todos los géneros literarios** he's dabbled in (*o* had a go at) all the literary genres; **yo no pico en esas cosas** I don't dabble in such things.
(**c**) (*pez*) to bite, take the bait; (*fig*) to rise to the bait; **por fin picó** he swallowed the bait eventually; **ha picado mucha gente** lots of people have fallen for it, it has caught on with lots of people.
(**d**) (*fig*) ~ **en** to border on, be akin to; **eso pica en frescura** that borders (*o* verges) on cheek*.
(**e**) (*Med*) to itch, sting; **me pican los ojos** my eyes hurt; **me pica la lengua** my tongue is smarting (*o* stinging); **me pica el brazo** my arm itches.
(**f**) (*Esp*: *sol*) to burn, scorch; **hoy sí pica el sol** the sun is really burning today.
(**g**) (*Aer, Orn*) to dive.
(**h**) ~ **muy alto** to aim too high, be over-ambitious.
(**i**) (*Aut*) to pink.
3 picarse *vr* (**a**) (*ropa*) to get moth-eaten; (*sustancia*) to get holes in it; (*muela*) to decay.
(**b**) (*vino etc*) to turn sour, go off; (*fruta etc*) to spoil, go rotten.
(**c**) (*mar*) to get choppy.
(**d**) (*persona*) to take offence, get piqued; to get cross; to bridle (*por* at); (*emborracharse*) to get tipsy; **el que se pica, ajos come** if the cap fits, wear it.
(**e**) ~ **con algo** to get a longing for, get an obsession about; to take a strong liking to.
(**f**) ~ **de puntual** to take a pride in being punctual, make a strong point of punctuality; ~ **de caballero** to boast of being a gentleman.
(**g**) ~ **de pecho** (*Carib*) to become consumptive.
(**h**) (*: *inyectarse*) to give o.s. a shot (of drugs)*, shoot up‡.
picarazado *adj* (*Carib*) pockmarked.
picardear [1a] **1** *vt*: ~ **a uno** to get sb into bad habits, lead sb into evil ways.
2 *vi* (*jugar*) to play about; (*dar guerra*) to play up, be mischievous.
3 picardearse *vr* to get into evil ways, go to the bad.
Picardía *nf* Picardy.
picardía *nf* (**a**) (*cualidad*) villainy, knavery; slyness, craftiness; naughtiness.
(**b**) (*una* ~) dirty trick; naughty thing (to do), mischievous act.

(**c**) (*grosería*) rude thing (to say), naughty word; (*insulto*) insult; **le gusta decir ~s a la gente** he likes saying naughty things to people.
picaresca *nf* (**a**) (*Liter*) (genre of the) picaresque novel. (**b**) (*astucia*) guile; chicanery, subterfuge; **la ~ española** Spanish guile, Spanish wiliness. (**c**) (*hampa*) (criminal) underworld.
picaresco *adj* (**a**) (*travieso*) roguish, rascally. (**b**) (*Liter*) *novela* picaresque, of roguery.
pícaro 1 *adj* (**a**) (*pillo*) villainous, knavish; (*taimado*) sly, crafty; (*travieso*) naughty, mischievous.
(**b**) (*precoz*) *etc* precocious, knowing, (*esp*) sexually aware before the proper age.
(**c**) (*hum*) naughty, wicked; **¡este ~ siglo!** what naughty times we live in!; **tiene inclinación a los ~s celos** she gives way to that wicked jealousy.
2 *nm* (**a**) (*granuja*) villain, knave, scoundrel, rogue, rascal; (*ladino*) sly sort; (*niño*) rascal, scamp; **¡~!** you rascal!
(**b**) (*Liter*) *pícaro* rogue.
picarón *nm* (**a**) rogue. (**b**) (*And, Cono Sur, Méx Culin*) fritter.
picaruelo *adj mirada etc* roguish, naughty, sly; **me dio una mirada picaruela** she gave me a roguish look.
picatoste *nm* fried bread.
picaza *nf* magpie.
picazo *nm* peck; jab, poke.
picazón *nf* (**a**) (*comezón*) itch; (*ardor*) sting, stinging feeling; smart, smarting. (**b**) (*fig*) (*disgusto*) annoyance, pique; (*remordimiento*) uneasy feeling, pang of conscience.
píccolo *nm* piccolo.
pícea *nf* spruce.
picia* *nf* prank, escapade.
pick-up [pi'kap *o* pi'ku] *nm* pick-up.
picnic *nm* (**a**) (*excursión*) picnic.
(**b**) (*cesta*) picnic basket, picnic set.
pico *nm* (**a**) (*Orn*) beak, bill; (*Ent etc*) beak; (*hum*: *boca*) mouth, lips; **callar** (*o* **cerrar**) **el ~‡** to shut one's trap‡, keep one's trap shut‡; **darle al ~*** to talk a lot; **darse el ~*** (*besar*) to kiss; (*fig*) to hit it off; **hincar el ~*** (*morir*) to peg out‡; (*ceder*) to give up, give in; **tener buen ~‡** to like one's grub‡.
(**b**) (*punta*) corner, peak, sharp point; (*de mesa, página*) corner; **sombrero de tres ~s** cocked hat, three-cornered hat; **andar** (*o* **irse**) **de ~s pardos*** to go for a good time.
(**c**) (*de jarra etc*) lip, spout.
(**d**) (*Téc*) pick, pickaxe.
(**e**) (*Geog*) peak, summit; pinnacle of rock.
(**f**) **y ~** and a bit; **son las 3 y ~** it's just after 3; **tiene 50 libros y ~** he has 50-odd books; **quédese con el ~** keep what's left over; **me costó un ~** it cost me quite a bit.
(**g**) (*Orn*: *especie*) woodpecker.
(**h**) (*: *labia*) talkativeness; **ser un ~ de oro, tener buen** (*o* **mucho**) **~** to have the gift of the gab*, be a great talker; **irse del ~** to talk too much; **perderse por el ~** to harm o.s. by saying too much.
(**i**) (*Naipes*) spade.
(**j**) (*And, CAm, Méx*: *beso*) kiss.
(**k**) (*And, Cono Sur***) prick**.
(**l**) (‡: *de droga*) fix‡, shot*; **darse el ~** to give o.s. a fix‡.
picolargo* *adj* (*Cono Sur*) (*respondón*) pert, saucy; (*murmurador*) backbiting; (*intrigante*) intriguing, scheming.
picoleto‡ *nm* (*Esp*) Civil Guard.
picón* 1 *adj* (**a**) (*And, Carib*: *respondón*) cheeky*. (**b**) (*And, Carib*: *quisquilloso*) touchy. (**c**) (*Carib*: *burlón*) mocking. **2** *nm*, **picona** *nf* (*And*) gossip, telltale.
picor *nm* = **picazón** (**a**).
picoreto *adj* (*And, CAm, Carib*) loose-tongued, indiscreet.
picoso *adj* (**a**) pockmarked. (**b**) (*LAm*: *picante*) hot, spicy.
picota *nf* (**a**) (*gen*) pillory; (*fig*) **poner a uno en la ~** to pillory sb.
(**b**) (*Arquit*) point, top; (*Geog*) peak.
(**c**) (*Bot*) bigarreau cherry.
(**d**) (‡: *nariz*) hooter‡, nose.
picotada *nf*, **picotazo** *nm* peck; sting, bite; **tener mala picotada** (*fig*) to be bad-tempered.
picotear [1a] **1** *vt* to peck. **2** *vi* (**a**) (*al comer*) to nibble, pick. (**b**) (*: *parlotear*) to chatter, gas*, gab*. **3 picotearse*** *vr* to squabble.
picotero 1 *adj* chattering, gossipy, talkative. **2** *nm*, **picotera** *nf* gossip, chatterer, gasbag*.
picotón *nm* (*And, Cono Sur*) peck.
picto 1 *adj* Pictish. **2** *nm*, **picta** *nf* Pict. **3** *nm* (*Ling*) Pictish.
pictograma *nm* pictogram.
pictóricamente *adv* pictorially.
pictórico *adj* (**a**) (*gen*) pictorial.
(**b**) *escena etc* worth painting; picturesque.
(**c**) *talento etc* artistic; **tiene dotes pictóricas** she has artistic gifts, she has talent for painting.
picú *nm* record player.
picúa *nf* (*Carib*) (**a**) (*cometa*) small kite. (**b**) (*comerciante*) sharp businessman. (**c**) (*puta*) prostitute.
picuda *nf* (**a**) (*Orn*) woodcock. (**b**) (*Carib*: *pez*) barracuda.
picudo *adj* (**a**) (*puntiagudo*) pointed, with a point; *jarra* with a spout; *persona* long-nosed, sharp-nosed.
(**b**) (*) = **picotero 1**.
(**c**) (*Carib*) *V* **cursi**.
(**d**) (*Méx**: *astuto*) crafty, clever.
piculina *nf* (*Esp*) tart‡, whore.
picure *nm* (**a**) (*And*) (*fugitivo*) fugitive; (*gandul*) slacker. (**b**) (*Carib*) spicy sauce.
picurearse* [1a] *vr* (*And, Carib*) to scarper‡.
picha[1] *nf* (*Méx*) blanket; (*hum*) mistress.
picha[2] *nf* (**) prick**.
pichado *adj* (*Cono Sur*) easily embarrassed.
pichana *nf* (*And, Cono Sur*) broom.
pichanga *nf* (**a**) (*And*) broom. (**b**) (*Cono Sur Dep*) friendly soccer match. (**c**) (*Cono Sur Culin*) tray of cocktail snacks.
pichango *nm* (*Cono Sur*) dog.
piche *nm* (**a**) (*CAm*: *avaro*) miser, skinflint.
(**b**) (*And, Cono Sur*: *Zool*) (*kind of*) armadillo.
(**c**) (*Carib, Cono Sur*: *miedo*) fright.
(**d**) (*And*: *empujón*) shove.
(**e**) (*And*: *suero*) whey.
(**f**) (*And*: *rojo*) red.
pichel *nm* tankard, mug; (*Méx*) water jug.
pichi[1]**‡ 1** *adj* smart, elegant. **2** *nm* (**a**) Madrid man in traditional dress. (**b**) (*Cos*) light knitted dress. (**c**) (*en oración directa*) mate*, man*.
pichi[2]** *nm*: **hacer ~** (*And, Cono Sur*) to have a pee**.
pichi[3] *nm* (*prenda*) pinafore dress.
pichicata* *nf* (*LAm*) cocaine powder; (*Cono Sur*) (*droga*) hard drugs; (*inyección*) shot*; fix‡.
pichicatero, -a* *nm/f* (*And*) drug addict.
pichicato *adj* (*LAm*) mean, miserly.
pichicote *adj* (*And*) mean, miserly.
pichichi *nm* top goal-scorer.
pichilingo *nm* (*Méx*) lad, kid*.
pichincha *nf* (*And, Cono Sur*) (*ganga*) bargain; (*precio*) bargain price; (*trato*) good deal; (*suerte*) lucky break.
pichingo *nm* (*CAm*) jar, vessel; (*pey*) piece of junk.
pichintún *nm* (*Cono Sur*) dash, smidgin*.
pichirre* *adj* (*And, Carib*) mean, stingy.
picholear* [1a] *vi* (**a**) (*CAm, Cono Sur*: *jaranear*) to have a good time. (**b**) (*CAm, Méx*: *apostar*) to have a flutter*.
pichón 1 *nm* (**a**) (*Orn*) young pigeon; (*Culin*) pigeon; (*LAm*) chick, young bird; **~ de barro** clay pigeon; **sí, ~** yes, darling.
(**b**) (*LAm*) (*novato*) novice, greenhorn; tyro; (*Dep*) young player, inexperienced player.
(**c**) **un ~ de hombre** (*Cono Sur*) a well-bred man.
2 pichona *nf*: **sí, ~** yes, darling.
pichonear [1a] **1** *vt* (**a**) (*Cono Sur, Méx**: *engañar*) to swindle, con*.
(**b**) (*And, CAm*: *pillar*) to catch out; (*matar*) to kill, murder.
(**c**) (*Cono Sur*) = **pinchar**.
(**d**) (*And, CAm*: *tener prestado*) to borrow, use temporarily; to occupy temporarily.
2 *vi* (*And, Cono Sur, Méx**: *triunfar*) to win an easy victory.
pichoso *adj* (*Carib*) dirty.
pichula** *nf* (*And*) cock**, prick**.
pichuleador *nm* (*Cono Sur*) moneygrubber.
pichulear* [1a] *vi* (**a**) (*Cono Sur*) (*negociar*) to be a small-time businessman; (*ser mercenario*) to be mercenary, be greedy for money. (**b**) (*CAm, Méx*: *gastar poco*) to be careful with one's money.
pichuleo* *nm* (**a**) (*Cono Sur*) meanness. (**b**) (*CAm, Méx*: *negocio*) small business, retail business.
pichulina** *nf* willie**.
PID *nm abr de* **proceso integrado de datos** integrated data processing, IDP.
pídola *nf* leapfrog.
pie *nm* (**a**) (*Anat etc*) foot; **~ de atleta** athlete's foot; **~ de**

cabra crowbar; **~s de cerdo** (*Culin*) pig's trotters; **~s planos** flat feet; **ligero de ~s** light-footed, quick; **a ~** on foot; **ir a ~** to go on foot, walk; **a cuatro ~s** on all fours; **a ~ enjuto** dry-shod, (*fig*) without danger, without any risk; **a ~ firme** steadfastly; **a ~ juntillo, a ~s juntillos** with both feet together, (*fig*) *creer* firmly, absolutely; **con el ~ bien sentado** calmly, thoughtfully; with due care; **con ~s de plomo** warily, gingerly; **andar con ~s de plomo** to go very carefully; **con un ~ en el hoyo** with one foot in the grave; **entrar con buen ~** (*o* **con ~ derecho**) to get off to a good start; **hacer algo con los ~s** to bungle sth, make a mess of sth; **levantarse con el ~ izquierdo** (*fig*) to get up on the wrong side of the bed; **estar de ~** to be standing (up); **ponerse de** (*o* **en**) **~** to stand up, get up, rise; **caer de ~** (*fig*) to fall on one's feet, be lucky; **nacer de ~** to be born with a silver spoon in one's mouth, be born lucky; **cojear del mismo ~** to have the same faults; **saber de qué ~ cojea uno** to know sb's weak spots (*o* weaknesses); **de ~s a cabeza** from head to foot, from top to toe; **soldado de a ~** (*Hist*) foot-soldier; **de a ~** (*fig*) common, ordinary; **en ~** standing; upright; **ganado en ~** cattle on the hoof; **mantenerse en ~** to remain upright; **la duda sigue en ~** the doubt remains; **las víctimas salieron por su ~** those affected were able to leave unassisted (*o* without help); **irse** (*o* **salir**) **por ~s** to make off; **argumento sin ~s ni cabeza** pointless argument, absurd argument; unintelligible argument; **asentar el ~** to make a cautious start; **buscar tres ~s al gato** to split hairs, quibble; to look for trouble; **no dar ~ con bola** to do everything wrong, be no good at anything; **déle el ~ y se tomará la mano** give him an inch and he'll take a yard; **se le fueron los ~s** he slipped, he stumbled; **no hace ~** he's out of his depth; **parar los ~s a uno** to curb sb, clip sb's wings; to stop sb going too far; to take sb down a peg; **poner el ~** to tread, put one's foot; **poner el ~ en el acelerador** to step on the gas*; (*fig*) to speed things up, step up the pace; **poner los ~s en** (*fig*) to set foot in; **sacar los ~s del plato** to abandon all restraint; to kick over the traces; **volverse ~s atrás** to retrace one's steps.

(**b**) (*Mat*) foot; **~ cuadrado** square foot; **~ cúbico** cubic foot; **tiene 6 ~s de largo** it is 6 feet long.

(**c**) (*Bot*) trunk, stem; (*de rosa etc*) root, stock, stand; (*de vaso*) stem; (*de estatua*) foot, base; (*de cama, colina, escalera, página etc*) foot, bottom; (*de carta, documento*) ending; (*de foto, grabado*) colophon, caption; **~ de autor** byline; **~ de imprenta** imprint; **al ~ del monte** at the foot (*o* bottom) of the mountain; **a los ~s de la cama** at the foot of the bed; **al ~ de fábrica** cost price, ex-works; **al ~ de la letra** *citar etc* literally, verbatim; *copiar* exactly, word for word; *cumplir* impeccably, down to the last detail; **al ~ de la página** at the foot of the page; **al ~ de la obra** (*Com*) delivered, including delivery charges; **a ~ de obra** on the spot; **estar a ~ de obra** to be on site, be on the job; **a ~ de ese edificio** next to that building, right beside that building; **estar al ~ del cañón** to be ready to act; **morir al ~ del cañón** to die in harness.

(**d**) (*Teat*) cue.

(**e**) (*de vino etc*) sediment.

(**f**) (*fig*) (*causa*) motive, basis; (*pretexto*) pretext; **dar ~ a** to give cause for; **dar ~ para que uno haga algo** to give sb a motive for doing sth; **tomar ~ para hacer algo** to use sth as a basis for action.

(**g**) (*fig*: *seguridad*) foothold; **no hacer ~** to be out of one's depth; **perder el ~** to lose one's foothold, slip.

(**h**) (*fig*: *posición*) standing, footing; **en ~ de guerra** on a war footing; **estar sobre un** (**mismo**) **~ de igualdad** to be on an equal footing, be on equal terms (*con* with).

(**i**) (*Liter*) foot; measure, verse form.

(**j**) (*Cono Sur**: *enganche*) deposit, down payment.

(**k**) **~ de vía** (*CAm Aut*) indicator.

piecería *nf*, **piecerío** *nm* (*Mec*) parts.

piecero, -a *nm/f* tailor's cutter, garment worker.

piedad *nf* (**a**) (*Rel*) piety, devotion, devoutness; respect; **~ filial** filial respect.

(**b**) (*compasión*) pity; (*misericordia*) mercy; **¡por ~!** for pity's sake!; **mover a uno a ~** to move sb to pity, arouse compassion in sb; **tener ~ de** to take pity on; **¡ten un poco de ~!** show some sympathy!; **no tuvieron ~ de ellos** they showed them no mercy.

piedra 1 *nf* (**a**) (*gen*) stone; (*roca*) rock; (*de encendedor etc*) flint; (*Med*) stone; (*Met*) hailstone; hail; **un puente de ~** a stone bridge; **tener el corazón de ~** to be hard-hearted; **primera ~** foundation stone; **~ de afilar** hone; **~ de amolar** grindstone; **~ angular** (*lit, fig*) cornerstone; **~ arenisca** sandstone; **~ de cal, ~ caliza** limestone; **~ de escándalo** source of scandal; bone of contention; **~ filosofal** philosopher's stone; **~ fundamental** (*fig*) basis, cornerstone; **~ imán** lodestone; **~ miliar** milestone; **~ de molino** millstone; **~ poma** (*Méx*), **~ pómez** pumice (stone); **~ preciosa** precious stone; **~ de toque** touchstone; **~ de tropiezo** stumbling block; **a tiro de ~** within a stone's throw; **no dejar ~ sobre ~** to raze to the ground; **no dejar ~ por mover** to leave no stone unturned; **¿quién se atreve a lanzar la primera ~?** which of you shall cast the first stone?; **colocar la primera ~** to lay the foundation stone; **hablar ~s** (*And‡*) to talk through the back of one's head*; **pasar a uno por la ~** to put sb through the mill; **pasar a una por la ~**‡** to screw sb**‡; **quedarse de ~** to be thunderstruck, be rooted to the spot; **no soy de ~** I'm not made of stone, I do have feelings; **eso sería tirar ~s sobre su propio tejado** people who live in glass houses should not throw stones.

(**b**) (‡: *droga*) dope‡, pot‡.

(**c**) **en ~** (*Cono Sur Culin*) with hot sauce.

2 *nmf* (*Carib**: *pesado*) bore.

piel 1 *nf* (**a**) (*Anat*) skin; **estirarse la ~** to have a facelift, have cosmetic surgery.

(**b**) (*Zool*) skin, hide, pelt; fur; leather; **~ de ante** buckskin, buff, suède; **~ de becerro, ~ de ternera** calf, calfskin; **~ de cabra** goatskin; **~ de cerdo** pigskin; **~ de gallina** goosepimples; **~ de Suecia** suède; **~ de ternera** calfskin; **la ~ del toro** Spain; **abrigo de ~es** fur coat; **artículos de ~** leather goods; **una maleta de ~** a leather suitcase; **dejarse la ~** (*fig*) to give one's all.

(**c**) (*Bot*) skin, peel, rind.

2 *nmf*: **~ roja** redskin; **los ~es rojas** the redskins.

piélago *nm* (*liter*) (**a**) (*océano*) ocean, deep. (**b**) **un ~ de dificultades** (*fig*) a sea of difficulties.

pienso[1] *nm* (*Agr*) feed, fodder; (‡) grub‡; **~s** feeding stuffs.

pienso[2]: **¡ni por ~!** (†) never!, the very idea!

pierna *nf* (**a**) (*Anat*) leg; **~ artificial** artificial leg; **en ~s** bare-legged; **estirar las ~s** (*fig*) to stretch one's legs; *V* **dormir.**

(**b**) (*de letra*) stroke; (*con pluma*) downstroke.

(**c**) (*Cono Sur*) player; partner.

piernas* *nm invar* twit*, idiot.

piernicorto *adj* short-legged.

pierrot [pie'ro] *nm* pierrot.

pietista *adj* pietistic.

pieza 1 *nf* (**a**) (*gen*) piece; (*de tela*) piece, roll; **~ de museo** museum piece; **~ arqueológica** object, find; **~ de ropa** piece of clothing, article of clothing; **de una ~** in one piece; solid; *prenda* one-piece; **taladro y destornillador en una sola ~** combined drill and screwdriver; **Juan es una ~** (*LAm**) Juan is as honest as the day is long; **formar ~ única con** to be all of a piece with, (*Mec*) be integral with; **dejar a uno de una ~** to strike sb all of a heap; **quedarse de una ~** to be dumbfounded; **vender algo por ~s** to sell sth by the piece.

(**b**) (*Mec*) part; **~ de recambio, ~ de repuesto** (*LAm*) spare, spare part, extra (*US*).

(**c**) (*Fin*) coin, piece; **~ de oro** gold coin, gold piece.

(**d**) (*Ajedrez etc*) piece, man.

(**e**) (*Caza*) example; **cobró dos bellas ~s** he obtained (*o* shot *etc*) two fine specimens.

(**f**) (*Arquit*) room; **~ amueblada** furnished room; **~ de recibo** reception room.

(**g**) (*Mús*) piece, composition; (*Teat*) piece, work, play; **~ corta** sketch; **~ oratoria** speech.

(**h**) **~ de artillería** piece, gun.

(**i**) **~ de convicción** (*Jur*) exhibit, document, piece of evidence; (*fig*) convincing argument; **~ de examen** show-piece; point to bear in mind.

(**j**) **buena ~** rogue, villain.

2 *nm* (**a**) (‡: *camello*) drug pusher.

(**b**) **un dos ~s** a two-piece suit.

pífano *nm* fife.

pifia *nf* (**a**) (*Billar*) miscue, faulty shot, mis-hit.

(**b**) (*fig*: *error*) blunder, bloomer*.

(**c**) (*And, Cono Sur*) (*chiste*) joke; (*burla*) mockery; **hacer ~ de** (*bromear*) to make a joke of, joke about; (*burlarse*) to poke fun at.

(**d**) (*And*: *rechifla*) hissing, booing.

pifiador *adj* (*And, Cono Sur*) joking, mocking.

pifiar [1b] **1** *vt* (**a**) (*And, Cono Sur**: *arruinar*) to mess up, cock up‡, botch.

(**b**) (*And, Cono Sur, Ven*: *burlarse de*) to joke about,

mock; (*engañar*) to play a trick on.
(**c**) (*And, Cono Sur*: *chiflar*) to boo, hiss at.
(**d**) (*Méx*‡: *robar*) to nick‡, lift*.
2 *vi* (**a**) (*Cono Sur*) (*fracasar*) to fail, come a cropper*; (*en el juego*) to mess up one's game.
(**b**) (*And, CAm*) to be disappointed, suffer a setback.
(**c**) (*: *meter la pata*: *t* **~la**) to blunder, make a bloomer*.

pigmentación *nf* pigmentation.

pigmentado **1** *adj* pigmented; (*euf*) *persona* coloured. **2** *nm*, **pigmentada** *nf* (*euf*) coloured person.

pigmento *nm* pigment.

pigmeo, -a *adj, nm/f* pigmy.

pignorable *adj*: **objeto fácilmente** ~ a thing which it is easy to pawn.

pignorar [1a] *vt* to pawn.

pigricia *nf* (**a**) (*pereza*) laziness; sluggishness. (**b**) (*And, Cono Sur*) trifle, bagatelle; small bit, pinch.

pija[1]‡‡ *nf* prick‡‡.

pija[2]* *nf* upper-crust girl; stuck-up female*.

pijada *nf* = **chorrada.**

pijama *nm* pyjamas; ~ **de playa** beach pyjamas.

pijar‡‡ [1a] *vt* to fuck‡‡.

pije* *nm* (*Cono Sur*) toff*, fop.

pijo **1** *adj* (*) (**a**) (*engreído*) stuck-up*; posh*; yuppified*.
(**b**) (*quisquilloso*) fussy, demanding.
(**c**) (*tonto*) thick.
2 *nm* (**a**) (*: *mimado*) spoiled brat; posh youth; yuppy; upper-class twit*.
(**b**) (*: *tonto*) twit*, thickie*.
(**c**) (*Esp*‡‡) prick‡‡.
(**d**) (‡) **¡qué ~s!** hell's bells!*; **¿qué ~s haces aquí?** what in hell's name are you doing here?; **no te oyen ni** ~ they can't hear you at all.

pijolero‡ *adj* = **pijotero.**

pijotada* *nf* (*Méx*) (**a**) (*molestia*) nuisance, annoying thing. (**b**) (*dinero*) insignificant sum.

pijotear* [1a] *vi* (*And, Cono Sur, Méx*) to haggle.

pijotería* *nf* (**a**) (*molestia*) nuisance, small annoyance; (*petición*) trifling request, silly demand.
(**b**) (*LAm*) (*pequeña cantidad*) insignificant sum, tiny amount; (*bagatela*) trifle, small thing.
(**c**) (*LAm*: *tacañería*) meanness.

pijotero **1** *adj* (**a**) (‡: *molesto*) tedious, annoying; wretched; (‡: *condenado*) bloody‡, bleeding‡.
(**b**) (*LAm**: *tacaño*) mean.
(**c**) (*Cono Sur*: *no fiable*) untrustworthy.
2 *nm* (**a**) (*: *persona molesta*) drag, pain*; **¡no seas ~!** don't be such a pain!*
(**b**) (*tonto*) berk‡, twit*.

pijudo‡ *adj* (**a**) = **pijotero.** (**b**) (*CAm*: *muy bueno*) great*, terrific*.

pila[1] *nf* (**a**) (*montón*) heap, pile; stack; (*Arquit*) pile.
(**b**) (*) heap*; (*LAm**) **una ~ de** a heap of*, a lot of; **una ~ de años** very many years; **una ~ de ladrones** a whole lot of thieves; **tengo una ~ de cosas que hacer** I have heaps of things to do*.

pila[2] *nf* (**a**) (*fregadero*) sink; (*artesa*) trough; (*abrevadero*) drinking trough; (*de fuente*) basin; (*LAm*) fountain; **~ de cocina** kitchen sink.
(**b**) (*Ecl*: *t* ~ **bautismal**) font; **~ de agua bendita** holy water stoup; **sacar de ~ a uno** to act as godparent to sb.
(**c**) (*Elec*) battery; cell; **~ atómica** atomic pile; **~ botón** small battery; **~ seca** dry cell; **~ solar** solar battery; **aparato a ~(s)** battery-run apparatus, battery-operated apparatus; **cargar las ~s** (*fig*) to recharge one's batteries.
(**d**) (*Carib*) tap, faucet (*US*).
(**e**) **ponerse la** ~ (*CAm*‡) to put one's back into it.

pilado‡ *adj*: **está** ~ (*And*) (*seguro*) it's a cert*; (*fácil*) it's a cinch‡.

pilar[1] *nm* (**a**) (*poste*) post, pillar; (*mojón*) milestone.
(**b**) (*Arquit*) pillar; column, pier.
(**c**) (*fig*) prop, (chief) support, mainstay; **un ~ de la monarquía** a mainstay of the monarchy.

pilar[2] *nm* (*de fuente*) basin, bowl.

pilastra *nf* pilaster; (*Cono Sur*: *de puerta etc*) frame.

Pilatos *nm* Pilate.

pilatuna* *nf* (*LAm*) dirty trick.

pilatuno *adj* (*And*) manifestly unjust.

pilcha *nf* (**a**) (*Cono Sur*) garment, article of clothing; (*de caballo*) harness; **~s** old clothes; fine clothes. (**b**) (*Cono Sur**) mistress.

pilche *nm* (*And*) gourd, calabash.

píldora *nf* pill; **la** ~ the pill; **~ abortiva** abortion pill; **~ antibaby**, **~ anticonceptiva** contraceptive pill; **~ antifatiga** anti-fatigue pill, pep pill*; **~ del día siguiente** morning-after pill; **dorar la** ~ to sweeten the pill.

pildorazo* *nm* (*Mil*) burst of gunfire, salvo; (*Dep*) fierce shot.

pildorita *nf* (*Cono Sur*) small cocktail sausage.

pileta *nf* (**a**) (*gen*) basin, bowl; sink; trough; **~ de cocina** kitchen sink. (**b**) (*Cono Sur*) (*de baño*) wash-basin; **~ (de natación)** swimming-pool.

pilgua *nf* (*Cono Sur*) wicker basket.

pilier *nm* prop forward.

piligüe **1** *adj* (*CAm*) *fruta* shrivelled, empty. **2** *nmf* (*CAm, Méx*) poor devil.

pilila‡‡ *nf* dick‡‡, cock‡‡.

pililo *nm* (*Cono Sur*) tramp; ragged person.

pilintruca *nf* (*Cono Sur*) slut.

pilmama *nf* (*Méx*) (*nodriza*) wet-nurse; (*niñera*) nursemaid.

pilme *adj* (*Cono Sur*) very thin.

pilón[1] *nm* (**a**) (*gen*) pillar, post; (*Elec etc*) pylon; **~ de azúcar** sugar loaf. (**b**) (*de romana*) weight. (**c**) (*Carib Agr*) dump, store.

pilón[2] *nm* (**a**) (*abrevadero*) drinking trough; (*de fuente*) basin; (*Méx*) drinking fountain. (**b**) (*mortero*) mortar. (**c**) (*Cono Sur*) pannier. (**d**) (*Méx**: *propina*) tip.

piloncillo *nm* (*Méx*) powdered brown sugar.

pilongo *adj* thin, emaciated.

pilosidad *nf* hairiness.

piloso *adj* hairy.

pilotaje *nm* piloting; navigation; **fallo de** ~ navigational error.

pilotar [1a] *vt avión* to pilot; *coche* to drive; *barco* to steer, navigate; (*fig*) to guide, direct.

pilote *nm* (**a**) (*Arquit*) pile.
(**b**) (*CAm**: *fiesta*) party.

pilotear [1a] *vt* (**a**) = **pilotar.** (**b**) (*LAm*) *persona* to guide, direct; *negocio* to run, manage. (**c**) (*Cono Sur*) *persona* to exploit.

piloto **1** *nmf* (**a**) (*Aer*) pilot; **~ automático** automatic pilot; **~ de caza** fighter pilot; **~ de pruebas** test pilot; **segundo** ~ co-pilot.
(**b**) (*Náut*) first mate; navigator, navigation officer; **~ de puerto** harbour pilot.
(**c**) (*Aut*) (*esp* racing) driver.
(**d**) (*fig*) guide; (*en exploración*) pathfinder.
(**e**) (*Elec*) pilot light; (*Aut*) rear light, tail light; **~ de alarma** flashing light.
(**f**) (*Cono Sur*) raincoat.
2 *atr* pilot (*atr*); trial (*atr*); experimental; **casa** ~ model home, show house; **estudio** ~ pilot study; **planta** ~ pilot plant; *V* **luz.**

pilpinto *nm* (*And, Cono Sur*) butterfly.

pilsen *nf* (*Cono Sur*) (*any*) beer.

piltra‡ *nf* kip‡.

piltrafa *nf* (**a**) (*Culin*) useless bit of meat, skinny meat; **~s** offal, scraps.
(**b**) (*fig*) useless lump, worthless object; (*persona*) poor specimen, poor fish*, weakling.
(**c**) (*And, Cono Sur*) (*ganga*) bargain; (*suerte*) piece of luck; (*ganancia*) profit.
(**d**) **~s** (*LAm*) rags, old clothes.

piltrafiento *adj* (**a**) (*Cono Sur, Méx*: *harapiento*) ragged. (**b**) (*Cono Sur*: *marchito*) withered.

piltrafoso *adj* (*And*) ragged.

piltrafudo *adj* (*And*) weak, languid.

piltre **1** *adj* (**a**) (*And, Carib*) foppish. (**b**) (*Cono Sur*) *fruta* over-ripe; shrivelled, dried up; *persona* wizened. **2** *nmf* (*And**) snappy dresser*.

pilucho (*Cono Sur*) **1** *adj* half-naked; half-dressed. **2** *nm* (*de bebé*) cotton vest, dress.

pillada *nf* (**a**) (*trampa*) dirty trick. (**b**) (*Cono Sur*) surprise revelation; surprise encounter.

pillaje *nm* pillage, plunder.

pillar [1a] *vt* (**a**) (*Mil etc*) to pillage, plunder, sack.
(**b**) (*: *atrapar*) to grasp, seize, lay hold of; (*suj*: *perro*) to catch, worry; **la puerta le pilló el dedo** the door trapped his finger, he got his finger caught in the door; **el perro le pilló el pantalón** the dog seized his trouser leg (in its teeth).
(**c**) (*: *coger*) to catch; (*fig*: *sorprender*) to catch, catch out, catch in the act; **por fin le pilló la policía** the police nabbed him eventually*; **¡te he pillado!** got you!
(**d**) (*) *ganga, puesto etc* to get, land, lay hold of.
(**e**) (*) *significación* to grasp, catch on to.

(f) (*) (caballo) to knock down; (coche) to knock down, run over.

(g) (*) ~ una enfermedad to catch a disease; ~ una borrachera to get drunk.

(h) (Esp*) me pilla muy cerca it's right here; me pilla lejos it's too far for me; me pilla de camino it's on my way.

pillastre* nm scoundrel.

pillería nf (a) (trampa) dirty trick. (b) (banda) gang of scoundrels.

pillete nm young rascal, scamp.

pillín, -ina nm/f little rascal.

pillo 1 adj villainous, blackguardly; sly, crafty; niño naughty. 2 nm rascal, rogue, scoundrel; rotter*; (niño) rascal, scamp.

pilluelo nm = pillo; urchin.

PIM nmpl abr de Programas Integrados Mediterráneos.

pimentero nm (a) (Culin) pepperpot. (b) (Bot) pepper plant.

pimentón nm cayenne pepper, red pepper; paprika; ~ dulce sweet pepper, capsicum; ~ picante chili.

pimienta nf pepper; ~ inglesa allspice; ~ negra black pepper.

pimiento nm (a) (Culin) pepper, pimiento; ~ rojo red pepper; ~ verde green pepper; no se me de un ~, (no) me importa un ~ I don't care two hoots (de about). (b) (Bot) pepper plant. (c) (**) cunt**.

pimpante* adj (a) (encantador) charming, attractive; chic. (b) (pey: esp tan ~) smug, self-satisfied.

Pimpinela nm: el ~ escarlata the Scarlet Pimpernel.

pimpinela nf pimpernel.

pimpollo nm (a) (Bot) (serpollo) sucker, shoot; (arbolito) sapling; (capullo) rosebud. (b) (*) (niño) bonny child; (mujer) attractive woman; estar hecho un ~ (elegante) to look very smart; (parecer joven) to look very young for one's age.

pimpón nm ping-pong.

pimponista nmf ping-pong player.

PIN nm abr de producto interior neto net domestic product, NDP.

pinabete nm fir, fir tree.

pinacate nm (Méx) black beetle.

pinacoteca nf art gallery.

pináculo nm pinnacle.

pinar nm pinewood, pine grove.

pinaza nf pinnace.

pincel nm (a) (gen) paintbrush, artist's brush; estar hecho un ~ to be very smartly dressed. (b) (fig) painter.

pincelada nf brush-stroke; última ~ (fig) finishing touch.

pinciano (Esp) 1 adj of (o from) Valladolid. 2 nm, pinciana nf native (o inhabitant) of Valladolid; los ~s the people of Valladolid.

pincha¹* nf (Carib) job, spot of work.

pincha² nf (Cono Sur) hair-grip.

pincha³* nmf, pinchadiscos* nmf invar (Esp) disc-jockey, DJ.

pinchante adj grito etc piercing.

pinchar [1a] 1 vt (a) (gen) to prick, pierce, puncture; neumático to puncture; (Esp* Telec) to tap, bug*; (*: con navaja) to knife, stab; ni ~ ni cortar* to cut no ice; tener un neumático pinchado to have a puncture, have a flat tyre; ~ a uno (Med*) to give sb a jab* (o injection).

(b) (fig: estimular) to prod; hay que ~le he needs prodding; le pinchan para que se case they keep prodding him to get married.

(c) (fig) (herir) to wound, mortify; (provocar) to provoke, stir up.

(d) (Rad*) disco to play, put on.

2 vi (a) (*: perder) to fail, suffer a defeat, get beaten.

(b) (**) to screw**.

3 pincharse vr (a) (gen) to prick o.s.; (*: con droga) to give o.s. a jab*, give o.s. a fix‡.

(b) (neumático) to get punctured, go flat, burst.

pinchazo nm (a) (gen) prick; puncture (t Aut), flat (US Aut); (*: de droga) jab*, fix‡. (b) (fig) prod. (c) (Telec*) tap, bug*. (d) (*: derrota) defeat; (fracaso) comedown*, débâcle.

pinche 1 nm (a) (de cocina) kitchen-boy, scullion. (b) (Cono Sur) (oficinista) minor office clerk; (criminal) small-time criminal. (c) (Carib, Méx) rascal. (d) (And) bad horse, nag. (e) (Cono Sur) hatpin. 2 adj (a) (Méx‡: maldito) bloody‡, lousy‡. (b) (CAm*: tacaño) stingy, tight-fisted; (CAm, Méx*: miserable) wretched; todo por unos ~s centavos all for a few measly cents.

pinchito nm (Esp: gen pl) savoury, titbit (served at bar with aperitif).

pincho nm (a) (gen) point; (Bot) prickle, thorn; (aguijón) pointed stick, spike; (Cono Sur) spike, prickle; (‡: navaja) knife; (**) prick**. (b) (Culin) = pinchito; un ~ de tortilla a portion of omelette (on a stick); ~ moruno kebab.

pinchota‡ nmf user of drugs by injection.

pindárico adj Pindaric.

Píndaro nm Pindar.

pindonga* nf gadabout.

pindonguear* [1a] vi to gad about.

pinga nf (And, Carib, Méx**) prick**; (Carib) de ~* amazing, terrific*.

pingajo nm rag, shred; tag.

pinganilla* nm (a) (LAm) poor man with pretensions to elegance.

(b) en ~s (And, Méx: de puntillas) on tiptoe; (Méx) (en cuclillas) squatting; (poco firme) wobbly.

pinganillo adj (And) chubby.

pinganitos nmpl: estar en ~ to be well up, be well-placed socially; poner a uno en ~s to give sb a leg up (socially).

pingo nm (a) (harapo) rag, shred; (cabo) tag; (prenda) old garment, shabby dress; ~s (*: ropa) clothes; (*: trastos) odds and ends; no tengo ni un ~ que ponerme* I haven't a single thing I can wear; andar (o ir) de ~ to gad about; poner a uno como un ~ to abuse sb.

(b) (*) (marrana) slut; (puta) prostitute.

(c) (Cono Sur: caballo) horse; good horse; (Cono Sur, And: pey) worthless horse, nag.

(d) (Méx: niño) scamp; el ~ the devil.

(e) (Cono Sur: niño) lively child.

pingonear* [1a] vi to gad about.

pingorotear [1a] vi (LAm), pingotear [1a] vi (LAm) to skip about, jump.

ping-pong ['pimpon] nm ping-pong.

pinguchita* nf (Cono Sur) beanpole*.

pingucho (Cono Sur) 1 adj poor, wretched. 2 nm urchin, ragamuffin.

pingüe adj (a) (grasoso) greasy, fat. (b) (fig) abundant, copious; ganancia rich, fat; cosecha heavy, bumper, rich; negocio lucrative.

pingui* nm swank.

pingüino nm penguin.

pininos nmpl (esp LAm), pinitos nmpl: hacer ~ (niño) to toddle, take one's first steps; (enfermo) to start to get about again, to get back on one's feet again; (novato) to take one's first steps, try for the first time; hago mis ~ como pintor I play at painting, I dabble at painting.

pinja** nf (And) prick**.

pino¹ nm (Bot) pine, pine-tree; ~ albar Scots pine; ~ araucano monkey-puzzle (tree); ~ bravo, ~ marítimo, ~ rodeno cluster pine; ~ silvestre Scots pine; ~ de tea pitch-pine; vivir en el quinto ~ to live at the back of beyond; eso está en el quinto ~ that's terribly far away; hacer el ~, ponerse de ~ to stand on one's head; ponerle ~ (Cono Sur*) to make a great effort.

pino² nm (a) en ~ upright, vertical; standing. (b) ~s = pinitos.

pinocha nf pine needle.

pinol(e) nm (CAm, Méx) roasted maize flour; drink made of toasted maize.

pinolero, -a* nm/f (CAm) Nicaraguan.

pinrel* nm hoof*, foot.

pinsapo nm (Esp) Spanish fir.

pinta¹ nf (a) (punto) spot, dot; (Zool etc) spot, mark, marking; una tela a ~s azules a cloth with blue spots.

(b) (Naipes) spot (indicating suit); ¿a qué ~? what's trumps?, what suit are we in?

(c) (gota etc) drop, spot; drop of rain; (*) drink, drop to drink; una ~ de grasa a grease spot.

(d) (fig: aspecto) appearance, look(s); ¡a la ~! (Cono Sur) perfect!, that's fine!; estar a la ~ (Cono Sur) = tener ~; por la ~ by the look of it; tener ~ (Cono Sur) to be attractive; to be smart, be well-dressed; tener buena ~ (persona) to look good, look well; (comida) to look good; tener ~ de listo to look clever, have a bright look about one; tiene ~ de criminal he has a criminal look; tiene ~ de español he looks Spanish, he looks like a Spaniard; ¿qué ~ tiene? what does he look like?; tirar ~* to impress, be impressive; no se le vio ni ~ (LAm*) there wasn't a sign (o trace) of him.

(e) (*: persona inútil) worthless creature.

(f) (And, Carib, Cono Sur: Zool etc: colorido etc) colouring, coloration; (LAm: señal) birthmark; (CAm: pintada) graffito.

(**g**) (*And, Cono Sur*) (*juego*) draughts; (*dados*) dice.

(**h**) (*Cono Sur Min*) high-grade ore.

(**i**) **hacer** ~ (*Méx*), **irse de** ~ (*CAm*) to play truant.

(**j**) **ser de la** ~ (*Carib: euf*) to be coloured.

pinta² *nf* (*medida inglesa*) pint.

pintada¹ *nf* (*Orn*) guinea-fowl.

pintada² *nf* graffiti, daub; slogan.

pintado 1 *adj* (**a**) (*moteado*) spotted; (*pinto*) mottled, dappled; (*fig*) many-coloured, colourful; (*LAm*) black and white.

(**b**) (*) **podría pasarle al más** ~ it could happen to anybody; **lo hace como el más** ~ he does it with (*o* as well as) the best.

(**c**) **me sienta que ni** ~, **viene que ni** ~* it comes just right; it suits me a treat.

(**d**) (*LAm*) like, identical; **el niño salió** (*o* **está**) ~ **al padre** the boy looks exactly like his father, the boy is the spitting image of his father; **ni** ~ **se le verá por aquí** (*Méx*‡) you won't catch sight of him round here.

2 *nm* (**a**) (*con pintura*) painting; (*Téc*) coating; ~ **de campo** marking-out of the pitch. (**b**) wine and vermouth cocktail.

pintalabios *nm invar* lipstick.

pintar [1a] **1** *vt* (**a**) (*gen*) to paint; *letra, letrero etc* to draw, make; ~ **algo de azul** to paint sth blue.

(**b**) (*fig*) to paint, depict, describe; **lo pinta todo muy negro** (*o* **de negro**) he paints it all very black.

(**c**) ~**la*** to put it on, show off.

(**d**) (*) **no pinta nada** he cuts no ice, he doesn't count; he has no say; **¿qué pinta?** (*de qué sirve*) what's it for?; (*qué hace*) what does he do?; **pero ¿qué pintamos aquí?** but what on earth are we doing here?

(**e**) (*LAm: zalamear*) to flatter.

2 *vi* (**a**) (*gen*) to paint; **'ojo, (que) pinta'** (*aviso*) 'wet paint'; ~ **como querer** to daydream, indulge in wishful thinking.

(**b**) (*Bot*) to ripen, turn red.

(**c**) **esto pinta mal*** this looks bad, I don't like the look of this.

(**d**) **pintan corazones** hearts are trumps.

3 pintarse *vr* (**a**) (*maquillarse*) to use make-up; to put on make-up, (*pey*) paint o.s.

(**b**) ~**las solo para algo** to be a dab hand at sth*.

(**c**) (*LAm*‡: *escaparse*) to scarper‡.

pintarraj(e)ar* [1a] *vti* to daub.

pintarrajo* *nm* daub.

pintas* *nm invar* ugly customer*; scruffily dressed person.

pintear [1a] *vi* to drizzle, spot with rain.

pintiparado *adj* (**a**) (*idéntico*) identical (*a* to). (**b**) **me viene (que ni)** ~ it comes just right, it's just what the doctor ordered.

pintiparar [1a] *vt* to compare.

pinto *adj* (**a**) (*LAm*) (*moteado*) spotted; (*con manchas*) mottled, dappled; (*marcado*) marked (*esp* with black and white); (*abigarrado*) motley, colourful; *tez* blotchy.

(**b**) (*Carib*) (*listo*) clever; (*pey*) sharp, shrewd.

(**c**) (*Carib: borracho*) drunk.

Pinto *nm*: **estar entre** ~ **y Valdemoro** (*Esp**) (*dudoso*) to be in two minds; (*borracho*) to be tipsy.

pintor, -a *nm/f* (**a**) painter; ~ **de brocha gorda** house painter, (*fig*) bad painter, dauber; ~ **decorador** house painter, interior decorator; ~ **de suelo** pavement artist. (**b**) (*Cono Sur*: fachendoso*) swank*.

pintoresco *adj* picturesque.

pintoresquismo *nm* picturesqueness.

pintura *nf* (**a**) (*gen*) painting; (*fig*) painting, depiction, description; **ne lo podía ver ni en** ~ she couldn't stand the sight of him.

(**b**) (*una* ~) painting; ~ **a la acuarela**, ~ **a la aguada** watercolour; ~ **al óleo** oil painting; ~ **al pastel** pastel drawing; ~ **rupestre** cave painting.

(**c**) (*material*) paint; ~ **a la cola**, ~ **al temple** distemper, (*Arte*) tempera; ~ **emulsionada** emulsion paint.

pinturero 1 *adj* flashy, flashily dressed. **2** *nm*, **pinturera** *nf* show-off*, dandy.

pinza *nf* (*t* ~**s**) (*de ropa*) clothes-peg, clothespin (*US*); (*de depilar etc*) tweezers; (*Med*) forceps; (*Téc: tenazas*) pincers; (*Zool*) claw; ~**s de azúcar** sugar tongs; ~ **de pelo** (*Carib*) hair grip; **no se lo sacan ni con** ~**s** wild horses won't drag it out of him.

pinzón *nm* finch; ~ **vulgar** chaffinch; ~ **real** bullfinch.

piña 1 *nf* (**a**) (*Bot*) pine-cone.

(**b**) (*t* ~ **de América**, ~ **de las Indias**) pineapple.

(**c**) (*fig*) group; cluster, knot; (*pey*) clique, closed circle.

(**d**) (*Carib, Méx*) hub.

(**e**) (*: *golpe*) punch, bash*; **darse** ~**s** to fight, exchange blows.

(**f**) (*Méx: de revólver*) chamber.

(**g**) (*And**) **¡qué** ~**!** bad luck!; **estar** ~ to be unlucky.

2 *nmf* (*CAm*‡) homosexual, poof‡.

piñal *nm* (*LAm*) pineapple plantation.

piñar* *nm* (*Méx*) lie.

piñata¹‡ *nf* ivories*, teeth.

piñata² *nf* (*Cono Sur*) brawl, scrap*.

piñatería *nf* (*Cono Sur*) armed hold-up.

piño¹‡ *nm* ivory*, tooth.

piño² *nm* (*Cono Sur*) lot, crowd.

piñón¹ *nm* (*Bot*) pine-nut, pine-seed; **estar a partir un** ~ to be bosom pals (*con* with)*.

piñón² *nm* (*Orn, Téc*) pinion; **quedarse a** ~ **fijo** to have a mental block; **seguir a** ~ **fijo** to go on in the same old way, be stuck in one's old ways.

piñonate *nm* candied pine-nut.

piñonear [1a] *vi* to click.

piñoneo *nm* click.

piñoso* *adj* (*And*) unlucky.

PIO *nm* (*Esp*) *abr de* **Patronato de Igualdad de Oportunidades** ≃ Equal Opportunities Commission.

Pío *nm* Pius.

pío¹ *adj caballo* piebald, dappled.

pío² *adj* (**a**) (*Rel*) pious, devout; (*pey*) sanctimonious; excessively pious. (**b**) (*compasivo*) merciful.

pío³ *nm* (**a**) (*Orn*) cheep, chirp; **no decir ni** ~ not to breathe a word; **¡de esto no digas ni** ~**!** you keep your mouth shut about this!; **irse sin decir ni** ~ to go off without a word.

(**b**) **tener el** ~ **de algo*** to long for sth.

piocha 1 *nf* (**a**) (*joya*) jewel (worn on the head). (**b**) (*LAm: piqueta*) pickaxe. (**c**) (*Méx*) goatee. **2** *adj* (*Méx*) nice.

piojería *nf* (**a**) (*lugar*) lousy place, verminous place. (**b**) (*pobreza*) poverty. (**c**) (*: *miseria*) tiny amount, very small portion.

piojo *nm* (**a**) (*Zool*) louse; ~ **resucitado*** jumped-up fellow, vulgar parvenu; **dar el** ~ (*Méx**) to show one's nasty side; **estar como** ~**s en costura** to be packed in like sardines.

(**b**) (*And*) gambling den.

piojoso *adj* (**a**) (*gen*) lousy, verminous; (*fig*) dirty, ragged.

(**b**) (*fig*) mean.

piojuelo *nm* louse.

piola 1 *nf* (**a**) (*LAm*) (*soga*) rope, tether; (*And, Carib: cuerda*) cord, string, twine; (*maguey*) agave.

(**b**) (*Cono Sur***) cock**.

2 *adj* (*Cono Sur**) (*listo*) bright; (*taimado*) sly; (*servicial*) helpful; (*bueno*) great*, terrific*; (*elegante*) classy*, smart.

piolet [pio'le] *nm, pl* **piolets** [pio'les] ice-axe.

piolín *nm* (*LAm*) cord, twine.

pionco *adj* (**a**) (*Cono Sur*) naked from the waist down. (**b**) (*Méx: en cuclillas*) squatting. (**c**) (*Méx*) *caballo* short-tailed.

pionero 1 *adj* pioneering. **2** *nm*, **pionera** *nf* pioneer.

piorrea *nf* pyorrhoea.

pipa¹ *nf* (**a**) (*de fumar*) pipe; **fumar una** ~, **fumar en** ~ to smoke a pipe.

(**b**) (*de vino*) cask, barrel; (*medida*) pipe.

(**c**) (*Bot*) pip, seed, edible sunflower seed.

(**d**) (*Mús*) reed.

(**e**) (*LAm*: barriga*) belly.

(**f**) (*And, CAm Bot*) green coconut.

(**g**) (‡: *pistola*) rod‡, pistol; (*ametralladora*) machine-gun.

(**h**) **pasarlo** ~* to have a great time*.

pipa*² *nm* (*Mús*) assistant; (*mozo de carga*) porter; (*utillero*) boy, mate.

pipear‡ [1a] **1** *vt* to look at. **2** *vi* to look.

pipero¹, -a *nmf* street vendor.

pipero² *nm* (**a**) (*estante*) pipe-rack. (**b**) (*fumador*) pipe-smoker.

pipeta *nf* pipette.

pipi‡ *nm* (*Mil*) squaddie*, recruit; (*novato*) new boy.

pipí‡ *nm* pee**, piss**, (*entre niños*) wee-wee‡; **hacer** ~ to have a pee**, go wee-wee‡.

pipián *nm* (*CAm, Méx*) (*salsa*) thick chili sauce; (*guiso*) meat cooked in thick chili sauce.

pipiar [1c] *vi* to cheep, chirp.

pipiciego *adj* (*And*) short-sighted.

pipil* *nm* (*CAm: hum*) Mexican.

pipiolero* *nm* (*Méx*) crowd of kids*.

pipiolo, -a* *nm/f* (*joven*) youngster; (*LAm*: *chico*) little boy, little girl; (*fig*: *novato*) novice, greenhorn, tyro. **(b)** (*Carib, Cono Sur*: *tonto*) fool. **(c)** **~s** (*CAm*) money.

pipirigallo *nm* sainfoin.

pipiripao *nm* **(a)** (*) slap-up do*, spread*. **(b)** **de** ~ (*LAm*) worthless.

pipo 1 *adj* (*And, Carib*) potbellied; **estar** ~ (*Carib*) to be bloated.

2 *nm* **(a)** (*Carib: niño*) child.

(b) (*And, Carib*: *empleado*) crooked employee*.

(c) (*And*: *golpe*) punch, bash*.

(d) (*And*: *licor*) contraband liquor.

pipón *adj* (*And, Carib, Cono Sur*) (*barrigón*) potbellied; (*después de comer*) bloated.

piporro *nm* **(a)** (*instrumento*) bassoon.

(b) (*persona*) bassoonist.

pipote *nm* keg, cask; (*And*) dustbin.

pipudo‡ *adj* great*, super*.

pique[1] *nm* **(a)** (*resentimiento*) pique, resentment; (*inquina*) ill will; (*rencor*) grudge; rivalry, competition; self-respect; **estar de** ~ to have a grudge, be at loggerheads; **tener un ~ con uno** to have a grudge against sb.

(b) **estar a ~ de** + *infin* to be on the point of + *ger*; to be in danger of + *ger*; **estuvo a ~ de hacerlo** he very nearly did it.

(c) **echar a** ~ *barco* to sink; (*fig*) to wreck, ruin; **irse a** ~ to sink, founder; (*esperanza, familia etc*) to be ruined.

(d) (*LAm*: *rebote*) bounce, rebound.

(e) (*CAm, Cono Sur Min*) mineshaft; (*Méx*) drill, well.

(f) (*Cam, Cono Sur*: *sendero*) trail, narrow path.

(g) (*And*: *insecto*) jigger flea.

pique[2] *nm* (*Naipes*) spades.

pique[3]‡ *nm* (*de droga*) fix‡, shot*.

piquera *nf* **(a)** (*de tonel, colmena*) hole, vent. **(b)** (*CAm, Méx*: *taberna*) dive‡. **(c)** (*Carib*: *de taxis*) taxi rank.

piquero *nm* **(a)** (*Hist*) pikeman. **(b)** (*And, Cono Sur*) miner. **(c)** (‡) pickpocket.

piqueta *nf* pick, pickaxe.

piquetazo *nm* (*LAm*) (*tijeretazo*) snip, small cut; (*mordida*) peck; (*de abeja etc*) sting, bite.

piquete *nm* **(a)** (*pinchazo*) prick, jab, slight wound.

(b) (*agujero*) small hole (*in clothing*).

(c) (*Mil*) squad, party; (*de huelguistas*) picket; picket line; **~ de ejecución** firing-squad; **~ informativo** picket; **~ móvil, ~ volante** flying picket.

(d) (*Cono Sur*) yard, small corral.

(e) (*And*) picnic.

(f) (*Carib*) street band.

piquin *nm* **(a)** (*And*: *galán*) boyfriend. **(b)** (*Cono Sur**) (*pizca*) pinch, dash. **(c)** (*Cono Sur*: *persona*) irritable sort.

piquiña *nf* **(a)** (*And, Carib*) = **picazón. (b)** (*Carib*: *envidia*) envy.

pira[1] *nf* pyre.

pira[2]‡ *nf*: **hacer ~, irse de** ~ to clear off*; (*Escol*) to cut class*, go off and amuse o.s.

pirado‡ **1** *adj* (*tonto*) crazy; (*drogado*) high (on drugs)‡. **2** *nm*, **pirada** *nf* nutcase‡; druggy‡.

piragua *nf* canoe.

piragüismo *nm* canoeing.

piragüista *nmf* canoeist; oarsman.

piramidal *adj* **(a)** pyramidal. **(b)** (*And**) terrific*, tremendous*.

pirámide *nf* pyramid.

Píramo *nm* Pyramus.

piraña *nf* (*LAm*) piranha.

pirarse* [1a] *vr* (*t* **pirárselas**) (*largarse*) to beat it*, clear out*; (*Escol*) to cut class*; (*And*) to escape from prison; (*Méx*) to peg out‡.

pirata 1 *nm/f* **(a)** pirate; **~ aéreo** hijacker. **(b)** (*fig*) hard-hearted person. **(c)** (*: *Liter etc*) plagiarist, borrower of other people's ideas (*etc*). **(d)** (*: *granuja*) rogue, scoundrel; (*Com*) cowboy, shark, sharp operator; (*Inform*) hacker. **2** *adj* pirate; illegal; unauthorized; **disco** ~ bootleg record; **edición** ~ pirated edition; **emisora** ~ pirate radio station.

piratear [1a] **1** *vt* (*Aer*) to hijack; (*esp Mús*) to pirate; *libro* to pirate; (*Inform*) to hack into. **2** *vi* to buccaneer, practise piracy; (*fig*) to steal.

pirateo *nm*, **piratería** *nf* piracy; (*fig*) theft, stealing; (*de disco*) pirating; bootlegging; (*Inform*) hacking; **~ aérea** hijacking; **~s** depredations.

pirático *adj* piratical.

piraya *nf* (*LAm*) piranha.

pirca *nf* (*LAm*) dry-stone wall.

pire‡ *nm* (*drogas*) trip‡.

pirenaico *adj* Pyrenean.

pirético *adj* pyretic.

piretro *nm* pyrethrum.

pirgua *nf* (*And, Cono Sur*) shed, outhouse.

piri‡ *nm* grub‡, nosh‡.

pirineísta *nmf* mountaineer (who climbs in the Pyrenees).

Pirineo *nm*, **Pirineos** *nmpl* Pyrenees; **el ~ catalán** the Catalan (part of the) Pyrenees.

pirineo *adj* Pyrenean.

pirinola* *nf* (*Méx*) kid*, child.

piripez* *nf*: **coger una** ~ to get merry.

piripi* *adj*: **estar** ~ to be merry.

piritas *nfpl* pyrites.

pirlán *nm* (*And*) doorstep.

piro‡ *nm*: **darse el** ~ to beat it*; **darse el ~ de** to escape from.

piro... *pref* pyro...

pirófago, -a *nm/f* fire-eater.

piromanía *nf* pyromania.

pirómano, -a *nm/f* arsonist, fire-raiser, pyromaniac.

piropear [1a] *vt* to pay an amorous compliment to, make a flirtatious remark to.

piropo *nm* **(a)** (*cumplido*) amorous compliment, flirtatious remark; **echar ~s a = piropear.**

(b) (*piedra*) garnet; ruby.

(c) (*And**) ticking-off*.

piroso* *adj* lewd, dirty.

pirotecnia *nf* pyrotechnics; firework display (*t fig*).

pirotécnico *adj* pyrotechnic, firework (*atr*).

pirrar* [1a], **pirriar** [1b] **1** *vt*: **le pirraba el cine** the cinema really turned him on*. **2 pirr(i)arse** *vr*: **~ por** to rave about, be crazy about.

pírrico *adj*: **victoria pírrica** Pyrrhic victory.

Pirro *nm* Pyrrhus.

pirucho *nm* **(a)** (*CAm*) (ice-cream) cone (*o* cornet). **(b)** (*Cono Sur* Pol*) Peronist.

pirueta *nf* **(a)** (*gen*) pirouette; (*cabriola*) caper. **(b)** (*fig*) remark which helps somebody out of an awkward situation; neat recovery. **(c)** **hacer ~s** (*fig*) to perform a balancing act (*between two policies etc*).

piruetear [1a] *vi* to pirouette; to caper.

pirula[1]‡ *nf* **(a)** (*Anat*) willy‡. **(b)** **hacer la ~ a** (*molestar*) to upset, annoy; (*jugarla*) to play a dirty trick on; (*embaucar*) to cheat, do down*.

piruleta *nf* lollipop.

pirulí *nm* **(a)** lollipop. **(b)** (**‡) prick**‡. **(c)** **el P~*** Madrid television tower.

pirulo (*Cono Sur*) **1** *nm*: **tiene 40 ~s**‡ he's forty. **2** *nm*, **pirula**[2] *nf* (*chico*) slim child.

pis‡ *nm* = **pipí.**

pisa *nf* **(a)** (*de uvas*) treading. **(b)** (*: *zurra*) beating.

pisada *nf* footstep, footfall, tread; (*huella*) footprint.

pisadera *nf* (*And*) carpet.

pisadero *nm* (*Méx*) brothel.

pisado *nm* treading (of grapes).

pisapapeles *nm invar* paperweight.

pisar [1a] **1** *vt* **(a)** (*gen*) to tread (on), walk on; (*por casualidad*) to step on; (*dañando*) to flatten, crush, trample (on, underfoot); *uvas etc* to tread; *tierra* to tread down; **~ el acelerador** to step on the accelerator, press the accelerator; **~ (el coche) a fondo** to put one's foot down*; **'no ~ el césped'** 'keep off the grass'; **no volvimos a ~ ese sitio** we never set foot in that place again.

(b) (*Mús*) *tecla* to play, strike, press; *cuerda* to hold down.

(c) (*edificio etc*) to lie on, cover (part of).

(d) (*fig*) (*atropellar*) to trample on, walk all over; (*desatender*) to disregard; (*maltratar*) to abuse; **no se deja ~ por nadie** he doesn't let anybody trample over him.

(e) (*: *robar*) to pinch*, steal; **A le pisó la novia a B** A pinched B's girl*; **~ una baza a uno** to trump sb's trick; **otro le pisó el puesto** sb got in first and collared the job*; **el periódico le pisó la noticia** the newspaper got in first with the news.

(f) (*And*) *hembra* to cover; (*CAm***‡) to fuck**‡, screw**‡.

2 *vi* **(a)** (*andar*) to tread, step, walk; **hay que ~ con cuidado** you have to tread carefully.

(b) (*fig*) **~ fuerte** to act determinedly; to make a strong showing, make a real impression; **entró (***o* **vino) pisando fuerte** she made a strong start; she made her position clear from the start, she showed she was not going to stand any nonsense; **ir pisando huevos** to tread carefully.

3 pisarse *vr* (*Cono Sur*) to be mistaken.
pisaverde *nm* fop.
pisca *nf* (**a**) (*Méx*) maize harvest, corn harvest (*US*). (**b**) (*And*: *prostituta*) prostitute.
piscador *nm* (*Méx*) harvester.
piscar [1g] *vi* (*Méx*) to harvest maize (*o* corn (*US*)).
piscicultura *nf* fish-farming.
piscifactoría *nf* fish-farm.
piscigranja *nf* (*LAm*) fish-farm.
piscina *nf* (**a**) (*Dep*) swimming-pool; ~ **climatizada** heated swimming-pool; ~ **cubierta** indoor swimming-pool; ~ **olímpica** Olympic-length pool. (**b**) (*tanque*) fishpond, fishtank.
Piscis *nm* (*Zodíaco*) Pisces.
pisco[1] *nm* (*And*) (**a**) (*Orn*) turkey. (**b**) (*fig*) fellow, guy* (*US*).
pisco[2] *nm* (*LAm*) strong liquor.
piscoiro* *nm*, **piscoira** *nf* (*Cono Sur**) bright child.
piscolabis *nm invar* (**a**) snack. (**b**) (*CAm, Méx*) money.
pisicorre *nm* (*Carib*) small bus.
piso *nm* (**a**) (*suelo*) floor; flooring.
(**b**) (*Arquit*) storey, floor; (*de autobús, barco*) deck; (*de cohete*) stage; (*de pastel*) layer; ~ **alto** top floor; ~ **bajo** ground floor, first floor (*US*); **primer** ~ first floor, second floor (*US*); **un edificio de 8** ~**s** an 8-storey building; **viven en el quinto** ~ they live on the fifth floor; **autobús de dos** ~**s** double-decker bus; **ir en el** ~ **de arriba** to travel on the top deck, travel upstairs.
(**c**) (*apartamento*) flat, apartment (*US*); ~ **franco** (*Esp*), ~ **de seguridad** safe house, hide-out; **poner un** ~ **a una** (*Esp*) to set a woman up in a flat.
(**d**) (*Aut*: *de neumático*) tread.
(**e**) (*de zapato*) sole; **poner** ~ **a un zapato** to sole a shoe.
(**f**) (*Min*) set of workings; (*Geol*) layer, stratum.
(**g**) (*Cono Sur*) (*taburete*) stool; (*banco*) bench.
(**h**) (*estera*) mat; (*Cono Sur, Méx*: *tapete*) table runner; (*And, Cono Sur*: *alfombra*) long narrow rug; ~ **de baño** bathmat.
pisón *nm* (**a**) (*herramienta*) ram, rammer. (**b**) (*LAm*) = **pisotón** (**b**). (**c**) (*Cono Sur*: *mortero*) mortar.
pisotear [1a] *vt* (**a**) (*gen*) to tread down, trample (on, underfoot); to stamp on. (**b**) (*fig*) to trample on; *ley etc* to abuse, disregard.
pisoteo *nm* treading, trampling; stamping.
pisotón *nm* (**a**) (*gen*) stamp on the foot. (**b**) (*: *Periodismo*) newspaper scoop, reporting scoop.
pispar* [1a] **1** *vt* (‡: *robar*) to nick‡, steal. **2** *vi* (*Cono Sur*) to keep watch, spy.
pisporra *nf* (*CAm*) wart.
pista *nf* (**a**) (*Zool y fig*) track, trail; (*fig*: *indicio*) clue; (*de cinta*) track; ~ **falsa** false trail, false clue; (*en discusión etc*) red herring; **estar sobre la** ~ to be on the scent; **estar sobre la** ~ **de uno** to be on sb's trail, be after sb; **seguir la** ~ **de uno** to be on sb's track, trail sb; to shadow sb; **la policía tiene una** ~ **ya** the police already have a lead (*o* clue).
(**b**) (*Dep etc*) track, course; (*cancha*) court; (*Aut*) carriageway; (*CAm*: *avenida*) avenue; (*de esquí*) run, slope; (*de circo etc*) floor, arena; (*Inform, Mús*) track; ~ **de aprendizaje** nursery slope; ~ **de aterrizaje** runway; landing-strip; ~ **de atletismo** athletics track, running track; ~ **de baile** dance-floor; ~ **de bolos** bowling-alley; ~ **de carreras** racetrack; ~ **de ceniza** dirt track; **reunión de** ~ **cubierta** indoor athletics meeting; ~ **de esquí** ski-run; ~ **forestal** forest trail; ~ **de hielo** ice-rink; ~ **de hierba** grass court; ~ **de patinaje** skating-rink; ~ **de tenis** tennis-court; ~ **de tierra batida** clay court; **atletismo en** ~ track events.
pistacho *nm* pistachio.
pistero *adj* (*CAm*) mercenary, fond of money.
pistilo *nm* pistil.
pisto *nm* (**a**) (*Med*) chicken broth.
(**b**) (*Culin Esp*) fried vegetable hash.
(**c**) (*fig*: *revoltijo*) mixture, hotchpotch.
(**d**) **a** ~**s** little by little; sparingly.
(**e**) **darse** ~* to show off, swank*, shoot a line*.
(**f**) (*And, CAm*‡) dough‡, money.
(**g**) (*And*: *de revólver*) barrel.
(**h**) (*Méx*‡) shot of liquor*.
pistola *nf* (**a**) (*Mil*) pistol; (*Téc*) spray gun; ~ **de agua** water pistol; ~ **ametralladora** submachine-gun, tommy-gun; ~ **engrasadora,** ~ **de engrase** grease-gun; ~ **de juguete** toy pistol; ~ **de pintar,** ~ **rociadora de pintura** paint spray, spray gun. (**b**) (*Culin*) long loaf. (**c**) (‡‡) prick‡‡.
pistolera *nf* (**a**) holster; **salir de** ~**s** to get out of a tight spot. (**b**) (*Anat**) ~**s** flabby thighs.
pistolerismo *nm* gun law, rule by terror.
pistolero *nm* gunman, gangster; ~ **a sueldo** hired killer.
pistoleta *nf* (*And, Cono Sur*) small pistol.
pistoletazo *nm* pistol shot; (*Dep, fig*) starting signal.
pistolete *nm* pocket pistol.
pistolo‡ *nm* soldier.
pistón *nm* (**a**) (*Mec*) piston. (**b**) (*Mús*) key; (*LAm*: *corneta*) bugle, cornet. (**c**) (*CAm, Méx*) corn tortilla. (**d**) **de** ~* = **pistonudo.**
pistonudo* *adj* smashing*, terrific*.
pistudo *adj* (*CAm*) rich.
pita *nf* (**a**) (*Bot*) agave; (*fibra*) pita fibre, pita thread; (*esp Chile, Peru*) string; **enredar la** ~ (*LAm**) to stir things up. (**b**) (*CAm*) ~**s** lies.
pitada *nf* (**a**) (*silbido*) whistle; (*rechifla*) hiss. (**b**) (*LAm**: *de cigarrillo*) puff, drag*. (**c**) (*: *salida inoportuna*) silly remark.
pitador, -a *nm/f* (*LAm*) smoker.
Pitágoras *nm* Pythagoras.
pitandero, -a *nm/f* (*Cono Sur*) smoker.
pitanza *nf* (**a**) (*ración*) dole, daily ration; (‡) grub‡. (**b**) (*: *precio*) price. (**c**) (*Cono Sur*) bargain; profit.
pitar [1a] **1** *vt* (**a**) *silbato* to blow; *partido* to referee; **el árbitro pitó falta** the referee whistled for a foul.
(**b**) *árbitro etc* to whistle at, boo; *actor, obra* to hiss, give the bird to*.
(**c**) (*LAm**) to smoke.
2 *vi* (**a**) (*silbar*) to whistle, blow a whistle; (*rechiflar*) to hiss, boo; (*Aut*) to sound one's horn; **pitó el árbitro** the referee blew (his whistle).
(**b**) (*LAm**) to smoke; to puff.
(**c**) (*) (*funcionar*) to work (well); (*dar resultados*) to give (good) results; **esto no pita** this is no good, this doesn't work; **la tele no pita** the telly is on the blink*; ~ **bien** to give a good account of o.s.; **salir pitando** to beat it*; **salió pitando para X*** he went off at top speed to X.
3 pitarse‡ *vr* to beat it*.
pitarra‡ *nf* grub‡, food.
pitay *nm* (*And, Cono Sur*) rash.
pitazo *nm* (*And, Méx*) whistle, hoot; **dar el** ~ **a uno** (*Carib**) to tip sb the wink*.
pítcher [pitʃer] *nm* (*CAm Béisbol*) pitcher.
pitear [1a] *vi* (*LAm*) = **pitar 2** (**a**).
pitido *nm* whistle.
pitilla *nf* (*Cono Sur*) string.
pitillera *nf* cigarette case.
pitillo *nm* (**a**) (*: *cigarrillo*) cigarette; **echarse un** ~ to have a smoke. (**b**) (*And, Carib*: *pajita*) drinking-straw.
pítima *nf* (**a**) (*Med*) poultice. (**b**) **coger una** ~‡ to get plastered‡.
pitiminí *nm*: **de** ~ (*fig*) trifling, trivial.
pitinsa* *nf* (*CAm*) overalls.
pitiyanqui‡ *nmf*, **pitiyanki**‡ *nmf* (*Carib*) Yankee-lover.
pito *nm* (**a**) (*silbato*) whistle; (*Aut*) horn, hooter; (*Ferro etc*) whistle, hooter; **tener voz de** ~ to have a squeaky voice.
(**b**) ~ **real** (*Orn*) green woodpecker.
(**c**) (*LAm Zool*) tick.
(**d**) (*: *cigarrillo*) cigarette; (*LAm*: *pipa*) pipe.
(**e**) (‡‡: *pene*) prick‡‡.
(**f**) ~ **de ternera** (*LAm*) steak sandwich.
(**g**) (*locuciones*) ~**s flautos*** tomfoolery, absurdities; **cuando** ~**s, flautas** it's always the same, one way or another it always happens; **cuando no es por** ~**s es por flautas** if it isn't one thing it's another; **entre** ~**s y flautas** what with one thing and another; ~ ~ **colorito** ≈ eeny meeny mainy mo; (*fig*) haphazard method of making decisions; **no se me da un** ~, **(no) me importa un** ~* I don't care two hoots (**de** about); **en este asunto no toca** ~ he's got nothing to do with this matter; **tocarse el** ~‡ to do damn-all‡, be bone-idle; **me tomaron por el** ~ **del sereno** (*Esp*) they thought I was something the cat had brought in; **no vale un** ~ it's not worth tuppence.
pitón[1] *nm* (*Zool*) python.
pitón[2] *nm* (*bulto*) bump, lump, protuberance; (*Zool*) budding horn; (*Bot*) sprig, young shoot; (*de jarra etc*) spout; (*LAm*: *de manguera*) nozzle; **pitones** (‡: *senos*) tits‡; ~ **de roca** sharp point of rock.
pitonisa *nf* (*adivinadora*) fortune-teller; (*bruja*) witch, sorceress.
pitopausia‡ *nf* male menopause.
pitorrearse* [1a] *vr*: ~ **de** to tease, make fun of.
pitorreo* *nm* teasing, joking; **estar de** ~ to be in a joking

mood.
pitorro *nm* spout.
pitote* *nm* fuss, row.
pitra *nf* (*Cono Sur*) rash.
pituco* (*Cono Sur*) **1** *adj* stuck-up*, toffee-nosed*. **2** *nm* toff*.
pitufa‡ *nf* bird‡, chick*.
pitufo‡ *nm* (**a**) (*Pol*) career politician. (**b**) (*Méx*) cop*, policeman.
pituitario *adj* pituitary; **glándula pituitaria** pituitary (gland).
pituto* *nm* (*Cono Sur*) (**a**) (*enchufe*) useful contact, connection. (**b**) (*chapuza*) odd job; moonlighting*.
piuco *adj* (*Cono Sur*) timid, scared.
piular [1a] *vi* to cheep, chirp.
pivote *nm* pivot.
píxide *nf* pyx.
pixtón *nm* (*CAm*) thick tortilla.
piyama *nm* (*t f*) (*LAm*) pyjamas.
pizarra *nf* (**a**) (*piedra*) slate; (*esquisto*) shale. (**b**) (*Escol etc*) blackboard; (*Cono Sur: tablero*) notice board.
pizarral *nm* slate quarry; shale bed.
pizarrín *nm* slate pencil.
pizarrón *nm* (*LAm Escol*) blackboard; (*Dep*) scoreboard.
pizarroso *adj* slaty.
pizca *nf* (**a**) (*partícula*) pinch, spot; (*migaja*) crumb; **una ~ de sal** a pinch of salt. (**b**) (*fig*) spot, speck, trace, jot; **ni ~** not a bit, not a scrap; **no tiene ni ~ de verdad** there's not a jot of truth in it. (**c**) (*Méx*) maize harvest.
pizcar [1g] *vt* to pinch, nip.
pizco *nm* pinch, nip.
pizcucha *nf* (*CAm*) kite (*toy*).
pizote *nm* (*CAm Zool*) coati(-mundi).
pizpireta* *nf* bright girl, lively (little) girl; smart little piece‡.
pizpireto* *adj* bright, lively, cheerful, saucy.
pizza *nf* (*Culin*) pizza.
PJ *nm* (*Argentina*) *abr de* **Partido Justicialista** *Peronist party*.
p.j. *nm abr de* **partido judicial**.
PL *nm abr de* **Parlamento Latinoamericano**.
placa *nf* (**a**) (*gen*) plate; (*lámina*) thin piece of material, (thin) sheet; tab; (*conmemorativa*) plaque, tablet; (*de horno*) plate; (*de dientes*) dental plate, denture; (*LAm Aut*) number-plate; (*Inform*) board; **~ conmemorativa** commemorative plaque; **~ giratoria** (*Ferro*) turntable; **~ de hielo** icy patch; **~ de matrícula** number-plate; **~ del nombre** nameplate; **~ de silicio** silicon chip; **~ solar** (*de techo*) solar panel; (*de pared*) radiator.
(**b**) (*Fot: t* **~ fotográfica**) plate; **~ esmerilada** focusing screen.
(**c**) (*esp LAm Mús*) gramophone record, phonograph record (*US*).
(**d**) (*distintivo*) badge, insignia.
(**e**) (*LAm*) (*erupción*) blotch, skin blemish; (*de dientes*) tartar.
placaje *nm* (*Rugby*) tackle.
placaminero *nm* persimmon.
placar [1g] *vt* (*Rugby*) to tackle.
placard [pla'kar] *nm* (*Cono Sur*) built-in cupboard.
pláceme *nm* congratulations, message of congratulations; **dar el ~ a uno** to congratulate sb.
placenta *nf* placenta.
placentero *adj* pleasant, agreeable.
placentino (*Esp*) **1** *adj* of Plasencia. **2** *nm*, **placentina** *nf* native (*o* inhabitant) of Plasencia; **los ~s** the people of Plasencia.
placer[1] **1** *nm* (**a**) (*gen*) pleasure; (*contento*) enjoyment, delight; **a ~** at one's pleasure; as much as one wants; **es un ~ +** *infin* it is a pleasure to + *infin*; **con mucho ~, con sumo ~** with great pleasure; **tengo ~ en +** *infin* it is my pleasure to + *infin*, I have pleasure in + *ger*.
(**b**) (*deleite*) pleasure; **los ~es del ocio** the pleasures of idleness; **darse a los ~es** to give o.s. over to pleasures.
2 [2w] *vt* (*liter*) to please; **me place poder +** *infin* I am gratified to be able to + *infin*.
placer[2] *nm* (**a**) (*Geol, Min*) placer. (**b**) (*Náut*) sandbank. (**c**) (*And Agr*) ground prepared for sowing; plot, patch; (*Carib*) field.
placero, -a *nm/f* (**a**) (*Com*) stallholder, market trader. (**b**) (*fig*) loafer, gossip.
placeta *nf* (*Cono Sur*) plateau.
plácidamente *adv* placidly.
placidez *nf* placidity.
plácido *adj* placid.

plaf *interj* bang!; crash!; smack!
plaga *nf* (**a**) (*Agr Zool*) pest, (*Bot*) blight; **~ del jardín** garden pest; **~ de la vid** pest of vines, pest on the vine; **~s forestales** pests on timber, forest pests.
(**b**) (*Med, de langostas etc*) plague; (*fig*) scourge; calamity, disaster; blight; **aquí la sequía es una ~** drought is a menace here; **una ~ de gitanos** a plague of gipsies.
(**c**) (*fig*) glut, abundance; **ha habido una ~ de lechugas** there has been a glut of lettuces.
(**d**) (*Med*) affliction, grave illness.
plagar [1h] **1** *vt* to infest, plague; to fill; **han plagado la ciudad de carteles** they have covered (*o* plastered) the town with posters; **un texto plagado de errores** a text full of errors, a text riddled with errors; **esta sección está plagada de minas** this part has mines everywhere.
2 plagarse *vr*: **~ de** to become infested with.
plagiar [1b] *vt* (**a**) *idea, libro etc* to plagiarize; *producto* to pirate, copy illegally. (**b**) (*LAm: secuestrar*) to kidnap.
plagiario, -a *nm/f* (*V* **plagio**) (**a**) plagiarist. (**b**) (*LAm*) kidnapper.
plagio *nm* (**a**) (*copia*) plagiarism; (*de producto*) piracy, illegal copying. (**b**) (*LAm: secuestro*) kidnap(ping).
plaguicida *nm* pest-control substance, insecticide.
plajo‡ *nm* fag‡, gasper‡.
plan *nm* (**a**) (*proyecto*) plan; scheme; (*intención*) idea, intention; **~ de desarrollo** development plan; **~ de jubilación** pension plan; **~ quinquenal** five-year plan; **~ de vuelo** flight plan; **mi ~ era comprar otro nuevo** my idea was to buy a new one; **realizar su ~** to put one's plan into effect.
(**b**) (***: *idea*) (idea for an) activity, amusement; **ha sido un ~ muy pesado** it turned out to be a very tedious kind of amusement; **tengo un ~ estupendo para mañana** I've got a splendid idea about what to do tomorrow; **no es ~, tampoco es ~** that's not a good way to go about it, that's not a good idea, that's not on*.
(**c**) (***: *aventura*) date; (*pey*) affair; (*persona*) date; boyfriend, girlfriend; **buscar ~** to try to pick somebody up*; **¿tienes ~ para esta noche?** are you booked for tonight?, have you a date for tonight?; **tiene un ~ con la mujer del alcalde** he's having an affair with the mayor's wife; **aquí hay ~** I'm in with a chance here; **estar en ~** to be in the mood; **ponerse en ~** to get in the mood.
(**d**) (*programa*) programme; **~ de estudios** curriculum, syllabus; **~ básico/de bachiller** (*CAm Escol*) basic secondary/advanced secondary curriculum.
(**e**) (*Med*) régime; course of treatment; **estar a ~** to be on a course of treatment.
(**f**) (*Agrimen*) level; height.
(**g**) **a todo ~*** with great ceremony; in a very posh way*, sparing no expense.
(**h**) **no me hace ~* +** *infin* it doesn't suit me to + *infin*.
(**i**) (*sistema*) set-up, system, arrangement; (*base*) basis, footing; (*actitud*) attitude; **chaparros en ~ disperso** scattered showers; **en ~ económico** in an economical way, on the cheap; **en ese ~** in that way; at that rate; **como sigas en ese ~** if you go on like that; **si te pones en ese ~** if that's your attitude; **no puedo con este ~ de esperar** I can't stand this business of waiting; **está en un ~ imposible** it's on an impossible basis, it's an impossible set-up; **en ~ de** as; on a basis of; **lo hicieron en ~ de broma** they did it for a laugh; **vamos en ~ de turismo** we're going as tourists; **no puedo porque estoy en ~ de viaje** I can't because I'm all set to go away; **unos jóvenes en ~ de divertirse** some youngsters out for a good time; **está en ~ de rehusar** he's in a mood to refuse, he's likely to refuse at the moment; **el negocio es en ~ timo** the deal is really a fraud; **lo hizo en ~ bruto** (*Esp*) he did it in a brutal way; **viven en ~ pasota** (*Esp*) they live like hippies.
(**j**) (*Cono Sur, Méx: de barco etc*) flat bottom.
(**k**) (*LAm: llano*) level ground; plain; (*Cono Sur: falda de cerro*) foothills.
(**l**) (*And, CAm, Carib: de espada etc*) flat.
plana *nf* (**a**) (*hoja*) sheet (of paper), page; (*Escol*) writing exercise, copywriting; (*Tip*) page; **~ de anuncios** advertisement page; **en primera ~** on the front page; **noticias de primera ~** front-page news; **corregir** (*o* **enmendar**) **la ~ a uno** to put sb right, (*pey*) find fault with sb; to improve upon sb's efforts; **escribir una ~ de castigo** to write 50 (*etc*) lines (as a punishment).
(**b**) **~ mayor** (*Mil*) staff; (*fig*) persons in charge; (*) top brass*, big shots*.
(**c**) (*Téc*) trowel.
planazo *nm* (**a**) **se dio un ~** (*LAm**) he fell flat on his face.
(**b**) (*Carib: trago*) shot of liquor.

plancton *nm* plankton.
plancha *nf* (**a**) (*lámina*) plate, sheet; (*losa*) slab; (*Tip*) plate; (*Náut*) gangway; (*Med*) dental plate; **hacer la ~** (*bañista*) to float.
(**b**) (*utensilio*) iron; (*acto*) ironing; pressing; (*ropa planchada*) ironed clothes; (*ropa para planchar*) clothes to be ironed, ironing; **~ eléctrica** electric iron; **~ a** (*o* **de**) **vapor** steam iron.
(**c**) (*Culin*) grill; (*Cono Sur*) griddle pan; **a la ~** grilled.
(**d**) (*ejercicio*) press-up.
(**e**) (*: *metedura de pata*) gaffe, blunder; **hacer una ~, tirarse una ~** to drop a clanger‡, put one's foot in it; **pasar ~** (*Cono Sur*) to have an embarrassing time.
(**f**) (*Dep*) dive; **entrada en ~** sliding tackle; **cabecear en ~** to do a diving header; **lanzarse en ~** to dive (for the ball), dive headlong.
planchada *nf* (*LAm*) (**a**) (*desembarcadero*) landing stage. (**b**) = **plancha** (**e**).
planchado 1 *adj* (**a**) *ropa* ironed; (*traje*) pressed.
(**b**) (*Culin*) pressed; **jamón ~** pressed ham.
(**c**) (*CAm, Cono Sur**: *elegante*) very smart, dolled up*.
(**d**) (*And, Carib, Cono Sur**: *sin dinero*) broke*.
(**e**) (*Méx*) (*listo*) clever; (*valiente*) brave.
2 *nm* ironing; pressing; (*Cono Sur*) panel-beating; **dar un ~ a** to iron; to press; **prenda que no necesita ~** non-iron garment.
planchar [1a] **1** *vt* (**a**) *ropa* to iron; *traje* to press; **prenda de no ~** non-iron garment.
(**b**) (*LAm**) to flatter, suck up to*.
(**c**) (*Méx**: *dejar plantado*) to stand up*.
2 *vi* (**a**) to iron, do the ironing.
(**b**) (*LAm**: *no bailar*) to sit out (a dance), be a wallflower.
(**c**) (*Cono Sur**) (*meter la pata*) to drop a clanger‡; (*ponerse en ridículo*) to make oneself look ridiculous.
planchazo* *nm* = **plancha** (**e**).
planchear [1a] *vt* to plate.
plancheta *nf* (**a**) (*Agrimen*) plane table. (**b**) **echárselas de ~*** to show off, swank*.
planchón *nm* (*Cono Sur*) snowcap; ice field.
planeador *nm* glider.
planeadora *nf* (**a**) (*niveladora*) leveller, bulldozer. (**b**) (*Náut*) speedboat, powerboat.
planear [1a] **1** *vt* (*proyectar*) to plan; **~ hacer algo** to plan to do sth. **2** *vi* (*Aer*) to glide; (*fig*) to hover (*sobre* over), hang (*sobre* over).
planeo *nm* gliding; (*un ~*) glide.
planeta *nm* planet; **el ~ rojo** the red planet, Mars.
planetario 1 *adj* planetary. **2** *nm* planetarium.
planicie *nf* (*llanura*) plain; (*llano*) flat area, level ground; (*superficie plana*) flat surface.
planificación *nf* planning; (*Inform*) scheduling; **~ de familia, ~ familiar** family planning; **~ urbana** town planning.
planificador 1 *adj* planning (*atr*). **2** *nm* **planificadora** *nf* planner.
planificar [1g] *vt* to plan.
planilla *nf* (**a**) (*esp LAm*) (*lista*) list; (*papelito*) slip of paper; (*tabla*) table, tabulation; (*nómina*) payroll; (*sujetapapeles*) clipboard.
(**b**) (*And, Cono Sur*) (*formulario*) form, application form; (*Fin*) (*cuenta*) account; (*cuenta de gastos*) expense account.
(**c**) (*And, CAm, Méx*) voting slip (*o* paper); (*nómina de electores*) electoral roll; (*candidatos*) ticket.
planimetría *nf* surveying, planimetry.
plan(n)ing ['planin] *nm, pl* **plan(n)ings** ['planin] agenda, schedule, plan.
plano 1 *adj* (**a**) (*gen*) flat, level, even; (*plano*) plane (*t Mat, Mec*); (*liso*) smooth; **caer de ~** to fall flat.
(**b**) (*fig*) **de ~**: **le daba el sol de ~** the sun shone directly on it; the sun was directly over it; **confesar de ~** to make a full confession; **rechazar algo de ~** to turn sth down flat, reject sth outright; *V* **cortar**.
2 *nm* (**a**) (*Mat, Mec*) plane; **~ focal** focal plane; **~ inclinado** inclined plane.
(**b**) (*fig*) plane; position, level; **de distinto ~ social** of a different social level; **están en un ~ distinto** they're on a different plane.
(**c**) (*Cine, Fot*) shot; **~ corto** close-up; **~ largo** long shot; **primer ~** foreground; close-up; **un primer ~ de la famosa actriz** a close-up of the famous actress.
(**d**) (*Aer*) plane; wing; **~ de cola** tailplane.
(**e**) (*Arquit, Mec etc*) plan; (*Geog*) map; (*de ciudad*) map, street plan; **~ acotado** contour map; **levantar el ~ de** *país* to survey, map, make a map of; *edificio etc* to draw up the designs for.
(**f**) (*de espada*) flat.
planta[1] *nf* (**a**) (*Anat*) sole of the foot; **asentar sus ~s en** to establish oneself in.
(**b**) (*Arquit*: *plano*) ground plan; **construir un edificio de** (**nueva**) **~** to build a completely new building, rebuild from the foundations up.
(**c**) (*Arquit*: *piso*) floor, storey; **~ baja** ground floor, first floor (*US*); **una ventana de la ~ baja** a downstairs window, a ground-floor window; **~ noble** suite for functions.
(**d**) (*Baile, Esgrima*) position (of the feet).
(**e**) **de buena ~** *hombre* well-built; *mujer* shapely; **tener buena ~** (*hombre*) to have a fine physique; (*mujer*) to be good-looking.
(**f**) (*Tec*) plant; **~ de ensamblaje** assembly plant; **~ piloto** pilot plant; **~ potabilizadora** waterworks, water treatment plant.
(**g**) (*proyecto*) plan, programme, scheme.
(**h**) **echar ~s*** to bluster; to threaten.
planta[2] *nf* (*Bot*) plant; **~ de interior** indoor plant, house plant; **~ de maceta** pot-plant; **~ trepadora** climbing plant.
plantación *nf* (**a**) (*acto*) planting. (**b**) (*plantas*) plantation; **~ de tabaco** tobacco plantation.
plantado* *adj* (**a**) **dejar a uno ~** to leave sb suddenly, leave sb in mid-sentence; to leave sb in the lurch, leave sb high and dry; **dejar ~ al novio** (*dar calabazas*) to jilt one's fiancé; (*en una cita*) to stand one's boyfriend up*; **ella dejó ~ a su marido** she left her husband.
(**b**) **bien ~** *hombre* well-built; *mujer* shapely; good-looking.
plantador *nm* (**a**) (*Agr*) dibber. (**b**) (*persona*) planter.
plantaje* *nm* (*And, Carib*) looks.
plantar [1a] **1** *vt* (**a**) (*Bot*) to plant; (‡: *enterrar*) to bury.
(**b**) *poste etc* to put in; *monumento etc* to erect, set up; *tienda* to pitch; *creencia, reforma etc* to implant; *institución* to set up.
(**c**) *golpe* to plant (*en* on).
(**d**) *insulto* to offer, hurl.
(**e**) **~ a uno en la calle** to pitch sb into the street, chuck sb out; **~ a un obrero en la calle** to sack a workman*.
(**f**) (*) **~ a uno** to curb sb, check sb; **le planté para que no dijera más** I stopped him before he could say any more.
(**g**) (*) = **dejar plantado** (*V adj* (**a**)).
2 plantarse *vr* (**a**) (*resistir*) to stand firm, stay resolutely where one is; to plant o.s.; (*fig*) to stand firm, dig one's heels in, refuse to compromise; (*Naipes*) to stick; **35, y me planto** 35, and there I stop.
(**b**) (*caballo*) to balk, refuse.
(**c**) **~ en** to reach, get to; **en 3 horas se plantó en Sevilla** he got to Seville in 3 hours.
(**d**) (*And, CAm, Méx*:*) to doll o.s. up*.
plante *nm* (**a**) (*huelga*) stoppage, protest strike. (**b**) (*postura*) stand, agreed basis for resistance; (*programa*) common programme of demands.
planteamiento *nm* (*de problema*) posing, raising; (*aproximación*) approach.
plantear [1a] **1** *vt* (**a**) *creencia, reforma etc* to implant; *cambio* to get under way; *institución* to set up, establish.
(**b**) (*proponer*) to plan.
(**c**) *problema* to create, pose; *cuestión, dificultad* to raise; *debate, pleito etc* to start; **nos ha planteado muchos problemas** it has created a lot of problems for us; **se lo plantearé** I'll put it to him; I'll have it out with him; **~ la cuestión de confianza** (*Parl*) to ask for a vote of confidence; **el estudio plantea que ...** the study proposes that ...
2 plantearse *vr* (*pensar*) to think, reflect; **¡no me lo planteo!** I don't want to think about it!
planteo *nm* (**a**) (*Hort*) nursery.
(**b**) (*centro educativo*) training establishment.
(**c**) **~ de actores y actrices** leading actors and actresses.
(**d**) (*Cono Sur, Méx*: *personal*) staff, personnel.
plantificar [1g] **1** *vt* (*: *colocar*) to plonk down, dump down*. **2 plantificarse** *vr* (**a**) (*Carib, Cono Sur, Méx**) (*plantarse*) to plant o.s.; (*no ceder*) to stand firm, stand one's ground; **se plantificó en la puerta** he planted himself in the doorway, he stood there in the doorway. (**b**) (*Méx*: *ataviarse*) to get dolled up*.
plantilla *nf* (**a**) (*de zapato*) inner sole, insole; (*de media etc*) sole.
(**b**) (*Téc*) pattern, template; stencil.
(**c**) (*personas*) establishment, personnel; list, roster;

(*Dep*) team, squad; ~ **de personal** staff; **ser de** ~ to be established, be on the establishment.
plantillada* *nf* (*And*) bragging.
plantío *nm* (**a**) (*acto*) planting. (**b**) (*terreno*) plot, bed, patch.
plantista *nm* braggart.
plantón *nm* (**a**) (*Bot*) (*plántula*) seedling; (*esqueje*) cutting.
(**b**) (*: *espera*) long wait, tedious wait; **dar (un)** ~ **a uno** to stand sb up (on a date*); **estar de** ~ (*Mil*) to be on sentry duty; (*fig*) to be stuck, have to wait around; **tener a uno de** ~ to keep sb waiting around.
plántula *nf* seedling.
plañidera *nf* (paid) mourner.
plañidero *adj* mournful, plaintive.
plañir [3h] *vt* to mourn, grieve over.
plas[1] *interj* = **plaf**.
plas[2]‡ *nm* brother.
plasa‡ *nf* sister.
plasma *nm* plasma; ~ **sanguíneo** blood plasma.
plasmación *nf* shape, form.
plasmar [1a] **1** *vt* (*formar*) to mould, shape, form; (*crear*) to create; (*representar*) to represent, give visible (*o* concrete) form to. **2** *vi y* **plasmarse** *vr* to take shape, appear in solid form, acquire a definite form; ~ **en** to take the form of, emerge as, turn into.
plasta 1 *nf* (**a**) (*masa*) soft mass, lump; (*cosa aplastada*) flattened mass.
(**b**) (*: *desastre*) botch, mess; **es una** ~ **de edificio** it's a mess of a building; **el plan es una** ~ the plan is one big mess, the plan is a complete botch.
2 *nmf* (*: *pelmazo*) bore.
3 *adj invar* (*) boring.
plástica *nf* (art of) sculpture, modelling.
plasticar [1g] *vt* (*LAm*) *documento* to cover with plastic, seal in plastic, laminate.
plasticidad *nf* (**a**) (*lit*) plasticity. (**b**) (*fig*) expressiveness, descriptiveness; richness, evocative character.
plasticina ® *nf* Plasticine ®.
plástico 1 *adj* (**a**) (*gen*) plastic; **artes plásticas** plastic arts.
(**b**) (*fig*) *imagen etc* expressive, descriptive; *descripción* rich, poetic, evocative.
(**c**) **chico** ~ (*CAm**) young trendy.
2 *nm* (**a**) (*gen*) plastic; **es de** ~* it's fake, it's not for real*.
(**b**) (*Mús**) disc, record; **pinchar un** ~ to put a record on.
(**c**) (*Mil*) plastic explosive.
plastificación *nf* treatment with plastic, lamination.
plastificado *adj* treated with plastic, laminated.
plastificar [1g] *vt* (**a**) (*Téc*) = **plasticar**. (**b**) (*Mús*) to record, make a record of.
plastilina ® *nf* Plasticine ®.
plastrón *nm* (*LAm*) floppy tie, cravate.
plata *nf* (**a**) (*metal*) silver; (*vajilla*) silverware; (*Fin*) silver, silver coin(s); **como una** ~ shining bright, like a new pin.
(**b**) (*esp LAm*) (*dinero*) money; (*riqueza*) wealth; **apalear** ~, **pudrirse en** ~ to be rolling in money.
(**c**) **hablar en** ~ to speak bluntly, speak frankly.
(**d**) **La P**~ (*río*) the (River) Plate.
platacho *nm* (*Cono Sur*) *dish of raw seafood.*
platada *nf* (*LAm*) dish, plateful.
plataforma *nf* (**a**) (*gen*) platform; stage; ~ **de carga** loading platform; ~ **continental** continental shelf; ~ **espacial** space-station; ~ **giratoria** turntable; ~ **de lanzamiento** launching-pad; ~ **de perforación,** ~ **petrolera,** ~ **petrolífera** drilling rig, oil-rig.
(**b**) (*Pol*: *t* ~ **electoral**) platform; (*programa*) programme; (*de negociación*) package, offer, set of proposals; ~ **reivindicativa** set of demands.
platal *nm* (*LAm*) fortune; wealth.
platanal *nm,* **platanar** *nm,* **platanera** *nf* (*LAm*) banana plantation.
platanero 1 *adj* banana (*atr*). **2** *nm* (*CAm, Méx*) (*cultivador*) banana grower; (*comerciante*) dealer in bananas.
plátano *nm* (**a**) (*árbol*) plane, plane tree. (**b**) (*fruta*) banana; (*bananero*) banana tree. (**c**) (*llantén*) plantain. (**d**) (**‡) prick**‡.
platea *nf* (*Teat*) pit, orchestra (*US*).
plateado 1 *adj* (**a**) (*color*) silver; silvery; (*Téc*) silver-plated. (**b**) (*Méx*) wealthy. **2** *nm* silver-plating.
platear [1a] **1** *vt* (**a**) (*gen*) to silver; (*Téc*) to silver-plate.
(**b**) (*CAm, Méx*) to sell, turn into money.
2 *vi* to show silver; to turn silvery.
platense (*LAm*) **1** *adj* (**a**) = **rioplatense 1.** (**b**) (*de la ciudad*) of La Plata. **2** *nmf* (**a**) = **rioplatense 2.** (**b**) native (*o* inhabitant) of La Plata; **los ~s** the people of La Plata.
plateresco *adj* plateresque.
platería *nf* (**a**) (*arte*) silversmith's craft. (**b**) (*tienda*) silversmith's; (*joyería*) jeweller's.
platero, -a *nm/f* silversmith; (*joyero*) jeweller.
plática *nf* (*esp CAm, Méx*) talk, chat; (*Ecl*) sermon; **estar de** ~ to be chatting, be having a talk.
platicador* *adj* (*Méx*) chatty, talkative.
platicar [1g] *vi* (**a**) (*charlar*) to talk, chat. (**b**) (*Méx*) to say, tell.
platija *nf* plaice, flounder.
platilla *nf* (*Carib*) water melon.
platillo *nm* (**a**) (*Culin*) saucer; small plate; (*de limosnas*) collecting bowl; ~ **de balance** scale, pan (*of scales*); ~ **volante,** ~ **volador** flying saucer; **pasar el** ~ to pass the hat round, make a collection.
(**b**) **~s** (*Mús*) cymbals.
(**c**) (*CAm, Méx*) dish; **el tercer** ~ **de la comida** the third course of the meal.
platina *nf* (*de microscopio*) microscope slide; (*de tocadiscos*) deck; (*de casete*) tape deck; (*Tip*) platen.
platino 1 *nm* platinum; **~s** (*Aut*) contact points. **2** *como adj*: **rubia** ~ platinum blonde.
plato *nm* (**a**) (*Culin*) *utensilio* plate, dish; (*Téc*) plate; (*de balanza*) scale, pan; ~ **frutero** fruit-dish; ~ **giradiscos,** ~ **giratorio** turntable; ~ **hondo,** ~ **sopero** soup-dish; **del** ~ **a la boca se pierde la sopa** there's many a slip 'twixt cup and lip; **fregar** (*o* **lavar**) **los ~s** to wash the dishes, wash up; **pagar los ~s rotos** to pay for the damage, (*fig*) to carry the can*; *V* **nada**.
(**b**) (*contenido del* ~) plateful, dish; **un** ~ **de arroz** a dish of rice; **vender algo por un** ~ **de lentejas** to sell sth for a mess of pottage.
(**c**) (*Culin*) dish; course; ~ **combinado** set main course; ~ **dulce** sweet course; ~ **de fondo,** ~ **principal** main course; ~ **fuerte** (*principal*) main course; (*abundante*) heavy dish, meal in itself; (*fig*: *tema*) main topic, central theme; (*fig*: *punto fuerte*) strong point; ~ **precocinado** pre-cooked meal; ~ **preparado** ready-to-serve meal; **sopa y 4 ~s** soup and 4 courses; **es mi** ~ **favorito** it's my favourite dish (*o* meal); **comen del mismo** ~ they're great pals; **ser** ~ **de segunda mesa*** to be second-best; to feel neglected, play second fiddle; **no es** ~ **de mi gusto** (*fig*) it's not my cup of tea.
(**d**) **es un** ~ (*Cono Sur**) he's very dishy*.
(**e**) (*Cono Sur**) **¡qué ~!** what a laugh!, that's a good one!
plató *nm* (*Cine*) set; (*TV*) floor.
Platón *nm* Plato.
platón *nm* (*LAm*) (**a**) (*Culin*) large dish; serving dish. (**b**) (*palangana*) washbasin.
platónicamente *adv* platonically.
platónico *adj* platonic.
platonismo *nm* platonism.
platonista *nmf* platonist.
platudo* *adj* (*LAm*) rich, well-heeled*.
plausible *adj* (**a**) (*loable*) commendable, laudable, praiseworthy. (**b**) *razón etc* acceptable, admissible.
plausiblemente *adv* commendably, laudably.
playa *nf* (**a**) (*orilla*) shore, beach; **P~ Girón** (*Carib*) Bay of Pigs; **una** ~ **de arenas doradas** a beach of golden sands; **pasar el día en la** ~ to spend the day at (*o* on) the beach; **pescar desde la** ~ to fish from the beach.
(**b**) (*fig*) seaside; seaside resort; **ir a veranear a una** ~ to spend the summer at the seaside, go to the seaside for one's summer holidays.
(**c**) (*LAm*) (*llano*) flat open space; ~ **de carga y descarga** (*Ferro*) goods-yard; ~ **de estacionamiento** car-park, parking lot (*US*); ~ **de juegos** playground.
(**d**) **una** ~ **de** (*Carib**) loads of.
playera *nf* sports shirt, T-shirt.
playeras *nfpl* sandals, sandshoes; tennis shoes.
playero *adj* beach (*atr*).
playo *adj* (*Cono Sur, Méx*) gently sloping.
plaza *nf* (**a**) (*gen*) square; public square, open space; (*mercado*) market (place); ~ **de armas** parade ground; ~ **mayor** main square; ~ **de toros** bullring; **abrir** ~ to open a bullfight; **hacer la** ~ (*Esp*) to do the daily shopping; **regar la** ~ (*Esp**) to have a beer (as a starter).
(**b**) (*Com*) town, city, centre; **en esa** ~ there, in your town.

(**c**) (*espacio*) room, space; (*lugar*) place; (*en vehículo etc*) seat, place; **¡~!** make way!; **~ de atraque** berth, mooring; **abrir ~** to make way; **el avión tiene 90 ~s** the plane has 90 seats, the plane carries 90 passengers; **de dos ~s** (*Aut etc*) two-seater; **'no hay ~s'** 'no vacancies'; **~s hoteleras** hotel beds; **reservar una ~** to reserve a seat.

(**d**) (*puesto*) post, job; (*vacante*) vacancy; **cubrir una ~** to fill a job, appoint to a post; **sentar ~** (*Mil*) to enlist, sign on (*de* as).

(**e**) (*Mil*: *t* **~ fuerte**) fortress, fortified town.

plazo *nm* (**a**) (*tiempo*) time, period, term; (*término*) deadline, time limit; (*vencimiento*) date, expiry date; (*Com, Fin*) date; **~ de entrega** delivery time, delivery date; **~ previsto** specified period; **~ prudencial** reasonable time; **en un ~ de 6 meses** in the space of 6 months, in a period of 6 months; within a term of 6 months, before 6 months are up; **nos dan un ~ de 8 días** they allow us a week, they give us a week's grace; **¿cuándo vence el ~?** when is the payment due?, what is the time limit?; **se ha cumplido el ~** the time is up; **a ~** (*Com*) on credit; **a corto ~** (*adj*) *préstamo* short-dated, (*fig*) short-term; (*adv*) in the short term; **a largo ~** (*adj*) *préstamo* long-dated, (*fig*) long-term; (*adv*) in the long term; **a ~ medio** in the medium term; **es una tarea a largo ~** it's a long-term job.

(**b**) (*pago*) instalment, payment; **pagar el ~ de marzo** to pay the March instalment; **comprar a ~s** to buy on hire purchase, pay for in instalments.

plazoleta *nf*, **plazuela** *nf* small square.

pleamar *nf* high tide.

plebe *nf*: **la ~** the common people, the masses, the mass of the population; (*pey*) the plebs; the mob, the rabble.

plebeyez *nf* plebeian nature; (*fig*) coarseness, commonness.

plebeyo 1 *adj* plebeian; (*pey*) coarse, common. **2** *nm*, **plebeya** *nf* plebeian, commoner; (*pey*) plebeian.

plebiscito *nm* plebiscite.

plectro *nm* plectrum.

plegable *adj* pliable, that bends; *silla etc* folding, that folds up, collapsible.

plegadera *nf* paperknife.

plegadizo *adj* = **plegable 1**.

plegado *nm*, **plegadura** *nf* (**a**) (*acto*) folding; bending; creasing. (**b**) (*pliegue*) fold; crease.

plegamiento *nm* (*de camión*) jack-knifing.

plegar [1h *y* 1j] **1** *vt* to fold; to bend; to crease; (*Cos*) to pleat. **2** *vi* (*fig*) to fold up. **3 plegarse** *vr* (**a**) (*gen*) to bend; to crease. (**b**) (*fig*) to yield, submit (*a* to).

plegaria *nf* prayer.

pleitear [1a] *vi* (**a**) (*Jur*) to plead, conduct a lawsuit; to go to law (*con, contra* with; *sobre* over), indulge in litigation. (**b**) (*esp LAm*) to argue.

pleitesía *nf*: **rendir ~ a** to show respect for, treat respectfully, show courtesy to; (*LAm*) to pay tribute to.

pleitista 1 *adj* (*lit*) litigious; (*fig: reñidor*) quarrelsome, argumentative. **2** *nmf* (*lit*) litigious person; (*fig*) troublemaker; (*LAm: peleonero*) brawler.

pleitisto *adj* (*LAm*) quarrelsome, argumentative.

pleito *nm* (**a**) (*Jur*) lawsuit, case; **~s** litigation; **~ de acreedores** bankruptcy proceedings; **~ civil** civil action; **andar a ~s** to be engaged in lawsuits; **entablar ~** to bring an action, bring a lawsuit; **ganar el ~** to win one's case; **poner ~** to sue, bring an action; **poner ~ a uno** to bring an action against sb, take sb to court.

(**b**) (*fig*) dispute, feud; controversy; (*LAm*) quarrel, argument; (*pelea*) fight, brawl; **estar a ~ con uno** to be at odds with sb.

(**c**) **~ homenaje** homage.

plenamente *adj* fully; completely.

plenaria *nf* plenary (session).

plenario *adj* plenary, full.

plenilunio *nm* full moon.

plenipotenciario, -a *nm/f* plenipotentiary.

plenitud *nf* plenitude, fullness; abundance; **en la ~ de sus poderes** at the height of his powers.

pleno 1 *adj* full; complete; *poderes* full; *sesión* plenary, full; **en ~ día** in broad daylight; **en ~ verano** at the height of summer; **tiene frío en ~ verano** he's cold even though it's summer; **en plena rebeldía** in open revolt; **en plena vista** in full view; **le dio en plena cara** it hit him full in the face.

2 *nm* (**a**) (*Parl etc*) plenum, plenary session; **reunirse en ~** to hold a full meeting.

(**b**) (*quinielas*) maximum correct forecast.

(**c**) **en ~** *decidir etc* unanimously.

pleonasmo *nm* pleonasm.

pleonástico *adj* pleonastic.

plepa *nf* (**a**) (*persona enfermiza*) sickly person. (**b**) (*: *antipático*) unpleasant sort. (**c**) (*molesto*) pain*, nuisance.

pletina *nf* = **platina**.

plétora *nf* (*abundancia*) plethora, abundance; flood; (*exceso*) excess, surplus.

pletórico *adj* abundant; **~ de** abounding in, full of, brimming with; **~ de salud** bursting with health.

pleuresía *nf* pleurisy.

plexiglás ® *nm* Perspex ®, Plexiglass ® (*US*).

plexo *nm*: **~ solar** solar plexus.

pléyade 1 *nf* (*liter*) group, gathering. **2** *nmpl*: **P~s** Pleiades.

plica *nf* sealed envelope, sealed document; (*en concurso*) sealed entry.

pliego *nm* (**a**) (*hoja*) sheet; (*carpeta*) folder; (*Tip*) section, signature.

(**b**) (*carta etc sellada*) sealed letter, sealed document; **~ cerrado** (*Náut*) sealed orders; **~ de condiciones** details, specifications (*of a tender etc*); **~ de cargos** list of accusations; *V* **descargo**.

pliegue *nm* (**a**) (*gen*) fold, crease; (*Cos*) pleat, crease; tuck. (**b**) (*Geol etc*) fold.

plima *nf*: **flor de la ~** (*Cono Sur*) wisteria.

plin*: **¡a mí ~!** *excl* I couldn't care less!

Plinio *nm* Pliny; **~ el Joven** Pliny the Younger; **~ el Viejo** Pliny the Elder.

plinto *nm* plinth.

plisado *nm* pleating; (*un ~*) pleat.

plisar [1a] *vt* to pleat.

plomada *nf* (*Arquit etc*) plumb, plumb line; (*Náut*) lead; (*en red de pescar*) weights, sinkers.

plomar [1a] *vt* to seal with lead.

plomazo *nm* (**a**) (*CAm, Méx*) (*tiro*) shot; (*herida*) bullet wound. (**b**) (*) drag.

plombagina *nf* plumbago.

plomería *nf* (**a**) (*Arquit*) leading, lead roofing. (**b**) (*LAm*) (*sistema*) plumbing; (*taller*) plumber's workshop, plumber's shop.

plomero *nm* (*LAm*) plumber.

plomífero* *adj* boring.

plomizo *adj* (**a**) (*de plomo*) leaden, lead-coloured. (**b**) (*fig*) leaden.

plomo 1 *nm* (**a**) (*metal*) lead; **~ derretido** molten lead; **soldado de ~** tin soldier; **gasolina con ~** leaded petrol; **gasolina sin ~** unleaded petrol; **sacar ~ a** (*fig*) to make light of, play down.

(**b**) = **plomada**.

(**c**) (*de pesca*) weight, sinker; **a ~** plumb, true, vertical(ly); (*fig*) just right, exactly right; **caer a ~** to fall heavily, fall flat.

(**d**) (*Elec*) fuse; **se ha fundido el ~** it's fused; **se le fundieron los ~s** (*Esp**) he blew his top*.

(**e**) (*esp LAm: bala*) bullet, shot.

(**f**) (*) (*pesadez*) bore, dull affair; (*pelmazo*) drag.

(**g**) (*Méx: tiroteo*) gunfight.

2 *adj* (**a**) (*LAm*) lead grey, lead-coloured.

(**b**) **ponerse ~*** to get cross.

(**c**) (*: *pesado*) boring, dull.

plomoso *adj* (*CAm*) boring.

plotter ['ploter] *nm, pl* **plotters** ['ploter] (*Inform*) plotter.

plugo, pluguiere *etc V* **placer**[1].

pluma 1 *nf* (**a**) (*Orn*) feather; quill; (*adorno*) plume, feather; (*volante*) shuttlecock; **colchón de ~s** feather-bed; **hacer a ~ y a pelo** to be versatile, be ready to undertake anything.

(**b**) (*de escribir, fig*) pen; **~ atómica** (*Méx*) ball-point pen; **~ electrónica** light pen; **~ esferográfica** (*LAm*) ball-point pen; **~ estilográfica, ~ fuente** (*LAm*) fountain-pen; **y otras obras de su ~** and other works from his pen; **dejar correr la ~** to write spontaneously; **escribir a vuela ~** to write quickly, write without much thought.

(**c**) (*fig: caligrafía*) penmanship, writing.

(**d**) (*CAm: mentira*) fib, tale; hoax.

(**e**) (*Cono Sur*: puta*) prostitute.

(**f**) (*And, Carib, Cono Sur: grifo*) tap, faucet (*US*).

(**g**) (*Cono Sur: grúa*) crane, derrick.

(**h**) (*Esp*‡: *peseta*) one peseta.

(**i**) (*Esp*‡‡: *pene*) prick‡‡.

(**j**) (*Esp*‡: *maricón*) queer‡, poofter‡.

(**k**) (*Esp**: *periodista*) hack (journalist).

2 *nm* (*Dep*) featherweight.

plumada *nf* stroke of the pen; flourish.

plumado *adj* feathered, with feathers; *pollo* fledged.
plumafuente *nf* (*LAm*) fountain-pen.
plumaje *nm* (**a**) (*Orn*) plumage, feathers. (**b**) (*adorno*) plume, crest; bunch of feathers.
plumario, -a *nm/f* (*CAm, Méx*) (*periodista*) hack (journalist); (*: *funcionario*) penpusher.
plumazo *nm* (**a**) (*trazo*) stroke of the pen (*t fig*); **de un ~** with one stroke of the pen; (*Carib*) in a jiffy*; **es un cuento que escribió de un ~** it's a story which she tossed off.
(**b**) (*colchón*) feather mattress; (*almohada*) feather pillow.
plumbemia *nf* lead poisoning.
plúmbeo *adj* leaden.
plúmbico *adj* plumbic.
plumear [1a] **1** *vt* (*CAm, Méx**) to write, scribble. **2** *vi* (*Méx*‡) to be on the game*.
plumero 1 *nm* (**a**) (*para limpiar*) feather duster.
(**b**) (*adorno*) plume; bunch of feathers; **se le ve el ~*** you can see what he's really thinking, you can see what he's really like.
(**c**) (*portaplumas*) penholder.
(**d**) (*And*) plumber.
(**e**) (*Cono Sur*) powder-puff.
2 *adj* (*) camp, exaggeratedly homosexual.
plumier(e) *nm* pencil-case.
plumífero, -a 1 *nm/f* (*hum*) poor writer, hack; hack journalist. **2** *nm* quilted anorak.
plumilla 1 *nf* nib, pen-nib. **2** *nmf* (*Prensa*) hack journalist.
plumín *nm* nib, pen-nib.
plumista *nm/f* clerk, scrivener.
plumón *nm* (**a**) (*Orn*) down. (**b**) (*cama*) feather bed. (**c**) (*LAm*) felt-tip pen.
plumoso *adj* feathery, downy.
plural 1 *adj* (**a**) plural. (**b**) (*fig: esp LAm*) many, manifold, numerous; diversified. **2** *nm* plural; **en ~** in the plural.
pluralidad *nf* (**a**) (*gen*) plurality.
(**b**) **~ de votos** majority of votes.
(**c**) **una ~ de** a number of; numerous, diverse; **el asunto tiene ~ de aspectos** there are a number of sides to this question; **hay una alta ~ temática** there are many different themes; **existe una ~ de textos para esta asignatura** there is a duplication of textbooks for this course.
pluralismo *nm* pluralism.
pluralista 1 *adj* (**a**) (*gen*) pluralist; pluralistic. (**b**) (*polifacético*) many-sided, diverse. **2** *nmf* pluralist.
pluri... *pref* pluri...; many ...; multi...
plurianual *adj* lasting for several years, covering a number of years; long-term.
pluricultural *adj* multicultural.
pluridimensional *adj* multifaceted, many-sided.
pluriempleado 1 *adj* having more than one job. **2** *nm*, **pluriempleada** *nf* person having more than one job, moonlighter*.
pluriempleo *nm* having more than one job, moonlighting*.
plurifamiliar *adj*: **vivienda ~** house (*etc*) for several families.
pluriforme *adj* very diverse, diversified, multifaceted.
plurilingüe *adj* multilingual.
plurinacional *adj*: **estado ~** state consisting of several nationalities.
pluripartidismo *nm* multi-party system.
pluripartidista *adj*: **sistema ~** multi-party system.
plurivalencia *nf* many-sided value; diversity of uses (*etc*); wide applicability.
plurivalente *adj* having numerous values; having diverse uses (*etc*); widely applicable.
plus *nm* extra pay, bonus; **~ de antigüedad** long-service bonus; **~ de carestía de vida** cost-of-living bonus; **~ de nocturnidad** extra pay for unsocial hours; **~ de peligrosidad** danger-money; **~ salarial** bonus; **con 5 dólares de ~** with a bonus of 5 dollars.
pluscafé *nm* (*LAm*) liqueur.
pluscuamperfecto *nm* pluperfect, past perfect.
plusmarca *nf* record; **batir la ~** to break the record.
plusmarquista *nmf* record-holder; record-breaker; top scorer.
plusvalía *nf* appreciation, added value; unearned increment; capital gain; **impuesto de ~** tax on rise in value (of land *etc*).
Plutarco *nm* Plutarch.
pluto‡ *adj* (*And*) drunk, sloshed‡.
plutocracia *nf* plutocracy.
plutócrata *nmf* plutocrat.
plutocrático *adj* plutocratic.
Plutón *nm* Pluto.
plutonio *nm* plutonium.
pluvial *adj* rain (*atr*).
pluviometría *nf* rainfall, precipitation.
pluviométrico *adj* rainfall (*atr*); **media pluviométrica** average rainfall.
pluviómetro *nm* rain-gauge, pluviometer.
pluviosidad *nf* rainfall.
pluvioso *adj* rainy.
pluviselva *nf* rain-forest.
PM *nf abr de* **Policía Militar** Military Police, MP.
p.m. (**a**) *abr de* **post meridiem** post meridiem, p.m. (**b**) *abr de* **por minuto** per minute.
PMA *nm abr de* **Programa Mundial de Alimentos** World Food Programme, WFP.
PMM *nm abr de* **parque móvil de ministerios** official cars.
pmo *abr de* **próximo.**
PN *nmf* (*Esp*) *abr de* **profesor numerario, profesora numeraria.**
PNB *nm abr de* **producto nacional bruto** gross national product, GNP.
PNN 1 *nmf* (*Escol*) *abr de* **profesor no numerario, profesora no numeraria. 2** *nm* (*Econ*) *abr de* **producto nacional neto** net national product, NNP.
PNUD *nm abr de* **Programa de las Naciones Unidas para el Desarrollo** United Nations Development Programme, UNDP.
PNV *nm* (*Esp*) *abr de* **Partido Nacionalista Vasco.**
P.º *abr de* **Paseo** Avenue, Ave, Av.
p.o. *abr de* **por orden.**
población *nf* (**a**) (*habitantes*) population; **~ activa, ~ ocupada** working population; **~ flotante** floating population; **~ pasiva** non-working population, retired people. (**b**) (*ciudad*) town, city; (*pueblo*) village; (*Cono Sur*) small hamlet; main building and outbuildings. (**c**) (*Chile*) poor quarter, slum area, shanty-town.
poblacional *adj* population (*atr*); demographic; **estudio ~** population study.
poblacho *nm* **poblachón** *nm* dump, one-horse town.
poblada *nf* (**a**) (*And, Cono Sur* ††: *rebelión*) revolt, armed rising. (**b**) (*And, Cono Sur: multitud*) crowd.
poblado 1 *adj* (**a**) (*habitado*) inhabited.
(**b**) **poco ~** underpopulated, with a sparse population; **densamente ~** thickly populated; **la ciudad más poblada del país** the most populous city in the country.
(**c**) **~ de** peopled with, populated with; (*fig*) full of, filled with; covered with.
(**d**) *barba* big, thick; *cejas* bushy.
2 *nm* (*pueblo*) village; (*población*) town; (*lugar habitado*) inhabited place; (*Aut etc*) built-up area; **~ de absorción, ~ dirigido** new town, satellite town.
poblador(a) *nm/f* (**a**) (*colono*) settler, colonist; (*fundador*) founder; (*habitante*) inhabitant. (**b**) (*Chile*) slum-dweller.
poblano 1 *adj* (**a**) (*LAm*) village (*atr*), town (*atr*). (**b**) (*Méx*) of Puebla. **2** *nm*, **poblana** *nf* (**a**) (*LAm*) villager. (**b**) (*Méx*) native (*o* inhabitant) of Puebla.
poblar [1l] **1** *vt* (**a**) *lugar* to settle, people, colonize; *colmena, río etc* to stock (*de* with); *tierra* to plant (*de* with).
(**b**) (*habitar*) to people, inhabit; **los peces que pueblan las profundidades** the fish that inhabit the depths; **las estrellas que pueblan el espacio** the stars that fill space.
2 poblarse *vr* (**a**) (*gen*) to fill (*de* with); (*ir aumentando*) to fill up, become stocked (*de* with); (*irse cubriendo*) to become covered (*de* with).
(**b**) (*Bot*) to come into leaf.
pobo *nm* white poplar.
pobre 1 *adj* (*gen*) poor (*de, en* in); **¡~ de mí!** poor old me!; **¡~ de él!** poor fellow!; **¡~ de ti si te pillo!** it'll be tough on you if I catch you!
2 *nmf* (**a**) (*necesitado*) poor person; (*mendigo*) beggar, pauper; **un ~** a poor man; **los ~s** the poor, poor people.
(**b**) (*fig*) poor wretch, poor devil; **la ~ estaba mojada** the poor girl was wet through; **el ~ está fatal de los ojos*** he's terribly short-sighted, poor chap*.
pobremente *adv* poorly.
pobrería *nf*, **pobrerío** *nm* (*Cono Sur*) poor people.
pobrete 1 *adj* poor, wretched. **2** *nm*, **pobreta** *nf* poor thing, poor wretch.
pobretería *nf* (**a**) (*pobres*) poor people (*collectively*); (*reunión*) gathering of poor people. (**b**) (*pobreza*) poverty. (**c**) (*tacañería*) miserliness, meanness.

pobretón 1 *adj* terribly poor. **2** *nm* poor man.
pobreza *nf* (*gen*) poverty; (*estrechez*) work, penury; ~ **de espíritu** poorness of spirit, small-mindedness; ~ **no es vileza** poverty is not a crime.
poca *nm* (*LAm*), **pócar** *nm* (*Méx*) poker.
pocero *nm* well-digger.
pocerón *nm* (*CAm, Méx*) pool.
pocilga *nf* piggery, pigsty; (*fig*) pigsty.
pocillo *nm* small cup; (*LAm esp: de café*) coffee cup; (*Méx*) mug.
pócima *nf*, **poción** *nf* (*Farm*) potion, draught; (*Vet*) drench; (*fig*) brew, concoction, nasty drink.
poco 1 *adj* (**a**) (*sing*) (*gen*) little; (*pequeño*) small; (*escaso*) slight, scanty; too little, *p.ej.* **era ~ para él** it was too little for him; **con ~ respeto** with little respect, with scant respect; **de ~ interés** of small interest; **de poca extensión** of small extent, not extensive; **hay ~ queso** there isn't much cheese; **nos queda ~ tiempo** we haven't much time; **el provecho es ~** the gain is small; **con lo ~ que me quedaba** with what little I had left; **ya sabes lo ~ que me interesa** you know how little it interests me; **todas las medidas son pocas** any measure will be inadequate; **por si fuera ~** if it were just a small thing; **y por si eso fuera ~** and as if that were not enough; and to add insult to injury.

(**b**) (*pl*) **~s** few; too few, *p.ej.* **eran ~s para ella** there were too few of them for her; **unos ~s** a few, some; **~s de entre ellos** few of them; **~s niños saben que ...** few (*o* not many) children know that ...; **~s son los que ...** there are few who ...; **me quedan pocas probabilidades** I don't have much chance; **un canalla como hay ~s** a real rotter*, an absolute rotter*.

2 *adv* (**a**) (*no mucho*) little, not much; (*ligeramente*) only slightly; **cuesta ~** it doesn't cost much; **ahora trabaja ~** he only works a little now; **¡ ~ (que) hemos trabajado!*** I should jolly well say we've been working!*; **los estiman ~** they hardly value them at all; **~ a ~** little by little; **¡~ a ~!** gently!, easy there!; **~ más o menos** more or less; **ser para ~** to be weak, be characterless, be very negative; **tener a uno en ~** to think little of sb, have no use for sb; **tiene la vida en ~** he holds his life cheap.

(**b**) (*con adj: se traduce a menudo con prefijo* dis-, un-) **~ dispuesto a ayudar** disinclined to help; **~ amable** unkind; **~ inteligente** unintelligent; **ser poca cosa** to be unimportant.

(**c**) **por ~** almost, nearly; **por ~ me ahogo** I very nearly drowned.

(**d**) (*locuciones de tiempo*) **a ~** shortly (after), presently; **a ~ de haberlo firmado** shortly after he had signed it; **a ~ que corras, lo alcanzas** if you run now you'll catch it; **cada ~** every so often; **dentro de ~** shortly; soon after; **hace ~** a short while back, a short time ago.

(**e**) (*LAm*) **¿a ~?** not really!, you don't say!; **¿a ~ no?** (well) isn't it?; **¿a ~ crees que ...?** do you really imagine that ...?; **a ~ vas a decir que ...** maybe you're going to say that ...; **a ~ que pueda** if at all possible.

3 *nm*: **un ~** a little, a bit; **estoy un ~ triste** I am a little sad; **le conocía un ~** I knew him slightly; **un ~ de dinero** a little money, some money.
pocha¹ *nf* (*Culin*) pinto bean.
pocha² *nf* (*Cono Sur*) (*mentira*) lie; (*trampa*) trick.
poch(e)ar [1a] *vt* (*Culin*) to poach.
pochismo *nm* (*Méx pey*) *anglicism introduced into Spanish.*
pocho 1 *adj* (**a**) *color, flor* faded, discoloured; *persona* pale; *fruta* soft, overripe; withered.

(**b**) (*fig*) depressed, gloomy.

(**c**) (*Cono Sur*) (*gordito*) chubby; (*rechoncho*) squat.

2 *nm*, **pocha** *nf* (*Méx etc*) Mexican-American, Latino.
pochola* *nf* nice girl, attractive girl; (*en oración directa*) dear, darling.
pocholada* *nf* nice thing, pretty thing.
pocholo* 1 *adj* nice; pretty, attractive, cute. **2** *nm* pretty boy.
pocholez* *nf* gem, treasure; **el vestido es una ~** it's a dear little dress.
poda *nf* (**a**) (*acto*) pruning. (**b**) (*temporada*) pruning season.
podadera *nf* pruning knife, billhook; pruning shears, secateurs.
podadora *nf* (*Méx*) lawnmower.
podar [1a] *vt* (**a**) (*gen*) to prune; (*mondar*) to lop, trim (off).

(**b**) (*fig*) to prune, cut out.
podenco *nm* hound.
poder 1 [2s] *vi* (**a**) (+ *infin*: *capacidad*) can, to be able to; **puede venir** he can come, he is able to come; **no puede venir** he cannot come; **puede ser** maybe, it may be so; **puede ser que ...** + *subj* it may be that ...; maybe ...; **pudiera ser que** + *subj* it might be that ...; **puede que esté en la biblioteca** he may be in the library, perhaps he's in the library; **este vino no se puede beber** this wine is not fit to drink.

(**b**) (+ *infin*: *posibilidad*) may; **puede no venir** he may not come, it is possible that he won't come; **por lo que pudiera pasar** because of what might happen; **¡podías habérmelo dicho!** you might have told me!; **pudo hacerse daño** he might (*o* could) have hurt himself; **bien puedes pasar la noche aquí** you may perfectly well spend the night here.

(**c**) (*absoluto*) can; **¿puedo?** may I (help you)? **lo haré si puedo** I'll do it if I can; **no puedo** I can't; **¡puede!** who knows!, maybe!; **¿se puede?** may I?, may I come in?; do you mind?; **los que pueden** those who can, those who are able (to); **el dinero puede mucho** money can do anything, money talks; **él puede mucho en el partido** he has great influence in the party; **causas respecto a las cuales nada puede el fabricante** causes over which the manufacturer has no control; **¿tú puedes con eso?** can you manage that?; **no puedo con él** I can't stand him; **no puedo con la maleta** I can't manage the case; **no puedo más** I've had enough; I can't go on any longer; I'm exhausted; **no puede ser** it's impossible; **a más no ~** to the utmost; as hard as possible, for all one is worth; **es terco a más no ~** he's utterly obstinate, he's as obstinate as they come; **comió a más no ~** he ate to excess; **me gusta el cine a más no ~** I'm passionately fond of the cinema; **no ~ menos de** + *infin* not to be able to help + *ger*; to have no alternative but to + *infin.*

(**d**) **puede que vaya** I may go, I might go; **puede que tenga uno ya** he may have one already; **puede que sí** it may be, maybe; **puede que sí, puede que no** maybe yes, maybe no.

(**e**) (*) **A le puede a B** A can beat B; A is tougher than B; A is more than a match for B.

(**f**) (*CAm, Méx**) to annoy, upset; **me pudo esa broma** that joke upset me; **su actitud me pudo** his attitude got on my nerves.

2 *nm* (**a**) (*fuerza*) power; (*autoridad*) authority; (*posesión*) possession; **~ adquisitivo, ~ de compra** purchasing power; **~ de convocatoria** drawing power; **~ de negociación** bargaining power; **~ de recuperación** resilience, recuperative power; **a ~ de** by dint of; **un partido jugado de ~ a ~** a hard-fought game; **bajo el ~ de** in the hands of; under the power of; **estar** (*u* **obrar**) **en ~ de** to be in the hands of, be in the possession of; **pasar a ~ de** to pass to, pass into the possession of; **el dinero es ~** money is power; **tiene ~ para arruinarnos** he has the power to ruin us; **esa droga no tiene ~ contra la enfermedad** that drug has no power (*o* is not effective) against the disease.

(**b**) (*Mec*) (*potencia*) power; strength; (*capacidad*) capacity; **el ~ del motor** the power of the engine; **tiene ~ para levantar X kilos** it has the power to lift X kilos.

(**c**) (*Pol etc*) power; authority; **~ absoluto** absolute power; **~ civil** civil power; **gobierno de ~ compartido** power-sharing government; **cuarto ~** fourth estate (*the Press*); **~ ejecutivo** executive power; **los ~es fácticos** the powers that be; **~ legislativo** legislative power; **~ negro** black power; **~es públicos** public authorities; **¡el pueblo al ~!** power to the people!; **¡Smith al ~!** Smith for leader!; **estar en el ~, ocupar el ~** to be in power.

(**d**) (*Jur*) power of attorney, proxy; **plenos ~es** full power, full authority (to act); **por ~(es)** by proxy.

(**e**) (*LAm*: persona*) drug pusher.
poderhabiente *nmf* (*Jur*) proxy; attorney (*US*).
poderío *nm* (**a**) (*gen*) power; (*fuerza*) might; (*señorío*) authority, jurisdiction. (**b**) (*Fin*) wealth.
poderosamente *adv* powerfully.
poderoso *adj* powerful.
podiatría *nf* podiatry.
podio *nm* podium; (*Méx*) rostrum; **estar en el ~ de la actualidad** to be in the limelight, be the centre of current interest.
pódium *nm*, *pl* **pódiums** = **podio.**
podología *nf* chiropody.
podólogo, -a *nm/f* chiropodist.
podómetro *nm* pedometer.
podón *nm* billhook.
podre *nf* pus.
podredumbre *nf* (**a**) (*Med*) pus; rotten part, rot.

(**b**) (*cualidad*) rottenness, putrefaction; (*fig*: *corrupción*) rottenness, decay, corruption; (*vino*) ~ **noble** noble rot.

(**c**) (*fig*: *tristeza*) secret sorrow, secret sadness.

podrido 1 *adj* (**a**) (*gen*) rotten, bad; (*putrefacto*) putrid.

(**b**) (*fig*) rotten, corrupt; **está ~ por dentro** he's rotten inside; **están ~s de dinero*** they're filthy rich*.

(**c**) (*Cono Sur**: *harto*) fed-up*.

2 podrida *nf*: **armar la ~** (*Cono Sur**) to start a fight.

podrir [3a] = **pudrir**.

poema *nm* (**a**) (*gen*) poem, (*esp*) long poem. (**b**) (*fig*) **fue todo un ~** it was just like a fairy tale; it was all terribly romantic; (*hum*) it was a proper farce.

poemario *nm* book of poems.

poemático *adj* poetic.

poesía *nf* (**a**) (*gen*) poetry; **la ~ del Siglo de Oro** Golden Age poetry. (**b**) (*una ~*) poem, (*esp*) short poem, lyric.

poeta *nmf* (**a**) (*gen*) poet. (**b**) (*LAm*) writer, author, literary person.

poetastro *nm* poetaster.

poética *nf* poetics, art of poetry, theory of poetry.

poéticamente *adv* poetically.

poético *adj* poetic(al).

poetisa *nf* poetess, (woman) poet.

poetizar [1f] **1** *vt* to poeticize; to idealize; to turn into poetry, make poetry out of. **2** *vi* to write poetry.

pogrom(o) *nm* pogrom.

póker *nm* (*Naipes*) poker.

polaco 1 *adj* Polish. **2** *nm*, **polaca** *nf* Pole. **3** *nm* (**a**) (*Ling*) Polish. (**b**) (*CAm‡*: *policía*) cop*. **4** *nf* (*And, Cono Sur*: *blusa*) smock.

polaina *nf* (**a**) (*sobrecalza*) gaiter, legging. (**b**) (*And, CAm, Cono Sur*) (*molestia*) annoyance; (*chasco*) setback.

polar *adj* polar.

polaridad *nf* polarity.

polarización *nf* polarization.

polarizar [1f] **1** *vt* to polarize. **2 polarizarse** *vr* to polarize (*en torno a* around).

polca *nf* (**a**) (*Mús*) polka. (**b**) (*And*) blouse; (*And, Cono Sur*) long jacket. (**c**) (*: *jaleo*) fuss, to-do*.

polcata* *nf* row, shindy*.

polea *nf* pulley; (*Aut*) fan belt; (*Náut*) tackle, tackle block.

poleada *nf* (*CAm*) *hot drink made of milk and flour*.

polémica *nf* (**a**) (*gen*) polemics. (**b**) (*una ~*) polemic, controversy.

polémico *adj* polemic(al); controversial.

polemista *nmf* polemicist; debater, controversialist.

polemizar [1f] *vi* to indulge in a polemic, argue (*en torno a* about); **no quiero ~** I have no wish to get involved in an argument; **~ con uno en la prensa** to have a debate with sb in the press.

polemología *nf* war studies.

polen *nm* pollen.

polenta *nf* (**a**) (*And, Cono Sur*) (*maicena*) cornflour; (*sémola de maíz*) ground maize, polenta. (**b**) **tener ~** (*entusiasta*) to be enthusiastic; (*de calidad*) to be first-rate.

polera *nf* (*Cono Sur*) (*jersey*) polo neck jersey; (*camiseta*) T-shirt.

poli* 1 *nm* bobby*, copper*, cop*. **2** *nf*: **la ~** the cops*.

poli... *pref* poly..., many ...

poliandria *nf* polyandry.

poliándrico *adj* polyandrous.

polibán *nm* hip-bath.

policía 1 *nm* policeman; **~ femenino** policewoman; **~ de paisano** plain-clothes policeman (*V t* **2**(**a**)).

2 *nf* (**a**) (*organización*) police; police force; **~ antidisturbios** riot police; **~ de barrio, ~ de manzana** neighbourhood police; **~ fluvial** river police; **~ militar** military police; **~ montada** mounted police; **P~ Municipal** local police; **P~ Nacional** national police; **~ paralela** force of undercover police; **~ secreta** secret police; **~ de tráfico, ~ de tránsito** (*LAm*) traffic police.

(**b**) (*persona*) policewoman.

(**c**) (*administración*) administration, (good) government; (*orden público*) public order.

(**d**) (*cortesía*) courtesy, politeness.

(**e**) (*limpieza*) cleanliness.

policiaco, policíaco *adj* police (*atr*); *V* **novela**.

policial 1 *adj* police (*atr*). **2** *nm* (*CAm*) policeman.

policlínico *nm* (*t* **hospital ~**) general hospital.

policromo *adj*, **polícromo** *adj* polychromatic; many-coloured, colourful.

Polichinela *nm* Punch.

polideportivo *nm* sports centre, sports complex; leisure centre.

poliedro *nm* polyhedron.

poliéster *nm* polyester.

poliestireno *nm* polystyrene.

polietileno *nm* polythene, polyethylene (*US*).

polifacético *adj persona, talento etc* many-sided, versatile.

polifacetismo *nm* many-sidedness, versatility.

Polifemo *nm* Polyphemus.

polifonía *nf* polyphony.

polifónico *adj* polyphonic.

polifuncional *adj* multifunctional, having many uses.

poligamia *nf* polygamy.

polígamo 1 *adj* polygamous. **2** *nm* polygamist.

poligénesis *nf* polygenesis.

poligloto, -a *nm/f* (*t* **polígloto** *nm*, **políglota** *nmf*) polyglot.

poligonal *adj* polygonal.

polígono *nm* (**a**) (*Mat*) polygon.

(**b**) (*Esp*) (*solar*) site (for development), building lot; (*zona*) area; (*viviendas*) housing estate; **~ de descongestión** overspill area; **~ industrial** industrial estate; **~ residencial** housing estate; **~ de tiro** shooting-range; firing range, artillery range.

polígrafo, -a *nm/f* writer on a wide variety of subjects.

poliinsaturado *adj* polyunsaturated.

polilla *nf* (*lepidóptero*) moth, (*esp*) clothes moth; (*oruga*) grub, destructive larva; (*de los libros*) bookworm.

polímata *nmf* polymath.

polimerización *nf* polymerization.

polímero *nm* polymer.

poli-mili *nmf* member of the political-military wing of ETA.

polimorfismo *nm* polymorphism.

polimorfo *adj* polymorphic.

Polinesia *nf* Polynesia.

polinesio, -a *adj, nm/f* Polynesian.

polínico *adj* pollen (*atr*).

polinización *nf* pollination; **~ cruzada** cross-pollination.

polinizar [1f] *vt* to pollinate.

polinosis *nf* hay fever.

polio *nf* polio.

poliomielitis *nf* poliomyelitis.

pólipo *nm* polyp, polypus.

Polisario [poli'sarjo] *nm* (*t* **El Frente ~**) *abr de* **Frente Popular de Liberación del Sáhara y Río de Oro**.

polisemia *nf* polysemy.

polisémico *adj* polysemic.

polisílabo 1 *adj* polysyllabic. **2** *nm* polysyllable.

polisón *nm* (**a**) bustle. (**b**) (*) bottom.

polista *nmf* polo player.

politeísmo *nm* polytheism.

politeísta *adj* polytheistic.

politene *nm*, **politeno** *nm* polythene, polyethylene (*US*).

política[1] *nf* (**a**) (*Pol*) politics; **~ de pasillo**(**s**) lobbying; **la ~ ruritana en la posguerra** postwar Ruritanian politics; **meterse** (*o* **mezclarse**) **en la ~** to go in for politics, get mixed up in politics.

(**b**) (*programa*) policy; **~ agraria** farming policy, agricultural policy; **~ de cañonera** gunboat diplomacy; **~ económica** economic policy; **~ exterior** foreign policy; **~ de ingresos y precios, ~ de jornales y precios** prices and incomes policy; **~ de mano dura** strong-arm policy, tough policy; **~ presupuestaria** budget policy; **~ de silla vacía** refusal to take one's seat (in parliament), **~ de tierra quemada** scorched earth policy.

(**c**) (*tacto*) tact, skill; (*cortesía*) politeness; (*educación*) good manners.

políticamente *adv* politically.

politicastro *nm* (*pey*) politician, politico.

político 1 *adj* (**a**) (*Pol*) political.

(**b**) (*diplomático*) politic; (*juicioso*) tactful, skilful; (*cortés*) polite, well-mannered, courteous.

(**c**) (*reservado*) stiff, reserved, stand-offish.

(**d**) (*pariente*) in-law, *p.ej.* **padre ~** father-in-law; **es tío ~ mío** he's an uncle of mine by marriage; *V* **familia** *etc*.

2 *nm*, **política**[2] *nf* politician; **~ de café** armchair politician.

politicón* *adj* (**a**) (*Pol*) strongly political, keenly interested in politics. (**b**) (*ceremonioso*) very ceremonious, obsequious.

politiquear [1a] *vi* to play at politics, dabble in politics; to talk politics.

politiqueo *nm*, **politiquería** *nf* (*pey*) party politics, the political game; political gossip.

politiquero, -a *nm/f* (*pey*) politician, party politician; political intriguer.

politiqués *nm* political jargon, special style of political journalese.

politiquillo, -a *nm/f* minor politician.

politización *nf* politicization.

politizar [1f] *vt* to politicize.

politología *nf* political science, study of politics.

politólogo, -a *nm/f* specialist in politics, political expert.

politraumatismo *nm* multiple injuries.

poliuretano *nm* polyurethane.

polivalente *adj* many-sided; multi-faceted; having diverse aspects, having diverse applications; *avión* multi-role; *edificio* multi-purpose.

póliza *nf* **(a)** (*certificado*) certificate, voucher; (*Fin: giro*) draft; (*Fin: de seguro*) insurance certificate; insurance policy; **~ dotal** endowment policy; **~ de seguro(s)** insurance policy; **pagar una ~** to pay out on an insurance.
(b) (*impuesto*) tax stamp, fiscal stamp.

polizón *nm* **(a)** (*vago*) tramp, vagrant, bum (*US*). **(b)** (*Aer, Náut, etc*) stowaway; **viajar de ~** to stow away (*en* on).

polizonte* *nm* bobby*, copper*.

polo[1] *nm* **(a)** (*Geog*) pole; **P~ Norte** North Pole; **P~ Sur** South Pole; **~ magnético** magnetic pole, magnetic north; **de ~ a ~** from pole to pole.
(b) (*Elec*) pole; (*borne*) terminal; (*de enchufe*) pin, point; **~ negativo** negative pole; **~ positivo** positive pole; **una clavija de 4 ~s** a 4-pin plug.
(c) (*fig: centro*) pole; focus, centre; **~ de atracción** focus of interest, centre of attraction; **los dos generales son ~s opuestos** the two generals are at opposite extremes; **esto es el ~ opuesto de lo que dijo antes** this is the exact opposite of what he said before.
(d) (*fig: Com etc*) **~ de desarrollo, ~ de promoción** growth point; development area.
(e) **~ helado** iced lolly*.

polo[2] *nm* (*Dep*) polo; **~ acuático** water polo.

polo[3] *nm* (*suéter*) polo-necked sweater; (*niki*) T-shirt.

polola *nf* (*Cono Sur*) (*coqueta*) flirt, flirtatious girl; (*amiga*) girlfriend.

pololear [1a] (*And, Cono Sur*) **1** *vt* (*pretender*) to court; (*coquetear con*) to flirt with. **2** *vi* (*coquetear*) to flirt (*con* with); (*tener relación fija*) to be going steady* (*con* with); (*salir*) to go out together, date*.

pololeo *nm* (*And, Cono Sur*) **(a)** courting; flirting; dating*.
(b) (*chapuza*) small job, odd job.

pololo *nm* (*Cono Sur*) **(a)** (*Ent*) buzzing insect. **(b)** (*soso*) bore, tedious person; (*coqueto*) flirt; (*amigo*) boyfriend; (*pretendiente*) (persistent) suitor. **(c)** (*chulo*) pimp.

polonesa *nf* polonaise.

Polonia *nf* Poland.

poltrón *adj* idle, lazy.

poltrona *nf* **(a)** easy chair; (*del presidente*) director's chair. **(b)** (‡) cushy number‡, soft job.

poltronear [1a] *vi* (*Cono Sur, Méx*) to loaf around.

polución *nf* **(a)** pollution; **~ de la atmósfera** air pollution. **(b)** **~ nocturna** (*Esp*) nocturnal emission, wet dream.

polucionante *adj* polluting.

polucionar [1a] *vt* to pollute.

polvareda *nf* **(a)** (*polvo*) dust cloud, cloud of dust. **(b)** (*fig*) storm, fuss, rumpus; **levantar una ~** to create a storm (*o* a stir).

polvata** *nm* = **polvo (d)**.

polvera *nf* **(a)** (*gen*) powder compact, vanity case. **(b)** (*Méx*) = **polvareda.**

polvero *nm* **(a)** (*LAm*) = **polvareda. (b)** (*CAm*) handkerchief.

polvete‡ *nm* = **polvo (d)**.

polvillo *nm* **(a)** (*And, Cono Sur Agr*) blight. **(b)** (*And, Cono Sur*) tobacco refuse. **(c)** (*CAm*) leather for shoemaking. **(d)** (*And*) rice bran.

polvo *nm* **(a)** (*gen*) dust; **lleno de ~** dusty; dust-covered; **limpiar un mueble de ~, quitar el ~ de** (*o* **a**) **un mueble** to dust a piece of furniture; **hacer algo ~** to smash sth, ruin sth; **hacer ~ a uno** to shatter sb; to wear sb out; to depress sb; (*en discusión*) to flatten sb, crush sb; **estoy hecho ~** I'm worn out; **hacer morder el ~ a** to humiliate, crush; **matar el ~** to lay the dust; **sacudir el ~ a uno** to thrash sb; to beat sb up*; **aquellos ~s traen estos lodos** such are the consequences.
(b) (*Quím, Culin, Med etc*) powder (*frec* **~s**); (*: *droga*) cocaine, heroin; **~s** (*esp*) face-powder; **~(s) de arroz** rice powder; **~s de blanqueo** bleaching-powder; **~s de chile** chili powder; **~(s) de hornear, ~(s) de levadura** baking-powder; **~ dentífrico, ~s para dientes** tooth powder; **~s de picapica** itching powder; **~s de talco** talcum powder; **en ~** powdered, in powdered form; **ponerse ~s** to powder one's face.
(c) (*porción*) pinch; **un ~ de rapé** a pinch of snuff.
(d) (*Esp***) screw**; **echar un ~** to have a screw**; **está para un ~, tiene mucho ~** she's hot stuff‡.

pólvora *nf* **(a)** (*Mil*) gunpowder; **~ de algodón** guncotton; **no ha descubierto** (*o* **inventado**) **la ~** he'll never set the Thames (*o* world) on fire; **gastar la ~ en salvas** to waste time and energy; to make empty gestures; to make a great song and dance; **levantar ~** to make a stir; **oler a ~** to smell fishy*; **propagarse como la ~** to spread like wildfire.
(b) (*fuegos artificiales*) fireworks.
(c) (*fig: mal genio*) bad temper, crossness.
(d) (*fig: viveza*) life, liveliness.

polvorear [1a] *vt* to powder, dust, sprinkle (*de* with).

polvoriento *adj* **(a)** *superficie etc* dusty. **(b)** *sustancia* powdery.

polvorilla* *nmf* touchy person, bad-tempered person, grouch*.

polvorín *nm* **(a)** (*pólvora*) fine gunpowder.
(b) (*Mil*) powder magazine; (*fig*) powder-keg.
(c) (*Cono Sur: insecto*) gnat.
(d) (*Cono Sur, Méx*) = **polvorilla.**
(e) (*And, Carib: polvareda*) cloud of dust.

polvorón *nm* shortbread; (*LAm*) cake.

polvorosa* *nf* road; **poner pies en ~** to beat it*.

polvoroso *adj* dusty.

polvoso *adj* (*CAm*) = **polvoriento.**

polla *nf* **(a)** (*Orn*) pullet; chick; **~ de agua** moorhen.
(b) (*Naipes*) pool, kitty; (*And, CAm, Cono Sur*) stakes, pool; (*Cono Sur: lotería*) lottery.
(c) (*Esp*‡: *chica*) chick, bird‡.
(d) (*Esp***) prick**; **¡una ~!** get away!*; **¡ni qué ~s!** no way!*; **¿qué ~s quiere?** what the hell does he want?

pollaboba‡ *nm* berk‡, wimp*.

pollada *nf* (*Orn*) brood.

pollastre* *nm* = **pollo (b)**.

pollastro* *nm*, **pollastrón*** *nm* sly fellow.

pollera *nf* **(a)** (*criadero*) hencoop; (*gallinero*) chicken run; (*cesto*) basket for chickens. **(b)** (*And, Cono Sur*) skirt; (*Cono Sur Ecl*) soutane. **(c)** (*aparato*) walker.

pollería *nf* poulterer's (shop).

pollero *nm* **(a)** (*gen*) chicken farmer; poulterer. **(b)** (*LAm*) gambler. **(c)** (*Méx*) guide for illegal immigrants (to USA).

pollerudo *adj* (*Cono Sur*) **(a)** (*cobarde*) cowardly; (*chismoso*) backbiting, gossipy. **(b)** (*santurrón*) self-righteous, sanctimonious.

pollino, -a *nm/f* **(a)** donkey. **(b)** (*) ass, idiot.

pollita *nf* **(a)** young pullet. **(b)** **echar ~s** to tell lies.

pollito *nm* **(a)** (*Orn*) chick; **~ de un día** day-old chick. **(b)** (*) = **pollo (b)**.

pollo *nm* **(a)** (*Orn*) chicken; chick, young bird; (*Culin*) chicken; **~ asado** roast chicken; **echarse el ~** (*Cono Sur*) to pack up and go; **¡qué duquesa ni qué ~s en vinagre!*** duchess my foot!*; **¡ni eso ni ~s en vinagre!*** no way!*
(b) (*Esp**) (*joven*) young man; (*señorito*) elegant youth, playboy; **~ pera*** dandy; (*chanchullero*) spiv*, flash Harry*; **¿quién es ese ~?** who is that chap?*; **es un ~ nada más** he's only a youngster.
(c) (*Esp*‡: *esputo*) spittle, spit; **soltar un ~** to spit.
(d) (*Méx*) (would-be) illegal immigrant (to USA).

polluelo *nm* chick.

pom *nm* (*CAm*) incense.

poma *nf* **(a)** (*fig*) apple. **(b)** (*frasco*) scent bottle; (*Cono Sur*) small flask; (*And*) carafe. **(c)** (*Méx*) pumice (stone).

pomada *nf* **(a)** (*gen*) pomade, ointment; **estar en la ~*** (*metido*) to be mixed up in it, be involved; (*al tanto*) to be in the know.
(b) **la ~**‡ the cream, the top people, the nobs‡.
(c) **hacer algo ~** (*Cono Sur**) to break sth to bits.

pomar *nm* apple orchard.

pomelo *nm* **(a)** (*Esp*) grapefruit, pomelo. **(b)** (*Anat**) bottom, backside.

pómez *nf*: **piedra ~** pumice (stone).

pomo *nm* **(a)** (*Bot*) pome, fruit with pips. **(b)** (*frasco*) scent bottle. **(c)** (*de espada*) pommel; (*de puerta*) round knob, handle. **(d)** (*And*) powder-puff.

pompa *nf* **(a)** (*burbuja*) bubble; **~ de jabón** soap bubble.
(b) (*Náut*) pump. **(c)** (*fausto*) pomp, splendour; (*ostentación*) show, display; procession; (*boato*) pageant, pageantry; **~s fúnebres** funeral ceremony; funeral procession; **'P~s fúnebres'** 'Undertaker', 'Funeral Parlour'.

Pompeya *nf* Pompeii.

Pompeyo *nm* Pompey.
pompis* *nm invar* bottom, behind*.
pompo *adj* (*And*) blunt.
pomposamente *adv* splendidly, magnificently; majestically; (*pey*) pompously.
pomposidad *nf* splendour, magnificence; majesty; (*pey*) pomposity.
pomposo *adj* splendid, magnificent; majestic; (*pey*) pompous.
pómulo *nm* (*hueso*) cheekbone; (*mejilla*) cheek.
Poncio Pilato *nm* Pontius Pilate.
ponchada¹ *nf* bowlful of punch.
ponchada²* *nf* (*Cono Sur*) large quantity, large amount; **costó una ~** it cost a bomb*.
ponchadura *nf* (*Méx*) puncture.
ponchar [1a] **1** *vt* (*Carib, Méx*) (**a**) *billete** to punch. (**b**) *neumático* to puncture. **2** *vi* (*LAm**: *resistir*) to chafe at the bit.
ponche *nm* punch.
ponchera *nf* (**a**) (*para ponche*) punch bowl. (**b**) (*And, Carib, Méx*: *palangana*) washbasin; (*And*: *bañera*) bath. (**c**) (*Cono Sur**: *barriga*) paunch, beer gut*.
poncho¹ *adj* (**a**) (*vago*) lazy, indolent; (*tranquilo*) quiet, peaceable. (**b**) (*And*: *gordito*) chubby.
poncho² *nm* (**a**) (*LAm*) (*prenda*) poncho; (*frazada*) blanket. (**b**) (*fig*) **los de a ~** (*And**) the poor; **arrastrar el ~** (*LAm**) to be looking (*o* spoiling) for a fight; **estar a ~** (*And**) to be in the dark; **pisarle el ~ a uno** (*And*) to humiliate sb; **pisarse el ~** (*Cono Sur**) to be mistaken.
ponderación *nf* (**a**) (*contrapeso*) weighing, consideration; (*cuidado*) deliberation. (**b**) (*exageración*) high praise; **está sobre toda ~** it is too good for words. (**c**) (*Estadística*) weighting. (**d**) (*calma*) calmness, steadiness, balance.
ponderado *adj* (**a**) *carácter* calm, steady, balanced. (**b**) (*Estadística*) weighted; **media ponderada** weighted average.
ponderar [1a] *vt* (**a**) (*considerar*) to weigh up, consider.
(**b**) (*elogiar*) to praise highly, speak in praise of; **~ algo a uno** to speak warmly of sth to sb, tell sb how good sth is; **le ponderan de inteligente** they speak highly of his intelligence.
(**c**) (*Estadística*) to weight.
ponedero *nm* nest, nesting box.
ponedora *adj*: **gallina ~** laying hen, hen in lay; **ser buena ~** to be a good layer.
ponencia *nf* (**a**) (*comunicación*) (learned) paper, communication; report. (**b**) (*persona*) rapporteur.
ponente *nmf* speaker (*at a conference*), person giving a paper.
poner [2q] **1** *vt* (**a**) (*gen*) to put; (*colocar*) to place, set; *ropa, sombrero* to put on; *cuidado* to take, exercise (*en* in); *objeción* to raise; *mesa* to lay, set; (*Com*) *escaparate* to dress, arrange; *énfasis* to place (*en* on); **~ algo a secar al sol** to put sth (out) to dry in the sun; **~ la experiencia al servicio de** to put one's experience at the disposal of; **~ algo como ejemplo** to give (*o* quote) sth as an example, use sth as an illustration; **~ a uno por testigo** to cite sb as a witness; **~ algo en duda** to cast doubt on sth, call sth in question; **~ algo aparte** to put sth aside, put sth on one side.
(**b**) *huevo* to lay.
(**c**) *reloj etc* to adjust, set (right); **pone el reloj por esa campana** he sets his watch by that bell.
(**d**) *radio etc* to switch on, turn on, put on; **ponlo más fuerte** turn it up.
(**e**) *carta, telegrama* to send (*a* to).
(**f**) *problema* to set; *impuesto, multa* to impose (*a* on); *tarea* to give, assign (*a* to); **nos pone mucho trabajo** he gives us a lot of work.
(**g**) *tienda* to open, set up, establish; *casa* to fit up, equip; **han puesto la casa con todo lujo** they have fitted the house up most luxuriously.
(**h**) *dinero* to contribute, subscribe, give; (*en el juego*) to stake; (*Fin*) to put, invest; (*fig*) to contribute; *tiempo* to put, give; **yo pongo el dinero pero ella escoge** I put up the money but she chooses; **he puesto 5 minutos en firmarlo** it took me 5 minutes to sign it; **esto no pone nada para la solución del problema** this does not contribute at all towards solving the problem.
(**i**) *nombre* to give; **al niño le pusieron Luis** they called the child Louis; **¿qué nombre le van a ~?** what are they going to call him?, what name are they giving him?
(**j**) **~ a uno de cochino** to call sb a swine*.
(**k**) (*añadir*) to add; **pongo 3 más para llegar a 100** I'll add 3 more to make it 100.
(**l**) (*Teat*) *obra* to put on, do, perform; *película* to show, put on; to screen; **¿qué ponen en el cine?** what's on at the cinema?
(**m**) *emoción, miedo etc* to cause; **me pone miedo** it frightens me, it scares me.
(**n**) *lengua, palabras etc* to translate, put (*en* into); **puso el discurso en alemán** he translated the speech into German.
(**o**) (*suponer*) to suppose; **pongamos 120** let's say 120, let's put it at 120; **pongamos que ...** let us suppose that ...; **poniendo que ...** supposing that ... assuming that ...
(**p**) (*Telec*) **~ a X con Y** to connect X to Y, give X a line to Y; **póngame con el conserje** get me the porter, put me through to the porter; **le pongo en seguida** I'm trying to connect you.
(**q**) (*conciliar*) **~ a P bien con Q** to reconcile P and Q, make things up between P and Q; **~ a Z mal con A** to cause a rift between Z and A, make Z fall out with A.
(**r**) (+ *adj*) to make, turn; **si añades eso lo pones azul** if you add that you turn it blue; **la medicina le puso bueno** the medicine made him better; **la has puesto colorada** now you've made her blush; **para no ~le de mal humor** so as not to make him cross.
(**s**) **~ a uno a** + *infin* to set sb to + *infin*; to start sb + *ger*.
(**t**) (*en colocación*) **puso a su hija de sirvienta** she got her daughter a job as a servant; **puso a sus hijos a trabajar** she sent her children out to work; *V* **aprendiz**; *para otros usos y muchas locuciones, V el n.*
(**u**) **¡no pongo ni una!** (*Carib**) I just can't get it right!
2 *vi* (**a**) (*Orn*) to lay, lay eggs.
(**b**) **no pongo a la lotería** I don't go in for the lottery, I don't invest in the lottery.
3 ponerse *vr* (**a**) (*gen*) to put o.s., place o.s.; **se ponía debajo de la ventana** he used to stand under the window; *V* **cómodo** *etc.*
(**b**) **~ un traje** to put a suit on.
(**c**) **~ de barro** to get covered in mud.
(**d**) **~ de conserje** to take a job as a porter.
(**e**) **~ a** (*lugar*), **~ en** to reach, get to, arrive at; **en 2 horas se puso a su lado** in 2 hours he reached her side, in 2 hours he was at her side.
(**f**) (*sol etc*) to set.
(**g**) **~ delante** (*estorbar*) to get in the way; (*intervenir*) to intercede, intervene; (*dificultad*) to arise, come up; **destruye al que se le pone delante** he destroys anyone who gets in his way.
(**h**) **~ a bien con uno** to get on good terms with sb, (*pey*) get in with sb; **~ a mal con uno** to get on the wrong side of sb.
(**i**) **~ con uno** (*reñir*) to quarrel with sb; (*oponerse*) to oppose sb; (*competir*) to compete with sb, play (against) sb.
(**j**) (+ *adj*) to turn, get, become; **se puso serio** he became serious; **en el agua se pone verde** it turns green in the water; **¡no te pongas así!** don't be like that!; *V* **furioso** *etc.*
(**k**) **~ a** + *infin* to begin to + *infin*, set about + *ger*; to proceed to + *infin*; **se pusieron a gritar** they started to shout.
(**l**) **ponérselos a*** to be unfaithful to.
(**m**) (‡) to get high‡.
(**n**) (*LAm*) **se me pone que ...** it seems to me that ...
(**o**) **~ al teléfono** to go on the phone, go to the phone.
poney ['poni] *nm, pl* **poneys** ['ponis] pony.
ponga, pongo¹ *etc V* **poner.**
pongaje *nm* (*And, Cono Sur*) *domestic service which Indian tenants are obliged to give free.*
pongo² *nm* orang-outang.
pongo³ *nm* (*And, Cono Sur*) (**a**) (*criado*) Indian servant, Indian tenant. (**b**) (*Geog*) ravine.
poni *nm* pony.
ponible *adj vestido* wearable.
poniente 1 *adj* west, western. **2** *nm* (**a**) (*oeste*) west. (**b**) (*viento*) west wind.
ponja‡ (*And*) *adj, nmf* Jap*.
p.º n.º *nm abr de* **peso neto** net weight, nt. wt.
pontaje *nm*, **pontazgo** *nm* toll.
pontevedrés (*Esp*) **1** *adj* of Pontevedra. **2** *nm*, **pontevedresa** *nf* native (*o* inhabitant) of Pontevedra; **los pontevedreses** the people of Pontevedra.
pontificado *nm* papacy, pontificate.
pontifical *adj* papal, pontifical.

pontificar [1g] *vi* to pontificate (*t fig*).
pontífice *nm* pope, pontiff; **el Sumo P~** His Holiness the Pope.
pontificio *adj* papal, pontifical.
pontón *nm* (**a**) (*de puente etc*) pontoon; (*Aer: de hidroavión*) float. (**b**) (*puente*: *t* ~ **flotante**) pontoon bridge; bridge of planks. (**c**) (*Náut*) converted ship.
pony ['poni] *nm, pl* **ponys** ['ponis] pony.
ponzoña *nf* poison, venom; (*fig*) poison.
ponzoñoso *adj* poisonous, venomous; (*fig*) *ataque etc* venomous; *propaganda* poisonous; *costumbre, idea etc* harmful.
pool [pul] *nm, pl* **pools** [pul] (*Fin*) consortium.
pop 1 *adj* pop. **2** *nm* (**a**) (*Mús*) pop, pop music. (**b**) (*Arte*) pop artist. **3** *interj* bingo!*
popa *nf* (**a**) (*Náut*) stern; **a** ~ astern, abaft; **de** ~ **a proa** fore and aft, from stem to stern. (**b**) (‡: *culo*) stern‡, bottom.
popar [1a] *vt* (**a**) *niño etc* to spoil; (*fig*) to make a fuss of, flatter. (**b**) (*mofarse de*) to scorn, jeer at.
pope *nm* (**a**) (*Ecl*) priest of the Orthodox Church. (**b**) (*: *líder espiritual*) guru, spiritual leader; idol.
popelín *nm*, **popelina** *nf*, **poplín** *nm* (*LAm*) poplin.
popería* *nf* pop fans (*collectively*).
popero* 1 *adj*: **música popera** pop music. **2** *nm*, **popera** *nf* pop fan.
popi* 1 *adj* pop. **2** *nmf* pop fan.
popó‡ *nm* bottom, bum‡.
poporo *nm* (**a**) (*And, Carib: bulto*) bump, swelling. (**b**) (*Carib: porra*) truncheon, nightstick (*US*).
popote *nm* (*Méx*) (*tallo*) long thin stem; (*hierba*) tough grass used for making brooms; (*paja*) drinking-straw.
populachería *nf* cheap popularity, playing to the gallery.
populachero *adj* (*plebeyo*) common, vulgar; (*chabacano*) cheap; *discurso, política* rabble-rousing; *político* demagogic, who appeals to the lower orders, who plays to the gallery.
populacho *nm* populace, plebs, mob.
popular *adj* (**a**) (*ampliamente aceptado etc*) popular. (**b**) (*del pueblo*) *palabra etc* colloquial; *cultura etc* of the people; folk (*atr*).
popularidad *nf* popularity.
popularización *nf* popularization.
popularizar [1f] **1** *vt* to popularize. **2 popularizarse** *vr* to become popular.
populismo *nm* populism; populist policies.
populista *adj, nmf* populist.
populoso *adj* populous.
popurrí *nm* potpourri.
poquedad *nf* (**a**) (*escasez*) scantiness, paucity; (*pequeñez*) smallness; (*poca cantidad*) fewness. (**b**) (*una* ~) small thing, trifle; small quantity. (**c**) (*fig: timidez*) timidity.
póquer *nm* poker.
poquísimo *adj* (**a**) (*sing*) very little; hardly any, almost no. (**b**) (*pl*) **~s** very few, terribly few.
poquitín *nm* a little bit.
poquito *nm* (**a**) **un** ~ a little bit (*de* of); (*adv*) a little, a bit. (**b**) **a ~s** bit by bit; in dribs and drabs; **¡~ a poco!** gently!, easy there!
por *prep* (**a**) (+ *infin*) in order to; ~ **no llegar tarde** in order not to be late, so as not to arrive late; **lo hizo** ~ **complacerle** he did it to please her; **hablar ~ hablar** to talk just for talking's sake; **moverse** ~ **no estar quieto** to move about simply so as to have a change from sitting still; *V t* (**c**).

(**b**) (*objetivo*) for; **luchar** ~ **la patria** to fight for one's country; **trabajar** ~ **dinero** to work for money; **su amor** ~ **la pintura** his love for painting; **hazlo** ~ **mí** do it for me, do it for my sake; (**sí,**) **¿~?** (*LAm*) (yes,) why?, why do you ask?

(**c**) (*causa*) out of, because of, from; **fue** ~ **necesidad** it was from (*o* out of, because of) necessity; ~ **temor** from fear; ~ **temor a** for fear of; **lo hago** ~ **gusto** I do it because I like to; **no se realizó** ~ **escasez de fondos** it was not put into effect because of lack of money; ~ **venir tarde perdió la mitad** through coming late he missed half of it; **se hundió** ~ **mal construido** it collapsed because it was badly built; **le expulsaron** ~ **revoltoso** they expelled him as a troublemaker; **lo dejó** ~ **imposible** he gave it up as (being) impossible.

(**d**) (*evidencia*) ~ **lo que dicen** from what they say, judging by what they say; ~ **las señas no piensa hacerlo** judging by the signs he's not intending to do it.

(**e**) (*en cuanto a*) ~ **mí, que se vaya** so far as I'm concerned (*o* for myself, for my part) he can go.

(**f**) (*agente*) by; ~ **su propia mano** by his own hand; ~ **correo** by post, through the post; ~ **mar** by sea, by boat; ~ **sí mismo** by o.s.; **hablar** ~ **señas** to talk by signs, communicate by means of signs; **lo obtuve** ~ **medio de un amigo** I got it through a friend, I got it with the help of a friend.

(**g**) (*Mat*) **7** ~ **2 son 14** twice 7 is 14; **7** ~ **5 son 35** 5 times 7 is 35.

(**h**) (*modo*) in; by; (*según*) according to; ~ **centenares** by the hundred, by hundreds; ~ **orden** in order; **están dispuestos** ~ **tamaños** they are arranged according to size (*o* by sizes, in sizes); **punto** ~ **punto** point by point; **día** ~ **día** day by day.

(**i**) (*lugar*) by, by way of; (*a través de*) through; (*a lo largo de*) along; **ir a Bilbao** ~ **Santander** to go to Bilbao via Santander; ~ **el lado izquierdo** on (*o* along) the left side; **cruzar la frontera** ~ **Canfranc** to cross the frontier at Canfranc; ~ **la calle** along the street; ~ **la caña** through the pipe, along the pipe; ~ **todo el país** over the whole country, throughout the country; **llevar periódicos** ~ **las casas** to deliver papers round the houses; **pasar** ~ **Madrid** to pass through Madrid; to go via Madrid; **pasearse** ~ **el parque** to walk round the park, stroll through the park.

(**j**) (*tiempo*) ~ **la mañana** in the morning; during the morning; **no sale** ~ **la noche** he doesn't go out at night.

(**k**) (*presente y futuro*) for; **se quedarán** ~ **15 días** they will stay for a fortnight; **será** ~ **poco tiempo** it won't be for long.

(**l**) (*a cambio de*) for, in exchange for; **te doy éste** ~ **aquél** I'll swap you this one for that one; **le dieron uno nuevo** ~ **el viejo** they gave him a new one (in exchange) for the old one; **se vendió** ~ **15 dólares** it was sold for 15 dollars; **me dieron 13 francos** ~ **una libra** they gave me 13 francs for a pound; **ha puesto B** ~ **V** he has put B instead of V.

(**m**) (*de parte de*) **vino** ~ **su jefe** he came instead of (*o* in place of) his boss; **interceder** ~ **uno** to intercede for sb, intercede on sb's behalf; **hablo** ~ **todos** I speak on behalf of (*o* in the name of) everybody.

(**n**) (*como*) **contar a uno** ~ **amigo** to count sb as a friend; **no se admite** ~ **válido** it is not accepted as valid; *V* **tener, tomar** *etc.*

(**o**) (*razón*) **10 dólares** ~ **hora** 10 dollars an hour; **revoluciones** ~ **minuto** revolutions per minute; *V* **persona** *etc.*

(**p**) (*indicación aproximativa*) **eso está allá** ~ **el norte** that's somewhere up in the north; ~ **la feria** about carnival time, round about the carnival; *V* **fecha, Navidad** *etc.*

(**q**) ~ **difícil que sea** however hard it is, however hard it may be; ~ **mucho que lo quisieran** however much they would like to; *V* **más 1** (**e**).

(**r**) **ir a** ~ **uno** (*Esp*: buscar*) to go for sb, go and fetch sb; (*atacar*) to attack sb, go for sb; **¡a** ~ **ellos!** after them!, get them!; *V* **venir** ~ *etc.*

(**s**) ~ **qué** why; **¿~ qué?** why?
porcachón* *adj* filthy, dirty.
porcada* *nf* = **porquería.**
porcallón* *adj* filthy, dirty.
porcelana *nf* (*sustancia*) porcelain; (*loza*) china, chinaware; **tienda de** ~ china shop.
porcentaje *nm* percentage; proportion, ratio; rate; **un elevado** ~ **de** a high percentage of, a high proportion of; ~ **de accesos** (*Inform*) hit rate; **el** ~ **de defunciones** the death-rate; **trabajar a** ~ to work on a percentage basis.
porcentual *adj* percentage (*atr*).
porcentualmente *adv* in percentage terms, percentagewise; proportionately.
Porcia *nf* Portia.
porcino 1 *adj* porcine; pig (*atr*); **ganado** ~ pigs. **2** *nm* (**a**) (*animales*) pigs; (*lechón*) young pig; **carne de** ~ pork; pigmeat. (**b**) (*Med*) bump, swelling.
porción *nf* (**a**) (*gen*) portion; (*parte*) part, share; (*en recetas etc*) quantity, amount, part; (*de chocolate etc*) piece, segment; **una** ~ **de patatas** a helping of potatoes.

(**b**) **una** ~ **de** (*fig*) a number of; **tengo una** ~ **de cosas que hacer** I have a number of things to do; **tuvimos una** ~ **de problemas** we had quite a few problems.
porcuno *adj* pig (*atr*).
porche *nm* (**a**) (*tiendas etc*) arcade (*of shops, round square etc*). (**b**) (*de casa*) porch.
pordiosear [1a] *vi* to beg (*t fig*).
pordiosero, -a *nm/f* beggar.
porende *adv* (†† *o liter*) hence, therefore.

porfa* *interj* please.

porfía *nf* (**a**) (*persistencia*) persistence; (*terquedad*) obstinacy, stubbornness. (**b**) (*disputa*) dispute; (*contienda*) continuous struggle, continuous competition. (**c**) **a ~** in competition.

porfiadamente *adv* persistently; obstinately, stubbornly.

porfiado 1 *adj* (*insistente*) persistent; (*terco*) obstinate, stubborn. **2** *nm* (*LAm*) doll; manikin, dummy.

porfiar [1c] *vi* (*persistir*) to persist, insist; (*disputar*) to argue stubbornly, doggedly maintain one's point of view; **~ con uno** to argue with sb; **~ en algo** to persist in sth; **porfía en que es así** he insists that it is so, he will have it that it is so; **~ por** + *infin* to struggle obstinately to + *infin*.

pórfido *nm* porphyry.

porfión *adj* dogged, stubborn.

porfirismo *nm* porphyria.

porfirista *nmf* (*Méx*) supporter of Porfirio Díaz.

pormenor *nm* detail, particular.

pormenorizadamente *adv* in detail.

pormenorizado *adj* detailed.

pormenorizar [1f] **1** *vt* (*detallar*) to detail, set out in detail; (*particularizar*) to particularize; to describe in detail. **2** *vi* to go into detail, particularize.

porno* **1** *adj invar* porno*, pornographic. **2** *nm* porn*, pornography; **~ blando** soft porn; **~ duro** hard porn.

pornografía *nf* pornography.

pornográfico *adj* pornographic.

pornografista *nmf* pornographer.

poro¹ *nm* (*Anat*) pore.

poro² *nm* (*Méx*) leek.

poronga‡‡ *nf* (*Cono Sur*) prick‡‡, cock‡‡.

porongo *nm* (*Cono Sur*) gourd, calabash; (*fig*) nobody.

pororó *nm* (*Cono Sur*) popcorn.

porosidad *nf* porousness, porosity.

poroso *adj* porous.

porotal *nm* (*LAm*) (**a**) (*gen*) beanfield, bean patch. (**b**) (*fig*) **un ~ de*** a lot of, a whole heap of.

poroto *nm* (**a**) (*And, Cono Sur*) kidney bean; **~ verde** green bean, runner bean; **~s*** food, grub‡; **ganarse los ~** to earn one's daily bread; **no valer un ~** to be worthless. (**b**) (*Cono Sur*: *punto*) point; **anotarse un ~*** to make it. (**c**) (*Cono Sur**) (*niño*) kid*; (*débil*) weakling.

porpuesto *nm* (*Carib*) minibus, taxi.

porque *conj* (**a**) (+ *indic*) because; since, for. (**b**) (+ *subj*) so that, in order that.

porqué *nm* (**a**) (*motivo*) reason (*de* for), cause (*de* of); the whys and wherefores; **el ~ de la revolución** the factors that underlie the revolution; **'El ~ de los dichos'** 'Origins of our Sayings'; **no tengo ~ ir** there's no reason I should go.

(**b**) (*Fin*) amount, portion; **tiene mucho ~** he's got plenty of the ready*.

porquería *nf* (**a**) (*sustancia*) filth, muck, dirt; **me lo devolvieron cubierto de ~** they gave it back to me filthy all over; **estar hecho una ~** to be covered in muck, be dirty all over.

(**b**) (*cualidad*) nastiness; indecency.

(**c**) (*objeto*) small thing, trifle; **~s** old things, junk, lumber; **le regalaron alguna ~** they gave her some worthless present; **lo vendieron por una ~** they sold it for next to nothing.

(**d**) (*acto*) dirty trick, mean action; indecent act; **me han hecho una ~** they've played a dirty trick on me.

(**e**) (*Culin*) nasty food, awful meal; attractive but unwholesome dish.

(**f**) (*fig*: *basura*) rubbish; **una película de ~** (*LAm*) a rotten film*; **la novela es una ~** the novel is just rubbish; **escribió 3 ó 4 ~s** he wrote 3 or 4 rubbishy books.

porqueriza *nf* pigsty.

porquerizo *nm*, **porquero** *nm* pigman.

porra *nf* (**a**) (*palo*) stick, club, cudgel; (*de policía*) truncheon; (*Téc*) large hammer; (*Culin*) large club-shaped fritter; (‡: *nariz*) conk‡, nose; (‡‡: *pene*) prick‡‡.

(**b**) (*: *pesado*) bore.

(**c**) (*: *fachenda*) swank*, conceit; **gasta mucha ~** he's got loads of swank*.

(**d**) (*: *locuciones*) **¡~s!** bother!, dash it!*; (*a otro*) rubbish!; **¡una ~!** never!, no way!*; **¡a la ~!** (*fuera*) get out!, (*no hay tal*) no way!*, rubbish!; **¡a la ~ el ministro!** the minister can go to blazes!*; **mandar a uno a la ~** to chuck sb out, send sb packing; **¡vete a la ~!** go to blazes!*; **¡qué coche ni qué ~s!** car my foot!

(**e**) (*And, Cono Sur*: *mechón*) curl, forelock.

(**f**) (*CAm, Méx*: *Pol*: *pandilla*) political gang.

(**g**) (*Méx*) (*Dep*) fans; (*Teat*) claque.

(**h**) (*CAm*: *olla*) metal cooking-pot.

(**i**) (*juego*) sweep, sweepstake.

porracear* [1a] *vt* (*Carib, Méx*) to beat up.

porrada *nf* (**a**) (*porrazo*) thwack, thump, blow. (**b**) (*: *montón*) pile*, heap*; lot; **una ~ de** a whole heap of*, a lot of; **a ~s** in abundance, galore.

porrata‡ *nmf* pot smoker.

porrazo *nm* (**a**) (*golpe*) thwack, thump, blow; (*al caer*) bump. (**b**) **de ~** (*LAm*) in one go, at one blow; **de golpe y ~** suddenly.

porrear [1a] *vi* (**a**) (*machacar*) to go on and on, harp on a theme. (**b**) (‡: *droga*) to smoke pot‡.

porrería* *nf* (**a**) (*petición*) annoying request, footling demand. (**b**) (*necedad*) stupidity.

porrero‡, **-a** *nm/f* pot smoker‡.

porreta *nf* (**a**) (*Bot*) green leaf. (**b**) **en ~(s)*** stark naked.

porretada *nf* = **porrada** (**b**).

porrillo: **a ~** *adv* in abundance, by the ton.

porro* **1** *adj* stupid, oafish. **2** *nm* (**a**) idiot, oaf. (**b**) (*Esp*‡: *canuto*) joint‡; (*droga*) hash*. (**c**) (*And, Carib*: *baile*) *a folk dance*.

porrón¹ *adj* (*lerdo*) slow, stupid; (*soso*) dull; (*torpe*) sluggish.

porrón² *nm wine jar with a long spout*; **un ~ de*** a lot of; **me gusta un ~** I like it a lot.

porrón³ *nm* (*Orn*) pochard.

porrudo *adj* (**a**) (*abultado*) big, bulging. (**b**) (*Cono Sur*: *melenudo*) long-haired. (**c**) (*Cono Sur*) (*engreído*) big-headed.

porsiacaso *nm* (*Cono Sur*) knapsack.

port. *abr de* **portugués** Portuguese, Port.

porta *nf* (*Náut*) port, porthole.

porta(a)viones *nm invar* aircraft-carrier.

portabebés *nm invar* baby-carrier.

portabilidad *nf* portability.

portable 1 *adj* portable. **2** *nm* portable computer.

portabultos *nm invar* carrier.

portabustos *nm invar* (*Méx*) brassière, bra*.

portacargas *nm invar* (*caja*) crate; (*de bicicleta etc*) carrier.

portación *nf*: **~ de armas** carrying (of) a weapon.

portacoches *nm invar* car transporter.

portacontenedores *nm invar* container ship.

portacubiertos *nm invar* knifebox, cutlery box.

portacheques *nm invar* chequebook.

portada *nf* (**a**) (*Arquit*) main front; (*fachada*) facade; (*pórtico*) porch, doorway; (*portal*) carriage door, gateway. (**b**) (*Tip*) title page; (*de revista*) cover; (*de disco*) sleeve.

portadiscos *nm invar* record rack.

portado *adj*: **bien ~** well-dressed; well-behaved; respectable.

portador(a) *nm/f* carrier, bearer; (*Com, Fin*) bearer; payee; **páguese al ~** pay the bearer; **~ de gérmenes** germ carrier; **el ~ de esta carta** the bearer of this letter.

portaequipajes *nm invar* (*Aut etc*) boot, trunk (*US*); (*de techo*) luggage-rack, roof-rack, grid; (*de bicicleta*) carrier.

portaestandarte *nm* standard-bearer.

portafolio(s) *nm* briefcase, attaché case.

portafotos *nm invar* locket.

portafusil *nm* rifle sling.

portahachón *nm* torchbearer.

portal *nm* (**a**) (*zaguán*) vestibule, hall.

(**b**) (*pórtico*) porch, doorway; (*puerta principal*) street door, main door; (*de ciudad*) gate; **~es** arcade (*of shops, around square, etc*).

(**c**) (*Dep*) goal.

(**d**) (*Ecl*) **~ de Belén** Nativity scene, crèche.

portalada *nf* large doorway; imposing entrance; gate.

portalámpara(s) *nm invar* lamp-holder, socket.

portaligas *nm invar* suspender-belt, garter belt (*US*).

portalón *nm* (**a**) (*Arquit*) = **portalada**. (**b**) (*Náut*) gangway.

portamaletas *nm invar* (*Aut*) luggage-rack, roof-rack, grid.

portamanteo *nm* (*Esp*) travelling bag.

portaminas *nm invar* propelling pencil.

portamisiles *nm invar* missile-carrier.

portamonedas *nm invar* purse.

portante *nm*: **tomar el ~*** to clear off*.

portañuela *nf* fly (*of trousers*).

portaobjeto(s) *nm invar* slide; stage.

portapapeles *nm invar* briefcase.

portaplacas *nm invar* (*Fot*) plateholder.

portaplatos *nm invar* plate rack.

portapliegos *nm invar* (*And*) office boy.
portaplumas *nm invar* penholder.
portar [1a] **1** *vt* (*liter*) to carry, bear.
2 portarse *vr* (**a**) (*conducirse*) to behave, conduct o.s.; ~ **mal** to misbehave, behave badly; **se ha portado como un cochino** he has behaved like a swine; **se portó muy bien conmigo** he was very decent to me, he treated me very well.
(**b**) (*: *distinguirse*) to show up well, come through creditably.
(**c**) (*LAm*) to behave well.
portarretratos *nm invar* picture-frame, photograph frame.
portasenos *nm invar* (*LAm*) bra*.
portátil *adj* portable.
portatostadas *nm invar* toast rack.
portatrajes *nm invar* suit bag.
portaviandas *nm invar* lunch tin, dinner pail (*US*).
portavoz 1 *nm* (*altoparlante*) megaphone, loudhailer. **2** *nmf* spokesperson, spokesman; (*pey*) mouthpiece.
portazgo *nm* toll.
portazo *nm* bang (*of a door*), slam; **dar un** ~ to slam the door.
porte *nm* (**a**) (*Com*) (*acto*) carriage, transport; (*gastos*) (costs of) carriage, transport charges; (*Correos*) postage; ~ **por cobrar** freight forward; ~ **pagado** (*Com*) carriage paid, (*Correos*) post-paid; **franco de** ~ (*Com*) carriage free, (*Correos*) post-free.
(**b**) (*esp Náut*) capacity.
(**c**) (*conducta*) conduct, behaviour.
(**d**) (*comportamiento*) bearing, demeanour; (*presencia*) air, appearance; **de** ~ **distinguido** with a distinguished air.
porteador *nm* carrier; (*Alpinismo etc*) porter; (*Caza etc*) bearer.
portear[1] [1a] *vt* (*Com*) to carry, convey, transport.
portear[2] [1a] *vi* (**a**) (*puerta*) to slam, bang. (**b**) (*Cono Sur*) to get out in a hurry.
portento *nm* marvel, wonder, prodigy; **es un** ~ **de belleza** she is extraordinarily beautiful.
portentosamente *adv* marvellously, extraordinarily; extraordinarily well.
portentoso *adj* marvellous, extraordinary.
porteño 1 *adj* (*Argentina*) of Buenos Aires; (*Chile*) of Valparaíso. **2** *nm*, **porteña** *nf* (*Argentina*) native (*o* inhabitant) of Buenos Aires *o* (*Chile*) Valparaíso; **los ~s** the people of Buenos Aires *o* (*Chile*) Valparaíso.
porteo *nm* carriage, transport, conveyance.
portera *nf* portress.
portería *nf* (**a**) (*conserjería*) porter's lodge, porter's office. (**b**) (*Dep*) goal.
portero *nm* (**a**) (*conserje*) porter, janitor; doorman; (*guardián*) caretaker; ~ **automático,** ~ **eléctrico,** ~ **electrónico** answering device. (**b**) (*Dep*) goalkeeper.
portezuela *nf* (**a**) (*gen*) little door; (*de vehículo*) door; ~ **de la gasolina** fuel-filler door. (**b**) (*Cos*) pocket flap.
portezuelo *nm* (*Cono Sur Geog*) pass.
pórtico *nm* (**a**) (*portal*) portico, porch; (*fig*) gateway (*de* to). (**b**) (*de tiendas etc*) arcade.
portilla *nf* porthole.
portillo *nm* (**a**) (*abertura*) gap, opening; (*brecha*) breach; (*postigo*) wicket, wicket gate; (*puerta falsa*) side entrance, private door.
(**b**) (*Geog*) narrow pass.
(**c**) (*abolladura*) dent; (*saltadura*) chip.
(**d**) (*fig*: *punto débil*) weak spot, vulnerable point; (*para solución*) opening (*affording solution to a problem*).
pórtland *nm o f* (*esp LAm*) cement.
portón *nm* (*puerta grande*) large door; (*puerta principal*) main door; (*Aut*: *t* ~ **trasero**) hatch, hatchback, tailgate (*US*); (*LAm*: *de casa*) main door, street door; (*Cono Sur*) back door.
portorriqueño, -a *adj, nm/f* Puerto Rican.
portuario *adj* port (*atr*), harbour (*atr*); dock (*atr*); **trabajador** ~ docker.
Portugal *nm* Portugal.
portugués, -esa 1 *adj, nm/f* Portuguese. **2** *nm* (*Ling*) Portuguese.
portuguesismo *nm* portuguesism, word (*o* phrase *etc*) borrowed from Portuguese.
porvenir *nm* future; **en el ~, en lo** ~ in the future; **un hombre sin** ~ a man with no future, a man with no prospects; **le espera un brillante** ~ a brilliant future awaits him.
pos: en ~ **de** *prep* after, in pursuit of; **ir en** ~ **de** to chase (after), pursue; **ella va en** ~ **de triunfo** she's after success.
pos(t)... *pref* post...; after...
posada *nf* (**a**) (*hospedaje*) shelter, lodging; **dar** ~ **a** to give shelter to, take in. (**b**) (*mesón*) inn; (*pensión*) lodging house. (**c**) (*morada*) house, dwelling, abode. (**d**) (*CAm, Méx*) Christmas party.
posaderas* *nfpl* backside, buttocks.
posadero *nm* innkeeper.
posar [1a] **1** *vt carga* to lay down, put down; *mano etc* to place, put gently; ~ **los ojos en** to look vaguely at, glance idly at.
2 *vi* (*Arte, Cine, Fot*) to sit, pose.
3 posarse *vr* (**a**) (*ave, insecto*) to alight, settle, rest; (*ave*) to perch, sit; (*avión*) to land, come down; **el avión se encontraba posado** the aircraft was on the ground.
(**b**) (*líquido*) to settle, form sediment; (*polvo*) to settle.
posas* *nfpl* backside, buttocks.
posavasos *nm invar* dripmat, mat, coaster (*US*); (*de taberna*) beer-mat.
posbélico *adj* postwar.
poscombustión *nf*: **dispositivo de** ~ afterburner.
posconciliar *adj* post-conciliar, after Vatican II.
posconcilio *nm*: **los 20 años de** ~ the 20 years following Vatican II.
posdata *nf* postscript.
posdoctoral *adj* post-doctoral.
pose [pouz *o* 'pose] *nf* (**a**) (*Arte, Cine, Fot*) pose; (*Fot*) time exposure.
(**b**) (*fig*: *actitud*) attitude.
(**c**) (*fig*: *aplomo*) composure; poise.
(**d**) (*fig*) (*afectación*) pose; affectedness; (*postura afectada*) affected posture.
poseedor *nm*, **poseedora** *nf* owner, possessor; (*de puesto, récord*) holder.
poseer [2e] *vt* (*gen*) to have, possess, own; *ventaja* to have, enjoy; *mujer* to have; *lengua, tema* to know perfectly, have a complete mastery of; *puesto, récord* to hold.
poseído 1 *adj* (**a**) (*lit*) possessed (*por* by); (*fig*: *enloquecido*) maddened, crazed.
(**b**) **estar muy** ~ **de** to be very vain about, have an excessively high opinion of.
2 *nm*, **poseída** *nf*: **gritar como un** ~ to shout like one possessed.
posesión *nf* (**a**) (*gen*) possession; (*de puesto*) tenure, occupation; (*de lengua, tema*) complete knowledge, perfect mastery; **dar** ~ **a** to hand over to, make formal transfer to; **él está en** ~ **de las cartas** he is in possession of the letters; **las cartas están en** ~ **de su padre** the letters are in the possession of his father; **está en** ~ **del récord** he holds the record; **tomar** ~ to take over, enter upon office (*etc*); **tomar** ~ **de** to take possession of, take over; **tomar** ~ **de un oficio** to take up a post.
(**b**) (*una* ~) possession (*t Pol*); (*propiedad*) property; (*finca*) piece of property, estate.
(**c**) (*Cono Sur*) country estate; (*Carib*) ranch, estate.
posesionar [1a] **1** *vt*: ~ **a uno de algo** to hand sth over to sb. **2 posesionarse** *vr*: ~ **de** to take possession of, take over.
posesividad *nf* possessiveness.
posesivo *adj, nm* possessive.
poseso = **poseído.**
posestructuralismo *nm* post-structuralism.
posfechar [1a] *vt* to postdate.
posfranquismo *nm* period after the death of Franco (*1975*).
posfranquista *adj*: *p.ej.* **cultura** ~ post-Franco culture, culture since Franco.
posglacial *adj* postglacial.
posgrado *nm*: **curso de** ~ postgraduate course.
posgraduado, -a *adj, nm/f* postgraduate.
posguerra *nf* postwar period; **los años de la** ~ the postwar years; **en la** ~ in the postwar period, after the war.
posibilidad *nf* possibility; chance; **no existe** ~ **alguna de que venga** there is no possibility of his coming; **tiene pocas ~es** he hasn't much chance; **si hay la** ~ **de verlo** if there's a chance to see it; **cabe la** ~ there's always the chance; **estar en la** ~ **de** + *infin* to be in a position to + *infin*; **vivir por encima de sus ~es** to live above one's means.
posibilista 1 *adj* optimistic, positive. **2** *nmf* optimist, positive thinker.
posibilitar [1a] *vt* to make possible, facilitate, permit; to make feasible; ~ **que uno haga algo** to allow sb to do sth, make it possible for sb to do sth.
posible 1 *adj* possible; feasible; **una** ~ **tragedia** a possible tragedy; **todas las concesiones ~s** all possible concessions;

a serme ~ if I possibly can; **de ser** ~ if possible; **en lo** ~ as far as possible; **lo antes** ~ as soon as possible; as quickly as possible; **lo más frecuentemente** ~ as often as possible; **hacer** ~ **una cosa** to make sth possible; **hacer lo** ~ to do all that one can (*para o por* + *infin* to + *infin*); **es** ~ **que** + *subj* it is possible that ...; perhaps ...; **¿es ~?** surely not?; can it really be true?; **¿será** ~ **que haya venido?** can he really have come (after all)?; **¿será** ~ **que no haya venido?** surely he has come, hasn't he?; **si es** ~ if possible; **si me es** ~ if I possibly can; *V* **dentro, pronto** *etc.*

2 ~**s** *nmpl* (*medios*) means; (*fondos*) funds, assets; **vivir dentro de sus** ~**s** to live within one's means.

posiblemente *adv* possibly.

posición *nf* (**a**) (*gen*) position; (*status*) status, standing, social position; ~ **del misionero** missionary position; **estar en** ~ **de guardia** to be on guard (*contra* against); **perder posiciones** to fall away, lose strength.

(**b**) (*Dep*) position; (*en liga etc*) place, position; **posiciones de honor** first three places, medal positions; **terminar en primera** ~ to finish first; **ganó A con B en segunda** ~ A won with B in second place.

(**c**) (*LAm*: *puesto*) position, post, job.

posicionado *nm* positioning.

posicionamiento *nm* stance, attitude.

posicionar [1a] **1** *vt* to position. **2 posicionarse** *vr* (*fig*) to adopt an attitude, take up a stance; to define one's position, declare oneself.

posimperial *adj* post-imperial.

posimpresionismo *nm* post-impressionism.

posimpresionista *adj, nmf* post-impressionist.

posindustrial *adj* post-industrial.

positiva *nf* (*Fot*) positive, print.

positivamente *adv* positively.

positivar [1a] *vt foto* to develop.

positivismo *nm* positivism.

positivista *adj, nmf* positivist.

positivo 1 *adj* (*gen*) positive; (*Mat*) positive, plus; *idea* useful, practical, constructive; **es** ~ **que** ... it is good that ..., it is encouraging that ...; **el atleta dio** ~ the athlete failed a drugs test. **2** *nm* (**a**) (*Ling*) positive. (**b**) (*Fot*) positive, print. (**c**) (*Dep*) point.

pósito *nm* (**a**) (*granero*) (public) granary. (**b**) (*cooperativa*) cooperative, association; ~ **de pescadores** fishing cooperative.

positrón *nm* positron.

posma* *nmf* bore, dull person.

posmeridiano *adj* postmeridian, afternoon (*atr*).

posmodernismo *nm* postmodernism.

posmoderno *adj* postmodern.

posnatal *adj* postnatal.

poso *nm* sediment, deposit; dregs; ~**s de café** coffee grounds; ~**s de té** tea-leaves.

posol *nm* (*CAm*) *maize drink.*

posoperativo *adj* post-operative.

posoperatorio 1 *adj* post-operative. **2** *nm* post-operative period, period of recovery after an operation.

pososo *adj* (*CAm*) (*poroso*) porous, permeable; (*absorbente*) absorbent.

posparto 1 *adj* postnatal. **2** *nm* postnatal period.

posponer [2q] *vt* (**a**) (*subordinar*) ~ **A a B** to put A behind (*o* below) B; ~ **el amor propio al interés general** to subordinate one's self-respect to the general interest; ~ **a uno** to downgrade sb.

(**b**) (*aplazar*) to postpone.

posposición *nf* (**a**) (*gen*) postposition; relegation; subordination. (**b**) (*aplazamiento*) postponement. (**c**) (*Ling*) post-position.

pospositivo *adj* postpositive.

posquemador *nm* afterburner.

post... *pref* post...

posta 1 *nf* (**a**) (*caballos*) relay, team; (*etapa*) stage; (*parada*) staging post; **a** ~ on purpose, deliberately; **por la** ~ post-haste, as quickly as possible.

(**b**) (*Naipes*) stake.

(**c**) (*Culin*) slice; ~ **de pierna** (*CAm*) leg of pork.

(**d**) (*Caza*) slug, pellet.

(**e**) (*Cono Sur*) first-aid post.

2 *nm* courier.

postal 1 *adj* postal. **2** *nf* postcard; ~ **ilustrada** picture postcard.

postdata *nf* postscript.

poste *nm* (*gen*) post, pole; (*columna*) pillar; (*estaca*) stake; (*Dep*) post, upright; (*de ejecución*) stake; ~**s** (*Dep*) goalposts, goal; ~ **de cerca** fencing post; ~ **indicador** signpost; ~ **de llegada** winning post; ~ **de portería** goalpost; ~ **de salida** starting post; ~ **telegráfico** telegraph pole; ~ **del tendido eléctrico** electricity pylon; **dar** ~ **a uno*** to keep sb hanging about; **mover los** ~**s** (*fig*) to move the goalposts; **oler el** ~ to scent danger, see trouble ahead; to smell a rat.

postema *nf* (**a**) (*Med*) abscess, tumour; (*Méx*: *pus*) pus; (*Méx*: *divieso*) boil. (**b**) (*****: *pelmazo*) bore, dull person.

postemilla *nf* (*LAm*) gumboil.

póster *nm, pl* **pósteres** *o* **pósters** poster.

postergación *nf* (**a**) (*relegación*) passing over, ignoring. (**b**) (*retraso*) delaying; (*aplazamiento*) deferment, postponement.

postergar [1h] *vt* (**a**) *persona* to pass over, disregard; to ignore the seniority (*o* better claim) of. (**b**) (*esp LAm*) (*demorar*) to delay; (*aplazar*) to defer, postpone.

posteridad *nf* (**a**) posterity. (**b**) (*Esp**: *culo*) bottom.

posterior *adj* (**a**) (*lugar*) back, rear; posterior; *motor* rear-mounted.

(**b**) (*en orden*) later, following.

(**c**) (*tiempo*) later, subsequent; **ser** ~ **a** to be later than.

posterioridad *nf* later nature; **con** ~ later, subsequently; **con** ~ **a** subsequent to, later than.

posteriormente *adv* later, subsequently, afterwards.

postigo *nm* (**a**) (*puerta pequeña*) wicket, wicket gate; (*portillo*) postern; (*puerta falsa*) small door, side door. (**b**) (*contraventana*) shutter.

postillón *nm* postillion.

postín* *nm* (**a**) (*lujo*) elegance, luxury, poshness*; (*entono*) tone; **de** ~ posh*, swanky*, smart.

(**b**) (*fachenda*) side*, swank*; **darse** ~ to show off, swank*; **se da mucho** ~ **de que su padre es ministro** he swanks about his father being a minister*.

postinear* [1a] *vi* to show off, swank*.

postinero* *adj* (**a**) *persona* vain, conceited (*de* about); swanky*. (**b**) *traje etc* posh*, swish*.

postizas *nfpl* (*Esp*) (*small*) castanets.

postizo 1 *adj* false, artificial; *dientes* false; *cuello* detachable; *exterior etc* dummy; *sonrisa etc* false, phoney*, sham. **2** *nm* switch, false hair, hairpiece.

postor(a) *nm/f* bidder; **mayor** (*o* **mejor**) ~ highest bidder.

postración *nf* prostration; ~ **nerviosa** nervous exhaustion.

postrado *adj* (*t fig*) prostrate; ~ **por el dolor** prostrate with grief.

postrar [1a] **1** *vt* (**a**) (*derribar*) to cast down, overthrow; (*humillar*) to humble. (**b**) (*Med*: *debilitar*) to weaken, exhaust, prostrate. **2 postrarse** *vr* (*hincarse*) to prostrate o.s.

postre 1 *nm* (*t* ~**s**) sweet, sweet course; dessert; **¿qué hay de ~?** what is there for dessert?; **para** ~**(s)*** to crown it all, on top of all that; **llegar a los** ~**s** (*fig*) to come too late, come after everything is over.

2 *nf*: **a la** ~ at last, in the end; when all is said and done.

postremo *adj*, **postrero** *adj* (**postrer** *delante de nm sing*) last; rear, hindermost; **palabras postremas** dying words.

postrimerías *nfpl* (**a**) (*gen*) dying moments; (*último período*) final stages, closing stages; **en las** ~ **del siglo** in the last few years of the century, right at the end of the century.

(**b**) (*Ecl*) four last things.

postulación *nf* (**a**) (*proposición*) postulation. (**b**) (*colecta*) collection.

postulado *nm* postulate, proposition; assumption, hypothesis.

postulante *nmf* petitioner; (*Ecl*) postulant; (*Pol*) candidate; (*LAm*) applicant.

postular [1a] **1** *vt* (**a**) (*proponer*) to postulate.

(**b**) (*pedir*) to seek, demand; (*solicitar*) to petition for; (*pretender*) to claim; **en el artículo postula la reforma de ...** in the article he sets out demands for the reform of ...

(**c**) *dinero* to collect (for charity).

(**d**) (*CAm, Méx*) *candidato* to nominate.

2 *vi* (*LAm*) to apply.

3 postularse *vr* (*LAm Pol*) to stand.

póstumo *adj* posthumous.

postura *nf* (**a**) (*del cuerpo*) posture, position; stance; pose; (*sexual*) position; ~ **del loto** lotus position.

(**b**) (*fig*) attitude, position; stand; **adoptar una** ~ **poco razonable** to take an unreasonable attitude; **la** ~ **del gobierno en este asunto** the government's position in this matter; **tomar** ~ to adopt a stance.

(**c**) (*en subasta*) bid; (*en el juego*) bet, stake; **hacer una** ~ to lay a bet; to make a bid.

(**d**) (*Orn*: *acto*) egg-laying; (*huevos*) eggs (laid).
(**e**) (‡: *droga*) quantity of hash*; 1000-pesetas' worth of hash*.

postural *adj* postural.
posventa *adj* after-sales (*atr*); **servicio** (*o* **asistencia**) **de** ~ after-sales service.
pota¹* *nf* wreck, clunker (*US*).
pota²‡ *nf*: **echar la** ~ to puke‡, throw up.
potabilización *nf* purification.
potabilizadora *nf* water-treatment plant, waterworks.
potabilizar [1f] *vt*: ~ **el agua** to make the water drinkable.
potable *adj* (**a**) drinkable; **agua** ~ drinking water. (**b**) (*: *aceptable*) good enough, passable.
potaje *nm* (**a**) (*Culin*) broth; vegetable stew, stewed vegetables. (**b**) (*fig*) (*mezcla*) mixture; (*revoltijo*) jumble.
potar‡ [1a] *vi* to spew, throw up.
potasa *nf* potash.
potasio *nm* potassium.
pote *nm* (**a**) (*gen*) pot; (*tarro*) jar; (*jarra*) jug; (*Farm*) jar; (*Méx*: *lata*) tin, can; (*Méx*: *vasija*) mug; (*Hort*) flowerpot, pot; (*And, Carib*) flask; **a** ~ in plenty; *V* **beber**.
(**b**) (*prov*) stew.
(**c**) (*: *puchero*) pout, sulky look.
(**d**) **darse** ~* to show off, swank*.
(**e**) (*: *trago*) drink; **tomar unos** ~**s** to have a few drinks.

potear* [1a] *vi* to have a few drinks.
potencia *nf* (**a**) (*gen*) power; potency; ~ **electoral** voting power, power in terms of votes; ~ **de fuego** firepower; ~ **hidráulica** hydraulic power; ~ **muscular** muscular power, muscular strength; ~ **nuclear** nuclear power.
(**b**) (*Mec*) power; capacity; ~ (**en caballos**) horsepower; ~ **al freno** brake horsepower; ~ **real** effective power.
(**c**) (*Pol*) power; **las** ~**s** the Powers; **las grandes** ~**s** the great powers; ~ **colonial** colonial power; ~ **mundial** world power; **éramos una** ~ **naval** we used to be a naval power.
(**d**) (*Mat*) power.
(**e**) (*Rel*: *t* ~ **del alma**) faculty.
(**f**) **en** ~ potential, in the making; **es una guerra civil en** ~ it is a civil war in the making.

potenciador *adj*: ~ **de** favourable to, encouraging to.
potencial 1 *adj* potential. **2** *nm* (**a**) (*gen*) potential; ~ **comercial** market potential; ~ **ganador** earning potential; ~ **de ventas** sales potential. (**b**) (*Ling*) conditional.
potencialidad *nf* potentiality.
potencialmente *adv* potentially.
potenciamiento *nm* favouring, fostering, promotion; development; strengthening, boosting, reinforcement.
potenciar [1b] *vt* (*promover*) to favour, foster, promote; (*desarrollar*) to develop; (*mejorar*) to improve, (*Inform*) to upgrade; (*fortalecer*) to strengthen, boost, reinforce.
potentado *nm* potentate; (*fig*) tycoon; baron, magnate; big shot*.
potente *adj* (**a**) (*poderoso*) powerful. (**b**) (*: *grande*) big, mighty, strong; **un grito** ~ a great yell.
poteo* *nm* drinks, drinking; **ir de** ~ to go round the bars.
potestad *nf* power, authority, jurisdiction; ~ **marital** husband's authority; **patria** ~ paternal authority.
potestativo *adj* optional, not mandatory; permissive.
potingue* *nm* concoction, brew.
potito *nm* (**a**) (*Esp*) small jar, (*esp*) (jar of) baby food. (**b**) (*LAm*) backside, bottom.
poto *nm* (*And, Cono Sur*) (**a**) (*) (*trasero*) backside, bottom; (*fondo*) lower end. (**b**) (*Bot*) calabash; (*vasija*) earthenware jug.
potoco* *adj* (*And, Cono Sur*) squat.
potón (*Cono Sur*) **1** *adj* coarse. **2** *nm* rustic, peasant.
potosí *nm* fortune; **cuesta un** ~ it costs the earth; **vale un** ~ it's worth a fortune; **ella vale un** ~ she's a treasure; **en ese negocio tienen un** ~ they've got a gold mine in that business.
potra *nf* (**a**) (*Zool*) filly. (**b**) (*Med*) rupture, hernia. (**c**) (‡: *suerte*) luck, jam‡; **de** ~ by luck, luckily; **tener** ~ to be jammy‡, be lucky.
potranca *nf* filly, young mare.
potranco *nm* (*LAm*) colt, young horse.
potrear [1a] **1** *vt* (**a**) (*And, CAm*) to beat. (**b**) (*Carib, Méx*) *caballo* to break, tame. **2** *vi* (*CAm, Cono Sur*) to caper about, chase around.
potrero 1 *nm* (**a**) (*Agr*) pasture; paddock. (**b**) (*LAm*) (*de ganado*) cattle ranch; (*caballeriza*) stud farm, horse breeding establishment. (**c**) (*Cono Sur*: *parque*) playground; (*Méx*: *llanura*) open grassland. **2** *adj* (‡) jammy‡, lucky.
potrillo *nm* (**a**) (*Cono Sur*: *caballo*) colt. (**b**) (*Cono Sur*: *vaso*) tall glass. (**c**) (*And*: *canoa*) small canoe.
potro *nm* (**a**) (*Zool*) colt; ~ **de madera** vaulting-horse. (**b**) (*de tormento*) rack; (*cepo*) stocks; (*de herrar*) shoeing frame. (**c**) (*LAm Med*) hernia, tumour.
potroso‡ *adj* jammy‡, lucky.
poyo *nm* stone bench.
poza *nf* puddle, pool; (*Méx*: *de río*) pool, backwater; (*LAm*‡: *escupitajo*) gob‡ of spit.
pozanco *nm* puddle, pool.
pozo *nm* (**a**) (*de agua*) well; ~ **artesiano** artesian well; ~ **ciego,** ~ **negro** cesspool; ~ **de petróleo,** ~ **petrolífero** oil-well; ~ **de riego** well used for irrigation; ~ **séptico** septic tank; **caer en el** ~ (*fig*) to fall into oblivion.
(**b**) (*Geog*) deep pool, deep part (*of river*).
(**c**) (*Min*) shaft; pit, mine; ~ **de aire** air-shaft; ~ **de registro,** ~ **de visita** manhole; inspection hatch; ~ **de ventilación** ventilation shaft.
(**d**) (*Náut*) hold.
(**e**) (*fig*) **ser un** ~ **de ciencia** to be immensely learned; **es un** ~ **de maldad** he is utterly wicked.

pozol *nm* (*LAm*) = **posol.**
pozole *nm* (*Méx Culin*) maize stew.
PP (**a**) *nmpl abr de* **padres** Fathers, Frs. (**b**) *nm* (*Pol*) *abr de* **Partido Popular.**
P.P. (*Com*) *abr de* **porte pagado** carriage paid, C/P.
p.p. (*Jur*) *abr de* **por poder** per procurationem, by proxy, p.p.
PPM *nm* (*Esp*) *abr de* **Patronato de Protección de la Mujer.**
ppm *nfpl abr de* **partes por millón** parts per million.
PR *nm abr de* **Puerto Rico.**
práctica *nf* (*gen*) practice; (*método*) method; (*destreza*) skill; **en la** ~ in practice; ~ **establecida** standard practice; ~**s restrictivas** (**de la competencia**) restrictive practices; ~**s profesionales** professional training, practical training for a profession; ~**s de tiro** target practice; **la** ~ **hace maestro** practice makes perfect; **aprender con la** ~ to learn by practice; **hacer** ~ **de clínica** to do one's hospital training, walk the wards; **poner algo en** ~ to put sth into practice.
practicable *adj* (**a**) (*gen*) practicable; (*factible*) workable, feasible. (**b**) *camino etc* passable, usable. (**c**) (*Teat*) *puerta* that opens, that is meant to open.
prácticamente *adv* practically; **está** ~ **terminado** it's practically finished, it's almost finished.
practicante 1 *adj* (*Ecl*) practising. **2** *nmf* practitioner; (*Med*) medical assistant, doctor's assistant; (*Méx*) final year medical student; (*LAm*: *médico recién recibido*) houseman, intern (*US*). **3** *nm* (*enfermero*) male nurse.
practicar [1g] **1** *vt* (**a**) *habilidad, virtud etc* to practise, exercise.
(**b**) *actividad etc* to practise; *deporte* to go in for, play; *profesión* to practise; ~ **el francés con su profesor** to practise one's French with one's teacher.
(**c**) (*ejecutar*) to perform, carry out; *detención* to make.
(**d**) *agujero* to cut, make; to bore, drill.
2 *vi y* **practicarse** *vr*: ~ **en la enseñanza** to do teaching practice, do one's school practice.

practicidad *nf* practicality; effectiveness.
practicismo *nm* down-to-earth attitude, sense of realism.
práctico 1 *adj* (**a**) (*gen*) practical; *herramienta etc* handy; *casa etc* convenient; *ropa* sensible, practical; **no resultó ser muy** ~ it turned out to be not very practical; **resulta** ~ **vivir tan cerca de la fábrica** it's convenient (*o* handy) to live so close to the factory.
(**b**) *estudio, formación etc* practical.
(**c**) *persona* skilled, expert (*en* at); **ser muy** ~ **en** to be very skilled at, be very adept at.
2 *nm* (*Med*) practitioner; (*Náut*) pilot.

pradera *nf* (*prado*) meadow, meadowland; (*césped*) lawn; (*Canadá etc*) prairie; **unas extensas** ~**s** extensive grasslands.
pradería *nf* meadowlands, grasslands.
prado *nm* meadow, field; pasture; green grassy area; (*Cono Sur*) lawn.
Praga *nf* Prague.
pragmática *nf* (*Hist*) decree, proclamation.
pragmático *adj* pragmatic.
pragmatismo *nm* pragmatism.
pragmatista *nmf* pragmatist.
prángana* *adj invar* (*Méx*) poor.
pre... *pref* pre...
preacordar [1l] *vt* to reach a preliminary agreement on, make a draft agreement about.

preacuerdo *nm* preliminary agreement; outline (*o* draft) agreement.

prealarma *nf* alert; early warning.

preámbulo *nm* (**a**) (*de libro, discurso*) preamble, introduction. (**b**) (*pey*) evasive talk, annoying digression; **gastar ~s** to talk evasively, beat about the bush; **sin más ~s** without more ado.

preaviso *nm* forewarning, early warning.

prebenda *nf* (**a**) (*Ecl*) prebend. (**b**) (*: *oficio*) sinecure, soft job*; (*gaje*) perk*; **~s corporativas** business perks*.

prebendado *nm* prebendary.

preboste *nm* (**a**) (*Hist*) provost. (**b**) (*Pol*) chief, leader.

precalentamiento *nm* warm-up, warming-up.

precalentar [1j] **1** *vt* to preheat; to warm up. **2 precalentarse** *vr* (*Dep etc*) to warm up.

precandidato, -a *nm/f* candidate not yet formally nominated.

precariamente *adv* precariously.

precariedad *nf* precariousness.

precario 1 *adj* (*gen*) precarious; (*dudoso*) doubtful, uncertain; (*poco firme*) shaky; (*impredecible*) unpredictable. **2** *nm* precarious state; **dejar a uno en ~** to leave sb in a difficult situation; **estamos en ~** we are in difficult circumstances; **vivir en ~** to live from hand to mouth, scrape a living.

precaución *nf* (**a**) (*acto*) precaution; (*medida*) preventive measure; **extremar las precauciones** to be extra careful; **tomar precauciones** to take precautions.

(**b**) (*cualidad*) foresight; caution, wariness; **ir con ~** to go cautiously, proceed warily; **lo hicimos por ~** we did it to be on the safe side, we did it as a safety measure.

precautorio *adj* precautionary.

precaver [2a] **1** *vt* (*prevenir*) to guard against, try to prevent; (*anticipar*) to forestall; (*evitar*) to stave off.

2 precaverse *vr* to be on one's guard, take precautions, be forewarned; **~ contra** to guard against; **~ de** to be on one's guard against, beware of.

precavidamente *adv* cautiously, warily.

precavido *adj* cautious, wary.

precedencia *nf* (*gen*) precedence; (*prioridad*) priority; (*preeminencia*) greater importance, superiority.

precedente 1 *adj* (*anterior*) preceding, foregoing; (*primero*) former; **cada uno mejor que el ~** each one better than the one before.

2 *nm* precedent; **de acuerdo con el ~** according to precedent; **contra todos los ~s** against all the precedents; **sin ~(s)** unprecedented; unparalleled; **establecer un ~, sentar un ~** to establish (*o* set up) a precedent.

precedentemente *adv* earlier, at an earlier stage, previously.

preceder [2a] **1** *vt*: **~ a** (**a**) (*anteceder*) to precede, go before; **le precedía un coche** he was preceded by a car; **el título precede al nombre** the title goes before the first name.

(**b**) (*fig*) to have priority over; to take precedence over.

2 *vi* to precede; **todo lo que precede** all the preceding (part), all that which comes before.

preceptista *nmf* theorist.

preceptiva *nf* teaching, doctrine.

preceptivo *adj* compulsory, obligatory, mandatory; **es ~ utilizar el formulario** the application form must be used.

precepto *nm* precept; order, rule; **de ~** compulsory, obligatory.

preceptor(a) *nm/f* teacher; (private) tutor.

preceptorado *nm* tutorship.

preceptoral *adj* tutorial.

preceptuar [1e] *vt* to lay down, establish; to state as an essential requirement.

preces *nfpl* prayers, supplications.

preciado *adj* (**a**) (*estimado*) esteemed, valuable. (**b**) (*presuntuoso*) presumptuous.

preciarse [1b] *vr* to boast; **~ de algo** to pride o.s. on sth, boast of being sth; **~ de inteligente** to think o.s. clever, pride o.s. on one's intelligence; **~ de** + *infin* to boast of + *ger*.

precintado 1 *adj* sealed; (*Com*) prepackaged; *calle etc* sealed-off. **2** *nm* sealing; (*Com*) prepackaging.

precintar [1a] *vt* (*Com etc*) to seal; (*fig*) to seal off.

precinto *nm* seal; (*de aduana*) customs seal.

precio *nm* (**a**) (*gen*) price; (*costo*) cost; (*valor*) value, worth; (*de viaje*) fare; (*en hotel etc*) rate, charge; **~ de compra** purchase price; **~ al contado** cash price; **~ de coste** cost-price; **a ~ de coste, a ~ costo** at cost-price; **'a ~ de fábrica'** 'cost-price', 'at cost'; **~ en fábrica** price ex-factory; **~ de intervención** intervention price; **~ irrisorio, ~ de oportunidad, ~ de situación** (*LAm*) bargain price; **~ de lista** list price; **~ de mercado** market price; market value; **~ neto** net price; **~ obsequio** giveaway price; **~ de ocasión** bargain price; **~ orientativo** manufacturer's recommended price; **~ de pensión** school fees; **~ de referencia** suggested price; **a ~ de saldo** at a knockdown price; **~ de salida** starting price; **a** (*o* **por**) **un ~ simbólico** for a nominal (*o* token) sum; **~ tope** top price, ceiling price; **último ~** closing price; **~ de venta** sale price; **~ del viaje** fare (for the journey); **al ~ de** (*fig*) at the cost of; **lo hará a cualquier ~** he'll do it whatever the cost; **evítelo a cualquier ~** avoid it at all costs; **'no importa ~'** 'cost no object'; **poner** (*o* **señalar**) **~ a la cabeza de uno** to put a price on sb's head; **no tener ~** (*fig*) to be priceless.

(**b**) (*fig*) value, worth; **hombre de gran ~** a man of great worth.

preciosamente *adv* beautifully; charmingly.

preciosidad *nf* (**a**) (*excelencia*) preciousness; (*valor*) value, worth.

(**b**) (*pey*) preciosity.

(**c**) (*objeto*) beautiful thing; precious object; (*chica*) lovely girl; **es una ~** it's lovely, it's really beautiful; **¡oye, ~!*** hey, beautiful!

preciosismo *nm* (*Liter etc*) preciosity.

preciosista (*Liter etc*) **1** *adj* precious, affected. **2** *nmf* precious writer, affected writer (*etc*).

precioso *adj* (**a**) (*excelente*) precious; (*valioso*) valuable.

(**b**) (*exquisito*) pretty, lovely, beautiful; (*encantador*) charming; **una edición preciosa** a beautiful edition; **tienen un niño ~** they have a lovely child; **¿verdad que es ~?** isn't it lovely?

preciosura *nf* (*LAm*) = **preciosidad** (**c**).

precipicio *nm* (**a**) (*gen*) cliff, precipice.

(**b**) (*fig*: *abismo*) chasm, abyss; **tiene el ~ abierto a sus pies** the chasm yawns before him, he stands on the brink of disaster.

(**c**) (*fig*: *ruina*) ruin.

precipitación *nf* (**a**) (*prisa*) haste; (*imprudencia*) rashness; **con ~** hastily; rashly, precipitately. (**b**) (*Met*) precipitation, rainfall. (**c**) (*Quím*) precipitation.

precipitadamente *adv* headlong; hastily, suddenly; rashly, precipitately.

precipitado 1 *adj huida etc* headlong; *partida etc* hasty, sudden; *acto, conducta* hasty, rash, precipitate. **2** *nm* (*Quím*) precipitate.

precipitar [1a] **1** *vt* (**a**) (*arrojar*) to hurl down, cast down, throw (*desde* from).

(**b**) (*apresurar*) to hasten; (*acelerar*) to speed up, accelerate; (*motivar*) to precipitate; **aquello precipitó su salida** that affair hastened his departure; **la dimisión precipitó la crisis** the resignation precipitated (*o* brought on, sparked off) the crisis.

(**c**) (*Quím*) to precipitate.

2 precipitarse *vr* (**a**) (*arrojarse*) to throw o.s., hurl o.s. (*desde* from); (*lanzarse*) to launch o.s.

(**b**) (*correr*) to rush, dash; to dart; **~ a hacer algo** to rush to do sth, hasten to do sth; **~ sobre** (*ave etc*) to swoop on, pounce on; **~ sobre uno** to rush at sb, hurl o.s. on sb; **~ hacia un sitio** to rush towards a place.

(**c**) (*obrar impetuosamente*) to act rashly; **se ha precipitado rehusándolo** he acted rashly in rejecting it, it was rash of him to refuse it.

precipitoso *adj* (**a**) *lugar* precipitous, steep, sheer. (**b**) *acto etc* = **precipitado 1**.

precisa *nf* (**a**) (*CAm*: *urgencia*) urgency. (**b**) **tener la ~** (*Cono Sur**) to be on the ball.

precisado *adj*: **verse ~ a** + *infin* to be obliged (*o* forced) to + *infin*.

precisamente *adv* (**a**) (*con precisión*) precisely, in a precise way.

(**b**) (*justamente*) precisely, exactly, just; **¡~!** exactly!, precisely!; just so!; **~ por eso** for that very reason, precisely because of that; **~ fue él quien lo dijo** it so happens it was he who said it, as a matter of fact it was he who said it; **~ estábamos hablando de eso** we were just talking about that; **llegó ~ cuando nos íbamos** he arrived just as we were leaving; **yo no soy un experto ~** I'm not exactly an expert; **no es eso ~** it's not quite that, it's not really that.

precisar [1a] **1** *vt* (**a**) (*necesitar*) to need, require; **no precisa lavado** it needs no washing; **'vendedores precisa agencia internacional'** (*anuncio*) 'salesmen wanted by international agency'; **precisa que vengas** you must come; **no**

precisamos que el candidato tenga experiencia we do not insist (*o* demand) that the candidate should be experienced.
(**b**) (*determinar*) to determine exactly, fix; (*señalar*) to pinpoint, put one's finger on; *detalles etc* to specify, state precisely; **hay alguna rareza que no puedo ~** there is some oddity which I cannot pin down (*o* put my finger on).
2 *vi* (*ser necesario*) to be necessary; (*ser urgente*) to be urgent; **~ de algo** to need sth; **precisamos de más tiempo** we need more time.

precisión *nf* (**a**) (*exactitud*) precision; preciseness, accuracy, exactness; **instrumento de ~** precision instrument.
(**b**) **hacer precisiones** to define matters more closely, make matters more precise, clarify matters.
(**c**) (*necesidad*) need, necessity; **tener ~ de algo** to need sth, have need of sth; **verse en la ~ de** + *infin* to be obliged to + *infin*.
(**d**) (*Méx*) urgency.

preciso *adj* (**a**) (*exacto*) precise; exact, accurate; **una descripción precisa** a precise description.
(**b**) **en equel ~ momento** at that precise moment, at that very moment, just at that moment.
(**c**) (*necesario*) necessary, essential; **las cualidades precisas** the essential qualities, the requisite qualities; **tener el tiempo ~ para** + *infin* to have (just) enough time to + *infin*; **cuando sea ~** when it becomes necessary; **es ~ que lo hagas** it is essential that you should do it, you must do it; **es ~ tener coche** it is essential to have a car; **ser un Don P~** (*Cono Sur*) to believe o.s. to be indispensable.
(**d**) (*Carib*) conceited.

precitado *adj* above-mentioned.
preclaro *adj* (*liter*) illustrious.
precocidad *nf* precociousness, precocity; (*Bot etc*) earliness.
precocinado *adj* precooked.
precocinar [1a] *vt* to precook.
precognición *nf* foreknowledge; precognition.
precolombino *adj* pre-Columbian; **la América precolombina** America before Columbus.
preconcebido *adj* preconceived; **idea preconcebida** preconception.
preconcepción *nf* preconception.
preconciliar *adj* preconciliar, before Vatican II.
precondición *nf* precondition.
preconizable *adj* foreseeable.
preconización *nf* (**a**) (*recomendación*) recommendation; favouring. (**b**) (*de algo futuro*) visualizing.
preconizar [1f] *vt* (**a**) (*elogiar*) to praise.
(**b**) (*recomendar*) to recommend, advise.
(**c**) (*proponer*) to suggest, propose; to advocate.
precontrato *nm* pre-contract.
precordillera *nf* (*LAm*) Andean foothills.
precoz *adj* precocious; forward; *calvicie etc* premature; (*Bot, Med etc*) early.
precozmente *adv* precociously; prematurely; early.
precursor(a) *nm/f* predecessor, forerunner.
predación *nf* (*Bio*) predation; (*fig*) depredation, plundering.
predador *nm*, **predator** *nm* predator.
predecesor(a) *nm/f* predecessor.
predecir [3o] *vt* to predict, foretell, forecast.
predemocrático *adj* prior to the establishment of democracy (*esp* in Spain).
predestinación *nf* predestination.
predestinado *adj* predestined; **ser ~ a** + *infin* to be predestined to + *infin*.
predestinar [1a] *vt* to predestine.
predeterminación *nf* predetermination.
predeterminado *adj* predetermined.
predeterminar [1a] *vt* to predetermine.
prédica *nf* sermon; harangue; **~s** preaching (*t fig*).
predicación *nf* (**a**) (*gen*) preaching. (**b**) (*una ~*) = **prédica**.
predicado *nm* predicate.
predicador(a) *nm/f* preacher.
predicamento *nm* (**a**) (*dignidad*) standing, prestige; **no goza ahora de tanto ~** it has less prestige now, it is not so well thought of now. (**b**) (*LAm*) predicament.
predicar [1g] *vti* to preach.
predicativo *adj* predicative.
predicción *nf* prediction; forecast; **~ del tiempo** weather forecast(ing).
predicho *adj* aforementioned.
predigerido *adj* predigested.
predilección *nf* predilection; **tener ~ por** to have a predilection for; **predilecciones y aversiones** likes and dislikes.
predilecto *adj* favourite.
predio *nm* property, estate; (*LAm*) premises; site; **~ rústico** country estate; **~ urbano** town property.
predisponente *adj*: **factor ~ de** factor which causes a tendency towards.
predisponer [2q] *vt* to predispose; (*pey*) to prejudice, bias (*contra* against).
predisposición *nf* predisposition, inclination; (*pey*) prejudice, bias (*contra* against); (*Med*) tendency, predisposition (*a* to).
predispuesto *adj* predisposed; **ser ~ a los catarros** to have a tendency to get colds; **ser ~ al abatimiento** to be inclined to depression; **estar ~ contra uno** to be prejudiced against sb.
predocumento *nm* draft, preliminary paper.
predominante *adj* predominant; major; prevailing; (*Com*) *interés* controlling.
predominantemente *adv* predominantly.
predominar [1a] **1** *vt* (*preponderar*) to dominate, predominate over.
2 *vi* (**a**) (*dominar*) to predominate; (*prevalecer*) to prevail.
(**b**) **esta casa predomina a aquélla** this house is higher than that one.
predominio *nm* (*dominio*) predominance; (*preponderancia*) prevalence; (*influencia*) sway, ascendancy, influence; (*superioridad*) superiority.
preelectoral *adj*: **sondeo ~** pre-election survey, survey taken before the election.
preeminencia *nf* pre-eminence, superiority.
preeminente *adj* pre-eminent; superior.
preeminentemente *adv* pre-eminently.
preempción *nf* pre-emption.
preenfriar [1c] *vt* to precool.
pre(e)scoger [2c] *vt jugadores* to seed.
preescolar 1 *adj* preschool; **educación ~** preschool education, nursery education. **2** *nm* (*escuela*) nursery-school. **3** *nmf* child of nursery-school age.
preestrenar [1a] *vt* to preview, give a preview of.
preestreno *nm* preview, press view, private showing.
preexistencia *nf* pre-existence.
preexistente *adj* pre-existent, pre-existing.
preexistir [3a] *vi* to pre-exist, exist before.
prefabricado 1 *adj* prefabricated. **2** *nm* prefabricated building.
prefabricar [1g] *vt* to prefabricate.
prefacio *nm* preface, foreword.
prefecto *nm* prefect.
prefectura *nf* prefecture.
preferencia *nf* preference; **de ~** for preference, preferably; **localidad de ~** seat in a reserved section; **tratamiento de ~** preferential treatment; **mostrar ~ por** to show preference to, be biassed in favour of.
preferencial *adj* preferential
preferente *adj* (**a**) (*preferido*) preferred; (*preferible*) preferable. (**b**) (*Fin*) *acción* preference (*atr*); *impuesto, trato etc* preferential; priority (*atr*); *derecho* prior. (**c**) **clase ~** (*Aer*) club class.
preferentemente *adv* preferably.
preferible *adj* preferable (*a* to).
preferiblemente *adv* preferably.
preferido *adj* favourite; **es mi cantante ~** he's my favourite singer.
preferir [3i] *vt* to prefer; **~ té a café** to prefer tea to coffee; **¿cuál prefieres?** which do you prefer?; (*en bar etc*) **¿qué prefieres?** what will you have?; **prefiero ir a pie** I prefer to walk, I'd rather go on foot.
prefiguración *nf* foreshadowing, prefiguration.
prefigurar [1a] *vt* to foreshadow, prefigure.
prefijar [1a] *vt* (**a**) (*determinar*) to fix beforehand, arrange in advance, prearrange. (**b**) (*Ling*) to prefix (*a* to).
prefijo *nm* prefix; (*Telec*) **~ local** area code; **~ telefónico** dialling code.
pregón *nm* proclamation, announcement (*by town crier*); (*Com*) street cry, vendor's cry; **~ literario de un acto** speech (*etc*) about a forthcoming public ceremony.
pregonar [1a] *vt* (*proclamar*) to proclaim, announce; *secreto* to disclose, reveal; *mercancía* to cry, hawk, advertise verbally; *méritos etc* to praise publicly, proclaim (for all to hear).
pregonero *nm* (**a**) (*municipal*) town crier. (**b**) (*Méx*: *subastador*) auctioneer.
pregrabado *adj* prerecorded.
preguerra *nf* prewar period; **el nivel de la ~** the prewar

level; **en la** ~ in the prewar period, before the war.

pregunta *nf* question; ~ **capciosa,** ~ **indiscreta** catch question, loaded question; ~ **retórica** rhetorical question; ~ **sugestiva** (*Jur*) leading question; **andar** (*o* **estar**) **a la cuarta** ~* (*Esp**) to be broke*; **contestar a una** ~ to answer a question; **hacer una** ~ to ask (*o* put) a question; **estrechar a uno a** ~**s** to press sb closely with questions; **a** ~**s necias oídos sordos** ask a silly question (get a silly answer).

preguntar [1a] **1** *vt* to ask; to question, interrogate; ~ **algo a uno** to ask sb sth; ~ **si** to ask if, ask whether; **le fue preguntada su edad** he was asked his age; *V* **caber.**

2 *vi* to ask, inquire; ~ **por uno** to ask for sb, inquire for sb; ~ **por la salud de uno** to ask after sb's health, ask about sb's health.

3 preguntarse *vr* to wonder; **me pregunto si vale la pena** I wonder if it's worth while.

preguntón *adj* inquisitive.

prehispánico *adj* pre-Hispanic.

prehistoria *nf* prehistory.

prehistórico *adj* prehistoric.

preignición *nf* preignition.

preimpositivo *adj*: **beneficios** ~**s** pre-tax profits, profits before tax.

preinforme *nm* preliminary report.

prejubilación *nf* early retirement.

prejubilado, -a *nm/f* person who takes early retirement.

prejuiciado *adj* (*LAm*) prejudiced (*contra* against).

prejuicio *nm* (**a**) (*acto*) prejudgement. (**b**) (*parcialidad*) prejudice, bias (*contra* against); (*idea preconcebida*) preconception.

prejuzgar [1h] *vt* to prejudge.

prelación *nf* preference, priority.

prelado *nm* prelate.

preliminar *adj, nm* preliminary.

preludiar [1b] **1** *vt* (*anunciar*) to announce, herald; (*introducir*) to introduce; (*iniciar*) to start off. **2** *vi* (*Mús*) to tune up, play a few scales.

preludio *nm* (**a**) (*Mús, fig*) prelude (*de* to). (**b**) (*Mús*: *ensayo*) tuning up, practice notes, scales.

premamá *atr*: **vestido** ~ maternity dress.

premarital *adj* premarital.

prematrimonial *adj* premarital; before marriage; *V* **relación** (**c**).

prematuramente *adv* prematurely.

prematuro *adj* premature.

premedicación *nf* premedication.

premeditación *nf* premeditation; **con** ~ with premeditation, deliberately.

premeditadamente *adv* with premeditation, deliberately.

premeditado *adj* premeditated, deliberate; wilful; *insult etc* studied.

premeditar [1a] *vt* to premeditate; to plan, think out (in advance).

premenstrual *adj* premenstrual.

premiado 1 *adj novela etc* prize (*atr*), prize-winning. **2** *nm*, **premiada** *nf* prizewinner.

premiar [1b] *vt* (*recompensar*) to reward (*con* with); (*dar un premio a*) to give a prize to, make an award to; **salir premiado** to win a prize.

premier [pre'mjer] *nmf* prime minister, premier.

premio *nm* (**a**) (*recompensa*) reward, recompense; **como** ~ **a sus servicios** as a reward for his services.

(**b**) (*en concurso*) prize; award; (*persona*) prize-winner; ~ **de consolación** consolation prize; ~ **extraordinario** award (*of a degree etc*) with special distinction; ~ **gordo** first prize, big prize; **Gran P~** Grand Prix; ~ **en metálico** cash prize.

(**c**) (*Com, Fin*) premium; **a** ~ at a premium.

premioso *adj* (**a**) *vestido etc* tight.

(**b**) *orden etc* strict.

(**c**) *persona* (*al hablar*) tongue-tied, slow of speech; (*al escribir*) slow in writing; (*al moverse*) slow in movement, heavy, awkward.

(**d**) (*fig*) *estilo* difficult.

premisa *nf* premise.

premonición *nf* premonition.

premonitoriamente *adv* in a warning way, as a warning.

premonitorio *adj* indicative, warning, premonitory.

premunirse [3a] *vr* (*LAm*) = **precaverse.**

premura *nf* (**a**) (*presión*) pressure; **con** ~ **de tiempo** under (time) pressure, with very little time; **debido a** ~ **de espacio** because of pressure on space.

(**b**) (*prisa*) haste, urgency.

prenatal *adj* antenatal, prenatal.

prenavideño *adj* pre-Christmas, before Christmas.

prenda *nf* (**a**) (*garantía*) pledge; (*fig*) pledge, token; **dejar algo en** ~ to pawn sth; to leave sth as security; **en** ~ **de** as a pledge of, as a token of; **al buen pagador no le duelen** ~**s** a good payer is not afraid of giving guarantees; **a mí no me duelen** ~**s** I don't mind saying nice things about others, it doesn't worry me that I'm not as good as others; **no soltar** ~ to give nothing away, avoid committing o.s.; to give sb no chance (*o* opening).

(**b**) (*t* ~ **de vestir**) garment, article of clothing; ~**s deportivas** sports clothes, sportswear; ~ **interior** undergarment, piece of underclothing; ~**s de cama** bedclothes; ~**s de mesa** table linen.

(**c**) ~**s** (*fig*: *cualidades*) talents, gifts; (*t* **buenas** ~**s**) good qualities; **de todas** ~**s** first class, excellent.

(**d**) ~**s** (*juego*) forfeits; **pagar** ~ to pay a forfeit.

(**e**) (*joya*: *esp LAm*) jewel; ~**s** jewellery.

(**f**) (*: *en oración directa*) darling!, my treasure!; (*piropo*: *Esp**) **¡oye,** ~**!** hi, gorgeous!*

(**g**) **la** ~ (*Cono Sur*) one's sweetheart, one's lover.

prendar [1a] **1** *vt* (**a**) (*encantar*) to captivate, enchant; (*ganar la voluntad*) to win over; **volvió prendado con** (*o* **de**) **la ciudad** he came back enchanted with the town.

(**b**) (*Méx*: *empeñar*) to pawn.

2 prendarse *vr*: ~ **de** (*aficionarse*) to be captivated by, be enchanted with; to take a fancy to; ~ **de uno** (*liter*) to fall in love with sb.

prendedera *nf* (*And*) waitress.

prendedero *nm*, **prendedor** *nm* clasp, brooch.

prender [2a] **1** *vt* (**a**) *persona* to catch, capture; (*detener*) to arrest.

(**b**) (*Cos etc*) (*sujetar*) to fasten; (*con alfiler*) to pin, attach (*en* to); (*atar*) to tie, do up; ~ **el pelo con horquillas** to fix one's hair with hairpins, put clips in one's hair.

(**c**) (*esp LAm*) *fuego, horno etc* to light; *fósforo* to strike; *luz, TV etc* to switch on; *cigarrillo, vela* to light; *cuarto* to light up.

2 *vi* (**a**) (*engancharse*) to catch, stick; to grip; **el ancla prendió en el fondo** the anchor buried itself in the seabed, the anchor gripped firmly.

(**b**) (*fuego*) to catch; (*inyección*) to take; (*planta*) to take, take root; **el mal prendió más en la juventud** the evil spread most among young people, the evil infected youth most strongly.

3 prenderse *vr* (**a**) (*encenderse*) to catch fire (*en* on).

(**b**) (*mujer*) to dress up.

(**c**) (*Carib*) to get drunk.

prendería *nf* (*Esp*: *de cosas usadas*) secondhand (clothes) shop; (*de baratijas*) junkshop; (*de empeños*) pawnbroker's (shop).

prendero, -a *nm/f* secondhand (clothes) dealer, junk dealer; (*prestamista*) pawnbroker.

prendido 1 *adj* (**a**) **quedar** ~ to be caught (fast), be stuck; (*fig*) to be captivated. (**b**) (*Cono Sur Med*) constipated. (**c**) (*Méx*) dressed up. **2** *nm* (*adorno*) clip, brooch.

prendimiento *nm* (**a**) (*captura*) capture, seizure; arrest. (**b**) (*Cono Sur Med*) constipation.

prensa *nf* (**a**) (*Mec*) press; (*Tip*) press, printing press; (*de raqueta*) press, frame; ~ **de copiar** (*Fot*) printing frame; ~ **hidráulica** hydraulic press; ~ **rotativa** rotary press.

(**b**) (*fig*) **la P~** the press; ~ **amarilla** gutter press; ~ **del corazón,** ~ **del hígado** (*hum*) periodicals specializing in real-life romance stories; women's magazines; **aprobar un libro para la** ~ to pass a book for (the) press; **dar algo a la** ~ to publish sth; **entrar en** ~ to go to press; **estar en** ~ to be in press; **tener mala** ~ to have (*o* get) a bad press; **'libros en** ~**'** (*anuncio*) 'books in press', 'forthcoming publications'.

prensado *nm* (**a**) (*acto*) pressing. (**b**) (*lustre*) sheen, shine, gloss.

prensador *nm* press, pressing machine; ~ **de paja** straw baler.

prensaestopas *nm invar* packing gland.

prensaje *nm* (*Mús*) recording.

prensalimones *nm invar* lemon-squeezer.

prensar [1a] *vt* to press.

prensil *adj* prehensile.

preñada *adj* pregnant; (*Zool*) pregnant, with young; ~ **de 6 meses** 6 months pregnant.

preñado 1 *adj* (*fig*) (**a**) *muro* bulging, sagging.

(**b**) ~ **de** pregnant with, full of; **una situación preñada de peligros** a situation full of danger, a situation fraught with dangers; **ojos** ~**s de lágrimas** eyes filled with tears, eyes brimming with tears.

2 *nm* (*embarazo*) pregnancy.
preñar [1a] *vt* to get pregnant; (*Zool*) to impregnate, fertilize; (*fig*) to fill.
preñez *nf* pregnancy.
preocupación *nf* (**a**) (*cuidado*) worry, anxiety, concern, preoccupation.
(**b**) (*prejuicio*) prejudice.
(**c**) (*ofuscación*) preconception; (*inquietud*) unfounded fear, silly fear; (*noción*) notion, silly idea; **tiene la ~ de que su mujer le es infiel** he has an obsession that his wife is unfaithful to him.
(**d**) (*LAm*) special consideration, priority, preference.
preocupado *adj* worried, anxious, concerned, preoccupied.
preocupante *adj* worrying, disturbing.
preocupar [1a] **1** *vt* (**a**) (*inquietar*) to worry, preoccupy; to bother, exercise; **esto me preocupa muchísimo** this worries me greatly; **me preocupa cómo decírselo** I'm worried about how to tell him; **no le preocupa el qué dirán** public opinion doesn't bother him.
(**b**) (*influir*) to prejudice, influence.
2 preocuparse *vr* (**a**) (*inquietarse*) to worry, care (*de, por* about); (*ocuparse*) to concern o.s. (*de* about); **¡no se preocupe!** don't worry!, don't bother!; **no te preocupes por eso** don't worry about that; **no se preocupa en lo más mínimo** he doesn't care in the least.
(**b**) **yo me preocuparé de que esté listo** I'll see to it that everything is ready; **tú preocúpate de que todo esté listo** you ensure that (*o* see to it that) everything is ready.
(**c**) **~ de algo** (*LAm*) to give special attention to sth, give sth priority.
preolímpico 1 *adj*: **torneo ~** Olympic qualifying tournament. **2** *nm* (*concurso*) Olympic qualifying tournament (*o* round *etc*). **3** *nm*, **preolímpica** *nf* Olympic qualifier; athlete (*etc*) taking part in an Olympic qualifying tournament.
preparación *nf* (**a**) (*acto*) preparation; **~ de datos** data preparation; **estar en ~** to be in preparation.
(**b**) (*estado*) preparedness, readiness; **~ militar** military preparedness.
(**c**) (*formación*) training (*t Dep*); **le falta ~ matemática** he lacks mathematical training, he is not trained in maths.
(**d**) (*competencia*) competence; ability.
(**e**) (*Bio, Farm*) preparation.
(**f**) (*Cono Sur*: *bocadito*) appetizer.
preparado 1 *adj* (**a**) (*dispuesto*) prepared (*para* for); (*Culin*) ready to serve, ready cooked; **¡~s, listos, ya!** ready, steady, go! (**b**) (*competente*) competent, able; (*con título*) qualified; (*informado*) well-informed.
2 *nm* (*Farm*) preparation.
preparador(a) *nm/f* (**a**) (*Dep*) trainer, coach; (*de caballo*) trainer; **~ físico** fitness trainer. (**b**) (*de laboratorio etc*) assistant.
preparar [1a] **1** *vt* (**a**) (*disponer*) to prepare, get ready; (*Téc*) to prepare, process, treat.
(**b**) (*enseñar*) to teach, train; (*Dep*) to train, coach; **X le prepara a Y de física** X is coaching Y in physics.
2 prepararse *vr* (**a**) (*disponerse*) to prepare, prepare o.s., get ready; **~ a** + *infin*, **~ para** + *infin* to prepare to + *infin*, get ready to + *infin*.
(**b**) (*problema, tormenta etc*) to be brewing.
preparativo 1 *adj* preparatory, preliminary.
2 ~s *nmpl* (*aprestos*) preparations; (*disposiciones*) preliminaries; **hacer sus ~s** to make one's preparations (*para* + *infin* to + *infin*).
preparatorio 1 *adj* preparatory. **2 preparatoria** *nf* (*CAm, Méx Educ*) secondary school, high school (*US*).
pre-Pirineo *nm* Pyrenean foothills.
preponderancia *nf* preponderance; superiority.
preponderante *adj* preponderant; superior.
preponderar [1a] *vi* to preponderate; to dominate, prevail.
preponente *adj* (*And*: *jactancioso*) boastful, conceited.
preponer [2q] *vt* to place before.
preposición *nf* preposition.
preposicional *adj* prepositional.
prepósito *nm* (*Ecl*) prefect, superior.
prepotencia *nf* power, dominance, superiority; (*pey*) arrogance; abuse of power.
prepotente *adj* powerful, supreme; (*pey*) arrogant, overbearing, domineering; given to abusing power.
prepucio *nm* foreskin, prepuce.
prerrequisito *nm* prerequisite.
prerrogativa *nf* prerogative, right, privilege.
prerrománico *adj* pre-romanesque.
presa[1] *nf* (**a**) (*acto*) capture, seizure; **hacer ~** to seize.
(**b**) (*asimiento*) clutch, hold; **~ de pie** foothold; **hacer ~ en** to clutch (on to), seize; to get a hold on; **el fuego hizo ~ en la cortina** the fire set light to (*o* caught, began to burn) the curtain.
(**c**) (*objeto*) capture, catch, prize; (*Mil*) spoils, booty; loot; (*Náut*) prize; (*Orn*) prey; (*Zool*) prey, catch; **ave de ~** bird of prey; **ser ~ de** (*fig*) to be a prey to, be a victim of.
(**d**) (*Orn*) claw; (*Zool*) tusk, fang.
(**e**) (*de río etc*) dam; (*represa*) weir, barrage.
(**f**) (*Agr*) ditch, channel.
(**g**) (*esp LAm*) (*de comida*) piece of food; (*de carne*) piece of meat.
presagiador *adj* ominous.
presagiar [1b] *vt* to betoken, forebode, presage.
presagio *nm* omen, portent.
presbicia *nf* (*Med*) long-sightedness.
presbiopía *nf* presbyopia.
présbita *adj*, **présbite** *adj* (*Med*) long-sighted.
presbítera *nf* (woman) priest; (woman) minister.
presbiteriano, -a *adj, nm/f* Presbyterian.
presbiterio *nm* presbytery, chancel.
presbítero *nm* priest.
presciencia *nf* prescience, foreknowledge.
presciente *adj* prescient.
prescindencia *nf* (*LAm*) doing without, going without; (*abstención*) non-participation, abstention.
prescindente *adj* (*LAm*) non-participating.
prescindible *adj* dispensable; **y cosas fácilmente ~s** and things we can easily do without.
prescindir [3a] *vi*: **~ de** (*pasarse sin*) to do without, go without; (*deshacerse de*) to dispense with, get rid of; (*desatender*) to disregard; (*omitir*) to omit, (*pasar por alto*) overlook; **han prescindido del coche** they've given up their car, they've got rid of their car; **no podemos ~ de él** we can't manage without him; **prescindamos de todo aquello** let's forget about all that, let's leave all that aside.
prescribir [3a; *ptp* **prescrito**] **1** *vt* to prescribe. **2** *vi* (*plazo*) to expire, run out.
prescripción *nf* (**a**) (*Med*) prescription; **~ facultativa, ~ médica** medical prescription; **por ~ facultativa** on the doctor's orders. (**b**) (*Méx Jur*) legal principle.
prescriptivo *adj* prescriptive.
prescrito *adj* prescribed.
presea *nf* (**a**) (*liter*) jewel; treasure, precious thing. (**b**) (*LAm*) prize.
preselección *nf* (**a**) (*Dep*) seeding; (*de candidatos*) shortlist(ing). (**b**) (*Dep*: *personas*) squad.
preseleccionado, -a *nm/f* short-listed candidate; (*Dep*) squad member, member of the squad.
preseleccionar [1a] *vt* (*Dep*) to seed; *candidatos* to shortlist.
presencia *nf* presence; **~ de ánimo, ~ de mente** presence of mind; **en ~ de** in the presence of; **tener (buena) ~** to have a good presence, be impressive, have an impressive bearing.
presencial *adj*: **testigo ~** eyewitness.
presenciar [1b] *vt* (*asistir a*) to be present at; to attend; (*ver*) to see, witness, watch.
presentable *adj* presentable.
presentación *nf* (**a**) (*gen*) presentation; (*de personas*) introduction; **~ en directo, ~ en vivo** personal appearance; **~ de modelos** fashion parade, fashion show; **~ en (la) sociedad** coming-out, début. (**b**) (*LAm*) petition.
presentador(a) *nm/f* (*TV etc*) presenter; host, hostess.
presentar [1a] **1** *vt* (**a**) (*gen*) to present; to offer; to show, display; *armas, excusas, petición, prueba etc* to present; *dimisión* to tender; *moción* to propose, put forward; **presenta señales de deterioro** it shows signs of wear; **el coche presenta ciertas modificaciones** the car has certain modifications.
(**b**) (*Teat*) *obra* to perform, put on; *película* to show; *estrella* to present, feature; *espectáculo* (*TV etc*) to present, host, compère.
(**c**) *persona* to introduce; **le presento a Vd a mi hermana** may I introduce my sister to you?; **ser presentada en (la) sociedad** to come out, make one's début.
(**d**) **le presento mis consideraciones ...** (*en carta*) yours faithfully ...
(**e**) (*Com*) **~ al cobro, ~ al pago** to present for payment.
2 presentarse *vr* (**a**) (*comparecer*) to present o.s.; (*aparecer*) to appear (unexpectedly), turn up; **~ a la policía** to report to the police, (*criminal*) give o.s. up to the

police; **hay que ~ el lunes a las 9** you should report at 9 on Monday; **se presentó en un estado lamentable** he turned up in a dreadful state.

(**b**) (*hacerse conocer*) to introduce o.s. (*a* to); **~ en** (**la**) **sociedad** to come out, make one's début.

(**c**) (*candidato*) to run, stand; **~ a** *puesto* to put in for, apply for; **~ a** (*o* **para**) *examen* to sit (for), enter for.

(**d**) (*ofrecerse*) to present itself; (*mostrarse*) to show, appear; **el día se presenta muy hermoso** it looks like being a lovely day, there are prospects of a fine day; **se presentó un caso singular** a strange case came up.

presente 1 *adj* (**a**) *persona* present; **¡~!** present!, here!; **los ~s** those present; **los señores aquí ~s** the gentlemen here present; **estar ~ en** to be present at; **mejorando lo ~, salvando a los ~s** present company excepted.

(**b**) **la ~ carta, la ~** this letter; **le comunico por la ~** I hereby inform you.

(**c**) *tiempo* present; **hacer ~** to state, declare; **tener ~** to remember, bear in mind; **tennos ~** don't forget us; **ten muy ~ que** ... be sure to remember that ...; understand clearly that ...

(**d**) **'~'** (*LAm*: *en sobre*) 'by hand'.

2 *nm* (**a**) present; **al ~** at present; **hasta el ~** up to the present.

(**b**) (*Ling*) present (tense).

(**c**) (*regalo*) present, gift.

presentimiento *nm* premonition, presentiment; foreboding.

presentir [3i] *vt* to have a premonition of; **~ que** ... to have a premonition that ...

preservación *nf* protection, preservation.

preservar [1a] *vt* (**a**) (*proteger*) to protect, preserve (*contra* against, *de* from). (**b**) (*LAm*) to keep, preserve.

preservativo *nm* condom, sheath.

presi* *nmf* = **presidente**.

presidencia *nf* presidency; chairmanship; **P~** (*esp*: *oficina*) Prime Minister's office; **ocupar la ~** to preside, be in (*o* take) the chair.

presidenciable 1 *adj*: **ministro ~** minister who has the makings of a prime minister. **2** *nmf* possible candidate (*o* contender) for the prime ministership (*o* presidency).

presidencial *adj* presidential.

presidencialismo *nm* autocratic leadership; abuse of presidential power.

presidente *nmf* (*t* **presidenta** *nf*) (*de asociación, país, Taur*) president; (*de comité, reunión*) chairman *m*, chairwoman *f*, chairperson *mf*; (*Pol Esp*: *t* **P~ del Gobierno**) prime minister; (*Pol*: *de la cámara*) speaker; (*Jur*) presiding judge, presiding magistrate; (*LAm*) mayor; **~ de honor** honorary president; **~ vitalicio** president for life; **candidato a ~** presidential candidate.

presidiario *nm* convict.

presidio *nm* (**a**) (*cárcel*) prison, penitentiary; **echar a uno a ~** to put sb in prison.

(**b**) (*trabajos forzados*) hard labour, penal servitude.

(**c**) (*Pol*) praesidium.

(**d**) (*Mil*) garrison; fortress.

presidir [3a] **1** *vt* (**a**) (*gobernar*) to preside at, preside over; (*dirigir*) to take the chair at.

(**b**) (*fig*: *dominar*) to dominate, rule, be the dominant element in.

2 *vi* (*presidir*) to preside; (*dirigir*) to take the chair.

presilla *nf* (**a**) (*para cerrar*) fastener, clip. (**b**) (*lazo*) loop. (**c**) (*LAm*) shoulder badge, flash; (*Méx*) epaulette.

presintonía *nf* presetting, preprogram(m)ing.

presión *nf* (**a**) (*gen*) pressure; (*con mano etc*) press, squeeze; (*Fís, Met, Téc*) pressure; (*de explosión*) blast; **~ arterial, ~ sanguínea** blood pressure; **~ atmosférica** atmospheric pressure, air pressure; **a ~** under pressure; **de ~** (*Téc*) pressure (*atr*); **hacer ~** to press (*sobre* on).

(**b**) (*fig*) pressure; **~ fiscal, ~ impositiva** tax burden; **ejercer** (*o* **hacer**) **~ para que se haga algo** to press for sth to be done; **hay presiones dentro del partido** there are pressures within the party.

presionar [1a] **1** *vt* (**a**) (*pulsar*) to press.

(**b**) (*fig*) to press, put pressure on; **el ministro, presionado por los fabricantes, accedió** the minister, under pressure from the manufacturers, agreed.

2 *vi* to press; **~ para, ~ por** to press for; **~ para que sea permitido algo** to press for sth to be allowed.

preso 1 *ptp de* **prender**; **llevar ~ a uno** to take sb away under arrest; **estar ~ de un terror pánico** to be panic-stricken; **~ por mil, ~ por mil quinientos** (*Esp*) in for a penny, in for a pound.

2 *nm*, **presa**[2] *nf* convict, prisoner; **~ de conciencia** prisoner of conscience, political prisoner; **~ de confianza** trusty; **~ político** political prisoner; **~ preventivo** remand prisoner.

pressing ['presin] *nm* (*Dep*) pressure; = **presión** (**b**).

prestación *nf* (**a**) (*aportación*) lending, loan; (*subsidio*) benefit, payment; (*Méx*) fringe benefit, perk*; **~ de ayuda** giving of help; **~ de desempleo** unemployment benefit; **~ económico, ~ social** social security benefit; **~ por jubilación** retirement benefit; **~ personal** obligatory service (*of individual on communal work*).

(**b**) **~ de juramento** oath-taking, (ceremony of) swearing in.

(**c**) (*Aut, Mec*) feature, detail; **prestaciones** performance qualities.

(**d**) (*Inform*) capability.

prestado *adj*: **dar algo ~** to lend sth; **eso está ~** that is on loan; **pedir ~ algo, tomar ~ algo** to borrow sth; **vivir de ~** to live at somebody else's expense, live on what one can borrow.

prestador(a) *nm/f* lender.

prestamista *nmf* moneylender; pawnbroker.

préstamo *nm* (**a**) (*acto*) loan, lending, borrowing. (**b**) (*empréstito*) loan; **~ bancario** bank loan; **~ cobrable a la vista** call loan; **~ colateral, ~ pignoraticio** collateral loan; **~ con garantía** secured loan; **~ hipotecario** mortgage (loan). (**c**) (*Ling*) loanword.

prestancia *nf* (*distinción*) distinction, excellence; (*elegancia*) elegance, dignity.

prestar [1a] **1** *vt* (**a**) *dinero etc* to lend, loan.

(**b**) (*fig*) to lend, give; *apoyo, ayuda* to give; *atención* to pay (*a* to); *servicio* to do, render; *encanto etc* to lend.

(**c**) *juramento* to take, swear.

(**d**) (*LAm*: *pedir prestado*) to borrow (*a* from).

(**e**) (*Carib, Cono Sur*) to do good to, be good for; to suit; **no le prestó el viaje** the trip was not good for him.

2 *vi* (**a**) (*extenderse*) to give, stretch.

(**b**) **~ para** to be big enough for.

3 prestarse *vr* (**a**) **no se presta a esas maniobras** he does not lend himself to manoeuvres of that kind; **la situación se presta a muchas interpretaciones** the situation lends itself to many interpretations.

(**b**) **~ a** + *infin* to offer to + *infin*, volunteer to + *infin*.

(**c**) **~ de algo** (*Carib*) to borrow sth.

prestatario, -a *nm/f* borrower.

preste *nm* (*hum*) priest.

presteza *nf* speed, promptness; alacrity; **con ~** promptly, with alacrity.

prestidigitación *nf* conjuring, juggling; sleight of hand.

prestidigitador(a) *nm/f* conjurer, juggler.

prestigiado *adj* (*LAm*) worthy, estimable, prestigious.

prestigiar [1b] *vt* to give prestige (*o* distinction, status) to; (*dar fama a*) to make famous; (*honrar*) to honour (*con* with); (*realzar*) to enhance.

prestigio *nm* (**a**) (*fama*) prestige; (*honra*) face; (*reputación*) good name; **de ~** prestigious. (**b**) (*ensalmo*) (magic) spell. (**c**) (*truco*) trick.

prestigioso *adj* worthy, estimable, prestigious; reputable; famous.

presto 1 *adj* (**a**) (*rápido*) quick, prompt. (**b**) (*listo*) ready (*para* for). (**c**) (*Mús*) presto. **2** *adv* (*rápidamente*) quickly; (*en seguida*) at once, right away.

presumible *adj* presumable; probable; **es ~** it is to be presumed.

presumiblemente *adj* presumably.

presumido *adj* conceited.

presumir [3a] **1** *vt* (**a**) (*suponer*) to presume, conjecture, surmise; **~ que** ... to presume that ..., guess that ...

(**b**) (*And, Cono Sur*: *pretender*) to court; (*coquetear con*) to flirt with.

2 *vi* (**a**) **según cabe ~** as may be presumed, presumably.

(**b**) (*engreírse*) to be conceited; (*fachendear*) to give o.s. airs, swank*, show off; **para ~ ante las amistades** in order to show off before one's friends; **no presumas tanto** don't be so conceited; **~ de listo** to think oneself very smart, boast of being clever; **~ de experto** to pride oneself on being an expert; **~ demasiado de sus fuerzas** to overestimate one's strength.

presunción *nf* (**a**) (*conjetura*) supposition, presumption; (*sospecha*) suspicion. (**b**) (*cualidad*) conceit, presumption; pretentiousness.

presuntamente *adv* supposedly; **un hombre ~ rico** a supposedly rich man; **dos mujeres que ~ se dedican a esto**

two women (who are) presumed to devote themselves to this, two women (who are) suspected of devoting themselves to this.

presunto *adj* (*supuesto*) supposed, presumed; (*llamado*) so-called; *heredero* presumptive; *criminal* suspected, alleged; **el ~ asesino** the alleged murderer; **X, ~ implicado en ...** X, alleged to be concerned in ...; **estos ~s expertos** these so-called experts.

presuntuosamente *adv* conceitedly, presumptuously; pretentiously.

presuntuoso *adj* (*vanidoso*) conceited, presumptuous; (*pretencioso*) pretentious.

presuponer [2q] *vt* to presuppose.

presuposición *nf* presupposition.

presupuestal *adj* (*Méx etc*) budgetary, budget (*atr*).

presupuestar [1a] *vt* (*Fin*) to budget for; *gastos, ingresos* to reckon up, estimate for, estimate the cost of.

presupuestario *adj* budgetary, budget (*atr*).

presupuestívoro, -a *nm/f* (*LAm*: *hum*) public employee.

presupuesto *nm* (**a**) (*Fin*) budget; (*de obras, proyecto etc*) estimate; **~ operante** operating budget; **~ de ventas** sales budget.

(**b**) (*supuesto*) premise, assumption.

presurizado *adj* pressurized.

presurosamente *adv* quickly, promptly; hastily.

presuroso *adj* (*rápido*) quick, prompt, speedy; (*apresurado*) hasty; *paso etc* light, quick.

pretal *nm* (*esp LAm*) strap, girth.

pretecnología *nf* (*Escol*) practical subjects, technical courses.

pretemporada *nf* (*Dep*) pre-season (*t atr*).

pretenciosidad *nf* (**a**) pretentiousness; showiness. (**b**) (*LAm*) vanity, boastfulness.

pretencioso *adj* (**a**) (*vanidoso*) pretentious, presumptuous; showy. (**b**) (*LAm*: *presumido*) conceited, stuck-up*.

pretender [2a] *vt* (**a**) (*intentar*) ~ + *infin* to try to + *infin*, seek to + *infin*, endeavour to + *infin*; **pretendió convencerme** he sought to convince me; **han pretendido robarme** they have attempted to rob me; **¿qué pretende Vd decir con eso?** what do you mean by that?; **no pretendo ser feliz** it's not happiness I'm after.

(**b**) (*afirmar*) to claim; **~ ser rico** to claim to be rich, profess to be rich; **~ haber hecho algo** to claim to have done sth; **el libro pretende ser importante** the book tries to look (*o* make out that it is) important; **esto pretende poder curarlo todo** this purports to cure everything; **pretende que el coche le atropelló** he alleges that the car knocked him down.

(**c**) (*aspirar a*) to seek, try for; *puesto* to apply for; *honor* to aspire to; *objetivo* to aim at, try to achieve; **pretende llegar a ser médico** she hopes to become a doctor; **¿qué pretende Vd?** what are you after?; what do you hope to achieve.

(**d**) **~ que** + *subj* to expect that ..., suggest that ..., intend that ...; **él pretende que yo le escriba** he suggests that I should write to him, he wants me to write to him; **¿cómo pretende Vd que lo compre yo?** how do you expect me to buy it?

(**e**) *mujer* to woo, court; to seek the hand of.

pretendidamente *adv* supposedly; allegedly.

pretendido *adj* supposed, pretended; alleged.

pretendiente 1 *nm* (*gen*) suitor. **2** *nm*, **pretendienta** *nf* (*aspirante*) claimant; (*a puesto*) candidate, applicant (*a* for); (*a trono*) pretender (*a* to).

pretensado *adj* prestressed.

pretensión *nf* (**a**) (*reclamación, afirmación*) claim.

(**b**) (*objetivo*) aim, object; (*aspiración*) aspiration.

(**c**) (*pey*) pretension; exaggerated claim, false claim; **tener pretensiones de** to have pretensions to, lay claim to; **tener pocas pretensiones** to be undemanding, be content with very little; **tiene la ~ de que le acompañe yo** he expects me to go with him.

(**d**) (*LAm*) (*vanidad*) vanity; (*presunción*) presumption, arrogance.

pretensioso *adj* (*LAm*) = **pretencioso** (**b**).

preterir [3a] *vt* to leave out, omit, pass over.

pretérito 1 *adj* (**a**) (*Ling*) past. (**b**) (*fig*) past, former; **las glorias pretéritas del país** the country's former glories. **2** *nm* (*Ling*) preterite, past historic.

preternatural *adj* preternatural.

pretextar [1a] *vt* to plead, use as an excuse; **~ que ...** to plead that ..., allege that ..., claim that ...

pretexto *nm* (*gen*) pretext; (*disculpa*) excuse, plea; **a ~ de** on the pretext of; **bajo ningún ~** under no circumstances; **so ~ de** under pretext of; **tomar a ~** to use as an excuse.

pretil *nm* (**a**) (*parapeto*) parapet; (*baranda*) handrail, guardrail, railing. (**b**) (*And*) forecourt; (*Carib, Méx*: *banco*) bench; (*Méx*: *encintado*) kerb.

pretina *nf* (**a**) girdle, belt, waistband; (*And, Cono Sur*: *correa*) leather strap; (*Carib*: *bragueta*) flies, fly. (**b**) (*Elec*) cassette-player.

pretor *nm* (*Méx*) lower-court judge, magistrate.

pretoriano *adj*: **guardia pretoriana** praetorian guard.

preu* *nm* one-year pre-university course.

preuniversitario 1 *adj* pre-university; **curso ~** one-year pre-university course.

2 *nm*, **preuniversitaria** *nf student on a pre-university course*.

prevalecer [2d] *vi* (**a**) (*imponerse*) to prevail (*sobre* against, over); (*triunfar*) to triumph, win through; (*dominar*) to come to dominate. (**b**) (*prosperar*) to thrive; (*Bot*) to take root and grow.

prevaleciente *adj* prevailing, prevalent; dominant.

prevalerse [2p] *vr*: **~ de** to avail o.s. of; (*pey*) to take advantage of.

prevaricación *nf*, **prevaricato** *nm* (*Jur*) perversion of the course of justice.

prevaricar [1g] *vi* to pervert the course of justice.

preve* *nf* = **prevención** (**f**).

prevención *nf* (**a**) (*preparativo*) preparation; (*estado*) preparedness, readiness; **las prevenciones para la ceremonia** the preparations for the ceremony.

(**b**) (*acto de impedir*) prevention.

(**c**) (*cualidad*) foresight, forethought; **obrar con ~** to act with foresight.

(**d**) (*medida*) precaution; precautionary measure, safety measure; **de ~** precautionary; **medidas de ~** emergency measures, contingency plans; **hemos tomado ciertas prevenciones** we have taken certain precautions.

(**e**) (*prejuicio*) prejudice; **tener ~ contra uno** to have a prejudice against sb, be prejudiced against sb.

(**f**) (*comisaría*) police-station; (*Mil*) guardroom, guard-house.

prevenido *adj* (**a**) **ser ~** to be cautious; to be far-sighted.

(**b**) **estar ~** to be prepared, be ready; to be forewarned, be on one's guard (*contra* against); **hombre ~ vale por dos** forewarned is forearmed.

prevenir [3r] **1** *vt* (**a**) (*disponer*) to prepare, get ready, make ready (*para* for).

(**b**) (*proveer*) **~ a uno de algo** to provide sb with sth.

(**c**) (*impedir*) to prevent; (*alertar*) to alert; (*anticipar*) to forestall; **hay accidentes que no se pueden ~** some accidents cannot be avoided.

(**d**) (*advertir*) **~ a uno** to warn sb, forewarn sb, put sb on his guard (*contra* against, *de* about); **pudieron ~le a tiempo** they were able to warn him in time.

(**e**) (*prever*) to foresee, anticipate; to provide for; **más vale ~ que curar** prevention is better than cure.

(**f**) (*predisponer*) to prejudice, bias (*a favor de* in favour of, *en contra de* against).

2 prevenirse *vr* (**a**) (*disponerse*) to get ready, prepare; **~ para un viaje** to get ready for a trip; **~ de ropa adecuada** to provide o.s. with suitable clothing.

(**b**) **~ contra** to take precautions against, prepare for.

(**c**) **~ en contra de uno** to adopt a hostile attitude to sb.

preventivo *adj* preventive, precautionary; (*Med*) preventive.

prever [2u] *vt* (**a**) (*antever*) to foresee.

(**b**) (*anticipar*) to anticipate, envisage, visualize; (*proyectar*) to plan; (*tener en cuenta*) to make allowances for; (*establecer*) to provide for, establish; **la elección es prevista para ...** the election is planned for ...; **no teníamos previsto nada para eso** we had not made any allowance for that; **~ que ...** to anticipate that ..., envisage that ..., expect that ...; **la ley prevé que ...** the law provides that ..., the law establishes that ...; **ya lo preveía** I expected as much.

previamente *adv* previously.

previo 1 *adj* (**a**) (*gen*) previous, prior, earlier; *examen* preliminary; **autorización previa** prior authorization (*o* permission); **'previa cita'** 'by appointment only', 'appointment required'.

(**b**) *idea* preconceived, received, traditional.

2 *como prep* (**a**) (*tras*) after, following; **~ acuerdo de los otros** subject to the agreement of the others; **~ pago de los derechos** on payment of the fees.

(**b**) **~ a** before, prior to.

3 *nm* (*Cine*) playback.

previsible *adj* foreseeable; predictable.
previsiblemente *adv* predictably.
previsión *nf* (**a**) (*cualidad: clarividencia*) foresight, far-sightedness; (*prudencia*) caution.
(**b**) (*acto*) precaution, precautionary measure; **en ~ de** as a precaution against; in anticipation of.
(**c**) **caja de ~ social** social security.
(**d**) (*pronóstico*) forecast; **previsiones económicas** economic forecast; **~ meteorológica, ~ del tiempo** weather forecast(ing); **~ de ventas** sales forecast; **las previsiones del plan quinquenal** the forecasts of the five-year plan.
previsivo *adj* (*Méx*) = **previsor.**
previsor *adj* far-sighted; (*precavido*) prudent.
previsoramente *adv* (**a**) far-sightedly; prudently. (**b**) (*por si acaso*) just in case.
prez *nm o f* honour, glory.
PRI *nm* (*Méx*) *abr de* **Partido Revolucionario Institucional.**
pribar* [1a] *vti etc* = **privar²**.
prieta *nf* (*Cono Sur Culin*) black pudding.
prieto 1 *adj* (**a**) (*oscuro*) blackish, dark; (*LAm*) dark, swarthy; *mujer* brunette.
(**b**) (*tacaño*) mean.
(**c**) (*apretado*) tight, compressed, tightly packed; **un siglo ~ de historia** a century packed full of history, a century rich in history.
2 *nm* (*LAm: dado*) loaded dice.
prietuzco *adj* (*CAm, Carib, Méx*) blackish.
priísta *nmf* (*Méx Pol*) member of the PRI; *V* **PRI.**
prima *nf* (**a**) (*pariente*) cousin.
(**b**) (*de sueldo etc*) bonus, extra payment; (*de exportación etc*) subsidy; **~ por coste de vida** cost of living bonus; **~ de incentivo, ~ a la** (*o* **de**) **producción** incentive bonus; **~ de seguro** insurance premium; **~ por trabajos peligrosos** danger money.
(**c**) (*Ecl*) prime.
(**d**) (*Cono Sur*) **bajar la ~** to moderate one's language; **subir la ~** to use strong language.
primacía *nf* (**a**) (*primer lugar*) primacy, first place; (*prioridad*) priority; (*supremacía*) supremacy; **~ de paso** (*Aut*) priority, right of way; **tener la ~ entre** to be supreme among.
(**b**) (*Ecl*) primacy.
primada* *nf* piece of stupidity; silly mistake.
primado *nm* (*Ecl*) primate.
primadon(n)a *nf* prima donna (*t fig*).
primal 1 *adj* yearling. **2** *nm*, **primala** *nf* yearling.
primar [1a] **1** *vt* to give priority to; to place a high value on. **2** *vi* to occupy first place, be supreme; **~ sobre** to have priority over, take precedence over; to outweigh.
primaria *nf* (*t* **~s** *pl*) primary election(s).
primariamente *adv* primarily.
primariedad *nf* primacy.
primario *adj* primary; **escuela primaria** primary school.
primate 1 *adj* most important. **2** *nm* (**a**) (*Zool*) primate. (**b**) (*prócer*) important person, outstanding figure.
primavera 1 *nf* (**a**) (*estación*) spring; springtime (*t fig*). (**b**) (*Orn*) blue-tit. (**c**) (*Bot*) primrose. **2** *nm*: **ser un ~** (*Esp**) to be a simple soul.
primaveral *adj* spring (*atr*); spring-like.
prime* *adj* = **primero.**
primer *adj V* **primero.**
primera *nf* (**a**) (*Aut etc*) first gear, bottom gear.
(**b**) (*Ferro*) first class; **viajar en ~** to travel first.
(**c**) **de ~** first-class, first-rate; **comer de ~** to eat really well, have a first-class meal; **estar de ~** to feel fine.
(**d**) **~ de cambio** (*Com*) first of exchange; *V* **cambio** (**c**).
(**e**) **a las ~s de cambio** (*fig*) as soon as I turned my back; before you know where you are.
primeramente *adv* first, firstly; chiefly.
primerear [1a] *vi* (*Cono Sur: fig*) to land the first blow, get in first.
primerizo 1 *adj* green, inexperienced. **2** *nm*, **primeriza** *nf* novice, beginner.
primero 1 *adj* (**primer** *delante de nm sing*) (**a**) (*que precede*) first; (*anterior*) former; *página* first, front; **en los ~s años del siglo** in the early years of the century; **en los ~s años treinta** in the early thirties; **a ~s de siglo** at the start of the century, early in the century; **llegar el ~** to arrive first; **ser el ~ en** + *infin* to be the first to + *infin*; **venir a primera hora de la mañana** to come first thing in the morning.
(**b**) (*fig*) (*primordial*) first; (*principal*) prime; (*fundamental*) basic, fundamental; (*urgente*) urgent; *materia* raw; **lo ~ es que ...** the fundamental thing is that ...; **lo ~ es lo ~** first things first; **es nuestro primer deber** it is our first duty; **es el primer país en estos estudios** it is the foremost country in these studies.
2 *adv* (**a**) (*primeramente*) first.
(**b**) (*antes*) rather, sooner; **~ se quedará en casa que pedir permiso para salir** she'd rather stay at home than have to ask for permission to go out; **¡~ morir!** we'd rather die!
primicia *nf* (**a**) (*novedad*) novelty; (*estreno*) first appearance; **~ informativa** scoop. (**b**) **~s** first fruits (*t fig*).
primigenio *adj* primitive, original.
primitiva* *nf*: **la ~** = **lotería primitiva.**
primitivamente *adv* (**a**) (*al principio*) at first; originally, in earlier times. (**b**) (*de un modo primitivo*) primitively, in a primitive way.
primitivo *adj* (**a**) (*temprano*) early; (*original*) first, original; (*Arte*) primitive; **el texto ~** the original text; **quedan 200 de los ~s 850** there remain 200 from the original 850; **es una obra primitiva** it is an early work; **devolver algo a su estado ~** to restore sth to its original state.
(**b**) *color* primary.
(**c**) (*Fin*) *acción* ordinary.
(**d**) (*Hist etc*) primitive; uncivilized; **en condiciones primitivas** in primitive conditions.
primo 1 *adj* (**a**) (*Mat*) prime.
(**b**) *materia* raw.
2 *nm* (**a**) (*pariente*) cousin; **~ carnal, ~ hermano** first cousin; **ser ~s hermanos** (*fig*) to be extraordinarily alike; **le vino el ~ de América*** she started her period.
(**b**) (*) (*cándido*) fool; (*incauto*) dupe, sucker‡; **hacer el ~** to be easily taken in, be taken for a ride*; to carry the can*; **tomar a uno por ~** to do sb down*, take sb in*.
primogénito *adj* first-born.
primogenitura *nf* (*Jur*) primogeniture; (*patrimonio*) birthright.
primor *nm* (**a**) (*belleza*) exquisiteness, beauty; (*elegancia*) elegance; (*delicadeza*) delicacy.
(**b**) (*maestría*) care, skill; **hecho con ~** done most skilfully, delicately made.
(**c**) (*objeto*) fine thing, lovely thing; **hace ~es con la aguja** she makes lovely things with her needlework; **cose que es un ~** she sews beautifully, she sews in a way that is a delight to see; **hijos que son un ~** delightful children, charming children.
primordial *adj* basic, fundamental, essential; supreme; **esto es ~** this is top priority; **es de interés ~** it is of fundamental concern; **es ~ saberlo** it is essential to know it.
primordialidad *nf* overriding importance, essential nature; supremacy.
primordialmente *adv* basically, fundamentally.
primorosamente *adv* exquisitely, delicately, elegantly; neatly, skilfully.
primoroso *adj* exquisite, fine, delicate, elegant; neat, skilful.
prímula *nf* primrose.
princesa *nf* princess.
principado *nm* principality; **P~** (*Esp Pol*) Asturias.
principal 1 *adj* (**a**) (*más importante*) principal, chief, main; (*más destacado*) foremost; *piso* first, second (*US*); **lo ~ es** ... the main thing is to ...
(**b**) *persona* illustrious.
2 *nm* (**a**) (*persona*) head, chief, principal.
(**b**) (*Fin*) principal, capital.
(**c**) (*Teat*) dress circle.
principalmente *adj* principally, chiefly, mainly.
príncipe *nm* (**a**) prince; **~ azul** knight in shining armour, Prince Charming; **~ consorte** prince consort; **~ encantado** Prince Charming; **~ heredero** crown prince. (**b**) *V* **edición.**
principesco *adj* princely.
principiante 1 *adj* (*que comienza*) who is beginning; (*novato*) novice; (*inexperto*) inexperienced, green. **2** *nm*, **principianta** *nf* beginner; learner; novice.
principiar [1b] *vti* to begin; **~ a** + *infin* to begin to + *infin*, begin + *ger*; **~ con** to begin with.
principio *nm* (**a**) (*comienzo*) beginning, start; (*origen*) origin; (*primera etapa*) early stage; **al ~** at first, in the beginning; **a ~s de** at the beginning of; **a ~s del verano** at the beginning of the summer, early in the summer; **desde el ~** from the first, from the outset; **desde el ~ hasta el fin** from start to finish, from beginning to end; **en un ~** at first, to start with; **dar ~ a** to start off; **tener** (*o* **tomar**) **~ en** to start from, be based on.
(**b**) **~s** (*nociones*) rudiments, first notions; **'P~s de física'**

'Introduction to Physics', 'Outline of Physics'.

(**c**) (*moral*) principle; **el ~ de la legalidad** the force of law, the rule of law; **persona de ~s** man of principles; **en ~** in principle; **por ~** on principle, as a matter of principle; **es inmoral por ~** it is immoral in principle; **sin ~s** unprincipled.

(**d**) (*Filos*) principle; (*Quím*) element, constituent.

(**e**) (*esp Esp Culin*) entrée.

principote* *nm* (*fachendoso*) swank*, show-off*; (*arribista*) parvenu, social climber.

pringada *nf* bread dipped in gravy (*etc*).

pringado*, -a *nm/f* (**a**) (*víctima*) (innocent) victim; (*sin suerte*) unlucky person; (*infeliz*) poor devil, wretch; down-and-out; **el ~ del grupo** the odd man out, the loser.

(**b**) (*gafe*) bringer of bad luck.

(**c**) (*tonto*) fool, idiot; **¡no seas ~!** don't be an idiot!

pringao* *nm* = **pringado**.

pringar [1h] **1** *vt* (**a**) (*Culin*) to dip in fat (*etc*); *asado* to baste; **~ el pan en la sopa** to dip one's bread in the soup.

(**b**) (*ensuciar*) to dirty, soil (with grease); (*rociar*) to splash grease (*o* fat) on; (*esp LAm*) to splash.

(**c**) (**: herir*) **~ a uno** to wound sb, make sb bleed.

(**d**) (**: denigrar*) to blacken, run down*.

(**e**) (**: involucrar*) **~ a uno en un asunto** to involve sb in a matter; **están pringadas en esto unas altas personalidades** some top people are mixed up in this.

(**f**) (*Cono Sur*) *enfermedad* to give.

(**g**) (*Cono Sur**) *mujer* to put in the family way.

(**h**) **~la*** (*meter la pata*) to drop a brick*, make a boob*; **~la(s)** (*morir*) to peg out‡; **~la*‡** (*Med*) to get a dose of clap‡.

(**i**) **estar pringado‡** to be hooked (on drugs)*.

2 *vi* (**a**) (**: perder*) to take a beating, lose badly; to come a cropper*; **hemos pringado** we're done for.

(**b**) (*Mil etc*: trabajar*) to sweat one's guts out‡, slog away.

(**c**) **~ en*** to dabble in; to take a hand in, get mixed up in.

(**d**) (**: morir*) to peg out‡.

(**e**) (*CAm, Carib, Méx*: *lloviznar*) to drizzle.

3 pringarse *vr* (**a**) (*ensuciarse*) to get splashed, get soiled (*con, de* with).

(**b**) = **2** (**c**).

(**c**) (*) (*ganar por medios dudosos*) to make money on the side; (*sacar tajada*) to get a rake-off*; (*enriquecerse*) to make a packet*.

(**d**) **o nos pringamos todos, o ninguno*** either we all carry the can or none of us does*.

pringo *nm* (*LAm*) (*gota*) drop; (*pizca*) bit, pinch; **con un ~ de leche** with a drop of milk.

pringón 1 *adj* (*sucio*) dirty, greasy. **2** *nm* (**a**) grease stain, grease spot. (**b**) (‡) (*tajada*) rake-off*, (*ganancias*) packet*.

pringoso *adj* greasy; sticky.

pringue *nm* (*a veces f*) (**a**) (*Culin*) grease, fat, dripping.

(**b**) (*mancha*) grease stain, grease spot; (*suciedad*) (*any*) dirty object, sticky thing.

(**c**) (**: molestia*) nuisance; cause of trouble; **es un ~ tener que ...** it's a bind having to ...*

(**d**) (*CAm, Méx*: *salpicadura*) splash (of mud *etc*); (*And*: *quemadura*) burn.

(**e**) (‡: *dinero*) dosh‡, money.

(**f**) (‡: *policía*) **P~** Crime Squad.

print-out *nm* (*Inform*) printout.

prior *nm* prior.

priora *nf*, **prioresa** *nf* †† prioress.

priorato *nm* priory.

prioridad *nf* (*precedencia*) priority; (*antigüedad*) seniority, greater age; **~ de paso** (*Aut*) right of way; **tener ~** to have priority (*sobre* over).

prioritariamente *adv* (*primero*) as a priority, first; (*mayormente*) mainly, principally.

prioritario *adj* prior, priority (*atr*); main, principal; **un proyecto de carácter ~** a plan with top priority, a plan in the priority class; **lo ~es ...** the first thing (to do) is ...

priorizar [1f] **1** *vt* to give priority to, treat as a priority, prioritize. **2** *vi* to determine priorities.

prisa *nf* (*prontitud*) hurry, haste; (*rapidez*) speed; (*premura*) (sense of) urgency; **temporada de más ~(s)** rush period, busy period; **a ~, de ~** quickly, hurriedly; **a toda ~** as quickly as possible; **sin ~ pero sin pausa** in an unhurried way; **estar de ~** to be in a hurry; **voy con mucha ~** I'm in a great hurry; **correr ~** to be urgent; **¿te corre ~?** are you in a hurry?; **¿corren ~ estas cartas?** (*Esp*) are these letters urgent?, is there any hurry for these letters?; **dar ~ a uno, meter ~ a uno** to make sb get a move on; **darse ~** to hurry (up); **¡date ~!** hurry (up)!, come along!; **tener ~** to be in a hurry.

prisco 1 *adj* (*LAm**) simple. **2** *nm* (*esp Cono Sur*) apricot.

prisión *nf* (**a**) (*cárcel*) prison; **~ (de régimen) abierto** open prison; **~ de alta** (*o* **máxima**) **seguridad** top-security prison.

(**b**) (*encierro*) imprisonment; **~ domiciliaria** house-arrest; **~ mayor** (*Esp*) sentence of more than six years and a day; **~ menor** (*Esp*) sentence of less than six years and a day; **~ perpetua** life imprisonment; **~ preventiva** preventive detention; **cinco años de ~** five years' imprisonment, prison sentence of five years. (**c**) **prisiones** (*grillos*) shackles, fetters.

prisionero, -a *nm/f* prisoner (of war); **hacer ~ a uno** to take sb prisoner.

prisma *nm* (**a**) prism. (**b**) (*fig*) point of view, angle; perspective; **bajo** (*o* **desde**) **el ~ de** from the point of view of.

prismático 1 *adj* prismatic. **2 ~s** *nmpl* binoculars, field glasses.

pristinidad *nf* pristine nature, original quality.

prístino *adj* pristine, original.

priva‡ *nf*: **la ~** (*Esp*) the booze*, the drink.

privacidad *nf* privacy; secrecy.

privación *nf* (**a**) (*acto*) deprivation, deprival; **sufrir ~ de libertad** to suffer loss of liberty. (**b**) (*estado*) deprivation; want, privation; **privaciones** hardships, privations.

privadamente *adv* privately.

privado 1 *adj* (**a**) (*particular*) private; personal; **'~ y confidencial'** 'private and confidential'.

(**b**) (*LAm*: *alocado*) mad, senseless; (*Carib*) weak, faint.

2 *nm* (**a**) (*Pol*) favourite, protégé; (*Hist*) royal favourite, chief minister.

(**b**) **en ~** privately, in private.

privanza *nf* favour; **durante la ~ de Lerma** when Lerma was royal favourite, when Lerma was chief minister.

privar¹ [1a] **1** *vt* (**a**) (*despojar*) **~ a uno de algo** to deprive sb of sth, take sth away from sb; **~ a uno del conocimiento** to render sb unconscious; **le privaron del carnet de conducir** they suspended his driving licence, they took away his driving licence; **nos vemos privados de ...** we find ourselves without ..., we find ourselves bereft of ...

(**b**) (*prohibir*) **~ a uno de** + *infin* to forbid sb to + *infin*, prevent sb from + *ger*; **lo cual me privó de verlos** which prevented me from seeing them; **no me prives de verte** don't forbid me to come to see you, don't tell me not to come again.

(**c**) (*extasiar*) to delight, overwhelm.

2 *vi* (**a**) (*Pol*) to be in favour (at court).

(**b**) (*existir*) to obtain, be present; (*predominar*) to prevail; (**: estar de moda*) to be in fashion, be the thing; **la cualidad que más priva entre ellos** the quality which is most strongly present in them; **en ese período privaba la minifalda*** at that time miniskirts were in.

3 privarse *vr*: **~ de** (*abstenerse de*) to deprive o.s. of; (*renunciar*) to give up, go without, forgo; **no se privan de nada** they lack nothing, they have everything they want.

privar²‡ [1a] *vti* to booze*, drink.

privata‡ *nf* = **priva**.

privativo *adj* exclusive; **~ de** exclusive to; **esa función es privativa del presidente** that function is the president's alone; **la planta es privativa del Brasil** the plant is peculiar to Brazil, the plant is restricted to Brazil.

privatización *nf* privatization.

privatizar [1f] *vt* to privatize.

prive‡ *nf* = **priva**.

privilegiado 1 *adj* (*gen*) privileged; *memoria etc* exceptionally good. **2** *nm*, **privilegiada** *nf* privileged person; **los ~s** the privileged.

privilegiar [1b] *vt* to grant a privilege to; to favour.

privilegio *nm* (*gen*) privilege; concession; (*exención*) immunity, exemption; (*Jur*) sole right; (*Liter*) copyright; **~ fiscal** tax concession; **~ de invención** patent.

privota‡ *nmf* piss artist*‡, boozer‡.

pro 1 *nm y nf* (**a**) (*provecho*) profit, advantage; **los ~s y los contras** the pros and the cons, for and against; **buena ~ le haga** and much good may it do him; **en ~ de** for, on behalf of; for the benefit of.

(**b**) **de ~** (*bueno*) worthy; (*verdadero*) real, true; **hombre de ~** worthy man, honest man; **para los cinéfilos de ~** for real film buffs.

2 *prep* for, on behalf of; **campaña ~ paz** peace campaign; **asociación ~ ciegos** association for (aid to) the blind.

pro... *pref* pro-..., *p.ej.* **prosoviético** pro-Soviet.

proa *nf* (*Náut*) bow, bows; prow; (*Aer*) nose; **de ~** bow (*atr*), fore; **en la ~** in the bows; **poner la ~ a** (*Náut*) to head for, set a course for; (*fig*) to aim at; **poner la ~ a uno** to take a stand against sb, set o.s. against sb.

probabilidad *nf* (**a**) (*gen*) probability, likelihood; **según toda ~** in all probability.

(**b**) (*perspectiva*) chance, prospect; **~es** chances; **~es de vida** expectation of life; **hay pocas ~es de que venga** there is little prospect of his coming; **apenas tiene ~es** he hasn't much chance.

probable *adj* probable, likely; **es ~ que +** *subj* it is probable (*o* likely) that ...; **es ~ que no venga** he probably won't come; **lo dio como ~** he said it was likely.

probablemente *adv* probably.

probadamente *adv* provenly.

probado *adj remedio etc* proven.

probador *nm* (**a**) (*persona*) taster. (**b**) (*en tienda*) fitting room. (**c**) (*LAm*) tailor's dummy.

probanza *nf* proof, evidence.

probar [1l] **1** *vt* (**a**) *hecho, teoría etc* to prove; (*demostrar*) to show, demonstrate; (*asentar*) to establish; **~ que ...** to prove that ...

(**b**) *aparato, arma etc* to test, try (out); *ropa* to try on.

(**c**) *comida etc* to try, taste, sample; **prueba un poco de esto** try a bit of this; **no han probado nunca un buen jerez** they have never tasted a good sherry; **no lo pruebo nunca** I never touch it; **al ~ se ve el mosto** the proof of the pudding is in the eating.

2 *vi* (**a**) (*intentar*) to try; **¿probamos?** shall we try?, shall we have a go?; **~ no cuesta nada** there's no harm in trying; **~ a +** *infin* to try to + *infin*.

(**b**) **~ de = 1** (**c**).

(**c**) (*sentar*) to suit; **no me prueba (bien) el café** coffee doesn't agree with me; **le probó mal ese oficio** that trade did not suit him.

3 probarse *vr*: **~ un traje** to try a suit on.

probatorio *adj* (**a**) (*que testimonia*) evidential; **documentos ~s del crimen** documents in proof of the crime, documents which prove the crime. (**b**) (*convincente*) convincing.

probeta 1 *nf* test-tube; graduated cylinder. **2** *atr* test-tube (*atr*); artificial; experimental; **niño ~** test-tube baby.

probidad *nf* integrity, honesty, rectitude.

problema 1 *nm* (*gen*) problem; (*pega*) difficulty, snag; trouble; (*Méx*) accident, mishap; (*Mat*) problem; (*rompecabezas*) puzzle. **2** *atr* problem (*atr*); **niño ~** problem child.

problemática *nf* problems, questions; issues; (*conjunto*) set of problems.

problemático *adj* problematic.

problematizar [1f] *vt asunto* to make problematic; *persona* to burden with problems.

probo *adj* honest, upright.

probóscide *nf* proboscis.

procacidad *nf* (**a**) (*desvergüenza*) insolence, impudence; (*descaro*) brazenness. (**b**) (*indecoro*) indecency, obscenity.

procaz *adj* (**a**) (*atrevido*) insolent, impudent; (*descarado*) brazen. (**b**) (*obsceno*) indecent, obscene.

procedencia *nf* (**a**) (*fuente*) source, origin; provenance (*punto de partida*) provenance; point of departure; (*Náut*) port of origin. (**b**) (*propiedad*) properness; (*justicia*) justification, soundness; (*Jur*) propriety.

procedente *adj* (**a**) **~ de** coming from, proceeding from, originating in. (**b**) (*razonable*) reasonable; (*apropiado*) proper, fitting; (*Jur*) proper; duly established.

procedentemente *adv* properly, in a right and proper fashion.

proceder [2a] **1** *vi* (**a**) (*pasar*) to proceed; **~ a una elección** to proceed to an election; **~ contra uno** (*Jur*) to take proceedings against sb.

(**b**) **~ de** to come from, originate in; to flow from, spring from; **todo esto procede de su negativa** all this springs from his refusal; **estas patatas proceden de Israel** these potatoes come from Israel; **de donde procede que ...** (from) whence it happens that ...

(**c**) (*obrar*) to act; (*conducirse*) to proceed, behave; **ha procedido precipitadamente** he has acted hastily; **conviene ~ con cuidado** it is best to go carefully.

(**d**) (*ser apropiado*) to be right (and proper), be fitting; **si el caso procede** if the case warrants it; **no procede obrar así** it is not right to act like that; **táchese lo que no proceda** cross out what does not apply; **luego, si procede,** ... then, if appropriate, ...

(**e**) (*: *estar de moda*) to be in*, be in fashion.

2 *nm* course of action; behaviour, conduct.

procedimental *adj* procedural; (*Jur*) legal.

procedimiento *nm* (*gen*) procedure; (*sistema*) process; (*medio*) means, method; (*Jur*) proceedings; **un ~ para abaratar el producto** a method of making the product cheaper; **por un ~ deductivo** by a deductive process.

proceloso *adj* (*liter*) stormy, tempestuous.

prócer *nm* (*persona eminente*) worthy, notable; (*magnate*) important person; (*Pol*) great man, leader; (*LAm*) leader of the independence movement.

procesado[1] **1** *adj alimento* processed. **2** *nm* (*Téc*) processing.

procesado[2]**, -a** *nm/f* (*Jur*) accused (person).

procesador *nm* processor; **~ de datos** data processor; **~ de palabras, ~ de textos** word processor.

procesadora *nf* (*LAm*: *t* **~ de alimentos**) food processor.

procesal *adj* (**a**) (*Parl etc*) procedural. (**b**) (*Jur*) *costas etc* legal; *derecho* procedural.

procesamiento *nm* (**a**) (*gen*) processing. (**b**) (*Inform*) processing; **~ concurrente** concurrent processing; **~ de datos** data processing; **~ interactivo** interactive processing; **~ por lotes** batch processing; **~ simultáneo** simultaneous processing; **~ de textos** word processing. (**c**) (*Jur*) prosecution; trial.

procesar [1a] *vt* (**a**) (*Jur*: *juzgar*) to try, put on trial; to prosecute; (*demandar*) to sue, bring an action against. (**b**) (*Téc*) to process.

procesión *nf* procession; **la ~ va por dentro** still waters run deep; there is more in this than meets the eye; **la ~ le va por dentro** he's a quiet one; he keeps his troubles to himself; **una ~ de quejas** a never-ending series of complaints.

procesional *adj* processional.

procesionaria *nf* processionary moth (*o* caterpillar).

proceso *nm* (**a**) (*gen*) process; **~ mental** mental process; **~ de una enfermedad** course (*o* progress) of a disease.

(**b**) (*transcurso*) lapse of time; **en el ~ de un mes** in the course of a month.

(**c**) (*Jur*) (*juicio*) trial; prosecution; (*pleito*) action, lawsuit, proceedings; **~ verbal** (*escrito*) record; (*audiencia*) hearing; **abrir** (*o* **entablar, formar**) **~** to bring a suit (*a* against).

(**d**) (*Inform*) processing; **~ de datos** data processing; **~ de imágenes** image processing; **~ por lotes** batch processing; **~ prioritario** foreground processing; **~ no prioritario** background processing; **~ de textos** word processing.

proclama *nf* (**a**) (*gen*) proclamation; (*discurso*) address; (*Pol*) manifesto. (**b**) **~s** (*Ecl*) banns.

proclamación *nf* proclamation.

proclamar [1a] **1** *vt* (*publicar*) to proclaim. **2 proclamarse** *vr*: **~ rey** to proclaim o.s. king; **~ campeón** to become champion, win the championship.

proclive *adj*: **~ a** given to, inclined to.

proclividad *nf* proclivity, inclination.

procónsul *nm* proconsul.

procreación *nf* procreation, breeding.

procrear [1a] *vti* to procreate, breed.

procura *nf* (*esp LAm*) obtaining, getting; **en ~ de** in search of; **andar en ~ de algo** to be trying to get sth.

procuración *nf* (*Jur*) power of attorney; proxy.

procurador(a) *nm/f* (**a**) (*Jur*: *abogado*) attorney, ≈ solicitor. (**b**) (*Jur*: *apoderado*) proxy. (**c**) **~ en Cortes, ~ a Cortes** (*Pol Hist*) deputy, member of (the Spanish) parliament. (**d**) **~ general** attorney general.

procuraduría *nf* (**a**) lawyer's office; **~ (general)** (*Méx*) attorney general's office. (**b**) (costs of) legal representation.

procurar [1a] **1** *vt* (**a**) (*intentar*) **~ +** *infin* to try to + *infin*, endeavour to + *infin*; **procura conservar la calma** do try to keep calm; **procura que no te vean** take care not to let them see you, don't let them see you.

(**b**) (*conseguir*) to get, obtain; to secure; (*producir*) to yield, produce; **~ un puesto a uno** to get sb a job, find a job for sb; **esto nos procurará grandes beneficios** this will bring us great benefits, this will secure great benefits for us.

(**c**) (*lograr*) **~ +** *infin* to manage to + *infin*, succeed in + *ger*; **por fin procuró dominarse** eventually he managed to control himself.

2 procurarse *vr*: **~ algo** to secure sth for o.s.

procurón* *adj* (*Méx*) interfering, nosey*.

Procustes *nm*, **Procusto** *nm* Procrustes; **lecho de ~** Procrustes' bed.

prodigalidad *nf* (**a**) (*abundancia*) bounty; richness. (**b**) (*liberalidad*) lavishness, generosity. (**c**) (*derroche*) prodigality; (*despilfarro*) extravagance, wastefulness.

pródigamente *adv* (**a**) (*abundantemente*) bountifully; richly. (**b**) (*generosamente*) lavishly. (**c**) (*con prodigalidad*) prodigally; wastefully.

prodigar [1h] **1** *vt* (*disipar*) to lavish, give lavishly; (*despilfarrar*) (*pey*) to squander; **prodiga las alabanzas** he is lavish in his praise (*a* of); **nos prodigó sus atenciones** he was very generous in his kindnesses to us.

2 prodigarse *vr* to be generous with what one has, lay o.s. out to please; to be generous with one's time (*o* energies *etc*); (*dejarse ver*) to show o.s.; **no te prodigas que digamos** we don't see much of you to say the least.

prodigio 1 *nm* prodigy; wonder, marvel; **es un ~ de talento** he is wonderfully talented.

2 *atr*: **niño ~** child prodigy.

prodigiosamente *adv* prodigiously, marvellously.

prodigioso *adj* prodigious, marvellous.

pródigo 1 *adj* (**a**) (*exuberante*) bountiful; (*rico*) rich; (*fértil*) productive; **~ en** rich in, generous with; **la pródiga naturaleza** bountiful nature.

(**b**) (*liberal*) lavish, generous (*de* with); **ser ~ de sus talentos** to be generous in offering one's talents.

(**c**) (*derrochador*) prodigal; extravagant, wasteful; **hijo ~** prodigal son.

2 *nm*, **pródiga** *nf* (*manirroto*) spendthrift, prodigal.

producción *nf* (**a**) (*gen*) production; (*producto*) output; yield; **~ bruta** gross production; **~ en cadena** production-line assembly; **~ en serie** mass production. (**b**) (*objeto*) product; (*Cine*) production.

producir [3n] **1** *vt* (*gen*) to produce; (*hacer*) to make; (*dar, rendir*) to give, yield; (*motivar*) to cause, generate; *cambio etc* to bring about; *impresión* to give, cause; (*Fin*) *interés* to bear; **le produjo gran tristeza** it caused her much sadness; **¿qué impresión le produce?** how does it impress you?, what impression do you get from it?; **Ruritania no produce cohetes** Ruritania does not make rockets; **estos factores produjeron la revolución** these factors caused the revolution; **~ en serie** to mass-produce.

2 producirse *vr* (**a**) (*fabricarse*) to be produced, be made (*etc*).

(**b**) (*cambio etc*) to come about; (*dificultad, crisis*) to arise; (*accidente*) to happen, take place; (*disturbio etc*) to break out; **así se produjo la nueva creencia de que ...** in this way there arose the new belief that ...; **en ese momento se produjo una explosión** at that moment there was an explosion; **a no ser que se produzca un cambio** unless a change takes place, unless there is a change.

productividad *nf* productivity.

productivo *adj* productive; *negocio* profitable; **~ de interés** *bono etc* interest-bearing.

producto *nm* (*gen*) product (*t Mat*); production; (*Com, Fin*: *beneficio*) yield, profit; (*ingresos*) proceeds, revenue; **~s** products, (*Agr*) produce; **~ acabado, ~ terminado** finished product; **~s agrícolas** agricultural produce, farm produce; **~ alimenticio** foodstuff; **~s básicos** commodities; **~s de belleza** cosmetics; **~ bruto** gross (national) product; **~s de consumo** consumer goods; **~ derivado** by-product; **~ de desecho** waste product; **~s estancados** goods sold by state monopoly; **~ lácteo** dairy product; **~s de marca** branded goods; **~s perecederos** perishable goods; **~ secundario** by-product.

productor 1 *adj* productive, producing; **clase productora** those who produce; **nación productora** producer nation.

2 *nm*, **productora¹** *nf* (**a**) (*gen*) producer.

(**b**) (*obrero*) workman, labourer.

(**c**) (*Cine, TV*) producer; **~ asociado** associate producer; **~ ejecutivo** executive producer.

productora² *nf* (*Cine*) production company.

produje, produzco *etc V* **producir**.

proemio *nm* preface, introduction.

proeza *nf* (**a**) (*hazaña*) exploit, feat, heroic deed. (**b**) (*And, Méx*) boast.

profa* *nf* = **profesora**.

profanación *nf* desecration.

profanar [1a] *vt* (*violar*) to desecrate, profane; (*deshonrar*) to defile; **~ la memoria de uno** to blacken the memory of sb.

profano 1 *adj* (**a**) (*laico*) profane, secular.

(**b**) (*irrespetuoso*) irreverent.

(**c**) (*no experto*) lay; (*ignorante*) ignorant.

(**d**) (*indecente*) indecent, immodest.

2 *nm* layman; outsider; **soy ~ en música** I'm ignorant of music, I'm a layman in matters of music.

profe* *nm* = **profesor**.

profecía *nf* prophecy.

proferir [3i] *vt palabra, sonido* to utter; *indirecta* to drop, throw out; *suspiro* to fetch; *insulto* to hurl, let fly (*contra* at); *maldición* to utter.

profesar [1a] **1** *vt* (**a**) *admiración, creencia etc* to profess; to declare.

(**b**) *materia* to teach; (*Univ*) to hold a chair in.

(**c**) *profesión* to practise.

2 *vi* (*Ecl*) to take vows.

profesión *nf* (**a**) (*de fe etc*) profession, declaration; avowal; (*Ecl*) taking of vows.

(**b**) (*carrera*) career; profession; (*vocación*) calling, vocation; '~' (*en formulario*) 'occupation'; **abogado de ~, de ~ abogado** a lawyer by profession; **~ liberal** liberal profession.

profesional 1 *adj* professional; **no ~** non-professional. **2** *nmf* professional; **~ del amor** prostitute.

profesionalidad *nf* (*de asunto*) professional nature; (*actitud*) professionalism, professional attitude.

profesionalismo *nm* professionalism.

profesionalmente *adv* professionally.

profesionista *nmf* (*LAm*) professional.

profeso *adj* (*Ecl*) professed.

profesor(a) *nm/f* (**a**) (*gen*) teacher; instructor; **~ de esgrima** fencing master; **~ de esquí** ski(ing) instructor; **~ de gimnasia** gym instructor; **~ de natación** swimming instructor; **~ de piano** piano teacher; **~ robot** teaching machine.

(**b**) (*Escol*: *gen*) teacher; **~ (de instituto)** schoolmaster, schoolmistress; **~ de biología** biology teacher (*o* master, mistress).

(**c**) (*Univ*) (*jefe*) professor; (*subordinado*) lecturer; **~ adjunto** (*kind of*) assistant lecturer, associate professor (*US*); **~ agregado** assistant professor (*US*); *V* **numerario, número**; **~ titular** full professor; **es ~ de griego** he is professor of Greek, he is a lecturer in Greek; **nuestros ~es de universidad** our university teachers; **se reunieron los ~es** the staff met, the faculty met (*esp US*).

profesorado *nm* (**a**) (*profesión*) teaching profession; teaching, lecturing. (**b**) (*personas*) teaching staff, faculty (*esp US*). (**c**) (*cargo*) professorship.

profesoral *adj* professorial; teaching (*atr*).

profesoril *adj* donnish.

profeta *nm* prophet.

proféticamente *adv* prophetically.

profético *adj* prophetic.

profetisa *nf* prophetess.

profetizar [1f] *vti* to prophesy.

profiláctico 1 *adj* prophylactic. **2** *nm* prophylactic; (*condón*) condom.

profilaxis *nf* prophylaxis.

prófugo *nm* fugitive; (*Mil*) deserter; **~ de la justicia** fugitive from justice.

profundamente *adv* deeply, profoundly; *dormir* deeply, soundly.

profundidad *nf* (**a**) (*hondura*) depth; (*Mat*) depth, height; **la poca ~ del río** the shallowness of the river; **tener una ~ de 30 cm** to be 30 cm deep (*o* in depth).

(**b**) **las ~es del océano** the depths of the ocean.

(**c**) (*fig*) depth, profundity; **investigación en ~** in-depth investigation.

profundímetro *nm* depth gauge.

profundizar [1f] **1** *vt* (**a**) (*ahondar*) to deepen, make deeper.

(**b**) (*fig*) *tema* to study in depth, make a profound study of, go deeply into; *misterio* to fathom, get to the bottom of.

2 *vi* (**a**) **~ en** to penetrate into, enter.

(**b**) **~ en** (*fig*) = **1** (**b**).

profundo *adj* (**a**) (*hondo*) deep; **poco ~** shallow; **tener 20 cm de ~** to be 20 cm deep (*o* in depth); **¿cuánto tiene de ~?** how deep is it?

(**b**) (*fig*) *reverencia* low; *respiración, suspiro, voz* deep; *nota* low, deep; *sueño* deep, sound; *oscuridad* deep; *efecto, impresión etc* deep; *misterio, pensador* profound; **~ conocedor del arte** a very knowledgeable expert in the art; **en lo ~ del alma** in the depths of one's soul.

(**c**) **en la Francia profunda** in the French heartland; **en el Sussex ~** in deepest Sussex, deep in Sussex.

profusamente *adv* profusely; lavishly, extravagantly.

profusión *nf* profusion; wealth, extravagance.

profuso *adj* (*abundante*) profuse; (*extravagante*) lavish, extravagant.

progenie *nf* (**a**) (*hijos*) progeny, offspring; (*pey*) brood. (**b**) (*familia*) family, lineage.
progenitor *nm* (*antepasado*) ancestor; (*padre*) father; **~es** (*hum*) parents.
progenitura *nf* offspring.
programa *nm* (**a**) (*gen*) programme; scheme, plan; **~ coloquio** chat-show; **~ concurso** game show; **~ continuo** (*Cine*) continuous showing; **~ doble** (*Cine*) double bill; **~ de estudios** curriculum, syllabus; **~ de fomento de empleo** job creation scheme; **~ piloto** pilot scheme.
(**b**) (*Inform*) program; **~ de aplicación** application program; **~ fuente** source program; **~ objeto** object program; **~ verificador de ortografía** spell(ing) checker program.
(**c**) (*Cono Sur**: *amorío*) love-affair.
programable *adj* that can be programmed.
programación *nf* (*Inform*) programming; (*Rad, TV*) programme planning; (*en periódico etc*) programme guide, viewing guide; (*Ferro etc*) scheduling, timetabling.
programado *adj* programmed; *visita etc* planned.
programador(a) *nm/f* programmer; (*Inform*) programmer; **~ de aplicaciones** applications programmer; **~ de sistemas** systems programmer.
programar [1a] *vt* (**a**) (*gen*) to plan; (*detalladamente*) to draw up a programme for; (*Inform*) to programme; (*Ferro etc*) to schedule, timetable; (*TV*) to put on, show.
(**b**) (*fig*) *futuro etc* to shape, mould, determine.
programático *adj* programmatical.
progre* **1** *adj* (*marchoso*) trendy; (*Pol*) leftish, liberal; (*en lo sexual etc*) liberal, permissive (in outlook); *mujer* liberated.
2 *nmf* trendy; lefty* (*pey*); liberal; sexual liberal.
3 *nf* liberated woman.
progresar [1a] *vi* to progress, make progress.
progresía *nf* (*V* **progre**) (**a**) (*actitud etc*) trendiness; leftish outlook (*pey*), liberal outlook; permissiveness; liberated outlook. (**b**) **la ~** (*personas*) the trendies; the lefties*, the liberals; the sexual liberals; liberated women.
progresión *nf* progression; **~ aritmética** arithmetic progression; **~ geométrica** geometric progression.
progresista *adj, nmf* progressive.
progresivamente *adv* progressively; gradually, little by little.
progresividad *nf* progressiveness, progressive nature.
progresivo *adj* (*que avanza*) progressive; (*paulatino*) gradual; (*continuo*) continuous; (*Ling*) continuous.
progreso *nm* progress; advance; **~s** progress; **hacer ~s** to progress, make progress, advance.
prohibición *nf* prohibition (*de* of); ban (*de* on); embargo (*de* on); **levantar la ~ de** to remove the ban on, lift the embargo on.
prohibicionismo *nm* prohibitionism.
prohibicionista *adj, nmf* prohibitionist.
prohibir [3a] **1** *vt* to prohibit, forbid, stop, ban; **~ una droga** to prohibit a drug, ban a drug; **~ algo a uno** to forbid sb sth; **~ a uno** + *infin* to forbid sb to + *infin*; to stop sb + *ger*, ban sb from + *ger*; **'prohibido fumar'** 'no smoking'; **está prohibido fumar aquí** smoking is not allowed here, you can't smoke in here; **queda terminantemente prohibido** + *infin* it is strictly forbidden to + *infin*; **el chico tiene prohibido salir de casa** the boy is not allowed out.
2 prohibirse *vr*: **'se prohibe fumar'** 'no smoking'.
prohibitivo *adj* prohibitive.
prohibitorio *adj* prohibitory.
prohijar [1a] *vt* to adopt (*t fig*).
prohombre *nm* outstanding man, great man; leader.
prójima *nf* (**a**) (*gen*) woman of dubious character, loose woman. (**b**) **la ~*** my old woman*, the wife*.
projimidad *nf* (*And, Carib, Cono Sur*) (*compasión*) fellow feeling, compassion (for one's fellows); (*solidaridad*) solidarity.
prójimo *nm* (**a**) (*semejante*) fellow man, fellow creature; (*vecino*) neighbour; **nuestros ~s los animales** our fellow animals. (**b**) (*: *tío*) so-and-so*, creature.
prolapso *nm* prolapse.
prole *nf* offspring; (*pey*) brood, spawn; **padre de numerosa ~** father of a large family.
prolegómeno *nm* preface, introduction (*t fig*); **los ~s del partido** the early stages of the match; the pre-match ceremonies.
proletariado *nm* proletariat.
proletario, -a *adj, nm/f* proletarian.
proletarismo *nm* proletarianism.
proliferación *nf* proliferation; **~ de armas nucleares** proliferation of atomic weapons, spread of nuclear arms; **tratado de no ~** non-proliferation treaty.
proliferar [1a] *vi* to proliferate.
prolífico *adj* prolific (*en* of).
prolijamente *adv* long-windedly; tediously; with an excess of detail.
prolijidad *nf* prolixity, long-windedness; tediousness; excess of detail.
prolijo *adj* (**a**) (*extenso*) prolix, long-winded; (*pesado*) tedious; (*muy detallado*) excessively detailed; (*muy meticuloso*) excessively meticulous. (**b**) (*Cono Sur*: *incansable*) untiring. (**c**) (*LAm*: *pulcro*) smart, neat.
prologar [1h] *vt* to preface, write an introduction to; **un libro prologado por Ortega** a book with a preface by Ortega.
prólogo 1 *nm* (**a**) (*gen*) prologue (*de* to); (*preámbulo*) preface, introduction.
(**b**) (*fig*) prelude (*de* to).
2 *atr*: **etapa ~** preliminary stage, preparatory stage.
prolongación *nf* (**a**) (*acto*) prolongation, extension.
(**b**) (*de carretera etc*) extension; **por la ~ de la Castellana** along the new part of the Castellana, along the extension of the Castellana.
(**c**) (*Elec*) extension, flex.
prolongado *adj sobre, cuarto etc* long; *estancia, reunión etc* lengthy.
prolongar [1h] **1** *vt* (*alargar*) to prolong, extend; *línea* (*Mat*) to produce; *tubo etc* to make longer, extend; *reunión* to prolong.
2 prolongarse *vr* to extend; to go on; **la carretera se prolonga más allá del bosque** the road goes on (*o* extends, stretches) beyond the wood; **el paisaje se prolonga hasta lo infinito** the countryside stretches away to infinity; **la sesión se prolongó bastante** the meeting went on long enough, it was a pretty long meeting.
prom. *nm abr de* **promedio** average, av.
promedial *adj* average.
promedialmente *adv* on the average, as an average.
promediar [1b] **1** *vt* (**a**) *objeto etc* to divide into two halves, divide equally.
(**b**) (*Mat etc*) to work out the average of, average (out).
(**c**) (*tener promedio de*) to average; **la producción promedia 100 barriles diarios** production averages 100 barrels a day.
2 *vi* (**a**) (*mediar*) to mediate (*entre* between).
(**b**) **promediaba el mes** it was halfway through the month; **antes de ~ el mes** before the month is halfway through.
promedio *nm* (**a**) (*gen*) average; **el ~ de asistencia diaria** the average daily attendance; **el ~ es de 35 por 100** the average is 35%.
(**b**) (*de distancia etc*) middle, mid-point.
promesa *nf* **1** (*ofrecimiento*) promise; (*compromiso*) pledge; **~ de matrimonio** promise of marriage; **absolver a uno de su ~** to release sb from his promise; **faltar a una ~** to break a promise, go back on one's word.
2 *atr*: **jugador ~** promising player, bright hope among players.
promesante *nmf* (*Cono Sur*), **promesero, -a** *nm/f* (*And, Cono Sur*) pilgrim.
prometedor *adj*, **prometente** *adj* promising.
prometedoramente *adv* promisingly.
Prometeo *nm* Prometheus.
prometer [2a] **1** *vt* (*ofrecer*) to promise; (*comprometer*) to pledge; **~ hacer algo** to promise to do sth, (*Ecl*) to take a vow to do sth; **esto promete ser interesante** this promises to be interesting; **esto no nos promete nada bueno** this does not look at all hopeful for us, this promises to be pretty bad for us.
2 *vi* (*tener porvenir*) to have promise, show promise; **es un jugador que promete** he's a promising player, he's a player with promise.
3 prometerse *vr* (**a**) (*esperar*) to expect, promise o.s.; **~ algo bueno** to promise o.s. a treat; **prometérselas muy felices** to have high hopes; **nos habíamos prometido algo mejor** we had expected sth better; **se prometía que todo iba a ser fácil** he anticipated that everything was going to be easy.
(**b**) (*2 personas*) to get engaged; **se prometió con él en abril** she got engaged to him in April.
prometida *nf* fiancée.
prometido 1 *adj* (**a**) (*ofrecido*) promised. (**b**) *persona* engaged; **estar ~ con** to be engaged to. **2** *nm* (**a**) (*novio*) fiancé. (**b**) (*promesa*) promise.
prominencia *nf* (**a**) (*elevación*) protuberance; (*hinchazón*)

swelling, bump; (*de terreno*) rise. (**b**) (*fig*: *esp LAm*) prominence.

prominente *adj* (**a**) prominent, protuberant; that sticks out. (**b**) (*fig*) prominent.

promiscuidad *nf* (**a**) (*mezcla*) mixture, jumble, confusion; (*confusión*) confused nature. (**b**) (*ambigüedad*) ambiguity.

promiscuo *adj* (**a**) (*revuelto*) mixed (up), in disorder; *multitud, reunión* motley. (**b**) *sentido* ambiguous.

promisión *nf*: **tierra de ~** land of promise, promised land.

promoción *nf* (**a**) (*ascenso*) promotion, advancement, furtherance; (*Com, Dep etc*) promotion; **~ inmobiliaria** property development; **~ de ventas** sales promotion.

(**b**) (*profesional*) promotion; (*año*) class, year; **la ~ de 1995** the 1995 class; **fue de mi ~** he belonged to the same class as I did, he graduated (*o* got his commission *etc*) at the same time as I did.

(**c**) (*Com*: *ganga*) special offer.

promocional *adj* promotional.

promocionar [1a] **1** *vt* (*Com*) to promote; *persona* to give rapid promotion to, advance rapidly.

2 promocionarse *vr* to improve o.s., better o.s.

promontorio *nm* promontory, headland.

promotor(a) 1 *nm/f* promoter (*t Com*); pioneer; instigator, prime mover; (*Parl*: *de ley*) sponsor; **~ inmobiliario** property developer; **~ de ventas** sales promoter; **el ~ de los disturbios** the instigator of the rioting. **2** *nf* property development company.

promovedor(a) *nm/f* promoter; instigator.

promover [2h] *vt* (**a**) *proceso etc* to promote, advance, further; *intereses* to promote; *plan etc* to pioneer; (*Parl*) *ley* to sponsor; *acción* to begin, set on foot, get moving; *pleito* to bring.

(**b**) *escándalo etc* to cause; *disturbio* to instigate, stir up.

(**c**) (*ascender*) to promote (*a* to).

promulgación *nf* promulgation; (*fig*) announcement, publication.

promulgar [1h] *vt* to promulgate; (*fig*) to proclaim, announce publicly.

pronombre *nm* pronoun; **~ personal** personal pronoun; **~ posesivo** possessive pronoun; **~ reflexivo** reflexive pronoun.

pronominal *adj* pronominal.

pronosticación *nf* prediction, prognostication, forecasting.

pronosticador(a) *nm/f* forecaster; (*en carreras*) tipster.

pronosticar [1g] *vt* to predict, foretell, forecast, prognosticate.

pronóstico *nm* (**a**) (*gen*) prediction, forecast; (*presagio*) omen; (*en carreras*) tip; **~ del tiempo** weather forecast; **~s para el año nuevo** predictions for the new year, prognostications for the new year.

(**b**) (*Med*) prognosis; **de ~ leve** slight, not serious; **de ~ reservado** of uncertain gravity, of unknown extent, possibly serious.

prontamente *adv* quickly.

prontito* *adv* (**a**) double-quick; right away. (**b**) very early, nice and early.

prontitud *nf* (**a**) (*presteza*) speed, quickness, promptness. (**b**) (*viveza*) quickness, sharpness.

pronto 1 *adj* (**a**) (*rápido*) *respuesta etc* prompt, quick, (*esp Com*) early; *cura* speedy; *servicio* quick, rapid, prompt.

(**b**) *persona* quick, sharp; **de inteligencia pronta** of keen (*o* sharp) intelligence; **es ~ en las decisiones** he is quick about taking decisions; **estuvo muy ~ para resolverse** he was quick to make up his mind, he decided on the spot.

(**c**) (*Cono Sur*) (*dispuesto*) ready; **la comida está pronta** lunch is ready; **estar ~ para** + *infin* to be ready to + *infin*.

(**d**) (*Cono Sur**: *borracho*) tight*.

2 *adv* (**a**) (*rápidamente*) quickly, promptly, speedily; (*en seguida*) at once, right away; (*dentro de poco*) soon; **cuanto más ~ mejor** the sooner the better; **lo más ~ posible** as soon as possible, as quickly as possible; **tan ~ como** as soon as; **tan ~ ríe como llora** he no sooner laughs than he cries; **tan ~ como me lo traigan** as soon as they bring it to me; **¡~!** hurry!, get on with it!; **al ~** at first; **de ~** suddenly; unexpectedly, without warning; **¡hasta ~!** see you soon!; **por de ~, por lo ~** (*entretanto*) meanwhile, for the present; (*al menos*) at least, anyway; (*al principio*) for a start, for one thing.

(**b**) (*temprano*) early; **levantarse ~** to get up early; **todavía es ~ para hacerlo** it's too early yet to do it, it's too soon to be doing it yet; **todavía es ~ para decidir si ...** it's early days to decide whether to ...; **iremos a comer un poco ~** we'll go and lunch a bit early.

3 *nm* (*impulso*) urge, strong impulse; (*ocurrencia*) sudden feeling; **tener ~s de enojo** to be quick-tempered.

prontuario *nm* handbook, manual, compendium.

pronuncia *nf* (*Méx*) = **pronunciamiento.**

pronunciación *nf* pronunciation.

pronunciado *adj* (*marcado*) pronounced, strong; *curva etc* sharp; *rasgo etc* marked, noticeable.

pronunciamiento *nm* revolt, insurrection, military rising.

pronunciar [1b] **1** *vt* (**a**) (*Ling*) to pronounce; (*articular*) to make, utter.

(**b**) (*fig*) *discurso* to make, deliver; *brindis* to propose; **~ palabras de elogio para ...** to say a few words of tribute to ...; **pronunció unas palabras en las que ...** she said that ...

(**c**) (*Jur*) *sentencia* to pass, pronounce.

2 pronunciarse *vr* (**a**) (*declararse*) to declare o.s., state one's opinion; to make a pronouncement; **~ a favor de** to pronounce in favour of, declare o.s. in favour of; **~ sobre** to pronounce on, make a pronouncement about.

(**b**) (*Pol*) to revolt, rise, rebel.

(**c**) (*fig*: *hacerse más marcado*) to become (more) pronounced.

(**d**) (*: *soltar la pasta*) to cough up*, fork out*.

pronuncio *nm* (*And*) = **pronunciamiento.**

propagación *nf* propagation; (*fig*) propagation, spread(ing), dissemination.

propaganda *nf* (**a**) (*Pol etc*) propaganda. (**b**) (*Com*) advertising; **hacer ~ de un producto** to advertise a product.

propagandista *nmf* propagandist.

propagandístico *adj* propaganda (*atr*); (*Com*) advertising (*atr*).

propagar [1h] **1** *vt* (*Bio*) to propagate; (*fig*) to propagate, spread, disseminate. **2 propagarse** *vr* (*Bio*) to propagate; (*fig*) to spread, be disseminated.

propalación *nf* disclosure; dissemination.

propalar [1a] *vt* (*divulgar*) to divulge, disclose; (*diseminar*) to disseminate; (*publicar*) to publish an account of.

propano *nm* propane.

propasarse [1a] *vr* to go too far, overstep the bounds; (*sexualmente*) to take liberties, overstep the bounds of propriety.

propela *nf* (*Carib, Méx*) (*hélice*) propeller; (*fuerabordo*) outboard motor.

propelente *nm* propellent.

propender [2a] *vi*: **~ a** to tend towards, incline to; **~ a** + *infin* to tend to + *infin*, have a tendency to + *infin*.

propensión *nf* inclination, propensity, tendency (*a* to).

propenso *adj*: **~ a** inclined to; prone to, subject to; **ser ~ a** + *infin* to be inclined to + *infin*, have a tendency to + *infin*.

propi* *nf* = **propina.**

propiamente *adv* properly; really, exactly; *V* **dicho.**

propiciación *nf* propitiation.

propiciador(a) *nm/f* (*LAm*) sponsor.

propiciar [1b] *vt* (**a**) (*atraer*) to propitiate, to win over.

(**b**) (*favorecer*) to favour; to create a favourable atmosphere for; (*provocar*) to cause, give rise to; (*ayudar*) to aid; **tal secreto propicia muchas conjeturas** such secrecy causes a lot of speculation; **hecho que propició que el fuego llegara a ...** a fact which helped the fire to reach ...

(**c**) (*LAm*) to sponsor.

propiciatorio *adj* propitiatory.

propicio *adj* (*gen*) propitious, auspicious; *momento etc* favourable; *persona* kind, well-disposed, helpful.

propiedad *nf* (**a**) (*pertenencia*) possession, ownership; **~ colectiva** collective ownership; **ser de la ~ de** to be the property of, belong to; **una finca de la ~ del marqués** an estate belonging to the marquis; **ceder algo a uno en ~** to transfer sth completely to sb, transfer to sb the full rights over sth.

(**b**) (*objeto, tierras etc*) property; **~ particular** private property; **una ~** a property, a piece of property; **es ~ del municipio** it is the property of the town.

(**c**) (*Quím etc*) property; (*fig*) property, attribute.

(**d**) (*cualidad*: *lo apropiado*) propriety, properness; (*conveniencia*) suitability, appositeness; **discutir la ~ de una palabra** to discuss the appropriateness of a word.

(**e**) (*cualidad*: *exactitud*) accuracy, faithfulness; (*naturalidad*) naturalness; **lo reproduce con toda ~** he reproduces it faithfully.

(**f**) (*Com etc*) right(s); **~ industrial** patent rights; patents and trademarks; **~ intelectual, ~ literaria** copyright; **'es ~'** 'copyright'; **tener una plaza en ~** to have tenure.

(**g**) **hablar español con ~** (*expresarse bien*) to have a good command of Spanish; (*hablar correctamente*) to speak Spanish correctly, speak correct Spanish.

propietaria *nf* owner, proprietress.

propietario 1 *adj* proprietary. **2** *nm* owner, proprietor; (*Agr etc*) landowner.

propina *nf* (**a**) tip, gratuity; **dar algo de ~** to give sth extra, give sth as a bonus; **con dos más de ~** (*fig*) with two more into the bargain. (**b**) (*Mús*) encore.

propinar [1a] **1** *vt* (**a**) **~ a uno** to treat sb to a drink, buy sb a drink.

(**b**) (*****) *golpe* to deal, hit; *paliza* to give; **le propinó una serie de consejos** he gave him a lot of advice, he made him listen to several bits of advice.

2 propinarse *vr*: **~ algo** to treat o.s. to sth.

propincuidad *nf* propinquity, nearness, proximity.

propincuo *adj* near.

propio 1 *adj* (**a**) (*de uno*) own, of one's own; **con su propia mano** with his own hand; **lo vi con mis ~s ojos** I saw it with my own eyes; **los rizos son ~s** her curls are natural, her curls are her own; **lo hizo en beneficio ~** he did it for his own good; he did it in his own interest; **tienen casa propia** they have a house of their own; **ahora tiene una bicicleta suya propia** now she has a bicycle of her very own.

(**b**) (*particular*) peculiar (*de* to); (*especial*) special; (*típico*) characteristic, typical (*de* of); (*suyo* ~) of one's own; **una bebida propia del país** a typical drink of the country; **hace un sol ~ de país mediterráneo** this sunshine is more typical of a Mediterranean country; **fruta propia del tiempo** fruit in season; **eso es muy ~ de él** that's very characteristic of him; **tiene un olor muy ~** it has a very special smell, it has a smell of its own.

(**c**) (*apropiado*) proper; (*correcto*) correct, suitable, fitting (*para* for); **con los honores que le son ~s** with the honours which are proper (*o* due) to him; **ese bikini no es ~ para esta playa** that bikini is not suitable for this beach.

(**d**) (*mismísimo*) selfsame, very; **sus propias palabras** his very words; **me lo dijo el ~ ministro** the minister himself told me so; **yo haría lo ~ que tú** I'd do the same as you, I'd do exactly what you're doing.

(**e**) *sentido* proper, true; basic.

(**f**) **de ~** especially, deliberately, expressly; **al ~** (*CAm*) on purpose.

2 *nm* (*mensajero*) messenger.

proponente *nmf* proposer.

proponer [2q] **1** *vt idea, proyecto etc* to propose, put forward; to suggest; *teoría* to propound; *problema* to pose; to outline, put up (for discussion); *moción* to propose; *candidato* to propose, nominate, put forward; **~ a uno para una beca** to propose sb for a scholarship; **le propuse que fuéramos juntos** I proposed to him that we should go together.

2 proponerse *vr* (**a**) **~ hacer algo** to propose to do sth, plan to do sth, intend to do sth.

(**b**) (*pey*) **te has propuesto hacerme perder el tren** you set out deliberately to make me miss the train.

proporción *nf* (**a**) (*gen*) proportion; (*Mat etc*) ratio; (*relación*) relationship; (*porcentaje etc*) rate; **proporciones** proportions, (*fig*) dimensions; size, scope; **la ~ entre azules y verdes** the proportion of blues to greens; **en ~ con** in proportion to; **en una ~ de 5 a 1** in a ratio of 5 to 1; at a rate of 5 to 1; **estar fuera de ~** to be out of proportion; **guarda bien las proporciones** it remains in proportion; **esto no guarda ~ con lo otro** this is out of proportion to the rest; **una máquina de gigantescas proporciones** a machine of huge proportions (*o* size); **se desconocen las proporciones del desastre** the size (*o* extent, scope) of the disaster is unknown.

(**b**) (*oportunidad*) chance, opportunity, right moment.

(**c**) **proporciones** (*Méx*) wealth; **de proporciones** (*LAm*: *enorme*) huge, vast; (*Méx*: *rico*) wealthy.

proporcionadamente *adv* proportionately, in proportion.

proporcionado *adj* (**a**) (*que guarda relación*) proportionate (*a* to).

(**b**) (*adecuado*) medium, middling, just right; **de tamaño ~** of the right size.

(**c**) *forma* well-proportioned; **bien ~** well proportioned; shapely, of pleasing shape.

proporcional *adj* proportional.

proporcionalmente *adv* proportionally.

proporcionar [1a] *vt* (**a**) (*facilitar*) to give, supply, provide, furnish; to get, obtain (not without difficulty); (*fig*) to lend; **~ dinero a uno** to give sb money, supply sb with money; **esto le proporciona una renta anual de ...** this brings him in a yearly income of ...; **esto proporciona gran encanto a la narración** this lends (*o* gives) great charm to the story; **su tío le proporcionó el puesto** his uncle found him the job, his uncle helped him into the job.

(**b**) (*adaptar*) to adjust, adapt (*a* to).

proposición *nf* proposition; proposal; **~ de ley** proposed bill; **~ no de ley** motion.

propósito *nm* purpose; aim, intention, objective; **buenos ~s** good intentions; good resolutions; **¿cuál es su ~?** what is his aim?; **nuestro ~ es de** + *infin* our aim is to + *infin*; **hacer(se) el ~ de** + *infin* to form an intention to + *infin*, set o.s. the aim of + *ger*; **a ~** (*como adj*) appropriate, suitable, fitting (*para* for); *observación etc* relevant, apt; **a ~** (*como adv*) (*adrede*) intentionally, on purpose; (*de paso*) by the way, incidentally; **a ~ de** about, with regard to; **y a ~ de los toros ...** and talking of bulls ..., and while we're on the subject of bulls ...; **eso no viene a ~** that's not relevant, that's nothing to do with it; **de ~** on purpose, purposely, deliberately; **fuera de ~** irrelevant(ly), off the point, out of place; **mudar de ~** to change one's mind; **sin ~ fijo** aimless(ly), pointless(ly).

propuesta *nf* proposal; **~ salarial** pay offer; **a ~ de** at the proposal of, on the suggestion of.

propugnación *nf* advocacy.

propugnar [1a] *vt* (*proponer*) to advocate, propose, suggest; (*apoyar*) to defend, support.

propulsado *adj*: **~ a cohete** rocket-driven; **~ a chorro** jet-propelled.

propulsante *nm* fuel, propellent.

propulsar [1a] *vt* (**a**) (*Mec*) to drive, propel. (**b**) (*fig*) to promote, encourage.

propulsión *nf* propulsion; **~ a cohete** rocket propulsion; **~ a chorro, ~ por reacción** jet propulsion; **con ~ a chorro** jet-propelled.

propulsor 1 *nm* (*Téc*: *combustible*) propellent, fuel; (*motor*) motor, engine. **2** *nm*, **propulsora** *nf* (*persona*) promoter.

prorrata *nf* share, quota, prorate (*US*); **a ~** pro rata, proportionately.

prorratear [1a] *vt* to share out, apportion, distribute proportionately, prorate (*US*); **prorratearemos el dinero** we will share out the money pro rata.

prorrateo *nm* sharing (in proportion), apportionment; **a ~** pro rata, proportionately.

prórroga *nf* deferment; (*Com*) extension; (*Mil*) deferment; (*Jur*) stay (of execution), respite; (*Dep*) extra time.

prorrogable *adj* which can be extended.

prorrogación *nf* deferment, prorogation.

prorrogar [1h] *vt sesión etc* to prorogue, adjourn; *período* to extend; (*Mil*) to defer; (*Jur*) to grant a stay of execution to; *decisión etc* to defer, postpone; **prorrogamos una semana las vacaciones** we extended our holiday by a week.

prorrumpir [3a] *vi* to burst forth, break out; **~ en gritos** to start shouting; **~ en lágrimas** to burst into tears.

prosa *nf* (**a**) (*Liter*) prose.

(**b**) (*fig*) prosaic aspects, tedium; **la ~ de la vida** the humdrum aspects of life.

(**c**) (*****: *verborrea*) verbiage.

(**d**) (*Cono Sur*: *vanidad*) vanity, haughtiness.

(**e**) (*And, CAm*: *afectación*) pomposity, affectation.

prosador(a) *nm/f* (**a**) (*Liter*) prose writer. (**b**) (*****: *hablador*) chatterbox, great talker.

prosaicamente *adv* (**a**) (*gen*) prosaically. (**b**) (*fig*) prosaically; tediously, monotonously.

prosaico *adj* (**a**) (*Liter*) prosaic, prose (*atr*). (**b**) (*fig*) prosaic, prosy; (*monótono*) tedious, monotonous; (*corriente*) ordinary.

prosaísmo *nm* (*fig*) prosaic nature; tediousness, monotony; ordinariness.

prosapia *nf* lineage, ancestry; **una familia de (mucha) ~** a (very) illustrious family.

proscenio *nm* proscenium.

proscribir [3a; *ptp* **proscrito**] *vt* to prohibit, ban; *partido etc* to proscribe; *criminal* to outlaw; to banish; *tema etc* to ban; **~ un tema de su conversación** to banish a topic from one's conversation.

proscripción *nf* prohibition (*de* of), ban (*de* on); proscription; outlawing; banishment.

proscrito 1 *ptp de* **proscribir**. **2** *adj* (*prohibido*) banned; (*desterrado*) outlawed; proscribed; **un libro ~** a banned book. **3** *nm*, **proscrita** *nf* (*exiliado*) exile; (*bandido*) outlaw.

prosecución *nf* (*continuación*) continuation; (*de demanda*) pressing; (*caza*) pursuit.

proseguir [3d *y* 3k] **1** *vt* (*continuar*) to continue, carry on, go on with, proceed with; *demanda* to go on with, push, press; *investigación, estudio* to pursue.

2 *vi* (**a**) ~ **en** (*o* **con**) **una actitud** to continue in one's attitude, maintain one's attitude.

(**b**) (*condición etc*) to continue, go on; **prosiguió con el cuento** he went on with the story; **¡prosigue!** continue!; **prosigue el mal tiempo** the bad weather continues.

proselitismo *nm* proselytism.

proselitista *adj* proselytizing.

prosélito, -a *nm/f* proselyte.

prosificación *nf* (*texto*) prose version; (*acto*) rewriting as prose, turning into prose.

prosificar [1g] *vt* to rewrite as prose, write a prose version of.

prosista *nmf* prose writer.

prosodia *nf* prosody.

prosopopeya *nf* (**a**) (*Liter*) personification. (**b**) (*fig*) pomposity, affectation.

prospección *nf* exploration; (*Min*) prospecting (*de* for); ~ **de mercados** market research; ~ **del petróleo** prospecting for oil, drilling for oil.

prospeccionar [1a] *vt futuro* to look to, examine.

prospectiva *nf* fortune-telling; futurology.

prospectivo *adj* prospective; future-orientated.

prospecto *nm* prospectus; (*Com etc*) leaflet, sheet of instructions.

prospector, -ora *nm/f* prospector; ~ **de mercados** market researcher.

prósperamente *adv* prosperously; successfully.

prosperar [1a] *vi* to prosper, thrive, flourish; to be successful; (*idea etc*) to prosper.

prosperidad *nf* prosperity; success; **en época de** ~ in a period of prosperity, in good times; **desear a uno muchas ~s** to wish sb all success.

próspero *adj* (**a**) (*rico*) prosperous, thriving, flourishing; (*venturoso*) successful; **¡~ año nuevo!** happy new year! (**b**) **con próspera fortuna** with good luck, favoured by fortune.

próstata *nf* prostate.

prosternarse [1a] *vr* (*postrarse*) to prostrate o.s.; (*humillarse*) to bow low, bow humbly.

prostético *adj* (*Ling, Med*) prosthetic.

prostibulario *adj* brothel (*atr*).

prostíbulo *nm* brothel.

prostitución *nf* (*t fig*) prostitution.

prostituir [3g] **1** *vt mujer* to prostitute (*t fig*). **2 prostituirse** *vr* (**a**) to take up prostitution, become a prostitute. (**b**) (*fig*) to prostitute o.s.

prostituta *nf* prostitute; ~ **callejera** streetwalker.

prostituto *nm* male prostitute.

prosudo *adj* (*And, Cono Sur*) affected, pompous.

protagónico *adj papel* leading, major.

protagonismo *nm* (**a**) (*papel*) leading role; (*liderazgo*) leadership; **conceder el ~ al pueblo** to grant power to the people. (**b**) (*importancia*) prominence; (*iniciativa*) initiative; (*en sociedad*) taking an active part, being socially active; **afán de** ~ urge to be in the limelight; **tuvo poco** ~ he made little showing; he did not have much to do; **el tema adquiere gran ~ en este texto** the theme becomes a major one in this text. (**c**) (*defensa*) defence; (*apoyo*) support.

protagonista **1** *adj* important, leading, influential. **2** *nmf* protagonist; (*Liter etc, frec*) main character; hero, heroine.

protagonístico *adj* leading; **papel** ~ leading role.

protagonizar [1f] *vt* (**a**) (*Teat etc*) to take the chief role in, play the lead in. (**b**) *proceso, rebelión* to lead; *manifestación* to stage; *accidente* to figure in, be concerned in; **el mes ha estado protagonizado por ...** the month has been notable for ...; **una entrevista protagonizada por X** an interview whose subject was X.

proteaginosa *nf* protein product.

protección *nf* protection; ~ **civil** civil defence; ~ **de datos** data protection.

proteccionismo *nm* protectionism.

proteccionista **1** *adj* (*Esp*) *política* protectionist; *impuesto etc* protective. **2** *nmf* protectionist.

protector **1** *adj* protective, protecting. **2** *nm*, **protectora** *nf* protector; (*Liter etc*) patron; (*de tradición etc*) guardian; ~ **del pueblo** (*Esp*) ombudsman. **3** *nm*: ~ **solar** suntan oil.

protectorado *nm* protectorate.

proteger [2c] *vt* (*resguardar*) to protect (*contra* against, *de* from); (*escudar*) to shield; (*defender*) to defend; *artista, autor etc* to act as patron to; ~ **contra grabación** (*Inform*) to write protect.

protegida *nf* protégée.

protegido **1** *adj*: **especie protegida** protected species. **2** *nm* protégé.

proteico *adj* protean; many-sided, diverse.

proteína *nf* protein.

proteínico *adj* protein (*atr*); **contenido** ~ protein content.

protervidad *nf* wickedness, perversity.

protervo *adj* wicked, perverse.

protesta *nf* (**a**) (*queja*) protest; grumble; **bajo** ~ under protest. (**b**) (*de inocencia etc*) protestation; **hacer ~s de lealtad** to protest one's loyalty.

protestación *nf* protestation; ~ **de lealtad** protestation of loyalty, declaration of loyalty; ~ **de fe** profession of faith.

protestante *adj, nmf* Protestant.

protestantismo *nm* Protestantism.

protestar [1a] **1** *vt* (**a**) *inocencia etc* to protest, declare, avow; *fe* to profess.

(**b**) (*Fin*) **cheque protestado por falta de fondos** cheque referred to drawer (*R/D*).

2 *vi* (**a**) (*quejarse*) to protest (*contra, de* about, against; *de que* that); (*objetar*) to object, remonstrate; ~ **contra una demora** to protest about a delay; **¡protesto contra esa observación!** I resent that!, I object to that remark!

(**b**) ~ **de** *inocencia etc* to protest.

protesto *nm* (*LAm*) protest.

protestón* (*pey*) **1** *adj* given to protesting, perpetually moaning. **2** *nm*, **protestona** *nf* perpetual moaner, permanent protester.

proto... *pref* proto...

protocolario *adj* (**a**) (*exigido por el protocolo*) established by protocol, required by protocol. (**b**) (*fig: ceremonial*) formal.

protocolo *nm* (**a**) (*Pol*) protocol (*t Inform*). (**b**) (*fig*) protocol, social etiquette, convention. (**c**) (*fig*) **sin ~s** informal(ly); without formalities, without a lot of fuss. (**d**) (*Med*) medical record.

protón *nm* proton.

protoplasma *nm* protoplasm.

prototipo *nm* prototype.

protuberancia *nf* protuberance; (*fig: en estadística etc*) bulge.

protuberante *adj* protuberant.

prov. *nf abr de* **provincia** province, prov.

provecto *adj* aged; **de edad provecta** elderly.

provecho *nm* advantage, benefit, profit; (*Fin*) profit; **de** ~ *negocio* profitable; *actividad* useful; *persona* worthy, honest; **¡buen ~!** *phrase used to those at table, hoping they will enjoy their meal*; **¡buen ~ le haga!** and much good may it do him!; **en ~ de** to the benefit of; **en ~ propio** to one's own advantage, for one's own profit; **ese alimento no le hace ~ a uno** that food(stuff) doesn't do one any good; **sacar ~ de algo** to benefit from sth, profit by (*o* from) sth.

provechosamente *adv* advantageously, beneficially, profitably.

provechoso *adj* advantageous, beneficial, profitable; useful; (*Fin*) profitable.

proveedor(a) *nm/f* supplier, purveyor; dealer; **'P~es de la Real Casa'** 'By appointment to His (*o* Her) Majesty'; **consulte a su ~ habitual** consult your usual dealer.

proveeduría *nf* (*Cono Sur*) grocer's, grocery.

proveer [2e; *ptp* **provisto** *y* **proveído**] **1** *vt* (**a**) (*suministrar*) to provide, supply, furnish (*de* with).

(**b**) (*disponer*) to provide, get ready; ~ **todo lo necesario** to provide all that is necessary (*para* for).

(**c**) *vacante* to fill.

(**d**) *negocio* to transact, dispatch.

(**e**) (*Jur*) to decree.

2 *vi*: ~ **a** to provide for; ~ **a las necesidades de uno** to provide for sb's wants; ~ **a un vicio de uno** to pander to sb's vice.

3 proveerse *vr*: ~ **de** to provide o.s. with.

provenir [3r] *vi*: ~ **de** to come from, arise from, stem from; **esto proviene de no haberlo curado antes** this comes from (*o* is due to) not having treated it earlier.

Provenza *nf* Provence.

provenzal **1** *adj, nmf* Provençal. **2** *nm* (*Ling*) Provençal.

proverbial *adj* (*lit, fig*) proverbial.

proverbialmente *adv* proverbially.

proverbio *nm* proverb.

próvidamente *adv* providently.

providencia *nf* (**a**) (*cualidad*) foresight; (*prevención*) fore-

thought, providence; (**Divina**) **P~** (Divine) Providence.
(**b**) (*precauciones*) **~s** measures, steps; **dictar** (*o* **tomar**) **~s para** + *infin* to take steps to + *infin*.
(**c**) (*Jur*) ruling, decision.
providencial *adj* providential.
providencialmente *adj* providentially.
providente *adj*, **próvido** *adj* provident.
provincia *nf* province; **las P~s Vascongadas** the Basque Provinces, the Basque Country; **un pueblo de ~(s)** a provincial town, a country town.
provincial 1 *adj* provincial. **2** *nm*, **provinciala** *nf* (*Ecl*) provincial.
provincialismo *nm* (*Ling*) provincialism, dialect(al) word (*o* phrase *etc*).
provincianismo *nm* provincialism; **~ de cortas luces, ~ de vía estrecha** narrow provincialism, deadening provincialism.
provinciano 1 *adj* (**a**) (*gen, t pey*) provincial; (*rural*) country (*atr*).
(**b**) (*vasco*) Basque, of the Basque Provinces.
2 *nm*, **provinciana** *nf* (*V adj* (**a**)) (**a**) provincial; country dweller.
(**b**) (*vasco*) Basque.
proviniente *adj*: **~ de** coming from, arising out of.
provisión *nf* (**a**) (*acto*) provision.
(**b**) (*suministro*) provision, supply; **provisiones** provisions, supplies, stores.
(**c**) (*Fin*) **~ de fondos** financial cover; **cheque sin ~** bad cheque.
(**d**) (*medida*) (precautionary) measure, step.
provisional *adj* provisional.
provisionalidad *nf* provisional nature, temporary character.
provisionalmente *adv* provisionally.
provisionar [1a] *vt deuda* to cover, to make bad-debt provision for.
provisorio *adj* (*LAm*) provisional.
provista *nf* (*Cono Sur*) provisions, supplies.
provisto 1 *ptp de* **proveer**. **2** *adv*: **~ de** provided with, supplied with; having, possessing.
provocación *nf* provocation.
provocador 1 *adj* (*hostil*) provocative; (*irritante*) provoking. **2** *nm*, **provocadora** *nf* trouble-maker.
provocar [1g] **1** *vt* (**a**) *persona* to provoke; (*enojar*) to rouse, stir up (to anger *etc*); (*tentar*) to tempt, invite; **~ a uno a cólera** (*o* **indignación**) to rouse sb to fury; **~ a uno a lástima** to move sb to pity; **~ a uno a risa** to make sb laugh; **el mar provoca a bañarse** the sea tempts one to bathe, the sea invites one to go for a swim.
(**b**) *cambio etc* to bring about, lead to; *proceso* to promote; *explosión, protesta, guerra etc* to cause, spark off; *fuego* to cause, start (deliberately); *parto* to induce, bring on.
(**c**) (*mujer*) to rouse, stir, stimulate (sexually).
(**d**) (*LAm*: *gustar, apetecer*) **¿te provoca un café?** would you like some coffee?, do you fancy a coffee?; **¿qué le provoca?** what would you like?, what do you fancy?; **no me provoca la idea** the idea doesn't appeal to me, I don't fancy the idea; **¿por qué no vas? — no me provoca** why aren't you going? — I don't feel like it; **no me provoca estudiar hoy** I'm not in the mood for (*o* I don't feel like) studying today.
2 *vi* (*: *vomitar*) to be sick.
provocativo *adj* (**a**) (*gen*) provocative, provoking.
(**b**) *mujer* provocative, sexually stimulating; *vestido* daring, immodest; *ademán, risa etc* inviting.
proxeneta *nmf* pimp, procurer, (*f*) procuress.
proxenetismo *nm* procuring.
próximamente *adv* shortly, soon.
proximidad *nf* nearness, closeness, proximity.
próximo *adj* (**a**) (*cercano*) near, close; neighbouring; *pariente* close; **en fecha próxima** soon, at an early date; **estar ~ a** to be close to, be near; **estar ~ a** + *infin* to be on the point of + *ger*, be about to + *infin*.
(**b**) (*anterior, siguiente*) next; **el mes ~** next month; **el mes ~ pasado** last month; **el ~ 5 de junio** on 5th June next; **bajarán en la próxima** they will get off at the next stop.
proyección *nf* (**a**) (*acto, parte*) projection.
(**b**) (*Cine etc*: *acto*) showing; **el tiempo de ~ es de 35 minutos** the showing lasts 35 minutes, the film runs for 35 minutes.
(**c**) (*Cine, Fot*: *diapositiva*) slide, transparency.
(**d**) (*fig*) hold, sway, influence; **la ~ de los periódicos sobre la sociedad** the hold of newspapers over society, the influence which newspapers have on society.
proyectable *adj*: **asiento ~** (*Aer*) ejector seat.
proyectar [1a] *vt* (**a**) *objeto* to hurl, throw; *luz* to cast, shed, project; *chorro, líquido etc* to send out, give out; to direct (*hacia* at); *sombra* to cast.
(**b**) (*Cine, Fot*) to project; to screen, show.
(**c**) (*Mat etc*) to project.
(**d**) (*Arquit etc*) to plan; (*Mec*) to design; **está proyectado para** + *infin* it is designed to + *infin*.
(**e**) **~** + *infin* to plan to + *infin*.
proyectil *nm* projectile, missile; (*Mil*: *de cañón*) shell, (*con cohete*) missile; **~ de aire a aire** air-to-air missile; **~ balístico intercontinental** intercontinental ballistic missile; **~ (tele)dirigido** guided missile; **~ de iluminación** flare, rocket.
proyectista *nmf* planner; (*Aer, Aut, Téc etc*) designer; (*delineante*) draughtsman; (*Cine*) projectionist.
proyecto *nm* (**a**) (*Téc*) plan, design; project; (*Fin*) detailed estimate.
(**b**) (*fig*) plan; scheme, project; **~ piloto** pilot scheme; **cambiar de ~** to change one's plans; **tener ~s para** to have plans for; **tener algo en ~** to be planning sth; **tener sus ~s sobre algo** to have designs on sth.
(**c**) (*Parl*) **~ de declaración** draft declaration; **~ de ley** bill.
proyector *nm* (**a**) (*Cine*) projector; **~ de diapositivas** slide projector. (**b**) (*Mil etc*) searchlight; (*Teat*) spotlight; **~ antiniebla** foglamp.
prudencia *nf* wisdom, prudence; care; soundness, sound judgement.
prudencial *adj* (**a**) (*adecuado*) prudential; (*razonable*) sensible; **tras un intervalo ~** after a decent interval, after a reasonable time.
(**b**) *cantidad, distancia etc* roughly correct, more or less correctly guessed.
prudenciarse [1b] *vr* (*And, CAm, Méx*) (*ser cauteloso*) to be cautious; (*contenerse*) to hold back, control o.s.
prudente *adj* sensible, wise, prudent; *conductor etc* careful; *decisión etc* sensible, judicious, sound.
prudentemente *adv* sensibly, wisely, prudently; carefully; judiciously, soundly.
prueba *nf* (**a**) (*gen, t Mat*) proof; (*Jur*) proof, evidence; exhibit; **~s** (*Jur*) documents; **~ documental** documentary evidence; **~ indiciaria** circumstantial proof; **~ palpable** clear proof; **a la ~ me remito** the proof of the pudding is in the eating, the event will show; **en ~ de** in proof of; **en ~ de lo cual** in proof whereof; **en ~ de que no es así te lo ofrezco gratis** to prove that it isn't so I offer it to you free; **¿tiene Vd ~ de ello?** can you prove it?; do you have proof?
(**b**) (*fig*: *indicio*) proof, sign, token; **es buena ~** it's a good sign; **sin dar la menor ~ de ello** without giving the faintest sign of it.
(**c**) (*Téc etc*) test, trial; (*Quím etc*) experiment; **~s** (*Aer, Aut, Náut*) trials; **~ de acceso** entrance test; **~ de aptitud** aptitude test; **~ de campo** field trial; **~ por carretera** road trials; **~ clínica** clinical test; **~ de embarazo** pregnancy test; **~ de fuego** (*fig*) acid test; **~ de imagen, ~ de luces, ~ de pantalla** screen test; **~ de inteligencia** intelligence test; **~ nuclear** nuclear test; **~ de selectividad** entrance examination; **~ de tornasol** litmus test; **a ~** (*Téc*) on trial; (*Com*) on approval, on trial; **libertad a ~** (release on) probation; **ingresar con un nombramiento a ~** to take up a post for a probationary period; to come in with a probationary appointment; **a ~ de** proof against; **a ~ de agua** waterproof; **a ~ de bala** bulletproof; **a ~ de bombas** bombproof, shellproof; **a ~ de choques** shockproof; **a ~ de fallo** with a failsafe device; **a ~ de grasa** greaseproof; **a ~ de impericia, a toda ~** foolproof; **a ~ de ladrones** burglar-proof; **a ~ de lluvia** rainproof; **a ~ de ruidos** soundproof; **a ~ de viento** windproof; **poner a ~, someter a ~** to test, put to the test, try out; **poner a ~ los nervios de uno** to test sb's nerves; **poner a ~ la paciencia de uno** to try sb's patience; **hacer ~ de** to test, put to the test.
(**d**) (*de comida etc*: *acto*) testing, sampling; (*cantidad*) taste, sample.
(**e**) (*Cos*) fitting, trying on; **sala de ~s** fitting room.
(**f**) (*Tip*) **~s** proofs; **primeras ~s** first proofs, galleys; **~s de planas** page-proofs.
(**g**) (*Fot*) proof, print; **~ negativa** negative; **~ positiva** positive, print.
(**h**) (*Dep*) event; race; **~s** trials; **~ clasificatoria, ~ eliminatoria** heat; **~ de descenso** downhill run; **~ de**

obstáculos obstacle race; ~ **de relevos** relay race; ~ **contra reloj** time trial; ~ **de resistencia** endurance test; ~ **de vallas** hurdles, hurdles race.

(i) (*LAm*) circus act; (*And*: *función*) circus show, performance.

(j) (*Méx*) examination.

pruebista *nmf* (**a**) (*LAm*) (*acróbata*) acrobat; (*funámbulo*) tightrope walker; (*prestidigitador*) conjurer; (*malabarista*) juggler; (*contorsionista*) contortionist. (**b**) (*Cono Sur*: *de libros*) proofreader.

prurito *nm* (**a**) (*Med*) itch, pruritis.

(**b**) (*fig*) itch, urge; **tener el ~ de** + *infin* to have the urge to + *infin*; **por un ~ de exactitud** out of an excessive desire for accuracy, because of his urge (*o* eagerness) to get everything just right.

Prusia *nf* Prussia.

prusiano, -a *adj, nm/f* Prussian.

PS *nm* (*Pol gen*) *abr de* **Partido Socialista**; *p.ej.* **PSA** *abr de* **Partido Socialista Argentino**; **PST** *abr de* **Partido Socialista de los Trabajadores** *etc.*

pse..., psi...: *the Academy recommends the spellings* **se..., si...**; *all forms are pronounced* [se—, si—].

psefología *nf* psephology.

psefólogo, -a *nm* psephologist.

psic... *pref*, **psiqu...** *pref* psych...

psicoactivo *adj* psychoactive.

psicoafectivo *adj* mental, psychological.

psicoanálisis *nm* psychoanalysis.

psicoanalista *nmf* psychoanalyst.

psicoanalítico *adj* psychoanalytic(al); **diván** ~ psychiatrist's couch.

psicoanalizar [1f] *vt* to psychoanalyse.

psicocirugía *nf* psychosurgery.

psicodélico 1 *adj* psychedelic. **2** *nm* light show.

psicodinámica *nf* psychodynamics.

psicodrama *nm* psychodrama.

psicología *nf* psychology.

psicológicamente *adv* psychologically.

psicológico *adj* psychological.

psicólogo, -a *nm/f* psychologist.

psiconeurosis *nf invar* psychoneurosis.

psicópata *nmf* psychopath.

psicopático *adj* psychopathic.

psicopatología *nf* psychopathology.

psicopedagogo, -a *nm/f* educational psychologist.

psicoquinesis *nf* psychokinesis.

psicoquinético *adj* psychokinetic.

psicosis *nf invar* psychosis; ~ **puerperal** puerperal psychosis.

psicosomático *adj* psychosomatic.

psicoterapeuta *nmf* psychotherapist.

psicoterapia *nf* psychotherapy.

psicótico, -a *adj, nm/f* psychotic.

psicotrópico *adj* psychotropic, psychoactive.

Psique *nf* Psyche.

psique *nf* psyche.

psiquiatra, psiquíatra *nmf* psychiatrist.

psiquiatría *nf* psychiatry.

psiquiátrico 1 *adj* psychiatric. **2** *nm* mental hospital; psychiatric ward.

psíquico *adj* psychic(al); **enfermedades psíquicas** mental illnesses, psychological illnesses.

psitacosis *nf* psittacosis.

PSOE [pe'soe] *nm* (*Esp Pol*) *abr de* **Partido Socialista Obrero Español.**

Pta. *abr de* **Punta** Point, Pt.

pta. (**a**) (*Fin*) *abr de* **peseta.** (**b**) *abr de* **presidenta.**

ptas. *abr de* **pesetas.**

pte *abr de* **presidente.**

pterodáctilo [te-] *nm* pterodactyl.

ptmo. (*Com*) *abr de* **préstamo.**

ptomaína [to-] *nf* ptomaine.

ptomaínico [to-] *adj*: **envenenamiento** ~ ptomaine poisoning.

pts. *abr de* **pesetas.**

púa *nf* (**a**) (*punta*) sharp point; (*Bot, Zool*) prickle, spike, spine; (*de erizo*) quill; (*de peine*) tooth; (*de tenedor*) prong, tine; (*de gancho, alambre*) barb; (*Carib, Cono Sur*: *de gallo*) spur; (*Mús*) plectrum; (*Mús*) gramophone needle, phonograph needle (*US*). (**b**) (*Bot*) graft, cutting. (**c**) (‡) one peseta.

puaf* *interj* yuck!*

pub [pub, paß] *nm, pl* **pubs** [pub, paß] bar *m.*

púber 1 *adj* adolescent. **2** *nmf* adolescent child, child approaching puberty.

pubertad *nf* puberty.

pubescencia *nf* pubescence.

pubescente *adj* pubescent.

púbico *adj* pubic.

pubis *nm* pubis.

publicación *nf* publication.

públicamente *adv* publicly.

publicar [1g] *vt* (*gen*) to publish; (*difundir*) to publicize; *secreto etc* to make public, disclose, divulge.

publicidad *nf* (**a**) (*gen*) publicity; **dar ~ a** to publicize, give publicity to.

(**b**) (*Com*) advertising; ~ **directa** direct advertising; ~ **estática** (advertising on) hoardings; ~ **de lanzamiento** advance publicity, advertising campaign to launch a product; **hacer ~ por** to advertise; **se ha prohibido la ~ de cigarrillos** cigarette advertising has been banned.

publicista *nmf* publicist.

publicitar [1a] *vt* to publicize; (*Com*) to advertise.

publicitario 1 *adj* advertising (*atr*); publicity (*atr*). **2** *nm* advertising man, advertising agent.

público 1 *adj* public; **hacer** ~ to publish, make public; to publicize; to disclose.

2 *nm* (*concurrencia*) public; (*Mús, Teat etc*) audience; (*Dep*) spectators, crowd; (*de café etc*) clients, clientèle, patrons; (*de periódico*) readers, readership; **hay poco** ~ there aren't many people; **el ~ que se paseaba por la calle** the people who were strolling in the street; **hubo un ~ de 800** there was a crowd (*o* gathering, audience *etc*) of 800; **el gran** ~ the general public; **en** ~ in public.

public relations [pußlıkre'laʃonz] *nmf invar* public relations man/woman.

publirreportaje *nm* feature, special report.

pucará *nf* (*LAm Arqueol*) pre-Columbian fort.

puco *nm* (*And, Cono Sur*) earthenware bowl.

pucha[1] *nf* (**a**) (*Carib*) bouquet. (**b**) (*Méx*) ring-shaped loaf.

pucha[2]* *nf* (*LAm*: *euf* = *puta*); **¡(la) ~!** (*sorpresa*) well I'm damned (*o* blowed*)!; (*irritación*) drat!

puchana *nf* (*Cono Sur*) broom.

puchar‡ [1a] *vt* to speak, say.

puchera *nf* stew.

pucherazo* *nm* (*Esp*) electoral fiddle*; **dar** ~ to rig an election, fiddle the votes*.

puchero *nm* (**a**) (*Culin*: *olla*) cooking-pot. (**b**) (*Culin*: *guiso*) stew; (*fig*) food, daily bread; **apenas gana para el** ~ he hardly earns enough to eat. (**c**) (*: *mueca*) pout; **hacer ~s** to pout, make a face, screw up one's face.

puches *nmpl* (*Esp*) porridge, gruel.

puchica‡ *interj* (*And*) blast!*, damn!

puchito, -a* *nm/f* (*Cono Sur*) youngest child.

pucho* *nm* (**a**) (*colilla*) (*de cigarrillo*) fag-end‡; (*de puro*) cigar stub; (*cigarrillo*) fag‡.

(**b**) (*LAm*) (*resto*) scrap, left-over(s); dregs; (*Cos*) remnant; (*Fin*) coppers, small change; (*fig*: *nimiedad*) trifle, mere nothing; **a ~s** in dribs and drabs.

(**c**) (*And, Cono Sur*) youngest child.

pude *etc V* **poder.**

pudendo 1 *adj*: **partes pudendas** pudenda, private parts. **2** *nm* (*pene*) penis.

pudibundez *nf* false modesty, affected modesty; excess of modesty.

pudibundo *adj* affectedly modest; over-shy (*about sexual matters*), excessively modest; prudish.

pudicicia *nf* modesty; chastity.

púdico *adj* modest; chaste.

pudiendo *V* **poder.**

pudiente *adj* (*rico*) wealthy, well-to-do; (*poderoso*) powerful, influential; **las gentes menos ~s** the less well-off.

pudín *nm* pudding.

pudinga *nf* puddingstone.

pudor *nm* (**a**) (*recato*) modesty; (*timidez*) shyness; (*vergüenza*) (sense of) shame, (sense of) decency; **con** ~ modestly; discreetly; **tenía ~ de confesarlo** he was ashamed to confess it. (**b**) (*castidad*) chastity, virtue; **atentado al** ~ indecent assault.

pudorosamente *adv* (**a**) (*recatadamente*) modestly; shyly. (**b**) (*virtuosamente*) chastely, virtuously.

pudoroso *adj* (**a**) (*recatado*) modest; shy. (**b**) (*casto*) chaste, virtuous.

pudrición *nf* (**a**) (*proceso*) rotting. (**b**) (*lo podrido*) rot, rottenness; ~ **seca** dry rot.

pudridero *nm* rubbish heap, midden.

pudrimiento *nm* (**a**) (*proceso*) rotting. (**b**) (*lo podrido*) rot, rottenness.

pudrir [3a] **1** *vt* (**a**) (*descomponer*) to rot.

(**b**) (*: *molestar*) to upset, vex, annoy, exasperate.

2 *vi* (*fig*: *haber muerto*) to rot, be dead and buried.

3 pudrirse *vr* (**a**) (*corromperse*) to rot, decay; (*descomponerse*) to rot away.

(**b**) (*fig*) to rot, languish; **mientras se pudría en la cárcel** while he was languishing in jail; **te vas a ~ de aburrimiento** you'll die of boredom; **¡que se pudra!** let him rot!; **¡ahí** (*o* **así**) **te pudras!** (*Esp*‡) get away!*, not on your nelly!‡.

pueblada *nf* (*LAm*) (*motín*) riot; (*sublevación*) revolt, uprising; (*Cono Sur*: *multitud*) (*gen*) mob; (*de obreros*) gathering of workers.

pueblerino 1 *adj* countrified, small-town (*atr*); *persona* rustic, provincial. **2** *nm*, **pueblerina** *nf* rustic, country person, provincial.

pueblero (*LAm*) **1** *adj* town (*atr*), city (*atr*). **2** *nm* townsman, city dweller; (*pey*) city slicker.

pueblo *nm* (**a**) (*Pol etc*) people, nation; **~ elegido** chosen people; **el ~ español** the Spanish people; **hombre del ~** man of the people; **la voluntad del ~** the nation's will; **hacer un llamamiento al ~** to call on the people, call on the nation.

(**b**) (*plebe*) common people, lower orders; **~ de mala muerte** (*gente*) dregs of society.

(**c**) (*aldea*) village; (*población*) small town, country town; **~ fantasma** ghost town; **~ joven** (*LAm*: *euf*) shantytown.

puedo *etc V* **poder.**

puente 1 *nm* (**a**) (*lit, fig*) bridge; **~ aéreo** (*en crisis*) airlift; (*servicio*) airbus service, shuttle (service); **~ atirantado** suspension bridge; **~ de barcas, ~ de pontones** pontoon bridge; **~ colgante** suspension bridge; **~ giratorio** swing bridge; **~ grúa** bridge crane; **~ levadizo** drawbridge; **~ de peaje** tollbridge; **~ para peatones** footbridge; **tender un ~** (*fig*) to offer a compromise, go part-way to meet somebody's wishes; **tender ~s de plata a uno** to make it as easy as possible for sb.

(**b**) (*fig*: *de gafas, Mús etc*) bridge.

(**c**) (*Náut*: *t* **~ de mando**) bridge; (*cubierta*) deck; **~ del timón** wheelhouse.

(**d**) (*fig*) gap; hiatus; **habrá que salvar el ~ de una cosecha a otra** something will have to be done to fill the gap between one harvest and the next.

(**e**) **hacer ~*** to take a long weekend, take extra days off work between two public holidays.

(**f**) (*And*) collarbone.

2 *atr* temporary; provisional, transitional; that bridges the gap; **crédito ~, préstamo ~** bridging loan; **gabinete ~** caretaker government; **hombre ~** linkman; intermediary; **solución ~** temporary solution.

puentear* [1a] **1** *vt* (**a**) *autoridad etc* to bypass, pass over; **le puentearon con el ascenso** they passed him over for the promotion. (**b**) (*Fin*) to take out a bridging loan on. **2** *vi* to jump a grade (in the hierarchy), go up to the grade next but one.

puerca *nf* (**a**) (*cerda*) sow. (**b**) (*: *puta*) slut. (**c**) (*cochinilla*) woodlouse.

puercada *nf* (*And, CAm, Carib*) (*acto*) dirty trick; (*dicho*) obscene remark.

puerco 1 *nm* (**a**) (*cerdo*) pig, hog (*US*); (*jabalí*) wild boar; **~ espín** porcupine; **~ jabalí, ~ montés, ~ salvaje** wild boar, wild pig; **~ de mar** porpoise; **~ marino** dolphin; *V* **Martín.**

(**b**) (*) (*sinvergüenza*) pig; (*canalla*) swine*, rotter*.

2 *adj* (**a**) (*sucio*) dirty, filthy.

(**b**) (*asqueroso*) nasty, disgusting; (*grosero*) coarse.

(**c**) (*canallesco*) vile, rotten*, mean.

puericia *nf* boyhood.

puericultor(a) *nm/f* (*t* **médico ~**) paediatrician.

puericultura *nf* paediatrics.

pueril *adj* (**a**) (*gen*) childish, child (*atr*); **edad ~** childhood. (**b**) (*pey*) puerile, childish.

puerilidad *nf* puerility, childishness.

puerperal *adj* puerperal.

puerqueza *nf* (*Cono Sur*) (**a**) (*objeto*) dirty thing, filthy object. (**b**) (*trampa*) dirty trick. (**c**) (*Zool*) bug, creepy-crawly*.

puerro *nm* leek.

puerta *nf* door; gate; doorway; (*esp fig*) gateway (*de* to); (*Aer*) gate; (*Inform*) port, gate; (*Dep*) goal; **~ accesoria** side door; **~ de artistas** stage door; **~ (de) corredera, ~ deslizante** sliding door; **~ cortafuegos** fire-door; **~ de cristales** glass door; **~ chica** side door, private door; **entrar por la ~ chica*** to get in by the back door; **~ de embarque** boarding gate; **~ excusada** private door, side door; **~ giratoria** revolving door; **~ oscilante** swing door; **~ (de transmisión en) paralelo** (*Inform*) parallel port; **~ principal** front door; main entrance; **~ (de transmisión en) serie** (*Inform*) serial port; **~ de servicio** tradesmen's entrance; **~ trasera** back door; **~ ventana** French window; **~ vidriera** glass door, French window; **a ~ cerrada** behind closed doors; **a las ~s de la muerte** at death's door; **tenemos la guerra a las ~s** war is upon us, the threat of war is imminent; **coche de 2 ~s** (*t* **un dos ~s**) 2-door car; **coche de 4 ~s** 4-door car; **~s adentro** (*adv*) behind closed doors; (*adj*: *sirviente*) live-in; **política de ~s adentro** home policy, domestic policy; **lo que pasa de ~s afuera** (*fuera de casa*) what happens on the other side of one's door; (*en el extranjero*) what happens abroad, foreign affairs; **de ~s afuera se dice que ...** for public consumption it is being said that ...; **de ~ en ~** from door to door; **abrir la ~ a** (*fig*) to open the door to; **cerrarle todas las ~s a uno** to close off all avenues to sb; **coger la ~*** to leave in a huff; **dar con la ~ en las narices a uno** to slam the door in sb's face; **dar ~ a uno*** to chuck sb out; **dejar la ~ abierta a** (*fig*) to leave the door open for; **enseñar la ~ a uno** to show sb the door; **entrar por la ~ grande** to take a big step up; to find promotion (*etc*) easy; **estar en ~s** to be imminent; **estar hasta la ~** to be chock-a-block; **franquear las ~s a uno** (*Esp*) to welcome sb in; **pegarse una ~‡** to storm out, leave in a huff; **quedarse a la ~** to almost get a job; **querer poner ~s al campo** to try to stem the tide; **sacar de ~** to take a goal-kick; **salir por la ~ de los carros** (*apurado*) to leave in a hurry; (*destituido etc*) to leave in disgrace; **tomar la ~*** to leave, get out.

puertaventana *nf* shutter; French window.

puertear [1a] *vi* (*Cono Sur*) to make a dash for the exit.

puerto *nm* (**a**) (*gen*) port, harbour; (*de mar*) seaport; **~ comercial** trading port; **~ de contenedores** container port; **~ deportivo** yachting harbour, marina; **~ de escala** port of call; **~ de entrada** port of entry; **~ franco, ~ libre** free port; **~ de gran calado** deep-water port; **~ de origen** home port; **~ naval** naval port, naval harbour; **~ pesquero** fishing port; **entrar a ~, tomar ~** to enter port, come into port.

(**b**) (*fig*: *refugio*) haven, refuge; **llegar a ~** to solve a problem, get over a difficulty, come through safely.

(**c**) (*Geog*) pass.

(**d**) (*Inform*) gate, port; **~ (de transmisión en) paralelo** parallel port; **~ (de transmisión en) serie** serial port.

Puerto Rico *nm* Puerto Rico.

puertorriqueñismo *nm* word (*o* phrase *etc*) peculiar to Puerto Rico.

puertorriqueño, -a *adj, nm/f* Puerto Rican.

pues 1 *adv* (**a**) (*entonces*) then; (*bueno*) well, well then; (*así que*) so; **~ no voy** well I'm not going, in that case I'm not going; **¿no vas con ella, ~?** aren't you going with her after all?; so you're not going with her?; **llegó, ~, con 2 horas de retraso** so he arrived 2 hours late; **~ sí** well yes, why yes; certainly; **~ no** well no; not at all; **¡~ qué!** come now!; what else did you expect!; **¿~?** so?, well?; what next?

(**b**) (*vacilando*) **~ ... no sé** well ... I don't know.

(**c**) (*afirmación*) **¡~!** yes!, certainly!; *V* **ahora, bien** *etc.*

2 *conj* since, for; **cómpralo, ~ lo necesitas** buy it, since you need it; **nos marchamos, ~ no había más remedio** we left, since there was no alternative.

puesta *nf* (**a**) (*acto*) putting, placing; **~ en antena** (*TV*) showing; **~ al día** revision, updating; **~ en escena** staging; **~ de largo** coming-out (in society); **~ en libertad** freeing, release; **~ en marcha** (*acto*) starting; launch; (*dispositivo*) self-starter; **~ en práctica** putting into effect, implementation; **~ a punto** final preparation; perfection, fine-tuning.

(**b**) (*Astron*) setting; **~ del sol** sunset.

(**c**) (*Orn*) egg-laying; **una ~ anual de 300 huevos** an annual lay (*o* output) of 300 eggs.

(**d**) (*Naipes etc*) stake, bet.

(**e**) (*Cono Sur*) **¡~!** it's a tie!, it's a draw!; (*Carreras*) it's a dead heat!

puestero *nm* (**a**) (*LAm Com*) stallholder, market vendor. (**b**) (*Cono Sur*) (*mayoral*) farm overseer; (*agricultor*) small farmer, tenant farmer; (*trabajador*) ranch hand.

puesto 1 *ptp de* **poner.**

2 *adj* (**a**) **con el sombrero ~** with one's hat on, wearing a hat; **una mesa puesta para 9** a table laid for 9.

(**b**) (**bien**) **~** well dressed, smartly turned out.

(**c**) **tenerlos bien ~s** (*Esp*‡) to be a real man.

(**d**) **no está muy ~ en este tema** he's not very well up in these matters.

3 *nm* (**a**) (*lugar*) place; position; ~ **de amarre** berth, mooring; ~ **de honor** leading position; ~ **de trabajo** (*Inform*) work-station; **el ~ de la especie en la clasificación** the place of the species in the classification; **ocupa el tercer ~ en la liga** it is in third place in the league; **ceder el ~ a uno** to give up one's place to sb; **guardar** (*o* **mantener**) **su ~** to know one's place; to keep the proper distance.

(**b**) (*cargo*) ~ (**de trabajo**) post, position, job; **tiene un ~ de conserje** he has a post as a porter; **se crearán 200 ~s de trabajo** 200 new jobs will be created.

(**c**) (*Mil etc*) post; ~ **de control** checkpoint; ~ **de escucha** listening-post; ~ **fronterizo** border post; ~ **de observación** observation post; ~ **de policía** police post, police station; ~ **de socorro** first-aid post.

(**d**) (*Caza*) stand, place.

(**e**) (*Com*) stall; stand, booth; kiosk; pitch; ~ **callejero** street stall; ~ **de mercado** market-stall; ~ **de periódicos** newspaper stand.

(**f**) (*Cono Sur*) small farm.

4 ~ **que** *conj* since, as.

puf *interj* ugh!

puff [puf] *nm, pl* **puffs** [puf] pouffe.

pufo* *nm* (**a**) (*trampa*) trick, swindle; **dar el ~ a uno** to swindle sb.

(**b**) (*deuda*) debt.

(**c**) (*persona*) con man*.

púgil *nm* boxer.

pugilato *nm* boxing.

pugilista *nm* (*LAm*) boxer.

pugilístico *adj* boxing (*atr*).

pugío *nm* (*And, Cono Sur*) spring.

pugna *nf* battle, struggle, conflict; **entrar en ~ con** to clash with, come into conflict with; **estar en ~ con** to clash with, conflict with.

pugnacidad *nf* pugnacity, aggressiveness.

pugnar [1a] *vi* (**a**) (*luchar*) to fight; ~ **en defensa de** to fight in defence of; ~ **por** to fight for.

(**b**) (*esforzarse*) to struggle, fight, strive (*por* + *infin* to + *infin*); ~ **por no reírse** to struggle not to laugh.

(**c**) ~ **con** (*opinión etc*) to clash with, conflict with.

pugnaz *adj* pugnacious, aggressive.

puja *nf* (**a**) (*esfuerzo*) attempt, effort. (**b**) (*en subasta*) bid; ~ **de salida** opening bid. (**c**) **sacar de la ~ a uno** (*adelantarse*) to get ahead of sb; (*sacar de apuro*) to get sb out of a jam*. (**d**) (*And**) ticking-off*.

pujante *adj* (*fuerte*) strong, vigorous; (*potente*) powerful; (*enérgico*) pushful, forceful.

pujanza *nf* strength, vigour; power; pushfulness, forcefulness, drive.

pujar [1a] *vi* (**a**) (*en subasta*) to bid, bid up; (*Naipes*) to bid; ~ **en** (*o* **sobre**) **el precio** to bid the price up.

(**b**) (*esforzarse*) to struggle, strain; ~ **para hacer algo** to struggle to do sth; ~ **para adentro** (*CAm, Carib*) to grin and bear it.

(**c**) (*vacilar*) to falter, dither, hesitate.

(**d**) (*no encontrar palabras*) to struggle for words, be at a loss for words.

(**e**) (*hacer pucheros*) to be on the verge of tears.

(**f**) (*CAm*‡: *quejarse*) to moan, whinge*.

puje* *nm* (*And*) ticking-off*.

pujo *nm* (**a**) (*Med*) difficulty in relieving o.s., tenesmus.

(**b**) (*fig*; *ansia*) longing, strong urge; **sentir ~ de llorar** to be on the verge of tears; **sentir ~ de reírse** to have an uncontrollable urge to laugh.

(**c**) (*fig*: *intento*) attempt, try, shot; **~s** pretensions; **tiene ~s de caballero** he has pretensions to being a gentleman.

pulcramente *adv* neatly, tidily, smartly; exquisitely; delicately.

pulcritud *nf* neatness, tidiness, smartness; exquisiteness, delicacy.

pulcro *adj* (*aseado*) neat, tidy, smart; (*elegante*) smartly dressed, smartly turned out; (*exquisito*) exquisite; (*delicado*) dainty, delicate.

pulga *nf* (**a**) (*Zool*) flea.

(**b**) (*de juego*) tiddlywink; **juego de ~s** tiddlywinks.

(**c**) (*locuciones*) **un tío de malas ~s** a bad-tempered chap, a peppery individual; **tener malas ~s** to be bad-tempered, be violent, be unpredictable; **no aguantar ~s*** to stand no nonsense; **buscar las ~s a uno*** to tease sb, needle sb*; **hacer de una ~ un elefante** (*o* **camello**) to make a mountain out of a molehill; to exaggerate sb's defects.

(**d**) (*Inform*) bug.

pulgada *nf* inch.

pulgar *nm* thumb.

pulgarada *nf* (**a**) (*capirotazo*) flick, flip. (**b**) (*de rapé etc*) pinch.

Pulgarcito *nm* Tom Thumb.

pulgón *nm* plant louse; bug.

pulgoso *adj*, **pulguiento** *adj* (*LAm*) full of fleas, verminous.

pulguero‡ *nm* (*Esp*) kip‡, bed; (*CAm, Carib*) gaol.

pulidamente *adv* (**a**) (*con pulcritud*) neatly, tidily; (*con esmero*) carefully; (*refinadamente*) in a polished way; (*pey*) affectedly. (**b**) (*con cortesía*) courteously.

pulido 1 *adj* (*pulcro*) neat, tidy; (*limpio*) clean; (*esmerado*) careful; (*refinado*) polished, refined; (*pey*) over-nice, affected, finicky. **2** *nm* polish, polishing.

pulidor(a) *nm/f* polisher.

pulimentado *nm* polishing.

pulimentar [1a] *vt* (*pulir*) to polish; (*dar lustre a*) to put a gloss on, put a shine on; (*alisar*) to smooth.

pulimento *nm* (**a**) (*acto*) polishing; polish, shine; (*brillo*) gloss. (**b**) (*sustancia*) polish.

pulique *nm* (*CAm*) *dish of chilis and maize.*

pulir [3a] **1** *vt* (**a**) (*gen*) to polish; (*dar lustre a*) to put a gloss on, put a shine on.

(**b**) (*alisar*) to smooth; (*acabar*) to finish (off).

(**c**) (*fig*) to polish up, touch up, rub up; *persona* to polish up.

(**d**) (‡) (*robar*) to pinch*; (*vender*) to sell, flog‡; to sell off (cheap); (*gastar*) to blow*, spend.

2 pulirse *vr* (*fig*: *refinarse*) to acquire polish; (*acicalarse*) to spruce o.s. up.

pulmón *nm* (**a**) (*gen*) lung; ~ **de acero** iron lung; **a pleno ~** *respirar* deeply; *gritar* at the top of one's voice; *funcionar* full-blast, at full throttle. (**b**) **pulmones**‡ tits‡.

pulmonar *adj* pulmonary, lung (*atr*).

pulmonía *nf* pneumonia; ~ **doble** double pneumonia.

pulmotor *nm* iron lung.

pulóver *nm*, **pull-over** *nm* pullover.

pulpa *nf* pulp; soft mass; (*de fruta, planta*) flesh, soft part; (*Anat*) soft flesh; (*Cono Sur*) boneless meat, fillet; ~ **de madera** wood pulp; ~ **de papel** paper pulp.

pulpejo *nm* fleshy part, soft part.

pulpería *nf* (*And, CAm, Cono Sur*) (*tienda*) general store, food store; (*bar*) bar, tavern.

pulpero, -a *nm/f* (*And, CAm, Cono Sur*) (*comerciante*) storekeeper, grocer; (*tabernero*) tavernkeeper.

púlpito *nm* pulpit.

pulpo *nm* (**a**) (*Zool*) octopus. (**b**) (*Aut etc*) elastic strap.

pulposo *adj* pulpy; soft, fleshy.

pulque *nm* (*And, Méx*) *fermented drink made from maguey sap.*

pulquear [1a] (*Méx*) **1** *vi* to drink *pulque*. **2 pulquearse** *vr* to get drunk on *pulque*.

pulquería *nf* (*Méx*) bar, tavern, *pulque* shop.

pulquérrimo *adj superl de* **pulcro**.

pulsación *nf* (**a**) (*latido*) beat, pulsation; (*Anat*) throb(bing), beat(ing). (**b**) (*en máquina de escribir etc*) tap; (*de mecanógrafo, pianista*) touch. (**c**) (*Inform*) ~ **doble** strikeover.

pulsador *nm* button, push-button; (*Elec*) switch.

pulsar¹ [1a] **1** *vt* (**a**) *tecla etc* to strike, touch, tap; *botón, interruptor* to press; (*Mús*) to play.

(**b**) ~ **a uno** (*Med*) to take sb's pulse, feel sb's pulse.

(**c**) (*fig*) *opinión etc* to sound out, take, explore.

2 *vi* to pulsate; to throb, beat.

pulsar² *nm* pulsar; (*fig*) black hole.

pulsear [1a] *vi* (**a**) (*entre dos personas*) to arm-wrestle. (**b**) (*Cono Sur*) to aim at a target.

pulsera *nf* wristlet, bracelet; ~ **de pedida** (*Esp*) engagement bracelet; ~ **para reloj** watch strap; **reloj de ~** wristwatch.

pulsión *nf* urge, drive, impulse.

pulso *nm* (**a**) (*Anat*) pulse; **tomar el ~ a uno** to take sb's pulse, feel sb's pulse; **tomar el ~ a la opinión** to sound out opinion.

(**b**) (*Anat*: *muñeca*) wrist; (*fig*: *fuerza*) strength of wrist; (*fig*: *contienda*) trial of strength; battle of wills; showdown; **echar un ~** to arm-wrestle; **echar un ~ a** (*fig*: *contender con*) to have a trial of strength with; (*desafiar*) to challenge; **a ~** by sheer strength; with the strength of one arm; (*fig*) by sheer hard work; unaided, all alone; the hard way; **a ~ sudando** by the sweat of one's brow; **dibujo** (**hecho**) **a** ~ freehand drawing; **orquesta de** ~ **y púa** string orchestra; **ganar algo a** ~ to get sth the hard way; **levantar una silla a** ~ to lift a chair with one hand; **tomar un mueble a** ~ to lift a piece of furniture clean off the ground; **con** ~ **firme** with a firm hand.

(**c**) (*fig*: *firmeza*) steadiness, steady hand, firmness of touch; **tener** ~ (*Cono Sur*) to have a good aim.

(**d**) (*fig*: *tacto*) tact, good sense; **con mucho** ~ very sensibly; with great tact.

(**e**) (*And*) = **pulsera.**

pulular [1a] **1** *vt* (*LAm*) to infest, swarm in, overrun.

2 *vi* (*estar plagado*) to swarm (*de* with); (*fig*) to abound.

pululo* *adj* (*CAm*) short and fat.

pulverización *nf* (**a**) (*de sólidos*) pulverization. (**b**) (*de perfume, insecticida*) spray; spraying.

pulverizador *nm* spray, sprayer, spray-gun; ~ **nasal** inhaler.

pulverizar [1f] *vt* (**a**) *sustancia* to pulverize; (*reducir a polvo*) to powder, convert into powder. (**b**) *líquido, plantas etc* to spray. (**c**) (*fig*) *ciudad, enemigo* to pound, pulverize, smash.

pulverulento *adj* (**a**) *sustancia* powdered, powdery. (**b**) *superficie* dusty.

pull [pul] *nm* pullover.

pulla *nf* (**a**) (*injuria*) cutting remark, wounding remark; (*mofa*) taunt; (*indirecta*) dig. (**b**) (*obscenidad*) obscene remark, rude word.

pum *interj* bang!; thud!; pop!

puma *nf* puma.

puna *nf* (*LAm*) (**a**) (*Geog*) high Andean plateau, puna. (**b**) (*Med*) mountain sickness. (**c**) (*viento*) cold mountain wind.

punción *nf* (*Med*) puncture.

punch *nm* (**a**) (*puñetazo*) punch. (**b**) (*fig*) (*empuje*) vigour, strength, punch; (*agilidad*) agility. (**c**) **~es** (*CAm*) popcorn.

punchar [1a] *vt* (*LAm*) to punch.

punching ['punʃin] *nm* punchball.

punching-ball ['punʃinbal] *n* punchball; (*fig*) whipping-boy.

pundonor *nm* (*dignidad*) self-respect, pride; (*honra*) honour; face.

pundonoroso *adj* (*honrado*) honourable; (*escrupuloso*) punctilious, scrupulous.

punga‡ **1** *nf* (*Cono Sur*) thieving, nicking‡. **2** *nmf* (*Cono Sur*) pickpocket, thief.

pungir [3c] *vt* (**a**) (*punzar*) to prick, puncture; (*picar*) to sting. (**b**) (*hacer sufrir*) to cause suffering to.

punguista‡ *nm* (*And, Cono Sur*) (*carterista*) pickpocket; (*ladrón*) thief.

punible *adj* punishable.

punición *nf* punishment.

púnico *adj, nm* (*Ling*) Punic.

punitivo *adj*, **punitorio** *adj* punitive.

punki(e) *adj, nmf* punk.

punta 1 *nf* (**a**) (*extremo*) end; (*extremo puntiagudo*) tip, point, sharp end; (*de madera etc*) thin end; (*Geog*) point; headland; (*Cos*) dentelle; **~s de espárrago** asparagus tips; ~ **de lanza** spearhead (*t fig*); **con la** ~ **de la lengua** with the tip of one's tongue; **la** ~ **del iceberg** the tip of the iceberg; **la** ~ **de la lengua** the tip of one's tongue; ~ **del pie** toe; **a** ~ **de cuchillo** at knife-point; **a** ~ **de pistola** at gunpoint; **línea** ~ **a** ~ (*Telec*) direct line; **de** ~ on end; endways; **de** ~ **a** ~ from one end to the other; **ir de** ~ **en blanco** to be dressed up to the nines; **se la pusieron los pelos de** ~ her hair stood on end; **energía de** ~ peak power demand; **estoy hasta la** ~ **de los pelos con él*** I'm utterly fed up with him*; **ponerse de** ~ **en blanco** to get all dressed up; **sacar** ~ **a** to sharpen, point, put a point on; **sacar** ~ **a una observación** to read too much into a remark; **sacar** ~ **a una máquina** to get the most out of a machine; to use a machine in ways which were never intended.

(**b**) (*fig*: *elemento*) touch, trace; tinge; **tiene una** ~ **de loco** he has a streak of madness, he's a bit mad; **tiene sus ~s de filósofo** there's a little of the philosopher about him.

(**c**) (*fig*: *locuciones*) **a** ~ **pala*** by the ton; by the score; **lo tenemos a** ~ **pala*** we have loads of it; **andar** (*o* **estar**) **de** ~ to be at odds (*con* with); **estar de** ~ to be edgy; to be in a bad mood; **ponerse de** ~ **con uno** to fall out with sb; to adopt a hostile attitude to sb; **tener de** ~ **a uno** to be at daggers drawn with sb.

(**d**) (*Téc*: *clavo*) small nail.

(**e**) (*colilla*) stub, butt.

(**f**) (*Zool*: *de toro*) horn; (*de ciervo*) point, tine.

(**g**) (*Agr*: *vacas*) group of cows.

(**h**) (*Carib*: *tabaco*) best quality tobacco (leaf).

(**i**) (*Méx*: *arma*)) sharp weapon.

(**j**) (*Carib*: *mofa*) taunt, snide remark.

(**k**) (*LAm*: *grupo*) group, gathering; lot; **una** ~ **de** a lot of, a bunch of.

(**l**) **en** ~ (*CAm*) wholesale.

(**m**) (*Dep*) striker, forward; **media** ~ midfield player.

(**n**) **~s** (*Ballet*) points; ballet-shoes.

2 *atr* (*máximo*) top, maximum; (*más moderno*) latest; (*primero*) leading; (*de mayor carga*) peak; **horas** ~ peak hours, rush hours; **industrias** ~ sunrise industries; **tecnología** ~ latest technology, leading edge technology; **velocidad** ~ maximum speed, top speed.

3 *nm* (*Dep*) striker, forward.

puntada *nf* (**a**) (*Cos*) stitch; ~ **cruzada** cross-stitch; ~ **invisible** invisible mending; **dar unas ~s en** to put a few stitches in, stitch up; **no ha dado** ~ (*fig*) he hasn't done a stroke; he's done nothing at all about it.

(**b**) (*****: *indirecta*) hint; **pegar** (*o* **soltar**) **una** ~ to drop a hint.

(**c**) (*LAm Med*) stitch; (*dolor agudo*) sharp pain.

(**d**) (*Méx*) witty remark, witticism.

puntaje *nm* (*LAm*) score.

puntal *nm* (**a**) (*Arquit*) prop, shore, support; (*Agr*) prop; (*Téc*) strut, crosspiece; stanchion. (**b**) (*fig*) prop, support; chief supporter. (**c**) (*LAm*) snack.

puntapié *nm* kick; (*Rugby*) ~ **de bote pronto** drop kick; ~ **colocado** place kick; ~ **de saque** drop-out; **echar a uno a ~s** to kick sb out; **pegar un** ~ **a uno** to give sb a kick.

puntazo *nm* (*Taur*) jab (*with a horn*); (*LAm*) (*pinchazo*) jab, poke; (*puñalada*) stab; (*herida*) stab wound, knife wound.

punteado 1 *adj* (*moteado*) dotted, covered with dots; (*grabado con puntos*) stippled; *plumaje etc* flecked (*de* with); *diseño* of dots.

2 *nm* (**a**) (*V adj*) series of dots; stippling; flecking.

(**b**) (*Mús*) *punteado*, pizzicato.

puntear [1a] **1** *vt* (**a**) (*marcar con puntos*) to dot, cover (*o* mark) with dots; to stipple; to fleck.

(**b**) *artículos* to tick, put a mark against; (*LAm*) *lista* to check off.

(**c**) (*Cos*) to stitch (up).

(**d**) (*Mús*) to play pizzicato, pluck.

(**e**) (*Cono Sur*) *tierra* to fork over.

(**f**) (*Cono Sur*) *marcha etc* to head, lead.

2 *vi* (*Náut*) to luff.

punteo *nm* plucking.

puntera *nf* (**a**) (*de zapato*) toecap. (**b**) (*de lapicero*) pencil top. (**c**) (*****: *puntapié*) kick.

punterazo *nm* (*Dep*) powerful shot, drive.

puntería *nf* (**a**) (*el apuntar*) aim, aiming; **enmendar** (*o* **rectificar**) **la** ~ to correct one's aim; **hacer la** ~ **de un cañón** to aim a gun, sight a gun.

(**b**) (*fig*: *destreza*) marksmanship; **tener buena** ~ to be a good shot; **tener mala** ~ to be a bad shot.

puntero 1 *adj* (*primero*) top, leading; (*moderno*) up-to-date; **más** ~ (*sobresaliente*) outstanding, furthest ahead; (*último*) latest; **equipo** ~ top club.

2 *nm* (**a**) (*palo*) pointer; ~ **luminoso** light pen.

(**b**) (*Téc*) stonecutter's chisel.

(**c**) (*persona*) outstanding individual; leader, top man.

(**d**) (*LAm*) (*Dep*) leading team, team which is ahead; (*de rebaño*) leading animal; (*de desfile*) leader.

(**e**) (*LAm*: *de reloj*) hand.

puntiagudo *adj* sharp, sharp-pointed.

puntilla *nf* (**a**) (*Téc*) tack, brad.

(**b**) (*de pluma*) point, nib.

(**c**) (*Cos*) lace edging.

(**d**) (*Taur*) short dagger for giving the coup de grâce; **dar la** ~ to give the coup de grâce, finish off the bull.

(**e**) **de ~s** on tiptoe; **andar de ~s** to walk on tiptoe.

puntillismo *nm* pointillism.

puntillo *nm* (**a**) punctilio; (*pey*) exaggerated sense of honour, excessive amour propre. (**b**) (**‡**) **ligar un** ~ (*drogas*) to get high‡; (*bebida*) to get plastered‡.

puntilloso *adj* punctilious; (*pey*) touchy, sensitive.

punto *nm* (**a**) (*en diseño etc*) dot, spot; fleck; (*en plumaje etc*) spot, speckle; (*en carta, dominó*) spot, pip; **diseño a ~s** design of dots, pattern of dots.

(**b**) (*Tip*) point; (*t* ~ **final**) full stop; **dos ~s** colon; ~ **y coma** semicolon; ~ **de admiración**, ~ **de exclamación** exclamation mark; ~ **de interrogación** question mark, query; **~s suspensivos** dots, suspension points (...); **¡y** ~ (**final**)**!** and that's that!; ~ **acápite** (*LAm*) full stop, new paragraph; **'~ y aparte'** (*al dictar*) 'new paragraph'; **sin faltar ~ ni coma** accurately, faithfully; minutely; **hacer algo con ~s y comas** to get sth right down to the last detail; **poner los ~s sobre las íes** to dot the i's and cross the t's; **le puso los ~s sobre las íes** she corrected him, she drew attention to his inaccuracies.

(**c**) (*tanto*: *Dep*) point; (*en examen*) mark; (*en bolsa*) point; **con 8 ~s a favor y 3 en contra** with 8 points for and 3 against; **los dos están empatados a ~s** the two are level on points; **ganar a los ~s, vencer por ~s** to win on points.

(**d**) (*en discusión*) point; item, matter, question; **contestar ~ por ~** to answer point by point; **~ capital** crucial point, basic point; crux; **~s de consulta** terms of reference; points referred for decision (*o* report); **~s a tratar** matters to be discussed, agenda.

(**e**) **~ de taxis** taxi stand, cab rank.

(**f**) (*Mús*) pitch.

(**g**) (*Cos*) stitch; (*de tela*) mesh; (*en media*) ladder, run; (*Med*) stitch; **una herida que necesitó 10 ~s** a wound which needed 10 stitches; **~ del derecho** plain knitting; **~ de media** plain knitting; **~ del revés** purl; **hacer ~** to knit; **¡~ en boca!** mum's the word!, keep it under your hat!; **chaqueta de ~** knitted jacket.

(**h**) **~ de costado** (*Med*) stitch, pain in the side.

(**i**) (*agujero etc*) hole; **darse dos ~s en el cinturón** to let out one's belt, (*fig*) overeat; **calzar muchos ~s** to know a lot; **calzar pocos ~s** to know very little, be pretty dim.

(**j**) (*Com*) **~ de equilibrio** break-even point.

(**k**) (*Inform*) pixel; **~ de parada** break-point; **~ de referencia** benchmark.

(**l**) (*lugar etc*) spot, place, point; (*Geog*) point; (*Mat*) point; (*de proceso*) point, stage; (*de tiempo*) point, moment; **~ de apoyo** fulcrum; **~ de arranque** starting point; **~ de atraque** berth, mooring; **~ cardinal** cardinal point; **~ céntrico** central point; **~ ciego** (*Anat*) blind spot; **~ clave (de las defensas)** key point (in the defences); **~ de congelación** freezing-point; **~ de contacto** point of contact; **~ de control** checkpoint; **~ crítico** critical point, critical moment; **~ culminante** culminating moment; topmost point, limit; **~ débil, ~ flaco** weak spot, weak point; **~ de ebullición** boiling-point; **~ de fuga** vanishing point; **~ de fusión** melting-point; **~ de inflamación** flashpoint; **estar en el ~ de mira de uno** to be in sb's sights; **~ muerto** (*Mec*) dead centre; (*Aut etc*) neutral (gear); (*fig*) deadlock, stalemate; **las negociaciones están en un ~ muerto** the negotiations are deadlocked, there is stalemate in the talks; **hemos llegado a un ~ muerto** we have reached deadlock; **~ negro** (*Aut*) blackspot; (*Anat*) blackhead; (*fig*) blemish, defect; **~ neurálgico** (*Anat*) nerve centre; (*fig*) key point; **~ neutro** (*Mec*) dead centre; (*Aut etc*) neutral (gear); **~ de no** (*o* **sin**) **retorno** point of no return; **~ panorámico** viewpoint, vantage point; **~ de partida** starting point; **~ de penalti** penalty spot; **~ de referencia** point of reference; **~ de venta** point of sale; **~ de veraneo** summer resort, holiday resort; **~ de vista** point of view, viewpoint; criterion; **él lo mira desde otro ~ de vista** he looks at it from another point of view.

(**m**) (*locuciones etc + prep*) **a ~** ready; **con sus máquinas a ~ para disparar** with their cameras ready to shoot; **llegar a ~** to come just at the right moment; **al llegar a este ~** at this moment, at this stage; **saber algo a ~ fijo** to know sth for sure; **al ~** at once, instantly; **está a ~** it's ready; **estar a ~ de +** *infin* to be on the point of + *ger*, be about to + *infin*; **estar a ~ de caramelo** to be at the point of realization; **estar al ~*** (*LAm*) to be high (on drugs)‡; **poner a ~** (*fig*) to fine-tune; **poner un motor a ~** to tune an engine; **de todo ~** completely, absolutely; **bajar de ~** to decline, fall off, fall away; **subir de ~** to grow, increase; to get worse; **a las 7 en ~** at 7 sharp, at 7 on the dot, punctually at 7; **en ~ a** with regard to; **estar en su ~** (*Culin*) to be done to a turn; **una medida muy puesta en su ~** a very timely (*o* proper) measure; **para dejar las cosas en su ~** to be absolutely precise; **llegar a su ~ cumbre** to reach its peak; **pongamos las cosas en su ~** let's be absolutely clear about this; **poner algo en su ~** to bring sth to perfection; **hasta el ~ de +** *infin* to the extent of + *ger*; **hasta cierto ~** up to a point, to some extent; in a way; **hasta tal ~ que ...** to such an extent that ...

(**n**) (*Esp**) (*hombre*) bloke‡, guy*; (*pey*) rogue; **¡vaya (un) ~!, ¡está hecho un ~ filipino!** he's a right rogue!*

(**o**) (‡) **ligar un ~** *V* **puntillo (b)**.

puntuable *adj* ranking; championship (*atr*); **una prueba ~ para el campeonato** a race counting towards the championship.

puntuación *nf* (**a**) (*Ling, Tip*) punctuation.

(**b**) (*acto*: *Escuela etc*) marking; (*Dep*) scoring; **sistema de ~** system of scoring.

(**c**) (*Escuela*: *puntos*) mark(s); (*grado*) class, grade; (*Dep*) score.

puntual *adj* (**a**) *persona* (*fiable*) reliable, conscientious; (*rápido*) prompt; (*al acudir etc*) punctual.

(**b**) *llegada etc* punctual.

(**c**) *informe etc* reliable; precise; *cálculo* exact, accurate.

(**d**) (*concreto*) specific, concrete, precise.

puntualidad *nf* (**a**) (*seguridad*) reliability, conscientiousness; (*diligencia*) promptness; (*exactitud*) punctuality. (**b**) (*precisión*) precision; exactness, accuracy.

puntualización *nf* specification, detailed statement (*o* explanation *etc*).

puntualizador *adj* specific, detailed.

puntualizar [1f] *vt* (**a**) (*precisar*) to fix, specify, state in detail; (*determinar*) to settle, determine. (**b**) (*recordar*) to fix in one's mind (*o* memory).

puntualmente *adv* (*V n*) (**a**) reliably, conscientiously; promptly; punctually. (**b**) precisely, exactly, accurately.

puntuar [1c] **1** *vt* (**a**) (*Ling, Tip*) to punctuate. (**b**) (*valorar*) to evaluate, assess; *examen* to mark. **2** *vi* (**a**) (*Dep*: *valer*) to score, count; **eso no puntúa** that doesn't count. (**b**) (*marcar*) to score.

puntudo *adj* (*LAm*) sharp.

puntura *nf* puncture, prick.

punzada *nf* (**a**) (*puntura*) puncture, prick; jab.

(**b**) (*Med*) stitch; (*dolor*) twinge (of pain), shooting pain; (*espasmo*) spasm.

(**c**) (*fig*) pang, twinge (of regret *etc*).

(**d**) (*Carib**: *insolencia*) cheek*.

punzante *adj* (**a**) *dolor* shooting, sharp. (**b**) *herramienta etc* sharp. (**c**) (*fig*) *comentario etc* biting, caustic.

punzar [1f] **1** *vt* (**a**) (*pinchar*) to puncture, prick, pierce; (*Téc*) to punch; to perforate.

(**b**) (*fig*) to hurt, grieve; **le punzan remordimientos** he feels pangs of regret, his conscience pricks him.

2 *vi* (*dolor*) to shoot, stab; to sting.

punzó *adj* (*Carib, Cono Sur*) bright red.

punzón *nm* (*Téc*) punch; graver, burin; bodkin.

puñada *nf* punch, clout; **dar de ~s en** to punch, pound, beat on.

puñado *nm* handful (*lit, fig*); **a ~s** by handfuls; in plenty, galore; **me mola un ~‡** I like it a lot.

puñal *nm* dagger; **poner el ~ al pecho a uno** (*fig*) to hold a pistol to sb's head.

puñalada *nf* (**a**) (*golpe*) stab, thrust; (*herida*) stab wound; **~ de misericordia** coup de grâce; **~ trapera** stab in the back; dirty trick; *V* **coser**. (**b**) (*fig*) stab, grievous blow; **~ encubierta** stab in the back, treacherous thrust.

puñeta 1 *nf* (**a**) (‡) (*bobada*) silly thing; (*queja*) silly complaint; (*dicho*) stupid remark; (*bagatela*) silly trifle; **¡no me vengas con ~s!** don't come whining to me!; **perder el tiempo en ~s** to waste time on piddling trifles.

(**b**) (‡) **hacer la ~ a uno** to muck sb around, screw sb up‡; **me han hecho la ~** they've screwed it up for me‡.

(**c**) (**‡) **hacer ~s** to wank**‡; **¡(vete) a hacer ~s!** get stuffed!**‡; **mandar a uno a hacer ~s** to tell sb to get stuffed**‡.

(**d**) (‡: *otras locuciones*) **tengo un catarro de la ~** I've got a bloody awful cold‡; **ese conserje de la ~** that swine of a porter*; **fue un lío de ~s** it was one hell of a mess; **es un problema de ~** it's a devil of a problem; **no entiende ni ~** he doesn't understand a blind thing; **¡qué coche ni qué ~s!** what car?, car my foot!; **¿qué ~s le habrá pasado?** what in hell's name can have happened to her?; **viven en la quinta ~** they live in the middle of nowhere.

2 *interj* (‡) **¡~s!, ¡qué ~s!** (*enojo*) hell!; (*asombro*) bugger me!**‡, well I'm damned!; **¡una ~!** get away!*; **¡es enorme, ~!** it's bloody huge!‡; **¡escucha, ~!** you bloody well listen!‡

puñetazo *nm* punch; **a ~s** with (blows of) one's fists; **dar a uno de ~s** to punch sb; **andaba a ~s con las lágrimas** he was struggling to keep back his tears.

puñetería‡ *nf* bore, drag; = **puñeta (a)**.

puñetero *adj* (**a**) (‡: *condenado*) bloody**‡; lousy‡. (**b**) (*malévolo*) bloody-minded‡; (*nimio*) niggling, hair-splitting.

puño *nm* (**a**) (*Anat*) fist; **~ de hierro** knuckleduster; **a ~ cerrado** with one's clenched fist; **apretar los ~s** (*fig*) to struggle hard; **comerse los ~s** to be starving; **como un ~** (*pequeño*) tiny, very small; (*grande*) huge, enormous; *verdad etc* obvious (*V t* **verdad**); (*tangible*) tangible, visible; **mentiras como ~s** whopping great lies*; **de propio ~** in one's own handwriting; **de ~ y letra del poeta** in the poet's own handwriting; **meter a uno en un ~** to intimidate sb, cow sb; to bring sb under control; **su mujer le tiene en un ~** his wife's got him completely under her thumb.

(**b**) (*cantidad*) handful, fistful.

(**c**) (*Cos*) cuff.

(**d**) (*de espada*) hilt; (*de herramienta*) handle, haft, grip; (*de vasija*) handle; (*de puerta*) handle.

(**e**) (*fig*) **~s** strength; brute force; **es hombre de ~s** he's strong, he's tough; **ganar algo con los ~s** to get sth by sheer hard work; **hacer algo a ~s** to do sth by hand.

(**f**) (*fig*) **un ~ de casa** a tiny house, a very small house.

pupa *nf* (**a**) (*Med*) (*ampolla*) blister, pimple; (*úlcera*) lip sore, ulcer; (*palabra de niños*) sore, pain; **hacer ~ a uno** to hurt sb. (**b**) (*: *error*) gaffe, blunder. (**c**) (*Ent*) pupa.

pupas* *nmf* unpredictable person; (*gruñón*) moaner*.

pupila *nf* (**a**) (*Anat*) pupil. (**b**) (*en orfelinato*) inmate; (*pensionista*) boarder. (**c**) (*Jur*) ward. (**d**) (*: *puta*) prostitute. (**e**) (*perspicacia*) sharpness, intelligence; good sense.

pupilo *nm* (**a**) (*en orfelinato*) inmate; (*interno*) boarder. (**b**) (*Jur*) ward. (**c**) (*Dep**) player.

pupitre *nm (Escol etc)* desk; (*Inform*) console.

pupo *nm* (*And, Cono Sur*) navel.

pupón *adj* (**a**) (*Cono Sur, Méx**: *lleno de comida*) stuffed, full (up). (**b**) (*Cono Sur*‡: *barrigón*) pot-bellied, paunchy.

pupusa *nf* (*CAm*) (**a**) (*Culin*) stuffed tortilla. (**b**) (**) cunt**.

puque *nm* (*Méx*) (*podrido*) rotten, bad; (*débil*) weak, sickly; (*estéril*) sterile.

puquío *nm* (*And, Cono Sur*) spring, fountain.

Pura *nf abr de* **Purificación**.

puramente *adv* purely, simply.

pura-sangre *nmf, pl* **pura-sangres** thoroughbred.

puré *nm* purée, (thick) soup; **~ de guisantes** pea soup; (*fig*) peasouper*, thick fog; **~ de patata(s)** mashed potatoes, creamed potatoes; **~ de tomate** tomato paste; **estoy hecho ~*** I'm knackered*.

purear [1a] *vi* (*And*) to drink one's liquor neat.

pureta‡ **1** *adj* old, elderly. **2** *nmf* (**a**) (*viejo*) old crock, old geezer‡. (**b**) (*carca*) old square*.

pureza *nf* purity.

purga *nf* (**a**) (*Med*) purge, cathartic, purgative. (**b**) (*Pol*) purge. (**c**) (*Mec*) venting, draining, airing; **válvula de ~** vent.

purgación *nf* (**a**) (*Med*) purging, purgative. (**b**) (*de mujer*) menstruation.

purgante *nm* purgative.

purgar [1h] **1** *vt* (**a**) (*gen*) to purge, cleanse (*de* of); (*Mec*) to vent, drain, air; (*Pol*) to purge, liquidate.

(**b**) (*purificar*) to purify, refine.

(**c**) (*Med*) to purge, administer a purgative to.

(**d**) (*fig*) *pecado* to purge, expiate; *pasiones* to purge.

2 purgarse *vr* (**a**) (*Med*) to take a purge.

(**b**) (*fig*) **~ de** to purge o.s. of.

purgativo *adj* purgative.

purgatorio *nm* purgatory (*lit, fig*); **¡fue un ~!** it was purgatory!

puridad *nf* (*lit*) secrecy; **en ~** (*llanamente*) plainly, directly; (*secretamente*) in secret; (*estrictamente*) strictly, in the strict sense.

purificación *nf* purification.

purificador *nm*: **~ de agua** water filter; **~ de aire** air purifier, air filter.

purificar [1g] *vt* to purify; to cleanse; (*Téc*) to purify, refine.

purili‡ *nmf* old geezer‡.

Purísima *adj superl*: **la ~** the Virgin.

purismo *nm* purism.

purista *nmf* purist.

puritanismo *nm* puritanism.

puritano 1 *adj actitud etc* puritanical; *iglesia, tradición etc* puritan. **2** *nm,* **puritana** *nf* puritan.

puro 1 *adj* (**a**) *color, lengua, sustancia etc* pure; (*sin mezcla*) unadulterated; *oro* solid; *cielo* clear.

(**b**) (*fig*) pure, simple; sheer; *verdad* plain, simple; **de ~ aburrimiento** out of sheer boredom; **de ~ tonto** out of sheer stupidity; **por pura casualidad** by sheer chance; **por las puras*** (*Cono Sur*) just for the hell of it.

(**c**) (*moralmente*) pure, virtuous, chaste.

(**d**) (*Méx*: *solo*) only, just; **me queda una pura porción** I have just one ration left, I have only one ration left.

(**e**) (*And, Carib Méx*: *idéntico*) identical; **el hijo es ~ el padre** the son is exactly like his father.

2 *como adv*: **de ~ bobo** out of sheer stupidity; **de ~ cansado** out of sheer tiredness; **no se le ve el color de ~ sucio** it's so dirty you can't tell what colour it is; **cosas que se olvidan de ~ sabidas** things which are so well known that they get overlooked.

3 *nm* (**a**) (*cigarro*) cigar; **~ habano** Havana cigar.

(**b**) **a ~ de** by dint of, thanks only to.

(**c**) **meter un ~ a uno** (*Mil*‡) to put sb on a charge.

púrpura *adj invar, nf* purple.

purpurado *nm* (*Ecl*) cardinal.

purpurar [1a] *vt* to dye purple.

purpúreo *adj,* **purpurino** *adj* purple.

purpurina *nf* metallic paint (*gold, silver etc*).

purrela *nf* (**a**) (*vino malo*) bad wine, cheap wine, plonk*. (**b**) **una ~** (*fig*) a mere trifle, chicken feed.

purrete* *nm* (*Cono Sur*) kid*, child.

purulento *adj* purulent.

pus *nm* pus, matter.

puse *etc V* **poner**.

pusilánime *adj* fainthearted, pusillanimous.

pusilanimidad *nf* faintheartedness, pusillanimity.

pústula *nf* pustule, sore, pimple.

put [put] *nm, pl* **puts** [put] (*Golf*) putt.

puta *nf* (**a**) (*gen*) whore, prostitute; **¡la muy ~!** the slut!, the bitch!‡; **~ callejera** streetwalker; **casa de ~s** brothel; **ir de ~s** to go whoring. (**b**) (‡) **¡~!** bloody hell!‡, Jesus!**; **¡la ~!** (*sorpresa*) well I'm damned! (**c**) (*LAm Naipes*) jack.

2 *adj invar* (‡) bloody‡; bloody awful‡; **¡ni ~ idea!** I've no bloody idea!‡; **de ~ madre** (*adj*) (*bueno*) terrific*, smashing*; (*malo*) bloody awful‡; (*adv*) marvellously; **ella cocina de ~ madre** she's a bloody marvellous cook‡; **por toda la ~ calle** all along the bloody street‡; **¡qué ~ suerte!** (*mala*) what bloody awful luck!‡, (*buena*) what incredible luck!; **pasarlas ~s** to have a terrible time.

putada‡ *nf* dirty trick; **¡qué ~!** what a bloody shame‡!; **es una ~** it's a bloody nuisance‡.

putañear [1a] *vi* to go whoring, consort with prostitutes.

putañero 1 *adj* (**a**) (*que va de putas*) whoring.

(**b**) (*cachondo*) randy, oversexed.

2 *nm* whoremonger.

putativo *adj* putative, supposed.

puteada *nf* (*Cono Sur, Méx*) insult; (*palabrota*) swearword.

puteado‡ *adj* (**a**) (*maleado*) corrupted, perverted. (**b**) (*harto*) fed up*, browned off‡.

putear‡ [1a] **1** *vt* (**a**) (*malear*) to corrupt, pervert. (**b**) (*fastidiar*) to bugger about**, muck around. (**c**) (*maltratar*) to kick around, abuse, misuse; **uno está puteado** you get fed up (to the teeth)*. (**d**) (*enfadar*) to upset, send up the wall*. (**e**) (*LAm*: *insultar*) to swear at, curse. (**f**) (**) to screw. **2** *vi* (**a**) (*ir de putas*) to go whoring; (*ser puta*) to be on the game*. (**b**) (*padecer*) to have a rough time of it. **3 putearse** *vr* to go down the drain*.

puteo‡ *nm* : **ir de ~** (*Esp*) to go whoring.

putería *nf* (**a**) (*gen*) prostitution; life (*etc*) of the prostitute. (**b**) (*prostíbulo*) brothel. (**c**) (‡: *zalamería*) soft soap*.

puterío *nm* whoring, prostitution.

puticlub* [putɪ'klu] *nm* (*hum*) singles club, singles bar.

putilla‡ *nf* scrubber‡.

putiza‡ *nf* (*Méx*) brawl, set-to*.

puto‡ **1** *adj* bloody‡; bloody awful‡; (**no me hizo**) **ni ~ caso** she completely bloody ignored me‡; *V t* **puta 2**. **2** *nm* (**a**) (*prostituto*) male prostitute; (*homosexual*) queer‡, fairy‡. (**b**) (*insulto*) sod**.

putrefacción *nf* (**a**) (*acto*) rotting, putrefaction; decay. (**b**) (*materia*) rot, rottenness; **~ fungoide** dry rot; **sujeto a ~** *comestible etc* perishable.

putrefacto *adj* rotten, putrid; decayed.

putrescente *adj* rotting, putrefying, putrescent.

pútrido *adj* putrid, rotten.

putt [put] *nm, pl* **puts** [put] putt.

putter ['puter] *nm, pl* **putters** ['puter] putter.

puya *nf* (**a**) (*punta acerada*) goad, pointed stick; point; (*Taur*) point of the picador's lance. (**b**) (*Carib*) one cent.

puyar [1a] **1** *vt* (**a**) (*LAm*) to jab, wound, prick. (**b**) (*CAm, Carib**: *molestar*) to upset, needle*. **2** *vi* (*Carib*: *planta*) to shoot, sprout.

puyazo *nm* (*Taur*) jab with the lance.

puyero *nm* (*Carib*) pile of money; **divertirse un ~*** to have a great time*, have a whale of a time*.

puyo *nm* (*Cono Sur*) coarse woollen poncho.

puyón *nm* (**a**) (*And, Cono Sur*: *de gallo*) cock's spur; (*Méx*: *punta*) sharp point; (*Méx*: *espina*) prickle, spine, thorn;

(*And, CAm, Méx*: *renuevo*) shoot, bud. (**b**) (*And, CAm, Carib*: *pinchazo*) jab, prick.

puzcua *nf* (*Méx*) puffed maize.

puz(z)le ['puθle] *nm* puzzle (*t fig*).

PVP *nm abr de* **precio de venta al público.**

PYME *nf abr de* **Pequeña y Mediana Empresa** small and middle-sized businesses.

PYRESA [pi'resa] *nf abr de* **Prensa y Radio Española, Sociedad Anónima.**

Q

Q, q [ku] *nf* (*letra*) Q, q.
Qatar *nm* Qatar.
q.b.s.m. *abr de* **que besa sus manos** *courtesy formula.*
q.b.s.p. *abr de* **que besa sus pies** *courtesy formula.*
q.D.g. *abr de* **que Dios guarde** *courtesy formula.*
q.e.g.e. *abr de* **que en gloria esté** = R.I.P.
q.e.p.d. *abr de* **que en paz descanse** R.I.P.
QH *nf abr de* **quiniela hípica** *horse-racing totalizator.*
qm *abr de* **quintal(es) métrico(s)**.
qts *abr de* **quilates** carats, c.
quáker *nm* (*And*) porridge.
quantum ['kwantum] *nm, pl* **quanta** ['kwanta] (*Fís*) quantum.
quark *nm, pl* **quarks** quark.
quásar *nm* quasar.
que[1] 1 *rel pron* (**a**) (*persona: sujeto*) who, that; (*acusativo*) whom, that; (*pero a menudo se omite el relativo, p.ej.*) **la joven ~ invité** the girl I invited.

(**b**) (*cosa*) that, which; (*pero a menudo se omite el relativo, p.ej.*) **el coche ~ compré** the car I bought; **la cama en ~ pasé la noche** the bed in which I spent the night, the bed I spent the night in; **el día ~ ella nació** the day (that) she was born, the day when she was born; **la reunión a ~ yo asistí** the meeting I attended, the meeting I was at; **los disgustos ~ tiene que aguantar** the unpleasantness he has to put up with.

2 *pron rel* (*con artículo*) *V* **el[3], lo[4]**.

que[2] *conj* (**a**) (*tras verbo*) that; (*pero a menudo se omite, p.ej.*) **creo ~ va a venir** I think (that) he will come; **no sabía ~ tuviera coche** I didn't know he had a car; **decir ~ sí** to say yes; **la idea de ~ haya oro en Ruritania** the idea that there is gold in Ruritania; **estoy seguro de ~ lloverá** I am sure (that) it will rain; **¡~ si lo tengo!** of course I've got it!; **¡~ tenga que escuchar tales cosas!** why do I have to listen to such things?; **vergonzoso, ~ dice tu padre** shameful, as your father says; **¿~ no estabas allí?** (are you telling me) you weren't there?; *V* **claro, decir** *etc.*

(**b**) (*con verbo en subj*) that; **esperar ~ uno haga algo** to hope that sb will do sth; **querer ~ uno haga algo** to want sb to do sth; **alegrarse de ~ uno haya llegado** to be glad (that) sb has arrived; **no digo ~ sea traidor** I'm not saying (that) he's a traitor; **¡~ lo haga él!** let him do it!, get him to do it!; **¡~ entre!** let him come in!, send him in!; **¡~ venga pronto!** let's hope he comes soon.

(**c**) (*elíptico*) **¡a ~ no!** *etc*: *V* **no** (**a**); **tengo una sed ~ me muero** I'm dying of thirst.

(**d**) **el que** + *subj* the fact that ...; **el ~ tenga dos hermanas guapas no me interesa** the fact that he has two pretty sisters doesn't concern me; **el ~ quiera estar con su madre es natural** it is natural (that) he should want to be with his mother.

(**e**) (*resultado*) that; **soplaba tan fuerte ~ no podíamos salir** it was blowing so hard (that) we couldn't go out; **huele ~ es un asco** it smells disgusting; *V* **bendición, primor** *etc.*

(**f**) (*locuciones*) **siguió toca ~ toca** he just kept on playing, he played and played; **estuvieron habla ~ habla toda la noche** they talked and talked all night.

(**g**) (*ya que, porque*) for, since, because; **vine un poco pronto ~ está lloviendo** I came a bit early because it's raining; **¡vamos, ~ cierro!** off with you, (because) I'm closing!; **¡cuidado, ~ nos vamos!** hold tight, we're off!; **¡suélteme, ~ voy a gritar!** let go or I'll scream.

(**h**) (*comparación*) than; **yo ~ tú** if I were you, if I were in your place; *V* **más** *etc.*

qué 1 *pron interrog*: **¿~?** what?; **¿~ dijiste?** what did you say?; **no sé ~ quiere decir** I don't know what it means; **¿a ~?** why?; **¿a ~ has venido?** why have you come?, what have you come for?; **¿y a mí ~?** so what?, what has that got to do with me?; **¿y ~?** so what?, well?; **¿con ~ lo vas a pagar?** what are you going to pay with?; how are you going to pay it?; **¿de ~ le conoces?** how do you recognize him?; **¿en ~ lo notas?** in what way do you see that?; **ahí estaba el ~** that was the reason; **sin ~ ni para ~** without rhyme or reason; *V* **más, para** *etc.*

2 *adj* (**a**) (*interrog*); **¿~ libro?** what book?; which book?; **¿~ edad tiene?** what age is he?, how old is he?; **¿~ traje te vas a poner?** which suit are you wearing (*o* going to wear)?; **¿a ~ velocidad?** at what speed?, how fast?; **¿de ~ tamaño es?** what size is it?, how big is it?; **dime ~ libro buscas** tell me which book you are looking for.

(**b**) (*excl*) **¡~ día más espléndido!** what a glorious day!; **¡~ bonito!** (*lit*) isn't it pretty!, how pretty it is!; (*lit, iró*) very nice too! **¡~ asco!** how awful!, how revolting!; **¡~ susto!** what a scare!; **¡~ de cosas te diría!** what a lot I'd have to say to you!; **¡~ de gente había!** what a lot of people there were!

quebracho *nm* (*LAm*) (**a**) (*Bot*) quebracho; (*madera*) break-ax (*US*). (**b**) (*Téc*) extract used in leather-tanning.
quebrada *nf* (**a**) (*hondonada*) gorge, ravine; (*puerto*) gap, pass. (**b**) (*LAm: arroyo*) mountain stream.
quebradero *nm*: **~ de cabeza** headache, worry.
quebradizo *adj* (**a**) (*gen*) fragile, brittle, delicate; *hojaldre* short; *galleta etc* crumbly; *voz* weak.

(**b**) (*Med*) sickly, frail.

(**c**) (*muy sensible*) emotionally fragile, sensitive, readily upset.

(**d**) (*moralmente*) frail, easily tempted.

quebrado 1 *adj* (**a**) *terreno* broken, rough, uneven; *línea* irregular, zigzag.

(**b**) (*t* **~ de color**) *rostro* pale; *tez* pallid.

(**c**) (*Med*) ruptured.

(**d**) (*Fin*) bankrupt.

2 *nm* (**a**) (*Mat*) fraction.

(**b**) (*Fin*) bankrupt.

quebradora *nf* (*CAm Med*) dengue fever.
quebradura *nf* (**a**) (*grieta*) fissure, slit, crack. (**b**) (*Geog*) = **quebrada** (**a**). (**c**) (*Med*) rupture.
quebraja *nf* fissure, slit, crack.
quebrantadura *nf*, **quebrantamiento** *nm* (**a**) (*V* **quebrantar 1** (**a**), (**b**), (**c**)) (*acto*) breaking; cracking; weakening; forcing; violation; **~ de forma** (*Jur*) breach of normal procedure.

(**b**) (*estado*) exhaustion, exhausted state; broken health.

quebrantahuesos *nm invar* bearded vulture.
quebrantar [1a] **1** *vt* (**a**) (*romper*) to break; to crack; to shatter.

(**b**) *cimientos, furia, moral etc* to weaken; *resistencia* to break, weaken; *salud, posición* to undermine, shatter, destroy; *persona* to shatter, break.

(**c**) *cerradura* to force; *caja fuerte, sello* to break open; *cárcel* to break out of; *sagrado* to break into, violate; *terreno vedado etc* to trespass on.

(**d**) *ley, promesa* to break.

(**e**) *color* to tone down.

(**f**) (*LAm*) *caballo* to break in.

2 quebrantarse *vr* (*persona*) to be shattered, be broken (in health *etc*).

quebranto *nm* (**a**) (*daño*) damage, harm; (*pérdida*) severe loss. (**b**) (*agotamiento*) exhaustion, weakness; (*mala salud*) broken health; (*depresión*) depression. (**c**) (*aflicción*) sorrow, affliction.
quebrar [1j] **1** *vt* (**a**) (*romper*) to break, smash.

(**b**) *cuerpo* to bend (at the waist); (*torcer*) to twist.

(**c**) *carrera, formación, proceso etc* to interrupt; to alter the course of, interfere seriously with.

(**d**) *color* to tone down.

(**e**) *para diversos significados V* **quebrantar.**

2 *vi* (**a**) (*Fin*) to fail, go bankrupt.

(**b**) (*debilitarse*) to weaken.

(**c**) ~ **con uno** to break with sb.

3 quebrarse *vr* (**a**) to break, smash, get broken.

(**b**) (*Med*) to be ruptured; to have a rupture.

quebraza *nf* crack; (*Med*) crack (on the skin), chap.

quebrazón *nf* (**a**) (*LAm*: *de vidrio etc*) smashing, shattering. (**b**) (*Cono Sur*: *contienda*) quarrel.

quebroso *adj* (*And*) brittle, fragile.

queche *nm* smack, ketch.

quechua = **quichua.**

queda *nf* (*t* **toque de** ~) curfew.

quedada[1] †† *nf* (*CAm, Carib, Méx*) spinster, old maid.

quedada[2]* *nf* joke, tease; hoax.

quedado *adj* (*Cono Sur, Méx*) lazy.

quedar [1a] **1** *vi* (**a**) (*gen*) to stay, remain; **quedamos una semana** we stayed a week; ~ **atrás** to remain behind; to fall behind.

(**b**) (*en un estado*: + *prep*, + *adj*) to remain, be; ~ **asombrado** to be amazed; ~ **inmóvil** to remain (*o* be, stand *etc*) motionless; (*vehículo etc*) to remain stationary; ~ **de pie** to remain standing; ~ **ciego** to go blind; ~ **cojo** to go lame; **después de eso ha quedado en ridículo** as a result of that he made a fool of himself; **A pretendía que B quedara en ridículo** A was trying to make B look ridiculous; **ha quedado sin hacer** it remained undone, nothing was done about it; **el proyecto quedó sin realizar** the plan was never carried out; **ir quedando atrás** to fall behind; **con las reformas el edificio queda mejor** as a result of the alterations the building looks better; **la cosa queda así** there the matter rests, that's how the affair stands; **¿cuánto te quedo a deber?** how much do I owe you?; **quedó heredero del título** he became heir to the title, that made him heir to the title.

(**c**) (~ **bien** *etc*) ~ **bien** to come off well; to do o.s. justice; to make a good impression; ~ **bien con uno** to be on good terms with sb, stand well with sb; **por** ~ **bien** (so as) to make a good impression; ~ **mal** to do badly, come off badly; ~ **mal con uno** to be at odds with sb; **por no** ~ **mal** in order to do the right thing, so as not to cause any offence; **ha quedado como un canalla** he showed himself to be a rotter*, he was shown up as the rotter he is*.

(**d**) (*lugar*) to be; **eso queda muy lejos** that's a long way (away); **queda un poco más al oeste** it is (*o* lies) a little further west; **esa cuestión queda fuera de nuestros límites** that matter lies (*o* falls, is) outside the bounds of our inquiry.

(**e**) (*sobrar*) to remain, be left; **quedan 6** there are 6 left; **me quedan 6** I have 6 left; **nos queda poco dinero** we haven't much money left; **no quedan más que escombros** there is nothing left but rubble; **ya no queda motivo para ello** there is no longer any reason for it; **no me queda otro remedio** I have no alternative (left).

(**f**) (*faltar*) to be ... still; **quedan pocos días para la fiesta** only a few days remain till the party, there are only a few days to go to (*o* left till) the party; **nos quedan 12 kms para llegar al pueblo** there are still 12 kms to go to the village.

(**g**) **¿cómo quedamos entonces?** what's the arrangement then?

(**h**) ~ **con uno** (*citarse*) to arrange to meet sb, make a date with sb; (*flirtear*) to give sb the eye* (*o* the come-on*); (*burlarse de*) to poke fun at sb; ~ **de verse con uno** (*LAm*) to arrange to meet sb.

(**i**) ~ **en** to turn out to be, result in, end up as; **todo ese trabajo quedó en nada** all that work came to nothing; **las discusiones quedaron en un informe más** the discussions merely resulted in one more report.

(**j**) ~ **en** + *infin* (*t* ~ **de,** *Méx*) to agree to + *infin*, arrange to + *infin*; ~ **en que** ... to agree that ...; **¿en qué quedamos?** what do we decide to do then?

(**k**) ~ **por** + *infin* to be still to be + *ptp*, remain to be + *ptp*; **las cartas quedan aún por escribir** the letters are still to be written; **eso queda todavía por estudiar** that remains to be studied, that still has to be studied.

(**l**) ~ + *ger* to be + *ger*, go on + *ger*; **él quedaba trabajando en casa** he went on working at home.

2 quedarse *vr* (**a**) *en sentidos básicos*, = **1** (**a**) *y* (**b**), *p.ej.* ~ **atrás** to remain behind; to fall behind; (*sentidos adicionales*) to stay on, stay behind, linger (on); ~ **en una pensión** to stay at a boarding-house, put up at a boarding-house; ~ **con unos amigos** to stay with some friends; **se me queda pequeña esta camisa** this shirt has got too small for me, I've outgrown this shirt; ~ **sin** to find o.s. out of, run out of; **nos hemos quedado sin café** we've run out of coffee; ~ **sin empleo** to lose one's job; ~ **helado** (*fig*) to be scared stiff.

(**b**) (*mar, viento*) to fall calm.

(**c**) ~ **con** (*retener*) to keep, hold on to, retain; to acquire, get hold of; (*fig*) to take, prefer; **se quedó con mi pluma** he kept my pen, he walked off with my pen; **quédese con la vuelta** keep the change; **el vencedor se queda con todo** winner takes all; **entre A y B, me quedo con B** if I have to choose between A and B, I'll take B; **así que me quedé con el más tonto de los tres** so I got left with the stupidest of the three.

(**d**) ~ **con uno** (*: *estafar*) to swindle sb, cheat sb; (*tratar de engañar*) to try to fool sb; (*convencer*) to win sb round, talk sb round; **¿quieres quedarte conmigo?** are you trying to kid me?*

(**e**) ~ **con uno** (*Esp**: *tomar el pelo*) to take the mickey out of sb‡, pull sb's leg*.

(**f**) ~ **con uno** (*Esp**: *mirar*) to give sb the come-hither look, look invitingly at sb.

(**g**) ~ **con uno** (*Esp**: *aburrir*) to bore the pants off sb*.

(**h**) (*locuciones*) **no se queda con la cólera dentro** he can't control his anger, he can't keep his anger bottled up; ~ **en nada** to come to nothing; **no se quedó en menos** he was not to be outdone.

(**i**) (*Cono Sur*) (*miembro*) to become paralysed; (*persona*) to die, pass away (*euf*).

(**j**) ~ + *ger* to be + *ger*, go on + *ger*; **se nos quedó mirando asombrado** he stood (*etc*) looking at us in amazement.

3 *vt* (‡) **me quedo este paraguas** I'll take this umbrella; **así que me lo quedé** so I took it; **me la quedo** (*acepto*) I'll buy it*, I'll stay with it*.

quedito *adv* very softly, very gently.

quedo 1 *adj* (**a**) (*inmóvil*) still. (**b**) *voz* quiet, soft, gentle; *paso etc* soft. **2** *adv* softly, gently; **¡~!** gently now!

quedón‡ *adj* (*Esp*) (**a**) (*guasón*) jokey, waggish. (**b**) (*ligón*) flirtatious, fond of the opposite sex.

quehacer *nm* job, task; **~es** (**domésticos**) household jobs, chores; **agobiado de** ~ overburdened with work; **atender a sus ~es** to go about one's business; **tener mucho** ~ to have a lot to do.

queja *nf* (**a**) (*gen*) complaint; (*protesta*) protest; grumble, grouse*; (*rencor*) grudge, resentment; (*Jur*) protest; **una** ~ **infundada** an unjustified complaint; **presentar** ~ **de uno** to make a complaint about sb; **tener** ~ **de uno** to have a complaint to make about sb; **tengo** ~ **de ti** I've a bone to pick with you.

(**b**) (*quejido*) moan, groan; ~ **de dolor** groan of pain.

quejadera *nf* (*And, Méx*), **quejambre** *nf* (*And, Méx*) moaning.

quejarse [1a] *vr* (**a**) (*gen*) to complain (*de* about, of); (*refunfuñar*) grumble (*de* about, at); (*protestar*) to protest (*de* about, at); ~ **de que** ... to complain (about the fact) that ...; ~ **a un oficial** to complain to an official.

(**b**) (*gemir*) to moan, groan; to whine.

quejica* *nmf*, **quejicas*** *nmf invar*, **quejicoso, -a*** *nm/f* = **quejón.**

quejido *nm* moan, groan; whine; **dar ~s** to moan, groan; to whine.

quejigal *nm*, **quejigar** *nm* gall-oak grove.

quejigo *nm* gall-oak.

quejón* 1 *adj* grumbling, complaining. **2** *nm*, **quejona** *nf* grumbler, constant complainer, misery*.

quejoso *adj persona* complaining; *tone* querulous, whining; plaintive.

quejumbre *nf* moan, groan.

quejumbroso *adj* = **quejoso.**

quela‡ *nf*, **quel(i)**[1]‡ *nm* house; **ir a** ~ to go home.

queli[2]‡ *nm* mate, pal*.

quelite *nm* (*CAm, Méx*) (*verduras*) greens, vegetables; (*renuevo*) shoot, tip, green part; **poner a uno como un** ~ (*Méx**) to make mincemeat of sb.

quelonia *nf* (*Carib*) turtle.

quelpo *nm* kelp.

quema *nf* (**a**) (*acto*) fire; burning, combustion; (*Méx*) burning-off (of scrub). (**b**) (*Cono Sur*: *vertedero*) rubbish-dump. (**c**) (*Méx: fig*) danger. (**d**) **hacer** ~ to hit the target.

quemable *adj* inflammable.

quemado 1 *adj* (**a**) (*gen*) burned, burnt; **aquí huele a** ~ I smell something burning in here; **esto sabe a** ~ this has a burnt taste. (**b**) *persona* (*agotado*) burned out, finished;

(*resentido*) bitter; **espía ~** spy who has had his cover blown. (**c**) (*moralmente, políticamente*) discredited. (**d**) (*Cono Sur*: *muy oscuro*) very dark. **2** *nm* (**a**) (*acto*) burning; (*Med*) cauterization; (*nuclear*) burn-out. (**b**) (*LAm*) burnt field.

quemador *nm* burner; hob; (*LAm*: *mechero*) lighter; **~ de gas** gas burner.

quemadura *nf* (**a**) (*gen*) burn; (*con líquido*) scald; (*por el sol*) sunburn; (*de fusible*) blowing, blow-out; **~ de primer grado** first-degree burns. (**b**) (*Bot: por helada*) cutting; withering. (**c**) (*Bot: tizón*) smut.

quemar [1a] **1** *vt* (**a**) to burn (*t Culin; por ácido, sol*); to burn up; to set on fire, kindle; to scorch; (*con líquido*) to scald; *fusible* to blow, burn out.

(**b**) *plantas* (*helada*) to cut, wither, burn.

(**c**) (*fig*) *fortuna etc* to burn up, squander; *persona* to burn out; *organismo, gobierno* to damage, affect seriously; *suma* to spend quickly, get through in no time; *recursos* to use up, exhaust; *precios* to slash, cut; *géneros* to sell off cheap.

(**d**) (*fig*: *molestar*) to annoy, upset; **estar muy quemado** to be very hurt; **estar quemado con** (*o* **por**) **algo** to be sick and tired of sth.

(**e**) (*CAm, Méx*: *denunciar*) to denounce, inform on.

(**f**) (*Carib, Méx*: *estafar*) to swindle.

(**g**) (*Carib*: *con arma de fuego*) to shoot.

2 *vi* (**a**) to be burning hot; **esto está que quema, está quemando** it's burning hot; **es una especia que quema en la lengua** it's a spice that tastes really hot, it's a spice that burns the tongue.

(**b**) (*piel*) to get tanned.

3 quemarse *vr* (**a**) (*hacerse daño*) to burn o.s.; (*consumirse*) to burn up, burn away; (*edificio etc*) to burn down; (*ropa etc*) to scorch, get scorched; (*con el sol*) to get sunburnt; **~ con la sopa** to burn one's mouth on the soup; **¡que me quemo!*** I'm scorching!, I'm terribly hot.

(**b**) (*en juego*) to get warm; **¡que te quemas!** you're getting warm!

(**c**) (*fig*: *agotarse*) to burn o.s. out, exhaust o.s.

(**d**) (*fig*: *inquietarse*) to fret.

(**e**) (*Carib, Cono Sur*: *deprimirse*) to get depressed.

(**f**) (*moralmente, políticamente*) to be discredited, lose credibility.

quemarropa: **a ~** *adv* (*lit, fig*) point-blank.

quemazón *nf* (**a**) (*gen*) burn; burning, combustion; (*CAm, Carib, Méx*) fire.

(**b**) (*calor*) intense heat.

(**c**) (*Med*) burning sensation; (*fig*) itch; smarting, sting.

(**d**) (*fig*: *dicho*) cutting remark, wounding thing (to say).

(**e**) (*fig*: *rencor*) pique, resentment, annoyance.

(**f**) (*Com*) bargain sale, cut-price sale.

(**g**) (*And, Cono Sur*: *espejismo*) mirage (*on the pampas*).

quemón, -ona‡ *nm/f* (*Méx*) dope smoker‡.

quena *nf* (*And, Cono Sur*) Indian flute.

queo¹‡ *nm* (*Esp*) house.

queo²* *nm*: **dar el ~** to shout a warning.

quepis *nm invar* kepi.

quepo *etc V* **caber.**

queque *nm* (*And*) *various types of cake*; (*CAm, Méx*) bun, cake.

querella *nf* (**a**) (*queja*) complaint. (**b**) (*Jur*: *acusación*) charge, accusation; (*proceso*) suit, case. (**c**) (*controversia*) dispute, controversy.

querellado, -a *nm/f* defendant.

querellante 1 *adj*: **parte ~ = 2. 2** *nmf* (*Jur*) plaintiff.

querellarse [1a] *vr* (**a**) (*quejarse*) to complain. (**b**) (*Jur*) to file a complaint, bring an action (*ante* before, *contra, de* against).

querencia *nf* (**a**) (*Zool*) lair, haunt; (*Taur*) (bull's) favourite spot; (*fig*) favourite spot, home ground, haunt; **buscar la ~** to home, head for home.

(**b**) (*Zool*: *instinto*) homing instinct; (*fig*: *nostalgia*) longing for home, homesickness.

querendón (*LAm*) **1** *adj* affectionate, loving, of an affectionate nature. **2** *nm*, **querendona** *nf* (*favorito*) favourite, pet; (*amante*) lover.

querer [2t] **1** *vti* (**a**) (*desear*) to want, wish (for); **¿cuál quieres?** which one do you want?; **no quiero más** I don't want any more; **hablaremos otro día, ¿quieres?** we'll talk another day, shall we?; **pero ¡que quieres!** but what do you expect?; **¿qué más quieres?** what more do you want?; **¡qué mas quisiera yo!** would that I could!, my wishes entirely!; **¿quiere un café?** would you like some coffee?; **¿cuánto quieren por el coche?** how much do they want for the car?, what are they asking for the car?; **como Vd quiera** as you wish, as you please; **ven cuando quieras** come when you like; **quiera o no, quiera que no** willy-nilly, whether he (*etc*) likes it or not; **hace lo que quiere** she does what she wants; **¡lo que quieras!** anything you say!; have it your own way!; **lo hizo queriendo*** he did it deliberately; **lo hizo sin ~** he didn't mean to do it, he did it inadvertently, he did it by mistake; **~ es poder** where there's a will there's a way; **¡está como quiere!** (*Esp‡*) she's a bit of all right!‡

(**b**) (+ *verbo*) **~ hacer algo** to want to do sth, wish to do sth; **~ que uno haga algo** to want sb to do sth; **no quiso pagar** he didn't want to pay; he refused to pay; **no queremos vender** we're not about to sell; **ha querido quedarse en casa** he preferred to stay at home, he decided to stay at home; **quiso hacerlo pero no pudo** he tried to do it but couldn't; **¿quiere abrir la ventana?** would you mind opening the window?, please open the window; **¿qué quieres que te diga?** how should I put it?, what can I say?; **más quiero** + *infin* I would rather + *infin*, I would prefer to + *infin*; **mejor quisiera** + *infin* I would rather + *infin*; **la ley quiere que seamos buenos** the law requires us to be good; **este crítico quiere que Góngora haya sido loco** this critic tries to make out that Góngora was mad, this critic would have us believe that Góngora was mad; **la tradición quiere que ...** tradition has it that ...; **éste quiere que le rompan la cabeza*** this fellow is asking for a crack on the head*.

(**c**) (*absoluto*) **¡no quiero!** I won't!, I refuse!; **sí quiero** (*matrimonio*) I will; **'él no quiere venir' ... '¡sí (que) quiero!'** 'he doesn't want to come' ... 'but I do!'; **lo hago porque quiero** I do it because I want to; **pero no quiso** but he refused; but he was unwilling; **¿quiere?** do you want some?, would you like some?

(**d**) (*requerir*) to need, demand; **tal traje quiere un sombrero ancho** that dress needs a big hat to go with it; **¡esto quiere unas copas!** we must have a drink on that!, that deserves a drink to celebrate it!

(**e**) (*impersonal*) **quería amanecer** dawn was about to break; **parece que quiere llover** it looks like rain, it seems that it's trying to rain.

(**f**) (*amar*) to love; to like; **~ bien a uno** to be fond of sb; **¡te quiero, bobo!** I love you, you idiot!; **en la oficina le quieren mucho** he is well liked at the office; **¿no me quieres siquiera un poquito?** don't you like me just a little bit?; **hace tiempo que te quiero** I've been in love with you for a long time; **hacerse ~ por uno** to endear o.s. to sb; **¡por lo que más quieras!** by all that's sacred!; (*arrancando pétalos etc*) **me quiere ... no me quiere** she loves me ... she loves me not.

(**g**) **como quiera** *etc: V* **comoquiera, dondequiera.**

2 *nm* love, affection; **tener ~ a** to be fond of.

querida *nf* (**a**) (*persona amada*) darling, beloved; **¡sí, ~!** yes, darling! (**b**) (*amante*) mistress, lover.

querido 1 *adj* (*amado*) dear, darling, beloved; (*en carta*) dear; **nuestra querida patria** our beloved country.

(**b**) (*And*) nice.

2 *nm* (**a**) (*persona amada*) darling, beloved; **¡sí, ~!** yes, darling!; **el ~ de las musas** the darling of the muses.

(**b**) (*amante*) lover.

querindongo, -a *nm/f* lover.

quermes, quermés *nf* kermes.

querosén *nm*, **queroseno** *nm*, **querosín** *nm* (*LAm*) kerosene, paraffin.

querúbico *adj* cherubic.

querubín *nm* cherub.

quesadilla *nf* (*torta*) cheesecake; (*Méx*) folded tortilla.

quesera *nf* (**a**) (*persona*) dairymaid; cheesemaker. (**b**) (*plato*) cheesedish.

quesería *nf* (**a**) (*tienda*) dairy; (*fábrica*) cheese factory. (**b**) (*quesos*) cheeses; dairy products.

quesero 1 *adj* cheese (*atr*); **la industria quesera** the cheese industry. **2** *nm* dairyman; cheesemaker.

quesillo *nm* (*CAm*) *tortilla with cream cheese filling.*

queso *nm* (**a**) cheese; **~ azul** blue cheese; **~ de bola** Dutch cheese; **~ crema, ~ de nata** cream cheese; **~ helado** ice-cream brick; **~ de puerco** (*Méx*) jellied pork; **~ rallado** grated cheese; **darla a uno con ~*** to swindle sb, pull a fast one on sb. (**b**) **~s** (**‡**: *pies*) plates‡, feet.

quetzal *nm* (**a**) quetzal (*Guatemalan unit of currency*). (**b**) (*ave*) quetzal.

quevedos *nmpl* pince-nez.

quey *nm* (*And*) cake.

quiá *interj* (*Esp* †) surely not!

quíbole* *interj* (*Méx*): **¿~?** how's things?

quicio *nm* upright, jamb; **estar fuera de ~** (*fig*) to be out of joint; **sacar a uno de ~** (*fig*) to irritate sb, get on sb's nerves; to get sb worked up; **estas cosas me sacan de ~** these things make me see red.
quico* *nm*: **ponerse como el ~** (*Esp*) (*comer mucho*) to stuff o.s.; (*engordar*) to get as fat as a pig.
quiche *nm* quiche.
quichua 1 *adj, nmf* Quechua. **2** *nm* (*Ling*) Quechua.
quichuismo *nm* Quechuan word (*o* expression).
quichuista *nm* (**a**) (*LAm*: *especialista*) Quechua specialist. (**b**) (*And, Cono Sur*: *hablante*) Quechua speaker.
quid *nm* core, crux; **dar en el ~** to hit the nail on the head; **he aquí el ~ del asunto** here we have the nub of the matter.
quídam *nm* (**a**) (*alguien*) somebody, somebody or other. (**b**) (*pey*) nobody, nonentity.
quiebra *nf* (**a**) (*grieta*) crack, fissure; slit.
(**b**) (*Fin*) bankruptcy; failure; (*Econ*) slump, crash, collapse; (*fig*) failure; risk of failure; **dar en ~, ir a la ~** to go bankrupt; **es una cosa que no tiene ~** it just can't go wrong, it's a venture that carries no risk.
quiebre *nm* breaking, rupture.
quiebro *nm* (**a**) (*Taur etc*) dodge, swerve; avoiding action; **dar el ~ a uno** (*fig*) to dodge sb. (**b**) (*Mús*) grace note(s), trill.
quien *pron rel* (**a**) (*sujeto*) who, (*ac*) whom; **la señorita con ~ hablaba** the young lady to whom I was talking, the young lady I was talking to; **las personas con ~es estabas** the people you were with; **esta señora es a ~ tienes que dar el recado** this is the lady to whom you are to give the message.
(**b**) (*indefinido*) **~ dice eso es tonto** whoever says that is a fool; **~ lo sepa, que lo diga** *o* **que lo diga ~ lo sepa** let whoever knows it speak up about it; **~ habla más trabaja menos** he who talks most works least; **contestó como ~ no quería** he answered as if he was reluctant to; **hay ~ no lo acepta** there are some who do not accept it; **no hay ~ lo aguante** nobody can stand him.
(**c**) **~ más, ~ menos tiene sus problemas** everybody has problems; **cada ~** each one, every one.
quién *pron interrog* (*sujeto*) who, (*ac*) whom; **¿~ es?** who is it?; who's there?; (*Telec*) who's calling?; **'¿Q~ es ~?'** 'Who's Who?'; **¿a ~ lo diste?** to whom did you give it?, who did you give it to?; **¿a ~ le toca jugar?** whose turn is it to play?, whose go is it?; **¿con ~ estabas anoche?** who were you with last night?; **¿de ~ es la bufanda esa?** whose scarf is that?, who does that scarf belong to?; **¡~ pudiese!** if only I could!; **¿~ de ustedes lo reconoce?** which of you recognizes it?; **no sé ~ lo dijo primero** I don't know who said it first.
quienquiera *pron indef, pl* **quienesquiera** whoever; **le cazaremos ~ que sea** we'll catch him whoever he is.
quietismo *nm* quietism.
quietista *nmf* quietist.
quieto *adj* (**a**) (*inmóvil*) still; motionless; **¡~!** (*a perro*) down boy!; **¡~!, ¡estáte ~!** (*a niño*) keep still!, stop fidgeting!; behave yourself!; **dejar ~ a uno** to leave sb alone; **estar ~ como un poste** (*o* **una estatua**) to stand stock-still.
(**b**) *carácter* calm, staid, placid.
quietud *nf* stillness; quietude; calm.
quif *nm* hashish.
quihubo‡ *excl* (*Méx*) how's it going?
quijada *nf* jaw, jawbone.
quijotada *nf* quixotic act.
quijote *nm* quixotic person; dreamer, hopelessly unrealistic person, do-gooder*; well-meaning busybody; **Don Q~** Don Quixote.
quijotería *nf* (**a**) = **quijotismo.** (**b**) = **quijotada.**
quijotescamente *adv* quixotically.
quijotesco *adj* quixotic.
quijotismo *nm* quixotism.
quil. *abr de* **quilates** carats, c.
quilar** [1a] *vt* (*Esp*) to screw**.
quilatar [1a] *vt* = **aquilatar.**
quilate *nm* carat.
quilco *nm* (*Cono Sur*) large basket.
quiligua *nf* (*Méx*) large basket.
quilo¹ *nm* (*Anat*) chyle; **sudar el ~*** to have a tough time; to slave, slog.
quilo² *nm* kilo, kilogramme.
quilo... = **kilo...**
quilombear‡ [1a] *vi* (*Cono Sur*) to go whoring.
quilombera‡ *nf* (*Cono Sur*) whore.
quilombero‡ *adj* (*Cono Sur*) rowdy.
quilombo‡ *nm* (**a**) (*And, Cono Sur*: *burdel*) brothel. (**b**) (*And, Cono Sur*: *lío*) row, set-to*. (**c**) (*And, Carib*) (*lugar apartado*) out-of-the-way spot; (*choza*) rustic hut, shack.
quiltrear* [1a] *vt* (*Cono Sur*) to annoy.
quiltro *nm* (*Cono Sur*) (**a**) (*perrito*) lapdog; (*callejero*) stray dog, mongrel. (**b**) (*: *tipo pesado*) pest, nuisance.
quilla¹ *nf* (*Náut*) keel; **colocar la ~ de un buque** to lay down a ship; **dar de ~** to keel over.
quilla² *nf* (*LAm*) cushion.
quillango *nm* (*And, Cono Sur*) fur blanket.
quimba *nf* (**a**) (*And, Carib*: *zapato*) sandal. (**b**) (*And*: *mueca*) grimace. (**c**) **~s** (*And*) (*dificultades*) difficulties; (*deudas*) debts.
quimbo *nm* (*Carib*) knife, machete.
quimera *nf* (**a**) (*Mit*) chimera.
(**b**) (*alucinación*) hallucination; (*noción*) fancy, fantastic idea; (*sueño*) impossible notion, pipe dream.
(**c**) (*sospecha*) unfounded suspicion; **tener la ~ de que ...** to suspect quite wrongly that ...
(**d**) (*riña*) quarrel.
quimérico *adj* fantastic, fanciful; *esperanza, proyecto etc* impossible.
quimerista 1 *adj* (**a**) (*pendenciero*) quarrelsome; (*ruidoso*) rowdy. (**b**) (*soñador*) dreamy. **2** *nmf* (*V adj*) (**a**) quarrelsome person; rowdy, brawler. (**b**) dreamer, visionary.
quimerizar [1f] *vi* to indulge in fantasy, indulge in pipe dreams.
química¹ *nf* chemistry; **~ inorgánica** inorganic chemistry; **~ orgánica** organic chemistry.
químico 1 *adj* chemical. **2** *nm*, **química²** *nf* chemist.
quimioterapia *nf* chemotherapy.
quimono *nm* kimono.
quimoterapia *nf* chemotherapy.
quina *nf* quinine, Peruvian bark; **tragar ~*** to have to put up with it.
quincalla *nf* (**a**) (*gen*) hardware, ironmongery. (**b**) (*una ~*) trinket.
quincallería *nf* ironmonger's (shop), hardware store (*US*).
quincallero, -a *nm* ironmonger, hardware dealer (*US*).
quince 1 *adj* fifteen; (*fecha*) fifteenth; **~ días** (*frec*) fortnight; **dar ~ y raya a uno** to be able to beat sb hollow (*en* at), be more than a match for sb (*en* at).
2 *nm* fifteen.
quinceañero 1 *adj* fifteen-year old, (*frec*) teenage. **2** *nm*, **quinceañera** *nf* fifteen-year old, (*frec*) teenager.
quinceavo *adj, nm* fifteenth.
quincena *nf* (**a**) (*quince días*) fortnight. (**b**) (*condena*) fortnight's imprisonment. (**c**) (*pago*) fortnightly pay.
quincenal *adj* fortnightly.
quincenalmente *adv* fortnightly, once a fortnight.
quinceno *adj* fifteenth.
Quincuagésima *nf* Quinquagesima Sunday.
quincuagésimo *adj* fiftieth.
quincha *nf* (*LAm*) wall (*o* roof *etc*) made of rushes and mud.
quinchar [1a] *vi* (*LAm*) to build walls (*etc*) of *quincha.*
quincho *nm* (*Cono Sur*: *choza*) mud hut; (*And, Cono Sur*: *cerco*) mud fence; (*Cono Sur*: *restaurán*) steak restaurant.
quindécimo *adj* fifteenth.
quinfa *nf* (*And*) sandal.
quingentésimo *adj* five-hundredth.
quingo *nm* (*And*) twist, turn; **~s** zigzag.
quinguear [1a] *vi* (*And*) to twist, turn; to zigzag.
quiniela *nf* pools coupon; **~s** football pool(s); **~ hípica** horse-racing totalizator; **hacer ~s** to do the pools.
quinielista *nmf* punter, participant in a football pool.
quinielístico *adj* pools (*atr*); **boleto ~** pools coupon; **peña quinielística** pools syndicate.
quinientos *adj* five hundred; **en el ~** in the sixteenth century; **volvió a las quinientas*** she got back at some unearthly hour.
quinina *nf* quinine.
quinqué *nm* (**a**) (*lámpara*) oil lamp. (**b**) (*: *astucia*) know-how, shrewdness; **tener mucho ~** to know what's going on, know what the score is*.
quinquenal *adj* quinquennial; **plan ~** five-year plan.
quinquenalmente *adv* every five years.
quinquenio *nm* quinquennium, five-year period.
quinqui* *nm* (*bandido*) bandit, gangster; (*delincuente*) delinquent, criminal; (*vendedor*) small-time dealer, tinker.
quinta *nf* (**a**) (*casa*) villa, country house; (*LAm*) small estate on the outskirts of a town.
(**b**) (*Mil*) draft, call-up; **la ~ de 1998** the 1998 call-up, the class called up in 1998; **ser de la ~ de uno** to be the

same age as sb; **entrar en ~s** to reach the call-up age; to be called up.

(**c**) (*Mús*) fifth.

quintacolumnista *nmf* fifth columnist.

quintada* *nf* rag, trick.

quintaescencia *nf* quintessence.

quintaesencial *adj* quintessential.

quintal *nm* (*Castilla*) *measure of weight,* = *46 kg*; ~ **métrico** = *100 kg.*

quintar [1a] *vt* (*Mil*) to call up, conscript, draft (*US*).

quintería *nf* farmhouse.

quintero *nm* (*dueño*) farmer; (*bracero*) farmhand, labourer.

quinteto *nm* quintet(te).

quintilla *nf* (*Liter: Hist*) *a five-line stanza.*

quintillizo *nm*, **quintilliza** *nf* quintuplet.

Quintín *nm*: **se armó la de San ~*** all hell broke loose; **se va a armar la de San ~** there will be an almighty row*; **costó la de San ~*** it cost a bomb*.

quinto 1 *adj* fifth. **2** *nm* (**a**) (*Mat*) fifth. (**b**) (*Mil*) conscript, national serviceman. (**c**) (*: *juego*) bingo. (**d**) (*Méx Fin*) nickel. (**e**) (*botellín*) small bottle of beer.

quintuplicar [1g] **1** *vt* to quintuple. **2 quintuplicarse** *vr* to quintuple.

quíntuplo 1 *adj* quintuple, fivefold. **2** *nm* quintuple; **X es el ~ de Y** X is five times the size of Y.

quinzavo = **quinceavo.**

quiña *nf* (*And*), **quiñadura** *nf* (*And*) scratch.

quiñar* [1a] *vt* (*And*) to scratch.

quiñazo *nm* (*LAm*) smash, collision.

quiño *nm* (*LAm*: *puñetazo*) punch.

quiñón *nm* piece of land, plot of land.

quiñonero *nm* part-owner (of a piece of land).

quiosco *nm* (*Com*) kiosk, stand, stall; (*de jardín*) summerhouse, pavilion; (*de parque*: *t* ~ **de música**) bandstand; ~ **de necesidad** public lavatory; ~ **de periódicos** news-stand.

quiosquero, -a *nm/f* proprietor of a news-stand, newspaper seller.

quipe *nm* (*And*) knapsack, rucksack, backpack (*US*).

quipu *nm* (*And Hist*) quipu (*system used by the Incas to record information using knotted strings*).

quiqui** *nm* screw**.

quiquiriquí *nm* cock-a-doodle-doo.

quirico *nm* (*Carib*) (*criado*) servant; (*mensajero*) messenger; (*ladrón*) petty thief.

quirófano *nm* operating theatre.

quirógrafo *nm* (*Méx*) IOU.

quirología *nf* palmistry.

quiromancia *nf* palmistry.

quiromántico, -a *nm/f* palmist.

quiromasaje *nm* massage.

quirúrgicamente *adv* surgically; **intervenir ~ a uno** to operate on sb.

quirúrgico *adj* surgical.

quise *etc V* **querer.**

quisicosa* *nf* puzzle, conundrum.

quisling ['kizlin] *nm, pl* **quislings** ['kizlin] quisling.

quisque* *nm*: **cada ~, todo ~** every man-Jack; **como cada ~** like everyone else; **ni ~** not a living soul.

quisqui* *nm*: **ser un ~** to be a fusspot*; to have a mania for details.

quisquilla *nf* (**a**) (*bagatela*) trifle, triviality.

(**b**) (*pega*) slight snag, minor difficulty.

(**c**) (*sofisterías*) **~s** quibbles, quibbling, hair-splitting; **¡déjate de ~s!** stop fussing!; don't quibble!; **pararse en ~s** to bicker; to quibble.

(**d**) (*Zool*) shrimp.

(**e**) (**) cunt**.

quisquilloso *adj* (**a**) (*sensible*) touchy, oversensitive; (*irritable*) irritable; (*delicado*) pernickety*, choosy*, fussy. (**b**) (*sofístico*) quibbling, hair-splitting.

quiste *nm* cyst.

quisto *adj*: **bien ~, mal ~** *V* **bienquisto, malquisto.**

quita *nf* (**a**) *de deuda* release (from a debt); (*LAm*: *descuento*) rebate. (**b**) **de ~ y pon** *V* **quitapón.**

quitaesmalte *nm* nail-polish remover.

quitagusto *nm* (*And*) intruder, gatecrasher.

quitalodos *nm invar* boot-scraper.

quitamanchas *nm invar* (**a**) (*líquido etc*) cleaning material, stain remover. (**b**) (*Esp*: *persona*) dry cleaner; (*tienda*) dry-cleaner's (shop).

quitamiedos *nm invar* (*Esp*) handrail.

quitamotas* *nm invar* creep‡, toady.

quitanieves *nm invar* snowplough.

quitapelillos* *nm invar* creep‡, toady.

quitapenas‡ *nm invar* (*pistola*) pistol, rod‡ (*US*); (*navaja*) knife, chiv‡.

quitapesares *nm invar* comfort; distraction.

quitapiedras *nm invar* (*Ferro*) cowcatcher.

quitapintura *nf* paint-remover, paint-stripper.

quitapón: de ~ detachable, removable.

quitar [1a] **1** *vt* (**a**) (*gen*) to take away, remove; *ropa etc* to take off; *mancha* to remove, get rid of, get out; *dolor etc* to relieve, stop, kill; *felicidad* to destroy; *vida* to take; (*Mec*) *pieza* to remove, take out, take off; *mesa* to clear; *abuso, dificultad, obstáculo* to remove, do away with, put an end to; *tiempo* to take (up); *molestia, inquietud* to save, prevent; (*Mat*) to take away, subtract; *valor etc* to reduce; (*robar*) to remove, steal; **quitando el postre comimos bien** apart (*o* aside) from the dessert we had a good meal; ~ **extensión a un campo** to reduce the size of a field; ~ **importancia a un acontecimiento** to diminish the importance of an event; **no quita nada de su valor** it does not detract at all from its value; **me quita mucho tiempo** it takes up a lot of my time; **le van a ~ ese privilegio** they are going to take that privilege away from him; **le quitaron la cartera en el tren** he had his wallet stolen on the train; **me quitó las ganas de comer** it took away my appetite; **el café me quita el sueño** coffee stops me sleeping; **quitando 3 ó 4, van a ir todos** except for 3 or 4 everybody is going; *V* **medio, mesa.**

(**b**) *golpe* to avert, ward off; (*Esgrima*) to parry.

(**c**) (*impedir*) ~ **a uno de hacer algo** to stop sb doing sth, prevent sb (from) doing sth; **esto no quita que tú tenías la culpa** this doesn't mean it wasn't your fault; **eso no quita para que me ayudes** that doesn't stop you helping me, that is no bar to your helping me.

(**d**) (‡) *dinero* to make.

2 *vi* (**a**) **¡quita!, ¡quita de ahí!** get away!, not a bit of it!

(**b**) **ni quito ni pongo** I'm not saying one thing or the other; I'm strictly neutral; **ni me quita ni me pone** it doesn't bother me.

3 quitarse *vr* (**a**) (*retirarse*) to remove o.s.; to withdraw (*de* from); ~ **de la vista de uno** to remove o.s. from sb's sight; **esa mancha de vino no se quita** that wine stain won't come off (*o* come out); **¡quítate de ahí!** come (*o* get) out of there!, off with you!; **me quito** (*And**) I'm off, I must be going; *V* **medio** *etc.*

(**b**) ~ **algo de encima** to get rid of sth; to cast sth off, shake sth off; ~ **la ropa** to take off one's clothing; ~ **una jaqueca andando** to walk off a headache.

(**c**) ~ **de un vicio** to give up a vice, wean o.s. away from a bad habit; ~ **del tabaco** to give up smoking; **se me ha quitado el gusto de fumar** I've lost my taste for smoking; ~ **la preocupación** to stop worrying; **quitémonos de tonterías** let's stop being silly.

quitasol *nm* sunshade, parasol.

quitasueño *nm* worry, problem.

quite *nm* (**a**) (*acto*) removal.

(**b**) (*Esgrima*) parry.

(**c**) (*movimiento*) dodge, sidestep, swerve; (*Taur*) *manoeuvre whereby bullfighters draw the bull away from an injured colleague, horse etc.* **estar al ~** to be ready to go to somebody's aid; **hacer el ~ a uno** (*Cono Sur*) to avoid somebody; **esto no tiene ~** there's no help for it.

(**d**) (*LAm Dep*) tackle.

quiteño 1 *adj* of (*o* from) Quito. **2** *nm*, **quiteña** *nf* native (*o* inhabitant) of Quito; **los ~s** the people of Quito.

quitrín *nm* (*CAm, Carib, Cono Sur*) trap (*vehicle*).

quizá(s) [ki'θa(s)] *adv* perhaps, maybe.

quórum ['kworum] *nm, pl* **quórums** ['kworum] quorum; **constituir ~** to constitute (*o* make up) a quorum.

R

R, r ['ere] *nf* (*letra*) R, r.

R. (**a**) (*Rel*) *abr de* **Reverendo** Reverend, Rev. (**b**) *abr de* **Real** royal. (**c**) *abr de* **remite, remitente** sender.

rabada *nf* hindquarter, rump.

rabadán *nm* head shepherd.

rabadilla *nf* (*Anat*) coccyx; (*Culin*: *de pollo*) parson's nose; (*) rear*, tail*.

rábano *nm* radish; **~ picante** horseradish; **¡un ~!*** get away!; **no se me da un ~, (no) me importa un ~** I don't care two hoots (*de* about); **tomar el ~ por las hojas** to get hold of the wrong end of the stick, bark up the wrong tree.

rabear [1a] *vi* (*perro*) to wag its tail.

rabelasiano *adj* Rabelaisian.

rabí *nm* (*delante de nombre*) rabbi.

rabia *nf* (**a**) (*Med*) rabies.

(**b**) (*fig*: *ira*) fury, rage, anger; bad feeling; **¡qué ~!** isn't it infuriating!; **me da ~** it maddens me, it infuriates me, it makes my blood boil; **tener ~ a uno** to have a grudge against sb, have it in for sb; **el maestro le tiene ~** the teacher has it in for him, the teacher doesn't like him; **tomar ~ a** to take a dislike to.

(**c**) (*LAm*) **con ~** extremely, terribly; **llueve con ~** it's raining with a vengeance; **es fea con ~** she's terribly ugly.

rabiadero *nm* (*And*) fit of rage.

rabiar [1b] *vi* (**a**) (*Med*) to have rabies.

(**b**) (*fig*: *sufrir*) to suffer terribly, be in great pain; **estaba rabiando de dolor de muelas** she had raging toothache.

(**c**) (*fig*) **esto quema** (*o* **pica**) **que rabia** this is hot enough to burn your mouth; **este cóctel está que rabia*** this cocktail has got a real kick to it*.

(**d**) (*fig*: *enfadarse*) to rage, rave, be furious; **~ contra** to storm at, rave about; **hacer ~ a uno** to rouse sb to a fury; **las cosas así le hacen ~** things like that make him see red; **está que rabia** he's hopping mad, he's furious; **¡para que rabies!** so there!; just to turn you green with envy.

(**e**) (*fig*: *anhelar*) **~ por algo** to long for sth, be dying for sth; **~ por** + *infin* to be dying to + *infin*.

(**f**) **me gusta a ~*** I'm terribly fond of it.

rabiasca *nf* (*Carib*) fit of temper.

rabieta* *nf* fit of temper; paddy*, pet, tantrum*; **tomarse una ~** to get cross, fly into a rage.

rabietas* *nmf invar* touchy sort, bad-tempered person.

rabillo *nm* (**a**) (*Anat*) small tail.

(**b**) (*Bot*) leaf stalk.

(**c**) (*punta*) tip; (*ángulo*) corner; (*parte delgada*) thin part; (*tira*) thin strip of material; **mirar con el ~ del ojo** to look out of the corner of one's eye.

rabimocho *adj* (*And, Carib, Méx*) short-tailed.

rabínico *adj* rabbinical.

rabino *nm* rabbi; **gran ~** chief rabbi.

rabión *nm* (*t* **rabiones**) rapids.

rabiosamente *adv* (*fig*) furiously; terribly, violently; rabidly.

rabioso *adj* (**a**) (*Med*) rabid, suffering from rabies; **perro ~** (*fig*) mad dog.

(**b**) (*fig*: *furioso*) *enfado* furious; *dolor* terrible, raging, violent; *aficionado etc* rabid; *sabor* hot; **poner ~ a uno** to enrage sb.

(**c**) (*fig*: *enorme*) huge, vast; **de rabiosa actualidad** highly topical.

rabo *nm* (**a**) (*Anat*) tail; **~ de toro** (*Culin*) oxtail; **con el ~ entre las piernas** crestfallen, dejected; **queda el ~ por desollar** we've still got the most difficult part to do.

(**b**) (*fig*) tail, train, hanging part; = **rabillo** (**b**) *y* (**c**).

(**c**) **~ verde** (*CAm*) dirty old man.

rabón *adj* (**a**) *animal* short-tailed; bobtailed; tailless.

(**b**) (*LAm*: *pequeño*) short, small.

(**c**) (*Cono Sur*: *desnudo*) stark naked.

(**d**) (*Carib, Cono Sur*) *cuchillo* damaged.

(**e**) (*Méx*: *desgraciado*) down on one's luck.

rabona *nf* (**a**) **hacer ~** (*ausentarse*) to play truant. (**b**) (*LAm*) camp-follower.

rabonear [1a] *vi* (*LAm*) to play truant.

rabosear [1a] *vt* to mess up, rumple, crumple.

rabotada *nf* rude remark; coarse expression.

rabudo *adj* long-tailed.

raca*[1] *nf* (*CAm*) mummy*.

raca‡[2] *nm* (*Aut*) crate*, old car.

racanear* [1a] *vi* (*trabajo*) to slack; to swing the lead; (*jugar mal*) to have a bad spell; (*con dinero*) to be stingy.

racaneo* *nm*, **racanismo*** *nm* slackness, idleness; stinginess.

rácano* 1 *adj* (**a**) (*vago*) bone-idle. (**b**) (*tacaño*) stingy, mean. (**c**) (*artero*) sly, artful. **2** *nm* (**a**) (*vago*) slacker, idler; **hacer el ~** to slack; to swing the lead*. (**b**) (*tacaño*) mean devil. (**c**) (*Aut*) crate*, old car.

RACE ['raθe] *nm abr de* **Real Automóvil Club de España** ≃ Royal Automobile Club, RAC.

racial *adj* racial, race (*atr*); **odio ~** race hatred.

racimo *nm* bunch, cluster; (*Bot*) raceme.

raciocinación *nf* ratiocination.

raciocinar [1a] *vi* to reason.

raciocinio *nm* (**a**) (*facultad*) reason. (**b**) (*acto*) reasoning.

ración *nf* (**a**) (*Mat*) ratio. (**b**) (*porción*) portion, helping; **raciones** (*Mil*) rations; **~ de hambre** starvation wage; **~ de reserva** emergency ration; iron ration; **darse una ~ de vista** to have a good look. (**c**) (*Ecl*) prebend.

racional *adj* (**a**) (*Mat, Filos etc*) rational. (**b**) rational, reasonable, sensible.

racionalidad *nf* rationality.

racionalismo *nm* rationalism.

racionalista *adj, nmf* rationalist.

racionalización *nf* rationalization.

racionalizador *adj* rationalizing; streamlining.

racionalizar [1f] *vt* to rationalize; (*Com*) to streamline.

racionalmente *adv* rationally, reasonably, sensibly.

racionamiento *nm* rationing.

racionar [1a] *vt* (**a**) (*limitar*) to ration; **estar racionado** to be rationed, be on the ration. (**b**) (*repartir*) to ration out, share out.

racionero *nm* (*Ecl*) prebendary.

racionista *nmf* (**a**) (*gen*) person living on an allowance. (**b**) (*actor*) (*Teat*) player of bit parts; ham*, third-rate actor (*o* actress).

racismo *nm* racialism, racism.

racista 1 *adj* racial, racialist. **2** *nmf* racist.

raco* *nm* (*CAm*) daddy*.

racha *nf* (**a**) (*Met*) gust of wind; squall.

(**b**) (*fig*: *serie*) string, series; run; **buena ~** piece of luck, stroke of luck, lucky break; **mala ~** piece of bad luck; unlucky spell, spell when everything goes wrong; **a ~s** by fits and starts; **estar de ~** to be in luck; (*Dep*) to be in form.

rache *nm* (*Carib*) zip.

racheado *adj viento* gusty, squally.

rachi‡ *nm* night.

rachir [3h] *vt* (*Cono Sur*) to scratch.

rachoso *adj* (*Cono Sur*) ragged.

rada *nf* (*Náut*) roads, roadstead; natural bay.

radar *nm* (*sistema*) radar; (*estación*) radar station.

radárico *adj* radar (*atr*).

radiación *nf* (**a**) (*Fís*) radiation; **~ solar** solar radiation; sun's rays; **~ ultravioleta** ultraviolet radiation. (**b**) (*Rad*) broadcasting.

radiactividad *nf* radioactivity.
radiactivo *adj* radioactive.
radiado *adj* **(a)** (*Bot etc*) radiate. **(b)** (*Rad*) radio (*atr*), broadcast; **en una interviú radiada** in a radio interview.
radiador *nm* radiator.
radial *adj* **(a)** (*Mec etc*) radial. **(b)** (*Aut*) road (*atr*). **(c)** (*LAm*: *Rad*) radio (*atr*), broadcasting (*atr*); **comedia ~** radio play.
radiante *adj* (*Fís y fig*) radiant; **estaba ~** she was radiant (*de* with).
radiar[1] [1b] *vt* **(a)** (*Fís etc*) to radiate; to irradiate. **(b)** (*Rad*) to broadcast. **(c)** (*Med*) to treat with X-rays.
radiar[2] [1b] *vt* (*LAm*) (*borrar*) to delete, cross off (a list); (*expulsar*) to expel; (*suprimir*) to remove.
radical 1 *adj* radical. **2** *nm* **(a)** (*Ling, Mat*) root; square-root sign. **(b)** (*Quím*) radical. **3** *nmf* (*Pol*) radical.
radicalidad *nf* radical nature; (*Pol*) radicalism.
radicalismo *nm* radicalism.
radicalizar [1f] **1** *vt* to radicalize. **2 radicalizarse** *vr* **(a)** (*Pol*) to be radicalized, become more radical. **(b)** (*situación etc*) to worsen, deteriorate.
radicalmente *adv* radically.
radicar [1g] **1** *vi* **(a)** (*Bot y fig*) to take root.
(b) (*estar*) to be, be situated, lie.
(c) (*dificultad etc*) **~ en** to lie in.
2 radicarse *vr* to establish o.s., put down one's roots (*en* in).
radícula *nf* (*Bot*) radicle.
radicha *nmf* (*Cono Sur*) radical.
radicheta* *nf* (*Cono Sur*: *hum*) radical.
radio[1] *nm* **(a)** (*Mat*) radius; **~ de acción** sphere of jurisdiction, extent of one's authority; (*Aer*) range; **un avión de largo ~ de acción** a long-range aircraft; **~ de giro** turning circle; **en un ~ de 10 km alrededor de la ciudad** within a radius of 10 km round the city.
(b) (*de rueda*) spoke.
(c) (*Anat*) radius.
(d) (*Quím*) radium.
(e) (*Rad**: *mensaje*) wireless message.
(f) (*LAm*) = **radio**[2].
radio[2] *nf* **(a)** (*gen*) radio, wireless; broadcasting; **R~ Eslobodia** Radio Slobodia; **~ libre** pirate radio; **~ macuto*** the grapevine; **~ pirata** pirate radio (station); **por ~** by radio, on the radio, over the radio; **hablar por ~** to talk on the radio.
(b) (*aparato*) radio (set), wireless (set).
radio... *pref* radio...
radioactivo *adj* = **radiactivo**.
radioaficionado, -a *nm/f* radio ham*, amateur radio enthusiast.
radioastronomía *nf* radio astronomy.
radiobaliza *nf* radio beacon.
radiobiología *nf* radiobiology.
radiocaptar [1a] *vt emisora* to listen in to, pick up.
radiocarbono *nm* radiocarbon.
radiocasete *nm o f* radiocassette (player).
radiocomunicación *nf* radio contact, contact by radio.
radiodespertador *nm* clock radio.
radiodifundir [3a] *vt* to broadcast.
radiodifusión *nf* broadcasting.
radiodifusora *nf* (*LAm*) radio station, transmitter.
radioemisora *nf* radio station, transmitter.
radioenlace *nm* radio link.
radioescucha *nmf* listener.
radiofaro *nm* radio beacon.
radiofonía *nf* radio, wireless.
radiofónico *adj* radio (*atr*).
radiogoniómetro *nm* direction finder.
radiografía *nf* **(a)** (*gen*) radiography, X-ray photography. **(b)** (*una ~*) radiograph, X-ray photograph (*o* picture).
radiografiar [1c] *vt* **(a)** (*Med*) to X-ray. **(b)** (*Rad*) to radio, send by radio.
radiográfico *adj* X-ray (*atr*).
radiograma *nm* wireless message.
radiogramola *nf* (*Esp*) radiogram; **~ tragamonedas, ~ tragaperras** jukebox.
radioisótopo *nm* radioisotope.
radiola *nf* (*And*) radiogram.
radiolocación *nf* radiolocation.
radiología *nf* radiology.
radiólogo, -a *nm/f* radiologist.
radionovela *nf* radio series.
radiooperador(a) *nm/f* (*LAm*) radio operator, wireless operator.
radiopatrulla *nm* patrol-car.
radiorreceptor *nm* radio (set), wireless (set), receiver; **~ de contrastación** monitor set.
radioscopia *nf* radioscopy.
radioso *adj* (*LAm*) radiant.
radiotécnica[1] *nf* radio engineering.
radiotécnico, -a[2] *nm/f* radio engineer.
radiotelefonía *nf* radiotelephony.
radioteléfono *nm* radiotelephone.
radiotelegrafía *nf* radiotelegraphy, wireless (telegraphy).
radiotelegrafista *nmf* radio operator, wireless operator.
radiotelescopio *nm* radiotelescope.
radioterapeuta *nmf* radiotherapist.
radioterapia *nf* radiotherapy.
radioyente *nmf* listener.
radón *nm* radon.
RAE *nf* (*Esp*) *abr de* **Real Academia Española**.
raedera *nf* scraper; spokeshave.
raedura *nf* **(a)** (*acto*) scrape, scraping; (*Med*) abrasion, graze. **(b) ~s** scrapings, filings.
raer [2y] **1** *vt* **(a)** (*gen*) to scrape; (*quitar*) to scrape off; (*borrar*) to erase; (*Med*) to abrade, graze; to chafe; *paño etc* to fray.
(b) *contenido* to level off, level with the brim.
2 raerse *vr* to chafe; (*paño*) to fray.
raf *nm* (*Golf*) rough.
Rafael *nm* Raphael.
ráfaga *nf* **(a)** (*Met*) gust, squall; sudden blast.
(b) (*de tiros*) burst.
(c) (*de intuición, luz*) flash; **dar ~s de luces a** to flash one's headlights at.
(d) (*And, Cono Sur*: *racha*) run of luck; **estar de** (*o* **en**) **(mala) ~** to have a spell of bad luck.
rafaguear [1a] **1** *vt* to direct a burst of machine-gun fire at. **2** *vi* to fire a burst with a machine-gun.
rafañoso* *adj* (*Cono Sur*) (*sucio*) dirty; (*ordinario*) coarse, common.
rafia *nf* raffia.
RAH *nf* (*Esp*) *abr de* **Real Academia de la Historia**.
raicear [1a] *vi* (*CAm, Carib*) to take root.
raicero *nm* (*LAm*) mass of roots, root system.
raid [raid] *nm, pl* **raids** [raid] **(a)** (*Mil*) raid, attack; expedition; (*plaga*) attack, infestation.
(b) (*de policía*) police raid; (*de criminales*) criminal raid.
(c) (*esfuerzo*) attempt, endeavour; (*empresa*) enterprise; (*hazaña*) heroic undertaking.
(d) (*Dep*) endurance test; (*Aer*) long-distance flight; (*Aut*) rally drive; transcontinental expedition by car.
(e) (*Méx Aut*) lift; **pedir ~** to hitch a lift.
raído *adj* **(a)** *paño* frayed, threadbare; *persona, prenda* shabby. **(b)** (*fig*) shameless.
raigambre *nf* (*a veces m*) **(a)** (*Bot*) mass of roots; root system.
(b) (*fig*) (*tradición*) tradition; (*antecedentes*) antecedents, history; **una familia de fuerte ~ local** a family with deep roots in the area; **tienen ~ liberal** they have a liberal tradition.
raigón *nm* (*Bot*) thick root, stump; (*Anat*) root, stump.
rail, raíl *nm* rail; **~ electrizado** electrified rail, live rail.
Raimundo *nm* Raymond.
raíz 1 *nf* **(a)** (*Bot etc*) root; **arrancar algo de ~** to root sth out completely, destroy sth root and branch; **cortar un peligro de ~** to nip a danger in the bud; **echar raíces** to take root (*t fig*).
(b) (*Mat*) root; **~ cuadrada** square root; **~ cúbica** cube root.
(c) (*Ling*) root.
(d) (*fig*) root, origin; **a ~ de** immediately after, immediately following; as a result of.
2 *atr* root (*atr*); **causa ~** root cause; **fuente ~** principal source.
raja *nf* **(a)** (*hendedura*) slit, split; (*grieta*) crack; (*abertura*) gash, chink.
(b) (*pedacito*) sliver, splinter, thin piece; (*de limón etc*) slice.
(c) (******) cunt******.
(d) **sacar ~*** to get a rake-off*, get a share.
(e) **tener ~** (*Carib*) to have Negro blood.
(f) **estar en la ~** (*And**) to be broke*.
(g) **~s** (*Méx Culin*) pickled green pepper.
rajá *nm* rajah.
rajada *nf* **(a)** (*Cono Sur*: *huida*) flight, hasty exit. **(b)** (*Méx*) (*cobardía*) cowardly act; (*el retroceder*) backing down,

going back on one's word.
rajado* *nm* (**a**) (*canalla*) swine*. (**b**) (*cobarde*) coward.
rajador *adj* (*Cono Sur*) fast.
rajadura *nf* = **raja** (**a**) *y* (**b**).
rajamacana* *nm* (*Carib*) (**a**) (*trabajo duro*) tough job. (**b**) (*persona*) (*dura*) tough character; (*terca*) stubborn person. (**c**) (*experto*) expert. (**d**) **a ~** = **a rajatabla.**
rajante* *adj* (*Cono Sur*) (*perentorio*) peremptory, sharp; (*inmediato*) immediate.
rajar [1a] **1** *vt* (**a**) (*hender*) to split, crack; to cleave; to slit; *fruta etc* to slice; *tronco etc* to chop (up), split; *neumático etc* to slash; *persona* to stab.
(**b**) (*LAm*: *difamar*) to slander, run down.
(**c**) (*LAm*‡ *Univ*) to flunk*.
(**d**) (*And, Carib*) (*aplastar*) to crush, defeat; (*arruinar*) to ruin; (*fastidiar*) to annoy.
(**e**) (*Cono Sur**) *obrero* to fire*.
(**f**) (*Carib**: *fastidiar*) to pester, bug*.
2 *vi* (**a**) (*hablar*) to chatter, talk a lot; (*jactarse*) to brag; (*And*: *chismear*) to gossip.
(**b**) (*LAm*: *salir*) to rush off, rush out.
3 rajarse *vr* (**a**) (*henderse*) to split, crack.
(**b**) (*) (*desistir*) to back out (*de* of); (*acobardarse*) to get cold feet; (*desdecirse*) to go back on one's word; **¡me rajé!** that's enough for me!, I'm quitting!
(**c**) (*And, Carib, Cono Sur*) (*huir*) to run away; to bolt; (*irse*) to rush off; **salir rajando** to go off at top speed.
(**d**) (*And, Cono Sur*: *equivocarse*) to be mistaken.
(**e**) (*Carib*: *emborracharse*) to get drunk.
(**f**) (*And, CAm, Carib, Cono Sur*: *ser pródigo*) to splash out*.
rajatabla: **a ~** *adv* (*estrictamente*) strictly, rigorously; (*exactamente*) exactly; (*imparcialmente*) without fear or favour, (*a toda costa*) at all costs; (*pase lo que pase*) regardless (of the consequences), by hook or by crook; **cumplir las órdenes a ~** to carry out one's orders to the letter; **pagar** (*etc*) **a ~** (*LAm*) to pay (*etc*) on the dot, pay (*etc*) promptly.
rajatablas* *nm invar* (*And, Carib*) ticking-off*.
raje* *nm* (*Cono Sur*) firing*, sacking*; **al ~** in a hurry; **dar el ~ a uno** to fire sb*; **tomar(se) el ~** to beat it*; to rush off.
rajita *nf* (*Culin*) (thin) slice.
rajo *nm* (*LAm*) tear, rip.
rajón 1 *adj* (**a**) (*Andalucía, LAm*: *liberal*) generous, lavish, free-spending.
(**b**) (*Andalucía, CAm, Méx*) (*cobarde*), cowardly; (*pesimista*) readily disheartened; (*Méx*: *de poca confianza*) unreliable.
2 *nm* (**a**) (*LAm*: *rajo*) tear, rip.
(**b**) (*Andalucía, CAm, Méx*: *remolón*) quitter.
(**c**) (*CAm, Méx*) (*matón*) bully; (*jactancioso*) braggart.
(**d**) (*And, Méx*: *chismoso*) gossip, telltale.
rajonada *nf* (*CAm*) (**a**) (*baladronada*) boast, brag; (*jactancia*) bragging. (**b**) (*ostentación*) ostentation.
rajuñar [1a] *vt* (*Cono Sur*) = **rasguñar.**
RAL *nf abr de* **red de área local** local area network, LAN.
rala *nf* (*And*) birdlime.
rale *nm* (*Cono Sur*) wooden bowl, wooden dish.
ralea *nf* (*pey*) kind, sort, breed; **de esa ~** of that ilk; **de baja ~** evil, wicked; wretched.
ralear [1a] *vi* to become thin, become sparse; to thin out; to become less dense.
ralentí *nm* (**a**) (*Cine*) slow motion; **al ~** in slow motion. (**b**) (*Aut*) neutral; **estar al ~, funcionar al ~** to be ticking over.
ralentización *nf* slowing down, deceleration; (*Econ etc*) slowing down.
ralentizar [1f] *vti* to slow down.
ralo 1 *adj pelo etc* thin, sparse; *tela* loosely woven; *bosque* open; *aire* rare, rarified; (*Cono Sur*) insubstantial, lacking body. **2** *adv*: **~-~** (*Cono Sur*) sometimes.
rallado *adj queso etc* grated.
rallador *nm* grater.
rallar [1a] *vt* (**a**) (*Culin*) to grate. (**b**) (*: *dar dentera a*) to grate on; to annoy, needle*. (**c**) (*Carib*: *provocar*) to goad.
rallo *nm* (*Culin*) grater; (*Téc*) file, rasp.
rallón *adj* (*And*) bothersome, irritating.
rally(e) ['rali] *nm* (**a**) (*Aut*) rally; (*concurso*) contest, competition; (*reunión*) gathering. (**b**) (*Fin*) rally.
rallye-paper *nm* paper chase.
rama *nf* (**a**) (*Bot etc*) branch; **en ~** *algodón, seda* raw; *libro* unbound; **~ de olivo** olive branch; **andarse por las ~s** to beat about the bush; to get bogged down in details; **poner algo en la última ~** to leave sth till last; to consider sth unimportant.
(**b**) (*LAm*‡) pot‡, hash*.
(**c**) **mi ~** (*Esp**) the wife*, my better half.
ramada *nf* (**a**) (*de árbol*) branches, foliage. (**b**) (*LAm*: *cobertizo*) shed, hut; shelter (*o* covering *etc*) made of branches; (*Cono Sur*) festival stall.
ramadán *nm* Ramadan.
ramaje *nm* branches, foliage.
ramal *nm* (**a**) (*de soga*) strand (of a rope); (*de caballo etc*) halter. (**b**) (*fig*) off-shoot; (*Aut*) branch, branch road; (*Ferro*) branch line.
ramalazo *nm* (**a**) (*azote*) lash; (*verdugón*) weal, bruise, mark left by a lash; (*cicatriz*) scar.
(**b**) (*fig*) (*dolor*) stab of pain, sharp pain; (*depresión*) fit of depression, (*pesar*) sudden grief; (*golpe*) blow; (*locura*) fit of madness.
(**c**) (*fig*: *Met*) gust of wind; lash of rain.
ramazón *nf* (*CAm, Cono Sur, Méx*) antler, horns.
rambla *nf* (**a**) (*arroyo*) watercourse; stream, torrent. (**b**) (*Esp*: *avenida*) avenue. (**c**) (*LAm*) (*paseo marítimo*) promenade; (*muelle*) quayside.
ramera *nf* whore.
ramificación *nf* ramification.
ramificarse [1g] *vr* to ramify, divide, branch (out).
ramillete *nm* (**a**) (*de flores*) bouquet, bunch of flowers, posy; (*llevado en el vestido*) corsage; (*Bot*) cluster. (**b**) (*fig*: *selección*) collection; choice bunch, select group.
ramita *nf* twig, sprig; (*flores*) spray.
ramo *nm* (**a**) (*de árbol*) (*t fig*) branch; (*ramillete*) bunch of flowers, bouquet.
(**b**) (*fig*) branch; (*Com*) section, department; (*de géneros*) line; **el ministro del ~** the appropriate minister, the minister concerned with this; **es del ~ de la alimentación** he's in the food business; **es del ~** (*: *homosexual*) he's one of them*.
(**c**) (*Med*; *t* **~s**) touch; **tiene ~s de loco** he has a streak of madness.
ramojo *nm* brushwood.
Ramón *nm* Raymond.
ramonear [1a] *vt* (**a**) *árboles* to lop, lop the twigs of. (**b**) (*ovejas*) to browse on.
rampa *nf* ramp, incline; **~ de la basura, ~ de desperdicios** refuse chute; **~ de lanzamiento** launching-ramp; (*fig*) springboard; **~ móvil** mobile launching-pad.
rampla *nf* (*Cono Sur*) trailer.
ramplón *adj* common, coarse, uncouth.
ramplonería *nf* commonness, coarseness, uncouthness.
rana *nf* (**a**) (*Zool*) frog; **~ toro** bullfrog; **no es ~** (*fig*) he's no fool, he knows his stuff*; **pero salió ~*** but he turned out badly, but he was a big disappointment; **cuando las ~s críen pelo** when pigs learn to fly; **¡hasta que las ~s críen pelo!** if I never see you again it'll be too soon! (**b**) (*LAm*) *game of throwing coins into the mouth of an iron frog.*
rancidez *nf*, **ranciedad** *nf* (**a**) (*madurez*) age, mellowness; (*pey*) rankness, rancidness; mustiness. (**b**) (*fig*) great age, antiquity; (*pey*) antiquatedness.
rancio 1 *adj* (**a**) *vino* old, mellow; *comestible* (*pey*) rank, rancid, stale; musty.
(**b**) (*fig*) *linaje* ancient; *tradición etc* very ancient, time-honoured; (*pey*) antiquated, old-fashioned; **esas dos rancias** those two old girls.
2 *nm* = **rancidez.**
rancontán *adv* (*And, CAm, Carib*) in cash.
ranchada *nf* (**a**) (*CAm*: *canoa*) canoe. (**b**) (*Cono Sur*: *cobertizo*) shed, hut.
ranchar [1a] *vi* (**a**) (*Cono Sur, Méx*: *vagar*) to wander from farm to farm. (**b**) (*And, Carib, Méx*) (*pasar la noche*) to spend the night; (*establecerse*) to settle. (**c**) (*Carib*: *obstinarse*) to persist.
ranchear [1a] **1** *vt* (*Carib, Méx*) (*saquear*) to loot, pillage; (*robar*) to rob. **2** *vi* (**a**) (*LAm*: *formar rancho*) to build a camp, make a settlement. (**b**) (*And, Cono Sur*: *comer*) to have a meal.
ranchera *nf* (**a**) (*Méx*) *typical Mexican song.* (**b**) (*Carib*) station wagon.
ranchería *nf* (**a**) (*Cono Sur*) = **ranchería.** (**b**) (*And*: *de rancho*) labourers' quarters, bunkhouse (*US*). (**c**) (*Carib*: *taberna*) poor country inn. (**d**) (*Carib*: *chabolas*) shanty-town.
ranchería *nm* (*LAm*) settlement.
ranchero 1 *adj* (*Méx*) (**a**) (*rudo*) uncouth; (*ridículo*) ridiculous, silly. (**b**) **es muy ~** (*conocedor del campo*) he's a real countryman. (**c**) **huevos ~s** fried eggs in a hot chili and tomato sauce; **música ranchera** ≃ country and western

music. **2** *nm* (**a**) (*LAm*: *jefe de rancho*) rancher, farmer; (*Méx*) peasant. (**b**) (*cocinero*) mess cook.
ranchitos *nmpl* (*Carib*) shanty town.
rancho *nm* (**a**) (*choza*) hut, thatched hut; (*And*: *cobertizo*) shed; (*And*: *casa de campo*) country house, villa; (*Carib*: *chabola*) shanty, shack; **~s** (*And, Carib*) shanty town.
(**b**) (*Náut*) crew's quarters.
(**c**) (*LAm*: *granja*) ranch, large farm; (*Méx*) small farm.
(**d**) (*de gitanos etc*) camp, settlement; (*Méx*) village.
(**e**) (*Mil etc*) mess, communal meal; (*pey*) bad food, grub‡; **asentar el ~** to prepare a meal; (*fig*) to get things organized, settle in; **hacer ~** to make room; **hacer el ~** to have a meal; **hacer ~ aparte** to set up on one's own, go one's own way, keep to oneself.
(**f**) (*Cono Sur*: *sombrero*) straw hat.
rand [ran] *nm, pl* **rands** [ran] rand.
randa¹ *nf* (*Cos*) lace, lace trimming.
randa²* *nm* (*ladrón*) pickpocket, petty thief; (*sospechoso*) suspicious character, prowler.
randar‡ [1a] *vt* to nick‡, rip off‡.
randevú *nm* (*Cono Sur*) rendez-vous.
randevuses *nmpl* (*Cono Sur*) courtesies.
ranfaña* *nm* (*And, Cono Sur*) scruff*.
ranfañoso* (*And, Cono Sur*) **1** *adj* shabby, scruffy. **2** *nm* scruff.
ranfla *nf* (*And, Méx*) ramp, incline.
ranga *nf* (*And*) nag, old horse.
rango¹ *nm* (**a**) (*categoría*) rank; (*status*) standing, status, class; **de ~** of high standing, of some status; **de alto ~** high-ranking. (**b**) (*LAm*) (*lujo*) luxury; (*pompa*) pomp, splendour.
rango² *nm* (*And*) = **ranga.**
rangosidad* *nf* (*Cono Sur*) generosity.
rangoso* *adj* (*CAm, Carib, Cono Sur*) generous.
Rangún *nm* Rangoon.
ránking ['raŋkin] *nm, pl* **ránkings** ['raŋkin) ranking, ranking list, ranking order; classification; (*And Mús*) hit parade.
rantifuso *adj* (*Cono Sur*) (**a**) (*sucio*) dirty, grubby; (*ordinario*) common. (**b**) (*sospechoso*) suspicious.
ranúnculo *nm* ranunculus; (*esp Esp*) buttercup.
ranura *nf* groove; slot; **~ de expansión** (*Inform*) expansion slot.
rap *nm* rap (music); **hacer ~** to rap; **música ~** rap (music).
rapacidad *nf* rapacity, greed.
rapadura *nf* (**a**) (*afeitado*) shave, shaving; (*corte de pelo*) close haircut. (**b**) (*LAm*) (*azúcar*) brown sugar; (*caramelo*) *sweet made of milk and syrup*.
rapapolvo* *nm* ticking-off*; **echar un ~ a uno** to give sb a ticking-off*, tick sb off*.
rapar [1a] *vt* (**a**) *barba* to shave; *pelo* to crop, cut very close. (**b**) (*arrebatar*) to snatch; (*) to pinch*.
rapaz¹ 1 *adj* (*ávido*) rapacious, greedy; (*ladrón*) thieving; (*Zool*) predatory; (*Orn*) raptorial, of prey. **2** *nf* (*Zool*) predatory animal; (*Orn*) bird of prey.
rapaz² *nm* lad, youngster; kid*; **sí, ~** yes, my lad.
rapaza *nf* lass, girl.
rape¹ *nm* (**a**) (*afeitado*) quick shave; (*corte de pelo*) close haircut; **al ~** cut close. (**b**) (*: *bronca*) ticking-off*.
rape² *nm* (*Zool*) anglerfish.
rapé *nm* snuff.
rápida *nf* (*Méx*) chute.
rápidamente *adv* rapidly, fast, quickly, swiftly.
rapidez *nf* rapidity, speed; speediness, swiftness.
rápido 1 *adj* (**a**) (*gen*) rapid, fast, quick, swift; *tren* fast, express.
(**b**) (*And, Carib, Cono Sur*) *campo* fallow; *paisaje* fallow; flat, open.
(**c**) (*Carib*) *tiempo* clear.
2 *adv* (*) quickly; **¡y ~, eh!** and make it snappy!*
3 *nm* (**a**) (*Ferro*) express.
(**b**) (*And, Carib, Cono Sur*: *campo*) open country.
(**c**) **~s** rapids.
rapiña *nf* robbery (with violence); *V* **ave.**
rapiñar [1a] *vt* to steal.
raposa *nf* (**a**) fox (*t fig*), vixen. (**b**) (*Carib*) carrier bag.
raposera *nf* foxhole.
raposero *adj*: **perro ~** foxhound.
raposo *nm* (**a**) (*zorro*) fox, dog fox. (**b**) (*And, Carib*: *mocoso*) kid*.
rap(p)el *nm* abseiling; **a ~** by abseiling; **hacer ~** to abseil (down *etc*).
rap(p)elar [1a] *vi* to abseil (down *etc*).
rapsodia *nf* rhapsody.
rapsódico *adj* rhapsodic.
raptar [1a] *vt* to kidnap, abduct; to carry off.
rapto *nm* (**a**) (*secuestro*) kidnapping, abduction; carrying-off. (**b**) (*fig*: *impulso*) sudden impulse; **en un ~ de celos** in a sudden fit of jealousy. (**c**) (*fig*: *éxtasis*) ecstasy, rapture.
raptor(a) *nm/f* kidnapper.
raque¹ *nm* beachcombing; **andar al ~** to beachcomb, go beachcombing.
raque² *nm* (*Carib*) bargain.
raquear¹ [1a] *vi* to go beachcombing.
raquear² [1a] *vt* (*Carib*) to rob, hold up.
Raquel *nf* Rachel.
raquero, -a *nm/f* beachcomber.
raqueta *nf* racquet; **~ de nieve** snowshoe.
raquetazo *nm* shot, hit, stroke.
raquítico *adj* (**a**) (*Med*) rachitic; *árbol etc* weak, stunted. (**b**) (*fig*) small, inadequate, miserly.
raquitis *nf*, **raquitismo** *nm* rickets.
raramente *adv* rarely, seldom.
rarefacción *nf* rarefaction.
rareza *nf* (**a**) (*cualidad*) rarity, rareness, scarcity.
(**b**) (*objeto*) rarity.
(**c**) (*fig*) oddity, peculiarity; eccentricity; **tiene alguna ~** there's something odd about him; **tiene sus ~s** he has his peculiarities, he has his little ways.
raridad *nf* rarity.
rarificar [1g] *vt* to rarefy.
rarífico *adj* (*Cono Sur*) = **raro** (**b**).
raro *adj* (**a**) (*poco frecuente*) rare, scarce, uncommon; **son ~s los que saben hacerlo** very few people know how to do it; **con alguna rara excepción** with rare exceptions.
(**b**) (*extraño*) odd, peculiar, strange; (*excéntrico*) eccentric; (*notable*) notable, remarkable; **de rara perfección** of rare perfection, of remarkable perfection; **es ~ que ...** it is odd that ..., it is strange that ...; **¡qué ~!** how (very) odd!; **¡(qué) cosa más rara!** how strange!, most odd!; **es un hombre muy ~** he's a very odd man.
(**c**) (*Fís*) rare, rarefied.
ras *nm* levelness, evenness; **~ con ~** level, on a level; flush; **a ~ de** level with; flush with; **volar a ~ de tierra** to fly (almost) at ground level.
rasado *adj* level; **cucharada rasada** level teaspoonful.
rasante 1 *adj* low; **tiro ~** low shot; **vuelo ~** low-level flight. **2** *nm* slope; **cambio de ~** (*Aut*) brow of a hill.
rasar [1a] **1** *vt* (**a**) *contenido* to level (with the rim).
(**b**) (*casi tocar*) to skim, graze; **la bala pasó rasando su sombrero** the bullet grazed his hat.
(**c**) = **arrasar.**
2 rasarse *vr* (*cielo*) to clear.
rasca¹‡ *nf* (*And, CAm, Carib*) drunkenness.
rasca²* *adj* (*Cono Sur*) tacky*, inferior.
rascacielos *nm invar* skyscraper.
rascadera *nf* scraper; (*de caballo*) currycomb.
rascado *adj* (**a**) (*LAm*: *borracho*) drunk. (**b**) (*CAm*: *casquivano*) feather-brained.
rascador *nm* (**a**) (*Téc*) scraper; file, rasp. (**b**) (*de pelo*) ornamental hairclasp.
rascaespalda *nf* backscratcher.
rascamoño *nm* (**a**) = **rascador** (**b**). (**b**) (*Bot*) zinnia.
rascapies *nm invar* (*And*) firecracker.
rascar [1g] **1** *vt* (**a**) (*raer*) to scrape, rasp; (*quitar*) to scrape off; *cabeza etc* to scratch.
(**b**) (*Mús*: *hum*) to scrape, scratch away.
(**c**) (*: *descubrir*) to sniff out, smell out, find out about.
2 *vi* (*Cono Sur*: *picar*) to itch.
3 rascarse *vr* (**a**) to scratch, scratch o.s.
(**b**) (*LAm**: *emborracharse*) to get drunk.
(**c**) **~ juntos** (*CAm, Cono Sur*) to band together (for a criminal purpose); **~ la barriga, ~ la panza** (*Méx, Cono Sur*) to take it easy; **no ~ con uno** (*And*) not to hit it off with sb.
rascatripas *nmf invar* fiddler, third-rate violinist.
rasco *adj* (*Cono Sur*) common, low; low-class.
rascón¹ *adj* (**a**) (*amargo*) sharp, sour (to taste). (**b**) (*Méx*: *pendenciero*) quarrelsome.
rascón² *nm* (*Orn*) water rail.
rascuache *adj* (*CAm, Méx*) (*pobre*) poor, penniless; (*desgraciado*) wretched; (*ridículo*) ridiculous, in bad taste; (*grosero*) coarse, vulgar; (*tacaño*) mean, tightfisted.
rascucho *adj* (*Cono Sur*) drunk.
RASD *nf abr de* **República Árabe Saharaui Democrática** Democratic Saharan Arab Republic.
raseado *adj* level; **cucharada raseada** level teaspoonful.
rasear [1a] *vt* (**a**) (*casi tocar*) to skim, graze. (**b**) (*nivelar*)

to level (off). (**c**) *balón* to play low, play along the ground.

rasera *nf* (*Culin*) fish slice.

rasero 1 *adj* low, level. **2** *nm* strickle; **medir dos cosas con el mismo ~** to treat two things alike.

rasete *nm* satinet(te).

rasgado *adj* (**a**) *ventana* wide; deep, which reaches to the floor; *ojos* wide; almond-shaped; *boca* wide, big. (**b**) (*LAm*: *franco*) outspoken. (**c**) (*And*: *generoso*) generous.

rasgadura *nf* tear, rip, slash.

rasgar [1h] *vt* (**a**) (*gen*) to tear, rip, slash; *papel* to tear up, tear to pieces. (**b**) = **rasguear**.

rasgo *nm* (**a**) (*de pluma*) stroke, flourish; (*adorno*) adornment; (*raya*) dash; **~s** characteristics (*of one's handwriting*); **a grandes ~s** (*fig*) with broad strokes, in outline; briefly; broadly speaking.

(**b**) **~s** (*Anat*) features; **de ~s enérgicos** of energetic appearance, with an energetic look.

(**c**) (*fig*: *característica*) characteristic, feature, trait; **~s característicos** typical features; **~s distintivos** distinctive features.

(**d**) (*acto*) generous deed; noble gesture; **~ de ingenio** flash of wit; stroke of genius.

(**e**) (*Cono Sur*: *acequia*) irrigation channel.

(**f**) (*Cono Sur*) (*terreno*) plot (of land); (*trozo*) piece, portion.

rasgón *nm* tear, rent.

rasguear [1a] *vt* (**a**) (*Mús*) to strum. (**b**) (*escribir*) to write with a flourish; (*fig*) to write.

rasguñadura *nf* (*LAm*) scratch.

rasguñar [1a] *vt* (**a**) (*gen*) to scratch. (**b**) (*Arte*) to sketch, draw in outline.

rasguño *nm* (**a**) (*gen*) scratch; **salir sin un ~** to come out of it without a scratch. (**b**) (*Arte*) sketch, outline drawing.

rasmillón *nm* (*Cono Sur*) scratch.

raso 1 *adj* (**a**) (*llano*) flat, level; (*despejado*) clear, bare, open; (*liso*) smooth; *silla* backless; **aprobado ~** bare pass (mark).

(**b**) *cielo* clear; **está ~** the sky is clear, the weather is clear.

(**c**) *contenido* level (with the brim); **una cucharada rasa** a level teaspoonful.

(**d**) *pelota, vuelo etc* very low, almost at ground level; **fusila el gol por ~** he scores with a low shot.

(**e**) **soldado ~** private.

2 *adv*: **tirar ~** (*Dep*) to shoot low.

3 *nm* (**a**) (*Cos*) satin.

(**b**) (*campo llano*) flat country; (*abierto*) open country; **al ~** in the open.

raspa *nf* (**a**) (*Bot*: *de cebada*) beard; (*de uva*) stalk.

(**b**) (*de pez*) fishbone, (*esp*) backbone.

(**c**) (*) sharp-tongued woman; (*criada*) servant.

(**d**) (*LAm**: *reprimenda*) scolding; dressing-down*.

(**e**) (*Carib, Méx*: *azúcar*) brown sugar.

(**f**) (*Cono Sur*: *herramienta*) rasp.

(**g**) **ni de ~** (*And*) under no circumstances, no way.

(**h**) (*CAm, Méx*: *burla*) joke.

(**i**) (*LAm*: *chusma*) riffraff.

raspada* *nf* (*Carib, Méx*) scolding; dressing-down*.

raspado 1 *adj* (*CAm, Carib*) shameless; **lo pasé ~** I just scraped through. **2** *nm* water ice.

raspador *nm* scraper, rasp; (*Méx Culin*) grater.

raspadura *nf* (**a**) (*acto*) scrape, scraping, rasping. (**b**) **~s** scrapings; filings. (**c**) (*raya*) scratch, mark; (*borradura*) erasure. (**d**) (*LAm*: *azúcar*) brown sugar.

raspante *adj vino* sharp, rough.

raspar [1a] **1** *vt* (**a**) (*gen*) to scrape; (*limar*) to rasp, file; (*alisar*) to smooth (down); (*quitar*) *etc* to scrape off, remove by scraping; *superficie* to scratch; *piel* to chafe; to graze; *palabra* to erase, scratch out.

(**b**) (*fig*: *casi tocar*) to skim, graze; to scrape past.

(**c**) **este vino raspa la boca** this wine tastes sharp.

(**d**) (*) to pinch*.

(**e**) (*Carib**: *matar*) to kill.

(**f**) (*Carib, Méx*: *regañar*) to scold, tell off*.

(**g**) (*Méx*: *maltratar*) to say unkind things to, make wounding remarks to.

2 *vi* (**a**) (*manos*) to be rough.

(**b**) (*vino*) to be sharp, have a rough taste.

(**c**) (*Carib**) (*irse*) to leave, go off; (*morir*) to die.

raspear [1a] **1** *vt* (*And, Cono Sur**) to tick off*. **2** *vi* (*pluma*) to scratch.

raspón *nm* (**a**) (*rasguño*) scratch, graze; (*LAm*) (*abrasión*) abrasion; (*cardenal*) bruise.

(**b**) (*LAm**: *regaño*) scolding; ticking-off*.

(**c**) (*Méx**: *dicho*) cutting remark.

(**d**) (*And*: *sombrero*) straw hat.

rasponear* [1a] *vt* (*And*) to scold; to tick off*.

rasposo *adj* (**a**) sharp-tasting, rough. (**b**) (*Méx*) joking, teasing. (**c**) (*Cono Sur*) (*raído*) scruffy, threadbare; (*miserable*) wretched.

rasqueta *nf* (*LAm*) scraper, rasp; (*de caballo*) currycomb.

rasquetear [1a] *vt* (*LAm*) *caballo* to brush down; (*Cono Sur*) to scrape.

rasquiña *nf* (*LAm*) itch.

rastacuerismo *nm* (*LAm*) (*ambición social*) social climbing; (*tren de vida*) rich living; (*ostentación*) ostentation, display.

rastacuero† *nm* (*LAm*) upstart, parvenu.

rastafario, -a *adj, nm/f* Rastafarian.

rastra *nf* (**a**) (*Agr*) (*rastrillo*) rake; (*grada*) harrow.

(**b**) = **rastro**; = **ristra**.

(**c**) (*de transporte*) sledge (*for moving heavy objects*); (*carga pesada*) weighty object, thing being pulled along.

(**d**) (*de pesca*) trawl; dredge; **pescar a la ~** to trawl.

(**e**) (*Cono Sur*: *cinturón*) *gaucho's thick leather belt.*

(**f**) (*Méx*: *puta*) prostitute.

(**g**) (*fig*) (*consecuencia*) unpleasant consequence, disagreeable result; (*castigo*) punishment; (*merecido*) deserts.

(**h**) **a ~s** by dragging, by pulling; (*fig*) unwillingly; **avanzar a ~s** to crawl (along), drag oneself along; **llevar un piano a ~s** to pull a piano along; **andar a ~s** (*fig*) to have a difficult time of it, suffer hardships.

rastreable *adj* traceable.

rastreador *nm* (**a**) (*persona*) tracker. (**b**) (*Náut*: *t* **barco ~**) trawler; **~ de minas** minesweeper.

rastrear [1a] **1** *vt* (**a**) (*seguir*) to track, trail, follow the trail of; *satélite* to track; (*localizar*) to track down, trace, run to ground; **~ el monte** to comb the woods; **~ los archivos** to trawl through the files.

(**b**) (*sacar a la superficie*) to dredge (up), drag (up); *pesca* to trawl; *minas* to sweep.

2 *vi* (**a**) (*Agr*) to rake, harrow.

(**b**) (*Pesca*) to trawl.

(**c**) (*Aer*) to skim the ground; to fly low, hedgehop.

rastreo *nm* (**a**) (*gen*) dredging, dragging; (*pesca*) trawling. (**b**) (*de satélite*) tracking.

rastrerismo‡ *nm* (*LAm*) toadying, bootlicking*.

rastrero *adj* (**a**) (*Zool*) creeping, crawling; (*Bot*) creeping.

(**b**) *vestido etc* trailing, hanging close to the ground; (*Aer*) *vuelo* very low.

(**c**) (*fig*) *conducta* mean, despicable; *método* low; *disculpa* abject, humble; *persona* cringing; soapy*, bootlicking*, fawning.

rastrillada *nf* (*Cono Sur*) track, trail.

rastrillar [1a] **1** *vt* (**a**) (*Agr*) (*gen*) to rake; (*recoger*) to rake up, rake together; (*alisar*) to rake smooth.

(**b**) *lino etc* to dress.

(**c**) (*LAm*) *fusil* to fire; *fósforo* to strike.

(**d**) (*CAm, Méx*) *pies* to drag.

2 *vi* (**a**) (*And, Carib, Cono Sur*: *errar el tiro*) to miss; (*Carib, Cono Sur*: *disparar*) to fire, shoot.

(**b**) (*Cono Sur**: *robar*) to shoplift.

rastrillazo *nm* (*CAm*) (*sueñecito*) light sleep; (*piscolabis*) light meal, snack.

rastrillero*, -a *nm/f* (*Cono Sur*) shoplifter.

rastrillo *nm* (**a**) (*Agr etc*) rake.

(**b**) (*Téc*) hackle, flax comb.

(**c**) (*de cerradura, llave*) ward.

(**d**) (*Mil*) portcullis; (*Arquit etc*) spiked gate.

(**e**) (*Ferro*) **~ delantero** cowcatcher.

(**f**) (*Com*) jumble sale; charity fête; (*And*) barter; deal.

rastro *nm* (**a**) (*Agr etc*) (*rastrillo*) rake; (*grada*) harrow.

(**b**) (*huella*) track, trail; mark on the ground; (*pista*) scent; (*de cohete etc*) track, course; (*de tormenta*) path; **perder el ~** to lose the scent; **seguir el ~ de uno** to follow sb's trail.

(**c**) (*fig*) trace, sign; **desaparecer sin dejar ~** to vanish without trace; **no quedaba ni ~ de ello** not a trace of it was to be seen.

(**d**) (*matadero*) slaughterhouse; **el R~** *secondhand market in Madrid.*

rastrojear [1a] *vi* (*LAm*) to glean; (*animales*) to feed in the stubble.

rastrojera *nf* stubble field.

rastrojero *nm* (**a**) (*Cono Sur*: *campo*) stubble field. (**b**) (*Cono Sur Aut*) jeep. (**c**) (*Méx*: *maíz*) maize (*o* corn *US*) stalks (*used as fodder*).

rastrojo *nm* (**a**) (*de campo*) stubble; (*Cono Sur*: *terreno cultivado*) ploughed field. (**b**) **~s** waste, remains, leftovers.

rasura *nf* (**a**) (*llanura*) flatness, levelness; (*lisura*) smoothness. (**b**) (*afeitado*) shave, shaving; (*Téc*) scrape, scraping. (**c**) **~s** scrapings; filings.

rasurado *nm* shave.

rasurador *nm*, **rasuradora** *nf* (electric) shaver, electric razor.

rasurar [1a] **1** *vt* (**a**) (*afeitar*) to shave. (**b**) (*Téc*) to scrape. **2 rasurarse** *vr* to shave.

rata 1 *nf* rat. **2** *nm* (*) (**a**) (*ladrón*) sneak thief. (**b**) (*tacaño*) mean devil.

rataplán *nm* drumbeat, rub-a-dub.

ratear[1] [1a] **1** *vt* to steal, pilfer; to filch. **2** *vi* to crawl, creep (along).

ratear[2] [1a] *vt* (**a**) (*repartir*) to share out. (**b**) (*reducir*) to reduce proportionately.

ratera *nf* (*Méx*) rat-trap.

ratería *nf* (**a**) (*gen*) petty larceny, small-time thieving, pilfering. (**b**) (*una* ~) theft. (**c**) (*cualidad*) crookedness, dishonesty.

raterismo *nm* (*LAm*) thieving.

ratero 1 *adj* thievish, light-fingered. **2** *nm* (*carterista*) pickpocket; (*ladrón*) sneak thief, small-time thief; (*Méx*: *de casas*) burglar.

raticida *nm* rat poison.

ratificación *nf* ratification; confirmation; support.

ratificar [1g] *vt tratado etc* to ratify; *noticia etc* to confirm; *opinión* to support; ~ **que** ... to confirm that ...

rating ['ratin] *nm, pl* **ratings** ['ratin] rating; (*Náut*) class; (*TV etc*) popularity rating.

ratio *nm* (*a veces f*) ratio.

Ratisbona *nf* Regensburg, Ratisbon.

rato *nm* (**a**) (short) time, while; spell, period; **un** ~ (*como adv*) a while, a time; **un buen ~, largo** ~ a long time, a good while; **~s libres, ~s de ocio** leisure, spare time, free time; **a ~s** at times, from time to time; **a ~s perdidos** at (*o* in) odd moments; **al ~ viene** (*LAm**) he'll be here in a moment; **al poco** ~ shortly after; **de a ~s** (*Cono Sur*) from time to time; **dentro de un** ~ in a little while; **hace ~ que se fue** (*LAm**) he's been gone a while, he left a while ago; **¡hasta cada** (*o* **el**) **~!** (*LAm**), **¡hasta otro ~!*** so long!; **matar el ~, pasar el** ~ to kill time, pass the time, while away the time; **pasar un buen** ~ to have a good time; **pasar** (*o* **llevarse**) **un mal** ~ to have a bad time of it, have a rough time; **dar malos ~s a uno** to give sb a hard time of it; to cause sb a lot of worry; **hay para** ~ there's still a long way to go; **tener sus ~s** (*persona*) to have one's moments; **tenemos para** ~ we've still a lot to do, we're still far from finished; **¿vas a tardar mucho ~?** will you be long?

(**b**) (*) **es un ~ difícil** it's a bit tricky; **pesan un** ~ they weigh a bit; **sabe un ~ de matemáticas** she knows a heck of a lot of maths*.

ratón *nm* (**a**) (*Zool*) mouse; **~ de archivo, ~ de biblioteca** bookworm; ~ **almizclero** muskrat; **mandar a uno a capar ratones‡** to tell sb to go to blazes*.

(**b**) (*Carib*: *petardo*) squib, cracker.

(**c**) (*Carib**: *resaca*) hangover*.

(**d**) (*: *pelusa*) ball of fluff.

(**e**) (*Inform*) mouse.

ratonar [1a] *vt* to gnaw, nibble.

ratonera *nf* (**a**) (*trampa*) mousetrap. (**b**) (*agujero*) mousehole. (**c**) (*And, Cono Sur*: *barrio bajo*) hovel, slum; (*Carib*: *tienda*) ranch store. (**d**) (*fig*) trap; **caer en la** ~ to fall into a trap.

ratonero *nm*: ~ **común** buzzard.

RAU *nf abr de* **República Árabe Unida** United Arab Republic, UAR.

raudal *nm* (**a**) (*torrente*) torrent, flood. (**b**) (*fig*) plenty, abundance; great quantity; **a ~es** in abundance, in great numbers; **entrar a ~es** to pour in, come flooding in.

raudo *adj* swift; rushing, impetuous.

ravioles *nmpl* ravioli.

raya[1] *nf* (**a**) (*gen*) line; streak; (*en piedra etc*) scratch, mark; (*en mano*) line; (*en diseño, tela*) stripe, pinstripe; ~ **magnética** magnetic stripe; ~ **de puntos** dotted line; ~ **en negro** black line; **a ~s** striped.

(**b**) (*del pelo*) parting; (*del pantalón*) crease; **hacerse la** ~ to part one's hair.

(**c**) (*límite*) line, boundary, limit; (*Dep*) line, mark; **hacer** ~ (*fig*) to be outstanding (*en* in); **mantener a ~ a uno** to keep sb at bay; to keep sb in line; **pasar de la** ~ to overstep the mark, go too far; **poner a** ~ to check, hold back; **tener a** ~ to keep off, keep at bay, keep in check, control.

(**d**) (*Tip*) line, dash; (*Telec*) dash.

(**e**) (*Méx* ††: *sueldo*) pay, wages.

(**f**) (‡: *droga*) fix‡, dose.

raya[2] *nf* (*pez*) ray, skate.

rayadillo *nm* (*Cos*) striped material, (*esp*) blue-and-white striped material.

rayado 1 *adj* (**a**) *papel* ruled; *cheque* crossed; *diseño, tela* striped; (*Téc*) *fusil etc* rifled. (**b**) (*And, Cono Sur**: *loco*) cracked, crazy. (**c**) (*Cono Sur**: *fanático*) extreme, fanatical. **2** *nm* (**a**) ruling, ruled lines; crossing; stripes, striped pattern; (*Téc*) rifling. (**b**) (*Carib Aut*) no parking area.

rayador *nm* (**a**) (*Méx* ††: *contador*) paymaster, accountant. (**b**) (*Cono Sur*: *árbitro*) umpire. (**c**) (*Cono Sur*) = **rallador.**

rayano *adj* (**a**) (*lindante*) adjacent, contiguous; (*fronterizo*) border *atr*. (**b**) ~ **en** bordering on.

rayar [1a] **1** *vt* (**a**) *papel* to line, rule lines on; *cheque* to cross; *piedra etc* to scratch, score, mark; *texto* to underline, underscore; *error* to cross out; (*como diseño*) to stripe, streak; (*Téc*) to rifle.

(**b**) (*Méx*: *pagar*) to pay (his wages to).

(**c**) (*Cono Sur*) = **rallar.**

(**d**) (*LAm*) *caballo* to spur on.

2 *vi* (**a**) ~ **con** to border on, be next to, be adjacent to.

(**b**) ~ **en** (*fig*) to border on, verge on; **esto raya en lo increíble** this verges on the incredible, this is well-nigh incredible; ~ **en los sesenta** to be nearly sixty, be pushing sixty.

(**c**) (*arañar*) to scratch, make scratches; **este producto no raya al fregar** this product scrubs without scratching.

(**d**) **al ~ el alba** at break of day, at first light.

(**e**) (*Méx*: *cobrar*) to draw one's wages.

3 rayarse *vr* (**a**) (*objeto*) to get scratched.

(**b**) (*And*: *ver realizados sus deseos*) to see one's wishes fulfilled; (*Méx*: *enriquecerse*) to get rich.

(**c**) (*And, Cono Sur**: *enojarse*) to get angry.

(**d**) (*Cono Sur**: *enloquecer*) to go crazy.

rayero *nm* (*Cono Sur*) linesman, line judge.

rayo[1] *nm* (**a**) (*de luz*) ray, beam; shaft (of light); ~ **láser** laser beam; ~ **de luna** moonbeam; ~ **de la muerte** death ray; ~ **de partículas** stream of particles; ~ **de sol,** ~ **solar** sunbeam, ray of sunlight; **~s catódicos** cathode rays; **~s cósmicos** cosmic rays; **~s gamma** gamma rays; **~s infrarrojos** infrared rays; **~s luminosos** light rays; **~s ultravioleta** ultraviolet rays; **~s X** X-rays.

(**b**) (*Téc*) spoke.

(**c**) (*Met*) lightning, flash of lightning; thunderbolt; **¡~s!*** dammit!*; **¿qué ~s es eso?*** what in hell's name is that?*; **cayó un ~ en la torre** the tower was struck by lightning; **huele/sabe a ~s*** it smells/tastes awful; **como un** ~ like lightning, like a shot; **la noticia cayó como un** ~ the news was a bombshell; **entrar como un** ~ to dash in; **salir como un** ~ to dash out; **pasar como un** ~ to rush past, flash past; **echar ~s y centellas** to rage, fume; **¡que le parta un ~!*, ¡mal ~ le parta!*** damn him!; **¡que me parta un** ~ (**si lo sé**)! I'm damned if I know; **¡a los demás que les parta un ~!** and the rest of them can go to hell!

(**d**) (*fig*: *desgracia*) blow, misfortune.

(**e**) (*fig*: *persona*) fast worker; **es un** ~ he's like lightning.

rayo[2] *etc V* **raer.**

rayón *nm* rayon.

rayuela *nf* pitch-and-toss; (*LAm*) hopscotch.

raza[1] *nf* (**a**) (*gen*) race; (*de animal*) breed, strain; (*estirpe*) stock; (*Bio*) race; ~ **blanca** white race; ~ **humana** human race; ~ **negra** black race; **de ~, de pura** ~ *caballo* thoroughbred; *perro etc* pedigree. (**b**) (*And**) cheek*, impudence; **¡qué tal ~!** some cheek!*, what a cheek!*

raza[2] *nf* (**a**) (*grieta*) crack, slit, fissure; (*en tela*) run. (**b**) (*rayo*) ray of light.

razano *adj* (*And*) thoroughbred.

razón *nf* (**a**) (*facultad*) reason; **hacer que uno entre en ~, meter** (*o* **poner**) **a uno en** ~ to make sb see sense; **avenirse a razones, meterse en** ~ to see sense, listen to reason; **perder la** ~ to lose one's reason, go out of one's mind; **muy puesto en** ~ very reasonable; **¡eso es ponerse en ~!** that's better!, now you're talking!

(**b**) (*lo correcto*) right, rightness; (*justicia*) justice; **con ~ o sin ella** rightly or wrongly; **le asiste la** ~ he has right on his side; **cargarse de** ~ to have right fully on one's side; **quiero cargarme de ~ antes de ...** I want to be sure of my case before ...; **dar la ~ a uno** to agree that sb is right, prove sb right; to side with sb; **tener ~** to be right; **no tener ~** to be wrong; **tener plenamente ~ en** + *infin* to be fully justified in + *ger*; **tratar de quitar a uno la ~** to try to put sb in the wrong.

(**c**) (*motivo*) reason, motive, cause; '**~: Princesa 4**' 'inquiries to 4 Princesa Street'; 'for further details, apply to 4 Princesa Street'; **~ que le sobra** she's only too right, she can say that again; **¿cuál es la ~?** what is the reason?; **la ~ por qué** the reason why; **la ~ por la que lo hizo** the reason why he did it, the reason for his doing it; **~ de estado** reasons of state; **~ de más** all the more reason (*para* + *infin* to + *infin*); **~ de ser** raison d'être; **con ~** with good reason; **¡con ~!** naturally!; **con ~ o sin ella** rightly or wrongly; **en ~ de** with regard to; **no atiende a razones** he'll not listen to reason, he's not open to argument; **dar ~ de** to give an account of, report on; to give information about; to deal with; to give some idea of, convey; **nadie me daba ~ de ella** nobody could tell me anything about her; **dar ~ de sí** to give an account of o.s.; **tener ~ para** + *infin* to have cause to + *infin*.

(**d**) (*Com*) **~ social** trade name, firm's name.

(**e**) (*: *recado*) message; **mandar a uno ~ de que haga algo** to send sb a message telling him to do sth.

(**f**) (*Mat*) ratio, proportion; rate; **a ~ de 5 a 7** in the ratio of 5 to 7; **a ~ de 8 por persona** at the rate of 8 per head; **abandonan el país a ~ de 800 cada año** they are leaving the country at the rate of 800 a year; **en ~ directa con** in direct ratio to.

razonabilidad *nf* reasonableness.

razonable *adj* reasonable.

razonablemente *adv* reasonably.

razonado *adj* reasoned; *cuenta etc* itemized, detailed.

razonamiento *nm* reasoning.

razonar [1a] **1** *vt* (**a**) (*gen*) to reason, argue. (**b**) *problema etc* to reason out. (**c**) *cuenta* to itemize. **2** *vi* (**a**) (*argüir*) to reason, argue. (**b**) (*hablar*) to talk (together).

raz(z)ia ['raθia] *nf* raid.

raz(z)iar [raθi'ar] *vi* to raid.

RCE *nf* (*Rad*) *abr de* **Radio Cadena Española.**

RCN *nf* (*Méjico, Colombia*) *abr de* **Radio Cadena Nacional.**

RD *nm abr de* **Real Decreto.**

RDA *nf* (*Hist*) *abr de* **República Democrática Alemana** German Democratic Republic, GDR.

Rdo. *abr de* **Reverendo.**

re *nm* (*Mús*) D; **~ mayor** D major.

re... (**a**) (*prefijo*) re...

(**b**) (*prefijo intensivo*) very, awfully, terribly, *p.ej.* **rebueno** very good, jolly good*; **reguapa** awfully pretty; **resalada** (*Esp*) terribly attractive; **¡rebomba!** (*Esp*) how utterly amazing!; **¡rediez!** (*Esp*) well I'm damned!

reabastecer [2d] **1** *vt* (*t* **~ de combustible, ~ de gasolina**) to refuel. **2 reabastecerse** *vr* to refuel.

reabastecimiento *nm* refuelling.

reabrir [3a; *ptp* **reabierto**] **1** *vt* to reopen; **~ las heridas** to open old wounds. **2 reabrirse** *vr* to reopen.

reacción *nf* (**a**) (*gen*) reaction (*a, ante* to; *t Med*); response (*a* to); **~ en cadena** chain reaction; **~ nuclear** nuclear reaction; **la ~ blanca** the white backlash.

(**b**) (*Pol*) reaction.

(**c**) (*Téc*) **avión a** (*o* **de**) **~** jet plane; **propulsión por ~** jet propulsion.

reaccionar [1a] *vi* (**a**) (*gen*) to react (*a, ante* to; *contra* against; *sobre* on); to respond (*a* to); **¿cómo reaccionó?** how did she take it? (**b**) (*sobreponerse*) to pull oneself together.

reaccionario, -a *adj, nm/f* reactionary.

reacio *adj* stubborn; reluctant; **ser ~ a, estar ~ a** to be opposed to, resist (the idea of), be unwilling to accept (the need for); **estar ~ a** + *infin* to be unwilling to + *infin*.

reacondicionamiento *nm* reconditioning; reorganization, restructuring.

reacondicionar [1a] *vt* to recondition; *organismo* to reorganize, restructure.

reactivación *nf* reactivating; (*Econ*) recovery, upturn.

reactivar [1a] *vt* to reactivate.

reactivo *nm* reagent.

reactor *nm* (**a**) (*Fís*) reactor; **~ de agua a presión** pressurized-water reactor; **~ enfriado por gas** gas-cooled reactor; **~ generador, ~ reproductor** breeder reactor; **~ nuclear** nuclear reactor. (**b**) (*Aer*) (*motor*) jet engine; (*avión*) jet plane; **~ ejecutivo** executive jet.

readaptación *nf* readaptation; readjustment; **~ profesional** industrial retraining; **~ social** social rehabilitation; assimilation into society.

readmisión *nf* readmission.

readmitir [3a] *vt* to readmit.

readquirir [3a] *vt poder etc* to recover, regain.

reafirmación *nf* reaffirmation; reassertion.

reafirmar [1a] *vt* to reaffirm; to reassert.

reagrupación *nf* regrouping.

reagrupar [1a] **1** *vt* to regroup. **2 reagruparse** *vr* to regroup.

reagudizarse [1f] *vr* (*Med*) to become acute again, recrudesce.

reaje‡ *nm* (*Cono Sur*) mob, rabble.

reajustar [1a] **1** *vt* to readjust; (*Pol*) to reshuffle; *precios etc* (*euf*) to increase, put up. **2 reajustarse** *vr* to readjust.

reajuste *nm* readjustment; (*fig*) readjustment, reappraisal; **~ agonizante, ~ doloroso** agonizing reappraisal; **~ ministerial** cabinet reshuffle; **~ de precios** (*euf*) rise in prices, price increase; **~ salarial** wage increase.

real[1] *adj* (*verdadero*) real.

real[2] **1** *adj* (**a**) (*del rey*) royal.

(**b**) (*fig*) royal; grand, splendid; *V* **moza** *etc.*

2 *nm* (**a**) (*Hist*) (*Mil*) army camp; (*de feria*) fairground; (a)**sentar sus ~es** to settle down; to establish o.s.

(**b**) (*Fin Hist*) *coin of 25 céntimos, one quarter of a peseta*; **costó 6 ~es** it cost $1\frac{1}{2}$ pesetas; **está sin un ~*, no tiene un ~*** he hasn't a bean*.

3 ~es *nmpl* (*Méx**) cash, dough‡.

reala *nf* (*CAm, Méx*) rope.

realada *nf* (*Méx*) roundup, rodeo.

realar [1a] *vt* (*Méx*) *ganado* to round up.

realce *nm* (**a**) (*Téc*) raised work, embossing.

(**b**) (*Arte*) highlight.

(**c**) (*fig*) (*esplendor*) lustre, splendour; (*importancia*) importance, significance; (*aumento*) enhancement; **dar ~ a** to add lustre to, enhance the splendour of; to highlight; **un asunto sin ~** a matter of no importance.

realengo *adj* (**a**) (*LAm*) *animal* stray, lost, ownerless. (**b**) (*Méx, Carib*) (*ocioso*) idle; (*libre*) free, unattached.

realeza *nf* royalty.

realidad *nf* (*gen*) reality; (*verdad*) truth; **la ~ de la política** the realities of politics; **atengámonos a la ~** let's face the facts; **en ~** in fact, really, actually; **la ~ es que ...** the fact of the matter is that ...

realimentación *nf* (*Rad, Inform etc*) feedback; (*Aer etc*) refuelling.

realineamiento *nm* realignment.

realinear [1a] *vt* to realign.

realísima *nf V* **gana.**

realismo *nm* realism; **~ mágico** magic realism.

realista 1 *adj* realistic. **2** *nmf* realist.

realizable *adj* (**a**) *bienes etc* realizable. (**b**) *objetivo* attainable; *plan* practical, feasible.

realización *nf* (**a**) (*Fin*) realization; (*venta*) sale, selling-up; (*liquidación*) clearance sale; **~ de beneficios** profit-taking. (**b**) (*acto*: *V vt* (**b**)) realization; fulfilment, carrying out; achievement. (**c**) (*Cine, TV*) production; (*Rad*) broadcast. (**d**) (*Ling*) performance.

realizado *adj* (*V vt, vr*); **sentirse ~** to feel fulfilled.

realizador(a) *nm/f* (*TV etc*) director.

realizar [1f] **1** *vt* (**a**) (*Fin*) *bienes* to realize; *existencias* to sell off, sell up; *beneficios* to take.

(**b**) *objetivo etc* to attain, achieve, realize; *promesa* to fulfil, carry out; *plan* to carry out, put into effect.

(**c**) *viaje etc* to make; *visita* to carry out; *expedición, vuelo etc* to undertake, make; *compra* to make.

(**d**) **~ que ...** (*LAm*) to realize that ...

2 realizarse *vr* (**a**) (*sueño etc*) to come true; (*esperanza*) to materialize; (*plan*) to be carried out.

(**b**) (*persona*) to fulfil o.s.; **~ como persona** to fulfil one's aims in life.

realmente[1] *adv* (*en efecto*) really; (*de hecho*) in fact, actually.

realmente[2] *adv* (*fig*) royally.

realquilar [1a] *vt* to sublet, sublease; to relet.

realzar [1f] *vt* (**a**) (*Téc*) to emboss, raise. (**b**) (*Arte*) to highlight. (**c**) (*fig*) to enhance, heighten, add to.

reanimación *nf* revival (*t fig*); resuscitation.

reanimar [1a] **1** *vt* (**a**) (*lit*) to revive; to resuscitate. (**b**) (*fig*) to revive, encourage, stimulate; to give new life to. **2 reanimarse** *vr* to revive; to acquire new life.

reanudación *nf* renewal; resumption.

reanudar [1a] *vt* to renew; *cuento, viaje etc* to resume.

reaparecer [2d] *vi* to reappear; to return; to recur.
reaparición *nf* reappearance; return; recurrence.
reapertura *nf* reopening.
reaprovisionamiento *nm* replenishment, restocking.
reaprovisionar [1a] *vt* to replenish, restock.
rearmar [1a] **1** *vt* to rearm. **2 rearmarse** *vr* to rearm.
rearme *nm* rearmament.
reasegurar [1a] *vt* to reinsure; to underwrite.
reaseguro *nm* reinsurance; underwriting.
reasumir [3a] *vt* to resume, reassume.
reata *nf* (**a**) (*cuerda*) rope (*joining string of pack animals*); (*LAm*: *lazo*) rope, lasso; (*LAm*: *correa*) strap; (*And*: *tira de algodón*) strip of cotton cloth.
(**b**) (*caballos*) string (of horses *etc*), pack train; **de ~** in single file, one after the other; (*fig*) submissively.
(**c**) (*And, Carib, Méx*: *de flores*) flowerbed, border.
(**d**) (*Méx*: *enrejado*) bamboo screen.
(**e**) (*Méx***) prick**; cock**; **echar ~** to fuck**.
reavivar [1a] *vt* to revive.
rebaja *nf* lowering, lessening, reduction; (*Com*) discount, rebate; (*en saldo*) reduction; **'~s'** 'sale'; **las ~s** the sales; **~s de marzo** spring sales; **'grandes ~s'** 'big reductions'.
rebajamiento *nm* (**a**) = **rebaja.** (**b**) **~ de sí mismo** self-abasement.
rebajar [1a] **1** *vt* (**a**) *tierra etc* to lower, lower the level of.
(**b**) *precio* to reduce, lower, cut (down); *valor* to detract from, reduce; **~ el precio a uno en un 5 por 100** to give sb a discount of 5%, knock 5% off the price for sb.
(**c**) *intensidad etc* to lessen, diminish; *color* to tone down; *sonido* to turn down, reduce; *calor* to lessen; (*LAm*) *droga* to cut.
(**d**) *persona etc* to humble; to bring down a peg or two, deflate; *ventajas etc* to decry, disparage; **llamarlo así es ~lo de categoría** calling it by that name reduces its (real) importance, calling it that makes it less important than it is.
2 rebajarse *vr*: **~ ante uno** to bow before sb; **~ a +** *infin* to humble o.s. sufficiently to + *infin*; to stoop to + *ger*, descend to + *ger*, condescend to + *infin*.
rebaje *nm* (**a**) (*Téc*) recess; groove. (**b**) (*acto*) lowering; (*Econ, Fin*) cut.
rebajo *nm* recess; (*Téc*) rabbet.
rebalsa *nf* pool, puddle.
rebalsar [1a] **1** *vt* (**a**) *agua* to dam (up), block. (**b**) (*LAm*) *orillas etc* to burst, overflow. **2 rebalsarse** *vr* to form a pool (*o* lake); to become dammed up.
rebanada *nf* (**a**) (*Culin*) slice. (**b**) (*Méx*: *pestillo*) latch.
rebanar [1a] *vt* (*Culin*) to slice, cut in slices; *árbol etc* to slice through, slice down; *miembro etc* to slice off.
rebañar [1a] *vt* (**a**) *restos* to scrape up, scrape together; to sweep up, sweep into a pile; **logró ~ ciertos fondos** he managed to scrape some money together; **~ el plato del arroz** to scrape a dish clean of rice.
(**b**) **~ una tienda de joyas** (*fig*) to clear a shop of jewellery, clean out all the jewellery from a shop.
rebaño *nm* flock, herd; (*fig*) flock.
rebasar [1a] *vt* (*t vi*: **~ de**) (*en calidad, número*) to exceed, surpass; (*en carrera, progreso*) to overtake, leave behind; (*Aut*) to overtake, pass; *punto* to pass, go beyond; (*Náut*) to sail past; *límite de tiempo* to exceed; (*agua*) to overflow, rise higher than; **han rebasado ya los límites razonables** they have already gone beyond all reasonable limits; **la cifra no rebasa de mil** the number does not exceed a thousand.
rebatible *adj* (**a**) *argumento* easily refuted. (**b**) *silla* tip-up.
rebatinga *nf* (*CAm, Méx*) = **rebatiña.**
rebatiña *nf* (*LAm*) scramble, rush; **les echó caramelos a la ~** he threw sweets so that they could scramble for them; **andar a la ~ de algo** to scramble for sth, fight over sth; (*fig*) to argue fiercely over sth.
rebatir [3a] *vt* (**a**) *ataque* to repel; *golpe* to parry, ward off.
(**b**) *argumento etc* to reject, rebut, refute; *tentación* to resist; *sugerencia* to reject.
(**c**) *suma* to reduce; *descuento* to deduct, knock off.
rebato *nm* (*Mil*: *alarma*) alarm, warning of attack, call to arms; (*ataque*) surprise attack; **llamar** (*o* **tocar**) **a ~** (*t fig*) to sound the alarm.
rebautizar [1f] *vt* to rechristen.
Rebeca *nf* Rebecca.
rebeca *nf* cardigan.
rebeco *nm* chamois, ibex.
rebelarse [1a] *vr* to revolt, rebel, rise; **~ contra** (*fig*) to rebel against.
rebelde 1 *adj* (**a**) (*gen*) rebellious; mutinous; **el gobierno ~** the rebel government; **ser ~ a** (*fig*) to be in revolt against, rebel against; to resist.
(**b**) *niño etc* unruly; unmanageable, uncontrollable; stubborn; *problema etc* difficult; *tos etc* persistent, hard to cure; *sustancia* difficult to work, awkward to treat.
(**c**) (*Jur*) defaulting; in contempt of court.
2 *nmf* (**a**) (*Mil, Pol*) rebel.
(**b**) (*Jur*) defaulter; person in contempt of court.
rebeldía *nf* (**a**) rebelliousness; defiance, disobedience; **estar en plena ~** to be in open revolt.
(**b**) (*Jur*) default; contempt of court; **caer en ~** to be in default; to be in contempt of court; **fue juzgado en ~** he was sentenced by default.
rebelión *nf* revolt, rebellion, rising.
rebelón *adj caballo* hard-mouthed.
rebencudo *adj* (*Carib*) stubborn.
rebenque *nm* (*LAm*) riding-crop, whip.
rebenquear* [1a] *vt* (*LAm*) to whip.
reblandecer [2d] *vt* to soften.
reblandecido* *adj* (*And*) (*loco*) soft in the head; (*senil*) senile.
reblandecimiento *nm* softening; **~ cerebral** softening of the brain.
reble‡ *nm* bum‡, bottom.
rebobinado *nm* rewind(ing).
rebobinar [1a] *vt* to rewind.
rebojo *nm* crust, piece (of bread).
rebolichada *nf* (*Méx*) opportunity.
rebolludo *adj* thickset, chunky*.
reborde *nm* ledge; (*Téc*) flange, rim; border.
rebosadero *nm* overflow.
rebosante *adj*: **~ de** (*t fig*) brimming with, overflowing with.
rebosar [1a] *vi* (**a**) (*líquido, recipiente*) to overflow, run over; **el café rebosa de la taza** the coffee cup is running over, the coffee is running over the cup; **llenar una sala a ~** to fill a room to overflowing.
(**b**) (*abundar*) to abound, be plentiful; **allí rebosa el mineral** the mineral abounds there, a lot of the mineral is found there; **le rebosa la alegría** merriment bubbles out of him.
(**c**) **~ de, ~ en** to overflow with, be brimming with; **~ de salud** to be bursting with health, be brimming with health; **ellos rebosan en dinero** they have pots of money.
reboso *nm* (*Carib, Cono Sur*) driftwood.
rebotado* *nm* (*sacerdote*) ex-priest; (*monje*) former monk.
rebotar [1a] **1** *vt* (**a**) *pelota* to bounce; *ataque* to repel; *rayos etc* to send back, turn back, cause to bounce off.
(**b**) *clavo* to clinch.
(**c**) *persona* to annoy; to put out, upset.
(**d**) (*And, Méx*) *agua* to muddy, stir up.
2 *vi* (**a**) (*pelota etc*) to bounce; to rebound (*de* off); (*bala*) to ricochet (*de* off), glance (*de* off). (**b**) (*fig*) to bounce back, recover.
rebote *nm* bounce, rebound; **de ~** on the rebound; (*fig*) indirectly, as an indirect consequence.
rebozado 1 *adj* (*Culin*) fried in batter (*o* breadcrumbs *etc*). **2** *nm* batter.
rebozar [1f] **1** *vt* (**a**) *cabeza, cara* to muffle up, wrap up. (**b**) (*Culin*) to roll in batter (*o* breadcrumbs *etc*), fry in batter. **2 rebozarse** *vr* to muffle (o.s.) up.
rebozo *nm* (**a**) (*mantilla etc*) muffler, wrap; (*LAm*: *chal*) shawl. (**b**) (*fig*: *disfraz*) disguise; dissimulation; **de ~** secretly; **sin ~** (*adv*) openly, frankly, (*adj*) plain, straight; aboveboard.
rebrotar [1a] *vi* to break out again, reappear.
rebrote *nm* new outbreak, reappearance; (*Econ*) upsurge, (sudden) rise.
rebufar [1a] *vi* to snort loudly.
rebufo *nm* loud snort.
rebujo *nm* (*maraña*) mass, knot, tangle, ball; (*paquete*) badly-wrapped parcel.
rebultado *adj* bulky.
rebullicio *nm* hubbub, uproar; agitation.
rebullir [3a] **1** *vt* (*Méx*) to stir up. **2** *vi y* **rebullirse** *vr* to stir, begin to move; to show signs of life.
rebumbio* *nm* (*Méx*) racket, din, hubbub.
rebusca *nf* (**a**) (*busca*) search.
(**b**) (*Agr*) gleaning.
(**c**) (*restos*) leavings, left-overs, remains.
(**d**) (*And, Cono Sur*) (*negocio*) small business; (*: *negocio ilegal*) shady dealing, illicit trading; (*ganancia*) profit on the side.
rebuscado *adj palabra* recherché; out-of-the-way; *estilo*

studied, elaborate; (*LAm*: *afectado*) affected, stuck-up*.

rebuscar [1g] **1** *vt* (**a**) *objeto etc* to search carefully for, search out; (*Agr*) to glean.

(**b**) *lugar* to search carefully; *montón etc* to search through, rummage in.

2 *vi* to search carefully; (*Agr*) to glean.

3 rebuscarse* *vr* (**a**) (*And, Cono Sur*) to look for work.

(**b**) (*And**) to live on one's wits.

rebuznar [1a] *vi* to bray.

rebuzno *nm* bray; braying.

recabar [1a] *vt* (**a**) (*obtener*) to obtain by entreaty, manage to get (*de* from); *fondos* to collect.

(**b**) (*reclamar*) to claim as of right, assert one's claim to.

(**c**) (*solicitar*) to ask for, apply for; (*exigir*) to demand, insist on.

recadero *nm* (*mensajero*) messenger; (*repartidor*) errand boy, deliveryman; (*trajinante*) carrier.

recado *nm* (**a**) (*mensaje*) message; errand; (*regalo*) gift, small present; **coger** (*o* **tomar**) **un** ~ (*Telec etc*) to take a message; **dejar** ~ to leave a message; **enviar a uno a un** ~ to send sb on an errand; **mandar** ~ to send word; **salir a hacer un** ~, **salir a un** ~ (*Méx*) to go out on an errand.

(**b**) (*compras*) provisions, daily shopping.

(**c**) (*equipo*) equipment, materials; ~ **de escribir** writing case, set of writing materials.

(**d**) (*LAm*: *montura*) saddle and trappings, riding gear.

(**e**) (*Carib*: *saludos*) greetings; **déle ~s a su familia** give my regards to his family.

recaer [2n] *vi* (**a**) (*Med*) to suffer a relapse.

(**b**) (*criminal etc*) to fall back, relapse (*en* into); to backslide.

(**c**) ~ **en** (*elección etc*) to fall on, fall to; (*legado*) to pass to; (*deber*) to devolve upon; (*premio*) to go to; **las sospechas recayeron sobre el conserje** suspicion fell on the porter; **este peso recaerá más sobre los pobres** this burden will bear most heavily on the poor; **la acusación recayó sobre él mismo** the charge recoiled upon him.

(**d**) (*Arquit*) ~ **a** to look out on, look over.

recaída *nf* relapse (*en* into); backsliding.

recalar [1a] **1** *vt* to saturate, soak. **2** *vi* (**a**) (*Náut*) to sight land, reach port. (**b**) (*) to end up (*en* at). (**c**) ~ **a uno** (*LAm*) to go to sb for help.

recalcar [1g] **1** *vt* (**a**) *contenido* to press down, press in, squeeze in; *recipiente* to cram, stuff (*de* with).

(**b**) (*fig*) to stress, emphasize; to make great play with; ~ **algo a uno** to insist on sth to sb; ~ **a uno que** ... to tell sb emphatically that ...

2 *vi* (*Náut*) to list, heel.

3 recalcarse *vr*: ~ **un hueso** (*LAm*) to dislocate a bone.

recalcitrante *adj* recalcitrant.

recalcitrar [1a] *vi* (**a**) (*echarse atrás*) to take a step back (the better to resist). (**b**) (*resistir*) to resist, be stubborn, refuse to take heed.

recalentado *adj* warmed-up (*t fig*).

recalentamiento *nm* (**a**) overheating; ~ **global** global warming. (**b**) (*Culin etc*) warming-up, reheating.

recalentar [1j] **1** *vt* (**a**) (*gen*) to overheat. (**b**) *comida etc* to warm up, reheat. **2 recalentarse** *vr* to become overheated, get too hot.

recalmón *nm* lull.

recamado *nm* embroidery.

recamar [1a] *vt* to embroider.

recámara *nf* (**a**) (*cuarto*) side room; (*vestidor*) dressing room; (*And, CAm, Méx*) bedroom.

(**b**) (*de cañón*) breech, chamber.

(**c**) (*fig*: *cautela*) caution, wariness; reserve; **tener mucha** ~ to be on the careful side, be wary by nature.

recamarera *nf* (*Méx*) chambermaid.

recambiar [1b] *vt pieza* to change over.

recambio *nm* (*Mec*) spare; (*de pluma*) refill; ~**s** spares, spare parts, extras (*US*); **neumático de** ~ spare tyre.

recañí‡ *nf* window.

recapacitar [1a] **1** *vt* to think over, reflect on. **2** *vi* to think things over, reflect.

recapitulación *nf* recapitulation, summing-up, summary.

recapitular [1a] *vti* to recapitulate, sum up, summarize.

recargable *adj* rechargeable.

recargado *adj* (**a**) (*sobrecargado*) overloaded. (**b**) *adorno, estilo etc* overelaborate.

recargar [1h] *vt* (**a**) (*cargar demasiado*) to overload; to overload on one side, unbalance.

(**b**) (*Fin*) to put an additional charge on, increase (the price of, the tax on *etc*).

(**c**) (*Jur*) *sentencia* to increase.

(**d**) (*Téc*) to reload, recharge; *pila* to recharge.

(**e**) (*fig*) to overload (*de* with); ~ **a uno de deberes** to overload sb with duties; ~ **el café de azúcar** to put too much sugar in the coffee, make the coffee too sweet; ~ **un diseño de adornos** to overload a pattern with decoration.

recargo *nm* (**a**) (*nueva carga*) new burden; (*aumento de carga*) extra load, additional load.

(**b**) (*Fin*) extra charge, surcharge; increase.

(**c**) (*Jur*) new charge, further charge; increase of sentence.

(**d**) (*Med*) rise in temperature.

recatado *adj* (**a**) *mujer* modest, shy, demure. (**b**) (*prudente*) cautious, circumspect.

recatar [1a] **1** *vt* to hide.

2 recatarse *vr* (**a**) (*ocultarse*) to hide o.s. away (*de* from).

(**b**) (*ser discreto*) to act discreetly; **sin** ~ openly.

(**c**) (*ser prudente*) to be cautious; (*vacilar*) to hesitate; ~ **de algo** to fight shy of sth; **no se recata ante nada** nothing daunts her.

recato *nm* (**a**) (*modestia*) modesty, shyness, demureness. (**b**) (*cautela*) caution, circumspection; reserve, restraint; **sin** ~ openly, unreservedly.

recatón *nm* (*And*) miner's pick.

recauchutado *nm* (**a**) (*neumático*) retread. (**b**) (*proceso*) retreading, remoulding.

recauchutar [1a] *vt neumático* to retread, remould.

recaudación *nf* (**a**) (*acto*) collection; recovery. (**b**) (*cantidad*) takings, sum taken, income; (*Dep*) gate, gate money. (**c**) (*oficina*) tax office.

recaudador(a)[1] *nm/f*: ~ **de contribuciones** tax collector.

recaudadora[2] *nf* (*And*) tax office.

recaudar [1a] *vt impuestos* to collect; *dinero* to collect, take (in), receive; *deuda* to recover.

recaudería *nf* (*Méx*) greengrocer's shop.

recaudo *nm* (**a**) (*Fin*) collection.

(**b**) (*Jur*) surety, security.

(**c**) (*cuidado*) care, protection; (*precaución*) precaution; **estar a buen** ~ to be in safekeeping; **poner algo a buen** ~ to put sth in a safe place.

(**d**) (*CAm, Cono Sur, Méx*: *especias*) spices, condiments.

(**e**) (*CAm, Cono Sur, Méx*: *legumbres*) daily supply of fresh vegetables.

recebo *nm* gravel.

recechar [1a] *vt caza* to stalk.

rececho *nm* stalking; **cazar a** (*o* **en**) ~ to stalk.

rechechor(a) *nm/f* stalker.

recelar [1a] **1** *vt*: ~ **que** ... to suspect that ..., fear that ...

2 *vi y* **recelarse** *vr*: ~ **de** to suspect, fear, distrust; ~ + *infin* to be afraid of + *ger*.

recelo *nm* (*suspicacia*) suspicion; (*temor*) fear, apprehension; (*desconfianza*) distrust, mistrust.

receloso *adj* suspicious, distrustful; apprehensive.

recensión *nf* recension; review.

recepción *nf* (**a**) (*acto*) reception, receiving; (*Rad*) reception; (*en academia etc*) admission.

(**b**) (*ceremonia*) reception.

(**c**) (*cuarto*) drawing room; (*de hotel*) reception, reception desk.

recepcionar [1a] *vt* (*esp LAm*) to receive, accept.

recepcionista *nmf* (hotel) receptionist, desk clerk (*US*).

receptación *nf* (crime of) receiving.

receptáculo *nm* receptacle; holder.

receptar [1a] *vt* (*Jur*) to receive.

receptividad *nf* receptivity.

receptivo *adj* receptive.

receptor 1 *nm* (**a**) (*Téc*) receiver; ~ **de control** (*TV*) monitor; ~ **de televisión** television receiver, television set; **descolgar el** ~ (*Telec*) to pick up the receiver. (**b**) (*Dep*) catcher. **2** *nm*, **receptora** *nf* person who receives a transplant.

recesar [1a] *vi* (*LAm, Pol*) to recess, go into recess.

recesión *nf* (*Com, Fin*) recession; slump; (*de precios*) slide, fall.

recesivo *adj* (*Bio*) recessive; (*Econ*) recession (*atr*), recessionary.

receso *nm* (**a**) (*LAm Parl*) recess. (**b**) (*descanso*) coffee break; **hacer un** ~ to pause, stop. (**c**) ~ **económico** downturn in the economy.

receta *nf* (*Culin*) recipe (*de* for); (*Med*) prescription.

recetar [1a] *vt* (**a**) (*Med*) to prescribe. (**b**) (*CAm, Méx*) *golpe* to deal out, hit.

recetario *nm* collection of recipes, recipe book.
recial *nm* rapids.
reciamente *adv* strongly; severely; intensely; loudly.
recibí *nm* 'received with thanks', receipt; **poner el ~ en** to sign one's receipt on.
recibidero *adj* receivable.
recibido *adj* (*LAm*) *persona* qualified.
recibidor[1] *nm* (*de casa*) entrance hall.
recibidor[2] *nm*, **recibidora** *nf* (*persona*) receiver, recipient.
recibimiento *nm* (**a**) (*acto*) reception, welcome; **dispensar a uno un ~ apoteósico** to give sb an enthusiastic welcome.
(**b**) (*antecámara*) anteroom. vestibule, lobby; (*hall*) hall; (*sala*) reception room.
recibir [3a] **1** *vt* (**a**) (*gen*) to receive; **'recibido'** (*Rad*) 'message received'.
(**b**) (*acoger*) *persona* to welcome, receive, greet; to go and meet; *propuesta etc* to receive; to welcome, greet; **~ a uno con los brazos abiertos** to welcome sb with open arms; **el torero recibe al toro** the bullfighter awaits the bull's charge; **le recibió el ministro** the minister received him, the minister granted him an interview; **la oferta fue mal recibida** the offer was badly received; **reciba un saludo de ...** (*en carta*) Yours sincerely ...
(**c**) (*Univ*) *título etc* to receive, take.
2 *vi* to receive; to entertain; **reciben mucho en casa** they entertain at home a good deal; **la baronesa recibe los lunes** the baroness receives visitors on Mondays, the baroness's 'at home' day is Monday.
3 recibirse *vr* (*LAm*) to qualify; (*Univ*) to graduate; **~ de** to qualify as; to graduate in; *V* **abogado**; **~ de doctor** to take one's doctorate, receive one's doctor's degree; **~ de médico** to graduate in medicine (*o* as a doctor).
recibo *nm* (**a**) = **recibimiento** (**a**) *y* (**b**); **estar de ~** (*vestido etc*) to be ready for collection; (*persona*) to be dressed, be ready to receive (visitors); **no es de ~** it is not acceptable, it is intolerable (*que* that).
(**b**) (*Com*) receipt; (*factura*) bill, account; **de la luz** electricity bill; **acusar ~** to acknowledge receipt (*de* of).
reciclado 1 *adj* recycled. **2** *nm* recycling; retraining.
reciclaje *nm*, **reciclamiento** *nm* (*V vt*) recycling; retraining; modification, adjustment.
reciclar [1a] **1** *vt* (*Téc*) to recycle; *persona* to retrain; *plan* to modify, adjust. **2 reciclarse** *vr* (*fig*) to retrain; to go on a refresher course; (*rejuvenecerse*) to rejuvenate oneself.
recidiva *nf* (*Med*) relapse.
reciedumbre *nf* strength, toughness; solidity; severity, harshness; loudness.
recién *adv* (**a**) newly, recently (+ *ptp*).
(**b**) (*LAm*) just, only just; **~ se acordó** (*apenas*) she only just remembered; **~ me lo acaban de decir** they've only just told me; **~ ahora** right now, this very moment; **~ aquí** right here, just here; **~ llego** I've (only) just arrived; **~ llegó** he has (only) just arrived, he arrived not long ago.
recién casado *adj* newly-wed; **los ~s** the newly-weds.
recién hecho *adj* newly-made.
recién llegado 1 *adj* newly arrived. **2** *nm*, **recién llegada** *nf* newcomer, new person; (*en fiesta etc*) latecomer.
recién nacido 1 *adj* newborn. **2** *nm*, **recién nacida** *nf* newborn child.
recién puesto *adj huevo* new-laid.
reciente *adj* recent; *pan etc* new, fresh, newly-made.
recientemente *adv* recently.
Recife *nm* Recife; (††) Pernambuco.
recinto *nm* (*cercado*) enclosure; (*zona*) precincts; (*lugar*) area, spot, place; **~ amurallado** walled enclosure; **~ ferial** trades fair pavilion; **~ fortificado** fortified place; strongpoint; **dentro del ~ universitario** on the university campus.
recio 1 *adj* (**a**) (*fuerte*) *cuerda etc* thick, strong; *persona* strong, tough, robust; *tierra* solid; *prueba etc* tough, demanding, severe.
(**b**) *voz* loud.
(**c**) *tiempo* harsh, severe.
(**d**) (*veloz*) swift, fast, quick.
(**e**) **en lo más ~ del combate** in the thick of the fight; **en lo más ~ del invierno** in the depths of winter.
2 *adv golpear* hard; *soplar* hard, strongly; *pasar etc* swiftly; *cantar, gritar* loud, loudly.
recipiendario, -a *nm/f* newly-elected member.
recipiente *nm* (**a**) (*persona*) recipient. (**b**) (*vaso etc*) recipient, container, vessel.
recíproca *nf* (*Mat*) reciprocal.
reciprocación *nf* reciprocation.
recíprocamente *adv* reciprocally, mutually.
reciprocar [1g] *vt* to reciprocate.
reciprocidad *nf* reciprocity; mutual character; **usar de ~** to reciprocate.
recíproco *adj* (**a**) (*mutuo*) reciprocal, mutual. (**b**) (*inverso*) inverse. (**c**) **a la recíproca** vice versa; **estar a la recíproca** to be ready to respond.
recitación *nf* recitation.
recitado *nm* recitation; (*Mús*) recitative.
recital *nm* (*Mús*) recital; (*Liter*) reading; **~ de poesías** poetry reading.
recitar [1a] *vt* to recite.
recitativo *nm* recitative.
reclamable *adj* reclaimable.
reclamación *nf* (**a**) (*gen*) reclamation. (**b**) (*reivindicación*) claim, demand; **~ salarial** wage claim. (**c**) (*objeción*) objection; (*queja*) complaint, protest; **formular una ~** to make (*o* lodge) a complaint.
reclamar [1a] **1** *vt* (**a**) (*exigir*) to claim, demand (*de* from); **~ algo para sí** to claim sth for o.s.; **~ su porción de la herencia** to claim one's share of the estate; **esto reclama toda nuestra atención** this demands our full attention.
(**b**) **~ a uno ante los tribunales** (*Jur*) to take sb to court, file a suit against sb.
2 *vi* to protest (*contra* against), complain (*contra* about); **~ contra una sentencia** (*Jur*) to appeal against a sentence.
3 reclamarse *vr* to proclaim o.s., declare o.s.; **~ de** to claim to be, describe o.s. as.
reclame *nm y f* (*LAm*) advertisement; **mercadería de ~** loss leader.
reclamo *nm* (**a**) (*Orn*) call, bird call; (*Caza*) decoy, lure.
(**b**) (*a persona*) call; **acudir al ~** to answer the call.
(**c**) (*Tip*) catchword.
(**d**) (*fig*: *aliciente*) inducement, lure, attraction; (*Com*) (*anuncio*) advertisement; (*slogan*) advertising slogan; (*editorial*) publisher's blurb.
(**e**) (*Jur*) claim.
(**f**) (*afirmación*) claim, statement.
(**g**) (*LAm*: *protesta*) complaint, protest.
reclinable *adj*: **asiento ~** reclining seat.
reclinar [1a] **1** *vt* to lean, recline (*contra* against, *sobre* on). **2 reclinarse** *vr* to lean; to recline, lean back.
reclinatorio *nm* (*Ecl*) prie-dieu.
recluir [3g] **1** *vt* to shut away; to confine; (*Jur*) to imprison. **2 recluirse** *vr* to shut o.s. away.
reclusión *nf* (**a**) (*acto*) seclusion; (*Jur*) imprisonment, confinement; **~ mayor** imprisonment in conditions of maximum security; **~ perpetua** life imprisonment. (**b**) (*cárcel*) place of imprisonment, prison.
recluso 1 *adj* imprisoned; **población reclusa** prison population. **2** *nm*, **reclusa** *nf* (**a**) *solitario* recluse. (**b**) (*Jur*) prisoner; **~ de confianza** trusty; **~ preventivo** prisoner on remand.
recluta 1 *nf* (*acto*) recruitment. **2** *nmf* (*persona*) recruit.
reclutamiento *nm* recruitment; conscription.
reclutar [1a] *vt* (**a**) (*Mil*) to recruit (*t fig*). (**b**) (*Cono Sur*) *ganado* to round up; *obrero* to contract, hire.
recobrar [1a] **1** *vt* to recover, get back, retrieve; *ciudad, fugitivo etc* to recapture; *amistad etc* to win back; *tiempo* to make up (for).
2 recobrarse *vr* (**a**) (*Med*) to recover, convalesce, get better; (*volver en sí*) to come to, regain consciousness.
(**b**) (*fig*) to collect o.s.
recobro *nm* recovery, retrieval; recapture.
recocer [2b *y* 2h] **1** *vt* (**a**) (*Culin*: *calentar*) to cook again, warm up; (*cocer demasiado*) to overcook.
(**b**) (*Metal*) to anneal.
(**c**) (*Cono Sur*: *cocer*) to cook.
2 recocerse *vr* (*) to be eaten up inside, suffer a lot.
recocina *nf* scullery.
recochinearse* [1a] *vr*: **~ de uno** (*Esp*) to take the mickey out of sb*.
recodar [1a] *vi* to twist, turn; to form a bend.
recodo *nm* turn, bend; elbow; loop.
recogedor *nm* (**a**) (*Agr*: *persona*) picker, harvester; gleaner; **~ de basura** dustman. (**b**) (*herramienta*) rake, scraper; (*recipiente*) pan.
recogepelotas *nmf invar* ballboy, ballgirl.
recoger [2c] **1** *vt* (**a**) *objeto caído* to pick up; *objetos dispersos* to gather (up), gather together; (*Dep*) *pelota* to gather, stop, field; *detalle, información etc* to pick up, come across; *cuentos, romances etc* to collect; *basura etc* to

collect, pick up, take; **el informe recoge que** ... the report says that ...

(**b**) *dinero etc* to collect, get together; *sellos etc* to collect.

(**c**) *periódico etc* to take up, call in, seize; **las autoridades recogieron todos los ejemplares** the authorities took up all the copies; **van a ~ las monedas antiguas** they are going to call in the old coins.

(**d**) (*Agr*) *cosecha* to harvest, get in; *fruta* to pick; (*fig*) to harvest, reap; to get as one's reward; **no recogió más que censuras** all he got was criticisms; **de todo esto van a ~ muy poco** they won't get much back out of all this.

(**e**) *agua etc* to absorb, take up; *polvo* to gather; (*en recipiente*) to collect.

(**f**) *cuerda, velas* to take in; *alas* to fold; *cuernos etc* to draw in; *falda* to roll up, lift, gather up; *mangas* to roll up; (*Cos*) to take in, reduce, shorten.

(**g**) *ropa lavada* to take in, get in; *aparato, platos etc* to put away.

(**h**) (*ir a buscar*) *persona* to get, fetch, come for; (*en coche*) to pick up; **te vendremos a ~ a las 8** we'll come for you at 8 o'clock; **me recogieron en la estación** they picked me up at the station.

(**i**) *necesitado* to take in, shelter.

2 recogerse *vr* (*retirarse*) to withdraw, retire; (*ir a casa*) to go home; (*acostarse*) to go to bed; (*refugiarse*) to take shelter; (*ir aparte*) to go off alone (to meditate *etc*).

recogida *nf* (**a**) (*retiro*) withdrawal, retirement.

(**b**) (*Agr*) harvest; (*de basura, correo etc*) collection; **~ de basuras** rubbish collection; **~ de datos** (*Inform*) data collection; **~ de equipajes** (*Aer*) baggage reclaim; **hay 6 ~s diarias** there are 6 collections daily.

(**c**) (*Méx Agr*) round-up; (*Cono Sur: de policía*) sweep, raid.

recogido 1 *adj* (**a**) *vida* quiet; *escenario, lugar* secluded; *carácter* modest, retiring, (*pey*) shy, inhibited; **ella vive muy recogida** she lives very quietly.

(**b**) (*pequeño*) small; (*apretado*) bunched up, tight.

2 *nm* tuck, gathering.

recogimiento *nm* (**a**) (*Agr etc: acto*) harvesting, picking; collection; gathering.

(**b**) (*acto: retiro*) withdrawal, retirement; (*Fin*) retrenchment.

(**c**) (*estado*) absorption, concentration; seclusion; quietness.

(**d**) (*Ecl*) recollection.

(**e**) (*Ecl: cualidad*) devotion, devoutness.

recolección *nf* (**a**) (*Agr etc*) harvesting, picking; collection; gathering.

(**b**) (*época*) harvest time, picking season.

(**c**) (*Liter*) compilation; summary.

(**d**) (*Ecl*) retreat.

(**e**) **~ de basura** (*esp LAm*) rubbish collection.

recolectar [1a] *vt* = **recoger** (**d**).

recolector(a) *nm/f* (*Agr*) picker; (*liter etc*) collector.

recoleto *adj persona* quiet, retiring; *calle* peaceful, quiet; (*aislado*) isolated.

recolocación *nf* relocation.

recolocar [1g] *vt* to relocate.

recomendable *adj* recommendable; laudable; advisable; **poco ~** inadvisable.

recomendación *nf* (**a**) (*indicación*) recommendation; (*sugerencia*) suggestion.

(**b**) (*elogio*) praise.

(**c**) (*escrito*) reference, testimonial; **carta de ~** letter of introduction (*para* to); **tiene muchas recomendaciones** he is strongly recommended to us, (*fig*) there's a lot to be said for him.

(**d**) (*Ecl*) **~ del alma** prayers for the dying.

recomendado *adj* (*LAm Correos*) registered.

recomendar [1j] *vt* (**a**) (*indicar*) to recommend; (*sugerir*) to suggest; (*aconsejar*) to advise; **~ a uno que haga algo** to recommend sb to do sth, advise sb to do sth; **se lo recomiendo** I recommend it to you.

(**b**) (*confiar*) to entrust, confide (*a* to).

(**c**) (*elogiar*) to praise, commend.

(**d**) (*LAm Correos*) to register.

recomendatorio *adj* recommendatory; **carta recomendatoria** letter of introduction (*para* to).

recomenzar [1f *y* 1j] *vti* to begin again, recommence.

recomerse [2a] *vr* to bear a secret grudge, harbour resentment.

recompensa *nf* recompense, reward; compensation (*de una pérdida* for a loss); **en ~ de** in return for, as a reward for.

recompensar [1a] *vt* to reward, recompense (*por* for); to compensate (*algo* for sth).

recomponer [2q] **1** *vt* (**a**) (*Téc*) to mend, repair; (*Tip*) to reset. (**b**) *persona** to dress up, doll up*. **2 recomponerse*** *vr* to dress up, doll o.s. up*.

recompra *nf* repurchase, buying back.

recomprar [1a] *vt* to repurchase, buy back.

reconcentrar [1a] **1** *vt* (**a**) *atención etc* to concentrate (*en* on), devote (*en* to).

(**b**) *personas etc* to bring together.

(**c**) *solución* to make more concentrated; to reduce the volume of, compress, increase the density of.

(**d**) *emoción* to hide.

2 reconcentrarse *vr* (**a**) to concentrate hard, become totally absorbed.

(**b**) *emoción* to harbour, conceal in one's heart.

reconciliable *adj* reconcilable.

reconciliación *nf* reconciliation.

reconciliar [1b] **1** *vt* to reconcile. **2 reconciliarse** *vr* to become (*o* be) reconciled.

reconcomerse [2a] *vr* to bear a secret grudge, harbour resentment.

reconcomio *nm* (**a**) (*rencor*) grudge, resentment. (**b**) (*deseo*) urge, longing, itch. (**c**) (*sospecha*) suspicion.

recóndito *adj* recondite; **en lo más ~ de** in the depths of; **en lo más ~ del corazón** in one's heart of hearts; **en lo más ~ de mi ser** deep inside me.

reconducir [3n] *vt* (**a**) *persona* to take back, bring back (*a* to).

(**b**) (*Jur*) to renew, extend.

reconfortante 1 *adj* comforting; cheering; heartwarming. **2** *nm* (*LAm*) tonic; pick-me-up.

reconfortar [1a] **1** *vt* (*confortar*) to comfort; (*animar*) to cheer, encourage; (*Med*) to strengthen. **2 reconfortarse** *vr*: **~ con** to fortify o.s. with.

reconocer [2d] *vt* (**a**) (*gen*) to recognize (*por* by); (*distinguir*) to identify, know, tell, distinguish (*por* by); **se le reconoce por el pelo** you can recognize him by his hair.

(**b**) (*aceptar*) to recognize (*por* as); *firma, gobierno, hijo etc* to recognize; **no le reconocieron por jefe** they did not recognize (*o* accept) him as their leader; **le reconocen por inteligente** they agree that he is intelligent; **reconoció al niño por suyo** he recognized that the child was his, he recognized the child as his.

(**c**) (*admitir*) *cualidad, deber, derecho etc* to recognize, admit, acknowledge; **~ los hechos** to face the facts; **~ que** ... to admit that ...; to realize that ...; **reconozco que no existen pruebas de ello** I realize that there is no proof of it; **hay que ~ que no es normal** one must admit that it isn't normal; **por fin reconocieron abiertamente que era falso** eventually they openly admitted that it was untrue.

(**d**) *regalo, servicio etc* to be grateful for.

(**e**) (*registrar*) *persona* to search; *equipaje etc* to search, inspect, examine; *terreno* to survey; (*Mil*) to reconnoitre, spy out; (*Med*) to examine.

reconocible *adj* recognizable.

reconocido *adj* (**a**) *jefe etc* recognized, accepted. (**b**) **quedar ~** to be grateful.

reconocimiento *nm* (**a**) recognition; identification; **~ de firma** (*Méx*) authentication of a signature; **~ óptico de caracteres** optical character recognition; **~ de la voz** speech recognition.

(**b**) recognition, admission, acknowledgement.

(**c**) gratitude; **en ~ de** in gratitude for.

(**d**) search(ing); inspection, examination; survey; (*Mil*) reconnaissance; (*Med*) examination, check-up; **~ físico** physical examination; **~ médico** medical examination; **vuelo de ~** reconnaissance flight.

reconquista *nf* reconquest; recapture; **la R~** the Reconquest (of Spain).

reconquistar [1a] *vt* (**a**) (*Mil*) *territorio* to reconquer; *ciudad, posición* to recapture (*a* from). (**b**) (*fig*) *estima etc* to recover, win back.

reconsideración *nf* reconsideration.

reconsiderar [1a] *vt* to reconsider.

reconstitución *nf* reconstitution, reforming; reconstruction.

reconstituir [3g] *vt* to reconstitute, reform; *crimen, escena* to reconstruct.

reconstituyente *nm* tonic, restorative, pick-me-up.

reconstrucción *nf* reconstruction; reshuffle.

reconstruir [3g] *vt* (*gen*) to reconstruct; *gobierno* to reshuffle.

recontar [1l] *vt* (**a**) *cantidad* to recount, count again; to count up carefully. (**b**) *cuento* to retell, tell again.
recontra* (**a**) (*LAm*: *prefijo intensivo*) extremely, terribly; *p.ej.* **recontracaro** terribly dear, **recontrabueno** really good; **estoy ~cansado** I'm terribly tired. (**b**) **¡~!** *interj* (*euf*) well I'm ...!*
reconvención *nf* (**a**) *reproches* reprimand; expostulation, remonstrance. (**b**) (*Jur*) counterclaim.
reconvenir [3r] *vt* (**a**) (*reprender*) to reprimand; (*tratar de convencer a*) to expostulate with, remonstrate with. (**b**) (*Jur*) to counterclaim.
reconversión *nf* reconversion; restructuring, reorganization; streamlining; **~ industrial** (*euf*) industrial rationalization; **~ profesional** industrial retraining.
reconvertir [3i] *vt* to reconvert (*en* to); to restructure, reorganize; to streamline; (*euf*) *industria* to rationalize; **~ profesionalmente** to retrain for industry, give industrial retraining to.
recopa *nf* cup-winners' cup.
recopilación *nf* summary; compilation; (*Jur*) code; **la R~** *Spanish law code of 1567*; **la Nueva R~** *Spanish law code of 1775*; **~ de datos** (*Inform*) data collection.
recopilador(a) *nm/f* compiler.
recopilar [1a] *vt* (**a**) (*reunir*) to compile, gather, collect (together); (*resumir*) to summarize. (**b**) *leyes* to codify.
record, récord [re'kor, 'rekor] **1** *adj invar* record; **cifras ~** record quantities; **en un tiempo ~** in a record time.
2 *nm, pl* **records, récords** [re'kor, 'rekor] record; **batir** (*o* **establecer**) **el ~** to break the record.
recordable *adj* memorable.
recordación *nf* recollection; remembrance; **de feliz ~** of happy memory; **de infeliz** (*o* **triste**) **~** of unhappy memory; **digno de ~** memorable.
recordar¹ [1l] **1** *vt* (**a**) (*acordarse de*) to remember; to recollect, recall; **no lo recuerdo** I don't remember it; **recuerda haberlo dicho** he remembers saying it.
(**b**) (*traer a la memoria*) to recall; to call up, evoke (memories of), bring to mind; **esto recuerda aquella escena de la película** this recalls that scene in the film; **la frase recuerda a Garcilaso** the phrase is reminiscent of Garcilaso, the phrase has echoes of Garcilaso.
(**c**) (*acordar a otro*) to remind; **~ algo a uno** to remind sb of sth; **~ a uno que haga algo** to remind sb to do sth; **recuérdale que me debe 5 dólares** remind him that he owes me 5 dollars.
(**d**) (*Cono Sur, Méx**: *despertar*) to awaken, wake up.
2 *vi* to remember; **no recuerdo** I don't remember; **que yo recuerde** as far as I can remember; **creo ~, si mal no recuerdo** if my memory serves me right; *V* **desde.**
3 recordarse *vr* (**a**) **~ que** ... to remind o.s. that ...
(**b**) (*Cono Sur, Méx**: *despertar*) to wake up.
(**c**) (*And, Carib, Cono Sur*: *volver en sí*) to come to, come round.
recordar² [1l] *vt* (*CAm, Carib, Méx*) *voz etc* to record.
recordativo *adj* reminiscent; **carta recordativa** reminder.
recordatorio *nm* (**a**) (*gen*) reminder; *recuerdo* memento. (**b**) (*tarjeta*) in memoriam card. (**c**) **esto te servirá de ~** let this be a lesson to you.
recordman *nm, pl* **recordmans** (*titular*) record-holder; (*campeón*) champion; (*jugador destacado*) outstanding player (*etc*).
recorrer [2a] *vt* (**a**) (*pasar por*) *lugar, zona* to go over, go across, go through, traverse; *país* to cross, tour, travel; (*buscadores*) to cover, range, scour; *distancia* to travel, cover, do; (*Mec*) to travel (along); **~ una provincia a pie** to go over a province on foot, have a walking tour through a province; **~ un escrito** to run one's eye over a document, look through a document; **en 14 días los Jones han recorrido media Europa** the Jones have done half Europe in a fortnight.
(**b**) (*registrar*) to look over, go over, survey; to check; to search.
(**c**) (*Mec etc*) to repair, mend; to overhaul.
(**d**) *sillas etc* to move along, put closer together; (*Tip*) *letras* to take over.
recorrido *nm* (**a**) (*viaje*) run, journey; (*ruta*) route, course, path; (*distancia*) distance covered, distance travelled; (*de golf, saltos; de repartidor etc*) round; (*de émbolo etc*) stroke; **el ~ del primer día fue de 450 km** the first day's run was 450 kms; **un ~ en 5 bajo par** a round in 5 under par; **tren de largo ~** long-distance train; **~ de aterrizaje** (*Aer*) landing run; **~ electoral** (*Pol*) campaign trail.
(**b**) (*Mec etc*) repair; overhaul.
(**c**) (*) detailed reprimand.
recortable *nm* cut-out.
recortada *nf* sawn-off shotgun.
recortado 1 *adj* (**a**) *borde* jagged; uneven, irregular. (**b**) (*CAm, Carib*: *chaparro*) short and stocky. (**c**) (*CAm, Carib**: *necesitado*) broke*. **2** *nm* (*And, Carib, Cono Sur*) sawn-off rifle, pistol.
recortar [1a] **1** *vt* (**a**) *exceso* to cut away, cut off, cut back, trim; *pelo* to trim; *grabado, recorte etc* to cut out; *escopeta* to saw off.
(**b**) (*Arte*) to draw in outline.
(**c**) (*fig*) to cut out, remove, suppress; *plantilla* to cut, cut back; *víveres etc* to cut down.
2 recortarse *vr* to stand out, be outlined, be silhouetted (*en, sobre* against).
recorte *nm* (**a**) (*acto*) cutting, trimming; (*de pelo*) trim; (*para economizar*) cutback (*de* in).
(**b**) (*de juguete*) cut-out.
(**c**) **~s** trimmings, clippings; **~s de periódico, ~s de prensa** newspaper cuttings, press clippings; **álbum de ~s** scrapbook; **el libro está hecho de ~s** the book is a scissors-and-paste job.
(**d**) (*CAm**: *comentario*) nasty remark.
recoser [2a] *vt* to patch up, darn.
recosido *nm* patch, darn.
recostable *adj*: **asiento ~** reclining seat.
recostado *adj* reclining, recumbent; **estar ~** to be lying down.
recostar [1l] **1** *vt* to lean (*en* on). **2 recostarse** *vr* (**a**) (*reclinar*) to recline, lie back; to lie down. (**b**) (*fig*) to have a short rest.
recotín* *adj* (*Cono Sur*) restless.
recova *nf* (**a**) (*negocio*) poultry business, dealing in poultry; (*mercado*) poultry market.
(**b**) (*And, Cono Sur*: *mercado*) food market; (*And*: *carnicería*) butcher's (shop).
(**c**) (*Cono Sur Arquit*) arcade, covered corridor (*along the front of a house*); porch.
recoveco *nm* (**a**) (*de calle etc*) turn, bend.
(**b**) (*en casa*) nook, odd corner; cubbyhole.
(**c**) (*fig*: *complejidades*) **~s** ins and outs; **el asunto tiene muchos ~s** it's a very complicated matter, the affair has lots of pitfalls.
(**d**) (*fig*: *subterfugios*) **~s** subterfuges, devious ways; **sin ~s** plainly, frankly.
recovero, -a *nm/f* poultry dealer.
recreación *nf* (**a**) recreation. (**b**) = **recreo.**
recrear [1a] **1** *vt* (**a**) (*crear de nuevo*) to recreate.
(**b**) (*divertir*) to amuse, divert, entertain.
2 recrearse *vr* to enjoy o.s.; to amuse o.s., entertain o.s. (*con* with); **~ viendo los infortunios de otros** to take pleasure in (*o* gloat over) others' misfortunes.
recreativo 1 *adj* recreative; recreational; **instalaciones recreativas** recreational facilities.
2 *nm* games arcade.
recrecer [2d] **1** *vt* to increase. **2** *vi* (**a**) (*crecer*) to increase, grow. (**b**) (*volver a ocurrir*) to happen again. **3 recrecerse** *vr* to cheer up, recover one's spirits.
recreo *nm* (**a**) (*gen*) recreation, relaxation; (*diversión*) amusement. (**b**) (*Escuela*) break, playtime, recreation.
recriminación *nf* (**a**) (*gen*) recrimination; **~ mutua** mutual recrimination. (**b**) (*Jur*) countercharge.
recriminar [1a] **1** *vt* (**a**) (*reprochar*) to reproach. (**b**) (*Jur*) to countercharge. **2** *vi* to recriminate. **3 recriminarse** *vr* to reproach each other, indulge in mutual recrimination.
recrudecer [2d] *vi y* **recrudecerse** *vr* to recrudesce, break out again; to worsen.
recrudecimiento *nm*, **recrudescencia** *nf* recrudescence, new outbreak, upsurge.
recrudescente *adj* recrudescent.
recta *nf* straight line; **la ~** (*Dep*) the straight; **~ final, ~ de llegada** home straight; (*fig*) closing stages, final stage; final dash.
rectal *adj* rectal.
rectangular *adj* = **rectángulo 1.**
rectángulo 1 *adj* rectangular, oblong; *triángulo etc* right-angled. **2** *nm* rectangle, oblong.
rectificable *adj* rectifiable; **fácilmente ~** easily rectified, easy to put right.
rectificación *nf* rectification; correction.
rectificador(a) *nm/f* (*Mec*) rectifier.
rectificar [1g] **1** *vt* (**a**) *carretera etc* to straighten (out).
(**b**) (*Mec etc*) to rectify; to balance; *cilindro* to rectify, rebore.
(**c**) *cálculo etc* to rectify, correct; *conducta* to change,

reform.

2 *vi* to correct oneself; **'No, eran 4', rectificó** 'No', he said, correcting himself, 'there were 4'; **rectifique, por favor** please see that this is put right.

rectilíneo *adj* rectilinear.

rectitud *nf* (**a**) (*gen*) straightness. (**b**) (*fig*) rectitude, honesty, uprightness.

recto 1 *adj* (**a**) *línea etc* straight; *ángulo* right; *componente etc* upright; *curso* straight, direct, unswerving; **la flecha fue recta al blanco** the arrow went straight to the target; **siga todo ~** go straight on.

(**b**) (*fig*) *persona* honest, upright; *juez etc* fair, just, impartial; *juicio* sound; *intención* lawful, proper.

(**c**) (*fig*) *sentido* literal, proper, basic; **en el sentido ~ de la palabra** in the proper sense of the word.

(**d**) (*Ling*) *caso* nominative.

2 *nm* (*Anat*) rectum.

rector 1 *adj persona* leading; governing, managing; *idea, principio* guiding, governing; **los deberes ~es del régimen** the régime's guiding principles; **una figura ~a** an outstanding figure, a leading figure.

2 *nm*, **rectora** *nf* (**a**) head, chief, leader; principal.

(**b**) (*Univ*: *t* **~ magnífico**) rector, president (*US*), (*aprox*) vice-chancellor.

rectorado *nm* (*Univ*) (**a**) (*oficio*) rectorship, presidency (*US*), (*aprox*) vice-chancellorship. (**b**) (*oficina*) rector's office.

rectorar [1a] *vt* (*CAm*) to rule, govern, direct.

rectoría *nf* = **rectorado** (**a**) *y* (**b**).

recua *nf* mule train, train of pack animals; **una ~ de chiquillos** a bunch of kids*.

recuadro *nm* (*Tip*) inset; (*Esp*: *de formulario*) box.

recubrir [3a; *ptp* **recubierto**] *vt* to cover (*con, de* with); to coat (*con, de* with).

recuento *nm* (*acto*) count, recount; (*inventario*) inventory, survey; **~ de espermas** sperm count; **~ polínico** pollen count; **hacer el ~ de** to make a survey of, draw up an inventory of; to count up, reckon up.

recuerdo 1 *adj* (*And**) awake.

2 *nm* (**a**) (*memoria*) memory; recollection; reminiscence; **'R~s de la vida de hace 80 años'** 'Reminiscences of life 80 years ago'; **contar los ~s** to reminisce; **entrar en el ~, pasar al ~** (*euf*) to pass away; **guardar un feliz ~ de uno** to have happy memories of sb.

(**b**) (*regalo*) souvenir, memento, keepsake; **'R~ de Mallorca'** 'A souvenir from Majorca'; **toma esto como ~** take this as a keepsake.

(**c**) (*: *joya*) jewel, piece of jewellery.

(**d**) (*saludo*) **~s** regards, best wishes; **¡dale ~s míos!** give him my regards!, remember me to him!; **os manda muchos ~s para todos** he sends you all his warmest regards.

recuero *nm* muleteer.

recuesto *nm* slope.

reculada *nf* (**a**) (*lit*) backward movement; (*de fusil*) recoil. (**b**) (*Méx*) retreat; (*fig*) backing down, weakening.

recular [1a] *vi* (**a**) (*animal, vehículo*) to go back, back; (*cañón*) to recoil; (*ejercito etc*) to fall back, retreat.

(**b**) (*fig*) to back down, weaken (in one's resolve).

reculativa *nf* (*Méx*) = **reculada** (**b**).

reculón *nm* (**a**) (*LAm*) = **reculada**. (**b**) **andar a reculones** to go backwards.

recuperable *adj* recoverable, retrievable.

recuperación *nf* recovery, recuperation, retrieval; **~ de datos** data retrieval; **~ de informaciones** information retrieval; **~ de tierras** land reclamation.

recuperar [1a] **1** *vt* (**a**) (*recobrar*) to recover, recuperate, retrieve; (*Inform*) to retrieve; *pérdida* to recoup; *tiempo* to make up; *tierras* to reclaim; *fuerzas* to restore, repair.

(**b**) (*Téc*) *residuos etc* to reclaim, process for re-use.

2 recuperarse *vr* (*Med etc*) to recover, recuperate.

recuperativo *adj* recuperative.

recurrencia *nf* (**a**) (*Med*) recurrence. (**b**) (*apelación*) recourse, appeal.

recurrente 1 *adj* recurrent. **2** *nmf* (*Jur*) appellant.

recurrir [3a] **1** *vt* (*Jur*) to appeal against. **2** *vi* (**a**) **~ a** *medio etc* to resort to, have recourse to; to fall back on; *persona* to turn to, appeal to. (**b**) (*Jur*) to appeal (*a* to; *contra, de* against).

recurso *nm* (**a**) (*gen*) recourse, resort; (*medio*) means; (*expediente*) expedient; **como último ~** as a last resort.

(**b**) **~s** (*Fin etc*) resources; means; **~s ajenos** (*Fin*) borrowed capital; **~s económicos** economic resources; **~s naturales** natural resources; **~s no renovables** non-renewable resources; **la familia está sin ~s** the family has nothing to fall back on.

(**c**) (*Jur*) appeal; **interponer ~ contra** to lodge an appeal against.

recusante *adj, nmf* recusant.

recusar [1a] *vt* (**a**) (*rechazar*) to reject, refuse. (**b**) (*Jur*) to challenge.

rechace *nm* (**a**) rejection. (**b**) (*Dep*) rebound.

rechazamiento *nm* (**a**) repelling, beating off; driving back; reflection. (**b**) rejection; refusal; resistance.

rechazar [1f] *vt* (**a**) *persona* to push back, push away; *ataque* to repel, beat off; *enemigo* to throw back, drive back; *luz etc* to reflect, turn back; *agua etc* to throw off.

(**b**) *acusación, idea, moción* to reject; *oferta* to reject, refuse, turn down; *tentación* to resist; (*Med*) *corazón etc* to reject.

rechazo *nm* (*rebote*) bounce, rebound; (*de cañón*) recoil; (*Med*) rejection; (*fig*) repulse, rebuff; **de ~** on the rebound; (*bala*) as it glanced off, as it ricocheted; (*fig*) in consequence, as a result.

rechifla *nf* (**a**) (*silbido*) whistling; (*siseo*) hissing; (*abucheo*) booing; (*Teat*) catcall. (**b**) (*fig*) mockery, derision.

rechiflar [1a] **1** *vt* to whistle at, hiss, boo. **2** *vi* to whistle, hiss. **3 rechiflarse** *vr* (**a**) (*de broma*) to take things as a huge joke; **~ de** to make a fool of. (**b**) (*Cono Sur*: *enojarse*) to get cross, lose one's temper.

rechín *nm* (*And*) piece of burnt food; **huele a ~** I can smell food burning.

rechinamiento *nm* creaking, grating; squeaking; clanking, clattering; humming, whirring; grinding, gnashing.

rechinar [1a] **1** *vi* (**a**) (*gen*) to creak, grate; to squeak; (*madera, puerta etc*) to creak; (*máquina*) to clank, clatter; (*piezas sin lubricar*) to grate; (*motor*) to hum, whirr; (*dientes*) to grate, grind, gnash; **hacer ~ los dientes** to grind one's teeth, gnash one's teeth.

(**b**) (*fig*) to do (*o* accept *etc*) something with an ill grace.

(**c**) (*) (*And, Cono Sur, Méx*: *rabiar*) to rage, fume; (*Carib*: *quejarse*) to grumble; (*Carib*: *contestar*) to answer back.

2 *vt* (*CAm Culin*) to burn, overcook.

3 rechinarse *vr* (**a**) (*CAm, Méx*) to burn, overcook.

(**b**) (*Cono Sur**) to get furious, lose one's temper.

rechinido *nm*, **rechino** *nm* = **rechinamiento**.

rechonchez *nf* stockiness; plumpness.

rechoncho *adj* thickset, stocky, squat; plump.

rechupete*: **de ~ 1** *adj* splendid, jolly good*; *comida* delicious, scrumptious*.

2 *adv* splendidly, jolly well*; **me ha salido de ~** it turned out marvellously for me; **pasarlo de ~** to have a fine time.

red *nf* (**a**) (*Pesca etc*) net; (*Dep*) net; (*del pelo*) hairnet; (*malla*) mesh, meshes; (*Ferro*) rack; (*cerca*) fence; (*reja*) grille; **~ de alambre** wire mesh, wire-netting; **~ barredera** trawl; **~ metálica** metal screen; **~ de seguridad** safety net.

(**b**) (*fig*) network, system; (*Elec, cañerías etc*) mains, supply system; grid; (*de almacenes etc*) chain; **~ de área extendida** extended area network; **~ de área local** local area network; **~ de comunicaciones** communications network; **~ de conmutación de circuito** circuit switching network; **~ de distribución** distribution network; **~ de emisoras** radio network; **~ de espionaje** spy network; spy ring; **~ ferroviaria** railway network, railway system; **~ informática, ~ informativa** information network; **~ local** local network; **~ rastreadora, ~ de rastreo** tracking network; **~ de transmisión de datos** data network; **~ vascular** vascular system; **~ vial** road network; **funciona a (la) ~** it works from the mains; **con agua de la ~** with mains water, with water from the mains; **estar conectado con la ~** to be connected to the mains.

(**c**) (*fig*: *trampa*) snare, trap; **aprisionar a uno en sus ~es** to have sb firmly caught in one's toils, have sb well and truly snared; **caer en la ~** to fall into the trap; **tender una ~ para uno** to set a trap for sb.

redacción *nf* (**a**) (*acto*) writing, redaction; editing. (**b**) (*fraseología*) wording. (**c**) (*oficina*) newspaper office. (**d**) (*personas*) editorial staff. (**e**) (*Escuela*) composition; (*Univ*) essay.

redactar [1a] *vt* (**a**) (*escribir*) to write; to draft, draw up; (*expresar*) to word, express; **una carta mal redactada** a badly-worded letter. (**b**) *periódico etc* to edit.

redactor, -a *nm/f* (**a**) (*escritor*) writer, drafter. (**b**) (*director*) editor; sub-editor.

redada *nf* (**a**) (*acto*) cast, casting, throw. (**b**) (*de policía*) sweep, raid. (**c**) (*cantidad*) catch, haul (*t fig*).

redaje *nm* (*And*) (*red*) net; (*maraña*) mess, tangle.

redaño *nm* (**a**) (*Anat*) mesentery; caul. (**b**) **~s*** guts, pluck.

redargüir [3g] **1** *vt* (**a**) (*Jur*) to impugn, hold to be invalid. (**b**) **~ que** ... to argue on the other hand that ... **2** *vi* to turn an argument against its proposer.

redecilla *nf* hairnet.

rededor: **al ~** *V* **alrededor**.

redemocratización *nf* return to democracy, reestablishment of democracy.

redención *nf* redemption.

redentor 1 *adj* redeeming. **2** *nm* redeemer; **R~** Redeemer, Saviour; **meterse a ~** to intervene (with the best intentions).

redescubrir [3a; *ptp* **redescubierto**] *vt* to rediscover.

redesignar [1a] *vt* (*Inform*) to rename.

redespachar [1a] *vt* (*Cono Sur Com*) to send on, forward (directly).

redicho *adj* affected, overrefined, stilted.

redil *nm* sheepfold.

redimensionamiento *nm* remodelling; rationalization; streamlining, cutting back.

redimensionar [1a] *vt* (**a**) (*Econ etc*) to remodel; (*euf*) to rationalize, streamline, cut back.

(**b**) (*disminuir*) to play down.

redimible *adj* redeemable.

redimir [3a] *vt* to redeem (*t Fin, fig*); *cautivo* to ransom; *esclavo* to purchase the freedom of.

rediós* *interj* good God!

redistributivo *adj* redistributive; **programa ~** programme for the redistribution of wealth (*etc*).

rédito *nm* interest, yield, return.

redituable *adj* (*Cono Sur*) profitable.

redituar [1e] *vt* to yield, produce, bear.

redivivo *adj* new; revived, resuscitated.

redoba *nf* (*Méx Mús*) *wooden board hung round neck and used as a percussion instrument*.

redoblado *adj* (**a**) (*Mec*) *pieza* reinforced, extra strong; *persona* stocky, thickset. (**b**) *celo etc* redoubled. (**c**) *paso* double-quick.

redoblante *nm* (long-framed) side drum.

redoblar [1a] **1** *vt* (**a**) *papel etc* to bend back, bend over, bend down; *clavo* to clinch.

(**b**) *celo, esfuerzo etc* to redouble.

(**c**) (*Bridge*) to redouble.

2 *vi* (*Mús*) to play a roll on the drum; (*trueno*) to roll, rumble.

redoble *nm* (*Mús*) drumroll, drumbeat; (*de trueno*) roll, rumble.

redoma *nf* (**a**) (*frasco*) flask, phial. (**b**) (*Cono Sur*: *de pez*) fishbowl. (**c**) (*Carib Aut*) roundabout, traffic circle (*US*).

redomado *adj* (**a**) (*taimado*) sly, artful. (**b**) *pícaro etc* complete, utter, out-and-out.

redomón *adj* (**a**) (*Méx*) *caballo* wild, unbroken; *persona* (*inexperto*) untrained, unskilled; (*torpe*) slow, dense; (*ordinario*) crude, rough. (**b**) (*LAm*) *caballo* half-trained.

redonda *nf* (**a**) (*Mús*) semibreve.

(**b**) (*Tip*) roman, rounded characters, ordinary letters.

(**c**) **en muchas millas a la ~** for many miles round about; **se olía a un kilómetro a la ~** you could smell it a mile off.

(**d**) (‡: *droga*) pill.

redondear [1a] **1** *vt* (**a**) (*lit*) to round, round off. (**b**) (*fig*: *completar*) to round off. (**c**) *cifra* to round up (*t* **~ por arriba, ~ por defecto**), round down (*t* **~ por abajo, ~ por exceso**). (**d**) (*complementar*) to top up. **2 redondearse** *vr* (**a**) (*enriquecerse*) to acquire money, become wealthy. (**b**) (*librarse de deudas*) to get clear of debts.

redondel *nm* (**a**) (*Taur*) bullring, arena. (**b**) (*: *círculo*) ring, circle; **~ de humo** smoke-ring. (**c**) (*Aut*) roundabout, traffic circle (*US*).

redondez *nf* roundness; **en toda la ~ de la tierra** in the whole wide world.

redondilla *nf* (*Liter Hist*) quatrain.

redondo 1 *adj* (**a**) *forma* round; rounded; **3 m en ~** 3 metres round; **¿cuánto tiene de ~?** how far is it round?; **caer ~** to fall in a heap; (*dormido*) to fall asleep; (*borracho*) to pass out; **girar en ~** to turn right round; **rehusar en ~** to give a flat refusal, refuse flatly.

(**b**) *cantidad, cifra* round; **en números ~s** in round numbers, in round figures.

(**c**) *viaje* round.

(**d**) *negativa etc* straight, flat, square; *afirmación etc* blunt.

(**e**) *negocio etc* complete, finished; successful; **todo le ha salido ~** it all went well for him; **el negocio era ~** the business was really profitable; **será un negocio ~** it will be a really good deal; **triunfo ~** complete success.

(**f**) *vino* full, rounded.

(**g**) (‡) AC/DC‡, bisexual.

(**h**) (*Méx**) (*lerdo*) dense*, thick*; (*débil*) weak.

2 *nm* (**a**) (*Mús**) disc, record.

(**b**) (*Culin*) rumpsteak.

(**c**) (‡) bisexual.

redopelo *nm* (**a**) (*) scrap*, rough-and-tumble. (**b**) **a ~** = **a contrapelo**; **una lógica a ~** logic stood on its head, logic in reverse; **traer al ~ a uno** to treat sb very badly, ride roughshod over sb.

redor: **en ~** *V* **alrededor**.

redro *adv* behind; backwards.

redrojo *nm* (**a**) (*Bot*) late fruit, withered fruit.

(**b**) (*Cono Sur*: *exceso*) rest, remainder.

(**c**) (*Méx**: *harapos*) rags.

redropelo = **redopelo**.

reducción *nf* (**a**) (*gen*) reduction; (*disminución*) diminution, lessening (*de* of); cut, cutback (*de* in); **~ del activo** divestment. (**b**) (*Med*) setting. (**c**) (*LAm Hist*) settlement of Christianized Indians.

reduccionismo *nm* reductionism.

reducible *adj* reducible.

reducido *adj* (**a**) (*gen*) reduced; (*limitado*) limited; *número etc* small; *ingresos, recursos* limited, small; *espacio* confined, limited; *precio* reduced. (**b**) **quedar ~ a** to be reduced to.

reducir [3n] **1** *vt* (**a**) *cantidad, número etc* to reduce; to diminish, lessen, cut (down); *discurso etc* to cut down, abridge; *tamaño* to reduce, cut down; *actividad, intervención etc* to limit (*a* to); (*Aut*) to change down; **~ algo al absurdo** to make sth seem ridiculous.

(**b**) (*Mat etc*) to reduce (*a* to), convert (*a* into); **~ las millas a kilómetros** to convert miles into kilometres; **~ los dólares en pesetas** to change dollars into pesetas; to express dollars as pesetas; **~ una casa a escombros** to reduce a house to rubble; **todo lo reduce a cosas materiales** he reduces everything to material terms.

(**c**) *país etc* to subdue; *persona peligrosa* to overpower; *rebeldes* to overcome, bring under control; *fortaleza* to reduce; **~ a uno al silencio** to silence sb, reduce sb to silence; **~ a uno a la obediencia** to bring sb to heel.

(**d**) (*Med*) *hueso* to set.

2 reducirse *vr* (**a**) to diminish, lessen, fall, be reduced (*a* to).

(**b**) (*Fin*) to economize.

(**c**) **~ a** to come down to, amount to no more than; **el escándalo se redujo a un simple chisme** the scandal amounted to nothing more than a piece of gossip; **~ a** + *infin* to come down to + *ger*, find o.s. reduced to + *ger*.

reductible *adj* (*Cono Sur, Méx*) reducible.

reductivo *adj régimen etc* slimming.

reducto *nm* (*Mil y fig*) redoubt; **el último ~ de** the last redoubt of.

reduje *etc V* **reducir**.

redundancia *nf* redundancy, superfluity; **valga la ~** forgive the repetition.

redundante *adj* redundant, superfluous.

redundar [1a] *vi*: **~ en** to redound to; **~ en beneficio de** to be to the advantage of.

reduplicación *nf* reduplication; redoubling.

reduplicar [1g] *vt* to reduplicate; *esfuerzo etc* to redouble.

reedición *nf* reissue, reprint(ing).

reedificación *nf* rebuilding.

reedificar [1g] *vt* to rebuild.

reeditar [1a] *vt* to reissue, republish, reprint.

reeducación *nf* re-education; **~ profesional** industrial retraining.

reeducar [1g] *vt* to re-educate; **~ profesionalmente** to give industrial retraining to.

reelección *nf* re-election.

reelegible *adj* eligible for re-election.

reelegir [3c *y* 3k] *vt* to re-elect.

reembalar [1a] *vt* to repack.

reembolsable *adj* repayable; refundable, returnable; (*Fin*) **no ~** *valores* irredeemable; *depósito* non-returnable, not refundable.

reembolsar [1a] **1** *vt persona* to reimburse; to repay; *dinero* to repay, pay back; *depósito* to refund, return.

2 reembolsarse *vr* to reimburse o.s.; **~ una cantidad**

to recover a sum.
reembolso *nm* reimbursement; repayment, refund; **enviar algo contra** ~ to send sth cash on delivery (*abr*: *COD*).
reemisor *nm* booster station.
reemplazable *adj* replaceable.
reemplazante *nmf* (*Méx*) replacement, substitute.
reemplazar [1f] *vt* to replace (*con* with, *por* by).
reemplazo *nm* (**a**) replacement. (**b**) (*Mil*) reserve; annual draft of recruits; **de** ~ reserve (*atr*), from the reserve.
reemprender [2a] *vt* to resume.
reencarnación *nf* reincarnation.
reencarnar [1a] **1** *vt* to reincarnate. **2** *vi* to be reincarnated.
reencauchado *nm* (*LAm Aut*) retread, remould.
reencauchar [1a] *vt* (*LAm Aut*) to retread, remould.
reencender [1j] *vt* to light again, rekindle.
reencuadernar [1a] *vt* to rebind.
reengancharse [1a] *vr* to re-enlist, sign on again.
reentrada *nf* re-entry.
reenvasar [1a] *vt* to repack, rewrap.
reenviar [1c] *vt* (*hacer seguir*) to forward, send on; (*devolver*) to send back.
reenvío *nm* cross-reference.
reestatificación *nf* renationalization.
reestatificar [1g] *vt* to renationalize.
reestrenar [1a] *vt* (*Teat*) to revive, put on again; (*Cine*) to reissue.
reestreno *nm* (*Teat*) revival; (*Cine*) reissue.
reestructuración *nf* restructuring, reorganizing.
reestructurar [1a] *vt* to restructure, reorganize.
reevaluación *nf* reappraisal.
reevaluar [1e] *vt* to reappraise.
reexaminación *nf* re-examination.
reexaminar [1a] *vt* to re-examine.
reexpedir [3k] *vt* to forward; to redirect.
reexportar [1a] *vt* to re-export.
REF *nm* (*Esp Econ*) *abr de* **Régimen económico fiscal**.
Ref.ª *abr de* **referencia** reference, ref.
refacción *nf* (**a**) (*comida*) light refreshment, refection.
(**b**) (*LAm Arquit, Mec*) repair(s).
(**c**) (*LAm Agr*: *gastos*) running costs.
(**d**) (*Carib, Méx*) (*préstamo*) short-term loan, (*subvención*) financial assistance.
(**e**) (*Méx Mec*) **refacciones** spares, spare parts.
refaccionar [1a] *vt* (**a**) (*LAm Arquit, Mec*) to repair. (**b**) (*LAm*: *subvencionar*) to finance, subsidize.
refaccionaria *nf* (*LAm*) repair shop.
refajo *nm* (*enagua*) flannel underskirt; (*falda*) short extra skirt; (*combinación*) slip.
refalar* [1a] (*Cono Sur*) **1** *vt* (**a**) ~ **algo a uno** to take sth from (*u* off) sb.
(**b**) (*hurtar*) to steal.
2 refalarse* *vr* (**a**) ~ **los zapatos** to kick off one's shoes.
(**b**) (*huir*) to make off, beat it*; (*resbalar*) to slip.
refalón* *nm* (*Cono Sur*) slip, fall.
refaloso* *adj* (*Cono Sur*) (**a**) (*resbaladizo*) slippery. (**b**) (*tímido*) shy, timid.
refectorio *nm* refectory.
referencia *nf* (**a**) (*gen*) reference; **con** ~ **a** with reference to; **hacer** ~ **a** to refer to, allude to; ~ **cruzada** cross-reference; ~ **multiple** general cross-reference.
(**b**) (*informe*) account, report; ~ **bancaria** banker's reference; **una** ~ **completa del suceso** a complete account of what took place.
referenciar [1b] *vt* to index.
referendo *nm* referendum.
referéndum *nm, pl* **referéndums** referendum.
referente *adj*: ~ **a** relating to, about, concerning.
referí *nmf* (*LAm*) referee, umpire.
referible *adj*: ~ **a** referable to.
referido *adj* (**a**) above-mentioned. (**b**) **discurso** ~ reported speech.
referir [3i] **1** *vt* (**a**) (*contar*) to recount, report; to tell; ~ **que ...** to say that ..., tell how ..., relate how ...
(**b**) ~ **al lector a un apéndice** to refer the reader to an appendix.
(**c**) (*relacionar*) to refer, apply, relate; **todo lo refiere a su teoría favorita** he refers (*o* relates) everything to his favourite theory; **han referido el cuadro al siglo XVII** they have referred the picture to the 17th century.
(**d**) ~ **a** (*Fin*) to convert into, express in terms of.
(**e**) (*CAm*: *insultar*) to abuse, insult.
(**f**) ~ **algo a uno en cara** (*Méx*) to throw sth in sb's face.
2 referirse *vr*: ~ **a** to refer to; **me refiero a lo de anoche** I refer to what happened last night; **por lo que se refiere a eso** as for that, as regards that.
refilón: **de** ~ *adv* obliquely, slantingly, aslant; **el sol da de** ~ the sun strikes obliquely, the sun comes slanting in; **mirar a uno de** ~ to take a sideways glance at; to take a quick look at.
refinación *nf* refining.
refinado *adj* refined, distinguished.
refinador *nm* refiner.
refinadura *nf* refining.
refinamiento *nm* refinement; **con todos los ~s modernos** with all the modern refinements; ~ **por pasos** (*Inform*) stepwise refinement.
refinanciar [1b] *vt* to refinance.
refinar [1a] *vt* (**a**) (*Téc*) to refine. (**b**) (*fig*) *sistema etc* to refine, perfect; *estilo etc* to polish.
refinería *nf* refinery.
refino 1 *adj* extra fine, pure, refined. **2** *nm* refining.
refirmar [1a] *vt* (*LAm*) to reaffirm.
refistolería *nf* (*V adj*) (**a**) (*CAm*) scheming nature; scheming, troublemaking.
(**b**) (*Méx*: *presunción*) vanity.
(**c**) (*Carib**) boot-licking*; oiliness.
refistolero *adj* (**a**) (*CAm*) (*mañoso*) intriguing, scheming; (*dañoso*) mischievous. (**b**) (*Carib*: *pedante*) pedantic. (**c**) (*Carib**: *zalamero*) greasy, oily.
reflación *nf* reflation.
reflacionar [1a] *vt* to reflate.
reflector *nm* (**a**) (*gen*) reflector. (**b**) (*Elec*) spotlight; (*Aer, Mil*) searchlight.
reflejar [1a] **1** *vt* (**a**) (*lit*) to reflect. (**b**) (*fig*) to reflect, mirror, show, reveal. **2 reflejarse** *vr* to be reflected (*t fig*).
reflejo 1 *adj* (**a**) *luz* reflected.
(**b**) *movimiento* reflex.
(**c**) (*Ling*) *verbo* reflexive.
2 *nm* (**a**) (*imagen*) reflection; **mirar su** ~ **en el agua** to look at one's reflection in the water.
(**b**) (*fig*) reflection.
(**c**) (*Anat etc*) reflex; (*condicionado*) reflex action; **perder ~s** (*fig*) to lose one's touch.
(**d**) **~s** gleam, glint; (*en el pelo*) highlight; streaks; **tiene ~s metálicos** it has a metallic glint.
(**e**) (*tratamiento del pelo*) rinse; streak; **darse un** ~ **azul** to give one's hair a blue rinse.
reflexión *nf* (**a**) (*Fís*) reflection. (**b**) (*fig*) reflection; thought; meditation; **con** ~ on reflection; **sin** ~ without thinking; **mis reflexiones sobre el problema** my reflections on the problem; **hacer reflexiones** to meditate, philosophize.
reflexionar [1a] **1** *vt* to reflect on, think about, think over.
2 *vi* to reflect (*en, sobre* on); (*antes de obrar*) to think, pause, reflect; **¡reflexione!** you think it over!, think for a moment!
reflexivamente *adv* (**a**) (*Ling*) reflexively. (**b**) *obrar* thoughtfully, reflectively.
reflexivo *adj* (**a**) (*Ling*) reflexive. (**b**) *persona etc* thoughtful, reflective. (**c**) *acto* considered.
reflotar [1a] *vt* to refloat; (*fig*) to relaunch, re-establish.
refluir [3g] *vi* to flow back.
reflujo *nm* ebb, ebb tide.
refocilación *nf*, **refocilamiento** *nm* huge enjoyment, great pleasure; (*pey*) unhealthy pleasure, cruel pleasure; coarse merriment.
refocilar [1a] **1** *vt* (*encantar*) to give great pleasure to; (*divertir*) to amuse hugely, amuse in a coarse way; (*alegrar*) to cheer up.
2 *vi* (*Cono Sur**: *relámpago*) to flash.
3 refocilarse *vr* (**a**) (*divertirse*) to enjoy o.s. hugely; (*pey*) to enjoy o.s. in a coarse way; ~ **con algo** to enjoy sth hugely, have a fine time with sth; ~ **viendo lo que sufre otro** to gloat over sb else's sufferings.
(**b**) (*alegrarse*) to cheer up no end.
refocilo *nm* (**a**) = **refocilación**. (**b**) (*Cono Sur**: *rayo*) lightning, flash of lightning.
reforma *nf* (**a**) reform; reformation; improvement; **R~** (*Ecl*) Reformation; **la R~** (*Méx Pol*) *19th century reform movement*; ~ **agraria** land reform.
(**b**) (*Arquit etc*) **~s** alterations, repairs, improvements; **'cerrado por ~s'** 'closed for repairs'.
reformación *nf* reform, reformation.
reformado *adj* reformed.

reformador(a) *nm/f* reformer.

reformar [1a] **1** *vt* (**a**) (*gen*) to reform; (*modificar*) to change, alter; (*mejorar*) to improve; (*reorganizar*) to reorganize; *abuso etc* to correct, put right; *texto* to revise.

(**b**) (*formar de otro modo*) to re-form.

(**c**) (*Arquit etc*) to alter, repair; to improve; to redecorate; (*Mec*) to mend, repair; (*Cos*) to alter.

2 reformarse *vr* to reform, mend one's ways.

reformatear [1a] *vt* (*Inform*) to reformat.

reformatorio *nm* reformatory; ~ **de menores** remand home.

reformismo *nm* reforming policy, reforming attitude.

reformista 1 *adj* reforming. **2** *nmf* reformist, reformer.

reforzador *nm* (*Elec*) booster; (*Fot*) intensifier.

reforzamiento *nm* reinforcement, strengthening.

reforzar [1f *y* 1l] *vt* (**a**) (*Arquit etc*) to reinforce, strengthen; (*Mil*) to reinforce; (*Elec etc*) to boost, raise, step up; *dosis* to increase; (*Fot*) to bring up, intensify.

(**b**) (*fig*) *resistencia etc* to strengthen, buttress, bolster up; *persona* to encourage.

refracción *nf* refraction.

refractar [1a] *vt* to refract.

refractario *adj* (**a**) (*Téc*) fireproof, heat-resistant; (*Culin*) ovenproof.

(**b**) (*fig*) refractory, recalcitrant; stubborn; **ser ~ a una reforma** to resist a reform, be opposed to a reform; **ser ~ a las lenguas** to be hopeless where languages are concerned.

refractivo *adj* refractive.

refractor *nm* refractor.

refrán *nm* proverb, saying; **como dice el** ~ as the saying goes.

refranero *nm* collection of proverbs.

refraniento *adj* (*Cono Sur*) much given to quoting proverbs.

refregar [1h *y* 1j] *vt* (**a**) (*frotar*) to rub (hard), brush (repeatedly); to scrub.

(**b**) (*fig*) ~ **algo a uno** to rub sth in; to harp on about sth to sb.

refregón *nm* (**a**) (*acto*) rub(bing), brush(ing); scrub(bing). (**b**) (*señal*) mark left by rubbing (*etc*).

refrenar [1a] *vt* (**a**) *caballo* to rein back, rein in; to hold back. (**b**) (*fig*) to curb, restrain, hold in check.

refrendar [1a] *vt* (**a**) (*firmar*) to endorse, countersign; (*autenticar*) to authenticate; (*aprobar*) to give one's approval to; *pasaporte* to stamp. (**b**) (*: *repetir*) to do again, repeat; *comida* to order more of, have a second helping of. (**c**) (*Méx*) to redeem (from pawn).

refrendo *nm* endorsement; counter-signature; authentication; approval.

refrescante *adj* refreshing, cooling.

refrescar [1g] **1** *vt* (**a**) (*gen*) to refresh; (*enfriar*) to cool (down).

(**b**) *memoria* to refresh; *conocimientos* to brush up, polish up.

(**c**) *acto* to repeat; *enemistad etc* to renew.

2 *vi* (**a**) (*Met*) to get cooler, cool down.

(**b**) (*persona*) to refresh o.s.; (*salir*) to take the air, go out for a walk.

(**c**) (*beber*) to take some refreshment, have a drink.

(**d**) (*Méx Med*) to get better.

3 refrescarse *vr* (**a**) = *vi* (*esp* **b**).

(**b**) (*And, esp Colombia*) to have tea.

refresco *nm* cool drink, soft drink, non-alcoholic drink; **~s** refreshments; **'R~s'** 'Refreshments'.

refresquería *nf* (*LAm*) refreshment stall.

refri* *nm* (*Méx*) fridge*, refrigerator.

refriega *nf* scuffle, set-to*; affray, brawl.

refrigeración *nf* refrigeration; (*Mec*) cooling; air conditioning; ~ **por agua** water-cooling; ~ **por aire** air-cooling.

refrigerado *adj* cooled; *cinema, room etc* air-conditioned; ~ **por agua** water-cooled; ~ **por aire** air-cooled.

refrigerador *nm* refrigerator; cooling unit, cooling system.

refrigeradora *nf* (*LAm*) refrigerator.

refrigerante 1 *adj* cooling, refrigerating. **2** *nm* (*Quím*) refrigerant, coolant.

refrigerar [1a] *vt* to cool, refresh; (*Téc*) to refrigerate; (*Mec*) to cool; *sala* to air-condition.

refrigerio *nm* (**a**) (*piscolabis*) snack; (*bebida*) cooling drink. (**b**) (*fig*) relief.

refrior *nm* chill (in the air).

refrito 1 *adj* (**a**) (*Culin*) refried; over-fried. (**b**) (*fig*) revised, rehashed. **2** *nm* rehash, revised version.

refucilar [1a] *vi* (*And, Cono Sur*) = **refocilar 2.**

refucilo *nm* (*Cono Sur*) = **refocilo** (**b**).

refuerzo *nm* (**a**) (*acto*) strengthening; reinforcement. (**b**) (*Téc*) brace, support. (**c**) **~s** (*Mil*) reinforcements. (**d**) (*fig: ayuda*) aid.

refugiado, -a *adj, nm/f* refugee.

refugiarse [1b] *vr* to take refuge; to shelter (*en* in); to go into hiding; ~ **en un país vecino** to flee to a neighbouring country, seek asylum in a neighbouring country.

refugio *nm* (**a**) (*gen*) refuge, shelter; asylum; (*Ecl*) sanctuary; (*fig*) refuge, haven; **acogerse a un** ~ to take refuge, shelter (*en* in); to seek sanctuary.

(**b**) (*edificio*) refuge, shelter; (*Esp Aut*) street island; ~ **alpino,** ~ **de montaña** mountain hut; ~ **antiaéreo** air-raid shelter; ~ **antiatómico,** ~ **antinuclear** fallout shelter; ~ **de caza** hunting lodge; ~ **subterráneo** underground shelter; dugout.

refulgencia *nf* brilliance, refulgence.

refulgente *adj* brilliant, refulgent.

refulgir [3c] *vi* to shine (brightly).

refundición *nf* (**a**) (*acto*) revision, recasting. (**b**) (*texto etc*) new version, adaptation; revision.

refundidor(a) *nm/f* reviser, adapter.

refundir [3a] **1** *vt* (**a**) (*Téc*) to recast.

(**b**) (*Liter etc*) to adapt; to revise, rewrite; to remodel.

(**c**) (*And, CAm, Méx: perder*) to lose, mislay.

(**d**) (*Cono Sur: arruinar*) to ruin, crush; (‡) *candidato* to plough‡.

(**e**) (*CAm: guardar*) to keep carefully.

2 refundirse *vr* (*And, CAm, Méx*) to get lost, be mislaid.

refunfuñar [1a] *vi* (*gruñir*) to growl, grunt; (*quejarse*) to grumble.

refunfuño *nm* growl, grunt; grumble.

refunfuñón* 1 *adj* growling, grunting; grumbling, grouchy*. **2** *nm*, **refunfuñona** *nf* grumbler, groucher*.

refutable *adj* refutable; **fácilmente** ~ easily refuted.

refutación *nf* refutation.

refutar [1a] *vt* to refute.

regadera *nf* (**a**) (*gen*) sprinkler; (*Hort*) watering-can. (**b**) (*Méx*) shower. (**c**) (*Esp**) **estar como una ~, ser una ~*** to be crazy, be as mad as a hatter.

regadío *nm* (*t* **tierra de** ~) irrigated land, irrigation land; **cultivo de** ~ crop that grows on irrigated land, crop that needs irrigation.

regadizo *adj* irrigable.

regador *nm* (*Cono Sur*) watering can.

regadura *nf* sprinkling, watering; (*Agr*) irrigation.

regala *nf* gunwale.

regaladamente *adv* *vivir* in luxury; **comer** ~ to eat extremely well.

regalado *adj* (**a**) *vida etc* of luxury; (*cómodo*) comfortable, pleasant; (*pey*) soft.

(**b**) (*delicado*) dainty, delicate.

(**c**) (*Com, Fin*) free, given away; **me lo dio medio** ~ he gave it to me for a song; **no lo quiero ni** ~ I won't have it at any price, I don't want it even as a present.

(**d**) **hace su regalada gana** (*LAm**) she does exactly what she likes.

regalar [1a] **1** *vt* (**a**) (*dar*) to give, present; to give away; ~ **algo a uno** to give sb sth, make sb a present of sth; **en su jubilación le regalaron este reloj** they gave him this clock on his retirement, they presented him with this clock on his retirement; **están regalando plumas** they're giving pens away, they're issuing pens free; **regaló el balón** (*Dep*) he gave the ball away.

(**b**) *persona* to treat royally, make a great fuss of; (*pey*) to indulge, pamper; ~ **a uno con un banquete** to entertain sb to a dinner, (*menos formal*) treat sb to a dinner; **le regalaron con toda clase de atenciones** they regaled him with all manner of hospitality, they lavished attentions on him.

2 regalarse *vr* (**a**) (*darse gusto*) to indulge o.s., pamper o.s.; to do o.s. well.

(**b**) ~ **con** to regale o.s. with.

regalía *nf* (**a**) **~s** (*del rey*) royal prerogatives.

(**b**) (*fig: privilegio*) privilege, prerogative; (*Fin*) perquisite, bonus.

(**c**) (*And, CAm, Carib: regalo*) gift, present.

(**d**) (*Liter, Mús*) **~s** (*derechos*) royalty; (*avance*) advance payment.

(**e**) (*Carib: excelencia*) excellence, goodness.

regaliz *nm*, **regaliza** *nf* liquorice, licorice; ~ **de palo** stick of liquorice.

regalo *nm* (**a**) (*gen*) gift, present; ~ **de boda** wedding present; ~ **de Navidad,** ~ **de Reyes** Christmas present; **entrada**

de ~ complimentary ticket; **estuche de ~** presentation case.
(**b**) (*fig*: *placer*) pleasure; (*comestible*) treat, delicacy, dainty; **es un ~ para el oído** it's a treat to listen to.
(**c**) (*fig*: *comodidad*) luxury, comfort.

regalón *adj* (**a**) *niño* spoiled, pampered; *persona* comfort-loving, (*pey*) soft, lapped in luxury.
(**b**) *vida* of luxury, comfortable; (*pey*) soft.
(**c**) (*LAm*) **es el ~ de su padre** he's the apple of his father's eye, he's his daddy's pet.
(**d**) (*And*: *obsequioso*) fond of giving presents.

regalonear [1a] **1** *vt* (*Cono Sur*: *mimar*) to spoil, pamper.
2 *vi* (*Cono Sur*: *dejarse mimar*) to allow o.s. to be pampered.

regañada* *nf* (*CAm, Méx*) = **regaño.**

regañadientes: a ~ *adv* unwillingly, reluctantly.

regañado *adj*: **estar ~ con uno** to be at odds with sb.

regañar [1a] **1** *vt* to scold; to tell off*, reprimand; to nag (at).
2 *vi* (**a**) (*perro*) to snarl, growl.
(**b**) (*persona*) to grumble, grouse*; to nag.
(**c**) (*2 personas*) to fall out, quarrel.

regañina *nf* = **regaño** (**b**).

regaño *nm* (**a**) (*gruñido*) snarl, growl; (*mueca*) scowl; (*queja*) grumble, grouse*. (**b**) (*reprimenda*) scolding; telling-off*; **merecerse un ~** to get a telling off*.

regañón *adj* grumbling, grouchy*; irritable; *mujer* nagging, shrewish.

regar [1h *y* 1j] **1** *vt* (**a**) *planta* to water; *tierra* to water, irrigate; *calle* to water, hose (down), wash; *herida etc* to wash, bathe (*con, de* with); (*con insecticida etc*) to spray (*con, de* with); **~ la garganta** to spray one's throat; **~ un plato con vino** to have wine with a dish, accompany a dish with wine; **regó la carta con lágrimas** she bathed the letter in tears.
(**b**) (*Geog*: *río*) to water; (*mar*) to wash, lap against; **una costa regada por un mar tranquilo** a coast washed by a calm sea.
(**c**) (*fig*: *esparcir*) to sprinkle, strew (in all directions), scatter; **iba regando monedas** he was dropping money all over the place.
(**d**) (*And, CAm**) (*derramar*) to spill; (*derribar*) to knock over, knock down.
(**e**) (*Carib*: *pegar*) to hit.
2 *vi* (**a**) (*Carib**: *bromear*) to joke; **está regando** she's having us on.
(**b**) (*Carib*: *actuar sin pensar*) to act rashly.
(**c**) **~la** (*Méx*‡: *fracasar*) to screw it up‡, make a mess of it.
3 regarse *vr* (**a**) (*CAm, Méx*: *dispersarse*) to scatter (in all directions).
(**b**) (*Carib**: *enfadarse*) to get cross.
(**c**) (*LAm*: *ducharse*) to shower, take a shower.

regata[1] *nf* (*Agr*) irrigation channel.

regata[2] *nf* (*Náut*) race, boat-race; regatta.

regate *nm* (**a**) (*desvío*) swerve, dodge; (*Dep*) dribble. (**b**) (*fig*) dodge, ruse.

regatear[1] [1a] *vi* (*Náut*) to race.

regatear[2] [1a] **1** *vt* (**a**) (*Com*) *objeto, trato* to haggle over, bargain over; *precio* to try to beat down.
(**b**) *provisión etc* to be mean with, economize on; to give (*o* issue *etc*) sparingly; **su padre no le regatea dinero** her father does not keep her short of money; **aquí regatean el vino** they are mean with their wine here; **no hemos regateado esfuerzo para** + *infin* we have spared no effort to + *infin*.
(**c**) (*fig*: *negar*) to deny, refuse to allow; **no le regateo buenas cualidades** I don't deny his good qualities.
2 *vi* (**a**) (*Com*) to haggle, bargain; (*fig*) to bicker.
(**b**) (*desviarse*) to swerve, dodge; to duck; (*Dep*) to dribble.
3 regatearse *vr*: **~ algo** (*LAm*) to haggle over sth.

regateo *nm* (**a**) (*Com*) haggling, bargaining. (**b**) (*Dep*) dribbling.

regatista *nmf* (*sailing*) competitor; yachtsman, yachtswoman.

regato *nm* pool.

regatón[1] *nm* (*de bastón*) tip, ferrule.

regatón[2] **1** *adj* (*Com*) haggling; (*fig*) bickering, niggling, argumentative. **2** *nm* (*Carib**: *restos*) dregs. **3** *nmf* (*Méx**: *comerciante*) small-time dealer.

regazo *nm* (*t fig*) lap.

regencia *nf* regency.

regeneración *nf* (**a**) (*gen*) regeneration. (**b**) (*Téc*) reclaiming, reclamation.

regenerado *adj* regenerate.

regenerador *adj* regenerative.

regenerar [1a] *vt* (**a**) (*gen*) to regenerate. (**b**) (*Téc*) to reclaim, process for re-use.

regentar [1a] *vt* (**a**) *cátedra etc* to occupy, hold; *puesto* to hold temporarily; *hotel etc* to run, manage, administer; (*fig*) *destinos etc* to guide, preside over. (**b**) (*: *dominar*) to domineer, boss.

regente 1 *adj* (**a**) *príncipe etc* regent.
(**b**) *director etc* managing.
2 *nmf* (*t* **regenta** *f*) (**a**) (*Pol*) regent.
(**b**) (*de fábrica, finca*) manager; (*Esp Farm*) chief pharmacist; (*Tip*) foreman.
(**c**) (*Méx*: *alcalde*) mayor of Mexico City.

regiamente *adv* regally.

regicida *nmf* regicide (*person*).

regicidio *nm* regicide (*act*).

regidor 1 *adj principio* governing, ruling. **2** *nm* (**a**) (*Teat*) stage manager. (**b**) (*Hist*) alderman.

regiego = **rejego.**

régimen *nm, pl* **regímenes** (**a**) (*Pol*) régime; rule; **el ~ anterior** (*esp*) Franco's rule, the Franco period; **antiguo ~** ancien régime; **~ marioneta** puppet régime; **~ del terror** reign of terror; **bajo el ~ del dictador** under the dictator's régime (*o* rule).
(**b**) (*Med esp Esp*) diet (*t* **~ alimenticio**); **~ lácteo** milk diet; **estar a ~** to be on a diet; **poner a uno a ~** to put sb on a diet; **ponerse a ~** to go on a diet.
(**c**) (*reglas*) rules, set of rules, régime, system; (*manera de vivir*) way of life; **prisión de ~ abierto** open prison; **he cambiado de ~** I have changed my whole way of life, I have made myself a new set of rules.
(**d**) (*Ling*) government.

regimentación *nf* regimentation.

regimiento *nm* (**a**) (*Pol etc*) administration, government, organization. (**b**) (*Mil*) regiment. (**c**) (*LAm**: *gentío*) mass, crowd.

Reginaldo *nm* Reginald.

regio 1 *adj* (**a**) royal, regal; kingly. (**b**) (*fig*) royal; splendid, majestic. (**c**) (*Cono Sur*) super*, brilliant*. **2** *interj* (*LAm**) great!*, terrific!*

regiomontano (*Méx*) **1** *adj* of (*o* from) Monterrey. **2** *nm*, **regiomontana** *nf* native (*o* inhabitant) of Monterrey.

región *nf* (**a**) (*Geog etc*) region; district, area, part; (*Pol*) region. (**b**) (*Anat*) region, tract.

regional *adj* regional.

regionalismo *nm* regionalism.

regionalista *adj, nmf* regionalist.

regir [3c *y* 3k] **1** *vt* (**a**) *país etc* to rule, govern; *colegio etc* to run, be in charge of, be at the head of; *empresa* to manage, run, control.
(**b**) (*Jur, Ling etc*) to govern; **según el reglamento que rige estos casos** according to the statute which governs these cases; **ese verbo rige el dativo** that verb takes the dative; **los factores que rigen los cambios del mercado** the factors which govern (*o* determine, control) changes in the market.
2 *vi* (**a**) (*Jur*) to be in operation, be in force, apply; (*precio*) to be in force; (*condición etc*) to prevail, obtain; **esa ley ya no rige** that law no longer applies; **el mes que rige** the present month, the current month; **cuando estas condiciones ya no rijan** when these conditions no longer obtain.
(**b**) (*Mec*) to work, go; **el timbre no rige** the bell doesn't work.
(**c**) **no ~*** to have a screw loose*, be not all there*.
3 regirse *vr*: **~ por** to be ruled by, be guided by, go by; to follow.

regista *nmf* (*Cine*) producer.

registrado *adj* registered.

registrador(a)[1] **1** *nm/f* (**a**) (*persona*) recorder, registrar. (**b**) **~ de sonido** (*TV*) sound recordist. **2** *nm*: **~ de vuelo** flight recorder.

registradora[2] *nf* (*Com*) cash register.

registrar [1a] **1** *vt* (**a**) (*anotar etc*) to register, record; to enter; to file; **~ un libro** to mark one's place in a book.
(**b**) (*Esp Mús etc*) to record; **~ la voz en una cinta** to record one's voice on tape.
(**c**) *equipaje, lugar, persona* to search; *archivo, documento* to survey, inspect; *cajón* to look through; **lo hemos registrado todo de arriba abajo** we have searched the whole place from top to bottom; **¡a mí que me registren!*** search me!*

(**d**) (*Méx*) *correo* to register.

2 registrarse *vr* (**a**) (*persona*) to register; (*en hotel*) to check in, sign in.

(**b**) (*hecho etc*) to be recorded; (*ocurrir*) to happen; **se han registrado algunos casos de tifus** a few cases of typhus have been reported; **no se ha registrado nunca nada parecido** nothing of the kind has ever been recorded before; **el cambio que se ha registrado en su actitud** the change which has occurred in his attitude.

registro *nm* (**a**) (*acto*) registration, recording.

(**b**) (*libro*) register; visitor's book; (*Inform*) record; ~ **catastral,** ~ **de la propiedad inmobiliaria** land registry; ~ **de defunciones** register of deaths; ~ **electoral** voting register, electoral roll; ~ **de hotel** hotel register; ~ **lógico** logical record; ~ **de matrimonios** register of marriages; ~ **mercantil** business register; ~ **de nacimientos** register of births; ~ **parroquial** parish register; **capacidad de** ~ storage facility, recording capacity; **firmar el** ~ to sign the register.

(**c**) (*lista*) list, roll, record; (*apunte*) note; ~ **de erratas** list of errata.

(**d**) (*entrada*) entry (in a register).

(**e**) (*oficina*) registry, record office; ~ **civil** registry office; ~ **de patentes y marcas** patents office; ~ **de la propiedad** land registry (office).

(**f**) (*búsqueda*) search; (*inspección*) survey, inspection; ~ **domiciliario** search of a house; ~ **policiaco** police search; **orden de** ~ search warrant; **practicar un** ~ to make a search (*en* of).

(**g**) (*Mús etc*: *grabación*) recording; **es un buen** ~ **de la sinfonía** it is a good recording of the symphony.

(**h**) (*Mús*) (*timbre*) register; (*del órgano*) stop; (*del piano*) pedal; **salir por** (*o* **adoptar**) **un** ~ **muy raro** (*fig*) to adopt a very odd tone, adopt a most inappropriate attitude; **mira por qué** ~ **nos sale ahora** look what he's coming out with now; **tocar todos los** ~**s** (*fig*) to pull out all the stops.

(**i**) (*Téc*) manhole, manhole cover; (*de fuego*) damper; inspection plate, inspection hatch.

(**j**) (*de libro*) bookmark.

(**k**) (*de reloj*) regulator.

(**l**) (*Tip*) register; **estar en** ~ to be in register.

(**m**) (*And, Cono Sur*: *tienda*) wholesale textiles store.

regla *nf* (**a**) (*instrumento*) ruler, rule; ~ **de cálculo** slide rule; ~ **de un pie** foot-rule; ~ **T,** ~ **en T** T-square.

(**b**) (*ley etc*) rule; regulation; (*Dep etc*) rule; (*científico*) law, principle; norm; ~**s del juego** rules of the game (*t fig*), laws of the game; ~**s de la circulación** traffic regulations; ~**s para el uso de una máquina** instructions for the use of a machine; **no hay** ~ **sin excepción** every rule has its exception; **ser de** ~ to be the rule, be usual, be the norm; **salir de** ~ to overstep the mark; to be abnormal, have abnormal features; **en** ~ in order; **es un español en toda** ~ he's a real Spaniard, he's a Spaniard through and through; **todo está en** ~ everything is in order; all is as it should be; **hacer algo en toda** ~ to do sth properly, do sth by the book; **poner algo en** ~ to put sth straight; **no tenía los papeles en** ~ his papers were not in order; **por** ~ **general** generally, usually, as a rule; on the average; **hacerse una** ~ **de** + *infin* to make it a rule to + *infin*.

(**c**) (*Mat*) rule; law; ~ **de 3** rule of 3; **¿por qué** ~ **de tres ...?** (*Esp**) why on earth ...?

(**d**) (*Ecl*) rule, order; **viven según la** ~ **benedictina** they live according to the Benedictine rule.

(**e**) (*Med*) period.

(**f**) (*fig*: *moderación*) moderation, restraint; **comer con** ~ to eat in moderation.

reglable *adj* adjustable.

reglaje *nm* (**a**) (*Mec*) checking, overhaul; adjustment; ~ **en altura** (*en anuncios de coches*) height adjustment; ~ **de neumáticos** wheel alignment. (**b**) (*Mil*) correction (of aim).

reglamentación *nf* (**a**) (*acto*) regulation. (**b**) (*reglas*) rules, regulations (*collectively*).

reglamentar [1a] *vt* to regulate; to make rules for, establish regulations for.

reglamentariamente *adv* in due form, according to the rules; properly.

reglamentario *adj* regulation (*atr*), obligatory, set; (*estatuario*) statutory; (*apropiado*) proper, due; **pistola reglamentaria** standard issue pistol; **en el traje** ~ in the regulation dress; **en la forma reglamentaria** in due form, in the properly established way; **es** ~ + *infin* the law requires that ..., the regulation makes it obligatory to + *infin*.

reglamento *nm* (*reglas*) rules, regulations (*collectively*); (*de reunión, sociedad*) standing order(s); (*municipal etc*) by-law; (*de profesión*) code of conduct; ~ **de aduana** customs regulations; ~ **del tráfico** rule of the road; **pistola de** ~ standard issue pistol.

reglar [1a] **1** *vt* (**a**) *línea, papel etc* to rule.

(**b**) (*Mec*) to check, overhaul; to adjust; (*Mil*) *puntería* to correct.

(**c**) (*fig*) to regulate, make regulations for.

2 reglarse *vr*: ~ **a** to abide by, conform to; ~ **por** to be guided by; to follow.

regleta *nf* (*Tip*) space.

regletear [1a] *vt* (*Tip*) to space out.

regocijadamente *adv* merrily; joyously, joyfully; exultantly.

regocijado *adj* (**a**) *carácter* jolly, cheerful, merry. (**b**) *estado, humor* merry; joyous, joyful; exultant.

regocijar [1a] **1** *vt* to gladden, delight, cheer (up); **un cuento que regocijó a todos** a story which made everyone laugh; **crear un personaje para** ~ **a los niños** to create a character to amuse children; **la noticia regocijó a la familia** the news delighted the family, the news filled the family with joy.

2 regocijarse *vr* (**a**) (*alegrarse*) to rejoice, be glad, express one's happiness (*de, por* about, at).

(**b**) (*reírse*) to laugh; ~ **con un cuento** to laugh at a story.

(**c**) (*pasarlo bien*) to make merry, have a merry time, celebrate.

(**d**) (*pey*) to exult; ~ **por un desastre ajeno** to exult in sb else's misfortune.

regocijo *nm* (**a**) (*alegría*) joy, happiness; rejoicing; delight, elation; gaiety, merriment.

(**b**) (*pey*) exultation; unhealthy pleasure, cruel delight (*por* in).

(**c**) ~**s** festivities, rejoicings, celebrations; ~**s navideños** Christmas festivities; ~**s públicos** public rejoicings.

regodearse [1a] *vr* (**a**) (*: *bromear*) to crack jokes*; to indulge in coarse humour.

(**b**) (*deleitarse*) to be glad, be delighted; ~ **haciendo algo** to enjoy o.s. hugely doing sth; (*pey*) ~ **con,** ~ **en** to gloat over, take a cruel delight in; ~ **porque otro está sufriendo** to be perversely glad that sb else is suffering.

(**c**) (*LAm**: *ser exigente*) to be fussy, be hard to please.

regodeo *nm* (**a**) joking; coarse humour. (**b**) delight; huge enjoyment; (*pey*) cruel delight, perverse pleasure.

regodeón (*LAm*) **1** *adj* (**a**) (*exigente*) fussy, hard to please. (**b**) (*egoísta*) self-indulgent.

2 *nm* pet.

regodiente *adj* (*And*) fussy, hard to please.

regojo *nm* (**a**) (*pan*) piece of left-over bread. (**b**) (*: *persona*) ti(t)ch*.

regoldar* [1l] *vi* to belch.

regordete *adj persona* chubby, plump; *manos etc* fat.

regosto *nm* longing, craving (*de* for).

regresar [1a] **1** *vt* (*LAm*) to give back, send back, return. **2** *vi* to come back, go back, return. **3 regresarse** *vr* (*LAm*) = **2.**

regresión *nf* regression; (*fig*) retreat; backward step.

regresivo *adj movimiento* backward; (*fig*) regressive, retrogressive, backward; downward.

regreso *nm* return; **viaje de** ~ return trip, homeward journey; **emprender el** ~ **a** to return to, come back to; **estar de** ~ to be back, be home.

regro *adj* (*Carib*) great*, fabulous*.

regüeldo *nm* belch, belching.

reguera *nf* (**a**) (*Agr*) irrigation channel. (**b**) (*Náut*) cable, mooring rope, anchor chain.

reguero *nm* (**a**) (*Agr*) irrigation ditch; (*LAm*: *surco*) furrow.

(**b**) (*pista*) track; (*señal*) streak, line, mark; (*de sangre etc*) trickle; (*de pólvora etc*) train; (*de humo, vapor*) trail; **propagarse como un** ~ **de pólvora** to spread like wildfire.

reguío *nm* (*And*) = **riego.**

regulable *adj* adjustable.

regulación *nf* (**a**) (*gen*) regulation; adjustment; control; ~ **de la natalidad** birth-control; ~ **del tráfico** traffic control; ~ **del volumen sonoro** (*Rad*) volume control. (**b**) (*euf*: *reducción*) reduction; ~ **de empleo** dismissal, redundancy; reduction of the workforce; ~ **de jornada** cut in working hours; ~ **de plantilla** staff cut; reduction of the workforce.

regulador 1 *adj* regulating, regulatory. **2** *nm* (*Mec*) regulator, throttle, governor; (*Rad etc*) control, knob, button;

~ **de intensidad** dimmer, dimmer switch; ~ **de volumen** volume control.
regular 1 *adj* **(a)** *(gen, t Ecl, Mat, Mil)* regular; *(normal)* normal, usual, customary; *(corriente)* ordinary; *vida etc* regular, orderly, well-organized; **a intervalos ~es** at regular intervals; **tiene un latido ~** it has a regular beat.
(b) *(fig: mediano)* regular; middling, medium, average; fair; *(pey)* fair, so-so, not too bad; **es una novela ~** it's an average sort of novel, it's a fair novel; **de tamaño ~** medium-sized, fair-sized; **'¿cómo es el profesor?' ... '~'** 'what's the teacher like?' ... 'not too bad', 'nothing special'.
(c) por lo ~ as a rule, generally.
2 *adv* **(*) estar ~** to be all right, be so-so; **'¿qué tal estás?' ... '~'** 'how are you?' ... 'so-so' (*o* 'all right', 'can't complain').
3 [1a] *vt* **(a)** *(gen)* to regulate, control; *(ley etc)* to govern; *tráfico* to control, direct; *precio etc* to control.
(b) *(Mec etc)* to adjust, regulate; *reloj* to put right; *despertador* to set.
(c) *(Méx)* to calculate.
regularcillo* *adj* = **regular 1 (b)**.
regularidad *nf* regularity; **con ~** regularly.
regularización *nf* regularization; standardization.
regularizar [1f] *vt* to regularize; to standardize, bring into line.
regularmente *adv* regularly.
régulo *nm* kinglet, petty king.
regurgitación *nf* regurgitation.
regurgitar [1a] *vt* to regurgitate.
regustado *adj* *(Carib)* well-satisfied.
regustar [1a] *vt* *(Carib, Méx)* to taste, relish, savour.
regusto *nm* *(t fig)* aftertaste; **queda siempre el ~** it leaves a bad taste in the mouth.
rehabilitación *nf* **(a)** *(de persona)* rehabilitation; *(en puesto)* reinstatement; *(de quebrado)* discharge. **(b)** *(Arquit etc)* restoration; *(Mec)* overhaul.
rehabilitar [1a] *vt* **(a)** to rehabilitate; to reinstate; *quebrado* to discharge. **(b)** to restore, renovate; to overhaul.
rehacer [2r] **1** *vt* **(a)** *(volver a hacer)* to redo, do again; *(repetir)* to repeat.
(b) *(recrear)* to remake; *(reparar)* to mend, repair; *(renovar)* to refurbish, renew, do up.
2 rehacerse *vr* **(a)** *(Med)* to recover; to regain one's strength; *(fig: reponerse)* to recover one's calm (*o* self esteem *etc*); **~ de** to get over, recover from.
(b) *(Mil)* to re-form; to rally.
rehecho *adj* thickset, chunky; *(fig: descansado)* rested.
rehén *nm* hostage.
rehenchir [3l] *vt* to fill, stuff, pack (*de* with).
rehilar [1a] *vi* **(a)** *(temblar)* to quiver, shake. **(b)** *(flecha etc)* to hum.
rehilete *nm* **(a)** *(flecha)* dart; *(Taur)* banderilla. **(b)** *(volante)* shuttlecock. **(c)** *(fig: comentario)* dig, cutting remark, taunt, barb.
rehogar [1h] *vt* *(Culin)* to sauté, toss in oil.
rehostia‡ 1 *interj* damn it! **2** *nf*: **es la ~** it's altogether too much; it's the bloody end‡; **él se cree que es la ~** he thinks he's the best thing since sliced bread*.
rehuir [3g] *vt* to shun, avoid; to shrink from; **~ +** *infin* to avoid + *ger*, shrink from + *ger*.
rehusar [1a] **1** *vt* to refuse, decline; **~ hacer algo** to refuse to do sth. **2** *vi* to refuse (*t caballo*).
reidero* *adj* amusing, funny.
reidor *adj* merry, laughing.
reilón *adj* *(Carib)* *(que se ríe)* given to laughing a lot, giggly; *(alegre)* merry.
reimplantar [1a] *vt* to re-establish, reintroduce.
reimponer [2q] *vt* to reimpose.
reimpresión *nf* reprint(ing).
reimprimir [3a] *vt* to reprint.
reina 1 *nf* **(a)** queen (*t Ajedrez, Ent etc*); **~ de belleza** beauty-queen; **~ claudia** *(Bot)* greengage; **~ de la fiesta** carnival queen; **~ madre** queen mother; **~ mora** *(juego)* hopscotch; **~ viuda** dowager queen. **(b)** (**‡**: *droga*) pure heroin. **2** *atr* top, ultimate; **prueba ~** ultimate test.
reinado *nm* reign; **bajo el ~ de** in the reign of.
Reinaldos *nm* Reginald.
reinante *adj* **(a)** *(lit)* reigning. **(b)** *(fig)* prevailing.
reinar [1a] *vi* **(a)** *(Pol)* to reign, rule.
(b) *(fig: prevalecer)* to reign; to prevail, be general; **reinan las bajas temperaturas** there are low temperatures everywhere; **reina una confusión total** total confusion reigns; **entre la población reinaba el descontento** unrest was rife in the population, there was widespread discontent in the population.
reincidencia *nf* *(acto)* relapse (*en* into); *(tendencia)* recidivism.
reincidente *nmf* recidivist; hardened offender; backslider.
reincidir [3a] *vi* to relapse (*en* into); *(criminal)* to repeat an offence; *(pecador etc)* to backslide.
reincorporar [1a] **1** *vt* to reincorporate (*a* in), reunite (*a* to).
2 reincorporarse *vr*: **~ a** to rejoin; **~ al trabajo** to return to work.
reindustrialización *nf* restructuring of industry.
reingresar [1a] *vi*: **~ en** to re-enter.
reingreso *nm* re-entry (*en* into).
reinicializar [1f] *vt* *(Inform)* to reset.
reiniciar [1b] *vt* to begin again; to resume.
reinicio *nm* new beginning; resumption.
reino *nm* kingdom; **el R~ Unido** the United Kingdom.
reinona‡ *nf* fairy‡.
reinoso, -a *nm/f* **(a)** *(And: del interior)* inlander, inhabitant of the interior *(esp of the cold eastern upland)*. **(b)** *(Carib)* Colombian.
reinserción *nf*: **~ social, ~ en la sociedad** social rehabilitation, assimilation into society.
reinsertado, -a *nm/f* former terrorist now socially rehabilitated.
reinsertar [1a] **1** *vt* to rehabilitate, assimilate into society.
2 reinsertarse *vr*: **~ en la sociedad** to resume an ordinary social life.
reinstalar [1a] *vt* to reinstall; *persona* to reinstate.
reintegrable *adj* *depósito* returnable, refundable.
reintegración *nf* **(a)** *rehabilitación* reinstatement (*a* in). **(b)** *(Fin)* refund, repayment, reimbursement. **(c)** *(vuelta)* return (*a* to).
reintegrar [1a] **1** *vt* **(a)** *(completar)* to make whole again, reintegrate.
(b) *persona* to reinstate (*a* in).
(c) *(Fin)* **~ a uno una cantidad** to refund (*o* repay, pay back) a sum to sb, reimburse sb for a sum; **ha sido reintegrado de todos sus gastos** he has been reimbursed in full for all his expenses.
(d) *suma* to pay back.
(e) *documento* to attach a fiscal stamp to.
2 reintegrarse *vr* **(a) ~ a** to return to.
(b) ~ de una cantidad to recover a sum, recoup a sum, secure repayment of a sum; **~ de los gastos** to reimburse o.s. for one's expenses.
reintegro *nm* **(a)** *(Fin)* refund, repayment, reimbursement; *(de cuenta bancaria)* withdrawal. **(b)** *(lotería)* return of one's stake. **(c)** *(sello)* (cost of a) fiscal stamp.
reinversión *nf* reinvestment.
reinvertir [3i] *vt* to reinvest.
reír [3l] **1** *vt* to laugh at; **todos le ríen los chistes** everybody laughs at his jokes.
2 *vi* **(a)** *(lit)* to laugh; **sólo para hacer ~** just to make people laugh, just for a laugh; **¡no me hagas ~!** don't make me laugh!; **~ como un loco** to laugh like a hyena; **el que ríe al último ríe mejor** he who laughs last laughs longest.
(b) *(fig: ojos etc)* to laugh, sparkle, be merry; *(campo, mañana, naturaleza)* to smile, be bright.
3 reírse *vr* **(a)** *(lit)* to laugh (*con, de* about, at, over); **~ con uno** to laugh at sb's jokes; **~ de uno** to laugh at sb, make fun of sb; **¿se ríe Vd de mí?** are you laughing at me?; **¡déjeme que me ría!** that's a good one!; **~ el último** to have the last laugh; **fue para ~** it was utterly absurd; *V* **echar** *etc*.
(b) **(*)** to split, come apart; **la chaqueta se me ríe por los codos** my jacket is out at the elbows; **estos zapatos se ríen** these shoes are coming apart.
reiteración *nf* reiteration, reaffirmation; repetition; *(Com)* **llamada de ~** follow-up call; **visita de ~** follow-up visit.
reiteradamente *adv* repeatedly.
reiterado *adj* repeated.
reiterar [1a] *vt* to reiterate, reaffirm; to repeat.
reiterativo *adj* reiterative; *(pey)* repetitive, repetitious.
reivindicable *adj* recoverable (at law).
reivindicación *nf* **(a)** *(reclamación)* claim (*de* to); *(queja)* grievance; **~ salarial** wage claim. **(b)** *(justificación)* vindication; *restauración* restoration of rights. **(c)** *(Jur)* recovery.
reivindicar [1g] **1** *vt* **(a)** *(reclamar)* to claim (the right to), claim as of right; to assert one's claim to; *(intentar cobrar)* to make a bid to recover; **~ un atentado** to claim re-

sponsibility for an outrage.

(**b**) *reputación etc* to vindicate; (*restaurar*) to restore; (*cobrar*) to win back; to restore one's rights.

(**c**) (*Jur*) *derecho* to recover.

(**d**) (*LAm**: *exigir*) to demand.

2 reivindicarse *vr* (*LAm*) to vindicate o.s.; to restore one's reputation.

reja *nf* (**a**) grating, grid, gridiron; (*de ventana*) bars, grille; (*Ecl*) screen; **estar entre ~s** to be behind bars; **meter a uno entre ~s** to put sb behind bars.

(**b**) (*Agr*) **~ del arado** ploughshare.

(**c**) (*LAm**: *cárcel*) prison, nick‡.

(**d**) (*Méx Cos*) darn, darning.

(**e**) (*Cono Sur Agr*) cattle truck.

rejado *nm* grille, grating.

rejeada *nf* (*And, CAm*) thrashing.

rejear [1a] *vt* (*CAm*) to jail, put in jail.

rejego 1 *adj* (**a**) (*Méx*) (*salvaje*) wild, untamed; (*fig*: *revoltoso*) troublesome, unruly; obstinate. (**b**) (*Méx*: *lento*) slow, sluggish. **2** *nm* (*CAm*) stud bull.

rejiego *adj* (*Carib, Méx*) = **rejego.**

rejilla *nf* (**a**) (*reja*) grating, grille; lattice; screen; (*Rad*) grille; (*Ferro*) luggage-rack; (*Méx Aut*) luggage-rack, roof-rack; (*de mueble*) wickerwork; **silla de ~** wicker chair.

(**b**) (*brasero*) small stove, footwarmer.

(**c**) (*Cono Sur*: *fresquera*) meat safe.

rejo *nm* (**a**) (*punta*) spike, sharp point.

(**b**) (*Ent*) sting.

(**c**) (*Bot*) radicle.

(**d**) (*fig*) strength, vigour, toughness.

(**e**) (*LAm*: *látigo*) whip; (*Carib*: *tira*) strip of raw leather.

(**f**) (*Carib*: *porra*) stick, club; **~ tieso** brave person.

(**g**) (*And*) (*ordeño*) milking; (*vacas*) herd of cows.

rejón *nm* pointed iron bar; spike; (*Taur*) lance.

rejoneador *nm* (*Taur*) *mounted bullfighter who uses the lance.*

rejonear [1a] (*Taur*) **1** *vt* to wound the bull with the lance. **2** *vi* to fight the bull on horseback with the lance.

rejoya *nf* (*Geog CAm*) deep valley.

rejudo *adj* (*And, Carib*: *pegajoso*) sticky, viscous; (*Carib*: *líquido*) runny.

rejugado *adj* (**a**) (*And, Carib*: *astuto*) cunning, sharp. (**b**) (*CAm*: *tímido*) shy.

rejunta *nf* (*Cono Sur, Méx*) round-up, rodeo.

rejuntar [1a] *vt* (**a**) (*Cono Sur*: *recoger*) to collect, gather in. (**b**) (*Méx*) *ganado* to round up. (**c**) (*Cono Sur*) *suma* to add up.

rejuvenecedor *adj* rejuvenating; (*fig*) refreshing, stimulating.

rejuvenecer [2d] **1** *vt* to rejuvenate. **2 rejuvenecerse** *vr* to be rejuvenated, become young again.

rejuvenecimiento *nm* rejuvenation.

relación *nf* (**a**) (*gen*) relation, relationship (*con* to, with); **relaciones** relations, relationship; **la ~ entre X y Z** the relationship between X and Z; **sus relaciones con el jefe** his relations with the boss; **buenas relaciones** good relations; **relaciones amistosas** friendly relations; **relaciones carnales** (*o* **sexuales**) sexual relations; **relaciones comerciales** business connections, trade relations; **relaciones empresariales, relaciones laborales** industrial relations; **Ministerio de Relaciones Exteriores** Foreign Ministry; **relaciones humanas** human relations, (*como sección, profesión*) personnel management; **estar en buenas relaciones con** to be on good terms with; **mantener relaciones con** to keep in touch with; **romper las relaciones con** to break off relations with; **con ~ a, en ~ a** in relation to; **un aumento de 3 por cien con ~ al año anterior** an increase of 3% over the previous year; *V t* **relaciones públicas.**

(**b**) (*Mat*) ratio; proportion; **~ de compresión** compression ratio; **en una ~ de 7 a 2** in a ratio of 7 to 2; **guardar cierta ~ con** to bear a certain relation to; **no guardar ~ alguna con** to be out of all proportion to, bear no relation whatsoever to.

(**c**) **relaciones** (**amorosas**) courting, courtship; affair; **relaciones formales** engagement; **relaciones ilícitas** illicit sexual relations; **relaciones prematrimoniales** premarital sex, sex before marriage; **llevan varios meses de relaciones** they've been going out (*o* courting) for some months; their affair has been going on for some months; **A está en** (*o* **tiene**) **relaciones con B** A and B are going out together, A and B are courting; A and B are having an affair.

(**d**) **relaciones** (*personas*) acquaintances; (*esp*) influential friends, contacts, connections; **para eso conviene tener relaciones** for that it helps to have contacts; **tener** (**buenas**) **relaciones** to be well connected, have powerful friends.

(**e**) (*narración*) account, report; story; (*de dificultades etc*) tale, recital; **hizo una larga ~ de su viaje** he gave a lengthy account of his trip.

(**f**) (*lista*) list; (*informe*) record, (official) return.

(**g**) (*Teat*) long speech.

relacionado *adj* (**a**) related; **un tema ~ con Lorca** a subject that has to do with Lorca, a subject that concerns Lorca; **A está íntimamente ~ con B** A is closely connected with B; A is much bound up with B.

(**b**) **una persona relacionada** (*LAm*), **una persona bien relacionada** a well-connected person.

relacional *adj*: **estudio ~** study of (human) relationships.

relacionar [1a] **1** *vt* (**a**) (*asociar*) to relate (*con* to), connect (*con* with).

(**b**) (*hacer constar*) to list.

2 relacionarse *vr* (**a**) **es hombre que se relaciona** he's a man with (powerful) connections.

(**b**) (*dos cosas etc*) to be connected, be related.

(**c**) (*formar amistades*) to make contacts, get to know people; to get in the swim; **~ con uno** to get to know sb; to get into touch with sb.

(**d**) **en lo que se relaciona con** as for, with regard to.

relaciones públicas 1 *nmf invar* (*persona*) public relations officer, publicity agent. **2** *nfpl* (*acto etc*) public relations.

relai(s) [re'le] *nm* (*Elec*) relay.

relajación *nf* (**a**) (*sosiego*) relaxation. (**b**) (*acto*) relaxation; slackening, loosening; weakening. (**c**) (*fig*: *diversión*) relaxation, amusement. (**d**) (*fig*: *moral*) laxity, looseness. (**e**) (*Med*) hernia, rupture.

relajado *adj* (**a**) (*sosegado*) relaxed. (**b**) (*inmoral*) dissolute, loose. (**c**) (*Med*) ruptured.

relajadura *nf* (*Méx Med*) hernia, rupture.

relajante 1 *adj* (**a**) *ejercicio etc* relaxing. (**b**) (*Med*) laxative. (**c**) (*Cono Sur*) *comida* sickly, sweet and sticky. (**d**) (*repugnante*) revolting, disgusting. **2** *nm* laxative.

relajar [1a] **1** *vt* (**a**) (*sosegar*) to relax.

(**b**) (*aflojar*) to relax; to slacken, loosen; (*debilitar*) to weaken.

(**c**) (*fig*: *moralmente*) to weaken, corrupt, make lax.

(**d**) (*LAm*: *comida*) to cloy, sicken, disgust.

(**e**) (*Carib*) (*hacer mofa*) to mock, deride; (*escarnecer*) to poke fun at.

2 relajarse *vr* (**a**) (*sosegarse*) to relax; **conviene relajarte más** you should relax more, you should take more time for relaxation.

(**b**) (*aflojarse*) to relax; to slacken, loosen; (*debilitarse*) to weaken.

(**c**) (*fig*: *moralmente*) to become dissolute, go to the bad; (*moralidad etc*) to become lax.

(**d**) (*Med*) **~ un tobillo** to sprain one's ankle, lose the feeling in an ankle; **~ un órgano** to rupture an organ.

relajo *nm* (*esp LAm*) (**a**) (*libertinaje*) laxity, dissipation, depravity; (*indecencia*) lewdness.

(**b**) (*acto inmoral*) immoral act; (*acto indecente*) indecent act.

(**c**) (*bullicio*) boisterous gathering; (*fiesta*) lewd party; (*desorden*) commotion, disorder; (*lío*) fuss, row.

(**d**) (*chiste*) rude joke; (*trastada*) practical joke; (*mofas*) derision; **cuento de ~** blue joke; **echar algo a ~** to make fun of sth.

(**e**) (*Méx*: *opción fácil*) easy ride, soft option.

(**f**) (*: *descanso*) rest, break.

relajón *adj* (**a**) (*Carib*) (*mofador*) mocking; (*: *obsceno*) dirty. (**b**) (*Méx*: *depravado*) depraved, perverse.

relamer [2a] **1** *vt* to lick repeatedly.

2 relamerse *vr* (**a**) (*animal*) to lick its chops; (*persona*) to lick one's lips (*t* **~ los labios**).

(**b**) **~ con algo** (*fig*) to relish sth, smack one's lips over sth; (*pey*) to gloat over sth.

(**c**) (*fig*: *jactarse*) to brag.

(**d**) (*fig*: *maquillarse*) to paint one's face.

relamido *adj* (**a**) (*remilgado*) prim and proper; (*afectado*) affected; (*muy elegante*) overdressed, dolled-up*. (**b**) (*CAm, Carib**) shameless, cheeky*.

relámpago 1 *nm* lightning, flash of lightning; (*fig*) flash; **~ difuso** sheet lightning; **como un ~** as quick as lightning, in a flash.

2 *atr* lightning; **guerra ~** blitzkrieg; **viaje ~** lightning trip; **visita ~** rushed visit, rapid visit, flying visit.

relampagucear [1a] *vi* (*Carib, Méx*) to twinkle; to flicker;

to gleam.
relampaguceo *nm* (*Carib, Méx*) twinkle; flicker, gleam.
relampagueante *adj* flashing.
relampaguear [1a] *vi* (**a**) (*gen*) to lighten; to flash; **relampagueó toda la noche** the lightning was flashing all night, there was lightning all night.
(**b**) (*Carib*) (*parpadear*) to twinkle, flicker; (*brillar*) to gleam, shine.
relampagueo *nm* (**a**) (*gen*) flashing. (**b**) (*Carib*) (*parpadeo*) twinkle, flicker; (*brillo*) gleam, shine.
relampuso *adj* (*Carib*) shameless, brazen.
relance *nm* (*Cono Sur*) (**a**) = **piropo** (**a**). (**b**) **de ~** (*al contado*) in cash.
relanzamiento *nm* relaunch(ing).
relanzar [1f] *vt* (**a**) *plan etc* to relaunch. (**b**) (*rechazar*) to repel, repulse.
relatar [1a] *vt* to relate, tell; to report.
relativamente *adv* relatively.
relativismo *nm* relativism.
relativista 1 *adj* relativistic. **2** *nmf* relativist.
relativizar [1f] *vt* to play down, (seek to) diminish the importance of.
relativo 1 *adj* relative (*t Ling*); **~ a** relative to; regarding, relating to. **2** *nm* (*Ling*) relative.
relato *nm* story, tale; account, report.
relator(a) *nm/f* teller, narrator; (*Jur*) court reporter.
relatoría *nf* post of court reporter.
relauchar* [1a] *vi* (*Cono Sur*) to skive off‡.
relax [re'las] *nm* (*Esp*) (**a**) (*sosiego*) (state of) relaxation; (*descanso*) rest, break; **hacer ~** to relax; **vamos a hacer un poco de ~** let's take a break.
(**b**) (*euf*) sexual services; (*anuncio*) **'R~'** 'Massage'.
relé *nm* (*Elec*) relay.
releer [2e] *vt* to reread.
relegación *nf* (**a**) (*gen*) relegation. (**b**) (*Hist*) exile, banishment.
relegar [1h] *vt* (**a**) (*gen*) to relegate; **~ algo al olvido** to banish sth from one's mind; to consign sth to oblivion. (**b**) (*desterrar*) to exile, banish.
relente *nm* night dew.
releso *adj* (*Cono Sur*) stupid, thick*.
relevación *nf* (**a**) (*gen*) relief (*t Mil*); replacement. (**b**) (*Jur*) exoneration; release (*de* from).
relevante *adj* (**a**) (*destacado*) outstanding. (**b**) (*pertinente*) relevant.
relevar [1a] *vt* (**a**) (*Téc*) to emboss; to carve (*o* paint *etc*) in relief.
(**b**) (*Mil*) *guardia* to relieve; *colega* to replace, substitute for.
(**c**) **~ a uno de una obligación** to relieve sb of a duty, free sb from an obligation; **~ a uno de la culpa** to exonerate sb, free sb from blame; **~ a uno de** + *infin* to free sb from the obligation to + *infin*.
(**d**) **~ a uno de un cargo** to relieve sb of his post, replace sb in his post; **ser relevado de su mando** to be relieved of one's command.
relevista *nmf* relay runner; relay swimmer.
relevo *nm* (**a**) (*Mil*: *acto*) relief, change; (*personas*) relief; **~ de la guardia** changing of the guard; **~ de los tiros** change of horses; **tomar el ~** to take over. (**b**) (*Dep*) **~s** relay (race); **400 metros ~s** 400 metres relay.
reliar [1c] *vt cigarrillo* to roll.
relicario *nm* (**a**) (*Ecl*) shrine; reliquary. (**b**) (*medallón*) locket.
relieve *nm* (**a**) (*Arte, Téc*) relief; raised work, embossing; raised part; **alto ~** high relief; **bajo ~** bas-relief; **en ~** raised pattern, embossed pattern, pattern in relief; **película en ~** stereoscopic film, three-dimensional (*abr*: *3-D*) film; **estampar en ~, grabar en ~** to emboss.
(**b**) (*importancia*) importance, prominence; (*status*) social standing; **un personaje de ~** an important man, a man of some importance; **dar ~ a** to enhance; to give prominence to, bring out; **poner algo de ~** to emphasize (the importance of), point out the interest of, stress the qualities of.
(**c**) **~s** (*restos*) left-overs.
religión *nf* (**a**) (*Rel*) religion.
(**b**) (*fig*) religion, cult; **tiene la ~ de la promesa** he believes utterly in keeping his word.
(**c**) (*religiosidad*) religiousness; (*piedad*) religious sense, piety.
(**d**) (*Ecl*) the religious life, religion; **entrar en ~** to take vows, enter a religious order.
religiosa *nf* nun.
religiosamente *adv* religiously.
religiosidad *nf* religiosity, religiousness; (*fig*) religiousness.
religioso 1 *adj* religious (*t fig*). **2** *nm* religious, member of a religious order, monk.
relimpio *adj* absolutely clean; spick and span.
relinchada *nf* (*Méx*) = **relincho.**
relinchar [1a] *vi* to neigh, whinny, snort.
relincho *nm* neigh(ing), whinny(ing), snort(ing).
reliquia *nf* (**a**) (*Ecl*) relic; (*Méx*) (votive) offering.
(**b**) (*tesoro etc*) relic; **~s** relics, remains; (*vestigios*) traces, vestiges; **~ de familia** heirloom, family treasure.
(**c**) (*Med*) **~s** after-effects, lingering effects, resultant weakness.
reloj [re'lo] *nm* (*grande*) clock; (*de bolsillo, de pulsera*) watch; (*Téc*) clock, meter; **~ de arena** sandglass, hourglass; **~ automático** timer, timing mechanism; **~ biológico** biological clock; **~ de bolsillo** pocket watch; **~ de caja** grandfather clock; **~ de carillón** chiming clock; **~ de cuco** cuckoo-clock; **~ despertador** alarm-clock; **~ digital** digital watch; **~ eléctrico** electric clock; **~ de estacionamiento** parking meter; **~ de fichar** time-clock; **~ de la muerte** (*Ent*) deathwatch beetle; **~ de pie** grandfather clock; **~ parlante** talking clock; **~ de pulsera** wristwatch; **~ registrador** time-clock; **~ de sol** sundial; **como un ~** like clockwork; **estar como un ~** to be regular; to be as fit as a fiddle; **marchar como un ~** to go like clockwork; **contra (el) ~** against the clock.
relojear [1a] *vt* (*Cono Sur*) (**a**) *carrera* to time. (**b**) (*: *vigilar*) to spy on, keep tabs on; (*controlar*) to check, keep a check on.
relojería *nf* (**a**) (*arte*) watchmaking, clockmaking. (**b**) (*tienda*) watchmaker's (shop). (**c**) (*t* **aparato de ~**) clockwork; **bomba de ~** time-bomb; **mecanismo de ~** timing device.
relojero *nm* watchmaker, clockmaker.
reluciente *adj* (**a**) (*brillante*) shining, brilliant; glittering, gleaming, sparkling; bright. (**b**) *persona* (*pulcro*) sleek; (*gordo*) well-fed; (*de buen aspecto*) healthy-looking.
relucir [3f] *vi* (**a**) (*brillar*) to shine; to glitter, gleam, sparkle; to be bright. (**b**) **siempre saca a ~ sus éxitos** he's always bringing up (*o* harping on) his triumphs.
relujar [1a] *vt* (*CAm, Méx*) *zapatos* to shine.
relumbrante *adj* brilliant, dazzling; glaring.
relumbrar [1a] *vi* to shine brilliantly, be bright; to dazzle; to glare.
relumbrón *nm* (**a**) flash; sudden glare. (**b**) (*fig*) flashiness, ostentation; **joyas de ~** flashy jewellery; **vestirse de ~** to dress flashily, dress to kill.
rellano *nm* (*Arquit*) landing.
rellena *nf* (*LAm*) black pudding; (*CAm*) *type of turnover.*
rellenable *adj* refillable; reusable.
rellenado *nm* refill; replenishment; (*Aer etc*) refuelling.
rellenar [1a] **1** *vt* (**a**) (*volver a llenar*) to refill, replenish; (*Aer etc*) to refuel.
(**b**) (*llenar completamente*) to fill up; to pack, stuff, cram (*de* with); (*Culin*) to stuff; (*Cos etc*) to pad; *espacios etc* to fill in; *formulario* to fill in, fill up.
2 rellenarse *vr* to stuff o.s. (*de* with).
rellenito *adj persona* plump.
relleno 1 *adj* (**a**) (*lleno*) packed, stuffed, crammed (*de* with); very full, full right up (*de* of); (*Culin*) stuffed (*de* with).
(**b**) *persona* plump; *cara* full.
(**c**) (*rellenado*) **envíe el cupón debidamente ~ a ...** send the completed coupon to ...
2 *nm* (**a**) (*gen*) filling; (*Arquit*) plaster filling; (*Culin*) stuffing; (*Cos*) padding; wadding; (*Mec*) packing; (*de caramelo*) **~ blando** soft centre; **~ duro** hard centre; **frases** (*etc*) **de ~** padding, stuffing.
(**b**) (*And*: *vertedero*) tip, dump.
remachado *adj* (*And*) quiet, reserved.
remachador *nm* riveter.
remachar [1a] **1** *vt* (**a**) (*Téc*) *clavo etc* to clinch; *metales* to rivet.
(**b**) (*fig*) *aspecto* to hammer home, drive home; to stress; *caso* to tie up, finish; **para ~lo todavía** to clinch matters; to make it entirely certain.
2 remacharse* *vr* (*And*) to remain stubbornly silent.
remache *nm* (**a**) (*Téc*) rivet. (**b**) (*acto*) clinching; riveting.
(**c**) (*And*: *terquedad*) stubbornness, obstinacy.
remada *nf* stroke.
remador(a) *nm/f* rower.
remaduro *adj* (*LAm*) overripe.

remalo *adj* (*LAm*) really bad.
remalladora *nf* mender, darner.
remallar [1a] *vt* to mend, darn.
remandingo *nm* (*Carib*) row, uproar; scandal.
remanente 1 *adj* remaining; (*Fís*) remanent; (*Com etc*) surplus. **2** *nm* remainder; (*Com, Fin*) retained earnings; balance; (*de producción*) surplus.
remangar = **arremangar.**
remango* *adj* lively, energetic, vigorous.
remangue* *nm* liveliness, energy, vigour; go; **hacer algo con ~** to do sth energetically, tackle sth vigorously.
remansarse [1a] *vr* to form a pool; to become stagnant.
remanso *nm* (**a**) (*de río*) pool; backwater. (**b**) (*fig*) quiet place, peaceful area; **un ~ de paz** an oasis of peace, a haven of peace.
remaque *nm* (*Cine*) remake.
remar [1a] *vi* (**a**) (*Náut*) to row. (**b**) (*fig*) to toil, struggle; to suffer hardships.
remarcable *adj* remarkable.
remarcación *nf* (*Com*) mark-up.
remarcar [1g] *vt* (**a**) (*observar*) to notice, observe, remark on. (**b**) (*distinguir*) to distinguish. (**c**) (*subrayar*) to emphasize, underline. (**d**) *precio* to mark up.
rematadamente *adv* terribly, hopelessly; **~ mal** terribly bad; **es ~ tonto** he's utterly stupid.
rematado *adj* (**a**) (*inútil*) hopeless; (*total*) complete, out-and-out; **es un loco ~** he's a raving lunatic; **es un tonto ~** he's an utter fool. (**b**) (*Esp*) *niño* very naughty.
rematador *nm* (**a**) (*Dep*) goal-scorer. (**b**) (*And, Cono Sur*) auctioneer.
rematadora *nf* auction house, auctioneer's.
rematante *nm* highest bidder.
rematar [1a] **1** *vt* (**a**) (*matar*) *persona* to finish off; to kill off; *animal* to shoot dead, kill instantly; *animal herido* to put out of its misery.
(**b**) (*fig*) *trabajo etc* to finish off, bring to a conclusion; *proceso* to finish, round off; *abuso* to put an end to; *bebida etc* to finish up, drink (*etc*) the last of; (*Cos*) to cast off.
(**c**) (*Arquit etc*) to top, be at the very top of, crown.
(**d**) (*Com: vender*) to sell off cheaply, sell at a bargain price.
(**e**) **~ algo a uno** (*Com: en subasta*) to knock sth down to sb (*en* for).
(**f**) (*LAm*) (*en subasta, comprar*) to buy at an auction, (*vender*) to sell at auction; (*CAm, Méx: vender*) to sell.
(**g**) (*Cono Sur*) *caballo* to pull up.
2 *vi* (**a**) (*terminar*) to end, finish off; **remató con un par de chistes** he finished with a couple of jokes.
(**b**) **~ en** to end in, come to; **es del tipo que remata en punta** it's the sort which comes to a point; **fue una situación que remató en tragedia** it was a situation which ended in tragedy.
(**c**) (*Dep*) to shoot, score; **~ de cabeza** to head a goal.
remate *nm* (**a**) (*acto*) finishing (off); killing off; (*Dep*) shot; **equipo sin ~** a team with no finishing power.
(**b**) (*cabo*) end; (*punta*) tip, point; (*Arquit*) top, crest; (*de mueble etc*) ornamental top.
(**c**) (*fig*) conclusion; finishing touch; **de ~** = **rematado** (**a**); **para ~** to crown it all, on top of all that; **por ~** finally, as a finishing touch; **poner ~ a** to cap; to put the finishing touch to, round off.
(**d**) (*Com: postura*) highest bid.
(**e**) (*Com: venta*) sale (by auction); (*Bridge*) bidding, auction.
rematista *nm* (*And, Carib*) auctioneer.
rembolsar *etc* = **reembolsar.**
remecer [2d] **1** *vt* to rock, swing (to and fro); (*Méx*) to shake; to wave. **2 remecerse** *vr* to rock, swing (to and fro).
remedar [1a] *vt* to imitate, copy; (*pey*) to ape; (*burlándose*) to ape, mimic.
remediable *adj* remediable, that can be remedied; **fácilmente ~** easy to remedy, easily remedied.
remediar [1b] *vt* (**a**) (*poner remedio a*) to remedy; *daño, pérdida* to make good, repair; (*compensar*) to make up for; *abuso* to correct, put right, put a stop to; **llorando no remedias nada** you won't do any good by crying.
(**b**) *necesidades etc* to meet, help with; *necesitado* to help (out); *persona en peligro* to help, save.
(**c**) (*evitar*) to avoid, prevent; **sin poder ~lo** without being able to prevent it; **a ver si lo remediamos** let's see if we can do anything about it; **no poder ~ el echarse a reír** not to be able to help laughing.
remedio *nm* (**a**) (*gen*) remedy (*t Med*; *contra* against); (*Med*) cure; (*ayuda*) help; **~ casero** ordinary remedy, simple domestic remedy; **~ heroico** extreme remedy; (*fig*) extreme measure; **como último ~** as a last resort; **sin ~** inevitable; irremediable; **es un tonto sin ~** he's a hopeless idiot, he's so stupid he's past redemption; **no se podía encontrar ni para un ~** it couldn't be had for love nor money; **¡ni por un ~!*** not on your life!; **no hay más ~** there's no help for it, there's nothing one can do, there's no other way; **no hay más ~ que** + *infin* the only thing is to + *infin*; **no hay ~ para él** it's all up with him, he's had it; **esto no tiene ~** it is unavoidable; there's nothing one can do about it; it's beyond repair; **él no tiene ~** he's hopeless, he's past redemption; **¿qué ~ tengo?** what else can I do?; **no tener más ~ que** + *infin* to have no alternative but to + *infin*; **poner ~ a un abuso** to correct an abuse, put a stop to an abuse; **ruego que se ponga ~** I hope something can be done about it.
(**b**) (*alivio*) relief, help; **buscar ~ en su aflicción** to look for some relief in one's distress.
(**c**) (*Jur*) remedy, recourse.
(**d**) (*CAm, Méx Med*) medicine.
remedo *nm* imitation, copy; (*pey*) poor imitation, travesty, parody.
rememorar [1a] *vt* (*liter*) to remember, recall.
remendar [1j] *vt* (**a**) (*Cos*) to mend, repair; to patch, darn. (**b**) (*fig*) to correct.
remendón *nm* cobbler.
remera *nf* (*Cono Sur*) T-shirt.
remero *nm* (**a**) (*persona*) oarsman. (**b**) (*máquina*) rowing machine.
remesa *nf* remittance; shipment, consignment; **~ de fondos** (*Méx Com*) (financial) settlement.
remesar [1a] *vt dinero* to remit, send; *mercancías* to send, ship, consign.
remeter [2a] *vr* to put back; *camisa, ropa de cama etc* to tuck in.
remezón *nm* (*LAm*) earth tremor, slight earthquake.
remiendo *nm* (**a**) (*acto*) mending; patching.
(**b**) (*parche etc*) mend; patch, darn; **a ~s** piecemeal; **echar un ~ a** to patch, put a patch on.
(**c**) (*fig*) correction; (*Med*) improvement.
(**d**) (*Zool*) spot, patch.
remilgado *adj* prudish, prim; affected; finicky, fussy, particular, overnice; squeamish, oversensitive; **don R~*** (*Esp hum*) Lord Muck*.
remilgarse [1h] *vr* to react prudishly; to show one's affectation; to be fussy; to be squeamish.
remilgo *nm* (**a**) (*gazmoñería*) prudery, primness; (*afectación*) affectation; (*melindre*) fussiness; (*sensibilidad*) squeamishness, excess of sensitivity.
(**b**) (*mueca*) prim look; simper; smirk; **hacer ~s a** to react in a prudish (*etc*) way to; **él no hace ~s a ninguna clase de trabajo** he won't turn up his nose at any kind of work.
(**c**) **don R~s** (*: *hum*) Lord Muck*.
remilgoso *adj* (*LAm*) = **remilgado.**
reminiscencia *nf* reminiscence.
remirado *adj* (**a**) (*prudente*) cautious, circumspect, careful; (*pey*) overcautious. (**b**) (*pey*) (*gazmoño*) prudish; (*afectado*) affected, over-nice; (*melindroso*) fussy, pernickety*.
remirar [1a] **1** *vt* to look at again; to look hard at. **2 remirarse** *vr* to be extra careful (*en* about), take great pains (*en* over).
remise *nm o f* (*Cono Sur*) hired car, taxi.
remisión *nf* (**a**) (*envío*) sending; (*LAm*) shipment, consignment.
(**b**) (*referencia*) reference (*a* to).
(**c**) (*aplazamiento*) postponement; adjournment.
(**d**) (*disminución*) remission (*t Med*); slackening.
(**e**) (*Ecl*) forgiveness, remission.
remiso *adj* (**a**) *persona* slack, slow (to obey), remiss; **mostrarse ~** to be reluctant; **estar ~ a** + *infin* to be reluctant to + *infin*, be unwilling to + *infin*. (**b**) *movimiento* slow, sluggish.
remisor(a) *nm/f* (*LAm Com*) sender.
remite *nm* sender's name and address (*written on back of envelope*).
remitente *nmf* sender.
remitido *nm* (**a**) (*en periódico*) paid insert. (**b**) (*Méx: consignación*) shipment, consignment.
remitir [3a] **1** *vt* (**a**) (*Correos: enviar*) to send; *dinero* to remit; (*Com*) to send, ship, consign.
(**b**) *lector, usuario* to refer (*a* to).

(**c**) (*aplazar*) to postpone; *sesión* to adjourn.

(**d**) ~ **una decisión a uno** to leave a decision to sb, refer a matter to sb for a decision.

(**e**) (*Ecl*) *pecados* to forgive, pardon.

2 *vi* (**a**) (*disminuir*) to slacken, diminish, let up.

(**b**) **'remite: X ...'** (*en sobre*) 'sender: X ...'

3 remitirse *vr*: **a las pruebas me remito** the proof of the pudding is in the eating.

remo *nm* (**a**) (*Náut*) oar; **a ~ y vela** (*fig*) speedily; **cruzar un río a ~** to row across a river; **pasaron los cañones a ~** they rowed the guns across.

(**b**) (*Dep*) rowing; **practicar el ~** to row, go in for rowing.

(**c**) (*Anat*) arm, leg; (*Orn*) wing.

(**d**) (*fig*) toils, hardships; **andar al ~** to work like a (galley) slave.

remoción *nf* (**a**) (*gen*) removal. (**b**) (*de persona*: *esp LAm*) sacking*, dismissal.

remodelación *nf* remodelling; (*renovación*) refurbishment; (*Aut*) restyling; (*Pol*) reshuffle, restructuring; **~ ministerial** cabinet reshuffle.

remodelar [1a] *vt* to remodel; (*Aut*) to restyle; (*Pol*) to reshuffle, restructure.

remojar [1a] *vt* (**a**) (*gen*) to steep, soak (*en* in); (*bañar*) to dip (*en* in, into); (*sin querer*) to soak, drench (*con* with); *galleta etc* to dip, dunk (*en* in).

(**b**) (*) *suceso* to celebrate with a drink.

(**c**) (*Méx**: *sobornar*) to bribe.

remojo *nm* (**a**) (*gen*) steeping, soaking; drenching; (*galleta*) dip, dipping; **dejar la ropa en ~** to leave clothes to soak; **poner los garbanzos a ~** to put chickpeas in to soak.

(**b**) (*Carib, Méx*) (*regalo*) gift, present; (*propina*) tip.

remojón *nm* (**a**) (*gen*) soaking, drenching; **darse un ~*** to go in for a dip. (**b**) (*Culin*) piece of bread soaked in milk (*etc*).

remolacha *nf* (*t* **~ de mesa, ~ roja**) beet, beetroot; **~ azucarera** sugar beet.

remolcable *adj* that can be towed.

remolcador *nm* (*Náut*) tug; (*Aut*) tow car, breakdown lorry.

remolcar [1g] *vt* to tow, tow along; to take in tow; (*Ferro*) to pull.

remoledor* *adj* (*And, Cono Sur*) roistering, party-going.

remoler [2h] **1** *vt* (**a**) (*moler*) to grind up small. (**b**) (*And, CAm*: *fastidiar*) to annoy, pester. **2** *vi* (*Cono Sur, And**) to live it up*.

remolienda* *nf* (*And, Cono Sur*) party, wild time*.

remolinar(se) [1a], **remolinear(se)** [1a] = **arremolinarse.**

remolino *nm* (**a**) (*agua*) swirl, eddy; (*en río*) whirlpool; (*de aire*) whirl; disturbance; (*viento*) whirlwind; (*de humo, polvo*) whirl, cloud.

(**b**) (*de pelo*) tuft.

(**c**) (*de gente*) crowd, throng, crush, moving mass.

(**d**) (*fig*) commotion.

remolón 1 *adj* (**a**) (*terco*) stubborn; (*difícil*) awkward, cantankerous. (**b**) (*vago*) slack, lazy. **2** *nm*, **remolona** *nf* stubborn individual; slacker, shirker; **hacerse el ~** = **remolonear.**

remolonear [1a] *vi* (**a**) (*estar resuelto*) to be stubborn, refuse to budge; to hold out on sb. (**b**) (*no trabajar*) to slack, shirk.

remolque *nm* (**a**) (*acto*) towing; **a ~** on tow, being towed; **ir a ~** to be on tow; **llevar un coche a ~** to tow a car; **lo hizo a ~** (*fig*) he did it reluctantly; they had to push him to do it, he did it because somebody made him; **dar ~ a** to tow, take in tow.

(**b**) (*Náut*: *cable*) towrope; cable, hawser; (*Aut etc*) towrope.

(**c**) (*vehículo etc*: *Aut*) tow; (*caravana*) trailer, caravan; (*Náut*) ship on tow.

remonda‡ *nf*: **¡es la ~!** this is the end!; it's sheer hell!

remonta *nf* (**a**) (*Cos etc*) mending, repair. (**b**) (*Mil*) remount, supply of cavalry horses; cavalry horses; cavalry depot.

remontada *nf* (*fig*) recovery.

remontar [1a] **1** *vt* (**a**) *media* to mend (a ladder in); *zapato* to mend, repair, resole.

(**b**) **~ el vuelo** to soar (up).

(**c**) *río etc* to go up.

(**d**) *obstáculo* to negotiate, get over, surmount.

(**e**) (*Mil*) *caballería* to remount.

(**f**) *reloj* to wind.

(**g**) (*Caza*) *animales* to frighten away.

(**h**) **~ un gol** (*Dep*) to pull a goal back.

2 remontarse *vr* (**a**) (*Aer, Orn etc*) to rise, soar; (*edificio*) to soar, tower; (*fig*) to soar; **~ en alas de la imaginación** to take flight on the wings of fantasy.

(**b**) **~ a** (*Fin*) to amount to.

(**c**) (*en el tiempo*) **~ a** to go back to; **sus recuerdos se remontan al siglo pasado** her memories go back to the last century; **este texto se remonta al siglo XI** this text dates from (*o* back to) the 11th century; **tenemos que remontarnos a los mismos orígenes** we must get back to the very origins.

remonte *nm* ski-lift.

remoquete *nm* (**a**) (*puñetazo*) punch. (**b**) (*fig*: *comentario*) cutting remark, dig. (**c**) (*apodo*) nickname; **poner ~ a uno** to give sb a nickname. (**d**) (*) (*coqueteo*) flirting, spooning*; (*pretendiente*) suitor.

rémora *nf* (**a**) (*Zool*) remora. (**b**) (*fig*) drawback; hindrance.

remorder [2h] **1** *vt persona* to grieve, distress; to cause remorse to; *conciencia* to prick; *mente* to afflict, prey upon.

2 remorderse *vr* to suffer (*o* show) remorse; to suffer inwardly, harbour a grudge (*o* jealousy *etc*).

remordimiento *nm* remorse, regret (*t* **~s**); **tener ~s** to feel remorse, suffer pangs of conscience.

remotamente *adv* (**a**) *parecerse, recordar* vaguely, slightly; **no se le parece ni ~** he doesn't look even remotely like him. (**b**) *pensar etc* vaguely, tentatively.

remotidad* *nf* (*CAm*) remote spot, distant place.

remoto *adj* remote; **¡ni por lo más ~!*** not on your life!; **no tengo lo más ~*** I haven't the faintest.

remover [2h] *vt* (**a**) *tierra etc* to turn over, dig up; *objetos* to move round, change over, shift about; *cóctel etc* to shake; *sopa etc* to stir (round); *sentimientos* to disturb, upset; **~ un asunto** to turn a matter over, go into a matter again; **~ el pasado** to stir up the past; to rake up the past; **~ un proyecto** to revive a scheme; **~ cielo y tierra, ~ Roma con Santiago** to move heaven and earth.

(**b**) (*quitar*) *obstáculo etc* to remove; (*Med*) to excise, cut out; *persona* to discharge, remove (from office); (*esp LAm*) to sack*, fire*.

removimiento *nm* removal.

remozado *nm* rejuvenation; renovation.

remozamiento *nm* rejuvenation; renovation.

remozar [1f] **1** *vt persona etc* to rejuvenate; *aspecto etc* to brighten up, polish up; *organización etc* to give a new look to, give a face-lift to; *edificio, fachada* to renovate.

2 remozarse *vr* to be rejuvenated; to look much younger; **la encuentro muy remozada** I find her looking much younger.

remplazar *etc* = **reemplazar** *etc.*

rempujar* [1a] *vt* to keep at it, persist.

rempujón* *nm* shove, push.

remuda *nf* change, alteration; replacement; **~ de caballos** change of horses; **~ (de ropa)** change of clothes, spare clothes.

remudar [1a] *vt* to remove; to change, alter; to replace.

remuneración *nf* remuneration.

remunerado *adj*: **trabajo mal ~** badly-paid job.

remunerador *adj* remunerative; rewarding, worthwhile; **poco ~** unremunerative.

remunerar [1a] *vt* to remunerate; to pay; to reward.

remunerativo *adj* remunerative.

renacentista *adj* Renaissance (*atr*).

renacer [2d] *vi* (**a**) (*gen*) to be reborn; (*Bot*) to appear again, come up again.

(**b**) (*fig*) to revive; to acquire new vigour (*o* life); **hacer ~** to revive; **hoy me siento ~** today I feel renewed, I feel I am coming to life again today; **sentían ~ la esperanza** they felt new hope.

renaciente *adj* renascent.

renacimiento *nm* rebirth, revival; **R~** Renaissance.

renacuajo *nm* (**a**) (*Zool*) tadpole. (**b**) (*) shrimp; (*pey*) runt, little squirt*.

renal *adj* renal, kidney (*atr*).

Renania *nf* Rhineland.

renano *adj* Rhenish, Rhine (*atr*).

rencilla *nf* (**a**) (*riña*) quarrel; (*enemistad*) feud; **~s** dissension; arguments, bickering. (**b**) (*rencor*) bad blood; ill will; grudge; **me tiene ~** he's got it in for me, he bears me a grudge.

rencilloso *adj* quarrelsome.

renco *adj* lame.

rencor *nm* rancour, bitterness; ill feeling, resentment; spitefulness; **guardar ~** to bear malice, have a grudge (*a* against); **no le guardo ~** I bear him no malice.

rencorosamente *adv* (*V adj*) (**a**) spitefully, maliciously. (**b**) resentfully; bitterly.

rencoroso *adj* (**a**) (*malicioso*) (*ser*) spiteful, nasty, malicious. (**b**) (*resentido*) (*estar*) resentful; (*amargado*) bitter, embittered.

rendición *nf* (**a**) (*Mil etc*) surrender; **~ incondicional** unconditional surrender. (**b**) (*Fin*) yield, profit(s), return. (**c**) (*Cono Sur*) (*Com*) trading balance; (*Fin*: *t* **~ de cuentas**) balance.

rendidamente *adv* submissively; obsequiously; humbly, devotedly.

rendido *adj* (**a**) (*sumiso*) submissive; (*servil*) obsequious; *admirador* humble, devoted. (**b**) **estar ~** (**de cansancio**) to be exhausted, be all in.

rendidor *adj* (*LAm*) highly productive; (*Fin*) highly profitable.

rendija *nf* (**a**) crack, cleft, crevice; chink; aperture. (**b**) (*fig*) rift, split. (**c**) (*Jur*) loophole.

rendimiento *nm* (**a**) (*parte útil*) usable part, proportion of usable material.

(**b**) (*Mec*) efficiency, performance; (*capacidad*) capacity; (*producción*) output; **el ~ del motor** the performance of the engine; **aumentar el ~ de una máquina** to increase the output of a machine; **funcionar a pleno ~** to work all-out, work at full throttle.

(**c**) (*Fin*) yield, profit(s), return; **~ del capital** return on capital; **ley del ~ decreciente** law of diminishing returns.

(**d**) (*cualidad*) (*sumisión*) submissiveness; (*servilismo*) obsequiousness; (*devoción*) devotion; **su ~ total a la voluntad de ella** his complete submissiveness to her will.

(**e**) (*agotamiento*) exhaustion.

rendir [3k] **1** *vt* (**a**) (*producir*) to produce, yield, bear; *producto, total etc* to produce; *beneficios etc* to yield; *interés* to bear.

(**b**) (*vencer*) *enemigo* to defeat, conquer, overcome; *país* to conquer, subdue; *fortaleza* to take, capture, reduce.

(**c**) *persona* to exhaust, tire out; **le rindió el sueño** sleep overcame him.

(**d**) *voluntad* to subject to one's own will, dominate, assume control of; **logró ~ el albedrío de la joven** he came to dominate the young woman's will completely; **había que ~ su entereza** he had to overcome his honest doubts, he had to fight down his moral objections.

(**e**) (*devolver*) to give back, return; (*entregar*) to hand over; (*Mil*) to surrender; (*Mil*) *guardia* to hand over; (*Esp**) to vomit, bring up.

(**f**) (*Com*) *factura* to send.

(**g**) (*Mil*) *bandera* to dip; *armas* to lower, reverse.

(**h**) *tributo* to pay; *homenaje* to do, pay; *gracias* to give; **~ culto a** to worship; (*fig*) to pay homage to, pay tribute to.

(**i**) **~ examen** (*Cono Sur*) to sit (*o* take) an exam.

2 *vi* (**a**) (*producir*) to yield, produce; to be profitable, give good results; **el negocio no rinde** the business doesn't pay; **este año ha rendido poco** it has done poorly this year; **la finca rinde para mantener a 8 familias** the estate produces enough to keep 8 families; **trabajo, pero no rindo** I work hard, but without much to show for it.

(**b**) (*LAm*: *durar*) to last longer, keep going.

(**c**) (*LAm*: *henchirse*) to swell up (in the cooking *etc*).

3 rendirse *vr* (**a**) (*ceder*) to yield (*a* to); (*Mil*) to surrender; (*entregarse*) to give o.s. up; **~ a la evidencia** to bow before the evidence; **~ a la fuerza** to yield to violence; **~ a la razón** to yield to reason.

(**b**) (*cansarse*) to wear o.s. out, exhaust o.s.

renditivo *adj* (*Cono Sur*) productive; profitable.

renegado 1 *adj* (**a**) (*traidor*) renegade; (*Ecl*) apostate.

(**b**) (*****) (*brusco*) gruff; (*malhumorado*) cantankerous, bad-tempered.

2 *nm*, **renegada** *nf* (**a**) renegade; (*Ecl*) apostate; (*Pol*) turncoat.

(**b**) (*****) bad lot, nasty piece of work.

renegar [1h *y* 1j] **1** *vt* (**a**) (*negar*) to deny vigorously, deny repeatedly.

(**b**) (*odiar*) to abhor, detest.

2 *vi* (**a**) (*apostatar*) to turn renegade, go over to the other side, be a traitor; (*Ecl*) to apostatize.

(**b**) **~ de** (*abandonar*) to forsake, disown; (*renunciar*) to renounce, give up; **~ de su familia** to disown one's family; **~ de la amistad de uno** to break completely with sb; **reniego de ti** I want nothing more to do with you.

(**c**) **~ de** (*odiar*) to abhor, detest.

(**d**) (*jurar*) to curse, swear; (*Rel*) to blaspheme.

(**e**) (*quejarse*) to grumble; to protest, complain.

(**f**) (*And, Méx*) (*enojarse*) to get angry, get upset; (*gritar*) to shout, rage.

(**g**) (*And, Cono Sur, Méx*: *protestar*) to protest.

renegociar [1b] *vt* to renegotiate.

renegón* *adj* grumbling, cantankerous, grouchy*.

renegrido *adj* (*LAm*) very black, very dark.

RENFE, Renfe ['renfe] *nf* (*Ferro*) *abr de* **Red Nacional de los Ferrocarriles Españoles.**

renglón *nm* (**a**) (*línea*) line (of writing); **a ~ seguido** in the very next line, (*fig*) straight after, without a break; **escribir un ~ a, poner unos renglones a** to drop a line to; **leer entre renglones** to read between the lines; **estos pobres renglones** these humble jottings.

(**b**) (*Com etc*) item (of expenditure).

(**c**) (*LAm Com*) (*género*) line of goods; (*departamento*) department, area.

rengo *adj* (*LAm*) lame, crippled.

rengue‡ *nm* train.

renguear [1a] *vi* (**a**) (*LAm*: *cojear*) to limp, hobble. (**b**) (*Cono Sur*: *perseguir*) to pursue a woman.

renguera *nf* (*LAm*) limp, limping; lameness.

reniego *nm* (**a**) (*juramento*) curse, oath; (*Rel*) blasphemy, blasphemous remark.

(**b**) (*queja*) grumble; complaint.

reno *nm* reindeer.

renombrado *adj* renowned, famous.

renombre *nm* (**a**) (*fama*) renown, fame; **de ~** renowned, famous. (**b**) (*apellido*) surname.

renovable *adj* renewable.

renovación *nf* (**a**) (*gen*) renewal; renovation; **~ espiritual** spiritual renewal; **~ de la suscripción** renewal of one's subscription; **~ urbana** urban renewal.

(**b**) (*Arquit etc*) renovation; restoration; redecoration.

(**c**) (*Pol etc*) reorganization, remodelling, transformation.

renovado *adj* renewed, redoubled; **con renovada energía** with renewed energy.

renoval *nm* (*Cono Sur, Méx*) area of young trees.

renovar [1l] *vt* (**a**) (*gen*) to renew; *aviso etc* to renew, repeat; *abono* to renew.

(**b**) (*Arquit etc*) to renovate; to restore; *cuarto* to redecorate.

(**c**) (*Pol etc*) to reorganize, remodel, transform.

renquear [1a] *vi* (**a**) (*cojear*) to limp, hobble. (**b**) (*****: *ir tirando*) to get along, manage with difficulty. (**c**) (*motor*) to splutter. (**d**) (*****: *vacilar*) to dither.

renta *nf* (**a**) (*ingresos*) income; (*interés etc*) interest, return, yield; **política de ~s** incomes policy; **~ devengada** earned income; **~ disponible** disposable income; **~ gravable, ~ imponible** taxable income; **~ nacional** national income; **~ bruta nacional** gross national income; **~s públicas** revenue; **~ del trabajo** earned income; **~ vitalicia** annuity; **título de ~ fija** fixed-interest bond; **valores de ~ fija** fixed-yield securities; **tiene ~s particulares** she has a private income; **vivir de sus ~s** to live on one's private income.

(**b**) (*deuda*) public debt, national debt.

(**c**) (*alquiler, esp LAm*) rent; **'casa de ~'** 'house to let'.

(**d**) (*Dep*) lead, advantage.

rentabilidad *nf* (*V adj*) profitability; cost-effectiveness.

rentabilizar [1f] *vt* to make (more) profitable; to promote; to exploit to the full, (*pey*) cash in on.

rentable *adj* profitable; (*de coste-beneficio favorable*) cost-effective, economic; **no ~** unprofitable; uneconomical; **el avión no es ~** the aircraft is not an economic proposition; **la línea ya no es ~** the line is no longer economic (to run).

rentado *adj* (*Cono Sur*) *trabajo* paid.

rentar [1a] **1** *vt* (**a**) (*rendir*) to produce, yield. (**b**) (*LAm*) *casa* to let, rent out, rent. **2 rentarse** *vr*: **'se renta'** (*Méx*) 'to let'.

rentero, -a *nm/f* tenant farmer.

rentista *nmf* (**a**) (*accionista*) stockholder, person who lives on income from shares, (*como miembro de clase*) rentier; (*que vive de sus rentas*) person of independent means. (**b**) (*experto*) financial expert.

rentístico *adj* financial.

renuencia *nf* (**a**) *persona* unwillingness, reluctance. (**b**) *objeto etc* awkwardness.

renuente *adj* (**a**) *persona* unwilling, reluctant. (**b**) *sustancia* awkward, difficult.

renuevo *nm* (**a**) (*acto*) renewal. (**b**) (*Bot*) shoot, sprout.

renuncia *nf* renunciation; resignation; relinquishment; abdication.

renunciar [1b] **1** *vt* (*t vi*: **~ a**) *derecho etc* to renounce (*en* in favour of), surrender, relinquish; *hábito, proyecto etc* to give up; *demanda* to drop, waive; *puesto, responsabilidad* to resign; *trono* to abdicate (*en* in favour of); **~ a hacer algo** to give up doing sth, stop doing sth.

2 *vi* (*Naipes*) to revoke.

renuncio *nm* **(a)** (*Naipes*) revoke. **(b) coger a uno en un ~** to catch sb in a fib, catch sb out.

reñidamente *adv luchar etc* bitterly, hard, stubbornly.

reñidero *nm*: **~ de gallos** cockpit.

reñido *adj* **(a)** *batalla, concurso* bitter; **un partido ~** a hard-fought game; a bitter struggle; **en lo más ~ de la batalla** in the thick of the fight.

(b) estar ~ con uno to be at odds with sb, be on bad terms with sb; **está ~ con su familia** he has fallen out with his family.

(c) estar ~ con (*principio etc*) to be at variance with, be divorced from, be in opposition to.

reñidor *adj* quarrelsome.

reñir [3h *y* 3k] **1** *vt* **(a)** (*regañar*) to scold; (*reprender*) to tell off, reprimand (*por* for).

(b) *batalla* to fight, wage.

2 *vi* (*disputar*) to quarrel, fall out (*con* with); (*pelear*) to fight, scrap, come to blows; **ha reñido con su novio** she's fallen out with her boyfriend; she's broken it off with her fiancé; **se pasan la vida riñendo** they spend their whole time quarrelling; **riñeron por cuestión de dinero** they quarrelled about (*o* over) money.

reo¹ *nmf* **(a)** (*delincuente*) culprit, offender; criminal; (*Jur*) accused, defendant; **~ de Estado** person accused of a crime against the state; **~ de muerte** person under sentence of death.

(b) (*Cono Sur*: *vagabundo*) tramp, bum (*US*).

reo² *nm* (*pez*) sea-trout.

reoca‡ *nf*: **es la ~** (*Esp*) (*bueno*) it's the tops*; (*malo*) it's the pits‡.

reojo: mirar a uno de ~ to look at sb out of the corner of one's eye; (*fig*) to look askance at sb, look dubiously at sb.

reordenación *nf* realignment.

reordenar [1a] *vt* to realign.

reorganización *nf* reorganization.

reorganizar [1f] **1** *vt* to reorganize; to reshuffle. **2 reorganizarse** *vr* to reorganize.

reorientación *nf* reorientation; new direction; readjustment.

reorientar [1a] *vt* to reorientate; to give a new direction to; to readjust.

reóstato *nm* rheostat.

repaminonda‡ *nf*: **es la ~** (*Esp*) it's the tops*.

repanchigarse [1h] *vr*, **repantigarse** [1h] *vr* to lounge, sprawl, loll (back); **estar repanchigado en un sillón** to loll back in a chair.

reparable *adj* repairable.

reparación *nf* **(a)** (*acto*) repairing, mending.

(b) (*Téc*) repair; **'reparaciones en el acto', 'reparaciones instantáneas'** 'repairs while you wait'; **efectuar reparaciones en** to carry out repairs to.

(c) (*fig*) amends, reparation, redress.

reparador 1 *adj* **(a)** *persona* critical, faultfinding.

(b) *comida* fortifying, strengthening, restorative; *sueño* refreshing.

2 *nm* (*Téc*) repairer.

3 *nm*, **reparadora¹** *nf* (*criticón*) carping critic, faultfinder.

reparadora² *nf*: **~ de calzados** (*Méx*) shoe repairer's.

reparar [1a] **1** *vt* **(a)** (*Téc*) to repair, mend.

(b) *energías etc* to repair, restore; *fortunas* to retrieve.

(c) *ofensa etc* to make amends for; *daño, pérdida* to make good; *consecuencia* to undo.

(d) *golpe* to parry.

(e) *observar* to observe, notice.

(f) (*Cono Sur*: *imitar*) to mimic, imitate.

2 *vi* **(a)** (*notar*) **~ en** to observe, notice, note, see; **no reparó en la diferencia** he didn't notice the difference; **sin ~ en que ya no funcionaba** without noticing that it was no longer working.

(b) ~ en (*hacer caso de*) to pay attention to, take heed of; (*considerar*) to consider; **no ~ en las dificultades** to take no heed of the difficulties, refuse to consider the difficulties; **repara en lo que vas a hacer** reflect on what you are going to do; **sin ~ en los gastos** heedless of expense, regardless of the cost; **no ~ en nada** to stop at nothing.

(c) (*CAm, Méx*: *caballo*) to rear, buck.

3 repararse *vr* **(a)** to check o.s., restrain o.s.

(b) (*CAm, Méx*: *caballo*) to rear, buck.

reparista *adj* (*And, CAm, Carib*), **reparisto** *adj* (*CAm, Carib*) = **reparón 1**.

reparo *nm* **(a)** (*Téc*) repair; (*Arquit etc*) restoration.

(b) (*Esgrima*) parry; (*fig*: *protección*) defence, protection.

(c) (*Med*) remedy; restorative.

(d) (*objeción*) objection; (*crítica*) criticism; (*duda*) doubt; **poner ~s** to raise objections (*a* to); to criticize, express one's doubts; (*pey*) to find fault (*a* with).

(e) (*escrúpulo*) hesitation; scruple, doubt; **no tuvo ~ en** + *infin* he did not hesitate to + *infin*; he did not scruple to + *infin*.

(f) (*CAm, Méx*: *caballo*) bucking, rearing; **tirar un ~** to rear, buck.

reparón 1 *adj* carping, critical, faultfinding. **2** *nm*, **reparona** *nf* critic, faultfinder.

repartición *nf* **(a)** (*distribución*) distribution; sharing out, division. **(b)** (*Cono Sur Admin*) government department, administrative section. **(c)** (*LAm Pol*: *de tierras*) redistribution.

repartida *nf* (*CAm, Cono Sur*) = **repartición (a)**.

repartido *nm* (*Correos*) delivery; (*de lechero etc*) round.

repartidor *nm* distributor; (*Com*) roundsman, deliveryman; **~ de leche** milkman; **~ de periódicos** paperboy.

repartija* *nf* share-out, carve-up*.

repartimiento *nm* distribution; division; (*de impuestos*) assessment.

repartir [3a] **1** *vt* (*distribuir*) to distribute; (*dividir entre varios*) to divide (up), share (out); to parcel out; *trabajos* to allot, assign; *tierras* to parcel up, divide, split up; *país* to partition; *folletos, premios etc* to give out, hand out; *comida* to serve out; *bebidas, vasos* to hand round; *dividendo* to declare, pay out; *cartas, leche, pan, periódicos etc* to deliver; *cartas* to deal; (*Teat*) *papeles* to cast; *castigos* to issue, impose, mete out; **el premio está muy repartido** the prize is shared among many; **las cartas están repartidas en 4 palos** the cards are distributed among 4 suits; **los diamantes están repartidos 4-3** the diamonds are split 4-3; **las guarniciones están repartidas por toda la costa** the garrisons are distributed all round the coast, there are garrisons dotted about all along the coast.

2 repartirse *vr* to be distributed, be shared out (*etc*); **'se reparte a domicilio'** 'home delivery service'.

reparto *nm* **(a)** (*acto*) = **repartición (a)**.

(b) (*distribución*) distribution (*t Bridge*); **un ~ poco uniforme** a very uneven distribution.

(c) (*Com, Correos*) delivery.

(d) (*Teat*: *acto*) casting; (*lista*) cast, cast list.

(e) (*CAm, Carib, Méx*: *solar*) building site, building lot (*US*); (*LAm*: *urbanización*) housing estate, real estate development (*US*).

(f) ~ de utilidades (*Fin*) profit sharing.

repasador *nm* (*Cono Sur*) dishcloth.

repasar [1a] *vt* **(a)** *lugar* to pass (by) again; *calle* to go along again; **pasar y ~ una calle** to go up and down a street repeatedly.

(b) ~ la plancha por una prenda to give a garment another iron.

(c) (*Cos*) to sew, sew up, darn; to mend.

(d) (*Mec*) to check, overhaul.

(e) *cuenta etc* to check; *texto* to revise, re-examine; *notas* to go over again; to read through rapidly, flick through; *lección* to revise; *publicación etc* to put the finishing touches to, polish up.

(f) (*Cono Sur*) *platos etc* to dust, polish; *mueble* to polish; *ropa* to brush (down).

repasata* *nf* ticking-off*.

repaso *nm* (*gen*) review, revision; check; (*Cos*) mending; (*Mec*) checkup, overhaul; (*lectura*) rapid reading, quick re-reading; **~ general** general overhaul; **curso de ~** revision course, refresher course; **ropa de ~** mending, darning; **dar un ~ a una lección** to revise a lesson; **los técnicos daban el último ~ al cohete** the technicians were giving the rocket a final check; **pegar un buen ~ a uno*** to give sb a proper ticking-off*.

repatear‡ [1a] *vt*: **ese tío me repatea** (*Esp*) that chap gets on my wick‡, that chap turns me right off*.

repatriación *nf* repatriation.

repatriado 1 *adj* repatriated. **2** *nm*, **repatriada** *nf* repatriate, repatriated person.

repatriar [1b] **1** *vt* to repatriate; *criminal etc* to deport; to send home, send back to one's country of origin; **van a ~ el famoso mármol** they are going to send the famous marble back to its original country.

2 repatriarse *vr* to return home, go back to one's own country.

repe*¹ **1** *adj* repeated, duplicated; **un sello que tengo ~** a duplicate stamp I have, a stamp I have twice over; **los tengo ~s** I've got stacks*. **2** *nmf* (*Univ*) student who is repeating a course. **3** *nf* (*TV etc*) repeat (of a programme).

repe² *nm* (*And*) mashed bananas with milk.

repechar [1a] *vi*: **~ contra** (*Méx*) to lean (one's chest) against.

repecho *nm* (**a**) (*vertiente*) sharp gradient, steep slope; **a ~** uphill. (**b**) (*Carib, Méx*: *parapeto*) parapet. (**c**) (*Méx*: *refugio*) shelter, refuge, hut.

repela *nf* (*And, CAm*) gleaning (of coffee crop).

repelar [1a] **1** *vt* (**a**) (*pelar completamente*) to leave completely bare, shear; *hierba* to nibble, crop; *uñas* to clip.
(**b**) **~ a uno** to pull sb's hair.
(**c**) (*Méx*: *criticar*) to raise objections to, call into question.
(**d**) (*Méx**: *reprender*) to scold, tell off*.
2 repelarse *vr* (*Cono Sur*) to feel remorse.

repelencia *nf* revulsion, disgust.

repelente 1 *adj* (**a**) (*asqueroso*) repellent, repulsive, disgusting. (**b**) (*LAm**: *impertinente*) cheeky*, insolent; (*Méx**: *fastidioso*) annoying, irritating. **2** *nm* (insect) repellent.

repeler [2a] **1** *vt* (**a**) *enemigo etc* to repel, repulse, drive back; *persona* to push away.
(**b**) **este material repele el agua** this material is water-repellent; **la pared repele la pelota** the wall sends the ball back, the ball bounces off the wall.
(**c**) *idea, oferta* to reject.
(**d**) (*fig*) to repel, disgust, fill with repulsion.
2 repelerse *vr*: **los dos se repelen** the two are (mutually) incompatible.

repelo *nm* (**a**) (*pelo*) hair out of place, hair (*etc*) that sticks up; (*en madera*) snag, knot; (*Anat*) hangnail.
(**b**) (*: *riña*) tiff, slight argument.
(**c**) (*fig*) aversion.
(**d**) (*And, Méx*) (*baratijas*) junk, bric-a-brac; (*trapo*) rag, tatter.

repelón 1 *adj* (*Méx*) grumbling, grumpy.
2 *nm* (**a**) (*tirón*) tug (at one's hair).
(**b**) (*Cos*) ruck, snag.
(**c**) (*pedacito*) small bit, tag, pinch.
(**d**) (*de caballo*) dash, short run.
(**e**) (*Méx*: *reprimenda*) telling-off*, scolding.

repelús* *nm* inexplicable fear; **me da ~** it gives me the willies‡, it gives me the shivers.

repeluz: **en un ~** *adv* (*Cono Sur*) in a flash, in an instant.

repeluzno* *nm* nervous shiver, slight start of fear.

repellar [1a] *vt* (**a**) (*Arquit*) to plaster, stucco; (*LAm*: *enjalbegar*) to whitewash. (**b**) (*Carib*: *menear*) to wriggle, wiggle.

repello *nm* (**a**) (*LAm*: *jalbegue*) whitewash(ing). (**b**) (*Carib etc*: *en baile*) wiggle, grind.

repensar [1j] *vt* to rethink, reconsider, think out again.

repente *nm* (**a**) (*movimiento*) sudden movement, start, jerk; (*fig*) sudden impulse; **~ de ira** fit of anger.
(**b**) **de ~** (*de pronto*) suddenly; (*sin avisar*) unexpectedly; (*de golpe*) all at once.
(**c**) (*Méx Med*) (*acceso*) fit; (*desmayo*) fainting fit.

repentinamente *adv* suddenly; unexpectedly; **torcer ~** to turn sharply, make a sharp turn.

repentino *adj* (**a**) (*súbito*) sudden; (*imprevisto*) unexpected; *cambio* sudden, swift; *curva, vuelta* sharp. (**b**) **tener repentina compasión** to be quick to pity.

repentización *nf* sight-reading; ad-lib*, improvisation.

repentizar [1f] *vi* (*Mús*) to sight-read; (*en discurso etc*) to ad-lib, improvise.

repentón* *nm* violent start.

repera* *nf*: **es la ~** it's the tops*.

repercusión *nf* (**a**) (*sonido*) (*gen*) repercussion; (*reverberación*) reverberation; echo.
(**b**) (*fig*: *consecuencia*) repercussion; **repercusiones** repercussions, after-effects; **las repercusiones de esta decisión** the repercussions of this decision; **de amplia ~, de ancha ~** far-reaching; **tener ~(es) en** to have repercussions on.

repercutir [3a] **1** *vt* (*And*) to contradict.
2 *vi* (**a**) (*objeto*) to rebound, bounce off; (*sonido*) to re-echo; to reverberate, go on sounding (*o* beating *etc*).
(**b**) (*fig*) **~ en** to have repercussions on, have effects on, have an effect on.
(**c**) (*Méx*: *oler mal*) to smell bad, stink.
3 repercutirse *vr* to reverberate.

reperiquete *nm* (*Méx*) (**a**) (*baratija*) cheap jewellery. (**b**) (*baladronada*) brag, boast.

repertoriar [1b] *vt* to catalogue, list.

repertorio *nm* (**a**) (*lista*) list, index, compendium; (*catálogo*) catalogue. (**b**) (*Teat*) repertoire; repertory. (**c**) (*Inform*) repertoire.

repesca *nf* (**a**) (*Univ*) repeat exam. (**b**) (*Dep**) play-off (for third place); second chance to qualify.

repescar [1g] *vt* to give a second chance to.

repeso *nm* (*And*) bonus, extra.

repetición *nf* (**a**) (*gen*) repetition; recurrence. (**b**) (*Teat etc*) encore; **pedir la ~ de una canción** to encore a song. (**c**) **fusil de ~** repeater rifle.

repetidamente *adv* repeatedly.

repetido *adj* repeated; (*numeroso*) numerous; *sello etc* duplicate; **el tan ~ aviso** the oft-repeated warning; **repetidas veces** repeatedly, over and over again, many times.

repetidor *nm* (*Rad, TV*) booster, booster station.

repetidora *nf* repeater rifle.

repetir [3l] **1** *vt* (*gen*) to repeat; (*volver a decir*) to say again; (*volver a hacer*) to do again; (*Teat*) to repeat as an encore, sing (*etc*) again; *lección* to recite, rehearse, go over; *sonido* to echo; *grabación* to repeat, play back; **le repito que es imposible** I repeat that it is impossible, I tell you again it is impossible; **los niños repiten lo que hacen las personas mayores** children imitate adults, children ape their seniors.
2 *vi* (**a**) (*gen*) to repeat; **el pepino repite mucho** cucumber keeps coming back, cucumber gives one bad hiccups.
(**b**) **~ de un plato** to have a second helping of a dish.
3 repetirse *vr* (**a**) (*persona*) to repeat o.s.
(**b**) (*suceso*) to recur; **¡ojalá no se repita esto!** I hope this won't happen again!

repicado *nm* copying of (video) tapes, video piracy.

repicar [1g] **1** *vt* (**a**) *carne etc* to chop up small.
(**b**) (*picar*) to prick (again).
(**c**) *campanas* to ring, peal (merrily).
(**d**) **~ gordo un acontecimiento*** to celebrate an event in style.
(**e**) *cinta* to copy, pirate.
2 repicarse *vr* to boast (*de* about, of).

repintar [1a] **1** *vt* (*volver a pintar*) to repaint; (*pintar de prisa*) to paint hastily, paint roughly. **2 repintarse** *vr* to pile the make-up on.

repipi* *adj* (*esnob*) posh*; (*afectado*) la-di-da*, affected; arty*; (*precoz*) precocious, knowing for one's years; (*engreído*) stuck-up*; **es una niña ~** she's a little madam, she's an insufferably affected child.

repipiez* *nf* poshness*; affectation; artiness*; precociousness; stuck-up ways*.

repique *nm* (**a**) (*Mús*) peal(ing), ringing; chime. (**b**) (*: *riña*) tiff, squabble.

repiquete *nm* (**a**) (*Mús*) merry peal(ing). (**b**) (*Mil*) clash. (**c**) (*Cono Sur Orn*) trill, song. (**d**) (*And*: *resentimiento*) pique, resentment.

repiquetear [1a] **1** *vt* (**a**) *campanas* to peal joyfully, ring merrily.
(**b**) *mesa, tambor etc* to tap, beat rapidly, drum lightly on.
2 *vi* (**a**) (*Mús*) to peal out, ring.
(**b**) (*máquina*) to clatter.
3 repiquetearse‡ *vr* to exchange insults, slag one another off‡.

repiqueteo *nm* (**a**) (*Mús*) joyful peal(ing), merry ringing. (**b**) (*en mesa etc*) tapping, drumming; (*de máquina*) clatter.

repisa *nf* ledge, shelf; (wall) bracket; **~ de chimenea** mantelpiece; **~ de ventana** windowsill.

replana *nf* (*And*) underworld slang.

replantar [1a] *vt* to replant.

replantear [1a] *vt cuestión* to raise again, reopen.

replantigarse [1h] *vr* (*LAm*) = **repanchigarse.**

repleción *nf* repletion.

replegable *adj* folding, that folds (up); (*Aer*) *tren de aterrizaje* retractable.

replegar [1h *y* 1j] **1** *vt* (*doblar*) to fold over; (*de nuevo*) to fold again, refold; *tren de aterrizaje* to retract, draw up.
2 replegarse *vr* (*Mil*) to withdraw, fall back (in good order; *sobre* on).

repletar [1a] **1** *vt* to fill completely, stuff full, pack tight. **2**

repletarse *vr* to eat to repletion.
repleto *adj* (**a**) (*lleno*) replete, full up; ~ **de** filled with, absolutely full of, crammed with; **la plaza estaba repleta de gente** the square was solid with people; **una colección repleta de rarezas** a collection containing innumerable rarities.
(**b**) **estar** ~ (*persona*) to be full up (*with food*), be replete.
(**c**) *aspecto* sleek, well-fed.
réplica *nf* (**a**) (*respuesta*) answer; retort, rejoinder; (*refutación*) rebuttal; (*Jur*) answer to a charge; ~**s** backchat; **dejar a uno sin ~s** to leave sb speechless. (**b**) (*Arte*) replica, copy.
replicar [1g] *vi* to answer, retort, rejoin; (*pey*) to argue, answer back; **¡no repliques!** don't answer back!, I don't want any backchat!
replicón* *adj* argumentative; cheeky, saucy.
repliegue *nm* (**a**) (*pliegue*) fold, crease. (**b**) (*Mil*) withdrawal, retirement.
repoblación *nf* (*gente*) repopulation, repeopling; (*objetos*) restocking; ~ **forestal** (re)afforestation.
repoblar [1l] *vt país, zona* to repopulate, repeople; *río etc* to restock; (*Bot*) to (re)afforest, plant trees on.
repollo *nm* cabbage.
repollonco* *adj* (*Cono Sur*), **repolludo*** *adj* tubby*, chunky*.
reponer [2q] **1** *vt* (**a**) (*devolver a su lugar*) to replace, put back; *persona* to reinstate; *combustible, surtido etc* to replenish; (*Fin*) to plough back, reinvest; *objeto dañado etc* to replace, pay for (the replacement of).
(**b**) (*Teat*) to revive, put on again; (*TV*) to repeat.
(**c**) (*contestar*) to reply (*que* that).
2 reponerse *vr* (*Med etc*) to recover; ~ **de** to recover from, get over.
reportaje *nm* report, article, news item; ~ **gráfico** illustrated report, story in pictures.
reportar [1a] **1** *vt* (**a**) (*traer*) to bring, fetch, carry.
(**b**) *beneficio etc* to obtain.
(**c**) (*producir*) to give, bring; **esto le habrá reportado algún beneficio** this will have brought him some benefit; **esto le habrá reportado 2 millones** it must have landed him 2 million; **la cosa no le reportó sino disgustos** the affair brought him nothing but trouble.
(**d**) (*fig: moderar*) to check, restrain.
(**e**) (*LAm*) (*informar*) to report; (*denunciar*) to denounce, accuse; (*notificar*) to notify, inform.
2 *vi* (*LAm: a cita*) to turn up (for an appointment).
3 reportarse *vr* (**a**) (*controlarse*) to control o.s.; to calm down; **¡repórtate!** control yourself!
(**b**) (*CAm, Méx: presentarse*) to present o.s., be present.
reporte *nm* (*CAm, Méx*) report, piece of news.
reportear [1a] **1** *vt* (**a**) *suceso* to report (on). (**b**) (*LAm*) to interview (for the purpose of writing an article); to photograph (for the press). **2** *vi* to report; to work as a journalist.
reportero, –a *nm/f* reporter; ~ **gráfico** news photographer, press photographer.
reposabrazos *nm invar* armrest.
reposacabeza(s) *nm invar* headrest.
reposacodos *nm invar* elbow-rest.
reposadamente *adv* quietly; gently, restfully; unhurriedly, calmly.
reposadera *nf* (*CAm*) drain, sewer.
reposado *adj* (*tranquilo*) quiet; (*descansado*) gentle, restful; (*sin prisa*) unhurried, calm.
reposapiés *nm invar* footrest.
reposaplatos *nm invar* tablemat.
reposar [1a] **1** *vt*: ~ **la comida** to let one's meal go down, settle one's stomach.
2 *vi* (*descansar*) to rest, repose; (*dormir*) to sleep; (*muerto*) to lie, rest.
3 reposarse *vr* (*líquido*) to settle.
reposera *nf* (*LAm*) deckchair, garden chair.
reposición *nf* (**a**) (*gen*) replacement. (**b**) (*Fin*) ploughing-back, reinvestment. (**c**) (*Teat*) revival; (*TV*) repeat. (**d**) (*Med y fig*) recovery.
repositorio *nm* repository.
reposo *nm* rest, repose; ~ **absoluto** (*Med*) complete rest; **guardar** ~ (*Med*) to rest, stay in bed.
repostada *nf* (*CAm*) rude reply, sharp answer.
repostadero *nm* refuelling stop.
repostaje *nm* refuelling, filling up.
repostar [1a] **1** *vt surtido etc* to replenish, renew; ~ **combustible,** ~ **gasolina** (*Aer*) to refuel, (*Aut*) to fill up (with petrol).
2 *vi* to refuel.
3 repostarse *vr* to replenish stocks, take on supplies; ~ **de combustible** to refuel.
repostería *nf* (**a**) (*tienda*) confectioner's (shop), cake shop. (**b**) (*arte*) confectionery; (art of) pastrymaking. (**c**) (*despensa*) larder, pantry.
repostero, –a *nm/f* (**a**) (*cocinero*) confectioner, pastrycook. (**b**) (*And: estantería*) kitchen shelf unit; (*cuarto*) pantry.
repostón* *adj* (*CAm, Méx*) rude, surly.
repregunta *nf* (*Jur*) cross-examination, cross-questioning.
repreguntar [1a] *vt* (*Jur*) to cross-examine, cross-question.
reprender [2a] *vt* to reprimand, tell off*, take to task; *niño* to scold; ~ **algo a uno** to reprimand sb for sth; to criticize sb about sth, reproach sb for sth.
reprensible *adj* reprehensible.
reprensión *nf* reprimand, rebuke; scolding; criticism, reproach.
represa *nf* (**a**) (*captura*) recapture. (**b**) (*represión*) repression; (*parada*) check, stoppage. (**c**) (*presa*) dam; (*vertedero*) weir; (*estanque*) pool, lake; (*Carib, Cono Sur*) reservoir; ~ **de molino** millpond.
represalia *nf* reprisal; **como ~ por** as a reprisal for; **tomar ~s** to take reprisals, retaliate (*contra* against).
represaliado, –a *nm/f* victim of a reprisal; person victimized.
represaliar [1b] *vt* to take reprisals against; to victimize.
represar [1a] *vt* (**a**) (*Náut*) to recapture. (**b**) (*reprimir*) to repress; (*parar*) to check, put a stop to; (*refrenar*) to restrain. (**c**) *agua* to dam (up); (*fig*) to stem.
representable *adj* (*Teat*): **la obra no es** ~ the play cannot actually be staged, it is not a play for the stage.
representación *nf* (**a**) (*gen*) representation; ~ **diplomática** diplomatic representation; embassy; ~ **proporcional** proportional representation; **en ~ de** representing, as a representative of; **por** ~ by proxy; **hacer representaciones a** to make representations to; **tener la ~ exclusiva de** (*Com*) to be sole agent for.
(**b**) (*Teat*) (*función*) performance; production; (*de un actor*) playing, acting; **una serie de 350 representaciones** a run of 350 performances.
(**c**) (*fig: status*) importance, standing; **hombre de** ~ man of some standing.
(**d**) ~ **visual** (*Inform*) visual display.
representante *nmf* (**a**) (*Com, Pol etc*) representative; (*Teat*) agent. (**b**) (*Teat: actor*) performer, actor, actress.
representar [1a] **1** *vt* (**a**) (*gen*) to represent; to act for; (*simbolizar*) to stand for, symbolize; (*expresar*) to express, depict.
(**b**) (*Teat*) *obra* to perform, put on, do; to produce; *papel* to act, play, take.
(**c**) *edad etc* to look; **representa unos 55 años** he looks about 55, from his appearance he's about 55; **ella no representa los años que tiene** she doesn't look her age; **el conserje no representaba ser muy listo** the porter didn't seem to be any too intelligent; **ese traje no representa lo que has gastado en él** that suit does not look as though it's worth what you paid for it.
(**d**) *detalles, hechos etc* to state, explain; to enumerate; to express; ~ **una dificultad a uno** to represent a difficulty to sb, explain a snag to sb; **representa que lo vendió por ...** he claims that he sold it for ...
(**e**) (*significar*) to mean; *amenaza* to pose, constitute; **tal acto representaría la guerra** such an act would mean war.
2 representarse *vr*: ~ **una escena** to imagine a scene, picture a scene to o.s.; ~ **una solución** to envisage a solution; **se me representa la cara que pondrá** I can just imagine his face.
representatividad *nf* representativeness; representative nature.
representativo *adj* representative.
represión *nf* repression; suppression.
represivo *adj*, **represor** *adj* repressive.
reprimenda *nf* reprimand, rebuke.
reprimido 1 *adj* repressed. **2** *nm*, **reprimida** *nf* repressed person.
reprimir [3a] **1** *vt* to repress, suppress; (*refrenar*) to curb, check; *bostezo, risa etc* to suppress, hold in, smother; *rebelión etc* to suppress.
2 reprimirse *vr*: ~ **de** + *infin* to stop o.s. from + *ger*.
reprisar [1a] *vt* (*CAm, Cono Sur, Méx*) *obra* to revive, put on again.
reprise[1] *nf* (*Teat*) revival.
reprise[2] [re'pris] *nm* (*a veces f*) (*Aut*) acceleration.

repristinación *nf* restoration to its original state.
repristinar [1a] *vt* to restore to its original state.
reprobable *adj* blameworthy, to be condemned, reprehensible.
reprobación *nf* reproval, reprobation; blame; condemnation; **escrito en ~ de ...** written in condemnation of ...
reprobador *adj mirada etc* reproving, disapproving.
reprobar [1l] *vt* (**a**) (*censurar*) to reprove, condemn; (*culpar*) to blame; (*condenar*) to damn. (**b**) *candidato* to fail.
reprobatorio *adj* = **reprobador.**
réprobo *adj* (*Ecl*) damned.
reprocesado *nm*, **reprocesamiento** *nm* reprocessing.
reprocesar [1a] *vt* to reprocess.
reprochabilidad *nf* blameworthiness, culpability.
reprochable *adj* blameworthy, culpable.
reprochar [1a] **1** *vt* to reproach; to condemn, censure; **~ algo a uno** to reproach sb for sth; **le reprochan (por) su descuido** they reproach him for his negligence.
2 reprocharse *vr* to reproach o.s.; **no tienes nada que reprocharte** you have nothing to reproach yourself for (*o* about).
reproche *nm* reproach (*a* for); reflection (*a* on); **es un ~ a su honradez** it is a reflection on his honesty; **nos miró con ~** he looked at us reproachfully.
reproducción *nf* reproduction.
reproducir [3c] **1** *vt* to reproduce; (*Bio*) to reproduce, breed.
2 reproducirse *vr* (**a**) to reproduce; to breed.
(**b**) (*condiciones etc*) to be reproduced; (*suceso*) to happen again, recur; **se le han reproducido los síntomas** the symptoms have recurred; **si se reproducen los desórdenes** if the disorders happen again.
reproductor *adj* reproductive.
reprografía *nf* reprography.
reprogramar [1a] *vt* to reprogram(me); *deuda etc* to reschedule.
reps *nm* (*tela*) rep.
reptar [1a] *vi* to creep, crawl; to snake along.
reptil 1 *adj* reptilian. **2** *nm* reptile.
república *nf* republic; **~ bananera** banana republic; **R~ Dominicana** Dominican Republic; **R~ Árabe Unida** United Arab Republic; **Segunda R~** Second Spanish Republic.
republicanismo *nm* republicanism.
republicano, -a *adj, nm/f* republican.
repudiación *nf* repudiation.
repudiar [1b] *vt mujer, violencia etc* to repudiate; (*desconocer*) to disown, disavow; *herencia* to renounce.
repudio *nm* repudiation.
repudrir [3a] **1** *vt* (**a**) (*pudrir*) to rot.
(**b**) (*fig*) to gnaw at, eat up, devour.
2 repudrirse *vr* to suffer inwardly, suffer gnawing doubts (*etc*); to eat one's heart out, pine away.
repuesto 1 *ptp de* **reponer**.
2 *nm* (**a**) (*provisión*) stock, store; (*abastecimiento*) supply.
(**b**) (*reemplazo*) replacement; (*de pluma*) refill.
(**c**) (*Aut, Mec*) spare, spare part, extra (*US*); **rueda de ~** spare wheel; **y llevamos otro de ~** and we have another as a spare (*o* in reserve).
(**d**) (*Esp*: *mueble*) sideboard, buffet.
repugnancia *nf* (**a**) (*asco*) disgust, loathing, repugnance; (*aversión*) aversion (*hacia, por* to).
(**b**) (*moral*) repugnance.
(**c**) (*desgana*) reluctance; **lo hizo con ~** he did it reluctantly.
(**d**) (*Filos*) opposition, incompatibility.
repugnante *adj* disgusting, loathsome, revolting.
repugnar [1a] **1** *vt* (**a**) (*dar asco a*) to disgust, revolt, nauseate; to fill with loathing; **ese olor me repugna** that smell revolts me, I loathe that smell; **me repugna tener que mirarlo** I hate having to watch it, I loathe having to watch it.
(**b**) (*odiar*) to hate, loathe; **siempre repugnaba el engaño** he always hated deceit.
(**c**) (*contradecir*) to contradict.
2 *vi* (**a**) (*ser asqueroso*) to be disgusting, be revolting.
(**b**) = **3.**
3 repugnarse *vr* to conflict, be in opposition; to contradict each other; **las dos teorías se repugnan** the two theories are not compatible, the two theories contradict each other.
repujar [1a] *vt* to emboss, work in relief.
repulgado *adj* affected.
repulgar [1h] *vt* (**a**) (*Cos*) to hem, edge. (**b**) (*Culin*) to crimp.
repulgo *nm* (**a**) (*Cos*) hem; hemstitch. (**b**) (*Culin*) crimping, fancy edging, decorated border; **~s de empanada** silly scruples.
repulido *adj* (**a**) *objeto* polished, repolished. (**b**) (*fig*) *persona* dressed up, dolled up*; spick and span, very smart.
repulir [3a] **1** *vt* (**a**) *objeto* to polish up; to repolish (*t fig*).
(**b**) (*fig*) *persona* to dress up; to spruce up.
2 repulirse *vr* (*fig*) to dress up, doll o.s. up*; to smarten up.
repulsa *nf* (**a**) (*Mil*) check. (**b**) (*fig*: *rechazo*) rejection, refusal; rebuff; **sufrir una ~** to meet with a rebuff. (**c**) (*fig*) (*censura*) strong condemnation; (*reprimenda*) severe reprimand.
repulsar [1a] *vt* (**a**) (*Mil*) to repulse; to check. (**b**) (*fig*) *solicitud* to reject, refuse; *oferta, persona* to rebuff. (**c**) (*fig*: *condenar*) to condemn in strong terms.
repulsión *nf* (**a**) = **repulsa.** (**b**) (*emoción*) repulsion, disgust, aversion. (**c**) (*Fís*) repulsion.
repulsivo *adj* disgusting, revolting, loathsome.
repunta *nf* (**a**) (*Geog*) point, headland. (**b**) (*indicio*) sign, indication, hint. (**c**) (*resentimiento*) pique. (**d**) (*disgusto*) slight upset, tiff. (**e**) (*LAm Agr*) round-up. (**f**) (*And*: *riada*) sudden rise (*of a river*), flash flood.
repuntar [1a] **1** *vt* (*Cono Sur, Méx*) *ganado* to round up.
2 *vi* (**a**) (*marea*) to turn.
(**b**) (*LAm*) (*manifestarse*) to (begin to) make itself felt, give the first signs; (*persona*) to turn up unexpectedly.
(**c**) (*LAm*: *río*) to rise suddenly; (*Cono Sur*) to rise to its previous level.
3 repuntarse *vr* (**a**) (*vino*) to begin to sour, turn.
(**b**) (*persona*) to get cross.
(**c**) (*2 personas*) to fall out, have a tiff.
repunte *nm* (**a**) (*Náut*) turn of the tide; (*de río*) level; rise. (**b**) (*LAm Agr*) round-up. (**c**) (*Fin*) rise in share prices; (*Econ*) upturn, recovery.
reputación *nf* reputation; standing.
reputado *adj* (*t* **bien ~**) highly reputed, reputable.
reputar [1a] *vt* (*gen*) to repute; (*estimar*) to esteem; (*considerar*) to deem, consider; **~ a uno de** (*o* **por**) **inteligente** to consider sb intelligent; **le reputan no apto para el cargo** they think him unsuitable for the post; **una colección reputada en mucho** a highly esteemed collection.
requebrar [1j] *vt* to say nice things to, flatter, compliment; **~ a una de amores** to court sb.
requemado *adj* scorched; parched; *piel* tanned, bronzed; *comida* overdone.
requemar [1a] **1** *vt* (**a**) (*fuego etc*) to scorch; *planta* to parch, scorch, dry up; *piel* to tan; *comida* to overdo, burn; *lengua* to burn, sting.
(**b**) (*fig*) *sangre* to inflame, set afire.
2 requemarse *vr* (*V vt*) (**a**) to scorch; to parch, get parched, dry up; to tan; to burn.
(**b**) (*fig*) to harbour resentment, smoulder with indignation (*etc*).
requenete *adj* (*Carib*), **requeneto** *adj* (*And, Carib*) = **rechoncho.**
requerimiento *nm* (**a**) (*petición*) request; (*demanda*) demand; (*llamada*) summons (*t Jur*); **a ~ de** at the request of. (**b**) (*notificación*) notification.
requerir [3i] **1** *vt* (**a**) (*necesitar*) to need, require; **esto requiere cierto cuidado** this requires some care.
(**b**) (*pedir*) to request, ask, invite; **~ a uno para que haga algo** to ask sb to do sth.
(**c**) (*mandar traer*) to send for, call for; (*buscar*) to hunt around for; (*con dedos*) to feel for; *persona* to send for, summon; **el ministro requirió sus gafas** the minister sent for his spectacles; **el ministro le requirió para que lo explicara** the minister summoned him to explain it.
(**d**) (*t* **~ de amores a**) *mujer* = **requebrar.**
2 *vi*: **~ de** (*LAm*) to need, require.
requesón *nm* cottage cheese; curd(s).
requete...* *prefijo intensivo, p.ej.* **requeteguapa** quite extraordinarily pretty; **me parece requetebién** it seems absolutely splendid to me; **lo tendré muy requetepensado** I'll think it over very thoroughly; **una joven requetemonísima** a fabulously attractive girl*; **una requetesuperminifalda** an ultrashort miniskirt.
requeté *nm* (**a**) (*Hist*) Carlist militiaman. (**b**) (*) he-man*, tough guy*.
requiebro *nm* amorous compliment, flirtatious remark.
réquiem *nm, pl* **réquiems** requiem.
requilorios *nmpl* (**a**) (*trámites*) tedious formalities, red

tape; petty conditions.

(**b**) (*adornos*) silly adornments, unnecessary frills.

(**c**) (*preliminares*) time-wasting preliminaries; (*rodeos*) roundabout way of saying something.

(**d**) (*elementos dispersos*) bits and pieces.

requintar [1a] **1** *vt* (**a**) (*LAm*) *cuerda* to tighten, make taut.

(**b**) ~ **a uno** (*And, Méx*) to impose one's will on sb, push sb around.

(**c**) (*And: insultar*) to abuse, swear at.

2 *vi* (*Carib: parecerse*) to resemble each other.

requisa *nf* (**a**) (*inspección*) survey, inspection. (**b**) (*Mil*) requisition. (**c**) (*LAm: confiscación*) seizure, confiscation.

requisar [1a] *vt* (**a**) (*Mil*) to requisition. (**b**) (*LAm: confiscar*) to seize, confiscate. (**c**) (*Cono Sur: registrar*) to search.

requisición *nf* (**a**) (*Mil*) requisition. (**b**) (*Cono Sur, Méx: embargo*) seizure, requisition. (**c**) (*Cono Sur, Méx: registro*) search.

requisito *nm* requirement, requisite; qualification; ~ **previo** prerequisite; **llenar los ~s** to fulfil the requirements; **tener los ~s para un cargo** to have the essential qualifications for a post.

requisitoria *nf* demand; (*LAm Jur*) examination, interrogation; (*orden*) writ.

res *nf* (**a**) (*animal*) beast, animal; ~ **lanar** sheep; ~ **vacuna** cow, bull, ox; **100 ~es** 100 animals, 100 head of cattle. (**b**) (*Méx: carne*) steak; beef. (**c**) (*Cono Sur*) body.

resabiado *adj* cunning, crafty; that has learned his lesson; *caballo* vicious.

resabiarse [1b] *vr* to acquire a bad habit, get into evil ways.

resabido *adj* (**a**) *dato* thoroughly well known; **lo tengo sabido y ~** of course I know all that perfectly well. (**b**) *persona* pretentious, pedantic, know-all.

resabio *nm* (**a**) (*dejo*) nasty taste (in the mouth), unpleasant aftertaste; **tener ~s de** (*fig*) to smack of. (**b**) (*vicio*) bad habit, unpleasant way; (*de caballo*) vicious nature.

resabioso *adj* (*And, Carib*) = **resabiado.**

resaca *nf* (**a**) (*Náut*) undertow, undercurrent; backward movement (of the waves).

(**b**) (*: *después de beber*) hangover*.

(**c**) (*fig*) reaction, backlash; **la ~ blanca** the white backlash.

(**d**) (*And, CAm, Méx*: aguardiente*) strong liquor; bad liquor.

(**e**) (*Cono Sur: en playa*) line of driftwood and rubbish (*left by the tide*).

(**f**) (*Cono Sur*: personas*) dregs of society.

(**g**) (*Carib: paliza*) beating.

(**h**) **la ~** (*Méx*) the very essence; (*iró*) the hardened criminal.

resacado* 1 *adj* (*Méx*) (*tacaño*) mean, stingy; (*débil*) weak; (*estúpido*) stupid; **es lo ~** (*Méx*) it's the worst of its kind. **2** *nm* (*And*) (contraband) liquor.

resacar [1g] *vt* (*And, Méx*) to distil (a second time).

resacoso* 1 *adj* hung-over*. **2** *nm*, **resacosa** *nf* person with a hangover*.

resalado *adj* lively, vivacious, attractive; *V* **re...**

resaltable *adj* notable, noteworthy.

resaltante *adj* (*LAm*) outstanding.

resaltar [1a] *vi* (**a**) (*salir*) to jut out, stick out, stick up, project.

(**b**) (*rebotar*) to bounce, rebound.

(**c**) (*fig*) to stand out; to be outstanding; **hacer ~ algo** to throw sth into relief, set sth off (*contra* against a background of); (*fig*) to emphasize sth; **~ como una mosca en la leche** to stick out like a sore thumb.

resalte *nm* projection.

resalto *nm* (**a**) (*saliente*) projection. (**b**) (*rebote*) bounce, rebound.

resanar [1a] *vt* to restore, repair, make good.

resaquero *adj* (*LAm*) = **remolón 1.**

resarcimiento *nm* repayment; indemnification, compensation.

resarcir [3b] **1** *vt* (*pagar*) to repay; (*compensar*) to indemnify, compensate; **~ a uno de una cantidad** to repay sb a sum; **~ a uno de una pérdida** to compensate sb for a loss.

2 resarcirse *vr*: **~ de** to make up for, compensate o.s. for; to retrieve.

resbalada *nf* (*LAm*) slip.

resbaladero *nm* slippery place; (*de parque etc*) slide, chute.

resbaladilla *nf* (*LAm*) slide, chute.

resbaladizo *adj* slippery.

resbalar [1a] **1** *vt* (**a**) (*sin querer*) to slip, slip up (*en, sobre* on); (*deslizarse*) to slide, slither (*por* along, down); (*Aut etc*) to skid; **el embrague resbala** the clutch is slipping; **le resbalaban las lágrimas por las mejillas** tears were trickling down her cheeks.

(**b**) (*fig: fallar*) to slip up, make a slip.

(**c**) (*) **me resbala** its leaves me cold; **las críticas le resbalan** criticism runs off him like water off a duck's back.

2 resbalarse *vr* (**a**) = **1.** (**b**) (‡: *rajarse*) to cop out‡.

resbalón *nm* (**a**) slip; slide, slither; skid. (**b**) (*fig*) slip, error; **dar un ~** to slip up.

resbalosa *nf a Peruvian dance.*

resbaloso *adj* (**a**) (*LAm: resbaladizo*) slippery. (**b**) (*Méx*: coqueta*) flirtatious, coquettish.

rescatar [1a] **1** *vt* (**a**) *cautivo* to ransom; *ciudad etc* to recapture, recover; *prenda* to redeem; *póliza* to surrender.

(**b**) (*salvar*) to save, rescue.

(**c**) *dinero, posesión etc* to get back, recover, regain possession of.

(**d**) *tiempo perdido* to make up; *delitos* to atone for, redeem, expiate.

(**e**) *tierras* to reclaim.

(**f**) (*Méx*: revender*) to resell.

2 *vi* (*And*) to peddle goods from village to village.

rescate *nm* (*V vt*) (**a**) ransom; recapture, recovery; redemption.

(**b**) rescue; **operaciones de ~** rescue operations; **acudir** (*o* **venir**) **al ~ de** to go (*o* come) to the rescue of.

(**c**) recovery.

(**d**) atonement, expiation.

(**e**) reclamation; **~ de terrenos** land reclamation.

rescindible *adj*: **contrato ~ por ambas partes** a contract that can be cancelled by either side.

rescindir [3a] *vt contrato etc* to rescind, cancel; *privilegio* to withdraw; *puestos de trabajo* to cut back.

rescisión *nf* cancellation; withdrawal; cutback.

rescoldo *nm* (**a**) (*lit*) embers, hot ashes. (**b**) (*fig*) lingering doubt, scruple; **avivar el ~** (*fig*) to stir up the dying embers.

rescontrar [1l] *vt* (*Com, Fin*) to offset, balance.

resecar¹ [1g] **1** *vt* (*secar*) to dry off, dry thoroughly; (*quemar*) to parch, scorch, burn. **2 resecarse** *vr* to dry up, get too dry.

resecar² [1g] *vt* (*Med*) to cut out, remove; to resect.

resección *nf* resection.

reseco *adj* (**a**) (*lit*) very dry, too dry; parched. (**b**) (*fig*) skinny, lean.

reseda *nf*, **resedá** *nf* (*LAm*) mignonette.

resellarse* [1a] *vr* to switch parties, change one's views.

resembrado *nm* re-sowing, re-seeding.

resembrar [1j] *vt* to re-sow, re-seed.

resentido *adj* resentful; bitter; sullen; **es un ~** he's bitter, he's got a chip on his shoulder, he feels hard done by.

resentimiento *nm* resentment; bitterness.

resentirse [3i] *vr* (**a**) **~ con algo, ~ por algo** (*t* **estar resentido por algo**) to resent sth, be offended about sth, feel bitter about sth.

(**b**) (*debilitarse*) to remain weak, be weakened, suffer; **con los años se resintió su salud** his health suffered (*o* was affected) over the years; **los cimientos se resintieron con el terremoto** the foundations were weakened by the earthquake; **sin que se resienta el dólar** without the dollar being affected.

(**c**) **~ de** *defecto* to suffer from, labour under; *consecuencias etc* to feel the effects of; **me resiento todavía del golpe** I can still feel the effects of the injury.

reseña *nf* (**a**) (*resumen*) outline, account, summary; (*Liter*) review; (*Dep etc*) report (*de* on), account (*de* of).

(**b**) (*descripción*) brief description (*for identification purposes*).

(**c**) (*Mil*) review.

(**d**) (*Cono Sur: esp Chile*) procession held on Passion Sunday.

reseñable *adj* (**a**) *ofensa* for which one can be booked. (**b**) (*destacado*) noteworthy, notable; worth mentioning.

reseñante *nmf* (*Liter*) reviewer.

reseñar [1a] *vt* (**a**) (*describir*) to describe (*for identification purposes*); (*narrar*) to write up, write a brief account of; (*Liter*) to review; *partido* to report on.

(**b**) *delincuente* to book.

reseñista *nmf* (*Liter*) reviewer.

resero *nm* (*And, CAm, Cono Sur*) cowboy, herdsman; (*comerciante*) cattle dealer.

reserva *nf* (**a**) (*acto*) reservation; **la ~ de asientos no se paga** there is no charge for seat reservation (*o* for reserving seats).

(**b**) (*provisión, surtido*) reserve (*t Com*); stock, holding; **~ para amortización, ~ para depreciaciones** depreciation allowance; **~ en metálico** cash reserves; **~s monetarias** financial reserves; **~s ocultas** hidden reserves; **~ de oro** gold reserve; **las ~s mundiales de petróleo** world reserves of oil, world stocks of oil; **de ~** spare, reserve (*atr*), emergency (*atr*); **tener algo de ~** to have sth in reserve, keep sth for an emergency.

(**c**) (*Geog etc*) reserve, reservation; **~ de caza** game reserve; **~ de indios** Indian reservation; **~ natural** nature reserve.

(**d**) (*Mil*) reserve.

(**e**) (*cualidad*) reserve; discretion, reticence; (*pey*) coldness, distance.

(**f**) (*secreto*) privacy; **con ~** in confidence; **escribir con la mayor ~** to write in the strictest confidence; **'absoluta ~'** (*anuncio*) 'strictest confidence'.

(**g**) (*salvedad*) reserve, reservation; **~ mental** mental reservation; **con ciertas ~s** with certain reservations; **hay que tomar esa noticia con ~** that news should be taken with reservations; **sin ~(s)** unreservedly, without qualification.

(**h**) **a ~ de** except for; **a ~ de que** ... unless ..., unless it should turn out that ...

reservación *nf* reservation.

reservadamente *adv* confidentially, privately.

reservado 1 *adj* (**a**) *asiento etc* reserved; **'~s todos los derechos'** 'all rights reserved'.

(**b**) *actitud, persona* reserved; discreet, reticent; (*pey*) cold, distant.

(**c**) *asunto etc* confidential, private.

2 *nm* (*en restaurante etc*) private room; (*Ferro*) reserved compartment.

reservar [1a] **1** *vt* (**a**) (*gen*) to reserve; (*guardar*) to keep, keep in reserve, set aside; *asientos etc* to reserve, book; **lo reserva para el final** he's keeping it till last; **ha reservado lo mejor para sí** he has kept the best part for himself.

(**b**) (*ocultar*) to conceal; (*callar*) to keep to oneself, refuse to tell; *opinión etc* to reserve; **prefiero ~ los detalles** I prefer to keep the details to myself.

2 reservarse *vr* to save o.s. (*para* for); to keep up one's strength; to bide one's time; **no bebo porque me reservo para más tarde** I'm not drinking because I have to be fit for later on.

reservista *nmf* reservist.

reservón* *adj* excessively reserved; cagey*, close; very quiet.

resfriado 1 *adj* (**a**) **estar ~** to have a cold. (**b**) (*Cono Sur**) indiscreet, loud-mouthed. **2** *nm* cold; chill; **coger un ~** to catch a cold.

resfriar [1c] **1** *vt* (**a**) (*gen*) to cool, chill.

(**b**) (*fig*) *ardor* to cool.

(**c**) **~ a uno** (*Med*) to give sb a cold.

2 *vi* (*Met*) to turn cold.

3 resfriarse *vr* (**a**) (*Med*) to catch (a) cold.

(**b**) (*fig: relaciones*) to cool off.

resfrío *nm* (*LAm*) cold.

resguardar [1a] **1** *vt* to protect, shield (*de* from); to safeguard.

2 resguardarse *vr* (**a**) (*protegerse*) to defend o.s., protect o.s.; to safeguard o.s.

(**b**) (*obrar con cautela*) to go warily, proceed with caution.

resguardo *nm* (**a**) (*protección*) defence, protection; safeguard; **servir de ~ a uno** to be a protection to sb; **~ de consigna** cloakroom check.

(**b**) (*Com etc*) (*vale*) voucher, certificate; (*garantía*) guarantee; (*recibo etc*) slip, check, cover note, receipt; (*de cheque*) stub; (*de consigna etc*) ticket.

(**c**) (*Náut*) sea room; safe distance.

residencia *nf* (**a**) (*gen*) residence; (*Univ*) hall of residence, hostel; **~ para ancianos, ~ para jubilados** rest home, old people's home; **~ canina** dogs' home, kennels; **~ sanitaria** hospital; **~ secundaria, segunda ~** second home. (**b**) (*Jur*) investigation, inquiry. (**c**) **~ vigilada** (*And*) house arrest.

residencial 1 *adj* residential. **2** *nm* (*And*) small hotel, boarding-house. **3** *nf* estate, housing development; (*CAm*) residential area.

residenciar [1b] **1** *vt* (*Jur*) to conduct a judicial inquiry into, investigate. **2 residenciarse** *vr* to take up residence, establish o.s., settle.

residente 1 *adj* resident; **no ~** non-resident. **2** *nmf* resident; **no ~** non-resident.

residir [3a] *vi* (**a**) (*gen*) to reside, live, dwell.

(**b**) (*fig*) **~ en** to reside in, lie in; to consist in; **la autoridad reside en el gobernador** authority rests with the governor; **la dificultad reside en que** ... the difficulty lies in the fact that ...

residual *adj* residual, residuary; **aguas ~es** sewage.

residuo *nm* residue; (*Mat*) remainder; (*Quím etc*) residuum; **~s** (*restos*) remains; (*basura*) refuse, waste; rubbish; (*sobras*) left-overs; (*Téc*) waste products; **~s nucleares** nuclear waste; **~s radiactivos** radioactive waste; **~s sólidos** solid waste; **~s tóxicos** toxic waste.

resignación *nf* resignation.

resignadamente *adv* resignedly, with resignation.

resignado *adj* resigned.

resignar [1a] **1** *vt* to resign, give up, renounce; *mando* to hand over (*en* to); *puesto* to resign.

2 resignarse *vr* to resign o.s. (*a, con* to); **~ a** + *infin* to resign o.s. to + *ger*.

resina *nf* (**a**) resin. (**b**) (*Méx*) torch (of resinous wood).

resinoso *adj* resinous.

resistencia *nf* (**a**) (*gen*) resistance; stand; **la R~** (*Pol*) the Resistance; **~ a la enfermedad** resistance to disease; **~ pasiva** passive resistance; **oponer ~ a** to resist, oppose, stand out against.

(**b**) (*del cuerpo etc*) endurance, stamina; (*fuerza*) strength; staying power; (*dureza*) toughness; (*de tela etc*) strength, toughness; **el maratón es una prueba de ~** the marathon is a test of endurance; **la ~ que necesitan tener los montañistas** the toughness (*o* stamina) which mountaineers need.

(**c**) (*oposición*) opposition; (*renuencia*) unwillingness (*para* + *infin* to + *infin*); **luchar con la ~ de sus colegas** to fight against the opposition of one's colleagues, try to overcome the hostility of one's colleagues.

resistente 1 *adj* resistant (*a* to); *tela etc* strong, tough; hard-wearing; (*Bot*) hardy; **~ al calor** resistant to heat, heat-resistant; **~ al fuego** fireproof; **hacerse ~** (*Med*) to build up a resistance (*a* to). **2** *nmf* resistance fighter.

resistible *adj* resistible.

resistir [3a] **1** *vt* (**a**) *peso* to bear, support; *presión etc* to bear, withstand.

(**b**) *enemigo* to resist; *ataque* to resist, withstand; to stand up to; *propuesta* to resist, oppose, make a stand against; *tentación* to resist.

(**c**) *agotamiento, decepción etc* to put up with, endure, withstand; **no puedo ~ este frío** I can't bear (*o* stand) this cold; **no lo resisto un momento más** I'm not putting up with this a moment longer.

(**d**) **~ la mirada de uno** to stare back at sb; to stare sb out.

2 *vi* (**a**) (*gen*) to resist; (*luchar*) to struggle; (*combatir*) to put up a fight, fight back; (*seguir resistiendo*) to hold out.

(**b**) (*durar*) to last, still go on, endure; **el coche resiste todavía** the car is still going; **el equipo no puede ~ mucho tiempo más** the team can't last out much longer; **no podíamos ~ del cansancio** we were so tired we couldn't go on any longer.

3 resistirse *vr* (**a**) = **2** (**a**).

(**b**) **~ a** + *infin* to refuse to + *infin*, find it hard to + *infin*, resist + *ger*; to be unwilling to + *infin*, be reluctant to + *infin*; **no me resisto a citar algunos versos** I can't resist quoting a few lines; **me resisto a creerlo** I refuse to believe it, I find it hard to believe; **se me resiste pasar sin saludarle** I cannot possibly pass by without calling on him.

(**c**) **se le resiste la química** he can't get on with chemistry, chemistry comes very hard to him.

resma *nf* ream.

resobado *adj* (*fig*) hackneyed, trite, well-worn.

resobar [1a] *vt* (**a**) (*manosear*) to finger, paw; to muck about*. (**b**) (*fig*) *tema* to work to death.

resobrino, -a *nm/f* first cousin once removed.

resol *nm* glare of the sun; reflected sunlight.

resolana *nf* (*LAm*) (**a**) (*luz del sol*) sunlight. (**b**) = **resol.** (**c**) = **resolano.**

resolano *nm* suntrap, sunny place.

resoltarse [1l] *vr* (*And*) to overstep the mark.

resolución *nf* (**a**) (*decisión*) decision; **~ fatal** decision to take one's own life; **tomar una ~** to take a decision.

(**b**) (*de problema: acto*) solving; (*respuesta*) solution; **un**

problema de ~ nada fácil a problem which it is not easy to (re)solve.

(**c**) (*Parl etc*) resolution; motion; **~ judicial** legal ruling.

(**d**) (*cualidad*) resolution, resolve, determination; decisiveness; **obrar con ~** to act with determination, act boldly.

(**e**) **en ~** in a word, in short, to sum up.

(**f**) (*Inform*) **alta ~** high resolution; **baja ~** low resolution.

(**g**) (*Cono Sur: terminación*) finishing, completion.

resolutivo *adj* decisive.

resoluto *adj* = **resuelto 2.**

resolver [2h; *ptp* **resuelto**] **1** *vt* (**a**) *problema* to solve, resolve; *crimen* to solve; *duda* to settle; *asunto* to decide, settle; *modo de obrar* to decide on; **crimen sin ~** unsolved crime.

(**b**) (*Quím*) to dissolve.

(**c**) *cuerpo de materiales etc* to analyse, divide up, resolve (*en* into).

2 *vi* (**a**) to resolve, decide; **~ a favor de uno** to resolve in sb's favour.

(**b**) **~ hacer algo** to resolve to do sth.

3 resolverse *vr* (**a**) (*problema etc*) to resolve itself, work out.

(**b**) **~ en** to resolve itself into; to be transformed into; **todo se resolvió en una riña más** in the end it came down to one more quarrel.

(**c**) (*decidir*) to decide, make up one's mind; **~ a** + *infin* to resolve to + *infin*; **~ por algo** to decide on sth; **hay que ~ por el uno o el otro** you'll have to make up your mind one way or the other.

resollar [1l] *vi* (**a**) (*respirar*) to breathe heavily, breathe noisily; (*jadear*) to puff and blow; to wheeze.

(**b**) (*fig*) **escuchar sin ~** to listen without saying a word in reply, listen scarcely daring to breathe; **hace tiempo que no resuella** he has given no sign of life for some time, it's a long time since we heard from him.

resonador *nm* resonator.

resonancia *nf* (**a**) (*repercusión*) resonance; (*eco*) echo. (**b**) (*fig: consecuencia*) wide importance, widespread effect; **tener ~** to have repercussions, cause a stir, have a considerable effect.

resonante *adj* (**a**) (*lit*) resonant; ringing, echoing, resounding. (**b**) (*fig*) *éxito etc* tremendous, resounding.

resonar [1l] *vi* to resound, ring, echo (*de* with).

resondrar* [1a] *vi* (*And*) to tell off*, tick off*.

resongar [1a] *vt* (*LAm*) = **rezongar.**

resoplar [1a] *vt* = **resollar**; (*de ira etc*) to snort; to pant.

resoplido *nm* (**a**) (*respiración*) heavy breathing, noisy breathing; (*jadeo*) puff, puffing; (*resuello*) wheeze; (*bufido*) snort; **dar ~s** to breathe heavily, puff; (*de motor*) to chug, puff; to labour.

(**b**) (*fig*) sharp answer.

resorber [2a] *vt* to reabsorb.

resorción *nf* resorption, reabsorption.

resorte *nm* (**a**) (*muelle*) spring.

(**b**) (*cualidad*) elasticity; springiness, resilience.

(**c**) (*fig*) (*medio*) means, expedient; (*enchufe*) contact; (*influencia*) influence; **tocar ~s** to pull strings; **tocar todos los ~s** to mobilize all one's influential friends, bring influence to bear from all sides.

(**d**) (*LAm: gomita*) elastic band.

(**e**) (*LAm*) (*responsabilidad*) responsibility; (*incumbencia*) concern; (*Jur*) authority; jurisdiction; **no es de mi ~** it's not my concern.

respaldar [1a] **1** *vt* (**a**) *documento* to endorse.

(**b**) (*fig*) to back, support.

(**c**) (*LAm*) (*asegurar*) to ensure; (*garantizar*) to guarantee, safeguard.

(**d**) (*Inform*) to back up.

2 respaldarse *vr* (**a**) to lean back, sprawl, loll (*contra* against, *en* on).

(**b**) **~ con, ~ en** (*fig*) to take one's stand on, base o.s. on.

respaldo *nm* (**a**) (*de silla etc*) back.

(**b**) (*Hort*) wall.

(**c**) (*de documento*) back; (*firma etc*) endorsement; **firmar al ~, firmar en el ~** to sign on the back.

(**d**) (*fig*) support, backing; (*esp LAm*) (*ayuda*) help; (*garantía*) guarantee; **operación de ~** back-up operation, support operation.

respectar [1a] *vt* to concern, relate to; **por lo que respecta a** as for, with regard to.

respectivamente *adv* respectively.

respective‡ *nmf*: **mi ~** (*Esp*) my other half (*spouse*).

respectivo 1 *adj* respective. **2 en lo ~ a** *como prep* as regards, with regard to.

respecto *nm*: **al ~** in the matter, with regard to the subject under discussion; **a ese ~** on that score; **no sé nada al ~** I know nothing about it; **bajo ese ~** in that respect; (**con**) **~ a, ~ de** with regard to, in relation to; (**con**) **~ a mí** as for me.

respetabilidad *nf* respectability.

respetable 1 *adj* respectable. **2** *nm*: **el ~** (*Teat*) the audience; (*hum*) the public, ≃ the great British sporting public.

respetablemente *adv* respectably.

respetar [1a] *vt* to respect; **hacerse ~** to win respect; (*establecerse*) to establish o.s., win a proper position; (*imponerse*) to impose one's will.

respeto *nm* (**a**) (*consideración*) respect, regard, consideration; **~ a la opinión ajena** respect for other people's opinions; **~ de sí mismo** self-respect; **~ a la conveniencia, ~s humanos** respect for the conventions, consideration for the susceptibilities of others; **por ~ a** out of consideration for; **¡un ~!** show some respect!; watch what you're saying!; **campar por sus ~s** to act independently, strike out on one's own; (*pey*) to show no consideration for others, be entirely self-centred; **faltar al ~, perder el ~** to be disrespectful (*a* to).

(**b**) **~s** respects; **presentar sus ~s a** to pay one's respects to.

(**c**) **de ~** best, reserve (*atr*); special; **cuarto de ~** best room; **estar de ~** to be all dressed up.

respetuosamente *adv* respectfully.

respetuosidad *nf* respectfulness.

respetuoso *adj* respectful.

réspice *nm* (**a**) (*respuesta*) sharp answer, curt reply. (**b**) (*reprimenda*) severe reprimand.

respingado *adj nose* snub, turned-up.

respingar [1h] **1** *vi* (**a**) (*caballo*) to shy, balk; to start.

(**b**) (*fig*) to kick, show oneself unwilling, dig one's heels in.

(**c**) = **2.**

2 respingarse *vr* (*vestido*) to ride up, curl up.

respingo *nm* (**a**) (*sobresalto*) shy; start; (*de dolor*) wince; **dar un ~** to start, jump.

(**b**) (*fig*) gesture of disgust; flounce.

(**c**) (*Cos*) **la chaqueta me hace un ~ aquí** the jacket rides up here.

(**d**) (*fig*) = **réspice** (**a**) *y* (**b**).

respingón *adj nariz* snub, turned-up.

respingona *nf traditional Castilian dance.*

respirable *adj* breathable.

respiración *nf* (**a**) (*gen*) breathing, respiration; (*una ~*) breath; **~ artificial, ~ mecánica** artificial respiration; **~ boca a boca** kiss of life, mouth-to-mouth resuscitation; (*fig*) revitalization; **contener la ~** to hold one's breath; **quedarse sin ~** (*lit*) to be out of breath; (*fig*) to be knocked all of a heap; **llegar sin ~** to arrive exhausted.

(**b**) (*ventilación etc*) ventilation.

respiradero *nm* (**a**) (*Téc*) vent, valve. (**b**) (*fig*) respite, breathing space.

respirador *nm* breathing tube, snorkel.

respirar [1a] **1** *vt* (**a**) to breathe; *gas etc* to breathe in, inhale.

(**b**) **respira confianza** she exudes (*o* oozes) confidence.

2 *vi* (**a**) (*gen*) to breathe; to draw breath; **~ con dificultad** to breathe with difficulty, gasp for breath; **sin ~** without a break, without respite; **paramos durante 5 minutos para ~** we stopped for 5 minutes to get our breath back.

(**b**) (*fig: después de esfuerzo, choque etc*) to breathe again; **¡respiro!** that's a relief! **no dejar ~ a uno** to keep on at sb, badger sb, make sb's life a misery; **no poder ~** to be all in; to be up to one's eyes (with work *etc*).

(**c**) **no ~** (*fig*) to say absolutely nothing; **estuvo escuchándole sin ~** he listened to him in complete silence; **los niños le miraban sin ~** the children watched him with bated breath.

(**d**) (*ventilarse*) to be ventilated.

respiratorio *adj* respiratory; breathing (*atr*).

respiro *nm* (**a**) (*gen*) breathing. (**b**) (*fig*) respite, breathing space; (*descanso*) rest; (*Com etc*) extension of time, period of grace; (*Jur*) suspension; reprieve.

respis *nm* = **réspice.**

resplandecer [2d] *vi* (**a**) (*relucir*) to shine; to gleam, glitter, glow; to blaze. (**b**) (*fig*) to shine; **~ de felicidad** to shine with happiness, be radiant with happiness.

resplandeciente *adj* (**a**) (*brillante*) shining; gleaming, glittering, glowing; blazing. (**b**) (*fig*) radiant (*de* with).

resplandor *nm* (**a**) (*brillantez*) brilliance, brightness, radiance; gleam, glitter, glow; blaze. (**b**) (*Cono Sur, Méx*) = **resolana.** (**c**) (*Méx*) (*luz del sol*) sunlight; (*resol*) warmth of the sun; (*brillo*) glare.

responder [2a] **1** *vt* to answer; to reply to; **pero él me responde con injurias** but he answers me with insults.

2 *vi* (**a**) (*gen*) to answer, reply; (*eco*) to answer; **~ a una pregunta** to answer a question.

(**b**) (*fig*) to reply, respond; **~ con grosería a una cortesía** to return rudeness for courtesy, answer a courteous request rudely.

(**c**) (*replicar*) to answer back.

(**d**) **~ a** *necesidad* to answer, obey; *mandos etc* to obey; *situación, tratamiento etc* to respond to; **la cápsula no responde a los mandos** the capsule is not obeying the controls; **pero no respondió a tal tratamiento** but he did not respond to such treatment.

(**e**) (*sustancia*) to be workable, be easily worked.

(**f**) (*corresponder etc*) to correspond (*a* to); **~ a una descripción** to fit a description, agree with a description; **la obra no responde al título** the book is not what the title implies.

(**g**) **~ de** to be responsible for; to answer for; **yo no respondo de lo que hagan mis colegas** I am not responsible for what my colleagues may do; **yo no respondo de lo que pueda pasar** I cannot answer for the consequences; **en estas circunstancias, ¿quién responde?** who is responsible in these circumstances?

(**h**) **~ por uno** to vouch for sb, guarantee sb.

(**i**) **~ al nombre de** to be called, go by the name of.

respondida *nf* (*LAm*) reply.

respondón *adj* cheeky, insolent.

responsabilidad *nf* responsibility; liability; **~ civil** public liability (insurance); **~ contractual** contractual liability; **~ objetiva** (*Jur*) strict liability; **~ solidaria** joint responsibility; **de ~ limitada** limited liability (*atr*); **bajo mi ~** on my responsibility; **cargo de ~** position of responsibility.

responsabilizar [1f] **1** *vt*: **~ a uno** to make sb responsible; (*encargar*) to put sb in charge; **~ a uno de un desastre** to hold sb responsible for a disaster, place the blame for a disaster on sb.

2 responsabilizarse *vr* to make o.s. responsible (*de* for); to acknowledge one's responsibility; to take charge; **~ de un atentado** to claim responsibility for an outrage.

responsable 1 *adj* (**a**) (*gen*) responsible (*de* for); **la persona ~** the person in charge; **la policía busca a los ~s** the police are hunting for those responsible; **hacer a uno ~** to hold sb responsible (*de* for); **hacerse ~ de algo** to assume responsibility for sth; to acknowledge one's responsibility for sth; **no me hago ~ de lo que pueda pasar** I take no responsibility for what may happen.

(**b**) (*ante otro*) accountable, answerable; **ser ~ ante uno de algo** to be answerable to sb for sth.

2 *nmf*: *p.ej.* **~ de prensa** press secretary.

responso *nm* (*Rel*) prayer for the dead.

responsorio *nm* (*Ecl*) response.

respuesta *nf* answer, reply; response; **~ inmune, ~ inmunitaria** immune response.

resquebra(ja)dura *nf* crack, split, cleft.

resquebrajar [1a] **1** *vt* to crack, split. **2 resquebrajarse** *vr* to crack, split.

resquebrar [1j] *vi* to begin to crack.

resquemar [1a] *vt* (**a**) (*lit*) to burn slightly; (*Culin*) to scorch, burn; *lengua* to burn, sting; *planta* to parch, dry up. (**b**) (*fig*) to cause bitterness to, upset.

resquemor *nm* (**a**) (*sensación*) burn, sting, stinging feeling; (*Culin*) scorching, burnt taste. (**b**) (*fig*: *resentimiento*) resentment, bitterness; (*enojo*) concealed anger; (*sospecha*) secret suspicion.

resquicio *nm* (**a**) (*abertura*) chink, crack.

(**b**) (*fig*) (*posibilidad*) chance, possibility; (*oportunidad*) opening, opportunity.

(**c**) (*And, Carib*: *vestigio*) vestige, trace.

(**d**) (*Carib*: *pedacito*) little bit, small piece.

resta *nf* (*Mat*) (**a**) (*acto*) subtraction. (**b**) (*residuo*) remainder.

restablecer [2d] **1** *vt* to re-establish; to restore. **2 restablecerse** *vr* (*Med*) to recover.

restablecimiento *nm* re-establishment; restoration; (*Med*) recovery.

restallar [1a] *vi* to crack; to click one's tongue; to crackle.

restallido *nm* (*de látigo*) crack; (*de lengua*) click; (*de papel etc*) crackle.

restante *adj* remaining; **lo ~** the rest, the remainder; **los ~s** the remaining ones, the rest, those that are left (over).

restañar [1a] *vt* to stanch, stop (the flow of).

restañasangre *nm* bloodstone.

restar [1a] **1** *vt* (**a**) (*quitar*) to take away, reduce; (*descontar*) to deduct; (*Mat*) to take away, subtract (*de* from); **~ autoridad a uno** to take away authority from sb, reduce sb's authority; **le restó importancia** he did not give it much importance.

(**b**) (*Dep*) *pelota, saque* to return.

2 *vi* to remain, be left; **restan 3 días para terminarse el plazo** there are 3 days left before the period expires; **ahora sólo me resta** + *infin* it only remains for me now to + *infin*.

restauración *nf* (**a**) restoration; **la R~** (*Esp*) *the restoration of the Spanish monarchy* (*1873*). (**b**) (*Com*) **la ~** the restaurant industry; **la ~ rápida** the fast-food industry.

restaurador(a) 1 *nm/f* (**a**) (*Arte etc*) restorer. (**b**) (*Com*) restauranteur, restaurant owner. **2** *nm*: **~ del cabello** hair-restorer.

restaurán *nm*, **restaurante** [resto'ran] *nm* restaurant.

restaurar [1a] *vt* to restore.

restinga *nf* sandbar, shoal, mudbank.

restitución *nf* return; restoration.

restituir [3g] **1** *vt* (**a**) (*devolver*) to return, give back, restore (*a* to). (**b**) (*Arquit etc*) to restore. **2 restituirse** *vr*: **~ a** to return to, go back to, rejoin.

resto *nm* (**a**) (*lo que queda*) rest, remainder; (*Mat*) remainder; **~s** remains; (*Culin*) left-overs, scraps; (*Náut etc*) wreckage; (*escombros*) debris, rubble; **~s de edición** remainders; **~s humanos** human remains; **~s mortales** mortal remains; **~ de serie** remainder, remaindered item; **~s de serie** (*fig*) left-overs.

(**b**) (*Dep*) return (of a ball *o* of service); (*persona*) receiver; **estar al ~** to be ready to return service.

(**c**) (*apuesta*) stake; **a ~ abierto** with no limit on stakes; (*fig*) without limit; **echar el ~*** to stake all one's money; (*fig*) to go all out, go the whole hog; **echar el ~ por** + *infin* to do one's utmost to + *infin*.

restorán *nm* restaurant.

restregar [1h *y* 1j] *vt* (**a**) (*fregar*) to scrub; to rub (hard). (**b**) (*mueble etc*) to rub on, rub against.

restricción *nf* restriction; limitation; restraint; **restricciones eléctricas** electricity cuts; **~ mental** mental reservations; **restricciones presupuestarias** budgetary constraints; **~ salarial** wage-restraint; **sin ~ de** without restrictions as to, with no limitation upon; **hablar sin restricciones** to talk freely.

restrictivo *adj* restrictive, limiting.

restrillar [1a] **1** *vt* (*And, Carib*) *látigo* to crack. **2** *vi* (*Carib*: *madera*) to crack, creak.

restringido *adj* restricted, limited.

restringir [3c] *vt* to restrict, limit (*a* to).

resucitación *nf* resuscitation.

resucitador *nm* (*Med*) respirator.

resucitar [1a] **1** *vt* (**a**) (*lit*) to resuscitate, revive.

(**b**) (*fig*) to revive; to resurrect, give a new existence to.

2 *vi* (**a**) (*lit*) to revive, return to life.

(**b**) (*fig*) to be resuscitated, be resurrected; to revive.

resudar [1a] *vti* to sweat a little; (*recipiente etc*) to leak slightly.

resueltamente *adv* resolutely, with determination; boldly; steadfastly.

resuelto 1 *ptp de* **resolver.**

2 *adj* (*decidido*) resolute, resolved, determined; (*audaz*) bold; (*firme*) steadfast; **estar ~ a algo** to be set on sth; **estar ~ a** + *infin* to be determined to + *infin*.

resuello *nm* (**a**) (*aliento*) breath; (*respiración*) breathing; **corto de ~** short of breath, short-winded; **sumir el ~ a uno** (*LAm*‡) to bump sb off‡.

(**b**) (*jadeo*) puff; (*respiración difícil*) heavy breathing; (*ruidoso*) wheeze.

(**c**) **meter a uno el ~ en el cuerpo** (*dar un susto a*) to put the wind up sb*, give sb a nasty fright; (*quitar los humos a*) to puncture sb's vanity.

(**d**) (*LAm*) breathing space; (*descanso*) rest; **tomar un ~** to take a breather.

(**e**) (‡: *dinero*) bread‡, money.

resulta *nf* result; **de ~s de** as a result of; **estar a ~s de** (*esp Esp*) to keep track of, keep up-to-date with.

resultado *nm* (*gen*) result; (*conclusión*) outcome, sequel;

(*efecto*) effect; **~s** (*Com, Fin*) results; **dar ~** to produce results.
resultante *adj* resultant, consequential.
resultar [1a] *vi* (**a**) (*ser*) to be; (*llegar a ser*) to prove (to be), turn out (to be); **me resulta simpático** I like him, he's nice; **si resulta (ser) verdadero** if it proves (to be) true; **el conductor resultó muerto** the driver was killed; **resultó (ser) el padre de mi cocinera** he turned out to be my cook's father, it emerged that he was my cook's father; **la casa nos resulta muy pequeña** we find the house very small; **resulta difícil decidir si ...** it is difficult to decide whether ...; **este trabajo está resultando un poco aburrido** this job is turning out to be a bit boring; **resulta que ...** it follows that ...; it seems that ..., it emerges that ...; **ahora resulta que no vamos** now it turns out that we're not going; **resulta que no me gusta** the thing is that I don't like it; **resulta de todo esto que no lo podemos pagar** it follows from all this that we can't afford it.
(**b**) **~ de** to result from; (*derivarse de*) to stem from; (*verse en*) to be evident from; **de ese negocio resultaron 4 más** from that deal there resulted 4 others, that deal produced 4 more; **me resultan 8 menos que a ti** that leaves me with 8 less than you.
(**c**) (*seguir*) to ensue; **con lo que después resultó** with what ensued, with what happened in consequence.
(**d**) (*salir bien*) to turn out well; **resultó de lo mejor** it worked out very well; **no resultó** it didn't work; **no me resultó muy bien aquello** that didn't work out very well for me; **este tema no me resulta** I can't get along with this subject.
(**e**) (*Fin*) to cost, work out at, amount to; **la serie completa nos resultó en 50 dólares** the complete set cost us 50 dollars; **entre unos y otros resultan 800 pesetas** all together they amount to 800 pesetas.
(**f**) (*****: *ser prudente*) **~** + *infin* to be best to + *infin*, be wise to + *infin*; **no resulta dejar el coche fuera** it's best not to leave the car outside, it's not a good idea to leave the car outside.
(**g**) (*parecer bien*) to look well, have a pleasing effect; **esa corbata no resulta con ese traje** that tie doesn't go with the suit.
resultón* *adj* (**a**) (*agradable*) pleasing; (*impresionante*) impressive, that makes a good impression. (**b**) *hombre, mujer* attractive (to the opposite sex).
resumen 1 *nm* summary, résumé; abstract; **en ~** (*en conclusión*) to sum up; (*brevemente*) in short. **2** *atr*: **comparencia ~** brief concluding appearance; **exposición ~** summary; **programa ~** programme in summary form.
resumidero *nm* (*LAm*) = **sumidero.**
resumir [3a] **1** *vt* (*recapitular*) to sum up; (*condensar*) summarize; (*reducir*) to abridge, shorten, cut down.
2 resumirse *vr* (**a**) **la situación puede resumirse en pocas palabras** the situation can be summed up in a few words.
(**b**) **~ en** to be reduced to, come down to, boil down to; **todo se resumió en algunos porrazos** the affair amounted to no more than a few punches.
resunta *nf* (*And*: *resumen*) summary.
resurgimiento *nm* resurgence; revival.
resurgir [3c] *vi* (**a**) (*reaparecer*) to reappear, revive; (*resucitar*) to be resurrected. (**b**) (*fig*) to acquire a new spirit, pick up again; (*Med*) to recover.
resurrección *nf* resurrection.
retablo *nm* (*Ecl*) (**a**) reredos, altarpiece. (**b**) (*Méx*) exvoto, votive offering.
retacada *nf* (*Billar*) foul stroke.
retacado *adj* (*Méx*) full.
retacarse* [1g] *vr* (*Cono Sur*) to dig one's heels in; to go back on a promise (*etc*).
retacear [1a] *vt* (*Cono Sur*) *dinero etc* to give grudgingly, give bit by bit.
retacitos *nmpl* (*CAm*) confetti.
retacón *adj* (*And, Cono Sur**) short and fat, squat.
retachar [1a] *vti* (*LAm*) to bounce (back).
retador 1 *adj* challenging; defiant. **2** *nm*, **retadora** *nf* (*LAm Dep*) challenger.
retaguardia *nf* (**a**) (*Mil etc*) rearguard; **a ~** in the rear; **3 millas a ~** 3 miles to the rear, 3 miles further back. (**b**) (*Anat**) rear*, bottom.
retahíla *nf* string, series; (*de insultos etc*) volley, stream.
retajado (*Cono Sur*) **1** *adj* (*Zool*) castrated, gelded. **2** *nm*, **retajada** *nf* (******) wanker******.
retajar [1a] *vt* (**a**) to cut out, cut round. (**b**) (*LAm*) to castrate, geld.
retal *nm* remnant, piece left over.
retaliación *nf* (*LAm*) retaliation.
retallones *nmpl* (*Carib*) left-overs.
retama *nf* (*Bot*), **retamo** *nm* (*LAm Bot*) broom.
retar [1a] *vt* (**a**) (*desafiar*) to challenge; to defy. (**b**) (*reprender*) to reprimand, tell off; (*regañar*) to scold. (**c**) (*Cono Sur**: *insultar*) to insult, abuse; **~le a uno algo** to throw sth in sb's face.
retardación *nf* retardation, slowing down; delaying; (*Mec*) deceleration.
retardar [1a] *vt* to slow down, slow up, retard; *marcha, progresos etc* to hold up, retard; *tren etc* to delay, make late; *reloj* to put back.
retardatriz *adj* (*f*) *acción etc* delaying.
retardo *nm* delay; time lag.
retazar [1f] *vt* (*cortar*) to cut up, snip into pieces; (*dividir*) to divide up; *leña* to chop.
retazo *nm* (**a**) (*Cos etc*) remnant; (*recorte*) snippet; (*trocito*) bit, piece, fragment; **~s** (*Liter etc*) snippets, bits and pieces; (*fragmentos*) disjointed fragments. (**b**) (*Carib*) bargain.
RETD *nf* (*Esp Telec*) *abr de* **Red Especial de Transmisión de Datos.**
rete... *prefijo intensivo* very ..., *p.ej.* **retebién** very well, terribly well; **una persona retefina** a terribly refined person.
retemblar [1j] *vi* to shudder, shake (*de* at, with).
retemplar [1a] *vt* (*And, CAm, Cono Sur*) to cheer up, revive.
retén *nm* (**a**) (*Téc*) stop, catch; lock; (*Aut*) oil-seal. (**b**) (*reserva*) reserve, store. (**c**) (*puesto de policía*) police post; (*control*) checkpoint, roadblock; (*pelotón*) post of armed men kept in reserve for an emergency; (*Mil*) reserves, reinforcements; **hombre de ~** reserve; **estar de ~** to be on call. (**d**) (*Carib*) remand home; detention centre.
retención *nf* (**a**) (*gen*) retention (*t Med*). (**b**) (*Fin*) deduction, stoppage (of pay *etc*); **~ a cuenta** deduction at source; **~ fiscal** retention for tax purposes. (**c**) (*Aut*) stoppage, hold-up, back-up. (**d**) (*Telec*) hold facility.
retener [2k] *vt* (*gen*) to retain; to keep (back), hold back; (*Fin*) to deduct; to withhold (part of); *atención* to hold; *memoria* to retain; *artículo prestado* to keep, hold on to; *tesoros, víveres* to hoard; **~ a uno preso** to keep sb in detention.
retenida *nf* guy-rope.
retentiva *nf* memory, capacity for remembering.
retentivo *adj* retentive.
reteñir [3h *y* 3k] *vt* to redye.
reticencia *nf* (**a**) (*sugerencia*) insinuation, (malevolent) suggestion; (*trascendencia*) implication; (*ironía*) irony, sarcasm. (**b**) (*engaño*) half-truth, misleading statement. (**c**) (*reserva*) reticence, reserve. (**d**) (*renuencia*) unwillingness, reluctance.
reticente *adj* (**a**) (*insinuador*) insinuating; (*irónico*) ironical, sarcastic; full of (unpleasant) implications. (**b**) (*reservado*) deceptive, misleading. (**c**) reticent, reserved. (**d**) (*desinclinado*) unwilling, reluctant; **estar** *o* **ser ~ a** to be unwilling for, be resistent to; **se mostró ~ a aceptar** she was unwilling to accept, she was reluctant to accept; **se declara ~ a la política** he says he doesn't like the idea of politics.
rético, -a 1 *adj, nm/f* Romansch. **2** *nm* (*Ling*) Romansch.
retícula *nf* (*Ópt*) reticle; (*Fot*) screen.
reticular *adj* reticulated.
retículo *nm* reticle; net, network; (*de medir etc*) grid.
retina *nf* retina.
retintín *nm* (**a**) (*tilín*) tinkle, tinkling; (*tintineo*) jingle, jangle; (*del oído*) ringing. (**b**) (*fig*) sarcastic tone; **decir algo con ~** to say sth sarcastically.
retinto *adj* (*LAm*) *tez* very dark.
retiñir [3a] *vi* to tinkle; to jingle, jangle; (*en el oído*) to go on ringing (in one's ears).
retirada *nf* (**a**) (*Mil*) retreat, withdrawal; **batirse en ~, emprender la ~** to (begin to) retreat.
(**b**) (*de dinero, embajador etc*) withdrawal; **~ de tierras de la producción** taking of land out of cultivation.
(**c**) (*refugio*) retreat, safe place, place of refuge.
retiradamente *adv vivir* quietly, in seclusion.
retirado *adj* (**a**) *vida* quiet; *lugar* remote, secluded, quiet. (**b**) *oficial etc* retired. (**c**) **la tiene retirada** (*Esp*) he keeps her as his mistress.
retirar [1a] **1** *vt* (**a**) (*mover*) *silla etc* to move away, move back; (*quitar*) to put away, take away, remove; *tentáculo etc* to draw in; *cortina, mano etc* to draw back; *tapa* to take off; (*Mec*) *pieza* to take out, remove; (*Mil*) *fuerzas* to with-

draw; ~ **tierras de la producción** to take land out of cultivation, set land aside.

(**b**) (*Fin*) to withdraw (*de* from), take out; *embajador* to recall, withdraw; *atleta, caballo* to scratch.

(**c**) *moneda, sello etc* to withdraw (from circulation); *permiso* to withdraw, cancel; (*Aut*) *carnet* to suspend, confiscate, take away.

(**d**) (*jubilar*) to retire, pension off.

(**e**) *acusación, palabras* to withdraw.

2 retirarse *vr* (**a**) (*apartarse*) to move back, move away (*de* from); (*Mil*) to retreat, withdraw; ~ **ante un peligro** to shrink back from a danger; **no se retire** (*Telec*) don't hang up.

(**b**) (*Dep*) to retire; to scratch.

(**c**) (*recluirse*) to go into seclusion, go off into retreat, withdraw from active life; (*jubilarse*) to retire (*de* from); **se retiró a vivir a Mallorca** he went off to live in Majorca, he retired to Majorca; **cuando me retire de los negocios** when I retire from business.

(**d**) (*después de cenar etc*) to retire (to one's room *o* to bed), go off to bed.

retiro *nm* (**a**) (*acto*) retirement; withdrawal; (*Dep*) retirement; scratching; (*de dinero etc*) withdrawal; ~ **prematuro** early retirement.

(**b**) (*estado*) retirement; **un oficial en** ~ an officer in retirement, a retired officer.

(**c**) (*Fin*) retirement pay, pension.

(**d**) (*lugar*) quiet place, secluded spot; (*apartamiento*) seclusion; retreat; **vivir en el** ~ to live in seclusion; live quietly.

(**e**) (*Ecl*) (*t* ~**s**) retreat.

reto *nm* (**a**) (*desafío*) challenge; (*amenaza*) threat, defiant statement (*etc*). (**b**) (*Cono Sur*: *reprimenda*) telling off, scolding. (**c**) (*Cono Sur*: *insulto*) insult.

retobado *adj* (**a**) (*LAm*: *salvaje*) *animal* wild, untamed; *persona* wild, unruly; (*rebelde*) rebellious; (*terco*) obstinate; (*hosco*) sullen; (*caprichoso*) unpredictable, capricious.

(**b**) (*And, CAm, Méx**) (*gruñón*) grumbling; (*descarado*) saucy, cheeky*.

(**c**) (*And, Cono Sur*: *taimado*) cunning, crafty.

(**d**) (*And‡*: *ofendido*) cheesed-off‡, offended.

retobar [1a] **1** *vt* (**a**) (*LAm*) (*forrar o cubrir*) to line (*o* cover) with leather; (*And, Cono Sur*) *etc* to line (*o* cover) with leather (*o* sacking *o* oilcloth).

(**b**) (*And*) *pieles* to tan.

2 *vi y* **retobarse** *vr* (*LAm*) (*obstinarse*) to be stubborn, dig one's heels in; (*quejarse*) to grumble, protest.

retobo *nm* (**a**) (*LAm*) (*forro*) lining; (*cubierta*) covering; (*Cono Sur*: *hule etc*) sacking, oilcloth, wrapping material.

(**b**) (*LAm*) (*terquedad*) stubbornness; (*protesta*) grumble, moan; (*capricho*) whim.

(**c**) (*And, CAm Agr*) old stock, useless animals; (*fig*) (*persona*) useless person; (*objeto*) worthless object; (*trastos*) junk, rubbish.

(**d**) (*LAm*: *resabio*) aftertaste.

retobón *adj* (*Cono Sur*) = **retobado** (**a**).

retocar [1g] **1** *vt* (**a**) *foto etc* to retouch, touch up. (**b**) *grabación* to play back. **2 retocarse** *vr* (*Esp*) to redo one's make-up.

retomar [1a] *vt* to take up again.

retoñar [1a] *vi* (**a**) (*Bot*) to sprout, shoot. (**b**) (*fig*) to reappear, recur.

retoño *nm* (**a**) (*Bot*) sprout, shoot, new growth. (**b**) (*: *niño*) kid*.

retoque *nm* (**a**) (*acto*) retouching, touching-up; (*último trazo*) finishing touch. (**b**) (*Med*) symptom, sign, indication.

retorcer [2b *y* 2h] **1** *vt* (**a**) *brazo etc* to twist; *cuello, manos, ropa lavada* to wring; *hebras* to twine (together).

(**b**) (*fig*) *argumento* to turn, twist; *sentido* to twist, force.

2 retorcerse *vr* (**a**) (*cuerda etc*) to get into knots, twist up, curl up.

(**b**) ~ **el bigote** to twirl one's moustache.

(**c**) (*persona*) to writhe; to squirm; ~ **de dolor** to writhe in pain, squirm with pain; ~ **de risa** to double up with laughter.

retorcido *adj* (**a**) *estilo* involved. (**b**) *método, persona* crafty, devious.

retorcijón *nm* (*LAm*) = **retortijón**.

retorcimiento *nm* (**a**) twisting; wringing; entwining; writhing.

(**b**) (*fig*: *complejidad*) involved nature.

(**c**) (*fig*: *astucia*) craftiness, deviousness.

retórica *nf* (**a**) (*lit*) rhetoric; (*pey*) affectedness, windiness, grandiloquence. (**b**) (*) ~**s** (*palabrería*) hot air, mere words; (*sofisterías*) quibbles.

retóricamente *adv* rhetorically.

retórico 1 *adj* rhetorical; (*pey*) affected, windy; grandiloquent. **2** *nm* rhetorician.

retornable *adj* returnable; **envase no** ~ non-returnable empty.

retornar [1a] **1** *vt* (**a**) (*devolver*) to return, give back. (**b**) (*devolver a su lugar*) to replace, return to its place. (**c**) (*mover*) to move back. **2** *vi* to return, come back, go back.

retorno *nm* (**a**) (*vuelta*) return; **'R~ a Brideshead'** 'Brideshead Revisited'; ~ **hacia atrás** flashback. (**b**) (*recompensa*) reward; (*pago*) repayment; (*cambio*) exchange, barter; (*de regalo, servicio etc*) return. (**c**) (*Elec*) ~ **terrestre** earth wire, ground wire (*US*). (**d**) (*Méx Aut*) turning place; **'~ prohibido'** 'No U turns'. (**e**) (*Inform*) ~ **del carro** carriage return; ~ (**del carro**) **automático** wordwrap, word wraparound.

retorsión *nf* = **retorcimiento** (**a**).

retorta *nf* (*Quím*) retort.

retortero *nm*: **andar al** ~ to bustle about, have heaps of things to do; **andar al** ~ **por algo** to crave for sth; **andar al** ~ **por uno** to be madly in love with sb; **llevar** (*o* **traer**) **a uno al** ~ to have sb under one's thumb; to keep sb constantly on the go; (*fig*) to push sb around.

retortijón *nm* rapid twist; ~ **de estómago** gripe, stomach cramp.

retostar [1l] *vt* to burn, overcook.

retozar [1f] *vi* to romp, frolic, frisk about; to gambol.

retozo *nm* (**a**) (*holgorio*) romp, frolic, (*jugueteo*) gambol; ~**s** romping, frolics; gambolling. (**b**) ~ **de la risa** giggle, titter, suppressed laugh.

retozón *adj* (**a**) (*juguetón*) playful, frolicsome, frisky. (**b**) *risa* bubbling.

retracción *nf* retraction, retractation.

retractable *adj* retractable.

retractación *nf* retraction, recantation.

retractar [1a] **1** *vt* to retract, withdraw. **2 retractarse** *vr* to retract, recant; **me retracto** I take that back; **me retracto de la acusación hecha** I withdraw the accusation.

retráctil *adj* (*Aer etc*) retractable; (*Bio*) retractile.

retraer [2o] **1** *vt* (**a**) *garras etc* to draw in, retract.

(**b**) (*volver a traer*) to bring back, bring again.

(**c**) (*fig*) to dissuade; to keep away.

2 retraerse *vr* to withdraw, retire, retreat (*de* from); to stay away; ~ **a** to take refuge in; ~ **de** (*fig*) (*retirarse de*) to withdraw from; (*renunciar a*) to give up; (*evitar*) to avoid, shun, stay away from.

retraído *adj* retiring, shy, reserved; (*pey*) aloof, unsociable.

retraimiento *nm* (**a**) (*acto*) withdrawal, retirement; (*estado*) seclusion. (**b**) (*cualidad*) retiring nature, shyness, reserve; (*pey*) aloofness. (**c**) (*lugar*) refuge, retreat.

retranca *nf* (*LAm*) brake.

retrancar [1g] **1** *vt* (*LAm*) to brake. **2 retrancarse** *vr* (**a**) (*LAm*: *frenar*) to brake, apply the brakes. (**b**) (*Méx*: *fig*) to come to a halt, seize up.

retransmisión *nf* repeat (broadcast), rebroadcast.

retransmitir [3a] *vt mensaje* to relay, pass on; (*Rad, TV*) to repeat, rebroadcast, retransmit; (*en vivo*) to broadcast live, do an outside broadcast of.

retrasado *adj* (**a**) **estar** ~ (*industria, persona etc*) to be behind, be behindhand, lag behind; **está ~ en química** he is behind in chemistry, he has a lot to make up in chemistry; **vamos ~s en la producción** we lag behind in production, our production is lagging; **estar ~ en los pagos** to be behind in one's payments, be in arrears.

(**b**) **estar** ~ (*reloj*) to be slow; **tengo el reloj 8 minutos** ~ my watch is 8 minutes slow.

(**c**) *país* backward, underdeveloped; *actitud etc* antiquated, old-fashioned.

(**d**) *comida etc* unused, left over; **tengo trabajo** ~ I have work piling up, I am behindhand in my work.

(**e**) (*Med*) subnormal, mentally retarded.

retrasar [1a] **1** *vt* (**a**) (*demorar*) to delay, put off, postpone; (*retardar*) to retard, slow down; to hold up.

(**b**) *reloj* to put back.

2 *vi y* **retrasarse** *vr* (*reloj*) to be slow; (*persona, tren etc*) to be late, be behind time; (*en estudios, producción etc*) to lag behind; (*producción etc*) to decline, fall away.

retraso *nm* (**a**) (*demora*) delay; (*intervalo*) time lag; (*tardanza*) slowness, lateness; **llegar con** ~ to be late, arrive late; **llegar con 25 minutos de ~** to be 25 minutes late; **llevo un ~ de 6 semanas** I'm 6 weeks behind (with my work *etc*).

(**b**) (*de país*) backwardness, backward state, underdevelopment.

(**c**) **~ mental** (*Med*) subnormality, mental deficiency.

(**d**) **~s** (*Com, Fin*) (*de pagos*) arrears; (*deudas*) deficit, debts.

retratar [1a] **1** *vt* (**a**) to portray; (*Arte*) to paint a picture of, paint the portrait of; (*Fot*) to photograph, take a picture of; **hacerse ~** (*Arte*) to have one's portrait painted; (*Fot*) to have one's photograph taken (as a portrait).

(**b**) (*fig: representar*) to portray, depict, describe.

2 retratarse *vr* (**a**) (*Arte*) to have one's picture painted; (*Fot*) to have one's photograph taken.

(**b**) (*) *dinero* to pay (up), fork out*; to let people see the colour of one's money.

retratería *nf* (*LAm*) photographer's (studio).

retratista *nmf* (*Arte*) portrait painter; (*Fot*) photographer.

retrato *nm* (**a**) (*Arte*) portrait; (*Fot*) photograph, portrait.

(**b**) (*fig: descripción*) portrayal, depiction, description.

(**c**) (*fig: semejanza*) likeness; **ser el vivo ~ de** to be the very image of.

retrato-robot *nm, pl* **retratos-robot** identikit picture, photofit picture.

retrechería *nf* (**a**) (*: *truco*) dodge*, wheeze*, crafty trick; (*hum*) rascally trick.

(**b**) (*: *encantos*) **~s** winning ways, charming ways.

(**c**) (*: *atractivo*) charm, attractiveness.

(**d**) (*V adj* (**c**)) meanness; deceitfulness; suspicious nature.

retrechero *adj* (**a**) (*) (*dado a trucos*) full of dodges*; (*astuto*) wily, crafty; (*hum*) rascally.

(**b**) (*: *encantador*) winning, charming, attractive.

(**c**) (*LAm*) (*tacaño*) mean; (*tramposo*) unreliable, deceitful; (*sospechoso*) suspicious.

retreparse [1a] *vr* to lean back; to sprawl, loll, lounge.

retreta *nf* (**a**) (*Mil*) retreat; (*exhibición*) tattoo, display. (**b**) (*LAm Mús*) open-air band concert. (**c**) (*LAm: serie*) series, string.

retrete *nm* lavatory.

retribución *nf* (**a**) (*pago*) pay, payment; (*recompensa*) reward; compensation. (**b**) (*Téc*) compensation.

retribuido *adj trabajo* paid; *puesto* salaried, that carries a salary; **un puesto mal ~** a badly paid post.

retribuir [3g] *vt* (**a**) (*pagar*) to pay; (*compensar*) to reward, compensate. (**b**) (*LAm*) *favor etc* to repay, return.

retro* **1** *adj invar moda etc* backward-looking; revivalist; (*Pol*) reactionary. **2** *nm* (*Pol*) reactionary.

retro... *pref* retro...

retroacción *nf* feedback.

retroactivamente *adv* retroactively, retrospectively.

retroactivo *adj* retroactive, retrospective; **ley de efecto ~** retrospective law; **un aumento ~ desde abril** a rise backdated to April; **dar efecto ~ a un pago** to backdate a payment.

retroalimentación *nf* feedback.

retroalimentar [1a] *vt* to feed back.

retrocarga: de ~ breechloading; **arma de ~** breechloader.

retroceder [2a] *vi* (**a**) (*moverse atrás*) to move back; (*retirarse*) to draw back, stand back; (*ir atrás*) to go backwards; (*volver atrás*) to turn back; (*Mil*) to fall back, retreat; (*cañón*) to recoil; (*agua, nivel, precio etc*) to fall, go down, (*Tip*) to backspace; **retrocedió unos pasos** he went back a few steps; **la policía hizo ~ a la multitud** the police forced the crowd back, the police pushed the crowd back.

(**b**) (*fig*) to back down; to give up; to flinch (*ante un peligro* from a danger); **no ~** to stand firm.

retroceso *nm* (**a**) (*movimiento hacia atrás*) backward movement; drawing back; (*Mil*) withdrawal, retreat; (*de cañón*) recoil; **cañón sin ~** recoil-less gun.

(**b**) (*fig*) backing down.

(**c**) (*Com, Fin*) recession (of trade), slump, depression; (*de apoyo, precio etc*) fall, decline.

(**d**) (*Med*) renewed attack, new outbreak.

(**e**) (*Tip*) backspace.

retrocohete *nm* retrorocket.

retrocuenta *nf* count-down.

retrogradación *nf* retrogression.

retrógrado *adj* retrograde, retrogressive; (*Pol etc*) reactionary.

retrogresión *nf* retrogression.

retronar [1l] *vi* = **retumbar**.

retropropulsión *nf* retropropulsion; (*Aer*) jet propulsion.

retroproyector *nm* overhead projector.

retrospección *nf* retrospection.

retrospectiva *nf* (**a**) (*Arte*) retrospective (exhibition). (**b**) **en ~** with hindsight.

retrospectivamente *adv* retrospectively; in retrospect.

retrospectivo *adj* retrospective; **escena retrospectiva** flashback; **mirada retrospectiva** backward glance, look back (*a* at).

retrotraer [2o] *vt* to carry back (in time), take back; **retrotrajo su relato a los tiempos del abuelo** he carried his tale back into his grandfather's day; **ahora podemos ~ su origen al siglo XI** now we can take its origin further back to the 11th century; **piensa ~ el problema a su origen** he hopes to trace the problem back to its origin.

retroventa *nf* resale; **precio de ~** resale price.

retrovirus *nm invar* retrovirus.

retrovisión *nf* (**a**) hindsight. (**b**) (*Cine*) flashback (technique).

retrovisor 1 *adj*: **espejo ~** = **2**. **2** *nm* driving mirror, rear-view mirror; wing mirror.

retrucar [1g] *vt* (**a**) *argumento* to turn against its user. (**b**) (*prov, LAm*) to retort; **le retruqué diciendo que ...** I retorted to him that ... (**c**) (*Billar*) to kiss.

retruécano *nm* pun, play on words.

retruque *nm* (**a**) (*And, Cono Sur*) sharp retort, brusque reply. (**b**) **de ~** (*Cono Sur, Méx*) on the rebound; as a consequence, as a result.

retumbante *adj* (**a**) booming, rumbling; resounding. (**b**) (*fig*) bombastic.

retumbar [1a] *vi* (*artillería, trueno etc*) to boom, roll, thunder, rumble; (*pasos, voz*) to echo, resound; to reverberate; **la cascada retumbaba a lo lejos** the waterfall boomed (*o* roared) in the distance; **la caverna retumbaba con nuestros pasos** the cave echoed with our steps; **sus palabras retumban en mi cabeza** his words still echo in my mind.

retumbo *nm* boom, roll, thunder, rumble; echo; reverberation.

reuma *nm*, **reúma** *nm* rheumatism.

reumático *adj* rheumatic.

reumatismo *nm* rheumatism.

reumatoide(o) *adj* rheumatoid.

reunificación *nf* reunification.

reunificar [1g] *vt* to reunify.

reunión *nf* (**a**) (*asamblea*) meeting, gathering; (*fiesta*) social gathering, party; (*Pol*) meeting; rally; (*Dep*) meeting; **~ (en la) cumbre** summit meeting; **~ ilícita** unlawful assembly; **~ informativa** press conference; **~ plenaria** plenary session.

(**b**) (*encuentro*) reunion.

reunir [3a] **1** *vt* (**a**) (*juntar*) *partes etc* to reunite, join (together); **~ dos cuartos** to knock two rooms together, make one room out of two.

(**b**) (*recoger*) *cosas dispersas etc* to gather (together), get together, put together; *datos etc* to assemble, collect, gather; *recursos* to pool; *colección* to make; *dinero* to collect; *fondos* to raise; (*ahorrar*) to save (up); **los 4 reunidos no valen lo que él** the 4 of them together are not as good as he is; **la producción de los demás países reunidos no alcanzará al nuestro** the production of the other countries put together will not come up to ours.

(**c**) *personas* to assemble, bring together, invite together; **reunió a sus amigos para discutirlo** he assembled his friends to talk it over; **está** (*o* **se encuentra**) **reunida** (*Esp*) she's in a meeting.

(**d**) *cualidades* to combine; *condiciones* to have, possess; **~ esfuerzos** to join forces; **la casa reúne la comodidad con la economía** the house combines comfort with economy.

2 reunirse *vr* (**a**) (*unirse*) to unite, join together; (*de nuevo*) to reunite.

(**b**) (*personas*) to meet, gather, assemble; to get together; **~ para** + *infin* to get together to + *infin*; **~ con uno para una excursión** to join sb for an outing.

(**c**) (*circunstancias*) to conspire (*para* + *infin* to + *infin*).

reutilizable *adj* reusable.

reutilización *nf* reuse; recycling.

reutilizar [1f] *vt* to reuse.

reválida *nf* (*Escol etc*) resit.

revalidar [1a] *vt* (**a**) (*confirmar*) to confirm, ratify. (**b**) (*Escol etc*) to resit.

revalor(iz)ación *nf* revaluation; reassessment.

revalorar [1a] *vt*, **revalorizar** [1f] *vt* to revalue; to reassess.

revaluación *nf* (*Fin*) revaluation.
revaluar [1e] *vt* (*Fin*) to revalue.
revancha *nf* (**a**) revenge; **en ~** in retaliation; **tomar su ~** to get one's revenge, get one's own back. (**b**) (*Dep*) return match; (*Boxeo*) return fight. (**c**) (*fig*) revision, reassessment.
revanchismo *nm* revanchism.
revanchista *adj, nmf* revanchist.
revejido *adj* (*And*) weak, feeble.
revelación 1 *nf* revelation (*t fig*); disclosure; **fue una ~ para mí** it was a revelation to me. **2** *atr* surprise (*atr*); **el coche ~ de 1998** the surprise car of 1998; **el diputado ~ del año** the surprise of the year among members.
revelado *nm* (*Fot*) developing.
revelador 1 *adj* revealing; telltale. **2** *nm* (*Fot*) developer.
revelar [1a] *vt* (**a**) (*gen*) to reveal; *secreto* to disclose; (*mostrar*) to betray, show; (*delatar*) to give away. (**b**) (*Fot*) to develop.
revendedor(a) *nm/f* (*al por menor*) retailer; (*pey*) speculator; (*de calle etc*) vendor, hawker, seller; (*Dep, Teat etc*) ticket tout.
revender [2a] *vt* (*volver a vender*) to resell; (*al por menor*) to retail; (*pey*) to speculate in; (*por la calle etc*) to hawk; *entradas* to tout.
revendón *nm* (*And*) middleman.
revenirse [3r] *vr* (**a**) (*encogerse*) to shrink.
(**b**) (*comida*) to go bad, go off; (*vino etc*) to sour, turn.
(**c**) (*enlucido etc*) to dry out; to give off moisture.
(**d**) (*Culin*) to get tough; get leathery.
(**e**) (*fig*: *ceder*) to give way (at last).
reventa 1 *nf* resale; speculation; hawking; touting; **precio de ~** resale price. **2** *nmf* (*persona*) ticket tout.
reventadero *nm* (**a**) (*terreno áspero*) rough ground; (*escarpado*) steep terrain. (**b**) (*fig*: *trabajo*) tough job, heavy work, grind. (**c**) (*And, Cono Sur, Méx*: *hervidero*) bubbling spring. (**d**) (*Cono Sur*) = **rompiente**.
reventador(a) *nm/f* (**a**) (*en mitín etc*) troublemaker, heckler. (**b**) (*ladrón*) safebreaker.
reventar [1j] **1** *vt* (**a**) *globo etc* to burst, explode, pop; *neumático, tubo etc* to burst; *barrera etc* to break, smash; **tengo una cubierta reventada** I have a puncture, I have a flat tyre, I have a flat (*US*).
(**b**) *caballo* to flog, ride hard, ride to death; *persona* to work to death, overwork, exhaust.
(**c**) (*) *proyecto etc* to sink, ruin; (*Teat etc*) *obra* to hiss off the stage; *orador* to heckle, barrack; *asamblea* to disturb, disrupt, break up.
(**d**) (*: *perjudicar*) to do down, do serious harm to.
(**e**) (*: *fastidiar*) to annoy, rile*; **me revienta tener que ponérmelo** it riles me to have to wear it.
2 *vi* (**a**) (*globo etc*) to burst, pop, go off pop; to explode; (*granada, neumático, tubo etc*) to burst; (*contenido*) to burst forth, burst out.
(**b**) (*ola*) to break.
(**c**) (*: *morir*) to peg out‡.
(**d**) **~ de** (*fig*) to be bursting with; **me revienta de aburrimiento** it bores me to tears; **~ de gordo** to be as fat as a pig; **~ de indignación** to be bursting with indignation; **casi reventaba de ira** he almost exploded with anger; **~ de risa** to burst out laughing, split one's sides; **~ de ganas de decirlo todo** to be bursting to tell all about it; **~ por algo** to crave sth; **~ por** + *infin* to be bursting to + *infin*, be dying to + *infin*.
3 reventarse *vr* (**a**) = **2** (**a**).
(**b**) (*caballo*) to die of overwork, die of exhaustion; (*en carrera*) to blow up; (*: *persona*) to slog away, sweat one's guts out‡.
(**c**) (*: *morir*) to peg out‡; **se revienta trabajando** he's killing himself with work.
reventazón *nf* (**a**) (*Cono Sur*: *colina*) low ridge. (**b**) (*Méx*: *de estómago*) flatulence. (**c**) (*Méx*: *fuente*) bubbling spring.
reventón *nm* (**a**) (*estallido*) burst, bursting; explosion; (*Aut*) puncture, blow-out, flat (*US*); **dar un ~** to burst, explode.
(**b**) (*: *muerte*) death (from overeating); **dar un ~** to peg out‡.
(**c**) (*pendiente*) steep slope; (*subida*) tough climb.
(**d**) (*) (*esfuerzo*) killing effort; (*trabajo*) toil, slog; **le dio un ~ al caballo** he flogged his horse, he half-killed his horse; **darse un ~, pegarse un ~** to slog, flog o.s., sweat one's guts out‡ (*para* + *infin* to + *infin*).
(**e**) (*apuro*) jam, difficulty.
(**f**) (*Cono Sur Min*) outcrop of ore.
(**g**) (*Cono Sur*: *estallido*) explosion, outburst; (*Med*) relapse.
(**h**) (*CAm*: *empujón*) shove, push.
(**i**) (*Méx**) party, binge*.
rever [2u] *vt* (**a**) to see again, look again at. (**b**) (*Jur*) *sentencia* to review; *pleito* to retry.
reverberación *nf* reverberation.
reverberador *nm* reverberator.
reverberar [1a] *vi* (**a**) (*luz*) to play, be reflected; (*superficie*) to shimmer, shine; (*nieve etc*) to glare; **la luz reverberaba en el agua** the light played (*o* danced) on the water; **la luz del farol reverberaba en la calle** the lamplight lay in a pool on the street, the lamplight was reflected on the street.
(**b**) (*sonido*) to reverberate.
reverbero *nm* (**a**) (*de luz*) play, reflection; shimmer, shine; glare; **el ~ de la nieve** the glare of the snow, the dazzle of the snow.
(**b**) (*de sonido*) reverberation.
(**c**) (*reflector*) reflector (*t Aut*).
(**d**) (*LAm*: *cocinilla*) small spirit stove.
(**e**) (*Carib**: *licor*) cheap liquor.
reverdecer [2d] **1** *vt* (*fig*) to renew, reawaken. **2** *vi* (**a**) (*Bot*) to grow green again. (**b**) (*fig*) to come to life again, revive, acquire new vigour.
reverencia *nf* (**a**) (*gen*) reverence. (**b**) (*inclinación*) bow, curtsy; **hacer una ~** to bow, curtsy. (**c**) (*título*) **R~** (*t* **Su R~, Vuestra R~**) Your Reverence.
reverencial *adj* reverential.
reverenciar [1b] *vt* to revere, venerate.
reverencioso *adj* reverent, respectful.
reverendísimo *adj* Most Reverend.
reverendo *adj* (**a**) (*estimado*) respected, revered.
(**b**) (*Ecl*) reverend; **el ~ padre X** Reverend Father X.
(**c**) (*: *solemne*) solemn.
(**d**) (*LAm**: *inmenso*) big, tremendous*, awful; **un ~ imbécil** an awful idiot.
reverente *adj* reverent.
reverentemente *adv* reverently.
reversa *nf* (*LAm Aut*) reverse.
reversible *adj* reversible.
reversión *nf* reversion.
reversionario *adj* reversionary.
reverso *nm* back, other side; wrong side; (*de moneda*) reverse; **el ~ de la medalla** (*fig*) the other side of the coin; the exact opposite.
revertir [3i] *vi* (**a**) (*posesión*) to revert (*a* to).
(**b**) **~ a su estado primitivo** to revert to its original state.
(**c**) **~ en** to end up as, come to be.
(**d**) **~ en beneficio de** to be to the advantage of; **~ en perjuicio de** to be to the detriment of.
revés *nm* (**a**) (*dorso*) back; (*contrahaz*) other side, wrong side; (*lado inferior*) underside; **el ~ de la medalla** (*fig*) the other side of the coin.
(**b**) (*golpe*) backhand (blow *o* shot *etc*); slap, swipe; (*Dep*) backhand; **~ cruzado** cross-court backhand.
(**c**) (*fig*) reverse (*t fig*), setback; **sufrir un ~** to suffer a setback; **los reveses de la fortuna** the blows of fate.
(**d**) **al ~** the wrong (*o* other) way round; upside down; *vestido etc* inside out; **y al ~** and vice versa; **entender algo al ~** to get hold of the wrong end of the stick; to have quite a different idea; **todo nos salió al ~** it all turned out wrong for us; **al ~ de lo que se cree** contrary to what is believed; **al ~ de lo corriente** against the usual practice, contrary to what normally happens; **llevar algo del ~** to wear sth the wrong way round (*o* inside out); **volver algo del ~** to turn sth round (the other way); to turn sth inside out.
revesado *adj* (**a**) *asunto* complicated, involved. (**b**) *niño etc* unruly, uncontrollable.
revesero *adj* (*And*) treacherous.
revestimiento *nm* (*Téc*) coating, facing, covering; lining; (*de carretera*) surface; (*Mil*) revetment; **~ antiadherente** non-stick coating.
revestir [3k] **1** *vt* (**a**) *ropa* to put on, don; to wear.
(**b**) (*Téc*) (*cubrir*) to coat, face, cover (*de* with); (*forrar*) to line (*de* with); *tubo etc* to sheathe (*de* in); (*fig*) *suelo etc* to carpet (*de* with).
(**c**) (*fig*) (*encubrir*) to cloak, disguise (*de* in); *persona* to invest (*con, de* with); *cuento etc* to adorn (*de* with); **revistió su acto de generosidad** he gave his action an appearance of generosity.
(**d**) *cualidad, importancia* to have, possess; **el acto revestía gran solemnidad** the ceremony had great dignity,

the ceremony was a very solemn one.

2 revestirse *vr* (**a**) (*Ecl*) to put on one's vestments.

(**b**) (*fig*: *ponerse*) to deck o.s. in, put on; **los árboles se revisten de hojas** the trees put their leaves on again.

(**c**) ~ **con**, ~ **de** (*fig*) *autoridad etc* to be invested with, have; *cualidad etc* to arm o.s. with; **se revistió de valor y fue a hablarle** he screwed up his courage and went to speak to her; *V t* **paciencia.**

(**d**) (*fig*) (*apasionarse*) to get carried away; (*engreírse*) to be vain, be haughty.

reviejo *adj* very old; *niño* wise beyond his years; old before his time.

revientapisos *nm invar* burglar, housebreaker.

revirado* *adj* (*Cono Sur*) (**a**) (*de mal genio*) bad-tempered, irritable; (*revoltoso*) unruly, wild. (**b**) (*loco*) crazy.

revirar [1a] **1** *vt* to turn (round), twist (round). **2 revirarse** *vr* (**a**) (*Carib, Cono Sur*) (*rebelarse*) to rebel. (**b**) (*Cono Sur*: *enloquecer*) to go crazy. (**c**) ~ **contra uno** (*Carib, Cono Sur*) to turn on sb.

revirón 1 *adj* (*CAm, Carib*) disobedient, rebellious, unruly. **2** *nm* (*CAm, Carib, Méx*) rebellion, revolt.

revisación *nf* (*Cono Sur*), **revisada** *nf* (*LAm*) = **revisión.**

revisar [1a] *vt* (**a**) *apuntes, texto etc* to revise, look over, go through; *edición* to revise; *cuenta* to check; to audit; (*Jur*) to review; *teoría etc* to re-examine, review.

(**b**) (*Mil*) *tropas* to review.

(**c**) (*Mec*) to check, overhaul; (*Aut*) to service.

revisión *nf* (**a**) (*repaso*) revision; check, checking; (*revista*) re-examination, review; ~ **aduanera** customs inspection; ~ **de cuentas** audit; ~ **de sueldos** salary review. (**b**) (*Mec*) check, overhaul; (*Aut*) service.

revisionismo *nm* revisionism.

revisionista *adj, nmf* revisionist.

revisor(a) *nm/f* reviser; inspector; (*Ferro*) ticket collector, inspector, conductor (*US*); ~ **de cuentas** auditor; ~ **de guión** (*Cine, TV*) script editor.

revista *nf* (**a**) (*acto*: *examen*) review, revision; (*inspección*) inspection; (*Jur*) retrial; **pasar ~ a** to review, revise, re-examine.

(**b**) (*Mil*) review, inspection; (*Náut*) review; **pasar ~ a** to review, inspect.

(**c**) (*periódico*) review, journal, magazine; ~ **comercial** trade paper; ~ **cómica** comic; ~ **del corazón** magazine of real-life romance stories; women's magazine; ~ **de destape** girlie magazine; ~ **gráfica** illustrated paper; ~ **juvenil** teenage magazine; ~ **literaria** literary review; ~ **de modas** fashion paper; ~ **para mujeres** women's magazine; ~ **semanal** weekly review.

(**d**) (*Liter*: *sección*) section, page; ~ **de libros** book review section, literary page; ~ **de toros** bullfighting page, section of bullfight reports.

(**e**) (*Teat*) revue; variety show, vaudeville show (*US*).

(**f**) (*And*: *del pelo*) trim.

revistar [1a] *vt* (*Mil*) to review, inspect; (*Náut*) to review.

revistero, -a 1 *nm/f* reviewer, critic; contributor; ~ **deportivo** sporting journalist; ~ **literario** literary critic, book reviewer. **2** *nm* (*mueble*) magazine rack.

revitalizador 1 *adj* revitalizing. **2** *nm* stimulant.

revitalizante *adj* revitalizing, invigorating.

revitalizar [1f] *vt* to revitalize.

revival 1 *nm* (*Mús etc*) revival; (*de persona*) comeback. **2** *atr*: **canción ~** revived hit song, hit song from the past; **prenda ~** garment enjoying a new popularity.

revivificar [1g] *vt* to revitalize.

revivir [3a] **1** *vt suceso etc* to revive memories of; (*vivir de nuevo*) to relive, live again; *sospecha* to revive. **2** *vi* to revive, be revived; to come to life again; **hacer ~ = 1.**

revocación *nf* revocation, repeal; reversal.

revocar [1g] *vt* (**a**) *decisión* to revoke, repeal; to cancel; to reverse; *persona* to remove from his post, axe.

(**b**) *humo etc* to send in a different direction, blow back, blow the wrong way.

(**c**) (*disuadir*) to dissuade (*de* from).

(**d**) (*Arquit*) (*enlucir*) to plaster, stucco; (*encalar*) to whitewash.

revocatoria *nf* (*LAm*) revocation, repeal.

revoco *nm* (**a**) = **revocación.** (**b**) = **revoque.**

revolar [1l] *vi* (*alzar el vuelo*) to take to flight again; (*revolotear*) to flutter about, fly around.

revolcadero *nm* (*Zool*) mudhole, mudbath.

revolcar [1g *y* 1l] **1** *vt* (**a**) (*derribar*) *persona* to knock down, knock over, send flying; (*Taur*) to knock down and trample on.

(**b**) (*) *adversario* to floor, crush; to wipe the floor with*.

(**c**) *orgulloso* to deflate, puncture.

(**d**) (*Esp‡ Univ*) to plough*.

2 revolcarse *vr* (**a**) (*persona*) to roll about, flounder about; to turn over and over; (*animal*) to wallow; (*: *amantes*) to have a romp in the hay; ~ **en la tumba** to turn over in one's grave; ~ **en los vicios** to wallow in vice.

(**b**) (*fig*) to dig one's heels in.

revolcón* *nm* fall, tumble; (*Fin*) slump; **dar un ~ a uno** (*fig*) to floor sb, crush sb; to wipe the floor with sb*; to deflate sb.

revolear [1a] **1** *vt* (*Cono Sur, Méx*) *lazo* to whirl, twirl. **2** *vi* to fly round.

revolera *nf* whirl, twirl.

revolica *nf* (*CAm*) confusion.

revolotear [1a] *vi* to flutter, fly about; to flit; to wheel, circle; to hover.

revoloteo *nm* fluttering; flitting; wheeling, circling; hovering.

revoltijo *nm*, **revoltillo** *nm* (**a**) (*confusión*) jumble, confusion; (*desorden*) mess, litter; (*fig*) mess; ~ **de huevos** scrambled eggs. (**b**) (*CAm, Cono Sur, Méx*) bundle.

revoltoso 1 *adj* rebellious, unruly, turbulent; *niño* naughty, uncontrollable. **2** *nm*, **revoltosa** *nf* (*rebelde*) rebel; (*Pol*) troublemaker, agitator; (*manifestante*) rioter.

revoltura *nf* (**a**) (*LAm*: *confusión*) confusion, jumble. (**b**) (*Méx*: *mezcla*) mixture; (*Culin*) scrambled eggs with vegetables; (*Arquit*) mortar, cement.

revolución *nf* (**a**) (*Téc*) revolution; **revoluciones por minuto** revolutions per minute. (**b**) (*Pol etc*) revolution; **R~ Cultural** Cultural Revolution; **R~ Industrial** Industrial Revolution; ~ **islámica** Islamic revolution; **R~ de Octubre** October Revolution; ~ **de palacio** palace revolution; **R~ Verde** Green Revolution.

revolucionar [1a] *vt* (**a**) *industria, moda etc* to revolutionize, cause a revolution in.

(**b**) *persona* to arouse intense excitement in, rouse to a pitch of excitement.

(**c**) (*Pol*) to stir up, sow discontent among; to rouse to revolt.

revolucionario, -a *adj, nm/f* revolutionary.

revoluta *nf* (*CAm*) revolution.

revolvedora *nf* (*Cono Sur, Méx*) concrete mixer.

revolver [2h; *ptp* **revuelto**] **1** *vt* (**a**) (*mover*) *objetos* to move about; (*poner al revés*) to turn round, turn over, turn upside-down; (*Culin*) to turn over; *tierra* to turn over, turn up, dig over; *recipiente* to shake; *líquido etc* to stir; *papeles etc* to look through; to rummage through, rummage among; (*Méx*) to revolve, turn around; **~la** (*fig*) to mess everything up; **¡deja de ~!, ¡no revuelvas!** (*a niño*) stop messing about with things!, stop fidgeting!

(**b**) (*desordenar*) to disturb, disarrange, mix up, mess up; **han revuelto toda la casa** they've messed up the whole house, they've turned the whole house upside-down.

(**c**) (*indagar*) to go into, inquire into, investigate; ~ **algo en la cabeza** to turn sth over in one's mind.

(**d**) (*Pol etc*) to stir up, rouse, cause unrest among; *persona* to provoke, rouse to anger; ~ **Eslobodia con Ruritania** to stir up trouble between Slobodia and Ruritania; ~ **al secretario con el jefe** to get the secretary into trouble with his boss.

(**e**) (*volver*) *ojos, caballo etc* to turn.

(**f**) (*envolver*) to wrap up.

(**g**) (*And*) to weed.

2 *vi*: ~ **en una maleta** to rummage (about) in a case, hunt through the contents of a case; ~ **en los bolsillos** to feel in one's pockets, fumble in one's pockets.

3 revolverse *vr* (**a**) (*volverse*) to turn (right) round; to turn over; (*en cama*) to toss and turn; (*con dolor*) to writhe, squirm; (*Astron*) to revolve; ~ **al enemigo** to turn to face the enemy; **se revolvía en su silla** he was fidgeting about on his chair; he was squirming uncomfortably on his chair.

(**b**) (*fig*) ~ **contra uno** to turn on sb, turn against sb, attack sb.

(**c**) (*sedimento*) to be stirred up, be disturbed; (*líquido*) to become cloudy.

(**d**) (*Met*) to break, turn stormy.

(**e**) (*And**: *prosperar*) to get a lucky break, have a change of fortunes; (*pey*) to look after Number One.

revólver *nm* revolver.

revoque *nm* (**a**) (*acto*) plastering; whitewashing. (**b**) (*materia*) (*enlucido*) plaster, stucco; (*cal*) whitewash.

revuelco *nm* fall, tumble; wallow(ing).

revuelo *nm* (**a**) flutter(ing).

(**b**) (*fig*) (*conmoción*) stir, commotion, disturbance; (*jaleo*) row, rumpus; **de ~** incidentally, in passing; **armar** (*o* **levantar** *etc*) **un gran ~** to cause a great stir.

revuelta *nf* (**a**) (*vuelta*) turn; **dar vueltas y ~s a algo** to go on turning sth over and over.

(**b**) (*de carretera etc*) bend, turn.

(**c**) (*fig*) (*conmoción*) commotion, disturbance; (*jaleo*) fuss; (*riña*) quarrel, row; (*Pol*) disturbance, riot; (*motín*) revolt.

(**d**) (*And*) weeding.

revuelto 1 *ptp de* **revolver.**

2 *adj* (**a**) *objetos* mixed up, in disorder, confused; *huevos* scrambled; *agua* cloudy, muddy; *mar* rough; *tiempo* unsettled, changeable; stormy; **todo estaba ~** everything was in disorder, everything was upside-down; **los tiempos están ~s** the times are out of joint, these are disturbed times; **viven ~s los animales y las personas** people and animals live on top of each other.

(**b**) *carácter* (*revoltoso*) unruly; (*inquieto*) restless, discontented; *niño etc* mischievous, naughty; *población* rebellious, mutinous; **la gente está revuelta por tales abusos** people feel mutinous about such scandals, people are properly on the boil about such abuses.

(**c**) *asunto* complicated, involved.

3 *nm* (**a**) **~ de huevos** mixed eggs and vegetables; **~ de morcilla** dish of mixed blood-sausage and vegetables.

(**b**) (*And*) must, grape juice.

revulsar [1a] *vt* (*Méx**) to vomit, throw up.

revulsionar [1a] *vt*: **~ a uno** to turn sb's stomach.

revulsivo *nm* (**a**) (*Med*) enema, revulsive. (**b**) (*fig*) nasty but salutary shock.

rey *nm* (**a**) king (*t Ajedrez, Naipes y fig*); **los ~es** (*frec*) the king and queen; royalty; **los R~es Católicos** the Catholic Monarchs (*Ferdinand and Isabella of Aragon and Castile*); **~ de armas** king of arms; **a ~ muerto ~ puesto** off with the old, on with the new; **ni ~ ni roque** no-one at all, not a single living soul; **lo mismo me da ~ que roque** it's all the same to me.

(**b**) (*Rel*) **los R~es** (**Magos**) the Magi, the Three Wise Men; (*fecha*) Twelfth Night, Epiphany; **nos veremos por R~es** we'll meet after Christmas; **¿qué te han traído los R~es?** ≃ what did Father Christmas bring you?

reyerta *nf* quarrel; fight, brawl, affray.

reyezuelo *nm* (**a**) petty king, kinglet. (**b**) (*Orn*) **~** (**sencillo**) goldcrest.

rezaga *nf* (*LAm*) = **zaga.**

rezagado 1 *adj* (**a**) **quedar ~** (*quedar atrás*) to be left behind; (*llevar retraso*) to be late, be behindhand; (*en pagos, progresos etc*) to fall behind, be backward.

(**b**) **carta rezagada** (*And, Méx*) unclaimed letter.

2 *nm*, **rezagada** *nf* latecomer; loiterer, dawdler; (*Mil*) straggler.

rezagamiento *nm* falling behind, lagging behind; (*fig*) backwardness.

rezagar [1h] **1** *vt* (**a**) (*dejar atrás*) to leave behind; to outpace, outdistance.

(**b**) (*aplazar etc*) to postpone.

2 rezagarse *vr* (*quedar atrás*) to stay behind, fall behind, get left behind; to lag (behind); (*ir despacio*) to loiter, dawdle; to straggle; **nos rezagamos en la producción** we are falling behind in production.

rezago *nm* (**a**) (*géneros*) left-over goods (*etc*); (*sobra*) unused material, material which is left over; (*Cono Sur*) (*mercancías*) unsold (*o* remaindered) goods; (*ganado*) cattle rejected at the abattoir.

(**b**) (*vacas dispersas*) group of straggling cattle.

(**c**) (*And, Méx Correos*) unclaimed letters.

rezar [1f] **1** *vt* (**a**) *oración* to say.

(**b**) (*pedir*) to call for, plead for; **el periódico reza agua** the paper says we need rain.

2 *vi* (**a**) (*Rel*) to pray (*a* to); to say one's prayers; to be at prayer.

(**b**) (*texto*) to read, say, run, go; **el anuncio reza así** the notice reads as follows.

(**c**) (*****: *quejarse*) to grumble.

(**d**) **~ con*** to concern, have to do with; **eso no reza conmigo** that has nothing to do with me; that doesn't apply to me.

rezo *nm* (**a**) (*un ~*) prayer(s); devotions; (*oficio*) daily service; **estar en el ~** to be at prayer. (**b**) (*acto, gen*) praying.

rezondrada* *nf* (*And*) telling off*, scolding.

rezondrar [1a] *vt* (*And*) = **rezongar.**

rezongador *adj* = **rezongón.**

rezongar [1h] **1** *vt* (*CAm, Cono Sur*) to tell off, scold. **2** *vi* to grumble; to mutter; to growl.

rezongo *nm* (**a**) (*quejido*) grumble, moan. (**b**) (*CAm*) (*reprimenda*) reprimand; (*regaño*) scolding.

rezongón *adj* grumbling, grouchy*, cantankerous.

rezumar [1a] **1** *vt* to ooze, exude; to leak.

2 *vi* (**a**) (*contenido*) to ooze (out), seep, leak out; (*recipiente*) to ooze, leak.

(**b**) (*fig*) to ooze; **le rezuma el orgullo** he oozes pride; **le rezuma el entusiasmo** he is bursting with enthusiasm, he overflows with enthusiasm.

3 rezumarse *vr* (**a**) = **2** (**a**).

(**b**) (*fig*) to leak out, become known.

RFA *nf* (*Hist*) *abr de* **República Federal Alemana** West Germany, FRG.

RFE *nf abr de* **Revista de Filología Española.**

ría[1] *etc V* **reír.**

ría[2] *nf* estuary; **R~s Altas** northern coast of Galicia; **R~s Bajas** southern coast of Galicia.

riachuelo *nm* brook, stream; **~s de gente** crowds of people.

Riad *nm* Riyadh.

riada *nf* flood (*t fig*); **hasta aquí llegó la ~** that's how bad things were.

ribazo *nm* steep slope, steep bank.

ribera *nf* (**a**) (*de lago, río*) bank; (*de mar*) beach, shore; (*zona*) riverside.

(**b**) (*Agr*) irrigated plain.

(**c**) (*Cono Sur, Méx*) (*de campo*) riverside community; (*chabolas*) shanty town, slum quarter.

riberano *adj* (*LAm*) = **ribereño.**

ribereño 1 *adj* riverside (*atr*); coastal; (*Jur*) riparian. **2** *nm*, **ribereña** *nf* person who lives near a river; riverside dweller.

ribete *nm* (**a**) (*Cos*) edging, border, trimming.

(**b**) (*fig*: *adorno*) addition, adornment; **~s** (*de cuento*) embellishments, trimmings, personal touches.

(**c**) **~s** (*fig*: *elementos*) touch, quality; **tiene sus ~s de pintor** he has some pretensions to being a painter, he is not without some of the painter's talents.

ribetear [1a] *vt* to edge, border, trim (*de* with).

ribo *nm* (*And*) (*de río*) bank; (*de mar*) shore.

riboflavina *nf* riboflavin.

ricacho* *nm*, **ricachón*** *nm* fabulously rich man; nouveau riche; (*Pol*: *pey*) well-heeled bourgeois*, dirty capitalist.

ricamente *adv* (**a**) (*lit*) richly.

(**b**) (*fig*) **muy ~, tan ~** very well, jolly well*; **comeremos tan ~** we'll have a really good meal; **he dormido tan ~** I've slept splendidly; **viven muy ~ sin él** they manage perfectly well without him.

Ricardo *nm* Richard.

ricino *nm* castor-oil plant; **aceite de ~** castor oil.

ricito *nm* ringlet, kiss-curl.

rico 1 *adj* (**a**) (*Fin*) rich, wealthy; **llueva sobre el más ~** to him that hath shall be given.

(**b**) (*fig*) *suelo, vena etc* rich; **~ de, ~ en** rich in.

(**c**) *joya etc* valuable, precious; *muebles etc* luxurious, sumptuous, valuable; *tela* fine-quality, rich.

(**d**) (*sabroso*) delicious, tasty; *fruta* luscious; **estos pasteles son riquísimos** these cakes are exceptionally tasty, these cakes are really lovely.

(**e**) (*****) *niño* bonny; cute, lovely; (*en oración directa*: *a marido etc*) **¡~!** darling!; **¡oye, ~!*** hey, man!*; **¡que no, ~!** (*Esp*) no way, mate!* **¡oye, rica!** (*Esp*) hey, beautiful!; hullo, gorgeous!*; **¡qué ~ está el pequeño!** isn't he a lovely baby!; **¡qué ~!** (*iró*) isn't that just splendid?; **está muy rica la tía‡** she's a bit of all right‡.

2 *nm*, **rica** *nf* rich person; wealthy man, wealthy woman; **nuevo ~** nouveau riche.

rictus *nm* (involuntary) curl of the lip, rictus; (*de desprecio*) sneer; (*de burla*) grin; **~ de dolor** wince of pain; **~ de amargura** bitter smile.

ricura* *nf* (**a**) (*lo sabroso*) tastiness, delicious quality,

(**b**) (*chica*) smashing girl*; **¡oye, ~!** hey, beautiful!; hullo, gorgeous*.

(**c**) **¡qué ~ de pastel!** isn't this a lovely cake?; what a smashing cake!*; **¡qué ~ de criatura!** what a lovely baby!

ridi* 1 *adj* ridiculous; **¡no seas ~!** don't be ridiculous! **2** *nm*: **hacer el ~** to make a fool of oneself.

ridículamente *adv* ridiculously, absurdly.

ridiculez *nf* absurdity.

ridiculización *nf* mockery; parody.

ridiculizador *adj*, **ridiculizante** *adj* mocking, derisive.

ridiculizar [1f] *vt* to ridicule, deride; to mock, guy, parody.
ridículo 1 *adj* ridiculous, absurd, ludicrous.
2 *nm* (**a**) **hacer el ~** to make o.s. ridiculous, make a fool of o.s.
(**b**) ridicule; **exponerse al ~** to lay o.s. open to ridicule; **poner a uno en ~** to ridicule sb, make a fool of sb; **ponerse en ~** to make o.s. ridiculous, make a fool of o.s.
riego *nm* (*aspersión*) watering; (*Agr*) irrigation; (*fig*) sprinkling; **~ por aspersión, ~ por goteo** watering by spray, watering by sprinklers; **la política del ~ en esta provincia** irrigation policy in this province.
riel *nm* (**a**) (*Ferro*) rail; **~es** rails, track, permanent way. (**b**) (*Téc*) ingot.
rielar [1a] *vi* (*poét*) to shimmer; to glitter, gleam.
rielazo* *nm* (*CAm*) blow, smack.
rielero *nm* (*Méx*) railwayman.
rienda *nf* rein; (*fig*) restraint, moderating influence; **a ~ suelta** at top speed; (*fig*) without the least restraint; violently; **aflojar las ~s** to let up; **dar ~ suelta a** to give free rein to; **dar ~ suelta al llanto** to weep uncontrollably; **dar ~ suelta a los deseos** to indulge one's desires freely; **dar ~ suelta a uno** to give sb a free hand; **empuñar las ~s** to take charge; **llevar las ~s** to be in charge, be in control; **soltar las ~s** to relinquish control; to take off the brakes; to kick over the traces; **tener a uno a ~ corta** to keep a tight rein on sb.
riente *adj* (**a**) (*risueño*) laughing, merry. (**b**) (*fig*) *paisaje etc* bright, pleasant.
riesgo *nm* risk, danger; **con ~ de** at the risk of; **seguro a** (*o* **contra**) **todo ~** comprehensive insurance; **grupos de ~** groups at risk; **correr ~ de** + *infin* to run the risk of + *ger*, be in danger of + *ger*.
riesgoso *adj* risky, dangerous.
rifa *nf* (**a**) (*lotería*) raffle. (**b**) (*riña*) quarrel, dispute, fight.
rifar [1a] **1** *vt* to raffle; **~ algo para fines benéficos** to raffle sth for charity.
2 *vi* to quarrel, fight.
3 rifarse* *vr* (**a**) **~ algo** to quarrel over sth, fight for sth; **~ el amor de una** to vie for sb's love.
(**b**) (*CAm*: *arriesgarse*) to take a risk.
rifeño 1 *adj* Riffian, of the Riff. **2** *nm*, **rifeña** *nf* Riffian.
rififí* *nm* (**a**) (*acto*) burglary, robbery, (*esp*) bank robbery. (**b**) burglar, robber, bank-robber.
rifir(i)rafe* *nm** shindy*, row.
rifle *nm* rifle; (*Dep*) sporting rifle; (*Caza*) hunting gun; **~ de repetición** repeater rifle.
riflero 1 *adj* (*Cono Sur, Méx*) *tirador* ace, crack. **2** *nm* (**a**) (*Mil*) rifleman. (**b**) (*Cono Sur, Méx*: *tirador*) marksman, crack shot.
rígidamente *adv* (*V adj*) (**a**) rigidly, stiffly. (**b**) (*fig*) rigidly. (**c**) (*fig*) strictly, sternly, harshly. (**d**) woodenly.
rigidez *nf* (*V adj*) (**a**) rigidity, stiffness; **~ cadavérica** rigor mortis. (**b**) (*fig*) rigidity; inflexibility. (**c**) (*fig*) strictness, sternness, harshness. (**d**) woodenness.
rígido *adj* (**a**) (*tieso*) rigid, stiff; **quedarse ~** to go rigid; (*aterirse*) to get stiff (with cold).
(**b**) (*fig*: *actitud*) rigid, inflexible, unadaptable.
(**c**) (*fig*: *moralmente*) strict, stern (*con, para* towards), harsh, unbending.
(**d**) *mirada, cara* wooden, expressionless.
rigor *nm* (**a**) severity, harshness; strictness; toughness, stringency.
(**b**) (*Met*) harshness, severity; **el ~ del verano** the worst of the summer, the hottest part of the summer; **los ~es del clima** the rigours of the climate.
(**c**) (*severidad*) rigour; (*exigencia*) exacting nature; (*precisión*) accuracy, meticulousness; **con todo ~ científico** with complete scientific rigour; **una edición hecha con el mayor ~ crítico** an edition produced with absolute meticulousness.
(**d**) **ser de ~** (*esencial*) to be de rigueur, be absolutely essential; **después de los saludos de ~** after the customary greetings; **me dio los consejos de ~** he gave the expected advice, he gave me the advice which he felt he had to; **en ~** strictly speaking.
(**e**) **un ~ de cosas** (*And*) a whole lot of things.
(**f**) **dar un ~ a uno** (*Cono Sur**: *paliza*) to give sb a hiding*.
rigorismo *nm* strictness, severity; austerity.
rigorista 1 *adj* strict. **2** *nmf* strict disciplinarian; strict observer (*de* of), stickler (*de* for).
rigue *nm* (*CAm Culin*) tortilla.
rigurosamente *adv* (**a**) (*severamente*) severely, harshly; (*estrictamente*) strictly; stringently.
(**b**) (*con precisión*) rigorously; accurately, meticulously.
(**c**) **un estudio ~ científico** an absolutely scientific study; **eso no es ~ exacto** that is not strictly accurate, that is not wholly true.
rigurosidad *nf* rigour, harshness, severity.
riguroso *adj* (**a**) *actitud, disciplina etc* severe, harsh; *aplicación etc* strict; *medida* severe, tough, stringent; **su tratamiento ~ de los empleados** his harsh treatment of the employees.
(**b**) (*Met*) harsh, severe, hard; extreme.
(**c**) *estudio, método etc* rigorous; exacting; accurate; meticulous.
(**d**) (*liter*) cruel; **los hados ~s** the cruel fates.
rija *nf* quarrel, dispute, fight.
rijio *nm* (**a**) (*CAm*) = **rijo**. (**b**) (*CAm, Méx*) spirit, spirited temperament (*of a horse*).
rijioso *adj* (*CAm, Méx*) = **rijoso**.
rijo *nm* lustfulness, sensuality; randiness*.
rijosidad *nf* (**a**) (*sensibilidad*) touchiness, susceptible nature; quarrelsomeness. (**b**) (*deseo sexual*) lustfulness, sensuality; randiness*.
rijoso *adj* (**a**) (*sensible*) touchy, susceptible; (*peleador*) quarrelsome. (**b**) (*cachondo*) lustful, sensual; randy*. (**c**) (*caballo*) in rut.
rila *nf* (**a**) (*And, Méx*: *de carne*) gristle. (**b**) (*And*: *excremento*) bird droppings.
rilado‡ **1** *adj* knackered*, shagged out‡. **2** *nm* coward.
rilarse‡ [1a] *vi* (**a**) (*agotarse*) to knacker o.s.*, get shagged out‡. (**b**) (*rajarse*) to back out, fall down on the job; to get cold feet. (**c**) (*asustarse*) to be dead scared. (**d**) (*temblar*) to shiver. (**e**) (*peerse*) to fart**.
rima *nf* (**a**) (*gen*) rhyme; **~ imperfecta** assonance, half-rhyme; **~ interna** internal rhyme; **~ perfecta** full rhyme; **octava ~** ottava rima; **tercia ~** terza rima. (**b**) **~s** poems, verse, poetry.
rimado *adj* rhymed, rhyming.
rimador(a) *nm/f* rhymester.
rimar [1a] *vti* to rhyme (*con* with).
rimbombancia *nf* (**a**) resonance, echo. (**b**) (*fig*) pomposity, bombast. (**c**) (*fig*) showiness, flashiness.
rimbombante *adj* (**a**) (*resonante*) resounding, echoing. (**b**) (*fig*: *pomposo*) pompous, bombastic. (**c**) (*fig*: *ostentoso*) showy, flashy.
rimbombar [1a] *vi* to resound, echo, boom.
rimel *nm*, **rímel** *nm*, **rimmel** *nm* mascara, eye-shadow.
rimero *nm* stack, pile, heap.
Rin *nm* Rhine.
rin *nm* (*And*) (*teléfono*) public telephone (using tokens); (*ficha*) token (for telephone).
rincón *nm* (**a**) (*gen*) (inside) corner. (**b**) (*fig*) corner, nook; (*retiro*) retreat; niche. (**c**) (*Agr*: *esp LAm*) patch of ground.
rinconada *nf* corner.
rinconera *nf* (**a**) (*mueble*) corner-piece (of furniture); (*armario*) corner-cupboard, dresser. (**b**) (*Arquit*) wall between corner and window.
rinche *adj* (*And, Cono Sur*) full to the brim, brimming over.
ringla *nf*, **ringle** *nm*, **ringlera** *nf* row, line; (*Agr*) swath.
ringorrango *nm* (**a**) (*en escritura*) flourish. (**b**) **~s** (*adornos*) frills, buttons and bows, useless adornments.
ringuelete *nmf* (**a**) (*Cono Sur, And*: *inquieto*) rolling stone (*fig*). (**b**) (*And*) (*rehilete*) dart; (*molinillo*) toy windmill.
ringueletear [1a] *vi* (*And, Cono Sur*) = **callejear**.
rinitis *nf*: **~ alérgica** hay fever.
rinoceronte *nm* rhinoceros.
rintoso‡ *nm* (*Carib*) skiver‡, shirker.
riña *nf* (*disputa*) quarrel, argument; (*pelea*) fight, brawl, scuffle; **~ de gallos** cockfight; **~ de perros** dogfight(ing).
riñón *nm* (**a**) (*Anat*) kidney; (*más general*) lower part of the back; **~ artificial** artificial kidney; **me costó un ~*** it cost me a bomb*; **tener riñones*** to have guts, be tough; **tener el ~ bien cubierto*** to be well-heeled*.
(**b**) (*fig*) heart, core; innermost part; **aquí en el ~ de Castilla** here in the very heart of Castile.
riñonada* *nf*: **me costó una ~** it cost the earth.
riñonera *nf* money belt, money pouch.
riñonudo* *adj* full of guts, tough.
río[1] **1** *nm* (*gen*) river; (*fig*) stream, torrent; **~ abajo** downstream; **~ arriba** upstream; **un ~ de gente** a stream of people, a flood of people; **es un ~ de oro** it's a gold mine; **a ~ revuelto, ganancia de pescadores** there are bound to be pickings for some, it's an ill wind that blows nobody any good; **cuando el ~ suena, agua lleva, cuando el ~ suena, piedras trae** there's no smoke without fire. **2** *atr* lengthy,

long-lasting; epic; (*pey*) interminable; **novela ~** saga; **programa ~** blockbuster of a programme; **serie ~** long-running series.
río², **rió** *etc V* **reír.**
Río de la Plata *nm* River Plate.
Rioja *nf*: **La ~** La Rioja.
rioja *nm* Rioja, Riojan wine.
riojano 1 *adj* Riojan, of La Rioja. **2** *nm*, **riojana** *nf* Riojan. **3** *nm* (**a**) (*vino*) Rioja. (**b**) (*Ling*) Riojan dialect.
riolada* *nf* flood, stream.
rioplatense 1 *adj* of the River Plate region. **2** *nmf* native (*o* inhabitant) of the River Plate region; **los ~s** the people of the River Plate region.
riostra *nf* brace, strut.
Ripalda *nm* catechism of Jerónimo Ripalda; (*fig*) bible, handbook.
ripiado *adj* (**a**) (*And*: *harapiento*) ragged. (**b**) (*Carib*: *pobre*) wretched, down-at-heel.
ripiar [1b] *vt* (**a**) (*Arquit*) to fill with rubble. (**b**) (*And, Carib*) (*cortar*) to shred, cut into shreds; (*desmenuzar*) to crumble. (**c**) (*And, Carib*: *despilfarrar*) to squander. (**d**) (*And*) *persona* to leave badly off; *dos personas* to mix up. (**e**) (*Méx*: *espigar*) to glean. (**f**) (*Carib*: *pegar*) to hit.
ripiería *nf* (*And*) mob, populace.
ripio *nm* (**a**) (*basura*) refuse, waste; (*Arquit*) rubble; debris; (*Cono Sur*) roadstone.
(**b**) (*Liter*) padding, word (*o* phrase) put in to fill up the line; (*fig*) padding, verbiage, empty words; **no perder ~** not to miss a trick, to miss nothing of what is going on.
ripioso *adj* (*And, Carib*) ragged.
riquerío *nm*: **el ~** (*Cono Sur**) rich people (*collectively*).
riqueza *nf* (**a**) (*bienes*) wealth, riches; **~ imponible** taxable wealth; **vivir en la ~** to live in luxury. (**b**) (*fig*: *cualidad*) richness.
riquiña *nf* (*Carib*) sewing basket.
riquiñeque *nm* (*And*) quarrel.
risa *nf* (*una ~*) laugh; (*gen, t ~s*) laughter; **hubo ~s** there was laughter; **no es cosa de ~** it's no laughing matter; **¡qué ~!** how very funny!, what a joke!; **el libro es una verdadera ~** the book is a laugh from start to finish; **~s enlatadas** canned laughter; **~ retozona** suppressed giggle, titter; **ahogarse** (*o* **caerse, descoserse, desternillarse, mondarse, morirse**) **de ~** to split one's sides laughing, die laughing*; **causar ~ a uno, mover** (*o* **provocar**) **a uno a ~** to make sb laugh; **entrar ganas de ~** to feel like laughing; **la ~ va por barrios** you'll all get your turn, every dog has his day; **soltar la ~** to burst out laughing; **tomar algo a ~** to take sth as a joke, laugh sth off.
risco *nm* (**a**) (*inclinado*) cliff, crag; steep rock. (**b**) **~s** (*terreno áspero*) rough parts, difficult pieces.
riscoso *adj* steep, craggy.
risible *adj* ludicrous, laughable.
risión *nf* derision, mockery; **ser un objeto de ~** to be a laughing-stock.
risotada *nf* guffaw, loud laugh.
rispiar [1b] *vi* (*CAm*) to rush off.
rispidez *nf* (**a**) coarseness, uncouthness. (**b**) roughness, sharpness.
ríspido *adj* (*esp LAm*) (**a**) (*maleducado*) coarse, uncouth. (**b**) (*áspero*) rough, sharp.
risquería *nf* (*Cono Sur*) craggy place.
ristra *nf* string (*t fig*); **una ~ de ajos** a string of garlic.
ristre *nm*: **en ~** at the ready, all set; *V* **lanza.**
risueñamente *adv* smilingly; cheerfully.
risueño *adj* (**a**) *cara* smiling; **muy ~** smiling all over, with a big smile, wreathed in smiles.
(**b**) *temperamento etc* cheerful, sunny, gay; *paisaje etc* smiling, pleasant.
(**c**) *perspectiva* bright, favourable.
RITD *nf* (*Telec*) *abr de* **Red Iberoamericana de Transmisión de Datos.**
rítmico *adj* rhythmic(al).
ritmo *nm* (**a**) (*Mús etc*) rhythm.
(**b**) (*fig*) rhythm; rate, pace; speed; **~ cardíaco** pulse-rate; **~ de crecimiento, ~ de expansión** rate of growth; **~ de publicación** rate of publication; **~ de vida** pace of life; lifestyle, way of life; **el trabajo se mantiene a un ~ intenso** the work is going on at a rapid rate (*o* pace); **trabajar a ~ lento** to go slow; **de acuerdo con el ~ de las estaciones** in keeping with the rhythm of the seasons.
rito *nm* rite, ceremony; **~ iniciático** initiation rite; **~s de paso** rites of passage.
ritual *adj, nm* ritual; **de ~** ritual, customary.
ritualismo *nm* ritualism.
ritualista 1 *adj* ritualistic, ritual. **2** *nmf* ritualist.
ritualizado *adj* ritualized; (*fig*) familiar; stereotyped, fixed.
rival 1 *adj* rival, competing. **2** *nmf* rival, competitor; contender; **el eterno ~** (*fig*) the old enemy.
rivalidad *nf* rivalry, competition.
rivalizar [1f] *vi* to vie, compete, contend; **~ con** to rival, compete with; **los dos rivalizan en habilidad** they rival each other in skill.
rizado *adj pelo* curly; *superficie* ridged, crinkly; *terreno* undulating; *mar* choppy.
rizador *nm* curling iron, hair-curler.
rizadura *nf* ripple.
rizar [1f] **1** *vt pelo* to curl; to ruffle; *superficie* to ridge, crinkle; *agua* to ripple, ruffle; *V* **rizo¹ 2** (**b**). **2 rizarse** *vr* (*agua*) to ripple; **~ el pelo** to perm one's hair.
rizo¹ 1 *adj curly.* **2** *nm* (**a**) (*de pelo*) curl, ringlet; (*en superficie*) ridge; (*en agua*) ripple. (**b**) (*Aer*) loop; **hacer el ~, rizar el ~** to loop the loop; (*fig*) to split hairs.
rizo² *nm* (*Náut*) reef; **tomar ~s** to reef in (the sails).
rizoma *nm* rhizome.
R.M. *abr de* **Reverenda Madre** Reverend Mother.
Rma. *abr de* **Reverendísima** *courtesy title.*
Rmo. *abr de* **Reverendísimo** Right Reverend, Rt. Rev.
RNE *nf* (*Rad*) *abr de* **Radio Nacional de España.**
R.O. *abr de* **Real Orden** royal order.
roano 1 *adj* roan. **2** *nm* roan (horse).
robacarros *nmf invar* (*LAm*) car thief.
robacarteras *nmf invar* pickpocket.
robalo *nm*, **róbalo** *nm* sea-bass.
robar [1a] *vt* (**a**) *dueño* to rob; *objeto* to steal (*a* from); *casa etc* to break into, burgle; *cajafuerte* to break open, break into, rifle (the contents of); **~ algo a uno** to steal sth from sb, rob sb of sth; **en ese negocio me han robado** I was cheated in that deal; **X robó el balón a Y** X stole the ball from Y.
(**b**) *persona* to kidnap, abduct.
(**c**) (*fig*) *atención etc* to steal, capture; *interés* to command; *paciencia* to exhaust; *tranquilidad* to destroy; *vida* to take; **~ el corazón a uno** to steal sb's heart; **tuve que ~ 3 horas al sueño** I had to use up 3 hours when I should have been sleeping.
(**d**) (*río*) to carry away.
(**e**) (*Naipes*) to draw, take (from the pile).
Roberto *nm* Robert.
robinsón *nm* castaway.
roblar [1a] *vt* to rivet, clinch.
roble *nm* oak, oak tree; **de ~** oak (*atr*), oaken; **de ~ macizo** of solid oak.
robledal *nm*, **robledo** *nm* oakwood.
roblón *nm* rivet.
roblonar [1a] *vt* to rivet.
robo *nm* (**a**) (*un ~*) theft; (*gen*) robbery, theft, thieving; **~ a mano armada** armed robbery; **~ con allanamiento, ~ con escalamiento, ~ con escalo, ~ en vivienda** housebreaking, burglary; **~ relámpago** smash-and-grab raid; **~ en la vía pública** highway robbery; **¡esto es un ~!** this is sheer robbery!
(**b**) (*cosa robada*) stolen article, stolen goods.
robot [ro'ßo] **1** *nm, pl* **robots** [ro'ßo] (**a**) robot. (**b**) (*fig*) puppet, tool. **2** *atr* stereotyped; identikit (*atr*).
robótica *nf* robotics.
robotización *nf* robotization; automation.
robotizar [1f] *vt* to automate; (*fig*) to turn into a robot.
robustecer [2d] **1** *vt* to strengthen. **2 robustecerse** *vr* to grow stronger.
robustez *nf* strength, toughness, robustness.
robusto *adj* strong, tough, robust.
roca *nf* (**a**) rock; **en ~ viva** in(to) the living rock; **la R~** the Rock (of Gibraltar). (**b**) **ser firme como una ~** (*fig*) to be as solid as a rock. (**c**) (**‡**: *droga*) crack.
rocalla *nf* small stones, pebbles; stone chippings.
rocalloso *adj* pebbly, stony.
rocambolescamente *adv* bizarrely, in a bizarre fashion; ornately, over-elaborately.
rocambolesco *adj* (*raro*) odd, bizarre; *estilo* ornate, baroque, over-elaborate.
rocanola *nf* jukebox.
rocanrol *nm* rock-'n'-roll.
roce *nm* (**a**) (*acto*) rub, rubbing; (*Téc*) friction; (*fig*: *Pol etc*) friction.
(**b**) (*señal*) rub, mark of rubbing; (*en la piel*) graze, chafing mark.
(**c**) (*) (*contacto*) close contact; (*familiaridad*) fa-

miliarity; (*disgusto*) brush; **tener ~ con** to be in close contact with, have a lot to do with; **tuvo algún ~ con la autoridad** he had a few brushes with the law.
rociada *nf* (**a**) (*aspersión*) shower, spray, sprinkling; (*en bebida etc*) dash, splash; (*Agr*) spray.
(**b**) (*fig*: *de piedras*) shower; (*de balas*) hail; (*de perdigones*) scatter; (*de insultos*) hail, stream, torrent.
rociadera *nf* watering can.
rociado *nm* sprinkling; (*Agr*) spraying.
rociador *nm* spray; sprinkler; **~ de moscas** fly spray.
rociar [1c] **1** *vt* to sprinkle, spray (*de* with); (*de lodo etc*) to spatter, bespatter (*de* with); (*de balas*) to spray (*de* with).
2 *vi*: **empieza a ~** the dew is beginning to fall; **rocía esta mañana** there is a dew this morning.
rocín *nm* (**a**) (*caballo*) hack, nag, poor horse; (*Cono Sur*) riding horse; (*And*) draught ox. (**b**) (*: *persona*) lout, ignorant fellow.
rocinante *nm* broken-down old horse.
rocío *nm* (**a**) (*Met*) (*de noche*) dew; (*llovizna*) light drizzle. (**b**) (*fig*) sprinkling; dew; drops of condensation (*etc*).
rockero 1 *adj* rock (*atr*); **música rockera** rock music; **es muy ~** he's a real rock fan. **2** *nm*, **rockera** *nf* (*cantante*) rock singer; (*músico*) rock musician; (*aficionado*) rock fan.
rococó *adj, nm* rococo.
rocola *nf* (*LAm*) jukebox.
rocosidades *nfpl* rocky places.
rocoso *adj* rocky.
rocote *nm*, **rocoto** *nm* (*LAm*) large pepper, large chili.
Rochela *nf*: **La ~** La Rochelle.
rochela* *nf* (*And, Carib*) rowdy party; (*alboroto*) din, racket.
rochelear* [1a] *vi* (*And, Carib*) (*juguetear*) to play about; (*ir de juerga*) to go out on the town.
rochelero* *adj* (*And, Carib*: *ruidoso*) unruly, rowdy; (*Carib*: *travieso*) mischievous, naughty.
roda¹ *nf* (*Náut*) stem.
roda²‡ *nm* (*Aut*) crate*, car.
rodaballo *nm* turbot; **~ menor** brill.
rodada *nf* (**a**) (*de rueda*) rut, wheel track. (**b**) (*Cono Sur, Méx*: *caída*) fall (from a horse).
rodadero *nm* (*And*) cliff, precipice.
rodado 1 *adj* (**a**) *tráfico* wheeled, on wheels.
(**b**) *piedra etc* rounded; **esto vino ~** this just happened (without my having to do anything); by luck the chance came up; **salir** (*o* **venir**) **~** to go smoothly.
(**c**) *caballo* dappled.
(**d**) *estilo* well-rounded, fluent.
(**e**) (*fig*: *experimentado*) experienced.
2 *nm* (*Cono Sur*) (wheeled) vehicle.
rodadura *nf* (**a**) (*acto*) roll, rolling. (**b**) (*rodada*) rut. (**c**) (*de neumático*: *t* **banda de ~**) tread.
rodaja *nf* (**a**) (*ruedecilla*) small wheel; (*disco*) small disc; (*de mueble*) castor. (**b**) (*de pan, fruta etc*) slice; **limón en ~s** sliced lemon.
rodaje *nm* (**a**) (*Téc*) wheels, set of wheels. (**b**) (*Cine*) shooting, filming. (**c**) (*Aut*) running-in; **'en ~'** 'running in'. (**d**) (*And*: *impuesto*) vehicle tax, road tax (*Brit*). (**e**) (*fig*) **período de ~** initial phase; **poner en ~** to launch. (**f**) (*experiencia*) experience; know-how.
rodamiento *nm* (**a**) **~ a bolas, ~ de bolas** ball-bearing. (**b**) (*Aut*: *de neumático, t* **banda de ~**) tread.
Ródano *nm* Rhône.
rodante 1 *adj* rolling; **material ~** rolling stock. **2** *nm* (‡: *coche*) crate*, car; (*carro*) cart.
rodapié *nm* skirting board, baseboard (*US*); (*estera*) doormat.
rodar [1l] **1** *vt* (**a**) *vehículo* to wheel (along); *objeto* to roll, drag (along).
(**b**) (*viajar por*) to travel, go over; **ha rodado medio mundo** he's been round half the world.
(**c**) *coche* (*en carreras*) to race, drive; *coche nuevo* to run in.
(**d**) (*Cine*) to shoot, film.
(**e**) (*Inform*) *programa* to run.
(**f**) (*Carib*) (*agarrar*) to seize; (*encarcelar*) to imprison.
(**g**) **~ (a patadas)** (*LAm*) to knock over, kick over.
(**h**) (*LAm*) *ganado etc* to round up.
2 *vi* (**a**) (*ir rodando*) to roll (*por* along, down, over *etc*); (*sobre ruedas*) to go, run, travel; (*Aut*) to go, drive; **~ de suelo** (*Aer*) to taxi; **se oía el ~ de los carros** one could hear the rumbling of the tanks; **~ por la escalera** to fall downstairs, go tumbling down the stairs; **echarlo todo a ~** (*fig*) to mess it all up, spoil everything; to throw one's hand in.
(**b**) (*girar etc*) to go round, turn, rotate.
(**c**) (*persona*) **andar** (*o* **ir**) **rodando** to move about (from place to place); (*gandulear*) to roll around, drift; **no hace más que ir rodando** he just drifts about; **me han hecho ir rodando de acá para allá** they kept shunting me about from place to place.
(**d**) (*fig*: *existir todavía*) to be still going, exist still; **no sabía que ese modelo rodaba todavía por esos mundos** I didn't know that model was still about.
(**e**) **~ por uno** to be at sb's beck and call, dance attendance on sb.
(**f**) (*Cine*) to shoot, film; **llevamos 2 meses de ~ en Méjico** we've spent 2 months filming in Mexico.
(**g**) (*Cono Sur*: *caballo*) to stumble, fall.
Rodas *nf* Rhodes.
rodear [1a] **1** *vt* (**a**) (*gen*) to surround (*de* by, with); (*encerrar*) to ring, encircle, enclose, shut in; (*brazos, ropa etc*) to encircle, enclose; **los soldados rodearon el edificio** the soldiers surrounded the building; **le rodeó el cuello con los brazos** she threw her arms round his neck.
(**b**) (*LAm*) *ganado* to round up.
2 *vi* (**a**) *ruta* to go round, go by an indirect route; to make a detour.
(**b**) (*fig*) to beat about the bush.
3 rodearse *vr* (**a**) **~ de** to surround o.s. with.
(**b**) (*volverse*) to turn round; (*en la cama*) to turn over (and over), toss and turn.
rodela *nf* (**a**) (*Hist*: *escudo*) buckler, round shield. (**b**) (*Cono Sur*: *rosca*) padded ring (*for carrying loads on one's head*).
rodenticida *nm* rat-poison.
rodeo *nm* (**a**) (*ruta indirecta*) long way round, roundabout way; (*desvío*) detour; **dar un ~** to make a detour.
(**b**) (*escape*) dodge; (*fig*) dodge, stratagem, subterfuge.
(**c**) (*en discurso*) circumlocution; (*evasión*) evasion; **andarse con ~s, ir por ~s** to beat about the bush; **no andarse con ~s, dejarse de ~s** to talk straight, stop beating about the bush; **hablar sin ~s** to speak out plainly.
(**d**) (*LAm*) round-up, rodeo (*US*).
rodera *nf* rut, wheel track.
Rodesia *nf* (*Hist*) Rhodesia.
rodesiano, -a *adj, nm/f* (*Hist*) Rhodesian.
rodete *nm* (**a**) (*de pelo*) coil, bun; (*de grasa*) roll; (*para llevar carga*) pad. (**b**) (*de cerradura*) ward.
rodilla *nf* (**a**) (*Anat*) knee; **de ~s** kneeling; **caer de ~s** to fall on one's knees; **doblar** (*o* **hincar**) **la ~** to kneel down; (*fig*) to bow, humble oneself, bend the knee (*ante* to); **estar de ~s** to kneel, be kneeling (down); **hincarse de ~s, ponerse de ~s** to kneel (down); **pedir algo de ~s** to ask for sth on bended knee; **poner de ~s a un país** to bring a country to its knees.
(**b**) (*para llevar carga*) pad.
(**c**) (*paño*) floorcloth, mop.
rodillazo *nm* push with the knee; **dar un ~ a** to knee.
rodillera *nf* (**a**) (*protección*) knee guard; (*remiendo*) kneepad, patch on the knee. (**b**) (*bolsa*) baggy part (*in knee of trousers*). (**c**) (*para llevar carga*) pad.
rodillo *nm* (*gen*) roller; (*Culin*) rolling pin; (*Tip*) ink roller; (*de máquina de escribir*) cylinder, roller; (*exprimidor*) mangle; (*Agr*) roller; **~ pastelero** rolling-pin; **~ pintor** paint roller; **~ de vapor** steamroller.
rodillón *nm* (*And‡*) old geezer*.
rodillona *nf* (*Carib‡*: *solterona*) old maid; (*And‡*: *bruja*) old bag*.
rodio *nm* rhodium.
rododendro *nm* rhododendron.
Rodrigo *nm* Roderick; **~ el último godo** Roderick, the last of the Goths.
rodrigón *nm* (*Agr*) stake, prop, support.
Rodríguez *nm*: **estar de ~** (*Esp*) to be a grass widower, be bacheloring it (*US*), be left on one's own.
roedor 1 *adj* (**a**) (*Zool*) gnawing. (**b**) (*fig*) *remordimiento etc* gnawing, ever-present, nagging. **2** *nm* rodent.
roer [2z] *vt* (**a**) *comida* to gnaw; (*mordiscar*) to nibble at; *hueso* to gnaw, pick.
(**b**) *metal* to corrode, eat away, eat into.
(**c**) (*fig*) *capital etc* to eat into bit by bit.
(**d**) (*fig*: *remordimiento etc*) to gnaw, nag, torment.
rogación *nf* (**a**) petition. (**b**) **rogaciones** (*Ecl*) rogations.
rogar [1h *y* 1l] **1** *vt* (**a**) *persona* to beg; to plead with; *cosa* to ask for, beg for, plead for; **~ a uno** + *infin* to ask sb to + *infin*, beg sb to + *infin*; **~ que** + *subj* to ask that ...; **ruegue a este señor que nos deje en paz** please ask this gentleman to leave us alone.

(**b**) (*Rel*) to pray.

2 *vi* (**a**) (*pedir*) to beg, plead; **hacerse ~** to have to be coaxed, be unwilling to agree; to play hard to get; **no se hace de ~** he doesn't have to be asked twice.

(**b**) (*Rel*) to pray.

3 rogarse *vr*: **'se ruega la mayor puntualidad'** 'please be punctual'; **'se ruega no fumar'** 'please do not smoke'.

rogativas *nfpl* (*Ecl*) rogations.

rogatoria *nf* (*LAm*) request, plea.

roja‡ *nf* 2000-peseta note.

rojamen* *nm*: **el ~** the reds, the commies*.

rojear [1a] *vi* (**a**) (*volverse rojo*) to redden, turn red.

(**b**) (*tirar a rojo*) to be reddish; (*mostrarse rojo*) to show red, look red.

rojeras* *nmf invar* red, commie*.

rojerío* *nm*: **el ~** the reds, the commies*.

rojete *nm* rouge.

rojez *nf* redness; (*en la piel*) blotch.

rojigualdo *adj* red-and-yellow (*colours of the Spanish flag*).

rojillo 1 *adj* (*Pol*) pink; (*fig*) suspicious, subversive. **2** *nm*, **rojilla** *nf* pinko*, leftie*.

rojizo *adj* reddish; ruddy.

rojo 1 *adj* (**a**) (*gen*) red; ruddy; **~ burdeos** maroon, dark red; **~ cereza** cherry-red; **~ sangre** blood-red; **~ teja** brick-red; **poner ~ a uno** to make sb blush; **ponerse ~** to turn red, blush; **ponerse ~ de la ira** to be fighting mad.

(**b**) *pelo* red; sandy.

(**c**) (*Pol*) red; (*entre nacionalistas en España, 1936 y después*) Republican.

2 *nm* (**a**) (*gen*) red, red colour; **calentar al ~** to make red-hot; **la atmósfera está al ~ vivo** the atmosphere is electric; **la emoción está al ~ vivo** excitement is at fever pitch; **un semáforo en ~** a red light.

(**b**) **~ de labios** rouge, lipstick.

(**c**) (*Pol*) red; Republican (*V* **1 c**).

rojura *nf* redness.

rol *nm* (**a**) (*lista*) list, roll; (*catálogo*) catalogue; (*Náut*) muster. (**b**) (*Teat y fig*) role, part. (**c**) (*Méx*) **dar un ~** to take a walk.

rola* 1 *nf* (*Carib*: *comisaría*) police-station. **2** *nmf* (*Cono Sur*: *matón*) lout; (*zonzo*) thickhead*, dope*.

Rolando *nm* Roland.

rolar [1a] **1** *vt* (**a**) (*And, Cono Sur*) to touch on, mention (in conversation); **la conversación roló la religión** the conversation touched on religion.

(**b**) (*And, Cono Sur*) to associate with, be in contact with.

(**c**) (*Méx*: *pasar*) to pass from hand to hand.

2 *vi* (**a**) (*Náut*: *viento*) to veer round.

(**b**) (*Cono Sur*: *ser arribista*) to be a social climber.

(**c**) (*And, Cono Sur*: *hablar*) to talk, converse (*con* with); (*And, Cono Sur*: *alternar con*) to associate, be in contact (*con* with).

Roldán *nm* Roland.

roldana *nf* pulley wheel.

rolo *nm* (*LAm*) stick, truncheon.

rollazo* 1 *adj* dead boring*. **2** *nm* deadly bore.

rollista* *nmf* (*pesado*) bore; (*mentiroso*) liar; (*chismoso*) gossip.

rollístico* *adj* dead boring*.

rollizo *adj* (**a**) *objeto* round, cylindrical. (**b**) *persona* plump; stocky; *niño* chubby; *mujer* plump, buxom.

rollo 1 *adj invar* boring, tedious.

2 *nm* (**a**) (*gen*: *de paño, papel, película*) roll; (*de cuerda*) coil; (*Hist*) scroll; **en ~** rolled, rolled up; *madera* whole, uncut.

(**b**) (*Culin*: *rodillo*) rolling-pin.

(**c**) (*madera*) round log, uncut log.

(**d**) (*Culin*: *empanada etc*) roll.

(**e**) (*Anat**) roll of fat.

(**f**) (*Esp**) (*cosa pesada*) bore; (*discurso*) boring speech; (*explicación*) tedious explanation, lengthy justification; (*sermón*: *fig*) sermon; (*conferencia*) lecture; (*cuento*) tale, story; **~ macabeo, ~ patatero** deadly bore, awful drag; **la conferencia fue un ~** the lecture was an awful bore; **¡menudo ~ nos colocó!** some sermon he gave us!; **¡qué ~ más pobre!** what awful rubbish!; **nos soltó el ~ de siempre** he gave us the usual stuff*; **cortar el ~** to stop the flow (of talk *etc*), break in, interrupt; **estar de ~** to be doing something dead boring*.

(**g**) (*Esp**) (*asunto*) thing, affair; (*actividad*) activity; (*negocio*) business; **está metido en muchos ~s** he's stuck into so many things*; **no sabemos de qué va el ~** we're not in the picture*, we don't know what the score is*; **tirarse el ~** to shoot a line*.

(**h**) (*Esp**) (*contracultura*) alternative culture, alternative life-style, life-style of young people; **darle al ~** to go in for an alternative life-style; **montarse el ~** to organize one's life-style; **traerse un mal ~** to adopt a false life-style; **tener un ~ muy bueno** to have style.

(**i**) (*Esp**) (*ambiente*) ambience, atmosphere; **el ~ madrileño** the Madrid scene*; **me va el ~** I like this scene*, I'm having a great time*; **se estableció un buen ~ entre los dos** they really hit it off, they got a good scene going between them*.

(**j**) **largar el ~** (*And, Cono Sur**: *vomitar*) to be sick, throw up.

(**k**) **~ de pelo** (*Carib*) (hair) curler, roller.

Roma *nf* Rome; **~ no se construyó en un día** Rome was not built in a day; **por todas partes se va a ~** all roads lead to Rome; *V* **remover** (**a**).

romadizo *nm* (*resfriado*) head cold; (*permanente*) catarrh; (*Carib*: *reuma*) rheumatism.

romana *nf* steelyard; **cargar la ~** (*Cono Sur**) to heap the blame on somebody else.

romance 1 *adj lengua* Romance.

2 *nm* (**a**) (*Ling*) Romance language; (*castellano*) Spanish, Spanish language; **hablar en ~** (*fig*) to speak plainly.

(**b**) (*Liter*) ballad.

(**c**) (*: *amorío*) romance, love-affair.

(**d**) (*: *amante*) lover; (*de antes*) old flame*.

romancear [1a] **1** *vt* to translate into Spanish. **2** *vi* (*Cono Sur*) (**a**) (*charlar*) to waste time chatting. (**b**) (*galantear*) to flirt.

romancero *nm* collection of ballads; **el R~** the Spanish ballads (*collectively*).

romancístico *adj* ballad (*atr*).

romaní *adj, nm/f* Romany, gipsy.

Romania *nf* Romance countries, Romance-speaking regions.

románico *adj* (**a**) (*Ling*) Romance. (**b**) (*Arquit*) Romanesque, Romanic; (*en Inglaterra*) Norman.

romanizar [1f] **1** *vt* to romanize. **2 romanizarse** *vr* to become romanized.

romano, -a 1 *adj, nm/f* Roman. **2** *nm* (*Esp‡*) cop*.

romanó *nm* (*Ling*) Romany.

románticamente *adv* romantically.

romanticismo *nm* romanticism.

romántico, -a *adj, nm/f* romantic.

romaza *nf* dock, sorrel.

rombal *adj* rhombic.

rombo *nm* rhomb, rhombus; (*TV*) diamond (*warning of sexually explicit scene*); (*en diseño etc*) diamond, diamond shape.

romboidal *adj* rhomboid.

romboide *nm* rhomboid.

Romeo *nm* Romeo.

romereante *nmf* (*And, Carib*) pilgrim.

romería *nf* (**a**) (*Ecl*) pilgrimage; gathering at a local shrine; **ir en ~** to go on a pilgrimage; (*fig*) to go in throngs, go thronging. (**b**) (*fig*: *excursión*) trip, excursion; (*feria*) fair, (*baile*) open-air dance; (*fiestas*) festivities. (**e**) (*Aut*) queue (of cars); slow procession.

romero¹ *nm*, **romera** *nf* pilgrim.

romero² *nm* (*Bot*) rosemary.

romo *adj* (**a**) (*gen*) blunt; *persona* snub-nosed. (**b**) (*fig*) dull, lifeless.

rompecabezas *nm invar* (**a**) (*gen*) puzzle; (*acertijo*) riddle; (*juego*) jigsaw (puzzle). (**b**) (*fig*) puzzle; problem, teaser, headache.

rompecorazones *nmf invar* breaker of hearts.

rompedero 1 *adj* breakable, delicate, fragile. **2** *nm*: **~ de cabeza** (*Cono Sur*) puzzle, brain teaser.

rompedora-cargadora *nf* (*Min*) power-loader.

rompehielos *nm invar* icebreaker.

rompehuelgas *nm invar* strikebreaker, blackleg.

rompenueces *nm invar* nutcrackers.

rompeolas *nm invar* breakwater.

rompepelotas‡ *nm invar* ball-breaker‡.

romper [2a; *ptp* **roto**] **1** *vt* (**a**) *juguete, plato etc* to break, smash, shatter; *barrera, cerca etc* to break down, break through; to breach; *cuerda etc* to snap, break; *paño, papel* to tear (up), rip (up); *niebla, nubes* to break through.

(**b**) (*gastar*) to wear out, wear a hole in.

(**c**) *olas* (*rompeolas*) to break the force of; (*barco*) to cleave.

(**d**) (*roturar*) to break (up), plough.

(**e**) (*Mil*) *línea etc* to break (through); *V* **fila**.

(**f**) *ayuno, continuidad, silencio, sucesión etc* to break.

(**g**) *contrato, pacto* to break; *amistad, relaciones* to break off.

(**h**) (*Mil*) ~ **el fuego** to open fire; ~ **las hostilidades** to start hostilities.

2 *vi* (**a**) (*olas*) to break.

(**b**) (*capullo*) to open, burst.

(**c**) (*guerra*) to break out.

(**d**) (*diente*) to break through; (*sol*) to break through, appear, begin to shine; (*alba, día*) to break; ~ **entre** to burst one's way through; ~ **por** to break through.

(**e**) ~ **a** + *infin* to start (suddenly) to + *infin*; ~ **a proferir insultos** to begin to pour forth abuse; ~ **a llorar** to burst into tears; **luego rompió a hacer calor** then it suddenly began to get hot.

(**f**) ~ **en llanto** to burst into tears.

(**g**) ~ **con uno** to fall out with sb, break with sb; **ha roto con su novio** she has broken it off with her fiancé.

(**h**) **de rompe y rasga** brash, tearaway, impetuous; full of self-confidence; utterly inconsiderate; **rompe por todo** he presses on regardless; **quien rompe paga** one must pay the consequences.

3 romperse *vr* to break, smash; to snap; to tear, rip; to wear out; **no te vayas a** ~ don't be so fussy; you're not that delicate.

rompestómagos* *nm invar* vile concoction.

rompiente *nm* reef, shoal.

rompimiento *nm* (**a**) (*acto*) breaking, smashing; (*de cristal, porcelana*) shattering; (*de muro etc*) breaching; (*de madera*) snapping; (*de tela, papel*) tearing; ~ **de aguas** downpour.

(**b**) (*abertura*) opening, breach; (*grieta*) crack.

(**c**) (*acto*: *fig*) break (*con* with); ~ **de contacto** (*Mil*) disengagement; ~ **de relaciones** breaking-off of relations.

(**d**) ~ **de hostilidades** outbreak of hostilities.

romplón: de ~ *adv* (*CAm, Méx*) off the cuff, on the spur of the moment.

rompope *nm* (*CAm, Méx*) eggnog.

Rómulo *nm* Romulus.

ron *nm* rum.

ronca *nf* (**a**) (*Zool*) (*sonido*) roar (*of rutting stag*); (*época*) rutting season. (**b**) (*fig*) threat; **echar ~s** to bully, threaten.

roncadoras *nfpl* (*LAm*) large spurs.

roncar [1g] *vi* (**a**) (*estando dormido*) to snore. (**b**) (*ciervo, mar, viento*) to roar. (**c**) (*amenazar*) to threaten, bully; (*And, Cono Sur**) to be bossy, domineer; to be jealous of one's authority.

roncear [1a] **1** *vt* (**a**) (*pedir repetidas veces*) to cajole, pester, keep on at. (**b**) (*LAm*) = **ronzar**[1]. (**c**) (*LAm*: *espiar*) to keep watch on, spy on. **2** *vi* (**a**) (*Náut*) to move slowly. (**b**) (*trabajar a desgana*) to work (*etc*) unwillingly; (*gandulear*) to slack, kill time.

roncería *nf* (**a**) (*desgana*) unwillingness. (**b**) (*lisonja*) cajolery.

roncero *adj* (**a**) (*Náut*) slow, slow-moving, sluggish.

(**b**) (*desganado*) unwilling; (*gandul*) slack, slow; **estar** ~ to find reasons for shirking work (*etc*).

(**c**) (*gruñón*) grumpy, grouchy*.

(**d**) (*cobista*) smooth, smarmy*.

(**e**) (*And, CAm, Cono Sur*) (*taimado*) sly, sharp; (*entrometido*) nosey*, meddling.

ronco *adj persona* hoarse; *voz* throaty, husky; *sonido* harsh, raucous.

roncón* *adj* (*And, Carib*) boastful, bragging.

roncha *nf* (**a**) (*cardenal*) bruise, weal, welt; (*hinchazón*) swelling; **hacer** ~ (*Cono Sur**) to create an impression; **levantar** ~ (*Carib**) to pass a dud cheque*; **sacar ~*** to cause an upset. (**b**) (*rodaja*) slice.

ronda *nf* (**a**) (*esp Hist*) night patrol, night watch; (*de policía*) beat; (*personas*) watch, patrol, guard; **ir de** ~ to go the rounds, do one's round.

(**b**) (*Mús*) group of serenaders.

(**c**) (*de bebidas, negociaciones etc*) round; **pagar una** ~ to pay for a round.

(**d**) (*Naipes*) hand, round, game; (*en concurso*) round; (*Golf*) round.

(**e**) (*Mil*) sentry walk.

(**f**) (*Aut*: *t* ~ **de circunvalación**) outer road, ringroad.

(**g**) (*Cono Sur*: *juego*) ring-a-ring-a-roses.

(**h**) **en** ~ (*Cono Sur*) in a ring, in a circle.

rondalla *nf* (**a**) (*Mús*) band of street musicians. (**b**) (*ficción*) fiction, invention.

rondana *nf* (*LAm*) pulley; winch.

rondar [1a] **1** *vt* (**a**) (*Mil etc*) to patrol; (*inspeccionar*) to inspect, go the rounds of; (*fig*) to haunt, frequent, hang about; ~ **la calle a una joven** to hang about the street where a girl lives.

(**b**) *persona* to hang round; (*acosar*) to harass, pester; *chica* to court.

(**c**) *luz* (*mariposa*) to flutter round, fly about.

(**d**) **me está rondando un catarro** (*fig*) I've got a cold hanging about.

(**e**) **el precio ronda los mil dólares** the price is nearly a thousand dollars; **rondaba los 30 años** he was about 30.

2 *vi* (*policía*) to patrol, go on patrol, go the rounds; (*fig*) to prowl round, go up and down, hang about; to roam the streets after dark; (*Mús*) to go serenading.

rondín[1] *nm* (*And, Cono Sur*) night watchman.

rondín[2] *nm* (*And Mús*) harmonica, mouth organ.

rondó *nm* (*Liter*) rondeau; (*Mús*) rondo.

rondón: de ~ *adv* unexpectedly; unannounced, without warning; **entrar de** ~ to rush in; (*en fiesta*) to crash a party*.

ronquear [1a] *vi* to be hoarse, talk hoarsely.

ronquedad *nf*, **ronquera** *nf* hoarseness; huskiness.

ronquido *nm* snore; snoring; (*fig*) roar(ing); snort.

ronronear [1a] *vi* to purr.

ronroneo *nm* purr.

ronzal *nm* halter.

ronzar[1] [1f] *vt* (*Náut*) to move with levers, lever along.

ronzar[2] [1f] **1** *vt* to munch, crunch, eat noisily. **2** *vi* to crunch.

roña 1 *nf* (**a**) (*Vet*: *de oveja*) scab, (*de perro*) mange; (*Bot*) rust.

(**b**) (*mugre*) crust of dirt, filth, grime; (*en metal*) rust.

(**c**) (*Bot*) pine bark.

(**d**) (*fig*: *peligro moral*) moral danger, contagion.

(**e**) (*fig*: *tacañería*) meanness, stinginess.

(**f**) (*estratagema*) stratagem.

(**g**) (*Carib, Méx*) (*envidia*) envy; (*inquina*) grudge, ill will.

(**h**) (*And*: *Med*) feigned illness.

(**i**) **jugar a la** ~ to play for fun, play without money stakes.

2 *nmf* (*) skinflint.

3 *adj invar* (*CAm, Cono Sur*) mean, stingy.

roñería *nf* meanness, stinginess.

roñica* *nmf* skinflint.

roñoso *adj* (**a**) (*Vet*) scabby, mangy.

(**b**) (*sucio*) dirty, filthy, grimy; rusty; (*fig*: *inútil*) broken down, useless.

(**c**) (*fig*: *tacaño*) mean, tight.

(**d**) (*And*: *tosco*) unpolished, coarse.

(**e**) (*And*: *tramposo*) tricky, slippery.

(**f**) (*Carib, Méx*) (*rencoroso*) bitter, resentful; (*hostil*) hostile.

ropa *nf* (*gen*) clothes, clothing; (*vestido*) dress; ~ **amplia** loose-fitting clothes; ~ **blanca** linen; ~ **blanca de mujer** lingerie; ~ **de cama** bed linen, bed-clothes; ~ **hecha** ready-made clothes; ~ **interior,** ~ **íntima** (*LAm*) underwear, underclothes; ~ **interior térmica** thermal underwear; ~ **lavada,** ~ **por lavar** washing; ~ **de mesa** table linen; ~ **planchada** ironing; ~ **sucia** dirty clothes, washing; ~ **usada** used clothing, secondhand clothes; ~ **vieja** (*Méx Culin*) meat stew; **a quema** ~ point-blank; **hay** ~ **tendida** be careful what you say, walls have ears; **guardar la** ~ to speak cautiously; **la** ~ **sucia se lava en casa** (*fig*) dirty linen should not be washed in public; **tentarse la** ~ to think long and hard (before doing anything); **no tocar la** ~ **a uno** not to touch a hair of sb's head, keep one's hands off sb; *V* **ligero, nadar,** *etc.*

ropaje *nm* (**a**) (*vestiduras*) gown, robes, ceremonial garb; **~s** (*Ecl*) vestments.

(**b**) (*fig*) drapes, drapery.

(**c**) (*pey*) (*raro*) odd garb; (*excesivo*) heavy clothing, excessive amount of clothes.

(**d**) (*Liter*) trappings, rhetorical adornments.

ropalócero *nm* butterfly.

ropavejería *nf* old-clothes shop.

ropavejero, -a *nm/f* old-clothes dealer.

ropería *nf* (**a**) (*tienda*) clothier's, clothes shop. (**b**) (*negocio*) clothing trade.

ropero 1 *adj* for clothes, clothes (*atr*); **armario** ~ = **2** (**b**).

2 *nm* (**a**) (*persona*) clothier.

(**b**) (*mueble*) wardrobe, clothes cupboard.

ropita *nf* baby clothes.

ropón *nm* (*de ceremonia*) long robe; (*bata*) loose coat, housecoat.

roque[1] *nm* (*Ajedrez*) rook, castle.

roque[2]* *adj*: **estar** ~ to be asleep; **quedarse** ~ to fall asleep.

roquedal *nm*, **roquedo** *nm* rocky place.

roqueño *adj* (**a**) (*rocoso*) rocky. (**b**) (*duro*) hard as rock, rock-like, flinty; (*fig*) rock-solid.

roquero = **rockero.**

ro-ro *nm* car ferry, roll-on/roll-off ferry.

rorro *nm* (**a**) (*: *niño*) baby, kid*. (**b**) (*Méx*) fair blue-eyed person; (*muñeca*) doll.

Rosa *nf* Rose.

rosa 1 *nf* (**a**) (*Bot*) rose; ~ **almizcleña** musk-rose; ~ **laurel** rosebay, oleander; ~ **palo** rosewood; **no hay** ~ **sin espinas** there's no rose without a thorn; **un cutis como una** ~ a skin as soft as silk; **estar como una** ~ to be fresh and clean; to feel as fresh as a daisy; **estar como las propias** ~**s** to feel entirely at ease; **florecer como** ~ **en mayo** to blossom, flourish.

(**b**) **de** ~, **color de** ~ pink, rose, rose-coloured; **vestidos color de** ~ pink dresses; *V t* **color.**

(**c**) (*Anat*) red spot, red mark, birthmark.

(**d**) (*Arquit*) rose window.

(**e**) ~ **náutica,** ~ **de los vientos** compass (card), compass rose.

(**f**) ~**s** (*Culin*) popcorn.

2 *adj invar* pink, rose, rose-coloured; **revista** ~ magazine of sentimental stories.

rosáceo *adj* = **rosado 1.**

rosado 1 *adj* pink, rosy, roseate; (*fig*) *panorama* favourable, rosy. **2** *nm* (*vino*) rosé.

rosal *nm* (**a**) (*planta*) rosebush, rosetree; ~ **silvestre** wild rose, dog rose; ~ **de China,** ~ **japonés** japonica. (**b**) (*Carib, Cono Sur*: *rosaleda*) rosebed, rosegarden.

rosaleda *nf* rosebed, rosegarden.

rosario *nm* (**a**) (*Rel*) rosary; chaplet, beads; **acabar como el** ~ **de la aurora** (*o* **del alba**) to end up in confusion, end with everybody falling out; **rezar el** ~ to say one's rosary, tell one's beads.

(**b**) (*Agr*) chain of buckets (*of a waterwheel*).

(**c**) (*Anat**) backbone.

(**d**) (*fig*) string, series; **un** ~ **de maldiciones** a string of curses.

(**e**) (*Arquit*) beading.

rosbif *nm* roast beef.

rosca *nf* (**a**) (*de humo etc*) coil, spiral, ring; (*Culin*) ring, ring-shaped roll; **estaba hecho una** ~ he was all curled up in a ball; **comerse una** ~‡ to make it (with a woman)‡; **no comerse una** ~‡ to get absolutely nowhere (*con* with); **no me como** (*o* **jalo**) **una** ~‡ I don't understand a word of it.

(**b**) (*de tornillo*) thread; (*de espiral*) turn; **hacer la** ~ **a uno*** to suck up to sb*; **pasarse de** ~ (*tornillo*) to have a crossed thread; (*fig*) to go too far, overdo it.

(**c**) (*Anat*) (*hinchazón*) swelling; (*de grasa*) roll of fat.

(**d**) (*Cono Sur*: *para llevar carga*) pad.

(**e**) (*Cono Sur*: *Naipes*) (circle of) card players.

(**f**) (*Cono Sur*) (*discusión*) noisy argument; (*jaleo*) uproar, commotion; **se armó una** ~ there was uproar.

(**g**) **tirarse una** ~ (*Esp* Univ*) to plough*.

(**h**) (*And Pol*) ruling clique.

rosco[1] *nm* (*LAm Com*) middleman.

rosco[2] *nm* (**a**) (*Culin*) doughnut. (**b**) (‡: *Univ*) zero, nought.

roscón *nm* ring-shaped cake.

rosedal *nm* (*Cono Sur*) = **rosaleda.**

Rosellón *nm* Roussillon.

róseo *adj* rosy, roseate.

roseta *nf* (**a**) (*Bot*) small rose.

(**b**) (*Dep etc*) rosette.

(**c**) (*de regadera*) rose, nozzle.

(**d**) (*Anat*) red spot (on the cheek).

(**e**) (*Cono Sur*) prickly fruit, burr.

(**f**) (*And, Cono Sur*: *de espuela*) rowel.

(**g**) ~**s** (**de maíz**) (*Culin*) popcorn.

rosetón *nm* (**a**) (*Arquit*) rose; rose window. (**b**) (*Dep etc*) rosette.

rosicler *nm* dawn pink, rosy tint of dawn.

rosita *nf* (**a**) (*Bot*) small rose. (**b**) (*Cono Sur*: *pendiente*) earring. (**c**) **de** ~ (*And, Méx*) free, gratis; **andar de** ~ (*Cono Sur, Méx*) to be out of work. (**d**) ~**s** (*Culin*) popcorn.

rosquero* *adj* (*Cono Sur*) quarrelsome.

rosquete *nm* (**a**) (*And, CAm*: *bollo*) bun. (**b**) (*And*‡) queer‡.

rosquilla *nf* (**a**) (*de humo*) ring. (**b**) (*Ent*) grub, small caterpillar. (**c**) (*Culin*) ring-shaped pastry, doughnut; **venderse como** ~**s** to sell like hot cakes.

rosticería *nf* = **rotisería.**

rostizado *adj* roast.

rostizar [1a] *vt* to spit-roast.

rostro *nm* (**a**) (*Anat*) face (*para locuciones, compárese* **cara**); **retrato de** ~ **entero** full-face portrait. (**b**) (*Náut*: *Hist*) beak. (**c**) (*Zool, Hist etc*) rostrum.

rostropálido, -a *nm/f* paleface.

rotación *nf* (*gen*) rotation; (*una* ~) turn, revolution; (*Téc*: *de producción etc*) turnover; ~ **de cultivos** rotation of crops; ~ **de existencias** (*Com*) turnover of stock; ~ **de la tierra** rotation of the earth.

rotacional *adj* rotational.

rotar [1a] *vt* (*Inform*) to rotate.

rotariano *adj y nm* (*LAm*) = **rotario.**

rotario, -a *adj, nm/f* Rotarian.

rotativamente *adv* by turns.

rotativo 1 *adj* rotary, revolving; *prensa* rotary. **2** *nm* (**a**) (*Tip*) rotary press. (**b**) (*periódico*) newspaper. (**c**) (*luz*) revolving light. (**d**) (*Cono Sur Cine*) continuous performance.

rotatorio *adj puesto* rotating; **la secretaría será rotatoria** the secretaryship will rotate.

rotería *nf* (*Cono Sur*) (**a**) (*plebe*) common people, plebs. (**b**) (*truco*) dirty trick; (*dicho*) coarse remark.

rotisería *nf* (*Cono Sur, Méx*) grillroom, steak restaurant; eating-house.

roto 1 *ptp de* **romper.**

2 *adj* (**a**) (*gen*) broken, smashed; *vestido etc* torn; ragged; *vida* shattered, destroyed; wasted; **estar** ~ **de cansancio** to be exhausted.

(**b**) (*fig*) debauched, dissipated.

(**c**) (*Cono Sur*) bad-mannered.

3 *nm* (**a**) (*en vestido*) hole, torn piece, worn part; **nunca falta un** ~ **para un descosido** you can always find a companion in misfortune; birds of a feather flock together.

(**b**) (*Cono Sur*: *pobre*) poor wretch, down-and-out; (*iró*) fop, toff*.

(**c**) (*And, Cono Sur*‡: *chileno*) *nickname given to a Chilean*; **el** ~ **chileno** the Chilean man in the street.

(**d**) (*And*: *mestizo*) half-breed.

rotograbado *nm* rotogravure.

rotonda *nf* (*Arquit*) rotunda; circular gallery; (*Ferro*) engine shed, roundhouse; (*Cono Sur Aut*) roundabout, traffic circle (*US*).

rotor *nm* rotor.

rotoso *adj* (**a**) (*LAm*: *harapiento*) ragged, shabby. (**b**) (*And, Cono Sur**: *ordinario*) low-life, common.

rótula *nf* (**a**) (*Anat*) kneecap. (**b**) (*Mec*) ball-and-socket joint.

rotulación *nf* (**a**) (*escritura*) labelling; lettering. (**b**) (*profesión*) sign painting.

rotulador *nm* felt-tip pen, marking pen.

rotular [1a] *vt objeto* to label, put a label (*o* ticket *etc*) on; *mapa etc* to letter, inscribe; *carta, documento* to head, entitle.

rotulata *nf* (**a**) (*etiquetas*) labels, inscriptions *etc* (*collectively*). (**b**) (*) = **rótulo.**

rotulista *nmf* sign painter.

rótulo *nm* (*etiqueta*) label, ticket, tag; (*en museo etc*) label; (*título*) heading, title; (*en mapa etc*) lettering; inscription; (*letrero*) sign, notice; (*Com*) sign; (*cartel*) placard, poster; ~ **luminoso** illuminated sign; ~ **de salida** (*TV*) credits.

rotundamente *adv negar* flatly, roundly; *afirmar, expresar acuerdo etc* emphatically.

rotundidad *nf* (*V adj*) (**a**) rotundity. (**b**) forthrightness; clearness, convincing nature. (**c**) well-rounded character, expressiveness.

rotundo *adj* (**a**) (*redondo*) round. (**b**) *negativa etc* flat, round, forthright; *victoria* clear, convincing; **me dio un 'sí'** ~ he gave me an emphatic 'yes'. (**c**) *estilo* well-rounded, expressive.

rotura *nf* (**a**) (*acto*) breaking *etc* (*V* **rompimiento** (**a**)); ~ **de servicio** break of service.

(**b**) (*abertura*) opening, breach; (*grieta*) crack; (*en tela*) tear, rip, hole.

(**c**) (*acto*: *fig*) break (*con* with); ~ **de relaciones** breaking-off of relations.

roturación *nf* breaking-up, ploughing.

roturar [1a] *vt* to break up, plough.

rough [ruf] *nm*: **el** ~ (*Golf*) the rough.

roya *nf* (*Bot*) rust, blight.

roza *nf* (**a**) (*Arquit*) groove, hollow (*in a wall*). (**b**) (*prov, Cono Sur*) weeds. (**c**) (*Méx*: *matas*) brush, stubble. (**d**)

(*And*) planting in newly-broken ground. (**e**) (*CAm*: *tierra limpia*) cleared ground.

rozado *adj* worn, grazed.

rozador *nm* (*Carib*) machete.

rozadura *nf* mark of rubbing, chafing mark; (*Med*) abrasion, graze, sore place.

rozagante *adj* (**a**) *vestido etc* showy, gorgeous; striking. (**b**) (*fig*) proud.

rozamiento *nm* (**a**) (*gen*) rubbing, chafing; (*Mec*) friction; wear. (**b**) **tener un ~ con uno*** to have a slight disagreement with sb.

rozar [1f] **1** *vt* (**a**) (*frotar*) to rub (on), rub against; (*raer*) to scrape (on); to chafe; (*Mec*) to grate on, cause friction with; (*Med*) to chafe, graze; (*tocar ligeramente etc*) to graze, shave, touch lightly; (*ave*) *superficie* to skim; **~ a uno al pasar** to brush past sb.
(**b**) (*arrugar*) to rumple, crumple; (*ensuciar*) to dirty.
(**c**) (*fig*) to touch on, border on; **es cuestión que roza la política** it's partly a political question.
(**d**) (*Arquit*) to make a groove (*o* hollow) in.
(**e**) (*Agr*) *hierba* to graze, crop, nibble.
(**f**) (*Agr*) *tierra* to clear.
2 *vi* (**a**) **~ en** = **1** (**a**).
(**b**) **~ con** (*fig*) = **1** (**c**).
3 rozarse *vr* (**a**) **~ el cuello** to rub (*o* wear, chafe) one's collar; **~ los puños** to graze one's knuckles.
(**b**) (*ajarse*) to get worn, get rubbed (*etc*).
(**c**) (*: *tropezar*) to trip over one's own feet.
(**d**) **~ con*** to hobnob with, rub shoulders with, mix with.
(**e**) **~ en un sonido** to stutter over a sound, have trouble pronouncing a sound.

roznar[1] [1a] *vti* = **ronzar**.

roznar[2] [1a] *vi* (*burro*) to bray.

roznido *nm* bray(ing).

R.P. *abr de* **Reverendo Padre** Reverend Father.

r.p.m. *nfpl abr de* **revoluciones por minuto** revolutions per minute, rpm.

rrollo‡ *nm* = **rollo** (**g**), (**h**), (**i**).

RRPP *nfpl abr de* **relaciones públicas** public relations, PR.

Rte. (*Correos*) *abr de* **remite, remitente** sender.

RTVE *nf* (*TV*) *abr de* **Radiotelevisión Española**.

rúa *nf* (*prov*) street.

Ruán *nm* Rouen.

ruana *nf* (*And, Carib*) ruana, poncho, wool cape.

ruanetas *nmf invar* (*And*) peasant.

ruano *adj y nm* = **roano**.

rubeola *nf*, **rubéola** *nf* German measles, rubella.

rubí *nm* ruby; (*de reloj*) jewel.

rubia *nf* (**a**) (*gen*) blonde; **~ de bote, ~ de frasco, ~ oxigenada** peroxide blonde; **~ ceniza** ash blonde; **~ miel** honey blonde; **~ platino** platinum blonde. (**b**) (*Aut*) estate car, station wagon (*US*). (**c**) (*Fin**) one peseta.

rubiales *nmf invar* blond(e), fair-headed person; **R~** Goldilocks.

rubiato 1 *adj* fa[illegible]lond(e). **2** *nm*, **rubiata** *nf* fair-haired person, blond(e[illegible]

Rubicón *nm* Rubicon; **pasar el ~** to cross the Rubicon.

rubicundo *adj* (**a**) *cara, persona* ruddy, rubicund. (**b**) (*rojizo*) reddish.

rubiez *nf* blondness.

rubio 1 *adj* (**a**) *pelo, persona* fair, fair-haired, blond(e); *animal, pelo de animal etc* light-coloured, golden. (**b**) **tabaco ~** = **2**. **2** *nm* Virginian tobacco.

rublo *nm* rouble.

rubor *nm* (**a**) (*color*) bright red. (**b**) (*en la cara*) blush, flush; **causar ~ a una** to make sb blush (*t fig*). (**c**) (*fig*) bashfulness; shame.

ruborizado *adj* blushing; flushed; (*avergonzado*) ashamed.

ruborizante *adj* blush-making.

ruborizar [1f] **1** *vt* (*t fig*) to cause to blush, make blush. **2 ruborizarse** *vr* to blush, flush, redden (*de* at).

ruboroso *adj* (**a**) **ser ~** to have a tendency to blush, blush easily. (**b**) **estar ~** to blush, be blushing, have a flush; (*fig*) to feel bashful.

rúbrica *nf* (**a**) (*señal*) red mark. (**b**) (*de la firma*) paraph, flourish. (**c**) (*título*) title, heading, rubric; **bajo la ~ de** under the heading of. (**d**) **de ~** = **de rigor**; *V* **rigor**.

rubricar [1g] *vt* to sign with a flourish, sign with one's paraph; *documento* to initial; (*en sentido lato*) to sign and seal.

rubro *nm* (**a**) (*LAm*: *título*) heading, title; (*Tip*) headline; section heading.
(**b**) (*LAm*: *de cuenta*) book-keeping (entry).
(**c**) (*LAm*: *sección*) section, department (*of a business*).
(**d**) **~ social** (*Cono Sur*) trading name, company name.

ruca *nf* (**a**) (*Cono Sur*: *cabina*) hut, cabin. (**b**) (*Méx*: *soltera*) old maid.

rucio 1 *adj caballo* grey, silver-grey; *persona* grey-haired; (*Cono Sur*) fair, blond(e). **2** *nm* grey (horse).

ruco *adj* (**a**) (*CAm, Méx*) (*usado*) worn-out; (*agotado*) exhausted. (**b**) (*And, Méx*: *viejo*) old.

rucho *adj* (*And*) (**a**) rough. (**b**) *fruta* overripe.

ruda *nf* rue.

rudamente *adv* simply, plainly; (*pey*) roughly, coarsely.

rudeza *nf* (**a**) (*simplicidad*) simplicity; plainness; (*pey*) roughness, coarseness, commonness. (**b**) (*estupidez*: *t* **~ de entendimiento**) stupidity.

rudimental *adj*, **rudimentario** *adj* rudimentary.

rudimento *nm* (**a**) (*Anat etc*) rudiment. (**b**) **~s** rudiments.

rudo *adj* (**a**) *madera etc* rough; (*sin labrar*) unpolished, unworked.
(**b**) (*Mec*) *pieza* stiff.
(**c**) *persona* (*sencillo*) simple, uncultured; (*llano*) plain; (*pey*) rough, coarse, common.
(**d**) *golpe* hard.
(**e**) (*estúpido*) simple, stupid.

rueca *nf* distaff.

rueda *nf* (**a**) (*Mec etc*) wheel; (*neumático*) tyre; (*de mueble*) roller, castor; **~ de agua, ~ hidráulica** waterwheel; **~ de alfarero** potter's wheel; **~s de aterrizaje** (*Aer*) landing wheels; **~ de atrás** rear wheel, back wheel; **~ de cadena** sprocket wheel; **~ dentada** cog, cogwheel; gearwheel; **~ de la fortuna** wheel of fortune; **~ impresora** daisy-wheel; **~ libre** freewheel; **~ de molino** millwheel; **~ motriz** driving-wheel; **~ de paletas** paddle wheel; **~ de recambio** spare wheel; **~ de trinquete** ratchet wheel; **comulga con ~s de molino** he'd swallow anything; he's pretty thick*; **chupar ~** to bide one's time; **ir sobre ~s*** to go for a spin*; (*fig*) to go smoothly; to go with a swing.
(**b**) (*círculo*) circle, ring; **en ~** in a ring; **~ de identificación, ~ de presos** identity parade; **~ informativa, ~ de prensa** press-conference.
(**c**) (*Culin*) slice, round.
(**d**) (*de torneo*) round.
(**e**) (*Hist*) rack.
(**f**) (*pez*) sunfish.
(**g**) (*Orn*: *de pavón*) spread tail; **hacer la ~** to spread its tail; **hacer la ~ a una** (*fig*) to court sb; **hacer la ~ a uno** (*fig*) to play up to sb, ingratiate o.s. with sb.
(**h**) **dar ~ (en)** (*Carib Aut*) to drive (around).

ruedecilla *nf* small wheel; roller, castor.

ruedero *nm* wheelwright.

ruedo *nm* (**a**) (*revolución*) turn, rotation. (**b**) (*contorno*) edge, circumference; (*borde*) border; (*de falda*) hem, bottom. (**c**) (*Taur*) bullring, arena; (*Pol etc*) ring. (**d**) (*esterilla*) (round) mat. (**e**) (*Cono Sur*: *suerte*) luck, gambler's luck.

ruego *nm* request, entreaty; **a ~ de** at the request of; **accediendo a los ~s de ...** in response to the requests of ...; (*en orden del día*) **'~s y preguntas'** 'any other business'.

rufián *nm* (**a**) (*coime*) pimp, pander. (**b**) (*gamberro*) lout, hooligan; (*canalla*) scoundrel.

rufiancete *nm* villain, rogue.

rufianería *nf*, **rufianismo** *nm* pimping, procuring; (*Jur*) living off immoral earnings.

rufianesca *nf* criminal underworld.

rufianesco *adj* (**a**) pimping, pandering. (**b**) loutish; villainous.

rufo *adj* (**a**) (*pelirrojo*) sandy-haired, red-haired; (*rizado*) curly-haired. (**b**) (*) (*satisfecho*) smug, self-satisfied; (*engreído*) cocky*, boastful.

rugbista *nm* rugby player.

rugby ['rugbi] *nm* rugby.

rugido *nm* roar; bellow; howl; **~ de dolor** howl of pain; **~ de tripas** intestinal rumblings, collywobbles*.

rugir [3c] *vi* (**a**) (*león etc*) to roar; (*toro*) to bellow; (*mar*) to roar; (*tormenta, viento*) to roar, howl, rage; (*persona*) to roar; (*tripas*) to rumble; **~ de dolor** to roar with pain, howl with pain. (**b**) (‡: *oler mal*) to pong‡, stink.

rugoso *adj* (*arrugado*) wrinkled, creased; (*desigual*) ridged; (*áspero*) rough.

ruibarbo *nm* rhubarb.

ruido *nm* (**a**) (*gen*) noise, sound; (*alboroto*) din, row; (*lo ruidoso*) noisiness; **~ blanco** white noise; **~ de fondo** background noise; **~ de sables** (*fig*) sharpening of knives; **sin ~** quietly, soundlessly, without making a noise; **no hagas ~** don't make a sound; **no hagas tanto ~** don't make such a noise; **mucho ~ y pocas nueces** much ado about nothing; **es más el ~ que las nueces** there's a lot of talk but nothing much gets done.

(**b**) (*fig*) (*escándalo*) commotion, stir; (*jaleo*) fuss; row, rumpus; (*grito*) outcry; **hacer ~, meter ~** to cause a stir, be a sensation; to have repercussions; to cause an outcry; **quitarse de ~s** to keep out of trouble.

ruidosamente *adv* (*V adj*) (**a**) noisily, loudly. (**b**) (*fig*) sensationally.

ruidoso *adj* (**a**) (*estrepitoso*) noisy, loud. (**b**) (*fig*) *noticia* sensational; much talked-of.

ruin 1 *adj* (**a**) (*vil*) *persona* mean, despicable, low, contemptible; *trato* (*injusto*) mean, shabby; (*cruel*) heartless, callous.

(**b**) (*tacaño*) mean, stingy.

(**c**) (*pequeño*) small, weak.

(**d**) *animal* vicious.

2 *nm* mean person (*etc*); **en nombrando al ~ de Roma, luego asoma** talk of the devil!; well, look who's here!

ruina *nf* (**a**) (*Arquit etc*) ruin; **~s** ruins, remains; **estar hecho una ~** to be a wreck; to be a shadow of one's former self.

(**b**) (*colapso*) collapse; **amenazar ~** to threaten to collapse, be about to fall down.

(**c**) (*fig*) ruin, destruction; (*de imperio*) fall, decline; (*de persona*) ruin, downfall; (*de esperanzas*) destruction; **será mi ~** it will be the ruin of me; **la empresa le llevó a la ~** the venture ruined him (financially).

(**d**) (*Jur*‡) bird‡, prison sentence.

ruindad *nf* (**a**) (*cualidad*) meanness, lowness; shabbiness; callousness. (**b**) (*acto*) mean act, low trick, piece of villainy.

ruinoso *adj* (**a**) (*Arquit*) ruinous; tumbledown. (**b**) (*Fin etc*) ruinous, disastrous.

ruiseñor *nm* nightingale.

rula *nf* (*And, CAm*) hunting knife.

rular‡ [1a] *vt droga* to pass round.

rulemán *nm* (*Cono Sur*) ball-bearing, roller bearing.

rulenco, rulengo *adj* (*Cono Sur*) weak, underdeveloped.

rulero *nm* (*And*) hair curler, roller.

ruleta *nf* roulette; **~ rusa** Russian roulette.

ruletero *nm* (*CAm, Méx*) (*taxista*) taxi driver, cab driver; (*camionero*) lorry driver.

rulo¹ *nm* (**a**) (*pelota*) ball, round mass. (**b**) (*rodillo*) roller; (*Culin*) rolling pin. (**c**) (*del pelo*) hair-curler. (**d**) (*Cono Sur*) (natural) curl.

rulo² *nm* (*Cono Sur*) well-watered ground.

rulota *nf* caravan, trailer (*US*).

ruma* *nf* (*LAm*) heap, pile.

Rumania *nf*, **Rumanía** *nf* Romania.

rumano, -a 1 *adj, nm/f* Romanian. **2** *nm* (**a**) (*lengua nacional*) Romanian. (**b**) (*: *lenguaje*) special language, jargon; (*argot*) slang.

rumba¹ *nf* (**a**) (*Mús*) rumba. (**b**) (*Carib*: *fiesta*) party, celebration.

rumba² *nf* (*Cono Sur*) = **ruma**.

rumbar [1a] **1** *vt* (*LAm*) to throw. **2** *vi* (**a**) (*And*: *zumbar*) to buzz. (**b**) (*And, Cono Sur*: *orientarse*) to get one's bearings. **3 rumbarse** *vr* (*And*) to make off, go away.

rumbeador *nm* (*And, Cono Sur*) pathfinder, tracker.

rumbear [1a] *vi* (**a**) (*LAm Mús*) to dance the rumba.

(**b**) (*LAm*) (*seguir un rumbo*) to follow a direction; (*orientarse*) to find one's way, get one's bearings.

(**c**) (*LAm*) to go out on the town, go on a binge*.

(**d**) (*Méx*: *en bosque*) to clear a path (through undergrowth).

rumbero 1 *adj* (**a**) (*And, Cono Sur*) tracking, pathfinding.

(**b**) (*Carib*: *juerguista*) party-going, fond of a good time.

2 *nm* (*And*) (*en bosque etc*) pathfinder, guide; (*de río*) river pilot.

rumbo¹ *nm* (**a**) (*camino*) route, direction; (*Náut*) course; bearing; **con ~ a** in the direction of; **ir con ~ a** to be heading for, be going in the direction of, be bound for; (*Náut*) to be bound for; **corregir el ~** to correct one's course; **hacer ~ a** (*o* **hacia**) to head for; **poner ~ a** (*Náut*) to set a course for.

(**b**) (*fig*) (*tendencia*) course of events; (*conducta*) line of conduct; **~ nuevo** new departure; **los nuevos ~s de la estrategia occidental** the new lines of western strategy; **tomar ~ nuevo** to set off on a different tack, change one's approach; **los acontecimientos vienen tomando un ~ sensacional** events are taking a sensational turn.

(**c**) (*fig*) (*liberalidad*) generosity, lavishness; (*boato*) lavish display; (*ostentación*) showiness, pomp; **de mucho ~** = **rumboso**; **viajar con ~** to travel in style, travel in state.

(**d**) (*CAm**: *fiesta*) party, binge*.

(**e**) (*Cono Sur*: *herida*) cut (on the head).

rumbo² *nm* (*And Orn*) hummingbird.

rumbón* *adj* = **rumboso**.

rumbosidad *nf* lavishness.

rumboso *adj* (**a**) *persona* generous, lavish; free-spending. (**b**) *regalo* lavish; *boda etc* big, splendid, slap-up*.

rumia *nf*, **rumiación** *nf* rumination.

rumiante *adj, nm* ruminant.

rumiar [1b] **1** *vt* (**a**) (*masticar*) to chew. (**b**) (*fig*) *asunto* to chew over; to brood over, ponder (over). **2** *vi* (**a**) (*pensar*) to chew the cud. (**b**) (*fig*) to ruminate, brood, ponder; (*pey*) to take too long to make up one's mind.

rumor *nm* (**a**) (*murmullo*) murmur, mutter; (*ruido sordo*) confused noise, low sound; (*de voces*) buzz; (*de agua*) murmur. (**b**) (*fig*) rumour.

rumoreado *adj* rumoured.

rumorearse [1a] *vr*: **se rumorea que** ... it is rumoured that ...

rumoreo *nm* murmur(ing).

rumorología *nf* rumours; gossip.

rumorólogo, -a *nm/f* scandal-monger.

rumorosidad *nf* noise level.

rumoroso *adj* full of sounds; *arroyo etc* murmuring, musical.

runa¹ *nf* rune.

runa² *nm* (*LAm*) Indian.

runcho *adj* (**a**) (*And*) (*ignorante*) ignorant; (*obstinado*) stubborn. (**b**) (*CAm*) mean.

rundir [3a] (*Méx*) **1** *vt* (*guardar*) to keep; (*ocultar*) to hide, put away. **2** *vi* to become drowsy. **3 rundirse** *vr* to fall fast asleep.

rundún *nm* (*Cono Sur*) hummingbird.

runfla* *nf*, **runflada*** *nf* (*LAm*) (*masa*) mass, (*montón*) lot, heap; (*multitud*) crowd; (*pandilla*) gang (of kids*).

rúnico *adj* runic.

runrún *nm* (**a**) *de voces* sound of voices, buzz of conversation, murmur. (**b**) (*fig*: *rumor*) rumour, buzz. (**c**) (*de máquina etc*) whirr.

runrunearse [1a] *vr*: **se runrunea que** ... it is rumoured that ...

runruneo *nm* = **runrún** (**a**).

ruñir [3h] *vti* (*And, Méx*) = **roer**; (*Carib*) = **roer** (**a**), (**b**).

rupestre *adj* rock (*atr*); **pintura ~** cave painting; **planta ~** rock plant.

rupia *nf* rupee; (‡) one peseta.

ruptor *nm* contact-breaker.

ruptura *nf* (*fig*) rupture; (*escisión*) split; (*de contrato etc*) breaking; (*de relaciones*) breaking-off; **~ matrimonial** breakdown of a marriage.

rural 1 *adj* rural, country (*atr*). **2** *nm* (**a**) (*Cono Sur*) estate car, station wagon (*US*). (**b**) **los ~es** (*Méx Hist*) the rural police.

Rusia *nf* Russia; **~ Soviética** Soviet Russia.

ruso, -a 1 *adj, nm/f* Russian. **2** *nm* (*Ling*) Russian.

rústica *nf*: **en ~** unbound, in paper covers; **libro en ~** paperback (book).

rusticidad *nf* (**a**) (*gen*) rusticity, rural character. (**b**) (*ordinariez*) coarseness, uncouthness; (*grosería*) crudity; (*descortesía*) unmannerliness.

rústico 1 *adj* (**a**) (*del campo*) rustic, rural, country (*atr*). (**b**) (*pey*: *tosco*) coarse, uncouth; (*grosero*) crude; (*sin educación*) unmannerly.

2 *nm* rustic, peasant, yokel.

ruta *nf* route; (*Cono Sur*) road; (*fig*) course, course of action; **~ aérea** air route, airway; **R~ Jacobea** Way of St James (*pilgrim road to Santiago de Compostela*).

rutero *adj* road (*atr*).

rutilante *adj* (*liter*) shining, sparkling, glowing.

rutilar [1a] *vi* (*liter*) to shine, sparkle, glow.

rutina *nf* routine; **~ diaria** daily routine, daily round; **por** (*o* **de**) **~** as a matter of course, as a matter of routine; (*fig*) from force of habit.

rutinariamente *adv* in a routine way; unimaginatively.

rutinario *adj* (**a**) (*ordinario*) *procedimiento* routine; ordinary, everyday. (**b**) *persona* ordinary; unimaginative; *creencia etc* unthinking, automatic.

rutinero 1 *adj* who sticks to routine; ordinary; unimaginative. **2** *nm*, **rutinera** *nf* person who sticks to routine; ordinary sort, unimaginative person.

rutinizarse [1f] *vr* to become routine, become normal.

S

S, s ['ese] *nf* (*letra*) S, s.
S (**a**) *abr de* **sur** South, S. (**b**) (*Rel*) *abr de* **San, Santa, Santo** Saint, St. (**c**) *abr de* **septiembre** September, Sept. (**d**) (*Cine*) **película S** *abr de* **película porno** pornographic film.
s. (**a**) *abr de* **siglo** century, c. (**b**) *abr de* **siguiente** following, foll.
s/ (*Com*) *abr de* **su, sus.**
S.ª *abr de* **Sierra** Mountains, Mts.
S.A. (**a**) (*Com*) *abr de* **Sociedad Anónima** Limited, Ltd; public limited company, plc; (*US*) Corporation, Corp., Incorporated, Inc. (**b**) *abr de* **Su Alteza** His Highness, Her Highness, H.H.
sáb. *abr de* **sábado** Saturday, Sat.
sábado *nm* Saturday; (*judío*) Sabbath; **S~ de Gloria, S~ Santo** Easter Saturday; **hacer ~** to have a good clean-up, do the weekly clean.
sábalo *nm* (*pez*) shad.
sabana *nf* (*LAm*) savannah.
sábana *nf* (**a**) (*de cama*) sheet; (*Ecl*) altar cloth; **~ de agua** sheet of rain; **la S~ Santa de Turín** the Holy Shroud of Turin; **encontrar las ~s*** to hit the hay*; **estirarse más de lo que dan de sí las ~s** to bite off more than one can chew, over-reach oneself; **se le pegan las ~s** he loves his sleep; he's bad about getting up; **ponerse uno en la ~** to strike it lucky.
(**b**) (*Fin*‡) 1000-peseta note; **media ~** 500-peseta note; **~ verde** 10000-peseta note.
sabandija *nf* (**a**) (*insecto*) bug, insect, creepy-crawly*, creature; **~s** bugs, vermin. (**b**) (*fig*) wretch, louse‡.
sabanear [1a] **1** *vt* (**a**) (*CAm*: *agarrar*) to catch.
(**b**) (*CAm*: *halagar*) to flatter.
(**c**) (*CAm, Carib*: *perseguir*) to pursue, chase.
2 *vi* (*LAm*) to travel across a plain; to round up cattle on the savannah, scour the plain for cattle.
sabanero (*LAm*) **1** *adj* plain (*atr*), savannah (*atr*); of (*o* from) the plains (*o* savannah). **2** *nm*, **sabanera** *nf* plainsman, plainswoman.
3 *nm* (*CAm**: *matón*) bully, thug.
sabanilla *nf* small sheet, piece of cloth; (*Ecl*) altar cloth; (*Cono Sur*) bedspread.
sabañón *nm* chilblain.
sabara *nf* (*Carib*) light mist, haze.
sabatario, -a *adj, nm/f* sabbatarian.
sabateño *nm* (*Carib*) boundary stone.
sabático *adj* sabbatical; (*del sábado*) Saturday (*atr*).
sabatino *adj* Saturday (*atr*).
sabedor *adj*: **ser ~ de** to know about; to be aware of.
sabelotodo* *nm invar* know-all.
saber [2m] **1** *vti* (**a**) (*gen*) to know; **~ de** to know about, be aware of; to know of; **desde hace 6 meses no sabemos nada de él** we haven't heard from him for 6 months, it's 6 months since we had news of him; **un 5 por ciento 'no sabe, no contesta'** there were 5% 'don't knows'; **lo sé** I know; **sin ~lo yo** without my knowledge; **hacer ~ algo a uno** to inform sb of sth, let sb know about sth.
(**b**) (*en pretérito, frec*) to find out, learn; to hear, get to know; (*darse cuenta*) to realize; **cuando lo supe** when I heard about it; **lograron ~ el secreto** they managed to learn the secret.
(**c**) (*locuciones*) **a ~** namely; **a ~ dónde lo tiene guardado** I wonder where he has it hidden away; **a ~ si realmente lo compró** I wonder whether he really did buy it; **es a ~** namely, that is to say; **¡haberlo sabido!** if only I'd known!; **¡yo qué sé!; ¡qué sé yo!** how should I know!, search me!*; **demasiado sé que ...** I know only too well that ...; **tú sabrás (lo que haces)** I suppose you know (what you're doing); **¡no lo sabes bien!*** not half!*; **que yo sepa** as far as I know; **que sepamos** as far as we know; **ya lo sabía yo** I thought as much; **un no sé qué** a certain something; **un no sé qué de afectado** a certain (element of) affectation; **nos sirvió no sé qué vino** he gave us some wine or other; **A y B y no sé qué** (*o* **cuántos**) A and B and so forth; **¿tú qué sabes?** what do you know about it?; **vete a ~** your guess is as good as mine; **¡vete a ~!** God knows!; **¡vete a ~ de dónde ha venido!** goodness only knows where he came from!; **cualquiera sabe si ...** it's anybody's guess whether ...; **¿sabe?*** you know?*, you know what I mean?*; **costó muy caro, ¿sabe Vd?** it was very dear, you know; **¿quién sabe?** who knows?, who can tell?, who's to say?; **sepa Vd, para que lo sepa** let me tell you, just for your information; **cada uno sabe dónde le aprieta el zapato** everyone knows his own weaknesses; **no sabía dónde meterse** he didn't know what to do with himself; **no ~ ni papa** not to know the first thing about something; **no ~ a qué quedarse** to be in a dilemma; *V* **cuánto, más, convenir, Briján** *etc.*
(**d**) **~ +** *infin* to know how to + *infin*, can + *infin*; **sé conducir** I can drive, I know how to drive; **¿sabes nadar?** can you swim?; **tiene que ~ contenerse** he must know how to control himself, he must be able to control himself.
(**e**) **~ +** *infin* (*movimiento*): **~ ir a un sitio** to know one's way to a place; **no sabe todavía andar por la ciudad** he still doesn't know his way about the town.
(**f**) **~ +** *infin* (*LAm*: *tener costumbre*) to be in the habit of + *ger*; **no sabe venir por aquí** he doesn't usually come this way, he's not in the habit of coming along here.
2 *vi*: **~ a** to taste of, taste like; (*fig*) to smack of; **esto sabe a queso** this tastes of cheese; **esto sabe mal, sabe a demonio(s)** this tastes awful; **le sabe mal que otro la saque a bailar** it upsets him that anybody else should ask her to dance, he doesn't like other people dancing with her.
3 saberse *vr* (**a**) **se sabe que ...** it is known that ..., we know that ...; **no se sabe** it's not known, nobody knows; **¿se puede ~ si ...?** may one inquire whether ...?; **¿quién es Vd, si puede ~?** who are you, may I ask?; **tiene que perder sépase cuánto tiempo para recuperarlo** he has to waste goodness knows how much time getting it back; **sépase que ...** let it be known that ...
(**b**) **se supo que ...** it was learnt that ..., it was discovered that ...; **por fin se supo el secreto** finally the secret was revealed.
4 *nm* (**a**) knowledge, learning; **~ popular** folk wisdom; **según mi leal ~ y entender** to the best of my knowledge, as far as I can honestly tell.
(**b**) **~ hacer** know-how.
sabiamente *adv* (**a**) (*eruditamente*) learnedly; expertly.
(**b**) (*prudentemente*) wisely, sensibly.
sabichoso* *adj* (*Carib*) = **sabihondo.**
sabidillo, -a* *nm/f* know-all.
sabido 1 *ptp de* **saber**; **es ~ que ...** it is well known that ...; **como es ~** as we know, as is well known.
2 *adj* (**a**) = **consabido.**
(**b**) (*iró*) highly knowledgeable, learned.
(**c**) **de ~** (*por supuesto*) for sure, certainly.
(**d**) (*And*) lively, mischievous, saucy.
sabiduría *nf* wisdom; learning, knowledge; **~ popular** popular knowledge; folklore.
sabiendas: a ~ *adv* (*sabiendo*) knowingly; (*con intención*) consciously, deliberately; **a ~ de que ...** knowing full well that ..., in the full knowledge that ...
sabihondo* 1 *adj* know-all, pedantic. **2** *nm*, **sabihonda** *nf* know-all, self-proclaimed expert; smart Aleck*; pedant.
sabio 1 *adj* (**a**) (*docto*) learned; expert; (*iró*) know-all.
(**b**) (*juicioso*) wise, sensible, judicious; **más ~ que Salomón** wiser than Solomon.
(**c**) *acto, decisión etc* wise, sensible.

(**d**) *animal* trained.

2 *nm*, **sabia** *nf* learned man, learned woman; wise person; scholar, expert, savant; (*Hist*) sage; **de ~s es rectificar** it takes a wise man to recognize that he was wrong; **¡hay que escuchar al ~!** (*iró*) just listen to the professor!

sablazo *nm* (**a**) (*herida*) sword wound; (*golpe*) slash with a sword.

(**b**) (*: *gorronería*) sponging*; **dar un ~, pegar un ~** to make a touch* (*de* for); **dar un ~ a uno** to touch sb for a loan*, to scrounge money off sb*; **vivir de ~s** to live by sponging*.

(**c**) **la cuenta fue un ~** the bill was astronomical.

sable[1] *nm* sabre, cutlass.

sable[2] *nm* (*Her*) sable.

sablear* [1a] **1** *vt*: **~ algo a uno** to scrounge sth from sb*. **2** *vi* (*por costumbre*) to live by sponging*; (*dar un sablazo*) to ask for a loan.

sablista* *nmf* sponger*, cadger.

sabor *nm* taste, flavour; savour, savouriness; (*fig*) flavour; **con ~ a** (*o* **de**) **queso** with a cheese flavour(ing), cheese-flavoured; **con ligero ~ arcaico** with a slightly archaic flavour (to it); **sin ~** tasteless; **le deja a uno mal ~ de boca** (*fig*) it leaves a nasty taste in the mouth.

saborcillo *nm* slight taste.

saborear [1a] **1** *vt* (**a**) *comida* to savour, relish (the savour of); (*probar*) to taste; (*deleitarse con*) to enjoy.

(**b**) (*dar sabor a*) to flavour, add a flavour to.

(**c**) (*fig*) to relish, enjoy; **~ el triunfo** to enjoy one's triumph, relish one's victory (to the full).

2 saborearse *vr* (**a**) to smack one's lips (in anticipation).

(**b**) **~ algo** (*fig*) to relish the thought of sth.

saborete *nm* slight taste.

saborizante *nm* flavouring.

sabotaje *nm* sabotage.

saboteador *nm* saboteur.

sabotear [1a] *vt* to sabotage (*t fig*).

Saboya *nf* Savoy.

saboyano 1 *adj* of Savoy. **2** *nm*, **saboyana** *nf* native (*o* inhabitant) of Savoy; **los ~s** the people of Savoy.

sabré *etc V* **saber.**

sabrosera *nf* (*LAm*) tasty thing, titbit.

sabroso *adj* (**a**) *comida* (*rico*) tasty, delicious; (*agradable*) nice, pleasant, agreeable.

(**b**) (*Esp Culin*) slightly salty.

(**c**) (*fig*) *libro etc* solid, meaty.

(**d**) (*fig*) *cuento, chiste etc* salty, racy, daring.

(**e**) (*And, Carib*: *agradable*) lovely, nice, pleasant.

(**f**) (*And, Carib, Méx*: *parlanchín*) talkative.

(**g**) (*Méx*: *fanfarrón*) bigheaded, stuck-up.

sabrosón* *adj* (**a**) (*LAm*) = **sabroso** (**a**). (**b**) (*And*: *parlanchín*) talkative, chatty.

sabrosura *nf* (*LAm*) (**a**) (*de comida*) tastiness. (**b**) (*fig*) pleasantness, delightfulness, sweetness; delight, enjoyment.

sabueso *nm* (**a**) (*Zool*) bloodhound. (**b**) (*fig*) sleuth.

saburra *nf* coat, fur (*on tongue etc*).

saburroso *adj lengua* coated, furred.

saca[1] *nf* (**a**) big sack; **~ de correo(s)** mailbag. (**b**) (*LAm*) (moving) herd of cattle.

saca[2] *nf* (*acto*) taking out; withdrawal; (*Com*) export; **~ carcelaria** illegal removal of a prisoner from prison (for execution); **estar de ~** (*Com*) to be on sale; (*fig*) to be at the right age to marry.

sacabocados *nm invar* (*Téc*) punch.

sacabotas *nm invar* bootjack.

sacabuche *nm* sackbut.

sacabullas* *nm* (*Méx*) bouncer*.

sacaclavos *nm invar* nail-puller, pincers.

sacacorchos *nm invar* corkscrew.

sacacuartos *nm invar* = **sacadineros.**

sacada *nf* (*And, Cono Sur*) = **sacadura.**

sacadera *nf* (*Pesca*) landing-net.

sacadineros *nm invar* (**a**) (*baratija*) cheap trinket. (**b**) (*diversión*) money-wasting spectacle, worthless sideshow (*etc*); (*truco criminal*) small-time racket. (**c**) (*persona*) cheat.

sacador(a) *nm/f* (*Tenis*) server.

sacadura *nf* (*And, Cono Sur*) extraction.

sacafaltas *nmf invar* faultfinder.

sacamanchas *nm invar* cleaning material, stain remover.

sacamuelas *nmf invar* (**a**) (*hum*: *dentista*) tooth-puller; (*Med*) charlatan, quack. (**b**) (*parlanchín*) chatterer.

sacaniguas *nm invar* (*And*) squib, Chinese cracker.

sacapuntas *nm invar* pencil sharpener.

sacar [1g] *vt* (**a**) (*gen*) to take out, get out; to pull out, draw out, extract; (*Quím*) to extract; *carbón etc* to mine, bring up; (*del bolsillo etc*) to get out; *arma* to draw; *dinero* (*de banco*) to draw out, withdraw; (*borrar etc*) to remove, exclude; **~ fuera a uno** to chuck sb out, get rid of sb.

(**b**) (*fig*: *extraer*) to get (out); **~ una información a uno** to get information out of sb; **los datos están sacados de 2 libros** the data is taken from 2 books; **~ un secreto a uno** to get (*o* worm) a secret out of sb; **¿de dónde has sacado esa idea?** where did you get that idea?; **no conseguirán ~le nada** they'll get nothing out of him; **lo que se saca de todo esto es que ...** what I gather from all this is that ..., the result of this is that ...

(**c**) *mancha etc* to remove, get out, get off.

(**d**) (*Tenis*) to serve; (*Fútbol*) to throw in.

(**e**) *parte del cuerpo* to stick out, put out, thrust out; **~ la barbilla** to stick one's chin out; **~ la lengua** to put (*o* stick) one's tongue out; **~ la mano** (*Aut etc*) to put one's hand out.

(**f**) *prenda de vestir* (*Cos*) to let out.

(**g**) *ropa etc* (*esp LAm*) to take off; **~ la funda a un fusil** to take the cover off a rifle.

(**h**) *entradas etc* to get; *reservas* to make, book.

(**i**) *solución* to reach, obtain, get; *conclusión* to draw.

(**j**) (*producir*) *obra* to produce, make; *producto* to make; *novela etc* to bring out, publish; *modelo nuevo* to bring out; *moda* to create; *canción etc* to compose, make up; **aquí sacan 200 coches diarios** they make 200 cars a day here; **he sacado 20 páginas de notas** I've made 20 pages of notes; **para** (*o* **con**) **este propósito han sacado unos versos** they've made up some verses about this.

(**k**) (*Fot*) to take; *copia* to make, have made; **saca buen retrato** he takes well; **nos quiso ~ una foto** he wanted to take a photo of us; **no tenía la intención de ~ ese coche** I didn't mean to include that car in the photograph.

(**l**) (*obtener*) *beneficio, legado, premio etc* to get; to receive; *ganancia* to make; (*fig*) to derive (*de* from); **sacó el premio gordo** he got (*o* won) the big prize; **así no vas a ~ nada** you won't get anything that way; **sacó un buen número para la lotería** he drew a good number for the lottery; **la sociedad saca una ganancia de ...** the company makes a profit of ...

(**m**) (*Parl etc*) to elect; **han sacado 35 diputados** they have got 35 members elected; **por fin sacaron presidente a X** they finally elected X (as) president.

(**n**) *cualidad etc* to show; **por fin en esto sacó su habilidad** in this he finally showed (*o* demonstrated *o* proved) his skill; **~ faltas a uno** to point out sb's defects.

(**o**) *lustre etc* to put on, bring up, bring out; **~ los colores a la cara de uno** to bring the colour to sb's cheeks, put some colour into sb's cheeks.

(**p**) (*en periódico etc*) to mention, put; **no me vayas a ~ en tu discurso** don't mention me in your speech; **le han sacado en el periódico** they've put him in the paper.

(**q**) (*) **le saca 10 cm a su hermano** he is 10 cm taller than his brother, he has an advantage in height of 10 cm over his brother; **al terminar la carrera le sacaba 10 metros al adversario** at the end of the race he was 10 metres ahead of his rival.

(**r**) **~ adelante** *niño* to bring up; *licenciado etc* to produce, turn out; *negocio* to carry on, go on with; **~ a una adelante*** to get a girl in the family way.

(**s**) **~ a uno de sí** to infuriate sb.

(**t**) (*And, CAm*: *lisonjear*) to flatter, fawn on.

(**u**) (*And, Méx*) **~ algo a uno** to reproach sb for sth, throw sth back in sb's face.

2 sacarse* *vr* (**a**) (*Méx*) to leave, go away; **¡sáquese de aquí!** get out of here!

(**b**) (*LAm*) **~ la ropa** to take off one's clothes.

sacarina *nf* saccharin(e).

sacarino *adj* saccharine.

sacatín *nm* (*And*) still.

sacerdocio *nm* priesthood.

sacerdotal *adj* priestly.

sacerdote *nm* priest; **~ obrero** worker priest; **sumo ~** high priest.

sacerdotisa *nf* priestess.

saciado *adj*: **~ de** sated with; (*fig*) steeped in, saturated in, full of.

saciar [1b] **1** *vt* (**a**) *hambre etc* to satisfy, satiate, sate; (*sed*) to quench.

(**b**) (*fig*) *deseos etc* to appease; *curiosidad, anhelo etc* to satisfy; *ambición* to fulfil, more than satisfy.

2 saciarse *vr* to satiate o.s.; to be satiated (*con, de* with).

saciedad *nf* satiation, satiety; **demostrar algo hasta la ~** to prove sth up to the hilt; **repetir algo hasta la ~** to repeat sth over and over again.

saco[1] *nm* **(a)** (*bolso*) bag; (*costal*) sack; (*Mil*) kitbag; (*medida*) bagful; sackful; **~ de arena** (*Mil*) sandbag, (*Dep*) punchball; **~ de dormir, ~ manta** sleeping-bag; **~ de mano, ~ de noche, ~ de viaje** travelling bag; **~ postal** mailbag, postbag; **~ terrero** sandbag; **a ~s** (*fig*) by the ton; **la petición cayó en ~ roto** the appeal fell on deaf ears; **eso es echarlo en ~ roto** that's like throwing it down the drain; **no echar algo en ~ roto** to be careful not to forget sth; **no es** (*o* **no parece**) **~ de paja** he can't be written off as unimportant; **lo tenemos en el ~*** we've got it in the bag*; **tomar a una por el ~*‡** to screw sb*‡; **mandar a uno tomar por el ~*‡** to tell sb to get stuffed*‡.

(b) (*Anat*) sac.

(c) (*) **ser un ~ de gracia** to be very witty; **es un ~ de picardías** he's full of tricks; **ser un ~ de huesos** (*LAm*) to be a bag of bones.

(d) (*prenda*) long coat, loose-fitting jacket; (*LAm*) coat, jacket; (*And*) jumper; (*Cono Sur*) woman's overcoat.

(e) (‡) 1000-peseta note; **medio ~** 500-peseta note.

(f) (‡: *cárcel*) nick‡, prison.

saco[2] *nm* (*Mil*) sack; **entrar a ~ en** to sack, loot, plunder.

sacón 1 *adj* **(a)** (*CAm*‡) (*soplón*) sneaky; (*cobista*) flattering, soapy*.

(b) (*LAm: entrometido*) nosey*, prying.

2 *nm*, **sacona** *nf* (‡) **(a)** (*CAm: zalamero*) flatterer, creep‡.

(b) (*LAm: entrometido*) nosey-parker*.

3 *nm* (*Cono Sur*) woman's outdoor coat.

saconear* [1a] *vt* (*CAm*) to flatter, soap up*.

saconería* *nf* **(a)** (*CAm: zalamería*) flattery, soft soap*. **(b)** (*LAm: curiosidad*) prying.

sacral *adj* religious, sacral; totemic.

sacralización *nf* (*hum*) consecration, canonization.

sacralizar [1f] *vt* (*hum*) to consecrate, canonize; to give official approval to.

sacramental *adj* **(a)** (*Ecl*) sacramental. **(b)** (*fig*) ritual, ritualistic; time-honoured; **pronunció las palabras ~es** he spoke the time-honoured words.

sacramentar [1a] *vt* to administer the last sacraments to.

sacramento *nm* sacrament; **el Santísimo S~** the Blessed Sacrament; **recibir los ~s** to receive the last sacraments.

sacrificar [1g] **1** *vt* **(a)** (*gen*) to sacrifice (*t fig*; *a* to).

(b) *animal* (*para carne*) to slaughter; *animal doméstico* to put down, destroy, put to sleep.

2 sacrificarse *vr* to sacrifice o.s.; to make a sacrifice.

sacrificio *nm* **(a)** (*gen, t fig*) sacrifice; **el ~ de la misa** the sacrifice of the mass. **(b)** (*de animal*) slaughter(ing); putting down, painless destruction.

sacrilegio *nm* sacrilege.

sacrílego *adj* sacrilegious.

sacristán *nm* verger, sacristan; sexton.

sacristía *nf* **(a)** (*Ecl*) vestry, sacristy. **(b)** (‡) (*bragueta*) flies; (*horcajadura*) crotch.

sacro[1] *adj* sacred, holy.

sacro[2] *nm* (*Anat*) sacrum.

sacrosanto *adj* most holy; (*fig*) sacrosanct.

sacuara *nf* (*And Bot*) bamboo plant.

sacudida *nf* **(a)** (*gen*) shake, shaking; (*tirón*) jerk; (*choque*) jolt, jar, bump; (*de terremoto*) shock; (*de explosión*) blast; (*de la cabeza*) jerk, toss; **~ eléctrica** electric shock; **dar una ~ a una alfombra** to beat a carpet; **el coche avanzaba dando ~s** the car moved forward in a series of jolts, the car went jerkily forwards; **la ~ de la bomba llegó hasta aquí** the blast of the bomb was felt as far away as this.

(b) (*fig*) violent change; sudden jolt; (*Pol etc*) upheaval; **hay que darle una ~** he needs a jolt.

sacudido *adj* **(a)** (*brusco*) ill-disposed, unpleasant; (*difícil*) intractable. **(b)** (*resuelto*) determined.

sacudidura *nf*, **sacudimiento** *nm* = **sacudida.**

sacudir [3a] **1** *vt* **(a)** *árbol, edificio, miembro, persona, tierra etc* to shake; *persona* (*como castigo*) to beat, thrash; *ala etc* to flap, move up and down; *alfombra* to beat; *colchón* to shake (the dust out of); *cuerda etc* to jerk, tug; *pasajero, vehículo etc* to shake, jolt, jar, bump; to rock (to and fro); *cabeza* to jerk, toss.

(b) (*quitar*) *moscas etc* to chase away, brush off; *carga* to shake off.

(c) (*conmover*) to shake; **una tremenda emoción sacudió a la multitud** a great wave of excitement ran through the crowd; **~ a uno de su depresión** to shake sb out of his depression; **~ los nervios a uno** to shatter sb's nerves.

(d) **~ a uno** (*: *pegar*) to belt sb*, to beat sb up*.

(e) **~ dinero a uno*** to screw money out of sb.

2 sacudirse *vr*: **~ (de) un peso** to shake off a burden, get rid of a burden; **por fin se le han sacudido** they've finally got rid of him; **el caballo se sacudía las moscas con la cola** the horse brushed off the flies with its tail.

sacudón *nm* (*LAm*) violent shake, severe jolt; (*fig*) shake-up, upheaval.

sacha *adj invar* (*LAm*) **(a)** (*fingido*) false, sham; **~ médico** quack. **(b)** (*desmañado*) bungling, unskilled; **~ carpintero** clumsy carpenter.

sachadura *nf* weeding.

sachar [1a] *vt* to weed.

sacho *nm* weeding hoe.

sádico 1 *adj* sadistic. **2** *nm*, **sádica** *nf* sadist.

sadismo *nm* sadism.

sadista *nmf* sadist.

sado* *adj* = **sadomasoquista.**

sadoca‡ *nmf* = **sadomasoquista.**

sadomasoquismo *nm* sadomasochism.

sadomasoquista 1 *adj* sadomasochistic. **2** *nmf* sadomasochist.

saeta *nf* **(a)** (*Mil*) arrow, dart.

(b) (*de reloj*) hand; (*de brújula*) magnetic needle.

(c) (*Mús*) *sacred song in flamenco style sung during Holy Week processions.*

(d) (*Rel*) ejaculatory prayer.

saetera *nf* (*Mil*) loophole.

saetín *nm* **(a)** (*de molino*) millrace. **(b)** (*Téc*) tack, brad.

safado *adj* (*LAm*) = **zafado.**

safagina *nf*, **safajina** *nf* (*And*) uproar, commotion.

safari *nm* safari; **estar de ~** to be on safari; **contar ~s*** to shoot a line*.

safo‡ *nm* hankie*, handkerchief.

saga *nf* **(a)** (*Liter*) saga. **(b)** (*fig*) clan, dynasty; family.

sagacidad *nf* shrewdness, cleverness, sagacity; astuteness.

sagaz *adj* **(a)** (*listo*) shrewd, clever, sagacious; (*astuto*) astute. **(b)** *perro* keen-scented.

sagazmente *adv* shrewdly, cleverly, sagaciously; astutely.

Sagitario *nm* (*Zodíaco*) Sagittarius.

sagrado 1 *adj* sacred, holy (*t fig*); *escritura, órdenes etc* holy. **2** *nm* sanctuary, asylum; **acogerse a ~** to seek sanctuary.

sagrario *nm* shrine; tabernacle, sacrarium.

sagú *nm* sago.

Sahara *nm*, **Sáhara** *nm* ['saxara] Sahara.

saharaui 1 *adj* Saharan. **2** *nm/f* Saharan, native (*o* inhabitant) of the Sahara; **los ~s** the people of the Sahara.

sahariana[1] *nf* safari jacket.

sahariano, -a[2] *adj, nm/f* = **saharaui.**

Sahel *nm* Sahel.

sahumadura *nf* = **sahumerio.**

sahumar [1a] *vt* (*incensar*) to perfume (with incense); (*fumigar*) to smoke, fumigate.

sahumerio *nm* **(a)** (*acto*) perfuming with incense. **(b)** (*humo*) aromatic smoke; (*sustancia*) aromatic substance.

S.A.I. *abr de* **Su Alteza Imperial** His (*o* Her) Imperial Highness, H.I.H.

saibó *nm* (*LAm*), **saibor** *nm* (*And, Carib*) sideboard.

saín *nm* **(a)** (*grasa*) animal fat, grease; *de pescado* fish oil (*used for lighting*). **(b)** (*en la ropa*) dirt, grease.

sainete *nm* **(a)** (*Culin*) seasoning, sauce; (*fig*) titbit, delicacy, pleasant adornment, nice extra.

(b) (*fig*) spice, relish, tastiness.

(c) (*Teat*) one-act farce (*o* comedy); comic sketch, skit.

sainetero, -a *nm/f*, **sainetista** *nmf* writer of farces (*etc*).

sajar [1a] *vt* (*Med*) to cut open, lance.

sajín* *nm* (*CAm*), **sajino*** *nm* (*CAm*) underarm odour, smelly armpits.

sajón, -ona *adj nm/f* Saxon.

Sajonia *nf* Saxony.

sajornar [1a] *vt* (*Carib*) to pester, harrass.

sal[1] *nf* **(a)** (*gen*) salt; **~ amoníaca** sal ammoniac; **~es** (**aromáticas**) smelling-salts; **~es de baño** bath-salts; **~ de cocina, ~ común, ~ gorda** kitchen salt, cooking salt; **~ de eno** (*CAm*) fruit-salts, liver-salts; **~ de fruta(s)** fruit-salts; **~ gema** rock salt; **~ de la Higuera** Epsom salts; **~ de mesa** table salt; **~ es minerales** mineral salts; **~ volátil** sal volatile.

(b) (*Esp: fig*) salt; (*gracia*) wit, wittiness; (*encanto*) charm, liveliness; ~ **de la tierra** salt of the earth; **esto es la ~ de la vida** this is the spice of life; **tiene mucha ~** he's a great wit, he's very amusing, he's good company; **ella tiene mucha ~** she's delightful, she's absolutely charming.

(**c**) (*fig*: *LAm*) misfortune, piece of bad luck.

sal² *V* **salir.**

sala *nf* (**a**) (*de casa*: *t* ~ **de estar**) drawing-room; (*cuarto grande*) (large) room; (*edificio público*) hall; (*Teat*) house, auditorium; (*Jur*) court; (*Med*) (hospital) ward, section; ~ **de alumbramiento** labour ward; ~ **de autoridades** (*Aer*) VIP lounge; ~ **de banderas** guardroom; ~ **capitular** chapterhouse, meeting room; ~ **de lo civil** civil court; ~ **de conciertos** concert-hall; ~ **de conferencias** lecture-room, lecture-hall; ~ **de lo criminal** criminal court; ~ **de embarque** (*Aer*) departure lounge; ~ **de espectáculos** concert-room, hall; (*teatro*) theatre; (*cine*) cinema; ~ **de espera** waiting-room; ~ **de fiestas** dance-hall; nightclub; ~ **de juntas** (*Com*) boardroom; ~ **de justicia** lawcourt; ~ **de lectura** reading room; ~ **de máquinas** (*Náut*) engine-room; ~ **de muestras** showroom; ~ **de operaciones** operating theatre; ~ **de partos** labour ward; ~ **de prensa** press room; ~ **de pruebas** fitting room; ~ **de recibo** parlour; ~ **de salidas** (*Aer*) departure lounge; ~ **de subastas** saleroom, auction-room; ~ **del trono** throneroom; ~ **de urgencias** casualty department; ~ **X** cinema showing 'adult' films; **deporte en ~** indoor sport, indoor game.

(**b**) (*muebles*) suite of drawing-room (*etc*) furniture.

salacidad *nf* salaciousness, prurience.

sala-cuna *nf, pl* **salas-cuna** (*Cono Sur*) day-nursery.

saladar *nm* salt marsh, saltings.

saladería *nf* (*Cono Sur*) meat-salting plant.

saladito *nm* (*Cono Sur*) nibble, (bar) snack.

salado *adj* (**a**) (*Culin*) salt, salty; savoury; *agua* salt; **muy ~** very salty, over-salted.

(**b**) (*Esp*: *fig*) (*gracioso*) witty, amusing; (*vivo*) lively; (*encantador*) charming, attractive, cute; *lenguaje* rich, racy; **es un tipo muy ~** he's a very amusing chap, he's a very lively sort; **¡qué ~!** how amusing!, (*iró*) very droll!, wasn't that clever of you?

(**c**) (*LAm*: *desgraciado*) unlucky, unfortunate.

(**d**) (*Cono Sur*) *artículo* dear, expensive; *precio* very high.

salamanca *nf* (*Cono Sur*) (**a**) (*cueva*) cave, grotto; (*lugar oscuro*) dark place. (**b**) (*brujería*) witchcraft, sorcery.

salamandra *nf* salamander.

salamanqués = **salmantino.**

salamanquesa *nf* lizard, gecko.

salame‡ *nm* (*Cono Sur*) idiot, thickhead*.

salami *nm* salami.

salar 1 *nm* (*And, Cono Sur*) (*mina*) salt mine; (*yacimiento*) salt pan.

2 [1a] *vt* (**a**) (*Culin*) *plato* to put salt in, add salt to.

(**b**) (*Culin*: *para conservar*) to salt, cure.

(**c**) (*And*) *ganado* to feed salt to.

(**d**) (*LAm*) (*arruinar*) to ruin, spoil; (*gafar*) to bring bad luck to, jinx*; (*maldecir*) to curse, wish bad luck on.

(**e**) (*CAm, Carib*: *deshonrar*) to dishonour.

salarial *adj* wage (*atr*); **reclamación ~** wage-claim.

salario *nm* wages, pay; (*LAm*) salary; ~ **base** basic wage; ~ **de hambre,** ~ **de miseria** starvation wage; pittance; ~ **inicial** starting salary; ~ **mínimo interprofesional** guaranteed minimum wage.

salaz *adj* salacious, prurient.

salazón *nf* (**a**) (*acto*) salting. (**b**) (*carne*) salted meat; (*pescado*) salted fish. (**c**) (*CAm, Carib, Méx*) bad luck.

salazonera *nf* salting plant (*for salting fish*).

salbeque *nm* (*CAm*) knapsack, backpack (*esp US*).

salbute *nm* (*Méx*) stuffed tortilla.

salceda *nf,* **salcedo** *nm* willow plantation.

salcochar [1a] *vt* to boil in salt water.

salchicha *nf* sausage.

salchichería *nf* pork butcher's (shop).

salchichón *nm* (salami-type) sausage.

salchipapa *nf* (*And*) (kind of) kebab.

saldar [1a] *vt* (**a**) *cuenta* to pay; *deuda* to pay off. (**b**) (*fig*) *diferencias* to settle, resolve; *V* **cuenta.** (**c**) *existencias* to sell off, sell up; *libros* to remainder.

saldo *nm* (**a**) (*acto*) settlement; payment.

(**b**) (*balance*) balance (*t fig*); ~ **acreedor,** ~ **a favor,** ~ **positivo** credit balance; ~ **activo** active balance; ~ **del banco,** ~ **de cuentas** bank statement; ~ **deudor,** ~ **en contra,** ~ **negativo** debit balance, adverse balance; ~ **final** final balance; ~ **vencido** balance due; **el ~ es a su favor** (*fig*) the balance is in his favour, on balance he comes off best.

(**c**) (*Com*: *liquidación*) clearance sale; **precio de ~** bargain price.

(**d**) (*restos*) remnant(s), remainder, left-over(s).

saledizo 1 *adj* projecting. **2** *nm* projection; overhang; **en ~** projecting, overhanging.

salera *nf* (*Cono Sur*) = **salina.**

salero *nm* (**a**) (*Culin*: *de mesa*) salt cellar. (**b**) (*reserva*) salt store. (**c**) (*Agr*) salt lick. (**d**) (*Esp*: *fig*) (*gracia*) wit, wittiness; (*encanto*) charm; (*sesapil*) sex appeal, allure, glamour. (**e**) (*Cono Sur*) = **salina.**

saleroso* *adj* = **salado** (**b**).

saleta *nf* small room; vestibule.

salida *nf* (**a**) (*acto*) leaving, going out, exit; emergence; (*viaje*) outing; (*Aer, Ferro etc*) departure; (*Astron*) rising; (*de gas etc*) leak, escape; (*Dep*) start; (*Golf*) drive; (*Teat*: *a escena*) appearance, entry, coming-on; (*Teat*: *para recibir aplausos*) curtain-call; **'S~s'** (*Ferro etc*) 'Departures'; ~ **al campo,** ~ **de campo** field trip; ~ **lanzada** running start, flying start; ~ **parada** standing start; ~ **del sol** sunrise; **oferta de ~** opening bid; **precio de ~** starting price; **la ~ fue triste** leaving was sad, our departure was sad; **a la ~ del trabajo** on leaving work; **a la ~ del teatro** as we (*etc*) came out of the theatre; **para García, dos orejas y ~ en hombros** (*Taur*) García won two ears and was carried out shoulder-high; **dar la ~** (*Dep*) to give the signal to start; **tomar la ~** (*Dep*) to line up (for the start); to start (*t fig*).

(**b**) (*Mil*) sally, sortie; (*Aer*) sortie.

(**c**) (*Naipes*) lead; **si la ~ es a trébol** if the lead is in clubs.

(**d**) (*Téc*: *producción*) output, production; (*Fin*: *inversion*) outlay; (*Inform*) output; ~ **impresa** (*Inform*) hard copy.

(**e**) (*lugar etc*) exit, way out; (*Mec*) outlet, vent, valve; (*Geog*) outlet; **'S~'** 'Exit', 'Way Out'; ~ **de artistas** (*Teat*) stage door; ~ **de emergencia,** ~ **de urgencia** emergency exit; ~ **de incendios** fire-exit; **dar ~ a su indignación** to vent one's anger; **tener ~ a** (*Arquit*) to lead to, open on to, (*Geog*) have an outlet to.

(**f**) (*fig*) (*solución*) way out; (*escapatoria*) pretext, loophole; (*truco*) dodge; **es una ~ cómoda** it's a simple solution; **no hay ~** there's no way out of it; **no tenemos otra ~ que firmarlo** there's nothing we can do but sign it, we have no option but to sign it; **dio con una ~ ingeniosa** he hit upon a clever way out; **es sólo una ~** it's only a pretext.

(**g**) (*fig*: *resultado*) issue, result, outcome.

(**h**) (*fig*: *argumento*) argument, counter-argument.

(**i**) (*Com*) (*venta*) sale; (*posibilidad de venta*) sales outlet, opening; **dar ~ a** to sell, place, find an outlet for; **tener ~** to sell well; **el bikini no tiene ~ en Groenlandia** bikinis don't sell in Greenland; **tener una ~ difícil** to be a hard sell; **tener una ~ fácil** to have a ready market, be a soft sell.

(**j**) (*saliente*) projection, protuberance.

(**k**) (*prenda*) ~ **de baño** bathing robe; beach robe; ~ **de cama** dressing gown; ~ **de teatro** evening wrap.

(**l**) (*Com*) (*de cuenta*: *gen*) item; (*cargo*) debit entry.

(**m**) (*chiste*) crack*, joke, witty remark; piece of repartee; **tener ~s** to be amusing, be full of wisecracks; to have amusing ideas.

(**n**) (*fig*: *comentario*) ~ **de pie de banco,** ~ **de tono,** ~ **de bombero,** ~ **de torero** inept remark, ill-judged remark.

salido *adj* (**a**) (*gen*) projecting, sticking out; *ojos* bulging. (**b**) (*Esp**: *cachondo*) randy*, lustful; **estar ~** to be in the mood, feel randy*; (*Zool*) **estar salida** to be on heat. (**c**) (*) (*osado*) daring; (*pey*) foolishly confident, reckless.

salidor *adj* (*Carib, Cono Sur*) (*andariego*) restless, roving; (*fiestero*) party-going; (*entusiasta*) lively, enthusiastic; (*Carib*: *buscapleitos*) argumentative.

saliente 1 *adj* (**a**) (*Arquit etc*) projecting, protuberant; raised, overhanging; *rasgo* prominent.

(**b**) (*fig*) salient; outstanding.

(**c**) *sol* rising.

(**d**) *miembro etc* outgoing, retiring.

2 *nm* projection; (*de carretera etc*) shoulder; (*Mil*) salient.

salina *nf* (*mina*) salt mine; (*depresión*) salt pan; **~s** (*fábrica*) saltworks; (*saladar*) salt flats.

salinera *nf* (*And, Carib*) = **salina.**

salinidad *nf* salinity; saltness, saltiness.

salinización *nf* (*acto*) salinization; (*estado*) salinity.

salinizar [1f] **1** *vt* to salinify, make salty. **2 salinizarse** *vr* to become salty.

salino *adj* saline; salty.

salir [3q] **1** *vi* (**a**) (*gen: persona*) to come out, go out (*de* of); to leave; to appear, emerge (*de* from); to get out (*de* of), escape (*de* from); **salimos a la calle** we went out into the street, we went out; ~ **a ver algo** to go out to see sth; ~ **de** to leave; **al** ~ **del cine** on leaving the cinema, when we (*etc*) came out of the cinema; **lo buscaremos al** ~ **de aquí** we'll look for it on the way out of here; **¿de dónde has salido?** where did you spring from?; ~ **del coma** to emerge from a coma; ~ **del enojo** to get over one's anger; ~ **de un apuro** to get out of a jam; ~ **de un puesto** to leave one's post, give up one's post; **este año sale de presidente** this year he ceases to be chairman, he gives up the chairmanship this year; **por fin salió de pobre** he finally left poverty behind him; ~ **para** to leave for.

(**b**) (*gen: objetos etc*) to come out; to emerge, appear; (*Astron*) to rise, come up; (*Bot*) to appear, come up, show; (*revista etc*) to come out, appear, be published; (*moda etc*) to come in; (*mancha, suciedad*) to come off, come out; **el agua sale aquí** the water comes out here; **le salió un diente** he cut a tooth; **esta calle sale a la plaza** this street comes out in the square, this street leads to the square; **el vino sale de la uva** wine comes from grapes; **el anillo no le sale del dedo** the ring won't come off her finger, she can't get the ring off her finger; **le salió la satisfacción a la cara** satisfaction showed in his face; **la noticia salió en el periódico de ayer** the news came out in yesterday's paper; **por fin salió la causa de todo ello** eventually the reason for the whole thing came to light; **¡ya salió aquello!** so that was it!, so now we know!; **cuando salga la ocasión** when the opportunity comes up (*o* arises, presents itself); **si sale un puesto apropiado** if the right job comes up; **no le sale novio** she doesn't seem to be able to get a young man; ~ **por la tele*** to appear on the telly*; **no sale ningún hombre en la peli*** there's not a man to be seen in the movie; ~ **adelante** to do well, make progress, get on.

(**c**) (*resultar etc*) to turn out; to prove, be, turn out to be; **salga lo que salga** (*o* **saliere**) come what may; regardless of the consequences; whatever turns up; **si sale cierto** if it proves (to be) true; **la prueba salió positiva** the test proved positive; **la criada nos salió muy trabajadora** the girl turned out to be very hard-working; **el conserje salió un sinvergüenza** the porter turned out to be a rogue; **si sale cara** (*al echar moneda*) if it comes down heads; **este crucigrama no me sale** this crossword won't work out, I can't do this crossword; **le salen los problemas sin dificultad** he works problems out with no trouble at all; ~ **a** (*precio*) to come to, amount to, work out at; **el traje le salió muy caro** the suit worked out very expensive for him; **esto nos va a** ~ **carísimo** this is going to cost us a fortune; **me sale a menor precio que a ti** it's working out cheaper for me than it is for you; ~ **ganando** to gain, be the gainer; to come out on top; to emerge as the winner; to gain on a deal; ~ **perdiendo** to lose, be the loser; to lose on a deal; ~ **bien** (*persona*) to succeed, make good; to do well; (*en examen*) to pass; (*fiesta etc*) to go off well; ~ **mal** (*persona*) to fail, do badly, come unstuck; (*en examen*) to fail; (*fiesta etc*) to be a failure; **les salió mal el proyecto** the scheme miscarried, the plan went badly for them; ~ **con la suya*** to get one's own way.

(**d**) (*Teat: t* ~ **a escena**) to enter, come on; **sale vestido de policía** he comes on dressed as a policeman; **'sale el rey'** (*acotación*) 'enter the king'.

(**e**) (*autobús, tren etc*) to leave, depart; (*Náut*) to sail; **sale a las 8** it leaves at 8; ~ **para** to leave for.

(**f**) ~ **con** (*novios*) to go out with, date (*US*); **salen juntos desde hace 2 años** they've been going out (*o* around) together for two years.

(**g**) (*huevo, pollito*) to hatch.

(**h**) (*Arquit etc*) to project, jut out; to stick out; to overhang; **sale un poco más cada día** it comes out a little further each day; **el balcón sale unos 2 metros** the balcony projects about 2 metres.

(**i**) (*número de lotería etc*) to come up, win (a prize); (*Pol: t* ~ **elegido**) to be elected, win; **salió alcalde por 3 votos** he was elected mayor by 3 votes.

(**j**) (*Naipes*) to lead; (*Ajedrez*) to have first move; (*Dep*) to start; ~ **con un as** to lead an ace; ~ **de triunfo** to lead a trump, play a trump.

(**k**) **y ahora sale con esto** (*decir*) and now he comes out with this.

(**l**) ~ **por uno** to come out in defence of sb, stick up for sb.

(**m**) ~ **con un propósito** to carry out a plan; ~ **con una pretensión** to succeed in a claim; **ella sale con todo el trabajo** she manages to keep up with all the work; she is fully up to all the work.

(**n**) (*parecerse*) ~ **a** to take after; **salió a su padre** he took after his father, he was exactly like his father.

(**o**) (*Fin*) ~ **a los gastos de uno** to meet (*o* pay, defray) sb's expenses; ~ **por uno** to back sb financially; to stand security for sb.

(**p**) (*Inform*) to quit, exit.

2 salirse *vr* (**a**) (*gen*) = **1**; **el camión se salió de la carretera** the lorry left (*o* ran off) the road; ~ **del tema** to wander from the point; to make a digression, go outside one's subject; **se salió del partido** he left the party; ~ **con la suya** to have it one's own way.

(**b**) (*animal, ave etc*) to escape (*de* from), get out (*de* of); (*aire, líquido etc*) to leak out; to overflow; (*al hervir*) to boil over; (*recipiente, río*) to leak; to overflow; **el barril se sale** (*Esp*) the barrel is leaking.

(**c**) (*Mec*) to become disconnected; ~ **de la vía** (*Ferro*) to leave the rails, jump the track.

(**d**) ~ **de costumbre** to break with custom, depart from tradition; ~ **de lo normal** to go beyond what is normal; ~ **de los límites** to go beyond the limits.

(**e**) ~ **de un compromiso** to get out of an obligation.

salita *nf* small room; (*Teat*) small auditorium.

salitre *nm* saltpetre, nitre.

salitrera *nf* (*fábrica*) nitre works; (*mina*) nitrate fields.

saliva *nf* saliva, spit; **gastar** ~ (*fig*) to waste one's breath (*en* on); **tragar** ~ to swallow one's feelings; to swallow hard.

salivación *nf* salivation.

salivadera *nf* (*Andalucía, Cono Sur*) spittoon, cuspidor (*US*).

salival *adj* salivary.

salivar [1a] *vi* to salivate; (*LAm*) to spit.

salivazo *nm* gobbet of spit; **arrojar un** ~ to spit.

salivera *nf* (*Cono Sur*) spittoon, cuspidor (*US*).

salmantino 1 *adj* of (*o* from) Salamanca. **2** *nm*, **salmantina** *nf* native (*o* inhabitant) of Salamanca; **los** ~**s** the people of Salamanca.

salmear [1a] *vi* to sing psalms.

salmo *nm* psalm.

salmodia *nf* (**a**) (*Ecl*) psalmody. (**b**) (*: *canturreo*) monotonous singing; drone, singsong.

salmodiar [1b] *vi* (**a**) (*Ecl*) to sing psalms. (**b**) (*) to drone, sing monotonously; to chant.

salmón *nm* salmon.

salmonela *nf* salmonella.

salmonelosis *nf* salmonellosis, salmonella food-poisoning.

salmonero *adj*: **río** ~ salmon river.

salmonete *nm* red mullet.

salmuera *nf* pickle, brine.

salobre *adj* salt, salty; *agua* salt, brackish.

saloma *nf* (*Náut*) sea shanty, sea song; (*de trabajo*) working song.

Salomé *nf* Salome.

Salomón *nm* Solomon.

salomónicamente *adv* with the wisdom of Solomon.

salomónico *adj*: **juicio** ~ judgement of Solomon.

salón *nm* (**a**) (*de casa*) drawing-room, lounge; (*Arte e Hist*) salon; (*sala pública*) hall, assembly-room; (*Náut*) saloon; (*de colegio etc*) common-room; (*Com*) show, trade fair, exhibition; ~ **de actos** assembly-room, hall; ~ **del automóvil** motor show; ~ **de baile** ballroom, dance-hall; ~ **de belleza** beauty-parlour; ~ **de demostraciones** showroom; ~ **de fiestas** dance-hall; ~ **de fumar** smoking room; ~ **de masaje** massage parlour; ~ **náutico** boat show; ~ **de los pasos perdidos*** waiting-room; ~ **de pintura** art exhibition, art gallery; ~ **de reuniones** conference room; ~ **de sesiones** assembly hall; (*Pol*) chamber; ~ **de té** tearoom; **juego de** ~ parlour game.

(**b**) (*muebles*) suite of drawing-room furniture.

saloncillo *nm* (*Teat etc*) private room; restroom.

salonero *n* (*And*) waiter.

salpicadera *nf* (*Méx*) mudguard.

salpicadero *nm* (*Aut*) dashboard.

salpicado 1 *adj* (**a**) ~ **de** splashed with, spattered with; sprinkled with; **un diseño** ~ **de puntos rojos** a pattern with red dotted about in it; **una llanura salpicada de granjas** a plain with farms dotted about on it, a plain dotted with farms.

(**b**) **un discurso** ~ **de citas latinas** a speech sprinkled with Latin quotations, a speech full of Latin quotations.

(**c**) (*Cono Sur, Méx*) *animal* spotted, dappled, mottled.

2 *nm* (**a**) (*acto*) splashing, spattering. (**b**) (*diseño*) sprinkle.

salpicadura *nf* (**a**) (*acto*) splashing, spattering; sprinkling; flecking. (**b**) (*mancha etc*) splash, spatter; sprinkle; dot, fleck. (**c**) (*fig*) spatter, peppering; sprinkling.

salpicar [1g] *vt* (**a**) (*de lodo, pintura etc*) to splash, spatter (*de* with); (*de agua etc*) to sprinkle (*de* with); *flores etc* to scatter, strew (about); *diseño, tela* to dot, fleck (*de* with); **~ un coche de barro** to splash a car with mud, splash mud over a car; **~ agua sobre el suelo** to sprinkle water on the floor; **la multitud de islas que salpican el océano** the host of islands dotted about the ocean; **este asunto salpica al gobierno** the government has got egg on its face over this affair.

(**b**) (*fig*) *conversación, oración etc* to sprinkle, interlard (*de* with); to pepper (*de* with).

salpicón *nm* (**a**) = **salpicadura**. (**b**) (*Culin*) salmagundi. (**c**) (*And: jugos mixtos*) cold mixed fruit juice.

(**d**) (*And, Cono Sur*) raw vegetable salad.

(**e**) **~ de mariscos** seafood cocktail.

salpimentar [1a] *vt* (**a**) (*Culin*) to season, add salt and pepper to. (**b**) (*fig*) to season, improve, sweeten (*de* with).

salpiquear [1a] *vt* (*And, Carib*) = **salpicar**.

salpresar [1a] *vt* to salt (down).

salpreso *adj* (*Culin*) salted, salt.

salpullido *nm* (**a**) (*Med*) rash, skin disease. (**b**) (*picadura*) fleabite; (*hinchazón*) swelling (from a bite). (**c**) (*fig*) problem, tricky situation.

salsa *nf* (**a**) (*gen*) sauce; (*para asado*) gravy; (*para postre*) sauce; (*para ensalada*) dressing; **~ de ají** chili sauce; **~ holandesa** hollandaise sauce; **~ mahonesa, ~ mayonesa** mayonnaise; **~ de soja** soy sauce; **~ de tomate** tomato sauce, ketchup; **~ tártara** tartar sauce; **cocerse en su propia ~** to stew in one's own juice; **estar en su ~** to be in one's element, be absolutely at home.

(**b**) (*fig*) seasoning, spice; appetizer; **es la ~ de la vida** it's the spice of life.

(**c**) (⁑: *ambiente*) scene*; **la ~ madrileña** the Madrid scene*.

(**d**) **música ~** salsa music.

salsera[1] *nf* sauce boat; gravy boat.

salsero 1 *adj* (*Mús*) salsa-loving; **ritmo ~** salsa rhythm. **2** *nm*, **salsera**[2] *nf* salsa music player.

salsifí *nm* salsify.

saltabanco *nm* (**a**) (*Hist*) quack, mountebank. (**b**) = **saltimbanqui**.

saltado *adj* (**a**) (*loza etc*) **estar ~** to be chipped, be damaged; **la corona tiene varias piedras saltadas** the crown has several stones missing. (**b**) *ojos* bulging.

saltador 1 *nm* (*comba*) skipping rope. **2** *nm*, **saltadora** *nf* (*atleta*) jumper; (*en agua*) diver; **~ de altura** high-jumper; **~ de longitud** long-jumper; **~ de pértiga** polevaulter.

saltadura *nf* chip.

saltamontes *nm invar* grasshopper.

saltante *adj* (*And, Cono Sur*) outstanding, noteworthy.

saltaperico *nm* (*Carib*) squib, firecracker.

saltar [1a] **1** *vt* (**a**) *muro, obstáculo etc* to jump (over), leap (over), vault.

(**b**) (*quitar*) to remove; **le saltó 3 dientes** he knocked out 3 of his teeth; **me has saltado un botón** you've torn off one of my buttons.

(**c**) (*fig: omitir*) to skip, miss out, leave out; **saltó un párrafo entero** he skipped a whole paragraph.

2 *vi* (**a**) (*persona etc*) to jump, leap, spring (*a* on to, into; *por, por encima de* over); to vault; to bound; (*niño*) to hop, skip; to gambol; **~ a la silla** to leap into the saddle; **~ al agua** to jump (*o* dive, plunge) into the water; **~ de la cama** to leap out of bed; **~ de alegría** to jump with joy, jump for joy; **~ en una silla** to jump up on (to) a chair; **~ en tierra** to leap ashore; **~ en paracaídas** to jump, come down by parachute; **~ por una ventana** to jump out of a window, leap from a window; **~ sobre uno** to pounce on sb; **hacer ~ un caballo** to jump a horse, make a horse jump.

(**b**) (*Inform*) to jump; (*fig: en discurso etc*) to skip about, skip from one subject to another.

(**c**) (*pelota*) to bounce, fly up; (*resorte*) to unroll suddenly; (*líquido*) to spurt up, shoot up; (*lágrimas*) to well up; (*cantidad, cifra*) to leap (up); **~ a la mente** to leap to one's mind; **estar a la que salta** to watch out for an opportunity, look for an opening; to live for the day; **la mayoría ha saltado a 900 votos** the majority has shot up (*o* leaped up) to 900 votes.

(**d**) (*desprenderse*) (*pieza*) to come off, fly off; (*corcho*) to blow out, pop out; (*astilla etc*) to fly off; (*botón*) to come off; (*madera etc*) to crack, snap, break; (*resorte*) to break; (*recipiente*) to crack; (*explosivo*) to explode, burst; **hacer ~ un edificio** to blow a building up; **hacer ~ una trampa** to spring a trap; **hacer ~ la banca** to break the bank.

(**e**) (*fig: de ira*) to explode, blow up.

(**f**) **~ con una patochada** (*fig*) to come out with a ridiculous (*o* foolish) remark.

(**g**) (*fig*) **~ de un puesto** to surrender a post, give up a job; **hacer ~ a uno de un puesto** to boot sb out of a job.

(**h**) **~ atrás** (*Bio*) to revert (to type).

3 saltarse *vr* (**a**) **~ un párrafo** to skip a paragraph; **me he saltado dos renglones** I've left out a couple of lines; **~ un semáforo en rojo*** to jump (*o* shoot) the lights*; *V* **1** (**c**).

(**b**) **~ todas las reglas** to break all the rules.

(**c**) (*pieza, botón etc*) to come off, fly off; *V* **2** (**d**).

saltarín 1 *adj* restless; full of movement, always on the go; (*pey*) unstable, volatile. **2** *nm*, **saltarina** *nf* dancer.

salteado *adj* (*Culin*) sauté.

salteador *nm* (*t* **~ de caminos**) holdup man; (*Hist*) highwayman, footpad.

salteamiento *nm* highway robbery, holdup.

saltear [1a] **1** *vt* (**a**) (*atracar*) to hold up; (*robar*) to rob, assault, attack; (*sorprender*) to take by surprise.

(**b**) (*fig: duda etc*) to assail.

(**c**) (*Culin*) to sauté.

2 *vi* to work (*etc*) fitfully, do sth by fits and starts; **lo leyó salteando** he read bits of it here and there.

salteña *nf* (*And*) meat pie.

salterio *nm* (**a**) (*Ecl*) psalter; (*Bib*) Book of Psalms. (**b**) (*Mús*) psaltery.

saltimbanqui *nm* (*malabarista*) juggler; (*acróbata*) acrobat; (*volatinero*) tightrope walker, mountebank; (*fig*) playboy.

salto *nm* (**a**) (*gen*) jump, leap; bound, spring; vault; hop, skip; (*al agua*) jump, dive, plunge; (*sobre víctima*) pounce; **~ a ciegas, ~ en el vacío** leap in the dark; **el gran ~ (hacia) adelante** the great leap forward; **un vuelo de tres ~s** (*Aer*) a flight in three hops; **a ~s** by jumping, in a series of jumps; (*fig*) by fits and starts; **avanzar a ~s** to jump along, go hopping along; **de un ~** at one bound, with one jump; **subió de un ~** he jumped up; **bajó de un ~** he jumped down; **en un ~** (*fig*) in a jiffy*; **en dos ~s estoy de vuelta*** I'll be back in a moment; **dar un ~, pegar un ~** to jump (with fright *etc*); **dar un ~ por la casa de alguien** to drop by sb's house; **me daba ~s el corazón** my heart was pounding; **hacer el ~*** to be unfaithful; **pegar el ~ a*** to be unfaithful to, cuckold; **vivir a ~ de mata** (*pobre*) to live from hand to mouth, keep one's head just above water; (*fugitivo*) to keep one jump ahead of justice; **escapar a ~ de mata** to flee headlong; **hacer algo a ~ de mata** to do sth thoughtlessly, do sth unmethodically; **el libro fue su ~ a la fama** the book marked his leap to fame.

(**b**) (*Dep: acto*) jump; (*al agua*) dive; **~ de altura** high jump; high dive; **~ de ángel** swallow-dive; **~ de cabeza** header; **~ de carpa** jack-knife dive; **~ a la** (*o* **con**) **garrocha, ~ con** (*o* **de**) **pértiga** polevault; **~ de longitud** long-jump; **~ mortal** somersault; **~ ornamental** fancy dive; **~ de palanca** high dive; **~ de trampolín** springboard dive; **triple ~** triple jump; hop, step and jump.

(**c**) **~ atrás** (*Bio*) throwback, reversion to type.

(**d**) (*Geol*) fault; chasm, rift.

(**e**) (*fig*) (*diferencia, vacío*) gap; jump; (*sección etc omitida*) passage skipped, part missed; **aquí hay un ~ de 50 versos** there is a gap here of 50 lines; **de él al otro hermano hay un ~ de 9 años** there is a gap of 9 years between him and the other brother, there are 9 years between him and the other brother.

(**f**) (*barricada*) barricade; (*barrera*) human barrier, line; (*Dep: barra etc*) jump; (*cerca*) fence; (*valla*) hurdle, obstacle; **~ de agua** water-jump.

(**g**) **~ de agua** (*Geog*) waterfall, cascade; (*Tec*) chute.

(**h**) **~ de cama** négligé, peignoir.

(**i**) **a** (*o* **al**) **~** (*Carib*) in cash.

(**j**) (*Inform*) jump; **~ de línea** line feed; **~ de línea automática** wordwrap; **~ de página** form feed.

saltón 1 *adj* (**a**) *ojos* bulging, popping; *dientes* prominent, protruding.

(**b**) (*LAm*) undercooked, half-cooked.

2 *nm* grasshopper; (*Méx*) young locust.

saltona *nf* (*Cono Sur*) young locust.

salubre *adj* healthy, salubrious.

salubridad *nf* (**a**) (*sanidad*) healthiness, salubrity, salubriousness. (**b**) (*estadística*) health statistics.

salud *nf* (**a**) (*Med*) health; state of health; ~ **ambiental** environmental health; ~ **mental** mental health; ~ **ocupacional** health at work; **estar bien de** ~ to be in good health; **estar mal de** ~ to be in bad health; **¿cómo vamos de ~?** how are we today?; **mejorar de** ~ to improve in health, get better; **devolver la ~ a uno** to give sb back his health, restore sb to health.

(**b**) (*fig*) health; welfare, wellbeing; **la ~ moral de la nación** the country's moral welfare; **curarse en** ~ to see one's own defects, put one's own house in order; (*precaverse*) to be prepared, take precautions.

(**c**) (*brindis*) **¡~!, ¡a su ~!, ¡~ y pesetas!** good health!, here's to you!, here's luck!; **beber a la ~ de** to drink to the health of.

(**d**) (*LAm*: *al estornudar*) **¡~!** bless you!

(**e**) (*Rel*) salvation; state of grace.

saludable *adj* (**a**) (*Med*) healthy. (**b**) (*fig*) salutary, good, beneficial; **un aviso ~** a salutary warning.

saludador(a) *nm/f* quack doctor.

saludar [1a] *vt* (**a**) (*gen*) to greet; (*hacer reverencia a*) to bow to; (*quitarse el sombrero a*) take off one's hat to; **ir a ~ a uno** to go and say hullo to sb, drop in to see sb; **salude de mi parte a X** give my regards to X; **no ~ a uno** to cut sb, refuse to acknowledge sb.

(**b**) (*en carta*) **le saluda atentamente** yours faithfully.

(**c**) (*Mil*) to salute.

(**d**) (*fig*) to salute, hail, welcome.

saludo *nm* (**a**) (*gen*) greeting; bow; **negar el ~ a uno** to cut sb, ignore sb.

(**b**) (*en carta*) **~s** best wishes, greetings, regards; **un ~ afectuoso, un ~ cordial** yours sincerely; **os envía muchos ~s** he sends you warmest regards; **atentos ~s** best wishes; **un ~ cariñoso a Jane** warm regards to Jane; **~s respetuosos** respectfully yours.

(**c**) (*Mil*) salute.

Salustio *nm* Sallust.

salutación *nf* greeting, salutation.

salva[1] *nf* (**a**) (*Mil etc*) salute, salvo; (*fig*: *de aplausos*) storm, volley; **~ de advertencia** warning shots. (**b**) (*saludo*) greeting. (**c**) (*promesa*) oath, solemn promise.

salva[2] *nf* (*bandeja*) salver, tray.

salvabarros *nm invar* mudguard.

salvación *nf* (**a**) (*gen*) rescue, delivery (*de* from), salvation. (**b**) (*Rel*) salvation; **~ eterna** eternal salvation.

salvada *nf* (*LAm*) = **salvación** (**a**).

salvado *nm* bran.

Salvador *nm* (**a**) **el ~** (*Rel*) the Saviour. (**b**) **El ~** (*Geog*) El Salvador.

salvador(a) *nm/f* rescuer, saviour; (*de playa*) life-saver.

salvadoreñismo *nm* word (*o* phrase *etc*) peculiar to El Salvador.

salvadoreño, -a *adj, nm/f* Salvadorian.

salvaguardar [1a] *vt* to safeguard; (*Inform*) to backup, make a backup copy of.

salvaguardia *nf* safe-conduct; (*fig*) safeguard.

salvajada *nf* savage deed, piece of savagery; barbarity, atrocity; brutal act.

salvaje 1 *adj* (**a**) (*Bot, Zool etc*) wild; *huelga* wildcat; *construcción etc* unauthorized, uncontrolled; *tierra* wild, uncultivated. (**b**) *pueblo, tribu etc* savage. (**c**) (*LAm**) terrific*, smashing*. **2** *nmf* savage (*t fig*).

salvajería *nf* = **salvajada.**

salvajez *nf* = **salvajismo.**

salvajino *adj* (**a**) (*gen*) wild, savage. (**b**) **carne salvajina** meat from a wild animal.

salvajismo *nm* savagery.

salvamanteles *nm invar* tablemat.

salvamento *nm* (**a**) (*acto*) rescue; delivery; salvage; (*fig*) salvation; **de ~** life-saving (*atr*); rescue (*atr*); **bote de ~** lifeboat; **operaciones de ~** rescue operations; **~ y socorrismo** life-saving.

(**b**) (*refugio*) place of safety, refuge; haven.

salvaplatos *nm invar* tablemat.

salvar [1a] **1** *vt* (**a**) *persona etc* to save, rescue (*de* from); *barco* to salvage; *apariencias* to save, keep up; **me salvó la vida** he saved my life; **apenas salvaron nada del incendio** they hardly rescued anything from the fire; **~ a uno de tener que** + *infin* to save sb from having to + *infin*.

(**b**) (*Rel*) to save.

(**c**) *barrera, línea, montañas, río etc* to cross; *rápidos* to shoot; *arroyo* to jump across, jump over, clear; *dificultad* to overcome, resolve; *obstáculo* to get round, negotiate.

(**d**) *distancia* to cover, do, travel; **el tren salva la distancia en 2 horas** the train covers the distance in 2 hours.

(**e**) (*excluir*) to except, exclude.

(**f**) (*árbol, edificio etc*) to rise above.

(**g**) (*nivel del agua etc*) to reach, rise as high as; **el agua salvaba el peldaño más alto** the water came up to the topmost step.

(**h**) (*Cono Sur*) *examen* to pass.

2 salvarse *vr* (**a**) to save o.s., escape (*de* from); **¡sálvese el que** (*o* **quien**) **pueda!** every man for himself!

(**b**) (*Rel*) to save one's soul, be saved.

salvavidas 1 *nm invar* lifebelt. **2** *adj* life-saving (*atr*); **bote ~** lifeboat; **cinturón ~** lifebelt; **chaleco ~** life-jacket.

salvedad *nf* reservation, qualification, proviso; **con la ~ de que** ... with the proviso that ...; **hacer una ~** to make a qualification.

Salvi *nm forma familiar de* **Salvador.**

salvia *nf* (*Bot*) sage.

salvilla *nf* salver, tray; (*Cono Sur*) cruet.

salvo 1 *adj* safe; *V* **sano.**

2 *adv y prep* (**a**) except (for), save; barring; **~ aquellos que ya contamos** except for those we have already counted; **de todos los países ~ de Ruritania** from all countries except Ruritania.

(**b**) **a ~** safely; out of danger; **a ~ de** safe from; **en ~** out of danger, in a safe place; **dejar algo a ~** to make an exception of sth, leave sth out of it; **para dejar a ~ su reputación** in order to keep his reputation safe; **poner algo a ~** to put sth in a safe place, put sth out of harm's way; **ponerse a ~** to escape, reach safety; **nada ha quedado a ~ de sus ataques** nothing has been safe from his attacks.

3 ~ que, ~ si *conj* unless ...; except that ...; **iré ~ que me avises al contrario** I'll go unless you tell me not to.

salvoconducto *nm* safe-conduct.

salvohonor *nm* (*hum*) backside.

samaritano, -a *adj, nm/f* Samaritan; **buen ~** good Samaritan.

samaruco *nm* (*Cono Sur*) hunter's pouch, gamebag.

samba *nf* samba.

sambenito *nm* (*Hist*) sanbenito; (*fig*) dishonour, disgrace, infamy; **le colgaron el ~ de fascista** they branded him a fascist; **le colgaron el ~ de haberlo hecho** they attached to him the stigma of having done it; **echar el ~ a otro** to pin the blame on somebody else; **quedó con el ~ toda la vida** he was disgraced for life.

sambumbia *nf* (**a**) (*And, Carib, Méx*: *bebida*) watery drink (*: *mazamorra*) mush, hash.

(**b**) (*Carib*) drink of sugar-cane syrup, water and peppers; (*Méx*: *de ananás*) pineapple drink; (*Méx*: *hordiate*) barleywater drink.

(**c**) (*And*: *trasto*) old thing, battered object; **volver algo ~** to smash sth to pieces.

sambutir [3a] *vt* (*Méx*) (‡: *meter a fuerza*) to stick in, stuff in; (*: *hundir*) to sink in, shove in.

samotana *nf* (*CAm*) row, uproar, racket.

samovar *nm* samovar.

sampablera *nf* (*Carib*: *jaleo*) racket, row.

sampán *nm* sampan.

Samuel *nm* Samuel.

samurear [1a] *vi* (*Carib*) to walk with bowed head.

San *nm* (*apocopated form of* **santo**) saint; **San Juan** Saint John, (*escrito en general*) St John; **cerca de San Martín** near St Martin's (church); **se casarán por San Juan** they'll get married sometime in midsummer (*estrictamente*, round about St John's Day); *V t* **santo, Juan,** *etc.*

sanable *adj* curable, susceptible to treatment.

sanaco *adj* (*Carib*) silly.

sanalotodo *nm* cure-all, universal remedy.

sanamente *adv* healthily; wholesomely.

sananería *nf* (*Carib*) stupid remark, silly comment.

sanar [1a] **1** *vt* to heal; to cure (*de* of). **2** *vi* (*persona*) to recover, get well; (*herida*) to heal.

sanativo *adj* healing, curative.

sanatorio *nm* sanatorium; (private) nursing-home.

San Bernardo *nm* St Bernard.

sanción *nf* sanction; punishment, penalty; **sanciones comerciales** trade sanctions; **~ disciplinaria** punishment, disciplinary measure; **sanciones económicas** economic sanctions; **imponer sanciones** to impose sanctions; **levantar sanciones a uno** to lift sanctions against sb.

sancionable *adj* punishable.

sancionado, -a *nm/f* guilty person; **los ~s** (*Pol*) those who have been punished for a political offence, those guilty of political crimes.

sancionar [1a] *vt* (**a**) (*castigar*) to sanction; (*Jur*) to

penalize. (**b**) (*permitir*) sancionar, permitir.
sancionatorio *adj* (*Jur*) penal, penalty (*atr*).
sancochado *nm* (*And*) = **sancocho**.
sancochar [1a] *vt* to parboil; (*CAm, Méx*) to throw together, rustle up*.
sancocho *nm* (**a**) (*comida malguisada*) undercooked food; (*carne*) parboiled meat. (**b**) (*LAm*: *guisado*) stew (of meat, yucca *etc*). (**c**) (*CAm, Carib, Méx*: *lío*) fuss; confusion; row (**d**) (*Carib*: *bazofia*) pigswill.
San Cristóbal *nm* (**a**) (*Ecl*) St Christopher. (**b**) (*Geog*) St Kitts.
sancho *nm* (**a**) (*prov*) pig. (**b**) (*Méx*: *carnero*) ram, (*cordero*) lamb; (*macho cabrío*) billygoat; (*animal abandonado*) orphan animal, suckling.
sandalia *nf* sandal.
sándalo *nm* sandal, sandalwood.
sandez *nf* (**a**) (*cualidad*) foolishness. (**b**) (*acto, dicho*) stupid thing, piece of stupidity; **decir sandeces** to talk nonsense; **fue una ~ obrar así** it was silly to do that.
sandía *nf* watermelon.
sandío *adj* foolish, silly, stupid.
sanduche *nm* (*And*) sandwich.
sandunga *nf* (**a**) (*) (*atractivo*) charm; (*gracia*) wit. (**b**) (*And, Carib, Cono Sur, Méx*: *juerga*) party, binge*.
sandunguero* *adj* charming; witty, amusing.
sandwich [saŋ'gwitʃ, sam'bitʃ] *nm, pl* **sandwichs** *o* **sandwiches** sandwich.
sandwichera *nf* toasted sandwich maker.
saneamiento *nm* (**a**) (*alcantarillado*) draining; drainage (system), sanitation; sewerage.
(**b**) (*fig*) remedy; ending; cleaning-up.
(**c**) (*garantía*) guarantee; insurance.
(**d**) (*compensación*) compensation, indemnification.
(**e**) (*Com, Fin*) restructuring, reorganization, streamlining.
sanear [1a] *vt* (**a**) *tierra* to drain; *casa* to remove the dampness from; (*Téc*) to instal drainage (*o* sewerage) in, lay sewers in.
(**b**) (*fig*) *daño* to remedy, repair; *abuso* to end; *centro de vicio* to clean up, purge.
(**c**) (*garantizar*) to guarantee; (*asegurar*) to insure.
(**d**) (*Jur*) *comprador* to compensate, indemnify.
(**e**) (*Com, Fin*) *capital, compañía* to restructure, reorganize, streamline.
sanfasón: a la ~ *adv* (*LAm*) unceremoniously, informally; (*pey*) carelessly.
sanfermines *nmpl* festivities in celebration of San Fermín (*Pamplona*).
sanforizar [1f] ® *vt* to Sanforize ®.
sango *nm* (*And Culin*) yucca and maize pudding.
sangradera *nf* (**a**) (*Med*) lancet. (**b**) (*Agr*: *acequia*) irrigation channel; (*desagüe*) sluice, outflow.
sangradura *nf* (**a**) (*Anat*) inner angle of the elbow. (**b**) (*Med*) (*incisión*) cut made into a vein; (*sangría*) bleeding, blood-letting. (**c**) (*Cono Sur*) outlet, drainage channel.
sangrante *adj* (**a**) *herida, persona* bleeding. (**b**) (*fig*) *injusticia etc* crying, flagrant.
sangrar [1a] **1** *vt* (**a**) (*Med*) to bleed.
(**b**) (*Agr etc*) *tierra* to drain, drain the water from; *agua* to drain off, let out, allow to drain away; *árbol* to tap; *horno* to tap.
(**c**) (*Tip*) to indent.
(**d**) (*) to filch, filch from.
2 *vi* (**a**) (*t fig*) to bleed.
(**b**) (*fig*) **estar sangrando** (*ser actual*) to be still fresh, be very new still; (*ser obvio*) to be obvious; **aún sangra la humillación** the humiliation still rankles.
sangre *nf* blood (*t fig*); **~ azul** blue blood; **~ fría** sangfroid, coolness; (*pey*) callousness; **a ~ fría** in cold blood, callously; **mala ~** bad blood; **pura ~** (*nmf*) thoroughbred; **~ vital** lifeblood; **a ~** by animal power, by horsepower; **a ~ caliente** in the heat of the moment; **a ~ y fuego** by fire and sword; **es de ~ de reyes** he has royal blood, he is of the blood royal; **fue de ~ de conquistadores** he was descended from conquistadors; **le bulle la ~ (en las venas)** he is full of youthful vigour, he is bursting with energy; **esto chorrea ~** this cries out to heaven; **chupar la ~ a uno** (*fig*) to exploit sb, suck out sb's lifeblood; to bleed sb white; **dar su ~** to give one's blood; **echar ~** to bleed (*de* from); **echar ~ por los ojos** to be furious; **encender** (*o* **quemar, revolver**) **la ~ a uno** to infuriate sb, make sb's blood boil; **freír la ~ a uno*** to rile sb*, needle sb*; **hacerse mala ~** to get upset; to fret; **se me heló la ~** my blood froze, my blood ran cold; **llegar a la ~** to come to blows; **la ~ no llegará al río** it's not as bad as all that; **sin que la ~ llegue al río** without disastrous results, without going to extremes; **no creo que llegue la ~ al río** I don't think it will be too disastrous; **lo lleva en la sangre** it runs in her blood; **sudar ~** to undergo hardships; to slog, toil; **tener la ~ gorda** (*o* **de horchata**), **no tener ~ en las venas** (*ser frío*) to be excessively phlegmatic, be unemotional, be stone cold; (*ser pesado*) to be dull, be boring.
sangregorda* *nmf* bore.
sangría *nf* (**a**) (*Med*) bleeding, bloodletting; **~ suelta** excessive flow of blood; (*fig*) outflow, drain, continuous loss.
(**b**) (*Anat*) inner angle of the elbow.
(**c**) (*Agr*) (*acequia*) irrigation channel; (*desagüe*) outlet, outflow; (*zanja*) ditch; (*drenaje*) drainage.
(**d**) (*Téc*) (*acto*) tapping (*of a furnace*); (*metal fundido*) stream of molten metal.
(**e**) (*Culin*) sangría, (*aprox*) fruit cup.
(**f**) (*Tip*) indentation.
sangrientamente *adv* bloodily.
sangriento *adj* (**a**) *herida* bleeding.
(**b**) *arma, ropa etc* bloody, bloodstained, gory.
(**c**) *batalla* bloody.
(**d**) (*liter*) blood-red.
(**e**) (*fig*) *injusticia etc* crying, flagrant; *insulto* deadly; *chiste* cruel.
sangrigordo *adj* (*Carib*) (*aburrido*) tedious, boring; (*insolente*) rude, insolent.
sangriligero *adj* (*LAm*), **sangriliviano** *adj* (*LAm*) pleasant, nice, congenial.
sangripesado *adj* (*LAm*), **sangrón** *adj* (*Carib, Méx*‡), **sangruno** *adj* (*Carib*) (*grosero*) rude; (*desagradable*) unpleasant, nasty; (*aburrido*) boring, tiresome; (*obstinado*) obstinate, pig-headed; (*triste*) miserable.
sanguarañas *nfpl* (*And**) circumlocutions, evasions.
sangüich *nm* (*Esp*) sandwich.
sanguijuela *nf* leech (*t fig*).
sanguinario *adj* bloodthirsty, cruel, callous.
sanguíneo *adj* (**a**) (*Anat*) blood (*atr*); **vaso ~** blood vessel. (**b**) (*fig*: *color*) blood-red.
sanguinolento *adj* (**a**) *herida* bleeding; *ropa etc* bloody, blood-stained; streaked (*o* tinged) with blood; *ojos* bloodshot.
(**b**) (*Culin*) underdone, rare.
(**c**) (*fig*: *color*) blood-red.
sanidad *nf* (**a**) (*gen*) health, healthiness; (*fig*) salubrity.
(**b**) (*asunto público*) public health; (*aguas residuales etc*) sanitation; (**Ministerio de**) **S~** Ministry of Health; **~ pública** public health (department); **inspector de ~, oficial de ~** sanitary inspector.
sanitaría *nf* (*Cono Sur*) plumber's (shop).
sanitario 1 *adj condiciones* sanitary; *centro etc* health (*atr*); sanitation (*atr*). **2** *nm* (**a**) (*Med*) stretcher bearer. (**b**) **~s** *pl* bathroom fittings. (**c**) **~s** *pl* (*wáter*) toilets; (*Méx*) toilet.
San Lorenzo *nm*: **el** (**Río**) **~** the St Lawrence.
sano *adj* (**a**) (*Med etc*) healthy; fit; *madera, órgano etc* sound; *fruta* good; **cortar por lo ~** to take extreme measures, go right to the root of the trouble; to cut one's losses.
(**b**) *clima etc* healthy; *comida* good, wholesome.
(**c**) *objeto* whole, intact, undamaged; **~ y salvo** safe and sound; **esa silla no es muy sana** that chair is not too strong; **no ha quedado plato ~ en toda la casa** there wasn't a plate left whole (*o* unbroken) in the house.
(**d**) (*fig*) (*sin vicios*) (morally) healthy, wholesome; *doctrina, enseñanza* sound; *deseo* earnest, sincere; *objetivo etc* worthy.
sansalvadoreño 1 *adj* of San Salvador. **2** *nm*, **sansalvadoreña** *nf* native (*o* inhabitant) of San Salvador; **los ~s** the people of San Salvador.
sánscrito *adj, nm* Sanskrit.
sanseacabó*: **y ~** and that's the end of it, and there's no more to be said.
Sansón *nm* Samson; **es un ~** he's tremendously strong.
santa *nf* saint; *V* **santo.**
Santa Bárbara *nf* Santa Barbara.
santabárbara *nf* (*Náut*) magazine.
santamente *adv*: **vivir ~** to live a saintly (*o* holy) life.
santanderino (*Esp*) **1** *adj* of Santander. **2** *nm*, **santanderina** *nf* native (*o* inhabitant) of Santander; **los ~s** the people of Santander.
santateresa *nf* (*Ent*) praying mantis.
santería *nf* (**a**) (*LAm*: *tienda*) *shop selling religious images, prints etc.* (**b**) (*) = **santidad.** (**c**) (*Carib Rel*) *religion of*

African origin.

santero 1 *nm* (*LAm*) *maker* (*o seller*) *of religious images, prints etc.* **2** *nm,* **santera** *nf* person excessively devoted to the saints.

Santiago *nm* St James.

santiaguero, -a* *nm/f* (*Cono Sur*) faith-healer.

santiagués = **santiaguino.**

santiaguino 1 *adj* of Santiago de Chile. **2** *nm,* **santiaguina** *nf* native (*o* inhabitant) of Santiago de Chile; **los ~s** the people of Santiago de Chile.

santiamén* *nm*: **en un ~** in a jiffy*, in no time at all.

santidad *nf* holiness, sanctity; saintliness; **su S~** His Holiness.

santificación *nf* sanctification.

santificar [1g] *vt* (**a**) (*gen*) to sanctify, make holy, hallow; *lugar* to consecrate; *fiesta* to keep; **santificado sea Tu Nombre** hallowed be Thy Name. (**b**) (*: *perdonar*) to forgive.

santiguada *nf* sign of the Cross; act of crossing oneself.

santiguar [1i] **1** *vt* (**a**) (*persignar*) to make the sign of the Cross over; to bless.

(**b**) (*LAm*: *sanear*) to heal (by blessing).

(**c**) (*: *pegar*)to slap, hit.

2 santiguarse *vr* (**a**) to cross o.s., make the sign of the Cross.

(**b**) (*: *exagerar*) to make a great fuss, react in an exaggerated way, overdo the emotion.

santísimo *adj superl* (most) holy; **hacer la santísima a uno*** (*jorobar*) to drive sb up the wall*; (*perjudicar*) to do sb down*.

santo 1 *adj* (**a**) (*gen*) holy; sacred; *tierra* holy, consecrated; *persona* saintly; *mártir* blessed.

(**b**) (*fig*) *remedio etc* wonderful, miraculous.

(**c**) (*: *total*) utter, complete; blessed; **~ y bueno** well and good; **todo el ~ día** the whole livelong day; the whole blessed day; **y él con su santa calma** and he utterly unmoved, and he so completely calm; *V* **voluntad** *etc.*

2 *nm* (**a**) (*Ecl*) saint; **~ patrón, ~ titular** patron saint; **S~ Domingo** (*Ecl*) St Dominic; (*Geog*) Santo Domingo, Dominican Republic; **S~ Tomás** St Thomas; *V t* **San.**

(**b**) (*locuciones*) **¿a qué ~?** what on earth for?; **¿a ~ de qué ...?** why on earth ...?; **¡por todos los ~s!** for pity's sake!; **no es ~ de mi devoción** I'm not very keen on him; **alzarse con el ~ y la limosna*** to clear off with the whole lot*; **comerse los ~s*** to be terribly devout; **desnudar a un ~ para vestir otro** to rob Peter to pay Paul; **se le fue el ~ al cielo** he forgot what he was about to say (*o* do *etc*), he clean forgot; he was day-dreaming; **¡que se te va el ~ al cielo!** you're miles away!; **llegar y besar el ~** to pull it off at the first attempt; **nacer con el ~ de espaldas** to be born unlucky; **poner a uno como un ~*** to give sb a telling-off*; **quedarse para vestir ~s** to be left on the shelf; **tener el ~ de cara*** to have tremendous luck*; **tener el ~ de espaldas*** to have bad luck.

(**c**) (*fig*: *persona*) saint; **es un ~** he's a saint; **estaba hecho un ~** he was terribly sweet.

(**d**) (*día*) saint's day; **~ y seña** (*Mil*) password; (*fig*) watchword, slogan; **mañana es mi ~** tomorrow is my saint's day, tomorrow is my name day (*celebrated in Spain etc as equivalent to a birthday*).

(**e**) (*Cono Sur Cos*) patch, darn.

santón* *nm* (*hum*) big shot*, big wheel*.

santoral *nm* calendar of saints' days.

santuario *nm* (**a**) (*Rel*) sanctuary, shrine; (*lugar seguro*) sanctuary. (**b**) (*And, Carib*) (*ídolo*) native idol; (*tesoro*) buried treasure.

santulario *adj* (*Cono Sur*) = **santurrón.**

santurrón 1 *adj* sanctimonious; hypocritical. **2** *nm,* **santurrona** *nf* sanctimonious person; hypocrite.

saña *nf* (**a**) (*furor*) anger, rage, fury; (*crueldad*) cruelty; (*fig*) fury, viciousness. (**b**) (‡: *cartera*) wallet.

sañero‡ *nm* (*Esp*) pickpocket.

sañoso *adj* = **sañudo.**

sañudamente *adv* angrily, furiously; cruelly; viciously.

sañudo *adj* furious, enraged; cruel; *golpe etc* vicious, cruel.

sapaneco *adj* (*CAm*) plump, chubby.

sáparo *nm* (*And*) wicker basket.

sapo¹ *nm* (**a**) (*Zool*) toad; (*fig*: *Zool*) small animal, bug, creature; (*persona*) ugly creature; thick-set individual; **echar ~s y culebras** to produce a stream of abuse, curse and swear.

(**b**) (*prov, LAm*) *game of throwing coins into the mouth of an iron toad.*

(**c**) (*CAm, Carib*‡: *soplón*) informer, grass‡; (*Cono Sur*‡) soldier.

sapo² *adj* (*And, CAm, Cono Sur*: *astuto*) cunning, sly; (*Cono Sur*: *hipócrita*) hypocritical, two-faced; (*CAm, Carib*) telltale, gossipy.

saporro *adj* (*And, CAm*) chubby, plump.

sapotear [1a] *vt* (*And*) to finger, handle.

saque *nm* (**a**) (*acto*: *Tenis*) service, serve; **~ de banda** (*Fútbol*) throw-in, (*Rugby*) line-out; **~ de castigo** penalty kick; **~ de esquina** corner-kick; **~ de falta** free kick; **~ de honor** guest appearance; **~ inicial** kick-off; **~ libre** free kick; **~ de mano** (*LAm Dep*) throw-in; **~ de portería, ~ de puerta** goal-kick.

(**b**) (*Tenis*: *persona*) server.

(**c**) **tener buen ~** to eat heartily, be a good trencherman.

saqueador *nm* looter.

saquear [1a] *vt* (*Mil*) to sack; (*robar*) to loot, plunder, pillage; (*fig*) to rifle, ransack; to turn upside down.

saqueo *nm* sacking; looting, plundering; (*fig*) rifling, ransacking.

saquito *nm* small bag; sachet; **~ de papel** paper bag.

S.A.R. *abr de* **Su Alteza Real** His (*o* Her) Royal Highness, H.R.H.

sarampión *nm* measles.

sarao *nm* (**a**) (*fiesta*) soirée, evening party. (**b**) (*: *lío*) fuss, to-do*.

sarape *nm* (*Méx*) blanket.

sarasa‡ *nm* pansy‡, fairy‡.

saraviado *adj* (*And*) spotted, mottled; *persona* freckled.

sarazo (*LAm*) = **zarazo.**

sarazón *adj* (*Méx*) = **zarazo.**

sarcasmo *nm* sarcasm; **es un ~ que ...** it is ludicrous that ...

sarcásticamente *adv* sarcastically.

sarcástico *adj* sarcastic.

sarcófago *nm* sarcophagus.

sarcoma *nm* sarcoma.

sardina *nf* sardine; pilchard; **~ arenque** herring; **~ noruega** brisling; **como ~s en lata** (packed) like sardines.

sardinero *adj* sardine (*atr*).

sardo, -a *adj, nm/f* Sardinian.

sardónico *adj* (*esp LAm*) sardonic; ironical, sarcastic.

sargazo *nm* (*Carib*) seaweed.

sargentear [1a] **1** *vt* (*Mil*) to command; (*) to boss about. **2** *vi* (*) to be bossy, boss people about.

sargento *nm* sergeant; (*pey**) bossy female.

sargentona* *nf* tough mannish woman.

sargo *nm* bream.

sari *nm* sari.

sarita *nf* (*And*) straw hat.

sarmentoso *adj* (**a**) *planta* twining, climbing. (**b**) *dedos etc* long and thin; gnarled.

sarmiento *nm* vine shoot.

sarna *nf* (*Med*) itch, scabies; (*Vet*) mange.

sarniento *adj* (*CAm, Méx*), **sarnoso** *adj* (**a**) (*Med*) itchy, infected with the itch; (*Vet*) mangy. (**b**) (*fig*) weak, feeble. (**c**) (*And, Cono Sur**: *despreciable*) contemptible, lousy‡, wretched.

sarpullido *nm* = **salpullido.**

sarraceno, -a *adj, nmf* Saracen.

sarracina *nf* (**a**) (*disputa*) quarrel; (*pelea*) brawl, free fight.

(**b**) (*matanza*) mass slaughter; (*fig*) wholesale destruction; **han hecho una ~** (*Univ**) they've ploughed almost everybody*.

Sarre *nm* Saar.

sarrio *nm* Pyrenean mountain goat.

sarro *nm* (**a**) (*gen*) incrustation, deposit; (*en dientes*) tartar, scale, plaque; (*en caldera, lengua*) fur. (**b**) (*Bot*) rust.

sarroso *adj* incrusted; covered with tartar; furred, furry.

sarta *nf,* **sartal** *nm,* **sartalada** *nf* (*Cono Sur*) (*serie*) string, series; (*fila*) line, row; (*fig*) string; **una ~ de mentiras** a pack of lies.

sartén *nf* (*m en LAm*) frying-pan; **coger la ~ por donde quema** to act rashly; **saltar de la ~ y dar en la brasa** to jump out of the frying pan into the fire; **tener la ~ por el mango** to be the master, rule the roost; to hold all the cards.

sarteneja *nf* (*And, Méx*) dried-out pool; (*Méx*) (*bache*) pothole; (*tierra seca*) cracked soil, parched soil.

sasafrás *nm* sassafras.

sastra *nf* seamstress.

sastre *nm* (**a**) tailor; **~ de teatro** costumier; **hecho por ~** tailor-made. (**b**) (*prenda*) tailor-made costume.

sastrería *nf* (**a**) (*oficio*) tailoring, tailor's trade. (**b**) (*tienda*) tailor's (shop).

Satán *nm*, **Satanás** *nm* Satan.

satánico *adj* satanic; devilish, fiendish.

satelitario *adj* satellite (*atr*).

satélite 1 *nm* (**a**) (*Astron*) satellite; ~ **artificial** artificial satellite; ~ **de comunicaciones** communications satellite; ~ **espía** spy satellite; ~ **meteorológico** weather satellite.

(**b**) satellite; minion; (*esbirro*) henchman; (*compañero*) crony.

2 *atr* satellite; **ciudad** ~ satellite town; **país** ~ satellite country.

satén *nm* sateen.

satín *nm* (*LAm*) sateen, satin.

satinado 1 *adj* glossy, shiny. **2** *nm* gloss, shine.

satinar [1a] *vt* to gloss, make glossy.

sátira *nf* satire.

satíricamente *adv* satirically.

satírico *adj* satiric(al).

satirizar [1f] *vt* to satirize.

sátiro *nm* satyr.

satisfacción *nf* (**a**) (*gen*) satisfaction; ~ **laboral,** ~ **profesional** job satisfaction; **a** ~ **de** to the satisfaction of; **a su entera** ~ to his complete satisfaction; **con** ~ **de todos** to the general satisfaction.

(**b**) (*de ofensa*) satisfaction, redress; (*disculpa*) apology; **pedir** ~ **a uno** to demand an apology from sb, demand satisfaction from sb.

(**c**) ~ **de sí mismo** self-satisfaction, smugness.

satisfacer [2s] **1** *vt* (**a**) (*gen*) to satisfy; (*éxito etc*) to gratify, please; *necesidad, solicitud* to meet, satisfy; *deuda, sueldo etc* to pay; (*Com*) *letra de cambio* to honour; *gastos* to meet.

(**b**) *culpa* to expiate; *pérdida* to make good.

(**c**) ~ **a uno de** (*o* **por**) **una ofensa** to give sb satisfaction for an offence.

2 satisfacerse *vr* (**a**) (*gen*) to satisfy o.s., be satisfied; ~ **con muy poco** to be content with very little.

(**b**) (*resarcirse*) to obtain redress, obtain satisfaction; (*vengarse*) to take revenge.

satisfactoriamente *adv* satisfactorily.

satisfactorio *adj* satisfactory.

satisfecho *adj* (**a**) (*gen*) satisfied; content(ed); **darse por** ~ **con algo** to declare o.s. satisfied (*o* content) with sth; **dejar** ~**s a todos** to satisfy everybody; **quedarse** ~ (*comida*) to be full.

(**b**) (*t* ~ **consigo mismo,** ~ **de sí mismo**) self-satisfied, smug; conceited; **nos miró** ~ he looked at us smugly.

sativa *nf* (*Cono Sur*) marijuana.

satrústegui* *interj* well!, well I'm blowed!*

satsuma *nf* satsuma.

saturación *nf* saturation; permeation.

saturado *adj* saturated.

saturar [1a] *vt* to saturate; to permeate; ~ **el mercado** to flood the market; **estos aeropuertos son los más saturados** these airports are the most crowded (*o* overused).

saturnales *nfpl* Saturnalia.

saturnino *adj* saturnine.

Saturno *nm* Saturn.

sauce *nm* willow (tree); ~ **de Babilonia,** ~ **llorón** weeping willow.

saucedal *nm* willow plantation.

saúco *nm* (*Bot*) elder.

saudí, saudita *adj, nmf* Saudi.

Saúl *nm* Saul.

sauna *nf* (*m en LAm*) sauna.

saurio *nm* saurian.

savia *nf* sap.

saxífraga *nf* saxifrage.

saxo* *nm* (*Mús*) sax*; (*persona*) saxist.

saxofón, saxófono 1 *nm* (*instrumento*) saxophone. **2** *nmf* (*persona*) saxophonist.

saxofonista *nmf* saxophonist.

saya *nf* (**a**) (*falda*) skirt; (*enaguas*) petticoat; (*vestido*) dress. (**b**) (*And: mujer*) woman.

sayal *nm* coarse woollen cloth.

sayo *nm* (**a**) smock, tunic; loose garment, long loose gown. (**b**) (*Esp*) **cortar un** ~ **a uno** to gossip about sb, talk behind sb's back; **¿qué** ~ **se me corta?** what are they saying about me?

sayón *nm* (**a**) (*Jur*) executioner. (**b**) (*fig*) cruel henchman; (*) ugly customer*.

sayuela *nf* (*Carib*) long shirt, smock.

sazo* *nm* hankie*.

sazón 1 *nf* (**a**) (*Agr*) good heart; proper condition (*of land*) for planting, tilth.

(**b**) (*de fruta*) ripeness, maturity; **en** ~ ripe, ready (to eat); (*fig*) opportunely; **fuera de** ~ at the wrong moment, inopportunely.

(**c**) (*liter*) time, moment, season; **a la** ~ then, at that time.

(**d**) (*Culin*) flavour.

2 *adj* (*And, CAm, Méx*) ripe.

sazonado *adj* (**a**) *fruta etc* ripe; mellow; *plato* tasty. (**b**) ~ **de** (*Culin*) seasoned with, flavoured with. (**c**) (*fig*) witty.

sazonar [1a] **1** *vt* (**a**) *fruta* to ripen, bring to maturity. (**b**) (*Culin*) to season, flavour (*de* with). (**c**) (*Carib*) to sweeten. **2** *vi* to ripen.

s/c (*Com*) (**a**) *abr de* **su casa** your firm. (**b**) *abr de* **su cuenta** your account.

scalextric *nm* complicated traffic interchange, spaghetti junction*.

scooter [es'kuter] *nm* motor scooter.

scotch [es'kotʃ] *nm* adhesive tape.

script [es'kri] *nf, pl* **scripts** [es'kri] script-girl.

schop [tʃop] *nm* (*Cono Sur*) (*vaso*) mug, tankard; (*cerveza*) keg beer.

SD *nf* (*Pol*) (**a**) *abr de* **Social Democracia.** (**b**) *abr de* **Solidaridad Democrática.**

Sdo. (*Com*) *abr de* **Saldo** balance, bal.

SE *abr de* **sudeste** south-east, SE.

S.E. *abr de* **Su Excelencia** His (*o* Her) Excellency, H.E.

se¹ *pron reflexivo* (**a**) (*sing: m*) himself, (*f*) herself, (*de cosa*) itself, (*de Vd*) yourself; (*pl*) themselves, (*de Vds*) yourselves; **se está lavando, está lavándose** he's washing, he's washing himself; **se retira** he withdraws; **se tiró al suelo** she threw herself to the ground; **¡siéntese!** sit down.

(**b**) (*recíproco*) each other, one another; **se ayudan** they help each other; **se miraron el uno al otro** they looked at one another; **no se hablan** they are not on speaking terms, they don't speak; **procuran no verse** they try not to meet each other.

(**c**) (*gen*) oneself; **conviene lavarse después del uso** it is advisable to wash after use.

(**d**) (*dativo*) **se ha comprado un sombrero** he has bought himself a hat, he has bought a hat for himself; **se rompió la pierna** he broke his leg; **han jurado no cortarse la barba** they have sworn not to cut their beards.

(**e**) (*uso impersonal: se traduce frec por la voz pasiva, por* one, some *o* people) **se compró hace 3 años** it was bought 3 years ago; **se comprende que ...** it can be understood that ..., it is understandable that ...; **no se sabe por qué** it is not known why; **en esa parte se habla galés** in that area Welsh is spoken, in that area people speak Welsh; **en ese hotel se come realmente bien** the food is really good in that hotel, you eat (*o* one eats) really well in that hotel; **se hace cuando se puede** one does it when one can; **se avisa a los interesados que ...** those concerned are informed that ...; **'véndese: solar ...'** (*anuncio*) 'for sale: plot ...'; **'véndese coche'** (*anuncio*) 'car for sale'.

se² *pron personal* (*que corresponde a* **le, les**) **se lo arrancó** he snatched it from her; **voy a dárselo** I'll give it to him; **se lo buscaré** I'll look for it for you; **no se lo agradecerán** they won't thank you for it.

sé *V* **saber, ser.**

SEA ['sea] *nm* (*Esp Agr*) *abr de* **Servicio de Extensión Agraria.**

sea *etc V* **ser.**

SEAT, Seat ['seat] *nf* (*Esp Com*) *abr de* **Sociedad Española de Automóviles de Turismo.**

sebear [1a] *vt* (*Carib*) to inspire love in; to court.

sebo *nm* (**a**) (*grasa*) grease, fat; (*para velas*) tallow; (*Culin*) suet.

(**b**) (*) *gordura* fat; (*mugre*) grease, filth, grime.

(**c**) **hacer** ~ (*Cono Sur*) to idle, loaf; **dar** ~ **a** (*And*) to pester; **hacer** (*o* **volver**) ~ **a** (*Carib*) to crush, ruin; **helarse a uno el** ~* (*fracasar*) to come a cropper*; (*morir*) to peg out**.

sebón *adj* (*And, CAm, Cono Sur*) idle, lazy.

seboso *adj* (**a**) (*gen*) greasy, fatty; (*de vela*) tallowy; (*de comida*) suety. (**b**) (*: *mugriento*) greasy, filthy, grimy.

Sec. *abr de* **Secretario** secretary, sec.

seca *nf* (**a**) (*Agr*) drought; (*Met*) dry season. (**b**) (*Náut*) sandbank.

secadero *nm* (**a**) (*lugar*) drying place; drying shed. (**b**) (*And: terreno*) dry plain, scrubland.

secado *nm* drying.

secador *nm* (**a**) (*lugar*) place where clothes are hung to dry. (**b**) ~ **de cabello,** ~ **para el pelo** hair-drier; ~ **centrífugo** spin-drier.

secadora *nf* drier, clothes drier; ~ **centrífuga** spin-drier; (*CAm, Méx*) ~ **de cabello** hair-drier.
secamente *adv* (*V adj* (**c**)) brusquely, sharply, curtly; drily.
secano *nm* (**a**) (*Agr*: *t* **tierra de** ~) dry land, dry region; unirrigated land; **cultivo de** ~ crop for dry farming.
(**b**) (*Náut*) (*banco de arena*) sandbank; (*islote*) small sandy island.
secante[1] **1** *adj* (**a**) *viento etc* drying; **papel** ~ = **2**. (**b**) (*Cono Sur*: *latoso*) tedious, irritating. **2** *nm* blotting paper, blotter.
secante[2] *nf* (*Mat*) secant.
secapelos *nm invar* hair drier.
secar [1g] **1** *vt* (**a**) (*gen*) to dry, dry up, dry off; *plato, superficie* to wipe dry; *lágrimas* to dry; *frente* to wipe, mop; *líquido derramado* to mop up; *tinta* to blot; *planta* to dry up, wither.
(**b**) (*fig*) (*fastidiar*) to annoy, vex; (*aburrir*) to bore.
2 secarse *vr* (**a**) (*ropa lavada etc*) to dry, dry off; (*río*) to dry up, run dry; (*planta*) to dry up, wither, wilt; (*persona*) to dry o.s., get dry (*con una toalla* on a towel, with a towel).
(**b**) (*herida*) to close up, heal up.
(**c**) (*: *adelgazar*) to get thin.
(**d**) (*: *t* ~ **de sed**) to have a raging thirst.
secarral *nm* dry plain, arid area.
secarropa *nm* clothes-horse.
sección *nf* (**a**) (*Arquit, Mat etc*) section; (*t* ~ **transversal**) cross-section; ~ **cónica** conic section; ~ **longitudinal** longitudinal section; ~ **vertical** vertical section.
(**b**) (*fig*) section; (*de almacén, compañía*) division, department, branch; ~ **de contactos** personal column (containing offers of marriage *etc*); ~ **de cuerdas** string section; ~ **deportiva** sports section, sports page; ~ **económica** financial pages.
(**c**) (*Mil*) section, platoon.
seccional *adj* sectional.
seccionar [1a] *vt* (*dividir*) to divide up, divide into sections; (*cortar*) to cut (off); (*disecar*) to dissect; ~ **la garganta a uno** to cut sb's throat.
secesión *nf* secession.
secesionista *adj, nmf* secessionist.
seco *adj* (**a**) (*gen*) dry; *fruta etc* dried; *planta* dried up, withered, dead; *batería, clima, época, lago, vino* dry; **estar en** ~ (*Náut y fig*) to be high and dry.
(**b**) (*flaco*) thin, skinny.
(**c**) *carácter* (*frío*) cold; (*antipático*) disagreeable; (*brusco*) blunt; *actitud, respuesta etc* brusque, sharp, curt; *estilo* plain, bare, flat, inexpressive; *explicación* plain, unvarnished; *estudio, tema* dry.
(**d**) *golpe, ruido etc* dull; *tos* dry.
(**e**) (*puro*) bare; *coñac* neat; **vivir a pan** ~ to live on bread alone, eat only bread; **tiene el sueldo** ~ he has just his salary; **estar** ~* to be broke*.
(**f**) **dejar a uno** ~ (*matar*) to kill sb stone-dead; (*atolondrar*) to dumbfound sb; **quedarse** ~ to be dumbfounded.
(**g**) **a secas: habrá pan a secas** there will be just bread; **decir algo a secas** to say sth curtly, say sth abruptly; **se llama Rodríguez a secas** he is called plain Rodríguez, he is just called Rodríguez.
(**h**) **en** ~: **callarse en** ~ to stop talking suddenly; to stop talking at once; **frenar en** ~ to brake sharply. pull up sharply; **parar en** ~ to stop dead, stop suddenly.
(**i**) (*LAm*: *golpe*) slap, smack.
secoya *nf* redwood, sequoia.
secre* *nmf* = **secretario**.
secreción *nf* secretion.
secreta 1 *nf* secret police; plain-clothes police. **2** *nm* secret policeman; plain-clothes policeman.
secretamente *adv* secretly.
secretar [1a] *vt* to secrete.
secretaría *nf* (**a**) (*plantilla*) secretariat. (**b**) (*oficina*) secretary's office. (**c**) (*cargo*) secretaryship. (**d**) (*Méx Pol*) Ministry, Department of State (*US*).
secretariado *nm* (**a**) (*plantilla*) secretariat. (**b**) (*cargo*) secretaryship. (**c**) (*LAm*: *curso*) secretarial course. (**d**) (*LAm*: *profesión*) career as a secretary, profession of secretary.
secretario, -a *nm/f* (**a**) secretary; ~ **adjunto** assistant secretary; ~ **general** general secretary, (*Pol*) secretary general; ~ **de imagen** public relations officer; ~ **municipal** town clerk; ~ **particular** personal secretary, private secretary; ~ **de prensa** press secretary; ~ **de rodaje** script clerk. (**b**) (*Méx Pol*) Minister (of State), Secretary of State (*US*).
secretear [1a] *vi* (**a**) (*conversar*) to talk confidentially, exchange secrets. (**b**) (*cuchichear*) to whisper unnecessarily; to whisper ostentatiously.
secreter *nm* writing-desk.
secretismo *nm* (excessive) secrecy.
secreto 1 *adj* (**a**) (*gen*) secret; (*escondido*) hidden; *información* secret, confidential, (*Mil*) classified; **alto** ~ top secret; **todo es de lo más** ~ it's all highly secret.
(**b**) *persona* secretive.
2 *nm* (**a**) (*un* ~) secret; ~ **de confesión** confessional secret; ~ **de estado** state secret; ~ **de fabricación** industrial secret; ~ **de Polichinela,** ~ **a voces** open secret; **debido al** ~ **sumarial** (*o* **del sumario**) because the matter is sub judice; **la juez ha levantado el** ~ **sumarial sobre el caso** the judge has lifted the ban on reporting the case; **estar en el** ~ to be in on the secret; **guardar un** ~ to keep a secret; **hacer** ~ **de algo** to be secretive about sth.
(**b**) (*cualidad*) secrecy; ~ **de correspondencia** sanctity of the mails; **de** (*o* **en**) ~ in secret, secretly, in secrecy; **lo han hecho con mucho** ~ they have done it in great secrecy.
(**c**) (*cajón*) secret drawer.
(**d**) (*de cerradura*) combination.
secta *nf* sect; denomination.
sectario 1 *adj* sectarian; denominational; **no** ~ non-sectarian, non-denominational.
2 *nm*, **sectaria** *nf* follower, devotee; member; (*Ecl*) sectarian, member of a sect (*o* denomination).
sectarismo *nm* sectarianism.
sector *nm* sector; (*de opinión etc*) section; ~ **privado** private sector; ~ **público** public sector; ~ **terciario** tertiary sector, service industries, service sector.
sectorial *adj* local, regional; relating to a particular sector (*o* industry *etc*).
sectorialmente *adv* locally, regionally; in a way which relates to a particular sector (*o* industry *etc*).
secuaz *nm* follower, supporter; (*pey*) underling, hireling.
secuela *nf* (**a**) (*consecuencia*) consequence; sequel. (**b**) (*Méx Jur*) proceedings, prosecution.
secuencia *nf* (*Cine, Ling etc*) sequence.
secuencial *adj* sequential.
secuencialmente *adv* sequentially, in sequence.
secuenciar [1b] *vt* to arrange in sequence.
secuestración *nf* (**a**) (*Jur*) sequestration. (**b**) = **secuestro.**
secuestrador(a) *nm/f* kidnapper; ~ **aéreo** hijacker.
secuestrar [1a] *vt* (**a**) *niño* to kidnap; *persona* to kidnap, abduct; (*Aer*) to hijack. (**b**) (*Jur*) *artículos* to seize, confiscate.
secuestro *nm* (**a**) (*rapto*) kidnapping, abduction; (*Aer*) hijack(ing). (**b**) (*Jur*) seizure, confiscation.
secular *adj* (**a**) (*Ecl*) secular; lay. (**b**) (*que dura 100 años*) century-old; (*fig*: *antiguo*) centuries-old, age-old, ancient; **según una tradición** ~ according to an age-old tradition.
secularización *nf* secularization.
secularizar [1f] *vt* to secularize.
secundar [1a] *vt* to second, help, support; *huelga* to take part in, join.
secundario *adj* secondary; minor, of lesser importance; **actor** ~ supporting actor.
secundinas *nfpl* afterbirth.
secuoia, secuoya *nf* (*LAm*) = **secoya.**
sed *nf* thirst; thirstiness; (*Agr*) thirst, drought, dryness; (*fig*) thirst, lust, longing (*de* for); ~ **inextinguible,** ~ **insaciable** unquenchable thirst; **apagar la** ~ to quench one's thirst; **tener** ~ to be thirsty; **tener mucha** ~ to be very thirsty; **tener** ~ **de** (*fig*) to thirst for, long for.
seda *nf* (**a**) (*gen*) silk; ~ **artificial** artificial silk; ~ **de coser** sewing silk; ~ **dental** dental floss; ~ **floja** floss silk; ~ **hilada** spun silk; ~ **en rama** raw silk; **como una** ~ (*adj*) as smooth as silk, beautifully smooth; *persona* very meek, very sweet-tempered; (*adv*) smoothly; **de** ~ silk (*atr*); silken, silky; **hacer** ~‡ to sleep, kip‡.
(**b**) (*Zool*) bristle.
sedación *nf* sedation.
sedal *nm* fishing-line.
sedán *nm* (*Aut*) saloon, sedan (*US*).
sedante 1 *adj* (*Med*) sedative; (*fig*) soothing, calming. **2** *nm* sedative.
sedar [1a] *vt* to sedate.
sedativo *adj* sedative.
sede *nf* (**a**) (*de gobierno*) seat; (*de sociedad*) headquarters, central office; (*Dep*) venue; ~ **diplomática** diplomatic quarter (of a city); ~ **social** head office, central office;

headquarters. (**b**) (*Ecl*) see; **Santa S~** Holy See.

sedentario *adj* sedentary.

sedentarismo *nm* (**a**) sedentary nature. (**b**) (*Med*) sedentary lifestyle; lack of exercise.

sedente *adj estatua* seated.

sedeño *adj* (**a**) (*sedoso*) silken, silky. (**b**) (*Zool*) bristly.

sedería *nf* (**a**) (*cría*) silk raising; (*manufactura*) silk manufacture, sericulture; (*comercio*) silk trade. (**b**) (*géneros*) silks, silk goods.

sedero 1 *adj* silk (*atr*); **industria sedera** silk industry. **2** *nm*, **sedera** *nf* silk dealer; draper, haberdasher.

SEDIC [se'ðik] *nf abr de* **Sociedad Española de Documentación e Información Científica.**

sedicente *adj*, **sediciente** *adj* self-styled; so-called, would-be.

sedición *nf* sedition.

sedicioso 1 *adj* seditious; mutinous, rebellious. **2** *nm*, **sediciosa** *nf* subversive element, disloyal individual; rebel; troublemaker.

sediente *adj*: **bienes ~s** (*Jur*) real estate.

sediento *adj* (**a**) (*lit, t Agr*) thirsty. (**b**) (*fig*) thirsty, eager (*de* for).

sedimentación *nf* sedimentation.

sedimentar [1a] **1** *vt* (**a**) (*depositar*) to deposit. (**b**) (*fig*) to calm, quieten. **2 sedimentarse** *vr* (**a**) (*depositarse*) to settle. (**b**) (*fig*) to calm down, quieten down.

sedimentario *adj* sedimentary.

sedimento *nm* sediment, deposit.

sedosidad *nf* silkiness.

sedoso *adj* silky, silken.

seducción *nf* (**a**) (*acto*) seduction. (**b**) (*cualidad*) seductiveness; charm, allure; lure, fascination.

seducir [3o] **1** *vt* (**a**) *mujer* to seduce.

(**b**) (*fig*) (*moralmente*) to lead on, seduce from one's duty; (*sobornar*) to bribe.

(**c**) (*fig: cautivar*) to charm, attract, captivate, fascinate; **seduce a todos con su simpatía** she captivates everyone with her charm; **la teoría ha seducido a muchos** the theory has attracted many people; **no me seduce la idea** I don't like the idea, I'm not taken with the idea.

2 *vi* to be charming, be fascinating; **es una película que seduce** it's a captivating film.

seductivo *adj* = **seductor 1.**

seductor 1 *adj* (**a**) seductive. (**b**) (*fig*) (*encantador*) charming, captivating, fascinating; *idea etc* tempting. **2** *nm* seducer.

Sefarad *nf* (*historia de los judíos*) Spain; (*fig*) homeland.

sefardí 1 *adj* Sephardic. **2** *nmf* Sephardi, Sephardic Jew(ess); **sefardíes** Sephardim.

sefardita = **sefardí.**

segable *adj cosecha* ready to cut.

segadera *nf* sickle.

segador *nm* harvester, reaper.

segadora *nf* (**a**) (*persona*) harvester, reaper. (**b**) (*Mec*) mower, reaper, mowing machine; **~ de césped** lawnmower.

segadora-atadora *nf* binder.

segar [1h *y* 1k] vt (**a**) (*Agr*) *trigo etc* to reap, cut, harvest; *heno, hierba* to mow, cut; *otro objeto* to cut off.

(**b**) (*fig*) to mow down.

(**c**) (*fig*) *esperanzas etc* to ruin, destroy; **~ la juventud de uno** to cut sb off in his prime.

seglar 1 *adj* secular, lay. **2** *nmf* layman, laywoman.

segmento *nm* segment; (*Com, Fin*) sector, group; **~ de émbolo** piston ring.

segoviano 1 *adj* of (*o* from) Segovia. **2** *nm*, **segoviana** *nf* native (*o* inhabitant) of Segovia; **los ~s** the people of Segovia.

segregación *nf* (**a**) (*gen*) segregation; **~ racial** racial segregation. (**b**) (*Anat*) secretion.

segregacionista *nmf* segregationist, supporter of racial segregation.

segregar [1h] *vt* (**a**) (*gen*) to segregate, separate. (**b**) (*Anat*) to secrete.

seguida *nf* (**a**) (*método normal*) normal way (of doing sth); (*ritmo*) proper rhythm, habitual speed; **coger la ~** to get into the swing of it, get into the proper way (of doing sth).

(**b**) **a ~ = seguidamente; de ~** uninterruptedly, straight off; at once; **en ~** at once, right away; **en ~ termino** I've very nearly finished, I shan't be long now; **en ~ tomó el avión para Madrid** he immediately caught the plane to Madrid.

seguidamente *adv* (**a**) (*sin parar*) uninterruptedly, straight off, without a break; continuously. (**b**) (*inmediatamente después*) immediately after, next; **dijo ~ que ...** he went on at once to say that ...

seguidista *adj* copycat (*atr*).

seguido 1 *adj* (**a**) *línea etc* continuous, unbroken.

(**b**) *camino, ruta etc* straight.

(**c**) **~s** consecutive, successive; **5 días ~s** 5 days running; **5 blancos ~s** 5 bull's-eyes in a row, 5 consecutive bull's-eyes.

(**d**) (*largo*) long-lasting; **una enfermedad muy seguida** a very lengthy illness, a long drawn-out illness.

(**e**) **todos sus hijos son muy ~s** she had all her children one after the other.

2 *adv* (**a**) (*directo*) straight; **vaya Vd todo ~** just keep straight on; **por aquí ~** straight on past here.

(**b**) (*detrás*) after; **ese coche iba primero y ~ el mío** that car was in front and mine was immediately behind it.

(**c**) (*LAm*) often; **le gusta visitarnos ~** she likes to visit us often.

3 *nm*: **a ~** then, next, right away.

seguidor(a) *nm/f* follower; (*Dep*) fan, follower, supporter.

seguimiento *nm* (**a**) (*caza*) chase, pursuit; (*continuación*) continuation; (*Med*) follow-up; monitoring; (*TV*) report, follow-up; **estación de ~** tracking-station; **ir en ~ de** to go in pursuit of, chase (after). (**b**) **el ~ de la huelga** the support for the strike.

seguir [3d *y* 3l] **1** *vt* (**a**) (*gen*) to follow; to follow on, come next to, come after.

(**b**) *caza* to chase, pursue; to hound; *pista* to follow; *satélite* to track; *pasos* to dog; *pista* (*de crimen*) to follow up; *mujer* to court.

(**c**) *autoridad, inclinación, jefe, orden, texto etc* to follow; *consejo* to follow, adopt, take; (*Med*) to follow up, monitor; **~ los acontecimientos de cerca** to monitor events closely.

(**d**) *carrera, rumbo* to follow, pursue.

(**e**) **~ su camino** to continue on one's way.

2 *vi* (**a**) (*venir después*) to follow; to follow on, come next, come after; **y los que siguen** and the next ones, and those that come next; **como sigue** as follows.

(**b**) (*continuar*) to continue, to carry on, go on; to proceed; **sigue** (*en carta*) PTO, (*en libro, TV*) continued; **¡siga!** go on!; (*And*) come in!; **¡síguele!** (*Méx*) go on!; **siga a la derecha** keep to the right; **~ con una idea** to go on with an idea; **sigue en su sitio** it is still in its place; **sigue en Caracas** he is still in Caracas; **seguía en su error** he continued in his error; **~ adelante** to go on, carry on; to go straight on; (*Aut*) to drive on, go straight ahead; **siga Vd adelante hasta Toboso** go straight ahead as far as Toboso; **~ por un camino** to carry on along a path; **hacer ~ una carta** to forward a letter; **¿cómo sigue?** how is he?; **sigue bien, que siga Vd bien** I hope you keep well, look after yourself.

(**c**) (*con adj o n etc*) to be still, go on being; **sigue enfermo** he's still ill; **si el tiempo sigue bueno** if the weather continues (*o* stays) fine; **sigue tan misterioso como antes** it's still as mysterious as ever; **sigue soltera** she's still single; **sigue sin poderlo comprar** he is still unable to buy it; **sigo sin comprender** I still don't understand.

(**d**) **~** + *ger* to go on + *ger*, keep (on) + *ger*; **sigue lloviendo** it's still raining; **sigue siendo lo mismo** it's still the same, it remains unchanged; **siguió mirándola** he went on looking at her; **siguió sentado** he stayed sitting down, he remained seated.

3 seguirse *vr* (**a**) (*venir después*) to follow; **una cosa se sigue a otra** one thing follows another.

(**b**) (*deducirse etc*) to follow, ensue, happen in consequence; **de esto se sigue que ..., síguese que ...** it follows that ...

según 1 *adv* (*) according to circumstances; **~ (y) como, ~ y conforme** it all depends; **'¿lo vas a comprar?' — '~'** 'are you going to buy it?' — 'it all depends'.

2 *prep* (**a**) (*gen*) according to; (*de acuerdo con*) in accordance with, in line with; **~ el jefe** according to the boss; **~ este mapa** according to this map; **obrar ~ las instrucciones** to act in accordance with one's instructions; **~ lo que dice** from what he says, according to what he says; **~ lo que se decida** according to what is decided; **iremos o no, ~ el tiempo** we'll go or not, depending on the weather; **eso es ~ el dinero de que se disponga** that depends on what money is available; **~ parece** it would seem so.

(**b**) **está ~ lo dejaste** it is just as you left it.

3 *conj* as; **~ me consta** as I know for a fact; **~ esté el tiempo** depending on the weather; **~ que vengan 3 ó 4** depending on whether 3 or 4 come.

segunda *nf* (**a**) (*Mús*) second. (**b**) (*intención*) second meaning, veiled meaning; **decir algo con** ~**(s)** to say sth with an implied second meaning. **(c)** (*Aut*) second gear. **(d) viajar en** ~ (*Ferro*) to travel second class.

segundar [1a] **1** *vt* **(a)** (*repetir*) to do again. **(b)** (*Cono Sur*) *golpe* to return. **(c)** (*Méx*) to earth up. **2** *vi* to come second, be in second place.

segundero *nm* second hand (*of a watch*).

segundo 1 *adj* second; *educación* secondary; *intención* double.

2 *nm* **(a)** (*gen*) second; second one; (*Mil etc*) second in command, second in authority; (*Náut*) first mate; (*Boxeo*) second; ~ **de a bordo** (*fig*) second in command; right-hand man; **sin** ~ unrivalled.

(b) (*tiempo*) second.

(c) (*Méx Teat etc*) ~**s** upstairs seats.

segundón 1 *nm* second son, younger son. **2** *nm*, **segundona** *nf* (*fig*) second-class citizen.

segur *nf* (*hoz*) sickle; (*hacha*) axe.

seguramente *adv* **(a)** *con certeza etc* for sure, with certainty.

(b) (*muy probablemente*) surely; ~ **tendrán otro** surely they'll have another, they must have another; ~ **van a estar contentos** no doubt they'll be pleased; **'¿lo va a comprar?' — '**~**'** 'is he going to buy it?' — 'I should think so'.

(c) (*probablemente*) probably, possibly; ~ **llegarán mañana** they'll probably arrive tomorrow.

seguridad *nf* **(a)** (*lo salvo*) safety; security; safeness; (*Mil, Pol*) security; ~ **en la carretera,** ~ **vial** road safety; ~ **ciudadana** law and order; ~ **colectiva** collective security; ~ **contra incendios** fire precautions; ~ **industrial** industrial safety, safety at work; ~ **social** social security; (*contribución*) national insurance (contribution); **de** ~ safety (*atr*), *p.ej.* **cinturón de** ~ safety belt; **con la mayor** ~ with (*o* in) complete safety; **para mayor** ~ to be on the safe side, for safety's sake; **estar en** ~ to be in a safe place.

(b) (*certeza*) certainty; **en la** ~ **de su victoria** in the certainty of winning, being sure of winning; **con toda** ~ with complete certainty, for sure; **no lo sabemos con** ~ we don't know for sure; **tener la** ~ **de que ...** to have the certainty that ..., be sure that ...; **tengan Vds la** ~ **de que ...** rest assured that ...

(c) (*t* ~ **en sí mismo**) confidence, self-confidence.

(d) (*fiabilidad*) trustworthiness; reliability.

(e) (*firmeza*) firmness; stability, steadiness.

(f) (*Jur*) security, surety.

seguro 1 *adj* **(a)** (*a salvo*) safe; secure; **un puerto** ~ a safe harbour; **está más** ~ **en el banco** it's safer in the bank; **lo más** ~ **es** + *infin* the safest thing is to + *infin*, the best thing is to + *infin*; **lo más** ~ **es que no quieren** it's highly likely they don't want to, most probably they don't want to; **conviene atenerse a lo** ~ it's best to be on the safe side.

(b) *método, resultado etc* sure, certain; (*inevitable*) bound to come, certain to happen; **ir a una muerte segura** to go to certain death; **es** ~ **que ...** it is certain that ...; **en estas investigaciones no hay nada** ~ nothing is certain in these researches.

(c) (*cierto*) sure, certain; **¿estás** ~**?** are you sure?; **estar** ~ **de** to be sure of; **estar** ~ **de que ...** to be sure that ...

(d) estar ~ **de sí mismo** to be confident, be self-confident, be sure of o.s.

(e) (*de fiar*) *amigo etc* firm, sure, trustworthy; *fuente etc* reliable, dependable, trustworthy.

(f) (*firme*) *objeto* firm; firmly fastened, securely tied (*etc*); stable, steady; *fecha etc* firm, definite.

(g) (*LAm: honesto*) honest, straight.

(h) (*probable*) probable, possible.

2 *adv* **(a)** for sure; **todavía no lo ha dicho** ~ he still hasn't said for sure.

(b) ¡~! sure!, I'm sure it is! (*etc*).

3 *nm* **(a)** (*dispositivo*) safety device; (*de cerradura*) tumbler; (*Mil*) safety catch; (*Téc*) catch, pawl, lock, stop.

(b) (*fig*) safety, certainty, assurance; **a buen** ~**, de** ~ surely; truly; **en** ~ in a safe place; **sobre** ~ safely, without risk; **ir sobre** ~ to be on safe ground.

(c) (*Com, Fin*) insurance; ~ **de desempleo,** ~ **de paro** unemployment benefit; **S**~ **de Enfermedad** ≃ National Health Insurance; ~ **de incendios** fire insurance; ~ **multiriesgo** multirisk insurance; ~ **mutuo** mutual insurance; ~ **social** social insurance, social security; ~ **contra terceros** third-party insurance; ~ **a** (*o* **contra**) **todo riesgo** comprehensive insurance; ~ **de vida,** ~ **sobre la vida** life insurance.

(d) (*Méx: alfiler*) safety pin.

seibó *nm* (*And, Carib*) sideboard.

seis 1 *adj* six; (*fecha*) sixth; **las** ~ six o'clock. **2** *nm* six.

seiscientos 1 *adj* six hundred; **en el** ~ in the seventeenth century. **2** *nm* (*Aut*) small car.

seísmo *nm* tremor, shock, earthquake.

seisporocho *nm* (*Carib*) *a Venezuelan folk dance.*

SEL *nf abr de* **Sociedad Española de Lingüística.**

selección *nf* **(a)** (*gen*) selection; ~ **biológica,** ~ **natural** natural selection; ~ **múltiple** multiple choice. **(b)** (*Dep*) team, side. **(c)** (*Liter, Mús*) **selecciones** selections.

seleccionable *adj* eligible.

seleccionado *nm* team.

seleccionador(a) *nm/f* (*Dep*) selector; team manager.

seleccionar [1a] *vt* to pick, choose, select.

selectividad *nf* **(a)** selectivity. **(b)** (*Univ*) entrance examination.

selectivo *adj* selective.

selecto *adj* **(a)** (*en calidad*) select, choice, fine; *club etc* select, exclusive. **(b)** (*Liter*) *obras* selected.

selenizaje *nm* moon-landing.

selenizar [1f] *vi* to land on the moon.

self* *nm*, **self-service** *nm* self-service restaurant.

seltz [selθ, sel]: **agua (de)** ~ seltzer (water).

selva *nf* (*bosque*) forest, woods; (*jungla*) jungle; **S**~ **Negra** Black Forest.

selvático *adj* **(a)** (*de la selva*) woodland (*atr*), sylvan; (*de la jungla*) jungle (*atr*); (*fig: rústico*) rustic. **(b)** (*Bot etc*) wild.

selvoso *adj* wooded, well-wooded.

sellado 1 *adj* sealed; stamped, franked. **2** *nm* **(a)** (*acto*) sealing; stamping. **(b)** (*Cono Sur*) stamps, stamp duty.

selladora *nf* primer, sealant.

selladura *nf* **(a)** (*sello*) seal. **(b)** (*acto*) sealing; stamping.

sellar [1a] *vt* **(a)** *documento, carta* to seal. **(b)** *pasaporte etc* to stamp. **(c)** (*marcar*) to brand. **(d)** (*cerrar*) *labios, pacto* to seal; *calle* to seal off.

sello *nm* **(a)** (*personal, de rey etc*) seal; (*administrativo*) (official *etc*) stamp; signet; (*LAm: en reverso de moneda*) tails; ~ **real** royal seal; ~ **de caucho,** ~ **de goma** rubber stamp.

(b) (*señal*) impression, mark; stamp; (*Com*) brand, seal; (*Mús: t* ~ **discográfico**) record label; recording company; (*Liter*) publishing house; ~ **fiscal** revenue stamp; **lleva el** ~ **de esta oficina** it carries the stamp of this office.

(c) (*Esp Correos*) stamp; ~ **aéreo** airmail stamp; ~ **conmemorativo** commemorative stamp; ~ **de correo** postage stamp; ~ **de urgencia** express-delivery stamp; **no pega ni un** ~* he's useless, he's a waste of space.

(d) (*Med*) cachet, wafer.

(e) (*fig: t* ~ **distintivo**) hallmark, stamp; **lleva el** ~ **de su genialidad** it carries the hallmark of his genius.

S.Em.ª *abr de* **Su Eminencia** His Eminence, H.E.

semaforazo* *nm* robbery (of occupants of a car) at traffic lights.

semáforo *nm* (*Náut etc*) semaphore; (*Ferro*) signal; (*Aut*) traffic-lights; ~ **sonoro** pelican crossing.

semana *nf* week; ~ **inglesa** working week of 5½ days; ~ **laboral** working week; **S**~ **Santa** Holy Week; **entre** ~ during the week; **vuelo de entre** ~ midweek flight.

semanal *adj* weekly.

semanalmente *adv* weekly, each week.

semanario 1 *adj* weekly. **2** *nm* (*revista*) weekly (magazine).

semanero, -a *nm/f* (*LAm*) weekly-paid worker; worker specially engaged for a week's work.

semántica *nf* semantics.

semántico *adj* semantic.

semblante *nm* (*Liter Anat*) face, visage; (*exterior*) face, appearance; (*perspectiva*) outlook; (*aspecto*) aspect; **alterar** (*o* **demudar**) **el** ~ **a uno** to make sb look alarmed, upset sb; **componer el** ~ to regain one's composure; **mudar de** ~ to change colour; **el caso lleva otro** ~ **ahora** the matter looks different now; **tener buen** ~ (*salud*) to look well; (*humor*) to be in a good mood.

semblantear [1a] *vt* **(a)** (*CAm, Cono Sur, Méx*) *persona* to look straight in the face, look deeply into the eyes of.

(b) (*CAm Méx: examinar*) to study, examine, look at.

semblanza *nf* biographical sketch.

sembradera *nf* seed drill.

sembradío *nm* = **sembrío.**

sembrado *nm* sown field.

sembrador(a) 1 *nm/f* (*persona*) sower. **2** *nf* (*Agr*) seed drill.

sembradura *nf* sowing.

sembrar [1k] *vt* (**a**) (*Agr*) *campo, semilla* to sow; ~ **de** to sow with.

(**b**) ~ **minas en un estrecho,** ~ **un estrecho de minas** (*Náut*) to mine a strait, lay mines in a strait.

(**c**) (*fig*) *objetos* to sprinkle, scatter about, spread around; *superficie* to sprinkle, strew (*de* with); *discordia* to sow; *noticia* to spread; **el que siembra recoge** one reaps what one has sown.

(**d**) (*Méx*) *jinete* to throw; (*derribar*) to knock down.

sembrío *nm* (*LAm*) land prepared for sowing.

semejante 1 *adj* (**a**) (*parecido*) similar; ~**s** alike, similar, the same; ~ **a** like; **es ~ a ella en el carácter** she is like her in character; **son muy ~s** they are very much alike.

(**b**) (*Mat*) similar.

(**c**) (*tal*) such; **nunca hizo cosa ~** he never did such a thing, he never did anything of the kind; **¿se ha visto frescura ~?** did you ever see such cheek?*.

(**d**) (*Cono Sur, Méx*) huge, enormous.

2 *nm* (**a**) (*ser humano*) fellow man, fellow creature; **nuestros ~s** our fellow men.

(**b**) **no tiene ~** (*equivalente*) it has no equal, there is nothing to equal it.

semejanza *nf* similarity, resemblance; **a ~ de** like, as; ~ **de familia** family likeness; **tener ~ con** to look like, resemble, bear a resemblance to.

semejar [1a] **1** *vi* to seem like, resemble, seem to be. **2 semejarse** *vr* to look alike, be similar, resemble each other; ~ **a** to look alike, resemble.

semen *nm* semen.

semental 1 *adj* stud, breeding (*atr*). **2** *nm* (*Zool*) sire, stud animal; (‡: *hombre*) stud‡.

sementera *nf* (**a**) (*acto*) sowing. (**b**) (*época*) seedtime, sowing season. (**c**) (*tierra*) sown land, sown field. (**d**) (*fig*) hotbed (*de* of), breeding ground (*de* for).

semestral *adj* half-yearly, biannual.

semestralmente *adv* half-yearly, biannually.

semestre *nm* (**a**) (*seis meses*) period of six months; (*US: Univ etc*) semester. (**b**) (*Fin*) half-yearly payment.

semi... *pref* semi..., half-...

semiacabado *adj* (*Com*) half-finished.

semialfabetizado *adj* semiliterate.

semiautomático *adj* semiautomatic.

semibola *nf* (*Bridge*) small slam.

semibreve *nf* semibreve.

semicircular *adj* semicircular.

semicírculo *nm* semicircle.

semiconductor *nm* semiconductor.

semiconsciente *adj* semiconscious, half-conscious.

semiconsonante *nf* semiconsonant.

semicorchea *nf* semiquaver.

semicualificado *adj* semiskilled.

semicultismo *nm* half-learned word.

semiculto *adj* half-learned.

semicupio *nm* (*CAm, Carib*) hip-bath.

semiderruido *adj* half-ruined, half-collapsed.

semidesconocido *adj* virtually unknown.

semidesierto *adj* half-empty.

semidesnatado *adj* semi-skimmed.

semidesnudo *adj* half-naked.

semidiós *nm* demigod.

semidormido *adj* half-asleep.

semidúplex *adj* (*Inform*) half duplex.

semielaborado *adj* half-finished.

semiexperto *adj* semiskilled.

semifallo *nm* (*Bridge*) singleton (*a* in).

semifinal *nf* semifinal.

semifinalista *nmf* semifinalist.

semifracaso *nm* partial failure, near failure.

semiinconsciente *adj* semiconscious.

semilla *nf* (**a**) (*Bot, t fig*) seed; ~ **de césped** grass seed. (**b**) (*Cono Sur*) brad, tack. (**c**) (*Cono Sur: niño*) baby, small child; **la ~*** the kids (*collectively*).

semillero *nm* (**a**) (*terreno*) seedbed; nursery; (*caja*) seed-box.

(**b**) (*fig*) hotbed (*de* of), breeding ground (*de* for); **un ~ de delincuencia** a hotbed of crime; **la decisión fue un ~ de disgustos** the decision caused a host of troubles, the decision became a battleground of controversy.

semimedio *nm* (*Boxeo*) welterweight.

seminal *adj* seminal.

seminario *nm* (**a**) (*Agr*) seedbed; nursery. (**b**) (*Ecl*) seminary. (**c**) (*Univ etc*) seminar.

seminarista *nm* seminarist.

seminuevo *adj* (*Com*) nearly new; pre-owned (*US*).

semioficial *adj* semi-official.

semiología *nf* semiology.

semiolvidado *adj* half-forgotten.

semioruga *nf* (*t* **camión ~**) half-track.

semioscuridad *nf* half-darkness; gloom.

semiótica *nf* semiotics.

semiótico *adj* semiotic.

semipesado *adj* (*Boxeo*) light-heavyweight.

semiprecioso *adj* semiprecious.

semisalado *adj agua* brackish.

semiseparado *adj* semidetached.

semisótano *nm* semibasement.

semita 1 *adj* Semitic. **2** *nmf* Semite.

semítico *adj* Semitic.

semitono *nm* semitone.

semivacío *adj* half-empty.

semivocal *nf* semivowel.

semivolea *nf* half-volley.

sémola *nf* semolina.

semoviente *adj*: **bienes ~s** livestock.

sempiterno *adj* everlasting.

sen *nm*, **sena** *nf* (*Bot, Med*) senna.

Sena *nm* Seine.

senado *nm* senate; (*fig*) assembly, gathering.

senador(a) *nm/f* senator.

senatorial *adj* senatorial.

sencillamente *adv* simply; **es ~ imposible** it's simply impossible.

sencillez (*V adj*) *nf* (**a**) simplicity, plainness. (**b**) simplicity, straightforwardness. (**c**) naturalness, unaffectedness, lack of sophistication; (*pey*) simplicity; (*LAm*) foolishness.

sencillo 1 *adj* (**a**) (*gen*) simple, plain, unadorned; *costumbres, estilo, ropa etc* simple.

(**b**) *asunto, problema* simple, easy, straightforward; **es muy ~** it's very simple.

(**c**) *persona* natural, unaffected, unsophisticated; (*pey*) simple, (*LAm*) foolish.

(**d**) *billete, flor, hilo etc* single.

2 *nm* (**a**) (*disco*) single. (**b**) (*LAm*: *moneda*) small change, loose change.

senda *nf* path, track; (*fig*) path; (*Aut*) lane.

senderismo *nm* trekking.

sendero *nm* path, track.

sendos *adj pl* one each, each; **les dio ~ libros** she gave them each a book; **los criados recibieron ~ regalos** each servant received a present; **con sendas peculiaridades** each with its own peculiarity.

Séneca *nm* Seneca.

senectud *nf* old age.

Senegal *nm*: **El ~** Senegal.

senegalés, -esa *adj, nm/f* Senegalese.

senescencia *nf* ageing.

senil *adj* senile.

senilidad *nf* senility.

seno *nm* (**a**) (*Anat*) bosom, bust; **~s** breasts; ~ **(frontal)** frontal sinus; ~ **materno** womb; (*fig*) bosom; **en el ~ de Abrahán** on Abraham's bosom; **morir en el ~ de la familia** to die in the bosom of one's family; **lo escondió en su ~** she hid it in her bosom, she put it down the front of her dress.

(**b**) (*hueco*) hollow, cavity; (*Náut*) trough (*between waves*); (*Met*) trough.

(**c**) (*Geog: ensenada*) small bay, inlet; (*golfo*) gulf.

(**d**) (*fig*) refuge, haven.

(**e**) (*de club etc*) headquarters; (*fig*) heart, core; **el ~ del movimiento** the heart of the movement.

(**f**) (*Mat*) sine.

SENPA ['senpa] *nm* (*Esp*) *abr de* **Servicio Nacional de Productos Agrarios.**

sensación *nf* (**a**) (*gen*) sensation, feeling; (*impresión*) sense; feel; **una ~ de placer** a feeling of pleasure; **tengo una ~ de inutilidad** I have a feeling of being useless.

(**b**) (*fig*) sensation; **causar ~, hacer ~** to cause a sensation.

sensacional *adj* sensational.

sensacionalismo *nm* sensationalism.

sensacionalista *adj* sensationalist.

sensacionalizar [1f] *vt* to sensationalize.

sensatamente *adv* sensibly.

sensatez *nf* good sense, sensibleness.

sensato *adj* sensible.

sensibilidad *nf* sensitivity (*a* to), sensitiveness; sensibility; ~ **artística** artistic feeling, sensitivity to art.
sensibilización *nf* sensitizing.
sensibilizado *adj* sensitized.
sensibilizar [1f] *vt* to sensitize; (*fig*) to alert (*a* about, to), make aware (*a* of).
sensible 1 *adj* (**a**) (*que siente*) feeling, sentient; (*que reacciona*) sensitive (*a* to); (*Med*) *lugar* sensitive, tender, sore; (*Fot*) sensitive; **un aparato muy** ~ a very sensitive (*o* delicate) piece of apparatus; **una placa** ~ **a la luz** a plate sensitive to light; **es muy** ~ **a los cambios de temperatura** it is very sensitive to changes in temperature.
(**b**) *carácter* sensitive (*a* to); responsive (*a* to); impressionable, emotional, easily hurt.
(**c**) *cambio etc* perceptible, appreciable, noticeable; *diferencia etc* tangible, palpable; *golpe* heavy; *pérdida* heavy, considerable; **una** ~ **mejoría** a noticeable improvement, a marked improvement.
(**d**) (*capaz*) ~ **de** capable of; ~ **de mejora** capable of improvement, having a capacity for improvement.
(**e**) **soy** ~ **del honor que se me hace** I am conscious of the honour being done me.
(**f**) (*lamentable*) regrettable, lamentable; **es muy** ~ it is highly regrettable; **es** ~ **que** ... it is regrettable that ...
2 *nf* (*Mús*) leading note.
sensiblemente *adv* perceptibly, appreciably, noticeably; markedly; ~ **más** substantially more.
sensiblería *nf* sentimentality; mushiness, sloppiness; squeamishness.
sensiblero *adj* sentimental; mushy, sloppy; squeamish.
sensitiva *nf* (**a**) (*Bot*) mimosa. (**b**) (*: *persona*) highly sensitive person, delicate flower.
sensitivo *adj* (**a**) *órgano etc* sense (*atr*). (**b**) *ser etc* sentient; sensitive.
sensor *nm* sensor; ~ **de calor** heat sensor; ~ **de fin de papel** paper-out sensor.
sensorial *adj* sensorial, sensory.
sensorio *adj* sensory.
sensual *adj* (**a**) (*sexual*) sensual; (*sensorio*) sensuous. (**b**) (*esp LAm*) alluring, sexy.
sensualidad *nf* (**a**) sensuality; sensuousness. (**b**) (*esp LAm*) attractiveness, allure, sexiness.
sensualismo *nm* sensualism.
sensualista *nmf* sensualist.
sentada *nf* (**a**) (*gen*) sitting; **de una** ~, **en una** ~ at one sitting. (**b**) (*Pol etc*) sit-down (protest); sit-in.
sentadera *nf* (**a**) (*LAm*) seat (*of a chair etc*). (**b**) (*Méx**) ~**s** backside.
sentadero *nm* seat.
sentado *adj* (**a**) (*gen*) **estar** ~ to sit, be sitting (down), be seated; **permanecer** ~ to remain seated.
(**b**) (*fig*) settled, established; firm; **dar algo por** ~ to take sth for granted, assume sth; **dejar algo** ~ to establish sth firmly; **dejar** ~ **que** ... to lay down that ..., have it clearly understood that ...
(**c**) (*fig*) *carácter* solid, sensible, steady; sedate.
sentador *adj* (*Cono Sur*) *vestido* smart, elegant.
sentadura *nf* (*en piel*) sore; (*en fruta*) mark.
sentar [1k] **1** *vt* (**a**) *persona* to sit, seat.
(**b**) *objeto* to place (firmly), settle (in its place); ~ **el último ladrillo** to tap the last brick into place; ~ **las costuras** to press the seams; ~ **las bases** to lay the foundations.
(**c**) ~ **una suma en la cuenta de uno** (*Com*) to put a sum down to sb's account.
(**d**) (*fig*) *base, cimientos* to lay, establish, create; *principio* to set up, establish; *precedente* to lay down, set up.
(**e**) (*And, Carib*) *persona* to crush, squash.
(**f**) (*And*) *caballo* to rein in (*o* pull up) sharply.
2 *vti* (**a**) (*ropa etc*) to suit; to fit; to look well on, be becoming to; **ese peinado le sienta horriblemente*** that hair style doesn't suit her one little bit*, she looks awful with that hairdo*.
(**b**) (*comida*) ~ **bien a** to agree with; ~ **mal a** to disagree with; **no me sientan las gambas** prawns disagree with me.
(**c**) (*fig*) ~ **bien** to go down well; ~ **mal** to go down badly, produce a bad impression; **le ha sentado mal que lo hayas hecho tú** he took it badly that you should do it, he didn't like your doing it; **a mí me sienta como un tiro*** it suits me like a hole in the head.
3 sentarse *vr* (**a**) (*persona*) to sit, sit down; to seat o.s.; to settle o.s.; **siéntese** (do) sit down, take a seat; **sentémonos aquí** let's sit (down) here; **se sentó a comer** she sat down to eat.
(**b**) (*sedimento etc*) to settle.
(**c**) (*tiempo etc*) to settle (down); to become steady, stabilize.
(**d**) (*Arquit*) to settle.
(**e**) (*zapato etc*) to leave a mark, rub.
sentencia *nf* (**a**) (*Jur*) sentence; (*fig*) decision, ruling; opinion; ~ **de muerte** death sentence; **dictar** ~, **pronunciar** ~ to pronounce sentence.
(**b**) (*Liter*) maxim, saying; dictum.
(**c**) (*Inform*) statement.
sentenciar [1b] **1** *vt* (**a**) (*Jur*) to sentence (*a* to). (**b**) (*LAm*) ~ **a uno** to swear revenge on sb. **2** *vi* to pronounce, give one's opinion.
sentenciosamente *adv* (*V adj*) (**a**) pithily. (**b**) sententiously.
sentenciosidad *nf* (**a**) pithiness; oracular nature. (**b**) sententiousness.
sentencioso *adj* (**a**) *dicho* pithy; oracular. (**b**) *persona* sententious.
sentidamente *adv* (*V adj*) (**a**) regretfully. (**b**) sincerely, with great feeling.
sentido 1 *adj* (**a**) (*lamentable*) regrettable; deeply felt; **una pérdida muy sentida** a deeply felt loss, a most regrettable loss.
(**b**) *compasión etc* sincere, deeply felt, keen; **le doy mi más** ~ **pésame** I offer my deepest sympathy.
(**c**) *carácter* sensitive, tender, easily wounded.
(**d**) (*Méx*) (*de buen oído*) having good hearing, sharp-eared.
(**e**) (*Méx*: *resentido*) bitter.
2 *nm* (**a**) (*del cuerpo*) sense; **los cinco** ~**s** the five senses; ~ **del olfato** sense of smell; ~ **del color** sense of colour; ~ **del humor** sense of humour; ~ **de la medida**, ~ **de las proporciones** sense of proportion; ~ **de los negocios** business sense; ~ **de orientación** sense of direction; **sexto** ~ sixth sense; **no tiene** ~ **del ritmo** he has no sense of rhythm; **sin** ~ senseless, unconscious; **aguzar el** ~ to prick up one's ears; **costar un** ~* to cost the earth; **embargar los** ~**s a uno** to enrapture sb; **perder el** ~ to lose consciousness; **poner los cinco** ~**s en algo** to give one's whole attention to sth; **quitar el** ~ **a uno** to take one's breath away; **recobrar el** ~ to regain consciousness.
(**b**) (*juicio*) sense; discernment, judgement; **buen** ~ good sense; ~ **común** common sense; **tener** ~ **para distinguir algo** to have enough sense to distinguish sth.
(**c**) (*Ling*) sense, meaning; **doble** ~ double meaning; ~ **figurado** figurative sense; **en el buen** ~ **de la palabra** in the best sense of the word; **en el** ~ **amplio, en** ~ **lato** in the broad sense; **en el** ~ **estricto** in the strict sense; **en cierto** ~ in a sense; **en todos los** ~**s** in every sense; **en este** ~ in this respect; **en tal** ~ to this effect; **en el** ~ **de que** ... to the effect that ...; **sin** ~ meaningless; **cobrar** ~ to begin to make sense; **no le encuentro ningún** ~ I can't make any sense of it; **tener** ~ to make sense; **no tiene** ~ **que lo haga él** it doesn't make any sense for him to do it; **la vida no tiene** ~ **para él** life has no meaning for him; **tomar algo en buen** (*o* **mal**) ~ to take sth the right (*o* wrong) way.
(**d**) (*sensibilidad etc*) feeling; **leer con** ~ to read with feeling; **tener** ~ **de la música** to have a feeling for music.
(**e**) (*Geog*) direction; way; **'~ único'** 'one way (street)'; **en** ~ **contrario, en** ~ **opuesto** in the opposite direction, the other way; **en el** ~ **de las agujas del reloj** clockwise; **en** ~ **contrario al de las agujas del reloj** anticlockwise; **algo en este** ~ (*fig*) something along these lines; **iban en** ~ **inverso al nuestro** they were travelling in the opposite direction to us.
(**f**) (*Méx*: *oreja*) ear.
sentimental *adj* (**a**) (*gen*) sentimental; emotional; *mirada* soulful. (**b**) *asunto, vida etc* love (*atr*); *V* **aventura**.
sentimentalismo *nm* sentimentality.
sentimentaloide* *adj* sugary, over-sentimental; mushy, soppy*.
sentimentero *adj* (*Carib, Méx*) = **sensiblero**.
sentimiento *nm* (**a**) (*emoción*) feeling, emotion, sentiment; **un** ~ **de insatisfacción** a feeling of dissatisfaction; **buenos** ~**s** fellow feeling, sympathy; **herir los** ~**s de uno** to hurt (*o* wound) sb's feelings.
(**b**) (*sentido*) sense; ~ **del deber** sense of duty; ~ **de la responsabilidad** sense of responsibility.
(**c**) (*pesar*) regret, grief, sorrow; **con profundo** ~ with profound regret; *V* **acompañar**.
sentina *nf* (**a**) (*Náut*) bilge; (*en ciudad*) sewer, drain. (**b**)

(*fig*) sink, sewer.

sentir [3i] **1** *vt* (**a**) (*gen*) to feel; (*percibir*) to perceive, sense; (*esp LAm: oír*) to hear; (*oler*) to smell; *emoción* to feel; *dignidad, responsabilidad etc* to feel, be aware of, realize; *música, pintura etc* to feel, have a feeling for; **~ un dolor** to feel a pain; **~ el ruido de un coche** to hear the noise of a car; **sin ~ el frío** without feeling the cold; **~ ganas de** + *infin* to feel an urge to + *infin*; **lo siento ajeno a mí** I feel it is foreign to me, I feel detached from it; **siente la profesión como un sacerdocio** he feels the profession like a sacred calling; **dejarse ~, hacerse ~** to let itself be felt; **se deja ~ el frío** it's beginning to feel cold.

(**b**) *enfermedad etc* to feel the effects of, suffer from the aftermath of.

(**c**) (*lamentar*) to regret, be sorry for; **lo siento** I'm sorry; **¡lo siento muchísimo!, ¡cuánto lo siento!** I'm very sorry!, I'm so sorry!; **sintió profundamente esa pérdida** he felt (*o* regretted, mourned *etc*) that loss deeply; **~ que ...** to regret that ..., be sorry that ...; **sentiré que me obligue Vd a venderlo** I shall be sorry if you force me to sell it; **siento no haberlo hecho antes** I am sorry not to have done it before; **siento molestarle** I'm sorry to bother you.

2 *vi* (**a**) (*gen*) to feel; **estaba que ni oía ni sentía** he was in such a state that he could neither hear nor feel anything; **sin ~** without noticing, quite inadvertently; imperceptibly, so quickly (*o* smoothly *etc*) that one does not notice.

(**b**) (*lamentar*) to feel sorry; **dar que ~** to give cause for regret.

3 sentirse *vr* (**a**) (*gen*) to feel; **~ pesimista** to feel pessimistic; **~ herido** (*fig*) to feel hurt; **~ mal(o)** to feel ill, feel bad; **~ como en su casa** to feel at home; **~ en ridículo** to feel ridiculous; **~ actor** to feel o.s. to be an actor.

(**b**) (*Med*) **~ del costado** to have a pain in one's side; **~ del paludismo** to suffer from malaria.

(**c**) (*ofenderse*) to be offended, feel resentful (*de* about, at); **~ de una observación** to take offence at a remark.

(**d**) (*LAm: enfadarse*) to get cross, get angry; **~ con uno** to fall out with sb.

(**e**) (*recipiente*) to crack.

4 *nm* opinion, judgement; **a mi ~, en mi ~** in my opinion; **compartir el ~ de** to share the view of, echo the opinion of.

sentón *nm* (**a**) (*CAm, Méx: caída*) heavy fall. (**b**) **dar un ~ a** (*And*) *caballo* to rein in suddenly; **dar un ~** (*Méx: caerse*) to fall on one's backside.

seña *nf* (**a**) (*del cuerpo etc*) mark, distinguishing mark; **~s** description; **~s de identidad, ~s particulares** identifying marks, distinguishing marks; **~s personales** personal description; **~s mortales** sure signs; **las ~s son mortales** the signs are unmistakable; **dar las ~s de uno** to give a personal description of sb.

(**b**) (*indicio etc*) sign; (*fig*) sign, token; secret sign; (*Mil*) password; **por las ~s** so it seems; **por más ~s** just to prove it, to clinch matters; into the bargain, moreover; **dar ~s de** to show signs of; **hablar por ~s** to talk by signs, communicate by means of signs; **hacer una ~ a uno** to make a sign to sb; **hacer una ~ a uno para que** + *subj* to signal to sb to + *infin*.

(**c**) **~s** (*Correos*) address.

señá *nf* = **señora**.

señal *nf* (**a**) (*gen*) sign; (*síntoma*) symptom; (*indicio*) token, indication; **en ~ de** as a token of, as a sign of, in sign of; **es buena ~** it's a good sign; **dar ~es de** to show signs of; **hacer la ~ de la cruz** to make the sign of the Cross; **hacer ~es de humo** to send up smoke-signals; (*****) to talk on the phone.

(**b**) (*Com, Fin*) token payment; deposit; pledge; **dejar una suma en ~** to leave a sum as a deposit.

(**c**) (*con la mano*) sign, signal; **~ de la victoria** victory sign, V-sign; **dar la ~ de** (*o* **para**) to give the signal for; **hacer una ~ a uno** to make a sign to sb; **hacer una ~ grosera** to make a rude sign; **al hacerse una ~ predeterminada** at a prearranged signal.

(**d**) (*seña*) mark; (*vestigio*) trace, vestige; sign; (*Med*) scar, mark; (*en animal*) mark, marking; brand; (*Geog*) landmark; (*Liter*) bookmark; **sin la menor ~ de** without the least trace of, without the slightest sign of; **no quedaba ni ~** there wasn't the slightest trace of it; **lo hicieron sin dejar ~** they did it without leaving a trace.

(**e**) (*Aut, Ferro etc*) signal; **~ de alto, ~ de stop** stop sign; **~ de auxilio, ~ de socorro** distress-signal; **~ de carretera, ~ de tránsito, ~ vertical** roadsign; **~ horizontal** road marking; **~es luminosas, ~es de tráfico** traffic-lights, traffic-signals; **~ de peligro** danger-signal.

(**f**) (*Rad*) signal; **~ horaria** time signal.

(**g**) (*Telec*) signal, tone; buzz; **~ de llamada** calling signal; **~ para marcar** dialling tone; **~ de ocupado** (*o* **comunicando**) engaged tone, busy signal (*US*).

(**h**) (*LAm*) earmark.

señala *nf* (*Cono Sur*) earmark.

señaladamente *adv* (**a**) (*especialmente*) especially. (**b**) (*claramente*) clearly, plainly.

señalado *adj* (**a**) **estar ~ como** to be marked down as, be known to be.

(**b**) **dejar ~ a uno** to scar sb permanently.

(**c**) (*claro*) distinct, clear, plain.

(**d**) *día, favor etc* special; *persona* distinguished, notable, (*pey*) notorious.

señalador *nm* bookmark.

señalar [1a] **1** *vt* (**a**) (*significar*) to mark; to denote, betoken; **señalan la llegada de la primavera** they announce the arrival of spring; **eso señaló el principio del descenso** that marked the start of the decline.

(**b**) *papel etc* to mark; to stamp; *persona* to mark (for life), scar (permanently); (*Med*) to leave a scar on; (*LAm*) *ganado* to brand.

(**c**) *carretera etc* to put up signs on; *ruta* to signpost.

(**d**) (*con el dedo*) to point to, point out, indicate; (*fig*) to show, indicate; (*aguja de reloj etc*) to show, point to, say; **iba señalando los edificios importantes** he went round pointing out the interesting buildings; **tuve que ~le varios errores** I had to point out several mistakes to him.

(**e**) (*en conversación*) to allude to; (*pey*) to criticize.

(**f**) *fecha, precio etc* to fix, settle; *tarea* to set; *persona* to appoint; **¿qué precio ha señalado al cuadro?** what price has he put on the picture?; **se negó a ~me hora** he refused to offer me an appointment, he refused to arrange a time to meet.

2 señalarse *vr* to make one's mark (*como* as); to distinguish o.s. (*por* by, by reason of), achieve distinction.

señalero *nm* (*Cono Sur*) signalman.

señalización *nf* (*acto*) signposting; (*sistema*) system of signs (*o* signals), signal code; **~ horizontal** markings on the road; **~ vertical** (system of) roadsigns.

señalizador *nm* roadsign, signpost.

señalizar [1f] *vt carretera etc* to put up signs on; *ruta* to signpost.

señero *adj* (**a**) (*solo*) alone, solitary. (**b**) (*sin par*) unequalled, outstanding.

señor 1 *nm* (**a**) man; (*caballero*) gentleman; **le espera un ~** there's a gentleman waiting to see you; **es todo un ~** he's a real gentleman; **dárselas de ~** to put on airs; **hacer el ~** to lord it; **quiere parecer un ~** he tries to look like a gentleman.

(**b**) (*de bienes*) owner, master; (*de criados*) master; (*fig*) master; **el ~ de la casa** the master of the household; **¿está el ~?** is the master in?; **no es ~ de sus pasiones** he cannot control his passions.

(**c**) (*delante de apellido*) Mister (*se escribe siempre* Mr); **es para el Sr Meléndez** it's for Mr Meléndez; **los ~es Poblet** the Poblets, Mr and Mrs Poblet; **Señor Don Jacinto Benavente** (*en sobre*) Mr J. Benavente, J. Benavente Esq.

(**d**) (*delante de cargo profesional: no se traduce*) **el ~ alcalde** the mayor; **el ~ cura** the priest; **el ~ presidente** the president (*pero V* (**e**)).

(**e**) (*en oración directa*) sir (*pero frec no se traduce*); (*a noble*) my lord; **~es** (*en discurso*) gentlemen; **¡mire Vd, ~!** look here!; **¡oiga Vd, ~!** I say!; **~ alcalde** Mr Mayor; **~ director ...** (*de periódico*) Dear Sir ...; **sí, ~ guardia** (*Esp*) yes, officer; **~ juez** my Lord; **~ presidente** Mr Chairman, Mr President; **¡no ~!** (*fig*) not a bit of it!, never!, absolutely not!; **¡sí ~!** (*fig*) yes indeed!, I should jolly well think it is!*, it certainly does! (*etc*); **pues sí ~** well that's how it is.

(**f**) (*Com etc*) **muy ~ mío** Dear Sir; **muy ~es nuestros** Gentlemen.

(**g**) (*Hist*) noble, lord; **~ feudal** feudal lord; lord of the manor; **~ de la guerra** warlord; **~ de horca y cuchillo** (*fig*) despot.

(**h**) (*Rel*) **El S~** The Lord; **Nuestro S~** Our Lord; **S~ de los Ejércitos** Lord of Hosts; **recibir al S~** to take communion.

(**i**) **los ~es‡** the fuzz‡, the police.

2 *adj* (*****) (**a**) (*señoril*) posh*; **un coche muy ~** a really posh car*.

(**b**) (*verdadero, grande*) real, really big; **una casa para**

un ~ ~ a house for a gentleman who really is a gentleman; **eso es un ~ melón** now that really is a melon, that's some melon; **fue una ~a herida** it was a real big wound*.

señora *nf* (**a**) (*gen*) lady; **~ de compañía** chaperon; companion; **le espera una ~** there's a lady waiting to see you.

(**b**) (*de bienes*) owner, mistress; **¿está la ~?** is the lady of the house at home?

(**c**) (*esposa*) wife; **mi ~** my wife; **el jefe y su ~** the boss and his wife; **la ~ de Smith** Mrs Smith.

(**d**) (*en oración directa: pero frec no se traduce*) madam, (*a noble*) my lady; **¡~s y señores!** ladies and gentlemen!; **sí, ~** yes, madam; **¡oiga Vd, ~!** I say!

(**e**) **muy ~ mía** (*Com etc*) Dear Madam.

(**f**) **Nuestra S~** (*Rel*) (*para católicos*) Our Lady, (*para protestantes*) the Virgin (Mary).

(**g**) (*Esp‡*) fuzz‡, police; secret police.

señorear [1a] **1** *vt* (**a**) (*gobernar*) to rule, control; (*pey*) to domineer, lord it over.

(**b**) (*edificio*) to dominate, soar above, tower over.

(**c**) *pasiones* to master, control.

2 señorearse *vr* (**a**) (*dominarse*) to control o.s.

(**b**) (*darse humos*) to adopt a lordly manner.

(**c**) **~ de** to seize, seize control of.

señoría *nf* (**a**) (*dominio*) rule, sway. (**b**) (*títulos*) **su S~** (*t* **vuestra S~**) your lordship, his lordship, your ladyship, her ladyship; my lord, my lady.

señorial *adj*, **señoril** *adj* lordly; aristocratic; noble, majestic, stately.

señorío *nm* (**a**) (*Hist*) manor, feudal estate; domain.

(**b**) (*fig: dominio*) rule, sway, dominion (*sobre* over).

(**c**) (*cualidad*) lordliness; majesty, stateliness.

(**d**) (*) (*personas*) distinguished people; (*pey*) toffs*, nobs‡.

señorita *nf* (**a**) (*gen*) young lady.

(**b**) (*delante de nombre o apellido*) Miss.

(**c**) (*en oración directa, no se traduce*) **¿qué busca Vd, ~?** what are you looking for?

(**d**) (*LAm: profesora*) schoolteacher.

señorito 1 *nm* (**a**) (*gen*) young gentleman; (*en lenguaje de criados*) master, young master. (**b**) (*pey*) rich kid*. **2** *adj* (*hum**) lordly; high-class, classy*; (excessively) genteel.

señorón* *nm* big shot*.

señuelo *nm* (**a**) (*lit*) decoy. (**b**) (*fig*) bait, lure. (**c**) (*And, Cono Sur: buey*) leading ox.

seo *nf* (*Aragón*) cathedral.

sep. *nm abr de* **septiembre** September, Sept.

separable 1 *adj* separable; (*Mec etc*) detachable, removable. **2** *nm* pull-out feature, supplement.

separación *nf* (**a**) (*acto etc*) separation; division; (*Mec*) removal; (*de puesto*) removal, dismissal (*de* from); **~ (del matrimonio)**, **~ judicial** legal separation; **~ racial** racial segregation; **~ del servicio** (*Mil*) discharge.

(**b**) (*distancia*) gap, distance.

separadamente *adv* separately.

separado *adj* separated; separate; (*Mec*) detached; **vive ~ de su mujer** he is separated from his wife, he doesn't live with his wife; **por ~** (*aparte*) separately; (*uno por uno*) individually, one by one; (*Correos*) under separate cover; **firmar una paz por ~** to sign a separate peace.

separador *nm* (**a**) separator. (**b**) (*Inform*) delimiter.

separadora *nf* (*Inform*) burster.

separar [1a] **1** *vt* (**a**) *objeto* to separate (*de* from); *silla etc* to move away (*de* from), take away, remove; **~ un trozo de pan** to put aside a piece of bread.

(**b**) *peleadores etc* to separate, pull apart, keep apart; *palabras, sílabas* to divide; *conexión* to sever, cut; *cartas etc* to sort (out); **saber ~ las buenas de las malas** to know how to separate (*o* tell, distinguish) the good ones from the bad; **los negocios le separan de su familia** business keeps him away from his family.

(**c**) (*Mec*) *pieza* to detach, remove (*de* from).

(**d**) (*destituir*) to remove, dismiss (*de* from); **ser separado del servicio** (*Mil*) to be discharged.

2 separarse *vr* (**a**) (*fragmento*) to come away, detach itself (*de* from); (*componentes*) to come apart; (*Pol*) to secede.

(**b**) (*persona*) to leave, go away, withdraw; **~ de un grupo** to leave a group; to part company with a group; **no quiere ~ de sus libros** she and her books are inseparable; **se ha separado de todos sus amigos** he has cut himself off from all his friends; **me separé de ella a las 11** I left her at 11; **se ha separado de su mujer** he has left his wife.

(**c**) (*Jur*) to withdraw (*de* from).

separata *nf* offprint.

separatismo *nm* separatism, separatist tendency.

separatista *adj, nmf* separatist.

separo *nm* (*Méx*) cell.

sepelio *nm* burial.

sepia *nf* (**a**) (*Zool*) cuttlefish. (**b**) (*Arte etc*) sepia.

sepsis *nf* sepsis.

sept. *abr de* **septiembre** September, Sept.

septentrión *nm* north.

septentrional *adj* north, northern.

septeto *nm* septet.

septicemia *nf* septicaemia.

séptico *adj* septic.

se(p)tiembre *nm* September.

septillizo, -a *nm/f* septuplet.

séptimo *adj, nm* seventh.

septuagenario 1 *adj* septuagenarian, seventy-year-old. **2** *nm*, **septuagenaria** *nf* septuagenarian, person in his (*o* her) seventies.

septuagésimo *adj* seventieth.

séptuplo *adj* sevenfold.

sepulcral *adj* sepulchral; (*fig*) sepulchral, gloomy, dismal.

sepulcro *nm* tomb, grave; (*esp Bib*) sepulchre; **~ blanqueado** whited sepulchre.

sepultación *nf* (*Cono Sur*) burial.

sepultar [1a] *vt* (**a**) (*enterrar*) to bury; (*fig: en mina etc*) to bury, entomb; **quedaban sepultados en la caverna** they were trapped in the cave, they were cut off in the cave.

(**b**) (*fig: esconder*) to hide away, bury, conceal.

sepultura *nf* (**a**) (*acto*) burial; **dar ~ a** to bury; **dar cristiana ~ a uno** to give sb a Christian burial; **recibir ~** to be buried.

(**b**) (*tumba*) grave, tomb.

sepulturero *nm* gravedigger, sexton.

sequedad *nf* (**a**) (*gen*) dryness. (**b**) (*fig*) bluntness; brusqueness, curtness; plainness, bareness (*V* **seco**).

sequerío *nm* (*prov*) dry place, dry field.

sequía *nf* (**a**) (*falta de lluvias*) drought; (*época*) dry season.

(**b**) (*prov, And*) thirst.

sequiar [1c] *vi* (*Cono Sur*) to inhale.

séquito *nm* (**a**) (*comitiva*) retinue, suite, entourage.

(**b**) (*Pol etc*) group of supporters, adherents, devotees.

(**c**) (*de sucesos*) train; aftermath; **con todo un ~ de calamidades** with a whole train of disasters.

SER [ser] *nf* (*Rad*) *abr de* **Sociedad Española de Radiodifusión.**

ser [2v] **1** *vi* (**a**) (*gen: absoluto, de carácter, identidad, etc*) to be; **~ o no ~** to be or not to be; **es difícil** it's difficult; **él es pesimista** he's a pessimist, he's a pessimistic sort; **soy ingeniero** I'm an engineer; **soy yo** it's me, it is I (*liter*); (*Telec*) **¡soy Pedro!** this is Peter, Peter here, Peter speaking; **somos seis** there are six of us; **el gran pintor que fue Goya** the great painter (known to us as) Goya; **¿quién es?** who is it?; who's there?; (*Telec*) who's calling?; **es él quien debiera hacerlo** it is he who should do it, he's the one who ought to do it; **¿qué ha sido?** what happened?, what is going on?; **libros, como ~ diccionarios** (*LAm*) books, for example (*o* such as) dictionaries.

(**b**) (*origen*) **~ de** to be from, come from; **ella es de Calatayud** she's from Calatayud; **estas naranjas son de España** these oranges come from Spain; **¿de dónde es Vd?** where are you from?

(**c**) (*sustancia*) **~ de** to be (made) of; **es de piedra** it is of stone, it is made of stone, it's a stone one.

(**d**) (*possesión*) **~ de** to belong to; **éste es suyo** this is his; **el parque es del municipio** the park belongs to the town; **esta tapa es de otra caja** this top belongs to another box; **¿de quién es este lápiz?** whose is this pencil?, who does this pencil belong to?

(**e**) (*destino*) **¿qué será de mí?** what will become of me?; **¿qué ha sido de él?** what has become of him?, what happened to him?; **el trofeo fue para Rodríguez** the trophy went to Rodríguez; **el sexto hoyo fue para García** the sixth hole went to García; **después ella fue su mujer** later she became his wife.

(**f**) (*lo adecuado*) **esas finuras no son para mí** those niceties are not for me; **ese coche no es para correr mucho** that car isn't made to go very fast; **esa manera de hablar no es de una dama** that talk does not come well from a lady, one does not expect to hear a lady say such things.

(**g**) (*hora*) **es la una** it is one o'clock; **son las 7** it is 7 o'clock; **serán las 8** it must be about 8 o'clock; **serían las 9 cuando llegó** it must have been about 9 when he arrived; *V* **hora** *etc.*

(**h**) (*uso especial del imperfecto, en juegos*) **yo era la reina** pretend I was the queen, let's pretend I'm the queen.

(**i**) (*uso especial del pretérito: cargos*) **presidente que fue de Ruritania** ex-president of Ruritania, former(ly) president of Ruritania.

(**j**) (*uso especial del futuro: hipótesis*) **¿será posible?** is it possible?, can it really be so? (*y V* **posible**); **¡serás burro!** can you really be so stupid?; **serán delincuentes** they must be criminals.

(**k**) (*corresponde a* estar) **soy en todo con Vd** I entirely agree with you, I'm with you all the way; **en un momento soy con Vd** I'll be with you in a moment.

(**l**) (~ **de** + *infin*) **es de creer que** ... it may be assumed that ...; and yet ...; in spite of the fact that ..., even though the truth of the matter is that ...; **es de desear que** ... it is to be wished that ...; **es de esperar que** ... it is to be hoped that ...; **era de ver** it was worth seeing, you ought to have seen it.

(**m**) (*locuciones con indic*) **siendo así que** ... since ...; **¡o somos o no somos!*** let's get on with it!, make your minds up!; **érase que se era, érase una vez** once upon a time (there was); **a no ~ por** but for; were it not for, had it not been for; **a no ~ que** ... unless ...; **¡ahí fue ella!** what a row there was!, you should have heard the fuss!; **es que no pude** but I couldn't; **es que no quiero** but I don't want to; **¿cómo es que ...?** how is it that ...?, how does it happen that ...?; **¡cómo ha de ~!** what else do you expect!; **hizo como quien es** he acted as one might expect, he did what one could expect of him; **con ~ ella su madre** even though she is his mother, despite the fact that she's his mother; **de no ~ esto así** if it were not so, were it not so; **no vaya a ~ que** ... unless.

(**n**) (*locuciones con subj*) **¡sea!** agreed!, all right!; **o sea** ... that is to say ..., or rather ..., in other words; **sea ... sea** ... either ... or, whether ... or whether; **sea lo que sea** (*o* **fuere**) be that as it may; **no sea que** ... lest ..., in case ..., for fear that ...; **hable con algún abogado que no sea Pérez** speak to some lawyer other than Pérez, consult any lawyer you like except Pérez.

2 *forma la voz pasiva*: **fue construido** it was built; **ha sido asaltada una joyería** there has been a raid on a jeweller's; **será fusilado** he will be shot; **está siendo estudiado** it is being examined.

3 *nm* (*ente*) being; (*existencia*) life; (*esencia*) essence; ~ **humano** human being; ~ **imaginario** imaginary being; **S~ Supremo** Supreme Being; ~ **vivo** living creature, living organism; **la que le dio su ~** she who gave him life, she who brought him into the world; **en lo más íntimo de su ~** in his inmost being, deep within himself.

sera *nf* pannier, basket.

seráficamente *adv* angelically, like an angel.

seráfico *adj* (**a**) (*angélico*) angelic, seraphic. (**b**) (*: *humilde*) poor and humble.

serafín *nm* (**a**) (*gen*) seraph; (*fig*) angel; cherub. (**b**) (*Carib: broche*) clip, fastener.

serape *nm* (*Méx*) = **sarape.**

serbal *nm*, **serbo** *nm* service tree, sorb; rowan, mountain ash.

Serbia *nf* Serbia.

serbio 1 *adj* Serbian. **2** *nm*, **serbia** *nf* Serb. **3** *nm* (*Ling*) Serbo-Croat.

serbocroata 1 *adj, nmf* Serbo-Croatian. **2** *nm* (*Ling*) Serbo-Croat.

serenamente *adv* (**a**) *con calma* calmly, serenely. (**b**) *tranquilamente* peacefully, quietly.

serenar [1a] **1** *vt* (**a**) (*calmar*) to calm; (*tranquilizar*) to quieten, pacify.

(**b**) *líquido* to clarify.

2 *vi* (*And**) to drizzle.

3 serenarse *vr* (**a**) (*persona etc*) to calm down, grow calm; to compose o.s.

(**b**) (*mar*) to grow calm; (*tiempo*) to clear up.

(**c**) (*líquido*) to clear, settle.

serenata *nf* serenade.

serendipismo *nm* serendipity.

serenera *nf* (*And, CAm, Carib*) cape, wrap.

serenero *nm* (*Cono Sur*) (*pañuelo*) headscarf; (*chal*) wrap, cape.

serenidad *nf* (**a**) (*calma*) calmness, serenity. (**b**) (*tranquilidad*) peacefulness, quietness.

sereno 1 *adj* (**a**) *persona* calm, serene, unruffled.

(**b**) *tiempo* settled, fine; *cielo* cloudless, clear.

(**c**) *ambiente* calm, peaceful, quiet.

(**d**) **estar ~*** to be sober.

2 *nm* (**a**) (*rocío*) night dew, night dampness; **dormir al ~** to sleep out in the open; **le perjudica el ~** the night air is bad for her.

(**b**) (*Esp: persona*) night watchman.

sereta *nf* builder's bucket, basket.

seriado *adj* mass-produced.

serial *nm* serial; ~ **radiofónico** radio serial; ~ **televisivo** television serial.

serialización *nf* serialization.

seriamente *adv* seriously.

seriar [1b] *vt* (**a**) (*poner en serie*) to arrange in series, arrange serially. (**b**) (*producir*) to mass-produce. (**c**) (*TV etc*) to make a serial of, serialize.

sericultura *nf* silk raising, sericulture.

serie *nf* series (*t Bio, Elec, Mat*); set, sequence, succession; (*Liter, Rad etc*) series, serial; (*de sellos*) set; (*de inyecciones*) course; ~ **eliminatoria** heats; **una ~ inacabable de** an endless series of; **arrollado en ~** (*Elec*) series-wound; **fabricación en ~** mass production; **fabricar** (*o* **producir**) **en ~** to mass-produce; **casas construidas en ~** mass-produced houses; **matanzas en ~** mass murders; **fuera de ~** out of order, not in the proper sequence; (*fig*) special; **un fuera de ~** a person out of the ordinary, an extraordinary person; **artículos fuera de ~** (*Com*) goods left over, remainders, remnants; **tamaño de ~** (*Com*) stock size, regular size; **equipamiento de ~** standard equipment; **modelo de ~** (*Aut etc*) standard model; **esta adición es de ~ en el coche** this addition is now standard on the car; **artículo de ~** mass-produced article; **ser de la ~ B*** to be one of them* (*homosexual*); **película de la ~ B*** gay film.

seriedad *nf* (**a**) (*gen*) seriousness; (*gravedad*) gravity, solemnity; (*formalidad*) staidness; **hablar con ~** to speak seriously, speak in earnest.

(**b**) (*dignidad*) dignity; properness; (*sensatez*) seriousness, (sense of) responsibility; **falta de ~** frivolity; irresponsibility.

(**c**) (*en negocio etc*) reliability, dependability, trustworthiness; straightness, honesty; fair-mindedness.

(**d**) (*en crisis etc*) gravity, seriousness.

serigrafía *nf* silkscreen printing; **una ~** a silkscreen print.

serimiri *nm* (*prov*) drizzle.

serio *adj* (**a**) *actitud, expresión, persona etc* serious; grave, solemn; staid; **ponerse ~** to look serious, adopt a solemn expression (*etc*); **se quedó mirándome muy ~** he looked at me very seriously, he stared gravely at me; **pareces muy ~** you're looking very serious.

(**b**) (*formal*) *actitud, persona etc* dignified; (*decente*) proper; (*responsable*) serious, responsible; **el negro es el único color ~ para esto** black is the only proper colour for this; **un traje ~** a formal suit; **poco ~** undignified; frivolous, not to be taken seriously; **es una persona poco seria** he's an irresponsible sort, he's rather a silly individual.

(**c**) (*de fiar etc*) *persona* reliable, dependable, trustworthy; responsible; fair-minded; *negocio, trato* straight, honest; **poco ~** unreliable; irresponsible; **es una casa seria** it's a reliable firm.

(**d**) *estudio, libro etc* serious.

(**e**) (*grave*) etc grave, serious; **esto se pone ~** this is getting serious.

(**f**) **en ~** seriously; **hablo perfectamente en ~** I'm perfectly serious, I'm in dead earnest; **¿lo dices en ~?** do you really mean it?; **tomar un asunto en ~** to take a matter seriously.

sermón *nm* sermon (*t* *); **el S~ de la Montaña** the Sermon on the Mount.

sermonear* [1a] **1** *vt* to lecture, read a lecture to. **2** *vi* to sermonize.

sermoneo* *nm* lecture, sermon.

sermonero* *adj* given to sermonizing.

sernambí *nm* (*And, Carib*) inferior rubber.

serología *nf* serology.

serón *nm* pannier, large basket; (*de bebé*) cot.

seronegativo *adj* seronegative.

seropositivo *adj* seropositive.

seroso *adj* serous.

serpa *nf* (*Bot*) runner.

serpear [1a] *vi*, **serpentear** [1a] *vi* (**a**) (*Zool*) to wriggle; to creep. (**b**) (*fig*) (*camino*) to wind, snake, twist and turn; (*río*) to wind, meander.

serpenteante *adj* (*fig*) winding, twisting; meandering.

serpenteo *nm* (**a**) (*Zool*) wriggling; creeping. (**b**) (*fig*) winding, twisting; meandering.

serpentín *nm* coil.

serpentina *nf* (**a**) (*Min*) serpentine. (**b**) (*de papel*) streamer.
serpentino *adj* snaky, sinuous; winding, meandering; serpentine.
serpiente *nf* (*culebra*) snake; (*Mit etc*) serpent; **la S~** the (European monetary) Snake; **~ de anteojos** cobra; **~ boa** boa constrictor; **~ de cascabel** rattlesnake; **~ de mar** sea-serpent; **~ pitón** python; **~ de verano** silly story, non-story (*used to fill papers in the slack season*); **~ de vidrio** slow-worm.
serpol *nm* wild thyme.
serpollo *nm* sucker, shoot.
serrado *adj* serrated; toothed; jagged, uneven, rough.
serraduras *nfpl* sawdust.
serrallo *nm* seraglio, harem.
serrana[1] *nf* = **serranilla.**
serranía *nf* (**a**) mountainous area, hilly country; range of mountains. (**b**) (*Méx*) wood, forest.
serraniego *adj* = **serrano.**
serranilla *nf 15th-century verse-form.*
serrano 1 *adj* (**a**) (*Geog*) highland (*atr*), hill (*atr*), mountain (*atr*).
(**b**) (*fig*) coarse, rustic.
(**c**) **partida serrana** (*Esp*) dirty trick.
2 *nm*, **serrana**[2] *nf* highlander.
serrar [1j] *vt* to saw (off, up).
serrería *nf* sawmill.
serrín *nm* sawdust.
serrote *nm* (*Méx*) = **serrucho.**
serruchar [1a] *vt* (*LAm*) to saw (off, up).
serrucho *nm* (**a**) saw, handsaw.
(**b**) (*Carib*: *puta*) whore.
(**c**) **hacer un ~** (*And, Carib*) to split the cost.
Servia *nf etc* = **Serbia** *etc.*
servible *adj* serviceable, usable.
servicial 1 *adj* helpful, obliging. **2** *nm* (*And*: *t* **serviciala** *nf*) servant.
servicialidad *nf* helpfulness, obliging nature.
servicio *nm* (**a**) (*gen*) service; **¿su ~, señor?** your order, sir?; **a su ~** at your service; **al ~ de** in the service of; **estar al ~ de** to be in the service of; **estar al ~ del gobierno** to be on government service; **estar de ~** to be serviceable, be in service; **entrar en ~** to come into service; **tiene 8 camiones en ~** he has 8 lorries in service; **hacer un ~ para uno** to do sb a service; **te ha hecho un flaco ~** he's done you a poor service.
(**b**) (*Mil etc*) service; **~ activo** active service; **~ militar** military service; **apto para el ~** fit for military service; **en condiciones de ~** operational; **entrar de ~** to go on duty; **estar de ~** to be on duty; **estar fuera de ~, estar libre de ~** to be off duty; **prestar ~** to serve, see service (*de* as).
(**c**) **~s de administración** management services; (**~** *individual*) **~ aduanero, ~ de aduana** customs service; **~ de asistencia, ~ de atención** after-sales service; **~s en autopista** motorway services; **~ comunitario** community service; **~ consultivo** advisory service; **~ de contraespionaje** secret service; **~ doméstico** domestic service; domestic help; (*personas*) servants; **~ a domicilio** delivery service; **'~ a domicilio'** 'we deliver'; **~ de entrega** delivery service; **~ de guardia** (*Aut*) breakdown service, emergency service; **~ de incendios** fire-service; **~ de información** (*Mil*), **~ de inteligencia** intelligence service; **~ médico** medical service; **~ de megafonía** public address system; **~s mínimos** essential services (*maintained during strike*), skeleton services; **~ de orden** (*Pol*) marshals, stewards; **~ permanente** round-the-clock service; **~s postales** postal services; **~ posventa** after-sales service; **~s públicos** public services; **~ secreto** secret service; **~s sociales** social services; welfare work; **~ social sustitutorio** community service in place of military service; **~ de transportes** transport service.
(**d**) (*Culin etc*) service, set; **~ de café** coffee-set; **~ de mesa** set of dishes, (*esp*) dinner-service; **~ de tocador** toilet set.
(**e**) (*euf*: *wáter*) toilet; (*Esp*: *orinal*) chamberpot; **~s** (*de casa*) services, (*euf*) sanitation; **'S~s'** (*letrero*) 'Toilets'; **'Todos ~s'** (*anuncio*) 'all main services'.
(**f**) (*Ecl*) service; **~ divino** divine service.
(**g**) (*en hotel etc*) service, service charge; **~ incluido** service charge included.
(**h**) (*Tenis*) serve, service; **romper el ~ de uno** to break sb's service.
(**i**) (*de policía*) job, case, inquiry.
(**j**) (*Fin*) servicing (of a debt).
servidor(a) *nm/f* (**a**) (*criado*) servant; **un ~** (*yo mismo*) yours truly*, my humble self; **aquí me tiene al ~ para lo que se le ofrezca** I am always at your service, please count on me for whatever it may be; **¡~ de Vd!** at your service!
(**b**) **¡~!** (*Esp*: *en clase etc*) present!
(**c**) (*en cartas*) **su seguro ~, atento y s.s.** (= *seguro servidor*) yours faithfully.
(**d**) **'~'** (*LAm*: *formal*) 'your servant', 'at your service'.
servidumbre *nf* (**a**) (*estado*) servitude; **~ de la gleba** serfdom.
(**b**) (*fig*) compulsion.
(**c**) (*Jur*) obligation; **~ de paso** right of way.
(**d**) (*personas*) servants, staff.
servil *adj* (**a**) (*gen*) slave (*atr*), serf's; *trabajo etc* menial. (**b**) *actitud etc* servile; obsequious, grovelling; *imitación etc* slavish.
servilismo *nm* servility; obsequiousness; slavishness.
servilla *nf* slipper, pump.
servilleta *nf* serviette, napkin.
servilletero *nm* serviette ring, napkin holder.
servir [3l] **1** *vt* (**a**) (*gen*) to serve; to do a favour to, oblige; **~ a Dios** to serve God; **~ a la patria** to serve one's country; **dígame en qué puedo ~le** tell me in what way I can be of service, tell me how I can help you; **para ~le** at your service; **para lo que me va a ~** for all the good it will do me; **ser servido de** + *infin* to be pleased to + *infin.*
(**b**) (*en restaurante*) to wait on, serve.
(**c**) (*Com*) *cliente* to serve; *pedido* to attend to, fill; *libro* (*en biblioteca*) to issue; *programa* (*TV*) to show, put on, present; **¿ya le sirven, señora?** are you being attended to, madam?; **el libro está servido** the book is out, the book is in use.
(**d**) (*Culin*) *comida* to serve (out *o* up); **~ patatas a uno** to serve sb with potatoes, help sb to potatoes; **la cena está servida** dinner is served; **~ vino a uno** to pour out wine for sb.
(**e**) *cargo* to hold, fill; *responsabilidad* to carry out.
(**f**) *cañón* to man; *máquina* to tend, mind, man.
(**g**) (*Tenis etc*) to serve; *cartas* to deal.
(**h**) (‡: *detener*) to nick‡, arrest.
2 *vi* (**a**) (*gen*) to serve; (*criado*) to be in service; **sirvió 10 años** he served 10 years, he did 10 years; **está sirviendo** (*Mil*) he's doing his military service; **para ~ a Vd** at your service.
(**b**) (*camarero*) to serve, wait (*a* at, on).
(**c**) (*ser útil*) to serve (*de* as, for); to be of use, be useful; **eso no sirve** that's no good, that won't do; **~ en lugar de** to do duty for; **~ de guía** to act as guide, serve as a guide; **no sirve de nada que vaya él** it's no use his going; **~ para** to be good for, be used for; **no sirve para nada** it's no use at all, it's utterly useless; **él no sirve para nada** he's a dead loss; **yo no serviría para futbolista** I shouldn't be any good as a footballer.
(**d**) **~ del palo** (*Naipes*) to follow suit.
3 servirse *vr* (**a**) (*en la mesa*) to serve o.s., help o.s.; **se sirvió patatas** he helped himself to potatoes; **se sirvió café** he poured himself some coffee; **¡sírvete más!** have some more!; **¿no te sirves más ensalada?** wouldn't you like more salad?; **¿qué se sirven?** (*LAm*) what are you going to have?
(**b**) **~ de algo** to make use of sth, use sth; to put sth to use.
(**c**) **~** + *infin* to be kind enough to + *infin*; to deign to + *infin*, condescend to + *infin*; **sírvase sentarse** please sit down, would you like to sit down?; **sírvase darme su dirección** could you give me your address, please?; **si la señora se sirve pasar por aquí** if madam would care to come this way.
servo *nm* servo.
servo... *pref* servo...
servoasistido *adj* servoassisted.
servodirección *nf* power steering.
servofrenos *nmpl* power-assisted brakes.
sésamo *nm* sesame; **¡~ ábrete!** open sesame!
sesapil *nm* sex-appeal.
sesear [1a] *vt to pronounce* c (*before* e, i) *and* z [θ] *as* [s] (*a feature of Andalusian and much LAm pronunciation*).
sesenta *adj* sixty; sixtieth; **los** (**años**) **~** the sixties.
sesentañera *nf* woman of about sixty.
sesentañero *nm* man of about sixty.
sesentón 1 *adj* sixty-year old, sixtyish. **2** *nm*, **sesentona** *nf* person of about sixty.
seseo *nm pronunciation of* c (*before* e, i) *and* z [θ] *as* [s].

sesera *nf* (*Anat*) brainpan; (*) brains, intelligence.
sesgado *adj* (**a**) slanted, slanting, oblique; leaning; awry, askew; *pelota* swerving, sliced. (**b**) (*fig*) biased, slanted.
sesgar [1h] *vt* (**a**) (*inclinar*) to slant, slope, place obliquely; (*ladear*) to put askew, twist to one side; *pelota* to swerve, cut, slice.
(**b**) (*Cos*) to cut on the slant, cut on the bias.
(**c**) (*Aut*) to cut across, cut in on.
(**d**) (*fig*) *reportaje etc* to bias, slant.
sesgo *nm* (**a**) (*inclinación*) slant, slope; (*torcimiento*) warp, twist, twisted position; (*Cos*) bias; (*de pelota*) swerve, slice; **estar al ~** to be aslant, be awry; **cortar algo al ~** to cut sth on the bias.
(**b**) (*fig*) direction; twist, turn; **ha tomado otro ~** it has taken a new turn.
(**c**) (*: *truco*) dodge*.
sésil *adj* sessile.
sesión *nf* (**a**) (*Parl etc*) session, sitting, meeting; (*Inform*) session; **~ de preguntas al gobierno** question-time; **~ de trabajo** (*acto*) working period; (*grupo*) working party; (*de gimnasio*) work-out; **~ secreta** secret session; **abrir la ~** to open the meeting; **celebrar una ~** to hold a meeting; **levantar la ~** to close the meeting, adjourn.
(**b**) (*Teat*) show, performance; **~ de espiritismo** séance; **~ de prestidigitación** conjuring show, exhibition of conjuring; **~ de lectura de poesías** poetry reading.
(**c**) (*Cine*) showing; **~ continua** continuous showing; **iremos a la segunda ~** we'll go to the second house; **hay 3 sesiones diarias** there are 3 showings a day.
sesionar [1a] *vi* to sit; to be in session; to hold a meeting.
seso *nm* (**a**) (*Anat*) brain; **~s** (*Culin*) brains.
(**b**) (*fig*) brains, sense, intelligence; **calentarse los ~s, devanarse los ~s, estrujarse los ~s** to rack one's brains; **perder el ~** to go off one's head (*por* over); **eso le tiene sorbido el ~** he's crazy about it.
sesquicentenario *nm* 150th anniversary, sesquicentenary.
sesquipedal *adj* sesquipedalian.
sestear [1a] *vi* to take a siesta, have a nap.
sesteo *nm* (*LAm*) siesta, nap.
sesudamente *adv* sensibly, wisely.
sesudo *adj* (**a**) (*juicioso*) sensible, wise. (**b**) (*inteligente*) brainy. (**c**) (*Cono Sur: terco*) stubborn, pig-headed.
set *nm, pl* **set** *o* **sets** (*Tenis*) set.
set. *abr de* **setiembre** September, Sept.
seta *nf* (**a**) mushroom; **~ venenosa** toadstool. (**b**) (**) cunt**.
setecientos *adj* seven hundred; **en el ~** in the eighteenth century.
setenta *adj* seventy; seventieth; **los (años) ~** the seventies.
setentañera *nf* woman of about seventy.
setentañero *nm* man of about seventy.
setentón 1 *adj* seventy-year old, seventyish. **2** *nm*, **setentona** *nf* person of about seventy.
setero 1 *adj* mushroom (*atr*). **2** *nm*, **setera** *nf* mushroom gatherer.
setiembre *nm* September.
seto *nm* (**a**) (*cercado*) fence; **~ vivo** hedge. (**b**) (*Carib: pared*) dividing wall, partition.
setter *nm, pl* **setters** [se'ter] setter.
SEU ['seu] *nm* (*Hist*) *abr de* **Sindicato Español Universitario.**
seudo... *pref* pseudo...
seudohistoria *nf* pseudohistory.
seudónimo 1 *adj* pseudonymous. **2** *nm* pseudonym; pen name, nom de plume.
Seúl *nm* Seoul.
s.e.u.o. *abr de* **salvo error u omisión** errors and omissions excepted, E.&O.E.
severamente *adv* (*V adj* (**a**), (**c**)) (**a**) severely, harshly; strictly.
(**b**) severely; grimly, sternly.
severidad *nf* (*V adj* (**a**), (**c**)) (**a**) severity, harshness; strictness; stringency. (**b**) severity; grimness, sternness.
severo *adj* (**a**) *carácter etc* severe, harsh; *disciplina* strict; *crítica, castigo* harsh; *padre etc* strict, harsh; *condiciones* harsh, stringent; **ser ~ con uno** to be hard on sb, treat sb harshly.
(**b**) *invierno etc* severe, harsh, hard; *frío* bitter.
(**c**) *cara, expresión* severe; grim, stern; *estilo, vestido etc* severe.
seviche *nm* = **cebiche.**
Sevilla *nf* Seville.
sevillanas *nfpl* (**a**) (*melodía*) *popular Sevillian tune*. (**b**) (*baile*) *typical Sevillian dance*.
sevillano 1 *adj* Sevillian, of Seville. **2** *nm*, **sevillana** *nf* Sevillian, native (*o* inhabitant) of Seville.
sexagenario 1 *adj* sexagenarian, sixty-year old. **2** *nm*, **sexagenaria** *nf* sexagenarian, person in his (*o* her) sixties.
sexagésimo *adj* sixtieth.
sexar [1a] *vt pollitos* to sex.
sexenio *nm* (*Méx Pol*) (six-year) presidential term.
sexería *nf* sex shop.
sexi = **sexy.**
sexismo *nm* sexism.
sexista *adj, nmf* sexist.
sexo *nm* sex; **el bello ~** the fair sex; **el ~ débil** the gentle sex; **el ~ femenino** the female sex; **el ~ fuerte** the stronger sex; **el ~ masculino** the male sex; **~ en grupo** group sex; **~ oral** oral sex; **de ambos ~s** of both sexes; **sin ~** sexless; **hablar del ~ de los ángeles** to talk in a pointless way, indulge in pointless discussion.
sexofobia *nf* aversion to sex.
sexología *nf* sexology.
sexólogo, -a *nm/f* sexologist.
sextante *nm* sextant.
sexteto *nm* sextet(te).
sextillizo, -a *nm/f* sextuplet.
sexto *adj, nm* sixth.
séxtuplo *adj* sixfold.
sexual *adj* sexual; sex (*atr*); **vida ~** sex life.
sexualidad *nf* (**a**) (*gen*) sexuality. (**b**) (*sexo*) sex; **determinar la ~ de** to determine the sex of.
sexualmente *adv* sexually.
sexy [sesi] **1** *adj invar* (*a veces pl* **sexys**) *mujer* sexy, full of sex-appeal; *libro, escena etc* warm, hot; **película ~** pornographic film; **~ show** adult show, nude show. **2** *nm* sexiness, sex-appeal. **3** *nf* nude artiste; stripper.
s.f. *abr de* **sin fecha** no date, n.d.
s/f (*Com*) *abr de* **su favor** your favour.
SGAE *nf abr de* **Sociedad General de Autores de España.**
SGEL [se'xel] *nf abr de* **Sociedad Española General de Librería.**
SGR *nf abr de* **sociedad de garantía recíproca.**
sgte(s). *abr de* **siguiente**(**s**) following, foll.
shock [ʃok] *nm, pl* **shock** *o* **shocks** [ʃok] (*Med*) shock.
short [ʃor] *nm, pl* **shorts** [ʃor] shorts.
show [tʃo, ʃou] *nm* (**a**) (*Teat etc*) show; spectacle. (**b**) (*farsa*) farce, masquerade. (**c**) (*: *jaleo*) fuss, bother; display of bad temper; **menudo ~ hizo** (*Esp*) he made a great song-and-dance about it.
si[1] *conj* (**a**) if; **~ lo quieres te lo doy** if you want it I'll give it to you; **~ me lo pedía se lo daba** if he asked me for it I gave it to him; **~ me lo hubiese pedido se lo hubiera dado** if he had asked me for it I would have given it to him; **~ lo sé te lo digo*** if I had known about it I would have told you.
(**b**) (*en pregunta indirecta*) if, whether; **me pregunto ~ vale la pena** I wonder whether (*o* if) it's worth the trouble; **no sé ~ hacerlo o no** I don't know whether to do it or not; **hablaban de ~ hacerlo o no** they were talking about whether to do it or not; **que ~ lavar los platos, que ~ limpiar el suelo, que ~ ...** what with washing up and sweeping the floor and ...
(**c**) (*locuciones etc*) **~ no** if not; otherwise, or else; **¿~ vendrá?** I wonder if he'll come?; **¿~ será verdad?** what if it's true?; **¿~ nos lo roban?** what if somebody steals it?, suppose it gets stolen?; **lleva un revólver por ~ (acaso) resulta útil** he carries a gun in case it should come in handy; **¡por ~ eso fuera poco!** as if that wasn't enough!; **¡~ fuera verdad!** if only it were true!; **¡~ viniese pronto!** I wish he'd come!; **¡~ (es que) acabo de llamar!** but I've only just phoned you!; **¡~ no está!** but it isn't there!; **¡~ no sabía que estabas allí!** but I didn't know you were there!; **¡~ es el cartero!** why, it's the postman!
si[2] *nm* (*Mús*) B; **~ mayor** B major.
sí[1] **1** *adv* (**a**) (*afirmativo*) yes; indeed, certainly; **él no quiere pero yo ~** he doesn't want to but I do; **ellos no van pero nosotros ~** they aren't going but we are; **~, pero menos** (*iró*) that's a bit much, that's pushing things a bit; **~ pues** (*LAm*) of course; **creo que ~** I think so; **¡que ~, hombre!** I tell you it is! (*etc*); **está de que ~*** he seems likely to agree; **¡(pues) ~ que estoy yo para bromas!** (*iró*) I should say I'm in the mood for jokes!; **por ~ o por no** in any case, just in case; **porque ~** because that's the way it is; because I say so; **lo hizo porque ~** he did it because he just felt like doing it; he did it because he thought it had to be done; (*pey*) he did it out of sheer cussedness; **una semana ~ y otra no** in alternate weeks, every other week.

(**b**) (*énfasis*) **¿sí?** oh?, really?, is that so?; **ella ~ vendrá** she will certainly come, she is sure to come; **ellos ~ tienen uno** they certainly have one; **¡~ que lo es!** I'll say it is!, you're dead right there!; **¡eso ~ que no!** never!, not on your life!

2 *nm* consent, agreement; **dar el ~** to agree, consent; (*mujer*) to accept a proposal; **todavía no tengo el ~** I have not yet received his consent, he still hasn't said yes.

sí² *pron reflexivo* (**a**) (*sing*) (*m*) himself, (*f*) herself, (*de objeto*) itself, (*de Vd*) yourself, (*gen*) o.s.; (*pl*) themselves, (*de Vds*) yourselves; **~ mismo** himself *etc*; **lo quieren todo para ~** they want the whole lot for themselves; **no lo podrá hacer por ~ solo** he won't be able to do it by himself; **conviene guardarlo para ~** it's best to keep it to o.s.; **se ríe de ~ misma** she laughs at herself; **no lo tiene en ~ misma** she doesn't have it in her.

(**b**) (*recíproco*) each other; **cambiaron una mirada entre ~** they exchanged a look, they gave each other a look.

(**c**) (*locuciones*) **de ~** in itself; spontaneously; **el problema es bastante difícil de ~** the problem is difficult enough in itself; **de por ~** in itself; per se; separately, individually; **estar en ~** to be in one's right mind; **pensar entre ~, pensar para ~** to think to o.s.; **estar fuera de ~** to be beside o.s.; **estar sobre ~** (*alerta*) to be on one's guard; (*engreído*) to be puffed up with conceit; *V* **decir, volver** *etc*.

Siam *nm* Siam.

siamés, -esa *adj nm/f* Siamese.

sibarita 1 *adj* sybaritic, luxury-loving; epicurean. **2** *nmf* sybarite, lover of luxury; epicure, bon vivant.

sibarítico *adj* sybaritic, luxury-loving; epicurean.

sibaritismo *nm* sybaritism, love of luxury; epicureanism.

Siberia *nf* Siberia.

siberiano, -a *adj nm/f* Siberian.

sibil *nm* (*cueva*) cave; (*sótano*) vault, underground store; (*de trigo*) corn-storage pit.

Sibila *nf* Sibyl.

sibila *nf* sibyl.

sibilante *adj, nf* sibilant.

sibilino *adj* sibylline.

sic... *pref* = **psic...**, *p.ej., para* **sicología** *V* **psicología.**

sicalipsis *nf* eroticism, suggestiveness; pornography.

sicalíptico *adj* erotic, suggestive; pornographic.

sicario *nm* hired assassin.

Sicilia *nf* Sicily.

siciliano, -a 1 *adj, nm/f* Sicilian. **2** *nm* (*Ling*) Sicilian.

sicofanta *nm*, **sicofante** *nm* sycophant.

sicomoro *nm*, **sicómoro** *nm* sycamore, sycamore tree.

sicote* *nm* (*LAm*) foot odour.

SIDA ['siða] *nm abr de* **síndrome de inmuno-deficiencia adquirida** acquired immuno-deficiency syndrome, AIDS; **~ declarado** full-blown AIDS.

sidatorio *nm* AIDS clinic.

sidecar ['saikar] *nm* sidecar.

sideral *adj*, **sidéreo** *adj* (**a**) astral, sidereal; space (*atr*). (**b**) (*fig*) *coste etc* astronomic.

siderometalúrgico *adj* iron and steel (*atr*).

siderurgia *nf* iron and steel industry.

siderúrgico 1 *adj* iron and steel (*atr*). **2 siderúrgica** *nf* iron and steel works.

sídico *adj* AIDS (*atr*).

sidoso 1 *adj* relating to AIDS, AIDS (*atr*). **2** *nm*, **sidosa** *nf* AIDS sufferer.

sidra *nf* cider.

sidrería *nf* cider bar.

sidrero 1 *adj* cider (*atr*). **2** *nm*, **sidrera** *nf* cider-maker.

sidrina *nf* cider.

siega *nf* (**a**) (*acto*) reaping, harvesting; mowing. (**b**) (*época*) harvest (time).

siembra *nf* (**a**) (*acto*) sowing; **patata de ~** seed potato. (**b**) (*época*) sowing time.

siembre *nm* (*Carib*) sowing.

siempre 1 *adv* (**a**) (*gen*) always; all the time; ever; (*LAm*) still; (*Méx*) in the end, eventually; **como ~** as usual, as always; **la hora de ~** the usual time; **somos amigos de ~** we're old friends; **es la historia de ~, es lo de ~** it's the same thing as it always is, it's the same old story; **desde ~** always; **lo vienen haciendo así desde ~** they've always done it this way; **¡hasta ~!*** see you!*; **para ~, por ~** for ever; for good (and all); **por ~ jamás** for ever and ever.

(**b**) (*LAm*) (*seguramente*) certainly, definitely; (*sin embargo*) still, in any case; **~ sí me voy** I'm going anyway; **~ no** (*Méx*) certainly not; **~ sí** certainly, of course.

2 *conj*: **~ que ...** (**a**) (+ *indic*) whenever; each time that ..., as often as ...

(**b**) (+ *subj*; *t* **~ y cuando ...**) provided that ...

siempreverde *adj* evergreen.

sien *nf* (*Anat*) temple.

siena¹ *nf* sienna.

siena²‡ *nf* (*Esp*) mug‡, face.

sierpe *nf* snake, serpent.

sierra *nf* (**a**) (*Téc*) saw; **~ de arco, ~ para metales** hacksaw; **~ de cadena** chainsaw; **~ de calados, ~ de calar** fretsaw; **~ circular** circular saw; **~ de espigar** tenon saw; **~ mecánica** power saw; **~ de vaivén** jigsaw.

(**b**) (*Geog*) mountain range, sierra; **la ~ madrileña** the hills close to Madrid; **van a la ~ a pasar el fin de semana** they're off to the mountains for the weekend.

(**c**) (*Méx Pez*) swordfish.

Sierra Leona *nf* Sierra Leone.

siervo, -a *nm/f* slave; **~ de la gleba** serf.

siesta *nf* (**a**) (*parte del día*) hottest part of the day, afternoon heat.

(**b**) (*sueñecito*) siesta, nap; **dormir la ~, echarse una ~, tomar una ~** to have one's afternoon nap, have a doze.

siestecita *nf* nap, doze.

siete¹ 1 *adj* seven; (*fecha*) seventh; **las ~** seven o'clock; **hablar más que ~** to talk nineteen to the dozen. **2** *nm* seven.

siete²‡ *nm* (*LAm*: *euf*) bum‡, backside.

sietecueros *nm invar* (*LAm*) gumboil, whitlow.

sietemesino *adj niño* premature; (*fig*) half-witted.

sífilis *nf* syphilis.

sifilítico, -a *adj, nm/f* syphilitic.

sifón *nm* (**a**) (*Téc*) trap, U-bend; siphon. (**b**) (*de agua*) siphon (of soda water); **whisky con ~** whisky and soda. (**c**) (*And*: *cerveza*) (bottled) beer. (**d**) (*Geol*) flooded underground chamber; underground stream.

sifrino *adj* (*Carib*) stuck-up*, full of airs and graces.

sig. *abr de* **siguiente** following, f.

siga *nf* (*Cono Sur*) pursuit; **ir a la ~ de algo** to chase after sth.

sigilo *nm* (*secreto*) secrecy; (*discreción*) discretion; (*pey*) stealth; slyness; **~ sacramental** secrecy of the confessional; **con mucho ~** with great secrecy.

sigilosamente *adv* secretly; discreetly; (*pey*) stealthily, slyly.

sigiloso *adj* secret; discreet; (*pey*) stealthy, sly.

sigla *nf* (*símbolo*) symbol; (*abreviatura*) abbreviation; acronym (*p.ej.* NATO, CAMPSA).

siglo *nm* (**a**) century; **S~ de las Luces** Age of Enlightenment (*18th century*); **~ de oro, ~ dorado** (*Mit*) golden age; **S~ de Oro** (*de España*) Golden Age (*Spain*: *about 1492-1650*); **los ~s medios** the Middle Ages; **el jugador del ~** the player of the century.

(**b**) (*fig*: *época*) age, time, times.

(**c**) (*fig*: *largo tiempo*) age(s); **hace un ~ que no le veo** I haven't seen him for ages.

(**d**) **por los ~s de los ~s** (*Rel*) world without end.

(**e**) (*Ecl*) **el ~** the world; worldly affairs; **retirarse del ~** to withdraw from the world, become a monk.

signar [1a] **1** *vt* (**a**) (*sellar*) to seal; (*marcar*) to put one's mark on.

(**b**) (*firmar*) to sign.

(**c**) (*Rel*) to make the sign of the Cross over.

2 signarse *vr* to cross o.s.

signatario, -a *adj, nm/f* signatory.

signatura *nf* (**a**) (*Mús, Tip*) signature. (**b**) (*de biblioteca*) catalogue number, press mark.

significación *nf* significance, importance; (*sentido*) meaning.

significado 1 *adj* well-known; outstanding.

2 *nm* (*importancia*) significance; (*de palabra etc*) meaning; **su ~ principal es ...** its chief meaning is ...; **una palabra de ~ dudoso** a word of uncertain meaning.

significante *adj* (*esp LAm*) significant.

significar [1g] **1** *vt* (**a**) (*palabra etc*) to mean; to signify (*t fig*); **¿qué significa 'nabo'?** what does 'nabo' mean?; **50 dólares significan muy poco para él** 50 dollars doesn't mean much to him; **significará la ruina de la sociedad** it will mean the ruin of the company; **él no significa gran cosa en estos asuntos** he doesn't count for much in these matters.

(**b**) (*expresar*) to make known, express (*a* to); **le significó la condolencia de la familia real** he expressed (*o* conveyed) the royal family's sympathy to him.

2 significarse *vr* (**a**) (*distinguirse*) to become known, make a name, become famous (*o* notorious); **~ como** to become known as, be recognized as.

(**b**) to declare o.s., take sides; **no ~** to refuse to take sides.

significativamente *adv* significantly; meaningfully.

significativo *adj* (**a**) (*gen*) significant; *mirada etc* meaning, expressive; **es ~ que ...** it is significant that ...; **calcularlo a 3 cifras significativas** to work it out to 3 significant figures. (**b**) (*influyente*) important, influential.

signo *nm* (**a**) (*gen*) sign; (*Mat*) sign, symbol; (*de analfabeto*) mark; **~ de admiración** exclamation mark; **~ de la cruz** sign of the Cross; **~ igual** equals sign; **~ de interrogación** question-mark; **~ (de) más, ~ de sumar** plus sign; **~ (de) menos** minus sign; **~ positivo** positive sign; **~ postal** postage-stamp; **~s de puntuación** punctuation marks; **~ de los tiempos** sign of the times; **~ de la victoria** victory sign, V-sign; **~ del zodíaco** sign of the zodiac; **bajo el ~ de** (*fig*) marked by, in the spirit of.

(**b**) (*fig*: *tendencia*) tendency; **una situación de ~ alentador** an encouraging situation; *V* **mercado.**

sigo *etc V* **seguir.**

sigs. *abr de* **siguientes** following, ff.

siguiente *adj* following; next; **dijo lo ~** he said the following; **¡que pase el ~!** next please!; **el día ~, al día ~** the following day, next day.

sij *nmf, pl* **sijs** Sikh.

sijolaj *nm* (*CAm Mús*) clay whistle, type of ocarina.

sílaba *nf* syllable.

silabario *nm* spelling book.

silabear [1a] *vt* to syllabify, syllabicate, divide into syllables; to pronounce syllable by syllable.

silabeo *nm* syllabification, syllabication, division into syllables.

silábico *adj* syllabic.

silba *nf* hissing, catcalls; **armar una ~, dar una ~** (**a**) to hiss.

silbar [1a] **1** *vt* (**a**) *melodía* to whistle; *silbato etc* to blow.

(**b**) *comedia, orador etc* to hiss.

2 *vi* (**a**) (*Mús*) to whistle; (*Anat*) to wheeze; (*viento*) to whistle; (*bala*) to whistle, whine; (*flecha etc*) to whizz, swish, hum.

(**b**) (*Teat etc*) to hiss, catcall, boo.

silbatina *nf* (*And, Cono Sur*) hissing, booing.

silbato *nm* whistle.

silbido *nm*, **silbo** *nm* whistle, whistling; hiss; wheeze; whine, whizz, swish, hum; **~ de oídos** ringing in the ears.

silenciador *nm* silencer.

silenciar [1b] **1** *vt* (**a**) *suceso etc* to hush up; *hecho etc* to keep silent about, pass over in silence. (**b**) *persona etc* to silence. (**c**) (*Téc*) to silence. **2 silenciarse** *vr*: **se silenció el asunto** the matter was hushed up; **se silenció su labor** a veil of silence was drawn over his work.

silencio 1 *nm* (**a**) (*gen*) silence; (*calma*) quiet, hush; **¡~!** silence!, quiet!; **~ administrativo** policy of doing nothing about a matter; **en ~** in silence; **en el ~ más absoluto** in dead silence; **entregar algo al ~** to cast sth into oblivion; **guardar ~** to keep silent, say nothing (*sobre* about); **había un ~ sepulcral** it was as quiet as the grave, there was a deathly silence; **imponer ~ a uno** to make sb be quiet; to force sb to remain silent; **mantener el ~ radiofónico** to keep radio silence; **pasar algo en ~** to pass over sth in silence; **reducir al ~** *persona* to silence, reduce to silence; *artillería* to silence.

(**b**) (*Mús*) rest.

2 *adj* (*And, CAm, Méx*) (*silencioso*) silent, quiet; (*tranquilo*) still.

silenciosamente *adv* silently, quietly; soundlessly; noiselessly.

silencioso 1 *adj* silent, quiet; soundless; *máquina* silent, noiseless. **2** *nm* silencer, muffler.

silense *adj* (*Esp*) of Silos, of Santo Domingo de Silos.

silente *adj* silent, noiseless.

sílex *nm* silex, flint.

sílfide *nf* (*t fig*) sylph.

silfo *nm* sylph.

silicato *nm* silicate.

sílice *nf* silica.

silíceo *adj* siliceous.

silicio *nm* silicon.

silicona *nf* silicone.

silicosis *nf* silicosis.

silo *nm* (*Agr*) silo; (*sótano*) underground store; (*depósito*) storage pit; (*Mil*) silo, bunker.

silogismo *nm* syllogism.

silogístico *adj* syllogistic.

silueta *nf* silhouette; (*de edificio*) outline; (*de ciudad*) skyline; (*de persona*) figure; (*Arte*) silhouette, outline drawing; **en ~** in silhouette.

siluetear [1a] *vt* to outline; (*fig*) to shape, mould.

silvático *adj* = **selvático.**

silvestre *adj* (*Bot*) wild; (*fig*) rustic, rural.

silvicultor(a) *nm/f* forestry expert.

silvicultura *nf* forestry.

silla *nf* (**a**) (*asiento*) seat; chair; **~ alta** high chair; **~ de balanza, ~ de hamaca** (*LAm*) rocking-chair; **~ eléctrica** electric chair; **~ giratoria** swivel chair; **~ de manos** sedan chair; **~ plegable, ~ plegadiza, ~ de tijera** folding chair, folding stool, camp-stool; **~ de ruedas** wheelchair; **política de la ~ vacía** policy of not taking one's seat (*in parliament etc*); **calentar la ~** to stay too long, overstay one's welcome; **movieron la ~ para que cayese** (*fig*) they pulled the rug out from under him.

(**b**) (*t* **~ de montar**) saddle.

sillar *nm* block of stone, ashlar.

sillería *nf* (**a**) (*sillas*) chairs, set of chairs; (*Teat etc*) seating; (*Ecl*) choir-stalls. (**b**) (*taller*) chairmaker's workshop. (**c**) (*Arquit*) masonry, ashlar work.

sillero *nm* (**a**) (*artesano*) chairmaker. (**b**) (*Cono Sur*: *caballo*) horse, mule.

silleta *nf* (**a**) (*silla pequeña*) small chair; (*LAm*: *silla*) seat, chair; (*LAm*: *taburete*) low stool. (**b**) (*Med*) bedpan.

sillico *nm* chamberpot; commode.

sillín *nm* saddle, seat.

sillita *nf* small chair; **~ de ruedas** pushchair.

sillón *nm* (**a**) (*butaca*) armchair; easy chair; (*LAm*) rocking-chair; **~ de lona** deckchair; **~ de orejas, ~ orejero** wingchair; **~ de ruedas** wheelchair.

(**b**) (*de montar*) woman's saddle, sidesaddle.

SIM [sim] *nm* (*Esp*) *abr de* **Servicio de Investigación Militar.**

sima *nf* abyss, chasm; pit; deep fissure, pothole.

Simbad *nm* Sinbad; **~ el marino** Sinbad the sailor.

simbiosis *nf* symbiosis.

simbiótico *adj* symbiotic.

simbólicamente *adv* symbolically.

simbólico *adj* symbolic(al); token (*atr*).

simbolismo *nm* symbolism.

simbolista *adj, nmf* symbolist.

simbolizar [1f] *vt* (*gen*) to symbolize; (*representar*) to represent, stand for, be a token of; (*ser ejemplo de*) to typify.

símbolo *nm* symbol; **~ de los apóstoles, ~ de la fe** Creed.

simbología *nf* (**a**) (*símbolos*) symbols (*collectively*); system of symbols. (**b**) (*estudio*) study of symbols.

simbombo *adj* (*Carib*) cowardly.

simetría *nf* symmetry; (*fig*) harmony.

simétricamente *adv* symmetrically; (*fig*) harmoniously.

simétrico *adj* symmetrical; (*fig*) harmonious.

simetrizar [1f] *vt* to make symmetrical; (*fig*) to bring into line, harmonize.

símico *adj* = **simiesco.**

simiente *nf* seed.

simiesco *adj* simian, apish.

símil 1 *adj* similar. **2** *nm* comparison; (*Liter*) simile.

similar *adj* similar.

similitud *nf* similarity, resemblance, similitude.

similor *nm* pinchbeck; **de ~** (*fig*) pinchbeck, showy but valueless; fake, sham.

simiñaca *nf* (*Carib*) tangle, mess.

simio *nm* ape, simian.

Simón *nm* Simon.

simonía *nf* simony.

simpatía *nf* (**a**) (*gen*) liking; (*afecto*) affection; **~ hacia, ~ por** liking for; **~s y antipatías** likes and dislikes; **coger ~ a uno** to take to sb, take a liking to sb; **ganarse la ~ de todos** to win everybody's affection, come to be well liked by everybody; **tener ~ a** to like; **tener mucha ~** to be likeable, nice; **no le tenemos ~ en absoluto** we don't like him at all; **no tiene ~s en el colegio** nobody at school likes him, he has no friends at school.

(**b**) (*de ambiente etc*) friendliness, warmth, congeniality; (*de lugar, persona etc*) charm, attractiveness, likeableness; **la famosa ~ andaluza** that well-known Andalusian charm.

(**c**) (*solidaridad*) fellow feeling; mutual support, solidarity, sympathy; (*comprensión*) understanding; **explosión por ~** secondary explosion; **mostrar su ~ por** to show one's support for, show one's solidarity with.

(**d**) (*compasión*) sympathy, compassion.

simpático *adj persona* nice, likeable, genial, pleasant; (*bondadoso*) kind; (*encantador*) charming, attractive; *ambiente etc* congenial, agreeable; **¡qué policía más ~!** what a nice policeman!; **no le hemos caído muy ~s** she didn't much take to us; **siempre procura hacerse ~** he's always trying to ingratiate himself; **me es ~ ese muchacho** I like that lad.

simpatizante *nmf* sympathizer (*de* with).

simpatizar [1f] *vi* (**a**) (*2 personas*) to get on (well together); **pronto simpatizaron** they hit it off at once, they soon became friends.

(**b**) **~ con** to get on well with, take to, hit it off with; to be congenial to.

simplada *nf* (*And, CAm*) (*cualidad*) simplicity, stupidity; (*acto etc*) stupid thing (to do *o* to say).

simple 1 *adj* (**a**) (*gen*) simple; (*sin adornos*) uncomplicated, unadorned, bare; (*Ling, Quím etc*) simple; (*Bot*) single; *método etc* simple, easy, straightforward.

(**b**) (*delante de n: puro*) mere; pure, sheer; alone; **por ~ descuido** through sheer (*o* pure) carelessness; **es cosa de una ~ plumada** it's a matter of a mere stroke of the pen; **me basta con tu ~ palabra** your word alone is good enough for me; **somos ~s aficionados** we're just amateurs.

(**c**) (*delante de n: corriente*) ordinary; **un ~ soldado** an ordinary soldier; **un ~ abogado** a solicitor of little importance.

(**d**) *persona* simple, simple-minded, innocent; (*crédulo*) gullible; (*pey*) foolish, silly.

2 *nm* (**a**) (*persona*) simpleton.

(**b**) (*And: licor*) liquor.

(**c**) **~s** (*Bot*) simples.

(**d**) **~s** (*Tenis*) singles.

simplemente *adv* (*V adj* (**a**), (**b**)) (**a**) simply. (**b**) simply, merely; purely.

simpleza *nf* (**a**) (*cualidad*) simpleness, simple-mindedness; gullibility; (*pey*) foolishness.

(**b**) (*una ~*) silly thing (to do *etc*); **~s** nonsense.

(**c**) (*fig*) trifle, small thing; **se contenta con cualquier ~** she's happy with any little thing; **se enojó por una ~** he got annoyed over nothing.

simplicidad *nf* simplicity, simpleness.

simplificable *adj* simplifiable.

simplificación *nf* simplification.

simplificar [1g] *vt* to simplify.

simplista *adj* simplistic.

simplón 1 *adj* simple, gullible. **2** *nm*, **simplona** *nf* simple soul, gullible person.

simplote = **simplón**.

simposio *nm* symposium.

simulación *nf* simulation; make-believe; (*pey*) pretence; **~ por ordenador** computer simulation.

simulacro *nm* (**a**) (*ídolo*) simulacrum; image, idol. (**b**) (*apariencia*) semblance; (*fingimiento*) sham, pretence; **un ~ de ataque** a mock attack; **un ~ de combate** a sham fight; **~ de incendio** fire-practice, fire-drill; **~ de salvamento** (*Náut*) boat-drill.

simulado *adj* simulated; (*fingido*) feigned; mock, sham.

simulador *nm* simulator; **~ de vuelo** flight simulator.

simular [1a] *vt* to simulate; (*fingir*) to feign, sham.

simultáneamente *adv* simultaneously.

simultanear [1a] *vt*: **~ dos cosas** to do two things simultaneously; **~ A con B** to contrive to do A at the same time as B, fit in A and B at the same time, synchronize A and B; **jugar con 16 tableros simultaneados** to play 16 boards simultaneously.

simultaneidad *nf* simultaneousness.

simultáneo *adj* simultaneous.

simún *nm* (*viento*) simoom; (*tempestad de arena*) sandstorm.

sin 1 *prep* (**a**) (*gen*) without; with no ...; apart from, not counting, not including; **~ nosotros** without us; **costó 5 dólares ~ los gastos de envío** it cost 5 dollars not counting postage and packing; **salió ~ sombrero** he went out without a hat (*o* hatless); **me he quedado ~ cerillas** I've run out of matches; **~ compromiso** without obligation; **~ protección contra el sol** with no protection against the sun.

(**b**) **~** + *infin* without + *ger*, *p.ej.* **~ verlo** without seeing it; **~ verlo yo** without my seeing it; **¡~ empujar!** don't push!, stop pushing!; **las 2 y el padre ~ venir** 2 o'clock and father hasn't come home yet; (*frec se traduce por 'un'* + *ptp, p.ej.*) **~ lavar** unwashed, **~ pagar** unpaid.

2 ~ que *conj* without + *ger*; **~ que lo sepa él** without his knowing; **entraron ~ que nadie les observara** they came in without anyone seeing them.

sinagoga *nf* synagogue.

Sinaí *nm* Sinai.

sinalefa *nf* elision.

sinalefar [1a] *vt* to elide.

sinapismo *nm* (**a**) (*Med*) mustard plaster; **hay que ponerle un ~*** he needs gingering up.

(**b**) (*fig*) bore; nuisance, pest.

sinarquismo *nm* (*Méx Pol*) Sinarquism (*Mexican fascist movement of the 1930s*).

sinarquista *nm* (*Méx Pol*) Sinarquist.

sinceramente *adv* sincerely.

sincerarse [1a] *vr* (*justificarse*) to vindicate o.s.; (*decir la verdad*) to tell the truth, be honest; **~ a, ~ con** to open one's heart to; to square o.s. with, give a full explanation to; **~ ante el juez** to justify one's conduct to the judge; **~ de su conducta** to explain one's conduct, justify one's conduct.

sinceridad *nf* sincerity; **con toda ~** in all sincerity.

sincero *adj* sincere.

síncopa *nf* (**a**) (*Ling*) syncope. (**b**) (*Mús*) syncope, syncopation.

sincopar [1a] **1** *vt* to syncopate. **2 sincoparse** *vr* (*corazón*) to miss a beat.

síncope *nm* (**a**) (*Ling*) syncope. (**b**) (*Med*) syncope; (*desmayo*) fainting fit, queer turn, blackout.

sincopizarse [1f] *vr* to have a fainting fit, have a blackout.

sincorbatismo *nm* habit of going without a tie.

sincretismo *nm* syncretism.

sincronía *nf* synchronous character; simultaneity.

sincrónico *adj* synchronous; (*Téc*) synchronized; *sucesos etc* simultaneous, coincidental; (*Ling*) synchronic.

sincronismo *nm* synchronism; simultaneity; (*de fechas etc*) coincidence.

sincronización *nf* synchronization.

sincronizadamente *adv* simultaneously.

sincronizador *nm* timer.

sincronizar [1f] *vt* to synchronize (*con* with).

síncrono *adj* synchronous.

sincrotrón *nm* synchrotron.

sindicación *nf* (**a**) (*de obreros*) unionization. (**b**) (*Prensa*) syndication. (**c**) (*LAm Jur*) charge, accusation.

sindical *adj* union (*atr*), trade-union (*atr*); (*Pol*) syndical.

sindicalismo *nm* trade(s) unionism; (*Pol*) syndicalism.

sindicalista 1 *adj* union (*atr*), trade-union (*atr*); (*Pol*) syndicalist. **2** *nmf* trade(s) unionist; (*Pol*) syndicalist.

sindicalizar [1f] **1** *vt* to unionize. **2 sindicalizarse** *vr* to form a union.

sindicar [1g] **1** *vt* (**a**) *obreros* to unionize, form into a trade(s) union. (**b**) (*LAm*) to charge, accuse.

2 sindicarse *vr* (*obrero*) to join a union; (*obreros*) to form themselves into a union.

sindicato *nm* (**a**) (*gen*) syndicate; **casarse por el ~*** to have a shotgun wedding. (**b**) (*de obreros*) trade(s) union, labor union (*US*).

sindicatura *nf* (*Fin*) syndicate.

síndico, -a *nm/f* trustee; (*Jur*) official receiver.

síndrome *nm* syndrome; **~ de abstinencia** withdrawal symptoms; **~ de Down** Down's syndrome; **~ premenstrual** premenstrual tension; **~ tóxico** poisoning.

sinécdoque *nf* synecdoche.

sinecura *nf* sinecure.

sine die *adv* sine die.

sinergía *nf* synergy.

sinfín *nm* (**a**) = **sinnúmero**. (**b**) (*Téc*) conveyor-belt; spiral conveyor.

sinfonía *nf* (**a**) symphony. (**b**) (*Carib Mús*) harmonica, mouth-organ.

sinfónico *adj* symphonic; **orquesta sinfónica** symphony orchestra.

sinfonieta *nf* sinfonietta.

sinfonola *nf* (*LAm*) jukebox.

Singapur *nm* Singapore.

singar [1h] **1** *vt* (*Carib**) to pester, annoy. **2** *vi* (*CAm, Carib***) to fuck**, screw**.

singladura *nf* (*Náut*) (*recorrido*) day's run; (*día*) nautical day (*from noon to noon*).

single *nm* (*Mús*) single.

singlista *nmf* (*LAm Dep*) singles player.

singón *nm* (*Carib, Méx*) womanizer, philanderer.

singuisarra* *nf* (*And, Carib*) row, racket.

singular 1 *adj* (**a**) (*Ling*) singular.

(**b**) **combate ~** single combat.

(**c**) (*fig*) outstanding, exceptional; (*pey*) singular, peculiar, odd.

2 *nm* (*Ling*) singular; **en ~** in the singular; (*fig*) **en ~** in particular; **se refiere a él en ~** it refers to him in particular; **que hable él en ~** let him speak solely for himself.

singularidad *nf* singularity, peculiarity, oddity.

singularizar [1f] **1** *vt* to single out; to refer specifically to.
2 singularizarse *vr* (*distinguirse*) to distinguish o.s., stand out, excel; (*llamar la atención*) to be conspicuous; (*ser el solo*) to be the odd one out; ~ **con uno** to single sb out for special treatment.

singularmente *adv* (**a**) (*extrañamente*) singularly, peculiarly, oddly. (**b**) (*especialmente*) especially.

sinhueso* *nf* tongue; **soltar la** ~ to shoot one's mouth off*.

siniestrado, -a 1 *adj* involved in an accident; damaged, wrecked, crashed; **la zona siniestrada** the affected area, the disaster zone. **2** *nm/f* victim (of an accident *etc*), person who has suffered a loss (*o* damage).

siniestralidad *nf* accident rate.

siniestro 1 *adj* (**a**) (*liter*) left.
(**b**) (*fig*) (*funesto*) sinister; (*de mal agüero*) ominous; (*maligno*) evil, malign.
(**c**) (*fig: nefasto*) fateful, disastrous.
2 *nm* (**a**) natural disaster, catastrophe, calamity; accident; ~ **marítimo** shipwreck, disaster at sea. (**b**) (*Fin*) insurance claim, claim on an accident (*etc*) insurance policy; ~ **total** total loss, total write-off.

sinnúmero *nm*: **un ~ de** a great many, no end of, a huge number of.

sino¹ *nm* fate, destiny.

sino² *conj* (**a**) but; **no son 8 ~ 9** there are not 8 but 9; **no cabe otra solución ~ que vaya él** there is no other solution but that he should go; **no lo hace sólo para sí ~ para todos** he's not doing it only for himself but for everybody.
(**b**) (*salvo*) except, save; only; **todos aplaudieron ~ él** everybody except him applauded; **no te pido ~ una cosa** I ask only (*o* but) one thing of you; **no deseo ~ verte** my sole wish is to see you; **no lo habría dicho ~ en broma** he could only have said it jokingly, he wouldn't have said it except as a joke.

sino... *pref* Chinese ..., Sino...

sínodo *nm* synod.

sinología *nf* Sinology.

sinólogo, -a *nm/f* Sinologist.

sinonimia *nf* synonymy.

sinónimo 1 *adj* synonymous (*con with*). **2** *nm* synonym.

sinopsis *nf invar* synopsis.

sinóptico *adj* synoptic(al); **cuadro ~**, diagram, chart.

sinovitis *nf*: ~ **del codo** tennis elbow.

sinrazón *nf* wrong, injustice, outrage.

sinsabor *nm* (**a**) (*disgusto*) trouble, unpleasantness. (**b**) (*dolor*) sorrow; (*inquietud*) uneasiness, worry.

sinsentido *nm* absurdity, the absurd.

sinsilico* *adj* (*Méx*) stupid, thick*.

sinsombrerismo *nm* hatlessness, custom of going hatless.

sinsonte *nm* mockingbird.

sinsostenismo *nm* bralessness, habit of going without a bra.

sinsustancia* *nmf* idiot.

sintáctico *adj* syntactic(al).

sintagma *nm* syntagma, syntagm.

Sintasol ® *nm* (*a kind of*) lino.

sintaxis *nf* syntax.

síntesis *nf invar* synthesis; ~ **de la voz humana** voice (*o* speech) synthesis.

sintéticamente *adv* synthetically.

sintético *adj* synthetic(al).

sintetizador *nm* synthesizer; ~ **de la voz humana** voice (*o* speech) synthesizer.

sintetizar [1f] *vt* to synthesize; (*resumir*) to summarize, sum up.

sintoísmo *nm* Shintoism.

síntoma *nm* symptom; sign, indication.

sintomático *adj* symptomatic.

sintomatizar [1f] *vt* to typify, characterize, be symptomatic of.

sintonía *nf* (**a**) (*acto: Elec*) syntony; (*Rad*) tuning. (**b**) (*Mús, Rad*) signature tune.

sintonización *nf* (*Rad*) tuning.

sintonizado *nm* tuning.

sintonizar [1f] *vt* (*Elec*) to syntonize; (*Cine*) to synchronize; (*Rad*) *emisora* to tune (in) to; to pick up, receive.

sinuosidad *nf* (**a**) (*gen*) sinuosity; waviness. (**b**) (*curva*) bend, curve, wave; **las ~es del camino** the windings of the road, the bends in the road. (**c**) (*fig*) deviousness.

sinuoso *adj* (**a**) *camino etc* winding, sinuous; *línea* wavy; *rumbo* devious. (**b**) (*fig*) *medio, persona etc* devious.

sinusitis *nf* sinusitis.

sinvergonzón‡ *nm* rotter*, swine‡.

sinvergüencería *nf* (**a**) (*cualidad*) villainy; rottenness; shamelessness. (**b**) (*acto*) = **sinvergüenzada.**

sinvergüenza *nmf* (**a**) (*pillo*) scoundrel, villain, rascal; (*canalla*) rotter*; ¡~! (*hum*) you villain! (**b**) (*descarado*) shameless person.

sinvergüenzada *nf* (*LAm*) villainous trick, rotten thing (to do)*.

sinvergüenzura *nf* (*LAm*) shamelessness.

Sión *nm* Zion.

sionismo *nm* Zionism.

sionista *adj, nmf* Zionist.

sipo *adj* (*And*) pockmarked.

sipotazo *nm* (*CAm*) slap (in the face), punch.

siqu... *pref* = **psiqu...**, *p.ej. para* **siquiatría** *V* **psiquiatría.**

siquiera 1 *adv* (**a**) (*por lo menos*) at least; **una vez ~** once at least, just once; **dame un abrazo ~** at least give me a hug; **deja ~ trabajar a los demás** at least let the others work; ~ **come un poquito** (*LAm*) at least eat a bit.
(**b**) **ni ~, ni ... ~** not even, not so much as; **ni él ~ vino** not even he came; **ella ni me miró ~** she didn't even look at me; **ni ~ probó la sopa** he hardly touched the soup.
2 *conj* (**a**) (*aunque*) even if, even though; **ven ~ sea por pocos días** do come even if only for a few days.
(**b**) ~ **venga, ~ no venga** whether he comes or not.

Siracusa *nf* Syracuse.

sirena *nf* (**a**) (*Mit*) siren; mermaid; ~ **de la playa** bathing beauty. (**b**) (*Téc*) siren, hooter; ~ **de buque** ship's siren; ~ **de niebla** foghorn.

sirga *nf* (*Náut*) towrope.

sirgar [1h] *vt* to tow.

sirgo *nm* (piece of) twisted silk.

Siria *nf* Syria.

sirimba *nf* (*Carib*) faint, fainting fit.

sirimbo *adj* (*Carib*) silly.

sirimbombo *adj* (*Carib*) (*débil*) weak; (*tímido*) timid.

sirimiri *nm* (*prov*) drizzle.

siringa *nf* (*LAm*) rubber tree.

siringal *nm* (*LAm*) rubber plantation.

Sirio *nm* Sirius.

sirio, -a *adj, nm/f* Syrian.

sirla‡ *nf* (**a**) (*arma*) chiv‡, knife. (**b**) (*atraco*) hold-up, armed robbery, stick-up‡.

sirlero‡ *nm* armed robber, hold-up man.

siró *nm* (*Carib*) syrup.

siroco *nm* sirocco.

sirope *nm* (*LAm*) syrup.

sirsaca *nf* seersucker.

sirte *nf* shoal, sandbank.

sirvienta *nf* servant, maid.

sirviente *nm* servant; waiter.

sisa *nf* (**a**) (*robo*) petty theft; (*ganancia*) dishonest profit (*made by a servant*); (*tajada*) cut, percentage*; **~s** pilfering, petty thieving. (**b**) (*Cos*) dart; armhole.

sisal *nm* sisal; sisal plant.

sisar [1a] *vt* (**a**) *artículos* to thieve, pilfer, filch; *persona* to cheat; *cuenta* to cheat on. (**b**) (*Cos*) to put darts in, take in.

sisear [1a] *vti* to hiss.

siseo *nm* hiss(ing).

Sísifo *nm* Sisyphus.

sísmico *adj* seismic.

sismo *nm* = **seísmo.**

sismografía *nf* seismography.

sismógrafo *nm* seismograph.

sismología *nf* seismology.

sismólogo, -a *nm/f* seismologist.

sisón¹ 1 *adj* thieving, light-fingered. **2** *nm,* **sisona** *nf* petty thief.

sisón² *nm* (*Orn*) little bustard.

sistema *nm* system; method; ~ **de alarma** alarm system; ~ **binario** binary system; ~ **de calefacción** heating (system); ~ **de diagnosis** diagnostic system; ~ **experto** expert system; ~ **de facturación** invoicing system; ~ **de gestión de base de datos** database management system; ~ **impositivo,** ~ **tributario** taxation, tax system; ~ **inmunitario,** ~ **inmunológico** immune system; ~ **de lógica compartida** shared logic system; **S~ Monetario Europeo** European Monetary System; ~ **montañoso** mountain range; ~ **nervioso** (**central**) (central) nervous system; ~ **operativo** operating system; ~ **operativo de disco** disk operating system; ~ **pedagógico** teaching method; ~ **rastreador** tracking system; ~ **de seguridad** security system; **trabajar con** ~ to work systematically, work methodically;

yo por ~ lo hago así I make it a rule to do it this way.
sistemática *nf* systematics.
sistemáticamente *adv* systematically.
sistematicidad *nf* systematic nature.
sistemático *adj* systematic.
sistematización *nf* systematization.
sistematizar [1f] *vt* to systematize.
sitiador *nm* besieger.
sitial *nm* seat of honour; ceremonial chair.
sitiar [1b] *vt* to besiege, lay siege to; (*fig*) to surround, hem in.
sitio *nm* (**a**) (*lugar*) place; spot; part; site, location; **real ~** royal country house; **en cualquier ~** anywhere; **en todos los ~s** everywhere, all over; **en el mejor ~ de la ciudad** in the best part of the city; **cambiar de ~** to shift, move; **cambiar de ~ con uno** to change places with sb; **dejar a uno en el ~** to kill sb (on the spot); **así no vas a ningún ~** you'll get nowhere doing that; **poner a uno en su ~** (*fig*) to put sb firmly in his place; **quedarse en el ~** to die instantly, die on the spot.
(**b**) (*espacio*) room, space; **¿hay ~?** is there any room?; **hay ~ de sobra** there's plenty of room; **hacer ~** to make room (*a uno* for sb); **te haremos ~** we'll make room for you.
(**c**) (*empleo*) job, post.
(**d**) (*Mil*) siege; **en estado de ~** in a state of siege; **levantar el ~** to raise the siege; **poner ~ a** to besiege.
(**e**) (*CAm, Cono Sur*: *solar*) building site, vacant lot (*US*).
(**f**) (*Carib, Méx Agr*) small farm, smallholding.
(**g**) (*LAm*) (*parada*) taxi rank, cab rank (*US*); **carro de ~** taxi, cab (*US*).
sito *adj* situated, located (*en* at, in).
situación *nf* (**a**) (*gen*) situation, position; (*status*) position, standing; **~ B** (*Mil y fig*) retirement; **~ económica** financial position; **~ límite** extreme situation; **crearse una ~** to attain a position of financial security, make good; **estar en ~ de** + *infin* to be in a position to + *infin*.
(**b**) **precio de ~** (*LAm*) bargain price.
situado *adj* (**a**) (*gen*) situated, placed. (**b**) **estar ~** (*Fin*) to be financially secure, be well placed.
situar [1e] **1** *vt* (**a**) (*gen*) to place, put, set; *edificio etc* to locate, situate, site; (*Mil*) to post, station; **sitúan esta etapa en el siglo XIII** they place this stage in the 13th century; **esto le sitúa entre los mejores** this places him among the best.
(**b**) (*Fin*) (*invertir*) to place, invest; (*depositar en banco*) to bank; (*destinar*) to set aside; to assign, earmark; **~ una pensión para uno** to settle an income on sb; **ha venido situando fondos en el extranjero** he has been placing money in accounts abroad.
2 situarse *vr* to get a position; to establish o.s., do well for o.s.
siútico *adj* (*Cono Sur*) = **cursi.**
siutiquería *nf* (*Cono Sur*) = **cursilería.**
skay [es'kai] *nm* imitation leather.
sketch [es'ketʃ] *nm, pl* **sketches** [es'ketʃ] (*Teat*) sketch.
S.L. (**a**) (*Com*) *abr de* **Sociedad Limitada** Limited Company, Ltd. (**b**) *abr de* **Sus Labores** self-employed (*V t* **labor** (**a**)).
slalom [ez'lalom] *nm* slalom; **~ gigante** giant slalom.
slam [ez'lam] *nm* (*Bridge*) slam; **gran ~** grand slam; **pequeño ~** little slam.
slip [ez'lip] *nm, pl* **slips** [ez'lip] (*Esp*) briefs, pants; (*LAm*) bathing-trunks.
s.l. ni f. (*Tip*) *abr de* **sin lugar ni fecha** no place or date, n.p. or d.
slogan [ez'loɣan] *nm, pl* **slogans** [ez'loɣan] slogan.
slot [es'lot] *nm*: **~ de expansión** (*Inform*) expansion slot.
S.M. (**a**) *nf* (*Esp Rel*) *abr de* **Sociedad Marianista.** (**b**) *abr de* **Su Majestad** His (*o* Her) Majesty, HM.
smash [ez'mas] *nm* (*Tenis*) smash.
SME *nm abr de* **Sistema Monetario Europeo** European Monetary System, EMS.
SMI *nm abr de* **salario mínimo interprofesional.**
smog [ez'smo] *nm* smog.
smoking [ez'mokin] *nm, pl* **smokings** [ez'mokin] dinner-jacket, tuxedo (*US*).
s/n *abr de* **sin número** no number.
snack [ez'nak] *nm, pl* **snacks** [ez'nak] (*merienda etc*) snack; (*cafetería*) snackbar.
s.n.m. *abr de* **sobre el nivel del mar** (height) above sea-level.
snob [ez'noß] *etc* = **esnob** *etc.*
SO *abr de* **suroeste** south-west, SW.
so[1] *prep* under; *V* **capa** *etc.*
so[2] *interj* (**a**) (*para parar*) whoa! (**b**) (*LAm*: *¡silencio!*) quiet!, shut up!* (**c**) (*Carib*) (*a animal*) shoo!
so[3] *como interj* (*contraction of* señor): **¡~ indecente!** you swine!; **¡~ burro!** you idiot!, you great oaf!
s/o (*Com*) *abr de* **su orden** your order.
soba *nf* (**a**) (*amasar*) kneading. (**b**) (*) (*bofetada*) slap, punch; (*paliza*) hiding*; **dar ~ a uno** to wallop sb*. (**c**) (*: *reprimenda*) telling-off*.
sobacal *adj* underarm (*atr*).
sobaco *nm* (*Anat*) armpit; (*Cos*) armhole; **lo pasó por el ~*** he dismissed it, he totally disregarded it.
sobado *adj* (**a**) *ropa* worn, shabby; (*ajado*) rumpled, crumpled, messed up; *libro* well-thumbed, dog-eared.
(**b**) (*fig*) *tema* well-worn; *chiste* hoary, corny*.
(**c**) (*Culin*) *hojaldre* short.
(**d**) (*Cono Sur**: *enorme*) big, huge.
sobador *nm* (**a**) (*And, Méx**: *Med*) bonesetter; quack. (**b**) (*And, Carib, Méx*: *lisonjero*) flatterer.
sobajar [1a] *vt* (**a**) (*gen*) to crush, rumple, mess up. (**b**) (*And, Méx*: *humillar*) to humiliate, demean.
sobajear [1a] *vt* (*LAm*) (*apretar*) to squeeze, press; (*desordenar*) to mess up.
sobandero *nm* (*And, Carib*) bonesetter; (*And*) quack.
sobaquera *nf* (**a**) (*Cos*) armhole. (**b**) (*pistolera*) shoulder holster. (**c**) (*CAm, Carib*: *olor*) underarm odour.
sobaquero *adj*: **funda sobaquera** shoulder holster.
sobaquina *nf* underarm odour.
sobar [1a] **1** *vt* (**a**) *tela etc* to handle, finger, dirty (with one's fingers); *ropa etc* to crush, rumple, crumple, mess up; *masa* to knead; *masilla etc* to squeeze (in the hands), soften; *músculo* to massage, rub.
(**b**) *persona* to fondle, feel (amorously); (*pey*) to finger, paw*, lay hands on.
(**c**) (*LAm*) *hueso* to set.
(**d**) (*And*: *despellejar*) to skin, flay.
(**e**) (*: *pegar*) to wallop*.
(**f**) (*: *molestar*) to pester; to annoy.
(**g**) (*And, Carib, Méx*: *lisonjear*) to flatter.
(**h**) (*CAm, Méx*: *reprender*) to tell off*.
2 *vi* (‡) to kip‡, sleep.
3 sobarse *vr* (*amantes*) to pet*, fondle, cuddle.
sobasquera *nf* (*CAm, Carib, Méx*) = **sobaquina.**
sobeo *nm* fondling, caresses, love-play.
soberanamente *adv* (*fig*) supremely.
soberanía *nf* sovereignty.
soberano 1 *adj* (**a**) (*Pol etc*) sovereign.
(**b**) (*fig*) supreme.
(**c**) (*) real, really big; **una soberana paliza** a real walloping*.
2 *nm*, **soberana** *nf* sovereign; **los ~s** the king and queen, the royal couple.
soberbia *nf* (**a**) (*orgullo*) pride; (*altanería*) haughtiness, arrogance.
(**b**) (*fig*) magnificence, grandeur, pomp.
(**c**) (*ira*) anger; (*malhumor*) irritable nature.
soberbio *adj* (**a**) (*orgulloso*) proud; haughty, arrogant. (**b**) (*fig*) magnificent, grand, superb; **¡~!** splendid! (**c**) (*enojado*) angry; irritable. (**d**) (*) = **soberano** (**c**).
sobeta‡ *adj invar*: **estar ~, quedarse ~** to be kipping‡.
sobijo *nm* (**a**) (*And, CAm*) = **soba.** (**b**) (*And*) (*desolladura*) skinning, flaying.
sobijón *nm* (*CAm*) = **sobijo.**
sobón* *adj* (**a**) (*que soba*) too free with one's hands, given to pawing*; (*fig*) fresh*, too familiar by half; *amantes* mushy, wet*; **¡no seas ~!** get your hands off me!, stop pawing me!*
(**b**) (*gandul*) lazy, workshy.
(**c**) (*And**: *adulón*) soapy*, greasy.
sobornable *adj* bribable, venal.
sobornar [1a] *vt* to bribe, suborn; to buy off; (*hum*) to get round.
soborno *nm* (**a**) (*un ~*) bribe; (*el ~*) bribery, graft. (**b**) (*And, Cono Sur*) (*sobrecarga*) extra load; (*prima*) extra, bonus; extra charge; **de ~** extra, in addition.
sobra *nf* (**a**) (*excedente*) excess, surplus; **~s** leavings, leftovers, scraps; (*Cos*) remnants.
(**b**) **de ~** spare, surplus, extra; **aquí tengo de ~** I've more than enough here, I've got plenty (and to spare) here; **tengo tiempo de ~** I've got plenty of time; **tuvo motivos de ~** he had plenty of justification, he was more than justified; **lo sé de ~** I know it only too well; **aquí estoy de ~** I'm not needed here; I'm in the way here.
sobradamente *adv* too; amply; over...; *saber* only too

well; **con eso queda ~ satisfecho** he is only too happy with that, with that he is more than fully satisfied.

sobradero *nm* overflow pipe.

sobradillo *nm* penthouse.

sobrado 1 *adj* (**a**) (*más que suficiente*) more than enough; (*excesivo*) superfluous, excessive; (*muy abundante*) superabundant; **hay tiempo ~** there's plenty of time; **motivo más que ~ para** + *infin* all the more reason to + *infin*; **tuvo razón sobrada** he was amply justified; **sobradas veces** repeatedly.

(**b**) **estar ~ de algo** to have more than enough of sth, be well provided with sth.

(**c**) (*rico*) wealthy; **no anda muy ~** he's not very well off.

(**d**) (*atrevido*) bold, forward.

(**e**) (*Cono Sur*: *enorme*) colossal.

(**f**) **darse de ~** (*And**) to be full of oneself.

2 *adv* too, exceedingly.

3 *nm* (**a**) attic, garret.

(**b**) **~s** (*Andalucía, Cono Sur*: *restos*) left-overs.

sobrador* *adj* (*Cono Sur*) stuck-up*, conceited.

sobrancero *adj* unemployed.

sobrante 1 *adj* (*que sobra*) spare, remaining, extra, surplus; *obrero* redundant.

2 *nm* (**a**) (*lo que sobra*) surplus, remainder; (*Com, Fin*) surplus; (*saldo*) balance in hand.

(**b**) **~s** odds and ends.

3 *nmf* redundant worker, person made redundant.

sobrar [1a] **1** *vt* to exceed, surpass.

2 *vi* (*quedar de más*) to remain, be left (over), be (to) spare; (*ser más que suficiente*) to be more than enough; (*ser superfluo*) to be superfluous; **por este lado sobra** there's too much on this side; **no es que sobre talento** it's not that there's a surplus of talent; **todo lo que has dicho sobra** all that you've said is quite unnecessary; **nos sobra tiempo** we have plenty (*o* lots *o* heaps) of time; **al terminar me sobraba medio metro** I had half a metre left over when I finished; **veo que aquí sobro** I see that I'm not needed here; I see that I'm in the way; **más vale que sobre que no que falte** better too much than too little.

sobrasada *nf* Majorcan sausage.

sobre[1] *nm* (**a**) (*gen*) envelope; **~ de primer día** (**de circulación**) first-day cover; **~ de paga, ~ de pago** pay-packet; **~ de sellos** packet of stamps. (**b**) (**‡**: *cama*) kip‡, bed; **meterse en el ~** to hit the hay*.

sobre[2] *prep* (**a**) (*lugar*) on, upon; (*encima de*) on top of; over, above; **está ~ la mesa** it's on the table; **volamos ~ Cádiz** we're flying over Cadiz; **prestar juramento ~ la Biblia** to swear on the Bible.

(**b**) (*cantidad etc*) over, over and above; more than; (*además de*) in addition to, on top of, besides; **un aumento ~ el año anterior** an increase over last year; **10 dólares ~ lo estipulado** 10 dollars over and above what was agreed; **~ todas mis obligaciones hay una nueva** on top of all my duties here comes another; **crimen ~ crimen** crime upon crime; **~ ser traidor es asesino** in addition to being a traitor he is a murderer.

(**c**) **estar ~ uno** (*fig*) (*acosar*) to keep on at sb; (*vigilar*) to keep constant watch over sb; **quiere estar ~ todos** he wants to control everyone.

(**d**) (*Fin etc*) on; **un préstamo ~ una propiedad** a loan on a property; **un tributo ~ las medias** a tax on stockings.

(**e**) (*cifras*) about; **~ las 6** at about 6 o'clock; **ocupa ~ 20 páginas** it fills about 20 pages, it occupies roughly 20 pages.

(**f**) (*porcentaje*) in, out of; **3 ~ 100** 3 in a 100, 3 out of every 100.

(**g**) (*tema*) about, on; **un libro ~ Tirso** a book about Tirso.

(**h**) (*comparaciones*) **si medimos julio ~ julio** if we measure this July against last July, if we compare this July with last July.

sobre... *pref* super..., over...

sobreabundancia *nf* superabundance, overabundance.

sobreabundante *adj* superabundant, overabundant.

sobreabundar [1a] *vi* to superabound (*en* in, with), be very abundant.

sobreactuación *nf* overacting.

sobreactuar [1e] *vi* to overact.

sobrealimentación *nf* overfeeding.

sobrealimentado *adj* (*Mec*) supercharged.

sobrealimentador *nm* supercharger.

sobrealimentar [1a] *vt* (**a**) *persona etc* to overfeed. (**b**) (*Mec*) to supercharge.

sobreañadido *adj* additional; (*pey*) superfluous.

sobreañadir [3a] *vt* to give in addition, add (as a bonus); to superinduce.

sobrecalentamiento *nm* overheating (*t fig*).

sobrecalentar [1j] *vt* to overheat (*t fig*).

sobrecama *nm* bedspread.

sobrecaña *nf* (*Vet*) splint.

sobrecapacidad *nf* overcapacity, excess capacity.

sobrecapitalización *nf* overcapitalization.

sobrecarga *nf* (**a**) (*carga*) extra load; (*peso*) excess weight; (*fig*) new burden.

(**b**) (*Com*) surcharge; (*Correos*) surcharge, overprint(ing); **~ de importación** import surcharge.

(**c**) (*cuerda*) rope.

sobrecargar [1h] *vt* (**a**) *camión etc* to overload; (*Elec*) to overcharge; *persona* to weigh down, overburden (*de* with); **~ el mercado** (*Cono Sur*) to glut the market.

(**b**) (*Com*) to surcharge; (*Correos*) to surcharge, overprint (*de* with).

sobrecargo *nm* (*Náut*) supercargo, purser.

sobrecejo *nm* (**a**) (*ceño*) frown. (**b**) (*Arquit*) lintel.

sobreceño *nm* frown.

sobrecito *nm* (*LAm*) sachet.

sobrecoger [2c] **1** *vt* (*sobresaltar*) to startle, take by surprise; (*asustar*) to scare, frighten.

2 sobrecogerse *vr* (**a**) (*asustarse*) to be startled, start (*a* at, *de* with); to get scared, be frightened.

(**b**) (*quedar impresionado*) to be overawed (*de* by); **~ de emoción** to be overcome with emotion.

sobrecontrata *nf* overbooking.

sobrecontratar *vti* to overbook.

sobrecoste *nm* extra charges; extra costs.

sobrecubierta *nf* outer cover; (*de libro*) jacket.

sobredicho *adj* aforementioned.

sobredimensionado *adj* (**a**) extra large; (*pey*) excessively large, oversized. (**b**) **estar ~ de** to have a surplus (*o* excess) of, have too much of.

sobredimensionamiento *nm* (*tamaño*) excessive size; (*de personal etc*) excessive number; overmanning; (*aumento*) increase in size, expansion.

sobredorar [1a] *vt* to gild; (*fig*) to gloss over.

sobredosis *nf invar* overdose.

sobre(e)ntender [2g] **1** *vt* to understand; (*adivinar*) to guess, deduce, infer.

2 sobre(e)ntenderse *vr*: **aquí se sobre(e)ntienden dos palabras** here two words are understood; **se sobre(e)ntiende que** ... it is implied that ..., one infers that ...

sobre(e)sfuerzo *nm* superhuman effort; (*Med*) overstrain.

sobre(e)stimación *nf* overestimate.

sobre(e)stimar [1a] *vt* to overestimate.

sobre(e)xcitación *nf* overexcitement.

sobre(e)xcitado *adj* overexcited.

sobre(e)xcitar [1a] **1** *vt* to overexcite. **2 sobre(e)xcitarse** *vr* to get overexcited.

sobre(e)xponer [2q] *vt* to overexpose.

sobre(e)xposición *nf* (*Fot*) overexposure.

sobrefunda *nf* (*CAm*) pillowslip, pillowcase.

sobregirar [1a] *vti* to overdraw.

sobregiro *nm* overdraft.

sobrehumano *adj* superhuman.

sobreimpresión *nf* (*Correos*) overprint(ing).

sobreimpresionar [1a] *vt* to overprint.

sobreimprimir [3a] *vt* (*Correos*) to overprint.

sobrellevar [1a] *vt peso* to carry, help to carry, help with; *carga de otro* to ease; *desastre, enfermedad, problemas etc* to bear, endure; *faltas ajenas* to be tolerant towards.

sobremanera *adv* exceedingly.

sobremarca *nf* (*Bridge*) overbid; raise (in a suit).

sobremarcha *nf* (*Aut*) overdrive.

sobremesa *nf* (**a**) (*mantel*) table cover.

(**b**) (*postre*) dessert.

(**c**) (*período etc del postre*) sitting on after a meal; **conversación de ~** table talk; **charla de ~** after-dinner speech; **lámpara de ~** table lamp; **orador de ~** after-dinner speaker; **ordenador de ~** desktop computer; **programa de ~** (*TV*) afternoon programme; **un cigarro de ~** an after-dinner cigar, a postprandial cigar; **estar de ~** to sit round the table after dinner; **hablaremos de eso de ~** we'll talk about that after dinner.

(**d**) (*de mueble*) desktop.

sobrenadar [1a] *vi* to float.

sobrenatural *adj* supernatural; (*misterioso*) weird, unearthly; **lo ~** the supernatural; **ciencias ~es** occult

sciences; **vida ~** life after death.
sobrenombre *nm* by-name, extra name; nickname.
sobrentender *etc* = **sobre(e)ntender** *etc*.
sobrepaga *nf* extra pay, bonus.
sobreparto *nm* confinement after childbirth; **dolores de ~** after-pains; **morir de ~** to die in childbirth.
sobrepasar [1a] **1** *vt* (*gen*) to exceed, surpass, outdo; *límite* to exceed; *esperanzas etc* to surpass; *rival, récord* to beat; *pista* (*Aer*) to overshoot. **2 sobrepasarse** *vr* = **propasarse**.
sobrepelo *nm* (*Cono Sur*) saddlecloth.
sobrepelliz *nf* surplice.
sobrepesca *nf* over-fishing.
sobrepeso *nm* (*carga*) extra load; (*de paquete, persona*) excess weight, overweight.
sobrepoblación *nf* overcrowding.
sobreponer [2r] **1** *vt* (**a**) (*objeto*) to put on top (*en* of), superimpose (*en* on), add (*en* to).
(**b**) **~ A a B** (*persona*) to give A preference over B, give more weight to A than to B.
2 sobreponerse *vr* (**a**) (*recobrar la calma*) to master o.s., pull o.s. together; (*triunfar*) to win through, pull through, overcome adversity (*etc*); to pull o.s. together.
(**b**) **~ a una enfermedad** to pull through an illness; **~ a un rival** to triumph over a rival; **~ a un enemigo** to overcome an enemy; **~ a un susto** to get over a fright, recover from a fright.
sobreprecio *nm* surcharge; increase in price.
sobreproducción *nf* overproduction.
sobreprotección *nf* over-protection.
sobreprotector *adj* over-protective.
sobrepuerta *nf* lintel.
sobrepuesto *adj* added, superimposed.
sobrepujar [1a] *vt* to outdo, excel, surpass; **sobrepuja a todos en talento** he excels all the rest in talent.
sobrereacción *nf* over-reaction.
sobrereserva *nf* overbooking.
sobrereservar [1a] *vti* to overbook.
sobrero 1 *adj* extra, spare. **2** *nm* (*Taur*) spare bull, reserve bull.
sobresaliente 1 *adj* (**a**) (*Arquit etc*) projecting; overhanging.
(**b**) (*fig*) outstanding, excellent; (*Univ etc*) *calificación* first class.
2 *nmf* substitute; (*Teat*) understudy.
3 *nm* (*Univ etc*) first class (mark), distinction.
sobresalir [3r] *vi* (**a**) (*Arquit etc*) to project, jut out; to overhang; to stick out, protrude; to stick up, stand up; to be conspicuous.
(**b**) (*fig*) to stand out, be outstanding, excel.
sobresaltar [1a] **1** *vt* to startle, scare, frighten. **2 sobresaltarse** *vr* to start, be startled (*con, de* at).
sobresalto *nm* (*sorpresa*) start; (*susto*) scare; (*conmoción*) sudden shock; **de ~** suddenly.
sobresanar [1a] *vi* (*Med*) to heal superficially; (*fig*) to conceal itself, hide its true nature.
sobrescrito *nm* (*señas*) address; (*inscripción*) superscription.
sobreseer [2e] **1** *vt*: **~ una causa** (*Jur*) to stop a case, stay a case. **2** *vi*: **~ de** to desist from, give up.
sobreseído *adj*: **causa sobreseída** (*Jur*) case dismissed.
sobresello *nm* double seal.
sobrestante *nm* (*capataz*) foreman, overseer; (*gerente*) site manager.
sobresueldo *nm* bonus.
sobretasa *nf* surcharge.
sobretiempo *nm* (*LAm*) overtime.
sobretiro *nm* (*Méx*) offprint.
sobretítulo *nm* (*Prensa*) general title, general heading.
sobretodo *nm* overcoat.
sobrevaloración *nf* overvaluation; (*fig*) overrating.
sobrevalorar [1a] *vt* to overvalue; (*fig*) to overrate, put too high a value on.
sobrevenir [3s] *vi* (*ocurrir*) to happen (unexpectedly), come up, supervene; (*resultar*) to follow, ensue.
sobrevirar [1a] *vi* to oversteer.
sobreviviente = **superviviente**.
sobrevivir [3a] *vi* to survive; **~ a** *accidente, desastre etc* to survive; *persona* to survive, outlive; (*durar más tiempo que*) to outlast.
sobrevolar [1m] *vt* to fly over, overfly.
sobrevuelo *nm* overflying; **permiso de ~** permission to overfly.
sobriedad *nf* soberness; moderation, restraint; quietness; plainness.
sobrina *nf* niece.
sobrinanieta *nf* great-niece.
sobrino *nm* nephew.
sobrinonieto *nm* great-nephew.
sobrio *adj* (*templado*) sober; (*moderado*) moderate, temperate, restrained; *color* quiet; *estilo, moda etc* plain, sober; **ser ~ en la bebida** to be temperate in one's drinking habits; **ser ~ de palabras** to speak with restraint.
sobros *nmpl* (*CAm*) left-overs, scraps.
soca[1] *nf* (**a**) (*And*) (*de arroz*) young shoots of rice; (*de tabaco*) top leaf of tobacco plant, high quality tobacco leaf.
(**b**) (*CAm**: *embriaguez*) drunkenness.
soca[2]* *nm*: **hacerse el ~** to act dumb*.
socaire *nm* (*Náut*) lee; **al ~** to leeward; **al ~ de** (*fig*) enjoying the protection of; using ... as an excuse; **estar** (*o* **ponerse**) **al ~** (*fig*) to shirk, dodge the column*.
socaliña 1 *nf* (*astucia*) craft, cunning; (*porfía*) clever persistence. **2** *nmf* (*) twister, swindler.
socaliñar [1a] *vt* to get by a swindle.
socaliñero *adj* crafty, cunning; cleverly persistent.
socapa* *nf* dodge, subterfuge; **a ~** surreptitiously.
socapar [1a] *vt*: **~ a uno** (*And, Méx**) to cover up for sb.
socar [1g] **1** *vt* (*CAm*) (**a**) (*comprimir*) to press down, squeeze, compress.
(**b**) (*: *enojar*) to annoy, upset.
2 *vi* (*CAm*) to make an effort.
3 socarse *vr* (*CAm*) (**a**) (*emborracharse*) to get drunk.
(**b**) **~ con uno** to fall out (*o* squabble) with sb.
socarrar [1a] *vt* to scorch, singe.
socarrón *adj* (**a**) (*sarcástico*) sarcastic, ironical; *humor* sly.
(**b**) (*taimado*) crafty, cunning.
socarronería *nf* (**a**) (*sarcasmo*) sarcasm, irony; sly humour. (**b**) (*astucia*) craftiness, cunning.
socava *nf*, **socavación** *nf* undermining.
socavar [1a] *vt* (**a**) (*excavar*) to undermine; to dig under, dig away; (*agua*) to hollow out. (**b**) (*fig*) to sap, undermine.
socavón *nm* (**a**) (*Min*) gallery, tunnel; (*hueco*) hollow; (*cueva*) cavern; (*en la calle*) hole. (**b**) (*Arquit etc*) subsidence, sudden collapse.
socia* *nf* (*Esp*) whore.
sociabilidad *nf* sociability, friendliness; gregariousness; conviviality.
sociable *adj* *persona* sociable, friendly; *animal* social, gregarious; *reunión etc* convivial.
sociablemente *adv* sociably; gregariously; convivially.
social 1 *adj* (**a**) (*gen*) social. (**b**) **acuerdo ~, pacto ~** wages agreement; **paz ~** industrial harmony, agreement between employers and unions. (**c**) (*Com, Fin*) company (*atr*), company's; *V* **capital, razón. 2 ~es*** *nmpl* (*Escol*) social studies.
socialdemocracia *nf* social democracy.
socialdemócrata *nmf* social democrat.
socialdemocrático *adj* social democratic.
socialismo *nm* socialism.
socialista 1 *adj* socialist(ic). **2** *nmf* socialist.
socialización *nf* socialization; nationalization.
socializar [1f] *vt* to socialize; to nationalize.
socialmente *adv* socially.
sociata‡ *adj, nmf* socialist.
sociedad *nf* (**a**) (*gen*) society; **los males de la ~ actual** the ills of contemporary society; **~ benéfica** welfare state; **~ de consumo** consumer society; **~ del ocio** leisure society; **~ opulenta** affluent society; **~ permisiva** permissive society; **hacer ~** to join forces.
(**b**) (*asociación*) society, association; (*cuerpo*) body; **~ científica, ~ docta** learned society; **~ gastronómica** dining club; **~ inmobiliaria** building society; **S~ de Jesús** Society of Jesus; **S~ de las Naciones** League of Nations; **~ secreta** secret society; **~ de socorro mutuo** friendly society, provident society.
(**c**) (*Com, Fin*) company; partnership; **~ anónima** limited liability company, corporation; **~ anónima laboral** workers' cooperative; **Góngora y Quevedo S~ Anónima** (*abr* SA) Góngora and Quevedo Limited (Incorporated *US*); **~ de cartera, ~ de control** holding company; **~ en comandita** limited partnership; **~ mercantil** company, trading company.
(**d**) (*mundo elegante*) society; **alta ~, buena ~** (high) society; **notas de ~** gossip column, column of society news; **entrar en ~, presentarse en (la) ~** to come out, make one's début.
(**e**) **~ conyugal** marriage partnership.

societal *adj* societal.
socio *nmf* (*t* **socia**) (**a**) (*gen*) associate; (*de club*) member; (*de sociedad docta etc*) fellow; **se ruega a los señores ~s ...** members are asked to ...; **~ honorario, ~ de honor** honorary member; **~ numerario, ~ de número** full member; **~ vitalicio** life member.
(**b**) (*Com, Fin*) partner; **~ activo** active partner; **~ capitalista, ~ comanditario, ~ pasivo** sleeping partner, silent partner (*US*).
(**c**) (*: *amigo*) buddy, mate*; (*coime*) pimp.
socio... *pref* socio...
sociobiología *nf* sociobiology.
socioeconómico *adj* socioeconomic.
sociolingüística *nf* sociolinguistics.
sociolingüístico *adj* sociolinguistic.
sociología *nf* sociology.
sociológico *adj* sociological.
sociólogo, -a *nm/f* sociologist.
sociopolítico *adj* sociopolitical.
sociosanitario *adj* public health (*atr*).
soco 1 *adj* (**a**) (*CAm*: *borracho*) drunk, tight*.
(**b**) = **zoco 1.**
2 *nm* (**a**) (*And Anat, Bot*) stump.
(**b**) (*And*: *cuchillo*) short blunt machete.
(**c**) = **zoco 2.**
socola *nf* (*And, CAm*) clearing of land.
socolar [1a] *vt* (**a**) (*And, CAm*) *tierra* to clear, clear of scrub.
(**b**) (*And*) *trabajo etc* to bungle, do clumsily.
socollón *nm* (*CAm, Carib*) violent shaking.
socollonear [1a] *vt* (*CAm*) to shake violently.
socón‡ *adj* (*CAm*) studious, swotty*.
soconusco *nm* (**a**) (*chocolate*) (*Carib*) chocolate; (*CAm, Méx*) high quality chocolate. (**b**) (*Carib**: *trato*) shady deal, dirty business.
socorrer [2a] *vt persona* to help; *necesidad* to relieve, meet, help with; *ciudad* to relieve; *expedición etc* to bring aid to.
socorrido *adj* (**a**) *tienda etc* well-stocked. (**b**) *objeto etc* handy; useful. (**c**) *persona* helpful, obliging, cooperative. (**d**) (*fig*: *probado*) well-tried; (*corriente*) ordinary, usual, common; *frase* well-worn.
socorrismo *nm* life-saving.
socorrista *nmf* lifeguard, life-saver.
socorro *nm* (**a**) (*ayuda*) help, aid, assistance; relief (*t Mil*); **¡~!** help!; **~s mutuos** mutual aid; **trabajos de ~** relief work, rescue work.
(**b**) (*Cono Sur*: *pago adelantado*) advance payment, sub*.
socoyote *nm* (*Méx*) smallest child.
Sócrates *nm* Socrates.
socrático *adj* Socratic.
socrocio *nm* (*Med*) plaster.
socucha *nf*, **socucho** *nm* (*Cono Sur, Méx*) (*cuartito*) poky little room, den; (*casucha*) hovel, slum.
soche *nm* (*And*) tanned sheepskin (*o* goatskin).
soda *nf* (**a**) (*Quím*) soda. (**b**) (*bebida*) soda water.
sodio *nm* sodium.
Sodoma *nm* Sodom.
sodomía *nf* sodomy.
sodomita *nm* sodomite.
sodomizar [1f] *vt* to sodomize.
SOE *nm* (*Esp*) *abr de* **Seguro Obligatorio de Enfermedad.**
soez *adj* dirty, rude, obscene.
sofá *nm* sofa, settee.
sofá-cama *nm*, **sofá-nido** *nm* studio couch, sofa-bed.
sofero *adj* (*And*) huge, enormous.
Sofia *nf*, **Sofía¹** *nf* Sophia.
Sofía² *nf* (*Geog*) Sofia.
sofión *nm* (*bufido*) angry snort; (*reprimenda*) sharp rebuke; (*réplica*) sharp retort.
sofisma *nm* sophism.
sofista *nmf* sophist; (*fig*) quibbler.
sofistería *nf* sophistry.
sofisticación *nf* sophistication; (*pey*) affectation, over-refinement.
sofisticado *adj* sophisticated; (*pey*) affected, over-refined.
sofístico *adj* sophistic(al); false, fallacious.
soflama *nf* (**a**) (*fuego*) dull glow, flicker. (**b**) (*sonrojo*) blush. (**c**) (*fig*: *arenga*) fiery speech, harangue. (**d**) (*fig**) (*engaño*) deceit; (*halagos*) cajolery, blarney. (**e**) (*Méx*: *chisme*) piece of trivia, bit of gossip.
soflamar [1a] *vt* (**a**) (*quemar*) to scorch; (*Culin*) to singe. (**b**) *persona* to shame, make blush. (**c**) (*: *engañar*) to deceive, swindle; (*halagar*) to cajole, blarney.
sofocación *nf* (**a**) (*gen*) suffocation. (**b**) (*fig*) = **sofoco** (**b**).
sofocado *adj*: **estar ~** (*fig*) to be out of breath; to feel stifled; to be hot and bothered; to be upset.
sofocante *adj* stifling, suffocating.
sofocar [1g] **1** *vt* (**a**) *persona* to suffocate, stifle.
(**b**) *incendio* to smother, put out; *rebelión etc* to crush, put down; *epidemia* to stop.
(**c**) (*fig*) **~ a uno** (*hacer sonrojar*) to make sb blush; (*avergonzar*) to put sb to shame; (*azorar*) to embarrass sb; (*enojar*) to anger sb, get sb worked up, provoke sb, upset sb.
2 sofocarse *vr* (**a**) (*ahogarse*) to suffocate, stifle; (*jadear*) to get out of breath, (begin to) pant; (*no poder respirar*) to choke.
(**b**) (*fig*) to blush; to feel embarrassed; to get angry, get worked up, get upset, upset o.s.; **no vale la pena de que te sofoques** it's not worth upsetting yourself about it.
(**c**) (*CAm, Méx*: *preocuparse*) to worry, be anxious.
Sófocles *nm* Sophocles.
sofoco *nm* (**a**) (*gen*) suffocation; stifling sensation; **~ de calor** hot flush.
(**b**) (*fig*) (*azoro*) embarrassment; (*ira*) anger, rage, feeling of indignation.
(**c**) **pasar un ~** to have an embarrassing time.
sofocón* *nm* shock, nasty blow; **se le dio un ~** he really blew up*, he got really worked up; **llevarse un ~** to have a sudden shock.
sofoquina* *nf* (**a**) (*calor*) stifling heat; **hace una ~** it's stifling hot. (**b**) = **sofocón.**
sofreír [3l; *ptp* **sofrito**] *vt* to fry lightly.
sofrenada *nf* (**a**) sudden check, sudden jerk on the reins. (**b**) (*) ticking-off*.
sofrenar [1a] *vt* (**a**) *caballo* to rein back sharply. (**b**) (*fig*) to restrain, control. (**c**) (*: *echar una bronca*) to tick off*.
sofrito *adj* lightly fried.
sofrología *nf* sleep therapy.
software ['sofwer] *nm* software; **~ de aplicación** application software; **~ del sistema** system software; **~ del usuario** user software.
soga *nf* (*gen*) rope, cord; (*de animal*) halter; (*del verdugo*) hangman's rope; **dar ~ a uno** to make fun of sb; **echar la ~ tras el caldero** to chuck it all up*, throw in one's hand; **estar con la ~ al cuello** to be in imminent danger, be in a real fix*; **hablar de** (*o* **mentar**) **la ~ en casa del ahorcado** to say something singularly inappropriate; **no hay que hablar de** (*o* **mentar**) **la ~ en casa del ahorcado** there's a time and a place for everything; **hacer ~** to lag behind.
soguear [1a] *vt* (**a**) (*And, CAm, Cono Sur*: *atar*) to tie with a rope; (*Carib*: *lazar*) to lasso. (**b**) (*Carib*: *domesticar*) to tame. (**c**) (*And**: *burlarse*) to make fun of.
soguero *adj* (*Carib*) tame.
sois *V* **ser.**
soja *nf* soya; **semilla de ~** soya bean.
sojuzgar [1h] *vt* (*vencer*) to conquer; to subdue; (*tiranizar*) to rule despotically.
sol¹ *nm* (**a**) (*gen*) sun; (*luz solar*) sunshine, sunlight; **~ artificial** sunlamp; **~ naciente** rising sun; **~ poniente** setting sun; **como un ~** as bright as a new pin; **día de ~** sunny day; **de ~ a ~** from sunrise to sunset; **dejar algo al ~** to leave sth in the sun; **tostarse al ~** to sit in the sun, acquire a sun tan; **arrimarse al ~ que más calienta** to know which side one's bread is buttered; to climb on the bandwagon; **no dejar a uno ni a ~ ni a sombra** to chase sb all over, pester sb continually; **mirar algo a contra ~** to look at sth against the light; **hay ~, hace ~** it is sunny, the sun is shining; **salga el ~ por donde quiera** come what may; press on regardless; **tomar el ~, tumbarse al ~** to sun o.s., sunbathe, bask.
(**b**) (*Fin*) sol (*Peruvian unit of currency*).
(**c**) (*Carib**) **~ y luna** machete, cane knife.
(**d**) (*) **¡es un ~!** he's great!*, he's the greatest!*; **el niño es un ~** he's a lovely child.
(**e**) (*: *bebida*) glass of brandy and anisette.
sol² *nm* (*Mús*) G; **~ mayor** G major.
solada *nf* sediment.
solado *nm* tiling, tiled floor.
solamente *adv* only; solely; just.
solana *nf* (*sitio*) sunny spot, suntrap; (*en casa*) sun-lounge, sun gallery.
solanera *nf* scorching sunshine; (*Med*) (*quemadura*) sunburn; (*insolación*) sunstroke.
solano *nm* east wind.
solapa *nf* (**a**) (*de chaqueta*) lapel; (*de bolsillo, libro, sobre*) flap. (**b**) (*fig*) pretext.
solapadamente *adv* slyly, in an underhand way, by under-

hand means.

solapado *adj* (*furtivo*) sly, underhand, sneaky; (*evasivo*) evasive; (*secreto*) undercover.

solapamiento *nm* overlapping.

solapante *adj* overlapping.

solapar [1a] **1** *vt* (**a**) (*lit*) to overlap.

(**b**) (*fig*) to cover up, cloak, keep dark.

2 *vi* to overlap (*con* with).

3 solaparse *vr* to overlap; **se ha solapado** it has got covered up, it has got hidden underneath.

solapo *nm* (**a**) (*Cos*) lapel; overlap. (**b**) **a ~*** = **solapadamente**.

solar¹ *nm* (**a**) (*Arquit*) lot, piece of ground, site; **~ para edificaciones** building site.

(**b**) (*casa*) ancestral home, family seat; (*fig*: *familia*) family, lineage, line.

(**c**) (*CAm, Carib*: *corral*) patio, yard.

(**d**) (*And, Carib*: *tugurio*) tenement house.

solar² [1m] *vt suelo* to floor, tile; *zapato* to sole.

solar³ *adj* solar, sun (*atr*).

solariego *adj* (**a**) **casa solariega** family seat, ancestral home. (**b**) (*Hist*) *familia* ancient and noble; *derechos etc* manorial; **tierras solariegas** demesne.

solario *nm* sunbed; solarium.

solárium *nm* solarium.

solaz *nm* (*descanso*) recreation, relaxation; (*consuelo*) solace, spiritual relief.

solazar [1f] **1** *vt* (*divertir*) to provide relaxation for; (*consolar*) to console; (*alegrar*) to comfort, cheer. **2 solazarse** *vr* to enjoy o.s., relax.

solazo* *nm* = **solanera**.

solazoso *adj* restful; recreative, relaxing; leisure (*atr*).

soldada *nf* pay; salary; (*Mil*) service pay.

soldadera *nf* (*Méx Hist*) camp-follower.

soldadesca *nf* (**a**) (*profesión*) military profession, military. (**b**) (*pey*) (brutal and licentious) soldiery.

soldadesco *adj* soldierly.

soldadito *nm*: **~ de plomo** tin soldier.

soldado¹ *nmf* soldier; **~ de infantería** infantryman; **~ de marina** marine; **~ de plomo** tin soldier; **~ de primera** lance-corporal; **~ raso** private; **una joven ~** a young woman soldier.

soldado² *adj juntura etc* welded; **totalmente ~** welded throughout.

soldador *nm* (**a**) (*Téc*) soldering iron. (**b**) (*persona*) welder.

soldadura *nf* (**a**) (*sustancia*) solder. (**b**) (*acto*) soldering, welding; **~ autógena** welding. (**c**) (*juntura*) soldered joint, welded seam.

soldar [1m] **1** *vt* (**a**) (*Téc*) to solder, weld.

(**b**) (*unir*) to join, unite; (*cementar*) to cement; *partes diversas* to weld together; *disputa* to patch up.

2 soldarse *vr* (*huesos*) to knit (together).

soleado *adj* sunny.

solear [1a] *vt* (*dejar al sol*) to put in the sun; (*blanquear*) to bleach.

solecismo *nm* solecism.

soledad *nf* (**a**) (*estado*) solitude; (*aislamiento*) loneliness. (**b**) (*duelo*) grieving, mourning. (**c**) (*lugar*) lonely place; **~es** wilderness.

solejar *nm* = **solana**.

solemne *adj* (**a**) (*serio*) solemn; (*ceremonioso*) dignified, impressive. (**b**) (*) *mentira* downright; *disparate* utter; *error* complete, terrible.

solemnemente *adv* solemnly; impressively.

solemnidad *nf* (**a**) (*cualidad*) solemnity; impressiveness; formality, gravity, dignity.

(**b**) (*acto*) solemnity, solemn ceremony; **~es** solemnities.

(**c**) **~es** (*hum*) (bureaucratic) formalities.

(**d**) **pobre de ~*** miserably poor, penniless.

solemnización *nf* solemnization, celebration.

solemnizar [1f] *vt* to solemnize, celebrate.

solenoide *nm* solenoid.

soler [2h; *defectivo*] vi (**a**) **~** + *infin* to be in the habit of + *ger*, be accustomed to + *infin*, be wont to + *infin*; **suele pasar por aquí** he usually comes this way; **solíamos ir todos los años** we used to go every year; **como se suele** as is normal, as is customary; **¿beber? pues no suele** drink? well he doesn't usually.

(**b**) (*Cono Sur*: *ocurrir*) to occur rarely, happen only occasionally.

solera *nf* (**a**) (*puntal*) prop, support; (*plinto*) plinth.

(**b**) (*de cuneta etc*) bottom.

(**c**) (*piedra de molino*) lower millstone.

(**d**) (*Méx*: *baldosa*) flagstone.

(**e**) (*Cono Sur*: *de acera*) kerb.

(**f**) (*carácter*) inherited character, collective character; traditional nature; **éste es país de ~ celta** this is a country of basically Celtic character; **es de ~ de médicos** he comes from a line of doctors; **vino de ~** sherry; older wine (for blending); **es un barrio con ~** it is a typically Spanish (*etc*) quarter, it is a quarter with lots of character.

solería *nf* flooring.

soleta *nf* (**a**) (*Cos*) patch, darn.

(**b**) (*: *mujer*) shameless woman.

(**c**) (*) **dar ~ a uno** to chuck sb out; **tomar ~** to beat it*; **dejar a uno en ~s** (*And*) to leave sb penniless.

(**d**) (*Méx Culin*) wafer, ladyfinger.

solevantamiento *nm* (**a**) pushing up, raising. (**b**) (*Pol*) rising; upheaval.

solevantar [1a] *vt* (**a**) *objeto* to push up, raise, heave up. (**b**) (*Pol etc*) to rouse, stir up.

solfa *nf* (**a**) (*Mús*) solfa; (*signos*) musical notation; (*fig*) music.

(**b**) (*: *paliza*) tanning*.

(**c**) **poner a uno en ~*** to make sb look ridiculous, hold sb up to mockery.

solfear [1a] *vt* (**a**) (*Mús*) to solfa. (**b**) (*: *zurrar*) to tan*. (**c**) (*: *reprender*) to tick off*. (**d**) (*Cono Sur**: *hurtar*) to nick‡, swipe‡.

solfeo *nm* (**a**) (*Mús*) solfa, singing of scales, voice practice; **clase de ~** singing lesson. (**b**) (*: *paliza*) tanning*; ticking-off*.

solicitación *nf* request; solicitation; canvassing.

solicitante *nmf* applicant; petitioner.

solicitar [1a] *vt* (**a**) *permiso etc* to ask for, request, seek; *aprobación* to seek; *puesto* to apply for; *apoyo* to solicit, canvass for; *votos* to canvass; **~ algo a uno** to ask sb for sth, request sth of sb.

(**b**) *atención, interés* to attract (*t Fís*).

(**c**) *persona* to pursue, chase after, try to attract; *mujer* to court; **le solicitan en todas partes** he is in great demand all over, he is much sought after, he's very popular.

solícito *adj* (*diligente*) diligent, careful; (*preocupado*) solicitous, concerned (*por* about, for); (*afectuoso*) affectionate.

solicitud *nf* (**a**) (*cualidad*) diligence, care; solicitude, concern; affection.

(**b**) (*acto*) request (*de* for); petition; application (*de un puesto* for a post); **a ~** on request; **~ de extradición** request for extradition; **~ de pago** (*Com*) demand note; **presentar una ~** to put in an application, make an application; **denegar** (*o* **desestimar** *etc*) **una ~** to refuse a request, reject an application.

sólidamente *adv* solidly.

solidariamente *adv* jointly, mutually.

solidaridad *nf* solidarity; **por ~ con** (*Pol etc*) out of sympathy with, out of solidarity with.

solidario *adj* (**a**) *obligación etc* mutually binding, jointly shared, shared in common; *participación etc* joint, common; *persona* jointly liable; **responsabilidad solidaria** joint liability.

(**b**) **hacerse ~ de** to sympathize with, declare one's solidarity with; **hacerse ~ de una opinión** to echo an opinion.

solidarizarse [1f] *vr*: **~ con** to declare one's solidarity with, affirm one's support for, line up with; **me solidarizo con esa opinión** I share that view.

solideo *nm* (*Ecl*) calotte, skullcap.

solidez *nf* solidity; hardness.

solidificación *nf* solidification; hardening.

solidificar [1g] **1** *vt* to solidify, harden. **2 solidificarse** *vr* to solidify, harden.

sólido 1 *adj* (**a**) (*gen*) solid (*t Mat, Fís*); (*duro*) hard.

(**b**) (*Téc etc*) solidly made; well built; *zapatos etc* stout, strong; *color* fast.

(**c**) (*fig*) solid, sound; firm, stable, secure; *base, moralidad, principio etc* sound.

2 *nm* solid.

soliloquiar [1b] *vi* to soliloquize, talk to oneself; to meditate aloud.

soliloquio *nm* soliloquy, monologue.

solimán *nm* corrosive sublimate; (*fig*) poison.

solio *nm* throne.

solipsismo *nm* solipsism.

solista *nmf* soloist.

solitaria[1] *nf* (*Zool*) tapeworm.

solitario 1 *adj* (**a**) *persona, vida* lonely, solitary; **vivir ~** to live alone.

(**b**) *lugar* lonely, desolate; bleak; **a tal hora la calle está solitaria** at such a time the street is deserted (*o* empty).

2 *nm*, **solitaria**[2] *nf* recluse; hermit; solitary person.

3 *nm* (**a**) (*Naipes*) patience, solitaire.

(**b**) (*diamante*) solitaire.

(**c**) **en ~** alone, on one's own; single-handed; **ir en ~** to go it alone, do something unaided; **vuelta al mundo en ~** solo (sailing) trip round the world; **tocar en ~** to play solo.

solito* *adj*: **estar ~** to be all alone, be on one's own.

sólito *adj* usual, customary.

soliviantar [1a] *vt* (**a**) (*amotinar*) to stir up, rouse (to revolt).

(**b**) (*enojar*) to anger; (*irritar*) to irritate, exasperate.

(**c**) (*inquietar*) to worry, cause anxiety to; **le tienen soliviantado los celos** he is eaten up with jealousy.

(**d**) (*causar anhelos a*) to fill with longing; (*dar esperanzas a*) to buoy up with false hopes; (*engreír*) to make vain, fill with conceit; **anda soliviantado con el proyecto** he has tremendous hopes for the scheme.

soliviar [1b] **1** *vt* to lift, push up. **2 soliviarse** *vr* to half rise, partly get up; to get up on one elbow.

solo 1 *adj* (**a**) (*uno*) single, sole; (*único*) one; unique; **hay una sola dificultad** there is just one difficulty; **con esta sola condición** with this single condition; **su sola preocupación es ganar dinero** his one concern is to make money; **no hubo ni una sola objeción** there was not a single objection; **es ~ en su género** it is unique of its kind.

(**b**) (*solitario*) alone; lonely; by o.s.; **venir ~** to come alone; **pasa los días ~ en su cuarto** he spends the days alone in his room; **iré ~** I'll go alone; **estos días me siento muy ~** I feel very lonely nowadays; **dejar ~ a uno** to leave sb all alone; **tendremos que comer pan ~** we shall have to eat plain bread, we shall have to eat bread and nothing with it; **se quedó ~ a los 7 años** he was left an orphan (*o* alone in the world) at 7; **se queda ~ en contar mentiras** there's nobody to touch him when it comes to telling lies; **lo hace como él ~** he does it as no-one else can.

(**c**) **a solas** alone, by oneself; **lo hizo a solas** he did it (all) by himself; **volar a solas** to fly solo; **vuelo a solas** solo flight.

(**d**) (*Mús*) solo; **cantar ~** to sing solo.

2 *nm* (**a**) (*Mús*) solo; **un ~ para tenor** a tenor solo.

(**b**) (*Naipes*) patience, solitaire.

(**c**) (*Cono Sur*: *lata*) tedious conversation.

sólo *adv* only, solely, merely, just; **~ quería verlo** I only (*o* just) wanted to see it; **es ~ un teniente** he's only a lieutenant, he's merely a lieutenant; **no ~ A sino también B** not only A but also B; **~ que ...** except that ...; but for the fact that ...; **ven aunque ~ sea para media hora** come even if it's just for half an hour; **con ~ que sepas tocar algunas notas** even if you only know how to play a few notes; **con ~ que estudies dos horas diarias** by studying for as little as two hours a day; **tan ~** only, just.

solomillo *nm* sirloin.

solomo *nm* sirloin; loin of pork.

solón *nm* (*Carib*) scorching heat, very strong sunlight.

solsticio *nm* solstice; **~ de estío** summer solstice; **~ de invierno** winter solstice.

soltar [1m] **1** *vt* (**a**) (*dejar ir*) to let go of; (*dejar caer*) to drop; to release; *nudo* to undo, untie; *amarra* to cast off; *hebilla etc* to undo, unfasten, loosen; *embrague* (*Aut*) to release, disengage; *freno* to release, take off; *cuerda etc* to loosen, slacken; to pay out; *cuerda trabada etc* to free; *agua* to let out, run off; *cautivo* to release, let go, set free; *animales* to let out, turn out, turn loose; to set free; *presa* to let go of; (*) *dinero* to cough up*; *puesto, privilegio etc* to give up; **¡suéltame, querido!** let go of me, dear!; **¡suélteme, señor!** unhand me, sir! (*liter*); **no quiere ~ el puesto por nada del mundo** he won't give up the job for anything.

(**b**) *estornudo, risa, exclamación etc* to let out; *suspiro* to fetch, heave; *blasfemia etc* to utter, come out with, let fly; *indirecta* to drop; *verdad* to let out, let slip; **¡suelta!** out with it!, spit it out!; **soltó un par de palabrotas** he came out with a couple of rude words, he let fly a couple of obscenities; **les volvió a ~ el mismo sermón** he read them the same lecture all over again.

(**c**) *golpe* to deal, strike, let fly.

(**d**) (*culebra*) *piel* to cast, slough.

(**e**) *dificultad* to solve; *duda* to resolve; *objeción etc* to satisfy, deal with.

(**f**) (*And*: *ceder*) to cede, give, hand over.

2 soltarse *vr* (**a**) (*cordón, nudo etc*) to come undone, come untied; (*costura etc*) to come unstitched; (*animal etc*) to get loose, break loose, free itself; to escape; (*Mec*: *pieza*) to work loose; to come off, fly off, fall off; **~ de las manos de uno** to escape from sb's clutches; **se le soltó un grito** a cry escaped him, he let out a yell; **no se vaya a ~ el perro** don't let the dog get out (*o* get loose *etc*); **~ del estómago** to have diarrhoea.

(**b**) (*fig*: *independizarse*) to achieve one's independence, win freedom.

(**c**) (*fig*: *perder el control*) to lose control (of o.s.); **~ a su gusto** to let fly, let o.s. go.

(**d**) (*fig*: *adquirir pericia etc*) to become expert, acquire real proficiency; (*en un idioma*) to become fluent.

(**e**) **~ a** + *infin* to begin to + *infin*.

(**f**) **~ con una idea absurda** to come up with a silly idea; **~ con una contribución de 50 dólares** to come up with a 50-dollar contribution; **por fin se soltó con algunos peniques** he eventually parted with a few coppers.

soltera *nf* single woman, unmarried woman, spinster; **apellido de ~** maiden name; **la señora de X, de ~ Z** Mrs X, née Z; Mrs X, whose maiden name was Z.

solterear [1a] *vi* (*Cono Sur*) to stay single.

soltería *nf* (*gen*) single state, unmarried state; (*de hombre*) bachelorhood, (*de mujer*) spinsterhood.

soltero 1 *adj* single, unmarried; **madre soltera** unmarried mother. **2** *nm* bachelor, unmarried man.

solterón *nm* confirmed bachelor, old bachelor.

solterona *nf* spinster, maiden lady; (*pey*) old maid; **tía ~** maiden aunt.

soltura *nf* (**a**) (*de cuerda etc*) looseness, slackness; (*Mec*) looseness; (*de miembros*) agility, nimbleness, ease of movement, freedom of action.

(**b**) (*Med*: *t* **~ de vientre**) looseness of the bowels, diarrhoea.

(**c**) (*en hablar etc*) fluency, ease; **habla árabe con ~** he speaks Arabic fluently.

(**d**) (*pey*) shamelessness; licentiousness; dissipation.

solubilidad *nf* solubility.

soluble *adj* (**a**) (*Quím*) soluble; **~ en agua** soluble in water.

(**b**) *problema* solvable, that can be solved.

solución *nf* (**a**) (*Quím*) solution.

(**b**) (*de problema etc*) solution; answer (*de* to); **~ final** final solution; **~ salomónica** compromise solution; **esto no tiene ~** there's no answer to this, there's no solution to this one.

(**c**) (*Teat*) dénouement.

(**d**) **~ de continuidad** break in continuity, interruption.

solucionar [1a] *vt* to solve; to resolve, settle.

solucionista *nmf* solver.

solvencia *nf* (**a**) (*Fin*: *estado*) solvency.

(**b**) (*Fin*: *acto*) settlement, payment.

(**c**) (*fig*) reliability; trustworthiness; (*Fin*) financial standing; **~ moral** character; **de toda ~ moral** of excellent character, completely trustworthy; **fuentes de toda ~** completely reliable sources.

(**d**) (*reputación*) solid reputation; (*valor*) recognized worth.

(**e**) (*Cono Sur*: *aptitud*) ability, competence; (*brillantez*) brilliance.

solventar [1a] *vt* (**a**) *cuenta, deuda* to settle, pay. (**b**) *dificultad* to resolve; *asunto* to settle.

solvente 1 *adj* (**a**) (*Fin*) solvent, free of debt. (**b**) (*fig*) reliable, trustworthy; *fuente etc* reliable. (**c**) (*fig*) respectable, worthy. (**d**) (*Cono Sur*: *hábil*) able, gifted, talented; brilliant. **2** *nm* (*Quím*) solvent.

solysombra* *nf* = **sol**[1] (**e**).

solla *nf* plaice.

sollamar [1a] *vt* to scorch, singe.

sollastre *nm* rogue, villain.

sollo *nm* sturgeon.

sollozar [1f] *vi* to sob.

sollozo *nm* sob; **decir algo entre ~s** to sob sth.

somalí *adj, nmf* Somali.

Somalia *nf* Somalia; (*Hist*) Somaliland.

somanta *nf* beating, thrashing.

somantar [1a] *vt* to beat, thrash.

somatada *nf* (*CAm*) blow, punch.

somatar [1a] (*CAm*) **1** *vt* (**a**) (*zurrar*) to beat, thrash; (*pegar*) to punch.

(**b**) to sell off cheap.

2 somatarse *vr* to fall and hurt o.s., knock o.s. about

badly.
somatén *nm* (**a**) (*alarma*) alarm; **tocar a ~** to sound the alarm. (**b**) (*: *jaleo*) uproar, confusion.
somático *adj* somatic; physical.
somatizar [1f] *vt* (**a**) to externalize, express externally. (**b**) (*fig*) to characterize.
somatón *nm* (*CAm*) = **somatada.**
sombra *nf* (**a**) (*proyectada por objeto*) shadow; (*protección etc*) shade; (*Arte*) shaded part, shaded area, dark part; **~ de ojos** eyeshadow; **~s** shadows, darkness; **~s chinescas** shadow play, shadow pantomime; **luz y ~** light and shade; **lugar de ~** shady spot; **a la ~ de** in the shade of; (*fig*) under the protection of; thanks to the support of; (*pey*) under the cloak of; **estar a la ~** to be in the shade; (*) to be inside‡; **dar ~, hacer ~** to give shade; to cast a shadow; **dar ~ a** to shade; **hacer ~ a uno** (*fig*) to put sb in the shade; **hacer ~** (*Boxeo*) to shadow box; **no quiere que otros le hagan ~** he doesn't want to be overshadowed by anybody else, he refuses to tolerate any rivals; **se ha constituido en ~ de sí mismo** he is a shadow of his former self; **quedar en la ~** (*fig*) to stay in the background, remain on the sidelines; **dirigente en la ~** shadow leader; **gobierno en la ~** shadow cabinet.
(**b**) **~s** (*fig*) (*oscuridad*) darkness, obscurity; (*ignorancia*) ignorance; (*pesimismo*) sombreness, pessimism.
(**c**) (*fantasma*) shade, ghost.
(**d**) (*mancha etc*) dark patch, stain; (*fig*) stain, blot; **es una ~ en su carácter** it is a stain on his character.
(**e**) (*fig: vestigio*) shadow; sign, trace, bit; **sin ~ de avaricia** without a trace of greed; **sin ~ de duda** without a shadow of doubt; **no se fía ni de su ~** he doesn't even trust his own shadow; **no tiene ni ~ de talento** he hasn't the least bit of talent; **tiene una ~ de parecido con su tío** he has a faint resemblance to his uncle; **ni por ~** by no means; not in the least bit.
(**f**) (*suerte*) luck; **tener buena ~** to be lucky; **ser de mala ~** to be unlucky.
(**g**) (*atractivo*) charm; (*gracia*) wit; (*talento*) talent, aptitude; **tiene mucha ~ para contar chistes** she's got a great talent for telling jokes; **tener buena ~** to be likeable, have lots of charm; **tener mala ~** to be a nasty piece of work; to have an unfortunate effect (on people *etc*); **el cuento tiene (buena) ~** it's a good story.
(**h**) (*CAm, Cono Sur: quitasol*) parasol, sunshade; (*CAm, Méx*) (*toldo*) awning; (*pórtico*) porch.
(**i**) (*CAm, Cono Sur: para escribir*) guidelines.
(**j**) (*Dep*) shadow-boxing.
(**k**) (*: *persona*) shadow, tail*.
sombraje *nm*, **sombrajo** *nm* shelter from the sun; **hacer ~s** to get in the light.
sombreado 1 *adj* shady. **2** *nm* (*Arte etc*) shading; hatching.
sombreador *nm*: **~ de ojos** eyeshadow.
sombrear [1a] *vt* to shade; (*Arte etc*) to shade; to hatch; (*maquillar*) to put eyeshadow on.
sombrerera *nf* (**a**) (*persona*) milliner. (**b**) (*caja*) hatbox. (**c**) (*And, Carib*) hatstand.
sombrerería *nf* (**a**) (*sombreros*) hats, millinery. (**b**) (*tienda*) hat shop; (*fábrica*) hat factory.
sombrerero *nm* (**a**) (*fabricante*) hatter, hatmaker. (**b**) (*And, Cono Sur*) hatstand.
sombrerete *nm* (**a**) (*sombrero*) little hat. (**b**) (*de hongo*) cap. (**c**) (*Téc*) bonnet; (*de cubo etc*) cap; (*de chimenea*) cowl.
sombrero *nm* (**a**) hat; headgear; **~ ancho, ~ jarano** (*Méx*) broad-brimmed Mexican hat; **~ apuntado** cocked hat; **~ de bola** (*Méx*), **~ hongo** bowler (hat); **~ de candil, ~ de tres picos** cocked hat, three-cornered hat; **~ de copa, ~ de pelo** (*LAm*) top hat; **~ flexible** soft hat, trilby; **~ gacho** slouch hat; **~ de jipijapa** Panama hat; **~ de paja** straw hat; **~ safari** safari hat; **~ tejano** stetson, ten-gallon hat*; **quitarse el ~ a** (*fig*) to take off one's hat to.
(**b**) (*Bot*) cap.
sombríamente *adv* sombrely; dismally; gloomily.
sombrilla *nf* parasol, sunshade.
sombrío 1 *adj* (**a**) *lugar* shaded, (too much) in the shade, dark.
(**b**) (*fig*) *lugar* sombre, sad, dismal; *persona* gloomy; *perspectiva etc* sombre.
2 *nm* (*Méx*) shady place.
someramente *adv* superficially.
somero *adj* superficial; shallow.
someter [2a] **1** *vt* (**a**) *país* to conquer; *persona* to subject to one's will, force to yield.
(**b**) **~ una decisión a lo que se resuelva en una reunión** to make one's decision depend on what is resolved in a meeting; **~ su opinión a la de otros** to subordinate one's opinion to that of others.
(**c**) *informe etc* to present, submit (*a* to); to send in; **~ algo a la aprobación de uno** to submit sth for sb's approval; **~ un trabajo a la censura** to send a work to the censor.
(**d**) **~ un asunto a una autoridad** to refer a matter to an authority for decision.
(**e**) **~ a** *prueba etc* to put to, subject to; **~ una sustancia a la acción de un ácido** to subject a substance to the action of an acid; *V* **prueba** *etc*.
2 someterse *vr* (**a**) (*rendirse*) to give in, yield, submit; **~ a la mayoría** to give way to the majority.
(**b**) **~ a una operación** to undergo an operation; **~ a un tratamiento con drogas** to have treatment with drugs.
sometico *adj* (*And*), **sometido** *adj* (*And, CAm*) = **entrometido.**
sometimiento *nm* (**a**) (*estado*) submission, subjection. (**b**) (*acto*) presentation, submission; reference.
somier [so'mjer] *nm, pl* **somiers** spring mattress.
somnambulismo *nm* sleepwalking, somnambulism.
somnámbulo, -a *nm/f* sleepwalker, somnambulist.
somnífero 1 *adj* sleep-inducing. **2** *nm* sleeping pill.
somnílocuo 1 *adj* given to talking in one's sleep. **2** *nm*, **somnílocua** *nf* person who talks in his (*o* her) sleep.
somnolencia *nf* sleepiness, drowsiness, somnolence.
somnolento *adj* = **soñoliento.**
somorgujar [1a] **1** *vt* to duck; to plunge, dip, submerge. **2 somorgujarse** *vr* to dive, plunge (*en* into).
somormujo *nm* grebe; **~ menor** dabchick.
somos *V* **ser.**
son[1] *nm* (**a**) (*gen*) sound; (*sonido agradable*) pleasant sound, sweet sound; **a ~ de** to the sound of; **a los ~es de la marcha nupcial** to the sounds (*o* strains) of the wedding march.
(**b**) (*fig: rumor*) rumour; **corre el ~ de que ...** there is a rumour going round that ...
(**c**) (*fig: estilo etc*) manner, style; **¿a qué ~ ...?, ¿a ~ de qué ...?** why ...?; **en ~ de** as, like, in the manner of; by the way of; **en ~ de broma** as a joke; **en ~ de guerra** in a warlike fashion; **lo dijo en ~ de riña** he said it as though he was trying to pick a quarrel; **no vienen en ~ de protesta** they're not coming in a protesting mood; **por este ~** in this way; **sin ~** for no reason at all; *V* **bailar.**
(**d**) (*Carib*) *Cuban folk song and dance.*
(**e**) **~ huasteca** (*Méx*) *folk song from Veracruz.*
son[2] *V* **ser.**
sonado *adj* (**a**) (*comentado*) talked-of; (*famoso*) famous; (*sensacional*) sensational; (*escandoloso*) scandalous; **un crimen muy ~** a particularly ghastly crime, a most notorious crime; **un suceso muy ~** a much talked-of event, an event which made a great stir.
(**b**) **hacer una (que sea) sonada** to do something really frightful; to cause a major scandal.
(**c**) **estar ~*** to be crazy; (*Boxeo*) to be punch-drunk.
sonaja *nf* little bell; (*Cono Sur*) (*Mús*) rattle, maracas; (*juguete*) rattle.
sonajera *nf* (*Cono Sur*), **sonajero** *nm* rattle.
sonanta‡ *nf* guitar.
sonante *adj* audible; resounding; tinkling, jingling; *V* **contante.**
sonar[1] [1m] **1** *vt* (**a**) *moneda, timbre* to ring; *trompeta etc* to play, blow; *sirena* to blow.
(**b**) **~ (las narices) a un niño** to blow a child's nose.
2 *vi* (**a**) (*gen*) to sound, make a noise; (*hacerse oír*) to sound out, make itself heard, be heard; (*Mús*) to play; (*timbre*) to ring; (*reloj*) to chime, strike; **han sonado las 10** it has struck 10; **le estaban sonando las tripas** his stomach was rumbling; **~ a cascado** to sound cracked; **~ a hueco** to sound hollow.
(**b**) (*Ling*) to be sounded, be pronounced; **la h de 'hombre' no suena** the h in 'hombre' is not pronounced (*o* is silent); **en esa región 'fue' suena casi como 'juez'** in that area 'fue' sounds (*o* is pronounced) almost like 'juez'.
(**c**) (*fig: parecer etc*) to sound; **esas palabras suenan extrañas** those words sound strange; **no me suena bien** it sounds all wrong to me; **no le ha sonado muy bien aquello** that did not make a good impression on him, he wasn't very well impressed with that; **me suena a camelo** (*Esp*) it sounds like a hoax to me; **se llama Anastasio, así como suena** he's called Anastasius, just like I'm telling you; **ni ~ ni tronar** not to count.

(**d**) (*fig*: *ser mencionado*) to be talked of; **es un nombre que suena** it's a name that's in the news, it's a name that people are talking about; **no quiere que suene su nombre** he doesn't want his name mentioned; **el asunto no ha sonado para nada en la reunión** the matter did not come up at all at the meeting.

(**e**) (*fig*: *ser conocido*) to sound familiar, seem familiar; **no me suena el nombre** the name doesn't ring a bell with me; **me suena ese coche** that car looks familiar.

(**f**) (*Cono Sur**) (*fracasar*) to come a cropper*, blow it‡; (*resentirse*) to suffer consequences, begin to feel it; (*perder*) to lose (in a game); (*ser despedido*) to lose one's job; (*morir*) to peg out‡; (*enfermar*) to suffer a mental illness.

(**g**) **hacer ~ a uno** (*Cono Sur**) to thrash sb within an inch of his life; (*derrotar*) to defeat sb.

3 sonarse *vr* (**a**) (*t* **~ las narices**) to blow one's nose.

(**b**) **se suena que ...** it is rumoured that ...

sonar[2] *nm* sonar.

sonata *nf* sonata.

sonda *nf* (**a**) (*acto*) sounding. (**b**) (*Náut*) lead; (*Téc*) bore, drill; (*Med*) probe; **~ acústica** echo-sounder; **~ espacial** space probe.

sondaje *nm* (*Náut*) sounding; (*Téc*) boring, drilling; **conversaciones de ~** exploratory talks; **organismo de ~** public opinion poll, institute of public opinion.

sond(e)ar [1a] *vt* (*Náut*) to sound, take soundings of; (*Med*) to probe, sound; (*Téc*) to bore, bore into, drill; (*fig*) *terreno etc* to explore; *misterio* to plumb, delve into, inquire into; *intenciones, persona etc* to sound out.

sondeo *nm* sounding; (*Téc*) boring, drilling; (*fig*) poll, inquiry, investigation; (*Pol etc*) feeler, overture, approach; **~ de audiencia** audience research; **~ de opinión** opinion poll.

sonería *nf* (*de reloj*) chimes.

soneto *nm* sonnet.

songa *nf* (**a**) (*Carib*: *sarcasmo*) sarcasm, irony. (**b**) (*Méx*: *grosería*) dirty joke, vulgar remark. (**c**) **a la ~(~)** (*And, CAm, Cono Sur**) slyly, underhandedly.

songo 1 *adj* (**a**) (*And, Méx**: *estúpido*) stupid, thick*. (**b**) (*And, Méx**: *taimado*) sly, crafty. **2** *nm* (*And*) buzz, hum.

sónico *adj* sonic, sound (*atr*).

sonidista *nmf* sound engineer.

sonido *nm* sound.

sonista *nmf* (*Cine, TV*) sound engineer, sound recordist.

sonoboya *nf* sonar buoy.

sonoridad *nf* sonority, sonorousness.

sonorizar [1f] (*Ling*) **1** *vt* to voice. **2 sonorizarse** *vr* to voice, become voiced.

sonoro *adj* (**a**) (*gen*) sonorous; (*ruidoso*) loud, resonant, resounding; *versos etc* sonorous; *cueva etc* echoing; *voz* rich.

(**b**) (*Ling*) voiced.

(**c**) **banda sonora** sound-track; **efectos ~s** sound effects.

sonotone *nm* hearing-aid.

sonreír [3m] **1** *vi* (**a**) to smile; **~ a uno** to smile at sb, beam at sb; **~ de un chiste** to smile at a joke; **~ forzadamente** to force a smile.

(**b**) (*fig*) **le sonríe la fortuna** fortune smiles upon him; **el porvenir le sonríe** he has a bright future.

2 sonreírse *vr* to smile.

sonriente *adj* smiling.

sonrisa *nf* smile; **~ amarga** bitter smile, wry smile; **~ forzada** forced smile.

sonrojante *adj* embarrassing.

sonrojar [1a] **1** *vt*: **~ a uno** to make sb blush. **2 sonrojarse** *vr* to blush, flush (*de* at).

sonrojo *nm* (**a**) (*rubor*) blush. (**b**) (*dicho etc*) offensive word, naughty remark (that brings a blush).

sonrosado *adj* rosy, pink.

sonrosarse [1a] *vr* to turn pink.

sonsacar [1g] *vt* (*obtener*) to get by cunning; (*quitar*) to remove surreptitiously; *criado etc* to entice away; (*engatusar*) to wheedle, cajole; **~ a uno** to pump sb for information; **~ un secreto a uno** to worm a secret out of sb.

sonsear [1a] *vi* (*Cono Sur*) = **zoncear**.

sonsera *nf*, **sonsería** *nf* (*LAm*) = **zoncera** *etc*.

sonso *adj* (*LAm*) = **zonzo**.

sonsonete *nm* (**a**) (*golpecitos*) tap, tapping; (*traqueteo*) rattle; (*cencerreo*) jangling; (*ruido monótono*) monotonous din.

(**b**) (*voz*) monotonous delivery, singsong (voice), chant.

(**c**) (*copla etc*) jingle, rhyming phrase.

(**d**) (*tono mofador*) mocking undertone.

sonsoniche *nm* (*Carib*) = **sonsonete**.

sonza *nf* (**a**) (*Carib*: *astucia*) cunning, deceit. (**b**) (*Méx*: *sarcasmo*) sarcasm, mockery.

soñación* *nf*: **¡ni por ~!** not on your life!

soñado *adj* (**a**) (*gen*) dreamed-of, that one has dreamed of; **el hombre ~** one's ideal man, one's dream man; Mr Right.

(**b**) (*) **hemos encontrado un sitio que ni ~** we've found an absolutely perfect spot; **me va que ni ~** it suits me a treat*.

soñador 1 *adj* dreamy. **2** *nm*, **soñadora** *nf* dreamer.

soñar [1l] *vti* (*t fig*) to dream; **~ con algo** to dream of sth; **soñé contigo anoche** I dreamed about you last night; **soñaba con una lavadora** she dreamed of (one day) having a washing machine; **~ con** + *infin*, **~ en** + *infin* to dream of + *ger*; **~ que ...** to dream that ...; **~ despierto** to daydream; **~ en voz alta** to talk in one's sleep; **¡ni ~lo!*** not on your life!; **nunca me lo hubiera soñado** I'd never have believed it.

soñarra *nf*, **soñarrera** *nf*, **soñera** *nf* (**a**) (*modorra*) drowsiness, deep desire to sleep. (**b**) (*sueño*) deep sleep.

soñolencia *nf* = **somnolencia**.

soñolientamente *adv* sleepily, drowsily.

soñoliento *adj* sleepy, drowsy, somnolent.

sopa *nf* (**a**) (*caldo*) soup; **~ de cebolla** onion soup; **~ de cola** (*CAm*) oxtail soup; **~ chilena** (*And*) corn and potato soup; **~ de fideos, ~ de pastas** noodle soup; **~ de letras** morass of political parties (*known by initials*); **~ de sobre** packet soup; **~ de verduras** vegetable soup; **comer** (*o* **andar a, vivir a**) **la ~ boba** to scrounge one's meals*, live on other people; **poner a uno como ~ de Pascua*** to give sb a ticking-off*; **los encontramos hasta en la ~** they're everywhere, they're ten a penny.

(**b**) (*pan mojado etc*) sop; **~s de leche** bread and milk; **dar ~s con honda a uno** to be streets ahead of sb; **estar como una ~*** to be tight*; **estar hecho una ~** to be sopping wet.

(**c**) (*Méx*: *t* **~ seca**) second course.

(**d**) (*: *resaca*) hangover*; **quitar la ~ a uno** to sober sb up; **quitarse la ~** to sober up.

sopaipilla *nf* (*And, Cono Sur Culin*) fritter.

sopapear [1a] *vt* (**a**) (*golpear*) to punch, bash*; to slap; (*sacudir*) to shake violently. (**b**) (*maltratar*) to maltreat; (*insultar*) to insult.

sopapié *nm* (*And*) kick.

sopapina *nf* series of punches, bashing*.

sopapo *nm* punch, thump.

sopar* [1a] (*Cono Sur*) **1** *vt pan etc* to dip, dunk. **2** *vi* to meddle.

sopear [1a] *vt* (*Cono Sur*) to dunk, dip, moisten.

sopenta: **cenar a la ~** to sup very late.

sopera *nf* soup tureen.

sopero 1 *adj* (**a**) **plato ~ = 2**.

(**b**) (*And*: *curioso*) nosey*, gossipy.

2 *nm* soup plate.

sopesar [1a] *vt* (**a**) (*levantar*) to try the weight of, try to lift. (**b**) (*fig*) *palabras* to weigh, consider; *situación* to weigh up.

sopetón *nm* (**a**) (*golpe*) punch.

(**b**) **de ~** suddenly, unexpectedly; **entrar de ~** to pop in, drop in; **entrar de ~ en un cuarto** to burst into a room, appear unexpectedly in a room.

sopimpa *nf* (*Carib*) series of punches; beating, bashing*.

soplacausas* *nmf invar* incompetent lawyer.

soplado 1 *adj* (**a**) (*limpio*) clean; (*pulcro*) extra smart, overdressed; (*afectado*) affected; (*engreído*) stuck-up*. (**b**) **estar ~*** to be tight*. (**c**) (*Cono Sur**) **ir ~** to drive very fast. **2** *nm* (*Téc*) air-cooling; **~ de vidrio** glass-blowing.

soplador *nm* (**a**) (*t* **~ de vidrio**) glass blower. (**b**) (*ventilador*) fan, ventilator. (**c**) (*fig*) troublemaker. (**d**) (*And, CAm Teat*) prompter.

soplagaitas* *nmf invar* idiot, twit*.

soplamocos *nm invar* (**a**) (*puñetazo*) punch, bash*. (**b**) (*Méx*: *comentario*) put-down.

soplapollas‡‡ *nmf invar* berk‡, prick‡‡.

soplar [1a] **1** *vt* (**a**) *polvo etc* to blow away, blow off; *superficie* to blow on; *vela* to blow out; *globo* to blow up, inflate; *vidrio* to blow; *cenizas, fuego* to blow on.

(**b**) (*fig*: *musa etc*) to inspire.

(**c**) **~ a uno** (*respuesta*) to whisper to sb; (*ayudar a recordar*) to prompt sb, help sb along; (*CAm Teat*) to prompt; **~ a X algo referente a Y** to tell X sth to Y's discredit.

(**d**) (*: *delatar*) to split on*.

(**e**) (‡: *birlar*) to pinch*, nick‡.

(**f**) (‡: *cobrar*) to charge, rush‡, sting*; **¿cuánto te so-**

plaron? what did they rush you?‡; **me han soplado 8 dólares** they stung me for 8 dollars*.

(**g**) (*) *golpe* to deal, fetch.

2 *vi* (**a**) (*persona, viento*) to blow; to puff; **¡sopla!*** well I'm blowed!*

(**b**) (‡: *delatar*) to split*, squeal‡.

(**c**) (‡: *beber*) to drink, booze*.

(**d**) (**‡: *copularse*) to screw**‡.

3 soplarse *vr* (**a**) (*) ~ **una docena de pasteles** to wolf a dozen cakes; **se sopla un litro entero** he knocks back a whole litre*.

(**b**) (*: *engreírse*) to get conceited.

(**c**) ~ **de uno*** to split on sb*, sneak on sb*.

soplete *nm* (**a**) (*lit*) blowlamp, torch; ~ **oxiacetilénico** oxy-acetylene burner; ~ **soldador** welding torch. (**b**) (*Cono Sur*) = **soplo** (**c**).

soplido *nm* strong puff, blast.

soplo *nm* (**a**) (*con la boca*) blow, puff; (*de viento*) puff, gust; (*Téc*) blast; **la semana pasó como** (*o* **en**) **un** ~ the week sped by, the week seemed no more than an instant.

(**b**) (‡) (*aviso*) tip, tip-off, secret warning; (*pronóstico*) tip; (*denuncia*) denunciation, informing; **dar el** ~ to tell tales; to split*, squeal‡; to inform; **ir con el** ~ **al director** to take one's tales to the headmaster, go and split to the head*.

(**c**) (*) (*chismoso*) telltale, talebearer, sneak; (*de policía etc*) informer, grass‡.

(**d**) ~ **cardíaco,** ~ **al corazón** heart murmur.

soplón, -ona *nm/f* (**a**) (*) = **soplo** (**c**). (**b**) (*: *policía*) (*Méx*) cop*; (*And*) member of the secret police. (**c**) (*CAm Teat*) prompter.

sopón *adj* (*Carib*) interfering.

soponcio *nm* queer turn, dizzy spell; (*fig*) upset.

sopor *nm* (*Med*) drowsiness; (*fig*) torpor, lethargy.

soporífero, soporífico 1 *adj* sleep-inducing; (*fig*) soporific. **2** *nm* nightcap; (*Med*) sleeping-pill, sleeping-draught.

soportable *adj* bearable.

soportal *nm* (**a**) (*pórtico*) porch; portico. (**b**) ~**es** arcade; colonnade.

soportante *adj* supportive.

soportar [1a] *vt* (**a**) (*Arquit etc*) to bear, carry, support, hold up; *presión etc* to resist, withstand. (**b**) (*fig: aguantar*) to stand, bear, endure, put up with.

soporte *nm* (**a**) (*gen*) support; (*pedestal*) base, stand, mounting; (*de repisa*) holder, bracket. (**b**) (*Her*) supporter. (**c**) (*fig*) pillar, support. (**d**) (*Inform*) medium; ~ **de entrada** input medium; ~ **físico** hardware; ~ **lógico** software; ~ **de salida** output medium.

soprano *nf* soprano.

soquete *nm* (*LAm*) sock, ankle sock.

sor *nf* (**a**) (*delante de nombre*) Sister; **S~ María** Sister Mary. (**b**) **una** ~* a nun.

sorber [2a] *vt* (**a**) (*con los labios*) to sip; to suck up; ~ **por una paja** to drink through a straw; ~ **por las narices** to sniff (in, up); (*Med*) to inhale.

(**b**) (*esponja*) to soak up, absorb, suck up; (*papel secante*) to dry up; (*con trapo*) to mop up.

(**c**) (*fig: mar*) to suck down, swallow up.

(**d**) (*fig*) *palabras* to drink in.

sorbete *nm* (**a**) sherbet; iced fruit drink, water-ice; (*CAm*) ice-cream. (**b**) (*Carib, Cono Sur: pajita*) drinking-straw. (**c**) (*Méx: sombrero*) top hat.

sorbetera *nf* ice-cream freezer.

sorbetería *nf* (*CAm*) ice-cream parlour (*o* shop).

sorbetón *nm* gulp, mouthful.

sorbito *nm* sip.

sorbo *nm* (*gen*) sip; (*trago*) gulp, swallow; (*por las narices*) sniff; **un** ~ **de té** a sip of tea; **beber a** ~**s** to sip; **tomar de un** ~ to down in one, to drink in one gulp.

sorche‡ *nm*, **sorchi‡** *nm* soldier.

sordamente *adv* dully, in a muffled way.

sordera *nf* deafness.

sordidez *nf* (**a**) (*suciedad*) dirt, dirtiness, squalor. (**b**) (*tacañería*) meanness.

sórdido *adj* (**a**) (*sucio*) dirty, squalid. (**b**) *palabra etc* nasty, dirty. (**c**) (*tacaño*) mean.

sordina *nf* (**a**) (*Mús*) mute, muffle, damper. (**b**) **a la** ~ on the quiet, surreptitiously, by stealth.

sordo 1 *adj* (**a**) *persona* deaf; ~ **como una tapia** as deaf as a post, stone deaf; **quedarse** ~ to go deaf; **a la sorda, a sordas** on the quiet, surreptitiously, by stealth; **mostrarse** ~ **a, permanecer** ~ **a** (*fig*) to remain deaf to; **se quedó** ~ **a sus súplicas** he was unmoved by her entreaties.

(**b**) *máquina etc* quiet, noiseless; *ruido* dull, muffled; *dolor* dull; (*Ling*) voiceless; *emoción, ira* suppressed, inward.

2 *nm*, **sorda** *nf* deaf person; **hacerse el** ~ to pretend not to hear, turn a deaf ear.

sordociego 1 *adj* blind and deaf. **2** *nm*, **sordociega** *nf* blind and deaf person.

sordomudez *nf* deaf-muteness.

sordomudo 1 *adj* deaf and dumb. **2** *nm*, **sordomuda** *nf* deaf-mute.

sorgo *nm* sorghum.

soriano 1 *adj* (*Esp*) of Soria. **2** *nm*, **soriana** *nf* native (*o* inhabitant) of Soria; **los** ~**s** the people of Soria.

soriasis *nf* psoriasis.

Sorlinga, Sorlingen: **Islas** *nfpl* ~ Scilly Isles.

sorna *nf* (**a**) (*malicia*) slyness; (*sarcasmo*) sarcasm, sarcastic tone; **con** ~ slyly, mockingly, sarcastically. (**b**) (*lentitud*) slowness; (*deliberación*) (humorous) deliberation.

sornar‡ [1a] *vi* to kip‡, sleep.

sorocharse [1a] *vr* (**a**) (*And, Cono Sur*) = **asorocharse.** (**b**) (*Cono Sur: ponerse colorado*) to blush.

soroche *nm* (**a**) (*LAm Med*) mountain sickness, altitude sickness. (**b**) (*Cono Sur: rubor*) blush(ing). (**c**) (*And, Cono Sur Min*) galena, natural lead sulphide.

sorprendente *adj* surprising; amazing; startling; **no es** ~ **que** ... it is hardly surprising that ..., it is small wonder that ...

sorprender [2a] **1** *vt* (**a**) (*gen*) to surprise; (*asombrar*) to amaze; (*sobresaltar*) to startle.

(**b**) (*Mil etc*) to surprise; (*coger desprevenido*) to catch unawares, take by surprise; *conversación* to overhear; *secreto* to find out, discover; *escondrijo* to come across; ~ **a uno en el hecho** to catch sb in the act.

2 *vi*: **sorprende observar cómo lo hace** it's surprising to see how he does it; **sorprende la delicadeza de su verso** the delicacy of her poetry is surprising.

3 sorprenderse *vr* to be surprised (*de* at), be amazed (*de* at); **no me sorprendería de que fuera así** I shouldn't be surprised if it were like that; **se sorprendió mucho** he was very surprised.

sorpresa 1 *nf* (**a**) (*emoción*) surprise; amazement; **causar** ~ **a, producir** ~ **a** to surprise; **con gran** ~ **mía, para mi** ~ much to my surprise, to my great surprise.

(**b**) (*acto*) surprise; **¡qué** ~**!, ¡vaya** ~**!** what a surprise!; **coger a uno de** ~ to take sb by surprise, come as a surprise to sb.

(**c**) (*regalo*) surprise.

(**d**) (*Mil*) surprise attack; **coger por** ~ to surprise.

2 *atr* surprise (*atr*); **ataque** ~ surprise attack; **inspección** ~ spot check; **regalo** ~ mystery present; **resultado** ~ surprise result, unexpected result; **sobre** ~ mystery envelope; **visita** ~ unannounced visit.

sorpresivamente *adv* surprisingly; suddenly, unexpectedly, without warning.

sorpresivo *adj* (*sorprendente*) surprising; (*repentino*) sudden, (*imprevisto*) unexpected.

sorrajar [1a] *vt* (*Méx*) (*golpear*) to hit; (*herir*) to wound.

sorrasear [1a] *vt* (*Méx*) to part-roast (*o* grill).

sorrongar [1h] *vi* (*And*) to grumble.

sorrostrigar [1h] *vt* (*And*) to pester, annoy.

sortario *adj* (*Carib*) lucky, fortunate.

sortear [1a] **1** *vt* (**a**) (*gen*) to draw lots for, decide by lot; to draw out of a hat; (*rifar*) to raffle (for charity); (*Dep etc*) *lados* to toss up for.

(**b**) *obstáculo* to dodge, avoid; to get round; to manage to miss, swerve past; **el torero sorteó al toro** the bullfighter eluded the bull; **el esquiador sorteó muy bien las banderas** the skier swerved round the flags skilfully; **aquí hay que** ~ **el tráfico** one has to dodge the traffic here.

(**c**) (*fig*) *dificultad* to avoid; to get round, overcome; *pregunta* to handle, deal with (skilfully).

2 *vi* to draw lots; (*con moneda*) to toss, toss up.

sorteo *nm* (**a**) (*lotería etc*) draw, drawing lots; (*rifa*) raffle; (*Dep*) toss; **ganar el** ~ to win the toss; **esto se realizará mediante** ~ this shall be determined by lot. (**b**) (*el evitar*) dodging, avoidance; swerving.

sortija *nf* (**a**) (*anillo*) ring; ~ **de compromiso,** ~ **de pedida** engagement ring; ~ **de sello** signet ring. (**b**) (*bucle*) curl, ringlet.

sortilegio *nm* (**a**) (*brujería*) sorcery; (*adivinación*) fortunetelling; (*vaticinio*) magical prediction. (**b**) (*un* ~) spell, charm (*t fig*).

sos (*Argentina*) = **sois**; *V* **ser**.

sosa *nf* soda; ~ **cáustica** caustic soda.

sosaina* 1 *adj* dull. **2** *nmf* dull person.

sosco *nm* (*And*) bit, piece.
sosegadamente *adv* quietly, calmly, peacefully; gently.
sosegado *adj* (**a**) (*tranquilo*) quiet, calm, peaceful; (*apacible*) gentle. (**b**) *persona* calm, sedate, steady.
sosegar [1h *y* 1k] **1** *vt* (*calmar*) to calm, quieten; (*arrullar*) to lull; *ánimos etc* to reassure; *dudas, temores* to allay.
2 *vi* to rest.
3 sosegarse *vr* to calm down, become calm; to quieten down.
soseras* *adj* = **soso** (**b**).
sosería *nf* (**a**) (*insipidez*) insipidness. (**b**) (*fig*) dullness; flatness, colourlessness. (**c**) **es una** ~ it's boring, it's terribly dull*.
sosiego *nm* (**a**) (*de lugar, ambiente etc*) calm(ness), quiet(ness); peacefulness. (**b**) (*de persona*) calmness, sedateness, steadiness, composure; **hacer algo con** ~ to do sth calmly.
soslayar [1a] *vt* (**a**) (*ladear*) to put across, put sideways, place obliquely. (**b**) (*fig*) *dificultad* to get round; *pregunta* to dodge, sidestep; *encuentro* to avoid.
soslayo: al ~, **de** ~ *adv* obliquely, sideways, aslant; **mirada de** ~ sidelong glance; **mirar de** ~ to look out of the corner of one's eye (at); (*fig*) to look askance (at), look down one's nose (at).
soso *adj* (**a**) (*Culin*) (*insípido*) tasteless, insipid; (*sin sal*) unsalted; (*sin azúcar*) unsweetened. (**b**) (*fig*) dull, uninteresting, flat, colourless.
sospecha *nf* suspicion.
sospechar [1a] **1** *vt* to suspect. **2** *vi*: ~ **de** to suspect, be suspicious of, have one's suspicions about.
sospechosamente *adv* suspiciously.
sospechoso 1 *adj* suspicious; suspect; suspected; **todos son ~s** everybody is under suspicion; **es ~ de desafecto al régimen** he is suspected of being hostile to the régime, it is suspected that he is hostile to the régime; **tiene amistades sospechosas** some of his acquaintances are suspect.
2 *nm*, **sospechosa** *nf* suspect.
sosquín *nm* (*Carib*) (**a**) (*ángulo*) wide corner, obtuse angle. (**b**) (*golpe*) backhander, unexpected blow.
sosquinar [1a] *vt* (*Carib*) to hit (*o* wound *etc*) unexpectedly.
sostén *nm* (**a**) (*Arquit etc*) support, prop; stand; pillar, post.
(**b**) (*prenda*) brassière, bra.
(**c**) (*alimento*) sustenance, food, nourishment.
(**d**) (*fig*) support, pillar, mainstay; **el principal ~ del gobierno** the mainstay of the government; **el único ~ de su familia** the sole support of his family.
sostener [2l] **1** *vt* (**a**) (*Arquit etc*) to hold up, support; to prop up; *carga* to carry; *peso* to bear; (*persona*) to hold up, hold on to; **¡sostén!** hold this!; **los dos sosteníamos la cuerda** we were both holding the rope; **la cinta le sostiene el pelo** the ribbon keeps her hair in place.
(**b**) (*fig*) *persona* to support, back; (*ayudar*) to help; (*defender*) to defend; **su partido le sostiene en el poder** his party keeps him in power; **esta manifestación de apoyo sirve para ~me** this demonstration of support strengthens my resolve; **le sostienen los nervios** his nerves keep him going.
(**c**) (*con alimentos*) to sustain, keep going.
(**d**) (*Mús*) *nota* to hold.
(**e**) (*fig*) *acusación etc* to maintain; *opinión* to stand by, stick to, uphold; *promesa* to stand by; *proposición, teoría* to maintain; *presión* to keep up, sustain; *resistencia* to strengthen, boost, bolster up; **sostenella y no emendalla** firm defence of a decision (*etc*).
(**f**) (*fig*) *lucha, posición, velocidad etc* to keep up, maintain.
(**g**) (*Fin*) to maintain, pay for; *gastos* to meet, defray.
(**h**) ~ **la mirada de uno** to stare sb out; to look sb in the eye without flinching.
2 sostenerse *vr* (**a**) (*lit*) to hold o.s. up, support o.s.; (*mantenerse en pie*) to stand up; **apenas podía ~ de puro cansado** he was so utterly tired he could hardly stand.
(**b**) (*fig*) (*ganarse la vida*) to support o.s.; (*continuar*) to keep (o.s.) going; (*resistir*) to last out; ~ **en el poder** to stay in power; ~ **vendiendo corbatas** to support o.s. by selling ties.
(**c**) (*fig*: *continuar*) to continue, remain; **el mercado se sostiene firme** the market remains firm, the market continues steady; **se sostiene el régimen lluvioso** rainy conditions prevail.
sostenible *adj* sustainable.
sostenidamente *adv* steadily, continuously.
sostenido 1 *adj* (**a**) (*continuo*) steady, continuous; *esfuerzo* sustained; (*prolongado*) prolonged. (**b**) (*Mús*) sharp. **2** *nm* (*Mús*) sharp.
sostenimiento *nm* (**a**) (*mantenimiento*) support; holding up; maintenance; upholding; strengthening; bolstering. (**b**) (*Fin*) maintenance; (*alimentos*) sustenance.
sota[1] *nf* (**a**) (*Naipes*) jack, knave; **de ~, caballo y rey** first-rate, top-class. (**b**) (*) (*descarada*) hussy, brazen woman; (*puta*) whore.
sota[2] *nm* (*Cono Sur**) overseer, foreman.
sotabanco *nm* (**a**) (*desván*) attic, garret. (**b**) (*Cono Sur*: *cuartucho*) poky little room.
sotabarba *nf* double chin, jowl.
sotacura *nm* (*And, Cono Sur*) curate.
sotana *nf* (**a**) (*Ecl*) cassock, soutane. (**b**) (*: *paliza*) hiding*.
sotanear* [1a] *vt* to tick off*.
sótano *nm* (*de casa*) basement; (*bodega*) cellar; (*de banco etc*) vault.
Sotavento: **Islas** *nfpl* **de** ~ Leeward Isles.
sotavento *nm* lee, leeward; **a** ~ to leeward; **de** ~ leeward (*atr*).
sotechado *nm* shed.
soterradamente *adv* in an underhand way.
soterramiento *nm* excavation; **obras de** ~ excavations, underground works.
soterrar [1j] *vt* to bury; (*fig*) to bury, hide away.
soto *nm* (**a**) (*matorral*) thicket; (*arboleda*) grove, copse. (**b**) (*And*) (*en la piel*) rough lump, bump; (*nudo*) knot.
sotobosque *nm* undergrowth.
sotreta *nf* (*And, Cono Sur*) (**a**) (*caballo*) horse; (*brioso*) frisky horse; (*viejo*) useless old nag. (**b**) (*persona*) loafer, idler; bum (*US*).
soturno *adj* taciturn, silent; unsociable.
soviet [so'ßie] *nm*, *pl* **soviets** [so'ßie] soviet.
soviético 1 *adj* Soviet (*atr*). **2** *nm*: **los ~s** the Soviets, the Russians.
soy *V* **ser**.
S.P. *nm* (**a**) (*Rel*) *abr de* **Santo Padre** Holy Father. (**b**) (*Esp Aut*) *abr de* **Servicio Público**. (**c**) (*Admin*) *abr de* **Servicio Postal**.
spárring [es'parin] *nm* sparring partner.
spi* [es'pi] *nm* spinnaker.
spleen [es'plin] *nm* = **esplín**.
SPM *nm abr de* **síndrome premenstrual** premenstrual tension, PMT.
sponsor [espon'sor] *nm*, *pl* **sponsors** [espon'sor] sponsor.
sport [es'por] **1** *nm* sport; **camiseta** ~ sleeveless vest; **chaqueta** (**de**) ~ sports coat; **vestido de** ~ wearing sports clothes; (*fig*) casually dressed; **hacer algo por** ~ to do sth (just) for fun.
2 de ~ *adv* (*con aplomo*) casually, nonchalantly; (*alegremente*) merrily; (*en broma*) for fun, as a joke; just for laughs.
spot [es'pot] *nm*, *pl* **spots** [es'pot] (**a**) (*TV*) slot, space; ~ **electoral** party political broadcast; ~ **publicitario** commercial, ad*. (**b**) (*Cono Sur Elec*) spotlight.
spray [es'prai] *nm*, *pl* **sprays** [es'prai] spray, aerosol.
sprint [es'prin] *nm*, *pl* **sprints** [es'prin] (**a**) (*Dep*) sprint; (*fig*) sprint, sudden dash; burst of speed; **tengo que hacer un** ~ I must dash, I must get a move on. (**b**) (*fig*: *t* ~ **final**) final dash, last-minute rush.
sprintar [esprin'tar] [1a] *vi* to sprint.
sprínter [es'printer] *nmf* sprinter.
squash [es'kwas] *nm* squash.
Sr. *abr de* **Señor** Mister, Mr.
Sra. *abr de* **Señora** Mistress, Mrs.
S.R.C. *abr de* **se ruega contestación** please reply, RSVP.
Sres., Srs. *abr de* **Señores** Messieurs, Messrs.
Sria., Srio. *abr de* **Secretaria, Secretario** secretary, sec.
Sri Lanka *nm* Sri Lanka.
Srta. *abr de* **Señorita** Miss.
SS *abr de* **Santos, Santas** Saints, SS.
S.S. (**a**) (*Rel*) *abr de* **Su Santidad** His Holiness, H.H. (**b**) *nf abr de* **Seguridad Social** ≃ Social Security. (**c**) *abr de* **Su Señoría** His Lordship, Her Ladyship.
ss. *abr de* **siguientes** following, foll.
s.s. *abr de* **seguro servidor** *courtesy formula*.
SSE *abr de* **sudsudeste** south-south-east, SSE.
SSI *nm abr de* **Servicio Social Internacional** International Social Service, ISS.
SS.MM. *abr de* **Sus Majestades** their Royal Highnesses.
SSO *abr de* **sudsudoeste** south-south-west, SSW.
SSS *nm abr de* **servicio social sustitutorio**.

s.s.s. *abr de* **su seguro servidor** *courtesy formula.*
Sta. *abr de* **Santa** Saint, St.
staccato [csta'kato] *adv, adj invar* staccato.
staff [es'taf] *nm, pl* **staffs** [es'taf] (**a**) (*equipo*) (*Mil*) staff, command; (*Pol*) ministerial team. (**b**) (*individuo*) top executive. (**c**) (*Cine, Mús*) credits, credit titles.
stage [es'teiʒ] *nm* period, phase.
stagflación [estagfla'θjon] *nf* stagflation.
Stalin [es'talin] *nm* Stalin.
stand [es'tan] *nm, pl* **stands** [es'tan] stand.
standar(d) [es'tandar] *adj y nm etc V* **estándar** *etc.*
standing [es'tandin] *nm* standing; rank, category; **de alto ~** high-class, high-ranking; *piso etc* luxury, top quality.
stárter [es'tarter] *nm* (**a**) (*Aut: aire*) choke; (*LAm: arranque*) starting-motor; ignition. (**b**) (*LAm Dep*) starter; (*puerta*) starting-gate.
statu quo [es'tatu kwo] *nm* status quo.
status [es'tatus] *nm invar* status.
Sto. *abr de* **Santo** Saint, St.
stock [es'tok] *nm, pl* **stocks** [es'tok] (*Com*) stock, supply.
stop [es'top] *nm* (*Aut*) stop sign, halt sign.
store [es'tor] *nm* sunblind, awning.
stress [es'tres] *nm* stress.
su *adj pos* (**a**) (*sing*) (*de él*) his; (*de ella*) her; (*de objeto*) its; (*impersonal*) one's; (*de Vd*) your. (**b**) (*pl*) (*de ellos, de ellas*) their; (*de Vds*) your.
suampo *nm* (*CAm*) swamp.
suato* *adj* (*Méx*) silly.
suave 1 *adj* (**a**) *superficie* smooth, even; *piel, pasta etc* smooth.
(**b**) *color, curva, movimiento, reprimenda, viento etc* gentle; *aire* soft, mild, sweet; *clima* mild; *trabajo* easy; *operación mecánica* smooth, easy; *música, voz* soft, sweet, mellow; *ruido* soft, gentle, quiet; *olor* sweet; *sabor* smooth, mild; *droga* soft; **~ como el terciopelo** (*fig*) smooth as silk.
(**c**) *persona, carácter* gentle; meek, docile; **estuvo muy ~ conmigo** he was very sweet to me, he was very helpful to me, he behaved very nicely to me.
(**d**) (*Cono Sur, Méx*) (*enorme*) vast, huge; (*destacado*) outstanding.
(**e**) (*Méx*‡) (*atractivo*) good-looking, fanciable*; (*estupendo*) great*, fabulous*; ¡~! great idea*!, right on*! (*US**), you bet!
(**f**) **dar la ~** (*LAm*) to flatter.
2 *adv* (**a**) (*LAm*) *sonar etc* softly, quietly.
(**b**) (*Méx*) **toca ~** she plays beautifully.
suavemente *adv* smoothly; gently; softly, sweetly.
suavidad *nf* smoothness, evenness; gentleness; softness, mildness; sweetness.
suavización *nf* (**a**) smoothing; softening. (**b**) softening, tempering; relaxation.
suavizador *nm* razor strop.
suavizar [1f] *vt* (**a**) (*alisar*) to smooth (out, down); (*ablandar*) to soften; *pasta etc* to make smoother; *navaja* to strop; *cuesta etc* to ease, make more gentle; *color* to tone down; *tono* to soften.
(**b**) *persona* to mollify, soften, make gentler; *carácter* to mellow; *severidad* to soften, temper; *medida* to relax.
sub... *pref* sub..., under...; **subprivilegiado** underprivileged, **subvalorar** to undervalue; **la selección española ~-21** the Spanish under-21 team.
suba *nf* (*CAm, Cono Sur*) rise (in prices).
subacuático *adj* underwater.
subalimentación *nf* underfeeding, undernourishment.
subalimentado *adj* underfed, undernourished.
subalpino *adj* subalpine.
subalterno 1 *adj importancia etc* secondary; *personal etc* minor, auxiliary. **2** *nm,* **subalterna** *nf* subordinate.
subarbustivo *adj* shrubby.
subarrendador(a) *nm/f* subtenant.
subarrendar [1k] *vt* to sublet, sublease.
subarrendatario, -a *nm/f* subtenant.
subarriendo *nm* subtenancy, sublease.
subártico *adj* subarctic.
subasta *nf* (**a**) (*venta*) auction, sale by auction; **~ a la baja** Dutch auction; **poner en** (*o* **sacar a**) **pública ~** to put up for auction, sell at auction.
(**b**) (*Com: oferta de obras*) tender.
(**c**) (*Naipes*) auction.
subastador(a)[1] *nm/f* auctioneer.
subastadora[2] *nf* (*casa*) auction-house.
subastar [1a] *vt* to auction, auction off, sell at auction.
subcampeón, -ona *nm/f* runner-up.
subcomisario, -a *nm/f* deputy superintendent.
subcomisión *nf* subcommittee.
subconjunto *nm* (*Inform*) subset; (*Pol*) subcommittee; (*Zool*) subspecies.
subconsciencia *nf* subconscious.
subconsciente 1 *adj* subconscious. **2** *nm*: **el ~** the subconscious; **~ colectivo** collective subconscious; **en el ~** in the subconscious.
subconscientemente *adv* subconsciously.
subcontinente *nm* subcontinent.
subcontrata *nf* subcontract.
subcontratación *nf* subcontracting.
subcontratista *nmf* subcontractor.
subcontrato *nm* subcontract.
subcultura *nf* subculture.
subcutáneo *adj* subcutaneous.
subdesarrollado *adj* underdeveloped.
subdesarrollo *nm* underdevelopment.
subdirección *nf* section, subdepartment.
subdirector(a) *nm/f* subdirector, assistant manager, deputy manager; **~ de biblioteca** sub-librarian, under-librarian.
subdirectorio *nm* subdirectory.
súbdito, -a *adj, nm/f* (*Pol*) subject.
subdividir [3a] **1** *vt* to subdivide. **2 subdividirse** *vr* to subdivide.
subdivisión *nf* subdivision.
sube *nm* (*LAm*): **~ y baja** see-saw; **dar un ~ a uno** to give sb a hard time.
subempleado *adj* underemployed.
subempleo *nm* underemployment.
subespecie *nf* subspecies.
subestación *nf* substation.
subestimación *nf* underestimation; undervaluation; understatement.
subestimar [1a] *vt capacidad, enemigo etc* to underestimate, underrate; *objeto, propiedad* to undervalue; *argumento* to understate.
subexposición *nf* under-exposure.
subexpuesto *adj* under-exposed.
subfusil *nm* automatic rifle.
subgénero *nm* (*Liter*) minor genre; (*Zool*) subspecies.
subgerente *nmf* assistant director.
subgrupo *nm* subgroup; (*Pol*) splinter group.
subibaja *nm* seesaw.
subida *nf* (**a**) (*de montaña etc*) climb, climbing; ascent; **una ~ en globo** a balloon ascent; **en la ~ había muchas flores** there were a lot of flowers on the way up; **es una ~ difícil** it's a tough climb.
(**b**) (*de cantidad, precio etc*) rise, increase (*de* in); raising; (*en escalafón*) promotion (*a* to); **~ salarial** wage increase; **esto va de ~** this is increasing, this is on the increase; **el calor va de ~** it's getting hotter.
(**c**) (*cuesta*) slope, hill; (*en nombres de calles*) rise, hill.
subido *adj* (**a**) *precio etc* high. (**b**) *color* bright, strong, intense; high; *olor* strong; *V* **color.** (**c**) *persona* vain, proud.
subienda *nf* (*And*) shoal.
subilla *nf* awl.
subíndice *nm* (*Inform*) subscript.
subinquilino, -a *nm/f* subtenant.
subir [3a] **1** *vt* (**a**) *objeto* to raise, lift up; to put up; to take up, get up; *cabeza etc* to raise; **que me suban los equipajes** please see that my luggage is brought up (*o* taken up); **lo subieron a la repisa** they put it up on the rack.
(**b**) *calle, cuesta etc* to go up; *escalera* to climb, mount, ascend.
(**c**) *persona* to promote (*a* to).
(**d**) (*Arquit*) to build, raise, put up; **~ una pared** to build a wall.
(**e**) *precio, sueldo etc* to raise, put up, increase; *artículo en venta* to put up the price of.
(**f**) (*Mús*) to raise the pitch of.
2 *vi* (**a**) (*gen*) to go up, come up; to move up; to climb; (*a caballo etc*) to get on, mount; (*a vehículo*) to get in, get on; **le subieron los colores a la cara** she blushed; **el vino me sube a la cabeza** wine goes to my head; **~ a caballo** to mount, get on one's horse; **~ al tren** to get into the train, get on to the train; **seguíamos subiendo** we went on climbing; **bajar es peor que ~** coming down is worse than going up; **¡sube pronto!** come up quickly!
(**b**) (*marea, mercurio, muro, río etc*) to rise.
(**c**) **~ a** (*Fin*) to amount to.
(**d**) (*persona: fig*) to be promoted (*a* to), rise, move up.
(**e**) (*precio, valor etc*) to rise, increase, go up; (*epidemia etc*) to spread; (*fiebre etc*) to get worse; **sigue subiendo la**

bolsa the market is still rising.

3 subirse *vr* (**a**) (*a un árbol etc*) to get up, climb (*a* on to); to go up, rise; ~ **al tren** to get on the train; **el niño se le subió a las rodillas** the child climbed on to her knees; **se me sube el vino a la cabeza** wine goes to my head; *V* **tono** *etc.*

(**b**) (*fig*) (*engreírse*) to get conceited; (*descararse*) to become bolder; (*portarse mal*) to forget one's manners.

(**c**) (*Bot*) to run to seed.

súbitamente *adv* suddenly; unexpectedly.

súbito 1 *adj* (**a**) (*repentino*) sudden; (*imprevisto*) unexpected. (**b**) (*: *precipitado*) hasty, rash. (**c**) (*: *irritable*) irritable. **2** *adv* (*t* **de** ~) suddenly; unexpectedly.

subjefatura *nf* local (police) headquarters.

subjetivamente *adv* subjectively.

subjetivar [1a] *vt*, **subjetivizar** [1f] *vt* to subjectivize, perceive in subjective terms.

subjetividad *nf* subjectivity.

subjetivismo *nm* subjectivism.

subjetivo *adj* subjective.

subjuntivo 1 *adj* subjunctive. **2** *nm* subjunctive (mood).

sublevación *nf* revolt, rising; (*Mil*) mutiny; (*de cárcel*) riot.

sublevar [1a] **1** *vt* (**a**) (*amotinar*) to rouse to revolt, stir up a revolt among.

(**b**) (*fig*) to upset, put out, irritate; to rouse to fury.

2 sublevarse *vr* to revolt, rise, rebel.

sublimación *nf* sublimation.

sublimado *nm* (*Quím*) sublimate.

sublimar [1a] *vt* (**a**) *persona* to exalt, praise. (**b**) *deseos etc* to sublimate. (**c**) (*Quím*) to sublimate.

sublime *adj* (**a**) sublime; (*elevado*) noble, lofty, grand; **lo** ~ the sublime. (**b**) (*liter*) high, tall, lofty.

sublimemente *adv* sublimely.

sublimidad *nf* sublimity.

subliminal *adj*, **subliminar** *adj* subliminal.

subliteratura *nf* third-rate literature, pulp writing.

submarinismo *nm* underwater exploration, diving; (*pesca*) underwater fishing.

submarinista 1 *adj*: **exploración** ~ underwater exploration. **2** *nmf* underwater fisherman, underwater diver (*o* explorer *etc*); frogman.

submarino 1 *adj* underwater, submarine; **pesca submarina** underwater fishing. **2** *nm* (**a**) (*Náut*) submarine. (**b**) (*Pol etc*) infiltrator; undercover man.

submundo *nm* underworld.

subnormal 1 *adj* subnormal. **2** *nmf* subnormal person.

subnormalidad *nf* subnormality, mental handicap.

suboficial *nmf* non-commissioned officer.

subordinación *nf* subordination.

subordinado 1 *adj* subordinate; **X queda ~ a Y** X is subordinate to Y. **2** *nm*, **subordinada** *nf* subordinate.

subpárrafo *nm* subparagraph.

subproducto *nm* by-product; spin-off.

subprograma *nm* subprogramme.

subrayable *adj* worth emphasizing; **el punto más** ~ the point which should particularly be noted, the most important point.

subrayado 1 *adj* underlined; (*en bastardilla*) italicized, in italics. **2** *nm* underlining; italics; **el ~ es mío** my italics, the italics are mine.

subrayar [1a] *vt* (**a**) to underline; (*poner en bastardilla*) to italicize, put in italics. (**b**) (*fig*) to underline, emphasize.

subrepticiamente *adv* surreptitiously.

subrepticio *adj* surreptitious.

subrogación *nf* substitution, replacement.

subrogante (*Cono Sur*) *adj*, *nmf* substitute.

subrogar [1h] *vt* to substitute (for), replace (with).

subrutina *nf* subroutine.

subsahariano *adj* sub-Saharan.

subsanable *adj* (*perdonable*) excusable; (*reparable*) repairable; **un error fácilmente** ~ an error which is easily rectified; **un obstáculo difícilmente** ~ an obstacle which is hard to overcome.

subsanar [1a] *vt falta* to overlook, excuse; *daño, defecto* to repair, make good; *error* to rectify, put right; *deficiencia* to make up for; *dificultad, obstáculo* to get round, overcome.

subscr... *pref* = **suscr...**

subsecretaría *nf* undersecretaryship.

subsecretario, -a *nm/f* undersecretary.

subsector *nm* subsection, subsector.

subsecuente *adj* subsequent.

subsede *nf* (*Dep*) secondary venue.

subsidiar [1b] *vt* to subsidize.

subsidiariedad *nf* subordination, subsidiary nature; complementary nature.

subsidiario *adj* subsidiary; complementary.

subsidio *nm* (**a**) (*subvención*) subsidy, grant; (*ayuda*) aid, financial help; benefit; ~ **de desempleo,** ~ **de paro** unemployment benefit; ~ **de enfermedad** sick benefit, sick-pay; ~ **de exportación** export subsidy; ~ **familiar** family allowance; ~ **de huelga** strike pay; ~ **de natalidad** maternity benefit; ~ **de vejez** old-age pension.

(**b**) (*And*: *inquietud*) anxiety, worry.

subsiguiente *adj* subsequent.

subsistema *nm* subsystem.

subsistencia *nf* subsistence; sustenance; **salario de** ~ subsistence wage.

subsistente *adj* lasting, enduring; surviving; **una costumbre aún** ~ a still surviving custom.

subsistir [3a] *vi* (**a**) (*malvivir*) to subsist, live (*con, de* on); (*perdurar*) to survive, last out, endure; **todavía subsiste el edificio** the building still stands; **es una creencia que subsiste** it is a belief which still exists; **sin ayuda económica no podrá ~ el colegio** the college will not be able to survive without financial aid.

(**b**) (*And*: *vivir juntos*) to live together.

subsónico *adj* subsonic.

subsótano *nm* basement.

subst... *pref* = **sust...**

subsuelo *nm* subsoil.

subsumir [3a] *vt* to subsume.

subte* *nm* (*Cono Sur*) tube, underground.

subteniente, -enta *nm/f* sub-lieutenant, second lieutenant.

subterfugio *nm* subterfuge.

subterráneo 1 *adj* underground, subterranean.

2 *nm* (**a**) (*túnel*) underground passage; (*almacén*) underground store (*o* cellar *etc*).

(**b**) (*LAm Ferro*) underground, subway (*US*).

subtexto *nm* subtext.

subtitulado *nm* subtitling.

subtitular [1a] *vt* to subtitle.

subtítulo *nm* subtitle (*t Cine*), subheading.

subtropical *adj* subtropical.

suburbano 1 *adj* suburban. **2** *nm* suburban train.

suburbial *adj* suburban; (*pey*) slum (*atr*).

suburbio *nm* (**a**) (*afueras*) suburb, outlying area. (**b**) (*barrio bajo*) slum quarter; (*chabolas*) shantytown.

subvención *nf* subsidy, subvention, grant; ~ **estatal** state subsidy; **subvenciones agrícolas** agricultural subsidies.

subvencionar [1a] *vt* to subsidize, aid.

subvenir [3s] *vi*: ~ **a** *gastos* to meet, defray; *necesidades etc* to provide for; **con eso subviene a sus vicios** with that he pays for his vices; **así subviene a la escasez de su sueldo** in that way he makes up for his low salary.

subversión *nf* (**a**) (*gen*) subversion.

(**b**) (*una* ~) revolution; **la ~ del orden establecido** the overthrow of the established order.

subversivo *adj* subversive.

subvertir [3i] *vi* (*minar*) to subvert; (*derrocar*) to overthrow, undermine; (*perturbar*) to disturb.

subyacente *adj* underlying.

subyacer [2x] *vt* to underlie.

subyugación *nf* subjugation.

subyugador *adj*, **subyugante** *adj* dominating; (*fig*) captivating, enchanting.

subyugar [1h] *vt* (**a**) *país etc* to subjugate, subdue; *enemigo* to overpower; *voluntad etc* to dominate, gain control over.

(**b**) (*fig*) to captivate, charm.

succión *nf* suction.

succionar [1a] *vt* (*sorber*) to suck; to apply suction to; (*Téc*) to absorb, soak up, suck up.

sucedáneo 1 *adj* substitute, ersatz. **2** *nm* substitute (food).

suceder [2a] **1** *vti* (**a**) (*pasar*) to happen; **pues sucede que no vamos** well it happens we're not going; **no le había sucedido eso nunca** that had never happened to him before; **suceda lo que suceda** come what may, whatever happens; **¿qué sucede?** what's going on?, whatever's all this?; **lo que sucede es que ...** the fact is that ..., the trouble is that ...; **lo más que puede ~ es que ...** the worst that can happen is that ...; **llevar algo por lo que pueda ~** to take sth just in case; **lo mismo sucede con éste que con el otro** it's the same with this one as it is with the other.

(**b**) (*seguir*) to succeed, follow; (*heredar*) to inherit; ~ **a uno en un puesto** to succeed sb in a post; ~ **al trono** to succeed to the throne; ~ **a una fortuna** to inherit a fortune; **al otoño sucede el invierno** winter follows autumn; **a este cuarto sucede otro mayor** a larger room leads off this

one, a large room lies beyond this one.
2 sucederse *vr* to follow one another.

sucesión *nf* (**a**) (*gen*) succession (*a* to); (*secuencia*) sequence, series; ~ **apostólica** apostolic succession; **una ~ de acontecimientos** a succession of events, a series of happenings; **en rápida ~** in quick succession; **la princesa ocupa el quinto puesto en la línea de ~ al trono** the princess is fifth in the line of succession to the throne.
(**b**) (*herencia*) inheritance; (*bienes*) estate; **derechos de ~** death duty.
(**c**) (*hijos*) issue, offspring; **morir sin ~** to die without issue.

sucesivamente *adv* successively, in succession; **y así ~** and so on.

sucesivo *adj* (*subsiguiente*) successive, following; (*consecutivo*) consecutive; **3 días ~s** 3 days running, 3 successive days; **en lo ~** henceforth, in future; (*desde entonces*) thereafter, thenceforth.

suceso *nm* (**a**) (*acontecimiento*) event, happening; (*incidente*) incident; (*en periódico*) **capítulo de ~s** *section of accident and crime reports.*
(**b**) (*resultado*) issue, outcome; **buen ~** happy outcome.

sucesor(a) *nm/f* successor; heir.

suciamente *adv* (**a**) (*gen*) dirtily, filthily. (**b**) (*fig*) vilely, meanly; obscenely, unfairly.

suciedad *nf* (**a**) (*sustancia*) dirt, filth, grime; (*cualidad*) dirtiness; filthiness. (**b**) (*fig*) vileness, meanness; obscenity; unfairness. (**c**) (*una ~*) dirty act; filthy remark; obscenity.

sucintamente *adv* succinctly, concisely, briefly.

sucinto *adj* (**a**) *declaración etc* succinct, concise, brief. (**b**) *prenda* short, brief, scanty.

sucio 1 *adj* (**a**) (*gen*) dirty; (*mugriento*) filthy, grimy; (*manchado*) grubby, soiled; *color* dirty; blurred, smudged; *bosquejo etc* rough, messy; *lengua* coated, furred.
(**b**) (*fig*) *conducta* vile, mean, despicable; *acto, palabra etc* dirty, filthy, obscene; *jugada* foul, dirty; *táctica* unfair.
(**c**) *conciencia* bad.
(**d**) *precio, sueldo* gross.
2 *adv*: **jugar ~*** to play unfairly, indulge in dirty play.
3 *nm* (*And*) smut, bit of dirt.

suco¹ *adj* (*And*) muddy, swampy.

suco² *adj* (*And*) (*rojizo*) bright red; (*rubio*) blond, fair; (*anaranjado*) orange.

sucre *nm* sucre (*Ecuadorian unit of currency*).

sucrosa *nf* sucrose.

sucucho *nm* (*Carib*) = **socucho**.

suculencia *nf* tastiness, richness; succulence, lusciousness, juiciness.

suculento *adj* (*sabroso*) tasty, rich; (*jugoso*) succulent, luscious, juicy.

sucumbir [3a] *vi* to succumb (*a* to).

sucursal *nf* (*oficina*) branch, branch office; (*filial*) subsidiary.

sucusumuco: **a lo ~** *adv* (*And, Carib*) pretending to be stupid, feigning stupidity.

suche 1 *adj* (*Carib**) sharp, bitter. **2** *nm* (**a**) (*Cono Sur**: *grano*) pimple. (**b**) (*Cono Sur**: *funcionario*) penpusher. (**c**) (*Cono Sur‡*: *coime*) pimp.

súchil *nm* (*LAm*) *an aromatic flowering tree.*

sucho *adj* (*And*) maimed, paralytic, crippled.

sud *nm* (*esp LAm*) south.

sudaca* *adj, nmf* (*pey*) South American.

sudadera *nf* (*CAm, Méx*) sweatshirt.

sudado *nm* (*And*) stew.

Sudáfrica *nf* South Africa.

sudafricano, -a *adj, nm/f* South African.

Sudamérica *nf* South America.

sudamericano, -a *adj, nm/f* South American.

Sudán *nm* Sudan.

sudanés, -esa *adj, nm/f* Sudanese.

sudar [1a] **1** *vt* (**a**) (*gen*) to sweat; **~ a chorros*** to drip with sweat; *V* **sangre** *etc.*
(**b**) (*Bot etc*) to ooze, give out, give off; (*recipiente*) to ooze; (*pared etc*) to sweat, give off.
(**c**) *ropa etc* to make sweaty, make damp with sweat.
(**d**) (*) **~lo** to sweat it out; **~ un aumento de sueldo** to sweat for a rise in pay, work hard for some extra money; **ha sudado el premio** he really sweated to get the prize; **~ la gota gorda** to sweat blood.
(**e**) (*) *dinero* to cough up*, part with.
(**f**) **es un asunto que me la suda*** it's a matter which bores the pants off me*.
2 *vi* to sweat; **hacer ~ a uno** (*fig*) to make sb sweat.

sudario *nm* shroud.

sudestada *nf* (*Cono Sur*) = **surestada**.

sudeste 1 *adj parte* south-east, south-eastern; *dirección* south-easterly; *viento* south-east, south-easterly. **2** *nm* (**a**) (*Geog*) south-east. (**b**) (*viento*) south-east wind.

sudista 1 *adj* southern. **2** *nmf* Southerner.

sudoeste 1 *adj parte* south-west, south-western; *dirección* south-westerly; *viento* south-west, south-westerly. **2** *nm* (**a**) (*Geog*) south-west. (**b**) (*viento*) south-west wind.

sudón *adj* (*LAm*) sweaty.

sudor *nm* sweat; (*fig*: *t* **~es**) sweat, toil, labour; **con el ~ de su frente** by the sweat of one's brow; **estar bañado en ~** to be dripping with sweat.

sudoración *nf* (*Med*) sweating.

sudoriento *adj*, **sudoroso** *adj*, **sudoso** *adj* sweaty, sweating; covered with sweat; **trabajo sudoroso** thirsty work, work that makes one sweat a lot.

Suecia *nf* Sweden.

suecia *nf* suède.

sueco¹ 1 *adj* Swedish.
2 *nm*, **sueca** *nf* Swede.
3 *nm* (*Ling*) Swedish.

sueco²* *nm*: **hacerse el ~** to pretend not to hear (*o* understand); to act dumb, not let on*.

suegra *nf* mother-in-law.

suegro *nm* father-in-law; **~s** parents-in-law, in-laws.

suela *nf* (**a**) (*de zapato*) sole; (*trozo de cuero*) piece of strong leather; **media ~** half sole; (*fig*) patch, botch; (*fig*) temporary remedy; temporary relief; **A no le llega a la ~ del zapato a B** A can't hold a candle to B; **un pícaro de siete ~s** a proper rogue; **duro como la ~ de un zapato** tough as leather, tough as old boots.
(**b**) **~s** (*Ecl*) sandals; **de siete ~s** utter, downright.
(**c**) (*Pez*) sole.
(**d**) (*LAm Téc*) washer.

suelazo* *nm* (*LAm*) (*caída*) heavy fall, nasty bump; (*golpe*) blow, punch.

sueldo *nm* (*gen*) pay; (*mensual*) salary; (*semanal*) wage; **~ atrasado** back pay; **~ de hambre** starvation wage; **asesino a ~** hired assassin, contract killer; **estar a ~** to be on a salary, earn a salary; **estar a ~ de una potencia extranjera** to be in the pay of a foreign power.

suelear* [1a] *vt* (*Cono Sur*) to throw, chuck.

suelo *nm* (**a**) (*tierra*) ground; (*superficie*) surface; **~ natal, ~ patrio** native land, native soil; **arrastrar** (*o* **poner** *o* **tirar**) **por los ~s** to blacken, run down, speak ill of; **caer al ~** to fall to the ground; **caerse al ~** (*fig*) to fail, collapse; **echar al ~** *edificio* to demolish; *esperanzas* to dash; *plan* to ruin; **echarse al ~** to hurl o.s. to the ground; to fall on one's knees; **echarse por los ~s** (*fig*) to grovel; **estar por el ~*** to feel very low; **los precios están por el ~** prices are at rock bottom; **esos géneros están por los ~s** those goods are dirt cheap; **irse al ~** to fall through; **medir el ~** to fall full-length; **tirarse por los ~s*** to roll in the aisles (with laughter)*; **venirse al ~** (*fig*) to fail, collapse, be ruined.
(**b**) (*de cuarto etc*) floor; flooring.
(**c**) (*Cono Sur*: *tierra*) ground, soil, earth; **~ vegetal** topsoil.
(**d**) (*de pan, vasija etc*) bottom.

sueltista *nmf* (*LAm*) freelance journalist.

suelto 1 *adj* (**a**) (*libre*) free; (*no atado*) untied, undone; *pieza etc* detached, unattached, separate; *cabo, hoja, tornillo* loose; (*sin trabas*) unhampered; *prenda etc* loose, loose-fitting; **~ de lengua** (*hablador*) talkative; (*respondón*) cheeky, given to answering back; (*soplón*) not to be trusted with secrets; (*obsceno*) foulmouthed; **~ de vientre** loose; **el libro tiene dos hojas sueltas** the book has two pages loose; **llevas ~s los cordones** your shoelaces are undone; **el perro anda ~** the dog is loose; **su marido anda ~** her husband is on the loose; **lo ató con el cabo ~** he tied it up with the free (*o* loose) end; **lo dejamos ~** we leave it untied, we leave it free; **iba con el pelo ~** she had her hair down.
(**b**) *fragmento, pasaje etc* detached, isolated; individual; (*Com*: *no envasado*) loose, in bulk; (*desparejado*) odd; *número, volumen* odd, single; **es un trozo ~ de la novela** it's a separate piece from the novel, it's an isolated passage from the novel; **son 3 poesías sueltas** these are 3 separate poems; **los tomos no se venden ~s** the volumes are not sold singly (*o* separately); **hay un calcetín ~** there is one odd sock; **una mesa con números ~s de revistas** a table with odd copies of magazines.
(**c**) (*en movimiento*) free, easy; (*ágil*) light; quick, agile, unhampered; *estilo* fluent, free, flowing; **está muy ~ en in-**

glés his English is fluent.

(**d**) (*moralmente*) free and easy; (*atrevido*) daring; (*licencioso*) licentious, lax.

(**e**) (*Liter*) *verso* blank.

2 *nm* (**a**) (*Fin*) change, loose change, small change.

(**b**) (*Tip*) paragraph; (*en periódico*) item, note, short article.

sueñera* *nf* (*LAm*) drowsiness, sleepiness.

sueño *nm* (**a**) (*el dormir*) sleep; ~ **eterno** eternal rest; ~ **invernal** (*Zool*) winter sleep; ~ **pesado,** ~ **profundo** deep sleep, heavy sleep; **coger el** ~, **conciliar el** ~ to get to sleep; **descabezar un** ~, **echarse un** ~ to have a nap; **dormir el** ~ **de los justos** to sleep the sleep of the just; **pasar una noche sin** ~ to have a sleepless night; **perder el** ~ **por algo** to lose sleep over sth; **tengo** ~ **atrasado** I haven't had much sleep lately; **tener el** ~ **ligero** to be a light sleeper; **tener el** ~ **pesado** (*o* **profundo**) to be a heavy sleeper.

(**b**) (*somnolencia*) sleepiness, drowsiness; **caerse de** ~ to be so sleepy one can hardly stand; **espantar el** ~ to struggle to keep awake; **tener** ~ to be sleepy; **sentirse con** ~ to feel sleepy; **se me ha quitado el** ~ I'm not sleepy any more.

(**c**) (*lo soñado*) dream (*t fig*); **¡ni en ~s!, ¡ni por ~!** not on your life!; **es su** ~ **dorado** it's the dream of his life, it's his great dream; **es un** ~ **hecho realidad** it's a dream come true; **estar entre ~s** to be half asleep; **ver algo en** (*o* **entre**) **~s** to see sth in a dream; **vive en un mundo de ~s** she lives in a dream world; **tiene una casa que es un** ~ she has a real dream of a house, she has a real dream-house.

suero *nm* (**a**) (*Med*) serum. (**b**) whey; ~ **de la leche** buttermilk.

suertaza* *nf* great stroke of luck.

suerte *nf* (**a**) (*destino*) fate, destiny; (*azar*) chance, fortune; **por** ~ by chance, as it happened; **abandonado a su** ~ left to one's own devices; **confiar algo a la** ~ to leave sth to chance; **dejar a uno a su** ~ to abandon sb to his fate; **la** ~ **que les espera** the fate which awaits them; **quiso la** ~ **que ...** as fate would have it ..., as luck would have it ...; **seguir la** ~ **a uno** to keep track of sb; **tentar a la** ~ to tempt fate; **unirse a la** ~ **de uno** to throw in one's lot with sb, make common cause with sb.

(**b**) (*elección*) lot; **caber en** ~ **a uno, caer en** ~ **a uno** to fall to sb, fall to sb's lot; **no me cupo tal** ~ I had no such luck; **echaron ~s entre los 4** the 4 of them drew lots, the 4 of them tossed up; **lo echaron a ~s** they drew lots for it, they tossed up for it; **la** ~ **está echada** the die is cast.

(**c**) (*fortuna*) luck; **buena** ~ luck, good luck; **¡buena ~!** good luck!; **¡~, y al toro!*** the best of luck to you!; **mala** ~ bad luck, hard luck; ~ **perra*** bad luck, rotten luck; **hombre de** ~ lucky man; **un número de mala** ~ an unlucky number; **por** ~ luckily, fortunately; **dar** ~, **traer** ~ to bring luck; **trae mala** ~ **escupir allí** it's unlucky to spit there; **estar de** ~ to be in luck; **probar** ~ to try one's luck; **tener** ~ to be lucky; to have a piece of luck; **¡que tengas ~!** good luck!, I wish you luck!, and the best of luck!; **tuvo una** ~ **loca*** he was fantastically lucky; **tuvo la** ~ **de que hacía buen tiempo** he was lucky that it was fine.

(**d**) (*condición*) lot; state, condition; **mejorar de** ~ to improve one's lot.

(**e**) (*billete de lotería*) lottery ticket.

(**f**) (*especie*) sort, kind; **es una** ~ **de** it is a kind of; **no podemos seguir de esta** ~ we cannot go on in this way; **de otra** ~ otherwise, if not; **de** ~ **que ...** in such a way that ..., so that ...; **¿de** ~ **que no hay más dragones?** so there are no more dragons?

(**g**) (*Taur*) stage, part (of the bullfight); ~ **de varas** *opening section* (*of play with the capes*).

suertero 1 *adj* (*LAm*) lucky. **2** *nm*, **suertera** *nf* (*And, CAm*) seller of lottery tickets.

suertoso *adj* (*And*) lucky.

suertudo *adj* lucky.

sueste *nm* (**a**) (*Náut*: *sombrero*) sou'wester. (**b**) (*LAm*: *viento*) south-east wind.

suéter *nm* sweater.

Suetonio *nm* Suetonius.

Suez *nm* Suez; **Canal de** ~ Suez Canal.

suficiencia *nf* (*V adj*) (**a**) sufficiency; adequacy; **una** ~ **de ...** enough ...; **a** ~ sufficiently, adequately.

(**b**) competence; suitability, fitness; adequacy; capacity; (*Escol*) proficiency; **demostrar su** ~ to prove one's competence, show one's capabilities.

(**c**) (*pey*) self-importance; superiority; condescension; smugness, self-satisfaction, complacency; *V* **aire.**

suficiente *adj* (**a**) (*bastante*) enough, sufficient (*para* for); (*adecuado*) adequate.

(**b**) *persona* competent; (*idóneo*) suitable, fit; (*adecuado*) adequate; (*capaz*) capable; (*Escol*) proficient.

(**c**) (*pey*) (*engreído*) self-important; superior; (*desdeñoso*) condescending; (*satisfecho de sí*) smug, self-satisfied, complacent.

suficientemente *adv* sufficiently, adequately.

sufijo *nm* suffix.

suflé *nm* soufflé.

sufragáneo *adj* suffragan.

sufragar [1h] **1** *vt* (**a**) (*ayudar*) to aid, help, support.

(**b**) *gastos* to meet, defray, cover; *proyecto etc* to pay for, defray the costs of.

2 *vi* (*LAm*) to vote (*por* for).

sufragio *nm* (**a**) (*voto*) vote; **los ~s emitidos a favor de X** the votes cast for X.

(**b**) (*derecho de votar*) suffrage; franchise; ~ **universal** universal suffrage.

(**c**) (*apoyo*) help, aid.

(**d**) (*Ecl*) suffrage.

sufragista *nf* suffragette.

sufrible *adj* bearable.

sufrido 1 *adj* (**a**) *persona* (*duro*) tough; (*paciente*) long-suffering, patient.

(**b**) *tela etc* hard-wearing, long-lasting, tough; *color* that does not show the dirt, that wears well.

(**c**) *marido* complaisant.

2 *nm* complaisant husband.

sufridor 1 *adj* suffering. **2** *nm* (**a**) (*persona*) sufferer. (**b**) (*And*) saddlecloth.

sufrimiento *nm* (**a**) (*estado*) suffering; misery, wretchedness.

(**b**) (*cualidad*) toughness; patience; tolerance; **tener** ~ **en las dificultades** to be patient in hard times, bear troubles patiently.

sufrir [3a] **1** *vt* (**a**) (*gen*) to suffer; *accidente, ataque* to have, suffer; *consecuencias, desastre, revés etc* to suffer; *cambio* to undergo, experience; *pérdida* to suffer, sustain; *operación* to have, undergo.

(**b**) (*soportar*) to bear, stand, put up with; **no sufre la menor descortesía** he won't tolerate the slightest rudeness; **A no le sufre a B** A can't stand B.

(**c**) (*sostener*) to hold up, support.

(**d**) *examen, prueba* to take, undergo.

2 *vi* to suffer; ~ **de** to suffer from, suffer with; **sufre de reumatismo** she suffers from (*o* with) rheumatism; **sufre mucho de los pies** she suffers a lot with her feet; **aprender a** ~ **silenciosamente** to learn to suffer in silence.

sugerencia *nf* suggestion.

sugerente *adj* full of suggestions, rich in ideas, thought-provoking; *escena etc* evocative.

sugerible *adj* = **sugestionable.**

sugerimiento *nm* suggestion.

sugerir [3i] *vt* (*gen*) to suggest; (*insinuar*) to hint, hint at; *pensamiento etc* to prompt; ~ **que ...** to suggest that ...

sugestión *nf* (**a**) (*sugerencia*) suggestion; (*insinuación*) hint; (*estímulo*) prompting, stimulus; **las sugestiones del corazón** the promptings of the heart; **un sitio de muchas sugestiones** a place rich in associations.

(**b**) (*autosugestión*) autosuggestion, self-hypnotism.

(**c**) (*poder*) fascination (for others), hypnotic power, power to influence others; **emanaba de él una fuerte** ~ a strong hypnotic power flowed from him.

sugestionable *adj* impressionable, suggestible; open to influence, readily influenced.

sugestionar [1a] **1** *vt* to influence, dominate the will of, hypnotize; to exercise a powerful fascination over; ~ **a uno para que haga algo** to influence sb to do sth.

2 sugestionarse *vr* to indulge in autosuggestion; **es probable que se haya dejado** ~ **por ...** he may have allowed himself to be influenced by ...; **te lo has sugestionado** you've talked yourself into it.

sugestivo *adj* (**a**) (*estimulante*) stimulating, thought-provoking; (*evocador*) evocative. (**b**) (*atractivo*) attractive; (*fascinante*) fascinating.

suicida 1 *adj, atr* suicidal; **comando** ~ suicide squad; **conductor** ~ suicidal driver; **piloto** ~ suicide pilot, kamikaze pilot.

2 *nmf* suicidal case, person with a tendency to suicide; (*muerto*) person who has committed suicide; **es un** ~ **conduciendo** he's a maniac behind the wheel.

suicidado, -a *nm/f* person who commits suicide.

suicidar [1a] **1** *vt* (*iró*) to murder, assassinate (so as to convey an impression of suicide), fake the suicide of. **2 suicidarse** *vr* to commit suicide, kill oneself.
suicid(i)ario *adj* suicidal.
suicidio *nm* suicide.
suiche *nm* (**a**) (*LAm, Elec*) switch. (**b**) (*Carib Aut*) ignition key.
Suiza *nf* Switzerland.
suiza[1] *nf* (**a**) (*CAm, Carib: juego*) skipping, skipping game.
(**b**) (*And, CAm: paliza*) beating.
suizo[1], **-a**[2] *adj, nm/f* Swiss.
suizo[2] *nm* (*Culin*) bun.
suje* *nm* bra*.
sujeción *nf* (**a**) (*estado*) subjection. (**b**) (*acto*) fastening; seizure; (*fig*) subjection (*a* to); **con ~ a** subject to.
sujetacorbata *nm* tiepin.
sujetador *nm* fastener; (*para pelo*) clip, pin, grip; (*para papeles*) clip; (*de pluma*) clip; (*prenda*) brassiere, bra; **~ de libros** book-end.
sujetalibros *nm invar* book-ends.
sujetapapeles *nm invar* paperclip.
sujetar [1a] **1** *vt* (**a**) (*dominar*) *nación* to subdue, conquer; to hold down; keep down, keep under; to exercise control over; *precio etc* to keep down, hold down; **~ A a B** to put A under B's authority, subordinate A to B.
(**b**) (*agarrar*) to seize, clutch, lay hold of; (*sostener*) to hold, (*fuertemente*) to hold tight; *persona* to hold down, keep hold of; (*Téc*) to fasten; (*con clavo*) to nail down; (*con cola*) to stick down; (*con tornillo*) to screw down (*etc*); *pelo etc* to keep in place, hold in place; *papeles etc* to fasten together.
2 sujetarse *vr*: **~ a** (*someterse a*) to subject o.s. to; *regla* to abide by; *circunstancias etc* to act in accordance with, recognize the limitations of; *autoridad* to submit to; **~ a** + *infin* to agree to + *infin*, give way before the necessity of + *ger*.
sujeto 1 *adj* (**a**) (*fijo*) fastened, secure; (*firme*) firm; (*ajustado*) tight; **la cuerda está bien sujeta** the rope is securely fastened.
(**b**) **~ a** subject to; (*propenso a*) liable to; **~ a la aprobación de** subject to the approval of; **~ a derechos** subject to duty, dutiable; **estar ~ a cambios inesperados** to be liable to sudden changes.
(**c**) **tener a alguien ~** to keep sb under supervision.
2 *nm* (**a**) (*Ling*) subject.
(**b**) (*persona*) individual; (*Med etc*) subject, case; (*) fellow, character*, chap*; **un ~ sospechoso** a suspicious character*; **buen ~** good chap*.
sulfamida *nf* sulphonamide.
sulfato *nm* sulphate; **~ amónico** ammonium sulphate; **~ de cobre** copper sulphate; **~ de hierro** iron sulphate; **~ magnésico** magnesium sulphate; **~ potásico** potassium sulphate.
sulfurado* *adj* cross, angry.
sulfurar [1a] **1** *vt* (**a**) (*Quím*) to sulphurate.
(**b**) (*) to annoy, rile*.
2 sulfurarse *vr* (*) to get mad*, see red, blow up*.
sulfúreo *adj* sulphurous.
sulfúrico *adj* sulphuric.
sulfuro *nm* sulphide.
sulfuroso *adj* sulphurous.
sultán *nm* sultan.
sultana *nf* sultana.
sultanato *nm* sultanate.
suma 1 *nf* (**a**) (*Mat: acto*) adding (up), addition; (*cantidad*) total, sum; (*de dinero*) sum; **'~ y sigue'** (*en cuenta*) 'carried forward'; (*) and it's still going on; **~ global** lump sum; **en ~** in short; **hacer ~s** to add up, do addition.
(**b**) (*fig: resumen*) summary; essence; **una ~ de perfecciones** perfection itself; **es la ~ y compendio de todas las virtudes** she is the personification of all the virtues.
2 *nm*: **un ~ y sigue de grandes aportaciones al mundo del automóvil** a whole host of great contributions to the world of cars.
sumador *nm* (*Inform*) adder circuit.
sumadora *nf* adding machine.
sumamente *adv* extremely, exceedingly, highly.
sumar [1a] **1** *vt* (**a**) (*Mat*) to add (up), total; (*fig: resumir*) to summarize, sum up.
(**b**) (*recoger*) to collect, gather.
(**c**) **la cuenta suma 6 dólares** the bill adds up to (*o* comes to, amounts to, works out at) 6 dollars.
2 *vi* to add up.
3 sumarse *vr*: **~ a un partido** to join a party; **~ a una protesta** to associate o.s. with a protest, join in a protest.
sumariamente *adv* summarily.
sumario 1 *adj* brief, concise; (*Jur*) summary; **información sumaria** summary proceedings. **2** *nm* (**a**) (*resumen*) summary. (**b**) (*Jur*) indictment.
Sumatra *nf* Sumatra.
sumergible 1 *adj* submersible; that can go under water. **2** *nm* submarine.
sumergido *adj* (**a**) submerged, sunken. (**b**) (*ilegal*) illegal, unauthorized; **economía sumergida** black economy; **tratos ~s** black-market deals.
sumergimiento *nm* submersion, submergence.
sumergir [3c] **1** *vt* (**a**) (*gen*) to submerge; (*hundir*) to sink; (*bañar*) to immerse, dip, plunge (*en* in).
(**b**) (*fig*) to plunge (*en* into).
2 sumergirse *vr* (**a**) (*gen*) to submerge, sink beneath the surface; (*submarino etc*) to dive.
(**b**) **~ en** (*fig*) to immerse o.s. in, become absorbed in.
sumersión *nf* (**a**) (*gen*) submersion, submergence; immersion. (**b**) (*fig*) absorption (*en* in).
sumidero *nm* (**a**) (*cloaca*) drain, sewer; (*fregadero*) sink; (*Téc*) sump; (*And, Carib*) cesspool, cesspit.
(**b**) (*Carib: tremedal*) quagmire.
(**c**) (*fig*) drain; **es el gran ~ de las reservas** it is the chief drain on our reserves.
sumiller *nm* wine-waiter.
suministrador(a) *nm/f* supplier.
suministrar [1a] *vt artículos, información etc* to supply, furnish, provide; *persona* to supply; **me ha suministrado muchos datos** he has given me a lot of data, he has supplied me with a lot of information.
suministro *nm* (*provisión*) supply; (*acto*) supplying, furnishing, provision; **~s** (*Mil*) supplies; **~s de combustible** fuel supply.
sumir [3a] **1** *vt* (**a**) (*hundir*) to sink, plunge, submerge; (*mar, olas*) to swallow up, suck down.
(**b**) (*fig*) to plunge (*en* into); **el desastre le sumió en la tristeza** the disaster plunged him into sadness.
(**c**) (*And, Cono Sur, Méx: abollar*) to dent.
2 sumirse *vr* (**a**) (*objeto*) to sink; (*agua etc*) to run away, disappear.
(**b**) (*boca, pecho etc*) to sink, be sunken, become hollow.
(**c**) **~ en el estudio** to become absorbed in one's work; **~ en la tristeza** to plunge into grief, give o.s. over entirely to one's grief.
(**d**) (*LAm*) (*encogerse*) to cower, cringe; (*desanimarse*) to lose heart; (*callar*) to fall silent from fear, clam up.
(**e**) **~ el sombrero** (*LAm*) to pull one's hat down over one's eyes.
sumisamente *adv* submissively, obediently; unresistingly; uncomplainingly.
sumisión *nf* (**a**) (*acto*) submission. (**b**) (*cualidad*) submissiveness, docility.
sumiso *adj* (*dócil*) submissive, docile, obedient; (*que no resiste*) unresisting; (*que no se queja*) uncomplaining.
sumo[1] *adj* (**a**) (*supremo*) great, extreme, supreme; **con suma dificultad** with the greatest (*o* utmost) difficulty; **con suma indiferencia** with supreme indifference; **con suma destreza** with consummate skill.
(**b**) (*en rango*) high, highest; **~ sacerdote** high priest; *V* **pontífice; la suma autoridad** the highest authority, the supreme authority.
(**c**) **a lo ~** at most.
sumo[2] *nm* sumo (wrestling).
sunco *adj* (*And*) = **manco.**
sungo *adj* (*And*) Negro; (*de piel liso*) with a shiny skin; (*tostado*) tanned.
suní, sunita *adj, nmf* Sunni.
suntuario *adj* sumptuary.
suntuosamente *adj* sumptuously, magnificently; lavishly, richly.
suntuosidad *nf* sumptuousness, magnificence; lavishness.
suntuoso *adj* sumptuous, magnificent; lavish, rich.
sup. *abr de* **superior** superior, sup.
supeditar [1a] **1** *vt* (**a**) (*subordinar*) to subordinate (*a* to); **tendrá que ser supeditado a lo que decidan ellos** it will have to depend on what they decide.
(**b**) (*sojuzgar*) to subdue; (*oprimir*) to oppress, crush.
2 supeditarse *vr*: **~ a** (*subordinarse*) to make o.s. subordinate to, come to depend on; (*ceder*) to give way to, allow o.s. to be overridden by; **no voy a supeditarme a su capricho** I am not going to depend on her whims.
super... *pref* super..., over... (**a**) **superambicioso** overambitious; **superatraco** major hold-up; **superdesarrollo**

overdevelopment.

(**b**) *prefijo de adj*: *equivale frec a superlativo*: **supercaro** impossibly expensive; **superfamoso** extremely famous; **superreservado** excessively shy; **un texto supercomentado** a text which has so often been commented on.

súper 1 *adj* (*) super*. **2** *adv* (*) really well, real good*. **3** *nm* (**a**) (*Aut*) four-star petrol. (**b**) (*Com*) supermarket.

superable *adj dificultad* surmountable, that can be overcome; *tarea etc* that can be performed; **un obstáculo difícilmente** ~ an obstacle not easily surmounted.

superabundancia *nf* superabundance.

superabundante *adj* superabundant.

superación *nf* (**a**) (*acto*) overcoming, surmounting; transcending; excelling. (**b**) (*mejora*) improvement, doing better; *V* **afán**.

superar [1a] **1** *vt* (**a**) *rival* to surpass, excel (*in* en), beat, do better than; *adversario* to overcome; *esperanzas* to exceed; *límite, punto* to go beyond, transcend; *récord* to break; **las escenas superan a toda imaginación** the scenes are more extraordinary than anyone could imagine, the scenes defeat one's imagination; ~ **a uno en brillantez** to outshine sb; **superó 2 veces la marca de los 200 metros** she twice broke the 200-metre record.

(**b**) *dificultad* to overcome, surmount; *prueba* to pass.

(**c**) *etapa, período* to get past, leave behind, emerge from; **ya hemos superado lo peor** we're over the worst now.

2 superarse *vr* to do extremely well, excel o.s.

superávit *nm invar* surplus.

superavitario *adj* surplus (*atr*).

supercarburante *nm* high-grade fuel.

supercarretera *nf* superhighway.

supercola *nf* superglue.

superconductividad *nf* superconductivity.

superconductor 1 *adj* superconductive. **2** *nm* superconductor.

superconsumo *nm* overconsumption.

supercopa *nf* cup-winners' cup.

supercotizado *adj* much sought-after, in very great demand.

superchería *nf* fraud, trick, swindle.

superchero *adj* fraudulent; sham, bogus.

superdirecta *nf* (*Aut*) overdrive.

superdotado 1 *adj* extremely gifted. **2** *nm*, **superdotada** *nf* extremely gifted person.

superego *nm* superego.

superempleo *nm* overemployment,

superentender [2g] *vt* to supervise, superintend.

supererogación *nf* supererogation.

superestrella *nf* superstar.

superestructura *nf* superstructure.

superferolítico* *adj* (**a**) (*afectado*) affected; (*muy refinado*) excessively refined. (**b**) (*delicado*) overnice, finicky, choosy*.

superficial *adj* (**a**) *medida etc* surface (*atr*), of the surface; *herida etc* superficial, flesh (*atr*). (**b**) (*fig*) *interés, mirada etc* superficial; (*breve*) brief, perfunctory; *carácter* superficial, shallow; (*frívolo*) facile.

superficialidad *nf* superficiality; shallowness.

superficialmente *adv* superficially.

superficie *nf* (**a**) (*gen*) surface; (*cara*) face; (*exterior*) outside; (*del mar etc*) surface; ~ **inferior** lower surface, underside; ~ **de rodadura** (*Aut*) tread; **el ave rozó la** ~ the bird skimmed the surface; **el submarino salió a la** ~ the submarine surfaced, the submarine came to the surface; **ruta de** ~ surface route, land (*o* sea) route.

(**b**) (*medidas etc*) area; ~ **útil** useful area, usable space; **se regará una** ~ **de 200 hectáreas** an area of 200 hectares will be irrigated; **todo quedó destruido en una extensa** ~ everything was destroyed over a wide area.

(**c**) (*fig*) surface, outward appearance.

(**d**) (*Com*) **gran** ~ superstore.

superfino *adj* superfine.

superfluamente *adv* superfluously.

superfluidad *nf* superfluity.

superfluo *adj* superfluous.

superfosfato *nm* superphosphate.

superhombre *nm* superman.

superíndice *nm* (*Inform*) superscript.

superintendencia *nf* supervision, superintendence.

superintendente *nmf* supervisor, superintendent; overseer; (*Com*) shop walker, floorwalker (*US*); ~ **de división** sectional head.

superior 1 *adj* (**a**) (*posición*: *más alto*) upper; (*el más alto*) uppermost, top; (*más elevado*) higher; *clase* upper; *estudio* advanced, higher; **labio** ~ upper lip; **vive en el piso** ~ he lives on the upper (*o* top) floor; **viven en el piso** ~ **al mío** they live on the floor above mine; **un estudio de nivel** ~ **a los existentes** a study on a higher plane than the present ones.

(**b**) (*en calidad etc*) superior, better; **ser** ~ **a** to be superior to, be better than; **de calidad** ~ of superior quality.

(**c**) (*en número*) higher, greater, larger; **cualquier número** ~ **a 12** any number above (*o* higher than) 12.

(**d**) (*en actitud*) superior; condescending, patronizing.

2 *nm* superior; **mis ~es** my superiors, those above me (in rank); (*fig*) my betters.

superiora *nf* mother superior.

superioridad *nf* superiority.

superitar [1a] *vt* (*And, Cono Sur*) (**a**) (*superar*) to overcome. (**b**) (*aventajar*) to improve.

superlativo *adj, nm* superlative.

superlujo *nm*: **hotel de** ~ super-luxury hotel; **tiene categoría de** ~ it is in the super-luxury class.

supermercado *nm* supermarket.

superministro, -a *nm/f* minister with an overall responsibility, senior minister, overlord.

supermoda *nf*: **vestido de** ~ high-fashion dress.

supernumerario, -a *adj, nm/f* supernumerary.

superordenador *nm* supercomputer.

superpetrolero *nm* supertanker.

superpoblación *nf* overpopulation, excess of population; overcrosing, congestion.

superpoblado *adj país, región* overpopulated; *barrio etc* overcrowded, congested.

superponer [2q] *vt* to superimpose, superpose, put on top.

superposición *nf* superposition.

superpotencia *nf* superpower, great power.

superproducción *nf* overproducton.

superprotector *adj* over-protective.

supersecreto *adj* top secret.

supersensible *adj* ultra-sensitive.

supersimplificación *nf* oversimplification.

supersónico *adj* supersonic.

supersoplón, -ona‡ *nm/f* supergrass‡.

superstición *nf* superstition.

supersticiosamente *adv* superstitiously.

supersticioso *adj* superstitious.

supertalla *nf* (*Cos*) outsize.

supervalorar [1a] *vt* to overvalue, overstate; (*Com, Fin*) to overvalue.

superventa 1 *adj* best-selling. **2** *nf* best-seller, best-selling article. **3** *nmf* (*persona*) top salesperson.

supervigilancia *nf* (*LAm*) supervision.

supervisar [1a] *vt* to supervise.

supervisión *nf* supervision.

supervisor(a) *nm/f* supervisor; (*f*: *de hospital*) matron.

supervivencia *nf* survival; ~ **de los más aptos,** ~ **de los mejor dotados** survival of the fittest.

superviviente 1 *adj* surviving. **2** *nmf* survivor.

superyo *nm* superego.

supino *adj, nm* supine.

súpito *adj* (**a**) = **súbito**. (**b**) (*And*: *atónito*) dumbfounded.

suplantación *nf* (**a**) (*gen*) supplanting; (*de persona*) impersonation. (**b**) (*And*: *falsificación*) forgery.

suplantar [1a] *vt* (**a**) (*gen*) to supplant; (*hacerse pasar por otro*) to take the place of (fraudulently), impersonate. (**b**) (*And*: *falsificar*) to falsify, forge.

suplefaltas *nmf invar* (**a**) (*chivo expiatorio*) scapegoat. (**b**) (*suplente*) substitute, stopgap, fill-in.

suplemental *adj* supplementary.

suplementario *adj* supplementary; extra, additional; **empleo** ~, **negocio** ~ sideline; **tren** ~ extra train, relief train; **tiempo** ~ overtime.

suplementero *nm* (*Cono Sur*) newsboy, news vendor.

suplemento *nm* (**a**) (*gen*) supplement; (*Ferro etc*) excess fare, supplement. (**b**) (*revista etc*) ~ **a** (*o* **en**) **color** colour supplement; ~ **dominical** Sunday supplement; ~ **separable** pull-out supplement.

suplencia *nf* (*LAm*) substitution, replacement.

suplente 1 *adj* substitute, deputy; reserve; **maestro** ~ supply teacher.

2 *nmf* substitute, deputy; replacement; (*Dep*) substitute, reserve.

supletorio 1 *adj* supplementary; extra, reserve, additional; stopgap (*atr*); **con la ventaja supletoria de que ...** with the additional advantage that ...; **llevar una lámpara supletoria** to take a spare bulb. **2** *nm* (*Telec*) extension.

súplica *nf* request; entreaty, supplication; (*Jur*) petition; **~s** entreaties, pleading; **acceder a las ~s de uno** to grant sb's request; **se publica a ~(s) de ...** it is published at the request of ...

suplicante 1 *adj tono etc* imploring, pleading. **2** *nmf* applicant; (*Jur*) petitioner, supplicant.

suplicar [1g] **1** *vt* (**a**) *cosa* to beg (for), plead for, implore.

(**b**) *persona* to beg, plead with, implore; **~ a uno no hacer algo** to implore sb not to do sth.

(**c**) (*Jur*) to appeal to, petition (*de* against).

2 suplicarse *vr*: **'se suplica cerrar la puerta'** 'please shut the door'.

suplicio *nm* (*tortura*) torture; (*Hist*) (*castigo*) punishment; (*ejecución*), execution; (*fig*) torment, torture; (*mental*) anguish; (*sufrimiento*) ordeal; **~ de Tántalo** torments of Tantalus; **es un ~ tener que escucharle** it's torture having to listen to him.

suplir [3a] **1** *vt* (**a**) *necesidad, omisión* to supply; *falta* to make good, make up for; *palabra etc que falta* to supply; to understand.

(**b**) (*sustituir*) **~ A con B** to replace A by B, substitute B for A; **suplen el aceite con grasa animal** they replace olive oil by animal fat.

2 *vi*: **~ a, ~ por** to replace, take the place of, substitute for, do duty for; **suple en el equipo al portero lesionado** he's replacing the injured goalkeeper in the team.

suponer [2r] **1** *vt* (**a**) (*dar por sentado*) to suppose, assume; **supongamos que ...** let us suppose (*o* assume) that ...; **supongo que sí** I suppose so; **era de ~ que ...** it was to be expected that ...; **con las dificultades que son de ~** with all the difficulties that one might expect.

(**b**) (*imaginarse*) to think, imagine; (*adivinar*) to guess; **ya puedes ~ lo que ella sufría** you can just imagine how she was suffering; **Vd puede ~ lo que pasó** you can guess what happened; **no puedes ~ lo bruto que es** you can't begin to imagine what a lout he is; **es un ~** I was only thinking aloud, of course that's just guesswork.

(**c**) (*atribuir*) to attribute; to credit (with); **le supongo unos 60 años** I give him (an age of) about 60; **se le supone una gran antigüedad** it is thought to be very ancient, it is credited with great antiquity; **hubo poco público y se ve que el equipo no tenía tanta 'fuerza' como se le suponía** there were few spectators and it is clear that the team did not have the 'pull' it was credited with.

(**d**) (*significar*) to mean, imply; (*acarrear*) to involve, entail; **el traslado le supone grandes gastos** the move involves a lot of expense for him; **tal distancia no supone nada yendo en coche** that distance doesn't amount to anything in a car; **esa cantidad supone mucho para ellos** that amount means a lot to them.

2 *vi* to have authority, count (for a lot); **casi no supone en la organización** he hardly counts for anything in the organization.

suposición *nf* (**a**) (*supuesto*) supposition, assumption, surmise. (**b**) (*autoridad*) authority; (*distinción*) distinction. (**c**) (*calumnia*) slander; (*engaño*) imposture.

supositorio *nm* suppository.

supra... *pref* supra...

supradicho *adj* aforementioned.

supranacional *adj* supranational.

supremacía *nf* supremacy.

supremo *adj* supreme.

supresión *nf* (*V vt*) suppression; abolition; removal, elimination; cancellation, lifting; deletion, omission; banning.

supresivo *adj* suppressive.

supresor *nm* (*Elec*) suppressor.

suprimido *adj libro etc* suppressed, banned.

suprimir [3a] *vt crítica, rebelión etc* to suppress; *costumbre, derecho, institución etc* to abolish; *dificultad, obstáculo, residuos* to remove, eliminate; *restricciones* to cancel, lift; *detalle, pasaje etc* to delete, cut out, omit; *libro etc* to suppress, ban.

supuestamente *adv* supposedly; allegedly.

supuesto 1 *ptp de* **suponer**.

2 *adj* (**a**) (*aparente*) supposed, ostensible; (*pretendido*) self-styled; (*según se afirma*) alleged; **el ~ jefe del movimiento** the self-styled leader of the movement; **bajo un nombre ~** under an assumed name, under a false name.

(**b**) **dar por ~ algo** to take sth for granted; **demos por ~ que ...** let us take it for granted that ...

3 ~ que *conj* (*ya que*) since; (*dado que*) granted that; (*pues*) inasmuch as.

4 *nm* (**a**) (*hipótesis*) assumption, hypothesis; **~ previo** prior assumption; **en el ~ de que** (+ *subj*) on the assumption that ...

(**b**) **¡por ~!** of course!, naturally! **pero ¡por ~!** (*LAm*) please do!, you're welcome!

supuración *nf* suppuration.

supurar [1a] *vi* to suppurate, discharge, fester.

sur 1 *adj parte* south, southern; *dirección* southerly; *viento south, southerly*.

2 *nm* (**a**) south; **en la parte del ~** in the southern part; **al ~ de León** to the south of Leon, on the south side of Leon; **eso cae más hacia el ~** that lies further (to the) south.

(**b**) (*viento*) south wind.

sura *nm* sura.

Suráfrica *nf* = **Sudáfrica.**

surafricano = **sudafricano.**

Suramérica *nf* = **Sudamérica.**

suramericano = **sudamericano.**

surazo *nm* (*And, Cono Sur*) strong southerly wind.

surcar [1g] *vt* (**a**) *tierra* to plough (through), furrow; *superficie* (*cortar*) to cut, score, groove; (*rayar*) to make lines across; **una superficie surcada de ...** a surface lined with ..., a surface criss-crossed with ...

(**b**) (*fig*) *agua, olas* to cut through, cleave; **los barcos que surcan los mares** (*liter*) the ships which ply the seas; **las aves que surcan los aires** (*liter*) the birds which ride the winds.

surco *nm* (*Agr etc*) furrow; (*de rueda*) rut, track; (*en metal etc*) groove, score, line; (*de disco*) groove; (*Anat*) wrinkle; (*en agua*) track, wake; **echarse al ~** *persona perezosa* to sit down on the job; (*terminar*) to knock off*, think one has done enough.

surcoreano, -a *adj, nm/f* South Korean.

sureño 1 *adj* southern. **2** *nm*, **sureña** *nf* Southerner.

surero *nm* (*And*) cold southerly wind.

surestada *nf* (*Cono Sur*) wet south-easterly wind.

sureste = **sudeste.**

surf *nm* surfboarding; **~ a vela** windsurfing.

surfista *nmf* surfboarder.

surgencia *nf*, **surgimiento** *nm* rise; emergence.

surgir [3c] *vi* (**a**) (*aparecer*) to arise, emerge, spring up, appear; (*líquido*) to spout (out), spurt (up), gush (forth); (*en niebla etc*) to loom up; (*persona*) to appear unexpectedly; (*dificultad*) to arise, come up, crop up; **la torre surge en medio del bosque** the tower rises (*o* soars) up in the middle of the woods; **han surgido varios problemas** several problems have arisen.

(**b**) (*Náut*) to anchor.

suriano *adj* (*Méx*) southern.

surmenage, surmenaje *nm* (*trabajo excesivo*) overwork; (*estrés*) stress, mental fatigue; (*crisis*) nervous breakdown.

suroeste = **sudoeste.**

surrealismo *nm* surrealism.

surrealista 1 *adj* surrealist(ic). **2** *nmf* surrealist.

surtido 1 *adj* (**a**) (*variado*) mixed, assorted, varied.

(**b**) **estar bien ~ de** to be well supplied with, have good stocks of; **estar mal ~ de** to be badly off for.

2 *nm* (selección) selection, assortment, range; (*existencias*) supply, stock; **gran ~** large assortment, wide range; **artículo de ~** article from stock.

surtidor *nm* (**a**) (*chorro*) jet, spout; (*fuente*) fountain. (**b**) **~ de gasolina** petrol pump. (**c**) (*LAm*: *de droga*) drug pusher.

surtir [3a] **1** *vt* (**a**) (*suministrar*) to supply, furnish, provide; **~ a uno de combustible** to supply sb with fuel; **~ el mercado** to supply the market; **~ un pedido** to fill an order.

(**b**) *efecto* to have, produce; *V* **efecto** (**a**).

2 *vi* to spout, spurt (up), rise.

3 surtirse *vr*: **~ de** to provide o.s. with.

surto *adj* anchored.

suruca *nf* (*Carib*) (**a**) (*algazara*) din, uproar. (**b**) (*borrachera*) drunkenness.

suruco** *nm* (*Cono Sur*) crap**, shit**.

surumbático *adj* (*LAm*) = **zurumbático.**

surumbo *adj* (*CAm*) = **zurumbo.**

surumpe *nm* (*And*) inflammation of the eyes (*caused by snow glare*), snow blindness.

surupa *nf* (*Carib*) cockroach, roach (*US*).

suruví *nm* (*Cono Sur*) catfish.

survietnamita *adj, nmf* South Vietnamese.

susceptibilidad *nf* (**a**) (*V adj* (**b**)) susceptibility (*a* to);

sensitivity; touchiness; impressionable nature.

(**b**) **~es** susceptibilities; **ofender las ~es de uno** to offend sb's susceptibilities.

susceptible *adj* (**a**) **~ de** capable of; **~ de mejora**(**r**) capable of improvement, open to improvement; **~ de sufrir daño** liable to suffer damage.

(**b**) *persona* susceptible; (*sensible*) sensitive; (*quisquilloso*) touchy; (*impresionable*) impressionable.

suscitar [1a] *vt rebelión etc* to stir up; *conflicto, escándalo, revuelo etc* to make, cause, provoke; *debate* to start; *duda, problema* to raise; *interés, sospechas* to arouse; *consecuencia* to cause, give rise to, bring with it.

suscribir [3a; *ptp* **suscrito**] **1** *vt* (**a**) *contrato, petición etc* to sign; *promesa* to make, agree to, ratify.

(**b**) *opinión* to subscribe to, endorse.

(**c**) (*Fin*) *acciones etc* to take out an option on; *seguro* to underwrite.

(**d**) **~ a uno a una revista** to enter sb as a subscriber to a journal, put sb on the subscription list of a journal; **A le suscribió a B por 100 dólares** A put B down for a 100-dollar contribution.

2 suscribirse *vr* to subscribe (*a* to, for); **¿te vas a suscribir?** are you going to subscribe?; **~ a una revista** to take out a subscription for a magazine (*o* journal).

suscripción *nf* subscription; **por ~ popular** by public subscription; **abrir una ~** to take out a subscription; **cerrar su ~** to cancel one's subscription.

suscriptor(a) *nm/f* subscriber.

Suso *nm familiar form of* **Jesús**.

susodicho *adj* above-mentioned.

suspender [2a] *vt* (**a**) *objeto* to hang, hang up, suspend (*de* from, on).

(**b**) (*fig*) *pago, trabajo etc* to stop, suspend; *reunión, sesión* to adjourn; *proceso etc* to interrupt; **~ hasta más tarde** to put off till later, postpone for a time.

(**c**) (*Univ etc*) *candidato, asignatura* to fail.

(**d**) (*fig: pasmar*) to astound, astonish; to fill with wonder, cause to marvel.

suspense *nm* suspense.

suspensión *nf* (**a**) (*acto*) hanging (up), suspension.

(**b**) (*Aut, Mec*) suspension; **~ hidráulica** hydraulic suspension; **con ~ independiente** with independent suspension.

(**c**) (*fig*) stoppage, suspension; adjournment; interruption; postponement; (*Jur*) stay; **~ de empleo** suspension (from work) on full pay; **~ de empleo y sueldo** suspension without pay; **~ de fuego, ~ de hostilidades** ceasefire, cessation of hostilities; **~ de pagos** suspension of payments.

(**d**) (*pasmo*) astonishment; wonderment; (*Liter, Teat etc*) suspense.

suspensivo *adj*: **puntos ~s** dots, suspension points.

suspenso 1 *adj* (**a**) (*colgado*) hanging, suspended; hung (*de* from).

(**b**) (*Univ etc*) *candidato* failed.

(**c**) (*fig*) **estar ~, quedarse ~** (*pasmarse*) to be astonished, be amazed; (*maravillarse*) to be filled with wonder; (*aturdirse*) to be bewildered, be baffled.

2 *nm* (**a**) (*Univ etc*) fail, failure.

(**b**) (*esp LAm*) suspense; **estar en ~, quedar en ~** to be in suspense, be pending; (*Jur: ley*) to be suspended, be in abeyance; (*pleito*) to stand over, be postponed.

suspensores *nmpl* (*LAm*) braces, suspenders (*US*).

suspensorio 1 *adj* suspensory. **2** *nm* jockstrap; (*Med*) suspensory (bandage).

suspicacia *nf* suspicion, mistrust.

suspicaz *adj* suspicious, distrustful.

suspirado *adj* longed-for, yearned for.

suspirar [1a] *vi* (*t fig*) to sigh (*por* for).

suspiro *nm* (**a**) (*gen*) sigh; (*fig*) sigh, breath, rustle, whisper; **~ de alivio** sigh of relief; **deshacerse en ~s** to sigh deeply, heave a great sigh; **exhalar el último ~** to breathe one's last. (**b**) (*LAm Culin*) meringue.

sustancia *nf* (*gen*) substance; (*esencia*) essence; (*materia*) matter; **~** (**de carne**) (*Culin*) stock; **~ gris** (*Anat*) grey matter; **en ~** in substance, in essence; **sin ~** lacking in substance; (*poco profundo*) shallow, superficial.

sustancial *adj* (**a**) (*lit*) substantial; (*fundamental*) essential, vital, fundamental. (**b**) = **sustancioso**.

sustancialmente *adv* (*V adj*) substantially; essentially, vitally, fundamentally.

sustancioso *adj discurso etc* solid; meaty; *comida* solid, substantial; (*nutritivo*) nourishing.

sustantivar [1a] *vt* to use as a noun.

sustantivo 1 *adj* substantive; (*Ling*) substantival, noun (*atr*). **2** *nm* noun, substantive; **~ contable** count-noun; **~ no contable** mass noun.

sustentabilidad *nf* viability.

sustentable *adj* viable, sustainable.

sustentación *nf* sustenance; support; (*Aer*) lift.

sustentar [1a] **1** *vt* (**a**) *objeto* to hold up, support, (bear the weight of).

(**b**) (*alimento*) to sustain, nourish, feed, keep going.

(**c**) (*fig*) *esperanza etc* to sustain, keep going, buoy up.

(**d**) *idea, teoría* to maintain, uphold, defend.

2 sustentarse *vr*: **~ con** to sustain o.s. with, subsist on; **~ de esperanzas** to sustain o.s. with hopes, live on hopes; **~ del aire** to live on air.

sustento *nm* (*apoyo*) support; (*alimento*) sustenance, food; (*mantenimiento*) maintenance; (*fig*) livelihood; **ganarse el ~** to earn one's living, earn a livelihood; **es el ~ principal de la institución** it is the lifeblood of the institution.

sustitución *nf* substitution (*por* for), replacement (*por* by).

sustituible *adj* replaceable; expendable.

sustituir [3g] **1** *vt* to substitute, replace; **~ A por B** to substitute B for A, replace A by B, replace A with B, put A in place of B; **tendremos que ~ el neumático pinchado** we shall have to change (*o* replace) the flat tyre; **le quieren ~** they want to remove him, they want him replaced.

2 *vi* to substitute; to deputize; **~ a** to replace; to substitute for, deputize for; **los sellos azules sustituyen a los verdes** the blue stamps are replacing the green ones.

sustitutivo 1 *adj* substitute; **géneros propios ~s de los importados** home-produced goods in substitution of (*o* to replace) imported ones. **2** *nm* substitute (*de* for); **es un ~ del café** it is a coffee substitute.

sustituto, -a *nm/f* substitute, replacement; deputy.

sustitutorio *adj* substitute, replacement (*atr*); equivalent; *V* **servicio** (**c**).

susto *nm* (**a**) (*gen*) fright, scare; **¡qué ~!** what a scare!; **caerse del ~** to be frightened to death; **dar un ~ a uno** to give sb a fright (*o* scare); **darse un ~, pegarse un ~*** to have a fright, give o.s. a fright; **no gana para ~s*** she never gets a moment's peace; **este año no ganamos para ~s*** it's been one blow after another this year; **meter un ~ a uno*** to put the wind up sb*.

(**b**) (*And: crisis nerviosa*) nervous breakdown.

(**c**) **el ~** (*hum*: en restaurante*) the bill.

sustracción *nf* (**a**) (*acto*) removal; (*Mat*) subtraction, taking away; deduction; extraction. (**b**) (*robo*) theft; **~ de menores** child abduction.

sustraer [2p] **1** *vt* (**a**) (*llevarse*) to remove, take away; (*Mat*) to subtract, take away; (*descontar*) to deduct; *agua etc* to extract.

(**b**) (*robar*) to steal; *persona* to abduct.

2 sustraerse *vr*: **~ a** (*evitar*) to avoid; (*apartarse de*) to withdraw from, contract out of; **~ a** + *infin* to avoid + *ger*, get out of + *ger*; **no pude sustraerme a la tentación** I could not resist the temptation.

sustrato *nm* substratum.

susurrante *adj* (*fig*) (*viento*) whispering; (*arroyo*) murmuring; (*follaje*) rustling.

susurrar [1a] **1** *vi* (**a**) (*persona*) to whisper; **~ al oído de uno** to whisper to sb, whisper in sb's ear.

(**b**) (*fig*) (*viento*) to whisper; (*insecto*) to hum; (*arroyo*) to murmur; (*hojas*) to rustle.

2 susurrarse *vr*: **se susurra que ...** it is being whispered that ..., it is rumoured that ...

susurro *nm* (**a**) (*cuchicheo*) whisper. (**b**) (*V vi* (**b**)) whisper; hum, humming; murmur; rustle.

sutil *adj* (**a**) *hebra, hilo etc* fine, delicate, tenuous; *rodaja* thin; *tela* (*fino*) thin, light; (*suave*) very soft; *aire* thin; *olor* delicate; subtle; *brisa etc* gentle. (**b**) *diferencia* fine, subtle, nice. (**c**) *mente, persona* sharp, keen, observant; subtle; *observación* subtle.

sutileza *nf* (**a**) (*cualidad*) fineness, delicacy; thinness; subtlety, subtleness; sharpness, keenness. (**b**) (*una* ~) subtlety; (*pey*) artifice, artful deceit.

sutilizar [1f] **1** *vt* (**a**) *objeto* (*reducir*) *etc* to thin down, fine down; (*fig: pulir*) to polish, perfect; (*fig: perfeccionar*) to refine (upon).

(**b**) *concepto etc* (*pey*) to quibble about, split hairs about.

2 *vi* (*pey*) to quibble, split hairs.

sutura *nf* suture.

suturar [1a] *vt* to suture; to stitch.

suyo *adj y pron pos* **1** (*tras verbo* **ser** *o con artículo*) (**a**) (*de él*) his, (*de ella*) hers, (*de cosa*) its, (*de uno mismo*) one's; (*de Vd*) yours; **es ~, es el ~** it is his (*etc*); **¿es ~ esto?** is this yours?; **lo** ~ (what is) his, what belongs to him; **los ~s** (*parientes*) his people, his relations, his family; (*partidarios*) his people, his supporters.

(**b**) (*de ellos, de ellas*) theirs; (*de Vds*) yours.

2 (*tras n*) (**a**) (*de él*) of his, (*de ella*) of hers; (*de la cosa misma*) of its own, (*de uno mismo*) of one's own; (*de Vd*) of yours; **no es amigo** ~ he is no friend of hers.

(**b**) (*de ellos, de ellas*) of theirs; (*de Vds*) of yours.

3 *adj y pron* (*locuciones*): **de** ~ in itself, per se; intrinsically; on its own; **eso es muy** ~ that's just like him, that's typical of him; **él es un hombre muy** ~ (*reservado*) he's a man who keeps very much to himself; (*quisquilloso*) he's a very fussy sort; **él pesa lo ~*** he's really heavy, he weighs a bit; **aguantar lo** ~ to shoulder one's burden; to put up with a lot; **eso cae de** ~ that's obvious, that goes without saying; **estar en lo mejor ~*** to be on top form, be in one's best form; **hizo suyas mis palabras** he echoed my words, he supported what I had said; **hacer de las suyas** to get up to one's old tricks; **ir a la suya, ir a lo** ~ to go one's own way; (*pey*) to act selfishly, think only of o.s.; **salirse con la suya** to get one's way; (*en discusión*) to carry one's point; **valorar lo** ~ to be worth one's keep; **cada cual a lo** ~ it's best to mind one's own business.

svástica *nf* swastika.

swing [es'win] *nm* (**a**) (*Mús*) swing. (**b**) (*Golf*) swing.

T

T, t [te] *nf* (*letra*) T, t.
t. *nm*(*pl*) *abr de* **tomo(s)** volume(s), vol(s).
TA *nf abr de* **traducción automática** automatic translation, A.T.
taba *nf* (*Anat*) anklebone; (*juego*) knucklebones, jackstones (*US*); **menear las ~s*** to bustle about; to get cracking*, get moving.
tabacal *nm* (*LAm*) (*sembrío*) tobacco field; (*plantación*) tobacco plantation.
Tabacalera *nf Spanish state tobacco monopoly.*
tabacalera *nf* (*Méx*) cigarette factory.
tabacalero 1 *adj* tobacco (*atr*). **2** *nm* (*en tienda*) tobacconist; (*cultivador*) tobacco grower; (*comerciante*) tobacco merchant.
tabaco 1 *nm* (**a**) (*gen*) tobacco; (*cigarrillos*) cigarettes, (*puro*) cigar (*esp LAm*); (*Bot*) tobacco plant; **~ amarillo, ~ americano** Virginian tobacco; **~ de hebra** loose tobacco; **~ de mascar** chewing tobacco; **~ negro** dark tobacco; **~ de pipa** pipe-tobacco; **~ en polvo** snuff; **~ en rama** leaf tobacco; **~ rubio** Virginian tobacco; **~ turco** Turkish tobacco; **¿tienes ~?** have you any cigarettes?; **se me acabó el ~** I've run out of cigarettes, I had nothing left to smoke; **se le acabó el ~** (*Cono Sur**) he ran out of dough‡; **estar de mal ~** (*CAm**) to be in a bad mood; **estaba hecho ~** (*: *persona*) he was all in; (*objeto*) it was all torn to pieces; **quitar el ~ a uno‡** to do sb in‡.
(**b**) (*LAm*‡: *droga*) reefer‡, joint‡.
(**c**) (*Carib**: *golpe*) slap, smack.
2 *adj* (*LAm*) dusty brown.
tabacón‡ *nm* (*Méx*) marijuana, grass‡.
tabalada *nf* bump, heavy fall.
tabalear [1a] **1** *vt* to rock; to swing. **2** *vi* to drum (with one's fingers), tap.
tabaleo *nm* rocking; swinging; drumming, tapping.
tabanco *nm* (**a**) (*CAm*: *desván*) attic. (**b**) (*Méx*: *puesto*) stall.
tábano *nm* horsefly, gadfly.
tabaqueada* *nf* (*Méx*) (*paliza*) beating-up*; (*pelea*) fist-fight.
tabaquear [1a] *vi* (*And*) to smoke.
tabaquera *nf* (*para tabaco*) tobacco-jar; (*para rapé*) snuff-box; (*de pipa*) bowl; (*LAm*) (*bolsa para tabaco*) tobacco-pouch; (*para puros*) cigar-case; (*para cigarrillos*) cigarette-case.
tabaquería *nf* (**a**) (*tienda*) tobacconist's (shop), cigar store (*US*) (**b**) (*Carib*: *fábrica*) cigar factory.
tabaquero 1 *adj* (*LAm*) tobacco (*atr*). **2** *nm* (*en tienda*) tobacconist; (*cultivador*) tobacco grower; (*comerciante*) tobacco merchant.
tabaquismo *nm* addiction to tobacco, tobacco habit.
tabaquito *nm* (*LAm*) small cigar.
tabarra* *nf* nuisance, bore; **dar la ~** to be a nuisance, be a bore; **dar la ~ a uno** to get on sb's nerves, annoy sb.
tabasco *nm* Tabasco ®.
tabear [1a] *vi* (*Cono Sur*) to chat, gossip; to gossip about a person not present.
taberna *nf* bar, pub; (*Hist*) tavern; (*Cono Sur*) gambling-den; (*Carib*) small grocery shop.
tabernáculo *nm* tabernacle.
tabernario *adj lenguaje etc* rude, dirty, coarse, tavern (*atr*).
tabernero *nm* (*dueño*) publican, landlord; (*mozo*) barman, bartender.
tabicar [1g] **1** *vt puerta* to wall up; *cuarto* to partition off; *nariz* to stop up.
2 tabicarse *vr* to get stopped up.
tabicón *nm* (*Méx*) breeze block.
tabique *nm* (*pared*) thin wall, partition (wall); (*Méx*: *ladrillo*) brick.
tabla 1 *nf* (**a**) (*de madera*) plank, board; (*estante*) shelf; (*de piedra etc*) slab; (*Arte*) panel; (*Carib*) shop counter; **~ deslizadora, ~ de surf, ~ a vela, ~ de windsurf** surfboard, windsurfing board; **~ de dibujo** drawing-board; **~ de esmeril** emery board; **~ de lavar** washboard; **~ de picar** chopping board; **~ de planchar** ironing-board; **~ de quesos** cheeseboard; **~ de salvación** (*fig*) last resort, sole hope; thing that saves one's life; **~ del suelo** floorboard; **es lo que canta** (*o* **marca**) **la ~** it's the rule, it's what the book says; **escaparse** (*o* **salvarse**) **en una ~** to have a narrow escape, have a close shave; **estar en las ~s** (*Carib*) to be destitute; **hacer ~ rasa de** to disregard utterly, sweep aside, ride roughshod over; **lo hizo por ~s*** she (only) just managed it, she very nearly didn't manage it.
(**b**) **~s** (*Taur*) boards, fence.
(**c**) **~s** (*Teat*) boards, stage; **coger ~s** to gain acting experience; (*fig*) to get the hang of it; **pisar las ~s** to walk the stage; **salir a las ~s** to go on the stage, become an actor; **tener ~s** to have a good stage presence; **tener muchas ~s** (*fig*) to be an old hand, be an expert.
(**d**) **~s** (*Ajedrez*) draw; tie; (*fig*) stalemate, deadlock; **~s por ahogado** stalemate; **hacer ~s, quedar (en) ~s** to draw, reach a drawn position; (*fig*) to reach stalemate, be deadlocked; **el partido quedó ~s** the game was a draw, the game was drawn.
(**e**) (*Anat*) flat area, wide part.
(**f**) (*Agr*) plot, patch, bed.
(**g**) (*Cos*) broad pleat.
(**h**) (*Com*) meat stall.
(**i**) (*fig*) table, list, chart; (*Dep*: *t* **~ clasificatoria**) table, league table; (*Mat*) table; (*Tip*) table, index; (*Inform*) array; **~s actuariales** actuarial tables; **~ de decisiones** decision table; **~ de ejercicios, ~ de gimnasia** exercise routine, set of exercises; **~ de logaritmos** table of logarithms; **~ de materias** table of contents; **~ de multiplicar** multiplication table; **~ salarial** wage scale; **~ trazadora** plotter; **~ de valores** set of values.
(**j**) (*And*) **cantarle las ~s a uno** to tell it to sb straight; **salir con las ~s** to fail.
2 *nm* (‡) queer‡, fairy‡.
tablada *nf* (*Cono Sur*) slaughterhouse.
tablado *nm* (*suelo*) plank floor, boards; (*plataforma*) stand, stage, platform; (*de baile*) dance-floor; (*Hist*) scaffold; (*Teat*) stage.
tablaje *nm*, **tablazón** *nf* planks, planking, boards.
tablao *nm* (= **tablado**) flamenco show; dance-floor (for flamenco dancing).
tablear [1a] *vt* (**a**) *madera* to cut into boards (*o* planks).
(**b**) (*Agr*) *tierra* to divide up into plots.
(**c**) *terreno* to level off; (*Cono Sur*) *masa* to roll out.
(**d**) (*Cos*) to pleat.
tablero *nm* (**a**) (*de madera*) board(s), plank(s); panel; (*de mármol etc*) slab; (*Escol etc*) blackboard; (*Com*) counter; (*de juegos*) board; (*Cono Sur*: *de anuncios*) notice-board, bulletin board (*US*); (*Elec*) switchboard; **~ de ajedrez** chessboard; **~ de dibujo** drawing-board; **~ de gráficos** (*Inform*) graph pad; **~ de instrumentos, ~ de mandos** instrument panel, (*Aut*) dashboard; **~ posterior** tailboard.
(**b**) (*Agr*) bed(s), plot(s).
(**c**) (*garito*) gambling-den.
tableta *nf* (**a**) (*de madera*) small board; block; (**b**) (*de escribir*) writing-pad. (**c**) (*Med*) tablet; (*de chocolate*) bar, stick.
tabletear [1a] *vi* to rattle, clatter; (*ametralladora*) to rattle.
tableteo *nm* rattle, clatter.
tablilla *nf* (**a**) small board; (*Med*) splint. (**b**) (*Méx*) bar (of chocolate).

tablista *nmf* windsurfer.
tabloide *nm* tabloid.
tablón *nm* (**a**) plank, beam; ~ **de anuncios** notice board, bulletin board (*US*).
(**b**) (*) **coger un ~, pillar un ~** to get tight*.
(**c**) (*LAm Agr*) plot, bed.
tablonazo *nm* (*Carib*) trick, swindle.
tabú 1 *adj invar* taboo; **varias palabras ~** several taboo words. **2** *nm, pl* ~**s** (*o* ~**es**) taboo.
tabuco *nm* (*chabola*) slum, shack; (*cuarto*) tiny room, poky little room.
tabulación *nf* (*Inform*) tabbing.
tabulador *nm* (*Inform*) tab.
tabular [1a] **1** *vt* to tabulate; (*Inform*) to tab; to tabulate. **2** *adj* tabular.
taburete *nm* stool.
tacada *nf* (*Billar*) stroke; (*serie de puntos*) break; **de una ~** (*fig*) all at once; all in one go.
tacana *nf* (**a**) (*And, Cono Sur Agr*) cultivated hillside terrace. (**b**) (*Cono Sur, Méx: de mortero*) pestle. (**c**) (*Cono Sur*‡: *policía*) fuzz‡, police.
tacanear [1a] *vt* (*Cono Sur*) to tread down; to pound, crush.
tacañería *nf* (*V adj*) (**a**) meanness, stinginess. (**b**) craftiness.
tacaño *adj* (**a**) (*avaro*) mean, stingy. (**b**) (*astuto*) crafty.
tacar [1g] *vt* (*And*) (**a**) (*disparar*) to shoot at. (**b**) (*llenar*) to fill, pack tightly (*de* with).
tacataca* *nm* baby-walker.
tacita *nf* small cup; **la T~ de Plata** (*affectionate name for*) Cadiz; **como una ~ de plata** as bright as a new pin.
tácitamente *adv* tacitly.
Tácito *nm* Tacitus.
tácito *adj* tacit; *comentario etc* unspoken; *ley* unwritten; (*Ling*) unexpressed, understood.
taciturnidad *nf* taciturnity, silent nature; moodiness, sullenness; glumness.
taciturno *adj* taciturn, silent; moody, sullen, sulky; glum.
tacizo *nm* (**a**) (*And, Carib* : *hacha*) narrow-bladed axe. (**b**) (*And*: *celda*) small prison cell.
taco[1] *nm* (**a**) (*de fusil etc*) wad, wadding; (*tarugo*) wooden peg; (*tapón*) stopper, plug, bung; **~ de salida** (*Dep*) starting block.
(**b**) (*de bota*) stud; (*LAm: de zapatos*) heel; (*CAm Dep*) football boot.
(**c**) (*para escribir*) pad; (*calendario*) calendar; (*de billetes etc*) book of travel tickets (*o* coupons *etc*); (*de cheque etc*) stub; (*Cono Sur*) desk calendar; **~ de papel** writing-pad, pad of notepaper.
(**d**) (*Billar*) cue.
(**e**) (*Mil Hist*) ramrod.
(**f**) (*fusil de juguete*) popgun.
(**g**) (*) (*bocado*) snack, bite; (*trago*) swig of wine*.
(**h**) (*Esp**: *palabrota*) rude word, swearword; **dice muchos ~s** he swears a lot; **soltar un ~** to swear.
(**i**) (*: *lío*) tangle, mess; **armarse un ~, hacerse un ~** to get into a mess, get all tied up; **dejar a uno hecho un ~** to flatten sb (in an argument).
(**j**) (‡: *año*) **tener 16 ~s** to be 16 (years old); **cumple 5 ~s** he's doing 5 years' bird‡.
(**k**) (*Cono Sur, Méx: obstáculo*) obstruction, blockage; (*Aut*) traffic jam.
(**l**) (*Méx Culin*) rolled tortilla, taco.
(**m**) (*Cono Sur*: *chaparro*) short stocky person.
(**n**) (*CAm, Carib*: *preocupación*) worry, anxiety; fear.
(**o**) **darse ~s** (*CAm, Méx**) to give o.s. airs.
taco[2] **1** *adj* (*Carib*) (**a**) (*currutaco*) foppish. (**b**) (*emprendedor*) bold, enterprising. **2** *nm* (**a**) (*CAm, Carib, Méx*) fop, dandy; **darse ~** to put on airs. (**b**) (*And**) big shot*.
tacógrafo *nm* tacograph.
tacómetro *nm* tachometer.
tacón *nm* (**a**) heel; **~ (de) aguja** stiletto heel; **tacones altos** high heels; **de ~ alto** high-heeled. (**b**) (‡) purse.
taconazo *nm* (*golpecito*) heel tap; (*patada*) kick with one's heel, blow with the heel; ~**s** (*Mil*) heel-clicking; **entró y dio un ~** he came in and clicked his heels.
taconear [1a] **1** *vt* (*Cono Sur*) to pack tight, fill right up.
2 *vi* (**a**) (*dar golpecitos*) to tap (*o* stamp) with one's heels; (*Mil etc*) to click one's heels; (*caminar ruidosamente*) to walk noisily on one's heels; (*con arrogancia*) to strut.
(**b**) (*: *apresurarse*) to bustle about.
taconeo *nm* tapping (*o* stamping) with one's heels; heel-clicking; noisy walking on one's heels; strutting.
tacote‡ *nm* (*Méx*) marijuana, grass‡.
táctica *nf* tactics; (*una* ~) tactic, move; (*gámbito*) gambit; **~ de cerrojo** stonewalling, negative play.
tácticamente *adv* tactically.
táctico 1 *adj* tactical. **2** *nm* tactician; (*Dep*) coach.
táctil *adj* tactile.
tacto *nm* (**a**) (*sentido*) touch, sense of touch; (*de mecanógrafa etc*) touch.
(**b**) (*acto*) touch, touching; feel; **ser áspero al ~** to feel rough, be rough to the touch.
(**c**) (*cualidad*) feel; **tiene un ~ viscoso** it has a sticky feel (to it).
(**d**) (*fig*) tact; **tener ~** to be tactful.
tacuacín *nm* (*Méx*) sloth.
tacuaco *adj* (*Cono Sur*) chubby.
tacuache *nm* (*Carib*) fib, lie.
tacuche 1 *nm* (*Méx*) bundle of rags. **2** *adj* worthless.
tacha[1] *nf* (**a**) (*Téc*) large tack, brad, stud. (**b**) (*LAm*) = **tacho**.
tacha[2] *nf* flaw, blemish, defect; **sin ~** perfect, flawless; **poner ~ a** to find fault with.
tachadura *nf* erasure, correction.
tachar [1a] *vt* (**a**) (*borrar*) to cross out, erase; (*corregir*) to correct.
(**b**) (*criticar*) to criticize, attack, find fault with; (*Jur*) *testigo* to challenge; **~ a uno de incapaz** to accuse sb of being incompetent.
tachero *nm* (*Cono Sur*) tinsmith.
tachines‡ *nmpl* (*Esp*) (*pies*) plates‡, feet; (*zapatos*) shoes.
tacho *nm* (*LAm*) (*caldero*) boiler, large boiling pan; (*para azúcar*) sugar pan, sugar evaporator; (*balde*) bucket, pail; (*arcón*) bin, container; (*Cono Sur*) washbasin; **~ de basura, ~ para la basura** dustbin, garbage can (*US*); **~ para lavar la ropa** clothes boiler; **irse al ~** (*Cono Sur**) to be ruined, fail.
tachón[1] *nm* (**a**) (*Téc*) large stud, ornamental stud, boss.
(**b**) (*Cos*) trimming.
tachón[2] *nm* erasure, stroke, crossing-out.
tachonado *adj*: **~ de estrellas** star-studded, star-spangled.
tachonar [1a] *vt* to stud, adorn with studs; (*Cos*) to trim; (*fig*) to stud (*de* with).
tachoso *adj* defective, faulty.
tachuela *nf* (**a**) (*clavito*) tack, tintack; (*en vestido*) stud; (*LAm: chincheta*) drawing-pin; (*Carib*) long pin; **me hace ~s** it gives me goosepimples.
(**b**) (*Aut*) speed ramp, sleeping policeman.
(**c**) (*And, Carib*: *recipiente*) metal pan; (*Carib, Méx*: *taza*) metal cup, dipper.
(**d**) (*CAm, Cono Sur, Méx*) (*persona*) short stocky person; (*pey*) runt.
TAE *nf abr de* **tasa anual efectiva** (*o* **equivalente**) annual percentage rate, APR.
tafetán *nm* (**a**) taffeta; **~ adhesivo, ~ inglés** sticking plaster. (**b**) **tafetanes** (*fig*) flags; (*) frills, buttons and bows.
tafia *nf* (*LAm*) rum.
tafilete *nm* morocco leather.
tagarnia* *nf*: **comer hasta la ~** (*And, CAm*) to stuff o.s.*.
tagarnina *nf* (**a**) (*puro*) (cheap) cigar. (**b**) (*Méx*) leather tobacco pouch. (**c**) (*And, CAm, Méx**) drunkenness; **agarrar una ~*** to get tight*.
tagarote *nm* (**a**) (*Zool*) sparrowhawk. (**b**) (*: *persona*) tall shabby person. (**c**) (*: *empleadillo*) lawyer's clerk, penpusher. (**d**) (*CAm**) big shot*.
tagua *nf* (*And*) ivory palm.
tahalí *nm* swordbelt.
Tahití *nm* Tahiti.
tahona *nf* (*panadería*) bakery, bakehouse; (*molino*) flour-mill.
tahonero *nm* baker; miller.
tahur *nm* gambler; (*pey*) cardsharper, cheat.
taifa* *nf* gang, crew; gang of thieves.
Tailandia *nf* Thailand.
tailandés, -esa 1 *adj, nm/f* Thai. **2** *nm* (*Ling*) Thai.
taima *nf* (**a**) (*astucia*) slyness, craftiness, slickness. (**b**) (*Cono Sur**: *terquedad*) obstinacy, pigheadedness.
taimado *adj* (**a**) (*astuto*) sly, crafty, slick. (**b**) (*hosco*) sullen. (**c**) (*And*: *perezoso*) lazy.
taimarse [1a] *vr* (**a**) (*volverse taimado*) to get sly, adopt crafty tactics. (**b**) (*amostazarse*) to go into a huff, sulk; (*obstinarse*) to be obstinate, dig one's heels in.
taita *nm* (**a**) (*) (*padre*) dad, daddy; (*tío*) uncle.
(**b**) (*Cono Sur etc*) *in direct address, term of respect used before a name.*
(**c**) (*Cono Sur*) (*matón*) tough, bully; (*pendenciero*)

quarrelsome person.

(**d**) (*coime*) pimp.

Taiwán *nm* Taiwan.

taiwanés, -esa *adj, nm/f* Taiwanese.

taja *nf* cut.

tajada *nf* (**a**) (*Culin*) slice; slab, chunk.

(**b**) (*Fin**) rake-off*; **sacar** ~ to get one's share, get something out of it; to get a rake-off*, take one's cut; (*fig*) to look after Number One.

(**c**) (*Med*) hoarseness.

(**d**) (‡) **coger una** ~, **pillar una** ~ to get tight*.

(**e**) (*tajo*) cut, slash; **¡te haré ~s!*** I'll cut you up!

tajadera *nf* (**a**) (*hacha*) chopper; (*cincel*) cold chisel. (**b**) (*tajadero*) chopping block.

tajadero *nm* chopping block.

tajado *adj peña* sheer.

tajador *nm* (*And*) pencil sharpener.

tajalán 1 *adj* (*Carib*) lazy. **2** *nm*, **tajalana** *nf* idler, layabout.

tajaleo* *nm* (*Carib*) (**a**) (*comida*) food, grub‡. (**b**) (*pelea*) row, brawl.

tajaloseo* *nm* (*Carib*) row.

tajamar *nm* (**a**) (*Náut*) stem; (*de puente*) cutwater. (**b**) (*CAm, Cono Sur: muelle*) mole; (*And, Cono Sur: presa*) dam, dike.

tajante *adj* (**a**) sharp, cutting.

(**b**) (*fig*) incisive, sharp, emphatic; *distinción etc* sharp; **contestó con un 'no'** ~ he answered with an emphatic 'no'; **una crítica** ~ **del gobierno** some sharp criticism of the government; **es una persona** ~ he's an incisive person.

tajantemente *adv* (*fig*) incisively, sharply, emphatically.

tajar [1a] *vt* to cut, slice, chop.

tajarrazo *nm* (*CAm, Méx*) slash, wound; (*fig*) damage, harm.

tajeadura *nf* (*Cono Sur*) long scar.

tajear* [1a] *vt* (*LAm*) to cut up, chop; to slash.

Tajo *nm* Tagus.

tajo *nm* (**a**) (*acto, herida*) cut, slash; **darse un** ~ **en el brazo** to cut one's arm; **tirar ~s a uno** to slash at sb.

(**b**) (*Geog*) cut, cleft; (*precipicio*) steep cliff, sheer drop.

(**c**) (*zona*) working area; (*: *empleo*) work, job; (*: *oficina, fábrica etc*) workplace; **largarse al ~*** to get off to work, go back on the job; **¡vamos al ~!*** let's get on with it!

(**d**) (*filo*) cutting edge.

(**e**) (*Culin*) chopping block; (*Hist*) block (*for executions*).

(**f**) (*taburete*) small three-legged stool.

tajón *nm* (*Méx*) slaughterhouse.

tal 1 *adj* such; ~ **cosa** such a thing; **~es cosas** such things; **no hay** ~ **cosa** there's no such thing; **con** ~ **atrevimiento** with such boldness; **con un resultado** ~ with such a result; **el** ~ **país no existió nunca** such a country never existed; **necesitas tanto dinero para** ~ **cosa** you need so much money for such-and-such a thing; ~ **día hace 10 años** on the corresponding day 10 years ago; **un** ~ **García** a man called García, one García; **el** ~ **cura** this priest, this priest we were talking about; (*pey*) this priest person.

2 *pron* (*persona*) such a one, sb; (*cosa*) such a thing, sth; **el** ~ this man (*etc*) I mentioned, this man we're talking about; such a person; **una** ~ (*euf*) a prostitute; **no haré** ~ I won't do anything of the sort; **¡no hay ~!** nothing of the sort!; **en la calle de** ~ in such-and-such a street; **es jefe de** ~ **y** ~ he's the boss of this and that; ~ **como** such as; ~ **como es, todavía vale algo** such as it is, it is still worth sth; **y como ~, tiene que pagar los derechos** and as such, he has to pay the fees; **se para aquí** ~ **cual autocar** an odd coach stops here, a coach stops here occasionally; **vive en** ~ **o cual hotel** he lives in such-and-such a hotel; **son** ~ **para cual** they're two of a kind; **sí** ~ yes indeed, yes of course; ~ **hay que lo piensa** there are some who think so; **hablábamos de que si** ~ **que si cual** we were talking about this that and the other; **había ruritanos y eslobodos y** ~ there were Ruritanians and Slobodians and such (*o* such like, others of that kind); **fuimos al cine y** ~ we went to the pictures and that kind of thing.

3 *adv* so; in such a way; ~ **como** just as; **estaba** ~ **como lo dejé** it was just as I had left it; ~ **cual** (*adv*) just as it is; **es** ~ **cual siempre deseaba** it is just what he had always wanted; **ella sigue** ~ **cual** (*regular*) she's so-so, she's middling fair; (*sin cambio*) she hasn't changed; ~ **la madre, cual la hija** like mother, like daughter; **tomaremos algo ligero** ~ **que una tortilla*** we'll have sth light such as an omelette; **¿qué ~?** how goes it?, how's things?; **¿qué** ~ **es?** what's she like?; **¿qué** ~ **estás?** how are you?; **¿qué** ~ **estoy?** how do I look?; **¿qué** ~ **el partido?** what was the game like?, how did the game go?; **¿qué** ~ **tu tío?** how's your uncle?; **¿qué** ~ **del profesor?** what's the news of the professor?; **¿qué** ~ **te gusta?** what do you think of it?, how do you like it? **¿qué** ~ **si lo compramos?** how about buying it?, suppose we buy it?; *V t* **cual** *para otras comparaciones*.

4 *conj*: **con** ~ (**de**) **que** ... provided (that) ..., on condition that ...; **con** ~ **de no volver nunca** on condition that he (*etc*) never comes back; **no importa el frío con** ~ **de ir bien abrigado** the cold doesn't matter if you're well wrapped up.

tala *nf* (**a**) *acto*) tree felling, wood cutting; (*fig*) havoc, destruction. (**b**) (*Carib: hacha*) axe. (**c**) (*Carib: huerto*) vegetable garden. (**d**) (*Cono Sur: pasto*) grazing.

talabarte *nm* sword belt.

talabartería *nf* (**a**) (*taller*) saddlery, harness-maker's shop. (**b**) (*LAm: tienda*) leather-goods shop.

talabartero *nm* saddler, harness maker.

talacha *nf*, **talache** *nm* (*Méx*) mattock.

taladradora *nf* drill; ~ **de fuerza** power drill; ~ **neumática** pneumatic drill.

taladrar [1a] *vt* (**a**) (*gen*) to bore, drill, punch, pierce; *billete* to punch; *lóbulo* to pierce.

(**b**) (*fig: dolor, ruido*) to pierce; **un ruido que taladra los oídos** an ear-splitting noise; **es un ruido que taladra** it's a shattering noise.

taladro *nm* (**a**) (*herramienta*) drill; auger, gimlet; borer; ~ **de billetes** ticket punch; ~ **mecánico** power drill; ~ **neumático** pneumatic drill. (**b**) (*agujero*) drill hole.

talaje *nm* (**a**) (*Cono Sur: pasto*) pasture. (**b**) (*Cono Sur, Méx: pastoreo*) grazing.

tálamo *nm* marriage bed.

talamoco *adj* (*And*) albino.

talante *nm* (**a**) (*voluntad*) mood, disposition, frame of mind; (*humor*) will, willingness; (*tendencia*) tendency; **estar de buen** ~ to be in a good mood, be in the right frame of mind; **hacer algo de buen** ~ to do sth willingly; **recibir a uno de buen** ~ to give sb a warm welcome; **estar de mal** ~ to be in a bad mood; **responder de mal** ~ to answer with an ill grace, answer bad-temperedly.

(**b**) (*aspecto*) mien, look, appearance.

talar [1a] *vt* (**a**) *árbol* to fell, cut down. (**b**) (*fig*) to lay waste, devastate. (**c**) (*Prov, LAm: podar*) to prune.

talco *nm* talcum powder; (*Min*) talc.

talcualillo* *adj* so-so, middling, fair.

talega *nf* (**a**) (*bolsa*) sack, bag. (**b**) (*pañal*) baby's nappy, diaper (*US*). (**c**) **~s** (*fig*) money. (**d**) **~s** (**‡) balls**‡.

talegada *nf*, **talegazo** *nm* heavy fall, severe bump.

talego *nm* (**a**) (*bolsa grande*) big sack, long sack, poke. (**b**) (*: *persona*) fat person, lump. (**c**) **tener ~*** to have money stashed away*; **no tengo** ~ I'm broke*. (**d**) (‡: *droga*) small bar of hash*. (**e**) (‡: *cárcel*) nick‡, jail. (**f**) (*Fin*‡) 1000 pesetas; **medio** ~ 500 pesetas.

taleguilla *nf* bullfighter's breeches.

talejo *nm* (*And*) paper bag.

talento *nm* (**a**) talent; ability, gift; **~s** talents; accomplishments. (**b**) (*Bib*) talent.

talentoso *adj* talented, gifted.

talero *nm* (*Cono Sur*) whip.

Talgo ['talɣo] *nm* (*Ferro*) *abr de* **tren articulado ligero Goicoechea-Oriol** (*Inter-city high-speed train*).

talidomida *nm* thalidomide.

talismán *nm* talisman.

talmente* *adv* (*tal*) so, in such a way; (*tan*) to such an extent; (*exactamente*) exactly, literally; **la casa es** ~ **una pocilga** the house is such a pigsty, the house is literally a pigsty.

Talmud *nm* Talmud.

talmúdico *adj* Talmudic.

talón *nm* (**a**) (*Anat*) heel; (*de zapato etc*) heel; ~ **de Aquiles** Achilles' heel; **pisar los talones a uno** to be on sb's heels, follow close behind sb; (*fig*) to run sb very close.

(**b**) (*Aut*) flange, rim.

(**c**) (*Com etc*) stub, counterfoil; (*Ferro*) luggage receipt; (*cheque*) cheque; ~ **en blanco** blank cheque; ~ **sin fondos** bad cheque; ~ **al portador** bearer cheque, cheque payable to bearer.

talonador *nm* (*Rugby*) hooker.

talonar [1a] *vt* (**a**) (*Rugby*) to heel. (**b**) (*en carrera*) to be hard on the heels of.

talonario 1 *adj*: **libro** ~ = **2**. **2** *nm* receipt book; book of tickets, book of counterfoils; ~ (**de cheques**) cheque book.

talonear [1a] **1** *vt* (**a**) (*Dep*) to heel. (**b**) (*LAm*) *caballo* to dig one's heels into, spur along. **2** *vi* (**a**) (*precipitarse*) to walk briskly, hurry along. (b) (*Méx: prostituta*) to walk the streets, ply her trade.

talonera *nf* heel-pad; (*And*) heel.

talquina* *nf* (*Cono Sur*) deceit, treachery.

talud *nm* slope, bank; (*Geol*) talus.

talla[1] *nf* (a) (*t* **obra de** ~) (*Arte: esp de madera*) carving; (*escultura*) sculpture; (*grabado*) engraving.

(b) (*altura: de persona*) height, stature; (*fig*) stature; (*de prenda*) size, fitting; **camisas de todas las ~s** shirts in all sizes; **tener poca** ~ to be short, be on the short side; **ha crecido de** ~ (*fig*) he has grown in stature; (*fig*) **dar la** ~ to set the standard; **no dio la** ~ he didn't measure up (to the task), he wasn't up to it.

(c) (*vara*) measuring rod.

(d) (*Med*) gallstones operation.

(e) (*Naipes*) hand.

(f) (*Jur*) reward (*for capture of a criminal*); **poner a uno a** ~ to offer a reward for the capture of sb.

talla[2] *nf* (a) (*CAm: mentira*) fib, lie. (b) (*Cono Sur*) (*chismes*) gossip, chitchat; (*piropo*) compliment; **echar ~s** to put on airs; **echar ~(s) a uno** to tease somebody; **echar ~s a una** to pay a compliment to a woman. (c) (*And: paliza*) beating. (d) (*Méx*: pelea*) set-to*, squabble.

tallado 1 *adj* (a) carved; sculpted; engraved.

(b) **bien** ~ shapely, well-formed; **mal** ~ misshapen.

2 *nm* carving; sculpting; engraving; ~ **en madera** woodcarving.

tallador *nm* (a) carver; sculptor; engraver. (b) (*LAm*) dealer, banker.

tallar[1] [1a] **1** *vt* (a) *madera etc* to carve, shape, work; *piedra* to sculpt; *metal* to engrave; *joya* to cut.

(b) *persona* to measure (the height of).

(c) (*Naipes*) to deal.

2 *vi* (*Naipes*) to deal, be banker.

tallar[2] [1a] **1** *vt* (a) (*And: fastidiar*) to bother, annoy.

(b) (*And: azotar*) to beat.

2 *vi* (*Cono Sur*) (*chismear*) to chat, gossip; to gossip maliciously; (*amantes*) to whisper sweet nothings.

tallarín *nm* (a) (*Culin*) noodle.

(b) (*And*: galón*) stripe.

talle *nm* (a) (*Anat, Cos*) waist; ~ **de avispa** wasp waist.

(b) (*Cos etc: medidas*) waist and chest measurements; (*número*) size, fitting.

(c) (*tipo: de mujer*) figure; (*de hombre*) build, physique; **de ~ esbelto** with a slim figure; **tiene buen** ~ she has a good figure.

(d) (*fig*) (*aspecto*) look, appearance; (*contorno*) outline.

(e) (*CAm, Cono Sur: corpiño*) bodice.

taller *nm* (*Téc*) workshop; (*fábrica*) mill, factory; (*Arte*) studio; (*Cos*) workroom; (*en lenguaje sindical*) shop; ~ **agremiado** union shop, closed shop; ~ **de coches** car repair shop, garage (for repairs); **~es gráficos** printing works; ~ **de máquinas** machine-shop; ~ **mecánico** garage (for repairs); ~ **de montaje** assembly-shop; ~ **de reparaciones** repair shop; ~ **de trabajo** (*en congreso etc*) workshop.

tallero *nm* (*LAm*) (a) (*verdulero*) vegetable merchant, greengrocer. (b) (*embustero*) liar.

tallista *nm* = **tallador** (a), (*esp*) wood carver.

tallo *nm* (a) (*Bot*) stem, stalk; (*de hierba*) blade, sprig; shoot.

(b) (*And: repollo*) cabbage.

(c) **~s** (*LAm*) vegetables, greens.

(d) (*Culin*) crystallized fruit.

talludito* *adj* grown-up; quite old; **el actor es ~ ya para este papel** the actor is getting on a bit now for this rôle; **la talludita actriz X** actress X, no longer as young as she was.

talludo *adj* (a) (*Bot*) tall; *persona* big, tall, lanky; (*fig*) grown-up; **ya eres una talluda** you're a big girl now, you're too big for that at your age; **es una talluda ya** (*pey*) she's not exactly a youngster, she's no spring chicken.

(b) (*CAm, Méx*) *fruta etc* tough, (*duro*) leathery; (*difícil de pelar*) hard to peel.

(c) (*CAm, Méx*) **es un viejo ~*** he's old but there's life in him yet; **es una máquina talluda*** it's an old machine but it still serves its purpose.

taltuza *nf* (*CAm*) raccoon.

tamal *nm* (a) (*LAm Culin*) tamale.

(b) (*Cono Sur*) bundle of clothing; (*Méx*) pile, bundle.

(c) (*LAm*) (*trampa*) fraud, trick, hoax; (*intriga*) intrigue; **hacer un** ~ to prepare a trick, set a trap.

tamalero (*LAm*) **1** *adj* (a) fond of tamales. (b) (*intrigante*) intriguing, fond of intrigue. **2** *nm*, **tamalera** *nf* tamale maker, tamale seller.

tamango *nm* (*Cono Sur*) (a) (*zapato*) sandal. (b) (*vendas*) bandages.

tamañito *adj*: **dejar a uno** ~ to make sb feel very small; to crush sb, flatten sb (in an argument); **me quedé** ~ I felt about so high; I felt utterly bewildered.

tamaño 1 *adj* (a) (*tan grande*) so big, such a big; (*tan pequeño*) so small, such a small; **parece absurdo que cometiera ~ error** it seems absurd that he should make so grave an error (*o* such a great error); **una piedra tamaña como una naranja** a stone as big as an orange. (b) (*LAm*) huge, colossal.

2 *nm* size; ~ **de bolsillo** pocket-size; **una foto ~ carnet** a passport-size photo; **de ~ extra, de ~ extraordinario** outsize, extra large; ~ **familiar** family-size; ~ **gigante** king-size, vast; **de ~ natural** full-size, life-size; **ser del mismo ~, tener el mismo** ~ to be the same size; **¿de qué ~ es?** what size is it?, how big is it?

támara *nf* date-palm; **~s** dates, cluster of dates.

tamarindo *nm* (a) (*Bot*) tamarind. (b) (*Méx*‡) traffic policeman, traffic cop (*).

tamarisco *nm*, **tamariz** *nm* tamarisk.

tambache *nm* (*Méx*) (*de ropa*) bundle of clothes; (*bulto*) big package.

tambaleante *adj* staggering, tottering; unsteady; swaying.

tambalearse [1a] *vr* (*LAm: t* **tambalear**) (*persona*) to stagger, totter, reel; to zigzag; to wobble (from side to side); (*vehículo*) to lurch, sway; (*mueble*) to wobble; **ir tambaleándose** to stagger along; to lurch along, sway about (as one walks *etc*).

tambar [1a] *vt* (*And*) to swallow.

tambarria* *nf* (*And, CAm*) binge*, booze-up*.

tambero *nm* (*Cono Sur*) (*fondista*) innkeeper; (*granjero*) dairy farmer.

también *adv* also, as well, too; besides; **¿Vd ~?** you too?; **y bebe** ~ and he drinks as well, he also drinks; **no sólo A sino ~ B** not only A but also B; **'¿y es guapa?' ... '~'** 'and is she pretty?' ... 'she's that as well'; **los ~ parados X y Z** X and Z, who are also out of work.

tambo *nm* (a) (*And*††: *taberna*) country inn, roadside inn. (b) (*Cono Sur: corral*) milking yard. (c) (*Cono Sur: burdel*) brothel.

tambocha *nf* (*LAm*) red ant.

tambor *nm* (a) (*Mús, Téc*) drum; (*botella*) bottle; (*Arquit, Cos*) tambour; (*Anat*) eardrum; ~ **de tostar café** coffee roaster; ~ **del freno** brake-drum; ~ **magnético** (*Inform*) magnetic drum; **venir** (*o* **salir**) **a ~ batiente** to come out with flying colours, emerge in triumph.

(b) (*Mús: persona*) drummer; ~ **mayor** drum-major.

(c) (*Carib, Méx: tela*) burlap, sackcloth.

tambora *nf* (a) (*Mús*) (*tambor*) bass drum; (*Méx*) brass band. (b) (*Carib*: mentira*) lie, fib.

tamboril *nm* small drum.

tamborilada *nf*, **tamborilazo** *nm* (*batacazo*) bump on one's bottom; (*sacudida*) severe jolt; (*espaldarazo*) slap on the shoulder.

tamborilear [1a] **1** *vt* (*) to praise up, boost. **2** *vi* (*Mús*) to drum, play the drum; (*con dedos*) to drum with one's fingers; (*lluvia*) to patter, drum.

tamborileo *nm* drumming; patter(ing).

tamborilero, -a *nm/f* drummer.

tambre *nm* (*And*) dam.

tamegua *nf* (*CAm, Méx*) weeding, cleaning.

tameguar [1d] *vt* (*CAm, Méx*) to weed, clean.

Tamerlán *nm* Tamburlaine.

Támesis *nm* Thames.

tamil *adj, nmf* Tamil.

tamiz *nm* sieve.

tamizar [1f] *vt* to sieve, sift.

tamo *nm* fluff, down, dust; (*Agr*) dust; chaff.

tampa *nf* (*Cono Sur*) matted hair.

támpax ['tampɑks] *nm, pl* **támpax** ['tampaks] ® (*LAm*) Tampax ®, tampon.

tampiqueño 1 *adj* of (*o* from) Tampico. **2** *nm*, **tampiqueña** *nf* native (*o* inhabitant) of Tampico.

tampoco *adv* neither, not ... either; nor; **ni A ni B** ~ neither A nor B, not A nor B either; **yo ~ lo compré, yo no lo compré** ~ I didn't buy one either; **ni yo** ~ nor I; **'¿lo sabes tú?' ... '~'** 'do you know?' ... 'No, I don't either'; **'pero ¿vendrás a la fiesta?' ... '~'** 'but you'll be coming to the party?' ... 'No, I shan't come to that either'.

tampón 1 *nm* (*Med*) tampon; (*Téc*) plug; (*Elec, Inform etc*) buffer; ~ **de entintar** inking-pad. **2** *atr*: **parlamento** ~ rubber-stamp parliament. (b) **sistema** ~ buffer system; **zona** ~ buffer zone.

tamuga *nf* (a) (*CAm*) (*lío*) bundle, pack; (*mochila*) knapsack. (**b**) (*LAm*‡) joint‡, reefer‡.

tan *adv* (**a**) so; ~ **rápido** so fast; ~ **rápidamente** so fast; **no es buena idea comprar un coche** ~ **grande** it's not a good idea to buy such a big car; **¡qué idea** ~ **rara!** what an odd notion!; **A es** ~ **feo como B** A is as ugly as B; **es** ~ **caro que nadie puede comprarlo** it's so expensive that nobody can afford it; **no te esperaba** ~ **pronto** I wasn't expecting you so soon; **de** ~ **rico resulta incomible** it's so rich that one can't eat it; ~ **es así que** ... so much so that ...; ~ **sólo** just.

(**b**) (*Méx*) **¿qué** ~ **grande es?** how big is it?; **¿ qué** ~ **grave está el enfermo?** how ill is the patient?; **¿qué** ~ **lejos?** how far?

tanaca *nf* (*And*) slut.

tanaceto *nm* tansy.

tanaco *adj* (*Cono Sur*) foolish, silly.

tanate *nm* (*CAm, Méx*) (**a**) (*cesta*) basket, pannier. (**b**) **~s** (*fig*) odds and ends, bits and pieces, gear.

tanatorio *nm* morgue.

tanda *nf* (**a**) (*serie etc*) series, set; batch; (*de huevos etc*) layer; (*de inyecciones*) course, series; (*de ladrillos*) course; (*de golpes*) series; ~ **de penaltis** series of penalties, penalty shoot-out.

(**b**) (*turno de trabajo*) shift, turn, spell; (*tarea*) job; task, piece of work; (*de riego*) turn (to use water); (*personas*) shift, relay; gang; ~ **de noche** nightshift, spell of night work; **ahora estás de** ~ now it's your turn.

(**c**) (*Billar etc*) game; (*Béisbol*) innings.

(**d**) (*LAm Teat*) show, performance; (*Cono Sur: farsa*) farce; (*Cono Sur: comedia musical*) musical; **primera** ~ first show, early performance.

tándem *nm* tandem; duo, pair, partnership; **en** ~ (*Elec*) in tandem; (*fig*) jointly, in association, together.

tanga[1] *nf* (*a veces m*) tanga, G-string.

tanga[2]‡ *nm* (*chulo*) pimp.

tangada‡ *nf* trick, swindle.

tanganear [1a] *vt* (*And, Carib*) to beat.

tanganillas: en ~ *adv* unsteadily; (*fig*) uncertainly, dubiously; unsafely.

tanganillo *nm* prop, wedge, temporary support.

tangar‡ [1h] *vt* to swindle; ~ **algo a uno** to do sb out of sth.

tangencial *adj* tangential; (*fig*) oblique.

tangencialmente *adv* tangentially; (*fig*) obliquely.

tangente *nf* tangent; **salirse por la** ~ (*fig: hacer una digresión*) to go off at a tangent; (*esquivar una pregunta*) to dodge the issue, give an evasive answer.

Tánger *nm* Tangier(s).

tangerino 1 *adj* of Tangier(s). **2** *nm*, **tangerina** *nf* native (*o* inhabitant) of Tangier(s); **los ~s** the people of Tangier(s).

tangibilidad *nf* tangibility.

tangible *adj* tangible; (*fig*) tangible, concrete.

tango *nm* tango.

tanguear [1a] *vi* (**a**) (*LAm: bailar*) to tango. (**b**) (*And: borracho*) to reel drunkenly.

tanguero, -a *nm/f*, **tanguista** *nmf* tango dancer.

tánico *adj* tannic; **ácido** ~ tannic acid.

tanino *nm* tannin.

tano* *nm* (*Cono Sur: pey*) Italian.

tanque *nm* (**a**) (*gen*) tank; water store, reservoir; (*Mil*) tank; (*Aut*) tanker, tanker lorry; ~ **de cerebros,** ~ **de ideas** think-tank. (**b**) (*Esp*‡) handbag.

tanquero *nm* (*Carib*) (*Náut*) tanker; (*Aut*) tanker, tank wagon.

tanqueta *nf* small tank, armoured car.

tanquista *nm* (*Mil*) member of a tank-crew.

tanta *nf* (*And*) maize bread.

tantán *nm* gong; tomtom.

tantarán *nm*, **tantarantán** *nm* (**a**) (*de tambor*) drumbeat, rub-a-dub. (**b**) (*) (*golpe*) hefty punch; (*sacudida*) violent shaking.

tanteada *nf* (**a**) (*LAm*) = **tanteo.** (**b**) (*Méx*) (*mala pasada*) dirty trick; (*estafa*) hoax, swindle.

tanteador 1 *nm* scoreboard. **2** *nm*, **tanteadora** *nf* (*persona*) scorer.

tantear [1a] **1** *vt* (**a**) *número, total, valor etc* to reckon (up), work out roughly, try to calculate, guess; *tela, cantidad etc* to size up, take the measure of; *peso* to feel, get the feel of, try the weight of; (*fig*) to weigh up, consider carefully.

(**b**) (*poner a prueba*) to test, try out; (*sondear*) to probe; *intenciones, persona* to sound out; ~ **si la superficie está bien segura** to test the surface to see if it is safe, see if the surface is safe.

(**c**) (*Arte*) to sketch in, draw the outline of.

(**d**) (*Dep*) to keep the score of.

(**e**) (*CAm, Méx: acechar*) to lie in wait for.

(**f**) (*Méx*) (*estafar*) to swindle; (*burlarse*) to make a fool of, take for a ride*.

2 *vi* (**a**) (*Dep*) to score, keep (the) score.

(**b**) (*LAm: ir a tientas*) to grope, feel one's way; **¡tantee Vd!** what do you think?

tanteo *nm* (**a**) reckoning, rough calculation, guesswork; weighing up, careful consideration; **a** ~, **por** ~ by guesswork.

(**b**) test(ing), trial; trial and error; **al** ~ by trial and error; **conversaciones de** ~ exploratory talks.

(**c**) (*Dep*) scoring.

tantico*: un ~ *adv* a bit, quite a bit; **es un** ~ **difícil** it's a wee bit awkward*.

tantísimo *adj superl* so much; **~s** so many; **había tantísima gente** there was such a crowd, there were so many people; **te lo he dicho tantísimas veces** I've told you lots of times.

tanto 1 *adj* so much, as much; so many, as many; **tiene** ~ **dinero como yo** he has as much money as I have; **tiene** ~ **dinero que no sabe qué hacer con él** he has so much money he doesn't know what to do with it; **hay ~s sellos verdes como azules** there are as many green stamps as (there are) blue ones; **hubo tanta manzana** there were so many apples; **es uno de ~s** it's one of many, it's one of a number; **quedan por ver otros ~s candidatos** there are as many candidates again still to be seen; **se dividen el trabajo en otras tantas porciones** they divide up the work into a like number of parts; **20 y ~s** 20-odd; **treinta y ~s** thirty-something; **tiene 40 y ~s años** he's over 40; **hay ciento y ~s concursantes** there are 100-odd competitors; **a ~s de marzo** on such-and-such a day in March; **a ~s de ~s** on such-and-such a day in this or that month; **a las tantas de la madrugada** at some time in the small hours; **volver a casa a las tantas** to come home terribly late; **estar fuera hasta las tantas** to stay out until all hours; **yo no sé qué ~s de libros hay** I don't know how many books there are.

2 *adv* so much, as much; **permanecer** ~ to stay so long; **trabajar** ~ to work so hard; **venir** ~ to come so often; **él gasta** ~ **como yo** he spends as much as I do; **gastó** ~ **que se quedó sin dinero** he spent so much that he ran out of money; ~ **A como B** both A and B; ~ **como eso** ... I don't think it's as bad as all that, I think you're exaggerating; ~ **como estafador, no** well, not really a swindler; I wouldn't go so far as to call him a swindler; ~ **como corre va a perder la carrera** with all his carry-on he'll end up with no qualifications; ~ **como habla no dice más que tonterías** all his talk is just hot air; **es** ~ **más difícil** it is all the more difficult; **es** ~ **más loable cuanto que** ... it is all the more praiseworthy because ...; ~ **mejor** all the better, so much the better (*para* for); ~ **peor** so much the worse; **¡y ~!** and how!, I'll say it is! (*etc*); ~ **es así que** ... so much so that ..., so much is this the case that ...; ~ **si viene como si no viene** whether he comes or whether he doesn't; **en** ~, **entre** ~ meanwhile, meantime; **no es para** ~ it's not as bad as all that; there's no need to make such a fuss; **por** ~, **por lo** ~ so, therefore; **¡ni** ~ **así!** not a scrap!; **¡ni** ~ **ni tan calvo!, ¡ni** ~ **ni tan poco!** don't exaggerate!, it's not that bad!; **no le tengo ni** ~ **así de lástima** I haven't a scrap of pity for him; **¿qué** ~ **será?** (*LAm*) how much (is it)?

3 *conj*: **con** ~ **que** ... provided (that) ...; **en** ~ **(que)** ... while ...; until ...; **hasta** ~ **que** ... until (such time as) ...

4 *nm* (**a**) (*Com, Fin etc*) certain amount, so much; ~ **alzado** agreed price; overall estimate; **por un** ~ **alzado** for a lump sum; at a flat rate; ~ **por palabra** rate per word, so much a word; ~ **por ciento** percentage; rate; **un** ~ **por cada semana de trabajo** so much for each week's work; **al** ~ at the same price; **las máquinas costaron otro** ~ the machines cost as much again (*o* the same again).

(**b**) (*Dep : punto*) point; (*gol*) goal; (*ficha*) counter, chip; ~ **en contra** point against; ~ **a favor** point for; ~ **del honor** consolation goal; **apuntar los ~s** to keep score; **apuntarse un** ~ to score a point; (*fig*) to stay one up.

(**c**) **estar al** ~ to be fully informed; to know the score (*fig*); **estar al** ~ **de los acontecimientos** to be fully abreast of events, be in touch with events; **poner a uno al** ~ to give sb the news (*de* about), put sb in the picture (*de* about).

(**d**) **al** ~ **de** because of; **al** ~ **de que** ... because of the fact that ...; with the excuse that ..., on the pretext that ...

(**e**) **algún** ~, **un** ~ (*como adv*) rather, somewhat; **estoy**

un ~ cansado I'm rather tired; **es un ~ difícil** it's a bit awkward.

Tanzanía *nf* Tanzania.

tañar‡ [1a] *vt* to grasp, understand; **~ a uno** to twig what sb is saying.*

tañer [2f] **1** *vt* (*Mús*) to play; *campana* to ring; **2** *vi* to drum with one's fingers.

tañido *nm* (*Mús*) sound; strains, notes; (*de campana*) ringing, pealing.

T/año *abr de* **toneladas por año.**

TAO *nf abr de* **traducción asistida por ordenador** computer-assisted translation, CAT.

tapa *nf* (**a**) (*de caja, olla*) lid; cover, top, (*de botella*) cap; (*de libro*) cover; (*de cilindro*) head; **~ de registro** manhole cover, inspection cover; **~ de los sesos** brainbox, skull; (**libro de**) **~ dura** hardback (book); **levantarse la ~ de los sesos** to blow one's brains out.
(**b**) (*de zapato*) heelplate.
(**c**) (*de canal*) sluicegate.
(**d**) (*Esp Culin*) dish of hors d'oeuvres; snack, delicacy (*taken at the bar counter with drinks*); **ir de ~s** *V* **tapeo.**
(**e**) (*And Culin*) rumpsteak.
(**f**) (*Méx Aut*) hubcap.
(**g**) (*Carib**: *comisión*) commission.

tapa(a)gujeros* *nm invar* (**a**) (*Arquit*) jerry-builder. (**b**) (*fig*) stand-in, substitute.

tapabarro *nm* (*And, Cono Sur*) mudguard.

tapaboca *nf*, **tapabocas** *nm invar* (**a**) (*manotada*) slap. (**b**) (*prenda*) muffler.

tapaboquetes *nm invar* stopgap.

tapacubos *nm invar* hubcap.

tapada *nf* (**a**) **un gay de ~*** a closet gay*.
(**b**) (*mentira*) lie.

tapadera *nf* (**a**) (*tapa*) lid, cover; cap. (**b**) (*fig*: *de organización*) cover, front (organization) (*de* for); (*de espía*) cover.

tapadero *nm* stopper.

tapadillo: de ~ *adv* secretly, stealthily.

tapado 1 *adj* (**a**) (*Cono Sur*) *animal* all one colour.
(**b**) (*And*) (*vago*) lazy, slack; (*ignorante*) ignorant.
2 *nm* (**a**) (*And, Cono Sur*: *tesoro*) buried treasure.
(**b**) (*CAm, Cono Sur*) (*abrigo de mujer*), woman's coat; (*de niño*) child's coat; (*Méx*: *chal*) headscarf, shawl.
(**c**) (*And, CAm Culin*) dish of plantain and barbecued meat.
(**d**) (*Pol*) officially-backed candidate.

tapagrietas *nm invar* filler.

tapalcate *nm* (*CAm, Méx*) (*objeto*) piece of junk, useless object; (*persona*) useless person.

tapalodo *nm* (*And, Carib*) mudguard.

tapanca *nf* (**a**) (*And, Cono Sur*) (*de caballo*) horse trappings; (*LAm*: *gualdrapa*) saddle blanket. (**b**) (*Cono Sur**: *culo*) backside.

tapaojo *nm* (*LAm*: *venda*) blindfold, bandage (over the eyes); (*parche*) patch.

tapaporos *nm invar* primer.

tapar [1a] **1** *vt* (**a**) (*gen*) to cover, cover up (*de* with); *olla, recipiente* to put the lid on; *botella* to put the cap on, put the stopper in, stopper, cork; *cara* to cover up, hide; to muffle up; (*en cama*) to wrap up; *tubo etc* to stop (up), block (up), obstruct; *agujero* to plug; (*Arquit*) to fill up, wall up, wall in; (*LAm*) *diente* to fill; *objeto* to hide; *vista* to obstruct, block; **el árbol tapa el sol a la ventana** the tree keeps the sunlight off the window, the tree prevents the sun from reaching the window; **el muro nos tapaba el viento** the wall protected us from the wind; **el atleta se encontraba tapado** the athlete was shut in (*o* boxed in).
(**b**) (*fig*) *derrota etc* to cover up, conceal; *fugitivo* to hide, conceal; *criminal* to cover up for.
(**c**) (*And*: *aplastar*) to crush, flatten; (*chafar*) to rumple.
(**d**) (*And*: *insultar*) to abuse, insult.
2 taparse *vr* (**a**) to wrap (o.s.) up, (*esp*) to wrap up warmly (in bed). (**b**) (*: *con sombrero*) to put one's hat on.

tapara *nf* (*Carib*) calabash, gourd.

táparo *nm* (*And*) (**a**) (*yescas*) tinderbox. (**b**) (*tuerto*) one-eyed person; (*fig*) dolt.

taparrabo *nm*, **taparrabos** *nm invar* (swimming) trunks; (*oriental etc*) loincloth.

tapatío 1 *adj* of Guadalajara. **2** *nm*, **tapatía** *nf* native (*o* inhabitant) of Guadalajara; **los ~s** the people of Guadalajara.

tapayagua *nf* (*CAm, Méx*), **tapayagüe** *nm* (*Méx*) (*nubarrón*) stormcloud; (*llovizna*) drizzle.

tape* *nm* (*Carib*) cover.

tapear [1a] *vi V* **tapeo.**

tapeo* *nm*: **ir de ~** (*Esp*) to go round the bars (eating snacks).

tapeque *nm* (*And*) equipment for a journey.

tapera *nf* (*LAm*) (*casa*) ruined house; (*pueblo*) abandoned village.

taperujarse* [1a] *vr* to cover up one's face.

tapesco *nm* (*CAm, Méx*) (*armazón*) bedframe; (*cama*) camp bed.

tapete *nm* (*alfombrita*) rug; (*de mesa*) table runner, table cover; **~ verde** card table; **estar sobre el ~** (*fig*) to be under discussion; **poner un asunto sobre el ~** to put a matter up for discussion.

tapetusa *nf* (*And*) contraband goods, contraband liquor.

tapia *nf* (**a**) garden wall; mud wall, adobe wall. (**b**) (‡) partner.

tapial *nm* = **tapia.**

tapialera *nf* (*And*) = **tapia.**

tapiar [1b] *vt* to wall in; *ventana* to block up; (*fig*) to block, stop up.

tapicería *nf* (**a**) (*arte*) tapestry making; upholstery. (**b**) (*tapiz*) tapestry; (*tapices*) tapestries, hangings; (*de coche, mueble etc*) upholstery.

tapiñar‡ [1a] *vt* to scoff*, eat.

tapioca *nf* tapioca.

tapir *nm* tapir.

tapisca *nf* (*CAm, Méx*) maize harvest, corn harvest (*US*).

tapiscar [1g] *vt* (*CAm*) *maíz* to harvest.

tapita* *como adj*: **estar ~** (*Carib*) to be as deaf as a post.

tapiz *nm* (*de pared*) tapestry; (*de suelo*) carpet; **~ volador** magic carpet.

tapizado *nm* tapestries; carpeting; upholstery.

tapizar [1f] *vt* (**a**) *pared* to hang with tapestries; *mueble* to upholster, cover; *coche* to upholster; *suelo* to carpet, cover.
(**b**) (*fig*) to carpet (*con, de* with).

tapón 1 *adj* (*CAm, Cono Sur*) tailless.
2 *nm* (**a**) (*de botella*) stopper, cap, top; (*corcho*) cork; (*Téc*) plug, bung, wad; (*para el oído*) ear-plug; (*Aut*) filler-cap; (*Med*) tampon; (*Méx Elec*) fuse; **~ de corona, ~ de rosca** screw top; **al primer ~, zurrapa*** well, the first shot was a failure.
(**b**) (*: *persona*) chubby person.
(**c**) (*estorbo*) obstacle, hindrance; (*Aut* *) slowcoach*.
(**d**) (*Aut*: *t* **~ circulatorio**) traffic-jam.

taponar [1a] *vt botella* to stopper, cork, put the cap on; *tubo* to plug, stop up, block; (*Dep*) to block, stop; (*Med*) to tampon; **~ los oídos** to stop up one's ears.

taponazo *nm* (*de corcho*) pop.

tapujar* [1a] **1** *vt* to cheat, con*. **2 tapujarse** *vr* to muffle o.s. up.

tapujo* *nm* (**a**) (*embozo*) muffler.
(**b**) (*engaño*) deceit, humbug; (*subterfugio*) subterfuge, dodge*; (*secreto*) secrecy; **sin ~s** honestly, openly, above-board; without beating about the bush; **andar con ~s** to behave deceitfully, be involved in some shady business; **llevan no sé qué ~ entre manos** they're up to some dodge or other*.

taquear [1a] **1** *vt* (*LAm*: *llenar*) to fill right up, pack tight (*de* with); *arma* to fire.
2 *vi* (**a**) (*And, Cono Sur, Méx*: *jugar al billar*)) to play billiards.
(**b**) (*Carib*: *vestirse*) to dress in style.
(**c**) (*Méx*: *comer tacos*) to have a snack.
3 taquearse *vr* (*And*) to get rich.

taquería *nf* (**a**) (*Carib*) cheek. (**b**) (*Méx*) taco restaurant, taco stall.

taquete *nm* (*Méx*) plug, bung.

taquicardia *nf* abnormally rapid heartbeat, tachycardia.

taquigrafía *nf* shorthand, stenography.

taquigráficamente *adv*: **tomar un discurso ~** to take a speech down in shorthand.

taquigráfico *adj* shorthand (*atr*).

taquígrafo, -a *nm/f* shorthand writer, stenographer.

taquilla *nf* (**a**) (*Ferro*) booking-office, ticket-office; ticket-window; (*Teat*) box-office.
(**b**) (*Teat*: *recaudación*) takings; (*Dep etc*) gate-money, proceeds.
(**c**) (*carpeta*) file; (*archivador*) filing-cabinet; (*armario*) locker.
(**d**) (*CAm*) (*bar*) bar; (*tienda*) liquor store.
(**e**) (*And, CAm, Cono Sur*: *clavo*) tack.

taquillaje *nm* (*Teat etc*) takings, box-office receipts; (*Dep*) gate-money, gate.

taquillero 1 *adj* popular, successful (at the box-office); **ser ~** to be good (for the) box-office, be a draw, be popular; **función taquillera** box-office success, big draw; **el actor más ~ del año** the actor who has been the biggest box-office draw of the year.

2 *nm*, **taquillera** *nf* clerk, ticket clerk.

taquimeca *nf*, **taquimecanógrafa** *nf* shorthand typist.

taquímetro *nm* (*Aut*) speedometer; (*Agrimensura*) tachymeter.

taquito *nm* (*Culin*) small slice.

tara¹ *nf* (**a**) (*Com*) tare.

(**b**) (*fig*) defect, blemish.

tara² *nf* tally stick.

tarabilla 1 *nf* (**a**) latch, catch. (**b**) (*: *charla*) chatter. **2** *nmf* (*) (*hablador*) chatterbox; (*casquivano*) featherbrained person; (*inútil*) useless individual, dead loss.

tarabita *nf* (**a**) (*de cinturón, hebilla*) tongue. (**b**) (*And*) cable of a rope bridge (*with hanging basket for carrying passengers across ravines*).

taracea *nf* inlay, marquetry.

taracear [1a] *vt* to inlay.

tarado 1 *adj* (**a**) (*Com etc*) damaged, defective, imperfect; *animal etc* maimed, weak. (**b**) (*Cono Sur*) *persona* (*mutilado*) physically impaired, crippled; (*raro*) odd, eccentric. (**c**) (*LAm**) (*idiota*) stupid; (*loco*) crazy. **2** *nm*, **tarada*** *nf* idiot, cretin.

tarambana(s) *nmf* (**a**) (*casquivano*) harum-scarum, fly-by-night; (*estrafalario*) crackpot; (*no fiable*) unreliable person. (**b**) (*parlanchín*) chatterbox.

taranta *nf* (**a**) (*And, Cono Sur Zool*) tarantula. (**b**) (*And, CAm*: *locura*) mental disturbance, madness; (*CAm*) bewilderment. (**c**) (*Méx*: *embriaguez*) drunkenness.

tarantear [1a] *vi* (*Cono Sur*: *hacer algo imprevisto*) to do something unexpected; (*cambiar*) to chop and change a lot; (*hacer cosas raras*) to behave strangely, be eccentric.

tarantela *nf* tarantella.

tarantín *nm* (**a**) (*CAm, Carib Culin*) kitchen utensil. (**b**) (*Carib*: *patíbulo*) scaffold. (**c**) (*Carib*: *puesto*) stall. (**d**) **tarantines** (*Carib**), odds and ends.

taranto *adj* (*And*) dazed, bewildered.

tarántula *nf* tarantula.

tarar [1a] *vt* (*Com*) to tare.

tarareable *adj*: **melodía ~** catchy tune, tune that you can hum.

tararear [1a] *vti* to hum.

tararí* 1 *adj* (*Esp*) crazy. **2** *interj* no way!*, you must be joking!

tarasca *nf* (**a**) (*monstruo*) carnival dragon, monster.

(**b**) (*fig*) (*comilón*) glutton; (*sumidero de recursos*) person who is a drain on one's resources.

(**c**) (*: *mujer*) old hag, old bag*; termagant.

(**d**) (*And, CAm, Cono Sur*: *boca*) big mouth.

tarascada *nf* (**a**) (*mordisco*) bite; snap. (**b**) (*: *réplica*) tart reply, snappy answer.

tarascar [1g] *vt* to bite, snap at.

tarasco *nm* (*And*) bite, nip.

tarascón *nm* (*LAm*) bite, nip.

tarasquear [1a] *vt* (*CAm, Cono Sur, Méx*) to bite, snap at; to bite off.

tardanza *nf* (**a**) (*lentitud*) slowness. (**b**) (*demora*) delay.

tardar [1a] *vi* (**a**) (*tomar mucho tiempo*) to take a long time, be long; (*llegar tarde*) to be late; (*retardarse*) to delay, linger (on); **a más ~, a todo ~** at the latest; **aquí tardan mucho** they are very slow here, they take a long time here; **he tardado un poco debido a la lluvia** I'm a bit late because of the rain, I took longer (to get here) because of the rain; **tardamos 3 horas de A a B** we took 3 hours (to get) from A to B; **escribiré sin ~** I'll write without delay.

(**b**) **~ a** + *infin* to delay + *ger*, be slow to + *infin*; **no tardes a hacerlo** don't put off doing it.

(**c**) **~ en** + *infin* to be slow to + *infin*, take a long time to + *infin*, be long in + *ger*; to be late in + *ger*; **tardó mucho en repararlo** he took a long time to repair it; **tardó 3 horas en encontrarlo** it took him 3 hours to find it, he spent 3 hours looking for it; **no tardes en informarme** tell me at once, inform me without delay; **¿cuánto tardaremos en terminarlo?** how long shall we take to finish it?; **el público no tardó en reaccionar** the spectators were not slow to react.

tarde 1 *adv* late; (*demasiado ~*) too late; **un poco más ~** a little later; **de ~ en ~** from time to time; **~ o temprano** sooner or later; **se hace ~** it's getting late; **es ~ para eso** it's too late for that.

2 *nf* (*primeras horas*) afternoon; (*últimas horas*) evening, early evening; **¡buenas ~s!** good afternoon!; good evening!; **a la ~** in the evening; by evening; **en la ~ de hoy** this afternoon, this evening; **por la ~** in the afternoon, in the evening; **función de la ~** matinée; **de la ~ a la mañana** overnight, during the night; (*fig*) in no time at all.

tardecer [2d] *vi* = **atardecer.**

tardecica *nf*, **tardecita** *nf* evening, approach of night, dusk.

tardecito *adv* (*LAm*) rather late.

tardíamente *adv* late, belatedly; too late.

tardío *adj* (*gen*) late; (*atrasado*) overdue, belated, slow to arrive (*etc*); *fruta, patata etc* late.

tardo *adj* (**a**) (*lento*) slow, sluggish; dilatory. (**b**) (*lerdo*) slow (of understanding), dull, dense; **~ de oído** hard of hearing.

tardo... *pref* late, *p.ej.* **tardorromano** late Roman; **el tardofranquismo** the last years of the Franco régime.

tardón* *adj* (**a**) (*lento*) slow; dilatory. (**b**) (*lerdo*) dim.

tarea *nf* (*gen*) job, task; (*faena*) chore; (*trabajo asignado*) set piece of work, stint, amount of work set; (*de colegial*) homework; (*Inform*) task; **~ de ocasión** chore; **~ suelta** odd job; **todavía me queda mucha ~** I've still got a lot left to do; **es una ~ poco grata** it's not a very satisfying job; **¡~ te mando!*** you've got a job on there!; you'll have your work cut out!

tareco *nm* (*And*) old thing, piece of junk; **~s** (*fig*) things, gear, odds and ends.

tarifa *nf* (*precio*) tariff; (*tasa*) rate; (*lista de precios*) price list, list of charges; (*en vehículo*) fare; **~ de agua** water rate, water charges; **~ de anuncios** advertisement rates; **~ nocturna** (*Telec*) cheap rate; **~ de suscripción** subscription rate; **~ turística** tourist class, tourist rates.

tarifar [1a] **1** *vt* to price. **2** *vi* to fall out, quarrel.

tarifario *adj* price (*atr*); rate (*atr*); tariff (*atr*).

tarificación *nf* metering.

tarificar [1g] *vt* (*Telec*) to meter.

tarima *nf* (*plataforma*) platform; (*estrado*) low dais; (*soporte*) stand; (*banquillo*) low bench.

tarimaco *nm* (*Carib*) = **tareco.**

tarja¹ *nf* tally, tally stick.

tarja² *nf* (*: *golpe*) swipe, bash*.

tarjar [1a] *vt* (**a**) to keep a tally of, notch up. (**b**) (*And, Cono Sur*: *tachar*) to cross out.

tarjeta *nf* card; **~ amarilla** (*Dep*) yellow card; **~ bancaria** bank-card; **~ de circuitos impresos** printed circuit board; **~ comercial** business card; **~ de crédito** credit-card; **~ de embarque** boarding-pass; **~ de expansión** expansion board; **~ de felicitaciones, ~ de saludo** greetings card; **~ de gráficos** graphics card; **~ de identidad** identity card; **~ inteligente** smart card; **~ de lector** reader's ticket; **~ de multifunción** multifunction card; **~ de Navidad, ~ navideña** Christmas card; **~ perforador** punched card; **~ de periodista** press card; **~ postal** postcard; **~ de presentación** business card; **~ de respuesta** reply card; **~ de respuesta pagada** reply-paid postcard; **~ roja** (*Dep*) red card; **~ telefónica** phonecard; **~ verde** green card; **~ de visita** visiting card, calling card (*US*); **dejar ~** to leave one's card; **pasar ~** to send in one's card.

tarjetear [1a] *vt*: **~ a un jugador** to show a card to a player.

tarpón *nm* tarpon.

tarquín *nm* mud, slime, ooze.

tarra‡ *nmf* old geezer‡.

tarraconense 1 *adj* of Tarragona. **2** *nmf* native (*o* inhabitant) of Tarragona; **los ~s** the people of Tarragona.

tarrajazo *nm* (**a**) (*And, Carib*: *suceso*) unpleasant event. (**b**) (*CAm*) (*golpe*) blow; (*herida*) wound.

tarramenta *nf* (*Carib, Méx*) horns.

tarrayazo *nm* (**a**) (*And, Carib, Méx*) (*de red*) cast (of a net). (**b**) (*Carib*: *golpe*) violent blow.

tarrear [1a] *vt* (*Carib*) to cuckold.

tarrina *nf* small container; pot, jar; (*de helado*) tub.

tarro *nm* (**a**) (*pote*) pot, jar.

(**b**) (*) **comer el ~ a uno** (*engañar*) to put one over on sb*; (*lavar el cerebro*) to brainwash sb; **comerse el ~** (*Esp*) to think hard, rack one's brains.

(**c**) (*And, Cono Sur*) (*lata*) tin, can; (*bidón*) drum; **arrancarse con los ~s*** to run off with the loot*.

(**d**) (*Carib, Cono Sur, Méx*: *cuerno*) horn.

(**e**) (*And*††: *chistera*) top hat.

(**f**) (*Cono Sur*: *chiripa*) stroke of luck, fluke.

(**g**) (*Carib*: *del marido*) cuckolding.

(**h**) (*Carib*: *asunto*) difficult matter, complicated affair.

tarsana *nf* (*LAm*) soapbark.
tarso *nm* tarsus.
tarta *nf* (a) (*pastel*) cake; (*torta*) tart; flan, sponge; ~ **de bodas,** ~ **nupcial** wedding cake; ~ **de cumpleaños** birthday-cake; ~ **de frutas** fruit-cake; ~ **de queso** cheesecake; ~ **de Reyes** Christmas cake; **repartir la** ~ **nacional** to divide up the national cake. (b) (*Inform*) pie-chart.
tártago *nm* (a) (*Bot*) spurge.
(b) (*: *desgracia*) mishap, misfortune.
(c) (*: *trastada*) practical joke.
tartaja 1 *adj* stammering, tongue-tied. **2** *nmf* stammerer.
tartajear [1a] *vi* to stammer.
tartajeo *nm* stammer(ing).
tartajoso, -a *adj, nm/f* = **tartaja**.
tartalear [1a] *vi* (a) (*al andar*) to walk in a daze; to stagger, reel. (b) (*al hablar*) to stammer, be stuck for words.
tartamudear [1a] *vi* to stutter, stammer.
tartamudeo *nm* stutter(ing), stammer(ing).
tartamudez *nf* stutter, stammer, speech defect.
tartamudo 1 *adj* stuttering, stammering. **2** *nm*, **tartamuda** *nf* stutterer, stammerer.
tartán *nm* tartan.
tartana *nf* trap, light carriage.
tartancho *adj* (*And, Cono Sur*) = **tartamudo.**
Tartaria *nf* Tartary.
tartárico *adj* tartaric; **ácido** ~ tartaric acid.
tártaro[1] *nm* (*Quím etc*) tartar.
tártaro[2]**, -a** *adj, nm/f* Tartar.
tartera *nf* cake-tin.
Tarteso *nm* Tartessus; (*Biblia*) Tarshish.
tarugo 1 *adj* (a) (*esp LAm*) stupid.
(b) (*Carib*) fawning.
2 *nm* (a) (*pedazo de madera*) lump, chunk (of wood *etc*); (*clavija*) wooden peg; (*tapón*) plug, stopper; (*pan*) chunk of stale bread; (*adoquín*) wooden paving block.
(b) (*Carib**: *susto*) fright, scare.
(c) (*esp LAm*: *imbécil*) chump*, blockhead.
(d) (*Méx*: *miedo*) fear, anxiety.
(e) (‡) backhander*.
tarumba* *adj invar:* **volver** ~ **a uno** to get sb all mixed up; to daze sb, fog sb; **volverse** ~ to get all mixed up, get completely bewildered; **esa chica me tiene** ~ I'm crazy about that girl.
tasa *nf* (a) (*acto*) valuation; estimate, appraisal.
(b) (*medida, norma*) measure, standard, norm.
(c) (*precio, tipo*) fixed price, official price, standard rate; ~ **de aeropuerto** airport tax; ~ **de basuras** rubbish-collection charge; ~ **de cambio** exchange rate; ~ **de crecimiento,** ~ **de desarrollo** growth rate; ~ **de descuento bancario** bank rate; ~ **de desempleo** level of unemployment; ~ **de instrucción** tuition fee; ~ **de interés** rate of interest; ~ **de nacimiento,** ~ **de natalidad** birthrate; ~ **de paro** level of unemployment; ~ **de rendimiento** rate of return; **sin** ~ boundless, limitless; unstinted; **gastar sin** ~ to spend like there's no tomorrow.
tasable *adj* ratable.
tasación *nf* valuation, assessment; (*fig*) appraisal; ~ **pericial** expert valuation; ~ **de un artículo** fixing of a price for an article.
tasadamente *adv* sparingly.
tasador(a) *nm/f* valuer; ~ **de averías** average adjuster; ~ **de impuestos** tax appraiser.
tasajear [1a] *vt* (*LAm*) (a) (*cortar*) to cut, slash. (b) *carne* to jerk.
tasajo *nm* (a) (*carne de vaca*) dried beef, jerked beef; (*carne*) (*any*) piece of meat. (b) (*And*: *persona*) tall thin person.
tasajudo *adj* (*LAm*) tall and thin.
tasar [1a] *vt* (a) *artículo* to fix a price for, price (*en* at); (*regular*) to regulate; *trabajo etc* to rate (*en* at).
(b) (*fig*) to value, appraise, assess (*en* at).
(c) (*restringir*) to limit, put a limit on, restrict; ration; (*escatimar*) to be sparing with, (*pey*) be mean with, stint; **les tasa a los niños hasta la leche** she even rations her children's milk.
tasca* *nf* (*Esp*) bar; **ir de** ~**s** to go on a crawl round the bars*.
tascar [1g] *vt* (a) *lino etc* to swingle, beat. (b) *hierba* to munch, champ; *freno* to champ at; (*And*: *masticar*) to chew, crunch.
Tasmania *nf* Tasmania.
tasquear* [1a] *vi* (*Esp*) to go drinking, go round the bars.
tasqueo* *nm*: **ir de** ~ (*Esp*) = **tasquear.**
tata 1 *nm* (a) (*Murcia, LAm**: *padre*) dad, daddy. (b) (*LAm*) = **taita** (b). **2** *nf* (a) (*: *niñera*) nanny, nursemaid; (*chacha*) maid. (b) (*LAm*: *hermana menor*) younger sister.
tatarabuelo *nm* great-great-grandfather; **los** ~**s** one's great-great-grandparents.
tataranieto *nm* great-great-grandson.
tatas: andar a ~ (*hacer pinitos*) to toddle; (*ir a gatas*) to crawl, get down on all fours.
tate[1] *interj* (*sorpresa*) good heavens!; well well!; (*admiración*) bravo!; (*ira*) come now!; watch your step!; (*dándose cuenta*) so that's it!; oh I see!; (*aviso*) look out!
tate[2]‡ *nm* hash*, pot‡.
tato* *nm* (*Cono Sur*) younger brother.
tatole* *nm* (*Méx*) plot.
tatuaje *nm* (a) (*dibujo*) tattoo. (b) (*acto*) tattooing.
tatuar [1d] *vt* to tattoo.
tauca *nf* (*And*) (a) (*objetos*) heap of things. (b) (*bolsa*) large bag.
taumaturgo *nm* miracle-worker; (*fig*) wonder-worker.
taurinamente *adv* in bullfighting terms.
taurino *adj* bullfighting (*atr*); **el negocio** ~ the bullfighting business; **leía una revista taurina** he was reading a bullfighting magazine.
Tauro *nm* (*Zodíaco*) Taurus.
taurofobia *nf* dislike of bullfighting.
taurófobo, -a *nm/f* opponent of bullfighting.
taurómaco 1 *adj* bullfighting (*atr*). **2** *nm* bullfighting expert.
tauromaquia *nf* (art of) bullfighting, tauromachy.
tauromáquico *adj* bullfighting (*atr*).
tautología *nf* tautology.
tautológico *adj* tautological.
TAV *nm abr de* **tren de alta velocidad** high-velocity train, HVT.
taxativamente *adv* in a restricted sense, specifically.
taxativo *adj* (*restringido*) limited, restricted; *sentido* particular, concrete; specific.
taxi *nm* taxi, cab, taxicab.
taxidermia *nf* taxidermy.
taxidermista *nmf* taxidermist.
taxímetro *nm* taximeter, clock.
taxista *nmf* (a) taxidriver, cabby. (b) (*: *chulo*) pimp.
taxonomía *nf* taxonomy.
taxonomista *nmf* taxonomist.
taza *nf* (a) cup; (*contenido*) cupful; ~ **de café** cup of coffee; ~ **para café** coffee cup, cup for coffee.
(b) (*de fuente*) basin, bowl; (*de lavabo*) bowl; (*Cono Sur*: *palangana*) washbasin; ~ **de noche** (*Cono Sur*: *euf*) chamberpot; ~ **del wáter** lavatory pan.
tazado *adj ropa* frayed, worn; *persona* shabby.
tazar [1f] **1** *vt* (a) (*cortar*) to cut; to cut up, divide. (b) (*desgastar*) to fray. **2 tazarse** *vr* to fray.
tazón *nm* (*taza*) large cup; (*cuenco*) bowl, basin; (*prov*) washbasin.
TBC *nm abr de* **tren de bandas en caliente** hot-strip mill.
TC *nm abr de* **Tribunal Constitucional** Constitutional Court.
TDV *nf abr de* **tabla deslizadora a vela** windsurfing board.
te *pron pers* (a) (*ac*) you; (††, *a Dios*) thee.
(b) (*dativo*) (to) you; (††, *a Dios*) (to) thee; **te he traído esto** I've brought you this, I've brought this for you; **¿te duele mucho el brazo?** does your arm hurt much?
(c) (*reflexivo*) (to) yourself; (††, *a Dios*) (to) thyself; **te vas a caer** you'll fall; **te equivocas** you're wrong; **¡cálmate!** calm yourself!
té *nm* (a) (*planta, bebida*) tea; (*reunión*) tea party; **dar un** ~ to give a tea party. (b) **dar el** ~ **a uno*** to bore sb to tears.
tea *nf* (a) (*antorcha*) torch; (*astillas*) firelighter. (b) (‡: *cuchillo*) chiv‡, knife.
teatral *adj* (a) theatre (*atr*); dramatic; **obra** ~ dramatic work; **temporada** ~ theatre season.
(b) (*fig*) theatrical, dramatic; (*pey*) histrionic, stagey.
teatralidad *nf* theatricality; drama; sense of the theatre, stage sense; (*pey*) showmanship; histrionics, staginess.
teatralizar [1f] *vt* to stage; to dramatize.
teatro *nm* (a) (*gen*) theatre; **el** ~ (*como profesión*) the theatre, the stage, acting; ~ **del absurdo,** ~ **de lo absurdo** theatre of the absurd; ~ **de aficionados** amateur theatre, amateur theatricals; ~ **de calle** street theatre; ~ **de la ópera** opera-house; ~ **de repertorio** repertory theatre; ~ **de títeres** puppet theatre; ~ **de variedades** variety theatre, music-hall, vaudeville theater (*US*); **escribir para el** ~ to write for the stage; **en el** ~ **es una persona muy distinta**

she's a very different person on the stage; **hacer que se venga abajo el** ~ to bring the house down.

(**b**) (*Liter*) drama, plays; **el** ~ **de Cervantes** Cervantes' plays, Cervantes' dramatic works; **selecciones del** ~ **del siglo XVIII** selections from 18th century drama.

(**c**) (*de suceso*) scene; (*Mil*) theatre; ~ **de guerra,** ~ **de operaciones** theatre of war, front.

(**d**) (*fig*) **hacer** ~ to exaggerate, act affectedly; **ella tiene mucho** ~ she's terribly dramatic, she's given to histrionics.

(**e**) (*LAm*: *cine*) cinema, movies.

Tebas *nm* Thebes.

tebeo *nm* (children's) comic; **eso está más visto que el** ~ that's old hat; ~ **de terror** horror comic.

tebeoteca *nf* collection of comics.

TEC *nfpl abr de* **toneladas equivalentes de carbón** equivalent tons of coal.

teca[1] *nf* teak.

teca[2]* *nf* (*Esp*) disco.

tecla[1] *nf* (*Mús, de máquina de escribir etc*) key; **dar en la** ~* to get it right; to get the hang of sth; **dar en la** ~ **de** + *infin** to fall into the habit of + *ger*; **hay que tocar muchas** ~**s a la vez*** there are too many things to think about all together; **no le queda ninguna** ~ **por tocar** there's nothing else left for him to try; ~ **de anulación** cancel key; ~ **de borrado** delete key; ~ **de cambio** shift-key; ~ **de control** control key; ~**s de control direccional del cursor** cursor control keys; ~ **del cursor** cursor key; ~ **de desplazamiento** scroll key; ~ **de edición** edit key; ~ **con flecha** arrow key; ~ **de función** function key; ~ **de iniciación** booting-up switch; ~ **programable** user-defined key; ~ **de retorno** return key; ~ **de tabulación** tab key.

teclado *nm* (*Mús, de máquina de escribir etc*) keyboard, keys; (*de órgano*) manual; ~ **numérico** numeric keypad; **marcación por** ~ push-button dialling.

tecle *adj* (*Cono Sur*) weak, sickly.

teclear [1a] **1** *vt* (**a**) (*LAm*) *instrumento* to play clumsily, mess about on; *máquina de escribir* to use clumsily.

(**b**) (*) *problema* to approach from various angles.

2 *vi* (**a**) (*Mús*) to strum, thrum, play a few chords.

(**b**) (*: *con dedos*) to drum, tap (with one's fingers).

(**c**) (*Cono Sur*: *estar enfermo*) to be weak, be ill.

(**d**) (*Cono Sur*: *ser pobre*) to be very poor.

(**e**) (*And, Cono Sur*: *negocio*) to be going very badly.

tecleo *nm* (**a**) (*Mús*) fingering, playing; touch; strumming, thrumming. (**b**) (*: *con dedos*) drumming, tapping.

tecleteo *nm* = **tecleo.**

teclista *nmf* (*Inform*) keyboard operator, key-puncher; (*Mús*) keyboard player.

teclo 1 *adj* (*And*) old. **2** *nm*, **tecla**[2] *nf* old man/woman.

técnica[1] *nf* (*gen*) technique; technology; (*método*) method; (*destreza*) craft, skill.

técnicamente *adv* technically.

tecnicidad *nf* technicality, technical nature.

tecnicismo *nm* (**a**) technical nature. (**b**) (*Ling*) technical term, technicality.

técnico 1 *adj* technical. **2** *nm*, **técnica**[2] *nf* technician; expert, specialist; (*Dep*) trainer, coach; ~ **informático** computer programmer; ~ **de mantenimiento** maintenance engineer; ~ **de sonido** sound engineer; ~ **de televisión** television engineer, television repairman; **es un** ~ **en la materia** he's an expert on the subject.

tecnicolor ® *nm* Technicolor ®; **en** ~ in Technicolor.

tecnificar [1g] **1** *vt* to make more technical. **2** **tecnificarse** *vr* to become more technical.

tecno... *pref* techno....

tecnocracia *nf* technocracy.

tecnócrata *nmf* technocrat.

tecnocrático *adj* technocratic.

tecnología *nf* technology; ~ **de alimentos** food technology; **alta** ~, ~ **(de) punta** high technology, advanced technology; ~ **de estado sólido** solid-state technology; ~ **de la información** Information Technology, IT.

tecnológico *adj* technological.

tecnólogo, -a *nm/f* technologist.

teco* *adj* (*CAm, Méx*) drunk.

tecolote 1 *adj* (**a**) (*CAm*) *color* reddish-brown. (**b**) (*CAm, Méx*: *borracho*) drunk. **2** *nm* (**a**) (*CAm, Méx Orn*) eagle owl. (**b**) (*Méx*‡: *policía*) policeman, cop*.

tecomate *nm* (*Méx*) (**a**) (*Bot*) gourd, calabash. (**b**) (*recipiente*) earthenware cup.

tecorral *nm* (*Méx*) dry-stone wall.

tectónica *nf* tectonics.

tecuán 1 *adj* (*CAm, Méx*) greedy, voracious. **2** *nm* monster.

techado *nm* roof, covering; **bajo** ~ under cover, indoors.

techar [1a] *vt* to roof (in, over).

techo *nm* (**a**) (*exterior*) roof; (*interior*) ceiling; (‡) lid‡, hat; ~ **corredizo,** ~ **solar** (*Aut*) sunroof; **bajo** ~ under cover, indoors; **tenis bajo** ~ indoor tennis; **sin** ~ *casa* roofless; *persona* homeless. (**b**) (*Aer*) ceiling. (**c**) (*fig*) limit, ceiling, upper limit; peak; (*Fin*) ceiling; **ha tocado** ~ it has reached its ceiling (*o* limit).

techumbre *nf* roof.

tedio *nm* (**a**) (*aburrimiento*) boredom, tedium. (**b**) (*falta de interés*) lack of interest; (*depresión*) depression; (*vaciedad*) sense of emptiness; **a mí no me produce sino** ~ it just depresses me.

tedioso *adj* boring, tedious; wearisome; depressing.

tefe *nm* (**a**) (*And*) (*cuero*) strip of leather, (*tela*) strip of cloth. (**b**) (*And*: *cicatriz*) scar on the face.

tegumento *nm* tegument.

Teherán *nm* Teheran.

tehuacán *nm* (*Méx*) mineral water.

Teide *nm*: **el (Pico de)** ~ Teide, Teyde.

teísmo *nm* theism.

teísta 1 *adj* theistic. **2** *nmf* theist.

teja[1] *nf* tile; **por fin le cayó la** ~ (*Cono Sur*) finally the penny dropped; **pagar a toca** ~ to pay cash; to pay on the nail; **de** ~**s abajo** in this world, in the natural way of things; **de** ~**s arriba** in the next world; up aloft; with God's help.

teja[2] *nf* (*Bot*) lime (tree).

tejadillo *nm* top, cover.

tejado *nm* roof, tiled roof; (*fig*) housetop; **tiene el** ~ **de vidrio** he himself is open to the same charge, he lives in a glass house and should not throw stones.

tejamaní *nm*, **tejamanil** *nm* (*LAm*) roofing board, shingle.

tejano, -a 1 *adj, nm/f* Texan. **2** **tejanos** *nmpl* (*vaqueros*) jeans.

tejar [1a] *vt* to tile, roof with tiles.

Tejas *nm* Texas.

tejaván *nm* (*LAm*) shed; (*cobertizo*) corridor; (*galería*) gallery; (*choza*) rustic dwelling.

tejavana *nf* (*cobertizo*) shed; (*tejado*) shed roof, plain tile roof.

tejedor(a) *nm/f* (**a**) (*artesano*) weaver. (**b**) (*And, Cono Sur*: *intrigante*) intriguer, meddler.

tejedura *nf* (**a**) (*acto*) weaving. (**b**) (*textura*) weave, texture.

tejeduría *nf* (**a**) (*arte*) (art of) weaving. (**b**) (*fábrica*) textile mill.

tejemaneje* *nm* (**a**) (*actividad*) bustle; (*jaleo*) fuss, to-do*; **se trae un tremendo** ~ **con sus papeles** he's making a tremendous to-do with his papers*, he's getting all worked up with his papers.

(**b**) (*intriga*) intrigue, shady business.

tejer [2a] **1** *vt* (**a**) (*Cos*) to weave; to make; *telaraña* to make, spin; *capullo* to spin; (*esp LAm*: *tricotar*) to knit; (*coser*) to sew; (*hacer de ganchillo*) to crochet.

(**b**) (*fig*) *complot* to weave; *cambio etc* to bring about little by little; *escándalo, mentira etc* to fabricate.

2 *vi*: ~ **y destejer** to chop and change, blow hot and cold.

tejerazo *nm*: **el** ~ the coup attempted by Col. Tejero on 23 February 1981.

tejeringo *nm* (*prov*) fritter.

tejido *nm* (**a**) (*tela*) weave, woven material; web; fabric; ~**s** textiles; ~ **de punto** knitting; knitted fabric; **un** ~ **de intrigas** a web of intrigue. (**b**) (*textura*) weave, texture. (**c**) (*Anat*) tissue; ~ **conjuntivo** connective tissue.

tejo[1] *nm* (**a**) (*aro*) ring, quoit; **echar los** ~**s** (*fig*) to set one's cap at somebody, make a play for somebody. (**b**) (*juego*) hopscotch. (**c**) (*Esp**) 5 peseta piece.

tejo[2] *nm* (*Bot*) yew (tree).

tejoleta *nf* bit of tile, shard; brickbat.

tejón *nm* badger.

tejudo *nm* label (*on spine of book*).

tel. *abr de* **teléfono** telephone, Tel.

tela *nf* (**a**) (*gen*) cloth, fabric, material; ~ **de cebolla** onion skin; ~**s del corazón** (*fig*) heartstrings; ~ **cruzada** twill; ~ **metálica** wire netting; ~ **mosquitera** mosquito net(ting); ~ **de saco** sackcloth; **en** ~ (*Tip*) clothbound.

(**b**) (*LAm Arte*) painting.

(**c**) (*Ent etc*) web; ~ **de araña** spider's web, cobweb.

(**d**) (*en líquido*) skin, film.

(**e**) (*Bot*) skin.

(**f**) (*Fin*‡) dough‡, money; **sacudir** (*o* **soltar**) **la** ~ to cough up*.

(**g**) (*fig*: *materia*) subject, matter; **hay ~ que cortar, hay ~ para rato** there's plenty of material, there's lots to talk about; it's a long job; it's a tricky business; **el asunto trae mucha ~** it's a complicated matter; **hay ~ de eso*** there's lots of that; **tiene ~*** there's a lot to it.

(**h**) **poner algo en ~ de juicio** to question, call in question, cast doubt on.

(**i**) (*And*: *tortilla*) thin maize pancake.

telabrejos *nmpl* (*LAm*) things, gear, odds and ends.
telanda* *nf* brass*, money.
telar *nm* (**a**) loom; **~es** (*fig*) textile mill. (**b**) (*Teat*) gridiron.
telaraña *nf* spider's web, cobweb.
tele* *nf* telly*; **salir en** (*o* **por**) **la ~** to be on telly*, be on the box*.
tele... *pref* tele...
teleadicto, -a* *nm/f* telly-addict*.
telealarma *nf* alarm (system).
telebaby *nm, pl* **telebabys** cable-car.
telebanco *nm* cash-dispenser.
telebrejos *nmpl* (*Méx*) = **telabrejos.**
telecabina *nf* cable-car.
telecámara *nf* television camera.
telecargar [1h] *vt* (*Inform*) to download.
telecomando *nm* remote control.
telecomedia *nf* television comedy show.
telecomunicación *nf* telecommunication.
teleconferencia *nf* teleconference; teleconferencing.
telecontrol *nm* remote control.
telecopia *nf* fax system; fax message.
telecopiadora *nf* fax copier.
telediario *nm* television news-bulletin.
teledifusión *nf* telecast.
teledirigido *adj* remote-controlled, radio-controlled.
telef. *abr de* **teléfono** telephone, Tel.
telefacsímil *nm*, **telefax** *nm* fax system; fax message.
teleférico *nm* ski lift; cable railway, cableway.
telefilm *nm, pl* **telefilms, telefilme** *nm* telefilm.
telefonazo *nm* telephone call; **te daré un ~** I'll give you a ring, I'll call you up.
telefonear [1a] *vti* to telephone.
telefonema *nm* telephone message.
telefonía *nf* telephony.
Telefónica *nf*: **la ~** *Spanish national telephone company.*
telefónicamente *adv* by telephone; **fue amenazado ~** he received threats by telephone.
telefónico *adj* telephonic; telephone (*atr*).
telefonillo *nm* portable telephone.
telefonista *nmf* (telephone) operator, telephonist.
teléfono *nm* telephone, phone; (*número*) telephone number; **~ árabe*** bush telegraph*, grapevine*; **~ de la esperanza** helpline; **~ sin hilos, ~ inalámbrico, ~ móvil** cordless telephone, mobile phone; **~ interior** house phone, interphone; **~ móvil de coche** car-phone; **~ rojo** hot line; **~ de socorro** (*Aut*) emergency telephone; **está hablando por ~** he's on the phone; **llamar a uno al** (*o* **por**) **~** to telephone sb, phone sb, ring sb up, call sb (up); **te llaman al ~** you're wanted on the phone.
telefoto(grafía) *nf* telephoto.
telefotográfico *adj* telephoto (*atr*).
telegenia *nf* telegenic quality.
telegénico *adj* telegenic.
telegrafía *nf* telegraphy.
telegrafiar [1c] *vti* to telegraph.
telegráfico *adj* telegraphic; telegraph (*atr*).
telegrafista *nmf* telegraphist.
telégrafo *nm* telegraph; **~ óptico** semaphore.
telegrama *nm* telegram; **poner un ~ a uno** to send sb a telegram.
teleimpresor *nm*, **teleimpresora** *nf* teleprinter.
teleinformático *adj* telematic.
telele *nm* fainting fit, queer turn; **le dio un ~** he came over queer.
telemandado *adj* remote-controlled.
telemando *nm* remote control.
telemática *nf* data transmission, telematics.
telemático *adj* telematic.
telemedida *nf* telemetry.
telemedir [3k] *vt* (*Inform*) to telemeter.
telémetro *nm* rangefinder.
telengues *nmpl* (*CAm*) things, gear, odds and ends.
telenovela *nf* television serial, soap-opera.
telenque *adj* (*Cono Sur*) weak, feeble.
teleobjetivo *nm* telephoto lens, zoom-lens.
teleología *nf* teleology.
telépata *nmf* telepathist.
telepate *nm* (*CAm*) bedbug.
telepáticamente *adv* telepathically.
telepático *adj* telepathic.
teleproceso *nm* teleprocessing.
telequinesia *nf* telekinesis.
telerregulación *nf* adjustment by remote control.
telescopar [1a] **1** *vt* to telescope. **2 telescoparse** *vr* to telescope.
telescópico *adj* telescopic.
telescopio *nm* telescope.
teleserie *nf* television serial, soap-opera.
telesilla *nm* ski lift, chair lift.
telespectador(a) *nm/f* viewer.
telesquí *nm* ski lift.
teletex *nm*, **teletexto** *nm* teletext.
teletipista *nmf* teletypist, teleprinter operator.
teletipo *nm* teletype, teleprinter.
teletratamiento *nm* teleprocessing.
teletubo *nm* cathode-ray tube, television tube.
televidente *nmf* viewer, televiewer.
televisar [1a] *vt* to televise.
televisión *nf* television; **~ por cable** cable television; **~ en color(es)** colour television; **~ comercial** commercial television; **~ matinal** breakfast television; **~ pagada** pay-television, pay-TV; **~ por satélite** satellite television; **hacer ~** to be doing television, be working in television, be engaged in television work; **mirar la ~** to watch television; **salir en** (*o* **por**) **la ~** to be on television.
televisivo 1 (**a**) *adj* television (*atr*); **serie televisiva** television serial (*o* series). (**b**) (*de interés ~*) televisual; *persona* telegenic. **2** *nm*, **televisiva** *nf* television personality.
televisor *nm* television set.
televisual *adj* television (*atr*).
télex *nm invar* telex.
telón *nm* (*Teat*) curtain; **~ de acero** (*Pol*) iron curtain; **~ de boca** front curtain; **~ de fondo, ~ de foro** backcloth, backdrop; **~ metálico** fire-curtain; **~ de seguridad** safety curtain.
telonero *nm* (*Teat*) first turn, curtain-raiser; (*Mús*) support band, support act.
telúrico *adj* of the earth, telluric; (*fig*) earthy; **tendencias telúricas** back-to-nature tendencies.
tema 1 *nm* (**a**) theme; subject, topic; (*Mús*) theme, motif; (*Arte*) subject; **~ de actualidad** current issue; **~s de actualidad** current affairs; **~s verdes** green issues; **el ~ de su discurso** the theme (*o* subject) of his speech; **es un tema muy manoseado** it's a subject which has often been discussed; **pasar del ~*** to dodge the issue; **las autoridades tienen ~ de meditación** the authorities have food for thought, the authorities have sth to think about; **tienen tema para un rato** they have plenty to talk about.

(**b**) (*Ling*) stem.

2 *nf* (**a**) (*idea fija*) fixed idea, mania, obsession; **tener ~** to be stubborn. (**b**) (*inquina*) ill will, unreasoning hostility; **tener ~ a uno** to have a grudge against sb.
temar [1a] *vi* (*Cono Sur*) (**a**) (*tener idea fija*) to have a mania, be obsessed. (**b**) (*tener inquina*) to bear ill will; **~ con uno** to have a grudge against sb.
temario *nm* (*temas*) set of themes, collection of subjects; (*programa*) programme; (*oposiciones*) topics to be examined; (*asignaturas, etc*) curriculum; (*de junta*) agenda, subjects for discussion.
temascal *nm* (*CAm, Méx*) bathroom; (*fig*) hot place, oven.
temática *nf* (collection of) themes, subjects; range of topics.
temático *adj* (**a**) (*gen*) thematic. (**b**) (*Ling*) stem (*atr*). (**c**) (*And*: *poco prudente*) injudicious, tasteless.
tembladera *nf* (**a**) (*****) violent shaking; trembling fit. (**b**) (*LAm*) = **tembladeral.**
tembladeral *nm* (*Cono Sur, Méx*) quagmire.
temblar [1j] *vi* (**a**) (*persona*: *de miedo*) to tremble, shake; (*de frío*) to shiver; (*edificio etc*) to shake, quiver, shudder; **~ de frío** to shiver with cold; **~ de miedo** to tremble with fright; **~ ante una escena** to shudder at a sight; **~ como un azogado** to shake like a leaf, tremble all over; **dejar una botella temblando*** to use most of a bottle, make a bottle look pretty silly.

(**b**) (*fig*) to tremble; **tiemblo de pensar en lo que pueda ocurrir** I tremble (*o* shudder) to think what may happen; **~ por su vida** to fear for one's life.
tembleque* *nm* (**a**) violent shaking, shaking fit; **le entró un ~** he began to shake violently, he got the shakes. (**b**)

(*LAm*: *persona*) weakling.
temblequeante *adj andar* doddery, wobbly, tottering; *voz* quivering, tremulous.
temblequear* [1a] *vi* to shake violently, be all of a quiver; to wobble.
temblequera *nf* (**a**) shaking; wobbling. (**b**) (*And, Carib*) (*miedo*) fear; (*temblor*) trembling.
temblón 1 *adj* trembling, shaking; tremulous; **álamo ~** = **2**. **2** *nm* aspen.
temblor (**a**) *nm* trembling, shaking; shiver, shivering, shudder, shuddering; **le entró un ~ violento** he began to shake violently. (**b**) (*LAm*: *t* **~ de tierra**) earthquake.
tembloroso *adj* trembling, tremulous; quivering; shivering; **con voz temblorosa** in a shaky voice, in a tremulous tone; **~ de sugerencias** alive with suggestions, bursting with suggestions.
tembo *adj* (*And*) featherbrained, stupid.
temer [2a] **1** *vt* (**a**) to fear, be afraid of; to dread; to go in awe of; **~** + *infin* to fear to + *infin*; **~ a Dios** to fear God.
(**b**) (*fig*) **temo que lo ha perdido** I'm afraid he has lost it, I fear he has lost it; **teme que no vaya a volver** she's afraid he won't come back.
2 *vi* to be afraid; **no temas** don't be afraid, (*fig*) don't worry; **~ por la seguridad de uno** to fear for sb's safety.
3 temerse *vr* = **1** (**b**).
temerariamente *adv* rashly, recklessly; hastily.
temerario *adj acto, persona* rash, reckless; *juicio etc* hasty, rash.
temeridad *nf* (**a**) (*cualidad*) rashness, recklessness; hastiness. (**b**) (*acto*) rash act, folly.
temerón 1 *adj* bullying, ranting, loud-mouthed. **2** *nm* bully, ranter.
temerosamente *adv* timidly, fearfully.
temeroso *adj* (**a**) (*tímido*) timid; (*miedoso*) fearful, frightened. (**b**) **~ de Dios** God-fearing, full of the fear of God. (**c**) (*espantoso*) dread, frightful.
temible *adj* fearsome, dread, frightful; *adversario etc* redoubtable.
temor *nm* (*miedo*) fear, dread; (*recelo*) suspicion, mistrust; **~ a** fear of; **~ de Dios** fear of God; **por ~** from fear; **por ~ a** for fear of; **sin ~ a** fearless of; regardless of.
témpano *nm* (**a**) (*t* **~ de hielo**) ice floe; **quedarse como un ~** * to be chilled to the marrow.
(**b**) (*Mús*: *tamboril*) small drum, kettledrum.
(**c**) (*Mús*: *parche*) drumhead.
(**d**) (*Arquit*) tympan.
(**e**) **~ de tocino** (*Culin*) flitch of bacon.
temperadero *nm* (*LAm*) summer resort.
temperado *adj* (*And*) = **templado.**
temperamental *adj* (**a**) temperamental. (**b**) (*: *fuerte*) vigorous, forceful, strong.
temperamento *nm* (**a**) (*naturaleza*) temperament, nature, disposition.
(**b**) (*constitución*) constitution.
(**c**) (*genio*) temperament; **tener ~** to have a temperament, be temperamental.
(**d**) (*Pol etc*) compromise.
(**e**) (*LAm*) (*clima*) climate, weather; (*verano*) summer; **ir de ~** to spend a (summer) holiday .
temperancia *nf* temperance, moderation.
temperante (*LAm*) **1** *adj* teetotal. **2** *nmf* teetotaller, abstainer.
temperar [1a] **1** *vt* (*moderar*) to temper, moderate; (*calmar*) to calm; (*aliviar*) to relieve. **2** *vi* (*And, Carib*: *veranear*) to spend the summer, summer; (*cambiar de aires*) to have a change of air.
temperatura *nf* temperature; **a ~ (de) ambiente** at room temperature.
temperie *nf* (state of the) weather.
tempestad *nf* storm (*t fig*); **~ de arena** sandstorm; **~ de nieve** snowstorm; **~ de polvo** dust-storm; **~ en un vaso de agua** storm in a teacup; **levantar una ~ de protestas** to cause a storm of protests.
tempestivo *adj* timely.
tempestuoso *adj* stormy (*t fig*).
templado 1 *adj* (**a**) (*moderado*) moderate, restrained; (*en comer*) frugal; (*en beber*) of sober habits, abstemious.
(**b**) (*algo caliente*) (pleasantly) warm; *agua* lukewarm; *clima* mild, temperate; (*Geog*) *zona* temperate.
(**c**) (*Mús*) in tune, well-tuned.
(**d**) (*) (*franco*) bold, forthright; (*valiente*) courageous.
(**e**) (*: *listo*) *niño* bright, lively; (*CAm, Méx*: *hábil*) able, competent.
(**f**) (*And*: *severo*) severe.
(**g**) (*And, Carib**: *borracho*) tipsy.
(**h**) **estar ~** (*And, Cono Sur*) to be in love.
2 *nm* (*Téc*) tempering, hardening.
templanza *nf* (**a**) *cualidad* moderation, restraint; frugality; abstemiousness. (**b**) (*Met*) mildness.
templar [1a] **1** *vt* (**a**) (*gen*) to temper; to moderate, soften; *ira* to restrain, control; *clima* to make mild; *calor* to reduce; *solución* to dilute.
(**b**) *agua, cuarto* to warm up (slightly).
(**c**) (*Mús*) to tune (up).
(**d**) (*Mec*) to adjust; *tornillo etc* to tighten up; *resorte etc* to set properly.
(**e**) *acero* to temper, harden.
(**f**) (*Arte*) *colores* to blend.
(**g**) (*And*: *derribar*) to knock down; (*CAm*) (*golpear*) to hit; (*pegar*) to beat; (*And*‡: *matar*) to kill, bump off‡.
(**h**) (*Carib***) to screw**, fuck**.
2 *vi* (**a**) (*frío etc*) to moderate.
(**b**) (*Carib*: *huir*) to flee.
3 templarse *vr* (**a**) (*persona*) to be moderate, be restrained, act with restraint; **~ en la comida** to eat frugally.
(**b**) (*agua*) to warm up, get warm.
(**c**) (*And, CAm*‡: *morir*) to die, kick the bucket‡.
(**d**) (*Carib*: *huir*) to flee; **templárselas** (*Carib, Méx*: *huir*) to flee.
(**e**) (*And, Carib*: *emborracharse*) to get drunk.
(**f**) (*Cono Sur*: *enamorarse*) to fall in love.
(**g**) (*Cono Sur*: *excederse*) to go too far, overstep the mark.
(**h**) **templárselas** (*And*) to stand firm.
templario *nm* Templar.
temple *nm* (**a**) (*Téc*) temper; tempering.
(**b**) (*Mús*) tuning.
(**c**) (*Met*) state of the weather, temperature.
(**d**) (*humor*) mood; **estar de mal ~** to be in a bad mood.
(**e**) (*espíritu*) spirit, temper, mettle; (*LAm*: *valentía*) courage, boldness.
(**f**) (*pintura*) distemper; (*Arte*) tempera; **pintar al ~** to distemper; (*Arte*) to paint in tempera.
(**g**) (*LAm**: *enamoramiento*) infatuation.
templete *nm* (**a**) (*quiosco*) pavilion; kiosk; **~ de música** bandstand.
(**b**) (*Rel*: *templo*) small temple; (*santuario*) shrine; (*nicho*) niche.
templo *nm* (*masónico, pagano, fig*) temple; (*Ecl*) church, chapel; **~ metodista** Methodist chapel; **~ protestante** Protestant church; **como un ~** (*esp LAm*) (*grande*) huge, tremendous; (*excelente*) first-rate, excellent.
tempo *nm* tempo (*t fig*).
temporada *nf* time, period, spell; (*Met*) spell; (*del año, social, Dep etc*) season; **~ alta** high season; **~ baja** low season; **~ de fútbol** football season; **~ de ópera** opera season; **~ de exámenes** examination period; **~ de lluvias** rainy spell; rainy season; **en plena ~** at the height of the season; **por ~s** on and off; **estar fuera de ~** to be out of season.
temporadista *nmf* (*Carib*) holiday-maker.
temporal 1 *adj* (**a**) temporary; *trabajador* temporary, casual; seasonal.
(**b**) (*Ecl etc*) temporal; **poder ~** temporal power.
2 *nm* (**a**) (*tormenta*) storm; (*período de lluvia*) rainy weather, spell of rough weather; **capear el ~** (*t fig*) to weather the storm, ride out the storm.
(**b**) (*Carib*: *persona*) shady character.
temporalmente *adv* temporarily.
temporáneo *adj* temporary.
temporario *adj* (*LAm*) temporary.
témporas *nfpl* ember days.
temporero 1 *adj obrero* temporary, casual. **2** *nm*, **temporera** *nf* casual worker.
temporizador 1 *adj*: **mecanismo ~** = **2**. **2** *nm* timing device, timer.
temporizar [1f] *vi* to temporize.
tempozonte *adj* (*Méx*) hunchbacked.
tempranal *adj planta, tierra etc* early.
tempranear [1a] *vi* (**a**) (*LAm*: *madrugar*) to get up early. (**b**) (*Cono Sur Agr*) to sow early.
tempranero *adj* (**a**) (*Bot*) early. (**b**) *persona* early, early-rising.
temprano 1 *adj* (**a**) *fruta etc* early.
(**b**) *años* youthful; *obra, período etc* early.
2 *adv* (*gen*) early; (*demasiado ~*) too early, too soon; **lo más ~ posible** as soon as possible.

tenacidad *nf* (*V adj*) (**a**) toughness. (**b**) tenacity. (**c**) ingrained nature; persistence; stubbornness.
tenacillas *nfpl* (*para azúcar*) sugar tongs; (*para pelo*) curling tongs; (*Med etc*) tweezers, forceps; (*para velas*) snuffers.
tenamaste 1 *adj* (*CAm, Méx*) stubborn. **2** *nm* (**a**) (*CAm, Méx*: *piedra*) cooking stone. (**b**) (*CAm*) = **cachivache**.
tenaz *adj* (**a**) *materia* tough, durable, resistant.
(**b**) *persona* tenacious.
(**c**) *mancha etc* hard to remove, that sticks fast; *suciedad* ingrained; *dolor* persistent; *creencia, resistencia etc* stubborn.
tenaza *nf* (**a**) (*Bridge*) squeeze (*a* in). (**b**) **~s** (*Téc*) pliers, pincers; tongs; (*Med*) forceps; **unas ~s** a pair of pliers (*etc*); **avance en ~** pincer movement.
tenazmente *adv* tenaciously; stubbornly.
tenazón: a ~, de ~ *adv* suddenly; *disparar* without taking aim.
tenca[1] *nf* (*pez*) tench.
tenca[2] *nf* (*Cono Sur*) lie, swindle.
tencal *nm* (*Méx*) wicker box, wicker poultry cage.
tencha* *nf* (*CAm*) prison.
tendajo *nm* = **tendejón**.
tendal *nm* (**a**) (*toldo*) awning.
(**b**) (*Agr*) sheet spread to catch olives (*when shaken from the tree*).
(**c**) (*LAm*) (*montón*) heap, lot, abundance; (*objetos etc desparramados*) lot of scattered objects (*o* bodies *etc*); (*desorden*) confusion, disorder; **un ~ de** a lot of, a whole heap of.
(**d**) (*Cono Sur Agr*) shearing shed; (*And, Carib*: *fábrica*) brickworks, tileworks; (*And, CAm*) sunny place for drying coffee.
(**e**) (*And*: *campo*) flat open field.
tendalada *nf* (*LAm*) = **tendal**.
tendalera *nf* mess, litter (of scattered objects).
tendear [1a] *vi* (*Méx*) to go window-shopping.
tendedera *nf* (**a**) (*CAm, Carib, Méx*: *cuerda*) clothes-line. (**b**) (*And*) = **tendal**.
tendedero *nm* (*lugar*) drying place; (*cuerda*) clothes-line, frame for drying clothes.
tendejón *nm* small shop; stall, booth.
tendencia *nf* tendency; trend; inclination; **~ imperante** dominant trend, prevailing tendency; **~ del mercado** (*Fin*) run of the market, price movement; **la ~ hacia el socialismo** the tendency (*o* trend) towards socialism; **una palabra con ~ a quedarse arcaica** a word tending to become archaic; **tener ~ a** + *infin* to have a tendency to + *infin*, tend to + *infin*, be inclined to + *infin*; **tener ~s de zurdo** to have a tendency towards left-handedness.
tendenciosidad *nf* tendentiousness.
tendencioso *adj* tendentious.
tendente *adj*: **una medida ~ a** + *infin* a measure tending to + *infin*; a measure designed to + *infin*.
ténder *nm* (*Ferro*) tender.
tender [2g] **1** *vt* (**a**) (*estirar*) to stretch; (*extender, desplegar*) to spread, spread out, extend, lay out; *pintura etc* to put on, apply; *mantel* to lay, spread; **tendieron el cadáver sobre el suelo** they stretched the corpse out on the floor.
(**b**) *ropa lavada* to hang out; *cuerda etc* to stretch (*a* to, *de* from), hang (*de* from); *mano* to stretch out, reach out; *ferrocarril, puente* to build; *cable, vía* to lay.
(**c**) *arco* to draw; *trampa* to set (*a* for).
(**d**) (*LAm*) **~ la cama** to make the bed; **~ la mesa** to lay the table.
2 *vi*: **~ a** to tend to, tend towards, have a tendency towards; **~ a** + *infin* to tend to + *infin*; **las plantas tienden a la luz** plants grow (*o* turn) towards the light; **el color tiende a verde** the colour tends towards green; **ella tiende al pesimismo** she has a tendency to be pessimistic.
3 tenderse *vr* (**a**) (*echarse*) to lie down, stretch (o.s.) out.
(**b**) (*fig*) to let o.s. go; to give up, let things go, stop bothering.
(**c**) (*caballo*) to run at full gallop.
(**d**) (*Naipes*) to lay down.
tenderete *nm* (**a**) (*para ropa lavada*) = **tendedero**. (**b**) (*puesto de mercado*) stall, market booth; (*carretón*) barrow. (**c**) (*Com*: *géneros*) display of goods for sale (*etc*); (*fig*) litter (of objects), mess.
tendero, -a *nm/f* shopkeeper, (*esp*) grocer.
tendida *nf* (*Cono Sur*: *de caballo*) shy, start.
tendido 1 *adj* (**a**) (*tumbado*) lying down; (*llano*) flat.
(**b**) *galope* fast, flat out.
2 *nm* (**a**) (*Arquit*) coat of plaster.
(**b**) (*ropa lavada*: *t* **~s**) washing, clothes (hung out to dry).
(**c**) (*Taur*) front rows of seats.
(**d**) (*de cable, vía*) laying; (*cables*) wires.
(**e**) (*Culin*) batch of loaves.
(**f**) (*And, Méx*: *ropa de cama*) bedclothes.
(**g**) (*CAm, Carib*: *cuerda*) long tether, rope.
(**h**) (*And, Méx*: *puesto de mercado*) stall, booth.
tendinoso *adj* sinewy.
tendón *nm* tendon, sinew; **~ de Aquiles** Achilles' tendon.
tendré *etc V* **tener**.
tenducho *nm* poky little shop.
tenebrosidad *nf* (*V adj*) (**a**) darkness; gloom(iness). (**b**) (*fig*) gloominess, dimness, blackness. (**c**) (*fig*) sinister nature, shadiness. (**d**) (*fig*) obscurity.
tenebroso *adj* (**a**) (*oscuro*) dark; (*sombrío*) gloomy, dismal. (**b**) (*fig*) *perspectiva etc* gloomy, dim, black. (**c**) (*pey*) *complot etc* sinister, dark; *pasado etc* shady. (**d**) (*fig*) *estilo etc* obscure.
tenedor 1 *nm* (**a**) (*Culin*) fork. (**b**) **restaurante de 5 ~es** ≃ five-star restaurant, top-class restaurant.
2 *nm*, **tenedora** *nf* (*Com, Fin etc*) holder, bearer; **~ de acciones** shareholder; **~ de libros** book-keeper; **~ de obligaciones** bondholder; **~ de póliza** policyholder.
teneduría *nf*: **~ de libros** book-keeping.
tenencia *nf* (**a**) (*de casa, apartamento etc*) tenancy, occupancy; (*de puesto*) tenure; (*de propiedad*) possession; **~ ilícita de armas** illegal possession of weapons.
(**b**) (*oficio*) deputyship; **~ de alcaldía** post of deputy mayor.
(**c**) (*Mil*) lieutenancy.
tener [2k] **1** *vt* (**a**) (*gen*) to have; to have got; to possess; **~ ojos azules** to have blue eyes; **hemos tenido muchas dificultades** we have had a lot of difficulties; **hoy no tenemos clase** we have no class today, we are not having a class today; **¿tienes una pluma?** have you got a pen?; **¿tiene Vd permiso para esto?** do you have permission for this?, have you (got) permission for this?; **va a ~ un niño** she's going to have a baby; **tiene un tío en Venezuela** he has an uncle in Venezuela; **tiene muchas preocupaciones encima** he has a lot of worries, he is burdened with anxieties; **el cargo tiene una buena retribución** the post carries a good salary; **de bueno no tiene nada** there's nothing good about it; **ya saben dónde me tienen** you always know where you can find me; *V* **particular, suerte** *etc*.
(**b**) (*locuciones con ciertos n*) **~ 7 años** to be 7, be 7 years old; **~ hambre** to be hungry; **~ mucha sed** to be very thirsty; **~ calor** to be hot; **~ mucho frío** to be very cold; *para más detalles, V* **celos, cuidado, ganas, miedo** *etc*.
(**c**) (*medidas*) **~ 5 cm de ancho** to be 5 cm wide; *V* **ancho, largo** *etc*.
(**d**) *objeto* to hold; (*agarrar*) to hold on to, hold up, grasp; (*llevar*) to carry, bear; **ten esto** take this, hold on to this; **¡ten!, ¡tenga!** here you are!; catch!; **lo tenía en la mano** he was holding it in his hand; he was carrying it in his hand; **los dos que tenían la bandera** the two who were carrying the flag.
(**e**) (*recipiente*) to hold, contain; **una caja para ~ el dinero** a box to hold the money, a box to keep (*o* put) the money in.
(**f**) *promesa* to keep.
(**g**) (*sentimiento*) to have, profess (*a* for); **~ gran admiración a uno** to have (a) great admiration for sb; **le tengo mucho cariño** I'm very fond of him; *V* **cariño** *etc*.
(**h**) (*pensar, considerar*) to think, consider, deem; **~ a bien** + *infin* to see fit to + *infin*, deign to + *infin*; to think it proper to + *infin*; **~ a menos** + *infin* to consider it beneath o.s. to + *infin*; **~ a uno en más** to think all the more of sb; **te tendrán en más estima** they will hold you in higher esteem; **~ para sí que ...** to think that ...; **~ a uno por** + *adj* to think sb + *adj*, consider sb to be + *adj*, deem sb to be + *adj*; **no quiero que me tengan por informal** I don't want them to think me unreliable; **le tengo por poco honrado** I consider him to be rather dishonest; **lo tienen por cosa cierta** they believe it to be true; **ten por seguro que ...** rest assured that ...; *V* **más, mucho** *etc*; *V* **gala, honra** *etc*.
(**i**) (+ *adj*) **procura ~ contentos a todos** he tries to keep everybody happy; **me tiene perplejo la falta de noticias** the lack of news perplexes me, I am bewildered by the absence of news; *V* **cuidado, frito** *etc*.

(j) (+ *infin*) **no tengo nada que deciros** I have nothing to tell you; **tengo trabajo que hacer** I have work to do.

(k) ~ **que** + *infin* to have to + *infin*, must + *infin*; **tengo que comprarlo** I have to buy it; **tenemos que marcharnos** we have to leave, we must go; **así tiene que ser** it has to be this way; **¡tú tenías que ser!** it would be you!, it had to be you!

(l) (+ *ptp*) **tenemos alquilado un piso** we have rented a flat; **tenía el sombrero puesto** he had his hat on; **te lo tengo dicho muchas veces** I've told you hundreds of times; **yo no le tengo visto** I've never set eyes on him; **nos tenían preparada una sorpresa** they had prepared a surprise for us; **teníamos andados unos 10 kilómetros** we had walked (*o* covered) some 10 kilometres.

(m) (*locuciones*) **¿qué tienes?** what's the matter with you?; **¿(conque) ésas tenemos?** so that's it!; so that's the game, is it?; here we go again!; **no ~las todas consigo** to be worried, feel uneasy; **no las tengo todas conmigo de que lo haga** I'm none too sure that he'll do it; **quien tuvo retuvo** it's gone for good, I've said goodbye to that; **ten con ten** (*como n*) good sense, tact; ability to find a middle way; ~ **todas las de ganar** to hold all the winning cards, look like a winner; ~ **todas las de perder** to be fighting a losing battle, look like losing.

(n) (*LAm*) **tengo 4 años aquí** I've been here for 4 years; **tenía 5 años sin verlo** I hadn't seen him for 5 years; **tienen 3 meses de no cobrar** they haven't been paid for 3 months, it's 3 months since they've been paid; **este cadáver tiene un mes de muerto** this corpse has been dead for a month; **¿cuánto tiempo tiene manejando este coche?** (*Méx*) how long have you been driving this car?

(o) **~lo** (******: *eyacular*) to come ******.

2 tenerse *vr* (a) (*estar de pie*) to stand, stand up; **la muñeca se tiene de pie** the doll stands up; ~ **firme** to stand upright; (*fig*) to stand firm; **no poder** ~ (*cansado*) to be all in, be tired out; (*borracho*) to be incapable (with drink).

(b) ~ **sobre algo** to lean on sth, support o.s. on sth.

(c) (*fig*: *dominarse*) to control o.s.; to stop in time.

(d) ~ **por** to consider o.s. to be, think o.s.; **se tiene por muy listo** he thinks himself very clever; ~ **en mucho** to have a high opinion of o.s.; (*fig*) to be dignified; to be incapable of a mean action.

teneraje *nm* (*LAm*) calves.

tenería *nf* tannery.

Tenerife *nm* Tenerife.

tenga, tengo *etc V* **tener.**

tenguerengue‡ *nm* (*Carib*) hovel.

tenia *nf* tapeworm.

tenida *nf* (a) (*LAm*) (*reunión*) meeting, session; (*de masones*) meeting of a masonic lodge. (b) (*Cono Sur*: *vestido*) suit, dress; (*Mil*) uniform; ~ **de gala,** ~ **de noche** evening dress; ~ **de luto** mourning.

tenienta *nf* (woman) lieutenant; (*Hist*) lieutenant's wife.

teniente 1 *nm* lieutenant; (*ayudante*) deputy; ~ **de alcalde** deputy mayor; ~ **coronel** lieutenant-colonel; ~ **fiscal** assistant prosecutor; ~ **general** lieutenant-general; ~ **de navío** lieutenant. **2** *adj*: **estar ~‡** to be deaf.

tenis *nm* (a) (*juego*) tennis; ~ **de mesa** table-tennis. (b) (*pl*: *zapatos*) tennis-shoes; **colgar los ~‡** to peg out‡. (c) (*construcción*) set of tennis-courts.

tenista *nmf* tennis-player.

tenístico *adj* tennis (*atr*).

tenor[1] *nm* (*Mús*) tenor.

tenor[2] *nm* tenor; meaning, sense, purport; **el ~ de esta declaración** the sense of this statement, the tenor of this declaration; **a este ~** like this, in this fashion; **a ~ de** on the lines of, like; (*Com*) in accordance with.

tenorio *nm* ladykiller, Don Juan.

tensado *nm* tensioning; tension.

tensamente *adv* tensely.

tensar [1a] *vt* to tauten; *arco* to draw.

tensión *nf* (a) (*física*) tension, tautness; (*Mec*) stress, strain; rigidity; ~ **superficial** surface tension.

(b) (*Fís*: *de gas etc*) pressure.

(c) (*Elec*) voltage; tension; **alta** ~ high tension; **cable de alta** ~ high-tension cable.

(d) (*Anat*) ~ **arterial** blood-pressure; **tener ~*, tener la ~ alta** to have high blood-pressure; **tomarse la** ~ to have one's blood-pressure taken.

(e) (*Med*) tension; (*estrés*) strain, stress; ~ **excesiva** (over)strain; ~ **nerviosa** nervous strain; ~ **premenstrual** premenstrual tension, PMT.

(f) (*fig*) tension, tenseness; ~ **racial** racial tension; **la ~ de la situación política** the tenseness of the political situation.

tensionado *adj* tense, in a state of tension.

tensional *adj* tense, full of tension.

tensionar [1a] *vt* (a) to tense, tauten. (b) (*fig*) *adversario* to put pressure on; *relaciones* to put a strain on.

tenso *adj* (a) (*estirado*) tense, taut.

(b) (*fig*) tense; strained; **es una situación muy tensa** it is a very tense situation; **las relaciones entre los dos están muy tensas** relations between the two are very strained.

tensor 1 *adj* tensile. **2** *nm* (*Téc*) guy, strut; (*Anat*) tensor; (*de cuello*) stiffener; (*Med*) chest-expander.

tentación *nf* (a) (*gen*) temptation; **resistir** (a) **la ~** to resist temptation; **no puedo resistir** (a) **la ~ de** + *infin* I can't resist the temptation of + *ger*; **vencer la** ~ to overcome temptation.

(b) (*****: *objeto*) tempting thing; **las gambas son mi** ~ I can't resist prawns; **¡eres mi ~!** you'll be the ruin of me!

tentáculo *nm* tentacle; feeler.

tentador 1 *adj* tempting. **2** *nm* tempter.

tentadora *nf* temptress.

tentar [1j] *vt* (a) (*tocar*) to touch, feel; (*Med*) to probe; **ir tentando el camino** to feel one's way, grope one's way along.

(b) (*probar*) to try, test, try out; (*emprender*) to undertake, venture on; ~ (a) **hacer algo** to try to do sth, attempt to do sth.

(c) (*atraer*: *t Rel*) to tempt; (*seducir*) to attract, lure, entice; **me tentó con una copita de anís** she tempted me with a glass of anise; **no me tienta nada la idea** the idea doesn't attract me at all; ~ **a uno a hacer algo** to tempt sb to do sth; **ella podría estar tentada también a probarlo** she might be tempted to try it too.

tentativa *nf* (*intento*) attempt; (*esfuerzo*) effort; (*Jur*) criminal attempt; ~ **de asesinato** attempted murder; ~ **de robo** attempted robbery; ~ **de suicidio** suicide attempt.

tentativo *adj* tentative.

tentebonete* *nm* (*puesto*) cushy job‡, plum; (*gaje*) perk*.

tentempié* *nm* snack, bite.

tenue *adj* (a) *palo etc* thin, slim, slender; *alambre* fine.

(b) (*fig*) tenuous; insubstantial, slight; *aire, olor* thin; *neblina* light; *línea* faint; *sonido* faint, weak; *relación etc* slight, tenuous; *estilo* simple.

tenuidad *nf* (*V adj*) (a) thinness, slimness, slenderness; fineness.

(b) tenuousness; slightness; thinness; lightness; faintness; simplicity.

(c) (*una* ~) triviality.

teñir [3h *y* 3k] *vt* (a) (*con tinte*) to dye; (*colorar*) to tinge, colour; to stain; ~ **una prenda de azul** to dye a garment blue; **el jersé ha teñido los pañuelos** the jersey has come out on the handkerchiefs.

(b) (*Arte*) *color* to darken.

(c) (*fig*) to tinge (*de* with); **una poesía teñida de añoranza** a poem tinged with longing.

teocali *nm* (*Méx*) teocalli, Aztec temple.

teocracia *nf* theocracy.

teocrático *adj* theocratic.

teodolito *nm* theodolite.

teología *nf* theology; ~ **de la liberación** liberation theology.

teológico *adj* theological.

teólogo *nm* theologian.

teorema *nm* theorem.

teorético *adj* (*LAm*) theoretic(al).

teoría *nf* theory; ~ **atómica** atomic theory; ~ **cuántica,** ~ **de los cuanta** quantum theory; ~ **de la información** information theory; ~ **de la relatividad** theory of relativity; **en** ~ in theory, theoretically.

teóricamente *adv* theoretically, in theory.

teoricidad *nf* theoretical nature.

teórico 1 *adj* theoretic(al). **2** *nm*, **teórica** *nf* theorist.

teorización *nf* theorizing.

teorizante *nmf* theoretician, theorist; (*pey*) theorizer.

teorizar [1f] *vi* to theorize.

teosofía *nf* theosophy.

teosófico *adj* theosophical.

teósofo, -a *nm/f* theosophist.

tepalcate *nm* (*CAm, Méx*) (a) (*vasija*) earthenware jar; (*fragmento*) fragment of pottery, shard. (b) (*cachorro*) piece of junk.

tepalcatero, -a *nm/f* (*Méx*) potter.

tepe *nm* sod, turf, clod.

tepetate *nm* (*CAm, Méx*) (a) (*residuo*) slag. (b) (*caliza*) limestone.

tepocate *nm* (*CAm, Méx*) (a) (*guijarro*) stone, pebble. (b)

(*: *niño*) kid*.
teporocho* *adj* (*Méx*) tight*, drunk.
tequi‡ *nm* car.
tequila *nf* (*Méx*) tequila.
tequilero* *adj* (*Méx*) tight*, drunk.
tequío *nm* (*CAm, Méx*) (*molestia*) trouble; (*fardo*) burden; (*daño*) harm, damage.
tequioso *adj* (*CAm, Méx*: *V n*) burdensome; harmful; annoying, bothersome.
TER [ter] *nm abr de* **Tren Español Rápido** ≈ *inter-city high-speed train.*
terapeuta *nmf* therapist.
terapéutica *nf* therapeutics; therapy.
terapéutico *adj* therapeutic(al).
terapia *nf* therapy; ~ **aversiva,** ~ **por aversión** aversion therapy; ~ **de choque** (*fig*) shock treatment; ~ **electroconvulsiva** electroconvulsive therapy; ~ **de electrochoque** electroshock therapy; ~ **de grupo** group therapy; ~ **laboral,** ~ **ocupacional** occupational therapy, work therapy; ~ **lingüística** speech therapy; ~ **táctil** touch therapy.
tercamente *adv* obstinately, stubbornly.
tercena *nf* (**a**) (*Méx*:††) government warehouse. (**b**) (*And*: *carnicería*) butcher's (shop).
tercenista *nm* (*And*) butcher.
tercer *adj V* **tercero.**
tercera *nf* (**a**) (*Mús*) third. (**b**) (*pey*) go-between, procuress.
tercería *nf* (*arbitración*) mediation, arbitration; (*buenos oficios*) good offices; (*pey*) pimping, procuring.
tercermundismo *nm* attitudes (*o* policies *etc*) akin to those of a third-world country; backwardness, underdevelopment.
tercermundista 1 *adj* third-world (*atr*); under-developed. **2** *nm* third-world country.
tercero 1 *adj* (**tercer** *delante de nm sing*) third; **Tercer Mundo** Third World; **a la tercera va la vencida** third time lucky; **un hotel de** ~ a third-class hotel.
2 *nm* (**a**) (*árbitro*) mediator, arbitrator; (*Jur*) third person, third party; ~ **en discordia** three's a crowd.
(**b**) (*pey*) pimp, pander, procurer.
tercerola *nf* (*Carib*) shotgun.
terceto *nm* (**a**) (*Mús*) trio. (**b**) (*Liter*) tercet, triplet.
terciada *nf* (*LAm*) plywood.
terciado (**a**) **azúcar terciada** brown sugar.
(**b**) **llevar algo** ~ to wear sth diagonally (*o* across one's chest *etc*); **con el sombrero** ~ with his hat on the slant, with his hat at a rakish angle.
(**c**) **está** ~ **ya** a third of it has gone (*o* been used *etc*) already.
terciana *nf* tertian (fever).
terciar [1b] **1** *vt* (**a**) (*Mat*) to divide into three.
(**b**) (*Agr*) to plough a third time.
(**c**) (*inclinar*) to slant, slope; *faja etc* to wear (diagonally) across one's chest; *sombrero etc* to tilt, wear on the slant, put on at a rakish angle.
(**d**) (*And, Cono Sur, Méx*) to hoist on to (*o* carry on) one's shoulder.
(**e**) (*LAm*) *vino etc* to water down; (*Méx*: *mezclar*) to mix, blend.
2 *vi* (**a**) (*completar el número*) to fill in, stand in, make up the number.
(**b**) ~ **en** to take part in, join in; **yo terciaré con el jefe** I'll have a word with the boss; ~ **entre dos rivales** to mediate between two rivals.
3 terciarse *vr* (**a**) **si se tercia una buena oportunidad** if a good chance presents itself (*o* comes up); **si se tercia, él también sabe hacerlo** on occasion he knows how to do it too, in the right circumstances he can manage it too.
(**b**) **si se tercia alguna vez que yo pase por allí** if I should happen sometime to go that way.
terciario *adj* tertiary.
tercio *nm* (**a**) (*tercera parte*) third; **dos ~s** two thirds.
(**b**) (*Mil Hist*) regiment, corps; ~ **extranjero** foreign legion; ~ **de la guardia civil** division of the civil guard.
(**c**) (*Taur*) stage, part (of the bullfight).
(**d**) **hacer buen** ~ **a uno** to do a service for sb; to serve sb well, be useful to sb; **hacer mal** ~ **a uno** to do sb a bad turn; **estar mejorado en** ~ **y quinto** to come out of it very well.
(**e**) (*LAm*) pack, package, bale.
(**f**) (*Carib**: *hombre*) fellow, guy*.
terciopelo *nm* velvet.
terco *adj* (**a**) (*obstinado*) obstinate, stubborn; ~ **como una mula** as stubborn as a mule. (**b**) *material* hard, tough, hard to work. (**c**) (*And*: *duro*) harsh, unfeeling; indifferent.
Tere *nf forma familiar de* **Teresa.**
tere *adj* (*And*) *niño* weepy, tearful.
terebrante *adj dolor* sharp, piercing.
tereco *nm* (*And*) = **tereque.**
Terencio *nm* Terence.
tereque *nm* (*And, Carib*) (**a**) = **cachivache.** (**b**) **~s** things, gear*, odds and ends.
Teresa *nf* T(h)eresa.
teresiano *adj*: **las obras teresianas** the works of Saint Teresa (of Ávila).
tergiversación *nf* (**a**) (*falseamiento*) distortion, misrepresentation. (**b**) (*vacilación*) prevarication.
tergiversar [1a] **1** *vt* (*torcer*) to distort, twist (the sense of), misrepresent. **2** *vi* (*no resolverse*) to prevaricate; (*vacilar*) to chop and change, blow hot and cold.
terliz *nm* ticking.
termal *adj* thermal.
termalismo *nm* hydrotherapy, bathing at a spa.
termalista 1 *adj* spa (*atr*). **2** *nmf* person who visits a spa.
termas *nfpl* hot springs, hot baths.
termes *nm invar* termite.
termia *nf* (gas) therm.
térmica *nf* thermal, hot-air current.
térmico *adj* thermic, heat (*atr*); *cristal etc* heated; *ropa* thermal.
terminación *nf* (**a**) (*acto*) ending, termination. (**b**) (*conclusión*) ending, conclusion. (**c**) (*Ling*) ending, termination. (**d**) (*Téc*) finish, finishing.
terminacho *nm* (*de palabra*) (*fea*) ugly word; (*incorrecta*) incorrect word, malapropism, linguistic monstrosity; (*malsonante*) nasty word, rude word.
terminado *nm* (*Téc*) finish, finishing.
terminajo *nm* = **terminacho.**
terminal 1 *adj* terminal. **2** *nm* (*Elec, Inform*) terminal; ~ **de computadora,** ~ **informático** computer terminal; ~ **interactivo** interactive unit; ~ **de vídeo** video terminal. **3** *nf* (*Aer, Ferro etc*) terminal; (*LAm Ferro etc*) terminus; ~ **de carga** freight terminal; ~ **de contenedores** container terminal; ~ **de pasajeros,** ~ **de viajeros** passenger terminal.
terminante *adj* (*definitivo*) final, decisive, definitive; *decisión* final; *contestación* categorical, conclusive; *negativa* flat, forthright; *prohibición* strict.
terminantemente *adv* finally, decisively, definitively; categorically, conclusively; flatly; strictly; **queda** ~ **prohibido** + *infin* it is strictly forbidden to + *infin.*
terminar [1a] **1** *vt* to end; to conclude; to finish, complete.
2 *vi* (**a**) (*forma, objeto etc*) to end, finish; **termina en punta** it ends in a point, it comes to a point; **esto va a** ~ **en tragedia** this will end in tragedy.
(**b**) (*acabar*) to end (up), finish; to stop; (*Inform*) to quit; **al** ~ **el acto se fueron todos** at the end of the ceremony everyone went off; **¡hemos terminado!** that's an end of the matter!; ~ **de hacer algo** to finish doing sth; to stop doing sth; **cuando termine de hablar** when he finishes speaking; **terminaba de salir del baño** she had just got out of the bath; **terminó de llenar el vaso con helado** he topped (*o* filled) the glass up with ice-cream; ~ **por hacer algo** to end (up) by doing sth; **terminó marchándose enfadado** he ended up by going off in a huff, he finally went off very cross; **terminó diciendo que** ... he ended by saying that ..., he said in conclusion that ...
3 terminarse *vr* to end, come to an end, draw to a close, stop.
terminista *nmf* (*Cono Sur*) pedant.
término *nm* (**a**) (*fin*) end, finish, conclusion; **dar** ~ **a** to finish off, conclude; **llevar a** ~ to carry out; **llevar a feliz** ~ to carry through to a happy conclusion; **poner** ~ **a** to put an end to, put a stop to.
(**b**) (*de tierra etc*) boundary, limit; (*mojón*) boundary-stone.
(**c**) (*Ferro etc*) terminus.
(**d**) (*Pol*) area, district; (*Jur*) jurisdiction; ~ **municipal** township; **tiene mucho** ~ he has a big patch (to look after).
(**e**) (*Teat*) **primer** ~ downstage; **segundo** ~ middle distance; **último** ~ upstage.
(**f**) (*Mat, Filos*) term; ~ **medio** middle term; average; (*fig*) compromise, middle way; happy medium; **de** ~ **medio** average; **por** ~ **medio** on the average; **tendrán que buscar un** ~ **medio** they will have to look for a

compromise (*o* middle way); **en primer ~** firstly; primarily; **en último ~** in the last analysis; as a last resort, if there is no other way out.

(**g**) (*plazo etc*) term, time, period; **en el ~ de 10 días** within a period of 10 days.

(**h**) (*de argumento etc*) point; **invertir los ~s** to stand an argument on its head; (*fig*) to switch things round completely, turn a situation upside down.

(**i**) (*Ling*) term; **~s de intercambio** terms of trade; **según los ~s del contrato** according to the terms of the contract; **en ~s generales** generally speaking; **en ~s reales** in real terms; **en ~s sencillos** in simple terms; **en otros ~s** in other words; **en ~s de la productividad** in terms of productivity; **se expresó en ~s conciliatorios** he expressed himself in conciliatory terms.

(**j**) **estar en buenos ~s con uno** to be on good terms with sb.

terminología *nf* terminology.

terminológico *adj* terminological.

terminólogo, -a *nm/f* specialist in technical terminology.

termita *nf*, **termite** *nm* termite.

termo *nm* (*botella*) thermos (bottle, flask); (*calentador*) water-heater.

termo... *pref* thermo...

termoaislante *adj* heat-insulating.

termodinámica *nf* thermodynamics.

termodinámico *adj* thermodynamic.

termoeléctrico *adj* thermoelectric.

termoiónico *adj* thermionic.

termómetro *nm* thermometer.

termonuclear *adj* thermonuclear.

termopar *nm* thermocouple.

termopila *nf* thermopile.

Termópilas *nfpl*: **Las ~** Thermopylae.

termos *nm invar* = **termo.**

termostático *adj* thermostatic.

termostato *nm* thermostat.

termotanque *nm* (*Cono Sur*) immersion heater.

terna *nf* list of three candidates (*among whom a final choice is made*), shortlist.

ternario *adj* ternary.

terne 1 *adj* (**a**) (*fuerte*) tough, strong, husky; (*pey*) bullying. (**b**) (*terco*) stubborn; **~ que ~** out of sheer stubbornness.

2 *nm* (**a**) bully, tough*. (**b**) (*Cono Sur*) rogue.

ternejo *adj* (*And*) spirited, vigorous.

ternera *nf* (**a**) (*Agr*) calf, heifer calf. (**b**) (*Culin*) veal.

ternero *nm* calf, bull calf.

ternerón *adj* (**a**) (*: *compasivo*) soft-hearted. (**b**) (*Cono Sur, Méx*) *mozo* overgrown, big.

terneza *nf* (**a**) (*cualidad*) tenderness. (**b**) **~s** (*palabras*) nice things, endearments, tender words.

ternilla *nf* gristle, cartilage; (*CAm, Carib, Méx*) cartilage of the nose.

ternilloso *adj* gristly, cartilaginous.

terno *nm* (**a**) (*grupo de tres*) set of three, group of three; trio; (*traje*) three-piece suit; (*Carib*: *joyas*) necklace set.

(**b**) (*: *palabrota*) curse, swearword; **echar** (*o* **soltar**) **~s** to curse, swear.

ternura *nf* (**a**) (*cualidad*) tenderness; fondness; affection. (**b**) (*palabra*) endearment, tender word.

ternurismo *nm* sentimentality.

ternurista *adj* sentimental.

Terpsícore *nf* Terpsichore.

terquedad *nf* (**a**) (*obstinación*) obstinacy, stubbornness. (**b**) (*dureza*) hardness, toughness. (**c**) (*And*: *severidad*) harshness, lack of feeling; indifference.

terracota *nf* terracotta.

terrado *nm* (**a**) terrace; flat roof. (**b**) (‡: *cabeza*) bonce‡, head.

terraja *nf* diestock.

terral 1 *nm* (*LAm*) cloud of dust. **2** *adj*: **viento ~** wind from the land.

Terranova *nf* Newfoundland.

terranova *nm* Newfoundland dog.

terraplén *nm* (**a**) (*Ferro etc*) embankment; (*Agr*) terrace; (*Mil*) rampart, bank, earthwork; mound. (**b**) (*cuesta*) slope, gradient.

terraplenar [1a] *vt terreno* to (fill and) level (off); (*Agr*) to terrace; *hoyo* to fill in; (*elevar*) to bank up, raise.

terrario *nm* terrarium.

terrateniente *nmf* landowner.

terraza *nf* (**a**) (*Arquit*) (*techo*) flat roof; (*balcón*) balcony; (*terraza*) terrace. (**b**) (*Agr*) terrace. (**c**) (*Hort*) flowerbed, border, plot. (**d**) (*Culin*) two-handled glazed jar. (**e**) (*café*) pavement café. (**f**) (‡: *cabeza*) nut‡, head.

terrazo *nm* terrazzo.

terregal *nm* (*LAm*: *terrón*) clod, hard lump of earth; (*Méx*: *tierra*) loose earth, dusty soil; (*polvareda*) cloud of dust.

terremoto *nm* earthquake.

terrenal *adj* earthly, worldly.

terreno 1 *adj* terrestrial; earthly, worldly.

2 *nm* (**a**) (*gen, Geol etc*) terrain; (*tierra, suelo*) soil, earth, ground, land; (*Agr*) soil, land; **los accidentes del ~** the characteristics of the terrain, the features of the landscape; **~ abonado para el vicio** hotbed of vice, breeding-ground of vice; **en todos los ~s** in any place you care to name; **un coche para todo ~** a car for every type of surface, a car for all conditions; **sobre el ~** on the spot; **hay que fiarse del hombre sobre el ~** you have to trust the man on the spot; **resolveremos el problema sobre el ~** we will solve the problem as we go along; **ceder ~, perder ~** to give ground, lose ground (*a, ante* to); **ganar ~** to gain ground; **llegar al ~** to arrive on the scene, get to the spot; **medir el ~** (*fig*) to see how the land lies; **minar** (*o* **socavar**) **el ~ a uno** to undermine sb's position; **preparar el ~** (*fig*) to pave the way (*a* for); **vencer a uno en su propio ~** to defeat sb on his home ground.

(**b**) (*un ~*) piece of land, piece of ground; (*para construcción*) plot, lot, site; (*Agr*) plot, field, patch; (*Dep*) field, pitch, ground; **~ beneficial** (*Ecl*) glebe, glebe land; **~ de camping** campsite; **~ de fútbol** football ground, football pitch; **~ de juego** field of play, pitch; **~ de pasto** pasture; **~ de pruebas** testing-ground; **un ~ plantado de patatas** a field planted with potatoes; **vender unos ~s** to sell some land; **repartir ~ a los campesinos** to distribute land to the peasants.

(**c**) (*fig*) field, sphere; **en el ~ de la química** in the field of chemistry; **eso no es mi ~** that's not (in) my field.

térreo *adj* earthen; earthy.

terrero 1 *adj* (**a**) (*de la tierra*) earthy; (*de tierra*) of earth. (**b**) *vuelo* low, skimming. (**c**) (*fig*) humble. **2** *nm* pile, heap; (*Min*) dump.

terrestre *adj* (*gen*) terrestrial; (*de la tierra*) earthly; ground (*atr*), land (*atr*); *ruta* land (*atr*), overland (*atr*); *fuerzas* (*Mil*) ground (*atr*).

terrible *adj* terrible, dreadful, awful.

terriblemente *adv* terribly, dreadfully, awfully.

terrier *nm* terrier.

terrífico *adj* terrifying.

terrina *nf* terrine.

territorial *adj* territorial.

territorialidad *nf* territoriality.

territorio *nm* territory; **~ bajo mandato** mandated territory.

terrón *nm* (**a**) (*Geol*) clod, lump, sod. (**b**) (*de azúcar, harina etc*) lump; **azúcar en ~** lump sugar. (**c**) (*Agr*) field, patch; **terrones** (*fig*) land.

terronera *nf* (*And*) terror, fright.

terror *nm* terror; **~ pánico** panic.

terrorífico *adj* terrifying, frightening.

terrorismo *nm* terrorism.

terrorista *adj, nmf* terrorist.

terroso *adj* earthy.

terruño *nm* (**a**) (*tepe*) lump, clod. (**b**) (*parcela*) plot, piece of ground; (*fig*) native soil, home (ground); **apego al ~** attachment to one's native soil.

terso *adj* (**a**) (*liso*) smooth; (*y brillante*) glossy, polished, shining; **piel tersa** smooth skin, soft skin. (**b**) *estilo* smooth, polished, flowing.

tersura *nf* (*V adj*) (**a**) smoothness; glossiness, polish, shine. (**b**) smoothness, flow.

tertulia *nf* (**a**) (*reunión informal*) social gathering, regular informal gathering; (*en café etc*) group, circle, set; **~ literaria** literary circle, literary gathering; **estar de ~** to talk, sit around talking; **hacer ~** to get together, meet informally and talk; **hoy no hay ~** there's no meeting today, the group is not meeting today.

(**b**) (*sala*) clubroom, games room.

(**c**) (*Cono Sur*: *galería*) gallery; (*Carib*: *palcos*) boxes.

Tertuliano *nm* Tertullian.

tertuliano, -a *nm/f* member of a social gathering (*etc*).

tertuliar [1b] *vi* (*LAm*) to attend a social gathering; to get together, meet informally and talk.

terylene ® *nm* Terylene ®.

Tesalia *nf* Thessaly.

tesar [1j] *vt* to tauten, tighten up.

tesauro *nm* thesaurus.

tescal *nm* (*Méx*) stony ground.
tesela *nf* tessera.
Teseo *nm* Theseus.
tesina *nf* minor thesis, dissertation (*for first degree*).
tesis *nf invar* thesis.
tesitura *nf* attitude, frame of mind.
teso *adj* taut, tight; tense.
tesón *nm* insistence; tenacity, persistence; firmness; **resistir con** ~ to resist firmly, resist staunchly.
tesonero *adj* (*LAm*) tenacious, persistent.
tesorería *nf* treasurership, office of treasurer.
tesorero, -a *nm/f* treasurer.
tesoro *nm* (**a**) (*dineral*) treasure; hoard; ~ **escondido** buried treasure; secret hoard; **valer un** ~ to be worth a fortune; (*persona*) to be a real treasure.
(**b**) (*Fin, Pol etc*) treasury; **T~ público** Exchequer, Treasury.
(**c**) (*Fin: pagaré*) treasury bond.
(**d**) (*Liter*) thesaurus.
(**e**) (*fig*) treasure; **¡sí, ~!** yes, darling!, **el libro es un ~ de datos** the book is a mine of information; **es un ~ de recuerdos** it is a treasure-house of memories; **tenemos una cocinera que es todo un ~** we have a real gem of a cook, we have a cook who is a real treasure.
Tespis *nm* Thespis.
test [tes] *nm, pl* **tests** [tes] test; ~ **de comprensión** comprehension test; ~ **de embarazo** pregnancy test.
testa *nf* (**a**) (*cabeza*) head; ~ **coronada** crowned head. (**b**) (*: *inteligencia*) brains; (*sentido común*) gumption*.
testador *nm* testator.
testadora *nf* testatrix.
testaduro *adj* (*Carib*) = **testarudo.**
testaferro *nm* (**a**) (*persona*) figurehead; front man. (**b**) (*Com*) dummy.
testamentaria *nf* executrix.
testamentaría *nf* (**a**) (*acto*) execution of a will. (**b**) (*bienes*) estate.
testamentario 1 *adj* testamentary. **2** *nm* executor.
testamento *nm* (**a**) (*gen*) will, testament; **hacer ~, otorgar ~** to make one's will.
(**b**) **Antiguo T~** Old Testament; **Nuevo T~** New Testament.
(**c**) (*) screed.
testar[1] [1a] *vi* to make a will.
testar[2] [1a] *vt* (*And*) to underline.
testar[3] [1a] *vt coche, producto* to test.
testarada* *nf*, **testarazo*** *nm* bump on the head; bang, bash*; **darse una testarada** to bump one's head, give o.s. a bang on the head.
testarudez *nf* stubbornness, pigheadedness.
testarudo *adj* stubborn, pigheaded.
testear [1a] (*LAm*) **1** *vt* to test. **2** *vi* to do a test, undergo a test.
testera *nf* front, face; (*Zool*) forehead.
testero *nm* (**a**) = **testera.** (**b**) (*de cama*) bedhead. (**c**) (*Arquit*) wall.
testes *nmpl* testes.
testiculamen** *nm* balls**, equipment*.
testículo *nm* testicle.
testificación *nf* (**a**) testification. (**b**) = **testimonio.**
testificar [1g] **1** *vt* (**a**) (*atestiguar*) to attest; (*dar testimonio de*) to testify to, give evidence of. (**b**) (*fig*) to attest, testify to. **2** *vi* to testify, give evidence; ~ **de** = **1** (**a**).
testigo 1 *nmf* (**a**) (*Jur etc*) witness; ~ **de cargo** witness for the prosecution; ~ **de descargo** witness for the defence; ~ **de Jehová** Jehovah's witness; ~ **del novio** ≃ best man; ~ **ocular,** ~ **presencial,** ~ **de vista** eyewitness; ~ **pericial** expert witness; **poner a uno por** ~ to cite sb as a witness.
(**b**) (*en experimento*) control; (*Geol*) sample core.
(**c**) (*en carrera de relevos*) baton.
(**d**) (*Aut*) ~ **luminoso** warning light.
2 *atr*: **grupo** ~ control group; **sujeto** ~ particular case, case used as an example.
testimonial *adj* token, nominal.
testimonialmente *adv* as a token gesture; nominally; (*fig*) half-heartedly.
testimoniar [1b] *vt* to testify to, bear witness to; (*fig*) to show, demonstrate.
testimonio *nm* testimony, evidence; affidavit; ~ **de oídas** hearsay evidence; **falso** ~ perjured evidence; **dar** ~ to testify (*de* to), give evidence (*de* of); **en ~ de mi afecto** as a token (*o* mark) of my affection.
testosterona *nf* testosterone.
testuz *nm* (*frente*) forehead; (*nuca*) nape (of the neck).
teta 1 *nf* (*de biberón*) teat; (*pezón*) nipple; (*) breast; **dar (la)** ~ **a** to suckle, breast-feed; **quitar la** ~ **a** to wean; **niño de** ~ baby still at the breast; **mejor que ~ de monja*** really great*. **2** *adj invar*: **estar** ~ (*Esp**) to be really great*.
tetamen* *nm* big bust, lots of bosom.
tétanos *nm* tetanus.
tete* *nm* (*Cono Sur*) mess, trouble.
tetelque *adj* (*CAm, Méx*) sharp, bitter.
tetera[1] *nf* teapot; tea urn; ~ **eléctrica** electric kettle.
tetera[2] *nf* (*Méx*) (*biberón*) feeding bottle; (*vasija*) vessel with a spout.
tetero *nm* (*And, Carib*) feeding bottle.
tetilla *nf* (**a**) (*Anat: de hombre*) nipple. (**b**) (*de biberón*) rubber teat.
tetina *nf* teat.
Tetis *nf* Thetis.
tetón[1] *nm* (*en neumático etc*) bubble, swelling.
tetón[2]* *adj* (*Cono Sur*) stupid, thick*.
tetona* *adj* busty*.
tetracilíndrico *adj*: **motor** ~ four-cylinder engine.
tetracloruro *nm* tetrachloride; ~ **de carbono** carbon tetrachloride.
tetraedro *nm* tetrahedron.
tetrágono *nm* tetragon.
tetrámetro *nm* tetrameter.
tetramotor *adj* four-engined.
tetrarreactor *nm* four-engined jet plane.
tetratlón *nm* tetrathlon.
tétrico *adj pensamiento* gloomy, dismal; *humor* gloomy, pessimistic; sullen; *luz* dim, wan.
tetuda* *adj* busty*.
tetunte *nm* (*CAm*) bundle.
teutón, -ona *nm/f* Teuton.
teutónico *adj* Teutonic.
teveo *nm* = **tebeo.**
textil 1 *adj* textile. **2** (**a**) **~es** *nmpl* textiles. (**b**) (*hum**) non-naturist, person who wears a swimsuit.
texto *nm* text; **grabado fuera de** ~ full-page illustration.
textual *adj* (**a**) (*de texto*) textual. (**b**) (*fig*) exact; literal; **son sus palabras ~es** those are his exact words.
textualmente *adv* (**a**) (*de texto*) textually. (**b**) (*fig*) exactly; literally; **dice ~ que** ... he says (and I quote his own words) that ...
textura *nf* texture (*t fig*).
tez *nf* complexion, skin; colouring.
tezontle *nm* (*Méx*) volcanic rock.
Tfno., tfno. *abr de* **teléfono** telephone, Tel.
TGV *nm abr de* **tren de gran velocidad** ≃ Advanced Passenger Train, APT.
ti *pron* (*tras prep*) you; yourself; (††, *a Dios*) thee, thyself; **es para** ~ it's for you; **¿lo has comprado para ~?** did you buy it for yourself?; **esto no se refiere a** ~ this doesn't refer to you.
tía *nf* (**a**) (*pariente*) aunt; ~ **abuela** great-aunt; **¡no hay tu ~!*** nothing doing!; **¡cuéntaselo a tu ~!*** pull the other one!*
(**b**) *delante de nombre en tono respetuoso, no se traduce*: **unos dulces para la ~ Dulcinea** some sweets for Dulcinea.
(**c**) (*) (*mujer*) woman; (*chica*) bird*, chick*; ~ **buena** smashing girl*; **¡oye, ~ buena!** hi, gorgeous!*; **las ~s piensan así** that's the way women think.
(**d**) (*: *puta*) whore.
(**e**) (*: *bruja*) old bat*, old bag*.
(**f**) **la ~*** (**María** *etc*) the curse (of Eve).
tiamina *nf* thiamine.
tiangue *nm* (*CAm*) small market; booth, stall.
tianguis *nm* (*CAm, Méx*) market.
TIAR [ti'ar] *nm abr de* **Tratado Interamericano de Asistencia Recíproca.**
tiarrón* *nm* big chap*, huge fellow.
tiarrona* *nf* big girl, hefty wench*.
tibante *adj* (*And*) haughty.
tibe *nm* (*And, Carib*) whetstone.
Tíber *nm* Tiber.
Tiberio *nm* Tiberius.
tiberio* 1 *adj* (*CAm, Méx*) sloshed*. **2** *nm* (**a**) (*jaleo*) uproar, row; (*pelea*) set-to*. (**b**) (*CAm, Méx*) binge*.
Tibet *nm*: **El** ~ Tibet.
tibetano, -a 1 *adj, nm/f* Tibetan. **2** *nm* (*Ling*) Tibetan.
tibia *nf* tibia.
tibiarse [1b] *vr* (*CAm, Carib*) to get cross.
tibieza *nf* (**a**) (*de sustancia*) lukewarmness, tepidness. (**b**) (*fig*) lukewarmness; coolness, lack of enthusiasm.
tibio *adj* (**a**) *agua etc* lukewarm, tepid.

(**b**) (*fig*) *fe, persona etc* lukewarm; cool, unenthusiastic; **estar ~ con uno** to be cool to sb, behave distantly towards sb.

(**c**) **poner ~ a uno** to hurl abuse at sb, give sb a verbal battering; to say dreadful things about sb.

(**d**) (*CAm, Carib*) cross, angry.

tibor *nm* large earthenware jar; (*Carib*) chamber pot; (*Méx*) gourd.

tiburón *nm* (**a**) shark; **~ de río** pike. (**b**) (*) go-getter*, unscrupulous person; (*en bolsa*) secret purchaser of shares; (*Cono Sur*) wolf*, Don Juan.

tic *nm, pl* **tics** [tik] (**a**) tap; click; tick, tick-tock. (**b**) (*Med*: *t* **~ nervioso**) tic.

Ticiano *nm* Titian.

tico*, -a *adj, nm/f* (*CAm*) Costa Rican.

tictac *nm* (*de reloj*) tick, tick-tock; (*de corazón*) beat; (*de máquina de escribir*) tapping, tip-tap; **hacer ~** to tick; to beat, go pit-a-pat; to tip-tap.

tiempecito *nm* (*LAm*) (spell of) very bad weather.

tiemple *nm* (**a**) (*Cono Sur: galanteo*) love-making, courting. (**b**) (*Cono Sur: amante*) lover. (**c**) (*LAm: enamoramiento*) infatuation.

tiempo *nm* (**a**) (*gen*) time; **breve ~** short while; **~ del bocadillo** teabreak; **~ compartido** timeshare; time-sharing; **~ libre** spare time, free time, leisure; **~ máquina** machine time; **~ muerto** (*Dep*) time out; (*fig*) breather, breathing-space; **~ real** real time; **~ de respuesta** response time; **a ~** in time, in good time, early; at the right time; **a un ~, al mismo ~** at the same time; **a su debido ~** in due course; **al poco ~** very soon, soon after; **a ~ que ..., al ~ que ...** at the time that ..., while ...; **al mismo ~ que ...** at the same time as ...; **trabajo a ~ parcial** part-time work; **trabajar a ~ completo** to work full-time; **cada cierto ~** every so often; **con ~** in time, in good time, early; **con el ~** eventually, in time; **cuánto ~, ¿eh?*** long time no see!; **¿cuánto ~ se va a quedar?** how long is he staying?; **de ~ en ~** from time to time; **de algún ~ a esta parte** for some time past; **una costumbre de mucho ~** a long-standing custom; **fuera de ~** at the wrong time; **necesito más ~** I need longer, I need more time; **no puede quedarse más ~** he can't stay any longer; **mucho ~** a long time, a long while; **todo el ~** all the time; **el ~ es de oro** time is money; time is precious; **el ~ lo es todo** time is everything, time is of the essence; **es ~ perdido hablar con él** it's a waste of time talking to him; **andando el ~** in due course, in time; in the fullness of time; **el ~ apremia** time presses; **dar ~ al ~** to consider all the possibilities; to let matters take their course; **darse buen ~** to have a good time; **el ~ dirá** time will tell; **apenas dispongo de mi ~** I can scarcely call my time my own; **engañar el ~, matar el ~** to kill time; **ganar ~** to save time; **hacer ~** to while away the time, kill time; to mark time; **hace mucho ~** a long time ago; **hace bastante ~ que lo compré** I bought it a good while ago; **desde hace mucho ~** for a long time; **hace mucho ~ que no voy** I haven't been for a long time; **perder el ~** to waste time; to fool around; **sería simplemente perder el ~** it would be just a waste of time; **sin perder ~** without delay; **sacar ~ para hacer algo** to take time out to do sth; **tener ~ para** to have time for.

(**b**) (*específico, limitado*) time, period, age; **~s modernos** modern times; **a través de los ~s** through the ages; **en ~ de los griegos** in the time of the Greeks; **en estos ~s nuestros** in this day and age; **en los ~s que corremos** in these dreadful times; **en mis ~s** in my day; **en los buenos ~s** in the good old days; **en mis buenos ~s** when I was in my prime; **en otro ~** formerly; once upon a time; **en los últimos ~s** recently, lately, in recent times; **en ~ de Maricastaña, en ~ del rey que rabió** way back, long ago; in the good old days; **estar en el ~ de las vacas flacas** to have fallen on hard times; **los ~s están revueltos** the times are out of joint, these are disturbed times; **hay que ir con los ~s** one must keep abreast of the times.

(**c**) (*de niño*) age; **A y B son del mismo ~** A and B are the same age; **¿cuánto** *o* **qué** (*LAm*) **~ tiene el pequeño?** how old is the child?

(**d**) (*Dep*) half; **primer ~** first half.

(**e**) (*Mús: compás*) tempo, time.

(**f**) (*Mús: de sinfonía etc*) movement.

(**g**) (*Ling*) tense; **~ compuesto** compound tense; **en ~ presente** in the present tense.

(**h**) (*Met*: *t* **~ atmosférico**) weather; **si dura el mal ~** if the bad weather continues; **hace buen ~** it's fine, the weather is good, the weather is fine; **¿qué ~ hará mañana?** what will the weather be like tomorrow?; **a mal ~, buena cara** one must make the best of a bad job.

(**i**) (*Náut*) stormy weather, rough weather.

(**j**) (*Mec*) cycle; **motor de 2 ~s** two-stroke engine.

tienda *nf* (**a**) (*Com*) shop, store; (*esp*) grocer's; (*Carib, Cono Sur: mercería*) draper's, clothier's; **~ de coloniales, ~ de comestibles, ~ de ultramarinos** (*Esp*) grocer's (shop), grocery (*US*); **~ por departamento** (*Carib*) department store; **~ de deportes** sports shop; **~ libre de impuestos** duty-free shop; **~ de regalos** gift-shop; **ir de ~s** to go shopping; **poner ~** to set up shop.

(**b**) (*Náut etc*) awning; **~ de campaña** tent; **~ de oxígeno** oxygen tent.

tienta *nf* (**a**) (*Med*) probe.

(**b**) (*habilidad*) cleverness; (*astucia*) astuteness.

(**c**) **a ~s** (*a ciegas*) gropingly, blindly; **andar a ~s** to grope one's way along, feel one's way; (*fig*) to feel one's way; **decir algo a ~s** to throw out a remark at random, say sth to see what effect it has.

(**d**) (*Taur*) trial, test.

tiento *nm* (**a**) (*sensación física*) feel, feeling, touch; (*Fin**) touch*, tickle*; (*: *amoroso*) pass*; **a ~** by touch; gropingly; (*fig*) uncertainly; **echar un ~ a una chica*** to make a pass at a girl*, try it on with a girl*; **a 40 dólares nadie le echó un ~** at 40 dollars nobody was biting, at 40 dollars he didn't get a tickle*; **perder el ~** to lose one's touch.

(**b**) (*fig*) (*tacto*) tact; (*prudencia*) care; (*cautela*) wariness, circumspection; **ir con ~** to go carefully, go cautiously.

(**c**) (*Arte etc*) steadiness of hand, steady hand.

(**d**) (*Zool*) feeler, tentacle; (*Circo*) balancing pole; (*de ciego*) blind man's stick.

(**e**) (*Mús*) preliminary flourish, scale, notes played in tuning up.

(**f**) (*: *puñetazo*) blow, punch; **dar ~s a uno** to hit sb.

(**g**) (*: *trago*) swig*; **dar un ~** to take a swig* (*a* from).

(**h**) (*Cono Sur: tira*) thong of raw leather, rawhide strap.

tiernamente *adv* tenderly.

tierno *adj* (*gen*) tender; soft; *pan etc* new, fresh.

tierra *nf* (**a**) (*Astron: el mundo*) earth, world.

(**b**) (*superficie*) land; **~ firme** mainland; terra firma, dry land; **~ de nadie** no-man's land; **~ quemada** scorched earth; **~ adentro** inland; (*LAm*) interior, remote area; **por ~** by land, overland; **¡~ a la vista!** land!; **besar la ~** to fall flat; **caer a ~** to fall down; **caer por ~** (*t fig*) to fall to the ground; **dar con algo en ~** to drop sth; to knock sth over; (*fig*) to overthrow sth; **echar a ~** to demolish, pull down; to raze to the ground; **echar** (*o* **tirar**) **algo por ~** to ruin sth, upset sth; **perder ~** (*perder el pie*) to lose one's footing; (*en agua*) to get out of one's depth; **poner un avión en ~** to land a plane; **poner ~ por medio** to get out quick, get as far away as possible; **saltar en** (*o* **a**) **~** (*desde barco*) to leap ashore; **tocar ~** (*Aer*) to touch down; **tomar ~** (*Aer*) to land, come down; (*Náut*) to reach harbour; **venirse a** (*o* **por**) **~** to collapse.

(**c**) (*Geol etc*) land, soil, earth, ground; **~ de batán** fuller's earth; **~ batida** (*Dep*) clay (court); **~ de brezo** peat; **~ vegetal** topsoil; **echar ~ a un asunto** to hush an affair up; to forget about a matter; **echar ~ a uno** (*Cono Sur, Méx*) to speak damagingly of sb.

(**d**) (*Agr*) land; **~s** lands, estate(s); **~ baldía** wasteland; **~ de labor** agricultural land; **~ de pan llevar** arable land, corn-growing land; **en cualquier ~ de garbanzos** all over; **heredó unas ~s en la provincia** he inherited some land in the province.

(**e**) (*Pol etc*) country; **su ~** one's own country, one's native land; one's own region, one's home area; **~ natal** native land; **~ prometida, ~ de promisión** land of promise, promised land; **ver ~s** to see the world; **vamos a nuestra ~ a pasar las Navidades** we go home for Christmas; **no es de estas ~s** he's not from these parts; **¿tienen tractores en tu ~?** do they have tractors where you come from?, do they have tractors in your part of the world?

(**f**) (*Elec*) earth, ground (*US*); **conectar un aparato a ~** to earth a piece of apparatus, ground a piece of apparatus (*US*).

(**g**) (*LAm: polvo*) dust.

tierra-aire *atr*: **misil ~** surface-to-air missile.

tierrafría *nmf* (*And*) highlander.

tierral *nm* (*LAm*), **tierrazo** *nm* (*LAm*) cloud of dust.

Tierra Santa *nf* Holy Land.

tierra-tierra *atr*: **misil ~** surface-to-surface missile.

tierrero *nm* (*LAm*) cloud of dust.

tierruca *nf* native land, native heath.

tieso 1 *adj* (**a**) (*rígido*) stiff, rigid; (*erecto*) erect; (*tenso*) taut; **con las orejas tiesas** with its ears pricked; **quedarse** ~ (*fig*) (*de frío*) to be frozen stiff; (‡: *muerto*) to peg out‡.

(**b**) (*fig*) (*sano*) fit; (*vivo*) sprightly; (*alegre*) chirpy*; **le encontré muy ~ a pesar de su enfermedad** I found him very cheerful in spite of his illness.

(**c**) (*fig*) (*estirado*) stiff (in manner); (*rígido*) rigid (in attitude); ~ **como un ajo** as stiff as a poker; **me recibió muy ~** he received me very stiffly.

(**d**) (*) (*orgulloso*) proud; (*presumido*) conceited, stuck-up*; (*satisfecho*) smug; ~ **de cogote** haughty; **iba tan ~ con la novia al brazo** he was walking so proudly with his girl on his arm.

(**e**) (*terco*) stubborn; (*firme*) firm, confident; ~ **que** ~ as stubborn as they come; **ponerse ~ con uno** to stand one's ground, insist on one's rights; (*pey*) to be stubborn with sb; **tenerlas tiesas con uno** to put up a firm resistance to sb, stand up for o.s.

(**f**) **estar** ~ (*Fin**) to be broke*.

(**g**) **estar** ~ (*: *parado*) to be out of work.

2 *adv* strongly, energetically, hard.

tiesto *nm* (**a**) (*Hort*) flowerpot. (**b**) (*casco*) shard, piece of pottery. (**c**) (*Cono Sur*) (*vasija*) pot, vessel; (*orinal*) chamberpot.

tiesura *nf* (**a**) (*rigidez*) stiffness, rigidity; erectness; tautness. (**b**) (*fig*) stiffness; rigidity. (**c**) (*) conceit. (**d**) (*terquedad*) stubbornness; (*confianza*) firmness, confidence.

tifiar‡ [1b] *vt* (*Carib*) to nick‡, lift*.

tifitifi* *nm* (*Carib*) theft.

tifo *nm* typhus; ~ **de América** yellow fever; ~ **asiático** cholera; ~ **de Oriente** bubonic plague.

tifoidea *nf* (*t* **fiebre** ~) typhoid.

tifón *nm* (**a**) (*huracán*) typhoon. (**b**) (*tromba*) waterspout. (**c**) (*Méx Min*) outcrop of ore.

tifus *nm* (**a**) (*Med*) typhus; ~ **exantemático** spotted fever; ~ **icteroides** yellow fever.

(**b**) (*Teat**) persons having complimentary tickets (*o* free seats); claque; **entrar de** ~ to get in free.

tigra *nf* (*LAm Zool*) female tiger; (*jaguar*) female jaguar; **ponerse como una ~ parida** (*And, Cono Sur**) to fly off the handle*.

tigre *nm* (**a**) (*Zool*) tiger; (*LAm*) jaguar; ~ **de Bengala** Bengal tiger; ~ **de colmillo de sable** sabre-toothed tiger; ~ **de papel** paper tiger. (**b**) (*And*: *café*) black coffee with a dash of milk; (*And*: *combinado*) cocktail. (**c**) (‡: *wáter*) bog‡, loo*; **esto huele a ~** this pongs‡, this smells awful.

tigrero 1 *adj* (*Cono Sur*) brave.

2 *nm* (*LAm*) jaguar hunter.

tigresa *nf* tigress.

tigridia *nf* tiger lily.

tigrillo *nm* (*LAm*) *member of the cat tribe, eg* ocelot, lynx.

Tigris *nm* Tigris.

tigrón* *nm* (*Carib*) bully, braggart.

tigüila *nf* (*Méx*) trick, swindle.

tija *nf* (*Aut*) shank.

tijera *nf* (**a**) (*de bicicleta*) fork; (*LAm*) scissors; **meter la ~ en** to cut into.

(**b**) (*LAm Zool*) claw, pincer.

(**c**) (*: *persona*) gossip; **ser una buena ~, tener buena ~** to be a great gossip; to have a sharp tongue; to indulge constantly in backbiting, be a scandalmonger.

(**d**) **de** ~ folding; **escalera de** ~ steps, step-ladder; **silla de** ~ folding chair, folding stool, camp stool.

(**e**) **es un trabajo de** ~ it's a scissors-and-paste job.

tijeral *nm* (*Cono Sur Orn*) stork.

tijeras *nfpl* scissors; (*Hort etc*) shears, clippers; ~ **de coser** sewing scissors; ~ **podadoras**, ~ **de podar** secateurs; ~ **para las uñas** nail-scissors; **unas** ~ a pair of scissors (*etc*), some scissors (*etc*).

tijereta *nf* (**a**) (*Ent*) earwig. (**b**) (*Bot*) vine tendril. (**c**) (*Dep*) scissors kick, overhead kick.

tijeretada *nf*, **tijeretazo** *nm* snip, snick, small cut.

tijeretear [1a] **1** *vt* to snip, snick, cut. **2** *vi* (**a**) (*entrometerse*) to meddle. (**b**) (*CAm, Cono Sur, Méx*: *chismear*) to gossip, backbite.

tijereteo *nm* (**a**) (*lit*) snipping, snicking, cutting. (**b**) (*fig*) meddling. (**c**) (*CAm, Cono Sur, Méx*: *chismes*) gossiping, backbiting.

tila *nf* (**a**) (*Bot*) lime tree. (**b**) (*Culin*) lime(-blossom) tea. (**c**) (‡: *droga*) hash*, pot‡.

tildar [1a] *vt* (**a**) (*Tip*) to put an accent on; to put a tilde over. (**b**) (*fig*) ~ **a uno de** + *adj* to brand sb as (being) + *adj*, stigmatize sb as (being) + *adj*.

tilde *gen nf* (**a**) (*Tip*) accent (´), tilde (˜). (**b**) (*fig*: *defecto*) blemish, defect, flaw. (**c**) (*fig*) (*bagatela*) triviality; (*pizca*) jot, bit; **en una ~*** in a jiffy*.

tilichera *nf* (*CAm, Méx*) hawker's box, glass-covered box.

tilichero *nm* (*CAm, Méx*) hawker, pedlar, peddler (*US*).

tiliches *nmpl* (*CAm, Méx*) trinkets; belongings; (*pey*) junk.

tilín *nm* (**a**) tinkle, ting-a-ling.

(**b**) (*) **hacer** ~ to be well liked; **me hace** ~ I like it, I go for it*; **no me hace** ~ it doesn't appeal to me; **tener** ~ to be nice, be attractive, have a way with people; **tener algo al** ~ (*Carib*) to have sth at one's fingertips.

(**c**) **en un** ~ (*And, Carib, Cono Sur*: *) in a flash.

tilinches* *nmpl* (*Méx*) rags.

tilingada* *nf* (*Cono Sur, Méx*) silly thing (to do *etc*).

tilingo* (*And, Cono Sur, Méx*) **1** *adj* silly, stupid. **2** *nm* fool.

tilinguear* [1a] *vi* (*And, Cono Sur, Méx*) to act the fool, do (*etc*) silly things.

tilinguería* *nf* (*And, Cono Sur, Méx*) (**a**) (*estupidez*) silliness, stupidity. (**b**) **~s** nonsense.

tilintar [1a] *vt* (*CAm*) to stretch, tauten.

tilinte *adj* (*CAm*) (**a**) (*tenso*) tight, taut. (**b**) (*elegante*) elegant. (**c**) (*repleto*) replete.

tilma *nf* (*Méx*) blanket, cape.

tilo *nm* (**a**) (*Bot*) lime, lime tree. (**b**) (*Cono Sur*) = **tila** (**b**).

tiloso* *adj* (*CAm*) dirty, filthy.

timador(a) *nm/f* swindler, trickster.

timar [1a] **1** *vt* (**a**) *propiedad* to steal.

(**b**) *persona* to swindle, play a confidence trick on, con*; **le timaron la herencia** they swindled him out of the inheritance.

2 timarse* *vr* to make eyes at each other; ~ **con uno** (*amorosamente*) to make eyes at sb, ogle sb; (*engatusar*) to play sb along, lead sb on.

timba *nf* (**a**) (*en juego de azar*) hand. (**b**) (*garita*) gambling den. (**c**) (*CAm, Carib, Méx*) pot-belly. (**d**) (*Carib*) **esto tiene** ~ it's a sticky business.

timbal *nm* (**a**) (*Mús*) small drum, kettledrum. (**b**) (*Culin*) meat pie. (**c**) **~es** (**‡) balls**‡.

timbembe* *adj* (*Cono Sur*) weak, trembling.

timbiriche *nm* (*Carib, Méx*) small shop.

timbrar [1a] *vt* (**a**) (*estampillar*) to stamp; (*sellar*) to seal. (**b**) (*Correos*) to postmark.

timbrazo *nm* ring; **dar un** ~ to ring the bell.

timbre *nm* (**a**) (*Com, Fin*) fiscal stamp, revenue stamp; *sello* seal; (*Fin*) stamp duty.

(**b**) (*Méx Correos*) postage stamp.

(**c**) (*LAm*: *descripción*) personal description; description of goods (*etc*).

(**d**) (*fig*) ~ **de gloria** mark of honour; action (*etc*) which is to one's credit.

(**e**) (*Elec etc*) bell; ~ **de alarma** alarm bell; **tocar el** ~ to ring the bell.

(**f**) (*Mús etc*) timbre; ~ **nasal** (*Ling*) nasal timbre, twang.

timbrear [1a] *vi* to ring (the bell).

timbusca *nf* (*And*: *sopa*) thick soup; (*plato rústico*) spicy local dish.

tímidamente *adv* timidly, shyly, nervously; bashfully.

timidez *nf* timidity, shyness, nervousness; bashfulness.

tímido *adj* timid, shy, nervous; bashful.

timo *nm* (*estafa*) swindle, confidence trick, confidence game (*US*); (*broma*) gag, hoax; **dar un ~ a uno** to swindle sb; to hoax sb.

timón *nm* (**a**) (*Aer, Náut*) rudder; helm; ~ **de deriva**, ~ **de dirección** (*Aer*) rudder; ~ **de profundidad** (*Aer*) elevator; **poner el ~ a babor** to turn to port, port the helm.

(**b**) (*de carruaje*) pole; (*de arado*) beam.

(**c**) (*fig*) helm; **coger el ~, empuñar el** ~ to take the helm, take charge.

(**d**) (*And Aut*) steering-wheel.

timonear [1a] **1** *vt* (*LAm*) (*dirigir*) to direct, manage; (*guiar*) to guide. **2** *vi* to steer; (*And Aut*) to drive.

timonel *nm* (*Náut*) steersman, helmsman; (*de bote de carreras*) cox.

timonera *nf* wheelhouse.

timonería *nf* (*Náut*) rudders, steering mechanisms; (*Ferro*) linkage.

timonero *nm* = **timonel.**

timorato *adj* (**a**) (*tímido*) timorous, feeble-spirited, small-minded. (**b**) (*mojigato*) prudish. (**c**) (*Rel*) God-fearing; (*pey*) excessively pious; sanctimonious.

Timoteo *nm* Timothy.

tímpano *nm* (**a**) (*Anat*) tympanum, eardrum. (**b**) (*Arquit*) tympanum. (**c**) (*Mús*) small drum, kettledrum; **~s** (*de orquesta*) tympani.

tina *nf* (*recipiente*) vat, tub; (*bañera*) bathtub; ~ **de lavar**

washtub.
tinaco *nm* (*And, Méx*: *vasija*) tall earthenware jar; (*Méx*: *cisterna*) water tank.
tinaja *nf* large earthen jar.
tinca *nf* (**a**) (*Cono Sur*: *capirotazo*) flip, flick. (**b**) (*And*) bowls. (**c**) (*Cono Sur**: *pálpito*) hunch.
tincada *nf* (*Cono Sur*) hunch.
tincanque *nm* (*Cono Sur*) = **tinca** (**a**).
tincar* [1g] *vt* (*Cono Sur*) (**a**) (*dar un capirotazo a*) to flip, flick. (**b**) (*presentir*) to have a hunch about. (**c**) (*apetecer*) to like, fancy; **me tinca** I like him (*etc*); **no me tinca** I don't like the idea, I don't fancy it.
tincazo *nm* (*Cono Sur*) = **tinca** (**a**).
tinctura *nf* tincture.
tinerfeño 1 *adj* of Tenerife. **2** *nm*, **tinerfeña** *nf* native (*o* inhabitant) of Tenerife; **los ~s** the people of Tenerife.
tinga* *nf* (*Méx*) row, uproar.
tingar [1h] *vt* (*And*) to flip, flick.
tinglado *nm* (**a**) (*tablado*) platform; (*cobertizo*) shed, covering.
(**b**) (*fig*) set-up, system; (*pey*) trick; plot, intrigue; **armar un ~** to lay a plot; **conocer el ~** to see through it, see sb's little game; **está metida en el ~ del espiritismo*** she's into the spiritualism thing; **montar el ~** to get going, set up in business; **montar su ~*** to do one's own thing*.
tingo *nm*, **tingue** *nm* (*And*) = **tinca** (**a**).
tinieblas *nfpl* (**a**) (*oscuridad*) darkness, dark; (*sombras*) shadows; (*tenebrosidad*) gloom.
(**b**) (*fig*) confusion, fog; black ignorance; **estamos en ~ sobre sus proyectos** we are in the dark about his plans, we are entirely ignorant of what he plans to do.
tino[1] *nm* (**a**) (*habilidad*) skill, knack; feel; (*seguridad*) (sureness of) touch; (*conjeturas*) (good) guesswork, (good) reckoning; (*Mil*) (accurate) aim, (good) marksmanship; **a ~** gropingly; **a buen ~** by guesswork; **coger el ~** to get the feel of it, get the hang of it.
(**b**) (*fig*) (*tacto*) tact; (*juicio*) good judgement; (*perspicacia*) insight, acumen; **sin ~** foolishly; aimlessly; **obrar con mucho ~** to act wisely, act with great good sense; **perder el ~** to act foolishly, go off the rails; **sacar de ~ a uno** to bewilder sb; to exasperate sb, infuriate sb.
(**c**) (*fig*: *moderación*) moderation; **sin ~** immoderately; **comer sin ~** to eat to excess; **gastar sin ~** to spend recklessly.
tino[2] *nm* (**a**) (*tina*) vat; (*de piedra*) stone tank. (**b**) (*lagar*) winepress; (*de aceite*) olive press.
tinoso *adj* (*And*) (*hábil*) skilful, clever; (*juicioso*) sensible; (*moderado*) moderate; (*diplomático*) tactful.
tinque *nm* (*Cono Sur*) = **tinca** (**a**).
tinta *nf* (**a**) (*Tip etc*) ink; **~ china** Indian ink; **~ de imprenta** printer's ink, printing ink; **~ indeleble, ~ de marcar** marking ink; **~ invisible, ~ simpática** invisible ink; **con ~** in ink; **sudar ~*** to slog, slave; **saber algo de buena ~** to know sth on good authority.
(**b**) (*Tec*) dye.
(**c**) (*de pulpo*) dye, ink.
(**d**) (*Arte*) colour; **~s** (*fig*) tints, shades, hues; **media ~** half-tone, tint; **medias ~s** (*fig*) (*medidas*) half measures; (*ideas*) half-baked ideas; (*respuestas*) inadequate answers; **presentar una situación bajo ~s muy negras** to paint a situation very black; **cargar las ~s** to exaggerate.
tintado 1 *adj vidrio* tinted. **2** *nm* tinting.
tinte *nm* (**a**) (*acto*) dyeing.
(**b**) (*Quím*) dye, dyestuff; stain.
(**c**) (*Com*) dyer's (shop); dry-cleaning establishment, dry cleaner's.
(**d**) (*fig*: *matiz*) tinge, colouring; **sin el menor ~ político** without the slightest political colouring, devoid of all political character.
(**e**) (*fig*: *barniz*) veneer, gloss, light covering; **tiene cierto ~ de hombre de mundo** he has a slight touch of the man of the world about him.
tinterillo *nm* (**a**) (*empleado*) penpusher, small-time clerk. (**b**) (*LAm*: *abogado*) shyster lawyer*.
tintero *nm* (**a**) (*lit*) inkpot, inkwell; inkstand; **lo dejó en el ~, se le quedó en el ~** (*fig*) he clean forgot about it; **no deja nada en el ~** she leaves nothing unsaid. (**b**) (*LAm*: *plumas etc*) writing materials, desk set.
tintillo *nm* (*Cono Sur*) red wine.
tintín *nm* tinkle, tinkling; ting-a-ling; jingle; clink, chink.
tintinear [1a] *vi* (*campanilla*) to tinkle; (*timbre*) to go ting-a-ling; (*cadena etc*) to jingle; (*tazas etc*) to clink, chink.
tintineo *nm* = **tintín**.
tinto 1 *adj* (**a**) (*teñido*) dyed; (*manchado*) stained; tinged; **~ en sangre** stained with blood, bloodstained. (**b**) *vino* red. **2** *nm* (**a**) (*vino*) red wine. (**b**) (*And*) black coffee.
tintorera *nf* shark; (*And, CAm, Méx*) female shark.
tintorería *nf* (**a**) (*arte*) dyeing. (**b**) (*Téc*: *fábrica*) dyeworks; (*tienda*) dyer's (shop). (**c**) (*de lavar en seco*) dry cleaner's.
tintorero *nm* (**a**) (*que tiñe*) dyer. (**b**) (*que lava en seco*) dry cleaner.
tintorro* *nm* plonk*, cheap red wine.
tintura *nf* (**a**) (*acto*) dyeing.
(**b**) (*Quím*) dye, dyestuff; (*Téc*) stain; (*Farm*) tincture; **~ de tornasol** litmus; **~ de yodo** iodine.
(**c**) (*fig*) smattering; thin veneer.
tinturar [1a] *vt* (**a**) (*teñir*) to dye; to tinge. (**b**) **~ a uno** (*fig*) to give sb a rudimentary knowledge, teach sb superficially.
tiña *nf* (**a**) (*Med*) ringworm. (**b**) (*fig*: *pobreza*) poverty. (**c**) (*fig*: *tacañería*) meanness.
tiñoso *adj* (**a**) (*Med*) scabby, mangy. (**b**) (*fig*: *miserable*) poor, wretched. (**c**) (*fig*: *tacaño*) mean.
tío *nm* (**a**) uncle; **~ abuelo** great-uncle; **~ carnal** real uncle; **mi ~ Eduardo** my uncle Edward; **T~ Sam** Uncle Sam; **mis ~s** (*frec*) my uncle and aunt.
(**b**) *delante de nombre en tono respetuoso, no se traduce*: **ha muerto el ~ Francisco** Francis has died.
(**c**) (*Esp**) (*viejo*) old fellow; (*sujeto*) fellow, chap*, guy*; **los ~s** guys*, men; **¿quién es ese ~?** who's that chap?*; **ese ~ del sombrero alto** that chap with the tall hat*; **¡qué ~!** what a fellow!; (*pey*) isn't he a so-and-so?*; **~ legal** good sort*; **es un ~ grande, es un ~ con toda la barba** he's a great guy*.
tiovivo *nm* roundabout, merry-go-round.
tipa[1] *nf* (*And, Cono Sur*) large wicker basket.
tipa[2]* *nf* dame*, chick*; (*pey*) bitch‡, cow‡.
tipaza* *nf*: **es una ~** she's got a smashing figure*.
tipazo* *nm* (*grande*) tall chap*, big guy*; (*arrogante*) arrogant fellow; (*And*: *persona importante*) bigwig.
tipear [1a] *vti* (*LAm*) to type.
tipejo*, -a *nm/f* queer fish*, odd sort; bad lot*.
tiperrita *nf* (*Carib*) typist.
tipiadora *nf* (**a**) (*máquina*) typewriter. (**b**) (*persona*) typist.
típicamente *adv* typically; characteristically.
tipicidad *nf* genuineness, authenticity.
típico *adj* (**a**) (*característico*) typical; characteristic.
(**b**) (*pintoresco*) quaint, picturesque; (*lleno de color local*) full of local colour; (*folklórico*) rich in folklore, full of folkloric interest; (*tradicional*) traditional; (*regional*) regional; (*de interés turístico*) of interest to tourists; **baile ~** regional dance, national dance; **es la taberna más típica de la ciudad** it's the most picturesque pub in town; **unas jóvenes con su ~ peinado** some girls with their hair done in the traditional (and local) fashion; **no hay que perderse tan típica fiesta** you shouldn't miss a festivity so rich in local colour and tradition.
tipificar [1g] *vt* (**a**) (*ser típico de*) to typify; to characterize. (**b**) (*clasificar*) to class, consider (*como* as).
tipismo *nm* quaintness, picturesqueness; local colour; folkloric interest; traditionalism; regional character; **estoy harto de tanto ~ bobo** I'm fed up with all this nonsensical local colour and traditionalism.
tiple 1 *nm* (**a**) (*persona*) treble, boy soprano. (**b**) (*voz*) soprano (voice). **2** *nf* soprano.
tipo 1 *nm* (**a**) (*gen*) type; (*norma*) norm, standard; (*pauta*) pattern, model; **un sombrero ~ Bogart** a Bogart-style hat, a hat like Bogart's; **una joven ~ Marilyn** a girl in the Marilyn mould; **un vehículo ~ jeep** a jeep-type vehicle.
(**b**) (*clase*) type, sort, kind; **un nuevo ~ de bicicleta** a new kind of bicycle; **de otro ~ pero del mismo precio** of a different type but at the same price.
(**c**) (*Liter etc*) type, character.
(**d**) (*: *hombre*) fellow, chap*, guy*; **dos ~s sospechosos** two suspicious characters*; **un ~ que yo conozco** a fellow I know; **¿quién es ese ~?** who's that chap*?
(**e**) (*Com, Fin*) rate; **~ bancario, ~ de descuento** bank rate; **~ de cambio** exchange rate, rate of exchange; **~ impositivo** tax coding, tax bracket; tax rate; **~ de interés** interest rate; **~ (de) oro** gold standard; **~ de seguro** insurance rates.
(**f**) (*Anat*: *de hombre*) build, physique; (*de mujer*) figure; **él tiene buen ~** he's well built; **ella tiene buen ~** she has a good figure; **tener mal ~** to be misshapen.
(**g**) (*Tip*: *t ~s*) type; **~ de datos** data type; **~ gótico** Gothic type, black letter; **~ de letra** typeface, font; **~**

menudo small print.

(**h**) (*) **aguantar el ~, mantener el ~** to hold out; to put up with a lot; **jugarse el ~** to risk one's neck.

2 *atr* standard; ordinary, average, typical; representative; **dos conductores ~** two average drivers; **lengua ~** standard language.

tipografía *nf* (**a**) (*arte*) typography; printing. (**b**) (*taller*) printing works; (*imprenta*) printing press.

tipográfico *adj* typographical; printing (*atr*).

tipógrafo, -a *nm/f* typographer; printer.

tipología *nf* typology.

tiposo *adj* (*And*) ridiculous, eccentric.

típula *nf* cranefly, daddy-long-legs.

tique *nm* = **tíquet**.

tiquear [1a] *vt* (*Cono Sur*) to punch.

tíquet ['tike] *nm, pl* **tíquets** ['tike], **tiquete** *nm* (*LAm*) ticket; (*en tienda*) cash slip; (*And*: *etíqueta*) label.

tiquitique* *nm*: **estar en el ~** to be gossiping.

tiquismiquis *nmpl* (**a**) (*escrúpulos*) silly scruples; (*detalles*) fussy details; (*quejas*) silly objections.

(**b**) (*cortesías*) affected courtesies, bowing and scraping.

(**c**) (*riñas*) bickering, squabbles.

(**d**) (*molestias*) minor irritations, pinpricks.

tira[1] **1** *nf* (**a**) strip; long strip, narrow strip; band; (*de papel*) slip of paper; **~ (cómica)** comic strip; **~ de películas** film strip; **~ publicitaria** flysheet, leaflet. (**b**) **la ~ de*** lots of, masses of; **estoy desde hace la ~ de tiempo** I've been here for absolute ages; **eso fue hace la ~** that was ages ago.

2 *nm*: **~ y afloja** (**a**) (*cautela*) prudence, caution; (*tacto*) tact.

(**b**) (*lucha*) tug-of-war (*fig*); (*concesiones*) give and take, mutual concessions; **3 horas de ~** 3 hours of touch and go.

tira[2]‡ **1** *nm* (*And, Cono Sur*) cop*. **2** *nf*: **la ~** the cops*, the fuzz‡; (*Uruguay*) the secret police.

tirabuzón *nm* (**a**) (*sacacorchos*) corkscrew; **sacar algo a uno con ~** (*fig*) to drag sth out of sb. (**b**) (*rizo*) curl, ringlet. (**c**) (*Natación*) twist, corkscrew.

tirachinas *nm invar* catapult.

tirada *nf* (**a**) (*acto*) cast, throw; (*Caza*) shoot; **~ de patos** duck shoot.

(**b**) (*distancia*) distance; (*tramo*) stretch; (*Cos*) length; (*fig*) series, number; time; (*Liter*) stanza; sequence; epic laisse; **de una ~** at one go, in a stretch; **lo recitó todo de una ~** he recited the whole lot straight off, he reeled the lot off; **estuvo con nosotros una ~ de días** he spent a number of days with us; **de B a C hay una ~ de 18 kms** from B to C there is a stretch of 18 kms.

(**c**) (*Tip*: *acto*) printing, edition; (*cantidad*) print-run; **~ aparte** offprint, reprint.

(**d**) (*LAm*: *discurso*) boring speech, tedious discourse.

(**e**) (*Cono Sur*: *indirecta*) hint.

(**f**) (*Carib*: *mala pasada*) dirty trick.

(**g**) (‡: *puta*) whore, slut.

tiradera *nf* (**a**) (*CAm, Carib, Cono Sur*) (*faja*) sash; (*correa*) belt, strap; (*Carib*: *de caballo*) harness strap, trace. (**b**) (*And, CAm**: *mofa*) taunt.

tiradero *nm* (*Méx*) tip, rubbish-dump; (*fig*) mess; **esta casa es un ~** this house is a tip*.

tirado *adj* (**a**) (*Náut*) rakish; *escritura* cursive.

(**b**) **estar ~*** (*Com*) to be dirt-cheap; to be a glut on the market; (*tarea etc*) to be very simple; **esa asignatura está tirada** that subject is dead easy*. (**c**) **quedarse ~** to be left in the lurch.

tirador *nm* (**a**) (*persona*) marksman, shot; shooter; (*CAm, Méx*) hunter; **~ apostado** sniper; **~ certero** sharpshooter; **~ de élite** marksman.

(**b**) (*puño*) handle, knob, button; (*de puerta*) doorknob; (*Elec*) cord; **~ de campanilla** bellrope, bellpull.

(**c**) (*tirachinas*) catapult.

(**d**) (*Arte, Téc*: *pluma*) drawing-pen.

(**e**) (*And, Cono Sur*: *cinturón*) wide gaucho belt.

(**f**) **~es** (*And, Cono Sur*) braces, suspenders (*US*).

tiragomas *nm invar* catapult.

tiraje *nm* (**a**) (*Tip*) (*impresión*) printing; (*cantidad*) print run. (**b**) (*CAm, Cono Sur, Méx*: *de chimenea*) chimney flue.

tiralevitas *nm invar* bootlicker*; creep‡.

tiralíneas *nm invar* drawing-pen, ruling pen.

tiranía *nf* tyranny.

tiránicamente *adv* tyrannically.

tiranicida *nm* tyrannicide (*person*).

tiranicidio *nm* tyrannicide (*act*).

tiránico *adj* tyrannical; despotic; *amor* possessive, domineering; *atracción* irresistible, all-powerful.

tiranizar [1f] *vt* to tyrannize, rule despotically; to domineer.

tirano 1 *adj* tyrannical, despotic; domineering. **2** *nm*, **tirana** *nf* tyrant, despot. **3** *nm* (*Méx**) cop*.

tirantas *nfpl* (*And, Méx*) braces, suspenders (*US*).

tirante 1 *adj* (**a**) *cuerda etc* tight, taut; tensed; drawn tight.

(**b**) *relaciones, situación etc* tense, strained; **las cosas andan algo ~s** things are rather strained.

(**c**) (*Fin*) tight.

2 *nm* (**a**) (*Arquit*) tie, brace, crosspiece; (*Mec*) brace, stay, strut.

(**b**) (*de arreos*) trace; (*de vestido*) shoulder strap; **~s** braces, suspenders (*US*); **vestido sin ~s** strapless dress.

tirantear [1a] *vt* (*CAm, Cono Sur*) to stretch.

tirantez *nf* (**a**) (*tensión*) tightness, tautness; tension.

(**b**) (*fig*) tension, strain; **la ~ de las relaciones con Eslobodia** the strained relations with Slobodia, the tense state of relations with Slobodia; **ha disminuido la ~** the tension has lessened.

(**c**) (*Fin*) tightness; stringency.

tirar [1a] **1** *vt* (**a**) (*lanzar*) to throw; to hurl, fling, cast, sling; (*sin querer*) to drop; (*volcar*) to knock over, knock down; *edificio* to pull down; *tiro* to fire, shoot; *cohete* to fire, launch; *bomba* to drop; **el aparato tira el proyectil a 2000 metros** the machine throws the projectile 2000 metres; **estaban tirando la fruta con palos largos** they were knocking the fruit down with long poles; **el viento ha tirado la valla** the wind has knocked the fence down; **me tiró un beso** she blew me a kiss.

(**b**) *basura etc* to throw away; to chuck out; *fortuna* to waste, squander; **estos calcetines están para ~los** these socks are ready to be thrown away; **hay que ~ los podridos** the rotten ones ought to be thrown out; **has tirado el dinero comprando eso** you've thrown your money away buying that.

(**c**) *alambre* to draw out.

(**d**) *línea* to draw, trace, rule.

(**e**) (*Tip*) to print, run off.

(**f**) *golpe etc* to give, deal, fetch; **~ una coz a uno** to give sb a kick; **~ un mordisco a uno** to give sb a bite; **~ tajos a uno** to slash at sb.

(**g**) (*And*: *usar*) to use; to work with; **~ brazo** to swim.

(**h**) (*And, Carib, Cono Sur*: *acarrear*) to cart, haul, transport.

(**i**) **~la de** to fancy oneself as, pose as.

2 *vi* (**a**) (*Mil etc*) to shoot (*a* at), fire (*a* at, on); **~ a matar** to shoot to kill; **~ con bala** to use live ammunition; **¡no tires!** don't shoot.

(**b**) **~ de** *objeto* to pull, tug; *carro etc* to draw (along), haul; *cuerda etc* to pull (on), tug (at); *cartera, pañuelo etc* to pull out, take out (suddenly), yank out; *espada* to draw; **~ de la manga de uno** to tug at sb's sleeve; **tire de ese cabo** pull that end; **este vestido tira un poco de aquí** this dress is a bit tight here; **tiraron de cuchillos** they drew their knives; **'~', 'tirad'** (*Esp*), **'tire'** (*LAm*) (*en puerta etc*) 'pull'; **el motor no tira** the engine is sluggish.

(**c**) (*imán etc*) to draw, attract; (*fig*) to draw, pull, have a pull; to appeal; **no le tira el estudio** study does not attract him; **la patria tira siempre** one's native land always exerts a powerful pull.

(**d**) (*chimenea etc*) to draw.

(**e**) (*Esp**) **ir tirando** to get along, manage; **vamos tirando** we manage, we keep going; **esos zapatos tirarán todavía otro invierno** those shoes will last out another winter.

(**f**) (*: *ir*) to go; **tire Vd adelante** go straight on; **¡tira (adelante)!** get on with it!; **~ a la derecha** to turn right; to keep right; **~ por una calle** to turn down a street, go off along a street.

(**g**) **~ a** (*tender*) to tend to, tend towards; **~ a rojo** to have some red in it, have a touch of red about it; **~ a viejo** to be getting old, be elderly; **~ a su padre** to take after one's father, resemble one's father; **él tira más bien a cuidadoso** he's on the careful side; **tira a hacerse servir** he tends to make others wait on him; **~ para médico** to have inclinations towards a medical career, feel like becoming a doctor, be attracted towards a career in medicine.

(**h**) **~ a** (*proponerse*) to aim at being, work to become; (*pey*) to intrigue to become; **~ a** + *infin* to aim to + *infin*; (*pey*) to intrigue in order to + *infin*, go surreptitiously to work to + *infin*.

(**i**) (*Dep*: *a portería etc*) to shoot; (*jugar*) to go, play, have one's turn; **tira tú ahora** it's your go now; **tiró fuera**

de la portería he shot wide of the goal; **¡tira!** shoot!

(j) **a todo ~** at the most; **nos queda gasolina para 20 kms a todo ~** we have only enough petrol for 20 kms at the outside (*o* at the most); **llegará el martes a todo ~** he'll arrive on Tuesday at the latest.

(k) (**) to screw**.

3 tirarse *vr* (a) (*lanzarse*) to throw o.s., hurl o.s.; **~ al agua** to dive (*o* plunge) into the water; **~ al suelo** to throw o.s. to the ground; **~ por una ventana** to throw o.s. out of a window; to jump from a window; **~ por un risco** to throw o.s. over a cliff; **~ en paracaídas** to parachute (down), (*en emergencia*) bale out; **~ en la cama** to lie down on one's bed; **~ sobre uno** to rush at sb, spring on sb.

(b) (*fig*) to cheapen o.s., demean o.s.; to waste o.s. in an unworthy job.

(c) **~ a una**** (*t* **tirársela**) to screw sb**.

(d) **me tiré mucho tiempo haciéndolo** I spent a lot of time doing it, it took me a lot of time to do it.

(e) (*: *irse*) **~ a otra parte** to clear off somewhere else*.

tirilla *nf* (a) band, strip; (*Cos*) neckband. (b) (*Cono Sur*) shabby dress, ragged garment.

tirillas* *nmf* (a) (*sin importancia*) unimportant person, nobody; **¡vete, ~!** get along, little man! (b) (*pequeño*) undersized individual, runt.

tirillento *adj* (*LAm*) ragged, shabby.

tirita *nf* (*Cos*) tag, tape (*for name, on clothing*); (*Med*) (sticking) plaster, bandaid (*US*).

tiritaña* *nf* mere trifle.

tiritar [1a] *vi* (a) to shiver (*de* with).

(b) (*) **dejaron el pastel tiritando** they almost finished the cake off; **este plato ha quedado tiritando** there isn't much left of this dish.

tiritón *nm* shiver.

tiritona *nf* shivering (fit).

Tiro *nm* Tyre.

tiro *nm* (a) (*lanzamiento*) throw.

(b) (*Mil etc*) shot; (*ruido*) sound of a shot, report; (*impacto*) impact of a shot, hit; (*señal*) bullet mark; (*gen*) shooting, firing; **~ con arco** archery; **~ al blanco** target practice, shooting practice; **~ de escopeta, ~ de fusil** gunshot; **~ al (o de) pichón** clay-pigeon shooting; **~ al plato** trap-shooting; **cañón de ~ rápido** quick-firing gun; **descargar un ~** to fire a shot; **errar el ~** to miss, miss with one's shot; **se oyó un ~** a shot was heard; **se pegó un ~** he shot himself; **le pegó un ~ a su novio** she shot her lover; **¡que le peguen cuatro ~s!** he ought to be shot!; **le salió el ~ por la culata** the scheme (*etc*) backfired; **hacer ~ a** (*fig*) to have designs on, aim at; **no lo haría ni a ~s** I wouldn't do it for love nor money; **esperar a ver por dónde van los ~s** to wait and see which way the wind is blowing; **liarse a ~s con** (*fig*) to get involved in a violent argument with; **matar a uno a ~s** to shoot sb (dead); **tendrán que decidirlo a ~s** they'll have to shoot it out; **me cae (o sienta) como un ~** I need it like I need a hole in the head.

(c) (*Dep*) shot; drive; **~ de aproximación** (*Golf*) approach shot; **~ libre** (*fútbol*) free kick; (*básquet*) free throw; **~ a gol** shot at goal; **~ de revés** backhand drive; **parar un ~** to stop a shot.

(d) (*Mil etc*: *alcance*) range; **a ~ de fusil** within gunshot; **a ~ de piedra** within a stone's throw; **estar a ~** to be within range; (*fig*) to be accessible; **si se pone a ~ se lo diré** if he comes my way I'll tell him; **ponerse a ~*** (*mujer*) to offer herself.

(e) (*campo de tiro*) rifle-range; (*galería de tiro*) shooting-gallery.

(f) (*caballos etc*) team of horses (*etc*); **caballo de ~** cart-horse, draught horse.

(g) (*Cos*) length (of cloth *etc*); **andar de ~s largos** to be all dressed up, be very smartly turned out.

(h) (*cuerda*) rope, cord; (*cadena*) chain; (*de timbre*) bellpull; (*de arreos*) trace, strap; **~s** (*Mil*) swordbelt; **~s** (*Cono Sur*) braces, suspenders (*US*).

(i) (*Arquit*) flight of stairs.

(j) (*de chimenea etc*) draught; (*Min*) shaft; **~ de mina** mineshaft.

(k) (*fig*: *revés*) blow; setback.

(l) (*fig*) (*ataque*) veiled attack; (*alusión*) damaging allusion.

(m) (*fig*: *broma*) trick, hoax; practical joke.

(n) (*fig*) (*robo*) petty theft; (*engaño*) petty deceit.

(o) (*And, Cono Sur, Méx*: *canica*) marble.

(p) (*Cono Sur Carreras*) distance, course.

(q) (*Méx*) (*número*) issue; (*edición*) edition.

(r) (*Cono Sur*: *indirecta*) hint.

(s) (*Carib*: *astucia*) craftiness, cunning.

(t) (*CAm, Cono Sur*: *locuciones*) **al ~** at once, right away; **a ~ de** + *infin* about to + *infin*, on the point of + *ger*; **de a ~** completely; **del ~** consequently; **hacer algo de un ~** to do sth in one go.

(u) **~ de cuerda, ~ de soga** tug-of-war.

tiroideo *adj* thyroid.

tiroides *nf* (*t* **glándula ~**) thyroid (gland).

Tirol *nm*: **El ~** the Tyrol.

tirolés, -esa *adj, nm/f* Tyrolese.

tirón[1] *nm* (a) (*acción brusca*) pull, tug, sudden jerk; hitch; (*Pol etc*) shake-up; **~ (de bolsos)** bag-snatching; **~ de orejas** (*fig*) reminder; rebuke, reprimand; **dar un ~ a** to pull at, tug at; to jerk suddenly; **le dieron un ~ al bolso** they snatched her bag; **me lo arrancó de un ~** she suddenly jerked it away from me; **el coche se movía a tirones** the car moved along in a series of jerks, the car went jerkily forward; **pegar un ~ a*** to shoot up.

(b) (*fig*) **de un ~** all at once; in one go, straight off, without a break; **leyó la novela de un ~** she read the novel straight through; **se lo bebió de un ~** he drank it down in one go; **trabajan 10 horas de un ~** they work 10 hours at a stretch.

(c) **ganar el ~ a uno** (*Cono Sur**) to steal a march on sb, beat sb to it.

(d) (*fuerza de atracción*) pull, power, attraction.

tirón[2] *nm* (*persona*) tyro, novice.

tirona* *nf* whore.

tironear [1a] *vt* (*LAm*) = **tirar 2 (b)**.

tironero *nm*, **tironista** *nm* bag-snatcher.

tirotear [1a] **1** *vt* to shoot at, fire on; to blaze away at; to snipe at; (*y matar etc*) to shoot, shoot down. **2 tirotearse** *vr* to exchange shots; to blaze away at each other.

tiroteo *nm* (*tiros*) firing, shooting, exchange of shots; (*escaramuza*) skirmish; (*batalla*) gunfight; (*con policía*) shoot-out; **~ cruzado** crossfire.

Tirreno *adj* : **Mar ~** Tyrrhenian Sea.

tirria *nf* dislike; ill will; **tener ~ a** to dislike, have a grudge against.

tisaje *nm* weaving.

tisana *nf* tisane, infusion.

tísico 1 *adj* consumptive, tubercular. **2** *nm*, **tísica** *nf* consumptive.

tisiqu(i)ento *adj* (*Cono Sur*) (*Med*) consumptive; (*fig*) pale and thin.

tisis *nf* consumption, tuberculosis.

tisú *nm, pl* **tisus** lamé, tissue.

tisular *adj* tissue (*atr*).

tít. *abr de* **título** title.

tita* *nf* auntie*, aunty*.

titán *nm* Titan.

titánico *adj* titanic.

titanio *nm* titanium.

titeador* *adj* (*And, Cono Sur*) mocking, derisive.

titear* [1a] *vt* (*And, Cono Sur*) to mock, scoff at; to make fun of.

titeo* *nm* (*And, Cono Sur*) mockery, scoffing; **tomar a uno para el ~** to scoff at sb; to make fun of sb.

títere 1 *nm* (a) puppet, marionette; **~s** puppets; (*espectáculo*) puppet show; (*arte*) puppetry; **~ de guante** glove puppet; **no dejar ~ con cabeza** to turn everything upside down; to break up everything in sight; to spare no-one.

(b) (*fig*) puppet; (*instrumento*) cat's-paw; (*débil, soso*) weak person, colourless individual; (*poco fiable*) untrustworthy person; (*de aspecto raro*) odd-looking person.

2 *atr*: **gobierno ~** puppet government.

titi **1** *nm* bloke*, chap*; (*en oración directa*) man. **2** *nf* bird*, chick* (*US*).

tití *nm* (*LAm*) capuchin (monkey).

titilar [1a] *vi* (*párpado etc*) to flutter, tremble; (*estrella, luz*) to twinkle.

titipuchal* *nm* (*Méx*) (noisy) crowd.

titiritaña *nf* (*Méx*) (a) (*espectáculo*) puppet show. (b) (*fig*) piece of trivia; **de ~** sickly.

titiritero, -a *nm/f* (*que maneja títeres*) puppeteer; (*acróbata*) acrobat; (*malabarista*) juggler; (*artista de circo*) circus artist.

tito* *nm* uncle.

Tito Livio *nm* Livy.

titubeante *adj* (a) tottery; *mueble etc* shaky, unsteady. (b) stammering; halting. (c) hesitant.

titubear [1a] *vi* (**a**) (*al andar*) to totter; to stagger; (*mueble etc*) to be unstable, be shaky, be unsteady; (*borracho*) to reel.

(**b**) (*Ling*) to stammer; to falter.

(**c**) (*vacilar*) to hesitate, vacillate; **no ~ en** + *infin* not to hesitate to + *infin*.

titubeo *nm* (*V v*) (**a**) tottering; staggering; instability, shakiness, unsteadiness.

(**b**) (*Ling*) stammering; faltering.

(**c**) hesitation, vacillation; **proceder sin ~s** to act resolutely, act without hesitation.

titulación *nf* (*Univ*) (system of) degrees and diplomas.

titulado 1 *adj* (**a**) *libro etc* entitled.

(**b**) *persona* titled.

(**c**) *persona* (*Univ etc*) with a degree, having a degree; qualified; (*Téc etc*) trained, skilled.

2 *nm*, **titulada** *nf* (*Univ*) graduate.

titular 1 *adj* titular, official; *campeón* reigning; defending.

2 *nm* (*Tip*: *t* **~es**) headline.

3 *nmf* (*de puesto*) holder, occupant; (*jefe*) head; (*Dep*) regular player, first-team player; (*LAm Dep*) captain; (*Ecl*) incumbent; (*de pasaporte, récord etc*) holder; (*de coche etc*) owner.

4 *vt* [1a] to title, entitle, call.

5 titularse *vr* (**a**) (*llamarse*) to be entitled, be called; to call o.s., style o.s. (**b**) (*Univ*) to graduate.

titularidad *nf* (**a**) (*propiedad*) ownership; **empresa de ~ pública** publicly-owned company. (**b**) (*Fin*) bond. (**c**) (*Dep*) first(-team) place, top spot. (**d**) (*Pol*: *puesto*) ministerial post; (*período*) term of office, tenure; **durante la ~ de Bush** during Bush's period of office.

titulillo *nm* (*Tip*) running title, page heading; (*Prensa*) subhead, section heading; **andar en ~s*** to watch out for every little thing.

titulitis *nf* (*hum*) mania for employing graduate personnel; obsession with acquiring an academic degree.

título *nm* (**a**) (*gen*) title; (*Jur etc*) section heading; (*artículo*) article; (*de presupuesto*) item; (*Tip*) title; (*de periódico*) headline; **~s de crédito** credits, credit titles; **a ~ de** by way of; in the capacity of; **a ~ de curiosidad** as a matter of interest; **el dinero fue a ~ de préstamo** the money was given as a loan, the money was by way of being a loan; **nos lo dijo a ~ de noticia alentadora** he told us it as being a cheering piece of news; **a ~ no exclusivo detallamos ...** for purposes of illustration we specify the following ...; **a ~ personal** for one's own part, personally, in a personal way; **a ~ póstumo** posthumously.

(**b**) (*de persona*) title; **~ de nobleza, ~ nobiliario** title of nobility.

(**c**) (*fig*: *noble*) titled person; **casarse con un ~** to marry a titled person, marry into the nobility.

(**d**) (*calificación profesional*) professional qualification; (*diploma*) diploma, certificate; (*Univ*) degree; (*fig*) qualification; (*Carib Aut*) driving licence; **~s** qualifications, credentials; **con ~ superior** with higher education; **~ universitario** university degree; **maestro sin ~** unqualified teacher; **obtener un ~** to obtain a qualification; to take a degree; **tener los ~s para un puesto** to have the qualifications for a job.

(**e**) (*de carácter etc*) quality; **no es precisamente un ~ de gloria para él** it is not exactly a quality on which he can pride himself; **tiene varios ~s honrosos** he has several noble qualities, he has a number of worthy attributes.

(**f**) (*Jur*) title; **~ de propiedad** title deed.

(**g**) (*Fin*) bond; **~ al portador** bearer bond; **~ de renta fija** fixed-interest security; **~ de renta variable** variable-yield security.

(**h**) (*fig*: *derecho*) right; **con justo ~** rightly; **¿con qué ~?** by what right?; **tener ~ de** + *infin* to be entitled to + *infin*, have the right to + *infin*; **le sobran ~s para hacerlo** he has every right to do it.

tiza *nf* (**a**) (*para escribir*: *t Billar*) chalk; (*de zapatos*) whitening; **una ~** a piece of chalk. (**b**) (*And*) exaggeration.

tizar [1f] *vt* (*Cono Sur*) to plan; to design, model; (*And*) *traje* to mark out for cutting.

tizate *nm* (*CAm, Méx*) chalk.

Tiziano *nm* Titian.

tizna *nf* black, grime.

tiznado‡ *nm* (*pey*) darkie‡.

tiznajo* *nm* black mark, dirty smear.

tiznar [1a] **1** *vt* (**a**) (*ennegrecer*) to blacken, black; (*manchar*) to smudge, soil, stain, spot; (*untar*) to smear (*de* with).

(**b**) (*fig*) to stain, tarnish; to defame, blacken.

2 tiznarse *vr* (**a**) **~ la cara con un corcho quemado** to blacken one's face with burnt cork.

(**b**) (*mancharse*) to get smudged, get soiled (*etc*).

(**c**) (*CAm, Cono Sur, Méx**: *emborracharse*) to get drunk.

tizne *nm* (**a**) (*hollín*) soot; (*mancha negra*) black smear, blackening; (*mugre*) grime; smut. (**b**) (*fig*) stain.

tiznón *nm* smut, speck of soot; smudge.

tizo *nm* burning piece of wood, brand.

tizón *nm* (**a**) (*tea*) burning piece of wood, brand; half-burned piece of wood. (**b**) (*Bot*) smut. (**c**) (*fig*: *mancha*) stain.

tizonazos *nmpl* (*fig*) pains of hell.

tizonear [1a] *vt fuego* to poke, stir.

tizos‡ *nmpl* dabs‡, fingers.

tlacanear* [1a] *vt* (*Méx*) to feel up‡.

tlacote *nm* (*Méx*) growth, tumour.

tlacual‡ *nm* (*Méx*) (**a**) (*comida*) food; meal. (**b**) (*olla*) cooking pot.

tlachique *nm* (*Méx*) unfermented *pulque*.

tlapalería *nf* (*Méx*) (*ferretería*) ironmonger's, hardware store; (*papelería*) stationer's.

tlapiloya‡ *nf* (*Méx*) clink‡, jail.

tlapisquera *nf* (*Méx*) shed, barn, granary.

tlecuil *nm* (*Méx*) brazier.

T.m., Tm, tm *abr de* **tonelada(s) métrica(s)** metric ton(s).

toa *nf* (*LAm*) hawser, rope, towrope.

toalla *nf* towel; **~ de baño** bath-towel; **~ de playa, ~ playera** beach-towel; **~ de rodillo** roller towel; **arrojar** (*o* **tirar**) **la ~** to throw in the towel.

toallero *nm* towel-rail.

toba‡ *nf* (**a**) (*colilla*) dog-end‡. (**b**) (*puñetazo*) punch, bash*.

tobar [1a] *vt* (*And*) to tow.

tobera *nf* nozzle.

tobillera *nf* (**a**) ankle-sock. (**b**)(*) teenager, bobbysoxer* (*US*).

tobillero *nm* ankle-sock; (*Dep*) ankle-guard.

tobillo *nm* ankle.

tobo *nm* (*Carib*) bucket.

tobogán *nm* (**a**) (*trineo*) toboggan. (**b**) (*de feria*) switch-back; **~ gigante** roller-coaster. (**c**) (*para niños*) children's slide; (*en piscina*) chute, slide; **~ acuático** water-slide.

toc *adv*: **¡~ ~!** (*en puerta*) rat-a-tat!; knock, knock!

toca[1] *nf* (*sombrero*) headdress; (*de mujer*) bonnet; toque; **~s de viuda** widow's weeds.

toca[2] *nmf* (*LAm*) = **tocayo.**

tocacasete *nm* cassette recorder.

tocadiscos *nm invar* record player, phonograph (*US*); **~ automático** auto-change record player; **~ tragamonedas, ~ tragaperras** jukebox.

tocado[1] *adj* (**a**) *fruta* bad, rotten; *carne etc* tainted, bad; **estar ~** (*Dep*) to be injured; **estar ~ de la cabeza** to be weak in the head.

(**b**) **una creencia tocada de heterodoxia** a belief tainted with heterodoxy.

(**c**) **estar ~ de piedad** to be all piety, have got religion.

tocado[2] **1** *adj*: **~ con un sombrero de paja** wearing a straw hat, with a straw hat on his head.

2 *nm* (**a**) (*sombrero*) headdress, headgear, hat.

(**b**) (*peinado*) coiffure, hair-do.

(**c**) (*atavío*) toilet.

tocador[1] *nm* (**a**) (*mueble*) dressing table; **jabón de ~** toilet soap; **juego de ~** toilet set.

(**b**) (*neceser*) toilet case.

(**c**) (*cuarto*) boudoir, dressing room; **~ de señoras** ladies' room.

tocador[2](a) *nm/f* (*Mús*) player.

tocadorista *nmf* (*Cine, TV*) dresser.

tocamientos *nmpl* (sexual) molestation.

tocante 1 : **~ a** *prep* with regard to, about; **en lo ~ a** so far as concerns, as for. **2** *adj* (*Cono Sur*) moving, touching.

tocar[1] [1g] **1** *vt* (**a**) (*gen*) to touch; to feel; to handle; *timbre* to touch, press; **~ las cosas de cerca** to experience things for oneself, learn about things at first hand; **sin ~ un pelo de su ropa** without laying a finger on her; **¡no me toques!** don't touch me!; **que nadie toque mis papeles** don't let anyone touch my papers, don't interfere with my papers.

(**b**) (*2 objetos*) to touch, be touching; **la mesa toca la pared** the table touches the wall, the table is up against the wall.

(**c**) (*Mús*) to play; *campana* to ring; to toll, peal; *tambor* to play, beat; *trompeta* to play, blow, sound; *sirena etc* to sound; *disco, cinta* to play; *hora* to chime, strike; **~ la generala** (*Mil*) to sound the call to arms; **~ la retirada** to sound the retreat.

(**d**) (*Arte*) to touch up.

(**e**) (*fig*: *conmover*) to touch; ~ **el corazón de uno** to touch sb's heart.

(**f**) *obstáculo etc* to hit, strike, collide with, run into; (*Náut*) to go aground on, run on to; (*Caza*) to hit, wing; *blanco etc* to hit.

(**g**) *tema* to touch on, refer to, allude to; **no tocó para nada esa cuestión** he didn't refer to that matter at all.

(**h**) *consecuencias* to suffer, undergo, come in for; **él tocará las consecuencias de todo esto** he will suffer the consequences of all this.

(**i**) (*afectar*) to concern, affect; **esto no te toca a ti** this doesn't concern you; **ello me toca de cerca** it concerns me closely; **por lo que a mí me toca** as far as I'm concerned.

(**j**) (*) to be related to; **X no le toca para nada a Y** X is not related at all to Y, X is no relation to Y.

2 *vi* (**a**) ~ **a una puerta** to knock on (*o* at) a door.

(**b**) **tocan a misa** they are ringing the bell for mass; **ese timbre toca a fuego** that bell sounds the fire alarm; **¡a pagar tocan!** it's time to pay up!

(**c**) **~le a uno** to fall to sb, fall to sb's lot; to fall to sb's share; **les tocó un dólar a cada uno** each one got a dollar as his share; **¿les tocará algo de herencia?** will they get anything under the will?; **le ha tocado otro premio** he has won another prize; **te toca jugar** it's your turn (to play), it's your go; **¿a quién le toca?** whose turn is it?; **¿a quién le toca pagar esta vez?** whose turn is it to pay this time?; **le toca a Vd reprenderle** it is up to you to reprimand him.

(**d**) (*impersonal*) **no toca hacerlo hasta el mes que viene** it's not due to be done until next month; **ahora toca torcer a la derecha** now you have to turn right, now there's a right turn coming up.

(**e**) (*Náut*) ~ **en** to call at, touch at; **el barco no toca en Barcelona** the ship does not call at Barcelona.

(**f**) (*fig*) ~ **en** to border on, verge on; **esto toca en locura** this verges on madness.

3 tocarse *vr* (**a**) to touch each other, be in contact.

(**b**) **tocárselas*** to beat it*.

(**c**) **tocársela** (*Esp*⁂: *masturbarse*) to wank⁂; (*fig*) not to do a stroke (of work).

(**d**) (*LAm*⁑: *drogarse*) to be on drugs.

tocar[2] [1g] **1** *vt pelo* to do, arrange, set. **2 tocarse** *vr* to cover one's head, put on one's hat.

tocata* *nf* record-player.

tocateja: **a** ~ *adv* on the nail.

tocayo, -a *nm/f* (**a**) (*gen*) namesake. (**b**) (*And*: *amigo*) friend.

tocinillo *nm*: ~ **de cielo** pudding made with egg yolk and syrup.

tocino *nm* (*t* ~ **de panceta**) bacon; salt pork; ~ **veteado** streaky bacon.

toco[1]**, -a** *nm/f* (*CAm*) = **tocayo.**

toco[2] *nm* (*Carib*) = **tocón.**

toco[3]⁑ *nm* : **costó un** ~ (*Cono Sur*) it cost a hell of a lot.

tocoginecología *nf* obstetrics.

tocoginecólogo, -a *nm/f* obstetrician.

tocología *nf* obstetrics.

tocólogo, -a *nm/f* obstetrician.

tocolotear [1a] *vi* (*Carib Naipes*) to shuffle (the cards).

tocomocho* *nm* con*, swindle.

tocón[1] **1** *adj* (**a**) (*And*: *sin rabo*) tailless; (*Carib*: *sin cuernos*) hornless. (**b**) = **sobón. 2** *nm* (*Anat, Bot*) stump.

tocón[2]* *nm* person given to excessive touching; (*fig*) dirty old man.

tocuyo *nm* (*And, Cono Sur*) coarse cotton cloth.

toche *nm* (*Méx*) hare.

tochimbo *nm* (*And*) smelting furnace.

tocho* *nm* big fat book, tome; mass of reading matter.

todavía *adv* still, yet; ~ **no** not yet; ~ **en 1980** as late as 1980, right up to 1980; ~ **no lo ha encontrado** he still has not found it, he has not found it yet; **está nevando** ~ it is still snowing; **es** ~ **más inteligente que su hermano** he is still (*o* yet) more intelligent than his brother.

(**b**) (*LAm*: *no obstante*) nonetheless, nevertheless.

todo 1 *adj* (**a**) (*gen*) all; (*entero*) whole, entire; (*cada*) every; ~ **el bosque** all the wood, the whole wood, the entire wood; **el universo** ~ the whole universe; **lo sabe** ~ **Madrid** all Madrid knows it, the whole of Madrid knows it; **lo golpeó con toda su fuerza** he hit him with his full strength, he hit him with all his might; **a toda velocidad** at full speed, at top speed; **con toda prisa** in all haste, with all speed; **en toda España** all over Spain, throughout Spain; **en toda España no hay más que 5** there are only 5 in the whole of Spain; ~ **lo demás** all the rest, all else; **~s vosotros** all of you; **~s los libros** all the books; **todas las semanas** every week; **viene ~s los martes** he comes every Tuesday; ~ **el que quiera ...** everyone who wants to ...; whoever wants to ...; **~s los que quieran ...** all those who want to ...; ~ **lo que ves aquí** all that you see here; ~ **lo que necesites** whatever you need; **con toda su inteligencia** with all his intelligence; in spite of all his intelligence; **de todas todas*** the whole lot, all of them without exception; **¡te digo que sí de todas todas!** (*Esp*) I tell you it jolly well is!*; **es verdad de todas todas** it's absolutely true; *V* **cuanto** *etc.*

(**b**) (*negativo*) **en** ~ **el día** not once all day; **en toda la noche he dormido** I haven't slept all night; **en toda España lo encuentras** you won't find it anywhere in Spain; **dio un portazo por toda respuesta** his only response was to slam the door.

(**c**) (*locuciones*) **es** ~ **un hombre** he's every inch a man; **es** ~ **un palacio** it's a real palace; **es** ~ **un héroe** he's a real hero; **la hija es toda su madre** the daughter is exactly like her mother; **tiene toda la nariz de su abuela** her nose is exactly like her grandmother's; **el niño estaba** ~ **ojos** the child was all eyes; **ese hombre es** ~ **ambición** that man is all ambition (and nothing else); **a** ~ **esto** (*entretanto*) meanwhile; (*de pasada*) by the way.

2 *adv* (**a**) all, entirely, completely; **estaba** ~ **rendido** he was completely worn out; **para las 8 estará** ~ **hecho** it will be completely finished by 8 o'clock; **lleva un vestido** ~ **roto** she's wearing a dress that's all torn.

(**b**) **puede ser** ~ **lo sencillo que Vd quiera** it can be as simple as you wish; *V* **más** *etc.*

3 *conj* **con** ~ **y** (*LAm*) in spite of; **el equipo, con** ~ **y estar integrado por buenos jugadores ...** the team, in spite of being (*o* for all that it is) made up of good players ...

4 *nm y pron* (**a**) all, everything; **~s** everybody; every one of them; **el** ~ the whole; **en un** ~ together, as a whole; **~s y cada uno** all and sundry; **lo comió** ~ he ate it all; **lo han vendido** ~ they've sold it all, they've sold the lot; ~ **lo sabemos** we know everything; ~ **o nada** all or nothing; ~ **es** (*o* **son**) **reveses** it's all setbacks, there's nothing but troubles; **y luego** ~ **son sonrisas** and then it's all smiles; ~ **cabe en él** he is capable of anything; **ser el** ~ to be the most important thing; (*: *persona*) to be the mainstay; to run the show, dominate everything; **y** ~ and so on, and what not; **tienen un coche nuevo y** ~ they have a new car and everything; **los zapatos, viejos y** ~**, durarán otro año** these shoes, old though they are, will last another year; **andando rápidamente y** ~**, no llegaron a tiempo** even though they walked quickly they still didn't get there in time; *V* **jugarse** *etc.*

(**b**) (*locuciones con prep*) **ir a** ~ to go forward resolutely, be prepared to do or die; **ante** ~ first of all, in the first place; primarily; **a pesar de** ~ even so, in spite of everything; all the same; **con** ~ still, however; in spite of everything; **de** ~ **como en botica** everything under the sun; **de** ~ **hay en este mundo de Dios, de** ~ **hay en la viña del Señor** it takes all sorts to make a world; **le llamaron de** ~ they called him every name under the sun; **del** ~ wholly, completely; **no es del** ~ **verdad** it is not entirely true, it is not quite true; **no es del** ~ **malo** it is not wholly bad; **después de** ~ after all; **está en** ~* he's on the ball, he doesn't miss a trick; **para** ~ all-purpose; **por** ~ all in all; **sobre** ~ especially; above all, most of all.

todopoderoso *adj* almighty, all-powerful; **el T~** the Almighty.

todoterreno 1 *nm invar* jeep, (type of) Land Rover ®, all-purpose vehicle. **2** *atr* multi-purpose; adaptable; *persona* for all seasons.

tofo *nm* (*Cono Sur*) white clay; fireclay.

toga *nf* (*Hist*) toga; (*Jur etc*) gown, robe; (*Univ*) gown; **tomar la** ~ to qualify as a lawyer.

togado, -a *nm/f* lawyer.

Togo *nm* Togo.

Togolandia *nf* Togoland.

togolés, -esa *adj, nm/f* Togolese.

toilette [tua'le] *nf* (*Cono Sur*) toilet, lavatory.

toisón *nm* : ~ **(de oro)** Golden Fleece.

tojo[1] *nm* (*Bot*) gorse, furze.

tojo[2] *adj* (*And*) twin.

Tokio, Tokío *nm* Tokyo.

tol *nm* (*CAm*) gourd.

tolda *nf* (**a**) (*And, Carib*: *tela*) canvas.

(**b**) (*And*) (*tienda*) tent, improvised hut; (*refugio*) shelter; (*de barco*) awning.

(**c**) (*Carib*: *bolsa grande*) large sack.
(**d**) (*Carib*: *cielo nublado*) overcast sky.
(**e**) **él es de la ~ Acción Democrática** (*Carib Pol*) he belongs to Acción Democrática.

toldería *nf* (*And, Cono Sur*) Indian village, camp of Indian huts.

toldillo *nm* (*And, Carib*) mosquito net.

toldo *nm* (**a**) (*de playa etc*) sunshade, awning; (*de tienda*) sunblind; (*entoldado*) marquee; (*encerado etc*) cover, cloth, tarpaulin.
(**b**) (*And, Cono Sur*: *choza*) Indian hut; (*Méx*: *tienda*) tent.
(**c**) (*And, Carib*) mosquito net.
(**d**) (*Méx Aut*) hood, top (*US*).
(**e**) (*fig*) pride, haughtiness.

tole[1]* *nm* (**a**) (*t* **toletole**: *disturbio*) hubbub, commotion, uproar; (*protesta*) outcry; **levantar el ~** to kick up a fuss; **venir a uno con el ~** to badger sb about something, complain perpetually about something.
(**b**) (*t* **toletole**: *chismes*) gossip, rumour; (*campaña difamatoria*) slander campaign.
(**c**) **coger el ~, tomar el ~** to get out, pack up and go.

tole[2] *nm* (*And*) track, trail.

toledano 1 *adj* Toledan, of Toledo; *V t* **noche. 2** *nm*, **toledana** *nf* Toledan, inhabitant (*o* native) of Toledo; **los ~s** the people of Toledo.

tolempo *nm* (*And*) = **lempo.**

tolerable *adj* tolerable.

tolerancia *nf* (**a**) tolerance; toleration. (**b**) (*Mec*) tolerance.

tolerante *adj* tolerant.

tolerantismo *nm* religious toleration.

tolerar [1a] *vt* (*gen*) to tolerate; (*aguantar*) to bear, endure, put up with; (*permitir*) to allow; **no se puede ~ esto** this cannot be tolerated; **no tolera que digan eso** he won't allow them to say that, he won't put up with their saying that; **su madre le tolera demasiado** his mother spoils him, his mother lets him get away with too much; **su estómago no tolera los huevos** eggs don't agree with him; **el cosmonauta toleró muy bien esta situación difícil** the cosmonaut stood up very well to this awkward situation; **el puente no tolera el peso de los tanques** the bridge will not support the weight of the tanks.

tolete *nm* (**a**) (*Náut*) tholepin. (**b**) (*LAm*: *palo*) short club, stick, cudgel. (**c**) (*And, Carib*: *pedazo*) piece, bit. (**d**) (*And*: *balsa*) raft.

toletole *nm* (**a**) (*Cono Sur**: *jaleo*) row. (**b**) (*And*: *terquedad*) obstinacy, persistence. (**c**) (*Carib**) (*vida alegre*) high life; (*vagabundeo*) roving life; *V t* **tole**[1] (**b**).

Tolomeo *nm* Ptolemy.

Tolón *nm* Toulon.

toloncho *nm* (*And*) piece of wood.

tolondro 1 *adj* scatterbrained. **2** *nm* (*Med*) bump, lump, swelling.

tolondrón *adj, nm* = **tolondro.**

Tolosa (de Francia) *nf* Toulouse.

tolosarra 1 *adj* of Tolosa (*Navarre*). **2** *nmf* native (*o* inhabitant) of Tolosa (*Navarre*); **los ~s** the people of Tolosa.

tolteca 1 *adj* Toltec. **2** *nmf* Toltec.

tolva *nf* (**a**) (*recipiente*) hopper; chute. (**b**) (*Cono Sur, Méx*: *Ferro*) hopper wagon, hopper car (*US*). (**c**) (*Méx Min*) shed for storing ore.

tolvanera *nf* dustcloud.

tolla *nf* (**a**) (*pantano*) marsh, quagmire. (**b**) (*Carib, Méx*: *abrevadero*) drinking trough.

tollina* *nf* hiding*; bashing*.

toma *nf* (**a**) (*gen*) taking; **~ de beneficios** profit-taking; **~ de conciencia** (*conocimiento*) awareness; increasing awareness; (*el darse cuenta*) realization; **~ de contacto** initial contact; first approach; **~ de decisiones** decision-making, decision-taking; **~ de declaración** taking of evidence; **~ de hábito** (*Ecl*) taking of vows; **~ de posesión** taking over; (*de presidente*) taking up of office, inauguration; **~ de tierra** (*Aer*) landing, touchdown; (*Elec*) earth (wire).
(**b**) (*Mil*) capture, taking; seizure.
(**c**) (*cantidad*) amount, portion; (*Med*) dose; (*de bebé*) feed; **~ de rapé** pinch of snuff.
(**d**) (*Mec etc*) (*entrada*) inlet, intake; (*salida*) outlet; (*de agua etc*) tap, outlet; (*Elec*) (*enchufe*) plug, socket; (*cable*) lead; (*borne*) terminal; **~ de agua** source of water supply; **~ de aire** air-inlet, air-intake; **~ de antena** (*Rad*) aerial socket; **~ de corriente, ~ de fuerza** power point, plug; **~ directa** (*Aut*) top gear; **~ de tierra** earth wire, ground wire (*US*).
(**e**) (*Cine, TV*) take, shot; **~ directa** live shot; live broadcast.
(**f**) (*LAm*: *acequia*) irrigation channel; (*CAm*: *arroyo*) brook.

tomacorriente *nm* (*Elec*) plug.

tomada *nf* (*LAm Elec*) plug.

tomadero *nm* (**a**) (*asidero*) handle. (**b**) (*entrada*) inlet, intake; (*grifo*) tap.

tomado *adj* (**a**) (*t* **~ de orín**) rusty. (**b**) *voz* (*LAm*) hoarse. (**c**) **estar ~** to be drunk.

tomador 1 *adj* (*LAm**) drunken, boozy‡. **2** *nm* (**a**) (*Com*) drawee. (**b**) (*: *ladrón*) thief; **~ del dos, ~ del pico** pickpocket. (**c**) (*LAm*: *bebedor*) drunkard, boozer‡.

tomadura *nf* = **toma** (**a**) *y* (**b**); **~ de pelo*** (*burla*) hoax; deception, rip-off‡; (*guasa*) leg-pull*; (*mofa*) mockery; (*insulto*) abuse.

tomaína *nf* ptomaine.

tomante‡ *nm* queer‡.

tomar [1a] **1** *vt* (**a**) (*gen*) to take; to accept; to get, acquire; *aire, baño, curva, decisión, medida, oportunidad, paso, ruta, sol, temperatura etc* to take; *armas, pluma etc* to take up; *actitud* to adopt, take up; to strike; *aspecto, forma etc* to take on; *pelota* to catch, stop; *catarro* to take, get, catch; *hábito* to get into, fall into, acquire; *negocio* to take over; *lección* to have; *nombre* to take, adopt; *criado* to take on, engage; *fuerza* to get, gain, acquire; *billete* to take, get, buy; **¡toma!** here you are!, here!, catch!; **¡tómate ésa!** take that!; **es a ~ o a dejar** it's take it or leave it; **~ y dejar pasajeros** to take up and set down passengers; **~ a uno por policía** to take sb for a policeman, think that sb is a policeman; **~ a uno por loco** to think sb mad; **¿por quién me toma Vd?** what do you take me for?, who do you think I am?; **~ algo sobre sí** to take sth upon o.s.; *V* **mal, serio** *etc.*
(**b**) (*Mil*) to take, capture; to seize; (*ocupar*) to occupy, take over.
(**c**) (*Culin*) to eat, drink, have; **~ el pecho** to suck, feed at the breast; **tomamos unas cervezas** we had a few beers; **¿qué quieres ~?** what will you have?, what would you like?
(**d**) *autobús, tren etc* to take.
(**e**) (*Cine, Fot, TV*) to take; (*Cine*) to shoot; **~ una foto de** to take a photo of.
(**f**) *apuntes* to take; *discurso etc* to take down; **~ por escrito** to write down; **~ en taquigrafía** to take down in shorthand; **~ en cinta** to record on tape.
(**g**) *afecto, asco etc* to acquire, take (*a* to); *V* **cariño** *etc.*
(**h**) (*dominar*) to overcome; **le tomaron ganas de reír** she was overcome by an urge to laugh.
(**i**) **~la con uno** to pick a quarrel with sb; **tenerla tomada con uno** to have a down on sb*, adopt a consistently hostile attitude to sb.
(**j**) (*And*: *molestar*) to upset, annoy.
(**k**) (‡) *mujer* to have.
2 *vi* (**a**) (*Bot*) to take, take root; (*injerto*) to take.
(**b**) **~ a la derecha** to go off to the right, turn right; **~ por una calle** to go off along a street, turn down a street.
(**c**) (*LAm*: *beber*) to drink; **estaba tomando en varios bares** he was drinking in a number of bars.
(**d**) (*) **tomó y lo rompió** he went and broke it; **tomó y se fue** off he went, he upped and went *.
(**e**) **toma y daca** (*como n*) give and take; (*pey*) mutual concessions (for selfish reasons), horse-trading, logrolling; **más vale un ~ que dos te daré** a bird in the hand is worth two in the bush.
(**f**) **¡toma!** well!; there!, fancy that!; I told you so!; (*a perro*) here boy!; **¡toma ya!** believe it or not!
3 tomarse *vr* (**a**) to take; **~ la venganza por su mano** to take vengeance with one's own hands; **no te lo tomes así** don't take it that way; **se lo sabe tomar bien** he knows how to take it, he can take it in his stride; **se tomó unas vacaciones larguísimas** he took tremendously long holidays; **se tomó un tremendo disgusto** he received a very severe blow; **se tomó 13 cervezas seguidas** he drank down 13 beers one after the other.
(**b**) **~ por** to think o.s., consider o.s. to be; **¿por quién se toma aquel ministro?** who does that minister think he is?
(**c**) **~ (de orín)** to get rusty.

Tomás *nm* Thomas; **~ Moro** Thomas More.

tomatal *nm* (**a**) (*sembrío*) tomato bed, tomato field. (**b**) (*LAm*: *planta*) tomato plant.

tomate *nm* (**a**) tomato; **ponerse como un ~** to turn as red as a beetroot. (**b**) (‡: *jaleo*) fuss, row, to-do*; (*pelea*) set-to*; (*pega*) snag, difficulty; **¡qué ~!** what a mess!; **esto tiene ~** this is tough, this is a tough one.

tomatera¹ *nf* (**a**) (*planta*) tomato plant. (**b**) (*Cono Sur**: *juerga*) drunken spree; rowdy party.
tomatero, -a² *nm/f* (*cultivador*) tomato grower; (*comerciante*) tomato dealer.
tomavistas *nm invar* film camera, cine-camera.
tombo‡ *nm* (*And*) fuzz‡, police.
tómbola *nf* tombola.
tomillo *nm* thyme; ~ **salsero** garden thyme.
tominero *adj* (*Méx*) mean.
tomismo *nm* Thomism.
tomista *adj, nmf* Thomist.
tomiza *nf* esparto rope.
tomo¹ *nm* (*libro*) volume; **en 3 ~s** in 3 volumes.
tomo² *nm* (*bulto*) bulk, size; (*fig*) importance; **de ~ y lomo** utter, out-and-out; **un canalla de ~ y lomo** a real swine*.
tomografía *nf* scanner.
tomo-homenaje *nm, pl* **tomos-homenaje** homage volume, Festschrift.
tomón *adj* (*And*) teasing, jokey.
tompiate *nm* (*Méx*) (*canasta*) basket (*of woven palm leaves*); (*bolsa*) pouch (*of woven palm leaves*).
ton: **sin ~ ni son 1** *adv* for no particular reason; without rhyme or reason. **2** *adj argumento etc* hopelessly confused.
tonada *nf* (**a**) (*Mús*) tune, song, air. (**b**) (*LAm*: *acento*) accent, local peculiarity, typical intonation. (**c**) (*Carib*) (*embuste*) fib; (*juego de palabras*) pun.
tonadilla *nf* little tune; merry tune, light-hearted song.
tonal *adj* tonal.
tonalidad *nf* (**a**) (*Mús*) key; tonality; (*Rad*) tone; **~ mayor** major key; **~ menor** minor key; **control de ~** tone control.
(**b**) (*Arte*) shade; colour scheme; **una bella ~ de verde** a beautiful shade of green; **cambiar la ~ de un cuarto** to change the colour scheme of a room.
tonel *nm* (**a**) barrel, cask, vat, keg; (**b**) (*: *persona*) fat lump.
tonelada *nf* ton; **~ americana, ~ corta** short ton; **~ inglesa, ~ larga** long ton, gross ton; **~ métrica** metric ton; **~ de registro** register ton; **un buque de 30.000 ~s de registro bruto** a ship of 30,000 gross register tons.
tonelaje *nm* tonnage.
tonelería *nf* cooperage, barrel-making.
tonelero *nm* cooper.
tonelete *nm* (**a**) (*tonel*) cask, keg. (**b**) (*falda*) short skirt.
Tonete *nm forma familiar de* **Antonio**.
tonga *nf* (**a**) layer, stratum; (*de ladrillos*) course. (**b**) (*Carib, Méx*: *montón*) pile. (**c**) (*And, Aragón, Cono Sur*) (*tarea*) job, task; (*tanda*) spell of work. (**d**) (*And*: *siesta*) nap.
tongada *nf* layer; coat, covering.
tongo¹ *nm* (*Dep etc*) fixing, throwing of a game (*o* fight *etc*); **¡hay ~!** it's been fixed!, it's been rigged!; **hubo ~ en las elecciones** the elections were rigged.
tongo² *nm* (*Cono Sur*) (**a**) (*sombrero*) bowler hat. (**b**) (*bebida*) rum punch.
tongonearse [1a] *vr* (*LAm*) = **contonearse**.
tongoneo *nm* (*LAm*) = **contoneo**.
tongorí *nm* (*And, Cono Sur*) (*hígado*) liver (of cow *etc*); (*menudencias*) offal; (*bofe*) lights.
tongoy *nm* (*LAm*) bowler hat.
Toni *nm forma familiar de* **Antonio**.
tónica *nf* (**a**) (*Mús*: *t fig*) tonic; keynote; **es una de las ~s del estilo moderno** it is one of the keynotes of the modern style. (**b**) (*fig*: *tendencia*) tone, trend, tendency. (**c**) (*bebida*) tonic, tonic water.
tonicidad *nf* tonicity.
tónico 1 *adj* (**a**) (*Mús*) tonic; (*Ling*) *sílaba* tonic, stressed, accented. (**b**) (*Med*: *t fig*) tonic, invigorating, stimulating. **2** *nm* tonic (*t fig*).
tonificador *adj*, **tonificante** *adj* invigorating, stimulating.
tonificar [1g] *vt* to tone up; to invigorate, fortify.
tonillo *nm* (**a**) (*monótono*) singsong, monotone, monotonous voice. (**b**) (*mofador*) sarcastic tone, mocking undertone. (**c**) (*peculiar*) (local) accent.
tono *nm* (**a**) (*Mús*) tone; (*altura*) pitch; (*tonalidad*) key; **~ mayor** major key; **~ menor** minor key; **estar a ~** to be in key; **estar a ~ con** (*fig*) to be in tune with.
(**b**) (*de voz etc, t fig*) tone; **~ de marcar** (*Telec*) dialling tone; **~ de voz** tone of voice; **a este ~** in the same fashion, in the same vein; **en ~ bajo** in low tones; **en ~ de enojo** in an angry tone; **bajar el ~** to lower one's voice; (*fig*) to change one's tune, quieten down; **cambiar el** (*o* **de**) **~** to change one's tune; **subir de ~** to get louder, increase in volume; **la expresión tiene un ~ despectivo** the expression has a pejorative tone; **la discusión tomó un ~ áspero** the discussion took on a harsh tone.
(**c**) (*social etc*) tone; **buen ~** tone, good tone; **una familia de ~** a good family, a family of some social standing; **de buen ~** elegant, fashionable; (*hum*) genteel, refined; **de mal ~** common, coarse; **eso no es de ~** that's not done, that's not nice; **fuera de ~** inappropriate; **dar el ~** to set the tone; **darse ~** to put on airs; **ponerse a ~** (*portarse bien*) to behave o.s.; (*conformarse*) to toe the line; (*: *en la onda*) to get with it*; **subirse de ~** to get more haughty (*o* angry), take a more arrogant (*o* indignant) line; **no venir a ~** to be inappropriate, be out of place.
(**d**) (*Mús*: *diapason*) tuning fork.
(**e**) (*Mús*: *corredera*) slide.
(**f**) (*Anat, Med*) tone.
(**g**) (*de color*) shade, hue; **~ pastel** pastel shade.
tonsura *nf* tonsure.
tonsurado *adj* tonsured.
tonsurar [1a] *vt* to clip, shear; (*Ecl*) to tonsure.
tontada *nf* = **tontería**.
tontaina* *nmf* idiot, dimwit*.
tontamente *adv* foolishly, stupidly.
tontear* [1a] *vi* (**a**) (*hacer el tonto*) to fool about, act the fool; to talk nonsense. (**b**) (*amorosamente*) to flirt.
tontera *nf* (*LAm*) = **tontería**.
tontería *nf* (**a**) (*cualidad*) silliness, foolishness, stupidity.
(**b**) (*una ~*) (*cosa*) silly thing; (*acto*) foolish act; (*dicho*) stupid remark; **~s** nonsense, rubbish; **¡déjate de ~s!** stop that nonsense!, quit fooling!; **dejémonos de ~s** let's be serious; **hacer una ~** to do a silly thing, do sth silly; **no es ninguna ~** it's not such a bad idea; it's not just a small thing, it's more serious than you think.
(**c**) (*fig*: *bagatela*) triviality; **lo vendió por una ~** he sold it for a song; **estima cualquier ~ de ese autor** he values any little thing by that writer.
(**d**) (*fig*: *escrúpulo*) silly scruple; **~s** display of delicacy (*o* squeamishness *etc*).
tonto 1 *adj* (**a**) (*necio*) silly, foolish, stupid; (*Med*) imbecile; (*) *chica* stuck-up*; **¡qué ~ soy!** how silly of me!; **¡no seas ~!** don't be silly!; **es lo bastante ~ como para** + *infin* he's fool enough to + *infin*; **es más ~ que Abundio*** he's as thick as two short planks*; **dejar a uno ~** to dumbfound sb.
(**b**) *amante* silly, soft, mushy.
(**c**) **a tontas y a locas** anyhow, unsystematically, haphazardly; **hablar a tontas y a locas** to talk without rhyme or reason; **lo hace a tontas y a locas** he does it just anyhow, he does it any old how; **repartir golpes a tontas y a locas** to hit out wildly, hit out blindly.
2 *nm*, **tonta** *nf* fool, idiot; (*Med*) imbecile; **¡~!** you idiot!; **soy un ~** I'm an idiot, I must be crazy; **~ del bote, ~ de capirote, ~ de remate** prize idiot, utter fool; **~ del lugar** village idiot; **~ útil*** stooge*; **hacer(se) el ~** to act the fool, play the fool.
3 *nm* (**a**) (*Circo, Teat*) clown, funny man.
(**b**) (*And, CAm, Cono Sur*: *palanca*) jemmy.
(**c**) (**‡**) cunt**‡**.
tontón¹, -ona* *nm/f* = **tonto 2**.
tontón²* *nm* (*vestido premamá*) smock, maternity dress.
tontorrón*, -ona* *nm/f* dimwit*.
tontura *nf* = **tontería** (**a**).
tontureco *adj* (*CAm*) = **tonto 1**.
tonudo* *adj* (*Cono Sur*) classy*.
tony ['toni] *nm* (*LAm**) clown.
toña‡ *nf* (**a**) (*puñetazo*) bash*, punch; (*patada*) kick. (**b**) **pillarse una ~** (*Esp*) to get plastered‡.
top* 1 *adj* top, best; leading; (*Com*) best-selling, leading.
2 *nm invar* (**a**) (*vestido*) top.
(**b**) top person; leading personality; **el ~ del ~** la crème de la crème; **el ~ de la gama** the best in its range.
topacio *nm* topaz.
topadora *nf* (*LAm*) bulldozer.
topar [1a] **1** *vt* (**a**) (*Zool*) to butt, horn.
(**b**) *persona* to run into, come across, bump into; *objeto* to find, come across; **le topé por casualidad en el museo** I happened to bump into him in the museum.
(**c**) (*And, Cono Sur, Méx*: *apostar*) to bet, stake.
2 *vi* (**a**) **~ contra, ~ en** to run into, hit, bump into, knock against.
(**b**) **~ con** = **1** (**b**); **~ con un obstáculo** to run up against an obstacle, encounter an obstacle.
(**c**) **la dificultad topa en eso** that's where the trouble lies, there's the rub.
(**d**) (*Méx*: *reñir*) to quarrel.
3 toparse *vr* = **2** (**b**).

tope[1] **1** (**a**) *como adj invar* top, maximum; **edad ~ para un puesto** maximum (*o* minimum) age for a job; **fecha ~** closing date, last date; **precio ~** top price, ceiling price; **sueldo ~** top salary, maximum salary.
(**b**) *adj* (*) great*, super*; **~ guay** clean over the top*.
2 *nm* (**a**) (*cabo*) end; (*límite*) top, maximum, limit; (*techo*) ceiling; (*Náut*) top, masthead; **al ~** end to end; **hasta el ~** to the brim, to the limit; **estar hasta los ~s** (*Náut*) to be overloaded, be loaded to the gunwales; (*fig*: *t* **estar a ~**) to be full to bursting; **voy a estar a ~** I'm going to be up to the eyes (with work *etc*); **estoy hasta los ~s*** I'm utterly fed up*; **ir a ~** to go flat out; **trabajar a ~** to work flat out, work to the limit; **vivir a ~** to live life to the full.
(**b**) (*Náut*: *persona*) lookout.
(**c**) (*And, Cono Sur*: *cumbre*) peak, summit.
(**d**) (*LAm*) (*saliente*) protuberance; (*obstáculo*) impediment; (*Méx Aut*) speed ramp, sleeping policeman.
tope[2] *nm* (**a**) (*golpe*) bump, knock, bang; (*con cabeza*) butt; (*Aut*) collision.
(**b**) (*fig*) (*riña*) quarrel; (*pelea*) scuffle.
(**c**) (*Mec etc*) catch, stop, check; (*Ferro*) buffer; (*Aut*) bumper; (*de revólver*) catch; **~ de tabulación** tab stop.
(**d**) (*fig*: *pega*) snag, difficulty; **ahí está el ~** that's just the trouble.
(**e**) (‡) burglary, breaking and entering.
topera *nf* (**a**) molehill. (**b**) (‡) tube, metro.
topero‡ *nm* burglar.
toperol *nm* (*Cono Sur, Méx*) brass tack.
topetada *nf* butt, bump, bang, collision.
topetar [1a] *vt* (**a**) (*golpear*) to butt, bump. (**b**) (*fig*) to bump into.
topetazo *nm* = **topetada.**
topetear [1a] *vt* (*And*) = **topetar.**
topetón *nm* = **topetada.**
tópico **1** *adj* (*Med*) for external application.
2 *nm* (**a**) (*lugar común*) commonplace, platitude; cliché; catch-phrase.
(**b**) (*LAm*) topic, subject.
topillo[1] *nm* (*Méx*) trick, swindle.
topillo[2] *nm* (*Zool*) vole.
topista‡ *nm* burglar.
top-less *nm* habit of going topless; topless bathing; topless entertainment; **ir en ~, practicar el ~** to go topless.
topo[1] *nm* (**a**) (*Zool*) mole. (**b**) (*fig*: *torpe*) clumsy person, blunderer. (**c**) (*espía*) mole, spy, inside informer. (**d**) (*Mec*) mole, tunnelling machine.
topo[2] *nm* (*LAm*) large pin.
topo[3] *nm* (*And*) measurement of distance of 1.5 leagues.
topocho[1] *adj* (*Carib*) plump, chubby.
topocho[2] *nm* (*Carib Bot*) plantain.
topografía *nf* topography.
topográfico *adj* topographic(al).
topógrafo, -a *nm/f* topographer; surveyor.
topolino **1** *nf* (**a**) teenager, bobbysoxer (*US*). (**b**) (*Aut*) small car (*Fiat 500 cc*). **2** *nmpl*: **~s** wedge-heeled shoes.
topón *nm* (*LAm*) = **topetada.**
toponimia *nf* (**a**) (*nombres*) toponymy, place-names. (**b**) (*estudio*) study of place-names.
topónimo *nm* place-name.
toposo *adj* (*Carib*) meddlesome.
toque *nm* (**a**) (*acto*) touch; **dar los primeros ~s a** to make a start on; **dar el último ~ a** to put the finishing touch to; **dar un** (*o* **el**) **~ a uno** (*estimular*) to give sb a prod; (*avisar*) to pass the message to sb, tip the wink to sb*; **faltan algunos ~s para completarlo** it needs a few touches to finish it off.
(**b**) (*Arte*) touch; dab (of colour); **~ de luz** light, highlight.
(**c**) (*Quím*) test; assay; **dar un ~ a** to test; *persona* to sound out.
(**d**) (*Mús*) (*de campana*) peal, chime; (*de reloj*) stroke; (*de timbre*) ring; (*de tambor*) beat; (*de sirena*) hoot, blast; (*Mil*) bugle call; **~ de atención** (*fig*) warning note; **~ de diana** reveille; **~ de difuntos** passing bell, knell; **~ de oración** call to prayer; **~ de queda** curfew; **~ de retreta** tattoo; **~ de silencio** ≈ lights out; **al ~ de las doce** on the stroke of twelve; **dar el ~ a uno** (*visitar*) to drop in on sb; (*Telec*) to give sb a ring.
(**e**) (*fig*: *quid*) crux; essence, heart of the matter; **ahí está el ~** that's the crux of the matter.
(**f**) (*And*: *vuelta*) turn.
toquetear [1a] *vt* (**a**) (*manosear*) to touch repeatedly, handle, keep fingering. (**b**) (*Mús*) to mess about on, play idly. (**c**) (‡: *amorosamente*) to fondle, feel up‡, touch up‡.
toqueteo‡ *nm* fondling, feeling up‡.
toquido *nm* (*CAm, Méx*) = **toque.**
toquilla *nf* headscarf; knitted shawl, woollen bonnet; (*And*) straw hat.
torácico *adj* thoracic.
torada *nf* herd of bulls.
tórax *nm* thorax.
torbellino *nm* (**a**) (*viento*) whirlwind; (*polvareda*) dust cloud. (**b**) (*fig*) whirl. (**c**) (*fig*: *persona*) whirlwind.
torcaz *adj*: **paloma ~** wood pigeon, ring dove.
torcecuello *nm* (*Orn*) wryneck.
torcedor *nm* (**a**) (*Téc*) spindle. (**b**) (*fig*) torture, torment.
torcedura *nf* (**a**) (*gen*) twist(ing); (*Med*) sprain, strain, wrench. (**b**) (*vino*) weak wine.
torcer [2b *y* 2h] **1** *vt* (**a**) (*gen*) to twist; (*doblar*) to bend; *madera etc* to warp; *miembro* to twist, wrench, put out; *músculo* to strain; *tobillo* to sprain, twist; *ojos* to turn, squint; *pelota* to spin, cut.
(**b**) *cuello, manos, ropa* to wring; *hebras, cuerda* to plait.
(**c**) (*fig*) *decisión, sucesos, tendencia* to influence, affect; *voluntad* to bend; *pensamientos* to turn (*de* from); *persona* to dissuade, turn (*de* from).
(**d**) (*fig*) *justicia* to pervert; *persona* to corrupt, bribe.
(**e**) (*fig*) *sentido* to twist, pervert, distort.
2 *vi* (**a**) (*camino, vehículo, viajero*) to turn; **el coche torció a la izquierda** the car turned left; **al llegar allí tuerza Vd a la derecha** when you reach there turn right.
(**b**) (*pelota*) to spin; to swerve.
3 torcerse *vr* (**a**) to twist; to bend; to warp.
(**b**) **~ un pie** to twist one's foot, sprain one's foot.
(**c**) (*fig*: *perverterse*) to go astray, be perverted; (*Med etc*) to suffer in one's development; (*suceso*) to take a strange turn; (*esperanzas, proyecto etc*) to go all wrong, go awry; **si no se tuerce** as long as nothing turns up to prevent it.
(**d**) (*leche, vino*) to turn sour.
torcida *nf* wick.
torcidamente *adv* (**a**) (*gen*) in a twisted way, crookedly. (**b**) (*fig*) deviously, in a crooked way.
torcido **1** (*gen*) *adj* (**a**) twisted; bent; *camino etc* crooked, twisty, full of turns; **el cuadro está ~** the picture is askew, the picture is not straight; **llevaba el sombrero algo ~** he had his hat on not quite straight.
(**b**) (*fig*) devious, crooked.
(**c**) (*And, CAm, Carib**: *desgraciado*) unlucky.
2 *nm* (*de seda etc*) twist.
torcijón *nm* (**a**) sudden twist. (**b**) = **retortijón.**
torcimiento *nm* = **torcedura.**
tordillo **1** *adj* dappled, dapple-grey. **2** *nm* dapple.
tordo **1** *adj* dappled, dapple-grey. **2** *nm* (*Orn*) thrush.
torear [1a] **1** *vt* (**a**) *toro* to fight, play.
(**b**) (*fig*: *esquivar*) to dodge, avoid.
(**c**) (*fig*) (*mantener a raya*) to keep at bay; (*embromar*) to tease, draw on; (*dar largas a*) to put off, keep guessing.
(**d**) (*fig*) (*acosar*) to plague; (*confundir*) to confuse.
(**e**) (*CAm, Cono Sur*) *animal* to provoke, enrage; (*Cono Sur, Méx*) *persona* to infuriate.
(**f**) (*And, Cono Sur*: *perro*) to bark furiously at.
2 *vi* (**a**) (*Taur*) to fight, fight bulls; to be a bullfighter; **toreó bien Suárez** Suárez fought well; **no volverá a ~** he will never fight again; **el muchacho quiere ~** the boy wants to be a bullfighter.
(**b**) (*) to spin it out, procrastinate.
(**c**) (*And, Cono Sur*: *ladrar*) to bark furiously.
toreo *nm* (**a**) (*Taur*) (art of) bullfighting. (**b**) (*Méx*: *alambique*) illicit still.
torera[1] *nf* (**a**) (*chaqueta*) short tight jacket. (**b**) **saltarse un deber a la ~** to disregard a duty; **saltarse una ley a la ~** to flout a law.
torería *nf* (**a**) (*toreros*) (class of) bullfighters; (*mundo del toreo*) bullfighting world. (**b**) (*Carib, CAm*: *broma*) prank.
torero, -a[2] *nm/f* bullfighter; **hacer una de ~*** to say sth wholly off the point; **un problema que no se lo salta un ~** a huge problem.
torete *nm* (**a**) (*animal*) small bull, young bull. (**b**) (*fig*: *niño*) strong boy, robust child; (*pey*) rough child; bad-tempered boy.
toril *nm* bullpen.
torio *nm* thorium.
torito* *nm* (*And Ent*) bluebottle.
tormenta *nf* (**a**) storm; **~ de arena** sandstorm; **~ de cerebros** brainstorm(ing); **~ de polvo** dust-storm.
(**b**) (*fig*: *tempestad*) storm; turmoil, upheaval; **~ en un vaso de agua** storm in a teacup; **sufrió una ~ de celos** she

suffered a great pang of jealousy; **desencadenó una ~ de pasiones** it unleashed a storm of passions.
(**c**) (*fig*) (*desgracia*) misfortune; (*revés*) reverse, setback.
tormento *nm* torture; (*fig*) torture, torment; anguish, agony; **dar ~ a** to torture; (*fig*) to torment, plague; **darse ~** to torment o.s.; **estos zapatos son un ~** these shoes are agony; **sus dos hijos son un ~ perpetuo** her two sons are a perpetual torment to her.
tormentoso *adj* stormy (*t fig*).
tormo *nm* lump, mass.
torna *nf* (**a**) (*vuelta*) return.
(**b**) **volver las ~s a uno** to turn the tables on sb; **se han vuelto las ~s** now it's all changed, now the boot's on the other foot.
tornada *nf* return.
tornadera *nf* pitchfork, winnowing fork.
tornadizo 1 *adj* changeable; fickle. **2** *nm*, **tornadiza** *nf* (*Hist*) renegade.
tornado *nm* tornado.
tornar [1a] **1** *vt* (**a**) (*devolver*) to give back, return.
(**b**) (*transformar*) to change, alter, transform (*en* into).
2 *vi* (**a**) (*volver*) to go back, come back, return.
(**b**) **~ a hacer algo** to do sth again; **tornó a llover** it began to rain again; **tornó a estudiar el problema** he returned to the study of the problem.
(**c**) **~ en sí** to regain consciousness, come to.
3 tornarse *vr* (**a**) (*volver*) to return.
(**b**) (*volverse*) to turn, become.
tornasol *nm* (**a**) (*Bot*) sunflower. (**b**) (*Quím*) litmus; **papel de ~** litmus paper. (**c**) (*fig*) sheen, iridescence.
tornasolado *adj* iridescent, sheeny; full of different lights; *tela* shot.
tornasolar [1a] **1** *vt* to make iridescent, put a sheen on. **2 tornasolarse** *vr* to be (*o* become) iridescent, show different lights.
tornavía *nf* (*Ferro*) turntable.
tornavoz *nf* baffle; sounding board; (*de púlpito*) sounding board, canopy; **hacer ~** to cup one's hands to one's mouth.
torneado 1 *adj* (**a**) (*Téc*) turned (on a lathe). (**b**) *brazo etc* shapely, delicately curved; pleasingly rounded. **2** *nm* turning.
tornear [1a] *vt* to turn (on a lathe).
torneo *nm* tournament, competition; (*Hist*) tourney, joust; **~ de tenis** tennis tournament; **~ por equipos** team tournament.
tornero, -a *nm/f* machinist, turner, lathe operator.
tornillería *nf* bolts; nuts and bolts.
tornillo *nm* (**a**) (*gen*) screw; bolt; **~ de banco** vice, vise (*US*), clamp; **~ sin fin** worm gear; **apretar los ~s a uno** to apply pressure on sb, put the screws on sb*; **le falta un ~*** he has a screw loose*.
(**b**) **hacer ~** (*Mil*) to desert.
(**c**) (*Cono Sur**: *frío*) bitter cold.
torniquete *nm* (**a**) (*gen*) turnstile. (**b**) (*Med*) tourniquet.
torniscón *nm* (**a**) (*apretón*) pinch, squeeze. (**b**) (*manotada*) slap on the face; smack on the head, cuff.
torno *nm* (**a**) (*Téc*: *cabrestante*) winch, windlass; drum; winding machine.
(**b**) (*Téc*: *de tornear*) lathe; **~ de banco** vice, vise (*US*), clamp; **~ de tornero** turning lathe; **labrar a ~** to turn on the lathe.
(**c**) (*Téc*) **~ de alfarero** potter's wheel; **~ de asador** spit; **~ de hilar** spinning wheel.
(**d**) (*freno etc*) brake.
(**e**) (*de rió*) (*curva*) bend; (*rabiones*) race, rapids.
(**f**) **en ~ a** round, about; **se reunieron en ~ suyo** they gathered round her; **todo estaba inundado en muchos kilómetros en ~** for many miles all round everything was flooded; **en ~ a este tema** on this theme, about this subject; **polemizar en ~ a un texto** to argue about a text.
toro *nm* (**a**) (*Zool*) bull; **~ bravo, ~ de lidia** fighting bull; **a ~ pasado** with hindsight, in retrospect; **coger el ~ por los cuernos, irse a la cabeza del ~** to take the bull by the horns; **echar** (*o* **soltar**) **el ~ a uno*** to give sb a severe dressing-down*; **hacer un ~*** (*Teat*) to stand in for somebody; **esto está hecho para que nos coja el ~** the dice are loaded against us; **pillar el ~ a uno*** to get sb into a corner (*in an argument*).
(**b**) (*fig*) strong man, he-man*; solidly-built man; tough guy*; **ser ~ corrido** to be an old hand at it, be an old fox.
(**c**) **los ~s** (*función*) bullfight; (*arte*) (art of) bullfighting; **este año no habrá ~s** there will be no bullfight this year; **ir a los ~s, ir de ~s** to go to the bullfight; **no me gustan los ~s** I don't like bullfighting; **ciertos son los ~s** it turns out that it's true; **ver los ~s desde la barrera** to be able to take an independent view, remain uncommitted; to sit on the fence.
(**d**) **hacer ~s*** to play truant, cut class.
(**e**) **T~** (*Zodíaco*) Taurus.
torombolo* *adj* (*Carib*) (*gordito*) plump; (*barrigón*) potbellied.
toronja *nf* grapefruit.
toronjil *nm* balm, (*esp*) lemon balm.
toronjo *nm* grapefruit tree.
torpe *adj* (**a**) *persona* (*desmañado*) clumsy, awkward; (*poco ágil*) slow, ungainly; *movimiento* slow, sluggish, heavy.
(**b**) *llave etc* stiff.
(**c**) *persona* (*lerdo*) dense, dim, slow-witted.
(**d**) (*fig*) (*vil*) morally vile; (*nada honrado*) dishonest, dishonourable.
(**e**) (*fig*: *obsceno*) crude, obscene.
torpear [1a] *vi* (*Cono Sur*) to be dishonest, behave dishonourably.
torpedear [1a] *vt* to torpedo; (*fig*) *proyecto* to torpedo; **~ a uno con preguntas** to bombard sb with questions.
torpedeo *nm* (*fig*) bombardment.
torpedero *nm* torpedo boat.
torpedo *nm* torpedo.
torpemente *adv* (*V adj*) (**a**) clumsily, awkwardly; slowly, sluggishly, heavily.
(**b**) stiffly.
(**c**) slow-wittedly.
(**d**) (*fig*) vilely, dishonestly.
(**e**) (*fig*) crudely, obscenely.
torpeza *nf* (*V adj*) (**a**) clumsiness, awkwardness; slowness, ungainliness; sluggishness, heaviness.
(**b**) stiffness.
(**c**) denseness, dimness, slowness of wit.
(**d**) (*fig*) moral vileness; dishonesty.
(**e**) (*fig*) crudeness, obscenity.
(**f**) (*una ~*) mistake, error of taste, lack of tact; **fue una ~ mía** it was tactless of me; **fue una ~ más** it was yet another instance of tastelessness.
torpón *adj* (*Cono Sur*) = **torpe.**
torrado *nm* (**a**) (*Anat*‡) bonce‡, head. (**b**) **~s** (*Culin*) toasted chickpeas.
torrar [1a] **1** *vt* (**a**) (*Culin*) to toast, roast. (**b**) (‡: *robar*) to pinch*, nick‡. **2 torrarse** *vr* to go off to sleep.
torre *nf* (**a**) (*Arquit etc*) tower; (*Rad, TV etc*) mast, tower; (*de pozo de petróleo*) derrick; (*de oficinas, viviendas*) tower block; **T~ de Babel** Tower of Babel; **~ de alta tensión, ~ de conducción eléctrica** electricity pylon; **~ de control** (*Aer*) control tower; **~ del homenaje** keep; **~ de marfil** ivory tower; **~ de observación** observation tower, watchtower; **~ de perforación** drilling rig; **~ de refrigeración** cooling-tower; **~ (de) vigía** (*Náut*) crow's-nest, (*de submarino*) conning-tower; **~ de vigilancia** watchtower.
(**b**) (*Ajedrez*) rook, castle.
(**c**) (*Aer, Mil, Náut*) turret; (*Mil*) watchtower; **~ de mando** (*de submarino*) conning-tower.
(**d**) (*Carib, Méx*: *chimenea*) factory chimney.
(**e**) **dar en la ~** (*Méx*) to hit where it hurts most.
torrefacción *nf* toasting, roasting.
torrefacto *adj* high roast.
torreja *nf* (*LAm*) (fried) slices of fruit and vegetables; (*Cono Sur*) slice of fruit.
torrencial *adj* torrential.
torrencialidad *nf* torrential nature.
torrencialmente *adv* torrentially, in a torrent; in great quantities.
torrente *nm* (**a**) (*río etc*) rushing stream, mountain stream, torrent; **llover a ~s** to rain cats and dogs, rain in torrents.
(**b**) (*Anat*: *t* **~ circulatorio, ~ sanguíneo**) bloodstream.
(**c**) (*fig*) stream, torrent, rush, flood; onrush; **~ de palabras** torrent of words, rush of words; **~ de voz** loud strong voice.
torrentera *nf* gully, watercourse.
torrentoso *adj* (*LAm*) *río* torrential, rushing; *lluvia* torrential.
torreón *nm* tower; (*Arquit*) turret.
torrero *nm* lighthouse keeper.
torreta *nf* (**a**) (*Aer, Mil, Náut*) turret; (*de submarino*) conning-tower; **~ de observación, ~ de vigilancia** watchtower. (**b**) (*Elec*) pylon, mast.
torrezno *nm* rasher, slice of bacon.
tórrido *adj* torrid.

torrificar [1g] *vt* (*Méx*) *café* to toast, roast.
torrija *nf* French toast.
torsión *nf* (*torcedura*) twist(ing); warp(ing); (*Mec*) torsion, torque.
torsional *adj* torsional.
torso *nm* (*Anat*) torso; (*Arte*) head and shoulder; (*Escultura*) bust.
torta *nf* (**a**) (*pastel*) cake; tart, flan; (*hojuela*) pancake; (*Méx*) sandwich; (*fig*) cake, flat mass, round lump; **la ~ costó un pan** it worked out dearer than expected, (*fig*) it was more trouble than it was worth; **eso es ~s y pan pintado** it's child's play, it's a cinch‡; **no entendió ni ~*** he didn't understand a word of it; **¡ni ~!*** I haven't a clue!*, not the foggiest!*; **nos queda la ~** (*fig*) there's a lot left over.
(**b**) (*Esp*‡) **agarrar una ~** to get plastered‡; **estar con la ~** to be all at sea, be totally bemused.
(**c**) (*CAm, Méx*: *t* **~ de huevos**) omelet(te).
(**d**) (*Tip*) fount.
(**e**) (*: *puñetazo*) punch, sock*; (*caída*) crash, fall; **liarse a ~s** to get involved in a punch-up*.
(**f**) (*CAm, Méx***) cunt**.
tortazo* *nm* slap, punch, sock*; **pegarse el ~** to get hurt, have a bad accident.
tortear [1a] **1** *vt* (*Cono Sur*) *masa* to flatten, roll; (*CAm, Méx*) *tortilla* to shape (with the palms of one's hands). **2** *vi* (*Méx*) to clap, applaud.
tortero *adj* (*And*) round and flat, disc-shaped.
tortícolis *nf invar* crick in the neck, stiff neck.
tortilla *nf* (**a**) (*de huevo*) omelet(te); **~ a la española, ~ de patatas** Spanish potato omelette; (*fig*) **cambiar** (*o* **volver**) **la ~ a uno** to turn the tables on sb; **se le volvió la ~** it came out all wrong for him, his luck let him down; **se ha vuelto la ~** now the boot is on the other foot; **hacer algo una ~** to smash sth up; **hacer a uno una ~*** to beat sb up*; **van a hacer el negocio una ~** they're sure to mess the deal up.
(**b**) (*CAm, Méx*: *de maíz*) flat maize pancake, tortilla.
(**c**) (**) lesbian intercourse, lesbian practices.
tortillera *nf* (**a**) (*CAm, Méx*) tortilla seller. (**b**) (**) dyke‡, lesbian.
tortita *nf* pancake.
tórtola *nf* turtledove.
tortoleo *nm* (*Méx*) billing and cooing.
tórtolo *nm* (**a**) (*Orn*) (male) turtledove. (**b**) (*amante*) lovebird, loverboy; **~s*** pair of lovers, lovebirds.
tortuga *nf* tortoise; **~ (marina)** turtle.
tortuguismo *nm* (*Méx Ind*) go-slow.
tortuoso *adj* (**a**) (*camino etc*) winding, tortuous, full of bends. (**b**) (*fig*) devious.
tortura *nf* torture (*t fig*).
torturado, -a *nm/f* torture victim.
torturar [1a] *vt* to torture.
toruno *nm* (**a**) (*CAm*: *semental*) stud bull; (*Cono Sur*: *toro viejo*) old bull; (*Cono Sur*: *buey*) ox. (**b**) (*Cono Sur*: *hombre*) fit old man.
torvisca *nf*, **torvisco** *nm* spurge flax.
torvo *adj* grim, stern, fierce.
torzal *nm* cord, twist (of silk); (*Cono Sur*) plaited rope.
tos *nf* cough; coughing; **acceso de ~** coughing fit; **~ ferina** whooping cough.
toscamente *adv* coarsely, roughly, crudely.
Toscana *nf*: **La ~** Tuscany.
toscano, -a 1 *adj, nm/f* Tuscan. **2** *nm* (**a**) (*Ling*) Tuscan; (*Hist*) Italian. (**b**) (*puro*) (a kind of) cigar.
tosco *adj* coarse, rough, crude (*t fig*).
tosedera *nf* (*LAm*) nagging cough.
toser [2a] **1** *vt* (*fig*) (**a**) **no le tose nadie, no hay quien le tosa** nobody can compete with him, he's in a class by himself.
(**b**) **a mí no me tose nadie** I'll not stand for that, I'm not taking that from anybody.
2 *vi* to cough.
tosido *nm* (*CAm, Cono Sur, Méx*) cough.
tósigo *nm* poison.
tosquedad *nf* coarseness, roughness, crudeness (*t fig*).
tostada *nf* (**a**) toast, piece of toast; (*Méx*: *tortilla*) fried tortilla; (*CAm*: *plátano*) toasted slice of banana; **una ~ de*** a lot of, masses of; **hace una ~ de años*** ages ago; **se olía la ~*** you could tell there was trouble coming.
(**b**) (*) **dar una ~ a uno, pegar una ~ a uno** to put one over on sb*, cheat sb.
(**c**) (*Cono Sur*: *conversación*) long boring conversation.
tostado 1 *adj* (**a**) (*Culin*) toasted. (**b**) *color* dark brown, ochre, burnt; *persona, piel* (*t* **~ por el sol**) brown, tanned, sunburnt. **2** *nm* tan.
tostador *nm* toaster; roaster; **~ eléctrico, ~ de pan** electric toaster.
tostadora *nf* toaster.
tostadura *nf* (*de café*) roasting.
tostar [1l] **1** *vt* (**a**) *pan etc* to toast; *café* to roast; (*Culin*) to brown.
(**b**) *persona, piel* to tan.
(**c**) **~ a uno** (*Carib, Cono Sur*:*) to tan sb's hide*.
(**d**) (*Carib, Cono Sur*: *proseguir*) to continue vigorously, push on with.
(**e**) (*Méx*) (*ofender*) to offend; (*perjudicar*) to harm, hurt; (*matar*) to kill.
2 tostarse *vr* (*t* **~ al sol**) to tan, brown, get brown.
tostelería *nf* (*CAm*) cake shop.
tostón *nm* (**a**) (*Culin*: *cubito*) small cube of toast, crouton; (*tostada*) toast dipped in oil; (*garbanzo*) toasted chickpea.
(**b**) (*Culin*: *lechón*) roast sucking-pig.
(**c**) (*Culin*: *tostada quemada*) piece of bread (*etc*) toasted too much.
(**d**) (*) (*lata*) bore, boring thing; (*discurso*) long boring speech; (*cuento*) tedious tale; **dar el ~** to be a bore, get on everybody's nerves; to be a nuisance.
(**e**) (*: *comedia etc*) bad play (*o* film *etc*), dreadful piece of work.
(**f**) (*Carib*: *banana*) slice of fried green banana.
(**g**) (*Méx**) 50-cent piece.
tostonear* [1a] *vti* (*Méx*) to sell at bargain prices.
total 1 *adj* (**a**) total; whole, complete; utter, sheer; *anestésico* general; **una revisión ~ de su teoría** a complete revision of his theory; **ha sido una calamidad ~** it was an utter disaster. (**b**) (*: *excelente*) smashing*, brilliant*; **es un libro ~** it's a super book*.
2 *adv* (*en resumen*) in short, all in all; (*así que*) and so; (*al fin*) when all is said and done; **~ que ...** to cut a long story short ..., the upshot of it all was that ...; **~, usted manda** well, you're the boss, after all; **~ que no fuimos** so we didn't go after all.
3 *nm* (**a**) (*Mat*) (*suma*) total, sum; (*totalidad*) whole; **~ de comprobación** hash total; **el ~ de la población** the whole (of the) population; **en ~** in all.
(**b**) **en ~** (*fig*) = **2**.
(**c**) (*Com*) total; **~ debe** debit total; **~ haber** assets total.
totalidad *nf* whole; totality; **en su ~** as a whole, in its entirety; **la ~ de los obreros** all the workers; **la casi ~ de ellos, la práctica ~ de ellos** nearly all of them; **la ~ de la población** the whole (of the) population; **pero el hombre en su ~ se nos escapa** but the whole man eludes us.
totalitario *adj* totalitarian.
totalitarismo *nm* totalitarianism.
totalizador 1 *adj* all-embracing, all-encompassing. **2** *nm* totalizator.
totalizar [1f] **1** *vt* to totalize, add up. **2** *vi* to total, add up to; to come to, amount to.
totalmente *adv* totally, wholly, completely.
totazo *nm* (**a**) (*And*: *explosión*) bursting, explosion. (**b**) (*And, Carib*: *golpe*) bang on the head.
totear [1a] (*And, Carib*) **1** *vi* to burst, explode. **2 totearse** *vr* (*reventar*) to burst; (*agrietarse*) to crack, split.
tótem *nm, pl* **tótems** *o* **tótemes** totem.
totémico *adj* totemic.
totemismo *nm* totemism.
totopo *nm*, **totoposte** *nm* (*CAm, Méx*) fried tortilla.
totora *nf* (*LAm*) reed.
totoral *nm* (*LAm*) reedbed.
totoreco* *adj* (*CAm*) thick*, stupid.
totovía *nf* woodlark.
totuma *nf* (**a**) (*And, Carib Bot*) gourd, calabash. (**b**) (*Cono Sur*) (*cardenal*) bruise; (*chichón*) bump, lump. (**c**) (*And, Carib, Cono Sur*‡: *cabeza*) nut‡, head; **cortarse ~** (*Carib*) to get one's hair cut.
totumo *nm* (**a**) (*And, Carib*: *árbol*) calabash tree. (**b**) (*Cono Sur*: *chichón*) bump on the head.
touroperador(a) *nm/f* tour-operator.
toxicidad *nf* toxicity, poisonous nature; poisonous properties.
tóxico 1 *adj* toxic, poisonous. **2** *nm* poison, toxic.
toxicodependencia *nf* drug-addiction.
toxicodependiente *nmf* drug-addict.
toxicología *nf* toxicology.
toxicológico *adj* toxicological.
toxicólogo, -a *nm/f* toxicologist.
toxicomanía *nf* drug-addiction.

toxicómano 1 *adj* addicted to drugs. **2** *nm,* **toxicómana** *nf* drug addict.
toximia *nf* toxaemia.
toxina *nf* toxin.
toxinfección *nf* poisoning; ~ **alimentaria** food poisoning.
tozudez *nf* obstinacy.
tozudo *adj* obstinate.
traba *nf* (**a**) (*gen*) bond, tie; (*de mesa etc*) crosspiece; (*Mec*) clasp, clamp; (*de caballo*) hobble; (*de prisionero*) fetter, shackle; (*Cono Sur*) hair slide.
(**b**) (*fig: vínculo*) bond, link, tie; (*pey*) hindrance, obstacle; **~s** trammels, shackles; **desembarazado de ~s** free, unrestrained; **poner ~s a** to shackle; to restrain, check; **ponerse ~s** to place restrictions on o.s., limit one's own freedom to act.
(**c**) (*Carib, Méx: de gallos*) cockfight; cockpit.
trabacuenta *nm* mistake, miscalculation; **andar con ~s** to be engaged in endless controversies.
trabado *adj* (**a**) (*unido*) joined; (*vinculado*) linked; *discurso etc* coherent, well constructed. (**b**) (*fig*) strong, tough. (**c**) (*And: bizco*) cross-eyed. (**d**) (*Méx: tartamudo*) stammering.
trabajado *adj* (**a**) *persona* worn out, weary from overwork. (**b**) (*Arte etc*) carefully worked, elaborately fashioned; (*pey*) forced, strained, artificial.
trabajador 1 *adj* hard-working, industrious. **2** *nm,* **trabajadora** *nf* worker; labourer; (*Pol*) worker; ~ **autónomo** self-employed person; freelance; ~ **por cuenta ajena** employee, employed person; ~ **por cuenta propia** self-employed person; freelance; ~ **eventual** casual worker; ~ **portuario** docker; ~ **social** social worker.
trabajar [1a] **1** *vt* (**a**) *tierra* to work, till; *madera etc* to work; *masa* to knead; *ingredientes* to mix, stir, work in.
(**b**) *estudio, tema* to work at, work on; *aspecto, detalle* to give special attention to, work to bring out; *negocio, proyecto etc* to work at, carry forward, pursue, follow up; (*Com*) *géneros* to run a line in, deal particularly with, handle; **estoy trabajando el latín** I am working away at Latin; **es mi colega quien trabaja esos géneros** it is my colleague who handles that line; **el pintor ha trabajado muy bien los árboles** the painter has taken special care over the trees.
(**c**) *caballo* to train.
(**d**) *persona* to work, drive, push.
(**e**) *persona* (*fig*) to work on, get to work on, persuade; **trabaja a su tía para sacarle los ahorros** he's working on his aunt in order to get hold of her savings.
(**f**) *mente etc* to trouble, bother.
2 *vi* (**a**) (*gen*) to work (*de* as; *en* in, at); (*Teat etc*) to act, perform; ~ **mucho** to work hard; ~ **más** to work harder; ~ **como un buey** (*etc*) to work like a Trojan; ~ **como un condenado** to work like a slave; ~ **por horas** to be paid by the hour; to work part-time; ~ **al mínimo legal** to work to rule; ~ **a ritmo lento** to go slow; ~ **a tiempo parcial** to work part-time; ~ **por** + *infin* to strive to + *infin*; **hacer** ~ *dinero etc* to put to good use, make work; *agua, recursos etc* to harness.
(**b**) (*fig*) ~ **con uno para que** + *subj* to work on sb to + *infin*, persuade sb to + *infin*.
(**c**) (*fig: proceso, tiempo etc*) to work, operate; **el tiempo trabaja a nuestro favor** time is working for us.
(**d**) (*fig: árbol, suelo etc*) to bear, produce, yield.
trabajo *nm* (**a**) (*gen*) work; (*Mec*) work; (*un* ~) job, task; (*Arte, Liter etc*) work, piece of work; (*Inform*) job; ~ **autónomo** self-employment; ~ **de campo,** ~ **en el terreno** fieldwork; ~ **de clase** schoolwork; ~ **de chinos** hard slog; ~ **a destajo** piecework; ~ **a domicilio** work at home, outwork; ~ **en equipo** teamwork; ~ **eventual** casual work, temporary work; ~ **fijo** permanent job; ~ **excesivo,** ~ **intenso** overwork; **~s forzados** hard labour; ~ **intelectual** brainwork; ~ **manual** manual labour; **~s manuales** (*Escol etc*) handicraft; ~ **nocturno** night work; ~ **social** social work; ~ **sucio** dirty work; ~ **a turnos,** ~ **por turno** shift work; **ropa de** ~ working clothes; **los sin** ~ the unemployed; **estar sin** ~ to be out of a job, be unemployed; **hacer** ~ **lento** to go slow; **ir al** ~ to go to work.
(**b**) (*Pol*) labour; the workers, the working class.
(**c**) **Ministerio de T~** Ministry of Labour; **en T~ dicen que ...** at the Ministry of Labour they say that ...
(**d**) (*fig*) (*esfuerzo*) effort, labour; (*dificultad*) trouble; **~s** troubles, difficulties, hardships; **ahorrarse el** ~ to save o.s. the trouble; **tomarse el** ~ **de** + *infin* to take the trouble to + *infin*; **lo hizo con mucho** ~ he did it after a lot of trouble, it took him a lot of effort to do it; **le cuesta** ~ + *infin* he finds it hard to + *infin*, it is difficult for him to + *infin*; **dar** ~ to cause trouble; ~ **te doy,** ~ **te mando** it's no easy task, it's a tough job; **tener** ~ **de sobra para poder** + *infin* to have one's work cut out to + *infin*.
trabajosamente *adv* laboriously; painfully.
trabajoso *adj* (**a**) (*difícil*) hard, laborious; (*doloroso*) painful.
(**b**) (*Med*) pale, sickly.
(**c**) (*Cono Sur*) (*exigente*) exacting, demanding; (*astuto*) wily.
(**d**) (*And*) (*poco amable*) unhelpful; (*malhumorado*) bad-tempered, tetchy.
(**e**) (*Cono Sur: molesto*) annoying.
trabalenguas *nm invar* tongue-twister.
trabar [1a] **1** *vt* (**a**) (*unir*) to join, unite, link.
(**b**) (*agarrar*) to seize; to lay hold of, catch, grasp; (*sujetar*) to tie down; (*encadenar*) to shackle, fetter; (*Mec*) to clamp, fasten; to jam; *caballo* to hobble.
(**c**) (*Culin etc*) to thicken.
(**d**) *sierra* to set.
(**e**) (*fig*) *conversación, debate etc* to start (up); *batalla* to join, engage in; *amistad* to strike up.
(**f**) (*fig: impedir*) to impede, hinder, obstruct.
(**g**) (*CAm, Carib: engañar*) to deceive.
2 *vi* (*planta*) to take, strike; (*ancla etc*) to grip, hold.
3 trabarse *vr* (**a**) (*con cuerda etc*) to get entangled, get tangled up; (*mecanismo*) to lock, jam; to seize up; **se le traba la lengua** he gets tongue-tied, he stammers.
(**b**) (*LAm:* ~ *la lengua*) to get tongue-tied, stammer; (*Carib: perder el hilo*) to lose the thread (of what one is saying).
(**c**) (*t* ~ **de palabras**) to get involved in an argument; to wrangle, squabble.
trabazón *nf* (**a**) (*Téc*) joining, assembly; (*fig*) link, bond, (close) connection. (**b**) (*de líquido*) consistency; (*fig*) coherence.
trabilla *nf* (*tira*) small strap; (*broche*) clasp; (*de cinturón*) belt loop; (*puntada*) dropped stitch.
trabucar [1g] **1** *vt* to confuse, to jumble up, mix up, mess up; *palabras, sonidos* to switch over, misplace, interchange. **2 trabucarse** *vr* to get all mixed up.
trabuco *nm* (**a**) (*Hist*) catapult; (*t* ~ **naranjero**) blunderbuss; (*prov*) pop-gun.
(**b**) (******) prick******.
traca *nf* string of fireworks; (*fig*) series of noises; row, racket; **es de ~*** it's killingly funny.
trácala *nf* (**a**) (*And: gentío*) crowd, mob. (**b**) (*Carib, Méx: trampa*) trick, ruse. (**c**) (*Méx: tramposo*) trickster.
tracalada *nf* (**a**) (*LAm: gentío*) crowd; lot, mass; **una ~ de** a lot of, a huge amount of; **a ~s*** by the hundred. (**b**) (*Méx: trampa*) trick, ruse.
tracalero (*Carib, Méx*) **1** *adj* (*astuto*) crafty; (*tramposo*) sly, deceitful. **2** *nm* cheat, trickster.
tracamundana* *nf* (**a**) (*jaleo*) row, rumpus. (**b**) (*cambio*) swap, exchange.
tracatrá* *interj* no way!*, get away!*
tracción *nf* traction; haulage; (*Mec*) drive, traction; ~ **delantera** front-wheel drive; ~ **trasera** rear-wheel drive; ~ **integral,** ~ **total,** ~ **a las cuatro ruedas** four-wheel drive.
tracería *nf* tracery.
tracoma *nm* trachoma.
tractivo *adj* tractive.
tractor 1 *adj*: **rueda ~a** drive wheel. **2** *nm* tractor; ~ **agrícola** agricultural tractor, farm tractor; ~ **(de) oruga** caterpillar tractor.
tractorista *nmf* tractor-driver.
trad. *abr de* **traducido** translated, trans.
tradición *nf* tradition.
tradicional *adj* traditional.
tradicionalidad *nf* traditionality, traditional character.
tradicionalismo *nm* traditionalism.
tradicionalista *adj, nmf* traditionalist.
tradicionalmente *adv* traditionally.
tráding ['tradin] **1** *adj*: **empresa** ~ = **2**. **2** *nf* trading company.
traducción *nf* translation (*a* into, *de* from); (*fig*) rendering, interpretation; ~ **asistida por ordenador** computer-assisted translation; ~ **automática,** ~ **automatizada** automatic translation, machine translation; ~ **simultánea** simultaneous translation.
traducible *adj* translatable.
traducir [3n] **1** *vt* to translate (*a* into, *de* from); (*fig*) to render, interpret; to express. **2 traducirse** *vr*: ~ **en** (*fig*) to mean in practice; to entail, result in.

traductor(a) *nm/f* translator; ~ **jurado** official translator.

traer [2o] **1** *vt* (**a**) (*gen*) to bring, get, fetch; to carry; to take; **¡trae!, ¡traiga!** hand it over!, give it here!; **el muchacho que trae los periódicos** the lad who brings the papers; **¿has traído el dinero?** have you brought the money?

(**b**) (*llevar encima*) to wear; *objeto* to wear, carry, have about one.

(**c**) (*imán etc*) to draw, attract, pull.

(**d**) (*fig: causar*) to bring (about), cause; to involve; *consecuencias* to bring, have; ~ **consigo** to involve, entail; **nos trajo grandes perjuicios** it did us great harm, it caused a lot of trouble for us.

(**e**) (*periódico etc*) to carry, have, print; **este periódico no trae nada sobre el particular** this newspaper doesn't carry anything about the affair.

(**f**) *autoridad, razón etc* to adduce, bring forward; *V* **colación, cuento.**

(**g**) ~ + *adj etc* to have + *adj*, keep + *adj*; ~ **de cabeza a uno** to upset sb, bother sb; **el juego le trae perdido** gambling is his ruin; **la ausencia de noticias me trae muy inquieto** the lack of news is making me very anxious; *V* **frito, loco** *etc*.

(**h**) (*locuciones*) ~ **a mal a uno** (*maltratar*) to abuse sb, maltreat sb; (*irritar*) to upset sb; (*exasperar*) to exasperate sb; (*mandar de acá para allá*) to keep sb chasing about all over the place; ~ **y llevar a uno** to gossip about sb.

2 traerse *vr* (**a**) ~ **algo** to have sth (improper) on hand; to be planning sth (disreputable); **los dos se traen algún manejo sucio** the two of them are up to something shady.

(**b**) ~ **bien** to dress well; to behave properly; ~ **mal** to dress shabbily; to behave badly.

(**c**) ~**las** (*molestar*) to be annoying; (*ser difícil*) to be difficult, be awkward; (*ser excesivo*) to be excessive; **es un problema que se las trae** it's a difficult problem; **ese punto realmente se las trae** that point really is a sticky one; **hace un calor que se las trae** this heat is too much of a good thing; **tiene un padre que se las trae** she has an excessively severe father.

trafagar [1h] *vi* to bustle about; to be on the move, keep on the go.

tráfago *nm* (**a**) (*Com*) traffic, trade. (**b**) (*trabajo*) drudgery, toil; routine job. (**c**) (*ajetreo*) bustle, hustle, intense activity.

trafaguear [1a] *vi* (*Méx*) to bustle about, keep on the go.

traficante *nmf* trader, dealer (*en* in); ~ **de armas** arms dealer; ~ **de drogas** (drug) pusher.

traficar [1g] *vi* (**a**) (*Com*) to trade, deal (*con* with, *en* in); to buy and sell; (*pey*) to traffic (*en* in).

(**b**) ~ **con** (*pey*) to deal illegally in, do illegal business in.

(**c**) (*moverse mucho*) to be on the move, keep on the go; (*viajar*) to travel a lot.

tráfico *nm* (**a**) (*Com*) trade, business; (*esp pey*) traffic (*en* in); ~ **de estupefacientes,** ~ **en narcóticos** drug-traffic; ~ **de influencias** peddling of political favours.

(**b**) (*Aut, Ferro etc*) traffic; ~ **de carga** (*LAm*), ~ **de mercancías** goods traffic; ~ **por ferrocarril** rail traffic; ~ **rodado** road traffic, vehicular traffic; **T~ pide que ...** the Dirección General de Tráfico asks that ...

(**c**) (*LAm: tránsito*) transit, passage.

tragabalas *nm invar* (*Méx*) búlly, braggart.

tragadera‡ *nf* (*LAm*) slap-up do*, blow-out‡.

tragaderas *nfpl* (**a**) (*garganta*) throat, gullet.

(**b**) (*fig*) (*credulidad*) gullibility; (*tolerancia*) tolerance, broad-mindedness; **tener buenas** ~ (*crédulo*) to be gullible, be prepared to swallow anything; (*permisivo*) to be very easy-going, be prepared to put up with a lot, be excessively tolerant.

tragadero *nm* throat, gullet; **la comida fue un** ~ (*Méx**) we stuffed ourselves*.

tragador(a) *nm/f* glutton; ~ **de leguas*** great walker.

tragafuegos *nmf invar* fire-eater.

trágala* *nmf* (**a**) (*glotón*) glutton, greedy sort. (**b**) **cantar el** ~ **a uno** to mock sb's authority by doing precisely what he has forbidden. (**c**) **es el país del** ~ it's the country where you accept something whether you like it or not.

tragaldabas* *nmf invar* glutton, greedy sort.

tragaleguas* *nmf invar* quick walker, great walker.

tragalibros *nmf invar* (*lector*) bookworm; (*empollón*) swot*.

tragaluz *nm* skylight.

tragallón *adj* (*Cono Sur*) greedy.

tragamonedas *nm invar* = **tragaperras.**

tragantada* *nf* swig*, mouthful.

tragantón* *adj* greedy, gluttonous.

tragantona* *nf* (**a**) (*comida*) blow-out‡, slap-up meal*. (**b**) (*acto*) (act of) swallowing hard.

tragaperras *nm* (*a veces f*) *invar* slot-machine; (*en bar etc*) fruit-machine; *V t* **máquina, tocadiscos** *etc*.

tragar [1h] **1** *vt* (**a**) (*gen*) to swallow; to swallow down, drink up; (*pey: rápidamente etc*) to bolt, devour, swallow whole (*o* quickly); to gulp down, get down.

(**b**) (*absorber etc*) to absorb, soak up, drink in; *V t* **3.**

(**c**) *insultos, reprimenda* to have to listen to; *trampa etc* to swallow, fall for, be taken in by; *injusticia etc* to put up with; **hacer** ~ **algo a uno** to force sb to listen to sth; to force sb to swallow sth, make sb believe sth; **no le puedo** ~ I can't stand him, I can't stomach him.

2 *vi* (‡) to sleep around*, be free and easy.

3 tragarse *vr* (**a**) (*comer etc*) to swallow; to eat, get down; **se lo tragó entero** he swallowed it whole; **el perro se ha tragado un hueso** the dog has swallowed a bone; **eso me lo trago en dos minutos** I could eat that up in a couple of minutes.

(**b**) (*tierra etc*) to absorb, soak up; (*abismo, mar*) to swallow up, engulf; to suck down; *ahorros etc* to swallow up, use up, absorb.

(**c**) (*fig*) *hecho desagradable, cuento etc* to swallow; **se tragará todo lo que se le diga** he'll swallow whatever he's told; **ya se lo tenía tragado** he had already learned to live with the idea, he had already prepared himself for that happening; **se las tragó como ruedas de molino** he swallowed it hook, line and sinker; **el árbitro se tragó dos penaltis** the referee did not award two penalties, the referee overlooked two penalties.

tragasables *nmf invar* sword-swallower.

tragasantos *nmf invar* excessively pious person.

tragavenado *nm* (*And, Carib*) boa constrictor.

tragedia *nf* tragedy.

trágicamente *adv* tragically.

trágico 1 *adj* tragic(al); **lo ~ es que ...** the tragedy of it is that ..., the tragic thing about it is that ... **2** *nm* tragedian.

tragicomedia *nf* tragicomedy.

tragicómico *adj* tragicomic.

trago *nm* (**a**) (*cantidad etc*) drink, draught; (*bocado*) swallow, mouthful, swig*; sip; ~ **largo** long drink; **el ~ del estribo** one for the road; **beber algo de un ~** to drink sth at a gulp; **brindar el ~ a uno** (*LAm*) to stand sb a drink; **echarse un ~** to have a drink, have a swig*; **no vendría mal un ~ de vino** a drop of wine would not come amiss.

(**b**) (*bebida en general*) drink, drinking; (*LAm*) hard liquor; **ser demasiado aficionado al ~** to be too fond of the drink.

(**c**) (*fig*) **mal ~, ~ amargo** (*rato difícil*) hard time, rough time; (*golpe*) nasty blow; (*desgracia*) misfortune, calamity; **fue un ~ amargo** it was a cruel blow; **nos quedaba todavía el ~ más amargo** the worst of it was still to come.

(**d**) **hacer algo a ~s** to do sth bit by bit.

tragón *adj* greedy, gluttonous.

tragona‡ *adj* (*Esp*) easy, promiscuous.

traguear* [1a] **1** *vti* (*CAm, Méx: beber*) to drink; (*Carib*) to get sloshed*. **2 traguearse** *vr* (*And, CAm, Méx*) to get sloshed*.

trai *nm* (*Cono Sur: rugby*) try.

traición *nf* (*gen*) treachery; (*Jur etc*) treason; (*una ~*) betrayal, act of treason, treacherous act; **alta ~** high treason; **matar a uno a ~** to kill sb treacherously; **hacer ~ a uno** to betray sb.

traicionar [1a] *vt* to betray (*t fig*).

traicionero *adj* treacherous.

traída *nf* carrying, bringing; ~ **de aguas** water supply.

traído 1 *adj* (**a**) (*usado*) worn, old, threadbare. (**b**) ~ **y llevado** (*fig*) well-worn, trite, hackneyed. **2** *nmpl*: ~**s** (*And*) presents.

traidor 1 *adj persona* treacherous; *acto* treasonable. **2** *nm* traitor; betrayer; (*Teat*) villain, bad character.

traidora *nf* traitress; betrayer.

traidoramente *adv* treacherously, traitorously.

traiga *etc V* **traer.**

tráiler *nm, pl* **tráilers** (**a**) (*Cine*) trailer. (**b**) (*Aut: caravana*) caravan, trailer (*US*); (*de camión*) trailer, trailer unit.

traílla *nf* (**a**) (*Téc*) scraper, leveller; (*Agr*) harrow. (**b**) (*de perro*) lead, leash; (*azote*) lash. (**c**) (*equipo de perros*) team of dogs.

traillar [1a] *vt* to scrape; to level; (*Agr*) to harrow.

traína *nf*, **traiña** *nf* sardine-fishing net, dragnet.

trainera *nf* small fishing-boat.

Trajano *nm* Trajan.

traje[1] *etc V* **traer.**

traje[2] *nm* (*gen*) dress, costume; (*de hombre*) suit; (*esp And, Cono Sur: de mujer*) woman's dress; (*fig*) garb, guise; **~ de agua** wetsuit; **~ de baño** bathing-costume, swimming-costume, swimsuit; **~ de calle** lounge suit; **un policía en ~ de calle** a policeman in plain clothes; **~ de campaña** battle-dress; **~ de casa** casual dress; **~ de ceremonia, ~ de etiqueta** full dress; dress suit, evening dress; **~ de cóctel** cocktail dress; **~ de cuartel** (*Mil*) undress; **~ de época** period costume; **~ espacial** spacesuit; **en ~ de Eva** in her birthday suit; **~ de faena** fatigues; **~ hecho** ready-made suit; **~ (hecho) a la medida** made-to-measure suit; **~ isotérmico** wetsuit; **~ largo** evening gown; **~ de luces** bullfighter's costume; **~ de madera*** coffin, box*; **~ de malla** tights; **~ de montar** riding-habit; **~ de noche** evening dress; **~ de novia** wedding-dress, bridal gown; **~ de oficina** business suit; **~ de paisano** (*Esp*) civilian clothes; **~ pantalón** trouser suit; **~ de playa** sunsuit; **~ regional** regional costume, regional dress; **~ serio** business suit; **cortar un ~ a uno** to gossip about sb.

trajeado *adj*: **ir bien ~** to be well dressed, be well turned out; **estar ~ de** to be dressed in; (*hum*) to be got up in, be rigged out in; **estar bien ~ para la temporada** to be well equipped with clothes for the season.

trajear [1a] **1** *vt* to clothe, dress (*de* in); (*hum*) to get up, rig out (*de* in). **2 trajearse** *vr* to dress up; to provide o.s. with clothes.

trajelarse⁑ [1a] *vr*: **~ una botella*** to knock a bottle back*.

traje-pantalón *nm, pl* **trajes-pantalón** trouser suit.

traje-sastre *nm, pl* **trajes-sastre** tailor-made suit.

trajín *nm* (**a**) (*acarreo*) haulage, carriage, transport.

(**b**) (*) (*ir y venir*) coming and going, movement; (*ajetreo*) hustle, bustle, commotion; (*jaleo*) fuss.

(**c**) **trajines** (*: *actividades*) affairs, (suspicious) doings, goings-on; **trajines de la casa** household chores.

trajinado *adj tema etc* well-worked, overworked, trite.

trajinante *nm* (**a**) carrier, carter; haulage contractor. (**b**) (*pey**) person who indulges in a lot of useless activity.

trajinar [1a] **1** *vt* (**a**) (*acarrear*) to carry, cart; to transport.

(**b**) (*Cono Sur: estafar*) to swindle, deceive.

(**c**) (*Cono Sur: registrar*) to search.

(**d**) (⁑) to fuck⁑.

2 *vi* (*ajetrearse*) to bustle about; (*viajar*) to travel around a lot; (*moverse mucho*) to be on the go, keep on the move.

trajinería *nf* carriage; haulage.

trajinista *nmf* (*Carib, Cono Sur*) busybody, snooper.

tralla *nf* whipcord, whiplash; lash.

trallazo *nm* (**a**) (*de látigo*) crack of a whip; lash. (**b**) (*: *bronca*) telling-off*. (**c**) (*Dep*) fierce shot, hard shot.

trama *nf* (**a**) (*Téc*) weft, woof. (**b**) (*fig: vínculo*) connection, link; (*correlación*) correlation. (**c**) (*fig: complot*) plot, scheme, intrigue; (*Liter*) plot. (**d**) (*Tip*) shading; area.

tramar [1a] **1** *vt* (**a**) (*Téc*) to weave.

(**b**) (*fig*) to plan, plot; to scheme for, intrigue for; *complot* to lay, hatch; **están tramando algo** they're up to sth; **¿qué estarán tramando?** I wonder what they're up to?

2 tramarse *vr*: **algo se está tramando** (*fig*) there's sth afoot, there's sth going on.

trambucar [1g] *vi* (**a**) (*And, Carib: naufragar*) to be shipwrecked. (**b**) (*Carib**: *enloquecer*) to go out of one's mind, lose one's marbles⁑.

trambuque *nm* (*And*) shipwreck.

trámil *adj* (*Cono Sur*) awkward, clumsy.

tramitación (*V vt*) *nf* transaction; negotiation; steps, procedure; handling.

tramitar [1a] *vt* (*despachar*) to transact; (*negociar*) to negotiate; (*proseguir*) to proceed with, carry forward; (*manejar*) to handle.

trámite *nm* (*etapa*) step, stage; (*negocio*) transaction; **~s** (*procedimientos*) procedure; (*formalidades*) formalities; (*pey*) red tape; (*Jur*) proceedings; **~s de costumbre** usual channels; **~s oficiales** official channels; **~ de quejas** grievance procedure; **los ~s para la obtención de un visado** the procedure for obtaining a visa; **para acortar los ~s de costumbre lo hacemos así** in order to get it quickly through the usual procedure we do it this way; **hacer los ~s para un viaje** to make the arrangements for a journey; **el gobierno se limita a resolver asuntos de ~** the government is dealing only with ordinary ongoing business; **en ~** in hand; **lo tenemos en ~** we have the matter in hand, we are pursuing the matter; **el proyecto de ley está en ~ parlamentario** the bill is going through parliament; **'patente en ~'** 'patent applied for'.

tramo *nm* (**a**) section, stretch; (*de carretera etc*) section, length; (*de puente*) span; (*de escalera*) flight; **~ cronometrado** time trial. (**b**) (*Agr*) plot. (**c**) (*Fin*) share issue.

tramontana *nf* (**a**) (*viento*) north wind; (*dirección*) north. (**b**) (*fig: vanidad*) conceit, pride; (*lujo*) luxury. (**c**) **perder la ~*** to lose one's head.

tramontar [1a] **1** *vi* (*sol*) to sink behind the mountains. **2 tramontarse** *vr* to escape over the mountains.

tramoya *nf* (**a**) (*Teat*) piece of stage machinery. (**b**) (*estafa*) trick, scheme, swindle; (*parte oculta*) concealed part, secret part (of a deal). (**c**) **armar una ~*** to kick up a fuss.

tramoyar [1a] *vt* (*And, Carib*) to swindle.

tramoyero *adj* (*CAm, Carib*) tricky, sharp.

tramoyista *nm* (**a**) (*Teat*) scene shifter, stagehand. (**b**) (*estafador*) swindler, trickster; (*farsante*) humbug; (*impostor*) impostor; (*intrigante*) schemer.

trampa *nf* (**a**) (*escotilla*) trapdoor; hatch; (*bragueta*) fly.

(**b**) (*Caza etc*) trap; snare; (*Golf*) bunker; (*fig*) snare; catch, pitfall; **~ cazabobos, ~ explosiva** booby-trap; **~ de fuera de juego** offside trap; **~ mortal** deathtrap; **~ para ratas** rat-trap; **caer en la ~** to fall for it, fall into the trap; **coger a alguien en la ~** to catch sb red-handed; **hay ~** there's a catch in it; there's something fishy here*; **esto es sin ~ ni cartón** this is the real thing; **este juego no tiene ~ ni cartón** there are no catches in this game.

(**c**) (*juego de manos*) conjuring trick; **hacer ~s** to juggle, conjure.

(**d**) (*fig*) (*estafa*) trick, swindle, fraud; (*chanchullo*) wangle*, fiddle*; (*broma*) hoax; (*Fin etc*) racket; **hacer ~s** to cheat; to be on the fiddle*; **hicieron (una) ~ con los votos** they fiddled the voting*, they juggled with the votes; *V* **ley** (**a**).

(**e**) (*Com*) bad debt.

trampantojo* *nm* (*juego de manos*) sleight of hand, trick; (*fig: chanchullo*) fiddle*, cheat; (*método poco limpio*) underhand method.

trampear [1a] **1** *vt* to cheat, swindle. **2** *vi* (**a**) to cheat; to get money by false pretences. (**b**) (*ir tirando*) to manage, get by; (*vestido, zapatos etc*) to last out.

trampería *nf* = **tramposería.**

trampero 1 *adj* (*CAm, Cono Sur, Méx*) = **tramposo. 2** *nm* (**a**) (*persona*) trapper. (**b**) (*Cono Sur: trampa*) trap for birds.

trampilla *nf* (**a**) (*mirilla*) peephole. (**b**) (*escotilla*) trapdoor, hatchway; (*bragueta*) fly; **~ de carburante** filler-cap, fuel-cap.

trampista *nm* = **tramposo 2.**

trampolín *nm* (*de piscina*) springboard, diving-board; (*Dep*) trampoline; (*de esquí*) ski-jump.

trampón* *adj* crooked*.

tramposería *nf* crookedness*; guile, deceit.

tramposo 1 *adj* crooked*, tricky, swindling; **pregunta tramposa** catch question. **2** *nm*, **tramposa** *nf* crook*, twister, swindler; (*tahur*) cardsharper; (*Fin*) bad payer.

tranca *nf* (**a**) (*porra*) stick, cudgel, club; (*Méx**) **~s** legs. (**b**) (*viga*) beam, pole; (*de puerta, ventana*) bar. (**c**) = **tranquera** (**b**). (**d**) (*: *borrachera*) drunken spree, binge*; **tener una ~** (*LAm*) to be drunk. (**e**) (*Cono Sur: de escopeta etc*) safety-catch. (**f**) (*Carib*) dollar, peso. (**g**) (*Carib Aut*) traffic-jam. (**h**) (⁑: *pene*) prick⁑. (**i**) **a ~s y barrancas** with great difficulty, against many obstacles; through fire and water. (**j**) **saltar las ~s** (*Méx*) to rebel; to lose one's patience. (**k**) (*Cono Sur**) complex, neurosis.

trancada *nf* stride; **en dos ~s** in a couple of strides; (*fig*) in a couple of ticks.

trancantrulla *nf* (*Cono Sur*) trick, fraud.

trancaperros *nm invar* (*Carib*) row, scrap.

trancar [1g] **1** *vt* (**a**) *puerta, ventana* to bar. (**b**) (*Carib Aut etc*) to box in, block, shut in.

2 *vi* to stride along.

3 trancarse *vr* (**a**) (*Carib*) to get drunk. (**b**) (*Cono Sur, Méx Med*) to be constipated.

trancazo *nm* (**a**) (*golpe*) blow, bang (with a stick). (**b**) (*Med**) flu.

trance *nm* (**a**) (*momento difícil*) (difficult) moment, (awkward) juncture, (tough) situation; critical juncture, moment of peril; **~ mortal, último ~, postrer ~** last moments, dying moments; **a todo ~** at all costs; **estar en ~ de muerte** to be at the point of death, be at death's door; **estar en ~ de** + *infin* to be on the point of + *ger*, be in process of + *ger*; **puesto en tal ~** placed in such a situation.

(**b**) (*estado hipnótico*) hypnotic state; (*estado drogado*) drugged condition; (*de médium*) (spiritualistic) trance; (*Rel*) trance, ecstasy.

tranco *nm* (**a**) (*paso*) stride, big step; **a ~s*** pell-mell, hastily, in a rush; **andar a ~s** to walk with long strides, take big steps; **en dos ~s** in a couple of strides; (*fig*) in a couple of ticks.

(**b**) (*Arquit*) threshold.

tranque *nm* (*Cono Sur*) dam; reservoir.

tranquera *nf* (**a**) (*cercado*) palisade, fence. (**b**) (*LAm*: *para ganado*) cattle-gate.

tranquero *nm* (*And, Carib, Cono Sur*) = **tranquera** (**b**).

tranqui* **1** *excl* cool it!*, calm down! **2** *adj* = **tranquilo**.

tranquilamente *adv* calmly; peacefully; quietly.

tranquilidad (*V adj*) *nf* stillness, calmness, tranquillity; peacefulness; quietness; freedom from anxiety; unruffled state; **dijo con toda ~** he said calmly; **perder la ~** to lose patience; to get worked up.

tranquilino *nm* (*LAm*) drunkard.

tranquilizador *adj música etc* soothing; lulling; *hecho etc* reassuring.

tranquilizadoramente *adv* soothingly; reassuringly.

tranquilizante 1 *adj* = **tranquilizador**. **2** *nm* (*Med*) tranquillizer.

tranquilizar [1f] **1** *vt* to calm, quieten, still; *mente* to reassure, relieve, set at ease; *persona* to calm down; to reassure.

2 tranquilizarse *vr* to calm down; to stop worrying; **¡tranquilícese!** calm yourself!; don't worry!, never fear!

tranquilo *adj* (**a**) (*gen*) still, calm, tranquil; peaceful; quiet; *mar etc* calm; *mente* calm, free of worry, untroubled; *carácter, estado* calm, unruffled; **dejar a uno ~** to leave sb alone; **ir con la conciencia tranquila** to go with a clear conscience; **¡estad ~s!** don't worry!; keep calm!; **tú estáte ~ hasta que yo vuelva** you stay put till I come back, you just sit tight till I get back; **¡tú, ~!*** calm down!, take it easy!; **mientras no lo hagan, todos ~s** provided they don't do it, everyone's happy; **se quedó tan ~** he didn't bat an eyelid.

(**b**) (*pey*) thoughtless, unreliable, inconsiderate; **es un tío de lo más ~** he's an utterly inconsiderate chap.

tranquilla *nf* (**a**) (*pasador*) latch; pin. (**b**) (*en conversación*) trap, catch. (**c**) (*And*) hindrance, obstacle.

tranquillo* *nm* knack; **coger el ~ a un problema** to get the hang of a problem, find the knack of solving a problem.

tranquis* *adj*: **hacer algo en plan ~** to do sth on the quiet.

tranquiza *nf* (*And, Méx*) beating.

trans... *pref* trans...; *V t* **tras...**

Trans. (*Com*) *abr de* **transferencia** transfer.

transacción *nf* (**a**) (*Com etc*) transaction; deal, bargain; **~ comercial** business deal. (**b**) (*componenda*) compromise, compromise settlement; **llegar a una ~** to reach a compromise.

transandino *adj* trans-Andean.

transar[1] [1a] **1** *vt* (*Cono Sur*) to trade. **2** *vi* (*LAm*) = **transigir**.

transar[2] [1a] *vt* (*Méx*) to cheat, swindle, defraud.

transatlántico 1 *adj cable etc* transatlantic; *travesía* Atlantic; **los países ~s** the countries on the other side of the Atlantic. **2** *nm* (*Náut*) liner.

transbordador *nm* (**a**) (*Náut*) ferry; (*Aer*) shuttle; **~ para coches** car ferry; **~ espacial** space shuttle. (**b**) **puente ~** transporter bridge. (**c**) **~ funicular** cable railway.

transbordar [1a] **1** *vt* to transfer, move across, switch; (*Náut*) to tranship; (*a través de río etc*) to ferry across. **2** *vi y* **transbordarse** *vr* (*Ferro etc*) to change.

transbordo *nm* (**a**) (*traslado*) transfer; move, switch; (*Náut*) transhipment; ferrying. (**b**) (*Ferro etc*) change; **hacer ~, realizar ~** to change (*en* at).

transceptor *nm* transceiver.

transcribir [3a; *ptp* **transcrito**] *vt (copiar)* to transcribe; (*de alfabeto distinto*) to transliterate.

transcripción *nf* transcription; transliteration.

transcultural *adj* cross-cultural.

transculturización *nf* cross-cultural influence(s); transculturation.

transcurrir [3a] *vi* (**a**) (*tiempo*) to pass, go by, elapse; **han transcurrido 7 años** 7 years have passed.

(**b**) (*suceso etc*) to be, turn out; **la tarde transcurrió aburrida** the evening was boring; **las fiestas transcurren con gran alegría** the festivities are being held in a very happy atmosphere, the celebrations are turning out to be very merry.

transcurso *nm*: **~ del tiempo** course of time, passing of time, lapse of time; **en el ~ de 8 días** in the course of a week, in the space of a week; **en el ~ de los años** in the course of the years.

transecto *nm* transect.

transepto *nm* transept.

transeúnte 1 *adj* transient, transitory; *miembro etc* temporary. **2** *nmf* (*en la calle etc*) passer-by; (*no permanente*) temporary member (*o* inhabitant *etc*), non-resident.

transexual *adj, nmf* transsexual.

transexualidad *nf* transsexuality.

transexualismo *nm* transsexualism.

transferencia *nf* transference; (*Dep, Jur*) transfer; **~ bancaria** banker's order; bank transfer; **~ por cable, ~ cablegráfica** cable transfer; **~ de crédito** credit transfer; **~ electrónica de fondos** electronic funds transfer.

transferible *adj* transferable.

transferir [3i] *vt* (**a**) (*trasladar*) to transfer. (**b**) (*aplazar*) to postpone.

transfiguración *nf* transfiguration.

transfigurar [1a] *vt* to transfigure (*en* into).

transformable *adj* transformable; (*Aut*) convertible.

transformación *nf* transformation (*en* into); change, conversion (*en* into); change-over; (*Rugby*) conversion.

transformacional *adj* transformational.

transformador *nm* (*Elec*) transformer.

transformar [1a] *vt* to transform (*en* into); to change, convert (*en* into); (*Dep*) *penalti* to convert.

transformismo *nm* (**a**) (*Bio*) evolution, transmutation. (**b**) (*sexual*) transvestism.

transformista *nmf* (**a**) (*Teat*) quick-change artist(e). (**b**) (*sexual*) transvestite.

transfronterizo *adj* cross-border *atr*; **seguridad transfronteriza** cross-border security.

tránsfuga *nmf* (*Mil*) deserter; (*Pol*) (*de partido*) turncoat; (*de nación*) defector.

transfuguismo *nm* tendency to desert (*o* defect).

transfundir [3a] *vt* (**a**) *sangre etc* to transfuse. (**b**) *noticia* to tell, spread, disseminate.

transfusión *nf* transfusion; **~ de sangre** blood transfusion; **hacer una ~ de sangre a uno** to give sb a blood transfusion.

transgredir [3a: *defectivo*] *vti* to transgress.

transgresión *nf* transgression.

transgresor(a) *nm/f* transgressor.

transiberiano *adj* trans-Siberian.

transición *nf* transition (*a* to, *de* from); **período de ~** transitional period; **la ~** (*Esp Pol*) the transition to democracy in Spain after Franco's death (1975).

transicional *adj* transitional.

transido *adj*: **~ de angustia** beset with anxiety; **~ de dolor** racked with pain; **~ de frío** frozen to the marrow; **~ de hambre** overcome with hunger.

transigencia *nf* (**a**) (*acto*) compromise; yielding. (**b**) (*actitud etc*) accommodating attitude, spirit of compromise.

transigente *adj* accommodating, compromising; tolerant.

transigir [3c] **1** *vt*: **~ un pleito** (*Jur*) to settle (a suit) out of court.

2 *vi* (*llegar a un acuerdo*) to compromise (*con* with; *en cuanto a* on, about); (*ceder*) to give way, yield, make concessions; **~ en** + *infin* to agree to + *infin*; **yo no transijo con tales abusos** I cannot tolerate such abuses, I cannot compromise with such abuses; **hemos transigido con la demanda popular** we have bowed to the people's demand.

Transilvania *nf* Transylvania.

transistor *nm* transistor.

transistorizado *adj* transistorized.

transitable *adj camino etc* passable.

transitar [1a] *vi* to go, go from place to place, travel; **~ por** to go along, pass along.

transitivamente *adv* transitively.

transitivo *adj* transitive.

tránsito *nm* (**a**) (*acto*) transit, passage, movement; **'se prohíbe el ~'** 'no thoroughfare'; **estar de ~** to be in transit, be passing through; **el ~ de este camino presenta dificultades** this road has its problems, the going on this road is not easy.

(**b**) (*Aut etc*) movement, traffic; **~ rodado** wheeled traffic, vehicular traffic; **calle de mucho ~** busy street; **horas de máximo ~** rush hours, peak traffic hours.

(**c**) (*traslado*) move, transfer.

(**d**) (*Rel*) passing, death.

(**e**) (*parada*) stop; stopping place; **hacer** ~ to make a stop.

(**f**) (*pasillo*) passageway.

transitoriedad *nf* transience.

transitorio *adj (pasajero)* transitory; fleeting; (*provisional*) temporary; *período etc* transitional, of transition.

transliteración *nf* transliteration.

transliterar [1a] *vt* to transliterate.

translucidez *nf* translucence.

translúcido *adj* translucent.

transmarino *adj* overseas.

transmigración *nf* migration, transmigration.

transmigrar [1a] *vi* to migrate, transmigrate.

transmisibilidad *nf* (*Med*) contagiousness, ability to be transmitted.

transmisible *adj* transmissible; (*Med*) contagious.

transmisión *nf* (**a**) (*acto*) transmission; (*Jur etc*) transfer; ~ **de dominio** (*Jur*) transfer of ownership.

(**b**) (*Mec*) transmission.

(**c**) (*Elec*) transmission; (*Rad, TV*) transmission, broadcast(ing); ~ **en circuito** hookup; ~ **en diferido** recorded programme, repeat broadcast; ~ **exterior** outside broadcast; ~ **por satélite** satellite broadcasting.

(**d**) **transmisiones** (*Mil*) signals (corps).

(**e**) (*Inform*) ~ **de datos** data transmission; ~ **de datos en paralelo** parallel data transmission; ~ **de datos en serie** serial data transmission; **media** ~ **bidireccional** half duplex; **plena** ~ **bidireccional** full duplex.

transmisor 1 *adj* transmitting; **aparato** ~ transmitter; **estación** ~**a** transmitter. **2** *nm* transmitter.

transmisora *nf* transmitter; radio relay station.

transmisor-receptor *nm* transceiver; (*portátil*) walkie-talkie.

transmitir [3a] *vti* to transmit (*a* to); (*Rad, TV*) to transmit, broadcast; *posesiones* to pass on, hand down; (*Jur*) to transfer (*a* to); (*Med*) *enfermedad* to give, infect with; *gérmenes* to carry.

transmutable *adj* transmutable.

transmutación *nf* transmutation.

transmutar [1a] *vt* to transmute (*en* into).

transnacional 1 *adj* international, transnational; that crosses national borders. **2** *nf* multinational (company).

transoceánico *adj* transoceanic.

transparencia *nf* (**a**) transparency; clarity, clearness; ~ **informativa** willingness to disclose information. (**b**) (*Fot*) slide, transparency. (**c**) (*fig*) (*franqueza*) openness; (*como sistema*) open government.

transparentar [1a] **1** *vt* to reveal, allow to be seen; *emoción etc* to show, reveal, betray.

2 *vi* to be transparent; to allow the contents (*etc*) to show through.

3 transparentarse *vr* (**a**) (*vidrio etc*) to be transparent, be clear; (*objeto etc*) to show through, be able to be seen.

(**b**) (*fig*) to show clearly, become perceptible; **se transparentaba su verdadera intención** his real intention became plain, his true intention was betrayed.

(**c**) (*: *ropa*) to become threadbare, show what is underneath.

(**d**) (*: *persona*) to be dreadfully thin.

transparente 1 *adj* transparent; *aire* clear; *vestido* diaphanous, filmy; (*fig*) transparent, clear, plain. **2** *nm* curtain, blind, shade.

transpiración *nf* perspiration; (*Bot*) transpiration.

transpirar [1a] *vi* (**a**) (*sudar*) to perspire; (*Bot*) to transpire; (*líquido*) to seep through, ooze out. (**b**) (*fig*) to transpire, become known.

transpirenaico *adj*, **transpireneo** *adj ruta etc* trans-Pyrenean; *tráfico* passing through (*o* over) the Pyrenees; **la nación transpirenaica** the country on the other side of the Pyrenees.

transplantar *etc V* **trasplantar** *etc.*

transpondedor *nm* transponder.

transponer [2q] **1** *vt* (**a**) (*gen*) to transpose; (*cambiar de sitio*) to switch over, move about, change the places of.

(**b**) (*trasplantar*) to transplant.

(**c**) ~ **la esquina** to disappear round the corner.

2 *vi (desaparecer)* to disappear from view; (*ir más allá*) to go beyond, get past; (*sol*) to go down, go behind the mountain (*etc*).

3 transponerse *vr* (**a**) (*cambiar de sitio*) to change places.

(**b**) (*esconderse*) to hide, hide behind sth; (*sol*) to go down, go behind the mountain (*etc*).

(**c**) (*dormirse*) to doze (off).

transportable *adj* transportable; **fácilmente** ~ easily carried, easily transported.

transportación *nf* transportation.

transportador *nm* (**a**) (*Mec*) conveyor, transporter; ~ **de banda,** ~ **de correa** conveyor belt. (**b**) (*Mat*) protractor.

transportar [1a] **1** *vt* (**a**) (*acarrear*) to transport; to haul, carry, take; (*Náut*) to ship; (*cable etc*) to carry, transmit; **el avión podrá** ~ **400 pasajeros** the plane will be able to carry 400 passengers.

(**b**) *diseño etc* to transfer (*a* to).

(**c**) (*Mús*) to transpose.

2 transportarse *vr* (*fig*) to get carried away, be enraptured.

transporte *nm* (**a**) (*acto*) transport; haulage, carriage; ~**s** transport, transportation; (*empresa*) haulage business, transport company; removals company; ~ **por carretera** road transport; ~ **colectivo,** ~ **público** public transport; ~ **escolar** school buses; **Ministerio de T~s** Ministry of Transport.

(**b**) (*de diseño etc*) transfer.

(**c**) (*Náut*) transport, troopship.

(**d**) (*Méx**) vehicle.

(**e**) (*fig*) transport, rapture, ecstasy.

transportista *nm* (*Aer etc*) carrier; (*Aut*) haulier, haulage contractor; freight transporter.

transposición *nf* transposition (*t Mús*).

transustanciación *nf* transubstantiation.

transustanciar [1b] *vt* to transubstantiate.

transversal 1 *adj* transverse, cross; oblique; **calle** ~ cross street; **otra calle** ~ **de la calle mayor** another street which crosses the high street.

2 *nf* cross street.

transversalmente *adv* transversely, across; obliquely.

transverso *adj* = **transversal 1.**

transvestido, -a *adj, nm/f* transvestite.

transvestismo *nm* transvestism.

tranvía *nm* (*vehículo*) tram, tramcar, streetcar (*US*); (*ferro*) local train; (*sistema*) tramway.

trapacear [1a] *vi* to cheat, be on the fiddle*; to run a racket; to make mischief.

trapacería *nf* (**a**) (*trampa*) racket*, fiddle*, swindle; (**b**) (*chisme*) piece of gossip, malicious tale.

trapacero 1 *adj* dishonest, swindling. **2** *nm*, **trapacera** *nf* (**a**) (*tramposo*) cheat, swindler; racketeer. (**b**) (*chismoso*) gossip, mischief-maker.

trapacista *nm* = **trapacero 2.**

trapajoso *adj* (**a**) *ropa* shabby, ragged. (**b**) *pronunciación* defective; incorrect; *persona* who talks incorrectly; who has a speech defect.

trápala 1 *nf* (**a**) (*de caballo*) clatter, noise of hooves, clip-clop, hoofbeat. (**b**) (*: *jaleo*) row, uproar, shindy*. (**c**) (*: *trampa*) swindle. **2** *nm* (*garrulidad*) talkativeness, garrulity. **3** *nmf* (*) (**a**) (*parlanchín*) chatterbox. (**b**) (*tramposo*) cheat, trickster, swindler.

trapalear [1a] *vi* (**a**) (*caballo*) to clatter, beat its hooves, clip-clop; (*persona*) to clatter, go clattering along. (**b**) (*: *parlotear*) to chatter, jabber. (**c**) (*mentir*) to fib, lie; (*trampear*) to be on the fiddle*.

trapalero *adj* (*Carib*) = **trapalón.**

trapalón* *adj* (*mentiroso*) lying; (*tramposo*) dishonest, swindling.

trapalonear [1a] *vi* (*Cono Sur*) = **trapalear** (**c**).

trapatiesta* *nf* (*jaleo*) commotion, shindy*; (*pelea*) rough-house*.

trapaza *nf* = **trapacería.**

trapeador *nm* (*CAm, Cono Sur, Méx*) floor mop.

trapear [1a] *vt* (**a**) (*LAm*) *suelo* to mop. (**b**) (*CAm**) (*pegar*) to beat, tan*; (*fig*: *insultar*) to insult; (*fig*: *regañar*) to tick off*.

trapecio *nm* trapeze; (*Mat*) trapezium.

trapecista *nmf* trapeze artist(e).

trapería *nf* (**a**) (*trapos*) rags; (*ropa vieja*) old clothes. (**b**) (*tienda*) old-clothes shop; junk shop.

trapero *nm* ragman.

trapezoide *nm* trapezoid.

trapicar [1g] *vi* (*Cono Sur*) (*comida*) to taste very hot; (*herida etc*) to sting, smart.

trapichar [1a] *vt* (*And, Méx*) to smuggle (in); (*Carib*) to deal in.

trapiche *nm* (*de aceite*) olive-oil press; (*de azúcar*) sugar mill; (*And, Cono Sur*: *Min*) ore-crusher.

trapichear* [1a] **1** *vt* to deal in, trade in. **2** *vi* (**a**)

(*trampear*) to be on the fiddle*; (*andar en malos pasos*) to be mixed up in something shady; (*intrigar*) to plot, scheme. (**b**) (*Cono Sur*: *comerciar*) to scrape a living by buying and selling.
trapicheo* **1** *nm* fiddle*, shady deal. **2** *nmpl*: **~s** (**a**) (*Com*) dealing, trading; (*pey*: *trampas*) fiddles*, shady dealing; (*intrigas*) plots, schemes, tricks. (**b**) (*Cono Sur*: *comercio*) small-time business. (**c**) (*Méx*) clandestine affair.
trapichero *nm* (**a**) (*LAm*: *obrero*) sugar-mill worker. (**b**) (*And, Carib**: *entrometido*) busybody. (**c**) (*Cono Sur*:*: *Com*) small-time dealer.
trapiento *adj* ragged, tattered.
trapillo *nm*: **estar de ~, ir de ~** to be dressed in ordinary clothes, be informally dressed.
trapío *nm* (**a**) (*atractivo*) charm; (*garbo*) elegant carriage, attractive way of moving; **tener buen ~** to have a fine presence, carry o.s. elegantly, move beautifully; (*fig*) to have real class. (**b**) (*de toro*) fine appearance.
trapisonda* *nf* (**a**) (*jaleo*) row, commotion; shindy*; (*pelea*) brawl, scuffle. (**b**) (*estafa*) swindle; (*asunto sucio*) monkey business*, shady affair, fiddle*; (*intriga*) intrigue.
trapisondear* [1a] *vi* (*intrigar*) to scheme, plot, intrigue; (*trampear*) to be on the fiddle*.
trapisondeo* *nm*, **trapisondería*** *nf* scheming, plotting, intrigues; fiddling*, wangling*.
trapisondista* *nmf* schemer, intriguer; fiddler*, wangler*.
trapito *nm* (*trapo*) rag; **~s** (*: *ropa*) clothes; **~s de cristianar*** Sunday best, glad rags; **él y sus ~s** he and all his troubles.
trapo *nm* (**a**) (*paño*) rag; **dejar a uno hecho un ~, poner a uno como un ~** (*: *reprender*) to give sb a dressing-down*; to haul sb over the coals; (*en debate*) to flatten sb, give sb a battering; to shower abuse on sb.
(**b**) (*t* **~ del polvo**) duster; (*de limpiar*) rag, cleaning cloth; **~ de fregar** dishcloth; **pasar un ~ por algo** to give sth a wipe over (*o* down).
(**c**) (*Taur**) cape.
(**d**) (*: *vestidos*) **~s** (woman's) clothes, dresses; **gasta una barbaridad en ~s*** she spends an awful lot on clothes; **lavar los ~s sucios ante el mundo entero** to wash one's dirty linen in public; **trataron de ocultar los ~s sucios** (*fig*) they tried to sweep it under the carpet; **sacar los ~s** (**a relucir**) to let fly, tell a lot of home truths; to bring out all the skeletons in the cupboard.
(**e**) (*Náut*) canvas, sails; **a todo ~** with all sails set, under full sail; (*fig*) quickly; **llorar** (*etc*) **a todo ~** to cry (*etc*) uncontrollably.
(**f**) **soltar el ~** (**a llorar**) to burst into tears; **soltar el ~** (**a reír**) to burst out laughing, collapse in helpless laughter.
(**g**) (*: *velocidad*) speed; **a todo ~** at full speed, flat-out; **¡qué ~ llevaba!** what a lick he was going at!
traposiento *adj* (*And*) ragged.
traposo *adj* (**a**) (*And, Carib, Cono Sur*: *harapiento*) ragged. (**b**) (*Cono Sur*) = **trapajoso** (**b**). (**c**) (*Cono Sur*) *carne* tough, stringy.
trapujear [1a] *vi* (*CAm*) to smuggle.
trapujero *nm* (*CAm*) smuggler.
traque *nm* (**a**) crack, bang. (**b**) (*****) noisy fart*****.
tráquea *nf* trachea, windpipe.
traquear [1a] **1** *vti* = **traquetear.**
2 *vt* (**a**) (*CAm, Cono Sur, Méx*: *dejar huella*) to make deep tracks on.
(**b**) (*Carib*) *persona* to take about from place to place; (*Cono Sur*) *ganado* to switch from place to place.
(**c**) (*Carib*) (*probar*) to test, try out; (*entrenar*) to train.
3 *vi* (**a**) (*Cono Sur*: *frecuentar*) to frequent a place.
(**b**) (*Carib*: *beber*) to drink.
4 traquearse *vr* (*Carib*) to go out of one's mind.
traqueo *nm* = **traqueteo.**
traquetear [1a] **1** *vt* (**a**) *recipiente* to shake; *sillas etc* to rattle, bang about, make a lot of noise with.
(**b**) (*: *estropear*) to mess up, muck about with.
2 *vi* (**a**) (*cohete etc*) to crackle, bang; (*vehículo etc*) to rattle, jolt; (*ametrallador*) to rattle, clatter.
(**b**) (*Cono Sur, Méx*: *apresurarse*) to bustle about, go to and fro a lot; (*Cono Sur*: *cansarse*) to tire o.s. out at work.
traqueteo *nm* (**a**) (*V vt*) crackle, bang; rattle, rattling, jolting; clatter; **se le da el ~*** she likes to live it up*. (**b**) (*And, Carib, Méx*) (*ruido*) row, din; (*movimiento*) hustle and bustle, coming and going.
traquidazo *nm* (*Méx*) = **traquido.**
traquido *nm* (*de látigo*) crack; (*de disparo*) crack, bang, report.
traquinar [1a] *vi* (*Carib*) = **trajinar.**
tras[1] **1** *prep* (**a**) (*lugar*) behind; after; **día ~ día** day after day; **uno ~ otro** one after the other; **andar ~ algo, estar ~ algo** to be looking for sth, be on the track of sth; **andamos ~ un coche que han anunciado** we're after a car which has been advertised; **correr ~ uno, ir ~ uno** to chase (after) sb.
(**b**) (*al otro lado de*) across, beyond; **~ los Pirineos** beyond the Pyrenees; **~ el río** on the other side of the river.
(**c**) (*tiempo*) after.
(**d**) **~ de** + *infin* besides + *ger*, in addition to + *ger*.
(**e**) (*And, Méx*) **~ de** + *infin* after + *ger*; **~ de que** ... after ...
2 *nm* (*) bottom, backside.
tras[2] *interj*: **¡~, ~!** tap, tap!; knock, knock!
tras... *pref* trans...; *V t* **trans...**
trasalcoba *nf* dressing-room.
trasaltar *nm* retrochoir.
trasbocar* [1g] *vti* (*And, Cono Sur*) to throw up.
trasbucar [1g] *vt* (*Carib, Cono Sur*) to upset, overturn.
trasbuscar [1g] *vt* (*Cono Sur*) to search carefully.
trascendencia *nf* (**a**) (*importancia*) importance, significance, momentousness; far-reaching nature; implications, consequences; **encuentro sin ~** casual meeting; **discusión sin ~** discussion of no particular significance.
(**b**) (*Filos*) transcendence.
trascendental *adj* (**a**) (*importante*) important, significant, momentous; (*esencial*) vital; *consecuencias* far-reaching. (**b**) (*Filos*) transcendental.
trascendente *adj* = **trascendental.**
trascender [2g] *vi* (**a**) (*oler*) to smell (*a* of); **el olor de la cocina trascendía hasta nosotros** the smell of the kitchen floated across to us, the kitchen smell reached as far as us; **la carne trasciende a pasada** the meat smells bad.
(**b**) **~ a** (*fig*) to smack of, be suggestive of; to evoke, suggest; **en esta novela todo trasciende a romanticismo** everything in this novel smacks of romanticism; **de su gesto trasciende cierta serenidad** his expression suggests a certain calmness, a certain serenity shines through his expression.
(**c**) (*saberse*) to come out, leak out; **~ a** to become known to, spread to; **por fin ha trascendido la triste noticia** the sad news has come out at last; **no queremos que ello trascienda a los demás** we do not want this to be known to the others.
(**d**) (*propagarse*) to spread, have a wide effect; **~ a** to reach, get across to, have an effect on; **su influencia trasciende a los países más remotos** his influence extends to the most remote countries; **~ de** to go beyond, go outside of, go beyond the limits of.
trascocina *nf* scullery.
trascolar [1l] *vt* to strain.
trasconejarse* [1a] *vr* to get lost, be misplaced.
trascordarse [1l] *vr*: **~ algo** to forget sth, lose all memory of sth; **estar trascordado** to be completely forgotten.
trascoro *nm* retrochoir.
trascorral *nm* (**a**) inner yard. (**b**) (*: *culo*) bottom.
trascuarto *nm* back room.
trasegar [1h *y* 1j] **1** *vt* (**a**) (*cambiar de sitio*) to move about, switch round; *puestos* to reshuffle; *vino* (*para la mesa*) to decant; (*en bodega*) to rack, pour into another container (*o* bottle).
(**b**) (*trastornar*) to mix up; to upset, turn upside down.
(**c**) (*) *bebida* to knock back*, put down*.
2 *vi* (*) to drink, booze*.
trasera *nf* back, rear.
trasero **1** *adj* back, rear; hind; **motor ~** rear-mounted engine; **rueda trasera** back wheel, rear wheel. **2** *nm* (**a**) (*Anat*) bottom, buttocks; (*Zool*) hindquarters, rump. (**b**) **~s** (*antepasados*) ancestors.
trasfondo *nm* background; (*de crítica etc*) undertone, undercurrent.
trasgo *nm* (**a**) (*duende*) goblin, imp. (**b**) (*niño*) imp.
trashojar [1a] *vt libro* to leaf through, glance through.
trashumación *nf* transhumance, seasonal migration, move to new pastures.
trashumante *adj animales* migrating, on the move to new pastures; *persona, tribu* nomadic.
trashumar [1a] *vi* to make the seasonal migration, move to new pastures.
trasiego *nm* (*V v*) (**a**) move, switch; reshuffle; decanting; racking. (**b**) mixing; upset.

trasigar [1h] *vt* (*And*) to upset, turn upside down.
trasijado *adj* skinny.
traslación *nf* (**a**) (*Astron*) movement, passage; removal. (**b**) (*copia*) copy; copying. (**c**) (*Liter*) metaphor; figurative use.
trasladar [1a] **1** *vt* (**a**) (*mudar*) to move; (*quitar*) to remove; *persona* to move, change, transfer (*a* to).
(**b**) (*aplazar*) to postpone (*a* until), move (*a* to); *reunión* to adjourn (*a* to).
(**c**) (*copiar*) to copy, transcribe.
(**d**) *pensamiento, sentimiento etc* to translate; to express, interpret; to convey in a different form; ~ **su pensamiento al papel** to put one's thoughts on paper; ~ **una novela a la pantalla** to transfer a novel to the screen, interpret a novel as a film.
(**e**) (*Ling*) to translate (*a* into).
2 trasladarse *vr* to go, move (*a* to); to betake o.s. (*a* to); (*LAm*) to move (house); ~ **a otro puesto** to move to a new job, change to a new post; **los que se trasladan a la oficina en coche** those who go to their offices by car; **después nos trasladamos al bar** later we moved to the bar.
traslado *nm* (**a**) (*mudanza*) move; removal; (*cambio*) change, transfer. (**b**) (*copia*) copy; (*Jur*) notification; **dar ~ a uno de una orden** to give sb a copy of an order.
traslapar [1a] **1** *vt* to overlap. **2 traslaparse** *vr* to overlap.
traslapo *nm* overlap, overlay.
traslaticiamente *adv* figuratively.
traslaticio *adj* figurative.
traslucir [3f] **1** *vt* to show, reveal, betray; **dejar ~ algo** to hint at sth, suggest sth.
2 traslucirse *vr* (**a**) (*ser transparente*) to be translucent, be transparent.
(**b**) (*ser visible*) to show through, be perceptible.
(**c**) (*fig*) (*revelarse*) to reveal itself, be revealed; (*ser obvio*) to be plain to see; **en su cara se traslucía cierto pesimismo** a certain pessimism was revealed in his expression, a certain pessimism was written on his face.
(**d**) (*fig*: *saberse*) to leak out, come to light.
(**e**) (*fig*: *persona*) to reveal one's inmost thoughts, betray one's hidden feelings.
traslumbrar [1a] **1** *vt* to dazzle.
2 traslumbrarse *vr* (**a**) (*ser deslumbrado*) to be dazzled.
(**b**) (*ir y venir*) to appear and disappear suddenly, come and go unexpectedly; (*pasar rápidamente*) to flash across.
trasluz *nm* (**a**) (*luz difusa*) diffused light; (*luz reflejada*) reflected light, glint, gleam.
(**b**) **mirar algo al ~** to look at sth against the light.
(**c**) (*Carib*: *semblanza*) resemblance.
trasmano (**a**) **a ~** *adv* out of reach; (*fig*) out of the way, remote.
(**b**) **por ~** (*LAm*) *adv* secretly, in an underhand way.
trasminante *adj* (*Cono Sur*) *frío* bitter, piercing.
trasminarse [1a] *vr* to filter through, pass through.
trasmundo *nm* hidden world, secret world.
trasnochada *nf* (**a**) (*vigilia*) vigil, watch; (*noche sin dormir*) sleepless night.
(**b**) (*Mil*) night attack.
(**c**) (*noche anterior*) last night, previous night, night before.
trasnochado *adj* (**a**) *comida etc* stale, old; (*fig*) stale, obsolete, ancient; *proyecto etc* that has been too long in the preparation, that has been overtaken by events.
(**b**) *persona* wan, haggard, hollow-eyed.
trasnochador 1 *adj* given to staying up late; **son muy ~es** they turn in very late, they keep very late hours. **2** *nm*, **trasnochadora** *nf* night-bird (*fig*).
trasnochar [1a] **1** *vt problema* to sleep on.
2 *vi* (**a**) (*acostarse tarde*) to stay up late, go to bed late; (*no acostarse*) to stay up all night; (*no dormir*) to have a sleepless night; (*ir de juerga*) to have a night out, have a night on the tiles.
(**b**) **~ en un sitio** to spend the night in a place.
3 trasnocharse *vr* (*LAm*) = **2.**
trasoír [3p] *vti* to mishear.
trasojado *adj* haggard, hollow-eyed.
traspaís *nm* interior, hinterland.
traspalar [1a] *vt* to shovel about, move with a shovel.
traspapelar [1a] **1** *vt* to lose, mislay, misplace. **2 traspapelarse** *vr* to get mislaid.
traspapeleo *nm* misplacement.
traspar [1a] *vi* (*Méx*) to move house.
traspasar [1a] **1** *vt* (**a**) (*penetrar*) to pierce, penetrate, go through; to transfix; (*líquido*) to go through, come through, soak through; **la bala le traspasó el pulmón** the bullet pierced his lung; **~ a uno con una espada** to run sb through with a sword.
(**b**) (*fig*: *dolor, grito etc*) to pierce; to pain, grieve mortally; **un ruido que traspasa el oído** a noise which pierces your ear, a noise which drills into your ear; **ese grito me traspasó** that yell transfixed me; **la escena me traspasó el corazón** the scene pierced me to the core.
(**c**) *calle, río etc* to cross over.
(**d**) *límite* to go beyond, overstep; to transcend; **esto traspasa los límites de lo tolerable** this goes beyond the limits of what is tolerable.
(**e**) *ley* to break, infringe, transgress.
(**f**) *jugador, propiedad etc* to transfer; to sell, make over; (*Jur*) to convey; **'traspaso negocio'** (*anuncio*) 'business for sale'.
2 traspasarse *vr* to go too far, overstep the mark.
traspaso *nm* (**a**) (*venta*) transfer, sale; (*Jur*) conveyance.
(**b**) (*propiedad, bienes*) property transferred, goods (*etc*) sold; (*Jur*) property being conveyed; (*Esp Pol*) **~s** fields of competence and powers transferred to an autonomous region.
(**c**) (*Com, Dep*) transfer fee; (*de piso etc*) key money.
(**d**) (*fig*: *pena*) anguish, pain; grief.
(**e**) (*de ley*) infringement, transgression.
traspatio *nm* (*LAm*) backyard.
traspié *nm* (**a**) (*tropiezo*) slip, stumble, trip; **dar un ~** to slip, trip, stumble. (**b**) (*fig*) slip, blunder.
traspintarse [1a] *vr* (**a**) (*en papel*) to come through, show through. (**b**) (*****: *acabar mal*) to backfire, turn out all wrong.
trasplantado, -a *nm/f* transplant patient.
trasplantar [1a] **1** *vt* to transplant. **2 trasplantarse** *vr* to emigrate, uproot o.s.
trasplante *nm* (**a**) (*Bot*) transplanting. (**b**) (*Med*) transplant, transplantation; **~ de corazón** heart transplant; **~ hepático** liver transplant.
traspontín *nm* = **traspuntín.**
traspuesta *nf* (**a**) (*transposición*) transposition; (*cambio*) switching, changing over; removal.
(**b**) (*Geog*) rise.
(**c**) (*huida*) flight, escape; (*acto de esconderse*) hiding.
(**d**) (*patio*) backyard; (*dependencias*) outbuildings.
traspunte *nm* (*Teat*: *botones*) callboy; (*apuntador*) prompt, prompter.
traspuntín *nm* (**a**) (*asiento*) tip-up seat, folding seat. (**b**) (*****: *culo*) backside, bottom.
trasque *conj* (*LAm*) in addition to the fact that ..., besides being ...
trasquiladura *nf* shearing, clipping.
trasquilar [1a] *vt* (**a**) *oveja* to shear, clip; *pelo, persona* to crop. (**b**) (*****: *cortar*) to cut down, curtail, chop off.
trastabillar [1a] *vi* = **trastrabillar.**
trastabillón *nm* (*LAm*) stumble, trip.
trastada* *nf* (**a**) (*acto insensato*) stupid act, senseless act; (*travesura*) mischief, prank; (*broma pesada*) practical joke; (*grosería*) piece of bad behaviour.
(**b**) (*mala pasada*) dirty trick; **hacer una ~ a uno** to play a dirty trick on sb.
trastajo *nm* piece of junk.
trastazo *nm* bump, bang, thump.
traste[1] *nm* (**a**) (*Mús*) fret.
(**b**) **dar al ~ con algo** to ruin sth, spoil sth, mess sth up; **dar al ~ con una fortuna** to squander a fortune; **dar al ~ con los planes** to ruin one's plans; **esto ha dado al ~ con mi paciencia** this has exhausted my patience; **ir al ~** to fail, fall through, be ruined.
traste[2] *nm* (**a**) (*LAm*) = **trasto.** (**b**) (*Cono Sur**) bottom, backside.
trastear [1a] **1** *vt* (**a**) (*Mús*) to play.
(**b**) *objetos* (*mover*) to move around; (*desordenar*) to mess up, disarrange.
(**c**) (*Taur*) to play with the cape.
(**d**) *persona* (*manipular*) to lead by the nose, twist round one's little finger.
(**e**) *persona* (*entretener*) to keep waiting, keep at bay, keep dangling.
(**f**) (*Méx*‡: *acariciar*) to feel up‡, touch up‡.
2 *vi* (**a**) (*mover objetos*) to move things around; **~ con, ~ en** (*buscando*) to rummage among; (*manosear*) to fiddle with; (*desordenar*) to mess up, disarrange.
(**b**) (*And, CAm*: *mudar de casa*) to move house.
(**c**) (*conversar*) to make bright conversation.

3 trastearse *vr* (*And, Cono Sur*) to move house.

trastera *nf* (**a**) (*cuarto*) lumber room. (**b**) (*Méx: armario*) cupboard. (**c**) (*Carib*) heap of junk.

trastería *nf* (**a**) (*trastos*) lumber, junk. (**b**) (*tienda*) junk-shop. (**c**) = **trastada.**

trastero *nm* (**a**) (*cuarto*) lumber room; storage room. (**b**) (*Méx*) cupboard, closet (*US*). (**c**) (*Méx*‡: *culo*) backside. (**d**) (*CAm, Méx: para platos*) dishrack.

trastienda *nf* (**a**) back room (of a shop), room behind a shop; **obtener algo por la ~** to get sth under the counter; (*fig*) to get sth by underhand means.

(**b**) **tiene mucha ~** (*: *astucia*) he's a sharp one; he's a deep one, he hides a lot inside himself.

(**c**) (*Cono Sur, Méx**) backside.

trasto *nm* (**a**) (*mueble*) piece of furniture; (*utensilio*) household utensil; (*cosa inutil*) piece of lumber, piece of junk; (*olla etc*) old crock, old pot; **~s viejos** lumber, junk, rubbish; **tirarse los ~s a la cabeza** to have a blazing row.

(**b**) **~s** (*Teat*) (*decorado*) scenery; (*accesorios*) stage furniture, properties.

(**c**) (*: *avíos*) **~s** gear, tackle; **~s de matar** weapons; **~s de pescar** fishing tackle; **coger los ~s, liar los ~s** to pack up and go.

(**d**) (*: *persona*) useless individual, good-for-nothing; dead loss; nuisance; unreliable person; odd type*.

trastocar* [1g *y* 1l] *vt* = **trastrocar.**

trastornado *adj persona* mad, crazy; *mente* unhinged.

trastornar [1a] **1** *vt* (**a**) (*volcar*) to overturn, upset; to turn upside down; *objetos* to mix up, jumble up, turn upside down; *orden* to confuse, disturb.

(**b**) (*fig*) *ideas etc* to upset, confuse; *proyecto* to upset; *vida* to disturb, disorganize; *sentidos* to daze, confuse; *nervios* to shatter; *orden público etc* to disturb; *persona* (*molestar*) to upset, trouble, disturb; (*marear*) to make dizzy.

(**c**) (*volver loco*) *mente* to unhinge; *persona* to drive crazy, disturb mentally; **esa chica le ha trastornado** that girl has bowled him over, that girl is driving him crazy.

(**d**) (*: *encantar*) to delight; **la trastornan las joyas** she's crazy about jewels, she just lives for jewels.

2 trastornarse *vr* (**a**) (*proyecto etc*) to fall through, be ruined.

(**b**) (*persona*) to go crazy, go out of one's mind.

trastorno *nm* (**a**) (*acto*) overturning, upsetting; mixing up, jumbling up.

(**b**) (*fig: perturbación*) confusion, disturbance; (*molestia*) trouble, inconvenience; (*Pol*) disturbance, upheaval; **los ~s políticos de Eslobodia** the Slobodian political disturbances.

(**c**) (*Med*) upset, disorder; **~ digestivo, ~ estomacal** stomach upset.

(**d**) **~ mental** mental disorder, breakdown.

trastrabillar [1a] *vi* (**a**) (*tropezar*) to trip, stumble. (**b**) (*tambalearse*) to totter, reel, stagger. (**c**) (*trabarse la lengua*) to stammer, stutter.

trastrocar [1g *y* 1l] *vt* (**a**) *objetos* to switch over, change round; *orden* to reverse, invert. (**b**) (*transformar*) to change, transform.

trastrueco *nm,* **trastrueque** *nm* (*V vt*) (**a**) switch, changeover; reversal. (**b**) change, transformation.

trastumbar [1a] *vt* : **~ la esquina** (*Méx*) to disappear round (*o* turn) the corner.

trasudar [1a] *vi* to sweat a little.

trasudor *nm* slight sweat.

trasuntar [1a] *vt* (**a**) (*copiar*) to copy, transcribe. (**b**) (*resumir*) to summarize. (**c**) (*fig: mostrar*) to show, exude; **su cara trasuntaba serenidad** his face exuded calm.

trasunto *nm* (**a**) (*copia*) copy, transcription.

(**b**) (*fig: semejanza*) image, likeness; carbon copy; **fiel ~** exact likeness; faithful representation; **esto es un ~ en menor escala de lo que ocurrió ayer** this is a repetition on a smaller scale of what happened yesterday.

trasvasar [1a] *vt vino etc* to pour into another container, decant, transfer; *río* to divert; (*fig*) to move, shift, transfer.

trasvase *nm* pouring, decanting; diversion; (*fig*) movement, shift, transfer; (*fuga*) drain.

trasvasijar [1a] *vt* (*Cono Sur*) = **trasvasar.**

trasvolar [1l] *vt* to fly over, cross in an aeroplane.

trata *nf* (*t* **~ de esclavos, ~ de negros**) slave trade; **~ de blancas** white slave trade.

tratable *adj* (**a**) (*amable*) friendly, sociable, easy to get on with. (**b**) (*Cono Sur*) passable.

tratadista *nmf* writer (of a treatise); essayist.

tratado *nm* (**a**) (*Com etc*) agreement; (*Pol*) treaty, pact; **T~ de Adhesión** Treaty of Accession (to EC); **~ de paz** peace treaty; **T~ de Roma** Treaty of Rome; **T~ de Utrecht** Treaty of Utrecht.

(**b**) (*Liter*) treatise, tract; essay; **un ~ de física** a treatise on physics.

tratamiento *nm* (**a**) (*Med, Quím, Téc etc*) treatment; (*Téc*) processing; (*de persona, problema*) treatment, handling; management; **~ de choque** shock treatment; **~ de gráficos** graphics processing; **~ de la información** information processing; **~ de márgenes** margin settings; **~ médico** medical treatment; **~ con rayos X** X-ray treatment; **~ de textos** word-processing.

(**b**) (*título*) title, style (of address); **~ de tú** familiar address (*in 2nd person singular of verb*); **apear el ~ a uno** to drop sb's title, address sb without formality; **dar ~ a uno** to give sb his full title.

tratante *nmf* dealer, trader (*en* in).

tratar [1a] **1** *vt* (**a**) (*gen*) to treat, handle; **la tratan muy bien en esa pensión** they treat her well in that boarding house; **~ a alguien a patadas** (*o* **con la punta del pie**) to kick sb around (*t fig*); **hay que ~ los libros con cuidado** books should be handled carefully; **trata a todos con poca ceremonia** he treats everyone very unceremoniously.

(**b**) (*Med, Quím, Téc*) to treat (*con, por* with); (*Inform*) to process; **~ a uno con un nuevo fármaco** to treat sb with a new drug.

(**c**) **~ a uno** (*tener relaciones*) to have dealings with sb, have to do with sb, know sb; **le trato desde hace 6 meses** I have known him for 6 months.

(**d**) **~ a uno de tú** to address sb as 'tú' (*familiar 2nd person sing*); **¿cómo le hemos de ~?** how should we address him?, what ought we to call him?; **~ a uno de vago** to call sb idle.

2 *vi* (**a**) **~ de** (*libro etc*) to deal with, be about, discuss; (*personas, reunión*) to talk about, discuss; **este libro trata de las leyendas épicas** this book is about the epic legends; **ahora van a ~ del programa** they're going to talk about the programme now.

(**b**) **~ con** (*Com*) to deal in, trade in, handle.

(**c**) **~ con** *tema etc* to have to do with, deal with; *persona* to know, have dealings with, have contacts with; *enemigo* to negotiate with, treat with; **el geólogo trata con rocas** the geologist deals with rocks; **no tratamos con traidores** we do not treat with traitors, there can be no negotiations with traitors; **no había tratado con personas de esa clase** I had not had dealings with people of that class.

(**d**) **~ de** + *infin* to try to + *infin,* endeavour to + *infin.*

3 tratarse *vr* (**a**) (*1 persona*) **~ bien** to do o.s. well, live well; **ahora se trata con mucho cuidado** he looks after himself very carefully now.

(**b**) (*2 personas*) to treat each other, behave towards each other.

(**c**) (*2 personas*) **se tratan de usted** they address each other as 'usted' (*polite form of verb*); **¿aquí nos tratamos de tú o de usted?** are we on 'tú' or 'usted' terms here?; **¿cómo nos hemos de ~?** how should we address each other?

(**d**) **~ con uno** to have to do with sb, have dealings with sb.

(**e**) (*ser cuestión de*) **se trata de la nueva piscina** it's about the new pool, it's a question of the new pool; **se trata de aplazarlo un mes** it's a question of putting it off for a month; **¿de qué se trata?** what's it about?; what's up?, what's the trouble?; **ahora, tratándose de Vd ...** now, in your case ...; **si no se trata más que de eso** if there's no more to it than that, if that's all it is.

tratativas *nfpl* (*Cono Sur*) negotiations; steps, measures.

trato *nm* (**a**) (*entre personas*) intercourse, dealings; (*relación*) relationship; (*conocimiento*) acquaintance; **~ carnal, ~ sexual** sexual intercourse; **~ doble** double-dealing, dishonesty; **entrar en ~s con uno** to enter into relations (*o* negotiations) with sb; **no querer ~s con uno** to want no dealings with sb; **romper el ~ con uno** to break off relations with sb.

(**b**) (*de persona: t* **~s**) treatment; **~ preferente** priority treatment; **malos ~s** ill-treatment, rough treatment, ill-usage.

(**c**) (*manera de ser*) manner; (*conducta*) behaviour; **de fácil ~** easy to get on with; **de ~ agradable** pleasant, affable; **~ de gentes** = **don de gentes; tener buen ~** to be easy to get on with, have a pleasant manner, be affable.

(**d**) (*Com, Jur*) agreement, contract; deal, bargain; (*fig*) deal; **~s** dealings; **~ colectivo** collective bargaining; **~ comercial** business deal; **~ equitativo** fair deal, square deal; **~ preferente** preferential treatment; **¡~ hecho!** it's a deal!; **cerrar un ~** to do a deal, strike a bargain; **hacer buenos ~s a uno** to offer sb advantageous terms.

(**e**) (*Ling*) title, style of address; **dar a uno el ~ debido** to give sb his proper title.

(**f**) (*Méx*: *puesto*) market stall.

(**g**) (*Méx*: *negocio*) small business.

trauma *nm* (**a**) (*mental*) trauma. (**b**) (*lesión*) injury.

traumático *adj* traumatic.

traumatismo *nm* traumatism.

traumatizante *adj* traumatic.

traumatizar [1f] *vt* (*Med, Psic*) to traumatize; (*fig*) to shock, affect profoundly, shake to the core.

traumatología *nf* orthopedic surgery.

traumatólogo, -a *nm/f* orthopedic surgeon.

trauque *nm* (*Cono Sur*) friend.

travelín *nm* (*Cine*) travelling platform, dolly.

través 1 *nm* (**a**) (*Arquit*) crossbeam.

(**b**) (*Mil*) traverse; protective wall.

(**c**) (*curva*) bend, turn; (*inclinación*) slant; (*sesgo*) bias; (*deformación*) warp.

(**d**) (*fig*) reverse, misfortune; upset.

2 al ~ *adv* across, crossways; **de ~** across, crossways; obliquely; sideways; **con el sombrero puesto de ~** with his hat on askew; **hubo que introducirlo de ~** it had to be squeezed in sideways; **ir de ~** (*Náut*) to drift off course, be blown (*etc*) to the side; **mirar de ~** to squint; **mirar a uno de ~** to look at sb out of the corner of one's eye, (*fig*) look askance at sb.

3 a ~ de, al ~ de *prep* across; over; (*por medio de*) through; **un árbol caído a ~ de los carriles** a tree fallen across the lines; **lo sé a ~ de un amigo** I know about it through a friend.

travesaño *nm* (**a**) (*Arquit*) crosspiece, crossbeam; (*Dep*) crossbar.

(**b**) (*de cama*) bolster.

(**c**) (*CAm, Carib, Méx Ferro*) sleeper.

travesear [1a] *vi* (**a**) (*jugar*) to play around; (*ser travieso*) to play up, be mischievous, be naughty; (*pey*) to live a dissipated life.

(**b**) (*fig*: *hablar*) to talk wittily, sparkle.

(**c**) (*Méx*: *de jinete*) to show off one's horsemanship.

traveseo *nm* (*Méx*) display of horsemanship.

travesero 1 *adj* cross (*atr*); slanting, oblique. **2** *nm* bolster.

travesía *nf* (**a**) (*calle*) cross-street, short street which joins two others; (*de pueblo*) road that passes through a village.

(**b**) (*Náut*) crossing, voyage; (*Aer*) crossing; distance travelled, distance to be crossed; **~ del desierto** (*fig*) period in the wilderness.

(**c**) (*viento*: *Náut*) crosswind; (*Cono Sur*) west wind.

(**d**) (*en el juego*) amount won, amount lost.

(**e**) (*And, Cono Sur*: *desierto*) arid plain, desert region.

travestí 1 *nm* (*Teat*) (**a**) (*persona*) drag artist. (**b**) (*arte*) art of drag. **2** *nmf* transvestite.

travestido *adj* disguised, in disguise; *V t* **travestí**.

travestirse [3k] *vr* to dress in clothes of the other sex.

travestismo *nm* transvestism.

travesura *nf* (**a**) (*broma etc*) prank, lark, piece of mischief; escapade; **son ~s de niños** they're just childish pranks; **las ~s de su juventud** the wild doings of his youth, the waywardness of his young days.

(**b**) (*mala pasada*) sly trick.

(**c**) (*gracia*) wit, sparkle.

traviesa *nf* (**a**) (*Arquit*) tie, crossbeam, rafter.

(**b**) (*Ferro*) sleeper.

(**c**) (*Min*) cross-gallery.

(**d**) = **travesía** (**b**); *V* **campo**.

travieso *adj* (**a**) *niño* naughty, mischievous; *adulto* (*inquieto*) restless; (*vivo*) lively, (*voluble*) unpredictable; (*pey*) dissolute.

(**b**) (*listo*) bright, clever, shrewd; (*gracioso*) witty.

trayecto *nm* (**a**) (*camino*) road, route, way; (*tramo*) stretch, section; **destrozó un ~ de varios kilómetros** it destroyed a stretch several kilometres long; **final del ~** end of the line, terminus; **recorrer un ~** to cover a distance.

(**b**) (*viaje*: *de persona*) journey; (*de vehículo*) run, journey; (*de bala etc*) flight, trajectory; **comeremos durante el ~** we'll eat on the journey, we'll lunch on the way.

trayectoria *nf* (**a**) (*camino*) trajectory, path; **~ de vuelo** flightpath.

(**b**) (*fig*) course of development, evolution, path; **la ~ poética de Garcilaso** Garcilaso's poetic development; **la ~ actual del partido** the party's present line (*o* course, path).

traza *nf* (**a**) (*Arquit, Téc*) plan, design; (*disposición*) layout.

(**b**) (*aspecto etc*) looks, general appearance, air; **por las ~s, según las ~s** from all the signs, to judge by appearances; **llevar buena ~** to look well, seem impressive; (*proyecto etc*) to seem promising; **llevar** (*o* **tener**) **~s de** + *infin* to look like + *ger*; **esto tiene ~s de nunca acabar** this looks as though it will never end.

(**c**) (*medio*) means; (*pey*) trick, device, expedient; **darse ~** to find a way, get along, manage; **darse ~ para hacer algo, discurrir ~s para hacer algo** to contrive (schemes) to do sth, look for a way of achieving sth.

(**d**) (*habilidad*) skill, ability; **tener** (**buena**) **~ para hacer algo** to be skilful at doing sth; **para pianista tiene poca ~** she's not much of a pianist.

(**e**) (*Cono Sur*: *huella*) track, trail.

(**f**) (*Inform*) trace.

trazable *adj* traceable.

trazada *nf* line, course, direction; **cortar la ~ a uno** (*Aut*) to cut in on sb.

trazado 1 *adj*: **bien ~** shapely, well-formed; good-looking; **mal ~** ill-favoured, unattractive.

2 *nm* (**a**) (*Arquit, Téc*) plan, design; (*disposición*) layout; (*esbozo etc*) outline, sketch; (*de carretera*) line, route.

(**b**) (*fig*) lines, outline.

(**c**) (*And*: *cuchillo*) machete.

trazador 1 *adj* (*Mil, Fís*) tracer (*atr*); **bala ~a** tracer bullet; **elemento ~** tracer element.

2 *nm* (**a**) (*persona*) planner, designer.

(**b**) (*Fís*) tracer.

(**c**) (*Inform*) **~ gráfico, ~ de gráficos** plotter; **~ plano** flatbed plotter.

trazadora *nf* tracer, tracer bullet.

trazar [1f] *vt* (**a**) (*Arquit, Téc*) (*planificar*) to plan, design; (*disponer*) to lay out; *línea etc* to draw, trace; (*Arte*) to sketch, outline; *límites* to mark out; *curso, huella* to trace, plot, follow.

(**b**) (*fig*) *desarrollo, política etc* to lay down, mark out.

(**c**) (*fig*: *en discurso etc*) to trace, describe, explain, outline.

(**d**) *medios etc* to contrive, devise.

trazo *nm* (**a**) (*línea*) line, stroke; **~ discontinuo** broken line; **~ de lápiz** pencil stroke, pencil mark.

(**b**) (*esbozo*) sketch, outline; **~s** (*de rostro*) lines, features, cast; **de ~s enérgicos** vigorous-looking; **de ~s indecisos** with an indecisive look about him (*etc*).

(**c**) (*Arte*: *de ropaje*) fold.

TRB *nfpl abr de* **toneladas de registro bruto** gross register tons, GRT.

TRC *nm abr de* **tubo de rayos catódicos** cathode ray tube, CRT.

trébede(s) *nf, pl* **trébedes** trivet.

trebejos *nmpl* (**a**) (*avíos*) equipment, gear, things; **~ de cocina** kitchen utensils, kitchen things.

(**b**) (*Ajedrez*) chessmen.

(**c**) (*fig*) old-fashioned things.

trébol *nm* (**a**) (*Bot*) clover, trefoil. (**b**) (*Arquit*) trefoil. (**c**) **~es** (*Naipes*) clubs.

trebolar *nm* (*Cono Sur*) clover field, field covered in clover.

trece *adj* thirteen; (*fecha*) thirteenth; **estar** (*o* **mantenerse, seguir** *etc*) **en sus ~** to stand firm, stick to one's guns.

trecho *nm* (**a**) (*tramo*) stretch; (*distancia*) length, distance; (*de tiempo*) while; **andar un buen ~** to walk a good way, go on a good distance; **a ~s** in parts, here and there; intermittently; by fits and starts; **de ~ en ~** at intervals, every so often; **muy de ~ en ~** very occasionally, only once in a while.

(**b**) (*Agr*) plot, patch.

(**c**) (*: *pedazo*) bit, piece, part; **he terminado ese ~ de punto** I've finished that bit of knitting; **queda un buen ~ que hacer** there's still quite a bit to do.

trefilar [1a] *vt alambre* to draw (out).

tregua *nf* (**a**) (*Mil*) truce. (**b**) (*fig*) lull, respite, let-up; **sin ~** without respite; **dar ~s** (*dolor etc*) to come and go, let up from time to time; (*asunto*) not to be urgent; **no dar ~** to give no respite.

treinta *adj* thirty; (*fecha*) thirtieth; **los** (**años**) **~** the thirties.

treintañero 1 *adj* thirtyish, about thirty. **2** *nm*, **treintañera** *nf* person of about thirty, person in his (*o* her) thirties.

treintena *nf* thirty; about thirty.
treintón 1 *adj* thirty-year old, thirtyish. **2** *nm*, **treintona** *nf* person of about thirty.
trekking *nm* pony-trekking.
trematodo *nm* (*Zool*) fluke.
tremebundo *adj* terrible, frightening; *palabras etc* fierce, threatening, savage.
tremedal *nm* quaking bog.
tremendamente* *adv* tremendously*; awfully, terrifically*.
tremendismo *nm* crudeness, coarse realism; use of realism to shock.
tremendista 1 *adj* crude, coarsely realistic. **2** *nmf* coarsely realistic writer, writer who shocks by his realism.
tremendo *adj* (**a**) (*terrible*) terrible, dreadful, frightful.
(**b**) (*imponente*) imposing, awesome.
(**c**) (*: *asombroso*) tremendous*; awful, terrific*; **una roca tremenda de alta** a terrifically high rock*; **le dio una tremenda paliza** he gave him a tremendous beating*; **un error ~** a terrible mistake.
(**d**) (*) *persona* inventive, witty, entertaining; **es ~, ¿eh?** isn't he a scream?*, isn't he great?*
(**e**) **echar la tremenda** to speak angrily; **dar** (*o* **tomar**) **algo por la tremenda** to make a great fuss about sth.
trementina *nf* turpentine.
tremolar [1a] **1** *vt* (**a**) *bandera* to wave. (**b**) (*fig*) to show off, flaunt. **2** *vi* to wave, flutter.
tremolina* *nf* row, fuss, commotion; shindy*; **armar una ~** to start a row, make a fuss.
tremotiles *nmpl* (*And, Carib*) tools, tackle.
trémulamente *adv* tremulously; quaveringly; timidly.
trémulo *adj* quivering, tremulous; *voz* quavering; timid, small; *luz etc* flickering.
tren *nm* (**a**) (*Ferro*) train; **~ de alta velocidad** high-speed train; **~ ascendente** up train; **~ botijo*, ~ de excursión, ~ de recreo** excursion train; **~ de carga** goods train, freight train (*US*); **~ de cercanías** suburban train; **~ de contenedores** container train; **~ correo** slow train; (*Correos*) mailtrain; **~ de cremallera** funicular (railway); **~ descendente** down train; **~ directo** through train; **~ expreso** fast train; **~ de largo recorrido** long-distance train; **~ (de) mercancías** goods train, freight train (*US*); **~ mixto** passenger and goods train; **~ ómnibus** stopping train, local train, accommodation train (*US*); **~ de pasajeros** passenger train; **~ postal** mailtrain; **~ rápido** express (train); **~ suplementario** extra train, relief train; **cambiar de ~** to change trains; **coger un ~, tomar un ~** to catch a train; **coger el ~ (en marcha)** (*fig*), **subirse al ~** (*fig*) to climb (o jump) on the bandwagon; **tenemos libros para parar un ~*** we have loads of books; **está como (para parar) un ~** (*Esp**) she's hot stuff*, she looks terrific*; **ir en ~** to go by train; **perder el ~** (*fig*) to miss the boat.
(**b**) (*equipaje*) baggage; (*equipo*) outfit, equipment; **~ de viaje** equipment for a journey.
(**c**) (*Mec*) set; set of gears (*o* wheels *etc*); **~ de aterrizaje** (*Aer*) undercarriage, landing gear; **~ de bandas en caliente** hot-strip mill; **~ de laminación** rolling-mill; **~ de lavado** (*Aut*) carwash.
(**d**) (*Mil*) convoy.
(**e**) **~ de vida** life style; (*Fin*) rate of spending; **vivir a todo ~** to live in style, live expensively; **no pudo sostener ese ~ de vida** he could not keep up that style of living.
(**f**) (*velocidad*) speed; **a fuerte ~** at a rapid pace, fast; **forzar el ~** to force the pace; **ir a buen ~** to go at a good speed.
(**g**) (*LAm*) **en ~ de** in the process of, in the course of; **estamos en ~ de realizarlo** we are carrying it out; **estar en ~ de recuperación** to be on one's way to recovery.
(**h**) (*Carib*) (*taller*) workshop; (*empresa*) firm, company; **~ de mudadas** removal company; **~ de lavado** laundry.
(**i**) (*CAm, Méx*: *trajín*) coming and going; **~es** shady dealings.
(**j**) (*Cono Sur, Méx*: *tranvía*) tram, streetcar (*US*).
(**k**) (*Carib*: *majadería*) cheeky remark.
trena‡ *nf* clink‡, prison.
trenca *nf* duffle-coat.
trencilla 1 *nf* braid. **2** *nm* (*Dep*) referee.
trencillo *nm* braid.
tren-cremallera *nm, pl* **trenes-cremallera** funicular (railway).
trenista *nm* (**a**) (*Carib*) (*patrón*) owner of a workshop; (*gerente*) company manager. (**b**) (*Méx Ferro*) railwayman.
Trento *nm* Trent; **Concilio de ~** Council of Trent.
trenza *nf* (**a**) (*de pelo*) plait; pigtail, ponytail; tress; (*Cos*) braid; (*de pajas etc*) plait; (*de hilos*) twist; **~ postiza** switch, hairpiece; **encontrar a una en ~** to find a woman with her hair down.
(**b**) (*LAm*: *de cebollas etc*) string.
(**c**) **~s** (*Carib*) shoelaces.
(**d**) (*Culin*) plaited pastry.
(**e**) (*Cono Sur*: *recomendación*) recommendation, suggestion.
(**f**) (*Cono Sur*: *pelea*) hand-to-hand fight.
trenzado 1 *adj* plaited; braided; twisted together, intertwined. **2** *nm* (**a**) (*de pelo*) plaits. (**b**) (*Ballet*) entrechat.
trenzar [1f] **1** *vt pelo* to plait, braid; *pajas etc* to plait; *hilos etc* to twist (together), intertwine, weave.
2 *vi* (*bailadores*) to weave in and out; (*caballo*) to caper.
3 trenzarse *vr* (**a**) **~ en una discusión** (*LAm*) to get involved in an argument.
(**b**) (*And, Cono Sur**: *pelear*) to come to blows.
trepa[1] 1 *nf* (**a**) (*subida*) climb, climbing.
(**b**) (*voltereta*) somersault.
(**c**) (*Caza*) hide.
(**d**) (*ardid*) trick, ruse, deception.
(**e**) (*: *paliza*) tanning*.
2 *nmf* (‡) (*cobista*) creep‡; (*arribista*) social climber; **ser un ~*** to be on the make*.
trepa[2] *nf* (**a**) (*Téc*) drilling, boring. (**b**) (*Cos*) trimming. (**c**) (*de madera*) grain.
trepada *nf* climb; (*fig*) rise, ascent.
trepaderas *nfpl* (*Carib, Méx*) climbing-irons.
trepado *nm* (**a**) (*Téc*) drilling, boring. (**b**) (*de sello etc*) perforation.
trepador 1 *adj* (**a**) *planta* climbing, rambling.
(**b**) **este vino es bien ~** (*And**) this wine goes right to your head.
2 *nm* (**a**) (*Bot*) climber, rambler.
(**b**) (*: *persona*) social climber.
(**c**) (*Orn*) nuthatch.
(**d**) **~es** climbing-irons.
trepadora *nf* (*Bot*) climber, rambler.
trepanar [1a] *vt* to trepan.
trepar[1] [1a] *vti* to climb (*a* up), clamber up; to scale; (*Bot*) to climb (*por* up); **~ a un avión** to climb into an aircraft; **~ a un árbol** to climb (up) a tree.
trepar[2] [1a] *vt* (**a**) (*Téc*) to drill, bore. (**b**) (*Cos*) to trim.
trepe* *nm* telling-off*; **echar un ~ a uno** to tell sb off*.
trepetera* *nf* (*Carib*) hubbub, din.
trepidación *nf* shaking, vibration.
trepidante *adj* shaking, vibrating; (*fig*) shattering; *frío* extreme; *ruido etc* intolerable, shattering.
trepidar [1a] *vi* (**a**) (*temblar*) to shake, vibrate. (**b**) (*And, Cono Sur*: *vacilar*) to hesitate, waver; **~ en** + *infin* to hesitate to + *infin*.
treque *adj* (*Carib*) witty, funny.
tres 1 *adj* three; (*fecha*) third; **las ~** three o'clock; **como ~ y 2 son 5** as sure as sure can be, as sure as eggs is eggs; **de ~ al cuarto** cheap, poor quality; **ni a la de ~** on no account, not by a long shot; not by any manner of means; **no ve ~ en un burro** he's as blind as a bat.
2 *nm* three; **~ en raya** (*juego*) noughts and crosses.
trescientos *adj* three hundred.
tresillo *nm* (**a**) (*muebles*) three-piece suite. (**b**) (*Mús*) triplet.
tresnal *nm* (*Agr*) shock, stook.
treso *adj* (*Méx*) dirty.
treta *nf* (**a**) (*Esgrima*) feint. (**b**) (*fig*) (*truco*) trick; (*ardid*) ruse, stratagem; (*Com etc*) stunt, gimmick; **~ publicitaria** advertising gimmick.
tri... *pref* tri...; three-...
tríada *nf* triad.
trial 1 *nm* (*Dep*) trial. **2** *nf* trial motorcycle.
triangulación *nf* triangulation.
triangular 1 *adj* triangular; three-cornered. **2** [1a] *vt* to triangulate.
triángulo *nm* triangle (*t Mús*); **~ de aviso** warning triangle; **~ de las Bermudas** Bermuda Triangle.
triates *nmpl* (*Méx*) triplets.
triatlón *nm* triathlon.
tribal *adj* tribal.
tribalismo *nm* tribalism.
tribu *nf* tribe.
tribulación *nf* tribulation.
tribulete* *nm* trainee journalist.
tribuna *nf* (**a**) (*de orador*) platform, rostrum, dais; (*en*

mitin) platform.

(**b**) (*Dep etc*) stand, grandstand; ~ **cubierta** covered stand; ~ **libre**, ~ **pública** (*Parl*) public gallery, (*Prensa*) open forum, forum for debate; ~ **de la prensa** (*Parl*) press-gallery, (*Dep*) press-box.

(**c**) (*Ecl*) gallery; ~ **del órgano** organ loft.

(**d**) (*Jur*) ~ **del acusado** dock; ~ **del jurado** jury-box.

(**e**) (*fig*) political oratory, public speechmaking.

tribunal *nm* (**a**) (*Jur*) court; (*personas*) court, bench; ~ **constitucional** contitutional court; ~ **de familia** family court; **T~ de la Haya, T~ Internacional de Justicia** International Court of Justice; ~ **juvenil**, ~ **(tutelar) de menores** juvenile court; **T~ Supremo** High Court, Supreme Court (*US*); **en pleno** ~ in open court; **llevar a uno ante los ~es** to take sb to court.

(**b**) (*Pol, comisión investigadora etc*) tribunal.

(**c**) (*Univ*) (*examinadores*) board of examiners; (*de selección*) appointments committee.

(**d**) (*fig*) tribunal; forum; ~ **de la conciencia** one's own conscience; **el ~ de la opinión pública** the forum of public opinion.

(**e**) (*Cono Sur Mil*) court-martial.

tribuno *nm* tribune.

tributación *nf* (**a**) (*pago*) payment. (**b**) (*impuestos*) taxation; ~ **directa** direct taxation.

tributar [1a] **1** *vt* (**a**) (*Fin*) to pay. (**b**) (*fig*) *homenaje, respeto etc* to pay; *gracias* to give; *afecto etc* to have, show (*a* for). **2** *vi* (*pagar impuestos*) to pay taxes.

tributario 1 *adj* (**a**) (*Geog, Pol*) tributary.

(**b**) (*Fin*) tax (*atr*), taxation (*atr*); **privilegio** ~ tax concession; **sistema** ~ taxation, tax system.

2 *nm* tributary.

tributo *nm* (**a**) (*Hist: t fig*) tribute. (**b**) (*Fin*) tax.

tricampeón, -ona *nm/f* triple champion, three-times champion.

tricentenario *nm* tercentenary.

tricentésimo *adj* three hundredth.

triciclo *nm* tricycle.

tricófero *nm* (*And, Cono Sur, Méx*) hair restorer.

tricola *nf* (*Cono Sur*) knitted waistcoat.

tricolor 1 *adj* tricolour, three-coloured; **bandera** ~ = **2**. **2** *nm* tricolour.

tricornio *nm* three-cornered hat.

tricota *nf* (*LAm*) sweater.

tricotar [1a] *vti* to knit; **tricotado a mano** hand-knitted.

tricotosa *nf* knitting-machine.

trichina *nf* (*LAm*) trichina.

tridente *nm* trident.

tridentino *adj* Tridentine, of Trent; **Concilio T~** Council of Trent; **misa tridentina** Tridentine Mass.

tridimensional *adj* three-dimensional.

trienal *adj* triennial.

trienalmente *adv* triennially.

trienio *nm* (**a**) period of three years. (**b**) (*pago*) monthly bonus for each three-year period worked with the same employer.

trifásico 1 *adj* (*Elec*) three-phase, triphase. **2** *nm*: **tener ~*** to have pull, have influence.

triforio *nm* (*Ecl*) triforium, clerestory.

trifulca* *nf* row, shindy*.

trifulquero* *adj* rowdy, trouble-making.

trifurcarse [1g] *vr* to divide into three.

trigal *nm* wheat field.

trigésimo *adj* thirtieth.

trigo *nm* (**a**) (*Bot*) wheat; ~ **candeal** bread wheat; ~ **sarraceno** buckwheat; **de ~ entero** wholemeal; **no es ~ limpio** (*fig*) he's (*o* it's) dishonest; **no todo era ~ limpio** it wasn't completely aboveboard; it was a bit fishy*.

(**b**) **~s** wheat, wheat field(s); **meterse en ~s ajenos** to meddle in sb else's affairs; to trespass on sb else's subject (*etc*).

(**c**) (‡: *dinero*) dough‡, money.

trigonometría *nf* trigonometry.

trigonométrico *adj* trigonometric(al).

trigueño 1 *adj* (**a**) *pelo* corn-coloured, dark blonde. (**b**) *piel* light brown, golden-brown; (*LAm euf*) coloured. **2** *nm*, **trigueña** *nf* (*LAm euf*) coloured man, coloured woman.

triguero 1 *adj* wheat (*atr*). **2** *nm* (**a**) (*comerciante*) corn merchant. (**b**) (*tamiz*) corn sieve.

trila *nf*, **triles** *nmpl* (game of) 'find the lady'.

trilateral, trilátero *adj* trilateral, three-sided.

trilero *nm* card-sharp.

trilingüe *adj* trilingual.

trilita *nf* trinitrotoluene.

trilogía *nf* trilogy.

trilla *nf* (**a**) (*Agr*) threshing. (**b**) (*Carib, Cono Sur**: *paliza*) thrashing, beating. (**c**) (*Méx*: *senda*) track. (**d**) (*Carib*: *atajo*) short cut.

trillado 1 *adj* (**a**) (*Agr*) threshed.

(**b**) (*fig*) *camino* beaten, well-trodden.

(**c**) (*fig*) *tema* (*gastado*) trite, hackneyed, well-worn; (*conocido*) well-known; (*sencillo*) straightforward.

2 *nm* (**a**) (*fig*) thorough investigation. (**b**) (*Carib*) path, track.

trillador *nm* thresher.

trilladora *nf* threshing machine.

trilladura *nf* threshing.

trillar [1a] *vt* (**a**) (*Agr*) to thresh. (**b**) (*fig*) to use a lot, wear out by frequent use.

trillizo *nm*, **trilliza** *nf* triplet.

trillo *nm* (**a**) (*máquina*) threshing machine. (**b**) (*CAm, Carib*: *sendero*) path, track.

trillón *nm* trillion (*Brit*), quintillion (*US*).

trimarán *nm* trimaran.

trimestral *adj* quarterly, three-monthly; (*Univ*) termly.

trimestralmente *adv* quarterly, every three months.

trimestre *nm* (**a**) (*período de tiempo*) quarter, period of three months; (*Univ*) term. (**b**) (*Fin*) (*pago*) quarterly payment; (*alquiler*) quarter's rent (*etc*).

trinado *nm* (*Orn*) song, warble; (*Mús*) trill.

trinar [1a] *vi* (**a**) (*Mús*) to trill; (*Orn*) to sing, warble. (**b**) (*: *enfadarse*) to fume, be angry; (*Cono Sur*) to shout; **está que trina** he's hopping mad*.

trinca *nf* (**a**) (*tres*) group of three, set of three, threesome.

(**b**) (*And, Cono Sur*) (*pandilla*) band, gang; (*facción*) faction; (*complot*) plot, conspiracy.

(**c**) (*Carib, Méx*: *embriaguez*) drunkenness.

(**d**) (*Cono Sur*: *canicas*) marbles.

trincar[1] [1g] **1** *vt* (**a**) (*atar*) to tie up, tie firmly; (*Náut*) to lash.

(**b**) (*inmovilizar*) to pinion, hold by the arms; (‡: *detener*) to nick‡, arrest, lift*.

(**c**) (*agarrar*) to pick up, grab, lay hold of; (‡: *robar*) to nick‡.

(**d**) (**: *copularse*) to screw**.

(**e**) (‡: *matar*) to do in‡.

(**f**) (*CAm, Cono Sur, Méx*) to squeeze, press.

(**g**) (*Cono Sur**) **me trinca que** ... I have a hunch that ...

2 trincarse *vr*: ~ **a** + *infin* (*CAm, Méx*) to start to + *infin*, set about + *ger*.

trincar[2] [1g] *vt* (*romper*) to break up; (*tajar*) to chop up; *papel etc* to tear up.

trincar[3] [1g] **1** *vti* (*beber*) to drink. **2 trincarse** *vr* (*Carib, Méx**) to get drunk.

trinco *nm* (*Carib, Méx*) drunkard.

trincón‡ *adj* murderous.

trinchador *nm* carving-knife, carver.

trinchante *nm* (**a**) (*cuchillo*) carving-knife, carver; (*tenedor*) carving-fork. (**b**) (*mueble*) sidetable; (*Cono Sur*) sideboard.

trinchar [1a] *vt* (**a**) (*cortar*) to carve, slice, cut up. (**b**) (‡: *matar*) to do in‡.

trinche 1 *nm* (**a**) (*LAm*: *tenedor*) fork. (**b**) (*And, Cono Sur, Méx*: *mueble*) sidetable. (**c**) (*Méx Agr*) pitchfork. **2** *adj*: **pelo** ~ (*And*) frizzy hair.

trinchera *nf* (**a**) (*zanja*) trench, entrenchment; (*Mil*) trench; (*Ferro*) cutting; **guerra de ~s** trench warfare.

(**b**) (*prenda*) trenchcoat.

(**c**) (*LAm*: *cercado*) fence, stockade.

(**d**) (*Méx*: *cuchillo*) curved knife.

trinchete *nm* shoemaker's knife; (*And*) table knife.

trincho *nm* (*And*) (*parapeto*) parapet; (*zanja*) trench, ditch.

trineo *nm* sledge, sleigh; ~ **de balancín** bobsleigh; ~ **de perros** dog sleigh.

Trini *nf forma familiar de* **Trinidad**.

Trinidad *nf* (**a**) (*Rel*) Trinity. (**b**) (*Geog*) Trinidad.

trinidad *nf* (*fig*) trio, set of three.

trinitaria *nf* (*de jardín*) pansy; (*silvestre*) heart's-ease.

trinitrotolueno *nm* trinitrotoluene.

trino *nm* (*Orn*) warble; trill; (*Mús*) trill.

trinomio *adj, nm* trinomial.

trinque* *nm* liquor, booze*.

trinquetada *nf* (*Carib*) period of danger; (*And, Méx*) hard times.

trinquete[1] *nm* (*Mec*) pawl, trip, catch; ratchet.

trinquete[2] *nm* (**a**) (*Náut*) (*mástil*) foremast; (*vela*) foresail. (**b**) (*Dep*) pelota court.

trinquete[3] *nm* (*Méx*) (**a**) (*soborno*) bribe; (*asunto turbio*) shady deal, corrupt affair. (**b**) **es un ~ de hombre*** he really is a tough customer. (**c**) (*And*) small room.

trinquis* *invar* **1** *nm* drink, swig*. **2** *adj* (*Méx**) drunk, sloshed*.

trío *nm* trio.

tripa *nf* (**a**) (*Anat*) intestine, gut; **~s** (*Anat*) guts, insides*, innards*; (*Culin*) tripe; **me duelen las ~s** I have a stomach ache; **echar las ~s** to retch, vomit violently; **le gruñían las ~s** his tummy was rumbling*; **hacer de ~s corazón** to pluck up courage, screw up one's courage; **llenar la ~*** to eat well at somebody else's expense; **quitar las ~s a un pez** to gut a fish; **revolver las ~s a uno** (*fig*) to turn sb's stomach; **¡te sacaré las ~s!*** I'll tear your guts out!‡; **tener malas ~s** to be cruel.

(**b**) (*fig**: *vientre*) belly, tummy*; (*de mujer encinta*) bulge; **echar ~** to put on weight, start to get a paunch; **dejar a una con ~** (*Esp*) to get a girl in the family way; **estar con ~** (*Esp*) to be in the family way; **tener mucha ~** to be fat, be paunchy.

(**c**) (*de fruta*) core, seeds.

(**d**) (*Mec*) **~s*** innards*, works; parts; **sacar las ~s de un reloj** to take out the works of a watch.

(**e**) (*de vasija*) belly, bulge.

(**f**) (*Com, Jur etc*) file, dossier.

(**g**) (*Carib*: *de neumático*) inner tube.

tripartito *adj* tripartite.

tripe *nm* shag.

tripear* [1a] *vi* to stuff o.s.*, scoff*.

triperío *nm* (*And, Méx*) guts, entrails.

tripero* *adj* greedy.

tripi‡ *nm* LSD; dose of LSD.

tripicallos *nmpl* (*Culin Esp*) tripe.

tripitir [3a] *vt* to repeat again, do a third time.

triple 1 *adj* triple; threefold; (*de 3 capas*) of three layers (*o* thicknesses *etc*); **~ salto** triple jump.

2 *nm* (**a**) triple; **es el ~ de lo que era** it is three times what (*o* as big as) it was; **su casa es el ~ de grande que la nuestra** their house is three times bigger than ours. (**b**) (*Dep*) triple jump.

3 *adv*: **esta cuerda es ~ gruesa que ésa*** this string is three times thicker than that bit.

tripleta *nf* trio, threesome.

triplicado *adj* triplicate; **por ~** in triplicate.

triplicar [1g] **1** *vt* to treble, triple; **las pérdidas triplican las ganancias** losses are three times the profits. **2 triplicarse** *vr* to treble, triple.

trípode *nm* tripod.

Trípoli *nm* Tripoli.

tripón* 1 *adj* fat, potbellied. **2** *nm*, **tripona** *nf* (*Méx*) little boy, little girl; **los tripones** the kids*.

tríptico *nm* (**a**) (*Arte*) triptych. (**b**) (*formulario*) form in three parts, three-part document (**c**) (*Com*) folder, brochur, leaflet.

triptongo *nm* triphthong.

tripudo *adj* fat, potbellied.

tripulación *nf* crew.

tripulado *adj*: **vuelo ~** manned flight; **vuelo no ~** unmanned flight; **~ por** manned by.

tripulante *nm* crew member, crewman; **~s** crew, men.

tripular [1a] *vt* (**a**) *barco etc* to man. (**b**) (*Aut etc*) to drive. (**c**) (*Cono Sur*) to mix (up).

tripulina* *nf* (*Cono Sur*) row, brawl.

trique *nm* (**a**) (*ruido*) crack, sharp noise, swish.

(**b**) **a cada ~** at every moment; repeatedly.

(**c**) (*And, Méx*) trick, dodge.

(**d**) **~s** (*Méx**) things, gear, odds and ends.

(**e**) (*And, CAm*: *juego*) noughts and crosses.

triquina *nf* trichina.

triquinosis *nf* trichinosis.

triquiñuela *nf* trick, dodge; **~s** dodges, funny business; **es un tío ~s*** he's an artful old cuss*; **saber las ~s del oficio** to know the tricks of the trade, know all the dodges.

triquis *nmpl* (*Méx*) = **trique** (**d**).

triquitraque *nm* string of fire-crackers.

trirreactor *nm* tri-jet.

trirreme *nm* trireme.

tris *nm* (**a**) (*estallido*) crack; (*al rasgarse*) tearing noise.

(**b**) **está en un ~** it's touch and go; **estaba en un ~ que lo perdiera** he very nearly lost it, he was within an inch of losing it; **los dos coches evitaron el choque por un ~** the two cars avoided a collision by a hair's breadth.

(**c**) (*LAm*: *juego*) noughts and crosses.

trisar [1a] *vt* (*And, Cono Sur*) to crack; to chip.

trisca *nf* (**a**) (*crujido*) crunch, crushing noise. (**b**) (*jaleo*) uproar, rumpus, row. (**c**) (*Carib*) (*mofa*) mockery; (*chiste*) private joke.

triscar [1g] **1** *vt* (**a**) (*mezclar*) to mix, mingle; (*confundir*) to mix up.

(**b**) *sierra* to set.

(**c**) (*And, Carib*: *mofar*) to mock, joke about; to tease.

2 *vi* (**a**) (*patalear*) to stamp one's feet about.

(**b**) (*corderos etc*) to gambol, frisk about; (*personas*) to romp, play about.

triscón *adj* (*And*) hypercritical, overcritical.

trisecar [1g] *vt* to trisect.

trisemanal *adj* triweekly.

trisemanalmente *adv* triweekly, thrice weekly.

trisilábico *adj* trisyllabic, three-syllabled.

trisílabo 1 *adj* trisyllabic, three-syllabled. **2** *nm* trisyllable.

trisito *nm* (*And*) (*pizca*) pinch; (*pedacito*) scrap, piece.

trismo *nm* lockjaw.

Tristán *nm* Tristram, Tristan.

triste 1 *adj* (**a**) (*estado*) *persona* sad; (*desgraciado*) miserable; gloomy; sorrowful; *carácter* gloomy, melancholy; *aspecto, cara* sad-looking; **poner ~ a uno** to make sb sad, make sb unhappy, make sb miserable; **ponerse ~** to become sad; to look sad.

(**b**) *cuento, noticia etc* sad; *canción* sad, mournful; *paisaje* dismal, desolate, dreary; *cuarto etc* gloomy, dismal.

(**c**) (*fig*) sorry, sad; **hizo un ~ papel** he cut a sorry figure; **la ~ verdad es que ...** the sorry truth is that ...; **es ~ verle así** it is sad to see him like that, it grieves one to see him like that; **es ~ no poder ir, es ~ que no podamos ir** it's a pity we can't go.

(**d**) (*) *flor etc* old, withered.

(**e**) (*: *desgraciado*) miserable, wretched; single; **no queda sino una ~ peseta** there's just one miserable peseta left, there's just one poor little peseta left; **su padre es un ~ vigilante** his father is just a poor old watchman; **le mató algún ~ campesino** some wretched peasant killed him.

(**f**) (*LAm*: *pobre*) poor, valueless, wretched.

(**g**) (*And*: *tímido*) shy, timid.

2 *nm* (*And, Cono Sur*: *canción*) sad love song.

tristemente *adv* sadly; miserably; gloomily; sorrowfully; mournfully; **el ~ famoso lugar** the place which is well known for such unhappy reasons, the place which enjoys a sorry fame.

tristeza *nf* (*V adj* (**a**), (**b**)) (**a**) sadness; misery; gloom; sorrow; gloominess, melancholy. (**b**) dismalness, desolation, dreariness. (**c**) **~s*** (*noticias*) sad news; (*sucesos*) unhappy events. (**d**) (*Bot*) (type of) tree virus.

tristón *adj* rather sad; given to melancholy; pessimistic, gloomy.

tristura *nf* (*LAm*) = **tristeza**.

Tritón *nm* Triton.

tritón *nm* (*Zool*) newt.

trituración *nf* trituration; grinding, crushing.

triturador *nm*, **trituradora** *nf* (*Téc*) grinder, crushing machine; (*Culin*) mincer, mincing machine; **~ de basuras** waste-disposal unit; **~ (de papel)** shredder.

triturar [1a] *vt* to triturate; to grind, crush, pulverize.

triunfador 1 *adj* triumphant; (*ganador*) winning. **2** *nm*, **triunfadora** *nf* victor, winner.

triunfal *adj* (**a**) *arco etc* triumphal. (**b**) *grito, sonrisa etc* triumphant.

triunfalismo *nm* euphoria, excessive optimism; overconfidence; self-congratulation; smugness; **lo digo sin ~s** I say it without wishing to exult.

triunfalista *adj* euphoric, excessively optimistic; overconfident; self-congratulatory; smug.

triunfalmente *adv* triumphantly.

triunfante *adj* (**a**) triumphant; (*ganador*) winning; **salir ~** to come out the winner, emerge victorious. (**b**) (*jubiloso*) jubilant, exultant.

triunfar [1a] *vi* (**a**) (*gen*) to triumph (*de, sobre* over); (*ganar*) to win; (*salir victorioso*) to emerge victorious; (*tener éxito*) to be a success, be successful; **~ de los enemigos** to triumph over one's enemies; **~ en la vida** to succeed in life, make a success of one's life; **~ en un concurso** to win a competition.

(**b**) (*pey*) to exult (*de, sobre* over).

(**c**) (*Naipes*: *jugador*) to trump (in), play a trump.

(**d**) (*Naipes*: *ser triunfos*) to be trumps; **triunfan corazones** hearts are trumps.

triunfo *nm* (**a**) (*gen*) triumph; (*victoria*) win, victory; (*éxito*) success; **adjudicarse el ~** to win; **ha sido un verdadero ~** it has been a real triumph; **fue el sexto ~ consecutivo del equipo** it was the team's sixth consecutive win.

(**b**) (*Mús etc*) hit, success; **lista de ~s, lista del ~** hit parade, top ten (*o* twenty *etc*).

(**c**) (*Naipes*) trump; **6 sin ~s** 6 no-trumps; **palo del ~** trump suit, trumps; **tener todos los ~s en la mano** (*fig*) to hold all the trumps.

triunvirato *nm* triumvirate.

trivial *adj* trivial, trite, commonplace.

trivialidad *nf* (**a**) (*cualidad*) triviality, triteness.

(**b**) (*una ~*) trivial matter; trite remark (*etc*); **~es** trivia, trivialities; **decir ~es** to talk trivially, talk in platitudes.

trivialización *nf* trivializing; minimizing (the importance of), playing-down.

trivializar [1f] *vt* to trivalize; to minimize (the importance of), play down.

trivialmente *adv* trivially, tritely.

triza *nf* bit, fragment; shred; **hacer algo ~s** to smash sth to bits; to tear sth to shreds; **hacer ~s a uno** to wear sb out; to flatten sb, crush sb; **los críticos dejaron la obra hecha ~s** the critics pulled the play to pieces, the critics tore the play to shreds.

trizar [1f] *vt* to smash to bits; to tear to shreds.

troca *nf* (*Méx*) lorry, truck.

trocaico *adj* trochaic.

trocar [1g *y* 1l] **1** *vt* (**a**) (*Com*) to exchange, barter (*por* for).

(**b**) *dinero* to change (*en* into).

(**c**) (*cambiar*) to change (*con, por* for); (*intercambiar*) to interchange, switch round, move about; *palabras* to exchange (*con* with); **~ la alegría en tristeza** to change gaiety into sadness.

(**d**) (*confundir*) to mix up, confuse.

(**e**) *comida* to vomit.

(**f**) (*Cono Sur: vender*) to sell; (*And: comprar*) to buy.

2 trocarse *vr* to change (*en* into); to get switched round; to get mixed up.

trocear [1a] *vt* to cut up, cut into pieces.

trocha *nf* (**a**) (*senda*) by-path, narrow path; (*atajo*) short cut. (**b**) (*LAm Ferro*) gauge; **~ normal** standard gauge. (**c**) (*Cono Sur Aut*) lane (of a motorway). (**d**) (*And: trote*) trot. (**e**) (*And: porción*) portion, helping (of meat).

trochar [1a] *vi* (*And*) to trot.

troche: a ~ y moche, a trochemoche *adv correr etc* helter-skelter, pell-mell; *desparramarse etc* all over the place; *repartir, usar etc* haphazardly, unsystematically, regardless of distinctions.

trofeo *nm* (**a**) (*objeto*) trophy. (**b**) (*fig*) victory, success, triumph.

troglodita *nmf* (**a**) (*Hist*) cave dweller, troglodyte. (**b**) (*fig*) (*grosero*) brute, coarse person; (*huraño*) unsociable individual, recluse. (**c**) (*: *glotón*) glutton.

troica *nf* troika.

troja *nf* (*LAm*) = **troj(e)**.

troj(e) *nf* granary, barn.

trola[1]* *nf* fib, lie.

trola[2] *nf* (*And*) (*jamón*) slice of ham; (*cuero*) piece of raw hide; (*corteza*) piece of loose bark.

trole *nm* (**a**) (*Elec*) trolley, trolley pole. (**b**) (*Cono Sur Hist: autobús*) trolley bus.

trolebús *nm* trolley bus.

trolero* *nm* fibber, liar.

tromba *nf* whirlwind; **~ marina** waterspout; **~ terrestre** whirlwind, tornado; **~ de agua** violent downpour; **~ de polvo** column of dust; **entrar en ~** to come in in a torrent, come rushing in; **pasar como una ~** to go by like a whirlwind.

trombón 1 *nm* (*instrumento*) trombone. **2** *nmf* (*persona*) trombonist.

trombonista *nmf* trombonist.

trombosis *nf* thrombosis; (*t* **~ cerebral**) cerebral haemorrhage.

trome* *adj* (*And*) bright, smart.

trompa 1 *nf* (**a**) (*Mús*) horn; **~ de caza** hunting horn; **sonar la ~ marcial** to sound a warlike note, blow a martial trumpet.

(**b**) (*peonza*) humming-top; whipping-top.

(**c**) (*Ent*) proboscis; (*Zool*) trunk; (*: *nariz*) snout‡, hooter‡; (*LAm: labios*) thick lips, blubber lips; **¡cierra la ~!** (*CAm, Méx*‡) shut your trap‡!

(**d**) (*Anat*) tube, duct; **~ de Eustaquio** Eustachian tube; **~ de Falopio** Fallopian tube.

(**e**) (*Met*) = **tromba.**

(**f**) (*: *borrachera*) drunkenness; **cogerse** (*LAm*: **agarrarse**) **una ~** to get tight*.

(**g**) (*Méx Ferro*) cowcatcher.

2 *nm* (**a**) (*Mús*) horn player. (**b**) (*Cono Sur*: patrón*) boss, chief.

trompada *nf*, **trompazo** *nm* (**a**) (*choque*) bump, bang; head-on collision. (**b**) (*puñetazo*) punch, swipe. (**c**) (*Méx: zurra*) thrashing, beating-up*.

trompeadura *nf* (*LAm*) (**a**) (*choques*) bumping, banging. (**b**) (*puñetazos*) series of punches; (*paliza*) beating-up*.

trompear [1a] (*LAm*) **1** *vt* (**a**) (*chocar con*) to bump, bang into; to collide head-on with. (**b**) (*pegar*) to punch, thump. **2** *vi* (**a**) to spin a top. (**b**) = **3**. **3 trompearse** *vr* to exchange blows, fight.

trompeta 1 *nf* (**a**) (*instrumento*) trumpet; (*corneta*) bugle; (*fig*) clarion. (**b**) (‡: *droga*) reefer‡, joint‡. (**c**) (*Cono Sur Bot*) daffodil. **2** *nmf* (*Mús*) trumpeter; bugler. **3** *nm* (*) (*imbécil*) twit*; (*borracho*) drunk*, old soak*. **4** *adj* (*Méx**) sloshed*, tight*.

trompetazo *nm* (*Mús*) trumpet blast; (*fig*) blast, blare.

trompetear [1a] *vi* to play the trumpet.

trompeteo *nm* sound of trumpets, (*esp*) fanfare.

trompetero *nm* (*de orquesta*) trumpet player; (*Mil etc*) trumpeter; bugler.

trompetilla *nf* (**a**) (*t* **~ acústica**) ear trumpet. (**b**) (*Carib**) raspberry*.

trompetista *nmf* trumpet player, (jazz) trumpeter.

trompeto* *adj* (*Méx*) drunk.

trompezar [1f] *vi* (*LAm*) = **tropezar.**

trompezón *nm* (*LAm*) = **tropezón.**

trompicar [1g] **1** *vt* (**a**) (*tropezar*) to trip up.

(**b**) **~ a uno*** to fiddle sb's promotion*, promote sb improperly.

2 *vi* to trip up a lot, stumble repeatedly.

trompicón *nm* (**a**) (*tropiezo*) stumble, trip; **a trompicones** in fits and starts; with difficulty. (**b**) (*Carib: puñetazo*) blow, punch.

trompis* *nm invar* punch, bash*.

trompiza* *nf* (*And, Méx*) punch-up‡.

trompo *nm* (**a**) (*juguete*) spinning top; **~ de música** humming-top; **ponerse como un ~*** to eat to bursting point.

(**b**) (*LAm*) (*desmañado*) clumsy person; (*bailador*) rotten dancer*.

(**c**) (*Fin*‡) 1000-peseta note; **medio ~** 500-peseta note.

(**d**) (*Dep*) spin.

trompón *nm* (**a**) (*) (*choque*) bump, bang; (*puñetazo*) hefty punch, vicious swipe. (**b**) = **trompo** (**b**). (**c**) (*Bot: t* **narciso ~**) daffodil.

trompudo *adj* (*LAm*) thick-lipped, blubber-lipped.

tron‡ *nm* = **tronco** (**d**).

tronada *nf*, **tronadera** *nf* (*Méx*) thunderstorm.

tronado *adj* (**a**) (*viejo*) old, broken-down, useless. (**b**) **estar ~*** (*loco*) to be potty*; (*arruinado*) to be ruined. (**c**) **estar ~** (*CAm**) to be broke*. (**d**) **estar ~** (*LAm**) to be high (on drugs)‡.

tronamenta *nf* (*And, Méx*) thunderstorm.

tronar [1l] **1** *vt* (**a**) (*CAm, Méx*: fusilar*) to shoot, execute; (*pegar un tiro a*) to shoot.

(**b**) **la tronó** (*Méx**) he blew it‡, he messed it up.

2 *vi* (**a**) to thunder; (*cañones etc*) to thunder, rumble, boom; **por lo que pueda ~** just in case, to be on the safe side.

(**b**) (*Fin**) to go broke*; (*fracasar*) to fail, be ruined.

(**c**) **~ con uno*** to fall out with sb.

(**d**) (*fig: enfurecerse*) to rave, rage; **~ contra** to fulminate against, thunder against; to storm at.

3 tronarse* *vr* (**a**) (*CAm, Méx*) to shoot o.s., blow one's brains out. (**b**) (*LAm*) to take drugs.

tronazón *nf* (*CAm, Méx*) thunderstorm.

tronca‡ *nf* bird‡.

troncal *adj*: **línea ~** main line, trunk line; **materia ~** core subject.

troncar [1g] *vt* = **truncar.**

tronco *nm* (**a**) (*Bot*) (*de árbol*) trunk; (*de flor etc*) stem, stalk; (*leño*) log; (*LAm*) tree stump; **~ de Navidad** (*Culin*) yule log; **dormir como un ~** to sleep like a log; **estar hecho un ~** (*dormido*) to be sound asleep; (*inmóvil*) to be completely deprived of movement.

(**b**) (*Anat*) trunk.

(**c**) (**‡: *pene*) prick**‡.

(**d**) (‡) (*hombre*) bloke‡, chap*; (*amigo: en oración directa*) mate, chum*; **oye, ~** hey, friend; hey, brother*; **María y su ~** María and her bloke‡.

(**e**) (*Ferro*) main line, trunk line.

(**f**) (*de familia*) stock.
troncha *nf* (**a**) (*LAm*) (*tajada*) slice; (*trozo*) chunk, piece. (**b**) (*LAm**: *prebenda*) sinecure, soft job. (**c**) (*Méx*: *comida*) soldier's rations; meagre meal.
tronchado* **1** *nm* (*Méx*: *buen negocio*) gold mine (*fig*), prosperous business. **2** *adj* (*And*: *lisiado*) maimed, crippled.
tronchante* *adj* killingly funny.
tronchar [1a] **1** *vt* (**a**) (*talar*) to bring down; to chop down, lop off; (*cortar*) to cut up, cut off; (*hender*) to split, rend, smash.
(**b**) (*fig*) *vida* to cut off, cut short; *esperanzas etc* to shatter.
(**c**) (*: *cansar*) to tire out.
2 troncharse *vr* (**a**) (*árbol*) to fall down, split.
(**b**) (*: *cansarse*) to tire o.s. out.
(**c**) (*) ~ **de risa** to split one's sides laughing.
troncho **1** *adj* (*Cono Sur*) maimed, crippled. **2** *nm* (**a**) (*Bot*) stem, stalk (of cabbage *etc*). (**b**) (*Cono Sur*: *trozo*) piece, chunk. (**c**) (*And*: *enredo*) knot, tangle. (**d**) (**‡**) prick**‡**.
tronera **1** *nf* (**a**) (*Mil*) loophole, embrasure; (*Arquit*) small window.
(**b**) (*Billar*) pocket.
(**c**) (*Méx*: *chimenea*) chimney, flue.
2 *nmf* (*: *tarambana*) crazy person, harum-scarum.
3 *nm* (*: *libertino*) rake, libertine.
tronido *nm* (*Met*) thunderclap; (*explosión*) loud report, bang, detonation; boom; ~**s** thunder, booming.
tronío *nm* lavish expenditure, extravagance.
trono *nm* throne; (*fig: frec*) crown; **heredar el** ~ to inherit the crown; **subir al** ~ to ascend the throne, come to the throne; **nuestra lealtad al** ~ our loyalty to the crown.
tronquista *nmf* (*LAm*) lorry driver, truck driver (*US*).
tronzar [1f] *vt* (**a**) (*cortar*) to cut up; (*romper*) to split, rend, smash. (**b**) (*Cos*) to pleat. (**c**) (*) *persona* to tire out.
tropa *nf* (**a**) (*multitud*) troop, body, crowd; (*pey*) troop, mob.
(**b**) (*Mil*) army, military; ~**s** troops; ~**s de asalto**, ~ **de choque** storm-troops; **ser de** ~* to be in the army, be a soldier.
(**c**) (*Mil*: *soldados rasos*) men, rank and file, ordinary soldiers.
(**d**) (*LAm Agr*) flock, herd.
(**e**) (*Cono Sur*: *vehículos*) line of carts; stream of vehicles; line of cars.
(**f**) (*Méx**: *maleducado*) rude person; (*Carib**: *tonto*) dope*.
tropear [1a] *vt* (*Cono Sur*) to herd.
tropecientos* *adj pl* umpteen*.
tropel *nm* (**a**) (*multitud*) mob, crowd, throng. (**b**) (*revoltijo*) jumble, mess, litter. (**c**) (*prisa*) rush, haste; **acudir** (*etc*) **en** ~ to come in a mad rush, all rush together, come thronging in confusion.
tropelía *nf* (**a**) = **tropel** (**c**). (**b**) (*atropello*) outrage, abuse of authority, violent act; **cometer una** ~ to commit an outrage.
tropero *nm* (**a**) (*Cono Sur*) cowboy. (**b**) (*Méx*) boor.
tropezar [1f *y* 1j] **1** *vt* = *vi* (**b**).
2 *vi* (**a**) (*dar con los pies*) to trip, stumble (*con, contra, en* on, over); ~ **con** to run into, run up against.
(**b**) (*fig*: *topar*) ~ **con uno** to run into sb, bump into sb; ~ **con algo** to run across sth.
(**c**) ~ **con una dificultad** (*fig*) to run into a difficulty, run up against a difficulty.
(**d**) ~ **con uno** (*fig*: *reñir*) to have an argument with sb; to fall out with sb.
(**e**) (*fig*: *cometer un error*) to slip up, blunder; (*moralmente*) to slip, fall.
3 tropezarse *vr* to run into each other.
tropezón *nm* (**a**) (*traspié*) trip, stumble; **dar un** ~ to trip, stumble; **proceder a tropezones** to proceed by fits and starts; **hablar a tropezones** to talk jerkily, talk falteringly.
(**b**) (*fig*: *error*) slip, blunder; (*moral*) slip, lapse.
(**c**) (*Culin**) small piece of meat (*added to soup etc*).
tropical *adj* (**a**) tropical. (**b**) (*Cono Sur*: *melodramático*) rhetorical, melodramatic, highly-coloured.
tropicalismo *nm* (*Cono Sur*) rhetoric, melodramatic style, excessive colourfulness.
trópico *nm* (**a**) (*Geog*) tropic; ~**s** tropics; ~ **de Cáncer** Tropic of Cancer; ~ **de Capricornio** Tropic of Capricorn.
(**b**) (*Carib*) ~**s** hardships, difficulties; **pasar los** ~**s** to suffer hardships, have a hard time.
tropiezo *nm* (**a**) (*error*) slip, blunder; (*desliz moral*) moral lapse. (**b**) (*desgracia*) misfortune, mishap; (*revés*) setback; (*en el amor*) disappointment in love. (**c**) (*obstáculo*) obstacle, snag; stumbling block. (**d**) (*riña*) quarrel; tiff, argument.
tropilla *nf* (*Cono Sur*) drove, team.
tropo *nm* trope, figure of speech.
troquel *nm* (*Téc*) die.
troquelado *nm* (*Téc*) hot-die forging, punching; (*fig*) moulding, shaping.
troqueo *nm* trochee.
trosco, -a* *nm/f* Trot*, Trotskyist.
trotamundos *nm invar* globetrotter.
trotar [1a] *vi* (**a**) (*caballo etc*) to trot. (**b**) (*: *persona*) to travel about, chase around here and there; to hustle.
trote *nm* (**a**) (*de caballo etc*) trot; ~ **cochinero**, ~ **de perro** jogtrot; **ir al** ~ to trot, go at a trot; **irse al** ~ to go off in a great rush.
(**b**) (*) (*viajes*) travelling, chasing around; (*ajetreo*) bustle; **yo ya no estoy para esos** ~**s** I can't go chasing around like that any more; **tomar el** ~ to dash off.
(**c**) **de mucho** ~ *ropa* tough, hard-wearing; **chaqueta para todo** ~ a jacket for everyday use, a jacket for ordinary wear.
(**d**) (*: *asunto turbio*) ~**s** shady affair, dark doings; **meterse en malos** ~**s** to get mixed up in something improper.
(**e**) (*: *apuros*) ~**s** hardships; **andar en malos** ~**s** to have a rough time of it, suffer hardships.
trotskismo *nm* Trotskyism.
trotskista *adj, nmf* Trotskyist.
trovador *nm* troubadour.
Troya *nf* Troy; **aquí fue** ~ and now this is all you see, now there's nothing but ruins; **¡aquí fue** ~! * you should have heard the fuss!; **¡arda** ~! press on regardless!, never mind the consequences!
troyano, -a *adj, nm/f* Trojan.
troza *nf* log.
trozo *nm* (**a**) (*pedazo*) bit, piece; chunk; fragment; **a** ~**s** in bits, piecemeal; **es un** ~ **de pan*** he's a dear, he's a sweetie*. (**b**) (*Liter, Mús*) passage; section; ~**s escogidos** selections, selected passages.
trucaje *nm* (*Cine*) trick photography; special effects; (*fig*) rigging, fixing, fiddling*.
trucar [1g] **1** *vt* (*) (**a**) *resultado* to fix, rig; *baraja* to arrange (fraudulently); **las cartas estaban trucadas** (*fig*) the dice were loaded against us. (**b**) (*Aut*) *motor* to soup up*. **2** *vi* (*Billar*) to pocket the ball, pot.
truco *nm* (**a**) (*ardid*) trick, device, dodge; (*destreza*) knack; (*Cine*) trick effect, piece of trick photography; **arte de los** ~**s** conjuring; ~ **de naipes** card trick; ~ **publicitario** advertising stunt, publicity gimmick; **el tío tiene muchos** ~**s** the fellow is up to all the dodges; **coger el** ~ to get the knack, get the hang of it, catch on; **coger el** ~ **a uno** to see how sb works a trick; (*fig*) to catch on to sb's little game.
(**b**) ~**s** (*Billar*) billiards, pool.
(**c**) (*And, Cono Sur**: *puñetazo*) punch, bash*.
(**d**) (*Cono Sur Naipes*) *popular card game*.
truculento *adj* (*cruel*) cruel; (*horroroso*) horrifying, terrifying; (*extravagante*) full of extravagant effects.
trucha[1] *nf* (**a**) (*pez*) trout; ~ **arco iris** rainbow trout; ~ **marina** sea trout. (**b**) (*Téc*) crane, derrick.
trucha[2] *nf* (*CAm Com*) stall, booth.
trucha[3]* *nmf* tricky individual, wily bird; cheat.
truche‡ *nm* (*And*) snappy dresser*, dude* (*US*).
truchero[1] *nm* (*CAm*) hawker, vendor.
truchero[2] *adj* trout (*atr*); **río** ~ trout river.
truchimán *nm* (**a**) (*Hist*) interpreter. (**b**) (*) rogue, villain.
trucho *adj* (*And*) sharp, rascally.
trueco *nm* = **trueque**.
trueno *nm* (**a**) (*gen*) thunder; (*un* ~) clap of thunder, thunderclap; (*de cañón etc*) bang, boom, report.
(**b**) (*) (*tarambana*) wild youth, madcap; (*libertino*) rake.
(**c**) ~ **gordo*** finale (*of firework display*); (*fig*) big row, major scandal.
(**d**) (*Carib**: *juerga*) binge*, noisy party.
(**e**) (*And‡*) rod‡, gun.
(**f**) ~**s** (*Carib*) stout shoes.
trueque *nm* (**a**) (*cambio*) exchange; switch; (*Com*) barter; **a** ~ **de** in exchange for; in place of; **aun a** ~ **de perderlo** even at the cost of losing it. (**b**) ~**s** (*And Fin*) change.
trufa *nf* (**a**) (*Bot*) truffle. (**b**) (*: *cuento*) fib, story.
trufado *adj* stuffed with truffles.
trufar [1a] **1** *vt* (**a**) (*Culin*) to stuff with truffles. (**b**) (*:

estafar) to take in*, swindle. **2** *vi* (*) to fib, tell stories.
trufi* *nm* (*And*) taxi.
truhán *nm* (**a**) (*Hist*) jester, buffoon, funny man. (**b**) (*estafador*) rogue, crook*, swindler; (*charlatán*) mountebank.
truhanería *nf* (**a**) (*Hist*) buffoonery. (**b**) (*picardía*) roguery, crookedness, swindling.
truhanesco *adj* (**a**) buffoonish. (**b**) (*tramposo*) crooked*, dishonest.
truísmo *nm* truism.
truja‡ *nm* fag‡, gasper‡.
trujal *nm* (*de vino*) winepress; (*de aceite*) olive-oil press.
trujimán *nm* = **truchimán**.
trujis‡ *nm invar* fag‡, gasper‡.
trulla *nf* (**a**) (*bullicio*) bustle, commotion, noise. (**b**) (*multitud*) crowd, throng. (**c**) (*And: broma*) practical joke.
trullada *nf* (*Carib*) crowd, throng.
trullo‡ *nm* nick‡, jail.
truncado *adj* (*reducido*) truncated, shortened; (*incompleto*) incomplete.
truncamiento *nm* truncation, shortening; curtailing; cutting; mutilation.
truncar [1g] *vt* (**a**) (*acortar*) to truncate, shorten; *texto etc* to cut off; to cut short, curtail; *discurso* to cut, slash; *cita* to mutilate; *sentido* to affect, upset, destroy.
(**b**) (*fig*) *carrera, vida* to cut short; *esperanzas, proyecto* to ruin; *desarrollo* to stunt, check, seriously affect.
trunco *adj* (*reducido*) truncated, shortened; (*incompleto*) incomplete.
truquero (*LAm*) **1** *adj* tricky; gimmicky. **2** *nm*, **truquera** *nf* trickster.
truqui* *nm* = **truco** (**a**).
trusa *nf* (**a**) (*Carib*: *bañador*) bathing trunks. (**b**) (*And, Méx*) (*de hombre*) underpants; (*de mujer*) panties, knickers; (*de bebé*) pants.
trust [trus] *nm, pl* **trusts** [trus] (*Fin*) trust, cartel.
truzas* *nfpl* knickers.
Tte. *abr de* **teniente** Lieutenant, Lt.
TU *nm abr de* **tiempo universal** universal time, U.T.
tu *adj pos* your; (††, *a Dios*) thy.
tú *pron pers* (**a**) you; (††, *a Dios*) thou; **tratar a uno de ~ a ~** to treat sb on equal terms; **en el partido se mantuvo el ~ a ~** the game was between equals, the game was an equal struggle. (**b**) (‡) (*usado solo, en oración directa*) (*enfático*) you know, you see; (*rechazo*) no way!*, get away!*; (*insulto*) get lost!‡
tualé (*LAm*) **1** *nm* toilet, lavatory. **2** *nf* (*feminine*) toilet.
tubercular *adj* tubercular.
tubérculo *nm* (**a**) (*Bot*) tuber. (**b**) (*Anat, Med etc*) tubercle.
tuberculosis *nf* tuberculosis.
tuberculoso *adj* tuberculous, tubercular.
tubería *nf* (*tubos*) pipes, piping; tubes, tubing; (*oleoducto etc*) pipeline.
tubero *nm* plumber, pipe-fitter.
Tubinga *nf* Tübingen.
tubo *nm* (**a**) tube (*t Anat, TV etc*); pipe; (*LAm Telec*) handset, earpiece; **~ acústico** speaking-tube; **~ capilar** capillary; **~ de chimenea** chimneypot; **~ de desagüe** drainpipe, waste-pipe; **~ digestivo** alimentary canal; **~ de ensayo** test-tube; **~ de escape** exhaust (pipe); **~ fluorescente** fluorescent tube; **~ de humo** chimney, flue; **~ de imagen** television tube; **~ intestinal** intestine; **~ de lámpara** lamp glass; **~ lanzatorpedos** torpedo-tube; **~ de órgano** organ pipe; **~ de radio** wireless valve, tube (*US*); **~ de rayos catódicos** cathode-ray tube; **~ de respiración** breathing-tube; **~ de vacío** valve, vacuum tube (*US*); **pasar por el ~*** to knuckle under; **lo vendió por un ~*** he sold it for a packet*. (**b**) (‡) (*Ferro*) tube, underground; (*Telec*) phone, blower‡; (*cárcel*) nick‡.
tubular 1 *adj* tubular. **2** *nm* (*prenda*) roll-on.
tucán *nm*, **tucano** *nm* (*Carib, Cono Sur*) toucan.
Tucídedes *nm* Thucydides.
tuco¹ 1 *adj* (**a**) (*LAm*) (*mutilado*) maimed, limbless; (*manco*) lacking a finger (*o* hand). (**b**) (*CAm**: *achaparrado*) squat. **2** *nm* (*LAm Anat*) stump. **3** *nm*, **tuca** *nf* (*persona*) cripple.
tuco² *nm* (*And, Cono Sur*: *Ent*) glow-worm.
tuco³, -a *nm/f* (*CAm*: *tocayo*) namesake.
tuco⁴ *nm* (*And, Cono Sur Culin*) tomato sauce.
tucura *nf* (**a**) (*Cono Sur*: *langosta*) locust. (**b**) (*And*) (*libélula*) dragonfly; (*mantis*) praying mantis; (*saltamontes*) grasshopper. (**c**) (*fig*: *cura*) corrupt priest.
tucuso *nm* (*Carib*) hummingbird.
tudesco, -a *adj, nm/f* German.
tuerca *nf* nut; **~ mariposa** wingnut; **apretar las ~s a uno** to tighten the screws on sb.
tuerce‡ *nm* (*CAm*) misfortune, setback.
tuerto 1 *adj* (**a**) (*torcido*) twisted, bent, crooked.
(**b**) (*mutilado*) one-eyed, blind in one eye.
(**c**) **a tuertas** upside-down; back to front; **a tuertas o a derechas** (*con razón o sin ella*) rightly or wrongly; (*por fas o por nefas*) by hook or by crook; (*sin pensar*) thoughtlessly, hastily.
2 *nm*, **tuerta** *nf* one-eyed person, person blind in one eye.
3 *nm* (*injusticia*) wrong, injustice.
tuesta* *nf* (*Carib*) binge*.
tueste *nm* (*de café*) roasting.
tuétano *nm* (**a**) (*Anat*) marrow; (*Bot*) pith; **hasta los ~s** through and through, utterly, to the core; **enamorado hasta los ~s** head over heels in love.
(**b**) (*fig*) core, essence.
tufarada *nf* (*olor*) bad smell; (*racha de olor*) gust of foul smell, cloud of evil-smelling gas (*etc*).
tufillas* *nmf invar* bad-tempered person.
tufillo *nm* (*fig*) slight smell (*a of*).
tufo¹ *nm* (**a**) (*vapor*) vapour, gas, exhalation.
(**b**) (*olor*) bad smell, stink; (*de cuerpos*) body odour; (*halitosis*) bad breath; (*de cuarto etc*) fug; **se le subió el ~ a las narices** (*fig*) he got very cross.
(**c**) **~s*** swank*, conceit; **tener ~s** to be swanky*, be conceited.
tufo² *nm* (*de pelo*) curl, sidelock.
tugurio *nm* (*Agr*) shepherd's hut; (*chabola*) hovel, slum, shack; (*cuartucho*) poky little room; (*cafetucho*) den, joint‡; **~s** (*And*) slum quarter, shanty town.
tuja *nf* (*And*) hide-and-seek.
tul *nm* tulle, net.
tulenco *adj* (*CAm*) splay-footed.
tulipa *nf* lampshade.
tulipán *nm* tulip; (*And, Carib, Méx*) hibiscus.
tulipanero *nm*, **tulipero** *nm* tulip-tree.
tulis *nm invar* (*Méx*) highway robber, brigand.
tullida¹ *nf* (*Carib*) dirty trick.
tullido 1 *adj* crippled; paralysed, paralytic. **2** *nm*, **tullida²** *nf* cripple.
tullir [3h] *vt* (**a**) (*lisiar*) to cripple, maim; (*paralizar*) to paralyze. (**b**) (*fig*: *agotar*) to wear out, exhaust. (**c**) (*fig*: *maltratar*) to abuse, maltreat.
tumba¹ *nf* (*sepultura*) tomb, grave; **ser (como) una ~** to keep one's mouth shut; **llevar a uno a la ~** (*euf*) to carry sb off; **hablar a ~ abierta** to speak openly.
tumba² *nf* (**a**) (*sacudida*) shake, jolt; lurch.
(**b**) (*voltereta*) somersault.
(**c**) (*LAm*) (*tala*) felling of timber, clearing of ground; (*tierra*) ground cleared for sowing; (*claro*) forest clearing.
(**d**) (*Cono Sur*: *carne*) boiled meat of poor quality.
tumba³ *nf* (*Carib, Cono Sur*) African drum.
tumbacuartillos* *nm invar* old soak‡.
tumbacuatro *nm* (*Carib*) braggart.
tumbadero *nm* (*Carib, Méx*) (**a**) (*Agr*) ground cleared for sowing. (**b**) (*: *burdel*) brothel.
tumbadora *nf* (*Carib*) large conga drum.
tumbar [1a] **1** *vt* (**a**) (*derribar*) to knock down, knock over, knock to the ground; (*: *vino*) to lay out; (‡: *matar*) to do in‡.
(**b**) (**: *copularse*) to lay**, screw**.
(**c**) (*Univ**) to plough*.
(**d**) (*: *olor etc*) to lay out*, knock back*; (*impresionar etc*) to amaze, stun; **su presunción tumbó a todos** his conceit amazed everybody, his conceit knocked everybody sideways.
(**e**) (*LAm*) *árboles* to fell; *tierra* to clear.
2 *vi* (**a**) (*caerse*) to fall down.
(**b**) (*Náut*) to capsize.
(**c**) (*) **un olor que tumba** a smell which knocks you back*; **tiene una desfachatez que tumba de espaldas** his brazenness is enough to stun you.
3 tumbarse *vr* (**a**) (*acostarse*) to lie down; (*estirarse*) to stretch out; (*repantigarse*) to sprawl, loll; **estar tumbado, quedar tumbado** to lie, be lying down.
(**b**) (*trigo etc*) to go flat.
(**c**) (*fig*) to give up, decide to take it easy; to let o.s. go (*after achieving a success etc*).
tumbilla *nf* (*CAm*) wicker suitcase.
tumbo¹ *nm* (**a**) (*caída*) fall, tumble; (*sacudida*) shake, jolt; lurch; **dar un ~** to tumble; to jolt; to lurch; **dando ~s** (*fig*) with all sorts of difficulties, despite the upsets, after a lot

of setbacks.

(**b**) (*momento crítico*) critical moment.

tumbo² *nm* (*Hist*) monastic cartulary.

tumbón* *adj* slack, lazy, bone-idle.

tumbona *nf* (*butaca*) easy chair; (*de playa*) deckchair, beach chair (*US*).

tumefacción *nf* swelling, tumefaction.

tumefacto *adj* swollen.

tumescente *adj* tumescent.

tumido *adj* swollen, tumid.

tumor *nm* tumour, growth; ~ **cerebral** brain tumour; ~ **maligno** malignant growth.

túmulo *nm* tumulus, barrow, burial mound; (*Geog*) mound.

tumulto *nm* turmoil, commotion, uproar, tumult; (*Pol etc*) riot, disturbance; ~ **popular** popular rising.

tumultuario *adj* = **tumultuoso**.

tumultuosamente *adv* tumultuously; (*pey*) riotously; rebelliously.

tumultuoso *adj* tumultuous; (*pey*) riotous, disorderly; rebellious.

tuna¹ *nf* (*Bot*) prickly pear.

tuna² *nf* (**a**) (*Esp Mús*) student music group (*guitarists and singers*).

(**b**) (*vida picaresca*) rogue's life, vagabond life; (*fig*) merry life; **correr la** ~ to have a good time, live it up*.

(**c**) (*CAm: embriaguez*) drunkenness.

tunantada *nf* dirty trick, villainous act.

tunante *nm* rogue, villain, crook; ¡~! you villain!, (*a niño*) you young scamp!

tunantear [1a] *vi* to live a rogue's life, be a crook*.

tunantería *nf* (**a**) (*cualidad*) villainy, crookedness. (**b**) (*una* ~) villainy, dirty trick.

tunar [1a] *vi* to loaf, idle, bum around (*US*).

tunco (*CAm, Méx*) **1** *adj* (*lisiado*) maimed, crippled; (*manco*) one-armed. **2** *nm* (**a**) (*persona*) cripple. (**b**) (*Zool*) pig.

tunda¹ *nf* (*esquileo*) shearing.

tunda² *nf* (**a**) (*paliza*) beating, thrashing. (**b**) **darse una** ~ to wear o.s. out.

tundir¹ [3a] *vt paño* to shear; *hierba etc* to mow, cut.

tundir² [3a] *vt* (**a**) (*pegar*) to beat, thrash. (**b**) (*fig*) to exhaust, tire out.

tundra *nf* tundra.

tunear [1a] *vi* (**a**) (*vivir como pícaro*) to live a rogue's life. (**b**) (*gandulear*) to loaf, idle; (*divertirse*) to have a good time.

tunecino, -a *adj, nm/f* Tunisian.

túnel *nm* (**a**) tunnel; ~ **aerodinámico,** ~ **de pruebas aerodinámicas,** ~ **de viento** wind-tunnel; ~ **del Canal de la Mancha** Channel Tunnel; ~ **de lavado** car-wash; ~ **del tiempo** timewarp; ~ **de vestuarios** tunnel leading to the changing-rooms.

(**b**) (*fig*) dark passage; dark period. (**c**) (*Dep*) nutmeg kick (*o* pass *etc*).

tuneladora *nf* tunnelling machine.

tunelar [1a] *vi* to tunnel.

tunes *nmpl* (*And, CAm*) first steps (*of a child*); **hacer** ~ to toddle, start to walk, take one's first steps.

Túnez *nm* (*ciudad*) Tunis; (*Hist: país*) Tunisia.

tungo 1 *adj* (*And*) short, shortened; blunt. **2** *nm* (**a**) (*And: trozo*) bit, chunk. (**b**) (*Cono Sur Anat*) neck; jowl.

tungsteno *nm* tungsten.

túnica *nf* (**a**) (*gen*) tunic; (*vestido largo*) robe, gown, long dress; ~ **de gimnasia** gymslip. (**b**) (*Anat, Bot*) tunic.

Tunicia *nf* Tunisia.

túnico *nm* (*LAm*) shift, long undergarment.

túnido *nm* tuna (fish).

tuno *nm* (**a**) (*hum*) rogue, villain; scamp; **el muy** ~ the old rogue. (**b**) (*Mús*) member of a student *tuna* (*V* **tuna²** (**a**)).

tunoso *adj* (*And*) prickly.

tuntún: **al** (**buen**) ~ *adv* thoughtlessly, without due calculation; trusting to luck; haphazardly; **juzgar al buen** ~ to judge hastily, jump to conclusions.

tuntuneco* *adj* (*CAm, Carib*) stupid, dense*.

tuñeco *adj* (*Carib*) maimed, crippled.

tupamaro, -a *nm/f* (*Uruguay Pol*) Tupamaro.

tupé *nm* (**a**) (*peluca*) toupée, hairpiece. (**b**) (*: *caradura*) nerve*, cheek*.

tupi *nm* (*LAm*) Tupi (Indian).

tupia *nf* (*And*) dam.

tupiar [1b] *vt* (*And*) to dam up.

tupición *nf* (**a**) (*LAm*) (*obstrucción*) blockage, stoppage, obstruction; (*Med*) catarrh.

(**b**) (*LAm: multitud*) dense crowd, throng.

(**c**) (*And, Méx: vegetación*) dense vegetation.

(**d**) **una** ~ **de cosas** (*Cono Sur**) a lot of things.

(**e**) (*LAm: fig*) bewilderment, confusion.

tupido 1 *adj* (**a**) (*denso*) thick, dense; impenetrable; *tela* close-woven.

(**b**) (*LAm: obstruido*) blocked, stopped up, obstructed.

(**c**) (*: *estúpido*) dense*, dim*.

(**d**) (*Méx: frecuente*) common, frequent.

2 *adv* (*Méx*) (*con tesón*) persistently, steadily; (*a menudo*) often, frequently.

tupinambo *nm* Jerusalem artichoke.

tupir [3a] **1** *vt* (**a**) (*apretar*) to pack tight, press down, compact.

(**b**) (*LAm: obstruir*) to block, stop up, obstruct.

2 tupirse *vr* (**a**) (*: *comer mucho*) to stuff oneself*.

(**b**) (*LAm: desconcertarse*) to feel silly, get embarrassed.

turba¹ *nf* peat, turf.

turba² *nf* crowd, throng; swarm; (*pey*) mob; rabble.

turbación *nf* (**a**) (*disturbio*) disturbance. (**b**) (*alarma*) perturbation, worry, alarm; (*vergüenza*) embarrassment; (*confusión*) bewilderment, confusion; (*agitación*) trepidation.

turbado *adj* disturbed, worried, upset; embarrassed; bewildered.

turbador *adj* disturbing, alarming; embarrassing.

turbal *nm* peat bog.

turbamulta *nf* mob, rabble.

turbante *nm* (**a**) (*sombrero*) turban. (**b**) (*Méx Bot*) gourd, calabash.

turbar [1a] **1** *vt* (**a**) *orden, paz, razón etc* to disturb.

(**b**) *persona* (*inquietar*) to disturb, worry, alarm; (*desconcertar*) to disconcert; (*alterar*) to upset; (*azorar*) to embarrass; (*aturdir*) to bewilder.

(**c**) *agua etc* to stir up.

2 turbarse *vr* to be disturbed, get worried, become alarmed; to be embarrassed; to be bewildered, get confused, get all mixed up.

turbera *nf* peat bog.

turbiedad *nf* (*V adj*) (**a**) cloudiness, thickness.

(**b**) dimness, mistiness; disturbance; lack of clarity, confusion.

(**c**) turbulence.

(**d**) (*pey*) shadiness; dubious character.

turbina *nf* turbine; ~ **eólica** wind turbine; ~ **de gas** gas turbine; ~ **a** (*o* **de**) **vapor** steam-engine.

turbio 1 *adj* (**a**) *agua etc* cloudy, thick, turbid, muddy.

(**b**) *vista* dim, misty, blurred; disturbed; *asunto, lenguaje* unclear, confused.

(**c**) (*fig*) *período etc* restless, unsettled, turbulent.

(**d**) (*pey*) *negocio* shady; *método* dubious.

2 *adv*: **ver** ~ to have disturbed vision, not see clearly.

3 *nmpl*: **~s** sediment; sludge.

turbión *nm* (**a**) (*Met*) heavy shower, downpour; squall. (**b**) (*fig*) shower, torrent; swarm; (*de balas*) hail.

turbo 1 *nm invar* (*Mec*) turbo, turbocharger; (*coche*) turbocharged car. **2** *atr* turbo (*atr*).

turbo... *pref* turbo...

turboalimentado *adj* turbocharged.

turbocompresor *nm* turbo-compressor, (*diesel*) turbo-supercharger.

turbohélice 1 *nm* turboprop (aeroplane). **2** *atr* turboprop (*atr*).

turbonada *nf* (*Cono Sur*) sudden storm, squall.

turbopropulsado *adj* turboprop (*atr*).

turbopropulsor, turborreactor 1 *nm* turbojet (aeroplane). **2** *atr* turbojet (*atr*).

turbulencia *nf* (*V adj*) (**a**) turbulence; troubled nature, unsettled character; storminess.

(**b**) restlessness; unruliness, rebelliousness; disorderly state, mutinous state.

turbulento *adj* (**a**) *elementos, río etc* turbulent; *período* troubled, unsettled, turbulent; *reunión* stormy.

(**b**) *carácter* restless; unruly, rebellious; *niño* noisy, troublesome, unruly; *ejército etc* disorderly, mutinous.

turca‡**¹** *nf* booze-up‡, binge*; **coger** (*o* **pillar** *etc*) **una** ~ to get sozzled‡; **estar con la** ~ to be under the weather.

turco 1 *adj* Turkish. **2** *nm*, **turca²** *nf* (**a**) (*de Turquía*) Turk; **joven** ~ (*Pol*) young Turk. (**b**) (*LAm*) (*árabe*) Arab, (*sirio*) Syrian, (*de Medio Oriente*) Middle Easterner; (*buhonero*) pedlar, peddler (*US*), hawker. **3** *nm* (*Ling*) Turkish.

turcochipriota *adj, nmf* Turkish-Cypriot.

túrdiga *nf* thong, strip of leather.

Turena *nf* Touraine.
turf *nm* (**a**) **el ~** the turf, horse-racing. (**b**) (*LAm*†: *pista*) racetrack.
turfista 1 *adj* fond of horse-racing. **2** *nm* racing man.
turgencia *nf* turgidity.
turgente *adj*, **túrgido** *adj* turgid, swollen.
Turín *nm* Turin.
Turingia *nf* Thuringia.
turismo *nm* (**a**) (*gen*) tourism; (*excursionismo*) touring, sightseeing; (*industria*) tourist trade; **~ blanco** winter holidays, skiing holidays; **hacer ~** to go touring (abroad), go travelling as tourists; **ahora se hace más ~ que nunca** numbers of tourists are greater now than ever; **se desarrolla mucho el ~ en Eslobodia** facilities for tourists are being much developed in Slobodia; **el ~ constituye su mayor industria** the tourist trade is their biggest industry. (**b**) (*Aut*) (private) car.
turista *nmf* tourist; sightseer, visitor, holidaymaker, vacationist (*US*).
turístico *adj* tourist (*atr*).
turistizado *adj* touristy.
turma *nf* (**a**) (*Anat*) testicle. (**b**) (*Bot*) truffle; (*And*) potato.
túrmix *nf* (*a veces m*) mixer, blender.
turnar [1a] *vi y* **turnarse** *vr* to take (it in) turns; **ellos se turnan para usarlo** they take it in turns to use it.
turné *nm* tour, trip.
turno *nm* (**a**) (*lista*) rota; (*orden*) order (of priority).
(**b**) (*vez, oportunidad*) turn; (*tanda*) spell, period of duty; (*de día etc*) shift; (*en juegos*) turn, go; (*en reunión etc*) opportunity to speak; **~ de día** day shift; **~ de noche** nightshift; **~ de oficio** spell of court duty; **~ de preguntas** question-and-answer session; **~ rotativo** rotating shift; **por ~** in rotation, in turn; **por ~s** by turns; **trabajar por ~s** to work shifts; **trabajo de ~s** shift work(ing); **es su ~, es el primero en ~, le toca el ~** it's his turn (next); **esperar su ~** to wait one's turn, take one's turn; **cuando le llegue el ~** when her turn comes; **estar de ~** to be on duty; **estuvo con la querida de ~** he was with his girlfriend of the moment.
turolense 1 *adj* of Teruel. **2** *nmf* native (*o* inhabitant) of Teruel; **los ~s** people of Teruel.
turón *nm* polecat.
turqueo* *nm* (*CAm*) fight.
turquesa *nf* turquoise.
turquesco *adj* Turkish.
turquí *adj*: **color ~** indigo, deep blue.
Turquía *nf* Turkey.
turra‡ *nf* (*Cono Sur*) whore, prostitute.
turrón *nm* (**a**) nougat. (**b**) (*) cushy government job‡; sinecure, political plum.
turulato* *adj* dazed, stunned, flabbergasted; **quedó ~ con la noticia** he was stunned by the news.
tururú* 1 *adj*: **estar ~** to be crazy. **2** *interj* no way!*, you're joking!
tus¹ *interj* (*a perro*) good dog!, here boy!
tus²: **sin decir ~ ni mus** without saying a word; **no decir ~ ni mus** to remain silent, say nothing.
tusa *nf* (**a**) (*And, CAm, Carib*) (*mazorca*) cob of maize, corncob; (*cascabillo*) maize husk; (*Carib*: *cigarro*) cigar rolled in a maize leaf; (*Cono Sur*: *seda*) cornsilk.
(**b**) (*Cono Sur*: *crin*) horse's mane.
(**c**) (*Cono Sur*: *esquileo*) clipping, shearing.
(**d**) (*And*: *hoyo*) pockmark.
(**e**) (*And*††) (*susto*) fright; (*inquietud*) anxiety.
(**f**) (*CAm, Carib*: *puta*) whore.
(**g**) **no vale ni una ~** (*CAm, Carib**) it's worthless.
tusar [1a] *vt* (*LAm*) (*esquilar*) to cut, clip, shear; (*cortar*) to cut roughly, cut badly.
tuse *nm* (*Cono Sur*) = **tusa.**
tuso *adj* (**a**) (*And, Carib*: *esquilado*) cropped, shorn. (**b**) (*Carib*: *rabón*) docked, tailless. (**c**) (*And, Carib*: *picado de viruelas*) pockmarked.
tútano *nm* (*LAm*) = **tuétano.**
tute *nm a card game similar to bezique;* **darse un ~** to work extra hard, make a special effort.
tutear [1a] **1** *vt* (**a**) **~ a uno** to address sb as 'tú' (*familiar 2nd person sing*). (**b**) (*fig*) **~ a** to be on equal terms with. **2 tutearse** *vr*: **se tutean desde siempre** they have always addressed each other as 'tú', they have always been on familiar terms.
tutela *nf* (*Jur*) guardianship; (*fig*: *protección*) protection, tutelage; (*fig*: *guía*) guidance; **bajo ~** in ward; **estar bajo ~ jurídica** (*niño*) to be a ward of court; **estar bajo la ~ de** (*amparo*) to be under the protection of; (*auspicios*) to be under the auspices of.
tutelado, -a *nm/f* (*Univ etc*) pupil; (*Jur*) ward.
tutelaje *nm* (*LAm*) = **tutela.**
tutelar 1 *adj* tutelary; **genio ~** tutelary genius.
2 [1a] *vt* (*proteger*) to protect, guard; (*guiar*) to advise, guide; (*vigilar*) to supervise, oversee.
tuteo *nm* addressing a person as 'tú', familiar usage; **se ha extendido mucho el ~** the use of 'tú' has greatly increased.
tutilimundi *nm* (*LAm*) everybody.
tutiplé(n): **a ~** *adv dar etc* freely; *repartir* haphazardly, without discernment; *comer etc* hugely, to excess.
tutor *nm* (**a**) (*Jur*) guardian; (*Univ*) tutor; **~ de curso** form master. (**b**) (*Agr*) prop, stake.
tutora *nf* (*Jur*) guardian; (*Univ*) tutor; **~ de curso** form mistress.
tutoría *nf* (**a**) (*Jur*) guardianship. (**b**) (*Univ*) tutorial, class.
tutorial *adj* tutorial.
tutorizar [1f] *vt* = **tutelar 2.**
tutú *nm* tutu.
tutuma *nf* (*And, Cono Sur*) (**a**) (‡: *cabeza*) nut‡, head; (*bollo*) bump; (*joroba*) hump; (*moretón*) bruise. (**b**) (*fruta*) *type of cucumber.*
tutumito *nm* (*And, CAm*) idiot.
tuturuto 1 *adj* (**a**) (*CAm, Carib, Méx*: *borracho*) drunk. (**b**) (*And, CAm, Carib*) (*tonto*) stupid; (*aturdido*) dumbfounded, stunned. **2** *nm* (*Cono Sur*: *chulo*) pimp.
tuve *etc V* **tener.**
tuyo *adj y pron* yours, of yours; (††, *a Dios*) thy, of thine; **es ~, es el ~** it is yours; **lo ~** (what is) yours, what belongs to you; **cualquier amigo ~** any friend of yours; **los ~s** (*frec*) your people, your relations, your family.
tuza *nf* (*LAm Zool*) mole.
TV *nf abr de* **televisión** television, TV.
TVE *nf abr de* **Televisión Española.**
tweed [twi] *nm* tweed.

U

U, u [u] *nf* (*letra*) U, u; ~ **doble** (*Méx*) w; **curva en** ~ hairpin bend.
U *abr de* **Universidad** university, univ., U.
u *conj* (*delante de* **o**~, **ho**~) or; **siete** ~ **ocho** seven or eight.
ualabi *nm* wallaby.
UAM *nf* (**a**) (*Esp*) *abr de* **Universidad Autónoma de Madrid.** (**b**) (*Méx*) *abr de* **Universidad Autónoma Metropolitana.**
ubérrimo *adj* exceptionally fertile, marvellously productive, very rich; (*LAm*) abundant.
ubicación *nf* (**a**) (*acto*) placing; siting. (**b**) (*lugar*) whereabouts; place, position, location, situation.
ubicado *adj* (**a**) **una tienda ubicada en la calle X** a shop situated in X street. (**b**) **bien ubicada, ubicadísima** (*Méx*) well located, in a desirable location.
ubicar [1g] **1** *vt* (*esp LAm*) (**a**) (*colocar*) to place, put, locate, situate; *edificio* to site.

(**b**) (*encontrar*) to find, locate; **no hemos podido** ~ **al jefe** we haven't been able to get hold of the boss; **a ver si logras** ~**lo** let's see if you can track it down.

(**c**) (*fig*: *instalar*) to instal in a place (*o* post *etc*), fix up with a job.

(**d**) (*fig*: *clasificar*) to classify, place, judge.

2 *vi* to be, be situated, be located; to lie, stand.

3 ubicarse *vr* (**a**) = **2.**

(**b**) (*orientarse*) to find one's way about; (*Cono Sur*: *fig*) to appreciate one's situation.

(**c**) (*LAm*: *en un puesto*) to get a job, fix o.s. up with a job; (*establecerse*) to settle in, establish o.s.
ubicuidad *nf* ubiquity; **el don de la** ~ the gift for being everywhere at once.
ubicuo *adj* ubiquitous.
ubre *nf* udder; teat.
ubrera *nf* (*Med*) thrush.
UBS *nfpl* (*Esp*) *abr de* **Unidades Básicas de Salud.**
UCD *nf* (*Pol*) *abr de* **Unión de Centro Democrático.**
UCE *nf* (**a**) (*Fin*) *abr de* **Unidad de Cuenta Europea** European Currency Unit, ECU. (**b**) *abr de* **Unión de Consumidores de España.**
ucedista 1 *adj*: **política** ~ policy of UCD, UCD policy. **2** *nmf* member of UCD.
UCI *nf abr de* **unidad de cuidados intensivos** intensive care unit, ICU.
UCM *nf* (*Esp*) *abr de* **Universidad Complutense de Madrid.**
-uco, -uca *V* **Aspects of Word Formation in Spanish 2.**
UCP *nf abr de* **unidad central de proceso** central processing unit, CPU.
Ucrania *nf* Ukraine.
ucranio, -a, ucraniano, -a *adj, nm/f* Ukrainian.
ucronía *nf* uchronia, imaginary time.
ucrónico *adj* uchronic, imaginary.
-ucho, -ucha *V* **Aspects of Word Formation in Spanish 2.**
uchuvito* *adj* (*And*) drunk, tight*.
Ud. *pron abr de* **usted** you.
-udo *V* **Aspects of Word Formation in Spanish 2.**
Uds. *pron abr de* **ustedes** you.
UDV *nf abr de* **unidad de despliegue visual** visual display unit, VDU.
UEI *nf abr de* **Unidad Especial de Intervención** *special force of the Guardia Civil.*
-uelo, -uela *V* **Aspects of Word Formation in Spanish 2.**
UEM *nf abr de* **unión económica y monetaria** economic and monetary union, EMU.
UEP *nf abr de* **Unión Europea de Pagos** European Payments Union, EPU.
UEPS *abr de* **último en entrar, primero en salir** last in, first out, LIFO.
UER *nf abr de* **Unión Europea de Radiodifusión** European Broadcasting Union, EBU.
uf *interj* (*calor, cansancio*) phew!; (*repugnancia*) ugh!
ufanamente *adv* proudly; cheerfully; exultantly; (*pey*) conceitedly; boastfully; smugly.
ufanarse [1a] *vr* to boast; to be vain, be conceited; ~ **con,** ~ **de** to boast of, pride o.s. on, be vain about; to glory in.
ufanía *nf* (**a**) (*orgullo*) pride; (*pey*) vanity, conceit; boastfulness. (**b**) (*Bot*) = **lozanía.**
ufano *adj* (**a**) (*orgulloso*) proud; (*alegre*) gay, cheerful; exultant; (*pey*: *vanidoso*) vain, conceited; (*jactancioso*) boastful; (*altivo*) overweening; (*satisfecho*) smug; **iba muy** ~ **en el nuevo coche** he was going along so proudly in his new car; **está muy** ~ **porque le han dado el premio** he is very proud that they have awarded him the prize.

(**b**) (*Bot*) = **lozano.**
ufología *nf* study of unidentified flying objects, ufology.
ufólogo, -a *nm/f* student of unidentified flying objects, ufologist.
Uganda *nf* Uganda.
ugandés, -esa *adj, nm/f* Ugandan.
ugetista 1 *adj*: **política** ~ policy of the UGT, UGT policy. **2** *nmf* member of the UGT.
UGT *nf* (*Esp*) *abr de* **Unión General de Trabajadores.**
UIT *nf abr de* **Unión Internacional para las Telecomunicaciones** International Telecommunications Union, ITU.
ujier *nm* usher; doorkeeper, attendant.
-ujo, -uja *V* **Aspects of Word Formation in Spanish 2.**
úlcera *nf* ulcer, sore; ~ **de decúbito** bedsore; ~ **duodenal** duodenal ulcer; ~ **gástrica** gastric ulcer.
ulceración *nf* ulceration.
ulcerar [1a] **1** *vt* to make sore, make a sore on, ulcerate. **2 ulcerarse** *vr* to ulcerate; to fester.
ulceroso *adj* ulcerous; full of sores, covered with sores.
ule *nm* (*CAm, Méx*) = **hule 1** (**a**).
ulerear [1a] *vt* (*Cono Sur*) *masa* to roll out.
ulero *nm* (*Cono Sur*) rolling pin.
Ulises *nm* Ulysses.
ulpo *nm* (*And, Cono Sur*) maize gruel.
ulterior *adj* (**a**) *lugar* farther, further. (**b**) *tiempo etc* later, subsequent; eventual.
ulteriormente *adv* later, subsequently.
ultimación *nf* completion, conclusion.
ultimador(a) *nm/f* (*LAm*) killer, murderer.
últimamente *adv* (**a**) (*por último*) lastly, finally. (**b**) (*en último caso*) as a last resort. (**c**) (*recientemente*) recently, lately. (**d**) ¡~! (*LAm*) well I'm damned!, that's the absolute end!
ultimar [1a] *vt* (**a**) (*terminar*) to finish, complete, conclude; *detalles, preparativos* to finalize; *acuerdo* to conclude; **lo tengo ultimado** I have it in the final stages.

(**b**) (*LAm*) *persona* (*rematar*) to finish off, give the coup de grâce to; (*matar*) to kill, murder.
ultimato *nm,* **ultimátum** *nm, pl* **ultimátums** ultimatum.
ultimizar [1f] *vt* = **ultimar.**
último 1 *adj* (**a**) (*en orden, tiempo*) (*final*) last; (*más reciente*) latest, most recent; (*de dos*) latter; **éste** ~, **éstos** ~**s** the latter; **el** ~ **día del mes** the last day of the month; **a** ~**s del mes** in the latter part of the month, towards the end of the month; **las últimas noticias** the latest news; **en estos** ~**s años** in recent years, in the last few years; **llegó el** ~ he arrived last, he came last, he was last; (*en carrera*) he came (in) last; **hablar el** ~ to speak last, (*fig*) have the last word, have the final say; **reírse el** ~ to have the last laugh; **ser el** ~ **en** + *infin* to be the last to + *infin*; **estar a lo** ~ **de** to be nearly at the end of, have nearly finished; **estar en las últimas** (*: *moribundo*) to be about to peg out ‡; (*pobrísimo*) to be down and out, be on one's last legs; (*casi falto de*) to be down to one's last little bit (of a stock *etc*); **está dando las últimas** it's on its last legs; **por**

~ lastly, finally; **por última vez** for the last time.

(**b**) (*lugar*) furthest, most remote; (*más al fondo*) back; (*más alto*) top, topmost; (*más bajo*) lowest, bottom; **en el ~ rincón del país** in the furthest corner of the country; **un asiento de última fila** a seat in the back row; **el equipo en última posición** the team in the lowest position, the bottom team; **viven en el ~ piso** they live on the top floor.

(**c**) (*fig: extremo*) final, extreme, last; utmost; **la última solución** the final solution; **el ~ remedio** the ultimate remedy; **en ~ caso** as a last resort, in the last resort; **decir la última palabra** to have the final say.

(**d**) (*Com*) *precio* lowest, bottom; **dígame lo ~, dígame el ~ precio** tell me what your lowest price is.

(**e**) (*fig*) *calidad* finest, best, superior.

(**f**) (*****) **estar** (*o* **vivir**) **a la última** to be thoroughly with it*, be utterly up-to-date; **vestido a la última** dressed in the latest style; **tienen un coche que es lo ~** they have the very latest thing in cars; **¡es lo ~!** it's the greatest!*, it's tremendous!*; (*pey*) this is the end!; **viven en un pueblucho que es lo ~** they live in a dump which is unbelievably awful*; **pedirme eso encima ya es lo ~** for him to ask that of me as well really is the limit.

2 *adv* (*LAm*): **ahora ~** lately, recently.

ultra (*Pol*) **1** *adj* extreme, extremist; ultra-conservative. **2** *nmf* (*esp* right-wing) extremist; ultra-conservative.

ultra... *pref* ultra..., extra...

ultracongelación *nf* (*Esp*) (deep-)freezing.

ultracongelado *adj* (*Esp*) (deep-)frozen.

ultracongelador *nm* (*Esp*) deep-freeze, freezer.

ultraconservador(a) *adj, nm/f* ultra-conservative.

ultracorto *adj* ultra-short.

ultraderecha *nf* (*Pol*) extreme right(-wing).

ultraderechista 1 *adj* extreme right(-wing). **2** *nmf* extreme right-winger.

ultrafino *adj* ultrafine.

ultraísmo *nm revolutionary poetic movement of the 1920s (imagist, surrealist etc)*.

ultrajador *adj*, **ultrajante** *adj* outrageous; offensive; insulting.

ultrajar [1a] *vt* (**a**) (*gen*) to outrage; (*ofender*) to offend; (*insultar*) to insult, revile, abuse. (**b**) (*liter*) to spoil, to crumple, disarrange.

ultraje *nm* outrage; insult.

ultrajoso *adj* outrageous; offensive; insulting.

ultraligero *nm* microlight (aircraft).

ultramar *nm* countries beyond the seas, foreign parts; **de ~, en ~** overseas; **los países de ~** the overseas countries; **productos venidos de ~** products from overseas, goods from abroad; **pasó 8 años en ~** he spent 8 years overseas.

ultramarino 1 *adj* overseas; foreign; (*Com*) imported. **2 : ~s** *nmpl* (*Esp*) (**a**) (*género*) (imported) groceries, foodstuffs; **tienda de ~s** = (**b**). (**b**) **un ~s** (*tienda*) a grocer's (shop), a grocery (*US*).

ultramoderno *adj* ultramodern.

ultramontanismo *nm* ultramontanism.

ultramontano *adj, nm* ultramontane.

ultranza 1 : a ~ *adv*: **luchar a ~** to fight to the death; **lo quiere hacer a ~** he wants to do it at all costs (*o* come what may, regardless of the difficulties); **paz a ~** peace at any price.

2 : a ~ *adj* all-out, extreme; **revolucionario a ~** out-and-out revolutionary, utterly uncompromising revolutionary.

ultrapotente *adj* extra powerful.

ultrarrápido *adj* extra fast.

ultrarrojo *adj* = **infrarrojo.**

ultrasecreto *adj* top secret.

ultrasensitivo *adj* ultrasensitive.

ultrasofisticado *adj arma* highly sophisticated.

ultrasónico *adj* ultrasonic.

ultrasonido *nm* (*Fís*) ultrasound.

ultratumba *nf* what lies beyond the grave; **la vida de ~** life beyond the grave, life in the next world; **una voz de ~** a voice from beyond the grave.

ultravioleta *adj invar* ultraviolet; **rayos ~** ultraviolet rays.

ulular [1a] *vi* (*animal, viento*) to howl, shriek; (*búho*) to hoot, screech.

ululato *nm* howl, shriek; hoot, screech.

ulluco *nm* (*And, Cono Sur*) manioc.

umbilical *adj* umbilical.

umbral 1 *nm* (**a**) (*de entrada*) threshold; **pasar** (*o* **traspasar**) **el ~ de uno** to set foot in sb's house.

(**b**) (*fig: comienzo*) threshold; first step, beginning; **~ de la pobreza** poverty line; **estar en los ~es de** to be on the threshold of, be on the verge of, be on the point of; **eso está en los ~es de lo imposible** that borders (*o* verges) on the impossible.

2 *atr*: **libro de nivel ~** basic level textbook, book for the beginner's stage.

umbralada *nf* (*And, Cono Sur*), **umbralado** *nm* (*And, Cono Sur*), **umbraladura** *nf* (*And*) threshold.

umbrío *adj*, **umbroso** *adj* shady.

UMI *nf abr de* **unidad de medicina intensiva** intensive care unit, ICU.

un, una 1 *art indef* a, (*delante de vocal y h muda*) an.

2 *adj* one; **la una** one o'clock; **¡a la una, a las dos, a las tres!** (*en subasta*) going, going, gone!; (*Dep*) ready, steady, go!

3 *nm* one.

unánime *adj* unanimous.

unánimemente *adv* unanimously.

unanimidad *nf* unanimity; **por ~** unanimously.

uncial *adj, nf* uncial.

unción *nf* (**a**) (*Med*) anointing. (**b**) (*Ecl y fig*) unction.

uncir [3b] *vt* to yoke.

undécimo *adj* eleventh.

UNED [u'neð] *nf* (*Esp Escol*) *abr de* **Universidad Nacional de Educación a Distancia** ≈ Open University.

ungido *adj* anointed; **el U~ del Señor** the Lord's Anointed.

ungir [3c] *vt* (**a**) (*Med*) to anoint, put ointment on, rub with ointment. (**b**) (*Ecl*) to anoint.

ungüento *nm* ointment, unguent; (*fig*) salve, balm.

ungulado 1 *adj* ungulate, hoofed. **2** *nm* ungulate, hoofed animal.

uni... *pref* uni..., one-..., single-...

únicamente *adv* only; solely.

unicameral *adj* (*Pol*) single-chamber.

unicameralismo *nm* system of single-chamber government.

unicelular *adj* unicellular, single-cell.

unicidad *nf* uniqueness; oneness.

único *adj* (**a**) (*solo*) only; sole, single, solitary; unique; **hijo ~** only child; **sistema de partido ~** one-party system, single-party system; **la única dificultad es que ...** the only difficulty is that ...; **fue el ~ sobreviviente** he was the sole survivor; **es el ~ ejemplar que existe** it is the only copy (*o* specimen) in existence; **es lo ~ que nos hacía falta** (*iró*) that's all we needed; **este ejemplar es ~** this specimen is unique.

(**b**) (*fig*) unique; unusual, extraordinary.

unicolor *adj* one-colour, all one colour.

unicornio *nm* unicorn.

unidad *nf* (**a**) (*cualidad*) unity; oneness; togetherness; **~ de acción** (*Liter*) unity of action; **~ de lugar** (*Liter*) unity of place.

(**b**) (*Mat, Mil, Téc etc*) unit; (*Ferro*) coach, wagon; **~ de cola** (*Aer*) tail unit; **~ de cuenta europea** European currency unit; **~ de cuidados intensivos** intensive care unit; **~ monetaria** monetary unit; **~ móvil** (*TV*) mobile unit; **~ vecinal de absorción de Toboso** overspill town for Toboso; **~ de vigilancia intensiva** intensive care unit; **~ de visualización** visual display unit.

(**c**) **nueve dólares (la) ~** (*Com*) nine dollars each.

(**d**) (*Inform*) **~ central de proceso** central processing unit; **~ de cinta** tape unit; **~ de control** control unit; **~ de disco** disk drive, disk unit; **~ de discos flexibles** floppy disk drive; **~ de entrada** input device; **~ de información** bit (of information); **~ periférica** peripheral device; **~ central de procesamiento** central processing unit; **~ de salida** output device.

unidimensional *adj* one-dimensional; (*fig*) flat; restricted, limited.

unidireccional *adj*: **calle ~** one-way street.

unido *adj* (**a**) (*juntado*) joined (*por* by), linked (*por* by).

(**b**) (*fig*) united; **una familia muy unida** a very united family; **mantenerse ~s** to remain united, maintain their (*etc*) unity, keep together.

unifamiliar *adj* single-family (*atr*).

unificación *nf* unification.

unificar [1g] *vt* to unite, unify.

uniformado 1 *adj* uniformed. **2** *nm* man in uniform, (*esp*) policeman.

uniformar [1a] *vt* (**a**) (*igualar*) to make uniform; to level up; to standardize, make the same. (**b**) *persona* to put into uniform, provide a uniform for.

uniforme 1 *adj* (*gen*) uniform; *superficie etc* level, even, smooth; *velocidad etc* uniform, steady; regular. **2** *nm* uniform; **~ de campaña, ~ de combate** battledress; **~ de gala** full-dress uniform.

uniformemente *adv* uniformly.
uniformidad *nf* (*V* **uniforme 1**) uniformity; levelness, evenness, smoothness; steadiness; regularity.
uniformización *nf* standardization.
uniformizar [1f] *vt* = **uniformar**.
unigénito *adj* (*Rel*) only begotten; **el U~** the Only Begotten Son.
unilateral *adj* unilateral, one-sided.
unilateralismo *nm* unilateralism.
unilateralmente *adv* unilaterally.
unión *nf* **(a)** (*acto*) union, uniting, joining; **en ~ de** with, together with; **la ~ hace la fuerza** united we stand.
(b) (*cualidad*) unity; closeness, togetherness.
(c) (*Com, Pol etc*) union; (*Jur*) union, marriage; **en ~ con** with, together with, accompanied by; **~ aduanera** customs union; **~ consensual** common-law marriage; **~ monetaria** monetary union; **U~ Panamericana** Pan-American Union; **U~ Soviética** Soviet Union; **U~ Sudafricana** Union of South Africa; **vivir en ~ libre con** to live with.
(d) (*Mec*) joint, union; (*t* **punto de ~**) junction (*entre* between).
unipersonal *adj* for one (person); single, individual.
unir [3a] **1** *vt* **(a)** *objetos, piezas* to join, unite; (*atar*) to tie (*o* fasten, bolt *etc*) together; *persona* to unite; *familias* to unite (by marriage); *compañías, intereses etc* to merge, join; to pool; *cualidades* to combine (*a* with); **les une una fuerte simpatía** they are bound by a strong affection, there are bonds of affection between them.
(b) *líquidos etc* to mix; *masa, salsa etc* to mix thoroughly, make smooth; to beat (up).
2 *vi* (*ingredientes*) to mix well, make a smooth mixture.
3 unirse *vr* **(a)** (*2 personas etc*) to join together, unite; (*compañías*) to merge, combine; **~ en matrimonio** to marry, be united in marriage.
(b) ~ a to join; **~ con** to unite with, merge with; **se unen las ramas por encima** the branches meet overhead.
(c) (*ingredientes*) to mix well, cohere.
unisex(o) *adj* unisex.
unísono *adj* unisonous, on the same tone; *voces etc* in unison; **al ~** on the same tone; (*fig*) in unison, with one voice, in harmony, harmoniously; **al ~ con** (*fig*) in tune with, in harmony with.
unitario 1 *adj* unitary; (*Ecl*) Unitarian. **2** *nm*, **unitaria** *nf* Unitarian.
unitarismo *nm* Unitarianism.
univalente *adj* univalent.
univalvo *adj* univalve.
universal *adj* (*gen*) universal; (*mundial*) world (*atr*), world-wide; **historia ~** world history; **de fama ~** known all over the world, internationally famous; **una especie de distribución ~** a species with a world-wide distribution.
universalidad *nf* universality.
universalizar [1f] *vt* to universalize, make universal; to extend widely, bring into general use.
universalmente *adv* universally; all over the world.
universiada *nf* university games, student games.
universidad *nf* university; **U~ Nacional de Educación a Distancia** ≃ Open University (*Brit*); **~ laboral** technical college, college of advanced technology; **~ popular** extra-mural classes, extension courses.
universitario 1 *adj* university (*atr*); academic. **2** *nm*, **universitaria** *nf* (*profesor*) university teacher; (*estudiante*) university student; (*graduado*) university graduate.
universo *nm* universe; world.
unívoco *adj* unanimous, single-minded.
uno 1 *adj* **(a)** (*gen*) one; (*idéntico*) one and the same, identical; **es todo ~, es ~ y lo mismo** it's all one, it's all the same; **Dios es ~** God is one; **la verdad es una** truth is one and indivisible.
(b) ~s (*t* **~s cuantos**) some, a few; about, *p.ej.* **~s 80 dólares** about 80 dollars.
(c) ¡hubo una (*enfático*) **gente!** there were so many people!, you should have seen the people!; **se dio una** (*enfático*) **hostia en la pierna** he banged his leg terribly.
2 *pron* **(a)** (*gen*) one; *persona* somebody; **~ mismo** oneself; **ha venido ~ que dice que te conoce** sb who says he knows you came; **~s que estaban allí protestaron** some (people) who were there protested; **los ~s dicen que sí y los otros que no** some say yes and some say no; **es mejor hacerlo ~ mismo** it's better to do it o.s.
(b) cada ~ each one, every one; **cada ~ a lo suyo** everyone should mind his own business; **había 3 manzanas para cada ~** there were 3 apples each.
(c) (*sujeto indef*) one, you; **~ nunca sabe qué hacer** one never knows what to do; **~ necesita descansar** a man has to rest, you have to rest.
(d) uno(s) a otro(s) each other, one another; **se detestan ~s a otros** they hate each other; **se miraban fijamente el ~ al otro** they stared at each other; **~ tras otro** one after the other.
(e) (*locuciones*) **~ a ~, ~ por ~, de ~ en ~, de ~ en fondo** in single file, one by one; **a una** all together; **juntarlo todo en ~** to put it all together; **estar en ~** to be at one; **no gustará a más de ~** there are quite a few who will not like this; **una de dos** either one thing or the other; the choice is simple, it's a straight choice; **~ con otro salen a 3 dólares** on an average they work out at 3 dollars each; **el ~ y el otro están locos** they're both mad; **ser ~ de tantos** to be run of the mill; **para mí es ~ de tantos** so far as I'm concerned he's just one of many; in my view he's a very ordinary sort; **salen una que otra vez** they go out from time to time; **lo ~ por lo otro** it comes to the same thing, what you lose on the swings you gain on the roundabouts.
uno-equis-dos *nm* (*1-X-2*) (*fig*) football pool(s).
untadura *nf* **(a)** (*acto*) smearing, dabbing, rubbing; greasing; spreading. **(b)** (*Med*) ointment; (*Mec etc*) grease, oil. **(c)** (*mancha*) mark, smear, dab.
untar [1a] **1** *vt* **(a)** to smear, dab, rub (*con, de* with); (*Med*) to anoint, rub (*con, de* with); (*Mec etc*) to grease, oil; **~ su pan en la salsa** to dip one's bread in the gravy, soak one's bread in the gravy; **~ los dedos de tinta** to smear one's fingers with ink; **~ el pan con mantequilla** to spread butter on one's bread, put butter on one's bread.
(b) (**: sobornar*) to bribe, grease the palm of.
2 untarse *vr* **(a) ~ con, ~ de** to smear o.s. with.
(b) (*Fin**) to take a rake-off*, get a cut in the profits; to line one's pockets.
unto *nm* **(a)** (*materia blanda*) soft substance; (*Med*) ointment, unguent; (*Zool*) grease, (animal) fat. **(b)** (*Cono Sur: betún*) shoe-polish.
untuosidad *nf* greasiness, oiliness; stickiness.
untuoso *adj* greasy, oily, sticky.
untura *nf* = **untadura**.
uña *nf* **(a)** (*Anat*) (*de la mano*) nail, fingernail; (*del pie*) toenail; (*Zool etc*) claw; **~ encarnada** ingrowing nail; **ser ~ y carne** to be inseparable, be as thick as thieves; **largo de ~s** light-fingered, thieving; **estar de ~s con uno** to be at daggers drawn with sb; **caer en las ~s de uno** to fall into sb's clutches; **comerse las ~s** to bite one's nails; (*fig*) to get very impatient, get furious; (*LAm: pobre*) to be terribly poor; **se dejó las uñas en ese trabajo** he wore his fingers to the bone at that job; **enseñar** (*o* **mostrar, sacar**) **las ~s** (*t fig*) to show one's claws; **tener las ~s afiladas** to be light-fingered.
(b) (*pezuña*) hoof; **~ de caballo** (*Bot*) coltsfoot; **escapar a ~ de caballo** to ride off at full speed; **~ de vaca** (*Culin*) cow heel.
(c) (*de alacrán*) sting.
(d) (*Téc*) claw; nailpuller.
(e) (*de ancla*) fluke.
uñada *nf* nail mark; scratch.
uñalarga *nmf* (*LAm*) thief.
uñarada *nf* = **uñada**.
uñero *nm* **(a)** (*panadizo*) whitlow. **(b)** (*uña encarnada*) ingrowing nail. **(c)** (*Tip*) thumb-notch; **2 tomos con ~** 2 volumes with thumb index.
uñeta *nf* (*Cono Sur Mús*) plectrum.
uñetas *nmf invar* (*And, CAm*) thief.
uñetear [1a] *vt* (*Cono Sur*) to steal.
uñilargo *nm* (*And*), **uñón** *nm* (*And*) thief.
UOE *nf* (*Esp Mil*) *abr* de **Unidad de Operaciones Especiales**.
UPA *nf abr de* **Unión Panamericana** Pan-American Union, PAU.
upa[1] *nm* (*And*) idiot.
upa[2] *interj* up, up!
UPAE *nf abr de* **Unión Postal de las Américas y España**.
upar* [1a] *vt* **(a)** to lift up, lift in one's arms. **(b)** (*LAm*) = **aupar**.
uperización *nf* UHT treatment.
uperizado *adj*: **leche uperizada** UHT milk.
UPU *nf abr de* **Unión Postal Universal** Universal Postal Union, UPU.
Urales *nmpl* (*t* **Montes ~**) Urals.
uranio *nm* uranium; **~ enriquecido** enriched uranium.
Urano *nm* Uranus.

urbanícola *nmf* city-dweller.
urbanidad *nf* courtesy, politeness, urbanity.
urbanificar [1g] *vt* = **urbanizar.**
urbanismo *nm* (**a**) (*planificación*) town planning; (*desarrollo*) urban development. (**b**) (*Carib*) real-estate development.
urbanista *nmf* town planner.
urbanístico *adj* town-planning (*atr*); urban, city (*atr*).
urbanita *nmf* city dweller.
urbanizable *adj*: **tierras ~s** building land; **zona no ~** green belt, land designated as not for building.
urbanización *nf* (**a**) (*acto*) urbanization; urban development. (**b**) (*colonia etc*) housing estate, residential development.
urbanizado *adj* built-up.
urbanizadora *nf* property development company.
urbanizar [1f] *vt* (**a**) *tierra* to develop, build on, urbanize; to lay out and prepare for city development. (**b**) *persona* to civilize.
urbano *adj* (**a**) (*de la ciudad*) urban, town (*atr*), city (*atr*). (**b**) (*cortés*) courteous, polite, urbane.
urbe *nf* large city, metropolis; (*capital*) capital city; (*Esp*) **La U~** Madrid, the Capital.
urbícola *nmf* city dweller.
urco *nm* (*And, Cono Sur*) ram; (*****) alpaca.
urdimbre *nf* (**a**) (*en tela*) warp. (**b**) (*fig*) scheme, intrigue.
urdir [3a] *vt* (**a**) *tela* to warp. (**b**) (*fig*) to plot, scheme for, contrive.
urdu *nm* Urdu.
urea *nf* urea.
urente *adj* (*Med etc*) burning, stinging.
uréter *nm* ureter.
uretra *nf* urethra.
urgencia *nf* (**a**) (*gen*) urgency; (*presión*) pressure; (*prisa*) haste, rush; **con toda ~** with the utmost urgency, posthaste; **de ~** urgent, pressing; (*Correos*) express; **pedir algo con ~** to press for sth.
(**b**) (*emergencia*) emergency; **medida de ~** emergency measure; **salida de ~** emergency exit.
(**c**) (*necesidad*) pressing need; **en caso de ~** in case of necessity, if the need arises; **acudió a mí en una ~ de dinero** he came to me with a pressing need for money.
(**d**) **urgencias** *pl* (*Med*) casualty department.
urgente *adj* urgent; pressing; *exigencia etc* pressing, imperative, insistent; **carta ~** express letter; **pedido ~** rush order.
urgentemente *adv* urgently; imperatively, insistently.
urgir [3c] *vi* to be urgent, be pressing; **urge el dinero** the money is urgently needed; **me urge la respuesta** the reply is required with the utmost urgency; **el tiempo urge** time presses, time is short; **me urge terminarlo** I must finish it as soon as I can, I must finish it with the utmost speed; **me urge partir** I have to leave at once; **'Úrgeme vender: dos gatos ...'** (*anuncio*) 'Must be sold: two cats.'
úrico *adj* uric.
urinario 1 *adj* urinary. **2** *nm* urinal, public lavatory, comfort station (*US*).
urna *nf* (*gen*) urn; (*de cristal*) glass case; (*Pol etc*: *t* **~ electoral**) ballot-box; **al cierre de las ~s** when voting closed; **acudir a las ~s** to vote, go and vote, go to the polls.
uro *nm* aurochs.
urogallo *nm* capercaillie.
urogenital *adj* urogenital.
urología *nf* urology.
urólogo, -a *nm/f* urologist.
urpo *nm* (*Cono Sur*) = **ulpo.**
urraca *nf* (**a**) (*Orn*) magpie. (**b**) (*****) (*habladora*) chatterbox; (*chismosa*) gossip.
URSS [urs] *nf abr de* **Unión de Repúblicas Socialistas Soviéticas** Union of Socialist Soviet Republics, *USSR.*
ursulina *nf* (**a**) (*Rel*) Ursuline nun. (**b**) (*Esp**) goody-goody*.
urticaria *nf* urticaria, nettlerash.
Uruguay *nm*: **El ~** Uruguay.
uruguayismo *nm* word (*o* phrase *etc*) peculiar to Uruguay.
uruguayo, -a *adj, nm/f* Uruguayan.
USA *atr* United States, American; **dos aviones ~** two American planes.
usado *adj sello etc* used; *ropa* worn; secondhand; **muy ~** worn out, old, shabby.
usagre *nm* (*Med*) impetigo; (*Vet*) mange.
usanza *nf* usage, custom; **a ~ india, a ~ de los indios** according to the custom of the Indians, in the Indian fashion.
usar [1a] **1** *vt* (**a**) (*utilizar*) to use, make use of; *ropa* to wear; **sin ~** unused; **botella de ~ y tirar** disposable bottle.
(**b**) **~** + *infin* (*soler*) to be accustomed to + *infin*, to be in the habit of + *ger.*
2 *vi*: **~ de** to use, make use of.
3 usarse *vr* (*gen*) to be used, be in use; (*ropa*) to be worn; to be in fashion; (*práctica*) to be the custom; **la chistera ya no se usa** top hats are not worn nowadays, top hats are no longer in fashion.
usina *nf* (**a**) (*LAm*) factory, plant. (**b**) (*Cono Sur*: *de electricidad*) power-plant; (*de gas*) gasworks; (*de tranvías*) tram depot.
uslero *nm* (*Cono Sur*) rolling-pin.
USO ['uso] *nf* (*Esp*) *abr de* **Unión Sindical Obrera.**
uso *nm* (**a**) (*empleo*) use; **de ~ corriente** in everyday use; **objeto de ~ personal** article for personal use; **de ~ externo** (*Med*) for external application; **de un solo ~** disposable, to be used once only; **estar fuera de ~** to be out of use, be obsolete; **estar en ~** to be in use; **estar en buen ~** to be in good condition; **estar en el ~ de la palabra** to be speaking, have the floor; **hacer ~ de** to make use of; **hacer ~ de la palabra** to speak; **retirar algo del ~** to withdraw sth from service.
(**b**) (*Mec etc*) wear, wear and tear; **~ y desgaste** wear and tear; **deteriorado por el ~** worn.
(**c**) (*costumbre*) custom, usage; (*estilo, moda*) fashion, style; **es un ~ muy antiguo** it is a very ancient custom; **al ~** as is customary, in keeping with custom; **con bigotes al ~** with the usual sort of moustache, with the sort of moustache which was then fashionable; **un hombre al ~** an ordinary man; **al ~ de** in the style of, in the fashion of; **un libro hecho al ~ de los principiantes** a book written for beginners.
usted, *pl* **ustedes** *pron pers* (*gen abr* **Vd., Vds.**) you (*polite o formal address*); **el coche de ~** your car; **mi coche y el de ~** my car and yours; **para ~** for you; **sin ~** without you; **¡a ~!** (*dando gracias*) thank you!
usual *adj* usual, customary; ordinary; regular.
usualmente *adv* usually; ordinarily, regularly.
usuario, -a *nm/f* user; (*de biblioteca*) reader; **~ de la vía pública** road user; **~ final** end-user.
usufructo *nm* usufruct, use; **~ vitalicio** life interest (*de* in).
usufructuario, -a *nm/f* usufructuary.
usura *nf* usury; (*fig*) profiteering, racketeering.
usurario *adj* usurious.
usurear [1a] *vi* to lend money at an exorbitant rate of interest; (*fig*) to profiteer, run a racket.
usurero, -a *nm/f* usurer; (*fig*) profiteer, racketeer.
usurpación *nf* usurpation; seizure, illegal taking; (*fig*) encroachment (*de* upon), inroads (*de* into).
usurpador, -a *nm/f* usurper.
usurpar [1a] *vt corona, derechos etc* to usurp; *tierra etc* to seize, take illegally; (*fig*) to encroach upon, make inroads into.
usuta *nf* (*And*) = **ojota.**
utensilio *nm* tool, implement; (*Culin*) utensil; **~s de cirujano** surgeon's instruments; **~s para escribir** writing materials; **~s para pescar** fishing tackle; **~s de pintor** painter's materials; **con los ~s de su oficio** with the tools of his craft, with the equipment of his trade.
uterino *adj* uterine; **hermanos ~s** children born of the same mother; *V* **furor.**
útero *nm* womb, uterus; **~ alquilado, ~ de alquiler** surrogate motherhood.
útil 1 *adj* (**a**) (*gen*) useful; (*servible*) usable, serviceable; handy; **las plantas ~es para el hombre** the plants which are useful to man; **el coche es viejo pero todavía está ~** the car is old but it is still serviceable; **es muy ~ tenerlo aquí cerca** it's very handy having it here close by; **¿en qué puedo serle ~?** can I do anything for you?, can I be of any help?
(**b**) **día ~** working day, weekday.
(**c**) **~ para el servicio** (*Mil*) *persona* fit for military service, *vehículo etc* operational.
2 ~es *nmpl* tools, implements; tackle, equipment; **~es de chimenea** fire irons; **~es de labranza** agricultural implements.
utilería *nf* (*Cono Sur, Méx Teat*) properties, props*.
utilidad *nf* (**a**) (*cualidad de útil*) usefulness, utility; (*provecho*) benefit. (**b**) (*Com, Fin etc*) profit, benefit; **~es ocasionales** windfall profits; **~es** profits, earnings; **~es líquidas** net profits. (**c**) (*Inform*) utility.
utilitario 1 *adj* (**a**) (*gen*) utilitarian. (**b**) *coche, ropa etc*

utility (*atr*). **2** *nm* (**a**) (*Inform*) utility. (**b**) (*Aut*) small car, compact car (*US*).
utilitarismo *nm* utilitarianism.
utilitarista *nmf* utilitarian.
utilizable *adj* (*gen*) usable; serviceable; (*disponible*) fit for use, ready to use; (*Téc*) *residuos* reclaimable, useful.
utilización *nf* use, utilization; (*Tec*) reclamation.
utilizar [1f] *vt* to use, make use of, utilize; *fuerzas, recursos etc* to harness; (*Tec*) *residuos* to reclaim.
útilmente *adv* usefully.
utillaje *nm* (set of) tools; tackle, equipment.
utillero *nm* (plumber's *etc*) mate.
utopía *nf*, **utopia** *nf* Utopia.
utópico *adj* Utopian.
utopista *adj, nmf* Utopian.
utrículo *nm* utricle.
UV *adj abr de* **ultravioleta** ultraviolet, UV.
UVA *nf abr de* **unidad vecinal de absorción**.
uva *nf* (**a**) grape; ~ **blanca** white grape; ~ **de Corinto** currant; ~ **crespa,** ~ **espina** gooseberry; ~**s del diablo** (*Bot*) nightshade; ~ **de gato** (*Bot*) stonecrop; ~**s de mesa** dessert grapes; ~ **moscatel** muscatel grape; ~ **pasa** raisin; ~**s verdes** (*fig*) sour grapes; **de ~s a peras** very occasionally, once in a blue moon; **ir de ~s a peras** to switch the subject for no reason; **entrar a por ~s** (*fig*) to take the plunge; **estar de mala ~** (*Esp**) to be in a bad mood; **estar de mala ~ con uno** (*Esp**) to have it in for sb; **estar hecho una ~** to be drunk as a lord. (**b**) (*****) (*vino*) wine; (*bebida*) drink (*in general*). (**c**) (*Cono Sur*: *beso*) kiss. (**d**) **las doce ~s** twelve grapes eaten at midnight on New-Year's Eve; (*fig*) New-Year's Eve, New Year.
uve *nf* the (name of the) letter *v*; ~ **doble** the (name of the) letter *w*; **de forma de** ~ V-shaped; **escote en** ~ V-neck.
UVI ['uβi] *nf abr de* **unidad de vigilancia intensiva** intensive care unit, ICU.
úvula *nf* uvula.
uvular *adj* uvular.
uxoricidio *nm* wife-murder.
-uzo, -uza *V* **Aspects of Word Formation in Spanish 2**.

V

V, v ['uβe, (*LAm*) be'korta] *nf* (*letra*) V,v; ~ **doble** (*Esp*), **doble** ~ (*LAm*) W; ~ **de la victoria** V for victory; victory sign, V-sign; **escote en** ~ V-neck.
V. (**a**) *abr de* **Usted** you. (**b**) *abr de* **Visto** approved, passed, OK.
v. (**a**) (*Elec*) *abr de* **voltio(s)** volt(s), V. (**b**) *abr de* **ver, véase** vide, see, v. (**c**) (*Liter*) *abr de* **verso** line, l.
V.A. *abr de* **Vuestra Alteza** Your Highness.
va *etc V* **ir.**
vaca *nf* (**a**) (*Zool*) cow; ~ **de leche,** ~ **lechera** dairy cow, milking cow; (*LAm*: *fig*) good business, profitable deal; ~ **marina** manatee, sea cow; ~ **sagrada** (*t fig*) sacred cow; ~ **de San Antón** ladybird, ladybug (*US*); (**los años de**) **las ~s flacas** the lean years; (**los años de**) **las ~s gordas** the fat years, the boom years; **pasar las ~s gordas** (*fig*) to have a grand time of it.
(**b**) (*Culin*: *carne de vaca*) beef; (*cuero*) cowhide.
(**c**) (*LAm*) enterprise with profits on a pro rata basis.
(**d**) **hacer**(**se**) **la** ~ (*And*) to play truant, play hooky (*US*).
vacaburra* *nf* insult.
vacación *nf* vacation; **vacaciones** holiday(s), vacation; **vacaciones escolares** school holidays; **vacaciones pagadas, vacaciones retribuidas** holidays with pay; **estar de vacaciones** to be (away) on holiday; **hacer vacaciones** to take a day off; **marcharse de vacaciones** to go off on holiday.
vacacional *adj* vacation (*atr*), holiday (*atr*); **período** ~ holiday period.
vacacionista *nmf* holidaymaker, vacationer (*US*).
vacada *nf* herd of cows.
vacaje *nm* (*Cono Sur*) cows, cattle; herd of cows; (*Méx*) herd of beef cows.
vacante 1 *adj* vacant, empty, unoccupied; *puesto* vacant. **2** *nf* (**a**) vacancy, place, (unfilled) post; **proveer una** ~ to fill a post. (**b**) (*LAm*: *asiento*) empty seat.
vacar [1g] *vi* (**a**) (*puesto*) to fall vacant, become vacant; to remain unfilled.
(**b**) (*persona*) to cease work; to be idle.
(**c**) ~ **a,** ~ **en** to attend to, engage in, devote o.s. to.
(**d**) ~ **de** to lack, be without.
vacarí *adj* cowhide (*atr*).
vaccinio *nm* (*Esp*) bilberry; blueberry (*US*).
vaciadero *nm* (**a**) (*desaguadero*) sink, drain; sump. (**b**) (*vertedero*) rubbish tip, dumping ground.
vaciado 1 *adj* (**a**) *estatua etc* cast in a mould; *herramienta* hollow-ground; ~ **a troquel** die-cast. (**b**) (*Méx**: *estupendo*) great*, terrific*. **2** *nm* (**a**) (*objeto*) cast, mould(ing); ~ **de yeso** plaster cast. (**b**) (*acto*) hollowing out; excavation. (**c**) ~ **rápido** (*Aer*) jettisoning.
vaciar [1c] **1** *vt* (**a**) *recipiente* to empty (out); *vaso etc* to drain; *contenido* to empty out; *líquido* (*verter*) to pour, pour away; to run off; (*beber*) to drink up; (*Aer etc*) to jettison; **vació los bolsillos en la mesa** he emptied out his pockets on the table; **vació la leche en un vaso** he poured (*o* emptied) the milk into a glass; **lo vació todo sobre su cabeza** he poured the lot over his head.
(**b**) *madera, piedra etc* to hollow out; *estatua etc* to cast.
(**c**) *cuchillo etc* to grind, sharpen.
(**d**) *tema, teoría* to expound at length.
(**e**) *texto* to copy out.
2 *vi* (*río*) to flow, empty, run (*en* into).
3 vaciarse *vr* (**a**) to empty.
(**b**) (*: *t* ~ **por la lengua**) to blab, spill the beans*.
vaciedad *nf* (**a**) (*estado*) emptiness. (**b**) (*fig*) silliness; piece of nonsense; **~es** nonsense, rubbish.
vacila* *nm* tease, joker.
vacilación *nf* hesitancy, hesitation, vacillation; **sin vacilaciones** unhesitatingly.
vacilada* *nf* (*Méx*) (**a**) (*borrachera*) spree, binge*. (**b**) (*chiste*) joke; (*chiste verde*) dirty joke; **de** ~ as a joke, (just) for a laugh. (**c**) (*truco*) trick.
vacilante *adj* (**a**) *mano, paso* unsteady; *mueble* wobbly, tottery; *habla* faltering, halting; *memoria* uncertain. (**b**) *luz* flickering. (**c**) (*fig*) hesitant, uncertain, vacillating; indecisive, dithery.
vacilar [1a] **1** *vt* (**a**) (*Carib, Méx**: *burlarse*) to make fun of, tease.
(**b**) (*CAm**: *engañar*) to trick.
(**c**) (*) to mess about, make difficulties for; **¡no me vaciles!** stop messing me about!
2 *vi* (**a**) (*mueble etc*) to be unsteady; to wobble, rock, move, shake; (*persona*) to totter; to reel, stagger; to stumble; (*fig*: *moralidad etc*) to be indecisive, be collapsing; (*habla*) to falter; (*memoria*) to fail.
(**b**) (*luz*) to flicker.
(**c**) (*fig*) to hesitate, waver, vacillate; to hang back; **sin** ~ unhesitatingly; ~ **en** + *infin* to hesitate to + *infin*; ~ **entre dos posibilidades** to hesitate between two possibilities; **es un hombre que vacila mucho** he is a very indecisive man, he is a man who dithers a lot; **no vaciles en decírmelo** don't hesitate to tell me about it.
(**d**) (*fig*: *variar*) ~ **entre** to vary between; **un sabor que vacila entre agradable y desagradable** a taste which varies between nice and nasty, a taste which ranges from nice to nasty.
(**e**) ~ **con uno** (*: *guasearse*) to tease sb, take the mickey out of sb‡.
(**f**) ~ **con uno** (*: *hablar*) to talk pointlessly to sb, bore sb with one's talk.
(**g**) (*: *fachendear*) to talk big*, show off, swank*.
(**h**) (*CAm, Carib, Méx*‡) (*emborracharse*) to get plastered‡; (*ir de juerga*) to go on a spree; (*bromear*) to lark about*, have fun.
vacile* *nm* (**a**) (*duda*) hesitation. (**b**) (*guasa*) teasing, amusing talk; **estar de** ~ to chat, indulge in teasing talk. (**c**) (*guasón*) tease, joker.
vacilón* 1 *adj* (**a**) (*guasón*) teasing, jokey; (*CAm, Méx*) fun-loving; **estar** ~ to be in a jokey mood. (**b**) (*: *fachendón*) swanky*, stuck-up*. **2** *nm* (**a**) tease, joker. (**b**) poser*, show-off*. (**c**) (*Méx*) reveller, merrymaker; **andar de** ~ to be out on the town. (**d**) (*CAm, Méx*: *juerga*) party, revels; fun.
vacío 1 *adj* (**a**) (*gen*) empty; *puesto etc* vacant, unoccupied; unfilled; *piso* unfurnished; *papel* blank; ~ **de todo contenido serio** empty of any serious contents, devoid of any serious purpose; **el teatro estaba medio** ~ the theatre was half empty; **irse con las manos vacías** to leave empty-handed.
(**b**) (*fig*) (*insustancial*) insubstantial; (*superficial*) superficial; *charla etc* light, idle, frivolous; *esfuerzo* vain, useless.
(**c**) (*fig*) (*vanidoso*) vain; (*orgulloso*) proud.
(**d**) (*fig*: *ocioso*) idle, unemployed.
(**e**) **pan** ~ (*And, CAm, Carib*) bread alone, just bread, bread by itself.
2 *nm* (*gen*) emptiness; void; (*Fís*) vacuum; (*un* ~) empty space, gap; vacant place; (*hueco*) hollow; (*Anat*) side, flank, ribs; ~ **legislativo** gap in legislation; ~ **político** political vacuum; **han dejado un** ~ **para el nombre** they have left a space for the name; **se nota ahora un gran** ~ **en la familia** one is conscious now of a big gap in the family; **el libro llenará un** ~ the book will fill a gap; **empaquetado al** ~, **envasado al** ~ vacuum-packed; **el camión volvió de** ~ the lorry came back empty; **lo pedí pero tuve que marcharme de** ~ I asked for it but had to go

away empty-handed; **caer en el** ~ to fail, be ineffective, produce no result; **dar un golpe en** ~ to miss, fail to connect; **esta viga parece que está en el** ~ this beam seems to be unsupported, this beam seems to rest on nothing at all; **marchar en** ~ (*Mec*) to tick over; **tener un** ~ **en el estómago** to feel hungry; **hacer el** ~ **a uno** to send sb to Coventry, pretend that sb does not exist; to ignore sb.

vacuidad *nf* (**a**) emptiness. (**b**) (*fig*) vacuity; superficiality, frivolity; empty-headedness.

vacuna *nf* (**a**) (*sustancia*) vaccine; ~ **antigripal** flu vaccine. (**b**) (*LAm*: *acto*) vaccination.

vacunación *nf* (**a**) vaccination. (**b**) (*fig*) preparation; inuring; forearming.

vacunar [1a] **1** *vt* (**a**) (*Med*) to vaccinate (*contra* against). (**b**) (*fig*: *preparar*) to prepare; (*habituar*) to inure; (*prevenir*) to forearm. **2 vacunarse** *vr* to get (oneself) vaccinated.

vacuno 1 *adj* bovine; cow (*atr*); **ganado** ~ cattle. **2** *nm* (*ganado*) cattle; **carne de** ~ beef.

vacuo *adj* (**a**) (*vacío*) empty; vacant. (**b**) (*fig*) vacuous; superficial, frivolous, empty-headed.

vade *nm* (*Esp Escuela etc*) satchel, case.

vadeable *adj* (**a**) (*lit*) fordable, which can be forded. (**b**) (*fig*) not impossible, not insuperable.

vadear [1a] **1** *vt* (**a**) *río* to ford; *agua* to wade through, wade across.

(**b**) (*fig*) *dificultad* to surmount, get round, overcome.

(**c**) (*fig*) *persona* to sound out.

2 *vi* to wade; **cruzar un río vadeando** to wade across a river; **llegar a tierra vadeando** to wade ashore.

vademécum *nm, pl* **vademécums** (**a**) (*libro*) vademecum. (**b**) (*Escuela etc*) satchel, schoolbag.

vadera *nf* wide ford.

vado *nm* (**a**) (*de río*) ford. (**b**) (*Esp Aut*) garage entrance; (*letrero*) '~ **permanente**' 'Garage Entrance', 'Keep Clear'. (**c**) (*fig*: *salida*) way out, solution, expedient; **no hallar** ~ to see no way out, find no solution; **tentar el** ~ to look into possible solutions. (**d**) (*fig*: *respiro*) respite.

vagabundaje *nm* vagrancy.

vagabundear [1a] *vi* (*errar*) to wander, roam, rove; (*haraganear*) to loaf, idle, bum (*US*).

vagabundeo *nm* wandering, roving; tramp's life; loafing, idling, bumming (*US*).

vagabundo 1 *adj* (*errante*) wandering, roving; (*pey*) vagrant; vagabond; *perro* stray. **2** *nm*, **vagabunda** *nf* wanderer, rover; (*pey*) vagrant; vagabond, tramp, bum (*US*).

vagación *nf* (*Mec*) free play.

vagamente *adv* vaguely.

vagamundería *nf* (*LAm*) idleness, laziness.

vagamundero *adj* (*LAm*) idle, lazy.

vagancia *nf* (**a**) (*vagabundaje*) vagrancy. (**b**) (*gandulería*) idleness, laziness.

vagante *adj* (**a**) wandering, vagrant. (**b**) (*Mec*) free, loose.

vagar 1 [1h] *vi* (**a**) (*errar*) to wander (about), roam, rove; (*rondar*) to prowl about; (*pasearse*) to saunter up and down, wander about the streets; (*entretenerse*) to loiter; (*gandulear*) to idle, loaf, laze about; ~ **como alma en pena** to wander about like a lost soul.

(**b**) (*Mec*) to be free, be loose, move about.

2 *nm* (*tiempo libre*) leisure, free time; (*pereza*) idleness; (*calma*) lack of anxiety, freedom from worry; **andar de** ~ to be at leisure; to feel at ease.

vagido *nm* baby's first cry, cry of new-born baby.

vagina *nf* vagina.

vaginal *adj* vaginal.

vago 1 *adj* (**a**) (*gen*) vague; (*indistinto*) ill-defined, indistinct; indeterminate; (*Arte, Fot*) blurred.

(**b**) (*errabundo*) roving, wandering.

(**c**) (*gandul*) lazy, slack; (*poco fiable*) unreliable; (*ocioso*) idle, unemployed; *objeto* idle, unused; *espacio etc* empty.

(**d**) **en** ~ *mantenerse en pie etc* unsteadily; (*sin apoyo*) unsupported; *esforzarse* in vain; aimlessly, pointlessly; **dar golpes en** ~ to flail about, beat the air.

2 *nm* (**a**) (*vagabundo*) tramp, vagrant; (*pobre*) down-and-out.

(**b**) (*gandul*) idler, slacker; unreliable person; (*inútil*) useless individual, dead loss; **hacer el** ~ to loaf around.

vagón *nm* (*de pasajeros*) coach, carriage, car; (*de mercancías*) truck, wagon; car, van; ~ **cisterna**, ~ **tanque** tanker, tank wagon; ~ **de cola** guard's-van; (*fig*) rear, tail-end; ~ **directo** through carriage; ~ **de equipajes** luggage-van; ~ **de ganado,** ~ **de hacienda** (*Cono Sur*), ~ **de reja** (*Cono Sur*) cattle-truck; ~ **de mercancías** goods van, freight-car (*US*); ~ **mirador** observation car; ~ **postal** mailcoach, mailcar (*US*); ~ **de primera** first-class carriage; ~ **de segunda** second-class carriage; ~ **restaurante** dining-car; ~ **tolva** hopper.

vagonada *nf* truckload, wagonload.

vagoneta *nf* light truck.

vaguada *nf* watercourse, stream bed.

vaguear [1a] *vi* = **vagar 1.**

vaguedad *nf* (**a**) (*cualidad*) vagueness; indistinctness; indeterminacy. (**b**) (*una* ~) vague remark; woolly idea; **hablar sin** ~**es** to get straight to the point, speak with precision.

vaguería *nf* laziness, slackness; unreliability.

vaguitis* *nf* (*Esp*) congenital idleness.

vaharada *nf* (*soplo*) puff, gust of breath; (*olor*) whiff, reek; smell.

vahear [1a] *vi* (*echar vapor*) to steam; (*humear*) to fume, give off fumes, smoke; (*oler*) to whiff, reek, smell.

vahído *nm* dizzy spell, blackout.

vaho *nm* (**a**) (*vapor*) vapour, steam; (*en cristal etc*) mist, condensation; (*Quím etc*) fumes; (*aliento*) breath; (*olor*) whiff, reek, smell. (**b**) ~**s** (*Med*) inhalation.

vaina 1 *nf* (**a**) (*de espada etc*) sheath, scabbard; (*de herramienta*) sheath, case; (*de cartucho*) case.

(**b**) (*Bot*) (*de guisante etc*) pod; (*de nuez etc*) husk, shell; ~**s** (*judías*) green beans.

(**c**) (*pega*) problem, snag; (*LAm**: *molestia*) nuisance, bother; **¡qué** ~**!** what a nuisance!

(**d**) (*And*: *chiripa*) fluke, piece of luck.

(**e**) (*Cono Sur*: *estafa*) swindle.

(**f**) **echar** ~ (*Carib****) to screw***, fuck***.

2 *nm* (*) twit*, nitwit*.

3 *adj* (*LAm*) annoying.

vainica *nf* (*Cos*) hemstitch.

vainilla *nf* vanilla.

vainillina *nf* vanillin.

vainita *nf* (*LAm*) green bean.

vaivén *nm* (**a**) (*ir y venir*) to-and-fro movement, oscillation; (*mecerse*) rocking, backward and forward movement; (*balanceo*) swing(ing), sway(ing); (*sacudidas*) lurch(ing).

(**b**) (*de tráfico etc*) coming and going, constant movement.

(**c**) (*fig*: *de la suerte*) change of fortune; **vaivenes** ups and downs, vicissitudes.

(**d**) (*fig*: *Pol etc*) swing, seesaw, violent change of opinion.

vaivenear [1a] *vt* to oscillate; to rock, move backwards and forwards; to swing, sway.

vajear [1a] *vt* (*CAm, Carib, Méx*) (*culebra*) to fascinate, hypnotize; (*hechizar*) to bewitch; (*seducir*) to win over by flattery, seduce.

vajilla *nf* (*gen*) crockery, china; dishes; (*una* ~) service, set of dishes; ~ **de oro** gold plate; ~ **de porcelana** chinaware; **lavar la** ~ to wash up.

valdiviano 1 *adj* of Valdivia. **2** *nm*, **valdiviana** *nf* native (*o* inhabitant) of Valdivia; **los** ~**s** the people of Valdivia. **3** *nm typical Chilean dish of dried meat and vegetables.*

valdré *etc V* **valer.**

vale[1] *nm* (*Fin*) promissory note, IOU; (*recibo*) receipt; (*cupón*) voucher, coupon, warrant; (*LAm*: *cuenta*) bill, check (*US*); ~ **de comida,** ~ **(de) restaurante** luncheon voucher; ~ **de correo,** ~ **postal** money order; **dar el** ~ (*fig*) to O.K., pass as suitable; to give the go-ahead.

vale[2]* *nm* (*LAm*: *abr de* **valedor**) pal*, chum*, buddy (*US*); ~ **corrido** (*Carib*) old crony; **ser** ~ **con** (*And*) to be pals with*.

valedero *adj* valid; (*Jur*) binding; ~ **para 6 meses** valid for 6 months; ~ **hasta el día 16** valid until the 16th.

valedor *nm* (**a**) (*protector*) protector, guardian. (**b**) (*LAm*) = **vale**[2].

valedura *nf* (**a**) (*Méx*) (*ayuda*) help; (*protección*) protection; (*favor*) favour. (**b**) (*And, Carib*: *propina*) gift made by a gambler out of his winnings.

valemadrista* *adj* (*Méx*) indifferent, laid-back*; cynical.

valencia *nf* (*Quím*) valency.

valencianismo *nm* (**a**) (*Ling*) word (*o* phrase *etc*) peculiar to Valencia. (**b**) sense of the differentness of Valencia; (*Pol*) doctrine of (*o* belief in) Valencian autonomy.

valenciano, -a *adj, nm/f* **1** Valencian. **2** *nm* (*Ling*) Valencian.

valentía *nf* (**a**) (*valor*) bravery, courage; boldness; (*resolución*) resoluteness.

(**b**) (*pey*) boastfulness.

(**c**) (*acto*) brave deed, heroic exploit; bold act.
(**d**) (*pey: dicho*) brag, boast.

valentón 1 *adj* boastful; blustering, bullying; arrogant. **2** *nm* braggart; bluster, bully.

valentonada *nf* (*dicho*) boast, brag; piece of bluster; (*acto*) arrogant act.

valer [2p] **1** *vt* (**a**) (*proteger*) to aid, protect; (*servir*) to serve; (*ayudar*) to help, avail; **¡válgame (Dios)!** *V* **Dios; no le vale ser hijo del ministro** it's of no help to him being the minister's son, it doesn't help his case that he's the minister's son; **su situación privilegiada no le valió** his privileged position did not save him; **no le valdrán excusas** excuses won't help him, excuses will avail him nothing.

(**b**) (*Mat: ser igual a*) to equal, be equal to; (*sumar*) to amount to, come to; **la suma vale 99** the total comes to 99; **el ángulo B vale 38°** angle B is 38°; **en ese caso X vale 9** in that case X equals 9.

(**c**) (*causar*) to cause; (*ganar*) to earn; to win; (*costar*) to lose, cost; **el asunto le valió muchos disgustos** the affair caused him lots of trouble; **esa tontería le valió un rapapolvo** that piece of stupidity got (*o* earned) him a dressing-down; **son las cualidades que le valieron el premio** these are the qualities which won him the prize; **su ausencia le valió la pérdida del contrato** his absence lost (*o* cost) him the contract.

2 *vti* (**a**) (*Com, Fin*) to be worth; (*costar*) to cost, be priced at, be valued at; (*ser valioso*) to be valuable; (*fig: representar*) to be equivalent to, represent; **este libro vale 5 dólares** this book costs (*o* is worth) 5 dollars; **ésas valen 20 pesetas el kilo** those are 20 pesetas a kilo; **esta tela vale a 60 pesetas** this cloth costs 60 pesetas; **¿cuánto vale?** how much is it?; **¿vale mucho?** is it valuable?; **4 fichas azules valen por una negra** 4 blue counters are worth one black one; **cada cupón vale por un paquete** each coupon represents (*o* counts for) a packet.

(**b**) (*fig: tener valor*) to be worth; **no vale nada** it's worthless, it's rubbish; **no vale un higo** (*Esp*) it's not worth a brass farthing; **vale lo que pesa** it's worth its weight in gold; **esa mirada suya me valió un sinfín de palabras** that look of hers told me more (*o* was worth more to me) than a hundred words; **más vale así** it's better this way; **A vale más que B** A is better than B; **más vale tarde que nunca** better late than never; **más vale no hacerlo** it's better not to do it; **más vale que vayas tú** it would be better for you to go; **más vale que me vaya** I had better go; *V* **pena.**

(**c**) (*fig: persona*) to be worthy; to have one's merits (*o* qualities); **es un hombre que vale** he's a worthy man, he's a man of some quality, he has his points; **no vale para este trabajo** he's no good for this job; **no vale para nada** he's useless, he's a dead loss.

(**d**) **¡me vale (madre)!** (*Méx**) I don't give a damn!

3 *vi* (**a**) (*servir*) to be of use, be useful; (*bastar*) to do, be enough; **es viejo pero todavía vale** it's old but it still serves; **este sombrero me vale aún** this hat is still useful to me; **hay que tirar todo lo que no vale** we must throw out everything that is no use; **este trozo no me vale para hacer la cortina** this piece won't do to make the curtain.

(**b**) (*ser valedero*) to be valid; (*ser aplicable*) to be applicable, apply; (*en juegos*) to count, score; to be permitted; **¿vale?** is that all right?, will that do?; how about that?; **¡vale!** (*Esp*) that's right!, O.K.!*; that'll do!, that's enough!; **es una teoría que no vale ya** it is a theory which no longer holds; **esa sección no vale ahora** that section is not now applicable; **¡eso no vale!** that doesn't count!; that's not allowed!, you can't do that!; **ese tanto no vale** that point doesn't count; **no vale golpearlo segunda vez** you aren't allowed to have a second shot at it; **¡no hay 'querido' que valga!** it's no good saying 'darling' to me!, you can cut out the 'darling'!

(**c**) **hacer ~ su derecho** to assert one's right; **hacer ~ sus argumentos** to make one's arguments felt, establish the validity of one's arguments.

(**d**) **está un poco chiflado, valga la expresión** he's a bit cracked, so to speak; he's a bit cracked, for want of a better way of putting it.

4 valerse *vr* (**a**) **~ de** to make use of, avail o.s. of; to take advantage of; *derecho* to exercise.

(**b**) **~ por sí mismo** to help o.s., shift for o.s., manage by o.s.; **poder ~** to be able to manage; **no poder ~** to be helpless.

5 *nm* worth, value.

valeriana *nf* valerian.

valerosamente *adv* bravely, valiantly.

valeroso *adj* brave, valiant.

valet [ba'le] *nm, pl* **valets** [ba'le] (*Naipes*) jack, knave.

valetudinario, -a *adj, nm/f* valetudinarian.

valga *etc V* **valer.**

Valhala *nm* Valhalla.

valía *nf* (**a**) (*valor*) worth, value; **de gran ~** of great worth, very valuable; *persona* worthy, estimable. (**b**) (*fig: influencia*) influence.

validación *nf* validation; ratification.

validar [1a] *vt* to validate, give effect to; (*Pol etc*) to ratify.

validez *nf* validity; **dar ~ a** to validate, give effect to; (*Pol etc*) to ratify.

válido *adj* (**a**) valid (*hasta* until, *para* for). (**b**) (*Med*) strong, robust; fit.

valido *nm* (*Hist*) (royal) favourite.

valiente 1 *adj* (**a**) (*valeroso*) brave, valiant; (*audaz*) bold.

(**b**) (*pey*) boastful, blustering.

(**c**) (*fig*) fine, excellent; noble; strong; (*iró*) fine, wonderful; **¡~ amigo!** a fine friend you are!; **¡~ gobierno!** some government!, do you call this a government?

2 *nmf* (**a**) (*héroe*) brave man, brave woman; hero, heroine.

(**b**) (*pey*) braggart.

valientemente *adv* (*V adj*) (**a**) bravely, valiantly; boldly. (**b**) (*pey*) boastfully. (**c**) (*fig*) excellently; nobly; (*iró*) wonderfully.

valija *nf* (**a**) (*maleta*) case; (*LAm*) suitcase. (**b**) (*portamantas*) valise; (*cartera*) satchel; (*Correos*) mailbag; (*fig*) mail, post; **~ diplomática** diplomatic bag.

valijería *nf* (*Cono Sur*) travel-goods shop.

valimiento *nm* (**a**) (*valor*) value; benefit.

(**b**) (*Pol etc*) favour, protection; (*Hist*) position of royal favourite, status of the royal favourite; **~ con uno, ~ cerca de uno** influence with sb.

valioso *adj* (**a**) (*de valor*) valuable; (*útil*) useful, beneficial; (*estimable*) estimable. (**b**) (*rico*) wealthy; (*poderoso*) powerful.

valisoletano = **vallisoletano.**

valón, -ona *adj, nm/f* **1** Walloon. **2** *nm* (*Ling*) Walloon.

valona *nf* (**a**) (*And, Carib*) artistically trimmed mane; **hacer la ~** (*Carib*) to shave. (**b**) (*Méx*) = **valedura** (**a**).

valonar [1a] *vt* (*And*) to trim, cut; to shear.

valonearse [1a] *vr* (*CAm*) to lean from the saddle.

valor *nm* (**a**) (*gen*) value, worth; (*precio*) price; (*de moneda, sello*) value, denomination; (*Mat, Mús etc*) value; (*de palabras etc*) value, importance; meaning; (*tasa*) rate; **objetos de ~** valuables; **sin ~** worthless, valueless; **~ adquisitivo** purchasing power; **~ alimenticio** food value, nutritional value; **~ añadido** added value; (*Econ*) surplus value; profit; (*Com*) mark-up; **~ según balance, ~ en libros** book value; **~ calorífico** calorific value; **~ catastral** official valuation of property (for tax purposes); **~ comercial** commercial value; **'sin ~ comercial'** 'no commercial value'; **~ contable** asset value; **~ por defecto** default value; **~ de desecho** salvage value; **~ facial, ~ nominal** face-value, nominal value; **~ a la par** par value; **~ sentimental** sentimental value; **por ~ de** to the value of, for; **conceder ~ a, dar ~ a** to attach importance to; to value, esteem; **quitar ~ a** to minimize the importance of; **esas cosas ya no tienen ~ para mí** such things no longer have any importance for me, I no longer value such things; **se han medido ~es de 80 al m³** rates of 80 to the cubic metre have been recorded.

(**b**) (*fig*) great name, great figure; **Cervantes, máximo ~ nacional** Cervantes, one of our country's greatest figures; Cervantes, part of our great national heritage.

(**c**) **~es** (*Com, Fin*) securities, bonds; stock; (*And, Cono Sur*) assets; **~es en cartera, ~es habidos** investments, holdings, share portfolio; **~es fiduciarios** fiduciary issue, banknotes; **~es inmuebles** real estate; **~es de renta fija** fixed-interest securities; **~es de renta variable** variable-yield securities.

(**d**) (*valentía*) bravery, courage, valour; **~ cívico** (sense of) civic duty; **armarse de ~** to gather up one's courage.

(**e**) (**: caradura*) nerve*, cheek*; **¡qué ~!** of all the cheek!*; **tuvo el ~ de pedírmelo** he had the nerve to ask me for it*.

valoración *nf* (**a**) (*valuación*) valuation; (*fig*) assessment, appraisal. (**b**) (*Quím*) titration.

valorar [1a] *vt* (**a**) to value (*en* at); (*tasar*) to price; (*esp fig*) to assess, appraise; to rate; **~ mucho** to value highly, esteem; **~ poco** to attach little value to; (*anuncio*) **'se valorarán conocimientos de eslóbodo'** 'Knowledge of Slobodian an advantage'. (**b**) (*Quím*) to titrate.

valorización *nf* valuation; (*fig*) appraisal, assessment.
valorizar [1f] *vt* (**a**) = **valorar**. (**b**) (*And, Cono Sur: subir el precio de*) to put up the price of. (**c**) (*And: vender barato*) to sell cheaply.
Valquiria *nf* Valkyrie.
vals *nm* waltz.
valsar [1a] *vi* to waltz.
valse *nm* (**a**) (*LAm*) waltz. (**b**) (*Carib*) *Venezuelan folk dance.*
valsear [1a] *vi* (*LAm*) to waltz.
valuable *adj* (*LAm*) (**a**) (*valioso*) valuable. (**b**) (*calculable*) calculable.
valuación *nf* = **valoración** (**a**).
valuador(a) *nm/f* (*LAm*) valuer.
valuar [1e] *vt* = **valorar** (**a**).
valumen *nm* (**a**) (*Cono Sur Bot*) luxuriance, rankness. (**b**) (*Méx*) (*lío*) bundle; (*masa*) mass, bulk.
valumoso *adj* (**a**) (*CAm, Cono Sur*) luxuriant, rank. (**b**) (*And, CAm, Méx: voluminoso*) bulky. (**c**) (*Carib: vanidoso*) vain, conceited.
valva *nf* (*Bot, Zool*) valve.
válvula *nf* (*Mec etc*) valve; ~ **de admisión** inlet valve; ~ **de escape** exhaust valve; (*fig*) relief, escape; ~ **de purga** vent; ~ **de seguridad** safety valve.
valla *nf* (**a**) (*cercado*) fence; (*Mil*) barricade; palisade, stockade; (*Dep*) hurdle; ~ **de protección,** ~ **de seguridad** barrier; ~ **publicitaria** hoarding, billboard (*US*); **400 metros ~s** 400 metres hurdles.
(**b**) (*fig*) (*barrera*) barrier; (*límite*) limit; (*obstáculo*) obstacle, hindrance; **romper las ~s, saltar(se) la** ~ to disregard the social conventions, do away with social niceties; to burst through the barriers of convention.
(**c**) (*And, Carib, Méx: de gallos*) cockpit.
(**d**) (*And: zanja*) ditch.
valladar *nm* (**a**) = **valla** (**a**). (**b**) (*fig*) defence, barrier.
vallado 1 *adj* fenced. **2** *nm* (**a**) = **valla** (**a**). (**b**) (*Mil*) defensive wall, rampart. (**c**) (*Méx: zanja*) deep ditch.
vallar [1a] *vt* to fence in, put up a fence round, enclose.
valle *nm* (**a**) valley; vale, dale; ~ **de lágrimas** vale of tears. (**b**) **energía de** ~ off-peak power demand (*o* supply); **horas de** ~ off-peak hours.
vallero (*Méx*) **1** *adj* valley (*atr*). **2** *nm*, **vallera** *nf* valley dweller.
vallino *adj* (*And*) valley (*atr*).
vallisoletano 1 *adj* of Valladolid. **2** *nm*, **vallisoletana** *nf* native (*o* inhabitant) of Valladolid; **los ~s** the people of Valladolid.
vallista *nmf* hurdler.
vallisto *adj* (*Cono Sur, Méx*) valley (*atr*).
vallunco *adj* (*CAm*) rustic, peasant (*atr*).
vamos *etc V* **ir.**
vampi* *nf* = **vampiresa.**
vampiresa *nf* vamp.
vampirizar [1f] *vt* to sap, milk, bleed dry.
vampiro *nm* (**a**) (*Zool*) vampire. (**b**) (*fig*) vampire; exploiter, bloodsucker.
vanagloria *nf* vainglory.
vanagloriarse [1b] *vr* to boast; to be vain, be arrogant; ~ **de** to boast of; ~ **de** + *infin* to boast of + *ger*, boast of being able to + *infin.*
vanaglorioso *adj* vainglorious; vain, boastful, arrogant.
vanamente *adv* uselessly, vainly.
vanarse [1a] *vr* (*And, Carib, Cono Sur*) to shrivel up; (*fig*) to fall through, come to nothing, produce no results.
vandálico *adj* Vandal(ic); (*fig*) loutish, destructive.
vandalismo *nm* vandalism.
vándalo 1 *adj* Vandal(ic). **2** *nm*, **vándala** *nf* (*Hist*) Vandal; (*fig*) vandal.
vanguardia *nf* vanguard, van (*t fig*); **estar en la** ~ **del progreso** to be in the van of progress; **ir a la ~, ir en** ~ to be in the vanguard; to be foremost, be ahead, be in front; **un pintor de** ~ an ultramodern painter, a painter with a revolutionary style.
vanguardismo *nm* (*Arte, Liter etc*) avant-garde movement; ultramodern manner, revolutionary style; new tendency.
vanguardista 1 *adj* avant-garde; ultramodern, revolutionary; **coche de tecnología** ~ technically advanced car. **2** *nmf* avant-garde artist (*etc*).
vanidad *nf* (**a**) (*irrealidad*) unreality; (*sospecha*) groundlessness; (*inutilidad*) uselessness, futility; (*superficialidad*) shallowness; (*necedad*) inanity; (*falta de sentido*) pointlessness.
(**b**) (*presunción*) vanity; **por pura** ~ out of sheer vanity; **halagar la** ~ **de uno** to play up to sb's vanity.
(**c**) **~es** vanities.
vanidoso *adj* vain, conceited; smug.
vano 1 *adj* (**a**) (*irreal*) unreal, imaginary, vain; *temor etc* idle; *sospecha* groundless; *superstición* foolish, unreasonable.
(**b**) (*inútil*) vain, useless; *pasatiempo* idle; **en** ~ in vain; **no en** ~ not in vain.
(**c**) *persona* (*frívolo*) shallow, superficial; frivolous; *placer etc* empty, inane, pointless; *adorno* silly.
(**d**) *cáscara* empty, hollow.
2 *nm* (*Arquit*) space, gap.
vapor *nm* (**a**) (*gen*) vapour; (*Tec*) steam; (*Quím*) fumes; (*Met*) mist, haze; ~ **de agua** water vapour; **al** ~ by steam, (*fig*) very fast; **cocer un plato al** ~ to steam a dish; **a todo** ~ at full steam, (*t fig*) full-steam; **de** ~ steam (*atr*); **acumular** ~ to get steam up; **echar** ~ to give off steam, steam.
(**b**) (*Náut*) steamer, steamship; ~ **correo** mailboat; ~ **de paletas,** ~ **de ruedas** paddle-steamer; ~ **volandero** tramp steamer.
(**c**) (*Med*) giddiness, faintness; dizzy spell; **~es** vapours, hysteria.
vapora *nf* (**a**) (*barco*) steam launch. (**b**) (*Carib Ferro*) steam engine.
vapor(e)ar [1a] **1** *vt* to evaporate. **2** *vi* to give off vapour. **3 vapor(e)arse** *vr* to evaporate.
vaporización *nf* vaporization.
vaporizador *nm* vaporizer; spray.
vaporizar [1f] **1** *vt* to vaporize, convert into vapour; *perfume etc* to spray. **2 vaporizarse** *vr* to vaporize, turn into vapour.
vaporizo *nm* (*Carib, Méx*) (**a**) (*calor*) strong heat, steamy heat. (**b**) (*Med*) inhalation.
vaporoso *adj* (**a**) (*de vapor*) vaporous; steamy, misty; steaming. (**b**) *tela* light, airy, diaphanous.
vapulear [1a] *vt* (**a**) *alfombra etc* to beat; *persona* (*pegar*) to beat; (*azotar*) to thrash; flog; (*dar paliza a*) to beat up*. (**b**) (*fig*) to give a tongue-lashing to.
vapuleo *nm* (**a**) (*paliza*) beating; thrashing, flogging; beating-up. (**b**) (*fig*) tongue-lashing.
vaquerear [1a] *vi* (*And*) to play truant.
vaquería *nf* (**a**) (*lechería*) dairy. (**b**) (*LAm*) (*cuidado de ganado*) cattle farming, cattle tending; (*arte del vaquero*) craft of the cowboy. (**c**) (*And, Carib*) (*cubo*) milking pail; (*lechería*) milking shed. (**d**) (*Carib: ganado*) herd of dairy cows. (**e**) (*Carib: caza*) hunting with a lasso. (**f**) (*Méx: baile*) barn dance, country dance.
vaqueriza *nf* (*establo*) cowshed; (*corral*) cattle yard.
vaquerizo 1 *adj* cattle (*atr*). **2** *nm* cowman; herdsman.
vaquero 1 *adj* cattle (*atr*). **2** *nm* (**a**) (*que cuida ganado*) cowman; herdsman, cattle tender; (*en US, LAm*) cowboy. (**b**) (*LAm: lechero*) milkman. (**c**) (*And: ausente*) truant. (**d**) (*Carib: látigo*) rawhide whip. (**e**) **~s** (*pantalones*) jeans.
vaqueta 1 *nf* (**a**) (*cuero*) cowhide, leather. (**b**) (*Carib: de afeitarse*) razor strop. **2** *nm* (*Carib*) shifty sort.
vaquetón *adj* (**a**) (*Carib: poco fiable*) unreliable, shifty. (**b**) (*Méx*) (*lerdo*) dim-witted; (*flemático*) phlegmatic, slow. (**c**) (*Méx: descarado*) barefaced, brazen.
vaquetudo *adj* (*Carib, Méx*) = **vaquetón, baquetudo.**
vaquilla *nf* (*LAm*) (**a**) (*Agr*) heifer. (**b**) **~s** (*Taur*) amateur bullfight with young bulls.
vaquillona *nf* (*LAm*) heifer.
vara *nf* (**a**) (*palo*) stick, pole; (*barra*) rod, bar; (*Mec*) rod; (*de carro*) shaft; (*Bot*) branch, twig (stripped of its leaves), wand, switch; (*Bot*) central stem, main stalk; ~ **mágica,** ~ **de las virtudes** magic wand; ~ **de medir** yardstick, measuring rod; ~ **de oro,** ~ **de San José** goldenrod; ~ **de pescar** fishing rod.
(**b**) (*Pol etc*) wand (of office); sign of authority; ~ **alta** (*autoridad*) authority, power; (*influencia*) influence; (*dominio*) dominance; **doblar la** ~ **de la justicia** to pervert justice; **empuñar la** ~ to take over, take up office (*as mayor etc*); **tener (mucha)** ~ **alta, tener** ~ (*And*) to have great influence, be influential.
(**c**) (*Mat: prov, LAm*) ≈ yard (= *.836 m*, = *2.8 feet*).
(**d**) (*Taur: lanza*) lance, pike; (*herida*) wound with the lance; **poner ~s al toro** to wound the bull with the lance.
(**e**) (‡: *revés*) blow; upset, setback.
(**f**) **dar la ~*** to annoy, pester.
varada *nf* (**a**) (*lanzamiento*) launching. (**b**) (*encalladura*) stranding, running aground.
varadero *nm* dry dock.

varado 1 *adj* (**a**) (*Náut*) stranded; **estar ~** to be aground; to be beached.
(**b**) **estar ~*** (*Cono Sur*: *sin trabajo*) to be without regular work; (*CAm, Cono Sur, Méx*: *sin dinero*) to be broke*.
2 *nm* (*Cono Sur*) drifter, man without a regular job.
varadura *nf* stranding, running aground.
varajillo *nm* (*Carib*) liqueur coffee.
varal *nm* (**a**) (*palo*) long pole, stout stick; (*armazón*) framework of poles; (*puntal*) strut, support; (*de carro*) shaft; (*Teat*) batten. (**b**) (*: *persona*) thin person, lamppost.
varapalear [1a] *vt* (*fig*) to slate, tear to pieces.
varapalo *nm* (**a**) (*palo*) long pole. (**b**) (*golpe*) blow with a stick; (*paliza*) beating. (**c**) (*fig*: *regañada*) dressing-down*. (**d**) (*fig*: *revés*) setback, disappointment, blow.
varar [1a] **1** *vt* (**a**) (*botar*) to launch.
(**b**) (*llevar a la playa*) to beach, run up on the beach.
2 *vi y* **vararse** *vr* (**a**) (*Náut*) to be stranded, run aground.
(**b**) (*fig*) to get stuck, get bogged down; to come to a standstill; (*And, Cono Sur*) to stop; to stay.
varayoc *nm* (*And*) Indian Chief.
varazo *nm* blow with a stick.
varazón *nf* (*And, Carib, Méx*) sticks, bunch of sticks.
vardasca *nf* green twig; switch.
varé‡ *nm* (*Esp*) 100 pesetas.
varear [1a] *vt* (**a**) *persona* to beat, hit; *fruta* to knock down (with poles); *alfombra etc* to beat; *toro* to prick with the lance, goad, stir up. (**b**) (*Com*) *paño* to sell by the yard. (**c**) (*Cono Sur*: *hacer ejercicio*) to exercise, train.
varec *nm* kelp, wrack.
varejón *nm* (*Cono Sur*) (**a**) = **vardasca**. (**b**) (*palo*) stick, straight branch (stripped of leaves).
vareta *nf* (**a**) (*ramita*) twig, small stick; (*con liga*) lime twig for catching birds.
(**b**) (*Cos*) stripe.
(**c**) (*indirecta*) insinuation; (*pulla*) taunt; **echar ~s** to make insinuations.
(**d**) **estar de ~, irse de ~** (*Med*) to have diarrhoea.
varetazo *nm* (*Taur*) sideways thrust with the horn.
varga *nf* steepest part of a slope.
variabilidad *nf* variability.
variable 1 *adj* variable, changeable; (*Mat*) variable. **2** *nf* (*Mat*) variable.
variación *nf* variation (*t Mús*); **sin ~** without varying, unchanged.
variado *adj* varied; mixed; assorted; *colores, superficie* variegated.
variante 1 *adj* variant. **2** *nm* (**a**) **~s** (*Esp Culin*) pickled vegetables (*as hors d'oeuvres*). (**b**) (*And*) (*senda*) path; (*atajo*) short cut. **3** *nf* (**a**) variant. (**b**) (*Aut*) by-pass.
variar [1c] **1** *vt* (*cambiar*) to vary, change, alter; (*modificar*) to modify; *menu etc* to vary, introduce some variety into; *posiciones* to change round, switch about.
2 *vi* to vary; to change; **~ de opinión** to change one's mind; **varía de 3 a 8** it ranges from 3 to 8, it goes from 3 to 8; **este producto varía mucho de precio** this article varies a lot in price; **esto varía de lo que dijo antes** this differs from what he said earlier; **para ~** for a change; **para no ~** as usual, the same as always.
varicela *nf* chickenpox.
várices, varices *nfpl* varicose veins.
varicoso *adj* (**a**) *pierna etc* varicose. (**b**) *persona* suffering from varicose veins.
variedad *nf* (**a**) (*diversidad*) variety; variation; (*Bio*) variety. (**b**) (*Teat*) **~es** variety show; **teatro de ~es** variety theatre, music hall, vaudeville theater (*US*).
varietés *nmpl* (*Teat*) = **variedades**.
varilla *nf* (**a**) (*palito*) (thin) stick; (*Bot*) twig, wand, switch; (*Mec*) rod, bar; (*Aut*) dipstick; (*eslabón*) link; (*de rueda*) spoke; (*de corsé*) rib, stay; (*de abanico, paraguas*) rib; (*de gafas*) sidepiece, earpiece; (*Anat*) jawbone; **~ mágica, ~ de virtudes** magic wand; **~ de zahorí** divining rod.
(**b**) (*Méx*) cheap wares, trinkets.
(**c**) (*Carib‡*: *vaina*) nuisance, bother.
varillaje *nm* (*Mec*) rods, links, linkage; (*de abanico, paraguas*) ribs, ribbing.
varillar [1a] *vt* (*Carib*) *caballo* to try out, train.
vario *adj* (**a**) (*variado*) varied; (*de color*) variegated, motley.
(**b**) (*cambiable*) varying, variable, changeable; *persona* fickle.
(**c**) **~s** several, some; a number of; **hay varias posibilidades** there are several (*o* various) possibilities; **en ~s libros que he visto** in a number of books which I have seen; **los inconvenientes son ~s** there are several drawbacks.
varioloso *adj* pockmarked.
variopinto *adj* many-coloured, colourful; of diverse colours; **~s** (*fig*) diverse, miscellaneous; very mixed.
varita *nf* wand; **~ mágica, ~ de las virtudes** magic wand.
varón 1 *adj* male; **hijo ~** male child, boy, son.
2 *nm* (**a**) (*hombre*) man, male; adult male; (*fig*) worthy man, great man; **~ de Dios** saintly man; **santo ~** simple old man; **tuvo 4 hijos, todos varones** she had 4 children, all boys.
(**b**) (*And*: *marido*) husband.
(**c**) (*Cono, Sur, Méx*: *vigas*) beams, timber.
varona *nf*, **varonesa** *nf* mannish woman.
varonil *adj* (**a**) (*viril*) manly, virile; (*enérgico*) vigorous. (**b**) (*Bio*) male. (**c**) **una mujer de aspecto ~** a woman of mannish appearance.
Varsovia *nf* Warsaw.
vasallaje *nm* (*Hist*) vassalage; (*fig*) subjection, serfdom.
vasallo *nm* vassal.
vasar *nm* kitchen dresser.
vasco, -a *adj, nm/f* **1** Basque.
2 (*Ling*) Basque.
vascófilo, -a *nm/f* expert in Basque studies.
vascófono 1 *adj* Basque-speaking. **2** *nm*, **vascófona** *nf* Basque speaker.
vascofrancés 1 *adj*: **País V~** French Basque Country. **2** *nm*, **vascofrancesa** *nf* French Basque.
vascohablante 1 *adj* Basque-speaking. **2** *nmf* Basque speaker.
Vascongadas *nfpl*: **las ~** the Basque Provinces.
vascongado = **vasco.**
vascuence *nm* (*Ling*) Basque.
vascular *adj* vascular.
vase (= **se va**) *V* **ir.**
vasectomía *nf* vasectomy.
vaselina *nf* ® Vaseline ®, petroleum jelly; **poner ~*** to calm things down; to make things go smoothly.
vasera *nf* kitchen shelf, rack.
vasija *nf* vessel; container, receptacle.
vaso *nm* (**a**) (*Culin*) glass, tumbler; vessel; container; (*liter*) vase, urn; (*de pila*) cell; (*And*) small cup; (*And Aut*) hub-cap; **~ de agua** glass of water; **~ para vino** wine-glass; **~ de engrase** (*Mec*) grease cup; **~ de noche** chamberpot; **~ litúrgico, ~ sagrado** liturgical vessel; **ahogarse en un ~ de agua** to get worked up about nothing at all.
(**b**) (*cantidad*) glassful, glass.
(**c**) (*Anat*) vessel; tube, duct; **~ capilar** capillary; **~ sanguíneo** blood vessel.
(**d**) (*Zool*) hoof.
(**e**) (*Náut*) (*casco*) hull; (*barco*) boat, ship, vessel.
vasquismo *nm* sense of the differentness of the Basque Country; (*Pol*) doctrine of (*o* belief in) Basque autonomy.
vasquista 1 *adj* that supports (*etc*) Basque autonomy; **el movimiento ~** the movement for Basque autonomy; **la familia es muy ~** the family strongly supports Basque autonomy. **2** *nmf* supporter (*etc*) of Basque autonomy.
vástago *nm* (**a**) (*Bot*) shoot, sprout, bud.
(**b**) (*Mec*) rod; stem; **~ de émbolo** piston rod.
(**c**) (*hijo, descendiente*) scion, offspring.
(**d**) (*And, CAm, Carib*: *tronco*) trunk of the banana tree.
vastedad *nf* vastness, immensity.
vasto *adj* vast, huge, immense.
vataje *nm* wattage.
vate *nm* (**a**) (*Hist*) seer, prophet. (**b**) (*Liter*) poet, bard.
váter *nm* = **wáter.**
Vaticano *nm* Vatican; **la Ciudad del ~** Vatican City.
vaticano *adj* Vatican; papal.
vaticinador *nm* seer, prophet; forecaster.
vaticinar [1a] *vt* to prophesy, predict; to forecast.
vaticinio *nm* prophecy, prediction; forecast.
vatio *nm* watt.
vaya *etc V* **ir.**
VCL *nm abr de* **visualizador cristal líquido** liquid crystal display, LCD.
Vd. *pron abr de* **usted** you.
Vda. de *abr de* **viuda de** widow of.
Vds. *pron abr de* **ustedes** you.
V.E. *abr de* **Vuestra Excelencia** Your Excellency.
ve *nf* (*LAm*): **~ corta** (*o* **chica**) *name of the letter v*; **~ doble** *name of the letter w*.
vecinal *adj* (**a**) *camino etc* local; *impuesto* local, municipal; **padrón ~** list of residents. (**b**) (*LAm*: *vecino*) neighbour-

ing, adjacent.

vecindad *nf* (**a**) (*barrio*) neighbourhood, vecinity; (*LAm*: *barrio pobre*) inner-city slum.
(**b**) (*vecinos*) neighbours, neighbourhood; local community; (*habitantes*) residents (of a block of flats).
(**c**) (*proximidad*) nearness, proximity.
(**d**) (*Jur etc*) residence, abode; **declarar su ~** to state where one lives, give one's place of abode.

vecindario *nm* neighbourhood; local community, residents; (*estadística etc*) population, inhabitants.

vecino 1 *adj* (**a**) (*contiguo*) neighbouring, adjacent, adjoining; (*cercano*) near, nearby, close; *casa etc* next; **el garaje ~ del mío** the garage next to mine; **no aquí sino en el pueblo ~** not here but in the next village; **las dos fincas son vecinas** the two estates adjoin.
(**b**) (*fig*) alike, similar; **~ a** like, similar to.
2 *nm*, **vecina** *nf* (**a**) (*de al lado*) neighbour; **~ de rellano** ≃ next-door neighbour.
(**b**) (*habitante*) resident, inhabitant, citizen; **un pueblo de 800 ~s** a village of 800 inhabitants; **asociación de ~s** residents' association; **una vecina de la calle X** a resident in X street.

vector *nm* vector.

Veda *nm* Veda.

veda *nf* (**a**) (*acto*) prohibition; imposition of a close season. (**b**) (*temporada*) close season.

vedado *nm* preserve; **~ de caza** game preserve; **cazar** (*o* **pescar**) **en ~** to poach, hunt (*o* fish) illegally.

vedar [1a] *vt* (*prohibir*) to prohibit, forbid, ban; (*impedir*) to stop, prevent; *idea, plan etc* to veto; **~ a uno hacer algo** to forbid sb to do sth; to stop sb doing sth, prevent sb from doing sth.

vedeta *nf*, **vedette** [be'ðet] *nf* (**a**) (*Cine*) star; starlet; (*fig*: *número*) star turn, main attraction. (**b**) (*Méx*: *corista*) chorus-girl.

vedetismo *nm* insistence on being in the forefront, insistence on playing the star role; star quality; stardom.

védico *adj* Vedic.

vedija *nf* (**a**) (*lana*) tuft of wool. (**b**) (*greña*) mat of hair, matted hair.

vega *nf* (**a**) (*terreno*) fertile plain, rich lowland area; water meadow(s); (*And*) stretch of alluvial soil. (**b**) (*Carib*: *tabacal*) tobacco plantation.

vegetación *nf* (**a**) (*plantas*) vegetation. (**b**) (*acto*) growth, growing. (**c**) (*Med*) **vegetaciones adenoideas** adenoids.

vegetal 1 *adj* vegetable, plant (*atr*); **patología ~** plant pathology. **2** *nm* (**a**) plant, vegetable; **~es** (*CAm, Méx*) vegetables. (**b**) (*persona*) vegetable.

vegetar [1a] *vi* (**a**) (*Bot*) to grow. (**b**) (*fig*: *persona*) to vegetate, live like a vegetable; (*negocio*) to stagnate.

vegetarianismo *nm* vegetarianism.

vegetariano, -a *adj, nm/f* vegetarian.

vegetativo *adj* vegetative.

vegoso *adj* (*Cono Sur*) *tierra* soggy, damp.

veguero 1 *adj* lowland (*atr*), of the plain. **2** *nm* (**a**) (*agricultor*) lowland farmer. (**b**) (*Carib*) tobacco planter. (**c**) (*cigarro*) coarse cigar; (*Cono Sur*) good-quality Cuban tobacco, good cigar.

vehemencia *nf* vehemence; passion, impetuosity; fervour; eagerness, violence.

vehemente *adj* (**a**) (*insistente*) vehement; (*apasionado*) passionate, impetuous; *partidario etc* fervent, passionate; *deseo* strong, eager, violent; *orador* passionate, forceful.
(**b**) *señal, sospecha etc* strong.

vehicular [1a] *vt* to transport; to transmit, convey.

vehiculizar [1f] *vt* = **vehicular**.

vehículo *nm* (**a**) (*Aut etc*) vehicle; **~ astral, ~ cósmico** spacecraft; **~ de carga, ~ de transporte** goods vehicle; **~ carretero** road vehicle.
(**b**) (*fig*) vehicle (*de* for); (*Med*) carrier, transmitter (*de* of).

veinte *adj* twenty; (*fecha*) twentieth; **los** (**años**) **~** the twenties.

veintena *nf* twenty, a score; about twenty, about a score.

veintiañero 1 *adj* twentyish, about twenty. **2** *nm*, **veintiañera** *nf* person of about 20, person in his (*o* her) twenties.

veintipocos *adj pl* twenty-odd.

veintiuna *nf* (*Naipes*) pontoon.

vejación *nf* vexation, annoyance; **sufrir vejaciones** to suffer vexations.

vejamen *nm* (**a**) = **vejación**. (**b**) (*pasquín*) satire, lampoon; (*pulla*) shaft, taunt.

vejaminoso *adj* (*And, Carib*) irritating, annoying.

vejancón*, vejarrón* 1 *adj* ancient, doddery. **2** *nm* old chap*, old dodderer.

vejancona* *nf*, **vejarrona*** *nf* (decrepit) old woman.

vejar [1a] *vt* (*molestar*) to vex, annoy; (*mofarse de*) to scoff at; (*acosar*) to harass.

vejarano *adj*(*LAm* ††) ancient, doddery, decrepit.

vejatorio *adj* (*molesto*) vexatious, annoying; (*humillante*) humiliating, degrading; **es ~ para él tener que pedirlo** it is humiliating for him to have to beg for it.

vejestorio *nm*, **vejete** *nm* dodderer, gaffer, old crock.

vejez *nf* (**a**) old age; **¡a la ~, viruelas!** fancy that happening at his (*etc*) age!
(**b**) (*fig*: *displicencia*) peevishness; grouchiness*, grumpiness.
(**c**) (*fig*) (*cuento*) old story; (*noticia*) piece of stale news.

vejiga *nf* (**a**) (*Anat*) bladder; **~ de la bilis** gall-bladder; **~ natatoria** air bladder. (**b**) (*Med, en pintura etc*) blister.

vela[1] *nf* (**a**) (*despierto*) wakefulness, state of being awake; sleeplessness; **estar en ~** to be unable to get to sleep, be still awake; **pasar la noche en ~** to have a sleepless night, not sleep all night.
(**b**) (*vigilia*) vigil; (*trabajo nocturno*) evening work, night work; (*Mil*) (period of) sentry duty.
(**c**) (*candela*) candle; **~ de sebo** tallow candle; **no se le dará ~ en este entierro** he will not be given any say in this matter; **¿quién te ha dado ~ en este entierro?** who asked you to poke your nose in?; **encender una ~ a San Miguel y otra al diablo** to want to have it both ways; **quedarse a dos ~s** (*fig*) to be in the dark.
(**d**) (*Taur**) horn.
(**e**) **~s*** mucus, snot*.
(**f**) (*CAm, Carib, Méx*: *velorio*) wake.
(**g**) (*Cono Sur*: *molestia*) nuisance, bother; **¡qué ~!** what a nuisance!; **aguantar la ~** to put up with it for sb else's sake.
(**h**) (*Carib, Méx**: *bronca*) telling-off*; **aguantar la ~** to face the music.

vela[2] *nf* (*Náut*) sail; (*deporte*) sailing; **~ balón** spinnaker; **~ mayor** mainsail; **a toda ~, a ~s desplegadas** under full sail, (*fig*) vigorously, energetically, straining every nerve; **barco de ~** sailing ship; **estar a dos ~ s*** to be broke*; **estar entre dos ~s*, ir a la ~*** to be half-seas over; **arriar ~s, recoger ~s** (*fig*) to back down; to give up, chuck it up*; **darse a la ~, hacerse a la ~, largar las ~s** to set sail, get under way; **hacer ~** to go sailing; **ir como las ~s** (*Cono Sur*) to drive very fast; **plegar ~s** (*fig*) to slow down.

velación *nf* wake, vigil.

velada *nf* (evening) party, social gathering, soirée; **~ de boxeo** fight night, boxing evening; **~ musical** musical evening.

veladamente *adv* in a veiled way.

velado *adj* veiled (*t fig*); (*Fot*) fogged, blurred; *sonido* muffled.

velador *nm* (**a**) (*vigilante*) watchman, caretaker; (*Hist*) sentinel.
(**b**) (*candelero*) candlestick.
(**c**) (*mesa*) pedestal table; (*LAm*: *mesita*) night table.
(**d**) (*Cono Sur*: *lámpara*) night light.
(**e**) (*Méx*: *pantalla*) lampshade.

veladora *nf* (*LAm*: *vela*) candle; (*Méx*) table-lamp, bedside lamp; (*Ecl*) paraffin lamp.

velamen *nm* sails, canvas.

velar[1] [1a] **1** *vt* (**a**) (*vigilar*) to watch, keep watch over; *enfermo* to sit up with, stay by the bedside of.
(**b**) (*LAm*: *codiciar*) to look covetously at.
2 *vi* (**a**) (*no dormir*) to stay awake; to go without sleep; (*seguir sin acostarse*) to stay up, sit up at night; (*trabajar de noche*) to work late, do night duty; (*vigilar*) to keep watch, (*Ecl*) keep vigil.
(**b**) (*ser solícito*) to be solicitous; **~ por** (*cuidar*) to watch over, look after; (*proteger*) to guard, protect; **~ por que se haga algo** to see to it (*o* ensure) that sth is done; **no hay quien vele por sus intereses** there is nobody to watch over his interests.
(**c**) (*Náut*: *arrecife*) to appear.

velar[2] [1a] **1** *vt* (**a**) (*lit*) to veil. (**b**) (*fig*) to shroud, hide, veil. (**c**) (*Fot*) to fog, blur. **2 velarse** *vr* (**a**) (*esconderse*) to hide itself. (**b**) (*ojos*) to glaze over; (*Fot*) to fog, blur.

velar[3] *adj* (*Ling*) velar.

velarte *nm* (*Hist*) broadcloth.

velatorio *nm* funeral wake.

Velázquez *nm* Velázquez, Velasquez.

veleidad *nf* (**a**) (*cualidad*) fickleness, capriciousness, flightiness. (**b**) (*una ~*) whim, caprice; unpredictable mood;

strange fancy.

veleidoso *adj* fickle, capricious, flighty.

velero 1 *adj barco* fast. **2** *nm* **(a)** (*Náut*: *barco*) sailing ship.

(b) (*Aer*) glider. **(c)** (*Náut*: *persona*) sailmaker.

veleta 1 *nf* **(a)** weather-vane, weathercock. **(b)** (*Pesca*) float. **2** *nmf* (*persona*) weathercock, fickle person.

veletería *nf* (*Cono Sur*) chopping and changing, fickleness.

velís *nm*, **veliz** *nm* (*Méx*) (*pequeño*) overnight bag, valise; (*maleta*) suitcase; **velises, velices** cases, luggage, bags.

velo *nm* **(a)** (*gen*) veil; **tomar el ~** to take the veil, become a nun; **corramos un tupido ~ sobre esto** let us draw a discreet veil over this.

(b) (*fig*: *cobertura*) veil, light covering; shroud; film; (*en cristal*) mist; (*Fot*) fog, veiling.

(c) (*fig*: *pretexto*) pretext, cloak.

(d) (*fig*: *falta de claridad*) mental fog, confusion, lack of clarity.

(e) ~ del paladar (*Anat*) soft palate, velum.

velocidad *nf* **(a)** (*gen*) speed; (*Téc etc*) rate, pace, velocity; (*lo veloz*) speediness, swiftness; **~ adquirida** momentum; **de alta ~** high-speed; **~ de crucero, ~ económica** cruising speed; **~ máxima, ~ punta** maximum speed, top speed; **~ máxima de impresión** maximum print speed; **~ máxima permitida** speed-limit; **~ de obturación, ~ de obturador** shutter speed; **~ de transferencia** transfer rate; **a gran ~** at high speed; **a máxima ~, a toda ~** at full speed, at top speed; **¿a qué ~?** at what speed?, how fast?; **¿a qué ~ ibas?** what speed were you doing?; **cobrar ~** to pick up speed, gather speed; **disminuir ~, moderar la ~, perder ~** to slow down; **exceder la ~ permitida** to speed, exceed the speed-limit.

(b) (*Mec*) gear, speed; **primera ~, ~ corta** low gear, bottom gear, first gear; **segunda ~** second gear; **~es de avance** forward gears; **4 ~es hacia adelante** 4 forward gears.

velocímetro *nm* speedometer.

velocípedo *nm* velocipede.

velocista *nmf* sprinter.

velódromo *nm* cycle track.

velomotor *nm* (*Hist*) autocycle.

velón *nm* **(a)** (*lámpara*) oil lamp. **(b)** (*And, Cono Sur, Méx*: *vela*) thick tallow candle. **(c)** (*CAm**: *parásito*) sponger*, parasite. **(d)** (*And, Carib*) person who casts covetous glances.

velorio¹ *nm* **(a)** (*fiesta*) party, celebration; (*And, Carib, Cono Sur*) dull party, flat affair.

(b) (*esp LAm*: *de entierro*) wake, vigil for the dead; **~ del angelito** wake for a dead child.

velorio² *nm* (*Ecl*) (ceremony of) taking the veil.

veloz *adj* fast, quick, swift; **~ como un relámpago** as quick as lightning.

velozmente *adv* fast, quickly, swiftly.

vello *nm* (*Anat*) down, fuzz, hair; (*Bot*) down; (*en fruta*) bloom; (*en cuerna*) velvet; **~ púbico** pubic hair.

vellocino *nm* fleece; **V~ de Oro** Golden Fleece.

vellón¹ *nm* **(a)** (*lana*) fleece; (*piel*) sheepskin. **(b)** (*mechón*) tuft of wool.

vellón² *nm* **(a)** (*Téc*) copper and silver alloy. **(b)** (*CAm, Carib*: *moneda*) five-cent coin.

vellonera *nf* (*Carib*) jukebox.

vellosidad *nf* downiness, fuzziness, hairiness; fluffiness.

velloso *adj* downy, fuzzy, hairy; fluffy.

velludo 1 *adj* hairy, shaggy. **2** *nm* plush, velvet.

vena *nf* **(a)** (*Anat*) vein; **~ yugular** jugular vein.

(b) (*Min*) vein, seam, lode.

(c) (*en madera, piedra*) grain.

(d) (*Bot*) vein, rib.

(e) (*Geog*) underground stream.

(f) (*fig*: *disposición*) vein; mood, disposition; **~ de loco** streak of madness; oddity, mania; **coger a uno de** (*o* **en**) **~** to catch sb in the right mood; **le daba la ~ por ello** he took a fancy to it, the mood took him that way; **estar de** (*o* **en**) **~** to be in the vein, be in the mood (*para* for); to be in good form.

(g) (*fig*: *talento*) talent, promise; **tiene ~ de pintor** he has the makings of a painter, he shows a talent for painting.

venablo *nm* javelin, dart; **echar ~s** (*fig*) to burst out angrily.

venado *nm* **(a)** (*Zool*) deer, stag.

(b) (*Culin*) venison.

(c) (*Carib*: *piel*) deerskin.

(d) (*Carib*: *puta*) whore.

(e) (*And*: *contrabanda*) contraband.

(f) correr el ~, pintar el ~ (*CAm, Méx*) to play truant.

venal¹ *adj* (*Anat*) venous.

venal² *adj* **(a)** (*Com*) commercial, that can be bought (*o* sold). **(b)** (*pey*) venal, corrupt.

venalidad *nf* venality, corruptness.

venático *adj* rather crazy, a bit mad.

venatorio *adj* hunting (*atr*).

vencedor 1 *adj equipo, jugador* winning, victorious; *general etc* victorious, successful; *nación* conquering, victorious.

2 *nm*, **vencedora** *nf* winner, victor; conqueror.

vencejo¹ *nm* (*Orn*) swift.

vencejo² *nm* (*Agr*) straw plait, string (*used in binding sheaves*).

vencer [2b] **1** *vt* **(a)** (*derrotar*) *enemigo* to defeat, beat; to conquer, vanquish, overcome; (*Dep*) to beat; *rival* to outdo, surpass; *pasión etc* to master, control, fight down; *tentación* to overcome; (*sueño etc*) to overcome; **vence a todos en elegancia** he outdoes them all in elegance, he beats them all for elegance; **por fin le venció el sueño** finally sleep overcame him; **dejarse ~** to yield, give in; **no te dejes ~** don't give in, don't let yourself be beaten (by it).

(b) *dificultad, obstáculo* to overcome, surmount, get round.

(c) *soporte, rama etc* to break down, snap, prove too heavy for; **el peso de los libros ha vencido el anaquel** the weight of the books has broken the shelf.

(d) *cuesta, montaña* to get to the top of, reach the summit of.

2 *vi* **(a)** (*ganar*) to win; to win through, succeed, triumph; **¡venceremos!** we shall win!; we shall overcome!

(b) (*Com etc*: *plazo*) to expire, end; (*pago etc*) to fall due; (*bono*) to mature, become due for redemption; (*póliza etc*) to become invalid, cease to apply, expire.

3 vencerse *vr* **(a)** (*persona*) to control o.s.

(b) (*soporte etc*) to break, snap, collapse (under the weight); (*Cono Sur*) (*gastarse*) to wear out, get worn out; (*deshacerse*) to come apart. **(c) se venció el plazo** (*LAm*) the time's up.

vencido 1 *adj* **(a)** (*gen*) beaten, defeated; *equipo etc* losing; **¡ay de los ~s!** woe to the conquered!; **darse por ~** to give up, acknowledge defeat; **ir de ~** to be all in, be on one's last legs; **la enfermedad va de vencida** the illness is past its worst; **la tormenta va de vencida** the worst of the storm is over.

(b) (*Com etc*) mature; due, payable; **con los intereses ~s** with the interest which is due; **pagar por meses ~s** to pay at the end of the month.

(c) (*LAm*) *billete, permiso etc* out of date.

2 *adv*: **pagar ~** to pay in arrears, pay for the month (*etc*) which is past.

vencimiento *nm* **(a)** (*bajo peso*) breaking, snapping; collapse. **(b)** (*Com etc*) expiration; maturity; **al ~, a su ~** when it matures, when it falls due.

venda *nf* bandage.

vendaje¹ *nm* (*Med*) dressing, bandaging.

vendaje² *nm* **(a)** (*Com*) commission. **(b)** (*LAm*: *plus*) bonus, perk*.

vendar [1a] *vt* **(a)** *herida* to bandage, dress; *ojos etc* to cover, put a bandage over, tie a cloth (*etc*) round. **(b)** (*fig*) (*cegar*) to blind; (*engañar*) to hoodwink.

vendaval *nm* gale, strong wind, hurricane; (*fig*) storm.

vendedor 1 *adj* selling; (*Fin*) **corriente vendedora** selling tendency, tendency to sell. **2** *nm* seller, vendor; retailer; (*en tienda*) salesman; **~ ambulante** street seller; hawker, pedlar, peddler (*US*); **~ a domicilio** door-to-door salesman; **~ por teléfono** telephone salesperson.

vendedora *nf* seller; (*dependienta*) salesgirl, saleswoman.

vendeja *nf* **(a)** (*venta*) public sale. **(b)** (*géneros*) collection of goods offered for sale.

vendepatrias *nmf invar* traitor.

vender [2a] **1** *vt* **(a)** (*gen*) to sell; to market; **~ por las casas** to peddle round the houses; **~ al contado** to sell for cash; **~ al descubierto** to sell short; **~ al por mayor** to sell wholesale; **~ al por menor** to sell retail; **estar sin ~** to remain unsold; **¡a mí que las vendo!** you can't catch an old bird with chaff!, I'm not falling for that one!

(b) (*fig*) to sell, betray.

2 venderse *vr* **(a)** (*Com*) to sell; to be sold; **~ a, ~ por** to sell at, sell for; to fetch, bring in; **este artículo se vende muy bien** this article is selling very well; **'se vende'** (*anuncio*) 'for sale'; **'véndese coche'** (*anuncio*) 'car for sale'; **no se vende** not for sale.

(**b**) ~ **caro** (*fig*) to play hard to get, be terribly choosy about one's friends*.
(**c**) (*fig*: *traicionarse*) to betray o.s., give o.s. away.
vendí *nm* certificate of sale.
vendibilidad *nf* saleability; marketability.
vendible *adj* saleable; marketable.
vendimia *nf* (**a**) (*de uvas*) grape harvest, wine harvest; (*relativo a calidad, año*) year; **la ~ de 1999** the 1999 vintage. (**b**) (*fig*) big profit, killing.
vendimiador(a) *nm/f* vintager.
vendimiar [1b] *vt* (**a**) *uvas* to harvest, pick, gather. (**b**) (*fig*) to take a profit from, squeeze a profit out of, make a killing with. (**c**) (‡: *matar*) to bump off‡.
vendré *etc V* **venir.**
venduta *nf* (**a**) (*LAm*: *subasta*) auction, public sale.
(**b**) (*Carib*: *frutería*) greengrocer's (shop), fruiterer's (shop); (*abacería*) small grocery store.
(**c**) (*Carib*: *estafa*) swindle.
vendutero *nm* (**a**) (*LAm*: *en subasta*) auctioneer. (**b**) (*Carib*: *comerciante*) greengrocer, fruiterer.
Venecia *nf* Venice.
veneciano, -a *adj, nm/f* Venetian.
veneno *nm* poison, venom.
venenoso *adj* poisonous, venomous.
venera *nf* scallop; scallop shell.
venerable *adj* venerable.
veneración *nf* veneration; worship.
venerando *adj* venerable.
venerar [1a] *vt* to venerate, revere; to worship.
venéreo *adj* venereal; **enfermedad venérea** venereal disease.
venero *nm* (**a**) (*Min*) lode, seam. (**b**) (*fuente*) spring. (**c**) (*fig*) source, origin; **~ de datos** mine of information.
venezolanismo *nm* word (*o* phrase *etc*) peculiar to Venezuela.
venezolano, -a *adj, nm/f* Venezuelan.
Venezuela *nf* Venezuela.
vengador 1 *adj* avenging. **2** *nm*, **vengadora** *nf* avenger.
venganza *nf* vengeance, revenge; retaliation; **tomar ~ de uno** to take vengeance on sb.
vengar [1h] **1** *vt* to avenge. **2 vengarse** *vr* to take revenge (*de una ofensa* for an offence; *de uno, en uno* on sb), avenge o.s.; to retaliate (*en* against, on).
vengativo *adj espíritu, persona* vindictive; *acto* retaliatory.
vengo *etc V* **venir.**
venia *nf* (**a**) (*perdón*) pardon, forgiveness.
(**b**) (*permiso*) permission, consent; **con su ~** by your leave, with your permission; **casarse sin la ~ de sus padres** to marry without the consent of one's parents.
(**c**) (*LAm Mil*) salute.
venial *adj* venial.
venialidad *nf* veniality.
venida *nf* (**a**) (*llegada*) coming; arrival; (*vuelta*) return. (**b**) (*fig*) impetuosity, rashness.
venidero *adj* coming, future; **los ~s** future generations, posterity, our (*etc*) descendants; **en lo ~** in (the) future.
venir [3r] **1** *vi* (**a**) (*gen*) to come (*a* to, *de* from); to arrive; **¡ven!, ¡venga!** come along!; come on (now)!; **¡ven acá!** come (over) here!; **¡ahora vengo!** I'm coming!, I'll be right there!; **vino a vernos** she came to see us; **~ por** to come for; **no me vengas con historias** don't come telling tales to me; **hacer ~ a uno** to summon sb; to call sb, have sb fetched; **le hicieron ~ desde Londres** they fetched him (all the way) from London; **en el periódico viene una nota** there's a note about it in the press.
(**b**) (*suceder*) to come, happen; **le vino una desgracia** she had a mishap, sth untoward happened to her; **venga lo que venga** (*o* **viniere**) come what may; **con todo lo que vino después** with everything that happened afterwards, with all that ensued; **(estar a) ver ~** to wait and see what happens; to sit on the fence; **se puede ver ~ la noche** one can face the evening ahead; **le vinieron muchos problemas** he was beset by problems.
(**c**) (*tiempo*) ... **que viene** next ..., *p.ej.* **el mes que viene** next month.
(**d**) (*provenir*) to come; **~ de** to come from, proceed from, stem from; to originate in; **la finca le viene de su hermano** the estate comes to him from his brother; **de ahí vienen muchos males** many evils spring from that; **de ahí viene que** ... hence it is that ..., and so it is that ...; thus it follows that ...; **la relación de X con Y viene desde lejos** the association of X and Y goes back a long way.
(**e**) (*fig*: *ocurrir etc*) to come; **le vino la idea de** + *infin* he got the idea of + *ger*, the idea of + *ger* came to him; **sentía ~me sueño** I felt sleep coming over me; **me vinieron ganas de llorar** I felt like crying, I had an urge to cry; **le vino un gran dolor de cabeza** he got a terrible headache.
(**f**) **~ a** + *infin* to come to + *infin*, serve to + *infin*; **el desastre vino a turbar nuestra tranquilidad** the disaster served to destroy our peace; **viene a llenar un gran vacío** it serves to fill a large gap; **viene a cumplir lo que habíamos empezado** it helps to finish off what we had begun; **venimos a conocerle en Bolivia** we got to know him in Bolivia; **vino a dar en la cárcel** he ended up in jail; *V* **caso, menos** *etc.*
(**g**) **~ a ser: viene a ser lo mismo** it comes to (about) the same thing; **viene a ser 84 en total** it amounts to 84 in all, it comes to 84 all together; **viene a ser más difícil que nunca** it's turning out to be more difficult than ever.
(**h**) **~ bien** to come just right; to be suitable, be convenient; to fit; (*Bot*) to do well, grow nicely; **eso vendrá bien para el invierno** that will come in handy for the winter; **me vendría bien una copita** I could do with a drink; **no me viene muy bien aquello** that doesn't suit me all that well; **~ bien a** (*ropa*) to suit, look well on, fit, be right for; **el tapón viene justo a la botella** the stopper fits the bottle exactly; **el abrigo te viene algo pequeño** the coat is rather small on you; **te viene estrecho por las espaldas** it's too tight round your shoulders; **~ mal** to come awkwardly, be inconvenient (*a* for); **~ mal a** (*ropa*) to look wrong on, not fit.
(**i**) (*locuciones*) **¿a qué viene esto?** what's behind all this?; **¿a qué vienes?*** what do you want?, what are you doing here?; **¿a qué viene afligirte?** why get so worked up?, what's the point of distressing yourself?; **¡venga!*** (*dámelo*) let's have it!, hand it over!; (*vamos*) let's go!; (*hagámoslo*) let's do it!; **¡venga ya!*** (*déjalo*) come off it!*; **¡venga la pluma esa!** let's have (a look at) that pen!; **¡venga una canción!** let's have a song!; **venga a** (*o* **de**) **pedir** she keeps on asking; **venga de preguntas** with endless questions, asking questions all the time.
(**j**) (*en tiempos continuos*) **venían andando desde mediodía** they had been walking since midday; **viene gastando mucho** she has been spending a lot; **eso vengo diciendo** that's what I've been saying all along.
(**k**) (+ *ptp*) **vengo cansado** I'm tired; **venía hecho polvo** he was worn out.
2 venirse *vr* (**a**) (*vino*) to ferment; (*masa*) to work.
(**b**) **~ abajo, ~ al suelo, ~ a (la) tierra** to fall down, collapse, tumble down; (*fig*) to fail, collapse, be ruined.
(**c**) **se nos vino encima la guerra** the war came upon us; **parece que todo se nos viene encima a la vez** everything seems to be happening to us all at once; **cualquier cosita se le viene encima** any little thing gets him down.
(**d**) **lo que se ha venido en llamar** ... what we have come to call ...
(**e**) *V* **mano.**
(**f**) (*CAm*‡) to come‡.
venoso *adj* (**a**) *sangre* venous. (**b**) *hoja etc* veined, ribbed.
venta *nf* (**a**) (*Com*) sale; selling; marketing; **~ por balance, ~ postbalance** stocktaking sale; **~s brutas** gross sales; **~ al contado** cash sale; **~ por correo** mail-order selling; **~s al detalle** retail sales; **~s directas** direct selling; **~ a domicilio** door-to-door selling; **~s de exportación** export sales; **~ por inercia** inertia selling; **~ de liquidación** sale, clearance sale, closing-down sale; **~ a plazos, ~ por cuotas** hire purchase; **~ al (por) mayor** wholesale; **~ al (por) menor, ~ piramidal** pyramid selling; **~ pública** public sale, auction; **~s por teléfono** telephone sales; **precio de ~** sale price; **servicio de ~** sales department; **poner algo a la ~** to put sth on sale, put sth up for sale; to market a product; **estar de** (*o* **en**) **~** to be (up) for sale, be on the market.
(**b**) (*posada*) country inn.
(**c**) (*Carib, Méx*) small shop, stall; (*Cono Sur*: *de feria etc*) stall, booth.
ventada *nf* gust of wind.
ventaja *nf* (**a**) (*gen*) advantage; (*en carrera*) start, advantage; (*Tenis*) advantage; (*en apuestas*) odds; **es un plan que tiene muchas ~s** it is a plan that has many advantages; **me dio una ~ de 4 metros, me dio 4 metros de ~** he gave me 4 metres start; **me dio una ~ de 20 puntos** he gave me an advantage of 20 points, he handicapped himself by 20 points; **llevar (la) ~ a** to have the advantage over; to be ahead of; to be one up on; **la ~ que A le lleva a B es grande** A has a big advantage over B; **sacar ~ de** to derive profit from, (*pey*) use to one's own advantage.

(**b**) (*Fin*: *esp LAm*) profit, gain; **dejar buena ~** to bring in a good profit.

(**c**) **~s** (*en empleo*) extras, perks*; **~s supletorias** fringe benefits.

ventajear [1a] *vt* (*And, CAm*) (**a**) (*rebasar*) to outstrip, surpass; (*llevar ventaja a*) to get the advantage of. (**b**) (*mejorar*) to better, improve on. (**c**) (*preferir*) to prefer, give preference to. (**d**) **~ a uno** (*pey*) to beat sb to it, get the jump on sb*.

ventajero *adj* (*LAm*) = **ventajista.**

ventajismo *nm* (**a**) opportunism. (**b**) (*LAm*) cheek*, nerve*.

ventajista *adj* (*poco escrupuloso*) unscrupulous; (*egoísta*) self-seeking, grasping; (*taimado*) sly, treacherous.

ventajosamente *adv* advantageously; (*Fin*) profitably; **estar ~ colocado** to be well placed.

ventajoso *adj* (**a**) (*gen*) advantageous; (*Fin*) profitable. (**b**) (*LAm*) = **ventajista.**

ventana *nf* (**a**) (*gen*) window; **~s dobles** double glazing; **~ de guillotina** sash-window; **~ de la nariz** nostril; **~ salediza** bay window; **tirar algo por la ~** to throw sth out of the window; (*fig*) to throw sth away, fail to make any use of sth.

(**b**) (*And*: *claro de bosque*) forest clearing, glade.

ventanaje *nm* windows.

ventanal *nm* large window.

ventanear [1a] *vi* to be always at the window, be forever peeping out.

ventanilla *nf* (**a**) (*gen*) small window; (*de sobre, taquilla, Aut, Ferro etc*) window; (*Fin*) bank counter; (*fig*) administrative office, public office; **programa de ~ única** programme to simplify bureaucratic procedures; **pasar por ~** (*fig*) to seek (*o* obtain) official approval. (**b**) (*Anat*: *t* **~ de la nariz**) nostril.

ventanillero, -a *nm/f* counter-clerk.

ventanillo *nm* (*ventana*) small window; (*mirilla*) peephole.

ventarrón* *nm* gale, violent wind, blast.

ventear [1a] **1** *vt* (**a**) (*perro etc*) *aire* to sniff.

(**b**) *ropa etc* to air, put out to dry, expose to the wind.

(**c**) (*CAm, Méx*) *animal* to brand.

(**d**) (*Cono Sur*) *adversario* to get far ahead of, leave far behind.

(**e**) (*And, Carib*) (*abanicar*) to fan; (*Agr*) to winnow.

2 *vi* (*curiosear*) to snoop, pry, come poking about; (*investigar*) to inquire, investigate.

3 ventearse *vr* (**a**) (*henderse*) to split, crack; (*ampollarse*) to blister; (*secarse*) to get too dry, spoil.

(**b**) (*Anat*) to break wind.

(**c**) (*And, Carib, Cono Sur*: *estar mucho fuera*) to be outdoors a great deal.

(**d**) (*And, Carib*: *engreírse*) to get conceited.

ventero, -a *nm/f* innkeeper.

ventilación *nf* (**a**) (*gen*) ventilation; **sin ~** unventilated. (**b**) (*corriente*) draught, air. (**c**) (*ventilador*) ventilator, opening for ventilation. (**d**) (*fig*) airing, discussion.

ventilado *adj* draughty, breezy.

ventilador *nm* ventilator; fan; **~ eléctrico** electric fan.

ventilar [1a] **1** *vt* (**a**) *cuarto etc* to ventilate.

(**b**) *ropa etc* to air, put out to air, dry in the air.

(**c**) (*fig*) *asunto* to air, discuss, talk over.

(**d**) (*fig*) *asunto privado* to make public, reveal.

2 ventilarse *vr* (**a**) (*cuarto etc*) to ventilate, air.

(**b**) (*persona*) to get some air, take a breather.

(**c**) (*Esp***) **~ a una** to screw sb**.

(**d**) (‡: *matar*) **~ a uno** to do sb in‡.

ventisca *nf* blizzard, snowstorm.

ventiscar [1g] *vi*, **ventisquear** [1a] *vi* (*nevar*) to blow a blizzard, snow with a strong wind; (*nieve*) to drift.

ventisquero *nm* (**a**) (*tormenta*) blizzard, snowstorm. (**b**) (*montón*) snowdrift; (*barranco*) gully (*o* slope *etc*) where the snow lies.

vento‡ *nm* (*Cono Sur*) dough‡.

ventolada *nf* (*LAm*) strong wind, gale.

ventolera *nf* (**a**) (*ráfaga*) gust of wind, blast.

(**b**) (*juguete*) windmill.

(**c**) (*fig*) (*vanidad*) vanity, conceit; (*satisfacción*) smugness; (*arrogancia*) arrogance; (*jactancia*) boastfulness; **tiene mucha ~*** she's terribly big-headed*.

(**d**) (*fig*: *capricho*) whim, wild idea; **le dio la ~ de +** *infin* he suddenly took it into his head to + *infin*.

(**e**) (*Méx***) fart**.

ventolina *nf* (**a**) (*Náut*) light wind. (**b**) (*Cono Sur, Méx*) sudden gust of wind. (**c**) (*Cono Sur Med*) wind, flatulence.

ventorrillo *nm* (**a**) (*taberna*) small inn, roadhouse. (**b**) (*Carib, Méx*: *tienda*) small shop.

ventosa *nf* (**a**) (*agujero*) vent, airhole. (**b**) (*Zool*) sucker; (*Téc*) peg (*etc*) that adheres by suction, suction pad. (**c**) (*Med*) cupping glass.

ventosear [1a] *vi* to break wind.

ventosidad *nf* wind; flatulence, windiness.

ventoso 1 *adj* (**a**) (*Met*) windy. (**b**) (*Anat*) windy, flatulent. **2** *nm* (**a**) (*Esp‡*) burglar. (**b**) (*CAm***) fart**.

ventral *adj* ventral.

ventregada *nf* brood, litter.

ventrículo *nm* ventricle.

ventrílocuo, -a *nm/f* ventriloquist.

ventriloquia *nf* ventriloquism.

ventrudo *adj* fat, potbellied.

ventura *nf* (**a**) (*dicha*) happiness.

(**b**) (*suerte*) luck, (good) fortune; chance; **mala ~** ill luck; **por su mala ~** as ill luck would have it; **a la ~** at random; **ir a la ~** to go haphazardly, go without a fixed plan; **vivir a la ~** to live in a disorganized way; **todo lo hace a la ~** he does it all in a hit-or-miss fashion; **por ~** fortunately; perhaps, by chance, *p.ej.* **¿piensas ir, por ~?** are you by any chance thinking of going?; **echar la buena ~ a uno** to tell sb's fortune; **probar la ~** to try one's luck; **~ te dé Dios** I wish you luck; **viene la ~ a quien la procura** God helps them that help themselves.

venturero *adj* (**a**) (*Méx*) **cosecha venturera** second crop. (**b**) (*fig*) temporary; casual; irregular.

venturoso *adj* (*dichoso*) happy; (*afortunado*) lucky, fortunate.

Venus 1 *nf* Venus. **2** *nm* (*Astron*) Venus.

venus *nf* (*fig*) venery, love-making, sexual delights.

venusiano, -a *adj, nm/f* Venusian.

veo-veo *nm* (*juego*) I spy (with my little eye).

ver [2u] **1** *vti* (**a**) (*gén*) to see; (*esp LAm*) to look at, watch; **la vi bajar la escalera** I saw her come downstairs; **lo he visto hacer muchas veces** I have often seen it done; **no lo veo** I can't see it; **desde aquí lo verás** you can see it from here; **¡lo que ves!** can't you see?, it's there for you to see!; **no veo nada en contra de eso** I see nothing against it; **te veo muy triste** you look really sad; **~ y creer** seeing is believing; **~ y callar** it's best to keep one's mouth shut about this; **un coche que no veas*** a car like you never saw before; **ir a ~ a uno** to go to see sb, go and see sb; **voy a ~** I'll go and see; **¡a ~!** let's see!, let's have a look!, show me!; (*fig*) I say!, hey!; (*And Telec*) hullo?; **¿a ~?** what's all this?; **a ~ qué nos dices** let's see what you've got to say; **¡a ~ qué pasa!*** just you dare!; **a ~ si ...** I wonder if ...; **a ~ si acabas pronto** I hope you can finish this off quickly; **es de ~** it's worth seeing, you really should see it; **eso está por ~** that remains to be seen.

(**b**) (*fig*: *entender*) to see, understand; **¿ves?** do you see?, (do you) get it?; **¿viste?** (*Cono Sur*) right?, are you with me?; **lo veo** I see; **¡verás!** you'll see!; **veremos** we'll see (about that); **¿no ves que ...?** don't you see that ...?; **como vimos ayer en la conferencia** as we saw in the lecture yesterday; **como veremos más adelante** as we shall see later; **según voy viendo** as I am now beginning to see; **no veo claro por qué lo quiere** I don't really see why he wants it; **a mi modo de ver** in my view; as I see it.

(**c**) (*fig*: *indagar*) to look into, examine, inquire into; **lo veremos** we'll look into it.

(**d**) (*Jur*) *pleito* to try, hear.

(**e**) **~ de +** *infin* to see about + *ger*; to try to + *infin*.

(**f**) (*locuciones*) **¡para que veas!** so there!; **si te vi no me acuerdo** they (*etc*) just don't want to know; there was no recognition, there was not a hint of gratitude; **me lo estoy viendo de almirante** I can just imagine him as an admiral; **lo estaba viendo** it's just what I expected, one could see this coming; **parece que lo estoy viendo** I can picture it quite clearly; **dejarse ~** (*etc*) to show, become apparent; to begin to tell; (*persona*) to show up, show one's face; **no dejarse ~** to keep away; to lie low, stay hidden; **la preocupación se dejaba ~ en su cara** the worry showed in his face; **las vi y las deseé** I just managed it by a great effort, it was a sweat but I did it; **echar de ~ algo** to notice sth; **¡hay que ~!** it just goes to show!; **hacer ~ que ...** to point out that ..., prove that ...; **no le puedo ~** I hate the sight of him, I can't stand him; **tener que ~ con** to concern, have to do with; **A no tiene nada que ~ con B** A has nothing to do with B; A is irrelevant to B; **vamos a ~** let's see ..., let me see ...; **y Vd que lo vea** and the same to you; **¿por qué no lo compraste, vamos a ~?** why didn't you buy it, I'd like to know?; *V t* **visto.**

(**g**) (*LAm*: *locuciones*) **¡vieras aquello!, ¡hubieras visto**

aquello! you should have seen that!, if only you'd seen that!; **¡nos estamos viendo!** (*Méx*) (I'll) be seeing you!; **eso está en veremos** that's still a long way off, that's very much in the future; **lo dijo por ~** (*Carib*), **lo dijo de por ~** (*Cono Sur*) he said it just as a joke; **todo quedó en veremos** it was all left in the air.

2 verse *vr* **(a)** (*2 personas*) to see each other; to meet; **~ con uno** to see sb, have a talk (*o* interview) with sb; **vérselas con uno** to confront sb, have it out with sb; **ahora apenas nos vemos** we hardly see (anything of) each other nowadays.

(b) (*1 persona etc*) to see o.s., imagine o.s.; (*ser visto*) to be seen; **véase la página 9** see page 9; **se le veía mucho en el parque** he used to be seen a lot in the park; **desde aquí no se ve** you can't see it from here; **se ve que sí** so it seems, apparently; **ya se ve** naturally, plainly; **ya se ve que ...** it is obvious that ...; apparently, it's turned out that ...; **¿cuándo se vio nada igual?** did you ever see the like?; **no se ha visto un lío parecido** you never saw such a mess, it was the biggest mess ever; **eso ya se verá** that remains to be seen; **¡habráse visto!*** did you ever!*, of all the cheek!*, well I like that!; **¡que se vean los forzudos!** let's see how tough you are!; come on, you tough guys*!

(c) (*encontrarse*) to find o.s., be; **~ en un apuro** to be in a jam; **se veía en la cumbre de la fama** he was at the height of his fame.

(d) (*Jur*) **el proceso se verá en mayo** the case will be heard in May.

(e) (*LAm: parecer*) to seem; **te ves cansado** you look tired; **te vas a ver precioso así** you'll look lovely like that.

3 *nm* **(a)** (*aspecto*) looks, appearance; **de buen ~** good-looking, of agreeable appearance; **tener buen ~** to be good-looking; **no tiene mal ~** she's not bad-looking.

(b) a mi ~ in my view, as I see it.

(c) a más ~, hasta más ~ au revoir.

vera *nf* edge, verge, border; (*del río*) bank; **a la ~ de** near, beside, next to; **a la ~ del camino** beside the road, at the roadside; **se sentó a mi ~** he sat down beside me.

veracidad *nf* truthfulness, veracity.

veracruzano 1 *adj* of Veracruz. **2** *nm*, **veracruzana** *nf* native (*o* inhabitant) of Veracruz; **los ~s** the people of Veracruz.

veragua *nf* (*CAm*) mildew (*on cloth*).

veranda *nf* veranda(h).

veraneante *nmf* holidaymaker, (summer) vacationer (*US*).

veranear [1a] *vi* to spend the summer (holiday); **veranean en Jaca** they go to Jaca for the summer, they holiday in Jaca; **es un buen sitio para ~** it's a nice place for a summer holiday.

veraneo *nm* summer holiday; **lugar de ~, punto de ~** summer resort, holiday resort; **estar de ~** to be away on one's summer holiday; **ir de ~ a la montaña** to go off to spend one's summer holidays in the mountains.

veraniego *adj* **(a)** (*del verano*) summer (*atr*). **(b)** (*fig*) slight, trivial.

veranillo *nm* **(a) ~ de San Martín** Indian summer. **(b)** (*CAm*) dry spell in the rainy season; **~ de San Juan** (*Cono Sur*) = Indian summer.

verano *nm* **(a)** summer. **(b)** (*And, Méx*) dry season.

veranoso *adj* (*LAm*) dry.

veras *nfpl* **(a)** (*verdad*) truth, reality; (*cosas serias*) serious things; (*hechos*) hard facts; *V* **burla**.

(b) de ~ really, truly; sincerely; in earnest; **¿de ~?** really?, indeed?, is that so?; **lo siento de ~** I am truly sorry; **ahora me duele de ~** now it really does hurt me; **esto va de ~** this is serious; I'm in earnest; **ahora va de ~ que lo hago** now I really am going to do it; **esta vez va de ~** this time it's the real thing.

veraz *adj* truthful, veracious.

verbal *adj* verbal; oral.

verbalmente *adv* verbally; orally.

verbalizar [1f] *vt* to verbalize, express.

verbena *nf* **(a)** (*Bot*) verbena. **(b)** (*fiesta*) fair; (*de santo*) open-air celebration on the eve of a saint's day; (*baile*) open-air dance.

verbenero *adj* of (*o* relating to) a *verbena* (*V* **verbena (b)**); **alegría verbenera** fun of the fair; **música verbenera** fair-ground music.

verbigracia *adv* for example, eg.

verbo *nm* **(a)** (*Ling*) verb; **~ activo** transitive verb; **~ auxiliar** auxiliary verb; **~ defectivo** defective verb; **~ deponente** deponent verb; **~ finito** finite verb; **~ intransitivo, ~ neutro** intransitive verb; **~ reflexivo** reflexive verb; **~ transitivo** transitive verb.

(b) (*juramento*) curse, oath; **echar ~s** to swear, curse.

(c) (*Liter*) language, diction, style; **de ~ elegante** elegant in style.

(d) el V~ (*Rel*) the Word.

verborragia *nf*, **verborrea** *nf* logorrhoea, verbal diarrhoea; torrent of words.

verborreico *adj* verbose; prone to fits of verbal diarrhoea.

verbosidad *nf* verbosity, wordiness; verbiage.

verboso *adj* verbose, wordy.

verdad *nf* **(a)** (*gen*) truth; (*veracidad*) truthfulness; (*fiabilidad*) reliability, trustworthiness; **la ~ de su relato** the truthfulness of his tale, the reliability of his account; **la ~ amarga** the bitter truth; **la ~ lisa y llana** the plain truth; **la pura ~ es que ...** the plain truth is that ...; **a la ~** really, in truth; **de ~** (*adj*) real, proper, *p.ej.* **un héroe de ~** a real hero; (*adv*) really, properly, *p.ej.* **entonces la pegó de ~** then he really did hit her; **¿de ~?** really?; **en ~** really, truly; **pues, la ~ no sé** well, the truth is I don't know; well, truth to tell, I don't know; **decir la ~** to tell the truth; **la ~ sea dicha** truth to tell, in all truth; **a decir ~ ...** to tell the truth ...; **faltar a la ~** to lie, be untruthful; **hablar con ~** to speak truthfully; **hay una parte de ~ en esto** there is some truth in this.

(b) es ~ it is true, it is so; (*confesión*) yes; I'm afraid so; **eso no es ~** that is not true; **es ~ que ...** it is true that ...; **bien es ~ que ...** it is of course true that ..., it is certainly true that ...; **si bien es ~ que ...** even though ..., despite the fact that ...; **¿~?, ¿no es ~?** isn't it?, aren't you?, don't you? (*etc*), isn't that so?

(c) media ~, ~ a medias half-truth; **~ de Pero Grullo** (*Esp*), **~ de Perogrullo** (*Esp*) platitude, truism; **sigo la ~ de Pero Grullo** I follow accepted truth; **~es del barquero** plain truths; **es una ~ como un puño** it's as plain as a pikestaff; **decir cuatro ~es a uno** to tell sb a few home truths, give sb a piece of one's mind.

verdaderamente *adv* really, indeed; truly; **~, no sé** I really don't know; **un hombre ~ bueno** a truly good man; **es ~ triste** it's really sad.

verdadero *adj* **(a)** (*gen*) true, truthful; (*de fiar*) reliable, trustworthy.

(b) *persona* truthful.

(c) (*fig*) true, real, veritable; **es un ~ héroe** he's a real hero; **fue un ~ desastre** it was a real disaster, it was a veritable disaster; **es un ~ amigo** he's a true friend.

verde 1 *adj* **(a)** green; **~ botella** bottle-green; **~ lima** lime-green; **~ manzana** apple-green; **~ oliva** olive-green.

(b) *fruta etc* green, unripe; *planta* green; *legumbres* green, fresh; *madera* unseasoned; (*fig*) *proyecto etc* premature; **¡están ~s!** sour grapes!; **segar la hierba en ~** to cut the grass while it is still green.

(c) (*fig*) *persona* unduly amorous, randy* (despite one's advanced years); **viejo ~** randy old man*, dirty old man*; **viuda ~** merry widow.

(d) (*fig*) *canción, chiste etc* blue, smutty, scabrous, dirty.

(e) (*Pol*) green.

(f) (*locuciones*) **está ~*** (*inocente*) he's very green; (*ignorante*) he doesn't know a thing; **estar ~ de envidia** to be green with envy; **¡si piensan eso, están ~s!** if that's what they think, they've got another think coming!; **pasar las ~s y las maduras** to have a rough time of it; **poner ~ a uno** (*: *regañar*) to give sb a dressing-down*; (*insultar*) to abuse sb violently; (*denigrar*) to run sb down.

2 *nm* **(a)** (*color*) green, green colour.

(b) (*Bot*) (*hierba*) green, green grass; (*de árboles*) foliage; (*Agr*) green fodder; **sentarse en el ~** to sit on the grass.

(c) darse un ~ to eat a lot, eat one's fill (*de* of); **darse un ~ de conciertos** to have a surfeit of concerts, have one's fill of concerts.

(d) (**) 1000-peseta note.

(e) (*Cono Sur*) (*pasto*) grass, pasture; (*mate*) maté; (*ensalada*) salad.

(f) (*And*) plantain.

(g) (*Carib, Méx: campo*) country, countryside.

(h) (*Carib*: policía*) policeman.

3 *nmf* (*Pol*) Green; **los V~s** the Greens, the Green Party.

verdear [1a] *vi* **(a)** (*volverse verde*) to go green, turn green.

(b) (*tirar a verde*) to be greenish; (*mostrarse verde*) to show green, look green.

(c) (*Cono Sur*) to drink maté.

(d) (*Cono Sur Agr*) to graze.

verdecer [2d] *vi* to turn green, grow green; (*persona*) to go green.

verdegay *adj, nm* light green.
verdemar *adj, nm* sea-green.
verderón *nm* (**a**) (*Orn*) greenfinch. (**b**) (*Esp*‡) 1000-peseta note.
verdete *nm* verdigris.
verdiazul *adj* greenish-blue.
verdiblanco *adj* light green.
verdín *nm* (**a**) (*color*) bright green, fresh green. (**b**) (*Bot*) (*capa*) scum; (*musgo*) moss; (*verdete*) verdigris. (**c**) (*en la ropa etc*) green stain.
verdinegro *adj* dark green.
verdino *adj* bright green.
verdirrojo *adj* green and red.
verdolaga *nf*: **crecer como la ~** (*CAm*) to spread like wildfire.
verdón 1 *adj* (*Cono Sur*) (**a**) (*gen*) bright green. (**b**) *fruta* slow to ripen. **2** *nm* (**a**) (*Orn*) = **verderón**. (**b**) (*Cono Sur*: *cardenal*) bruise, welt.
verdor *nm* (**a**) (*color*) greenness; (*Bot*) verdure, lushness. (**b**) (*fig*: *t* **~es**) youthful vigour, lustiness.
verdoso *adj* greenish.
verdugo *nm* (**a**) (*Hist*) executioner; hangman.
(**b**) (*fig*) (*amo*) cruel master, slave-driver; (*tirano*) tyrant; (*atormentador*) tormentor.
(**c**) (*fig*: *tormento*) torment.
(**d**) (*látigo*) lash.
(**e**) (*cardenal*) weal, welt.
(**f**) (*Bot*) twig, shoot, sprout.
(**g**) (*arma*) slender rapier.
(**h**) (*de lana*) balaclava, woollen hood.
verdugón *nm* (**a**) (*cardenal*) weal, welt. (**b**) (*Bot*) twig, shoot, sprout. (**c**) (*And*: *rasgón*) rent, rip.
verdulera *nf* (**a**) (*comerciante*) greengrocer. (**b**) (*pey*) coarse woman, fishwife.
verdulería *nf* greengrocer's (shop).
verdulero *nm* greengrocer.
verdura *nf* (**a**) (*gen*) greenness; (*Bot*) greenery, verdure. (**b**) **~s** (*Culin*) greens, green vegetables, (*esp*) cabbage. (**c**) (*fig*) smuttiness, scabrous nature.
verdusco *adj* dark green, dirty green.
vereco* *adj* (*CAm*) cross-eyed.
verecundia *nf* bashfulness, sensitivity, shyness.
verecundo *adj* bashful, sensitive, shy.
vereda *nf* (**a**) path, lane; **entrar en ~** (*persona*) to toe the line; (*elemento*) to fall into place, fit into the normal pattern; **hacer entrar en ~ a uno, meter en ~ a uno** to make sb toe the line; **ir por la ~** (*fig*) to do the right thing; to keep to the straight and narrow.
(**b**) (*LAm*: *acera*) pavement, sidewalk (*US*).
(**c**) (*And*) (*pueblo*) village, settlement; (*zona*) section of a village.
(**d**) (*Méx*: *raya*) parting.
veredicto *nm* verdict; **~ de culpabilidad** verdict of guilty; **~ de inculpabilidad** verdict of not guilty.
veredón *nm* (*Cono Sur*) broad pavement, broad sidewalk (*US*).
verga *nf* (**a**) (*vara*) rod, stick; (*Náut*) yard, spar. (**b**) (*CAm**) **a ~** by hook or by crook; **por la ~ grande** miles away, at the back of beyond*. (**c**) (*Zool*) penis; (**‡) prick**‡, cock**‡; **me vale ~**‡** I don't give a toss**‡; **¡ni ~!** no way !*, you must be joking!
vergajo *nm* (**a**) (*Anat*: *de toro*) pizzle; (**‡) prick**‡; **dar un ~**‡** to have a screw**‡. (**b**) (*látigo*) lash, whip. (**c**) (*And**) swine*, rat*.
vergazo *nm*: **un ~ de** (*CAm**) lots of, loads of.
vergel *nm* (*liter*) (*jardín*) garden; (*huerto*) orchard.
vergonzante *adj* (**a**) (*avergonzado*) shamefaced; (*tímido*) bashful; **pobre ~** poor but too ashamed to beg openly. (**b**) (*vergonzoso*) shameful, shaming.
vergonzosamente *adv* (*V adj*) (**a**) bashfully, shyly; modestly. (**b**) shamefully, disgracefully.
vergonzoso *adj* (**a**) *persona* bashful, shy, timid; modest. (**b**) *acto, asunto etc* shameful, disgraceful, shocking; **es ~ que** ... it is disgraceful that ... (**c**) **partes vergonzosas** (*Anat*) private parts.
vergüenza *nf* (**a**) (*sentimiento*) shame; sense of shame, feelings of shame; **perder la ~** to lose all sense of shame, cast aside all restraints; **sacar a uno a la ~** to hold sb up to shame; **tener ~** to be ashamed; **tener ~ de** + *infin* to be ashamed to + *infin*; **si tuviera ~ no lo haría** if he had any shame he wouldn't do it.
(**b**) (*timidez*) bashfulness, shyness, timidity; (*azoramiento*) embarrassment; (*modestia*) (sexual) shame, modesty; **me da ~ decírselo** I feel too shy to say it to him, it embarrasses me to say it to him, it upsets me to say it to him; **sentir ~ ajena** to feel embarrassed on somebody else's account.
(**c**) (*escándalo*) disgrace; **¡qué ~!** what a disgrace!, what a scandal!; shame (on you)!; **el hijo es la ~ de su familia** the son is a disgrace to his family; **es una ~ que esté tan sucio** it's a disgrace that it should be so dirty.
(**d**) **~s** (*Anat*) private parts.
vericueto *nm* rough part, rough track, piece of difficult terrain.
verídico *adj* true, truthful.
verificable *adj* verifiable.
verificación *nf* (**a**) (*inspección*) check, checkup, inspection; (*prueba*) testing; verification; proving. (**b**) (*cumplimiento*) carrying out; performance; holding. (**c**) (*de profecía etc*) realization.
verificar [1a] **1** *vt* (**a**) (*Mec etc*) to check, inspect; to test; *resultados* to check (up on); *hechos* to verify, establish, substantiate; *testamento* to prove.
(**b**) *inspección etc* to carry out; *ceremonia* to perform; *elecciones* to hold.
2 verificarse *vr* (**a**) (*suceso etc*) to occur, happen; (*reunión etc*) to be held, take place.
(**b**) (*profecía etc*) to come true, prove true, be realized.
verija *nf* (**a**) (*Anat*) groin, genital region. (**b**) (*LAm*: *de caballo*) flank.
verijón* *adj* (*Méx*) idle, lazy.
veringo *adj* (*And*) nude, naked.
veringuearse [1a] *vr* (*And*) to undress.
verismo *nm* realism, truthfulness; factual nature.
verista *adj* realistic, true to life; factual.
verja *nf* (*reja*) grating, grille; (*cerca*) railing(s); (*puerta*) iron gate.
vermicida *nm* vermicide.
vermífugo *nm* vermifuge.
verminoso *adj* infected, wormy.
vermú *nm, pl* **vermús, vermut** [ber'mu] *nm, pl* **vermuts** [ber'mu] **1** *nm* vermouth. **2** *nf* (*And, Cono Sur Teat*) early performance.
vernáculo *adj* vernacular.
vernal *adj* spring (*atr*), vernal.
Verónica *nf* Veronica.
verónica *nf* (**a**) (*Bot*) veronica, speedwell. (**b**) (*Taur*) *a kind of pass with the cape.*
verosímil *adj* (*probable*) likely, probable; (*creíble*) credible.
verosimilitud *nf* likeliness, probability; credibility; (*Liter*) verisimilitude.
verosímilmente *adv* in a likely way; credibly.
verraco *nm* boar, male pig; (*And*) ram; (*Carib*) wild boar.
verraquear [1a] *vi* (**a**) (*gruñir*) to grunt. (**b**) (*niño*) to wail, howl with rage.
verraquera *nf* (**a**) (*enfado*) crying spell, fit of rage, tantrum. (**b**) (*Carib*: *borrachera*) drunken spell.
verruga *nf* (**a**) (*Anat, Bot*) wart. (**b**) (*latoso*) bore, pest, nuisance. (**c**) (*: *defecto*) fault, bad habit.
verrugoso *adj* warty, covered in warts.
versación *nf* (*Cono Sur, Méx*) expertise, skill.
versada *nf* (*LAm*) long tedious poem.
versado *adj*: **~ en** versed in, conversant with; expert in, skilled in.
versal (*Tip*) **1** *adj* capital. **2** *nf* capital (letter).
versalitas *nfpl* (*Tip*) small capitals.
Versalles *nm* Versailles.
versar [1a] *vi* (**a**) (*girar*) to go round, turn.
(**b**) **~ sobre** to deal with, discuss, be about; to turn on.
(**c**) (*Carib*: *versificar*) to versify, improvise verses.
(**d**) (*Carib*: *charlar*) to chat, talk.
(**e**) (*Méx**: *guasearse*) to tease, crack jokes.
versátil *adj* (**a**) (*Anat etc*) versatile, mobile, loose, easily turned. (**b**) (*fig*) versatile. (**c**) (*fig*: *pey*) fickle, changeable.
versatilidad *nf* (**a**) versatility, mobility, looseness, ease of movement. (**b**) (*fig*) versatility. (**c**) (*fig*: *pey*) fickleness, changeableness.
versículo *nm* (*Biblia*) verse.
versificación *nf* versification.
versificador(a) *nm/f* versifier.
versificar [1g] **1** *vt* to versify, put into verse. **2** *vi* to write verses, versify.
versión *nf* version; translation; adaptation; **~ (de) concierto** concert performance.
versionar [1a] *vt* (*traducir*) to translate; (*adaptar*) to adapt, make a new version of; (*Mús*) to adapt; to record a ver-

sion of.
vers.º *nm* (*Rel*) *abr de* **versículo** verse, v.
verso *nm* (**a**) (*gen*) verse; ~ **libre** free verse; ~ **suelto** blank verse; **teatro en** ~ verse drama.
(**b**) (*un* ~) line; **en el segundo** ~ **del poema** in the second line of the poem.
(**c**) **echar** ~ (*Carib, Méx**) to rabbit on*.
versus *prep* versus, against.
vértebra *nf* vertebra.
vertebración *nf* (*V vt*) (**a**) support. (**b**) structuring, essential structure.
vertebrado *adj, nm* vertebrate.
vertebrador *adj*: **fuerza ~a** unifying force, force making for cohesion; **columna ~a** central column; **soporte** ~ principal support.
vertebral *adj* vetebral.
vertebrar [1a] *vt* (**a**) (*apoyar*) to hold up, support. (**b**) (*estructurar*) to provide the backbone of, be the essential structure of.
vertedero *nm* (**a**) (*de basura*) rubbish dump, tip. (**b**) = **vertedor (a)**. (**c**) (*Cono Sur*: *pendiente*) slope, hillside.
vertedor *nm* (**a**) (*salida*) runway, overflow; (*desagüe*) drain, outlet; spillway. (**b**) (*Náut*) scoop, bailer. (**c**) (*cuchara etc*) scoop, small shovel.
verter [2g] **1** *vt* (**a**) *contenido, líquido etc* to pour (out); to empty (out); (*sin querer*) to pour, spill; *luz, sangre* to shed; *basura* to dump, tip, shoot; ~ **los granos del saco en el camión** to pour grain from a sack into a lorry; ~ **el café sobre el mantel** to spill (*o* upset) one's coffee on the tablecloth.
(**b**) *recipiente* to empty (out); to tip up; (*sin querer*) to upset.
(**c**) (*Ling*) to translate (*a* into).
2 *vi* (*río*) to flow, run (*a* into); (*pendiente etc*) to fall (*a* towards).
vertical 1 *adj* vertical; upright. **2** *nf* vertical; **en** ~ straight (up).
verticalidad *nf* (*posición*) vertical position; (*dirección*) vertical direction.
verticalmente *adj* vertically.
vértice *nm* (**a**) (*cúspide*) vertex, apex; top; ~ **geodésico** bench mark, survey point. (**b**) (*Anat*) crown of the head.
verticilo *nm* whorl.
vertido *nm* (**a**) (*acto*) spillage; dumping; pouring. (**b**) **~s** (*residuo*) waste; residue; effluent; **el** ~ **de residuos nucleares** the disposal of nuclear waste.
vertiente *nf* (**a**) (*declive*) slope. (**b**) (*fig*) (*lado*) side, aspect; (*punto de vista*) point of view, viewpoint. (**c**) (*And, Cono Sur, Méx*) spring, fountain.
vertiginosamente *adv* (*V adj*) (**a**) giddily, dizzily. (**b**) (*fig*) excessively; very rapidly; **los precios suben** ~ prices are rising rapidly, prices are spiralling up.
vertiginoso *adj* (**a**) (*Med*) giddy, dizzy, vertiginous. (**b**) (*fig*) *velocidad* dizzy, excessive; *subida etc* very rapid.
vértigo *nm* (**a**) (*Med*) giddiness, dizziness, vertigo; dizzy spell; **puede provocar ~s** it may cause giddiness; **bajar así me produce** ~ going down like that makes me dizzy.
(**b**) (*fig*) (*frenesí*) sudden frenzy; (*locura*) fit of madness, aberration; (*actividad*) intense activity; (*remolino*) whirl, maelstrom; **el** ~ **de los negocios** the frenzied rush of business; **el** ~ **de los placeres** the whirl of pleasures; **¡es el ~, tío!*** it's great, man!*
(**c**) (*Esp**) **de** ~: **con una velocidad de** ~ at a giddy speed; **fue un jaleo de** ~ it was an almighty row*; **tiene un talento de** ~ he has a fantastic talent*; **es de** ~ **cómo crece la ciudad** the city grows at a frenzied speed, the town spreads at a tremendous rate*.
vesania *nf* rage, fury; (*Med*) insanity.
vesánico *adj* raging, furious; (*Med*) insane.
vesícula *nf* vesicle; blister; ~ **biliar** gall-bladder.
vespa *nf* Vespa, motor scooter.
vespertino 1 *adj* evening (*atr*). **2** *nm* (*diario*) evening paper.
vespino *nm* small motorcycle.
vesr(r)e* *nm* (*Cono Sur*) backslang.
vestal *adj, nf* vestal.
veste *nf* (*liter*) garb.
vestíbulo *nm* vestibule, lobby, hall; (*Teat*) foyer.
vestiditos *nmpl* (*frec*) baby clothes.
vestido *nm* (**a**) (*gen*) dress, costume, clothing; **historia del** ~ history of costume.
(**b**) (*un* ~: *de mujer*) dress, frock; costume, suit; (*And, CAm, Cono Sur*: *de hombre*) suit; ~ **de debajo** undergarment; ~ **de encima** outer garment; ~ **isotérmico** wetsuit.
vestidor *nm* dressing-room.
vestidura *nf* (**a**) (*liter*) clothing, apparel.
(**b**) (*Ecl*) **~s** vestments; **~s sacerdotales** priestly vestments; **rasgarse las ~s** to tear one's hair.
vestigial *adj* vestigial.
vestigio *nm* vestige, trace; sign; **~s** remains, relics; **no quedaba el menor** ~ **de ello** there was not the slightest trace of it.
vestimenta *nf* (**a**) (*ropa*) clothing; (*pey*) gear, stuff*, things. (**b**) **~s** (*Ecl*) vestments.
vestir [3k] **1** *vt* (**a**) *cuerpo, persona* to dress (*de* in), clothe (*de* in, with); *estatua, superficie etc* to clothe, cover, drape (*de* in, with); *pared* to hang (*de* with); (*adornar*) to dress up, adorn, deck, embellish (*de* with); **estar vestido de** to be dressed in, be clad in; (*como disfraz*) to be dressed as; **vístame lentamente, que tengo prisa** more haste less speed.
(**b**) *ropa* (*ponerse*) to don, put on; (*llevar*) to wear; **vestía traje azul con sombrero** he was wearing a blue suit and a hat; **lo viste siempre** she always wears it.
(**c**) (*pagar la ropa de etc*) to clothe, pay for the clothing of.
(**d**) (*sastre*) to dress, make clothes for; **le viste un buen sastre** he has his clothes made at a good tailor's.
(**e**) *idea etc* to express (*de* in); *defecto etc* to conceal, cover up, disguise; ~ **el rostro de gravedad** to put on a serious expression.
2 *vi* (**a**) (*persona*) to dress; ~ **bien** to dress well; ~ **con elegancia** to dress smartly; ~ **de negro** to dress in black, wear black; ~ **de sport** to dress casually; ~ **de uniforme** to wear a uniform; **el mismo que viste y calza** the selfsame, the very same.
(**b**) (*ropa*) to look well, be right (for an occasion); **traje de (mucho)** ~ formal suit, (*pey*) suit that is too dressy; **el vestido negro viste más que el azul** the black dress is more formal (*o* suitable) than the blue one.
3 vestirse *vr* (**a**) (*persona*) to dress o.s., get dressed, put on one's clothes; (*fig*) to cover itself, become covered (*de* in); ~ **de azul** to wear blue, dress in blue; **el árbol se está vistiendo de verde** the tree is coming out in leaf, the tree is turning green; **le gusta vestirse en París** he likes to buy his clothes in Paris; **apenas gana para** ~ she hardly earns enough to keep her in clothes.
(**b**) (*fig*: *Med*) to get up again (after an illness).
(**c**) (*fig*) ~ **de cierta actitud** to adopt a certain attitude; ~ **de severidad** to adopt a severe tone (*etc*).
vestón *nm* (*Cono Sur*) jacket.
vestuario *nm* (**a**) (*ropa*) clothes, wardrobe; (*Teat*) wardrobe, costumes; (*Mil*) uniform.
(**b**) (*cuarto*: *Teat*) dressing-room, (*gen*) backstage area; (*en edificio público etc*) cloakroom; (*Dep*) changing-room; pavilion.
Vesubio *nm* Vesuvius.
veta *nf*(*Min*) seam, vein, lode; (*en madera*) grain; (*en carne, piedra etc*) streak, stripe.
vetar [1a] *vt* to veto; *socio* to blackball.
vetazo *nm* (*And*) lash.
veteada *nf* (*And*) flogging, beating.
veteado 1 *adj* veined; grained; streaked, striped (*de* with); *tocino* streaky. **2** *nm* veining; graining; streaks, markings.
vetear [1a] *vt* (**a**) (*gen*) to grain; to streak. (**b**) (*And*: *azotar*) to flog, beat.
veteranía *nf* (*status*) status (*o* dignity *etc*) of being a veteran; (*servicio*) long service; (*antigüedad*) seniority.
veterano 1 *adj* veteran. **2** *nm*, **veterana** *nf* veteran; (*fig*) old hand, old stager.
veterinaria[1] *nf* veterinary science, veterinary medicine.
veterinario, -a[2] *nm/f* veterinary surgeon, vet, veterinarian (*US*).
vetevé *nm* (*And*) sofa.
veto *nm* veto; **poner (su)** ~ **a** to veto; **tener** ~ to have a veto.
vetulio *nm* (*And*) old man.
vetustez *nf* (*liter*) great age, antiquity; (*iró*) venerable nature; hoariness.
vetusto *adj* (*liter*) very old, ancient, venerable; (*iró*) venerable, ancient; hoary.
vez *nf* (**a**) (*gen*) time, occasion; instance; **aquella** ~ **en Tánger** that time in Tangiers; **a veces** at times; **a la** ~ at a time, at the same time; **a la** ~ **que ...** at the same time as ...; **alguna ~, algunas veces** sometimes; **¿lo viste alguna ~?** did you ever see it?; **alguna que otra** ~ occasionally, now and again; **cada** ~ every time; **cada** ~ **que ...,** ~ **que ...** (*And*) (*como conj*) each time that ..., whenever ...; **cada** ~

más increasingly, more and more; **iba cada ~ más lento** it went slower and slower; **le encuentro cada ~ más inaguantable** he gets more and more unbearable; **contadas veces** seldom, rarely; **¿cuántas veces?** how often?, how many times?; **de ~ en cuando** now and again, from time to time, occasionally; **en veces** by fits and starts; with interruptions; **las más de las veces** most of the times, mostly, in most cases; **muchas veces** often; **otra ~** again; **pocas veces** seldom, rarely; **por esta ~** this time, this once; **rara ~** seldom, rarely; **repetidas veces** repeatedly, over and over again; **tal ~** perhaps; **toda ~ que ...** (*como conj*) since ...; although ...; in view of the fact that ...; **varias veces** several times; repeatedly.

(**b**) (*con número*) **una ~** once; **una ~ que** (*como conj*) once ...; as soon as ..., when ...; **una ~ dice que sí y otra que no** first he says yes and then he says no; **érase una ~** once upon a time (there was); **había una ~ una princesa** there was once a princess; **de una ~** in one go, all at once; outright; without a break, straight off; **¡acabemos de una ~!** let's get it over!, let's have done with it!; **una y otra ~** time and (time) again; **de una ~ para siempre** (*o* **por todas**) once and for all, for good; **dos veces** twice; **dos veces tanto** twice as much; **con una velocidad dos veces superior a la del sonido** at a speed twice that of sound; **tres veces** three times; **cien veces** hundreds of times, lots of times; **la primera ~ que le vi** the first time I saw him; **por primera ~** for the first time; **por última ~** for the last time; **por enésima ~** for the umpteenth time*; **no se permite golpearlo segunda ~** you can't hit it again, you aren't allowed a second shot at it.

(**c**) (*Mat*) **7 veces 9** 7 times 9.

(**d**) (*turno*) turn; **a su ~** in his turn; **en ~ de** instead of, in place of; **ceder la ~** to give up one's turn, (*en cola etc*) give up one's place; **cuando le llegue la ~** when his turn comes; **hacer las veces de** to take the place of, act for, stand in for; to serve as, do duty as; **pedir la ~** to speak out, establish one's rights.

veza *nf* vetch.

v.g. = **v.gr.**

v.gr. *abr de* **verbigracia** videlicet, namely, *viz.*

vía 1 *nf* (**a**) (*calle etc*) road; (*ruta*) route; track; (*And Aut*) lane (*of a motorway*); (*fig*) way; (*Rel etc*) way; **~ de acceso** access road; service road; **~ aérea** airway; lane; (*Correos*) airmail; **por ~ aérea** by air, (*Correos*) (by) airmail; **~ de agua** leak; **abrirse una ~ de agua** to spring a leak; **~ de circunvalación** bypass, ringroad; **~ de comunicación** communication route; **V~ Crucis** Way of the Cross; **~ de escape** escape route, way out; **~ férrea** railway; **~ fluvial** waterway; **V~ Láctea** Milky Way; **¡~ libre!** make way!, clear the way!; **dar ~ libre a** to give the go-ahead to; **~ marítima** sea route, seaway; **por ~ marítima** by sea; **~ pública** public thoroughfare; **~ romana** Roman road; **~ terrestre** overland route, (*Correos*) surface route; **por ~ terrestre** overland, by land, (*Correos*) by surface mail; **por ~ de** via, by way of; through; (*fig*) by way of, as, as a kind of; **dejar la ~ libre al desafuero** to leave the way open for abuse.

(**b**) (*Ferro*) track; line; (*ancho*) gauge; **~ ancha** broad gauge; **~ doble** double track; **de ~ estrecha** narrow-gauge (*atr*); **~ muerta** siding, (*fig*) dead end; **~ normal** standard gauge; **~ única** single track; **de ~ única** single-track (*atr*); **el tren está en la ~ 8** the train is at platform 8; **la estación tiene 18 ~s** the station has 18 platforms.

(**c**) (*Anat*) passage, tube; tract; **~s digestivas** digestive tract; **~s respiratorias** respiratory tract; **~s urinarias** urinary tract; **por ~ bucal** through the mouth, by mouth; **por ~ interna** (*Med*) internally.

(**d**) (*fig*) system; way, means; channel; **~s de hecho** physical violence, assault and battery; **~ judicial** process of law, legal means; **recurrir a la ~ judicial** to go to law, have recourse to the law; **por ~ oficial** through official channels; by official means; **tercera ~** middle way, compromise.

(**e**) (*fig*) **en ~s de** in process of; **un país en ~s de desarrollo** a developing country; **una especie en ~s de extinción** an endangered species, a species on the verge of extinction; **el asunto está en ~s de una solución** the matter is on its way to a solution, the question is in process of being solved.

2 *prep* (*Ferro etc*) via, by way of; through.

viabilidad *nf* (**a**) viability; feasibility. (**b**) (*Aut*) road conditions.

viabilizar [1f] *vt* to make viable.

viable *adj* viable; *plan etc* feasible.

viacrucis *nf* Way of the Cross; (*fig*) load of disasters, heap of troubles; **hacer la ~‡** ≈ to go on a pub-crawl*.

viada *nf* (*And*) speed.

viaducto *nm* viaduct.

viajante 1 *adj* travelling. **2** *nm* (*t* **~ de comercio**) commercial traveller, salesman; **~ en jabones** traveller in soap.

viajar [1a] *vi* (**a**) to travel (*t Com*); to journey; **ha viajado mucho** he has travelled a lot; **~ en coche** to go in a car, ride (in a car); **~ por Ruritania** to travel through (*o* across) Ruritania; to tour Ruritania. (**b**) (‡) to trip‡.

viajazo *nm* (**a**) (*Méx*: *empujón*) push, shove. (**b**) (*Carib*: *azote*) lash. (**c**) (*CAm**: *bronca*) telling-off*.

viaje[1] *nm* (**a**) (*gen*) journey; trip; (**~** *largo*) tour; (*Náut*) voyage; **el ~, los ~s** (*gen*) travel; **~ en coche** ride, trip by car; **~ en barco** boat trip, sail; **~ de buena voluntad** goodwill trip, goodwill mission; **~ de compras** shopping trip; **~ de ensayo** trial run; **~ de Estado** state visit; **~ de fin de curso** end-of-year trip; **~ de ida** outward journey, trip out; **~ de ida y vuelta** (*o* **ida y retorno**), **~ redondo** (*LAm*) round trip, journey there and back; **~ de negocios, ~ de trabajo** business trip; **~ de novios** honeymoon; **~ de recreo** pleasure trip; **¡buen ~!, ¡feliz ~!** bon voyage!, have a good trip!; **estar de ~** to be travelling, be on a trip.

(**b**) (*Com etc*: *carga*) load; cartload, cartful (*etc*); **un ~ de leña** a load of wood.

(**c**) (*Carib*: *vez*) time; **lo repitió varios ~s** he repeated it several times; **de un ~** (*Carib*) all in one go, at one blow; all at once.

(**d**) **echar un ~ a uno** (*CAm*) to give sb a telling-off*.

(**e**) (‡: *droga*) trip‡; **estar de ~** to be high‡, be on a trip‡; **ir de ~** to trip‡.

viaje[2]* *nm* (*tajada*) slash (with a razor); (*golpe*) bash*; (*puñalada*) stab; **tirar un ~ a uno** to take a slash at sb.

viajero 1 *adj* travelling; (*Zool*) migratory. **2** *nm*, **viajera** *nf* traveller; (*en vehículo, Ferro etc*) passenger; **¡señores ~s, al tren!** will passengers kindly board the train?

vial 1 *adj* road (*atr*); traffic (*atr*); **circulación ~** road traffic; **fluidez ~** free movement of traffic; **reglamento ~** (*control*) traffic control; (*código*) rules of the road, highway code; **seguridad ~** road safety, safety on the road(s).

2 *nm* road.

vialidad *nf* highway administration.

vianda *nf* (**a**) (*t* **~s**) food. (**b**) (*Carib*: *verduras*) vegetables. (**c**) (*And, Cono Sur*) lunch tin, dinner pail (*US*).

viandante *nmf* (*viajero*) traveller, wayfarer; (*en ciudad*) passer-by; pedestrian.

viaraza *nf* (*And, CAm, Cono Sur*) (**a**) (*enojo*) fit of anger (*o* temper); **estar con la ~** to be in a bad mood. (**b**) (*idea*) bright idea.

viario *adj* road (*atr*); **red viaria** road network; **sistema ~** transport system, system of communications.

viático *nm* (**a**) (*Hist*) food for a journey. (**b**) (*Fin*) travel allowance; **~s** travelling expenses. (**c**) (*Ecl*) viaticum.

víbora *nf* (**a**) viper (*t fig*). (**b**) (*Méx*: *cartera*) money belt.

viborear [1a] *vi* (**a**) (*Cono Sur*: *serpentear*) to twist and turn, snake along. (**b**) (*Carib Naipes*) to mark the cards.

vibración *nf* (**a**) (*temblor*) vibration; shaking; (*pulsación*) throbbing, pulsating. (**b**) (*Ling*) roll, trill. (**c**) (*Psic*) **vibraciones** vibrations, vibes*; **vibraciones negativas** bad vibes*.

vibracional *adj* vibratory.

vibrador *nm* vibrator.

vibráfono *nm* vibraphone.

vibrante 1 *adj* (**a**) (*gen*) vibrant, vibrating.

(**b**) (*Ling*) rolled, trilled.

(**c**) (*fig*) *voz, slogan etc* ringing; *reunión etc* exciting, lively; **~ de** ringing with, vibrant with.

2 *nf* (*Ling*) vibrant.

vibrar [1a] **1** *vt* (**a**) (*gen*) to vibrate; (*agitar*) to shake, rattle. (**b**) (*Ling*) to roll, trill. **2** *vi* to vibrate; to shake, rattle; (*pulsar*) to throb, beat, pulsate.

vibratorio *adj* vibratory.

viburno *nm* viburnum.

vicaria *nf* woman priest.

vicario *nm* (*Ecl*) curate; deputy; **~ general** vicar-general; **V~ de Cristo** Vicar of Christ (*the Pope*).

vice* *nmf* deputy; second in command; vice-president.

vice... *pref* vice...

vicealcalde, -esa *nm/f* deputy mayor.

vicealmirante *nm* vice-admiral.

vicecampeón, -ona *nm/f* runner-up.

viceconsejero, -a *nm/f* deputy minister in a regional government.

viceconsul *nmf* vice-consul.
vicedecano, -a *nm/f* subdean.
vicedirector(a) *nm/f* (*Com etc*) deputy director; (*Escol*) deputy headmaster, deputy headmistress; (*Prensa*) deputy editor.
vicegerente *nmf* assistant manager.
vicelíder *nmf* deputy leader.
viceministro, -a *nm/f* deputy minister.
Vicente *nm* Vincent.
vicepresidencia *nf* vice-presidency; vice-chairmanship.
vicepresidente *nmf* (*Pol*) vice-president; (*de comité etc*) vice-chairman.
vicetiple *nf* chorus-girl.
viceversa *adv* vice versa.
viciado *adj* (**a**) *aire* foul, thick, stale. (**b**) *texto* corrupt.
viciar [1b] **1** *vt* (**a**) *costumbres etc* to corrupt, pervert, subvert.
(**b**) (*Jur*) to nullify, invalidate.
(**c**) *texto* to corrupt, vitiate, falsify; to interpret erroneously.
(**d**) *sustancia* to adulterate; *aire* to make foul; *comida etc* to spoil, taint, contaminate.
(**e**) *objeto* to bend, twist, put out of shape; to warp.
2 viciarse *vr* (**a**) (*persona*) to take to vice, get depraved, become corrupted; *V t* **enviciarse.**
(**b**) (*objeto*) to warp, lose its shape.
vicio *nm* (**a**) *gen* vice; (*carácter vicioso*) viciousness, depravity.
(**b**) (*mala costumbre*) bad habit, vice; **el ~** (*droga*) the drug habit, drug addiction; **~ inveterado, ~ de origen** ingrained bad habit; **tiene el ~ de no contestar las cartas** he has the bad habit of not answering letters; **no le podemos quitar el ~** we can't get him out of the habit; **darse al ~** (*droga*) to take to drugs; **de ~, por ~** out of sheer habit; for no reason at all; **hablar de ~** to chatter away; **quejarse de ~** to complain for no reason at all; **eso tiene mucho ~*** that's very addictive.
(**c**) (*defecto*) defect, blemish; (*Jur etc*) error; (*Ling*) mistake, incorrect form; solecism; **adolece de ciertos ~s** it has a number of defects, there are certain things wrong with it.
(**d**) (*de superficie etc*) warp; (*de línea*) twist, bend.
(**e**) (*con niño*) excessive indulgence.
(**f**) (*Bot*) rankness, luxuriance, lushness.
(**g**) **estar de ~** (*LAm*) to be idle.
(**h**) **de ~*** very tasty; great*, super*.
viciosamente *adv* (**a**) viciously; dissolutely. (**b**) (*Bot*) rankly, luxuriantly.
viciosidad *nf* viciousness.
vicioso 1 *adj* (**a**) vicious; depraved, dissolute; *niño* spoiled.
(**b**) (*Mec etc*) faulty, defective.
(**c**) (*Bot*) rank, luxuriant, lush.
2 *nm*, **viciosa** *nf* (**a**) vicious person, depraved person.
(**b**) (*adicto*) addict, fiend.
vicisitud *nf* (*desgracia*) accident, upset, mishap; (*cambio*) sudden change; **~es** vicissitudes.
víctima *nf* (**a**) (*gen*) victim; (*fig, t de ave etc*) prey; **fue ~ de una estafa** she was the victim of a swindle; **es ~ de alguna neurosis** he is a prey to some neurosis; **hay pocas ~s mortales** there are not many dead; **no hay que lamentar ~s del accidente** there were no casualties in the accident.
(**b**) (*Hist*) sacrifice.
victimar [1a] *vt* (*herir*) to wound; (*matar*) to kill.
victimario, -a *nm/f* (**a**) (*gen*) person responsible for somebody's suffering (*o* accident *etc*).
(**b**) (*LAm*) person responsible for wounding (*o* killing), killer.
victimismo *nm* victimization; persecution.
victimizar [1f] *vt* to victimize.
Victoria *nf* Victoria.
victoria *nf* victory; triumph; **~ moral** moral victory; **~ pírrica** Pyrrhic victory.
victoriano *adj* Victorian.
victoriosamente *adv* victoriously.
victorioso *adj* victorious.
victrola *nf* (*LAm†*) gramophone, phonograph (*US*).
vicuña *nf* vicuna.
vichadero *nm* (*Cono Sur*) = **bichadero.**
vich(e)ar [1a] *vt* (*Cono Sur*) = **bichear.**
vid *nf* vine.
vid. *abr de* **vide** see.
vida *nf* (**a**) (*gen*) life; (*modo de vivir*) way of life; (*años de ~*) lifetime, life span; (*profesión etc*) livelihood; **tuvo una ~ ejemplar** he lived an exemplary life; **la ~ de estos edificios es breve** the life of these buildings is short; **así es la ~** such is life, that's life; **¿qué es de tu ~?** what's the news?; **este sol es la ~** this sunshine is a real tonic; **¡esto es ~!** this is living!; **¡es la ~!, ¡qué ~ ésta!** well, that's life!; **está escribiendo la ~ de Quevedo** he is writing the life (*o* a biography) of Quevedo.
(**b**) (*locuciones con prep*) **¡hermana de mi ~!** my dear sister!; **de por ~** for life, for the rest of one's life; **un amigo de toda la ~** a lifelong friend; **en ~** during his (*etc*) lifetime, while still alive; **en la ~, en mi ~** (*negativo*) never, never in my life; **entre ~ y muerte** at death's door; **¡por ~ de ... !** upon my soul!; **¡por ~ del chápiro verde!** I'll be darned!
(**c**) (*locuciones con adj etc*) **~ airada** criminal life; underworld; **de ~ airada** criminal; loose-living, immoral; **~ arrastrada** wretched life; **la ~ cotidiana** everyday life; **doble ~** double life; **~ eterna** everlasting life; **~ íntima** private life; **de ~ libre** loose-living, immoral; **mala ~** dissolute life; prostitution; **mujer de ~ alegre, mujer de mala ~** prostitute; **~ y milagros de uno*** full details about sb; **cuéntame tu ~ y milagros** tell me all about yourself; **la otra ~** the next life; the life to come; **~ perra, ~ de perros** dog's life, wretched life; **~ privada** private life; **~ sentimental** love-life; **~ útil** (*Com*) life span; (*Téc*) useful life.
(**d**) (*locuciones con verbo*) **estar con ~** to be still alive; **amargar la ~ a uno** to make sb's life a misery; **complicarse la ~** to make life difficult for o.s.; **cortar la ~ de uno** to cut sb off (in his prime); **darse buena ~, darse ~ de canónigo, darse la ~ padre*** to live well, live in style, do o.s. proud*; **dar la ~** to sacrifice one's life; **dar mala ~ a uno** to ill-treat sb, give sb a wretched time of it; **enterrarse en ~** to go into seclusion; **escapar con ~** to escape alive; **ganarse la ~** to make a living; **desde hace 5 años goza de mejor ~** she passed away 5 years ago; **hacer ~ marital** to live together (as man and wife); **hacer por la ~*** to eat; **no le va la ~ en esto** it's not as though his life depends on it; **meterse en ~s ajenas** to pry, snoop; to meddle; **pasar a mejor ~** (*euf*) to pass away; **pasar la ~ a tragos*** to have a miserable life; **pegarse la gran ~*, pegarse la ~ padre*** to live it up*, live the life of Riley; **perder la ~** to lose one's life; **quitar la ~ a uno** to take sb's life; **quitarse la ~** to kill o.s., do away with o.s.; **rehacer la ~** to start a new life; **tener siete ~s como los gatos** (*hum*) to have nine lives; **vender cara la ~** to sell one's life dearly.
(**e**) (*de ojos, mirada etc*) liveliness, brightness.
(**f**) (*en oración directa*) **¡~!, ¡~ mía!, ¡mi ~!** my darling!, my love!
(**g**) (**euf*) prostitution; **una mujer de la ~** a prostitute, a woman on the game*; **echarse a la ~** to take up prostitution; **hacer la ~** to be on the game*.
(**h**) (‡: *hachís*) pot‡, hash*.
videncia *nf* clairvoyance; fortune-telling.
vidente 1 *adj* sighted, able to see. **2** *nmf* (**a**) (*no ciego*) sighted person, person who can see. (**b**) (*profeta*) seer, prophet; clairvoyant(e). (**c**) (*TV*) viewer.
vídeo *nm* (*gen*) video; (*aparato*) video, video recorder; (*cinta*) video; **~ comunitario** community video; **~ doméstico** home video; **~ musical** music video; **~ promocional** promotional video; **cinta de ~** videotape; **película de ~** videofilm; **grabar en ~** to videotape, record.
vídeo... *pref* video ...
videoadicción *nf* video addiction.
videoadicto, -a *nm/f* video addict.
videoaficionado, -a *nm/f* video fan.
videocámara *nf* video camera.
videocasete *nm* video cassette.
videocasetera *nf* video cassette recorder.
videocine *nm* video films.
videocinta *nf* videotape.
videoclip *nm, pl* **videoclips** videoclip, video.
videoclub *nm, pl* **videoclubs** *o* **videoclubes** videoclub.
videoconferencia *nf* videoconference, teleconference.
videocopia *nf* pirate video.
videodisco *nm* video disc.
videofilm(e) *nm* videofilm.
videófono *nm* videophone.
videofrecuencia *nf* video frequency.
videograbación *nf* (*acto*) videotaping, video recording; (*cinta*) recording.
videograbadora *nf* video recorder.
videográfico *adj* video (*atr*).
videograma *nm* video recording, videogram, video.

videojuego *nm* video game.
videolibro *nm* video book.
videomarcador *nm* electronic scoreboard.
videopiratería *nf* video piracy.
videoproyector *nm* video projector.
videorregistrador *nm* video (tape-)recorder.
videorrevista *nf* video magazine.
videoteca *nf* video (film) library; videotape library.
videotelefonía *nf* videotelephony.
videoteléfono *nm* videophone.
videoterminal *nm* video terminal; video display unit.
videotex *nm* Videotex ®.
videotexto *nm* videotext.
vidorra* *nf* good life, easy life; **pegarse la ~** to live it up*.
vidorria *nf* (**a**) (*Cono Sur*: *vida alegre*) gay life, easy life. (**b**) (*And, Carib*: *vida triste*) miserable life.
vidriado 1 *adj* glazed. **2** *nm* (**a**) (*barniz*) glaze, glazing. (**b**) (*loza*) glazed earthenware.
vidriar [1b] **1** *vt* to glaze. **2 vidriarse** *vr* to become glazed.
vidriera *nf* (**a**) (*Ecl*: *t* **~ de colores**) stained glass window; (*t* **puerta ~**) glass door; glass partition.
(**b**) (*LAm*) (*escaparate*) shop window; (*vitrina*) showcase.
(**c**) (*Carib*) tobacco stall, tobacco kiosk.
vidriería *nf* (**a**) (*fábrica*) glassworks. (**b**) (*objetos*) glassware.
vidriero *nm* glazier.
vidrio *nm* (**a**) (*gen*) glass; **~ cilindrado** plate glass; **~ de color(es)**, **~ coloreado, ~ pintado** stained glass; **~ deslustrado** (*o* **esmerilado**) frosted glass, ground glass; **~ inastillable** laminated glass, splinter-proof glass; **~ plano** sheet glass; **~ tallado** cut glass; **bajo ~** under glass; **pagar los ~s rotos*** to carry the can*; **soplar ~*** to booze*.
(**b**) (*: *vaso*) glass; **tomar unos ~s** to have a few drinks.
(**c**) (*Cono Sur*: *botella*) bottle of liquor.
(**d**) (*LAm*: *ventanilla*) window.
vidrioso *adj* (**a**) (*gen*) glassy; (*como vidrio*) glass-like; (*frágil*) brittle, fragile, delicate.
(**b**) *ojo* glassy; fishy; *expresión, mirada* glazed; *superficie* slippery as glass, glassy.
(**c**) *persona* touchy, sensitive.
(**d**) *asunto* delicate.
vidurria *nf* (*And, Carib, Cono Sur*) = **vidorria**.
vieira *nf* scallop.
vieja *nf* (**a**) (*gen*) old woman.
(**b**) (*) **la ~** (*madre*) my mum*; **la ~** (*esposa*) my old woman*.
(**c**) (*Cono Sur*: *petardo*) cracker, squib.
(**d**) (*Méx*: *de cigarro*) cigar stub.
viejada *nf* (*Cono Sur*) group of old people.
viejales* *nm invar* old chap*.
viejera *nf* (**a**) (*Carib*: *vejez*) old age. (**b**) (*Carib*: *trasto*) bit of old junk.
viejo 1 *adj* (**a**) (*gen*) old; **~ como el mundo, más ~ que el cagar*** as old as the hills; **se cae de ~** (*persona*) he's so old he can hardly walk; (*objeto*) it's falling to bits (*o* pieces); **hacerse ~** to grow old, get old; **no parece más ~ de un día** he doesn't look a day older.
(**b**) **zapatero de ~** cobbler.
(**c**) **Plinio el V~** Pliny the Elder.
2 *nm* (**a**) (*persona*) old man; **el V~ de Pascua** (*LAm*) Father Christmas; *V* **verde**.
(**b**) (*) **el ~** (*padre*) my dad*; **mi ~** (*esposo*) my old man*; **los ~s** the old folks, my (*etc*) mum and dad*.
(**c**) (*LAm**: *amigo*) mate, pal*; (*en oración directa*) old chap*.
viejón *adj* (*And, Cono Sur, Méx*) elderly.
Viena *nf* Vienna.
vienés, -esa *adj, nm/f* Viennese.
viento *nm* (**a**) (*corriente de aire*) wind, breeze; **corre ~, hay ~, hace ~** it is windy, there is a wind; **hace mucho ~** it is very windy; **cuando sopla el ~** when the wind blows; **~s alisios** trade winds; **~ ascendente** up-current; **~ de cara** headwind; **~ de cola, ~ de espalda, ~ a favor, ~ trasero** tailwind; **~ colado** draught; **~ contrario, ~ de proa** headwind; **~ de costado** crosswind, sidewind; **~ de la hélice** slipstream; **~ huracanado** hurricane wind, violent wind; **~ lateral** sidewind; **~s nuevos** (*fig*) winds of change; **~ en popa** following wind; **ir ~ en popa** to go splendidly; to do extremely well; (*de negocio*) to prosper, boom; **~ portante** prevailing wind; **~ racheado** gusty wind, squally wind; **~ terral** land breeze; **estar lleno de ~** to be empty, have nothing inside; **beber los ~s por uno** to be crazy about sb; **echar a uno con ~ fresco*** to chuck sb out; **¡vete con ~ fresco!*** go to blazes!*, and good riddance!; **le mandé a tomar ~** I sent him packing; **publicar algo a los cuatro ~s** to tell all and sundry about sth, shout sth from the rooftops; **soplan ~s de fronda** there's trouble brewing; **sorber los ~s por uno** to be crazy about sb; **como el ~** like the wind; **contra ~ y marea** come hell or high water, come what may.
(**b**) (*Anat*) wind, flatulence.
(**c**) (*Mús*) wind; wind instruments, wind section.
(**d**) (*Caza*) scent.
(**e**) (*de perro*) keen scent, sense of smell.
(**f**) (*fig*: *vanidad*) conceit, vanity; **estar lleno de ~** to be puffed up (with conceit).
(**g**) (*de poste, tienda*) guy, guy-rope.
(**h**) (*And*: *de cometa*) strings of a kite.
(**i**) (*CAm, Carib Med*) rheumatism.
vientre *nm* (**a**) (*Anat*) (*estómago etc*) belly; (*matriz*) womb; **bajo ~** lower abdomen; **llevar un hijo en su ~** to carry a child in one's womb.
(**b**) (*intestino*) bowels; **~ flojo** looseness of the bowels; **descargar el ~, exonerar el ~, hacer de ~** to have a bowel movement.
(**c**) (*de animal muerto*) guts, entrails, offal.
(**d**) (*Zool*) foetus, unborn young.
(**e**) (*de vasija*) belly, wide part.
vier. *abr de* **viernes** *m* Friday, Fri.
viernes *nm invar* Friday; **V~ Santo** Good Friday.
Vietnam *nm* Vietnam; **~ del Norte** North Vietnam; **~ del Sur** South Vietnam.
vietnamita[1] 1 *adj, nmf* Vietnamese. **2** *nm* (*Ling*) Vietnamese.
vietnamita[2] *nf* (*máquina*) duplicator.
viga *nf* (*de madera*) balk, timber; (*Arquit*) beam, rafter; (*metal*) girder; **~ maestra** main beam; **~ transversal** crossbeam; **estar contando las ~s** (*fig*) to be gazing vacantly at the ceiling.
vigencia *nf* (**a**) (*ley etc*) operation; (*validez*) validity, applicability; (*de contrato etc*) term, life; **estar en ~** to be in force; to be valid, apply; **entrar en ~** to take effect, come into operation; **perder ~** to go out of use, be no longer applicable; **tener ~** to be valid, apply; to prevail.
(**b**) (*norma social*) social convention, norm of society.
vigente *adj* valid, applicable, in force; prevailing.
vigésimo *adj, nm* twentieth.
vigía 1 *nm* look-out, watchman; **los ~s** (*Náut*) the watch. **2** *nf* (**a**) (*Mil etc*) watchtower. (**b**) (*Geog*) reef, rock.
vigilancia *nf* vigilance, watchfulness; **burlar la ~ de uno** to escape sb's vigilance; **tener a uno bajo ~** to keep watch on sb, keep sb under observation.
vigilante 1 *adj* vigilant, watchful; alert.
2 *nm* (**a**) (*guardián*) watchman, caretaker; (*de cárcel*) warder; (*de trabajo*) supervisor; (*en tienda*) shopwalker, store detective; (*de museo*) keeper; **~ jurado** security guard; **~ de noche, ~ nocturno** night watchman.
(**b**) (*Cono Sur*: *policía*) policeman.
vigilantemente *adv* vigilantly, watchfully.
vigilar [1a] **1** *vt* (*velar por*) to watch, watch over; (*cuidar*) to look after, keep on eye on; *instalación, prisionero etc* to guard; *máquina* to tend; *frontera etc* to guard, police, patrol; *trabajo etc* to supervise, superintend; **~ a los niños para que no se hagan daño** to see that the children come to no harm; **~ la leche para que no se salga** to keep an eye on the milk so that it does not boil over.
2 *vi* to be vigilant, be watchful, stay alert; to keep watch; **~ por, ~ sobre** to watch over.
vigilia *nf* (**a**) (*estar sin dormir*) wakefulness, being awake; (*vigilancia*) watchfulness; **pasar la noche de ~** to spend a night without sleep, stay awake all night.
(**b**) (*trabajo*) night work, late work; time spent working late; (*estudio*) night-time study, lucubrations.
(**c**) (*Ecl*) vigil; abstinence; **día de ~** day of abstinence; **comer de ~** to fast, abstain from meat.
vigor *nm* (**a**) (*fuerza*) vigour; (*vitalidad*) vitality; (*resistencia*) toughness, stamina, hardiness; (*empuje*) drive; **con ~** vigorously.
(**b**) = **vigencia**; **en ~** in force; valid, applicable, operative; **entrar en ~** to take effect, come into force; **poner en ~** to put into effect, put into operation, enforce; *V* **mantenerse**.
vigorización *nf* strengthening; encouragement, stimulation; revitalization.
vigorizador *adj*, **vigorizante** *adj* invigorating; bracing; revitalizing; *medicina* tonic.

vigorizar [1f] *vt* to invigorate; to strengthen, encourage, stimulate; to revitalize.
vigorosamente *adv* vigorously; strongly, forcefully; strenuously.
vigoroso *adj* vigorous; strong, tough, forceful; *esfuerzo* strenuous; *protesta etc* vigorous, forceful; *niño* sturdy, strong.
viguería *nf* beams, rafters; girders, metal framework.
vigués 1 *adj* of Vigo. **2** *nm*, **viguesa** *nf* native (*o* inhabitant) of Vigo; **los vigueses** the people of Vigo.
vigueta *nf* joint, small beam.
VIH *nm abr de* **virus de la inmunodeficiencia humana** human immunodeficiency virus, HIV; ~ **positivo** HIV positive.
vihuela *nf* (*Hist*) *an early form of the guitar*.
vihuelista *nmf* (*Hist*) *vihuela* player.
vijúa *nf* (*And*) rock salt.
vikingo, -a *nm/f* Viking.
vil *adj persona* low, villainous, blackguardly; *acto* vile, foul, rotten; *conducta* despicable; *trato* unjust, shabby, mean.
vileza *nf* (**a**) (*cualidad*) low character, villainy; vileness, foulness; despicable nature; injustice, shabbiness, meanness.
(**b**) (*una* ~) vile act, base deed, villainy.
vilipendiar [1b] *vt* (*V n*) (**a**) to vilify, revile, abuse. (**b**) to despise, scorn.
vilipendio *nm* (**a**) (*denuncia*) vilification, abuse. (**b**) (*desprecio*) contempt, scorn; humiliation.
vilipendioso *adj* contemptible; humiliating.
vilmente *adv* villainously; vilely, foully; despicably; unjustly, shabbily, meanly.
vilo: **en** ~ *adv* (**a**) **en** ~ (up) in the air; suspended, unsupported; **sostener algo en** ~ to hold sth up.
(**b**) (*fig*) **estar en** ~, **quedar en** ~ to be left in the air, be left in suspense.
villa *nf* (**a**) (*romana etc*) villa. (**b**) (*pueblo*) small town; (*Pol*) borough, municipality; **la V**~ (**y Corte**) Madrid; ~ **miseria** slum quarter, shanty-town; ~ **olímpica** Olympic village.
Villadiego: **tomar las de** ~* to beat it quick*.
villanaje *nm* (**a**) (*status*) humble status, peasant condition. (**b**) (*personas*) peasantry, villagers.
villancico *nm* (Christmas) carol.
villanesco *adj* peasant (*atr*); village (*atr*), rustic.
villanía *nf* (**a**) (*Hist*) humble birth, lowly status.
(**b**) (*cualidad*) villainy, baseness.
(**c**) (*una* ~) = **vileza** (**b**).
(**d**) (*dicho*) obscene expression, filthy remark.
villano 1 *adj* (**a**) (*Hist*) peasant (*atr*); rustic.
(**b**) (*fig*: *grosero*) coarse.
(**c**) (*fig*: *vil*) villainous, base.
2 *nm*, **villana** *nf* (**a**) (*Hist*) villein, serf; (*esp fig*) peasant, rustic.
(**b**) (*fig*) rotter*, rat*, swine*.
(**c**) (*LAm*) villain.
villorrio *nm* one-horse town, dump*; (*LAm*) shantytown.
villista *nmf* (*Méx Pol*) supporter of Pancho Villa.
vinagre *nm* vinegar; ~ **de sidra** cider vinegar; ~ **de vino** wine vinegar.
vinagrera *nf* (**a**) (*recipiente*) vinegar bottle; ~**s** cruet stand. (**b**) (*LAm Med*) heartburn, acidity.
vinagreta *nf* (*Culin*: *t* **salsa** ~) vinaigrette (sauce).
vinagroso *adj* (**a**) (*amargo*) vinegary, tart. (**b**) (*fig*) *persona* bad-tempered, sour.
vinatería *nf* (**a**) (*tienda*) wine shop. (**b**) (*comercio*) wine trade.
vinatero, -a *nm/f* wine-merchant, vintner.
vinaza *nf* nasty wine, wine from the dregs.
vinazo *nm* strong wine.
vinculación *nf* (**a**) (*gen*) linking, binding; (*fig*) bond, link, connexion. (**b**) (*Jur*) entail.
vinculante *adj fallo* binding (*para* on).
vincular [1a] **1** *vt* (**a**) (*liar*) to link, bind, tie (*a* to); *esperanzas etc* to base, found (*en* on); ~ **su suerte a la de otro** to make one's fate depend on sb else's; **están estrechamente vinculados entre sí** they are closely bound together.
(**b**) (*Jur*) to entail.
2 vincularse *vr* to link o.s. (*a* to).
vínculo *nm* (**a**) (*gen*) link, bond, tie; ~ **de parentesco** family ties, ties of blood; **los** ~**s de la amistad** the bonds of friendship; **hay un fuerte** ~ **histórico** there is a strong historical link.
(**b**) (*Jur*) entail.
vincha *nf* (*And, Cono Sur*) hairband.
vindicación *nf* (**a**) (*gen*) vindication. (**b**) (*venganza*) vengeance, revenge.
vindicar [1g] **1** *vt* (**a**) (*vengar*) to avenge.
(**b**) (*justificar*) to vindicate.
(**c**) (*Jur*) = **reivindicar**.
2 vindicarse *vr* (**a**) (*vengarse*) to avenge o.s.
(**b**) (*justificarse*) to vindicate o.s.
vine *etc V* **venir**.
vineo* *nm*: **ir de** ~ to go boozing*.
vinería *nf* (*And, Cono Sur*) wine-shop.
vínico *adj* (*Quím*) wine (*atr*).
vinícola *adj industria etc* wine (*atr*); *región* wine-growing (*atr*); wine-making (*atr*).
vinicultor(a) *nm/f* wine-grower.
vinicultura *nf* wine-growing, wine production.
vinificable *adj* that can be made into wine, suitable for wine-making.
vinificación *nf* fermentation.
vinílico *adj* vinyl (*atr*).
vinilo *nm* vinyl.
vinillo *nm* thin wine, weak wine.
vino *nm* (**a**) wine; ~ **añejo** mellow wine, mature wine; ~ **del año** new wine, wine for early drinking; ~ **base** base; ~ **blanco** white wine; ~ **de la casa** house wine; ~ **corriente** ordinary wine, plonk*; ~ **espumoso** sparkling wine; ~ **generoso** strong wine, full-bodied wine; ~ **de Jerez** sherry; ~ **litúrgico,** ~ **de misa,** ~ **para consagrar** communion wine; ~ **de Málaga** Malaga (wine); ~ **de mesa** table wine; ~ **de Oporto** port (wine); ~ **de pasto** ordinary wine; ~ **peleón** coarse wine, plonk*; ~ **de postre** dessert wine; ~ **seco** dry wine; ~ **de solera** vintage wine; ~ **tinto** red wine; ~ **tranquilo** still wine; **aguar** (*o* **bautizar, cristianar**) **el** ~ to water the wine; **dormir el** ~ to sleep off a hangover*; **echar agua al** ~ (*fig*) to water down a statement; **tener buen** ~ to know how to carry one's liquor; **tener mal** ~ to get wild after a few drinks.
(**b**) (*recepción*) drinks, reception, party; ~ **de honor** official reception; (*Cono Sur*) special wine; **después de la conferencia hubo un** ~ there were drinks after the lecture.
vinolento *adj* boozy‡, fond of the bottle.
vinoso *adj sabor* like wine, vinous; *color* wine-coloured.
vinoteca *nf* collection of wines.
vinotería *nf* (*Méx*) wine-shop.
viña *nf* (**a**) (*viñedo*) vineyard. (**b**) (*Méx*) rubbish-dump.
viñador(a) *nm/f* vine grower; wine grower.
viñal *nm* (*Cono Sur*) vineyard.
viñatero, -a *nm/f* (*And, Cono Sur*) vine-grower; wine-grower.
viñedo *nm* vineyard.
viñeta *nf* (*Arte y fig*) vignette; (*Prensa*) cartoon, sketch, drawing; (*emblema*) emblem, badge, device.
viola *nf* (**a**) (*Bot*) viola. (**b**) (*Mús*) viola; (*Hist*) viol; ~ **de gamba** viola da gamba.
violáceo *adj* violet.
violación *nf* (*V vt*) (**a**) violation. (**b**) rape. (**c**) offence, infringement. (**d**) ~ **de contrato** (*Com*) breach of contract.
violado 1 *adj* violet. **2** *nm* violet (colour).
violador 1 *nm* rapist. **2** *nm*, **violadora** *nf* violator; offender (*de* against).
violar [1a] *vt* (**a**) *sagrado, territorio etc* to violate.
(**b**) *mujer* to rape.
(**c**) *ley etc* to break, offend against, infringe; *acuerdo, principio etc* to violate, break.
violencia *nf* (**a**) (*gen*) violence; (*fuerza*) force; (*Jur*) violence, assault; (*Pol*) rule by force; **no** ~ non-violence; **usar** ~ **para abrir una caja** to use force to open a box; **no se consigue nada con él usando la** ~ you will not achieve anything with him by using force; **amenazar** ~ to threaten violence, (*turba etc*) to turn ugly; **apelar a la** ~ to resort to violence, use force; **hacer** ~ **a** = **violentar** (**b**), (**c**).
(**b**) (*una* ~) unjust act, damaging act; outrage.
(**c**) (*azoramiento*) embarrassment; (*situación*) embarrassing situation; **si eso te cuesta** ~ if that embarrasses you; **estar con** ~ to be (*o* feel) embarrassed.
violentamente *adv* (*V adj*) (**a**) violently; furiously, wildly.
(**b**) awkwardly, unnaturally.
(**c**) embarrassingly, awkwardly.
(**d**) (*interpretación*) distortedly.
(**e**) (*LAm*) quickly.
violentar [1a] **1** *vt* (**a**) *puerta etc* to force; *rama etc* to bend, twist (out of shape); *casa* to break into, enter forcibly.
(**b**) *persona* to force, use force on, persuade forcibly; to subject to violence; (*Jur*) to assault.
(**c**) (*fig*) *principio* to violate, outrage.

(**d**) (*fig*) *sentido* to distort, twist, force.
2 violentarse *vr* to force o.s.
violentismo *nm* (*Cono Sur*) agitation; social unrest; political violence.
violento *adj* (**a**) (*gen*) violent; *esfuerzo etc* furious, wild; *discurso, medio, persona, temperamento etc* violent; *deporte* tough, physically demanding, (*pey*) rough; **mostrarse ~** to turn violent, offer violence.
(**b**) *postura etc* awkward, unnatural; cramped; *acto* unnatural, forced; **me es muy ~ consentir en ello** it goes against the grain with me to agree with it.
(**c**) *situación etc* embarrassing, awkward; **para mí todo esto es un poco ~** this is all a bit awkward for me.
(**d**) *estado de persona* embarrassed, awkward; **estar** (*o* **sentirse**) **~** to be (*o* feel) embarrassed; **me encuentro ~ estando con ellos** I feel awkward when I'm with them; **la discusión entre los dos me hacía estar ~** the argument between them made me feel embarrassed.
(**e**) (*fig*) *interpretación* forced, distorted.
(**f**) (*LAm*) quick, sudden; **tuvo que hacer un viaje ~** she had to make a sudden trip.
violeta 1 *nf* violet; **~ africana** African violet; **~ de genciana** gentian violet; **conservador a la ~** dyed-in-the-wool conservative. **2** *adj invar* violet.
violín 1 *nm* (**a**) (*instrumento*) violin.
(**b**) **~ de Ingres** spare-time occupation (*o* art, hobby *etc*) at which one shines.
(**c**) (*Carib*) bad breath.
(**d**) **de ~** (*Méx*) gratis, free.
(**e**) **embolsar el ~** (*Carib**) to get egg on one's face*; **meter ~ en bolsa** (*Cono Sur**) to be embarrassed; **pintar un ~*** (*Méx*) to make a rude sign; **tocar ~*** (*And*) to play gooseberry.
2 *nmf* (*persona*) violinist; **primer ~** first violin.
violinista *nmf* violinist.
violón 1 *nm* (*instrumento*) double bass; **tocar el ~*** to talk rot*. **2** *nmf* (*persona*) double bass player.
violonc(h)elista *nmf* cellist.
violonc(h)elo *nm* cello.
vip* *nm, pl* **vips** VIP.
viperino *adj* viperish.
vira[1] *nf* (*Mil etc*) dart.
vira[2] *nf* (*de zapato*) welt.
viracho *adj* (*Cono Sur*) cross-eyed.
virada *nf* (*Náut*) tack, tacking.
virago *nf* mannish woman.
viraje *nm* (**a**) (*Náut*) tack; turn, going about; (*de vehículo*) turn; swerve; (*de carretera etc*) bend, curve; **~ en horquilla** hairpin bend.
(**b**) (*fig*) change of direction; (*de política*) abrupt switch, volte-face; (*de votos*) swing.
(**c**) (*Fot*) toning.
virar [1a] **1** *vt* (**a**) (*Náut*) to put about, turn.
(**b**) (*Fot*) to tone.
(**c**) (*And, Cono Sur*) (*volver*) to turn round; (*invertir*) to turn over, turn upside down.
(**d**) (*Carib*: *azotar*) to whip.
2 *vi* (**a**) (*cambiar de dirección*) to change direction; (*Náut*) to tack; to turn, go about, put about; (*conductor, vehículo*) to turn; to swerve; **~ a estribor** to turn to starboard; **~ hacia el sur** to turn towards the south; **~ en redondo** to turn completely round; **tuve que ~ a la izquierda para no atropellarle** I had to swerve left to avoid hitting him.
(**b**) (*fig*) to change one's views, switch round; to veer (*a, hacia* to, towards); (*Pol:votos*) to swing; **~ en redondo** to switch round completely, veer round, make a complete volte-face; **el país ha virado a la derecha** the country has swung (to the) right.
(**c**) (*And, Cono Sur*) to turn.
3 virarse *vr* (*Carib*‡) to kick the bucket‡.
virgen 1 *adj* virgin; *cinta* blank; *película* unexposed.
2 *nf* virgin; **la V~** the Virgin; **la V~ de las Angustias** Our Lady of Sorrows; **la Santísima V~** the Blessed Virgin; **¡Santísima V~!** by all that's holy!; **es un viva la V~*** he doesn't give a damn, he doesn't care one little bit; **ser (devoto) de la V~ del Puño*** to be very tight-fisted; **se le apareció la V~*** he got his big chance, he struck lucky*.
virgencita *nf* (*frec*) small picture of the Virgin.
Vírgenes: Islas *nfpl* ~ Virgin Isles.
virgiliano *adj* Virgilian.
Virgilio *nm* Virgil.
virginal *adj* (**a**) (*gen*) maidenly, virginal. (**b**) (*Ecl*) of (*o* relating to) the Virgin.
virginidad *nf* virginity.
virgo *nm* virginity.
Virgo *nf* (*Zodíaco*) Virgo.
virguería *nf* (*adorno*) silly adornment, frill; (*objeto delicado*) pretty thing, delicately made object; (*fig*) **hacer ~s** to do clever things; **hacer ~s con algo** to be clever enough to handle sth well.
virguero* *adj* (**a**) (*bueno*) super*, smashing*. (**b**) (*elegante*) smart, nattily dressed*; (*exquisito*) pretty, delicately made. (**c**) (*hábil*) clever.
vírico *adj* viral, virus (*atr*); **enfermedad vírica** virus disease.
viril *adj* virile; manly; *V* **edad** *etc*.
virilidad *nf* (**a**) (*cualidad*) virility; manliness. (**b**) (*estado*) manhood.
virilizar [1f] **1** *vt* to make like a man, induce male characteristics in. **2 virilizarse** *vr* to become like a man, acquire male characteristics.
viringo *adj* (*And*) (**a**) (*desnudo*) bare, naked. (**b**) (*despellejado*) skinned. skinless.
viroca *nf*(*Cono Sur*) serious mistake.
virola *nf* (**a**) (*gen*) metal tip, ferrule; (*de lanza, herramienta etc*) collar. (**b**) (*Cono Sur, Méx*) (*argolla*) silver ring; (*disco*) metal disc (*fixed to harness etc as an adornment*).
virolento *adj* pockmarked.
virolo *adj* (*And*) cross-eyed.
virología *nf* virology.
virólogo, -a *nm/f* virologist.
virote *nm* (**a**) (*flecha*) arrow.
(**b**) (*Méx*: *pan*) bread roll.
(**c**) (*) (*señorito*) playboy; (*estirado*) stuffed shirt.
(**d**) (*And, Méx*: *tonto*) simpleton.
virreinato *nm* viceroyalty.
virrey *nm* viceroy.
virriondo‡ *adj* (*Méx*) (**a**) *animal* (*hembra*) on heat; (*macho*) in rut. (**b**) *persona* randy*, horny‡.
virtual *adj* (**a**) (*real*) virtual. (**b**) (*potencial etc*) potential; future, possible. (**c**) (*Fís*) apparent.
virtualidad *nf* potentiality; **tiene ciertas ~es** it has certain potentialities.
virtualmente *adj* virtually.
virtud *nf* (**a**) (*cualidad*) virtue; **~ cardinal** cardinal virtue.
(**b**) (*capacidad*) virtue, power; (*eficacia*) efficacy; **en ~ de** by virtue of, by reason of; **tener la ~ de** + *infin* to have the virtue of + *ger*, have the power to + *infin;* **una planta que tiene ~ contra varias enfermedades** a plant which is effective against certain diseases.
(**c**) (*Carib**‡) (*pene*) prick*‡; (*vagina*) cunt*‡.
virtuosamente *adv* virtuously.
virtuosismo *nm* virtuosity.
virtuosista *adj* virtuoso.
virtuoso 1 *adj* virtuous. **2** *nm* virtuoso.
viruela *nf* (**a**) (*Med*) smallpox. (**b**) **~s** pockmarks; **picado de ~s** pockmarked.
virulé: a la ~ *adj* (**a**) (*viejo*) old; (*estropeado*) damaged; (*torcido*) bent, twisted; (*raído*) shabby. (**b**) (*) *persona* cracked, potty*.
virulencia *nf* virulence.
virulento *adj* virulent.
virus *nm invar* virus (*t Inform*); **~ gripal** flu virus.
viruta *nf* **1** (**a**) (*Téc*) shaving; **~s de acero** steel wool. (**b**) (‡: *dinero*) bread‡, money. **2** *nm* (*t* **~s**) carpenter.
vis *nf*: **~ cómica** comic sense, sense of comedy; **tener ~ cómica** to be witty, sparkle.
visa *nm* (*f en LAm*) visa.
visado *nm* visa; permit; **~ de permanencia** residence permit; **~ de salida** exit visa; **~ de tránsito** transit visa; **~ turístico** tourist visa.
visaje *nm*(wry) face, grimace; **hacer ~s** to pull faces, grimace, smirk.
visar [1a] *vt* (**a**) *pasaporte* to visa. (**b**) *documento* to pass, approve, endorse.
visceral *adj* (*fig*) innate, fundamental; intense, profound, deep-rooted; **aversión ~** gut aversion; **sentimientos ~es** gut feelings.
visceralidad *nf* gut feelings, gut reaction; strong feelings.
visceralmente *adv* innately, fundamentally; intensely, profoundly.
vísceras *nfpl* viscera, entrails; (*fig*) guts, bowels.
visco *nm* birdlime.
viscosa *nf* viscose.
viscosidad *nf* (**a**) (*cualidad*) viscosity, stickiness; thickness. (**b**) (*Bot, Zool*) slime; sticky secretion.
viscoso *adj* viscous, sticky; *líquido* thick, stiff; *secreción* slimy.

visera *nf* (*Mil*) visor; (*de gorra*) peak; (*de jugador etc*) eyeshade; (*Carib*: *de caballo*) (horse's) blinkers; (*de estadio*) canopy; ~ **de béisbol** baseball cap.

visibilidad *nf* visibility; **la ~ es de 200 m** there is a visibility of 200 m; **la ~ queda reducida a cero** visibility is down to nil; **una curva de escasa ~** (*Aut*) a bend that leaves a driver with a poor view.

visible *adj* (**a**) (*gen*) visible.
(**b**) (*fig*) (*claro*) clear, plain; (*obvio*) evident, obvious.
(**c**) *persona* (*libre*) free (to receive a visit); **¿está ~ el profesor?** is the professor free?
(**d**) *persona* (*vestida*) decent, presentable; **¿estás ~?** are you decent?

visiblemente *adv* (**a**) (*lit*) visibly.
(**b**) (*fig*) clearly; evidently; **parecía crecer ~** it seemed to grow as one watched it, it seemed to get bigger before one's eyes.

visigodo 1 *adj* Visigothic. **2** *nm*, **visigoda** *nf* Visigoth.

visigótico *adj* Visigothic.

visillo *nm* (**a**) (*cortina*) lace curtain, net curtain. (**b**) (*antimacasar*) antimacassar.

visión *nf* (**a**) (*Anat*) vision, (eye)sight; **~ de túnel** tunnel vision; **perder la ~ de un ojo** to lose the sight in one eye.
(**b**) (*Rel etc*) vision; (*fantasía*) fantasy; (*ilusión*) illusion; **se le apareció en ~** it came to him in a vision; **ver ~es** to be seeing things, suffer delusions.
(**c**) (*vista*) view; **~ de conjunto** complete picture, overview, overall view; **su ~ del problema** his view of the problem.
(**d**) (*pey*) scarecrow, fright*; **ella iba hecha una ~** she looked a real fright*; **han comprado una ~ de cuadro** they've bought a frightful picture, they've bought an absolutely ghastly picture*.

visionado *nm* (**a**) viewing, inspection. (**b**) (*TV*) viewing-room.

visionador(a) *nm/f* (*Fot*) viewer.

visionar [1a] *vt* (**a**) (*Fot etc*) to view, have a viewing (*o* showing) of; (*TV*) to view, see; to preview. (**b**) (*entrever*) to glimpse; (*prever*) to foresee. (**c**) (*presenciar*) to witness.

visionario 1 *adj* (**a**) (*gen*) visionary.
(**b**) (*pey*) deluded, subject to hallucinations.
2 *nm*, **visionaria** *nf* (**a**) (*gen*) visionary.
(**b**) (*pey*) deluded person, crazy individual.

visir *nm* vizier; **gran ~** grand vizier.

visita *nf* (**a**) (*gen*) visit; (*breve*) call; **derecho de ~** right of search; **~ conyugal, ~ íntima** conjugal visit; **~ de cortesía, ~ de cumplido** formal visit, courtesy call; **~ de despedida** farewell visit; **~ de Estado** state visit; **~ de intercambio** exchange visit; **~ de médico*** very short call; **~ de pésame** call to express one's condolences; **~ relámpago** lightning visit, flying visit; **estar de ~ en** to be on a visit to; **hacer una ~, rendir una ~** to visit, pay a visit; **devolver una ~, pagar una ~** to return a visit; **tener ~** (*Med*) to have an appointment at the surgery.
(**b**) (*persona*) visitor, caller; **'no se admiten ~s'** 'no visitors allowed'; **hoy tenemos ~** we have visitors today.
(**c**) (*Carib Med*) enema.
(**d**) **tener la ~, tener ~s‡** to have the curse (of Eve).

visitación *nf* (*Ecl*) visitation.

visitador(a) 1 *nm/f* (**a**) (*visitante*) frequent visitor, person much given to calling.
(**b**) (*inspector*) inspector; (*Com, Med*) drug-company salesman.
2 visitadora *nf* (*LAm*) (*jeringa*) syringe; (*enema*) enema.

visitante 1 *adj* visiting **2** *nmf* visitor.

visitar [1a] **1** *vt* to visit; to call on, go and see; *ciudad, museo etc* to visit; (*oficialmente*) to visit; to inspect.
2 *vi*: **el médico está visitando** the doctor is holding his surgery.
3 visitarse *vr* (**a**) (*2 personas*) to visit each other.
(**b**) (*Med*) to attend the doctor's surgery.

visiteo *nm* frequent visiting, constant calling.

visitero 1 *adj* fond of visiting, much given to calling.
2 *nm*, **visitera** *nf* frequent visitor, constant caller.

visitón* *nm* long and boring visit; visitation.

vislumbrar [1a] *vt* (**a**) (*entrever*) to glimpse, catch a glimpse of, see briefly.
(**b**) (*fig*) to glimpse, see some slight possibility of; *solución etc* to begin to see; *futuro* to get a slight idea of, make a conjecture about; *hecho desconocido etc* to surmise.

vislumbre *nf* (**a**) (*vista*) glimpse, brief view.
(**b**) (*brillo*) gleam, glimmer.
(**c**) (*fig*) (*posibilidad*) glimmer; slight possibility; (*noción*) vague idea; (*conjetura*) conjecture; **tener ~s de** to get an inkling of, get a vague idea of.

viso *nm* (**a**) (*de metal*) gleam, glint.
(**b**) (*de tela*) **~s** sheen, gloss; shot-silk appearance; **negro con ~s azules** black with a bluish sheen, black with bluish lights in it; **hacer ~s** to shimmer.
(**c**) (*fig*: *aspecto*) appearance; **a dos ~s, de dos ~s** (*fig*) with a double purpose, two-edged; **hay un ~ de verdad en esto** this has the appearance of truth, there is an element of truth in this; **tiene ~s de ser puro cuento** it looks like being just a tale; **tenía ~ de nunca acabar** it seemed that it was never going to finish.
(**d**) (*Cos*) coloured undergarment (*worn under a filmy outer garment*).
(**e**) (*Geog*) viewpoint, vantage point.
(**f**) **ser persona de ~** to be somebody, have some standing.

visón *nm* mink.

visor *nm* (**a**) (*Mil*) sight; (*Aer*) bombsight; **~ nocturno** nightsight; **~ telescópico** telescopic sight. (**b**) (*Fot*: *t* **~ de imagen**) viewfinder.

víspera *nf* eve, day before, evening before; **~ de Navidad** Christmas Eve; **la ~ de, en ~ s de** on the eve of (*t fig*); **estar en ~s de** + *infin* to be on the point of + *ger*, be on the verge of + *ger*.

vista 1 *nf* (**a**) (*Anat*) sight, eyesight, vision; (*acto*) look, gaze, glance; **~ de águila, ~ de lince** very keen sight, eagle eye; **~ corta** short sight; **~ doble** double vision; second sight; **¡~ a la derecha!** (*Mil*) eyes right!
(**b**) (*gen*: *locuciones con prep*) **a primera ~** at first sight; on the face of it; **traducción hecha a primera ~** unseen translation; **a simple ~** with the naked eye; at a glance; **lo teníamos a la ~** we could see it, we had it before our eyes; **la parte que quedaba a la ~** the part that was visible (or uncovered); **no tenemos ningún cambio a la ~** we do not have any change in view; **a la ~ está** it's obvious, you can see for yourself; **está a la ~ que ...** . it is obvious that ...; **estar a la ~ de** to be within sight of; **a la ~ de muchas personas** in the presence of many people; **a la ~ de todo el mundo** openly, publicly, for all to see; **a la ~ de tal espectáculo** at the sight of such a scene, on beholding such a scene; **a la ~ de sus informes** in the light of his reports; **estaré a la ~ de lo que pase** I will keep an eye on developments; **yo me quedo a la ~ del fuego** I'll keep an eye on the fire; **con la ~ puesta en** with one's eyes (*fig*: thoughts) fixed on; **conocer a uno de ~** to know sb by sight; **en plena ~** in full view; **en ~ de** (*fig*) in view of; **en ~ de que ...** in view of the fact that ...; **¡hasta la ~!** au revoir!; so long!; **hasta donde alcanza la ~** as far as the eye can see; **no muy agradable para la ~** not a pretty sight, not nice to look at.
(**c**) (*gen*: *locuciones con verbo*) **aguzar la ~** to look sharp, look more carefully; **alzar la ~** to look up; (*fig*) to raise one's eyes to; **alzar la ~ a uno** (*fig*) to turn to sb for help; **apartar la ~** to look away, glance away; (*fig*) to turn a blind eye (*de* to); **no apartar la ~ de** to keep one's eyes glued to; **bajar la ~** to look down; to cast one's eyes down; **clavar la ~ en** to stare at, fix one's eyes on; to clap eyes on; **comer** (*o* **devorar**) **con la ~** to look angrily at; to look curiously at; to look lovingly (*pey*: lustfully) at; **dirigir la ~ a** to look at, look towards; to turn one's gaze on; **echar una ~ a** to take a look at: **fijar la ~ en** to stare at, fix one's eyes on; **hacer la ~ gorda** to pretend not to notice, turn a blind eye; **hacer la ~ gorda a** to wink at, close one's eyes to; **luz que hiere la ~** light that dazzles, light that hurts one's eyes; **leer con la ~** to read to o.s.; **medir a uno con la ~** to size sb up; **se me nubló la ~** my eyes clouded over; **pasar la ~ por** to look over, glance quickly at; **perder algo de ~** to lose sight of sth (*t fig*); **se pierde de ~** (*fig*) he's very sharp, he's terribly clever; **no perder a uno de ~** to keep sb in sight; **poner algo a la ~** to put sth on view; **recorrer algo con la ~** to run one's eye over sth; **salta a la ~** it hits you in the eye; **torcer la ~** to squint; **volver la ~** to look back (*t fig*); to look away; **nunca volvió la ~ atrás** he never looked back, he never had regrets about the past.
(**d**) **a la ~** (*esp Com*) at sight, on sight; **a 30 días ~** (*Com*) thirty days after sight; **a 5 años ~** 5 years from then; **dinero a la ~** (*Com*) money on call; **año ~ de las elecciones** a year before the elections.
(**e**) (*aspecto*) appearance, looks; **un coche con una ~ estupenda** a splendid-looking car; **de ~ poco agradable** of unattractive appearance, unprepossessing; **a la ~, no son pobres** from what one can see, they're not poor.

(**f**) (*fig*: *perspicacia*) foresight, perception; **ha tenido mucha ~** he was very far-sighted.

(**g**) (*fig*: *intención*) intention; **con ~s a una solución del problema** with a view to solving the problem.

(**h**) (*panorama etc*) view, scene, vista, panorama; **~s** (*de casa etc*) outlook; (*fig*) outlook, prospect; **la ~ desde el castillo** the view from the castle; **~ anterior, ~ frontal** front view; **con ~s a la montaña** with views across to the mountains; **con ~s al mar** overlooking the sea; **con ~s al oeste** facing west, with westerly aspect.

(**i**) (*Arte, Fot etc*) view; **~ fija** still; **frontal** front view; **~ de pájaro** bird's-eye view; **una tarjeta con una ~ de Venecia** a card with a view of Venice.

(**j**) (*Jur*) hearing; trial; **~ de una causa** hearing of a case; **~ oral** first hearing.

(**k**) **~s** (*Hist*) meeting, conference.

2 *nm* customs inspector.

vistar* [1a] *vt* (*LAm*) to have a look at, look over, look round.

vistazo *nm* look, glance; **de un ~** at a glance; **dar un ~*** to pop in, drop in; **dar un ~ a, echar un ~ a** to glance at, take a look at, have a quick look at.

vistillas *nfpl* viewpoint, height, high place.

visto 1 *ptp de* **ver**.

2 *ptp y adj* (**a**) **~ todo esto** in view of all this; **por lo ~** evidently, apparently; by the look of it; **ni ~ ni oído** like lightning; **cosa no vista, cosa nunca vista** an unheard-of thing; **lo fusilaron, ~ y no ~** they shot him just like that.

(**b**) **~ bueno** approved, passed, O.K.*.

(**c**) **está muy ~** it is very commonly worn (*o* used), one sees it about a lot; everyone's wearing it.

(**d**) **está ~ que ...** it is clear that ...; **estaba ~** it had to be, it was expected all along.

(**e**) **lo que está bien ~** what is socially acceptable, what is done; **eso está muy mal ~** that's not done, that is thought highly improper; **está muy mal ~ que una joven vaya sola** it is thought most improper for a girl to go alone.

3 : **~ que ...** *conj* seeing that ...; since ..., inasmuch as ...

4 : **~ bueno** *nm* approval, O.K.*, authorization; **dar su ~ bueno** to give one's approval.

vistosamente *adv* showily, colourfully; attractively; (*pey*) gaudily.

vistosidad *nf* showiness, colourfulness; attractiveness; (*pey*) gaudiness; spectacular nature, liveliness.

vistoso *adj ropa etc* showy, colourful; gay, attractive; (*pey*) gaudy; *partido etc* spectacular, lively.

Vístula *nm* Vistula.

visual 1 *adj* visual; **campo ~** field of vision. **2** *nf* (**a**) (*gen*) line of sight. (**b**) (*****: *vistazo*) look, glance; **echar una ~** to take a look (*a* at).

visualización *nf* (**a**) (*Inform*) display(ing); **pantalla de ~** display screen. (**b**) **~ radiográfica** (*Med*) scan(ning).

visualizador *nm* (*Inform*) display.

visualizar [1f] *vt* (**a**) (*LAm*: *divisar*) to see, make out, descry. (**b**) (*fig*: *imaginarse*) to visualize. (**c**) (*Inform*) to display. (**d**) **~ radiográficamente** (*Med*) to scan.

visualmente *adv* visually.

vital *adj* (**a**) life (*atr*), living (*atr*); **espacio ~** living space, (*Pol*) lebensraum; **fuerza ~** life force.

(**b**) (*fig*) vital, essential, fundamental; **de importancia ~** of vital importance.

(**c**) (*fig*) *persona* vital, full of vitality.

vitaliciamente *adv* for life.

vitalicio 1 *adj* life (*atr*); for life; **cargo ~** post held for life; **interés ~** life interest. **2** *nm* life annuity.

vitalidad *nf* vitality.

vitalizador *adj*: **acción ~a, efecto ~** revitalizing effect.

vitalizante *adj* revitalizing.

vitalizar [1f] *vt* (*esp LAm*) to vitalize; to revitalize.

vitamina *nf* vitamin.

vitaminado *adj* vitaminized, with added vitamins.

vitaminar [1a] *vt* to vitaminize, add vitamins to.

vitamínico *adj* vitamin (*atr*).

vitaminizado *adj* vitaminized, with added vitamins.

vitando *adj* to be avoided; to be condemned.

vitela *nf* vellum.

vitícola *adj* vine (*atr*), vine-growing (*atr*).

viticultor(a) *nm/f* (*cultivador*) vine grower; (*dueño*) proprietor of a vineyard

viticultura *nf* vine growing, viticulture.

vitivinicultura *nf* grape and wine-growing.

vitoco* *adj* (*Carib*) vain, stuck-up*.

vitola *nf* (**a**) (*de cigarro*) cigar band. (**b**) (*aire, aspecto*) looks, appearance, general air.

vitoquear* [1a] *vi* (*Carib*) to be conceited, swank*.

vítor 1 *interj* hurrah! **2** *nm* cheer; **entre los ~es de la multitud** among the cheers of the crowd; **dar ~es a** to cheer on.

vitorear [1a] *vt* to cheer, acclaim.

vitral *nm* stained-glass window.

vítreo *adj* glassy, vitreous; glass-like.

vitrificación *nf* vitrification.

vitrificar [1g] **1** *vt* to vitrify. **2 vitrificarse** *vr* to vitrify.

vitrina *nf* (**a**) (*aparador*) glass case, showcase; (*en casa*) display cabinet. (**b**) (*LAm*: *escaparate*) shop window.

vitriolo *nm* vitriol.

vitrola *nf* (*LAm*†) gramophone, phonograph (*US*).

vitualla *nf*, **vituallas** *nfpl* provisions, victuals.

vituperable *adj* reprehensible.

vituperación *nf* condemnation, censure.

vituperar [1a] *vt* to condemn, censure, inveigh against.

vituperio *nm* (**a**) (*condena*) condemnation; (*reproche*) reproach, censure; (*injuria*) insult; **~s** abuse, insults; vituperation. (**b**) (*deshonra*) stigma, dishonour.

vituperioso *adj* abusive; vituperative.

viuda *nf* (**a**) (*persona*) widow; **~ verde** merry widow. (**b**) (*And, Cono Sur*: *fantasma*) ghost. (**c**) (*And Culin*) fish stew. (**d**) (*Carib*: *cometa*) large kite.

viudedad *nf* (**a**) (*esp LAm*) widowhood. (**b**) (*Fin*) widow's pension.

viudez *nf* widowhood.

viudo 1 *adj* (**a**) widowed; **estar ~*** to be a grass widow(er). (**b**) **garbanzos ~s** (*Culin**) chick peas by themselves. **2** *nm* widower.

viva *nm* cheer; **dar un ~** to give a cheer; **prorrumpir en ~s** to start to cheer, burst out cheering.

vivac *nm, pl* **vivacs** bivouac.

vivacidad *nf* (**a**) (*vigor*) vigour. (**b**) (*personalidad*) liveliness, vivacity; keenness, sharpness; (*inteligencia*) brightness.

vivales* *nm invar* wide boy*, smooth operator.

vivamente *adv* in lively fashion; *describir, recordar etc* vividly; *protestar* sharply, strongly; *sentir* acutely, intensely; **lo siento ~** I am deeply sorry, I sincerely regret it; **se lo deseo ~** I sincerely hope he gets (*etc*) it.

vivaque *nm* bivouac.

vivaquear [1a] *vi* to bivouac.

vivar[1] *nm* (**a**) (*Zool*) warren. (**b**) (*estanque*) fishpond; (*criadero*) fish nursery.

vivar[2] [1a] *vt* (*LAm*) to cheer.

vivaracho *adj* (**a**) *persona* jaunty, lively, sprightly; vivacious; bouncy; (*atractivo*) superficially attractive; *ojos* bright, lively, twinkling. (**b**) (*Méx*) sharp, sly.

vivaz *adj* (**a**) (*de larga vida*) long-lived; (*duradero*) enduring, lasting; (*Bot*) perennial. (**b**) (*vigoroso*) vigorous. (**c**) (*vivo*) lively; (*listo*) keen, sharp, quick-witted.

vivencia *nf* (*t* **~s**) experience, knowledge gained from experience.

vivencial *adj* existential.

víveres *nmpl* provisions; (*esp Mil*) stores, supplies.

vivero *nm* (**a**) (*Hort etc*) nursery; (*semillero*) seedbed; (*de árboles*) tree nursery.

(**b**) (*de peces*: *estanque*) fishpond; (*criadero*) hatchery, fish nursery; (*Zool*) vivarium; **~ de ostras** oyster bed.

(**c**) (*fig*) breeding ground; (*pey*) hotbed; **es un ~ de discordias** it's a hotbed of discord.

viveza *nf* liveliness, vividness; brightness; sharpness; strength, depth, intensity; acuteness; **la ~ de su inteligencia** the sharpness of his mind; **la ~ de sus sentimientos** the strength of his feelings; the sincerity of his regret; **contestar con ~** to answer sharply, answer with spirit.

vividero *adj* habitable, inhabitable, that can be lived in.

vivido *adj* personally experienced; **un episodio ~ por el autor** an episode which the author himself lived (through).

vívido *adj* vivid, graphic.

vividor 1 *adj* (*pey*) sharp, clever; opportunistic; unscrupulous. **2** *nm* wide boy*.

vivienda *nf* (**a**) (*gen*) housing, accommodation; **escasez de ~s** housing shortage; **el problema de la ~** the housing problem.

(**b**) (*una ~*) dwelling, accommodation unit; (*piso*) flat, apartment (*US*), tenement; **~ campestre** small house in the country, cottage; **bloque de ~s** block of flats, block of tenements; **~ libre** (house *etc* with) freehold; **~s para obreros** workers' housing; **~ de protección oficial** ≈ council

house, council flat; **~s protegidas, ~s de renta limitada, ~s sociales** = council houses, public housing (*US*); **segunda ~** second home, holiday home.
viviente *adj* living; **los ~s** the living.
vivificador *adj*, **vivificante** *adj* life-giving; (*fig*) revitalizing.
vivificar [1g] *vt* (**a**) (*lit*) to give life to, vivify. (**b**) (*fig*) to revitalize, bring to life, bring new life to; to enliven.
vivillo *adj y nm* (*Cono Sur*) = **vividor**.
vivíparo *adj* viviparous.
vivir [3a] **1** *vt* to live through; to experience, go through; **los que hemos vivido la guerra** those of us who lived through the war; **ha vivido momentos de verdadera angustia** she went through moments of real agony.
2 *vi* (**a**) (*gen*) to live (*en* at, in); (*ser vivo*) to be alive; **~ bien** to live well, be prosperous; to live an honest life; (*2 personas*) to live happily together, live in harmony; **~ para ver** you live and learn; would you believe it?; that'll be the day!; **¡viva!** hurray!; **¡viva el rey!** long live the king!; hurray for the king!; **¿quién vive?** (*Mil*) who goes there?; **dar el quién vive a uno** to challenge sb; **~ como un pachá** to live like a prince; **saber ~** to know how to get the best out of life; **no dejar ~ a uno** to give sb no peace, harass sb; **no le dejan ~ los celos** she is eaten up with jealousy; **no vivo de intranquilidad** I'm worried to death; **ya no vivo de vergüenza** the shame of it is killing me; **y a pesar de todo eso vive todavía** and in spite of all that she's still alive today.
(**b**) (*Fin*) to live (*de* by, off, on); **~ muy justo** to be hard up*, have only just enough to live on; **~ dentro de los medios** to live within one's means; **~ por encima de sus posibilidades** to live beyond one's means; **~ de la pluma** to live by one's pen; **~ de las rentas** to live on one's private income; **no tienen con qué ~** they haven't enough to live on; **ganar lo justo para ~** to earn a bare living.
(**c**) (*fig*: *durar*) to last (out); **el abrigo no vivirá mucho** the coat won't last much longer.
(**d**) (*fig*: *memoria*) to live, remain.
3 *nm* life, way of life; living; **de mal ~** (*inmoral*) dissolute, loose-living; (*criminal*) criminal, delinquent.
vivisección *nf* vivisection.
vivito *adj*: **estar ~ y coleando** to be alive and kicking.
vivo 1 *adj* (**a**) (*gen*) living; live, alive; *carne* living, raw; *lengua* living; **los ~s y los muertos** the living and the dead; **los venden en ~** they sell them alive; **actuación en ~** live show, live performance; **transmitir algo en ~** to broadcast sth live; **le ha llegado al ~** it touched him on the raw, it really came home to him; **me dio** (*o* **hirió**) **en lo más ~** it got me on the raw, it cut me to the quick.
(**b**) (*fig*) *descripción* lively, vivid, graphic; *escena, memoria* vivid; *brillo etc* bright, sudden; *mirada, ojos, ritmo* lively; *movimiento, paso* quick, lively; *color* bright; rich, vivid; *filo* sharp; *protesta etc* sharp, strong; *emoción* strong, deep, intense; *dolor* sharp, acute; *genio* sharp, quick; *inteligencia* sharp, keen, acute; *ingenio* ready; *imaginación* lively; **¡~!** hurry up!; **describir algo al ~** (*o* **a lo ~**) to describe sth to the life, describe sth very realistically; **lo explica al ~** (*o* **a lo ~**) he explains it very expressively.
(**c**) *persona* (*listo*) sharp, clever; (*animado*) lively; (*pey*) sharp; (*esp LAm*) sly, crafty; unscrupulous; **pasarse de ~** to be too clever by half.
(**d**) (*Cono Sur*: *travieso*) naughty.
2 *nm* (*Cos*) trimming, edging, border.
vizcaíno, -a *adj, nm/f* Biscayan.
Vizcaya *nf* Biscay (*Spanish province*); **el Golfo de ~** the Bay of Biscay.
vizcondado *nm* viscounty.
vizconde *nm* viscount.
vizcondesa *nf* viscountess.
V.M. *abr de* **Vuestra Majestad** Your Majesty.
V.º B.º *abr de* **visto bueno** approval, O.K.
V.O. *nf abr de* **versión original** original version, undubbed version (of a film).
vocablo *nm* word; term; **jugar del ~** to make a pun, play on words.
vocabulario *nm* vocabulary.
vocación *nf* vocation, calling; **errar la ~** to miss one's vocation; **tener ~ por** to have a vocation for.
vocacional 1 *adj* vocational. **2** *nf* (*Méx Educ*) ≈ technical college.
vocal 1 *adj* vocal. **2** *nmf* member (of a committee *etc*); (*director*) director, member of the board of directors. **3** *nf* (*Ling*) vowel.
vocálico *adj* vocalic, vowel (*atr*).
vocalismo *nm* vowel system.
vocalista *nmf* vocalist, singer.
vocalizar [1f] **1** *vt* to vocalize. **2** *vt* (*Mús*) (*canturrear*) to hum; (*hacer prácticas*) to sing scales, practise. **3 vocalizarse** *vr* to vocalize.
vocalmente *adv* vocally.
vocativo *nm* vocative.
voceado *adj* vaunted, much-trumpeted.
voceador 1 *adj* loud, loud-mouthed, vociferous. **2** *nm* (**a**) (*pregonero*) town crier. (**b**) (*And, Méx*) newsboy, paperboy.
vocear [1a] **1** *vt* (**a**) *mercancías* to cry.
(**b**) (*llamar a*) to call loudly to, shout to, shout the name of.
(**c**) (*dar vivas a*) to cheer, acclaim.
(**d**) *secreto etc* to shout to all and sundry, shout from the rooftops; (*fig*) to proclaim; **su cara voceaba su culpabilidad** his face proclaimed his guilt.
(**e**) (*: *reivindicar*) to boast publicly about, lay public claim to.
2 *vi* to shout, yell, bawl.
vocejón *nm* loud voice, big voice.
voceo *nm* shouting, yelling, bawling.
voceras‡ *nm invar* loudmouth*.
vocería *nf*, **vocerío** *nm* (*griterío*) shouting, yelling; (*jaleo*) clamour, uproar, hullabaloo.
vocero, -a *nm/f* (*esp LAm*) spokesperson.
vociferación *nf* vociferation.
vociferador *adj* loud, loud-mouthed.
vociferar [1a] **1** *vt* (**a**) (*gritar*) to shout, scream, vociferate. (**b**) (*proclamar*) to proclaim boastfully. **2** *vi* to shout, yell, clamour.
vocinglería *nf* (**a**) (*griterío*) clamour, uproar. (**b**) (*cualidad*) loudness, noisiness; garrulity.
vocinglero *adj* (**a**) (*vociferador*) vociferous, loud, loud-mouthed. (**b**) (*hablador*) loquacious, garrulous. (**c**) (*fig*) blatant.
vodevil *nm* vaudeville (*US*), music-hall, variety show (*o* theatre).
vodevilesco *adj* music-hall (*atr*).
vodka *nf* (*a veces m*) vodka.
vodú *nm* (*LAm*) voodoo.
voduísmo *nm* (*LAm*) voodooism.
volada *nf* (**a**) (*vuelo*) short flight, single flight. (**b**) (*LAm*: *diversos sentidos*) = **bolada**.
voladizo *adj* (*Arquit*) projecting.
volado 1 *adj* (**a**) (*Tip*) superior, superscript.
(**b**) **estar ~** (*preocupado*) to be worried, feel anxious (*con* about); to be ill-at-ease; (*: *loco*)) to be crazy; (*LAm*: *despistado*) to be absent-minded; (*LAm*: *enamorado*) to be in love; (*LAm*: *soñador*) to be in a dreamy state.
(**c**) (*Cono Sur*) (*saledizo*) projecting; (*abultado*) protuberant, big.
(**d**) **~ de genio** (*Cono Sur, Méx*) quick-tempered.
2 *nm* (**a**) (*CAm*: *mentira*) fib, lie.
(**b**) (*Carib, Cono Sur Cos*) flounce, ruffle.
(**c**) (*Méx*: *juego*) game of heads or tails; **echar ~** to toss a coin.
(**d**) (*Méx*) (*aventura*) adventure; (*incidente*) incident, happening.
3 *adv* (*And, CAm, Méx*) in a rush, hastily.
volador 1 *adj* (**a**) flying.
(**b**) (*fig*) swift; fleeting.
2 *nm* (**a**) (*pez*) flying fish; (*calamar*) (*a species of*) squid.
(**b**) (*cohete*) rocket.
(**c**) (*And, CAm*: *molinillo*) toy windmill; (*Carib*: *cometa*) kite.
voladura *nf* (**a**) blowing up, demolition; blast; **~ controlada** controlled explosion. (**b**) (*Cos*) flounce, ruffle.
volandas: **en ~** *adv* (**a**) in the air, off the ground (**b**) (*fig*) swiftly, as if on wings; **¡voy en ~!** (*hum*) I fly!
volandera *nf* (**a**) (*piedra*) millstone, grindstone. (**b**) (*Mec*) washer. (**c**) (*: *mentirilla*) fib.
volandero *adj* (**a**) *pieza* loose, movable, not fixed; *cuerda, hoja etc* loose; *dolor* that moves about.
(**b**) (*fortuito*) random, casual; (*imprevisto*) unexpected.
(**c**) (*Orn*) fledged, ready to fly; (*fig*) *persona* restless.
volanta *nf* (**a**) (*And, Carib*: *rueda*) flywheel; large wheel. (**b**) (*Carib, Méx*: *carro*) break.
volantazo *nm* (*Aut*) sharp turn; (*fig*) sudden switch, sudden change of direction.
volante 1 *adj* (**a**) (*que vuela*) flying; *V* **escuadrón** *etc*.
(**b**) (*fig*) unsettled.

2 *nm* (a) (*Téc*) flywheel; (*de reloj*) balance.
(b) (*Aut*) steering wheel; **ir al ~** to be at the wheel, be driving.
(c) (*nota*) note; (*folleto*) pamphlet; **un ~ para el especialista** (*Med*) a referral to a specialist.
(d) (*Dep*: *objeto*) shuttlecock; (**juego del**) ~ badminton.
(e) (*Dep*: *jugador*) winger.
(f) (*Cos*) flounce, ruffle.
(g) (*LAm*) (*Aut*) driver; (*de carreras*) racing driver.

volantín 1 *adj* loose, unattached. 2 *nm* (a) (*sedal*) fishing line. (b) (*LAm*: *cometa*) kite. (c) (*And*: *cohete*) rocket. (d) (*LAm*: *voltereta*) somersault.

volantista *nmf* (*Aut*) driver; (*de carreras*) racing driver; (*pey*) roadhog, speed merchant*.

volantón 1 *adj* fledged, ready to fly. 2 *nm* fledgling.

volantusa *nf* (*LAm*) prostitute.

volantuzo* *nm* (*And*) snappy dresser*.

volapié *nm* (*Taur*) wounding thrust; **a ~** (*ave*) half walking and half flying; **de ~*** in a split second.

volar [1l] 1 *vt* (a) *edificio, puente etc* to blow up, demolish (with explosive); *mina* to explode; *roca* to blast.
(b) (*Caza*) to put up, put to flight, rouse; (*LAm*) to put to flight, chase off, repel.
(c) (*: *irritar*) to irritate, upset, exasperate.
(d) (*CAm*) **~ lengua** to talk, speak; **~ diente** to eat; **~ pata** to walk; **~ máquina** to type.
(e) (*Méx**: *robar*) to pinch*.
(f) (*Méx**: *estafar*) to swindle.
(g) (*Méx**: *coquetear con*) to flirt with.
2 *vi* (a) (*gen*) to fly; (*irse*) to fly away, fly off; to get blown away; **una alfombra que vuela** a carpet that flies, a flying carpet; **~ a solas** to fly solo; **echar a ~ una noticia** to spread a piece of news; **echarse a ~** (*fig*) to leave the parental nest.
(b) (*fig*: *tiempo*) to fly, pass swiftly; (*noticia*) to spread rapidly.
(c) (*fig*) (*correr*) to fly; to rush, hurry; (*coche etc*) to scorch, hurtle (along, past *etc*), go like the wind; **¡volando!** get a move on!; **voy volando** I'll go as quickly as I can; I must dash; **prepárame volando la cena** get my supper double-quick, please; **~ a** + *infin* to fly to + *infin*, rush to + *infin*.
(d) (*: *desaparecer*) to disappear, vanish, walk*; **han volado mis pitillos** my fags have walked*.
(e) (*LAm Naipes*) to bluff.
(f) (*: *droga*) to trip‡.
3 **volarse** *vr* (a) to fly away.
(b) (*LAm*: *enfadarse*) to get angry, lose one's temper.
(c) **~ algo** (*Méx*) to spirit sth away.

volate *nm* (a) (*And*: *confusión*) confusion, mess. (b) (*And*: *objetos*) lot of odd things. (c) **echar ~** (*Carib**: *desesperarse*) to throw up one's hands in despair.

volatería *nf* (a) (*Caza*) hawking, falconry; fowling.
(b) (*Orn*) birds; fowls; flock of birds.
(c) (*fig*: *pensamientos*) random thoughts, formless collection of ideas.
(d) (*And*: *fuegos artificiales*) fireworks.

volatero *nm* (*And*) rocket.

volátil *adj* (a) (*Quím*) volatile. (b) (*fig*) changeable, inconstant.

volatilidad *nf* (a) (*Quím*) volatility, volatile nature. (b) (*fig*) changeableness, inconstancy.

volatilizar [1f] 1 *vt* (a) (*Quím*) to volatilize, vaporize.
(b) (*fig*) to spirit away, cause to vanish.
2 **volatilizarse** *vr* (a) (*Quím*) to volatilize, vaporize.
(b) (*fig*) to vanish into thin air; **¡volatilízate!‡** get lost!‡

volatín *nm* (a) (*acrobacia*) acrobatics, tightrope walking. (b) = **volatinero**.

volatinero, -a *nm/f* acrobat, tightrope walker.

volcado *nm*: **~ de memoria** (*Inform*) dump.

volcán *nm* (a) volcano.
(b) (*And, Cono Sur*) (*torrente*) summer torrent; (*avalancha*) avalanche.
(c) (*CAm, Carib*: *montón*) pile, heap; **un ~ de cosas** a lot of things, a whole heap of things.
(d) (*Carib*: *estrépito*) deafening noise; confusion, hubbub.
(e) (*And*) breakdown; collapse, fall.

volcanada *nf* (*Cono Sur*) whiff.

volcanarse [1a] *vr* (*And*) to break down; to collapse, fall down.

volcánico *adj* volcanic.

volcar [1g *y* 1l] 1 *vt* (a) *recipiente* to upset, overturn, tip over, knock over; (*adrede*) to empty out; *contenido* to upset; to empty out; *camión etc* to tip; *carga* to dump, shoot; *coche etc* to overturn; *barco* to overturn, capsize, upset.
(b) **~ a uno** (*fig*: *marear*) to make sb dizzy, make sb's head swim.
(c) **~ a uno** (*fig*: *convencer*) to force sb to change his mind.
(d) (*fig*) (*irritar*) to irritate, exasperate; (*desconcertar*) to upset; (*embromar*) to tease.
(e) **estar volcado a un cometido** to be dedicated to a task.
(f) **estar volcado*** to be broke*.
2 *vi* (*coche etc*) to overturn.
3 **volcarse** *vr* (a) (*recipiente*) to be upset, get overturned; to tip over; (*coche etc*) to overturn; (*barco*) to capsize.
(b) (*fig*) to go out of one's way, be excessively kind; to be welcoming; **~ para** (*o* **por**) **conseguir algo** to do one's utmost to get sth; **~ por complacer a uno** to lean over backwards to satisfy sb.
(c) **~ en una actividad** to throw o.s. into an activity.

volea *nf* volley; **media ~** half-volley.

volear [1a] *vti* to volley; **~ por alto** to lob.

voleibol *nm* volleyball.

voleiplaya *nm* beachball, beach volleyball.

voleo *nm* (a) (*gen*) volley; **de un ~, del primer ~** (*rápidamente*) quickly; (*bruscamente*) brusquely, suddenly; (*de un golpe*) at one blow; **sembrar a** (*o* **al**) **~** to broadcast the seed, scatter the seed; **repartir algo a** (*o* **al**) **~** to distribute sth haphazardly.
(b) (*: *puñetazo*) punch, bash*.

volframio *nm* wolfram.

volibol *nm* volleyball.

volición *nf* volition.

volido *nm* (*LAm*) flight; **de un ~** quickly, at once.

volován *nm* vol-au-vent.

volquete *nm* (*carro*) tipcart; (*Aut*) dumping lorry, dumper, dump truck (*US*).

voltaico *adj* voltaic.

voltaje *nm* voltage.

voltario *adj* (*Cono Sur*) (a) (*cambiable*) fickle, changeable. (b) (*voluntarioso*) wilful, headstrong. (c) (*pulcro*) spruce, dapper.

volteada *nf* (a) (*Cono Sur Agr*) round-up. (b) (*CAm, Cono Sur, Méx Pol*) defection.

volteado *nm* (*And Mil*) deserter; (*Pol*) turncoat.

volteador(a) *nm/f* acrobat.

voltear [1a] 1 *vt* (a) (*volver al revés*) to turn over, roll over; (*invertir*) to turn upside down; (*dar vuelta a*) to turn round; *recipiente* to upset, overturn; (*LAm*) *espalda etc* to turn; (*Cono Sur, Méx*: *volcar*) to knock down; to knock over, spill.
(b) *campanas* to peal.
(c) (*lanzar al aire*) to throw into the air; (*toro*) to toss.
(d) (*esp LAm*) *lazo etc* to whirl, twirl.
(e) **~ a uno** (*And, Carib, Cono Sur*) to force sb to change his mind.
(f) (*Carib*: *buscar*) to search all over for.
2 *vi* (a) (*dar vueltas*) to roll over, go rolling over and over; (*Teat etc*) to somersault.
(b) (*LAm*: *torcer*) to turn (*a la derecha* to the right); (*volverse*) to turn round.
(c) (*LAm*) **~ a hacer algo** to do sth again.
(d) **volteó con mi amiga** (*Carib‡*) he went off with my girlfriend.
3 **voltearse** *vr* (*LAm*) (a) (*dar la vuelta*) to turn round; (*volcarse*) to overturn, turn over.
(b) (*Pol*) to change one's allegiance, go over to the other side; to change one's ideas.

voltereta *nf* somersault; roll, tumble; **~ lateral** cartwheel; **dar ~s** to turn somersaults, do cartwheels.

voltímetro *nm* voltmeter.

voltio *nm* (a) (*gen*) volt. (b) **darse un ~*** to take a stroll.

volubilidad *nf* fickleness, changeableness; unpredictability; instability.

voluble *adj* (a) (*Bot*) twining, clinging; climbing. (b) *persona* (*inconstante*) fickle, changeable; (*imprevisible*) erratic, unpredictable; (*inestable*) unstable.

volumen *nm* (a) (*gen*) volume; (*lo abultado*) bulk, bulkiness; (*masa*) mass; **~ (sonoro)** volume (of sound); **~ de negocios, ~ de ventas** amount of business done, volume of business, turnover; **~ de capital invertido** amount of capital invested; **una operación de mucho ~** a very substantial operation; **poner la radio a todo ~** to turn the

radio up full (*o* as loud as possible).
(**b**) (*tomo*) volume.
volumétrico *adj* volumetric.
voluminoso *adj* voluminous; sizeable, bulky, massive.
voluntad *nf* (**a**) (*gen*) will; (*resolución*: *t* **fuerza de** ~) willpower; (*volición*) volition; (*deseo*) wish, desire; (*intención*) intention; **buena** ~ goodwill; good intention, honest intention; **mala** ~ ill will, malice; evil intent; **última** ~ last wish, (*Jur*) last will and testament; ~ **débil** weak will, lack of willpower; ~ **divina** divine will; ~ **férrea**, ~ **de hierro** will of iron; ~ **popular** will of the people; **a** ~ at will; at one's discretion; *cantidad* as much as one likes; whatever you (*etc*) can afford, 'all donations gratefully received'; **se abre a** ~ it opens at will; **a** ~ **de uno** as one wishes; **por causas ajenas a mi** ~ for reasons beyond my control; **por** ~ **propia** of one's own volition, of one's own free will; **su** ~ **es** + *infin* his wish is to + *infin*; **no lo dije con** ~ **de** + *infin* I did not say so with any wish to + *infin*, I did not say it with any intention of + *ger*; **hacer su santa** ~ to do exactly as one pleases, have one's own way at all costs; **hace falta** ~ **para escucharlo hasta el final** you need a strong will to sit right through it; **ganar(se) la** ~ **de uno** to win sb over; to dominate sb's will; **tener** ~ **de ganar** to have the will to win; **no tener** ~ **propia** to have no will of one's own; **no tiene** ~ **para dejar de beber** he hasn't the willpower to give up drinking; **reiterar su** ~ **de** + *infin* to reaffirm one's intention to + *infin*; **le viene** ~ **de** + *infin* he feels a need to + *infin*, he feels like + *ger*.
(**b**) (*: *afecto*) fondness, affection; **tener** ~ **a** to be fond of, feel affection for.
voluntariamente *adv* voluntarily.
voluntariedad *nf* wilfulness, unreasonableness.
voluntario 1 *adj* (**a**) (*gen*) voluntary. (**b**) (*Mil*) voluntary; *fuerza etc* volunteer. **2** *nm*, **voluntaria** *nf* volunteer; **alistarse** (*u* **ofrecerse**) to volunteer (*para* for).
voluntariosamente *adv* (**a**) (*pey*) wilfully, unreasonably. (**b**) (*con buenas intenciones*) dedicatedly, in a well-intentioned way.
voluntarioso *adj* (**a**) (*pey*) headstrong, wilful, unreasonable. (**b**) (*bienintencionado*) dedicated, willing, well-intentioned.
voluntarismo *nm* headstrong nature, wilfulness; arbitrariness.
voluntarista *adj* headstrong, wilful; *decisión etc* arbitrary.
voluptuosamente *adv* voluptuously; sensually.
voluptuosidad *nf* voluptuousness; sensuality.
voluptuoso 1 *adj* voluptuous; sensual. **2** *nm*, **voluptuosa** *nf* voluptuary; sensualist.
voluta *nf* (**a**) (*Arquit*) scroll, volute. (**b**) (*de humo*) spiral, column.
volvedor 1 *adj*: **este caballo es** ~ (*And, Carib*) this horse always finds its way home.
2 *nm* (**a**) (*llave inglesa*) wrench; (*destornillador*) screwdriver.
(**b**) (*And*: *plus*) bonus, extra.
volver [2h; *ptp* **vuelto**] **1** *vt* (**a**) *objeto* (*gen*) to turn, turn round; (*poner boca abajo*) to turn over, turn upside down; (*poner al revés*) to turn back to front; *cabeza, espalda* to turn; (*Culin*) to turn (over); (*Cos*) to turn; *tierra* to turn over; *ojos* to turn (*a* on, towards), cast (*a* on); *arma* to aim (*a* at), turn (*a* on); ~ **un calcetín** to turn a sock inside out; **tener a uno vuelto como un calcetín** (*o* **media**) to have got sb where one wants him; ~ **el pensamiento a Dios** to turn one's thoughts to God; **me volvió la espalda** he turned his back on me (*V t* **espalda**); ~ **la proa al viento** to turn the bow into the wind; ~ **la vista atrás** to look back.
(**b**) *página* to turn (over); *puerta, ventana* (*abrir*) to push open, swing open; (*cerrar*) to close, pull to, swing to.
(**c**) *manga etc* to roll up.
(**d**) *objeto lanzado etc* to turn back, send back, return; *comida* to bring up; *imagen* to reflect.
(**e**) (*: *devolver*) to return, give back, send back; *vuelta* to give; *visita* to repay, return; ~ **algo a su lugar** to return sth to it place, put sth back (in its place); ~ **bien por mal** to return good for evil.
(**f**) (*transformar*) to change, turn, transform; (+ *adj*) to turn, make, render; ~ **la casa a su estado original** to restore a house to its original state; **vuelve fieras a los hombres** it turns men into wild beasts; **esto le vuelve furioso** this makes him mad; **todo lo volvió muy triste** it made it all very sad; **el ácido lo vuelve azul** the acid turns it blue; *V* **loco**.
(**g**) (*Ling*) to translate (*a* into).
2 *vi* (**a**) (*camino, viajero etc*) to turn (*a* to).
(**b**) (*regresar*) to return (*a* to, *de* from), come back, go back, get back; ~ **atrás** to go back, turn back; ~ **victorioso** to come back victorious, return in triumph; **volvió muy cansado** he got back tired out; ~ **a una costumbre** to revert to a habit; **volviendo ahora a mi tema** ... returning (*o* reverting) now to my theme ...
(**c**) ~ **a hacer algo** to do sth again; **han vuelto a pintar la casa** they have painted the house again; **he vuelto a salir con ella** I've started going out with her again.
(**d**) ~ **en sí** to come to, come round; regain consciousness; ~ **sobre sí** to give up an idea, change one's mind; ~ **por** to come out in defence (*o* support) of, stand up for.
3 volverse *vr* (**a**) (*persona*) to turn round, (*objeto*) to turn over, turn upside down, turn inside out; **se le volvió el paraguas** his umbrella turned inside out; **se volvió riendo a mí** she turned laughingly to me; **se volvió para mirarlo** he turned (round) to look at it; ~ **atrás** (*recordando*) to look back; (*desdecirse*) to back down, go back on one's word; ~ **contra uno** to turn against (*o* on) sb.
(**b**) = **2** (**b**); **vuélvete a buscarlo** go back and look for it.
(**c**) (+ *adj*) to turn, become, go, get; **se ha vuelto imposible** he has become quite impossible; **en el ácido se vuelve más oscuro** it turns darker in the acid; **todo se le vuelve dificultades** troubles come thick and fast for him; *V* **loco** *etc*.
(**d**) (*vino etc*) to go off, turn sour.
vomitado *adj persona* sickly; seedy.
vomitar [1a] **1** *vt* (**a**) (*devolver*) to vomit, bring up, throw up; ~ **sangre** to spit blood.
(**b**) (*fig*) *humo, llamas etc* to belch, belch forth; *lava* to spew, throw up, hurl out; *injurias* to hurl (*contra* at).
(**c**) (*fig*) *secreto* to tell reluctantly, finally come out with; *ganancias etc* to disgorge, shed.
2 *vi* (*devolver*) to vomit, be sick; **eso me da ganas de** ~ (*fig*) that makes me sick, that turns my stomach.
vomitera *nf* (*Carib*), **vomitina** *nf* vomiting, retching.
vomitivo 1 *adj* (**a**) (*Med*) emetic. (**b**) (*fig*) disgusting; *chiste etc* sick-making, repulsive. **2** *nm* (**a**) (*Med*) emetic. (**b**) (*Cono Sur*: *fastidio*) nuisance, bore.
vómito *nm* (**a**) (*acto*) vomiting, being sick; ~ **de sangre** spitting of blood. (**b**) (*materia*) vomit.
vomitona* *nf* bad sick turn.
voquible *nm* (*hum*) word.
VOR *nm abr de* **valor objetivo de referencia**.
voracear [1a] *vt* (*Cono Sur*) to challenge in a loud voice.
voracidad *nf* voracity, voraciousness.
vorágine *nf* whirlpool, vortex, maelstrom; (*fig*) maelstrom; whirl.
voraz *adj* (**a**) (*devorador*) voracious, ravenous; (*pey*) greedy. (**b**) (*fig*) *fuego* all-devouring, fierce. (**c**) (*Méx*: *audaz*) bold.
vorazmente *adv* voraciously, ravenously; greedily.
vórtice *nm* (**a**) (*agua*) whirlpool, vortex; (*viento*) whirlwind. (**b**) (*Met*) cyclone, hurricane.
vos *pron pers* (**a**) (††) you, ye††. (**b**) (*Cono Sur*) you (*sing*).
vosear [1a] *vt* (*Cono Sur*) to address as 'vos'.
voseo *nm* (*Cono Sur*) addressing a person as 'vos' (*familiar usage*).
Vosgos *nmpl* Vosges.
vosotros, vosotras *pron pers* (**a**) (*sujeto*) you.
(**b**) (*tras prep*) you; (*reflexivo*) yourselves; **entre** ~ among yourselves; **irán sin** ~ they'll go without you; **¿no pedís nada para** ~**?** are you not asking anything for yourselves?; **¿es de** ~**?** is it yours?
votación *nf* voting; vote; ~ **a mano alzada** show of hands; **por** ~ **popular** by popular vote; **por** ~ **secreta** by secret vote, by secret ballot; ~ **táctica** tactical voting; ~ **unánime** unanimous vote; **la** ~ **ha sido nutrida** voting has been heavy; **someter algo a** ~ to put sth to the vote, take a vote on sth.
votante 1 *adj* voting. **2** *nmf* voter.
votar [1a] **1** *vt* (**a**) (*Pol*) *candidato, partido* to vote for; *moción, proyecto de ley* to pass, approve (by vote); **Pérez fue el más votado** Pérez received the highest number of votes, Pérez got most votes.
(**b**) (*Ecl*) to vow, promise (*a* to).
2 *vi* (**a**) (*Pol etc*) to vote (*por* for).
(**b**) (*Ecl*) to vow, take a vow.
(**c**) (*echar pestes*) to curse, swear.
votivo *adj* votive.
voto *nm* (**a**) (*Pol etc*) vote; ~ **afirmativo** vote in favour; ~ **en blanco**, ~ **nulo** blank vote, spoiled ballot-paper; ~ **de calidad** casting vote; ~ **de censura** vote of censure, vote of no confidence; ~ **de conciencia** free vote; ~ **de confianza**

vote of confidence; ~ **por correo** postal vote; ~ **de desconfianza** vote of no confidence; ~ **fluctuante,** ~ **de los indicisos** floating vote; ~ **secreto** secret vote, secret ballot; **dar su** ~ to cast one's vote (*a* for), give one's vote (*a* to); **emitir su** ~ to cast one's vote, (*fig*) give one's opinion; **ganar por 7** ~**s** to win by 7 votes; **hubo 13** ~**s a favor y 11 en contra** there were 13 votes for and 11 against; **tener** ~ to have a vote.

(**b**) (*Ecl*: *promesa*) vow; ~ **de castidad** vow of chastity; ~ **de pobreza** vow of poverty; ~**s monásticos** monastic vows; **hacer** ~ **de** + *infin* to take a vow to + *infin.*

(**c**) (*Ecl*: *ofrenda*) ex voto.

(**d**) (*juramento*) oath, curse; (*palabrota*) swearword.

(**e**) (*deseos*) ~**s** wishes; good wishes; **mis mejores** ~**s por su éxito** my best wishes for its success; **hacer** ~**s por el restablecimiento de uno** to wish sb a quick recovery, hope that sb will get well; **hago** ~**s para que se remedie pronto** I pray that it may be speedily put right, I earnestly hope that something will soon be done about it.

voy *etc V* **ir**.

voye(u)r *nm* voyeur.

voye(u)rismo *nm* voyeurism.

voz *nf* (**a**) (*gen*) voice; ~ **argentina** silvery voice; ~ **empañada,** ~ **opaca** thin voice, voice weak with emotion; ~ **en off** voice-over; **la** ~ **de la conciencia** the voice of conscience, the promptings of conscience; **la** ~ **del pueblo** the voice of the people; **a una** ~ with one voice, unanimously; **a media** ~ in a low voice; **a** ~ **en cuello, a** ~ **en grito** at the top of one's voice; **de viva** ~ personally, in person; orally; **en alta** ~ loud(ly), in a loud voice; *V* **bajo**; **estar en** ~ to be in good voice; (*) to be fit, be ready for anything; **aclarar la** ~ to clear one's throat; **alzar la** ~**, levantar la** ~ to raise one's voice; **ahuecar la** ~ to adopt a serious tone, try to make o.s. sound impressive; **se me anudó la** ~ (**en la garganta**) I got a lump in my throat; **desanudar la** ~ to manage to speak again, find one's voice; **tener la** ~ **tomada** to be hoarse.

(**b**) (*Mús etc*: *sonido*) sound, note; (*de trueno etc*) noise; **la** ~ **del órgano** the sound of the organ, the strains of the organ.

(**c**) (*Mús*: *de cantante*) voice, part; **canción a cuatro voces** song for four voices, four-part song; **cantar a dos voces** to sing a duet; ~ **cantante** leading part; **llevar la** ~ **cantante** (*fig*) to be the boss, have the chief say.

(**d**) (*grito*) shout; yell; **voces** shouts, shouting, yelling; ~ **de mando** (*Mil*) command; **dar** (*o* **pegar**) **voces** to shout, call out, yell; **dale una** ~ give him a shout; **dar la** ~ **de alarma** to sound the alarm; **dar cuatro voces** to make a great fuss; **discutir a voces** to argue noisily; **llamar a uno a voces** to shout to sb; **está pidiendo a voces que se remedie** it's crying out (to heaven) to be put right.

(**e**) (*Naipes*) call.

(**f**) (*fig*: *rumor*) rumour; ~ **común** hearsay, gossip, rumour; **corre la** ~ **de que** ... there is a rumour going round that ...

(**g**) (*fig*: *en junta etc*) voice, say; vote, support; **asistir con** ~ **y voto** to be present as a full member; **tener** ~ **y voto** to be a full member, (*fig*) have a say; **no tener** ~ **en capítulo** to have no say in a matter; to have no influence, not count.

(**h**) (*Ling*: *vocablo*) word; **una** ~ **de origen árabe** a word of Arabic origin.

(**i**) (*Ling*: *forma*) voice; ~ **activa** active voice; ~ **pasiva** passive voice.

vozarrón *nm* loud voice, big voice.

VPO *nfpl abr de* **viviendas de protección oficial.**

vra., vro. *pron pos abr de* **vuestra, vuestro** your.

vto. (*Com*) *abr de* **vencimiento** due date, maturity.

vudú *nm* voodoo.

vuduísmo *nm* voodooism.

vuelapluma: **a** ~ *adv* quickly, without much thought.

vuelco *nm* (**a**) (*gen*) upset, overturning, spill; **dar un** ~ (*coche etc*) to overturn; (*barco*) to capsize.

(**b**) **mi corazón dio un** ~ my heart missed a beat; I had a presentiment.

(**c**) (*fig*) collapse; catastrophe, ruin; **este negocio va a dar un** ~ this business is heading for a catastrophe.

vuelillo *nm* lace, frill.

vuelo *nm* (**a**) (*gen*) flight; ~ **con alas delta,** ~ **libre** hang-gliding; ~ **a baja cota** low flying; ~ **a ciegas** blind flying, flying on instruments; ~ **charter** charter flight; ~ **de ensayo** test-flight; ~ **sin escalas,** ~ **sin etapas** non-stop flight; ~ **espacial** space-flight; ~ **con motor** powered flight; ~ **sin motor,** ~ **a vela** gliding; ~ **nacional** domestic flight; ~ **de órbita** orbital flight; ~ **en picado** dive; ~ **de prueba**(**s**) test-flight; ~ **rasante** ground flying; hedge-hopping; ~ **regular** scheduled flight; ~ **a solas** solo flight; **alzar el** ~**, levantar el** ~ to take flight, take off; (*fig*: *partir*) to dash off; (*fig**: *largarse*) to clear off*; (*fig*: *joven*) to leave the parental nest, spread one's wings; **se oía el** ~ **de una mosca** you could hear a pin drop; **remontar el** ~ to soar (up); **tocar las campanas a** ~ to peal the bells; **tomar** ~ to grow, develop; to assume great importance; **de un** ~**, en un** ~ rapidly.

(**b**) **al** ~: **cazar** (*o* **coger**) **algo al** ~ to catch sth in flight; (*fig*) to overhear sth in passing; **tirar al** ~ to shoot at a bird on the wing; **cogerlas** (*o* **pescarlas, pillarlas** *etc*) **al** ~ (*fig*) (*comprender*) to catch on immediately, get it at once*; (*ser listo*) to be pretty smart.

(**c**) (*Orn*: *t* ~**s**) (*plumas*) flight feathers; (*ala*) wing, wings; **de altos** ~**s** (*fig*) grandiose, ambitious, far-reaching; **cortar los** ~**s a uno** to clip sb's wings.

(**d**) (*Cos*: *de bocamangas*) lace, frill.

(**e**) (*Cos*: *de falda etc*) loose part; **el** ~ **de la falda** the spread of the skirt, the swirl of the skirt; **falda de mucho** ~ full skirt, wide skirt.

(**f**) (*Arquit*) projection, projecting part.

vuelta *nf* (**a**) (*gen*) turn; (*Astron, Mec etc*) revolution; **una** ~ **de la tierra** one revolution of the earth; ~ **al mundo** trip round the world; ~ **atrás** backward step (*t fig*); (*Cine etc*) flashback; **¡media** ~**!** (*Mil*) about turn!; ~ **en redondo** complete turn; **a** ~ **de** by dint of; **andar a** ~**s con** to be engaged in, be immersed in; **dar la** ~ **a una página** to turn a page; **dar la** ~ **al mundo** to go round the world; **el coche dio la** ~ the car turned over; **dar una** ~ **de campana** to overturn, turn completely over, somersault; **dar media** ~ (*Mil*) to face about; to turn half round; (*) to about-turn, walk out; **al llegar allí hay que dar media** ~ when you get there make a half turn; **dar** ~ **a una llave** to turn a key; **dar** ~ **a un coche** (*Esp*) to reverse a car, turn a car round; **el libro dio la** ~ **por muchas oficinas** the book went round a lot of offices; **dar la** ~ **a la tortilla** to change things completely; **dar la** ~ **a uno** (*CAm**) to con sb*; **dar** ~**s** to turn, revolve, go round; (*cabeza*) to spin, swim, be in a whirl; **dar** ~**s alrededor de un eje** to spin round an axle; **dar** ~**s alrededor de un planeta** to revolve round a planet, go round a planet; **dar** ~**s al calcetín** (*fig*) to try sth different ways; **dar** ~**s a una manivela** to turn (*o* wind, crank) a handle; **dar** ~**s a un botón** to turn a knob; **dar** ~**s a un asunto** to think a matter over, turn a matter over in one's mind; **le estás dando demasiadas** ~**s** you're worrying too much about it; **dar** ~**s a un palo entre los dedos** to twirl a stick in one's fingers; **no hay que darle** ~**s** that's the way it is, there's no mistake about it; **poner a uno de** ~ **y media*** (*insultar*) to heap abuse on sb; (*reprender*) to give sb a good telling-off*; **sacar la** ~ **a uno** (*And*) to cuckold sb.

(**b**) (*fig*) (*cambio*) turn, change; (*pey*) volte-face, reversal; ~ **de calcetín** complete turnaround; ~ **de la marea** turn of the tide; ~ **de tuerca** (*fig*) turn of the screw; twist; **las** ~**s de la vida** the ups and downs of life; **dar la** ~**, dar una** ~ to change right round, alter radically.

(**c**) (*de camino, río*) bend, curve, turn; ~ **cerrada** sharp turn, tight bend; **a la** ~ **de la esquina** round the corner; **en una** ~ **del río** at a bend in the river; **dar** ~**s** to twist and turn.

(**d**) (*de cuerda*) loop; coil; ~ **de cabo** (*Náut*) hitch.

(**e**) (*de elecciones, negociaciones, torneo etc*) round; (*en carrera*) lap, circuit; (*Golf*) round; ~ **ciclista** long-distance cycle race; **V**~ **de Francia** Tour de France; ~ **de honor** lap of honour; ~ **al ruedo** (*Taur*) *circuit of the ring made by a triumphant bullfighter*; **dio 3** ~**s al ruedo** he went round the ring 3 times; **segunda** ~ (*Univ*) repeat examinations, resits; **la segunda** ~ **de la Liga** the second half of the League programme.

(**f**) (*rodaja etc*) round, slice.

(**g**) (*Cos*) (*de puntos*) row of stitches; (*al hacer calceta*) row.

(**h**) (*Cos*) (*tira*) strip; (*guarnición*) facing; (*puño*) cuff; (*del pantalón*) turn-up, cuff (*US*).

(**i**) (*de papel, tela etc*) back, reverse, other side; (*de disco*) flip side; **a la** ~ on the next page, overleaf; **a la** ~ **de la esquina** round the corner; **a la** ~ **de varios años** after some years; **lo escribió a la** ~ **del sobre** he wrote it on the back of the envelope; **buscar las** ~**s a uno** to try to catch sb out; **no tiene** ~ **de hoja** there's no alternative; there are no two ways about it; there's no gainsaying it, it's unanswerable.

(**j**) (*acto*) return; (*Ferro etc*) return journey, homeward journey; **a ~ de correo** by return (of post); **a la ~** on one's return; **lo haré a la ~** I'll do it when I get back; **partido de ~** return match; **de ~, iremos a verlos** we'll go and see them on the way back; **estar de ~** to be back, be home (again); (*fig*) to have no illusions, know from experience; **el público está de ~ de todo** the public has seen it all before, the public knows all about it; **¡hasta la ~!** au revoir!, good-bye for now!; **envase sin ~** non-returnable bottle (*etc*).

(**k**) (*acto*) = **devolución.**

(**l**) (*Fin*: *t* **~s**) change; **quédese con la ~** keep the change.

(**m**) (*paseo*) stroll, walk; **dar una ~** to take a stroll, go for a walk.

(**n**) (*****: *paliza*) beating, tanning*.

vueltero *adj* (*Cono Sur*) *persona* difficult.

vuelto 1 *ptp de* **volver. 2** *nm* (*LAm*) change.

vuestro 1 *adj pos* your; (*tras n*) of yours, *p.ej.* **una idea vuestra** an idea of yours, one of your ideas; **lo ~** (what is) yours, what belongs to you.

2 *pron pos* yours, of yours; **es el ~** it is yours; **los ~s** (*frec*) your people, your relations, your family; your men, your side.

vulcanita *nf* vulcanite.

vulcanización *nf* vulcanization.

vulcanizar [1f] *vt* to vulcanize.

Vulcano *nm* Vulcan.

vulcanología *nf* vulcanology.

vulcanólogo, -a *nm/f* vulcanologist.

vulgar *adj* (**a**) *lengua* vulgar; *término* common, ordinary; *canción, cuento* popular; (*pey*) vulgar.

(**b**) *persona* ordinary, common; *modales, rasgos etc* coarse; **el hombre ~** the ordinary man, the common man.

(**c**) *suceso, vida etc* ordinary, everyday; (*rutinario*) humdrum; *observación etc* banal, trivial, commonplace; inane.

vulgaridad *nf* (**a**) (*cualidad*) (*ordinariez*) ordinariness, commonness; (*lo grosero*) coarseness; (*banalidad*) banality; (*trivialidad*) triviality; (*necedad*) inanity. (**b**) (*acto*) vulgarity, coarse thing; (*locución*) coarse expression. (**c**) **~es** banalities, trivialities, platitudes; inanities.

vulgarismo *nm* popular form (of a word); (*pey*) slang word, vulgarism, popular expression.

vulgarización *nf* (**a**) (*gen*) popularization; **obra de ~** popular work. (**b**) (*Ling*) translation into the vernacular.

vulgarizar [1f] *vt* (**a**) (*gen*) to popularize; to spread a knowledge of. (**b**) (*Ling*) to translate into the vernacular.

vulgarmente *adv* commonly, ordinarily; vulgarly; **A, llamado ~ B** A, popularly (*o* commonly) known as B.

Vulgata *nf* Vulgate.

vulgo 1 *nm* common people; (*pey*) lower orders, common herd; mob. **2** *adv*: **el mingitorio, ~ 'meadero'** the urinal, commonly (*o* popularly) known as the 'bog'.

vulnerabilidad *nf* vulnerability.

vulnerable *adj* vulnerable (*de* to).

vulneración *nf* infringement, contravention.

vulnerar [1a] *vt* (**a**) (*perjudicar*) to damage, harm; *costumbre, derecho etc* to interfere with, affect seriously. (**b**) *ley* to break, infringe, contravene.

vulpeja *nf* fox; vixen.

vulpino *adj* vulpine; (*fig*) foxy.

vulva *nf* vulva.

W

W, w ['uβe 'doβle, (*LAm*) 'doβle be] *nf* (*letra*) W, w.
walki-talki *nm* walkie-talkie.
Walkman ® *nm* Walkman ®.
wambas *nfpl* sandshoes.
wat, watt *nm* [bat, wat] watt.
wáter ['bater] *nm* lavatory, water closet.
waterpolista *nmf* water polo player.
waterpolo *nm* water polo.
wedge [weʒ] *nm* (*Golf*) wedge.
wélter ['belter] *nm* welterweight.
whisky ['wiski, 'gwiski] *nm* whisk(e)y; ~ **de malta** malt whisky.
windsurf ['winsurf] *nm* windsurfing.
windsurfista [winsur'fista] *nmf* windsurfer.
wolfram ['bolfram] *nm*, **wolframio** [bol'framjo] *nm* wolfram.

X

X, x ['ekis] *nf* (*letra*) X, x.
XDG *nf* (*Esp Pol*) *abr de* **Xunta Democrática de Galicia**.
xeno *nm* xenon.
xenofobia *nf* xenophobia.
xenófobo 1 *adj* xenophobic. **2** *nm*, **xenófoba** *nf* xenophobe.
xenón *nm* xenon.
xerocopia *nf* photocopy.
xerocopiar [1b] *vt* to photocopy.
xilófono *nm* xylophone.
xilografía *nf* (**a**) (*arte*) xylography. (**b**) (*una* ~) xylograph, wood engraving.
xilográfico *adj* xylographic.
Xunta *nf Galician autonomous government.*

Y

Y, y [i'ɣrjeɣa] *nf* (*letra*) Y, y.
y ...: *para algunas palabras escritas con* **y...** *en LAm, V t* **ll...**
y *conj* and; **¿~?** so?, well?; **¿~ eso?** why?, how so?*; **¿~ los demás?** what about the rest?
ya 1 *adv* (**a**) (*pasado*) already; **lo hemos visto ~** we've seen it already; **han dado las 8 ~** it's past 8 already; **~ en el siglo X** as long ago as the 10th century, as early as the 10th century; **~ no viene** he no longer comes, he doesn't come any more.
(**b**) (*presente*: *ahora*) now; (*en seguida*) at once, right away; (*pronto*) soon, presently; (*más adelante*) in due course; **~ veremos (eso)** we'll see (about) that; **~ es hora de irnos** it's time for us to go now; **~ viene el autobús** the bus is coming now, here's the bus; **~ se lo traerán** they'll bring it for you right away; **~ no lo volverás a ver** you won't see it any more; **~ arreglarán todo eso** they'll soon put all that right.
(**c**) (*como interj*) **¡~!** (*sí recuerdo*) of course!, that's it!, now I remember!; (*bien*) sure!; (*comprendo*) I understand!; (*por fin*) at last!, so you've managed it at last!; **¡~, ~!** yes, yes!; all right!; O.K.!*; **~, pero ...** yes, but ...
(**d**) (*enfático*: *no se suele traducir*) **¡~ voy!** coming!; **~ lo sé** I know; **~ se acabó** it's all over; **¿ ~ estás aquí otra vez?** are you here again?; **~ te llegará el turno a ti** your turn will come (don't you worry); **esto ~ es un robo** this really is robbery, you can't call this anything other than robbery; **~ gasta, ~** he really does spend a lot.
(**e**) (*LAm*) now; **~ mismo** right now; **desde ~** (*Esp*) (*a partir de ahora*) from now, (*fig*) of course.
2 *conj* (**a**) **~ por una cosa, ~ por otra** now for one thing, now for another; **~ dice que sí, ~ dice que no** first he says yes, then he says no; **~ te vas, ~ te quedas, me es igual** whether you go or stay is all the same to me.
(**b**) **no ~** not only; **no ~ aquí, sino en todas partes** not only here, but everywhere.
(**c**) **~ que ...** as ..., since ...; now that ..., seeing that ...; **~ que no ...** but not ...
yac *nm, pl* **yacs** [jak] yak.
yacaré *nm* (*LAm*) alligator.
yacente *adj estatua* reclining, recumbent.
yacer [2x] *vi* (*gen* ††) to lie; **aquí yace X** here lies X; **~ con** to sleep with.
yacija *nf* (**a**) (*cama*) bed; rough bed; **ser de mala ~** to sleep badly, be a restless sleeper; (*fig*) to be a vagrant, be a ne'er-do-well. (**b**) (*sepultura*) grave, tomb.
yacimiento *nm* (*Geol*) bed, deposit; (*arqueológico*) site; **~ petrolífero** oilfield.
yagua *nf* (*LAm*) royal palm; fibrous tissue from the wood of the royal palm.
yagual *nm*(*CAm, Méx*) padded ring (*for carrying loads on the head*).
yaguareté *nm*(*And, Cono Sur*) jaguar.
yaguré *nm* (*LAm*) skunk.
yaíta *adj* (*LAm*) = **ya**.
yak *nm, pl* **yaks** [jak] yak.
Yakarta *nf* Jakarta.
yámbico *adj* iambic.
yana *adj* (*And*) black.
yanacón, -ona *nm/f* (*And, Cono Sur*) (*aparcero*) Indian tenant farmer, Indian sharecropper; (*criado*) unpaid Indian servant.
yancófilo *adj* (*LAm*) pro-American, pro-United States.
yanqui 1 *adj* Yankee. **2** *nmf* Yank, Yankee.
yantar (†† *o hum*) **1** *nm* food. **2** [1a] *vt* to eat. **3** *vi* to have lunch.
yapa *nf* (**a**) (*LAm*) (*plus*) extra, extra bit, bonus; (*trago*) one for the road, last drink; **dar algo de ~** to add a bit, give sth as a bonus; (*fig*) to add sth for good measure.
(**b**) (*Carib, Méx*: *propina*) tip.
(**c**) (*Cono Sur Mec*) attachment, end piece.
yapada *nf* (*LAm*) extra, extra bit, bonus.
yapar [1a] (*LAm*) **1** *vt* (**a**) (*dar de más*) to give as a bonus, add as an extra. (**b**) (*extender*) to stretch; (*alargar*) to add a bit to, lengthen.
2 *vi* to add an extra, give an extra bit.
yarará *nm o f* (*And, Cono Sur*) rattlesnake.
yarda *nf* yard.
yate *nm* (*de vela*) yacht; (*de motor*) pleasure cruiser, motor cruiser.
yatista *nmf* yachtsman, yachtswoman.
yaya¹ *nm* (**a**) (*And, Carib, Cono Sur*) (*herida*) slight wound; (*cicatriz*) scar; (*dolor*) slight pain. (**b**) (*Carib*: *bastón*) stick, walking stick.
yaya²* *nf* nan, nana.
yaz *nm* jazz.
ye...: *para ciertas palabras, V* **hie...**, *p.ej. para* **yerra** *V* **hierra.**
yedra *nf* ivy.
yegua 1 *nf* (**a**) (*Zool*) mare; **~ de cría** breeding mare.
(**b**) (*And, Cono Sur*) (⁑: *pey*) old bag⁑; (*puta*) whore, slag⁑.
(**c**) (*And, CAm*: *de cigarro*) cigar stub.
2 *adj* (**a**) (*CAm, Carib*) (*tonto*) stupid; (*ordinario*) rough, coarse.
(**b**) (*Cono Sur*: *grande*) big, huge.
yeguada *nf* (**a**) (*caballeriza*) stud; (*Cono Sur*: *yeguas*) group of breeding mares. (**b**) (*CAm, Carib*: *estupidez*) piece of stupidity, foolish act (*etc*).
yeguarizo *nm* (*Cono Sur*) (**a**) (*de cría*) stud, group of breeding mares. (**b**) (*caballos gen*) horses.
yegüerío *nm* (*CAm, Carib*) = **yeguarizo** (**a**).
yelmo *nm* helmet.
yema *nf* (**a**) (*de huevo*) yolk; (*LAm*: *huevo*) egg; **~ mejida** egg flip.
(**b**) (*Bot*) leaf bud, eye; young shoot.
(**c**) **~ del dedo** (*Anat*) fingertip.
(**d**) (*fig*: *lo mejor*) best part.
(**e**) (*fig*: *pega*) snag; **dar en la ~** to put one's finger on the spot, hit the nail on the head.
(**f**) **en la ~ del invierno** (*fig*) in the dead of winter.
Yemen *nm* : **el ~** the Yemen.
yemenita *adj, nmf* Yemeni.
yen *nm, pl* **yens** *o* **yenes** yen.
yendo *V* **ir.**
yerba *nf* (**a**)=**hierba.**
(**b**) (*LAm*) green.
(**c**) (*And, Cono Sur*: *t* **~ mate, ~ de mate**) maté.
(**d**) (*: *marijuana*) marijuana, grass⁑.
yerbabuena *nf* (*LAm*) mint.
yerbal *nm* (*Cono Sur*), **yerbatal** *nm* (*And*) maté plantation.
yerbatero 1 *adj* pertaining to maté. **2** *nm* (**a**) (*LAm*) (*herbolario*) herbalist; (*curandero*) quack doctor. (**b**) (*Cono Sur*) (*comerciante*) dealer in maté; (*cultivador*) grower of maté.
yerbear [1a] *vi* (*Cono Sur*) to drink maté.
yerbera *nf* (*Cono Sur*) maté container.
yerbero *nm* (*LAm*) = **yerbatero.**
yermar [1a] *vt* to lay waste.
yermo 1 *adj* uninhabited; waste, uncultivated. **2** *nm* waste land; waste, wilderness.
yerna *nf* (*And, Carib*) daughter-in-law.
yerno *nm* son-in-law.
yernocracia* *nf* nepotism.
yeros *nmpl* lentils.
yerro *nm* error, mistake.
yersey *nm*, **yersi** *nm* jersey.
yerto *adj* stiff, rigid; **~ de frío** stiff with cold.

yesca *nf* (**a**) (*materia inflamable*) tinder; (*Cono Sur*: *piedra*) flint; **~s** tinderbox; **arder como si fuera ~** to burn like tinder.
(**b**) (*fig*) (*pábulo*) fuel; (*situación*) inflammable situation; (*grupo*) group (*etc*) which is easily inflamed.
(**c**) (*fig*: *Culin*) thirst-making food.
(**d**) (*And Fin*) debt.
yesería *nf* plastering, plasterwork.
yesero *nm* plasterer.
yeso *nm* (**a**) (*Geol*) gypsum.
(**b**) (*Arquit etc*) plaster; **~ mate** plaster of Paris; **dar de ~ a una pared** to plaster a wall.
(**c**) (*Arte etc*) plaster cast.
(**d**) (*Escuela*) chalk.
yesquero *nm* (*And, Carib*) cigarette lighter.
yeta* *nf* (*Méx, Cono Sur*) bad luck, misfortune.
yetar* [1a] *vt* (*Cono Sur*) to put a jinx on*, jinx*.
yeti *nm* yeti.
ye-yé⁑ **1** *adj* groovy⁑, trendy. **2** *nmf* groover⁑, trendy.
yíd(d)ish *nm* Yiddish.
yihad *nm* jehad.
yip *nm* jeep.
yirante* *nf* (*Cono Sur*) streetwalker.
yo *pron pers* (**a**) (*gen*) I; **soy ~** it's me, (*liter*) it is I. (**b**) **el ~** the self, the ego.
yod *nf* yod.
yodo *nm* iodine.
yodoformo *nm* iodoform.
yoga[1] *nm* yoga.
yoga[2] *nf* (*Méx*) dagger.
yogui *nm* yogi.
yogur *nm* (**a**) yoghurt; **mal ~** (*euf*) = **mala leche**. (**b**) (⁑: *coche de policía*) police-car, squad-car.
yogurtera *nf* (**a**) yoghurt-maker. (**b**) (⁑) (*Esp*) police-car, squad-car.
yol *nm* yawl.
yola *nf* gig, yawl; sailing boat; (*de carreras*) (racing) shell.
yonqui* *nmf* junkie*.
yoquei *nm* = **yóquey**.
yoquepierdismo* *nm* (*CAm*) self-interest, I'm-all-right-Jack attitude*.
yóquey *nmf, pl* **yóqueis** jockey.
yuca 1 *nf* (**a**) (*Bot*) yucca; (*LAm*) manioc root, cassava. (**b**) (*Carib*) poverty; **pasar ~** (*LAm*) to be poor. (**c**) (*And*: *comida*) food. (**d**) (*And*: *pierna*) leg. (**e**) (*And, CAm*: *mentira*) lie. **2** *adj* (*CAm*⁑: *difícil*) tough, hard.
yucateco 1 *adj* of Yucatan. **2** *nm*, **yucateca** *nf* native (*o* inhabitant) of Yucatan; **los ~s** the people of Yucatan.
yudo *nm* judo.
yugar [1a] *vi* (*CAm**) to slog away.
yugo *nm* yoke (*t fig*); **~ del matrimonio** marriage tie; **sacudir el ~** (*fig*) to throw off the yoke.
Yugo(e)slavia *nf* Yugoslavia, Jugoslavia.
yugo(e)slavo 1 *adj* Yugoslavian, Jugoslavian. **2** *nm*, **yugo(e)slava** *nf* Yugoslav, Jugoslav.
yuguero *nm* ploughman.
yugular 1 *adj* jugular. **2** [1a] *vt* to slaughter.
yungas *nfpl* (*And, Cono Sur*) hot valleys.
yungla *nf* jungle.
yunque *nm* (**a**) (*herramienta*) anvil. (**b**) (*fig*) (*estoico*) stoical person; (*trabajador*) tireless worker; **hacer de ~, servir de ~** to have to put up with hardships (*o* abuse *etc*).
yunta *nf* (**a**) (*bueyes*) yoke, team (of oxen). (**b**) **~s** (*esp LAm*) (*pareja*) couple, pair; (*gemelos*) cufflinks.
yuntero *nm* ploughman.
yuta *nf* (**a**) (*Cono Sur Bio*) slug. (**b**) **hacer la ~** (*And, Cono Sur*) to play truant.
yute *nm* jute.
yuxtaponer [2q] *vt* to juxtapose.
yuxtaposición *nf* juxtaposition.
yuyal *nm* (*Cono Sur*) scrub(land).
yuyerío *nm* (*And, Cono Sur*) (*malas hierbas*) weeds; (*plantas silvestres*) wild plants.
yuyero, -a *nm/f* (*Cono Sur*) herbalist.
yuyo *nm* (**a**) (*And, Cono Sur*) (*mala hierba*) weed; (*planta silvestre*) wild plant, useless plant; (*Cono Sur Med*) medicinal plant, herb; (*And*) herb flavouring; (*And*) cooking herb; **estar como un ~** (*Cono Sur*) to be wet*.
(**b**) (*And*: *emplasto*) herbal poultice.
(**c**) **~s** (*CAm*: *ampollas*) blisters on the feet.

Z

Z, z [θeta, (*esp LAm*) seta] *nf* (*letra*) Z, z.
zabordar [1a] *vi* to run aground.
zabullir [3h] *vi etc* = **zambullir** *etc*.
ZAC *nf abr de* **zona de atmósfera contaminada**.
zacapel(l)a *nf* rumpus*, row.
zacatal *nm* (*CAm, Méx*) pasture.
zacate *nm* (**a**) (*CAm, Méx*) (*hierba*) grass; (*heno*) hay, fodder. (**b**) (*Méx*: *trapo*) dishcloth.
zacatear [1a] (*CAm, Méx*) **1** *vt* to beat. **2** *vi* to graze.
zacatera *nf* (*CAm, Méx*) (*pasto*) pasture; (*almiar*) haystack.
zafacoca *nf* (**a**) (*LAm*) (*riña*) row, quarrel; (*pelea*) brawl. (**b**) (*Méx*: *paliza*) beating. (**c**) (*Carib*: *disturbio*) riot.
zafado *adj* (**a**) (*prov, LAm*: *descarado*) brazen, shameless; insolent. (**b**) (*Cono Sur*: *despierto*) alert, sharp, wide awake. (**c**) (*And, Méx*‡: *loco*) crazy, nuts‡.
zafadura *nf* (*LAm*) dislocation, sprain.
zafaduría* *nf* (*LAm*) (**a**) (*descaro*) cheek*, nerve*. (**b**) (*una* ~) bit of cheek*.
zafante *prep* (*Carib*) except (for).
zafar [1a] **1** *vt* (**a**) (*soltar*) to loosen, untie.
(**b**) *barco* to lighten; *superficie etc* to clear, free.
(**c**) (*LAm*: *excluir*) to exclude.
2 zafarse *vr* (**a**) (*huir*) to escape, run away; (*irse*) to slip away; (*soltarse*) to break loose; (*ocultarse*) to hide o.s. away.
(**b**) (*Mec*: *correa*) to slip off, come off.
(**c**) ~ **de** *persona* to get away from; to dodge, shake off; *deber, trabajo* to get out of, dodge; *acuerdo* to get out of, wriggle out of; *dificultad* to get round.
(**d**) (*) ~ **con algo** (*robar*) to pinch sth*; (*quedar sin castigo*) to get away with sth.
(**e**) ~ **un brazo** (*LAm*) to dislocate one's arm.
(**f**) (*CAm, Cono Sur*: *esquivar*) to dodge (a blow).
(**g**) (*And*‡: *volverse loco*) to go a bit crazy, to lose one's marbles‡.
zafarrancho *nm* (**a**) (*Náut*) clearing for action; ~ **de combate** call to action stations.
(**b**) (*fig*) havoc, destruction; mess; **hacer un** ~ to cause havoc; to break everything up; to make a dreadful mess.
(**c**) (*: *riña*) quarrel, row.
zafio *adj* coarse, uncouth.
zafiro *nm* sapphire.
zafo 1 *adj* (**a**) (*Náut*) clear; unobstructed. (**b**) (*ileso*) unharmed; (*intacto*) undamaged, intact; **salir ~ de** to come unscathed out of. (**c**) (*LAm*: *libre*) free. **2** *prep* (*CAm*: *excepto*) except (for).
zafón *nm* (*And*) slip, error.
zafra[1] *nf* oil jar, oil container.
zafra[2] *nf* (*esp LAm*) (*cosecha*) sugar harvest; (*fabricación*) sugar making.
zaga *nf* (**a**) rear; **a la ~, en ~** behind, in the rear; **dejar en ~** to leave behind, outstrip; **A ha quedado muy a la ~ de B** A is well behind B; **A no le va a la** (*o* **en**) **~ a B** A is every bit as good as B, A is in no way inferior to B; **no le va a la ~ a nadie** he is second to none. (**b**) (*Dep*) defence.
zagal *nm* boy, lad, youth; (*Agr*) shepherd boy.
zagala *nf* girl, lass; (*Agr*) shepherdess.
zagalejo *nm* lad; (*Agr*) shepherd boy.
zagalón *nm* big boy, strapping lad.
zagalona *nf* big girl, hefty wench*.
zagual *nm* paddle.
zaguán *nm* (**a**) (*entrada*) vestibule, hallway, entry. (**b**) (*CAm*: *garaje*) garage.
zaguero 1 *adj* (**a**) (*trasero*) rear, back; *carro* too heavily laden at the back; **equipo** ~ bottom team, team that is trailing. (**b**) (*fig*) slow, laggard. **2** *nm*, **zaguera** *nf* (*Dep*) back.
zahareño *adj* wild; shy, unsociable.
zaherimiento *nm* criticism; mortification; reprimand; reproach.
zaherir [3i] *vt* (*criticar*) to criticize sharply (*o* sarcastically), attack, lash; (*herir*) to wound, mortify; (*reprender*) to upbraid; ~ **a uno con algo** to reproach sb for sth, cast sth in sb's teeth.
zahiriente *adj* wounding, mortifying.
zahones *nmpl* chaps.
zahorí *nm* (*vidente*) seer, clairvoyant; (*que busca agua*) water diviner; (*fig*) highly perceptive person.
zahurda *nf* (**a**) (*Agr*) pigsty. (**b**) (*: *chabola*) hovel, shack.
zahurra *nf* (*And*) din, hullabaloo*.
zaino[1] *adj caballo* chestnut; *vaca* black.
zaino[2] *adj* (*pérfido*) treacherous; *animal* unreliable, vicious; **mirar a lo** (*o* **de**) ~ to look sideways, look shiftily.
zainoso *adj* (*Cono Sur*) treacherous.
Zaire *nm* Zaire.
zaireño, -a *adj, nm/f* Zairean.
zalagarda *nf* (**a**) (*Mil*) (*emboscada*) ambush, trap; (*ardid*) ruse; (*escaramuza*) skirmish; (*Caza*) trap. (**b**) (*ruido*) row, din; (*riña*) noisy quarrel; (*jaleo*) shindy*, hullabaloo*.
zalamerear [1a] *vi* (*And, Méx*) to flatter, cajole, wheedle.
zalamería *nf* (**a**) (*t* **~s**) flattery; cajolery, wheedling. (**b**) (*cualidad*) suaveness; oiliness, soapiness*.
zalamero 1 *adj* (*lisonjero*) flattering; (*mimoso*) cajoling, wheedling; (*fino*) suave; (*cobista*) oily, soapy‡. **2** *nm* flatterer; wheedler; suave person; oily sort, soapy individual*.
zalea *nf* sheepskin.
zalema *nf* salaam, deep bow; **~s** bowing and scraping, flattering courtesies.
zalenco *adj* (*Carib*) crippled, lame.
zalenquear [1a] *vi* (*And*) to limp.
zamarra *nf* (*piel*) sheepskin; (*chaqueta*) sheepskin jacket, fur jacket.
zamarrazo *nm* (*fig*) blow; setback; nasty jolt.
zamarrear [1a] *vt* (**a**) (*perro*) to shake, worry.
(**b**) (*) (*sacudir*) to shake up, knock around; (*empujar*) to shove around.
(**c**) (*: *en discusión*) to corner, beat, squash.
(**d**) (‡) to rob, pick the pocket of.
zamarro *nm* (**a**) (*piel*) sheepskin; (*chaqueta*) sheepskin jacket. (**b**) **~s** (*And, Carib*) chaps. (**c**) (*) (*rústico*) boor, yokel; (*taimado*) sly person.
zamba[1] *nf* (*esp LAm*) zamba (*a dance*).
zambada *nf* (*And*) group of half-breeds.
zambardo *nm* (**a**) (*Cono Sur*: *desmañado*) clumsy person. (**b**) (*Cono Sur*) (*desmaña*) clumsiness; (*daño*) damage, breakage. (**c**) (*Cono Sur**: *chiripa*) fluke.
zambeque (*Carib*) **1** *adj* silly. **2** *nm* (**a**) (*idiota*) idiot. (**b**) (*: *jaleo*) uproar, hullabaloo*.
zambequería *nf* (*Carib*) silliness.
zamberío *nm* (*And*) half-breeds* (*collectively*).
Zambeze *nm* Zambesi.
Zambia *nf* Zambia.
zambiano, -a *adj, nm/f* Zambian.
zambo 1 *adj* knock-kneed. **2** *nm*, **zamba**[2] *nf* (**a**) (*LAm*) half-breed (*of Negro and Indian parentage*). (**b**) (*And, Cono Sur*: *mulato*) mulatto.
zambomba *nf* (**a**) (*tambor*) *a kind of rustic drum*. (**b**) (*) ¡~! phew!
zambombazo *nm* (**a**) (*estallido*) bang, explosion. (**b**) (*golpe*) blow, punch.
zambombo *nm* boor, yokel.
zambra *nf* (**a**) (*de gitanos*) gipsy festivity. (**b**) (*: *jaleo*) uproar, shindy*; commotion.
zambrate *nm* (*CAm*), **zambrera** *nf* (*Carib*) row, commo-

tion.
zambucar [1g] *vt* to hide, tuck away, cover up.
zambuir [3g] *vi* (*And, Carib*) = **zambullir.**
zambullida *nf* dive, plunge; dip; ducking.
zambullir [3h] **1** *vt* (*en el agua*) to dip, plunge (*en* into); (*debajo del agua*) to duck (*en* under).
2 zambullirse *vr* (**a**) (*debajo del agua*) to dive, plunge (*en* into); to duck (*en* under).
(**b**) (*ocultarse*) to hide, cover o.s. up.
zambullón *nm* (*And, Cono Sur*) = **zambullida.**
zamorano 1 *adj* of Zamora. **2** *nm*, **zamorana** *nf* native (*o* inhabitant) of Zamora; **los ~s** the people of Zamora.
zampa *nf* (*Arquit*) pile.
zampabollos *nmf invar* (**a**) (*glotón*) greedy pig, glutton. (**b**) (*grosero*) coarse individual.
zampar [1a] **1** *vt* (**a**) (*ocultar*) to put away hurriedly (*en* in), whip smartly (*en* into); (*sumergir*) to dip, plunge (*en* into).
(**b**) (*arrojar*) to hurl, dash (*en* against, to); **lo zampó en el suelo** he dashed it to the floor.
(**c**) *comida* to gobble, wolf.
(**d**) (*LAm*) *golpe* to fetch, deal.
2 *vi* to gobble, eat voraciously.
3 zamparse *vr* (**a**) (*lanzarse*) to bump, crash, hurtle; **se zampó en medio del corro** he thrust himself roughly into the circle.
(**b**) (*fig: en fiesta etc*) to gatecrash, go along uninvited.
(**c**) ~ **en** to dart into, whip into, shoot into; **pero se zampó en el cine** but he shot into the cinema.
(**d**) ~ **algo** to wolf sth, tuck sth away*; **se zampó 4 porciones enteras** he wolfed 4 whole helpings.
zampatortas* *nmf invar* = **zampabollos.**
zampón* *adj* greedy.
zampoña *nf* panpipes.
zampuzar [1f] *vt* = **zambullir**; = **zampar.**
zanahoria 1 *nf* carrot (*t fig*). **2** *nm* (*Cono Sur**) (*imbécil*) idiot, nitwit*; (*desmañado*) clumsy oaf; (*pobre*) poor wretch.
zanate *nm* (*CAm, Méx Orn*) rook.
zanca *nf* (**a**) (*Orn*) shank. (**b**) (*Anat hum*) shank.
zancada *nf* stride; **alejarse a grandes ~s** to go off with big strides, stride away; **en dos ~s** (*fig*) (*rápidamente*) in a couple of ticks; (*fácilmente*) very easily.
zancadilla *nf* trip; (*fig*) stratagem, trick (*to get sb out of a job*); **echar la ~ a uno** to trip sb up; (*fig*) to put the skids under sb*, scheme to get sb out.
zancadillear [1a] *vt* to trip (up); (*fig*) to undermine, put the skids under.
zancajear [1a] *vi* to rush around.
zancajo *nm* (**a**) (*Anat, Cos*) heel; **A no le llega a los ~s a B** A can't hold a candle to B, A is much inferior to B. (**b**) (*: *enano*) dwarf, runt.
zancajón *adj* (*Méx*) (**a**) (*alto*) tall, lanky. (**b**) (*torpe*) clumsy, misshapen.
zancarrón *nm* (**a**) (*Anat*) leg bone; big bone. (**b**) (*: *viejo*) old bag of bones. (**c**) (*: *maestro*) ignorant teacher.
zanco *nm* stilt; **estar en ~s** (*fig*) to be well up, be in a good position.
zancón *adj* (**a**) (*de piernas largas*) long-legged. (**b**) (*CAm: alto*) lanky; clumsy-looking. (**c**) (*LAm*) *vestido* too short.
zancudero *nm* (*CAm, Carib, Méx*) swarm of mosquitoes.
zancudo 1 *adj* long-legged; **ave zancuda** wader, wading bird.
2 *nm* (*LAm*) mosquito.
zanfona *nf* hurdy-gurdy.
zangamanga* *nf* trick; funny business.
zanganada *nf* stupid remark, silly thing (to say).
zanganear [1a] *vi* (**a**) (*gandulear*) to idle, loaf; (*hacer el tonto*) to fool around, waste one's time. (**b**) (*decir disparates*) to make stupid remarks.
zángano *nm* (**a**) (*Ent*) drone. (**b**) (*fig: gandul*) drone; idler, slacker. (**c**) (*imbécil*) idiot, fool. (**d**) (*pesado*) bore. (**e**) (*CAm, Méx*: malvado*) rogue.
zangarriana *nf* (**a**) (*Med*) headache, migraine; minor upset. (**b**) (*fig*) blues, depression.
zangolotear [1a] **1** *vt* (*manosear*) to keep playing with, fiddle with; (*agitar*) to shake, jiggle.
2 *vi y* **zangolotearse** *vr* (**a**) (*ventana etc*) to rattle, shake.
(**b**) (*persona*) to fidget; to jiggle; to fiddle about, fuss around.
zangoloteo *nm* fiddling; shaking, jiggling; fidgeting; rattling.
zangolotino 1 *adj*: **niño ~** older boy with childish habits (*o clothes etc*); silly child. **2** *nm* youth, lad.
zangón *nm* big lazy lad, lazy lump*.
zanguanga* *nf* fictitious illness; **hacer la ~** to swing the lead*, malinger.
zanguango* 1 *adj* idle, slack. **2** *nm*, **zanguanga** *nf* slacker, shirker; malingerer.
zanja *nf* (**a**) (*fosa*) ditch; (*de drenaje*) drainage channel; (*foso*) trench; (*hoyo*) pit; (*tumba*) grave; **abrir las ~s** (*Arquit*) to lay the foundations (*de* for).
(**b**) (*LAm: barranco*) gully, watercourse.
(**c**) (*And: límite*) fence, low wall.
zanjar [1a] *vt* (**a**) (*gen*) to ditch, trench; to dig trenches in. (**b**) (*fig*) *dificultad, problema* to get around, surmount; *desacuerdo* to resolve, clear up.
zanjón *nm* (**a**) (*zanja profunda*) deep ditch. (**b**) (*Carib, Cono Sur*) (*risco*) cliff; (*barranco*) gully, ravine.
zanquear [1a] **1** *vt* (*CAm, Carib, Méx*) to hunt for. **2** *vi* (**a**) (*andar mal*) to waddle; to walk awkwardly. (**b**) (*ir rápidamente*) to stride along. (**c**) (*fig*) to rush about, bustle about.
zanquilargo *adj* long-legged, leggy.
zanquivano *adj* spindly-legged.
Zanzíbar *nm* Zanzibar.
zapa¹ *nf* sharkskin; shagreen.
zapa² *nf* (**a**) (*pala*) spade.
(**b**) (*Mil*) sap, trench.
zapador *nm* sapper.
zapallada *nf* (**a**) (*Cono Sur*) (*chiripa*) fluke; (*suerte*) lucky break; (*conjetura*) lucky guess (*etc*). (**b**) (*And: comentario*) silly remark.
zapallo *nm* (**a**) (*LAm Bot*) gourd, pumpkin. (**b**) (*Cono Sur*) = **zapallada** (**a**). (**c**) (*And: gordo*) fat person. (**d**) (*And, CAm*: tonto*) dope*, fool. (**e**) (*Cono Sur‡: cabeza*) nut‡.
zapallón* *adj* (*And, Cono Sur*) chubby, fat.
zapapico *nm* pick, pickaxe; mattock.
zapar [1a] *vti* to sap, mine.
zaparrazo *nm* claw, scratch.
zapata *nf* (**a**) boot. (**b**) (*Mec, Náut*) shoe; **~ de freno** brake shoe.
zapatazo *nm* (**a**) (*golpe dado con zapato*) blow with a shoe; (*caída, ruido*) thud; bump; bang; (*de pies*) stamping; pounding; (*Dep*) fierce kick, hard shot; **tratar a uno a ~s*** to treat sb very rudely. (**b**) (*Náut*) violent flapping of a sail.
zapateado *nm* (*gen*) tap dance; (*baile típico español*) zapateado.
zapatear [1a] **1** *vt* (**a**) (*dar golpecitos en*) to tap with one's foot.
(**b**) (*patear*) to kick, prod with one's foot.
(**c**) (*: *maltratar*) to ill-treat, treat roughly.
2 *vi* (**a**) (*dar golpecitos*) to tap with one's feet; (*bailar*) to tap-dance; (*conejo*) to thump.
(**b**) (*Náut: vela*) to flap violently.
zapatería *nf* (**a**) (*fabricación*) shoemaking. (**b**) (*tienda*) shoeshop; (*fábrica*) shoe factory, footwear factory.
zapatero 1 *adj* (**a**) shoemaking (*atr*). (**b**) *patatas etc* hard, undercooked; poor-quality.
2 *nm* shoemaker; **~ remendón, ~ de viejo** cobbler; **~, a tus zapatos** let the cobbler stick to his last.
zapatiesta* *nf* set-to*, shindy*.
zapatilla *nf* (**a**) (*para casa*) slipper; (*de baile*) pump; (*Dep*) trainer, training shoe, running shoe; **~s de clavos** spiked shoes; **~s de deporte** sports shoes; **~s de tenis** tennis-shoes. (**b**) (*Mec*) washer, gasket.
zapato *nm* shoe; **~s de color** brown shoes; **~s de cordones** lace-up shoes; **~s de golf** golf shoes; **~s de goma** (*LAm*), **~s de hule** (*Méx*) tennis-shoes, gymshoes, plimsolls; **~s de plataforma** platform shoes; **~s de salón** pumps; **~s de tacones altos** high-heeled shoes; **~s de tenis** tennis-shoes; **estaban como tres en un ~** they were packed in like sardines; **meter a uno en un ~** to bring sb to heel; **saber dónde aprieta el ~** to be alive to all the difficulties, have the right feeling about a situation; to know which side one's bread is buttered; to know where somebody's weakness lies.
zapatón *nm* big shoe; (*LAm*) overshoe, galosh.
zape 1 *interj* (**a**) (*a animal*) shoo! (**b**) (*sorpresa*) good gracious! **2** *nm* (‡) queer‡.
zapear [1a] *vt* (**a**) *gato etc* to shoo, scare away; *persona* to shoo away, get rid of. (**b**) (*And, CAm: espiar*) to spy on, watch.
zaperoco* *nm* (*Carib*) muddle, mess.
zapote *nm* (*LAm Bot*) sapodilla (plum), sapota.
zapoteca *adj, nmf* Zapotec.

zaque *nm* (a) (*de vino*) wineskin. (b) (‡: *borracho*) boozer‡, old soak‡.
zaquizamí *nm* (a) (*buhardilla*) attic, garret. (b) (*fig*: *cuartucho*) poky little room, hole; hovel.
zar *nm* tzar, czar.
zarabanda *nf* (a) (*Hist*) sarabande. (b) (*fig*) confused movement, rush, whirl. (c) (*Méx**: *paliza*) beating.
zaragata *nf* (a) (*: *ajetreo*) bustle, turmoil; (*jaleo*) hullabaloo*; (*riña*) row, set-to*. (b) **~s** (*Carib*) cajolery, wheedling.
zaragate *nm* (a) (*Cono Sur*: *malvado*) rogue, rascal; (*entrometido*) busybody. (b) (*Carib**: *zalamero*) flatterer, creep‡.
zaragatero 1 *adj* (*ruidoso*) rowdy, noisy; (*pendenciero*) quarrelsome. **2** *nm* rowdy, hooligan.
Zaragoza *nf* Saragossa.
zaragozano 1 *adj* of Saragossa. **2** *nm*, **zaragozana** *nf* native (*o* inhabitant) of Saragossa; **los ~s** the people of Saragossa.
zaramullo 1 *adj* (a) (*And, CAm, Carib*) (*afectado*) affected; (*engreído*) conceited; (*delicado*) finicky.
(b) (*And, Carib*: *divertido*) amusing, witty.
2 *nm* (a) (*And*: *tontería*) silly thing.
(b) (*And**) (*entrometido*) busybody; (*tonto*) fool.
zaranda *nf* (a) (*tamiz*) sieve. (b) (*Méx*: *carrito*) wheelbarrow. (c) (*Carib*: *juguete*) spinning top; (*Mús*) horn.
zarandajas* *nfpl* trifles, odds and ends, little things.
zarandear [1a] **1** *vt* (a) (*cribar*) to sieve, sift.
(b) (*: *sacudir*) to shake vigorously to and fro, shake up, toss about; (*empujar*) to shove, jostle, push around.
(c) (*: *dar prisa a*) *persona* to keep on the go, keep hustling about.
(d) (*LAm*: *balancear*) to swing, push to and fro; (*fig*) to abuse publicly.
2 zarandearse *vr* (a) (*prov, LAm*: *pavonearse*) to strut about.
(b) (*ir y venir*) to keep on the go, hustle about.
zarandillo *nm* active person, bustler; (*pey*) restless individual; (*niño*) fidget; **llevar a uno como un ~** to keep sb on the go.
zarapito *nm* (*t* ~ **real**) curlew.
zaraza *nf* printed cotton cloth, chintz.
zarazas *nfpl* rat poison.
zarazo *adj* (*LAm*) (a) *fruta* underripe. (b) (*: *bebido*) rather drunk, tight*.
zarcillo *nm* (a) (*pendiente*) earring. (b) (*Bot*) tendril. (c) (*Cono Sur, Méx Agr*) earmark.
zarco *adj* light blue.
zarigüeya *nf* opossum.
zarina *nf* tsarina.
zaroche *nm* (*LAm*) = **soroche**.
zarpa *nf* (a) (*Zool*) claw, paw; **echar la ~ a** to claw at, paw; (*: *agarrar*) to grab, lay hold of. (b) (*salpicadura*) splash of mud, smear of mud.
zarpada *nf* clawing; blow with the paw; **dar una ~ a** to claw, scratch; to hit with its paw.
zarpar [1a] *vi* to weigh anchor, set sail, get under way.
zarpazo *nm* (a) = **zarpada**. (b) (*fig*) thud; bang, bump. (c) **dar un ~*** to beat it quick*.
zarpear [1a] *vt* (*CAm, Méx*) to splash with mud.
zarrapastrón* *adj*, **zarrapastroso*** *adj* shabby, dirty, rough-looking.
zarria *nf* (a) (*salpicadura*) splash of mud, spattering of mud, smear of mud. (b) (*harapo*) rag, tatter.
zarza *nf* bramble, blackberry (bush).
zarzal *nm* bramble patch, clump of brambles.
zarzamora *nf* blackberry.
zarzaparrilla *nf* sarsaparilla.
zarzo *nm* (a) (*Agr etc*) hurdle; (*para construir*) wattle. (b) (*And*: *buhardilla*) attic.
zarzuela *nf* (a) (*Mús*) operetta, light opera, (Spanish-style) musical comedy. (b) **~ de mariscos** (*Culin Esp*) seafood casserole. (c) **(Palacio de) la Z~** *royal palace in Madrid*.
zarzuelista *nmf* composer of light opera, musical-comedy writer.
zas *interj* bang!, slap!; crash!; **le pegó un porrazo ..., ¡~! ... que ...** he gave him a swipe ... bang! ... which ...; **apenas habíamos puesto la radio y ... ¡~! ... se cortó la corriente** we had only just switched on the radio when ... click! ... and off went the current; **cayó ¡~! al agua** she fell right into the water.
zasca *excl* (a) bang!, crash! (b) (*como adv*) all of a sudden.
zascandil *nm* (a) (*casquivano*) featherbrained person; (*poco fiable*) unreliable person; (*frívolo*) frivolous individual.
(b) (*entrometido*) busybody.
zascandilear [1a] *vi* (a) (*obrar sin dar resultado*) to buzz about uselessly, fuss a lot; to behave frivolously, do featherbrained things. (b) (*entrometerse*) to pry, meddle.
zaya *nf* (*Carib*) whip.
zeda *nf* the (name of the) letter z.
Zenón *nm* Zeno.
zenzontle *nm* (*Cam, Méx*) mockingbird.
zepelín *nm* zeppelin.
zeta 1 *nf* the (name of the) letter z. **2** *nm* (*Aut*) police-car, Z-car.
Zetlandia: Islas *nfpl* **de ~** Shetland Isles.
ZID *nf abr de* **zona industrializada en declive**.
zigzag 1 *adj* zigzag. **2** *nm, pl* **zigzagues** zigzag (line *etc*); **relámpago en ~** forked lightning, chain lightning (*US*).
zigzagueante *adj* (*LAm*) zigzag (*atr*).
zigzaguear [1a] *vi* to zigzag.
zigzagueo *nm* zigzag, zigzagging movement.
Zimbabue *nm*, **Zimbabwe** *nm* Zimbabwe.
zimbabuo, -a *adj, nm/f* Zimbabwean.
zinc *nm* zinc.
zíngaro = **cíngaro**.
zipizape* *nm* set-to *, rumpus*; **armar un ~** to cause a rumpus; **los dos están de ~** the two of them are always squabbling.
zócalo *nm* (a) (*Arquit*: *pedestal*) plinth, base.
(b) (*de pared*) skirting board, baseboard (*US*); (*paneles*) panelling.
(c) (*Méx*) (*Mil*) parade ground; (*plaza*) town square; (*bulevar*) walk, boulevard; (*parque*) park.
zocato 1 *adj* (a) *fruta, legumbre* hard, rubbery; damaged. (b) *persona* left-handed. **2** *nm* (*And*: *pan*) stale bread.
zoclo *nm* = **zueco**.
zoco¹ 1 *adj* (a) (*zurdo*) left-handed. (b) (*And*: *manco*) one-armed; (*And, Carib, Cono Sur*: *tullido*) maimed, limbless. **2** *nm* (a) (*zurdo*) left-handed person. (b) (*Carib*: *tonto*) fool. (c) (*Cono Sur*: *puñetazo*) hefty punch.
zoco² *nm* (*Com*) (Arab) market, soq, souk.
zocotroco *nm* (*And, Cono Sur*) chunk, big lump; **~ de hombre*** hefty man*.
zodiaco *nm*, **zodíaco** *nm* zodiac.
zollenco *adj* (*Méx*) big and tough.
zollipar* [1a] *vi* to sob.
zombi *nm* zombie.
zona *nf* zone; belt, area; (*Inform*) area; **~ acuosa, ~ húmeda** wetland; **~ ancha** (*Dep*) midfield; **~ de batalla** battle zone; **~ catastrófica, ~ de desastre** disaster area; **~ común** communal area; **~ construida, ~ edificada** built-up area; **~ desnuclearizada** nuclear-free zone; **~ de ensanche** development area; **~ erógena** erogenous zone; **~ fronteriza** border area, border land; **~ de guerra** war-zone; **~ lumbar** lumbar region; **~ marginada** (*CAm*) slum area; **~ peatonal** pedestrian precinct; **~ de peligro** danger-area, danger-zone; **~ en penumbra, ~ de sombra** (*fig*) grey area; **~ de pruebas** testing-ground; **~ de tiendas** shopping centre; **~ tórrida** torrid zone; **~ verde** (*cinturón*) green belt; (*parque*) park, green area.
zonación *nf* zoning.
zonal *adj* zonal.
zoncear [1a] *vi* (*CAm, Cono Sur*) to behave stupidly.
zoncera *nf* (a) (*LAm*) = **zoncería**. (b) (*Cono Sur*) mere trifle; small amount; **costar una ~** to cost next to nothing; **comer una ~** to have a bite to eat.
zoncería *nf* silliness, stupidity; dullness; boredom, boring nature.
zonchiche *nm* (*CAm, Méx*) buzzard.
zonda *nf* (*And, Cono Sur*) hot northerly wind.
zonzo 1 *adj* (*esp LAm*) (*tonto*) silly, stupid; (*pesado*) boring, inane; (*Méx*) dazed, weary. **2** *nm* (*LAm*) idiot; bore, drag.
zonzoneco *adj* (*CAm*), **zonzoreco** *adj* (*CAm*), **zonzoreno** *adj* (*CAm*) stupid.
zoo *nm* zoo.
zoo... *pref* zoo...
zoología *nf* zoology.
zoológico 1 *adj* zoological. **2** *nm* zoo.
zoólogo, -a *nm/f* zoologist.
zoom [θum] *nm* (*objetivo*) zoom-lens; (*toma*) zoom shot.
zoomórfico *adj* zoomorphic.
zoomorfo *nm* zoomorph.
zooplancton *nm* zooplankton.
zoo-safari *nm* safari park.

zope *nm* (*CAm*) vulture.
zopenco* **1** *adj* dull, stupid.
2 *nm* clot‡, nitwit*.
zopilote *nm* (*LAm*) buzzard; (*) thief.
zopilotear [1a] *vt* (*Méx*) to eat greedily, wolf; (*fig*) to steal.
zopo *adj* crippled, maimed.
ZOPRE *nf abr de* **zona de promoción económica**.
zoquetada *nf* (*LAm*) stupidity.
zoquetazo *nm* (*Cono Sur, Méx*) swipe, punch.
zoquete *nm* (**a**) (*de madera*) block, piece, chunk (of wood).
(**b**) (*de pan*) crust of old bread.
(**c**) (*: *rechoncho*) squat person.
(**d**) (*) (*zopenco*) duffer, blockhead; (*patán*) lout, oaf.
(**e**) (*LAm: suciedad*) body dirt, human dirt.
(**f**) (*Carib, Méx*) (*puñetazo*) punch; (*trompada*) smack in the face.
zoquetillo *nm* shuttlecock.
zorenco *adj* (*CAm*) stupid.
Zoroastro *nm* Zoroaster.
zorra *nf* (**a**) (*animal*) fox; vixen. (**b**) (‡: *mujer*) whore, tart‡; ¡~! you slut! (**c**) **pillar una ~*** to get tight*.
zorral *adj* (**a**) (*And, CAm: molesto*) annoying. (**b**) (*And: obstinado*) obstinate.
zorrera *nf* (**a**) (*madriguera*) foxhole; (*fig: cuarto*) smoky room, room with a fug. (**b**) (*consternación*) dismay; (*inquietud*) worry, anxiety. (**c**) (*modorra*) drowsiness, lethargy.
zorrería *nf* (**a**) (*cualidad*) foxiness, craftiness. (**b**) (*una ~*) sly trick.
zorrero *adj* foxy, crafty.
zorrillo *nm* (*Cono Sur*), **zorrino** *nm* (*Cono Sur*) skunk.
zorro **1** *adj* (**a**) foxy, crafty.
(**b**) (‡) bloody**; **toda la zorra noche** the whole bloody night**; **no tengo ni zorra** (**idea**) I haven't a clue*.
2 *nm* (**a**) (*Zool*) fox, dog fox.
(**b**) (*piel*) fox-fur, foxskin; ~ **plateado** silver fox (fur).
(**c**) (*fig*) (*taimado*) old fox, crafty person, rascal; (*gandul*) slacker, shirker; **hacerse el ~** to act dumb; **estar hecho un ~** to be very drowsy; **estar hecho unos ~s*** to be all in, be done up; to be in an awful state.
(**d**) **~s** (*trapo*) duster.
zorrón *adj* sluttish.
zorruno *adj* foxy, fox-like.
zorrupia‡ *nf* tart‡, whore.
zorzal *nm* (**a**) (*Orn*) thrush. (**b**) (*fig*) (*listo*) shrewd person; (*taimado*) sly fellow. (**c**) (*Cono Sur*) (*tonto*) simpleton; (*inocente*) dupe, innocent person.
zorzalear* [1a] *vi* (*Cono Sur*) to sponge*.
zorzalero* *adj* (*Cono Sur*) sponging*, parasitical.
zorzalino* *adj*: **la vida zorzalina** the easy life.
zosco *nm* (*Carib*) idiot.
zotal *nm* ® disinfectant.
zote* **1** *adj* dense, dim, stupid. **2** *nm* dimwit*.
zozobra *nf* (**a**) (*Náut*) capsizing, overturning; sinking. (**b**) (*fig*) (*inquietud*) worry, anxiety; (*nerviosismo*) jumpiness, nervous state.
zozobrar [1a] *vi* (**a**) (*Náut*) (*peligrar*) to be in danger (of foundering); (*volcar*) to capsize, overturn; (*hundirse*) to founder, sink.
(**b**) (*fig: intención, proyecto*) to fail, come to naught, collapse; (*negocio*) to be ruined.
(**c**) (*fig: persona*) to be anxious, worry, fret.
zueco *nm* clog, wooden shoe.
zulo *nm* (*de armas*) cache; (*de documentos etc*) hiding-place.
zulú **1** *adj* (**a**) Zulu. (**b**) (*) thick*, stupid. **2** *nmf* (**a**) Zulu. (**b**) (*) idiot, dimwit*.
Zululandia *nf* Zululand.
zulla *nf* (human) excrement.
zullarse [1a] *vr* (*ensuciarse*) to dirty o.s.; (*ventosear*) to break wind.
zullón *nm* breaking wind.
zumaque *nm* sumac(h).
zumba *nf* (**a**) (*charla*) banter, chaff, teasing; humour; **dar ~ a, hacer ~ a** to rag, tease. (**b**) (*LAm: paliza*) beating. (**c**) (*Méx*) drunkenness.
zumbado* *adj* (**a**) **estar ~** to be crazy, be off one's head. **andar ~, ir ~** to be in a rush.
zumbador *nm* (**a**) (*Elec*) buzzer. (**b**) (*Carib, Méx Orn*) hummingbird.
zumbar [1a] **1** *vt* (**a**) *persona* to rag, tease.
(**b**) (*Univ**) to plough*.
(**c**) *golpe* to fetch, hit.
(**d**) (*LAm*) (*lanzar*) to throw, chuck*, toss; (*expulsar*) to chuck out.
(**e**) (‡: *robar*) to nick‡.
(**f**) (**) to fuck**.
2 *vi* (**a**) (*insecto*) to buzz, hum, drone; (*máquina*) to hum, whirr; (*zumbador*) to buzz; (*oídos*) to hum, sing, buzz; **me zumban los oídos** I have a buzzing in my ears (*V t* **oído**).
(**b**) (*: *quedar cerca*) to be very close; **no está en peligro ahora, pero le zumba** he's not actually in danger now, but it's not far away.
3 zumbarse *vr* (**a**) ~ **de** to rag, tease; to poke fun at.
(**b**) (*And, Carib**: *marcharse*) to clear off*.
(**c**) (*Carib: pasarse*) to overstep the mark.
(**d**) ~ **a una**** to screw sb**.
(**e**) **~la**** to wank**.
zumbido *nm* (**a**) *insecto* buzz(ing), hum(ming), drone; *máquina etc* whirr(ing); ~ **de oídos** buzzing in the ears, ringing in the ears. (**b**) (*: *puñetazo*) punch, biff*.
zumbo[1] *nm* (*And, CAm*) gourd, calabash.
zumbo[2] *nm* = **zumbido** (**a**).
zumbón **1** *adj persona* waggish, funny; *tono etc* teasing, bantering; (*pey*) sarcastic. **2** *nm* wag, joker, funny man; tease.
zumiento *adj* juicy.
zumo *nm* (**a**) juice; (*bebida*) juice, squash; ~ **de naranja** orange squash. (**b**) (*fig*) (solid) profit, (real) gain.
zumoso *adj* juicy.
zuncho *nm* metal band, hoop.
zupia *nf* (**a**) (*heces*) dregs; (*vino*) muddy wine; (*bebistrajo*) nasty drink, evil-tasting liquid. (**b**) (*fig: gente*) dregs; human trash. (**c**) (*And**: *aguardiente*) rough liquor.
ZUR *nf abr de* **zona de urgente reindustrialización**.
zurcido *nm* (**a**) (*acto*) darning, mending. (**b**) (*remiendo*) darn, mend, patch.
zurcidura *nf* = **zurcido**.
zurcir [3b] *vt* (**a**) (*Cos*) to darn, mend, sew up. (**b**) (*fig*) to join, combine, put together; *mentira* to concoct, think up. (**c**) (‡) **¡que las zurzan!** to blazes with them!; **¡que te zurzan!** get lost!‡
zurdazo *nm* (*golpe*) left-handed punch; (*tiro*) left-footed shot.
zurdear [1a] *vt* (*LAm*) to do with the left hand.
zurdo **1** *adj mano* left; *persona* left-handed; **a zurdas** with the left hand, (*fig*) the wrong way, clumsily; **no es ~** (*fig*) he's no fool; **ser ~ a algo** (*Carib**) to be bad at sth.
2 *nm*, **zurda** *nf* (**a**) (*gen*) left-handed person.
(**b**) (*Cono Sur Pol: pey*) lefty*, left-winger.
zurear [1a] *vi* (*paloma*) to coo.
zureo *nm* coo, cooing.
zuri‡ *nm* : **darse el ~** to clear out*.
zurito *nm* small glass (of beer).
zurra *nf* (**a**) (*Téc*) dressing, tanning.
(**b**) (*: *paliza*) tanning*, hiding*.
(**c**) (*: *trabajo*) hard grind*, drudgery.
(**d**) (*: *pelea*) roughhouse*.
zurrador *nm* tanner.
zurrapa *nf* (**a**) (*masa*) soft lump, dollop; (*mancha*) smudge, smear; (*hilo*) thread, stream (of dirt *etc*); **~s** dregs. (**b**) (*fig*) trash, muck, rubbish.
zurraposo *adj* full of dregs, thick, muddy.
zurrar [1a] *vt* (**a**) (*Téc*) to dress, tan.
(**b**) (*: *pegar*) to tan*, wallop*, lay into*.
(**c**) (*: *en discusión*) to sit heavily on*, flatten.
(**d**) (*: *criticar*) to lash into, criticize ferociously.
zurria* *nf* (**a**) (*And, CAm: paliza*) tanning*, hiding*. (**b**) (*And: multitud*) lot, crowd, mass.
zurriaga *nf* whip, lash.
zurriagar [1h] *vt* to whip, lash.
zurriagazo *nm* (**a**) (*azote*) lash, stroke, cut.
(**b**) (*fig*) (*revés*) severe blow, bad knock; (*mala suerte*) stroke of bad luck.
(**c**) (*fig: trato injusto*) piece of unjust (*o* harsh) treatment.
zurriago *nm* whip, lash.
zurribanda* *nf* = **zurra** (**b**) *y* (**d**).
zurriburri* *nm* (**a**) (*confusión*) turmoil, bustle, confusion; (*lío*) mess, mix-up; (*ruido*) hubbub. (**b**) (*persona*) worthless individual. (**c**) (*pandilla*) gang; (*turba*) rabble.
zurrón *nm* pouch, bag.
zurullo *nm*, **zurullón** *nm* (**a**) (*en líquido*) lump, hard bit.
(**b**) (**) turd**.
(**c**) (*persona*) lout, hooligan.
zurumato *adj* (*Méx*) (*turulato*) light-headed, woozy*; (*estúpido*) stupid.
zurumbanco *adj* (*CAm, Méx*) (**a**) = **zurumato**.

(**b**) (*****: *medio borracho*) half-drunk, half cut*****.

zurumbático *adj*: **estar ~** to be stunned, be dazed.

zurumbo *adj* (*CAm*) (**a**) = **zurumato**. (**b**) (*****: *medio borracho*) fuddled, stupid with drink.

zutano, -a *nm/f* (Mr, Mrs *etc*) So-and-so; **si se casa fulano con zutana** if Mr X marries Miss Y; *V* **fulano**.

ENGLISH~SPANISH DICTIONARY

DICCIONARIO INGLÉS~ESPAÑOL

A

A[1], a[1] [eɪ] *n* (**a**) (*letter*) A, a *f.* (**b**) (*Mus*) **A** la *m*; **A minor** la *m* menor; **No. 32A** (*house*) núm. 32 bis, núm. 32 duplicado; **to know a subject from A to Z** saber un tema de cabo a rabo; **to get from A to B** ir de A a B; **A for Andrew, A for Able** (*US*) A de Antonio. (**b**) **A-Level** *V* **advanced** (**b**); **A-line dress** vestido *m* de línea trapezoide; **A road** ≃ carretera *f* nacional; **'A' shares** acciones *fpl* de clase A; **A-side** cara *f* A; **A-test** prueba *f* de bomba atómica. (**c**) (*Scol*) sobresaliente.

A. *abbr of* **answer** respuesta *f.*

a[2] [eɪ, ə], **an** [æn, ən, n] (*before words starting with a vowel sound*) *indef art* (**a**) un, una.

(**b**) (*omitted in translation*) **half an hour** media hora; **a fine excuse!** ¡bonita disculpa!; **have you a passport?** ¿tiene Vd pasaporte?; **he is an engineer** es ingeniero; **what an idiot!** ¡qué idiota!; (*negative uses*) **I am not a doctor** yo no soy médico; **I haven't got a car** no tengo coche; **you don't stand a chance** no tienes posibilidad alguna; **without a doubt** sin duda; **without saying a word** sin decir palabra; (*apposition*) **the Duero, a Spanish river** el Duero, río de España.

(**c**) (*a certain*) **a Mr Smith called to see you** vino a verle un tal Sr Smith.

(**d**) (*distributive*) **2 apples a head** 2 manzanas por persona.

(**e**) (*rate*) **50 kilometres an hour** 50 kilómetros por hora; **£80 a week** 80 libras por semana; **3 times a month** 3 veces al mes; **she reads 3 books a week** lee 3 libros cada semana; **3 dollars a dozen** 3 dólares la docena.

a... *pref* a...; **atonal** atonal; **atypical** atípico.

a- *pref* (†† *or dialectal*): **everyone came a-running** todos acudieron corriendo; **it was a-snowing hard** estaba nevando mucho.

A1 ['eɪ'wʌn] *adj* de primera clase, de primera categoría; excelente; **to be ~ at Lloyd's** estar en excelentes condiciones, (*fig*) tener la máxima garantía; **to feel ~** estar muy bien.

A3 ['eɪ'θriː] *adj*: **~ size** (*paper*) papel *m* tamaño A3, doble folio *m*.

A4 ['eɪ'fɔːʳ] *adj*: **~ size** (*paper*) papel *m* tamaño A4, folio *m*.

AA *n* (**a**) (*Brit*) *abbr of* **Alcoholics Anonymous** Alcohólicos *mpl* Anónimos, A.A. (**b**) (*Brit Aut*) *abbr of* **Automobile Association** ≃ RACE *m*, Real Automóvil Club *m* de España. (**c**) (*US Univ*) *abbr of* **Associate in** (*or* **of**) **Arts** Profesor *m* numerario de letras. (**d**) (*Mil*) *abbr of* **anti-aircraft** antiaéreo.

AAA *n* (**a**) *abbr of* **Amateur Athletics Association** Asociación *f* de Atletismo Amateur. (**b**) (*US Aut*) *abbr of* **American Automobile Association** ≃ Real Automóvil Club *m* de España, RACE *m*.

Aachen ['ɑːxən] *n* Aquisgrán *m*.

AAF *n abbr of* **American Air Force** Fuerzas *fpl* Aéreas Americanas.

AAM *n abbr of* **air-to-air missile.**

AAR *abbr of* **against all risks** contra todo riesgo.

Aaron ['ɛərən] *nm* Aarón.

AAUP *n* (*US Univ*) *abbr of* **American Association of University Professors.**

AB (**a**) (*Naut*) *abbr of* **able-bodied seaman** marinero *m* de primera. (**b**) (*US Univ*) *abbr of* **Bachelor of Arts** Lic. en Fil. y Let. (**c**) (*Canada*) *abbr of* **Alberta.**

ABA *n* (**a**) *abbr of* **Amateur Boxing Association** Asociación *f* de Boxeo Amateur. (**b**) (*US*) *abbr of* **American Bankers Association.** (**c**) (*US*) *abbr of* **American Bar Association.**

aback [ə'bæk] *adv*: **to take ~** desconcertar, coger de improviso; **to be taken ~** quedar desconcertado; **I was quite taken ~ by the news** la noticia me causó gran sorpresa, la noticia me cogió de improviso.

abacus ['æbəkəs] *n, pl* **abacuses** *or* **abaci** ['æbəsaɪ] ábaco *m*.

abaft [ə'bɑːft] **1** *adv* a popa, en popa. **2** *prep* detrás de.

abalone [,æbə'ləʊnɪ] *n* (*US*) oreja *f* marina.

abandon [ə'bændən] **1** *vt* (**a**) (*leave*) abandonar, desamparar; salir de; descuidar; *old car etc* dejar tirado; **to ~ sb to his fate** abandonar a uno a su suerte; **~ ship!** ¡evacuar el barco!, ¡todos a los botes!

(**b**) (*give up*) renunciar a, abandonar; **the attempt had to be ~ed** hubo que renunciar a la tentativa; **the game was ~ed after 20 minutes' play** después de 20 minutos de juego se anuló el partido; **~ hope all ye who ...** abandonad la esperanza todos los que ...

2 *vr*: **to ~ o.s. to** abandonarse a, entregarse a.

3 *n* abandono *m*; libertad *f*, desenfado *m*, desenfreno *m*; **to dance with wild ~** abandonarse al éxtasis del baile, bailar desenfrenadamente; **to talk with gay ~** hablar con el mayor desenfado (*or* desparpajo).

abandoned [ə'bændənd] *adj* (**a**) (*deserted*) abandonado; desierto; *child* desamparado. (**b**) (*uninhibited*) libre, desenfadado; **in an ~ fashion** con abandono, desenfrenadamente. (**c**) (*vicious*) vicioso, entregado a los vicios. (**d**) **an ~ woman** una mujer perdida, una mujer de conducta dudosa.

abandonment [ə'bændənmənt] *n* (**a**) (*state*) desamparo *m*, abandono *m*; (*act*) acto *m* de desamparar, el abandonar (*etc*). (**b**) (*moral*) = **abandon 3.**

abase [ə'beɪs] **1** *vt* humillar, rebajar, degradar; envilecer, despreciar. **2** *vr*: **to ~ o.s.** humillarse; envilecerse.

abasement [ə'beɪsmənt] *n* humillación *f*, rebajamiento *m*, degradación *f*; envilecimiento *m*.

abashed [ə'bæʃt] *adj* avergonzado, confuso, corrido, desconcertado; **to be ~** quedar confuso; **to be ~ at** avergonzarse de; quedar desconcertado por; **he carried on not a bit ~** siguió sin dar la menor señal de vergüenza, siguió como si tal cosa.

abate [ə'beɪt] **1** *vt* disminuir, reducir; acabar con; (*Jur*) suprimir; *price* rebajar; *violence* mitigar, suavizar; *energy* debilitar; *enthusiasm* moderar; *pride* abatir.

2 *vi* disminuir, reducirse; ceder, menguar; (*violence, enthusiasm*) moderarse; (*wind*) calmarse, amainar; (*pain*) ceder; (*fever, flood, price*) bajar; (*courage*) desfallecer.

abatement [ə'beɪtmənt] *n* disminución *f*, reducción *f*; moderación *f*; (*Jur*) supresión *f*; (*of pain*) alivio *m*.

abattoir ['æbətwɑːʳ] *n* matadero *m*, camal *m* (*And*), picadero *m* (*And*).

abbacy ['æbəsɪ] *n* abadía *f*.

abbé ['æbeɪ] *n* abate *m*.

abbess ['æbɪs] *n* abadesa *f*.

abbey ['æbɪ] *n* abadía *f*; monasterio *m*, convento *m*, cenobio *m*; **~ church** iglesia *f* abacial; **Westminster A~** Abadía *f* de Westminster.

abbot ['æbət] *n* abad *m*.

abbreviate [ə'briːvɪeɪt] *vt* abreviar.

abbreviation [ə,briːvɪ'eɪʃən] *n* (*short form*) abreviatura *f*; (*act*) abreviación *f*.

ABC ['eɪbiː'siː] *n* (**a**) abecé *m*; abecedario *m*; (*fig*) abecé *m*; **~ of Politics** (*as title*) Introducción *f* a la política. (**b**) *abbr of* **Australian Broadcasting Commission.** (**c**) (*US*) *abbr of* **American Broadcasting Company.**

abdicate ['æbdɪkeɪt] **1** *vt throne* abdicar; *responsibility, rights* renunciar a; *principles* abdicar de. **2** *vi* abdicar (*in favour of* en, en favor de).

abdication [,æbdɪ'keɪʃən] *n* abdicación *f*; renuncia *f*.

abdomen ['æbdəmen, (*Med*) æb'dəʊmen] *n* abdomen *m*.

abdominal [æb'dɒmɪnl] *adj* abdominal.

abducent [æb'djuːsənt] *adj* abductor.

abduct [æb'dʌkt] *vt* raptar, secuestrar, plagiar (*LAm*).

abduction [æb'dʌkʃən] *n* rapto *m*, secuestro *m*, plagio *m* (*LAm*).

abductor [æb'dʌktəʳ] *n* raptor *m*, secuestrador *m*.

abed†† [ə'bed] *adv* en cama, acostado.

Aberdonian [ˌæbə'dəunɪən] **1** *adj* de Aberdeen. **2** *n* nativo *m*, -a *f* (*or* habitante *mf*) de Aberdeen.

aberrant [ə'berənt] *adj* aberrante; (*Bio etc*) anómalo, anormal.

aberration [ˌæbe'reɪʃən] *n* (*all senses*) aberración *f*.

abet [ə'bet] *vt criminal* incitar; ayudar; *crime* instigar; **to ~ sb in a crime** ser cómplice de uno en un crimen; **X, aided and ~ted by Y** X, persuadido y ayudado por Y; **accused of aiding and ~ting** acusado de ser cómplice en un crimen.

abetment [ə'betmənt] *n* incitación *f*, instigación *f*; (*Jur*) complicidad *f*.

abetter, abettor (*esp Jur*) [ə'betəʳ] *n* instigador *m*, -ora *f*; fautor *m*, -ora *f*; (*esp Jur*) cómplice *mf*.

abeyance [ə'beɪəns] *n*: **to be in ~** estar en suspenso; estar pendiente de aplicación; **to fall into ~** caer en desuso.

abhor [əb'hɔːʳ] *vt* aborrecer, abominar (de), detestar, odiar.

abhorrence [əb'hɒrəns] *n* (**a**) aborrecimiento *m*, detestación *f*; **violence fills me with ~** aborrezco la violencia; **to hold in ~** detestar. (**b**) (*object*) abominación *f*.

abhorrent [əb'hɒrənt] *adj* aborrecible, detestable, repugnante; **a thought ~ to common sense** un concepto repugnante al sentido común.

abide [ə'baɪd] (*irr*: *pret and ptp* **abode** *or* **abided**) **1** *vt* aguantar, soportar; **I can't ~ him** no le puedo ver; **I can't ~ a coward** aborrezco los cobardes; **I can't ~ tea** me da asco el té.

2 *vi* (*†† dwell*) morar; (*stay*) permanecer, continuar; **to ~ by** atenerse a, obrar de acuerdo con, guiarse por; *decision* respetar, atenerse a; *promise* cumplir; *rules of competition* ajustarse a, aceptar.

abiding [ə'baɪdɪŋ] *adj* permanente, perdurable.

ability [ə'bɪlɪtɪ] *n* habilidad *f*, capacidad *f*; talento *m*, aptitud *f*; **~ to pay** solvencia *f*, recursos *mpl*; **a boy of ~** un chico de talento; **he has great ~** tiene un gran talento (*for* para); **his ~ in French** su aptitud para el francés; **to the best of my ~** lo mejor que yo pueda (*or* sepa); **my ~ to do it depends on ...** el que yo lo haga depende de ...; **abilities** talento *m*, dotes *fpl*.

ab initio [ˌæbɪ'nɪʃɪəʊ] **1** *adv* ab initio, desde el principio. **2** *adj*: **~ learner** principiante *mf*.

abiotic [ˌeɪbaɪ'ɒtɪk] *adj* abiótico.

abject ['æbdʒekt] *adj* abyecto, vil; servil; abatido; *apology* rastrero; humilde; **an ~ liar** un mentiroso redomado; **to live in ~ poverty** vivir en la mayor miseria.

abjectly ['æbdʒektlɪ] *adv* abatidamente, vilmente; humildemente.

abjectness ['æbdʒektnɪs] *n* abyección *f*, vileza *f*; lo humilde.

abjure [əb'dʒʊəʳ] *vt* renunciar (a), abjurar.

ablative ['æblətɪv] **1** *adj* ablativo; **~ case** = 2. **2** *n* ablativo *m*; **~ absolute** ablativo *m* absoluto.

ablaze [ə'bleɪz] *adv and pred adj* en llamas, ardiendo; **the cinema was ~ in 5 minutes** en 5 minutos el cine estuvo envuelto en llamas; **the palace was ~ with light** brillaban todas las luces del palacio; **the garden was ~ with colour** resplandecía el jardín con sus flores multicolores; **to be ~ with excitement** estar emocionadísimo; **to be ~ with indignation** estar indignadísimo, estar encolerizado.

able ['eɪbl] *adj* (**a**) (*capable*) hábil, capaz, talentoso, competente; **~ to pay** solvente; **he's a very ~ man** es un hombre de mucho talento; **it's an ~ piece of work** es un trabajo sólido, es un trabajo competente; **~ seaman** marinero *m* de primera, marinero *m* patentado.

(**b**) (*in verb phrase*) **to be ~ to** + *infin* poder + *infin*; (*of acquired skills*) saber + *infin*, *eg* **you can go when you are ~ to swim** te permitiré ir cuando sepas nadar; **the child is nearly ~ to talk** el niño casi sabe hablar; **I was eventually ~ to escape** por fin pude escaparme, por fin logré escaparme; **come as soon as you are ~** ven en cuanto puedas.

-able *suffix* -able.

able-bodied ['eɪbl'bɒdɪd] *adj* sano, robusto; **~ seaman** marinero *m* de primera, marinero *m* patentado.

ablution [ə'bluːʃən] *n* (**a**) ablución *f*; **to perform one's ~s** (*hum*) lavarse; **to be at one's ~s** (*hum*) estar en el lavabo. (**b**) **~s** (*Mil**) servicios *mpl*.

ably ['eɪblɪ] *adv* hábilmente, con mucha habilidad.

ABM *n abbr of* **anti-ballistic missile.**

abnegate ['aebnɪgeɪt] *vt responsibility* eludir, evitar, rehuir; *one's religion* abjurar; **to ~ one's rights** renunciar a los derechos de uno.

abnegation [ˌæbnɪ'geɪʃən] *n* abnegación *f*.

abnormal [æb'nɔːməl] *adj* anormal; anómalo; irregular; deforme, mal formado.

abnormality [ˌæbnɔː'mælɪtɪ] *n* anormalidad *f*; irregularidad *f*; deformidad *f*.

abnormally [æb'nɔːməlɪ] *adv* anormalmente, de modo anormal; **an ~ formed bone** un hueso de formación anormal; **an ~ large sum** una cantidad descomunal.

Abo* ['æbəʊ] *n* (*Australia*) = **aboriginal.**

aboard [ə'bɔːd] **1** *adv* a bordo; **to go ~** embarcarse, ir a bordo; **to take ~** tomar a bordo, embarcar, cargar; **all ~!** (*Rail etc*) ¡señores viajeros, al tren! (*etc*); **life ~ is pleasant** es agradable la vida de a bordo.

2 *prep*: **~ the ship** a bordo del barco; **~ the train** en el tren.

abode [ə'bəʊd] **1** *pret and ptp of* **abide.**

2 *n* domicilio *m*, morada *f*; **place of ~** domicilio *m*; **right of ~** derecho *m* a domiciliarse; **of no fixed ~** sin domicilio fijo; **to take up one's ~** domiciliarse, establecerse.

abolish [ə'bɒlɪʃ] *vt* suprimir, abolir; anular, revocar; eliminar.

abolishment [ə'bɒlɪʃmənt] *n*, **abolition** [ˌæbəʊ'lɪʃən] *n* supresión *f*, abolición *f*; anulación *f*.

abolitionist [ˌæbəʊ'lɪʃənɪst] *n* abolicionista *mf*.

A-bomb ['eɪbɒm] *n abbr of* **atom bomb** bomba *f* atómica.

abominable [ə'bɒmɪnəbl] *adj* abominable; execrable; *taste, workmanship etc* detestable, pésimo; **the ~ snowman** el abominable hombre *m* de las nieves.

abominably [ə'bɒmɪnəblɪ] *adv* abominablemente; detestablemente, pésimamente; **to behave ~** comportarse de una manera detestable; **to be ~ rude to sb** ponerse sumamente grosero con uno; **he writes ~** escribe pésimamente.

abominate [ə'bɒmɪneɪt] *vt* abominar (de), detestar.

abomination [əˌbɒmɪ'neɪʃən] *n* abominación *f*.

aboriginal [ˌæbə'rɪdʒənl] **1** *adj* aborigen, indígena. **2** *n* aborigen *mf*, indígena *mf*.

aborigine [ˌæbə'rɪdʒɪnɪ] *n* aborigen *mf*.

abort [ə'bɔːt] **1** *vt* abortar; (*Comput*) interrumpir, detener prematuramente. **2** *vi* abortar, malparir; (*fig*) malograrse; (*Comput*) interrumpir el programa.

abortifacient [əˌbɔːtɪ'feɪʃənt] **1** *adj* abortivo. **2** *n* abortivo *m*.

abortion [ə'bɔːʃən] *n* (**a**) (*Med*) aborto *m* provocado, aborto *m* (criminal); **illegal ~** aborto *m* ilegal; **to have an ~** hacerse abortar; **to procure an ~** hacer abortar a una mujer; **~ clinic** clínica *f* de abortos; **~ law** ley *f* del aborto; **~ pill** píldora *f* abortiva. (**b**) (*creature*) engendro *m*; (*fig*) malogro *m*, fracaso *m*.

abortionist [ə'bɔːʃənɪst] *n* abortista *mf*.

abortive [ə'bɔːtɪv] *adj* (**a**) (*gen*) abortivo. (**b**) (*fig*) ineficaz, fracasado; malogrado; **to prove ~** fracasar, no dar resultado, malograrse.

abortively [ə'bɔːtɪvlɪ] *adv* (*try etc*) en vano; **the negotiations ended ~** las negociaciones fracasaron.

abound [ə'baʊnd] *vi* abundar (*in, with* de, en).

about [ə'baʊt] **1** *adv* (**a**) (*approximately*) alrededor de, más o menos; aproximadamente; **~ 20** unos 20, 20 más o menos; (*esp LAm*) como (unos) 20; **~ 7 years ago** hace unos 7 años; **~ 2 o'clock** a eso de las 2, sobre las 2; **~ a month** un mes poco más o menos, cosa de un mes; **he must be ~ 40** tendrá alrededor de 40 años; **it's ~ time you stopped** ya es hora de que lo dejes; **~ half** alrededor de la mitad; **it's just ~ finished** está casi terminado; **he's ~ the same** sigue más o menos igual; **that's ~ it, that's ~ right** eso es (más o menos); **that's ~ all I could find** eso es más o menos todo lo que podía encontrar.

(**b**) (*place*) **all ~** por todas partes; **to run ~** correr, correr por todas partes; **to walk ~** pasearse; ir y venir; *V* **play, turn** *etc*.

(**c**) (*with verb* to be) **to be ~ again** (*after illness*) estar levantado; **we were ~ early** nos levantamos temprano; **is anyone ~?** ¿hay alguien?; **is Mr Brown ~?** ¿está por aquí el Sr Brown?; **he must be ~ somewhere** debe de andar por aquí; **there's a thief ~** por aquí anda un ladrón; **there's a lot of measles ~** está dando el sarampión; **there isn't much money ~** hay poco dinero, la gente tiene poco dinero; **to be ~ to** + *infin* estar a punto de + *infin*, estar para + *infin*, estar por + *infin* (*LAm*); **nobody is ~ to sell it** nadie tiene la más mínima intención de venderlo.

2 *prep* (**a**) (*place*) alrededor de; **all ~ the house** (*outside*) por todos los alrededores de la casa, (*inside*) por todas partes de la casa; ~ **the fire** junto a la lumbre; **to walk ~ the house** andar por la casa; **to wander ~ the town** pasearse sin rumbo fijo por la ciudad; **you're ~ the house all day** pasas todo el día en casa; **to do jobs ~ the house** hacer las faenas domésticas; **he looked ~ him** miró a su alrededor; **I have no money ~ me** no llevo dinero encima.

(**b**) (*place*: *fig*) **he had a mysterious air ~ him** había algo misterioso en él; **there's sth ~ him (that I like)** tiene un no sé qué (que me gusta); **there's sth odd ~ it** aquí hay algo raro; **while you're ~ it** mientras lo estés haciendo; **and while I'm ~ it I'll talk to your father** y de paso charlaré con tu padre; **you've been a long time ~ it** has tardado bastante en hacerlo; **to be ~ one's business** atender a su negocio.

(**c**) (*relating to*) de, acerca de, sobre, con respecto a, respecto de; **a book ~ travel** un libro de viajes, un libro sobre los viajes; **I can tell you nothing ~ him** no le puedo decir nada acerca de él; **they fell out ~ money** riñeron por cuestión de dinero; **how ~ me?** ¿y yo?; **how ~ that book?** ¿y el libro ese?; **how ~ that?** ¿qué te parece?; **how ~ that!** (*amazement*) ¡toma!, ¡vaya!; **what ~ that book?** ¿y el libro ese?; **what ~ it?** (*what's your answer*) ¿quieres?; (*what of it*) ¿y qué?; **what ~ a song?** ¿queréis que os cante algo?; ¿por qué no nos cantas algo?; **what's that book ~?** ¿de qué trata ese libro?; **what's it all ~?** ¿de qué se trata?, ¿qué pasa?; **what are you ~?** ¿qué haces ahí?; ¿qué pretendes con eso?; **what did he talk ~?** ¿de qué habló?

about-face [ə'baʊt'feɪs], **about-turn** [ə,baʊt'tɜːn] **1** *n* (**a**) (*Mil*) media vuelta *f*. (**b**) (*fig*) cambio *m* radical de postura, giro *m* (brusco). **2** *vi* (**a**) (*Mil*) dar media vuelta. (**b**) (*fig*) cambiar radicalmente de postura.

above [ə'bʌv] **1** *adv* encima, por encima, arriba; (*in text*) arriba; **as ~** según lo dicho antes; **as set out ~** según lo arriba expuesto; **as I said ~** según dije ya; **from ~** desde encima, desde arriba; de lo alto; del cielo, de Dios; **orders from ~** órdenes *fpl* superiores, órdenes *fpl* de fuente superior; **the flat ~** el piso de arriba; **the air ~** el aire por encima; **those ~** (*superiors*) los de categoría superior; (*dead*) los que están en el cielo; (*gods*) los dioses.

2 *prep* (**a**) (*place*) encima de; ~ **my head** encima de mi cabeza; ~ **ground** sobre la tierra; **the Tagus ~ Toledo** el Tajo más arriba de Toledo; **2000 metres ~ sea level** 2000 metros sobre el nivel del mar.

(**b**) (*place*: *fig*) **he is ~ me in rank** tiene categoría superior a la mía; **to marry ~ one's class** casarse por encima de su clase; **I couldn't hear ~ the din** no podía oír con tanto ruido; **we are ~ that sort of thing** nosotros quedamos por encima de aquello; **it is ~ criticism** queda por encima de toda crítica; **it's ~ me** no lo entiendo, soy incapaz de entenderlo; **he is not ~ a bit of blackmail** es capaz de hacer un poco de chantaje.

(**c**) (*number*) más de; superior a; ~ **100** más de 100; **there were not ~ 40 people** no había más de 40 personas; **any number ~ 12** cualquier número superior a 12; **she can't count ~ 10** no sabe contar más allá de 10; **those now ~ 21** los ahora mayores de 21 años; **temperatures well ~ normal** temperaturas muy superiores a las normales.

3 *adj* susodicho, citado, arriba escrito, antedicho.

above-board [ə'bʌv'bɔːd] **1** *adv* abiertamente, sin rebozo. **2** *adj* legítimo, honrado.

above-mentioned [ə'bʌv'menʃənd] *adj* sobredicho, susodicho.

above-named [ə'bʌv'neɪmd] *adj* arriba mencionado.

Abp *abbr of* **Archbishop** arzobispo *m*.

abracadabra [,æbrəkə'dæbrə] *n* abracadabra *f*.

abrade [ə'breɪd] *vt* raer, raspar; desgastar.

Abraham ['eɪbrəhæm] *nm* Abrahán, Abraham.

abrasion [ə'breɪʒən] *n* raedura *f*, raspadura *f*; desgaste *m*; (*Med*) abrasión *f*.

abrasive [ə'breɪzɪv] *adj* (**a**) (*gen*) abrasivo. (**b**) (*fig*) *personality* difícil, agresivo, brusco; *tone* áspero, hiriente.

abrasiveness [ə'breɪzɪvnɪs] *n* (**a**) lo abrasivo. (**b**) (*fig*) agresividad *f*, brusquedad *f*; aspereza *f*.

abreast [ə'brest] *adv* de frente, de fondo; **to march 4 ~** marchar 4 de frente; marchar en columna de 4 en fondo; **he was walking ~ of the last two** caminaba a la par de los dos últimos; **to come ~ of** llegar a la altura de; **to be ~ of** (*fig*) estar al corriente de; **to keep ~ of** mantenerse al corriente de; **to keep ~ of the times** mantenerse al día.

abridge [ə'brɪdʒ] *vt book* compendiar, resumir, condensar; (*cut short*) abreviar, acortar.

abridged [ə'brɪdʒd] *adj* resumido, en resumen; abreviado.

abridgement [ə'brɪdʒmənt] *n* compendio *m*, resumen *m*; abreviación *f*.

abroad [ə'brɔːd] *adv* (**a**) (*in foreign parts*) en el extranjero, fuera; **to be ~** estar en el extranjero; **our army ~** nuestro ejército en el extranjero; **our debts ~** nuestras deudas en el exterior; **when the minister is ~** cuando el ministro está fuera del país; **to go ~** ir al extranjero; **he had to go ~** (*fleeing*) tuvo que salir del país; **troops brought in from ~** tropas traídas de fuera.

(**b**) (*outside*) fuera; fuera de casa; **there were not many ~ at that hour** había poca gente por las calles a aquella hora; **there is a rumour ~ that ...** corre un rumor de que ...; **it has got ~ that ...** se tiene noticia de que ..., (*falsely*) corre la voz de que ..., se ha divulgado la especie de que ...; **how did the news get ~?** ¿cómo se divulgó la noticia?

abrogate ['æbrəʊgeɪt] *vt* abrogar.

abrogation [,æbrəʊ'geɪʃən] *n* abrogación *f*.

abrupt [ə'brʌpt] *adj* (*sudden*) repentino, brusco; precipitado; *terrain* abrupto, escarpado; *style* cortado, lacónico; entrecortado; *manner of person* áspero, brusco; **he was very ~ with me** me trató sin miramientos.

abruptly [ə'brʌptlɪ] *adv* repentinamente, bruscamente; precipitadamente; **a cliff rose ~ before them** delante de ellos se alzaba un risco cortado a pico; **to leave ~** salir repentinamente; **everything changed ~** de pronto cambió todo.

abruptness [ə'brʌptnɪs] *n* brusquedad *f*; precipitación *f*; lo escarpado; lo cortado.

ABS *n abbr of* **antilock braking system** sistema *m* de frenos ABS, ABS *m*.

abscess ['æbsɪs] *n* absceso *m*.

abscond [əb'skɒnd] *vi* fugarse, huir (de la justicia), irse a hurtadillas; **to ~ with** alzarse con.

abseil ['æbsaɪl] *vi* (*also* **to ~ down**) hacer rappel, bajar en la cuerda; **he ~ed down the rock** hizo rappel bajando de la roca.

abseiling ['æbsaɪlɪŋ] *n* rappel *m*.

absence ['æbsəns] *n* (*of person*) ausencia *f*; (*of thing*) falta *f*, carencia *f*; **in the ~ of** *person* en ausencia de; *thing* a falta de; **to be sentenced in one's ~** ser condenado en ausencia; **signed in his ~** firmado por ausencia; **to be conspicuous by one's ~** brillar por su ausencia; **~ of mind** distracción *f*, despiste *m*.

absent 1 ['æbsənt] *adj* ausente (*from* de); (*fig*) distraído; **~ without leave** ausente sin permiso; **where liberty is ~** donde falta la libertad; **why were you ~ from class?** ¿por qué has faltado a la clase? **2** [æb'sent] *vr*: **to ~ o.s.** ausentarse (*from* de).

absentee [,æbsən'tiː] *n* ausente *mf*; **~ ballot** (*US*) voto *m* por correo; **~ landlord** absentista *mf*; **~ rate** nivel *m* de absentismo.

absenteeism [,æbsən'tiːɪzəm] *n* absentismo *m*.

absently ['æbsəntlɪ] *adv* distraídamente.

absent-minded ['æbsənt'maɪndɪd] *adj* distraído, despistado, volado (*LAm*).

absent-mindedly ['æbsənt'maɪndɪdlɪ] *adv* distraídamente, por distracción.

absent-mindedness ['æbsənt'maɪndɪdnɪs] *n* distracción *f*, despiste *m*.

absinth(e) ['æbsɪnθ] *n* (*Bot*) ajenjo *m*; (*drink*) absenta *f*.

absolute ['æbsəluːt] *adj* (*Gram, Math*) absoluto; *majority, monarch, power, zero etc* absoluto; *government* absolutista; *certainty, confidence etc* completo, total, pleno; *support* incondicional; *need* ineludible; *prohibition* terminante, total; *statement* tajante, categórico; *denial* rotundo; *alcohol* puro; *liar* redomado; **the ~** (*Philos*) lo absoluto; **the man's an ~ idiot** es un puro imbécil; **it's ~ rubbish!** ¡es puro disparate!; **it's the ~ end!** ¡es el colmo!; **~ monopoly** monopolio *m* total; **it's an ~ scandal** es simplemente escandaloso.

absolutely ['æbsəluːtlɪ] *adv rule etc* absolutamente; (*wholly*) completamente, totalmente; **~!** ¡perfectamente!, ¡eso es!; **~ not!** ¡de ninguna manera!; **that is ~ untrue** eso es totalmente falso; **it is ~ forbidden to** + *infin* queda terminantemente prohibido + *infin*; **I deny it ~** lo niego rotundamente (*LAm*: positivamente).

absolution [,æbsə'luːʃən] *n* absolución *f*; **to give ~ to sb** dar la absolución a uno, absolver a uno.

absolutism ['æbsəluːtɪzəm] *n* absolutismo *m*.

absolutist ['æbsəluːtɪst] **1** *adj* absolutista. **2** *n* absolutista *mf*.

absolve [əb'zɒlv] *vt* absolver (*from* de), perdonar.

absorb [əb'zɔːb] *vt* absorber; *shock etc* amortiguar; **the business ~s a lot of my time** el negocio me lleva mucho tiempo, el negocio me trae ocupadísimo; **she ~s chemistry readily** la química le entra con facilidad; **the country ~ed 1000 refugees** el país dio entrada a 1000 refugiados, el país acogió a 1000 refugiados; **the parent company ~s the losses made by the subsidiary** la compañía matriz absorbe las pérdidas de la filial; **to be ~ed in** (*fig*) estar absorto en, ensimismarse en; **to get ~ed in** (*fig*) engolfarse en, empaparse de, dedicarse de lleno al estudio de.

absorbable [əb'zɔːbəbl] *adj* absorbible.

absorbency [əb'zɔːbənsɪ] *n* absorbencia *f.*

absorbent [əb'zɔːbənt] *adj* absorbente; **~ cotton** (*US*) algodón *m* hidrófilo.

absorbing [əb'zɔːbɪŋ] *adj* absorbente, interesantísimo; **I find history very ~** me apasiona la historia.

absorption [əb'zɔːpʃən] *n* absorción *f* (*also fig, Comm*); **~ costing** cálculo *m* del costo de absorción.

abstain [əb'steɪn] *vi* abstenerse (*from* de); (*not vote*) abstenerse de votar; (*not drink*) abstenerse de las bebidas alcohólicas; **to ~ from comment** no ofrecer comentario.

abstainer [əb'steɪnəʳ] *n* (*also* **total ~**) abstemio *m*, -a *f*, abstinente *mf*, persona *f* que no bebe alcohol.

abstemious [əb'stiːmɪəs] *adj* sobrio, abstemio, moderado.

abstemiousness [əb'stiːmɪəsnɪs] *n* sobriedad *f*, moderación *f.*

abstention [əb'stenʃən] *n* abstención *f*; (*Parl*) abstención *f* de votar.

abstinence ['æbstɪnəns] *n* abstinencia *f* (*from* de); **total ~** abstinencia *f* total (*esp* de bebidas alcohólicas); **~ syndrome** síndrome *m* de abstinencia.

abstinent ['æbstɪnənt] *adj* abstinente.

abstract 1 ['æbstrækt] *adj* abstracto; **~ art** arte *m* abstracto; **~ noun** nombre *m* abstracto; **in the ~** en abstracto. **2** ['æbstrækt] *n* resumen *m*, sumario *m*. **3** [æb'strækt] *vt* (*remove*) extractar, quitar, separar; (*steal*) sustraer, robar; (*Chem*) extraer; *research publication* resumir, abstractar; *book* resumir, compendiar. **4** [æb'strækt] *vr*: **to ~ o.s.** abstraerse, ensimismarse.

abstracted [æb'stræktɪd] *adj* distraído, ensimismado.

abstractedly [æb'stræktɪdlɪ] *adv*: **she listened ~** escuchaba distraída.

abstraction [æb'strækʃən] *n* abstracción *f*; robo *m*; distraimiento *m*, ensimismamiento *m.*

abstruse [æb'struːs] *adj* recóndito, abstruso.

abstruseness [æb'struːsnɪs] *n* lo recóndito, carácter *m* abstruso.

absurd [əb'sɜːd] *adj* absurdo, ridículo, disparatado; **how ~!** ¡qué ridículo!; **don't be ~!** ¡no digas tonterías!; **you look ~ in that hat** se te ve ridículo con ese sombrero, con ese sombrero pareces ridículo; **the ~ thing is that ...** lo absurdo es que ...

absurdity [əb'sɜːdɪtɪ] *n* **(a)** (*an* ~) absurdo *m*, disparate *m*; locura *f*; **it would be an ~ to try** sería una locura intentarlo. **(b)** (*quality*) absurdidez *f*, absurdidad *f*, lo absurdo.

absurdly [əb'sɜːdlɪ] *adv* absurdamente, ridículamente, desproporcionadamente.

ABTA ['aebtə] *n abbr of* **Association of British Travel Agents** ≃ Asociación *f* Empresarial de Agencias de Viajes Españolas, AEDAVE *f.*

Abu Dhabi [ˌæbʊ'dɑːbɪ] *n* Abu Dhabi *m.*

abulia [ə'buːlɪə] *n* abulia *f.*

abundance [ə'bʌndəns] *n* abundancia *f*; **in ~** en abundancia, abundantemente, a granel; **we had an ~ of rain** llovió copiosamente; **we have a great ~ of plums** tenemos ciruelas en abundancia; **out of the ~ of his heart** de la plenitud de su corazón.

abundant [ə'bʌndənt] *adj* abundante (*in* en); copioso.

abundantly [ə'bʌndəntlɪ] *adv* abundantemente; copiosamente; **to make it ~ clear that ...** hacer constar con toda claridad que ...

abuse 1 [ə'bjuːs] *n* **(a)** (*insults*) improperios *mpl*, injurias *fpl*; **to heap ~ on sb** llenar a uno de injurias.

(b) (*misuse*) abuso *m*; (*physical*) malos tratos *mpl*; **~ of confidence, ~ of trust** abuso *m* de confianza; **child ~** maltrato *m* de los hijos; **sexual ~** abuso *m* sexual.

2 [ə'bjuːz] *vt* **(a)** (*revile*) maltratar (de palabra), injuriar, llenar de injurias; ultrajar (de palabra); **he roundly ~d the government** dijo mil improperios contra el gobierno.

(b) (*misuse*) abusar de; **he ~d his daughter** abusaba de su hija.

(c) (*mistreat*) maltratar.

Abu Simbel [ˌæbʊ'sɪmbl] *n* Abu Simbel *m.*

abusive [ə'bjuːsɪv] *adj* **(a)** (*insulting*) ofensivo, injurioso, insultante; **to be ~ to sb** decir cosas injuriosas a uno; **to become ~** empezar a soltar injurias (*to* contra). **(b)** *practice etc* abusivo.

abut [ə'bʌt] *vi* confinar, estar contiguo; **to ~ against, to ~ on** confinar con, lindar con; (*penthouse etc*) apoyarse en.

abutment [ə'bʌtmənt] *n* (*Archit*) estribo *m*, contrafuerte *m*; (*Carp*) empotramiento *m.*

abutting [ə'bʌtɪŋ] *adj* colindante, contiguo.

abuzz [ə'bʌz] *adj*: **the whole office was ~ with the news** toda la oficina comentaba la noticia.

abysmal [ə'bɪzməl] *adj* (*gen, liter*) abismal; (*fig*) profundo; **the most ~ ignorance** la ignorancia más profunda; **an ~ result** un malísimo resultado; **an ~ performance** una pésima actuación; **the play was ~** la obra fue una catástrofe; **to live in ~ poverty** vivir en la mayor miseria.

abysmally [ə'bɪzməlɪ] *adv* (*fig*) malísimamente, terriblemente; **~ bad** terriblemente malo.

abyss [ə'bɪs] *n* abismo *m*, sima *f.*

Abyssinia [ˌæbɪ'sɪnɪə] *n* Abisinia *f.*

Abyssinian [ˌæbɪ'sɪnɪən] **1** *adj* abisinio. **2** *n* abisinio *m*, -a *f.*

a/c **(a)** *abbr of* **account** cuenta *f*, cta. **(b)** (*US*) *abbr of* **account current** cuenta *f* corriente, c/c.

AC *n* **(a)** (*Elec*) *abbr of* **alternating current** corriente *f* alterna. **(b)** (*Aer*) *abbr of* **aircraftman** cabo *m* segundo de las fuerzas aéreas. **(c)** (*US Sport*) *abbr of* **Athletic Club** ≃ Club *m* Atlético, C.A.

acacia [ə'keɪʃə] *n* acacia *f.*

academe ['ækədiːm] *n* centro *m* de erudición, universidad *f*; (*fig*) vida *f* tranquila.

academia [ˌækə'diːmɪə] *n* el mundo erudito, el mundo de la erudición, (*esp*) la universidad.

academic [ˌækə'demɪk] **1** *adj* **(a)** (*Univ etc*) académico; universitario; escolar, docente; **~ advisor** (*US*) jefe *mf* de estudios; **~ dean** (*US*) decano *m*, -a *f*; **~ dress** vestidura *f* universitaria; **~ freedom** libertad *f* de cátedra; **~ interests** intereses *mpl* eruditos; **~ journal** revista *f* erudita; **~ officers** (*US*) personal *m* docente de centros de enseñanza; **~ rank** (*US*) rango *m* académico, jerarquía *f* académica; **~ staff** profesorado *m*, personal *m* docente; **~ year** año *m* universitario; **the boy is highly ~** el chico tiene gran aptitud intelectual; **he is an ~ painter** es un pintor académico. **(b)** (*gen pej*) *question* puramente teórico, sin trascendencia práctica; *argument* bizantino, poco provechoso, estéril; **the point is purely ~** la cuestión no tiene aplicación práctica.

2 *n* universitario *m*, -a *f*, catedrático *m*, -a *f* (*or* profesor *m*, -ora *f*) (de universidad).

academically [ˌækə'demɪkəlɪ] *adv* **(a) an ~ sound argument** un argumento intelectualmente sólido; **an ~ gifted child** un niño con altas dotes intelectuales; **~ the boy is below average** en los estudios el chico no llega al promedio. **(b) to argue ~** (*gen pej*) razonar de manera puramente teórica.

academicals [ˌækə'demɪkəlz] *npl* vestidura *f* universitaria.

academician [əˌkædə'mɪʃən] *n* académico *m*, -a *f.*

academy [ə'kædəmɪ] *n* academia *f*; (*Scot*) instituto *m* (de segunda enseñanza), colegio *m*; **military ~** academia *f* militar; **naval ~** escuela *f* naval; **~ of music** (*Brit*) conservatorio *m*; **~ for young ladies** colegio *m* para señoritas; **secretarial ~** escuela *f* de secretarias; **Royal A~ (of Arts)** Real Academia *f* (de Bellas Artes); **the Spanish A~** la Real Academia Española.

acanthus [ə'kænθəs] *n* acanto *m.*

ACAS ['eɪkæs] *n* (*Brit*) *abbr of* **Advisory Conciliation and Arbitration Service** ≃ Instituto *m* de Mediación, Arbitraje y Conciliación, IMAC *m.*

acc. **(a)** (*Fin*) *abbr of* **account** cuenta *f*. **(b)** (*Ling*) *abbr of* **accusative** acusativo *m.*

accede [æk'siːd] *vi* **(a) to ~ to** (*assent to*) *request* consentir en, acceder a; *suggestion* aceptar. **(b) to ~ to** (*gain, enter into*) *office, post* tomar posesión de, entrar en; *party* adherirse a; *throne* subir a; *treaty* firmar, adherirse a.

accelerate [æk'seləreɪt] **1** *vt* acelerar; impulsar, apresurar; **~d depreciation** depreciación *f* acelerada; **~d program** (*US Univ*) curso *m* intensivo. **2** *vi* acelerar.

acceleration [ækˌselə'reɪʃən] *n* aceleración *f*; **~ clause** provisión *f* para el vencimiento anticipado de una deuda.

accelerator [æk'seləreɪtəʳ] *n* (*Brit*) acelerador *m*, chancleta *f* (*Carib*), hierro *m* (*SC*); **to step on the ~** pisar el acelerador.

accent 1 ['æksənt] *n* **(a)** acento *m*; énfasis *m*; **~ mark** acento *m* ortográfico; **with a strong provincial ~** con fuerte acento de provincia; **in ~s of some surprise** en cierto tono de asombro. **(b) to put the ~ on** (*fig*) subrayar (la importancia de), recalcar; **this year the ~ is on bright**

colours este año están de moda los colores vivos; **the minister put the ~ on exports** el ministro recalcó la importancia de la exportación.

2 [æk'sent] *vt* acentuar.

accented [æk'sentɪd] *adj syllable* acentuado.

accentual [æk'sentjʊəl] *adj* acentual.

accentuate [æk'sentjʊeɪt] *vt* (**a**) (*gen*) acentuar. (**b**) (*fig*) subrayar (la importancia de), recalcar, dar énfasis a; aumentar.

accentuation [æk,sentjʊ'eɪʃən] *n* acentuación *f*.

accept [ək'sept] **1** *vt* aceptar (*also Comm*); aprobar; admitir; reconocer; recibir, acoger, dar acogida a; **the Academy ~s the word** la Academia aprueba la palabra; **the Academy ~ed the word in 1970** la Academia admitió la palabra en 1970; **to ~ orders** (*Comm*) admitir pedidos; **I do not ~ that way of doing it** no apruebo ese modo de hacerlo; **it is ~ed that ...** se reconoce que ...; **he was ~ed as one of us** pasaba por ser uno de nosotros, le acogieron como a uno de nosotros mismos.

2 *vi* aceptar, asentir.

acceptability [ək,septə'bɪlətɪ] *n* admisibilidad *f*.

acceptable [ək'septəbl] *adj* aceptable; admisible; adecuado, satisfactorio; (*welcome*) grato, oportuno; **tea is always ~** el té siempre agrada; **that would be most ~** eso me gustaría muchísimo; **that would not be ~ to the government** eso no le sería grato al gobierno; **that policy is not ~** esa política no es admisible; **it is not easy to find an ~ gift** no es fácil encontrar un regalo adecuado.

acceptance [ək'septəns] *n* aceptación *f* (*also Comm*); aprobación *f*; (buena) acogida *f*; **~ credit** crédito *m* de aceptación; **to meet with general ~** ser bien recibido por todos; **to win ~** lograr la aprobación.

acceptation [,æksep'teɪʃən] *n* acepción *f*.

accepted [ək'septɪd] *adj* aceptado; admisible; *fact, idea etc* corriente, reconocido, establecido; **it's the ~ thing** es la norma general, es cosa corriente; **he's an ~ expert** es un experto reconocido (como tal); **it is not a socially ~ habit** es costumbre no admisible en la buena sociedad.

acceptor [ək'septə^r] *n* aceptador *m*, -ora *f*; (*Comm*) aceptante *mf*.

access ['ækses] **1** *n* (**a**) (*entry etc*) acceso *m*, entrada *f*; (*Comput*) acceso *m*; **~ road** vía *f* de acceso; **of easy ~** asequible, de fácil acceso; *person* abordable, tratable; **to give ~ to a room** comunicar con una habitación; **this gives ~ to the garden** por aquí se sale al jardín; **to have ~ to the minister** poder libremente hablar con el ministro, tener libre acceso al ministro; **to obtain legal ~ to a property** conseguir una autorización legal para entrar en una propiedad; **he had ~ to the family papers** pudo leer los papeles de la familia, se le facilitaron los papeles de la familia.

(**b**) (*fig, Med*) acceso *m*, ataque *m*; **in an ~ of rage** en un arranque de cólera; **he had a sudden ~ of generosity** tuvo un repentino impulso de generosidad.

2 *vt* (*Comput*) entrar.

3 *attr*: **~ code** código *m* de acceso; **~ time** tiempo *m* de acceso.

accessibility [æk,sesɪ'bɪlɪtɪ] *n* accesibilidad *f*; lo asequible; carácter *m* abordable.

accessible [æk'sesəbl] *adj* accesible, asequible (*to* a); obtenible; *person* tratable, abordable; **he is not ~ to reason** no escucha la razón, hace oídos sordos a la razón; **she is not ~ to compassion** no es capaz de mostrar compasión; **the duke is not ~ to visitors** el duque no recibe visitas.

accession [æk'seʃən] *n* (**a**) (*entry etc*) acceso *m*, entrada *f* en posesión (*to* de); (*of king*) subida *f*, ascenso *m* (*to the throne* al trono); **~ to power** ascenso *m* al poder. (**b**) (*increase*) aumento *m*; (*new library book, exhibit etc*) (nueva) adquisición *f*; **a sudden ~ of strength** un aumento inesperado de fuerzas. (**c**) (*consent*) accesión *f*, adherencia *f* (*to a treaty* a un tratado).

accessory [æk'sesərɪ] **1** *adj* accesorio; secundario; **~ to** (*Jur*) cómplice *mf* de.

2 *n* (**a**) (*object*) accesorio *m*; **accessories** accesorios *mpl*; (*Aut etc, also of dress*) complementos *mpl*; **toilet accessories** artículos *mpl* de tocador.

(**b**) (*Jur*) cómplice *mf*; **~ after the fact** cómplice *m* encubridor, -ora *f*; **~ before the fact** cómplice *m* instigador, -ora *f*.

accidence ['æksɪdəns] *n* accidentes *mpl*.

accident ['æksɪdənt] *n* (**a**) (*mishap*) accidente *m*; percance *m*; **A~ (and Emergency) Unit** (*Aut*) puesto *m* de ayuda en carretera; **(road) ~ figures** (*or* **statistics**) cifras *fpl* (*or* estadísticas *fpl*) de accidentes (en carretera *etc*); **~ insurance** seguro *m* contra accidentes; **~ prevention** prevención *f* de accidentes; **~s will happen** hay accidentes que no se pueden prever; **to have an ~, to meet with an ~** sufrir un accidente.

(**b**) (*unforeseen event*) accidente *m*; **by ~** (*by chance*) por casualidad; (*unintentionally*) accidentalmente, sin querer, por descuido; **by some ~ I found myself there** me encontré allí sin saber cómo; **more by ~ than design** más por casualidad que por intención; **I'm sorry, it was an ~** lo siento, lo hice sin querer.

(**c**) (*Geol, Philos*) accidente *m*.

accidental [,æksɪ'dentl] **1** *adj* (**a**) (*casual*) accidental, fortuito; **~ death** muerte *f* por accidente. (**b**) (*incidental*) secundario, incidente. **2** *n* (*Mus*) accidente *m*.

accidentally [,æksɪ'dentəlɪ] *adv* (**a**) (*lit*) accidentalmente, por accidente; **he was ~ killed** fue muerto en accidente. (**b**) (*by chance*) por casualidad; sin querer, por descuido, por inadvertencia; **we met quite ~** nos encontramos por pura casualidad; **the liquids were ~ mixed** los líquidos se mezclaron por descuido.

accident-prone ['æksɪdənt,prəʊn] *adj* con tendencia a sufrir (*or* causar) accidentes.

acclaim [ə'kleɪm] **1** *vt* aclamar; (*applaud*) vitorear, ovacionar; **he was ~ed king** le aclamaron rey; **he was ~ed (as) the winner** le aclamaron por vencedor; **the play was ~ed** la obra fue muy aplaudida, la obra recibió muchos aplausos. **2** *n* aclamación *f*, aplausos *mpl*; **the book was met with ~** el libro tuvo una acogida entusiasta.

acclamation [,æklə'meɪʃən] *n* aclamación *f*, aplausos *mpl*; **amid the ~s of the crowd** entre los vítores de la multitud; **to be chosen by ~** ser elegido por aclamación.

acclimate [ə'klaɪmət] (*US*) = **acclimatize**.

acclimatization [ə,klaɪmətaɪ'zeɪʃən] *n*, (*US*) **acclimation** [,æklaɪ'meɪʃən] *n* aclimatización *f*, aclimatación *f*.

acclimatize [ə'klaɪmətaɪz] **1** *vt* aclimatar (*to* a). **2** *vi, vr*: **to ~ o.s., to become ~d** aclimatarse (*to* a).

acclivity [ə'klɪvɪtɪ] *n* subida *f*, cuesta *f*.

accolade ['ækəʊleɪd] *n* (**a**) premio *m*; honor *m*; galardón *m*; elogio *m* entusiasta. (**b**) (*Hist*) acolada *f*, espaldarazo *m*.

accommodate [ə'kɒmədeɪt] **1** *vt* (**a**) (*lodge, have room for*) *person* alojar, hospedar; *thing* tener espacio para, tener cabida para, contener; **can you ~ 4 people in July?** ¿tiene Vd habitaciones para 4 personas en julio?; **can you ~ 2 more in your car?** ¿caben 2 más en tu coche?; **this car ~s 6** este coche tiene 6 asientos.

(**b**) (*reconcile*) *differences* acomodar, concertar; *quarrel* componer, arreglar; *quarrellers* reconciliar.

(**c**) (*adapt*) acomodar, adaptar (*to* a), ajustar, ataviar (*LAm*).

(**d**) (*supply*) proveer (*with* de); **to ~ sb with a loan** facilitar un préstamo a uno.

(**e**) (*oblige*) complacer, hacer un favor a.

2 *vi* (*eye*) adaptarse (*to* a).

accommodating [ə'kɒmədeɪtɪŋ] *adj* servicial, complaciente, atento; (*pej*) acomodadizo, que a todo se aviene fácilmente.

accommodation [ə,kɒmə'deɪʃən] *n* (**a**) (*lodging*: *also* **~s** (*US*)) alojamiento *m*; (*rooms*) habitaciones *fpl*; '**~ to let**' 'se alquila habitación'; **have you any ~ available?** ¿tiene Vd habitación disponible?; **to book ~ in a hotel** reservar una habitación en un hotel; **~ address** dirección *f* por donde uno pasa a recoger cartas; **~ bureau** oficina *f* de hospedaje.

(**b**) (*space*) espacio *m*, sitio *m*; cabida *f*; **seating ~** plazas *fpl*, asientos *mpl*; **~ train** (*US*) tren *m* de cercanías; **there is standing ~ only** hay sitio solamente para estar de pie; **there is ~ for 20 passengers** hay sitio para 20 pasajeros; **the plane has limited ~** el avión tiene un número fijo de plazas.

(**c**) (*agreement*) acuerdo *m*, convenio *m*; **to reach an ~ with creditors** llegar a un acuerdo con los acreedores.

(**d**) (*adaptation*) acomodación *f*, adaptación *f*.

(**e**) (*loan*) crédito *m*, préstamo *m*; **~ bill, ~ note** (*Comm*) pagaré *m* de favor.

accompaniment [ə'kʌmpənɪmənt] *n* acompañamiento *m* (*also Mus*).

accompanist [ə'kʌmpənɪst] *n* acompañante *m*, -a *f*.

accompany [ə'kʌmpənɪ] **1** *vt* acompañar (*by, with* de; *also Mus, on* con, de); (*attach, enclose*) adjuntar, enviar adjunto; **he accompanied this with a grimace** al decir esto hizo una mueca.

2 *vr*: **to ~ o.s. on the piano** acompañarse del (*or* al, con el) piano.

accomplice [əˈkʌmplɪs] *n* cómplice *mf*.

accomplish [əˈkʌmplɪʃ] *vt* (*finish*) acabar, concluir; (*carry out*) llevar a cabo, hacer; (*bring about*) efectuar, lograr; *one's design* realizar; *prophecy* cumplir.

accomplished [əˈkʌmplɪʃt] *adj* (**a**) *person* experto, consumado, hábil, diestro. (**b**) *fact* consumado.

accomplishment [əˈkʌmplɪʃmənt] *n* (**a**) (*act*) conclusión *f*; efectuación *f*, logro *m*; realización *f*; cumplimiento *m*; **difficult of ~** de difícil consecución. (**b**) (*result*) logro *m*; triunfo *m*, hazaña *f*; **a great ~** una auténtica hazaña; **it's quite an ~ to** + *infin* exige mucho talento + *infin*; **her ~ in finishing the film although ill** su triunfo al terminar la película a pesar de estar enferma. (**c**) (*skill etc*) talento *m*; habilidad *f*; **~s** talentos *mpl*, prendas *fpl*, dotes *fpl*, méritos *mpl*.

accord [əˈkɔːd] **1** *n* (**a**) (*harmony*) acuerdo *m*, armonía *f*; **of one's own ~** espontáneamente, voluntariamente, por impulso propio; **with one ~** de común acuerdo; **to be in ~** estar de acuerdo (*with* con), estar en armonía (*with* con).

(**b**) (*treaty*) acuerdo *m*, convenio *m*.

2 *vt* conceder, otorgar (*to* a); *welcome* dar (*to* a).

3 *vi* concordar (*with* con), armonizar (*with* con).

accordance [əˈkɔːdəns] *n*: **in ~ with** conforme a, de conformidad con, con arreglo a, de acuerdo con.

according [əˈkɔːdɪŋ] *adv* (**a**) **~ as** según que, a medida que. (**b**) **~ to** según; (*in accordance with*) con arreglo a, conforme a; **~ to what he told me** según me dijo; **everything went ~ to plan** todo salió bien, todo resultó como se había previsto. (**c**) **it's all ~*** según, eso depende.

accordingly [əˈkɔːdɪŋlɪ] *adv* en conformidad, de acuerdo con esto; (**and**) **~** así pues, por consiguiente, por lo tanto.

accordion [əˈkɔːdɪən] *n* acordeón *m*.

accordionist [əˈkɔːdɪənɪst] *n* acordeonista *mf*.

accost [əˈkɒst] *vt* abordar, dirigirse a, entablar conversación con; (*prostitute*) abordar (con fines deshonestos); **he ~ed me in the street** se dirigió a mí en la calle; **he ~ed me for a light** se acercó a mí para pedir fuego.

accouchement [əˈkuːʃmɑ̃ːŋ] *n* parto *m*.

account [əˈkaʊnt] **1** *n* (**a**) (*Comm, Fin, fig*) cuenta *f*; computación *f*; (*invoice*) factura *f*; albarán *m*; (*statement of ~*) estado *m* de cuenta; **the A~** (*St Ex*) período *m* (de 15 días) al fin del cual se ajustan las cuentas; **~ balance** saldo *m* de una cuenta; **~s department** sección *f* de contabilidad; **~ payable** cuenta *f* a (*or* por) pagar; **~ receivable** cuenta *f* por cobrar; **~ rendered** cuenta *f* pasada; **(is it) cash or ~?** ¿en metálico o a cuenta?; **on ~** a cuenta; **payment on ~** pago *m* a cuenta; **could I have £50 on ~?** ¿puede Vd darme 50 libras anticipadas?; **on his ~** por él, por causa de él; de su parte; **on his own ~** por cuenta propia; **on ~ of** por, por causa de, por motivo de, debido a; *as conj* (*esp US**) porque, debido a que, *eg* **I couldn't do it on ~ of my back's sore** no he podido hacerlo porque me duele la espalda; **on that ~** por eso; **on no ~, not on any ~** de ninguna manera, bajo ningún concepto; **to bring sb to ~, to call sb to ~** pedir cuentas a uno; **to charge sth to sb's ~** cargar algo en cuenta a uno; **to close an ~** liquidar una cuenta; **they have the Blotto ~** ellos hacen la publicidad de Blotto; **to keep the ~s** llevar las cuentas; **to open an ~** abrir una cuenta; **to render an ~, to send an ~** pasar factura; **to settle an ~** liquidar una cuenta; **to settle ~s with sb** (*fig*) ajustar cuentas con uno; **to turn sth to ~** aprovechar algo, sacar provecho de algo; *V* **current, joint** *etc*.

(**b**) (*estimation*) importancia *f*; **of no ~, of little ~, of small ~** de poca importancia; **of some ~** de cierta importancia, de alguna consideración.

(**c**) (*report*) relato *m*, relación *f* (*of* de), informe *m* (*of* sobre); **by** (*or* **from**) **all ~s** a decir de todos, por lo que dicen todos; según todas las informaciones; **by** (*or* **according to**) **her own ~** por lo que dice ella; **to give an ~ of** dar cuenta de, informar sobre; **to give an ~ of o.s.** justificar su conducta; **to give a good ~ of o.s.** dar buena cuenta de sí; **to leave sth out of ~** no tomar algo en consideración; **to take sth into ~, to take ~ of sth** tener algo en cuenta, tener algo presente; **to take no ~ of** no tomar en cuenta, desestimar, desatender.

2 *vt* considerar, creer; **I ~ him a fool** considero que es tonto; **I ~ myself lucky** creo que tengo suerte; **he is ~ed an expert** se le considera un experto; **I should ~ it a favour if ...** agradecería que ...

◆**account for** *vt* (**a**) (*answer for*) responder de; (*explain*) dar cuenta de, dar razón de, justificar; representar; **that ~s for it** ésa es la razón, ha sido por eso; **I cannot ~ for it** no me lo explico; **how do you ~ for it?** ¿cómo lo explica Vd?; **everything is now ~ed for** todo está completo ya; **many are still not ~ed for** todavía no sabemos qué suerte han tenido muchos, seguimos ignorando lo que ha pasado a muchos; **there is no ~ing for tastes** sobre gustos no hay nada escrito; **children ~ for 5% of the audience** los niños representan el 5 por ciento de la audiencia.

(**b**) (*kill*) acabar con, matar; liquidar; **they ~ed for 3 stags** mataron 3 ciervos; **the ship ~ed for 3 enemy aircraft** el barco derribó 3 aviones enemigos; **one bomb ~ed for the power-station** una bomba acabó con la central eléctrica.

accountability [əˌkaʊntəˈbɪlətɪ] *n* responsabilidad *f*.

accountable [əˈkaʊntəbl] *adj* responsable (*for* de, *to* ante); explicable; **not ~ for one's actions** no responsable de los propios actos; **he is ~ only to himself** no reconoce más responsabilidad que ante sí mismo.

accountancy [əˈkaʊntənsɪ] *n* contabilidad *f*.

accountant [əˈkaʊntənt] *n* contable *mf*, contador *m*, -ora *f* (*esp LAm*); asesor *m*, -ora *f* fiscal (*or* de cuentas); (*in bank etc*) economista *mf*; **~'s office** contaduría *f*.

account-book [əˈkaʊntbʊk] *n* libro *m* de cuentas.

account-day [əˈkaʊntdeɪ] *n* día *m* de ajuste de cuentas.

accounting [əˈkaʊntɪŋ] *n* contabilidad *f*; teneduría *f* de libros; **~ period** período *m* contable, ejercicio *m* financiero.

accounting machine [əˈkaʊntɪŋməˌʃiːn] *n* máquina *f* de contabilidad, calculadora *f*.

accoutred, (*US*) **accoutered** [əˈkuːtəd] *ptp and adj* equipado (*with* de).

accoutrements, (*US*) **accouterments** [əˈkuːtrəmənts] *npl*, [əˈkuːtəmənts] *npl* equipo *m*, avíos *mpl*, arreos *mpl*.

accredit [əˈkredɪt] *vt* (**a**) (*credit*) atribuir (*to* a); **to ~ a quality to sb, to ~ sb with a quality** atribuir una cualidad a uno. (**b**) (*recognize*) reconocer (oficialmente); certificar, autorizar. (**c**) (*appoint*) acreditar (*an ambassador to a government* un embajador cerca de un gobierno).

accreditation [əˌkredɪˈteɪʃən] *n* reconocimiento *m* (oficial); autorización *f*; (*US Scol, Univ*) habilitación *f* de enseñanza; **~ officer** (*US Scol*) inspector *m*, -ora *f* de enseñanza.

accredited [əˈkredɪtɪd] *adj* autorizado, acreditado; **~ agent** agente *m* acreditado.

accretion [əˈkriːʃən] *n* aumento *m*, acrecentamiento *m*.

accrual [əˈkruːəl] *n* acumulación *f*.

accrue [əˈkruː] *vi* (*grow*) aumentar, acumularse; **to ~ from** proceder de; derivarse de; **to ~ to** corresponder a; **some benefit will ~ to you from this** de esto resultará algo a beneficio de Vd; **~d charges** gastos *mpl* vencidos; **~d income** renta *f* acumulada; **~d interest** interés *m* acumulado.

ACCT *n abbr of* **Association of Cinematograph, Television and Allied Technicians.**

acct *abbr of* **account** cuenta *f*, cta.

acculturate [əˈkʌltʃəˌreɪt] *vt* aculturar.

acculturation [əˌkʌltʃəˈreɪʃən] *n* aculturación *f*.

accumulate [əˈkjuːmjʊleɪt] **1** *vt* acumular, amontonar; acopiar, juntar. **2** *vi* acumularse, amontonarse; **~d depreciation** depreciación *f* acumulada.

accumulation [əˌkjuːmjʊˈleɪʃən] *n* (**a**) (*act*) acumulación *f*, amontonamiento *m*. (**b**) (*mass*) montón *m*, acopio *m*.

accumulative [əˈkjuːmjʊlətɪv] *adj* acumulativo.

accumulator [əˈkjuːmjʊleɪtə^r] *n* acumulador *m*.

accuracy [ˈækjʊrəsɪ] *n* exactitud *f*, precisión *f*; esmero *m*.

accurate [ˈækjʊrɪt] *adj number, observation etc* exacto, preciso, correcto; *copy* fiel; *answer* correcto, acertado; *shot* certero; *worker* exacto, esmerado; **to be strictly ~ ...** para decirlo con toda exactitud ...

accurately [ˈækjʊrɪtlɪ] *adv* exactamente, correctamente; fielmente; acertadamente; certeramente; con esmero.

accursed, accurst [əˈkɜːst] *adj* (*liter*) maldito; (*ill-fated*) infausto, desventurado; **~ be he who ...!** ¡maldito sea quien ...!, ¡mal haya quien ...!

accusal [əˈkjuːzl] *n* (*Jur*) acusación *f*.

accusation [ˌækjuˈzeɪʃən] *n* acusación *f*, cargo *m*; denuncia *f*, delación *f*.

accusative [əˈkjuːzətɪv] **1** *adj* acusativo; **~ case** = **2**. **2** *n* acusativo *m*.

accusatorial [əˌkjuːzəˈtɔːrɪəl] *adj*, **accusatory** [əˈkjuːzətərɪ] *adj* acusador.

accuse [əˈkjuːz] *vt* acusar (*of* de); denunciar, delatar; echar la culpa a, inculpar; **he stands ~d of ...** se le acusa de ...

accused [əˈkjuːzd] *n* acusado *m*, -a *f*.

accuser [əˈkjuːzə^r] *n* acusador *m*, -ora *f*, delator *m*, -ora *f*.

accusing [əˈkjuːzɪŋ] *adj* acusador, lleno de reproches.

accusingly [əˈkjuːzɪŋlɪ] *adv*: **she spoke ~** habló con tono acusador; **she looked at me** ~ me lanzó una mirada acusadora.

accustom [əˈkʌstəm] **1** *vt* acostumbrar, habituar (*to* a); **to be ~ed to** + *infin* acostumbrar + *infin*, soler + *infin*; estar hecho a + *infin*; **I'm not really ~ed to** + *ger* en realidad no tengo la costumbre de + *infin*, no estoy realmente acostumbrado a + *infin*; **to get ~ed to sth** acostumbrarse a algo, habituarse a algo; **to get ~ed to** + *ger* acostumbrarse a + *infin*; **don't worry, you'll get ~ed** no te preocupes, ya te acostumbrarás a esto.

2 *vr*: **to ~ o.s. to** acostumbrarse a; **to ~ o.s. to** + *ger* acostumbrarse a + *infin*.

accustomed [əˈkʌstəmd] *adj* acostumbrado, usual.

AC/DC [ˌeɪsiːˈdiːsiː] **1** *n abbr of* **alternating current/direct current** corriente *f* alterna/corriente *f* continua. **2** *adj*: **he's** ~‡ es bisexual.

ACE *n* (*US*) *abbr of* **American Council on Education**.

ace [eɪs] **1** *n* (**a**) (*all senses*) as *m*; **to be** (*or* **come**) **within an ~ of** estar a dos dedos de, estar a pique de; **to keep an ~ up one's sleeve, to have an ~ in the hole** (*US**) guardar un triunfo en la mano; guardarse un as en la manga; **to play one's ~** (*fig*) jugar su triunfo; **A~ bandage** (*US*) ® venda *f* elástica. (**b**) **he's ~s** (*US**) es fenomenal*.

2 *adj* (*) estupendo*, de aúpa*; **~ player** *etc* as *m*.

acephalous [əˈsefələs] *adj* acéfalo.

acerbic [əˈsɜːbɪk] *adj* acre, áspero (*also fig*).

acerbity [əˈsɜːbɪtɪ] *n* acritud *f*, aspereza *f*; (*fig*) aspereza *f*.

acetate [ˈæsɪteɪt] *n* acetato *m*.

acetic [əˈsiːtɪk] *adj* acético; **~ acid** ácido *m* acético.

acetone [ˈæsɪtəʊn] *n* acetona *f*.

acetylene [əˈsetɪliːn] *n* acetileno *m*; **~ burner, ~ lamp, ~ torch** soplete *m* oxiacetilénico; **~ welding** soldadura *f* oxiacetilénica.

ache [eɪk] **1** *n* dolor *m* (*also fig*); achaque *m*; **I have an ~ in my side** me duele el costado; **full of ~s and pains** lleno de goteras; **with an ~ in one's heart** con dolor del corazón.

2 *vi* (**a**) (*tooth etc*) doler; **my head ~s** me duele la cabeza; **it makes my head ~** me da un dolor de cabeza; **I ~ all over** tengo dolores por todas partes. (**b**) (*fig*) **it was enough to make your heart ~** era para romperle a uno el alma; **my heart ~s for you** lo siento en el alma; **I am aching for you** suspiro por ti; **I am aching to see you again** quiero tantísimo volver a verte; **I ~d to help him** quería con todo mi ser acudir en su auxilio, ansiaba tanto poder ayudarle, hubiera dado lo que fuera por ayudarle.

achievable [əˈtʃiːvəbl] *adj* alcanzable, realizable, factible; **an aim readily ~** un propósito fácil de alcanzar.

achieve [əˈtʃiːv] **1** *vt* lograr, conseguir, alcanzar, realizar; llevar a cabo; acabar; **he will never ~ anything** él no hará nunca nada; **what can you hope to ~ by that?** ¿qué esperas lograr con eso? **2** *vi* ir adelante, hacer progresos; realizar todo su potencial; **here is a man who has ~d** he aquí un hombre que ha llegado muy alto; **the children are not achieving as they should** los niños no hacen los progresos que debieran.

achievement [əˈtʃiːvmənt] *n* (**a**) (*act*) consecución *f*, realización *f*. (**b**) (*thing achieved*) éxito *m*, logro *m*; hazaña *f*; proeza *f*; conquista *f*; **that's quite an ~, that is no mean ~** eso representa un éxito nada despreciable; **among his many ~s** entre las muchas hazañas en su haber; **~ test** (*Brit Scol*) examen *m* de consecución.

achiever [əˈtʃiːvəʳ] *n* (*also* **high ~**) persona *f* que realiza su potencial; persona *f* que llega muy alto.

Achilles [əˈkɪliːz] *nm* Aquiles; **~' heel** talón *m* de Aquiles; **~' tendon** tendón *m* de Aquiles.

aching [ˈeɪkɪŋ] **1** *adj tooth etc* dolorido, que duele. (**b**) (*fig*) *heart etc* afligido. **2** *n* dolor *m*.

achromatic [ˌækrəʊˈmætɪk] *adj* acromático.

acid [ˈæsɪd] **1** *adj* (**a**) (*Chem*) ácido; **~ drops** (*Brit*) caramelos *mpl* ácidos; **~ rain** lluvia *f* ácida; **~ test** (*fig*) prueba *f* de fuego, prueba *f* decisiva; **~ test ratio** razón *f* de prueba de fuego; **to stand the ~ test** resistir a la prueba de fuego. (**b**) (*fig*) *comment etc* mordaz, punzante, áspero.

2 *n* (*Chem*) ácido *m*; (*: *drug*) ácido* *m*; **~ (house) music** música *f* acid*; **~ house party** fiesta *f* acid*.

acidhead* [ˈæsɪdhed] *n* adicto *m*, -a *f* al ácido.

acidic [əˈsɪdɪk] *adj* ácido.

acidifier [əˈsɪdɪfaɪəʳ] *n* acidulante *m*.

acidify [əˈsɪdɪfaɪ] **1** *vt* acidificar. **2** *vi* acidificarse.

acidity [əˈsɪdɪtɪ] *n* acidez *f*; (*of stomach*) acidez *f* de estómago, acedía *f*.

acidly [ˈæsɪdlɪ] *adv comment etc* mordazmente, ásperamente.

acidophilous [ˌæsɪˈdɒfɪləs] *adj* acidófilo.

acid-proof [ˈæsɪdpruːf] *adj*, **acid-resisting** [ˈæsɪdrɪˈzɪstɪŋ] *adj* a prueba de ácidos.

acidulant [əˈsɪdjʊlənt] *n* acidulante *m*.

acidulous [əˈsɪdjʊləs] *adj* acídulo.

ack-ack* [ˈækˈæk] *n* (*fire*) fuego *m* antiaéreo; (*guns*) artillería *f* antiaérea; **~ fire** fuego *m* antiaéreo; **~ gun** cañón *m* antiaéreo.

acknowledge [əkˈnɒlɪdʒ] **1** *vt* reconocer; *truth etc* confesar; *claim* admitir; *crime* confesarse culpable de; *favour* agradecer; *letter* acusar recibo de; *present* dar las gracias por; *greeting* contestar a; **to ~ defeat** darse por vencido; **to ~ receipt** acusar recibo (*of* de); **I ~ that ...** reconozco que ...; **to ~ sb as leader** reconocer a uno como jefe; **to ~ that sb is superior, to ~ sb as superior** reconocer que alguien es mejor.

2 *vr*: **to ~ o.s. beaten** darse por vencido, reconocer que uno ha perdido; **I ~ myself the loser** reconozco que he perdido; **she ~d herself in the wrong** reconoció que estaba equivocada (*or* era culpable).

acknowledged [əkˈnɒlɪdʒd] *adj*: **an ~ expert** un experto reconocido como tal; **a generally ~ fact** un hecho generalmente admitido.

acknowledgement [əkˈnɒlɪdʒmənt] *n* reconocimiento *m*; confesión *f*; agradecimiento *m*; contestación *f* (*of a greeting* a un saludo); (*Comm*) acuse *m* de recibo; **~s** (*in preface etc*) agradecimientos *mpl*; **in ~ of sb's help** en reconocimiento de la ayuda de uno, agradeciendo la ayuda de uno; **to make ~s** expresar su agradecimiento; **I wish to make public ~ of the help** quiero agradecer públicamente la ayuda; **to quote sb without ~** citar a uno sin mencionar la fuente.

ACLU *n abbr of* **American Civil Liberties Union**.

acme [ˈækmɪ] *n* colmo *m*, cima *f*; **~ of perfection** la suma perfección; **he is the ~ of good taste** es el buen gusto en persona.

acne [ˈæknɪ] *n* acné *f*.

acolyte [ˈækəʊlaɪt] *n* (*Rel*) acólito *m*, monaguillo *m*; (*fig*) seguidor *m*.

aconite [ˈækənaɪt] *n* acónito *m*.

acorn [ˈeɪkɔːn] *n* bellota *f*.

acoustic [əˈkuːstɪk] *adj* acústico; **~ coupler** acoplador *m* acústico.

acoustics [əˈkuːstɪks] *n sing and pl* acústica *f*.

acquaint [əˈkweɪnt] **1** *vt* (**a**) (*inform*) **to ~ sb with** avisar a uno de, informar a uno sobre; poner a uno al corriente de.

(**b**) (*know*) **to be ~ed** conocerse; **to be ~ed with** *person* conocer, *fact* saber, *situation* estar enterado de, estar al corriente de; **to become ~ed with** *person* (llegar a) conocer, *fact* saber, *situation* ponerse al tanto de.

2 *vr*: **to ~ o.s. with** informarse sobre, enterarse de, averiguar.

acquaintance [əˈkweɪntəns] *n* (**a**) (*knowledge*) conocimiento *m* (*with* de); familiaridad *f* (*with* con); trato *m* (*with* con); **a plumber of my ~** un fontanero que conozco; **I have not the honour of his ~** no tengo el honor de conocerle; **to have a nodding ~ with** conocer ligeramente; **it improves on ~** parece mejor después de conocido; **on closer** (*or* **further**) **~ it seems less attractive** al conocerlo mejor tiene menos atracción; **to make sb's ~** conocer a uno; **I am very glad to make your ~** tengo mucho gusto en conocerle; **he scraped ~ with Lord X** se las arregló para hacerse presentar a Lord X.

(**b**) (*person*) conocido *m*, -a *f*; **~s** personas *fpl* que uno conoce, relaciones *fpl*, amistades *fpl*; **an ~ of mine** una persona que yo conozco; **we're just ~s** nos conocemos ligeramente nada más; **we're old ~s** nos conocemos desde hace tiempo; **to have a wide circle of ~s** conocer a muchas personas.

acquaintanceship [əˈkweɪntənsʃɪp] *n* (**a**) (*knowledge*) conocimiento *m* (*with* de), familiaridad *f* (*with* con). (**b**) (*between two persons*) relaciones *fpl*.

acquiesce [ˌækwɪˈes] *vi* consentir (*in* en), asentir (*in* a), conformarse (*in* con); (*unwillingly*) someterse, doblegarse.

acquiescence [ˌækwɪˈesns] *n* consentimiento *m* (*in* en), asentimiento *m* (*in* a), conformidad *f* (*in* con); (*state*) aquiescencia *f*, resignación *f*.

acquiescent [ˌækwɪˈesnt] *adj* condescendiente, conforme; aquiescente; **he is ~ by nature** por su naturaleza se conforma con todo; **he was perfectly ~** se mostró completamente conforme.

acquire [əˈkwaɪəʳ] *vt* adquirir; obtener; conseguir; proporcionarse; *language etc* aprender; *territory, property* tomar (*from* a), tomar posesión de; *colour, tint* adquirir, tomar; *habit* contraer; **I seem to have ~d a strange um-**

brella parece que he tomado el paraguas de otro; **he ~d a fine tan** se dio un espléndido bronceado; **where did you ~ that?** ¿dónde conseguiste eso?; **she ~d many followers** se le pegaron muchos pretendientes; **to ~ a name for honesty** crearse una reputación de honrado; **to ~ a taste for** tomar gusto a, cobrar afición a.

acquired [ə'kwaɪəd] *adj character(istic), taste* adquirido.

acquirement [ə'kwaɪəmənt] *n* (**a**) adquisición *f*; obtención *f*, consecución *f*. (**b**) **~s** (*of knowledge*) conocimientos *mpl*.

acquisition [ˌækwɪ'zɪʃən] *n* adquisición *f*.

acquisitive [ə'kwɪzɪtɪv] *adj* codicioso.

acquisitiveness [ə'kwɪzɪtɪvnɪs] *n* codicia *f*.

acquit [ə'kwɪt] **1** *vt* absolver (*of* de), exonerar (*of* de), exculpar (*of* de); **he was ~ted on all charges** le absolvieron de todas las acusaciones.

2 *vr*: **to ~ o.s.** portarse; **how did he ~ himself?** ¿cómo se portó?, ¿cómo desempeñó el cometido?; **to ~ o.s. well** tener éxito, hacerlo bien, salir airoso; **to ~ o.s. of** *duty* desempeñar.

acquittal [ə'kwɪtl] *n* absolución *f*, exculpación *f*.

acre ['eɪkəʳ] *n* (= 40,47 *áreas*, 4047m^2) acre *m*; **God's ~** camposanto *m*; **the family's broad** (*or* **rolling**) **~s** las extensas fincas de la familia; **there are ~s of space for you to play in*** hay la mar de espacio para que juguéis; **I've got ~s of weeds*** tengo un montón de malas hierbas*.

acreage ['eɪkərɪdʒ] *n* superficie *f* (*or* extensión *f*) medida en *acres*; **the 1990 wheat ~** el área sembrada de trigo en 1990; **what ~ have you here?** ¿cuánto miden estos terrenos?, ¿qué extensión tiene esta tierra?; **they farm a large ~** cultivan unos terrenos muy extensos.

acrid ['ækrɪd] *adj* (**a**) *smell etc* acre, punzante. (**b**) (*fig*) áspero, desapacible.

Acrilan ['ækrɪlæn] ® *n* acrilán *m*.

acrimonious [ˌækrɪ'məʊnɪəs] *adj remark etc* áspero, cáustico, mordaz; *argument* amargo, reñido.

acrimoniously [ˌækrɪ'məʊnɪəslɪ] *adv* ásperamente, mordazmente; amargamente.

acrimony ['ækrɪmənɪ] *n* aspereza *f*, acrimonia *f*, acritud *f*; lo amargo, lo reñido.

acrobat ['ækrəbæt] *n* acróbata *mf*.

acrobatic [ˌækrəʊ'bætɪk] **1** *adj* acrobático. **2 ~s** *npl* acrobacia *f*; (*as profession*) acrobatismo *m*; (*Aer*) vuelo *m* acrobático.

acronym ['ækrənɪm] *n* sigla(s) *f(pl)*, acrónimo *m*.

acropolis [ə'krɒpəlɪs] *n* acrópolis *f*.

across [ə'krɒs] **1** *adv* (**a**) (*gen*) a través, al través, de través; **don't go round, go ~** no des la vuelta, ve al través; **shall I go ~ first?** ¿paso yo el primero?; **it's ~ from the post-office** está enfrente de Correos.

(**b**) (*from one side to the other*) de una parte a otra, de un lado a otro; **we shall have to cut it ~** tendremos que cortarlo por medio; **a plank had been laid ~** habían colocado una tabla encima; **he helped an old lady ~** ayudó a una señora mayor a cruzar la calle (*etc*).

(**c**) (*measurements*) **the plank is 10 cm ~** la tabla tiene 10 cm de ancho; **it's not very far ~** es corta la travesía; **how far is it ~?** (*river etc*) ¿cuántos metros tiene de ancho?; **how far is it ~ to the lighthouse?** ¿qué distancia hay desde aquí al faro?

(**d**) (*crossways*) a través, en cruz, transversalmente.

2 *prep* (**a**) (*gen*) a través de, al través de; **to go ~ a bridge** pasar por un puente; **the bridge ~ the Tagus** el puente sobre el Tajo; **with arms folded ~ his chest** con los brazos cruzados sobre el pecho; **a tree had fallen ~ the road** había caído un árbol a través de la carretera.

(**b**) (*on the other side of*) al otro lado de, del otro lado de; **~ the seas** allende el mar; **from ~ the sea** desde más allá del mar; **the lands ~ the sea** las tierras más allá del mar; **~ the street from our house** en el otro lado de la calle enfrente de nuestra casa; **he'll be ~ the water by now** ya estará al otro lado del mar.

(**c**) (*measurements*) **it is 12 km ~ the strait** el estrecho tiene 12 km de ancho.

across-the-board [ə'krɒsðə'bɔːd] *adj increase etc* global, general.

acrostic [ə'krɒstɪk] *n* acróstico *m*.

acrylic [ə'krɪlɪk] *adj* acrílico; **~ fibre** fibra *f* acrílica.

acrylonitrile [ˌækrɪləʊ'naitraɪl] *n* acrilonitrilo *m*.

ACT *n* (*US*) *abbr of* **American College Test** *examen que se hace al término de los estudios secundarios*.

act [ækt] **1** *n* (**a**) (*gen, liter*) acto *m*, acción *f*; obra *f*; **A~s of the Apostles** Hechos *mpl* de los Apóstoles; **~ of contrition** acto *m* de contrición; **~ of faith** acto *m* de fe; **~ of God** (caso *m* de) fuerza *f* mayor; **~ of justice** acción *f* de justicia; **~ of war** acción *f* de guerra; **an ~ of folly** una locura; **an ~ of treason** una traición; **we need ~s not words** queremos hechos no palabras; **I was in the ~ of writing to him** precisamente le estaba escribiendo (a él); **to catch sb in the ~** coger a uno en flagrante, coger a uno con las manos en la masa.

(**b**) (*Parl*) decreto *m*, ley *f*.

(**c**) (*Theat*: *division*) acto *m*.

(**d**) (*Theat*: *turn*) número *m*; **it's a hard ~ to follow** este número es tan bueno que será difícil repetirlo; **to get into** (*or* **in on**) **the ~*** introducirse en el asunto, lograr tomar parte; **to get one's ~ together*** organizarse, arreglárselas; **to put on an ~** (*fig*) fingir (el asco, el enojo *etc*).

2 *vt play* representar; *part* hacer; **to ~ the part of** hacer el papel de; **when I ~ed the Comendador** cuando yo hice (el papel) de Comendador; **to ~ the fool** hacer el tonto.

3 *vi* (**a**) (*Theat*) actuar, trabajar, representar; **I ~ed in my youth** de joven fui actor; **she's away ~ing in the provinces** está actuando en provincias; **never ~ with children or animals** no salgas nunca a escena con niños o animales; **to ~ in a film** tener un papel en una película; **have you ever ~ed?** ¿has hecho algún papel?; **who's ~ing in it?** ¿quién actúa?

(**b**) (*fig*) fingir; **he's only ~ing** lo está fingiendo nada más; **to ~ ill** hacerse enfermo.

(**c**) (*function*: *machine*) funcionar, marchar; (*person*) actuar; **the brakes did not ~** no funcionaron los frenos; **~ing in my capacity as chairman** de acuerdo con las funciones atribuidas a mi cargo de presidente; **he declined to ~** se negó a servir; **to ~ as** actuar de, hacer de, servir de; **it ~s as a safety valve** funciona como (una) válvula de seguridad; **he was ~ing as ambassador** estaba de embajador; **to ~ for sb** representar a uno; hablar por uno; hacer las veces de uno.

(**d**) (*behave*) actuar, obrar, comportarse; **he is ~ing strangely** se está comportando de una manera rara; **to ~ with caution** obrar con precaución; **she ~ed as if she was unwell** hacía como si estuviese enferma; **to ~ up to a principle** obrar con arreglo a un principio, seguir fiel a un principio.

(**e**) (*take action*) obrar, tomar medidas; **he ~ed to stop it** tomó medidas para impedirlo; **now is the time to ~** es hora ya de ponerse en acción; **he ~ed for the best** hizo lo que mejor le parecía; **to ~ on a suggestion** seguir una indicación; **to ~ on the evidence** obrar de acuerdo con los hechos.

(**f**) (*take effect*) surtir efecto, dar resultados; **the medicine is slow to ~** la medicina tarda en surtir efecto.

(**g**) (*affect*) **to ~ on** (*Mech*) impulsar, accionar; **to ~ on, to ~ upon** afectar (a), obrar sobre, tener resultados en; **the drug ~s upon the brain** la droga afecta al cerebro; **acids ~ upon metals** los ácidos atacan los metales.

◆**act out** *vt* representar; expresar; **to ~ out a macabre drama** (*fig*) representar (hasta el final) un drama macabro; **she is given to ~ing out her fantasies** tiene tendencia a hacer vivir sus fantasías en la realidad.

◆**act up*** *vi* (*person*) travesear, hacer de las suyas; (*car, machine*) funcionar mal, fallar.

actable ['æktəbl] *adj* representable.

acting ['æktɪŋ] **1** *adj* interino, suplente; provisional; en funciones.

2 *n* (**a**) (*Theat*: *of play*) representación *f*; (*by actor*) desempeño *m*, actuación *f*; interpretación *f*; **what was his ~ like?** ¿qué tal hizo el papel?; **this is ~ as it should be** esto se llama realmente ser actor (*or* actriz), así es el teatro de verdad.

(**b**) (*as profession*) profesión *f* de actor; **~ is not in my line** yo no soy actor; **she has done some ~** tiene alguna experiencia como actriz, ella ha hecho algunos papeles; **to go in for ~** hacerse actor.

actinic [æk'tɪnɪk] *adj* actínico.

actinium [æk'tɪnɪəm] *n* actinio *m*.

action ['ækʃən] *n* (**a**) (*gen*) acción *f*, acto *m*, hecho *m*; actuación *f*; **~!** ¡vamos!, ¡a ello!; **man of ~** hombre *m* de acción; **~-packed film** película *f* de acción; **~ painting** tachismo *m*; **~ replay** (*Brit TV*) repetición *f* (de la jugada *etc*); **he likes to be where the ~ is** le gusta estar en medio del bullicio; **I want to see some ~ here** quiero que todos pongan manos a la obra; **when shall we get some ~ on this?** ¿cuándo se hará algo en este asunto?; **~s speak louder than words** dicho sin hecho no trae provecho; **to judge sb by his ~s** juzgar a uno por sus hechos; **to suit the ~ to the word** unir la acción a la palabra; **to bring** (*or* **put**) **into ~** poner en movimiento; desplegar, poner en juego; **to go into ~** entrar en acción; empezar a funcionar; **to be out of ~** (*Mech*) no funcionar, estar parado, estar averiado; (*person*) estar inactivo, quedar fuera del juego; **'out of ~'** 'no funciona'; **to put out of ~** inutilizar, parar, destrozar; **the illness put him out of ~** la enfermedad le dejó fuera de combate; **he was out of ~ for months** durante meses estuvo sin poder hacer nada; **to take ~** tomar medidas; **to take no ~** no hacer nada.

(**b**) **a piece of the ~** (*: *Comm*) una parte de las ganancias, una tajada*.

(**c**) (*: *merry activity*) actividad *f*; bullicio *m*, animación *f*, diversión *f*; vida *f* alegre; **where's the ~ in this town?** ¿dónde hay vida en este lugar?; **there's hardly any ~ before dark** antes de la noche apenas hay animación.

(**d**) (*Mil*) acción *f*, batalla *f*; **killed in ~** muerto en acción, muerto en acto de servicio; **to see ~** servir, luchar; **~ stations!** ¡a sus puestos!; **to go to ~ stations** ir a sus puestos; **to go into ~** entrar en batalla.

(**e**) (*Mech etc*) mecanismo *m*; funcionamiento *m*; movimiento *m*; (*of horse*) marcha *f*.

(**f**) (*Jur*) demanda *f*, proceso *m*; **civil ~** demanda *f* civil; **to bring an ~** entablar demanda (*against* contra).

(**g**) (*Theat*: *of play*) argumento *m*, acción *f*.

actionable ['ækʃnəbl] *adj* justiciable, procesable.

activate ['æktɪveɪt] *vt* activar.

activator ['æktɪˌveɪtəʳ] *n* activador *m*.

active ['æktɪv] *adj* activo (*also Comm, Gram, Comput*); *personality etc* enérgico, vigoroso; **~ assets** bienes *mpl* activos; **~ balance** saldo *m* activo; **~ duty (AD)** (*US*) servicio *m* activo; (*Mil*) **~ list** escala *f* activa; **~ partner** socio *mf* activo; **~ population** población *f* activa; **~ service** servicio *m* activo; **to be on ~ service** estar en activo; **to die on ~ service** morir en acto de servicio; **~ volcano** volcán *m* en actividad; **we are giving it ~ consideration** lo estamos estudiando en serio; **to play an ~ part in** colaborar activamente en; **to take an ~ interest in** interesarse vivamente por.

actively ['æktɪvlɪ] *adv* activamente; enérgicamente, vigorosamente; vivamente.

activism ['æktɪvɪzəm] *n* activismo *m*.

activist ['æktɪvɪst] *n* activista *mf*.

activity [æk'tɪvɪtɪ] *n* actividad *f*; (*of personality*) energía *f*, vigor *m*; (*of busy scene*) movimiento *m*, bullicio *m*; **activities** actividades *fpl*; **all his business activities** todos sus intereses comerciales; **social activities** vida *f* social; **his activities were wide** tuvo una ancha esfera de actividad; **to be in full ~** estar en pleno vigor; **~ holiday** vacaciones *fpl* activas; **~ method** (*Scol*) método *m* de actividades.

actor ['æktəʳ] *n* actor *m*.

actress ['æktrɪs] *n* actriz *f*.

actual ['æktjʊəl] *adj* verdadero, real, efectivo; **~ loss** (*Comm*) pérdida *f* efectiva; **~ total loss** pérdida *f* total efectiva; **in ~ fact** en realidad; **let's take an ~ case** tomemos un caso concreto; **what were his ~ words?** ¿cuáles fueron sus palabras exactas?, ¿qué es lo que dijo, concretamente?; **is this the ~ book?** ¿es éste el mismo libro?; **what was the ~ price?** ¿cuál fue el precio real?; **there is no ~ contract** no hay contrato propiamente dicho; **there is a church but no ~ village** hay iglesia pero en realidad no hay pueblo.

actuality [ˌæktjʊ'ælɪtɪ] *n* realidad *f*; **in ~** en realidad.

actualize ['æktjʊəlaɪz] *vt* (**a**) (*make real*) realizar. (**b**) (*represent*) representar de manera realista, describir con realismo.

actually ['æktjʊəlɪ] *adv* (**a**) (*really*) realmente, en realidad, en efecto, efectivamente; **~ I am her husband** en realidad soy su marido; **those ~ present did not see it** los que en efecto asistían no lo vieron; **I wasn't ~ there** en realidad yo no estuve allí; **did you ~ see him?** ¿le vieron Vds realmente?; **what did he ~ say?** ¿qué es lo que dijo, exactamente?; **~, no pues no.**

(**b**) (*even*) **he ~ hit her** incluso llegó a pegarla; **we ~ caught a fish** hasta cogimos un pez.

(**c**) **that's not true ~** eso no es verdad, que digamos; **as for ~ working, he didn't** pues trabajar, como trabajar, no lo hizo; la verdad es que no trabajó nada.

actuarial [ˌæktjʊ'ɛərɪəl] *adj* actuarial; **~ tables** tablas *fpl* actuariales.

actuary ['æktjʊərɪ] *n* actuario *m*, -a *f* de seguros.

actuate ['æktjʊeɪt] *vt* (**a**) *person etc* mover, animar; estimular; **a statement ~d by malice** una declaración motivada por el rencor; **he was ~d by envy** la envidia le movió a ello. (**b**) (*Mech*) impulsar, accionar.

acuity [ə'kju:ɪtɪ] *n* acuidad *f*, agudeza *f*.

acumen ['ækjʊmen] *n* perspicacia *f*, tino *m*, agudeza *f*.

acupuncture ['ækjʊpʌŋktʃəʳ] *n* acupuntura *f*.

acupuncturist [ˌækjʊ'pʌŋktʃərɪst] *n* acupuntor *m*, -ora *f*, acupunturista *mf*.

acute [ə'kju:t] *adj* (*in most senses*) agudo; **~ accent** acento *m* agudo; **~ angle** ángulo *m* agudo; **~ appendicitis** apendicitis *f* aguda; **~ anxiety exists** existe una honda preocupación; **he has an ~ sense of the ridiculous** tiene un sentido agudo del ridículo; **that was very ~ of you** te has mostrado muy perspicaz.

acutely [ə'kju:tlɪ] *adv* agudamente; **I am ~ aware that** ... me doy cuenta cabal de que ...; **I feel my position ~** no se me oculta que es muy difícil mi situación.

acuteness [ə'kju:tnɪs] *n* agudeza *f*; perspicacia *f*.

AD (**a**) *adv abbr of* **Anno Domini** = *in the year of our Lord* año *m* de Cristo, A.C., después de Jesucristo, d. de J.C. (**b**) *n* (*US Mil*) *abbr of* **active duty** servicio *m* activo.

ad* [æd] *n abbr of* **advertisement.**

a.d. *abbr of* **after date** a partir de la fecha ...

adage ['ædɪdʒ] *n* adagio *m*, refrán *m*.

adagio [ə'dɑ:dʒɪəʊ] *n* adagio *m*.

Adam ['ædəm] *nm* Adán; **~'s ale** agua *f*; **~'s apple** nuez *f* (de la garganta *or* de Adán); **the old ~** la inclinación al pecado; **I don't know him from ~** no le conozco en absoluto.

adamant ['ædəmənt] *adj* firme, inexorable, inflexible; **he was ~** se mostró inflexible; **he was ~ in his refusal** reiteró inexorablemente su denegación; **we must remain totally ~** tenemos que mantenernos totalmente firmes.

adamantine [ˌædə'mæntaɪn] *adj* adamantino.

adapt [ə'dæpt] **1** *vt* (**a**) adaptar (*to* a); acomodar, ajustar (*to* a); **it is perfectly ~ed to its environment** se ajusta perfectamente a su ambiente.

(**b**) *text* arreglar, refundir; **a novel ~ed by X** una novela en versión de X; **a novel ~ed as a play** una novela en versión dramática; **~ed from the Spanish** basado en una obra española.

2 *vi and vr*: **to ~ (o.s.) to** adaptarse a, ajustarse a, conformarse con.

adaptability [əˌdæptə'bɪlɪtɪ] *n* adaptabilidad *f*; capacidad *f* para acomodarse (*or* ajustarse).

adaptable [ə'dæptəbl] *adj* adaptable; *person* capaz de acomodarse; **he's very ~** se acomoda en seguida a las circunstancias.

adaptation [ˌædæp'teɪʃən] *n* adaptación *f*; (*of text*) arreglo *m*, versión *f*, refundición *f*.

adapter, adaptor [ə'dæptəʳ] *n* (*Brit*) adaptador *m*.

adaption [æ'dæpʃən] *n* = **adaptation.**

adaptive [ə'dæptɪv] *adj* adaptivo.

ADC *n* (**a**) *abbr of* **aide-de-camp** edecán *m*. (**b**) (*US*) *abbr of* **Aid to Dependent Children** *ayuda a niños dependientes.*

add [æd] *vt* (**a**) (*Math*) sumar.

(**b**) (*join*) añadir, agregar (*to* a); (*to drink etc*) añadir, echar, sumar (*to* a); **we gave £100 and he ~ed the rest** nosotros dimos 100 libras y él contribuyó lo demás; **'~ salt to taste'** 'echar sal al gusto'.

(**c**) (*say further*) añadir, agregar; **he ~ed that** ... añadió que ...; **there's nothing to ~** no hay nada más que decir.

◆**add in** *vt* añadir, incluir.

◆**add on** *vt* añadir; poner además; **we ~ed two rooms on** hicimos construir dos habitaciones más; **you have to ~ 15 dollars on for the service** hay que poner 15 dólares más de servicio.

◆**add to** *vi* aumentar, acrecentar; realzar; **it only ~ed to our problems** no hizo sino aumentar nuestros problemas; **then to ~ to our troubles** ... luego para colmo de desgracias ...

◆**add together** *vt* sumar.

◆**add up 1** *vt* sumar. **2** *vi* sumar; **it doesn't ~ up** (*Math*) no se puede sumar correctamente; (*fig*) no tiene sentido, no tiene pies ni cabeza; **it all ~s up*** es lógico, tiene sentido; **it's beginning to ~ up*** la cosa nos deja ya entrever una solución, ya podemos empezar a atar cabos.

◆**add up to** *vi* (*Math*) sumar, ascender a; (*fig*) venir a ser, equivaler a, querer decir; **it doesn't ~ up to much*** es poca cosa, no tiene gran importancia.

added ['ædɪd] *adj* (**a**) añadido, adicional; **~ value** valor *m* añadido; **with ~ emphasis** con mayor énfasis, con más énfasis aún; **it's an ~ problem** es un problema más; **there is nothing ~** no hay nada añadido. (**b**) **~ to which ...** y además ...

addendum [ə'dendəm] *n*, *pl* **addenda** [ə'dendə] ad(d)enda *f*,

adición *f*, artículo *m* suplementario.
adder ['ædəʳ] *n* víbora *f*.
addict ['ædɪkt] *n* partidario *m*, -a *f*, entusiasta *mf*, fanático *m*, -a *f* (*of* de); (*Med*) adicto *m*, -a *f* (*and V* **drug** ~); **I'm a guitar** ~ me apasiona la guitarra; **I'm a detective story** ~ yo soy un apasionado de la novela policíaca.
addicted [ə'dɪktɪd] *adj*: **to be** ~ **to sth** ser adicto a algo; (*viciously*) estar enviciado con algo; **to be** ~ **to drugs** ser drogadicto; **to be** ~ **to** + *ger* ser apasionado de + *infin*, ser fanático de + *infin*; (*viciously*) tener el vicio de + *infin*; **to become** ~ **to sth** enviciarse con algo, entregarse a algo.
addiction [ə'dɪkʃən] *n* afición *f*; (*pej*) vicio *m*, dependencia *f*, hábito *m* morboso; (*to drugs*) adicción *f*, drogadicción *f*, drogodependencia *f*.
addictive [ə'dɪktɪv] *adj* adictivo, que conduce al hábito morboso, que crea dependencia.
adding machine ['ædɪŋmə,ʃiːn] *n* sumadora *f*.
Addis Ababa ['ædɪs'æbəbə] *n* Addis Abeba *m*.
addition [ə'dɪʃən] *n* (**a**) (*Math*) suma *f*, adición *f*; cálculo *m*; ~ **sign** signo *m* de sumar; **if my** ~ **is correct** si he hecho bien el cálculo; **to do** ~ hacer sumas.
(**b**) (*thing added*) adición *f*, añadidura *f*; adquisición *f*; **we made** ~**s to our stocks** aumentamos nuestras existencias; **these are our new** ~**s** éstas son nuestras nuevas adquisiciones; **this is a welcome** ~ **to our books on Ruritania** éste aumenta valiosamente nuestros libros sobre Ruritania; **there's been an** ~ **to the family** hay uno más en la familia; **in** ~ además; **in** ~ **to** además de.
additional [ə'dɪʃənl] *adj* adicional; complementario, supletorio; añadido; **we need** ~ **men** necesitamos más hombres; **it is an** ~ **reason to** + *infin* es razón de más para + *infin*; **this gave him** ~ **confidence** esto aumentó su confianza.
additionally [ə'dɪʃənlɪ] *adv* adicionalmente; por añadidura; **and** ~ y además; **this makes it** ~ **difficult for me** esto aumenta (aún) mis dificultades.
additive ['ædɪtɪv] *n* aditivo *m*.
additive-free ['ædɪtɪv'friː] *adj* sin aditivos.
addled ['ædld] *adj* huero, podrido; *brain* confuso, débil.
add-on ['ædɒn] *n* adicional *m*.
address [ə'dres] **1** *n* (**a**) (*of house etc*) señas *fpl*, dirección *f*; **business** ~ dirección *f* profesional, dirección *f* de la oficina (*etc*) de uno; **home** ~ dirección *f* particular; ~ **commission** (*Comm*) comisión *f* que se paga al agente fletador por su tarea de embarque; **she isn't at this** ~ **any more** ya no vive en esta casa; **they left no forwarding** ~ no dejaron dirección a la que pudiésemos hacer seguir las cartas.
(**b**) (*style*) tratamiento *m*, título *m*; **what form of** ~ **should I use?** ¿qué tratamiento debo darle?
(**c**) (*speech*) discurso *m*; (*lecture*) conferencia *f*; **election** ~, **electoral** ~ carta *f* electoral; **public** ~ **system** sistema *m* amplificador.
(**d**) (*Parl etc*) petición *f*, memorial *m*.
(**e**) (†: *skill*) destreza *f*, habilidad *f*.
(**f**) (†: *behaviour*) modales *mpl*; conducta *f*, comportamiento *m*.
(**g**) **to pay one's** ~**es to** hacer la corte a, pretender a.
(**h**) (*Comput*) dirección *f*; **absolute** ~ dirección *f* absoluta; **relative** ~ dirección *f* relativa.
2 *vt* (**a**) *letter, parcel, protest* dirigir (*to* a); **I** ~**ed it to your home** lo mandé a tu casa; **I haven't** ~**ed it yet** todavía no he puesto la dirección; **this is** ~**ed to you** esto viene con el nombre de Vd; **this letter is wrongly** ~**ed** en esta carta han puesto mal la dirección.
(**b**) *person* dirigirse a, dirigir la palabra a; *meeting* pronunciar un discurso ante; **to** ~ **the House** pronunciar un discurso en el Parlamento; **he** ~**ed us on politics** nos habló de política; **are you** ~**ing me?** ¿habla Vd conmigo?
(**c**) **to** ~ **sb as** dar a uno el tratamiento de; **to** ~ **sb by his proper title** dar el debido tratamiento a uno; **to** ~ **sb as 'tú'** tratar a uno de 'tú', tutear a uno.
(**d**) *problem etc* estudiar; aplicarse a.
3 *vr*: **to** ~ **o.s. to** *person* dirigirse a; *problem, task* aplicarse a.
address-book [ə'dresbʊk] *n* librito *m* de direcciones, agenda *f*.
addressee [,ædre'siː] *n* destinatario *m*, -a *f*; (*Comm*) consignatario *m*, -a *f*; **postage will be paid by the** ~ a franquear en destino.
addressing [ə'dresɪŋ] *n* (*Comput*) direccionamiento *m*; ~ **machine** máquina *f* de direcciones.
Addressograph [ə'dresəʊgrɑːf] ® *n* máquina *f* de direcciones, máquina *f* para dirigir sobres.
adduce [ə'djuːs] *vt* alegar, aducir, presentar.
adductor [ə'dʌktəʳ] *n* aductor *m*.
Adelaide ['ædeleɪd] *n* Adelaida *f*.
Aden ['eɪdn] *n* Adén *m*; **Gulf of** ~ Golfo *m* de Adén.
adenoidal ['ædɪnɔɪdl] *adj* adenoideo; **the child is** ~* el niño padece inflamación adenoidea; **he has an** ~ **tone** tiene una voz gangosa.
adenoids ['ædɪnɔɪdz] *npl* vegetaciones *fpl* adenoideas; (*) inflamación *f* adenoidea.
adept ['ædept] **1** *adj* experto, hábil, ducho (*at, in* en). **2** *n* experto *m*, -a *f*, perito *m*, -a *f*; **to be an** ~ **at** ser maestro en, ser ducho en; **he's an** ~ **at thieving** es un ladrón consumado.
adequacy ['ædɪkwəsɪ] *n* suficiencia *f*; idoneidad *f*, propiedad *f*.
adequate ['ædɪkwɪt] *adj* suficiente, adecuado; proporcionado; idóneo, propio; **to feel** ~ **to a task** sentirse con fuerzas para una tarea.
adequately ['ædɪkwɪtlɪ] *adv* suficientemente.
ADGA *n* (*US*) *abbr of* **Age Discrimination in Employment Act.**
adhere [əd'hɪəʳ] *vi* (**a**) pegarse (*to* a). (**b**) **to** ~ **to** (*fig*) *party, policy* adherirse a; *promise* cumplir; *rule* observar, atenerse a.
adherence [əd'hɪərəns] *n* adherencia *f*, adhesión *f* (*to* a); observancia *f* (*to a rule* de una regla).
adherent [əd'hɪərənt] **1** *adj* adhesivo. **2** *n* partidario *m*, -a *f*.
adhesion [əd'hiːʒən] *n* = **adherence.**
adhesive [əd'hiːzɪv] **1** *adj* adhesivo, pegajoso; ~ **plaster** esparadrapo *m*; ~ **tape** (*Brit*: *stationery*) cinta *f* adhesiva; (*Med*) esparadrapo *m*, scotch *m*. **2** *n* adhesivo *m*.
ad hoc [,æd'hɒk] *adj* ad hoc; ~ **committee** comité *m* ad hoc.
adieu [ə'djuː] **1** *interj* ¡adiós! **2** *n* (*pl* ~**s** *or* ~**x**) adiós *m*; **to bid** ~ **to** *person* despedirse de; *thing* renunciar a, separarse de, abandonar; **to make one's** ~**x** despedirse.
ad infinitum [,ædɪnfɪ'naɪtəm] *adv* ad infinitum, a lo infinito, hasta el infinito; hasta la saciedad; **it just carries on** ~ es inacabable, es cosa de nunca acabar; **it varies** ~ tiene un sinfín de variaciones; **and so (on)** ~ y así hasta el infinito.
ad interim ['æd'ɪntərɪm] **1** *adv* en el ínterin, interinamente. **2** *adj* interino.
adipose ['ædɪpəʊs] *adj* adiposo.
adiposity [,ædɪ'pɒsɪtɪ] *n* adiposidad *f*.
adjacent [ə'dʒeɪsənt] *adj* contiguo, inmediato (*to* a); *angle* adyacente.
adjectival [,ædʒek'taɪvəl] *adj* adjetivo, adjetival.
adjectivally [,ædʒek'taɪvəlɪ] *adv* adjetivamente.
adjective ['ædʒektɪv] *n* adjetivo *m*.
adjoin [ə'dʒɔɪn] **1** *vt* estar contiguo a, lindar con. **2** *vi* estar contiguo, colindar.
adjoining [ə'dʒɔɪnɪŋ] *adj* contiguo, vecino, colindante; **two** ~ **countries** dos países vecinos; **the** ~ **house** la casa de al lado; **in an** ~ **room** en un cuarto inmediato.
adjourn [ə'dʒɜːn] **1** *vt* (*postpone*) aplazar; prorrogar, diferir; *session* suspender, levantar; (*US*: *end*) terminar; **to** ~ **a discussion for a week** aplazar un debate por ocho días; **I declare the meeting** ~**ed** se levanta la sesión.
2 *vi* (**a**) (*meeting*) suspenderse; **the house then** ~**ed** luego se suspendió la sesión; **to stand** ~**ed** estar en suspenso.
(**b**) **to** ~ **to** trasladarse a, pasar a; **so we** ~**ed to the pub** así que nos trasladamos al bar.
adjournment [ə'dʒɜːnmənt] *n* (*postponement*) aplazamiento *m*; (*period of time*) suspensión *f*, clausura *f*.
adjudge [ə'dʒʌdz] *vt* *matter* juzgar, decidir; (*award juridically*) adjudicar; **to** ~ **that ...** estimar que ..., considerar que ...; **he was** ~**d the winner** se le decretó ganador, se le concedió la victoria; **to** ~ **sb guilty** declarar culpable a uno.
adjudicate [ə'dʒuːdɪkeɪt] **1** *vt* *claim* decidir, juzgar. **2** *vi* ser juez, sentenciar; **to** ~ **on a matter** fallar un asunto, ser árbitro en un asunto.
adjudication [ə,dʒuːdɪ'keɪʃən] *n* juicio *m*, sentencia *f*, decisión *f*; (*Comm*) adjudicación *f*; ~ **of bankruptcy** adjudicación *f* de quiebra; ~ **order** (*Jur*) orden *f* de adjudicación.
adjudicator [ə'dʒuːdɪkeɪtəʳ] *n* juez *mf*, árbitro *mf*.
adjunct ['ædʒʌŋkt] *n* adjunto *m*, accesorio *m*.
adjure [ə'dʒʊəʳ] *vt* ordenar solemnemente (*to do* hacer); suplicar, implorar.
adjust [ə'dʒʌst] **1** *vt* (*change*) modificar, cambiar; corregir; (*arrange*) arreglar; *machine* ajustar, graduar, regular; *differences* concertar, componer, resolver; *insurance claim* liquidar.
2 *vi and vr*: **to** ~ **to, to** ~ **o.s. to** adaptarse a; **we shall**

have to ~ tendremos que adaptarnos; **the boy is having trouble in ~ing** el niño tiene dificultad en adaptarse.
adjustability [ə,dʒʌstə'bɪlɪtɪ] *n* adaptabilidad *f.*
adjustable [ə'dʒʌstəbl] *adj* ajustable, graduable, regulable; ~ **spanner** llave *f* inglesa; **the date is** ~ podemos cambiar la fecha.
adjustment [ə'dʒʌstmənt] *n* modificación *f*, cambio *m*; arreglo *m*; reajuste *m*; (*Mech*) ajuste *m*, regulación *f*; (*of differences*) composición *f*; resolución *f*; (*personal*) adaptación *f*; (*Comm*) ajuste *m*, reajuste *m*; ~ **of prices** ajuste *m* de precios; ~ **of wages** reajuste *m* salarial; **financial** ~ arreglo *m* financiero; **social** ~ adaptación *f* social; **after** ~ **for inflation** después de tomar en cuenta la inflación; **we can always make an** ~ siempre podemos cambiarlo; **to make a small** ~ **in one's plans** modificar ligeramente sus proyectos.
adjutant ['ædʒətənt] *n* ayudante *m*; **A~ General** *general responsable del aparato administrativo.*
Adlerian [,æd'lɪərɪən] *adj* adleriano.
ad-lib* [æd'lɪb] **1** *adv* a voluntad, a discreción. **2** *adj comment etc* espontáneo; hecho sin pensar. **3** *vt* improvisar; decir (*etc*) espontáneamente. **4** *vi* improvisar, expresarse espontáneamente.
adman* ['ædmæn] *n, pl* **admen** ['ædmen] profesional *m* de la publicidad, publicista *m.*
admass ['ædmæs] *n parte de la población que está considerada como fácilmente influida por los actuales medios de la publicidad o propaganda comercial, conjunto de consumidores que tiene poco sentido crítico.*
admin. ['ædmin] (*Brit*) *abbr of* **administration** administración *f.*
administer [əd'mɪnɪstə^r] *vt* (**a**) administrar; dirigir, regir, gobernar; **~ed price** precio *m* fijado por el fabricante (*y que no puede ser variado por el detallista*). (**b**) *shock etc* dar, proporcionar; *punishment* aplicar. (**c**) **to** ~ **an oath to sb** tomar juramento a uno.
adminstrate [əd'mɪnɪstreɪt] *vt* administrar, dirigir.
administration [əd,mɪnɪs'treɪʃən] *n* (**a**) administración *f*; gobierno *m*, dirección *f*; gerencia *f.* (**b**) (*ministry*) gobierno *m.*
administrative [əd'mɪnɪstrətɪv] *adj* administrativo; ~ **assistant** ayudante *m* administrativo, ayudante *f* administrativa; ~ **court** (*US Jur*) tribunal *m* administrativo; ~ **expenses** gastos *mpl* administrativos; ~ **machinery** (*US Jur*) maquinaria *f* administrativa, aparato *m* administrativo; ~ **staff** personal *m* de administración.
administrator [əd'mɪnɪstreɪtə^r] *n* administrador *m*, -ora *f*; (*Jur*) albacea *mf.*
admirable ['ædmərəbl] *adj* admirable, digno de admiración, excelente; ~! ¡muy bien!
admirably ['ædmərəblɪ] *adv* admirablemente, de una manera digna de admiración.
admiral ['ædmərəl] *n* almirante *m.*
Admiralty ['ædmərəltɪ] *n* (*Brit*) Ministerio *m* de Marina, Almirantazgo *m*; **First Lord of the** ~ Ministro *m* de Marina; **a~ court** (*US*) tribunal *m* marítimo.
admiration [,ædmə'reɪʃən] *n* admiración *f.*
admire [əd'maɪə^r] *vt* admirar; (*express admiration for*) manifestar su admiración por, elogiar; **she was admiring herself in the mirror** se estaba mirando satisfecha en el espejo.
admirer [əd'maɪərə^r] *n* admirador *m*, -ora *f*; (*suitor*) enamorado *m*, pretendiente *m.*
admiring [əd'maɪərɪŋ] *adj look etc* admirativo, de admiración.
admiringly [əd'maɪərɪŋlɪ] *adv* con admiración; **he looked at her** ~ le lanzó una mirada llena de admiración; **to speak** ~ **of** hablar en términos elogiosos de.
admissibility [əd,mɪsə'bɪlɪtɪ] *n* admisibilidad *f.*
admissible [əd'mɪsəbl] *adj* admisible, aceptable.
admission [əd'mɪʃən] *n* (**a**) (*entry*) entrada *f* (*to* a, en); (*to academy, club etc*) ingreso *m* (*to* en); ~ **is free on Sundays** la entrada es gratuita los domingos; **'~ free'** 'entrada gratis'; **'no ~'** 'se prohíbe la entrada'; **we gained** ~ **by a window** logramos entrar por una ventana; ~ **fee** cuota *f* de entrada; **~s form** (*US Univ*) impreso *m* de matrícula; **~s office** (*US Univ*) secretaría *f.*
(**b**) (*acknowledgement*) confesión *f* (*of* de); **on his own** ~ por confesión propia; **it would be an** ~ **of defeat** sería reconocer nuestra derrota; **he made an** ~ **of guilt** se confesó culpable.
admit [əd'mɪt] *vt* (**a**) (*allow to enter*) dejar entrar, dar entrada a, hacer pasar (*LAm*); (*fig*) admitir, aceptar; **'children not ~ted'** 'no se admiten menores'; **ticket which ~s two** entrada *f* para dos personas; **to be ~ted to the Academy** ingresar en la Academia; **to be ~ted to hospital** ingresar en el hospital; **~ting office** (*US Med*) oficina *f* de ingresos.
(**b**) (*acknowledge*) reconocer, confesar; **it must be ~ted that** hay que reconocer que; **I** ~ **nothing!** ¡no tengo nada que confesar!; **it is hard, I** ~ es difícil, lo reconozco; **he ~ted himself beaten** reconoció que había sido vencido.
◆**admit of** *vt* admitir, dar lugar a, permitir; **it ~s of no other explanation** no cabe otra explicación.
◆**admit to** *vt crime* confesarse culpable de; **she ~s to doing it** confiesa haberlo hecho; **I** ~ **to feeling a bit ill** confieso que me siento algo mal.
admittance [əd'mɪtəns] *n* entrada *f*; derecho *m* de entrada; **he was refused** ~ se le negó la entrada; **I gained** ~ **by the window** logré entrar por la ventana; **'no ~'** 'se prohíbe la entrada'.
admittedly [əd'mɪtɪdlɪ] *adv* se reconoce que, es verdad que, de acuerdo que; **an** ~ **serious crime** un crimen que se reconoce como grave.
admixture [əd'mɪkstʃə^r] *n* mezcla *f*, adición *f*; (*fig*) dosis *f.*
admonish [əd'mɒnɪʃ] *vt* (*reprimand*) reprender, amonestar; (*warn*) amonestar, prevenir; (*advise*) aconsejar (*to do* hacer).
admonition [,ædməʊ'nɪʃən] *n* (*reproof*) reprensión *f*; (*warning*) amonestación *f*, advertencia *f*; (*advice*) consejo *m*, recomendación *f.*
admonitory [əd'mɒnɪtərɪ] *adj* admonitorio.
ad nauseam [,æd'nɔːsɪæm] *adv* hasta la saciedad; **he repeated it** ~ no se hartó de repetirlo, lo repitió incansablemente; **you've told me that** ~ ya me lo has dicho mil veces.
adnominal [,aed'nɒmɪnəl] **1** *adj* adnominal. **2** *n* adnominal *m.*
ado [ə'duː] *n*: **much** ~ **about nothing** mucho ruido y pocas nueces, nada entre dos platos; **without further ~, without more** ~ sin más (ni más).
adobe [ə'dəubɪ] *n* adobe *m.*
adolescence [,ædəʊ'lesns] *n* adolescencia *f.*
adolescent [,ædəʊ'lesnt] **1** *adj* adolescente. **2** *n* adolescente *mf*; joven *mf.*
Adolf, Adolph ['ædɒlf], **Adolphus** [ə'dɒlfəs] *nm* Adolfo.
Adonis [ə'dəʊnɪs] *nm* Adonis.
adopt [ə'dɒpt] *vt* adoptar; *candidate, report, motion* aprobar; *child* adoptar, prohijar; *suggestion* seguir, aceptar.
adopted [ə'dɒptɪd] *adj child* adoptivo, adoptado (*Mex*).
adoption [ə'dɒpʃən] *n* adopción *f*; **they have two children by** ~ tienen dos hijos adoptivos; **country of** ~ patria *f* adoptiva.
adoptive [ə'dɒptɪv] *adj* adoptivo.
adorable [ə'dɔːrəbl] *adj* adorable; encantador, mono*.
adoration [,ædɔː'reɪʃən] *n* adoración *f.*
adore [ə'dɔːrə^r] *vt* adorar.
adoring [ə'dɔːrɪŋ] *adj look* lleno de adoración; *parent etc* cariñoso.
adoringly [ə'dɔːrɪŋlɪ] *adv* con adoración.
adorn [ə'dɔːn] *vt* adornar, ornar, embellecer, engalanar.
adornment [ə'dɔːnmənt] *n* adorno *m*, decoración *f.*
ADP *n abbr of* **Automatic Data Processing** proceso *m* automático de datos.
adrenal [ə'driːnl] *adj* suprarrenal; ~ **gland** glándula *f* suprarrenal.
adrenalin(e) [ə'drenəlɪn] *n* (*Brit*) adrenalina *f*; **I feel the** ~ **rising** siento que me sube la adrenalina.
Adriatic (Sea) [,eɪdrɪ'ætɪk (siː)] *n* (Mar *m*) Adriático *m.*
adrift [ə'drɪft] *adv* a la deriva, al garete; **to be all** ~ (*fig*) ir a la deriva; estar desorientado; **to break** ~ (*accidentally*) perder las anclas, romper las amarras; (*deliberately*) cortar las amarras; **to come** ~ (*fig*) soltarse, desprenderse; **to cut a boat** ~ cortar las amarras de una barca; **something has gone** ~ algo ha fallado; **my bike has gone** ~ mi bici se ha extraviado; **to turn sb** ~ abandonar a uno a su suerte.
adroit [ə'drɔɪt] *adj* diestro, hábil, mañoso.
adroitly [ə'drɔɪtlɪ] *adv* diestramente, hábilmente.
adroitness [ə'drɔɪtnɪs] *n* destreza *f*, habilidad *f.*
ADT *n* (*US*) *abbr of* **Atlantic Daylight Time.**
adulate ['ædjʊleɪt] *vt* adular.
adulation [,ædjʊ'leɪʃən] *n* adulación *f.*
adulatory ['ædjʊleɪtərɪ] *adj* adulador.
adult ['ædʌlt] **1** *adj* adulto; maduro; mayor de edad, mayor; (*Cine etc*) apto para adultos; ~ **education** educación *f* de adultos. **2** *n* adulto *m*, -a *f*; persona *f* mayor (de edad); **'~s only'** (*exhibition etc*) '(sólo para) mayores'; (*Cine*)

'autorizada para los mayores de 18 años'.

adulterate [ə'dʌltəreɪt] *vt* adulterar.

adulteration [əˌdʌltə'reɪʃən] *n* adulteración *f*.

adulterer [ə'dʌltərəʳ] *n* adúltero *m*.

adulteress [ə'dʌltərɪs] *n* adúltera *f*.

adulterous [ə'dʌltərəs] *adj* adúltero.

adultery [ə'dʌltərɪ] *n* adulterio *m*.

adulthood [ə'dʌlthʊd] *n* adultez *f*, mayoría *f* de edad, edad *f* adulta.

adumbrate ['ædʌmbreɪt] *vt* bosquejar; (*foreshadow*) presagiar, anunciar.

adumbration [ˌædʌm'breɪʃən] *n* bosquejo *m*; presagio *m*, anuncio *m*.

ad val. *abbr of* **ad valorem**.

ad valorem [ædvə'lɔːrəm] *adv* conforme a su valor, por avalúo; ~ **tax** impuesto *m* según valor.

advance [əd'vɑːns] **1** *n* (**a**) (*Mil*) avance *m*; (*progress*) avance *m*, progreso *m*, adelanto *m*; **an important scientific** ~ un importante adelanto científico.

(**b**) (*loan*) anticipo *m*; préstamo *m*; **to get an** ~ **on one's salary** conseguir un anticipo de sueldo.

(**c**) (*in price, value*) alza *f*, aumento *m*; **any** ~ **on £5?** ¿alguien ofrece más de 5 libras?

(**d**) ~**s** primeros pasos *mpl*; insinuaciones *fpl*; (*amorous*) requerimiento *m* amoroso; **to accept** (*or* **respond favourably to**) **sb's** ~**s** aceptar las intenciones de uno; **to make** ~**s to a woman** requerir de amores a una mujer; **to make the first** ~**s** dar los primeros pasos.

(**e**) (*phrases with* in) **in** ~ por adelantado, de antemano; **to arrive in** ~ **of sb** llegar antes que uno; **to be in** ~ **of one's times** adelantarse a su época; **to book in** ~ reservar con anticipación; **to let sb know a week in** ~ avisar a uno con ocho días de anticipación; **to pay in** ~ pagar por adelantado; **to thank sb in** ~ anticipar las gracias a uno; **thanking you in** ~ dándole anticipadas gracias.

2 *adj* anticipado, adelantado; ~ **booking** reserva *f* anticipada; ~ **booking office** (*Brit*) despacho *m* de venta anticipada; ~ **copy** anticipo *m* editorial; ~ **deposit** paga y señal *f*; ~ **freight** flete *m* pagado; ~ **guard** avanzada *f*; ~ **man** (*US Pol*) responsable *m* de una campaña política; ~ **notice** previo aviso *m*; ~ **party** grupo *m* avanzado; (*Mil*) brigada *f* móvil; ~ **payment** anticipo *m*; ~ **post** puesto *m* de vanguardia; ~ **warning** = ~ **notice.**

3 *vt* (**a**) (*move forward*) avanzar, adelantar; *person* (*in rank*) ascender (*to* a).

(**b**) (*encourage*) promover, fomentar, ayudar.

(**c**) (*put forward*) *idea, opinion, theory* proponer (para la discusión), propugnar, exponer; *suggestion* hacer; *claim* presentar, formular.

(**d**) *money* anticipar; *loan* prestar; **he** ~**d me £50** me anticipó 50 libras.

4 *vi* (**a**) (*move forward*) avanzar, adelantarse; **she** ~**d across the room** avanzó a través del cuarto; **to** ~ **on sb** acercarse (de modo amenazador) a uno; **to** ~ **on a town** avanzar sobre una ciudad.

(**b**) (*fig*) avanzar, adelantarse; **the work is advancing quickly** el trabajo se está adelantando rápidamente.

(**c**) (*in rank*) ascender (*to* a).

(**d**) (*price*) subir.

advanced [əd'vɑːnst] *adj* (**a**) (*gen*) *ideas etc* avanzado; *machine etc* muy moderno; *student* adelantado; *study* superior, alto; ~ **maths** matemáticas *fpl* avanzadas; ~ **in years** de edad avanzada, entrado en años; **the corn is well** ~ el trigo está muy avanzado; **the season is well** ~ la estación está avanzada; ~ **gas-cooled reactor** reactor *m* refrigerado por gas de tipo avanzado.

(**b**) (*Brit Scol*) **A~ Level** ≈ bachillerato *m*; **to take 3 A~ Levels** presentarse como candidato en 3 asignaturas de *Advanced Level*; **she has an A~ Level in chemistry** tiene un título de *Advanced Level* en química.

advancement [əd'vɑːnsmənt] *n* (**a**) adelantamiento *m*, progreso *m*; fomento *m*. (**b**) (*in rank*) ascenso *m*.

advantage [əd'vɑːntɪdʒ] *n* (**a**) ventaja *f*; **it's no** ~ **to play first** el jugar primero no da ventaja; **to be to sb's** ~ ser ventajoso para uno; **to have the** ~ **of sb** llevar ventaja a uno; **I'm sorry, you have the** ~ **of me** lo siento, pero no recuerdo su nombre; **to have the** ~ **in numbers** llevar ventaja en cuanto al número; **to show to** ~ (*vi*) lucir, aparecer bajo una luz favorable; **to show sth off to best** ~ hacer que algo se vea bajo la luz más favorable; **to take** ~ **of** aprovechar(se de); sacar partido de; *kindness etc* abusar de; (*euph*) seducir; **to turn sth to (one's)** ~ sacar buen partido de algo; **'languages and shorthand an** ~**'** (*job advert*) 'serán méritos (*or* se valorarán) idiomas y taquigrafía'.

(**b**) (*Tennis*) ventaja *f*; (*Soccer*) ~ **rule** ley *f* de la ventaja.

advantaged [əd'vɑːntɪdʒd] *npl*: **the** ~ los privilegiados, los favorecidos.

advantageous [ˌædvən'teɪdʒəs] *adj* ventajoso, provechoso.

advantageously [ˌædvən'teɪdʒəslɪ] *adv* ventajosamente, provechosamente.

advent ['ædvənt] *n* advenimiento *m*, venida *f*, llegada *f*; **A~** (*Rel*) Adviento *m*.

adventitious [ˌædven'tɪʃəs] *adj* adventicio.

adventure [əd'ventʃəʳ] *n* aventura *f*; ~ **playground** parque *m* infantil.

adventurer [əd'ventʃərəʳ] *n* aventurero *m*.

adventuress [əd'ventʃərɪs] *n* aventurera *f*.

adventurism [əd'ventʃərɪzəm] *n* adventurismo *m*.

adventurous [əd'ventʃərəs] *adj person, character* aventurero, emprendedor; atrevido; *enterprise* peligroso, arriesgado, difícil; **we had a very** ~ **time getting here** las hemos pasado negras al venir aquí; **we need a more** ~ **slogan** necesitamos un eslogan más llamativo.

adventurously [əd'ventʃərəslɪ] *adv* con espíritu aventurero (*or* emprendedor); atrevidamente.

adverb ['ædvɜːb] *n* adverbio *m*.

adverbial [əd'vɜːbɪəl] *adj* adverbial.

adversarial [ˌædvɜː'sɛərɪəl] *adj*: ~ **procedure** procedimiento *m* de confrontación.

adversary ['ædvəsərɪ] *n* adversario *m*, -a *f*, contrario *m*, -a *f*.

adverse ['ædvɜːs] *adj* adverso, contrario, hostil (*to* a); desfavorable (*to* para); *balance* negativo, deudor; *effect, result* adverso.

adversely ['ædvɜːslɪ] *adv* desfavorablemente, negativamente; **to affect** ~ perjudicar.

adversity [əd'vɜːsɪtɪ] *n* infortunio *m*, desgracia *f*; **in times of** ~ en tiempos difíciles; **he knew** ~ **in his youth** de joven conoció la miseria; **companion in** ~ compañero *m* de desgracias.

advert[1] [əd'vɜːt] *vi*: **to** ~ **to** referirse a.

advert[2]* ['ædvɜːt] *n* (*Brit*) = **advertisement.**

advertise ['ædvətaɪz] **1** *vt* (**a**) publicar, anunciar; *weakness etc* exponer, revelar públicamente.

(**b**) (*Comm etc*) anunciar; **'as** ~**d on TV'** 'anunciado en TV'.

2 *vi* hacer publicidad, hacer propaganda; poner un anuncio (*in a paper* en un periódico; *for sth* solicitando algo); **to** ~ **for** buscar por medio de anuncios, solicitar; **it pays to** ~ la publicidad siempre rinde.

advertisement [əd'vɜːtɪsmənt] *n* anuncio *m*; ~ **column** columna *f* de anuncios, sección *f* de anuncios; ~ **rates** tarifas *fpl* de anuncios; **small** ~**s** (*Brit*) anuncios *mpl* por palabras, anuncios *mpl* económicos; **it's not much of an** ~ **for the place*** no dice mucho en favor de la ciudad (*etc*).

advertiser ['ædvətaɪzəʳ] *n* anunciante *mf*.

advertising ['ædvətaɪzɪŋ] **1** *n* publicidad *f*, propaganda *f*; (*adverts collectively*) anuncios *mpl*; **my brother's in** ~ mi hermano trabaja en la publicidad.

2 *attr*: ~ **agency** agencia *f* de publicidad; ~ **campaign** campaña *f* publicitaria; ~ **man** empresario *m* de publicidad; ~ **manager** jefe *m*, -a *f* de publicidad; ~ **matter** material *m* de publicidad; ~ **medium** medio *m* de publicidad; ~ **rates** tarifa *f* de anuncios.

advice [əd'vaɪs] *n* consejo *m*; (*report*) informe *m*, noticia *f*; (*Comm*) aviso *m*, notificación *f*; ~ **column** consultorio *m* sentimental; ~ **note** aviso *m* de mercancías, albarán *m*; ~ **of dispatch** nota *f* de consignación; **a piece of** ~ un consejo; **technical** ~ asesoramiento *m* técnico; **my** ~ **to you is** + *infin* te aconsejo + *infin*; **to ask for** ~**, to seek** ~ pedir consejos; **to take sb's** ~ seguir los consejos de uno; **to take legal** ~ consultar a un abogado; **to take medical** ~ consultar a un médico.

advisability [ədˌvaɪzə'bɪlɪtɪ] *n* conveniencia *f*, prudencia *f*.

advisable [əd'vaɪzəbl] *adj* aconsejable, conveniente, prudente; **it would be** ~ **to** + *infin* sería aconsejable + *infin*; **if you think it** ~ si te parece bien, si crees que es recomendable.

advise [əd'vaɪz] **1** *vt* (**a**) (*counsel*) aconsejar (*to do* hacer); (*as paid adviser, also technically*) asesorar; **what do you** ~ **me to do?** ¿qué me aconsejas (que haga)?

(**b**) (*recommend*) aconsejar, recomendar; **he** ~**s caution** él recomienda la prudencia; **the doctor** ~**s complete rest** el médico recomienda el descanso total.

(**c**) (*inform*) avisar, informar; advertir; (*Comm*) notificar; **to** ~ **sb of an event** informar a uno de un suceso; **to keep sb** ~**d of sth** tener a uno al corriente de algo; **keep me ~d** manténgame al corriente; **please ~ us of a convenient date** (*Comm*) ruego nos notifique una fecha conveniente; **we will ~ you of delivery in due course** les notificaremos la entrega en su momento.

2 *vi*: **he ~s against the plan** él aconseja en contra del plan; **he ~s against going** aconseja que no vayamos; **to ~ on** ser asesor en.

advised [əd'vaɪzd] *adj*: **well-~** prudente; **you would be well ~ to** + *infin* sería aconsejable + *infin*, harías bien en + *infin*; *V* **ill-~**.

advisedly [əd'vaɪzɪdlɪ] *adv* deliberadamente; **to speak ~** hablar con conocimiento de causa; **I say so ~** lo digo después de pensarlo bien.

advisement [əd'vaizmənt] *n* (*US*) consulta *f*, deliberación *f*; **~ counseling** guía *f* vocacional.

adviser, advisor [əd'vaɪzə^r] *n* consejero *m*, -a *f*; (*eg business ~, technical ~*) asesor *m*, -ora; *f* **legal ~** abogado *mf*, asesor *m* jurídico, asesora *f* jurídica; **spiritual ~** confesor *m*.

advisory [əd'vaɪzərɪ] *adj* consultivo; **~ board** junta *f* consultiva; **~ body** cuerpo *m* consultivo; **~ committee** (*US Pol*) comité *m* consultivo; **~ opinion** (*US Jur*) opinión *f* consultiva, opinión *f* asesoria; **~ service** servicio *m* consultivo; **in an ~ capacity** en calidad de asesor.

advocacy ['ædvəkəsɪ] *n* apoyo *m* (activo); (*Jur etc*) defensa *f*.

advocate 1 ['ædvəkɪt] *n* defensor *m*, -ora *f*, partidario *m*, -a *f*; (*Scot Jur*) abogado *mf*; **devil's ~** abogado *m* del diablo.

2 ['ædvəkeɪt] *vt* abogar por, recomendar; ser partidario de; **what do you ~?** ¿qué nos aconsejas?; **I ~ doing nothing** yo recomiendo no hacer nada.

advt *abbr of* **advertisement.**

adze, (*US*) **adz** [ædz] *n* azuela *f*.

AEA (**a**) *n* (*Brit*) *abbr of* **Atomic Energy Authority** Consejo *m* de Energía Nuclear.

(**b**) *n abbr of* **Association of European Airlines** Asociación *f* de Aerolíneas Europeas, AAE *f*.

AEC *n* (*US*) *abbr of* **Atomic Energy Commission.**

AEF *n* (*US*) *abbr of* **American Expeditionary Forces.**

Aegean Sea [iː'dʒiːən siː] *n* Mar *m* Egeo.

aegis ['iːdʒɪs] *n* égida *f*; **under the ~ of** (*protection*) bajo la tutela de; (*patronage*) patrocinado por.

aegrotat [iː'grəutæt] *n* (*Brit*) *título universitario que se concede al candidato que por enfermedad no ha podido presentarse a los exámenes.*

Aeneas [iː'niːæs] *nm* Eneas.

Aeneid ['iːnɪɪd] *n* Eneida *f*.

aeon, (*US*) **eon** ['iːən] *n* eón *m*; (*fig*) eternidad *f*.

aerate ['ɛəreɪt] *vt* airear; ventilar, oxigenar.

aerated ['ɛəreɪtɪd] *adj*: **~ water** gaseosa *f*.

aeration [ɛə'reɪʃən] *n* aireación *f*.

aerial ['ɛərɪəl] **1** *adj* aéreo; **~ beacon** aerofaro *m*; **~ cableway** teleférico *m*; **~ input*** (*US*) mensaje *m* recibido por antena; **~ ladder** (*US*) escalera *f* de bomberos; **~ photograph** aerofoto *f*; **~ photography** fotografía *f* aérea; **~ survey** reconocimiento *m* aéreo; **~ tanker** transportador *m* aéreo.

2 *n* (*esp Brit*) antena *f*; **~ (mast)** torre *f* de antena.

aerie ['ɛərɪ] *n* (*US*) = **eyrie**.

aero... ['ɛərəu] *pref* aero...

aerobatics [,ɛərəu'bætɪks] *npl* acrobacia *f* aérea.

aerobic [ɛə'rəubɪk] *adj shoes, dances* de aerobic, para aerobic.

aerobics [ɛə'rəubɪks] *n sing* aeróbica *f*, aerobic *m*, aerobismo *m* (*SC*).

aerodrome ['ɛərədrəum] *n* (*Brit*) aeródromo *m*.

aerodynamic ['ɛərəudaɪ'næmɪk] *adj* aerodinámico.

aerodynamics ['ɛərəudaɪ'næmɪks] *npl* aerodinámica *f*.

aero-engine ['ɛərəu,endʒɪn] *n* motor *m* de aviación.

aerofoil ['ɛərəufɔɪl] *n* plano *m* aerodinámico.

aerogram(me) ['ɛərəugræm] *n* (*air-letter*) aerograma *m*; (*radio message*) radiograma *m*.

aerolite ['ɛərəlaɪt] *n* aerolito *m*.

aeromodelling ['ɛərəu'mɒdlɪŋ] *n* aeromodelismo *m*.

aeronaut ['ɛərənɔːt] *n* aeronauta *mf*.

aeronautic(al) [,ɛərə'nɔːtɪk(əl)] *adj* aeronáutico.

aeronautics [,ɛərə'nɔːtɪks] *npl* aeronáutica *f*.

aeroplane ['ɛərəpleɪn] *n* (*Brit*) avión *m*; **model ~** aeromodelo *m*.

aerosol ['ɛərəsɒl] *n* aerosol *m*.

aerospace ['ɛərəuspeɪs] *attr* aeroespacial; **the ~ industry** la industria aeroespacial; **the ~ minister** el ministro encargado de asuntos aeroespaciales.

Aeschylus ['iːskɪləs] *nm* Esquilo.

Aesop ['iːsɒp] *nm* Esopo; **~'s Fables** Fábulas *fpl* de Esopo.

aesthete, (*US*) **esthete** ['iːsθiːt] *n* esteta *mf*.

aesthetic(al), (*US*) **esthetic(al)** [iːs'θetɪk(əl)] *adj* estético.

aesthetically, (*US*) **esthetically** [iːs'θetɪkəlɪ] *adv* estéticamente.

aestheticism, (*US*) **estheticism** [iːs'θetɪsɪzəm] *n* esteticismo *m*.

aesthetics, (*US*) **esthetics** [iːs'θetɪks] *npl* estética *f*.

AEU *n* (*Brit*) *abbr of* **Amalgamated Engineering Union** Sindicato *m* Mixto de Ingeniería.

a.f. *n* (**a**) *abbr of* **audio frequency** audiofrecuencia *f*. (**b**) (*Comm*) *abbr of* **advance freight** flete *m* pagado.

AFA *n* (*Brit*) *abbr of* **Amateur Football Association** Asociación *f* de Fútbol Amateur.

afar [ə'fɑː^r] *adv* (*also* **~ off**) lejos, en lontananza; **from ~** desde lejos.

AFB *n* (*US Mil*) *abbr of* **Air Force Base** Base *f* Aérea.

AFC *n* (**a**) (*Brit*) *abbr of* **Amateur Football Club** *or* **Association Football Club.** (**b**) *abbr of* **automatic frequency control** control *m* automático de frecuencia.

AFDC *n* (*US Admin*) *abbr of* **Aid to Families with Dependent Children** Ayuda *f* a familias con hijos menores de edad, Ayuda *f* familiar.

affability [,æfə'bɪlɪtɪ] *n* afabilidad *f*, amabilidad *f*.

affable ['æfəbl] *adj* afable, amable.

affably ['æfəblɪ] *adv* afablemente.

affair [ə'fɛə^r] *n* (**a**) (*event*) acontecimiento *m*; episodio *m*; caso *m*; **The Falklands ~** el asunto de las Malvinas, aquello (*or* lo) de las Malvinas; **the Irangate ~** el caso Irangate, el episodio de Irangate; **it was a strange ~** fue un asunto raro; **it will be a big ~** será un acontecimiento importante; **I have no liking for such ~s** no me gustan estas cosas.

(**b**) (*concern*) asunto *m*; **current ~s** actualidades *fpl*; **foreign ~s** asuntos *mpl* (*or* relaciones *fpl* (*LAm*)) exteriores; **~ of honour** lance *m* de honor; **~s of state** asuntos *mpl* de estado; **how are your ~s?** ¿qué tal van tus cosas?; **that's my ~** ésa es cosa mía, eso me toca únicamente a mí; **that's his ~** es asunto suyo, que se las arregle él; **to put one's ~s in order** arreglar sus asuntos personales.

(**c**) (*business*) **~s** negocios *mpl*; **man of ~s** hombre *m* de negocios.

(**d**) (*love* **~**: *also* **affaire**) aventura *f* amorosa; amorío *m*, lío *m*, enredo *m*; (*more serious*) amor *m*, amores *mpl*; (*considered poetically*) idilio *m*; (*seen as vulgar*) plan* *m*, ligue* *m*; **~ of the heart** aventura *f* sentimental; **to have an ~ with sb** andar en relaciones con uno; **he's always having ~s with his secretaries** siempre tiene plan con la secretaria de turno; **she ended the ~** ella terminó las relaciones.

affect [ə'fekt] *vt* (**a**) (*concern*) afectar (a), tener que ver con, influir en; (*harm*) perjudicar; (*Med*) interesar, afectar; **this will ~ everybody** esto afectará a todos; **it did not ~ my decision** no influyó en mi decisión; **it ~s me considerably** para mí tiene gran importancia; **a wound ~ing the right leg** una herida que interesa la pierna derecha; **his whole side was ~ed** todo su costado estaba afectado.

(**b**) (*move*) conmover, enternecer; **he seemed much ~ed** pareció muy emocionado, se conmovió mucho.

(**c**) (*like*) **she ~s bright colours** a ella le gustan los colores claros.

(**d**) (*feign*) **he ~s the rebel** se las echa de rebelde; **he ~ed indifference** afectó indiferencia; hizo ostentación de su indiferencia, fingió ser indiferente; **she ~ed to cry** ella fingió llorar.

affectation [,æfek'teɪʃən] *n* afectación *f*; amaneramiento *m*.

affected [ə'fektɪd] *adj* afectado; amanerado.

affectedly [ə'fektɪdlɪ] *adv* de manera afectada, en tono afectado, con afectación.

affecting [ə'fektɪŋ] *adj* conmovedor, enternecedor.

affection [ə'fekʃən] *n* afecto *m* (*for* a, *towards* hacia), cariño *m*; inclinación *f* (*for* a, hacia); **to have an ~ for** tener cariño a; **to transfer one's ~s** dar su amor a otro (*or* otra).

affectionate [ə'fekʃənɪt] *adj* cariñoso, afectuoso; **with ~ greetings** (*formula in letter*) afectuosamente; **your ~ nephew** con abrazos de tu sobrino, tu sobrino que te quiere.

affectionately [ə'fekʃənɪtlɪ] *adv* afectuosamente, cariñosamente; **~ yours, yours ~** (*formula in letter*) un abrazo cariñoso.

affective [ə'fektɪv] *adj* afectivo.

affectivity [,æfek'tɪvətɪ] *n* afectividad *f*.

affiance [ə'faɪəns] († *or hum*) **1** *vt* prometer en matrimonio (*to* a); **to be ~d** estar prometido (*to* a). **2** *vr*: **to ~ o.s. to** prometerse a.

affidavit [,æfɪ'deɪvɪt] *n* declaración *f* jurada, testificata *f*, afidávit *m*; **to swear an ~ (to the effect that)** (*Jur*) hacer una declaración jurada (que).

affiliate 1 [ə'fɪlɪeɪt] *vi*: **to ~ to, to ~ with** afiliarse a. **2** [ə'fɪlɪɪt] *n* afiliado *m*, filial *f*.

affiliated [ə'fɪlɪeɪtɪd] *adj company* filial, subsidiario; *member, society* afiliado.

affiliation [ə,fɪlɪ'eɪʃən] *n* **(a)** afiliación *f*; **political ~s** afiliaciones *fpl* políticas, relaciones *fpl* políticas; **the painting's ~s are with this school** el cuadro está relacionado con esta escuela.

(b) (*Jur*) paternidad *f*; **~ order** decreto *m* relativo a la paternidad; **~ proceedings** proceso *m* para determinar la paternidad.

affinity [ə'fɪnɪtɪ] *n* afinidad *f*; **A has certain affinities with B** entre A y B existe cierta afinidad; **I feel no ~ whatsoever with him** no nos une ningún lazo de simpatía.

affirm [ə'fɜːm] *vt* afirmar, asegurar, aseverar.

affirmation [,æfə'meɪʃən] *n* afirmación *f*, aseveración *f*.

affirmative [ə'fɜːmətɪv] *adj* afirmativo; **to answer in the ~** dar una respuesta afirmativa, contestar afirmativamente; **~ action** (*US Pol*) medidas *fpl* a favor de las minorías.

affirmatively [ə'fɜːmətɪvlɪ] *adv* afirmativamente.

affix 1 ['æfɪks] *n* afijo *m*. **2** [ə'fɪks] *vt signature etc* poner, añadir; *stamp* poner, pegar; *seal* imprimir; **to ~ a notice to the wall** pegar un anuncio en la pared.

afflict [ə'flɪkt] *vt* afligir; **the ~ed** los afligidos; **to be ~ed with** (*or* **by**) sufrir de, estar aquejado de.

affliction [ə'flɪkʃən] *n* **(a)** (*state*) aflicción *f*, congoja *f*; pena *f*; (*event etc*) mal *m*, infortunio *m*, desgracia *f*. **(b)** (*Med*) mal *m*; **the ~s of old age** los achaques de la vejez.

affluence ['æfluəns] *n* riqueza *f*, opulencia *f*; prosperidad *f*; **to live in ~** vivir con lujo.

affluent ['æfluənt] **1** *adj* rico, opulento, acaudalado; próspero; **the ~ society** la sociedad opulenta. **2** *n* **(a) the ~** los ricos. **(b)** (*Geog*) afluente *m*.

afflux ['æflʌks] *n* afluencia *f*; (*Med*) aflujo *m*.

afford [ə'fɔːd] *vt* **(a)** (*provide*) dar, proporcionar; **this ~s me a chance to speak** esto me da la oportunidad de hablar; **that ~ed me some relief** eso me proporcionó cierto alivio; **it ~s shade** da sombra.

(b) (*pay for*) **we can ~ it** tenemos con que comprarlo, podemos permitírnoslo; **can we ~ it?** ¿podemos hacer este gasto?, ¿tenemos bastante dinero (para comprarlo *etc*)?; **we can't ~ such things** tales cosas no están a nuestro alcance.

(c) (*spare, risk*) **I can't ~ the time to go** no tengo bastante tiempo para ir; **how much can you ~?** ¿cuánto estás dispuesto a gastar (*or* invertir *etc*)?; **we can ~ to wait** nos conviene esperar, bien podemos esperar; **an opportunity you cannot ~ to miss** una ocasión que no es para desperdiciar; **I can't ~ to be idle** no puedo permitirme el lujo de no hacer nada; **can we ~ the risk?** ¿podemos arriesgarlo?

affordable [ə'fɔːdəbl] *adj price* razonable; *purchase* posible, dentro de los medios del comprador.

afforest [æ'fɒrɪst] *vt* repoblar (de *or* con árboles).

afforestation [æ,fɒrɪs'teɪʃən] *n* repoblación *f* forestal.

afforested [æ'fɒrɪstɪd] *adj land* repoblado de árboles.

affray [ə'freɪ] *n* refriega *f*, reyerta *f*, riña *f*.

affreightment [ə'freɪtmənt] *n* fletamento *m*.

affricate ['æfrɪkət] **1** *adj* africado. **2** *n* africada *f*.

affright† [ə'fraɪt] *vt* asustar, espantar.

affront [ə'frʌnt] **1** *n* afrenta *f*, ofensa *f*; **to offer an ~ to** afrentar a. **2** *vt* afrentar, ofender; **he was much ~ed** se ofendió mucho.

Afghan ['æfgæn] **1** *adj* afgano. **2** *n* **(a)** afgano *m*, -a *f*. **(b)** (*dog*) perro *m* afgano.

Afghanistan [æf'gænɪstæn] *n* Afganistán *m*.

aficionado [ə,fɪsjə'nɑːdəʊ] *n* aficionado *m*, -a *f*.

afield [ə'fiːld] *adv*: **far ~** muy lejos; **countries further ~** países *mpl* más lejanos; **you'll have to go further ~ for that** para eso hará falta buscar más lejos; **we are exploring further ~ all the time** exploramos cada vez más lejos.

afire [ə'faɪəʳ] *adv and pred adj*: **to be ~** arder, quemar, estar en llamas; **to be ~ to help** anhelar ardientemente ayudar; *V also* **ablaze.**

aflame [ə'fleɪm] *adv and pred adj* en llamas; *V* **ablaze, afire.**

AFL-CIO *n* (*US*) *abbr of* **American Federation of Labor and Congress of Industrial Organizations.**

afloat [ə'fləʊt] *adv* a flote; en el mar; **the oldest ship ~** el barco más viejo que sigue a flote; **the largest navy ~** la mayor marina del mundo; **by a miracle we were still ~** por maravilla quedamos a flote; **to get a business ~** lanzar un negocio; **to keep ~** mantener(se) a flote (*also fig*); **to spend one's life ~** pasar toda la vida a bordo.

afoot [ə'fʊt] *adv*: **there is sth ~** algo se está tramando; **what's ~?** ¿qué están tramando?; **there is a plan ~ to remove him** existe un proyecto para apearle; **to set a scheme ~** poner un proyecto en práctica, poner una idea en movimiento.

aforementioned [ə,fɔː'menʃənd] *adj*, **aforenamed** [ə'fɔːneɪmd] *adj*, **aforesaid** [ə'fɔːsed] *adj* susodicho, mencionado, ya dicho.

aforethought [ə'fɔːθɔːt] *adj*: **with malice ~** con premeditación.

afoul [ə'faʊl] *adv* (*esp US*): **to run ~ of sb** enredarse con uno, indisponerse con uno; **to run ~ of a ship** chocar con un barco.

afraid [ə'freɪd] *adj* **(a) to be ~** tener miedo; **everyone was very ~** todos tenían mucho miedo, todos se espantaron mucho; **don't be ~** no tengas miedo, no temas; **to make sb ~** infundir miedo a uno; **to be ~ for sb** temer por uno; **to be ~ of** *person* tener miedo a; *thing* tener miedo de; **I'm ~ of hurting him** temo hacerle daño; **to be ~ to** + *infin* tener miedo de + *infin*, temer + *infin*; **he was ~ to speak** no se atrevía a hablar.

(b) (*polite regret*) **I'm ~ he's out** lo siento, pero no está; **I'm ~ I have to go now** siento tener que irme ahora; **I'm ~ he won't come** me temo que no venga; **I'm ~ not** lo siento pero no; **I'm ~ so!** lo siento, pero es así; **my car is not available, I'm ~** lamento que no disponga ahora de mi coche.

afresh [ə'freʃ] *adv* de nuevo, otra vez; **to do sth ~** volver a hacer algo; **to start ~** empezar de nuevo, reempezar, recomenzar.

Africa ['æfrɪkə] *n* África *f*.

African ['æfrɪkən] **1** *adj* africano. **2** *n* africano *m*, -a *f*.

African-American [,æfrɪkənə'merɪkən] *adj* afroamericano.

Afrikaans [,æfrɪ'kɑːns] *n* africaans *m*.

Afrikaner [,æfrɪ'kɑːnəʳ] **1** *adj* africánder. **2** *n* africánder *mf*.

Afro ['æfrəʊ] *adj*, *pref* afro; **~ hairstyle** peinado *m* afro; **to go ~** africanizarse.

Afro-American [,æfrəʊə,merɪkən] *adj* afroamericano.

Afro-Asian ['æfrəʊ'eɪʃən] *adj* afroasiático.

AFT *n* (*US*) *abbr of* **American Federation of Teachers.**

aft [ɑːft] *adv* (*Naut*) (*be*) en popa; (*go*) a popa.

after ['ɑːftəʳ] **1** *adv* **(a)** (*time, order*) después; **for weeks ~** durante varias semanas después; **long ~** mucho tiempo después; **soon ~** poco después.

(b) (*place*) detrás.

2 *prep* **(a)** (*time, order*) después de; **it was 20 ~ 3** eran las 3 y 20; **soon ~ eating it** poco después de comerlo; **do you put Lope ~ Calderón?** ¿crees que Lope le es inferior a Calderón?

(b) (*place, order*) detrás de; tras; **day ~ day** día tras día; **excuse ~ excuse, one excuse ~ another** excusas y más excusas; **one ~ the other** uno tras otro; **he ran ~ me with my umbrella** corrió tras de mí con mi paraguas; **~ you!** ¡pase Vd!, ¡Vd primero!; **~ you with the salt*** ¿me das la sal?

(c) (*in the manner of*) **this is ~ Goya** esto se pintó según el estilo de Goya; **~ the English fashion** a la (manera) inglesa; *V* **heart.**

(d) (*on account of*) **he is named ~ Churchill** se le llamó así por Churchill.

(e) (*idioms with* to be): **the police are ~ him** la policía le está buscando; la policía está detrás de él; **I have been ~ that for years** eso lo busco desde hace años; **what are you ~?** ¿qué pretendes con eso?; **they're all ~ the same thing** todos van a por lo mismo; **I see what you're ~** ya caigo; ya comprendo lo que quieres decir; (*hostile*) ya te he calado; **she's ~ a husband** va en pos de un marido; **she's ~ a special dress** busca un vestido especial.

3 *conj* después (de) que; una vez que.

4 *adj part* posterior, trasero, de atrás; (*Naut*) de popa; **in ~ years** en los años siguientes, años después.

5 *npl*: **~s** (*Brit**) postre *m*.

afterbirth ['ɑːftəbɜːθ] *n* placenta *f*, secundinas *fpl*.

afterburner ['ɑːftə,bɜːnəʳ] *n* dispositivo *m* de poscombustión.

aftercare ['ɑːftəkɛəʳ] *n* (*Med*) asistencia *f* postoperatoria; (*of prisoners*) asistencia *f* para ex-prisioneros.

afterdeck ['ɑːftədek] *n* cubierta *f* de popa.

after-dinner ['ɑːftə'dɪnəʳ] *adj* de sobremesa; **~ drink** copa *f* de después de la cena; **~ speech** discurso *m* de sobremesa.

after-effect ['ɑːftərɪfekt] *n* consecuencia *f*; secuela *f*; **~s** efectos *mpl*, repercusiones *fpl*.

afterglow ['ɑːftəgləʊ] *n* (*in sky*) arrebol *m*, resplandor *m* crepuscular; (*bodily*) sensación *f* de bienestar.

after-hours ['ɑːftə'aʊəz] **1** *adv* fuera de horas. **2** *adj*: **~ dealings** transacciones *fpl* fuera de horas.

afterlife ['ɑːftəlaɪf] *n* (*after death*) vida *f* futura; (*on earth*) vida *f* posterior, resto *m* de la vida.

aftermath ['ɑːftəmæθ] *n* consecuencias *fpl*, resultados *mpl*, secuelas *fpl*; resaca *f*; **in the ~ of the war** en las condiciones que resultaron de la guerra.

afternoon ['ɑːftə'nuːn] *n* tarde *f*; **good ~!** ¡buenas tardes!; **~ performance** función *f* de la tarde; **~ tea** ≃ merienda *f*; **~s he's generally out** por las tardes en general no está.

afterpains ['ɑːftə,peɪnz] *npl* dolores *mpl* de posparto.

after-sales service ['ɑːftəseɪlz'sɜːvɪs] *n* (*Brit*) servicio *m* posventa.

after-shave (lotion) ['ɑːftəʃeɪv('ləʊʃən)] *n* loción *f* para después del afeitado.

aftershock ['ɑːftə,ʃɒk] *n* (*of earthquake*) réplica *f*.

aftertaste ['ɑːftəteɪst] *n* dejo *m*, resabio *m*, gustillo *m*.

after-tax ['ɑːftə'tæks] *adj* después del impuesto; **~ profits** beneficios *mpl* postimpositivos.

afterthought ['ɑːftəθɔːt] *n* ocurrencia *f* tardía, idea *f* adicional.

after-treatment ['ɑːftətriːtmənt] *n* tratamiento *m* postoperatorio.

afterwards, (*esp US*) **afterward** ['ɑːftəwəd(z)] *adv* después, más tarde; **immediately ~** acto seguido; **long ~** mucho tiempo después; **shortly ~, soon ~** poco después.

afterworld ['ɑːftəwɜːld] *n* mundo *m* más allá.

A.G. *abbr of* **Attorney General**; *V* **attorney**.

again [ə'gen] *adv* (**a**) otra vez, nuevamente, de nuevo; *often translated by* volver a + *infin*, *eg* **he climbed up ~** volvió a subir; **would you do it all ~?** ¿lo volverías a hacer?; **~ and ~** una y otra vez, repetidas veces; **I've told you ~ and ~** te lo he dicho mil veces; **what was that joke ~?** ¿cómo era el chiste aquel (que acabas de contar)?; **never ~** nunca más; **I won't do it ever ~** no lo haré nunca más; **as much ~** otro tanto; **as many ~** otros tantos; **he is as old ~ as I am** me dobla la edad; **oh no, not ~!** ¡Dios mío, otra vez!; **what, you ~?** ¿tú otra vez (por aquí)?

(**b**) (*emphatic*: *besides, moreover*) además; por otra parte; **and ~, then ~** y además; **~, we just don't know** por otra parte, realmente no sabemos; **~, it may not be true** por otra parte, puede no ser verdad; **these are different ~** también éstos son distintos.

against [ə'genst] **1** *prep* (**a**) (*next to*) contra; (*close to*) al lado de, junto a, cerca de; **over ~ the church** enfrente de la iglesia; **~ the light** contra la luz, a contra sol; **he hit his head ~ the wall** se dio la cabeza contra la pared; **the hills stood out ~ the sunset** las colinas se destacaban sobre la puesta del sol; **to lean ~ a table** apoyarse en una mesa; **he leant the ladder ~ the wall** apoyó la escalera contra la pared.

(**b**) (*contrast*) **~ that, as ~ that** en contraste con eso; por otra parte; **6 today as ~ 7 yesterday** 6 hoy en comparación con 7 ayer.

(**c**) (*for*) **everything is ready ~ his arrival** todo está listo para su llegada.

(**d**) (*fig*) contra; en contra de; **he was ~ it** estaba en contra, se opuso a ello; **I see nothing ~ it** no veo nada en contra; **I spoke ~ the plan** hablé en contra del proyecto; **I know nothing ~ him** yo no sé nada que le sea desfavorable; **what have you got ~ me?** ¿por qué me guarda Vd rencor?; **it's ~ the law** lo prohíbe la ley; **it's ~ the rules** no lo permiten las reglas; **conditions are ~ us** las condiciones nos son desfavorables; **luck was ~ him** la suerte le era contraria; **to be up ~ it** estar en un aprieto; **now we're really up ~ it!** ¡ahora sí tenemos problemas!

(**e**) **refund available ~ this voucher** se devuelve el precio al presentar este comprobante.

2 *adv* en contra; **well, I'm ~** bueno, yo estoy en contra; **there were twenty votes ~** hubo veinte votos en contra.

Agamemnon [,ægə'memnən] *nm* Agamenón.

agape [ə'geɪp] *adj and adv* boquiabierto.

agar-agar [,eɪgə'eɪgəʳ] *n* gelatina *f*, agar-agar *m*.

agate ['ægət] *n* ágata *f*.

agave [ə'geɪvɪ] *n* agave *f*, pita *f*, maguey *m* (*LAm*).

age [eɪdʒ] **1** *n* (**a**) (*gen*) edad *f*; (*old ~*) vejez *f*, senectud *f*; **~ of consent** edad *f* núbil; **~ of discretion** edad *f* del juicio; **he is 20 years of ~** tiene 20 años; **when I was your ~** cuando yo era de su edad; **what ~ are you?** (*Brit*) ¿cuántos años tienes?; **be your ~!** ¡compórtate de acuerdo con tu edad!, ¡no seas niño!; **60 is no ~ at all** los sesenta no son nada; **to feel one's ~** sentirse viejo; **she doesn't look her ~** no representa los años que tiene; **~ is beginning to tell on him** los años empiezan a pesar sobre él; **at the ~ of 7** a la edad de 7 años; **at my ~** a la edad que yo tengo; **of ~** mayor de edad; **to be of an ~ to go alone** ser de edad para ir solo; **they are both of an ~** los dos tienen la misma edad; **to come of ~** llegar a la mayoría de edad; **over ~** demasiado viejo; **under ~** menor de edad; demasiado joven.

(**b**) (*period*) época *f*, era *f*, siglo *m*; **this is the ~ of the car** éste es el siglo del coche; **the ~ we live in** el siglo en que vivimos; **in the ~ of Queen Elizabeth** en la época (*or* en tiempos) de la reina Isabel; **atomic ~** era *f* atómica; **A~ of Enlightenment** Siglo *m* de las Luces; **A~ of Reason** Siglo *m* de la Razón; *V* **bronze, dark, middle** *etc*.

(**c**) (*: *long time*) siglo *m*, eternidad *f*, muchísimo tiempo *m*; **we waited an ~, we waited (for) ~s** esperamos una eternidad; **it's ~s since I saw him** hace años que no le veo.

2 *attr* etario; **~ discrimination** discriminación *f* por edad; **~ factor** factor *m* edad; **~ structure** estructura *f* etaria.

3 *vt* envejecer; *wine* criar, añejar.

4 *vi* envejecer(se); (*wine etc*) madurar, añejarse.

age-bracket ['eɪdʒ,brækɪt] *n* grupo *m* etario.

aged *adj* (**a**) ['eɪdʒɪd] (*old*) viejo, anciano. (**b**) [eɪdʒd]: **~ 15** de 15 años, que tiene 15 años.

ageful ['eɪdʒfəl] *adj* (*US*: *euph*) viejo, de edad.

age-group ['eɪdʒgruːp] *n* grupo *m* etario, grupo *m* de personas de la misma edad; **the 40 to 50 ~** el grupo que comprende los de 40 a 50 años; **children of the same ~** niños *mpl* de la misma edad; **to arrange people by ~s** clasificar las personas según su edad.

ag(e)ing ['eɪdʒɪŋ] **1** *adj* viejo, que envejece, que va para viejo. **2** *n* envejecimiento *m*, el envejecer; senescencia *f*; **the ~ process** el proceso de envejecer.

ageism ['eɪdʒɪzəm] *n* prejuicio *m* contra los viejos.

ageless ['eɪdʒlɪs] *adj* eternamente joven; perenne, inmemorial.

age-limit ['eɪdʒlɪmɪt] *n* edad *f* mínima *or* máxima; edad *f* tope; (*for retirement*) edad *f* de jubilación.

age-long ['eɪdʒlɒŋ] *adj* multisecular.

agency ['eɪdʒənsɪ] *n* (**a**) (*office*) agencia *f*; *V* **advertising** *etc*.

(**b**) (*of UN etc*) organismo *m*, oficina *f*; **A~ for International Development** Agencia *f* para el Desarrollo Internacional.

(**c**) (*Comm, Fin*) agencia *f*; *V* **sole** *etc*.

(**d**) **through the ~ of** por medio de, por la mediación de.

agenda [ə'dʒendə] *n* orden *m* del día, asuntos *mpl* a tratar, agenda *f*.

agent ['eɪdʒənt] *n* (**a**) (*representative*) representante *mf*, delegado *m*, agenciero *m*, -a *f* (*SC*); intermediario *m*; (*Jur*) apoderado *m*; (*Comm*) agente *m*, representante *m*, gestor *m*; (*Police etc*) agente *mf*; (*US*) jefe *m* de estación; *V* **publicity, sole** *etc*.

(**b**) (*Chem*) agente *m*; **chemical ~** agente *m* químico.

agentive ['eɪdʒəntɪv] *n* agentivo *m*.

agent provocateur ['æʒɑːprɒvɒkə'tɜːʳ] *n* agente *m* provocador.

age-old ['eɪdʒəʊld] *adj* secular, multisecular, antiquísimo.

age-range ['eɪdʒ,reɪndʒ] *n*: **the ~ of the group is wide** en el grupo hay personas de diversas edades; **children in the ~ 12 to 14** niños en edades comprendidas entre los 12 y los 14 años.

agglomeration [ə,glɒmə'reɪʃən] *n* aglomeración *f*.

agglutinate [ə'gluːtɪneɪt] **1** *vt* aglutinar. **2** *vi* aglutinarse.

agglutination [ə,gluːtɪ'neɪʃən] *n* aglutinación *f*.

agglutinative [ə'gluːtɪnətɪv] *adj* aglutinante.

aggrandize [ə'grændaɪz] *vt* agrandar, ampliar; aumentar; engrandecer.

aggrandizement [ə'grændɪzmənt] *n* agrandamiento *m*, ampliación *f*; engrandecimiento *m*.

aggravate ['ægrəveɪt] *vt* (**a**) agravar, empeorar. (**b**) (*) irritar, sacar de quicio.

aggravating ['ægrəveɪtɪŋ] *adj* (**a**) (*Jur*) agravante. (**b**) (*) irritante, molesto; **it's very ~** es para volverse loco; **don't be so ~** no seas pesado*; **he's an ~ child** es un niño molesto.

aggravation [,ægrə'veɪʃən] *n* (**a**) agravación *f*, empeoramiento *m*; (*Jur*) circunstancia *f* agravante; **robbery with ~** robo *m* agravado. (**b**) (*) irritación *f*.

aggregate 1 ['ægrɪgɪt] *adj* total, global; **~ corporation**

corporación *f* global.

2 ['ægrɪgɪt] *n* (**a**) agregado *m*, conjunto *m*; **in the ~** en conjunto, en total; **Barataria won 5-4 on ~** ganó Barataria por 5 a 4 en conjunto.

(**b**) (*Geol etc*) agregado *m*.

3 ['ægrɪgeɪt] *vt* agregar, juntar, reunir.

4 ['ægrɪgeɪt] *vi* ascender a, sumar.

aggression [ə'greʃən] *n* agresión *f*.

aggressive [ə'gresɪv] *adj* (**a**) agresivo. (**b**) (*zealous etc*) dinámico, enérgico, emprendedor.

aggressively [ə'gresɪvlɪ] *adv* (**a**) de manera agresiva. (**b**) con dinamismo, enérgicamente, con empuje.

aggressiveness [ə'gresɪvnɪs] *n* (**a**) agresividad *f*. (**b**) dinamismo *m*, energía *f*, empuje *m*.

aggressor [ə'gresəʳ] *n* agresor *m*, -ora *f*.

aggrieved [ə'griːvd] *adj* ofendido; apenado; **the ~ husband** el marido ofendido; **in an ~ tone** en un tono de queja; **he was much ~** se ofendió mucho; **to feel ~** ofenderse, resentirse (*at* por).

aggro* ['ægrəʊ] *n* (*Brit*) (**a**) (*violence*) violencia *f*, conducta *f* violenta; agresión *f*; (*hooliganism*) gamberrismo *m*. (**b**) (*hassle*) líos *mpl*, problemas *mpl*; **I'm not going, it's too much ~** no voy, es mucha lata*.

aghast [ə'gɑːst] *adj* horrorizado, pasmado; **to be ~** horrorizarse, pasmarse (*at* de); **we were all ~** todos quedamos pasmados.

agile ['ædʒaɪl] *adj* ágil.

agility [ə'dʒɪlɪtɪ] *n* agilidad *f*.

agin [ə'gɪn] *prep* (*Scot or hum*) = **against** (**d**); **to be** (*or* **take**) **~ a plan** oponerse a un proyecto.

aging ['eɪdʒɪŋ] = **ag(e)ing.**

agitate ['ædʒɪteɪt] **1** *vt* (**a**) (*shake*) agitar.

(**b**) (*perturb*) inquietar, perturbar; alborotar.

(**c**) *question* discutir acaloradamente.

2 *vi*: **to ~ against** hacer propaganda contra, hacer una campaña en contra de; **to ~ for** hacer propaganda por, hacer una campaña en pro de.

agitated ['ædʒɪteɪtɪd] *adj* inquieto, perturbado; **in an ~ tone** en tono inquieto; **to be very ~** estar muy inquieto (*about* por), estar en ascuas.

agitation [ˌædʒɪ'teɪʃən] *n* (**a**) (*state*) inquietud *f*, perturbación *f*; nerviosismo *m*. (**b**) (*Pol etc*) agitación *f*; propaganda *f*, campaña *f*.

agitator ['ædʒɪteɪtəʳ] *n* (**a**) agitador *m*, -ora *f*; alborotador *m*, -ora *f*, elemento *m* revoltoso. (**b**) (*Chem*) agitador *m*.

aglow [ə'gləʊ] *adv and pred adj* radiante, brillante; **to be ~ with** brillar de; **to be ~ with happiness** irradiar felicidad; *V also* **ablaze, afire.**

AGM *n abbr of* **annual general meeting** junta *f* anual.

Agnes ['ægnɪs] *nf* Inés.

agnostic [æg'nɒstɪk] **1** *adj* agnóstico. **2** *n* agnóstico *m*, -a *f*.

agnosticism [æg'nɒstɪsɪzəm] *n* agnosticismo *m*.

ago [ə'gəʊ] *adv*: **a week ~** hace una semana; **just a moment ~** hace un momento nada más; **a little while ~** hace poco; **long ~** hace mucho tiempo; **how long ~ was it?** ¿hace cuánto tiempo?; **no longer ~ than yesterday** ayer solamente, ayer nada más; **as long ~ as 1978** ya en 1978.

agog [ə'gɒg] *adj*: **to be ~** estar ansioso, sentir gran curiosidad; **the country was ~** el país estaba emocionadísimo, el país estaba pendiente de lo que pudiera pasar; **he was ~ to hear the news** tenía enorme curiosidad por saber las noticias; **to set ~** emocionar, infundir gran curiosidad a.

agonize ['ægənaɪz] **1** *vt* atormentar. **2** *vi*: **to ~ over** sufrir muchísimo a causa de, atormentarse con motivo de, experimentar grandes angustias por.

agonized ['ægənaɪzd] *adj* angustioso.

agonizing ['ægənaɪzɪŋ] *adj pain* atroz, muy agudo; *indecision, suspense* angustioso; *moment* de angustia; *reappraisal* agonizante, doloroso.

agonizingly ['ægənaɪzɪŋlɪ] *adv* (*V adj*) atrozmente; angustiosamente; dolorosamente; **~ slow** terriblemente lento.

agony ['ægənɪ] *n* (**a**) (*pain*) dolor *m* agudo, dolor *m* punzante; **I was in ~** sufría unos dolores horrorosos. (**b**) (*last ~, death ~*) agonía *f*. (**c**) (*mental anguish*) angustia *f*, aflicción *f*, congoja *f*; **to be in an ~ of impatience** impacientarse mucho; **to suffer agonies of doubt** ser atormentado por las dudas; **it was ~!*** ¡fue fatal!*; **the play was sheer ~*** la obra era una birria*; **~ aunt** (*Brit*) columnista *f* de la consulta sentimental; **~ column** sección *f* de anuncios personales; consultorio *m* sentimental.

agoraphobe ['ægərəfəʊb] *n* agorafóbico *m*, -a *f*.

agoraphobia [ˌægərə'fəʊbɪə] *n* agorafobia *f*.

AGR *n abbr of* **Advanced Gas-Cooled Reactor** reactor *m* refrigerado por gas de tipo avanzado.

agrarian [ə'grɛərɪən] *adj* agrario; **~ reform** reforma *f* agraria; **~ revolution** revolución *f* agraria.

agrarianism [ə'grɛərɪənɪzəm] *n* agrarismo *m*.

agree [ə'griː] **1** *vt* (**a**) (*consent*) **to ~ to do sth** consentir en hacer algo, quedar en hacer algo; **it was ~d to** + *infin* (*Parl etc*) se acordó + *infin*.

(**b**) (*admit*) reconocer; **I ~ I was too hasty** reconozco que lo hice con precipitación; **I ~ (that) it was foolish** reconozco que era tonto.

(**c**) (*have same opinion*) **everyone ~s it is so** todos están de acuerdo en que es así; **they ~d among themselves to do it** (todos) se pusieron de acuerdo para hacerlo; **it was ~d that** se resolvió que; (*Parl*) se acordó que; **it is ~d that ...** (*legal contracts*) se acuerda que ...; **we ~d to differ** aceptamos (amistosamente) la diferencia de opiniones.

(**d**) *plan, report, statement etc* aceptar, ponerse de acuerdo en, estar de acuerdo con; *price etc* convenir; **the plan was speedily ~d** el proyecto fue aceptado sin demora; **we ~d that yesterday** quedamos en eso ayer; **at a date to be ~d** en una fecha que queda por determinar; **'salary to be ~d'** 'sueldo a convenir'.

2 *vi* (**a**) (*have same opinion*) estar de acuerdo (*with* con, *that* en que); **to ~ with** *plan, policy* aprobar, estar de acuerdo con; **they ~d in finding the film a bore*** convinieron en que la película era una lata*; **I ~** estoy conforme; **I quite ~** estoy completamente de acuerdo; **he's an idiot, don't you ~?** es un imbécil, ¿no crees?; **I don't ~ with women playing football** no apruebo que las mujeres jueguen al fútbol, no acepto el fútbol femenino.

(**b**) (*come to terms*) ponerse de acuerdo (*with* con); consentir, asentir; **eventually he ~d** por fin consintió; **'it's impossible', she ~d** 'es imposible', asintió; **you'll never get him to ~** no lograrás nunca su consentimiento; **to ~ about, to ~ on** convenir en.

(**c**) **to ~ to** *plan, proposal* convenir en, aprobar; **I ~ to your marrying my niece** convengo en que Vd se case con mi sobrina; **he'll ~ to anything** se aviene a todo.

(**d**) (*be in harmony*) concordar, coincidir (*with* con); corresponder (*with* a); **these statements do not ~** estas declaraciones no concuerdan (*with each other* mutuamente); **his reasoning ~s with mine** su razonamiento concuerda con el mío.

(**e**) (*be in harmony: persons*) llevarse bien, entenderse; **we simply don't ~, that's all** es que no existe simpatía entre nosotros, no congeniamos.

(**f**) (*Gram*) concordar (*with* con).

(**g**) (*suit*) sentar bien a; **this heat does not ~ with me** este calor no me sienta bien; **garlic never ~s with me** el ajo nunca me sienta bien.

agreeable [ə'griːəbl] *adj* (**a**) (*pleasing*) agradable; *person* simpático, amable; **is that ~ to everybody?** ¿estamos de acuerdo todos?; **he was more ~ this morning** esta mañana se mostró más simpático. (**b**) (*willing*) **if you are ~** si estás de acuerdo, si quieres; **he was ~ to that** estaba conforme con eso, lo aprobó; **he is ~ to help** está dispuesto a ayudar.

agreeably [ə'grɪəblɪ] *adv* agradablemente.

agreed [ə'griːd] *adj plan etc* convenido; **as ~** según lo convenido; **at the ~ time** a la hora convenida; **~!** ¡de acuerdo!, ¡conforme(s)!

agreement [ə'griːmənt] *n* (**a**) (*treaty etc*) acuerdo *m*, pacto *m*, convenio *m*; (*Comm*) contrato *m*; **~ to differ** desacuerdo *m* amistoso; **by mutual ~** de común acuerdo, por acuerdo mutuo; **to come to** (*or* **reach**) **an ~** ponerse de acuerdo, llegar a un acuerdo; **to enter into an ~** firmar un contrato (*to* + *infin* para + *infin*); *V* **gentleman.**

(**b**) (*harmony*) concordancia *f*; correspondencia *f*; (*between persons*) conformidad *f*, armonía *f*; **in ~ with** de acuerdo con; conforme a; **to be in ~ on a plan** estar conformes en un proyecto; **to be in ~ with** estar de acuerdo con.

(**c**) (*Gram*) concordancia *f*.

agribusiness ['ægrɪˌbɪznɪs] *n* (*esp US*) comercio *m* en productos agrícolas, industria *f* agropecuaria.

agricultural [ˌægrɪ'kʌltʃərəl] *adj* agrícola; agropecuario; **~ college** escuela-granja *f* agrícola, escuela *f* de peritos agrícolas; **~ expert** (perito *m*, -a *f*) agrónomo *m*, -a *f*; **~ show** feria *f* agrícola, feria *f* de campo; **~ subsidy** subvención *f* agrícola.

agriculture ['ægrɪkʌltʃəʳ] *n* agricultura *f*; **Minister/Ministry of A~** (*Brit*), **Secretary/Department of A~** (*US*) Ministro *m*/ Ministerio *m* de Agricultura.

agricultur(al)ist [ˌægrɪˈkʌltʃər(əl)ɪst] *n* (*farmer*) agricultor *m*, -ora *f*; (*professional expert*) (perito *m*, -a *f*) agrónomo *m*, -a *f*.

agrobiologist [ˌægrəʊbaɪˈɒlədʒɪst] *n* agrobiólogo *m*, -a *f*.

agrobiology [ˌægrəʊbaɪˈɒlədʒɪ] *n* agrobiología *f*.

agrochemical [ˌægrəʊˈkemɪkəl] **1** *adj* agroquímico. **2** *n* sustancia *f* agroquímica.

agronomist [əˈgrɒnəmɪst] *n* agrónomo *m*, -a *f*.

agronomy [əˈgrɒnəmɪ] *n* agronomía *f*.

agroproduct [ˌægrəʊˈprɒdʌkt] *n* agroproducto *m*.

aground [əˈgraʊnd] *adv*: **to be ~** estar encallado, estar varado; **to run ~** (*vi*) encallar, varar, embarrancar; **to run a ship ~** varar un barco, hacer que encalle un barco.

agt (*Comm*) *abbr of* **agent** agente *m*.

ague [ˈeɪgjuː] *n* fiebre *f* intermitente.

AH *abbr of* **anno Hegirae**, = *from the year of the Hegira* desde el año de la Hégira, a.h.

ah [ɑː] *excl* ¡ah!

aha [ɑːˈhɑː] *excl* ¡ajá!

ahead [əˈhed] **1** *adv* **(a)** (*in space, order*) delante; **to be ~** estar delante; (*in race*) ir delante, ir ganando, llevar ventaja; **can you see who is ~?** ¿ves quién va al frente?; **straight ~** todo seguido; **full speed ~!** ¡avante todas!*, ¡avante a toda máquina!; **to draw ~, to pull ~** adelantarse (*of* a); **to get ~** (*fig*) adelantar, hacer progresos, abrirse camino; **she's keen to get ~** tiene ganas de ir adelante; **to go ~, to press ~, to push ~** ir adelante (*also fig*); continuar, avanzar; **to go ~ with one's plans** seguir adelante con sus proyectos; **this put Barataria 3 points ~** esto dio a Barataria 3 puntos de ventaja; **to send sb ~** enviar a uno por delante.

(b) (*in time*) hacia delante; **there's trouble ~** han de sobrevenir disgustos; ya se prevén dificultades; **there's a busy time ~** tendremos mucha tarea; **to look ~** tener en cuenta el futuro, mirar el futuro; **to plan ~** hacer proyectos para el futuro; **to think ~** pensar en el futuro.

2 (a) ~ of *prep* (*in space, order*) delante de; **to be ~ of** llevar ventaja a; **to get ~ of sb** adelantarse a uno; **you'll get there ~ of us** llegarás antes de nosotros.

(b) (*in time*) **to arrive ~ of time** llegar antes de la hora prevista; **to be 2 hours ~ of the next competitor** llevar 2 horas de ventaja sobre el rival más próximo; **we are 3 months ~ of schedule** llevamos 3 meses de adelanto sobre la fecha prevista; **to be ~ of one's time** anticiparse a su época; **the plane is ~ of its time** el avión va por delante de su tiempo; **Wagner was 2 centuries ~ of his time** Wagner se anticipó en 2 siglos a su época; **share prices rose ~ of the annual report** la cotización subió en anticipación del informe anual.

ahem [əˈhem] *excl* ¡ejem!

ahoy [əˈhɔɪ] *excl*: **~!, ~ there!** ¡oiga!; **~!** (*Naut*) ¡ah del barco!; **ship ~!** ¡barco a la vista!

AHQ *n abbr of* **Army Headquarters** cuartel *m* general del ejército.

AI *n* **(a)** *abbr of* **Amnesty International** Amnistía *f* Internacional. **(b)** *abbr of* **artificial insemination** inseminación *f* artificial. **(c)** *abbr of* **artificial intelligence** inteligencia *f* artificial, I.A. *f*.

aid [eɪd] **1** *n* **(a)** ayuda *f*, auxilio *m*, socorro *m*; asistencia *f*; **by** (*or* **with**) **the ~ of** con la ayuda de; **in ~ of** (*charity etc*) a beneficio de, pro; **what's all this in ~ of?*** (*Brit*) ¿qué motivo tiene esto?, ¿para qué sirve esto?; ¿a qué viene todo esto?; **to come to the ~ of** acudir en ayuda de, (*in argument*) salir en defensa de; **to give ~** prestar ayuda; **to give medical ~** dar asistencia médica; **to go to the ~ of a sinking ship** ir en auxilio de un barco que se hunde; *V* **economic, mutual** *etc*.

(b) (*person*) asistente *mf*.

(c) (*object*) ayuda *f*.

2 *vt* ayudar, auxiliar, socorrer; **~ed by darkness** al amparo de la noche; *V* **abet**.

A.I.D. *n* **(a)** (*US*) *abbr of* **Agency for International Development** Agencia *f* Internacional para el Desarrollo, AID *f*.

(b) *abbr of* **artificial insemination by donor** inseminación *f* artificial por donante anónimo.

aide [eɪd] *n* (*Mil*) edecán *m*; (*Pol etc*) hombre *m* de confianza.

aide-de-camp [ˌeɪddəˈkɑ̃ːŋ] *n*, *pl* **aides-de-camp** edecán *m*.

aide-mémoire [ˈeɪdmeɪˈmwɑː] *n*, *pl* **aides-mémoire,** *often* **aide-mémoires**, memorándum *m*.

AIDS, Aids [eɪdz] *n abbr of* **acquired immune** *or* **immuno-deficiency syndrome** síndrome *m* de inmuno-deficiencia adquirida, SIDA *m*; **~ campaign** campaña *f* anti-SIDA; **~ clinic** sidatorio *m*; **~ sufferer** sidoso *m*, -a *f*; **~ test** test *m* de SIDA, prueba *f* anti-SIDA; **~ victim** víctima *f* del SIDA.

aid station [ˈeɪdˌsteɪʃən] *n* (*US*) puesto *m* de socorro.

AIH *n abbr of* **artificial insemination by husband** inseminación *f* artificial por donante (esposo).

ail [eɪl] **1** *vt* afligir; **what ~s you?** ¿qué tienes?, ¿qué te pasa? **2** *vi* (*gen* **to be ~ing**) estar enfermo, estar sufriendo.

aileron [ˈeɪlərɒn] *n* alerón *m*.

ailing [ˈeɪlɪŋ] *adj* enfermo, achacoso; *industry etc* decadente, debilitado.

ailment [ˈeɪlmənt] *n* enfermedad *f*, achaque *m*, dolencia *f*.

aim [eɪm] **1** *n* **(a)** (*of weapon*) puntería *f*; **to have a good ~** tener buena puntería; **to miss one's ~** errar el tiro; **to take ~** apuntar (*at* a).

(b) (*fig*) propósito *m*, intención *f*, meta *f*, blanco *m*; **with the ~ of** + *ger* con miras a + *infin*, con la intención de + *infin*; **his one ~ is to** + *infin* su único propósito es de + *infin*; **to have no ~ in life** no saber qué hacer con su vida.

2 *vt gun* apuntar (*at* a); *missile, remark* dirigir (*at* a); *blow* asestar (*at* a); **he ~ed the pistol at me** me apuntó con la pistola.

3 *vi* **(a)** (*with weapon*) apuntar (*at* a).

(b) (*fig*) **to ~ at** apuntar a, aspirar a, pretender, ambicionar; tener la mira puesta en; **what are you ~ing at?** ¿qué intentas?, ¿qué es lo que pretendes?; **to ~ high** picar muy alto; **to ~ to** + *infin* aspirar a + *infin*, pretender + *infin*, tener la intención de + *infin*.

aimless [ˈeɪmlɪs] *adj* sin propósito fijo, sin objeto; *wandering etc* sin rumbo.

aimlessly [ˈeɪmlɪslɪ] *adv* a la ventura; a la buena de Dios; *wander etc* sin rumbo.

aimlessness [ˈeɪmlɪsnɪs] *n* falta *f* de propósito fijo, carencia *f* de objeto.

ain't‡ [eɪnt] = **am not, is not, are not; has not, have not.**

air [ɛəʳ] **1** *n* **(a)** aire *m*; **foul ~** aire *m* viciado; **fresh ~** aire *m* fresco; **he's a breath of fresh ~** es una persona con ideas nuevas; **to get some fresh ~** (salir a) respirar aire limpio; **to let in some fresh ~** airear la atmósfera; (*fig*) aclarar las cosas; **in the open ~** al aire libre; **by ~** en avión; (*Post*) por avión, por vía aérea; **war in the ~** guerra *f* aérea; **spring is in the ~** se presiente ya la llegada de la primavera, corren aires de primavera; **to throw sth into the ~** lanzar algo al aire; **to vanish into thin ~** evaporarse, desaparecer por completo; **one can't live on ~** no se vive de aire solo; **to clear the ~** airear la atmósfera; (*fig*) aclarar las cosas; **to fly through the ~** volar por los aires; **to have a change of ~** mudar de aires; **so we let the ~ out of his tyres** así que desinflamos sus neumáticos; **to take the ~** dar un paseo; **to take to the ~** (*bird*) alzar el vuelo; (*plane*) despegar.

(b) (*further fig phrases*) **to be in the ~** estar en el aire, estar en proyecto; **it's still very much in the ~** está todavía en el aire, queda todavía por resolver; **there's sth in the ~** algo se está tramando; **to give sb the ~** (*US**) despedir a uno, dar calabazas a uno*; **to go up in the ~*** (*angry*) ponerse negro*, subirse por las paredes*, (*excited*) no caber en sí de alegría; **to hang in the ~** estar en el aire, estar pendiente; **to leave sth in the ~** dejar algo en el aire, dejar algo en suspenso; **to walk on ~** no caber en sí de alegría; **it appeared out of thin ~** salió de la nada, apareció de no se sabe dónde; **he produces money out of thin ~** saca dinero de los aires.

(c) (*Rad, TV*) **to be on the ~** estar en el aire, hablar por radio; (*TV*) estar en antena; **we are on the ~ from 6 to 7** emitimos de 6 a 7; **to go on the ~** comenzar la emisión; **to go off the ~** cerrar la emisión; **to go out on the ~** salir al aire; **to put a programme on the ~** emitir un programa.

(d) (*Mus*) aire *m*, tonada *f*.

(e) (*appearance*) aire *m*, aspecto *m*; (*manner, mien*) porte *m*, ademán *m*; **~s and graces** afectación *f*, melindres *mpl*; **with an ~** con toda confianza, con aplomo, con garbo; **with an ~ of surprise** con aire de sorpresa; **he has a distinguished ~, he has an ~ of distinction about him** tiene un no sé qué de distinguido; **to give o.s. ~s, to put on ~s** presumir, darse tono.

2 *attr* aéreo; aeronáutico; atmosférico; **~ attack** ataque *m* aéreo; **~ cargo** carga *f* aérea; **~ carrier** aerolínea *f*; **~ consignment note** talón *m* de expedición por vía aérea; **~ express** (*US*) avión *m* de carga; **~ mass** masa *f* de aire; **~ pollution** contaminación *f* del aire, polución *f* de la atmósfera.

3 *vt* (**a**) *room etc* airear, ventilar; (*fig*) *idea, grievance* airear; **to ~ one's knowledge** lucir sus conocimientos, hacer alarde de sus conocimientos.

(**b**) (*US: Rad, TV*) *programme* emitir, radiar, radiodifundir.

(**c**) (*US: transport*) transportar por avión, aerotransportar.

air-alert ['ɛərə,lɜːt] *n* alerta *f* aérea.

airbag ['ɛəbæg] *n* (*Aut*) bolsa *f* de aire.

airbase ['ɛəbeɪs] *n* base *f* aérea.

airbed ['ɛəbed] *n* (*Brit*) colchón *m* neumático.

air-bladder ['ɛəblædəʳ] *n* (*Zool*) vejiga *f* natatoria.

airborne ['ɛəbɔːn] *adj* (**a**) aerotransportado (*also Mil*); *germ* transmitido por el aire; *seed* llevado por el aire; **~ troops** tropas *fpl* aerotransportadas.

(**b**) **to become ~** elevarse en los aires, subir, **we shall soon be ~** el avión despegará pronto; **suddenly we were ~** de pronto nos vimos en el aire; **we were ~ for 8 hours** volamos durante 8 horas.

airbrake ['ɛəbreɪk] *n* freno *m* neumático; (*Aer*) freno *m* aerodinámico.

airbrick ['ɛəbrɪk] *n* ladrillo *m* ventilador.

airbrush ['ɛəbrʌʃ] *n* aerógrafo *m*.

air-bubble ['ɛə,bʌbl] *n* burbuja *f* de aire.

airbus ['ɛəbʌs] *n* aerobús *m*; **~ service** puente *m* aéreo.

air-chamber ['ɛə,tʃeɪmbəʳ] *n* cámara *f* de aire.

air chief marshal [,ɛətʃiːf'mɑːʃəl] *n* (*Brit*) comandante *m* supremo de las Fuerzas Aéreas.

air commodore [,ɛə'kɒmədɔːʳ] *n* (*Brit*) general *m* de brigada aérea.

air-condition ['ɛəkən,dɪʃən] *vt* climatizar, refrigerar.

air-conditioned ['ɛəkən,dɪʃənd] *adj* climatizado, refrigerado, con aire acondicionado, con clima artificial.

air-conditioner ['ɛəkən,dɪʃənəʳ] *n* aparato *m* acondicionador del aire, acondicionador *m* del aire.

air-conditioning ['ɛəkən,dɪʃənɪŋ] *n* climatización *f*, refrigeración *f* (del aire), acondicionamiento *m* de aire; **cinema with ~** cine *m* climatizado.

air-cooled ['ɛəkuːld] *adj* refrigerado por aire.

air-corridor ['ɛə,kɒrɪdɔːʳ] *n* pasillo *m* aéreo.

air-cover ['ɛəkʌvəʳ] *n* (*Mil*) cobertura *f* aérea.

aircraft ['ɛəkrɑːft] *n* avión *m*; **~ industry** industria *f* aeronáutica.

aircraft-carrier ['ɛəkrɑːft,kærɪəʳ] *n* porta(a)viones *m*.

aircraftman ['ɛəkrɑːftmən] *n, pl* **aircraftmen** ['ɛəkrɑːftmen] (*Brit*) cabo *m* segundo (de las fuerzas aéreas).

aircrew ['ɛəkruː] *n* tripulación *f* de avión.

air-current ['ɛə,kʌrənt] *n* corriente *f* de aire.

air-cushion ['ɛəkʊʃən] *n* cojín *m* de aire, almohada *f* neumática; (*Aer*) colchón *m* de aire.

airdrome ['ɛə,drəʊm] *n* (*US*) aeródromo *m*.

airdrop ['ɛədrɒp] *n* entrega *f* (de víveres *etc*) por paracaídas.

airduct ['ɛədʌkt] *n* tubo *m* de aire; tubo *m* de ventilación.

Airedale ['ɛədeɪl] *n* (*also* **~ dog**) perro *m* Airedale.

air-fare ['ɛəfɛəʳ] *n* precio *m* del billete (por avión); tarifa *f* aérea.

airfield ['ɛəfiːld] *n* campo *m* de aviación, aeródromo *m*.

airflow ['ɛəfləʊ] *n* corriente *f* de aire.

airfoil ['ɛə,fɔɪl] *n* (*US*) = **aerofoil**.

air force ['ɛəfɔːs] *n* aviación *f*, fuerzas *fpl* aéreas; **~ base** (*Mil*) base *f* aérea; **A~ One** (*US*) avión *m* presidencial.

airframe ['ɛəfreɪm] *n* armazón *f* de avión.

air-freight ['ɛəfreɪt] *n* flete *m* por avión; mercancías *fpl* aerotransportadas; **~ terminal** terminal *f* de mercancías.

air-freshener ['ɛəfreʃnəʳ] *n* ambientador *m*.

airgun ['ɛəgʌn] *n* escopeta *f* de aire comprimido.

airhead‡ ['ɛa,hɛd] *n* cabeza *f* de serrín*, chorlito* *m*.

airhole ['ɛəhəʊl] *n* respiradero *m*.

air-hostess ['ɛə,həʊstɪs] *n* (*Brit*) auxiliar *f* de vuelo, azafata *f*, aeromoza *f* (*LAm*).

airily ['ɛərɪlɪ] *adv say etc* muy a la ligera, sin dar importancia a la cosa; (*behave*) de manera confiada, con aire satisfecho.

airiness ['ɛərɪnɪs] *n* (*of room etc*) (buena) ventilación *f*.

airing ['ɛərɪŋ] *n* (**a**) ventilación *f*; (*of clothes*) oreo *m*; **to go for an ~, to take an ~** dar un paseo (para tomar el fresco). (**b**) (*fig*) ventilación *f*; **to give a matter an ~** ventilar un asunto.

airing-cupboard ['ɛərɪŋ,kʌbəd] *n* (*Brit*) *cámara f de aire caliente* (*para secar la ropa*).

air-intake ['ɛər,ɪnteɪk] *n* toma *f* de aire, admisión *f* de aire.

airlane ['ɛəleɪn] *n* vía *f* aérea, pasillo *m* aéreo.

airless ['ɛəlɪs] *adj room* mal ventilado; *day* sin viento; **it's very ~ in here** aquí no hay aire.

airletter ['ɛəletəʳ] *n* carta *f* por correo aéreo, aerograma *m*.

airlift ['ɛəlɪft] **1** *n* puente *m* aéreo. **2** *vt* aerotransportar, transportar por avión.

airline ['ɛəlaɪn] *n* línea *f* aérea, aerolínea *f*, compañía *f* de aviación.

airliner ['ɛəlaɪnəʳ] *n* avión *m* de pasajeros.

airlock ['ɛəlɒk] *n* (*Mech*) esclusa *f* de aire; compartimiento *m* estanco; (*accidental*) bola *f* de aire.

airmail ['ɛəmeɪl] **1** *n* correo *m* aéreo, aeroposta *f* (*LAm*); **by ~** por avión, por vía aérea; **~ edition** edición *f* aérea; **~ letter** carta *f* por correo aéreo, aerograma *m*; **~ paper** papel *m* para avión; **~ stamp** sello *m* para correo aéreo; **~ sticker** etiqueta *f* de correo aéreo.

2 *vt* enviar por avión, enviar por correo aéreo.

3 *as adv*: **to send a letter ~** mandar una carta por avión.

airman ['ɛəmən] *n, pl* **airmen** ['ɛəmen] aviador *m*, piloto *m*.

air marshal ['ɛə'mɑːʃəl] *n* (*Brit*) mariscal *m* de aire.

air-mattress ['ɛə,mætrɪs] *n* colchón *m* neumático.

air-miss [,ɛə'mɪs] *n* incidente *m* aéreo, air-miss *m*, aproximación *f* peligrosa entre dos aviones.

airplane ['ɛəpleɪn] *n* (*US*) avión *m*.

air-pocket ['ɛə,pɒkɪt] *n* bache *m* (aéreo).

airport ['ɛəpɔːt] *n* aeropuerto *m*; **~ taxes** impuestos *mpl* de aeropuerto.

air-power ['ɛə,paʊəʳ] *n* poderío *m* aéreo.

air-pressure ['ɛə,preʃəʳ] *n* presión *f* atmosférica.

airproof ['ɛəpruːf] *adj* hermético.

air-pump ['ɛəpʌmp] *n* bomba *f* de aire.

air-purifier ['ɛə,pjʊərɪfaɪəʳ] *n* purificador *m* de aire.

air-raid ['ɛəreɪd] *n* ataque *m* aéreo; **~ precautions** precauciones *fpl* contra ataques aéreos; **~ shelter** refugio *m* antiaéreo; **~ warden** vigilante *m* contra ataques aéreos; **~ warning** alarma *f* antiaérea.

air-rifle ['ɛəraɪfl] *n* escopeta *f* de aire comprimido.

airscrew ['ɛəskruː] *n* (*Brit*) hélice *f* de avión.

air-sea ['ɛə'siː] *adj*: **~ base** base *f* aeronaval; **~ rescue** rescate *m* aeronaval.

air-shaft ['ɛəʃɑːft] *n* pozo *m* de ventilación.

airship ['ɛəʃɪp] *n* aeronave *f*, dirigible *m*.

air-show ['ɛəʃəʊ] *n* (*commercial*) feria *f* aérea; (*air display*) exhibición *f* aeronáutica.

air-shuttle ['ɛəʃʌtl] *n* puente *m* aéreo.

airsick ['ɛəsɪk] *adj*: **to be ~, to get ~** marearse (en un avión).

airsickness ['ɛəsɪknɪs] *n* mareo *m* (en un avión).

airspace ['ɛəspeɪs] *n* espacio *m* aéreo.

airspeed ['ɛəspiːd] *n* velocidad *f* aérea; **~ indicator** anemómetro *m*.

air-steward ['ɛə,stjʊəd] *n* auxiliar *m* de vuelo.

airstream ['ɛəstriːm] *n* corriente *f* de aire.

airstrike ['ɛəstraɪk] *n* ataque *m* aéreo.

airstrip ['ɛəstrɪp] *n* pista *f* de aterrizaje.

air-suspension [,ɛəsə'spenʃən] *n* (*Aut*) suspensión *f* neumática.

air-taxi ['ɛətæksɪ] *n* aerotaxi *m*.

air terminal ['ɛə,tɜːmɪnl] *n* terminal *f* (de aeropuerto).

airtight ['ɛətaɪt] *adj* hermético, estanco al aire.

airtime ['ɛə,taɪm] *n* (*Rad, TV*) tiempo *m* en antena.

air-to-air ['ɛətə,ɛəʳ] *adj missile* aire-aire.

air-to-sea ['ɛətə,siː] *adj missile* aire-mar.

air-to-surface ['ɛətə,sɜːfɪs] *adj missile* de aire a superficie, aire-tierra.

air-traffic ['ɛətræfɪk] *n* tráfico *m* aéreo; **~ control** control *m* de tráfico aéreo; **~ controller** controlador *m*, -ora *f* de tráfico aéreo.

air-valve ['ɛəvælv] *n* respiradero *m*.

air vent ['ɛəvent] *n* (*in building*) respiradero *m*; (*on dryer*) tobera *f* de aire caliente.

air vice marshal [,ɛəvaɪs'mɑːʃəl] *n* (*Brit*) general *m* de división de las Fuerzas Aéreas.

air-waves ['ɛəweɪvz] *npl* ondas *fpl* hertzianas (*or* radiofónicas).

airway ['ɛəweɪ] *n* (**a**) (*company*) línea *f* aérea, aerolínea *f*. (**b**) (*route*) ruta *f* aérea. (**c**) (*Anat*) vía *f* respiratoria. (**d**) (*Tech*) conducto *m* de ventilación.

air waybill ['ɛəweɪbɪl] *n* hoja *f* de ruta aérea.

airwoman ['ɛə,wʊmən] *n, pl* **airwomen** ['ɛə,wɪmɪn] aviadora *f*.

airworthiness ['ɛə,wɜːðɪnɪs] *n* aeronavegabilidad *f*.

airworthy ['ɛəwɜːðɪ] *adj* en condiciones de vuelo, aeronavegable.

airy ['ɛərɪ] *adj* (**a**) *place* de mucho viento; ventilado; (*large*) amplio, espacioso. (**b**) *cloth etc* ligero, diáfano; (*unsubstantial*) etéreo. (**c**) *step* ligero, alegre; *remark etc* dicho a la ligera, hecho sin dar importancia a la cosa; *behaviour* confiado, satisfecho.

airy-fairy* [ˌɛərɪˈfɛərɪ] *adj* (*Brit*: *light*) superficial; (*fanciful*) tontamente romántico, tontamente idealista; (*insubstantial*) sin sustancia; (*pretentious*) pretencioso, vacío.

aisle [aɪl] *n* nave *f* lateral; pasadizo *m*; (*Theat, also US*) pasillo *m*; **it had them rolling in the ~s*** los hizo desternillarse de risa*; **to lead one's bride up the ~** conducir a su novia al altar.

AISP *n abbr of* **Agricultural Income Subsidies Programme** Programa *m* de Ayudas a la Renta Agraria, PARA *m*.

aitch [eɪtʃ] *n nombre de la* h *inglesa*; **to drop one's ~es** no pronunciar las haches (*indicio clasista o de habla dialectal*).

Aix-la-Chapelle [ˈeɪkslæʃəˈpel] *n* Aquisgrán *m*.

Ajaccio [əˈjætʃɪəʊ] *n* Ajaccio *m*.

ajar [əˈdʒɑː^{r}] *adv* entreabierto, entornado; **to leave the door ~** no cerrar completamente (*Mex*: entrecerrar) la puerta.

Ajax [ˈeɪdʒæks] *nm* Áyax.

AK (*US*) *abbr of* **Alaska.**

a.k.a. *abbr of* **also known as** por otro nombre.

akimbo [əˈkɪmbəʊ] *adv*: **with arms ~** en jarras.

akin [əˈkɪn] *adj* (**a**) (*related by blood*) consanguíneo; **they are not ~** no tienen parentesco consanguíneo. (**b**) (*similar to*) relacionado (*to* con), análogo (*to* a), semejante (*to* a).

AL (*US*) *abbr of* **Alabama.**

ALA *n* (*US*) *abbr of* **American Library Association.**

Ala. (*US*) *abbr of* **Alabama.**

alabaster [ˈæləbɑːstə^{r}] **1** *n* alabastro *m*. **2** *adj* alabastrino.

alabastrine [ˌæləˈbæstraɪn] *adj* alabastrino.

à la carte [ælæˈkɑːt] *adv* a la carta.

alacrity [əˈlækrɪtɪ] *n* prontitud *f*, presteza *f*; **with ~** con la mayor prontitud.

Aladdin [əˈlædɪn] *nm* Aladino; **~'s lamp** lámpara *f* de Aladino.

Alans [ˈælənz] *npl* alanos *mpl*.

Alaric [ˈælərɪk] *nm* Alarico.

alarm [əˈlɑːm] **1** *n* (**a**) (*warning*) alarma *f*; **false ~** falsa alarma *f*; **~ call** voz *f* de alarma; **~ system** sistema *m* de alarma; **~s and excursions** sobresaltos *mpl*; **to give** (*or* **raise, sound**) **the ~** dar la alarma.

(**b**) (*emotion*) alarma *f*, sobresalto *m*; inquietud *f*, temor *m*; **~ and despondency** confusión *f* y desconcierto; **there was general ~** hubo una alarma general; **there was some ~ at this** esto produjo cierta inquietud, esto sobresaltó a la gente; **to cry out in ~** gritar alarmado; **to take ~** alarmarse, sobresaltarse.

(**c**) (*) (*clock*) despertador *m*; (*bell*) timbre *m* del despertador.

2 *vt* alarmar, sobresaltar; inquietar, asustar; **to be ~ed at** alarmarse de; **don't be ~ed** no te asustes, no te inquietes.

alarm-bell [əˈlɑːmbel] *n* timbre *m* de alarma.

alarm-clock [əˈlɑːmklɒk] *n* despertador *m*.

alarmed [əˈlɑːmd] *adj voice etc* sobresaltado, asustado.

alarming [əˈlɑːmɪŋ] *adj* alarmante.

alarmingly [əˈlɑːmɪŋlɪ] *adv* de modo alarmante; **~ high numbers** cifras *fpl* alarmantes.

alarmist [əˈlɑːmɪst] **1** *adj* alarmista, catastrofista. **2** *n* alarmista *mf*, catastrofista *mf*.

alarm-signal [əˈlɑːmˌsɪgnəl] *n* señal *f* de alarma.

alarum [əˈlærəm] *n* (††, *hum*) = **alarm 1.**

alas [əˈlæs] *excl* ¡ay!, ¡ay de mí!; **~, it is not so** desafortunadamente, no es así; **I must tell you, ~, that ...** tengo que decirte, y lo siento, que ...; **I have no money, ~** no tengo dinero, y esto es triste; **~ for Slobodia!** ¡ay de Eslobodia!

Alas. (*US*) *abbr of* **Alaska.**

Alaska [əˈlæskə] *n* Alaska *f*; **~ Highway** carretera *f* de Alaska; **~ Range** Cordillera *f* de Alaska.

Alaskan [əˈlæskən] **1** *adj* de Alaska. **2** *n* nativo *m*, -a *f* (*or* habitante *mf*) de Alaska.

alb [ælb] *n* (*Rel*) alba *f*.

Albania [ælˈbeɪnɪə] *n* Albania *f*.

Albanian [ælˈbeɪnɪən] **1** *adj* albanés. **2** *n* (**a**) albanés *m*, -esa *f*. (**b**) (*Ling*) albanés *m*.

albatross [ˈælbətrɒs] *n* (**a**) (*Orn*) albatros *m*. (**b**) (*Golf*) albatros *m*, menos tres *m*.

albeit [ɔːlˈbiːɪt] *conj* aunque, no obstante (que).

Albert [ˈælbət] *nm* Alberto.

Albigenses [ˌælbɪˈdʒensiːz] *npl* albigenses *mpl*.

Albigensian [ˌælbɪˈdʒensɪən] *adj* albigense.

albinism [ˈælbɪnɪzəm] *n* albinismo *m*.

albino [ælˈbiːnəʊ] **1** *adj* albino. **2** *n* albino *m*, -a *f*.

Albion [ˈælbɪən] *n* Albión *f*.

album [ˈælbəm] *n* álbum *m*.

albumen [ˈælbjʊmɪn] *n* (*Bot*) albumen *m*; (*Chem*) albúmina *f*.

albumin [ˈælbjʊmɪn] *n* albúmina *f*.

albuminous [ælˈbjuːmɪnəs] *adj* albuminoso.

alchemist [ˈælkɪmɪst] *n* alquimista *m*.

alchemy [ˈælkɪmɪ] *n* alquimia *f*.

alcohol [ˈælkəhɒl] *n* alcohol *m*.

alcoholic [ˌælkəˈhɒlɪk] **1** *adj* alcohólico. **2** *n* alcohólico *m*, -a *f*, alcoholizado *m*, -a *f*.

alcoholism [ˈælkəhɒlɪzəm] *n* alcoholismo *m*; **to die of ~** morir alcoholizado.

alcove [ˈælkəʊv] *n* hueco *m*, nicho *m*.

alder [ˈɔːldə^{r}] *n* aliso *m*.

alderman [ˈɔːldəmən] *n*, *pl* **aldermen** [ˈɔːldəmen] concejal *m*, -ala *f* (de categoría superior).

aldosterone [ælˈdɒstəˌrəʊn] *n* aldosterona *f*.

aldrin [ˈɔːldrɪn] *n* aldrina *f*.

ale [eɪl] *n* cerveza *f*.

aleatoric [ˌælɪəˈtɒrɪk] *adj*, **aleatory** [ˈeɪlɪətərɪ] *adj* aleatorio.

Alec [ˈælɪk] *nm familiar form of* **Alexander.**

alert [əˈlɜːt] **1** *adj* alerta (*invariable*: *eg* estaban alerta); vigilante; *character* listo; (*wide-awake*) despierto, despabilado; *expression* vivo.

2 *n* alerta *m*, alarma *f*; **bomb ~** aviso *m* de bomba; **to be on the ~** estar alerta, estar sobre aviso; **to put troops on the ~** poner las tropas sobre aviso.

3 *vt* alertar, poner sobre aviso, avisar; **he ~ed us to the possibility** nos avisó acerca de la posibilidad; **we are now ~ed to the dangers** ahora estamos sobre aviso en cuanto a los peligros.

alertness [əˈlɜːtnɪs] *n* vigilancia *f*; listeza *f*; lo despierto, lo despabilado; viveza *f*.

Aleutian [əˈluːʃən] *adj*: **~ Islands** Islas *fpl* Aleutianas.

Alex [ˈælɪks] *nm familiar form of* **Alexander.**

Alexander [ˌælɪgˈzɑːndə^{r}] *nm* Alejandro; **~ the Great** Alejandro Magno.

Alexandria [ˌælɪgˈzɑːndrɪə] *n* Alejandría *f*.

alexandrine [ˌælɪgˈzændraɪn] *n* alejandrino *m*.

Alf [ælf] *nm familiar form of* **Alfred.**

alfalfa [ælˈfælfə] *n* alfalfa *f*.

Alfred [ˈælfrɪd] *nm* Alfredo.

alfresco [ælˈfreskəʊ] **1** *adv* al aire libre. **2** *adj* de aire libre, al aire libre.

alga [ˈælgə] *n*, *pl* **algae** [ˈældʒɪ] alga *f*.

algebra [ˈældʒɪbrə] *n* álgebra *f*.

algebraic [ˌældʒɪˈbreɪɪk] *adj* algebraico.

Algeria [ælˈdʒɪərɪə] *n* Argelia *f*.

Algerian [ælˈdʒɪərɪən] **1** *adj* argelino. **2** *n* argelino *m*, -a *f*.

algicide [ˈældʒɪsaɪd] *n* algicida *m*.

Algiers [ælˈdʒɪəz] *n* Argel *m*.

algorithm [ˈælgəˌrɪðəm] *n* algoritmo *m*.

algorithmic [ˌælgəˈrɪðmɪk] *adj* algorítmico.

alias [ˈeɪlɪæs] **1** *adv* alias, por otro nombre. **2** *n* alias *m*; nombre *m* ficticio, seudónimo *m*.

alibi [ˈælɪbaɪ] **1** *n* coartada *f*; (*excuse*) excusa *f*, pretexto *m*. **2** *vt*: **to ~ sb** (*US*) proveer de una coartada a uno. **3** *vi* (*US*) buscar excusas (*for doing sth* por haber hecho algo).

Alice [ˈælɪs] *nf* Alicia; **~ in Wonderland** Alicia en el país de las maravillas; **~ through the Looking-Glass** Alicia en el país del espejo.

alien [ˈeɪlɪən] **1** *adj* (**a**) (*strange*) ajeno (*to* a), extraño (*to* a); **~ being** ser *m* extraterrestre. (**b**) (*of foreign country*) extranjero. **2** *n* extranjero *m*, -a *f*; (*fig*) extraño *m*, -a *f*.

alienate [ˈeɪlɪəneɪt] *vt* (**a**) (*Jur*) *property* enajenar, traspasar. (**b**) *friend* indisponerse con, alejar, ofender; apartar; *other people* ganarse la antipatía de; *sympathies* perder, enajenar. (**c**) (*Pol etc*) alienar, enajenar.

alienation [ˌeɪlɪəˈneɪʃən] *n* (**a**) (*Jur*) enajenación *f*, traspaso *m*. (**b**) (*of friend*) alejamiento *m*. (**c**) (*Med*) enajenación *f* mental. (**d**) (*Pol etc*) enajenación *f*, alienación *f*; **feelings of ~** (**from society**) sentimientos *mpl* de enajenación (social).

alienist [ˈeɪljənɪst] *n* (*US*) alienista *mf*.

alight[1] [əˈlaɪt] *adj* (**a**) **to be ~** (*fire*) arder, estar ardiendo, estar quemando; (*light*) estar encendido (*LAm*: prendido); **to keep a fire ~** mantener un fuego ardiendo; **to set ~** pegar fuego a, incendiar. (**b**) **~ with** (*fig*) encendido de, que brilla de.

alight[2] [əˈlaɪt] *vi* bajar, apearse (*from* de); (*from air*) posarse (*on* sobre); (*Aer*) aterrizar.

◆**alight on** *vt fact, idea* caer en la cuenta de, darse cuenta de.

align [ə'laɪn] **1** *vt* alinear. **2** *vr*: **to ~ o.s. with** ponerse al lado de, alinearse con.

alignment [ə'laɪnmənt] *n* alineación *f* (*also fig*); **to be in ~** estar alineados, estar en línea recta; **to be out of ~** estar fuera de alineación.

alike [ə'laɪk] **1** *adj* semejante, parecido, igual; **it's all ~ to me** todo me es igual; **you're all ~!** ¡todos sois iguales!; **to look ~** parecerse; **they all look ~ to me** yo no veo diferencia entre ellos, para mí todos son iguales.

2 *adv* del mismo modo, igualmente; **winter and summer ~** tanto en invierno como en verano, lo mismo en invierno como en verano; **to dress ~** vestir de modo idéntico; **to think ~** pensar del mismo modo.

alimentary [,ælɪ'mentərɪ] *adj* alimenticio; **~ canal, ~ tract** tubo *m* digestivo.

alimony ['ælɪmənɪ] *n* alimentos *mpl*, pensión *f* alimenticia.

alive [ə'laɪv] *adj* (**a**) vivo; **to be ~** estar vivo, vivir; **to be still ~** vivir todavía, estar todavía con vida; **~ and kicking** vivito y coleando; **dead or ~** vivo o muerto; **man ~!** (*excl*) ¡hombre!; **while ~ he did no harm** en vida no hizo daño a nadie; **he's the best footballer ~** es el mejor futbolista del mundo; **no man ~ could do better** no lo podría hacer mejor nadie; **she plays as well as any pianist ~** toca tan bien como cualquier pianista del mundo; **it's good to be ~!** ¡qué bueno es vivir!; **the scene came ~ as she described it** la escena se animaba (*or* vivificaba) al describirla ella; **to be buried ~** ser enterrado vivo; **to burn sb ~** quemar a uno vivo; **to bring a story ~** animar una narración; **to keep sb ~** conservar a uno con vida; **to keep a tradition ~** conservar una tradición; **to keep a memory ~** guardar fresco un recuerdo, hacer perdurar una memoria; **he managed to stay ~ on fruit** logró sobrevivir comiendo frutas.

(**b**) **~ with** (*insects etc*) lleno de, hormigueante en, rebosante de; **a book ~ with interest** un libro lleno de interés.

(**c**) (*fig*) activo, enérgico; **look ~!** ¡menearse!, ¡apúrate! (*LAm*).

(**d**) (*fig*) **~ to** sensible a, consciente de; **I am ~ to the danger** estoy consciente del peligro, me doy cuenta del peligro; **I am fully ~ to the fact that ...** no se me escapa que ..., no ignoro que ...; **I am fully ~ to the honour you do me** soy plenamente consciente del honor que se me hace.

alkali ['ælkəlaɪ] *n* álcali *m*.

alkaline ['ælkəlaɪn] *adj* alcalino.

alkalinity [,ælkə'lɪnɪtɪ] *n* alcalinidad *f*.

alkaloid ['ælkəlɔɪd] **1** *adj* alcaloideo. **2** *n* alcaloide *m*.

all [ɔːl] **1** *adj* (*sing*) todo, (*pl*) todos; **~ day** todo el día; **~ the time** todo el tiempo; **is that ~ the time it is!** ¡es ésa la hora tan sólo!; **~ (the) women** todas las mujeres; **~ Spain** toda España; **with ~ due speed** con toda prontitud; **books of ~ kinds** libros de todo tipo, libros de todos los tipos; **~ four of them were there** los cuatro estaban todos; **they chose him, of ~ people** le eligieron a él, como si no hubiera otros; **to choose this of ~ cars!** ¡elegir éste entre tantísimos coches!; **it's ~ done** todo está hecho; **he ate it ~** se lo comió todo; **and ~ that** y cosas así, y otras cosas por el estilo; **with bands and banners and ~ that** con bandas y banderas y qué sé yo qué más; **it's not as bad as ~ that** no es para tanto; **for ~ that** con todo, así y todo; **on ~ fours** a cuatro patas.

2 *pron* (**a**) (*sing*) todo *m*; **~ or nothing** todo o nada; **~ (that) I can tell you is ...** lo único que puedo decirte es ...; **~ is lost, it's ~ up** se acabó; **it's ~ up with him** no hay remedio para él; **that's ~** eso es todo, nada más; **is that ~?** ¿eso es todo?, ¿nada más?; **it cost him ~ of 50 dollars** le costó 50 dólares largos; **what with the rain and ~** con la lluvia y todo; **it was ~ I could do not to laugh** apenas pude contener la risa; **I did ~ that I could to stop him** hice lo posible para impedirle; **when ~ is said and done** en fin de cuentas.

(**b**) (*pl*) todos *mpl*, todas *fpl*; **~ of us** todos nosotros, nosotros todos; **~ of the women** todas las mujeres; **we are ~ going** vamos todos; **they were ~ present** todos estaban presentes.

(**c**) (*phrases with prep*) **above ~** sobre todo; **after ~** con todo, después de todo; al fin y al cabo; **did you speak at ~?** ¿dijiste algo?; **if I go at ~** si es que voy; **if it's at ~ possible** si hay la menor posibilidad; **not at ~** de ninguna manera, nada de eso; **not at ~!** (*answer to thanks*) ¡de nada!, ¡no hay de qué!; **not at ~ nice** nada agradable; **I'm not at ~ tired** no estoy cansado en lo más mínimo; **if she can sing at ~** si sabe cantar de alguna manera; **it rarely rains here if at ~** aquí llueve rara vez o nunca; **you mean she didn't sing at ~?** ¿quieres decir que no cantó siquiera?; **I don't know him at ~** no le conozco en absoluto; **for ~ I know** que yo sepa, quizá; **for ~ his boasting** a pesar de toda su jactancia; **50 men in ~** 50 hombres en total; **~ in ~** con todo, en resumen; **most of ~** más que nada, sobre todo; *V* **best, once** *etc*.

3 *n*: **my ~** todo lo que tengo, todo lo que es mío; **I would give my ~ to see it back** daría todo lo que tengo a cambio de verlo aquí; **to stake one's ~** arriesgar el todo por el todo.

4 *adv* (**a**) (*entirely*) completamente, enteramente, del todo; **dressed ~ in black** vestido enteramente de negro; **it's ~ dirty** está todo sucio; **~ along the street** todo a lo largo de la calle, por toda la calle; **~ of a sudden** de repente; **the time went ~ too quickly** pasó el tiempo demasiado rápidamente; **it's ~ too true** por desgracia es la misma verdad; **~ but** casi; **he ~ but died** casi murió, por poco se nos murió; **it's ~ but impossible** es casi imposible; **~ but 7** todos menos 7; *V* **over, same,** *etc*.

(**b**) (*in comparisons*) *V* **better, more.**

(**c**) (*in games*) **to draw 2-~** empatar a 2; **the score stands at 3-~** están empatados a 3 (goles), el marcador está a 3-3.

all- [ɔːl] *pref*: **~American** todo americano, típicamente americano, americano cien por cien; **~leather** todo cuero; **with an ~Chinese cast** con un reparto totalmente chino; **there will be an ~Spanish final** en la final figurarán únicamente españoles; **it's an ~woman show** es un espectáculo enteramente femenino.

Allah ['ælə] *nm* Alá.

all-around ['ɔːlə'raʊnd] *adj* (*US*) = **all-round.**

allay [ə'leɪ] *vt pain* aliviar; *fears, suspicion* aquietar, disipar.

all clear ['ɔːl'klɪə] *n* (*also* **~ signal**) cese *m* (*or* fin *m*) de alarma; (*fig*) visto *m* bueno, luz *f* verde; **~!** ¡fin del alerta!

allegation [,æle'geɪʃən] *n* aseveración *f*, aserto *m*; alegato *m*; acusación *f*.

allege [ə'ledʒ] *vt* declarar, afirmar, pretender (*that* que); (*with n*) alegar, pretextar; **he is ~d to be wealthy** se pretende que es rico; **he is ~d to be the leader** se dice que él es el jefe; **he absented himself alleging illness** se ausentó pretextando una enfermedad.

alleged [ə'ledʒd] *adj* supuesto, pretendido; presunto.

allegedly [ə'ledʒɪdlɪ] *adv* supuestamente, según se afirma.

allegiance [ə'liːdʒəns] *n* lealtad *f*; fidelidad *f*; **to owe ~ to** deber lealtad a; **to swear ~ to** jurar su lealtad a; **oath of ~** (*Brit*) juramento *m* de fidelidad.

allegoric(al) [,ælɪ'gɒrɪk(əl)] *adj* alegórico.

allegorically [,ælɪ'gɒrɪkəlɪ] *adv* alegóricamente.

allegorize ['ælɪgəraɪz] *vt* alegorizar.

allegory ['ælɪgərɪ] *n* alegoría *f*.

allegro [ə'legrəʊ] *n* alegro *m*.

alleluia [,ælɪ'luːjə] *n* aleluya *f*.

all-embracing ['ɔːlɪm'breɪsɪŋ] *adj* comprensivo, universal, global, general.

allergenic ['ælə,dʒenɪk] *adj* alergénico.

allergic [ə'lɜːdʒɪk] *adj* alérgico (*to* a); **to be ~ to** tener alergia a.

allergist ['ælədʒɪst] *n* alergista *mf*, alergólogo *m*, -a *f*.

allergy ['ælədʒɪ] *n* alergia *f* (*to* a); **~ clinic** clínica *f* de alergias; **total ~ syndrome** síndrome *m* de alergia total.

alleviate [ə'liːvɪeɪt] *vt* aliviar, mitigar.

alleviation [ə,liːvɪ'eɪʃən] *n* alivio *m*, mitigación *f*.

alley ['ælɪ] *n* callejuela *f*, callejón *m*; (*in park*) paseo *m*; (*Sport*) bolera *f*; **~ cat** gato *m* callejero, gata *f* callejera (*also *fig*); *V* **blind.**

alleyway ['ælɪweɪ] *n* = **alley.**

all-fired* ['ɔːlfaɪərd] (*US*) **1** *adj* excesivo; extremado; **in an ~ hurry** con muchísima prisa. **2** *adv* a más no poder.

All Fools' Day ['ɔːl'fuːlzdeɪ] *n* día *m* de inocentes (*en Inglaterra el 1 abril, en España el 28 diciembre*).

All Hallows' (Day) ['ɔːl'hæləʊz(deɪ)] *n* Día *m* de Todos los Santos (*1 noviembre*).

alliance [ə'laɪəns] *n* alianza *f*; **to enter into an ~ with** aliarse con.

allied ['ælaɪd] *adj* (**a**) (*Mil, Pol*) aliado; **the ~ nations** las naciones aliadas. (**b**) (*similar*) afín, conexo, parecido; **languages and ~ subjects** los idiomas y temas afines; **and other subjects ~ to this** y otros temas relacionados con éste.

alligator ['ælɪgeɪtə^r^] *n* caimán *m*.

all-important ['ɔːlɪm'pɔːtənt] *adj* sumamente importante, importantísimo.

all-in ['ɔːlɪn] *adj* (*Brit*) *sum, figure* global; *charge* todo incluido; *insurance policy* contra todo riesgo; ~ **wrestling** lucha *f* libre.
all-inclusive ['ɔːlɪn'kluːsiv] *adj* todo incluido; global; ~ **insurance policy** póliza *f* de seguro completa.
alliteration [əˌlɪtə'reɪʃən] *n* aliteración *f*.
alliterative [ə'lɪtərətɪv] *adj* aliterado.
all-metal ['ɔːl'metl] *adj* enteramente metálico.
all-night ['ɔːl'naɪt] *adj café, garage, etc* (que está) abierto toda la noche; *journey, party, vigil* que dura toda la noche; ~ **pass** (*Mil*) permiso *m* de pernocta; ~ **service** servicio *m* nocturno, servicio *m* que funciona toda la noche; ~ **showing** (*Cine*) sesión *f* continua nocturna.
allocate ['æləʊkeɪt] *vt* (**a**) (*allot*) asignar, señalar (*to* a). (**b**) (*apportion*) repartir, distribuir.
allocation [ˌæləʊ'keɪʃən] *n* (**a**) (*act: allotting*) asignación *f* (*also Comput*). (**b**) (*act: apportioning*) reparto *m*; distribución *f*. (**c**) (*share, amount*) ración *f*, cupo *m*, cuota *f*.
allomorph ['æləʊmɔːf] *n* alomorfo *m*.
allopathic [ˌæləʊ'pæθɪk] *adj* alopático.
allophone ['æləʊfəʊn] *n* alófono *m*.
allot [ə'lɒt] *vt* (**a**) (*assign*) asignar, adjudicar, dar, destinar (*to* a); **the space ~ted to each contributor** el espacio asignado a cada colaborador; **we finished in the time ~ted** hemos terminado en el tiempo previsto; **to ~ funds for a purpose** asignar (*or* destinar) fondos para un propósito; **he was ~ted the role of villain** le dieron el papel de malo. (**b**) (*share out*) repartir, distribuir.
allotment [ə'lɒtmənt] *n* (**a**) (*act*) asignación *f*; reparto *m*, distribución *f*. (**b**) (*share*) ración *f*, porción *f*, cuota *f*. (**c**) (*Brit: land*) parcela *f* (alquilada para el cultivo); ≈ huerto *m*.
all-out ['ɔːl'aʊt] **1** *adj supporter* acérrimo, incondicional; *effort* máximo, supremo; **to make an ~ attack on a problem** atacar un problema de frente; ~ **effort** esfuerzo *m* máximo; ~ **strike** huelga *f* general; ~ **war** guerra *f* total.
2 *adv* con todas sus fuerzas; a fondo; (*of speed*) a máxima velocidad; **to go ~** tirar la casa por la ventana; (*Sport*) emplearse a fondo; **to go ~ for the prize** volcarse por conseguir el premio; **we must go ~ to ensure it** hemos de desplegar todas nuestras fuerzas para asegurarlo.
all-over ['ɔːl'əʊvəʳ] **1** *adj* que tiene un diseño repetido sobre toda la superficie.
2 *n* (tela *f* con) diseño *m* repetido sobre toda la superficie.
allow [ə'laʊ] **1** *vt* (**a**) (*with n object*) permitir; (*grant*) dar, conceder, asignar; *discount* aplicar, dar; *allowance* pagar, dar; **you should ~ more space** conviene dejar más espacio; **~ yourself 3 hours for the journey** cuenta con 3 horas para el viaje; **~ 5 cm for shrinkage** tener en cuenta 5 cm perdidos por encogimiento; **how much should I ~ for expenses?** ¿cuánto debo prever para los gastos?; **it ~s very little time for meals** deja muy poco tiempo para comer; **the judge ~ed him £1000 costs** el juez le asignó 1000 libras en concepto de costas; **~ me!** ¡permítame!
(**b**) (*permit*) **to ~ sb to** + *infin* permitir a uno + *infin*, dejar a uno + *infin*, permitir que uno + *subj*; **smoking is not ~ed here** aquí no se permite fumar; **'no dogs ~ed'** 'se prohíbe dejar entrar a los perros'.
(**c**) *claim, request* admitir, aceptar; **to ~ that ...** reconocer que ..., confesar que ...; **he is ~ed to be strong** se reconoce que es fuerte; **even ~ing that to be so** aun admitiendo eso.
2 *vr*: **to ~ o.s. to be persuaded** dejarse persuadir; **she finally ~ed herself to say that ...** por fin se permitió decir que ...
◆**allow for** *vt* tener en cuenta, tomar en consideración; prever; **after ~ing for his costs** cuenta habida de sus gastos; **we should ~ for all possibilities** debemos tener presentes todas las posibilidades.
◆**allow in** *vt*: **to ~ sb in** dejar entrar a uno, permitir que uno entre.
◆**allow of** *vt* permitir; admitir; **the situation ~s of no delay** la situación no permite demora; **this ~s of no excuse** esto no admite disculpa.
◆**allow out** *vt*: **to ~ sb out** permitir que uno salga.
allowable [ə'laʊəbl] *adj* permisible; admisible; tolerable; lícito; *expense* deducible; ~ **against tax** desgravable.
allowance [ə'laʊəns] *n* (**a**) (*money etc assigned*) subsidio *m*, subvención *f*, pago *m*; paga *f*; pensión *f*; (*food*) ración *f*; (*esp US: pocket money*) dinero *m* de bolsillo; (*subsistence* ~) dietas *fpl*; **he has an ~ of £100 a month** tiene una subvención de 100 libras mensuales; **he makes his mother an ~** le concede una pensión a su madre.
(**b**) (*Comm, Fin: discount*) descuento *m*, rebaja *f*; **tax ~** desgravación *f* fiscal.
(**c**) (*concession*) concesión *f*; **one must make ~s** hay que hacer concesiones; hay que ser indulgente (*for him* con él); **to make ~s for the weather** tener en cuenta el tiempo.
(**d**) (*Mech*) tolerancia *f*.
(**e**) (*volume, weight*) margen *m*.
alloy[1] ['ælɔɪ] *n* aleación *f*, liga *f*; (*fig*) mezcla *f*; ~ **wheels** llantas *fpl* de aleación.
alloy[2] [ə'lɔɪ] *vt* alear, ligar.
all-pervading [ˌɔːlpə'veɪdɪŋ] *adj*, **all-pervasive** [ˌɔːlpə'veɪsɪv] *adj* omnipresente.
all-powerful ['ɔːl'paʊəfʊl] *adj* omnipotente, todopoderoso.
all-purpose ['ɔːl'pɜːpəs] *adj* universal, para todo uso, de uso múltiple.
all right [ˌɔːl'raɪt] **1** *adj* (**a**) (*satisfactory*) **it's ~** todo está bien, todo va bien; **yes, that's ~** sí, de acuerdo; sí, vale; **it's ~ with me** yo, de acuerdo; **it's ~ for you** no tienes de qué quejarte, tú no tienes problemas; **it's ~ for you to smile** tú bien puedes sonreír; **it will be ~ on the night** todo estará listo para el estreno; **I made it ~ with the cabby** lo arreglé con el taxista; **is it ~ for me to smoke?** ¿puedo fumar?; **is he ~ with the girls?** ¿se comporta bien con las chicas?; **is it ~ for me to take the dog?** ¿se me permite llevar al perro?; **are you ~ for Tuesday?** ¿estás libre (*or* podrás jugar, podrás venir, *etc*) el martes?; **he's ~ as a goalkeeper (but a lousy forward)** como portero vale (pero como delantero es un desastre); **well, he's ~** (*doubtful*) bueno, es regular; **let me tell you, our Joe is ~!*** ¡te digo que Pepe es tremendo!*; **she's a bit of ~‡** está buenísima‡.
(**b**) (*safe, well*) **she's ~ again now** está mejor, se ha repuesto ya; **it's ~, you can come out now** está bien, puedes salir ya.
(**c**) (*prosperous*) **we're ~ for the rest of our lives** no tendremos problema económico en el resto de la vida; **are you ~ for cigarettes?** ¿tienes buena cantidad de tabaco?
2 *adv*: **I can see ~, thanks** veo bien, gracias; **you'll get your money back ~** se te devolverá el dinero, eso es seguro; **he complained ~!** ¡ya lo creo que se quejó!; **'You say I was wrong. A~, but ...'** 'Dices que me equivoqué. Bien, pero ...'
3 *excl* (*approval*) ¡bueno!, ¡muy bien!; (*agreement*) ¡de acuerdo!; (*that's enough*) ¡basta ya!; (*exasperation*) ¡se acabó!
all-risks ['ɔːl'rɪsks] *attr*: ~ **insurance** seguro *m* contra todo riesgo.
all-round ['ɔːl'raʊnd] *adj success etc* completo; *improvement* general, en todos los aspectos; *view* amplio; *person* que hace de todo, hábil para todo, con talentos para todo.
all-rounder ['ɔːl'raʊndəʳ] *n* persona *f* (*esp* jugador *m*, -ora *f*) que hace de todo.
All Saints' Day ['ɔːl'seɪntsdeɪ] *n* Día *m* de Todos los Santos (*1 noviembre*).
All Souls' Day ['ɔːl'səʊlzdeɪ] *n* Día *m* de (los) Difuntos (*2 noviembre*).
allspice ['ɔːlspaɪs] *n* pimienta *f* inglesa, pimienta *f* de Jamaica.
all-star ['ɔːl'stɑː] *adj cast* todo estelar; ~ **performance, show with an ~ cast** función *f* de primeras figuras, función *f* estelar.
all-terrain vehicle [ˌɔːltəˌreɪn'viːɪkl] *n* vehículo *m* todo terreno.
all-the-year-round [ˌɔːlðəˌjɪə'raʊnd] *adj sport* que se practica todo el año; *resort* abierto todo el año.
all-time ['ɔːl'taɪm] *adj* sin precedentes, inaudito, nunca visto; **an ~ record** un récord nunca igualado; **exports have reached an ~ high** las exportaciones han alcanzado cifras nunca conocidas antes; **the pound is at an ~ low** la libra ha caído a su punto más bajo.
allude [ə'luːd] *vi*: **to ~ to** referirse a, aludir a.
allure [ə'ljʊəʳ] **1** *n* atractivo *m*, encanto *m*, fascinación *f*; aliciente *m*. **2** *vt* atraer, captarse la voluntad de, tentar; fascinar.
alluring [ə'ljʊərɪŋ] *adj* atractivo, seductor, tentador; fascinante.
allusion [ə'luːʒən] *n* alusión *f*, referencia *f* (*to* a); **he said in ~ to** dijo refiriéndose a.
allusive [ə'luːsɪv] *adj* (**a**) alusivo, referente (*to* a). (**b**) *style* lleno de alusiones.
alluvial [ə'luːvɪəl] *adj* aluvial.
alluvium [ə'luːvɪəm] *n* aluvión *m*, depósito *m* aluvial.
all-weather ['ɔːl'weðəʳ] *adj* para todo tiempo.
ally[1] **1** ['ælaɪ] *n* aliado *m*; **the Allies** los Aliados. **2** [ə'laɪ] *vr*:

to ~ o.s. to (*or* **with**) aliarse con; (*by marriage*) emparentar con.
ally² ['ælɪ] *n* bolita *f*, canica *f*.
alma mater ['ælmə'meɪtəʳ] *n* alma máter *f*.
almanac ['ɔːlmənæk] *n* almanaque *m*.
almighty [ɔːl'maɪtɪ] **1** *adj* (**a**) omnipotente, todopoderoso; **A~ God, God A~** Dios Todopoderoso.
(**b**) (*) terrible, imponente, enorme de grande*; **they made an ~ fuss** armaron un tremendo lío*; **he really is an ~ idiot** realmente es un terrible idiota; **I foresee ~ problems** preveo unos enormes problemas.
2 *n*: **the A~** el Todopoderoso.
3 *adv* (*) terriblemente, la mar de*; **an ~ loud bang** un estallido terriblemente fuerte; **that was ~ silly of you** en eso has sido la mar de tonto*.
almond ['ɑːmənd] **1** *n* (*fruit*) almendra *f*; (*tree*) almendro *m*; *V* **sugar**.
2 *attr* de almendra(s); **an ~ taste** un sabor a almendra.
almond-eyed ['ɑːmənd'aɪd] *adj* de ojos almendrados.
almond oil ['ɑːmənd,ɔɪl] *n* aceite *m* de almendra.
almond-shaped ['ɑːmənd,ʃeɪpt] *adj* almendrado.
almond tree ['ɑːməndtriː] *n* almendro *m*.
almoner ['ɑːmənəʳ] *n* (*Hist*) limosnero *m*; (*Brit Med*) oficial *mf* de asistencia social (adscrito a un hospital).
almost ['ɔːlməʊst] *adv* casi; **an ~ complete failure** un fracaso casi total; **we're ~ there** ya estamos al llegar, nos falta poco para llegar; **he ~ died on us** casi se nos murió, por poco se nos murió.
alms [ɑːmz] *n sing and pl* limosna *f*.
almsbox ['ɑːmzbɒks] *n* cepillo *m* para los pobres.
almshouse ['ɑːmzhaʊs] *n*, *pl* **almshouses** ['ɑːmz,haʊzɪz] hospicio *m*, asilo *m* para los pobres; casa *f* de beneficencia.
aloe ['æləʊ] *n* áloe *m*; **~s** (*juice*) acíbar *m*.
aloft [ə'lɒft] *adv* (*also* **up ~**) arriba, en lo alto; en vuelo; (*Naut*) en la arboladura.
alone [ə'ləʊn] **1** *adj* (**a**) solo; **to be ~** estar solo, estar a solas; **to be all** (*or* **quite**) **~** estar completamente solo; **am I ~ in thinking so?** ¿soy yo el único en pensar así?; **to go it ~** hacerlo solo, hacerlo sin ayuda de nadie.
(**b**) **to leave sb ~** dejar a uno solo; **we must not leave them ~ together** no hay que dejarlos solos; **to leave** (*or* **let**) **sb ~** (*fig*) no molestar a uno, dejar de molestar a uno, dejar a uno tranquilo; **leave me ~!** ¡déjame en paz!, ¡déjame estar! (*LAm*); **to leave** (*or* **let**) **sth ~** no tocar algo; **leave it ~!** ¡déjalo!, ¡no toques!; **just leave the plant ~ so that it will grow** deja la planta sin tocar para que crezca; **I advise you to leave that severely ~** te aconsejo no meterte de ninguna manera en eso.
(**c**) **let ~** (*as prep etc*) sin mencionar, sin tomar en cuenta; y no digamos; **he can't read, let ~ write** nada de escribir, no sabe leer siquiera; **one can't get into Slobodia, let ~ Ruritania** no se puede entrar en Eslobodia, ni menos en Ruritania.
2 *adv* solamente, sólo, únicamente; **it is mine ~** es todo mío; **a charm which is hers ~** un encanto que es únicamente suyo; **man cannot live by bread ~** no sólo de pan vive el hombre; **you ~ can do it** sólo tú puedes hacerlo.
along [ə'lɒŋ] **1** *adv*: **all ~** desde el principio, todo el tiempo; **~ with** junto con; **I'll be ~ in a moment** ahora voy; **she'll be ~ tomorrow** vendrá mañana; *V* **come** *etc*.
2 *prep* a lo largo de; por; **~ the river** a lo largo del río; **all ~ the street** todo lo largo de la calle; **we went ~ the tunnel** pasamos por el túnel; **it's ~ here** es por aquí; **somewhere ~ the way it fell off** en alguna parte del camino se cayó; **please sign ~ this line** por favor firme en este renglón; **we acted ~ the lines suggested** hemos obrado de acuerdo con las indicaciones que nos hicieron.
alongside [ə'lɒŋ'saɪd] **1** *adv* (*Naut*) al costado, costado con costado; **to bring a ship ~** acostar un buque; **to come ~** atracarse al costado.
2 *prep* junto a, al lado de; (*Naut*) al costado de; **to come ~ a ship** atracarse al costado de un buque; **the car stopped ~ me** el coche se paró a mi lado; **there's a stream ~ the garden** hay un arroyo al lado del jardín; **they have to work ~ each other** tienen que trabajar juntos; **how can these systems work ~ each other?** ¿cómo estos sistemas pueden funcionar en colaboración?
aloof [ə'luːf] **1** *adj character* reservado, frío; **he was very ~ with me** conmigo se mostró muy reservado; **she has always been somewhat ~** ella siempre ha guardado las distancias.
2 *adv*: **to keep ~, stand ~** mantenerse a distancia, mantenerse apartado (*from* de), guardar las distancias.
aloofness [ə'luːfnɪs] *n* reserva *f*, frialdad *f*.
alopecia [,æləʊ'piːʃə] *n* alopecia *f*.
aloud [ə'laʊd] *adv* en voz alta, alto.
alpaca [æl'pækə] *n* alpaca *f*.
alpenhorn ['ælpənhɔːn] *n* trompa *f* de los Alpes.
alpenstock ['ælpɪnstɒk] *n* alpenstock *m*, bastón *m* montañero.
alpha ['ælfə] *n* alfa *f*; (*Brit*: *Scol, Univ*) sobresaliente *m*; **~ particle** partícula *f* alfa.
alphabet ['ælfəbet] *n* alfabeto *m*.
alphabetic(al) [,ælfə'betɪk(əl)] *adj* alfabético.
alphabetically [,ælfə'betɪkəlɪ] *adv* alfabéticamente, en (*or* por) orden alfabético.
alphabetize ['ælfəbətaɪz] *vt* alfabetizar, poner en orden alfabético.
alphanumeric [,ælfənjuː'merɪk] *adj* alfanumérico; **~ character** carácter *m* alfanumérico; **~ field** campo *m* alfanumérico.
Alphonso [æl'fɒnsəʊ] *nm* Alfonso.
alpine ['ælpaɪn] **1** *adj* alpino, alpestre. **2** *n* planta *f* alpestre.
alpinist ['ælpɪnɪst] *n* alpinista *mf*.
Alps [ælps] *npl* Alpes *mpl*.
already [ɔːl'redɪ] *adv* ya; **that's enough ~!** (*US**) ¡basta!, ¡vale ya!, ¡ya está bien!
alright* [,ɔːl'raɪt] = **all right**.
Alsace ['ælsæs] *n* Alsacia *f*.
Alsace-Lorraine ['ælsæslə'reɪn] *n* Alsacia-Lorena *f*.
Alsatian [æl'seɪʃən] **1** *adj* alsaciano. **2** *n* alsaciano *m*, -a *f*; (*Brit*: *dog*) perro *m* lobo, (perro *m*) pastor *m* alemán.
also ['ɔːlsəʊ] *adv* también, además.
also-ran ['ɔːlsəʊræn] *n* (**a**) (*Sport*) caballo *m* (*or* competidor *m etc*) que no logra colocarse. (**b**) (*: *person*) fracasado *m*, -a *f*, cero *m* a la izquierda, perdedor *m*.
alt. *abbr of* **altitude** altura *f*.
Alta. (*Canada*) *abbr of* **Alberta**.
Altamira [,æltə'miːrə] *n*: **the ~ caves** las cuevas de Altamira.
altar ['ɒltəʳ] *n* altar *m*; (*pagan*) ara *f*; **high ~** altar *m* mayor; **to lead a girl to the ~** conducir a su novia al altar; **he sacrificed all on the ~s of his ambition** lo sacrificó todo en aras de su ambición.
altar-boy ['ɒltəbɔɪ] *n* acólito *m*, monaguillo *m*.
altar-cloth ['ɒltəklɒθ] *n* sabanilla *f*, paño *m* de altar.
altarpiece ['ɒltəpiːs] *n* retablo *m*.
altar-rail ['ɔːltə,reɪl] *n* comulgatorio *m*.
alter ['ɒltəʳ] **1** *vt* (**a**) (*change*) cambiar, modificar, (*esp for the worse*) alterar; *painting, speech etc* retocar; (*Archit*) reformar; *opinion, course etc* cambiar de; **then that ~s things** entonces la cosa cambia; **it has ~ed things for the better** ha mejorado las cosas, ha cambiado las cosas en sentido positivo; **circumstances ~ cases** el caso depende de las circunstancias; **I see no need to ~ my view** no veo ninguna necesidad de cambiar mi opinión.
(**b**) (*falsify*) *evidence etc* falsificar; *text* alterar.
(**c**) (*US*: *castrate*) castrar.
2 *vi* cambiar(se), mudarse; **I find him much ~ed** le veo muy cambiado; **to ~ for the better** mejorar, cambiarse en sentido positivo; **to ~ for the worse** empeorar, cambiarse en sentido negativo.
alteration [,ɒltə'reɪʃən] *n* cambio *m*, modificación *f*, (*esp for the worse*) alteración *f* (*in, to* de); **~s** (*Archit*) reformas *fpl*; (*to text, painting, speech etc*) retoques *mpl*; (*Sew*) arreglo *m* (*to* de).
altercation [,ɒltə'keɪʃən] *n* altercado *m*.
alter ego ['æltər'iːgəʊ] *n* álter ego *m*.
alternate 1 [ɒl'tɜːnɪt] *adj* (**a**) (*Bot, Math, Tech etc*) alterno; *movement* alternativo.
(**b**) (*every second*) alterno; **on ~ days** un día sí y otro no, cada dos días, los días alternos.
(**c**) (*US*) = **alternative**.
2 [ɒl'tɜːnit] *n* (*US*) suplente *mf*.
3 ['ɒltɜːneɪt] *vti* alternar.
alternately [ɒl'tɜːnɪtlɪ] *adv* alternativamente; por turno.
alternating ['ɒltɜːneɪtɪŋ] *adj* alterno; **~ current** corriente *f* alterna.
alternation [,ɒltɜː'neɪʃən] *n* alternación *f*; **in ~** alternativamente.
alternative [ɒl'tɜːnətɪv] **1** *adj* alternativo; otro; **the only ~ system** el único otro sistema; **have you any ~ candidate?** ¿no tienes otro candidato?; **~ energy** energías *fpl* alternativas; **~ medicine** medicina *f* alternativa; **the ~ society** la sociedad alternativa.
2 *n* alternativa *f*; posibilidad *f*; **I have no ~** no tengo

más remedio, no puedo hacer otra cosa; no me queda otra (*LAm*); **you have no ~ but to go** no tienes más remedio que ir; **what ~s are there?** ¿qué opciones hay?; **she chose the first ~** optó por la primera alternativa.

alternatively [ɒl'tɜːnətɪvlɪ] *adv* por otra parte, en cambio; si no ...; otra solución sería ...

alternator ['ɒltɜːneɪtə^r] *n* (*Brit*) alternador *m*.

although [ɔːl'ðəʊ] *conj* aunque; si bien; a pesar de que.

altimeter ['æltɪmiːtə^r] *n* altímetro *m*.

altitude ['æltɪtjuːd] *n* altura *f*, altitud *f*; **at these ~s** en estas alturas; **~ sickness** mal *m* de altura, soroche *m* (*LAm*).

alto ['æltəʊ] **1** *adj* alto; **~ saxophone** saxofón *m* alto; **to sing the ~ part** cantar la parte de contralto. **2** *n* contralto *mf*.

altocumulus [,æltəʊ'kjuːmjʊləs] *n, pl* **altocumuli** [,æltəʊ'kjuːmjʊlaɪ] altocúmulo *m*.

altogether [,ɔːltə'geðə^r] **1** *adv* **(a)** (*with everything included*) en conjunto, en total; **how many are there ~?** ¿cuántos hay en total?

(b) (*wholly*) enteramente; del todo; **we haven't ~ finished** no hemos terminado del todo; **I'm not ~ sure** no estoy del todo seguro; **this is ~ too hard** esto es demasiado difícil con mucho; **you're ~ wrong** Vd está completamente equivocado; **I'm not ~ satisfied with it** no estoy satisfecho del todo con ello, no me acaba de convencer.

(c) (*on the whole*) en general, en resumidas cuentas; en conjunto; **~ it was a good show** en general ha sido un éxito.

2 *n*: **in the ~*** desnudo, en cueros*, en pelota picada*.

altostratus [,æltəʊ'streɪtəs] *n, pl* **altostrati** [,æltəʊ'streɪtaɪ] altostrato *m*.

altruism ['æltrʊɪzəm] *n* altruismo *m*.

altruist ['æltrʊɪst] *n* altruista *mf*

altruistic [,æltrʊ'ɪstɪk] *adj* altruista.

ALU *n abbr of* **Arithmetical Logic Unit** unidad *f* lógica aritmética, ULP *f*.

alum ['æləm] *n* alumbre *m*.

aluminium [,æljʊ'mɪnɪəm] (*Brit*) *n*, **aluminum** [ə'luːmɪnəm] *n* (*US*) aluminio *m*; **~ foil** aluminio *m* doméstico.

alumnus [ə'lʌmnəs] *n, pl* **alumni** [ə'lʌmnaɪ]; **alumna** [ə'lʌmnə] *n, pl* **alumnae** [ə'lʌmnɪ] (*esp US*) graduado *m*, -a *f*; **~ association** asociación *f* de graduados.

alveolar [æl'vɪələ^r] *adj* alveolar.

alveolus [æl'vɪələs] *n, pl* **alveoli** [æl'vɪəlaɪ] alvéolo *m*, alveolo *m*.

always ['ɔːlweɪz] *adv* siempre.

Alzheimer's disease ['ælts,haɪməzdɪziːz] *n* enfermedad *f* de Alzheimer.

AM *n* **(a)** *abbr of* **Amplitude Modulation** amplitud *f* modulada, AM. **(b)** (*US*) *abbr of* **Artium Magister**; *V* **MA**.

am [æm] *V* **be**.

Am. **(a)** *abbr of* **America** América *f*. **(b)** *abbr of* **American** americano.

a.m. *adv abbr of* **ante meridiem** antes del mediodía, de la mañana.

AMA *n* (*US*) *abbr of* **American Medical Association** Colegio *m* Oficial de Médicos de América.

amalgam [ə'mælgəm] *n* amalgama *f*.

amalgamate [ə'mælgəmeɪt] **1** *vt* amalgamar; *companies etc* unir. **2** *vi* amalgamarse; unirse.

amalgamation [ə,mælgə'meɪʃən] *n* amalgamación *f*; unión *f*; (*Comm*) fusión *f*.

amanita [,æmə'naɪtə] *n* amanita *f*.

amanuensis [ə,mænjʊ'ensɪs] *n, pl* **amanuenses** [ə,mænjʊ'ensiːz] amanuense *mf*.

Amaryllis [,æmə'rɪlɪs] *nf* Amarilis.

amass [ə'mæs] *vt* amontonar, acumular.

amateur ['æmətə^r] **1** *n* amateur *mf*, aficionado *m*, -a *f* (*also pej*), no profesional *mf*.

2 *adj* **(a)** **~ dramatics** teatro *m* no profesional; **A~ Football Association** Asociación *f* de Fútbol Amateur; **~ status** condición *f* de amateur; **~ tennis** tenis *m* amateur, tenis *m* para aficionados; **I have an ~ interest in pottery** me interesa como aficionado la cerámica.

(b) (*pej*) = **amateurish**.

amateurish ['æmətərɪʃ] *adj* (*pej*) de (mero) aficionado; superficial, inexperto, torpe, chapucero.

amateurism ['æmətərɪzəm] *n* amateurismo *m*, estado *m* de aficionado; **~ in sport** deportes *mpl* para los no profesionales, deportes *mpl* de aficionados.

amatory ['æmətərɪ] *adj* amatorio, erótico.

amaze [ə'meɪz] *vt* asombrar, pasmar; **to be ~d** quedar estupefacto, quedar atónito; **to be ~d at** asombrarse de; **you ~ me!** ¡me admiras!, ¡me dejas patidifuso!

amazed [ə'meɪzd] *adj glance, expression* asombrado, lleno de estupor; **to be ~ at (seeing) sth** quedar asombrado de (ver) algo.

amazement [ə'meɪzmənt] *n* asombro *m*, sorpresa *f*, estupefacción *f*; **they looked on in ~** miraron asombrados; **the news caused general ~** la noticia causó un asombro general.

amazing [ə'meɪzɪŋ] *adj* asombroso, pasmoso; extraordinario.

amazingly [ə'meɪzɪŋlɪ] *adv* milagrosamente, por maravilla; extraordinariamente; **~ enough** aunque parece mentira; **she is ~ generous** es extraordinariamente generosa; **~, nobody was killed** por milagro, no hubo víctimas; **he did ~ well** tuvo un éxito formidable; **he is ~ fit for his age** su estado físico es extraordinario para un hombre de su edad.

Amazon[1] ['æməzən] *n* **(a)** (*Myth*) amazona *f*. **(b)** (*fig: also* **a~**) mujer *f* fuerte, atleta *f* (fuerte); (*US pej*) marimacho *m*.

Amazon[2] ['æməzən] *n* (*Geog*) Amazonas *m*; **~ basin** cuenca *f* del Amazonas; **~ jungle** selva *f* de Amazonas.

Amazonia [,æmə'zəʊnɪə] *n* Amazonia *f*.

Amazonian [,æmə'zəʊnɪən] *adj* amazónico.

ambassador [æm'bæsədə^r] *n* embajador *m*, -ora *f*; **the Spanish ~** el embajador de España.

ambassadorial [æm,bæsə'dɔːrɪəl] *adj* de embajador.

ambassadorship [æm'bæsədəʃɪp] *n* embajada *f*.

ambassadress [æm'bæsədrɪs] *n* embajadora *f*.

amber ['æmbə^r] **1** *n* ámbar *m*. **2** *adj* de ámbar; ambarino, color de ámbar; **~ light** (*Brit Aut*) luz *f* amarilla; **at ~** (*Aut*) en el amarillo.

ambergris ['æmbəgriːs] *n* ámbar *m* gris.

ambi... ['æmbɪ] *pref* ambi...

ambidextrous [,æmbɪ'dekstrəs] *adj* ambidextro.

ambience ['æmbɪəns] *n* ambiente *m*, atmósfera *f*.

ambient ['æmbɪənt] *adj* ambiente.

ambiguity [,æmbɪ'gjʊɪtɪ] *n* ambigüedad *f*.

ambiguous [æm'bɪgjʊəs] *adj* ambiguo.

ambiguously [æm'bɪgjʊəslɪ] *adv* ambiguamente, de forma ambigua.

ambiguousness [æm'bɪgjʊəsnɪs] *n* ambigüedad *f*.

ambit ['æmbɪt] *n* ámbito *m*.

ambition [æm'bɪʃən] *n* ambición *f*; **to have an ~ for sth** ambicionar algo; **to have an ~ to be a doctor** ambicionar ser médico.

ambitious [æm'bɪʃəs] *adj* ambicioso; **to be ~ for sth** ambicionar algo; **they are very ~ for their children** planean cosas grandes para sus hijos; **he was ~ to be the boss** ambicionaba llegar a ser el jefe.

ambitiously [æm'bɪʃəslɪ] *adv* ambiciosamente.

ambivalence [æm'bɪvələns] *n* ambivalencia *f*.

ambivalent [æm'bɪvələnt] *adj* ambivalente.

amble ['æmbl] **1** *n* (*of horse*) ambladura *f*, portante *m*, paso *m* de andadura; **to walk at an ~** (*person*) andar muy despacio, pasearse despacio.

2 *vi* (*horse*) amblar; ir a paso de andadura; (*person*) andar muy despacio; **to ~ along** pasearse despacio, caminar sin prisa; **the bus ~s along at 40 kph** el autobús va tranquilamente a 40 kph; **he ~d into my office at 10 o'clock** entró tranquilamente en mi oficina a las 10; **he ~d up to me** se me acercó despacio.

Ambrose ['æmbrəʊz] *nm* Ambrosio.

ambrosia [æm'brəʊzɪə] *n* ambrosía *f*.

ambulance ['æmbjʊləns] *n* ambulancia *f*; **~ driver, ~ man** ambulanciero *m*.

ambulatory [,æmbjʊ'leɪtərɪ] *adj* (*US Med*) no encamado.

ambush ['æmbʊʃ] **1** *n* emboscada *f*; **troops in ~** tropas *fpl* emboscadas; **to fall into an ~** caer en una emboscada; **to lay an ~ for** tender una emboscada a; **to lie in ~** estar emboscado (*for* para coger).

2 *vt* tender una emboscada a, coger (*LAm*: agarrar) por sorpresa; **to be ~ed** caer en una emboscada, ser cogido por sorpresa.

ameba [ə'miːbə] *n* (*US*) = **amoeba**.

ameliorate [ə'miːlɪəreɪt] **1** *vt* mejorar. **2** *vi* mejorar(se).

amelioration [ə,miːlɪə'reɪʃən] *n* mejora *f*, mejoramiento *m*, mejoría *f*.

amen ['ɑː'men] **1** *interj* amén; **~ to that** así sea, ojalá sea así. **2** *n* amén *m*.

amenable [ə'miːnəbl] *adj* **(a)** (*responsive, tractable*) sumiso, dócil, tratable; **~ to argument** flexible, que se deja convencer; **~ to discipline** sumiso, dispuesto a dejarse disciplinar; **~ to reason** que se deja convencer por la razón; **~ to treatment** (*Med*) susceptible de ser curado, curable. **(b)** (*Jur*) responsable (*for* de).

amend [ə'mend] *vt* enmendar; rectificar, corregir; modificar; reformar.
amendment [ə'mendmənt] *n* enmienda *f*; rectificación *f*, corrección *f*; **the Fifth A~** la Quinta Enmienda (de la Constitución de EE.UU.); **to invoke** (*or* **plead, take**) **the Fifth (A~)** negarse a dar testimonio bajo la protección de la Quinta Enmienda (*relativa a la autoincriminación*).
amends [ə'mendz] *npl*: **to make ~** dar cumplida satisfacción, compensarlo, enmendarlo; **to make ~ for sth** dar satisfacción por algo, enmendar algo, remediar algo; **I'll try to make ~ in future** trataré de dar satisfacción en el futuro.
amenity [ə'mi:nɪtɪ] *n* (**a**) (*pleasantness*) amenidad *f*. (**b**) (*pleasant feature*) atractivo *m*, cosa *f* agradable, ventaja *f*; **amenities** *pl* atractivos *mpl*, conveniencias *fpl*, comodidades *fpl*; **the amenities of life** las cosas agradables de la vida; **a house with all amenities** una casa con todo confort; **we are trying to improve the city's amenities** nos esforzamos por mejorar las instalaciones de la ciudad; **~ bed** (*Brit*) habitación *f* privada; **~ society** asociación *f* para la conservación del medio ambiente.
amenorrhoea, (*US*) **amenorrhea** [eɪ,menə'rɪə] *n* amenorrea *f*.
America [ə'merɪkə] *n* América *f*; (*ie USA*) Estados *mpl* Unidos; *V* **north** *etc*.
American [ə'merɪkən] **1** *adj* americano; (*ie of USA*) norteamericano, estadounidense; **~ cloth** hule *m*; **the ~ dream** el sueño americano; **~ English** inglés *m* americano; **football** fútbol *m* americano; **~ Indian** amerindio *m*, -a *f*; **~ leather** cuero *m* artificial; **~ Legion** *organización de veteranos de las dos guerras mundiales*; **~ plan** (*US*) (habitación *f* con) pensión *f* completa; **~ Spanish** español *m* de América.
2 *n* americano *m*, -a *f*; (*ie of USA*) norteamericano *m*, -a *f*, estadounidense *mf*.
Americana [ə,merɪ'kɑ:nə] *n* (*US*) *objetos, documentos etc pertenecientes a la herencia cultural norteamericana*.
americanism [ə'merɪkənɪzəm] *n* americanismo *m*.
americanization [ə,merɪkənaɪ'zeɪʃən] *n* americanización *f*.
americanize [ə'merɪkənaɪz] *vt* americanizar; **to become ~d** americanizarse.
americium [,æmə'rɪsɪəm] *n* americio *m*.
Amerind [,æmərɪnd] *n* amerindio *m*, -a *f*.
Amerindian [,æmə'rɪndɪən] **1** *adj* amerindio. **2** *n* amerindio *m*, -a *f*.
amethyst ['æmɪθɪst] *n* amatista *f*.
Amex ['æmeks] *n* (*US*) *abbr of* **American Stock Exchange**.
amiability [,eɪmɪə'bɪlɪtɪ] *n* afabilidad *f*, amabilidad *f*.
amiable ['eɪmɪəbl] *adj* afable, amable, simpático; bonachón; **he's an ~ idiot** es un imbécil simpático.
amiably ['eɪmɪəblɪ] *adv* afablemente, amablemente.
amicable ['æmɪkəbl] *adj* amistoso, amigable; **to reach an ~ settlement** llegar a un arreglo amistoso.
amicably ['æmɪkəblɪ] *adv* amistosamente, amigablemente.
amid [ə'mɪd] *prep* en medio de, entre.
amidships [ə'mɪdʃɪps] *adv* en medio del barco.
amidst [ə'mɪdst] *prep* = **amid**.
amino-acid [ə'mi:nəʊ,æsɪd] *n* aminoácido *m*.
amiss [ə'mɪs] **1** *adv* mal, fuera de lugar, fuera de propósito; **a little politeness would not come ~** no le vendría mal un poco de cortesía; **a cup of coffee would not come ~** me gustaría mucho una taza de café; **to take sth ~** llevar algo a mal; **don't take it ~, will you?** ¿no te vas a ofender, eh?; **don't take it ~ if I come too** no te ofendas si yo vengo también; **but he took it very ~** pero él se ofendió mucho.
2 *adj* malo; **there's sth ~** pasa algo malo, no va todo bien, (*with machine etc*) esto no marcha bien, esto funciona mal; **sth is ~ in your calculations** algo está mal en tu cálculo; **what's ~ with you?** ¿qué te pasa?; **is anything ~?** ¿pasa algo?; **we found nothing ~** no encontramos nada fuera de lugar; **to say sth ~** decir algo que no está bien, decir algo inoportuno; **it would not be ~ for him to say thank you** no le estaría mal dar las gracias.
amity ['æmɪtɪ] *n* concordia *f*, amistad *f*.
AMM *n abbr of* **antimissile missile** misil *m* antimisil.
Amman [ə'mɑ:n] *n* Ammán *m*.
ammeter ['æmɪtəʳ] *n* amperímetro *m*.
ammo* ['æməʊ] *n* = **ammunition**.
ammonal ['æmənəl] *n* amonal *m*.
ammonia [ə'məʊnɪə] *n* amoniaco *m*, amoníaco *m*; **liquid ~** amoníaco *m* líquido.
ammonium [ə'məʊnɪəm] *n*: **~ hydroxide** hidróxido *m* amónico; **~ sulphate** sulfato *m* amónico.
ammunition [,æmjʊ'nɪʃən] *n* (**a**) municiones *fpl*; **~ belt** cinturón *m* de municiones; **~ dump, ~ store** depósito *m* de municiones; **~ pouch** cartuchera *f*. (**b**) (*fig*) argumentos *mpl*, razones *fpl*.
amnesia [æm'ni:zɪə] *n* amnesia *f*.
amnesiac [æm'ni:zɪæk] *adj* amnésico.
amnesty ['æmnɪstɪ] **1** *n* amnistía *f*, indulto *m* general; **to give** (*or* **grant**) **an ~ to sb** amnistiar a uno; **A~ International** Amnistía *f* Internacional. **2** *vt* amnistiar, indultar.
amniocentesis [,æmnɪəʊsen'ti:sɪs] *n* amniocéntesis *f*.
amoeba, (*US*) **ameba** [ə'mi:bə] *n*, *pl* **amoebas** (*US* **amebas**), **amoebae** amiba *f*, ameba *f*.
amoebic [ə'mi:bɪk] *adj* amébico; **~ dysentery** disentería *f* amébica.
amok [ə'mɒk] *adv* = **amuck**.
among(st) [ə'mʌŋ(st)] *prep* entre, en medio de; **from ~** de entre; **~ the Ruritanians it is deemed a virtue** entre ruritanios se considera como una virtud; **he is ~ those who know** es de los que saben; **it is not ~ the names I have** no figura entre los nombres que tengo; **this is ~ the possibilities** esto figura en las posibilidades; **they quarrelled ~ themselves** riñeron entre sí; **one can say that ~ friends** eso se puede decir entre amigos.
amoral [eɪ'mɒrəl] *adj* amoral.
amorality [,eɪmɒ'rælɪtɪ] *n* amoralidad *f*.
amorous ['æmərəs] *adj* enamorado, enamoradizo; cariñoso; (*pej*: *man*) mujeriego; **he made ~ advances to his secretary** requebró de amores a su secretaria; **after two drinks she became quite ~** después de dos tragos se puso algo caliente*.
amorously ['æmərəslɪ] *adv* amorosamente.
amorphous [ə'mɔ:fəs] *adj* amorfo.
amortizable [ə'mɔ:tɪzəbl] *adj* amortizable; **~ loan** préstamo *m* amortizable.
amortization [ə,mɔ:tɪ'zeɪʃən] *n* amortización *f*.
amortize [ə'mɔ:taɪz] *vt* amortizar.
amount [ə'maʊnt] *n* (**a**) (*total*) suma *f*, importe *m*; **to the ~ of** hasta un total de; por la suma de, por el valor de; **debts to the ~ of £100** deudas *fpl* que suman 100 libras; **check in the ~ of $50** (*US*) cheque *m* por valor de 50 dólares.
(**b**) (*quantity*) cantidad *f*; **in small ~s** en pequeñas cantidades; **there is quite an ~ left** queda bastante; **I have any ~ of time** tengo mucho tiempo; **we used to drink any ~ of that** bebíamos grandes cantidades de eso; **we have had any ~ of trouble** hemos tenido un sinnúmero de problemas; **no ~ of arguing will help** es totalmente inútil discutir.
◆**amount to** *vt* (**a**) ascender a, sumar, subir a.
(**b**) (*fig*) equivaler a, significar, venir a ser; **it ~s to the same thing** es igual, viene a ser lo mismo; **this ~s to a refusal** esto equivale a una negativa; **it doesn't ~ to much** apenas es significativo, viene a ser poca cosa; **he'll never ~ to much** siempre será una nulidad, es un pobre hombre.
amour [ə'mʊəʳ] *n* amorío *m*, aventura *f* amorosa.
amour-propre ['æmʊə'prɒpr] *n* amor *m* propio.
amp [æmp] *n*, **ampere** ['æmpɛəʳ] *n* amperio *m*; **ampere-hour** amperio-hora *m* (*pl*: amperios-hora *mpl*); **a 13 amp plug** una clavija de 13 amperios.
ampersand ['æmpəsænd] *n el signo* & (*que significa* and).
amphetamine [æm'fetəmi:n] *n* anfetamina *f*.
amphibia [æm'fɪbɪə] *npl* anfibios *mpl*.
amphibian [æm'fɪbɪən] **1** *adj* anfibio. **2** *n* anfibio *m*.
amphibious [æm'fɪbɪəs] *adj* anfibio.
amphitheatre, (*US*) **amphitheater** ['æmfɪ,θɪətəʳ] *n* anfiteatro *m*.
Amphitryon [æm'fɪtrɪən] *nm* Anfitrión.
amphora ['æmfərə] *n*, *pl* **amphorae** ['æmfəri:] ánfora *f*.
ample ['æmpl] *adj* (**a**) (*large*) *room etc* amplio, ancho, espacioso, extenso; *garment* amplio, grande. (**b**) (*enough and to spare*) bastante, suficiente; **there is ~ room for it** hay más que suficiente espacio para él; **there was an ~ supply of food** había comida abundante; **she has ~ means** tiene medios más que suficientes; **we have ~ reason to believe that ...** tenemos razones sobradas para creer que ...; **thanks, I have ~** gracias, tengo bastante.
amplification [,æmplɪfɪ'keɪʃən] *n* amplificación *f* (*also Tech*); explicación *f*; desarrollo *m*.
amplifier ['æmplɪfaɪəʳ] *n* amplificador *m*.
amplify ['æmplɪfaɪ] *vt sound* amplificar (*also Rad*), aumentar; *statement etc* explicar, añadir comentarios a; *argument* desarrollar; **he refused to ~ his remarks** se negó a dar más comentarios.
amplitude ['æmplɪtju:d] *n* amplitud *f*.

amply ['æmplɪ] *adv* ampliamente; bastante, suficiente; abundantemente; **you were ~ justified** tuviste razón de sobra; **the room is ~ big enough** el cuarto es más que suficientemente grande; **we are ~ supplied with food** tenemos abundancia de comida.

ampoule, (*US*) **ampule** ['æmpu:l] *n* ampolla *f.*

amputate ['æmpjʊteɪt] *vt* amputar.

amputation [,æmpjʊ'teɪʃən] *n* amputación *f.*

amputee [,æmpjʊ'ti:] *n* persona *f* cuya pierna (*or* cuyo brazo) ha sido amputada (amputado).

Amsterdam [,æmstə'dæm] *n* Amsterdam *m.*

amt *abbr of* **amount** importe *m,* impte.

amuck [ə'mʌk] *adv*: **to run ~** enloquecer, desbocarse, desmandarse; (*fig*) conducirse como un loco, hacer locuras, mostrarse violento, atacar a ciegas.

amulet ['æmjʊlɪt] *n* amuleto *m.*

amuse [ə'mju:z] **1** *vt* (**a**) (*cause mirth to*) divertir, hacer reír; **this ~d everybody** hizo reír a todos; **we are not ~d** no nos cae en gracia; **to be ~d at** (*or* **by**) divertirse con, reírse con; **with an ~d expression** con gesto risueño. (**b**) (*entertain*) divertir, entretener, distraer; **to keep sb ~d** entretener a uno; **this should keep them ~d for years** esto deberá ocupar su atención por muchos años.

2 *vr*: **to ~ o.s.** distraerse (*doing* haciendo); **run along and ~ yourselves** idos a jugar; **you'll have to ~ yourselves for a while** tendréis que entreteneros (a vosotros mismos) por un rato; **we ~d ourselves a good deal** lo pasamos muy bien.

amusement [ə'mju:zmənt] *n* (**a**) (*amusing thing*) diversión *f,* entretenimiento *m*; **~s** (*in fairground*) máquinas *fpl* electrónicas, máquinas *fpl* tragaperras; **~ arcade** galería *f* de atracciones; **~ park** parque *m* de atracciones; **place of ~** sitio *m* de recreo.

(**b**) (*pastime*) pasatiempo *m,* recreo *m*; **a town with plenty of ~s** una ciudad que ofrece muchas diversiones; **it is for ~ only** es una diversión nada más; **they do it for ~ only** lo hacen sólo para divertirse, es un pasatiempo nada más.

(**c**) (*laughter*) risa *f,* regocijo *m*; **with a look of ~** con mirada risueña; **there was general ~ at this** al oír esto se rieron todos; **much to my ~** con gran regocijo mío; **to conceal one's ~** ocultar sus ganas de reír, aguantarse la risa.

amusing [ə'mju:zɪŋ] *adj* divertido, gracioso, entretenido.

amusingly [ə'mju:zɪŋlɪ] *adv* de modo divertido, graciosamente.

an [æn, ən, n] *indef art* = **a²**.

ANA *n* (*US*) (**a**) *abbr of* **American Newspaper Association.** (**b**) *abbr of* **American Nurses' Association.**

anabolic [ænə'bɒlɪk] *adj*: **~ steroid** esteroide *m* anabolizante.

anachronism [ə'nækrənɪzəm] *n* anacronismo *m.*

anachronistic [ə,nækrə'nɪstɪk] *adj* anacrónico.

anacoluthon [,aenəkə'lu:θɒn] *n* anacoluto *m.*

anaconda [,ænə'kɒndə] *n* anaconda *f.*

Anacreon [ə'nækrɪən] *nm* Anacreonte.

anaemia, (*US*) **anemia** [ə'ni:mɪə] *n* anemia *f.*

anaemic, (*US*) **anemic** [ə'ni:mɪk] *adj* (*Med*) anémico; (*fig*) soso, fofo, insípido, débil.

anaerobic, (*US*) **anerobic** [,ænɛə'rəubɪk] *adj* anaerobio.

anaesthesia, (*US*) **anesthesia** [,ænɪs'θi:zɪə] *n* anestesia *f.*

anaesthetic, (*US*) **anesthetic** [,ænɪs'θetɪk] **1** *adj* anestésico. **2** *n* anestésico *m*; **to be under an ~** estar anestesiado; **to give sb an ~, to put sb under an ~** anestesiar a uno.

anaesthetist, (*US*) **anesthetist** [æ'ni:sθɪtɪst] *n* anestesista *mf.*

anaesthetize, (*US*) **anesthetize** [æ'ni:sθɪtaɪz] *vt* anestesiar.

anagram ['ænəgræm] *n* anagrama *m.*

anal ['eɪnəl] *adj* anal.

analgesia [,ænæl'dʒi:zɪə] *n* analgesia *f.*

analgesic [,ænæl'dʒi:sɪk] **1** *adj* analgésico. **2** *n* analgésico *m.*

analog ['ænəlog] *n* (*US*) = **analogue.**

analogical [,ænə'lɒdʒɪkəl] *adj* analógico.

analogous [ə'næləgəs] *adj* análogo (*to, with* a); afín, semejante.

analogue, (*US*) **analog** ['ænəlɒg] *n* cosa *f* (*or* palabra *f etc*) análoga; **~ computer** ordenador *m* analógico.

analogy [ə'nælədʒɪ] *n* analogía *f*; afinidad *f,* semejanza *f*; **by ~ with, on the ~ of** por analogía con; **to argue from** (*or* **by**) **~** razonar por analogía; **to draw an ~ between** aducir una analogía entre.

analysand [ə'nælɪ,sænd] *n* sujeto *m* analizado, analizando *m.*

analyse, (*US*) **analyze** ['ænəlaɪz] *vt* (**a**) analizar. (**b**) (*esp US*) psicoanalizar.

analysis [ə'næləsɪs] *n, pl* **analyses** [ə'nælisi:z] (**a**) análisis *m*; **in the final** (*or* **last**) **~** en último término, en fin de cuentas. (**b**) (*esp US*) psicoanálisis *m.*

analyst ['ænəlɪst] *n* (**a**) analista *mf*; **public ~** jefe *mf* del laboratorio municipal. (**b**) (*esp US*) psicoanalista *mf.*

analytic(al) [,ænə'lɪtɪk(əl)] *adj* analítico.

analyze ['ænəlaɪz] *vt* (*US*) = **analyse.**

anapaest, (*US*) **anapest** ['ænəpi:st] *n* anapesto *m.*

anaphoric [,ænə'fɒrɪk] *adj* anafórico.

anarchic(al) [æ'nɑ:kɪk(əl)] *adj* anárquico.

anarchism ['ænəkɪzəm] *n* anarquismo *m.*

anarchist ['ænəkɪst] **1** *adj* anarquista. **2** *n* anarquista *mf.*

anarchy ['ænəkɪ] *n* anarquía *f.*

anathema [ə'næθɪmə] *n* (*Rel, fig*) anatema *m*; (*fig*) abominación *f*; **he is ~ to me** no le puedo ver, para mí es inaguantable; **the idea is ~ to her** para ella la idea es una abominación, la idea le resulta odiosa.

anathematize [ə'næθɪmətaɪz] *vt* anatematizar.

anatomical [,ænə'tɒmɪkəl] *adj* anatómico.

anatomist [ə'nætəmɪst] *n* anatomista *mf.*

anatomize [ə'nætəmaɪz] *vt* anatomizar; (*fig*) analizar minuciosamente.

anatomy [ə'nætəmɪ] *n* (**a**) anatomía *f,* estructura *f.* (**b**) (*surface of body*) cuerpo *m* humano; carnes *fpl*; (*****: *bottom*) nalgas *fpl,* posaderas *fpl.*

ANC *n abbr of* **African National Congress** Congreso *m* Nacional Africano.

ancestor ['ænsɪstəʳ] *n* antepasado *m,* -a *f*; **~s** *pl* antepasados *mpl,* abuelos *mpl,* ascendientes *mpl.*

ancestral [æn'sestrəl] *adj* ancestral, hereditario; **~ home** casa *f* solariega, solar *m.*

ancestress ['ænsɪstrɪs] *n* antepasada *f.*

ancestry ['ænsɪstrɪ] *n* ascendencia *f,* abolengo *m,* linaje *m,* estirpe *f.*

anchor ['æŋkəʳ] **1** *n* ancla *f,* áncora *f*; **to be** (*or* **lie, ride**) **at ~** estar al ancla, estar anclado; **to cast** (*or* **drop**) **~** echar anclas; **to weigh ~** levar anclas.

2 *vt* poner sobre el ancla; (*fig*) sujetar (*to* a), asegurar.

3 *vi* anclar, fondear.

anchorage ['æŋkərɪdʒ] *n* ancladero *m,* fondeadero *m*; **~ dues, ~ fee** anclaje *m.*

anchorite ['æŋkəraɪt] *n* anacoreta *mf.*

anchor-man ['æŋkəmæn] *n, pl* **anchor-men** ['æŋkəmen] (*TV*) hombre *m* ancla, presentador *m*; (*fig*) hombre *m* clave.

anchovy ['æntʃəvɪ] *n* (*live, fresh*) boquerón *m*; (*salted, tinned*) anchoa *f.*

ancient ['eɪnʃənt] **1** *adj* (**a**) antiguo; **in ~ days** en la antigüedad, hace muchísimo tiempo; **~ Greek** griego *m* antiguo; **~ history** historia *f* antigua; **that's ~ history!*** ¡eso pertenece a la historia!; **~ monument** (*Brit*) monumento *m* histórico; **~ Rome** Roma *f* clásica; **remains of ~ times** restos *mpl* de la antigüedad.

(**b**) (*hum*) *person* viejo, anciano; *clothing, object* muy viejo, anticuado, totalmente pasado de moda; **we went in his ~ car** fuimos en su antiquísimo coche; **he's getting pretty ~** va para viejo.

2 *n* (*hum*) viejo *m,* vejete *m*; **the ~s** los antiguos.

ancillary [æn'sɪlərɪ] *adj* subordinado (*to* a), ancilar, secundario; auxiliar; **~ staff** (*Brit Scol*) personal *m* auxiliar; **~ workers** personal *m* auxiliar.

and [ænd, ənd, nd, ən] *conj* (**a**) y, (*before* i-, hi-) e, *eg* franceses e ingleses, padre e hijo; **~?** ¿y después?, ¿y qué más?; **~/or** y/o; **better ~ better** cada vez mejor; **more ~ more** cada vez más.

(**b**) (*in numbers*) **a hundred ~ one** ciento uno; **two hundred ~ ten** doscientos diez; **five hours ~ twenty minutes** cinco horas veinte minutos; **ten dollars ~ fifty cents** diez dólares y (*or* con) cincuenta centavos.

(**c**) (*negative sense*) ni; **you can't buy ~ sell here** aquí no se permite comprar ni vender.

(**d**) (*repetition, continuation*) **she cried ~ cried** no dejaba de llorar, lloraba sin parar; **I rang ~ rang** llamé repetidas veces; **he talked ~ talked without effect** habló incansablemente pero sin lograr nada, por mucho que hablase no logró nada.

(**e**) (*before infins*) **come ~ see me** ven a verme; **try ~ do it** trata de hacerlo, hazlo si puedes; **wait ~ see** espera y verás.

Andalusia [,ændə'lu:zɪə] *n* Andalucía *f.*

Andalusian [,ændə'lu:zɪən] **1** *adj* andaluz. **2** *n* (**a**) andaluz *m,* -uza *f.* (**b**) (*Ling*) andaluz *m.*

Andean ['ændɪən] *adj* andino, de los Andes.
Andes ['ændi:z] *npl* Andes *mpl*.
andiron ['ændaɪən] *n* morillo *m*.
Andorra [,æn'dɔ:rə] *n* Andorra *f*.
Andorran [,æn'dɔ:rən] **1** *adj* andorrano. **2** *n* andorrano *m*, -a *f*.
Andrew ['ændru:] *nm* Andrés.
androcentric [,ændrəʊ'sɛntrik] *adj* androcéntrico.
androcentricity [,ændrəʊsɛn'trɪsɪtɪ] *n* androcentrismo *m*.
androgen ['ændrədʒən] *n* andrógeno *m*.
androgenic ['ændrə'dʒɛnɪk] *adj* androgénico.
androgynous [æn'drɒdʒɪnəs] *adj* andrógino.
android ['ændrɔɪd] *n* androide *m*.
Andromache [æn'drɒməkɪ] *nf* Andrómaca.
Andromeda [æn'drɒmɪdə] *nf* Andrómeda.
androsterone [æn'drɒstə,rəʊn] *n* androsterona *f*.
Andy ['ændɪ] *n familiar form of* **Andrew**.
anecdotal [,ænɪk'dəʊtəl] *adj* anecdótico.
anecdote ['ænɪkdəʊt] *n* anécdota *f*.
anemia [ə'ni:mɪə] *n* (*US*) = **anaemia**.
anemic [ə'ni:mɪk] *adj* (*US*) = **anaemic**.
anemone [ə'nemənɪ] *n* (*Bot, Zool*) anemone *f*, anémona *f*, anemona *f*.
anerobic [,ænɛə'rəʊbɪk] *adj* (*US*) = **anaerobic**.
aneroid ['ænərɔɪd] *adj* aneroide; ~ **barometer** barómetro *m* aneroide.
anesthesia [,ænɪs'θi:zɪə] *n* (*US*) = **anaesthesia**.
anesthesiologist [,ænɪs,θi:zɪ'ɒlədʒɪst] *n* (*US*) anestesista *mf*.
anesthetic [,ænɪs'θetɪk] *adj, n* (*US*) = **anaesthetic**.
anesthetist [æ'ni:sθɪtɪst] *n* (*US*) = **anaesthetist**.
anesthetize [æ'ni:sθɪtaɪz] *vt* (*US*) = **anaesthetize**.
anew [ə'nju:] *adv* de nuevo, otra vez; **to begin** ~ comenzar de nuevo, volver a comenzar, recomenzar.
angel ['eɪndʒəl] *n* (**a**) ángel *m*; **A~ of Darkness** ángel *m* de tinieblas; **I'm on the side of the ~s** yo estoy de parte de los ángeles; **talk of ~s!** hablando del ruin de Roma, por la puerta asoma; *V* **guardian**.
(**b**) (*: *person*) **yes, ~!** ¡sí, querida!, ¡sí, mi amor!; **she's an ~** es un ángel; **be an ~ and give me a cigarette** ¿me das un pitillo, amor?
(**c**) (*Fin**: *esp Theat*) caballo *m* blanco*, promotor *m*, -ora *f*.
Angeleno [,ændʒə'li:nəʊ] *n* habitante *mf* de Los Angeles.
angelfish ['eɪndʒəlfɪʃ] *n* angelote *m*, pez *m* ángel.
angelic(al) [æn'dʒelɪk(əl)] *adj* angélico.
angelica [æn'dʒelɪkə] *n* angélica *f*.
angelus ['ændʒɪləs] *n* ángelus *m*.
anger ['æŋgə[r]] **1** *n* cólera *f*, ira *f*; furia *f*; **words spoken in ~** palabras *fpl* furiosas; **to move** (*or* **rouse**) **sb to ~** provocar a uno a cólera, encolerizar a uno; **to speak in ~** hablar indignado, hablar coléricamente. **2** *vt* enojar, provocar, encolerizar.
angina [æn'dʒaɪnə] *n* angina *f*; ~ **pectoris** angina *f* del pecho.
angiosperm ['ændʒɪə,spɜ:m] *n* angiosperma *f*.
angle[1] ['æŋgl] **1** *n* (**a**) ángulo *m* (*also Math*); ~ **of climb** (*Aer*) ángulo *m* de subida; **it is leaning at an ~ of 80°** está ladeado en un ángulo de 80°; **to be at an ~ to** formar ángulo con; **to cut a pipe at an ~** cortar un tubo al sesgo; **to look at a building from a different ~** contemplar un edificio desde otro sitio, tener de un edificio una nueva perspectiva.
(**b**) (*fig*) punto *m* de vista; opinión *f*; criterio *m*; aspecto *m*; **look at it from my ~** considere la cosa desde mi punto de vista; **he has a different ~** tiene otro modo de enfocar la cuestión, en este asunto su criterio es distinto; **what's your ~ on this?** ¿tú qué opinas de esto?; **that's a new ~ to the problem** ése es un aspecto nuevo del problema; **to look at a problem from all ~s** estudiar un problema en todos sus aspectos.
2 *vt* (**a**) (*Sport*) *shot* ladear, sesgar, jugar en diagonal.
(**b**) *report etc* presentar bajo una luz especial; ajustar de acuerdo con intereses concretos; **this article is ~d towards non-specialists** este artículo se dirige preferentemente a los no especializados.
angle[2] [æŋgl] *vi* (**a**) pescar (con caña) (*for trout* truchas). (**b**) **to ~ for** (*fig*) ir a la caza de, tratar de pescar, intrigar para conseguir.
angle-iron ['æŋgl,aɪən] *n* hierro *m* angular.
Anglepoise ['æŋglpɔɪz] ® *n*: ~ **lamp** lámpara *f* de estudio.
angler ['æŋglə[r]] *n* pescador *m*, -ora *f* (de caña).
anglerfish ['æŋgləfɪʃ] *n* rape *m*.
Angles ['æŋglz] *npl* anglos *mpl*.
Anglican ['æŋglɪkən] **1** *adj* anglicano. **2** *n* anglicano *m*, -a *f*.
Anglicanism ['æŋglɪkənɪzəm] *n* anglicanismo *m*.
anglicism ['æŋglɪsɪzəm] *n* anglicismo *m*, inglesismo *m*.
anglicist ['æŋglɪsɪst] *n* anglicista *mf*.
anglicize ['æŋglɪsaɪz] *vt* dar forma inglesa a.
angling ['æŋglɪŋ] *n* pesca *f* (con caña).
Anglo* ['æŋgləʊ] *n* (*US*) blanco *m*, -a *f*, americano *m*, -a *f* (*de origen no hispano*).
Anglo... ['æŋgləʊ] *pref* anglo...; **~-American relations** relaciones *fpl* angloamericanas; **an ~-French project** un proyecto anglofrancés.
Anglo-Catholic ['æŋgləʊ'kæθlɪk] **1** *adj* anglocatólico. **2** *n* anglocatólico *m*, -a *f*.
Anglo-Catholicism ['æŋgləʊkə'θɒlɪsɪzəm] *n* anglocatolicismo *m*.
Anglo-Indian ['æŋgləʊ'ɪndɪən] **1** *adj* angloindio. **2** *n* angloindio *m*, -a *f*.
Anglo-Norman [,æŋgləʊ'nɔ:mən] **1** *adj* anglonormando. **2** *n* (**a**) anglonormando *m*, -a *f*. (**b**) (*Ling*) anglonormando *m*.
anglophile ['æŋgləʊfaɪl] *n* anglófilo *m*, -a *f*.
anglophobe ['æŋgləʊfəʊb] *n* anglófobo *m*, -a *f*.
anglophobia [,æŋgləʊ'fəʊbjə] *n* anglofobia *f*.
anglophone ['æŋgləʊfəʊn] **1** *adj* anglófono. **2** *n* anglófono *m*, -a *f*.
Anglo-Saxon ['æŋgləʊ'sæksən] **1** *adj* anglosajón. **2** *n* (**a**) anglosajón *m*, -ona *f*. (**b**) (*Ling*) anglosajón *m*.
Angola [æŋ'gəʊlə] *n* Angola *f*.
Angolan [æŋ'gəʊlən] **1** *adj* angoleño. **2** *n* angoleño *m*, -a *f*.
angora [æŋ'gɔ:rə] *n* angora *mf*.
angostura [,æŋgə'stjʊərə] *n* angostura *f*: ~ **bitters** ® bíter *m* de angostura.
Angoulême [ɑ:ŋgu'lɛm] *n* Angulema *f*.
angrily ['æŋgrɪlɪ] *adv* coléricamente, airadamente; **he protested ~** protestó colérico.
angry ['æŋgrɪ] **1** *adj* (**a**) enfadado, enojado, airado; **in an ~ voice** en tono colérico; **she gave me an ~ look** me miró enfadada; ~ **young man** (*Brit*) joven *m* airado; **to be ~** estar enfadado (*LAm*: enojado) (*about* por; *at, with* con); **you won't be ~ if I tell you?** no te vayas a ofender si te lo digo; **to get ~** enfadarse, ponerse furioso, indignarse; **this sort of thing makes me ~** estas cosas me sacan de quicio.
(**b**) (*fig*) *sea* bravo; *sky* tormentoso, borrascoso, que amenaza tormenta.
(**c**) (*Med*) inflamado.
2 *npl*: **the angries** los airados *mpl*.
angst [æŋst] *n* angustia *f*, congoja *f*.
angstrom ['æŋstrʌm] *n* angstrom *m*.
anguish ['æŋgwɪʃ] *n* (*bodily*) dolor *m* agudo, tormentos *mpl*; (*mental*) angustia *f*, congoja *f*; **to be in ~** padecer tormentos, sufrir lo indecible.
anguished ['æŋgwɪʃt] *adj* acongojado, afligido, angustiado.
angular ['æŋgjʊlə[r]] *adj* angular; *face etc* anguloso.
angularity [,æŋgjʊ'lærətɪ] *n* angularidad *f*; angulosidad *f*.
aniline ['ænɪli:n] *n* anilina *f*; ~ **dyes** colorantes *mpl* de anilina.
anima ['ænɪmə] *n* ánima *f*, alma *f*.
animal ['ænɪməl] **1** *attr* animal; ~ **fats** grasas *fpl* de animal; ~ **husbandry** cría *f* de animales; ~ **instinct** instinto *m* animal; ~ **kingdom** reino *m* animal; ~ **rights movement** movimiento *m* pro derechos de los animales; ~ **spirits** vitalidad *f*. **2** *n* animal *m*; (*horse etc*) bestia *f*; (*insect etc*) bicho *m*; **you ~!*** ¡animal!*, ¡bestia!*
animalcule [,ænɪ'mælkju:l] *n* animálculo *m*.
animality [,ænɪ'mælətɪ] *n* animalidad *f*.
animate 1 ['ænɪmɪt] *adj* vivo, que tiene vida. **2** ['ænɪmeɪt] *vt* animar, infundir vida a (*or* en); vivificar, estimular; alentar.
animated ['ænɪmeɪtɪd] *adj* animado; vivo, vivaz, vigoroso; *discussion* vivo; ~ **cartoon** dibujos *mpl* animados; **to become ~** animarse.
animatedly ['ænɪmeɪtɪdlɪ] *adv talk etc* animadamente.
animation [,ænɪ'meɪʃən] *n* animación *f*; vivacidad *f*, viveza *f*.
animator ['ænɪmeɪtə[r]] *n* (*Cine*) animador *m*, -ora *f*.
animism ['ænɪmɪzəm] *n* animismo *m*.
animist ['ænɪmɪst] **1** *adj* animista. **2** *n* animista *mf*.
animosity [,ænɪ'mɒsɪtɪ] *n* animosidad *f*, rencor *m*, hostilidad *f*.
animus ['ænɪməs] *n* odio *m*, rencor *m*.
anise ['ænɪs] *n* anís *m*.
aniseed ['ænɪsi:d] *n* anís *m*; (*strictly*) grano *m* de anís; ~ **ball** bombón *m* de anís.
anisette [,ænɪ'zet] *n* anisete *m*, anís *m* .
Anjou [ɑ:ŋ'ʒu:] *n* Anjeo *m*.
Ankara ['æŋkərə] *n* Ankara *f*.
ankle ['æŋkl] *n* tobillo *m*.

anklebone ['æŋklbəʊn] *n* hueso *m* del tobillo, taba *f*, astrágalo *m*.
ankle-deep ['æŋkl'di:p] *adv*: **to be ~ in water** estar metido hasta los tobillos en el agua; **the water is only ~** el agua llega a los tobillos nada más.
ankle joint ['æŋkldʒɔɪnt] *n* articulación *f* del tobillo.
ankle sock ['æŋklsɒk] *n* (*Brit*) escarpín *m*.
ankle strap ['æŋklstræp] *n* tirita *f* tobillera.
anklet ['æŋklɪt] *n* brazalete *m* para el tobillo, ajorca *f* para el pie; (*US*) calcetín *m* corto.
ankylosis [,æŋkɪ'ləʊsɪs] *n* anquilosis *f*.
Ann [æn] *nf* Ana; **~ Boleyn** Ana Bolena.
ann. (**a**) *abbr of* **annual**. (**b**) (*Fin*) *abbr of* **annuity**.
annalist ['ænəlɪst] *n* analista *mf*, cronista *mf*.
annals ['ænəlz] *npl* anales *mpl*, crónica *f*; **in all the ~ of crime** en toda la historia del crimen; **never in the ~ of human endeavour** nunca en la historia de los esfuerzos humanos.
Anne [æn] *nf* Ana; **Queen ~'s dead!*** eso no es noticia, eso lo tenemos archisabido.
anneal [ə'ni:l] *vt* recocer; templar.
annex [ə'neks] *vt* (**a**) *territory* anexar. (**b**) *document* adjuntar, añadir (*to* a).
annexation [,ænek'seɪʃən] *n* anexión *f*.
annexe, (*US*) **annex** ['æneks] *n* (**a**) (*building*) pabellón *m* separado, dependencia *f*, edificio *m* anexo. (**b**) (*to document*) apéndice *m*, anejo *m*.
annihilate [ə'naɪəleɪt] *vt* aniquilar.
annihilation [ə,naɪə'leɪʃən] *n* aniquilación *f*, aniquilamiento *m*.
anniversary [,ænɪ'vɜ:sərɪ] *n* aniversario *m*; **the Góngora ~ dinner** el banquete para festejar el aniversario de Góngora.
Anno Domini ['ænəʊ'dɒmɪnaɪ] *n* (*gen abbr* AD) (**a**) **~ 43** el año 43 después de Jesucristo; **the third century ~** el siglo tercero de Cristo. (**b**) (*) vejez *f*, edad *f*.
annotate ['ænəʊteɪt] *vt* anotar, comentar.
annotation [,ænəʊ'teɪʃən] *n* anotación *f*, apunte *m*, comentario *m*.
announce [ə'naʊns] *vt* anunciar; informar; proclamar; declarar; hacer saber, comunicar; **then he ~d 'I won't'** luego declaró 'No quiero'; **it is ~d from London that ...** se comunica desde Londres que ...; **we regret to ~ the death of X** lamentamos tener que participar la muerte de X.
announcement [ə'naʊnsmənt] *n* anuncio *m*; informe *m*; proclama *f*; notificación *f*; declaración *f*; aviso *m*; **~ of birth** (aviso *m*) natalicio *m*; **~ of death** (nota *f*) necrológica *f*.
announcer [ə'naʊnsəʳ] *n* (*Rad, TV*) locutor *m*, -ora *f*, presentador *m*, -ora *f*, speaker *mf*; (*at airport etc*) el (*or* la) que hace anuncios.
annoy [ə'nɔɪ] *vt* molestar, fastidiar, irritar; **to be ~ed** estar enfadado (*about* por; *at, with* con); **don't be ~ed if I can't come** no te enfades si no puedo venir; **is this man ~ing you, madam?** ¿le está molestando este hombre, señora?; **to get ~ed** enfadarse, molestarse, incomodarse; **it's no good getting ~ed with me** de nada sirve enfadarte conmigo.
annoyance [ə'nɔɪəns] *n* (**a**) (*state*) enojo *m*, irritación *f*; contrariedad *f*; disgusto *m*; **to my ~ I find that ...** con gran disgusto mío descubro que ... (**b**) (*cause, thing*) molestia *f*.
annoying [ə'nɔɪɪŋ] *adj* molesto, fastidioso, engorroso; *person* pesado, importuno; **how very ~!** ¡qué fastidio!; **it's ~ to have to** + *infin* me molesta tener que + *infin*, es una lata* tener que + *infin*.
annoyingly [ə'nɔɪɪŋlɪ] *adv* de modo fastidioso; pesadamente, importunamente; **and then, ~ enough ...** y luego, para fastidiarnos ...; **the radio was ~ loud** la radio nos molestó con su ruido; **he has an ~ loud voice** tiene una voz tan fuerte que molesta.
annual ['ænjʊəl] **1** *adj* anual; **~ general meeting** (*Brit*) junta *f* general (anual); **~ income** ingresos *mpl* anuales; **~ leave** vacaciones *fpl* (anuales); **~(ized) percentage rate** tasa *f* de interés anual; **~ premium** prima *f* anual; **~ rate** tipo *m* anual; **~ report** informe *m* anual, memoria *f* anual; **~ return** (*for tax*) declaración *f* anual; (*report*) informe *m* anual; **~ ring** anillo *m* anual, cerco *m* anual; **~ statement** informe *m* anual. **2** *n* (**a**) (*Bot*) planta *f* anual, anual *m*. (**b**) (*book*) anuario *m*.
annually ['ænjʊəlɪ] *adv* anualmente, cada año; **£500 ~** 500 libras al año.
annuity [ə'nju:ɪtɪ] *n* (*also* **life ~**) renta *f* vitalicia, pensión *f* vitalicia; anualidad *f*.
annul [ə'nʌl] *vt* anular, invalidar; cancelar; *marriage* anular; *law* revocar, abrogar.
annulment [ə'nʌlmənt] *n* anulación *f*, invalidación *f*, cancelación *f*; revocación *f*, abrogación *f*.
Annunciation [ə,nʌnsɪ'eɪʃən] *n* Anunciación *f*.
anode ['ænəʊd] *n* ánodo *m*.
anodize ['ænədaɪz] *vt* anodizar.
anodyne ['ænəʊdaɪn] **1** *adj* anodino. **2** *n* anodino *m*.
anoint [ə'nɔɪnt] *vt* untar; (*Eccl*) ungir.
anointing [ə'nɔɪntɪŋ] *n*: **~ of the sick** (*Rel*) unción *f* de los enfermos.
anomalous [ə'nɒmələs] *adj* anómalo.
anomaly [ə'nɒməlɪ] *n* anomalía *f*.
anon¹ [ə'nɒn] *adv* (**a**) luego, dentro de poco; **I'll see you ~** nos veremos luego. (**b**) (††) **ever and ~** a menudo, de vez en cuando.
anon² [ə'nɒn] *abbr* = **anonymous**.
anonymity [,ænə'nɪmɪtɪ] *n* (*in general*) anonimia *f*, anonimato *m*; (*particular case*) anónimo *m*; **to preserve one's ~** conservar el anónimo.
anonymous [ə'nɒnɪməs] *adj* anónimo; **~ letter** anónimo *m*; **he wishes to remain ~** no quiere que se publique su nombre, quiere conservar el anónimo.
anonymously [ə'nɒnɪməslɪ] *adv* anónimamente; **the book came out ~** salió el libro sin nombre de autor; **he gave £100 ~** dio 100 libras sin revelar su nombre.
anorak ['ænəræk] *n* anorac *m*, anorak *m*.
anorexia [,ænə'reksɪə] *n* anorexia *f*; **~ nervosa** anorexia *f* nerviosa.
anorexic [,ænə'reksɪk] **1** *adj* anoréxico. **2** *n* anoréxico *m*, -a *f*.
another [ə'nʌðəʳ] **1** *adj* (**a**) (*additional*) otro (*no art needed, eg* **~ man** otro hombre); **~ glass?** ¿otra copita?; **take ~ 5** toma 5 más; **in ~ 10 years** en otros 10 años; **we need ~ 2 men** necesitamos 2 hombres más; **not ~ minute!** ¡ni un minuto más!; **there are ~ 2 months to go** faltan todavía 2 meses; **without ~ word** sin decir una palabra más, sin más palabras.
(**b**) (*similar*) otro; **he's ~ Hitler** es otro Hitler, es un segundo Hitler; **there's not ~ painting like it** no hay otro cuadro como éste.
(**c**) (*different*) **come ~ day** venga otro día; **that is ~ matter altogether** eso es un asunto totalmente distinto.
2 *pron* otro *m*, otra *f*; **just such ~** otro tal; **many ~ would hate it** otros muchos lo detestarían; **~ would have done it this way** cualquier otro lo hubiera hecho de este modo; **taking one with ~ they're not bad** tomándolos en conjunto no son nada malos; **if not this time then ~** si no esta vez, pues otra.
3 *reflexive pron*: **they love one ~** (*2 persons*) se quieren (uno a otro), (*more than 2 persons*) se quieren unos a otros; **they don't speak to one ~** no se hablan.
A.N. Other [,eɪ,en'ʌðəʳ] *n* fulano* *m*, un tipo cualquiera*; '~' (*in list*) 'a concretar'.
Ansaphone ['ɑ:nsəfəʊn] ® *n* contestador *m* automático.
ANSI *n* (*US*) *abbr of* **American National Standards Institute**.
answer ['ɑ:nsəʳ] **1** *n* (**a**) (*to question etc*) contestación *f*, respuesta *f* (*to* a); (*Jur*) contestación *f* a la demanda, réplica *f*; **in ~ to** contestando a; **he smiled in ~** contestó con una sonrisa; **his only ~ was to smile** por toda respuesta, se sonrió; **I knocked but there was no ~** llamé pero no contestaron; **she's always got an ~** siempre tiene la respuesta pronta; **to know all the ~s** saberlo todo, ser una hacha*; **he's not exactly the ~ to a maiden's prayer** no es precisamente el hombre soñado.
(**b**) (*to problem*) solución *f* (*to* de); **what do you make the ~?** ¿qué solución tienes?; **my ~ is to do nothing** mi solución es no hacer nada, yo me propongo no hacer nada; **there is no easy ~** esto no se resuelve fácilmente; **it's the poor man's ~ to champagne** es lo que se sirve el pobre en lugar de champán.
(**c**) (*defence, reason*) **there must be an ~** debe de haber una razón, debe de haber una explicación; **he has an ~ to everything** lo justifica todo; **he has a complete ~ to the charges** puede probar su inocencia; **there is no ~ to the H-bomb** contra la bomba H no hay defensa posible.
2 *vt* (**a**) *charge, question etc* contestar a, responder a; *letter* contestar (a); **he ~ed not a word** no dijo palabra; **that should ~ your question** eso debe resolver (*or* satisfacer) sus dudas; **God will ~ our prayers** Dios escuchará nuestras oraciones; **our prayers have been ~ed** nuestras súplicas han sido oídas; **to ~ the bell, to ~ the door** acudir a la puerta, atender la puerta (*LAm*); **to ~ the telephone** contestar el teléfono; **to ~ one's name** contestar a su nombre; **to ~ a call for help** acudir a una llamada de socorro.

(**b**) *description, expectations* corresponder a, cuadrar con; *purpose* convenir para; *dream* realizar.
(**c**) **to ~ the helm** obedecer al timón.
3 *vi* (**a**) contestar, responder.
(**b**) **to ~ to** *description* corresponder a, cuadrar con; **the dog ~s to the name of Cipion** el perro atiende por Cipión.
(**c**) (*suffice*) servir, convenir.
◆answer back *vi* replicar; (*habitually*) ser respondón; **don't ~ back!** ¡no repliques!
◆answer for *vt thing* responder de, ser responsable de, *person* responder por; **I'll not ~ for the consequences** no me responsabilizo de las consecuencias; **he's got a lot to ~ for** tiene la culpa de muchas cosas.
answerable ['ɑːnsərəbl] *adj* (**a**) *question* que tiene contestación, *problem* que admite solución; **the question is not readily ~** la pregunta no tiene contestación fácil.
(**b**) (*responsible*) responsable; **to be ~ to sb for sth** ser responsable ante uno de algo; **he's not ~ to anyone** no tiene que dar cuentas a nadie.
answer-back ['ɑːnsə,bæk] *n*: **~ (code)** código *m* de respuesta.
answering ['ɑːnsərɪŋ] *attr*: **~ machine** contestador *m* automático; **~ service** servicio *m* de contestación automática.
ant [ænt] *n* hormiga *f*; **to have ~s in one's pants*** tener avispas en el culo*.
ANTA *n* (*US*) *abbr of* **American National Theater and Academy.**
antacid ['ænt'æsɪd] **1** *adj* antiácido. **2** *n* antiácido *m*.
antagonism [æn'tægənɪzəm] *n* antagonismo *m*; oposición *f*, hostilidad *f* (*to* a); rivalidad *f* (*between* entre).
antagonist [æn'tægənɪst] *n* adversario *m*, -a *f*, antagonista *mf*.
antagonistic [æn,tægə'nɪstɪk] *adj* antagónico; contrario, opuesto (*to* a); **I am not in the least ~ to the idea** yo no me opongo en lo más mínimo a la idea.
antagonize [æn'tægənaɪz] *vt* enemistarse con, provocar la enemistad de; **I don't want to ~ him** no quiero contrariarle; **he managed to ~ everybody** logró ponerse a malas con todos, logró suscitar el antagonismo de todos.
Antarctic [ænt'ɑːktɪk] **1** *adj* antártico; **~ Ocean** Océano *m* Antártico. **2** *n*: **the ~** el Antártico.
Antarctica [ænt'ɑːktɪkə] *n* Antártida *f*.
Antarctic Circle [ænt'ɑːktɪk'sɜːkl] *n* Círculo *m* Polar Antártico.
ante ['æntɪ] (*esp US*) **1** *n* apuesta *f*, tanto *m*; **to raise** (*or* **up**) **the ~** aumentar las apuestas. **2** *vt* apostar. **3** *vi* poner su apuesta.
◆ante up *vi* (*US**) pagar, apoquinar*.
ante... ['æntɪ] *pref* ante...
anteater ['ænt,iːtəʳ] *n* oso *m* hormiguero.
antecedent [,æntɪ'siːdənt] **1** *adj* antecedente. **2** *n* antecedente *m*; **~s** antecedentes *mpl*.
antechamber ['æntɪ,tʃeɪmbəʳ] *n* antecámara *f*, antesala *f*.
antedate ['æntɪ'deɪt] *vt* (**a**) (*in time*) preceder, ser anterior a; **text A ~s B by 50 years** el texto A es anterior a B en 50 años; **this building ~s the Norman conquest** este edificio se construyó antes de la conquista normanda.
(**b**) *cheque etc* antedatar, poner fecha anticipada a.
antediluvian ['æntɪdɪ'luːvɪən] *adj* antediluviano; (*fig*) viejísimo.
antelope ['æntɪləʊp] *n* antílope *m*.
antenatal ['æntɪ'neɪtl] *adj* prenatal, antenatal; **~ care** asistencia *f* prenatal; **~ clinic** clínica *f* de asistencia prenatal; **~ examination** reconocimiento *m* prenatal.
antenna [æn'tenə] *n*, *pl* **antennae** [æn'teniː] (*all senses*) antena *f*.
antepenult [,æntipɪ'nʌlt] *n* sílaba *f* antepenúltima.
antepenultimate ['æntɪpɪ'nʌltɪmɪt] *adj* antepenúltimo.
anterior [æn'tɪərɪəʳ] *adj* anterior (*to* a).
anteroom ['æntɪrʊm] *n* antesala *f*, antecámara *f*.
anthem ['ænθəm] *n* (*Eccl*) motete *m*; **national ~** himno *m* nacional.
anther ['ænθəʳ] *n* antera *f*.
ant-hill ['ænthɪl] *n* hormiguero *m*.
anthologist [æn'θɒlədʒɪst] *n* antologista *mf*.
anthologize [æn'θɒlədʒaiz] *vt works* hacer una antología de; *poem, author* incluir en una antología.
anthology [æn'θɒlədʒɪ] *n* antología *f*.
Anthony ['æntənɪ] *nm* Antonio.
anthracite ['ænθrəsaɪt] *n* antracita *f*.
anthrax ['ænθræks] *n* ántrax *m*.
anthropo... [,ænθrəʊpɒ] *pref* antropo...
anthropocentric [,ænθrəʊpəʊ'sentrɪk] *adj* antropocéntrico.
anthropoid ['ænθrəʊpɔɪd] **1** *adj* antropoide. **2** *n* antropoideo *m*.
anthropological [,ænθrəpə'lɒdʒikəl] *adj* antropológico.
anthropologist [,ænθrə'pɒlədʒɪst] *n* antropólogo *m*, -a *f*.
anthropology [,ænθrə'pɒlədʒɪ] *n* antropología *f*.
anthropomorphic [,ænθrəpəʊ'mɔːfɪk] *adj* antropomórfico.
anthropomorphism [,ænθrəʊpə'mɔːfɪzəm] *n* antropomorfismo *m*.
anthropophagi [,ænθrəʊ'pɒfəgaɪ] *npl* antropófagos *mpl*.
anthropophagous [,ænθrəʊ'pɒfəgəs] *adj* antropófago.
anthropophagy [,ænθrəʊ'pɒfədʒɪ] *n* antropofagia *f*.
anti... ['æntɪ] (**a**) *in compounds*: anti... (**b**) **he's rather ~*** está más bien opuesto; **she is ~ the whole idea*** ella está completamente en contra de la idea.
anti-abortion [,æntɪə'bɔːʃən] *adj*: **~ campaign** campaña *f* en contra del aborto, campaña *f* antiabortista.
anti-abortionist [,æntɪə'bɔːʃənɪst] *n* antiabortista *mf*.
anti-aircraft ['æntɪ'ɛəkrɑːft] *adj* antiaéreo; **~ gun** cañón *m* antiaéreo.
antiballistic ['æntɪbə'lɪstɪk] *adj*: **~ missile** mísil *m* antibalístico.
antibiotic ['æntɪbaɪ'ɒtɪk] **1** *adj* antibiótico. **2** *n* antibiótico *m*.
antibody ['æntɪ,bɒdɪ] *n* anticuerpo *m*.
antic ['æntɪk] *n* V **antics.**
Antichrist ['æntɪkraɪst] *n* Anticristo *m*.
anticipate [æn'tɪsɪpeɪt] *vt* (**a**) (*forestall*) *person* anticiparse a, adelantarse a; *event* anticiparse a, prevenir.
(**b**) (*foresee*) prever; **~d cost** (*Comm*) coste *m* previsto; **~d profit** beneficios *mpl* previstos; **as ~d** de acuerdo con lo previsto, según se había previsto; **you have ~d my wishes** Vd se ha anticipado (*or* adelantado) a mis deseos; **you have ~d my orders** Vd se ha anticipado a mis órdenes, (*wrongly*) Vd ha actuado sin esperar mis órdenes.
(**c**) (*expect*) esperar; contar con; (*look forward to*) prometerse; *pleasure* disfrutar de antemano; *pain* sufrir anticipadamente; **this is more than I ~d** esto es más de lo que esperaba; **the police ~d trouble** la policía contaba con algunos disturbios; **the ~d audience did not materialize** no apareció el público con que se había contado; **I ~ seeing her tomorrow** cuento con verla mañana; **to ~ that ...** prever que ..., calcular que ...; **do you ~ that this will be easy?** ¿crees que esto va a resultar fácil?; **we ~ that he will come in spite of everything** esperamos que venga a pesar de todo.
anticipation [æn,tɪsɪ'peɪʃən] *n* (**a**) (*forestalling*) anticipación *f*, prevención *f*.
(**b**) (*foresight*) previsión *f*, prevención *f*; **to act with ~** proceder con anticipación, obrar con previsión.
(**c**) (*foretaste*) anticipo *m*, anticipación *f*.
(**d**) (*expectation*) esperanza *f*, esperanzas *fpl*; **in ~ of a fine week** esperando una semana de buen tiempo; **it did not come up to our ~s** no correspondió a nuestras esperanzas, no alcanzó el nivel esperado; **I bought it in ~ of her visit** lo compré en previsión de su visita; **I thank you in ~** le doy las gracias anticipadas.
(**e**) (*advance excitement*) expectación *f*, ilusión *f*; **we waited with growing ~** esperábamos con creciente ilusión; **we waited in great ~** esperábamos muy ilusionados.
anticipatory [æn'tɪsɪpeɪtərɪ] *adj* anticipador; **~ breach of contract** violación *f* anticipadora de contrato.
anticlerical ['æntɪ'klerɪkl] **1** *adj* anticlerical. **2** *n* anticlerical *mf*.
anticlericalism ['æntɪ'klerɪklɪzəm] *n* anticlericalismo *m*.
anticlimactic ['æntɪklaɪ'mæktɪk] *adj* que marca un descenso de la emoción *etc*; decepcionante.
anticlimax ['æntɪ'klaɪmæks] *n* acontecimiento *m* (*etc*) que marca un descenso de la emoción *etc*; decepción *f*, chasco *m*; (*Rhetoric*) anticlímax *m*; **what an ~!** ¡qué decepción!; **the book ends in ~** la emoción desfallece hacia el fin de la novela, la novela termina de modo decepcionante; **the game came as an ~** el partido no correspondió con las esperanzas, el partido no alcanzó el nivel esperado.
anticlockwise ['æntɪ'klɒkwaɪz] (*Brit*) **1** *adj* sinistrorso. **2** *adv* sinistrórsum, en dirección contraria a la de las agujas del reloj.
anticoagulant ['æntɪkəʊ'ægjʊlənt] **1** *adj* anticoagulante. **2** *n* anticoagulante *f*.
anticorrosive ['æntɪkə'rəʊzɪv] *adj* anticorrosivo.
antics ['æntɪks] *npl* (*of clown*) bufonadas *fpl*, payasadas *fpl*; (*of child, animal*) gracias *fpl*, travesuras *fpl*; **he's up to his ~ again** ha vuelto a hacer de las suyas; **all his ~** todas sus payasadas.
anticyclone ['æntɪ'saɪkləʊn] *n* anticiclón *m*.
anticyclonic [,æntɪsaɪ'klɒnɪk] *adj* anticiclónico, anticiclonal.

anti-dandruff [ˌæntɪˈdændrəf] *adj* anticaspa.
anti-dazzle [ˈæntɪˈdæzl] *adj* antideslumbrante.
antidepressant [ˌæntɪdɪˈpresnt] **1** *adj* antidepresivo. **2** *n* antidepresivo *m.*
antidote [ˈæntɪdəʊt] *n* antídoto *m* (*against, for, to* contra).
anti-dumping [ˈæntɪˈdʌmpɪŋ] *attr*: ~ **duty** arancel *m* anti-dumping; ~ **measures** medidas *fpl* anti-dumping.
antifeminism [ˌæntɪˈfemɪnɪzəm] *n* antifeminismo *m.*
antifeminist [ˌæntɪˈfemɪnɪst] **1** *adj* antifeminista. **2** *n* antifeminista *mf.*
antifreeze [ˈæntɪˈfriːz] **1** *adj* anticongelante. **2** *n* anticongelante *m.*
anti-friction [ˈæntɪˈfrɪkʃən] *adj* antifriccional, contrafricción (*attr*).
antigen [ˈæntɪdʒən] *n* antígeno *m.*
anti-glare [ˈæntɪˈglɛəʳ] *adj* antideslumbrante.
Antigone [ænˈtɪgənɪ] *nf* Antígona.
anti-hero [ˈæntɪˌhɪərəʊ] *n* antihéroe *m.*
antihistamine [ˌæntɪˈhɪstəmɪn] **1** *adj* antihistamínico. **2** *n* antihistamínico *m.*
anti-inflationary [ˌæntɪɪnˈfleɪʃnərɪ] *adj* antiinflacionista.
anti-knock [ˈæntɪˈnɒk] *adj* antidetonante.
Antilles [ænˈtɪliːz] *npl* Antillas *fpl.*
anti-lock [ˈæntɪˈlɒk] *adj*: ~ **device** (*Aut*) dispositivo *m* antibloque.
antilogarithm [ˌæntɪˈlɒgərɪθəm] *n* antilogaritmo *m.*
antimacassar [ˈæntɪməˈkæsəʳ] *n* antimacasar *m.*
antimagnetic [ˌæntɪmægˈnetɪk] *adj* antimagnético.
antimalarial [ˌæntɪməˈlɛərɪəl] *adj* antipalúdico.
anti-marketeer [ˈæntɪˌmɑːkəˈtɪəʳ] *n* (*Brit Pol*) persona *f* contraria al Mercado Común.
antimatter [ˈæntɪˌmætəʳ] *n* antimateria *f.*
antimissile [ˈæntɪˈmɪsaɪl] *adj* antimisil.
antimony [ˈæntɪmənɪ] *n* antimonio *m.*
antinomy [ænˈtɪnəmɪ] *n* antinomia *f.*
antinuclear [ˈæntɪˈnjuːklɪəʳ] *adj* antinuclear.
Antioch [ˈæntɪɒk] *n* Antioquía *f.*
antiparasitic [ˌæntɪˌpaerəˈsɪtɪk] *adj* antiparasitario.
antipathetic [ˌæntɪpəˈθetɪk] *adj* antipático (*to* a); hostil (*to* a).
antipathy [ænˈtɪpəθɪ] *n* (**a**) (*feeling*) antipatía *f* (*between* entre; *to* por, hacia). (**b**) (*thing disliked*) aversión *f,* cosa *f* aborrecida.
antipersonnel [ˈæntɪpɜːsəˈnel] *adj* destinado a causar bajas.
antiperspirant [ˌæntɪˈpɜːspərənt] **1** *adj* antiperspirante. **2** *n* antiperspirante *m.*
antiphon [ˈæntɪfən] *n* antífona *f.*
antiphony [ænˈtɪfənɪ] *n* canto *m* antifonal.
antipodean [ænˌtɪpəˈdiːən] **1** *adj* de las antípodas; (*hum*) australiano. **2** *n* habitante *mf* de las antípodas; (*hum*) australiano *m,* -a *f.*
antipodes [ænˈtɪpədiːz] *npl* antípodas *mpl*; **the A~** (*esp hum*) Australia *f* (y Nueva Zelanda *f*).
antipope [ˈæntɪpəʊp] *n* antipapa *m.*
antiprotectionist [ˌæntɪprəˈtɛkʃənɪst] *adj* antiproteccionista.
antiquarian [ˌæntɪˈkwɛərɪən] **1** *adj* anticuario; ~ **bookseller** librero *m* especializado en libros antiguos; ~ **bookshop** librería *f* anticuaria; ~ **collection** colección *f* de antigüedades. **2** *n* (*collector*) aficionado *m,* -a *f* a antigüedades, coleccionista *mf* de antigüedades; (*dealer*) anticuario *m,* -a *f.*
antiquary [ˈæntɪkwərɪ] *n* = **antiquarian 2.**
antiquated [ˈæntɪkweɪtɪd] *adj* anticuado.
antique [ænˈtiːk] **1** *adj* antiguo, viejo; (*pej*) anticuado; decimonónico, caduco; *furniture etc* de época.
2 *n* antigüedad *f,* antigualla *f* (*also pej*); ~ **dealer** anticuario *m,* -a *f,* comerciante *mf* en antigüedades; ~ **shop** tienda *f* de antigüedades.
antiquity [ænˈtɪkwɪtɪ] *n* (*all senses*) antigüedad *f*; **antiquities** antigüedades *fpl*; **high** ~ remota antigüedad *f*; **in** ~ en la antigüedad, en el mundo antiguo.
antiracist [ˈæntɪˈreɪsɪst] **1** *adj* antirracista. **2** *n* antirracista *mf.*
antireligious [ˈæntɪrɪˈlɪdʒəs] *adj* antirreligioso.
anti-riot [ˈæntɪˈraɪət] *adj*: ~ **police** policía *f* antidisturbios.
anti-roll [ˈæntɪˈrəʊl] *adj*: (*Brit*) ~ **bar** barra *f* estabilizadora, barra *f* antivuelco, estabilizador *m*; ~ **device** estabilizador *m.*
antirrhinum [ˌæntɪˈraɪnəm] *n* antirrino *m.*
anti-rust [ˈæntɪˈrʌst] *adj* antioxidante, anticorrosión (*attr*).
antisegregationist [ˈæntɪsegrəˈgeɪʃənɪst] *adj* antisegregacionista.
anti-semite [ˈæntɪˈsiːmaɪt] *n* antisemita *mf.*
anti-semitic [ˈæntɪsɪˈmɪtɪk] *adj* antisemítico.
anti-semitism [ˈæntɪˈsemɪtɪzəm] *n* antisemitismo *m.*
antiseptic [ˌæntɪˈseptɪk] **1** *adj* antiséptico. **2** *n* antiséptico *m.*
anti-skid [ˈæntɪˈskɪd] *adj* antideslizante.
antislavery [ˈæntɪˈsleɪvərɪ] *adj* en contra de la esclavitud.
antisocial [ˈæntɪˈsəʊʃəl] *adj* antisocial.
anti-strike [ˈæntɪˈstraɪk] *adj* antihuelga.
anti-submarine [ˈæntɪsʌbməˈriːn] *adj* antisubmarino.
anti-tank [ˈæntɪˈtæŋk] *adj* antitanque.
anti-terrorist [ˈæntɪˈterərɪst] *adj*: ~ **brigade** brigada *f* antiterrorista.
anti-theft [ˌæntɪˈθeft] *adj*: ~ **device** sistema *m* anti-robo.
antithesis [ænˈtɪθɪsɪs] *n, pl* **antitheses** [ænˈtɪθɪsiːz] antítesis *f.*
antithetic(al) [ˌæntɪˈθetɪk(əl)] *adj* antitético.
antitoxin [ˈæntɪˈtɒksɪn] *n* antitoxina *f.*
anti-trust [ˈæntɪˈtrʌst] *adj* antimonopolista; ~ **law** ley *f* antimonopolios; ~ **legislation** legislación *f* antimonopolios.
antivivisectionism [ˈæntɪˌvɪvɪˈsekʃənɪzəm] *n* antiviviseccionismo *m.*
antivivisectionist [ˈæntɪˌvɪvɪˈsekʃənɪst] *n* antiviviseccionista *mf.*
anti-war [ˌæntɪˈwɔːʳ] *adj* antibelicista, antiguerra, pacifista.
anti-wrinkle [ˈæntɪˈrɪŋkl] *adj* antiarrugas.
antler [ˈæntləʳ] *n* cuerna *f*; ~**s** cuernas *fpl,* cornamenta *f.*
Antony [ˈæntənɪ] *nm* Antonio.
antonym [ˈæntənɪm] *n* antónimo *m.*
antsy‡ [ˈæntsɪ] *adj* (*US*) nervioso, inquieto.
Antwerp [ˈæntwɜːp] *n* Amberes *f.*
anus [ˈeɪnəs] *n* ano *m.*
anvil [ˈænvɪl] *n* yunque *m.*
anxiety [æŋˈzaɪətɪ] *n* (**a**) (*worry*) inquietud *f,* preocupación *f,* ansiedad *f*; **some ~ is felt about it** existe cierta inquietud sobre esto; **it is a great ~ to me** me preocupa muchísimo; **that child is a perpetual ~** ese niño me trae loco.
(**b**) (*eagerness*) ansia *f,* anhelo *m* (*for* de; *to do* de hacer, por hacer); **in his ~ to be off he forgot his case** tanto ansiaba partir que olvidó la maleta.
(**c**) (*Med*) ansiedad *f*; angustia *f*; ~ **neurosis** neurosis *f* de ansiedad.
anxious [ˈæŋkʃəs] *adj* (**a**) (*worried*) inquieto, preocupado, angustiado; **to be ~ about, to be ~ for** inquietarse por; **I'm very ~ about you** me tienes muy preocupado; **in an ~ voice** en un tono angustiado; **with an ~ glance** con una mirada inquieta, con una mirada llena de inquietud.
(**b**) (*causing worry*) **it is an ~ time** es un período de gran ansiedad; **you gave me some ~ moments** a ratos me causaste gran inquietud; **it was an ~ moment** fue un momento de ansiedad.
(**c**) (*eager*) deseoso (*for* de; *to do* de hacer); **he is ~ for success** ansía el triunfo, ambiciona el triunfo; **to be ~ to do** anhelar hacer, tener ganas de hacer, tener empeño en hacer; **I am very ~ that he should go** quiero a toda costa que vaya; **I'm not very ~ to go** tengo pocas ganas de ir; **she is ~ to see you before you go** se empeña en verte antes de que te vayas.
anxiously [ˈæŋkʃəslɪ] *adv* (**a**) con inquietud, de manera angustiada, con ansiedad. (**b**) con impaciencia.
anxiousness [ˈæŋkʃəsnɪs] *n* = **anxiety.**
any [ˈenɪ] **1** *adj* (**a**) algún, alguna; **if there are ~ tickets left** si queda alguna entrada; **he'll do it if ~ man can** lo hará si lo puede alguno.
(**b**) (*partitive: gen not translated*) **have you ~ money?** ¿tienes dinero?; **have you ~ bananas?** ¿hay plátanos?; **is there ~ man who ...?** ¿hay hombre que ...?
(**c**) (*any ... you like*) cualquier; ~ **day now** cualquier día; ~ **farmer will tell you** te lo dirá cualquier agricultor; **wear ~ hat (you like)** ponte el sombrero que quieras, ponte sombrero (no importa cuál); **he's not just ~ golfer** no es un golfista cualquiera; ~ **person who breaks the rules will be expelled** se expulsará a toda persona que viole las reglas; **take ~ two children** tome dos niños al azar, tome dos niños cualesquiera; **he should arrive at ~ moment now** deberá llegar de un momento a otro.
(**d**) (*negative sense*) ningún, ninguna; **I haven't ~ money** no tengo dinero; **I don't see ~ cows** no veo vaca alguna, no veo ninguna vaca.
2 *pron* (**a**) alguno, alguna; **if there are ~ who ...** si hay algunos que ...; **if ~ of you knows how to drive** si alguno de vosotros sabe conducir; **few, if ~** pocos, si es que los hay; pocos, si acaso alguno.
(**b**) (*any ... you like*) cualquiera; **take ~ you like** tome cualquiera; ~ **but her would have protested** cualquier persona que no fuera ella hubiera protestado.
(**c**) (*negative sense*) ninguno, ninguna; **I haven't ~ of**

them no tengo ninguno de ellos; **I have hardly ~ left** apenas me queda (alguno), ninguno apenas me queda.

3 *adv* (**a**) (*gen not translated*) **~ more** más; **don't wait ~ longer** no esperes más tiempo; **are there ~ others?** ¿hay otros?; **is he ~ better?** ¿está algo mejor?; **they didn't sing ~ too well** no han cantado bien que digamos; **I couldn't do that ~ more than I could fly** yo haría eso igual que podría volar.

(**b**) (*esp US**) **it doesn't help us ~** eso no nos ayuda para nada; **does she sing ~?** ¿sabe cantar de alguna manera?

anybody ['enɪbɒdɪ] *pron* (**a**) alguien, alguno; **did you see ~?** ¿vio a alguien?; **~ would have said he was mad** se hubiera dicho que estaba loco; **if ~ can manage it, he can** si lo puede alguno lo podrá él; **~ who wants to go back should go now** si alguno quiere volver que vuelva ahora; **I'll shoot ~ who moves** al primero que se mueva le mato.

(**b**) (**~ ...** *you like*) cualquiera; **~ will tell you the same** cualquiera te dirá lo mismo; **~ who invests in this** todo el que invierta en esto; **~ else would have laughed** cualquier otro se hubiera reído; **bring ~ you like** trae a quien quieras; **~ but Napoleon** todos menos Napoleón, todo el que no fuera Napoleón; **it's not available to just ~** no se hace asequible a todos sin distinción; **I'm not going to marry just ~** yo no me caso con un cualquiera; **it's ~'s guess!** ¡nadie lo sabe!; **it's ~'s race** esta carrera la podría ganar cualquiera; **he's not just ~, he's the boss** no es un cualquiera, es el jefe.

(**c**) (*negative sense*) nadie, ninguno; **I can't see ~** no veo a nadie; **hardly ~ came** apenas vino nadie.

(**d**) (*person of importance*) **is he ~?** ¿es una persona de importancia?; **he isn't ~ in this town** en este pueblo no es nadie, en este pueblo no cuenta para nada; **you must work harder if you want to be ~** tienes que trabajar más si quieres llegar a ser algo.

anyhow ['enɪhaʊ] *adv* (**a**) (*at any rate*) de todas formas, de todos modos, con todo; **~ it's not my fault** de todas formas yo no tengo la culpa.

(**b**) (*in spite of everything*) **I shall go ~** voy a pesar de todo, sin embargo voy.

(**c**) (*haphazard: also* **any old how***) **he leaves things just ~** deja sus cosas de cualquier modo; **I came in late and finished my essay off ~** volví tarde y terminé mi ensayo sin pensarlo mucho.

(**d**) (*in any way whatever*) no importa cómo; **do it ~ you like** hazlo del modo que quieras; **the door was locked and I couldn't get in ~** la puesta estaba cerrada y no había manera de entrar.

(**e**) (*by the way*) a propósito; **why are you going, ~?** por cierto, ¿por qué te vas?

anyone ['enɪwʌn] *pron* = **anybody**.

anyplace ['enɪpleɪs] *adv* (*US*) = **anywhere**.

anything ['enɪθɪŋ] *pron* (**a**) algo, alguna cosa; **is there ~ inside?** ¿hay algo dentro?; **are you doing ~ tonight?** ¿tienes compromiso para esta noche?; **have you heard ~ of them?** ¿tienes alguna noticia de ellos?; **it's as clean as ~*** está pero muy limpio*, está requetelimpio*; **~ else?** (*in shop etc*) ¿algo más?, ¿alguna cosita más?; **is there ~ in this idea?** ¿tiene algún valor esta idea?; **if ~ it's much better** es mucho mejor si cabe; **if ~ it's larger** si acaso, es algo más grande.

(**b**) (**~** *you like*) cualquier cosa; **he will give you ~ you ask for** te dará lo que pidas; **sing ~ you like** canta lo que quieras, canta cualquier cosa; **~ but that** todo menos eso; **~ but!** (*reply to question*) ¡nada de eso!; **~ else is ruled out** todo lo demás está excluido; **I'll read ~ else** leeré cualquier otra cosa; **I'm not buying just ~** yo no compro una cosa cualquiera; **it was ~ but pleasant** era todo menos que agradable; **I'd give ~ to know** daría cualquier cosa por saberlo.

(**c**) (*negative sense*) nada; **I can't see ~** no veo nada; **you haven't seen ~ yet** todavía no has visto nada; **he's not a minister or ~** no es ministro ni nada por el estilo; **can't ~ be done?** ¿no se puede hacer nada?; **we can't do ~ else** no podemos hacer otra cosa; **hardly ~** casi nada; **not for ~ in the world** por nada del mundo.

(**d**) **like ~*** hasta más no poder.

anytime ['enɪtaɪm] *adv V* **time**.

anyway ['enɪweɪ] *adv* = **anyhow**.

anywhere ['enɪweəʳ] *adv* (**a**) en todas partes, en (*or* a) cualquier parte, dondequiera; **~ in the world** en todas partes del mundo; en cualquier parte del mundo; **go ~ you like** vaya adonde quiera; **~ you go you'll see the same** dondequiera que vayas verás lo mismo; **~ else** en cualquier otra parte; **I'm not going to live just ~** yo no voy a vivir en un sitio cualquiera; **it's miles from ~** está en el quinto infierno; **it's not ~ near Castroforte** está bastante lejos de Castroforte; **do you see him ~?** ¿le ves en alguna parte?; **she leaves her things just ~** deja sus cosas en cualquier parte; **~ from 200 to 300** (*US*) entre 200 y 300.

(**b**) (*negative sense*) en (*or* a) ninguna parte; **I'm not going ~** yo no voy a ninguna parte; **he was first and the rest didn't come ~** él se clasificó primero y los demás quedaron muy por debajo; **that won't get you ~** así no llegas a ninguna parte; **we didn't go ~ special** no fuimos a ningún sitio especial.

Anzac ['ænzæk] *n abbr of* **Australia-New Zealand Army Corps** Fuerzas *fpl* Armadas de Australia y Nueva Zelanda.

A.O.(C.)B. *abbr of* **any other (competent) business** ruegos *mpl* y preguntas.

aorist ['ɛərɪst] *n* aoristo *m*.

aorta [eɪ'ɔːtə] *n* aorta *f*.

aortic [eɪ'ɔːtɪk] *adj* aórtico.

AP *n abbr of* **Associated Press** *agencia de prensa*.

apace [ə'peɪs] *adv* aprisa, rápidamente.

apache [ə'pætʃɪ] *n* apache *m*.

apart [ə'pɑːt] **1** *adv* (**a**) (*separated*) aparte, separadamente; **with one's feet ~** con los pies apartados; **posts set equally ~** postes *mpl* espaciados con regularidad, postes *mpl* colocados a intervalos iguales; **they stood a long way ~** estaban muy apartados (el uno del otro); **we live only three doors ~** vivimos a tres puertas de ellos; **the deaths were only three days ~** murieron con sólo tres días de diferencia; **they are living ~ now** ahora viven separados; **he lives ~ from his wife** vive separado de su mujer; **the house stands somewhat ~** la casa está algo aislada; **to hold o.s. ~** mantenerse aparte; **to keep ~** separar, mantener aislado (*from* de); **to tell ~** distinguir.

(**b**) (*aside*) **that ~** aparte de eso; **but joking ~** pero bromas aparte, pero en serio; **to set ~** guardar, reservar (*for* para), poner aparte.

(**c**) (*in pieces*) **to come ~, to fall ~** romperse, deshacerse; **to tear ~** hacer trizas, destrozar (*and V* **tear[1]**); *V* **take** *etc*.

2 ~ from *prep* aparte de; **but quite ~ from that** pero aparte de eso.

apartheid [ə'pɑːteɪt] *n* apartheid *m*, segregación *f* racial.

aparthotel [ə'pɑːthəʊ,tel] *n* apart(a)hotel *m*.

apartment [ə'pɑːtmənt] *n* (**a**) (*Brit: room*) cuarto *m*, aposento *m*; **~s** piso *m*, apartamento *m* (en una casa), departamento *m* (*LAm*).

(**b**) (*esp US*) piso *m*, apartamento *m*; **~ hotel** (*US*) pisos *mpl* con personal de servicio; **~ house** (*US*) casa *f* de pisos.

apathetic [,æpə'θetɪk] *adj* apático, indiferente; **to be ~ towards** ser indiferente a, no mostrar interés alguno en.

apathetically [,æpə'θetɪkəlɪ] *adv* con apatía, con indiferencia, sin entusiasmo.

apathy ['æpəθɪ] *n* apatía *f*, indiferencia *f* (*towards* a), falta *f* de interés (*towards* en).

APB *n* (*US*) *abbr of* **all points bulletin** *frase usada por la policía por 'descubrir y aprehender'*.

APC *n abbr of* **armoured personnel carrier**.

ape [eɪp] **1** *n* (**a**) mono *m* (*esp* los antropomorfos), simio *m*, antropoideo *m*; **you (great) ~!*** ¡bestia!*; **to go ~** (*US‡*) volverse loco, enloquecer. (**b**) (*fig*) mono *m* de imitación, imitador *m*, -ora *f*. **2** *vt* imitar, remedar.

Apennines ['æpɪnaɪnz] *npl* Apeninos *mpl*.

aperient [ə'pɪərɪənt] **1** *adj* laxante. **2** *n* laxante *m*.

apéritif [ə'perɪtɪv] *n* aperitivo *m*.

aperture ['æpətʃjʊəʳ] *n* abertura *f*, rendija *f*, resquicio *m*; (*Phot etc*) abertura *f*.

APEX ['eɪpeks] *n* (**a**) (*Brit*) *abbr of* **Association of Professional, Executive, Clerical and Computer Staff** Asociación *f* de Profesionales, Ejecutivos, Auxiliares Administrativos y Personal de Informática. (**b**) (*also* **apex**) *abbr of* **Advance Purchase Excursion**: **~ fare** precio *m* APEX; **~ ticket** billete *m* APEX.

apex ['eɪpeks] *n, pl* **apices** ['eɪpɪsiːz] ápice *m*; (*fig*) cumbre *f*.

aphasia [æ'feɪzɪə] *n* afasia *f*.

aphid ['eɪfɪd] *n* áfido *m*.

aphis ['eɪfɪs] *n, pl* **aphides** ['eɪfɪdiːz] áfido *m*.

aphorism ['æfərɪzəm] *n* aforismo *m*.

aphrodisiac [,æfrəʊ'dɪzɪæk] **1** *adj* afrodisíaco. **2** *n* afrodisíaco *m*.

Aphrodite [,æfrəʊ'daɪtɪ] *nf* Afrodita.

API *n* (*US*) *abbr of* **American Press Institute**.

apiarist ['eɪpɪərɪst] *n* apicultor *m*, -ora *f*.

apiary ['eɪpɪərɪ] *n* colmenar *m*.
apiculture ['eɪpɪkʌltʃəʳ] *n* apicultura *f*.
apiece [ə'piːs] *adv* cada uno; por persona, por cabeza; *eg* **they had a gun ~** tenía cada uno un revólver; **he gave them an apple ~** dio una manzana a cada uno; **the rule is a dollar ~** la regla es un dólar por persona.
aplenty [ə'plentɪ] *adv*: **there was food ~** había comida abundante, había abundancia de comida.
aplomb [ə'plɒm] *n* aplomo *m*, sangre *f* fría, serenidad *f*; **with the greatest ~** con la mayor serenidad, tan tranquilo.
APO *n* (*US*) *abbr of* **Army Post Office.**
Apocalypse [ə'pɒkəlɪps] *n* Apocalipsis *m*.
apocalyptic [əˌpɒkə'lɪptɪk] *adj* apocalíptico.
apocopate [ə'pɒkəpeɪt] *vt* apocopar.
apocope [ə'pɒkəʊpɪ] *n* apócope *f*.
Apocrypha [ə'pɒkrɪfə] *npl* libros *mpl* apócrifos de la Biblia.
apocryphal [ə'pɒkrɪfəl] *adj* apócrifo.
apodosis [ə'pɒdəʊsɪs] *n* apódosis *f*.
apogee ['æpəʊdʒiː] *n* apogeo *m*.
apolitical [ˌeɪpə'lɪtɪkəl] *adj* apolítico.
Apollo [ə'pɒleʊ] *nm* Apolo.
apologetic [əˌpɒlə'dʒetɪk] **1** *adj* (**a**) (*contrite*) lleno de disculpas; apenado, que tiene ademán de pedir perdón, que se deshace en disculpas; **with an ~ air** como si viniera a pedir perdón; **he was very ~ about it** dijo que lo sentía profundamente; **he was very ~ about his dress** se disculpó mucho por su traje. (**b**) (*vindicatory*) apologético. **2 ~s** *npl* apologética *f*.
apologetically [əˌpɒlə'dʒetɪkəlɪ] *adv* con aire del que pide perdón, en tono apenado; con muchas excusas, excusándose; **he said ~** dijo apenado.
apologia [ˌæpə'leʊdʒɪə] *n* apología *f*.
apologist [ə'pɒlədʒɪst] *n* apologista *mf*.
apologize [ə'pɒlədʒaɪz] *vi* disculparse (*for* de; *to* con), pedir perdón (*to* a); (*for absence etc*) presentar sus excusas; **never ~!** disculpas, ¡nunca!
apologue ['æpəlɒg] *n* apólogo *m*.
apology [ə'pɒlədʒɪ] *n* (**a**) disculpa *f*, excusa *f*; **letter of ~** carta *f* de disculpa; **please accept my apologies** le ruego me disculpe; **I demand an ~** reclamo una satisfacción, insisto en que Vd se disculpe; **to make** (*or* **offer**) **an ~** disculparse, presentar sus excusas (*for* por); **to send an ~** (*at meeting*) presentar sus excusas; **there are apologies from X and Y** se han excusado X y Y.
(**b**) (*Liter etc*) apología *f*.
(**c**) (*pej*) **an ~ for a house** una birria de casa*; **this ~ for a letter** ésta que apenas se puede llamar carta.
apophthegm ['æpəʊθem] *n* apotegma *m*.
apoplectic [ˌæpə'plektɪk] *adj* apopléctico; (*fig*) furioso; **to get ~** (*fig*) enfurecerse.
apoplexy ['æpəpleksɪ] *n* apoplejía *f*; **to have ~** (*fig*) reventar (de rabia *etc*).
apostasy [ə'pɒstəsɪ] *n* apostasía *f*.
apostate [ə'pɒstɪt] *n* apóstata *mf*.
apostatize [ə'pɒstətaɪz] *vi* apostatar (*from* de).
apostle [ə'pɒsl] *n* apóstol *m*; (*fig*) apóstol *m*, paladín *m*.
apostolate [ə'pɒstəlɪt] *n* apostolado *m*.
apostolic [ˌæpəs'tɒlɪk] *adj* apostólico; **~ succession** sucesión *f* apostólica.
apostrophe [ə'pɒstrəfɪ] *n* (**a**) (*sign*) apóstrofo *m*. (**b**) (*address*) apóstrofe *gen m*.
apostrophize [ə'pɒstrəfaɪz] *vt* apostrofar.
apothecary [ə'pɒθɪkərɪ] *n* (†) boticario *m*.
apotheosis [əˌpɒθɪ'əʊsɪs] *n, pl* **apotheoses** [əˌpɒθɪ'əʊsiːz] apoteosis *f*.
appal, (*US*) **appall** [ə'pɔːl] *vt* horrorizar, aterrar; repugnar; **everyone was ~led** se horrorizaron todos, todos quedaron consternados; **I was ~led by the news** me horrorizó la noticia.
Appalachians [ˌæpə'leɪʃənz] *npl* (Montes *mpl*) Apalaches *mpl*.
appalling [ə'pɔːlɪŋ] *adj* espantoso, horroroso; *taste etc* detestable, pésimo.
appallingly [ə'pɔːlɪŋlɪ] *adv* espantosamente, horrorosamente; detestablemente; **it was quite ~ bad** fue del todo horrible; **he's ~ self-centred** es terriblemente egocéntrico.
apparatus [ˌæpə'reɪtəs] *n* aparato *m*.
apparel [ə'pærəl] **1** *n* ropa *f*, vestidos *mpl*; indumentaria *f*; (*hum*) atavío *m*. **2** *vt* vestir (*in* de); (*hum*) trajear, ataviar (*in* de).
apparent [ə'pærənt] *adj* (**a**) (*seeming*) aparente; **more ~ than real** más aparente que real.
(**b**) (*clear*) claro, evidente, manifiesto; *heir* forzoso; **it is ~ that ...** está claro que ...; **it is becoming ~ that ...** ya se está viendo que ...; **their weakness became ~** se hizo patente su debilidad.
apparently [ə'pærəntlɪ] *adv* (*evidently*) por lo visto; (*seemingly*) según parece, al parecer.
apparition [ˌæpə'rɪʃən] *n* (**a**) (*act*) aparición *f*. (**b**) (*ghost*) fantasma *m*, aparecido *m*.
appeal [ə'piːl] **1** *n* (**a**) (*call*) llamamiento *m*; **a national ~ for funds** un llamamiento a todo el país para que contribuya dinero; **~ for charity** cuestación *f* para obras benéficas; **he made an ~ for calm** hizo un llamamiento para que se mantuviera la calma.
(**b**) (*petition*) súplica *f*, ruego *m*, petición *f*; **deaf to all ~s** impasible; **an ~ for help** una petición de socorro.
(**c**) (*Jur*) apelación *f*, recurso *m* (de casación); **~ committee** (*Sport etc*) comité *m* de apelación; **~ court** tribunal *m* de apelación; **~s procedure** procedimiento *m* de apelación; **without ~** inapelable; **there is no ~ against his decision** su fallo es inapelable; **to give notice of ~** entablar apelación; **to lodge an ~** apelar (*against* de).
(**d**) (*attraction*) atractivo *m*, encanto *m*, interés *m*; **the ~ of children** el encanto de los niños; **a book of general ~** un libro de interés para todos.
2 *vt* (*Jur*) **to ~ a case** apelar de una sentencia.
3 *vi* (**a**) (*call, beg*) **to ~ for** suplicar, reclamar; **I ~ for its return** ruego que se me devuelva; **he ~ed for silence** rogó que se callasen todos; **the authorities ~ed for calm** las autoridades hicieron un llamamiento para que se mantuviera la calma; **to ~ to sb for sth** suplicar algo a uno; **I ~ to you!** ¡se lo ruego!; **it's no good ~ing to me** de nada sirve acudir a mí; **to ~ to arms** recurrir a las armas; **to ~ to the country** (*Pol*) apelar al arbitrio de las urnas; **to ~ to sb's finer feelings** apelar a los sentimientos nobles de uno.
(**b**) (*Jur*) apelar (*against* de; *to* a), recurrir (*against* contra).
(**c**) (*attract*) atraer, tener atractivo para, interesar, gustar; **jazz does not ~ to me** el jazz no me gusta; **it ~s to the imagination** estimula la imaginación; **I don't think this will ~ much to the public** no creo que esto tenga atractivo para el público.
appealing [ə'piːlɪŋ] *adj* (**a**) (*begging*) suplicante. (**b**) (*attractive*) atrayente, atractivo, encantador, sugestivo.
appealingly [ə'piːlɪŋlɪ] *adv* de modo suplicante.
appear [ə'pɪəʳ] *vi* (**a**) (*present o.s.*) aparecer, mostrarse, presentarse; **he ~ed from behind a tree** salió de detrás de un árbol; **he ~ed without a tie** se presentó sin corbata; **the plane ~ed out of a cloud** el avión salió de una nube; **when the sun ~s** cuando se muestra el sol, cuando sale el sol; **the ghost ~s at midnight** el fantasma aparece a medianoche; **he ~ed from nowhere** salió de la nada; **as will ~ in due course** según se verá luego; **she ~ed as Ophelia** hizo el papel de Ofelia; **she ~ed in 'Fuenteovejuna'** hizo un papel en 'Fuenteovejuna'; **when are you going to ~ on TV?** ¿cuándo te vas a presentar en TV?, ¿cuándo vas a salir por la tele?*; **to ~ to sb** (*as vision*) aparecerse a uno.
(**b**) (*book etc*) salir a luz, publicarse, aparecer.
(**c**) (*Jur*) comparecer (*before* ante); **to ~ on a charge of murder** comparecer acusado de homicidio; **to ~ on behalf of sb, to ~ for sb** representar a uno.
(**d**) (*seem*) parecer; **he ~s tired** parece cansado; **how does it ~ to you?** ¿qué le parece esto?; **it ~s that ...** resulta que ..., parece que ...; **so it ~s, so it would ~** así parece; **in daylight it ~s red** a la luz del día se muestra rojo.
appearance [ə'pɪərəns] *n* (**a**) (*act of appearing*) aparición *f*; **~ money** pago *m* por presentarse; **to make an ~** aparecer, presentarse, dejarse ver; **to make one's first ~** aparecer por primera vez; estrenarse; **to make a personal ~** aparecer en persona; **to put in an ~** hacer acto de presencia.
(**b**) (*Jur*) comparecencia *f*; **to make an ~ in court** comparecer ante el tribunal.
(**c**) (*of book etc*) publicación *f*.
(**d**) (*Theat etc*) actuación *f*; presentación *f*; **his ~ in 'Don Mendo'** su actuación en 'Don Mendo'; **his ~ as Don Mendo** su actuación en el papel de Don Mendo; **cast in order of ~** personajes *mpl* en orden de aparición en escena.
(**e**) (*aspect*) apariencia *f*, aspecto *m*; **to have a dignified ~** tener aspecto solemne.
(**f**) **~s** (*seeming*) apariencias *fpl*; **~s are deceptive** las apariencias engañan; **to** (*or* **by**) **all ~s** al parecer, según

todos los indicios; **it had all the ~s of a rabbit** se parecía en todo a un conejo; **you shouldn't go by ~s** no hay que juzgar por las apariencias.

(**g**) (*face*) apariencias *fpl*; **for the sake of ~s** para salvar las apariencias; **to keep up ~s, save ~s** salvar las apariencias.

appease [ə'pi:z] *vt* apaciguar; aplacar; *hunger* satisfacer, saciar; *passion* mitigar; *person* satisfacer, dar satisfacción a; *angry person* desenojar, apaciguar; (*Pol*) apaciguar, contemporizar con.

appeasement [ə'pi:zmənt] *n* apaciguamiento *m*, pacificación *f*; (*Pol*) apaciguamiento *m*, contemporización *f*.

appellant [ə'pelənt] *n* apelante *mf*.

appellate [ə'pelɪt] *adj*: **~ court** (*US*) tribunal *m* de apelación.

appellation [,æpe'leɪʃən] *n* nombre *m*, título *m*; (*of wine*) denominación *f* de origen.

append [ə'pend] *vt* (*add*) añadir; (*attach, enclose*) adjuntar, enviar adjunto; *signature* poner; (*Comput*) anexionar (al final).

appendage [ə'pendɪdʒ] *n* añadidura *f*, apéndice *m*; (*fig*) pegote *m*.

appendectomy [,æpen'dektəmɪ] *n* apendectomía *f*.

appendicitis [ə,pendɪ'saɪtɪs] *n* apendicitis *f*.

appendix [ə'pendɪks] *n*, *pl* **appendices** [ə'pendɪsi:z] apéndice *m*.

apperception [,æpə'sepʃən] *n* percepción *f*; **~ test** (*US*) test *m* de percepción.

appertain [,æpə'teɪn] *vi*: **to ~ to** relacionarse con, tener que ver con.

appetite ['æpɪtaɪt] *n* (**a**) apetito *m*; **~ depressant** inhibidor *m* del apetito; **to eat with an ~** comer con buen apetito; **to have no ~** no tener apetito, no tener ganas; **to whet one's ~** abrir el apetito, despertar el apetito.

(**b**) (*fig*) deseo *m*, anhelo *m* (*for* de), ganas *fpl*; **they had no ~ for further fighting** ya no les apetecía seguir luchando, no tenían más ganas de luchar; **to spoil one's ~ for** quitar a uno las ganas de.

appetizer ['æpɪtaɪzə^r] *n* aperitivo *m*; tapa *f*.

appetizing ['æpɪtaɪzɪŋ] *adj* apetitoso.

applaud [ə'plɔ:d] **1** *vt* aplaudir; (*fig*) aplaudir, celebrar, elogiar. **2** *vi* aplaudir, palmotear.

applause [ə'plɔ:z] *n* aplausos *mpl*, aplauso *m*; (*fig*) aplausos *mpl*, aprobación *f*; **a round of ~ for X!** ¡un aplauso para X!; **there was loud ~** sonaron fuertes aplausos; **to win the ~ of** ganarse la aprobación de.

apple ['æpl] *n* (*fruit*) manzana *f*; (*tree*) manzano *m*; **~ of discord** manzana *f* de la discordia; **the ~ of one's eye** la niña de los ojos; **~s and pears** (*Brit‡*) escalera *f*; **the** (**Big**) **A~** (*US**) Nueva York *f*.

apple-blossom ['æpl,blɒsəm] *n* flor *f* del manzano.

apple-brandy [,æpl'brændɪ] *n* aguardiente *m* de manzana.

applecart ['æplkɑ:t] *n*: **to upset the ~** echarlo todo a rodar, desbaratar los planes.

apple-core ['æplkɔ:^r] *n* corazón *m* de manzana.

apple dumpling [,æpl'dʌmplɪŋ] *n postre a base de manzana asada y masa*.

apple fritter [,æpl'frɪtə^r] *n* manzana *f* rebozada.

apple-green ['æplgri:n] **1** *adj* verde manzana. **2** *n* verde *m* manzana.

applejack ['æpldʒæk] *n* (*US*) aguardiente *m* de manzana.

apple-orchard ['æpl,ɔ:tʃəd] *n* manzanar *m*, pomar *m*.

apple-pie ['æpl'paɪ] *n* tarta *f* de manzanas; **in ~ order** en perfecto orden; **to make sb an ~ bed** (*Brit*) hacerle la petaca a uno.

apple-sauce ['æpl'sɔ:s] *n* (**a**) compota *f* de manzanas. (**b**) (*US**) coba *f*.

apple-tart [,æpl'tɑ:t] *n* tarta *f* de manzana.

appliance [ə'plaɪəns] *n* aparato *m*, instrumento *m*, dispositivo *m*; (*Brit*: *fire ~*) coche *m* de bomberos; **electrical ~** (aparato *m*) electrodoméstico *m*.

applicability [,æplɪkə'bɪlɪtɪ] *n* aplicabilidad *f*.

applicable [ə'plɪkəbl] *adj* aplicable (*to* a); **a rule ~ to all** una regla que se aplica a todos; **this is not ~ to you** esto no se refiere a Vd; **delete what is not ~** táchese lo que no sea pertinente.

applicant ['æplɪkənt] *n* aspirante *mf*, candidato *m*, -a *f* (*for a post* a un puesto); suplicante *mf*, solicitante *mf*.

application [,æplɪ'keɪʃən] *n* (**a**) (*in most senses*) aplicación *f*; **for external ~ only** para uso externo.

(**b**) (*request*) solicitud *f*, petición *f* (*for* de, por); **~ form** hoja *f* de solicitud, formulario *m* de inscripción; **~(s) package, ~(s) software** paquete *m* de aplicación (*or* aplicaciones); **~(s) program** programa *m* de aplicaciones; **prices on ~** los precios, a solicitud; **~s in triplicate** las solicitudes por triplicado; **~ for shares** solicitud *f* de acciones; **are you going to put in an ~?** ¿te vas a presentar?; **to make an ~ for** solicitar; **to make an ~ to** dirigirse a; **to submit one's ~** presentar su solicitud; **details may be had on ~ to Z** para los detalles dirigirse a Z.

applicator ['æplɪkeɪtə^r] *n* aplicador *m*.

applied [ə'plaɪd] *adj* aplicado **~ linguistics** lingüística *f* aplicada; **~ mathematics** matemáticas *fpl* aplicadas; **~ science** ciencias *fpl* aplicadas.

appliqué [æ'pli:keɪ] *n* (*also* **~ lace, ~ work**) encaje *m* de aplicación.

apply [ə'plaɪ] **1** *vt* (*gen*) aplicar; *ointment, paint etc* aplicar; *brakes* poner, echar; *rule* emplear, recurrir a; (*Jur*) poner en vigor; **to ~ heat to a surface** (*Tech*) exponer una superficie al calor; (*Med*) calentar una superficie; **to ~ a match to** poner fuego (con una cerilla) a; **to ~ pressure** ejercer presión, presionar; **how can we best ~ this money?** ¿cómo podemos utilizar mejor este dinero?; **he applied his mind to the problem** se dedicó a resolver el problema.

2 *vi* (**a**) (*refer to*) ser aplicable, interesar, ser pertinente; **cross out what does not ~** táchese lo que no interese, táchese lo que no sea pertinente.

(**b**) (*request*) presentarse, ser candidato; **are you ~ing?** ¿te vas a presentar?; **please ~ at the office** diríjanse a la oficina, (*on notice*) dirigirse a la oficina; **to ~ to sb** dirigirse a uno, acudir a uno; **to ~ to sb for sth** dirigirse a uno pidiendo algo.

3 *vr*: **to ~ o.s. to** aplicarse a, dedicarse a.

◆**apply for** *vt* solicitar, pedir; *post* solicitar, presentarse a; **'Patent applied for'** 'Patente en trámite'.

◆**apply to** *vt* tener que ver con, ser aplicable a, referirse a; **the law applies to all** la ley comprende a todos.

appoggiatura [ə,pɒdʒə'tʊərə] *n* apoyatura *f*.

appoint [ə'pɔɪnt] *vt* (**a**) (*fix*) fijar, señalar (*for* para); **at the ~ed time** a la hora señalada.

(**b**) (*nominate*) nombrar (*to* a); **they ~ed him chairman** le nombraron presidente; **they ~ed him to do it** le nombraron para hacerlo.

(**c**) **well ~ed** bien amueblado.

appointee [əpɔɪn'ti:] *n* persona *f* nombrada.

appointive [ə'pɔɪntɪv] *adj* (*US*): **~ position** puesto *m* que se cubre por nombramiento.

appointment [ə'pɔɪntmənt] *n* (**a**) (*act of appointing*) nombramiento *m* (*to* a); **'By ~ to HRH'** 'Proveedores de S.A.R.'

(**b**) (*engagement*) cita *f*, compromiso *m*; (*at dentist's, hairdresser's etc*) hora *f*; **I have an ~ at 10** tengo una cita a las 10; **have you an ~ tonight?** ¿tienes compromiso para esta noche?; **have you an ~?** (*to caller*) ¿tiene Vd hora?; **to keep an ~** acudir a una cita; **to make an ~** (*2 or more persons*) darse una cita, citarse (*with* con); **to make an ~ for 3 o'clock** citarse para las 3; **to meet sb by ~** reunirse con uno de acuerdo con lo convenido.

(**c**) (*post*) puesto *m*, empleo *m*, colocación *f*; **~s board, ~s service** (*Univ etc*) oficina *f* de colocación; **~s bureau** agencia *f* de colocaciones; **'A~s Vacant'** 'ofrecen empleos'.

(**d**) **~s** (*furniture etc*) mobiliario *m*, moblaje *m*, equipo *m*.

apportion [ə'pɔ:ʃən] *vt* prorratear; repartir, distribuir; desglosar; **the blame is to be ~ed equally** todos tienen la culpa por partes iguales.

apportionment [ə'pɔ:ʃənmənt] *n* prorrateo *m*; repartición *f*, distribución *f*, desglose *m*; (*US Pol*) delimitación *f* de distritos (*or* condados).

apposite ['æpəzɪt] *adj* apropiado (*to* a); a propósito, oportuno.

apposition [,æpə'zɪʃən] *n* (**a**) (*of position*) yuxtaposición *f*. (**b**) (*Gram*) aposición *f*; **in ~** en aposición.

appraisal [ə'preɪzəl] *n* tasación *f*, valoración *f*, evaluación *f*; (*fig*) estimación *f*, apreciación *f*.

appraise [ə'preɪz] *vt* tasar, valorar, evaluar; (*Comm, Fin*) tasar; *staff* evaluar; (*fig*) estimar, apreciar.

appraiser [ə'preɪzə^r] *n* apreciador *m*, -ora *f*, evaluador *m*, -ora *f*; (*Comm, Fin*) tasador *m*, -ora *f*.

appraising [ə'preɪzɪŋ] *adj look etc* apreciativo.

appreciable [ə'pri:ʃəbl] *adj* sensible, perceptible; (*large*) considerable, importante; **an ~ sum** una cantidad importante; **an ~ loss** una pérdida sensible.

appreciably [ə'pri:ʃəblɪ] *adv* sensiblemente, perceptiblemente.

appreciate [ə'pri:ʃɪeɪt] **1** *vt* (**a**) (*estimate worth of*) apreciar, valorar, aquilatar.

(**b**) (*estimate correctly*) apreciar, saber valorar en su justo precio.

(**c**) (*esteem*) apreciar, tener en mucho, tener un alto concepto de; **he does not ~ music** no sabe apreciar la música, no entiende de música; **I am not ~d here** aquí no me estiman; **we much ~ your work** tenemos un alto concepto de su trabajo.

(**d**) (*understand*) comprender; hacerse cargo de; **I ~ your wishes** comprendo sus deseos; **yes, I ~ that** sí, lo comprendo; **to ~ that ...** comprender que ...; **we fully ~ that ...** comprendemos perfectamente que ...

(**e**) (*be grateful for*) agradecer; **I ~ the gesture** agradezco el detalle; **we should much ~ it if ...** agradeceríamos mucho que ... + *subj*.

(**f**) (*be sensitive to*) percibir; **the smallest change can be ~d on this machine** en esta máquina se percibe el más leve cambio.

2 *vi* aumentar(se) en valor, subir.

appreciation [əˌpriːʃɪ'eɪʃən] *n* (**a**) (*estimation*) aprecio *m*, apreciación *f*, estimación *f*; (*report*) aprecio *m*, informe *m*; (*obituary*) (nota *f*) necrológica *f*; (*praise*) elogio *m*; (*Liter etc*) crítica *f*.

(**b**) (*esteem*) aprecio *m*; **you have no ~ of art** no sabes apreciar el arte, no entiendes de arte.

(**c**) (*gratitude*) reconocimiento *m*, agradecimiento *m*; **as a token of my ~** en señal de reconocimiento; **she smiled her ~** sonrió agradecida.

(**d**) (*rise in value*) aumento *m* en valor, subida *f*.

appreciative [ə'priːʃɪətɪv] *adj* agradecido; *audience* atento, apreciativo; *comment* elogioso, de aprobación; **an ~ look** (*grateful*) una mirada llena de agradecimiento; (*admiring*) una mirada admirativa; **he was very ~ of what I had done** agradeció mucho lo que yo había hecho; **he is ~ of good wine** estima el buen vino.

appreciatively [ə'priːʃɪətɪvlɪ] *adv* (*V adj*) agradecidamente, con gratitud; atentamente; con aprobación; con admiración.

apprehend [ˌæprɪ'hend] *vt* (**a**) (*arrest*) prender, detener. (**b**) (*perceive*) percibir; comprender. (**c**) (*fear*) recelar.

apprehension [ˌæprɪ'henʃən] *n* (**a**) (*arrest*) prendimiento *m*, detención *f*.

(**b**) (*perception*) percepción *f*; comprensión *f*.

(**c**) (*fear*) recelo *m*, aprensión *f*; **my chief ~ is that ...** sobre todo me temo que ... + *subj*.

apprehensive [ˌæprɪ'hensɪv] *adj* aprensivo, inquieto; **to be ~ about, to be ~ for** temer por, inquietarse por; **to be ~ of danger** temer el peligro; **to be ~ that ...** recelar que ..., temer que ... + *subj*; **to grow ~** inquietarse.

apprehensively [ˌæprɪ'hensɪvlɪ] *adv* con aprensión.

apprentice [ə'prentɪs] **1** *n* aprendiz *m*, -iza *f*; (*fig*) novicio *m*, -a *f*, principiante *mf*, aprendiz *m*, -iza *f*; **~ electrician** aprendiz *m* de electricista. **2** *vt* poner de aprendiz (*to* con); **to be ~d to** estar de aprendiz con.

apprenticeship [ə'prentɪʃɪp] *n* aprendizaje *m*; **to serve one's ~** hacer su aprendizaje.

apprise [ə'praɪz] *vt* informar, avisar (*of* de); **I will ~ him of it** se lo diré; **I was never ~d of your decision** no se me comunicó nunca su decisión; **to be ~d of** estar al corriente de.

appro* ['æprəʊ] (*Comm*) *abbr of* **approval**; **on ~** a prueba.

approach [ə'prəʊtʃ] **1** *vt* (**a**) *place* acercarse a; aproximarse a.

(**b**) *subject etc* abordar, enfocar; **we must ~ the matter with care** tenemos que abordar el asunto con mucho cuidado; **it all depends on how we ~ it** depende de cómo enfocamos la cuestión; **I ~ it with an open mind** me lo planteo sin prejuicios.

(**c**) *person* abordar, dirigirse a; **a man ~ed me in the street** un hombre me abordó en la calle; **you should ~ the boss about that** Vd debiera dirigirse al jefe sobre aquello; **have you ~ed him yet?** ¿has hablado ya con él?; **he is difficult to ~** no es fácil abordarle.

(**d**) (*approximate to*) aproximarse a; parecerse a, ser semejante a; **here the colour ~es blue** aquí el color tira a azul; **she must be ~ing 50** debe de tener cerca de los 50, debe de ser casi cincuentona; **it was ~ing midnight** era casi medianoche; **the performance ~ed perfection** la interpretación era casi perfecta.

2 *vi* acercarse.

3 *n* (**a**) (*act*) acercamiento *m*; (*Golf*) aproximación *f*; **~ light** (*Aer*) baliza *f* de aproximación; **~ shot** (*Golf*) golpe *m* de aproximación; **we observed his ~** le vimos acercarse; **at the ~ of the enemy** al acercarse el enemigo; **at the ~ of night** al entrar la noche; **at the ~ of Easter** al acercarse la Pascua.

(**b**) (*to subject etc*) aproximación *f* (*to* a), enfoque *m* (*to* de), modo *m* de enfocar una cuestión, método *m* de abordar un problema; orientación *f*, actitud *f*; planteamiento *m*; **an ~ to Spanish history** una aproximación a la historia de España; **I don't like your ~ to this matter** no me gusta su modo de enfocar esta cuestión; **we must think of a new ~** tenemos que inventar otro método.

(**c**) (*access*) acceso *m* (*to* a); (*Aut*) carril *m* de aceleración; **~es** accesos *mpl*, (*Mil*) aproches *mpl*; **~ road** vía *f* de acceso; **the station ~es** las vías de acceso a la estación; **the northern ~es to Madrid** las rutas de acceso a Madrid por el norte; **easy of ~** asequible, de fácil acceso.

(**d**) (*advance*) propuesta *f*, proposición *f*; oferta *f*; **to make ~es to** dirigirse a, tratar de hablar con; hacer gestiones ante; **to make amorous ~es to** requerir de amores a.

approachable [ə'prəʊtʃəbl] *adj place* asequible; *person* abordable, tratable, accesible.

approaching [ə'prəʊtʃɪŋ] *adj* próximo, venidero; *car etc* que se acerca, que viene en dirección opuesta.

approbation [ˌæprə'beɪʃən] *n* aprobación *f*.

appropriate 1 [ə'prəʊprɪɪt] *adj* apropiado, conveniente, a propósito; adecuado; correspondiente; *moment etc* oportuno; *authority etc* competente; **~ for, ~ to** apropiado para; **whichever seems more ~** el que te parezca más apropiado; **would it be ~ for me to wear it?** ¿convendría que (yo) me lo pusiera?; **A, and where ~, B** A, y en su caso, B.

2 [ə'prəʊprɪeɪt] *vt* (**a**) (*take*) apropiarse.

(**b**) (*assign*) asignar, destinar (*for* a).

appropriately [ə'prəʊprɪɪtlɪ] *adv* apropiadamente, convenientemente; **he was ~ named Flint** tuvo el nombre apropiado de Flint; **in an ~ designed house** en una casa convenientemente distribuida; **~ respectful** con el debido respeto.

appropriateness [ə'prəʊprɪɪtnɪs] *n* propiedad *f*, conveniencia *f*.

appropriation [əˌprəʊprɪ'eɪʃən] *n* (**a**) apropiación *f*. (**b**) (*Comm, Fin*) apropiación *f*, asignación *f*; fondos *mpl*; (*US*) crédito *m*; **~ account** cuenta *f* de apropiaciones; (*US*) **~ bill** ley *f* financiera; **A~ Committee** (*US Pol*) Comité *m* de gastos de la Cámara de Representantes; **~ fund** fondo *m* de asignación.

approval [ə'pruːvəl] *n* aprobación *f*; consentimiento *m*; (*formal OK*) visto *m* bueno; **on ~** (*Comm*) a prueba; previa aceptación; **a look of ~** una mirada aprobatoria; **has this your ~?** ¿Vd ha aprobado esto?; **to meet with sb's ~** obtener la aprobación de uno; **he nodded his ~** asintió con la cabeza.

approve [ə'pruːv] **1** *vt* aprobar; **read and ~d** visto bueno.

2 *vi*: **she ~s** ella lo aprueba; **yes, I heartily ~** sí, estoy totalmente de acuerdo.

◆**approve of** *vt plan* aprobar, dar por bueno; *person* tener un buen concepto (*or* buena concepción de); *behaviour, idea* aprobar, ser partidario de; **they don't ~ of my fiancé** no les cae bien mi novio, mi novio no les resulta simpático; **we ~ of our new neighbours** nos agradan (*or* nos gustan) los nuevos vecinos; **I cannot ~ of your going** no puedo consentir en que vayas; **grandma doesn't ~ of women smoking** a la abuela no le gusta que fumen las mujeres; **she ~s of being punctual** estima la puntualidad; **I don't ~ of his conduct** no estoy de acuerdo con su conducta; **I don't ~ of your decision** no estoy de acuerdo con tu decisión; **he doesn't ~ of smoking or drinking** está en contra del tabaco y del alcohol.

approved [ə'pruːvd] *adj* aprobado, acreditado; **in the ~ fashion** del modo acostumbrado; **~ school** (*Brit*) correccional *m*, reformatorio *m*.

approving [ə'pruːvɪŋ] *adj* de aprobación, aprobatorio.

approvingly [ə'pruːvɪŋlɪ] *adv* con aprobación.

approx *abbr of* **approximately** aprox.

approximate 1 [ə'prɒksɪmɪt] *adj* aproximado. **2** [ə'prɒksɪmeɪt] *vi* aproximarse (*to* a).

approximately [ə'prɒksɪmətlɪ] *adv* aproximadamente, poco más o menos.

approximation [əˌprɒksɪ'meɪʃən] *n* aproximación *f*.

appt. (*US*) *abbr of* **appointment**.

appurtenance [ə'pɜːtɪnəns] *n* (*frec pl*) (*appendage*) dependencia *f*; (*accessory*) accesorio *m*; **the house and its ~s** la casa con sus dependencias.

Apr. *abbr of* **April** abril *m*, abr.

APR, apr *n abbr of* **annual(ized) percentage rate** tasa *f* de interés anual.

après-ski [ˌæpreɪ'skiː] **1** *n* après-ski *m*. **2** *attr* de après-ski.

apricot ['eɪprɪkɒt] *n* (*fruit*) albaricoque *m*, chabacano *m* (*Mex*), damasco *m* (*LAm*); (*tree*) albaricoquero *m*, chabacano *m* (*Mex*), damasco *m* (*LAm*).

April ['eɪprəl] *n* abril *m*; ~ **Fools' Day** día *m* de inocentes (*en Inglaterra el 1 abril*); **to make an ~ fool of sb** hacer una inocentada a uno; ~ **showers** lluvias *fpl* de abril.

a priori [eɪpraɪ'ɔːraɪ] **1** *adv* a priori. **2** *adj* apriorístico.

apron ['eɪprən] *n* (**a**) (*garment*) delantal *m*; (*workman's, mason's etc*) mandil *m*. (**b**) (*Aer*) pista *f*. (**c**) (*Theat*) proscenio *m*; ~ **stage** escena *f* saliente.

apron strings ['eɪprən'strɪŋz] *npl*: **to be tied to the ~ of** estar cosido a las faldas de.

apropos [ˌæprə'pəʊ] **1** *adv* a propósito. **2** *prep*: ~ **of** a propósito de. **3** *adj* oportuno.

apse [æps] *n* ábside *m*.

APT *n* (*Brit*) *abbr of* **Advanced Passenger Train** ≈ tren *m* de gran velocidad, TGV *m*.

apt[1] [æpt] *adj* (**a**) (*suitable*) apropiado, conveniente; *remark, reply* acertado, oportuno; *description* exacto, atinado, apto.

(**b**) (*tending*) **to be ~ to** + *infin* tener tendencia a + *infin*, ser propenso a + *infin*, ser susceptible de ~ *infin*; **to be rather ~ to** + *infin* tener cierta tendencia a + *infin*; **I am ~ to be out on Mondays** por regla general no estoy los lunes; **we are ~ to forget that** ... a menudo nos olvidamos que ..., es fácil que olvidemos que ...; **only children are ~ to be spoiled** a los hijos únicos casi siempre se les mima; **it is ~ to cause trouble** es probable que cause molestias.

(**c**) (*gifted*) talentoso, inteligente; **to be an ~ pupil** ser un alumno aprovechado.

apt[2] *abbr of* **apartment** apartamento *m*.

aptitude ['æptɪtjuːd] *n* aptitud *f* (*for, in* para), capacidad *f*, habilidad *f*; ~ **test** test *m* de aptitud.

aptly ['æptlɪ] *adv* oportunamente, acertadamente; **an ~ named plant** una planta de nombre apropiado.

aptness ['æptnɪs] *n* lo apropiado, propiedad *f*; lo acertado, oportunidad *f*, exactitud *f*.

Apuleius [ˌæpjə'lɪəs] *nm* Apuleyo.

aquafarming ['ækwəˌfɑːmɪŋ] *n* piscicultura *f*.

aqualung ['ækwəlʌŋ] *n* escafandra *f* autónoma.

aquamarine [ˌækwəmə'riːn] **1** *adj* (de color) verde mar. **2** *n* aguamarina *f*.

aquanaut ['ækwənɔːt] *n* submarinista *mf*.

aquaplane ['ækwəpleɪn] *n* hidroavión *m*.

Aquarian [ə'kwɛərɪən] *n* acuario *mf*.

aquarium [ə'kwɛərɪəm] *n*, *pl* **aquariums** *or* **aquaria** [ə'kwɛərɪə] acuario *m*.

Aquarius [ə'kwɛərɪəs] *n* (*Zodiac*) Acuario *m*.

aquatic [ə'kwætɪk] **1** *adj* acuático. **2** *n* (**a**) (*Bot*) planta *f* acuática; (*Zool*) animal *m* acuático. (**b**) **~s** (*Sport*) deportes *mpl* acuáticos.

aquatint ['ækwətɪnt] *n* acuatinta *f*.

aqueduct ['ækwɪdʌkt] *n* acueducto *m*.

aqueous ['eɪkwɪəs] *adj* ácueo, acuoso.

aquifer ['ækwɪfəʳ] *n* acuífero *m*.

aquiferous [ə'kwɪfərəs] *adj* acuífero.

aquiline ['ækwɪlaɪn] *adj* aguileño, aquilino.

Aquinas [ə'kwaɪnəs] *nm* Aquino; **St Thomas ~** Santo Tomás Aquino.

AR (**a**) (*Comm*) *abbr of* **account rendered** cuenta *f* girada. (**b**) (*for tax*) *abbr of* **annual return** declaración *f* anual. (**c**) (*report*) *abbr of* **annual return** informe *m* anual. (**d**) (*US*) *abbr of* **Arkansas.**

A/R *abbr of* **against all risks** contra todo riesgo.

Arab ['ærəb] **1** *adj* árabe. **2** *n* (**a**) árabe *mf*; *V* **street.** (**b**) (*horse*) caballo *m* árabe.

arabesque [ˌærə'besk] *n* arabesco *m*.

Arabia [ə'reɪbɪə] *n* Arabia *f*.

Arabian [ə'reɪbɪən] **1** *adj* árabe, arábigo; ~ **Desert** Desierto *m* Arábigo; ~ **Gulf**, ~ **Sea** Mar *m* de Omán; **The ~ Nights** Las mil y una noches. **2** *n* árabe *mf*.

Arabic ['ærəbɪk] **1** *adj* árabe, arábigo; ~ **numeral** número *m* arábigo. **2** *n* árabe *m*.

Arabist ['ærəbɪst] *n* arabista *mf*.

arabization [ˌærəbaɪ'zeɪʃən] *n* arabización *f*.

arable ['ærəbl] **1** *adj* cultivable, arable (*esp LAm*); ~ **farm** granja *f* agrícola; ~ **farming** agricultura *f*; ~ **land** = **2**. **2** *n* tierra *f* de labrantío.

arachnid [ə'ræknɪd] *n* arácnido *m*.

Aragon ['ærəgən] *n* Aragón *m*.

Aragonese [ˌærəgə'niːz] **1** *adj* aragonés. **2** *n* (**a**) aragonés *m*, -esa *f*. (**b**) (*Ling*) aragonés *m*.

Aramaic [ˌærə'meɪɪk] *n* arameo *m*.

arbiter ['ɑːbɪtəʳ] *n* árbitro *m*.

arbitrage [ˌɑːbɪ'trɑːʒ] *n* arbitraje *m*.

arbitrageur [ˌɑːbɪtræ'ʒɜː] *n* arbitrajista *m*.

arbitrarily ['ɑːbɪtrərɪlɪ] *adv* arbitrariamente.

arbitrariness ['ɑːbɪtrərɪnɪs] *n* arbitrariedad *f*.

arbitrary ['ɑːbɪtrərɪ] *adj* arbitrario; subjetivo; artificial.

arbitrate ['ɑːbɪtreɪt] **1** *vt* resolver, juzgar. **2** *vi* arbitrar (*in* en, *between* entre).

arbitration [ˌɑːbɪ'treɪʃən] *n* arbitraje *m*; **we want the claim to go to ~** queremos que la reclamación pase a una comisión de arbitraje; **the question was referred to ~** se confió el asunto a un juez árbitro (*or* a una comisión de arbitraje).

arbitrator ['ɑːbɪtreɪtəʳ] *n* juez árbitro *mf*.

arboreal [ɑːbɔːrɪəl] *adj* arbóreo.

arboretum [ˌɑːbə'riːtəm] *n* arboleda *f*.

arboriculture ['ɑːbərɪˌkʌltʃəʳ] *n* arboricultura *f*.

arbour, (*US*) **arbor** ['ɑːbəʳ] *n* cenador *m*, pérgola *f*, glorieta *f*.

arbutus [ɑː'bjuːtəs] *n* madroño *m*.

ARC *n* (**a**) *abbr of* **American Red Cross** Cruz *f* Roja Norteamericana. (**b**) (*Med*) *abbr of* **AIDS-related complex.**

arc [ɑːk] **1** *n* arco *m*. **2** *vi* arquearse, formar un arco.

arcade [ɑː'keɪd] *n* (*series of arches*) arcada *f*; (*round public square*) soportales *mpl*; (*with shops*) galería *f*.

Arcadia [ɑː'keɪdɪə] *n* Arcadia *f*.

Arcadian [ɑː'keɪdɪən] **1** *adj* árcade; arcádico. **2** *n* árcade *mf*.

Arcady ['ɑːkədɪ] *n* Arcadia *f*.

arcane [ɑː'keɪn] *adj* arcano; secreto, misterioso.

arch[1] [ɑːtʃ] **1** *n* (**a**) (*Archit*) arco *m*; (*vault*) bóveda *f*.

(**b**) (*Anat*) empeine *m*; (*dental*) arcada *f*, arco *m*; **fallen ~es** pies *mpl* planos.

2 *vt* (**a**) *back, body etc* arquear; *eyebrows* enarcar.

(**b**) **to ~ over** (*Archit*) abovedar.

3 *vi* arquearse, formar un arco; formar una bóveda.

arch[2] [ɑːtʃ] *adj* (*cunning*) astuto; (*roguish*) zumbón, picaruelo; *look, remark etc* malicioso, lleno de malicia; de complicidad; *woman* coqueta.

arch-[3] [ɑːtʃ] (*gen in compounds, V also below*) principal; consumado; archi-; *eg* **the ~criminal** el mayor de los criminales; **an ~hypocrite** un consumado hipócrita, un hipócrita de primer orden.

archaeological, (*esp US*) **archeological** [ˌɑːkɪə'lɒdʒɪkəl] *adj* arqueológico.

archaeologist, (*esp US*) **archeologist** [ˌɑːkɪ'ɒlədʒɪst] *n* arqueólogo *m*, -a *f*.

archaeology, (*esp US*) **archeology** [ˌɑːkɪ'ɒlədʒɪ] *n* arqueología *f*.

archaic [ɑː'keɪɪk] *adj* arcaico.

archaism ['ɑːkeɪɪzəm] *n* arcaísmo *m*.

archangel ['ɑːkˌeɪndʒəl] *n* arcángel *m*.

archbishop ['ɑːtʃ'bɪʃəp] *n* arzobispo *m*.

archbishopric [ɑːtʃ'bɪʃəprɪk] *n* arzobispado *m*.

archdeacon ['ɑːtʃ'diːkən] *n* arcediano *m*.

archdiocese ['ɑːtʃ'daɪəsɪs] *n* archidiócesis *f*.

archduke ['ɑːtʃ'djuːk] *n* archiduque *m*.

arched [ɑːtʃt] *adj* en forma de arco(s); arqueado; abovedado.

arch-enemy ['ɑːtʃ'enɪmɪ] *n* archienemigo *m*, -a *f*; (*devil*) el enemigo malo.

archeological [ˌɑːkɪə'lɒdʒɪkəl] *adj* (*esp US*) = **archaeological.**

archeologist [ˌɑːkɪ'ɒlədʒɪst] *n* (*esp US*) = **archaeologist.**

archeology [ˌɑːkɪ'ɒlədʒɪ] *n* (*esp US*) = **archaeology.**

archer ['ɑːtʃəʳ] *n* arquero *m*.

archery ['ɑːtʃərɪ] *n* tiro *m* con arco.

archetypal [ɑːkɪ'taɪpl] *adj* arquetípico.

archetype ['ɑːkɪtaɪp] *n* arquetipo *m*.

Archimedes [ˌɑːkɪ'miːdiːz] *nm* Arquímedes; **~' screw** rosca *f* de Arquímedes.

archipelago [ˌɑːkɪ'pelɪgəʊ] *n* archipiélago *m*.

archiphoneme ['ɑːkɪˌfəʊniːm] *n* archifonema *m*.

architect ['ɑːkɪtekt] *n* (**a**) arquitecto *mf* (*also* -a *f*). (**b**) (*fig*) artífice *m*; **the ~ of victory** el artífice de la victoria.

architectonic [ˌɑːkɪtek'tɒnɪk] *adj* arquitectónico.

architectural [ˌɑːkɪ'tektʃərəl] *adj* arquitectónico.

architecture ['ɑːkɪtektʃəʳ] *n* arquitectura *f*.

architrave ['ɑːkɪtreɪv] *n* arquitrabe *m*.

archive ['ɑːkaɪv] **1** *n* (*gen, Comput*) archivo *m*; ~ **file** fichero *m* archivado. **2** *vt* archivar.

archivist ['ɑːkɪvɪst] *n* archivero *m*, -a *f*, archivista *mf* (*LAm*).

archness ['ɑːtʃnɪs] *n* astucia *f*; picardía *f*; malicia *f*; coquetería *f*.

archway ['ɑːtʃweɪ] *n* arco *m*, arcada *f*.

arc lamp ['ɑːklæmp] *n* lámpara *f* de arco; (*in welding*) arco *m* voltaico.

arctic ['ɑːktɪk] **1** *adj* ártico; (*fig*) glacial; **A~ Circle** Círculo *m* Polar Ártico; **A~ Ocean** Océano *m* Glacial Ártico. **2** *n*: **the A~** el Ártico.

arc-welding ['ɑːk,weldiŋ] *n* soldadura *f* por arco.

ARD *n* (*US*) *abbr of* **acute respiratory disease.**

Ardennes [ɑː'dənz] *npl* Ardenas *fpl.*

ardent ['ɑːdənt] *adj* ardiente, vehemente, apasionado; *supporter* fervoroso; *desire* ardiente; *lover* apasionado.

ardently ['ɑːdəntlɪ] *adv* ardientemente, con vehemencia, apasionadamente; fervorosamente.

ardour, (*US*) **ardor** ['ɑːdəʳ] *n* ardor *m*; fervor *m*; vehemencia *f*; pasión *f*.

arduous ['ɑːdjʊəs] *adj* arduo, fuerte, riguroso; *climb, journey* penoso, arduo; *task* difícil, trabajoso.

arduously ['ɑːdjʊəslɪ] *adv* rigurosamente; penosamente; con dificultad.

arduousness ['ɑːdjʊəsnɪs] *n* rigor *m*, lo riguroso; lo penoso; lo arduo; dificultad *f*.

are [ɑːʳ] *V* **be.**

area ['ɛərɪə] *n* (**a**) (*Math, surface extent*) área *f*, superficie *f*; extensión *f*.

(**b**) (*Geog, space*) región *f*, zona *f*; (*Sport, eg goal* ~) área *f*; (*Comm*) zona *f*; **the London ~** la región londinense; **~ code** (*Brit Post*) código *m* postal; (*US Telec*) código *m* territorial, prefijo *m* (local); **~ manager** gerente *m* de zona; **~ office** oficina *f* regional; **~ representative** representante *mf* de (la) zona.

(**c**) (*Archit*) corral *m*, patio *m* (de sótano); **dining ~** comedor *m*.

(**d**) (*fig*) región *f*, zona *f*; ámbito *m*; terreno *m*, campo *m*; **I am not a specialist in this ~** no soy especialista en este campo; **~ of concern** motivo *m* de preocupación; **~ of disagreement** zona *f* de discrepancia; **~ of knowledge** sector *m* del saber; **~ of study** campo *m* de estudio.

arena [ə'riːnə] *n* anfiteatro *m*, redondel *m*, arena *f*; palenque *m*; (*Taur*) plaza *f*, ruedo *m*; (*Circus*) pista *f*; **the political ~** el ruedo político.

aren't [ɑːnt] = **are not.**

Argentina [,ɑːdʒən'tiːnə] *n* la Argentina.

Argentine ['ɑːdʒəntaɪn] **1** *adj* argentino. **2** *n* (**a**) (*person*) argentino *m*, -a *f*. (**b**) **the ~** la Argentina.

Argentinian [,ɑːdʒən'tɪnɪən] **1** *adj* argentino. **2** *n* argentino *m*, -a *f*.

Argie* ['ɑːdʒɪ] *n* (*pej*) = **Argentine.**

argon ['ɑːgɒn] *n* argón *m*.

Argonaut ['ɑːgənɔːt] *n* argonauta *m*.

argot ['ɑːgəʊ] *n* argot *m*.

arguable ['ɑːgjʊəbl] *adj* discutible; sostenible; defensible; **it is ~ whether ...** es dudoso si ...; **it is ~ that ...** se puede decir que ...

arguably ['ɑːgjʊəblɪ] *adv*: **it is ~ the best** se puede sostener que es el mejor.

argue ['ɑːgjuː] **1** *vt* (**a**) *case* sostener; *matter* razonar acerca de; *point* discutir; **a well ~d case** un argumento razonado; **how will you ~ the case?** ¿cómo va Vd a presentar el pleito?; **to ~ one's way out of a jam** salir de un apuro a fuerza de argumentos.

(**b**) (*point to*) argüir, indicar; **it ~s his untrustworthiness** esto sugiere que es poco confiable; **it ~s him to be untrustworthy** hace creer que es poco confiable.

(**c**) **to ~ that ...** sostener que ...; **I have heard it ~d that ...** he oído sostener que ...

(**d**) **to ~ sb into** + *ger* persuadir a uno a + *infin*; **to ~ sb out of** + *ger* disuadir a uno de + *infin*; **to ~ sb out of an idea** persuadir a uno a abandonar una idea.

2 *vi* (**a**) (*two persons*) discutir, disputar, polemizar, pelear(se) (*LAm*) (*about* acerca de, *with* con); **we ~d all night** pasamos toda la noche discutiendo; **don't ~!** ¡no discutas!, ¡no repliques!

(**b**) (*reason*) razonar, argüir, discurrir; **I ~ this way** yo pienso de este modo, yo razono así; **he ~s well** razona bien, presenta sus argumentos de modo convincente; **this ~s in his favour** esto habla en su favor; **it ~s well for him** es un indicio a su favor; **to ~ against** *person* hablar en contra de, *thing* alegar razones contra, combatir por argumentos; **to ~ for** abogar por.

◆argue out *vt problem* debatir a fondo, discutir a fondo.

argufy* ['ɑːgjʊfaɪ] *vi* discutir.

argument ['ɑːgjʊmənt] *n* (**a**) (*reason*) argumento *m* (*against* en contra de, *for* en pro de); **his ~ is that ...** él sostiene que ...; **there is a strong ~ in favour of** + *ger* hay un fuerte argumento para + *infin*; **I don't follow your ~** no comprendo su razonamiento; **to be open to ~** estar dispuesto a dejarse convencer.

(**b**) (*debate*) discusión *f*, disputa *f*, debate *m*; **there was a heated ~** hubo una discusión acalorada; **it is beyond ~** es indiscutible, queda fuera de toda duda; **for the sake of ~ ...** pongamos por caso ..., pongamos como hipótesis ...; **the conclusion is open to ~** la conclusión es discutible; **to have the better of an ~** salir airoso de un debate; **he had an ~ with a wall** (*hum*) tuvo un asunto con un muro; **let's not have any ~, I don't want any ~ about it** no discutamos; **you've heard only one side of the ~** te han contado solamente un lado del asunto.

(**c**) (*Jur*) alegato *m*.

(**d**) (*synopsis*) argumento *m*, resumen *m*.

argumentation [,ɑːgjʊmən'teɪʃən] *n* argumentación *f*, argumentos *mpl*.

argumentative [,ɑːgjʊ'mentətɪv] *adj* discutidor.

Argus ['ɑːgəs] *nm* Argos.

argy-bargy* ['ɑːdʒɪ'bɑːdʒɪ] *n* (*Brit*) discusión *f*, tiquismiquis *m*, dimes *mpl* y diretes.

aria ['ɑːrɪə] *n* aria *f*.

Arian ['ɛərɪən] **1** *adj* arriano. **2** *n* arriano *m*, -a *f*.

Arianism ['ɛərɪənɪzəm] *n* arrianismo *m*.

ARIBA [ə'riːbə] *n* (*Brit*) *abbr of* **Associate of the Royal Institute of British Architects** *socio del instituto de arquitectos.*

arid ['ærɪd] *adj* árido (*also fig*).

aridity [ə'rɪdɪtɪ] *n* aridez *f*.

Aries ['ɛəriːz] *n* (*Zodiac*) Aries *m*.

aright [ə'raɪt] *adv* correctamente, acertadamente; **if I heard you ~** si le oí bien; **if I understand you ~** si le entiendo correctamente; **to set ~** rectificar.

arise [ə'raɪz] (*irr*: *pret* **arose,** *ptp* **arisen**) *vi* (**a**) (†, *liter*) levantarse, alzarse; **~!** (*slogan*) ¡arriba!

(**b**) (*fig*) surgir; presentarse, producirse; **matters arising (from the last meeting)** asuntos *mpl* pendientes (de la última reunión); **difficulties have ~n** han surgido dificultades; **should the occasion ~** si se presenta la ocasión; **should need ~** si fuera preciso, si nos vemos en el caso; **a storm arose** se desencadenó un temporal; **a great clamour arose** se produjo un tremendo clamor; **the question does not ~** no hay tal, no existe ese problema; **the question ~s whether ...** se plantea el problema de si ...

(**c**) (*result*) **to ~ from** provenir de, resultar de; originarse en; **arising from this, can you say ...?** partiendo de esta base, ¿puede Vd decir ...?

arisen [ə'rɪzn] *ptp of* **arise.**

aristo* ['ærɪstəʊ] *n* aristócrata *mf*.

aristocracy [,ærɪs'tɒkrəsɪ] *n* aristocracia *f*.

aristocrat ['ærɪstəkræt] *n* aristócrata *mf*.

aristocratic [,ærɪstə'krætɪk] *adj* aristocrático.

Aristophanes [,ærɪs'tɒfəniːz] *nm* Aristófanes.

Aristotelian [,ærɪstə'tiːlɪən] *adj* aristotélico.

Aristotle ['ærɪstɒtl] *nm* Aristóteles.

arithmetic [ə'rɪθmətɪk] *n* aritmética *f*; **~ mean** media *f* aritmética.

arithmetical [,ærɪθ'metɪkəl] *adj* aritmético; **~ progression** progresión *f* aritmética.

arithmetician [ə,rɪθmə'tɪʃən] *n* aritmético *mf*.

Ariz. (*US*) *abbr of* **Arizona.**

Ark. (*US*) *abbr of* **Arkansas.**

ark [ɑːk] *n* arca *f*; **A~ of the Covenant** Arca *f* de la Alianza; **Noah's A~** Arca *f* de Noé; **it's out of the A~** viene del año de la nana.

arm¹ [ɑːm] *n* (**a**) (*Anat, fig*) brazo *m*; **~ in ~** del brazo, de bracete, cogidos del brazo; **with folded ~s** con los brazos cruzados; **with open ~s** con los brazos abiertos; **within ~'s reach** al alcance del brazo; **with his coat over his ~** con el abrigo sobre el brazo; **she came in on her father's ~** entró del brazo de su padre; **to chance one's ~** arriesgarse, aventurarse; **I'd give my right ~ to own it** daría todo lo que tengo por poseerlo; **to give sb one's ~** dar el brazo a uno; **he held it at ~'s length** lo tenía en la mano con el brazo extendido; **to keep sb at ~'s length** mantener a uno a distancia; **to pay an ~ and a leg for sth*** dar un ojo de la cara por algo; **this pushed them into the ~s of the Ruritanians** esto les obligó a buscar el apoyo de los ruritanios; esto les obligó a aliarse con los ruritanios; **to put one's ~ round sb** rodear a uno del brazo; **to put the ~ on sb** (*US**) presionar a uno; **to take sb in one's ~s** abrazar a uno; **please take my ~** toma el brazo; **to twist sb's ~** convencer a uno a la fuerza, presionar a uno; **the long ~ of the law** el brazo de la ley.

(**b**) (*of chair, crane, etc*) brazo *m*; (*of coat*) manga *f*; **~ of the sea** brazo *m* de mar.

(**c**) (*Comm etc*) sección *f*, división *f*, departamento *m*;

technical ~ sección *f* técnica, servicio *m* técnico.

arm² [ɑːm] **1** *n* (**a**) (*Mil*) arma *f*; **~s control** control *m* de armamento(s); **~s dealer** traficante *m* en armas; **~s factory** fábrica *f* de armas; **~s limitation** limitación *f* armamentística (*or* de armamentos); **~s manufacturer** fabricante *m* de armas; **~s race** carrera *f* de armamentos; **to be under ~s** estar sobre las armas; **to be up in ~s** poner el grito en el cielo (*about* a causa de); **to lay down one's ~s** rendir las armas; **to rise up in ~s** alzarse en armas; **to take up ~s** tomar las armas; **present ~s!** ¡presenten armas!; **order ~s!** ¡descansen armas!; **shoulder ~s!, slope ~s!** ¡armas al hombro!

(**b**) **~s** (*Her*) escudo *m*, blasón *m*.

2 *vt* (**a**) *person, nation* armar.

(**b**) *missile* cebar.

3 *vr*: **to ~ o.s.** armarse; **to ~ o.s. with arguments** pertrecharse de argumentos; **to ~ o.s. with patience** armarse de paciencia.

armada [ɑː'mɑːdə] *n* flota *f*, armada *f*; **the A~** la Invencible.

armadillo [,ɑːmə'dɪləʊ] *n* armadillo *m*.

Armageddon [,ɑːmə'gedn] *n* Armagedón *m*, lucha *f* suprema.

armament ['ɑːməmənt] *n* armamento *m*.

armature ['ɑːmətjʊəʳ] *n* (*Bot, Elec, Zool*) armadura *f*; (*of dynamo*) inducido *m*; (*supporting framework*) armazón *f*.

armband ['ɑːmbænd] *n* brazal *m*, brazalete *m*.

armchair ['ɑːmtʃɛəʳ] **1** *n* sillón *m*, butaca *f*. **2** *attr*: **~ general** general *m* de salón; **~ strategist** estratega *m* de gabinete, estratega *m* de café.

armed [ɑːmd] **1** *pret and ptp of* **arm²**. **2** *adj* armado; provisto de armas; **~ to the teeth** armado hasta los dientes; **~ conflict** conflicto *m* armado; **~ forces, ~ services** fuerzas *fpl* armadas; **~ neutrality** neutralidad *f* armada; **~ robbery** robo *m* a mano armada.

-armed [ɑːmd] *adj ending in compounds* de brazos ..., *eg* **strong~** de brazos fuertes; **one~** manco.

Armenia [ɑː'miːnɪə] *n* Armenia *f*.

Armenian [ɑː'miːnɪən] **1** *adj* armenio. **2** *n* (**a**) armenio *m*, -a *f*. (**b**) (*Ling*) armenio *m*.

armful ['ɑːmfʊl] *n* brazado *m*, brazada *f*.

armhole ['ɑːmhəʊl] *n* sobaquera *f*, sisa *f*.

armistice ['ɑːmɪstɪs] *n* armisticio *m*.

armlet ['ɑːmlɪt] *n* brazal *m*.

armor ['ɑːməʳ] *n* (*US*) = **armour**.

armorial [ɑː'mɔːrɪəl] *adj* heráldico; **~ bearings** escudo *m* de armas.

armour, (*US*) **armor** ['ɑːməʳ] **1** *n* (**a**) (*Mil, Zool, fig*) armadura *f*; (*steel plates*) blindaje *m*. (**b**) (*tank forces*) tanques *mpl*, fuerzas *fpl* blindadas. **2** *vt* blindar, acorazar.

armour-clad, (*US*) **armor-clad** ['ɑːməklæd] *adj*, **armoured,** (*US*) **armored** ['ɑːməd] *adj* blindado, acorazado; **~ car** (carro *m*) blindado *m*; **~ column** columna *f* blindada; **~ personnel carrier** vehículo *m* blindado para el transporte de tropas.

armourer, (*US*) **armorer** ['ɑːmərəʳ] *n* armero *m*.

armour-piercing, (*US*) **armor-piercing** ['ɑːmə,pɪəsɪŋ] *adj shell* perforante.

armour-plate, (*US*) **armor-plate** ['ɑːmə,pleɪt] *n* blindaje *m*.

armour-plated, (*US*) **armor-plated** ['ɑːmə'pleɪtɪd] *adj* blindado, acorazado.

armour-plating, (*US*) **armor-plating** ['ɑːmə'pleɪtɪŋ] *n* blindaje *m*.

armoury, (*US*) **armory** ['ɑːmərɪ] *n* armería *f*; arsenal *m*.

armpit ['ɑːmpɪt] *n* sobaco *m*, axila *f*.

armrest ['ɑːmrest] *n* apoyo *m* para el brazo, apoyabrazos *m*; (*of chair*) brazo *m*.

arm-wrestling ['ɑːm,reslɪŋ] *n* lucha *f* a pulso.

army ['ɑːmɪ] *n* ejército *m*; (*fig*) ejército *m*, multitud *f*; **~ chaplain** capellán *m* castrense; **~ corps** cuerpo *m* de ejército; **~ doctor** médico *m* militar; **~ life** vida *f* militar; **A~ list** lista *f* de oficiales del ejército; **~ of occupation** ejército *m* de ocupación; **~ slang** argot *m* militar; **to join the ~** hacerse soldado, engancharse, alistarse.

arnica ['ɑːnɪkə] *n* árnica *f*.

aroma [ə'rəʊmə] *n* aroma *m* (*of* a).

aromatic [,ærəʊ'mætɪk] *adj* aromático.

arose [ə'rəʊz] *pret of* **arise**.

around [ə'raʊnd] **1** *adv* (**a**) (*round about*) alrededor; a la redonda, *eg* **for 5 miles ~** en 5 millas a la redonda; **all ~** por todas partes, por todos lados.

(**b**) (*nearby*) cerca; por aquí; **is he ~?** ¿está por aquí?; **he must be somewhere ~** debe de andar por aquí; **he'll be ~ soon** estará dentro de poco; **there's a lot of flu ~** hay mucha gripe.

(**c**) **she's been ~*** (*travelled*) ha viajado mucho, ha visto mucho mundo; (*experienced*) tiene mucha experiencia; (*pej*) tiene historia.

2 *prep* (*esp US*) (**a**) (*round*) alrededor de, en torno de; **all ~ me** por todas partes alrededor de mí; **it's just ~ the corner** está a la vuelta de la esquina; **to go ~ the world** dar la vuelta al mundo; *V also* **about, round**.

(**b**) (*inside*) **to wander ~ the town** pasearse por la ciudad; **there were books all ~ the house** había libros en todas partes de la casa.

(**c**) (*approximately*) alrededor de; **~ 50** unos 50, 50 más o menos, alrededor de 50; **~ 2 o'clock** a eso de las 2; **~ 1950** alrededor de 1950.

arousal [ə'raʊzəl] *n* despertamiento *m*; (**sexual**) ~ excitación *f* (sexual), calentura *f*.

arouse [ə'raʊz] *vt* (**a**) (*wake up*) despertar. (**b**) (*fig*) mover, incitar, estimular, despertar; **it ~d great interest** despertó mucho interés; **it should ~ you to greater efforts** deberá incitarle a esforzarse más.

ARP *npl abbr of* **air-raid precautions** servicios *mpl* de defensa contra ataques aéreos.

arpeggio [ɑː'pedʒɪəʊ] *n* arpegio *m*.

arr. *abbr of* **arrives** llega.

arrack ['ærək] *n* arac *m*, aguardiente *m* de palma (*or* caña *etc*).

arraign [ə'reɪn] *vt* procesar, acusar (*before* ante).

arrange [ə'reɪndʒ] **1** *vt* (**a**) (*put in order*) arreglar, ordenar, disponer, organizar; **to ~ one's hair** arreglarse el pelo; **to ~ one's affairs** poner sus asuntos en orden; **how did we ~ matters last time?** ¿cómo lo organizamos la última vez?

(**b**) (*draw up*) disponer; **how is the room ~d?** ¿qué disposición tienen los muebles?

(**c**) (*Mus*) arreglar, adaptar.

(**d**) (*fix on, agree*) fijar, señalar; decidir, resolver; acordar; *meeting* organizar; *date* fijar; *plan, programme* acordar; **'to be ~d'** 'por determinar'; **I have ~d a surprise for tonight** he preparado una sorpresa para esta noche; **have you anything ~d for tomorrow?** ¿tienes planes para mañana?, ¿tienes compromiso mañana?; **a marriage has been ~d between** ... se ha concertado la boda de ...; **what did you ~ with him?** ¿cómo quedaron Vds con él?; **it was ~d that** ... se decidió que ...

2 *vi* (**a**) **to ~ for** prevenir, disponer; **I have ~d for you to go** he hecho los arreglos para que vaya Vd; **can you ~ for my luggage to be sent up?** por favor, que me suban los equipajes; **I ~d to meet him at the station** me cité con él en la estación; **I have ~d to see him tonight** quedamos en vernos esta noche, nos hemos dado una cita para esta noche; **can you ~ for him to replace you?** ¿te puedes hacer sustituir por él?

(**b**) **to ~ with sb to** + *infin* ponerse de acuerdo con uno para que + *subj*; **to ~ with sb that** ... convenir con uno en que ... + *subj*.

arranged [ə'reɪndʒd] *adj marriage* concertado (por los padres).

arrangement [ə'reɪndʒmənt] *n* (**a**) (*order, ordering*) arreglo *m*, orden *m*, disposición *f*; ordenación *f*; **flower ~** arreglo *m* floral.

(**b**) (*Mus*) arreglo *m*, adaptación *f*.

(**c**) (*agreement*) acuerdo *m*, convenio *m*; **to come to an ~** llegar a un acomodo; **we have an ~ with them** existe un acuerdo con ellos; **larger orders by ~** los pedidos de mayor cantidad previo arreglo; **salary by ~** (*advert*) sueldo a convenir; **by ~ with Covent Garden** con permiso de Covent Garden.

(**d**) (*plan, line of action*) plan *m*, medida *f*; **~s** (*preparations*) preparativos *mpl*; (*order of events*) programa *m*; **what are the ~s for your holiday?** ¿qué plan tienes para las vacaciones?; **we must make ~s to help them** tenemos que tomar medidas para ayudarles; **to make one's own ~s** obrar por cuenta propia; **if she doesn't like the idea she must make her own ~s** si no le gusta la idea que se las arregle sola; **all the ~s are made** todo está arreglado; **if this ~ doesn't suit you** si este plan no te conviene; **he has an ~ with his secretary** se entiende con su secretaria.

arranger [ə'reɪndʒəʳ] *n* (*Mus*) arreglador *m*, -ora *f*, arreglista *mf*.

arrant ['ærənt] *adj knave, liar etc* consumado, de siete suelas; **~ nonsense** puro disparate *m*.

array [ə'reɪ] **1** *n* (**a**) (*Mil*) orden *m*, formación *f*; **in battle ~** en orden de batalla; **in close ~** en filas apretadas.

(**b**) (*fig*) serie *f* impresionante, colección *f* imponente; **a fine ~ of flowers** un bello conjunto de flores; **a great ~ of**

hats una magnífica colección de sombreros.

(**c**) (*dress*) adorno *m*, atavío *m*.

(**d**) (*Comput*) matriz *f*, tabla *f*.

2 *vt* (*dress*) ataviar, engalanar (*in* de).

arrears [ə'rɪəz] *npl* (*sometimes sing*) atrasos *mpl*; ~ **of rent** atrasos *mpl* de alquiler; **in** ~ moroso, atrasado en pagos; **to be in** ~ **with one's correspondence** tener atrasos de correspondencia; **to get into** ~ atrasarse en los pagos; **to pay one month in** ~ pagar con un mes de retraso.

arrest [ə'rest] **1** *n* detención *f*; (*of goods*) secuestro *m*; **to be under** ~ estar detenido; **you're under** ~ queda Vd detenido; **to make an** ~ hacer una detención.

2 *vt* (**a**) (*Jur*) *criminal* detener, arrestar, capturar; *judgement* prorrogar.

(**b**) *attention* llamar.

(**c**) *growth, progress etc* detener, parar; atajar; (*hinder*) obstaculizar; **measures to** ~ **inflation** medidas *fpl* para detener la inflación; **~ed development** atrofia *f*, desarrollo *m* atrofiado.

arresting [ə'restɪŋ] *adj* llamativo, impresionante.

arrival [ə'raɪvəl] *n* (**a**) llegada *f*; (*fig*) advenimiento *m*; **'A~s'** (*Aer*) 'Llegadas'; ~ **platform** andén *m* de llegada; **on** ~ al llegar.

(**b**) (*person*) persona *f* que llega; **new** ~ recién llegado *m*, -a *f*, persona *f* que acaba de llegar; (*baby*) recién nacido *m*, -a *f*.

arrive [ə'raɪv] *vi* (**a**) llegar (*at, in* a); **to** ~ **(up)on the scene** llegar, aparecer, presentarse. (**b**) (*succeed*) triunfar, llegar (a ser alguien).

◆**arrive at** *vt decision, solution* llegar a; *perfection* lograr, alcanzar; **we finally ~d at a price** por fin convenimos en un precio; **they finally ~d at the idea of doing** ... finalmente llegaron a la decisión de hacer ...; **how did you** ~ **at this figure?** ¿cómo has llegado a esta cifra?

arriviste [ˌærɪ'viːst] *n* arribista *mf*.

arrogance ['ærəgəns] *n* arrogancia *f*, prepotencia *f* (*LAm*).

arrogant ['ærəgənt] *adj* arrogante, prepotente (*LAm*).

arrogantly ['ærəgəntlɪ] *adv* arrogantemente, con arrogancia, con prepotencia (*LAm*).

arrogate ['ærəʊgeɪt] *vt*: **to** ~ **sth to o.s.** arrogarse algo; *quality* atribuirse, apropiarse.

arrow ['ærəʊ] *n* flecha *f*.

arrowhead ['ærəʊhed] *n* punta *f* de flecha.

arrowroot ['ærəʊruːt] *n* arrurruz *m*.

arse** [ɑːs] (*esp Brit*) **1** *n* culo‡ *m*; **he can't tell his** ~ **from his elbow** confunde el culo con las témporas‡; **get off your** ~! ¡menearse!; **move** (*or* **shift**) **your** ~ córrete para allá.

2 *vi*: **to** ~ **about,** ~ **around** hacer el oso*.

arsehole** ['ɑːsheʊl] *n* (*esp Brit*) culo‡ *m*; (*person*) gilipollas‡ *m*.

arsenal ['ɑːsɪnl] *n* arsenal *m*.

arsenic ['ɑːsnɪk] *n* arsénico *m*.

arsenical [ɑː'senɪkl] *adj* arsénico, arsenical.

arson ['ɑːsn] *n* incendio *m* doloso, incendio *m* provocado, incendiarismo *m*.

arsonist ['ɑːsənɪst] *n* incendiario *m*, -a *f*, pirómano *m*, -a *f*.

art¹ [ɑːt] *n* (**a**) (*artistic*) arte *m* (*gen f in pl*); ~ **for ~'s sake** el arte por el arte; ~ **collection** colección *f* de arte; ~ **college** escuela *f* de Bellas Artes; ~ **deco** arte *m* deco; ~ **exhibition** exposición *f* de arte; ~ **gallery** museo *m* de pintura, pinacoteca *f*; ~ **nouveau** art *m* nouveau; ~ **paper** papel *m* cuché; ~ **school** escuela *f* de arte; ~ **student** estudiante *mf* de Bellas Artes.

(**b**) (*skill*) arte *m*; técnica *f*; (*quality*) habilidad *f*, destreza *f*; **~s and crafts** artes *fpl* y oficios; **A~s Council** (*Brit*) Consejería *f* de Cultura; **he's got it down to a fine** ~ ha perfeccionado su método.

(**c**) (*Univ*) **A~s** Filosofía *f* y Letras; **Faculty of A~s** Facultad *f* de Filosofía y Letras; **Bachelor of A~s** (*abbr* **BA**) Licenciado *m*, -a *f* en Filosofía y Letras; **Master of A~s** (*abbr* **MA**) Maestro *m*, -a *f* en Artes; **A~s degree** licenciatura *f* en Letras; **A~s student** estudiante *mf* de Letras.

(**d**) (*cunning*) arte *m*; astucia *f*; (*trick*) ardid *m*, maña *f*; **all her** ~ **of persuading** todo su arte de persuadir.

art²†† [ɑːt] *V* **be.**

artefact, (*esp US*) **artifact** ['ɑːtɪfækt] *n* artefacto *m*.

arterial [ɑː'tɪərɪəl] *adj* arterial; ~ **road** carretera *f* nacional.

arteriosclerosis [ɑː'tɪərɪəʊsklɪə'rəʊsɪs] *n* arteriosclerosis *f*.

artery ['ɑːtərɪ] *n* arteria *f* (*also fig*).

artesian [ɑː'tiːzɪən] *adj*: ~ **well** pozo *m* artesiano.

art-form ['ɑːtˌfɔːm] *n* medio *m* de expresión artística.

artful [ɑːtfʊl] *adj* mañoso, artero, astuto; (*skilful*) ingenioso.

artfully ['ɑːtfəlɪ] *adv* con mucha maña, astutamente; ingeniosamente.

artfulness ['ɑːtfʊlnɪs] *n* maña *f*, astucia *f*; ingenio *m*, artificio *m*.

arthritic [ɑː'θrɪtɪk] *adj* artrítico.

arthritis [ɑː'θraɪtɪs] *n* artritis *f*.

arthropod ['ɑːθrəpɒd] *n* artrópodo *m*.

Arthur ['ɑːθəʳ] *nm* Arturo; **King** ~ el rey Artús, el Rey Arturo.

Arthurian [ɑː'θjʊərɪən] *adj* arturiano, artúrico.

artichoke ['ɑːtɪtʃəʊk] *n* alcachofa *f*.

article ['ɑːtɪkl] **1** *n* (**a**) (*object*) artículo *m*, objeto *m*, cosa *f*; ~ **of clothing** prenda *f* de vestir; **~s of value** objetos *mpl* de valor.

(**b**) (*Press etc*) artículo *m*; colaboración *f*; reportaje *m*; (*learned*) artículo *m*.

(**c**) (*Jur etc*) artículo *m*; **~s of apprenticeship** contrato *m* de aprendizaje; **~s of association** (*Brit*) estatutos *mpl* de fundación (de una sociedad anónima); estatutos *mpl* sociales, escritura *f* social; ~ **of faith** artículo *m* de fe; **~s of incorporation** (*US*) carta *f* constitucional; ~ **of partnership** contrato *m* de asociación; **~s of war** (*US Mil Hist*) código *m* militar.

(**d**) (*Gram*) artículo *m*.

2 *vt apprentice* pactar, comprometer por contrato; **to be ~d to** estar de aprendiz con, servir bajo contrato a; **~d clerk** pasante *m*.

articulate 1 [ɑː'tɪkjʊlɪt] *adj* (**a**) *limb* articulado. (**b**) *speech* claro, distinto; *person* capaz de hablar; que se expresa bien, elocuente; **at 2 a child is hardly** ~ a los 2 años el niño es apenas capaz de hablar claramente; **he's not very** ~ no se expresa bien, no habla con confianza.

2 [ɑː'tɪkjʊleɪt] *vt* articular; *plan, goal* expresar claramente.

articulated [ɑː'tɪkjʊleɪtɪd] *adj*: ~ **lorry** camión *m* con remolque.

articulately [ɑː'tɪkjʊlɪtlɪ] *adv* fluidamente, con facilidad.

articulation [ɑːˌtɪkjʊ'leɪʃən] *n* articulación *f*.

articulatory [ɑː'tɪkjʊlətərɪ] *adj* articulatorio.

artifact ['ɑːtɪfækt] *n* (*esp US*) = **artefact.**

artifice ['ɑːtɪfɪs] *n* (*quality*) artificio *m*; (*ruse*) artificio *m*, ardid *m*, estratagema *f*.

artificial [ˌɑːtɪ'fɪʃəl] *adj* (**a**) artificial; *hair, teeth etc* postizo; ~ **insemination** inseminación *f* artificial; ~ **intelligence** inteligencia *f* artificial; ~ **light** luz *f* artificial; ~ **manure** abono *m* químico; ~ **respiration** respiración *f* artificial; ~ **silk** seda *f* artificial, rayón *m*.

(**b**) *person* afectado; *smile* forzado; *manner* artificial, poco natural; *grief etc* fingido, fabricado.

artificiality [ˌɑːtɪfɪʃɪ'ælɪtɪ] *n* artificialidad *f*; afectación *f*.

artificially [ˌɑːtɪ'fɪʃəlɪ] *adv* artificialmente; afectadamente, con afectación.

artillery [ɑː'tɪlərɪ] *n* artillería *f*.

artilleryman [ɑː'tɪlərɪmən], *pl* **artillerymen** [ɑː'tɪlərɪmen] artillero *m*.

artisan ['ɑːtɪzæn] *n* artesano *m*.

artist ['ɑːtɪst] *n* artista *mf*.

artiste [ɑː'tiːst] *n* (*Theat etc*) artista *mf* (de teatro *etc*); (*Mus*) intérprete *mf*.

artistic [ɑː'tɪstɪk] *adj* artístico; **she is very** ~ tiene mucho talento para el arte.

artistically [ɑː'tɪstɪkəlɪ] *adv* artísticamente; **to be** ~ **gifted** tener talento para el arte.

artistry ['ɑːtɪstrɪ] *n* arte *m*; talento *m* artístico, habilidad *f* artística, maestría *f*.

artless ['ɑːtlɪs] *adj* (**a**) natural, sencillo; ingenuo. (**b**) (*pej*) torpe, desmañado.

artlessly ['ɑːtlɪslɪ] *adv* ingenuamente.

artlessness ['ɑːtlɪsnɪs] *n* (**a**) naturalidad *f*, sencillez *f*; ingenuidad *f*. (**b**) desmaña *f*.

art-lover ['ɑːtˌlʌvəʳ] *n* aficionado *m*, -a *f* al arte.

artwork ['ɑːtwɜːk] *n* material *m* gráfico.

arty* ['ɑːtɪ] *adj style etc* ostentosamente artístico; seudoartístico; *clothing* afectado, extravagante; *person* de gusto muy afectado, que se las da de muy artista, repipi*.

arty-crafty* ['ɑːtɪ'krɑːftɪ] *adj,* (*US*) **artsy-craftsy*** ['ɑːtsɪ'krɑːftsɪ] *adj* ostentosamente artístico, afectadamente artístico.

A.R.V. *n* (*US*) *abbr of* **American Revised Version** *versión norteamericana de la Biblia*.

Aryan ['ɛərɪən] **1** *adj* ario. **2** *n* ario *m*, -a *f*.

AS (*US*) (**a**) *n abbr of* **Associate in** (*or* **of**) **Science**. (**b**) *abbr of* **American Samoa**.

as [æz, əz] *adv, conj and prep* (**a**) (*comparisons*) como: **he does** ~ **I do** hace como yo; ~ ... ~ tan ... como, *eg* ~ **tall**

~ tan alto como; ~ **quickly** ~ tan rápidamente como; **is it ~ big ~ all that?** ¿es en verdad tan grande?; **the same ~** el (*or* la, lo) mismo que; **such countries ~ France** países tales como Francia; **large books (such) ~ dictionaries** los libros grandes tales como los diccionarios; **he is not so silly ~ to do that** no es tan tonto como para hacer eso.

(**b**) (*comparisons: intensifying similes*) (~) **pale ~ death** pálido como un muerto; ~ **dead ~ a doornail** más muerto que mi abuela.

(**c**) (*comparisons*: as if *etc*) ~ **if,** ~ **though** como si + *subj*: ~ **if (he were) drunk** como si estuviera borracho; **it isn't ~ if he were poor** no es que sea pobre; **it isn't ~ if I didn't care** no es que me trajera sin cuidado; **he was — ~ it were — tired and emotional** estaba — por decirlo de alguna manera — cansado y exaltado; ~ **if to** + *infin* como para + *infin*.

(**d**) (*concessive*) **interesting ~ the book is** por interesante que sea el libro; **stupid ~ he is** aunque es estúpido; **be that ~ it may** sea como sea; **try ~ she would she couldn't lift it** por más que se esforzara no pudo levantarlo.

(**e**) (*in the capacity of*) como; ~ **a husband and father** como marido y padre; **Chaplin ~ Hitler** Charlot en el papel de Hitler; **I don't think much of him ~ an actor** no le estimo como (*or* en cuanto, en tanto que) actor; **she was often ill ~ a child** a menudo estuvo enferma de niña; **it's spelled with V ~ in Valencia** se escribe con V de Valencia; **we're going ~ tourists** vamos en plan de turismo; **he was there ~ adviser** estuvo en calidad de asesor.

(**f**) (*after certain verbs*) **to act ~** actuar de, estar de; **to be dressed ~** estar vestido de; *V also the verbs.*

(**g**) (*concerning*) ~ **for that,** ~ **to that,** ~ **regards that** en cuanto a eso, por lo que se refiere a eso, en lo que a eso atañe.

(**h**) (*manner*) como; ~ **often happens** como ocurre a menudo; **do ~ you wish** haz lo que quieras, haz como quieras; **to leave things ~ they are** dejar las cosas tal como están; **just ~ you are an engineer, (so) I am a doctor** como Vd es ingeniero yo soy médico; **her door is the first ~ you go up** su puerta es la primera según se sube; **you've got plenty ~ it is** tiene ya bastantes; ~ **it is we can do nothing** como están las cosas no podemos hacer nada.

(**i**) (*time*) **he came in ~ I was leaving** entró cuando yo salía, entró al salir yo; ~ **I was sitting there he came up** mientras yo estaba sentado allí él vino; ~ **she got older she got deafer** a medida que (*or* conforme) envejecía ensordecía más; ~ **I was passing the house** al pasar yo delante de la casa; ~ **from tomorrow** a partir de mañana; ~ **of last week** a partir de la semana pasada.

(**j**) (*result*) **he did it in such a way ~ to please everyone** lo hizo de tal modo que logró contentar a todos; *V* **so.**

(**k**) (*since*) ~ **I don't speak Arabic** como yo no hablo árabe; **I can't come ~ I have an appointment** no puedo venir pues (*or* ya que, porque) tengo un compromiso; ~ **we hadn't heard from you** al no tener noticias tuyas.

ASA *n* (*Brit*) (**a**) *abbr of* **Advertising Standards Authority** Asociación *f* de Normas Publicitarias. (**b**) *abbr of* **Amateur Swimming Association** *federación amateur de natación.* (**c**) (*US*) *abbr of* **American Standards Association** Asociación *f* Norteamericana de Normalización.

a.s.a.p. *adv abbr of* **as soon as possible.**

asbestos [æz'bestəs] *n* asbesto *m*, amianto *m*.

asbestosis [ˌæzbes'təusɪs] *n* asbestosis *f*.

ascend [ə'send] **1** *vt stairs, river* subir; *mountain* escalar, subir a; *throne* subir a, ascender a. **2** *vi* subir, ascender; (*soar*) elevarse, encaramarse.

ascendancy [ə'sendənsɪ] *n* ascendiente *m*, dominio *m* (*over* sobre).

ascendant [ə'sendənt] *n*: **to be in the ~** predominar, tener una influencia cada vez mayor, subir.

ascending [ə'sendɪŋ] *adj* ascendente; **in ~ order** en orden ascendente.

ascension [ə'senʃən] *n* ascensión *f*; **A~ Day** (Día *m* de) la Ascensión; **A~ Island** Isla *f* Ascensión.

ascent [ə'sent] *n* (*act*) subida *f*, ascensión *f*; (*slope*) cuesta *f*, pendiente *f*.

ascertain [ˌæsə'teɪn] *vt* averiguar, determinar, descubrir, indagar.

ascertainable [ˌæsə'teɪnəbl] *adj* averiguable, comprobable.

ascertainment [ˌæsə'teɪnmənt] *n* averiguación *f*, comprobación *f*.

ascetic [ə'setɪk] **1** *adj* ascético. **2** *n* asceta *mf*.

asceticism [ə'setɪsɪzəm] *n* ascetismo *m*.

ASCII *n abbr of* **American Standard Code for Information Interchange** código *m* estándar norteamericano para el intercambio de información.

ascorbic [ə'skɔːbɪk] *adj*: ~ **acid** ácido *m* ascórbico.

ascribable [əs'kraɪbəbl] *adj* atribuible (*to* a).

ascribe [ə'skraɪb] *vt* atribuir (*to* a).

ascription [ə'skrɪpʃən] *n* atribución *f*.

ASCU *n* (*US*) *abbr of* **Association of State Colleges and Universities.**

ASE *n* (*US*) *abbr of* **American Stock Exchange.**

ASEAN *n abbr of* **Association of South-East Asian Nations** Asociación *f* de Naciones del Sureste Asiático.

aseptic [eɪ'septɪk] *adj* aséptico.

asexual [eɪ'seksjuəl] *adj* asexual.

ASH [æʃ] *n abbr of* **Action on Smoking and Health** *organización anti-tabaco.*

ash¹ [æʃ] **1** *n* (*also* ~ **tree**) fresno *m*. **2** *attr* de fresno.

ash² [æʃ] *n* ceniza *f*; **~es** cenizas *fpl* (*also of dead*); **A~ Wednesday** Miércoles *m* de Ceniza; **the A~es** *trofeo imaginario de los partidos de críquet Australia-Inglaterra*; **to burn** (*or* **reduce**) **sth to ~es** reducir algo a cenizas.

ashamed [ə'ʃeɪmd] *adj*: **to be ~, to feel ~** avergonzarse, estar avergonzado, apenarse (*LAm*) (*at, of* de; *for* por; *of being* de ser); **I am ~ of you** me das vergüenza; **I was ~ to ask for money** me daba vergüenza pedir dinero; **I am ~ to say that ...** me avergüenza decir que ...; **your generosity makes me feel ~** su generosidad me produce vergüenza; **to be ~ of o.s.** tener vergüenza de sí; **you ought to be ~ of yourself!** ¿no te da vergüenza?, ¿no tienes vergüenza?

ashbin ['æʃbɪn] *n* cubo *m* de la basura, tarro *m* de basura (*LAm*).

ash blond(e) [æʃ'blɒnd] **1** *adj* rubio ceniza. **2** *n* rubia *f* ceniza.

ashcan ['æʃkæn] *n* (*US*) = **ashbin.**

ash-coloured, (*US*) **ash-colored** ['æʃkʌləd] *adj* ceniciento; color ceniza; *face* pálido.

ashen ['æʃn] *adj* (**a**) (*pale*) pálido, ceniciento. (**b**) (*Bot: of ash wood*) de fresno.

Ashkenazi [ˌæʃkə'nɑːzɪ] **1** *adj* askenazí. **2** *n, pl* **Ashkenazim** [ˌæʃkə'nɑːzɪm] askenazí *mf*.

ashlar ['æʃləʳ] *n* sillar *m*; (*also* ~ **work**) sillería *f*.

ashman ['æʃmæn] *n, pl* **ashmen** ['æʃmen] (*US*) basurero *m*.

ashore [ə'ʃɔːʳ] *adv* en tierra; **to be ~** estar en tierra; **to come ~, to go ~** desembarcar; **to put sb ~** desembarcar a uno, poner a uno en tierra.

ashpan ['æʃpæn] *n* cenicero *m*, cajón *m* de la ceniza.

ashram ['æʃrəm] *n* ashram *m*.

ashtray ['æʃtreɪ] *n* cenicero *m*.

ashy ['æʃɪ] *adj* cenizoso.

Asia ['eɪʃə] *n* Asia *f*; ~ **Minor** Asia *f* Menor.

Asian ['eɪʃn] **1** *adj* asiático; ~ **flu** gripe *f* asiática. **2** *n* asiático *m*, -a *f*.

Asiatic [ˌeɪsɪ'ætɪk] **1** *adj* asiático. **2** *n* asiático *m*, -a *f*.

aside [ə'saɪd] **1** *adv* aparte, a un lado; *V* **put, set** *etc.* **2** *prep* (*esp US*) ~ **from** aparte de. **3** *n* (*Theat*) aparte *m*; **to say sth in an ~** decir algo aparte.

asinine ['æsɪnaɪn] *adj* asnal; (*fig*) estúpido.

ask [ɑːsk] **1** *vt* (**a**) (*inquire, inquire of*) preguntar; **to ~ sb sth** preguntar algo a uno; **to ~ sb a question** hacer una pregunta a uno; **they ~ed me about my passport** me hicieron preguntas acerca de mi pasaporte; **they ~ed me about the new missile** me interrogaron sobre el nuevo mísil; **if you ~ me ...** para mí que ..., en mi opinión ...; **don't ~ me!** ¡yo qué sé!; **I ~ you!** (*despairing*) ¡vaya por Dios!; ¡lo que faltaba!; **~ed if this was true, she replied ...** preguntada si esto era cierto, contestó ...

(**b**) (*request, demand*) pedir; **to ~ sb a favour, to ~ a favour of sb** pedir un favor a uno; **I don't ~ much from you** lo que te pido es poco; **that's ~ing the impossible** eso es pedir lo imposible; **that's ~ing a lot** eso es mucho pedir; **to ~ that ...** pedir que ... + *subj*, rogar que ... + *subj*; **to ~ sb to do sth** pedir a uno que haga algo.

(**c**) (*invite*) invitar, convidar (*LAm*); **have they ~ed you?** ¿te han invitado?; **to ~ sb to dinner** invitar a uno a cenar.

2 *vi* (*inquire*) preguntar; (*request, demand*) pedir; **I was only ~ing** solamente era una simple pregunta; **it's ours for the ~ing** si lo pedimos nos lo dan, es nuestro con solo pedir; **~ing price** precio *m* a que se ofrece; **this is the third time of ~ing** (ésta) es la tercera vez que te lo pido; **now you're ~ing!** (*iro*) ¡vaya pregunta!

◆**ask about** *vt* preguntar por; pedir noticias de.

◆**ask after** *vt person* preguntar por, interesarse por; **to ~ after sb's health** interesarse por la salud de uno.

◆**ask along** *vt* invitar.

◆**ask back** *vt* (*for second visit*) volver a invitar; **to ~ sb**

back (*on reciprocal visit*) invitar a uno a que devuelva la visita.

◆**ask for** *vt* (**a**) (*inquire*) preguntar por.

(**b**) (*request*) pedir, reclamar; solicitar; **to ~ sb for sth** pedir algo a uno; **he ~ed for it*** se la buscó, bien merecido lo tiene; **to ~ for sth back** pedir que se devuelva algo; **how much are they ~ing for it?** ¿cuánto piden por él?; **to write ~ing for help** escribir pidiendo ayuda; *V* **trouble.**

◆**ask in** *vt* invitar a entrar, invitar a pasar.

◆**ask out** *vt*: **they never ~ her out** no le invitan nunca a salir (con ellos); **I'm ~ed out** estoy invitado; **the first time he ~ed her out** la primera vez que la invitó a salir con él; **I never dared to ~ her out** nunca me atreví a pedirle una cita.

◆**ask round** *vt* invitar.

askance [ə'skɑːns] *adv*: **to look ~** mirar de soslayo, mirar con recelo.

askew [ə'skjuː] *adv* sesgado, ladeado; oblicuamente; **the picture is ~** el cuadro está torcido.

aslant [ə'slɑːnt] **1** *adv* a través, oblicuamente. **2** *prep* a través de.

asleep [ə'sliːp] *adj* dormido; **to be ~** estar dormido; **to be fast ~, to be sound ~** estar profundamente dormido; **to fall ~** dormirse, quedar dormido.

ASLEF ['æzlef] *n* (*Brit*) *abbr of* **Associated Society of Locomotive Engineers and Firemen** *sindicato de maquinistas y fogoneros.*

ASM *n abbr of* **air-to-surface missile** misil *m* aire-tierra.

ASP *abbr of* **American Selling Price** precio *m* de venta en América.

asp [æsp] *n* áspid(e) *m*.

asparagus [əs'pærəgəs] *n* (*plant*) esparraguera *f*, espárrago *m*; (*as food*) espárragos *mpl*.

ASPCA *n* (*US*) *abbr of* **American Society for the Prevention of Cruelty to Animals.**

aspect ['æspekt] *n* aspecto *m* (*also Gram*); apariencia *f*; **to study all ~s of a question** estudiar una cuestión bajo todos sus aspectos; **seen from this ~** visto desde este lado; **a house with a southerly ~** una casa orientada hacia el sur.

aspen ['æspən] *n* álamo *m* temblón.

asperity [æs'perɪtɪ] *n* aspereza *f*.

aspersion [əs'pɜːʃən] *n* calumnia *f*; **to cast ~s on** difamar, calumniar.

asphalt ['æsfælt] **1** *n* (*material*) asfalto *m*; (*place*) pista *f* asfaltada, recinto *m* asfaltado; **~ jungle** desierto *m* de asfalto. **2** *vt* asfaltar.

asphyxia [æs'fɪksɪə] *n* asfixia *f*.

asphyxiate [æs'fɪksɪeɪt] **1** *vt* asfixiar. **2** *vi* morir asfixiado.

asphyxiation [æs,fɪksɪ'eɪʃən] *n* asfixia *f*.

aspic ['æspɪk] *n* gelatina *f*.

aspidistra [,æspɪ'dɪstrə] *n* aspidistra *f*.

aspirant ['æspɪrənt] *n* aspirante *mf*, candidato *m*, -a *f* (*to* a).

aspirate 1 ['æspərɪt] *adj* aspirado. **2** ['æspərɪt] *n* aspirada *f*. **3** ['æspəreɪt] *vt* aspirar; **~d H** H *f* aspirada.

aspiration [,æspə'reɪʃən] *n* (*all senses*) aspiración *f*.

aspire [əs'paɪər] *vi*: **to ~ to** aspirar a; ambicionar, anhelar; **we can't ~ to that** no aspiramos a tanto, nuestras pretensiones son más modestas; **he ~s to a new car** anhela tener un coche nuevo; **to ~ to** + *infin* aspirar a + *infin*, anhelar + *infin*, ambicionar + *infin*.

aspirin ['æsprɪn] *n* aspirina *f*.

aspiring [əs'paɪərɪŋ] *adj* ambicioso; en ciernes.

ass[1] [æs] *n* (**a**) asno *m*, burro *m*, -a *f*. (**b**) (* *fig*) burro *m*, imbécil *m*; **the man's an ~** es un imbécil; **don't be an ~!** ¡no seas imbécil!; **what an ~ I am!** ¡soy un imbécil!; **to make an ~ of o.s.** ponerse en ridículo.

ass[2]** [æs] *n* (*US*) culo* *m*; **to bust one's ~** ir de culo*; **to fall on one's ~** (*fig*) hacer el ridi*; **kiss my ~!** ¡vete a la mierda!**; ¡vete al carajo!**

assail [ə'seɪl] *vt* acometer, atacar; *task* acometer, emprender; **doubts began to ~ him** las dudas empezaron a asaltarle; **he was ~ed by critics** le atacaron los críticos; **a sound ~ed my ear** un ruido penetró en mis oídos.

assailant [ə'seɪlənt] *n* asaltador *m*, -ora *f*, agresor *m*, -ora *f*; **she did not recognize her ~s** no reconoció a los que la agredieron; **there were 4 ~s** eran 4 los agresores.

Assam [æ'sæm] *n* Assam *m*.

assassin [ə'sæsɪn] *n* asesino *m*.

assassinate [ə'sæsɪneɪt] *vt* asesinar.

assassination [ə,sæsɪ'neɪʃən] *n* asesinato *m*.

assault [ə'sɔːlt] **1** *n* (**a**) (*Mil etc*) asalto *m* (*on* sobre), ataque *m* (*on* a, contra); **~ course** pista *m* americana; **~ craft** barcaza *f* de asalto; **~ troops** tropas *fpl* de asalto; **to make** (*or* **mount**) **an ~ on** asaltar, hacer un ataque a.

(**b**) (*Jur etc*) atentado *m* (*on* a, contra), agresión *f*; violencia *f*; **~ and battery** maltrato *m* de palabra y obra, vías *fpl* de hecho; *V* **indecent, sexual.**

2 *vt* (**a**) (*Mil*) asaltar, atacar.

(**b**) (*Jur etc*) agredir; *woman* (tratar de) violar, atentar contra el pudor de.

assay [ə'seɪ] **1** *n* ensaye *m*; (*of gold*) ensaye *m*, aquilatamiento *m*; **~ mark** señal *f* de ensaye; **~ office** oficina *f* de ensaye. **2** *vt* (**a**) *metal etc* ensayar; *gold* ensayar, aquilatar; (*fig*) intentar, probar. (**b**) **to ~ to** + *infin* (*try*) intentar + *infin*.

assemblage [ə'semblɪdʒ] *n* (**a**) reunión *f*; colección *f*. (**b**) (*Mech*) montaje *m*; ensambladura *f*.

assemble [ə'sembl] **1** *vt* reunir, juntar; (*Parl*) convocar; (*Mech*) montar; ensamblar. **2** *vi* reunirse, juntarse; celebrar una sesión; **the ~d dignitaries** las dignidades reunidas, la reunión de dignidades.

assembler [ə'semblər] *n* ensamblador *m*.

assembly [ə'semblɪ] *n* (**a**) (*meeting*) reunión *f*; (*Pol etc*) asamblea *f*; (*people present*) concurrencia *f*, asistentes *mpl*; (*Brit Scol*) reunión *f* general de todos los alumnos. (**b**) (*Mech*) montaje *m*; ensamblaje *m*, ensamblado *m*. (**c**) (*Comput*) **~ language** lenguaje *m* ensamblador.

assembly-line [ə'semblɪlaɪn] *n* línea *f* de montaje, cadena *f* de montaje; **~ worker** trabajador *m*, -ora *f* en línea de montaje.

assemblyman [ə'semblɪmən] *n, pl* **assemblymen** [ə'semblɪmen] (*US*) miembro *m* de una asamblea.

assembly-plant [ə'semblɪ,plɑːnt] *n* planta *f* de montaje.

assembly-room [ə'semblɪrʊm] *n* sala *f* de fiestas.

assembly-shop [ə'semblɪʃɒp] *n* taller *m* de montaje.

assent [ə'sent] **1** *n* asentimiento *m*, consentimiento *m*, aprobación *f*; **royal ~** aprobación *f* real; **to nod one's ~** asentir con la cabeza. **2** *vi* consentir (*to* en), asentir (*to* a).

assert [ə'sɜːt] **1** *vt* afirmar, declarar; *claim* sostener, defender; *rights* hacer valer; *innocence* afirmar. **2** *vr*: **to ~ o.s.** imponerse, hacer valer sus derechos.

assertion [ə'sɜːʃən] *n* aserto *m*, afirmación *f*, declaración *f*.

assertive [ə'sɜːtɪv] *adj* asertivo.

assertively [ə'sɜːtɪvlɪ] *adv* de manera asertiva.

assertiveness [ə'sɜːtɪvnɪs] *n* asertividad *f*.

assess [ə'ses] *vt* valorar, apreciar; tasar, calcular (*at* en); enjuiciar, juzgar; *damages, tax* fijar (*at* en); (*Univ etc*) evaluar; *situation* apreciar; *amount* calcular; **how did you ~ this candidate?** ¿qué juicio formó sobre este candidato?; **how do you ~ your chances now?** ¿cómo evalúa sus posibilidades ahora?

assessable [ə'sesəbl] *adj* tasable, calculable; **~ income** ingresos *mpl* imponibles; **a theory not readily ~** una teoría difícil de enjuiciar.

assessment [ə'sesmənt] *n* (**a**) (*act*) valoración *f*; tasación *f*; enjuiciamiento *m*; (*opinion*) aprecio *m*, juicio *m*; evaluación *f*; **in my ~** a mi juicio; **continuous ~** evaluación *f* continua; **what is your ~ of the situation?** ¿cómo ve la situación? (**b**) (*for tax etc*) tasación *f*, imposición *f*; cálculo *m* del valor imponible, cálculo *m* de los ingresos imponibles.

assessor [ə'sesər] *n* asesor *m*, -ora *f*; (*US*: *of taxes etc*) tasador *m*, -ora *f*; **~'s office** oficina *f* municipal.

asset ['æset] *n* (**a**) (*advantage*) ventaja *f*; plus *m*, factor *m* positivo; **she is a great ~ in the department** es una persona valiosísima en el departamento.

(**b**) (*Fin etc*) posesión *f*; (*book-keeping item*) partida *f* del activo; **~s** activo *m*, haber *m*; fondos *mpl*; (**personal**) **~s** bienes *mpl* muebles; **~s in hand** activo *m* disponible, bienes *mpl* disponibles; **~s and liabilities** activo *m* y pasivo.

asset-stripper ['æset,strɪpər] *n* (*Fin*) *persona que compra empresas en crisis para vender sus bienes.*

asset-stripping ['æset,strɪpɪŋ] *n* (*Fin*) *compra de empresas en crisis para vender sus bienes.*

asseverate [ə'sevəreɪt] *vt* aseverar.

asseveration [ə,sevə'reɪʃən] *n* aseveración *f*.

asshole** ['æshəʊl] *n* (*US*) culo* *m*; (*person*) gilipollas* *m*.

assiduity [,æsɪ'djuːɪtɪ] *n* asiduidad *f*, diligencia *f*.

assiduous [ə'sɪdjʊəs] *adj* asiduo, diligente.

assiduously [ə'sɪdjʊəslɪ] *adv* asiduamente, diligentemente.

assign [ə'saɪn] **1** *vt* (**a**) (*allot*) asignar; *reason etc* señalar, indicar; *share, task* asignar, señalar; *date* señalar, fijar (*for* para); *room etc* destinar, señalar; *literary work etc* atribuir; *property* traspasar, ceder; **which is the room ~ed to me?** ¿qué habitación es la que me destinan a mí?; **the event is to be ~ed to 1600** hemos de referir el suceso al año 1600.

(**b**) *person* nombrar, destinar; designar; **they ~ed him to the Paris embassy** le nombraron para la embajada de París.

2 *n* (*Jur*) cesionario *m*, -a *f*.

assignation [ˌæsɪgˈneɪʃən] *n* (**a**) (*act*) asignación *f*; traspaso *m*; atribución *f*; nombramiento *m*, designación *f*. (**b**) (*task*) = **assignment (b)**. (**c**) (*appointment*) cita *f* (*esp* amorosa).

assignee [ˌæsaɪˈniː] *n* (*Jur*) = **assign 2**.

assignment [əˈsaɪnmənt] *n* (**a**) (*act*) asignación *f etc* (*V* **assignation**). (**b**) (*task*) cometido *m*, tarea *f*; misión *f*; (*Scol etc*) trabajo *m*.

assignor [ˌæsaɪˈnɔːʳ] *n* (*Jur*) cedente *mf*.

assimilate [əˈsɪmɪleɪt] **1** *vt* asimilar. **2** *vi* asimilarse.

assimilation [əˌsɪmɪˈleɪʃən] *n* asimilación *f*.

Assisi [əˈsiːzɪ] *n* Asís *m*.

assist [əˈsɪst] **1** *vt* ayudar; asistir; *development, progress etc* favorecer, estimular, fomentar; **~ed passage** pasaje *m* subvencionado; **to ~ sb out** ayudar a uno a salir; **we ~ed him to his car** le ayudamos a llegar a su coche.

2 *vi* ayudar; **to ~ in** tomar parte en, participar en; **to ~ in** + *ger* ayudar a + *infin*, contribuir a + *infin*.

assistance [əˈsɪstəns] *n* (**a**) ayuda *f*, auxilio *m*; **to be of ~ to, to give ~ to** ayudar a, prestar ayuda a; **can I be of ~?** ¿puedo ayudarle?; **to come to sb's ~** acudir en auxilio de uno, socorrer a uno.

(**b**) (*also* **national ~**, **public ~**) subsidio *m* (al necesitado).

assistant [əˈsɪstənt] **1** *adj* auxiliar; **~ manager** subdirector *m*; **~ master** profesor *m* de instituto; **~ mistress** profesora *f* de instituto; **~ principal** subdirector *m*, -ora *f*; **~ professor** (*US*) profesor *m* agregado, profesora *f* agregada; **~ secretary** vicesecretario *m*, -a *f*.

2 *n* ayudante *mf*, auxiliar *mf*; (*language* ~) auxiliar *mf* de conversación; *V* **laboratory, shop**.

assizes [əˈsaɪzɪz] *npl* (*Brit*) sesiones *fpl* jurídicas (regionales).

assn *abbr of* **association** asociación *f*.

assoc. (**a**) *abbr of* **association** asociación *f*. (**b**) *abbr of* **associate(d)** asociado.

associate 1 [əˈsəʊʃɪɪt] *adj* asociado; **~ director** subdirector *m*, -ora *f*; **A~ Justice** (*US*) juez *mf* asociado; **~ member** miembro *mf* correspondiente; **~ producer** (*TV etc*) productor *m* asociado, productora *f* asociada; **~ professor** (*US*) profesor *m* adjunto, profesora *f* adjunta.

2 [əˈsəʊʃɪɪt] *n* asociado *m*, -a *f*, colega *mf*; compañero *m*, -a *f*; (*in crime*) cómplice *mf*; (*member*) miembro *mf* correspondiente; (*Comm*) asociado *m*, -a *f*, socio *mf*, consocio *mf*; **Fred Bloggs and A~s** Fred Bloggs y Asociados; **~'s degree** (*US*) licenciatura *f*.

3 [əˈsəʊʃɪeɪt] *vt* asociar; relacionar; juntar, unir; **I don't wish to be ~d with it** no quiero tener nada que ver con ello; **was he ~d with that scandal?** ¿estuvo mezclado en ese escándalo?; **to be ~d with a plot** participar en un complot.

4 [əˈsəʊʃɪeɪt] *vi* asociarse (*with* con); juntarse, unirse; **to ~ in** participar juntamente en; **to ~ with** ir con, tratar con, frecuentar (la compañía de).

5 [əˈsəʊʃɪeɪt] *vr*: **to ~ o.s. with sb in a venture** participar con uno en una empresa, colaborar con uno en un proyecto; **I should like to ~ myself with that** quiero hacerme eco de aquello.

associated [əˈsəʊʃɪeɪtɪd] *adj* asociado; conexo, relacionado; *company* afiliado.

association [əˌsəʊsɪˈeɪʃən] *n* (**a**) (*relation*) asociación *f*; (*with person*) relación *f*, conexión *f*; **A in ~ with B** A conjuntamente con B; **to form an ~ with** relacionarse con, entrar en relaciones con; **by ~ of ideas** por asociación de ideas.

(**b**) (*body*) asociación *f*; **~ football** (*Brit*) fútbol *m*.

(**c**) **~s** (*memories*) recuerdos *mpl*; sugestiones *fpl*, connotaciones *fpl*; **the town has historic ~s** la ciudad es rica en recuerdos históricos; **the word has nasty ~s** la palabra tiene connotaciones feas.

associative [əˈsəʊʃɪətɪv] *adj*: **~ storage** almacenamiento *m* asociativo.

assonance [ˈæsənəns] *n* (*system*) asonancia *f*; (*word*) asonante *m*; **words in ~** palabras *fpl* asonantadas.

assonant [ˈæsənənt] **1** *adj* asonante. **2** *n* asonante *m*.

assonate [ˈæsəneɪt] *vi* asonar.

assort [əˈsɔːt] *vi* concordar (*with* con), convenir (*with* a); **it ~s ill with his character** no cuadra con su carácter; **this does not ~ with what you said** esto no concuerda con lo que dijo.

assorted [əˈsɔːtɪd] *adj* surtido, variado; **he dined with ~ ministers** (*hum*) cenó con este y con el otro ministro.

assortment [əˈsɔːtmənt] *n* variedad *f*, colección *f* variada; (*Comm*) surtido *m*; **quite an ~!** ¡aquí hay de todo!; **there was an ~ of guests** los invitados eran de lo más variado; **Peter was there with an ~ of girlfriends** estaba Pedro con una colección de amigas.

asst (**a**) *abbr of* **assistant** ayudante *mf*. (**b**) (*as adj*) auxiliar.

assuage [əˈsweɪdʒ] *vt feelings* calmar; *pain* aliviar; *passion* mitigar, suavizar; *desire* satisfacer; *appetite* saciar; *person* apaciguar, sosegar; **he was not easily ~d** no era fácil apaciguarle.

assume [əˈsjuːm] *vt* (**a**) *aspect, name, possession, importance, large proportions* tomar; *air* darse; *attitude* adoptar; *authority* (*unjustly*) apropiarse, arrogarse; *burden, control, responsibility* asumir; *power* tomar, ocupar.

(**b**) (*suppose*) suponer, dar por sentado; **to ~ that ...** suponer que ..., imaginar que ...; **let us ~ that ...** pongamos por caso que ...; **you resigned, I ~** dimitió Vd, me imagino; **you are assuming a lot** Vd supone demasiado, eso es mucho suponer; **assuming that ...** (*as conj*) en el supuesto de que ...

assumed [əˈsjuːmd] *adj* (**a**) *name etc* falso, fingido. (**b**) (*supposed*) presunto; **the ~ culprit** el presunto culpable.

assumption [əˈsʌmpʃən] *n* (**a**) (*act*) asunción *f*; el tomar, adopción *f*; apropiación *f*; **the A~** (*Rel*) la Asunción.

(**b**) (*supposition*) suposición *f*, supuesto *m*; presunción *f*; **we cannot make that ~** no podemos dar eso por sentado; **on the ~ that ...** suponiendo que ...; **to start from a false ~** partir de una base falsa.

(**c**) (*arrogance*) presunción *f*.

assurance [əˈʃʊərəns] *n* (**a**) (*guarantee*) garantía *f*, promesa *f*; **you have my ~ that ...** les aseguro que ...; **I can give you no ~ about that** no les puedo garantizar nada.

(**b**) (*confidence*) confianza *f*; aplomo *m*, serenidad *f*.

(**c**) (*certainty*) certeza *f*, seguridad *f*; **with the ~ that ...** con la seguridad de que ...; **to make ~ doubly sure** para mayor seguridad.

(**d**) (*Brit Fin*) seguro *m*; **~ company** compañía *f* de seguros.

assure [əˈʃʊəʳ] **1** *vt* (**a**) (*make certain*) asegurar, garantizar.

(**b**) (*Brit Fin*) asegurar; **his life is ~d for £500,000** su vida está asegurada en 500.000 libras.

(**c**) (*reassure*) asegurar; **I ~d him of my support** le afirmé mi apoyo; **you may rest ~d that ...** tenga la seguridad de que ...; **let me ~ you that ...** permita que le asegure que ...; **it is so, I ~ you** es así, se lo garantizo.

2 *vr*: **to ~ o.s. of sth** asegurarse de algo.

assured [əˈʃʊəd] **1** *adj* (**a**) (*self~*) confiado, sereno.

(**b**) (*certain*) seguro; **you have an ~ future** tienes un porvenir seguro.

2 *n*: **the ~** (*Fin*) el asegurado, la asegurada.

assuredly [əˈʃʊərɪdlɪ] *adv* seguramente, sin duda.

ass-wipe** [ˈæswaɪp] *n* (*US*) papel *m* de wáter*.

Assyria [əˈsɪrɪə] *n* Asiria *f*.

Assyrian [əˈsɪrɪən] **1** *adj* asirio. **2** *n* asirio *m*, -a *f*.

AST *n abbr of* **Atlantic Standard Time** *hora oficial de Nueva Escocia*.

aster [ˈæstəʳ] *n* aster *f*.

asterisk [ˈæstərɪsk] **1** *n* asterisco *m*. **2** *vt* señalar con un asterisco, poner un asterisco a.

astern [əˈstɜːn] **1** *adv* a popa, por la popa; **to fall ~** quedarse atrás; **to go ~** ciar, ir hacia atrás; **to make a boat fast ~** amarrar un barco por la popa.

2 *prep*: **~ of** detrás de.

asteroid [ˈæstərɔɪd] *n* asteroide *m*.

asthma [ˈæsmə] *n* asma *f*.

asthmatic [æsˈmætɪk] **1** *adj* asmático. **2** *n* asmático *m*, -a *f*.

astigmatic [ˌæstɪgˈmætɪk] *adj* astigmático.

astigmatism [æsˈtɪgmətɪzəm] *n* astigmatismo *m*.

astir [əˈstɜːʳ] *adv, adj*: **to be ~** estar activo, estar en movimiento; (*up and about*) estar levantado; **we were ~ early** nos levantamos temprano; **nobody was ~ at that hour** a tal hora todos estaban todavía en cama.

ASTM *n* (*US*) *abbr of* **American Society for Testing Materials**.

ASTMS *n* (*Brit*) *abbr of* **Association of Scientific, Technical and Managerial Staff** *sindicato de personal científico, técnico y directivo*.

astonish [əˈstɒnɪʃ] *vt* asombrar, pasmar; sorprender; **you ~ me!** ¡esto es asombroso!; **to be ~ed** asombrarse (*at* de), maravillarse (*at* de, con), quedarse asombrado (*at* de); **I am ~ed that ...** me asombra que + *subj*.

astonished [əˈstɒnɪʃt] *adj* estupefacto, pasmado.

astonishing [əˈstɒnɪʃɪŋ] *adj* asombroso, pasmoso; sorprendente; **I find it ~ that ...** me asombra que + *subj*.
astonishingly [əˈstɒnɪʃɪŋlɪ] *adv*: **~ easy** increíblemente fácil; **it was an ~ lovely scene** la escena era de una belleza totalmente inesperada; **~ enough** por milagro, por maravilla; **but, ~, he did not** pero, por maravilla, no lo hizo.
astonishment [əˈstɒnɪʃmənt] *n* asombro *m*, sorpresa *f*, estupefacción *f*; **to my ~** con gran sorpresa mía.
astound [əˈstaʊnd] *vt etc* = **astonish** *etc*.
astounded [əˈstaʊndɪd] *adj* pasmado, estupefacto; **I am ~** estoy pasmado.
astounding [əˈstaʊndɪŋ] *adj* asombroso, pasmoso; **~!** ¡esto es asombroso!; **I find it ~ that ...** me asombra que + *subj*.
astoundingly [əˈstaʊndɪŋlɪ] *adv V* **astonishingly**.
astrakhan [ˌæstrəˈkæn] *n* astracán *m*.
astral [ˈæstrəl] *adj* astral.
astray [əˈstreɪ] *adv*: **to go ~** extraviarse; (*fig: make a mistake*) equivocarse, (*morally*) descarriar, ir por mal camino; **to lead ~** llevar por mal camino; **I was led ~ by his voice** su voz me despistó.
astride [əˈstraɪd] **1** *adv* a horcajadas. **2** *prep* a caballo sobre, a horcajadas sobre.
astringency [əsˈtrɪndʒənsɪ] *n* astringencia *f*; (*fig*) adustez *f*, austeridad *f*.
astringent [əsˈtrɪndʒənt] *adj* astringente; (*fig*) adusto, austero.
astro... [æstrəʊ] *pref* astro...
astrolabe [ˈæstrəʊleɪb] *n* astrolabio *m*.
astrologer [əsˈtrɒlədʒəʳ] *n* astrólogo *m*, -a *f*.
astrological [ˌæstrəˈlɒdʒɪkəl] *adj* astrológico.
astrologist [əsˈtrɒlədʒɪst] *n* astrólogo *m*, -a *f*.
astrology [əsˈtrɒlədʒɪ] *n* astrología *f*.
astronaut [ˈæstrənɔːt] *n* astronauta *mf*.
astronautics [ˌæstrəʊˈnɔːtɪks] *n* astronáutica *f*.
astronomer [əsˈtrɒnəməʳ] *n* astrónomo *m*, -a *f*.
astronomical [ˌæstrəˈnɒmɪkəl] *adj* astronómico (*also fig*).
astronomy [əsˈtrɒnəmɪ] *n* astronomía *f*.
astrophysicist [ˌæstrəʊˈfɪzɪsɪst] *n* astrofísico *mf*.
astrophysics [ˈæstrəʊˈfɪzɪks] *n* astrofísica *f*.
Astroturf [ˈæstrəʊtɜːf] ® *n* césped *m* artificial.
Asturian [æˈstʊərɪən] **1** *adj* asturiano. **2** *n* (**a**) asturiano *m*, -a *f*. (**b**) (*Ling*) asturiano *m*.
Asturias [æˈstʊərɪæs] *n* Asturias *f*.
astute [əsˈtjuːt] *adj* listo, inteligente; sagaz; **that was very ~ of you** en eso has sido muy inteligente; **an ~ choice** una elección acertada.
astutely [əsˈtjuːtlɪ] *adv* inteligentemente, sagazmente.
astuteness [əsˈtjuːtnɪs] *n* inteligencia *f*; sagacidad *f*.
asunder [əˈsʌndəʳ] *adv*: **to put ~** separar; **to tear ~** hacer pedazos, romper en dos.
ASV *n* (*US*) *abbr of* **American Standard Version**.
Aswan [æsˈwɑːn] *n* Asuán *f*; **~ High Dam** Presa *f* de Asuán.
asylum [əˈsaɪləm] *n* (**a**) asilo *m*; **to afford** (*or* **give**) **~ to** (*place*) servir de asilo a, (*person*) dar asilo a; **to ask for political ~** pedir asilo político. (**b**) (*mental ~*) manicomio *m*, hospital *m* psiquiátrico.
asymmetric(al) [ˌeɪsɪˈmetrɪk(əl)] *adj* asimétrico.
asymmetry [eɪˈsɪmətrɪ] *n* asimetría *f*.
asymptomatic [æˌsɪmptəˈmætik] *adj* asintomático.
asynchronous [æˈsɪŋkrənəs] *adj* asíncrono.
AT *n abbr of* **automatic translation** traducción *f* automática, TA *f*.
at [æt] *prep* (**a**) (*position*) en; **~ the edge** en el borde; **~ the top** en la cumbre; **~ Toledo** en Toledo; **~ school** en la escuela; **~ sea** en el mar; **~ peace** en paz; **~ John's** en casa de Juan; **~ the hairdresser's** en la peluquería; **~ table** en la mesa; **to dry o.s. ~ the fire** secarse junto a la lumbre; **to stand ~ the door** estar a la puerta; **to be ~ the window** estar junto a la ventana; **he came in ~ the window** entró por la ventana; **to find a gap to go in ~** buscar un resquicio por donde entrar; **this is where it's ~*** aquí es donde tiene lugar (la reunión *etc*); aquí es lo importante, aquí es un buen rollo*.
(**b**) (*time, order, frequency*) **~ 4 o'clock** a las 4; **~ midday** a mediodía; **~ night** de noche, por la noche; **~ this season** en esta época del año; **~ Christmas** por Navidades; **~ a time like this** en un momento como éste; **two ~ a time** de dos en dos; **~ my time of life** con los años que tengo.
(**c**) (*price, rate*) **~ 5 dollars a pound** a 5 dólares la libra; **~ 4% interest** al 4 por 100 de interés; **~ a high price** a un precio elevado; **to go ~ 100 km an hour** ir a 100 km por hora.
(**d**) (*following, concerning*) **~ my request** a petición mía; **to awaken ~ the least sound** despertarse al menor ruido; **~ her cries** al escuchar sus gritos; **~ his suggestion** siguiendo su sugerencia, de acuerdo con su sugerencia; **boys ~ play** muchachos que juegan, los muchachos cuando juegan; **he's good ~ games** es bueno para los juegos; **I'm no good ~ that** no valgo para eso.
(**e**) (*with verb* to be) **to be ~ work** estar en el trabajo; **to be hard ~ it** estar trabajando con ahinco; **I've been ~ it for 3 hours** estoy ocupado en esto desde hace 3 horas; **what are you ~?** ¿qué haces ahí?; **while we're ~ it** mientras lo estamos haciendo; de paso; **you've been ~ me all day** has estado persiguiéndome todo el día; **she's ~ it again** está siempre con la misma canción, sigue con el mismo tema.
atavism [ˈætəvɪzəm] *n* atavismo *m*.
atavistic [ˌætəˈvɪstɪk] *adj* atávico.
ATC *n abbr of* **Air Training Corps** *cuerpo militar para la formación de aviadores*.
ate [eɪt] *pret of* **eat**.
atheism [ˈeɪθɪɪzəm] *n* ateísmo *m*.
atheist [ˈeɪθɪɪst] *n* ateo *m*, -a *f*.
atheistic [ˌeɪθɪˈɪstɪk] *adj* ateo, ateísta.
Athenian [əˈθiːnɪən] **1** *adj* ateniense. **2** *n* ateniense *mf*.
Athens [ˈæθɪnz] *n* Atenas *f*.
athirst [əˈθɜːst] *adj*: **to be ~ for** (*fig*) tener sed de.
athlete [ˈæθliːt] *n* atleta *mf*; **~'s foot** (*Med*) pie *m* de atleta.
athletic [æθˈletɪk] *adj* atlético; **~ coach** (*US*) profesor *m*, -ora *f* de Educación Física; **~ supporter** (*US*) hincha *mf*.
athleticism [æθˈletsɪzəm] *n* atletismo *m*.
athletics [æθˈletɪks] *n sing* (*Brit*) atletismo *m*; (*US*) deportes *mpl*.
at-home [ətˈhəʊm] *n* recepción *f* (en casa particular).
athwart [əˈθwɔːt] **1** *adv* de través, al través. **2** *prep* a través de.
atishoo [əˈtɪʃuː] *interj* ¡(h)achís!
Atlanticism [ətˈlæntɪsɪzəm] *n* atlantismo *m*.
Atlanticist [ətˈlæntɪsɪst] *adj, n* atlantista *mf*.
Atlantic (Ocean) [ətˈlæntɪk(ˈəʊʃən)] *n* (Océano *m*) Atlántico *m*.
Atlantis [ətˈlæntɪs] *n* Atlántida *f*.
atlas [ˈætləs] *n* atlas *m*; **A~** Atlas *m*, Atlante *m*; **A~ Mountains** el Atlas.
ATM *n abbr of* **automated teller machine** cajero *m* automático; **~ card** tarjeta *f* de cajero automático.
atmosphere [ˈætməsfɪəʳ] *n* atmósfera *f*; (*fig*) ambiente *m*; clima *m*, atmósfera *f*.
atmospheric [ˌætməsˈferɪk] *adj* atmosférico; ambiental; **~ pollution** contaminación *f* atmosférica; **~ pressure** presión *f* atmosférica.
atmospherics [ˌætməsˈferɪks] *npl* (*Rad*) interferencias *fpl* atmosféricas, parásitos *mpl*.
atoll [ˈætɒl] *n* atolón *m*.
atom [ˈætəm] *n* átomo *m*; **there is not an ~ of truth in it** eso no tiene ni pizca de verdad; **if you had an ~ of sense** si tuvieras una gota de sentido común; **to smash sth to ~s** hacer algo añicos.
atom-bomb [ˈætəm,bɒm] *n* bomba *f* atómica.
atomic [əˈtɒmɪk] *adj* atómico; **~ age** edad *f* atómica; **~ bomb** bomba *f* atómica; **~ clock** reloj *m* atómico; **~ energy** energía *f* nuclear; **A~ Energy Authority** Consejo *m* de Energía Nuclear; **~ nucleus** núcleo *m* atómico; **~ number** número *m* atómico; **~ particle** partícula *f* atómica; **~ physicist** físico *m*; **~ physics** física *f* atómica; **~ pile** pila *f* atómica; **~ power** (*nation*) potencia *f* atómica; **~ power station** central *f* nuclear; **~ structure** estructura *f* atómica; **~ theory** teoría *f* de los átomos; **~ warfare** guerra *f* atómica; **~ warhead** cabeza *f* atómica; **~ weight** peso *m* atómico.
atomic-powered [əˈtɒmɪkˈpaʊəd] *adj* impulsado por energía atómica.
atomize [ˈætəmaɪz] *vt* atomizar, pulverizar.
atomizer [ˈætəmaɪzəʳ] *n* atomizador *m*, pulverizador *m*.
atom-smasher [ˈætəm,smæʃəʳ] *n* acelerador *m* de partículas atómicas, rompeátomos *m*.
atonal [æˈtəʊnl] *adj* atonal.
atone [əˈtəʊn] *vi*: **to ~ for** expiar.
atonement [əˈtəʊnmənt] *n* expiación *f*; **Day of A~** Día *m* de la Expiación.
atonic [æˈtɒnɪk] *adj* átono.
atop [əˈtɒp] **1** *adv* encima. **2** *prep* encima de; sobre; en la cumbre de.
ATP *n abbr of* **Association of Tennis Professionals**.
atrocious [əˈtrəʊʃəs] *adj* atroz.
atrociously [əˈtrəʊʃəslɪ] *adv* atrozmente.

atrocity [ə'trɒsɪtɪ] *n* atrocidad *f.*
atrophy ['ætrəfɪ] **1** *n* atrofia *f.* **2** *vt* atrofiar. **3** *vi* atrofiarse.
att. (*Comm*) *abbr of* **attached** adjunto, anexo.
attaboy* ['ætə,bɔɪ] *interj* (*esp US*) ¡bravo!, ¡dale!
attach [ə'tætʃ] **1** *vt* (**a**) (*fasten*) sujetar; (*stick*) pegar; (*tie*) atar, liar; (*with pin etc*) prender; (*join*) unir; *seal* poner; *trailer etc* acoplar, enganchar; **he's ~ed*** (*married etc*) no está libre.
(**b**) (*in letter*) adjuntar; **the document is ~ed** enviamos adjunto el documento; **the ~ed letter** la carta adjunta; **please find ~ed details of ...** les adjuntamos detalles de ...
(**c**) (*fig*) *importance, value* dar, conceder (*to* a); **the salary ~ed to the post is ...** el sueldo que corresponde al puesto es ...; **to be ~ed to an embassy** estar agregado a una embajada; **there are no strings ~ed to this** esto es sin compromiso alguno, esto es libre de condiciones; **commission ~ed to the Ministry of ...** comisión *f* que depende del Ministerio de ...
(**d**) (*Jur*) *property* incautar, embargar.
(**e**) **to be ~ed to** *person etc* tener cariño a; *theory etc* estar apegado a; **they are very ~ed (to each other)** se quieren mucho.
2 *vi*: **to ~ to** corresponder a, pertenecer a; ser inherente en; **no blame ~es to you** no tienes culpa alguna; **certain duties ~ to this post** ciertas responsabilidades corresponden a este puesto.
3 *vr*: **to ~ o.s. to** *group* agregarse a, unirse a, entrar a formar parte de, (*pej*) pegarse a.
attaché [ə'tæʃeɪ] *n* agregado *m*, -a *f*; *V* **cultural** *etc.*
attaché case [ə'tæʃeɪkeɪs] *n* portafolio *m*, cartera *f*; maletín *m.*
attachment [ə'tætʃmənt] *n* (**a**) (*act*) atadura *f*; unión *f etc.*
(**b**) (*device*) accesorio *m*, dispositivo *m*; (*coupling*) acoplamiento *m.*
(**c**) (*affection*) cariño *m*, apego *m* (*to* a); (*loyalty*) adhesión *f.*
(**d**) (*Jur*) incautación *f*, embargo *m.*
attack [ə'tæk] **1** *n* (**a**) (*Mil etc*) ataque *m* (*on* a, contra, sobre), asalto *m*; (*criminal, on person*) atentado *m*, agresión *f*; **~ on sb's life** atentado *m* contra la vida de uno; **~ on the security of the state** atentado *m* contra la seguridad del estado; **~ is the best form of defence** la mejor defensa está en el ataque; **to be under ~** ser atacado; **to launch an ~** lanzar un ataque; **to leave o.s. open to ~** dejarse expuesto al ataque; **to return to the ~** volver al ataque.
(**b**) (*Med*) ataque *m*, acceso *m*; crisis *f*; dolencia *f* repentina; **an ~ of pneumonia** una pulmonía; **an ~ of nerves** una crisis nerviosa.
2 *vt* (**a**) (*Mil etc*) atacar; acometer; (*criminally*) agredir, asaltar; atentar contra; (*bull etc*) embestir; (*gratuitously*) emprenderla con; (*Med*) atacar, afectar; *opinion, theory* impugnar; **he was ~ed by doubts** le asaltaron dudas.
(**b**) (*fig*) *problem* acometer, tratar de resolver; *task* emprender, lanzarse a; **we must ~ poverty** debemos combatir la pobreza.
(**c**) (*Chem*) atacar; (*Med*) atacar, minar.
3 *vi* atacar.
attackable [ə'tækəbl] *adj* atacable, expuesto al ataque.
attacker [ə'tækəʳ] *n* agresor *m*, -ora *f*, asaltante *mf*, atacante *mf.*
attain [ə'teɪn] **1** *vt* alcanzar, lograr, conseguir. **2** *vi*: **to ~ to** llegar a.
attainable [ə'teɪnəbl] *adj* alcanzable, realizable.
attainder [ə'teɪndəʳ] *n* extinción *f* de los derechos civiles de un individuo.
attainment [ə'teɪnmənt] *n* (**a**) (*act*) logro *m*, consecución *f*, obtención *f*; **difficult of ~** de difícil consecución, de difícil realización. (**b**) **~s** dotes *fpl*, talento *m* (*in* para), conocimientos *mpl* (*in* de).
attempt [ə'tempt] **1** *n* (**a**) tentativa *f*, intento *m*, conato *m*; **at the first ~** en el primer intento; **to make an ~ to** + *infin* hacer una tentativa de + *infin*, intentar + *infin*; **he made two ~s at it** trató dos veces de lograrlo; **to make an ~ on the record** tratar de batir el récord; **to make an ~ on the summit** tratar de llegar a la cumbre; **we'll do it or die in the ~** lo haremos o moriremos en la demanda; **it was a good ~** fue un esfuerzo digno de alabanza; **this is my first ~** es la primera vez que lo intento; **we had to give up the ~** tuvimos que renunciar a la empresa.
(**b**) (*attack*) atentado *m* (*on sb's life* contra la vida de uno).
2 *vt* (**a**) probar, ensayar, intentar; tratar de efectuar (*or* conseguir *etc*); (*undertake*) emprender.
(**b**) **to ~ to** + *infin* intentar + *infin*, tratar de + *infin.*
attempted [ə'temptɪd] *adj*: **~ murder** tentativa *f* de asesinato, homicidio *m* frustrado; **~ suicide** intento *m* de suicidio.
attend [ə'tend] **1** *vt* (**a**) (*assist at*) asistir a; **a well-~ed meeting** una reunión muy concurrida.
(**b**) (*serve*) servir; (*accompany*) acompañar; (*Med*) atender, asistir; **a method ~ed by many risks** un método que comporta muchos riesgos; **the policy was ~ed by many difficulties** la política tropezó con muchas dificultades.
2 *vi* (**a**) (*pay attention*) prestar atención, poner atención (*LAm*).
(**b**) (*be present*) asistir.
◆**attend to** *vt* (*Comm*) *order* ejecutar; *one's task, one's business* ocuparse de, atender; *words, work, lesson, speech* prestar atención a, poner atención en (*LAm*); *advice* seguir; **to ~ to a customer** atender a un cliente; **are you being ~ed to?** (*in a shop*) ¿le atienden?, ¿le atiende alguien?; **I'll ~ to you in a moment** un momentito y estoy con Vd; **I'll ~ to you later** (*threatening*) luego me las arreglo con Vd.
◆**attend up(on)** *vt person* servir, estar al servicio de.
attendance [ə'tendəns] **1** *n* (**a**) (*act*) asistencia *f* (*at* a), presencia *f* (*at* en); **is my ~ necessary?** ¿debo asistir?, ¿es preciso que asista yo?; **to be in ~** asistir; estar de servicio; **to be in ~ on the minister** acompañar al ministro, formar parte del séquito del ministro; **to dance ~ on sb** esforzarse por complacer a uno, desvivirse por uno.
(**b**) (*Med*) asistencia *f.*
(**c**) (*those present*) concurrencia *f*, asistentes *mpl*; **what was the ~ at the meeting?** ¿cuántos asistieron a la reunión?; **we need an ~ of 1000** hace falta atraer a un público de 1000.
2 *attr*: **~ centre** (*Brit*) centro *m* (*or* prisión *f*) de régimen abierto; **~ fee** honorarios *mpl* por asistencia; **~ money** pago *m* por asistencia; **~ officer** (*Scol*) encargado *m*, -a *f* del control de asistencia; **~ order** (*Brit*) *orden que exige a los padres la asistencia de sus hijos en la escuela*; **~ sheet** lista *f* de clase.
attendant [ə'tendənt] **1** *adj* relacionado, concomitante; **the ~ crowd** la gente que asistía; **the ~ difficulties** las dificultades intrínsecas; **the ~ circumstances** las circunstancias concomitantes; **old age and its ~ ills** la vejez y los achaques correspondientes.
2 *n* acompañante *m*; (*servant*) sirviente *m*, -a *f*; (*Theat*) acomodador *m*, -ora *f*; (*in carpark, museum*) celador *m*, encargado *m*; **the prince and his ~s** el príncipe y su séquito.
attention [ə'tenʃən] *n* (**a**) atención *f*; **~ span** capacidad *f* de concentración; **(your) ~ please!** ¡su atención por favor!; **it requires daily ~** hay que atenderlo a diario; **it shall have my earliest ~** lo atenderé lo más pronto posible; **for the ~ of Mr X** a la atención del Sr X; **we were all ~** todos estábamos muy atentos; **to attract (*or* catch) sb's ~** llamar la atención de uno; **to call (*or* draw) sb's ~ to** llamar la atención de uno sobre; **to come to sb's ~** hacérsele presente a uno; **it has come to my ~ that ...** me han informado que ...; **to give (*or* pay) ~** prestar atención (*to* a); **he paid no ~** no hizo caso (*to that* de eso); **to pay special ~ to** fijarse de modo especial en; destacar; **to turn one's ~ to** pasar a considerar, pasar a estudiar.
(**b**) (*Mil*) **~!** ¡firme(s)!; **to come to ~** ponerse firme(s), cuadrarse; **to stand at (*or* to) ~** estar firme(s).
(**c**) **~s** (*kindnesses*) atenciones *fpl*, cortesías *fpl.*
attention-seeking [ə'tenʃən,si:kɪŋ] *adj* que busca (*or* intenta llamar) la atención.
attentive [ə'tentɪv] *adj* (**a**) (*heedful*) atento (*to* a). (**b**) (*polite*) atento, cortés, obsequioso (*to* con).
attentively [ə'tentɪvlɪ] *adv* atentamente; cortésmente.
attentiveness [ə'tentɪvnɪs] *n* atención *f*; cortesía *f.*
attenuate [ə'tenjʊeɪt] *vt* atenuar.
attenuating [ə'tenjʊeɪtɪŋ] *adj* atenuante.
attenuation [ə,tenjʊ'eɪʃən] *n* atenuación *f*, disminución *f.*
attest [ə'test] **1** *vt* atestiguar (*that* que); dar fe de; *signature* confirmar, autenticar; **~ed herd** (*Brit*) ganado *m* certificado. **2** *vi*: **to ~ to** dar fe de.
attestation [ætes'teɪʃən] *n* atestación *f*, testimonio *m*; confirmación *f*, autenticación *f.*
attic ['ætɪk] *n* desván *m*, ático *m*, buhardilla *f.*
Attila ['ætɪlə] *nm* Atila.
attire [ə'taɪəʳ] **1** *n* traje *m*, vestido *m*; (*hum*) atavío *m.* **2** *vt* vestir (*in* de); (*hum*) ataviar (*in* de).
attitude ['ætɪtju:d] *n* (**a**) (*of body*) actitud *f*, postura *f*; (*Art*) ademán *m.* (**b**) (*of mind*) actitud *f*; postura *f*; disposición *f*

de ánimo; **the government's ~ is negative** la postura del gobierno es negativa; **what is your ~ to this?** ¿cuál es su posición con respecto a esto?; **if that's your ~** si te pones en ese plan; **I don't like your ~** no me gusta su manera de enfocar esta cuestión (*or* su tono de voz *etc*); **to adopt** (*or* **strike, take up**) **an ~** adoptar una actitud, tomar una postura (estudiada). **(c)** (*: *bad* ~) **don't give me ~, girl!** ¡no te me pongas de morros, guapa!*.

attitudinize [ˌætɪ'tjuːdɪnaɪz] *vi* tomar posturas afectadas (*or* teatrales).

attorney [ə'tɜːnɪ] *n* **(a)** (*representative*) apoderado *m*, -a *f*. **(b)** (*US*: *also* **~-at-law**) abogado *mf*; *V* **district**. **(c) A~ General** (*Brit*) ≃ Presidente *m* del Consejo del Poder Judicial (*Sp*); (*US*) procurador *m* general (= Ministro *m* de Justicia).

attract [ə'trækt] *vt* atraer; *attention* llamar.

attraction [ə'trækʃən] *n* atracción *f*; (*attractive feature*) atractivo *m*; (*inducement*) aliciente *m*; **the ~ of the plan is that ...** el aspecto positivo del plan es que ...; **the film has the special ~ of featuring X** la película tiene la atracción especial de presentar a X; **the main ~ at the party was Y** el interés de la fiesta se cifraba en Y; **one of the ~s of the quiet life** uno de los encantos de la vida retirada; **spring ~s in Madrid** las diversiones de la primavera madrileña.

attractive [ə'træktɪv] *adj* atractivo; agradable; (*interesting*) atrayente, interesante; *idea, plan* sugestivo; *offer, price, salary* interesante; *prospect* halagüeño; *child, girl* mono, guapo, atractivo, lindo (*LAm*); **~ power** fuerza *f* atractiva.

attractively [ə'træktɪvlɪ] *adv* atractivamente; en forma atractiva; de modo atrayente; de modo sugestivo; de modo halagüeño; **an ~ designed garden** un jardín de trazado atractivo.

attractiveness [ə'træktɪvnɪs] *n* atracción *f*, atractivo *m*, atractividad *f*.

attributable [ə'trɪbjʊtəbl] *adj*: **~ to** atribuible a, imputable a.

attribute 1 ['ætrɪbjuːt] *n* atributo *m*. **2** [ə'trɪbjuːt] *vt* atribuir (*to* a); achacar (*to* a); **to what would you ~ this?** ¿cómo explicas esto?

attribution [ˌætrɪ'bjuːʃən] *n* atribución *f*.

attributive [ə'trɪbjʊtɪv] *adj* atributivo.

attrit [ə'trɪt] *vt*, **attrite** [ə'traɪt] *vt* desgastar, agotar.

attrition [ə'trɪʃən] *n* desgaste *m*; rozadura *f*, roce *m*; **war of ~** guerra *f* de agotamiento.

attune [ə'tjuːn] *vt* (*fig*): **to ~ to** armonizar con; **to be ~d to** estar en armonía con.

atty (*US*) *abbr of* **attorney**.

Atty Gen. *abbr of* **Attorney General**.

ATV *n abbr of* **all-terrain vehicle** vehículo *m* todo terreno.

atypical [ˌeɪ'tɪpɪkəl] *adj* atípico.

atypically [ˌeɪ'tɪpɪklɪ] *adv* atípicamente, de manera atípica.

aubergine ['əʊbəʒiːn] *n* (*esp Brit*) berenjena *f*.

auburn ['ɔːbən] *adj* castaño rojizo.

auction ['ɔːkʃən] **1** *n* subasta *f*, almoneda *f*, licitación *f*, remate *m* (*esp LAm*); (*Bridge*) subasta *f*; **~ bridge** bridge-remate *m*; **~ sale** subasta *f*; **to put up for ~, to sell at ~** subastar, poner (*or* vender) en pública subasta.

2 *vt* (*also* **to ~ off**) subastar, licitar (*LAm*), rematar (*esp LAm*).

auctioneer [ˌɔːkʃə'nɪəʳ] *n* subastador *m*, -ora *f*, licitador *m*, -ora *f* (*LAm*), rematador *m*, -ora *f* (*esp LAm*).

auction-room ['ɔːkʃənrʊm] *n* sala *f* de subastas.

aud. *abbr of* **audit, auditor**.

audacious [ɔː'deɪʃəs] *adj* audaz, atrevido; (*pej*) descarado.

audaciously [ɔː'deɪʃəslɪ] *adv* audazmente, atrevidamente; (*pej*) descaradamente.

audacity [ɔː'dæsɪtɪ] *n* audacia *f*, atrevimiento *m*; (*pej*) descaro *m*; **and you have the ~ to say that!** ¡y te atreves a decir eso!, ¡y me lo dices tan fresco!

audibility [ˌɔːdɪ'bɪlɪtɪ] *n* audibilidad *f*.

audible ['ɔːdɪbl] *adj* audible, perceptible, que se puede oír; **the speech was barely ~** apenas se podía oír el discurso; **there was an ~ gasp** se oyó un grito sofocado.

audibly ['ɔːdɪblɪ] *adv* de modo que se puede oír, de modo audible.

audience ['ɔːdɪəns] *n* **(a)** (*gathering*) auditorio *m*, público *m*, audiencia *f*; **it's got ~ appeal** tiene gancho con el público; **~ participation** participación *f* del público; **~ rating** (*TV*) índice *m* de audiencia; **~ research** sondeo *m* de opiniones; **there was a big ~** asistió un público numeroso; **those in the ~** los que formaban parte de la audiencia.

(b) (*interview*) audiencia *f* (*of, with* con); **~ chamber** sala *f* de audiencia; **to have an ~ of** (*or* **with**) ser recibido en audiencia por; **to receive sb in ~** recibir a uno en audiencia.

audio ['ɔːdɪəʊ] **1** *adj* de audio; **~ equipment** equipo *m* de audio; **~ recording** grabación *f* en audio; **~ system** sistema *m* audio, audiosistema *m*. **2** *n* audio *m*.

audio... ['ɔːdɪəʊ] *pref* audio...

audiofrequency [ˌɔːdɪəʊ'friːkwənsɪ] *n* audiofrecuencia *f*.

audiometer [ˌɔːdɪ'ɒmɪtəʳ] *n* audiómetro *m*.

audiotronic [ˌɔːdɪəʊ'trɒnɪk] *adj* audio-electrónico.

audiotyping ['ɔːdɪəʊˌtaɪpɪŋ] *n* mecanografía *f* por dictáfono.

audiotypist ['ɔːdɪəʊˌtaɪpɪst] *n* mecanógrafo *m*, -a *f* de dictáfono.

audio-visual [ˌɔːdɪəʊ'vɪzjʊəl] *adj* audiovisual; **~ aid** ayuda *f* audiovisual; **~ equipment** equipo *m* audiovisual; **~ method** método *m* audiovisual.

audit ['ɔːdɪt] **1** *n* revisión *f* de cuentas, intervención *f*; auditoría *f*. **2** *vt* **(a)** (*Fin*) revisar, intervenir, auditar. **(b) to ~ a course** (*US*) asistir a un curso como oyente.

auditing ['ɔːdɪtɪŋ] *n*: **~ of accounts** auditoría *f*, censura *f* de cuentas.

audition [ɔː'dɪʃən] **1** *n* audición *f*. **2** *vt* dar audición a; **he was ~ed for the part** le hicieron una audición para el papel. **3** *vi*: **he ~ed for the part** hizo una audición para el papel.

auditor ['ɔːdɪtəʳ] *n* **(a)** (*Fin*) censor *m*, -ora *f* de cuentas, interventor *m*, -ora *f*; (*internal*) auditor *m*, -ora *f*; **~'s report** informe *m* del auditor. **(b)** (*US Univ*) estudiante *mf* libre, oyente *mf*.

auditorium [ˌɔːdɪ'tɔːrɪəm] *n* auditorio *m*, sala *f*.

auditory ['ɔːdɪtərɪ] *adj* auditivo.

Audubon ['ɔːdəbɒn] *n*: **~ Society** (*US*) *sociedad para la conservación de la naturaleza*, ≃ ICONA *m*, ≃ ADENA *f*.

AUEW *n* (*Brit*) *abbr of* **Amalgamated Union of Engineering Workers** *sindicato mixto de trabajadores de ingeniería*.

Aug. *abbr of* **August** agosto *m*, ag.

Augean Stables [ɔː'dʒiːən'steɪblz] *npl* establos *mpl* de Augias.

aught [ɔːt] *n* (†, *liter*) algo, alguna cosa *f*; (*with negation*) nada; **if there is ~ I can do** si puedo hacer algo, si puedo ayudarles de algún modo; **for ~ I care he can ...** igual me da si él ...; **for ~ I know** que yo sepa.

augment [ɔːg'ment] **1** *vt* aumentar. **2** *vi* aumentar(se).

augmentation [ˌɔːgmen'teɪʃən] *n* aumento *m*.

augmentative [ɔːg'mentətɪv] *adj* aumentativo.

au gratin [əʊ'grætɛ̃] *adj* gratinado.

augur ['ɔːgəʳ] **1** *vt* augurar, pronosticar, anunciar; **it ~s no good** esto no nos promete nada bueno.

2 *vi*: **it ~s ill** es de mal agüero; **it ~s well** es de buen agüero (*for* para).

augury ['ɔːgjʊrɪ] *n* augurio *m*; presagio *m*; **to take the auguries** consultar los augurios.

August ['ɔːgəst] *n* agosto *m*.

august [ɔː'gʌst] *adj* augusto.

Augustan [ɔː'gʌstən] *adj* augustal; **the ~ age** (*Rome*) el siglo de Augusto, (*English*) la época neoclásica (del siglo XVIII).

Augustine [ɔː'gʌstɪn] *nm* Agustín.

Augustinian [ɔːgə'stɪnɪən] **1** *adj* agustino. **2** *n* agustino *m*, -a *f*.

Augustus [ɔː'gʌstəs] *nm* Augusto.

auk [ɔːk] *n* alca *f*; **little ~** mérgulo *m* marino.

auld [ɔːld] *adj* (*Scot* = *old*) **~ lang syne** tiempos *mpl* antiguos, los buenos tiempos de antaño; **A~ Reeky** Edimburgo.

aunt [ɑːnt] *n* tía *f*; **my ~ and uncle** mis tíos; **A~ Sally** blanco *m* (de insultos, críticas *etc*).

auntie*, aunty* ['ɑːntɪ] *n* tía *f*; **A~** (*Brit hum*) la BBC.

au pair ['əʊ'pɛə] **1** *adv* au pair. **2** *adj*: **~ girl** = **3**. **3** *n, pl* **au pairs** chica *f* au pair.

aura ['ɔːrə] *n* emanación *f*; (*atmosphere*) atmósfera *f*; **a mystic ~** un halo místico; **an ~ of doom** un halo fatídico.

aural ['ɔːrəl] *adj* aural, auditivo.

aureole ['ɔːrɪəʊl] *n* aureola *f*.

au revoir [ˌəʊrə'vwɑːʳ] *adv* hasta la vista.

auricle ['ɔːrɪkl] *n* aurícula *f*.

aurochs ['ɔːrɒks] *n* uro *m*, aurochs *m*.

aurora borealis [ɔː'rɔːrəbɔːrɪ'eɪlɪs] *n* aurora *f* boreal.

auspices ['ɔːspɪsɪz] *npl*: **under the ~ of** bajo los auspicios de, auspiciado por.

auspicious [ɔːs'pɪʃəs] *adj* propicio, favorable, de buen augurio; **to make an ~ start** comenzar felizmente (*or* favorablemente).

auspiciously [ɔːs'pɪʃəslɪ] *adv* propiciamente, favorablemente; **to start ~** comenzar felizmente (*or* favorablemente).

Aussie* ['ɒzɪ] = **Australian.**
austere [ɒs'tɪəʳ] *adj* austero.
austerely [ɒs'tɪəlɪ] *adv* austeramente.
austerity [ɒs'terɪtɪ] *n* austeridad *f.*
Australasia [,ɔːstrə'leɪzɪə] *n* Australasia *f.*
Australasian [,ɔːstrə'leɪzɪən] **1** *n* australasiano. **2** *adj* australasiano *m,* -a *f.*
Australia [ɒs'treɪlɪə] *n* Australia *f.*
Australian [ɒs'treɪlɪən] **1** *adj* australiano. **2** *n* australiano *m,* -a *f.*
Austria ['ɒstrɪə] *n* Austria *f.*
Austrian ['ɒstrɪən] **1** *adj* austríaco. **2** *n* austríaco *m,* -a *f.*
Austro-Hungarian ['ɒstrəʊhʌŋ'gɛərɪən] *adj* austro-húngaro.
AUT *n* (*Brit*) *abbr of* **Association of University Teachers** *sindicato de profesores de universidad.*
authentic [ɔː'θentɪk] *adj* auténtico.
authenticate [ɔː'θentɪkeɪt] *vt* autenticar; autentificar.
authentication [ɔː,θentɪ'keɪʃn] *n* autenticación *f.*
authenticity [,ɔːθen'tɪsɪtɪ] *n* autenticidad *f.*
author ['ɔːθəʳ] **1** *n* autor *m,* -ora *f;* ~! ~! (*Theat*) ¡que salga el autor!; **~'s copy** ejemplar *m* autógrafo, (*book*) ejemplar *m* del autor. **2** *vt* (*esp US*) escribir, componer.
authoress ['ɔːθərɪs] *n* autora *f.*
authoritarian [,ɔːθɒrɪ'tɛərɪən] **1** *adj* autoritario. **2** *n* autoritario *m,* -a *f.*
authoritarianism [,ɔːθɒrɪ'tɛərɪənɪzəm] *n* autoritarismo *m.*
authoritative [ɔː'θɒrɪtətɪv] *adj version etc* autorizado, autoritativo; *manner etc* autoritario.
authoritatively [ɔː'θɒrɪtətɪvlɪ] *adv* autoritativamente; autoritariamente.
authority [ɔː'θɒrɪtɪ] *n* (**a**) (*power*) autoridad *f;* **those in ~** los que tienen la autoridad; **who is in ~ here?** ¿quién manda aquí?; **in ~ over** al mando de; **on one's own ~** por su propia autoridad; **to do sth without ~** hacer algo sin tener autorización; **to give sb ~ to** + *infin* autorizar a uno para que + *subj*; **he had no ~ to do that** no tenía autoridad para hacer eso.
(**b**) (*competence*) autoridad *f;* **on the ~ of Plato** con la autoridad de Platón; **I have it on good ~ that ...** sé de buena tinta que ...; **to speak with ~** hablar con conocimiento de causa.
(**c**) (*person*) autoridad *f;* (*book*) obra *f* autoritaria, obra *f* clásica; **he is the greatest living ~** es la máxima autoridad actual; **he is an ~ on the subject** es un experto en la materia.
(**d**) (*official body*) autoridad *f;* **the authorities** las autoridades; **health ~** administración *f* sanitaria; **regional ~** autoridad *f* regional; **to apply to the proper authorities** dirigirse a la autoridad competente.
authorization [,ɔːθəraɪ'zeɪʃən] *n* autorización *f.*
authorize ['ɔːθəraɪz] *vt* autorizar; **to ~ sb to** + *infin* autorizar a uno para que + *subj*; **to be ~d to** + *infin* estar autorizado para + *infin*, tener autorización para + *infin*.
authorized ['ɔːθəraɪzd] *adj* autorizado; **~ agent** agente *m* oficial; **~ capital** capital *m* autorizado, capital *m* social; **~ distributor** distribuidor *m* autorizado; **A~ Version** Versión *f* Autorizada (de la Biblia).
authorship ['ɔːθəʃɪp] *n* (**a**) profesión *f* de autor. (**b**) (*of book etc*) autoría *f,* paternidad *f* literaria; **of unknown ~** de autor desconocido.
autism ['ɔːtɪzəm] *n* autismo *m.*
autistic [ɔː'tɪstɪk] *adj* autístico, autista.
auto[1]**...** ['ɔːtəʊ] *pref* auto...
auto[2] ['ɔːtəʊ] *n* (*US*) coche *m,* automóvil *m,* carro *m* (*LAm*); **~ repair** reparación *f* de automóviles; **A~ Show** Salón *m* del Automóvil; **~ worker** trabajador *m,* -ora *f* de la industria automovilística (*or* del automóvil).
autobank ['ɔːtəʊbæŋk] *n* cajero *m* automático.
autobiographic(al) ['ɔːtəʊ,baɪəʊ'græfɪk(əl)] *adj* autobiográfico.
autobiography [,ɔːtəʊbaɪ'ɒgrəfɪ] *n* autobiografía *f.*
autocade ['ɔːtəʊkeɪd] *n* caravana *f* de automóviles.
autochthonous [ɔː'tɒkθənəs] *adj* autóctono.
autocracy [ɔː'tɒkrəsɪ] *n* autocracia *f.*
autocrat ['ɔːtəʊkræt] *n* autócrata *mf.*
autocratic [,ɔːtəʊ'krætɪk] *adj* autocrático.
autocross ['ɔːtəʊkrɒs] *n* auto-cross *m.*
autocue ['ɔːtəʊkjuː] *n* (*Brit TV*) autocue *m,* chuleta* *f.*
autocycle ['ɔːtəʊsaɪkl] *n* velomotor *m,* ciclomotor *m.*
auto-da-fé ['ɔːtəʊdɑː'feɪ] *n* auto *m* de fe.
autogiro ['ɔːtəʊ'dʒaɪərəʊ] *n* autogiro *m.*
autograph ['ɔːtəgrɑːf] **1** *adj* autógrafo; **~ album** álbum *m* de autógrafos; **~ hunter** cazaautógrafos *mf.* **2** *n* (*manuscript*) autógrafo *m;* (*signature*) firma *f,* autógrafo *m.* **3** *vt* (*sign*) firmar; *book, photo etc* dedicar.
autohypnosis ['ɔːtəʊhɪp'nəʊsɪs] *n* autohipnosis *f.*
automat ['ɔːtəmæt] *n* (**a**) (*Brit*) máquina *f* expendedora. (**b**) (*US*) restaurante *m* de autoservicio.
automata [ɔː'tɒmətə] *npl of* **automaton.**
automate ['ɔːtəmeɪt] *vt* automatizar.
automated ['ɔːtə,meɪtɪd] *adj* automatizado; **~ teller, ~ telling machine** cajero *m* automático.
automatic [,ɔːtə'mætɪk] **1** *adj* automático; **~ data processing** proceso *m* automático de datos; **~ pilot** piloto *m* automático; **~ transmission** (*Aut*) transmisión *f* automática. **2** *n* (*pistol*) automática *f;* (*Brit Aut*) automático *m.*
automatically [,ɔːtə'mætɪkəlɪ] *adv* automáticamente.
automation [,ɔːtə'meɪʃən] *n* automatización *f.*
automatism [ɔː'tɒmətɪzəm] *n* automatismo *m.*
automaton [ɔː'tɒmətən] *n, pl* **automata** [ɔː'tɒmətə] autómata *m.*
automobile ['ɔːtəməbiːl] *n* (*esp US*) coche *m,* carro *m* (*LAm*), automóvil *m;* **~ industry** industria *f* del automóvil.
automotive [ɔːtə'məʊtɪv] *adj* automotor.
autonomous [ɔː'tɒnəməs] *adj* autónomo; autonómico.
autonomy [ɔː'tɒnəmɪ] *n* autonomía *f.*
autonymous [ɔː'tɒnɪməs] *adj* autónimo.
autopilot ['ɔːtəʊpaɪlət] *n* piloto *m* automático.
autopsy ['ɔːtɒpsɪ] *n* autopsia *f,* necropsia *f* (*LAm*).
autosuggestion ['ɔːtəʊsə'dʒestʃən] *n* (auto)sugestión *f.*
auto-teller ['ɔːtəʊ,teləʳ] *n* cajero *m* automático.
autotimer ['ɔːtəʊ,taɪməʳ] *n* programador *m* automático.
autumn ['ɔːtəm] *n* otoño *m.*
autumnal [ɔː'tʌmnəl] *adj* otoñal, de(l) otoño.
Auvergne [əʊ'vɛən] *n* Auvernia *f.*
auxiliary [ɔːg'zɪlɪərɪ] **1** *adj* auxiliar; **~ police** (*US*) cuerpo *m* de policía auxiliar; **~ staff** (*Brit Scol*) profesores *mpl* sustitutos, profesores *mpl* auxiliares; **~ verb** verbo *m* auxiliar. **2** *n* (*Gram*) verbo *m* auxiliar; (*Med etc*) ayudante *mf;* (*Mil*) **auxiliaries** tropas *fpl* auxiliares.
AV (**a**) *abbr of* **Authorized Version** (*of the Bible*). (**b**) *abbr of* **audio-visual.**
Av., Ave *abbr of* **Avenue** avenida *f,* Av., Avda.
av. *abbr of* **average** promedio *m,* prom.
a.v., a/v *abbr of* **ad valorem.**
avail [ə'veɪl] (*liter*) **1** *n*: **it is of no ~** es inútil; **to no ~** en vano, sin resultado; **to be of little ~** ser de poco provecho; **of what ~ is it to?** + *infin* ¿de qué sirve? + *infin.*
2 *vt* aprovechar, valer.
3 *vi*: **it ~s nothing to** + *infin* de nada sirve + *infin.*
4 *vr*: **to ~ o.s. of** aprovechar(se de), valerse de; acogerse a.
availability [ə,veɪlə'bɪlɪtɪ] *n* (**a**) disponibilidad *f.* (**b**) (*US*) validez *f.*
available [ə'veɪləbl] *adj* (**a**) disponible; asequible, aprovechable; **~ exclusively from Smith's** sólo se puede conseguir en Smith's; **further details are ~ from the secretary** puede obtenerse más información en secretaría; **is your latest catalogue ~?** ¿está listo su último catálogo?; **to make sth ~ to sb** poner algo a la disposición de uno; **is the manager ~?** ¿está libre el gerente?, ¿puedo pasar a ver al gerente?; **are you ~ next Thursday?** ¿estás libre el jueves que viene?; **the Minister is not ~ for comment** el Ministro no se ofrece a hacer comentarios; **this item is not ~ at the moment** no tenemos este artículo por el momento; **I am not ~ to visitors** no estoy para las visitas; **I'd like a seat on the first ~ flight** quiero una plaza en el primer vuelo que haya. (**b**) (*US*: *valid*) válido.
avalanche ['ævəlɑːnʃ] *n* alud *m,* avalancha *f;* (*fig*) torrente *m,* avalancha *f.*
avant-garde ['ævɑːŋ'gɑːd] **1** *adj* de vanguardia, nueva ola, ultramoderno. **2** *n* vanguardia *f,* nueva ola *f.*
avarice ['ævərɪs] *n* avaricia *f.*
avaricious [,ævə'rɪʃəs] *adj* avaro, avariento.
avdp. *abbr of* **avoirdupois.**
Ave. *abbr of* **avenue** avenida *f,* Av., Avda.
avenge [ə'vendʒ] **1** *vt* vengar. **2** *vr*: **to ~ o.s.** vengarse (*on* en).
avenger [ə'vendʒəʳ] *n* vengador *m,* -ora *f.*
avenging [ə'vendʒɪŋ] *adj* vengador.
avenue ['ævənjuː] *n* avenida *f;* (*fig*) vía *f,* camino *m;* **to explore every ~** tentar todas las vías.
aver [ə'vɜːʳ] *vt* afirmar, declarar, aseverar.
average ['ævərɪdʒ] **1** *adj* (**a**) (*Math*) medio, de término medio; **~ (daily) balance** saldo *m* medio (diario); **~ (due) date** fecha *f* media de vencimiento; **~ price** precio *m* medio; **~ quality** calidad *f* media; **wines of above ~ quality**

vinos *mpl* de calidad superior; **of ~ height** de regular estatura; **the ~ height of players** el promedio de talla de los jugadores (*or* por jugador).

(**b**) (*fig*) mediano, regular, corriente; **the ~ man** el hombre medio; **your ~ Ruritanian** el ruritanio corriente; **of ~ ability** de capacidad regular.

2 *n* (**a**) (*Math etc*) promedio *m*, término *m* medio; **on (the) ~, on an ~** por término medio; por regla general; **above ~** superior al promedio; **below ~** inferior al promedio; **to do an ~ of 150 kph** ir a un promedio de 150 kph; **to take an** (*or* **the**) **~ of** tomar el promedio de, calcular el promedio de. (**b**) (*Comm*) avería *f*; **~ adjuster** tasador *m* de averías; **~ bond** fianza *f* de averías; **~ statement** declaración *f* del tasador de averías.

3 *vt* (**a**) (*also* **to ~ out**: *find average of*) calcular el término medio de; prorratear.

(**b**) **we ~ 8 hours a day** trabajamos (*etc*) por regla general 8 horas diarias; **he ~d 140 all the way** hizo un promedio de 140 kph por todo el recorrido; **the sales ~ 200 a week** la venta media es de 200 ejemplares cada semana.

4 *vi* ser por término medio, resultar por término medio; ser por regla general.

◆**average down** *vt* promediar hacia abajo.

◆**average out 1** *vt* calcular el término medio de. **2** *vi*: **our working hours ~ out at 8 per day** trabajamos un promedio de 8 horas al día.

◆**average up** *vt* promediar hacia arriba.

averse [əˈvɜːs] *adj*: **to be ~ to** sentir repugnancia por, tener antipatía a; **to be ~ to** + *ger* tener pocas ganas de + *infin*, no estar dispuesto a + *infin*; **I am ~ to getting up early** soy enemigo de levantarme temprano; **I am not ~ to an occasional drink** no me repugna tomar algo de vez en cuando.

aversion [əˈvɜːʃən] *n* (**a**) (*feeling*) aversión *f* (*for, from, to* hacia), repugnancia *f* (*for, from, to* por); **~ therapy** terapia *f* por aversión, terapia *f* aversiva; **to feel an ~ for** sentir repugnancia por; **I have an ~ to him** me resulta antipático; **I took an ~ to it** empezó a repugnarme.

(**b**) (*hated thing*) cosa *f* aborrecida; **it is one of my ~s** es una de las cosas que me repugnan; *V* **pet**.

avert [əˈvɜːt] *vt eyes, thoughts* apartar (*from* de); *suspicion* desviar (*from* de); *possibility* evitar, quitar; *blow* impedir, desviar; *accident, illness, rebellion* prevenir.

aviary [ˈeɪvɪərɪ] *n* pajarera *f*, avería *f*.

aviation [ˌeɪvɪˈeɪʃən] *n* aviación *f*; **~ industry** industria *f* de la aviación; **~ spirit** gasolina *f* de aviación.

aviator [ˈeɪvɪeɪtəʳ] *n* aviador *m*, -ora *f*.

avid [ˈævɪd] *adj* ávido, ansioso (*for, of* de).

avidity [əˈvɪdɪtɪ] *n* avidez *f*, ansia *f*.

avidly [ˈævɪdlɪ] *adv* ávidamente, ansiosamente; **to read ~** leer con avidez.

Avignon [ˈævɪnjɒ] *n* Aviñón *m*.

avionics [ˌeɪvɪˈɒnɪks] *n sing* aviónica *f*.

avocado [ævəˈkɑːdəʊ] *n* (*Brit also* **~ pear**) aguacate *m*, palta *f* (*LAm*); **~ tree** aguacate *m*, palto *m* (*LAm*).

avocation [ˌævəʊˈkeɪʃən] *n* diversión *f*, distracción *f*, ocupación *f* accesoria; (*loosely*) vocación *f*.

avoid [əˈvɔɪd] *vt* evitar; guardarse de; *duty etc* eludir; *danger* salvarse de; **to ~** + *ger* evitar + *infin*; **he managed to ~ (hitting) the tree** evitó chocar con el árbol; **to ~ being seen** procurar no ser visto; **are you trying to ~ me?** ¿estás tratando de evitar hablar conmigo?; **I try to ~ him** procuro no tener nada que ver con él; **he ~s all his friends** huye de todos sus amigos; **it's to be ~ed like the plague** esto hay que evitarlo como la peste; **this way we ~ London** por esta ruta evitamos pasar por Londres; **to ~ sb's eye** evitar cambiar miradas con uno; **to ~ tax** (*legally*) evitar pagar impuestos, (*illegally*) defraudar al fisco.

avoidable [əˈvɔɪdəbl] *adj* evitable, eludible.

avoidance [əˈvɔɪdəns] *n* el evitar (*etc*), evitación *f*.

avoirdupois [ˌævədəˈpɔɪz] *n* (**a**) *sistema de pesos usado en países de habla inglesa* (1 *libra* = 16 *onzas* = 453,50 *gramos*). (**b**) (*: *overweight*) peso *m*, gordura *f*.

avow [əˈvaʊ] **1** *vt* reconocer, confesar, admitir. **2** *vr*: **he ~ed himself beaten** admitió que había perdido.

avowal [əˈvaʊəl] *n* confesión *f*; declaración *f*.

avowed [əˈvaʊd] *adj* declarado, abierto.

avowedly [əˈvaʊɪdlɪ] *adv* declaradamente, abiertamente.

AVP *n* (*US*) *abbr of* **assistant vice-president**.

avuncular [əˈvʌŋkjʊləʳ] *adj* como de tío; **~ advice** consejos *mpl* amistosos.

AWACS [eɪˈwæks] *n abbr of* **airborne warning and control system** AWACS *m*.

await [əˈweɪt] *vt* esperar, aguardar; **the fate that ~s him** la suerte que le espera; **we ~ your instructions** esperamos sus instrucciones; **we ~ your reply with interest** nos interesa mucho saber su respuesta; **a long ~ed event** un acontecimiento largamente esperado.

awake [əˈweɪk] **1** *adj* despierto; **to lie ~** quedar despierto, estar sin poder dormir; **to stay ~ all night** pasar toda la noche en vela; **the noise kept me ~** el ruido me impidió dormir; **coffee keeps me ~** el café me desvela.

2 (*irr*: *pret* **awoke**, *ptp* **awoken** *or* **awaked**) *vt* despertar.

3 *vi* despertar(se).

awaken [əˈweɪkən] **1** *vt* despertar (*also fig*); **to ~ sb to a danger** alertar a uno de un peligro.

2 *vi* (*also* **to ~ from sleep**) despertar(se); **to ~ from one's illusions** desilusionarse, quitarse las ilusiones; **to ~ to a danger** darse cuenta de un peligro.

awakening [əˈweɪknɪŋ] **1** *adj* (*fig*) naciente. **2** *n* el despertar, despertamiento *m*; **a rude ~** una sorpresa desagradable.

award [əˈwɔːd] **1** *n* (**a**) (*prize*) premio *m*; galardón *m*; (*Jur*) sentencia *f*, fallo *m*; (*Mil*) condecoración *f*.

(**b**) (*act of ~ing*) adjudicación *f*, concesión *f*; **pay ~** adjudicación *f* de aumento de salarios.

2 *vt* conceder, otorgar; *prize, damages etc* adjudicar, decretar; *medal* dar; (*Sport*) *penalty* decretar, señalar; **the prize is not being ~ed this year** este año el premio se ha declarado desierto.

award-winning [əˈwɔːdˌwɪnɪŋ] *adj* premiado.

aware [əˈwɛəʳ] *adj* (**a**) (*alert*) enterado; despierto; **politically ~** politizado; **sexually ~** enterado de lo sexual; **socially ~** educado en lo social.

(**b**) (*knowledgeable*) **to be ~ of** saber, estar enterado de, ser consciente de; **not that I am ~ of** (no) que yo sepa; **our employees are ~ of this advertisement** los empleados de la empresa han sido informados de este anuncio; **to be ~ that ...** saber que ..., ser consciente que ...; **I am fully ~ that ...** sé perfectamente que ...; **to become ~ of** darse cuenta de, enterarse de; **to make sb ~ of sth** hacer que uno se dé cuenta de algo.

awareness [əˈwɛənɪs] *n* conciencia *f*, conocimiento *m*; **sexual ~ in the young** los conocimientos sexuales de los jóvenes.

awash [əˈwɒʃ] *adj*: **the deck is ~** la cubierta está a flor de agua; **the house was ~** la casa estaba inundada; **we are ~ with applicants** estamos inundados de solicitudes.

away [əˈweɪ] **1** *adv* (**a**) (*at a distance*) **3 km ~** a 3 km (de aquí *or* de allí *or* de distancia); **X won with Y only 2 strokes ~** ganó X con Y a sólo 2 golpes de distancia; **~ in the distance** allá a lo lejos; **~ from the noise** lejos del ruido; **~ back in 1066** allá en 1066; **~!, ~ with you!** ¡vete!, ¡fuera de aquí!; **~ with him!** ¡fuera!, ¡que le lleven de aquí!; **~ with taxes!** ¡abajo los impuestos!; **to play ~** (*Sport*) jugar fuera de casa, jugar en campo ajeno; **they have won only 2 games ~** han ganado solamente dos partidos fuera (de casa).

(**b**) (*absent*) **to be ~ (from home)** estar fuera, estar ausente; **he's ~ for a week** pasa ocho días fuera; **he's ~ in Bognor** está en Bognor; **she was ~ before I could shout** se fue antes de que yo pudiese gritar; **I must ~** (*liter or hum*) tengo que marcharme.

(**c**) (*continuously*) sin parar; (*earnestly*) con ahínco; (*persistently*) con empeño; **he was grumbling ~** seguía quejándose; **to talk ~** hablar mucho, no parar de hablar; **talk ~!** ¡di lo que quieras!; **to work ~** seguir trabajando, trabajar sin parar.

(**d**) *V* **die, get** *etc*.

2 *adj*: **the ~ team** el equipo de fuera; **~ match** partido *m* fuera de casa; **~ win** victoria *f* fuera de casa.

awe [ɔː] **1** *n* temor *m* reverencial, pavor *m* y respeto; **to go** (*or* **be**) **in ~ of, hold in ~, stand in ~ of** tener temor reverencial a. **2** *vt* imponer respeto a; atemorizar; **in an ~d tone** con un tono de respeto y temor.

awe-inspiring [ˈɔːɪnˌspaɪərɪŋ] *adj*, **awesome** [ˈɔːsəm] *adj* imponente, pasmoso.

awe-struck [ˈɔːstrʌk] *adj* pasmado, atemorizado.

awful [ˈɔːfəl] *adj* (**a**) (*awesome*) tremendo, imponente, terrible, pasmoso.

(**b**) (*nasty etc*) horrible, malísimo, fatal; **how ~!** ¡qué horror!; **how ~ for you!** ¡lo que habrás sufrido!; **it was just ~** fue francamente horrible; **what ~ weather!** ¡qué tiempo más feo!; **his English is ~** tiene un inglés fatal*; **he's an ~ fool** es tonto de remate; **there were an ~ lot of people** había la mar de gente; **to feel ~** sentirse molesto, estar sobrecogido, (*ill*) sentirse muy mal; **I felt ~ about**

what had happened sentía muchísimo lo que había ocurrido; **you are ~!*** ¡eres una bestia!*

awfully ['ɔːflɪ] *adv* (**a**) (*badly*) terriblemente; pasmosamente; **she sings ~** canta terriblemente mal. (**b**) (*intensifying*) terriblemente; **it's ~ hard** es terriblemente difícil; **it's ~ funny** es divertidísimo, es la mar de divertido; **I'm ~ sorry** lo siento muchísimo; **thanks ~!** ¡muchísimas gracias!; **an ~ big car** un coche la mar de grande.

awfulness ['ɔːfʊlnɪs] *n* horror *m*, atrocidad *f*.

awhile [ə'waɪl] *adv* un rato, algún tiempo; **not yet ~** todavía no.

awkward ['ɔːkwəd] *adj* (**a**) (*inconvenient*) *problem, question* difícil; *situation* violento, difícil; *time* inoportuno; *task* delicado, desagradable; *shape* incómodo; *corner* peligroso; **it's ~ for me** es difícil para mí; **it's all a bit ~** todo esto es un poco violento (*or* molesto); **to come at an ~ time** llegar en un momento difícil; **to feel ~** sentirse molesto; **to make things ~ for sb** plantear problemas a uno, crear dificultades para uno.

(**b**) (*obstinate*) terco, difícil; (*unhelpful*) poco amable; **he's being ~** se muestra poco dispuesto a ayudar; está poniendo peros; **he's an ~ customer*** es un tipo difícil, es un sujeto de cuidado.

(**c**) (*clumsy*) desmañado, desgarbado, torpe; *phrasing* poco elegante; **the ~ squad** la sección de los bisoños; **to be at the ~ age** estar en la edad del pavo.

awkwardly ['ɔːkwədlɪ] *adv move, speak* con dificultad; **he expresses himself ~** se expresa mal, se expresa con poca elegancia; **he dances ~** baila torpemente; **we are ~ placed** estamos en una situación molesta.

awkwardness ['ɔːkwədnɪs] *n* (*V adj*) (**a**) dificultad *f*; violencia *f*; incomodidad *f*; molestia *f*. (**b**) terquedad *f*. (**c**) desmaña *f*, torpeza *f*.

awl [ɔːl] *n* lezna *f*, subilla *f*.

awning ['ɔːnɪŋ] *n* toldo *m*; (*of cart*) entalamadura *f*; (*Naut*) toldilla *f*; (*over window, at entrance*) marquesina *f*.

awoke [ə'wəʊk] *pret and ptp of* **awake**.

awoken [ə'wəʊkən] *ptp of* **awake**.

AWOL ['eɪwɒl] (*Mil*) *abbr of* **absent without leave** ausente sin permiso.

awry [ə'raɪ] *adv*: **with his hat on ~** con el sombrero torcido, con el sombrero ladeado; **to be ~** estar de través, estar al sesgo, estar puesto mal; **to go ~** salir mal, fracasar.

axe, (*US*) **ax** [æks] **1** *n* (**a**) hacha *f*; (*fig: blow*) golpe *m*; (*cut-back*) recorte *m*, reducción *f*; **when the ~ fell** cuando se descargó el golpe; **to have an ~ to grind** tener un interés creado; **I have no ~ to grind** no tengo ningún interés personal.

(**b**) **to give sb the ~** *employee* despedir a uno; *boyfriend* dejar plantado a uno; **I got the ~** (*employee*) me despidieron; (*boyfriend*) me dejó plantado.

2 *vt* (*fig*) *costs etc* reducir, recortar; *person* despedir; *staff* recortar.

axial ['æksɪəl] *adj* axial.

axiom ['æksɪəm] *n* axioma *m*.

axiomatic [,æksɪəʊ'mætɪk] *adj* axiomático.

axis ['æksɪs] *n, pl* **axes** ['æksiːz] eje *m*; (*Anat*) axis *m*; **the A~** (*Pol*) el Eje.

axle ['æksl] *n* eje *m*, árbol *m*, cardán *m* (*CAm*), flecha *f* (*Mex*).

ay(e) [aɪ] **1** *adv* (*esp Scot, N. England*) sí; **~ ~ sir!** sí mi capitán (*etc*). **2** *n* sí *m*; **to vote ~** votar sí; **the ~s have it** se ha aprobado la moción; **there were 50 ~s and 3 noes** votaron 50 a favor y 3 en contra.

ayatollah [aɪə'tɒlə] *n* imam *m*, ayatolá *m*, ayatollah *m*.

aye [eɪ] *adv*: **for ever and ~** (*Scot*) para siempre jamás.

AYH *n* (*US*) *abbr of* **American Youth Hostels**.

Aymara [,aɪmə'rɑː] **1** *adj* aimará. **2** *n* (**a**) aimará *mf*. (**b**) (*Ling*) aimará *m*.

AZ (*US*) *abbr of* **Arizona**.

azalea [ə'zeɪlɪə] *n* azalea *f*.

Azerbaijan [,æzəbaɪ'dʒɑːn] *n* Azerbaiyán *m*.

Azerbaijani [,æzəbaɪ'dʒɑːnɪ] **1** *adj* azerbaiyaní. **2** *n* azerbaiyaní *mf*.

Azores [ə'zɔːz] *npl* Azores *fpl*.

Aztec ['æztek] **1** *adj* azteca. **2** *n* azteca *mf*.

azure ['eɪʒə^r] **1** *adj* azul celeste. **2** *n* azul *m* celeste; (*Her*) azur *m*.

B

B, b [biː] *n* **(a)** (*letter*) B, b *f* (*Esp*), B larga, b larga (*LAm*). **(b)** **B** (*Mus*) si *m*; **B major** si *m* mayor; **B road** ≈ carretera *f* secundaria. **(c)** **B for Baker** B de Burgos; **number 7b** (*in house numbers*) séptimo segunda; **B-girl** (*US**) camarera *f* de barra. **(d)** (*Scol*) notable *m*. **(e)** (*Cine: also* **B-movie**) película *f* de la serie B.

b. *abbr of* **born** nacido, n.

B & B *n abbr of* **bed and breakfast** cama *f* con desayuno, alojamiento *m* y desayuno.

BA **(a)** *n* (*Univ*) *abbr of* **Bachelor of Arts** Lic. en Fil. y Let.
(b) *n abbr of* **British Academy**.
(c) *n abbr of* **British Association (for the Advancement of Science)**.
(d) (*Geog*) *abbr of* **Buenos Aires** Bs. As.
(e) *n* (*Brit Aer*) *abbr of* **British Airways**.

BAA *n abbr of* **British Airports Authority**.

baa [bɑː] **1** *n* balido *m*. **2** *interj* ¡bee! **3** *vi* balar.

baa-lamb* ['bɑːlæm] *n* corderito *m*, borreguito *m*.

babble ['bæbl] **1** *n* parloteo *m*; barboteo *m*; (*of stream*) murmullo *m*; **a ~ of voices arose** se oyó un ruido confuso de voces.
2 *vt* decir balbuceando.
3 *vi* barbullar, barbotear; (*talk to excess*) parlotear; (*tell secrets*) hablar indiscretamente; (*stream*) murmurar.

◆babble away, babble on *vi* hablar sin parar.

babbling ['bæblɪŋ] **1** *adj person* hablador; *baby* balbuceante; *stream* que murmura, músico. **2** *n* = **babble 1**.

babe [beɪb] *n* (*liter or hum*) criatura *f*; (*US‡*) chica *f*, (*in direct address*) ricura *f*, nena *f*; **~ in arms** niño *m*, -a *f* de pecho.

babel ['beɪbəl] *n* babel *m or f*; **Tower of B~** Torre *f* de Babel.

baboon [bə'buːn] *n* mandril *m*.

Babs [bæbz] *nf familiar form of* **Barbara**.

baby ['beɪbɪ] **1** *n* niño *m*, -a *f*, guagua *mf* (*LAm*); (*more sentimental*) bebé *mf*, crío *m*, -a *f*, rorro *m*, -a *f*, nene *m*, -a *f*; (*US‡*) chica *f*, (*in direct address*) ricura *f*, nena *f*; **she's having a ~ in May** va a tener un niño en mayo; **she's having the ~ in hospital** va a dar a luz en el hospital; **~ of the family** benjamín *m*; **don't be such a ~!** ¡no seas niño!; **that's not my ~*** eso no me toca a mí; **to be left holding the ~*** (tener que) pagar el pato*, cargar con el muerto*; **to throw out the ~ with the bathwater** actuar con un exceso de celo; **that ~ cost me a fortune** (*US**) ese chisme me costó una fortuna*.
2 *attr and adj*: **~ bonds** (*US*) bonos *mpl* depreciados; **~ boy** nene *m*; **~ break** interrupción *f* de las actividades profesionales por maternidad; **~ car** coche *m* pequeño; **~ clothes, ~ linen** ropita *f* de niño; **~ face** cara *f* de niño; **~ food(s)** comida *f* para niños, potitos* *mpl*; **~ girl** nena *f*; **~ hedgehog** cría *f* de erizo; **~ rabbit** conejito *m*; **~ seat** (*Aut*) sillita *f* (*or* asiento *m*) de seguridad para niños; **~ tender** (*US*) canguro *mf*; **~ tooth*** diente *m* de leche; **~ wipe** toallita *f* húmeda.

baby-batterer ['beɪbɪ,bætərəʳ] *n* persona *f* que maltrata a sus hijos.

baby-battering ['beɪbɪ,bætərɪŋ] *n* maltrato *m* de los hijos.

baby bed ['beɪbɪ,bed] *n* (*US*) cuna *f*.

baby-boom ['beɪbɪbuːm] *n* boom *m* de natalidad, boom *m* de nacimientos; explosión *f* demográfica.

baby-boomer ['beɪbɪ,buːməʳ] *n* niño *m* nacido (*or* niña *f* nacida) en época de un boom de natalidad (*esp* de los años 60).

Baby bouncer ['beɪbɪ,baʊnsəʳ] ® *n* columpio *m* para bebés.

baby buggy ['beɪbɪ,bʌgɪ] *n* (*US*), **baby carriage** ['beɪbɪ,kærɪdʒ] *n* (*esp US*) cochecito *m* de niño.

baby-doll pyjamas [,beɪbɪdɒlpɪ'dʒɑːməz] *n* picardía *f*, *camisón corto con pantalones a juego*.

baby grand ['beɪbɪ'grænd] *n* piano *m* de media cola.

babygrow ['beɪbɪ,grəʊ] *n* pijama *m* de una pieza.

babyhood ['beɪbɪhʊd] *n* infancia *f*.

babyish ['beɪbɪɪʃ] *adj* infantil.

Babylon ['bæbɪlən] *n*, **Babylonia** [,bæbɪ'ləʊnɪə] *n* Babilonia *f*.

Babylonian [,bæbɪ'ləʊnɪən] **1** *adj* babilónico; *person* babilonio. **2** *n* babilonio *m*, -a *f*.

baby-minder ['beɪbɪ,maɪndəʳ] *n* niñera *f*.

baby-sit ['beɪbɪsɪt] (*irr: V* **sit**) *vi* hacer de canguro, estar de canguro.

baby-sitter ['beɪbɪ,sɪtəʳ] *n* canguro *mf*.

baby-sitting ['beɪbɪ,sɪtɪŋ] *n* hacer *m* de canguro; **I can't pay for ~** no puedo pagar un canguro; **I hate ~** detesto hacer canguros.

baby-snatcher ['beɪbɪ,snætʃəʳ] *n* mujer *f* que roba un bebé.

baby talk ['beɪbɪtɔːk] *n* habla *f* infantil.

baby-walker ['beɪbɪ,wɔːkəʳ] *n* tacataca* *m*, andador *m*.

baccalaureate [,bækə'lɔːrɪɪt] *n* (*US*) bachillerato *m*.

baccarat ['bækərɑː] *n* bacará *m*, bacarrá *m*.

bacchanalia [,bækə'neɪlɪə] *npl* bacanales *fpl*; (*fig*) bacanal *f*.

bacchanalian [,bækə'neɪlɪən] *adj* bacanal, báquico.

Bacchic ['bækɪk] *adj* báquico.

Bacchus ['bækəs] *nm* Baco.

baccy* ['bækɪ] *n* tabaco *m*.

bachelor ['bætʃələʳ] *n* **(a)** (*unmarried man*) soltero *m*; **confirmed ~, old ~** solterón *m*; **~ flat** piso *m* (*LAm*: departamento *m*) de soltero; **~ girl** soltera *f* (que se dedica a una carrera); **~ party** guateque *m* para hombres solos.
(b) (*Univ*) licenciado *m*, -a *f* (*of* en); **B~ of Science** Licenciado *m*, -a *f* en Ciencias; **~'s degree** licenciatura *f*.

bachelorhood ['bætʃələhʊd] *n* soltería *f*, estado *m* de soltero, celibato *m*.

bacillary [bə'sɪlərɪ] *adj* bacilar.

bacillus [bə'sɪləs] *n*, *pl* **bacilli** [bə'sɪlaɪ] bacilo *m*.

back [bæk] **1** *adj* **(a)** (*not front*) trasero, de atrás; posterior; *view* desde atrás; **~ boiler** (*Brit*) caldera *f* pequeña (*detrás de una chimenea*); **~ burner** hornillo *m* trasero; **to put a problem on the ~ burner** (*fig*) dejar un problema para después, relegar un problema al segundo plano; **~ door** puerta *f* trasera; **~ door methods** métodos *mpl* poco ortodoxos; **by the ~ door** (*fig*) por enchufe, gracias al amiguismo; **~ garden** (*Brit*) jardín *m* detrás de la casa, huerto *m*; **~ matter** apéndices *mpl*; **~ pass** pase *m* atrás; **~ passage** (*euph*) recto *m*; **~ row** última fila *f*; **~ somersault** salto *m* mortal hacia atrás; **~ tooth** muela *f*; **~ wheel** rueda *f* trasera.
(b) (*overdue*) *issue, number* atrasado; *payment* retrasado; **~ rent** atrasos *mpl* de alquiler; **~ tax** impuestos *mpl* atrasados.
2 *adv* **(a)** (*place*) atrás, hacia atrás; **~!** ¡atrás!; **~ and forth** de acá para allá, de una parte a otra; **a house standing ~ from the road** una casa algo retirada de la carretera; **to make one's way ~** regresar; **to fly to Madrid and ~** ir en avión a Madrid y volver del mismo modo.
(b) (*time*) **~ in the 12th century** allá en el siglo XII; **as far ~ as 1900** ya en 1900; **some months ~** hace unos meses.
(c) (*with verb* to be) **to be ~** estar de vuelta; **when will he be ~?** ¿cuándo volverá?
3 *prep*: **~ of** (*US*) = **behind**.
4 *n* **(a)** (*Anat*) espalda *f*; (*of animal*) lomo *m*; **~ to ~** espalda con espalda; **~ to front** al revés; **at the ~ of** tras, detrás de; **what's at the ~ of it?** (*fig*) ¿qué motivo oculto tendrá esto?; **who's at the ~ of it?** ¿quién está detrás de esto?; **behind one's ~** a espaldas de uno, detrás de uno; **she wears her hair down her ~** el pelo le cae por la espalda; **with one's ~ to** de espaldas a; **his ~ is broad**

(*fig*) es capaz de soportarlo; **to be on one's ~** (*Med*) estar postrado (en la cama); **to carry sth on one's ~** llevar algo a cuestas; **he lay on his ~** estaba tumbado boca arriba; **to break one's ~** deslomarse; **to break the ~ of the work** terminar lo más difícil (*or* pesado) del trabajo, superar lo más difícil; **to get** (*or* **put**) **sb's ~ up** picar a uno; **to get off sb's ~*** dejar de fastidiar a uno*; **to have one's ~ to the wall** estar entre la espada y la pared; **to live off sb's ~** vivir a costa de uno; **to put one's ~ into it** arrimar el hombro; **put your ~s into it!** ¡dale!; **to scratch sb's ~*** hacer un favor a uno; **if you scratch my ~ I'll scratch yours*** favor con favor se paga; **to see the ~ of sb** librarse de uno; **we were glad to see the ~ of him** nos alegramos de que se fuera; **to shoot sb in the ~** matar a uno por la espalda; **to turn one's ~** volver las espaldas (*on* a).

(**b**) (*of chair*) respaldo *m*; (*spine of book*) lomo *m*; (*end of book*) final *m*; (*of coin*) reverso *m*; (*of knife*) lomo *m*; (*of cheque, document, hand, page*) dorso *m*; **I know Bognor like the ~ of my hand** conozco Bognor como la palma de la mano; **to sign on the ~** firmar al dorso; **the ship broke its ~** el barco se rompió por medio.

(**c**) (*furthest part*) fondo *m*; (*rear part*) parte *f* trasera; **at the ~ of the hall** en el fondo de la sala, al fondo de la sala; **at the ~ of beyond*** en el quinto pino*, en los quintos infiernos*; **in the ~ of the car** en la parte trasera del coche; **you'll have to sit in the ~** tendrás que ponerte detrás; **in ~ of the house** (*US*) detrás de la casa; **they keep the car round** (*or* **out**) **the ~** dejan el coche detrás de la casa (*etc*); **you'll have to ask round the ~** tendrás que preguntar ahí detrás.

(**d**) (*Sport*: *area*) defensa *f*; **the team is weak at the ~** el equipo es débil defensivamente.

(**e**) (*Sport*: *person*) defensa *mf*.

5 *vt* (**a**) (*support*) apoyar, respaldar; defender; favorecer.

(**b**) (*bet on*) apostar a.

(**c**) (*reverse*) *vehicle* dar marcha atrás a; *horse* recular; **she ~ed the car into the garage** hizo entrar el coche en el garaje marcha atrás; **he ~ed the car into a wall** al dar marcha atrás chocó con el muro.

6 *vi* (**a**) (*move backwards*) moverse atrás, retroceder; (*vehicle*) dar marcha atrás.

(**b**) (*wind*) cambiar, girar (en dirección contraria a las agujas del reloj).

◆**back away** *vi* retroceder, dar un paso (*or* varios pasos *etc*) hacia atrás.

◆**back down** *vi* volverse atrás, echarse atrás, rajarse*.

◆**back off** *vi* dar marcha atrás; (*US*: *withdraw*) retirarse; **~ off!** ¡lárgate!, ¡déjame estar!

◆**back on to** *vt*: **the house ~s on to the park** la parte trasera de la casa da al parque.

◆**back out 1** *vt vehicle* hacer salir marcha atrás.

2 *vi* (*vehicle*) salir marcha atrás; (*person*) salir reculando; (*fig*) retirarse, volverse atrás; **to ~ out of** (*fig*) retirarse de, renunciar a; no cumplir.

◆**back up 1** *vt* (**a**) *vehicle* dar marcha atrás a. (**b**) (*support*) apoyar, respaldar; defender. (**c**) (*US*: *delay*) demorar, retrasar. (**d**) (*Comput*) hacer una copia de apoyo de. **2** *vi* (**a**) dar marcha atrás, retroceder. (**b**) (*Comput*) hacer una copia de apoyo.

backache ['bækeɪk] *n* dolor *m* de espalda.

backbench ['bæk'bentʃ] *n* escaños *mpl* de los diputados que no son ministros; **~ opinions** opiniones *fpl* de los diputados corrientes.

backbencher ['bæk'bentʃəʳ] *n* (*Brit*) diputado *m*, -a *f* que no es ministro.

backbite ['bækbaɪt] **1** *vt* maldecir (*an absent person* de un ausente), hablar mal de. **2** *vi* murmurar.

backbiting ['bækbaɪtɪŋ] *n* murmuración *f*, maledicencia *f*.

backboard ['bækbɔːd] *n* (*US Sport*) tablero *m*.

backbone ['bækbəʊn] *n* espinazo *m*; (*fig*) (*guts*) firmeza *f*, agallas *fpl*; (*chief support*) espina *f* dorsal, piedra *f* angular; **a patriot to the ~** patriota hasta los tuétanos.

back-breaking ['bækbreɪkɪŋ] *adj* deslomador, matador.

backchat ['bæktʃæt] *n* réplicas *fpl*.

backcloth ['bækklɒθ] *n* (*Brit*) telón *m* de fondo.

backdate ['bæk'deɪt] *vt cheque etc* antedatar; *measure* dar efecto retroactivo a; **a pay rise ~d to April** un aumento salarial con efecto desde abril, un aumento retroactivo desde abril.

backdrop ['bækdrɒp] *n* telón *m* de foro.

-backed [bækt] *adj ending in compounds* (**a**) **low~ chair** silla *f* de respaldo bajo. (**b**) **rubber~ carpet** alfombra *f* con refuerzo de caucho.

backer ['bækəʳ] *n* (*Pol*) partidario *m*, -a *f*; (*Comm*) promotor *m*, impulsor *m*, caballo *m* blanco; (*Sport*) apostador *m*, -ora *f*.

backfire ['bæk'faɪəʳ] **1** *n* (*Aut*) petardeo *m*. **2** *vi* (*Aut*) petardear; (*fig*) salir el tiro por la culata; **the idea ~d** la idea perjudicó a sus propios inventores.

back-formation ['bækfɔːˌmeɪʃən] *n* derivación *f* regresiva.

backgammon ['bækˌgæmən] *n* backgamon *m*.

background ['bækgraʊnd] **1** *n* (**a**) (*gen*) fondo *m*; (*Art*) fondo *m*, último término *m*; **in the ~** al fondo, en el fondo, en último término; **against a dim ~** sobre un fondo oscuro; **to stay in the ~** mantenerse en segundo plano, no buscar la luz de la publicidad.

(**b**) (*of person*) antecedentes *mpl*, historial *m*, educación *f*; **what is his ~?** ¿cuáles son sus antecedentes?

(**c**) (*information*) antecedentes *mpl*; información *f* previa; **the ~ to the crisis** los antecedentes de la crisis; **to fill in the ~ for sb** poner a uno en antecedentes.

2 *attr*: **~ music** música *f* de fondo; **~ noise** ruido *m* de fondo; **~ reading** lecturas *fpl* preparatorias; **~ studies** estudios *mpl* del ambiente histórico (*etc*) (en que vivió un autor *etc*); **~ task** (*Comput*) tarea *f* secundaria.

backhand(ed) ['bæk'hænd(ɪd)] *adj* dado con la vuelta de la mano; (*fig*) irónico, equívoco; **~ drive, ~ shot, ~ stroke** revés *m*; **~ volley** (*Sport*) volea *f* de revés.

backhander ['bæk'hændəʳ] *n* (*Brit*) (**a**) (*Sport*) revés *m*. (**b**) (*) soborno *m*, coima *f* (*LAm*).

backing ['bækɪŋ] *n* apoyo *m*; garantía *f*; (*Comm*) respaldo *m*; (*funds*) reserva *f*; (*Mus*) apoyo *m*; **~ store** memoria *f* auxiliar.

backlash ['bæklæʃ] *n* reacción *f*, contragolpe *m*; (*Pol*) reacción *f* violenta; **the white ~** la resaca blanca.

backless ['bæklɪs] *adj dress* sin espalda, muy escotado por detrás.

back-line player ['bæklaɪnˌpleɪəʳ] *n* (*US*) defensa *m*.

backlog ['bæklɒg] *n* atrasos *mpl*; (*Comm*) reserva *f* de pedidos pendientes; (*work*) volumen *m* de trabajo acumulado.

back number ['bæk'nʌmbəʳ] *n* número *m* atrasado (de revista *etc*); (*fig*) cero *m* a la izquierda, nulidad *f*.

back-pack ['bækpæk] (*esp US*) **1** *n* mochila *f*. **2** *vi* viajar con mochila.

back-packer ['bækˌpækəʳ] *n* mochilero *m*, -a *f*, persona *f* que viaja con mochila.

back-packing ['bækˌpækɪŋ] *n*: **to go ~** viajar de mochila.

back pain ['bækˌpeɪn] *n* dolor *m* de espalda, dolor *m* lumbar.

back pay ['bækpeɪ] *n* atrasos *mpl* (de sueldo).

back-pedal ['bæk'pedl] *vi* contrapedalear; volverse atrás, echarse atrás; (*fig*) dar marcha atrás.

back-pedalling ['bækˌpedəlɪŋ] *n*: **~ is his speciality** dar marcha atrás es su especialidad.

back-rest ['bækrest] *n* respaldo *m*.

back room ['bæk'rʊm] *n* cuarto *m* interior, cuarto *m* trasero; (*fig*) lugar *m* donde se hacen investigaciones secretas; **~ boy** investigador *m*, inventor *m* (que hace el trabajo preliminar sin reclamar ningún reconocimiento público); (*Pol*) fontanero *m*.

back seat ['bæk'siːt] *n* asiento *m* trasero; **~ driver** pasajero *m*, -a *f* que molesta al conductor dándole consejos *etc*; **to take a ~** ceder su puesto, pasar a segundo plano.

backshift ['bækʃɪft] *n* turno *m* de tarde.

backside ['bæk'saɪd] *n* trasero *m*, culo *m*.

backslapping ['bækˌslæpɪŋ] *n* espaldarazos *mpl*; **mutual ~** bombo *m* mutuo.

backslash ['bækslæʃ] *n* barra *f* inversa.

backslide ['bæk'slaɪd] (*irr*: *V* **slide**) *vi* reincidir, volver a las andadas.

backslider ['bæk'slaɪdəʳ] *n* reincidente *mf*.

backsliding ['bæk'slaɪdɪŋ] *n* reincidencia *f*.

backspace [ˌbæk'speɪs] **1** *vt* retroceder. **2** *n* retroceso *m*, tecla *f* de retroceso.

backspin ['bækspɪn] *n* efecto *m* de retroceso.

backstage ['bæk'steɪdʒ] **1** *n* (*off-stage*) bastidores *mpl*, espacio *m* entre bastidores; (*dressing-rooms*) camarines *mpl*.

2 *adj* de bastidores.

3 *adv* entre bastidores.

backstairs ['bæk'stɛəz] **1** *npl* escalera *f* de servicio; **by the ~** (*fig*) por enchufe. **2** *attr* clandestino.

backstitch ['bækstɪtʃ] **1** *n* pespunte *m*. **2** *vt* pespuntar.

backstreet ['baekstriːt] **1** *n*: **the ~s** (*quiet*) las calles tranquilas, las calles apartadas del centro; (*poor*) las calles de los barrios bajos. **2** *attr*: **~ abortion** aborto *m* clandestino; ~ **abortionist** curandero *m*, -a *f* abortista, abortista *m* clandestino, abortista *f* clandestina.

backstroke ['bækstrəʊk] *n* braza *f* de espalda, crol *m* de espalda; **the 100 metres** ~ los 100 metros espalda.

back talk ['bæktɔːk] *n* (*US*) = **backchat.**

back-to-back ['bæktə'bæk] **1** *adj*: ~ **credit** créditos *mpl* contiguos; ~ **houses** casas *fpl* adosadas. **2** *adv*: **to sit** ~ sentarse (*or* estar sentados) espalda con espalda.

backtrack ['bæktræk] *vi* volver pies atrás; volverse atrás, echarse atrás.

back-up ['bækʌp] *n* (**a**) (*support*) apoyo *m*, respaldo *m*; reserva *f*; ~ **document** (*Comput*) copia *f* de seguridad, copia *f* de respaldo; ~ **lights** (*US*) luces *fpl* de marcha atrás; ~ **operation** operación *f* de apoyo; ~ **services** servicios *mpl* auxiliares. (**b**) (*Aut*) embotellamiento *m*, retención *f*.

backward ['bækwəd] *adj* (**a**) *motion etc* hacia atrás; ~ **and forward movement** movimiento *m* de vaivén. (**b**) (*retarded*) atrasado; (*shy*) tímido; **he's not** ~ **in coming forward** no peca de tímido; **he was not** ~ **in taking the money** no vaciló en tomar el dinero.

backwardation [ˌbækwə'deɪʃən] *n* retraso *m* en la entrega de acciones; (*fee*) prima *f* pagada por retraso en la entrega de acciones.

backward(s) ['bækwəd(z)] *adv* atrás, hacia atrás; (*back to front*) al revés; **to walk** ~ andar de espaldas; **to read sth** ~ leer algo para atrás; **to go** ~ **and forward** ir de acá para allá; **to know a subject** ~ saber un tema al dedillo; **I know this poem** ~ este poema lo tengo archisabido.

backward-looking ['bækwəd,lʊkɪŋ] *adj* nostálgico; reaccionario.

backwardness ['bækwədnɪs] *n* atraso *m*, estado *m* atrasado; timidez *f*.

backwash ['bækwɒʃ] *n* agua *f* de rechazo; (*fig*) reacción *f*, consecuencias *fpl*.

backwater ['bækwɔːtəʳ] *n* brazo *m* de río estancado, remanso *m*; (*fig*) lugar *m* atrasado, lugar *m* de agradable tranquilidad.

backwoods ['bækwʊdz] *npl* región *f* apartada (*freq* = Las Batuecas *in Spain*); ~ **community** comunidad *f* rústica.

backwoodsman ['bækwʊdzmən] *n*, *pl* **backwoodsmen** ['bækwʊdzmen] patán *m*, rústico *m*; (*Pol*) *miembro de la Cámara de los Lores que rara vez asiste al Parlamento*.

backyard ['bæk'jɑːd] *n* (*Brit*) patio *m* trasero, corral *m*, traspatio *m* (*LAm*); (*US*) jardín *m* trasero; **'Not in my ~'** (*slogan*) 'no lo [*residuos tóxicos etc*] quiero en mi patio'.

bacon ['beɪkən] *n* tocino *m* (entreverado, de panceta); ~ **and eggs** tocino *m* con huevos; **to bring home the** ~* sacarse el gordo; lograrlo, tener éxito; **to save one's** ~* salvar el pellejo.

bacteria [bæk'tɪərɪə] *npl of* **bacterium** bacterias *fpl*.

bacterial [bæk'tɪərɪəl] *adj* bacteriano.

bacteriological [bækˌtɪərɪə'lɒdʒɪkəl] *adj* bacteriológico.

bacteriologist [bækˌtɪərɪ'ɒlɒdʒɪst] *n* bacteriólogo *m*, -a *f*.

bacteriology [bækˌtɪərɪ'ɒlədʒɪ] *n* bacteriología *f*.

bacteriosis [ˌbæktɪərɪ'əʊsɪs] *n* bacteriosis *f*.

bacterium [bæk'tɪərɪəm] *n*, *pl* **bacteria** [bæk'tɪərɪə] bacteria *f*.

bad [bæd] **1** *adj* (**a**) (*wicked*) *person* malo, malvado; *habit* malo; *language* indecente; **he's a** ~ **one** es un mal sujeto; **he's not as** ~ **as he looks** es mejor persona de lo que parece; **you** ~ **boy!** ¡eres un niño malo!; **you** ~ **dog!** ¡qué asco de perro!; **it was very** ~ **of him to say that** ha hecho muy mal en decir eso.

(**b**) (*inferior etc*) malo; (*ill*) malo, enfermo; (*rotten*) podrido, dañado, pasado; (*harmful*) nocivo, dañoso; *accident, mistake, wound* grave; *air* viciado; *headache, pain* agudo, intenso; *smell* malo; *cheque* descubierto, sin fondos; *coin* falso; *debt* incobrable; *joke* de mal gusto, nada divertido; *law, treatment* injusto; *shot* errado; *tooth* cariado; *voting-paper* inválido; **my** ~ **leg** mi pierna lisiada; **it's not so** ~ no está tan mal; **I'm** ~ **about getting up** soy lento para levantarme; **to be** ~ **at French** ser malo en francés; **business is** ~ el negocio va mal; **not** ~ bastante bueno, nada malo; (*less enthusiastic*) regular; **not** ~! ¡muy bien!; **that's too** ~ es una pena; **it's really too** ~ **of you** te has comportado muy mal; **it would be** ~ **for you to** + *infin* sería poco aconsejable que tú + *subj*; **it's** ~ **for you** te hace daño; **what's** ~ **about it?** ¿qué hay de malo en ello?; **I feel** ~ me siento mal; **I feel** ~ **about it** lo lamento; **to go** ~ (*food etc*) echarse a perder, pasarse, alterarse; **to go from** ~ **to worse** ir de mal en peor; **she's got a** ~ **cold** tiene un resfriado muy fuerte; **I've got a** ~ **head** tengo un fuerte dolor de cabeza; **he looks** ~ tiene mal aspecto; **this is beginning to look** ~ esto se está poniendo feo; **to be taken** ~* caer enfermo; **to talk** ~ **Spanish** hablar mal el español; **to have a** ~ **trip** (*Drugs*‡) tener un mal viaje.

(**c**) (*esp US*‡: *great*; *comp* ~**der**, *superl* ~**dest**) guay‡.

2 *adv* (*) **he's got it** ~ (*hobby*) está obsesionado; (*love*) está enamorado como un tonto.

3 *n* lo malo; **I'm £5 to the** ~ he perdido 5 libras; **to be in** ~ **with sb** (*US*) estar a malas con uno, estar en la lista negra de uno; **to go to the** ~ echarse a perder, arruinarse; **to take the** ~ **with the good** aceptar lo malo con lo bueno.

baddie*, baddy* ['bædɪ] *n* (*Cine etc*; *often hum*) malo *m*.

baddish ['bædɪʃ] *adj* bastante malo, más bien malo.

bade [bæd] *pret of* **bid**.

badge [bædʒ] *n* divisa *f*, insignia *f*; (*worn on coat*) distintivo *m*; (*metal disc*) chapa *f*, placa *f*; (*fig*) señal *f*, indicio *m*; ~ **of office** distintivo *m*, insignia *f* de su función.

badger ['bædʒəʳ] **1** *n* tejón *m*. **2** *vt* acosar, atormentar (*for* para obtener); **stop** ~**ing me!** ¡no me fastidies!; **to** ~ **sb into doing sth** acosar a uno hasta que haga algo.

badinage ['bædɪnɑːʒ] *n* chanzas *fpl*, bromas *fpl*.

badlands ['bædlændz] *npl* (*US*) tierras *fpl* malas, tierras *fpl* desgastadas por la erosión (*región yerma, esp en los estados de Nebraska y Dakota del Sur*).

badly ['bædlɪ] *adv* (**a**) (*gen*) mal; **things are going** ~ las cosas van mal; **we came off** ~ **in the deal** salimos mal del negocio; **to be** ~ **off** andar (*or* estar) mal de dinero; **we are** ~ **off for coal** andamos mal de carbón; **how did he take it?** ... ~ ¿qué efecto le produjo la noticia? ... malísimo. (**b**) (*seriously*) **the** ~ **disabled** los severamente minusválidos; ~ **wounded** gravemente herido; **to be** ~ **beaten** sufrir una grave derrota; **to be** ~ **mistaken** equivocarse gravemente. (**c**) (*very much*) **it** ~ **needs painting** hace mucha falta pintarlo; **I need money** ~ tengo mucha necesidad de dinero, necesito urgentemente dinero; **I want it** ~ lo deseo muchísimo; **we** ~ **need another assistant** nos hace gran falta otro ayudante.

badman ['bædmæn], *pl* **badmen** ['bædmen] *n* (*esp US*) gángster *m*.

bad-mannered ['bæd'mænəd] *adj* sin educación, grosero.

badminton ['bædmɪntən] *n* bádminton *m*, (juego *m* del) volante *m*.

badmouth* ['bæd,maʊθ] *vt* (*US*) criticar, insultar; murmurar de.

badness ['bædnɪs] *n* (**a**) (*wickedness*) maldad *f*. (**b**) (*bad quality*) lo malo, mala calidad *f*.

bad-tempered ['bæd'tempəd] *adj* (*permanently*) de mal genio; (*temporarily*) de mal humor; *argument* fuerte; *tone etc* áspero, malhumorado.

BAe *abbr of* **British Aerospace**.

Baffin ['bæfɪn] *n*: ~ **Bay** Bahía *f* de Baffin; ~ **Island** Tierra *f* de Baffin.

baffle ['bæfl] **1** *n* (*also* ~ **plate**) deflector *m*; (*Rad*) pantalla *f* acústica.

2 *vt progress* impedir, estorbar; *mind etc* desconcertar; *person* dejar perplejo; *searchers* confundir; **at times you** ~ **me** a veces no te comprendo; **the problem** ~**s me** al problema no le veo solución alguna; **the police are** ~**d** la policía no tiene pista alguna; **the crime** ~**d the police for months** durante meses el crimen dejó perpleja a la policía; **it** ~**s description** es imposible describirlo.

bafflement ['bæflmənt] *n* perplejidad *f*; desconcierto *m*, confusión *f*.

baffling ['bæflɪŋ] *adj crime* de solución nada fácil, misterioso; *action* desconcertante, incomprensible; *problem* dificilísimo.

bag [bæg] **1** *n* (**a**) saco *m*; talega *f*; (*large sack*) costal *m*; (*handbag*) bolso *m*, cartera *f* (*LAm*); (*suitcase*) maleta *f*, valija *f* (*LAm*), veliz *m* (*Mex*); (*carried over shoulder*) zurrón *m*, mochila *f*; (*in dress*) bolsa *f*; (*in trousers*) rodillera *f*; ~**s under the eyes** ojeras *fpl*; **it's a mixed** ~ (* *fig*) es una mezcla de todo; **the whole** ~ **of tricks*** todo el rollo*; **he was like a** ~ **of bones** estaba como un saco de huesos; **it's in the** ~* es cosa segura, está en la talega; **we had the game nearly in the** ~* teníamos el partido casi en la mochila*; **it's not his** ~ (*US**) no es de su gusto; **to be left holding the** ~ (*US**) cargar con el mochuelo*; **to pack one's** ~**s** hacer las maletas; **to pack** ~ **and baggage** liar el petate; **they threw him out** ~ **and baggage** le pusieron de patitas en la calle con todo lo suyo.

(**b**) (*Hunting*) cacería *f*, caza *f*; **a good day's** ~ una buena cacería.

(**c**) ~**s*** (*baggage*) equipaje *m*.

(**d**) ~**s** (*Brit**: *trousers*) pantalones *mpl*.

(**e**) (*Brit**) ~**s of** la mar de*, un montón de*; **we've** ~**s**

of time tenemos tiempo de sobra.

(**f**) (*) **old** ~ bruja *f*, arpía *f*.

2 *vt* (**a**) (*also* **to** ~ **up**) ensacar; (*Hunting*) cazar, coger, capturar; (*shoot down*) derribar; (‡) birlar. (**b**) (*Brit**) tomar, apropiarse; reservar para sí; **I ~s that** eso pa' mí.

3 *vi* (*also* **to** ~ **out**) hacer bolsa.

bagatelle [ˌbægəˈtel] *n* bagatela *f*.

bagel [ˈbeɪgl] *n* (*Culin*) pan *m* ácimo; (*US*) *especie de bollo*.

bagful [ˈbægfʊl] *n* saco *m* (lleno).

baggage [ˈbægɪdʒ] *n* (**a**) (*luggage*) equipaje *m*; (*Mil*) bagaje *m*; ~ **allowance** (*Aer*) franquicia *f* de equipaje; ~ **car** (*US*) furgón *m* de equipajes; ~ **check** talón *m* de equipaje; ~ **(check)room** (*US*) consigna *f*; ~ **handler** despachador *m* de equipaje; ~ **locker** consigna *f* automática; ~ **reclaim** recogida *f* de equipajes; ~ **train** tren *m* de equipajes. (**b**) (*: ††) mujercilla *f*.

baggy [ˈbægɪ] *adj* muy holgado; que hace bolsa; *trousers* con rodilleras; abombachado.

Baghdad [ˌbægˈdæd] *n* Bagdad *m*.

bag lady* [ˈbægˌleɪdɪ] *n* indigente *f*, mujer *f* que vive con lo puesto*.

bagpiper [ˈbægpaɪpəʳ] *n* gaitero *m*.

bagpipes [ˈbægpaɪps] *npl* gaita *f*.

bag-snatcher [ˈbægˈsnætʃəʳ] *n* ladrón *m* de bolsos, tironista* *m*.

bag-snatching [ˈbægˌsnætʃɪŋ] *n* tirón *m* (de bolsos).

bah [bɑː] *interj* ¡bah!

Bahamas [bəˈhɑːməz] *npl* Islas *fpl* Bahamas, las Bahamas.

Bahrain [bɑːˈreɪn] *n* Bahrein *m*.

Bahraini [bɑːˈreɪnɪ] **1** *adj* bahreiní. **2** *n* bahreiní *mf*.

bail¹ [beɪl] (*Jur*) **1** *n* caución *f*, fianza *f*; **on** ~ bajo fianza; **he's out on** ~ está libre bajo fianza; **to be** (*or* **go, stand**) ~ **for** salir fiador por; **to jump one's ~*** fugarse estando bajo fianza; **to be released on** ~ ser puesto en libertad bajo fianza. **2** *vt* afianzar.

◆**bail out** *vt*: **to** ~ **sb out** obtener la libertad de uno bajo fianza; (*fig*) echar un cable a uno.

bail² [beɪl] *n* (*Cricket*) palito *m* corto.

bail³ [beɪl] *vt* (*Naut*) achicar.

◆**bail out 1** *vi* (*Aer*) lanzarse en paracaídas. **2** *vt* (*Naut*) = **bail³**.

bail-bond [ˌbeɪlˈbɒnd] *n* caución *f*, fianza *f*.

bailiff [ˈbeɪlɪf] *n* (*Jur*) alguacil *m*, corchete *m*; (*steward*) administrador *m*.

bain-marie [bɛ̃məˈri] *n* baño *m* de María.

bairn [beən] *n* (*Scot, N Eng*) niño *m*, -a *f*.

bait [beɪt] **1** *n* cebo *m*, carnada *f*; (*fig*) aliciente *m*, añagaza *f*; **he wouldn't rise to the** ~ no quería picar; **to swallow the** ~ tragar el anzuelo.

2 *vt hook, trap* cebar, poner cebo en; (*fig*) acosar, atormentar.

baize [beɪz] *n* bayeta *f*; **green** ~ tapete *m* verde.

bake [beɪk] **1** *vt* cocer al horno; *bricks etc* cocer; (*harden*) endurecer; **it's baking hot** hace un calor terrible; **a baking hot day** un día de calor asfixiante; **to** ~ **one's own bread** hornear su propio pan. **2** *vi*: **we were baking in the heat** estábamos asfixiados del calor.

baked [beɪkt] *adj* cocido al horno; ~ **beans** judías *fpl* en salsa de tomate; ~ **potatoes** patatas *fpl* (*LAm*: papas *fpl*) al horno.

bakehouse [ˈbeɪkhaʊs] *n*, *pl* **bakehouses** [ˈbeɪkhaʊzɪz] tahona *f*, panadería *f*.

baker [ˈbeɪkəʳ] *n* panadero *m*; **~'s (shop)** panadería *f*; **~'s dozen** docena *f* del fraile.

bakery [ˈbeɪkərɪ] *n* tahona *f*, panadería *f*.

Bakewell tart [ˌbeɪkwəlˈtɑːt] *n tarta hecha a base de almendras, mermelada y azúcar en polvo*.

baking [ˈbeɪkɪŋ] *n* cocción *f*; (*batch*) hornada *f*.

baking-chocolate [ˈbeɪkɪŋˌtʃɒklɪt] *n* (*US*) chocolate *m* fondant.

baking-dish [ˈbeɪkɪŋˌdɪʃ] *n* fuente *f* de hornear.

baking-pan [ˈbeɪkɪŋˌpæn] *n* = **baking-tin**.

baking-powder [ˈbeɪkɪŋˌpaʊdəʳ] *n* polvos *mpl* de levadura, polvo *m* de hornear.

baking-sheet [ˈbeɪkɪŋˌʃiːt] *n* = **baking-tray**.

baking-soda [ˈbeɪkɪŋˌsəʊdə] *n* bicarbonato *m* de sosa.

baking-tin [ˈbeɪkɪŋˌtɪn] *n* lata *f* para hornear.

baking-tray [ˈbeɪkɪŋˌtreɪ] *n* bandeja *f* de horno.

baksheesh [ˈbækʃiːʃ] *n* propina *f*.

bal. *abbr of* **balance** balance *m*.

Balaclava [ˌbæləˈklɑːvə] *n* (*Brit*: *also* ~ **helmet**) pasamontañas *m*.

balalaika [ˌbæləˈlaɪkə] *n* balalaica *f*.

balance [ˈbæləns] **1** *n* (**a**) (*state*) equilibrio *m*; ~ **of power** equilibrio *m* político; distribución *f* de fuerzas; ~ **of terror** equilibrio *m* del terror, equilibrio *m* armamentístico; **in** ~ en equilibrio, equilibrado; **when the** ~ **of his mind was disturbed** en un momento de obcecación; **to keep one's** ~ mantener el equilibrio; **to lose one's** ~ perder el equilibrio; **to throw sb off** ~ hacer que uno pierda el equilibrio, (*fig*) desconcertar a uno.

(**b**) (*scales*) balanza *f*; **to be** (*or* **hang**) **in the** ~ estar pendiente de un hilo; **to hold the** ~ tener una influencia decisiva.

(**c**) (*Comm*) balance *m*; (*statement*) balance *m*, estado *m* de cuentas; (*remainder*) resto *m*, saldo *m*; (*still to be paid over*) remanente *m*; (*credit* ~) saldo *m*; ~ **due** saldo *m* deudor; ~ **in hand** alcance *m*, sobrante *m*; ~ **of payments** balance *m* (*or* balanza *f*) de pagos; ~ **of trade** balance *m* (*or* balanza *f*) de comercio; **on** ~ pensándolo bien; **to strike a proper** ~ encontrar el punto medio.

(**d**) (*good sense*) buen sentido *m*, juicio *m*; serenidad *f*.

2 *vt* (**a**) equilibrar; (*make up for*) contrapesar (*with* con); **this has to be ~d against that** hay que pesar esto contra aquello.

(**b**) *account* saldar; *budget* nivelar; **to** ~ **the books** hacer balance, cerrar los libros.

3 *vi* (**a**) equilibrarse.

(**b**) (*Comm*) **now the account ~s** ahora está bien el balance de esta cuenta; **to make the budget** ~ nivelar el presupuesto.

4 *vr*: **to** ~ **o.s.** equilibrarse (*on* en).

◆**balance out 1** *vt* (*fig*) compensar. **2** *vi*: **the profits and losses** ~ **out** las ganancias y las pérdidas se compensan.

◆**balance up** *vt* finiquitar, saldar.

balanced [ˈbælənst] *adj* equilibrado.

balance-sheet [ˈbælənsʃiːt] *n* balance *m*, avanzo *m*.

balancing [ˈbælənsɪŋ] *n* (**a**) (*equilibrium*) ~ **on a high wire is not easy** mantener el equilibrio en la cuerda floja no es fácil; **to do a** ~ **act** (*Theat*) andar en la cuerda floja; (*fig*) hacer malabarismos (*between* con). (**b**) (*Comm, Fin*) ~ **of accounts** balance *m* de cuentas; ~ **of the books** balance *m* de los libros.

balcony [ˈbælkənɪ] *n* balcón *m*; (*covered*) mirador *m*; (*of block of flats*) galería *f*, terraza *f*; (*Theat*) paraíso *m*; **first** (*or* **second**) ~ (*US*) galería *f* superior.

bald [bɔːld] *adj* (**a**) calvo; *tyre* desgastado; ~ **patch** claro *m*; **as** ~ **as a coot** pelado como bola de billar; **to go** ~ quedarse calvo. (**b**) (*fig*) *style* escueto, desnudo; *statement* franco y sencillo.

balderdash [ˈbɔːldədæʃ] *n* tonterías *fpl*.

bald-headed [ˈbɔːldˈhedɪd] *adj* calvo; **to go** ~ **into*** lanzarse ciegamente a.

balding [ˈbɔːldɪŋ] *adj* parcialmente calvo.

baldly [ˈbɔːldlɪ] *adv* escuetamente, desnudamente.

baldness [ˈbɔːldnɪs] *n* (**a**) calvicie *f*. (**b**) (*fig*) lo escueto, desnudez *f*.

baldy* [ˈbɔːldɪ] *n* calvo *m*.

bale [beɪl] **1** *n* bala *f*; (*Agr*) paca *f*, fardo *m*. **2** *vt* (*also* **to** ~ **up**) embalar; (*Agr*) empacar.

◆**bale out** *vi* (*Aer*) lanzarse en paracaídas.

Bâle [bɑːl] *n* Basilea *f*.

Balearic [ˌbælɪˈærɪk] **1** *adj* balear. **2**: **the ~s,** ~ **Islands** *npl* los Baleares, Islas *fpl* Baleares.

baleful [ˈbeɪlfʊl] *adj influence* funesto, siniestro; *look* ceñudo, hosco.

balefully [ˈbeɪlfəlɪ] *adv look* tristemente; *say* funestamente, siniestramente.

baler [ˈbeɪləʳ] *n* (*Agr*) empacadora *f*, enfardadora *f*.

balk [bɔːk] **1** *n* (*Agr*) lomo *m*, caballón *m*; (*Billiards*) cabaña *f*; (*of timber*) viga *f*.

2 *vt* (*thwart*) burlar, impedir; (*miss*) perder, no aprovechar; **we were ~ed of the chance to see it** perdimos la oportunidad para verlo.

3 *vi* (*stop*) detenerse bruscamente; (*horse*) plantarse, repropiarse (*at* al ver); **he ~ed at this** se resistió a considerarlo, lo rechazó.

Balkan [ˈbɔːlkən] **1** *adj* balcánico. **2** *npl*: **the ~s** los Balcanes.

ball¹ [bɔːl] *n* (**a**) (*gen*) bola *f*; globo *m*, esfera *f*; (*eg tennis ball*) pelota *f*; (*eg football*) balón *m*; (*Mil*) bala *f*; (*of wool*) ovillo *m*; ~ **(and socket) joint** junta *f* articulada; **he's a real** ~ **of fire** es muy dinámico; **he's not exactly a** ~ **of fire** no se le nota exceso de dinamismo; **behind the eight** ~ (*US* fig*) en apuros; **that's the way the** ~ **bounces** (*US**) así es la vida, así son las cosas; **the** ~ **is with you** (*or* **in your court**) (*Brit fig*) ahora te toca a ti; **to be on the** ~ ser un hacha; estar al tanto; **you have to be on the** ~ **for this**

para esto hay que fijarse mucho; **to have a lot on the ~** (*US**) tener mucho talento; **to keep one's eye on the ~** (*fig*) no perder de vista lo principal del asunto; **to play ~** jugar a la pelota, (*fig*) cooperar (*with* con), ser acomodadizo; **to roll up into a ~** hacerse un ovillo; **to start** (*or* **set**) **the ~ rolling** empezar, hablar (*etc*) primero; poner las cosas en marcha.

(**b**) (*Anat***) cojón *m***, huevo** *m*; **~s!** ¡cojones!; **~s** (*Brit*: *nonsense*) tonterías *fpl*, pavadas *fpl*.

◆**ball up**** *vt* = **balls up****.

ball² [bɔːl] *n* (*dance*) baile *m* (*gen* de etiqueta); **we had a ~** (*US**) lo pasamos en grande*, nos divertimos una barbaridad*.

ballad ['bæləd] *n* balada *f*, (*Spanish*) romance *m*, corrido *m* (*LAm*).

ballade [bæ'lɑːd] *n* (*Mus*) balada *f*.

ballast ['bæləst] **1** *n* (*Naut and fig*) lastre *m*; (*Rail*) balasto *m*; **in ~** en lastre. **2** *vt* (*Naut*) lastrar; (*Rail*) balastar.

ball-bearing ['bɔːl'bɛərɪŋ] *n* bola *f*, cojinete *m* a (*or* de) bolas, rodamiento *m* a bolas, balero *m* (*Mex*), rulemán *m* (*Cono Sur*).

ballboy ['bɔːlbɔɪ] *n* recogedor *m* de pelotas.

ballcock ['bɔːlkɒk] *n* llave *f* de bola, llave *f* de flotador.

ballerina [ˌbælə'riːnə] *n* bailarina *f* (de ballet); **prima ~** primera bailarina *f*.

ballet ['bæleɪ] *n* ballet *m*, baile *m*.

ballet-dancer ['bæleɪˌdɑːnsər] *n* bailarín *m*, -ina *f* (de ballet).

ballet-shoes ['bæleɪˌʃuːz] *npl* zapatillas *fpl* de ballet.

ballet-skirt ['bæleɪˌskɜːt] *n* falda *f* de bailarina (*or* de ballet).

ball game ['bɔːlgeɪm] *n* (*US*) partido *m* de béisbol; (*fig*) **this is a different ~** esto es otro cantar, esto es algo muy distinto; **it's a whole new ~** todo ha cambiado.

ball girl ['bɔːlgɜːl] *n* recogedora *f* de pelotas.

ballistic [bə'lɪstɪk] *adj* balístico; **~ missile** misil *m* balístico.

ballistics [bə'lɪstɪks] *n sing* balística *f*.

balloon [bə'luːn] **1** *n* globo *m*, bomba *f* (*And*); (*in cartoons*) bocadillo *m*, globo *m*; **then the ~ went up*** luego se armó la gorda*; **that went down like a lead ~*** eso cayó como un jarro de agua fría. **2** *vi* subir en un globo; (*swell*) dispararse; (*sail etc*: *also* **to ~ out**) hincharse como un globo.

balloonist [bə'luːnɪst] *n* ascensionista *mf*, aeronauta *mf*.

ballot ['bælət] **1** *n* (*voting*) votación *f*; (*paper*) papeleta *f* (para votar); **to take a ~ on sth** someter algo a votación; **there will be a ~ for the remaining places** se sortearán las plazas restantes; **to vote by secret ~** votar en secreto.

2 *vt members etc* invitar a votar.

3 *vi* votar; **to ~ for** elegir (*or* determinar *etc*) por votación; **to ~ for** *tickets* rifar, sortear; **to ~ for a place** sortear un puesto.

ballot-box ['bælətbɒks] *n* urna *f* electoral; **~ stuffing** (*US*) fraude *m* electoral, pucherazo* *m*.

balloting ['bælətɪŋ] *n* votación *f*.

ballot-paper ['bælətpeɪpər] *n* papeleta *f* (para votar), boleta *f* (*LAm*).

ballpark ['bɔːlpɑːk] *n* (*US*) estadio *m* de béisbol; **~ estimate** cálculo *m* aproximado; **~ figure, ~ number** cifra *f* aproximada; **it's in the same ~** está en la misma categoría, se trata de lo mismo.

ball-point (pen) ['bɔːlpɔɪnt(pen)] *n* bolígrafo *m*, pluma *f* esferográfica (*LAm*), birome *f* (*Cono Sur*).

ballroom ['bɔːlrʊm] *n* salón *m* de baile; **~ dance, ~ dancing** baile *m* de salón.

balls-up** ['bɔːlzʌp] *n* (*Brit*) lío *m*; **he made a ~ of the job** la pifió en el trabajo*, lo escoñó todo*; *V also* **cock-up**.

◆**balls up**** *vt* estropear, joder**.

ball-up** ['bɔːlʌp] *n* (*US*) = **balls-up****.

bally‡ ['bælɪ] *adj* (*Brit*) puñetero‡.

ballyhoo* [ˌbælɪ'huː] *n* (*advertising*) propaganda *f* estrepitosa; (*noise*) ruido *m*, jaleo *m*, conmoción *f*.

balm [bɑːm] *n* bálsamo *m* (*also fig*).

balmy ['bɑːmɪ] *adj* (**a**) (*liter*) (*soothing*) balsámico; *breeze etc* suave, fragante. (**b**) (*Brit‡*) = **barmy**.

baloney‡ [bə'ləʊnɪ] *n* chorradas‡ *fpl*.

BALPA ['bælpə] *n abbr of* **British Airline Pilots' Association** ≃ Sindicato *m* Español de Pilotos de Líneas Aéreas, SEPLA *m*.

balsa ['bɔːlsə] *n* balsa *f*.

balsam ['bɔːlsəm] *n* bálsamo *m*.

Baltic ['bɔːltɪk] *adj*: **~ Sea** Mar *m* Báltico; **the ~ states** los estados bálticos; **one of the ~ ports** uno de los puertos del Mar Báltico.

balustrade [ˌbælə'streɪd] *n* balaustrada *f*, barandilla *f*.

bamboo [bæm'buː] *n* bambú *m*; **~ shoots** brotes *mpl* de bambú; **the B~ Curtain** el Telón de Bambú.

bamboozle* [bæm'buːzl] *vt* embaucar, capear; **she was ~d into buying it** se la engatusó para que lo comprara.

ban [bæn] **1** *n* prohibición *f* (*on* de); veda *f* (de caza); **to be under a ~** estar prohibido; **to put a ~ on** prohibir (el uso de), proscribir; **to raise the ~ on** levantar el entredicho a.

2 *vt* prohibir, proscribir; vedar; *person* excluir (*from* de); **B~ the Bomb Campaign** Campaña *f* contra la bomba; **he was ~ned from driving for life** le retiraron el carné de por vida; **the bullfighter was ~ned for 3 months** el torero fue inhabilitado para ejercer la profesión durante 3 meses.

banal [bə'nɑːl] *adj* banal, vulgar.

banality [bə'nælɪtɪ] *n* banalidad *f*, vulgaridad *f*.

banana [bə'nɑːnə] *n* plátano *m*, banana *f* (*esp LAm*); **~ boat** barco *m* bananero; **~ republic** república *f* bananera; **to be ~s‡** estar chalado‡; **to go ~s‡** perder la chaveta (*over* por).

banana-skin [bə'nɑːnəskɪn] *n* piel *f* de plátano; (*fig*) problema *m* no previsto, peligro *m* no sospechado.

banana tree [bə'nɑːnəˌtriː] *n* plátano *m*, banano *m*.

band¹ [bænd] *n* (**a**) (*strip of material*) banda *f*, tira *f*, faja *f*; (*ribbon*) cinta *f*; (*edging*) cenefa *f*, franja *f*; (*of cigar*) vitola *f*, faja *f*; (*of wheel*) fleje *m*; (*armband*) brazalete *m*; (*hatband*) cintillo *m*; (*of harness*) correa *f*; (*stripe*) lista *f*, raya *f*; (*of territory*) faja *f*; zona *f*.

(**b**) (*Rad*) banda *f*.

(**c**) (*of statistics, tax etc*) banda *f*, categoría *f*, clase *f*.

band² [bænd] *n* (**a**) (*Mus*) orquesta *f*; (*Mil Mus*) banda *f*, música *f*; (*brass ~*) charanga *f*, banda *f*; **then the ~ played*** (*US*) y se armó la gorda*.

(**b**) (*group*) grupo *m*; cuadrilla *f*; (*gang*) gavilla *f*, pandilla *f*.

◆**band together** *vi* juntarse, asociarse; (*pej*) apandillarse.

bandage ['bændɪdʒ] **1** *n* venda *f*, vendaje *m*. **2** *vt* (*also* **to ~ up**) vendar; **with a ~d hand** con una mano en vendas.

Band-Aid ['bændeɪd] ® *n* tirita *f*.

bandan(n)a [bæn'dænə] *n* pañuelo *m* de cabeza.

b. and b. *n abbr of* **bed and breakfast** cama *f* con desayuno, alojamiento *m* y desayuno.

bandbox ['bændbɒks] *n* sombrerera *f*.

banding ['bændɪŋ] *n* (*Brit Scol*) calificaciones *fpl* por letras.

bandit ['bændɪt] *n* bandido *m*.

banditry ['bændɪtrɪ] *n* bandolerismo *m*, bandidismo *m*.

bandmaster ['bændmɑːstər] *n* director *m* de banda.

bandolier [ˌbændə'lɪər] *n* bandolera *f*.

band-saw ['bændsɔː] *n* sierra *f* de cinta.

bandsman ['bændzmən] *n*, *pl* **bandsmen** ['bændzmen] músico *m* (de banda).

bandstand ['bændstænd] *n* quiosco *m* de música.

bandwagon ['bænd,wægən] *n*: **to climb** (*or* **jump**) **on the ~** subirse al carro.

bandy¹ ['bændɪ] *vt words, stories* cambiar; **don't ~ words with me!** ¡no replique Vd!

◆**bandy about** *vt*: **the story was bandied about that ...** se rumoreaba que ...; **his name was being bandied about** su nombre estaba en boca de todos.

bandy² ['bændɪ] *adj*, **bandy-legged** ['bændɪ'legd] *adj* estevado.

bane [beɪn] *n* (††) veneno *m*; (*fig*) plaga *f*, azote *m*; **it's the ~ of my life** será mi ruina.

baneful ['beɪnfʊl] *adj* nocivo; funesto, fatal.

banefully ['beɪnfəlɪ] *adv* nocivamente; funestamente, fatalmente.

bang [bæŋ] **1** *interj* ¡pum!; (*of a blow*) ¡zas!; **to go** (**off**) **~** hacer explosión, estallar; **~ went £5!** se acabaron ¡pum! las 5 libras.

2 *adv* (*) precisamente, exactamente; **~ in the middle** justo en el centro; **I ran ~ into a traffic-jam** me encontré de repente en un embotellamiento; **it hit him ~ on the ear** le dio en la oreja precisamente; **~ on!** ¡acertado!; **the answer was ~ on** (*Brit*) la respuesta era muy acertada; **she came ~ on time** (*Brit*) llegó a la hora exacta; **it was ~ on target** (*Brit*) dio en el mismo centro del blanco.

3 *n* (**a**) (*explosion*) estallido *m*, detonación *f*; (*of door*) portazo *m*; (*any loud noise*) golpe *m*, estrépito *m*; **the door closed with a ~** la puerta se cerró de golpe; **not with a ~ but a whimper** no con un estallido sino con un sollozo; **it started off with a ~*** empezó con muchísimo ímpetu; **it all went with a ~*** todo fue a las mil maravillas.

(**b**) (*blow*) golpe *m* (violento).

(**c**) (*also* **~s**) (*US*) flequillo *m*.

4 *vt* (**a**) (*explode*) volar, hacer estallar; *door* cerrar de golpe; *table etc* dar golpes en; (*strike*) golpear; **to ~ one's**

fist on the table dar un puñetazo en la mesa; **I ~ed his head on the table** di con su cabeza en la mesa.
(**b**) (**) joder**.
5 *vi* hacer explosión, estallar; hacer estrépito; **the balloons were ~ing** estallaban los globos; **to ~ on a door** dar golpes en una puerta; **downstairs a door ~ed** abajo se cerró de golpe una puerta.
6 *vr*: **he ~ed himself against the wall** dio consigo contra la pared.
◆**bang about, bang around** *vi* moverse ruidosamente.
◆**bang away** *vi* (*guns*) disparar estrepitosamente; (*workman*) martillear, dar martillazos; **she was ~ing away on the piano** aporreaba el piano.
◆**bang down** *vt receiver* colgar de golpe; **he ~ed it down on the table** lo arrojó violentamente sobre la mesa.
◆**bang into** *vt* chocar (violentamente) con; (*meet*) tropezar con, topar con.
◆**bang out** *vt tune* tocar ruidosamente.
◆**bang together** *vt heads* hacer chocar; **I'll ~ your heads together!** ¡voy a dar un coscorrón a los dos!; **the leaders should have their heads ~ed together** hay que obligar a los jefes a que lleguen a un acuerdo.
◆**bang up*** *vt* (**a**) (*ruin*) estropear. (**b**) (*prisoner*) encerrar (en su celda).
banger ['bæŋəʳ] *n* (**a**) (*firework*) petardo *m*.
(**b**) (*Brit*‡: *Aut*) cacharro *m*, coche *m* destartalado.
(**c**) (*Brit*‡: *Culin*) = **sausage.**
Bangkok [bæŋ'kɒk] *n* Bangkok *m*.
Bangladesh [ˌbæŋglə'deʃ] *n* Bangladesh *m*.
Bangladeshi [ˌbæŋglə'deʃɪ] **1** *adj* bangladesí. **2** *n* bangladesí *mf*.
bangle ['bæŋgl] *n* ajorca *f*, brazalete *m*, esclava *f* (*LAm*).
bang-up‡ ['bæŋʌp] *adj* (*US*) tope, guay‡.
banish ['bænɪʃ] *vt* desterrar (*also fig*); **to ~ a topic from one's conversation** proscribir un tema de su conversación.
banishment ['bænɪʃmənt] *n* destierro *m*.
banisters ['bænɪstəz] *npl* barandilla *f*, pasamanos *m*.
banjax‡ ['bændʒæks] *vt* (*US*) dar una paliza a.
banjo ['bændʒəʊ] *n, pl* **banjos** *or* **banjoes** banjo *m*.
bank[1] [bæŋk] **1** *n* (**a**) (*of river etc*) ribera *f*, orilla *f*, ribo *m* (*And*); (*small hill*) loma *f*; (*of earth*) terraplén *m*; (*sandbank*) banco *m*; (*of snow, clouds*) montón *m*; (*rise in road*) cuesta *f*; (*escarpment*) escarpa *f*; (*Rail*) terraplén *m*; (*of switches*) batería *f*, serie *f*; (*of phones etc*) equipo *m*, batería *f*; (*of oars*) hilera *f*.
(**b**) (*Aer*) inclinación *f* lateral.
2 *vt* (**a**) (*also freq* **to ~ up**) (*pile*) amontonar; *fire* cubrir.
(**b**) (*Aer*) ladear.
3 *vi* (**a**) (*Aer*) ladearse. (**b**) **to ~ up** (*clouds etc*) amontonarse.
bank[2] [bæŋk] (*Comm, Fin*) **1** *n* banco *m*; (*in games*) banca *f*; **B~ of England** Banco *m* de Inglaterra; **B~ of International Settlements** (*US*) Banco *m* Internacional de Pagos; **B~ of Spain** Banco *m* de España; **to break the ~** hacer saltar (*or* quebrar) la banca.
2 *attr* bancario; **~ acceptance** letra *f* de cambio; **~ account** cuenta *f* bancaria, cuenta *f* de banco; **~ balance** saldo *m*; **this won't be good for my ~ balance** esto no será bueno para mi situación financiera; **~ bill** (*Brit*) letra *f* de cambio, (*US*) billete *m* de banco; **~ charges** (*Brit*) comisión *f* por servicio bancario; **~ credit** crédito *m* bancario; **~ deposits** depósitos *mpl* bancarios; **~ draft** letra *f* de cambio; **~ giro** giro *m* bancario; **~ holiday** (*Brit*) día *m* festivo (*en que están cerrados los bancos y el comercio en general*); **~ loan** préstamo *m* bancario; **~ manager** director *m*, -ora *f* de banco; **~ rate** tipo *m* bancario, tasa *f* de descuento bancario; **~ run** (*US*) asedio *m* de un banco; **~ statement** estado *m* de cuentas; **~ transfer** transferencia *f* bancaria.
3 *vt* depositar, ingresar.
4 *vi*: **we ~ with Smith** tenemos la cuenta en el banco Smith.
◆**bank on** *vt* contar con; **don't ~ on it** sería prudente no contar con eso, no puedes estar tan seguro de eso.
bankable ['bæŋkəbl] *adj idea etc* válido, valedero.
bank-book ['bæŋkbʊk] *n* libreta *f* (de depósitos); (*in savings bank*) cartilla *f*.
bank-card ['bæŋkkɑːd] *n* tarjeta *f* bancaria.
bank-clerk ['bæŋkklɑːk] *n* (*Brit*) empleado *m*, -a *f* de banco.
banker ['bæŋkəʳ] *n* banquero *m*; **~'s draft** letra *f* bancaria; **~'s order** (*Brit*) orden *f* bancaria; **~'s reference** referencia *f* bancaria; **to be ~** (*at games*) tener la banca.
banking[1] ['bæŋkɪŋ] *n* (*of earth*) terraplén *m*, rampas *fpl*.
banking[2] ['bæŋkɪŋ] **1** *n* (*Comm, Fin*) banca *f*. **2** *attr* bancario; **~ account** cuenta *f* bancaria; **~ hours** horas *fpl* bancarias.
banking-house ['bæŋkɪŋhaʊs] *n, pl* **banking-houses** ['bæŋkɪŋhaʊzɪz] casa *f* de banca.
banknote ['bæŋknəʊt] *n* (*Brit*) billete *m* de banco.
bank-robber ['bæŋkˌrɒbəʳ] *n* ladrón *m* de banco.
bankroll ['bæŋkrəʊl] (*US*) **1** *n* fortuna *f*. **2** *vt* financiar.
bankrupt ['bæŋkrʌpt] **1** *adj* quebrado, insolvente; **to be ~** estar en quiebra; **to be ~ of ideas** estar totalmente falto de ideas; **to be declared ~** declararse en quiebra; **to go ~** quebrar, (*esp fraudulently*) hacer bancarrota.
2 *n* quebrado *m*; **~'s estate** activo *m* (*or* masa *f*) de la quiebra.
3 *vt* hacer quebrar, arruinar.
4 *vr*: **to ~ o.s. buying pictures** arruinarse comprando cuadros.
bankruptcy ['bæŋkrəptsɪ] *n* quiebra *f*, insolvencia *f*, (*esp fraudulent*) bancarrota *f*; (*fig*) falta *f* (*of* de); **~ court** (*Brit*) tribunal *m* de quiebras; **~ proceedings** juicio *m* de insolvencia; **moral ~** insolvencia *f* moral.
banner ['bænəʳ] *n* bandera *f*, estandarte *m*; (*carried in demonstration*) pancarta *f*; **~ headlines** titulares *mpl* sensacionales.
bannisters ['bænɪstəz] *npl* = **banisters.**
banns [bænz] *npl* amonestaciones *fpl*, banas *fpl* (*Mex*); **to call** (*or* **put up**) **the ~** correr (*or* leer) las amonestaciones.
banquet ['bæŋkwɪt] **1** *n* banquete *m*. **2** *vt* festejar, banquetear. **3** *vi* banquetear.
banqueting-hall ['bæŋkwɪtɪŋˌhɔːl] *n* comedor *m* de gala, sala *f* de banquetes.
banshee ['bæn'ʃiː] *n* (*Ir*) *hada que anuncia una muerte en la familia*.
bantam ['bæntəm] *n* gallinilla *f* de Bantam.
bantam-weight ['bæntəmweɪt] *n* peso *m* gallo.
banter ['bæntəʳ] **1** *n* burlas *fpl*, zumba *f*; comentarios *mpl* sin importancia. **2** *vt* chancearse con, tomar el pelo a. **3** *vi* chancearse, bromear.
bantering ['bæntərɪŋ] **1** *adj tone* de chanza. **2** *n* = **banter 1.**
Bantu [ˌbæn'tuː] *adj, n* bantú *mf*.
BAOR *n abbr of* **British Army of the Rhine.**
baptism ['bæptɪzəm] *n* (*in general*) bautismo *m*; (*act*) bautizo *m*; **~ of fire** bautismo *m* de fuego.
baptismal [bæp'tɪzməl] *adj* bautismal.
Baptist ['bæptɪst] *n* bautista *mf*; **the ~ Church** la Iglesia Bautista; **St John the ~** San Juan Bautista.
baptize [bæp'taɪz] *vt* bautizar (*also fig*); **he was ~d John** le bautizaron con el nombre de Juan.
bar [bɑːʳ] **1** *n* (**a**) (*gen, of metal, in harbour, Her*) barra *f*; (*on door*) tranca *f*; (*lever*) palanca *f*; (*of soap*) pastilla *f*; (*of chocolate*) pastilla *f*, tableta *f*; (*tavern*) bar *m*, cantina *f* (*CAm, Mex*); (*counter*) bar *m*, barra *f*, mostrador *m*; (*of public opinion*) tribunal *m*; (*Mus*) compás *m*; (*Jur*) **the B~** (*persons*) el colegio de abogados, (*profession*) el foro, la Barra (*Mex*), la abogacía; **prisoner at the ~** acusado *m*, -a *f*; **to be called to the B~** (*Brit*) recibirse de abogado; **to be behind ~s** estar entre rejas; **to put sb behind ~s** meter a uno entre rejas; **to spend 3 years behind ~s** pasar 3 años entre rejas. (**b**) (*hindrance*) obstáculo *m*, impedimento *m* (*to* para); (*ban*) prohibición *f* (*on* de); **it is a ~ to progress** es un obstáculo para el progreso.
2 *vt* (**a**) *door* atrancar; *road* obstruir. (**b**) (*fig*) *progress* impedir; (*ban*) prohibir; (*exclude*) excluir (*from* de); **to ~ sb from doing sth** prohibir a uno hacer algo; **to be ~red from a club** ser excluido de un club.
3 *prep* excepto, con excepción de; **all ~ 2** todos con excepción de 2; **~ none** sin excluir a ninguno, sin excepción; **it was all over ~ the shouting** con eso terminaba en efecto el asunto.
barb [bɑːb] *n* (**a**) (*of arrow, hook*) lengüeta *f*; (*of feather*) barba *f*; (*Zool*) púa *f*. (**b**) (*fig*) flecha *f*, dardo *m*; observación *f* mordaz.
Barbadian [bɑː'beɪdɪən] **1** *adj* de Barbados. **2** *n* nativo *m*, -a *f* (*or* habitante *mf*) de Barbados.
Barbados [bɑː'beɪdɒs] *n* Barbados *m*.
barbarian [bɑː'bɛərɪən] **1** *adj* bárbaro. **2** *n* bárbaro *m*, -a *f*.
barbaric [bɑː'bærɪk] *adj* bárbaro, barbárico; de ruda magnificencia.
barbarism ['bɑːbərɪzəm] *n* barbarie *f*; (*Gram*) barbarismo *m*.
barbarity [bɑː'bærɪtɪ] *n* barbaridad *f*.
barbarous ['bɑːbərəs] *adj* bárbaro.
barbarously ['bɑːbərəslɪ] *adv* bárbaramente.
Barbary ['bɑːbərɪ] *n* Berbería *f*; **~ ape** macaco *m*.
barbecue ['bɑːbɪkjuː] **1** *n* barbacoa *f*, asado *m* (*LAm*); **~**

sauce salsa *f* para barbacoa. **2** *vt* preparar en barbacoa.
barbed [bɑːbd] *adj arrow etc* armado de lengüetas; *criticism* incisivo, mordaz.
barbed wire ['bɑːbd'waɪəʳ] *n* alambre *m* de espino, (*Mil*) alambre *m* de púas; **barbed-wire entanglement** alambrada *f*; **barbed-wire fence** cercado *m* de alambrado (*or* de alambre de espino).
barbel ['bɑːbəl] *n* (*Anat*) barbilla *f*, cococha *f*; (*Fish*) barbo *m*.
barbell ['bɑːbel] *n* (*US Sport*) haltera *f*, pesas *fpl*.
barber ['bɑːbəʳ] *n* peluquero *m*, barbero *m*; **~'s** peluquería *f*; **The B~ of Seville** El barbero de Sevilla.
barbershop ['bɑːbəʃɒp] *n* (*US*) barbería *f*; **~ quartet** cuarteto *m* vocal armónico.
barbican ['bɑːbɪkən] *n* barbacana *f*.
barbitone ['bɑːbɪtəʊn] *n* barbitúrico *m*.
barbiturate [bɑː'bɪtjʊrɪt] *n* barbitúrico *m*.
barbs‡ [bɑːbz] *npl* (*Drugs*) barbitúricos *mpl*.
barcarol(l)e [ˌbɑːkə'rəʊl] *n* barcarola *f*.
Barcelona [ˌbɑːsə'ləʊnə] *n* Barcelona *f*.
bar-chart ['bɑːˌtʃɑːt] *n* cuadro *m* de barras.
bar-code ['bɑːˌkəʊd] *n* código *m* de barras.
bard [bɑːd] *n* bardo *m*; **the B~** (*Shakespeare*) el Vate; **the B~ of Avon** el Cisne del Avon.
bare [bɛəʳ] **1** *adj* desnudo; *head* descubierto; *landscape* pelado; *ground* raso; *room* (casi) desprovisto de muebles; *style* escueto, desnudo; **~ to the waist** desnudo hasta la cintura; **in one's ~ skin** en la misma piel; **with one's head ~** sin sombrero; **with the breasts ~** con los senos al desnudo; **with one's ~ hands** con las manos desnudas; **~ of** desprovisto de; **the trees are ~** los árboles están sin hojas; **the pantry is ~** la despensa está vacía; **the ~ bones (of a matter)** los puntos esenciales, lo esencial, el mínimo esencial; **to earn a ~ living** ganar lo justo para vivir; **the ~ minimum** lo justo, lo indispensable; **the ~ necessities** las cosas más indispensables; **there's a ~ chance** hay una remota posibilidad; **by a ~ majority** por una mayoría escasa; **the ~ thought frightens me** me horroriza sólo pensar en ello; **to lay ~** poner al descubierto, poner al desnudo.
2 *vt* desnudar; descubrir; **to ~ one's head** descubrirse; **the dog ~d its teeth** el perro mostró los dientes.
bareback ['bɛəbæk] *adv* a pelo, sin montura; **to ride ~** montar a pelo.
bare-bones ['bɛə'beʊnz] *adj* (*US*) muy limitado.
barefaced ['bɛəfeɪst] *adj* descarado, fresco; **a ~ lie** una mentira descarada; **it's ~ robbery** es un robo descarado.
barefoot(ed) ['bɛə'fʊt(ɪd)] *adj, adv* descalzo, con los pies desnudos.
bareheaded ['bɛə'hedɪd] *adj* descubierto, con la cabeza descubierta, sin sombrero.
barelegged ['bɛə'legɪd] *adj* en pernetas.
barely ['bɛəlɪ] *adv* **(a)** (*scarcely*) apenas; **~ possible** apenas posible; **it was ~ enough** casi no bastaba. **(b) a ~ furnished room** un cuarto escasamente amueblado.
bareness ['bɛənɪs] *n* desnudez *f*.
barf‡ [bɑːf] *vi* (*US*) arrojar*.
barfly* ['bɑːflaɪ] *n* (*US*) ≈ culo *m* de café*.
bargain ['bɑːgɪn] **1** *n* **(a)** (*agreement*) pacto *m*, trato *m*; (*business deal*) negocio *m*; (*advantageous deal*) negocio *m* ventajoso; **into the ~** por añadidura, además, y encima; **it's a ~!** ¡trato hecho!; **to drive a good ~** hacer un buen trato; **you drive a hard ~** Vd sabe regatear; **to make** (*or* **strike**) **a ~** cerrar un trato; **I'll make a ~ with you** hagamos un pacto.
(b) (*cheap thing*) ganga *f*; **~s** (*Comm*) artículos *mpl* de ocasión, oportunidades *fpl*; **it's a real ~** es una verdadera ganga.
2 *attr* de ocasión; **~ basement, ~ counter** sección *f* de rebajas; **~ offer** oferta *f* especial; **~ price** precio *m* de ganga, precio *m* de saldo; **~ sale** saldo *m*.
3 *vt*: **to ~ away** malvender, malbaratar.
4 *vi* negociar (*about* sobre, *for* para obtener, *with* con); (*haggle*) regatear; **I wasn't ~ing for that** yo no contaba con eso; **I wouldn't ~ on it** es mejor no contar con eso; **he got more than he ~ed for** le resultó peor de lo que esperaba.
bargain-hunter ['bɑːgɪnˌhʌntəʳ] *n* cazador *m*, -ora *f* de rebajas; **she's a real ~** siempre va a por saldos.
bargain-hunting ['bɑːgɪnˌhʌntɪŋ] *n* caza *f* de rebajas; **I enjoy ~** me gusta ir de rebajas.
bargaining ['bɑːgɪnɪŋ] *n* negociación *f*; (*haggling*) regateo *m*; **~ power** fuerza *f* en el negocio; **~ table** mesa *m* de negociaciones.
barge [bɑːdʒ] **1** *n* barcaza *f*; (*towed*) lancha *f* a remolque, gabarra *f*; (*ceremonial*) falúa *f*.
2 *vt* (*) empujar; (*Sport*) atajar.
◆**barge about** *vi* moverse pesadamente, dar tumbos.
◆**barge in** *vi* entrar sin pedir permiso, irrumpir; (*fig*) entrometerse; **to ~ in on a conversation** entrometerse en una conversación.
◆**barge into** *vt person* chocar contra, dar contra; *room* irrumpir en.
bargee [bɑː'dʒiː] *n* (*Brit*) gabarrero *m*.
bargepole ['bɑːdʒpəʊl] *n* bichero *m*; **I wouldn't touch it with a ~** no lo quiero ver ni de lejos.
bargirl* ['bɑːgɜːl] *n* (*US*) camarera *f* de barra.
barhopping ['bɑːˌhɒpɪŋ] *n* (*US*): **to go ~** ir de bar en bar, ir de copeo*.
baritone ['bærɪtəʊn] *n* barítono *m*.
barium ['bɛərɪəm] *n* bario *m*; **~ meal** sulfato *m* de bario.
bark[1] [bɑːk] (*Bot*) **1** *n* corteza *f*. **2** *vt tree* descortezar; *skin* raer, raspar.
bark[2] [bɑːk] **1** *n* ladrido *m*; (*) tos *f* fuerte, tos *f* molesta; **his ~ is worse than his bite** perro que ladra no muerde.
2 *vt*: **to ~ (out)** *order* escupir, dar en un tono muy brusco.
3 *vi* ladrar (*at* a); (*) toser; *V* **tree**.
bark[3] [bɑːk] *n* (*liter, Poet*) barco *m*.
barkeeper ['bɑːˌkiːpəʳ] *n* (*US*) tabernero *m*, -a *f*.
barking ['bɑːkɪŋ] *n* ladridos *mpl*, ladrar *m*.
barley ['bɑːlɪ] *n* cebada *f*.
barleyfield ['bɑːlɪfiːld] *n* cebadal *m*.
barley-sugar ['bɑːlɪˌʃʊgəʳ] *n* azúcar *m* cande.
barley-water ['bɑːlɪˌwɔːtəʳ] *n* (*esp Brit*) hordiate *m*.
barmaid ['bɑːmeɪd] *n* camarera *f*, moza *f* de taberna (*LAm*).
barman ['bɑːmən] *n, pl* **barmen** ['bɑːmen] barman *m*.
Bar Mitzvah, bar mitzvah [bɑː'mɪtsvə] *n* Bar Mitzvah *m*.
barmy‡ ['bɑːmɪ] *adj* (*Brit*) lelo, gilí*; **you must be ~!** ¿estás loco?
barn [bɑːn] *n* granero *m*, troje *f*; (*US*) establo *m*, cuadra *f*; (*US: for buses etc*) parque *m*, garaje *m*; **a great ~ of a house** una casa enorme, un caserón.
barnacle ['bɑːnəkl] *n* percebe *m*.
barndance ['bɑːnˌdɑːns] *n* (*esp US*) baile *m* campesino.
barndoor ['bɑːn'dɔːʳ] *n* puerta *f* de granero; **~ fowls** aves *fpl* de corral.
barney ['bɑːnɪ] *n* (*Brit*) bronca *f*.
barn-owl ['bɑːnˌaʊl] *n* lechuza *f*.
barnstorm ['bɑːnstɔːm] *vi* (*US*) hacer una campaña electoral por el campo.
barnyard ['bɑːnjɑːd] *n* corral *m*; **~ fowls** aves *fpl* de corral.
barometer [bə'rɒmɪtəʳ] *n* barómetro *m*.
barometric ['bærəʊ'metrɪk] *adj* barométrico; **~ pressure** presión *f* barométrica.
baron ['bærən] *n* **(a)** barón *m*; (*fig*) magnate *m*, potentado *m*. **(b) ~ of beef** solomillo *m*.
baroness ['bærənɪs] *n* baronesa *f*.
baronet ['bærənɪt] *n* baronet *m*.
baronetcy ['bærənɪtsɪ] *n* dignidad *f* del baronet.
baronial [bə'rəʊnɪəl] *adj* baronial.
barony ['bærənɪ] *n* baronía *f*.
baroque [bə'rɒk] **1** *adj* barroco; (*fig*) complicado; grotesco. **2** *n* barroco *m*.
barrack ['bærək] *vt* abuchear, dar bronca a; lanzar improperios a.
barracking ['bærəkɪŋ] *n* abucheo *m*, bronca *f*; improperios *mpl*.
barrack-room ['bærəkrʊm] **1** *n* dormitorio *m* de tropa. **2** *adj* cuartelero; **~ ballad** canción *f* cuartelera; **~ lawyer** protestón *m*, -ona *f*.
barracks ['bærəks] *npl* **(a)** (*Mil*) cuartel *m*; **to be confined to ~** estar bajo arresto en el cuartel, ser acuartelado.
(b) (*house*) caserón *m*; **a great ~ of a place** (*Brit*) una casa enorme, un caserón.
barrack-square ['bærək'skwɛəʳ] *n* plaza *f* de armas.
barracuda [ˌbærə'kjuːdə] *n* barracuda *f*.
barrage ['bærɑːʒ] *n* presa *f*; (*Mil*) cortina *f* de fuego, barrera *f* (de artillería); (*of balloons etc*) barrera *f*; **a ~ of noise** un estrépito; **a ~ of questions** un aluvión de preguntas; **there was a ~ of protests** estallaron ruidosamente las protestas.
barrage-balloon ['bærɑːʒbəˌluːn] *n* globo *m* de barrera.
barred [bɑːʳd] *adj window etc* enrejado, con reja.
barrel ['bærəl] *n* **(a)** tonel *m*, cuba *f*, barril *m*; (*of oil*) barril *m*; (*Tech*) cilindro *m*, tambor *m*; **to have sb over a ~*** tener a uno con el agua al cuello; **to scrape the (bottom of the) ~** rebañar las últimas migas.
(b) (*of gun, pen*) cañón *m*.

barrel-chested [ˈbærəlˈtʃestɪd] *adj* de pecho fuerte y grueso.
barrel-organ [ˈbærəl,ɔːgən] *n* organillo *m*.
barrel-vault [ˈbærəl,vɔːlt] *n* bóveda *f* de cañón.
barren [ˈbærən] *adj* estéril, árido; *woman* estéril; ~ **of** falto de, desprovisto de.
barrenness [ˈbærənnɪs] *n* esterilidad *f*, aridez *f*.
barrette [bəˈret] *n* (*US*) pasador *m* (para el pelo).
barricade [,bærɪˈkeɪd] **1** *n* barricada *f*. **2** *vt* barrear, cerrar con barricadas. **3** *vr*: **to ~ o.s. in a house** hacerse fuerte en una casa.
barrier [ˈbærɪəʳ] *n* barrera *f* (*also fig*: *to* a, para); ~ **cream** crema *f* protectora.
barring [ˈbɑːrɪŋ] *prep* excepto, salvo; **we shall be there ~ accidents** iremos si Dios quiere.
barrister [ˈbærɪstəʳ] *n* (*Brit*) abogado *mf* (*que tiene derecho a alegar en los tribunales superiores*).
bar-room [ˈbɑː,rʊm] *n* (*US*) bar *m*, taberna *f*; ~ **brawl** pendencia *f* de taberna.
barrow[1] [ˈbærəʊ] *n* (*Hist*) túmulo *m*.
barrow[2] [ˈbærəʊ] *n* carretilla *f*, carretón *m* de mano.
barrow-boy [ˈbærəʊbɔɪ] *n* vendedor *m* callejero.
barstool [ˈbɑː,stuːl] *n* taburete *m* (de bar).
Bart [bɑːt] (*Brit*) *abbr of* **Baronet.**
bartender [ˈbɑːtendəʳ] *n* barman *m*.
barter [ˈbɑːtəʳ] **1** *n* permuta *f*, trueque *m*. **2** *vt* permutar, trocar (*for* por, con); **to ~ away** malvender. **3** *vi* hacer negocios de trueque, cambiar unos géneros por otros.
Bartholomew [bɑːˈθɒləmjuː] *nm* Bartolomé.
barytone [ˈbærɪtəʊn] *n* viola *f* de bordón.
basal [ˈbeɪsl] *adj* (*lit, fig*) fundamental, básico, esencial; (*Physiol*) basal.
basalt [ˈbæsɔːlt] *n* basalto *m*.
base[1] [beɪs] **1** *n* base *f*; (*Archit*) basa *f*; (‡) cocaína *f* (para fumar); **to get to first ~** (*fig*) alcanzar la primera meta, dar el primer paso; **he's way off ~** (*US**) está totalmente equivocado.
2 *attr* base; ~ **camp** campamento *m* de base; ~ **coat** (*of paint*) primera capa *f*, capa *f* selladora; ~ **form** (*Ling*) base *f* derivativa; ~ **(lending) rate** tipo *m* de interés base; ~ **period** período *m* base.
3 *vt* basar, fundar (*on* en); **to be ~d on** estar basado en, fundarse en; (*Mil*) **we were ~d on Malta** tuvimos nuestra base en Malta; **the post will be ~d in Barcelona** la base del empleo será en Barcelona; **where are you ~d now?** ¿dónde estás establecido ahora?
4 *vr*: **I ~ myself on the following facts** me apoyo en los hechos siguientes.
base[2] [beɪs] *adj* bajo, infame, vil; *metal* bajo de ley, de baja ley.
baseball [ˈbeɪsbɔːl] *n* béisbol *m*.
baseboard [ˈbeɪsbɔːd] *n* (*US*) rodapié *m*.
-based [beɪst] *in compounds*: *eg* **a London~ company** una compañía con base en Londres; **shore~** con base en tierra.
Basel [ˈbɑːzəl] *n* Basilea *f*.
baseless [ˈbeɪslɪs] *adj* infundado.
baseline [ˈbeɪslaɪn] *n* (*Survey*) línea *f* de base; (*Tennis*) línea *f* de saque, línea *f* de fondo.
basely [ˈbeɪslɪ] *adv* (*V adj*) despreciablemente, bajamente, ruínmente.
baseman [ˈbeɪsmən] *n*, *pl* **basemen** [ˈbeɪsmen] (*Baseball*) hombre *m* de base.
basement [ˈbeɪsmənt] *n* sótano *m*.
baseness [ˈbeɪsnɪs] *n* bajeza *f*, vileza *f*.
bases [ˈbeɪsiːz] *npl of* **basis.**
bash* [bæʃ] **1** *n* (**a**) golpe *m*, palo *m*.
(**b**) (*fig*) intento *m*; **to have a ~ at** probar, intentar, echar un tiento a; **go on, have a ~!** ¡vamos, trátalo tú!
(**c**) (*party*) fiesta *f*, juerga *f*.
2 *vt* golpear; aporrear; *person* pegar, (*also* **to ~ about, to ~ up**) dar una paliza a.
3 *vi*: **to ~ away = to bang away.**
◆**bash in*** *vt door* echar abajo; *hat, car* abollar; *lid, cover* forzar a golpes, cargarse a golpes*; **to ~ sb's head in** aporrear a uno, mamporrear* a uno.
◆**bash on*** *vi* continuar (a pesar de todo); **~ on!** ¡adelante!
bashful [ˈbæʃfʊl] *adj* tímido, vergonzoso, apenado (*LAm*).
bashfully [ˈbæʃfəlɪ] *adv* tímidamente.
bashfulness [ˈbæʃfʊlnɪs] *n* timidez *f*, vergüenza *f*.
bashing* [ˈbæʃɪŋ] *n* tunda *f*, paliza *f*; **to give sb a ~** dar una paliza a uno; **the team took a real ~** el equipo recibió una paliza.
basic[1] [ˈbeɪsɪk] **1** *adj* básico (*also Chem*), fundamental; ~ **airman** (*US*) soldado *m* raso de la aviación; ~ **pay** sueldo *m* básico; ~ **rate** (*Fin*) interés *m* base; ~ **slag** escoria *f* básica; ~ **training** entrenamiento *m* básico; ~ **turn** (*ski*) giro *m* básico, giro *m* elemental; ~ **wage** salario *m* básico. **2** *n*: **the ~s** los fundamentos, los elementos básicos.
basically [ˈbeɪsɪklɪ] *adv* fundamentalmente, en el fondo, esencialmente.
basil [ˈbæzl] *n* albahaca *f*.
basilica [bəˈzɪlɪkə] *n* basílica *f*.
basilisk [ˈbæzɪlɪsk] *n* basilisco *m*.
basin [ˈbeɪsn] *n* (*in kitchen*) bol *m*, tazón *m*, cuenco *m*; (*washbasin*) jofaina *f*, palangana *f*; (*large fixed washbasin*) lavabo *m*; (*of fountain*) taza *f*; (*Geog*) cuenca *f*; (*of port*) dársena *f*.
basis [ˈbeɪsɪs] *n*, *pl* **bases** [ˈbeɪsiːz] base *f*; **on a daily ~** a base diaria; **on the ~ of** a base de; partiendo de una base de.
bask [bɑːsk] *vi* asolearse; **to ~ in the sun** tomar el sol; **to ~ in the heat** disfrutar del calor; **he ~s in flattery** le encantan los elogios.
basket [ˈbɑːskɪt] *n* cesta *f*; (*big*) cesto *m*; (*two-handled*) canasta *f*; (*hamper*) banasta *f*, capacho *m*; (*two-handled, for earth etc*) espuerta *f*; (*pannier*) sera *f*, serón *m*; (*of balloon*) barquilla *f*; ~ **case** (*US*) caso *m* desahuciado; ~ **chair** silla *f* de mimbre; ~ **of currencies** cesta *f* de monedas, canasta *f* de divisas.
basketball [ˈbɑːskɪtbɔːl] *n* baloncesto *m*, básket *m*.
basketball player [ˈbɑːskɪt,bɔːl,pleɪəʳ] *n* jugador *m*, -ora *f* de baloncesto.
basketwork [ˈbɑːskɪtwɜːk] *n* cestería *f*.
Basle [bɑːl] *n* Basilea *f*.
Basque [bæsk] **1** *adj* vasco. **2** *n* (**a**) vasco *m*, -a *f*. (**b**) (*Ling*) vasco *m*, vascuence *m*, euskera *m*.
Basque Country [ˈbæskˈkʌntrɪ] *n* País *m* Vasco, Euskadi *m*.
Basque Provinces [ˈbæskˈprɒvɪnsɪz] *npl* las Vascongadas.
bas-relief [ˈbæsrɪ,liːf] *n* bajorrelieve *m*.
bass[1] [beɪs] (*Mus*) **1** *adj* bajo; ~ **baritone** barítono *m* bajo; ~ **clef** clave *f* de fa; ~ **drum** bombo *m*; ~ **flute** flauta *m* contralto; ~ **guitar** guitarra *f* baja; ~ **horn** trompa *f* baja; ~ **strings** instrumentos *mpl* bajos de cuerda; ~ **trombone** trombón *m* bajo; ~ **tuba** tuba *f*; ~ **viol** viola *f* de gamba baja. **2** *n* (*voice, note*) bajo *m*; (*instrument*) contrabajo *m*.
bass[2] [bæs] *n* (*Fish*) róbalo *m*.
basset [ˈbæsɪt] *n* perro *m* basset.
bassist [ˈbeɪsɪst] *n* (*Mus*) bajista *mf*, bajo *m*.
bassoon [bəˈsuːn] *n* fagot *m*.
basso profundo [,bæsəʊprəˈfʊndəʊ] *n* bajo *m* profundo.
bastard [ˈbɑːstəd] **1** *adj* bastardo. **2** *n* bastardo *m*, -a *f*; **you ~!‡** ¡cabrón!‡; **you old ~!‡‡** ¡eh, hijoputa!‡‡; **that silly ~‡** ese memo‡; **all Slobodians are ~s‡** todos los eslobodios son cabrones‡; **this job is a real ~‡** esta faena es la monda‡.
bastardized [ˈbɑːstədaɪzd] *adj language* corrupto.
bastardy [ˈbɑːstədɪ] *n* bastardía *f*.
baste[1] [beɪst] *vt* (*Culin*) pringar.
baste[2] [beɪst] *vt* (**a**) (*Sew*) hilvanar. (**b**) (*: *beat*) dar de palos a.
basting [ˈbeɪstɪŋ] *n* (**a**) (*Sew*) hilván *m*. (**b**) (*: *beating*) paliza *f*, zurra *f*.
bastion [ˈbæstɪən] *n* bastión *m*, baluarte *m* (*also fig*).
Basutoland [bəˈsuːtəʊlænd] *n* (*Hist*) Basutolandia *f*.
BASW *n abbr of* **British Association of Social Workers** *sindicato de empleados de los servicios sociales*.
bat[1] [bæt] *n* (*Zool*) murciélago *m*; **old ~*** bruja* *f*; **to be ~s*, to have ~s in the belfry*** estar chiflado; **to go like a ~ out of hell*** ir como alma que lleva el diablo.
bat[2] [bæt] **1** *n* (**a**) (*eg cricket* ~) maza *f*, paleta *f*; (*Baseball*) bate *m*; **off one's own ~** por sí solo, por iniciativa propia; **right off the ~** (*US*) de repente, sin deliberación. (**b**) (*: *blow*) golpe *m*.
2 *vt* (*) golpear, apalear; (*US**: *fig*) **to ~ sth around** (*discuss*) discutir acerca de algo; **to ~ sth out** hacer algo a toda leche‡.
3 *vi* (*Baseball*) batear.
bat[3] [bæt] **1** *n*: **in the ~ of an eyelid** en un santiamén. **2** *vt*: **without ~ting an eyelid** (*Brit*), **without ~ting an eye** (*US*) sin inmutarse.
batch [bætʃ] *n* (**a**) colección *f*, serie *f*, grupo *m*, cantidad *f*, lote *m*, montoncito *m*; (*of papers*) lío *m*; (*Culin*) hornada *f*; ~ **production** producción *f* por lotes. (**b**) (*Comput*) lote *m*; **in ~ mode** en tratamiento por lotes; ~ **processing** tratamiento *m* por lotes, proceso *m* por lotes.
bated [ˈbeɪtɪd] *adj*: **with ~ breath** con aliento entrecortado.
bath [bɑːθ] **1** *n*, *pl* **baths** [bɑːðz] (**a**) (*container*) baño *m*,

bañera *f*, tina *f* (*LAm*); (*swimming pool*) piscina *f*. (**b**) (*act*) baño *m*; **to have** (*or* **take**) **a ~** tomar un baño, bañarse.

2 *vt* (*Brit*) bañar, dar un baño a.

3 *vi* (*Brit*) tomar un baño.

bathchair ['bɑːθtʃɛəʳ] *n* silla *f* de ruedas.

bathcube ['bɑːθkjuːb] *n* cubo *m* de sales para el baño.

bathe [beɪð] **1** *n* baño *m* (en el mar *etc*); **to go for a ~, to have a ~** ir a bañarse.

2 *vt* bañar; **to ~ the baby** (*US*) bañar al niño; **~d in tears** bañado en lágrimas.

3 *vi* bañarse.

bather ['beɪðəʳ] *n* bañista *mf*.

bathetic [bə'θetɪk] *adj* que pasa de lo sublime a lo trivial.

bathhouse ['bɑːθhaʊs] *n*, *pl* **bathhouses** ['bɑːθhaʊzɪz] baño *m*.

bathing ['beɪðɪŋ] *n* baños *mpl* (de mar *etc*), el bañarse; **'no ~'** 'prohibido bañarse'.

bathing-beauty ['beɪðɪŋ,bjuːtɪ] *n* sirena *f* (*or* belleza *f*) de la playa.

bathing-cap ['beɪðɪŋkæp] *n* gorro *m* de baño.

bathing-costume ['beɪðɪŋ,kɒstjuːm] *n* (*Brit*) traje *m* de baño, bañador *m*.

bathing-hut ['beɪðɪŋ,hʌt] *n* caseta *f* de playa.

bathing-machine ['beɪðɪŋmə,ʃiːn] *n* (*Hist*) caseta *f* de playa movible.

bathing-suit ['beɪðɪŋ,suːt] *n* traje *m* de baño, bañador *m*.

bathing-trunks ['beɪðɪŋ,trʌŋks] *n* (*Brit*) taparrabo *m*, bañador *m*.

bathing-wrap ['beɪðɪŋ,ræp] *n* albornoz *m*.

bathmat ['bɑːθmæt] *n* estera *f* de baño.

bathos ['beɪθɒs] *n* paso *m* de lo sublime a lo trivial.

bathrobe ['bɑːθrəʊb] *n* albornoz *m*, bata *f* de baño.

bathroom ['bɑːθrʊm] *n* cuarto *m* de baño, baño *m*; **~ cabinet** armario *m* de aseo; **~ fittings** aparatos *mpl* sanitarios; **~ scales** báscula *f* de baño.

bath-salts ['bɑːθsɒlts] *npl* sales *fpl* de baño.

bath-sheet ['bɑːθ,ʃiːt] *n* toalla *f* de baño.

bath-towel ['bɑːθtaʊəl] *n* toalla *f* de baño.

bathtub ['bɑːθtʌb] *n* (*esp US*) bañera *f*, baño *m*, bañadera *f* (*LAm*), tina *f* (*Mex*).

bathwater ['bɑːθwɔːtəʳ] *n* agua *f* del baño.

bathysphere ['bæθɪsfɪəʳ] *n* batisfera *f*.

batiste [bæ'tiːst] *n* batista *f*.

batman ['bætmən] *n*, *pl* **batmen** ['bætmen] (*Brit*) ordenanza *m*.

baton ['bætən] *n* (*Mil*) bastón *m*; (*Mus*) batuta *f*; (*in race*) testigo *m*; **~ charge** carga *f* con bastones; **~ round** bala *f* de goma.

batrachian [bə'treɪkɪən] *n* batracio *m*.

batsman ['bætsmən] *n*, *pl* **batsmen** ['bætsmen] (*Cricket*) bateador *m*.

battalion [bə'tælɪən] *n* batallón *m*.

batten ['bætn] **1** *n* alfarjía *f*, lata *f*, listón *m*; (*Naut*) junquillo *m*, sable *m*. **2** *vt*: **to ~ down the hatches** atrancar las escotillas (*also fig*).

◆batten on *vt* vivir (*etc*) a costa de, explotar, cebarse en.

batter[1] ['bætəʳ] *n* (*Culin*) batido *m* (para rebozar).

batter[2] ['bætəʳ] **1** *n* (*Baseball*) bateador *m*.

2 *vt person* apalear; (*of boxer*) magullar; (*of the elements*) embravecerse contra; (*Mil*) cañonear, bombardear; (*verbally etc*) criticar ásperamente, poner como un trapo.

◆batter (away) at *vt* dar grandes golpes en.

◆batter down, batter in *vt* derribar a palos.

battered ['bætəd] *adj* (*bruised*) magullado; (*damaged*) estropeado; maltrecho, malparado; *hat etc* ajado; **~ baby** niño *m* golpeado, niña *f* golpeada; **~ wife** mujer *f* maltratada.

battering ['bætərɪŋ] *n* (*blows*) paliza *f*; (*Mil*) bombardeo *m*; **the ~ of the waves** el golpear de las olas; **he got a ~ from the critics** los críticos le pusieron como un trapo.

battering-ram ['bætərɪŋræm] *n* ariete *m*.

battery ['bætərɪ] *n* (**a**) (*Mil*) batería *f*; **~ fire** fuego *m* de batería. (**b**) (*Elec*) (*dry*) pila *f*; (*wet*) batería *f*. (**c**) (*series*) serie *f*; (*of lights*) batería *f*, equipo *m*; (*of questions*) descarga *f*. (**d**) (*Agr*) batería *f*; **~ farming** cría *f* intensiva, cría *f* en batería; **~ hen** gallina *f* de criadero. (**e**) (*Jur*) violencia *f*, agresión *f*.

battery-charger ['bætərɪ,tʃɑːdʒəʳ] *n* cargador *m* de baterías.

battery-operated [,bætərɪ'ɒpəreɪtɪd] *adj* a pilas.

battery-set ['bætərɪ,set] *n* (*Rad*) radio *f* de pilas, transistor *m*.

battle ['bætl] **1** *n* (**a**) batalla *f*; **in ~ array, in ~ order** en formación (*or* en orden) de batalla; **to do ~** librar batalla (*with* con); **to do ~ for** luchar por; **to fight a ~** luchar; **the ~ was fought in 1346** se libró la batalla en 1346; **to join ~** trabar batalla.

(**b**) (*fig*) lucha *f* (*for control of* por el control de, *to control* por controlar); **~ royal** batalla *f* campal; (*among women*) pelotera *f*; **~ of wills** lucha *f* de voluntades; **~ of wits** duelo *m* de inteligencias; **confidence is half the ~** la confianza vale por la mitad de la batalla; **to fight a losing ~** ir perdiendo poco a poco, ir de vencida.

2 *vi* luchar (*against* contra, *for* por, *to do* por hacer); **the two armies ~d all day** los dos ejércitos se batieron todo el día; **to ~ against the wind** luchar contra el viento; **to ~ for breath** esforzarse por respirar; **to ~ on** seguir luchando.

battle-axe, (*US*) **battle-ax** ['bætlæks] *n* hacha *f* de combate; **old ~*** arpía *f*.

battlecruiser ['bætl,kruːzəʳ] *n* crucero *m* de batalla.

battlecry ['bætlkraɪ] *n* grito *m* de combate; (*fig*) lema *m*, consigna *f*.

battledore ['bætldɔːʳ] *n* raqueta *f* de bádminton; **~ and shuttlecock** *antiguo juego predecesor del bádminton.*

battledress ['bætldres] *n* traje *m* de campaña.

battlefield ['bætlfiːld] *n*, **battleground** ['bætlgraʊnd] *n* campo *m* de batalla.

battle-hardened ['bætl,hɑːdənd] *adj* endurecido por la lucha.

battlements ['bætlmənts] *npl* almenas *fpl*.

battle-scarred ['bætl,skɑːd] *adj* (*gen hum*) marcado por la lucha; deteriorado.

battleship ['bætlʃɪp] *n* acorazado *m*.

battle zone ['bætl,zəʊn] *n* zona *f* de batalla.

Battn *abbr of* **battalion** Bón, batallón *m*.

batty* ['bætɪ] *adj* lelo.

bauble ['bɔːbl] *n* chuchería *f*.

baud [bɔːd] *n* baudio *m*.

baudrate ['bɔːdreɪt] *n* velocidad *f* de transmisión.

baulk [bɔːlk] = **balk.**

bauxite ['bɔːksaɪt] *n* bauxita *f*.

Bavaria [bə'vɛərɪə] *n* Baviera *f*.

Bavarian [bə'vɛərɪən] **1** *adj* bávaro. **2** *n* bávaro *m*, -a *f*.

bawbee [bɔː'biː] *n* (*Scot and hum*) medio penique *m*.

bawd†† [bɔːd] *n* alcahueta *f*.

bawdiness ['bɔːdɪnɪs] *n* lo verde.

bawdy ['bɔːdɪ] *adj* verde.

bawdyhouse†† ['bɔːdɪhaʊs] *n*, *pl* **bawdyhouses** ['bɔːdɪhaʊzɪz] mancebía *f*.

bawl [bɔːl] **1** *vt*: **to ~ out** *song etc* cantar (*etc*) en voz muy fuerte; **to ~ sb out** echarle un rapapolvo a uno.

2 *vi* gritar, vocear, desgañitarse; hablar (*or* cantar *etc*) muy fuerte; **to ~ at** reñir en voz alta.

bay[1] [beɪ] *n* (*Bot*) laurel *m*.

bay[2] [beɪ] *n* (*Geog*) bahía *f*; (*small*) abra *f*; (*very large*) golfo *m*; **B~ of Biscay** Golfo *m* de Vizcaya.

bay[3] [beɪ] *n* (*Archit*) intercolumnio *m*; crujía *f*; (*Rail*) nave *f*; (*of window*) parte *f* salediza.

bay[4] [beɪ] **1** *n* (*bark*) ladrido *m*, aullido *m*; **at ~** acorralado; **to bring to ~** acorralar; **to keep at ~** mantener a raya. **2** *vi* ladrar, aullar.

bay[5] [beɪ] **1** *adj horse* bayo. **2** *n* caballo *m* bayo.

bayleaf ['beɪliːf] *n*, *pl* **bayleaves** ['beɪliːvz] (hoja *f* de) laurel *m*.

bayonet ['beɪənɪt] **1** *n* bayoneta *f*; **~ charge** carga *f* a la bayoneta; **~ practice** ejercicios *mpl* con bayoneta, prácticas *fpl* de bayoneta; **at ~ point** a punta de bayoneta; **with fixed ~s** con las bayonetas caladas. **2** *vt* herir (*or* matar) con la bayoneta.

Bayonne [baɪ'jɒn] *n* Bayona *f*.

bayou ['baɪjuː] *n* (*US*) pantanos *mpl*.

bay rum ['beɪ'rʌm] *n* ron *m* de laurel, ron *m* de malagueta.

bay window ['beɪ'wɪndəʊ] *n* (**a**) ventana *f* salediza, mirador *m*. (**b**) (*US**) barriga *f*.

bazaar [bə'zɑːʳ] *n* bazar *m*.

bazooka [bə'zuːkə] *n* bazuca *f*.

B.B. *n* (**a**) *abbr of* **Boys' Brigade** *organización parecida a los Boy Scouts.* (**b**) **~ gun** (*US*) carabina *f* de aire comprimido.

B.B.A. *n* (*US*) *abbr of* **Bachelor of Business Administration.**

BBB *n* (*US*) *abbr of* **Better Business Bureau.**

BBC *n abbr of* **British Broadcasting Corporation** la BBC.

bbl *abbr of* **barrels.**

BC (**a**) *adv abbr of* **Before Christ** a. de C. (**b**) *n* (*Canada*) *abbr of* **British Columbia.** (**c**) *n* (*Brit*) *abbr of* **British Coal.** (**d**) *n abbr of* **Bachelor of Commerce.**

BCD *n* (*Comput*) *abbr of* **binary-coded decimal** código *m* decimal binario.

BCG *n abbr of* **Bacillus Calmette-Guérin** *vacuna de la tuberculosis.*

BC-NET [ˌbiːsiːˈnet] *n abbr of* **Business Cooperation Network** Red *f* de Cooperación de Empresas.

B.Com. [ˌbiːˈkɒm] *n abbr of* **Bachelor of Commerce** Licenciado *m*, -a *f* en Comercio.

B/D *abbr of* **bank draft.**

b/d (*Fin*) *abbr of* **brought down** suma *f* parcial anterior.

BD *n* (**a**) (*Univ*) *abbr of* **Bachelor of Divinity** Licenciado *m*, -a *f* en Teología. (**b**) (*Fin*) *abbr of* **bills discounted** efectos *mpl* descontados.

bd (*Fin*) *abbr of* **bond** bono *m*, obligación *f*.

BDS *n* (*Univ*) *abbr of* **Bachelor of Dental Surgery** Licenciado *m*, -a *f* en Odontología.

B/E (**a**) *Fin abbr of* **bill of exchange** letra *f* de cambio. (**b**) (*Fin*) *abbr of* **Bank of England.**

be [biː] (*irr: pres* **am, is, are;** *pret* **was, were;** *ptp* **been**) **1** (*absolute*) **to ~ or not to ~** ser o no ser; **as things are** tal como están las cosas; **you're busy enough as it is** estás bastante ocupado ya; **some are and some aren't** algunos lo son y otros no; **let it ~!** ¡déjalo!; **let me ~!** ¡déjame en paz!

2 (*with noun, pronoun, numeral or verb complement* [*but V also* 7, 8, 9, 10 *below*]) ser; **I am a man** soy hombre; **he's a pianist** es pianista; **he was a communist** era comunista; **he will be pope** será papa; **I was a bullfighter for 2 days** durante 2 días fui torero; **it's a fact** es un hecho; **it is I, it's me** soy yo; **it's 8 o'clock** son las 8; **it's the 3rd of May** es el 3 de mayo; **seeing is believing** ver y creer.

3 (*with adj complement*) (**a**) (*when a permanent or essential quality is expressed*) ser; **I'm English** soy inglés; **she's tall** es alta; **it was very bad** fue malísimo; **I used to be poor but now I'm rich** antes era pobre pero ahora soy rico; **when I was young** cuando era joven; **when I'm old** cuando sea viejo.

(**b**) (*when a temporary or reversible state is indicated, also fig*) estar; **it's dirty** está sucio; **he's ill** está enfermo; **they're tired** están cansados; **the glass is empty** el vaso está vacío; **the pond is always full** el estanque siempre está lleno; **the symphony is full of tunes** la sinfonía está llena de melodías.

(**c**) (*of persons,* ser + *adj indicates a permanent quality of character,* estar + *adj indicates a more temporary mood or state*): **he's a cheerful sort** es alegre, **he's very cheerful** (*about sth*) está alegre; **he's always very smart** siempre es muy elegante, **you're very smart** (*today, for once*) ¡qué guapo estás!; **they're very happy together** son muy felices, **are you happy in your work?** ¿estás contento con tu trabajo?

(**d**) (+ *adj, impersonal*) ser; **it is possible that** ... es posible que ...; **is it certain that ...?** ¿es cierto que ...?

4 (*expressions of authorship, origin, possession, construction*) ser: **it's a Picasso** es de Picasso; **I'm from the south** soy del Sur; **it's mine** es mío; **it's of gold, it's a gold one** es de oro.

5 (*place, geographical location, temporary circumstances*) estar: **he's here** está aquí; **it's on the table** está en la mesa; **Burgos is in Spain** Burgos está en España; **the issue was in doubt** el resultado estaba en duda; **I'm in a jam** estoy en un aprieto; **to ~ on a journey** estar de viaje; **to ~ in a hurry** tener prisa; **to ~ in mourning** estar de luto.

6 (*health*) **how are you?** ¿cómo estás?; **how are you now?** ¿qué tal te encuentras ahora?; **I'm very well, thanks** estoy muy bien, gracias.

7 (*age*) **I'm 8** tengo 8 años; **how old are you?** ¿cuántos años tienes?

8 (*weather, temperatures, certain adjs*) **it is hot** (*weather*) hace calor; **I'm hot** tengo calor; **the water is hot** el agua está caliente; **it's sunny** hay sol; **it's foggy** hay niebla; **it's windy** hace viento; **to ~ hungry** tener hambre; **to ~ afraid** tener miedo.

9 (*certain expressions of time*) **we've been here a year** hace un año que estamos aquí, llevamos un año aquí; **it's a long time since I saw him** hace mucho tiempo que no le veo.

10 there is, there are hay; **there was, there were** había, hubo; **there has been, there have been** ha habido; **there may not ~ any** puede no haber ninguno.

11 (*idioms*) **so ~ it** así sea; **~ that as it may** sea como fuere; **what is it to you?** ¿a ti qué te importa?; **mother to ~** futura madre *f*; **my wife to ~** mi prometida, mi futura esposa; **what's it to ~?** (*in bar etc*) ¿qué vas a tomar?

12 (*call, come*) **has the postman been?** ¿ha venido el cartero?; **you've been and done it now!*** ¡la has hecho buena!; **that dog of yours has been and dug up my flowers!*** ¡el perro ese ha destrozado mis flores!

13 *v aux* (**a**) (*conditional sentences*) **if I were to say so** si dijera eso; **if I were you** yo en tu lugar, yo que tú.

(**b**) (*obligation*) **I am to do it** he de hacerlo; **he was to have come** tenía que venir; **what am I to say?** ¿qué he de decir?

(**c**) (*continuous tenses*) **to be** + *ger* estar + *ger, eg* **I was singing** estaba cantando, **were you waiting for me?** ¿me estabas esperando?; (*but a simple tense is used in such cases as*) **he is coming tomorrow** viene (*or* vendrá) mañana, **what are you doing?** ¿qué haces?, **I shall ~ seeing him** voy a verle, **will you ~ wanting more?** ¿vas a necesitar más?

(**d**) (**to be** + *ptp, passive*) ser + *ptp*: **the window was opened by the servant** la ventana fue abierta por el criado; **it is being studied** está siendo estudiado; (*but the passive is often replaced by a reflexive or active construction*) **the window was opened by the servant** la ventana la abrió el criado; **it is being studied** se está estudiando, está al estudio; **it is said that** se dice que, dicen que; **he was nowhere to ~ seen** no se le veía en ninguna parte; **what's to ~ done?** ¿qué hay que hacer?; **it is to ~ regretted that** es de lamentar que; **it is to ~ hoped that** es de esperar que; **it's a film not to ~ missed** es una película que no hay que perder.

(**e**) (**to be** + *ptp, state*) estar + *ptp*: **the window was open** la ventana estaba abierta; **it's made of wood** está hecho de madera; **the book is bereft of ideas** el libro está desprovisto de ideas.

beach [biːtʃ] **1** *n* playa *f*. **2** *vt* varar; *whale* embarrancar, encallar.

beachball [ˈbiːtʃˌbɔːl *n* pelota *f* de playa.

beach-buggy [ˈbiːtʃˌbʌgɪ] *n* buggy *m* (de playa).

beach-chair [ˈbiːtʃˌtʃɛəʳ] *n* (*US*) tumbona *f*.

beachcomber [ˈbiːtʃˌkəʊməʳ] *n* raquero *m*; (*US**) vago *m*, desocupado *m*.

beach-head [ˈbiːtʃhed] *n* cabeza *f* de playa.

beach-hut [ˈbiːtʃhʌt] *n* caseta *f* de playa.

beach pyjamas [ˈbiːtʃpɪˌdʒɑːməz] *npl* pijama *m* de playa.

beach umbrella [ˈbiːtʃʌmˌbrelə] *n* sombrilla *f*, parasol *m*, quitasol *m*.

beachwear [ˈbiːtʃwɛəʳ] *n* traje(s) *m*(*pl*) de playa.

beach-wrap [ˈbiːtʃˌræp] *n* bata *f*, batín *m* (de playa).

beacon [ˈbiːkən] *n* almenara *f*; (*in port*) faro *m*, fanal *m*; (*on aerodrome*) baliza *f*, aerofaro *m*; (*Rad*) radiofaro *m*; (*hill*) hacho *m*; **~ light** luz *f* de faro.

bead [biːd] *n* cuenta *f*; (*of glass*) abalorio *m*; (*of dew, sweat*) gota *f*; (*of gun*) mira *f* globular; **~s** sarta *f* de cuentas, collar *m*, (*Eccl*) rosario *m*; **to draw a ~ on** apuntar a; **to tell one's ~s** rezar el rosario.

beading [ˈbiːdɪŋ] *n* (*Archit*) astrágalo *m*, contero *m*.

beadle [ˈbiːdl] *n* (*Brit*) bedel *m*; (*Eccl*) pertiguero *m*.

beady [ˈbiːdɪ] *adj eyes* parecidos a dos gotas brillantes; pequeños y brillantes.

beady-eyed [ˈbiːdɪˈaɪd] *adj* de ojos pequeños y brillantes.

beagle [ˈbiːgl] *n* sabueso *m*, beagle *m*.

beak [biːk] *n* (**a**) pico *m*; (*****: *nose*) nariz *f* (corva); (*Naut*) rostro *m*; **~ of land** promontorio *m*. (**b**) (*Brit**) magistrado *m*.

beaked [biːkt] *adj* picudo.

beaker [ˈbiːkəʳ] *n* (*cup*) taza *f* alta; (*prehistoric*) vaso *m*; (*Chem*) vaso *m* de precipitación.

be-all [ˈbiːˈɔːl] *n* (*also* **~ and end-all**) único objeto *m*, única cosa *f* que importa; **he is the ~ of her life** él es lo único que le importa en la vida; **money is not the ~** el dinero no es lo único que vale, hay cosas que valen tanto como el dinero.

beam [biːm] **1** *n* (**a**) (*Archit*) viga *f*; travesaño *m*; (*of plough*) timón *m*; (*of balance*) astil *m*; (*Mech*) balancín *m*.

(**b**) (*Naut*) (*timber*) bao *m*; (*width*) manga *f*; **broad in the ~*** ancho de caderas, nalgudo; **on the port ~** a babor.

(**c**) (*of light*) rayo *m*; (*from beacon, lamp*) haz *m* de luz; (*from radio beacon*) haz *m* de radiofaro; (*smile*) sonrisa *f*, mirada *f* alegre, mirada *f* brillante; **~ lights** (*Aut*) luces *fpl* largas; **with a ~ of pleasure** con una sonrisa de placer; **to be on the ~*** seguir el buen camino; **to be off the ~*** estar despistado, estar equivocado.

2 *vt light, signal* emitir; **she ~ed her thanks at me** me lanzó una mirada agradecida.

3 *vi* (*shine*) brillar; (*smile*) sonreírse alegremente (*at* a).

beam-ends [ˈbiːmˈendz] *npl* (*Naut*) cabezas *fpl* de los baos (de un buque); **she was on her** ~ (*Naut*) el buque escoraba peligrosamente; **they are on their** ~ (*fig*) están en un grave aprieto, no tienen donde caerse muertos.

beaming ['bi:mɪŋ] *adj* sonriente, radiante.

bean [bi:n] *n* (**a**) (*plant*) (**broad**) ~ haba *f* gruesa; (**dwarf**) ~ judía *f*, enana *f*, fríjol *m*; (**runner**) ~ judía *f*, habichuela *f*.

(**b**) (*served as food*) ~**s** judías *fpl*; (*broad, haricot*) habas *fpl*; (*of coffee*) granos *mpl*.

(**c**) (*US**: *head, brain*) coco* *m*; **I haven't a** ~ (*Brit**) no tengo un céntimo; **not a** ~**!*** ¡nada en absoluto!; **I didn't make a** ~ **on the deal** no saqué ni un céntimo del negocio; **he doesn't know** ~**s about it** (*US**) no tiene ni zorra idea*; **to be full of** ~**s*** rebosar de vitalidad; **to spill the** ~**s‡** (*improperly*) tirar de la manta; (*tell all*) contarlo todo.

beanbag ['bi:nbæg] *n* (*for throwing*) *saquito que se usa para realizar ejercicios gimnásticos*; (*chair*) almohadón *m*, cojín *m*.

bean curd ['bi:nkɜ:d] *n* tofu *m*, tofú *m*.

beanfeast* ['bi:nfi:st] *n*, **beano*** ['bi:nəʊ] *n* (*Brit*: *party*) fiesta *f*, juerga *f*; (*meal*) comilona *f*.

beanpole ['bi:npəʊl] *n* emparrado *m*; (*) espárrago *m*; **he's a real** ~ está como un espárrago*.

beanshoots ['bi:nʃu:ts] *npl*, **beansprouts** ['bi:nspraʊts] *npl* (*Culin*) brotes *mpl* de soja, soja *f* germinada.

beanstalk ['bi:nstɔ:k] *n* judía *f*.

bear¹ [bɛəʳ] **1** *n* (**a**) oso *m*; **Great B**~ Osa *f* Mayor; **Little B**~ Osa *f* Menor; **to be like a** ~ **with a sore head** estar de un humor de perros. (**b**) (*Fin*) bajista *m*; ~ **market** mercado *m* bajista. **2** *vt*: **to** ~ **the market** hacer bajar el mercado vendiendo acciones especulativamente.

bear² [bɛəʳ] (*irr*: *pret* **bore**, *ptp* **borne**) **1** *vt* (**a**) (*carry*) llevar; *arms, date, inscription etc* llevar; *character, name, relation, responsibility* tener; *weight* sostener; *fruit* dar, producir; *interest* devengar; *child* parir, tener; *cost* pagar, correr con; *love etc* sentir, tener (*for* para); *grudge, ill will* guardar, tener (*against* a).

(**b**) (*stand up to*) *inspection etc* sufrir, resistir a; **it doesn't** ~ **close examination** no resiste a la inspección de cerca; **it doesn't** ~ **thinking about** da horror sólo pensar en ello; **the film will** ~ **a second viewing** la película vale la pena de verse por segunda vez.

(**c**) (*endure*) soportar, aguantar, resistir; **I can't** ~ **delays** yo no aguanto los retrasos; **I can't** ~ **him** no le puedo ver; **I can't** ~ **spiders** odio las arañas; **I can't** ~ **to look!** ¡no puedo mirar!; **can you** ~ **me to look at it?** ¿puedes dejarme verlo?; **I could** ~ **it no longer** ya no resistía más.

2 *vi* (**a**) **a tree that** ~**s well** un árbol que rinde bien.

(**b**) **the ship** ~**s north** el barco lleva dirección norte; **to** ~ **left** torcer a la izquierda.

(**c**) **it** ~**s hard on the old** esto pesa bastante sobre los viejos.

(**d**) **to bring a gun to** ~ **on** apuntar a; **to bring pressure to** ~ **on** ejercer presión sobre.

3 *vr*: **to** ~ **o.s.** comportarse, portarse.

◆**bear away** *vt* llevarse.

◆**bear down** *vt*: **borne down by adversity** derrotado por la adversidad.

◆**bear down upon** *vt* (**a**) (*ship*) correr sobre; (*person*) avanzar hacia, acercarse majestuosamente (*or* de manera amenazadora *etc*) a. (**b**) (*press*) pesar sobre.

◆**bear in** *vt*: **it was borne in on me that ...** iba comprendiendo que ...

◆**bear off** *vt* = **bear away**.

◆**bear on** *vt person* interesar; *subject* tener que ver con, referirse a.

◆**bear out** *vt* (**a**) (*carry*) llevar. (**b**) (*confirm*) confirmar, corroborar; **I can** ~ **that out** yo confirmo eso; **you will** ~ **me out that ...** estarás de acuerdo conmigo para decir que ...

◆**bear up** *vi* animarse; ~ **up!** ¡ánimo!; **I'm** ~**ing up, thanks** estoy regular, gracias.

◆**bear with** *vt* tener paciencia con, ser indulgente con.

bearable ['bɛərəbl] *adj* soportable, aguantable.

bear-cub ['bɛəkʌb] *n* osezno *m*.

beard [bɪəd] **1** *n* barba *f*; (*Bot*) arista *f*; **to have** (*or* **wear**) **a** ~ llevar barba. **2** *vt* desafiar.

bearded ['bɪədɪd] *adj* barbado; (*heavily*) barbudo.

beardless ['bɪədlɪs] *adj* barbilampiño, lampiño; *youth* imberbe.

bearer ['bɛərəʳ] *n* (*servant*) mozo *m*; (*Comm*) portador *m*, -ora *f*; (*of credentials, office, passport*) poseedor *m*, -ora *f*; ~ **cheque** cheque *m* al portador.

bear-garden ['bɛəˌgɑ:dn] *n* (*fig*) manicomio *m*, guirigay *m*, casa *f* de locos.

bear-hug ['bɛəhʌg] *n*: **he gave me a great** ~ me dio un abrazo de oso.

bearing ['bɛərɪŋ] *n* (**a**) (*of person*) porte *m*, comportamiento *m*; **soldierly** ~ porte *m* militar.

(**b**) (*relationship*) relación *f* (*on* con); **this has no** ~ **on the matter** esto no tiene que ver con el asunto.

(**c**) (*Mech*) cojinete *m*.

(**d**) (*Naut*) marcación *f*; **to get one's** ~**s** orientarse; **to lose one's** ~**s** desorientarse; **to take a** ~ marcarse; **to take one's** ~**s** orientarse.

(**e**) (*Her*) blasón *m*.

(**f**) **beyond all** ~ del todo inaguantable.

bearish ['bɛərɪʃ] *adj* pesimista; (*Fin*) (de tendencia) bajista.

bearskin ['bɛəskɪn] *n* piel *f* de oso; (*Mil*) gorro *m* militar (de piel de oso).

beast [bi:st] *n* (**a**) bestia *f*; ~ **of burden** bestia *f* de carga; **wild** ~ fiera *f*; **the king of** ~**s** el rey de los animales. (**b**) (*person*) animal *m*, bruto *m*, salvaje *m*; (*thing*) cosa *f* muy difícil; **you** ~**!** ¡animal!; **that** ~ **of a policeman** aquel bruto de policía; **what a** ~ **he is!** ¡qué bruto!; **this is a** ~ esto es horrible; **it's a** ~ **of a day** es un día horrible.

beastliness ['bi:stlɪnɪs] *n* bestialidad *f*.

beastly ['bi:stlɪ] **1** *adj* (**a**) bestial. (**b**) (*) detestable, horrible; condenado, maldito; **that was a** ~ **thing to do** aquello sí que fue cruel; **you were** ~ **to me** fuiste cruel conmigo; **where's that** ~ **book?** ¿dónde está el maldito libro ese?

2 *adv* (*Brit**): **it's** ~ **awkward** es terriblemente difícil; **it's** ~ **cold** hace un frío bestial.

beat [bi:t] **1** *n* (**a**) (*of heart*) latido *m*.

(**b**) (*Mus*) compás *m*, ritmo *m*; (*of drum*) redoble *m*; **music with a** ~ música *f* de ritmo fuerte.

(**c**) (*of policeman*) ronda *f*; **to be on the** ~ estar de ronda; **it's off my** ~ (*fig*) no es de mi competencia.

(**d**) (*Hunting*) batida *f*.

(**e**) (‡) beatnik *mf*; ~ **generation** generación *f* de los beatniks.

2 (*irr*: *pret* **beat**, *ptp* **beaten**) *vt* (**a**) (*strike*) golpear; *table, door* dar golpes en; *metal etc* batir, martillar; *person* pegar, (*as punishment*) dar una paliza a, mondar (*LAm*); *carpet* sacudir; (*Culin*) batir; *drum* tocar; *path* abrir; **to** ~ **time** (*Mus*) marcar el compás, llevar el compás; **he** ~ **him on the head** le dio un golpe en la cabeza; **he** ~ **him about the head** le dio una serie de golpes por la cabeza; **to** ~ **sb to death** matar a uno a palos; **the bird** ~ **its wings** el pájaro batió las alas; **to** ~ **it*** poner pies en polvorosa; ~ **it!*** ¡lárgate!

(**b**) (*Hunting*) ojear.

(**c**) (*defeat*) vencer, derrotar; *record* batir, superar, mejorar; **to** ~ **sb to it** ganar por la mano a uno, llegar antes que uno; **to** ~ **sb hollow** (*or* **hands down** (*Brit*) *or* **into a cocked hat**) cascar a uno, vencer a uno fácilmente; **he didn't know when he was** ~**en** en ningún momento quería darse por vencido; **to** ~ **the system** explotar el sistema.

(**d**) (*be better than*) sobrepasar, superar; **if you can't** ~ **them join them** si no puedes superarlos únete a ellos; **can you** ~ **that?** ¿has visto cosa igual?; **that** ~**s everything!** ¡eso es el colmo!

(**e**) (*mystify*) confundir; **the police confess themselves** ~**en** la policía confiesa no tener pista alguna; **the problem has me** ~**en** el problema me deja totalmente perplejo; **it** ~**s me how ...** no llego a comprender cómo ...

3 *vi* (*heart*) latir, pulsar; **the drums were** ~**ing** redoblaban los tambores; **to** ~ **on a door** dar golpes en una puerta; **the waves** ~ **on the shore** las olas azotaban la playa.

4 *adj* (*) hecho polvo*; *V also* **beaten**.

◆**beat about** *vi* (*Naut*) barloventear.

◆**beat back** *vt* rechazar.

◆**beat down** **1** *vt* (**a**) abatir, derribar a golpes; *corn* acamar; *opponent, resistance* vencer. (**b**) *price* conseguir rebajar (regateando); *seller* persuadir a que venda a precio más bajo.

2 *vi* (*sun*) picar, calentar mucho; (*rain*) llover con violencia.

◆**beat off** *vt* rechazar.

◆**beat out** *vt metal* martillar, formar a martillazos; *tune* tocar (con fuerte ritmo); *fire* apagar (a golpes).

◆**beat up** *vt* (**a**) (*Culin*) batir. (**b**) (*) *person* aporrear, dar una paliza a. (**c**) (*recruit*) *persons* reclutar; *customers* atraer; *help* asegurar.

beatbox ['bi:t,bɒks] *n* caja *f* de ritmos.

beaten ['bi:tn] **1** *ptp of* **beat**. **2** *adj* (**a**) *metal etc* batido, martillado; ~ **track** camino *m* trillado (*also fig*); **a village off the ~ track** un pueblo apartado; **to get off the ~ track** apartarse del camino trillado. (**b**) *team etc* derrotado, vencido.

beaten-up* [bi:tnʌp] *adj*: **a ~ car** un cacharro*, una birria de coche*.

beater ['bi:tə^r] *n* (**a**) (*Hunting*) ojeador *m*, batidor *m*. (**b**) (*Culin*) batidor *m*, batidora *f* (eléctrica).

beatific [,bi:ə'tɪfɪk] *adj* beatífico; **with a ~ smile** con una sonrisa de puro contento.

beatification [bi:,ætɪfɪ'keɪʃən] *n* beatificación *f*.

beatify [bi:'ætɪfaɪ] *vt* beatificar.

beating ['bi:tɪŋ] *n* (**a**) (*blows*) golpes *mpl*, golpeo *m*; (*of waves*) el batir, el azotar; (*punishment*) paliza *f*; **to get a ~** recibir una paliza.

(**b**) (*of heart*) latido *m*, pulsación *f*.

(**c**) (*Hunting*) ojeo *m*, batida *f*.

(**d**) (*defeat*) derrota *f*; **to take a ~** salir derrotado (*from* por), recibir una paliza (*at the hands of* a manos de); **that score will take some ~** será difícil superar ese total de puntos (*etc*).

beating-up [,bi:tɪŋ'ʌp] *n* paliza *f*.

beatitude [bi:'ætɪtju:d] *n* beatitud *f*; **the B~s** las Bienaventuranzas.

beatnik ['bi:tnɪk] *n* beatnik *mf*.

Beatrice ['bɪətrɪs] *nf* Beatriz.

beat-up* ['bi:tʌp] *adj* viejo, destartalado, ruinoso.

beau [bəʊ] **1** *adj*: **~ ideal** lo bello ideal; (*person*) tipo *m* ideal. **2** *n*, *pl* **beaux** [bəʊ] (*fop*) petimetre *m*, dandy *m*; (*ladies' man*) galán *m*; (*suitor*) pretendiente *m*; (*sweetheart*) novio *m*.

Beaufort scale ['bəʊfət'skeɪl] *n* escala *f* de Beaufort.

beaut* [bju:t] *n*: **it's a ~** es pistonudo*, es de primera.

beauteous ['bju:tɪəs] *adj* (*poet*) bello.

beautician [bju:'tɪʃən] *n* esteticista *mf*.

beautiful ['bju:tɪfʊl] *adj* hermoso, bello; precioso; **the ~ people** la gente guapa.

beautifully ['bju:tɪflɪ] *adv* (*fig*) maravillosamente, perfectamente; **that will do ~** así sirve perfectamente; **she plays ~** toca a la perfección.

beautify ['bju:tɪfaɪ] *vt* embellecer.

beauty ['bju:tɪ] **1** *n* (**a**) (*in general*) belleza *f*, hermosura *f*; (*concrete*) belleza *f*, *eg* **the beauties of Majorca** las bellezas de Mallorca; **the ~ of it is that ...** (*fig*) lo genial es que ...

(**b**) (*person*) belleza *f*, beldad *f*; (*thing, specimen*) ejemplar *m* hermoso; **it's a ~** es maravilloso; **that was a ~!** (*stroke etc*) ¡qué golpe más fino!; **isn't he a little ~?** (*child*) ¡mira qué rico está el niño!; **B~ and the Beast** la Bella y la Bestia.

2 *attr* de belleza; **~ editor** directora *f* de la sección de belleza; **~ products** productos *mpl* para la belleza.

beauty competition ['bju:tɪ,kɒmpɪ,tɪʃən] *n*, **beauty contest** ['bju:tɪ,kɒntest] *n* concurso *m* de belleza.

beauty consultant ['bju:tɪkən,sʌltənt] *n* esteticista *mf*.

beauty-cream ['bju:tɪkri:m] *n* crema *f* de belleza.

beauty-parlour ['bju:tɪ,pɑ:lə^r] *n* salón *m* de belleza.

beauty-queen ['bju:tɪkwi:n] *n* reina *f* de la belleza, miss *f*.

beauty-salon ['bju:tɪ,sælɒn] *n* = **beauty-parlour**.

beauty-sleep ['bju:tɪsli:p] *n* primer sueño *m*; **to lose one's ~** (*hum*) perder el tiempo en que uno debiera estar dormido.

beauty-spot ['bju:tɪspɒt] *n* (**a**) (*on face*) lunar *m* postizo. (**b**) (*in country*) sitio *m* pintoresco, lugar *m* de excepcional belleza natural.

beaver ['bi:və^r] **1** *n* castor *m*. **2** *vi*: **to ~ away** (*Brit*) trabajar diligentemente (*at* en).

becalm [bɪ'kɑ:m] *vt*: **to be ~ed** estar encalmado.

became [bɪ'keɪm] *pret of* **become**.

because [bɪ'kɒz] **1** *conj* porque; **~ I don't want to** porque no quiero; **~ he was ill he couldn't go** por estar enfermo no podía ir; **~ he has two cars he thinks he's somebody** como tiene dos coches se cree un personaje.

2 *prep*: **~ of** a causa de, debido a, por motivo de.

bechamel [,beɪʃə'mel] *n* (*also* **~ sauce**) besamel *f*.

beck[1] [bek] *n*: **to be at the ~ and call of** estar a disposición de, estar sometido a la voluntad de.

beck[2] [bek] *n* (*prov, NEng*) arroyo *m*, riachuelo *m*.

beckon ['bekən] **1** *vt* llamar con señas; (*fig*) llamar, atraer. **2** *vi*: **to ~ to** hacer señas a.

become [bɪ'kʌm] (*irr*: *V* **come**) **1** *vt* (*of clothes etc*) sentar a, favorecer; (*action etc*) convenir a; **that thought does not ~ you** ese pensamiento es indigno de ti.

2 *vi* (**a**) (*absolute*) **what has become of him?** ¿qué es de él?; **what will ~ of me?** ¿qué será de mí?; **what can have become of that book?** ¿adónde diablos se habrá metido aquel libro?

(**b**) (*followed by n*: *entering profession etc*) hacerse, (*by promotion etc*) llegar a ser, (*of material things*) transformarse en, convertirse en; **to ~ a soldier** hacerse soldado; **to ~ professor** llegar a ser catedrático; **he became king in 1911** subió al trono en 1911; **later this lady became his wife** después esta dama fue su esposa; **to ~ a father** ser padre; **the gas ~s liquid** el gas se convierte en líquido; **the building has become a cinema** el edificio se ha transformado en cine.

(**c**) (*followed by adj*) ponerse, volverse, (*by effort*) hacerse; **this is becoming difficult** esto se está poniendo difícil; **to ~ rich** hacerse rico; **to ~ mad** volverse loco; (*freq* to become + *adj is translated by a reflexive verb*) **to ~ red** ponerse rojo, enrojecerse; **to ~ ill** ponerse enfermo, enfermar; **to ~ angry** enfadarse; **he became quite blind** quedó totalmente ciego; **to ~ accustomed to** acostumbrarse a; **it became known that** se supo que, llegó a saberse que; **we became very worried** empezamos a inquietarnos muchísimo.

(**d**) (*of age*) **when he ~s 21** cuando llegue a tener 21 años, cuando cumpla los 21 años.

becoming [bɪ'kʌmɪŋ] *adj clothes* favorecedor, que sienta bien, que le va bien a uno; *action* decoroso, conveniente.

becomingly [bɪ'kʌmɪŋlɪ] *adv* de modo favorecedor; elegantemente; decorosamente, convenientemente; **~ dressed** elegantemente vestido.

becquerel [,bekə'rel] *n* becquerelio *m*.

B.Ed. [,bi:'ed] *n abbr of* **Bachelor of Education** licenciado *m*, -a *f* en pedagogía.

bed [bed] **1** *n* (**a**) cama *f*; (*of animal*) lecho *m*; **~ and board** comida *f* y casa, pensión *f* completa; **~ and breakfast** (*Brit*) cama *f* con desayuno, alojamiento *m* y desayuno; **~ of nails** cama *f* de clavos; **~ of roses** lecho *m* de rosas; **life isn't exactly a ~ of roses** la vida no es ningún lecho de rosas; **to get out of ~ on the wrong side, to get up on the wrong side of the ~** (*US**) levantarse por los pies de la cama, levantarse con el pie izquierdo; **to get into ~** meterse en la cama; **to give sb a ~ for the night** hospedar a uno una noche; **to go to ~** acostarse (*with* con); **to make the ~** hacer la cama; **you've made your ~ and you must lie on it** quien mala cama hace en ella se yace; **to put a child to ~** acostar a un niño; **to put a paper to ~** terminar la redacción de un número; **to stay in ~** (*ill*) guardar cama, (*lazy*) seguir en la cama; **to take to one's ~** encamarse.

(**b**) (*Geol*) capa *f*, estrato *m*, yacimiento *m*.

(**c**) (*Archit, Tech*) base *f*.

(**d**) (*of sea*) fondo *m*; (*of river*) cauce *m*, lecho *m*.

(**e**) (*of flowers*) macizo *m*, cuadro *m*, arriate *m*.

2 *vt* (**a**) (*Archit etc*) fijar, engastar.

(**b**) (*****) *woman* llevar a la cama, acostarse con.

◆**bed down** **1** *vt* (**a**) (*Archit*) = **bed 2** (**a**). (**b**) *children* acostar; *animals* hacer un lecho para. **2** *vi* hacerse una cama, acostarse.

◆**bed out** *vt plants* plantar en un macizo.

bedaub [bɪ'dɔ:b] *vt* embadurnar.

bedbath ['bedbɑ:θ] *n*, *pl* **bedbaths** ['bedbɑ:ðz]: **they gave him a ~** le lavaron en la cama.

bedbug ['bedbʌg] *n* chinche *gen f*.

bedclothes ['bedkləʊðz] *npl* ropa *f* de cama.

bedcover ['bedkʌvə^r] *n* = **bedspread**; **~s** ropa *f* de cama.

-bedded ['bedɪd] *adj ending in compounds*: **twin~ room** habitación *f* doble.

bedding ['bedɪŋ] *n* ropa *f* de cama; (*for animal*) lecho *m*.

Bede [bi:d] *nm* Beda; **the Venerable ~** el venerable Beda.

bedeck [bɪ'dek] *vt* adornar, engalanar.

bedevil [bɪ'devəl] *vt* endiablar; (*dog*) acosar; (*trouble*) fastidiar; **the problem is ~led by several factors** hay diversos factores que complican el problema; **the team has been ~led by injuries** el equipo ha sufrido mucho de lesiones.

bedfellow ['bedfeləʊ] *n* compañero *m*, -a *f* de cama; **they make strange ~s** hacen una pareja rara.

bedhead ['bedhed] *n* testero *m*, cabecera *f*.

bedjacket ['beddʒækɪt] *n* mañanita *f*.

bedlam ['bedləm] *n* (†† *or fig*) manicomio *m*; **it was sheer ~** la confusión era total; **~ broke out** se armó una algarabía espantosa.

bedlinen ['bedlɪnɪn] *n* ropa *f* de cama, sábanas *fpl*.

Bedouin ['bedʊɪn] **1** *adj* beduino. **2** *n* beduino *m*, -a *f*.

bedpan ['bedpæn] *n* chata *f*, silleta *f*, cuña *f*.

bedpost ['bedpəust] *n* columna *f* (*or* pilar *m*) de cama.
bedraggled [bɪ'drægld] *adj* ensuciado, mojado.
bedridden ['bedrɪdn] *adj* postrado en cama, encamado.
bedrock ['bedrɒk] *n* lecho *m* de roca, roca *f* sólida; (*fig*) fondo *m* de la cuestión; **to get down to ~** ir a lo fundamental.
bedroll ['bed,rəul] *n* petate *m*.
bedroom ['bedrʊm] *n* dormitorio *m*, alcoba *f*, habitación *f*, recámara *f* (*LAm*); **~ eyes*** ojos *mpl* seductores; **~ farce** farsa *f* de dormitorio; **~ slippers** pantuflas *fpl*; **~ suburb** (*US*) ciudad *f* colmena; ciudad *f* dormitorio; **~ suite** juego *m* de muebles para dormitorio; **3-~ flat** piso *m* de 3 habitaciones.
-bedroomed ['bed,rʊmd] *adj*: *eg* **a 5~ house** una casa con 5 dormitorios.
Beds [beds] *n abbr of* **Bedfordshire**.
bed-settee [,bedse'tiː] *n* sofá-cama *m*.
bedside ['bedsaɪd] **1** *n*: **to wait at the ~ of** esperar a la cabecera de.
2 *attr*: **~ lamp** lámpara *f* de noche; **~ rug** alfombrilla *f* de cama; **~ table** mesa *f* de noche; **to have a good ~ manner** tener mucho tacto con los enfermos.
bedsit* ['bedsɪt] *n*, **bedsitter** ['bed'sɪtəʳ] *n*, **bedsitting room** ['bed'sɪtɪŋrʊm] *n* (*Brit*) estudio *m*, salón *m* con cama, cuarto cama *m*, suite *m* (*LAm*).
bedsocks ['bedsɒks] *npl* calcetines *mpl* de cama.
bedsore ['bedsɔːʳ] *n* úlcera *f* de decúbito.
bedspread ['bedspred] *n* sobrecama *m*, cobertor *m*, cubrecama *f*.
bedstead ['bedsted] *n* cuja *f*, armazón *m* de cama.
bedstraw ['bedstrɔː] *n* (*Bot*) cuajaleche *m*, amor *m* de hortelano.
bedtime ['bedtaɪm] *n* hora *f* de acostarse; **~ story** cuento *m* (para hacer dormir a un niño).
bedwetting ['bedwetɪŋ] *n* enuresis *f*.
bedworthy* ['bed,wɜːðɪ] *adj* atractivo.
bee [biː] *n* (**a**) abeja *f*; **to have a ~ in one's bonnet** tener una idea fija, tener algo metido entre ceja y ceja; **he thinks he's the ~'s knees*** se cree el mar de listo (*or* de elegante *etc*). (**b**) (*esp US*) reunión *f* social de vecinos, círculo *m* social.
Beeb* [biːb] *n*: **the ~** (*Brit*) la BBC.
beech [biːtʃ] *n* haya *f*.
beech-grove ['biːtʃ,grəuv] *n* hayal *m*.
beechmast ['biːtʃmɑːst] *n* hayucos *mpl*.
beechnut ['biːtʃnʌt] *n* hayuco *m*.
beech-tree ['biːtʃtriː] *n* haya *f*.
beechwood ['biːtʃwʊd] *n* (**a**) (*group of trees*) hayedo *m*, hayal *m*. (**b**) (*material*) (madera *f* de) haya *f*.
bee-eater ['biː,iːtəʳ] *n* (*Orn*) abejaruco *m*.
beef [biːf] **1** *n* (**a**) carne *f* de vaca, carne *f* de res (*LAm*), vaca *f*. (**b**) (*) fuerza *f* muscular, corpulencia *f*. (**c**) (*US**) queja *f*. **2** *attr*: **~ cattle** ganado *m* vacuno de carne; **~ olive** *picadillo envuelto en una lonja de carne y cocinado en salsa*; **~ sausage** salchicha *f* de carne de vaca; **~ tea** caldo *m* de carne (para enfermos). **3** *vi* (*) quejarse (*about* de).
◆**beef up**‡ *vt essay, speech* reforzar, fortalecer.
beefburger ['biːf,bɜːgəʳ] *n* hamburguesa *f*.
beefcake* ['biːf,keɪk] *n* despliegue *m* de fuerza muscular masculina (*esp en fotos*).
beefeater ['biːf,iːtəʳ] *n* (*Brit*) alabardero *m* de la Torre de Londres.
beefsteak ['biːf'steɪk] *n* biftec *m*, bistec *m*, bife *m* (*SC*).
beefy* ['biːfɪ] *adj* fornido, corpulento.
beehive ['biːhaɪv] *n* colmena *f*.
beekeeper ['biːkiːpəʳ] *n* apicultor *m*, -ora *f*, colmenero *m*, -a *f*.
beeline ['biːlaɪn] *n*: **to make a ~ for** ir en línea recta hacia, salir disparado hacia.
Beelzebub [biː'elzɪbʌb] *nm* Belcebú.
been [biːn] *ptp of* **be**.
beep [biːp] *n* bip *m*.
beeper ['biːpəʳ] *n* (*US*) localizador *m*, busca* *m*.
beer [bɪəʳ] *n* cerveza *f*; **small ~** (*fig*) cosa *f* sin importancia, bagatela *f*; **we're only here for the ~** venimos en plan de diversión; **life isn't all ~ and skittles** (*Brit*) la vida no es un lecho de rosas.
beer-barrel ['bɪə,bærəl] *n* barril *m* de cerveza.
beer-belly* ['bɪə,belɪ] *n*, **beer-gut*** ['bɪə,gʌt] *n* curva *f* de la felicidad.
beer-bottle ['bɪə,bɒtl] *n* botella *f* de cerveza.
beer-can ['bɪə,kæn] *n* lata *f* de cerveza, bote *m*.
beerfest ['bɪə,fest] *n* (*US*) festival *m* cervecero.
beer-glass ['bɪə,glɑːs] *n* jarra *f* de cerveza.
beer-mat ['bɪə,mæt] *n* posavasos *m* (de taberna).
beery ['bɪərɪ] *adj smell* a cerveza; *person* muy aficionado a la cerveza; *party* donde se bebe mucha cerveza; **it was a ~ affair** allí se bebió una barbaridad.
beeswax ['biːzwæks] *n* cera *f* (de abejas).
beet [biːt] *n* = **beetroot**.
beetle ['biːtl] *n* escarabajo *m*, coleóptero *m*.
◆**beetle off*** *vi* marcharse.
beetroot ['biːtruːt] *n* (*Brit*) (raíz *f* de) remolacha *f*, betabel *m* (*LAm*), betarraga *f* (*LAm*).
beet sugar [biːt,ʃugəʳ] *n* azúcar *m* de remolacha.
befall [bɪ'fɔːl] (*irr*: *V* **fall**) **1** *vt* acontecer a. **2** *vi* acontecer; **whatever may ~** pase lo que pase.
befallen [bɪ'fɔːlən] *ptp of* **befall**.
befell [bɪ'fel] *pret of* **befall**.
befit [bɪ'fɪt] *vt* convenir a, venir bien a, corresponder a.
befitting [bɪ'fɪtɪŋ] *adj* conveniente, decoroso.
befog [bɪ'fɒg] *vt* (*fig*) *issue etc* entenebrecer; *person* ofuscar, confundir.
before [bɪ'fɔːʳ] **1** *adv* (**a**) (*place*) delante, adelante; **~ and behind** por delante y por detrás; **that chapter and the one ~** ese capítulo y el anterior.
(**b**) (*time*) antes; anteriormente; **a moment ~** un momento antes; **the day ~** el día anterior; **on this occasion and the one ~** en esta ocasión y la anterior.
2 *prep* (**a**) (*place*) delante de; (*in the presence of, faced with*) ante, en presencia de; **we still have 2 hours ~ us** tenemos todavía 2 horas por delante; **the problem ~ us** el problema que se nos plantea; **the task ~ us** la tarea que tenemos por delante.
(**b**) (*time*) antes de; **income ~ tax** renta *f* bruta; **profits ~ tax** beneficios *mpl* preimpositivos.
(**c**) (*rather than*) **I should choose this one ~ that** yo escogería éste antes que aquél; **death ~ dishonour!** ¡antes la muerte que el deshonor!
(**d**) (*with verb*) **~ going out** antes de salir.
3 *conj* antes (de) que.
beforehand [bɪ'fɔːhænd] *adv* de antemano, con anticipación; (*esp liter, admin*) con antelación.
befoul [bɪ'faul] *vt* ensuciar.
befriend [bɪ'frend] *vt* ofrecer amistad a; amparar, favorecer.
befuddle [bɪ'fʌdl] *vt* (*confuse*) atontar, confundir; (*make tipsy*) atontar.
befuddled [bɪ'fʌdld] *adj* aturdido; **~ with drink** atontado por la bebida.
beg [beg] **1** *vt* (**a**) pedir, suplicar, rogar (*from, of* a); **to ~ sb for sth** pedir algo a uno; **he ~ged my help** suplicó mi ayuda; **he ~ged me to help him** me suplicó que le ayudara; **he ~ged the book from me** rogó que le diese el libro; **I ~ you!** ¡se lo suplico!; *V* **question**.
(**b**) (*as beggar*) mendigar; pedir; **he ~ged a pound** pidió una libra.
2 *vi* (**a**) pedir, rogar; **to ~ for** pedir, solicitar; **I ~ to inform you that ...** tengo el gusto de informarle que ...
(**b**) (*as beggar*) mendigar, pedir por Dios, pedir limosna; **it's going ~ging** no hay candidato (*or* comprador), nadie lo quiere; **there's some cake going ~ging** hay un poco de tarta por terminar.
◆**beg off*** *vi* (*US*) pedir dispensa, escabullirse*.
began [bɪ'gæn] *pret of* **begin**.
beget [bɪ'get] (*irr*: *pret* **begot**, (*arch*) **begat**, *ptp* **begotten**) *vt* engendrar (*also fig*).
beggar ['begəʳ] **1** *n* (**a**) mendigo *m*, -a *f*, pordiosero *m*; **~s can't be choosers** a quien dan no escoge, los pobres no escogen. (**b**) (*) tío* *m*, sujeto* *m*; **lucky ~!*** ¡qué chorra tiene el tío!*.
2 *vt* (**a**) empobrecer, arruinar, reducir a la miseria. (**b**) (*fig*) excederse a; **it ~s description** supera toda descripción; **it ~s belief** resulta totalmente inverosímil.
beggarly ['begəlɪ] *adj* indigente; (*fig*) miserable, mezquino.
beggary ['begərɪ] *n* mendicidad *f*; miseria *f*; **to reduce to ~** reducir a la miseria.
begging ['begɪŋ] *n* mendicidad *f*; **~ letter** carta *f* en que se pide dinero.
begin [bɪ'gɪn] (*irr*: *pret* **began**, *ptp* **begun**) **1** *vt* comenzar, empezar; iniciar; (*undertake*) emprender; **the work will be begun tomorrow** mañana se iniciará el trabajo, mañana se dará principio al trabajo; **I was foolish ever to ~ it** hice mal en emprenderlo.
2 *vi* comenzar, empezar; **to ~ to** + *infin* comenzar (*or* empezar) a + *infin*; **to ~ talking** empezar a hablar; **it doesn't ~ to be possible** dista mucho de ser posible; **to ~ by saying** comenzar diciendo; **to ~ on** emprender, co-

menzar; **to ~ with sth** comenzar por (*or* con) algo; **to ~ with** (*as phrase*) en primer lugar, para empezar; **~ning from Monday** a partir del lunes.

beginner [bɪ'gɪnəʳ] *n* principiante *mf*; novato *m*, -a *f*.

beginning [bɪ'gɪnɪŋ] *n* **(a)** (*of speech, book, film etc*) principio *m*, comienzo *m*; **at the ~ of** al principio de; **at the ~ of the century** a principios del siglo; **from the ~** desde el principio; **from ~ to end** desde el principio hasta el final, de cabo a rabo; **in the ~** al principio; **the ~ of the end** el comienzo del fin; **to make a ~** empezar.

(b) (*origin*) origen *m*; **from small ~s** de orígenes modestos, de antecedentes humildes; **he had the ~s of a beard** tenía un asomo de barba.

begone†† [bɪ'gɒn] *interj* ¡fuera de aquí!

begonia [bɪ'gəʊnɪə] *n* begonia *f*.

begot [bɪ'gɒt] *pret of* **beget.**

begotten [bɪ'gɒtn] *ptp of* **beget; the only B~ Son** el Unigénito.

begrime [bɪ'graɪm] *vt* tiznar, ensuciar.

begrudge [bɪ'grʌdʒ] *vt* (*give*) dar de mala gana; (*envy*) tener envidia a; **I don't ~ him his success** no le envidio su éxito.

beguile [bɪ'gaɪl] *vt* (*delude*) engañar; (*charm away*) seducir, engatusar; *time etc* entretener; **to ~ sb into doing sth** persuadir (*or* engatusar) a uno a hacer algo.

beguiling [bɪ'gaɪlɪŋ] *adj* seductor, persuasivo, atractivo.

begun [bɪ'gʌn] *ptp of* **begin.**

behalf [bɪ'hɑːf] *n*: **on ~ of** de parte de; **on ~ of everybody** en nombre de todos; **a collection on ~ of orphans** una colecta en beneficio de los huérfanos, una colecta por huérfanos; **I interceded on his ~** intercedí por él; **don't worry on my ~** no te preocupes por mí.

behave [bɪ'heɪv] **1** *vi* (*person*) portarse (*to, towards* con), comportarse, conducirse; (*Mech etc*) comportarse, funcionar.

2 *vr*: **to ~ o.s.** (*esp of or to child*) portarse bien; **~ yourself!** ¡estáte formal!, ¡pórtate bien!; **if you ~ yourself (properly)** si te conduces debidamente.

behaviour, (*US*) **behavior** [bɪ'heɪvjəʳ] *n* conducta *f*, comportamiento *m*; (*Mech etc*) comportamiento *m*, funcionamiento *m*; **good ~** buena conducta *f*; **to be on one's best ~** portarse del mejor modo posible; **you must be on your best ~** tienes que portarte pero muy bien.

behavioural, (*US*) **behavioral** [bɪ'heɪvjərəl] *adj* conductual, conductista, behaviorístico.

behaviourism, (*US*) **behaviorism** [bɪ'heɪvjərɪzəm] *n* conductismo *m*, behaviorismo *m*.

behaviourist, (*US*) **behaviorist** [bɪ'heɪvjərɪst] **1** *adj* conductista, behaviorista.

2 *n* conductista *mf*, behaviorista *mf*.

behead [bɪ'hed] *vt* decapitar, descabezar.

beheld [bɪ'held] *pret and ptp of* **behold.**

behest [bɪ'hest] *n* (*liter*): **at the ~ of** por orden de.

behind [bɪ'haɪnd] **1** *adv* **(a)** (*in or at the rear*) detrás, por detrás; atrás; **to come from ~** venir desde atrás; **to follow close ~** seguir muy de cerca; **to attack sb from ~** atacar a uno por la espalda; **Pepe won with Paco only 2 strokes ~** ganó Pepe con Paco a sólo 2 golpes de distancia.

(b) (*with verb* to be) **to be a bit ~** estar algo atrasadillo; **to be ~ with one's work** estar atrasado en su trabajo, tener atrasos de trabajo.

2 *prep* (*at the back of, also fig*) detrás de; **what's ~ all this?** ¿qué hay detrás de todo esto?; **he has all of us ~ him** (*fig*) tiene el apoyo de todos nosotros; **we are much ~ them in technology** les somos muy inferiores en tecnología; **with his hands ~ his back** las manos en la espalda; **X is 9 points ~ Y** X tiene 9 puntos menos que Y; **Ruritania is well ~ Slobodia in production** Ruritania queda muy a la zaga de Eslobodia en la producción; **she has 4 novels ~ her** tiene 4 novelas en el haber; **it's all ~ us now** todo eso ha quedado ya detrás.

3 *n* (*****) trasero *m*, culo *m*.

behindhand [bɪ'haɪndhænd] *adv* atrasado, con retraso; **to be ~ with the rent** tener atrasos de alquiler.

behold [bɪ'həʊld] (*irr*: *V* **hold**) *vt* (*†† or liter*) contemplar; **~!** ¡fíjese bien!; **~ the results!** ¡he aquí los resultados!; *V* **lo.**

beholden [bɪ'həʊldən] *adj*: **to be ~ to** estar bajo una obligación a; estar agradecido a; **I don't want to be ~ to anybody** yo no quiero tener obligaciones con nadie.

beholder [bɪ'həʊldəʳ] *n* espectador *m*, -ora *f*, observador *m*, -ora *f*.

behove [bɪ'həʊv], (*US*) **behoove** [bɪ'huːv] *vt*: **it ~s him to +** *infin* le incumbe + *infin*.

beige [beɪʒ] **1** *adj* (color de) beige. **2** *n* beige *m*.

Beijing ['beɪ'dʒɪŋ] *n* Pekín *m*.

being ['biːɪŋ] *n* ser *m*; **in ~** existente; **to come** (*or* **be called** *or* **be brought**) **into ~** nacer, empezar a existir.

Beirut [beɪ'ruːt] *n* Beirut *m*.

bejewelled, (*US*) **bejeweled** [bɪ'dʒuːəld] *adj* enjoyado.

belabour, (*US*) **belabor** [bɪ'leɪbəʳ] *vt* apalear; (*fig*) criticar, dar un palo a.

belated [bɪ'leɪtɪd] *adj* atrasado, tardío.

belatedly [bɪ'leɪtɪdlɪ] *adv* con retraso.

belay [bɪ'leɪ] *vt* amarrar (dando vueltas en una cabilla).

belch [beltʃ] **1** *n* eructo *m*. **2** *vt* (*fig*: *also* **to ~ out**) vomitar, arrojar. **3** *vi* eructar.

beleaguered [bɪ'liːgəd] *adj* sitiado, asediado, cercado.

belfry ['belfrɪ] *n* campanario *m*.

Belgian ['beldʒən] **1** *adj* belga. **2** *n* belga *mf*.

Belgium ['beldʒəm] *n* Bélgica *f*.

Belgrade [bel'greɪd] *n* Belgrado *m*.

belie [bɪ'laɪ] *vt* desmentir, contradecir; *hopes etc* defraudar.

belief [bɪ'liːf] *n* **(a)** (*conviction*) creencia *f* (*that* de que); opinión *f*; **a man of strong ~s** un hombre de opiniones firmes; **contrary to popular ~ ...** al contrario de lo que muchos creen ...; **to the best of my ~** según mi leal saber y entender; **I did it in the ~ that ...** lo hice creyendo que ...; **it is my firm ~ that ...** creo firmemente que ...; **it passes ~, it is beyond ~** es increíble (*that* que).

(b) (*Rel etc*) fe *f*; **his ~ in God** su fe en Dios.

believable [bɪ'liːvəbl] *adj* creíble.

believe [bɪ'liːv] **1** *vt* creer; *ears, story* dar crédito a; **don't you ~ it!** ¡no lo creas!; **~ it or not, she bought it** aunque parece mentira, lo compró; **it was hot, ~ (you) me** hacía calor ¡y cómo!; **he is ~d to be abroad** se cree que está en el extranjero; **I couldn't ~ my eyes** no pude dar crédito a mis ojos; **do you really ~ the threat?** ¿crees de veras en la amenaza?; **I would never have ~d it of him** no le creía capaz de eso.

2 *vi* creer; **to ~ in God** creer en Dios; **we don't ~ in drugs** no aprobamos (el uso de) las drogas; **I ~ so** creo que sí; **I ~ not** creo que no.

believer [bɪ'liːvəʳ] *n* (*Rel*) creyente *mf*, fiel *mf*; (*supporter*) partidario *m*, -a *f*; **I am a ~ in letting things take their course** yo soy partidario de dejar que las cosas se desarrollen por sí mismas.

Belisha beacon [bɪ,lɪʃə'biːkən] *n* poste *m* luminoso (*de cruce de peatones*).

belittle [bɪ'lɪtl] *vt* despreciar, minimizar, conceder poca importancia a.

Belize [be'liːz] *n* Belice *m*.

Belizean [be'liːzɪən] **1** *adj* beliceño. **2** *n* beliceño *m*, -a *f*.

bell [bel] *n* (*church ~*) campana *f*; (*hand ~*) campanilla *f*; (*animal's*) cencerro *m*; (*on toy, dress etc*) cascabel *m*; (*electric*) timbre *m*; (*of trumpet*) pabellón *m*; (*Bot*) campanilla *f*; **2, 8** (*etc*) **~s** *las medias horas de cada guardia marítima*; **I'll give you a ~** (*Telec**) te llamaré; **that rings a ~** eso me suena; **it doesn't ring a ~ with me** no me suena; **he was saved by the ~** (*fig*) se salvó por los pelos.

belladonna [,belə'dɒnə] *n* (*Bot, Med*) belladona *f*; **~ lily** azucena *f* rosa.

bell-bottomed ['bel'bɒtəmd] *adj* acampanado, abocinado.

bellboy ['belbɔɪ] *n* botones *m*.

bellbuoy ['belbɔɪ] *n* boya *f* de campana.

belle [bel] *n* belleza *f*, beldad *f*; **the ~ of the ball** la reina del baile.

belles-lettres ['bel'letr] *npl* bellas letras *fpl*.

bellglass ['belglɑːs] *n* campana *f* de cristal.

bellhop ['belhɒp] *n* (*US*) botones *m*.

bellicose ['belɪkəʊs] *adj* belicoso.

bellicosity [,belɪ'kɒsɪtɪ] *n* belicosidad *f*.

belligerence [bɪ'lɪdʒərəns] *n*, **belligerency** [bɪ'lɪdʒərənsɪ] *n* beligerancia *f*; agresividad *f*.

belligerent [bɪ'lɪdʒərənt] **1** *adj* beligerante; *person, tone* agresivo. **2** *n* beligerante *m*.

belljar ['beldʒɑːʳ] *n* campana *f* de vidrio.

bellow ['beləʊ] **1** *n* bramido *m*; (*of person*) rugido *m*. **2** (*also* **to ~ out**) *vt* gritar, vociferar. **3** *vi* bramar; (*person*) rugir.

bellows ['beləʊz] *npl* fuelle *m*; **a pair of ~** un fuelle.

bellpull ['bel,pʊl] *n* campanilla *f*.

bellpush ['belpʊʃ] *n* botón *m* del timbre.

bellringer ['bel,rɪŋəʳ] *n* campanero *m*; (*as hobby*) campanólogo *m*, -a *f*.

bell-ringing ['bel,rɪŋɪŋ] *n* campanología *f*.

bellrope ['belrəʊp] *n* cuerda *f* de campana.

bell-shaped ['belʃeɪpt] *adj* acampanado, campaniforme.

bell-tent ['beltent] *n* pabellón *m.*
bell-tower ['bel,tauəʳ] *n* campanario *m.*
belly ['belɪ] **1** *n* vientre *m*; (*with offensive connotations*) barriga *f*, panza *f*, guata *f* (*And*); (*of vessel*) barriga *f*; **to go ~ up*** quebrar. **2** *vi* (*sail*: *also* **to ~ out**) hacer bolso, llenarse de viento.
bellyache ['belɪeɪk] **1** *n* dolor *m* de barriga, dolor *m* de tripas. **2** *vi* (‡) quejarse constantemente (*about* de).
bellyaching‡ ['belɪ,eɪkɪŋ] *n* quejas *fpl* constantes.
belly-button* ['belɪ,bʌtn] *n* ombligo *m.*
belly-dance ['belɪdɑːns] *n* danza *f* del vientre.
belly-dancer ['belɪ,dɑːnsəʳ] *n* danzarina *f* del vientre.
bellyflop ['belɪ,flɒp] *n* panzazo *m*; **to do a ~** dar (*or* darse) un panzazo.
bellyful ['belɪfʊl] *n* panzada *f*; **I've had a ~** estoy harto ya (*of* de).
belly-landing ['belɪ,lændɪŋ] *n* aterrizaje *m* de panza.
belly-laugh ['belɪlɑːf] *n* carcajada *f* (grosera), risotada *f.*
belong [bɪ'lɒŋ] *vi* (**a**) (*be the possession of*) pertenecer (*to* a); **who does this ~ to?** ¿a quién pertenece esto?, ¿de quién es esto?; **the countryside ~s to everyone** el campo es de todos.
(**b**) (*be incumbent on*) **that duty ~s to me** ese deber me corresponde.
(**c**) (*of membership etc*) **to ~ to a club** ser socio de un club; **to ~ to a party** ser miembro de un partido; **why don't you ~?** ¿por qué no te haces (*or* eres) socio?
(**d**) (*have rightful place*) **this ~s with that** éste va con aquél; **that card ~s under K** esa ficha debiera estar en la K; **where does this ~?** ¿esto dónde lo pongo?; **it ~s on the shelf** tiene un puesto en el estante; **it doesn't ~ here** aquí está mal colocado.
(**e**) (*be resident, be at ease*) **I ~ here** yo soy de aquí; **I feel I ~ here** aquí me siento cómodo, aquí me siento como en casa; **that feeling of not ~ing** esa sensación de estar fuera de su ambiente natural.
belongings [bɪ'lɒŋɪŋz] *npl* pertenencias *fpl*, bártulos *mpl*, cosas *fpl*; **personal ~** efectos *mpl* personales.
beloved [bɪ'lʌvɪd] **1** *adj* querido (*by, of* de). **2** *n* querido *m*, amada *f.*
below [bɪ'ləʊ] **1** *adv* abajo, (por) debajo; **that flat ~** ese piso de abajo; **the passage quoted ~** el pasaje abajo citado; **here ~** aquí abajo; en este mundo; **'see ~'** 'véase más abajo'; **it was 5 ~** la temperatura era de 5 grados bajo cero.
2 *prep* bajo, debajo de; (*fig*) inferior a; **temperatures ~ normal** temperaturas inferiores a las normales.
Belshazzar [bel'ʃæzəʳ] *nm* Baltasar; **~'s Feast** la Cena de Baltasar.
belt [belt] **1** *n* cinturón *m*, fajo *m* (*Mex*); (*Mech*) correa *f*, cinta *f*; (*Geog and fig*) zona *f*, región *f*; faja *f*; **a blow below the ~** un golpe bajo; **he has 3 novels under his ~** tiene 3 novelas en su haber; **to tighten one's ~** (*fig*) apretarse el cinturón; **it was a ~-and-braces job*** se tomaron todas las precauciones posibles.
2 *vt* (*) zurrar, dar una paliza a.
◆**belt along*** *vi* ir como una bala.
◆**belt down*** *vt* (*US*) *drink* cepillarse*.
◆**belt out*** **1** *vt* (*radio*) emitir muy fuerte; *song* cantar a todo pulmón, cantar a voz en grito; (*band*) tocar muy fuerte. **2** *vi* (*also* **to come ~ing out**) salir disparado.
◆**belt past** *vi* pasar como un rayo.
◆**belt up** *vi* (**a**) (*Aut*) abrocharse el cinturón.
(**b**) (*Brit*‡) callarse, cerrar el pico; **~ up!** ¡calla la boca!
beltway ['beltweɪ] *n* (*US*) carretera *f* de circunvalación.
bemoan [bɪ'məʊn] *vt* lamentar.
bemuse [bɪ'mjuːz] *vt* aturdir, confundir.
Ben [ben] *nm familiar form of* **Benjamin.**
ben [ben] *n* (*Scot*) montaña *f*; (*room*) cuarto *m* interior.
bench [bentʃ] *n* banco *m*; (*Sport*) banquillo *m*; (*court*) tribunal *m*; (*persons*) judicatura *f*; **to be on the ~** (*Jur*) ser juez, ser magistrado; **he's on the ~ today** hoy forma parte del tribunal.
benchmark ['bentʃmɑːk] *n* cota *f*, punto *m* topográfico; **~ price** precio *m* de referencia.
benchwarmer ['bentʃ,wɔːməʳ] *n* (*US*) calientabanquillos *m.*
bend [bend] **1** *n* curva *f*; recodo *m*, vuelta *f*; ángulo *m*; (*Her*) banda *f*; (*Naut*) gaza *f*; **~s** (*Med*) apoplejía *f* por cambios bruscos de presión; **to be round the ~** (*Brit*‡) estar chiflado; **to go round the ~** (*Brit*‡) volverse loco.
2 (*irr*: *pret and ptp* **bent**) *vt* encorvar; (*buckle*) doblar, torcer; (*cause to sag*) combar; *body, head* inclinar; *knee* doblar; *sail* envergar; *efforts, steps etc* dirigir (*to* a); **to ~ the rule for sb** ajustar la regla a beneficio de uno; **to ~ one's mind to a problem** aplicarse a un problema; **to ~ sb to one's will** doblar a uno a su voluntad.
3 *vi* encorvarse; (*buckle*) doblarse, torcerse; (*sag*) combarse; (*road*) torcer(se) (*to the left* a la izquierda).
◆**bend back** *vt* doblar hacia atrás.
◆**bend down** **1** *vt* doblar hacia abajo; *head* inclinar.
2 *vi* (*person*) encorvarse, inclinarse, agacharse.
◆**bend over** **1** *vt* doblar. **2** *vi* (*person*) inclinarse, encorvarse, doblarse (*LAm*); **to ~ over backwards** (*fig*) hacer lo imposible (*to + infin* por + *infin*).
bender‡ ['bendəʳ] *n*: **to go on a ~** ir de juerga, ir de borrachera.
beneath [bɪ'niːθ] *adv and prep* (**a**) = **below.** (**b**) (*fig*) **it is ~ him** es indigno de él; **it is ~ him to do such a thing** él es incapaz de hacer tal bajeza; **she married ~ her** se casó con un hombre de clase inferior.
Benedict ['benɪdɪkt] *nm* Benito; (*pope*) Benedicto.
Benedictine [,benɪ'dɪktɪn] **1** *adj* benedictino. **2** *n* benedictino *m.*
benediction [,benɪ'dɪkʃən] *n* bendición *f.*
benefaction [,benɪ'fækʃən] *n* (*gift*) beneficio *m.*
benefactor ['benɪfæktəʳ] *n* bienhechor *m*, benefactor *m.*
benefactress ['benɪfæktrɪs] *n* bienhechora *f*, benefactora *f.*
benefice ['benɪfɪs] *n* beneficio *m.*
beneficence [bɪ'nefɪsəns] *n* beneficencia *f.*
beneficent [bɪ'nefɪsənt] *adj* benéfico.
beneficial [,benɪ'fɪʃəl] *adj* provechoso, beneficioso.
beneficially [,benɪ'fɪʃəlɪ] *adv* provechosamente, beneficiosamente.
beneficiary [,benɪ'fɪʃərɪ] *n* beneficiario *m*, -a *f*; (*Eccl*) beneficiado *m.*
benefit ['benɪfɪt] **1** *n* beneficio *m*; provecho *m*, utilidad *f*; (*payment*) subsidio *m*; (*Theat, Sport*) beneficio *m*; **~ association, ~ society** (*esp US*) sociedad *f* de socorro mutuo, mutualidad *f*; **~ match** partido homenaje *m*, (partido *m* de) beneficio *m*; **~s package** paquete *m* de beneficios; **~ performance** función *f* benéfica; (función *f* de) beneficio *m*; **for the ~ of** a beneficio de; (**I may say**) **for your ~ that ...** (y agrego) para tu gobierno que ...; **to be to the ~ of** ser provechoso a; **to give sb the ~ of the doubt** dar a uno el beneficio de la duda; **to have the ~ of** tener la ventaja de; **to marry without ~ of clergy** casarse por lo civil; **to reap the ~ of** sacar el fruto de.
2 *vt* beneficiar, aprovechar.
3 *vi* aprovecharse; **to ~ by, to ~ from** sacar provecho de.
Benelux ['benɪlʌks] *n* Benelux *m*; **the ~ countries** los países del Benelux.
benevolence [bɪ'nevələns] *n* benevolencia *f.*
benevolent [bɪ'nevələnt] *adj* benévolo; *society* de socorro mutuo; **~ fund** fondos *mpl* benéficos.
benevolently [bɪ'nevələntlɪ] *adv* benévolamente, con benevolencia.
B.Eng. [,biː'eŋ] *n abbr of* **Bachelor of Engineering** licenciado *m*, -a *f* en Ingeniería.
Bengal [beŋ'gɔːl] *n* Bengala *f*; **~ tiger** tigre *m* de Bengala.
Bengali [beŋ'gɔːlɪ] **1** *adj* bengalí. **2** *n* bengalí *mf.*
Benghazi [ben'gɑːzɪ] *n* Bengasi *m.*
benighted [bɪ'naɪtɪd] *adj* (*fig*) ignorante.
benign [bɪ'naɪn] *adj* benigno (*also Med*).
benignant [bɪ'nɪgnənt] *adj* benigno (*also Med*); (*healthy*) saludable.
benignly [bɪ'naɪnlɪ] *adv* benignamente.
Benjamin ['bendʒəmɪn] *nm* Benjamín.
benny ['benɪ] *n* (*Drugs*‡) benzedrina *f.*
bent¹ [bent] *adj, pret and ptp of* **bend**; (**a**) (*curved, twisted*) encorvado; doblado, torcido.
(**b**) **on pleasure ~** empeñado en divertirse; **to be ~ on + *ger*** estar resuelto a + *infin*, estar empeñado en + *infin*; **to be ~ on a quarrel** estar resuelto a provocar una riña.
(**c**) (‡: *dishonest*) sospechoso; de tendencias criminales; (‡: *perverted*) pervertido; (‡: *homosexual*) invertido.
bent² [bent] *n* inclinación *f* (*to, towards, for* a); **to follow one's ~** seguir su inclinación; **to have a ~ towards** estar inclinado a.
benumb [bɪ'nʌm] *vt* entumecer; (*fig*) entorpecer; *mind etc* paralizar.
benumbed [bɪ'nʌmd] *adj* (*cold*) *person, fingers* entumecido; (*frightened, shocked*) paralizado.
Benzedrine ['benzɪdriːn] ® *n* benzedrina ® *f.*
benzene ['benziːn] *n* benceno *m.*
benzine ['benziːn] *n* bencina *f.*
bequeath [bɪ'kwiːð] *vt* legar.

bequest [bɪ'kwest] *n* legado *m*.
berate [bɪ'reɪt] *vt* censurar; reñir, regañar.
Berber ['bɜːbəʳ] **1** *adj* bereber. **2** *n* bereber *mf*.
bereave [bɪ'riːv] (*irr*: *pret and pp* **bereft**) *vt* privar (*of* de).
bereaved [bɪ'riːvd] *adj* afligido; **the ~** los afligidos; **with the thanks of his ~ family** con el agradecimiento de su desconsolada familia.
bereavement [bɪ'riːvmənt] *n* aflicción *f* (por la muerte de un pariente); pérdida *f*; luto *m*, duelo *m*.
bereft [bɪ'reft] *ptp*: **to be ~ of** (*act*) ser privado de, (*state*) estar desprovisto de.
beret ['bereɪ] *n* boina *f*; **The Red B~s** (*Mil*) los boinas rojas.
beriberi ['berɪ,berɪ] *n* beriberi *m*.
Bering Sea ['beɪrɪŋ'siː] *n* Mar *m* de Bering.
berk* [bɜːk] *n* tipo* *m*, tío* *m*; memo* *m*.
berkelium [bɜː'kiːlɪəm] *n* berkelio *m*.
Berks [bɑːks] *n abbr of* **Berkshire**.
Berlin [bɜː'lɪn] *n* Berlín *m*; (*attr*) berlinés; **the ~ Wall** el Muro *m* de Berlín; **East ~** Berlín Este; **West ~** Berlín Oeste.
Berliner [bɜː'lɪnəʳ] *n* berlinés *m*, -esa *f*.
berm [bɜːm] *n* (*US*) arcén *m*.
Bermuda [bɜː'mjuːdə] *n* Islas *fpl* Bermudas, las Bermudas; **~ shorts** bermudas *mpl*; **the ~ Triangle** el Triángulo *m* de las Bermudas.
Bern [bɜːn] *n* Berna *f*.
Bernard ['bɜːnəd] *nm* Bernardo.
Bernese [bɜː'niːz] *adj* bernés; **~ Alps, ~ Oberland** Alpes *mpl* Berneses.
berry ['berɪ] *n* baya *f*; (*of coffee*) grano *m*.
berserk [bə'sɜːk] *adj*: **to go ~** perder los estribos; ponerse como una fiera; volverse loco.
Bert [bɜːt] *nm familiar form of* **Albert, Herbert** *etc*.
berth [bɜːθ] **1** *n* (*place at wharf*) amarradero *m*; (*place in marina etc*) punto *m* de atraque; (*cabin*) camarote *m*; (*bunk*) litera *f*; (*) puesto *m*, lugar *m*; **to give sb a wide ~** evitar el encuentro de uno, huir el trato de uno. **2** *vti* atracar.
beryl ['berɪl] *n* berilo *m*.
beryllium [be'rɪljəm] *n* berilio *m*.
beseech [bɪ'siːtʃ] (*irr*: *pret and ptp* **besought**) *vt* suplicar (*for sth* algo, *to do* hacer).
beseeching [bɪ'siːtʃɪŋ] *adj* suplicante.
beseechingly [bɪ'siːtʃɪŋlɪ] *adv* en tono (*etc*) de súplica.
beset [bɪ'set] (*irr*: *V* **set**) *vt person* acosar, perseguir; *road* obstruir, dificultar; **a policy ~ with dangers** una política llena de peligros; **a way ~ with difficulties** un camino erizado de dificultades; **to be ~ by doubts** estar acosado por las dudas.
besetting [bɪ'setɪŋ] *adj* obsesionante; *sin* dominante.
beside [bɪ'saɪd] *prep* (**a**) (*at the side of*) cerca de, junto a, al lado de; **to be ~ o.s.** (*with anger*) estar fuera de sí, (*with anxiety*) volverse loco de inquietud.
(**b**) (*fig*) **whom can we set ~ him?** ¿con quién podemos compararle?; **what is that ~ victory?** y eso ¿qué importa en comparación con la victoria?
besides [bɪ'saɪdz] **1** *adv* además. **2** *prep* además de; (*with negation*) excepto, fuera de.
besiege [bɪ'siːdʒ] *vt* asediar, sitiar; **we are ~d with calls** nos están llamando incesantemente; **we were ~d with inquiries** hubo un torrente de preguntas.
besieger [bɪ'siːdʒəʳ] *n* sitiador *m*.
besmear [bɪ'smɪəʳ] *vt* embarrar, embadurnar.
besmirch [bɪ'smɜːtʃ] *vt* (*fig*) manchar, mancillar.
besom ['biːzəm] *n* escoba *f*.
besotted [bɪ'sɒtɪd] *adj* entontecido; **~ with alcohol** embrutecido por el alcohol; **~ with love** amartelado, atortolado; encaprichado, encalabrinado; **he is ~ with her** anda loco por ella.
besought [bɪ'sɔːt] *pret and ptp of* **beseech**.
bespatter [bɪ'spætəʳ] *vt* salpicar (*with* de).
bespeak [bɪ'spiːk] (*irr*: *V* **speak**) *vt* (**a**) (*engage*) apalabrar; *goods etc* encargar, reservar. (**b**) (*be evidence of*) indicar.
bespectacled [bɪ'spektɪkld] *adj* con gafas, que lleva gafas.
bespoke [bɪ'spəʊk] **1** *pret and ptp of* **bespeak**. **2** *adj* (*Brit*): **~ clothing** ropa *f* hecha a la medida; **~ tailor** sastre *m* que confecciona a medida.
bespoken [bɪ'spəʊkən] *ptp of* **bespeak**.
besprinkle [bɪ'sprɪŋkl] *vt* salpicar, rociar (*with* de); espolvorear (*with* de).
Bess [bes], **Bessie, Bessy** ['besɪ] *nf familiar forms of* **Elizabeth** (Isabelita); **Good Queen Bess** (*Brit*) la buena reina Isabel.
best [best] **1** *adj superl* (el, la) mejor; **the ~ one of all** el mejor de todos; **to know what is ~ for sb** saber lo que más le conviene a uno; **'~ by 31 May'** 'consumir de preferencia antes del 31 mayo', 'consumir preferentemente antes del 31 mayo'; **'~ before date'** fecha *f* de consumo preferente.
2 *adv superl* (lo) mejor; **as ~ I could** lo mejor que pude; **she did ~ of all in the test** ella hizo el test mejor que nadie; **I had ~ go** más vale que yo vaya; **I had ~ see him at once** sería aconsejable verle en seguida; **you know ~** Vd sabe mejor que yo; **Mummy knows ~** estas cosas las decide mamá, mamá sabe lo que más conviene; **when it comes to hotels I know ~** yo soy el más experto en asunto de hoteles; **to come off ~** salir ganando.
3 *n* (**a**) lo mejor; **the ~ of it is that ...** lo mejor del caso es que ...; **is that the ~ you can do?** y eso ¿es todo lo que Vd puede hacer?; **we have had the ~ of the day** el buen tiempo se acabó por hoy; **'my ~'** (*US*: *ending letter*), **'all the ~'** 'un abrazo'; **all the ~!** (*as farewell*) ¡que tengas suerte!; **all the ~ to Jim!** ¡recuerdos para Jim!
(**b**) (*phrases with prep*) **at ~, at the ~** a lo más, en el mejor de los casos; **the garden is at its ~ in June** es en junio cuando el jardín luce más; **he wasn't at his ~** no estuvo en forma; **it's boring at the ~ of times** en el mejor de los casos es aburrido; **it's all for the ~** todo conduce al bien a la larga; **I acted for the ~** obré con la mejor intención; **we drank of the ~** bebimos el mejor vino (*etc*); **I can sing with the ~ (of them)** yo canto como el que más.
(**c**) (*phrases with verb*) **to do one's ~** hacer todo lo posible, hacerlo lo mejor posible; **to do one's ~ to** + *infin* hacer todo lo posible para (*or* por) + *infin*; **I'll do it as ~ I can** lo haré lo mejor que pueda; **to get the ~ of it** salir ganando, imponerse; **to get the ~ of the bargain** llevarse la mejor parte, salir ganando; **in order to get the ~ out of the car** para obtener el máximo rendimiento del coche; **to have the ~ of both worlds** tenerlo todo, tener ventajas por ambas partes; **to look one's ~** mostrarse en todo su esplendor; **she's not looking her ~** está algo desmejorada; **to make the ~ of it** salir de un mal negocio lo mejor posible; **to play ~ of three** jugar al mejor de tres; **I try to think the ~ of him** procuro conservar mi buena opinión de él.
4 *vt* vencer.
bestial ['bestɪəl] *adj* bestial.
bestiality [,bestɪ'ælɪtɪ] *n* bestialidad *f*.
bestir [bɪ'stɜːʳ] *vr*: **to ~ o.s.** menearse.
best man [,best'mæn] *n*, *pl* **best men** [,best'men] (*at wedding*) padrino *m* de boda, testigo *m* del novio.
bestow [bɪ'stəʊ] *vt* (*grant*) otorgar (*on* a); (*give*) conceder, dar (*on* a); *affections* ofrecer (*on* a); *compliment* hacer (*on* a).
bestowal [bɪ'stəʊəl] *n* otorgamiento *m*; donación *f*; ofrecimiento *m*.
bestraddle [bɪ'strædl] *vt* montar a horcajadas, estar a horcajadas sobre; (*fig*) estar a caballo sobre.
bestrew [bɪ'struː] (*irr*: *V* **strew**) *vt things* desparramar, esparcir; *surface* sembrar, cubrir (*with* de).
bestridden [bɪ'strɪdn] *ptp of* **bestride**.
bestride [bɪ'straɪd] (*irr*: *V* **stride**) *vt horse* montar a horcajadas; *stream etc* cruzar de un tranco; (*fig*) dominar.
bestrode [bɪ'strəʊd] *pret of* **bestride**.
best-seller ['best'seləʳ] *n* bestseller *m*, éxito *m* de librería.
best-selling ['best'selɪŋ] *adj*: **our ~ line** nuestro producto de mayor venta, nuestro campeón de ventas; **for years it was the ~ car** durante años fue el coche que más se vendió.
bet [bet] **1** *n* apuesta *f*; (*sum*) postura *f*; **to lay** (*or* **make, put**) **a ~ on** apostar a; **it's a good ~ that he'll come** seguramente vendrá, es casi seguro que vendrá; **your best ~ is to come today** lo mejor que puedes hacer es venir hoy.
2 (*irr*: *pret and ptp* **bet** *or* **betted**) *vt* apostar (*on* a); **I ~ you a fiver that ...** te apuesto 5 libras a que ...; **I'll ~ you anything you like!** ¡apuesto lo que quieras!; **you ~ (your life)!** ¡ya lo creo!
3 *vi* apostar, jugar; **I ~ you can't!** ¡a que no puedes!; **I ~ it isn't!** ¡a que no!; **I don't ~** yo no juego; **don't ~ on it, I wouldn't ~ on it** eso no es tan seguro, no hay que contar con eso.
beta ['biːtə] *n* beta *f*.
betake [bɪ'teɪk] (*irr*: *V* **take**) *vr*: **to ~ o.s. to** dirigirse a, trasladarse a, acudir a.
betaken [bɪ'teɪkən] *ptp of* **betake**.
betel ['biːtəl] *n* betel *m*.
bête noire ['beɪt'nwɑːʳ] *n* bestia *f* negra, pesadilla *f*.
bethink [bɪ'θɪŋk] (*irr*: *V* **think**) *vr*: **to ~ o.s. of** acordarse de.

Bethlehem ['beθlɪhem] *n* Belén *m.*
bethought [bɪ'θɔːt] *pret and ptp of* **bethink**.
betide [bɪ'taɪd] *vti* acontecer; *V* **woe**.
betimes [bɪ'taɪmz] *adv* (*liter*) (*early*) temprano, al alba; (*quickly*) rápidamente; (*in good time*) a tiempo.
betoken [bɪ'təʊkən] *vt* presagiar, anunciar.
betook [bɪ'tʊk] *pret of* **betake**.
betray [bɪ'treɪ] *vt* (**a**) *person, country* traicionar; **to ~ sb to the enemy** vender a uno al enemigo; **his accent ~s him** su acento le traiciona; **his accent ~s him as a foreigner** su acento le acusa de extranjero.
(**b**) (*reveal*) *plot etc* revelar, delatar; *ignorance etc* hacer patente.
(**c**) (*show signs of*) dejar ver, dar muestras de, descubrir; **his face ~ed a certain surprise** su cara acusó cierto asombro.
betrayal [bɪ'treɪəl] *n* (*V vt*) (**a**) traición *f*; **~ of trust** abuso *m* de confianza. (**b**) revelación *f*. (**c**) descubrimiento *m*.
betrayer [bɪ'treɪəʳ] *n* traidor *m*, -ora *f*; **she killed her ~** mató a quien la traicionó.
betroth [bɪ'trəʊð] (*liter*) *vt* prometer en matrimonio (*to* a); **to be ~ed** (*act*) desposarse, (*state*) estar desposado.
betrothal [bɪ'trəʊðəl] *n* (*liter*) desposorios *mpl*, esponsales *mpl*.
betrothed [bɪ'trəʊðd] (*liter, hum*) **1** *adj* prometido. **2** *n, pl invar* prometido *m*, -a *f*.
better¹ ['betəʳ] **1** *adj comp* mejor; **~ and ~** cada vez mejor; **that's ~** eso va mejor; más vale así; **that's ~!** ¡bien!; **he's much ~** (*Med*) está mucho mejor; **it couldn't be ~** no podría ser mejor; **it is ~ to** + *infin* más vale + *infin*; **it would be ~ to** + *infin* más valdría + *infin*, sería aconsejable + *infin*; **she's no ~ than she ought to be** es una mujer que tiene historia; **to get ~** mejorar(se), (*Med*) mejorar(se), reponerse; **to go one ~** hacer mejor todavía (*than* que).
2 *adv comp* mejor; **all the ~, so much the ~** tanto mejor (*for* para); **to be all the ~ for** haber mejorado mucho a consecuencia de; **it would be all the ~ for a drop of paint** no le vendría mal una mano de pintura; **they withdrew the ~ to resist** se retiraron para poder resistir mejor; **they are ~ off than we are** son más acomodados que nosotros; **I had ~ go** más vale que yo vaya; **but he knew ~** pero él tuvo otra idea; **he thinks he knows ~** él cree que se lo sabe todo; **at his age he ought to know ~** a la edad que tiene debiera saberlo; **he knows ~ than the experts** él sabe más que los expertos; **to think ~ of it** mudar de parecer, cambiar de idea.
3 *n* (**a**) **my ~s** mis superiores.
(**b**) **it's a change for the ~** es un cambio beneficioso; **for ~ or worse** en la fortuna como en la adversidad; **to get the ~ of** vencer, quedar por encima de.
4 *vt* mejorar; *record, score* superar.
5 *vr*: **to ~ o.s.** mejorar su posición.
better² ['betəʳ] *n* apostador *m*, -ora *f*.
betterment ['betəmənt] *n* mejora *f*, mejoramiento *m*.
betting ['betɪŋ] **1** *adj* aficionado al juego; **I'm not a ~ man** yo no juego. **2** *n* juego *m*, el apostar.
betting-shop ['betɪŋ,ʃɒp] *n* (*Brit*) agencia *f* de apuestas.
betting-slip ['betɪŋslɪp] *n* (*Brit*) boleto *m* de apuestas.
betting-tax ['betɪŋ,tæks] *n* impuesto *m* sobre las apuestas.
Betty ['betɪ] *nf familiar form of* **Elizabeth** (Isabelita).
between [bɪ'twiːn] **1** *adv* (*also* **in ~**) en medio.
2 *prep* entre; **~ ourselves** entre nosotros; **~ you and me** entre tú y yo; **we bought it ~ 4 of us** lo compramos entre los 4; **they shared it ~ them** se lo repartieron; **~ now and May** de ahora a mayo; **the shops are shut ~ 2 and 4** las tiendas están cerradas de 2 a 4.
betweentimes [bɪ'twiːntaɪmz] *adv*, **betweenwhiles** [bɪ'twiːnwaɪlz] *adv* mientras, entretanto.
betwixt [bɪ'twɪkst] **1** *adv* en medio; **~ and between** entre lo uno y lo otro. **2** *prep* entre; en medio de.
bevel ['bevəl] **1** *adj* biselado. **2** *n* (*tool*: *also* **~ edge**) cartabón *m*, escuadra *f* falsa; (*surface*) bisel *m*. **3** *vt* biselar.
bevel-edged [,bevl'edʒd] *adj* biselado.
beverage ['bevərɪdʒ] *n* bebida *f*.
bevvy* ['bevɪ] *n* trago* *m*.
bevy ['bevɪ] *n* (*birds*) bandada *f*; (*women etc*) grupo *m*.
bewail [bɪ'weɪl] *vt* lamentar.
beware [bɪ'wɛəʳ] *vi* (**a**) tener cuidado; **to ~ of** precaverse de, tener cuidado con, guardarse de.
(**b**) **~!** ¡cuidado!, ¡atención!, ¡ojo!; **~ of the dog!** ¡ojo con el perro!, (*as notice*) 'perro peligroso'; **~ of pickpockets!** ¡ojo con los carteristas!; **~ of imitations** desconfíe de las imitaciones.
bewhiskered [bɪ'wɪskəd] *adj* bigotudo.
bewilder [bɪ'wɪldəʳ] *vt* aturdir, dejar perplejo, aturrullar, desconcertar.
bewildered [bɪ'wɪldəd] *adj person* desconcertado, perplejo, aturdido; **he gave me a ~ look** me miró perplejo.
bewildering [bɪ'wɪldərɪŋ] *adj* desconcertante.
bewilderingly [bɪ'wɪldərɪŋlɪ] *adv* de modo desconcertante; **a ~ complicated matter** un asunto tan complicado que desconcierta.
bewilderment [bɪ'wɪldəmənt] *n* aturdimiento *m*, perplejidad *f*.
bewitch [bɪ'wɪtʃ] *vt* hechizar (*also fig*).
bewitching [bɪ'wɪtʃɪŋ] *adj* hechicero, encantador.
bewitchingly [bɪ'wɪtʃɪŋlɪ] *adv* encantadoramente; **~ beautiful** encantadoramente hermoso.
beyond [bɪ'jɒnd] **1** *adv* más allá, más lejos; **next year and ~** el año que viene y después.
2 *prep* (**a**) (*in space, time*) más allá de; **~ the seas** allende los mares; **we can't see ~ 2010** no podemos ver más allá de 2010.
(**b**) (*over and above*) además de, fuera de.
(**c**) (*fig*) **the task is ~ him** la tarea es superior a sus fuerzas; **it's ~ me** está fuera de mi alcance, no lo entiendo; **it's ~ me to see how** no alcanzo a ver cómo; **this is getting ~ me** se me está haciendo imposible esto; **it's ~ a doubt** está fuera de toda duda; **it's ~ praise** queda por encima de todo elogio; **to go ~ one's authority** exceder a su autoridad.
3 *n*: **the great ~** el más allá.
bezique [bɪ'ziːk] *n juego de cartas que se juega con dos mazos.*
BF* *n* (*euph*) *abbr of* **bloody fool**.
b/f *abbr of* **brought forward** suma *f* del anterior.
BFPO *n* (*Brit Mil*) *abbr of* **British Forces Post Office**.
b/fwd = **b/f**.
b.h.p. *n abbr of* **brake horsepower** potencia *f* al freno.
Bhutan [buː'tɑːn] *n* Bután *m*.
bi... [baɪ] *pref* bi...
Biafra [bɪ'æfrə] *n* Biafra *f*.
Biafran [bɪ'æfrən] **1** *adj* de Biafra. **2** *n* nativo *m*, -a *f* (*or* habitante *mf*) de Biafra.
biannual [baɪ'ænjʊəl] *adj* semestral.
bias ['baɪəs] **1** *n* (**a**) (*Sew*) sesgo *m*, diagonal *f*; **to cut sth on the ~** cortar algo al sesgo.
(**b**) (*inclination*) propensión *f*, predisposición *f* (*to, towards* a); **to have a ~ towards** tener propensión a, estar inclinado a.
(**c**) (*prejudice*) pasión *f*, prejuicio *m* (*against* contra).
2 *vt* (*fig*) influir en, torcer; **to ~ sb against sth** predisponer a uno en contra de algo; **to be ~sed** tener prejuicio (*against* contra), ser partidario (*in favour of* de).
bias(s)ed ['baɪəst] *adj* parcial.
biathlon [baɪ'æθlən] *n* biatlón *m*.
bib [bɪb] *n* babero *m*, babador *m*; **in one's best ~ and tucker** acicalado, engalanado.
Bible ['baɪbl] *n* Biblia *f*; **the Holy ~** la Santa Biblia; **~ Belt** (*US*) *Estados del Sur ultraprotestantes*; **~ class** (*for confirmation etc*) catecismo *m*; **~ college** (*US*) colegio *m* evangelista; **~ school** (*US*) escuela *f* de enseñanza de la Biblia; **~ stories** historias *fpl* de la Biblia; **~ study** estudio *m* de la Biblia; **~ thumper** (*) fanático *m* religioso, fundamentalista *mf*.
Biblical ['bɪblɪkəl] *adj* bíblico.
biblio... ['bɪblɪəʊ] *pref* biblio...
bibliographer [,bɪblɪ'ɒgrəfəʳ] *n* bibliógrafo *m*, -a *f*.
bibliographic(al) [,bɪblɪəʊ'græfɪk(əl)] *adj* bibliográfico.
bibliography [,bɪblɪ'ɒgrəfɪ] *n* bibliografía *f*.
bibliomania [,bɪblɪəʊ'meɪnɪə] *n* bibliomanía *f*.
bibliometric [,bɪblɪəʊ'metrɪk] *adj* bibliométrico.
bibliometry [,bɪblɪ'ɒmɪtrɪ] *n* bibliometría *f*.
bibliophile ['bɪblɪəʊfaɪl] *n* bibliófilo *m*, -a *f*.
bibulous ['bɪbjʊləs] *adj* bebedor, borrachín.
bicameral [baɪ'kæmərəl] *adj* bicameral.
bicarb* [baɪ'kɑːb] *n*, **bicarbonate of soda** [baɪ'kɑːbənɪtəv'səʊdə] *n* bicarbonato *m* sódico.
bicentenary [,baɪsen'tiːnərɪ], (*US*) **bicentennial** [baɪsen'tenɪəl] **1** *adj* (de) bicentenario; **~ celebrations** celebraciones *fpl* de(l) bicentenario. **2** *n* bicentenario *m*.
biceps ['baɪseps] *n, pl invar* bíceps *m*.
bicker ['bɪkəʳ] *vi* reñir, altercar; (*stream*) murmurar.
bickering ['bɪkərɪŋ] *n* riñas *fpl*, altercados *mpl*.
bicuspid [baɪ'kʌspɪd] **1** *adj* bicúspide. **2** *n* bicúspide *m*.
bicycle ['baɪsɪkl] **1** *n* bicicleta *f*. **2** *vi* ir en bicicleta; **to ~ to Dover** ir en bicicleta a Dover. **3** *attr*: **~ chain** cadena *f* de bicicleta; **~ clip** pinza *f* para ir en bicicleta; **~ kick**

chilena *f*, tijereta *f*; ~ **lane**, ~ **track** carril *m* para ciclistas; ~ **pump** bomba *f* de bicicleta; ~ **rack** soporte *m* para bicicleta; ~ **shed** cobertizo *m* para bicicletas; ~ **touring** turismo *m* en bicicleta.

bid [bɪd] **1** *n* (**a**) (*at auction*) oferta *f*, postura *f*; (*Fin*) oferta *f*; ~ **price** precio *m* de oferta; **highest** ~ mejor postura *f*.
(**b**) (*Cards*) marca *f*; apuesta *f*, declaración *f*; **no** ~ paso.
(**c**) (*fig*) tentativa *f*, conato *m*; **to make a** ~ **for control of** tratar de asegurar el control de; **to make a** ~ **to** + *infin* hacer una tentativa de + *infin*.
2 (*irr*: *pret* **bade, bid,** *ptp* **bidden, bid**) *vt* (**a**) (*order*) ordenar, mandar; **to** ~ **sb to do sth** mandar a uno hacer algo.
(**b**) (*at auction*) licitar, ofrecer; **to** ~ **£10 for** ofrecer 10 libras por; **to** ~ **sb up to £12** hacer que uno siga haciendo posturas hasta 12 libras.
(**c**) (*Cards*) marcar, pujar, declarar.
(**d**) (*say*) **to** ~ **sb good-day** dar a uno los buenos días; **to** ~ **defiance to** desafiar a; *V* **adieu**.
3 *vi* (**a**) (*at auction*) **to** ~ **for** pujar por, hacer una oferta por; **to** ~ **up** pujar.
(**b**) **to** ~ **fair to** + *infin* prometer + *infin*, dar esperanzas de + *infin*.

biddable ['bɪdəbl] *adj* (**a**) obediente, sumiso. (**b**) (*Cards*) marcable.

bidden ['bɪdn] *ptp of* **bid**.

bidder ['bɪdə^r] *n* (**a**) (*at auction*) postor *m*, -ora *f*; (*Fin*) ofertante *mf*, postor *m*, -ora *f*; **highest** ~ mejor postor *m*.
(**b**) (*Cards*) declarante *mf*.

bidding ['bɪdɪŋ] *n* (**a**) (*order*) orden *f*, mandato *m*; **they did it at her** ~ lo hicieron cumpliendo su orden; **to do sb's** ~ cumplir el mandato de uno.
(**b**) (*at auction*) licitación *f*, ofertas *fpl*; **the** ~ **opened at £5** la primera oferta fue de 5 libras; **there was keen** ~ **for the picture** hubo una rápida serie de ofertas por el cuadro; **to raise** (*or* **up**) **the** ~ aumentar la licitación.
(**c**) (*Cards*) remate *m*, declaración *f*; **to open the** ~ abrir la declaración.
(**d**) (*Eccl*; *also* ~ **prayers**) oraciones *fpl* de los fieles.

biddy ['bɪdɪ] *n* († *or dial*) vieja bruja *f*.

bide [baɪd] *vt*: **to** ~ **one's time** esperar la hora propicia.

bidet ['biːdeɪ] *n* bidet *m*, bidé *m*.

bidirectional [baɪdɪ'rekʃənl] *adj* bidireccional.

biennial [baɪ'enɪəl] **1** *adj* bienal; (*Bot*) bianual. **2** *n* planta *f* bienal, bianual *m*.

bier [bɪə^r] *n* féretro *m*, andas *fpl*.

biff* [bɪf] **1** *n* bofetada *f*. **2** *vt* dar una bofetada a.

bifocal ['baɪ'fəʊkəl] **1** *adj* bifocal. **2** *n* lente *m* bifocal; ~**s** bifocales *mpl*.

bifurcate ['baɪfəkeɪt] *vi* bifurcarse.

big [bɪg] **1** *adj* (**a**) grande; abultado, voluminoso; importante; ~ **band** orquesta *f*, big band *f*; **the** ~ **bang** (*Fin, Phys*) el big bang *m*, la gran explosión *f*; ~ **bang theory** teoría *f* de la gran explosión; **B~ Ben** Big Ben *m*; **my** ~ **brother** mi hermano mayor; **B~ Brother is watching you** el Gran Hermano te vigila; ~ **cat** felino *m* mayor; ~ **city** ciudad *f* grande; ~ **city problems** problemas *mpl* de las grandes urbes; **the B~ Eight/Ten** (*US*) *las ocho/diez grandes universidades del Centro-Oeste*; ~ **end** (*Aut*) cabeza *f* (*or* pie *m*) de biela; **the B~ Four** (*Pol*) las cuatro Grandes (Potencias); (*Fin*) los cuatro Grandes (Bancos); ~ **game** (*Brit*) caza *f* mayor; ~ **game hunter** cazador *m*, -ora *f* de caza mayor; **the** ~ **house** la casa principal (de un pueblo *etc*); **the** ~ **match** el partido principal; **Mr B~** Número *m* Uno; ~ **noise**, ~ **shot** (*Brit**) pez *m* gordo*; **a** ~ **one** (*US‡*) un billete de 1.000 dólares; ~ **top** carpa *f*; **it's a** ~ **shame** es una terrible lástima; **that's** ~ **money** eso es mucho dinero; **when you're** ~ cuando seas mayor; **to earn** ~ **money** ganar mucho dinero; **to have** ~ **ideas** tener ideas grandiosas; **boots are** ~ **this year*** las botas están de moda este año; **to be** ~ **with child** estar encinta. (**b**) (*: *generous*) amable; generoso; **that's very** ~ **of you** eres muy amable; *V* **dipper²**, **name 1** (**c**) *etc*.
2 *adv* (*) **to go over** ~ tener un exitazo*; **to talk** ~ darse mucha importancia, fanfarronear, darse bombo; **to think** ~ hacer proyectos de gran envergadura.

bigamist ['bɪgəmɪst] *n* bígamo *m*, -a *f*.

bigamous ['bɪgəməs] *adj* bígamo.

bigamy ['bɪgəmɪ] *n* bigamia *f*.

big-boned [ˌbɪg'bəʊnd] *adj* de huesos grandes, huesudo.

biggish ['bɪgɪʃ] *adj* bastante grande.

bighead* ['bɪghed] *n* orgulloso *m*, -a *f*, engreído *m*, -a *f*.

bigheaded* ['bɪg'hedɪd] *adj* engreído.

big-hearted ['bɪg'hɑːtɪd] *adj* generoso.

bight [baɪt] *n* (**a**) (*Geog*) ensenada *f*, cala *f*; (*bend*) recodo *m*. (**b**) (*of rope*) gaza *f*, laza *f*.

bigmouth‡ ['bɪgmaʊθ] *n*, *pl* **bigmouths** ['bɪgmaʊðz] (*talkative*) bocazas‡ *mf*; (*gossipy*) chismoso *m*, -a *f*; (*treacherous*) soplón *m*.

big-mouthed ['bɪg'maʊθt] *adj* (**a**) de boca grande, de boca ancha, bocudo. (**b**) (‡) bocón; chismoso; soplón.

bigot ['bɪgət] *n* fanático *m*, -a *f*, intolerante *mf*.

bigoted ['bɪgətɪd] *adj* fanático, intolerante.

bigotry ['bɪgətrɪ] *n* fanatismo *m*, intolerancia *f*.

big-time* ['bɪg'taɪm] *adj* de rumbo, de muchas campanillas; importante, poderoso.

bigwig ['bɪgwɪg] *n* pez *m* gordo, señorón *m*.

bijou ['biːʒuː] *as adj*: '~ **residence for sale**' (*Brit*) 'residencia coquetona en venta'.

bike* [baɪk] **1** *n* bici* *f*; ~ **rack** (*US*) soporte *m* para bicicletas; **on your** ~**!*** ¡largo de aquí!*, ¡andando!* **2** *vi* ir en bicicleta, ir en moto.

biker* ['baɪkə^r] *n* motorista *mf*.

bikeshed ['baɪkʃed] *n* cobertizo *m* para bicicletas.

bikeway ['baɪkweɪ] *n* (*lane*) carril *m* de bicicletas; (*track*) pista *f* de ciclismo.

bikini [bɪ'kiːnɪ] *n* bikini *m*, biquini *m*.

bilabial [baɪ'leɪbɪəl] *adj, n* bilabial *f*.

bilateral [baɪ'lætərəl] *adj* bilateral.

bilberry ['bɪlbərɪ] *n* arándano *m*.

bile [baɪl] *n* bilis *f*; (*fig*) mal genio *m*, displicencia *f*.

bilge [bɪldʒ] *n* (**a**) (*Naut*) pantoque *m*; (*water*) aguas *fpl* de pantoque. (**b**) (‡) tonterías *fpl*.

bilge-water ['bɪldʒwɔːtə^r] *n* aguas *fpl* de pantoque.

bilharzia [bɪl'hɑːzɪə] *n*, **bilharziasis** [ˌbɪlhɑː'zaɪəsɪs] *n* bilharciasis *f*, bilarciasis *f*.

bilingual [baɪ'lɪŋgwəl] *adj* bilingüe.

bilingualism [baɪ'lɪŋgwəlɪzəm] *n* bilingüismo *m*.

bilious ['bɪlɪəs] *adj* bilioso (*also fig*); ~ **attack** trastorno *m* biliar; **to be** (*or* **feel**) ~ tener un trastorno biliar.

biliousness ['bɪlɪəsnɪs] *n* trastornos *mpl* biliares.

bilk [bɪlk] *vt* estafar, defraudar.

bill¹ [bɪl] **1** *n* (*bird's*) pico *m*; (*of anchor*) uña *f*; (*Agr*) podadera *f*, podón *m*; (*Geog*) promontorio *m*. **2** *vi*: **to** ~ **and coo** besuquearse, acariciarse.

bill² [bɪl] **1** *n* (**a**) (*esp Brit*) (*account*) cuenta *f*, adición *f* (*SC*); (*invoice*) factura *f*; **wages** ~ (*in industry*) coste *m* de salarios; ~**s discounted** efectos *mpl* descontados; ~**s payable** efectos *mpl* a pagar; ~**s receivable** efectos *mpl* a cobrar; **to foot the** ~ pagar la cuenta; correr con los gastos.
(**b**) (*Parl*) proyecto *m* de ley; ~ **of rights** declaración *f* de derechos, ley *f* fundamental; **to fill the** ~ llenar los requisitos, servir; **the** ~ **passed the Commons** (*Brit*) el proyecto de ley fue aprobado en la Cámara de los Comunes.
(**c**) (*US*: *banknote*) billete *m*; ~ (**of exchange**) letra *f* de cambio.
(**d**) (*notice*) cartel *m*; '**stick no** ~**s**' 'prohibido fijar carteles'.
(**e**) ~ **of fare** lista *f* (de platos), menú *m*; **clean** ~ **of health** (*Naut, fig*) patente *f* de sanidad; ~ **of lading** conocimiento *m* de embarque; ~ **of sale** escritura *f* de venta.
2 *vt* (**a**) (*Theat*) anunciar; **he is** ~**ed to appear next week** figura en el programa de la semana que viene.
(**b**) (*Comm*) **to** ~ **sb for sth** extender (*or* pasar) a uno la factura de algo; **you've** ~**ed me for 5 instead of 4** Vd ha puesto 5 y no 4 en la factura.

Bill [bɪl] *nm familiar form of* **William**; **the** (**Old**) ~ (*Brit‡*) la pasma‡, la policía; ~ **shop‡** comisaría *f*.

billboard ['bɪlbɔːd] *n* (*esp US*) cartelera *f*, valla *f* publicitaria.

billet¹ ['bɪlɪt] **1** *n* alojamiento *m*; (*) colocación *f*, puesto *m*. **2** *vt* alojar (*on* en casa de, a, con).

billet² ['bɪlɪt] *n* (*wood*) leño *m*.

billet-doux ['bɪleɪ'duː] *n*, *pl* **billets-doux** ['bɪleɪ'duː] carta *f* amorosa.

billeting ['bɪlətɪŋ] *n* acantonamiento *m*; ~ **officer** oficial *m* de acantonamiento.

billfold ['bɪlfəʊld] *n* (*US*) billetero *m*, cartera *f*.

billhook ['bɪlhʊk] *n* podadera *f*, podón *m*.

billiard-ball ['bɪlɪəd,bɔːl] *n* bola *f* de billar.

billiard-cue ['bɪlɪəd,kjuː] *n* taco *m*.

billiards ['bɪlɪədz] *n sing* billar *m*.

billiard(s) saloon ['bɪlɪəd(z)sə,luːn] *n* (*Brit*) salón *m* de billar, billares *mpl*.

billiard-table ['bɪlɪəd,teɪbl] *n* mesa *f* de billar.

billing[1] [ˈbɪlɪŋ] *n*: **to get top/second ~** (*Theat*) ser primero/segundo de cartel.

billing[2] [ˈbɪlɪŋ] *n*: **~ and cooing** besuqueo *m*, caricias *fpl*.

billion [ˈbɪlɪən] *n* billón *m*, (*US, now frequent in Britain*) mil millones *mpl*; **I've told you a ~ times** te lo he dicho infinidad de veces.

billionaire [ˌbɪlɪəˈnɛəʳ] *n* billonario *m*, -a *f*.

billow [ˈbɪləʊ] **1** *n* oleada *f*; **~s** las olas, el mar. **2** *vi* ondular, ondear.

◆**billow out** *vi* hincharse (de viento *etc*).

billowy [ˈbɪləʊɪ] *adj* ondoso; hinchado.

billposter [ˈbɪlˌpəʊstəʳ] *n*, **billsticker** [ˈbɪlˌstɪkəʳ] *n* cartelero *m*, pegador *m* de carteles.

Billy [ˈbɪlɪ] *nm familiar form of* **William**.

billy [ˈbɪlɪ] *n* (*US: also* **~ club**) porra *f*.

billy-can [ˈbɪlɪˌkæn] *n* cazo *m*.

billy goat [ˈbɪlɪgəʊt] *n* macho *m* cabrío.

billy-ho* [ˈbɪlɪhəʊ] *adv*: **like ~** hasta más no poder.

BIM *n abbr of* **British Institute of Management**.

bimbo‡ [ˈbɪmbəʊ] *n* jai‡ *f*, gachí‡ *f*; (*pej*) putilla *f*.

bimonthly [ˈbaɪˈmʌnθlɪ] **1** *adj* (*every 2 months*) bimestral; (*twice monthly*) bimensual, quincenal.
2 *adv* bimestralmente; bimensualmente, quincenalmente.
3 *n* revista *f* bimestral; revista *f* bimensual, revista *f* quincenal.

bin [bɪn] **1** *n* hucha *f*, arcón *m*; (*for bread*) caja *f*; (*Brit*: *for rubbish*) cubo *m*, tacho *m* (*LAm*); (*for litter*) papelera *f*. **2** *vt* tirar.

binary [ˈbaɪnərɪ] *adj* binario; **~ code** código *m* binario; **~ notation** notación *f* binaria; **~ number** número *m* binario; **~ system** sistema *m* binario.

bind [baɪnd] (*irr*: *pret and ptp* **bound**) **1** *vt* (**a**) (*tie*) atar, liar (*to* a); *hands* atar; *wound* vendar; (*Sew*) ribetear; *corn* agavillar; *book* encuadernar; (*Med*) estreñir; (*encircle*) rodear (*with* de), ceñir (*with* con, de); (*fig*) liar (*to* a), unir (*to* con).
(**b**) (*force*) obligar; **to ~ sb to do sth** obligar a uno a hacer algo; **to ~ sb to a promise** obligar a uno a cumplir su promesa; **to ~ sb apprentice to** poner a uno de aprendiz con; *V also* **bound**[1].
2 *vi* (*cement etc*) endurecerse; cuajarse; adherirse; (*parts of machine*) trabarse.
3 *n* (*Brit**) (*difficulty*) apuro *m*; situación *f* difícil; (*problem*) pega *f*, problema *m*; **the ~ is that ...** el problema es que ...; **it's a ~** es una lata*; **what a ~!** ¡qué lata!*; **to be in a ~** estar en apuros.

◆**bind on** *vt* prender.

◆**bind over** *vt* obligar a comparecer ante el magistrado; **to ~ sb over for 6 months** conceder a uno la libertad bajo fianza durante 6 meses; **to ~ sb over to** + *infin* imponer a uno el deber legal de + *infin*.

◆**bind together** *vt* atar, liar; (*fig*) vincular.

◆**bind up** *vt wound* vendar; *V* **bound**.

binder [ˈbaɪndəʳ] *n* (*Agr*) agavilladora *f*; (*file*) carpeta *f*; (*of book*) encuadernador *m*, -ora *f*.

bindery [ˈbaɪndərɪ] *n* taller *m* de encuadernación.

binding [ˈbaɪndɪŋ] **1** *adj* (**a**) *rule etc* obligatorio (*on* a, para); *promise* que hay que cumplir; *decision* vinculante (*on* para); **legally ~** de obligatoriedad jurídica. (**b**) (*Med*) que estriñe. **2** *n* (*of book*) encuadernación *f*; (*Sew*) ribete *m*.

bindweed [ˈbaɪndwiːd] *n* convólvulo *m*, enredadera *f*.

binge* [bɪndʒ] *n* (*drunken*) borrachera *f*; (*of eating*) comilona* *f*, exceso *m* gastronómico; **to go on a ~** ir de juerga.

bingo [ˈbɪŋgəʊ] **1** *n* (*game*) bingo *m*. **2** *excl* ¡premio!

bingo-hall [ˈbɪŋgəʊˌhɔːl] *n* bingo *m*.

bin-liner [ˈbɪnlaɪnəʳ] *n* bolsa *f* de la basura.

binnacle [ˈbɪnəkl] *n* bitácora *f*.

binocular [bɪˈnɒkjuləʳ] **1** *adj* binocular. **2** *npl*: **~s** gemelos *mpl*, binoculares *mpl*, prismáticos *mpl*, (*Mil*) anteojo *m* de campaña.

binomial [baɪˈnəʊmɪəl] **1** *adj* de dos términos. **2** *n* binomio *m*.

bint‡ [bɪnt] *n* jai‡ *f*.

binuclear [baɪˈnjuːklɪəʳ] *adj* binuclear.

bio... [ˈbaɪəʊ] *pref* bio...

bioactive [ˈbaɪəʊˈæktɪv] *adj* bioactivo.

biochemical [ˈbaɪəʊˈkemɪkəl] *adj* bioquímico.

biochemist [ˈbaɪəʊˈkemɪst] *n* bioquímico *mf*.

biochemistry [ˈbaɪəʊˈkemɪstrɪ] *n* bioquímica *f*.

biodegradable [ˌbaɪədɪˈgreɪdəbl] *adj* biodegradable.

biodegradation [ˌbaɪəʊˌdegrəˈdeɪʃən] *n* biodegradación *f*.

biodegrade [ˌbaɪədɪˈgreɪd] **1** *vt* biodegradar. **2** *vi* biodegradarse.

bioengineering [ˌbaɪəʊˌendʒɪˈnɪərɪŋ] *n* bioingeniería *f*.

biofeedback [ˌbaɪəʊˈfiːdbæk] *n* biofeedback *m*.

biofuel [ˈbaɪəʊfjʊəl] *n* combustible *m* biológico.

biogas [ˈbaɪəʊgæs] *n* biogás *m*.

biogenesis [ˌbaɪəʊˈdʒenɪsɪs] *n* biogénesis *f*.

biographee [baɪˈɒgrəˌfiː] *n* biografiado *m*, -a *f*.

biographer [baɪˈɒgrəfəʳ] *n* biógrafo *m*, -a *f*.

biographic(al) [ˌbaɪəʊˈgræfɪk(əl)] *adj* biográfico.

biography [baɪˈɒgrəfɪ] *n* biografía *f*.

biological [ˌbaɪəˈlɒdʒɪkəl] *adj* biológico; **~ clock** reloj *m* biológico; **~ warfare** guerra *f* biológica.

biologist [baɪˈɒlədʒɪst] *n* biólogo *m*, -a *f*.

biology [baɪˈɒlədʒɪ] *n* biología *f*.

biomass [ˈbaɪəʊˌmæs] *n* biomasa *f*.

biome [ˈbaɪəʊm] *n* biomedio *m*.

biomedical [ˌbaɪəʊˈmedɪkl] *adj* biomédico.

biometrics [ˌbaɪəˈmetrɪks] *n sing*, **biometry** [baɪˈɒmətrɪ] *n* biometría *f*.

bionic [baɪˈɒnɪk] *adj* biónico.

bionics [baɪˈɒnɪks] *n sing* electrónica *f* biológica.

bioorganic [ˌbaɪəʊɔːˈgænɪk] *adj* bioorgánico; **~ chemistry** química *f* bioorgánica.

biophysical [ˌbaɪəʊˈfɪzɪkəl] *adj* biofísico.

biophysicist [ˌbaɪəʊˈfɪzɪsɪst] *n* biofísico *m*, -a *f*.

biophysics [ˌbaɪəʊˈfɪzɪks] *n sing* biofísica *f*.

biopsy [ˈbaɪɒpsɪ] *n* biopsia *f*.

biorhythm [ˈbaɪəʊrɪðəm] *n* bioritmo *m*.

bioscopy [baɪˈɒskəpɪ] *n* bioscopia *f*.

biosensor [ˈbaɪəʊˈsensəʳ] *n* biosensor *m*.

biosphere [ˈbaɪəˌsfɪəʳ] *n* biosfera *f*.

biostatistics [ˈbaɪəʊstəˈtɪstɪks] *npl* bioestadística *f*.

biosynthesis [ˌbaɪəʊˈsɪnθɪsɪs] *n* biosíntesis *f*.

biosynthetic [ˌbaɪəʊˌsɪnˈθetɪk] *adj* biosintético.

biotechnological [ˌbaɪəˌteknəˈlɒdʒɪkəl] *adj* biotecnológico.

biotechnologist [ˌbaɪəʊtekˈnɒlədʒɪst] *n* biotecnólogo *m*, -a *f*.

biotechnology [ˌbaɪəʊtekˈnɒlədʒɪ] *n* biotecnología *f*.

biotic [baɪˈɒtɪk] *adj* biótico.

biotope [ˈbaɪəˌtəʊp] *n* biotopo *m*.

biotype [ˈbaɪəˌtaɪp] *n* biotipo *m*.

biowarfare [ˈbaɪəʊˈwɔːfɛəʳ] *n* guerra *f* bacteriológica.

bipartisan [ˌbaɪˈpɑːtɪzæn] *adj policy etc* que tienen en común los dos partidos, bipartido.

bipartite [baɪˈpɑːtaɪt] *adj* bipartido; *treaty etc* bipartito.

biped [ˈbaɪped] *n* bípedo *m*.

biplane [ˈbaɪpleɪn] *n* biplano *m*.

bipolar [baɪˈpəʊləʳ] *adj* bipolar.

bipolarize [baɪˈpəʊləraɪz] *vt* bipolarizar.

birch [bɜːtʃ] **1** *n* abedul *m*; (*for punishment*) palo *m*, férula *f*. **2** *vt* castigar con el palo.

birching [ˈbɜːtʃɪŋ] *n* flagelación *f*, azotamiento *m*.

birch-tree [ˈbɜːtʃtriː] *n* abedul *m*.

birchwood [ˈbɜːtʃwʊd] *n* bosque *m* de abedules.

bird [bɜːd] *n* (**a**) ave *f*, (*gen small*) pájaro *m*; **~ of ill omen** pájaro *m* de mal agüero; **~ of paradise** ave *f* del paraíso; **~ of passage** ave *f* de paso (*also fig*); **~ of prey** ave *f* de rapiña; **a little ~ told me** me lo ha dicho un pajarito; **they haven't yet told her about the ~s and the bees** todavía no le han explicado las cosas de la vida; **the ~s have flown** (*fig*) los pájaros han volado; **strictly for the ~s*** trivial, de poca monta, pal gato*.
(**b**) (*Theat**) **to get the ~** ganarse un abucheo, ser pateado; **to give sb the ~** abuchear a uno, patear a uno.
(**c**) (*proverbs*) **the early ~ catches the worm** al que madruga Dios le ayuda; **a ~ in the hand is worth two in the bush** más vale pájaro en mano que ciento volando; **~s of a feather flock together** Dios los cría y ellos se juntan; **they're ~s of a feather** son lobos de una camada; **to kill two ~s with one stone** matar dos pájaros de un tiro.
(**d**) (**: man*) tío* *m*, tipo* *m*; (‡: *girl*) chica *f*, jai‡ *f*; (*girlfriend*) amiguita *f*.
(**e**) (‡) **to do 2 years ~** pasar 2 años a la sombra‡.

bird-bath [ˈbɜːdbɑːθ] *n*, *pl* **bird-baths** [ˈbɜːdbɑːðz] pila *f* para pájaros.

birdbrain* [ˈbɜːdbreɪn] *n* casquivano *m*, -a *f*.

bird-brained* [ˈbɜːdbreɪnd] *adj* casquivano.

birdcage [ˈbɜːdkeɪdʒ] *n* jaula *f* de pájaro; (*large, outdoor*) pajarera *f*.

bird-call [ˈbɜːdkɔːl] *n* reclamo *m*.

bird-dog [ˈbɜːddɒg] *n* (*US*) perro *m* de caza.

bird-fancier [ˈbɜːdˌfænsɪəʳ] *n* pajarero *m*.

birdie [ˈbɜːdɪ] *n* (*Golf*) birdie *m*, menos uno *m*.

birdlike [ˈbɜːdlaɪk] *adj* como un pajarito.

birdlime ['bɜːdlaɪm] *n* liga *f.*
bird-nesting ['bɜːd,nestɪŋ] *n*: **to go ~** ir a buscar nidos.
bird-sanctuary ['bɜːd,sæŋktjʊərɪ] *n* reserva *f* para las aves.
birdseed ['bɜːdsiːd] *n* alpiste *m.*
bird's-eye view ['bɜːdzaɪ'vjuː] *n* vista *f* de pájaro.
birdshot ['bɜːdʃɒt] *n* perdigones *mpl.*
bird's-nest ['bɜːdznest] **1** *n* nido *m* de pájaro. **2** *vi* (*esp* **to go ~ing**) ir a buscar nidos.
bird-table ['bɜːd,teɪbl] *n mesita de jardín para poner comida a los pájaros.*
bird-watcher ['bɜːdwɒtʃə^r] *n* ornitólogo *m,* -a *f,* observador *m,* -a *f* de aves.
bird-watching ['bɜːd,wɒtʃɪŋ] *n* ornitología *f,* observación *f* de aves.
biretta [bɪ'retə] *n* birrete *m.*
Biro ['baɪrəʊ] ® *n* (*Brit*) (marca *f* de) bolígrafo *m.*
birth [bɜːθ] *n* nacimiento *m;* (*Med*) parto *m;* (*fig*) nacimiento *m,* origen *m,* comienzo *m;* **the ~ of an idea** el origen de una idea; **by ~** de nacimiento; **of humble ~** de origen humilde; **the village of his ~** el pueblo donde nació, su pueblo natal; **to give ~ to** dar a luz, parir, (*fig*) dar lugar a, ser el origen de; **to be in at the ~ of** (*fig*) asistir al nacimiento de.
birth-certificate ['bɜːθsə'tɪfɪkɪt] *n* partida *f* de nacimiento, fe *f* de bautismo.
birth-control ['bɜːθkən'trəʊl] *n* control *m* de natalidad; **method of ~** método *m* anticonceptivo; **~ pill** píldora *f* anticonceptiva.
birthday ['bɜːθdeɪ] *n* cumpleaños *m;* (*of event etc*) aniversario *m;* (*the Spaniard more commonly celebrates his*) día *m* del santo de uno, fiesta *f* onomástica; **on my 21st ~** cuando cumplí los 21 años; **in one's ~ suit** en cueros.
birthday-cake ['bɜːθdeɪ,keɪk] *n* tarta *f* de cumpleaños.
birthday-card ['bɜːθdeɪ,kɑːd] *n* tarjeta *f* de cumpleaños.
birthday-party ['bɜːθdeɪ,pɑːtɪ] *n* fiesta *f* de cumpleaños.
birthday-present ['bɜːθdeɪ'preznt] *n* regalo *m* de cumpleaños.
birthmark ['bɜːθmɑːk] *n* rosa *f,* antojo *m,* marca *f* de nacimiento.
birth-pill ['bɜːθ,pɪl] *n* píldora *f* anticonceptiva.
birthplace ['bɜːθpleɪs] *n* lugar *m* de nacimiento.
birth-rate ['bɜːθreɪt] *n* natalidad *f.*
birthright ['bɜːθraɪt] *n* derechos *mpl* de nacimiento; primogenitura *f;* (*fig*) patrimonio *m,* herencia *f;* **it is the ~ of every Englishman** pertenece por derecho natural a todo inglés, es el patrimonio de todo inglés; **to sell one's ~ for a mess of potage** vender su primogenitura por un plato de lentejas.
birthstone ['bɜːθstəʊn] *n* piedra *f* natalicia.
BIS *n* (*US*) *abbr of* **Bank of International Settlements** Banco *m* Internacional de Pagos, BIP *m.*
Biscay ['bɪskeɪ] *n* Vizcaya *f.*
biscuit ['bɪskɪt] *n* (**a**) (*Brit*) galleta *f.* (**b**) (*US*) bizcocho *m;* **that takes the ~!*** ¡eso es el colmo!
biscuit-barrel ['bɪskɪt,bærəl] *n* galletero *m.*
bisect [baɪ'sekt] *vt* bisecar.
bisection [baɪ'sekʃən] *n* (*Math*) bisección *f,* división *f* en dos partes; (*angle*) bisección *f.*
bisector [baɪ'sektə^r] *n* bisector *m.*
bisexual ['baɪ'seksjʊəl] **1** *adj* bisexual. **2** *n* bisexual *mf.*
bisexuality [baɪ,seksjʊ'ælɪtɪ] *n* bisexualidad *f.*
bishop ['bɪʃəp] *n* obispo *m,* -a *f;* (*Chess*) alfil *m;* **yes, B~** sí, Ilustrísima.
bishopric ['bɪʃəprɪk] *n* obispado *m.*
bismuth ['bɪzməθ] *n* bismuto *m.*
bison ['baɪsən] *n* bisonte *m.*
bisque [bɪsk] *n* (*Culin*) sopa *f* de mariscos; (*Sport*) ventaja *f;* (*Pottery*) bizcocho *m,* biscuit *m.*
bit[1] [bɪt] *n* (*horse's*) freno *m,* bocado *m;* (*of drill*) broca *f;* (*tool*) barrena *f;* **to get the ~ between one's teeth** desbocarse, rebelarse.
bit[2] [bɪt] **1** *n* (**a**) (*piece*) trozo *m,* pedacito *m,* porción *f.*
(**b**) (*noun phrases*) **a ~ of advice** un consejo; **a ~ of news** una noticia; **I had a ~ to eat** tomé un bocado; **I'll have a ~ of cake** tomaré un poco de tarta; **they have a ~ of money** tienen dinerillos; **to blow sth to ~s** hacer algo añicos; **to come to ~s** hacerse pedazos, romperse, desmontarse; **to do one's ~** contribuir, hacer la debida contribución, servir como se debe (a la patria *etc*); **he did his ~ in the war** durante la guerra aportó su granito de arena; **~s and pieces** trocitos *mpl,* retazos *mpl;* (*elements*) elementos *mpl* dispersos; (*Mech etc*) piezas *fpl,* componentes *mpl;* **my ~s and pieces** mis cosas, mis bártulos; **he tore the argument to ~s** hizo el argumento pedazos.
(**c**) (*adjectival uses*) **he's a ~ of a liar** es algo mentiroso; **I'm a ~ of a musician** yo sé algo de música; **I'm a ~ of a socialist** yo soy socialista hasta cierto punto; **it was a ~ of a shock** fue un golpe bastante duro; **I've a ~ of a cold** estoy ligeramente acatarrado; **it cost quite a ~ of money** costó bastante dinero; **it takes quite a ~ of my time** ocupa bastante tiempo; **this is a ~ of all right!*** ¡esto está muy bien!; **not a ~ of it!** ¡ni hablar!, ¡nada, nada!; **it's not a ~ of use** no sirve para nada en absoluto; **every ~ as good as** de ningún modo inferior a; **every ~ a man** todo un hombre; **to enjoy every ~ of sth** disfrutar algo totalmente.
(**d**) (*adverbial uses*) **~ by ~** poco a poco; **by** (*or* **in**) **~s and pieces** a retazos; **it's a ~ awkward** es un poco difícil; **it's a ~ much when ...** es intolerable cuando ...; **that's a ~ much!** ¡eso pasa de castaño oscuro!; **a ~ later** poco después, un poco más tarde; **wait a ~!** ¡espere un momento!, ¡un momento, por favor!; **I waited quite a ~** esperé bastante tiempo; **so I waited a ~** así que esperé un ratito; **it's a good ~ further than we thought** queda bastante más lejos de lo que creíamos; **a good ~ bigger** bastante más grande; **are you tired? ... not a ~!** ¿estás cansado? ... ¡en absoluto!; **she was thrilled to ~s** se extasió, se emocionó muchísimo.
(**e**) (*Comput*) bit *m,* bitio *m,* unidad *f* de información.
(**f**) **two ~s** (*US*) 25 centavos.
(**g**) (‡) tía* *f,* jai‡ *f.*
2 *adj* (*Theat*): **~ part** papel *m* pequeño.
bit[3] [bɪt] *pret of* **bite.**
bitch [bɪtʃ] **1** *n* (**a**) perra *f.*
(**b**) (‡: *woman*) lagarta *f,* zorra *f;* **you ~!** ¡lagarta!; **this car is a ~** este coche es la monda*; **it's a ~ of a problem** es un problema cojonudo*.
(**c**) (*US*‡) queja *f;* **what's your ~?** ¿de qué coño te quejas?‡
2 *vi* (‡) quejarse (*about* de).
bitchy* ['bɪtʃɪ] *adj* maldiciente, malicioso; de mal genio; rencoroso; *remark etc* malintencionado, horrible; **to be ~ to sb** tratar a uno con malevolencia.
bite [baɪt] **1** *n* (**a**) mordedura *f;* mordisco *m;* (*toothmark*) dentellada *f;* (*of bird, insect*) picadura *f;* **he wants another** (*or* **a second**) **~ at the cherry** quiere otra oportunidad, quiere probar otra vez; **to put the ~ on sb** (*US**) hacer cerrar el pico a uno*.
(**b**) (*food*) bocado *m;* (*snack*) bocado *m,* piscolabis *m;* **I've not had a ~ to eat** no he probado bocado; **will you have a ~ to eat?** ¿le traigo algo de comer?; **I'll get a ~ on the train** tomaré algo en el tren.
(**c**) **are you getting any ~s?** (*Fishing*) ¿están picando?
(**d**) (*fig*) mordacidad *f,* penetración *f;* garra *f;* **a novel with ~** una novela penetrante; **a speech with ~** un discurso tajante; **without any ~** sin garra.
2 (*irr: pret* **bit,** *ptp* **bitten**) *vt* morder; (*bird, fish, insect*) picar; (*acid*) corroer; (*Mech*) asir, trabar; **what's biting you?*** ¿qué mosca te ha picado?; **once bitten twice shy** el gato escaldado del agua fría huye; **to be bitten with*** estar contagiado con.
3 *vi* morder; picar; (*fish*) picar; (*fig*) tragar el anzuelo; (*fig*) hacer mella, surtir efecto, hacerse sentir; **the strike is beginning to ~** la huelga empieza a hacer mella; **to ~ at** tratar de morder; **to ~ into** *earth etc* devorar, tragar.
◆**bite back 1** *vt words* tragar, dejar sin decir.
2 *vi*: **but the dog bit back** pero el perro mordió a su vez.
◆**bite off** *vt* arrancar con los dientes; **to ~ off more than one can chew** abarcar más de lo que se puede apretar, abarcar mucho.
◆**bite on** *vt* morder; afirmar los dientes en.
◆**bite through** *vt string, thread* cortar; *tongue, tip* morderse; **he fell and bit through his tongue** al caerse se cortó la lengua de un mordisco.
biter ['baɪtə^r] *n*: **the ~ bit** el cazador, cazado.
biting ['baɪtɪŋ] *adj cold, wind* penetrante, cortante; *criticism etc* mordaz.
bitten ['bɪtn] *ptp of* **bite.**
bitter ['bɪtə^r] **1** *adj* amargo; *cold* penetrante, cortante; *battle* encarnizado; *enemy, hatred* implacable; *disappointment* agudo; *protest* amargo; *person* resentido; **~ aloes** amargante *m* para uñas, líquido *m* para no morderse las uñas; **~ lemon** limonada *f* ácida; **~ orange** naranja *f* amarga; **to carry on to the ~ end** continuar hasta el final (cueste lo que cueste); **to feel ~ about sth** resentirse por algo, tener rencor por motivo de algo.
2 *n* (*Brit*) cerveza *f* amarga.
bitterly ['bɪtəlɪ] *adv* amargamente; **it's ~ cold** hace un frío cortante; **he protested ~** se quejó amargamente; **I was ~**

disappointed sufrí una terrible decepción; **she spoke ~ of her experiences** habló con mucho rencor de sus experiencias.

bittern ['bɪtɜːn] *n* avetoro *m* (común).

bitterness ['bɪtənɪs] *n* (*taste*) amargor *m*; (*feelings*) amargura *f*; encarnizamiento *m*; implacabilidad *f*; agudeza *f*; **there is great ~ between them** entre ellos existe un odio implacable; **I accepted it without ~** lo acepté sin rencor; **I have no ~ towards you** no le guardo rencor.

bitters ['bɪtəz] *npl* bíter *m*.

bittersweet ['bɪtəswiːt] *adj* agridulce.

bitty ['bɪtɪ] *adj* (**a**) (*Brit*) poco coherente, descosido; en pedacitos. (**b**) (*US*) pequeñito.

bitumen ['bɪtjʊmɪn] *n* betún *m*.

bituminous [bɪ'tjuːmɪnəs] *adj* bituminoso.

bivalent ['baɪ'veɪlənt] *adj* bivalente.

bivalve ['baɪvælv] **1** *adj* bivalvo. **2** *n* (molusco *m*) bivalvo *m*.

bivouac ['bɪvʊæk] **1** *n* vivaque *m*, vivac *m*. **2** *vi* vivaquear.

bi-weekly ['baɪ'wiːklɪ] **1** *adj* (*every 2 weeks*) quincenal; (*twice weekly*) bisemanal.

2 *adv* quincenalmente; bisemanalmente.

3 *n* revista *f* quincenal; revista *f* bisemanal.

biz* [bɪz] *n abbr of* **business**; *V* **show.**

bizarre [bɪ'zɑːʳ] *adj event* extraño, raro; *appearance etc* estrafalario.

bk (**a**) *abbr of* **book** libro *m*, l. (**b**) *abbr of* **bank** Banco *m*, Bco.

bkcy *abbr of* **bankruptcy.**

bkg *abbr of* **banking.**

bkpt *abbr of* **bankrupt.**

B/L *abbr of* **bill of lading** conocimiento *m* de embarque.

BL *n* (**a**) *abbr of* **British Leyland.** (**b**) *abbr of* **British Library.** (**c**) *abbr of* **Bachelor of Law(s)** licenciado *m*, -a *f* en Leyes.

blab [blæb] **1** *vt* (*also* **to ~ out**) divulgar, soltar. **2** *vi* chismear; (*to police etc*) soplar.

black [blæk] **1** *adj* (**a**) negro; **~ arts** magia *f* negra; **~ ball** bola *f* negra; **~ bass** perca *f*; **~ belt** (*Sport*) cinturón *m* negro; **~ box** (*Aer*) caja *f* negra; **~ coffee** café *m* solo; **~ comedy** comedia *f* negra; **B~ Country** *región industrial de Birmingham y su comarca* (*Inglaterra*); **B~ Death** peste *f* negra; **~ economy** economía *f* sumergida, economía *f* negra; **~ eye** ojo *m* amoratado, ojo *m* a la funerala; **B~ Forest** Selva *f* Negra; **B~ Forest gâteau** *pastel de chocolate, nata y guindas;* **~ grouse** = **blackcock**; **~-headed gull** gaviota *f* de cabeza negra; **~ hole** (*Astron*) agujero *m* negro; **~ humour** humor *m* negro; **~ ice** *hielo invisible en la carretera*; **~ line** raya *f* en negro; **~ magic** magia *f* negra; **B~ Maria** (*Brit*) coche *m* celular, furgón *m* celular; **~ mark** señal *f* roja; (*fig*) nota *f* adversa, punto *m* negativo; **~ market** estraperlo *m*, mercado *m* negro; **~ marketeer** estraperlista *mf*; **~ pepper** pimienta *f* negra; **~ pudding** (*Brit*) morcilla *f*, moronga *f* (*Mex*); **B~ Rod** (*Brit Parl*) *dignatario de la Cámara de los Lores encargado de reunir a los Comunes en la apertura del Parlamento*; **~ sheep (of the family)** oveja *f* negra, garbanzo *m* negro; **(accident) ~ spot** (*Aut*) punto *m* negro; **~ tie** corbata *f* de lazo, corbata *f* de smoking; **'~ tie'** (*on invitation*) 'de etiqueta'; **B~ Watch** (*Brit Mil*) *regimiento escocés*; **~ and white photo** foto *f* en blanco y negro; **~ and white TV** TV *f* monocromo; **with a face as ~ as thunder** con cara de pocos amigos; **his face was ~ and blue** tenía la cara amoratada; **to swear ~ and blue** jurar por todo lo más santo (*that* que).

(**b**) (*negro*) **~ man** negro *m*; **~ woman** negra *f*; **B~ Africa** el Africa negra; **the ~ belt** (*US*) la zona *f* negra; **~ college** (*US*) *universidad para gente de color*; **B~ English** (*US*) *inglés hablado por los negros americanos*; **B~ Moslem** musulmán *m* negro; **B~ Nationalism** nacionalismo *m* negro; **B~ Panthers** Panteras *fpl* negras; **B~ Power** poder *m* negro; **B~ Studies** (*US*) *estudios de la cultura negra americana.*

(**c**) (*dark*) oscuro, tenebroso; **as ~ as pitch, as ~ as your hat** oscuro como boca de lobo.

(**d**) (*dirty*) sucio; (*with smoke*) negro, ennegrecido.

(**e**) (*Brit*: *trade union parlance*) **~ goods** géneros *mpl* sujetos a boicoteo; **to declare a product ~** boicotear un producto.

(**f**) (*fig*) (*wicked*) negro; (*angry*) negro, furioso; (*ominous*) negro, ominoso; *thought* malévolo; *rage* negro; *look* ceñudo, de desaprobación; *day, event* negro, funesto, aciago; *outlook* negro; *forecast* pesimista; **a ~ day on the roads** una jornada negra en las carreteras; **he is not as ~ as he is painted** no es tan malo como se cree; **things look pretty ~** la situación es desconsoladora; **things were looking ~ for him** la situación se le presentaba muy difícil.

2 *n* (**a**) (*colour*) negro *m*, color *m* negro; **a film in ~ and white** un film en blanco y negro; **I should like it in ~ and white** quisiera tenerlo por escrito; **there it is in ~ and white!** ¡ahí lo tiene en letras de molde!

(**b**) (*person*) negro *m*, -a *f*.

(**c**) (*mourning*) luto *m*; **to be in ~, to wear ~** estar de luto.

(**d**) (*darkness*) oscuridad *f*, noche *f*.

(**e**) **to stay in the ~** (*banking*) estar en números negros.

3 *vt* (**a**) ennegrecer; *shoes* limpiar, lustrar; **to ~ sb's eye** ponerle a uno el ojo a la funerala.

(**b**) (*Brit*: *trade union parlance*) boicotear.

◆**black out 1** *vt*: **to ~ out a house** apagar las luces de una casa, hacer que no sean visibles por fuera las luces de una casa; **the screen was ~ed out by the strike** (*TV*) debido a la huelga no había programas en la pantalla; **the storm ~ed out the city** la tormenta causó un apagón en la ciudad. **2** *vi* (*faint*) desmayarse, perder el conocimiento.

blackball ['blækbɔːl] *vt* dar bola negra a.

blackberry ['blækbərɪ] *n* (*fruit*) zarzamora *f*, mora *f*; (*plant*) zarza *f*.

blackberrying ['blæk,berɪɪŋ] *n*: **to go ~** ir a coger zarzamoras.

blackbird ['blækbɜːd] *n* mirlo *m*.

blackboard ['blækbɔːd] *n* pizarra *f*, encerado *m*.

blackcap ['blæk,kæp] *n* cucurra *f* capirotada.

black-coated ['blæk'kəʊtɪd] *adj*: **~ worker** oficinista *mf*.

blackcock ['blækkɒk] *n* gallo *m* lira.

blackcurrant [blæk'kʌrənt] *n* (*fruit*) casis *m*, grosella *f* negra; (*bush*) grosellero *m* negro.

blacken ['blækən] **1** *vt* ennegrecer; (*by fire*) calcinar; *face* tiznar de negro; (*fig*) denigrar, desacreditar. **2** *vi* ennegrecerse.

blackguard ['blægɑːd] **1** *n* pillo *m*, canalla *m*. **2** *vt* vilipendiar.

blackguardly ['blægɑːdlɪ] *adj* vil, canallesco.

blackhead ['blækhed] *n* comedón *m*, espinilla *f*.

black-hearted ['blæk'hɑːtɪd] *adj* malvado, perverso.

blacking ['blækɪŋ] *n* betún *m*.

blackish ['blækɪʃ] *adj* negruzco; (*wine parlance*) aguindado.

blackjack ['blækdʒæk] *n* (*esp US*) (**a**) (*truncheon*) cachiporra *f* (*con puño flexible*). (**b**) (*flag*) bandera *f* pirata. (**c**) (*game*) veintiuna *f*.

blackleg ['blækleg] (*Brit*) **1** *n* esquirol *m*. **2** *vi* ser esquirol, trabajar durante una huelga.

blacklegging ['blæk,legɪŋ] *n* esquirolaje *m*.

blacklist ['blæklɪst] **1** *n* lista *f* negra. **2** *vt* poner en la lista negra.

blackmail ['blækmeɪl] **1** *n* chantaje *m*; **it's sheer ~!** ¡es un chantaje! **2** *vt* chantajear, sacar dinero por chantaje a; **to ~ sb into doing sth** chantajear a uno para que haga algo; **he was ~ed into it** lo hizo obligado por el chantaje.

blackmailer ['blækmeɪləʳ] *n* chantajista *mf*.

blackness ['blæknɪs] *n* negrura *f*; (*darkness*) oscuridad *f*.

blackout ['blækaʊt] *n* (**a**) (*electrical*) apagón *m*. (**b**) (*Med*) amnesia *f* temporal, desmayo *m*. (**c**) (*of news*) bloqueo *m* informativo, apagón *m* informativo; **there was a media ~ at the request of the police** hubo un bloqueo informativo en los medios de comunicación a petición de la policía.

Black Sea ['blæk'siː] *n* Mar *m* Negro.

blackshirt ['blækʃɜːt] *n* camisa negra *mf*, fascista *mf*.

blacksmith ['blæksmɪθ] *n* herrero *m*; **~'s (forge)** herrería *f*.

blackthorn ['blækθɔːn] *n* endrino *m*.

bladder ['blædəʳ] *n* vejiga *f*.

blade [bleɪd] *n* (*of weapon etc*) hoja *f*; (*cutting edge*) filo *m*; (*sword*) espada *f*; (*of propeller*) paleta *f*, aleta *f*; (*of oar, hoe*) pala *f*; **a ~ of grass** una brizna de hierba.

blaeberry ['bleɪbərɪ] *n* arándano *m*.

blag⁑ [blæg] **1** *n* robo *m* a mano armada. **2** *vt* robar a mano armada.

blah* [blɑː] **1** *adj* (*US*) poco apetitoso. **2** *n* (**a**) (*words*) paja *f*, palabrería *f*; **and there was a lot more ~, ~, ~** y hubo mucho más bla, bla, bla. (**b**) **the ~s** (*US*) la depre*.

blamable ['bleɪməbl] *adj* censurable, culpable.

blame [bleɪm] **1** *n* culpa *f*; **to bear the ~** tener la culpa; **to lay** (*or* **put**) **the ~ for sth on sb** echar a uno la culpa de algo.

2 *vt* culpar, echar la culpa a; **to ~ sb for sth** echar a uno la culpa de algo; **to be to ~ for** tener la culpa de; **I am not to ~** yo no tengo la culpa; **who's to ~?** ¿quién tiene la culpa?; **you have only yourself to ~** tú eres el

único culpable; **and I don't ~ him** y lo comprendo perfectamente.
blameless ['bleɪmlɪs] *adj person* inocente (*of* de); *action* intachable, irreprochable.
blamelessly ['bleɪmlɪslɪ] *adv* inocentemente, intachablemente.
blameworthy ['bleɪmwɜːðɪ] *adj* censurable, culpable.
blanch [blɑːntʃ] **1** *vt* blanquear. **2** *vi* palidecer.
blancmange [blə'mɒnʒ] *n* ≈ crema *f* (de vainilla *etc*).
bland [blænd] *adj* suave.
blandish ['blændɪʃ] *vt* engatusar, halagar.
blandishments ['blændɪʃmənts] *npl* halagos *mpl*, lisonjas *fpl*.
blandly ['blændlɪ] *adv* suavemente.
blank [blæŋk] **1** *adj paper, space, cheque etc* en blanco; *tape* sin grabar, virgen; *wall* liso, sin adorno; *verse* suelto, blanco; *cartridge* sin bala, *shell* de fogueo; **to give sb a ~ cheque** dar a uno un cheque en blanco; (*fig*) dar carta blanca a uno (*to* + *infin* para + *infin*); **a ~ look** una mirada sin expresión, una mirada de incomprensión; **a ~ stare** una mirada vaga; **when I asked him he looked ~** cuando se lo pregunté puso la mirada en el vacío; **a look of ~ amazement** una mirada de profundo asombro; **in a state of ~ despair** en un estado de desesperación total; **my mind went ~** no pude recordar nada.
2 *n* (*space*) blanco *m*, espacio *m* en blanco; (*form*) formulario *m*, hoja *f*; (*coin*) cospel *m*; (*Mil*) cartucho *m* sin bala, granada *f* de fogueo; **to fire ~s** usar municiones de fogueo; **my mind was a complete ~** no pude recordar nada; **to draw a ~** no encontrar nada, no tener éxito alguno.
blanket ['blæŋkɪt] **1** *n* manta *f*, frazada *f* (*LAm*); (*fig*) manto *m*, capa *f*; **a ~ of snow** una manta de nieve; **~ bath = bedbath**; **~ stitch** punto *m* de aguja.
2 *adj* comprensivo, general; **~ agreement** acuerdo *m* comprensivo, acuerdo *m* general; **this insurance policy gives ~ cover** esta póliza de seguro es a todo riesgo.
3 *vt* (*fig*) cubrir (*in, with* de), envolver (*by, in, with* en).
blankly ['blæŋklɪ] *adv*: **he looked at me ~** me miró sin comprender.
blare [blɛəʳ] **1** *n* estrépito *m*, sonido *m* fuerte; (*of trumpet*) trompetazo *m*. **2** *vt*: **to ~ out** vociferar, anunciar a gritos; *music* tocar muy fuerte. **3** *vi* resonar, sonar muy fuerte.
blarney ['blɑːnɪ] **1** *n* coba *f*; labia *f*. **2** *vt* dar coba a.
blasé ['blɑːzeɪ] *adj* hastiado; de vuelta de todo; **he's very ~ about it** habla de ello en términos de hastío, habla con indiferencia de ello.
blaspheme [blæs'fiːm] *vi* blasfemar.
blasphemer [blæs'fiːməʳ] *n* blasfemador *m*, -ora *f*.
blasphemous ['blæsfɪməs] *adj* blasfemo.
blasphemously ['blæsfɪməslɪ] *adv* blasfemamente.
blasphemy ['blæsfɪmɪ] *n* blasfemia *f*.
blast [blɑːst] **1** *n* (**a**) (*of wind*) ráfaga *f*; (*of air*) soplo *m*; (*of sand, water*) chorro *m*.
(**b**) (*sound*) trompetazo *m*; (*of whistle etc*) toque *m*.
(**c**) (*explosive*) explosión *f*; onda *f* explosiva, onda *f* expansiva.
(**d**) (*of criticism etc*) tempestad *f*, oleada *f*.
(**e**) (*US**) fiesta *f*; **to have a ~*** organizar una fiesta; **to get a ~ out of sth*** pasárselo chachi con algo*.
2 *vt* (*with explosive*) volar; (*by lightning*) derribar, destruir; (*Mil*) bombardear; (*Bot*) marchitar, (*with blight*) añublar; (*fig*) arruinar; criticar duramente; (*US: verbally*) atacar verbalmente; **to ~ open** abrir con carga explosiva; **~ (it)!*** ¡maldición!
◆**blast away** **1** *vt* volar; quitar con explosivos. **2** *vi* (*gun*) seguir disparando; **they were ~ing away at the town** seguían bombardeando el pueblo.
◆**blast off** *vi* (*rocket*) (*also US**) despegar.
◆**blast out** *vt radio message etc* emitir a toda potencia; *tune* tocar (*etc*) a máximo volumen.
blasted* ['blɑːstɪd] *adj* condenado*, maldito.
blast-furnace ['blɑːst'fɜːnɪs] *n* alto horno *m*.
blasting ['blɑːstɪŋ] *n* (*Tech*) explosión *f* controlada; **'~ in progress'** 'explosión controlada en curso'; **to give sb a ~ for (having done) sth** dar una bronca a uno (*or* abroncar a uno) por (haber hecho) algo.
blast-off ['blɑːstɒf] *n* lanzamiento *m*, despegue *m*.
blatant ['bleɪtənt] *adj* (*shameless*) descarado; agresivo; (*noisy*) estrepitoso, vocinglero; *colour etc* chillón.
blatantly ['bleɪtəntlɪ] *adv* descaradamente.
blather ['blæðəʳ] **1** *n* disparates *mpl*. **2** *vi* charlatanear, decir tonterías.
blaze¹ [bleɪz] **1** *n* (**a**) (*with flames*) llamarada *f*, (*steady glow*) resplandor *m*; (*fire*) incendio *m*; (*bonfire*) hoguera *f*; **the garden is a ~ of colour** el jardín está radiante de color; **in a ~** en llamas; **in a ~ of anger** en un arranque de cólera; **in a ~ of publicity** bajo los focos de la publicidad, a bombo y platillo. (**b**) (*****) **like ~s** hasta más no poder, con todas sus fuerzas; **what the ~s ...?** ¿qué diablos ...?; **go to ~s!** ¡vete al diablo!, ¡vete a la porra!*
2 *vt*: **the news was ~d across the front page** la noticia venía con grandes titulares en la primera plana.
3 *vi* arder en llamas; (*fig*) brillar, resplandecer; **all the lights were blazing** brillaban todas las luces; **to ~ with anger** estar furioso, echar chispas.
◆**blaze abroad** *vt* (*liter*) *news etc* difundir.
◆**blaze away** *vi* (*soldiers*) seguir disparando rápidamente.
◆**blaze down** *vi*: **the sun was blazing down** brillaba implacable el sol, picaba muy fuerte el sol.
◆**blaze forth** *vi* (*liter, sun*) aparecer súbitamente; (*anger*) estallar.
◆**blaze out** *vi* (*fire*) llamear; (*sun*) resplandecer, relucir; (*light*) relucir; (*anger, hatred*) estallar.
◆**blaze up** *vi* (volver a) encenderse vivamente; (*fig*) estallar.
blaze² [bleɪz] **1** *n* (*on animal*) mancha *f*, estrella *f*; (*on tree*) señal *f* (hecha para servir de guía). **2** *vt*: **to ~ a trail** abrir un camino (*also fig*).
blazer ['bleɪzəʳ] *n* chaqueta *f* (de deporte, de colegio *etc*), chaquetilla *f*, blázer *m*.
blazing ['bleɪzɪŋ] *adj sun* abrasador; *light* brillante; *anger* irreprimible; *row* violento.
blazon ['bleɪzn] **1** *n* blasón *m*. **2** *vt* (*fig*) proclamar.
bleach [bliːtʃ] **1** *n* lejía *f*. **2** *vt* blanquear. **3** *vi* blanquearse.
bleachers ['bliːtʃəz] *npl* (*US*) gradas *fpl*.
bleaching-agent ['bliːtʃɪŋ,eɪdʒənt] *n* decolorante *m*.
bleaching-powder ['bliːtʃɪŋ,paʊdəʳ] *n* polvos *mpl* de blanqueo.
bleak¹ [bliːk] *n* (*fish*) breca *f*, albur *m*.
bleak² [bliːk] *adj landscape* desierto, desolador, inhóspito; (*treeless*) pelado; *weather* crudo; *smile* triste, adusto; *welcome* inhospitalario; *prospect* nada prometedor.
bleakly ['bliːklɪ] *adv look* desoladamente; *speak* tristemente, descorazonadoramente.
bleakness ['bliːknɪs] *n* (*of landscape*) desolación *f*; (*of room, furnishings*) frialdad *f*; (*of weather*) crudeza *f*, desapacibilidad *f*.
bleary ['blɪərɪ] *adj eye* legañoso.
bleary-eyed ['blɪərɪaɪd] *adj* de ojos legañosos; semidormido.
bleat [bliːt] **1** *n* balido *m*; (*****) queja *f*. **2** *vi* balar; (*fig*) quejarse tristemente (*about* de), gimotear.
bled [bled] *pret and ptp of* **bleed**.
bleed [bliːd] (*irr: pret and ptp* **bled**) **1** *vt* (*Med*) sangrar; (*fig*) desangrar; **to ~ sb white** desangrar a uno, sacarle el jugo a uno; **to ~ a country white** explotar despiadadamente un país.
2 *vi* sangrar; (*tree*) exudar; **to ~ to death** morir desangrado, morir de desangramiento; **to ~ for** sangrar de dolor por; **those who have bled for England** los que han vertido su sangre por Inglaterra; **my heart ~s for you** te compadezco mucho.
bleeder ['bliːdəʳ] *n* (*Med**) hemofílico *m*; (*Brit‡*) cabrón‡ *m*.
bleeding ['bliːdɪŋ] **1** *adj* (**a**) *wound etc* sangrante, sangriento, que sangra; *heart* dolorido; **~-heart liberal** (*US*) liberal *m* de gran corazón.
(**b**) (**‡**) puñetero‡, pijotero‡.
2 *adv* (**‡**) **~ awkward** condenadamente difícil‡.
3 *n* (*Med*) sangría *f*; desangramiento *m*, hemorragia *f*.
bleep [bliːp] **1** *n* bip *m*. **2** *vi* hacer bip, dar un bip.
bleeper ['bliːpəʳ] *n* localizador *m*, busca* *m*.
blemish ['blemɪʃ] **1** *n* tacha *f*, mancha *f*. **2** *vt* manchar.
blench [blentʃ] *vi* cejar, recular; palidecer.
blend [blend] **1** *n* mezcla *f*, combinación *f*; (*of drinks*) mezcla *f* (de varias cosechas).
2 *vt* mezclar, combinar, armonizar; *colours* casar.
3 *vi* combinarse, armonizarse; **to ~ in with** armonizarse con, formar un conjunto armonioso con; **to ~ into** transformarse poco a poco en.
blended ['blendɪd] *adj* mezclado.
blender ['blendəʳ] *n* (**a**) (*person*) catador *m*, -a *f*; **tea ~** catador *m*, -ora *f* de té. (**b**) (*Culin*) licuadora *f*.
bless [bles] *vt* bendecir; **to ~ o.s.** persignarse, santiguarse; **~ you!** (*on sneezing*) ¡Jesús!; **God ~ you!** ¡Dios te bendiga!; **well I'm ~ed!, God ~ my soul!** ¡caramba!; **I'm ~ed if I know** que me maten si lo sé; **they were ~ed with children** Dios les dio la bendición de los hijos; **she is ~ed with every virtue** la adornan mil virtudes; **I ~ the day I bought it** bendigo el día que lo compré.

blessed ['blesɪd] **1** *adj* (**a**) (*holy*) bendito, bienaventurado; (*beatified*) beato; **the B~ Virgin** la Santísima Virgen; **the B~ Sacrament** el Santísimo Sacramento; **~ be Thy Name** bendito sea Tu Nombre; **a day of ~ calm** un día de bendita tranquilidad.

(**b**) (*) santo; **the whole ~ day** todo el santo día; **where's that ~ book?** ¿dónde diablos estará el libro ese?; **we didn't find a ~ thing** encontramos maldita la cosa.

2 *npl*: **the B~** los bienaventurados.

blessedness ['blesɪdnɪs] *n* (*Rel*) bienaventuranza *f*, beatitud *f*, bendición *f*; (*happiness*) felicidad *f*.

blessing ['blesɪŋ] *n* (**a**) (*Rel*) bendición *f*.

(**b**) (*advantage*) beneficio *m*, ventaja *f*; **the ~s of electricity** los beneficios de la electricidad; **the ~s of science** los adelantos de la ciencia; **to count one's ~s** apreciar lo que uno tiene; **it's a ~ in disguise** no hay mal que por bien no venga; **it's a mixed ~** tiene su pro y su contra.

blest [blest] *adj and ptp* (*poet*) *of* **bless**.

blether ['bleðəʳ] = **blather**.

blew [bluː] *pret of* **blow**.

blight [blaɪt] **1** *n* (*Bot*) añublo *m*, tizón *m*, roya *f*, polvillo *m* (*LAm*); (*fig*) plaga *f*, infortunio *m*; desperfecto *m*, mancha *f*; **urban ~** desertización *f* urbana; **to cast a ~ on** (*or* **over**) arruinar.

2 *vt* (**a**) (*Bot*) añublar, atizonar. (**b**) (*fig*) arruinar, destruir; *hopes* arruinar; *urban scene* desertizar.

blighter‡ ['blaɪtəʳ] *n* (*Brit*) tío* *m*, sujeto* *m*; (*hum*) **you ~!** ¡cacho cabrón!‡; (**what a**) **lucky ~!** ¡es un chorrón!*

Blighty* ['blaɪtɪ] *n* (*Brit Mil* ††) Inglaterra *f*.

blimey‡ ['blaɪmɪ] *interj* (*Brit*) ¡caray!

blimp [blɪmp] *n* (**a**) (*Aer*) globo *m*. (**b**) (*Brit*) (*person*) reaccionario *m*, militarista *m*, patriotero *m*; **a** (**Colonel**) **B~** ≃ un carpetovetónico.

blimpish ['blɪmpɪʃ] *adj* reaccionario, militarista, patriotero.

blind [blaɪnd] **1** *adj* ciego (*also fig, Archit*; *to* a, para; *with* de); *corner* sin visibilidad; **~ alley** callejón *m* sin salida (*also fig*); **~ date** cita *f* a ciegas; **~ spot** (*Anat*) punto *m* ciego; (*fig*) debilidad *f*, punto *m* flojo; **~ in one eye** tuerto; **as ~ as a bat** más ciego que un topo; **a ~ man** un ciego; **it's a case of the ~ leading the ~** tan ciego el uno como el otro; **to be ~ to** no ver, (*deliberately*) hacer la vista gorda a; **he is ~ to all dangers** no comprende en absoluto los peligros; **he is ~ to her true character** se le oculta su verdadero carácter; **he took not a ~ bit of notice*** no hizo caso alguno, no le concedió la más mínima importancia; **to come up on the ~ side** (*Aut*) avanzar por el lado donde el conductor tiene la vista impedida; **to go ~** quedar ciego.

2 *n* (**a**) **the ~** *pl* los ciegos, los invidentes (*euph*).

(**b**) (*also* **Venetian ~**) persiana *f*; (*outside window*) toldo *m*.

(**c**) (*pretence*) pretexto *m*, subterfugio *m*; **it's all a ~** no es más que un pretexto.

(**d**) **to go on a ~**‡ ir de juerga*.

3 *adv*: **to fly ~** volar a ciegas; **to be ~ drunk*** estar como una cuba*; **he swore ~ that ...*** juró por todo lo más sagrado que ...

4 *vt* cegar; (*dazzle*) deslumbrar; **to be ~ed in an accident** quedar ciego después de un accidente; **to be ~ed by anger** estar cegado por la ira, estar ciego de ira.

blinder ['blaɪndəʳ] *n* (**a**) **to play a ~** (**of a match**)* jugar maravillosamente. (**b**) **~s** (*US*) anteojeras *fpl*.

blindfold ['blaɪn*d*fəʊld] **1** *adj* con los ojos vendados; *game of chess* a la ciega; **I could do it ~** sé hacerlo con los ojos cerrados. **2** *n* venda *f*. **3** *vt* vendar los ojos a.

blinding ['blaɪndɪŋ] *adj light* intenso, cegador, deslumbrante.

blindingly ['blaɪndɪŋlɪ] *adv*: **a ~ obvious fact** un hecho de meridiana claridad; **it is ~ obvious that ...** es meridianamente claro que ...

blindly ['blaɪndlɪ] *adv* a ciegas (*also fig*), ciegamente.

blind-man's buff ['blaɪn*d*mænz'bʌf] *n* gallina *f* ciega.

blindness ['blaɪndnɪs] *n* ceguera *f*, ceguedad *f*.

blindworm ['blaɪndwɜːm] *n* lución *m*.

blini(s) ['blɪnɪ(z)] *n* panqueque *m* ruso.

blink [blɪŋk] **1** *n* parpadeo *m*; (*gleam*) destello *m*; **to be on the ~*** funcionar mal, no pitar*.

2 *vt* guiñar, cerrar momentáneamente; **to ~ one's eyes** parpadear; **there is no ~ing the fact that ...** es imposible soslayar el hecho de que ...

3 *vi* parpadear, pestañear; (*light*) oscilar.

blinkered ['blɪŋkəd] *adj* (*fig*) ignorante; de miras estrechas, de cabeza cuadrada.

blinkers ['blɪŋkəz] *npl* (**a**) (*Brit*) anteojeras *fpl*. (**b**) (*Aut*) (luces *fpl*) intermitentes *mpl*.

blinking* ['blɪŋkɪŋ] *adj* maldito.

blip [blɪp] *n* (**a**) = **bleep**.

(**b**) (*fig*) irregularidad *f* momentánea; interrupción *f* temporal; **this is just a ~** esto es un mal momento que pasará pronto.

bliss [blɪs] *n* (*Rel*) bienaventuranza *f*; (*happy state*) felicidad *f*; (*fig*) éxtasis *m*, arrobamiento *m*; **the concert was ~!** ¡el concierto fue una gloria!; **what ~!** ¡qué dicha!, ¡qué encanto!; **isn't he ~?** ¡qué hombre más estupendo!

blissful ['blɪsfʊl] *adj* bienaventurado; (*happy*) feliz; (*fig*) deleitoso; (*) maravilloso, estupendo.

blissfully ['blɪsfəlɪ] *adv* felizmente *etc*; **to be ~ ignorant** vivir en la luna; **to be ~ ignorant** (*or* **unaware**) **of** estar completamente ajeno a, estar totalmente inconsciente de.

blister ['blɪstəʳ] **1** *n* ampolla *f*. **2** *vt* ampollar, causar ampollas en. **3** *vi* ampollarse.

blistering ['blɪstərɪŋ] *adj heat* abrasador; *criticism* feroz, devastador.

blister-pack ['blɪstə,pæk] *n* envase *m* en lámina al vacío.

blister-packed ['blɪstə,pækt] *adj* envasado en lámina al vacío.

blithe [blaɪð] *adj* alegre.

blithely ['blaɪðlɪ] *adv* alegremente.

blithering* ['blɪðərɪŋ] *adj*: **~ idiot** imbécil *mf*.

B.Lit(t) [,biː'lɪt] *n abbr of* **Bachelor of Letters**.

blitz [blɪts] **1** *n* guerra *f* relámpago; (*Aer*) bombardeo *m* aéreo; (*fig*) campaña *f* (*on* contra); **the B~** *el bombardeo alemán de Gran Bretaña en 1940-42*; **to have a ~ on** hacer campaña contra. **2** *vt* bombardear.

blitzkrieg ['blɪtskriːg] *n* guerra *f* relámpago.

blizzard ['blɪzəd] *n* ventisca *f*.

BLM *n* (*US*) *abbr of* **Bureau of Land Management**.

bloated ['bləʊtɪd] *adj* hinchado (*also fig*; *with* de), abotagado.

bloater ['bləʊtəʳ] *n* arenque *m* ahumado.

blob [blɒb] *n* (*drop*) gota *f*; (*blot*) borrón *m*; (*stain*) mancha *f*.

bloc [blɒk] *n* bloque *m*; **en ~** en bloque.

block [blɒk] **1** *n* (**a**) (*stone*) bloque *m*; (*wood*) zoquete *m*, tarugo *m*; (*for paving*) adoquín *m*; (*butcher's, executioner's*) tajo *m*; (*child's toy*) cubo *m*; (*of brake*) zapata *f*; (*of cylinder*) bloque *m*; (*Brit Typ*) molde *m*; (*Brit*: *writing pad*) bloc *m*; **~s** (*Sport*) taco *m* de salida; **on the ~** (*US**) a tocateja*; **~** (**and tackle**) aparejo *m* de polea; **~ diagram** diagrama *m* de bloques; **to knock sb's ~ off**‡ romper la crisma a uno.

(**b**) (*buildings*) manzana *f*, cuadra *f* (*LAm*); **~ of flats** (*Brit*) edificio *m* de pisos, bloque *m* de viviendas; **it's 5 ~s away** (*US*) eso queda a 5 calles (*LAm*: cuadras) de aquí; **to take a stroll round the ~** dar un paseo alrededor de la manzana (*LAm*: cuadra).

(**c**) (*quantity*) bloque *m*; **~ booking** reserva *f* en bloque; **~ grant** subvención *f* en bloque; **~ of seats** grupo *m* de asientos; **~ of shares** bloque *m* de acciones; **~ release** (*Brit Scol*) exención *f* (*or* descargo *m*) por estudios; **~ vote** voto *m* por representación.

(**d**) (*obstruction*) obstáculo *m*, estorbo *m*; **writer's ~** bloqueo *m* de escritor; **to have a mental ~** tener un bloqueo mental.

(**e**) (*Comput*) bloque *m*.

2 *adj*: **~ letter** mayúscula *f*, letra *f* de molde; **please write in ~ letters** escribir por favor en caracteres de imprenta.

3 *vt* obstruir, cerrar, atorar (*LAm*); *traffic, progress* estorbar, impedir; (*Parl*) *bill* bloquear; (*Comm*) *account* bloquear; (*Comput*) agrupar; **'road ~ed'** 'cerrado (por obras)'; **the line is ~ed in 4 places** la vía está cortada en 4 lugares; **my nose is ~ed** tengo la nariz taponada.

4 *vi* obstruirse, cerrarse.

◆**block in** *vt* (*sketch roughly*) esbozar.

◆**block off** *vt road etc* cortar; (*accidentally*) bloquear.

◆**block out** *vt* (*sketch roughly*) esbozar; (*suppress*) suprimir, tachar.

◆**block up** *vt* tapar, cegar; **his nose is all ~ed up** tiene la nariz congestionada.

blockade [blɒ'keɪd] **1** *n* bloqueo *m*; **to run the ~** forzar (*or* burlar) el bloqueo. **2** *vt* (*also US*: *traffic*) bloquear.

blockage ['blɒkɪdʒ] *n* obstrucción *f*; obstáculo *m*, estorbo *m*.

blockbuster ['blɒk,bʌstəʳ] *n* (*Mil*) bomba *f* revientamanzanas; (*fig*) suceso *m* (*etc*) fulminante; bomba *f*.

blockhead ['blɒkhed] *n* zopenco *m*, -a *f*; **you ~!** ¡imbécil!

blockhouse ['blɒkhaʊs] *n*, *pl* **blockhouses** ['blɒkhaʊzɪz] blocao *m*.

bloke‡ [bləʊk] *n* (*Brit*) tío* *m*, sujeto *m*; (*boyfriend*) amigo *m.*

blond(e) [blɒnd] **1** *adj* rubio, güero (*CAm, Mex*). **2** *n* rubio *m*, -a *f*, güero *m*, -a *f* (*CAm, Mex*).

blood [blʌd] **1** *n* (**a**) sangre *f*; (*family*) sangre *f*, linaje *m*; raza *f*; parentesco *m*; **~ royal** estirpe *f* regia; **bad ~** mala *f* leche, mala *f* uva; **this created** (*or* **made**) **bad ~ between them** esto causó rencores entre ellos; **in cold ~** a sangre fría; **that man of ~** aquel monstruo; **~ is thicker than water** la sangre es más espesa que el océano; **it's in the ~** lo lleva la masa de la sangre; **they're out for ~** están dispuestos a verter sangre; **he's after my ~** me tiene un odio mortal, (*hum*) quiere darme una paliza; **when my ~ is up** cuando me encolerizo; **to donate** (*or* **give**) **~** dar su sangre; **to draw ~** hacer que sangre uno, herir, (*fig*) herir en lo vivo; **he has X's ~ on his hands** tiene las manos manchadas con la sangre de X; **it makes my ~ boil** hace que se me queme la sangre, me saca de quicio; **we need new ~ in the company** hace falta gente nueva en la compañía; **my ~ ran cold** se me heló la sangre; **to scent ~, to smell ~** oler la sangre; **to shed one's ~** verter su sangre; **to shed** (*or* **spill**) **the ~ of** derramar la sangre de; **without shedding ~** sin efusión de sangre; **it's like trying to get ~ out of a stone** es como sacar agua de las piedras.

(**b**) (††: *person*) galán *m*.

2 *vt hound* iniciar; *new talent* fomentar, criar.

blood-and-thunder [ˈblʌdənˈθʌndəʳ] **1** *adj* aparatosamente violento, intencionadamente cruel; melodramático.

2 *n* violencia *f* aparatosa, crueldad *f* intencionada; melodrama *m*.

bloodbank [ˈblʌdbæŋk] *n* banco *m* de sangre.

bloodbath [ˈblʌdbɑːθ] *n*, *pl* **bloodbaths** [ˈblʌdbɑːðz] carnicería *f*, baño *m* de sangre.

blood-blister [ˈblʌd,blɪstəʳ] *n* ampolla *f* de sangre.

blood brother [ˈblʌd,brʌðəʳ] *n* hermano *m* de sangre.

blood-cell [ˈblʌdsel] *n* célula *f* sanguínea.

blood-clot [ˈblʌdklɒt] *n* coágulo *m* sanguíneo.

blood corpuscle [ˈblʌd,kɔːpʌsl] *n* glóbulo *m* sanguíneo.

bloodcount [ˈblʌdkaʊnt] *n* recuento *m* sanguíneo.

bloodcurdling [ˈblʌd,kɜːdlɪŋ] *adj* espeluznante, horripilante.

blood-donor [ˈblʌd,dəʊnəʳ] *n* donante *mf* de sangre.

blood-feud [ˈblʌdfjuːd] *n* odio *m* de sangre, enemistad *f* mortal (entre clanes, familias).

blood-group [ˈblʌdgruːp] *n* grupo *m* sanguíneo.

blood-grouping [ˈblʌd,gruːpɪŋ] *n* grupo *m* sanguíneo.

blood-heat [ˈblʌdhiːt] *n* temperatura *f* de la sangre.

bloodhound [ˈblʌdhaʊnd] *n* (**a**) sabueso *m*. (**b**) (*****) policía *m*, sabueso *m*.

bloodily [ˈblʌdɪlɪ] *adv* sangrientamente, con efusión de sangre; violentamente.

bloodiness [ˈblʌdɪnɪs] *n* (*lit*) lo sangriento *etc*.

bloodless [ˈblʌdlɪs] *adj* exangüe; (*lacking spirit*) soso; *revolt etc* incruento, sin efusión de sangre.

bloodlessly [ˈblʌdlɪslɪ] *adv* sin efusión de sangre.

blood-letting [ˈblʌd,letɪŋ] *n* (*Med*) efusión *f* de sangre, sangría *f*; (*fig*) sangría *f*, carnicería *f*.

bloodlust [ˈblʌdlʌst] *n* sed *f* de sangre.

blood-money [ˈblʌd,mʌnɪ] *n* dinero *m* manchado de sangre; precio *m* de la sangre.

blood-orange [ˈblʌd,ɒrɪndʒ] *n* naranja *f* sanguina.

blood-plasma [ˈblʌd,plæzmə] *n* plasma *m* sanguíneo.

blood-poisoning [ˈblʌd,pɔɪznɪŋ] *n* envenenamiento *m* de la sangre.

blood-pressure [ˈblʌd,preʃəʳ] *n* presión *f* sanguínea, tensión *f* arterial; **high ~** hipertensión *f*.

blood-pudding [,blʌdˈpʊdɪŋ] *n* (*US*) morcilla *f*.

blood-red [ˈblʌdˈred] *adj* sanguíneo, sanguinolento.

blood-relation [ˈblʌdrɪˈleɪʃən] *n* pariente *m* consanguíneo, parienta *f* consanguínea.

blood-relationship [,blʌdrɪˈleɪʃənʃɪp] *n* consanguinidad *f*; lazo *m* de parentesco.

blood-sausage [,blʌdˈsɒsɪdʒ] *n* (*US*) = **blood-pudding**.

bloodshed [ˈblʌdʃed] *n* efusión *f* de sangre; mortandad *f*.

bloodshot [ˈblʌdʃɒt] *adj* inyectado en (*or* de) sangre, sanguinolento.

blood-sports [ˈblʌdspɔːts] *npl* caza *f*.

bloodstain [ˈblʌdsteɪn] *n* mancha *f* de sangre.

bloodstained [ˈblʌdsteɪnd] *adj* manchado de sangre.

bloodstock [ˈblʌdstɒk] *n* caballos *mpl* de raza.

bloodstone [ˈblʌdstəʊn] *n* restañasangre *m*; sanguinaria *f*.

bloodstream [ˈblʌdstriːm] *n* corriente *f* sanguínea, sangre *f*.

bloodsucker [ˈblʌdsʌkəʳ] *n* (*fig*) sanguijuela *f*.

blood-test [ˈblʌdtest] *n* análisis *m* de sangre.

blood-thirstiness [ˈblʌd,θɜːstɪnɪs] *n* (*of person, animal*) sed *f* (*or* avidez *f*) de sangre; (*of book, of story*) violencia *f*.

bloodthirsty [ˈblʌdθɜːstɪ] *adj* sanguinario.

blood-transfusion [ˈblʌdtrænzˈfjuːʒən] *n* transfusión *f* de sangre.

blood-type [ˈblʌdtaɪp] *n* grupo *m* sanguíneo.

blood-vessel [ˈblʌd,vesl] *n* vaso *m* sanguíneo.

bloody [ˈblʌdɪ] **1** *adj* (**a**) *battle* sangriento, cruento; *steak* sanguinolento; *hands, dress* ensangrentado, manchado de sangre; **B~ Mary** María la Sangrienta, María Tudor; **~ mary** vodka *m* con jugo de tomate.

(**b**) (*Brit*⁑) puñetero‡, condenado*; **shut the ~ door!** ¡cierra la puerta, coño!‡; **that ~ dog!** ¡ese puñetero perro!‡; **you ~ idiot!** ¡gran imbécil!

2 *adv* (*Brit*‡) muy, terriblemente, condenadamente; **not ~ likely!** ¡ni hablar!; **he can ~ well do it himself** que lo haga él, ¡coño!‡

3 *vt* manchar de sangre; **with bloodied hands** con las manos ensangrentadas; **he was bloodied but unbowed** (*fig*) había sufrido pero no se daba por vencido.

bloody-minded‡ [ˈblʌdɪˈmaɪndɪd] *adj* (*Brit*) malintencionado; de mal genio, de malas pulgas; **to be ~ about a matter** mostrarse poco dispuesto a ayudar en un asunto, crear dificultades para la solución de un problema; **don't be so ~!** ¡no seas malintencionado!, ¡qué mala idea!

bloody-mindedness‡ [ˈblʌdɪˈmaɪndɪdnɪs] *n* mala intención *f*; mal genio *m*; mala disposición *f* (para ayudar *etc*); **it's just ~** (**on his part**) son ganas de joder⁑.

bloom [bluːm] **1** *n* flor *f*; floración *f*; (*fig*) perfección *f*; lozanía *f*; (*on fruit*) vello *m*; **in ~** en flor; **in full ~** en plena floración; **in the full ~ of youth** en la flor de la edad; **to come into ~** florecer.

2 *vi* florecer; (*fig*) prosperar, lozanear.

bloomer* [ˈbluːməʳ] *n* plancha* *f*.

bloomers [ˈbluːməz] *npl* pantalones *mpl* (de señora), bombachos *mpl*.

blooming [ˈbluːmɪŋ] (**a**) *adj* floreciente; lleno de salud. (**b**) (*euph**) = **bloody 1** (**b**).

blooper‡ [ˈbluːpəʳ] *n* (*US*) metedura *f* de pata.

blossom [ˈblɒsəm] **1** *n* flor *f*; **in ~** en flor.

2 *vi* florecer; **to ~ into** transformarse en, convertirse (algo inesperadamente) en; **to ~ out** alcanzar su plenitud, florecer, hacer eclosión.

blot [blɒt] **1** *n* borrón *m* (*also fig*); **a ~ on the family escutcheon** una mancha en el honor de la familia; **a ~ on the landscape** una cosa que afea el paisaje.

2 *vt* (*with ink*) manchar, emborronar; (*with blotter*) secar; *reputation* desacreditar.

3 *vi* (*pen*) echar borrones; (*ink*) correrse.

◆**blot out** *vt* oscurecer, tapar, hacer desaparecer; (*fig*) aniquilar; borrar (el recuerdo de).

◆**blot up** *vt ink* secar; *mist* beber, absorber.

blotch [blɒtʃ] *n* mancha *f*; (*on skin*) erupción *f*, rojez *f*.

blotchy [ˈblɒtʃɪ] *adj* manchado, lleno de manchas; *skin* lleno de manchas.

blotter [ˈblɒtəʳ] *n* secante *m* tipo rodillo, secafirmas *m*; (*sheet*) hoja *f* de papel secante.

blotting-pad [ˈblɒtɪŋ,pæd] *n* secante *m*.

blotting-paper [ˈblɒtɪŋ,peɪpəʳ] *n* papel *m* secante.

blotto‡ [ˈblɒtəʊ] *adj*: **to be ~** estar mamado‡.

blouse [blaʊz] *n* blusa *f*.

blouson [ˈbluːzɒn] *n* cazadora *f*.

blow[1] [bləʊ] *n* (**a**) golpe *m*; bofetada *f*; (**a ~ with** *may often be translated by the suffix* -azo, *eg*) **a ~ with a hammer** un martillazo, **a ~ with the fist** un puñetazo; **a ~ by ~ account** una narración pormenorizada; **at one ~** de un solo golpe; **to cushion** (*or* **soften**) **the ~** amortiguar el golpe; (*fig*) disminuir los efectos de un desastre (*etc*), hacer menos severo un impacto; **to deal** (*or* **strike**) **sb a ~** dar (*or* asestar) un golpe a uno; **to strike a ~ for freedom** dar un golpe por la libertad; **without striking a ~** sin violencia; **to come to ~s** venir a las manos.

(**b**) (*fig*) golpe *m*; **at one ~** de un golpe; de repente; **that's a ~!** ¡qué lástima!; **it is a cruel ~ for everybody** es un golpe cruel para todos; **the news came as a great ~** la noticia me *etc* causó un gran disgusto; **the affair was a ~ to his pride** la cosa le hirió en el amor propio; **it was a final ~ to our hopes** esto acabó de arruinar nuestras esperanzas; **on Monday the ~ fell** el lunes se descargó el golpe.

blow[2] [bləʊ] **1** *n* soplo *m*, soplido *m*.

2 (*irr*: *pret* **blew**, *ptp* **blown**) *vt* (**a**) (*of wind*) llevar; **the wind blew the ship towards the coast** el viento llevó el barco hacia la costa; **the wind has blown dust all over it** el viento lo ha cubierto todo de polvo; **to ~ open** *door* abrir de golpe, *safe* abrir con explosivos; **the wind blew the door**

shut el viento cerró la puerta de golpe; **to ~ a matter wide open** destapar un asunto.

(**b**) (*make by blowing*) *glass* soplar; *bubble* hacer, formar.

(**c**) *trumpet etc* tocar, sonar; *nose* sonarse; *kiss* tirar, enviar con la mano; *egg* vaciar (soplando); *organ* dar viento a; *whistle* pitar.

(**d**) (*destroy*) *fuse* fundir, quemar; *safe* abrir (con explosivos); **he blew a gasket** *or* (*US*) **his cork** *or* (*US*) **his stack** (*fig*) estaba que trinaba; **to ~ sb's cover** quitar la cobertura de uno; **to ~ sb's mind‡** barrer la mente de uno*, dejar a uno alucinado*; **to ~ it‡** cagarla‡; **now you've blown it!‡** ¡ya la has cagado!‡

(**e**) (*) *money* tirar, despilfarrar.

(**f**) (*) **~ me!, ~ it!, well I'm ~ed!** ¡caramba!; **I'll be ~ed if** ... que me cuelguen si ...; **~ the expense!** ¡al diablo con el gasto!

(**g**) **to ~ grass** (*Drugs‡*) fumar hierba.

3 *vi* (**a**) (*wind, whale*) soplar; (*siren etc*) sonar; (*puff and ~*) jadear, resoplar; **it's ~ing a gale** hace muchísimo viento; **to ~ on one's fingers** soplarse los dedos; **to ~ on one's soup** enfriar la sopa soplando; **to ~ open** abrirse de golpe; **the referee blew for a foul** el árbitro pitó para señalar falta.

(**b**) (*fuse*) fundirse, quemarse.

(**c**) (*: *leave*) irse; pirarla*; **I must ~** tengo que largarme*.

◆**blow about** *vt leaves etc* llevar de acá para allá.

◆**blow away 1** *vt* llevarse; arrancar; hacer desaparecer. **2** *vi* ser llevado (por el viento); ser arrancado (por el viento).

◆**blow down 1** *vt* derribar. **2** *vi* ser derribado (por el viento).

◆**blow in*** *vi* entrar de sopetón; llegar (inesperadamente).

◆**blow off** *vt* quitar, arrebatar; **to ~ the dust off a table** quitar el polvo de una mesa soplando.

◆**blow out 1** *vt* (**a**) *candle* apagar. (**b**) *cheeks* henchir. (**c**) **it blew out the window** rompió la ventana.

2 *vi* (**a**) (*candle etc*) apagarse. (**b**) (*tyre*) reventar; (*window*) romperse (con la fuerza del viento *etc*).

3 *vr*: **next day the storm had blown itself out** al día siguiente la tormenta se había calmado.

◆**blow over 1** *vt* derribar, volcar.

2 *vi* pasar; pasar al olvido, quedar olvidado; no tener consecuencias de importancia; (*storm*) pasar, calmarse.

◆**blow up 1** *vt* (**a**) *tyre* inflar. (**b**) *photo* ampliar. (**c**) (*with explosive*) volar, hacer saltar, explotar. (**d**) (*) (*with publicity*) dar bombo a; **to ~ sb up into a great novelist** hacer creer que alguien es gran novelista. (**e**) (*) **the boss blew the boy up** el jefe puso al chico como un trapo*.

2 *vi* (**a**) (*explosive*) estallar, explotar, explosionar; (*container*) estallar, reventar; (*) reventar (de ira). (**b**) **it's ~ing up for rain** con este viento tendremos lluvia; **now sth else has ~n up** ahora ha surgido otra cosa.

blow-drier ['bləʊ,draɪəʳ] *n* secador *m* de pelo.

blow-dry ['bləʊ,draɪ] *vt* secar con secador.

blower‡ ['bləʊəʳ] *n* teléfono *m*.

blowfly ['bləʊflaɪ] *n* moscarda *f*, mosca *f* azul.

blowgun ['bləʊ,gʌn] *n* (*US*) cerbatana *f*.

blowhole ['bləʊhəʊl] *n* (*of whale*) orificio *m* nasal; (*Tech*) sopladura *f*, venteadura *f*.

blow job*‡ ['bləʊdʒɒb] *n* francés*‡ *m*, felacio *f*.

blowlamp ['bləʊlæmp] *n* soplete *m*, lámpara *f* de soldar.

blown [bləʊn] **1** *ptp of* **blow²**. **2** *adj* (**a**) *flower* marchito. (**b**) *bridge etc* volado, destruido.

blow-out ['bləʊaʊt] *n* (**a**) (*Aut*) pinchazo *m*, pinchadura *f* (*Mex*); (*Elec*) quemadura *f*; (*of oil-well*) erupción *f*. (**b**) (‡: *meal*) banquetazo* *m*, comilona* *f*.

blowpipe ['bləʊpaɪp] *n* cerbatana *f*.

blowsy ['blaʊzɪ] = **blowzy**.

blow-torch ['bləʊtɔːtʃ] *n* soplete *m*.

blow-up ['bləʊʌp] *n* (**a**) (*Phot*) ampliación *f*. (**b**) (*) explosión *f* de ira; riña *f*, pelea *f* (*between* entre).

blowy ['bləʊɪ] *adj* ventoso; de mucho viento; **on a ~ day in March** un día de marzo de mucho viento; **it's ~ here** aquí hay mucho viento.

blowzy ['blaʊzɪ] *adj* desaliñado; de aspecto muy ordinario; (*red in face*) coloradote.

BLS *n* (*US*) *abbr of* **Bureau of Labor Statistics**.

BLT *n abbr of* **bacon, lettuce and tomato (sandwich)**.

blub* [blʌb] *vi* lloriquear.

blubber¹ ['blʌbəʳ] *n* grasa *f* de ballena.

blubber² ['blʌbəʳ] **1** *vt* decir lloriqueando. **2** *vi* lloriquear, llorar a lágrima viva.

blubbery ['blʌbərɪ] *adj* (*fat*) fláccido, fofo; **~ lips** labios *mpl* carnosos.

bludgeon ['blʌdʒən] **1** *n* cachiporra *f*. **2** *vt* aporrear; **to ~ sb into doing sth** (*fig*) coaccionar (*or* forzar) a uno a hacer algo.

blue [bluː] **1** *adj* (**a**) azul; *body, bruise* amoratado; (*Pol*) conservador; *blood* azul, noble; **~ with cold** amoratado de frío; **you can talk till you're ~ in the face*** puedes hablar hasta que revientes; **to go like a ~ streak** ir como un rayo; **to talk like a ~ streak*** hablar muy rápidamente; **~ baby** niño *m*, -a *f* azul, niño *m* cianótico, niña *f* cianótica; **~ blood** sangre *f* azul; **~ book** (*US Scol*) cuaderno *m* de exámenes; **~ cheese** queso *m* de tipo Roquefort, queso *m* de gusanos*; **~ chips, ~-chip securities** fianzas *fpl* fiables; **~ grass** (*US*) *hierba norteamericana usada como forraje*; **~ grass music** (*US*) *música folk de Kentucky*; **~ jeans** tejanos *mpl*, vaqueros *mpl*; **~ pencil** lápiz *m* negro (en la censura); **B~ Peter** (*Naut*) bandera *f* de salida; **~ shark** tiburón *m* azul; **~ whale** ballena *f* azul; **~ whiting** bacaladilla *f*.

(**b**) (*sad*) triste, deprimido, melancólico; **to feel ~** estar melancólico; **to look ~** tener aspecto triste.

(**c**) (*obscene*) verde, colorado (*LAm*); **~ film** película *f* porno.

2 *n* (**a**) azul *m*; (*Chem*) añil *m*; **the ~** (*sky*) el cielo, (*sea*) el mar; **to come out of the ~** venir como cosa llovida del cielo, bajar del cielo; (*bad news*) caer como una bomba; **he said out of the ~** dijo de repente, dijo inesperadamente.

(**b**) (*Pol*) conservador *m*, -ora *f*; *V* **true-blue**.

(**c**) **~s** melancolía *f*, murrias *fpl*, morriña *f*; (*Mus*) blues *m*.

(**d**) **Dark/Light B~** (*Brit Univ*) deportista *mf* representante de Oxford/de Cambridge.

3 *vt* (**a**) azular; *washing* añilar, dar azulete a. (**b**) (*Brit‡*) despilfarrar.

Bluebeard ['bluːbɪəd] *nm* Barba Azul.

bluebell ['bluːbel] *n* jacinto *m* silvestre; (*Scot*: *harebell*) campanilla *f*.

blueberry ['bluːberɪ] *n* (*US*) arándano *m*.

bluebird ['bluːbɜːd] *n* pájaro *m* azul, azulejo *m* (de América).

blue-blooded ['bluː'blʌdɪd] *adj* de sangre noble, linajudo.

bluebottle ['bluː,bɒtl] *n* moscarda *f*, mosca *f* azul.

blue-chip ['bluː'tʃɪp] *attr*: **~ company** empresa *f* que gestiona con inversión muy segura; **~ investment** inversión *f* en acciones de mucha demanda; inversión *f* asegurada.

blue-collar ['bluː,kɒləʳ] *attr*: **~ worker** manual *mf*.

blue-eyed ['bluː,aɪd] *adj* de ojos azules; **~ boy*** (*Brit*) favorito *m*, ojo *m* derecho.

bluejacket ['bluː,dʒækɪt] *n* marinero *m* (de buque de guerra).

bluejay ['bluːdʒeɪ] *n* (*US*) arrendajo *m* azul.

blueness ['bluːnɪs] *n* azul *m*, lo azul.

blue-pencil ['bluː'pensl] *vt* (*US*) tachar con lápiz negro (en la censura).

blueprint ['bluːprɪnt] *n* cianotipo *m*, ferroprusiato *m*; (*fig*) anteproyecto *m* (*for* de).

blue-sky ['bluːskaɪ] *attr* (*US*): **~ laws** legislación *f* para regular la emisión y venta de valores.

bluestocking ['bluː,stɒkɪŋ] *n* literata *f*, marisabidilla *f*.

bluetit ['bluːtɪt] *n* herrerillo *m* (común).

bluey ['bluːɪ] *adj* azulado.

bluff¹ [blʌf] **1** *adj* (**a**) *cliff etc* escarpado. (**b**) *person* brusco, francote. **2** *n* (*Geog*) risco *m*, peñasco *m*.

bluff² [blʌf] **1** *n* bluff *m*, blof *m* (*LAm*), farol *m*; **to call sb's ~** descubrirle a uno la fanfarronada, pillar a uno en un farol, coger a uno la palabra (*Sp*).

2 *vt* hacer un bluff a, engañar, intimidar con amenazas que no se pueden cumplir.

3 *vi* hacer un bluff, farolear, tirarse un farol.

bluffer ['blʌfəʳ] *n* farolero *m*.

bluish ['bluːɪʃ] *adj* azulado, azulino.

blunder ['blʌndəʳ] **1** *n* patochada *f*, metedura *f* de pata; error *m* garrafal.

2 *vi* hacer una patochada, tirarse una plancha.

◆**blunder about** *vi* andar a ciegas, andar a tontas y locas.

◆**blunder into** *vt* chocar con.

◆**blunder out** *vt* descolgarse con.

◆**blunder upon** *vt* tropezar con.

blunderbuss ['blʌndəbʌs] *n* trabuco *m*.

blunderer ['blʌndərəʳ] *n* torpe *m*, metelapata* *m*.

blundering ['blʌndərɪŋ] **1** *adj person* torpe, que mete la pata; *words, act* torpe. **2** *n* torpeza *f.*

blunt [blʌnt] **1** *adj* (**a**) *edge* embotado, desafilado; *point* despuntado; **with a ~ instrument** con un instrumento contundente. (**b**) *manner* directo, franco, abrupto; *statement* terminante, franco; *person* francote; **I will be ~ with you** voy a hablar con franqueza; **he was very ~ with me** conmigo no se mordió la lengua.
2 *vt* embotar (*also fig*), desafilar, despuntar.

bluntly ['blʌntlɪ] *adv* francamente; de modo terminante.

bluntness ['blʌntnɪs] *n* (**a**) embotadura *f.* (**b**) (*fig*) franqueza *f*, brusquedad *f.*

blur [blɜːʳ] **1** *n* contorno *m* borroso, impresión *f* imprecisa; **my mind was a ~** no me podía acordar claramente, todo se había vuelto borroso en mi mente.
2 *vt* hacer borroso, oscurecer, empañar, desdibujar; **a ~red photo** una foto desenfocada; **a ~red image** una imagen borrosa; **my eyes were ~red with tears** las lágrimas enturbiaban mi vista.
3 *vi* desdibujarse, hacerse borroso.

blurb [blɜːb] *n* anuncio *m* efusivo (de un libro), propaganda *f* publicitaria.

blurred [blɜːd] *adj* (**a**) *outline, photo etc* borroso, poco nítido. (**b**) *speech* incoherente, poco claro; *memory* borroso.

blurt [blɜːt] *vt*: **to ~ out** descolgarse con; *secret* revelar, dejar escapar impulsivamente.

blush [blʌʃ] **1** *n* rubor *m*, sonrojo *m*; (*glow*) color *m* de rosa; (*US*: *make-up*) colorete *m*; **the first ~ of dawn** la primera luz del alba; **in the first ~ of youth** en la inocencia de la edad juvenil; **at first ~** a primera vista; **it should not bring a ~ to the face of a bishop** no haría sonrojar a una hermana de la caridad; **to spare sb's ~es** (dejar de contar algo para) no ofender a uno.
2 *vi* ruborizarse, sonrojarse, ponerse colorado (*at* por, *with* de); **to ~ like a lobster** (*or* **tomato**) ponerse colorado como un pavo; **I ~ for you** me das vergüenza; **I ~ to +** *infin* me avergüenzo de + *infin*; **to make sb ~** sofocar a uno, hacer que uno se ruborice.

blusher ['blʌʃəʳ] *n* colorete *m.*

blushing ['blʌʃɪŋ] *adj* ruboroso; *bride* candoroso.

bluster ['blʌstəʳ] **1** *n* jactancia *f*; fanfarronadas *fpl*, bravatas *fpl.*
2 *vt*: **to ~ it out** defenderse echando bravatas, baladronear.
3 *vi* fanfarronear, echar bravatas.

blusterer ['blʌstərəʳ] *n* fanfarrón *m.*

blustering ['blʌstərɪŋ] *adj person* jactancioso, fanfarrón.

blustery ['blʌstərɪ] *adj wind* tempestuoso; *day* de mucho viento.

Blvd *abbr of* **boulevard** Bulevar *m*, Blvr.

BM *n* (**a**) *abbr of* **British Museum.** (**b**) *abbr of* **Bachelor of Medicine** licenciado *m*, -a *f* en medicina.

BMA *n abbr of* **British Medical Association.**

BMC *n abbr of* **British Medical Council.**

BMJ *n abbr of* **British Medical Journal.**

B.Mus. [ˌbiː'mʌs] *n abbr of* **Bachelor of Music.**

bn *abbr of* **billion.**

BNFL *n abbr of* **British Nuclear Fuels Limited.**

B/O (*Fin*) *abbr of* **brought over** suma *f* anterior.

BO *n* (**a**) (*euph*) *abbr of* **body odour** olor *m* a sudor. (**b**) (*US*) *abbr of* **box-office.**

b.o. (*Comm*) *abbr of* **buyer's option** opción *f* del comprador.

boa ['bəʊə] *n* (*snake, fur etc*) boa *f*; **~ constrictor** boa *f.*

Boadicea [ˌbəʊədɪ'sɪə] *nf* Boadicea.

boar [bɔːʳ] *n* verraco *m*, cerdo *m* (padre); **wild ~** jabalí *m*, coche *m* de monte (*Mex*).

board [bɔːd] **1** *n* (**a**) (*of wood*) tabla *f*, tablero *m*, tablón *m*; (*notice ~*) tablón *m*, tablero *m*; (*table*) mesa *f*; (*in bookbinding*) cartón *m*; (*for chess etc*) tablero *m*; (*Comput*) placa *f*, tarjeta *f*; **the ~s** (*Theat*) las tablas; **increase across the ~** aumento *m* global (*or* general *or* lineal); **in ~s** *book* en cartoné; **to sweep the ~** ganar todas las bazas, (*in election*) copar todos los escaños; **to tread the ~s** (*as profession*) ser actor, ser actriz, (*action*) salir a escena.
(**b**) (*provision of meals*) pensión *f*; **full ~** pensión *f* (completa); **~ and lodging** (*Brit*) comida *f* y casa, (*as advert*) comidas *fpl* y camas.
(**c**) (*Naut*) **on ~** a bordo; en el tren, en el autobús *etc*; **on ~ (the) ship** a bordo del barco; **to go on ~** embarcarse, ir a bordo; **to go by the ~** ser abandonado; **to take on ~** *idea etc* adoptar, asimilar.
(**d**) (*persons*) junta *f*, consejo *m* de administración; **~ of directors** junta *f* directiva; **~ of governors** (*Brit Scol*) consejo *m* (de escuela); **~ of inquiry** comisión *f* investigadora; **B~ of Trade** (*Brit*) Departamento *m* de Comercio y Exportación, (*US*) Cámara *f* de Comercio; **~ meeting** reunión *f* de la junta directiva.
2 *vt* (**a**) *ship* ir a bordo de, embarcarse en; *enemy ship* abordar; *bus, train* subir a. (**b**) *person* hospedar, dar pensión (completa) a.
3 *vi*: **to ~ with** hospedarse en casa de.

◆**board in** *vt* = **board up.**

◆**board out** *vt person* buscar alojamiento a; **he is ~ed out with relatives** vive con unos parientes (pagando la pensión).

◆**board up** *vt door, window* entablar.

boarder ['bɔːdəʳ] *n* huésped *m*, -eda *f*; (*Brit Scol*) interno *m*, -a *f.*

board-game ['bɔːdgeɪm] *n* juego *m* de mesa.

boarding ['bɔːdɪŋ] *n* entablado *m.*

boarding-card ['bɔːdɪŋˌkɑːd] *n* tarjeta *f* de embarque.

boarding-house ['bɔːdɪŋhaʊs] *n, pl* **boarding-houses** ['bɔːdɪŋˌhaʊzɪz] pensión *f*, casa *f* de huéspedes.

boarding-party ['bɔːdɪŋˌpɑːtɪ] *n* pelotón *m* de abordaje.

boarding-pass ['bɔːdɪŋˌpɑːs] *n* tarjeta *f* de embarque, pase *m* de embarque (*LAm*).

boarding-school ['bɔːdɪŋskuːl] *n* internado *m.*

boardroom ['bɔːdrʊm] *n* sala *f* de juntas.

boardwalk ['bɔːdwɔːk] *n* paseo *m* entablado.

boast [bəʊst] **1** *n* fanfarronada *f*, alarde *m*; **it is his ~ that ...** se jacta de que ...
2 *vt* enorgullecerse de poseer, ostentar.
3 *vi* jactarse; **to ~ about, to ~ of** jactarse de, hacer alarde de; **that's nothing to ~ about** eso no es motivo para vanagloriarse.

boasted ['bəʊstɪd] *adj* alardeado, cacareado.

boaster ['bəʊstəʳ] *n* jactancioso *m*, -a *f*, fanfarrón *m*, -ona *f*, presumido *m*, -a *f.*

boastful ['bəʊstfʊl] *adj* jactancioso, fanfarrón, presumido.

boastfully ['bəʊstfəlɪ] *adv* jactanciosamente.

boastfulness ['bəʊstfʊlnɪs] *n* jactancia *f.*

boasting ['bəʊstɪŋ] *n* jactancia *f*, fanfarronadas *fpl.*

boat [bəʊt] *n* (*gen*) barco *m*; (*large ship*) buque *m*, navío *m*; (*small*) barca *f*, embarcación *f*; (*racing eight, ship's ~*) bote *m*; **we're all in the same ~** todos estamos embarcados en la misma nave, todos remamos en la misma galera; **to burn one's ~s** quemar las naves; **to go by ~** ir en barco; **to launch** (*or* **lower**) **the ~s** botar los botes al agua; **to miss the ~** (*fig*) perder el tren; **to push the ~ out*** celebrar dispendiosamente; ir de parranda; tirar la casa por la ventana; **to rock the ~** (*fig*) hacer olas, perturbar el equilibrio.

boatbuilder ['bəʊtˌbɪldəʳ] *n* constructor *m* de barcos; **~'s (yard)** astillero *m.*

boatbuilding ['bəʊtˌbɪldɪŋ] *n* construcción *f* de barcos.

boat-deck ['bəʊtˌdek] *n* cubierta *f* de botes.

boater ['bəʊtəʳ] *n* canotier *m*, canotié *m.*

boatful ['bəʊtfʊl] *n* (*goods*) cargamento *m*; **the refugees arrived in ~s** llegaron barcos llenos de refugiados.

boat-hook ['bəʊthʊk] *n* bichero *m.*

boathouse ['bəʊthaʊs] *n, pl* **boathouses** ['bəʊthaʊzɪz] cobertizo *m* para botes.

boating ['bəʊtɪŋ] *n* canotaje *m*; **~ holiday/trip** vacaciones *fpl*/paseo *m* en barca.

boatload ['bəʊtləʊd] *n* barcada *f.*

boatman ['bəʊtmən] *n, pl* **boatmen** ['bəʊtmen] barquero *m.*

boat people ['bəʊtˌpiːpl] *npl refugiados que huyen en barco (esp de Vietnam).*

boat-race ['bəʊtreɪs] *n* regata *f*; **the B~ Race** *carrera anual de remo entre Oxford y Cambridge.*

boatswain ['bəʊsn] *n* contramaestre *m.*

boat-train ['bəʊttreɪn] *n* tren *m* que enlaza con un barco, tren *m* del barco.

boatyard ['bəʊtjɑːd] *n* astillero *m.*

Bob [bɒb] *nm familiar form of* **Robert**; **~'s your uncle!*** (*Brit*) ¡ya está!, ¡ya se acabó!

bob¹ [bɒb] **1** *n* (*of hair*) pelo *m* a lo garçon. **2** *vt hair* cortar a lo garçon.

bob²* [bɒb] *n, pl invar* (*Brit*) chelín *m.*

bob³ [bɒb] **1** *n* (*jerk*) sacudida *f*, meneo *m*, movimiento *m* brusco; (*curtsy*) reverencia *f* (breve).
2 *vi* menearse, agitarse.

◆**bob about** *vi* (*in wind etc*) bailar; (*on water*) fluctuar.

◆**bob down** *vi* agacharse; esconderse.

◆**bob to** *vi*: **to ~ to sb** hacer una reverencia a uno.

◆**bob up** *vi* levantarse; aparecer; (*fig*) surgir, presentarse inesperadamente; **to ~ up and down** subir y bajar; (*person*) levantarse y sentarse repetidas veces.

bob[4] [bɒb] *n* (*also* **bobsleigh**) bob *m*, bobsleigh *m*.
bobbin [ˈbɒbɪn] *n* carrete *m*, bobina *f* (*also Elec*); (*Sew*) canilla *f*.
bobble [ˈbɒbl] **1** *n* (**a**) borla *f*. (**b**) (*US**) pifia *f*. **2** *vt* (*US**) pifiar.
Bobby [ˈbɒbɪ] *nm familiar form of* **Robert**.
bobby* [ˈbɒbɪ] *n* guili* *m*, poli* *m*.
bobby pin [ˈbɒbɪˌpɪn] *n* (*US*) horquilla *f*, prendedor *m*.
bobbysocks* [ˈbɒbɪsɒks] *npl* (*US*) escarpines *mpl*.
bobbysoxer* [ˈbɒbɪsɒksəʳ] *n* (*US*) tobillera *f*.
bobcat [ˈbɒbkæt] *n* (*US*) lince *m*.
bobsled [ˈbɒbsled] *n*, **bobsleigh** [ˈbɒbsleɪ] *n* bob *m*, bobsleigh *m*.
bobtail [ˈbɒbteɪl] *n* cola *f* corta; animal *m* de cola corta, animal *m* rabón.
bobtailed [ˈbɒbteɪld] *adj* rabicorto.
Boccaccio [bɒˈkætʃɪəʊ] *nm* Bocacio.
Boche [bɒʃ] **1** *adj* (*pej*) alemán, tudesco. **2** *n* (*pej*) boche *m*, alemán *m*; **the ~** los alemanes.
bock beer [ˈbɒkˌbɪəʳ] *n* (*US*) cerveza *f* alemana.
bod* [bɒd] *n* (*Brit*) tío* *m*, individuo *m*.
bode [bəʊd] **1** *vt* presagiar; **it ~s no good** esto no nos promete nada bueno. **2** *vi*: **this ~s ill for** es mala señal para, es de mal agüero para.
bodge* [bɒdʒ] *vt* = **botch**.
bodice [ˈbɒdɪs] *n* corpiño *m*, almilla *f*.
-bodied [ˈbɒdɪd] *adj ending in compounds* de cuerpo ..., *eg* **small~** de cuerpo pequeño; **full~** *cry* fuerte, *wine* de mucho cuerpo.
bodily [ˈbɒdɪlɪ] **1** *adj* corpóreo, corporal; **~ harm** daños *mpl* corporales; **~ needs** necesidades *fpl* corporales. **2** *adv* (*in person*) en persona; (*as a whole*) en conjunto; **to lift sb ~** levantar a uno en peso.
bodkin [ˈbɒdkɪn] *n* (*Sew*) aguja *f* de jareta; (*Typ*) punzón *m*; (*for hair*: ††) espadilla *f*††.
body [ˈbɒdɪ] *n* (**a**) cuerpo *m*; (*corpse*) cadáver *m*; (*****) persona *f*; (*frame*) armazón *f*, bastidor *m*; (*Aut*) caja *f*, carrocería *f*; (*Astron, Chem*) cuerpo *m*; **~ and soul** (*as adv*) de todo corazón, con el alma; **the ~ politic** el estado; **~ repairs** (*Aut*) reparación *f* de la carrocería; **~ (repair) shop** taller *m* de reparaciones; **over my dead ~!** ¡sobre mi cadáver!; ¡bajo ningún concepto!; **to keep ~ and soul together** vivir justo, seguir viviendo; **her salary hardly keeps ~ and soul together** apenas si gana para vivir.
(**b**) (*corporation etc*) corporación *f*, cuerpo *m*.
(**c**) (*group*) grupo *m*, conjunto *m*; **a considerable ~ of evidence** una colección importante de datos; **there is a ~ of opinion that ...** hay quienes opinan que ...; **a large ~ of people** un nutrido grupo de personas; **main ~** grueso *m*; **the main ~ of his speech** la parte principal de su discurso; **in a ~** todos juntos, en bloque.
(**d**) (*of wine*) cuerpo *m*, volumen *m*.
body-bag [ˈbɒdɪˌbæg] *n* bolsa *f* para restos humanos.
body-blow [ˈbɒdɪˌbləʊ] *n* (*fig*) golpe *m* duro.
body-builder [ˈbɒdɪˌbɪldəʳ] *n* culturista *mf*.
body-building [ˈbɒdɪˌbɪldɪŋ] *n* culturismo *m*.
body count [ˈbɒdɪˌkaʊnt] *n* (*US*) número *m* de muertos; **to do a ~** (*of those present*) hacer un recuento de la asistencia; (*of dead*) hacer un recuento de los muertos.
bodyguard [ˈbɒdɪgɑːd] *n* (*man*) guardaespaldas *m*; (*royal*) guardia *f* de corps; (*men*) guardia *f* personal.
body-language [ˈbɒdɪˌlæŋgwɪdʒ] *n* lenguaje *m* gestual, gestualidad *f*.
body-lotion [ˈbɒdɪˌləʊʃən] *n* loción *f* corporal.
body-mike* [ˈbɒdɪmaɪk] *n* micrófono *m* escondido, micro* *m* de solapa.
body-odour, (*US*) **body-odor** [ˈbɒdɪˌəʊdəʳ] *n* olor *m* a sudor.
body-scanner [ˈbɒdɪˌskænəʳ] *n* escáner *m*.
body-search [ˈbɒdɪsɜːtʃ] **1** *n* registro *m* de la persona. **2** *vt* registrar (la persona de).
body-snatcher [ˈbɒdɪˌsnætʃəʳ] *n* (*Hist*) ladrón *m* de cadáveres.
body stocking [ˈbɒdɪˌstɒkɪŋ] *n*, **body suit** [ˈbɒdɪˌsuːt] *n* body *m*, bodi *m*.
body warmer [ˈbɒdɪˌwɔːməʳ] *n* chaleco *m* acolchado.
bodywork [ˈbɒdɪwɜːk] *n* (*Aut*) carrocería *f*.
Boer [ˈbəʊəʳ] **1** *adj* bóer. **2** *n* bóer *mf*.
Boer War [ˈbəʊəˌwɔːʳ] *n* Guerra *f* Bóer, Guerra *f* del Transvaal.
B. of E. *n abbr of* **Bank of England**.
boffin [ˈbɒfɪn] *n* (*Brit*) científico *m*, inventor *m*.
bog [bɒg] **1** *n* (**a**) pantano *m*, ciénaga *f*. (**b**) (*Brit*‡) meadero‡ *m*.
2 *vt*: **to get ~ged down** quedar atascado en el lodo, hundirse en el lodo; (*fig*) empantanarse, atrancarse (*in* en).
bogey [ˈbəʊgɪ] *n* (**a**) (*goblin*) duende *m*, trasgo *m*; (*bugbear*) pesadilla *f*; **that is our ~ team** ése es un equipo gafe para nosotros.
(**b**) (*Brit*‡: *policeman*) bofia‡ *m*.
(**c**) (*Rail*) bogie *m*, boga *f*.
(**d**) (*Golf*) bogey *m*, más uno *m*.
bogeyman [ˈbəʊgɪˌmæn] *n*, *pl* **bogeymen** [ˈbəʊgɪˌmen] coco *m*.
boggle [ˈbɒgl] **1** *vi* sobresaltarse, pasmarse; **don't just stand and ~** no te quedes ahí parado con la boca abierta; **the imagination ~s** la imaginación es incapaz de representárselo; **the mind ~s** nos quedamos pasmados; **to ~ at** vacilar ante, titubear ante. **2** *vt*: **to ~ the mind*** dejar alucinado.
boggy [ˈbɒgɪ] *adj* pantanoso.
bogie [ˈbəʊgɪ] *n* = **bogey**.
Bogotá [ˌbɒgəʊˈtɑː] *n* Bogotá *m*.
bog-paper‡ [ˈbɒgˌpeɪpəʳ] *n* (*Brit*) papel *m* higiénico, papel *m* de wáter.
bog-roll‡ [ˈbɒgrəʊl] *n* (*Brit*) rollo *m* de papel de wáter.
bogtrotter‡ [ˈbɒgˌtrɒtəʳ] *n* irlandés *m*, -esa *f*.
bogus [ˈbəʊgəs] *adj* falso, fraudulento; *person* fingido; (*of person's character*) artificial, afectado.
bogy [ˈbəʊgɪ] *n* = **bogey, bogie**.
Bohemia [bəʊˈhiːmɪə] *n* Bohemia *f*.
Bohemian [bəʊˈhiːmɪən] **1** *adj* bohemo; (*fig*) bohemio. **2** *n* bohemo *m*, -a *f*; (*fig*) bohemio *m*, -a *f*.
Bohemianism [bəʊˈhiːmɪənɪzəm] *n* bohemia *f*, vida *f* bohemia.
boil[1] [bɔɪl] *n* (*Med*) divieso *m*, furúnculo *m*, chupón *m* (*And*), postema *f* (*Mex*).
boil[2] [bɔɪl] **1** *n*: **to be on the ~** estar hirviendo; (*fig*) (*situation*) estar a punto de estallar, (*person*) estar furioso; **to bring to the** (*US*: **a**) **~** calentar hasta que hierva, llevar a ebullición; **to come to the** (*US*: **a**) **~** comenzar a hervir, (*fig*) entrar en ebullición; **to go off the ~** dejar de hervir.
2 *vt* hervir, hacer hervir, calentar hasta que hierva; (*Culin*) *liquid* hervir; *vegetables, meat* herventar, cocer; salcochar; *egg* pasar por agua.
3 *vi* (**a**) hervir; **to ~ dry** hervir hasta que se consume el caldo. (**b**) (*fig*) **it makes me ~** me hace rabiar; **to ~ with rage** estar furioso; **to ~ with indignation** estar indignado.
◆**boil away** *vi* (*evaporate completely*) evaporarse, reducirse (por ebullición).
◆**boil down** **1** *vt sauce etc* reducir por cocción; (*fig*) reducir a forma más sencilla. **2** *vi*: **~ down to** reducirse a; **it all ~s down to this** la cosa se reduce a lo siguiente.
◆**boil over** *vi* (**a**) (*liquid*) irse, rebosar. (**b**) (*fig*) desbordarse.
◆**boil up** *vi* (*lit*: *milk*) hervir, subir; **anger was ~ing up in him** estaba a punto de estallar de ira; **they are ~ing up for a real row** se están enfureciendo de verdad.
boiled [bɔɪld] *adj* hervido; **~ egg** huevo *m* pasado por agua; **~ potatoes** patatas *fpl* cocidas al agua; **~ shirt** camisa *f* de pechera; **~ sweet** (*Brit*) caramelo *m* con sabor a frutas.
boiler [ˈbɔɪləʳ] *n* (**a**) caldera *f*; (*Brit*: *for washing clothes*) caldero *m*, calefón *m* (*SC*). (**b**) (*Culin*) pollo *m* viejo (*que sólo sirve para hervir*).
boilerhouse [ˈbɔɪləhaʊs] *n*, *pl* **boilerhouses** [ˈbɔɪləhaʊzɪz] edificio *m* de la caldera.
boilermaker [ˈbɔɪləˌmeɪkəʳ] *n* calderero *m*.
boiler-room [ˈbɔɪlərʊm] *n* sala *f* de calderas.
boilersuit [ˈbɔɪləsuːt] *n* (*Brit*) mono *m*.
boiling [ˈbɔɪlɪŋ] **1** *adj* hirviendo (*invariable*), en ebullición. **2** *adv*: **it's ~ hot** (*weather*) hace un calor terrible; **on a ~ hot day** un día de mucho calor.
boiling-point [ˈbɔɪlɪŋpɔɪnt] *n* punto *m* de ebullición.
boisterous [ˈbɔɪstərəs] *adj wind* borrascoso; *behaviour* ruidoso, turbulento; *child* bullicioso, revoltoso; (*in high spirits*) muy alegre, de excelente humor; *meeting* nada tranquilo, alborotado; *welcome* tumultuoso.
boisterously [ˈbɔɪstərəslɪ] *adv* (*V adj*) bulliciosamente; ruidosamente.
bold [bəʊld] *adj* (*courageous*) valiente, audaz; (*excessively ~*) atrevido, osado, temerario; (*shameless*) descarado; *move, stroke* enérgico; *relief, contrast* fuerte; *headland* escarpado; *line* claro, vigoroso; **~ face** (*Typ*) negrita *f*; **~ type** (*Typ*) (caracteres *mpl* en) negrita *f*; **he came up as ~ as brass** se acercó tan fresco; **if I may make so ~** si Vd me lo permite; **if I may make so ~ as to** + *infin* si se me permite + *infin*.

boldly ['bəʊldlɪ] adv (V adj) audazmente; atrevidamente, con temeridad; descaradamente; enérgicamente; vigorosamente.

boldness ['bəʊldnɪs] n (V adj) audacia f, osadía f; temeridad f; descaro m; energía f; fuerza f, lo marcado.

bole [bəʊl] n tronco m.

bolero [bə'lɛərəʊ] n bolero m.

boletus [bəʊ'li:təs] n seta f.

Bolivia [bə'lɪvɪə] n Bolivia f.

Bolivian [bə'lɪvɪən] 1 adj boliviano. 2 n boliviano m, -a f.

boll [bəʊl] n (Bot) cápsula f.

bollard ['bɒləd] n (Brit) (at wharf) bolardo m, noray m; (Aut) poste m.

bollocking** ['bɒləkɪŋ] n: to give sb a right ~ poner a uno como un trapo*.

bollocks** ['bɒləks] npl (Brit) = ball[1] (b).

Bologna [bə'ləunjə] n Bolonia f.

bolognese [bɒlə'njeɪz] adj: ~ sauce salsa f boloñesa.

boloney‡ [bə'ləʊnɪ] n (US: sausage) tipo de salchicha; (nonsense) chorradas‡ fpl; = baloney.

Bolshevik ['bɒlʃəvɪk] 1 adj bolchevique. 2 n bolchevique mf.

Bolshevism ['bɒlʃəvɪzəm] n bolchevismo m, bolcheviquismo m.

Bolshevist ['bɒlʃəvɪst] 1 adj bolchevista. 2 n bolchevista mf.

bolshie*, bolshy* ['bɒlʃɪ] 1 n bolchevique mf. 2 adj (Pol) bolchevique; (fig) revoltoso; difícil; protestón*, contestón*.

bolster ['bəʊlstə^r] 1 n travesero m, cabezal m; (Tech) cojín m. 2 vt (also to ~ up) reforzar; (fig) alentar, dar aliento a.

bolt [bəʊlt] 1 n (a) (of door, rifle) cerrojo m; (of crossbow) cuadrillo m; (of cloth) rollo m; (Tech) perno m, tornillo m; (of thunder) rayo m; ~ from the blue suceso m inesperado, sorpresa f desagradable; like a ~ from the blue como una bomba; he has shot his ~ ha quemado su último cartucho.

(b) (dash) fuga f precipitada, salida f repentina; to make a ~ for it evadirse corriendo, fugarse repentinamente; he made a ~ for the door se precipitó hacia la puerta.

2 as adv: ~ upright rígido, erguido; to sit ~ upright (action) incorporarse de golpe.

3 vt (a) door echar el cerrojo a; (Tech) sujetar con tornillos, empernar; to ~ together unir con pernos.

(b) food engullir, comer rapidísimamente.

4 vi (escape) fugarse; (horse) desbocarse, dispararse; (rush) precipitarse; (US Pol) separarse del partido; to ~ past pasar como un rayo.

◆bolt in 1 vt (lock in) encerrar echando el cerrojo (or bajo cerrojo). 2 vi (rush in) entrar precipitadamente.

◆bolt on vt (Tech) asegurar con perno.

◆bolt out 1 vt (lock out) to ~ sb out dejar fuera a uno echando el cerrojo. 2 vi (rush out) salir de golpe.

bolt-hole ['bəʊlthəʊl] n refugio m.

bomb [bɒm] 1 n bomba f; ~ alert, ~ warning aviso m de bomba; ~ attack atentado m con bomba; ~ scare amenaza f de bomba; this car goes like a ~ (Brit*) este coche corre a toda pastilla (or va a toda hostia‡); it all went like a ~* (Brit) todo fue sobre ruedas*, todo fue a las mil maravillas*; it costs a ~* (Brit) cuesta un ojo de la cara*; he made a ~* se ganó un fortunón*.

2 vt bombardear; (US: fail) suspender.

3 vi (US) fracasar.

◆bomb along* vi ir como el demonio, ir muy rápido; we were ~ing along at 150 corríamos a 150.

◆bomb out vt house volar; the family was ~ed out (by terrorists) a la familia les volaron la casa; (by planes) a la familia les bombardearon la casa.

bombard [bɒm'bɑ:d] vt bombardear; (fig) asediar, llenar (with de); I was ~ed with questions me acribillaron a preguntas.

bombardier [,bɒmbə'dɪə^r] n bombardero m.

bombardment [bɒm'bɑ:dmənt] n bombardeo m.

bombast ['bɒmbæst] n ampulosidad f, rimbombancia f; (words) palabras fpl altisonantes; (boasts) bravatas fpl.

bombastic [bɒm'bæstɪk] adj altisonante, ampuloso, rimbombante; person jactancioso, farolero.

bombastically [bɒm'bæstɪklɪ] adv altilocuentemente, ampulosamente, rimbombantemente.

Bombay [bɒm'beɪ] n Bombay m; ~ duck (Culin) pescado seco utilizado en la elaboración del curry.

bomb-bay ['bɒm,beɪ] n compartimento m de bombas.

bomb-crater ['bɒm,kreɪtə^r] n cráter m de bomba.

bomb-disposal ['bɒmdɪs'pəʊzəl] n desactivación f de bombas, neutralización f de bombas; ~ expert técnico m de desactivación de bombas, artificiero m; ~ squad, ~ unit brigada f de bombas.

bomber ['bɒmə^r] n bombardero m; ~ command jefatura f de bombardeo; ~ jacket cazadora f de aviador; ~ pilot piloto m de bombardero.

bombing ['bɒmɪŋ] n bombardeo m.

bombproof ['bɒmpru:f] adj a prueba de bombas.

bombshell ['bɒmʃel] n obús m, granada f; it fell like a ~ cayó como una bomba; she was a real ~ era algo excepcional; a blond ~ una rubia despampanante*.

bomb-shelter ['bɒm,ʃeltə^r] n refugio m antiaéreo.

bombsight ['bɒmsaɪt] n mira f de bombardeo, visor m de bombardeo.

bomb-site ['bɒmsaɪt] n lugar m donde ha estallado una bomba; solar m arrasado por una bomba.

bona fide ['bəʊnə'faɪdɪ] adj genuino, auténtico, de fiar, fiable.

bona fides ['bəʊnə'faɪdɪz] n buena fe f; autenticidad f.

bonanza [bə'nænzə] n (US Min, fig) bonanza f.

bonce‡ [bɒns] n coco* m.

bond [bɒnd] n 1 n (a) (link) lazo m, vínculo m; ~s of friendship lazos mpl de amistad; the marriage ~ el vínculo del matrimonio.

(b) (Fin) bono m, obligación f; (bail, customs) fianza f; in ~ en depósito bajo fianza; ~ washing lavado m de bonos; to put goods into ~ poner mercancías en el almacén aduanero; to take goods out of ~ retirar mercancías del almacén aduanero.

(c) (Chem etc) enlace m.

(d) ~s (fetters) cuerdas fpl, cadenas fpl.

2 vt (also to ~ together) liar, vincular.

bondage ['bɒndɪdʒ] n esclavitud f, cautiverio m; (as fetish) bondage m.

bonded ['bɒndɪd] adj: ~ goods mercancías fpl en depósito de Aduanas; ~ warehouse almacén m aduanero.

bondholder ['bɒnd,həʊldə^r] n obligacionista mf, titular mf de bonos.

bonding ['bɒndɪŋ] n vinculación f.

bone [bəʊn] 1 n hueso m; (of fish) espina f; ~s (of dead) huesos mpl, (more respectfully) restos mpl mortales; ~ of contention manzana f de la discordia; close to the ~ joke verde, arriesgado; to feel sth in one's ~s tener una corazonada con respecto a algo, tener un presentimiento de algo; to work one's fingers to the ~ trabajar como un esclavo; to have a ~ to pick with sb tener que arreglar cuentas con uno; to make no ~s about + ger no vacilar en + infin; to make no ~s about sth no tener reparos en algo, no andarse con rodeos en (el asunto de) algo; he won't make old ~s no llega a viejo.

2 vt (a) meat deshuesar, fish quitar las espinas a. (b) (‡) birlar‡.

3 vi (*) to ~ up quemarse las cejas (on estudiando), empollar (on sobre).

bone china ['bəʊn'tʃaɪnə] n porcelana f fina.

boned [bəʊnd] adj meat deshuesado; fish sin espinas; corset de ballenas.

bone-dry ['bəʊn'draɪ] adj enteramente seco.

bonehead* ['bəʊnhed] n tonto m, -a f.

boneheaded* ['bəʊn'hedɪd] adj estúpido.

bone-idle ['bəʊn'aɪdl] adj muy gandul.

boneless ['bəʊnlɪs] adj (a) (Anat) sin hueso(s), deshuesado. (b) (fig) sin carácter, débil.

bone-marrow ['bəʊn,mærəʊ] n médula f ósea.

bonemeal ['bəʊnmi:l] n harina f de huesos.

boner* ['bəʊnə^r] n (US) plancha f, patochada f; to pull a ~ meter el cuezo*.

bone-shaker* ['bəʊn,ʃeɪkə^r] n (Aut etc) armatoste m, rácano m.

bonfire ['bɒnfaɪə^r] n hoguera f, fogata f; B~ Night (Brit) fiesta que se celebra en la noche del 5 noviembre en toda Gran Bretaña.

bongo ['bɒŋgəʊ] n (also ~ drum) bongó m.

bonhomie ['bɒnɒmi:] n afabilidad f.

bonk[1]* [bɒŋk] 1 n (blow) golpe m. 2 vt golpear, pegar.

bonk[2]* [bɒŋk] n: it went ~ hizo ¡pum!, se oyó un ruido sordo; things that go ~ in the night cosas que hacen ruidos misteriosos en la noche.

bonk[3]** [bɒŋk] vti joder**.

bonkers‡ ['bɒŋkəz] adj (Brit): to be ~ estar chalado*; to go ~ chalarse*.

bonking** ['bɒŋkɪŋ] n joder** m.

bon mot ['bɒn'məʊ] n dicho m agudo, chiste m, agudeza f.

Bonn [bɒn] *n* Bona *m*, Bonn *m*.
bonnet ['bɒnɪt] *n* (**a**) (*woman's*) gorra *f*, cofia *f*; (*large, showy*) papalina *f*, toca *f*; (*baby's*) gorro *m*; (*Scot's*) gorra *f* escocesa. (**b**) (*Brit Aut*) capó *m*.
bonny ['bɒnɪ] *adj* (*esp Scot*) bonito, rollizo.
bonsai ['bɒnsaɪ] *n* bonsai *m*.
bonus ['bəʊnəs] **1** *n* plus *m*; (*on wages*) sobrepaga *f*, bonificación *f*, prima *f*, suplemento *m*, abono *m* (*LAm*); (*insurance etc*) prima *f*; (*to shareholders*) dividendo *m* adicional.
2 *adj* adicional, extra; ~ **scheme** plan *m* de incentivos; ~ **shares,** ~ **stock** (*US*) acciones *fpl* gratuitas.
bony ['bəʊnɪ] *adj* huesudo; (*like bone*) óseo, huesoso; (*thin*) descarnado, flaco.
boo [buː] (*equivalents in Spain etc*) **1** *n* silbido *m*, rechifla *f*, pateo *m*; **he couldn't say** ~ **to a goose*** no dice ni mu.
2 *vt* abuchear, silbar, rechiflar, patear; **to** ~ **an actor** patear a un actor; **he was** ~**ed off the stage** tuvo que abandonar la escena a fuerza de pateo.
3 *vi* silbar.
boob* [buːb] **1** *n* (*mistake*) patochada *f*. **2** *vi* tirar una plancha.
boobies‡ ['buːbɪz] *npl* (*US*), **boobs‡** [buːbz] *npl* tetas* *fpl*.
booboo* ['buːbuː] *n* (*US*) patochada *f*.
boobtube ['buːbtjuːb] *n* (*US*: *TV set*) televisor *m*; (*sun top*) camiseta-tubo *f*.
booby ['buːbɪ] *n* bobo *m*.
booby hatch ['buːbɪˌhætʃ] *n* (*US‡*) casa *f* de locos.
booby-prize ['buːbɪpraɪz] *n* premio *m* al peor competidor.
booby-trap ['buːbɪtræp] **1** *n* trampa *f*; (*bomb*) trampa *f* explosiva, trampa *f* cazabobos, bomba *f* trampa. **2** *vt* poner trampa explosiva a; **the house had been** ~**ped** habían puesto una trampa explosiva en la casa.
booby-trapped ['buːbɪtræpt] *adj*: ~ **car** coche-bomba *m*; ~ **door** puerta *f* con sorpresa.
boogie-woogie ['buːgɪˌwuːgɪ] *n* bugui-bugui *m*.
booing ['buːɪŋ] *n* abucheo *m*, silbos *mpl*, rechifla *f*.
book [bʊk] **1** *n* (**a**) (*gen*) libro *m*; (*notebook*) libreta *f*, librito *m*; (*exercise book*) cuaderno *m*; (*of cheques, tickets*) (libro *m*) talonario *m*; (*of members*) registro *m*; (*of stamps*) taco *m*; **it's a closed** ~ **to me** para mí es un asunto misterioso; **the good** ~ la Biblia; **in my** ~ (*fig*) a mi modo de ver, en mi concepto; **to be in sb's good** ~**s** estar bien con uno; **to be in sb's bad** (*or* **black**) ~**s** estar mal con uno, estar en la lista negra de uno; **there's no such name on our** ~**s** no existe ese nombre en nuestro registro, no consta tal nombre en nuestros registros; **to bring sb to** ~ pedir cuentas a uno, llamar a uno a capítulo; **to go by the** ~ proceder según las reglas (*or* normas); **to make a** ~ **on** aceptar apuestas sobre; **to read sb like a(n open)** ~ conocer a uno a fondo; conocer a uno como la palma de la mano; **to suit sb's** ~ convenir a uno; **to throw the** ~ **at sb** acusar a uno de todo lo posible; castigar a uno con todo rigor; **that's one for the** ~**s** (*or* **for the** ~ (*US*)) es digno de ser enmarcado. (**b**) (*Comm, Fin*) **the** ~**s** los libros, las cuentas; el balance; **to close the** ~**s** cerrar los libros; **to cook the** ~**s*** falsificar las cuentas; **to keep the** ~**s** llevar las cuentas, llevar los libros; ~ **debts** deudas *fpl* contabilizadas; ~ **entry** apunte *m* en los libros de contabilidad; ~ **value** valor *m* en libros.
2 *vt* (*note down*) apuntar; (*Comm*) asentar (*to* en la cuenta de), *order* anotar; *room, place* reservar; (*Brit*) *ticket* sacar; *performer* contratar; *suspect* fichar*, reseñar; (*Sport*) *player* reseñar; **please** ~ **us in for Tuesday** le ruego reservarnos una habitación para el martes; **the hotel is** ~**ed up** todas las habitaciones del hotel están reservadas; **we are** ~**ed up all summer** no tenemos nada libre en todo el verano, lo tenemos todo reservado para todo el verano; **are you** ~**ed up for tonight?** ¿tienes compromiso para esta noche?
3 *vi*: **to** ~ **in** firmar el registro; tomar una habitación; reservar una habitación; ~ **well in advance** es aconsejable reservar con mucha anticipación; **to** ~ **through to** sacar un billete hasta.
bookable ['bʊkəbl] *adj seat etc* que se puede reservar (de antemano); (*Sport*) *offence* sujeto a tarjeta amarilla.
bookbinder ['bʊkˌbaɪndəʳ] *n* encuadernador *m*, -ora *f*.
bookbinding ['bʊkˌbaɪndɪŋ] *n* encuadernación *f*.
bookcase ['bʊkkeɪs] *n* librería *f*, estante *m* para libros, librero *m* (*Carib*).
book-club ['bʊkklʌb] *n* club *m* de lectores.
book-ends ['bʊkendz] *npl* sujetalibros *mpl*, soportalibros *mpl*.
book-fair ['bʊkfeəʳ] *n* feria *f* de libros.
bookie* ['bʊkɪ] *n* = **bookmaker**.
booking ['bʊkɪŋ] *n* (*esp Brit*) reserva *f*; contratación *f*; **he had 9** ~**s last year** (*Sport*) el año pasado se le tomó el nombre 9 veces, el año pasado recibió tarjeta amarilla 9 veces.
booking-clerk ['bʊkɪŋˌklɑːk] *n* (*Brit*) taquillero *m*, -a *f*.
booking-office ['bʊkɪŋˌɒfɪs] *n* (*Rail*) despacho *m* de billetes (*LAm*: boletos); (*Theat*) taquilla *f*.
bookish ['bʊkɪʃ] *adj learning* libresco; *person* estudioso, (*pej*) pedantesco.
book-jacket ['bʊkˌdʒækɪt] *n* sobrecubierta *f*.
book-keeper ['bʊkˌkiːpəʳ] *n* contable *mf*, contador *m*, -ora *f*, tenedor *m*, -ora *f* de libros.
book-keeping ['bʊkˌkiːpɪŋ] *n* teneduría *f* de libros; ~ **by double entry** contabilidad *f* por partida doble; ~ **by single entry** contabilidad *f* por partida simple.
book-learning ['bʊkˌlɜːnɪŋ] *n* saber *m* libresco, erudición *f*.
booklet ['bʊklɪt] *n* folleto *m*; (*learned*) opúsculo *m*; (*of tickets*) bono *m*.
book-lover ['bʊkˌlʌvəʳ] *n* bibliófilo *m*, -a *f*.
bookmaker ['bʊkmeɪkəʳ] *n* corredor *m* de apuestas, apostador *m* profesional.
bookmark ['bʊkmɑːk] *n* señal *f*, registro *m* (de libro).
bookmobile ['bʊkməʊˌbiːl] *n* (*US*) bibliobús *m*.
bookplate ['bʊkpleɪt] *n* ex libris *m*.
book-post ['bʊkpəʊst] *n* correo *m* de libros; tarifa *f* especial para libros.
bookrest ['bʊkrest] *n* atril *m*.
bookseller ['bʊkˌseləʳ] *n* librero *m*, -a *f*; ~**'s** librería *f*.
bookshelf ['bʊkʃelf] *n*, *pl* **bookshelves** ['bʊkʃelvz] anaquel *m* para libros, estantería *f*; ~**shelves** estante *m* para libros.
bookshop ['bʊkʃɒp] *n* librería *f*.
bookstall ['bʊkstɔːl] *n* (*Brit*) quiosco *m* de libros.
bookstore ['bʊkstɔːʳ] *n* (*US*) librería *f*.
book-token ['bʊkˌtəʊkən] *n* (*Brit*) vale *m* para comprar libros.
bookworm ['bʊkwɜːm] *n* polilla *f*; (*fig*) ratón *m* de biblioteca.
Boolean ['buːlɪən] *adj* booleano; ~ **algebra** álgebra *f* de Boole; ~ **logic** lógica *f* booleana.
boom[1] [buːm] *n* (**a**) (*Naut*) (*of jib*) botalón *m*, (*of mainsail*) botavara *f*; (*of crane*) aguilón *m*, brazo *m* (de grúa). (**b**) (*across harbour*) barrera *f*.
boom[2] [buːm] **1** *n* estampido *m*, trueno *m*.
2 *vt* (*also* **to** ~ **out**) tronar; anunciar (*etc*) muy fuerte.
3 *vi* (*also* **to** ~ **out**) hacer estampido, tronar; (*voice, radio, organ*) resonar, retumbar; (*gun*) retumbar.
boom[3] [buːm] **1** *n* boom *m*; alza *f* rápida (*in prices* de los precios); prosperidad *f* repentina (*in an industry* de una industria).
2 *adj*: ~ **economy** economía *f* de alza; ~ **market** mercado *m* de alza; ~ **town** ciudad *f* boom, ciudad *f* que disfruta de una prosperidad repentina; **in** ~ **conditions** en condiciones de prosperidad repentina.
3 *vi* (*prices*) estar en alza; (*commodity*) tener mucha demanda; (*industry, town*) gozar de boom, disfrutar de gran prosperidad.
boomerang ['buːməræŋ] **1** *n* bumerang *m*. **2** *adj* contraproducente, contrario a lo que se esperaba. **3** *vi* tener un resultado contraproducente (*on* para); **it** ~**ed on him** le salió el tiro por la culata.
booming[1] ['buːmɪŋ] *adj voice* resonante, retumbante.
booming[2] ['buːmɪŋ] *adj* (*Comm etc*) próspero, que goza de boom, floreciente.
boon[1] [buːn] *n* favor *m*; ventaja *f*, beneficio *m* (*to* para); **it would be a** ~ **if he went** nos alegraríamos si se fuera; **the new machine is a great** ~ la nueva máquina representa un gran adelanto; **the servant is a** ~ **to me** la criada me ayuda muchísimo; **it should be a** ~ **to humanity** ha de ser un beneficio para el género humano.
boon[2] [buːn] *adj*: ~ **companion** compañero *m*, -a *f* inseparable.
boondocks* ['buːndɒks] *npl* (*US*): **out in the** ~ en el quinto pino.
boondoggle* ['buːndɒgl] *vi* (*US*) enredar*.
boons* [buːnz] *npl* (*US*) = **boondocks**.
boor [bʊəʳ] *n* patán *m*, hombre *m* grosero.
boorish ['bʊərɪʃ] *adj* palurdo, grosero.
boorishly ['bʊərɪʃlɪ] *adv behave, speak* groseramente.
boorishness ['bʊərɪʃnɪs] *n* grosería *f*.
boost [buːst] **1** *n* (**a**) (*thrust etc*) empuje *m*, empujón *m*, estímulo *m*, ayuda *f*; **to give a** ~ **to** = **2**. (**b**) (*rise*: *esp US*) aumento *m*, subida *f*. **2** *vt* empujar (hacia arriba); *price*,

sales, total aumentar; *product* hacer publicidad por; *person* dar bombo a; *morale* reforzar; *process* estimular, fomentar, dar ímpetu a; (*Elec*) elevar.

booster[1] ['bu:stəʳ] **1** *n* (*Elec*) elevador *m* de tensión, elevador *m* de voltaje; (*Aer*) impulsor *m*, impulsador *m*; (*Mech*) aumentador *m* de presión; (*Rad*) repetidor *m*. **2** *attr* auxiliar; ~ **injection** revacunación *f*.

booster[2] ['bu:stəʳ] *n*, **booster rocket** ['bu:stə,rɒkɪt] *n* cohete *m* acelerador (*or* lanzador).

booster station ['bu:stə,steɪʃən] *n* repetidor *m*.

boot[1] [bu:t] **1** *n* (**a**) bota *f*; **now the ~ is on the other foot** (*Brit*) los papeles están trastrocados; **to die with one's ~s on** morir con las botas puestas; **to get** (*or* **be given**) **the ~*** ser despedido; **he's getting too big for his ~s** tiene muchos humos; **to give sb the ~*** poner a uno de patitas en la calle; **to lick sb's ~s** hacer la pelotilla a uno; **to put the ~ in*** emplear la violencia; (*fig*) obrar decisivamente.

(**b**) (*Brit Aut*) maletero *m*, baúl *m* (*LAm*), maletera *f* (*LAm*).

(**c**) (*: *blow*) puntapié *m*.

(**d**) (*US Aut*; *also* **Denver** ~) cepo *m*.

2 *vt* (**a**) (*kick*) dar un puntapié a; **to ~ out** poner de patitas en la calle.

(**b**) (*Comput*) arrancar, cebar, inicializar.

3 *vi* (*Comput*) arrancar, cebar, inicializar.

boot[2] [bu:t] *adv*: **to ~** (*liter*) además, por añadidura.

bootblack ['bu:tblæk] *n* limpiabotas *m*.

bootee [bu:'ti:] *n* borceguí *m*, bota *f* de lana.

booth [bu:ð] *n* (*in market*) puesto *m*; (*at fair*) barraca *f*; (*Telec, interpreter's, voting*) cabina *f*.

booting-up [,bu:tɪŋ'ʌp] *n* (*Comput*) operación *f* de cargo, iniciación *f*; ~ **switch** tecla *f* de iniciación.

bootlace ['bu:tleɪs] *n* cordón *m*.

bootleg ['bu:tleg] (*US*) **1** *adj*: ~ **whisky** whisky *m* de contrabando, whisky *m* ilegal. **2** *vi* contrabandear en licores (*etc*).

bootlegger ['bu:t,legəʳ] *n* (*US*) contrabandista *m* en licores.

bootlicker* ['bu:tlɪkəʳ] *n* lameculos‡ *m*.

bootlicking* ['bu:tlɪkɪŋ] **1** *adj* pelotillero*. **2** *n* pelotilleo* *m*.

bootmaker ['bu:tmeɪkəʳ] *n* zapatero *m* que hace botas.

boot-polish ['bu:t,pɒlɪʃ] *n* betún *m*, crema *f* para botas.

boots [bu:ts] *n sing* (*Brit*) limpiabotas *m* (de un hotel).

bootstrap ['bu:tstræp] *n* oreja *f*; **to pull oneself up by one's ~s** reponerse gracias a sus propios esfuerzos.

booty ['bu:tɪ] *n* botín *m*, presa *f*.

booze* [bu:z] **1** *n* (**a**) (*in general*) bebida *f*, alcohol *m*; (*in particular*) vino *m*, cerveza *f etc*; **to go on the ~** darse a la bebida.

(**b**) (*outing*) borrachera *f*; **to go on a ~** ir de juerga.

2 *vt* beber.

3 *vi* beber; emborracharse.

boozer‡ ['bu:zəʳ] *n* (**a**) (*person*) bebedor *m*, tomador *m* (*LAm*). (**b**) (*Brit*: *pub*) bar *m*, taberna *f*.

booze-up‡ ['bu:z,ʌp] *n* (*Brit*) bebezona‡ *f*.

boozy‡ ['bu:zɪ] *adj person* borracho, aficionado a la bebida; *party* donde se bebe bastante; *song etc* tabernario.

bop[1]* [bɒp] (*Mus*) **1** *n* bop *m*. **2** *vi* bailar.

bop[2]* [bɒp] *vt* (*US*: *hit*) cascar*.

bo-peep [bəʊ'pi:p] *n*: **to play ~** jugar tapándose la cara y descubriéndola de repente; **Little B~** *personaje de una poesía infantil, famoso por haber perdido sus ovejas.*

boracic [bə'ræsɪk] *adj* bórico.

borage ['bɒrɪdʒ] *n* borraja *f*.

borax ['bɔ:ræks] *n* bórax *m*.

Bordeaux [bɔ:'dəʊ] *n* Burdeos *m*; **b~** (*wine*) burdeos *m*.

bordello [bɔ:'deləʊ] *n* (*US*) casa *f* de putas.

border ['bɔ:dəʳ] **1** *n* borde *m*, margen *m*; (*Sew*) orla *f*, orilla *f*, cenefa *f*; (*Pol*) frontera *f*; (*Hort*) arriate *m*; **the B~** (*Brit*) *la frontera entre Inglaterra y Escocia.*

2 *attr area, town, ballad* fronterizo; *guard* de la frontera; ~ **dispute** disputa *f* fronteriza; ~ **incident** incidente *m* fronterizo; ~ **patrol** (*US*) patrulla *f* de fronteras; ~ **post** puesto *m* fronterizo.

3 *vt* (*Sew*) ribetear, orlar; **it is ~ed on the north by ...** confina en el norte con ...

◆**border on** *vt* lindar con, confinar con; (*fig*) rayar en, aproximarse a.

bordering ['bɔ:dərɪŋ] *adj* contiguo.

borderland ['bɔ:dəlænd] *n* zona *f* fronteriza.

borderline ['bɔ:dəlaɪn] **1** *n* línea *f* divisoria; (*Pol and fig*) frontera *f*. **2** *adj case etc* dudoso, incierto; ~ **case** caso *m* dudoso.

bore[1] [bɔ:ʳ] **1** *n* (**a**) (*tool*) taladro *m*, barrena *f*; (*Geol*) sonda *f*.

(**b**) (*hole*) agujero *m*, barreno *m*; (*of gun*) calibre *m*, alma *f*; (*of cylinder*) alesaje *m*; (*for oil*) perforación *f*.

2 *vt* taladrar, perforar, agujerear, barrenar; **to ~ a hole in** practicar un agujero en; **to ~ one's way through** abrirse un camino por; **wood ~d by insects** madera *f* carcomida.

3 *vi*: **to ~ for oil** hacer perforaciones en busca de petróleo.

bore[2] [bɔ:ʳ] **1** *n* (**a**) (*person*) pelmazo *m*, pesado *m*, -a *f*; **what a ~ he is!** ¡qué hombre más pesado!

(**b**) (*thing*) lata* *f*, rollo* *m*; **what a ~!** ¡qué rollo!*; **it's such a ~** es una lata*.

2 *vt* aburrir; fastidiar, molestar, dar la lata a*; **to be ~d, to get ~d** aburrirse; **to be ~d to death** (*or* **to tears, stiff**) aburrirse como una ostra; **to be ~d with** estar harto de.

bore[3] [bɔ:ʳ] *pret of* **bear**[2].

bore[4] [bɔ:ʳ] *n* (*tidal wave*) marea *f*.

boredom ['bɔ:dəm] *n* aburrimiento *m*, fastidio *m*.

borehole ['bɔ:həʊl] *n* perforación *f*.

Borgia ['bɔ:dʒjə] *n* Borja *m*.

boric ['bɔ:rɪk] *adj*: ~ **acid** ácido *m* bórico.

boring ['bɔ:rɪŋ] *adj* aburrido, pesado, latoso.

born [bɔ:n] **1** *ptp of* **bear**[2]; **to be ~** nacer; **I was ~ in 1927** nací en 1927; **a daughter was ~ to them** les nació una hija; **he wasn't ~ yesterday** es perro viejo; **evil is ~ of idleness** la pereza es madre de todos los vicios; **to be ~ again** renacer, volver a nacer.

2 *adj actor, artist etc* nato; *liar* innato; **a Londoner ~ and bred** londinense de casta y cuna; **in all my ~ days** en mi vida.

-born [-bɔ:n] *adj ending in compounds*: **British~** británico de nacimiento.

born-again ['bɔ:nə,gen] *adj* renacido, vuelto a nacer.

borne [bɔ:n] *ptp of* **bear**[2].

-borne [-bɔ:n] *suf* llevado por, traído por; *V* **water~** *etc*.

Borneo ['bɔ:nɪəʊ] *n* Borneo *m*.

boron ['bɔ:rɒn] *n* boro *m*.

borough ['bʌrə] *n* (*Brit*) municipio *m*; (*US*) distrito *m* municipal.

borrow ['bɒrəʊ] *vt* pedir prestado, tomar prestado (*from, of* a); *idea etc* adoptar, apropiarse; *word* tomar (*from* de); **may I ~ your car?** ¿me prestas tu coche?; **you can ~ it till I need it** te lo presto hasta que yo lo necesite.

borrower ['bɒrəʊəʳ] *n* él (la) que toma prestado; (*in library*) usuario *m*, -a *f*; (*Comm*) prestatario *m*, -a *f*.

borrowing ['bɒrəʊɪŋ] *n* préstamo(s) *m(pl)* (*from* de); ~ **power(s)** capacidad *f* de endeudamiento.

borstal ['bɔ:stl] *n* (*Brit*) reformatorio *m* de menores; ~ **boy** joven *m* delincuente (que ha pasado por el reformatorio).

borzoi ['bɔ:zɔɪ] *n* galgo *m* ruso.

Bosch [bɒʃ] *nm* El Bosco.

bosh* [bɒʃ] *n* tonterías *fpl*.

bo's'n ['bəʊsən] *n* = **boatswain**.

bosom ['bʊzəm] **1** *n* seno *m*, pecho *m*; (*of garment*) pechera *f*; **in the ~ of the family** en el seno de la familia; **to take sb to one's ~** acoger amorosamente a uno. **2** *attr friend* íntimo, inseparable.

bosomy ['bʊzəmɪ] *adj* tetuda*, de pecho abultado.

Bosphorus ['bɒsfərəs] *n* Bósforo *m*.

boss[1] [bɒs] *n* (*bulge*) protuberancia *f*; (*stud*) clavo *m*, tachón *m*; (*of shield*) ombligo *m*; (*Archit*) llave *f* de bóveda.

boss[2] [bɒs] **1** *n* jefe *m*; (*owner, employer*) patrón *m*, amo *m*; (*foreman*) capataz *m*; (*manager*) gerente *m*; (*US Pol*) cacique *m*; **I like to be my own ~** quiero mandar en mis asuntos, quiero controlar mis propias cosas; **I'm the ~ here** aquí mando yo; **OK, you're the ~** vale, tú mandas.

2 *vt* (*also* **to ~ about**) regentar, dar órdenes a, dominar.

3 *adj* (*US**) chulo*.

◆**boss around*** *vt person* mandonear.

boss-eyed [,bɒs'aɪd] *adj* bizco.

bossiness ['bɒsɪnɪs] *n* carácter *m* mandón, tiranía *f*.

bossy ['bɒsɪ] *adj* mandón, tiránico.

Bostonian [bɒs'təʊnɪən] *n* bostoniano *m*, -a *f*.

bosun ['bəʊsən] *n* = **boatswain**.

botanic(al) [bə'tænɪk(əl)] *adj* botánico.

botanist ['bɒtənɪst] *n* botánico *mf*, botanista *mf*.

botanize ['bɒtənaɪz] *vi* herborizar.

botany ['bɒtənɪ] *n* botánica *f*.

botch [bɒtʃ] **1** *n* chapuza *f*; **to make a ~ of** = **2**. **2** *vt* chapucear, chafullar; **to ~ it** arruinarlo, estropearlo; **to ~ up** remendar (chapuceramente).

both [bəʊθ] **1** *adj and pron* ambos, los dos; **I bought ~ books**

compré ambos libros; ~ **of them are nice** uno y otro son agradables; **we ~ went** fuimos los dos; ~ **of them** los dos; ~ **of us** nosotros dos.

2 *adv and conj*: ~ **A and B** tanto A como B; **he ~ plays and sings** canta y toca además; **I find it ~ impressive and vulgar** encuentro que es impresionante y vulgar a la vez.

bother ['bɒðəʳ] **1** *n* (**a**) molestia *f*, lata* *f*; **it's no ~** no es molestia; **it's such a ~ to clean** me molesta tener que limpiarlo, es muy incómodo limpiarlo; **I went to the ~ of finding one** me tomé la molestia de buscar uno; **what a ~!** ¡qué lata!*

(**b**) **he had a spot of ~ with the police** tuvo una dificultad con la policía; **do you have much ~ with your car?** ¿tienes muchas dificultades con el coche?

2 *vt* molestar, fastidiar, incomodar; poner nervioso; **does the noise ~ you?** ¿le molesta el ruido?; **does it ~ you if I smoke?** ¿le molesta que fume?; **stop ~ing me!** ¡no fastidies!; **please don't ~ me about it now** le ruego no molestarme con eso ahora; **I can't be ~ed** no quiero tomarme el trabajo (*to* + *infin* de + *infin*), no me da la gana (*to go* ir); **to get ~ed** desconcertarse, ponerse nervioso, perder la calma.

3 *vi*: **to ~ about, to ~ with** molestarse con, preocuparse por; **to ~ to** + *infin* tomarse la molestia de + *infin*.

4 *excl*: ~ (**it**) ¡porras!; ~ **that child!** ¡caray con el niño!

botheration [,bɒðə'reɪʃən] *interj* ¡porras!

bothersome ['bɒðəsəm] *adj* molesto.

Bothnia ['bɒθnɪə] *n*: **Gulf of ~** Golfo *m* de Botnia.

Botswana [bɒ'tswɑːnə] *n* Botsuana *f*.

bottle ['bɒtl] **1** *n* (**a**) botella *f*; (*of ink, scent*) frasco *m*; (*baby's*) biberón *m*, tetero *m* (*LAm*); **to hit the ~** beber mucho; **to take to the ~** darse a la bebida. (**b**) (*) valor *m*; descaro *m*; **to lose one's ~** rajarse*; **it takes a lot of ~ to** + *infin* hay que tener mucho valor para + *infin*.

2 *vt* embotellar; enfrascar.

◆**bottle out*** *vi* rajarse*; **they ~d out of doing it** se rajaron y no lo hicieron*.

◆**bottle up** *vt* embotellar; *emotion* reprimir, contener.

bottle-bank ['bɒtl,bæŋk] *n* banco *m* de botellas.

bottle-brush ['bɒtl,brʌʃ] *n* escobilla *f*, limpiabotellas *m*; (*Bot*) callistemon *m*.

bottled ['bɒtld] *adj*: ~ **beer** cerveza *f* de botella; ~ **water** agua *f* embotellada.

bottle-fed ['bɒtlfed] *adj* alimentado con biberón.

bottle-feed ['bɒtl,fiːd] *vt* (*irr*: *V* **feed**) criar con biberón.

bottle-green ['bɒtl'griːn] **1** *adj* verde botella. **2** *n* verde *m* botella.

bottleneck ['bɒtlnek] *n* (*fig*) cuello *m* de botella.

bottle-opener ['bɒtl,əʊpnəʳ] *n* abrebotellas *m*, destapador *m* de botellas, descapsulador *m*.

bottle-party ['bɒtl,pɑːtɪ] *n* guateque *m* al que cada invitado lleva su botella.

bottling ['bɒtlɪŋ] *n* embotellado *m*.

bottom ['bɒtəm] **1** *n* (*of cup, river, sea, box, garden*) fondo *m*; (*of stairs, hill, page*) pie *m*; (*of chair*) asiento *m*; (*of ship*) quilla *f*, casco *m*; (*Anat*) trasero *m*, culo *m*; **~s up!** ¡salud y pesetas!; **at ~** en el fondo; **at the ~ of the garden** en el fondo del jardín; **he's at the ~ of the class** es el último de la clase; **to be at the ~ of sth** (*fig*: *thing*) ser el motivo de algo, (*person*) ser el causante oculto de algo; **from the ~ of one's heart** de todo corazón; **the ~ has fallen out of the market** se han derrumbado los precios; **to get to the ~ of a matter** llegar al fondo de un asunto, desentrañar un asunto; **to go to the ~** (*Naut*) irse a pique; **to knock the ~ out of** desfondar; **to send a ship to the ~** hundir un buque; **to touch ~** (*lit*) tocar fondo; (*fig*) tocar fondo, llegar al punto más bajo.

2 *adj part* más bajo, inferior; (*last*) último; ~ **drawer** (*Brit*) ajuar *m* (de novia); ~ **floor** planta *f* baja; ~ **gear** primera *f* (velocidad *f*); ~ **half** mitad *f* de abajo, mitad *f* inferior; ~ **line** (*minimum*) mínimo *m* aceptable; (*essential point*) punto *m* fundamental; **the ~ line is he has to go** al fin y al cabo tenemos que despedirle; ~ **price** precio *m* más bajo; ~ **step** primer peldaño *m*; ~ **team** colista *m*.

◆**bottom out** *vi* (*figures etc*) tocar fondo.

bottomless ['bɒtəmlɪs] *adj* sin fondo, insondable.

bottommost ['bɒtəmməʊst] *adj* (el) más bajo; último.

botulism ['bɒtjʊlɪzəm] *n* botulismo *m*.

bouclé [buː'kleɪ] **1** *n* lana *f* rizada, ropa *f* rizada. **2** *adj* de lana rizada.

boudoir ['buːdwɑːʳ] *n* tocador *m*.

bouffant ['buːfɔːŋ] *adj hairdo* crepado.

bougainvillea [,buːgən'vɪlɪə] *n* buganvilla *f*.

bough [baʊ] *n* rama *f*.

bought [bɔːt] *pret and ptp of* **buy**; ~ **ledger** libro *m* de compras.

bouillon ['buːjɔːŋ] *n* caldo *m*; ~ **cube** cubito *m* de caldo.

boulder ['bəʊldəʳ] *n* canto *m* rodado.

boulevard ['buːləvɑːʳ] *n* bulevar *m*, zócalo *m* (*Mex*).

bounce [baʊns] **1** *n* (**a**) (re)bote *m*; **to catch a ball on the ~** coger una pelota de rebote.

(**b**) (*fig*: *swagger*) fanfarronería *f*, presunción *f*; (*energy*) energía *f*, dinamismo *m*; (*resilience*) capacidad *f* de recuperación.

2 *vt* (**a**) hacer (re)botar.

(**b**) (*: *eject*) plantar en la calle, poner de patitas en la calle.

(**c**) **I will not be ~d into it** no lo voy a hacer bajo presión, no permito que me presionen para hacerlo.

3 *vi* (**a**) (re)botar; **to ~ back, come bouncing back** (*fig*) recuperarse (de repente); **to ~ in** (*fig*) irrumpir (alegremente).

(**b**) (*: *cheque*) ser incobrable.

bouncer* ['baʊnsəʳ] *n* forzudo *m*, gorila *m*, sacabullas *m* (*Mex*) (*que echa a los alborotadores de un café etc*).

bouncing ['baʊnsɪŋ] *adj* robusto, fuerte.

bouncy ['baʊnsɪ] *adj* (**a**) *ball* de mucho rebote, que rebota fuertemente. (**b**) *person* enérgico; bullicioso, muy activo.

bound¹ [baʊnd] **1** *pret and ptp of* **bind**.

2 *adj* (**a**) **to be ~ for** (*Naut*) navegar con rumbo a, tener ... como puerto de destino, (*fig*) dirigirse a; **where are you ~ for?** ¿adónde se dirige Vd?

(**b**) (*obliged*) **to be ~ to** + *infin* (*sure*) estar seguro de + *infin*, (*must*) tener que + *infin*; **we are ~ to win** estamos seguros de ganar; **he's ~ to come** es seguro que vendrá, no puede dejar de venir; **it's ~ to happen** tiene forzosamente que ocurrir; **you're not ~ to go** no es que tengas que ir; **I am ~ to say that** ... tengo el deber de decir que ...; **I feel ~ to tell you that** ... me veo en la necesidad de decirte que ...; **they'll regret it, I'll be ~** se arrepentirán de ello, estoy seguro; **to be ~ by contract to sb** estar ligado por contrato a uno; **I feel ~ to him by gratitude** el agradecimiento me liga a él.

(**c**) (*linked*) **the problems are ~ together** existe una estrecha relación entre estos problemas; **they are ~ by close ties** entre ellos existen vínculos muy fuertes; **to be ~ up with** tener que ver con; estar estrechamente vinculado con; **they are ~ up in each other** están absortos el uno en el otro.

bound² [baʊnd] **1** *n* límite *m*; **out of ~s** fuera de los límites; **out of ~s to civilians** prohibido el paso a los civiles; **to put a place out of ~s** prohibir la entrada a un lugar; **it is within the ~s of possibility** cabe dentro de lo posible; **to keep sth within ~s** tener algo a raya; **to set ~s to one's ambitions** poner límites a sus ambiciones; **his ambition knows no ~s** su ambición no tiene límite.

2 *vt* limitar, deslindar; **a field ~ed by woods** un campo rodeado de bosque; **on one side it is ~ed by the park** por un lado confina con el parque.

bound³ [baʊnd] **1** *n* (*jump*) salto *m*; **at a ~, in one ~** de un salto.

2 *vt* saltar por encima de.

3 *vi* saltar; (*ball*) (re)botar; **to ~ forward** avanzar a saltos; **his heart ~ed with joy** su corazón daba brincos de alegría; **the number is ~ing up** el número aumenta rápidamente.

-bound [-baʊnd] *adj ending in compounds*: **to be London~** ir rumbo a Londres; **the south~ carriageway** la autopista dirección sur.

boundary ['baʊndərɪ] *n* límite *m*, lindero *m*; (*Sport*) banda *f*; (*Pol etc*) frontera *f*; **to make ~ changes** (*Brit Pol*) hacer cambios en las circunscripciones.

boundary-line ['baʊndərɪ,laɪn] *n* límite *m*, frontera *f*.

boundary-stone ['baʊndərɪ,stəʊn] *n* mojón *m*.

bounden ['baʊndən] *adj*: ~ **duty** obligación *f* ineludible.

bounder*† ['baʊndəʳ] *n* (*esp Brit*) sinvergüenza *m*, granuja *m*.

boundless ['baʊndlɪs] *adj* ilimitado.

bounteous ['baʊntɪəs] *adj*, **bountiful** ['baʊntɪfʊl] *adj crop etc* abundante; *person* liberal, generoso.

bounty ['baʊntɪ] *n* (**a**) (*generosity*) munificencia *f*, liberalidad *f*. (**b**) (*Mil*) premio *m* de enganche; (*Comm*) prima *f*, subvención *f*.

bouquet ['bʊkeɪ] *n* (**a**) (*of flowers*) ramo *m*, ramillete *m*. (**b**) (*of wine*) buqué *m*, nariz *f*.

Bourbon ['bʊəbən] **1** *n* Borbón *m*; **b~ (whiskey)** (*US*) whisky *m* americano. **2** *adj* borbónico.

bourgeois [ˈbʊəʒwɑː] **1** *adj* burgués. **2** *n* burgués *m*, -esa *f*.
bourgeoisie [ˌbʊəʒwɑːˈziː] *n* burguesía *f*.
bout [baʊt] *n* (*spell*) turno *m*, rato *m*; (*Med*) ataque *m*; (*Fencing*) asalto *m*; (*fight in general*) lucha *f*, combate *m*; (*boxing fixture*) encuentro *m*, match *m*; (*of drinking*) juerga *f* de borrachera.
boutique [buːˈtiːk] *n* boutique *f*; ~ **furniture** muebles *mpl* artesano.
bovine [ˈbəʊvaɪn] *adj* bovino; (*fig*) lerdo, estúpido.
bovver‡ [ˈbɒvəʳ] *n* (*Brit*) desorden *m*, alboroto *m*; violencia *f*; gamberrismo *m*; ~ **boots** *botas de suela gruesa usadas por los punkis*.
bow[1] [bəʊ] *n* (*Mil, Mus*) arco *m*; (*tie, knot*) lazo *m*; ~ **and arrow** arco *m* y flechas.
bow[2] [baʊ] **1** *n* inclinación *f*, reverencia *f*; **to make a** ~ inclinarse (*to* delante de), hacer una reverencia (*to* a); **to make one's** ~ presentarse, debutar; **to take a** ~ salir a recibir aplausos.
2 *vt head etc* inclinar, (*in shame*) bajar; (*fig*: *also* **to** ~ **down**) agobiar; **to** ~ **one's thanks** inclinarse en señal de agradecimiento.
3 *vi* inclinarse (*to* delante de), hacer una reverencia (*to* a); **to** ~ **and scrape** hacer zalamerías; **to** ~ **beneath** estar agobiado por; **to** ~ **to** inclinarse a, ceder ante, transigir con, someterse a; **to** ~ **to the inevitable** resignarse a lo inevitable.
◆**bow down 1** *vt* (*lit, fig*) doblegar. **2** *vi* doblegarse.
◆**bow out 1** *vt*: **to** ~ **sb out** despedir con cortesía al que sale. **2** *vi* retirarse.
bow[3] [baʊ] *n* (*Naut*) proa *f*; ~**s** proa *f*; **on the port** ~ a babor; **shot across the** ~**s** cañonazo *m* de advertencia.
Bow Bells [ˌbəʊˈbelz] *npl famoso campanario de Londres*; **born within the sound of** ~ nacido en la zona alrededor de Bow Bells (*definición del puro cockney londinense*).
bowdlerize [ˈbaʊdləraɪz] *vt* expurgar.
bowel [ˈbaʊəl] *n* intestino *m*; ~**s** intestinos *mpl*, vientre *m*, (*fig*) entrañas *fpl*; ~**s of the earth** entrañas *fpl* de la tierra; ~**s of compassion** compasión *f*; ~ **movement** evacuación *f* del vientre.
bower [ˈbaʊəʳ] *n* emparrado *m*, enramada *f*; cenador *m*.
bowing [ˈbəʊɪŋ] *n* (*Mus*) técnica *f* del arco; (*marked on score*) inicio *m* del golpe de arco; **his** ~ **was sensitive** su uso del arco era sensible; **to mark the** ~ indicar (*or* marcar) los movimientos del arco.
bowl[1] [bəʊl] *n* (*Culin*) escudilla *f*, tazón *m*; (*for washing*) jofaina *f*, palangana *f*; (*of spoon*) cuenco *m*; (*of fountain*) tazón *m*; (*of pipe*) hornillo *m*, cazoleta *f*; (*of WC*) taza *f* (de retrete); (*US Sport*) estadio *m*; (*Geog*) cuenca *f*.
bowl[2] [bəʊl] **1** *n* bola *f*, bocha *f*; ~**s** (*Brit*) juego *m* de las bochas, (*US*) boliche *m*.
2 *vt* rodar; (*Sport*) arrojar, lanzar, tirar (*LAm*).
3 *vi* (*Sport*) arrojar la pelota; jugar a las bochas.
◆**bowl along** *vi* correr, rodar rápidamente.
◆**bowl over** *vt* (**a**) tumbar, derribar, echar a rodar. (**b**) (*fig*) desconcertar, dejar atónito; **we were quite** ~**ed over by the news** la noticia nos desconcertó, la noticia nos sorprendió; **she** ~**ed him over** ella le dejó patidifuso.
bow-legged [ˈbəʊˌlegɪd] *adj* estevado, patiestevado; (*stance*) con las piernas en arco.
bowlegs [ˌbəʊˈlegz] *npl* piernas *fpl* arqueadas.
bowler[1] [ˈbəʊləʳ] *n* (*Brit Sport*) lanzador *m*, el que arroja la pelota; (*US Sport*) jugador *m*, -ora *f* de bolos.
bowler[2] [ˈbəʊləʳ] *n* (*Brit*: *also* ~ **hat**) hongo *m*, bombín *m*.
bowline [ˈbəʊlɪn] *n* bolina *f*.
bowling [ˈbəʊlɪŋ] *n* (*US*) bolos *mpl*, boliche *m* (*LAm*).
bowling-alley [ˈbəʊlɪŋˌælɪ] *n* bolera *f*, boliche *m* (*LAm*).
bowling-green [ˈbəʊlɪŋˌgriːn] *n* pista *f* para bochas.
bowling-match [ˈbəʊlɪŋˌmætʃ] *n* (*Brit*) concurso *m* de bochas.
bowman [ˈbəʊmən] *n*, *pl* **bowmen** [ˈbəʊmen] arquero *m*, (*cross-*~) ballestero *m*.
bowsprit [ˈbəʊsprɪt] *n* bauprés *m*.
bowstring [ˈbəʊstrɪŋ] *n* cuerda *f* de arco.
bow-tie [ˈbəʊˈtaɪ] *n* corbata *f* de lazo, pajarita *f*.
bow-window [ˈbəʊˈwɪndəʊ] *n* mirador *m*, ventana *f* salediza.
bow-wow [ˈbaʊˈwaʊ] *interj* ¡guau!
box[1] [bɒks] **1** *n* caja *f*, (*large*) cajón *m*; (*for money etc*) cofre *m*, arca *f*; (*for jewels etc*) estuche *m*; (*Racing, Theat*) palco *m*; (*Brit*: *road junction*) parrilla *f*; (*Typ*) recuadro *m*; (*on form, to be filled in*) casilla *f*; **the** ~* la caja boba*, la tele*; **we saw it on the** ~* lo hemos visto en la tele*; ~ **of matches** caja *f* de cerillas; (**post-office**) ~ apartado *m* de correos, casilla *f* (de correos) (*LAm*).
2 *vt* encajonar, poner en una caja; (*capture*) encerrar en una caja; **to** ~ **the compass** cuartear la aguja.
◆**box in** *vt* (**a**) *pipe etc* tapar, revestir (de madera *etc*).
(**b**) (*fig*) **to** ~ **sb in** encerrar a uno; cortar los vuelos a uno; **to feel** ~**ed in** sentirse encerrado; **to get** ~**ed in** (*Sport*) encontrarse tapado.
◆**box off** *vt* compartimentar.
◆**box up** *vt* poner en una caja; (*fig*) constreñir.
box[2] [bɒks] *n* (*Bot*) boj *m*.
box[3] [bɒks] **1** *n*: ~ **on the ear** cachete *m*. **2** *vt* boxear contra; **to** ~ **sb's ear** dar un cachete a uno. **3** *vi* boxear.
box camera [ˈbɒksˈkæmərə] *n* cámara *f* de cajón.
boxcar [ˈbɒksˌkɑːʳ] *n* (*US*) furgón *m*.
boxer [ˈbɒksəʳ] *n* boxeador *m*; (*dog*) boxer *m*; ~ **shorts** calzones *mpl*.
box-girder [ˈbɒksˌgɜːdəʳ] *n* viga *f* en forma de cajón, vigas *fpl* gemelas.
boxing [ˈbɒksɪŋ] *n* boxeo *m*.
Boxing Day [ˈbɒksɪŋdeɪ] *n* (*Brit*) *día en que se dan aguinaldos a los empleados, proveedores caseros etc* (*26 diciembre*).
boxing-gloves [ˈbɒksɪŋglʌvz] *npl* guantes *mpl* de boxeo.
boxing-match [ˈbɒksɪŋˌmætʃ] *n* partido *m* de boxeo.
boxing-ring [ˈbɒksɪŋˌrɪŋ] *n* cuadrilátero *m* (de boxeo).
box junction [ˈbɒksˌdʒʌŋkʃən] *n* (*Brit*) cruce *m* con parrilla.
box-number [ˈbɒksˌnʌmbəʳ] *n* apartado *m*, casilla *f* (*LAm*).
box-office [ˈbɒksɒfɪs] **1** *n* taquilla *f*; boletería *f* (*LAm*); **to be good** ~ ser taquillero, estar seguro de obtener un éxito. **2** *attr* taquillero; ~ **receipts** ingresos *mpl* de taquilla; ~ **success** éxito *m* de taquilla.
box-pleat [ˈbɒksˌpliːt] *n* tablón *m*.
boxroom [ˈbɒksrʊm] *n* (*Brit*) trastero *m*.
box-seat [ˈbɒksˌsiːt] *n* (*US*: *Theat*) asiento *m* de palco.
box-spring [ˈbɒksˈsprɪŋ] *n* muelle *m*.
boxwood [ˈbɒkswʊd] *n* boj *m*.
boy [bɔɪ] *n* (*small*) niño *m*; (*older, also apprentice etc, and affectionately of adult*) muchacho *m*, chico *m*; (*son*) hijo *m*; (*servant*) criado *m*; (*boyfriend*) amigo *m*, amiguito *m*; **García and his** ~**s in the national team** García y sus muchachos del equipo nacional; **the** ~**s in blue** (*Brit**) los policías, los marrones; **oh** ~! ¡vaya, vaya!; **old** ~ (*Brit*: *of school*) antiguo alumno *m*; (*) vejete *m*; **old** ~! ¡chico!; **old** ~ **network** (sistema *m* de) amiguismo *m*; **that's the** ~!, **that's my** ~! ¡bravo el chico!; **but my dear** ~! ¡pero hijo!; **I have known him from a** ~ le conozco desde chico; ~**s will be** ~**s** así son los chicos; juventud no conoce virtud; **my husband's out with the** ~**s** mi marido ha salido con sus amigotes; **he's one of the** ~**s now** ahora es un personaje; **it's all jobs for the** ~**s** ahora todo es puestos para los amigotes, todo es amiguismo; **to send a** ~ **to do a man's job** mandar un chico para hacer un trabajo de hombre.
boycott [ˈbɔɪkɒt] **1** *n* boicoteo *m*. **2** *vt* boicotear.
boyfriend [ˈbɔɪfrend] *n* amigo *m*, amiguito *m*; compañero *m*.
boyhood [ˈbɔɪhʊd] *n* juventud *f*, muchachez *f*.
boyish [ˈbɔɪɪʃ] *adj* juvenil, muchachil, de muchacho.
boy scout [ˌbɔɪˈskaʊt] *n* (muchacho *m or* niño *m*) explorador *m*.
B/P, b/p (*Comm*) *abbr of* **bills payable**.
BP *n abbr of* **British Petroleum.**
Bp *abbr of* **Bishop** obispo *m*, obpo.
BPS *npl abbr of* **bits per second** bits *mpl* por segundo.
B/R *abbr of* **bills receivable** obligaciones *fpl* por cobrar.
BR *n abbr of* **British Rail.**
Br *abbr of* **Brother** hermano *m*. (**b**) *abbr of* **British**.
bra* [brɑː] *n* sostén *m*, sujetador *m*.
brace [breɪs] **1** *n* (**a**) (*strengthening piece*) abrazadera *f*, refuerzo *m*; (*Archit*) riostra *f*, tirante *m*; (*for teeth*) banda *f*, corrector *m*; (*Naut*) braza *f*; (*tool*) berbiquí *m*; ~**s** (*Brit*) tirantes *mpl*, tiradores *mpl* (*LAm*); (*US*) corrector *m*; ~ **and bit** berbiquí *m* y barrena.
(**b**) (*Mus*) corchete *m*; (*Typ*) corchete *m* ({}).
(**c**) (*pair*) par *m*; **in a** ~ **of shakes*** en un decir Jesús.
2 *vt* asegurar, reforzar.
3 *vr*: **to** ~ **o.s.** prepararse para resistir (una sacudida *etc*); (*fig*) fortalecer su ánimo; **we** ~**d ourselves for bad news** nos preparamos para aguantar una noticia mala.
bracelet [ˈbreɪslɪt] *n* pulsera *f*, brazalete *m*.
bracing [ˈbreɪsɪŋ] *adj* tónico, vigorizante.
bracken [ˈbrækən] *n* helecho *m*.
bracket [ˈbrækɪt] **1** *n* (**a**) (*holding*) abrazadera *f*; (*supporting*) soporte *m*, puntal *m*; (*angle*) escuadra *f*; (*Archit*) ménsula *f*, repisa *f*; (*for gas*) mechero *m*.
(**b**) (*Typ*) **round** ~**s** () paréntesis *mpl* curvos; **square** ~**s** [] corchetes *mpl* rectos, paréntesis *mpl* cuadrados; <>

corchetes *mpl* agudos; { } corchetes *mpl*, llaves *fpl*; **in ~s** entre paréntesis.

(**c**) (*fig*) clase *f*, categoría *f*; **he's in the £200,000 a year ~** pertenece a la categoría de los que ganan 200,000 libras al año.

2 *vt* (**a**) (*join by brackets*) asegurar con ménsulas (*etc*).

(**b**) (*Typ*) poner entre paréntesis; **to ~ sth with sth else** agrupar algo con otra cosa.

◆**bracket off** *vt* excluir; poner aparte, separar; aislar.

◆**bracket together** *vt* agrupar, poner juntos.

brackish ['brækɪʃ] *adj* salobre, semisalado.

brad [bræd] *n* puntilla *f*, clavito *m*.

brae [breɪ] *n* (*Scot*) ladera *f* de monte, pendiente *f*.

brag [bræg] **1** *n* fanfarronada *f*, bravata *f*. **2** *vi* jactarse (*about, of* de; *that* de que), fanfarronear.

braggart ['brægət] *n* fanfarrón *m*, jactancioso *m*.

bragging ['brægɪŋ] *n* fanfarronadas *fpl*.

Brahman ['brɑːmən], **Brahmin** ['brɑːmɪn] *n* brahamán *m*, -ana *f*; bracmán *m*, -ana *f*.

Brahmaputra ['brɑːmə,puːtrə] *n* Brahmaputra *m*.

braid [breɪd] **1** *n* (**a**) (*of hair*) trenza *f*. (**b**) (*Mil*) galón *m*; (**gold**) ~ galón *m* de oro. **2** *vt* trenzar; *dress* galonear.

Braille [breɪl] **1** *n* Braille *m*. **2** *attr*: ~ **library** biblioteca *f* Braille.

brain [breɪn] **1** *n* (**a**) cerebro *m*; **~s** (*Anat, Culin*) sesos *mpl*; **to blow one's ~s out** pegarse un tiro, levantarse la tapa de los sesos.

(**b**) (*fig*) **~s** inteligencia *f*, cabeza *f*; capacidad *f*; **to beat one's ~s out*** romperse el coco*; **to cudgel** (*or* **rack**) **one's ~s** devanarse los sesos; **to get sth on the ~** dejarse obsesionar por algo; **to have sth on the ~** estar obsesionado por algo, no poder quitar algo de la cabeza; **to have ~s** ser inteligente; **to pick sb's ~s** exprimir a uno, explotar los conocimientos de uno; **to turn sb's ~** volver loco a uno.

2 *vt* (*) romper la crisma a.

brainchild ['breɪntʃaɪld] *n* parto *m* del ingenio, invento *m*.

brain-damage ['breɪn,dæmɪdʒ] *n* lesión *f* cerebral, lesión *f* medular.

brain-damaged ['breɪn,dæmɪdʒd] *adj*: **he was permanently ~ by meningitis** sufrió lesiones cerebrales por la meningitis; **the child was ~ for life** el niño quedó con lesiones medulares de por vida.

brain-dead ['breɪn,ded] *adj* clínicamente muerto.

brain-death ['breɪn,deθ] *n* muerte *f* clínica, muerte *f* cerebral.

brain-drain ['breɪn,dreɪn] *n* fuga *f* de cerebros.

brainless ['breɪnlɪs] *adj* estúpido, insensato.

brainpower ['breɪn,paʊəʳ] *n* fuerza *f* intelectual.

brain-scan ['breɪn,skæn] *n* exploración *f* cerebral mediante escáner.

brain-scanner ['breɪn,skænəʳ] *n* escáner *m* cerebral.

brainstorm ['breɪnstɔːm] *n* frenesí *m*; (*) idea *f* genial, idea *f* luminosa.

brains-trust ['breɪnz,trʌst] *n*, (*US*) **brain trust** ['breɪn,trʌst] *n* consultorio *m* intelectual; grupo *m* de peritos; (*TV etc*) jurado *m* de expertos.

brain-teaser ['breɪn,tiːzəʳ] *n* rompecabezas *m*.

brain-tumour, (*US*) **braintumor** ['breɪn,tjuːməʳ] *n* tumor *m* cerebral.

brainwash ['breɪnwɒʃ] *vt* lavar el cerebro a; **he was ~ed into believing that ...** le lavaron el cerebro para hacerle creer que ...

brainwashing ['breɪn,wɒʃɪŋ] *n* lavado *m* de cerebro.

brainwave ['breɪnweɪv] *n* idea *f* luminosa.

brainwork ['breɪnwɜːk] *n* trabajo *m* intelectual.

brainy ['breɪnɪ] *adj* muy inteligente, talentudo.

braise [breɪz] *vt* brasear.

brake¹ [breɪk] **1** *n* freno *m* (*also fig*); **to apply the ~s, put the ~s on** echar los frenos, frenar; **to put a ~ on** (*fig*) frenar, detener el progreso de.

2 *vti* frenar.

brake² [breɪk] *n* (*vehicle*) break *m*; (*estate car*) rubia *f*.

brake³ [breɪk] *n* (*Bot*) helecho *m*; (*thicket*) soto *m*.

brake-block ['breɪkblɒk] *n* pastilla *f* de frenos.

brake-drum ['breɪkdrʌm] *n* tambor *m* de freno.

brake-fluid ['breɪk,fluɪd] *n* líquido *m* para frenos.

brake-horsepower ['breɪk'hɔːspaʊəʳ] *n* potencia *f* al freno.

brake-lever ['breɪk,liːvəʳ] *n* palanca *f* de freno.

brake-lights ['breɪklaɪts] *n* = **braking-lights**.

brake-lining ['breɪk,laɪnɪŋ] *n* forro *m* del freno, guarnición *f* del freno.

brake-pad ['breɪkpæd] *n* pastilla *f* de frenos.

brake-pedal ['breɪk,pedl] *n* pedal *m* de freno.

brake-shoe ['breɪkʃuː] *n* zapata *f* del freno.

brakesman ['breɪksmən] *n*, *pl* **brakesmen** ['breɪksmen] encargado *m* del montacargos de la mina.

brake-van ['breɪkvæn] *n* furgón *m* de cola.

braking ['breɪkɪŋ] **1** *n* frenar *m*, frenaje *m*. **2** *attr* de frenar, de frenaje.

braking-distance ['breɪkɪŋ,dɪstəns] *n* distancia *f* recorrida después de frenar.

braking-lights ['breɪkɪŋ,laɪts] *npl* luces *fpl* de stop, luces *fpl* de frenado.

braking-power ['breɪkɪŋ,paʊəʳ] *n* potencia *f* al freno.

bramble ['bræmbl] *n* zarza *f*.

bran [bræn] *n* salvado *m*; ~ **tub** (*Brit*) sorteo *m* de regalos.

branch [brɑːntʃ] **1** *n* (*Bot*) rama *f*; (*fig*) ramo *m*, división *f*, sección *f*; (*Comm*) sucursal *f*; (*road, Rail*) ramal *m*; (*of river*) brazo *m*; (*US*: *of stream*) arroyo *m*; (*of family*) ramo *m*.

2 *vi* (*also* **to ~ out**) ramificarse, echar ramas.

◆**branch off** *vi* salir, separarse (*from* de); **we ~ed off at Medina** salimos de la carretera principal en Medina.

◆**branch out** *vi* (*fig*) extenderse, ensanchar el campo de sus operaciones (*etc*).

branch-line ['brɑːntʃlaɪn] *n* ramal *m*, línea *f* secundaria.

branch-manager ['brɑːntʃ'mænɪdʒəʳ] *n* director *m*, -ora *f* de sucursal.

branch-office ['brɑːntʃ,ɒfɪs] *n* sucursal *f*.

brand [brænd] **1** *n* (**a**) (*mark*) marca *f*; (*iron*) hierro *m* (de marcar).

(**b**) (*Comm*) marca *f*; ~ **awareness** conciencia *f* de una marca; ~ **image** imagen *f* de marca; ~ **loyalty** fidelidad *f* a una marca; ~ **name** nombre *m* de marca.

(**c**) (*fire ~*) tizón *m*, tea *f*.

2 *vt* (**a**) marcar (con hierro candente), ventear (*Mex*).

(**b**) (*fig*) **to ~ sb as** motejar a uno de, estigmatizar a uno de; **to ~ sth as** calificar algo de; **to be ~ed a liar** quedar por mentiroso; **it is ~ed in my memory** lo tengo grabado en la memoria. (**c**) **~ed goods** (*Comm*) artículos *mpl* de marca.

branding-iron ['brændɪŋ,aɪən] *n* hierro *m* (de marcar).

brandish ['brændɪʃ] *vt* blandir.

brand-new ['brænd'njuː] *adj* flamante, completamente nuevo, novísimo.

brandy ['brændɪ] *n* coñac *m*, brandy *m*; aguardiente *m*; ~ **butter** mantequilla *f* al coñac.

brash [bræʃ] *adj* (*rough*) inculto, tosco; (*cheeky*) descarado, respondón; (*rash*) impetuoso; (*unwise*) indiscreto; (*know-all*) presuntuoso.

brashly ['bræʃlɪ] *adv* (*V adj*) incultamente, toscamente; descaradamente, respondonamente; impetuosamente; indiscretamente; presuntuosamente.

brashness ['bræʃnɪs] *n* (*V adj*) incultura *f*, tosquedad *f*; descaro *m*; impetuosidad *f*; indiscreción *f*; presunción *f*.

Brasilia [brə'zɪljə] *n* Brasilia *f*.

brass [brɑːs] **1** *n* (**a**) (*metal*) latón *m*; **to get down to ~ tacks** ir al grano; **it's not worth a ~ farthing** no vale un ardite.

(**b**) (*plate*) placa *f* conmemorativa; (*Eccl*) plancha *f* sepulcral (de latón).

(**c**) (*Mus*) **the ~** el cobre, el bronce; ~ **band** banda *f*, charanga *f*.

(**d**) (*: *money*) pasta* *f*.

(**e**) **the top ~** (*Mil**) los jefazos*.

(**f**) (*: *nerve*) cara* *f*; **he had the ~ to ask me for it** tuvo la cara de pedírmelo.

2 *attr* de latón; ~ **neck*** cara* *f*, valor *m*.

3 *vt*: **to ~ off*** fastidiar; **to be ~ed off with sth*** tener algo hasta encima de la coronilla.

brass hat* ['brɑːs'hæt] *n* (*Mil*) jefazo* *m*.

brassière ['bræsɪəʳ] *n* sostén *m*, sujetador *m*.

brass knuckles [,brɑːs'nʌklz] *npl* (*US*) nudilleras *fpl*.

brass-rubbing [,brɑːs'rʌbɪŋ] *n* (*art, object*) calco *m* de plancha sepulcral (de latón).

brassy ['brɑːsɪ] *adj* de latón; *sound* desapacible, metálico; *person etc* descarado.

brat ['bræt] *n* mocoso *m*, crío *m*; ~ **pack** (*actors etc*) generación *f* de jóvenes artistas con éxito, (*pej*) niños *mpl* pijos*.

bravado [brə'vɑːdəʊ] *n* bravatas *fpl*, baladronadas *fpl*; **a piece of ~** una bravata; **out of sheer ~** de puro bravucón.

brave [breɪv] **1** *adj* (**a**) (*valiant*) valiente, valeroso; esforzado; bizarro; **as ~ as a lion** más fiero que un león.

(**b**) (*splendid*) magnífico, vistoso, garboso; **B~ New World** El nuevo mundo feliz.

2 *n* valiente *m*; (*Indian*) guerrero *m* indio.

3 *vt* desafiar, arrostrar; **to ~ the storm** aguantar la tempestad; **to ~ sb's anger** no amilanarse ante la ira de uno; **to ~ it out** defenderse sin confesarse culpable.

bravely ['breɪvlɪ] *adv* valientemente, con valor; (*fig*) vistosamente, airosamente.

bravery ['breɪvərɪ] *n* valor *m*, valentía *f*.

bravo ['brɑː'vəʊ] *interj* ¡bravo!

bravura [brə'vʊərə] *n* (**a**) arrojo *m*, brío *m*. (**b**) (*Mus*) virtuosismo *m*.

brawl [brɔːl] **1** *n* pendencia *f*, reyerta *f*; alboroto *m*. **2** *vi* armar pendencia, alborotar.

brawling ['brɔːlɪŋ] **1** *adj* pendenciero, alborotador. **2** *n* alboroto *m*.

brawn [brɔːn] *n* (*Brit*) carne *f* en gelatina; (*fig*) fuerza *f* muscular.

brawny ['brɔːnɪ] *adj* fornido, musculoso.

bray [breɪ] **1** *n* rebuzno *m*; (*laugh*) carcajada *f*. **2** *vi* rebuznar; (*trumpet*) sonar con estrépito.

braze [breɪz] *vt* soldar.

brazen ['breɪzn] **1** *adj* (*fig*) descarado, cínico; **~ lie** mentira *f* descarada.
2 *vt*: **to ~ it out** defenderse con argumentos descarados.

brazenly ['breɪznlɪ] *adv* descaradamente, con cinismo.

brazenness ['breɪzənnɪs] *n* descaro *m*, desvergüenza *f*.

brazier ['breɪzɪə^r] *n* brasero *m*.

Brazil [brə'zɪl] *n* el Brasil; **~ nut** nuez *f* del Brasil.

Brazilian [brə'zɪlɪən] **1** *adj* brasileño. **2** *n* brasileño *m*, -a *f*.

BRCS *n abbr of* **British Red Cross Society**.

breach [briːtʃ] **1** *n* (**a**) (*gap*) abertura *f*, brecha *f*; (*Mil*) brecha *f*. (**b**) (*fig*) violación *f*, infracción *f*; (*between friends: act*) rompimiento *m* de relaciones, (*state*) desavenencia *f*; (*Pol*) ruptura *f*; **~ of confidence** abuso *m* de confianza; **~ of contract** incumplimiento *m* de contrato; **~ of faith** (*or* **trust**) abuso *m* de confianza, infidencia *f*; **~ of the law** violación *f* de la ley; **~ of the peace** perturbación *f* del orden público; **~ of privilege** (*Parl*) abuso *m* del privilegio parlamentario; **~ of promise** incumplimiento *m* de la palabra de casamiento; **~ of security** fallo *m* de seguridad; **to be in ~ of a rule** incumplir una regla; **to fill the ~, to step into the ~** llenar el vacío; **to heal the ~** hacer las paces.
2 *vt* romper; (*Mil*) abrir brecha en.

bread [bred] *n* (**a**) pan *m* (*also fig*); **~ grains** granos *mpl* panificables; **to be on ~ and water** estar a pan y agua; **to break ~ with** sentarse a la mesa con; **to cast one's ~ on the waters** hacer el bien sin mirar a quién; **to earn one's daily ~** (*or* **one's ~ and butter**) ganarse el pan; **to know which side one's ~ is buttered** saber dónde aprieta el zapato; **man cannot live by ~ alone** no sólo de pan vive el hombre; **to take the ~ out of sb's mouth** quitar el pan de la boca de uno.
(**b**) (‡) guita‡ *f*, pasta* *f*, plata *f* (*LAm*).

bread-and-butter ['bredən'bʌtə^r] **1** *n* pan *m* con mantequilla; (*) pan *m* de cada día; **~ pudding** pudín *m* de pan y mantequilla.
2 *adj* corriente (y moliente), normal, regular; prosaico; de uso general; **~ letter** carta *f* de agradecimiento (*a una señora en cuya casa el invitado ha pasado varios días*).

breadbasket ['bred,bɑːskɪt] *n* cesto *m* para el pan; (‡) tripa* *f*.

breadbin ['bredbɪn] *n* caja *f* del pan, panera *f*.

breadboard ['bredbɔːd] *n* (*in kitchen*) tablero *m* para cortar el pan; (*Comput*) circuito *m* experimental.

breadbox ['bredbɒks] *n* (*US*) = **breadbin**.

bread-crumb ['bredkrʌm] *n* migaja *f*; **~s** (*Culin*) pan *m* rallado; **in ~s** empanado.

breaded ['bredɪd] *adj* empanado.

breadfruit ['bredfruːt] *n* fruto *m* del pan; **~ tree** árbol *m* del pan.

breadknife ['brednaɪf] *n*, *pl* **breadknives** ['brednaɪvz] cuchillo *m* para cortar el pan.

breadline ['bredlaɪn] *n* (*US*) cola *f* del pan; **to be on the ~** (*fig*) vivir en la mayor miseria.

bread-pudding [,bred'pʊdɪŋ] *n* pudín *m* de leche y pan.

breadth [bretθ] *n* anchura *f*; (*Naut*) manga *f*; (*fig*) amplitud *f*, extensión *f*; **to be 2 metres in ~** tener 2 metros de ancho.

breadthwise ['bretθwaɪz] *adv* de lado a lado.

breadwinner ['bred,wɪnə^r] *n* mantenedor *m*, -ora *f* de la familia.

break [breɪk] **1** *n* (**a**) (*breakage*) ruptura *f*, rompimiento *m*; (*between friends*) ruptura *f*; (*in voice*) quiebro *m*; sollozo *m*; (*in register of voice*) gallo *m*; (*in weather*) cambio *m*; **two ~s of service** (*Tennis*) dos servicios rotos; **at ~ of day** al amanecer; **to make a ~ with** cortar con; romper relaciones con.
(**b**) (*gap*) abertura *f*; (*crack*) grieta *f*; (*on paper etc*) espacio *m*, blanco *m*; (*of time*) intervalo *m*; (*in process*) interrupción *f*; (*in clouds*) claro *m*; (*holiday*) vacación *f*, (*one day*) asueto *m*; (*rest*) descanso *m*; (*at school*) período *m* de recreo; **~ in continuity** solución *f* de continuidad; **without a ~** sin interrupción, sin descansar; **to take a ~** descansar; **to take a weekend ~** ir a pasar el fin de semana fuera, hacer una escapada de fin de semana.
(**c**) (*vehicle*) break *m*, volanta *f* (*LAm*).
(**d**) (*chance*) oportunidad *f*; **lucky ~** chiripa *f*, racha *f* de suerte; **to give sb a ~** dar una oportunidad a uno, dejar de presionar a uno; **give me a ~!** ¡déjame un momento respirar!
(**e**) (*break-out*) evasión *f*, fuga *f*; **to make a ~ for it** tratar de evadirse.
(**f**) (*Billiards, Snooker*) tacada *f*; serie *f*.
2 (*irr*: *pret* **broke**, *ptp* **broken**) *vt* (**a**) (*smash, tear*) romper; *ground* roturar; *heart* partir; *record* batir, superar, mejorar; *code* descifrar; *conspiracy, ring* deshacer; **to ~ one's leg** romperse la pierna; *V* **back, heart** *etc*.
(**b**) (*fail to observe*) *appointment* no acudir a; *promise, word* faltar a, incumplir; *law, treaty* violar, infringir, quebrantar.
(**c**) (*weaken, vanquish*) *rebellion, strike* vencer; acabar con; *horse* domar, amansar; *rival* arruinar; *health* quebrantar; *bank* (*in gambling*) quebrar, hacer quebrar; (*morally*) abatir, vencer; **to ~ sb of a habit** lograr que uno abandone una costumbre, quitar a uno una costumbre.
(**d**) (*interrupt*) *silence, spell* romper; *custom* romper con; *journey* interrumpir; (*Elec*) interrumpir, cortar; **to ~ sb's service** (*Tennis*) romper el servicio del otro.
(**e**) (*leave*) *cover* abandonar, salir de; *jail* fugarse de; *ranks* salir de; *camp* ausentarse de.
(**f**) (*soften*) *impact, fall* amortiguar.
(**g**) *news* comunicar (*to* a).
(**h**) (*Naut*) *flag* desplegar.
(**i**) (*US*) **can you ~ me a 100-dollar bill?** ¿me puede cambiar un billete de 100 dólares?
3 *vi* (**a**) (*fall apart*) romperse, quebrarse, hacerse pedazos; (*machine*) estropearse; (*boil*) reventar; (*heart*) partirse; (*ranks, wave*) romperse.
(**b**) **to ~ free** soltarse; liberarse; *V* **loose**.
(**c**) (*news*) saberse, llegar a saberse; (*story*) revelarse; (*storm*) desencadenarse.
(**d**) (*weaken*) acabarse; debilitarse; (*voice*) mudar, cambiar, (*singing voice*) cascarse; (*heat wave*) terminar; (*weather*) cambiar (bruscamente); (*bank*) quebrar; (*health*) decaer (de repente).
(**e**) (*Boxing*) separarse.
(**f**) (*dawn*) romper; (*day*) apuntar.
(**g**) **to ~ even** salir sin ganar ni perder.
(**h**) (*Sport*: *ball*) torcerse, desviarse.

◆**break away** *vi* (**a**) (*piece*) desprenderse, separarse. (**b**) (*runner*) despegarse, salir del pelotón; (*at games*) escapar; **~ away from** *guard* evadirse de; *party* romper con.

◆**break down 1** *vt* (**a**) (*shatter*) derribar, romper, echar abajo; *resistance* acabar con, vencer; *alibi* probar la falsedad de. (**b**) *figures* analizar, descomponer, desglosar; clasificar.
2 *vi* (*Med*) perder la salud, sufrir un colapso; (*Aut*) averiarse, descomponerse (*LAm*); (*machine*) estropearse, dañarse, descomponerse (*LAm*); dejar de funcionar; (*negotiation, plan*) fracasar; (*person*) perder el control; romper a llorar.

◆**break forth** *vi* (*light, water*) surgir; (*storm*) estallar; **to ~ forth into song** romper a cantar.

◆**break in 1** *vt* (**a**) (*shatter*) forzar, romper.
(**b**) *recruit* desbastar, acostumbrar a la vida militar (*etc*); *horse* domar.
2 *vi* (*burglar*) forzar una entrada; (*in conversation*) cortar, interrumpir.

◆**break into** *vt* (**a**) **to ~ into a house** allanar una morada; **to ~ into the market** introducirse en el mercado, establecerse en el mercado.
(**b**) **to ~ into a run** echar a correr, empezar a correr; **to ~ into tears** romper a llorar.

◆**break off 1** *vt* (**a**) *piece* separar, desgajar. (**b**) *engagement, relations* romper; (*Mil*) *action* terminar.
2 *vi* (**a**) (*piece*) separarse, desprenderse, desgajarse.
(**b**) (*cease*) pararse repentinamente; dejar de hablar, interrumpirse; suspender el trabajo (*etc*).

◆**break out** *vi* (**a**) (*from prison*) escaparse, evadirse.

(**b**) (*fire, war, riot, argument*) estallar; (*noise*) hacerse oír; (*Med*) declararse; (*exclaim*) exclamar, gritar.
(**c**) **she broke out in spots** le salieron granos en la piel; **he broke out in a sweat** quedó cubierto de sudor.

◆**break through 1** *vt barrier* penetrar, atravesar, romper.
2 *vi* (**a**) (*water etc*) abrirse paso, abrirse (un) camino; **to ~ through to** *miners* llegar a, abrirse un camino hasta.
(**b**) (*inventor*) hacer un descubrimiento importante; abrirse paso, empezar a tener éxito.

◆**break up 1** *vt* (**a**) (*shatter*) romper, deshacer; *ship* desguazar; *estate* parcelar; *industry* desconcentrar; *camp* levantar; *meeting, organization* disolver; *gang* desarticular; *marriage* deshacer; **~ it up!** ¡basta ya!; ¡no quiero más follón!; **it's time we broke it up** es hora de irnos, es hora de terminar; **they broke the place up** destrozaron el local.
(**b**) (*divide*) dividir; separar.
(**c**) (*US**) hacer reír a carcajadas.
2 *vi* (**a**) (*shatter*) romperse, hacerse pedazos; desmenuzarse; (*ice*) romperse; (*in disorder*) disolverse; (*marriage*) deshacerse, romperse; (*federation, group*) desmembrarse, disgregarse; (*partnership*) romperse; (*weather*) cambiar; (*crowd*) dispersarse.
(**b**) (*Brit: end*) (*school*) terminar el curso, cerrarse (para las vacaciones); (*session*) levantarse, terminar.
(**c**) (*divide*) dividirse, desglosarse (*into* en).
(**d**) (*US**) reír a carcajadas.

◆**break with** *vt* romper con.

breakable ['breɪkəbl] *adj* frágil, quebradizo.

breakage ['breɪkɪdʒ] *n* rotura *f*.

breakaway ['breɪkəweɪ] **1** *adj group etc* disidente, separatista; **~ state** (*Pol*) estado *m* independizado. **2** *n* (*Sport*) escapada *f*.

break-dancer ['breɪk,dɑːnsəʳ] *n* bailarín *m*, -ina *f* de break.

break-dancing ['breɪk,dɑːnsɪŋ] *n* break *m*.

breakdown ['breɪkdaʊn] *n* (**a**) interrupción *f*; (*failure*) fracaso *m*, mal éxito *m*; (*Med*) colapso *m*, crisis *f* nerviosa; (*Aut etc*) avería *f*, pana *f*, descompostura *f* (*LAm*); **~ gang** (*Brit Aut*) equipo *m* de asistencia en carretera; **~ service** (*Brit Aut*) asistencia *f* en carretera, servicio *m* de averías; **~ truck, ~ van** (*Brit*) grúa *f*, camión *m* grúa.
(**b**) (*of numbers etc*) análisis *m*, descomposición *f*; desglose *m*; (*report*) informe *m* detallado.

breaker ['breɪkəʳ] *n* ola *f* grande, cachón *m*.

break-even [,breɪk'iːvən] *attr*: **~ chart** gráfica *f* del punto de equilibrio; **~ point** punto *m* de indiferencia.

breakfast ['brekfəst] **1** *n* desayuno *m*; **~ cereals** cereales *mpl* para el desayuno; **~ cup** taza *f* de desayuno; **~ room** habitación *f* del desayuno; **~ TV** televisión *f* matinal. **2** *vi* desayunar(se) (*off eggs, on eggs* huevos).

break-in ['breɪk,ɪn] *n* escalamiento *m*, (*loosely*) robo *m*.

breaking ['breɪkɪŋ] *n* rotura *f*, rompimiento *m*; **~ and entering** allanamiento *m* de morada.

breaking-point ['breɪkɪŋpɔɪnt] *n* punto *m* de ruptura, carga *f* de rotura; **to reach ~** llegar a la crisis, llegar al límite.

breaking-up [,breɪkɪŋ'ʌp] *n* (*meeting etc*) disolución *f*, levantamiento *m* (de la sesión); (*school, college*) fin *m* de las clases, fin *m* de curso.

breakneck ['breɪknek] *adj*: **at ~ speed** como alma que lleva el diablo.

breakout ['breɪkaut] *n* evasión *f*, fuga *f*.

break-point ['breɪk'pɔɪnt] *n* (*Tennis*) punto *m* de break; (*Comput*) punto *m* de interrupción.

breakthrough ['breɪkθruː] *n* (*Mil*) ruptura *f*; (*fig*) avance *m*, adelanto *m*, invento *m* decisivo; **to achieve a ~** hacer grandes progresos, hacer un descubrimiento importante.

break-up ['breɪkʌp] *n* disolución *f*, desintegración *f*, desmembración *f*; **~ value** (*Comm*) valor *m* en liquidación.

breakwater ['breɪk,wɔːtəʳ] *n* rompeolas *m*, espigón *m*.

bream [briːm] *n* (*sea* ~) besugo *m*.

breast [brest] **1** *n* (*Anat*) pecho *m*; (*woman's*) pecho *m*, seno *m*; (*of bird*) pechuga *f*; (*fig*) corazón *m*; **~ cancer** cáncer *m* de mama; **to beat one's ~** darse golpes de pecho; **to make a clean ~ of** confesar con franqueza; **to make a clean ~ of it** confesarlo todo, desembuchar. **2** *vt* (**a**) *waves etc* hacer cara a, arrostrar. (**b**) **to ~ the tape** romper la cinta, (*fig*) llegar a la meta.

breastbone ['brestbəʊn] *n* esternón *m*.

breast-fed ['brestfed] *adj* criado a pecho.

breast-feed ['brestfiːd] (*irr*: *V* **feed**) *vt* criar a los pechos; amamantar, dar el pecho a.

breast-feeding ['brest,fiːdɪŋ] *n* cría *f* a los pechos, amamantamiento *m*.

breast-high ['brest'haɪ] *adv* a la altura del pecho.

breastplate ['brestpleɪt] *n* peto *m*.

breast-pocket ['brest,pɒkɪt] *n* bolsillo *m* de pecho.

breast-stroke ['breststrəʊk] *n* braza *f* (de pecho).

breastwork ['brestwɜːk] *n* parapeto *m*.

breath [breθ] *n* aliento *m*, respiración *f*; (*esp visible in air*) hálito *m*; **bad ~** halitosis *f*; **the first ~ of spring** el primer viento suave que anuncia la primavera; **the least ~ of scandal** la más ligera sospecha de escándalo; **there's not a ~ of air stirring** no hay ni un soplo de aire; **the theatre was the ~ of life to her** el teatro era la misma vida para ella; **to bring a ~ of fresh air to** traer un soplo de aire refrescante a; **all in the same ~** de una tirada, todo al mismo tiempo; **in the very next ~** a renglón seguido; **out of ~** sofocado, jadeante, sin aliento; **to get out of ~** quedar sin aliento; **short of ~** corto de resuello; **under one's ~** a media voz, en voz baja; **to catch one's ~** suspender la respiración; **it made me catch my ~** (*fig*) me dejó pasmado; **to draw a deep ~** respirar a fondo; **to draw one's last ~** tomar el último aliento; **the best that ever drew ~** el mejor que se conoció jamás; **to gasp for ~** luchar por respirar; **to get one's ~ back** recuperar el aliento; **to go out for a ~ of air** salir a tomar el fresco; **to hold one's ~** contener la respiración; **to save one's ~** ahorrar las palabras; **to take a deep ~** respirar a fondo; **it took my ~ away** me dejó pasmado; **to waste one's ~** perder el tiempo (*on* hablando con), predicar en el desierto.

breathable ['briːðəbl] *adj air* respirable, que se puede respirar.

breathalyse, (*US*) **breathalyze** ['breθəlaɪz] *vt* someter a la prueba del alcoholímetro (*or* del alcohol).

Breathalyser, (*US*) **Breathalyzer** ['breθəlaɪzəʳ] ® *n* alcoholímetro *m*.

breathe [briːð] **1** *vt* respirar; *sigh* dar; *prayer* decir en voz baja; **to ~ air into a balloon** inflar un globo soplando; **it ~s the spirit of** late por todas partes el espíritu de.
2 *vi* respirar; (*noisily*) resollar; **to ~ again** respirar.

◆**breathe in** *vti* aspirar, respirar.

◆**breathe out 1** *vt* exhalar. **2** *vi* espirar.

breather* ['briːðəʳ] *n* respiro *m*, descanso *m*; **to give sb a ~** dejar que uno tome una pausa; **to go out for a ~** salir a descansar un momento.

breathing ['briːðɪŋ] *n* respiración *f*; **heavy ~** resuello *m*; **~ apparatus** respirador *m*.

breathing-space ['briːðɪŋspeɪs] *n* respiro *m*.

breathing-tube ['briːðɪŋtjuːb] *n* tubo *m* de respiración.

breathless ['breθlɪs] *adj* (**a**) falto de aliento, jadeante; **~ with excitement** sin aliento por la emoción; **a ~ confession** una confesión apresurada.
(**b**) **a ~ silence** un silencio lleno de expectación.

breathlessly ['breθlɪslɪ] *adv*: **to say ~** decir jadeante.

breathlessness ['breθlɪsnɪs] *n* falta *f* de aliento, dificultad *f* respiratoria.

breathtaking ['breθ,teɪkɪŋ] *adj sight* imponente, pasmoso; *speed* vertiginoso; *effrontery* pasmoso; **the view is ~** la vista corta la respiración.

breathtakingly ['breθ,teɪkɪŋlɪ] *adv*: **~ beautiful** tan hermoso que corta la respiración; **to go ~ fast** ir a una velocidad vertiginosa.

breath-test ['breθtest] **1** *n* prueba *f* del alcoholímetro (*or* del alcohol). **2** *vt* someter a la prueba del alcoholímetro.

bred [bred] *pret and ptp of* **breed**.

breech [briːtʃ] *n* recámara *f*.

breeches ['briːtʃɪz] *npl* calzones *mpl*; (**riding**) **~** pantalones *mpl* de montar; **~ buoy** boya *f* pantalón; **to wear the ~** llevar los pantalones, llevar los calzones.

breechloader ['briːtʃ,ləʊdəʳ] *n* arma *f* de retrocarga.

breed [briːd] **1** *n* raza *f*, casta *f*.
2 (*irr*: *pret and ptp* **bred**) *vt* criar, engendrar; (*as farmer*) criar; (*fig*) engendrar, producir; **town bred** criado en la ciudad; **they are bred for show** se crían para las exposiciones; **we ~ them for hunting** los criamos para la caza.
3 *vi* reproducirse, procrear; **they ~ like flies** (*or* **rabbits**) se multiplican como conejos.

breeder ['briːdəʳ] *n* (**a**) (*person*) criador *m*, -ora *f*; (*of cattle*) ganadero *m*. (**b**) (*animal*) criadero *m*, paridera *f*.

breeder reactor ['briːdəriː,æktəʳ] *n* reactor *m* reproductor.

breeding ['briːdɪŋ] *n* (**a**) (*Bio*) reproducción *f*. (**b**) (*of stock*) cría *f*. (**c**) (*of person*) crianza *f*, educación *f*; **bad ~, ill ~** mala crianza *f*, falta *f* de educación; **good ~** educación *f*, cultura *f*; **he has (good) ~** es una persona educada; **it shows bad ~** indica una falta de educación.

breeding-ground ['briːdɪŋ,graʊnd] *n* tierra *f* de cría; (*fig*) caldo *m* de cultivo (*of, for* de).

breeding-season ['briːdɪŋ,siːzn] *n* época *f* de reproducción.
breeks [briːks] *npl* (*Scot*) pantalones *mpl.*
breeze [briːz] **1** *n* brisa *f*; **to do sth in a ~** (*US**) hacer algo con los ojos cerrados; **to shoot the ~** (*US**) charlar; **it's a ~** (*US**) esto es coser y cantar. **2** *vi*: **to ~ in** entrar como Pedro por su casa; **to ~ through sth** (*US**) hacer algo con los ojos cerrados.
breeze-block ['briːzblɒk] *n* (*Brit*) bloque *m* de cemento; bovedilla *f.*
breezily ['briːzɪlɪ] *adv* jovialmente, despreocupadamente.
breezy ['briːzɪ] *adj* (**a**) *day, place* de mucho viento; **it is ~** hace viento. (**b**) *person's manner* animado, jovial, despreocupado.
Bren [bren] *n*: **~ gun** fusil *m* ametrallador; **~ (gun) carrier** vehículo *m* de transporte ligero (con fusil ametrallador).
brethren ['breðrɪn] *npl* (*irr pl of* **brother**: *esp Rel*) hermanos *mpl.*
Breton ['bretən] **1** *adj* bretón. **2** *n* (**a**) bretón *m*, -ona *f.* (**b**) (*Ling*) bretón *m.*
breve [briːv] *n* (*Mus, Typ*) breve *f.*
breviary ['briːvɪərɪ] *n* breviario *m.*
brevity ['brevɪtɪ] *n* brevedad *f.*
brew [bruː] **1** *n* (*hum*) poción *f*, brebaje *m.*
2 *vt beer* hacer, elaborar; *tea* hacer; (*fig: also* **to ~ up**) urdir, tramar.
3 *vi* (*fig*) prepararse; (*storm*) amenazar; **there's sth ~ing** algo se está tramando; **there's trouble ~ing** soplan vientos de fronda.
◆**brew up** *vi* preparar el té.
brewer ['bruːəʳ] *n* cervecero *m.*
brewery ['bruːərɪ] *n* cervecería *f*, fábrica *f* de cerveza.
brew-up ['bruːʌp] *n*: **let's have a ~** (*Brit**) vamos a tomar un té.
briar ['braɪəʳ] *n* (**a**) (*rose*) escaramujo *m*, rosa *f* silvestre; (*hawthorn*) espino *m*; (*bramble*) zarza *f*; (*heather*) brezo *m.* (**b**) (*pipe*) pipa *f* de brezo.
bribable ['braɪbəbl] *adj* sobornable.
bribe [braɪb] **1** *n* soborno *m*, cohecho *m*, mordida *f* (*Mex*), coima *f* (*LAm*); **to take a ~** dejarse sobornar (*from* por). **2** *vt* sobornar, cohechar, mojar (*LAm*), aceitar (*LAm*).
bribery ['braɪbərɪ] *n* soborno *m*, cohecho *m*, coima *f* (*LAm*).
bric-à-brac ['brɪkəbræk] *n* chucherías *fpl*, curiosidades *fpl.*
brick [brɪk] **1** *n* ladrillo *m*, tabique *m* (*LAm*); (*of ice cream*) bloque *m*; (*Brit: child's*) cubo *m*; **a ~ wall** una pared de ladrillos; **~s and mortar** (*fig*) construcción *f*, edificios *mpl*; (*fig*) inversión *f* sólida; resultados *mpl* tangibles; **he's a ~** (*†) es un buen chico; **be a ~ and lend it to me** (*†) préstamelo como buen amigo; **he came down on us like a ton of ~s** nos echó una bronca fenomenal; **to drop a ~*** (*Brit*) tirarse una plancha; **you can't make ~s without straw** sin paja ho hay ladrillos.
2 *attr* de ladrillo(s).
3 *vt* (*also* **to ~ up**) cerrar con ladrillos, tapar con ladrillos.
brickbat ['brɪkbæt] *n* trozo *m* de ladrillo; (*fig*) palabra *f* hiriente, crítica *f.*
brick-built ['brɪk,bɪlt] *adj* construido de ladrillos.
brickie* ['brɪkɪ] *n* albañil *m.*
brick-kiln ['brɪk,kɪln] *n* horno *m* de ladrillos.
bricklayer ['brɪkleɪəʳ] *n* albañil *m.*
brick-red ['brɪkred] **1** *adj* rojo ladrillo. **2** *n* rojo *m* ladrillo.
brickwork ['brɪkwɜːk] *n* enladrillado *m*, ladrillos *mpl.*
brickworks ['brɪkwɜːks] *n*, **brickyard** ['brɪk,jɑːd] *n* ladrillar *m.*
bridal ['braɪdl] *adj* nupcial.
bride [braɪd] *n* novia *f*; **the ~ and groom** los novios.
bridegroom ['braɪdgrʊm] *n* novio *m.*
bridesmaid ['braɪdzmeɪd] *n* dama *f* de honor.
bridge[1] [brɪdʒ] **1** *n* puente *m* (*also Mus*); (*Naut*) puente *m* de mando; (*of nose*) caballete *m*; **to burn one's ~s** quemar las naves; **we'll cross that ~ when we come to it** nos enfrentaremos con ese problema en su momento; **don't cross your ~s before you come to them** no adelantes los acontecimientos; **much water has flowed under the ~ since then** mucho ha llovido desde entonces; **we must rebuild our ~s** (*fig*) tenemos que restablecer las relaciones.
2 *vt* tender un puente sobre; *gap* llenar, salvar.
bridge[2] [brɪdʒ] *n* (*Cards*) bridge *m.*
bridge-building ['brɪdʒ,bɪldɪŋ] *n* construcción *f* de puentes; (*fig*) restablecimiento *m* de relaciones.
bridgehead ['brɪdʒhed] *n* cabeza *f* de puente (*also fig*).
bridge-party ['brɪdʒ,pɑːtɪ] *n* reunión *f* de bridge.
bridge-player ['brɪdʒ,pleɪəʳ] *n* jugador *m*, -ora *f* de bridge.
bridge-roll [,brɪdʒ'rəʊl] *n tipo de bollo.*
Bridget ['brɪdʒɪt] *nf* Brígida.
bridging-loan ['brɪdʒɪŋ,ləʊn] *n* (*Brit*) crédito *m* puente.
bridle ['braɪdl] **1** *n* brida *f*, freno *m.* **2** *vi*: **to ~ at** picarse por, ofenderse por.
bridle-path ['braɪdlpɑːθ] *n*, *pl* **bridle-paths** ['braɪdlpɑːðz] camino *m* de herradura.
brief [briːf] **1** *adj* breve, corto; (*fleeting*) fugaz, pasajero; *style* lacónico; **well, to be ~ ...** bueno, en resumen ...; bueno, para decirlo con pocas palabras ...; **please be as ~ as possible** explíquese con la mayor brevedad.
2 *n* (**a**) (*Eccl: papal*) breve *m.*
(**b**) (*Jur*) escrito *m*; **to go beyond one's ~** exceder las instrucciones; **to hold a ~ for** representar a; **to hold a watching ~ for sb** representar a un cliente a quien no interesa directamente un juicio; **to hold no ~ for** no aprobar, no apoyar; **to stick to one's ~** atenerse a las órdenes dadas.
(**c**) (*Brit**: *barrister*) abogado *mf.*
(**d**) **in ~** en resumen.
(**e**) **~s** (*man's*) calzoncillos *mpl*, (*woman's*) bragas *fpl.*
3 *vt* (*Mil etc*) dar órdenes a, dar instrucciones a; informar (de antemano); *barrister, lawyer* constituir; **she had been well ~ed** estaba bien informada.
briefcase ['briːfkeɪs] *n* cartera *f*, maletín *m*, portafolio *m* (*LAm*).
briefing ['briːfɪŋ] *n* reunión *f* en que se dan las órdenes (a la tripulación de un avión militar); órdenes *fpl*, instrucciones *fpl*; (*to press*) informe *m*, sesión *f* informativa; (*heading in press*) informaciones *fpl.*
briefly ['briːflɪ] *adv* brevemente; en resumen, en pocas palabras; **he was ~ ambassador in Lima** por poco tiempo fue embajador en Lima.
briefness ['briːfnɪs] *n* brevedad *f.*
brier ['braɪəʳ] *n* = **briar.**
brig [brɪg] *n* (*Naut*) bergantín *m.*
Brig. *abbr of* **Brigadier** general *m* de brigada.
brigade [brɪ'geɪd] *n* brigada *f*; (*fire etc*) cuerpo *m*; **one of the old ~** un veterano.
brigadier [,brɪgə'dɪəʳ] *n* (*Brit*) general *m* de brigada.
brigand ['brɪgənd] *n* bandido *m*, bandolero *m.*
brigandage ['brɪgəndɪdʒ] *n* bandidaje *m*, bandolerismo *m.*
bright [braɪt] *adj* **1** (**a**) claro, brillante, luminoso; *day* luminoso, de sol; *eyes* claro; *sun* brillante; *surface* lustroso; *colour* subido; *smile* radiante; **~ interval** período *m* de sol; **~ lights** (*US Aut*) luces *fpl* largas.
(**b**) (*clever*) listo, inteligente; ocurrente; *idea* luminoso; *conversation, remark* ingenioso; **that was ~ of you** en eso anduviste muy listo; **you're a ~ one!** ¡qué despiste tienes!; **the child's as ~ as a button** el niño es más listo que el hambre.
(**c**) (*cheerful*) alegre, animado, optimista.
(**d**) *prospect etc* prometedor, esperanzador; *hope* vivo, firme.
2 *adv*: **to get up ~ and early** levantarse tempranito.
brighten ['braɪtn] **1** *vt* (*also* **to ~ up**) (**a**) (*make shine*) abrillantar, lustrar. (**b**) *house* hacer más alegre, poner colores en; (*cheer*) alegrar.
2 *vi* (*also* **to ~ up**) (**a**) (*person*) animarse, alegrarse. (**b**) (*weather*) despejarse; (*prospect*) mejorar.
bright-eyed ['braɪt'aɪd] *adj* de ojos vivos.
brightly ['braɪtlɪ] *adv* (**a**) brillantemente; **the sun shone ~** el sol lucía brillantemente; **the fire burned ~** el fuego resplandecía. (**b**) ingeniosamente; *smile, look* radiantemente; *say, answer* con prontitud.
brightness ['braɪtnɪs] *n* (*V adj*) (**a**) claridad *f*; brillantez *f*, luminosidad *f*; lustre *m*; lo subido; **~ control** botón *m* de ajuste del brillo. (**b**) inteligencia *f*; viveza *f* de ingenio.
brill[1] [brɪl] *n* rodaballo *m* menor.
brill[2]‡ [brɪl] *adj* = **brilliant**; tremendo*, fantástico*; **~!** ¡fantástico!*
brilliance ['brɪljəns] *n*, **brilliancy** ['brɪljənsɪ] *n* brillo *m*, brillantez *f.*
brilliant ['brɪljənt] **1** *adj* brillante; *idea* genial, luminoso; *student etc* brillante, sobresaliente; *success* clamoroso, resonante, brillante; *wine* completamente límpido; (*) tremendo*, fantástico*; **~!** ¡fantástico! **2** *n* brillante *m.*
brilliantine [,brɪljən'tiːn] *n* brillantina *f.*
brilliantly ['brɪljəntlɪ] *adv* brillantemente (*also fig*).
Brillo pad ['brɪləʊ,pæd] ® *n* estropajo *m* de aluminio.
brim [brɪm] **1** *n* borde *m*; (*of hat*) ala *f.* **2** *vi*: **to ~ over** desbordarse, rebosar; **to ~ with** rebosar de.
brimful ['brɪm'fʊl] *adj* lleno hasta el borde; **~ of, ~ with** rebosante de.
brimstone ['brɪmstəʊn] *n* azufre *m.*

brindled ['brɪndld] *adj* manchado, mosqueado.
brine [braɪn] *n* salmuera *f*; (*fig*) mar *m or f*.
bring [brɪŋ] (*irr: pret and ptp* **brought**) **1** *vt* (**a**) *person, object, news, luck etc* traer; *person* llevar, conducir; **to ~ a matter to a conclusion** concluir un asunto, llevar un asunto a su desenlace; **it brought us to the verge of disaster** nos llevó al borde del desastre; **this brought him to his feet** esto hizo que se pusiera de pie, con esto se levantó; **he brought it upon himself** se lo buscó; **~ it over here** tráelo para acá; **~ it closer** acércalo; *V* **house, light, sense** *etc*.
(**b**) (*cause*) causar; traer, provocar; *profit etc* dar, producir; **you ~ nothing but trouble** no haces más que causarme molestias; **it brought tears to her eyes** con esto se le llenaron los ojos de lágrimas; **to ~ sth to happen** hacer que algo ocurra.
(**c**) (*Jur*) *charge* hacer, formular; *suit* entablar; **no charges will be brought** no se hará ninguna acusación; **the case was brought before the judge** la causa fue vista por el juez.
(**d**) **to ~ sb to do sth** inducir a uno a hacer algo, hacer que uno haga algo; **he was brought to see his error** le convencieron de su error; **it brought me to realize that ...** me hizo comprender que ...
2 *vr*: **to ~ o.s. to** + *infin* convencerse para + *infin*; cobrar suficiente ánimo para + *infin*; resignarse + *infin*.
◆**bring about** *vt* ocasionar, producir, causar; *change* efectuar.
◆**bring along** *vt* traer consigo, llevar consigo.
◆**bring away** *vt* llevarse.
◆**bring back** *vt* (**a**) volver a traer; volver con, traer de vuelta; *monarchy etc* restaurar; *thing borrowed* devolver; (*to life*) devolver la vida a.
(**b**) *memory* recordar, traer a la memoria.
◆**bring down** *vt* (**a**) *luggage etc* bajar.
(**b**) (*Mil, Hunting*) abatir, derribar; *government* derribar, derrocar.
(**c**) *price* rebajar, reducir.
◆**bring forth** *vt child* parir, dar a luz; (*fig*) producir.
◆**bring forward** *vt* (**a**) *proposal* proponer, presentar, suscitar.
(**b**) *date* adelantar.
(**c**) (*Comm*) pasar a otra cuenta; **brought forward** suma *f* del anterior.
◆**bring in** *vt* (**a**) (*carry in*) entrar, traer, introducir; *meal* servir; *harvest* recoger; *person* introducir, hacer entrar; *suspect* detener, llevar a la comisaría; **to ~ in the police** llamar a la policía; pedir la intervención de la policía; **~ him in!** ¡que entre!, ¡que pase!; **I was not brought into the matter at any stage** no me dieron voz en este asunto en ningún momento.
(**b**) *fashion, custom* introducir; (*Parl*) *bill* presentar.
(**c**) (*attract*) atraer; **this should ~ in the masses** esto deberá atraer a las masas.
(**d**) (*Fin*) *income* dar, producir.
(**e**) (*Jur*) *verdict* dar, pronunciar.
◆**bring off** *vt* lograr, conseguir; *success* obtener, realizar; *plan* llevar a cabo.
◆**bring on** *vt* (**a**) (*cause*) causar, acarrear.
(**b**) *growth* estimular, favorecer; *plant* hacer acelerar el desarrollo de.
(**c**) (*Theat*) presentar, introducir; hacer salir a la escena.
◆**bring out** *vt* (**a**) (*take out*) sacar; *argument* sacar a relucir; *product* lanzar, lanzar al mercado; *book* publicar, sacar a luz.
(**b**) (*emphasize*) subrayar, recalcar; *colour* hacer resaltar.
(**c**) *person* hacer menos reservado, ayudar a adquirir confianza.
◆**bring over** *vt* (**a**) *person* ir a buscar. (**b**) (*convert*) *person* convertir, convencer.
◆**bring round** *vt* (**a**) (*win over*) ganarse la voluntad de; convencer, convertir.
(**b**) (*Med*) hacer volver en sí.
◆**bring to** *vt* (**a**) (*Naut*) pairear, poner al pairo. (**b**) *unconscious person* reanimar.
◆**bring together** *vt* reunir; *enemies* reconciliar.
◆**bring under** *vt* (*fig*) someter.
◆**bring up** *vt* (**a**) (*carry*) subir; *person* hacer subir.
(**b**) *subject* sacar a colación, sacar a relucir; llamar la atención sobre.
(**c**) *person* criar, educar; **she was badly brought up** la criaron de manera poco satisfactoria; **he was brought up to believe that ...** le educaron en la creencia de que ...; **where were you brought up?** (*iro*) ¡cómo se ve que no has ido a colegios de pago!
(**d**) (*) arrojar, vomitar.
(**e**) **to ~ sb up short** parar a uno en seco.
(**f**) **to ~ up the rear** (*Mil*) cerrar la marcha.
(**g**) **to ~ sb up in court** (*Jur*) hacer que uno comparezca ante el magistrado.
(**h**) *V* **date**.
bring-and-buy sale [,brɪŋənd'baɪseɪl] *n* (*Brit*) tómbola *f* de beneficencia.
brink [brɪŋk] *n* borde *m*; **on the ~ of** (*fig*) + *n* en la antesala de + *n*; + *ger* a punto de + *infin*.
brinkmanship ['brɪŋkmənʃɪp] *n* política *f* de la cuerda floja, política *f* del borde del abismo.
briny ['braɪnɪ] **1** *adj* salado, salobre. **2** *n*: **the ~** (†, *hum*) el mar.
briquette [brɪ'ket] *n* briqueta *f*.
brisk [brɪsk] *adj* enérgico, vigoroso; *pace, sales* rápido; *trade etc* activo; *wind* fuerte; **business is ~** el negocio va bien; estos géneros (*etc*) se venden bien.
brisket ['brɪskɪt] *n* carne *f* de pecho (para asar).
briskly ['brɪsklɪ] *adv* enérgicamente; rápidamente; activamente.
briskness ['brɪsknɪs] *n* energía *f*; rapidez *f*; actividad *f*.
brisling ['brɪzlɪŋ] *n* espadín *m* (noruego).
bristle ['brɪsl] **1** *n* cerda *f*; (**pure**) **~ brush** cepillo *m* de púas. **2** *vi* (**a**) (*hair etc*) erizarse; (*animal*) erizar las cerdas; **to ~ with** (*fig*) estar erizado de. (**b**) (*fig*) ofenderse, irritarse (*at* por).
bristly ['brɪslɪ] *adj* cerdoso; **to have a ~ chin** tener la barba crecida.
Bristol ['brɪstəl] *n* (**a**) **~ board** cartulina *f*. (**b**) **b~s**‡ tetas* *fpl*.
Brit* [brɪt] *n* británico *m*, -a *f*, (*loosely*) inglés *m*, -esa *f*.
Britain ['brɪtən] *n* Gran Bretaña *f*, (*loosely*) Inglaterra *f*.
Britannia [brɪ'tænɪə] *n* Britania *f*, *figura que representa simbólicamente a Gran Bretaña*.
Britannic [brɪ'tænɪk] *adj*: **His** (*or* **Her**) **~ Majesty** su Majestad *f* Británica.
briticism ['brɪtɪsɪzəm] *n* (*US*) modismo *m* (*or* vocablo *m etc*) del inglés de Inglaterra.
British ['brɪtɪʃ] **1** *adj* británico, (*loosely*) inglés; **~ Council** (*in Spain etc*) Instituto *m* Británico; **~ English** inglés *m* hablado en Gran Bretaña, inglés *m* británico; **~ Legion** *organización de veteranos de las dos guerras mundiales*; **~ Museum** Museo *m* Británico; **the best of ~ (luck)!**‡ ¡y un cuerno!‡ **2** *n*: **the ~** los británicos, (*loosely*) los ingleses.
Britisher ['brɪtɪʃə^r] *n* (*US*) británico *m*, -a *f*, natural *mf* de Gran Bretaña.
British Isles ['brɪtɪʃ'aɪlz] *npl* Islas *fpl* Británicas.
Briton ['brɪtən] *n* británico *m*, -a *f*, (*loosely*) inglés *m*, -esa *f*.
Brittany ['brɪtənɪ] *n* Bretaña *f*.
brittle ['brɪtl] *adj* frágil, quebradizo.
brittleness ['brɪtlnɪs] *n* fragilidad *f*, lo quebradizo.
Bro. *n abbr of* **Brother** hermano *m*.
broach [brəʊtʃ] *vt cask* espitar; *bottle etc* abrir; *subject* comenzar a hablar de, mencionar por primera vez, abordar; **he didn't ~ the subject** no mencionó el punto, no sacó el tema a colación.
broad [brɔːd] **1** *adj* (**a**) ancho; extenso, amplio; **~ bean** haba *f* gruesa; **~ jump** (*US*) salto *m* de longitud; **3 metres ~** ancho de 3 metros; **it's as ~ as it is long** (*fig*) lo mismo da.
(**b**) (*fig*) ancho; *view* comprensivo; *mind* tolerante, liberal; *hint* claro, inconfundible; *accent* marcado, cerrado, fuerte; *story* verde; *sense of word* ancho, lato; *grin, smile* jovial; *range, spectrum* amplio, extenso; **~ daylight** plena luz *f* de día; **in ~ daylight** en (*or* a) pleno día.
2 *n* (*US*‡) tía* *f*.
broad-brimmed ['brɔːd'brɪmd] *adj hat* de ala ancha.
broadcast ['brɔːdkɑːst] **1** *adj* (*Agr*) sembrado a voleo; (*Rad*) radiodifundido, de (la) radio.
2 *adv* por todas partes.
3 *n* emisión *f*, programa *m*.
4 *vt* (*Agr*) sembrar a voleo; (*fig*) diseminar, divulgar; (*Rad*) emitir, radiar.
5 *vi* hablar (*or* tocar *etc*) por la radio.
broadcaster ['brɔːdkɑːstə^r] *n* conferenciante *mf* (*or* cronista *mf*) de radio; (*announcer*) locutor *m*, -ora *f*.
broadcasting ['brɔːdkɑːstɪŋ] **1** *n* radiodifusión *f*. **2** *attr* de radiodifusión.
broadcasting station ['brɔːdkɑːstɪŋ,steɪʃən] *n* emisora *f*.
broadcloth ['brɔːdklɒθ] *n* velarte *m*.
broaden ['brɔːdn] (*also* **to ~ out**) **1** *vt* ensanchar; **travel ~s**

the mind los viajes edifican el entendimiento. **2** *vi* ensancharse.
broadleaved [ˌbrɔːd'liːvd] *adj* de hoja ancha.
broadloom ['brɔːdluːm] *adj*: ~ **carpet** alfombra *f* sin costuras.
broadly ['brɔːdlɪ] *adv* extensamente; *smile* de modo jovial; **it is ~ true that ...** es en general verdad que ...; ~ **speaking** grosso modo, en general, hablando en términos generales.
broadly-based ['brɔːdlɪˌbeɪst] *adj* que cuenta con una base amplia, apoyado por sectores muy diversos; **a ~ coalition** una coalición que representa gran diversidad de intereses.
broad-minded ['brɔːd'maɪndɪd] *adj* de amplias miras, de criterio amplio, tolerante, liberal.
broad-mindedness ['brɔːd'maɪndɪdnɪs] *n* amplitud *f* de criterio, tolerancia *f*.
broadness ['brɔːdnɪs] *n* anchura *f*, extensión *f*; (*of accent*) lo cerrado.
broadsheet ['brɔːdʃiːt] *n* periódico *m* de gran formato.
broad-shouldered ['brɔːd'ʃəʊldəd] *adj* ancho de espaldas.
broadside ['brɔːdsaɪd] *n* (*side*) costado *m*; (*shots*) andanada *f*; (*abuse etc*) andanada *f* verbal; ~ **on** de costado; **to fire a ~** soltar (*or* disparar) una andanada (*also fig*).
broadsword ['brɔːdˌsɔːd] *n* sable *m*.
broadways ['brɔːdweɪz] *adv* a lo ancho, por lo ancho; con la parte ancha por delante; ~ **on to the waves** de costado a las olas.
brocade [brəʊ'keɪd] *n* brocado *m*.
broccoli ['brɒkəlɪ] *n* brécol *m*, bróculi *m*, broculí *m*.
brochure ['brəʊʃjʊəʳ] *n* folleto *m*.
brock [brɒk] *n* (*Brit*) tejón *m*.
brogue[1] [brəʊg] *n* (*shoe*) abarca *f*, zapato *m* de estilo inglés picado.
brogue[2] [brəʊg] *n* (*Ling*) acento *m* irlandés.
broil [brɔɪl] *vt* asar a la parrilla.
broiler ['brɔɪləʳ] *n* (**a**) (*chicken*) pollo *m* para asar. (**b**) (*US*: *grill*) parrilla *f*, grill *m*.
broiler-house ['brɔɪləˌhaʊs] *n*, *pl* **broiler-houses** ['brɔɪləˌhaʊzɪz] batería *f* de engorde.
broiling ['brɔɪlɪŋ] *adj*: **it's ~ hot** hace un calor sofocante.
broke [brəʊk] *pret of* **break**; **to be ~*** no tener un céntimo, estar sin blanca; **to go ~*** quebrar; **to go for ~*** echar el resto*, ir al límite.
broken ['brəʊkən] **1** *ptp of* **break**.
2 *adj ground* accidentado, quebrado; *tone* de desesperación; ~ **in health** deshecho, muy decaído; **in ~ Spanish** en castellano chapurreado; ~ **home** familia *f* desestructurada, familia *f* en la que se han divorciado (*or* separado) los padres; ~ **man** hombre *m* que no vale para nada; hombre *m* arruinado; ~ **reed** (*fig*) persona *f* quemada.
broken-down ['brəʊkən'daʊn] *adj* agotado; *machine* destartalado, desvencijado.
broken-hearted ['brəʊkən'hɑːtɪd] *adj* traspasado de dolor; **to be ~** tener el corazón partido.
brokenly ['brəʊkənlɪ] *adv say etc* en tono angustiado, con palabras entrecortadas.
broker ['brəʊkəʳ] *n* corredor *m*, bolsista *m*; agente *m* de negocios.
brokerage ['brəʊkərɪdʒ] *n*, **broking** ['brəʊkɪŋ] *n* corretaje *m*.
brolly* ['brɒlɪ] *n* (*Brit*) paraguas *m*.
bromide ['brəʊmaɪd] *n* (**a**) (*Typ*) bromuro *m*. (**b**) (*fig*: *platitude*) perogrullada *f*.
bromine ['brəʊmiːn] *n* bromo *m*.
bronchial ['brɒŋkɪəl] *adj* bronquial; ~ **asthma** asma *f* bronquial; ~ **tubes** bronquios *mpl*.
bronchitic [brɒŋ'kɪtɪk] *adj* bronquítico.
bronchitis [brɒŋ'kaɪtɪs] *n* bronquitis *f*.
bronchopneumonia [ˌbrɒŋkəʊnjuː'məʊnɪə] *n* bronconeumonía *f*.
broncho-pulmonary ['brɒŋkəʊ'pʌlmənərɪ] *adj* broncopulmonar.
bronchus ['brɒŋkəs] *n*, *pl* **bronchi** ['brɒŋkaɪ] bronquio *m*.
bronco ['brɒŋkəʊ] *n* (*US*) potro *m* cerril.
broncobuster* ['brɒŋkəʊˌbʌstəʳ] *n* (*US*) domador *m* de potros cerriles, domador *m* de caballos.
brontosaurus [ˌbrɒntə'sɔːrəs] *n* brontosauro *m*.
Bronx [brɒŋks] *n*: ~ **cheer** (*US**) pedorreta *f*.
bronze [brɒnz] **1** *n* bronce *m*. **2** *adj* de bronce; **B~ Age** Edad *f* de(l) Bronce; ~ **medal** medalla *f* de bronce; ~ **medallist** medallero *m*, -a *f* de bronce. **3** *vt* broncear. **4** *vi* broncearse.
bronzed [brɒnzd] *adj* bronceado.
brooch [brəʊtʃ] *n* alfiler *m* (de pecho), prendedor *m*; (*ancient*) fíbula *f*.
brood [bruːd] **1** *n* camada *f*, cría *f*; (*of chicks*) nidada *f*; (*of insects, first etc*) generación *f*; (*fig*) familia *f*, progenie *f*, (*pej*) prole *f*.
2 *adj*: ~ **mare** yegua *f* de cría.
3 *vi* (*also* **to ~ on**: *eggs*) empollar; (*fig*) meditar tristemente; **to ~ on, to ~ over** meditar tristemente; **you mustn't ~ over it** no debes dejarte obsesionar con eso; **disaster ~ed over the town** se cernía el desastre sobre la ciudad.
brooding ['bruːdɪŋ] *adj evil, presence etc* siniestro, amenazador.
broodings ['bruːdɪŋs] *npl* meditaciones *fpl*.
broody ['bruːdɪ] *adj* clueca; (*fig*) triste, melancólico.
brook[1] [brʊk] *n* arroyo *m*.
brook[2] [brʊk] *vt* (*liter*) aguantar, permitir.
brooklet ['brʊklɪt] *n* arroyuelo *m*.
broom [brʊm] *n* (**a**) escoba *f*, pichana *f* (*And*); **new ~** (*fig*) escoba *f* nueva. (**b**) (*Bot*) hiniesta *f*, retama *f*.
broomstick ['brʊmstɪk] *n* palo *m* de escoba.
Bros *abbr of* **Brothers** Hermanos *mpl*, Hnos.
broth [brɒθ] *n* caldo *m*.
brothel ['brɒθl] *n* prostíbulo *m*, casa *f* de putas, quilombo *m* (*LAm*).
brother ['brʌðəʳ] *n* hermano *m* (*also Eccl*); compañero *m*, camarada *m*; **hey, ~!*** ¡oye, amigo!*; **oh, ~!*** ¡santo cielo!; **X and his ~ teachers** X y sus colegas profesionales; **they're ~s under the skin** debajo de la piel son hermanos.
brotherhood ['brʌðəhʊd] *n* fraternidad *f*; (*religious, group*) hermandad *f*; cofradía *f*.
brother-in-law ['brʌðərɪnlɔː] *n*, *pl* **brothers-in-law** cuñado *m*, hermano *m* político.
brotherly ['brʌðəlɪ] *adj* fraternal.
brought [brɔːt] *pret and ptp of* **bring**.
brow [braʊ] *n* ceja *f*; (*forehead*) frente *f*; (*of hill*) cresta *f*, cumbre *f*, (*of cliff*) borde *m*; **to knit one's ~** fruncir las cejas.
browbeat ['braʊbiːt] *vt* intimidar (con amenazas) (*into doing sth* para que haga algo).
brown [braʊn] **1** *adj* moreno; marrón; *hair* castaño; (*tanned*) moreno, bronceado; **as ~ as a berry** muy moreno, muy bronceado; **to get ~** (*in sun*) ponerse moreno, morenearse, broncearse; ~ **ale** cerveza *f* negra; ~ **bread** pan *m* moreno; ~ **egg** huevo *m* moreno; ~ **paper** papel *m* de embalar, papel *m* de estraza; ~ **rice** arroz *m* integral; ~ **shoes** zapatos *mpl* marrones; ~ **sugar** azúcar *f* negra, azúcar *f* terciada.
2 *n* color *m* moreno (*etc*).
3 *vt* poner moreno *etc*; *skin* broncear; (*Culin*) dorar.
4 *vi* ponerse moreno (*etc*); (*skin*) ponerse moreno, morenearse, broncearse; (*Culin*) dorarse.
◆**brown off**⁑ *vt* (*Brit*): **to ~ sb off** fastidiar a uno; **I'm ~ed off** estoy hasta las narices (*with* de).
brownie ['braʊnɪ] *n* (**a**) (*fairy*) duende *m*; (*person*) *miembro joven de las Girl Guides*; **to earn** (*or* **get, win**) **~ points** apuntarse un tanto a favor, merecerse una notita favorable. (**b**) (*US*: *cookie*) pastelillo *m* de chocolate y nueces.
browning ['braʊnɪŋ] *n* (*Brit Culin*) aditamento *m* colorante.
brownish ['braʊnɪʃ] *adj* pardusco, que tira a moreno.
brownnose⁑ ['braʊnˌnəʊz] (*US*) **1** *n* lameculos* *mf*. **2** *vt* lamer el culo a⁑.
brownstone ['braʊnstəʊn] *n* (*US*) (casa *f* construida con) piedra *f* caliza de color rojizo.
browse [braʊz] **1** *n*: **to have a ~ (around)** curiosear; pasearse para ver cosas.
2 *vt grass* pacer, rozar; *trees* ramonear.
3 *vi* pacer; (*fig*) leer ociosamente; curiosear; **to spend an hour browsing in a bookshop** pasar una hora hojeando los libros en una librería.
◆**browse on** *vt* pacer.
brucellosis [ˌbruːsə'ləʊsɪs] *n* brucelosis *f*.
Bruges [bruːʒ] *n* Brujas *f*.
bruise [bruːz] **1** *n* contusión *f*, cardenal *m*, magulladura *f*, magullón *m*, moretón *m* (*esp LAm*). **2** *vt* contundir, magullar; *fruit* estropear.
bruiser* ['bruːzəʳ] *n* boxeador *m*.
bruising ['bruːzɪŋ] *adj experience* doloroso, penoso; *match* durísimo, violento.
bruit [bruːt] *vt*: **to ~ about** (††, *US*) rumorear.
Brum* [brʌm] *n* (*Brit*) *abbr of* **Birmingham**.
Brummie* ['brʌmɪ] *n* nativo *m*, -a *f* (*or* habitante *mf*) de Birmingham.
brunch* [brʌntʃ] *n* desayuno-almuerzo *m*.
brunette [bruː'net] **1** *adj* moreno. **2** *n* morena *f*.

brunt [brʌnt] *n*: **the ~ of the attack** lo más fuerte del ataque; **the ~ of the work** la mayor parte del trabajo; **to bear the ~ of** aguantar lo más recio de, llevar el peso de.
brush [brʌʃ] **1** *n* **(a)** *(act of brushing)* cepilladura *f*, cepillado *m*; **to give a coat a ~** cepillar un abrigo; **let's give it a ~** vamos a pasar el cepillo.
(b) *(implement)* cepillo *m*; *(large)* escoba *f*; *(shaving ~)* brocha *f*; *(currying ~, scrubbing ~)* bruza *f*; *(artist's)* pincel *m*; *(housepainter's)* brocha *f*; *(Elec)* escobilla *f*.
(c) *(fox's)* rabo *m*, hopo *m*.
(d) *(Bot)* broza *f*; maleza *f*, monte *m* bajo.
(e) *(Mil)* escaramuza *f*; *(fig)* encuentro *m*; **to have a ~ with sb** tener un roce con uno.
2 *vt* cepillar; *shoes etc* limpiar; *(in passing)* rozar al pasar.
◆**brush against** *vt* rozar al pasar.
◆**brush aside** *vt* rechazar, no hacer caso de; quitar importancia a.
◆**brush away** *vt* quitar (con un cepillo, con la mano *etc*).
◆**brush down** *vt* cepillar, limpiar; *horse* almohazar.
◆**brush off** *vt* **(a)** quitar (con un cepillo, con la mano *etc*). **(b) to ~ sb off*** mandar a uno a paseo; deshacerse de uno, zafarse de uno.
◆**brush past 1** *vt* pasar muy cerca de; rozar al pasar.
2 *vi* pasar muy cerca.
brush-off* ['brʌʃɒf] *n*: **to give sb the ~** mandar a uno a paseo*.
brush-stroke ['brʌʃstrəʊk] *n* pincelada *f*.
brush-up ['brʌʃ'ʌp] *n*: **to have a ~** lavarse y peinarse, arreglarse.
brushwood ['brʌʃwʊd] *n* maleza *f*, monte *m* bajo; *(faggots)* broza *f*, leña *f* menuda.
brushwork ['brʌʃwɜːk] *n* pincelada *f*, técnica *f* del pincel; **Turner's ~** la pincelada de Turner, la técnica del pincel de Turner.
brusque [bruːsk] *adj comment, manner etc* brusco, abrupto, áspero; *person* malhumorado; **he was very ~ with me** me trató con poca cortesía.
brusquely ['bruːsklɪ] *adv* bruscamente, abruptamente, ásperamente.
brusqueness ['bruːsknɪs] *n* brusquedad *f*, aspereza *f*; mal humor *m*; falta *f* de cortesía.
Brussels ['brʌslz] *n* Bruselas *f*; **~ sprouts** coles *fpl* de Bruselas.
brutal ['bruːtl] *adj* brutal.
brutality [bruː'tælɪtɪ] *n* brutalidad *f*.
brutalize ['bruːtəlaɪz] *vt* brutalizar.
brutally ['bruːtəlɪ] *adv* de manera brutal.
brute [bruːt] **1** *adj* brutal; *(unthinking)* bruto; **by ~ force** a fuerza bruta.
2 *n* bruto *m*; *(person)* bestia *f*, hombre *m* bestial; **you ~!** ¡bestia!; **it's a ~ of a problem** es un problema de los más feos.
brutish ['bruːtɪʃ] *adj* bruto.
Brutus ['bruːtəs] *nm* Bruto.
BS *n* **(a)** *(Brit) abbr of* **British Standard(s)**. **(b)** *(US) abbr of* **Bachelor of Science.**
bs (a) *(Comm) abbr of* **bill of sale**. **(b)** *(Comm, Fin) abbr of* **balance sheet.**
BSA *n (US) abbr of* **Boy Scouts of America.**
BSB *n abbr of* **British Sky Broadcasting.**
BSC *n abbr of* **Broadcasting Standards Council.**
B.Sc. *n abbr of* **Bachelor of Science.**
BSE *n abbr of* **bovine spongiform encephalopathy** encefalopatía *f* espongiforme bovina.
BSI *n (Brit) abbr of* **British Standards Institution.**
BST *n (Brit) abbr of* **British Summer Time.**
Bt *abbr of* **Baronet** baronet *m*.
BTA *n abbr of* **British Tourist Authority.**
bt fwd *abbr of* **brought forward** suma *f* del anterior.
BTU *n abbr of* **British Thermal Unit** Unidad *f* térmica británica.
bubble ['bʌbl] **1** *n* burbuja *f*, ampolla *f*; *(under paint etc)* ampolla *f*; *(in cartoon)* bocadillo *m*, globo *m*; **to blow ~s** hacer pompas; **the ~ burst** se deshizo la burbuja.
2 *vi* burbujear, borbotar.
◆**bubble over** *vi* desbordarse; **to ~ over with** rebosar de.
◆**bubble up** *vi (liquid)* burbujear, borbotear; *(excitement etc)* rebosar.
bubble and squeak [,bʌblənd'skwiːk] *n (Brit) carne picada frita con patatas y col.*
bubble-bath ['bʌbl,bɑːθ] *n, pl* **bubble-baths** ['bʌbl,bɑːðz] baño *m* de espuma, baño *m* de burbujas.
bubble-car ['bʌblkɑːʳ] *n* coche-cabina *m*, huevo *m*.
bubble-gum ['bʌblgʌm] *n* chicle *m* de globo, chicle *m* de burbuja.
bubble-memory ['bʌbl,memərɪ] *n* memoria *f* de burbuja.
bubble-pack ['bʌbl,pæk] *n*, **bubble-package** ['bʌbl,pækɪdʒ] *n* envasado *m* en lámina.
bubble-store ['bʌbl,stɔːʳ] *n* memoria *f* de burbuja.
bubbly ['bʌblɪ] **1** *adj* burbujeante, gaseoso. **2** *n* (*) champaña *m*.
bubonic [bjuː'bɒnɪk] *adj*: **~ plague** *n* peste *f* bubónica.
buccaneer [,bʌkə'nɪəʳ] **1** *n* bucanero *m*. **2** *vi* piratear.
Bucharest [,buːkə'rest] *n* Bucarest *m*.
buck [bʌk] **1** *adj (male)* macho; **~ nigger** *(Hist)* negrazo *m*; **~ private** *(US)* soldado *m* raso; **~ rabbit** conejo *m* (macho); **~ sergeant** *(US)* sargento *m* chusquero.
2 *n* **(a)** *(male)* macho *m*; *(deer)* gamo *m*; *(goat)* macho *m* cabrío; *(rabbit)* conejo *m* macho.
(b) (††) galán *m*, dandy *m*.
(c) *(US*)* dólar *m*; **to make a fast** (*or* **quick**) **~** hacer pasta rápidamente*.
(d) (*) **to pass the ~** echar a uno el muerto, escurrir el bulto; **the ~ stops here** yo soy el responsable.
3 *vt (esp US) rider* desarzonar; *system* vencer, desbaratar; **to ~ the market** *(Fin)* ir en contra del mercado; **to ~ the system** *(US)* oponerse al sistema; **to ~ the trend** ir en contra de la tendencia.
4 *vi* **(a)** *(horse)* corcovear, ponerse de manos.
(b) to ~ for sth *(US*)* buscar algo.
◆**buck up* 1** *vt* **(a)** *(hurry)* dar prisa a. **(b)** *(cheer)* animar, dar ánimos a; *V* **idea.**
2 *vi* **(a)** *(hurry)* darse prisa; **~ up!** ¡date prisa!; ¡espabílate!
(b) *(cheer up)* animarse, cobrar ánimos; **~ up!** ¡ánimo!; **we were very ~ed up** nos alegramos mucho.
bucket ['bʌkɪt] **1** *n* cubo *m*, balde *m*; *(child's)* cubito *m*; *(of waterwheel etc)* cangilón *m*; **to kick the ~‡** estirar la pata; **to rain ~s*** llover a cántaros; **to weep ~s*** llorar a mares.
2 *vi*: **it was ~ing down** llovía a cántaros.
bucketful ['bʌkɪtfʊl] *n* cubo *m* (lleno), balde *m* (lleno); **by the ~** a cubos, *(fig)* a montones, en grandes cantidades.
bucket-shop ['bʌkɪt,ʃɒp] *n* agencia *f* de viajes que vende barato.
buckle ['bʌkl] **1** *n* hebilla *f*.
2 *vt* **(a)** abrochar con hebilla.
(b) *(deform)* torcer, combar, encorvar.
3 *vi* torcerse, combarse, doblarse.
◆**buckle down to** *vt* dedicarse con empeño a, emprender en serio.
◆**buckle in** *vt*: **to ~ a baby in** abrochar el cinturón de un niño; **I was ~d in my seat** estaba en mi asiento con el cinturón abrochado.
◆**buckle on** *vt armour, sword* ceñirse.
◆**buckle to*** *vi* empezar a trabajar.
◆**buckle up** *vi (US)* ponerse el cinturón de seguridad.
buckra ['bʌkrə] *n (US pej)* blanco *m*.
buckram ['bʌkrəm] *n* bucarán *m*.
Bucks [bʌks] *n abbr of* **Buckinghamshire.**
bucksaw ['bʌksɔː] *n* sierra *f* de arco.
buckshee [bʌk'ʃiː] *(Brit‡)* **1** *adj* gratuito. **2** *adv* gratis.
buckshot ['bʌkʃɒt] *n* perdigón *m* zorrero, posta *f*.
buckskin ['bʌkskɪn] *n* cuero *m* de ante.
buckthorn ['bʌkθɔːn] *n* espino *m* cerval.
buck-tooth ['bʌk'tuːθ] *n* diente *m* saliente.
buck-toothed ['bʌk'tuːθt] *adj* de dientes salientes, dentón, dentudo.
buckwheat ['bʌkwiːt] *n* alforfón *m*, trigo *m* sarraceno.
bucolic [bjuː'kɒlɪk] **1** *adj* bucólico. **2** *n*: **the B~s** las Bucólicas.
bud¹ [bʌd] **1** *n* brote *m*, yema *f*, *(containing flower)* capullo *m*; **in ~** en brote; **to nip in the ~** cortar de raíz, salir al paso a.
2 *vt* injertar de escudete.
3 *vi* brotar, echar brotes.
bud² [bʌd] *n (US*)* = **buddy.**
Budapest [,bjuːdə'pest] *n* Budapest *m*.
Buddha ['bʊdə] *nm* Buda.
Buddhism ['bʊdɪzəm] *n* budismo *m*.
Buddhist ['bʊdɪst] **1** *adj* budista. **2** *n* budista *mf*.
budding ['bʌdɪŋ] *adj (fig)* en ciernes, en embrión.
buddleia ['bʌdlɪə] *n* budleia *f*.
buddy ['bʌdɪ] *n (esp US)* compañero *m*, amigote *m*, compadre *m (esp LAm)*, compinche *m*; *(in direct address)* chico, hijo; **they use the ~ system*** emplean el amiguismo, se ayudan mutuamente.
budge [bʌdʒ] **1** *vt* mover, hacer que se mueva; **I couldn't ~**

him an inch no pude hacerle cambiar de opinión en lo más mínimo.

2 *vi* moverse; bullir; menearse; **he didn't dare to ~** no osaba bullir; **he won't ~ an inch** no nos ofrece la más pequeña concesión.

◆**budge up** *vi* moverse un poco (para dejar espacio), correrse un poco a un lado (*etc*).

budgerigar [ˈbʌdʒərɪɡɑːʳ] *n* periquito *m* (australiano).

budget [ˈbʌdʒɪt] **1** *n* presupuesto *m*. **2** *attr* presupuestario; **~ account** cuenta *f* presupuestaria; **~ day** día *m* de la presentación del presupuesto; **~ plan** plan *m* presupuestario; **~ speech** discurso *m* en el que se presenta el presupuesto.

◆**budget for** *vt* presupuestar; (*fig*) tener en cuenta, contar con.

budgetary [ˈbʌdʒɪtrɪ] *adj* presupuestario; **~ control** control *m* presupuestario; **~ deficit** déficit *m* presupuestario; **~ policy** política *f* presupuestaria; **~ year** año *m* presupuestario.

budgeted [ˈbʌdʒɪtɪd] *adj*: **~ costs** costos *mpl* presupuestados.

budgeting [ˈbʌdʒɪtɪŋ] *n* elaboración *f* de un presupuesto, presupuesto *m*; **with careful ~** con buena administración.

budgie* [ˈbʌdʒɪ] *n* = **budgerigar.**

Buenos Aires [ˌbwenəsˈaɪərɪz] *n* Buenos Aires *m sing*.

buff[1] [bʌf] **1** *adj* color de ante. **2** *n* piel *f* de ante; **in the ~*** en cueros. **3** *vt* pulir, pulimentar.

buff[2]* [bʌf] *n* aficionado *m*, -a *f*; entusiasta *mf*; **film ~** cinéfilo *m*, -a *f*.

buffalo [ˈbʌfələʊ] *n*, *pl* **buffaloes** búfalo *m*; (*esp US*) bisonte *m*.

buffer[1] [ˈbʌfəʳ] *n* amortiguador *m* (de choques); (*Rail*: *on carriage*) tope *m*, (*fixed*) parachoques *m*; (*US Aut*) parachoques *m*; (*Comput*) memoria *f* intermedia, buffer *m*; **~ state** estado *m* tapón; **~ zone** espacio *m* amortiguador; **the plan suddenly hit the ~s** de pronto el plan chocó con los topes.

buffer[2] [ˈbʌfəʳ] *n*: **old ~** (*Brit*) mastuerzo *m*, carca* *m*.

buffering [ˈbʌfərɪŋ] *n* (*Comput*) almacenamiento *m* en memoria intermedia.

buffet[1] [ˈbʌfɪt] **1** *n* bofetada *f*; (*of sea, wind etc*) golpe *m*. **2** *vt* abofetear; (*of sea, wind etc*) golpear, llevar de aquí para allá, combatir.

buffet[2] [ˈbʊfeɪ] *n* aparador *m*; (*Rail*) cantina *f*, cafetería *f*; **~ lunch** buffet *m* libre, bufé *m* libre; **~ meal** comida *f* buffet, comida *f* fría; **~ supper** cena *f* fría.

buffet-car [ˈbʊfeɪkɑːʳ] *n* (*Brit*) coche-comedor *m*.

buffeting [ˈbʌfɪtɪŋ] *n* (*of sea etc*) el golpear; **to get a ~ from** sufrir los golpes de.

buffoon [bəˈfuːn] *n* bufón *m*, chocarrero *m*, payaso *m*.

buffoonery [bəˈfuːnərɪ] *n* bufonadas *fpl*.

bug [bʌɡ] **1** *n* (**a**) (*Ent*) chinche *f* (*also m*); (*any insect*) bicho *m*, sabandija *f*; **big ~*** señorón* *m*, pez *m* gordo.

(**b**) (*Med**) microbio *m*, bacilo *m*; **flu ~** virus *m* de la gripe; **to get the travel ~** entusiasmarse por los viajes, coger la manía de viajar; **he's got the painting ~** le ha dado por la pintura.

(**c**) (*: *defect, snag*: *esp US*) estorbo *m*, traba *f*, pega *f*; problema *m*; (*Comput*) duende *m**, fallo *m*, error *m*.

(**d**) (*: *Telec*) micrófono *m* oculto, aparato *m* auditivo escondido; (*Tech*) indicador *m* de posición.

2 *vt* (**a**) (*: *annoy*: *esp US*) molestar, fastidiar*; **what's ~ging you?*** ¿qué mosca te ha picado?

(**b**) (*: *Telec*) *phone* intervenir, pinchar*; *room* poner un micrófono oculto en; *person* escuchar clandestinamente a, pinchar el teléfono de*; **this phone is ~ged** este teléfono está pinchado*; **do you think this room is ~ged?** ¿crees que en esta habitación hay un micro oculto?*

◆**bug out**‡ *vi* (*US*) largarse.

bugaboo [ˈbʌɡəbuː] *n* (*US*) espantajo *m*, coco *m*.

bugbear [ˈbʌɡbɛəʳ] *n* pesadilla *f*, obsesión *f*.

bug-eyed* [ˌbʌɡˈaɪd] *adj*: **to be ~** mirar con los ojos saltones.

bug-free* [ˈbʌɡˈfriː] *adj* (*Comput*) sin errores, libre de duendes*.

bugger [ˈbʌɡəʳ] **1** *n* (**a**) (*Jur*) sodomita *m*.

(**b**) (**) mierda *m***, coño** *m*; **that silly ~** ese mierda**; **some poor ~** algún pobre hombre; **I don't give a ~!** ¡me importa un rábano!

2 *excl*: **~ (it)!**** ¡mierda!**

3 *vt* (**a**) (*Jur*) cometer sodomía con. (**b**) (**well**) **I'll be ~ed!** ¡coño!**; **lawyers be ~ed!** ¡que se jodan los abogados!**; **I'll be ~ed if I will** que me cuelguen si lo hago.

◆**bugger about, bugger around** (*Brit***) **1** *vt*: **to ~ sb about** fastidiar a uno.

2 *vi* perder el tiempo, no hacer nada; ocuparse en tonterías.

◆**bugger off** *vi* (*Brit***) largarse*; **~ off!** ¡vete a hacer puñetas!‡

◆**bugger up**** *vt*: **to ~ sth up** joder algo**.

bugger-all** [ˈbʌɡəˌɔːl] = **damn-all.**

buggery [ˈbʌɡərɪ] *n* sodomía *f*.

bugging* [ˈbʌɡɪŋ] *n* (*Telec*) intervención *f*; **~ device** micrófono *m* oculto.

buggy [ˈbʌɡɪ] *n* calesa *f*; (*US*) cochecillo *m* (de niño); (**baby**) **~** (*Brit*) cochecito *m* de niño; (*Golf*) cochecito *m*.

bughouse‡ [ˈbʌɡhaʊs] *n*, *pl* **bughouses** [ˈbʌɡˌhaʊzɪz] (*US*) casa *f* de locos, manicomio *m*.

bug-hunter* [ˈbʌɡhʌntəʳ] *n* entomólogo *m*, -a *f*.

bugle [ˈbjuːɡl] *n* corneta *f*, clarín *m*.

bugler [ˈbjuːɡləʳ] *n* corneta *m*.

bug-ridden [ˈbʌɡˌrɪdn] *adj*: **this house is ~** esta casa está llena de bichos; **this program is ~** este programa está lleno de errores.

build [bɪld] **1** *n* talle *m*, tipo *m*; **of powerful ~** fornido.

2 (*irr*: *pret and ptp* **built**) *vt* construir, edificar, hacer (*in*, *of* de); *ship* construir; *fire* preparar; *nest* hacer.

◆**build in** *vt cupboard etc* empotrar; (*Mech*) incorporar.

◆**build on 1** *vt* (*add*) añadir; **to ~ a garage on to a house** añadir un garaje a una casa; **the garage is built on to the house** la casa tiene un garaje anexo.

2 *vi* (*construct*) edificar sobre; **to ~ on a site** construir casas (*etc*) en un solar; **now we have a base to ~ on** ahora tenemos base en la que podemos construir.

◆**build up 1** *vt* (*Mech etc*) montar, armar; (*Med*) fortalecer; *company* fomentar, desarrollar; *sales*, *numbers* acrecentar; *reputation* crear para sí; *impression* crear; *stocks* acumular, formar; **the area was built up years ago** la zona fue urbanizada hace años. **2** *vi* desarrollarse; (*pressure*) aumentar; (*excitement*) crecer; (*picture*) perfilarse, formarse.

builder [ˈbɪldəʳ] *n* constructor *m* (*also fig*); (*contracting firm*) contratista *m*; aparejador *m*.

building [ˈbɪldɪŋ] *n* (**a**) edificio *m*; (*at exhibition*) pabellón *m*; **the Ruritanian B~** el pabellón de Ruritania.

(**b**) (*act*) construcción *f*; **~ block** (*toy*) bloque *m* de construcción; (*fig*) elemento *m* esencial, componente *m* básico; **~ contractor** contratista *m*; **~ industry** industria *f* de la construcción; **~ land** tierra *f* para construcción, terrenos *mpl* edificables; **~ lot, ~ plot** solar *m* (para construcción); **~ materials** material *m* de construcción; **~ permit** permiso *m* de obras; **~ site** solar *m* (para construcción), obra *f* (*LAm*); **~ society** (*Brit*) sociedad *f* de préstamo inmobiliario; **the ~ trade** (la industria de) la construcción; **~ worker** obrero *m* (*or* trabajador *m*) de la construcción; **~ works** obras *fpl* de construcción.

build-up [ˈbɪldʌp] *n* (**a**) (*of pressure*) aumento *m*; (*of gas*) acumulación *f*, concentración *f*; (*of forces*) concentración *f*.
(**b**) (*fig*) propaganda *f* previa; bombo *m*.

built [bɪlt] *pret and ptp of* **build.**

-built *adj ending in compounds*: **American~** de construcción americana; **brick~** construido de ladrillos.

built-in [ˈbɪltˈɪn] *adj* (*Archit*) empotrado; (*Mech*, *Rad etc*) interior, incorporado; **~ obsolescence** caducidad *f* programada, caducidad *f* calculada.

built-up [ˈbɪltˈʌp] *adj*: **~ area** zona *f* edificada.

bulb [bʌlb] *n* (*Bot*) bulbo *m*, camote *m* (*Mex*); (*Elec*) bombilla *f*, foco *m* (*LAm*), bombillo *m* (*And*), bujía *f* (*CAm*); (*of thermometer*) ampolleta *f*.

bulbous [ˈbʌlbəs] *adj* bulboso.

Bulgaria [bʌlˈɡɛərɪə] *n* Bulgaria *f*.

Bulgarian [bʌlˈɡɛərɪən] **1** *adj* búlgaro. **2** *n* (**a**) búlgaro *m*, -a *f*. (**b**) (*Ling*) búlgaro *m*.

bulge [bʌldʒ] **1** *n* bombeo *m*, pandeo *m*; protuberancia *f*; (*in statistics*) protuberancia *f*; **the ~ in the birth rate** el aumento (súbito y transitorio) de la natalidad.

2 *vi* bombearse, pandearse; sobresalir; (*pocket etc*) hacer bulto; **his pockets ~d with apples** sus bolsillos estaban atestados de manzanas; **their eyes ~d at the sight** se les saltaron los ojos al verlo.

bulging [ˈbʌldʒɪŋ] *adj*: **~ eyes** ojos *mpl* saltones; **~ pocket** bolsillo *m* muy lleno; **~ suitcase** maleta *f* que está para reventar.

bulimia [bjuːˈlɪmɪə] *n* bulimia *f*.

bulk [bʌlk] **1** *n* (**a**) bulto *m*, volumen *m*; masa *f*, mole *f*; **the enormous ~ of the ship** la enorme mole del buque; **he set his full ~ down in a chair** dejó caer todo el peso de su cuerpo en un sillón.

(**b**) (*Comm*) **in ~** a granel; (*unpackaged*) suelto; **to buy**

in ~ comprar en grandes cantidades.
(c) (*main part*) **the ~ of** la mayor parte de; **the ~ of those present** la mayor parte de los presentes; **the ~ of the army** el grueso del ejército.
2 *adj*: ~ **goods** mercancías *fpl* a granel; ~ **purchase** compra *f* de cantidad grande.
3 *vi*: **to ~ large** tener un puesto importante, ocupar un lugar importante.
bulk-buying ['bʌlk'baɪɪŋ] *n* compra *f* en grandes cantidades.
bulk carrier ['bʌlk,kærɪəʳ] *n* (buque *m*) granelero *m*.
bulkhead ['bʌlkhed] *n* (*Brit*) mamparo *m*.
bulkiness ['bʌlkɪnɪs] *n* volumen *m*, lo abultado.
bulky ['bʌlkɪ] *adj* voluminoso, abultado, grueso; *goods* de gran bulto.
bull[1] [bʊl] **1** *n* (**a**) (*Zool*) toro *m*; (*of elephant, whale*) macho *m*; **to be like a ~ in a china shop** comportarse como un elefante en una tienda de porcelana; **to take the ~ by the horns** coger (*LAm*: agarrar) el toro por los cuernos.
(**b**) (*Fin*) alcista *m*.
(**c**) (*Mil*‡) trabajos *mpl* rutinarios.
(**d**) (‡: *nonsense*) tonterías *fpl*; **to shoot the ~** decir chorradas*.
2 *adj* (**a**) (*Zool*) macho.
(**b**) (*Fin*) *market* alcista.
3 *vt* (*Fin*): **to ~ the market** hacer subir el mercado comprando acciones especulativamente.
bull[2] [bʊl] *n* (*Eccl*) bula *f*.
bull-calf ['bʊl,kɑːf] *n, pl* **bull-calves** ['bʊl,kɑːvz] becerro *m*.
bulldog ['bʊldɒg] *n* bul(l)dog *m*, (perro *m*) dogo *m*; **the ~ breed** los ingleses (*bajo su aspecto heroico y porfiado*); **~ clip** (*Brit*) pinza *f*.
bulldoze ['bʊldəʊz] *vt site* nivelar (con motoniveladora); *building* arrasar (con motoniveladora); *opposition* arrollar.
bulldozer ['bʊldəʊzəʳ] *n* motoniveladora *f*, aplanadora *f*, bulldozer *m*.
bullet ['bʊlɪt] *n* bala *f*; **to bite (on) the ~** resolverse, tomar una decisión heroica; **to go by like a ~** pasar como un rayo.
bullet-hole ['bʊlɪt,həʊl] *n* agujero *m* de bala.
bulletin ['bʊlɪtɪn] *n* anuncio *m*, parte *m*; (*journal*) boletín *m*.
bulletin board ['bʊlɪtɪnbɔːd] *n* (*US*) tablón *m* de anuncios; (*Comput*) tablero *m* de noticias.
bulletproof ['bʊlɪtpruːf] *adj* a prueba de balas; **~ glass** vidrio *m* antibalas.
bullet train ['bʊlɪt,treɪn] *n* tren *m* de gran velocidad (*japonés*).
bullet-wound ['bʊlɪtwuːnd] *n* balazo *m*.
bullfight ['bʊlfaɪt] *n* corrida *f* (de toros).
bullfighter ['bʊlfaɪtəʳ] *n* torero *m*, matador *m* de toros.
bullfighting ['bʊlfaɪtɪŋ] *n* toreo *m*; arte *m* de torear, tauromaquia *f*; **do you like ~?** ¿le gustan los toros?
bullfinch ['bʊlfɪntʃ] *n* camachuelo *m*.
bullfrog ['bʊlfrɒg] *n* rana *f* toro.
bullhorn ['bʊlhɔːn] *n* (*US*) megáfono *m*.
bullion ['bʊljən] *n* oro *m* en barras, plata *f* en barras.
bullish ['bʊlɪʃ] *adj* optimista; (*Fin*) (de tendencia) alcista.
bull-neck [,bʊl'nek] *n* cuello *m* de toro.
bull-necked ['bʊl'nekt] *adj* de cuello de toro.
bullock ['bʊlək] *n* toro *m* castrado, novillo *m* castrado.
bullring ['bʊlrɪŋ] *n* plaza *f* de toros.
bull's-eye ['bʊlzaɪ] *n* (*of target*) centro *m* del blanco, diana *f*; (*lantern*) linterna *f* sorda; (*Naut*) ojo *m* de buey; (*sweet*) *tipo de dulce*; **to score a ~** dar en el blanco, (*fig*) acertar.
bullshit‡* ['bʊlʃɪt] *n* = **bull 1 (c), (d)**.
bull terrier [,bʊl'terɪəʳ] *n* bulterrier *m*.
bully[1] ['bʊlɪ] **1** *n* (**a**) matón *m*, valentón *m*. (**b**) (*Brit Hockey*: *also* **~-off**) saque *m*. **2** *vt* intimidar, tiranizar; **to ~ sb into** + *ger* forzar a uno con amenazas a + *infin*.
◆**bully off** *vi* (*Brit Hockey*) sacar.
bully[2]* ['bʊlɪ] **1** *adj* de primera. **2** *interj*: **~ for you!** ¡bravo!
bully-beef ['bʊlɪ'biːf] *n* carne *f* de vaca conservada en lata.
bully-boy ['bʊlɪ,bɔɪ] *n* matón *m*, esbirro *m*; **~ tactics** táctica *f* de matón.
bullying ['bʊlɪɪŋ] **1** *adj person* abusón, matón, valentón; *attitude* amenazador; tiránico; propio de matón. **2** *n* intimidación *f*, abuso *m*.
bulrush ['bʊlrʌʃ] *n* (*rush*) junco *m*; (*reedmace*) anea *f*, espadaña *f*.
bulwark ['bʊlwək] *n* (*Mil and fig*) baluarte *m*; (*Naut*) macarrón *m*.
bum[1]‡ [bʌm] *n* (*Brit Anat*) culo *m*.
bum[2] [bʌm] (*US*) **1** *n* (*idler*) holgazán *m*; (*tramp*) vagabundo *m*; (*scrounger*) gorrón *m*; (*as term of general disapproval*) vago *m*; **you poor ~!** ¡tío tonto!; **to give sb the ~'s rush**‡ expulsar violentamente a uno; **to go** (*or* **live**) **on the ~** vivir de gorra, vagabundear.
2 *adj* (*US*) falso; **~ deal** negocio *m* turbio; **~ rap*** acusación *f* falsa; **~ steer*** bulo *m*, noticia *f* falsa.
3 *vt* (‡) mendigar, gorronear; **he ~med a cigarette off me** me gorroneó un pitillo.
4 *vi* (*also* **to ~ around**) holgazanear, vagabundear.
bumbag ['bʌmbæg] *n* (*Ski*) riñonera *f*.
bumble ['bʌmbl] *vi* (*walk unsteadily*) andar de forma vacilante, andar a tropezones; (*fig*) trastabillar.
bumblebee ['bʌmblbiː] *n* abejorro *m*.
bumbling ['bʌmblɪŋ] **1** *adj* (*inept*) inepto, inútil; (*muttering*) que habla a tropezones, que se atropella al hablar. **2** *n* divagación *f*.
bumf‡ [bʌmf] *n* (*Brit*) (**a**) papel *m* higiénico. (**b**) (*fig*) papeles *mpl*, papeleo *m*.
bummer‡ ['bʌməʳ] *n* (*esp US*) (*nuisance*) lata* *f*; (*bore*) rollo* *m*; (*disaster*) desastre *m*; **what a ~!** ¡qué desastre!, ¡qué horror!
bump [bʌmp] **1** *n* (**a**) (*blow*) golpe *m*, topetazo *m*; choque *m*; (*jolt of vehicle*) sacudida *f*; (*Aer*) rebote *m*; (*in falling*) batacazo *m*; **things that go ~ in the night** cosas que hacen ruidos misteriosos en la noche.
(**b**) (*swelling*) bollo *m*, abolladura *f*, protuberancia *f*; (*on skin*) chichón *m*, hinchazón *f*; (*on road*) bache *m*; **to have a ~ for** tener el don de, tener un sentido especial de.
2 *vt* chocar contra, topetar; **to ~ one's head** darse un golpe en la cabeza; **to ~ one's head on a door** dar con su cabeza contra una puerta.
3 *vi* (*vehicle*) dar sacudidas.
◆**bump against** *vt* chocar contra, topetar, dar contra.
◆**bump along** *vi* avanzar dando sacudidas.
◆**bump into** *vt* chocar contra, tropezar con; *person* topar; **fancy ~ing into you!** ¡qué casualidad encontrarle a Vd!
◆**bump off**‡ *vt* cargarse a*.
◆**bump up** *vt price* subir, aumentar.
◆**bump up against** *vt* tropezar con.
bumper ['bʌmpəʳ] **1** *n* (**a**) (*Aut*) parachoques *m*; **~ car** auto *m* de choque; **~ sticker** pegatina *f* de parachoques; **traffic is ~ to ~ as far as the airport** hay una caravana hasta el aeropuerto. (**b**) (*glass*) copa *f* llena. **2** *adj*: **~ crop** cosecha *f* abundante, cosechón *m*.
bumph‡ [bʌmf] *n* = **bumf**.
bumpkin ['bʌmpkɪn] *n* (*gen* **country ~**) patán *m*.
bump-start ['bʌmpstɑːt] **1** *n*: **to give a car a ~** empujar un coche para que arranque. **2** *vt* **V 1**.
bumptious ['bʌmpʃəs] *adj* engreído, presuntuoso.
bumpy ['bʌmpɪ] *adj surface* desigual; *road* accidentado, lleno de baches; *air* agitado; *journey* de muchas sacudidas.
bun [bʌn] *n* (**a**) (*bread*) bollo *m*; (*Brit*: *cake*) pastel *m*; **to have a ~ in the oven*** estar en estado. (**b**) (*hair*) rodete *m*, moño *m*.
bunch [bʌntʃ] **1** *n* manojo *m*, puñado *m*; (*of flowers*) ramo *m*, ramillete *m*; (*of grapes*) racimo *m*, (*of bananas*) racimo *m*, cacho *m*; (*of keys*) manojo *m*; (*set of people*) grupo *m*, (*pej*) pandilla *f*; **a ~ of times** (*US*) varias veces, muchas veces; **the best of a bad ~** el menos malo de una serie de malos; **they're an odd ~** son gente rara; **they're a ~ of traitors** son unos traidores; **to wear one's hair in ~es** (*Brit*) llevar coletas.
2 *vt* agrupar, juntar; **to be ~ed together** estar muy juntos unos a otros.
◆**bunch up 1** *vt* (**a**) *dress, skirt* arremangar. (**b**) **they sat ~ed up on the bench** se apretujaban en el banco. **2** *vi* apretujarse; ponerse más cerca unos de otros.
bundle ['bʌndl] **1** *n* (**a**) lío *m*, bulto *m*, fardo *m*; (*of sticks*) haz *f*; (*of papers*) legajo *m*; **he's a ~ of nerves** es un manojo de nervios, está hipertenso. (**b**) **to go a ~ on**‡ entusiasmarse mucho por; **to make a ~*** ganarse un pastón‡.
2 *vt*: **~ it all into the case** póngalo todo en la maleta no importa cómo.
◆**bundle off** *vt person* despachar; **he was ~d off to Australia** le despacharon para Australia.
◆**bundle out** *vt*: **to ~ sb out** botar a uno; **they ~d him out into the street** le pusieron de patitas en la calle.
◆**bundle up** *vt* liar, atar, envolver.
bun-fight* ['bʌn,faɪt] *n* té *m* (*servido para mucha gente*); merienda *f*.
bung [bʌŋ] **1** *n* tapón *m*.
2 *vt* (**a**) tapar con bitoque; (*gen*) cerrar, tapar; **to be ~ed up** estar obturado, estar obstruido; (*eye*) estar hinchado.

(**b**) (*Brit**) (*throw*) tirar, lanzar; ~ **it over** tíralo para acá.

(**c**) (***: *put*) poner, meter.

◆**bung in*** *vt* (*include*) añadir.

◆**bung out*** *vt* tirar, botar.

bungalow [ˈbʌŋgələʊ] *n* casa *f* de un solo piso, chalet *m*, bungalow *m*.

bunghole [ˈbʌŋhəʊl] *n* piquera *f*, boca *f* (de tonel).

bungle [ˈbʌŋgl] **1** *n* chapuza *f*. **2** *vt work* chapucear, hacer con los pies; **to** ~ **it** hacerlo malísimamente; desperdiciar la ocasión.

bungled [ˈbʌŋgld] *adj*: **a** ~ **job** una chapuza; **a** ~ **operation** una operación mal ejecutada.

bungler [ˈbʌŋgləʳ] *n* chapucero *m*.

bungling [ˈbʌŋglɪŋ] *adj* torpe, desmañado.

bunion [ˈbʌnjən] *n* juanete *m*.

bunk[1] [bʌŋk] *n* (*Naut*) litera *f*, camastro *m*; (*Rail*, *child's*) litera *f*; (*) cama *f*.

bunk[2]‡ [bʌŋk] **1** *n*: **to do a** ~ (*Brit*) = **2**. **2** *vi* huir, poner pies en polvorosa.

bunk[3]* [bʌŋk] *n* tonterías *fpl*, música *f* celestial; ~! ¡tonterías!; **history is** ~ la historia es un absurdo.

bunk-bed [ˈbʌŋkˈbed] *n* litera *f*.

bunker [ˈbʌŋkəʳ] **1** *n* (**a**) (*for coal*) carbonera *f*; (*Naut*) pañol *m* del carbón. (**b**) (*Mil*) refugio *m*, búnker *m*. (**c**) (*Golf*) búnker *m*, arena *f*.

2 *vt* (**a**) (*Naut*) proveer de carbón. (**b**) **to be ~ed** (*fig*) estar en un atolladero.

bunkhouse [ˈbʌŋkˌhaʊs] *n*, *pl* **bunkhouses** [ˈbʌŋkˌhaʊzɪz] (*US*) casa *f* de dormitorios (para trabajadores de hacienda).

bunkum* [ˈbʌŋkəm] *n* = **bunk**[3].

bunk-up* [ˌbʌŋkˈʌp] *n*: **to give sb a** ~ ayudar a uno a subir.

bunny [ˈbʌnɪ] *n* (**a**) conejito *m*. (**b**) (*girl*) tía *f* buena; ~ **girl** conejita *f*.

Bunsen [ˈbʌnsn] *n*: ~ **burner** mechero *m* Bunsen.

bunting[1] [ˈbʌntɪŋ] *n* (*Orn*) escribano *m*.

bunting[2] [ˈbʌntɪŋ] *n* (*decoration*) banderas *fpl*, empavesado *m*; (*cloth*) lanilla *f*.

buoy [bɔɪ, *US* buːɪ] **1** *n* boya *f*. **2** *vt channel* aboyar, señalar con boyas.

◆**buoy up** *vt person* mantener a flote; (*fig*) animar, alentar.

buoyancy [ˈbɔɪənsɪ] *n* lo boyante, capacidad *f* para flotar; (*Aer*) fuerza *f* ascensional; (*fig*) confianza *f*, optimismo *m*.

buoyant [ˈbɔɪənt] *adj* boyante, capaz de flotar; (*fig*) ilusionado, optimista; (*Comm*) con tendencia al alza.

buoyantly [ˈbɔɪəntlɪ] *adv* de modo boyante; (*fig*) de modo ilusionado, con optimismo.

BUPA [ˈbuːpə] *n abbr of* **British United Provident Association** *seguro médico privado*.

bur(r) [bɜːʳ] *n* erizo *m*.

burble [ˈbɜːbl] *vi* (*bubble*) burbujear, hervir; (*talk*) parlotear.

burbot [ˈbɜːbət] *n* lota *f*.

burden [ˈbɜːdn] **1** *n* (**a**) carga *f*; (*weight*) peso *m*.

(**b**) (*Naut*) arqueo *m*.

(**c**) (*fig*) carga *f*; fardo *m*; ~ **of proof** peso *m* de la prueba; **to be a** ~ **to sb** ser una responsabilidad molesta para uno; **he carries a heavy** ~ tiene que cargar con una gran responsabilidad; **to make sb's life a** ~ amargar la vida a uno.

(**d**) (*of speech etc*) tema *m* principal; (*of song*) estribillo *m*.

2 *vt* cargar (*with* de); **to be ~ed with** tener que cargar con; **don't** ~ **me with your troubles** no me vengas a mí con tus problemas.

burdensome [ˈbɜːdnsəm] *adj* gravoso, oneroso.

burdock [ˈbɜːdɒk] *n* (*Bot*) bardana *f*.

bureau [bjʊəˈrəʊ] *n*, *pl* **bureaux** [bjʊˈrəʊz] (**a**) (*esp Brit*: *desk*) escritorio *m*, buró *m*. (**b**) (*US*: *chest of drawers*) cómoda *f*. (**c**) (*office*) oficina *f*, agencia *f*, departamento *m*; (*of congress*) oficina *f*, mesa *f*; ~ **de change** caja *f* de cambio; ~ **of standards** (*US*) oficina *f* de pesos y medidas. (**d**) **Federal B**~ (*US*) Departamento *m* de Estado.

bureaucracy [bjʊəˈrɒkrəsɪ] *n* burocracia *f*.

bureaucrat [ˈbjʊərəʊkræt] *n* burócrata *mf*.

bureaucratic [ˌbjʊərəʊˈkrætɪk] *adj* burocrático.

burg [bɜːg] *n* (*US*, *often hum*) burgo *m*.

burgeon [ˈbɜːdʒən] *vi* (*Bot*) retoñar; (*fig*) empezar a prosperar (rápidamente); (*trade etc*) florecer.

burgeoning [ˈbɜːdʒənɪŋ] *adj* que empieza a prosperar (*or* florecer), en vías de expansión.

burger [ˈbɜːgəʳ] *n* (*US*) hamburguesa *f*.

burgess [ˈbɜːdʒɪs] *n* (*Brit*) ciudadano *m*, -a *f*; (*Parl* ††) diputado *m*, -a *f*.

burgh [ˈbʌrə] *n* (*Scot*) villa *f*.

burgher [ˈbɜːgəʳ] *n* (*Hist*) burgués *m*, -esa *f*; ciudadano *m*, -a *f*.

burglar [ˈbɜːgləʳ] *n* ladrón *m*, escalador *m*.

burglar-alarm [ˈbɜːglərəˌlɑːm] *n* alarma *f* antirrobo.

burglarize [ˈbɜːgləraɪz] *vt* (*US*) = **burgle**.

burglar-proof [ˈbɜːgləpruːf] *adj* a prueba de ladrones.

burglary [ˈbɜːglərɪ] *n* robo *m* en una casa, robo *m* con escalamiento, (*Jur*) allanamiento *m* de morada.

burgle [ˈbɜːgl] *vt* robar, escalar, allanar, desvalijar.

Burgundian [bɜːˈgʌndɪən] **1** *adj* borgoñón. **2** *n* borgoñón *m*, -ona *f*.

Burgundy [ˈbɜːgəndɪ] *n* Borgoña *f*; **b**~ vino *m* de Borgoña.

burial [ˈberɪəl] *n* entierro *m*.

burial-ground [ˈberɪəlgraʊnd] *n* cementerio *m*, camposanto *m*.

burial-mound [ˈberɪəlˌmaʊnd] *n* túmulo *m*.

burial-place [ˈberɪəlˌpleɪs] *n* lugar *m* de sepultura.

burial service [ˈberɪəlˌsɜːvɪs] *n* funerales *mpl*.

burial-vault [ˈberɪəlˌvɔːlt] *n* panteón *m* familiar, cripta *f*.

burlap [ˈbɜːlæp] *n* arpillera *f*.

burlesque [bɜːˈlesk] **1** *adj* burlesco, festivo, paródico; ~ **show** (*US*) revista *f* de estriptise. **2** *n* parodia *f*; (*US*) revista *f* de estriptise. **3** *vt* parodiar.

burly [ˈbɜːlɪ] *adj* fornido, membrudo, corpulento, anchote.

Burma [ˈbɜːmə] *n* Birmania *f*.

Burmese [bɜːˈmiːz] **1** *adj* birmano. **2** *n* birmano *m*, -a *f*.

burn[1] [bɜːn] **1** *n* (**a**) quemadura *f*. (**b**) (‡) tabaco *m*, cigarrillos *mpl*.

2 (*irr*: *pret and ptp* **burned** *or* **burnt**) *vt* quemar; *house etc* incendiar; *corpse* incinerar; *plants* (*by sun*) abrasar; *almonds etc* tostar; *fuel* funcionar con, utilizar como combustible; *mouth*, *tongue* quemar, escaldar; **to** ~ **one's hand** quemarse la mano; **to** ~ **a hole in sth** hacer un agujero en algo quemándolo; **to** ~ **sth to ashes** reducir algo a cenizas; **to** ~ **a house to the ground** incendiar y arrasar una casa; **to be ~ed alive** ser quemado vivo; **to be ~ed to death** morir abrasado; **with a face ~ed by the sun** con una cara tostada al sol; **it has a burnt taste** sabe a quemado.

3 *vi* (**a**) quemar(se), arder; (*catch fire*) incendiarse; (*light*, *gas*) estar encendido; (*smart*) escocer; **to** ~ **to death** morir abrasado.

(**b**) (*fig*) arder (*with* de, en); **to** ~ **to** + *infin* desear ardientemente + *infin*; **to** ~ **with desire for** desear ardientemente; **to** ~ **with impatience** consumirse de impaciencia.

◆**burn away** **1** *vt* quemar, consumir. **2** *vi* (**a**) (*be consumed*) consumirse. (**b**) (*go on burning*) seguir ardiendo, arder bien.

◆**burn down** **1** *vt* incendiar; destruir por incendio, quemar totalmente. **2** *vi* quedar destruido en un incendio, quemarse hasta los cimientos.

◆**burn off** *vt paint etc* quitar con la llama; *weeds* quemar.

◆**burn out** **1** *vt* (**a**) (*criminally*) incendiar; *person* incendiar la casa de.

(**b**) (*destroy*) reducir a cenizas, destruir con fuego.

(**c**) (*Elec*) fundir, quemar.

2 *vi* (**a**) (*go out*) consumirse, apagarse; (*Elec*) fundirse.

(**b**) (*fig*) apagarse.

3 *vr*: **to** ~ **o.s. out** quemarse.

◆**burn up** **1** *vt* (**a**) quemar, consumir.

(**b**) *crop* abrasar.

(**c**) *person* indignar, sacar de quicio.

2 *vi* (**a**) consumirse.

(**b**) (*burn brighter*) arder más.

3 *vr*: **to** ~ **o.s. up** (*fig*) quemarse.

burn[2] [bɜːn] *n* (*Scot*) arroyo *m*, riachuelo *m*.

burner [ˈbɜːnəʳ] *n* mechero *m*; (*on stove etc*) hornillo *m*, quemador *m*, fuego *m*.

burning [ˈbɜːnɪŋ] **1** *adj* (**a**) ardiente (*also fig*); **it's** ~ **hot** está que quema, hace un calor sofocante, el sol pica mucho. (**b**) *question* candente, palpitante. **2** *n* el quemar; **the** ~ **of the embassy during the riots** el incendio de la embajada durante los disturbios; **a smell of** ~ un olor a quemado.

burnish [ˈbɜːnɪʃ] *vt* bruñir.

burnoose, burnous(e) [bɜːˈnuːz] *n* albornoz *m*.

burnt [bɜːnt] *pret and ptp of* **burn**[1]; ~ **almonds** almendras *fpl* dulces tostadas; ~ **offering** holocausto *m*.

burnt-out [ˌbɜːntˈaʊt] *adj person* quemado.

burp* [bɜːp] **1** *n* eructo *m*. **2** *vi* eructar.

burr [bɜːʳ] *n* (*Bot*) erizo *m*.

burrow ['bʌrəʊ] **1** *n* madriguera *f*; (*rabbit's*) conejera *f*.
2 *vt* hacer madrigueras en; (*and undermine*) socavar, minar; **to ~ one's way into** abrirse camino cavando en, (*fig*) insinuarse en.
3 *vi* amadrigarse, hacer una madriguera; **to ~ into** hacer madrigueras en, horadar; (*fig*) investigar minuciosamente.
bursar ['bɜːsəʳ] *n* (*Univ etc*) tesorero *m*; (*of school*) administrador *m*, -ora *f*.
bursary ['bɜːsərɪ] *n* (*Univ*) beca *f*.
burst [bɜːst] **1** *n* reventón *m*; (*explosion*) estallido *m*, explosión *f*; (*of shots*) serie *f* de tiros, ráfaga *f* de tiros; **a ~ of applause** una salva de aplausos; **a ~ of speed** una arrancada; **a ~ of activity** un frenesí repentino de actividad; **in a ~ of anger** en un arranque de cólera.
2 (*irr: pret and ptp* **burst**) *vt balloon etc* reventar; *bubble* deshacer; *tyre* pinchar; *banks, dam, pipe* romper; **to ~ open a door** abrir de golpe una puerta.
3 *vi* (*balloon, boil, boiler*) reventar(se); (*bubble*) deshacerse; (*tyre*) pincharse; (*dam, pipe*) romperse; (*bomb etc*) estallar; (*heart*) partirse; (*storm*) desencadenarse; **he was ~ing to tell me** reventaba por decírmelo; **he was ~ing with impatience** reventaba de impaciencia; **I'm ~ing for the loo*** necesito urgentemente ir al wáter; **to ~ with laughter** reventar de risa; **London is ~ing with young people** Londres está que bulle de juventud; **to be full to ~ing** estar lleno a reventar; estar apretado a presión.
◆**burst forth** *vi* brotar, salir a chorro.
◆**burst in** *vi* entrar violentamente; **he ~ in on the meeting** irrumpió en la reunión.
◆**burst into** *vt* (**a**) **to ~ into a room** irrumpir en un cuarto.
(**b**) **to ~ into flames** estallar en llamas; **to ~ into song** romper a cantar; **to ~ into tears** deshacerse en lágrimas.
◆**burst out** *vi* (**a**) **to ~ out of a room** salir repentinamente de un cuarto; **to be ~ing out of a dress** no caber en un vestido.
(**b**) **to ~ out laughing** soltar la carcajada; **'No!', he ~ out** '¡No!', gritó con pasión.
◆**burst through** *vt barrier* romper (violentamente); **the sun ~ through the clouds** el sol brilló repentinamente por entre las nubes.
bursting ['bɜːstɪŋ] *n* (*Comput*) separación *f* de hojas.
burton ['bɜːtn] *n*: **it's gone for a ~*** (*broken etc*) se ha fastidiado*; (*lost*) se ha perdido; **he's gone for a ~** (*Brit Aer‡*) la palmó*.
Burundi [bə'rʊndɪ] *n* Burundi *m*.
bury ['berɪ] **1** *vt* enterrar (*also fig*); *body* enterrar, sepultar; *memory, matter* echar tierra sobre; (*Sport**) *opponents* cascar*; **to ~ a dagger in sb's heart** clavar un puñal en el corazón de uno; **to ~ one's face in one's hands** ocultar el rostro en las manos; **it's buried away in the library** está no sabemos dónde en la biblioteca, está en algún rincón de la biblioteca; **to be buried in thought** estar absorto en la meditación.
2 *vr*: **to ~ o.s. in the country** enterrarse en el campo; **the bullet buried itself in a tree** la bala se empotró en un árbol; **she buried herself in her book** se ensimismó con su lectura, se enfrascó en su libro.
bus [bʌs] **1** *n* (**a**) autobús *m*, colectivo *m* (*SC*), camión *m* (*Mex*); (*coach*) autocar *m*; **to go by ~** ir en autobús; **to miss the ~** perder el tren; **the house is (not) on a ~ route** la casa (no) se halla en el recorrido de un autobús. (**b**) (*) (*car*) cacharro* *m*; (*plane*) avión *m* viejo. (**c**) (*Comput*) bus *m*. **2** *vt* llevar en autobús. **3** *vi* (**a**) ir en autobús. (**b**) (*US: clear away dishes*) quitar los platos de la mesa.
busbar ['bʌzbɑːʳ] *n* (**a**) (*Comput*) bus *m*. (**b**) (*Tech*) barra *f* ómnibus.
busby ['bʌzbɪ] *n* (*Brit*) gorro *m* alto de piel negra.
bus-conductor ['bʌskən,dʌktəʳ] *n* cobrador *m*.
bus-conductress ['bʌskən,dʌktrɪs] *n* cobradora *f*.
bus-depot ['bʌs,depəʊ] *n* cochera *f* de autobuses.
bus-driver ['bʌs,draɪvəʳ] *n* chófer *m*.
bush[1] [bʊʃ] *n* (*Bot*) arbusto *m*; **the ~** (*Australia*) el monte, el despoblado; **to beat about the ~** andarse por las ramas, ir con rodeos.
bush[2] [bʊʃ] *n* (*Tech*) cojinete *m*.
bush-baby ['bʊʃ,beɪbɪ] *n* (*Zool*) lemúrido *m*.
bushed [bʊʃt] *adj* (**a**) (‡) (*puzzled*) perplejo, pasmado; (*exhausted*) agotado, hecho polvo*. (**b**) (*Australia*) perdido en la maleza.
bushel ['bʊʃl] *n medida de áridos*: *British = 36,36 litros, US = 35,24 litros.*
bush-fire ['bʊʃfaɪəʳ] *n* incendio *m* de monte.
bush-league ['bʊʃ,liːg] *adj* de calidad mediocre.
bushman ['bʊʃmən] *n*, *pl* **bushmen** ['bʊʃmen] bosquimano *m*, bosquimán *m*.
bushranger ['bʊʃ,reɪndʒəʳ] *n* (*Australia*) bandido *m*.
bush telegraph* ['bʊʃ'telɪgrɑːf] *n* teléfono *m* árabe*.
bushwhack ['bʊʃ,wæk] *vi* (*US*) abrirse camino por el bosque.
bushwhacker ['bʊʃ,wækəʳ] *n* (*US*) pionero *m*, -a *f*, explorador *m*, -ora *f*.
bushy ['bʊʃɪ] *adj plant* arbustivo; parecido a un arbusto; *ground* lleno de arbustos; *beard* poblado, espeso.
busily ['bɪzɪlɪ] *adv* activamente; enérgicamente; **everyone was ~ writing** todos escribían con ahínco; **he was ~ engaged in painting it** se ocupaba enérgicamente en pintarlo.
business ['bɪznɪs] **1** *n* (**a**) (*commerce in general*) comercio *m*, negocios *mpl*; **~ is ~** la cuenta es la cuenta, el comercio es una cosa seria; **~ before pleasure** primero es la obligación que la devoción; **~ as usual** (*general slogan*) los negocios como de costumbre; (*notice outside shop*) 'continúa la venta al interior'; **big ~** comercio *m* en gran escala; **kidnapping is big ~** los secuestros son un gran negocio; **~ is good at the moment** el negocio va bien por el momento; **he's in ~** se dedica al comercio; **he's in ~ in London** trabaja en una empresa comercial de Londres; **we're not in ~ to** + *infin* no es nuestro propósito + *infin*; **if we can find a car we're in ~*** si encontramos un coche todo empieza a rodar; **to be (away) on ~** estar (en viaje) de negocios; **to carry on ~ as** tener un negocio de; **to do ~ with** comerciar con; **to get down to ~** ir al grano, ir derecho a lo esencial; **to go into ~** dedicarse al comercio; **to go abroad on ~** ir al extranjero en viaje de negocios; **to go out of ~** quebrar; **the shop is losing ~** la tienda pierde clientela; **to put sb out of ~** hacer que uno quiebre; **to mean ~** hablar (*etc*) en serio; **to send sb about his ~** echar a uno con cajas destempladas; **to set up in ~ as** montar un negocio de; **to set sb up in ~** proveer a uno de un capital explotable.
(**b**) (*firm*) empresa *f*, casa *f*; **it's a family ~** es una empresa familiar.
(**c**) (*task, duty*) **that's my ~** eso me toca únicamente a mí; **it is my ~ to** + *infin* me corresponde + *infin*; **it's no ~ of mine** yo no tengo nada que ver con eso; **the dog did its ~*** el perro hizo sus necesidades; **you had no ~ to** + *infin* Vd no tenía ningún derecho a + *infin*; **what ~ have you to intervene?** ¿con qué derecho interviene Vd?; **they're working away like nobody's ~** están trabajando como demonios; **I will make it my ~ to tell him** yo me propongo decírselo, yo les aseguro que se lo diré; **mind your own ~** no se meta Vd donde no le llaman.
(**d**) (*one's trade, profession*) oficio *m*, ocupación *f*; **what ~ are you in?** ¿a qué se dedica Vd?; **he's got the biggest laugh in the ~** tiene la risa más fuerte que hay por aquí.
(**e**) (*affair*) cosa *f*, asunto *m*, cuestión *f*; **the Suez ~** el asunto de Suez, la cuestión Suez; **the ~ before the meeting** los asuntos a tratar; **I have ~ with the minister** tengo asuntos que tratar con el ministro; **it's a nasty ~** es un asunto desagradable; **did you hear about that ~ yesterday?** ¿le dijeron algo de lo que pasó ayer?; **what a ~ this is!** ¡qué lío!; **I can't stand this ~ of doing nothing** no puedo con este plan de no hacer nada; **any other ~** (*agenda*) ruegos *mpl* y preguntas.
(**f**) (*Theat*) acción *f*, gag *m*.
2 *adj, attr*: *connection, deal, quarter* comercial; *house* de comercio; *cycle* económico; **his ~ address** su dirección *f* profesional; **~ administration** (*as course*) administración *f* de empresas; **~ agent** agente *m* de negocios; **~ associate** socio *m*, -a *f*, asociado *m*, -a *f*; **~ card** tarjeta *f* comercial, tarjeta *f* de visita; **~ centre** centro *m* financiero; **~ college** escuela *f* de comercio; **~ consultancy** empresología *f*; **~ consultant** empresólogo *m*, -a *f*; **~ deal** trato *m* comercial; **~ end*** punta *f*; **~ expenses** gastos *mpl* del negocio, gastos *mpl* comerciales; **~ hours** horas *fpl* de oficina; **~ language** lenguaje *m* comercial; **~ lunch** comida *f* de negocios; **~ machines** máquinas *fpl* para la empresa; **~ management** dirección *f* empresarial; **~ manager** (*Theat*) secretario *m*, -a *f*; **~ premises** local *m* comercial; **~ school = business college**; **~ sense** olfato *m* para los negocios; **~ Spanish** español *m* comercial, español *m* para el comercio; **~ suit** traje *m* de oficina, traje *m* de calle; **(Faculty of) B~ Studies** (Facultad *f* de) Estudios *mpl* de la Empresa, (Facultad *f* de) Estudios *mpl* Empresariales; **~ trip** viaje *m* de negocios.
businesslike ['bɪznɪslaɪk] *adj* formal, metódico, serio,

práctico.
businessman ['bɪznɪsmæn] *n, pl* **businessmen** ['bɪznɪsmen] hombre *m* de negocios, empresario *m*; **small ~** pequeño empresario *m*.
businesswoman ['bɪznɪsˌwʊmən] *n, pl* **businesswomen** ['bɪznɪsˌwɪmɪn] mujer *f* de negocios, mujer *f* empresaria.
busk [bʌsk] *vi (Brit)* tocar música (en la calle).
busker ['bʌskər] *n (Brit)* músico *m*, -a *f* ambulante.
bus lane ['bʌsˌleɪn] *n (Brit)* carril *m* de autobús.
busload ['bʌsləʊd] *n* autobús *m* (lleno, completo); **they came by the ~** *(fig)* vinieron en masa, vinieron en tropel.
busman ['bʌsmən] *n, pl* **busmen** ['bʌsmen] conductor *m* (*or* cobrador *m*) de autobús; **~'s holiday** ocupación *f* del ocio parecida a la del trabajo diario.
bus-service ['bʌsˌsɜːvɪs] *n* servicio *m* de autobús.
bus-shelter ['bʌsˌʃeltər] *n* refugio *m* de espera, parada *f* cubierta, marquesina *f*.
bus(s)ing ['bʌsɪŋ] *n (US)* transporte *m* escolar.
bus-station ['bʌsˌsteɪʃən] *n* estación *f* de autobuses.
bus-stop ['bʌsstɒp] *n* parada *f* de autobús.
bust¹ [bʌst] *n (Anat: Art)* busto *m*; *(bosom)* pecho *m*, pechos *mpl*.
bust² [bʌst] **1** (*) *ptp of* **burst**; roto; inservible; **to go ~** *(Comm)* quebrar. **2** *vt* **(a)** (*) romper, estropear. **(b)** (‡) arrestar, detener; **the police ~ed him for drugs** la policía le detuvo por uso de drogas; **the police ~ed the place** la policía registró el local. **3** *vi* (*) romperse, estropearse. **4** *n (US*)* pifia *f*.
◆**bust up‡** **1** *vt marriage, friendship* romper. **2** *vi (friends)* reñir, pelearse.
bustard ['bʌstəd] *n* avutarda *f*.
buster* ['bʌstər] *n (in direct address)* macho*, tío*.
bus-ticket ['bʌsˌtɪkɪt] *n* billete *m* de autobús.
bustle¹ ['bʌsl] *n (Hist: dress)* polisón *m*.
bustle² ['bʌsl] **1** *n* movimiento *m*, actividad *f*; bullicio *m*, animación *f*; *(haste)* prisa *f*. **2** *vi* (*gen* **to ~ about**) menearse, apresurarse, ir y venir.
bustling ['bʌslɪŋ] *adj* activo, hacendoso; *crowd* apresurado, animado, bullicioso.
bust-up* ['bʌstʌp] *n* riña *f*.
busty* ['bʌstɪ] *adj* tetuda*.
busway ['bʌsweɪ] *n (US)* carril *m* de autobús.
busy ['bɪzɪ] **1** *adj* **(a)** *person* ocupado; atareado; activo; *(pej)* entrometido; **as ~ as a bee** muy activo, ocupadísimo; **are you ~?** ¿está ocupado?; **to be ~ at** (*or* **on, with**) estar ocupado en; **to be ~ doing sth** estar ocupado en hacer algo; **to get ~** empezar a trabajar, *(hurry)* menearse, darse prisa; **let's get ~!** ¡vamos!; **to keep ~** estar siempre ocupado; **to keep sb ~** ocupar a uno.
(b) *day* de muchas ocupaciones; ajetreado; **the busiest season is the autumn** la época de mayor actividad es el otoño.
(c) *place* (muy) concurrido, de mucho movimiento; *scene* animado, lleno de movimiento.
(d) *(esp US Telec)* **~ signal** señal *f* de comunicando; **to be ~** estar comunicando.
2 *vt* ocupar.
3 *vr*: **to ~ o.s. at** (*or* **in, with**) ocuparse en, estar ocupado con; **she busied herself with the children** ella se ocupó de los niños.
busybody ['bɪzɪbɒdɪ] *n* entrometido *m*, -a *f*, metijón *m*, -ona *f*.
but [bʌt] **1** *adv (only)* sólo, solamente, no más que; **all ~** casi; **nothing ~** nada más que; **he is ~ a servant** no es más que un criado; **he talks ~ little** habla muy poco; **if I could ~ speak to him** si solamente pudiese hablar con él; **had I ~ known** si lo hubiera sabido; **you can ~ try** en todo caso vale probarlo.
2 *prep and conj (except)* excepto, menos; salvo; **all ~ him** todos excepto él, todos salvo él; **the last ~ one** el penúltimo; **the last ~ three** el tercero antes del último; **~ for** a no ser por, si no fuera por; **there is nothing for it ~ to pay up** no hay más remedio que pagar; **one cannot ~ admire him** no se puede sino admirarle; **I'll do anything ~ sing** lo hago todo menos cantar.
3 *conj* **(a)** pero; **she was poor ~ she was honest** era pobre pero honrada; **~ it does move!** ¡pero sí se mueve!; **it never rains ~ it pours** llueve sobre mojado; **I never go there ~ I think of you** nunca voy allá sin pensar en ti.
(b) *(in statements of direct contradiction)* sino, *eg* **he's not English ~ Irish** no es inglés sino irlandés; **he didn't sing ~ he shouted** no cantó sino que gritó.
4 *n* pero *m*, objeción *f*; **there are no ~s about it** no hay pero que valga.
butane ['bjuːteɪn] *n* butano *m*; *(US: for camping)* camping gas *m*; **~ gas** gas *m* butano.
butch‡ [bʊtʃ] **1** *adj woman* marimacho; *man* macho. **2** *n (woman)* marimacho *m*; *(man)* macho *m*.
butcher ['bʊtʃər] **1** *n* **(a)** carnicero *m (also fig)*; **~'s (shop)** carnicería *f*. **(b)** *(US)* vendedor *m* de dulces. **(c) let's have a ~'s** *(Brit‡)* déjame verlo. **2** *vt* matar; *(fig)* dar muerte a, hacer una carnicería con.
butchery ['bʊtʃərɪ] *n* matanza *f*, carnicería *f*.
butler ['bʌtlər] *n* mayordomo *m*.
butt¹ [bʌt] *n (barrel)* tonel *m*; *(for rainwater)* tina *f*.
butt² [bʌt] *n (end)* cabo *m*, extremo *m*; extremo *m* más grueso; *(of gun)* culata *f*; *(of cigarette)* colilla *f*; *(US: cigarette)* colilla *f*, pito* *m*; *(US*: Anat)* culo *m*; **to work one's ~ off*** romperse los cuernos*.
butt³ [bʌt] *n (target)* blanco *m*; **~s** campo *m* de tiro al blanco; **to be a ~ for** ser el blanco de, ser el objeto de.
butt⁴ [bʌt] **1** *n (push with head)* cabezada *f*, topetada *f*.
2 *vt* dar cabezadas contra, topetar; **to ~ one's head against** dar con la cabeza contra; **to ~ one's way through** abrirse paso dando cabezadas.
◆**butt in** *vi* interrumpir; *(meddle)* entrometerse, meter baza, meter su cuchara.
◆**butt into** *vt conversation* meterse en; *meeting* interrumpir.
butt-end ['bʌtend] *n* = **butt²**.
butter ['bʌtər] **1** *n* mantequilla *f*; **~ wouldn't melt in his mouth** es una mosquita muerta. **2** *vt* untar con mantequilla.
◆**butter up** *vt (Brit*)* dar coba a*.
butterball ['bʌtəbɔːl] *n (US)* gordo *m*.
butter-bean ['bʌtəˌbiːn] *n (Bot)* judía *f* valenciana.
buttercup ['bʌtəkʌp] *n* ranúnculo *m*.
butter-dish ['bʌtəˌdɪʃ] *n* mantequillera *f*.
butter-fingered ['bʌtəˌfɪŋgəd] *adj* desmañado en coger la pelota *(etc)*.
butterfingers* ['bʌtəˌfɪŋgəz] *n sing* manos *m* de trapo, manos *m* de mantequilla; **~!** ¡premio!
butterfly ['bʌtəflaɪ] *n* mariposa *f*; **~ mind** mentalidad *f* frívola; **to have butterflies in the stomach** estar muy nervioso.
butterfly-knot ['bʌtəflaɪˌnɒt] *n* nudo *m* de lazo.
butterfly-net ['bʌtəflaɪˌnet] *n* manga *f* de mariposas.
butterfly-nut ['bʌtəflaɪˌnʌt] *n* tuerca *f* de mariposa.
butterfly-stroke ['bʌtəflaɪˌstrəʊk] *n* braza *f* de mariposa.
butter-icing [ˌbʌtər'aɪsɪŋ] *n* cobertura *f* de mantequilla.
butter-knife ['bʌtəˌnaɪf] *n, pl* **butter-knives** ['bʌtəˌnaɪvz] cuchillo *m* de mantequilla.
buttermilk ['bʌtəmɪlk] *n* suero *m* de leche, suero *m* de manteca.
butterscotch ['bʌtəskɒtʃ] *n dulce de azúcar terciado con mantequilla*.
buttery ['bʌtərɪ] *n* despensa *f*.
buttocks ['bʌtəks] *npl* nalgas *fpl*, cachas *fpl*.
button ['bʌtn] **1** *n (all senses)* botón *m*; **~s** *(esp Brit: person)* botones *m*; **on the ~*** *arrive* en punto; *(absolutely exact)* exacto.
2 *vt (also* **to ~ up**) abotonar, abrochar; **to ~ one's lip*** no decir ni mu.
3 *vi*: **it ~s in front** se abrocha por delante.
buttonhole ['bʌtnhəʊl] **1** *n* ojal *m*; *(Brit: flower)* flor *f* que se lleva en el ojal.
2 *vt* obligar a escuchar, abordar; **I was ~d by X** me vi obligado a detenerme en conversación con X.
buttonhook ['bʌtnhʊk] *n* abotonador *m*.
button mushroom [ˌbʌtn'mʌʃrʊm] *n* champiñón *m* pequeño.
button-through dress [ˌbʌtnˌθruː'dres] *n* vestido *m* abrochado por delante.
buttress ['bʌtrɪs] **1** *n* contrafuerte *m (also Geog)*; *(fig)* apoyo *m*, sostén *m*. **2** *vt* poner contrafuerte a; *(fig)* apoyar, reforzar.
butty* ['bʌtɪ] *n* bocadillo *m*.
buxom ['bʌksəm] *adj* rollizo, frescachón; tetuda*.
buy [baɪ] **1** *n* compra *f*; **a good ~** un buen negocio, una ganga, una buena compra; **this month's best ~** la ganga del mes.
2 *(irr: pret and ptp* **bought**) *vt* **(a)** comprar *(from, off* a); **money couldn't ~ it** no se puede comprar con dinero.
(b) *(bribe)* comprar, sobornar.
(c) (*: *believe*) creer, tragar; **he won't ~ that** eso no lo va a tragar; **all right, I'll ~ it** bueno, dime.
(d) he bought it‡ la palmó‡.
◆**buy back** *vt* volver a comprar.

◆buy forward *vi* comprar con antelación.
◆buy in *vt* (*Brit*) *foods* aprovisionarse de; (*Stock Exchange*) comprar; (*Fin*) comprar por cuenta del dueño.
◆buy into *vt company* comprar acciones de.
◆buy off *vt* comprar la benevolencia de; (*bribe*) sobornar.
◆buy out *vt partner* comprar la parte de.
◆buy up *vt* comprar todas las existencias de, acaparar.
buy-back ['baɪ,bæk] *adj*: ~ **option** opción *f* de recompra.
buyer ['baɪəʳ] *n* comprador *m*, -ora *f*; (*in store*) encargado *m* de compras; **~'s market** mercado *m* de compradores, mercado *m* de signo favorable al comprador.
buying ['baɪɪŋ] *n* compra *f*; ~ **power** poder *m* adquisitivo.
buy-out ['baɪaʊt] *n* compra *f* (de la totalidad de las acciones); **management** ~ compra *f* (de acciones) por los gerentes; **workers'** ~ compra *f* de una empresa por los trabajadores de la misma.
buzz [bʌz] **1** *n* (**a**) zumbido *m*. (**b**) (*: *rumour*) rumor *m*. (**c**) (*Telec**) llamada *f* (telefónica); **I'll give you a** ~ te llamaré. **2** *vt* (**a**) (*US Telec*) llamar. (**b**) (*Aer*) zumbar. **3** *vi* zumbar; **my ears are ~ing** me zumban los oídos; **the school ~ed with the news** todo el colegio comentaba la noticia.
◆buzz about, buzz around *vi* ir zumbando de acá para allá; (*fig*) ser muy activo, correr a todas partes.
◆buzz off* *vi* (*Brit*) largarse*, rajarse*; ~ **off!** ¡largo de aquí!*
buzzard ['bʌzəd] *n* ratonero *m* común, águila *f* ratonera.
buzz-bomb ['bʌzbɒm] *n* bomba *f* volante.
buzzer ['bʌzəʳ] *n* timbre *m*.
buzzing ['bʌzɪŋ] *n* zumbido *m*, zumbar *m*.
buzz-saw ['bʌz,sɔː] *n* (*US*) sierra *f* circular.
buzz-word ['bʌz,wɜːd] *n* palabra *f* que está de moda, cliché *m*.
b.v. *abbr of* **book value** valor *m* en libros.
B.V.M. *n abbr of* **Blessed Virgin Mary**.
by [baɪ] **1** *adv*: ~ **and** ~ más tarde, luego; ~ **and large** en general, por lo general.

2 *prep* (**a**) (*agent, by means of*) por; **a house built** ~ **X** una casa construida por X; ~ **one's own efforts** por sus propios esfuerzos; ~ **God** por Dios; **made** ~ **hand** hecho a mano; **to divide** ~ **5** dividir por 5; **he had 3 children** ~ **his first wife** tuvo 3 hijos con su primera mujer; **he is known** ~ **the name of** se le conoce con (*of pseudonym*: bajo) el nombre de; **he did it** ~ **himself** lo hizo por sí solo, lo hizo por sí mismo.

(**b**) (*manner*) ~ **air** en avión; por avión; ~ **cheque** por cheque; ~ **easy stages** en cortas etapas; ~ **leaps and bounds** a pasos agigantados; ~ **moonlight** a la luz de la luna; ~ **train** (*come*) en tren, (*send*) por ferrocarril; **to be** ~ **o.s.** estar solo.

(**c**) (*rate*) **hour** ~ **hour** hora tras hora, cada hora; ~ **the dozen** a docenas, por docenas; **2** ~ **2** de 2 en 2; **little** ~ **little** poco a poco; **to buy sth** ~ **the kilo** comprar algo por kilos; **to reduce sth** ~ **a third** reducir algo en una tercera parte; **we pay** ~ **the month** pagamos cada mes.

(**d**) (*in accordance with*) según, de acuerdo con; ~ **what you say** según lo que dices; **to be cautious** ~ **nature** ser de naturaleza cauteloso.

(**e**) (*time*) ~ **2 o'clock** para las 2; ~ **nightfall** antes del anochecer; ~ **then** para entonces, antes de eso; ~ **day** de día.

(**f**) (*place: next*) junto a, cerca de, al lado de; ~ **me** a mi lado; **north** ~ **west** norte por oeste; (*through, along*) por; **he came in** ~ **the window** entró por la ventana.

(**g**) (*measurement*) **6 metres** ~ **4** 6 metros por 4; **it's too short** ~ **a foot** falta un pie; **he missed** ~ **an inch** erró el tiro en una pulgada.

(**h**) (*with gerund*) ~ **working hard** trabajando mucho; **he ended** ~ **saying that ...** terminó diciendo que ...

3 *n*: ~ **the** ~ a propósito, por cierto.
bye¹ [baɪ] *n* **1** (*Golf etc*) bye *m*; **to have a** ~ pasar a la segunda eliminatoria por sorteo; **by the** ~ por cierto, a propósito. **2**: **bye-election** = **by-election**; **bye-law** = **by-law**.
bye²* [baɪ] *interj* = **bye-bye**.
bye-bye* ['baɪ'baɪ] **1** *interj* ¡adiós!, ¡hasta luego! **2** *n*: **to go ~s** dormirse, quedar dormido; **it's time to go ~s** es hora de acostarte.
by-election ['baɪɪ,lekʃən] *n* elección *f* parcial.
bygone ['baɪgɒn] **1** *adj* pasado. **2** *n*: **let ~s be ~s** lo pasado pasado está.
by-law ['baɪlɔː] *n* (*Brit*) estatuto *m*, reglamento *m* local (*or* suplementario).
by-line ['baɪlaɪn] *n* (*Press*) pie *m* de autor.
by-name ['baɪneɪm] *n* sobrenombre *m*; (*nickname*) apodo *m*, mote *m*.
BYOB* *abbr of* **bring your own bottle** trae botella.
bypass ['baɪpɑːs] **1** *n* (*Aut*) carretera *f* de circunvalación; (*Elec*) desviación *f*; ~ **operation** by-pass *m*, operación *f* de by-pass; ~ **surgery** cirugía *f* de by-pass.

2 *vt* evitar, evitar el contacto con; prescindir de; *town* evitar entrar en, pasar de largo; *lower official etc* puentear.
by-play ['baɪpleɪ] *n* (*Theat*) acción *f* aparte, escena *f* muda.
by-product ['baɪ,prɒdəkt] *n* subproducto *m*; (*Chem*) derivado *m*; (*fig*) consecuencia *f*.
byre ['baɪəʳ] *n* (*Brit*) establo *m*, vaquería *f*.
by-road ['baɪrəʊd] *n* camino *m* vecinal, carretera *f* secundaria.
bystander ['baɪ,stændəʳ] *n* espectador *m*, -ora *f*, circunstante *mf*, curioso *m*, -a *f*, mirón *m*, -ona *f*.
byte [baɪt] *n* byte *m*, octeto *m*.
byway ['baɪweɪ] *n* camino *m* apartado, camino *m* poco frecuentado; **the ~s of history** los aspectos poco conocidos de la historia.
byword ['baɪwɜːd] *n*: **to be a** ~ **for** (*Brit*) ser conocidísimo por, ser ... por antonomasia.
by-your-leave [,baɪ,jɔː'liːv] *n*: **without so much as a** ~ sin pedir permiso; sin decir nada, así por las buenas, sin más ni más.
Byzantine [baɪ'zæntaɪn] **1** *adj* bizantino. **2** *n* bizantino *m*, -a *f*.
Byzantium [baɪ'zæntɪəm] *n* Bizancio *m*.

C

C, c [siː] *n* (**a**) (*letter*) C, c *f*; **C for Charlie** C de Carmen. (**b**) **C** (*Mus*) do *m*; **C major** do *m* mayor.

C. (**a**) (*Liter*) *abbr of* **chapter** capítulo *m*, cap. (**b**) (*Geog*) *abbr of* **Cape** cabo *m*. (**c**) *abbr of* **centigrade** termómetro *m* centígrado. (**d**) (*Pol*) *abbr of* **Conservative** conservador *m*, -ora *f*.

c (**a**) (*US Fin*) *abbr of* **cent** centavo *m*. (**b**) *abbr of* **century** siglo *m*, S. (**c**) *abbr of* **circa, about** hacia, h. (**d**) (*Math*) *abbr of* **cubic** cúbico.

C & W *n abbr of* **Country and Western**; *V* **country**.

CA (*US Post*) *abbr of* **California**.

C.A. *n* (**a**) *abbr of* **chartered accountant**; *V* **chartered**. (**b**) *abbr of* **Central America** Centroamérica *f*.

C/A (**a**) *abbr of* **current account** cuenta *f* corriente, cta. cte. (**b**) *abbr of* **credit account** cuenta *f* a crédito.

CAA *n* (*Brit*) *abbr of* **Civil Aviation Authority** ≃ Aviación *f* Civil.

C.14 *n abbr of* **carbon 14**; ~ **dating** datación *f* por C-14.

CAB *n* (*Brit*) *abbr of* **Citizens' Advice Bureau** ≃ Servicio *m* de Información Ciudadana.

cab [kæb] *n* (*taxi*) taxi *m*; (††) cabriolé *m*, coche *m* de alquiler; (*of lorry etc*) cabina *f*.

cabal [kəˈbæl] *n* cábala *f*; camarilla *f*; cabildeo *m*.

cabaret [ˈkæbəreɪ] *n* cabaret *m*.

cabbage [ˈkæbɪdʒ] *n* (**a**) col *f*, berza *f*, repollo *m*; ~ **white** (**butterfly**) mariposa *f* de la col. (**b**) (*person*) vegetal *m*.

cab(b)ala [kəˈbɑːlə] *n* cábala *f*.

cabbalistic [ˌkæbəˈlɪstɪk] *adj* cabalístico.

cabbie, cabby* [ˈkæbɪ] *n*, **cabdriver** [ˈkæbdraɪvəʳ] *n* taxista *m*; (††) cochero *m*.

caber [ˈkeɪbəʳ] *n* (*Scot*) tronco *m*.

cabin [ˈkæbɪn] *n* (*hut*) cabaña *f*, barraca *f*; (*Naut*) camarote *m*; (*of lorry, plane*) cabina *f*; ~ **class** clase *f* de cámara; ~ **crew** tripulación *f* de pilotaje.

cabin-boy [ˈkæbɪnbɔɪ] *n* grumete *m*.

cabin-cruiser [ˈkæbɪnˌkruːzəʳ] *n* yate *m* de motor, motonave *f*.

cabinet [ˈkæbɪnɪt] *n* (**a**) (*cupboard*) armario *m*; (*for display*) vitrina *f*; (*Rad, TV*) caja *f*; **medicine** ~ botiquín *m*.
(**b**) (*Pol*) consejo *m* de ministros, gabinete *m*, ministros *mpl*; ~ **crisis** crisis *f* del gobierno; ~ **meeting** consejo *m* de ministros; ~ **minister** ministro *m*, -a *f*.

cabinetmaker [ˈkæbɪnɪtˌmeɪkəʳ] *n* ebanista *m*.

cabinetmaking [ˈkæbɪnɪtˌmeɪkɪŋ] *n* ebanistería *f*.

cable [ˈkeɪbl] **1** *n* (*Naut, Elec, Telec*) cable *m*; (*message*) cablegrama *m*; ~ **address** dirección *f* cablegráfica; ~ **television** televisión *f* por cable; ~ **transfer** transferencia *f* por cable, transferencia *f* cablegráfica.
2 *vti* cablegrafiar.

cable-car [ˈkeɪblkɑːʳ] *n* coche *m* de teleférico.

cablecast [ˈkeɪblˌkɑːst] **1** *n* emisión *f* de televisión por cable. **2** *vt* emitir por cable.

cablegram [ˈkeɪblgræm] *n* cablegrama *m*.

cable-railway [ˈkeɪblˈreɪlweɪ] *n* teleférico *m*, funicular *m* aéreo.

cable-stitch [ˈkeɪblstɪtʃ] *n* punto *m* de trenza.

cableway [ˈkeɪblweɪ] *n* teleférico *m*, funicular *m* aéreo.

cabman [ˈkæbmən] *n*, *pl* **cabmen** [ˈkæbmən] taxista *m*; (††) cochero *m*.

caboodle* [kəˈbuːdl] *n*: **the whole** ~ todo el rollo*.

caboose [kəˈbuːs] *n* (*US*) furgón *m* de cola.

cabrank [ˈkæbræŋk] *n*, **cabstand** [ˈkæbstænd] *n* parada *f* de taxis.

cacao [kəˈkɑːəʊ] *n* cacao *m*.

cache [kæʃ] **1** *n* (*hiding-place*) escondite *m*, escondrijo *m*; (*stores*) víveres *mpl* (*etc*) escondidos; (*of contraband, arms*) alijo *m*; ~ **memory** cache *m*, submemoria *f* ultrarrápida. **2** *vt* esconder, ocultar; acumular.

cachet [ˈkæʃeɪ] *n* caché *m*, cachet *m*.

cack-handed* [ˌkækˈhændɪd] *adj* (*Brit*) zurdo; (*fig*) torpe, desmañado.

cackle [ˈkækl] **1** *n* cacareo *m*; (*laughter*) risotada *f*; (*talk*) parloteo *m*; **cut the ~!*** ¡corta el rollo!*; ¡basta de cháchara! **2** *vi* cacarear; (*laugh*) reírse agudamente, desternillarse de risa; parlotear.

CACM *n abbr of* **Central American Common Market** Mercado *m* Común Centroamericano, MCCA *m*.

cacophonous [kəˈkɒfənəs] *adj* cacofónico.

cacophony [kæˈkɒfənɪ] *n* cacofonía *f*.

cactus [ˈkæktəs] *n*, *pl* **cacti** [ˈkæktaɪ] cactus *m*, cacto *m*.

CAD *n abbr of* **computer-aided design** diseño *m* asistido por ordenador, DAO *m*.

cad [kæd] *n* (*Brit*) sinvergüenza *m*, caradura *m*, canalla *m*; **you** ~! ¡canalla!

cadaster, cadastre [kəˈdæstəʳ] *n* catastro *m*.

cadaver [kəˈdeɪvəʳ] *n* (*esp US*) cadáver *m*.

cadaverous [kəˈdævərəs] *adj* cadavérico.

CADCAM [ˈkædˌkæm] *n abbr of* **computer-aided design and manufacture**.

caddie [ˈkædɪ] *n* cadi *m*, caddie *m*.

caddis fly [ˈkædɪsflaɪ] *n* frígano *m*.

caddish*† [ˈkædɪʃ] *adj* desvergonzado, canallesco; ~ **trick** canallada *f*.

caddy[1] [ˈkædɪ] *n* (**a**) cajita *f* para té. (**b**) (*US: shopping trolley*) carrito *m* de la compra.

caddy[2] [ˈkædɪ] *n* = **caddie**.

cadence [ˈkeɪdəns] *n* cadencia *f*; **the ~s of prose** el ritmo de la prosa.

cadenza [kəˈdenzə] *n* cadencia *f*.

cadet [kəˈdet] *m* (*Mil etc*) cadete *mf*; (*younger son*) hijo *m* menor.

cadet corps [kəˈdetˌkɔːʳ] *n* (*Brit: in school*) cuerpo *m* de alumnos que reciben entrenamiento militar; (*Police*) cuerpo *m* de cadetes.

cadet school [kəˈdetˌskuːl] *n* escuela *f* en la que se ofrece instrucción militar.

cadge [kædʒ] (*Brit*) **1** *vt* sacar de gorra, obtener mendigando, gorronear (*off* a); **he tried to ~ a lift** trató de conseguir que le llevaran gratis (en coche). **2** *vi* gorronear, vivir de gorra, sablear; **you can't ~ off me** es inútil pedirme cosas a mí.

cadger [ˈkædʒəʳ] *n* (*Brit*) gorrón *m*, -ona *f*, sablista *mf*.

Cadiz [kəˈdɪz] *n* Cádiz *m*.

cadmium [ˈkædmɪəm] *n* cadmio *m*.

cadre [ˈkædrɪ] *n* (*Mil etc*) cuadro *m*.

CAE *n abbr of* **computer-assisted engineering** ingeniería *f* asistida por computadora, IAC *f*.

caecum, (*US*) **cecum** [ˈsiːkəm] *n* (intestino *m*) ciego *m*.

Caesar [ˈsiːzəʳ] *nm* César.

Caesarean, (*US*) **Cesarean** [siːˈzɛərɪən] **1** *n* = **2**. **2** *adj* cesariano, cesáreo; ~ **operation,** ~ **section** (operación *f*) cesárea *f*.

caesium, (*US*) **cesium** [ˈsiːzɪəm] *n* cesio *m*.

caesura [sɪˈzjʊərə] *n* cesura *f*.

CAF, c.a.f. *n abbr of* **cost and freight** coste y flete *m*, C. y F.

café [ˈkæfeɪ] *n* café *m*, cafetería *f*.

cafeteria [ˌkæfɪˈtɪərɪə] *n* (restaurante *m* de) autoservicio *m*.

caff⁑ [kæf] *n* = **café**.

caffein(e) [ˈkæfiːn] *n* cafeína *f*.

caftan [ˈkæftæn] *n* caftán *m*.

cage [keɪdʒ] **1** *n* jaula *f*. **2** *vt* enjaular; **a ~d bird** un pájaro en jaula; **like a ~d tiger** como una fiera enjaulada.

cage bird [ˈkeɪdʒbɜːd] *n* pájaro *m* de jaula.

cagey* [ˈkeɪdʒɪ] *adj* cauteloso, reservado, reservón*; **he was very ~ about it** en eso anduvo con mucha reserva.

cagily* [ˈkeɪdʒɪlɪ] *adv* cautelosamente, con reserva.

caginess* ['keɪdʒɪnɪs] *n* cautela *f*, reserva *f*.
cagoule [kə'gu:l] *n* canguro *m*.
cahoots* [kə'hu:ts] *n*: **to be in ~ with sb** obrar de acuerdo con uno; confabularse con uno; **to go ~** entrar por partes iguales.
CAI *n abbr of* **computer-aided instruction** instrucción *f* asistida por ordenador, IAO *f*.
caiman ['keɪmən] *n* caimán *m*.
Cain [keɪn] *nm* Caín; **to raise ~** armar la gorda, protestar enérgicamente.
cairn [kɛən] *n* mojón *m*, montón *m* de piedras (*puesto en una cumbre o sobre una sepultura, etc*).
Cairo ['kaɪərəʊ] *n* el Cairo.
caisson ['keɪsən] *n* (*Mech*) cajón *m* hidráulico; (*Naut*) cajón *m* de suspensión; (*of dry-dock*) puerta *f* de dique; (*Mil*) cajón *m* de municiones.
cajole [kə'dʒəʊl] *vt* halagar, camelar; **to ~ sb into doing sth** halagar (*or* engatusar) a uno para que haga algo.
cajolery [kə'dʒəʊlərɪ] *n* halagos *mpl*, marrullería *f*, engatusamiento *m*.
Cajun ['keɪdʒən] **1** *adj* cajún; **~ cookery** cocina *f* tipo cajún. **2** *n* (**a**) cajún *mf*. (**b**) (*Ling*) cajún *m*.
cake [keɪk] **1** *n* (*large*) pastel *m*; tarta *f*; (*small*) pasta *f*, pastelillo *m*, queque *m* (*LAm*); (*sponge*) bizcocho *m*; (*of soap*) pastilla *f*; **it's a piece of ~*** es pan comido*, está tirado; **to want to have one's ~ and eat it** querer nadar y guardar la ropa; **the way the national ~ is divided** el modo de repartir la tarta (*or* el pastel) nacional; **to go** (*or* **sell**) **like hot ~s** venderse como pan bendito; **that takes the ~!*** ¡es el colmo!

2 *vt* endurecer; **a tyre ~d with mud** un neumático incrustado de lodo.

3 *vi* endurecerse, apelmazarse.
caked [keɪkt] **1** *pret and ptp of* **cake**. **2** *adj* endurecido.
cake-mix ['keɪkmɪks] *n* polvos *mpl* para hacer pasteles.
cakeshop ['keɪkʃɒp] *n* pastelería *f*.
cake-tin ['keɪktɪn] *n* (*Culin*) molde *m* para pastel; (*for keeping*) caja *f* de pastel.
Cal. *abbr of* **California**.
cal. *n abbr of* **calorie**.
calabash ['kæləbæʃ] *n* calabaza *f*.
calaboose* ['kæləbu:s] *n* (*US*) jaula *f**, cárcel *f*.
calamine ['kæləmaɪn] *n* calamina *f*.
calamitous [kə'læmɪtəs] *adj* calamitoso, desastroso.
calamity [kə'læmɪtɪ] *n* calamidad *f*, desastre *m*.
calcareous [kæl'kɛərɪəs] *adj* calcáreo.
calcicole ['kælsɪ,kəʊl] *n* calcícola *f*.
calcicolous [kæl'sɪkələs] *adj* calcícola.
calcification [,kælsɪfɪ'keɪʃən] *n* calcificación *f*.
calcifugous [kæl'sɪfjəgəs] *adj* calcífugo.
calcify ['kælsɪfaɪ] **1** *vt* calcificar. **2** *vi* calcificarse.
calcium ['kælsɪəm] *n* calcio *m*; **~ carbonate** carbonato *m* de calcio; **~ chloride** cloruro *m* de calcio.
calculable ['kælkjʊləbl] *adj* calculable.
calculate ['kælkjʊleɪt] **1** *vt* calcular; **~d to** + *infin* aprestado para + *infin*; **this is ~d to give him a jolt** esto tiene el propósito de darle una sacudida; **it is hardly ~d to help us** esto apenas será ventajoso para nosotros.

2 *vi* calcular; **to ~ on** contar con.
calculated ['kælkjʊleɪtɪd] *adj risk etc* calculado, premeditado, estudiado.
calculating ['kælkjʊleɪtɪŋ] *adj* astuto.
calculating machine ['kælkjʊleɪtɪŋmə,ʃi:n] *n* máquina *f* de calcular, calculadora *f*.
calculation [,kælkjʊ'leɪʃən] *n* cálculo *m*, cómputo *m*.
calculator ['kælkjʊleɪtə^r] *n* (*machine*) calculadora *f*; (*small*) minicalculadora *f*.
calculus ['kælkjʊləs] *n* cálculo *m*.
Calcutta [kæl'kʌtə] *n* Calcuta *f*.
calendar ['kæləndə^r] *n* (**a**) calendario *m*; (*Jur*) lista *f* (de pleitos); **university ~** (*Brit*) calendario *m* universitario; **~ month** mes *m* civil; **~ year** año *m* civil. (**b**) (‡) condena *f* de un año de prisión.
calf¹ [kɑ:f] *n*, *pl* **calves** [kɑ:vz] (*Zool*) ternero *m*, -a *f*, becerro *m*, -a *f*; (*of elephant*) cría *f*; (*of whale*) ballenato *m*; (*of seal etc*) cría *f*; (*skin*) piel *f* de becerro; **the cow is in** (*or* **with**) **~** la vaca está preñada; **to kill the fatted ~** festejar con mucho rumbo a un recién llegado, celebrar una fiesta de bienvenida.
calf² [kɑ:f] *n*, *pl* **calves** [kɑ:vz] (*Anat*) pantorrilla *f*.
calf love ['kɑ:flʌv] *n* amor *m* juvenil.
calfskin ['kɑ:fskɪn] *n* piel *f* de becerro.
caliber ['kælɪbə^r] *n* (*US*) = **calibre**.
calibrate ['kælɪbreɪt] *vt* calibrar.
calibrated ['kælɪbreɪtɪd] *adj* calibrado.
calibration [,kælɪ'breɪʃən] *n* calibración *f*.
calibre, (*US*) **caliber** ['kælɪbə^r] *n* calibre *m*; (*fig*) capacidad *f*, aptitud *f*, carácter *m*, valor *m*; **a man of his ~** un hombre de su calibre; **then he showed his real ~** luego demostró su verdadero valor.
calico ['kælɪkəʊ] *n* calicó *m*, indiana *f*.
Calif. *abbr of* **California**.
California [,kælɪ'fɔ:nɪə] *n* California *f*.
Californian [,kælɪ'fɔ:nɪən] **1** *adj* californiano. **2** *n* californiano *m*, -a *f*.
californium [,kælɪ'fɔ:nɪəm] *n* californio *m*.
calipers ['kælɪpəz] *npl* (*US*) = **callipers**.
caliph ['keɪlɪf] *n* califa *m*.
caliphate ['keɪlɪfeɪt] *n* califato *m*.
calisthenics [,kælɪs'θenɪks] *n* (*US*) = **callisthenics**.
CALL [kɔ:l] *n abbr of* **computer-assisted language learning** enseñanza *f* de lenguas asistida por ordenador.
call [kɔ:l] **1** *n* (**a**) (*gen*) llamada *f* (*also Mil*); (*cry*) grito *m*; (*of bird*) canto *m*, reclamo *m*; (*imitating bird's cry*) reclamo *m*, (*imitating animal's cry*) chilla *f*; (*Theat: summons to actor*) llamamiento *m*, (*curtain ~*) salida *f*; **~ loan** préstamo *m* cobrable a la vista; **~ of nature** (*euph*) necesidad *f* fisiológica; **~ option** opción *f* de compra a precio fijado; **the ~ of the unknown** la atracción de lo desconocido; **on ~** disponible, a su disposición; **money on** (*or* **at**) **~** dinero *m* a la vista; **within ~** al alcance de la voz; **they came at my ~** acudieron a mi llamada; **please give me a ~ at 7** hágame el favor de llamarme a las 7; **he's had a ~ to the Palace** le han llamado a palacio; **to have a close ~** escapar por un pelo, salvarse de milagro.

(**b**) (*Telec etc*) llamada *f*, llamado *m* (*LAm*); **to give sb a ~** llamar a uno; **to make a ~** llamar, hacer una llamada.

(**c**) (*visit*) visita *f*; **port of ~** puerto *m* de escala; **the boat makes a ~ at Vigo** el barco hace escala en Vigo; **to pay a ~ on sb** hacer una visita a uno.

(**d**) (*appeal, summons, invitation*) llamamiento *m*; **a ~ went to the fire brigade** se llamó a los bomberos; **the boat sent out a ~ for help** el barco emitió una llamada de socorro; **the minister sent out a ~ to the country to remain calm** el ministro hizo un llamamiento al país para que conservara la calma; **~ for a strike** convocatoria *f* de huelga; **~ for congress papers** convocatoria *f* de ponencias para un congreso; **to answer the ~** acudir al llamamiento; **to be on ~** estar de turno, (*doctor*) estar de guardia localizable, (*nurse*) estar de retén.

(**e**) (*need etc*) (*Comm*) demanda *f* (*for, on* de); **there isn't much ~ for these now** éstos tienen poca demanda ahora; **you had no ~ to say that** no había razón para que dijeras eso; **what ~ was there for you to intervene?** ¿qué necesidad había para que tú te entrometieras?

(**f**) (*claim*) **there are many ~s on my attention** son muchas las cosas que reclaman mi atención; **he has many ~s on his purse** tiene muchas obligaciones financieras.

(**g**) (*Bridge*) marca *f*, voz *f*; **whose ~ is it?** ¿a quién le toca?

2 *vt* (**a**) (*gen*) llamar; **did you ~?** ¿me llamaste?; **they ~ed me to see it** me llamaron para que lo viese; **please ~ me at 8** hágame el favor de llamarme a las 8.

(**b**) (*Telec*) llamar (por *or* al teléfono), telefonear (*esp LAm*); **London ~ed you this morning** esta mañana le llamaron (al teléfono) desde Londres; **I'll ~ you again tomorrow** volveré a llamarle mañana; **don't ~ us, we'll ~ you** no se moleste en llamar, nosotros le llamaremos.

(**c**) (*name*) llamar; **I'm ~ed Peter** me llamo Pedro; **what are you ~ed?** ¿cómo te llamas?; **what are they ~ing him?** ¿qué nombre le van a poner?; **they're ~ing the boy John** al niño le van a dar el nombre de Juan; **I ~ it an insult** yo digo que es un insulto; **I ~ed him a liar** le califiqué de mentiroso; **are you ~ing me a liar?** ¿dice Vd que yo soy un mentiroso?; **shall we ~ it £50?** ¿ponemos 50 libras?; **what time do you ~ this?** (*iro*) ¿qué hora crees que es?

(**d**) (*special uses*) *attention* llamar (*to* sobre); *meeting* convocar; *roll* pasar; *strike* declarar, convocar; *election* convocar; (*Bridge*) marcar; (*US*) *game* suspender; **to be ~ed to the Bar** (*Brit Jur*) recibirse de abogado; **to ~ sb as a witness** citar a uno como testigo; **he felt ~ed to do it** se creó llamado a hacerlo, se creó obligado a hacerlo; *V* **halt, name, question** *etc*.

3 *vi* (**a**) (*cry out*) llamar, dar voces, dar gritos.

(**b**) (*Telec*) **who is it ~ing?**, ¿quién llama?; ¿de parte de quién?; (*Rad*) **Madrid ~ing!** ¡aquí Radio Madrid!

(**c**) (*visit*) venir, hacer una visita.

♦**call aside** *vt* llamar aparte.
♦**call at** *vt house* visitar, pasar por; *port* hacer escala en.
♦**call away** *vt*: **he was ~ed away** tuvo que salir (*or* partir); se vio obligado a ausentarse (*from* de); **he was ~ed away on business** tuvo que ir a atender un negocio.
♦**call back 1** *vt* hacer volver; (*Telec*) llamar, volver a llamar.
2 *vi* volver, regresar (*LAm*); (*Telec*) volver a llamar.
♦**call down** *vt* (**a**) *blessings etc* pedir (*on* para); *curses* lanzar (*on* contra).
(**b**) (*US**) poner verde*.
♦**call for** *vt* (**a**) *person* venir por, venir a recoger.
(**b**) (*demand, require*) pedir, requerir, exigir; *food* pedir; **to ~ for help** pedir socorro (a voces); **this ~s for firm measures** esto exige unas medidas contundentes.
(**c**) (*US*) pronosticar, prever.
♦**call forth** *vt* sacar; *remark* inspirar; *protest* motivar, provocar.
♦**call in 1** *vt* (**a**) hacer entrar; *expert etc* llamar, hacer intervenir, pedir la ayuda de; *V* **receiver**.
(**b**) *old notes* retirar de la circulación; *book, loan* pedir la devolución de.
2 *vi* entrar, venir; dar un vistazo.
♦**call off** *vt* cancelar, suspender; *meeting, strike* desconvocar; *search* dar por terminado, suspender, abandonar; *dog* llamar.
♦**call out 1** *vt workers* llamar a la huelga; *rescue services* llamar.
2 *vi* (**a**) gritar, dar voces. (**b**) (*fig*) **this ~s out for universal condemnation** esto pide a gritos la condena de todos.
♦**call over** *vt* llamar; *names* pasar la lista de.
♦**call round** *vi*: **to ~ round to see sb** ir de visita a casa de uno, ir a ver a uno; **I'll ~ round in the morning** pasaré por ahí por la mañana.
♦**call together** *vt* convocar, reunir.
♦**call up** *vt* (**a**) hacer subir.
(**b**) (*esp US*: *Telec*) llamar.
(**c**) *memory* evocar; traer a la memoria.
(**d**) (*Mil*) llamar a filas, llamar al servicio militar.
♦**call (up)on** *vt* (**a**) (*visit*) *person* visitar, ir a ver.
(**b**) (*for a speech*) invitar a hablar; (*invoke*) invocar; **to ~ (up)on sb to do** (*invite*) convidar a uno a hacer; (*demand*) reclamar a uno que haga; **I now ~ (up)on Mr X to speak** ahora cedo la palabra al Sr. X; **to ~ (up)on sb for help** pedir ayuda a uno, acudir a uno pidiendo ayuda; **he ~ed (up)on the nation to be strong** hizo un llamamiento a la nación para que se mostrara fuerte.
callable ['kɔːləbəl] *adj* redimible, amortizable.
callback ['kɔːlbæk] *n* reclamación *f* (*de productos con defecto de origen*).
callbox ['kɔːlbɒks] *n* (*Brit*) cabina *f* telefónica.
callboy ['kɔːlbɔɪ] *n* (*Theat*) traspunte *m*; (*hotel*) botones *m*.
called-up ['kɔːldʌp] *adj*: **~ capital** capital *m* desembolsado.
caller ['kɔːləʳ] *n* visita *f*; (*Brit Telec*) comunicante *mf*; **~, please wait** espere por favor; **the first ~ at the shop** el primer cliente de la tienda.
callgirl ['kɔːlgɜːl] *n* prostituta *f*, chica *f* de cita.
calligraphic [ˌkælɪ'græfɪk] *adj* caligráfico.
calligraphy [kə'lɪgrəfɪ] *n* caligrafía *f*.
call-in ['kɔːlɪn] *n* (*also* **~ program**: *US*) (programa *m*) coloquio *m* (por teléfono).
calling ['kɔːlɪŋ] *n* vocación *f*, profesión *f*.
calling card ['kɔːlɪŋkɑːd] *n* (*US*) tarjeta *f* de visita, tarjeta *f* comercial.
callipers ['kælɪpəz] *npl* calibrador *m*; (*Med*) soporte *m*, corrector *m*.
callisthenics [ˌkælɪs'θenɪks] *n sing* calistenia *f*.
call letters ['kɔːlˌletəz] *npl* (*US*: *Telec*) letras *fpl* de identificación, indicativo *m*.
call money ['kɔːlmʌnɪ] *n* dinero *m* a la vista.
call-number ['kɔːlˌnʌmbəʳ] *n* número *m* de catalogación.
callosity [kæ'lɒsɪtɪ] *n* callo *m*, callosidad *f*.
callous ['kæləs] *adj* (**a**) insensible, cruel. (**b**) (*Med*) calloso.
calloused ['kæləsd] *adj* calloso, con callos.
callously ['kæləslɪ] *adv* cruelmente.
callousness ['kæləsnɪs] *n* insensibilidad *f*, crueldad *f*.
callow ['kæləʊ] *adj* inexperto, novato; *youth* imberbe.
call-sign ['kɔːlsaɪn] *n* (*Rad*) (señal *f* de) llamada *f*.
call-signal ['kɔːlˌsɪgnəl] *n* (*Telec*) codigo *m* de llamada.
call-up ['kɔːlʌp] *n* (*of reserves*) movilización *f*; (*conscription*) servicio *m* militar obligatorio; (*act of calling*) llamamiento *m* (a filas); **~ papers** notificación *f* de llamada a filas.
callus ['kæləs] *n* callo *m*.
calm [kɑːm] **1** *adj person, mind* tranquilo, sosegado; *weather* calmoso, sin viento; *sea* liso, en calma; **to keep ~** no emocionarse, conservar la tranquilidad; **keep ~, everybody!** ¡todos tranquilos!; ¡no se pongan nerviosos!; **to grow ~** calmarse, sosegarse.
2 *n* calma *f*, tranquilidad *f*; **the ~ before the storm** la calma antes de la tormenta.
3 *vt* (*also* **to ~ down**) calmar, tranquilizar.
4 *vi* (*also* **to ~ down**) calmarse, tranquilizarse; **~ down!** ¡cálmese!, (*to excited child*) ¡estáte quieto!
5 *vr*: **~ yourself!** ¡cálmese!
calming ['kɑːmɪŋ] *adj* calmante.
calmly ['kɑːmlɪ] *adv* con calma, tranquilamente.
calmness ['kɑːmnɪs] *n* calma *f*, tranquilidad *f*, sosiego *m*.
Calor gas ['kæləˌgæs] ® *n* (*Brit*) butano *m*.
caloric [ˌkə'lɒrɪk] *adj* calórico, térmico; **~ energy** energía *f* calórica, energía *f* térmica.
calorie ['kælərɪ] *n* caloría *f*; **~-conscious** cuidadoso con la línea.
calorific [ˌkælə'rɪfɪk] *adj* calorífico; **~ value** valor *m* calorífico.
calque [kælk] *n* calco *m* (*on* de).
calumniate [kə'lʌmnɪeɪt] *vt* calumniar.
calumny ['kæləmnɪ] *n* calumnia *f*.
Calvados ['kælvəˌdɒs] *n* Calvados *m*.
Calvary ['kælvərɪ] *n* Calvario *m*.
calve [kɑːv] *vi* parir (*la vaca*).
calves [kɑːvz] *npl of* **calf**[1] *and* **calf**[2].
Calvin ['kælvɪn] *nm* Calvino.
Calvinism ['kælvɪnɪzəm] *n* calvinismo *m*.
Calvinist ['kælvɪnɪst] **1** *adj* calvinista. **2** *n* calvinista *mf*.
Calvinistic [ˌkælvɪ'nɪstɪk] *adj* calvinista.
calypso [kə'lɪpsəʊ] *n* calipso *m*.
calyx ['keɪlɪks] *n, pl* **calyces** ['keɪlɪsiːz] cáliz *m*.
CAM *n abbr of* **computer-aided manufacture** fabricación *f* asistida por ordenador, FAO *f*.
cam [kæm] *n* leva *f*.
camaraderie [ˌkæmə'rɑːdərɪ] *n* compañerismo *m*, camaradería *f*.
camber ['kæmbəʳ] **1** *n* combadura *f*; convexidad *f*; (*of road*) peralte *m*. **2** *vt* combar, arquear. **3** *vi* combarse, arquearse.
Cambodia [kæm'bəʊdɪə] *n* Camboya *f*.
Cambodian [kæm'bəʊdɪən] **1** *adj* camboyano. **2** *n* camboyano *m*, -a *f*.
cambric ['keɪmbrɪk] *n* batista *f*.
Cambs *abbr of* **Cambridgeshire**.
camcorder ['kæmkɔːdəʳ] *n* cámara *f* de vídeo y audio, cámcorder *m*.
came [keɪm] *pret of* **come**.
camel ['kæməl] *n* camello *m*.
camel-hair ['kæməlˌheəʳ] *n*, **camel's-hair** ['kæməlzˌheəʳ] *n* pelo *m* de camello.
camellia [kə'miːlɪə] *n* camelia *f*.
cameo ['kæmɪəʊ] *n* camafeo *m*.
camera ['kæmərə] *n* (**a**) máquina *f* (fotográfica); (*Cine, TV*) cámara *f*; **~ crew** equipo *m* de cámara; **to be on ~** estar enfocado; **we shall be on ~ in 30 seconds** entramos en cámara dentro de 30 segundos. (**b**) (*Jur*) **in ~** en secreto, a puerta cerrada.
cameraman ['kæmərəmæn] *n, pl* **cameramen** ['kæmərəmen] cámara *m*.
camera-ready ['kæmərəˌredɪ] *adj*: **~ copy** material *m* preparado para la cámara.
camera-shy ['kæmərəˌʃaɪ] *adj*: **to be ~** cohibirse en presencia de la cámara.
camerawork ['kæmərəˌwɜːk] *n* (*Cine*) uso *m* de la cámara.
Cameroon [ˌkæmə'ruːn] *n* Camerún *m*.
camisole ['kæmɪsəʊl] *n* camisola *f*.
camomile ['kæməʊmaɪl] *n* camomila *f*; **~ tea** (infusión *f* de) manzanilla *f*.
camouflage ['kæməflɑːʒ] **1** *n* camuflaje *m*. **2** *vt* camuflar.
camp[1] [kæmp] **1** *n* (**a**) campamento *m*, campo *m*; **to make ~, to pitch ~** poner el campamento, armar la tienda, acampar(se); **to break ~, to strike ~** levantar el campamento.
(**b**) (*Pol etc*) grupo *m*, facción *f*; **to have a foot in both ~s** tener intereses en ambos partidos (*etc*).
2 *vi* acampar(se); (*) alojarse temporalmente; **to go ~ing** hacer camping, ir a veranear (*etc*) con la tienda; **to ~ out on the beach** pasar la noche en la playa.
camp[2]* [kæmp] **1** *adj* (**a**) (*affected*) afectado (y divertido), exagerado; (intencionadamente) teatral; sensible, elegante; (*Liter etc*) afectado, amanerado.

(**b**) (*effeminate*) afeminado; (*openly gay*) (abiertamente) homosexual.

2 *n* (**a**) afectación *f* divertida, exageración *f*, teatralidad *f* intencionada; (*Liter etc*) amaneramiento *m*.

(**b**) afeminación *f*; homosexualidad *f* (abierta).

3 *vt*: **to ~ it up** parodiarse a sí mismo; comportarse ostentosamente de modo raro; guasearse, hacer el tonto.

campaign [kæm'peɪn] **1** *n* campaña *f*; **~ trail** recorrido *m* electoral; **~ worker** colaborador *m*, -ora *f* en una campaña política.

2 *vi* (*Mil*) luchar; servir; hacer campaña; **to ~ against** hacer campaña en contra de; **to ~ for** hacer campaña a favor de.

campaigner [kæm'peɪnəʳ] *n* (*fig*) paladín *m*, partidario *m*, -a *f* (*for* de), propagandista *mf* (*for* por); **old ~** veterano *m*, -a *f*.

campanile [ˌkæmpə'niːlɪ] *n* campanario *m*.

campanologist [ˌkæmpə'nɒlədʒɪst] *n* campanólogo *m*, -a *f*.

campanology [ˌkæmpə'nɒlədʒɪ] *n* campanología *f*.

campbed ['kæmp'bed] *n* (*Brit*) cama *f* de campaña, cama *f* plegable, catre *m* (*LAm*).

camp-chair ['kæmp'tʃɛəʳ] *n* silla *f* plegadiza.

camper ['kæmpə] *n* (**a**) (*person*) campista *mf*. (**b**) (*Aut*: *esp US*) autocaravana *f*, campero *m* (*LAm*).

campfire ['kæmp'faɪə] *n* hoguera *f* de campamento; (*of scouts*) reunión *f* alrededor de la hoguera.

camp-follower ['kæmpˌfɒləʊəʳ] *n* (*fig*) simpatizante *mf*; (*Mil*††: *prostitute*) prostituta *f*; (*civilian worker*) trabajador *m* civil.

campground ['kæmpgraʊnd] *n* (*US*) cámping *m*.

camphor ['kæmfəʳ] *n* alcanfor *m*.

camphorated ['kæmfəreɪtɪd] *adj* alcanforado.

camping ['kæmpɪŋ] *n* cámping *m*.

Camping gas ['kæmpɪŋˌgæs] ® *n* (*Brit*: *gas*) gas *m* butano; (*US*: *stove*) cámping gas ® *m*.

camping-ground ['kæmpɪŋgraʊnd] *n*, **camping-site** ['kæmpɪŋsaɪt] *n* (terreno *m* de) cámping *m*.

camping-van ['kæmpɪŋˌvæn] *n* camioneta-casa *f*.

campion ['kæmpɪən] *n* colleja *f*.

campsite ['kæmpsaɪt] *n* cámping *m*; campamento *m*.

camp-stool ['kæmpstuːl] *n* taburete *m* plegable.

camp-stove ['kæmp'stəʊv] *n* hornillo *m* de campista.

campus ['kæmpəs] *n* campus *m*.

camshaft ['kæmʃɑːft] *n* árbol *m* de levas.

can[1] [kæn] (*irr*: *conditional and pret* **could**; *defective*) *vi* (**a**) (*be able to*) poder; **if I ~** si puedo; **we can't go swimming today** hoy no podemos ir a bañarnos; **that cannot be!** ¡eso no puede ser!, ¡es imposible!; **he will do all he ~** hará lo posible (to + *infin* por + *infin*); **I could have screamed** estuve para lanzar un grito; **it could have been a wolf** podía ser un lobo; **I reckon you could have got a job last year** creo que podías obtener un trabajo el año pasado; **'have another helping' — 'I really couldn't'** '¿otra ración?' — 'no puedo'.

(**b**) (*with verbs of perception, not translated*) **I ~ hear it** lo oigo; **I couldn't see it anywhere** no lo veía en ninguna parte; **I can't understand why** no comprendo por qué.

(**c**) (*of acquired skills, know how to*) saber, *eg* **~ you swim?** ¿sabes nadar?

(**d**) (*have permission to*) poder, *eg* **~ I go now?** ¿puedo irme ahora?

(**e**) (*with emphasis*) **you cannot be serious!** ¿lo dices en serio?; **but he can't be dead!** ¡pero no es posible que esté muerto!; **he can't possibly have been wrong** no es posible que se haya equivocado; **he can't have said that** no puede haber dicho eso; **you could have told me!** ¡podías habérmelo dicho!; **how ~ you say that?** ¿cómo te atreves a decir eso?; **where ~ she be?** ¿dónde demonios puede estar?

(**f**) (*comparisons*) **I'm doing it as well as I ~** lo hago lo mejor que puedo; **as cheap as ~ be** lo más barato posible; **as big as big ~ be** lo más grande posible.

can[2] [kæn] **1** *n* lata *f*, bote *m*; (*for petrol etc*) bidón *m*; (*of film*) lata *f*, cartucho *m*; (*US*‡: *toilet*) wáter *m*; (*US*‡: *prison*) chirona‡ *f*; (*US*: *buttocks*) culo‡ *m*; **~ of worms*** problema *m* (*etc*) peliagudo; **it's in the ~*** está en el bote*; (**to be left**) **to carry the ~*** pagar el pato*.

2 *vt* conservar en lata; enlatar, envasar; (*US*‡) *employee* despedir; **~ it!** (*US*‡) ¡cállate!; *V also* **canned**.

Canaan ['keɪnən] *n* Canaán *m*.

Canaanite ['keɪnənaɪt] *n* canaanita *mf*.

Canada ['kænədə] *n* el Canadá.

Canadian [kə'neɪdɪən] **1** *adj* canadiense. **2** *n* canadiense *mf*.

canal [kə'næl] *n* canal *m*; (**alimentary ~**) tubo *m* digestivo; **the C~ Zone** (*Brit*: *Suez*) la zona del Canal de Suez; (*US*: *Panama*) la zona del Canal de Panamá.

canalization [ˌkænəlaɪ'zeɪʃən] *n* canalización *f*.

canalize ['kænəlaɪz] *vt* canalizar.

canapé ['kænəpeɪ] *n* (*Culin*) canapé *m*.

canard [kæ'nɑːd] *n* filfa *f*, bulo *m*, noticia *f* falsa.

Canaries [kə'nɛərɪz] *npl* Las Canarias.

canary [kə'nɛərɪ] *n* canario *m*.

Canary Islands [kə'nɛərɪˌaɪləndz] *npl* Islas *fpl* Canarias.

canary seed [kə'nɛərɪˌsiːd] *n* alpiste *m*.

canary yellow [kəˌnɛərɪ'jeləʊ] *adj* amarillo canario.

canasta [kə'næstə] *n* canasta *f*.

Canberra ['kænbərə] *n* Canberra *f*.

cancan ['kænkæn] *n* cancán *m*.

cancel ['kænsəl] **1** *vt* cancelar; suprimir; *flight, holiday, party* suspender; *permission etc* retirar; *stamp* matar, inutilizar; **they ~ each other out** se anulan mutuamente.

2 *vi* (*Math*) **to ~ out** destruirse, anularse.

cancel key ['kænsəlkiː] *n* teclado *m* de anulación.

cancellation [ˌkænsə'leɪʃən] *n* cancelación *f*; supresión *f*; suspensión *f*; el retirar; (*Post*: *mark*) matasellos *m*, (*act*) inutilización *f*.

Cancer ['kænsəʳ] *n* (*Zodiac*) Cáncer *m*.

cancer ['kænsəʳ] *n* cáncer *m*; **~ causing** cancerígeno; **~ patient** canceroso *m*, -a *f*; **~ research** investigación *f* del cáncer; **~ specialist** cancerólogo *m*, -a *f*, oncólogo *m*, -a *f*; **~ stick** (*Brit*‡) pito* *m*, fumata‡ *m*.

cancerous ['kænsərəs] *adj* canceroso; **to become ~** cancerarse.

candelabra [ˌkændɪ'lɑːbrə] *n* candelabro *m*.

C and F (*Comm*) *abbr of* **Cost and Freight** costo *m* y flete.

candid ['kændɪd] *adj* franco, sincero, abierto; **~ camera** cámara *f* indiscreta; **to be quite ~** hablando con franqueza.

candidacy ['kændɪdəsɪ] *n* (*esp US*) candidatura *f*.

candidate ['kændɪdeɪt] *n* (*applicant*) aspirante *mf* (*for* a), solicitante *mf* (*for* de); (*for election, examinee, Pol, etc*) candidato *m*, -a *f* (*for* a); (*in competitive exams*) opositor *m*, -ora *f* (*for a post* a un puesto).

candidature ['kændɪdətʃəʳ] *n* (*Brit*) candidatura *f*.

candidly ['kændɪdlɪ] *adv* francamente, con franqueza.

candidness ['kændɪdnɪs] *n* franqueza *f*.

candied ['kændɪd] *adj* azucarado; **~ fruits** frutas *fpl* escarchadas; **~ peel** piel *f* almibarada, cascas *fpl* almibaradas.

candle ['kændl] *n* vela *f*, cera *f* (*And*); candela *f*; (*Eccl*) cirio *m*; **to burn the ~ at both ends** consumir la vida, hacer de la noche día; **you can't hold a ~ to him** no llegas a la suela de su zapato.

candle-end ['kændlˌend] *n* cabo *m* de vela.

candle-grease ['kændlgriːs] *n* cera *f* derretida.

candlelight ['kændllaɪt] *n* luz *f* de una vela; **by ~** a la luz de una vela.

candlelit ['kændllɪt] *adj* alumbrado por velas; **a ~ supper for two** una cena para dos con velas.

Candlemas ['kændlməs] *n* Candelaria *f* (*2 febrero*).

candlepower ['kændlˌpaʊəʳ] *n* bujía *f*.

candlestick ['kændlstɪk] *n* (*single*) candelero *m*; (*low*) palmatoria *f*; (*large, ornamental*) candelabro *m*; (*processional*) cirial *m*.

candlewick ['kændlwɪk] *n* (**a**) pabilo *m*, mecha *f* (de vela).

(**b**) (*cloth*) tela *f* de algodón afelpada, chenille *f*.

can-do* [ˌkæn'duː] *adj* (*US*) dinámico.

candour, (*US*) **candor** ['kændəʳ] *n* franqueza *f*.

candy ['kændɪ] **1** *n* azúcar *m* cande; (*US*) caramelo *m*, bombón *m*, dulce *m*, golosina *f* (*LAm*). **2** *vt* azucarar, garapiñar.

candy-floss ['kændɪflɒs] *n* (*Brit*) algodón *m* azucarado.

candy store ['kændɪstɔː] *n* (*US*) bombonería *f*, confitería *f*.

candy-striped ['kændɪˌstraɪpt] *adj* a rayas multicolores.

cane [keɪn] **1** *n* (*Bot*) caña *f*; (*sugar~*) caña *f* de azúcar; (*stick*) bastón *m*; (*for punishment*) palmeta *f*, vara *f*; (*in furnishings*) mimbre *f*; **~ sugar** azúcar *m* de caña.

2 *vt* castigar con palmeta, azotar.

canine ['kænaɪn] **1** *adj* canino; **~ tooth** diente *m* canino, colmillo *m*. **2** *n* (*dog*) perro *m*, can *m*; (*tooth*) canino *m*, colmillo *m*.

caning ['keɪnɪŋ] *n* castigo *m* con palmeta; **to give sb a ~** castigar a uno con la palmeta, (*fig*) dar una paliza a uno.

canister ['kænɪstəʳ] *n* lata *f*, bote *m*; (*of gas*) bombona *f*; (*smoke-bomb*) bote *m* (de humo).

canker ['kæŋkəʳ] **1** *n* (*Med*) llaga *f* gangrenosa; úlcera *f* en la boca; (*Bot*) cancro *m*; (*fig*) cáncer *m*.

2 *vt* ulcerar; (*fig*) corromper.

3 *vi* ulcerarse; (*fig*) corromperse.

cankerous ['kæŋkərəs] *adj* ulceroso.
cannabis ['kænəbɪs] *n* (*Bot*) cáñamo *m* (índico); (*drug*) canabis *m*.
canned ['kænd] *adj food* en lata, de lata; *music* grabado, enlatado; ~ **foods** conservas *fpl* alimenticias; **to be ~‡** estar ajumado*, estar tomado* (*LAm*).
cannelloni [ˌkænɪ'ləʊnɪ] *npl* canelones *mpl*.
cannery ['kænərɪ] *n* fábrica *f* de conservas.
cannibal ['kænɪbəl] **1** *adj* antropófago. **2** *n* caníbal *mf*, antropófago *m*.
cannibalism ['kænɪbəlizəm] *n* canibalismo *m*.
cannibalistic [ˌkænɪbə'lɪstɪk] *adj* canibalesco.
cannibalize ['kænɪbəlaɪz] *vt* (*fig*) canibalizar.
canning ['kænɪŋ] *n* enlatado *m*; ~ **factory** fábrica *f* de conservas; ~ **industry** industria *f* conservera.
cannon ['kænən] **1** *n* (**a**) cañón *m*; (*collectively*) artillería *f*. (**b**) (*Brit Billiards*) carambola *f*.
2 *vi* (*Brit Billiards*) hacer carambola.
◆**cannon into** *vt* chocar violentamente con.
◆**cannon off** *vt* rebotar contra.
cannonade [ˌkænə'neɪd] *n* cañoneo *m*.
cannonball ['kænənbɔːl] *n* bala *f* de cañón.
cannon-fodder ['kænənˌfɒdəʳ] *n* carne *f* de cañón.
cannon-shot ['kænənʃɒt] *n* cañonazo *m*, tiro *m* de cañón; (*ammunition*) bala *f* de cañón; **within ~** al alcance de un cañón.
cannot ['kænɒt] *negative of* **can¹**.
canny ['kænɪ] *adj* (*esp Scot*) astuto.
canoe [kə'nuː] **1** *n* canoa *f*, chalupa *f* (*LAm*); (*sporting*) piragua *f*. **2** *vi* ir en canoa.
canoeing [kə'nuːɪŋ] *n* piragüismo *m*.
canoeist [kə'nuːɪst] *n* piragüista *mf*.
canon ['kænən] *n* (**a**) canon *m*; criterio *m*; ~ **law** derecho *m* canónico. (**b**) (*person*) canónigo *m*.
canonical [kə'nɒnɪkəl] *adj* canónico.
canonization [ˌkænənaɪ'zeɪʃən] *n* canonización *f*.
canonize ['kænənaɪz] *vt* canonizar.
canonry ['kænənrɪ] *n* canonjía *f*.
canoodle* [kə'nuːdl] *vi* besuquearse*.
can-opener ['kænəʊpnəʳ] *n* abrelatas *m*.
canopy ['kænəpɪ] *n* dosel *m*, toldo *m*; (*over bed*) cielo *m*; (*Archit*) baldaquín *m*; (*over tomb*) doselete *m*; **the ~ of heaven** la bóveda celeste.
cant¹ [kænt] **1** *n* (*slope*) inclinación *f*, sesgo *m*; (*of crystal etc*) bisel *m*. **2** *vt* inclinar, sesgar. **3** *vi* inclinarse, ladearse.
◆**cant over** *vi* volcar.
cant² [kænt] **1** *n* (**a**) (*special language*) jerga *f*. (**b**) (*hypocritical talk*) hipocresías *fpl*, camándulas *fpl*; tópicos *mpl*; gazmoñería *f*. **2** *vi* camandulear.
can't [kɑːnt] = **cannot**.
Cantab [kæn'tæb] *adj* (*Brit*) *abbr of* **Cantabrigiensis, of Cambridge**.
Cantabrian [kæn'tæbrɪən] *adj* cantábrico.
cantaloup ['kæntəluːp] *n* cantalupo *m*.
cantankerous [kæn'tæŋkərəs] *adj* arisco, malhumorado, irritable.
cantata [kæn'tɑːtə] *n* cantata *f*.
canteen [kæn'tiːn] *n* (**a**) (*restaurant*) cantina *f*, comedor *m*. (**b**) (*bottle*) cantimplora *f*. (**c**) (*of cutlery*) juego *m*.
canter ['kæntəʳ] **1** *n* medio galope *m*; **to go for a ~** pasearse a caballo; **to win in a ~** (*Brit fig*) ganar fácilmente. **2** *vi* ir a medio galope.
Canterbury ['kæntəbərɪ] *n* Cantórbery *m*; ~ **Tales** Cuentos *mpl* de Cantórbery.
cantharides [kæn'θærɪdiːz] *npl* polvo *m* de cantárida.
canticle ['kæntɪkl] *n* cántico *m*; **the C~s** el Cantar de los Cantares.
cantilever ['kæntɪliːvəʳ] *n* viga *f* voladiza; ~ **bridge** puente *m* voladizo.
canting ['kæntɪŋ] *adj* hipócrita.
canto ['kæntəʊ] *n* canto *m*.
canton ['kæntɒn] *n* cantón *m*.
cantonal ['kæntənl] *adj* cantonal.
Cantonese [ˌkæntə'niːz] **1** *adj* cantonés. **2** *n* (**a**) cantonés *m*, -esa *f*. (**b**) (*Ling*) cantonés *m*.
cantonment [kən'tuːnmənt] *n* acantonamiento *m*.
Canuck‡ [kə'nʊk] *n* (*a Canadian, pej a French Canadian*) canuck *mf*.
Canute [kə'njuːt] *nm* Canuto.
canvas ['kænvəs] *n* (**a**) lona *f*; (*Naut*) velamen *m*, velas *fpl*; ~ **chair** silla *f* de lona; ~ **shoes** calzado *m* de lona; (*rope-soled*) alpargatas *fpl*; **under ~** en tiendas de campaña. (**b**) (*Art*) lienzo *m*.
canvass ['kænvəs] **1** *n* (**a**) (*inquiry*) sondeo *m*.
(**b**) (*for votes*) solicitación *f*; **to make a door-to-door ~** ir solicitando votos de puerta en puerta.
2 *vt* (**a**) *possibility, question* discutir, hacer que se discuta, someter a una discusión pública.
(**b**) *opinion* sondear; hacer una encuesta de.
(**c**) *votes* solicitar; *voter* solicitar el voto de; *district* hacer campaña en; *orders* solicitar; *purchaser* solicitar pedidos de.
(**d**) (*US*) *votes* escudriñar.
3 *vi*: **to ~ for** solicitar votos por, hacer campaña a favor de; **to go out ~ing** salir a solicitar votos.
canvasser ['kænvəsəʳ] *n* (*Pol*) representante *mf* electoral; (*Comm*) corredor *m*, -ora *f*.
canvassing ['kænvəsɪŋ] *n* solicitación *f* (de votos).
canyon ['kænjən] *n* cañón *m*.
CAP *n abbr of* **Common Agricultural Policy** Política *f* Agraria Común, PAC *f*.
cap [kæp] **1** *n* (**a**) (*hat*) gorra *f*; (*Univ*) bonete *m*; (*servant's etc*) cofia *f*; ~ **and gown** toga *f* y bonete; **to come ~ in hand to sb** venir a uno con el sombrero en la mano; **if the ~ fits wear it** el que se pica ajos come; **to put on one's thinking ~** calarse las gafas, ponerse a pensar; **to set one's ~ at sb** proponerse conquistar a uno; **he's got his ~ for England, he's an England ~** (*Brit*) es miembro de la selección nacional inglesa.
(**b**) (*lid*) tapa *f*, tapón *m*; (*of gun*) cápsula *f*; (*of pen*) capuchón *m*; (*on chimney*) caballete *m*; (*Mech*) casquete *m*; (*contraceptive*) diafragma *m*.
(**c**) (*percussion ~*) cápsula *f* (fulminante).
2 *vt* (**a**) *hill etc* coronar; *work* terminar, poner remate a; *oil-well* encapuchar, tapar.
(**b**) (*surpass*) exceder, superar; **see if you can ~ that story** a ver si cuentas un chiste mejor que ése; **I can ~ that** yo sé algo mejor sobre el mismo asunto; **to ~ it all** para colmo de desgracias.
(**c**) *expenditure* restringir, imponer un límite a; *council etc* restringir los gastos de, imponer un límite presupuestario a.
(**d**) **to be ~ped for Ruritania** jugar en el equipo nacional de Ruritania.
cap. (*Typ*) *abbr of* **capital** mayúscula *f*, may.
capability [ˌkeɪpə'bɪlɪtɪ] *n* capacidad *f*, aptitud *f*.
capable ['keɪpəbl] *adj* capaz, competente; **to be ~ of** ser capaz de; **it's ~ of some improvement** se puede mejorar en algo.
capably ['keɪpəblɪ] *adv* competentemente.
capacious [kə'peɪʃəs] *adj room* grande, extenso, espacioso; *container* de mucha cabida, grande, capaz; *dress* ancho, holgado.
capacitor [kə'pæsɪtəʳ] *n* capacitor *m*.
capacity [kə'pæsɪtɪ] *n* (**a**) (*ability to contain*) capacidad *f*; cabida *f*; (*Aut*) cilindrada *f*; (*carrying ~*) capacidad *f* de cargo; **filled to ~** totalmente lleno, lleno a rebosar; ~ **audience** lleno *m*; ~ **booking** reserva *f* total; **there was a ~ crowd** hubo un lleno completo; **what is the ~ of this hall?** ¿cuántos caben en esta sala?; **to work at full ~** dar el pleno rendimiento.
(**b**) (*ability*) capacidad *f*; aptitud *f*; **her capacities** su talento, su aptitud; **her ~ for research** su aptitud para la investigación; **it is beyond my capacities now** supera ya a mis fuerzas; **to the extent of my ~** hasta donde yo pueda, en la medida de mis fuerzas.
(**c**) (*status*) calidad *f*; **in my ~ as treasurer** en mi calidad de tesorero, como tesorero que soy; **in what ~ were you there?** ¿en calidad de qué estabas allí?
caparison [kə'pærɪsn] **1** *n* caparazón *m*, gualdrapa *f*; (*of person*) vestido *m* rico, galas *fpl*; (*harness etc*) equipo *m*.
2 *vt* engualdrapar; **gaily ~ed** brillantemente enjaezado, (*fig*) brillantemente vestido.
cape¹ [keɪp] *n* (*Geog*) cabo *m*, promontorio *m*; **the C~** (*esp*) el Cabo de Buena Esperanza; ~ **honeysuckle** madreselva *f* siempreviva, bignonia *f* del Cabo.
cape² [keɪp] *n* (*cloak*) capa *f*; (*short*) capotillo *m*, esclavina *f*; (*oilskin*) chubasquero *m*; (*Taur*) capote *m*.
Cape Canaveral [ˌkeɪpkə'nævərəl] *n* Cabo *m* Cañaveral.
Cape Coloureds ['keɪp'kʌlədz] *npl personas de padres racialmente mixtos* (*que habitan en la provincia del Cabo*).
Cape Horn ['keɪp'hɔːn] *n* Cabo *m* de Hornos.
Cape of Good Hope ['keɪpəvgʊd'həʊp] *n* Cabo *m* de Buena Esperanza.
Cape Province ['keɪp'prɒvɪns] *n* Provincia *f* del Cabo.
caper¹ ['keɪpəʳ] *n* (*Bot*) alcaparra *f*.
caper² ['keɪpəʳ] **1** *n* (**a**) (*of horse*) cabriola *f*; **to cut ~s**

hacer cabriolas.

(**b**) (*fig*) (*prank*) travesura *f*; (*) lío *m*, embrollo *m*; **that was quite a** ~ eso sí que fue un número*; **I don't bother with taxes and all that** ~ no me molesto con contribuciones y cosas así; **how did your Spanish** ~ **go?** ¿qué tal el viajecito por España?

2 *vi* (**a**) (*horse*) hacer cabriolas; (*other animal*) brincar, corcovear; (*child*) juguetear, correr y brincar; **to** ~ **about** brincar, juguetear.

(**b**) (*) ir, correr; **he went ~ing off to Paris** se marchó a París como si tal cosa.

Cape Town ['keɪptaʊn] *n* El Cabo, Ciudad *f* del Cabo.

Cape Verde Islands ['keɪp'vɜːd'aɪləndz] *npl* Islas *fpl* de Cabo Verde.

capful ['kæpfʊl] *n*: **one** ~ **to 4 litres of water** un tapón por cada cuatro litros de agua.

capillarity [,kæpɪ'lærɪtɪ] *n* capilaridad *f*.

capillary [kə'pɪlərɪ] **1** *adj* capilar. **2** *n* vaso *m* capilar.

capital ['kæpɪtl] **1** *adj* (**a**) (*Jur*) capital; ~ **offence** delito *m* capital; ~ **punishment** pena *f* de muerte; ~ **sentence** condena *f* a la pena de muerte.

(**b**) (*essential*) capital, primordial; **of** ~ **importance** de importancia primordial.

(**c**) (*chief*) capital; ~ **city** capital *f*; ~ **letter** mayúscula *f*; ~ **Q** Q *f* mayúscula; ~ **ship** acorazado *m*; **it was farce with a** ~ **F** fue una farsa con F mayúscula.

(**d**) (*) magnífico, estupendo; ~! ¡magnífico!

2 *n* (**a**) (*money*) capital *m*; ~ **account** (*Fin, Econ etc*) cuenta *f* de capital; ~ **allowances** amortizaciones *fpl*; ~ **assets** activo *m* fijo, activo *m* inmovilizado; ~ **expenditure** inversiones *fpl*; ~ **gain(s)** plusvalía *f*; ~ **gains tax** impuesto *m* sobre la plusvalía; ~ **goods** bienes *mpl* de equipo, bienes *mpl* de capital; ~ **intensive** intensivo de capital; ~ **investment** inversión *f* de capital; ~ **levy** impuesto *m* sobre el capital; ~ **outlay** desembolso *m* de capital; ~ **reserves** reservas *fpl* de capital; ~ **spending** capital *m* adquisitivo; ~ **stock** (*capital*) capital *m* social, capital *m* comercial; (*shares*) acciones *fpl* de capital; ~ **sum** capital *m*; ~ **transfer tax** impuesto *m* sobre plusvalía de cesión; **to make** ~ **out of** (*fig*) aprovechar, sacar partido de.

(**b**) (*city*) capital *f*.

(**c**) (*Archit*) capitel *m*.

(**d**) (*Typ*) mayúscula *f*; **~s** (*large*) versales *fpl*, (*small*) versalitas *fpl*; **please write in ~s** escribir en letras de imprenta.

capitalism ['kæpɪtəlɪzəm] *n* capitalismo *m*.

capitalist ['kæpɪtəlɪst] **1** *adj* capitalista. **2** *n* capitalista *mf*.

capitalistic [,kæpɪtə'lɪstɪk] *adj* capitalista.

capitalization [kə,pɪtəlaɪ'zeɪʃən] *n* capitalización *f*.

capitalize [kə'pɪtəlaɪz] **1** *vt* (**a**) capitalizar. (**b**) (*Typ*) *word* escribir (*or* imprimir) con mayúscula; *letter* convertir en mayúscula. **2** *vi*: **to** ~ **on** aprovechar, sacar partido de, capitalizar.

capitation [,kæpɪ'teɪʃən] *n* capitación *f*; impuesto *m* por cabeza; ~ **grant** subvención *f* por capitación.

Capitol ['kæpɪtɒl] *n* (*US*) Capitolio *m*.

capitulate [kə'pɪtjʊleɪt] *vi* capitular (*to* ante), rendirse, entregarse (*to* a); (*fig*) ceder, conformarse.

capitulation [kə,pɪtjʊ'leɪʃən] *n* capitulación *f*, rendición *f*.

capon ['keɪpən] *n* capón *m*.

cappuccino [,kæpə'tʃiːnəʊ] *n* capuchino *m*.

caprice [kə'priːs] *n* capricho *m*.

capricious [kə'prɪʃəs] *adj* caprichoso, caprichudo.

capriciously [kə'prɪʃəslɪ] *adv* caprichosamente.

Capricorn ['kæprɪkɔːn] *n* (*Zodiac*) Capricornio *m*.

caps [kæps] *npl* (*Typ*) *abbr of* **capital letters** mayúsculas *fpl*, may.

capsicum ['kæpsɪkəm] *n* pimiento *m*.

capsize [kæp'saɪz] **1** *vt* volcar; (*Naut*) hacer zozobrar, tumbar. **2** *vi* volcarse, dar una vuelta de campana; (*Naut*) zozobrar.

capstan ['kæpstən] *n* cabrestante *m*.

capsule ['kæpsjuːl] *n* (*all senses*) cápsula *f*.

Capt. *abbr of* **Captain** capitán *m*.

captain ['kæptɪn] **1** *n* capitán *m*; (*Sport*) capitán *m*, -ana *f*; ~ **of industry** gran industrial *m*, magnate *m*.

2 *vt* capitanear, ser el capitán de; **a team ~ed by Grace** un equipo capitaneado por Grace.

captaincy ['kæptənsɪ] *n* capitanía *f*.

caption ['kæpʃən] **1** *n* (*heading*) encabezamiento *m*, título *m*; (*to cartoon etc*) leyenda *f*, pie *m*; (*to photo*) pie *m* de foto; (*in film*) subtítulo *m*. **2** *vt* titular; poner un pie a.

captious ['kæpʃəs] *adj* criticón, reparón.

captivate ['kæptɪveɪt] *vt* cautivar, encantar.

captivating ['kæptɪveɪtɪŋ] *adj* cautivante, encantador, delicioso.

captive ['kæptɪv] **1** *adj* cautivo; ~ **audience** público *m* cautivo; ~ **balloon** globo *m* cautivo; ~ **market** mercado *m* cautivo. **2** *n* cautivo *m*, -a *f*.

captivity [kæp'tɪvɪtɪ] *n* cautiverio *m*; cautividad *f*; **bred in** ~ criado en cautividad.

captor ['kæptə^r] *n* apresador *m*, -ora *f*.

capture ['kæptʃə^r] **1** *n* (**a**) (*act*) apresamiento *m*, captura *f*; (*of city etc*) toma *f*, conquista *f*; (*Comput*) captura *f*, recogida *f*.

(**b**) (*thing captured*) presa *f*.

2 *vt person* prender; apresar; *specimen etc* capturar; *animal* coger; *city etc* tomar, conquistar; (*Comm*) *market* conquistar, acaparar; (*fig*) captar; *attention* llamar, atraer; *interest* ocupar; (*Art etc*) captar, reproducir, representar fielmente; (*Comput*) capturar, recoger.

capuchin ['kæpjʊʃɪn] *n* (**a**) (*cowl*) capucho *m*. (**b**) (*Zool*) mono *m* capuchino. (**c**) **C**~ (*Eccl*) capuchino *m*.

car [kɑː^r] *n* (*Aut*) coche *m*, automóvil *m*, carro *m* (*LAm*), máquina *f* (*Carib*); (*tramcar*) tranvía *m*; (*US Rail*) vagón *m*, coche *m*; (*of cable railway*) coche *m*; (*of lift*) caja *f*; (*of balloon etc*) barquilla *f*; ~ **accident** accidente *m* de circulación; ~ **allowance** extra *m* por uso de coche propio; ~ **boot (sale)** (*Brit*) *mercadillo que se organiza en un aparcamiento y en el que se exponen las mercancías en el maletero del coche;* ~ **industry** industria *f* del automóvil; ~ **insurance** seguro *m* del automóvil; ~ **journey** viaje *m* en coche; ~ **licence** permiso *m* de circulación; ~ **number** (*Brit*) matrícula *f*; ~ **radio** radio *f* de coche, autorradio *f*; ~ **rental** alquiler *m* de coches; ~ **sleeper** (*Rail*) *tren coche-cama que transporta automóviles*; ~ **worker** trabajador *m*, -ora *f* de la industria del automóvil.

Caracas [kə'rækəs] *n* Caracas *m*.

carafe [kə'ræf] *n* jarro *m*.

caramel ['kærəməl] *n* caramelo *m*; azúcar *m* quemado; ~ **cream** flan *m*.

carapace ['kærəpeɪs] *n* carapacho *m*.

carat ['kærət] *n* quilate *m*; **18-~ gold** oro *m* de 18 quilates.

caravan ['kærəvæn] **1** *n* (**a**) (*gipsies'*) carricoche *m*, carromato *m*; (*Brit Aut*) caravana *f*, remolque *m*, tráiler *m* (*LAm*); (*Aut*: *camper*) autocaravana *f*; (*of camels*) caravana *f*; ~ **site** cámping *m* para caravanas. (**b**) (*US*) = **convoy 1**. **2** *vi*: **to go ~ing** ir de vacaciones en caravana, viajar en caravana.

caravanette [,kærəvə'net] *n* (*Brit*) caravana *f* pequeña, rulota *f* pequeña.

caravel [kærə'vel] *n* carabela *f*.

caraway ['kærəweɪ] *n* alcaravea *f*; ~ **seed** carvi *m*.

carbide ['kɑːbaɪd] *n* carburo *m*.

carbine ['kɑːbaɪn] *n* carabina *f*.

carbohydrate ['kɑːbəʊ'haɪdreɪt] *n* hidrato *m* de carbono; (*starch in food*) fécula *f*.

carbolic [kɑː'bɒlɪk] *adj*: ~ **acid** ácido *m* carbólico, ácido *m* fénico.

car-bomb ['kɑː,bɒm] *n* coche-bomba *m*.

carbon ['kɑːbən] *n* (*Chem*) carbono *m*; (*Elec, paper*) carbón *m*; ~ **copy** copia *f* al carbón; **he's a** ~ **copy of my uncle** está calcado a mi tío; **~-date** datar mediante la prueba del carbono 14; ~ **dating** datación *f* por C-14; ~ **dioxide** dióxido *m* de carbono; ~ **fibre** fibra *f* de carbono; ~ **monoxide** monóxido *m* de carbono; ~ **ribbon** cinta *f* mecanográfica de carbón; ~ **tetrachloride** tetracloruro *m* de carbono.

carbonaceous [,kɑːbə'neɪʃəs] *adj* carbonoso.

carbonate ['kɑːbənɪt] *n* carbonato *m*.

carbonated ['kɑːbəneɪtɪd] *adj*: ~ **drink** gaseosa *f*; ~ **water** agua *f* mineral.

carbonic [kɑː'bɒnɪk] *adj*: ~ **acid** ácido *m* carbónico.

carboniferous [,kɑːbə'nɪfərəs] *adj* carbonífero.

carbonization [,kɑːbənaɪ'zeɪʃən] *n* carbonización *f*.

carbonize ['kɑːbənaɪz] **1** *vt* carbonizar. **2** *vi* carbonizarse.

carbon-paper ['kɑːbən,peɪpə^r] *n* papel *m* carbón, papel *m* carbónico (*LAm*).

carborundum [,kɑːbə'rʌndəm] *n* carborundo *m*.

carboy ['kɑːbɔɪ] *n* bombona *f*, garrafón *m*, damajuana *f*.

carbuncle ['kɑːbʌŋkl] *n* (**a**) (*ruby*) carbúnculo *m*, carbunco *m*. (**b**) (*Med*) carbunc(l)o *m*, grano *m*.

carburation [,kɑːbjʊ'reɪʃən] *n* carburación *f*.

carburettor [,kɑːbjʊ'retə^r] *n*, (*US*) **carburetor** carburador *m*.

carcass ['kɑːkəs] *n* cadáver *m* de animal, res *f* muerta; (*frame*) armazón *f*; (*) cuerpo *m*.

car-chase ['kɑːtʃeɪs] *n* persecución *f* de (*or* por) un coche; **there followed a ~ along the motorway** se persiguió luego al coche por la autopista.

carcinogen [kɑː'sɪnədʒen] *n* carcinógeno *m*.

carcinogenic [ˌkɑːsɪnə'dʒenɪk] *adj* cancerígeno, carcinogénico.

carcinoma ['kɑːsɪ'nəʊmə] *n*, *pl* **carcinomas** *or* **carcinomata** [ˌkɑːsɪ'nəʊmətə] carcinoma *m*.

card¹ [kɑːd] (*Tech*) **1** *n* carda *f*. **2** *vt* cardar.

card² [kɑːd] **1** *n* (**a**) (*playing* ~) carta *f*, naipe *m*; (*Post*) tarjeta *f* (postal), postal *f*; (*visiting* ~) tarjeta *f* (de visita); (*index* ~) ficha *f*; (*member's, press* ~) carnet *m*, carné *m*; (*at dance, race*) programa *m*; (*piece of cardboard*) cartulina *f*; **to play ~s** jugar a las cartas; **to lose money at ~s** perder el dinero jugando a las cartas.

(**b**) (*idioms*) **isn't he a ~?** ¡qué gracia tiene el tío!, ¡qué tipo más salado!; **like a house of ~s** como un castillo de naipes; **it is quite on** (*or* (*US*) **in**) **the ~s that** ... es perfectamente posible que ... + *subj*; **to ask for one's ~s** (*Brit*) dejar su puesto, renunciar; **to get one's ~s** (*Brit*) ser despedido; **to have a ~ up one's sleeve** quedar a uno todavía un recurso; **to hold all the ~s** tener los triunfos en la mano; **to lay one's ~s on the table** poner las cartas boca arriba; **if you play your ~s properly** si obras con el debido cuidado.

2 *vt* (*US*): **to ~ sb*** verificar los papeles de identidad de uno.

cardboard ['kɑːdbɔːd] *n* cartón *m*, cartulina *f*; **~ box** caja *f* de cartón.

card-carrying member [ˌkɑːdˌkærɪɪŋ'membəʳ] *n* miembro *mf* de (*or* con) carnet.

card-catalogue ['kɑːdˌkætəlɒg] *n* catálogo *m* de fichas, fichero *m*.

card-game ['kɑːdgeɪm] *n* juego *m* de naipes, juego *m* de cartas.

cardholder ['kɑːdˌhəʊldəʳ] *n* (*political party, organization*) miembro *mf* de carnet; (*library*) socio *mf* (de una biblioteca); (*restaurant etc*) asiduo *m*; (*credit cards*) titular *mf* (de tarjeta de crédito).

cardiac ['kɑːdɪæk] *adj* cardíaco; **~ arrest** paro *m* cardíaco.

cardigan ['kɑːdɪgən] *n* rebeca *f*; cárdigan *m*.

cardinal ['kɑːdɪnl] **1** *adj* cardinal; **~ number** número *m* cardinal; **~ points** puntos *mpl* cardinales; **~ sin** pecado *m* capital. **2** *n* cardenal *m*.

card-index 1 ['kɑːdˌɪndeks] *n* fichero *m* (de tarjetas). **2** [ˌkɑːd'ɪndeks] *vt* fichar, catalogar.

cardio... ['kɑːdɪəʊ] *pref* cardio....

cardiogram ['kɑːdɪəʊˌgræm] *n* cardiograma *m*.

cardiograph ['kɑːdɪəʊˌgræf] *n* cardiógrafo *m*.

cardiological [ˌkɑːdɪə'lɒdʒɪkəl] *adj* cardiológico.

cardiologist [ˌkɑːdɪ'ɒlɪdʒɪst] *n* cardiólogo *m*, -a *f*.

cardiology [ˌkɑːdɪ'ɒlədʒɪ] *n* cardiología *f*.

cardiovascular [ˌkɑːdɪəʊ'væskjʊləʳ] *adj* cardiovascular.

card-phone ['kɑːdˌfəʊn] *n* (*Brit*) *cabina que funciona con una tarjeta de crédito telefónico*.

card-reader ['kɑːdˌriːdəʳ] *n* lector *m* de fichas.

card-sharp ['kɑːdˌʃɑːp] *n*, **card-sharper** ['kɑːdˌʃɑːpəʳ] *n* fullero *m*, tahur *m*.

card-stacker ['kɑːdˌstækəʳ] *n* depósito *m* de descarga de fichas.

card-table ['kɑːdˌteɪbl] *n* mesa *f* de baraja, tapete *m* verde.

card-trick ['kɑːdˌtrɪk] *n* truco *m* de naipes.

card-vote ['kɑːdˌvəʊt] *n* voto *m* por delegación, voto *m* de grupo.

CARE [kɛəʳ] *n* (*US*) *abbr of* **Cooperative for American Relief Everywhere**.

care [kɛəʳ] **1** *n* (**a**) (*anxiety*) cuidado *m*; inquietud *f*, solicitud *f*; **full of ~s** lleno de inquietudes; **he has many ~s** son muchas las cosas que le preocupan; **he hasn't a ~ in the world** no tiene problema alguno; **the ~s of State** las responsabilidades de un cargo oficial, las preocupaciones y fatigas del gobierno.

(**b**) (*carefulness*) cuidado *m*, esmero *m*, atención *f*; (*gingerliness*) delicadeza *f*; **'with ~!'** '¡atención!', '¡cuidado!'; **convicted of driving without due ~ and attention** declarado culpable de conducir sin la debida precaución; **have a ~, sir!** ¡mire Vd lo que está diciendo!; **to take ~** tener cuidado; **take ~ !** ¡(ten) cuidado!, ¡ojo!; (*as farewell*) ¡cuídate!; **to take ~ of** cuidar de, *valuable object* guardar, custodiar, *thing to be done* encargarse de; **I'll take ~ of him*** yo me encargo de él; **that can take ~ of itself** eso se resolverá por sí mismo; **that takes ~ of that** con eso todo queda arreglado; **she can take ~ of herself** ella sabe cuidar a sí misma; **I'll take ~ of this** (*bill etc*) esto corre de mi cuenta; **to take good ~ of o.s.** cuidarse mucho; **to take ~ to** + *infin* cuidar de que + *subj*, asegurarse de que + *subj*; **he doesn't take enough ~ to** + *infin* no pone bastante cuidado en + *infin*; **to take ~ not to** + *infin* guardarse de + *infin*; **take ~ not to drop it!** ¡ten cuidado, no lo dejes caer!

(**c**) (*charge*) cargo *m*, custodia *f*; (*Med etc*) asistencia *f*; **~ of** (*on letter*) en casa de; **to be in the ~ of** estar bajo la custodia de; **he is in the ~ of Dr X** le asiste el doctor X, le atiende el doctor X; **the child was taken into ~** el niño fue internado en un centro de protección de menores.

2 *vi* (**a**) (*feel interest, anxiety etc*) interesarse, preocuparse; **we need more people who ~** necesitamos más gente que se preocupe por los demás, necesitamos más personas que se interesen por los prójimos; **to ~ about** preocuparse de (*or* por), tener interés en, interesarse por; **to ~ deeply about sb's fate** preocuparse hondamente por la suerte de uno; **that's all he ~s about** es lo único que le interesa; **what do I ~ ?** ¿qué se me da a mí?, ¡maldito lo que me importa!; **as if I ~d!** y a mí ¿qué?; **I couldn't ~ less!** (*Brit*) eso me trae sin cuidado; **I could ~ less** (*US*) eso me trae sin cuidado; **for all I ~ you can take it** por mí te lo puedes llevar; **I don't ~** me es igual, no me importa; **I don't ~ twopence!** (*or* **a fig, hoot, jot, rap** *etc*) ¡me importa un comino!; **I don't ~ either way** me da lo mismo; **I don't ~ what people say** me trae sin cuidado lo que diga la gente; **who ~s?** ¿qué más da?

(**b**) (*like, want*) **to ~ to** + *infin* querer + *infin*, tener ganas de + *infin*; **if you ~ to** si quieres; **would you ~ to tell me?** ¿quieres decírmelo?; **would you ~ to take a walk?** ¿te apetece dar un paseo?; **would you ~ to take your hat off?** ¿tendrías inconveniente en quitarte el sombrero?

◆**care for** *vt* (**a**) (*like*) tener afecto a, sentir cariño por; (*amorously*) sentirse atraído por; **I don't much ~ for him** no me resulta simpático; **I know he ~s for you a lot** sé que te tiene mucho cariño; **I don't ~ for the idea** no me hace gracia la idea; **I don't ~ for coffee** no me gusta el café; **would you ~ for a walk?** ¿te apetece dar un paseo?; **would you ~ for a drink?** ¿quieres tomar algo?

(**b**) (*look after*) cuidar; atender; **well ~d for** (bien) cuidado, bien atendido.

careen [kə'riːn] **1** *vt* carenar. **2** *vi* inclinarse, escorar.

career [kə'rɪəʳ] **1** *n* profesión *f*, carrera *f* (profesional); **~s adviser** (*or* **officer**) (*Brit*), **~(s) counselor** (*US*), **~s teacher** (*Brit Scol*) *persona encargada de la guía vocacional de los alumnos*; **~ diplomat** diplomático *m*, -a *f* de carrera; **~ girl** mujer *f* dedicada a su profesión; **~s guidance** (*Brit*) guía *f* vocacional; **~s office** *oficina de guía vocacional*; **~ prospects** perspectivas *fpl* de futuro; **~s service** servicio *m* de consejería profesional.

2 *vi* (*also* **to ~ along**) correr a toda velocidad; **to ~ down the street** correr calle abajo; **to ~ into a wall** estrellarse contra un muro.

careerist [kə'rɪərɪst] *n* ambicioso *m*, -a *f*, arribista *mf*.

carefree ['kɛəfriː] *adj* despreocupado, libre de preocupaciones, alegre, inconsciente.

careful ['kɛəfʊl] *adj* (**a**) cuidadoso; cauteloso, prudente; **~!** ¡cuidado!, ¡ojo!; **to be ~** tener cuidado; **be ~!** ¡ten cuidado!; **one can't be too ~** nunca se peca por demasiado cuidadoso; **we must be very ~ here** en esto conviene andar con pies de plomo; **be ~ what you say to him** ten cuidado con lo que le dices; **we shall lose it if we're not ~** lo perderemos si no tenemos cuidado; **to be ~ of** tener cuidado con; **to be ~ to** + *infin* poner diligencia en + *infin*, asegurarse cuidadosamente de que + *subj*; **he was ~ to say that ...** dijo de modo particular que ...

(**b**) (*painstaking*) esmerado, cuidadoso; competente, concienzudo.

(**c**) (*with money*) económico, ahorrativo; (*pej*) tacaño.

carefully ['kɛəfəlɪ] *adv* (*V adj*) (**a**) con cuidado, cuidadosamente; **we must go ~ here** en esto conviene andar con pies de plomo; **I have to spend ~** tengo que pensar mucho en lo que gasto; **he replied ~** contestó con cautela. (**b**) con esmero, esmeradamente; competentemente, concienzudamente.

carefulness ['kɛəfəlnɪs] *n* (*V adj*) (**a**) cuidado *m*; prudencia *f*, cautela *f*. (**b**) esmero *m*, cuidado *m*. (**c**) economía *f*; (*pej*) tacañería *f*.

care label ['kɛəˌleɪbl] *n* (*on garment*) etiqueta *f* de instrucciones de lavado.

careless ['kɛəlɪs] *adj* descuidado; negligente; (*inattentive*) poco atento; (*thoughtless*) irreflexivo, imprudente; *stroke* hecho a la ligera; *appearance* descuidado, desaliñado; (~ *of others*) indiferente, insensible (*of* a); **~ driving**

conducción *f* negligente; **that was very ~ of you** en eso fuiste muy imprudente.
carelessly ['kɛəlɪslɪ] *adv* descuidadamente; a la ligera.
carelessness ['kɛəlɪsnɪs] *n* descuido *m*; falta *f* de atención; desaliño *m*; indiferencia *f* (*of* a); **through sheer ~** por simple descuido, por simple falta de atención.
caress [kə'res] **1** *n* caricia *f*. **2** *vt* acariciar.
caret ['kærət] *n* signo *m* de intercalación (‸).
caretaker ['kɛə,teɪkəʳ] *n* (*Brit*) vigilante *m*; (*in museum etc*) guardián *m*; (*of flats*) portero *m*, conserje *m*, celador *m*, curador *m*; **~ government** gobierno *m* de transición.
careworn ['kɛəwɔːn] *adj person* agobiado de preocupaciones; *face, frown* preocupado, lleno de ansiedad.
carfare ['kɑːfɛəʳ] *n* (*US*) pasaje *m*, precio *m* (del billete).
car-ferry ['kɑː,ferɪ] *n* transbordador *m* para coches, ferry *m*.
cargo ['kɑːgəʊ] *n* cargamento *m*, carga *f*.
cargo-boat ['kɑːgəʊbəʊt] *n* barco *m* de carga, carguero *m*.
cargo-plane ['kɑːgəʊ,pleɪn] *n* avión *m* de carga.
car-hire ['kɑːhaɪəʳ] *n* alquiler *m* de coches; **~ firm** empresa *f* de alquiler de coches.
carhop ['kɑːhɒp] *n* (*US*) camarero *m*, -a *f* de un restaurante 'drive-in'.
Caribbean [,kærɪ'biːən] *adj* caribe, caribeño.
Caribbean Sea [,kærɪ'biːən'siː] *n* Mar *m* Caribe.
caribou ['kærɪbuː] *n* caribú *m*.
caricature ['kærɪkətjʊəʳ] **1** *n* caricatura *f*; (*in newspaper*) dibujo *m* cómico; **it was a ~ of a ceremony** fue una parodia de ceremonia. **2** *vt* caricaturizar.
caricaturist [,kærɪkə'tjʊərɪst] *n* caricaturista *mf*, dibujante *mf*.
CARICOM ['kærɪ,kɒm] *n abbr of* **Caribbean Community and Common Market** Comunidad *f* y Mercado Común del Caribe, CMCC *f*.
caries ['kɛərɪiːz] *n* caries *f*.
carillon [kə'rɪljən] *n* carillón *m*.
caring ['kɛərɪŋ] **1** *adj* afectuoso, bondadoso; humanitario; **the ~ professions** las profesiones de dedicación humanitaria; **the ~ society** la sociedad humanitaria. **2** *n* (*care*) cuidado *m*; (*affection*) afecto *m*, cariño *m*; (*help*) ayuda *f*, auxilio *m*.
carious ['kɛərɪəs] *adj* cariado.
Carlism ['kɑːlɪzəm] *n* carlismo *m*.
Carlist ['kɑːlɪst] **1** *adj* carlista. **2** *n* carlista *mf*.
Carmelite ['kɑːməlaɪt] **1** *adj* carmelita. **2** *n* carmelita *mf*.
carmine ['kɑːmaɪn] **1** *adj* carmín, de carmín. **2** *n* carmín *m*.
carnage ['kɑːnɪdʒ] *n* carnicería *f*, mortandad *f*, matanza *f*.
carnal ['kɑːnl] *adj* carnal; **to have ~ knowledge of** tener ayuntamiento carnal con.
carnation [kɑː'neɪʃən] *n* clavel *m*.
carnival ['kɑːnɪvəl] *n* carnaval *m*; fiesta *f*, feria *f*; (*US*) parque *m* de atracciones; **~ queen** reina *f* de la fiesta.
carnivore ['kɑːnɪvɔːʳ] *n* carnívoro *m*.
carnivorous [kɑː'nɪvərəs] *adj* carnívoro.
carob ['kærəb] *n* (*bean*) algarroba *f*; (*tree*) algarrobo *m*.
carol ['kærəl] **1** *n* villancico *m*. **2** *vi* cantar alegremente.
Carolingian [kærə'lɪnʒɪən] *adj* carolingio.
carotid [kə'rɒtɪd] *n* (*also* **~ artery**) carótida *f*.
carousal [kə'raʊzəl] *n* jarana *f*, parranda *f*, juerga *f*.
carouse [kə'raʊz] *vi* jaranear, estar de parranda, estar de juerga.
carousel [,kæruː'sel] *n* (*merry-go-round*) caballitos *mpl*, tiovivo *m*, carrusel *m*; (*Phot*) bombo *m* de diapositivas; (*at airport*) cinta *f* de equipajes.
carp¹ [kɑːp] *n* carpa *f*.
carp² [kɑːp] *vi* criticar (sin motivo); **to ~ at, to ~ about** quejarse (sin motivo) de, murmurar de.
car-park ['kɑːpɑːk] *n* (*Brit*) aparcamiento *m*, parking *m*, estacionamiento *m* (*LAm*).
Carpathians [kɑː'peɪθɪənz] *npl* Montes *mpl* Cárpatos.
carpenter ['kɑːpɪntəʳ] *n* carpintero *m*.
carpentry ['kɑːpɪntrɪ] *n* carpintería *f*.
carpet ['kɑːpɪt] **1** *n* alfombra *f*; moqueta *f*; **~ square, ~ tile** loseta *f*; **to be on the ~*** tener que aguantar un rapapolvo*; **to roll out the red ~ for sb** recibir a uno con todos los honores debidos; **they tried to sweep it under the ~** trataron de ocultar los trapos sucios, quisieron echar tierra sobre el asunto.
2 *vt* alfombrar; (*fig*) alfombrar, cubrir, revestir (*with* de); **to ~ sb*** echar un rapapolvo a uno*.
carpet-bag ['kɑːpɪt,bæg] *n* (*US*) maletín *m*, morral *m*.
carpetbagger ['kɑːpɪt,bægəʳ] *n* (*US*) aventurero *m* político, explotador *m* político (venido de fuera).
carpet-bomb ['kɑːpɪt,bɒm] *vt* arrasar con bombas.
carpet-bombing ['kɑːpɪt,bɒmɪŋ] *n* bombardeo *m* de arrasamiento.
carpeted ['kɑːpɪtɪd] *adj floor* alfombrado, enmoquetado; **~ with** (*fig*) cubierto de.
carpet-slippers ['kɑːpɪt,slɪpəz] *npl* zapatillas *fpl*.
carpeting ['kɑːpɪtɪŋ] *n* alfombrado *m*, tapizado *m*; moqueta *f*.
carpet-sweeper ['kɑːpɪt,swiːpəʳ] *n* (*mechanical*) máquina *f* para barrer alfombras; (*vacuum-cleaner*) aspiradora *f*.
car-phone ['kɑːfəʊn] *n* teléfono *m* móvil (de coche).
carping ['kɑːpɪŋ] *adj* criticón, reparón.
carpool ['kɑːpuːl] *n* (*US*) coches *mpl* de uso compartido, uso *m* compartido de coches.
carport ['kɑːpɔːt] *n* garaje *m* abierto, cobertizo *m* para coche.
carriage ['kærɪdʒ] *n* (**a**) (*Brit Rail*) vagón *m*, coche *m*; (*horse-drawn*) carruaje *m*, coche *m*; (*gun* **~**) cureña *f*; (*of typewriter etc*) carro *m*; **~ return** retorno *m* del carro.
(**b**) (*bearing*) andares *mpl*, modo *m* de andar, porte *m*.
(**c**) (*Brit: act of carrying*) transporte *m*; (*Comm*) porte *m*; **~ forward** al precio de cotización (el comprador paga el coste del porte); **~ free** franco de porte; **~ inwards** pagos *mpl* por porte de mercancías compradas; **~ outwards** flete *m* de ida; **~ paid** porte pagado.
carriage-drive ['kærɪdʒdraɪv] *n* calzada *f*.
carriage trade ['kærɪdʒ,treɪd] *n* (*US*) sector *m* de transporte de mercancías.
carriageway ['kærɪdʒweɪ] *n* (*Brit*) carretera *f*; calzada *f*.
carrier ['kærɪəʳ] *n* (**a**) (*person*) transportista *m*; (*company*) empresa *f* de transportes; (*Aer*) aerotransportista *m*, aerolínea *f*.
(**b**) (*Med*) portador *m*, -ora *f* (de enfermedad).
(**c**) (*basket etc*) portaequipajes *m*; (*on cycle*) parrilla *f*.
(**d**) (*Naut*) portaaviones *m*.
carrier-bag ['kærɪə'bæg] *n* (*Brit*) saco *m* (de plástico), bolsa *f*.
carrier-pigeon ['kærɪə,pɪdʒən] *n* paloma *f* mensajera.
carrion ['kærɪən] *n* carroña *f*; inmundicia *f*; **~ crow** corneja *f* negra.
carrot ['kærət] *n* zanahoria *f*.
carroty ['kærətɪ] *adj* pelirrojo.
carrousel [,kæruː'sel] *n* (*US*) = **carousel**.
carry ['kærɪ] **1** *n* (*of ball, shot*) alcance *m*.
2 *vt* (**a**) (*transport*) llevar; traer; transportar, acarrear; *disease* transmitir, ser portador de; (*in mind*) retener; *authority etc* tener, revestir; **as fast as his legs could ~ him** lo más rápidamente posible, a todo correr; **this bus carries 60 passengers** este autobús tiene asientos para 60 personas; **he carries our lives in his hands** lleva nuestras vidas en sus manos; **to ~ one's audience with one** (*fig*) captarse al auditorio.
(**b**) (*have on one's person*) llevar encima, tener consigo.
(**c**) (*involve*) *consequence* acarrear, tener como consecuencia; (*Fin*) *interest* llevar, producir; *guarantee* tener, llevar; *responsibility* conllevar; *interpretation* encerrar, llevar implícito; prestarse a; *meaning* tener; **the offence carries a fine of £100** el delito es castigado por una multa de 100 libras.
(**d**) (*support*) *burden* sostener; *crop* producir, llevar.
(**e**) (*Comm*) *stock* tener en existencia; *article* tener, tratar en; **~ing charge** costo *m* de géneros no en venta (almacenados *etc*).
(**f**) (*extend*) extender, prolongar; **to ~ sth too far** llevar algo al exceso.
(**g**) (*win*) *position* tomar, conquistar; (*Parl*) *seat* ganar; *proposition* hacer aceptar; *motion* aprobar; **to ~ all before one** triunfar, vencer todos los obstáculos, arrollarlo todo.
(**h**) (*newspaper etc*) *story* llevar, imprimir; informar sobre; **this journal does not ~ reviews** esta revista no tiene reseñas.
(**i**) (*Math*) llevar.
(**j**) *child* estar encinta de.
3 *vi* (*reach*) alcanzar, llegar; (*sound*) oírse; **she has a voice which carries** tiene una voz que se oye bastante lejos.
4 *vr*: **to ~ o.s.** portarse; **to ~ o.s. well** andar con garbo, tener buena presencia.
◆**carry about** *vt* llevar consigo; llevar de acá para allá.
◆**carry along** *vt* llevar; (*flood, water*) arrastrar.
◆**carry away** *vt* (**a**) llevarse; (*kidnap*) secuestrar.
(**b**) (*fig*) arrebatar, inspirar, entusiasmar; **to get carried away** exaltarse, emocionarse (demasiado), entusiasmarse (demasiado); extralimitarse.
◆**carry back** *vt* (*lit*) *things* traer; (*Fin*) cargar (sobre cuentas anteriores); **that music carries me back to the 60s** esa música me hace recordar los 60.

◆**carry down** *vt* bajar.
◆**carry forward** *vt* (*Comm*) pasar a cuenta nueva; **carried forward** suma y sigue.
◆**carry off** *vt* (**a**) llevarse; llevar a la fuerza; *prize* alzarse con, arramblar con; *election* ganar; **she carried it off splendidly** salió muy airosa de la prueba.
(**b**) (*kill*) matar, llevar a la tumba.
◆**carry on 1** *vt work* continuar, proseguir; *business* poseer, llevar, ser dueño de.
2 *vi* (**a**) (*continue*) continuar; seguir adelante; **we ~ on somehow** vamos tirando; **if you ~ on like that** si sigues así; **~ on!** ¡adelante!, ¡sigue!, (*in talking*) ¡prosigue!
(**b**) (*) (*complain*) quejarse, protestar; murmurar (*about* de); (*protest*) protestar amargamente (*about* de, por).
(**c**) (*) (*insist*) insistir, machacar; (*argue*) discutir; armar un follón*; **you do ~ on!** ¡dale que dale!; **don't ~ on so!** ¡no machaques!
(**d**) **to ~ on with sb*** (*lovers*) tener un plan con uno*.
◆**carry out** *vt* (**a**) *order, promise, threat* cumplir; *intention* realizar; *plan* llevar a cabo, poner por obra.
(**b**) *repair* hacer; *test* verificar; *work* realizar, llevar a cabo.
◆**carry over** *vt* (**a**) posponer; guardar para después.
(**b**) (*Comm*) pasar a cuenta nueva.
◆**carry through** *vt* (**a**) *plan* llevar a cabo, ejecutar.
(**b**) *person* sostener hasta el fin; **to ~ sb through a crisis** ayudar a uno a superar una crisis; **the stock will ~ us through the winter** las existencias nos bastarán durante todo el invierno.
◆**carry up** *vt* subir.
carryall ['kæriːɔːl] *n* (*US*) cesto *m* grande; = **hold-all.**
carry-back ['kærɪbæk] *n* (*Fin*) traspaso *m* al período anterior.
carrycot ['kærɪkɒt] *n* (*Brit*) cuna *f* portátil, capazo *m*.
carrying-on ['kærɪɪŋ'ɒn] *n* (**a**) continuación *f*; prosecución *f*.
(**b**) (*) plan *m*, relaciones *fpl* amorosas (ilícitas).
carry-on* [ˌkærɪ'ɒn] *n* aspaviento *m*, conmoción *f*, alharaca *f*; lío* *m*; riña *f*, pelea *f*; **what a ~!** ¡qué follón!*; **there was a great ~ about the tickets** se armó un tremendo lío a causa de los billetes*; **did you ever see such a ~?** ¿se ha visto un embrollo igual?
carry-out ['kærɪˌaʊt] **1** *adj meal etc* para llevar. **2** *n* (*food*) comida *f* para llevar; (*drink*) bebida *f* para llevar.
carry-over ['kærɪ'əʊvə^r] *n* (*surplus*) sobrante *m*; resto *m*, remanente *m*; (*Comm*) suma *f* anterior (para traspasar), suma *f* que pasa de una página (de cuenta) a la siguiente; (*St Ex*) aplazamiento *m* de pago hasta el próximo día de ajuste de cuentas.
car-sick ['kɑːˌsɪk] *adj*: **to be ~, to get ~** marearse (en el coche).
car-sickness ['kɑːˌsɪknɪs] *n* mareo *m* (*al ir en coche*); **to suffer ~** marearse (en el coche).
cart [kɑːt] **1** *n* carro *m*, carreta *f*; (*heavy*) carretón *m*; (*hand~*) carretilla *f*, carro *m* de mano; (*US*) carrito *m* de la compra, carrito *m* de supermercado; **to be in the ~*** estar en un atolladero; **to put the ~ before the horse** poner el carro delante de los bueyes.
2 *vt* llevar, acarrear, carretear; (*) llevar (con gran dificultad).
◆**cart away, cart off** *vt* llevarse.
cartage ['kɑːtɪdʒ] *n* acarreo *m*, porte *m*.
carte blanche ['kɑːt'blɑ̃ːnʃ] *n* carta *f* blanca; **to give sb ~** dar carta blanca a uno.
cartel [kɑː'tel] *n* cartel *m*.
carter ['kɑːtə^r] *n* carretero *m*.
Cartesian [kɑː'tiːzɪən] **1** *adj* cartesiano. **2** *n* cartesiano *m*.
Carthage ['kɑːθɪdʒ] *n* Cartago *f*.
Carthaginian [ˌkɑːθə'dʒɪnɪən] **1** *adj* cartaginés. **2** *n* cartaginés *m*, -esa *f*.
cart-horse ['kɑːthɔːs] *n* caballo *m* de tiro.
Carthusian [kɑː'θjuːzɪən] **1** *adj* cartujo. **2** *n* cartujo *m*.
cartilage ['kɑːtɪlɪdʒ] *n* cartílago *m*.
cartilaginous [ˌkɑːtɪ'lædʒɪnəs] *adj* cartilaginoso.
cartload ['kɑːtləʊd] *n* carretada *f* (*also fig*); **by the ~** a carretadas, a montones.
cartographer [kɑː'tɒgrəfə^r] *n* cartógrafo *m*, -a *f*.
cartographic(al) [ˌkɑːtəʊ'græfɪk(əl)] *adj* cartográfico.
cartography [kɑː'tɒgrəfɪ] *n* cartografía *f*.
carton ['kɑːtən] *n* envase *m*, caja *f* de cartón, cartón *m*.
cartoon [kɑː'tuːn] *n* (*newspaper*) dibujo *m* cómico, caricatura *f*; (*Art*) cartón *m*; (*film*) dibujos *mpl* animados; (*strip*) tira *f* cómica.
cartoonist [ˌkɑː'tuːnɪst] *n* dibujante *mf*, caricaturista *mf*.
cartridge ['kɑːtrɪdʒ] *n* cartucho *m* (*also Comput*); (*for pen*) recambio *m*.
cartridge-belt ['kɑːtrɪdʒbelt] *n* cartuchera *f*, canana *f*.
cartridge-case ['kɑːtrɪdʒkeɪs] *n* cartucho *m*.
cartridge-paper ['kɑːtrɪdʒˌpeɪpə^r] *n* papel *m* guarro (de acuarela).
cartridge-player ['kɑːtrɪdʒˌpleɪə^r] *n* lector *m* de cartucho.
cart-track ['kɑːttræk] *n* (*rut*) carril *m*, rodada *f*; (*road*) camino *m* (para carros).
cartwheel ['kɑːtwiːl] *n* rueda *f* de carro; (*fig*) voltereta *f* lateral, rueda *f*.
cartwright ['kɑːtraɪt] *n* carretero *m*.
carve [kɑːv] *vt meat* trinchar; *stone* esculpir, tallar, labrar; *name on tree etc* grabar; **to ~ one's way through** abrirse a la fuerza un camino por.
◆**carve out** *vt piece of wood* tallar; *piece of land* limpiar; *statue, figure* esculpir; *tool* tallar; **to ~ out a career for o.s.** labrarse un porvenir.
◆**carve up** *vt country* dividir, repartir entre los vencedores; desmembrar; *person* (*) coser a puñaladas.
carver ['kɑːvə^r] *n* (**a**) (*person*) (*Culin*) trinchador *m*; (*Art*) escultor *m*, -ora *f*, tallista *mf*. (**b**) **~s** cubierto *m* de trinchar.
carvery ['kɑːvərɪ] *n* restaurante *m* que se especializa en asados.
carve-up* ['kɑːvˌʌp] *n* división *f*, repartimiento *m*; (*Pol etc*) arreglo *m*.
carving ['kɑːvɪŋ] *n* (*Culin*) arte *m* de trinchar; (*Art*) escultura *f*, obra *f* de talla.
carving-knife ['kɑːvɪŋnaɪf] *n*, *pl* **carving-knives** ['kɑːvɪŋnaɪvz] trinchante *m*.
car-wash ['kɑːwɒʃ] *n* tren *m* (*or* túnel *m*) de lavado (de coches).
Casablanca [ˌkæsə'blæŋkə] *n* Casablanca *f*.
cascade [kæs'keɪd] **1** *n* cascada *f*, salto *m* de agua; (*fig*) chorro *m*; torrente *m*. **2** *vi* caer en cascada.
case[1] [keɪs] **1** *n* (**a**) (*container*) caja *f*; (*packing~*) cajón *m*; (*Brit: suitcase*) maleta *f*, valija *f* (*LAm*), veliz *m* (*Mex*); (*for jewels, spectacles etc*) estuche *m*; (*for scissors etc*) vaina *f*; (*of watch*) caja *f*; (*for guitar etc*) funda *f*; (*of window*) marco *m*, bastidor *m*; (*of cartridge*) cartucho *m*, vaina *f*, cápsula *f*; (*showcase*) vitrina *f*.
(**b**) (*Typ*) caja *f*; **lower ~** caja *f* baja; **upper ~** caja *f* alta.
2 *vt* (**a**) encajonar; enfundar; **~d in concrete** revestido de hormigón.
(**b**) (**‡**) *house etc* estudiar la situación de (con intención de robar).
case[2] [keɪs] *n* (**a**) (*instance*) caso *m* (*also Med*); asunto *m*; **a fever ~** un caso de fiebre; **a hospital ~** un caso para el hospital, un enfermo que tendrá que ser trasladado al hospital; **a ~ in point** un ejemplo que hace al caso; **it's a sad ~** es un caso triste; **it's a hopeless ~** (*Med*) es un caso desahuciado; **it's a ~ for the police** éste es asunto para la policía; **it's a ~ of ...** se trata de ...; **it's a clear ~ of murder** es un claro caso de homicidio; **he's working on the train-robbery ~** está haciendo investigaciones sobre el robo del tren; **he's a ~*** es un caso, es un tipo raro*.
(**b**) (*argument, reasoning*) **there seems to be a ~ for reform** parece que hay razones para reformarlo; **there is a ~ for saying that ...** puede decirse razonablemente que ...; **there is a ~ for that attitude** hay argumentos en favor de esa actitud; **that alters the ~** eso cambia la cosa; **I understand that is not the ~** tengo entendido que no es así; **if that is the ~, such being the ~** si las cosas son así; **as the ~ may be** según el caso.
(**c**) (*with prep*) **in ~ he comes** por si viene, (en) caso de que venga; **in ~ of** en caso de; **in your ~** en tu caso; **as in the ~ of** como en el caso de; **in most ~s** en la mayoría de los casos; **in any ~** en todo caso, de todas formas; **just in ~** por si acaso, por lo que pueda ocurrir, por si las moscas; **in such a ~** en tal caso; **in that ~** en ese caso.
(**d**) (*Jur*) causa *f*, pleito *m*, proceso *m*; **the ~ for the defence** la defensa, el conjunto de razones alegadas por el acusado; **the ~ for the prosecution** la acusación, el conjunto de acusaciones alegadas por el fiscal; **the Dreyfus ~** el proceso de Dreyfus, (*more loosely*) el asunto Dreyfus; **there is no ~ to answer** no hay acusación para contestar; **to have a good** (*or* **strong**) **~** tener argumentos fuertes (*for* para); **to make the ~ for doing nothing** exponer las razones para no hacer nada; **to make out a ~** exponer un argumento; **to make out a good ~** presentar argumentos convincentes (*for* para); **all right, you have made your ~** bien, Vd ha justificado su posición; **to put** (*or* **state**) **one's**

~ presentar sus argumentos; **to rest one's ~** terminar la presentación de su alegato.

(**e**) (*Gram*) caso *m*.

casebook ['keɪsbʊk] *n* diario *m*, registro *m*.

case-file ['keɪsfaɪl] *n* historial *m*.

case grammar ['keɪs,græmə^r] *n* gramática *f* de caso.

case-hardened ['keɪs,hɑːdnd] *adj* cementado; (*fig*) insensible, poco compasivo.

case-history ['keɪs'hɪstərɪ] *n* historia *f*, historial *m*, antecedentes *mpl*; **what is the patient's ~?** ¿cuál es la historia médica del enfermo?; **I'll give you the full ~** le contaré la historia con todos los detalles.

case-law ['keɪs'lɔː] *n* jurisprudencia *f*.

casement ['keɪsmənt] *n* ventana *f* a bisagra; (*frame*) marco *m* de ventana.

case-study ['keɪs,stʌdɪ] *n* estudio *m* de casos (prácticos).

case-system ['keɪs,sɪstəm] *n* sistema *m* de casos.

casework ['keɪswɜːk] *n* asistencia *f* social individualizada, trabajo *m* social con individuos.

caseworker ['keɪs,wɜːkə^r] *n* asistente *mf* social.

cash [kæʃ] **1** *n* dinero *m* contante; efectivo *m*, metálico *m*; (*) dinero *m*, plata *f* (*LAm*); (*cashdesk*) caja *f*; **~ account** cuenta *f* de caja; **~ advance** adelanto *m*; **~ card** tarjeta *f* de dinero; **~ crop** cultivo *m* comerciable; **~ deficit** déficit *m* de caja; **~ discount** descuento *m* por pronto pago (*or* por pago al contado); **~ down, for ~** al contado; **~ income** ingresos *mpl* al contado; **~ offer** oferta *f* de pago al contado; **~ order** pedido *m* al contado; **~ payment, ~ terms** pago *m* al contado; **~ price** precio *m* al contado; **~ prize** premio *m* en metálico; **~ ratio** coeficiente *m* de caja; **~ receipts** total *m* cobrado; **~ reduction = ~ discount**; **~ reserves** reservas *fpl* en metálico; **~ sale** venta *f* al contado; **~ squeeze** restricciones *fpl* económicas; **~ transaction** transacción *f* al contado; **~ in hand** (*in till*) efectivo *m* en caja; **~ on delivery** entrega *f* contra reembolso; **'~ with order'** 'enviar dinero con pedido'; **in ~** en metálico, en efectivo; **to be out of ~** estar sin blanca; **I haven't any ~ on me** no llevo dinero conmigo; **to pay ~ for** pagar al contado.

2 *vt cheque* cobrar, hacer efectivo; *coupon* (*also* **to ~ in**) canjear; **to ~ sb a cheque** pagar a uno en metálico a cambio de su cheque, cambiarle a uno un cheque.

◆**cash in** *vt bonds, savings certificates* vender.

◆**cash in on*** *vt* sacar partido de, aprovechar.

◆**cash up** *vi* contar el dinero recaudado (al cerrar la tienda *etc*).

cash-and-carry ['kæʃən'kærɪ] **1** *n* almacén *m* de venta al por mayor. **2** *adj goods, business* de venta al por mayor.

cashbook ['kæʃbʊk] *n* libro *m* de caja.

cashbox ['kæʃbɒks] *n* caja *f*.

cashdesk ['kæʃdesk] *n* caja *f*.

cash-dispenser ['kæʃdɪs,pensə^r] *n* (*Brit*) cajero *m* automático.

cashew [kæ'ʃuː] *n* (*also* **~ nut**) anacardo *m*, marañón *m*.

cash-flow ['kæʃ,fləʊ] *n* flujo *m* de fondos, cash-flow *m*; **~ problems** problemas *mpl* de cash-flow.

cashier [kæ'ʃɪə^r] **1** *n* cajero *m*, -a *f*. **2** *vt* (*Mil*) separar del servicio, degradar, destituir.

cashless ['kæʃlɪs] *adj*: **the ~ society** la sociedad sin dinero.

cashmere [kæʃ'mɪə^r] *n* cachemir *m*, cachemira *f*.

cashpoint ['kæʃ,pɔɪnt] *n* cajero *m* automático.

cash-register ['kæʃ,redʒɪstə^r] *n* caja *f* registradora.

casing ['keɪsɪŋ] *n* caja *f*, cubierta *f*, envoltura *f*; revestimiento *m*, carcasa *f* reforzada.

casino [kə'siːnəʊ] *n* casino *m* (de juego).

cask [kɑːsk] *n* tonel *m*, barril *m*, barrica *f*.

casket ['kɑːskɪt] *n* cajita *f*, cofrecito *m*, estuche *m*, arquilla *f*; (*US*) ataúd *m*, féretro *m*.

Caspian Sea ['kæspɪən,siː] *n* Mar *m* Caspio.

Cassandra [kə'sændrə] *nf* Casandra.

cassava [kə'sɑːvə] *n* mandioca *f*, tapioca *f*.

casserole ['kæsərəʊl] *n* (*Brit*) cacerola *f*; (*food*) cazuela *f*.

cassette [kæ'set] *n* casete *f*, cassette *f*.

cassette-deck [kə'set,dek] *n* platina *f* a cassette.

cassette-player [kæ'set,pleɪə^r] *n* casete *m*, cassette *m*, tocacasete *m*, tocacintas *m*.

cassette-recorder [kə'setrɪ,kɔːdə^r] *n* cassette *f* grabadora.

Cassius ['kæsɪəs] *nm* Casio.

cassock ['kæsək] *n* sotana *f*.

cassowary ['kæsəweərɪ] *n* casuario *m*.

cast [kɑːst] **1** *n* (**a**) (*throw*) echada *f*.

(**b**) (*Tech*) pieza *f* fundida.

(**c**) (*mould*) forma *f*, molde *m*; (*plaster ~*) vaciado *m*; escayola *f*; **~ of features** facciones *fpl*, fisonomía *f*; **~ of mind** temperamento *m*; genio *m*; **leg in ~** pierna *f* enyesada, pierna *f* escayolada.

(**d**) (*Theat*) reparto *m*; **~ (and credits)** (*US*: *Cine, TV*) reparto *m*.

(**e**) (*in eye*) estrabismo *m*.

2 *vt* (**a**) (*throw*) echar, lanzar, arrojar; *anchor, net* echar.

(**b**) (*throw*: *fig*) *blame, glance, lots* echar; *eyes* volver (*on* a, hacia); *light* arrojar (*on* sobre); *shadow* proyectar; *doubt* suscitar (*on* acerca de); *vote* dar, emitir; *horoscope* hacer; *spell* echar.

(**c**) (*shed*) *skin* mudar; (*lose*) perder.

(**d**) (*Tech*: *in mould*) vaciar; (*Metal*) fundir.

(**e**) (*Theat*) *parts* repartir; *part* asignar; **to ~ an actor in the part of** dar a un actor el papel de; **he was ~ as the fool** le dieron el papel del gracioso; **we shall ~ the play on Tuesday** repartiremos los papeles de la obra el martes.

3 *vi* (*Fishing*) lanzar, arrojar.

◆**cast about, cast around** *vi*: **to ~ about for** buscar, andar buscando.

◆**cast aside** *vt* desechar.

◆**cast away** *vt* desechar, tirar; abandonar; **to be ~ away** (*Naut*) naufragar; quedar desamparado; **to be ~ away on an island** naufragar y arribar en una isla.

◆**cast back 1** *vt*: **to ~ one's thoughts back to** rememorar. **2** *vi* volver.

◆**cast down** *vt* (**a**) derribar; *eyes* bajar.

(**b**) (*fig*) desanimar; **to be ~ down** estar deprimido.

◆**cast in** *vt, vi*: **to ~ in (one's lot) with sb** compartir el destino de uno.

◆**cast off 1** *vt* (**a**) desechar, abandonar; *burden* deshacerse de, quitarse de encima; *clothing* quitarse; *wife* repudiar; *mistress* dejar.

(**b**) (*Knitting*) terminar, cerrar los puntos de.

2 *vi* (**a**) (*Naut*) soltar las amarras, desamarrar.

(**b**) (*Knitting*) rematar.

◆**cast on** *vt* (*Knitting*) echar los puntos de.

◆**cast out** *vt* arrojar, echar fuera de sí, expulsar.

◆**cast up** *vt* (**a**) echar; vomitar. (**b**) *account* sumar.

castanet [,kæstə'net] *n* castañuela *f*.

castaway ['kɑːstəweɪ] *n* náufrago *m*, -a *f*.

caste [kɑːst] *n* casta *f*; **to lose ~** desprestigiarse.

castellated ['kæstəleɪtɪd] *adj* almenado.

caster ['kɑːstə^r] *n* = **castor¹** *and* **castor²**.

castigate ['kæstɪgeɪt] *vt* reprobar, condenar, censurar.

castigation [,kæstɪ'geɪʃən] *n* reprobación *f*, censura *f*.

Castile [kæs'tiːl] *n* Castilla *f*.

Castilian [kæs'tɪlɪən] **1** *adj* castellano. **2** *n* (**a**) castellano *m*, -a *f*. (**b**) (*Ling*) castellano *m*.

casting ['kɑːstɪŋ] **1** *adj*: **~ vote** voto *m* de calidad. **2** *n* (**a**) (*Tech*) pieza *f* fundida, pieza *f* de fundición. (**b**) (*Theat*) reparto *m*.

casting-couch ['kɑːstɪŋ,kaʊtʃ] *n* (*Cine*: *hum*) diván *m* del director (del reparto).

cast-iron ['kɑːst'aɪən] **1** *adj* hecho de hierro fundido; (*fig*) fuerte, duro; *will* férreo, inflexible; *case* sólido, convincente; *excuse* inatacable. **2** *n* hierro *m* colado, hierro *m* fundido.

castle ['kɑːsl] **1** *n* castillo *m*; (*Chess*) torre *f*, roque *m*; **to build ~s in the air** construir castillos en el aire.

2 *vi* (*Chess*) enrocar.

castling ['kɑːslɪŋ] *n* enroque *m*.

cast-off ['kɑːstɒf] **1** *adj clothing etc* de desecho.

2 *n* persona *f* (*or* cosa) abandonada, persona *f* (*or* cosa) desechada, plato *m* de segunda mesa; **~s** ropa *f* de desecho.

castor¹ ['kɑːstə^r] *n* (*at table*: *sugar*) azucarero *m*; (*salt*) salero *m*; **~s** convoy *m*, vinagreras *fpl*.

castor² ['kɑːstə^r] *n* (*wheel*) ruedecilla *f*, castor *m*.

castor-oil ['kɑːstər'ɔɪl] *n* aceite *m* de ricino; **~ plant** ricino *m*.

castor sugar ['kɑːstə'ʃʊgə^r] *n* (*Brit*) azúcar *m* extrafino.

castrate [kæs'treɪt] *vt* castrar.

castration [kæs'treɪʃən] *n* castración *f*.

casual ['kæʒjʊəl] **1** *adj* (**a**) (*happening by chance*) fortuito, accidental, casual; **a ~ glance** una mirada al azar; **a ~ stroll** un paseo sin rumbo fijo; **in a ~ conversation I had with him** en una conversación sin trascendencia que tuve con él, en una conversación que por casualidad tuve con él; **a ~ meeting** un encuentro fortuito.

(**b**) (*offhand*) despreocupado; **a ~ remark** una observación hecha a la ligera; **in a ~ manner** con afectada indiferencia; **he tried to sound ~** se esforzó por parecer tranquilo; **to assume a ~ air** hacer como si nada; **he was**

very ~ about it no daba importancia a la cosa.

(**c**) *clothing* informal; corriente; de sport.

(**d**) *labour* temporero, eventual; **~ earnings** ingresos *mpl* ocasionales; **~ worker** jornalero *m*, temporero *m*.

2 *n* hincha *m* violento que viste ropa cara.

3 ~s *npl* traje *m* de sport, ropa *f* de estar por casa.

casually ['kæʒjʊəlɪ] *adv* (**a**) (*by chance*) por casualidad, de manera fortuita.

(**b**) (*offhandedly*) de manera despreocupada; con aire de indiferencia, con aire de naturalidad; **he said ~** dijo con mucha tranquilidad; **I was ~ watching them** los miraba un poco distraído; **I said it quite ~** lo dije sin darle importancia.

casualness ['kæʒjuəlnɪs] *n* despreocupación *f*.

casualty ['kæʒjʊəltɪ] *n* (**a**) (*Mil*) baja *f*; **~ list** lista *f* de bajas; **casualties** pérdidas *fpl*; **there were heavy casualties** hubo muchas bajas.

(**b**) (*in accident*) víctima *f*, herido *m*, muerto *m*; **casualties** víctimas *fpl*; **fortunately there were no casualties** por fortuna no hubo víctimas; **a ~ of modern society** una víctima de la sociedad moderna; **~ department** sección *f* de accidentes; **~ list** lista *f* de víctimas; **~ ward** sala *f* de accidentes.

casuist ['kæzjʊɪst] *n* casuista *mf*; (*pej*) sofista *mf*.

casuistry ['kæzjʊɪstrɪ] *n* casuística *f*; (*pej*) sofismas *mpl*, razonamiento *m* falaz.

CAT *n* (**a**) *abbr of* **computer-assisted translation** traducción *f* asistida por ordenador, TAO *f*. (**b**) *abbr of* **College of Advanced Technology**.

cat [kæt] *n* (**a**) gato *m*, (*she-~*) gata *f*; **to be like a ~ on hot bricks** estar como gato sobre ascuas; **to fight like ~ and dog** pelearse como gato y perro; **he hasn't a ~ in hell's chance** no tiene la más mínima posibilidad; **to lead a ~ and dog life** vivir como perros y gatos; **to let the ~ out of the bag** descubrir el pastel, tirar de la manta; **he looked like something the ~ had brought in** estaba hecho un desastre; **to rain ~s and dogs** llover a cántaros; **to see which way the ~ jumps** esperar a ver de qué lado caen las peras; **to set the ~ among the pigeons** meter los perros en danza; **there isn't room to swing a ~** aquí no cabe un alfiler; **he thinks he's the ~'s pyjamas** (*or* **whiskers**)* se cree la mar de listo*; **when the ~'s away the mice will play** cuando el gato no está bailan los ratones. (**b**) (*US**) tío*, tipo* *m*. (**c**) (††*Naut*) azote *m*.

cataclysm ['kætəklɪzəm] *n* cataclismo *m*.

cataclysmic [,kætə'klɪzmɪk] *adj* de cataclismo.

catacombs ['kætəku:mz] *npl* catacumbas *fpl*.

catafalque ['kætəfælk] *n* catafalco *m*.

Catalan ['kætəlæn] **1** *adj* catalán. **2** *n* (**a**) catalán *m*, -ana *f*. (**b**) (*Ling*) catalán *m*.

cataleptic [,kætə'leptɪk] **1** *adj* cataléptico. **2** *n* cataléptico *m*, -a *f*.

catalogue, (*US*) **catalog** ['kætəlɒg] **1** *n* catálogo *m*; (*of cards*) fichero *m*; (*US*: *pamphlet, also prospectus* (*Scol*)) folleto *m*; **a whole ~ of complaints** toda una serie de quejas. **2** *vt* catalogar, poner en un catálogo; **it is not catalog(u)ed** no consta en el catálogo.

Catalonia [,kætə'ləʊnɪə] *n* Cataluña *f*.

Catalonian [,kætə'ləʊnɪən] = **Catalan**.

catalyse, (*US*) **catalyze** ['kætəlaɪz] *vt* catalizar.

catalysis [kə'tælɪsɪs] *n* catálisis *f*.

catalyst ['kætəlɪst] *n* catalizador *m*.

catalytic [,kætə'lɪtɪk] *adj* catalítico; **~ converter** catalizador *m*.

catamaran [,kætəmə'ræn] *n* catamarán *m*.

cat-and-mouse ['kætn'maʊs]: **to play a ~ game with sb** jugar al gato y ratón con uno.

catapult ['kætəpʌlt] **1** *n* (*Hist and Aer*) catapulta *f*; (*boy's*) tirador *m*, tiragomas *m*, tirachinas *m*. **2** *vt* (**a**) (*Aer*) catapultar. (**b**) (*fig*) **he was ~ed into fame** le llegó muy súbitamente la fama.

cataract ['kætərækt] *n* (*Geog and Med*) catarata *f*.

catarrh [kə'tɑ:ʳ] *n* catarro *m*.

catastrophe [kə'tæstrəfɪ] *n* catástrofe *f*.

catastrophic [,kætə'strɒfɪk] *adj* catastrófico.

catatonic [,kætə'tɒnɪk] **1** *adj* catatónico. **2** *n* catatónico *m*, -a *f*.

cat-basket ['kæt,bɑ:skɪt] *n* (*for carrying*) cesto *m* para llevar el gato; (*for sleeping*) cesto *m* del gato.

catbird ['kætbɜ:d] *attr*: **to be in the ~ seat** (*US**) sentirse seguro.

cat-burglar ['kætbɜ:gləʳ] *n* (ladrón *m*) balconero *m*.

catcall ['kætkɔ:l] **1** *n* silbo *m*, silbido *m*, rechifla *f*. **2** *vi* silbar.

catch [kætʃ] **1** *n* (**a**) (*act of catching*) cogida *f*.

(**b**) (*thing caught*) presa *f*, captura *f*; (*fish*: *quantity caught*) pesca *f*, captura *f*, cantidad *f* de peces cogidos; **he's a good ~*** (*in marriage*) es un buen partido; **he's a good ~ for the team** es un buen recluta para el equipo.

(**c**) (*Brit*: *of lock, on door*) pestillo *m*; (*Brit*: *of box, window*) cerradura *f*; (*small flange*) fiador *m*.

(**d**) (*Mus*) canon *m*.

(**e**) (*trick*) trampa *f*; **there must be a ~ here somewhere** aquí debe de haber trampa; **the ~ is that ...** la dificultad es que ...; **a question with a ~ to it, ~ question** pregunta *f* de pega, pregunta *f* tramposa; **~ 22 situation** situación *f* de callejón sin salida, círculo *m* vicioso.

(**f**) (*Sport*) catch-can *m*, lucha *f*.

(**g**) **with a ~ in one's voice** con la voz entrecortada.

2 (*irr*: *pret and ptp* **caught**) *vt* (**a**) (*capture*) coger (*Sp*), agarrar, atrapar; (*grasp*) asir; *ball* recoger (*Sp*), coger (*Sp*), parar, agarrar (*LAm*); *attention* captar; *cold* coger (*Sp*); **~!** ¡cógelo! (*Sp*), ¡toma!; **to be caught like a rat in a trap** estar en una trampa sin salida; **I tried to ~ you on the phone** traté de hablar contigo por teléfono; **you've caught me at a bad moment** me has pillado en un mal momento; **when can I ~ you next?** ¿cuándo te convendrá hablar de esto?, ¿me das hora para volver a hablar de esto?

(**b**) (*surprise*) sorprender, coger (*Sp*); coger en una falta (*Sp*); **they caught him stealing apples** le pillaron mientras robaba manzanas; **you'll not ~ me doing it** no hay peligro de que yo lo haga; **we never caught them at it** no los sorprendimos nunca en flagrante; **we were caught by the snow** nos sorprendió la nieve; **we'll not be caught like this again** no volveremos a caer en esta trampa; **he was caught off stride** (*US**) le cogieron (*LAm*: agarraron) con la guardia baja.

(**c**) *bus, train etc* coger (*Sp*), tomar.

(**d**) (*be in time for*) **to ~ the post** llegar antes de la recogida del correo; **we only just caught the train** por poco perdimos el tren; **hurry if you want to ~ it** date prisa si quieres llegar a tiempo.

(**e**) (*entangle*) **I caught my fingers in the door** pillé los dedos en la puerta; **I caught my coat on that nail** mi chaqueta se enganchó en ese clavo; **I caught my head on that beam** di con la cabeza contra esa viga.

(**f**) (*Med*) coger (*Sp*), contagiarse de; *habit* adquirir, adoptar.

(**g**) (*perceive*) *likeness* captar; *meaning* comprender; *flavour* percibir; (*hear*) oír, llegar a oír; **I didn't quite ~ you** no oí bien lo que dijiste; **to ~ the mood of the times** definir el espíritu de la época; **the painter has caught her expression** el pintor ha sabido captar su gesto.

(**h**) **to ~ sb a blow** pegar un golpe a uno; **the stone caught him on the ear** la piedra le dio en la oreja; **she caught me one on the nose** me pegó en la nariz.

(**i**) *breath* suspender.

(**j**) (*) **to ~ it** merecerse una regañina (*from* de); **you'll ~ it!** ¡las vas a pagar!; **he caught it good and proper** todo se le vino encima, se le cargaron por las buenas.

(**k**) (*receive*) **this room ~es the morning sun** este cuarto recibe el sol de la mañana; **the light was ~ing her hair** la luz brillaba en su pelo.

3 *vi* (**a**) (*fire*) encenderse, prenderse; (*Culin*) quemarse.

(**b**) (*entangle*) engancharse (*on* en); (*Tech*) engranar, (*improperly*) rozar, ludir (*on* con), prender (*on* en).

◆**catch at** *vt* tratar de coger (*LAm*: agarrar), asir.

◆**catch on** *vi* (**a**) (*see the joke*) caer, percibir lo gracioso del cuento; (*tumble to*) caer en la cuenta; (*get the knack*) coger el truco; **to ~ on to** comprender.

(**b**) (*become popular*) hacerse popular, alcanzar gran popularidad, afirmarse en el gusto del público; **it never really caught on** no logró establecerse de verdad.

◆**catch out** *vt* (*esp Brit*) sorprender, pillar, cazar; coger en una falta (*Sp*); **we were caught out by the rise in the dollar** nos cogió desprevenidos la subida del dólar; **you won't ~ me out again like that** no me vas a pillar así otra vez.

◆**catch up 1** *vt* (**a**) *person etc* alcanzar, llegar al nivel de.

(**b**) *weapon etc* asir.

(**c**) **we were caught up in the traffic** nos vimos bloqueados por el tráfico; **a society caught up in change** una sociedad afectada por cambios.

2 *vi* ponerse al día; hacer los atrasos de trabajo (*etc*); ponerse al nivel de los demás; **to ~ up on one's sleep** recuperar los atrasos de sueño; **to ~ up with** *person* alcanzar; *news etc* ponerse al corriente de; *work* poner al día, cubrir los atrasos de.

catch-all ['kætʃ,ɔːl] **1** *adj regulation, clause etc* general; ~ **phrase** frase *f* para todo. **2** *n algo que sirve para todo.*

catcher ['kætʃəʳ] *n* (*Baseball*) apañador *m*, receptor *m*.

catching ['kætʃɪŋ] *adj* (*Med*) contagioso; (*fig*) pegajoso, atrayente, cautivador.

catchment ['kætʃmənt] *n:* ~ **area** zona *f* de captación; ~ **basin** cuenca *f*.

catchpenny ['kætʃ,penɪ] *adj* llamativo (y barato); hecho para venderse al instante; ~ **solution** solución *f* atractiva (pero poco recomendable).

catch-phrase ['kætʃfreɪz] *n* tópico *m*; muletilla *f*; slogan *m*; (*Rad etc*) frase *f* típica.

catchword ['kætʃwɜːd] *n* (*Typ*) reclamo *m*; (*Theat*) pie *m*; (*catch-phrase*) tópico *m*.

catchy ['kætʃɪ] *adj* (**a**) (*Mus*) pegadizo, atractivo, fácil de recordar. (**b**) *question* tramposo.

catechism ['kætɪkɪzəm] *n (manual)* catecismo *m*; (*instruction*) catequismo *m*, catequesis *f*.

catechize ['kætɪkaɪz] *vt* catequizar.

categoric(al) [,kætɪ'gɒrɪk(əl)] *adj* categórico, terminante; *refusal* rotundo.

categorically [,kætɪ'gɒrɪkəlɪ] *adv state etc* de modo terminante; *refuse* rotundamente.

categorization [,kætɪgəraɪ'zeɪʃən] *n* categorización *f*.

categorize ['kætɪgəraɪz] *vt* clasificar; **to ~ sth as** calificar algo de, clasificar algo como.

category ['kætɪgərɪ] *n* categoría *f*.

cater ['keɪtəʳ] *vi* (**a**) **to ~ for** abastecer a, proveer comida a; (*fig*) atender a, proveer a; satisfacer; servir, ofrecer servicios a; **we ~ for group bookings** atendemos a las reservas de grupos; **this magazine ~s for the under-21s** esta revista se dirige a los sub-21; **to ~ for all tastes** atender a todos los gustos.

(**b**) (*US*) **to ~ to** transigir con, hacer concesiones a.

cater-cornered ['keɪtə'kɔːnəd] (*US*) **1** *adj* diagonal. **2** *adv* diagonalmente.

caterer ['keɪtərəʳ] *n* abastecedor *m*, -ora *f*, proveedor *m*, -ora *f*.

catering ['keɪtərɪŋ] *n* abastecimiento *m*; servicio *m* de comidas, servicio *m* de comedor; ~ **company** empresa *f* de hostelería; ~ **industry**, ~ **trade** restaurantería *f*, hostelería *f*; **a career in ~** una carrera en la hostelería.

caterpillar ['kætəpɪləʳ] *n* oruga *f*, gusano *m*; ~ **track**, ~ **tread** (rodado *m* de) oruga *f*; ~ **tractor** tractor *m* oruga.

caterwaul ['kætəwɔːl] *vi* chillar, aullar, maullar.

caterwauling ['kætə,wɔːlɪŋ] *n* chillidos *mpl*, aullidos *mpl*.

catfish ['kætfɪʃ] *n, pl invar* siluro *m*, bagre *m*, perro *m* del norte.

catflap ['kætflæp] *n* gatera *f*.

catgut ['kætgʌt] *n* cuerda *f* de tripa; (*Med*) catgut *m*.

Cath. (**a**) *abbr of* **Cathedral** catedral *f*. (**b**) *abbr of* **Catholic** católico.

Catharine ['kæθərɪn] *nf* Catalina.

catharsis [kə'θɑːsɪs] *n* catarsis *f*.

cathartic [kə'θɑːtɪk] **1** *adj* (*Med*) catártico, purgante; (*Liter*) catártico. **2** *n* purgante *m*.

cathedral [kə'θiːdrəl] *n* catedral *f*; ~ **city** ciudad *f* episcopal; ~ **church** iglesia *f* catedral.

Catherine ['kæθərɪn] *nf* Catalina; ~ **wheel** (*firework*) rueda *f* catalina.

catheter ['kæθɪtəʳ] *n* catéter *m*.

catheterize ['kæθɪtə,raɪz] *vt bladder, person* entubar.

cathode ['kæθəʊd] *n* cátodo *m*; ~ **rays** rayos *mpl* catódicos; ~ **ray tube** tubo *m* de rayos catódicos.

Catholic ['kæθəlɪk] **1** *adj* católico. **2** *n* católico *m*, -a *f*.

catholic ['kæθəlɪk] *adj* (**a**) católico. (**b**) (*fig*) liberal, de amplias miras; de gustos eclécticos; *taste* amplio.

Catholicism [kə'θɒlɪsɪzəm] *n* catolicismo *m*.

cathouse‡ ['kæthaʊs] *n, pl* **cathouses** ['kæthaʊzɪz] (*US*) casa *f* de putas.

Cathy ['kæθɪ] *nf familiar form of* **Catharine, Catherine**.

catkin ['kætkɪn] *n* amento *m*, candelilla *f*.

cat-lick* ['kætlɪk] *n* mano *f* de gato; **to give o.s. a ~** lavarse a lo gato.

catlike ['kætlaɪk] *adj* felino, gatuno.

catmint ['kætmɪnt] *n*, (*US*) **catnip** ['kætnɪp] *n* hierba *f* gatera, nébeda *f*.

catnap ['kætnæp] *n* siestecita *f*, sueñecito *m*.

Cato ['keɪtəʊ] *nm* Catón.

cat-o'nine-tails ['kætə'naɪnteɪlz] *n* azote *m* (con nueve ramales).

cat's-cradle ['kæts,kreɪdl] *n* (juego *m* de la) cuna *f*.

cat's-eyes ['kæts,aɪz] *npl* (*Brit Aut*) catafotos *mpl*.

cat's-paw ['kætspɔː] *n* instrumento *m*.

catsuit ['kætsuːt] *n* traje *m* de gato.

catsup ['kætsəp] *n* (*US*) salsa *f* de tomate, catsup *m*.

cat's whisker [,kæts'wɪskaʳ] *n* (*Rad*) cable *m* antena.

cattiness ['kætɪnɪs] *n* malicia *f*, rencor *m*.

cattle ['kætl] *npl* ganado *m*, ganado *m* vacuno, vacas *fpl*.

cattle-breeder ['kætl,briːdəʳ] *n* criador *m* -ora *f* de ganado.

cattle-breeding ['kætl,briːdɪŋ] *n* crianza *f* de ganado.

cattle-crossing ['kætl,krɒsɪŋ] *n* paso *m* de ganado.

cattle drive ['kætl,draɪv] *n* (*US*) recogida *f* de ganado.

cattle egret ['kætl'iːgrɪt] *n* garcilla *f* bueyera.

cattle-grid ['kætl,grɪd] *n* (*Brit*) rejilla *f* de retención (de ganado).

cattleman ['kætlmæn] *n, pl* **cattlemen** ['kætlmen] ganadero *m*.

cattle-market ['kætl,mɑːkɪt] *n* mercado *m* ganadero (*or* de ganado); (*also fig*) feria *f* de ganado.

cattle-raising ['kætlreɪzɪŋ] *n* ganadería *f*.

cattle rustler ['kætlrʌsləʳ] *n* (*US*) ladrón *m* de ganado, cuatrero *m*.

cattle-shed ['kætl,ʃed] *n* establo *m*.

cattle-show ['kætlʃəʊ] *n* feria *f* de ganado.

cattle-truck ['kætltrʌk] *n* (*Aut*) camión *m* ganadero; (*Brit Rail*) vagón *m* para ganado.

catty ['kætɪ] *adj* malicioso, rencoroso.

Catullus [kə'tʌləs] *nm* Catulo.

CATV *n abbr of* **community antenna television**.

catwalk ['kætwɔːk] *n* pasadizo *m*, pasarela *f*.

Caucasian [kɔː'keɪzɪən] **1** *adj* (*by race*) caucásico; (*Geog*) caucasiano. **2** *n* (*by race*) caucásico *m*, -a *f*; (*Geog*) caucasiano *m*, -a *f*.

Caucasus ['kɔːkəsəs] *n* Cáucaso *m*.

caucus ['kɔːkəs] *n* (*Brit Pol*) camarilla *f* (política), junta *f* secreta; (*US Pol*) reunión *f* de un partido; jefes *mpl* de un partido, comité *m* directivo.

caudal ['kɔːdl] *adj* caudal.

caught [kɔːt] *pret and ptp of* **catch**.

cauldron ['kɔːldrən] *n* caldera *f*, calderón *m*.

cauliflower ['kɒlɪflaʊəʳ] *n* coliflor *f*; ~ **cheese** coliflor *f* con queso; ~ **ear** oreja *f* deformada por los golpes.

caulk [kɔːk] *vt* calafatear.

causal ['kɔːzəl] *adj* causal.

causality [kɔː'zælɪtɪ] *n* causalidad *f*.

causation [kɔː'zeɪʃən] *n* causalidad *f*.

causative ['kɔːzətɪv] *adj* causativo.

cause [kɔːz] **1** *n* (**a**) causa *f*, motivo *m*, razón *f*; **lost ~** causa *f* perdida, causa *f* imposible; **with good ~** con razón; **to be the ~ of** ser causa de, causar, motivar; **there's no ~ for alarm** no hay para qué asustarse; **in the ~ of liberty** por la libertad; **it's all in a good ~** todo esto tiene un propósito noble; **to die in a good ~** morir por una causa noble; **to give ~ for complaint** dar motivo de queja; **you have ~ to be worried** Vd tiene buen motivo para inquietarse; **to make common ~ with** hacer un frente común con, hacer causa común con; **to show ~** aducir argumentos convincentes; **to take up sb's ~** apoyar la campaña de uno, acudir a la defensa de uno.

(**b**) (*Jur*) causa *f*, pleito *m*.

2 *vt* causar, motivar, provocar; originar; **to ~ an accident** causar un accidente; **to ~ sb to do sth** hacer que uno haga algo.

cause célèbre [,kɔːzseɪ'lebr] *n* pleito *m* célebre, caso *m* célebre.

causeway ['kɔːzweɪ] *n* calzada *f* elevada; carretera *f* elevada; (*in sea*) arrecife *m*.

caustic ['kɔːstɪk] *adj* cáustico; ~ **soda** sosa *f* cáustica.

cauterize ['kɔːtəraɪz] *vt* cauterizar.

caution ['kɔːʃən] **1** *n* (**a**) cautela *f*, prudencia *f*; **'~!'** (*Aut*) '¡cuidado!', '¡precaución!'; **to throw ~ to the winds** abandonar la prudencia.

(**b**) (*warning*) advertencia *f*, amonestación *f*.

(**c**) (*) **he's a ~** (*odd*) es un tío muy raro, (*amusing*) es un tío divertidísimo.

2 *vt* amonestar (*against* contra).

cautionary ['kɔːʃənərɪ] *adj tale* de escarmiento, aleccionador.

cautious ['kɔːʃəs] *adj* cauteloso, prudente, precavido; cauto; **to make a ~ statement** hacer una declaración prudente; **to play a ~ game** jugar con mucha prudencia.

cautiously ['kɔːʃəslɪ] *adv* cautelosamente, con cautela.

cautiousness ['kɔːʃəsnɪs] *n* cautela *f*, prudencia *f*.

cavalcade [,kævəl'keɪd] *n* cabalgata *f*; (*fig*) desfile *m*.

cavalier [,kævə'lɪəʳ] **1** *adj* arrogante, desdeñoso; *treatment* sin miramientos.

2 *n* caballero *m*; (††) galán *m*; (*Brit Hist*) *partidario del Rey en la Guerra Civil inglesa (1641-49)*.
cavalierly [ˌkævəˈlɪəlɪ] *adv* arrogantemente, desdeñosamente; sin miramientos.
cavalry [ˈkævəlrɪ] *n* caballería *f*; ~ **charge** carga *f* de caballería; ~ **officer** oficial *m* de caballería; ~ **twill** *tela asargada utilizada para confeccionar pantalones*.
cavalryman [ˈkævəlrɪmən] *n, pl* **cavalrymen** [ˈkævəlrɪmen] soldado *m* de caballería.
cave¹ [keɪv] **1** *n* cueva *f*, caverna *f*. **2** *vi*: **to ~ in** derrumbarse, hundirse; (*fig*) ceder, rendirse.
cave² [ˈkeɪvɪ] *interj*: ~! (*Brit Scol*:*) ¡ojo!, ¡ahí viene!; **to keep** ~ estar a la mira.
caveat [ˈkævɪæt] *n* advertencia *f*; (*Jur*) advertencia *f* de suspensión; **to enter a** ~ hacer una advertencia.
cave-dweller [ˈkeɪvˌdweləʳ] *n* cavernícola *mf*, troglodita *mf*.
cave-in [ˈkeɪvɪn] *n* (*of roof etc*) derrumbe *m*, derrumbamiento *m*; (*of pavement etc*) socavón *m*.
caveman [ˈkeɪvmæn] *n, pl* **cavemen** [ˈkeɪvmen] cavernícola *m*, troglodita *m*; hombre *m* de las cavernas; (*vaguely*) hombre *m* prehistórico; (*hum and iro*) machote *m*.
cave-painting [ˈkeɪvˌpeɪntɪŋ] *n* pintura *f* rupestre.
caver [ˈkeɪvəʳ] *n* espeleólogo *m*, -a *f*.
cavern [ˈkævən] *n* caverna *f*.
cavernous [ˈkævənəs] *adj* cavernoso.
caviar(e) [ˈkævɪɑːʳ] *n* caviar *m*.
cavil [ˈkævɪl] **1** *n* reparo *m*. **2** *vi* sutilizar, critiquizar; **to ~ at** poner peros a, critiquizar sin motivo.
caving [ˈkeɪvɪŋ] *n* espeleología *f*.
cavity [ˈkævɪtɪ] *n* cavidad *f*, hueco *m*, hoyo *m*; (*of tooth*) caries *f*; **nasal cavities** fosas *fpl* nasales; ~ **wall** doble pared *f*.
cavort [kəˈvɔːt] *vi* dar cabrioladas; (*fig*) divertirse ruidosamente.
cavy [ˈkeɪvɪ] *n* conejillo *m* de Indias, cobaya *m*.
caw [kɔː] **1** *n* graznido *m*. **2** *vi* graznar.
cawing [ˈkɔːɪŋ] *n* graznidos *mpl*, el graznar.
cayenne [ˈkeɪen] *n* (*also* ~ **pepper**) pimienta *f* de chile.
cayman [ˈkeɪmən] *n* caimán *m*.
CB (**a**) *n abbr of* **Companion (of the Order) of the Bath** *título honorífico británico*. (**b**) (*Mil*) *abbr of* **confined to barracks** (*men*) arresto *m* menor en cuartel; (*officers*) arresto *m* en banderas. (**c**) *attr*: ~ **Radio** *abbr of* **Citizens' Band Radio** banda *f* ciudadana.
CBC *n abbr of* **Canadian Broadcasting Corporation.**
CBE *n abbr of* **Commander of the Order of the British Empire** *título honorífico británico*.
CBI *n abbr of* **Confederation of British Industry** ≃ Confederación *f* Española de Organizaciones Empresariales, CEOE *f*.
CBS *n* (*US*) *abbr of* **Columbia Broadcasting System.**
CC *n abbr of* **County Council.**
c.c. (**a**) *npl* (*Math*) *abbr of* **cubic centimetres** centímetros *mpl* cúbicos. (**b**) (*Comm*) *abbr of* **carbon copy.**
CCA *n* (*US*) *abbr of* **Circuit Court of Appeals** tribunal *m* de apelación itinerante.
CCC *n* (*US*) *abbr of* **Commodity Credit Corporation.**
CCTV *n abbr of* **closed-circuit television.**
CCU *n* (*US*) *abbr of* **coronary care unit** unidad *f* de cuidados cardiológicos.
CD *n* (**a**) *abbr of* **Corps Diplomatique** Cuerpo *m* Diplomático, CD. (**b**) *abbr of* **Civil Defence (Corps)** defensa *f* civil. (**c**) (*US Pol*) *abbr of* **congressional district.** (**d**) *abbr of* **compact disk** disco *m* compacto. (**e**) (*Pol*) *abbr of* **Conference on Disarmament.**
CDC *n* (*US*) *abbr of* **center for disease control.**
CDI *adj abbr of* **compact disk interactive.**
Cdr (*Brit Naut, Mil*) *abbr of* **commander** Comandante *m*; ~ **R. Thomas** (*on envelope*) Cdte. R. Thomas.
CD-ROM [ˌsiːdiːˈrɒm] *n abbr of* **compact disk read-only memory.**
CDT *n* (*US*) *abbr of* **Central Daylight Time.**
CDV *n abbr of* **compact disk video.**
CE *n abbr of* **Church of England** Iglesia *f* Anglicana.
cease [siːs] **1** *vt* suspender, cesar; **to ~ work** suspender el trabajo, terminar de trabajar.
2 *vi* cesar; **to ~ (from)** + *ger*, **to ~ to** + *infin* dejar de + *infin*, cesar de + *infin*.
ceasefire [ˌsiːsˈfaɪəʳ] *n* cese *m* de hostilidades, alto *m* el fuego; ~ **line** línea *f* del alto el fuego.
ceaseless [ˈsiːslɪs] *adj* incesante, continuo.
ceaselessly [ˈsiːslɪslɪ] *adv* incesantemente, sin cesar.
Cecil [ˈsesl] *nm* Cecilio.
Cecily [ˈsɪsɪlɪ] *nf* Cecilia.
cecum [ˈsiːkəm] *n* (*US*) = **caecum.**
CED *n* (*US*) *abbr of* **Committee for Economic Development.**
cedar [ˈsiːdəʳ] *n* cedro *m*; ~ **wood** madera *f* de cedro.
cede [siːd] *vt* ceder (*to* a).
cedilla [sɪˈdɪlə] *n* cedilla *f*.
CEEB *n* (*US*) *abbr of* **College Entry Examination Board.**
ceiling [ˈsiːlɪŋ] *n* techo *m* (*also Aer*); cielo *m* raso; (*fig*) límite *m*, punto *m* más alto; ~ **price** precio *m* tope; **to fix a ~ for, to put a ~ on** fijar el límite de, señalar el punto más alto de; **to hit the ~*** subirse por las paredes*; **he has not yet reached his ~** se desarrollará todavía algo más, ha de ser mejor aún.
celandine [ˈseləndaɪn] *n* celidonia *f*.
celeb* [sɪˈleb] *n* famoso *m*, -a *f*.
celebrant [ˈselɪbrənt] *n* celebrante *m*.
celebrate [ˈselɪbreɪt] **1** *vt* celebrar; festejar; *marriage* solemnizar; *happy event* celebrar, señalar con una fiesta; *anniversary etc* conmemorar; **we're celebrating his arrival** estamos celebrando su llegada; **what are you celebrating?** ¿qué festejáis?, ¿qué motivo tiene esta fiesta?; **he ~d his birthday by scoring 2 goals** celebró su cumpleaños marcando 2 goles.
2 *vi* divertirse, estar (*or* ir) de parranda.
celebrated [ˈselɪbreɪtɪd] *adj* célebre, famoso.
celebration [ˌselɪˈbreɪʃən] *n* celebración *f*; (*party*) fiesta *f*, guateque *m*; (*public rejoicing*) festividad *f*; **~s** (*of anniversary etc*) conmemoraciones *fpl*; **in ~ of** en conmemoración de.
celebratory [ˌselɪˈbreɪtərɪ] *adj event etc* de celebración; **let's have a ~ dinner** vamos a ofrecer una cena para celebrarlo.
celebrity [sɪˈlebrɪtɪ] *n* (*all senses*) celebridad *f*.
celeriac [səˈlerɪæk] *n* apio *m* nabo.
celerity [sɪˈlerɪtɪ] *n* celeridad *f*.
celery [ˈselərɪ] *n* apio *m*, panil *m* (*SC*).
celestial [sɪˈlestɪəl] *adj* celestial.
celibacy [ˈselɪbəsɪ] *n* celibato *m*.
celibate [ˈselɪbɪt] **1** *adj* célibe. **2** *n* célibe *mf*.
cell [sel] *n* (*of prison, monastery*) celda *f*; (*Bio, Pol*) célula *f*; (*of bees*) celda *f*, celdilla *f*; (*Elec*) elemento *m*, vaso *m*, pila *f*; (*Pol, of terrorists etc*) célula *f*; ~ **biology** biología *f* celular.
cellar [ˈseləʳ] *n* sótano *m*; (*for wine*) bodega *f*; **to keep a good ~** tener buena bodega.
cellist [ˈtʃelɪst] *n* violonchelista *mf*.
cello [ˈtʃeləʊ] *n* violonchelo *m*.
Cellophane [ˈseləfeɪn] ® *n* celofán *m*.
cellphone [ˈselˌfəʊn] *n* = **cellular telephone.**
cellular [ˈseljʊləʳ] *adj* celular; ~ **telephone** teléfono *m* celular.
cellulitis [ˌseljuˈlaɪtɪs] *n* celulitis *f*.
celluloid [ˈseljʊlɔɪd] *n* celuloide *m*.
cellulose [ˈseljʊləʊs] *n* celulosa *f*.
Celsius [ˈselsɪəs] *adj* celsius, centígrado.
Celt [kelt, selt] *n* celta *mf*.
Celtiberia [ˌkeltaɪˈbɪərɪ] *n* Celtiberia *f*.
Celtiberian [ˌkeltaɪˈbɪərɪən] **1** *adj* celtibérico. **2** *n* celtíbero *m*, -a *f*.
Celtic [ˈkeltɪk, ˈseltɪk] **1** *adj* celta, céltico. **2** *n* (*Ling*) céltico *m*.
cembalo [ˈtʃembələʊ] *n* clavicordio *m*, clave *m*.
cement [səˈment] **1** *n* cemento *m*; (*glue*) cola *f*, pegamento *m*; ~ **mixer** hormigonera *f*. **2** *vt* cementar; cubrir (*or* revestir *etc*) de cemento; (*fig*) fortalecer, reforzar, consolidar.
cementation [ˌsiːmenˈteɪʃən] *n* cementación *f*.
cemetery [ˈsemɪtrɪ] *n* cementerio *m*.
cenotaph [ˈsenətɑːf] *n* cenotafio *m*.
censer [ˈsensəʳ] *n* incensario *m*.
censor [ˈsensəʳ] **1** *n* censor *m*, -ora *f*. **2** *vt* censurar; (*delete*) tachar, suprimir.
censorious [senˈsɔːrɪəs] *adj* hipercrítico, criticón.
censorship [ˈsensəʃɪp] *n* censura *f*.
censurable [ˈsenʃərəbl] *adj* censurable.
censure [ˈsenʃəʳ] **1** *n* censura *f*. **2** *vt* censurar.
census [ˈsensəs] *n* censo *m*; empadronamiento *m*; **to take a ~ of** levantar el censo de.
cent [sent] *n* (*Canada, US*) centavo *m*; **I haven't a ~** no tengo un céntimo.
cent. (**a**) *abbr of* **centigrade.** (**b**) *abbr of* **central.** (**c**) *abbr of* **century.**
centaur [ˈsentɔːʳ] *n* centauro *m*.
centenarian [ˌsentɪˈneərɪən] **1** *adj* centenario. **2** *n* centenario *m*, -a *f*.

centenary [sen'tiːnərɪ] *n* centenario *m*; **the ~ celebrations for ...** las festividades para celebrar el centenario de ...
centennial [sen'tenɪəl] (*esp US*) **1** *adj* centenario. **2** *n* centenario *m*.
center ['sentəʳ] *etc* (*US*) = **centre** *etc*.
centesimal [sen'tesɪməl] *adj* centesimal.
centigrade ['sentɪgreɪd] *adj* centígrado; **30 degrees ~** 30 grados centígrados.
centigram(me) ['sentɪgræm] *n* centigramo *m*.
centilitre, (*US*) **centiliter** ['sentɪ,liːtəʳ] *n* centilitro *m*.
centime ['sɑ̃ːntiːm] *n* céntimo *m*.
centimetre, (*US*) **centimeter** ['sentɪ,miːtəʳ] *n* centímetro *m*.
centipede ['sentɪpiːd] *n* ciempiés *m*.
central ['sentrəl] *adj* central; (*in town etc*) céntrico; **~ bank** banco *m* central; **~ government** gobierno *m* central; **~ heating** calefacción *f* central; **~ locking** cierre *m* centralizado; **~ processing unit** unidad *f* procesadora central, unidad *f* central de proceso; **~ reservation** (*Brit Aut*) mediana *f*; **of ~ importance** de la mayor importancia, primordial; **it is ~ to our policy** es un punto clave de nuestra política.
Central African Republic [,sentrəl,æfrɪkənrɪ'pʌblɪk] *n* República *f* Centroafricana.
Central America ['sentrələ'merɪkə] *n* Centroamérica *f*.
Central American ['sentrələ'merɪkən] **1** *adj* centroamericano. **2** *n* centroamericano *m*, -a *f*.
Central European ['sentrəl,jʊərə'piːən] **1** *adj* centroeuropeo. **2** *n* centroeuropeo *m*, -a *f*.
centralism ['sentrəlɪzm] *n* (*Pol*) centralismo *m*.
centralization [,sentrəlaɪ'zeɪʃən] *n* centralización *f*.
centralize ['sentrəlaɪz] *vt* centralizar; concentrar, reunir en un centro.
centralized ['sentrəlaɪzd] *adj* centralizado.
centrally ['sentrəlɪ] *adv organize etc* centralmente; **~-heated** con calefacción central; **~ planned economy** economía *f* de planificación central.
centre, (*US*) **center** ['sentəʳ] **1** *n* centro *m*; núcleo *m*; (*of chocolate*) relleno *m*; (*Sport*) centro *m* (*also kick*); **~ of attraction** centro *m* de atracción; **~ of gravity** centro *m* de gravedad; **~ of intrigue** centro *m* de intrigas.
2 *attr* central; del centro; **~ court** pista *f* central; **~ parties** partidos *mpl* centristas, partidos *mpl* del centro; **~ spread** artículo *m* de doble página central; **~ vowel** vocal *f* media.
3 *vt* centrar; *ball* pasar al centro; (*fig*) concentrar (*on* en).
4 *vi:* **to ~ (a)round, to ~ in, to ~ on** concentrarse en, estar concentrado en, tener por centro, (*hopes etc*) cifrarse en.
centre-back ['sentə'bæk] *n* defensa *m* centro, escoba *m*.
centre-board, (*US*) **center-board** ['sentəbɔːd] *n* orza *f* de deriva.
-centred, (*US*) **-centered** ['sentəd] *in compounds* centrado en, basado en; *eg* **home~** centrado en el hogar.
centrefold, (*US*) **centerfold** ['sentə,fəʊld] *n* entrepágina *f*.
centre-forward ['sentə'fɔːwəd] *n* delantero *m* centro.
centre-half ['sentə'hɑːf] *n, pl* **centre-halves** ['sentə'hɑːvz] medio *m* centro.
centrepiece, (*US*) **centerpiece** ['sentəpiːs] *n* centro *m* de mesa; (*fig*) atracción *f* principal, objeto *m* (*etc*) de mayor interés.
centrifugal [sen'trɪfjʊgəl] *adj* centrífugo.
centrifuge ['sentrɪfjuːʒ] **1** *n* centrífuga *f*. **2** *vt* centrifugar.
centripetal [sen'trɪpɪtl] *adj* centrípeto.
centrist ['sentrɪst] **1** *adj* centrista. **2** *n* centrista *mf*.
centuries-old ['sentjʊrɪz,əʊld] *adj* secular.
centurion [sen'tjʊərɪən] *n* centurión *m*.
century ['sentjʊrɪ] *n* siglo *m*; (*cricket etc*) cien carreras *fpl* (*etc*); **in the 20th ~** en el siglo veinte.
CEO *n* (*US*) *abbr of* **Chief Executive Officer**.
ceramic [sɪ'ræmɪk] *adj* cerámico.
ceramics [sɪ'ræmɪks] *n sing* cerámica *f*.
cereal ['sɪərɪəl] **1** *adj* cereal. **2** *n* cereal *m*; **~s** (*crops, cornflakes*) cereales *mpl*.
cerebellum [,serɪ'beləm] *n* cerebelo *m*.
cerebral ['serɪbrəl] *adj* cerebral; intelectual; **~ palsy** parálisis *f* cerebral.
cerebration [,serɪ'breɪʃən] *n* meditación *f*, actividad *f* mental.
cerebrum ['serəbrəm] *n* cerebro *m*.
ceremonial [,serɪ'məʊnɪəl] **1** *adj* ceremonial; de ceremonia, de gala. **2** *n* ceremonial *m*.
ceremonially [,serɪ'məʊnɪəlɪ] *adv* con ceremonia.
ceremonious [,serɪ'məʊnɪəs] *adj* ceremonioso.
ceremoniously [,serɪ'məʊnɪəslɪ] *adv* ceremoniosamente.
ceremony ['serɪmənɪ] *n* ceremonia *f*; **to stand on ~** hacer ceremonias, ser etiquetero, estar de cumplido; **let's not stand on ~** dejémonos de cumplidos.
cerise [sə'riːz] **1** *adj* (de) color de cereza. **2** *n* cereza *f*.
CERN [sɜːn] *n abbr of* **Conseil Européen pour la Recherche Nucléaire** Consejo *m* Europeo para la Investigación Nuclear.
cert* [sɜːt] *n* (*Brit*) *abbr of* **certainty; it's a (dead) ~** es cosa segura; **he's a (dead) ~ for the job** sin duda le darán el puesto.
cert. *abbr of* **certified** certificado.
certain ['sɜːtən] *adj* **(a)** (*of things*) seguro, cierto; **it is ~ that ...** es seguro que ..., es cierto que ...; **it is ~ death to go there** ir allí es buscarse una muerte segura.
(b) (*of person*) seguro; **are you ~?** ¿estás seguro?; **I am ~ of it** estoy seguro de ello; **I am ~ that...** estoy seguro de que...; **we are ~ of his support** estamos seguros de tener su apoyo; **he is ~ to be there** es seguro que estará allí; **be ~ to call on him** no dejes de visitarle; **you don't sound very ~** no pareces estar muy seguro.
(c) (*a particular*) cierto; **to quote a ~ book** citar cierto libro; **to see a ~ man** ver a cierto hombre; **a ~ Mr Smith** un tal Sr Smith; **on a ~ day in May** cierto día de mayo; **he left on a ~ Tuesday** se marchó uno de tantos martes; **~ of our leaders** algunos de nuestros líderes.
(d) (*phrases*) **we don't know for ~** no sabemos a ciencia cierta; **to make ~ of** asegurarse de; **I'll make ~** lo averiguaré; **I'll make it as ~ as I can** lo haré todo lo seguro que pueda ser; **this should make victory ~** esto ha de asegurarnos la victoria; **you should make ~ of your facts** conviene comprobar los datos.
certainly ['sɜːtənlɪ] *adv* **(a)** **~!** ¡desde luego!, ¡por supuesto!, ¡naturalmente!; **~ madam!** ¡con mucho gusto, señora!, ¡cómo Vd quiera, señora!; **~ not!** ¡de ninguna manera!, ¡ni hablar!
(b) **it is ~ true that...** desde luego es verdad que...; **you may ~ take the car** desde luego que puedes tomar el coche; **I shall ~ be there** es seguro que asistiré, estaré allí sin falta; **you ~ did that well** eso sí que lo hiciste bien; **the meat is ~ tough** la carne sí es dura; **and ~ the Germans had more planes** y por cierto los alemanes tenían más aviones.
certainty ['sɜːtəntɪ] *n* certeza *f*, certidumbre *f*; seguridad *f*; **in the ~ of being able to go** con la certeza de poder ir; **there is no ~ about it** sobre esto no hay seguridad alguna; **his ~ was alarming** su convicción era desconcertante; **faced with the ~ of disaster** ante la inevitabilidad del desastre; **it's a ~** es cosa segura; **we know for a ~ that ...** sabemos a ciencia cierta que ...; **we can't know with complete ~** no lo podemos saber a ciencia cierta.
Cert. Ed. *n abbr of* **Certificate of Education.**
certifiable [,sɜːtɪ'faɪəbl] *adj* **(a)** certificable. **(b)** (*Med*) demente, que padece tal demencia que hay que encerrarle en un manicomio.
certificate [sə'tɪfɪkɪt] *n* certificado *m*; (*academic etc*) título *m*; (*of birth etc*) partida *f*, acta *f* (*Mex*); **~ of airworthiness** certificado *m* de aeronavegabilidad; **~ of baptism** partida *f* de bautismo; **~ of birth** partida *f* de nacimiento; **~ of death** partida *f* de defunción; **~ of deposit** certificado *m* de depósito; **~ of incorporation** escritura *f* de constitución (de una sociedad anónima); **~ of marriage** partida *f* de casamiento; **~ of origin** certificado *m* de origen; **C~ of Secondary Education** (*Brit Scol*) ≃ Título *m* de BUP.
certificated [sə'tɪfɪkeɪtɪd] *adj* titulado, diplomado.
certification [,sɜːtɪfɪ'keɪʃən] *n* certificación *f*.
certified ['sɜːtɪfaɪd] *adj document* certificado, atestiguado; (*in profession*) titulado, diplomado; **~ copy** copia *f* certificada; **~ mail** (*US*) correo *m* certificado; **~ public accountant** experto *m*, -a *f* contable.
certify ['sɜːtɪfaɪ] *vt* certificar; atestiguar, dar fe de; **certified as a true copy** confirmada como copia auténtica; **to ~ that...** declarar que...; **to ~ sb insane** declarar loco a uno.
certitude ['sɜːtɪtjuːd] *n* certidumbre *f*.
cerumen [sɪ'ruːmen] *n* cerumen *m*.
cervical ['sɜːvɪkəl] *adj* cervical; **~ cancer** cáncer *m* cervical; **~ smear test** diagnosis *f* citológica del cuello uterino, frotis *m* cervical.
cervix ['sɜːvɪks] *n, pl* **cervices** ['sɜːvɪsiːz] cuello *m* del útero.
Cesarean (*US*) = **Caesarean.**
cesium ['siːzɪəm] (*US*) = **caesium.**
cessation [se'seɪʃən] *n* cesación *f*, suspensión *f*; **~ of hostilities** cese *m* de hostilidades.

cession [ˈseʃən] *n* cesión *f*.

cesspit [ˈsespɪt] *n*, **cesspool** [ˈsespu:l] *n* pozo *m* negro; (*fig*) sentina *f*.

CET *n abbr of* **Central European Time**.

cetacean [sɪˈteɪʃɪən] **1** *adj* cetáceo. **2** *n* cetáceo *m*.

Ceylon [sɪˈlɒn] *n* (*Hist*) Ceilán *m*.

Ceylonese [sɪlɒˈni:z] (*Hist*) **1** *adj* ceilanés. **2** *n* ceilanés *m*, -esa *f*.

CF, cf *n abbr of* **cost and freight** costo *m* y flete.

C/F *abbr of* **carried forward** suma y sigue.

cf. *abbr of* **confer, compare** confróntese, cfr.

c/f, c/fwd *abbr of* **carried forward** suma y sigue.

CG *n* (*US*) *abbr of* **coastguard.**

cg *abbr of* **centigram(s), centigramme(s)** centigramo(s) *m*(*pl*), cg.

CH *n* (*Brit*) *abbr of* **Companion of Honour** *título honorífico*.

ch *abbr of* **central heating** calefacción *f* central, cal. cen.

ch. (**a**) (*Liter*) *abbr of* **chapter** capítulo *m*, cap. (**b**) (*Fin*) *abbr of* **cheque** cheque *m*, ch. (**c**) (*Rel*) *abbr of* **church** iglesia *f*.

cha-cha-(cha) [ˈtʃɑ:ˈtʃɑ:(ˈtʃɑ:)] *n* cha-cha-cha *m*.

Chad [tʃæd] **1** *n* Chad *m*; **Lake ~** Lago *m* Chad. **2** *adj* chadiano.

chador [ˈtʃʌdəʳ] *n* chador *m*.

chafe [tʃeɪf] **1** *vt* (**a**) (*rub*) rozar, raer.
(**b**) (*warm*) calentar frotando.
2 *vi* desgastarse (*against, on* contra); (*fig*) irritarse, impacientarse; **to ~ at, to ~ under** (*fig*) impacientarse por, irritarse debido a.

chaff [tʃɑ:f] **1** *n* barcia *f*, ahechaduras *fpl*, paja *f* menuda; (*waste*) desperdicios *mpl*; (*fig*) zumbas *fpl*, chanzas *fpl*, burlas *fpl*; (*Mil*) paja *f* metálica.
2 *vt* zumbarse de, tomar el pelo a.

chaffinch [ˈtʃæfɪntʃ] *n* pinzón *m* (vulgar).

chafing-dish [ˈtʃeɪfɪŋdɪʃ] *n* calientaplatos *m*.

chagrin [ˈʃægrɪn] **1** *n* mortificación *f*, desazón *f*, disgusto *m*; **to my ~** con gran disgusto mío. **2** *vt* mortificar, disgustar.

chain [tʃeɪn] **1** *n* cadena *f* (*also fig*); **~ of command** cadena *f* de mando; **~ of mountains** cordillera *f*; **in ~s** en cadenas; **to pull the ~** tirar del cordón. **2** *vt* encadenar.

◆**chain up** *vt animal* encadenar.

chain-gang [ˈtʃeɪngæŋ] *n* grupo *m* de prisioneros encadenados.

chain-letter [ˈtʃeɪn,letəʳ] *n* carta *f* que circula en cadena (*con promesa de una ganancia cuantiosa para los que la hacen seguir según las indicaciones*).

chain lightning [ˈtʃeɪnˈlaɪtnɪŋ] *n* (*US*) relámpagos *mpl* en zigzag.

chainmail [ˈtʃeɪnˈmeɪl] *n* cota *f* de malla.

chainpump [ˈtʃeɪnpʌmp] *n* bomba *f* de cangilones.

chain-reaction [ˈtʃeɪnri:ˈækʃən] *n* reacción *f* en cadena, reacción *f* eslabonada.

chainsaw [ˈtʃeɪn,sɔ:] *n* sierra *f* de cadena.

chain-smoke [ˈtʃeɪn,sməʊk] *vi* fumar un pitillo tras otro.

chain-smoker [ˈtʃeɪnsməʊkəʳ] *n* fumador *m*, -ora *f* que fuma un pitillo tras otro.

chain-stitch [ˈtʃeɪnstɪtʃ] *n* (*sew*) punto *m* de cadeneta, cadeneta *f*.

chain-store [ˈtʃeɪnstɔ:ʳ] *n* tienda *f* (*or* sucursal *f*) de una cadena.

chair [tʃɛəʳ] **1** *n* (**a**) silla *f*; (*Univ*) cátedra *f*; (*of meeting*) presidencia *f*; **to address the ~** dirigirse al presidente; **to be in the ~, to take the ~** presidir (*at a meeting* una reunión); **won't you take a ~?** ¿quiere sentarse?; **the ~** (*US electric ~*) la silla eléctrica.
(**b**) (*person*) presidente *m*, -a *f*.
2 *vt* (**a**) *person* llevar a hombros; **they ~ed him off the ground** le sacaron a hombros del campo.
(**b**) *meeting* presidir.

chairback [ˈtʃɛəbæk] *n* respaldo *m*.

chairlift [ˈtʃɛəlɪft] *n* telesilla *m*.

chairman [ˈtʃɛəmən] *n*, *pl* **chairmen** [ˈtʃɛəmen] presidente *m*, -a *f*; **~'s report** informe *m* del presidente.

chairmanship [ˈtʃɛəmənʃɪp] *n* (*post*) presidencia *f*; (*art*) arte *m* de presidir reuniones.

chairoplane [ˈtʃɛərəʊ,pleɪn] *n* silla *f* colgante.

chairperson [ˈtʃɛə,pɜ:sn] *n* presidente *m*, -a *f*.

chairwarmer* [ˈtʃɛə,wɔ:məʳ] *n* (*US*) calientasillas *mf*.

chairwoman [ˈtʃɛə,wʊmən] *n*, *pl* **chairwomen** [ˈtʃɛə,wɪmɪn] presidenta *f*.

chaise longue [ˈʃeɪzˈlɔ̃:ŋ] *n* tumbona *f*.

chalet [ˈʃæleɪ] *n* chalet *m*, chalé *m*.

chalice [ˈtʃælɪs] *n* cáliz *m*.

chalk [tʃɔ:k] **1** *n* (*Geol*) creta *f*; (*for writing*) tiza *f*, gis *m* (*LAm*); **by a long ~** (*Brit fig*) de lejos; **not by a long ~** (*Brit fig*) ni con mucho; **they're as different as ~ and cheese** (*persons*) se parecen (*or* son) como el día y la noche.
2 *vt* marcar (*or* dibujar *etc*) con tiza.

◆**chalk up** *vt* apuntar, anotar; atribuir (*to* a).

chalkboard [ˈtʃɔ:kbɔ:d] *n* (*US*) pizarra *f*.

chalkface [ˈtʃɔ:kfeɪs] *n*: **the teacher at the ~** el maestro en su clase, el profesor delante de la pizarra; **those at the ~** los que enseñan.

chalkpit [ˈtʃɔ:kpɪt] *n* cantera *f* de creta.

chalktalk* [ˈtʃɔ:ktɔ:k] *n* (*US*) charla *f* ilustrada en la pizarra.

chalky [ˈtʃɔ:kɪ] *adj* cretáceo; gredoso, cretoso.

challenge [ˈtʃælɪndʒ] **1** *n* (*to duel*) desafío *m*, reto *m*; (*of sentry*) quién vive *m*; (*Jur*) recusación *f*; **the ~ of new ideas** el reto de las nuevas ideas; **the ~ of the 21st century** el reto del siglo XXI, las posibilidades del siglo XXI; **Vigo's ~ for the league leadership** la tentativa que hace el Vigo para tomar el liderato de la liga; **this is a ~ to us all** esto es un reto a todos nosotros; **to issue a ~ to sb** desafiar a uno; **to take up a ~** aceptar un desafío.
2 *vt* (*to duel*) desafiar, retar; (*sentry*) dar el quién vive a; (*Jur*) recusar; *fact, point* poner en duda, cuestionar, expresar dudas acerca de; contestar; *speaker* hablar en contra de; **to ~ sb to** + *infin* desafiar a uno a que + *subj*; **I ~ you to name her** a ver si Vd se atreve a decir su nombre; **I ~ that conclusion** creo que esa conclusión no es acertada.

challenger [ˈtʃælɪndʒəʳ] *n* desafiador *m*, -ora *f*; (*competitor*) aspirante *mf*, concursante *mf*; (*opponent*) contrincante *mf*.

challenging [ˈtʃælɪndʒɪŋ] *adj* desafiante; *tone* de desafío; *speech etc* estimulante, provocador; *book* sugestivo, lleno de sugestiones; *task* arduo; **it's a ~ job** es un puesto que constituye un reto.

chamber [ˈtʃeɪmbəʳ] *n* (**a**) (*room*) cámara *f*; aposento *m*, sala *f*; (*Pol*) cámara *f*; **~s** (*Jur*) despacho *m*, bufete *m*; (*Brit: lodgings*) aposentos *mpl*; **~ of commerce** cámara *f* de comercio. (**b**) (*of gun*) recámara *f*. (**c**) (*Mus*) **~ concert** concierto *m* de cámara; **~ music** música *f* de cámara; **~ orchestra** orquesta *f* de cámara.

chamberlain [ˈtʃeɪmbəlɪn] *n* chambelán *m*, gentilhombre *m* de cámara.

chambermaid [ˈtʃeɪmbəmeɪd] *n* camarera *f*, sirvienta *f*, recamarera *f* (*Mex*).

chamberpot [ˈtʃeɪmbəpɒt] *n* orinal *m*, vaso *m* de noche.

chambray [ˈtʃæmbreɪ] *n* (*US*) = **cambric.**

chameleon [kəˈmi:lɪən] *n* camaleón *m*.

chamfer [ˈtʃæmfəʳ] **1** *n* chaflán *m*, bisel *m*. **2** *vt* chaflanar, biselar.

chammy [ˈʃæmɪ] *n* gamuza *f*.

chamois *n* (**a**) [ˈʃæmwɑ:] (*Zool*) gamuza *f*. (**b**) [ˈʃæmɪ] (*also* **~ leather**) gamuza *f*.

chamomile [ˈkæməʊmaɪl] *n* = **camomile.**

champ[1] [tʃæmp] *vt* (*also vi*: **to ~ at**) morder, mordiscar; *bit* tascar, morder; **to be ~ing at the bit** (*fig*) estar impaciente por algo, morirse por algo.

champ[2]* [tʃæmp] *n* = **champion.**

Champagne [ʃæmˈpeɪn] *n* Champaña *f*.

champagne [ʃæmˈpeɪn] *n* champán *m*, champaña *m*; **~ breakfast** desayuno *m* con champán; **~ cup, ~ glass** copa *f* de champán.

champion [ˈtʃæmpɪən] **1** *adj* (**a**) campeón; **a ~ athlete** un atleta campeón.
(**b**) (*) magnífico; **~!** ¡estupendo!
2 *n* (**a**) campeón *m*, -ona *f*.
(**b**) (*of a cause*) defensor *m*, -ora *f*, paladín *m*.
3 *vt* defender, apoyar, abogar por.

championship [ˈtʃæmpɪənʃɪp] *n* (**a**) campeonato *m*. (**b**) (*of cause*) defensa *f*.

chance [tʃɑ:ns] **1** *adj* fortuito, casual; imprevisto; (*random*) aleatorio.
2 *n* (**a**) (*luck, fortune, fate*) casualidad *f*; azar *m*; suerte *f*; **game of ~** juego *m* de azar; **the ~s of war** la fortuna de la guerra; **~ was against him** la suerte le fue contraria; **~ ordained that ...** la suerte quiso que ...; **it cannot have been a matter of ~** esto no habrá tenido nada de casual; **by ~** por casualidad; **by sheer ~** por pura casualidad; **do you by any ~ have a pen?** ¿tienes por casualidad una pluma?; **to leave things to ~** dejar las cosas al azar; **to leave nothing to ~** obrar con la mayor previsión, no dejar nada imprevisto.
(**b**) (*opportunity*) ocasión *f*, oportunidad *f*; **now's our ~!** ya nos toca el turno, nos ha llegado la vez; **~ would be a fine thing!** ¡ojalá tuviera la oportunidad!; **this is my big ~**

ésta es la oportunidad que venía esperando; **you'll never get another ~ like this** la suerte nunca te deparará otra ocasión como ésta; **give me a ~ to show what I can do** déme la oportunidad de mostrar si soy capaz; **give me a ~ won't you?** ¡déjame un momento en paz!; **to give sb another ~** darle otra oportunidad a uno; **he has had every ~** le hemos dado todas las oportunidades posibles; **to have an eye for the main ~** mirar por su propio provecho; **to let the ~ slip by** perder la ocasión; **to waste one's ~s** desperdiciar las ocasiones.

(**c**) (*possibility*) posibilidad *f*, probabilidad *f*; **the ~s are that ...** lo más probable es que + *subj*; **there is no ~ of that** eso es imposible; **there's one ~ in ten** hay una posibilidad sobre diez; **it's a long ~** eso es poco probable; **to be in with a ~** tener algunas posibilidades; **to have a fair ~ of** + *ger* tener buenas probabilidades de + *infin*; **he hasn't a ~** no tiene posibilidad alguna; **I never had a ~ in life** la suerte no me ha favorecido jamás en la vida; **to stand a ~** tener posibilidades; **you don't stand a ~** no tienes posibilidad alguna.

(**d**) (*risk*) riesgo *m*; **to take a ~** arriesgarse, probar fortuna; **to take no ~s** obrar con la mayor previsión, no dejar nada imprevisto; **that's a ~ we shall have to take** tendremos que tomar ese riesgo.

3 *vt* (**a**) (*risk*) arriesgar; probar; **to ~ it** probarlo, aventurarse; **shall we ~ it?** ¿probaremos?; *V* **arm[1]**.

(**b**) (*happen*) **it ~d that ...** aconteció que ...; **if it ~s that ...** si resulta que ...; **I ~d to see him** le vi por casualidad.

4 *vi*: **to ~ upon** encontrar por casualidad, tropezar con, topar con.

chancel [ˈtʃɑːnsəl] *n* coro *m* y presbiterio.

chancellery [ˈtʃɑːnsərɪ] *n* cancillería *f*.

chancellor [ˈtʃɑːnsələʳ] *n* canciller *m*; **C~ of the Exchequer** (*Brit*) Ministro *m*, -a *f* de Hacienda; **Lord C~** *jefe de la administración de la justicia en Inglaterra y Gales, y presidente de la Cámara de los Lores.*

chancery [ˈtʃɑːnsərɪ] *n* (*Jur*) chancillería *f* (††), tribunal *m* de equidad; **ward in ~** pupilo *m*, -a *f* bajo la protección del tribunal.

chancre [ˈʃæŋkəʳ] *n* chancro *m*.

chancy* [ˈtʃɑːnsɪ] *adj* arriesgado; dudoso.

chandelier [ˌʃændəˈlɪəʳ] *n* araña *f* (de luces).

chandler [ˈtʃɑːndləʳ] *n* velero *m*.

change [tʃeɪndʒ] **1** *n* (**a**) cambio *m*; modificación *f*; transformación *f*; (*of skin etc*) muda *f*; **~ of address** cambio *m* de domicilio; **~ of clothes** cambio *m* (*or* muda *f LAm*) de ropa; **~ of front** cambio *m* de frente; **~ of heart** cambio *m* de sentimiento, cambio *m* de idea; **~ of horses** relevo *m* de los tiros; **~ of life** menopausia *f*; **~ of ownership** cambio *m* de dueño; **~ of scene** (*Theat*) mutación *f*; **for a ~** para variar un poco; **it's a ~ for the better** es una mejora; **to get no ~ out of sb** no conseguir sacar nada a uno; **to make a ~ of direction** cambiar de dirección; **the day out made a refreshing ~** el día fuera de casa nos dio un buen cambio de aire; **to resist ~** resistirse a las innovaciones; **to ring the ~s on sth** hacer algo de diversas maneras.

(**b**) (*money*) (*small coins*) moneda *f* suelta, suelto *m*, sencillo *m* (*LAm*), feria *f* (*Mex*); (*for a larger coin*) cambio *m*; (*money returned*) vuelta *f*, vuelto *m* (*LAm*); **to give sb ~ for a £10 note** cambiar a uno un billete de 10 libras; (**you may**) **keep the ~** quédese con la vuelta (*LAm*: el vuelto).

2 *vt* cambiar (*for* por), trocar; reemplazar; modificar; transformar (*into* en); *clothes, colour, gear, mind etc* cambiar de, mudar de; **to ~ pounds into dollars** cambiar libras en dólares; **can you ~ this note for me?** ¿me hace el favor de cambiar este billete?; **I find him much ~d** le veo muy cambiado; **to ~ a baby, to ~ a nappy** cambiar el pañal de un bebé.

3 *vi* cambiar(se), mudar; transformarse (*into* en); (*Rail etc*) hacer transbordo, cambiar de tren (*etc*); **all ~!** ¡cambio de tren!; **you haven't ~d a bit!** ¡no has cambiado en lo más mínimo!

◆**change down** *vi* (*Aut*) cambiar a una velocidad inferior.

◆**change over 1** *vt* cambiar, trocar. **2** *vi* cambiar (*to* a).

◆**change up** *vi* (*Aut*) cambiar a una velocidad superior.

changeability [ˌtʃeɪndʒəˈbɪlɪtɪ] *n* lo cambiable, mutabilidad *f*; inconstancia *f*, lo cambiadizo; variabilidad *f*.

changeable [ˈtʃeɪndʒəbl] *adj* cambiable, mudable; inconstante, cambiadizo; *weather* variable.

changeless [ˈtʃeɪndʒlɪs] *adj* inmutable.

changeling [ˈtʃeɪndʒlɪŋ] *n* niño *m* sustituido por otro, niña *f* sustituida por otra.

change machine [ˈtʃeɪndʒməˌʃiːn] *n* máquina *f* de cambio.

changeover [ˈtʃeɪndʒˌəʊvəʳ] *n* cambio *m*.

change purse [ˈtʃeɪndʒpɜːs] *n* (*US*) monedero *m*.

changing [ˈtʃeɪndʒɪŋ] **1** *adj* cambiante; mudable, variable; **a ~ world** un mundo en perpetua evolución. **2** *n*: **~ of the guard** relevo *m* de la guardia.

changing-room [ˈtʃeɪndʒɪŋrʊm] *n* (*Brit*) vestuario *m*.

channel [ˈtʃænl] **1** *n* canal *m* (*also TV*); (*of a river*) cauce *m*; (*strait*) estrecho *m*; (*fig*) conducto *m*, medio *m*; (*irrigation* ~) acequia *f*, canal *m* de riego; **~ of distribution** vía *f* de distribución, canal *m* de distribución; **the** (**English**) **C~** el Canal (de la Mancha); **the C~ Tunnel** el túnel del Canal de la Mancha; **by the usual** (*or* **proper**) **~s** por las vías de costumbre, por los conductos normales; **green ~** (*Customs*) pasillo *m* verde; **red ~** (*Customs*) pasillo *m* rojo.

2 *vt* acanalar; (*fig*) encauzar, dirigir (*into* a, por).

◆**channel off** *vt* (*lit, fig*) *water, energy, resources* canalizar.

Channel Islands [ˈtʃænəlˌaɪləndz] *npl*, **Channel Isles** [ˈtʃænəlˌaɪlz] *npl* Islas *fpl* Normandas, Islas *fpl* Anglonormandas, Islas *fpl* del Canal (de la Mancha).

chant [tʃɑːnt] **1** *n* canto *m*; (*Rel*: *plain* ~) canto *m* llano; (*fig*) sonsonete *m*; (*by demonstrators etc*) grito *m*, eslogan *m*. **2** *vt* cantar (el canto llano); *praises* cantar; *slogan* gritar (rítmicamente), corear, entonar; (*fig*) salmodiar, recitar en tono monótono. **3** *vi* (*Rel*) cantar (el canto llano); (*at demonstration etc*) gritar (rítmicamente).

chantey [ˈʃæntɪ] *n* (*US*) saloma *f*.

chaos [ˈkeɪɒs] *n* caos *m*, desorden *m*.

chaotic [keɪˈɒtɪk] *adj* caótico, desordenado.

chap[1] [tʃæp] **1** *n* grieta *f*, hendedura *f*. **2** *vt* agrietar. **3** *vi* agrietarse.

chap[2] [tʃæp] *n* (*Anat*) mandíbula *f*; (*cheek*) mejilla *f*.

chap[3]* [tʃæp] *n* tío* *m*, tipo* *m*, pájaro* *m*; **a ~ I know** un tío que conozco; **he's a nice ~** es buen chico, es buena persona; **he's very deaf, poor ~** es muy sordo, el pobre; **how are you, old ~?** ¿qué tal, amigo?; **be a good ~ and say nothing** sé buen chico y no digas nada.

chap. *abbr of* **chapter** capítulo *m*, cap.

chapel [ˈtʃæpəl] **1** *n* capilla *f*; (*Protestant etc*) templo *m*; (*Typ*) personal *m* de una imprenta. **2** *as adj*: **people here are very ~** la gente aquí son metodistas (*etc*) muy firmes; **I'm not ~ myself** yo mismo no soy practicante.

chaperon(e) [ˈʃæpərəʊn] **1** *n* acompañanta *f* (de señorita), carabina *f**. **2** *vt* acompañar (a una señorita).

chaplain [ˈtʃæplɪn] *n* capellán *m*.

chaplaincy [ˈtʃæplənsɪ] *n* capellanía *f*.

chaplet [ˈtʃæplɪt] *n* guirnalda *f*, corona *f* de flores; (*necklace*) collar *m*; (*Eccl*) rosario *m*.

chapped [tʃæpt] *adj skin* agrietado.

chappy* [ˈtʃæpɪ] *n* = **chap[3]**.

chaps [tʃæps] *npl* (*US*) zahones *mpl*, chaparreras *fpl*.

chapter [ˈtʃæptəʳ] *n* (**a**) capítulo *m*; **~ of accidents** serie *f* de desgracias; **with ~ and verse** con pelos y señales, con todo lujo de detalles; **he can quote you ~ and verse** él lo sabe citar con todos sus pelos y señales.

(**b**) (*Eccl*) cabildo *m*.

chapterhouse [ˈtʃæptəhaʊs] *n*, *pl* **chapterhouses** [ˈtʃæptəhaʊzɪz] sala *f* capitular.

char[1] [tʃɑːʳ] *vt* carbonizar, chamuscar.

char[2] [tʃɑːʳ] *n* (*Brit*‡) té *m*.

char[3] [tʃɑːʳ] **1** *n* (*Brit**) = **charlady**. **2** *vi* limpiar, trabajar como asistenta.

char-à-banc [ˈʃærəbæŋ] *n* (†) autocar *m*.

character [ˈkærɪktəʳ] *n* (**a**) (*nature of thing*) carácter *m*, naturaleza *f*, índole *f*, calidad *f*; (*moral ~ of person*) carácter *m*; **~ assassination** defamación *f*, asesinato *m* moral; **~ reference** informe *m*, referencia *f*; **to be in ~** ser característico, ser conforme al tipo; **to be out of ~ with** disonar de, desentonar con; **to bear a good ~** tener una buena reputación; **to have a bad ~** tener mala fama; **to give sb a good ~** dar a uno una recomendación satisfactoria.

(**b**) (*personage in novel, play etc*) personaje *m*; (*rôle*) papel *m*; **'Six C~s in Search of an Author'** 'Seis personajes en busca de autor'; **the play has 8 ~s** la obra tiene 8 personajes; **chief ~** protagonista *mf*; **~ actor** actor *m* de carácter; **~ actress** característica *f*; **in the ~ of** en el papel de; **that is more in ~** eso es más característico; **~ part** papel *m* de carácter; **~ sketch** esbozo *m* de carácter.

(**c**) (*energy, determination*) carácter *m*; **a man of ~** un hombre de carácter; **he lacks ~** le falta carácter.

(**d**) (*) tipo* *m*, sujeto* *m*; **a ~ I know** un tipo que yo conozco; **he's quite a ~** es un tipo pintoresco, es un original; **he's a very odd ~** es un tipo muy raro.

(**e**) (*Bio, Comput, Typ etc*) carácter *m*; ~ **code** código *m* de caracteres; ~ **set** juego *m* de caracteres; ~ **space** espacio *m* (de carácter).

characteristic [ˌkærɪktəˈrɪstɪk] **1** *adj* característico (*of* de). **2** *n* característica *f*, carácter *m*; peculiaridad *f*; distintivo *m*, señal *f* distintiva.

characteristically [ˌkærɪktəˈrɪstɪkəlɪ] *adv* característicamente, de modo característico.

characterization [ˌkærɪktəraɪˈzeɪʃən] *n* caracterización *f*.

characterize [ˈkærɪktəraɪz] *vt* caracterizar.

characterless [ˈkærɪktəlɪs] *adj* sin carácter.

charade [ʃəˈrɑːd] *n* (*game*: *also* ~**s**) charada *f*; (*fig*) payasada *f*, farsa *f*, comedia *f*.

charcoal [ˈtʃɑːkəʊl] *n* carbón *m* vegetal; (*Art*) carboncillo *m*; ~ **drawing** dibujo *m* al carbón, dibujo *m* al carboncillo.

charcoal-burner [ˈtʃɑːkəʊlˌbɜːnəʳ] *n* carbonero *m*.

charcoal-grey [ˌtʃɑːkəʊlˈgreɪ] *adj* gris marengo.

charge [tʃɑːdʒ] **1** *n* (**a**) (*explosive, electrical*) carga *f*.

(**b**) (*attack*) carga *f*, ataque *m*, asalto *m*; (*of bull*) embestida *f*; (*Sport*) placaje *m*, atajo *m*.

(**c**) (*Jur etc*) acusación *f*, cargo *m*; **to appear on a ~ of** comparecer acusado de; **to beat the ~*** ser absuelto; **to bring** (*or* **lay**) **~s against** hacer acusaciones contra, levantar expediente contra (*LAm*); **to give sb in ~** entregar a uno a la policía; **to lay o.s. open to the ~ of ...** dejarse expuesto a la acusación de ...; **to return to the ~** volver al cargo, repetir la acusación.

(**d**) (*price*) precio *m*, coste *m*; (*professional*) honorarios *mpl*; ~ **account** cuenta *f* para compras a crédito, cuenta *f* abierta; ~ **card** tarjeta *f* de cuenta; **free of ~** gratis; **~ for admission** precio *m* de entrada; **'no ~ for admission'** 'entrada gratis', 'entrada gratuita'; **there's no ~** esto no se cobra, esto es gratuito; **is there a ~ for delivery?** ¿se paga el transporte?; **to be a ~ upon** cargarse en cuenta a; **to make a ~ for sth** cobrar por algo; **to reverse the ~s** (*Telec*) cobrar al número llamado, llamar a cobro revertido.

(**e**) (*responsibility*) responsabilidad *f*; (*office*) cargo *m*; (*task*) encargo *m*, cometido *m*; **the person in ~** la persona responsable; **to be in ~** mandar; **who is in ~ here?** ¿quién manda aquí?; **to be in ~ of** estar encargado de; **to be in the ~ of** correr a cargo de; **to take ~ of** hacerse cargo de, encargarse de; *men, expedition etc* asumir el mando de.

(**f**) (*person etc cared for*) **the teacher and her ~s** la maestra y sus alumnos; **the nurse and her ~s** la enfermera y sus enfermos.

(**g**) (*order*) orden *f*, instrucción *f*.

(**h**) (*Her*) blasón *m*.

2 *vt* (**a**) (*fill*) cargar (*also Mil, Elec*; *with* de).

(**b**) (*attack*) atacar, cargar contra; (*bull etc*) embestir; atajar.

(**c**) (*Jur etc*) acusar (*with* de).

(**d**) *price* pedir; *price, person* cobrar (a); **to ~ 3% commission** cobrar un 3 por cien de comisión; **what are they charging for it?** ¿cuánto piden por él?; **what did they ~ you for it?** ¿cuánto te cobraron?.

(**e**) (*record as debt*: *also* **to ~ up**) **to ~ sth (up) to sb, to ~ sth (up) to sb's account** cargar algo en cuenta a uno; **~ it to my card** cárguelo a mi tarjeta; **cash or ~?** (*US*) ¿al contado o a crédito?

(**f**) (*order*) **to ~ sb to do sth** ordenar a uno hacer algo; **to ~ sb with a mission** confiar una misión a uno; **I am ~d with the task of** + *ger* me han encargado el deber de + *infin*.

3 *vi* (**a**) (*Mil*) atacar, cargar; (*bull*) embestir; **to ~ down upon** cargar sobre, precipitarse sobre; **to ~ into** *wall* chocar contra; *crowd, meeting* irrumpir en; *fray* lanzarse a (participar en).

(**b**) (*make pay*) cobrar, (*a lot*) cobrar mucho.

◆**charge up** *vt* (**a**) = **charge 2 (e)**. (**b**) *battery* cargar.

chargeable [ˈtʃɑːdʒəbl] *adj* (**a**) ~ **with** (*Jur*) *person* acusable de. (**b**) ~ **to** a cargo de.

charged [tʃɑːdʒd] *adj* (*Elec*) cargado, con carga.

chargé d'affaires [ˈʃɑːʒeɪdæˈfɛəʳ] *n* encargado *m* de negocios.

chargehand [ˈtʃɑːdʒhænd] *n* (*Brit*) capataz *m*.

charge-nurse [ˈtʃɑːdʒˌnɜːs] *n* (*Brit*) enfermero *m*, -a *f* jefe.

charger [ˈtʃɑːdʒəʳ] *n* (*horse*) corcel *m*, caballo *m* de guerra; (*Elec*) cargador *m*.

charge-sheet [ˈtʃɑːdʒˌʃiːt] *n* ≃ hoja *f* (*or* impreso *m*) de cargos.

charily [ˈtʃɛərɪlɪ] *adv* cuidadosamente, cautelosamente; parcamente, con parquedad.

chariot [ˈtʃærɪət] *n* carro *m* (romano, de guerra *etc*).

charioteer [ˌtʃærɪəˈtɪəʳ] *n* auriga *m*.

charisma [kæˈrɪzmə] *n* carisma *m*.

charismatic [ˌkærɪzˈmætɪk] *adj* carismático.

charitable [ˈtʃærɪtəbl] *adj* (**a**) *person* caritativo; *remark, view* comprensivo, compasivo. (**b**) *purpose, trust, society* benéfico; ~ **institution** institución *f* benéfica, institución *f* de beneficencia.

charitably [ˈtʃærɪtəblɪ] *adv* caritativamente; con caridad; con compasión.

charity [ˈtʃærɪtɪ] *n* (**a**) caridad *f*; (*sympathy*) comprensión *f*, compasión *f*; **out of ~** por caridad; **~ begins at home** la caridad bien entendida empieza por uno mismo; **to live on ~** vivir de limosnas.

(**b**) (*organization*) sociedad *f* benéfica; **~ appeal** cuestación *f* para obras benéficas; **to raffle sth for ~** rifar algo para fines benéficos; **all proceeds go to ~** todo el importe se destina a obras benéficas; **most of it goes to ~** la mayor parte está destinada a obras de beneficencia.

(**c**) (*act*) **it would be a ~ if ...** sería una obra de caridad si ...

charlady [ˈtʃɑːleɪdɪ] *n* (*Brit*) asistenta *f*, mujer *f* de la limpieza.

charlatan [ˈʃɑːlətən] *n* charlatán *m*; (*Med*) charlatán *m*, curandero *m*.

Charlemagne [ˈʃɑːləmeɪn] *nm* Carlomagno.

Charles [tʃɑːlz] *nm* Carlos.

charleston [ˈtʃɑːlstən] *n* charlestón *m*.

charley horse* [ˈtʃɑːlɪhɔːs] *n* (*US*) calambre *m*.

Charlie [ˈtʃɑːlɪ] *nm* (**a**) Carlitos; ~ **Chaplin** Charlot. (**b**) ~‡ imbécil *m*; **he must have looked a proper ~!** (*Brit*) ¡debía parecer un verdadero gilipollas!‡; **I felt a right ~!** (*Brit*) me sentí como un gilipollas‡.

Charlotte [ˈʃɑːlət] *nf* Carlota.

charm [tʃɑːm] **1** *n* (**a**) (*gen*) encanto *m*, atractivo *m*, hechizo *m*; **~s** (*of woman*) atractivo *m*, hechizos *mpl*; **he has great ~** tiene mucho encanto, tiene un fuerte atractivo; **typical Spanish ~** la típica simpatía española; **to turn on the ~** ponerse fino, deshacerse en finuras.

(**b**) (*spell*) hechizo *m*, (*recited*) ensalmo *m*.

(**c**) (*object*) amuleto *m*; dije *m*.

2 *vt* hechizar, encantar, seducir; **we were ~ed by Granada** nos encantó Granada.

◆**charm away** *vt* hacer desaparecer como por magia, llevarse misteriosamente.

charm bracelet [ˈtʃɑːmˌbreɪslɪt] *n* brazalete *m* amuleto.

charmer [ˈtʃɑːməʳ] *n* hombre *m* (*etc*) encantador.

charming [ˈtʃɑːmɪŋ] *adj* encantador; *person* encantador, simpático; *present, remark etc* fino, gentil; **~!** (*iro*) ¡qué simpático!; **how ~ of you!** ¡qué detalle!

charmingly [ˈtʃɑːmɪŋlɪ] *adv* de modo encantador; con finura; **a ~ simple dress** un vestido sencillo pero muy mono.

charm-school* [ˈtʃɑːmˌskuːl] *n* = **finishing school**.

charnel-house [ˈtʃɑːnlhaʊs] *n*, *pl* **charnel-houses** [ˈtʃɑːnlhaʊzɪz] osario *m*.

charred [tʃɑːd] *adj* carbonizado, chamuscado.

chart [tʃɑːt] **1** *n* tabla *f*, cuadro *m*, esquema *m*, gráfico *m*; (*graph*) gráfica *f*; (*of discs*) lista *f*; (*Naut*) carta *f* de navegación; **the ~s*** los cuarenta (principales); ~ **topper*** éxito *m* discográfico.

2 *vt* (*record*) poner en una carta; (*outline*) explorar; (*on graph etc*) mostrar, representar, registrar; **the diagram ~s the company's progress** el diagrama muestra el progreso de la compañía; **to ~ a course** trazar un derrotero, planear una ruta.

charter [ˈtʃɑːtəʳ] **1** *n* (**a**) carta *f*; (*of city, bill of rights*) fuero *m*; (*of company*) carta *f* de privilegio; **royal ~** cédula *f* real.

(**b**) (*hire*) alquiler *m*; fletamiento *m*; ~ **flight** vuelo *m* chárter; ~ **plane** avión *m* chárter.

2 *vt* (**a**) estatuir; dar carta de privilegio a.

(**b**) *bus etc* alquilar; *plane, ship* fletar.

chartered [ˈtʃɑːtəd] *adj* *person* diplomado; *company* legalmente constituido; ~ **accountant** (*Brit, Canada*) censor *m* jurado de cuentas, censora *f* jurada de cuentas, contador *m* público, contadora *f* pública (*LAm*).

Chartism [ˈtʃɑːtɪzəm] *n* (*Hist*) cartismo *m*.

Chartist [ˈtʃɑːtɪst] *n*: **the ~s** (*Hist*) los cartistas.

charwoman [ˈtʃɑːˌwʊmən] *n*, *pl* **charwomen** [ˈtʃɑːˌwɪmɪn] = **charlady**.

chary [ˈtʃɛərɪ] *adj* cuidadoso, cauteloso, reservado; **to be ~ of** + *n* ser avaro de + *n*, ser parco en + *n*; **to be ~ of** + *ger* evitar + *infin*, no prestarse de buena gana a + *infin*.

chase[1] [tʃeɪs] **1** *n* persecución *f*; (*hunt*) caza *f*; **to give ~ to**

dar caza a, perseguir; **to join in the ~ for sth** unirse a los que buscan algo.

2 *vt* (*follow*) perseguir; (*hunt*) cazar; *girl etc* perseguir, dar caza a; **to ~ sb for money** reclamar dinero a uno.

3 *vi* correr, precipitarse.

◆**chase after** *vt* ir tras, (*fig*) correr tras.

◆**chase away** *vt* ahuyentar.

◆**chase down** *vt* (*US*) = **chase up.**

◆**chase off** *vt* ahuyentar.

◆**chase out** *vt* echar fuera.

◆**chase up** *vt* buscar, tratar de localizar; investigar, tratar de aclarar; **I'll ~ him up** se lo voy a recordar.

chase² [tʃeɪs] *vt metal* grabar, adornar grabando, cincelar.

chaser ['tʃeɪsəʳ] *n* bebida *f* tomada inmediatamente después de otra distinta, *p.ej.* copita *f* de licor.

chasm ['kæzəm] *n* (*Geog*) sima *f*, abismo *m*, grieta *f*; (*fig*) abismo *m*, fosa *f*.

chassis ['ʃæsɪ] *n* chasis *m*.

chaste [tʃeɪst] *adj* casto.

chastely ['tʃeɪstlɪ] *adv* castamente.

chasten ['tʃeɪsn] *vt* castigar, corregir, escarmentar.

chastened ['tʃeɪsnd] **1** *pret and ptp of* **chasten. 2** *adj* (*by experience etc*) escarmentado; *tone etc* sumiso; **they seemed much ~** parecían haberse arrepentido.

chasteness ['tʃeɪstnɪs] *n* castidad *f*.

chastening ['tʃeɪsnɪŋ] *adj experience etc* aleccionador.

chastise [tʃæs'taɪz] *vt* castigar.

chastisement ['tʃæstɪzmənt] *n* castigo *m*.

chastity ['tʃæstɪtɪ] *n* castidad *f*.

chasuble ['tʃæzjʊbl] *n* casulla *f*.

chat [tʃæt] **1** *n* charla *f*, plática *f* (*LAm*); **to have a ~ with** charlar con; **I'll have a ~ with him** hablaré con él. **2** *vi* charlar, platicar (*LAm*) (*to, with* con).

◆**chat up** *vt* (*Brit**) *girl* ligar*, enrollarse con*; *influential person* dar jabón a*.

chatline ['tʃætlaɪn] *n* teléfono *m* del placer.

chat-show ['tʃæt,ʃəʊ] *n* (*Brit TV*) programa *m* de entrevistas (informales), tertulia *f* (de TV); **~ host/hostess** presentador *m*, -ora *f* de programa de entrevistas.

chattels ['tʃætlz] *npl* bienes *mpl* muebles; (*loosely*) cosas *fpl*, enseres *mpl*.

chatter ['tʃætəʳ] **1** *n* (*talk*) charla *f*, parloteo *m*; (*of birds*) parloteo *m*; (*of teeth*) castañeteo *m*.

2 *vi* (*person*) charlar, parlotear; (*birds*) parlotear; (*monkeys*) chillar; (*teeth*) castañetear; **she does ~ so** es muy habladora; **stop ~ing!** ¡silencio!

chatterbox ['tʃætəbɒks] *n*, **chatterer** ['tʃætərəʳ] parlanchín *m*, -ina *f*, charlatán *m*, -ana *f*, platicón *m*, -ona *f* (*Mex*), tarabilla *mf*.

chatty ['tʃætɪ] *adj person* hablador, locuaz; *style* familiar; *letter* afectuoso y lleno de noticias; *article* de tono familiar.

chauffeur ['ʃəʊfəʳ] **1** *n* chófer *m*, chofer *m* (*LAm*). **2** *vt* llevar en coche (*to the station* a la estación); actuar de chófer para.

chauffeur-driven ['ʃəʊfə,drɪvən] *adj*: **~ car** coche *m* con chófer.

chauvinism ['ʃəʊvɪnɪzəm] *n* chauvinismo *m*, patriotería *f*; **male ~** machismo *m*, falocracia *f*.

chauvinist ['ʃəʊvɪnɪst] **1** *adj* chauvinista, patriotero; **male ~ pig** falócrata *m*, cerdo *m* machista. **2** *n* chauvinista *mf*, patriotero *m*, -a *f*.

chauvinistic [,ʃəʊvɪ'nɪstɪk] *adj* (*of race, sex etc*) chauvinista; (*jingoistic*) patriotero.

Ch.E. (*esp US*) (**a**) *abbr of* **Chemical Engineer.** (**b**) *abbr of* **Chief Engineer.**

cheap [tʃiːp] **1** *adj* barato; *ticket etc* económico; (*fig*) de mal gusto, cursi, chabacano; *trick* malo; **~ labour** mano *f* de obra barata; **~ money** préstamos *mpl* obtenidos a bajo interés, créditos *mpl* a tipos de interés bajos; **it's ~ at the price** a ese precio resulta económico; **that's pretty ~** eso es poco recto, eso se llama no jugar limpio; **to feel ~** sentirse humillado, sentir vergüenza; **to hold ~** tener en poco; **to make o.s. ~** hacer cosas indignas de sí, aplebeyarse; **to make a product ~er** abaratar un producto.

2 *adv* barato; *V* **cheaply.**

3 *n* (*****) **on the ~** barato; **to do sth on the ~** hacer algo con el mínimo de gastos, hacer algo en plan económico; **to get sth on the ~** obtener algo a precio reducido.

cheapen ['tʃiːpən] **1** *vt* abaratar. **2** *vi* abaratarse. **3** *vr*: **to ~ o.s.** hacer cosas indignas de sí, aplebeyarse.

cheapie* ['tʃiːpɪ] **1** *adj* de barato*. **2** *n* (*ticket, meal etc*) ganga *f*.

cheap-jack ['tʃiːpdʒæk] **1** *adj* de bajísima calidad, malísimo; muy mal hecho. **2** *n* baratillero *m*.

cheaply ['tʃiːplɪ] *adv* barato; a precio económico; **you got off ~** te has librado barato, podía haberte sido peor.

cheapness ['tʃiːpnɪs] *n* lo barato, baratura *f*.

cheapo* ['tʃiːpəʊ] **1** *adj* baratejo, de (a) perrona, perronero. **2** *n* perronero* *m*.

cheapshot‡ ['tʃiːpʃɒt] *vt*: **to ~ sb** (*US*) hablar mal de uno.

cheapskate* ['tʃiːpskeɪt] *n* (*US*) canalla *m*; tacaño *m*, roñoso *m*.

cheat [tʃiːt] **1** *n* (**a**) trampa *f*, fraude *m*; **it was a ~** fue un timo, hubo trampa; **there's a ~ in it somewhere** aquí hay trampa.

(**b**) (*person*) tramposo *m*, -a *f*, petardista *mf*; (*at cards*) fullero *m*.

2 *vt person* defraudar, timar, embaucar; **to ~ sb out of sth** estafar algo a uno; **to feel ~ed** sentirse defraudado.

3 *vi* (*in exam etc*) hacer trampas.

◆**cheat on** *vt* (*esp US*) engañar.

cheating ['tʃiːtɪŋ] *n* trampa *f*, fraude *m*; (*at cards*) fullerías *fpl*.

check¹ [tʃek] **1** *n* (**a**) (*halt, setback*) parada *f* (súbita); (*Mil*) repulsa *f*; (*to plans*) contratiempo *m*, revés *m*; (*restraint*) restricción *f* (*on* de); (*obstacle*) impedimento *m* (*on* para), estorbo *m* (*on* a); **~s and balances in a constitution** (*US*) frenos *mpl* y equilibrios de una constitución; **to act as a ~ on** (*restrain*) refrenar, (*impede*) ser un estorbo a; **to hold** (*or* **keep**) **in ~** contener, tener a raya; **to suffer a ~** sufrir un revés.

(**b**) (*Chess*) jaque *m*; **in ~** en jaque; **continuous ~** tablas *fpl* por jaque continuo.

(**c**) (*check-up*) control *m*, inspección *f*, verificación *f* (*on* de); (*Mech etc*) repaso *m*; (*Med*) chequeo *m*, reconocimiento *m* general; **~ digit** dígito *m* de control; **to keep a ~ on** controlar.

(**d**) (*token*) (*counterfoil*) talón *m*; (*at cloakroom*) número *m*, billete *m*, boleto *m*; (*in games*) ficha *f*; (*US: invoice*) factura *f*; (*US: cheque*) cheque *m*; (*bill for food*) nota *f*, cuenta *f*; **to cash** (*or* **hand**) **in one's ~s** (*US‡*) estirar la pata, palmarla*.

2 *interj* (**a**) **~!** (*Chess*) ¡jaque! (**b**) (*US**: *O.K.*) ¡vale!

3 *vt* (**a**) *motion* parar, detener; *spread etc* restringir, tener a raya, refrenar; (*be an obstacle to*) impedir, estorbar; *attack* rechazar.

(**b**) (*Chess*) dar jaque a.

(**c**) (*also* **to ~ out**) (*examine*) controlar, examinar, inspeccionar; *facts* comprobar; *document* compulsar, revisar; (*count*) llevar la cuenta de, contar; (*Mech*) revisar, repasar; *baggage* (*US*) facturar; *tickets, passports* comprobar; **to ~ a copy against the original** cotejar una copia con el original; **'~ against delivery'** (*on text of speech*) 'comprobar el texto definitivo'; **~ the state of him!** ¡mira cómo viene!

4 *vi* (**a**) (*make sure*) = **~ up.** (**b**) (*agree*) concordar, estar de acuerdo (*with* con); **that ~s with our results here** eso concuerda con nuestros resultados aquí.

5 *vr*: **to ~ o.s.** detenerse, refrenarse.

◆**check in 1** *vt baggage* facturar, chequear (*LAm*).

2 *vi* (*Aer*) presentarse, facturar el equipaje; (*hotel*) firmar el registro, (*fig*) llegar, entrar.

◆**check off** *vt list* marcar; (*count*) contar; **to ~ items off on a list** comprobar artículos en una lista.

◆**check on** *vt information, time etc* verificar; **to ~ on sb** investigar a uno.

◆**check out 1** *vt* (**a**) *accounts etc* verificar, chequear (*LAm*). (**b**) *luggage* recoger, llevar (fuera). (**c**) (*look at, inspect*) mirar, controlar.

2 *vi* (**a**) pagar y marcharse, (*loosely*) salir, marcharse. (**b**) = **check¹ 4** (**b**).

◆**check over** *vt* revisar, escudriñar.

◆**check up** *vi* comprobar; hacer una investigación; informarse; **to ~ up on** comprobar, verificar; investigar; investigar los antecedentes (*or* la lealtad *etc*) de.

◆**check with** *vi* consultar a.

check² [tʃek] **1** *n* (*in pattern*) cuadro *m*; (*cloth*) paño *m* a cuadros. **2** *adj* a cuadros; **~ suit** traje *m* a cuadros.

checkbook ['tʃekbʊk] *n* (*US*) = **chequebook.**

checked [tʃekt] *adj*, **checkered** ['tʃekəd] *adj* (*US*) a cuadros; = **chequered.**

checker ['tʃekəʳ] *n* verificador *m*; (*US*: *in supermarket*) cajero *m*, -a *f*; (*in cloakroom*) encargado *m*, -a *f* de guardarropa.

checkerboard ['tʃekəbɔːd] *n* (*US*) tablero *m* de damas.

checkers ['tʃekəz] *n* (*US*: *game*) damas *fpl*.

check-in ['tʃekɪn] **1** *n* (*Aer*: *also* **~ desk**) mostrador *m* de

facturación, mostrador *m* de embarque. **2** *attr*: ~ **desk** (*Aer*) mostrador *m* de facturación, mostrador *m* de embarque; **your ~ time is an hour before departure** su hora de facturación es una hora antes de la salida.
checking ['tʃekɪŋ] *n* control *m*, comprobación *f*; ~ **account** (*US*) cuenta *f* corriente.
checking-in [ˌtʃekɪŋ'ɪn] *n* (*Aer*) facturación *f*.
checklist ['tʃeklɪst] *n* lista *f* de chequeo, catálogo *m*.
checkmate ['tʃek'meɪt] **1** *n* mate *m*, jaque *m* mate; (*fig*) callejón *m* sin salida, situación *f* irresoluble. **2** *vt* dar mate a; **to be ~d** (*fig*) estar en un callejón sin salida.
check-out ['tʃekaʊt] **1** *n* (*Comm*) caja *f*. **2** *attr*: ~ **counter** caja *f* (de supermercado); ~ **girl** cajera *f* (de supermercado); ~ **time** hora *f* de salida (de un hotel).
checkpoint ['tʃekpɔɪnt] *n* (punto *m* de) control *m*.
checkroom ['tʃekrʊm] (*US*) *n* guardarropa *m*; (*Rail*) consigna *f*; (*euph*) lavabo *m*.
check-up ['tʃekʌp] *n* comprobación *f*, verificación *f*; examen *m*; (*Med*) chequeo *m*, reconocimiento *m* general.
cheddar ['tʃedəʳ] *n queso parecido en textura y sabor al manchego.*
cheek [tʃiːk] **1** *n* (**a**) mejilla *f*, carrillo *m*; (*: *buttock*) nalga *f*; ~ **by jowl** codo a codo, codo con codo (*with* con); **they were dancing ~ to ~** bailaban muy apretados; **to turn the other ~** poner la otra mejilla.
(**b**) (*) descaro *m*, frescura* *f*, impertinencia *f*; **what a ~!, of all the ~!** ¡qué caradura!*, ¡qué frescura!*; **to have the ~ to** + *infin* tener el valor de + *infin*, descararse a + *infin*.
2 *vt* (*Brit**) decir cosas descaradas a, portarse como un fresco con*.
cheekbone ['tʃiːkbəʊn] *n* pómulo *m*.
cheekily* ['tʃiːkɪlɪ] *adv* descaradamente, con frescura*.
cheekiness* ['tʃiːkɪnɪs] *n* descaro *m*, frescura *f*, impertinencia *f*.
cheeky* ['tʃiːkɪ] *adj* descarado, fresco*, impertinente.
cheep [tʃiːp] **1** *n* pío *m*; **we couldn't get a ~ out of him** no dijo ni pío. **2** *vi* piar.
cheer [tʃɪəʳ] **1** *n* (**a**) (*applause*) grito *m* de entusiasmo; **~s** aplausos *mpl*, aclamaciones *fpl*; vítores *mpl*, vivas *fpl*; **there were loud ~s at this** en esto hubo fuertes aplausos; **to give three ~s for** vitorear a, aclamar a; **three ~s for the general!** ¡viva el general!
(**b**) (*state of mind*) humor *m*; **what ~?** ¿qué tal?; **~s!** (*esp Brit**) (*thanks*) ¡gracias!; (*toast*) ¡salud y pesetas!; **be of good ~!** (*liter*) ¡ánimo!
2 *vt* (**a**) (*also* **to ~ up**) alegrar, animar; **I was much ~ed by the news** me alegró mucho la noticia.
(**b**) (*applaud*) aplaudir, aclamar, vitorear.
3 *vi* aplaudir, gritar con entusiasmo.
◆**cheer on** *vt* animar con aplausos.
◆**cheer up** **1** *vt* alegrar, animar. **2** *vi* cobrar ánimo, alegrarse; ~ **up!** ¡anímate!
cheerful ['tʃɪəfʊl] *adj* alegre; de buen humor.
cheerfully ['tʃɪəfʊlɪ] *adv* alegremente.
cheerfulness ['tʃɪəfʊlnɪs] *n* alegría *f*; buen humor *m*.
cheerily ['tʃɪərɪlɪ] *adv* alegremente, jovialmente; de modo acogedor.
cheering ['tʃɪərɪŋ] **1** *adj news etc* bueno, esperanzador. **2** *n* aplausos *mpl*, aclamaciones *fpl*, vítores *mpl*, vivas *fpl*.
cheerio ['tʃɪərɪ'əʊ] *interj* (*esp Brit*) ¡hasta luego!; (*toast*) ¡salud y pesetas!
cheer-leader ['tʃɪəˌliːdəʳ] *n* (*esp US*) animador *m*, -ora *f*; organizador *m*, -ora *f* de los aplausos.
cheerless ['tʃɪəlɪs] *adj* triste, sombrío.
cheery ['tʃɪərɪ] *adj* alegre, jovial; *room etc* acogedor.
cheese [tʃiːz] **1** *n* (**a**) queso *m*; **hard ~!‡** ¡mala pata! (**b**) (‡) **big ~, head ~** (*person*) pez *m* gordo, jefazo *m*, -a *f*, personaje *m*.
2 *vt* (**a**) (‡) dejar, poner fin a; ~ **it!** (*US*) ¡déjalo!; ¡ojo, que viene gente!; **let's ~ it** dejémoslo; vámonos.
(**b**) **to ~ sb off‡** fastidiar a uno*; **I'm ~d off** (*Brit‡*) estoy hasta las narices* (*with this* con esto).
cheeseboard ['tʃiːzbɔːd] *n* plato *m* de quesos.
cheeseburger ['tʃiːzˌbɜːgəʳ] *n* hamburguesa *f* con queso.
cheesecake ['tʃiːzkeɪk] *n* quesadilla *f*; (*) *fotos, dibujos etc de chicas atractivas en traje o actitud incitante.*
cheesecloth ['tʃiːzklɒθ] *n* estopilla *f*.
cheesedish ['tʃiːzdɪʃ] *n* quesera *f*.
cheeseparing ['tʃiːzˌpɛərɪŋ] **1** *adj* tacaño. **2** *n* economías *fpl* pequeñas.
cheesy ['tʃiːzɪ] *adj* (**a**) caseoso, como queso; que huele (*or* sabe) a queso. (**b**) (*US‡*) horrible, sin valor. (**c**) *grin* de hiena.
cheetah ['tʃiːtə] *n* leopardo *m* cazador.
chef [ʃef] *n* jefe *m* de cocina, (primer) cocinero *m*.
chef-d'œuvre [ʃɛdœvrə] *n*, *pl* **chefs-d'œuvre** [ʃɛdœvrə] obra *f* maestra.
Chekhov ['tʃekɒf] *nm* Chejov.
chemical ['kemɪkəl] **1** *adj* químico; ~ **agent** agente *m* químico; ~ **engineer** ingeniero *m* químico; ~ **warfare** guerra *f* química; ~ **weapon** arma *f* química. **2** *n* sustancia *f* química, producto *m* químico.
chemically ['kemɪkəlɪ] *adv* químicamente, por medios químicos.
chemise [ʃə'miːz] *n* camisa *f* de señora.
chemist ['kemɪst] *n* (*scientist*) químico *mf* (*also* -a *f*); (*Brit*: *pharmacist*) farmacéutico *m*, -a *f*; **~'s (shop)** (*Brit*) farmacia *f*; **all-night ~'s** farmacia *f* de guardia, farmacia *f* de turno.
chemistry ['kemɪstrɪ] *n* química *f*; ~ **laboratory** laboratorio *m* de química; ~ **set** juego *m* de química; **the ~ between them is right** (*fig*) tienen buena química.
chemotherapy ['keməʊ'θerəpɪ] *n* quimioterapia *f*.
cheque, (*US*) **check** [tʃek] *n* cheque *m*, talón *m* (bancario); **bad ~** cheque *m* sin fondos, cheque *m* sin provisión; **to make out a ~, to write a ~** extender un cheque (*for £100* de 100 libras, por 100 libras; *to Rodríguez* a favor de Rodríguez); **to pay by ~** pagar por (*or* con) cheque.
chequebook, (*US*) **checkbook** ['tʃekbʊk] *n* talonario *m* (de cheques), libreta *f* de cheques; ~ **journalism** periodismo *m* por talonario.
cheque-card ['tʃek,kɑːd] *n* (*Brit*) (*also* **cheque guarantee card**) tarjeta *f* de identidad bancaria.
chequered, (*US*) **checkered** ['tʃekəd] *adj cloth etc* a cuadros; ajedrezado; (*fig*) *career* accidentado, lleno de vicisitudes, lleno de altibajos; *collection* variado.
chequers, (*US*) **checkers** ['tʃekəz] *n* damas *fpl*.
cherish ['tʃerɪʃ] *vt* querer, apreciar; cuidar, proteger; mimar; *hope etc* abrigar, acariciar.
cherished ['tʃerɪʃt] *adj memory etc* precioso, entrañable; *privilege* apreciado.
cheroot [ʃə'ruːt] *n* puro *m* (cortado en los dos extremos).
cherry ['tʃerɪ] **1** *adj* (de) color rojo cereza. **2** *n* (*fruit*) cereza *f*; (*tree, wood*) cerezo *m*; (*colour*) rojo *m* cereza; ~ **brandy** aguardiente *m* de cerezas; ~ **laurel** laurel *m* cerezo.
cherry-red ['tʃerɪ'red] *adj* (de) color rojo cereza.
cherry-tree ['tʃerɪtriː] *n* cerezo *m*.
cherub ['tʃerəb] *n* (**a**) querubín *m*, angelito *m*. (**b**) (*Rel*) *pl* **cherubim** ['tʃerəbɪm] querubín *m*.
cherubic [tʃe'ruːbɪk] *adj* querúbico.
chervil ['tʃɜːvɪl] *n* perifollo *m*.
chess [tʃes] *n* ajedrez *m*; ~ **tournament** torneo *m* de ajedrez.
chessboard ['tʃesbɔːd] *n* tablero *m* de ajedrez.
chessman ['tʃesmæn] *n*, *pl* **chessmen** ['tʃesmen] pieza *f*, trebejo *m*, ficha *f*.
chessplayer ['tʃespleɪəʳ] *n* ajedrecista *mf*.
chess-set ['tʃes,set] *n* (juego *m* de) ajedrez *m*.
chest [tʃest] *n* (**a**) (*Anat*) pecho *m*; tórax *m*; ~ **trouble** enfermedad *f* del pecho; **to get sth off one's ~*** desahogarse, confesar algo de una vez; **to have a cold on the ~** tener el pecho resfriado.
(**b**) (*box*) cofre *m*, arca *f*, cajón *m*; ~ **of drawers** cómoda *f*.
chest cold ['tʃes*t*,kəʊld] *n* resfriado de pecho.
chesterfield ['tʃestəfiːld] *n* (*esp US*) sofá *m*.
chest expander ['tʃestɪk,spændəʳ] *n* tensor *m*, extensor *m*.
chest freezer ['tʃest'friːzəʳ] *n* congelador *m* de arcón.
chest infection ['tʃestɪn,fekʃən] *n* infección *f* bronquial.
chestnut ['tʃesnʌt] **1** *adj* (*also* ~ **brown**) castaño.
2 *n* (**a**) (*fruit*) castaña *f*; (*tree, wood*) castaño *m*.
(**b**) (*horse*) caballo *m* castaño.
(**c**) (*) (*joke*) chiste *m* viejo.
chestnut-tree ['tʃesnʌttriː] *n* castaño *m*.
chest pain ['tʃes*t*,peɪn] *n* dolor *m* de pecho.
chest specialist ['tʃes*t*,speʃəlɪst] *n* especialista *mf* de pecho.
chesty ['tʃestɪ] *adj* (*Brit*) *person* que tiene el pecho resfriado (*or* congestionado); (*permanently*) enfermizo del pecho; ~ **cough** tos *f* que afecta al pecho.
cheval glass [ʃə'vælglɑːs] *n* psique *f*.
chevron ['ʃevrən] *n* (*Mil*) galón *m*; (*Her*) cheurón *m*.
chew [tʃuː] *vt* mascar, masticar.
◆**chew on** *vt* (*fig*) *facts, problems* rumiar.
◆**chew out** *vt* (*US*) = **chew up (b)**.
◆**chew over** *vt*: **to ~ sth over** rumiar algo.

◆**chew up** *vt* (**a**) (*damage*) estropear. (**b**) (‡) *person* echar una bronca a.
chewing-gum ['tʃuːɪŋgʌm] *n* chicle *m*, goma *f* de mascar.
chewy ['tʃuːɪ] *adj* fibroso, correoso.
chiaroscuro [kɪ,ɑːrəs'kʊərəʊ] *n* claroscuro *m*.
chic [ʃiːk] **1** *adj* elegante. **2** *n* chic *m*, elegancia *f*.
chicanery [ʃɪ'keɪnərɪ] *n* embustes *mpl*, sofismas *mpl*; **a piece of ~** un sofisma, una superchería, una triquiñuela.
Chicano [tʃɪ'kɑːnəʊ] **1** *adj* chicano. **2** *n* chicano *m*, -a *f*.
chichi ['ʃiːʃiː] *adj* afectado, extravagante.
chick [tʃɪk] *n* pollito *m*, polluelo *m*; (*US**) chavala *f*.
chickadee ['tʃɪkədiː] *n* carbonero *m*.
chicken ['tʃɪkɪn] **1** *n* gallina *f*, pollo *m*; (*as food*) pollo *m*; **to be ~*** dejarse intimidar, acobardarse, cejar; **to play ~*** jugar a quién es más valiente; **she's no ~** ya no es tan pollita, ya no es tan pichona; **it's a ~ and egg situation** es aquello de la gallina y el huevo; **the ~s are coming home to roost** ahora se ven las consecuencias; **don't count your ~s before they're hatched** no hagas las cuentas de la lechera.
2 *vi*: **to ~ out*** amedrentarse, rajarse; dejarse intimidar; **to ~ out of** retirarse miedoso de, zafarse de.
chicken-farmer ['tʃɪkɪn,fɑːməʳ] *n* avicultor *m*, -ora *f*.
chicken-farming ['tʃɪkɪn,fɑːmɪŋ] *n* avicultura *f*.
chickenfeed ['tʃɪkɪnfiːd] *n* pienso *m* para gallinas; (*) minucias *fpl*, bagatelas *fpl*; **it's ~ to him** para él es una bagatela.
chicken-hearted ['tʃɪkɪn,hɑːtɪd] *adj* cobarde, gallina.
chicken liver ['tʃɪkɪn,lɪvəʳ] *n* hígado *m* de pollo.
chickenpox ['tʃɪkɪnpɒks] *n* varicela *f*.
chicken-run ['tʃɪkɪnrʌn] *n* corral *m*, gallinero *m*.
chicken-wire ['tʃɪkɪn,waɪəʳ] *n* tela *f* metálica, alambrada *f*.
chickpea ['tʃɪkpiː] *n* garbanzo *m*.
chickweed ['tʃɪkwiːd] *n* pamplina *f*.
chicory ['tʃɪkərɪ] *n* (*in coffee*) achicoria *f*; (*in salad*) escarola *f*.
chide [tʃaɪd] (*irr: pret* **chid**, *ptp* **chidden** *or* **chid**) *vt* (*liter*) reprender.
chief [tʃiːf] **1** *adj* principal, primero, mayor, capital; **~ constable** (*Brit*) jefe *m* de policía; **C~ Executive** (*Brit local government*) director *m*, -ora *f*; (*US Pol*) jefe *m* del Ejecutivo; primer mandatario *m*; **~ inspector** (*Brit Police*) inspector *m* jefe; **~ justice** (*US*) presidente *m*, inspectora *f* jefe del Tribunal Supremo; **~ superintendent** (*Brit Police*) comisario *m* jefe.
2 *n* jefe *m*; jerarca *m*; (*of tribe*) jefe *m*, cacique *m*; (*: *boss*) jefe *m*; **yes, ~!** ¡sí, patrón!; **~ of staff** jefe *m* del estado mayor; **~ of state** jefe *m* de estado; **... in ~** ... en jefe.
chiefly ['tʃiːflɪ] *adv* principalmente, sobre todo.
chieftain ['tʃiːftən] *n* jefe *m*, cacique *m*.
chiffchaff ['tʃɪftʃæf] *n* mosquitero *m* común.
chiffon ['ʃɪfɒn] *n* gasa *f*.
chignon ['ʃiːnjɔ̃ːŋ] *n* moño *m*.
chihuahua [tʃɪ'wɑːwɑː] *n* chihuahua *m*.
chilblain ['tʃɪlbleɪn] *n* sabañón *m*.
child [tʃaɪld] *n*, *pl* **children** ['tʃɪldrən] niño *m*, -a *f*; (*as offspring*) hijo *m*, -a *f*; **~ abuse** abuso *m* (sexual) de niños; **~ battering** maltrato *m* de los hijos; **~ benefit** *ayuda familiar por hijos;* **~ guidance** psicopedagogía *f*; **~ guidance centre** centro *m* psicopedagógico; **~ labour** trabajo *m* de menores; **~ lock** (*on door*) seguro *m* para niños; **~ prodigy** niño *m*, -a *f* prodigio; **~ welfare** asistencia *f* infantil, protección *f* a la infancia; **children's home** asilo *m* de niños; **children's literature** literatura *f* infantil; **to be with ~** estar encinta; **to get sb with ~** dejar a una encinta; **I have known him from a ~** le conozco desde niño.
childbearing ['tʃaɪld,beərɪŋ] **1** *attr*: **~ women** las mujeres fecundas, las mujeres que producen hijos; **women of ~ age** las mujeres de edad para tener hijos.
2 *n* (*act*) parto *m*; (*as statistic*) natalidad *f*.
childbed ['tʃaɪldbed] *n* parturición *f*.
childbirth ['tʃaɪldbɜːθ] *n* parto *m*; alumbramiento *m*; **to die in ~** morir de sobreparto.
childcare ['tʃaɪldkeəʳ] *n* cuidado *m* de los niños; **~ services** servicios *mpl* de asistencia al niño.
childhood ['tʃaɪldhʊd] *n* niñez *f*, infancia *f*; **to be in one's second ~** estar en su segunda infancia; **from ~** desde niño.
childish ['tʃaɪldɪʃ] *adj* (**a**) (*slightly pej*) pueril, aniñado; infantil, achiquillado (*Mex*); **don't be so ~!** ¡no seas niño! (**b**) *disease etc* infantil; **~ ailment** enfermedad *f* de la infancia.
childishly ['tʃaɪldɪʃlɪ] *adv* de modo pueril; **she behaved ~** se portó como una niña.
childishness ['tʃaɪldɪʃnɪs] *n* puerilidad *f*.
childless ['tʃaɪldlɪs] *adj* sin hijos.
childlike ['tʃaɪldlaɪk] *adj* como de niño, infantil.
child-minder ['tʃaɪld,maɪndəʳ] *n* (*Brit*) niñera *f*.
child-minding ['tʃaɪld,maɪndɪŋ] *n* cuidado *m* de niños.
child-proof ['tʃaɪld,pruːf] *adj* a prueba de niños; **~ (door) lock** cerradura *f* de seguridad para niños.
children ['tʃɪldrən] *npl of* **child**.
child-resistant ['tʃaɪld,rɪzɪstənt] *adj* = **child-proof**.
child's-play ['tʃaɪldzpleɪ] *n* (*fig*): **it's ~** es cosa de coser y cantar (*to* para).
Chile ['tʃɪlɪ] *n* Chile *m*.
Chilean ['tʃɪlɪən] **1** *adj* chileno. **2** *n* chileno *m*, -a *f*.
chili ['tʃɪlɪ] *n* (*Brit*) chile *m*, ají *m* (*SC*); **~ powder** polvos *mpl* de chile; **~ sauce** salsa *f* de ají.
chill [tʃɪl] **1** *adj* frío.
2 *n* (**a**) frío *m*; **a ~ of horror** un estremecimiento de horror; **to cast a ~ over** enfriar el ambiente de; verter un jarro de agua fría sobre; **to take the ~ off** *liquid, room* calentar un poco.
(**b**) (*Med*) escalofrío *m*; resfriado *m*; **to catch a ~** resfriarse.
3 *vt* enfriar; (*with fear etc*) helar; *meat etc* congelar; **to be ~ed to the bone** estar helado hasta los huesos.
◆**chill out*** *vi* (*esp US*) descansarse, relajarse; **~ out, man!** ¡tranqui tronco!*
chill(i)ness ['tʃɪl(ɪ)nɪs] *n* frío *m*; (*fig*) frialdad *f*.
chilling ['tʃɪlɪŋ] *adj* (*fig*) escalofriante.
chilly ['tʃɪlɪ] *adj* (**a**) frío; (*fig*) frío, glacial; **it is (very) ~** hace (mucho) frío; **I am feeling ~** tengo frío. (**b**) (*sensitive to cold*) friolento, friolero.
chime [tʃaɪm] **1** *n* (*set*) juego *m* de campanas, carillón *m*; (*peal*) repique *m*, campanada *f*; **~ clock** (*US*) reloj *m* de carillón.
2 *vt* repicar; **to ~ six** dar las seis.
3 *vi* repicar, sonar; **to ~ in** hablar inesperadamente, (*pej*) entrometerse; **to ~ in with** decir inesperadamente; (*harmonize*) estar en armonía con.
chimera [kaɪ'mɪərə] *n* quimera *f*.
chimerical [kaɪ'merɪkəl] *adj* quimérico.
chiming ['tʃaɪmɪŋ] **1** *adj*: **~ clock** reloj *m* de carillón. **2** *n* repiqueteo *m*, campanadas *fpl*.
chimney ['tʃɪmnɪ] *n* chimenea *f*; (*of lamp*) tubo *m* de lámpara; (*Mountaineering*) olla *f*, chimenea *f*.
chimney-breast ['tʃɪmnɪ,brest] *n* manto *m* de chimenea.
chimney-corner ['tʃɪmnɪ,kɔːnəʳ] *n* rincón *m* de la chimenea.
chimneypiece ['tʃɪmnɪ,piːs] *n* repisa *f* de chimenea.
chimneypot ['tʃɪmnɪpɒt] *n* (cañón *m* de) chimenea *f*.
chimney-stack ['tʃɪmnɪstæk] *n* fuste *m* de chimenea.
chimney-sweep ['tʃɪmnɪswiːp] *n* deshollinador *m*, limpiachimeneas *m*.
chimp* [tʃɪmp] *n* = **chimpanzee.**
chimpanzee [,tʃɪmpæn'ziː] *n* chimpancé *m*.
chin [tʃɪn] **1** *n* barba *f*, barbilla *f*, mentón *m*; **to keep one's ~ up** no desanimarse; **keep your ~ up!** ¡ánimo!; **to take it on the ~** (* *fig*) encajar el golpe. **2** *vt* (*) (*punch*) dar una hostia a*; (*reprimand*) echar un rapapolvo a*. **3** *vi* (*US**) charlar.
China ['tʃaɪnə] *n* China *f*; **~ Sea** Mar *m* de China; **~ tea** té *m* de China.
china[1] ['tʃaɪnə] *n* porcelana *f*, (*loosely*) loza *f*; **~ cabinet** vitrina *f* de la porcelana; **~ clay** coalín *m*, barro *m* de porcelana, arcilla *f* figulina.
china[2]‡ ['tʃaɪnə] *n* amigo *m*, compinche *m*; **here you are, my old ~** toma, macho*.
Chinaman ['tʃaɪnəmən] *n*, *pl* **Chinamen** ['tʃaɪnəmen] (*pej in US*) chino *m*.
Chinatown ['tʃaɪnətaʊn] *n* (*US*) barrio *m* chino.
chinaware ['tʃaɪnəweəʳ] *n* porcelana *f*.
chinch (bug) ['tʃɪntʃ(bʌg)] *n* (*US*) chinche *m or f* de los cereales.
chinchilla [tʃɪn'tʃɪlə] *n* chinchilla *f*.
chin-chin* [,tʃɪn'tʃɪn] *excl* ¡chin-chin!
Chinese ['tʃaɪ'niːz] **1** *adj* chino; **~ lantern** farolillo *m*; **~ leaves** (*US*) col *f* china; **~ puzzle** (*fig*) rompecabezas *m*. **2** *n* (**a**) chino *m*, -a *f*. (**b**) (*Ling*) chino *m*.
Chink* [tʃɪŋk] *n* (*‡ *in US*) chino *m*, -a *f*.
chink[1] [tʃɪŋk] *n* (*slit*) grieta *f*, hendedura *f*, resquicio *m*; **~ in one's armour** punto *m* débil, talón *m* de Aquiles.
chink[2] [tʃɪŋk] **1** *n* (*sound*) sonido *m* metálico, tintineo *m*. **2** *vt* hacer sonar. **3** *vi* sonar (a metal), tintinear.
chintz [tʃɪnts] *n* cretona *f*.
chintzy ['tʃɪntsɪ] *adj* (**a**) *style* de oropel. (**b**) (*US*‡: *mean*) garrapo‡.
chin-ups ['tʃɪnʌps] *npl*: **to do ~** hacer contracciones.

chinwag* ['tʃɪnwæg] *n* charla *f*; **to have a ~** charlar, echar un párrafo.

chip [tʃɪp] **1** *n* (**a**) (*splinter*) astilla *f*, pedacito *m*; (*of stone*) lasca *f*; **he's a ~ off the old block** de tal palo tal astilla; **to have a ~ on one's shoulder** ser un resentido.

(**b**) **~s** (*Culin*) (*Brit*) patatas *fpl* fritas, papas *fpl* (*LAm*) fritas (a la española); (*US*: *also* **potato ~**) patatas *fpl* fritas, papas *fpl* (*LAm*) fritas (a la inglesa).

(**c**) (*break, mark*) saltadura *f*; (*on rim of vessel*) desportilladura *f*.

(**d**) (*Cards*) ficha *f*; **to hand in one's ~s*** palmarla*; **he's had his ~s*** se acabó para él; **when the ~s are down** en la hora de la verdad.

(**e**) (*Comput*) chip *m*, micropastilla *f*, pastilla *f*, microplaquete *m*, circuito *m* integrado.

(**f**) (*Golf*) chip *m*.

2 *vt* (**a**) astillar, desportillar; *surface* picar; *sculpture* cincelar.

(**b**) (*) tomar el pelo a.

3 *vi* astillarse; (*surface*) picarse, desconcharse.

◆**chip away 1** *vt paint etc* desconchar. **2** *vi* (*paint etc*) caer a pedazos; **to ~ away at** *authority, lands* ir usurpando; *law, decision* reducir paulatinamente el alcance de.

◆**chip in*** *vi* (**a**) (*interrupt*) cortar, interrumpir (*with* diciendo). (**b**) (*contribute*) contribuir (*with* con).

◆**chip off** *vt* = **chip away**.

chip-based ['tʃɪp,beɪst] *adj*: **~ technology** tecnología *f* a base de micropastillas.

chipboard ['tʃɪpbɔːd] *n* cartón-madera *m*.

chipmunk ['tʃɪpmʌŋk] *n* ardilla *f* listada.

chipolata [,tʃɪpə'lɑːtə] *n* (*Brit*) salchicha *f* pequeña.

chipper* ['tʃɪpəʳ] *adj* (*US*) alegre, contento.

chippings ['tʃɪpɪŋz] *npl* gravilla *f*; **'loose ~'** 'gravilla suelta'.

chippy* ['tʃɪpɪ] *n* (**a**) (*US*) tía* *f*, fulana* *f*. (**b**) (*Brit*) pescadería *f*.

chip shop ['tʃɪpʃɒp] *n* pescadería *f*.

chiropodist [kɪ'rɒpədɪst] *n* (*Brit*) pedicuro *m*, -a *f*, podólogo *m*, -a *f*.

chiropody [kɪ'rɒpədɪ] *n* (*Brit*) pedicura *f*, podología *f*.

chiropractor ['kaɪrəʊ,præktəʳ] *n* quiropráctico *m*.

chirp [tʃɜːp] **1** *n* pío *m*, gorjeo *m*; (*of cricket*) chirrido *m*. **2** *vi* piar, gorjear; (*cricket*) chirriar.

chirpy* ['tʃɜːpɪ] *adj* alegre, animado.

chirrup ['tʃɪrəp] = **chirp**.

chisel ['tʃɪzl] **1** *n* (*for wood*) formón *m*, escoplo *m*; (*for stone*) cincel *m*. **2** *vt* (**a**) escoplear; cincelar. (**b**) (*) timar, estafar.

chiseller, (*US*) **chiseler** ['tʃɪzləʳ] *n* gorrón *m*.

chit[1] [tʃɪt] *n*: **a ~ of a girl** una muchachita no muy crecida.

chit[2] [tʃɪt] *n* nota *f*, esquela *f*; vale *m*.

chitchat ['tʃɪttʃæt] *n* chismes *mpl*, habladurías *fpl*.

chitterlings ['tʃɪtəlɪŋz] *npl* menudos *mpl* de cerdo (comestibles).

chitty ['tʃɪtɪ] *n* = **chit**[2].

chiv‡ [tʃɪv] *n* chori‡ *m*, navaja *f*.

chivalresque [ʃɪvəl'resk] *adj*, **chivalric** [ʃɪ'vælrɪk] *adj* caballeresco.

chivalrous ['ʃɪvəlrəs] *adj* caballeroso.

chivalrously ['ʃɪvəlrəslɪ] *adv* caballerosamente.

chivalry ['ʃɪvəlrɪ] *n* (*institution*) caballería *f*; (*spirit*) caballerosidad *f*.

chive [tʃaɪv] *n* cebollino *m*.

chivvy ['tʃɪvɪ] *vt* (*Brit**) perseguir, atormentar, acosar; **to ~ sb into doing sth** no dejar en paz a uno hasta que haga algo.

◆**chivvy up** *vt person* espabilar.

chloral ['klɔːrəl] *n* cloral *m*.

chlorate ['klɔːreɪt] *n* clorato *m*.

chloric ['klɔːrɪk] *adj* clórico; **~ acid** ácido *m* clórico.

chloride ['klɔːraɪd] *n* cloruro *m*; **~ of lime** cloruro *m* de cal.

chlorinate ['klɒrɪneɪt] *vt* clorinar, clorar, tratar con cloro.

chlorinated ['klɒrɪneɪtɪd] *adj*: **~ water** agua *f* clorinada.

chlorination [,klɔːrɪ'neɪʃən] *n* cloración *f*, tratamiento *m* con cloro.

chlorine ['klɔːriːn] *n* cloro *m*; **~ monoxide** monóxido *m* de cloro; **~ nitrate** nitrato *m* de cloro.

chlorofluorocarbon ['klɔːrəʊ'fluərəʊ'kɑːbən] *n* clorofluorocarbono *m*.

chloroform ['klɒrəfɔːm] **1** *n* cloroformo *m*. **2** *vt* cloroformizar, cloroformar (*LAm*).

chlorophyl(l) ['klɒrəfɪl] *n* clorofila *f*.

choc* [tʃɒk] *n* = **chocolate**.

choc-ice ['tʃɒkaɪs] *n* helado *m* de chocolate.

chock [tʃɒk] **1** *n* calzo *m*, cuña *f*. **2** *vt* calzar, acuñar, poner calzos a.

chock-a-block ['tʃɒkə'blɒk] *adj*, **chock-full** ['tʃɒk'fʊl] *adj* de bote en bote; **~ of, ~ with** atestado de, totalmente lleno de.

chocker‡ ['tʃɒkəʳ] *adj*: **to be ~** estar harto (*with* de).

chocolate ['tʃɒklɪt] *n* **1** (*in bar, for drinking*) chocolate *m*; **a ~** una chocolatina, un bombón; **a box of ~s** una caja de bombones (*or* chocolatinas).

2 *attr* de chocolate; **~ biscuit** galleta *f* de chocolate; **~ éclair** relámpago *m* de chocolate.

3 *adj* color (de) chocolate.

chocolate-box ['tʃɒklɪt,bɒks] *adj look, picture* de postal de Navidad.

choice [tʃɔɪs] **1** *adj* selecto, escogido; *quality, wine etc* fino.

2 *n* (*act of choosing*) elección *f*, selección *f*; (*thing chosen*) preferencia *f*; (*between 2 or more possibilities*) opción *f*, alternativa *f*; (*range to choose from*) surtido *m*, serie *f* de posibilidades; **for ~** preferentemente; **he did it but not from ~** lo hizo pero de mala gana; **the house of my ~** mi casa predilecta; **the prince married the girl of his ~** el príncipe se casó con la joven que había elegido; **it's your ~, the ~ is yours** Vd elige; **it was not a free ~** no estuvo libre para elegir a su gusto; **we have a wide ~** (*Comm*) tenemos un gran surtido; **you have a wide ~** tienes muchas posibilidades; **to have no ~** no tener alternativa, no tener opción; **he had no ~ but to go** no tuvo más remedio que ir; **to take one's ~** elegir; **take your ~!** ¡lo que quieras!

choir ['kwaɪəʳ] *n* (**a**) coro *m*; coros *mpl*; orfeón *m*; coral *f*. (**b**) (*Archit*) coro *m*.

choirboy ['kwaɪəbɔɪ] *n* niño *m* de coro.

choirmaster ['kwaɪə,mɑːstəʳ] *n* director *m* de coro, maestro *m* de coros.

choir-practice ['kwaɪə,præktɪs] *n* ensayo *m* de coro.

choirschool ['kwaɪə,skuːl] *n escuela primaria para niños cantores*.

choir-stall ['kwaɪəstɔːl] *n* silla *f* de coro.

choke [tʃəʊk] **1** *n* (*Mech*) obturador *m*, cierre *m*; (*Aut*) estárter *m*, ahogador *m* (*Mex*), chok(e) *m* (*LAm*).

2 *vt pipe etc* atascar, tapar, obstruir; *person* (*to death*) estrangular, ahogar, sofocar; **a ~d cry** un grito ahogado; **in a voice ~d with emotion** en una voz embargada (*or* empañada) por la emoción; **a street ~d with traffic** una calle atestada de tráfico; **a canal ~d with weeds** un canal atascado de hierbas.

3 *vi* (*also* **to ~ to death**) sofocarse; (*over food*) atragantarse; no poder respirar; **to ~ on a bone** atragantarse con un hueso; **to ~ with laughter** desternillarse de risa.

◆**choke back** *vt* contener, ahogar.

◆**choke down** *vt rage, sobs* ahogar.

◆**choke off** *vt supply, suggestions etc* cortar; *discussion* cortar por lo sano; *person* cortar; **to ~ sb off*** echar un rapapolvo a uno*; hacer callar a uno; desanimar a uno, disuadir a uno.

◆**choke up 1** *vt pipe, drain* obstruir. **2** *vi* (**a**) (*pipe, drain*) atascarse. (**b**) (*person*) quedarse sin habla.

choked* ['tʃəʊkt] *adj* cortado.

choker ['tʃəʊkəʳ] *n* (**a**) (*Mech*) obturador *m*. (**b**) (*necklace*) gargantilla *f*; (*hum*) cuello *m* alto.

choking ['tʃəʊkɪŋ] **1** *adj* asfixiador, asfixiante. **2** *n* ahogo *m*, asfixia *f*.

choky‡ ['tʃəʊkɪ] *n* (*prison*) trena‡ *f*; (*cell*) unidad *f* de aislamiento.

cholera ['kɒlərə] *n* cólera *m*.

choleric ['kɒlərɪk] *adj* colérico.

cholesterol [kə'lestərɒl] *n* colesterol *m*.

chomp* [tʃɒmp] *vti* mascar.

choose [tʃuːz] (*irr: pret* **chose**, *ptp* **chosen**) **1** *vt* (**a**) elegir, escoger; *candidate* elegir; *team etc* seleccionar; **he was chosen leader** fue elegido caudillo.

(**b**) **to ~ to** + *infin* optar por + *infin*; **if I don't ~ to** si no quiero; **I'll do it when I ~ (to)** lo haré cuando me dé la gana; **he cannot ~ but (to) go** no tiene más remedio que ir; **you cannot ~ but admire it** no puedes menos de admirarlo; **there is nothing to ~ between them** no les veo diferencia alguna.

2 *vi*: **to ~ between** elegir entre; **there are 5 kinds to ~ from** a elegir entre 5 tipos, hay 5 clases de las que se puede elegir.

choos(e)y* ['tʃuːzɪ] *adj* melindroso, delicado; **he's a bit ~ about it** en esto es algo difícil de contentar; **I'm ~ about whom I go out with** yo no salgo con un cualquiera; **in his**

position he can't be ~ en su posición no le permite darse el lujo de escoger.

chop¹ [tʃɒp] **1** *n* (**a**) (*Culin*) chuleta *f*. (**b**) (*blow*) golpe *m* cortante; **he's for the ~*** le van a despedir; **this programme is for the ~*** este programa se va a suprimir; **to get the ~*** ser despedido; **to give sb the ~*** despedir a uno. **2** *vt* (**a**) (*cut*) cortar, tajar; **to ~ one's way through** abrirse camino a tajadas. (**b**) *person* despedir. (**c**) *ball* cortar.

◆**chop at** *vt* tratar de tajar.

◆**chop down** *vt* talar.

◆**chop off** *vt* tronchar, separar; (*fig*) recortar, reducir.

◆**chop up** *vt* desmenuzar; *meat* picar.

chop² [tʃɒp] *vi*: **to ~ and change** (*person*) cambiar constantemente de opinión (*etc*).

chopper ['tʃɒpəʳ] *n* (**a**) (*for cutting*) hacha *f*; (*butcher's*) tajadera *f*, cuchilla *f*. (**b**) (*Aer**) helicóptero *m*. (**c**) (*US**: *motorbike*), (*Brit*: *cycle*) chópper *f*.

chopping-block ['tʃɒpɪŋblɒk] *n*, **chopping board** ['tʃɒpɪŋ,bɔːd] *n* tajadera *f*, tajo *m*.

chopping-knife ['tʃɒpɪŋ,naɪf] *n*, *pl* **chopping-knives** ['tʃɒpɪŋ,naɪvz] tajadera *f*.

choppy ['tʃɒpɪ] *adj sea* picado, agitado.

chops [tʃɒps] *npl* (*Anat*) boca *f*, labios *mpl*; **to lick one's ~** relamerse, chuparse los dedos.

chopsticks ['tʃɒpstɪks] *npl* palillos *mpl* (de los chinos).

chop suey [,tʃɒp'suɪ] *n* chop suey *m*.

choral ['kɔːrəl] *adj* coral; **~ society** orfeón *m*.

chorale [kɔ'rɑːl] *n* coral *m*.

chord [kɔːd] *n* (*string, Anat, Math*) cuerda *f*; (*group of notes, sound*) acorde *m*; **we must strike a common ~** tenemos que encontrar un punto común; **this struck a responsive ~ with everyone** esto produjo una reacción positiva de todos; **to strike the right ~** acertar el tono.

chore [tʃɔːʳ] *n* faena *f*, tarea *f*, tarea *f* necesaria pero falta de interés, trabajo *m* rutinario; **~s** (*at home*) quehaceres *mpl* domésticos.

choreograph ['kɒrɪə,græf] *vt* coreografiar.

choreographer [,kɒrɪ'ɒgrəfəʳ] *n* coreógrafo *m*, -a *f*.

choreographic [,kɒrɪəʊ'græfɪk] *adj* coreográfico.

choreography [,kɒrɪ'ɒgrəfɪ] *n* coreografía *f*.

chorister ['kɒrɪstəʳ] *n* corista *mf*; (*US*) director *m*, -a *f* de un coro.

chortle ['tʃɔːtl] **1** *n* risa *f* alegre. **2** *vi* reírse alegremente; (*pej*) reírse satisfecho (*over* por).

chorus ['kɔːrəs] **1** *n* (*Mus*) coro *m*; (*of chorus girls*) conjunto *m*; (*repeated words*) estribillo *m*; **~ line** línea *f* de coro; **a ~ of praise greeted the book** el libro recibió la aprobación de todos, el libro se mereció las alabanzas de todos; **a ~ of shouts greeted this** todos gritaron a la vez al oír esto; **in ~** en coro; **to sing in ~** cantar en coro; **to join in the ~** cantar el estribillo.

2 *vt* cantar (*etc*) en coro; (*answer*) contestar todos con una voz.

chorus-girl ['kɔːrəsgɜːl] *n* corista *f*, conjuntista *f*, chica *f* de conjunto.

chose [tʃəʊz] *pret of* **choose.**

chosen ['tʃəʊzn] **1** *ptp of* **choose. 2** *adj* preferido, predilecto; **the ~ people** el pueblo escogido; **one of the ~** uno de los elegidos; **their ~ representative** su representante elegido.

chough [tʃʌf] *n* chova *f* (piquirroja).

chow¹ [tʃaʊ] *n* (*dog*) chow-chow *m*, perro *m* chino.

chow²⁑ [tʃaʊ] *n* comida *f*.

chowder ['tʃaʊdəʳ] *n* (*US*) estofado *m* con almejas y pescado; (*soup*) sopa *f* de pescado.

Chris [krɪs] *nm familiar form of* **Christopher.**

Christ [kraɪst] *nm* Cristo; **~!** ¡Dios mío!

christen ['krɪsn] *vt* bautizar (*also fig*).

Christendom ['krɪsndəm] *n* cristiandad *f*.

christening ['krɪsnɪŋ] *n* bautizo *m*, bautismo *m*; **~ gown, ~ robe** faldón *m* bautismal.

Christian ['krɪstɪən] **1** *adj* cristiano; *name* de pila, de bautismo. **2** *n* cristiano *m*, -a *f*.

Christianity [,krɪstɪ'ænɪtɪ] *n* cristianismo *m*.

Christianize ['krɪstɪənaɪz] *vt* cristianizar.

Christlike ['kraɪstlaɪk] *adj* como Cristo.

Christmas ['krɪsməs] **1** *n* Navidad *f*; (*ie ~ period*) Navidades *fpl*; **at ~** por Navidades; **merry ~!** ¡felices Pascuas!

2 *attr* navideño, de Navidad; **~ box** (*Brit*) aguinaldo *m*; **~ cake** tarta *f* de Reyes; **~ card** crisma *m*, tarjeta *f* de Navidad; **~ carol** villancico *m*; **~ club** club *m* de ahorros (que los reparte por Navidades); **~ Day** día *m* de Navidad; **~ Eve** Nochebuena *f*; **~ Island** Isla *f* Christmas; **~ party** fiesta *f* de Navidad; **~ present** regalo *m* de Navidad; **~ pudding** pudín *m* de Navidad; **~ rose** eléboro *m* negro; **~ stocking** ≈ zapatos *mpl* de Reyes; **~ time** Navidades *fpl*, Pascua *f* de Navidad; **~ tree** árbol *m* de Navidad.

Christopher ['krɪstəfəʳ] *nm* Cristóbal.

chromatic [krə'mætɪk] *adj* cromático.

chromatogram [krəʊ'mætə,græm] *n* cromatograma *m*.

chromatography [,krəʊmə'tɒgrəfɪ] *n* cromatografía *f*.

chrome [krəʊm] *n* cromo *m*; **~ steel** acero *m* al cromo, acerocromo *m*; **~ yellow** amarillo *m* de cromo.

chromium ['krəʊmɪəm] *n* cromo *m*.

chromium-plated ['krəʊmɪəm,pleɪtɪd] *adj* cromado.

chromium-plating ['krəʊmɪəm,pleɪtɪŋ] *n* cromado *m*.

chromosomal [,krəʊmə'səʊməl] *adj* cromosomático, cromosómico.

chromosome ['krəʊməsəʊm] *n* cromosoma *m*.

chronic ['krɒnɪk] *adj* (**a**) crónico; (*fig*) constante, permanente. (**b**) (*) horrible, malísimo; insufrible; **I had toothache sth ~** me dolían las muelas horriblemente.

chronically ['krɒnɪkəlɪ] *adv*: **to be ~ sick** sufrir una enfermedad crónica; **beer is ~ scarce** hay una escasez permanente de cerveza.

chronicle ['krɒnɪkl] **1** *n* crónica *f*; **C~s** (*Bib*) Crónicas *fpl*. **2** *vt* historiar; registrar, describir.

chronicler ['krɒnɪkləʳ] *n* cronista *mf*.

chronological [,krɒnə'lɒdʒɪkəl] *adj* cronológico.

chronologically [,krɒnə'lɒdʒɪkəlɪ] *adv* por orden cronológico.

chronology [krə'nɒlədʒɪ] *n* cronología *f*.

chronometer [krə'nɒmɪtəʳ] *n* cronómetro *m*.

chrysalis ['krɪsəlɪs] *n* crisálida *f*.

chrysanthemum [krɪ'sænθəməm] *n* crisantemo *m*.

chub [tʃʌb] *n* cacho *m*.

chubby ['tʃʌbɪ] *adj* rechoncho, gordinflón, regordete; *face* mofletudo.

chuck¹ [tʃʌk] **1** *n* (**a**) (*throw*) tiro *m*, echada *f*. (**b**) **~ under the chin** mamola *f*. (**c**) (⁑) **to get the ~** ser despedido. **2** *vt* (**a**) (*throw*) lanzar, arrojar; (*pass, hand*) echar. (**b**) (*give up*) abandonar; **~ it!** ¡basta ya!, ¡déjalo!; **I'm thinking of ~ing it (in)** estoy pensando en dejarlo todo; **so I had to ~ it** así que tuve que abandonarlo. (**c**) **to ~ sb under the chin** dar la mamola a uno.

◆**chuck away** *vt old clothes, books* tirar, botar (*LAm*); *money* despilfarrar; *chance* desperdiciar.

◆**chuck in*** *vt* = **chuck up 1.**

◆**chuck out** *vt rubbish* tirar, botar (*LAm*); *person* poner de patitas en la calle; *person from work etc* despedir, dar el pasaporte a*.

◆**chuck up 1** *vt* (*) abandonar, renunciar a. **2** *vi* (*US⁑*: *vomit*) arrojar*.

chuck² [tʃʌk] = **chock.**

chuck³ [tʃʌk] *n* (**a**) (*also* **~ steak**) bistec *m* de pobre. (**b**) (*US⁑*) manduca⁑ *f*; **~ wagon** carromato *m* de provisiones.

chucker-out* ['tʃʌkər'aʊt] *n* (*Brit*) forzudo *m* (*que echa a los alborotadores de un café etc*).

chuckle ['tʃʌkl] **1** *n* risita *f*, risa *f* sofocada; **we had a good ~ over that** nos reímos bastante con eso. **2** *vi* reírse entre dientes, soltar una risita; **to ~ at, to ~ over** reírse con.

chuddar ['tʃʌdəʳ] *n* chador *m*.

chuffed [tʃʌft] *adj* (*Brit**) contento, alegre; **he was pretty ~ about it** estaba la mar de contento por eso.

chug [tʃʌg] *vi* hacer ruidos explosivos repetidos; (*Rail*) resoplar; **the train ~ged past** pasó el tren resoplando.

◆**chug along** *vi* (*car, train*) avanzar haciendo chuf-chuf.

chum* [tʃʌm] **1** *n* compinche *m*, compañero *m*, cuate *m* (*Mex*); (*child*) amiguito *m*, -a *f*; (*in direct address*) amigo; **to be great ~s** ser íntimos amigos; **to be ~s with sb** ser amigo de uno.

2 *vi*: **to ~ up** hacerse amigos; **to ~ up with sb** hacerse amigo de uno.

chummy* ['tʃʌmɪ] *adj* familiar, muy afable; **they're very ~** son muy amigos; **he's very ~ with the boss** es muy amigo del jefe; **he got ~ with the boss** se hizo amigo del jefe.

chump* [tʃʌmp] *n* (**a**) (*head*) cabeza *f*; **to be off one's ~** estar chiflado. (**b**) (*idiot*) imbécil *m*, melón *m*; **you ~!** ¡imbécil!

chunk [tʃʌŋk] *n* (*of bread, cheese etc*) pedazo *m*, trozo *m*; pedazo *m* grueso; cantidad *f* considerable.

chunky* ['tʃʌŋkɪ] *adj person* fornido; *object* sólido, macizo.

Chunnel ['tʃʌnl] *n* (*hum*) túnel *m* bajo el Canal de la Mancha.

chunter* ['tʃʌntəʳ] *vi* murmurar; (*complain*) quejarse; **to ~ on about** seguir quejándose de.

church [tʃɜːtʃ] *n* iglesia *f*; (*esp non-Catholic*) templo *m*; **C~**

of England Iglesia *f* Anglicana; **C~ and State** Iglesia *f* y Estado; **~ fathers** Padres *mpl* de la Iglesia; **~ hall** sacristía *f*; **~ service** oficio *m*, culto *m*, servicio *m*; **to go to ~** (*Protestant*) ir al oficio, asistir al culto, (*Catholic*) ir a misa; **to go into the ~** hacerse cura (*or* pastor *etc*).
churchgoer ['tʃɜːtʃ,gəʊəʳ] *n* fiel *mf* (que practica una religión).
churchman ['tʃɜːtʃmən] *n*, *pl* **churchmen** ['tʃɜːtʃmən] (**a**) (*priest*) sacerdote *m*, eclesiástico *m*. (**b**) (*member*) fiel *m* practicante.
churchwarden ['tʃɜːtʃ'wɔːdn] *n* capillero *m*.
churchwoman ['tʃɜːtʃ,wʊmən] *n*, *pl* **churchwomen** ['tʃɜːtʃ,wɪmɪn] fiel *f* practicante.
churchy* ['tʃɜːtʃɪ] *adj* beato; que va mucho a la iglesia, que toma muy en serio las cosas de la iglesia.
churchyard ['tʃɜːtʃjɑːd] *n* cementerio *m*, camposanto *m*.
churl [tʃɜːl] *n* (*fig*) patán *m*.
churlish ['tʃɜːlɪʃ] *adj person* poco afable, grosero, hosco; *remark* nada amistoso; **it would be ~ not to thank him** sería muy maleducado no darle las gracias.
churlishly ['tʃɜːlɪʃlɪ] *adv* groseramente, sin educación.
churlishness ['tʃɜːlɪʃnɪs] *n* grosería *f*, hosquedad *f*; conducta *f* (*etc*) poco amistosa; mala educación *f*.
churn [tʃɜːn] **1** *n* (*for milk*) lechera *f*; cántara *f* de leche; (*for butter*) mantequera *f*.
2 *vt butter* batir (*or* hacer) en una mantequera; (*fig*: *also* **to ~ up**) revolver, agitar, remover.
3 *vi* revolverse, agitarse; **my stomach ~ed** se me revolvió el estómago.
◆**churn out** *vt* producir en serie, producir en masa.
chute [ʃuːt] *n* (**a**) (*Tech*) tolva *f*, vertedor *m*, rampa *f* de caída; (*Brit*: *in playground, swimming-pool*) tobogán *m*. (**b**) (*: *Aer*) paracaídas *m*.
chutney ['tʃʌtnɪ] *n* chutney *m* (*condimento a base de frutas de la India*).
chutzpa(h)* ['xʊtspə] *n* (*US*) cara *f* dura.
CI *abbr of* **Channel Islands** Islas *fpl* del Canal (de la Mancha).
C.I. *n abbr of* **Consular Invoice** factura *f* consular.
CIA *n* (*US*) *abbr of* **Central Intelligence Agency.**
ciao* [tʃaʊ] *interj* ¡chao!
cicada [sɪ'kɑːdə] *n* cigarra *f*.
Cicero ['sɪsərəʊ] *nm* Cicerón.
Ciceronian [,sɪsə'rəʊnɪən] *adj* ciceroniano.
CID *n* (*Brit*) *abbr of* **Criminal Investigation Department**; **~ man, ~ officer** policía *m* (*or* oficial *m*) del Departamento de Investigación Criminal.
cider ['saɪdəʳ] *n* sidra *f*; **~ apple** manzana *f* de sidra; **~ vinegar** vinagre *m* de sidra.
cider-press ['saɪdəpres] *n* lagar *m* para hacer sidra.
CIF, c.i.f. *n abbr of* **cost, insurance and freight** coste, seguro y flete, c.s.f.
cig* [sɪg] *n* = **cigarette.**
cigar [sɪ'gɑːʳ] *n* puro *m*, cigarro *m*.
cigar-case [sɪ'gɑːkeɪs] *n* cigarrera *f*.
cigarette [,sɪgə'ret] *n* cigarrillo *m*, pitillo *m*, cigarro *m*.
cigarette-ash [sɪgə'ret,æʃ] *n* ceniza *f* de cigarrillo.
cigarette-card [,sɪgə'retkɑːd] *n* cromo *m* (coleccionable).
cigarette-case [,sɪgə'ret,keɪs] *n* pitillera *f*, petaca *f*.
cigarette-end [,sɪgə'ret,end] *n* colilla *f* (de cigarrillo).
cigarette-holder [,sɪgə'ret,həʊldəʳ] *n* boquilla *f*.
cigarette-lighter [,sɪgə'ret,laɪtəʳ] *n* mechero *m*, encendedor *m*.
cigarette-paper [,sɪgə'ret,peɪpəʳ] *n* papel *m* de fumar.
cigar-holder [sɪ'gɑː,həʊldəʳ] *n* boquilla *f* de puro.
cigar-lighter [sɪ'gɑː,laɪtəʳ] *n* (*Aut*) encendedor *m* de puro.
cigar-shaped [sɪ'gɑːʃeɪpt] *adj* en forma de puro.
ciggy* ['sɪgɪ] *n* = **cigarette.**
C.-in-C. *n abbr of* **Commander-in-Chief.**
cinch‡ [sɪntʃ] *n*: **it's a ~** es facilísimo, está chupado‡, es un chollo‡.
cinchona [sɪŋ'kəʊnə] *n* quino *m*; **~ bark** quina *f*.
cinder ['sɪndəʳ] *n* carbonilla *f*; **~s** cenizas *fpl*; **to be burned to a ~** quedar carbonizado.
cinder block ['sɪndəblɒk] *n* (*US*) ladrillo *m* de cenizas.
Cinderella [,sɪndə'relə] *nf* la Cenicienta; **it's the ~ of the arts** es la hermana pobre de las artes.
cinder track ['sɪndətræk] *n* pista *f* de ceniza.
cine-camera ['sɪnɪ'kæmərə] *n* (*Brit*) cámara *f* cinematográfica.
cine-film ['sɪnɪ,fɪlm] *n* (*Brit*) película *f* de cine.
cinema ['sɪnəmə] *n* cine *m*; **~ complex** cine *m* multisalas.
cinema-going ['sɪnəmə,gəʊɪŋ] **1** *n*: **~ is very popular among the young** el ir al cine es muy popular entre los jóvenes. **2** *adj*: **the ~ public** el público aficionado al cine.
Cinemascope ['sɪnəməskəʊp] ® *n* Cinemascope ® *m*.
cinematic [,sɪnɪ'mætɪk] *adj* cinemático.
cinematograph [,sɪnɪ'mætəgrɑːf] *n* (*Brit*) cinematógrafo *m*.
cinematographer [,sɪnəmə'tɒgrəfəʳ] *n* (*US*) cinematógrafo *m*, -a *f*.
cinematography [,sɪnəmə'tɒgrəfɪ] *n* cinematografía *f*.
cine-projector [,sɪnɪprə'dʒektəʳ] *n* (*Brit*) proyector *m* de películas.
cinerary ['sɪnərərɪ] *adj* cinerario.
cinnabar ['sɪnəbɑːʳ] *n* cinabrio *m*.
cinnamon ['sɪnəmən] *n* canela *f*.
cipher ['saɪfəʳ] **1** *n* (**a**) (*o, zero*) cero *m*; (*any number, initials*) cifra *f*; (*Arabic numeral*) cifra *f*, número *m*; **he's a mere ~** (*fig*) es un cero a la izquierda. (**b**) (*secret writing*) cifra *f*, código *m*; **in ~** cifrado, en cifra, en clave. (**c**) (*monogram*) monograma *m*. **2** *vt code, calculations, communications* cifrar; (*Math*) calcular.
circa ['sɜːkə] *prep* hacia; **~ 1500** hacia (el año) 1500.
circadian [sə'keɪdɪən] *adj* circadiano; **~ cycle** ciclo *m* circadiano.
circle ['sɜːkl] **1** *n* (**a**) círculo *m*; (*Brit Theat*) anfiteatro *m*; (*set of people*) círculo *m*, grupo *m*; **an inner ~ of ministers** un grupo interior de ministros; **John and his ~** Juan y sus amigos, Juan y su peña; **the wheel has come full ~** la rueda ha dado una vuelta completa; **we're going round in ~s** (*fig*) estamos en un círculo vicioso.
(**b**) **~s** (*fig*): **in certain ~s** en ciertos medios; **in business ~s** en círculos comerciales; **to move in fashionable ~s** frecuentar la buena sociedad; **to go round in small ~s** perderse en detalles nimios; **it had us running round in ~s** nos hizo dar vueltas sin orden ni concierto.
2 *vt* (*be round*) cercar, rodear; (*move round*) girar alrededor de, dar la vuelta a; *part of body* ceñir, rodear; **the lion ~d its prey** el león se movió alrededor de la presa; **the cosmonaut ~d the earth** el cosmonauta dio la vuelta al mundo; **the aircraft ~d the town twice** el avión dio dos vueltas sobre la ciudad.
3 *vi* dar vueltas.
circlet ['sɜːklɪt] *n* anillo *m*; adorno *m* en forma de círculo.
circuit ['sɜːkɪt] **1** *n* (*Elec etc*) circuito *m*; (*tour*) gira *f*; (*track*) pista *f*; (*lap by runner*) vuelta *f*; (*Brit Jur, approx*) distrito *m*. **2** *attr*: **~ board** tarjeta *f* de circuitos; **~ court** (*US*) tribunal *m* superior; **~ switching network** red *f* de conmutación de circuito.
circuit-breaker ['sɜːkɪt,breɪkəʳ] *n* cortacircuitos *m*.
circuitous [sɜː'kjʊɪtəs] *adj* tortuoso, indirecto.
circuitry ['sɜːkɪtrɪ] *n* circuitería *f*, sistema *m* de circuitos.
circular ['sɜːkjʊləʳ] **1** *adj* circular; **~ saw** sierra *f* circular; **~ tour** viaje *m* redondo. **2** *n* circular *f*.
circularity [,sɜːkjʊ'lærɪtɪ] *n* circularidad *f*.
circularize ['sɜːkjʊləraɪz] *vt* enviar circulares a.
circulate ['sɜːkjʊleɪt] **1** *vt* poner en circulación; *letter, papers etc* hacer circular; *news* anunciar por circular. **2** *vi* circular.
circulating ['sɜːkjʊleɪtɪŋ] *adj* circulante; **~ assets** activo *m* circulante; **~ capital** capital *m* circulante; **~ library** (*US*) biblioteca *f* circulante; **~ medium** medios *mpl* monetarios.
circulation [,sɜːkjʊ'leɪʃən] *n* circulación *f*; (*number of papers printed*) tirada *f*; **~ of the blood** circulación *f* de la sangre; **he's in ~ again, he's back in ~** ha vuelto a circular; **to put into ~** poner en circulación.
circulatory [,sɜːkjʊ'leɪtərɪ] *adj* circulatorio.
circum... *pref* circun..., circum...
circumcise ['sɜːkəmsaɪz] *vt* circuncidar.
circumcision [,sɜːkəm'sɪʒən] *n* circuncisión *f*.
circumference [sə'kʌmfərəns] *n* circunferencia *f*.
circumflex ['sɜːkəmfleks] *n* circunflejo *m*; **~ accent** acento *m* circunflejo.
circumlocution [,sɜːkəmlə'kjuːʃən] *n* circunloquio *m*, rodeo *m*.
circumnavigate [,sɜːkəm'nævɪgeit] *vt* circunnavegar.
circumnavigation ['sɜːkəm,nævɪ'geiʃən] *n* circunnavegación *f*.
circumscribe ['sɜːkəmskraɪb] *vt* circunscribir; limitar, restringir.
circumspect ['sɜːkəmspekt] *adj* circunspecto, prudente.
circumspection [,sɜːkəm'spekʃən] *n* circunspección *f*, prudencia *f*.
circumspectly ['sɜːkəmspektlɪ] *adv* prudentemente.
circumstance ['sɜːkəmstəns] *n* (**a**) circunstancia *f*; **in** (*or* **under**) **the ~s** en las circunstancias; **in no ~s, under no ~s** de ninguna manera, bajo ningún concepto; **owing to ~s beyond our control** debido a circunstancias ajenas a nues-

tra voluntad; **~s alter cases** las circunstancias cambian los casos; **were it not for the ~ that** ... si no fuera por la circunstancia de que ...; *V* **pomp**.

(**b**) (*economic situation*) **to be in easy ~s** estar acomodado; **to be in narrow** (*or* **reduced**) **~s** estar estrecho; **what are your ~s?** ¿cuál es su situación económica?; **if the family ~s allow it** si lo permite la situación económica de la familia.

circumstantial [ˌsɜːkəm'stænʃəl] *adj report* detallado, circunstanciado; **~ evidence** prueba *f* indiciaria.

circumstantiate [ˌsɜːkəm'stænʃɪeɪt] *vt* probar refiriendo más detalles, corroborar, confirmar.

circumvent [ˌsɜːkəm'vent] *vt* burlar; *difficulty, obstacle* salvar, evitar.

circumvention [ˌsɜːkəm'venʃən] *n* acción *f* de burlar (*or* salvar); **the ~ of this obstacle will not be easy** no va a ser fácil salvar este obstáculo.

circus ['sɜːkəs] *n* circo *m*; (*in town*) plaza *f* redonda, glorieta *f*.

cirrhosis [sɪ'rəʊsɪs] *n* cirrosis *f*.

cirrocumulus [ˌsɪrəʊ'kjuːmjʊləs] *n, pl* **cirrocumuli** [ˌsɪrəʊ'kjuːmjʊlaɪ] cirrocúmulo *m*.

cirrostratus [ˌsɪrəʊ'strɑːtəs] *n, pl* **cirrostrati** [ˌsɪrəʊ'strɑːtaɪ] cirrostrato *m*.

cirrus ['sɪrəs] *n, pl* **cirri** ['sɪraɪ] cirro *m*.

cissy* ['sɪsɪ] *n* = **sissy**.

Cistercian [sɪs'tɜːʃən] **1** *adj* cisterciense; **~ Order** Orden *f* del Císter. **2** *n* cisterciense *m*.

cistern ['sɪstən] *n* tanque *m*, depósito *m*; (*of WC*) cisterna *f*, depósito *m*; (*for hot water*) termo *m*; (*for rainwater*) aljibe *m*, cisterna *f*.

citadel ['sɪtədl] *n* ciudadela *f*; (*in Spain, freq*) alcázar *m*; (*fig*) reducto *m*.

citation [saɪ'teɪʃən] *n* cita *f*; (*Jur*) citación *f*; (*Mil*) mención *f*, citación *f*; **~ index** índice *m* de citación.

cite [saɪt] *vt* citar; (*Mil*) mencionar, citar.

citizen ['sɪtɪzn] *n* ciudadano *m*, -a *f*; (*in counting inhabitants etc*) habitante *mf*, vecino *m*, -a *f*; (*national*) súbdito *m*, -a *f*; **C~s' Band** (*Rad*) banda *f* ciudadana.

citizenry ['sɪtɪznrɪ] *n* ciudadanos *mpl*, ciudadanía *f*.

citizenship ['sɪtɪznʃɪp] *n* ciudadanía *f*.

citric ['sɪtrɪk] *adj*: **~ acid** ácido *m* cítrico.

citron ['sɪtrən] *n* (*fruit*) cidra *f*; (*tree*) cidro *m*.

citrus ['sɪtrəs] *n*: **~ fruits** agrios *mpl*, cítricos *mpl*.

city ['sɪtɪ] **1** *n* ciudad *f*; **the C~** (*Brit*: *London*) *el centro bursátil y bancario*.

2 *attr* municipal, de la ciudad; **~ center** (*US*), **~ centre** centro *m* de la ciudad; **~ council** concejo *m* municipal, ayuntamiento *m*; **~ desk** (*Brit*) sección *f* de noticias financieras (de un periódico); (*US*) sección *f* de noticias de la ciudad (de un periódico); **~ dweller** ciudadano *m*, -a *f*; **~ editor** redactor *m* encargado de las noticias financieras, redactora *f* encargada de las noticias financieras; **~ fathers** prohombres *mpl* de la ciudad; **~ hall** palacio *m* municipal; (*US*) ayuntamiento *m*; **~ limits** perímetro *m* urbano; **~ manager** administrador *m*, -ora *f* municipal; **~ news** (*Brit*) noticias *fpl* financieras; (*US*) noticias *fpl* de la ciudad; **~ plan** (*US*) plano *m* de la ciudad; **~ planner** (*US*) urbanista *mf*; **~ planning** (*US*) urbanismo *m*; **~ slicker*** capitalino *m*.

cityscape ['sɪtɪskeɪp] *n* (*US*) paisaje *m* urbano.

city-state ['sɪtɪˌsteɪt] *n* ciudad-estado *f*.

civet ['sɪvɪt] *n* algalia *f*.

civic ['sɪvɪk] *adj* cívico; municipal; **~ centre** (*Brit*) conjunto *m* de edificios municipales.

civics ['sɪvɪks] *npl* cívica *f*; (*as course*) educación *f* cívica.

civies* ['sɪvɪz] *npl* (*US*) = **civvies**.

civil ['sɪvl] *adj* (**a**) civil; **~ defence** protección *f* civil; **~ disobedience** resistencia *f* pasiva; **~ engineer** ingeniero *m* de caminos, canales y puertos; **~ engineering** ingeniería *f* civil; **~ law** derecho *m* civil; **~ liberties** libertades *fpl* civiles; **C~ List** (*Brit*) *presupuesto de la casa real aprobado por el parlamento*; **~ marriage** matrimonio *m* civil; **~ rights** derechos *mpl* civiles; **~ servant** funcionario *m*, -a *f* (del Estado); **~ service** cuerpo *m* de funcionarios (del Estado); **~ status** estado *m* civil; **~ war** guerra *f* civil. (**b**) (*polite*) cortés, atento; amable; **he was very ~ to me** fue muy cortés conmigo; **that's very ~ of you** es Vd muy amable; **be more ~!** ¡hable con más educación!

civilian [sɪ'vɪlɪən] **1** *adj* (de) paisano; civil. **2** *n* civil *mf*, paisano *m*, -a *f*.

civility [sɪ'vɪlɪtɪ] *n* (**a**) (*politeness*) cortesía *f*; urbanidad *f*; amabilidad *f*; **lack of ~** falta *f* de educación. (**b**) (*polite remark*) cortesía *f*, cumplido *m*.

civilization [ˌsɪvɪlaɪ'zeɪʃən] *n* civilización *f*.

civilize ['sɪvɪlaɪz] *vt* civilizar.

civilized ['sɪvɪlaɪzd] *adj* civilizado.

civilizing ['sɪvɪlaɪzɪŋ] *adj influence etc* civilizador.

civilly ['sɪvɪlɪ] *adv* cortésmente, atentamente.

civism ['sɪvɪzəm] *n* civismo *m*.

civvies* ['sɪvɪz] *npl* traje *m* civil; **in ~** vestido de civil.

civvy* ['sɪvɪ] *adj*: **~ street** (*Brit*) la vida civil.

CKD *adj abbr of* **completely knocked down**; *V* **knock down**.

cl *abbr of* **centilitre**(**s**) centilitro(s) *m*(*pl*), cl.

clack [klæk] *vi* (*chatter*) charlar, chismear; **this will make the tongues ~** esto será tema para los chismosos.

clad [klæd] (††) **1** *pret and ptp of* **clothe**. **2** *adj*: **~ in** vestido de.

cladding [klædɪŋ] *n* (*Tech*) revestimiento *m*.

claim [kleɪm] **1** *n* (**a**) (*gen, demand*) reclamación *f*; (*formally stated*) petición *f*; (*wage ~*) reivindicación *f* salarial; **to have a ~ on sb** tener motivo para reclamar contra uno; **I think this has a ~ on your attention** creo que esto merece su atención; **I have many ~s on my time** son muchas las cosas que ocupan el tiempo de que dispongo; **to lay ~ to** reclamar; **he put in a ~ for a rise** pidió un aumento de sueldo.

(**b**) (*Jur*) demanda *f* (*for* de); (*insurance ~*) demanda *f*, reclamación *f*; **to put in a ~ for** entablar demanda de; **to state a ~** presentar una demanda; **you have no legal ~** Vd no tiene derecho legal alguno.

(**c**) (*pretension*) pretensión *f*; afirmación *f*, declaración *f*; **his ~ turned out to be untrue** su declaración resultó ser falsa; **that's a big ~ to make** eso es mucho decir; **to make large ~s for an invention** pretender que un invento tiene grandes ventajas.

(**d**) (*Min*) pertenencia *f*, concesión *f*.

2 *vt* (**a**) (*demand as one's due*) reclamar, exigir; *benefit* solicitar; **to ~ the right to vote** reclamar (*or* reivindicar) el derecho de votar; **to ~ sth from sb** reclamar algo a uno; **sth else ~ed her attention** otra cosa mereció su atención; **death ~ed him** se lo llevó la muerte.

(**b**) (*Jur*) demandar; **to ~ damages from sb** reclamar a uno por daños y perjuicios.

(**c**) (*profess, assert*) pretender; reivindicar; **XYZ has ~ed responsibility for the bomb** XYZ ha reivindicado la colocación de la bomba; **to ~ kinship with sb** afirmar ser pariente de uno; **he ~s to be her son** afirma ser su hijo; **he ~s to have seen her** afirma haberla visto; **to ~ that** ... sostener que ..., afirmar que ...; **that's ~ing a lot** eso es mucho decir.

3 *vi* presentar una reclamación, presentar una demanda (*for* de).

claimant ['kleɪmənt] *n* (*of benefit etc*) solicitante *mf*; (*Jur*) demandante *mf*; (*to throne*) pretendiente *m*, -a *f*.

claim form ['kleɪmˌfɔːm] *n* (*Admin*) (*for benefit*) impreso *m* de solicitud; (*for expenses*) impreso *m* de demanda de gastos.

clairvoyance [kleə'vɔɪəns] *n* clarividencia *f*.

clairvoyant(e) [kleə'vɔɪənt] *n* clarividente *mf*, vidente *mf*.

clam [klæm] **1** *n* (**a**) almeja *f*; **~ chowder** (*US*) sopa *f* de almejas. (**b**) (*US*‡: *dollar*) dólar *m*. **2** *vi*: **to ~ up*** callarse como un muerto.

clambake ['klæmbeɪk] *n* (*US*) merienda *f* en la playa (*or* en el campo); (*) fiesta *f*.

clamber ['klæmbəʳ] **1** *n* subida *f*. **2** *vi* trepar, subir gateando (*over* sobre, *up* a).

clammy ['klæmɪ] *adj* frío y húmedo, pegajoso.

clamorous ['klæmərəs] *adj* clamoroso, vociferante, ruidoso.

clamour, (*US*) **clamor** ['klæməʳ] **1** *n* clamor *m*, clamoreo *m*, griterío *m*. **2** *vi* clamorear, vociferar; **to ~ for** clamar por, pedir a voces.

clamp [klæmp] **1** *n* (**a**) (*brace*) abrazadera *f*; (*Aut: on parked car*) cepo *m*; (*in laboratory etc*) grapa *f*; (*Carp*) tornillo *m* de banco, cárcel *f*.

(**b**) (*Agr*) ensilado *m*, montón *m*.

2 *vt* (**a**) (*secure*) afianzar (*or* sujetar *etc*) con abrazadera; **he ~ed it in his hand** lo agarró con la mano; **he ~ed his hand down on it** lo sujetó firmemente con la mano. (**b**) *car* poner un cepo en.

3 *vi*: **to ~ down on** (*fig*) tratar de acabar con, restringir, reprimir; apretar los tornillos a.

clamp-down ['klæmpdaʊn] *n* restricción *f* (*on* de); prohibición *f* (*on* de).

clan [klæn] *n* clan *m* (*also fig*).

clandestine [klæn'destɪn] *adj* clandestino.

clang [klæŋ] **1** *n* sonido *m* metálico fuerte, estruendo *m*. **2** *vt* hacer sonar. **3** *vi* sonar, hacer estruendo; **the gate ~ed**

shut la puerta se cerró ruidosamente.
clanger‡ ['klæŋəʳ] *n* (*Brit*) plancha* *f*, metida *f* de pata* (*LAm*); **to drop a ~** tirarse una plancha*, meter la pata*.
clangorous ['klæŋgərəs] *adj* estrepitoso, estruendoso.
clangour, (*US*) **clangor** ['klæŋgəʳ] *n* estruendo *m*.
clank ['klæŋk] **1** *n* sonido *m* metálico seco, golpeo *m* metálico.
2 *vt* hacer sonar.
3 *vi* sonar, hacer estruendo, rechinar metálico; **the train went ~ing past** pasó el tren con estruendo.
clannish ['klænɪʃ] *adj* exclusivista, con fuerte sentimiento de tribu.
clansman ['klænzmən] *n*, *pl* **clansmen** ['klænzmen] miembro *m* del clan.
clap[1] [klæp] **1** *n* (*on shoulder*) palmoteo *m*; (*of the hands*) palmada *f*; **~ of thunder** trueno *m* (seco), estampido *m* (seco) de trueno.
2 *vt* (**a**) (*with hands*) *person, play, announcement* aplaudir; **to ~ one's hands** batir las manos, dar palmadas, batir palmas; **to ~ sb on the back** dar a uno una palmada en la espalda.
(**b**) (*place*) poner; **he ~ped his hat on** se encasquetó el sombrero; **to ~ eyes on** clavar la vista en; **to ~ a hand over sb's mouth** tapar a uno la boca con la mano; **to ~ sth shut** cerrar algo de golpe; **to ~ sb in jail** encarcelar a uno, meter a uno en la cárcel.
3 *vi* aplaudir.
clap[2]‡ [klæp] *n* (*Med*) gonorrea *f*.
clapboard ['klæpbɔːd] *n* (*US*) chilla *f*, tablilla *f*.
clapped-out* [ˌklæpt'aʊt] *adj car etc* anticuado; desvencijado; inútil; *mine* agotado.
clapper ['klæpəʳ] *n* badajo *m*; **to go like the ~s** (*Brit**) correr como un loco.
clapperboard ['klæpəˌbɔːd] *n* (*Cine*) claqueta *f*.
clapping ['klæpɪŋ] *n* aplausos *mpl*.
claptrap* ['klæptræp] *n* pavadas* *fpl*, burradas* *fpl*.
claque [klæk] *n* claque *f*.
claret ['klærət] *n* vino *m* tinto (*esp* de Burdeos); (*colour*) burdeos *m*.
clarification [ˌklærɪfɪ'keɪʃən] *n* aclaración *f*.
clarify ['klærɪfaɪ] *vt* aclarar.
clarinet [ˌklærɪ'net] *n* clarinete *m*.
clarinettist [ˌklærɪ'netɪst] *n* clarinetista *mf*.
clarion ['klærɪən] *n* (toque *m* de) trompeta *f*; **~ call** llamada *f* fuerte y sonora.
clarity ['klærɪtɪ] *n* claridad *f*.
clash [klæʃ] **1** *n* (**a**) (*noise*) estruendo *m*, fragor *m*.
(**b**) (*conflict*) choque *m*; enfrentamiento *m*; (*Mil*) encuentro *m*; (*of opinions etc*) desacuerdo *m*, conflicto *m*; **~ of dates** coincidencia *f* de fechas; **~ of wills** lucha *f* de voluntades; **timetable ~** incompatibilidad *f* de horas.
2 *vt* batir, golpear.
3 *vi* (*Mil*) encontrarse, batirse; (*be opposed*) pugnar (con), estar en pugna, chocar; (*persons*) pelearse, reñir; enfrentarse (uno con otro); (*colours*) desentonar; (*dates*) coincidir; (*opinions*) estar en desacuerdo.
clasp [klɑːsp] **1** *n* (*fastener*) broche *m*, corchete *m*; (*of box, necklace etc*) cierre *m*; (*of book*) broche *m*, manecilla *f*; **with a ~ of the hand** con un apretón de manos.
2 *vt* (*fasten*) abrochar; (*embrace*) abrazar; *hand* apretar, estrechar; (*in one's hand*) tener asido, agarrar; **to ~ sb to one's bosom** estrechar a uno contra el pecho.
claspknife ['klɑːspnaɪf] *n*, *pl* **claspknives** ['klɑːspnaɪvz] navaja *f*.
class [klɑːs] **1** *n* clase *f*; **first ~** primera clase *f*; **lower ~es** clase *f* baja; **middle ~es** clase *f* media; **upper ~** clase *f* alta; **~ of degree** (*Brit Univ*) categoría *f* del título; **~ of '92** (*esp US*) promoción *f* del '92; **a good ~ novel** una novela de buena calidad; **it's just not in the same ~** no hay comparación entre los dos; **it's in a ~ by itself** no tiene igual, es único en su género; **she's certainly got ~** ella sí que tiene clase.
2 *attr* clasista, de clase(s); **~ distinction** distinción *f* de clases; **~ list** (*Scol*) lista *f* de clase; (*Univ*) lista *f* de estudiantes aprobados para la licenciatura; **~ society** (*Pol*) sociedad *f* clasista; **~ struggle** lucha *f* de clases; **~ teacher** (*Brit*) tutor *m*, -a *f*; **~ war(fare)** = **~ struggle**.
3 *vt* clasificar.
class-conscious ['klɑːs'kɒnʃəs] *adj* que tiene conciencia de clase.
class-consciousness ['klɑːs'kɒnʃəsnɪs] *n* conciencia *f* de clase.
classic ['klæsɪk] **1** *adj* clásico. **2** *n* (*person*) autor *m* clásico; (*work*) obra *f* clásica; (*Sport*) carrera *f* clásica; **the ~s** los clásicos, las obras clásicas; **~s** (*Univ etc*) clásicas *fpl*.
classical ['klæsɪkəl] *adj* clásico; **~ scholar** erudito *m*, -a *f* en lenguas clásicas.
classicism ['klæsɪsɪzəm] *n* clasicismo *m*.
classicist ['klæsɪsɪst] *n* clasicista *mf*.
classifiable ['klæsɪfaɪəbl] *adj* clasificable.
classification [ˌklæsɪfɪ'keɪʃən] *n* clasificación *f*.
classified ['klæsɪfaɪd] *adj* (**a**) *information* secreto, reservado. (**b**) **~ advertisement** anuncio *m* por palabras.
classify ['klæsɪfaɪ] *vt* (**a**) clasificar (*in, into* en; *under letter B* en la B). (**b**) *information* clasificar como secreto, reservar.
classless ['klɑːslɪs] *adj society* sin clases.
classmate ['klɑːsmeɪt] *n* (*Brit*) compañero *m*, -a *f* de clase, condiscípulo *m*, -a *f*.
classroom ['klɑːsrʊm] *n* aula *f*, clase *f*.
classy* ['klɑːsɪ] *adj* de buen tono, muy pera*.
clatter ['klætəʳ] **1** *n* ruido *m*, estruendo *m*; (*of plates*) choque *m*; (*of hooves*) chacoloteo *m*; (*of train*) triquitraque *m*; (*hammering*) martilleo *m*.
2 *vi* hacer ruido, hacer estruendo; (*hooves, feet*) chacolotear; **to come ~ing down** caer ruidosamente; **to ~ down the stairs** bajar ruidosamente la escalera.
Claudius ['klɔːdɪəs] *nm* Claudio.
clause [klɔːz] *n* cláusula *f*; (*Gram*) oración *f*; cláusula *f*.
claustrophobia [ˌklɔːstrə'fəʊbɪə] *n* claustrofobia *f*.
claustrophobic [ˌklɔːstrə'fəʊbɪk] **1** *adj* claustrofóbico. **2** *n* claustrófobo *m*, -a *f*.
clavichord ['klævɪkɔːd] *n* clavicordio *m*.
clavicle ['klævɪkl] *n* clavícula *f*.
claw [klɔː] **1** *n* (*Zool*) garra *f*, zarpa *f*, (*of cat*) uña *f*, (*of lobster*) pinza *f*; (*Tech*) garfio *m*, gancho *m*; **~s** (*) dedos *mpl*, mano *f*; **to get one's ~s into** (*attack*) atacar con rencor; (*dominate*) dominar, tener los sesos sorbidos a; **to get one's ~s on** agarrarse de (*or* a); **get your ~s off that!** ¡fuera las manos!; **to show one's ~s** sacar las uñas.
2 *vt* arañar; (*tear*) desgarrar.
◆**claw at** *vt* arañar; (*tear*) desgarrar.
◆**claw back** *vt* volver a tomar, tomar otra vez para sí.
clawback ['klɔːbæk] *n* (*Econ*) *desgravación fiscal obtenida por devolución de impuestos*.
claw-hammer ['klɔːˌhæməʳ] *n* martillo *m* de orejas, martillo *m* de carpintero.
clay [kleɪ] *n* arcilla *f*; **~ court** pista *f* de lodo, pista *f* de tierra batida; **~ pigeon** plato *m* de barro; (*fig: victim*) víctima *f*; **~ pigeon shooting** tiro *m* al plato; **~ pipe** pipa *f* de cerámica; **~ pit** pozo *m* de arcilla.
clayey ['kleɪɪ] *adj* arcilloso.
clean [kliːn] **1** *adj* (**a**) (*not dirty*) limpio; aseado; (*unobstructed*) despejado; **as ~ as a new pin** tan limpio como un espejo; **he's ~** (*US*‡) no lleva arma; **to come ~**‡ confesarlo todo, desembuchar*.
(**b**) (*pure etc*) limpio, decente; inocente; *life* sano; *joke etc* que no ofende; *reputation* bueno, sin tacha; *game* limpio; *player* honrado; **to do a ~ copy** hacer una copia en limpio; **to have a ~ record** no tener nota adversa (en su historial); **'must have ~ driving licence'** 'imprescindible tener carnet de conducir sin nota de sanción'; **Mr C~** Señor Manos Limpias; *V* **bill**[2] **1** (**e**), **party 1** (**c**).
(**c**) (*clear-cut*) neto, distinto, bien definido; (*shapely*) bien formado, elegante; (*adroit*) diestro, elegante; **~ lines** contornos *mpl* elegantes.
2 *adv* enteramente; **he cut ~ through it** lo cortó de un golpe; **it cuts ~ across tradition** esto corta netamente con la tradición; **to get ~ away** escaparse sin dejar rastro; **I ~ forgot** se me olvidó por completo; **the fish jumped ~ out of the net** el pez saltó fuera de la red.
3 *n* limpia *f*, limpieza *f*; **to give the car a ~** limpiar el coche.
4 *vt* limpiar; asear; *streets* barrer; (*dry-clean*) limpiar en seco.
◆**clean down** *vt* limpiar.
◆**clean off** *vt surface etc* limpiar; *dirt* quitar limpiando.
◆**clean out** *vt* (**a**) limpiar; **to ~ out a box** limpiar (el interior de) una caja.
(**b**) (*: *in robbery*) limpiar.
(**c**) (*: *fleece*) **we were ~ed out** nos dejaron sin blanca, quedamos limpios*.
◆**clean up 1** *vt* (**a**) *room* limpiar, asear.
(**b**) (*morally*) limpiar; reformar; *act, play* suprimir los pasajes verdes de; **they're trying to ~ up TV** tratan de hacer más decentes los programas de TV.
(**c**) **we ~ed up £500*** sacamos 500 libras de ganancia.
2 *vi* (**a**) **to ~ up after sb** limpiar lo que ha dejado (*or* ensuciado) otro; **to ~ up after a party** limpiar después de

un party.

(**b**) (*) hacer una pingüe ganancia, ponerse las botas*; **he ~ed up on that deal** sacó una buena ganancia de ese negocio.

clean-cut ['kli:n'kʌt] *adj* (**a**) claro, bien definido, preciso; *outline* nítido. (**b**) *person* de buen parecer; de tipo elegante.

cleaner ['kli:nəʳ] *n* (**a**) (*person*) limpiador *m*, -ora *f*, asistenta *f*, mujer *f* de la limpieza; **~'s** (**shop**) tintorería *f*, lavandería *f*; **we'll take them to the ~'s*** les dejaremos sin blanca, les dejaremos limpios*. (**b**) (*household* ~) producto *m* para la limpieza.

cleaning ['kli:nɪŋ] *n* limpia *f*, limpieza *f*; **~ fluid** líquido *m* de limpieza; **~ lady, ~ woman** asistenta *f*, mujer *f* de la limpieza, limpiadora *f*.

clean-limbed [ˌkli:n'lɪmd] *adj* bien proporcionado.

cleanliness ['klenlɪnɪs] *n* limpieza *f* (habitual), aseo *m*.

clean-living [ˌkli:n'lɪvɪŋ] *adj* de vida sana.

cleanly[1] ['klenlɪ] *adj* limpio, aseado.

cleanly[2] ['kli:nlɪ] *adv* limpiamente; (*adroitly*) diestramente, con destreza.

cleanness ['kli:nnɪs] *n* limpieza *f*, aseo *m*.

clean-out ['kli:naʊt] *n* limpieza *f*.

cleanse [klenz] *vt* limpiar (*of* de).

cleanser ['klenzəʳ] *n* agente *m* de limpieza, producto *m* (químico) para la limpieza.

clean-shaven ['kli:n'ʃeɪvn] *adj* sin barba ni bigote, todo afeitado.

cleansing ['klenzɪŋ] **1** *adj* (*for complexion*) limpiador; (*fig*) purificador; **~ cream** crema *f* desmaquilladora; **~ department** departamento *m* de la limpieza; **~ lotion** loción *f* limpiadora. **2** *n* limpieza *f*.

clean-up ['kli:nʌp] *n* limpia *f*, limpieza *f*.

clear [klɪəʳ] **1** *adj* (**a**) (*transparent, audible, distinct, unambiguous, obvious*) claro; *sky, surface* despejado; *air* transparente; *conscience* limpio, tranquilo; *mind* penetrante, despejado; *majority* absoluto, neto; *round* (*Sport*) sin penalizaciones; **as ~ as crystal** más claro que el agua; **as ~ as day** más claro que el sol; **as ~ as mud*** nada claro; **it is ~ that ...** está claro que ...; **is that ~?** ¿comprendido?; **to make o.s. ~** explicarse bien, explicarse claramente; **do I make myself ~?** ¿entiende?, ¿estamos?; **I think I've got it pretty ~** creo que lo entiendo bastante bien; **I wish to make it ~ that ...** quiero subrayar que ..., quiero dejar bien sentado que ...; **a ~ case of murder** un caso evidente de homicidio.

(**b**) (*certain*) **I'm not ~ whether** yo no sé a punto fijo si; **I'm not very ~ about this** no tengo una idea muy clara de esto; **he was perfectly ~ that he did not intend to go** dijo de modo tajante que no pensaba ir; **are we ~ that we want this?** ¿estamos seguros de que queremos esto?

(**c**) (*complete*) entero, completo; **3 ~ days** 3 días completos; **£3 ~ profit** una ganancia neta de 3 libras; **to win by a ~ head** ganar por una cabeza larga.

(**d**) (*free*) **~ of** libre de; **to be ~ of debt** estar libre de deudas.

2 *adv* claramente; **I can hear you loud and ~** te oigo perfectamente; **to get ~ away** escaparse sin dejar rastro alguno; **to jump ~** quitarse de en medio de un salto; **to get ~ of** deshacerse de; **when we get ~ of London** cuando estemos fuera de Londres; **to steer ~ of** evitar cualquier contacto con; **stand ~ of the doors!** ¡atención a las puertas!

3 *n* (**a**) **to be in the ~** (*of debt*) estar libre de deudas; (*of suspicion*) quedar fuera de toda sospecha; (*of danger*) estar fuera de peligro. (**b**) **message in ~** mensaje *m* no cifrado.

4 *vt* (**a**) (*remove obstacles from*) *place, road* despejar, limpiar; desescombrar; *pipe* desatascar; *wood* desmontar; *land* limpiar; *court, hall* desocupar, desalojar (de público *etc*); *postbox* recoger las cartas de; (*Sport*) *ball* despejar; **to ~ the table** quitar la mesa; **to ~ a space for** hacer sitio para; *V* **way**.

(**b**) (*clarify*) *liquid* aclarar, clarificar; *blood* purificar; *bowels* purgar; *head* despejar; **to ~ one's throat** carraspear, aclarar la voz.

(**c**) (*find innocent*) absolver (*of* de); demostrar la inocencia de; **you will have to be ~ed by Security** será preciso que le acredite la Seguridad; **the plan will have to be ~ed with the director** el plan tendrá que ser aprobado por el director; **we've already ~ed it with him** hemos obtenido ya su visto bueno.

(**d**) (*jump over*) salvar, saltar por encima de; (*avoid touching*) pasar sin rozar; **to ~ 2 metres** saltar 2 metros; **the plane just ~ed the roof** el avión por poco no tocó el tejado; **this part has to ~ that by at least 1 centimetre** entre esta pieza y aquélla tiene que haber un espacio de 1 centímetro al menos.

(**e**) *cheque* pasar por un banco, (*in clearing-house*) compensar; *account, stock, debt* liquidar; *profit* sacar (una ganancia de); *conscience* descargar; (*of Customs*) despachar, dejar pasar; **he ~ed £50 on the deal** ganó 50 libras en el negocio; **we have just about ~ed our costs** estamos a punto de cubrir los gastos; **she ~s £500 a week** se saca 500 libras a la semana; **'half-price to ~'** 'liquidación a mitad de precio'.

(**f**) (*Comput*) despejar.

5 *vi* (*liquid*) aclararse, clarificarse; (*weather*) despejarse; (*Sport*) despejar.

6 *vr*: **to ~ o.s. of a charge** probar su inocencia de una acusación.

◆**clear away 1** *vt* quitar (de en medio); *dishes* retirar.

2 *vi* (**a**) (*dishes*) quitar los platos, quitar la mesa.

(**b**) (*mist*) disiparse.

◆**clear off 1** *vt debt* pagar, liquidar.

2 *vi* (*) irse, largarse*; desaparecer; **~ off!** ¡lárgate!, ¡fuera de aquí!

◆**clear out 1** *vt place* limpiar; vaciar; desescombrar; *objects* quitar.

2 *vi* (*) = **clear off 2**.

◆**clear up 1** *vt* (**a**) *crime* esclarecer; *mystery* aclarar; *doubt* resolver, aclarar, disipar; *difficulty* aclarar; *business* despachar.

(**b**) (*tidy*) limpiar, asear; (*arrange*) arreglar, poner en orden.

2 *vi* (**a**) (*weather*) aclararse, despejarse; (*problem*) resolverse; (*illness*) curarse, terminar.

(**b**) (*tidy*) limpiar, ordenar las cosas.

clearance ['klɪərəns] *n* (**a**) (*of road etc; also Sport*) despeje *m*; (*of land*) desmonte *m*, roza *f*.

(**b**) (*Tech*) espacio *m* (libre), espacio *m* muerto; separación *f*, holgura *f*; (*distance above ground*) luz *f* libre.

(**c**) (*by Customs*) despacho *m* de aduana; (*by Security*) acreditación *f*; (*Fin*) compensación *f*; **~ for take-off** autorización *f* para despegar; **~ sale** liquidación *f*, realización *f* (*LAm*).

clear-cut ['klɪə'kʌt] *adj* claro, bien definido, neto, nítido.

clear-eyed [ˌkli:r'aɪd] *adj* de ojos claros; (*fig*) clarividente.

clear-headed ['klɪə'hedɪd] *adj* de mentalidad lógica, perspicaz, inteligente, sereno.

clear-headedness ['klɪə'hedɪdnɪs] *n* mentalidad *f* lógica, perspicacia *f*, inteligencia *f*, serenidad *f*.

clearing ['klɪərɪŋ] **1** *n* (**a**) (*in wood*) claro *m*; *V also* **clearance**. (**b**) (*Fin*) liquidación *f*. **2** *attr*: **~ account** cuenta *f* de compensación; **~ cheque** cheque *m* de compensación.

clearing-bank ['klɪərɪŋbæŋk] *n*, **clearing-house** ['klɪərɪŋhaʊs] *n*, *pl* **clearing-houses** ['klɪərɪŋˌhaʊzɪz] (*Brit*) cámara *f* (*or* banco *m*) de compensación.

clearly ['klɪəlɪ] *adv* (**a**) claramente. (**b**) (*at start of sentence*) desde luego; (*as answer*) sin duda, naturalmente.

clearness ['klɪənɪs] *n* claridad *f*.

clear-out ['klɪəraʊt] *n*: **to have a good ~** limpiarlo todo, despejarlo todo.

clear-sighted ['klɪə'saɪtɪd] *adj* clarividente, perspicaz.

clear-sightedness ['klɪə'saɪtɪdnɪs] *n* clarividencia *f*, perspicacia *f*.

clearway ['klɪəweɪ] *n* (*Brit*) carretera *f* en la que está prohibido parar.

cleat [kli:t] *n* abrazadera *f*, listón *m*, fiador *m*.

cleavage ['kli:vɪdʒ] *n* escisión *f*, división *f*; (*in dress*) escote *m*.

cleave[1] [kli:v] (*irr*: *pret* **clove** *or* **cleft**, *ptp* **cloven** *or* **cleft**) *vt* partir, hender, abrir por medio; *water* surcar.

cleave[2] [kli:v] *vi*: **to ~ to** adherirse a, no separarse de; **to ~ together** ser inseparables.

cleaver ['kli:vəʳ] *n* cuchilla *f* de carnicero.

clef [klef] *n* clave *f*.

cleft [kleft] **1** *pret and ptp of* **cleave**[1]. **2** *adj*: **~ palate** fisura *f* del paladar, palatosquisis *f*. **3** *n* grieta *f*, hendedura *f*.

cleg [kleg] *m* tábano *m*.

clematis ['klemətɪs] *n* clemátide *f*.

clemency ['klemənsɪ] *n* clemencia *f*.

Clement ['klemənt] *nm* Clemente.

clement ['klemənt] *adj* clemente, benigno.

clementine ['kleməntaɪn] *n* clementina *f*.

clench [klentʃ] *vt teeth, fist* apretar, cerrar; **the ~ed fist** el puño cerrado; = **clinch**.

Cleopatra [ˌkli:ə'pætrə] *nf* Cleopatra.

clerestory ['klɪəˌstɔːrɪ] *n* triforio *m*.
clergy ['klɜːdʒɪ] *n* clero *m*.
clergyman ['klɜːdʒɪmən] *n*, *pl* **clergymen** ['klɜːdʒɪmen] clérigo *m*; (*specifically Anglican*) sacerdote *m* anglicano; (*Protestant minister*) pastor *m*.
cleric ['klerɪk] *n* eclesiástico *m*, clérigo *m*.
clerical ['klerɪkəl] *adj* (**a**) oficinista, oficinesco, de oficina; ~ **error** error *m* de pluma, error *m* de copia; ~ **grades** (*Civil Service etc*) oficinistas *mpl*; ~ **staff** personal *m* de oficina; ~ **work** trabajo *m* de oficina; ~ **worker** oficinista *mf*. (**b**) (*Eccl*) clerical; ~ **collar** alzacuello(s) *m*.
clericalism ['klerɪkəˌlɪzəm] *n* clericalismo *m*.
clerihew ['klerɪhjuː] *n* *estrofa inglesa de 4 versos, de carácter festivo*.
clerk [klɑːk, (*US*) klɜːrk] **1** *n* (**a**) oficinista *mf*, empleado *m*, -a *f*, secretario *m*, -a *f*; (*in bank*) funcionario *m*, -a *f*; (*in hotel*) recepcionista *mf*; (*esp US*) dependiente *m*, -a *f*, vendedor *m*, -ora *f*; (*Jur*) escribano *m*; ~ **of works** maestro *m* de obras. (**b**) (*Eccl*: *also* ~ **in holy orders**) clérigo *m*.
2 *vi* (*US*) trabajar como dependiente.
clerkship ['klɑːkʃɪp, (*US*) 'klɜːrkʃɪp] *n* empleo *m* de oficinista; (*Jur*) escribanía *f*.
clever ['klevəʳ] *adj* inteligente, listo; *move, speech etc* hábil; *invention, parody, trick, etc* ingenioso; **to be ~ at** ser listo en, tener aptitud para; **he is very ~ with his fingers** es muy hábil con los dedos, tiene mucha destreza manual; **she is very ~ with cars** entiende de coches, tiene mano para los coches; **that was ~ of you** lo hiciste muy bien, (*you were right*) has acertado; **that's ~, isn't it?** ¿es ingenioso, eh?; **to be too ~ by half** pasarse de listo; **he was too ~ for us** fue demasiado astuto para nosotros; **he tries to be too ~** se esfuerza por parecer ingenioso; ~ **Dick*** sabelotodo *m*.
clever-clever* ['klevəˌklevəʳ] *adj* sabihondo; **he's very ~** es un siete ciencias.
cleverly ['klevəlɪ] *adv* hábilmente; ingeniosamente; con destreza.
cleverness ['klevənɪs] *n* inteligencia *f*; habilidad *f*; ingenio *m*; destreza *f*.
clew [kluː] *n* (*US*) = **clue**.
cliché ['kliːʃeɪ] *n* cliché *m*, tópico *m*, frase *f* hecha, lugar *m* común.
click [klɪk] **1** *n* golpecito *m* seco; (*of gun*) piñoneo *m*; (*of heels*) taconeo *m*; (*of tongue*) chasquido *m*; (*of typewriter etc*) tecleo *m*.
2 *vt tongue etc* chasquear; **to ~ one's heels** taconear, hacer sonar los talones.
3 *vi* (**a**) (*gun*) piñonear; sonar con un golpecito seco; (*typewriter etc*) teclear.
(**b**) (*) (*succeed*) tener suerte, lograrlo; (*2 persons*) congeniar, gustarse inmediatamente; (*sexually*) ligar; (*product, invention*) tener éxito.
(**c**) **suddenly it ~ed** de repente caí en la cuenta, de repente me di cuenta.
◆**click on** *vi* (**a**) (*: *understand*) = **3** (**c**). (**b**) (*Comput*) pulsar el ratón.
clicking ['klɪkɪŋ] *n* chasquido *m*.
client ['klaɪənt] *n* cliente *mf*; **my ~** (*in court*) mi defendido.
clientèle [ˌkliːɑ̃ːnˈtel] *n* clientela *f*.
cliff [klɪf] *n* risco *m*, precipicio *m*; (*sea* ~) acantilado *m*.
cliff-dweller* ['klɪfˌdweləʳ] *n* (*US*) *persona que habita en un bloque*.
cliff-hanger ['klɪfˌhæŋəʳ] *n* película *f* (*etc*) melodramática, película *f* (*etc*) de suspense; **the election was a ~** el resultado de la elección siguió muy incierto hasta el final.
cliff-hanging ['klɪfˌhæŋɪŋ] *adj* muy emocionante (por su final dudoso y apasionante), que tiene a todos pendientes de su resultado; *drama* de suspense.
climacteric [klaɪ'mæktərɪk] **1** *adj* climactérico. **2** *n* período *m* climactérico.
climactic [klaɪ'mæktɪk] *adj* culminante.
climate ['klaɪmɪt] *n* clima *m*; (*fig*) ambiente *m*; ~ **of opinion** opinión *f* general.
climatic [klaɪ'mætɪk] *adj* climático; ~ **change** cambio *m* climático.
climatological [ˌklaɪmətə'lɒdʒɪkəl] *adj* climatológico.
climatologist [ˌklaɪmə'tɒlədʒɪst] *n* climatólogo *m*, -a *f*.
climatology [ˌklaɪmə'tɒlədʒɪ] *n* climatología *f*.
climax ['klaɪmæks] **1** *n* punto *m* culminante, colmo *m*, apogeo *m*, (*of play etc*) clímax *m*; (*sexual*) orgasmo *m*; **to reach a ~** llegar a su punto álgido, alcanzar una cima de intensidad. **2** *vi* llegar a un (*or* su) clímax.
climb [klaɪm] **1** *n* subida *f*, escalada *f*, ascenso *m*; **it was a stiff ~** la subida fue penosa.
2 *vt tree, wall etc* trepar a; *staircase* subir, subir por; *mountain* subir a, escalar.
3 *vi* (**a**) subir, trepar; (*aircraft, price, road, sun*) subir; **the path ~s higher yet** la senda sigue subiendo todavía; **to ~ to power** subir al poder.
◆**climb down 1** *vt*: **to ~ down a tree** bajar de un árbol; **to ~ down a cliff** bajar por un precipicio.
2 *vi* (**a**) bajar. (**b**) (*fig*) volverse atrás, rajarse, desdecirse; darse por vencido.
◆**climb into** *vt*: **to ~ into an aircraft** subir a un avión; **to ~ into a tree** trepar a un árbol.
◆**climb out** *vi* salir trepando.
◆**climb out of** *vt* salir trepando de.
◆**climb over** *vt*: **to ~ over a wall** franquear una tapia.
◆**climb up 1** *vt*: **to ~ up a rope** trepar por una cuerda; **to ~ up a cliff** trepar por un precipicio.
2 *vi* subir, trepar.
climb-down ['klaɪmdaʊn] *n* vuelta *f* atrás, retroceso *m*.
climber ['klaɪməʳ] *n* montañista *mf*, alpinista *mf*, escalador *m*, -ora *f*, andinista *mf* (*LAm*); (*fig*) arribista *mf*, trepador *m*, -ora *f*; (*Bot*) trepadora *f*, enredadera *f*.
climbing ['klaɪmɪŋ] **1** *n* montañismo *m*, alpinismo *m*, andinismo *m* (*LAm*).
2 *adj* (*Bot*) trepador.
climbing-frame ['klaɪmɪŋˌfreɪm] *n estructura metálica en la cual los niños juegan trepando*.
climbing-irons ['klaɪmɪŋaɪənz] *npl* garfios *mpl*.
clime [klaɪm] *n* (*liter*) clima *m*; región *f*.
clinch [klɪntʃ] **1** *n* abrazo *m*; (*Boxing*) clinch *m*; **to go into a ~** abrazarse.
2 *vt* (**a**) (*secure*) afianzar; *nail* remachar, roblar.
(**b**) (*fig*) resolver de una vez, decidir; *argument* remachar; *deal* cerrar; **to ~ matters** para remacharlo todavía; **that ~es it** eso es concluyente; ¡ni una palabra más!; = **clench**.
clincher ['klɪntʃəʳ] *n*: **that was the ~** eso fue el punto clave, eso fue el argumento irrebatible.
clinching ['klɪntʃɪŋ] *adj argument* decisivo, irrebatible.
cling [klɪŋ] (*irr*: *pret and ptp* **clung**) *vi*: **to ~ to** adherirse a, pegarse a, quedar pegado a; *life* aferrarse a; *person* agarrarse a, abrazarse a, quedar abrazado a; *person pursued* no separarse de; *opinion* seguir fiel a, aferrarse a; **they clung to one another** quedaron abrazados; **a dress that ~s to the figure** un vestido que se pega al cuerpo.
Clingfilm ['klɪŋfɪlm] ® *n*, **clingwrap** ['klɪŋræp] *n* plástico *m* para envolver.
clinging ['klɪŋɪŋ] *adj dress* ceñido, muy ajustado; *person* pegajoso; *odour* tenaz; ~ **vine** (*US fig*) lapa* *mf*.
clinic ['klɪnɪk] *n* clínica *f*; centro *m* médico (privado); (*of hospital*) dispensario *m*.
clinical ['klɪnɪkəl] *adj* (**a**) clínico; ~ **thermometer** termómetro *m* clínico. (**b**) (*fig*) clínico, aséptico, frío.
clinically ['klɪnɪkəlɪ] *adv* (**a**) clínicamente; ~ **dead** clínicamente muerto. (**b**) (*fig*) de manera clínica, de manera aséptica, fríamente.
clinician [klɪ'nɪʃən] *n* médico *m*, -a *f* de clínica.
clink[1] [klɪŋk] **1** *n* tintín *m*, sonido *m* metálico; (*of glasses*) choque *m*. **2** *vt* hacer sonar, hacer tintinar; *glasses* chocar. **3** *vi* tintinar.
clink[2]‡ [klɪŋk] *n* trena‡ *f*.
clinker ['klɪŋkəʳ] *n* escoria *f* de hulla.
clinker-built ['klɪŋkəˌbɪlt] *adj* (*Naut*) de tingladillo.
clip[1] [klɪp] **1** *n* (**a**) (*cut with scissors*) tijeretada *f*; (*shearing*) esquila *f*, esquileo *m*; (*wool*) cantidad *f* de lana esquilada; (*Cine*) fotograma *m*.
(**b**) (*blow*) golpe *m*, cachete *m*; **at a** (**fast**) ~ (*US*) a toda pastilla.
2 *vt* (**a**) (*cut*) cortar; (*cut to shorten*) acortar; *wool* trasquilar, esquilar; *coin* cercenar; *ticket* picar; *wings* cortar; *words* comerse, abreviar; (*US*) *news story etc* recortar.
(**b**) (*hit*) golpear, dar un cachete a.
◆**clip off** *vt* cortar, quitar cortando.
◆**clip out** *vt* recortar.
clip[2] [klɪp] **1** *n* (*clamp*) grapa *f*; (*for papers*) sujetapapeles *m*, broche *m* (*LAm*); (*of pen*) sujetador *m*; (*of cyclist*) pinza *f*; (*for hair*) prendido *m*, horquilla *f*, clip *m*; (*brooch*) alfiler *m* de pecho, clip *m*, abrochador *m* (*LAm*).
2 *vt* sujetar.
◆**clip on 1** *vt brooch* sujetar; *document etc* sujetar con un clip. **2** *vi*: **it ~s on here** se fija aquí (con clip).
◆**clip together** *vt* unir.
clipboard ['klɪpˌbɔːd] *n* tablilla *f* con sujetapapeles.
clip-clop ['klɪp'klɒp] *n* ruido *m* de los cascos del caballo.

clip-joint* ['klɪpˌdʒɔɪnt] *n* (*US*) bar *m* (muy caro).
clip-on ['klɪpɒn] *adj badge etc* para prender, con prendedor.
clipped [klɪpt] *adj accent* abrupto; *style* sucinto; *hair* corto.
clipper ['klɪpəʳ] *n* (*Naut*) clíper *m*.
clippers ['klɪpəz] *npl* (*for hair*) maquinilla *f* (para el pelo); (*Hort*) tijeras *fpl* podadoras.
clippie* ['klɪpɪ] *n* (*Brit*) cobradora *f* (de autobús).
clipping ['klɪpɪŋ] *n* (*from newspaper*) recorte *m*; (*of cloth*) retazo *m*.
clique [kliːk] *n* pandilla *f*, camarilla *f*, peña *f*.
cliquey ['kliːkɪ] *adj*, **cliquish** ['kliːkɪʃ] *adj* exclusivista.
cliquishness ['kliːkɪʃnɪs] *n* exclusivismo *m*.
clitoris ['klɪtərɪs] *n* clítoris *m*.
Cllr *abbr of* **Councillor.**
cloak [kləuk] **1** *n* capa *f*, manto *m*; (*fig*) pretexto *m*; **under the ~ of** so capa de, al amparo de. **2** *vt* encapotar; (*cover*) cubrir (*in, with* de); (*fig*) encubrir, disimular.
cloak-and-dagger ['kləukən'dægəʳ] *adj* clandestino, propio de agente secreto; *play* de capa y espada; *story* de agentes secretos, de espías.
cloakroom ['kləukrum] *n* guardarropa *m*; (*Brit Rail*) consigna *f*; (*Brit euph*) aseos *mpl*, lavabo *m*, servicios *mpl*, baño *m* (*LAm*).
clobber‡ ['klɒbəʳ] **1** *n* (*dress*) ropa *f*, traje *m*; (*Brit*: *gear*) bártulos *mpl*, trastos *mpl*. **2** *vt* (*defeat*) cascar*; (*beat up*) dar una paliza a.
cloche [klɒʃ] *n* campana *f* de cristal.
clock [klɒk] **1** *n* (**a**) reloj *m*; (*dial*) esfera *f*, cuadrante *m*; (*of taxi*) taxímetro *m*; (*Aut*: *speedometer*) velocímetro *m*, (*milometer*) cuentakilómetros *m*; **it's only got 60 miles on the ~** este coche ha hecho solamente 60 millas; **this will put the ~ back 50 years** esto nos hará retroceder a la situación de hace 50 años; **you can't put the ~ back** no se puede detener el progreso; **against the ~** contra (el) reloj; **we have surveillance round the ~** tenemos vigilancia de veinticuatro horas, tenemos vigilancia permanente; **to sleep round the ~** dormir doce horas seguidas; **the garage is open around the ~** el garaje está abierto las veinticuatro horas; **to do sth by the ~** hacer algo con precisión de reloj; **to keep one's eyes on** (*or* **watch**) **the ~** mirar mucho el reloj (ansiando abandonar el trabajo).
(**b**) (‡) jeta *f*.
2 *vt* (**a**) registrar; **she ~ed 4 minutes for the mile** hizo la milla en 4 minutos; **we ~ed 80 m.p.h.** alcanzamos una velocidad de 80 millas por hora.
(**b**) (*Brit‡*: *hit*) **he ~ed him one** le dió un bofetón*.
(**c**) (*Brit‡*: *see*) guipar‡, calar‡.
◆**clock in** *vi* fichar, picar, (*loosely*) llegar al trabajo.
◆**clock off** *vi* fichar la salida, (*loosely*) terminar el trabajo.
◆**clock on** *vi* = **clock in.**
◆**clock out** *vi* = **clock off.**
◆**clock up** *vt* acumular; **he ~ed up 250 miles** (*Aut*) recorrió 250 millas.
clockmaker ['klɒkˌmeɪkəʳ] *n* relojero *m*.
clock radio [ˌklɒk'reɪdɪəu] *n* radio-despertador *m*.
clock repairer ['klɒkrɪˌpɛərəʳ] *n* relojero *m*.
clocktower ['klɒkˌtauəʳ] *n* torre *f* de reloj.
clock-watcher ['klɒkˌwɒtʃəʳ] *n* persona *f* que mira mucho el reloj (ansiando abandonar el trabajo).
clockwise ['klɒkwaɪz] **1** *adj* dextrorso. **2** *adv* dextrorsum, en la dirección de las agujas del reloj.
clockwork ['klɒkwɜːk] **1** *n* aparato *m* de relojería; **to go like ~** ir como un reloj. **2** *attr* de cuerda; **~ train** tren *m* de cuerda; **C~ Orange** La Naranja Mecánica.
clod [klɒd] *n* (**a**) terrón *m*. (**b**) (*person*) patán *m*; **you ~!** ¡bestia!
clodhopper ['klɒdˌhɒpəʳ] *n* patán *m*.
clog [klɒg] **1** *n* zueco *m*, chanclo *m*. **2** *vt* (*also* **to ~ up**) atascar, obstruir. **3** *vi* (*also* **to ~ up**) atascarse, obstruirse.
cloister ['klɔɪstəʳ] *n* claustro *m*.
cloistered ['klɔɪstəd] *adj* conventual; **to live a ~ life** (*fig*) llevar una vida de ermitaño.
clonal ['kləunəl] *adj* clónico.
clone [kləun] **1** *n* clon *m*; (*Comput*) clónico *n*. **2** *vt* clonar.
cloning ['kləunɪŋ] *n* clonación *f*, clonaje *m*.
close[1] [kləus] **1** *adv* cerca; **~ by** muy cerca; **~ by sth, ~ to sth** cerca de algo; **to be ~ together** estar muy juntos, estar muy cerca uno(s) de otro(s); **to come ~** acercarse; **that comes ~ to an insult** eso equivale casi a un insulto; **the runners finished very ~** llegaron los atletas casi a la par; **to fit ~** ajustarse al cuerpo (*etc*); **to follow ~ behind sb** seguir muy de cerca a uno; **to keep ~ to the wall** ir arrimado a la pared; **to look at sth ~ up** (*or* **to**) mirar algo de cerca; **it's ~ on 6 o'clock** son casi las 6; **he must be ~ on 50** estará frisando en los 50; **according to sources ~ to the police** según fuentes allegadas a la comisaría.
2 *adj* (**a**) (*near*) cercano, próximo; (**~** *together*) apretados, arrimados unos a otros; densos; *connection, contact, friendship* estrecho, íntimo; *friend* íntimo; *relation* cercano; *resemblance* casi completo, muy estrecho; *imitation* arrimado; **a ~ circle of friends** un estrecho círculo de amigos; **~ combat** combate *m* cuerpo a cuerpo; **they are very ~** son muy amigos; **he was the ~st thing to a real worker among us** entre nosotros él tenía más visos de ser un obrero auténtico.
(**b**) (*compact*) *weave* compacto, tupido; *print* compacto; *formation* cerrado.
(**c**) (*strict*) *control* estricto, rígido; *confinement, watch* estricto, severo; *attention* concienzudo; *argument, questioning, study* detallado, minucioso; *translation* fiel, exacto; **to keep a ~ eye** (*or* **watch**) **on sth** vigilar algo con mucho cuidado.
(**d**) (*airless*) *atmosphere* sofocante; *weather* pesado, bochornoso; *room* mal ventilado.
(**e**) (*nearly equal*) *election, finish, result* muy reñido; *scores* casi iguales.
(**f**) (*secretive*) reservado; (*mean*) tacaño.
(**g**) **~ season** veda *f*.
(**h**) (*Ling*) *vowel* cerrado.
(**i**) (*Fin*) **~ company** (*Brit*), **~ corporation** (*US*) sociedad *f* exclusiva, compañía *f* propietaria.
3 *n* recinto *m*.
close[2] [kləuz] **1** *n* fin *m*, final *m*, conclusión *f*; **at the ~** al final; **at the ~ of day** a la caída de la tarde; **at the ~ of the year** al fin del año; **to bring sth to a ~** terminar algo, concluir algo; **to draw to a ~** tocar a su fin, estar terminando.
2 *vt* (*shut*) cerrar; (*end*) concluir, terminar; *hole etc* tapar, obstruir; *breach, gap* cerrar; *deal, list, sale* cerrar; *ceremony, debate* clausurar; *account* (*Comm*) saldar; *bank account* cerrar, finiquitar; *ranks* apretar; **'road ~d'** 'carretera cerrada', 'cerrado el paso'.
3 *vi* (*shut*) cerrarse; (*end*) concluir(se), terminar(se); **Pooleys ~d $2 up** los Pooley habían subido $2 al cierre; **the crowd ~d round him** se agolpó la multitud en torno suyo; **the clouds ~d round the peak** las nubes envolvieron la cumbre; **the waters ~d round it** lo rodearon las aguas.
◆**close down 1** *vt* cerrar (definitivamente), clausurar. **2** *vi* cerrarse (definitivamente); (*Brit Rad*) cerrar la emisión.
◆**close in 1** *vt* cercar, rodear. **2** *vi* (*person*) acercarse, ir acercándose; **the days are closing in** los días son cada vez más cortos; **night was closing in** se cerraba ya la noche; **to ~ in on sb** rodear a uno, cercar a uno.
◆**close off** *vt road etc* cerrar; *supply* cortar; *access* bloquear.
◆**close on** *vt* (**a**) (*get nearer to*) acercarse a. (**b**) (*US*) = **close in on**; *V* **close in 1.**
◆**close out** *vt* (*US*: *Fin*) liquidar.
◆**close up 1** *vt* cerrar del todo. **2** *vi* (*flower*) cerrarse del todo; (*people*) arrimarse más, ponerse más cerca unos de otros; (*ranks*) apretarse; (*wound*) cicatrizarse.
◆**close with** *vt*: **to ~ with sb** cerrar con uno.
close-cropped ['kləus'krɒpt] *adj* (cortado) al rape, rapado.
closed [kləuzd] **1** *pret and ptp of* **close. 2** *adj car, circuit etc* cerrado; *mind* de miras estrechas; *society* exclusivista, cerrado; *session, hearing* a puerta cerrada; **~ primary** (*US Pol*) *elección primaria reservada a los miembros de un partido*; **~ season** (*US*) veda *f*; **~ shop** coto *m* cerrado; *V* **book** *etc*.
closed-circuit ['kləuzd'sɜːkɪt] *adj*: **~ television** circuito *m* interno de televisión, televisión *f* por circuito cerrado.
close-down ['kləuzdaun] *n* (*Brit Rad*) cierre *m*; (*by strike etc*) cierre *m*, paralización *f*.
close-fisted ['kləus'fɪstɪd] *adj* tacaño.
close-fitting ['kləus'fɪtɪŋ] *adj* ceñido, ajustado.
close-grained [ˌkləus'greɪnd] *adj wood* tupido.
close-harmony singing [ˌkləusˌhɑːmənɪ'sɪŋɪŋ] *n* canto *m* en estrecha armonía.
close-knit ['kləusnɪt] *adj* muy unido, bien ensamblado, homogéneo.
closely ['kləuslɪ] *adv* (*exactly*) fielmente, exactamente; (*carefully*) atentamente; **~ packed** *case* atestado.
closeness ['kləusnɪs] *n* (**a**) (*nearness*) proximidad *f*; cercanía *f*; (*of connection*) intimidad *f*. (**b**) (*of translation*) fidelidad *f*. (**c**) (*of room*) mala ventilación *f*; (*of weather*) pesantez *f*, lo bochornoso. (**d**) (*of election etc*) lo muy reñido. (**e**) (*secretiveness*) reserva *f*; (*meanness*) tacañería

f.

close-run [ˌkləʊs'rʌn] *adj*: ~ **race** carrera *f* muy reñida.

close-set ['kləʊsˌset] *adj eyes* muy juntos.

closet ['klɒzɪt] **1** *n* (**a**) wáter *m*, lavabo *m*; (*US*: *cupboard*) armario *m*, (*for clothes*) ropero *m*. (**b**) **to come out of the** ~ (*US*) anunciarse públicamente, hacerse público, darse a conocer. **2** *attr* (*esp US*) secreto, tapado; ~ **gay** gay *m* de tapada. **3** *vt*: **to be ~ed with** estar encerrado con.

close-up ['kləʊsʌp] *n* primer plano *m*; ~ **lens** teleobjetivo *m*.

closing ['kləʊzɪŋ] **1** *n* cierre *m*; clausura *f*. **2** *adj*, *attr*: ~ **date** fecha *f* tope, fecha *f* límite; ~ **entry** (*in account*) asiento *m* de cierre; ~ **price** (*Fin*) cotización *f* de cierre; ~ **speech** discurso *m* de clausura; **in the** ~ **stages** en las últimas etapas; ~ **time** (*Brit*) hora *f* de cerrar; **his** ~ **words were ...** sus palabras finales eran ...

closing-down ['kləʊzɪŋ'daʊn] *n* cierre *m*; ~ **sale** venta *f* de liquidación.

closure ['kləʊʒəʳ] *n* (*close-down*) cierre *m*; (*end*) fin *m*, conclusión *f*; (*Parl*) clausura *f*.

clot [klɒt] **1** *n* (**a**) (*Culin etc*) grumo *m*, cuajarón *m*; (*Med*) embolia *f*; ~ **of blood** coágulo *m* sanguíneo; ~ **on the brain** embolia *f* cerebral.

(**b**) (*Brit*‡) papanatas* *m*; **you** ~! ¡bobo!

2 *vi* cuajarse, coagularse; **~ted cream** nata *f* espesa, nata *f* cuajada.

cloth [klɒθ] *n*, *pl* **cloths** [klɒθs, klɒðz] (*material*) paño *m*, tela *f*; (*for cleaning*) trapo *m*; (*table-*) mantel *m*; **the** ~ (*Eccl*) el clero; **a man of the** ~ un clérigo; ~ **cap** (*Brit*) gorra *f* de paño; **bound in** ~ encuadernado en tela; **to lay the** ~ poner la mesa.

clothbound ['klɒθˌbaʊnd] *adj*: ~ **book** libro *m* en tela.

clothe [kləʊð] *vt* vestir (*in*, *with* de); (*fig*) cubrir, revestir (*in*, *with* de).

cloth-eared ['klɒθɪəd] *adj* sordo como una tapia.

clothed [kləʊðd] *adj* vestido.

clothes [kləʊðz] *npl* ropa *f*, vestidos *mpl*.

clothes-basket ['kləʊðzˌbɑːskɪt] *n* canasta *f* de la ropa sucia.

clothes-brush ['kləʊðzbrʌʃ] *n* cepillo *m* de la ropa.

clothes-drier, clothes-dryer ['kləʊðzˌdraɪəʳ] *n* secadora *f*.

clothes-hanger ['kləʊðzˌhæŋəʳ] *n* percha *f*.

clothes-horse ['kləʊðzˌhɔːs] *n* (tipo *m* de) tendedero *m*; (*US**: *model*) modelo *mf*; **she's a** ~ (*US**) está obsesionada con sus trapos*.

clothes-line ['kləʊðzlaɪn] *n* (cuerda *f* de) tendedero *m*, tendedera *f* (*LAm*).

clothes-moth ['kləʊðzmɒθ] *n* polilla *f*.

clothespeg ['kləʊðzpeg] *n*, (*US*) **clothespin** ['kləʊðzpɪn] *n* pinza *f*.

clothespole ['kləʊðzpəʊl] *n*, **clothesprop** ['kləʊðzprɒp] *n* palo *m* de tendedero.

clothes-rack ['kləʊðzˌræk] *n* tendedero *m*.

clothes-rope ['kləʊðzrəʊp] *n* = **clothes-line**.

clothes-shop ['kləʊðzʃɒp] *n* tienda *f* de modas.

clothier ['kləʊðɪəʳ] *n* ropero *m*, (*tailor*) sastre *m*; **~'s** (**shop**) pañería *f*, ropería *f*, (*tailor's*) sastrería *f*.

clothing ['kləʊðɪŋ] **1** *n* ropa *f*, vestidos *mpl*; **article of** ~ prenda *f* de vestir.

2 *attr*: ~ **industry** industria *f* textil; ~ **shop** pañería *f*, ropería *f*, (*tailor's*) sastrería *f*; **the** ~ **trade** la industria de la confección.

clotting agent ['klɒtɪŋˌeɪdʒənt] *n* agente *m* coagulante.

cloud [klaʊd] **1** *n* nube *f* (*also fig*); (*storm-~*) nubarrón *m*; **to be under a** ~ estar desacreditado; **to leave under a** ~ ser despedido bajo sospecha; **to be up in the ~s** estar en las nubes; **every** ~ **has a silver lining** no hay mal que por bien no venga; **to be on** ~ **9** estar en el séptimo cielo.

2 *vt* anublar (*also fig*).

3 *vi* (*also* **to** ~ **over**) nublarse (*also fig*).

cloudberry ['klaʊdbərɪ] *n* (*US*) camemoro *m*.

cloudburst ['klaʊdbɜːst] *n* chubasco *m* (violento), aguacero *m* fuerte.

cloud-cuckoo land [ˌklaʊd'kʊkuːˌlænd] *n*, (*US*) **cloudland** ['klaʊdlænd] *n*: **to be in** ~ estar en Babia, estar en las Batuecas, vivir en la luna.

cloudiness ['klaʊdɪnɪs] *n* lo nublado, lo nuboso; lo turbio.

cloudless ['klaʊdlɪs] *adj* sin nubes, despejado.

cloudy ['klaʊdɪ] *adj* nublado, nuboso; *liquid* turbio; *glass* empañado; **partly** ~ con nubes alternas; **it is** ~ el cielo está nublado.

clout[1] [klaʊt] **1** *n* (**a**) (*blow*) tortazo *m*. (**b**) (*) influencia *f*, fuerza *f* (política *etc*). **2** *vt* dar un tortazo a.

clout[2] [klaʊt] *n*: **ne'er cast a** ~ **till May be out** hasta el cuarenta de mayo no te quites el sayo.

clove[1] [kləʊv] *n* (*spice*) clavo *m* de especia; ~ **of garlic** diente *m* de ajo.

clove[2] [kləʊv] *pret of* **cleave**[1].

clove-hitch ['kləʊvhɪtʃ] *n* ballestrinque *m*.

cloven ['kləʊvn] *ptp of* **cleave**[2]; ~ **hoof** pata *f* hendida.

cloven-footed [ˌkləʊvn'fʊtɪd] *adj animal* de pezuña hendida; *devil* con pezuña.

clover ['kləʊvəʳ] *n* trébol *m*; **to be in** ~ estar en Jauja, vivir a cuerpo de rey.

cloverleaf ['kləʊvəliːf] *n*, *pl* **cloverleaves** ['kləʊvəliːvz] hoja *f* de trébol; (*Aut*) cruce *m* en trébol.

clown [klaʊn] **1** *n* payaso *m*, clown *m*; (*boor*) patán *m*; **to make a** ~ **of o.s.** hacer el ridículo. **2** *vi* (*also* **to** ~ **about, to** ~ **around**) hacer el payaso; **stop ~ing!** ¡déjate de tonterías!

clowning ['klaʊnɪŋ] *n* payasadas *fpl*.

clownish ['klaʊnɪʃ] *adj* clownesco.

cloy [klɔɪ] *vti* empalagar.

cloying ['klɔɪɪŋ] *adj* empalagoso.

cloyingly ['klɔɪɪŋlɪ] *adv* de manera empalagosa; ~ **sweet** tan dulce que empalaga.

C.L.U. *n* (*US*) *abbr of* **Chartered Life Underwriter**.

club [klʌb] **1** *n* (**a**) (*stick*) porra *f*, cachiporra *f*, garrote *m*; (*golf~*) palo *m*.

(**b**) (*Cards*) **~s** tréboles *mpl*, (*in Spanish pack*) bastones *mpl*.

(**c**) (*association*) club *m*; (*for gaming etc*) casino *m*; ~ **car** (*US*: *Rail*) coche *m* club; ~ **class** clase *f* club; ~ **member** socio *m*, -a *f*; ~ **sandwich** *bocadillo vegetal con pollo y bacón*; ~ **soda** (*US*) agua *f* de sifón; ~ **steak** (*US*) bistec *m* culer; **to be in the** ~ (*hum*) estar en estado; **he put her in the** ~ él la dejó encinta.

2 *vt* aporrear; **to** ~ **sb to death** matar a uno a porrazos.

3 *vi*: **to** ~ **together** pagar a escote; **we ~bed together to buy it for him** entre todos se lo compramos.

clubbable* ['klʌbəbl] *adj* sociable.

club-foot ['klʌb'fʊt] *n* pie *m* zopo.

club-footed ['klʌbˌfʊtɪd] *adj* con el pie zopo.

clubhouse ['klʌbhaʊs] *n*, *pl* **clubhouses** ['klʌbˌhaʊzɪz] (*Golf etc*) chalet *m*, chalé *m*, casa *f* (de) club.

clubroom ['klʌbrʊm] *n* salón *m*, sala *f* de reuniones.

cluck [klʌk] **1** *n* (**a**) (*of hen*) cloqueo *m*. (**b**) (*with tongue*) chasquido *m* (de la lengua). **2** *vi* (**a**) cloquear. (**b**) chasquear con la lengua.

◆**cluck over** *vt*: **she ~ed over the children** con los niños estaba como la gallina con sus polluelos.

clue [kluː] **1** *n* indicio *m*; (*in a crime etc*) pista *f*; (*of crossword*) indicación *f*; **I haven't a ~*** no tengo ni idea; **he hasn't a ~*** es un pobre hombre, tiene un tremendo despiste; **can you give me a ~?** ¿me das una pista? **2** *vt* (‡) **to** ~ **sb up** (*US*: **in**) informar a uno; poner a uno al tanto; **to be all ~d up** (*US*: **in**) estar bien informado, estar al tanto.

clueless* ['kluːlɪs] *adj* (*Brit*) estúpido; despistado; desorientado.

clump[1] [klʌmp] *n* (*of trees*) grupo *m*; (*of plant*) mata *f*, macizo *m*.

clump[2] [klʌmp] **1** *n* (*noise of feet*) pisadas *fpl* fuertes. **2** *vi* pisar fuerte, ir pisando fuerte.

clumsily ['klʌmzɪlɪ] *adv* torpemente; pesadamente; toscamente, chapuceramente.

clumsiness ['klʌmzɪnɪs] *n* torpeza *f*, desmaña *f*; tosquedad *f*.

clumsy ['klʌmzɪ] *adj* torpe, desmañado; (*in movement*) desgarbado, pesado; (*inartistic*) tosco, chapucero.

clung [klʌŋ] *pret and ptp of* **cling**.

Cluniac ['kluːnɪæk] **1** *adj* cluniacense. **2** *n* cluniacense *m*.

clunk [klʌŋk] **1** *n* (**a**) (*sound*) sonido *m* metálico sordo. (**b**) (*US*‡) cabezahueca *mf*. **2** *vi* (*make sound*) sonar a hueco.

clunker‡ ['klʌŋkəʳ] *n* (*US*) cacharro* *m*.

cluster ['klʌstəʳ] **1** *n* grupo *m*; (*Bot*) racimo *m*. **2** *vi* agruparse, apiñarse; (*Bot*) arracimarse; **to** ~ **round sb** reunirse en torno de uno, apiñarse alrededor de uno.

cluster-bomb ['klʌstəˌbɒm] *n* bomba *f* de dispersión, bomba *f* de racimo.

clutch[1] [klʌtʃ] **1** *n* (**a**) (*grasp*) apretón *m*; **to make a** ~ **at sth** tratar de agarrar algo.

(**b**) **to fall into sb's ~es** caer en las garras de uno; **to get sth out of sb's ~es** hacer que uno ceda la posesión (*or* se desprenda) de algo.

(**c**) (*Aut*) embrague *m*, cloche *m* (*LAm*); (*pedal*) pedal *m* de embrague; **to disengage the** ~ desembragar; **to let in** (*or* **engage**) **the** ~ embragar.

(**d**) (*US**: *crisis*) crisis *f*.

2 *vt* tener asido en la mano; sujetar, apretar, empuñar; **he ~ed her to his heart** la estrechó contra el pecho.

3 *vi*: **to ~ at** agarrarse a, tratar de asir; **he ~ed at my hand** trató de coger mi mano; **to ~ at a hope** aferrarse a una esperanza.

clutch[2] [klʌtʃ] *n* (*of eggs*) nidada *f*.

clutter [ˈklʌtəʳ] **1** *n* desorden *m*, confusión *f*; **a ~ of shoes** un montón de zapatos. **2** *vt* llenar desordenadamente, atestar; **to be ~ed up with** estar atestado de.

CM (*US Post*) *abbr of* **North Mariana Islands**.

cm *abbr of* **centimetre(s)** centímetro(s) *m*(*pl*), cm.

Cmdr *abbr of* **Commander**.

CNAA *n* (*Brit*) *abbr of* **Council for National Academic Awards**.

CND *n abbr of* **Campaign for Nuclear Disarmament** Campaña *f* pro Desarme Nuclear.

CNN *n* (*US*) *abbr of* **Cable News Network**.

CO (**a**) *n* (*Brit*) (*V* **Commonwealth**) *abbr of* **Commonwealth Office** *Ministerio de relaciones con la Commonwealth*. (**b**) *n* (*Mil*) *abbr of* **Commanding Officer**. (**c**) *n abbr of* **conscientious objector** objetor *m* de conciencia. (**d**) (*US Post*) *abbr of* **Colorado**.

Co. (**a**) [keʊ] *n* (*Comm*) *abbr of* **company** compañía *f*, Cía, S.A.; **Mrs Thatcher and ~** (*pej*) La Thatcher y compañía. (**b**) *abbr of* **county** condado *m*.

c/o (**a**) *abbr of* **care of** en casa de, c/d; al cuidado de, a/c. (**b**) (*Comm*) *abbr of* **cash order** orden *f* de pago al contado.

co... *pref* co...

coach [kəʊtʃ] **1** *n* (**a**) (*gen*) coche *m*; (††: *stage~*) diligencia *f*; (*ceremonial*) carroza *f*; (*Rail*) coche *m*, vagón *m*; (*Aut*) autocar *m*, coche *m* de línea, camión *m* (*Méx*), autobús *m* (*LAm*).

(**b**) (*Sport*) entrenador *m*, -ora *f*, preparador *m*, -ora *f*, instructor *m*, -ora *f*; (*Golf*) maestro *m*, -a *f*; (*tutor*) profesor *m*, -ora *f* particular.

2 *vt team* entrenar, preparar; *student* enseñar, preparar; **to ~ sb in French** enseñar francés a uno; **to ~ sb in a part** ensayar un papel a uno.

coachbuilder [ˈkəʊtʃˌbɪldəʳ] *n* (*Brit Aut*) carrocero *m*.

coachbuilding [ˈkəʊtʃˈbɪldɪŋ] *n* (*Brit*) construcción *f* de carrocerías.

coach-driver [ˈkəʊtʃˌdraɪvəʳ] *n* conductor *m*, -ora *f* de autocar.

coachload [ˈkəʊtʃləʊd] *n* autocar *m* (lleno); **they came by the ~** vinieron en masa, vinieron hordas de ellos.

coachman [ˈkəʊtʃmən] *n*, *pl* **coachmen** [ˈkəʊtʃmen] cochero *m*.

coach-operator [ˈkəʊtʃˌɒpəreɪtəʳ] *n* compañía *f* de autocares.

coach station [ˈkəʊtʃˌsteɪʃən] *n* estación *f* de autocares.

coach-trip [ˈkəʊtʃtrɪp] *n* excursión *f* en autocar, viaje *m* en autocar.

coachwork [ˈkəʊtʃwɜːk] *n* (*Brit*) carrocería *f*.

coagulant [kəʊˈægjʊlənt] *n* coagulante *m*.

coagulate [kəʊˈægjʊleɪt] **1** *vt* coagular. **2** *vi* coagularse.

coagulation [kəʊˌægjʊleɪʃən] *n* coagulación *f*.

coal [kəʊl] **1** *n* carbón *m*; hulla *f*; **a ~** un pedazo de carbón; **to carry ~s to Newcastle** ir a vendimiar y llevar uvas de postre; **to haul sb over the ~s** echar una bronca a uno; **to heap ~s of fire on sb's head** avergonzar a uno devolviéndole bien por mal.

2 *attr*: **~ industry** industria *f* del carbón; **~ measures** depósitos *mpl* de carbón.

3 *vi* (*Naut*) tomar carbón.

coal-black [ˈkəʊlˈblæk] *adj* negro como el carbón.

coal-bunker [ˈkəʊlˌbʌŋkəʳ] *n* carbonera *f*.

coal-burning [ˈkəʊlˌbɜːnɪŋ] *adj* que quema carbón.

coal-cellar [ˈkəʊlˌseləʳ] *n* carbonera *f*.

coaldust [ˈkəʊldʌst] *n* polvillo *m* de carbón, cisco *m*.

coalesce [ˌkəʊəˈles] *vi* fundirse; unirse, incorporarse.

coalescence [ˌkəʊəˈlesəns] *n* fusión *f*; unión *f*, incorporación *f*.

coalface [ˈkəʊlfeɪs] *n* frente *m* de (arranque de) carbón.

coalfield [ˈkəʊlfiːld] *n* yacimiento *m* de carbón; (*large area*) cuenca *f* minera, cuenca *f* carbonífera.

coal fire [ˌkəʊlˈfaɪəʳ] *n* hogar *m* de carbón.

coal-fired [ˌkəʊlˈfaɪəd] *adj* que quema carbón.

coalgas [ˈkəʊlgæs] *n* gas *m* de hulla.

coal-hod [ˈkəʊlhɒd] *n* cubo *m* de carbón.

coalition [ˌkəʊəˈlɪʃən] *n* coalición *f*; **~ government** gobierno *m* de coalición.

coalman [ˈkəʊlmən] *n*, *pl* **coalmen** [ˈkəʊlmən], **coal merchant** [ˈkəʊlˌmɜːtʃənt] *n* carbonero *m*.

coalmine [ˈkəʊlmaɪn] *n* mina *f* de carbón.

coalminer [ˈkəʊlˌmaɪnəʳ] *n* minero *m* de carbón.

coalmining [ˈkəʊlˌmaɪnɪŋ] *n* minería *f* de carbón.

coal oil [ˈkəʊlˌɔɪl] *n* (*US*) parafina *f*.

coalpit [ˈkəʊlpɪt] *n* mina *f* de carbón, pozo *m* de carbón.

coal-scuttle [ˈkəʊlˌskʌtl] *n* cubo *m* para carbón.

coal strike [ˈkəʊlˌstraɪk] *n* huelga *f* de mineros.

coal-tar [ˈkəʊlˈtɑːʳ] *n* alquitrán *m* mineral.

coaltit [ˈkəʊltɪt] *n* carbonero *m* garrapinos.

coalyard [ˈkəʊljɑːd] *n* patio *m* del carbón.

coarse [kɔːs] *adj* (**a**) (*of texture*) basto, burdo; *sand etc* grueso; (*badly-made*) tosco, torpe; *hands* calloso, poco elegante, *skin* áspero, poco fino. (**b**) *character, laugh, remark* ordinario, grosero; *joke* verde; **~ fishing** pesca *f* de agua dulce (excluyendo salmón y trucha).

coarse-grained [ˈkɔːsgreɪnd] *adj* de grano grueso; (*fig*) tosco, basto.

coarsely [ˈkɔːslɪ] *adv* toscamente; groseramente.

coarsen [ˈkɔːsn] **1** *vt person* volver basto, poner grosero, embastecer. **2** *vi* embastecerse.

coarseness [ˈkɔːsnɪs] *n* (**a**) basteza *f*; tosquedad *f*; falta *f* de finura, falta *f* de elegancia. (**b**) ordinariez *f*, grosería *f*; lo verde.

coast [kəʊst] **1** *n* costa *f*; litoral *m*; **the ~ is clear** ya no hay peligro.

2 *vi* (*Aut etc*) llanear; (*on sledge, cycle etc*) deslizarse cuesta abajo; **to ~ along** (*Aut*) llanear; (*fig*) avanzar sin esfuerzo, (*pej*) gandulear.

coastal [ˈkəʊstəl] *adj* costero, costanero; **~ defences** defensas *fpl* costeras; **~ traffic** (*Naut*) cabotaje *m*.

coaster [ˈkəʊstəʳ] *n* (**a**) (*Naut*) buque *m* costero, barco *m* de cabotaje; (*US*) trineo *m*. (**b**) (*dripmat*) posavasos *m*.

coastguard [ˈkəʊstgɑːd] *n* guardacostas *m*; **~ station** puesto *m* de guardacostas; **~ vessel** guardacostas *m*.

coastline [ˈkəʊstlaɪn] *n* litoral *m*.

coat [kəʊt] **1** *n* (**a**) (*jacket*) chaqueta *f*, americana *f*, saco *m* (*LAm*); (*overcoat*) abrigo *m*; (*chemist's etc*) bata *f*; **~ of arms** escudo *m* (de armas); **~ of mail** cota *f* de malla; **to cut one's ~ according to one's cloth** adaptarse a las circunstancias; **to turn one's ~** chaquetear, cambiar de chaqueta.

(**b**) (*animal's*) pelo *m*, lana *f*.

(**c**) (*layer*) capa *f*; **~ of paint** mano *f* de pintura.

2 *vt* cubrir, revestir (*with* de); (*with a liquid*) bañar (*with* en); **to ~ sth with paint** dar una mano de pintura a algo.

coated [ˈkəʊtɪd] *adj tongue* saburral.

coat-hanger [ˈkəʊtˌhæŋəʳ] *n* percha *f*, colgador *m*, gancho *m* (*LAm*).

coating [ˈkəʊtɪŋ] *n* capa *f*, baño *m*; (*of paint etc*) mano *f*.

coatstand [ˈkəʊtstænd] *n* perchero *m*.

coat-tails [ˈkəʊtteɪlz] *npl* faldón *m*; **to ride on sb's ~** salir adelante gracias al favor de uno, lograr el éxito a la sombra de uno.

co-author [ˈkəʊˌɔːθəʳ] **1** *n* coautor *m*, -ora *f*. **2** *vt* (*US*) escribir conjuntamente, componer en colaboración.

coax [kəʊks] *vt* halagar, mimar; **to ~ sth out of sb** sonsacar algo a uno; **to ~ sb into doing sth** halagar a uno para que haga algo; **she likes to be ~ed** se hace rogar; **to ~ sb along** mimar a uno.

coaxial [ˌkəʊˈæksɪəl] *adj* coaxial; **~ cable** cable *m* coaxial.

coaxing [ˈkəʊksɪŋ] **1** *adj* mimoso. **2** *n* mimos *mpl*, halagos *mpl*.

coaxingly [ˈkəʊksɪŋlɪ] *adv* mimosamente.

cob [kɒb] *n* (**a**) (*swan*) cisne *m* macho. (**b**) (*horse*) jaca *f* fuerte. (**c**) (*loaf*) pan *m* redondo. (**d**) (*nut*) avellana *f*. (**e**) (*maize*) mazorca *f*.

cobalt [ˈkəʊbɒlt] *n* cobalto *m*; **~ blue** azul *m* de cobalto; (*colour*) azul *m* cobalto; **~ bomb** bomba *f* de cobalto.

cobber* [ˈkɒbəʳ] *n* (*Australia*) amigo *m*, compañero *m*; (*in direct address*) amigo.

cobble [ˈkɒbl] *vt* (**a**) (*also* **to ~ up**) *shoes* remendar. (**b**) *street* empedrar con guijarros, enguijarrar.

◆**cobble together** *vt* (*pej*) ensamblar, juntar (de modo poco satisfactorio); arreglar (provisionalmente).

cobbled [ˈkɒbld] *adj*: **~ street** calle *f* adoquinada.

cobbler [ˈkɒbləʳ] *n* zapatero *m* remendón.

cobblers [ˈkɒbləz] *npl* (*Brit*) (**a**) (*Anat***) cojones** *mpl*. (**b**) (*fig**) chorradas* *fpl*.

cobbles [ˈkɒblz] *npl*, **cobblestones** [ˈkɒblstəʊnz] *npl* guijarros *mpl*, enguijarrado *m*.

cobra [ˈkəʊbrə] *n* cobra *f*.

cobweb [ˈkɒbweb] *n* telaraña *f*; **to blow** (*or* **clear**) **the ~s away** (*fig*) despejar la mente.

cocaine [kəˈkeɪn] *n* cocaína *f*; **~ addict** cocainómano *m*, -a

f; ~ **addiction** cocainomanía *f*.
coccyx ['kɒksɪks] *n* cóccix *m*.
cochineal ['kɒtʃɪni:l] *n* cochinilla *f*.
cochlea ['kɒklɪə] *n*, *pl* **cochleae** ['kɒklɪi:] cóclea *f*, caracol *m* óseo.
cock [kɒk] **1** *n* (**a**) (*cockerel*) gallo *m*; (*other male bird*) macho *m*; ~ **of the walk** gallito *m* del lugar; **old ~!*** ¡amigo!, ¡viejo!
(**b**) (*tap*) grifo *m*, espita *f*; (*Anat***) polla** *f*.
(**c**) (*of gun*) martillo *m*; **to go off at half** ~ (*plan*) ponerse por obra sin la debida preparación.
2 *vt* (**a**) *gun* amartillar; *head* ladear; *ears* aguzar; **to ~ one's eye at** mirar con intención a, guiñar el ojo a; **to keep one's ears ~ed** mantenerse alerta, aguzar las orejas.
(**b**) **to ~ sth up‡** joder algo‡.
cockade [kɒ'keɪd] *n* escarapela *f*.
cock-a-doodle-doo ['kɒkədu:dl'du:] *interj* ¡quiquiriquí!
cock-a-hoop ['kɒkə'hu:p] *adj*: **to be** ~ estar jubiloso, estar más contento que unas pascuas.
cockamamie* [,kɒkə'meɪmɪ] *adj* (*US*) pijotero*.
cock-and-bull ['kɒkən'bʊl] *adj*: ~ **story** cuento *m*, camelo *m*, cuento *m* chino.
cockatoo [,kɒkə'tu:] *n* cacatúa *f*.
cockchafer ['kɒk,tʃeɪfəʳ] *n* abejorro *m*.
cockcrow ['kɒkkrəʊ] *n* canto *m* del gallo; **at** ~ al amanecer.
cocked [kɒkt] *adj*: ~ **hat** sombrero *m* de tres picos; **to knock sth into a ~ hat** ser netamente superior a algo, dar quince y raya a algo.
cocker ['kɒkəʳ] *n* (*also* ~ **spaniel**) cocker *m*.
cockerel ['kɒkrəl] *n* gallito *m*, gallo *m* joven.
cock-eyed* ['kɒkaɪd] *adj* (**a**) (*squinting*) bizco. (**b**) (*fig*) incomprensible; estúpido, estrafalario.
cockfight ['kɒkfaɪt] *n*, **cockfighting** ['kɒk,faɪtɪŋ] *n* pelea *f* de gallos.
cockiness* ['kɒkɪnɪs] *n* engreimiento *m*, presunción *f*.
cockle ['kɒkl] *n* (*Zool*) berberecho *m*; **to warm the ~s of the heart** dar grandísimo contento a uno.
cockleshell ['kɒklʃel] *n* concha *f* de berberecho; (*boat*) cascarón *m* de nuez.
cockney ['kɒknɪ] *n habitante de ciertos barrios populares de Londres; dialecto de estos barrios*; (*loosely*) londinense *mf* (nativo, de clase popular).
cockpit ['kɒkpɪt] *n* (*Aer*) cabina *f* (del piloto); carlinga *f*; (*for cockfight*) cancha *f*, reñidero *m* de gallos, palenque *m* (*LAm*); (*fig*) ruedo *m*, campo *m* de batalla; **the ~ of Europe** Bélgica *f* (*escenario de muchos combates*).
cockroach ['kɒkrəʊtʃ] *n* cucaracha *f*.
cockscomb ['kɒkskəʊm] *n* cresta *f* de gallo.
cock sparrow [,kɒk'spærəʊ] *n* gorrión *m* macho.
cocksure ['kɒk'ʃʊəʳ] *adj* presumido, presuntuoso.
cocktail ['kɒkteɪl] *n* combinado *m*, copetín *m*, cóctel *m* (*also fig*); ~ **bar** bar *m*; ~ **dress** vestido *m* de cóctel; ~ **lounge** salón *m* de cóctel; ~ **onion** cebolla *f* perla; ~ **sausage** salchichita *f* de aperitivo.
cocktail-cabinet ['kɒkteɪl,kæbɪnɪt] *n* mueble-bar *m*.
cocktail-party ['kɒkteɪl,pɑ:tɪ] *n* cóctel *m*.
cocktail-shaker ['kɒkteɪl,ʃeɪkəʳ] *n* coctelera *f*.
cock-teaser** [kɒk,ti:zəʳ] *n* calientapollas** *f*.
cock-up‡ ['kɒkʌp] *n* lío* *m*, embrollo *m*; **there's been a ~ over my passport** me han armado un follón con el pasaporte*; **to make a ~ of sth** joder algo‡.
cocky* ['kɒkɪ] *adj* engreído, hinchado.
cocoa ['kəʊkəʊ] *n* cacao *m*; (*drink*) chocolate *m*; ~ **bean** grano *m* de cacao.
coconut ['kəʊkənʌt] *n* coco *m*; ~ **matting** estera *f* de hojas de cocotero; ~ **oil** aceite *m* de coco; ~ **palm**, ~ **tree** cocotero *m*; ~ **shy** tiro *m* al coco.
cocoon [kə'ku:n] **1** *n* capullo *m*. **2** *vt* envolver.
COD *abbr of* **cash on delivery** (*Brit*), **collect on delivery** (*US*) contra reembolso.
cod [kɒd] *n* bacalao *m*.
coda ['kəʊdə] *n* coda *f*.
coddle ['kɒdl] *vt* mimar, hacer mimos a.
code [kəʊd] **1** *n* (**a**) (*Jur etc*) código *m*; (*Telec*) prefijo *m*, código *m*; (*Comput*) código *m*; ~ **of practice** código *m* de práctica. (**b**) (*cypher*) clave *f*, cifra *f*; (*of Morse etc*) alfabeto *m*; **in** ~ en cifra. **2** *vt* cifrar, poner en cifra, poner en clave.
codebook ['kəʊdbʊk] *n* libro *n* de códigos.
coded ['kəʊdɪd] *adj* en cifra, en clave (*also fig*).
code-dating ['kəʊd'deɪtɪŋ] *n* fechación *f* en código.
codeine ['kəʊdi:n] *n* codeína *f*.
code-letter ['kəʊd,letəʳ] *n* letra *f* de código.
code-name ['kəʊdneɪm] **1** *n* nombre *m* en clave. **2** *vt* dar nombre en clave a; **the operation was ~d Clavileño** la operación tuvo el nombre en clave de Clavileño.
code-number ['kəʊd,nʌmbəʳ] *n* (*Tax*) índice *m* de desgravación fiscal.
codeword ['kəʊdwɜ:d] *n* palabra *f* en clave.
codex ['kəʊdeks] *n*, *pl* **codices** ['kɒdɪsi:z] códice *m*.
codfish ['kɒdfɪʃ] *n*, *pl invar* bacalao *m*.
codger* ['kɒdʒəʳ] *n*: **old** ~ sujeto *m*, vejete *m*.
codices ['kɒdɪ,si:z] *npl of* **codex**.
codicil ['kɒdɪsɪl] *n* codicilo *m*.
codify ['kəʊdɪfaɪ] *vt* codificar.
coding ['kəʊdɪŋ] *n* (*of telegram, message*) codificación *f*; (*Comput*) codificación *f*; ~ **sheet** hoja *f* de programación.
cod-liver oil ['kɒdlɪvər'ɒɪl] *n* aceite *m* de hígado de bacalao.
codpiece ['kɒdpi:s] *n* (*Hist*) bragueta *f*.
co-driver ['kəʊdraɪvəʳ] *n* copiloto *mf*.
codswallop‡ ['kɒdzwɒləp] *n* (*Brit*) chorradas‡ *fpl*.
coed* ['kəʊ'ed] **1** *adj* mixto. **2** *n* alumna *f* de un colegio mixto. **3** *adj abbr of* **coeducational**.
co-edition ['kəʊɪ,dɪʃən] *n* edición *f* conjunta.
coeducation ['kəʊ,edjʊ'keɪʃən] *n* coeducación *f*, educación *f* mixta.
coeducational ['kəʊ,edjʊ'keɪʃənl] *adj* mixto.
coefficient [,kəʊɪ'fɪʃənt] *n* coeficiente *m*.
coelacanth ['si:ləkænθ] *n* celacanto *m*.
coerce [kəʊ'ɜ:s] *vt* forzar, obligar (*into doing sth* a hacer algo), coaccionar.
coercion [kəʊ'ɜ:ʃən] *n* coacción *f*, coerción *f*, compulsión *f*; **under** ~ obligado a ello, a la fuerza.
coercive [kəʊ'ɜ:sɪv] *adj* coactivo, coercitivo.
coeval [kəʊ'i:vəl] **1** *adj* coetáneo (*with de*), contemporáneo (*with* de), coevo. **2** *n* coetáneo *m*, -a *f*, contemporáneo *m*, -a *f*.
coexist ['kəʊɪg'zɪst] *vi* coexistir (*with* con), convivir (*with* con).
coexistence ['kəʊɪg'zɪstəns] *n* coexistencia *f*, convivencia *f*.
coexistent ['kəʊɪg'zɪstənt] *adj* coexistente.
co-extensive [,kəʊɪk'stensɪv] *adj* de la misma extensión (*with* que).
C of C *n abbr of* **Chamber of Commerce**.
C of E *abbr n of* **Church of England** Iglesia *f* Anglicana; **to be ~*** ser anglicano.
coffee ['kɒfɪ] *n* café *m*; **white** ~ (*Brit*), ~ **with milk** (*or* **cream**) (*US*) café *m* con leche.
coffee-bar ['kɒfɪbɑ:ʳ] *n* (*Brit*) cafetería *f*, café *m*.
coffee-bean ['kɒfɪbi:n] *n* grano *m* de café.
coffee-break ['kɒfɪ,breɪk] *n* tiempo *m* del bocadillo.
coffee-cake ['kɒfɪ,keɪk] *n* (*Brit*) pastel *m* de café.
coffee-coloured, (*US*) **coffee-colored** ['kɒfɪ,kʌləd] *adj* (de) color café.
coffee-cup ['kɒfɪkʌp] *n* taza *f* para café.
coffee-filter ['kɒfɪ,fɪltəʳ] *n* filtro *m* de café.
coffee-grounds ['kɒfɪgraʊndz] *npl* poso *m* de café.
coffee-house ['kɒfɪhaʊs] *n*, *pl* **coffee-houses** ['kɒfɪ,haʊzɪz] café *m*.
coffee-machine ['kɒfɪmə,ʃi:n] *n* (*small*) máquina *f* de café, cafetera *f*; (*vending machine*) máquina *f* expendedora de café.
coffee-maker ['kɒfɪ,meɪkəʳ] *n* máquina *f* de café, cafetera *f*.
coffee-mill ['kɒfɪmɪl] *n* molinillo *m* de café.
coffee morning ['kɒfɪ,mɔ:nɪŋ] *n* tertulia *f* formada para tomar el café por la mañana.
coffee percolator ['kɒfɪ,pɜ:kəleɪtəʳ] *n* = **coffee-maker**.
coffee plantation ['kɒfɪplɑ:n,teɪʃən] *n* cafetal *m*.
coffeepot ['kɒfɪpɒt] *n* cafetera *f*.
coffee-service ['kɒfɪ,sɜ:vɪs] *n*, **coffee-set** ['kɒfɪ,set] *n* servicio *m* de café.
coffee shop ['kɒfɪʃɒp] *n* (*shop*) tienda *f* especializada en variedades de café; (*café*) café *m*.
coffee-spoon ['kɒfɪspu:n] *n* cucharilla *f* de café.
coffee-table ['kɒfɪ,teɪbl] *n* mesita *f* baja; ~ **book** libro *m* de gran formato (bello e impresionante).
coffee-whitener ['kɒfɪ,waɪtnəʳ] *n* leche *f* en polvo.
coffer ['kɒfəʳ] *n* cofre *m*, arca *f*; (**a**) **~s** (*fig*) tesoro *m*, fondos *mpl*; reservas *fpl*. (**b**) (*Archit*) artesón *m*.
cofferdam ['kɒfədæm] *n* ataguía *f*.
coffin ['kɒfɪn] *n* ataúd *m*, cajón *m* (*SC*).
C of I *n abbr of* **Church of Ireland**.
co-founder ['kəʊ'faʊndəʳ] *n* cofundador *m*, -ora *f*.
C of S *n abbr of* **Church of Scotland**.
cog [kɒg] *n* diente *m*; (*wheel*) rueda *f* dentada; **to be just a ~ in a machine** ser solamente una pieza de un mecanismo.
cogency ['kəʊdʒənsɪ] *n* fuerza *f*, lógica *f*, convicción *f*.
cogent ['kəʊdʒənt] *adj* fuerte, lógico, convincente, sólido.

cogently ['kəʊdʒəntlɪ] *adv* lógicamente, de modo convincente, con argumentos sólidos.
cogitate ['kɒdʒɪteɪt] *vti* meditar, reflexionar.
cogitation [ˌkɒdʒɪ'teɪʃən] *n* meditación *f*, reflexión *f*.
cognac ['kɒnjæk] *n* coñac *m*.
cognate ['kɒgneɪt] **1** *adj* cognado (*with* con); afín. **2** *n* cognado *m*.
cognition [kɒg'nɪʃən] *n* cognición *f*.
cognitive ['kɒgnɪtɪv] *adj* cognitivo, cognoscitivo; ~ **modelling** modelización *f* cognoscitiva.
cognizance ['kɒgnɪzəns] *n* conocimiento *m*; **to be within one's ~** ser de la competencia de uno; **to take ~ of** tener en cuenta.
cognizant ['kɒgnɪzənt] *adj*: **to be ~ of** saber, estar enterado de.
cognoscenti [ˌkɒnəʊ'ʃentɪ] *npl* expertos *mpl*, peritos *mpl*.
cogwheel ['kɒgwiːl] *n* rueda *f* dentada.
cohabit [kəʊ'hæbɪt] *vi* cohabitar.
cohabitation [ˌkəʊhæbɪ'teɪʃən] *n* cohabitación *f*.
cohere [kəʊ'hɪəʳ] *vi* adherirse, pegarse; (*ideas etc*) formar un conjunto sólido, ser consecuentes.
coherence [kəʊ'hɪərəns] *n* coherencia *f*.
coherent [kəʊ'hɪərənt] *adj* coherente; lógico, comprensible.
coherently [kəʊhɪərəntlɪ] *adv* coherentemente; lógicamente, comprensiblemente.
cohesion [kəʊ'hiːʒən] *n* cohesión *f*.
cohesive [kəʊ'hiːsɪv] *adj* cohesivo; unido.
cohesiveness [kəʊ'hiːsɪvnɪs] *n* cohesión *f*.
cohort ['kəʊhɔːt] *n* cohorte *f*.
COHSE ['kəʊzɪ] *n* (*Brit*) *abbr of* **Confederation of Health Service Employees** *confederación de trabajadores de la seguridad social*.
COI *n* (*Brit*) *abbr of* **Central Office of Information.**
coif [kɔɪf] *n* cofia *f*.
coiffeur [kwɒ'fɜːʳ] *n* peluquero *m*.
coiffure [kwɒ'fjʊəʳ] *n* peinado *m*.
coil [kɔɪl] **1** *n* rollo *m*; (*of rope etc*) aduja *f*; (*of snake*) anillo *m*; (*of smoke*) espiral *f*; (*of still etc*) serpentín *m*; (*Elec*) bobina *f*, carrete *m*; (*contraceptive*) espiral *f* (intrauterina).
2 *vt* arrollar, enrollar; *rope* (*Naut*) adujar.
3 *vi* arrollarse, enrollarse.
◆**coil up 1** *vt* arrollar, enrollar.
2 *vi* (*snake*) enroscarse; (*smoke*) subir en espiral.
coiled [kɔɪld] *adj* arrollado, enrollado.
coin [kɔɪn] **1** *n* moneda *f*; **to pay sb back in his own ~** pagar a uno en (*or* con) la misma moneda; **to toss a ~** echar a cara o cruz.
2 *vt money* acuñar; *word etc* acuñar, inventar, idear; **he must be ~ing money** debe de estar acuñando dinero, el negocio ha de ser un río de oro para él.
coinage ['kɔɪnɪdʒ] *n* (*system*) moneda *f*, sistema *m* monetario; (*act*) acuñación *f*; (*of word etc*) invención *f*.
coinbox ['kɔɪnbɒks] *n* (*Telec*) depósito *m* de monedas.
coincide [ˌkəʊɪn'saɪd] *vi* coincidir (*with* con); (*agree*) estar de acuerdo (*with* con).
coincidence [kəʊ'ɪnsɪdəns] *n* coincidencia *f*; (*chance*) casualidad *f*; **what a ~!** ¡qué casualidad!
coincidental [kəʊˌɪnsɪ'dentl] *adj* coincidente; (*by chance*) fortuito, casual.
coincidentally [ˌkəʊɪnsɪ'dentəlɪ] *adv* por casualidad, casualmente; **not ~, we** ... no es una casualidad que nosotros ... + *subj*.
coin-op* ['kɔɪnˌɒp] *n abbr of* **coin-operated laundry** lavandería *f* que funciona con monedas.
coin-operated ['kɔɪn'ɒpəreɪtɪd] *adj* que funciona con monedas.
coinsurance [ˌkəʊɪn'ʃʊərəns] *n* coaseguro *m*, seguro *m* copartícipe.
coinsurer [ˌkəʊɪn'ʃʊərəʳ] *n* coasegurador *m*.
coitus ['kɔɪtəs] *n* coito *m*.
Coke* [kəʊk] ® *n* Coca-Cola ® *f*, cola* *f*, colas* *fpl*.
coke¹ [kəʊk] *n* coque *m*.
coke²‡ ['kəʊk] *n* (*Drugs*) coca‡ *f*.
Col. (**a**) *abbr of* **Colonel** coronel *m*. (**b**) (*US*) *abbr of* **Colorado.**
col. *abbr of* **column** columna *f*, col.
COLA *n* (*US*) *abbr of* **cost-of-living adjustment** reajuste *m* salarial de acuerdo con el costo de la vida.
colander ['kʌləndəʳ] *n* colador *m*, escurridor *m*.
cold [kəʊld] **1** *adj* (**a**) frío (*also fig*); **as ~ as charity** frío como un mármol; **my feet are ~ as ice** tengo los pies helados; **to be ~** (*person*) tener frío, (*thing*) estar frío, (*weather*) hacer frío; **to be very ~** (*person*) tener mucho frío, (*thing*) estar muy frío, (*weather*) hacer mucho frío; **to get ~** (*thing*) enfriarse, (*weather*) empezar a hacer frío; **he's got them ~*** (*audience*) los tiene en el bolsillo; **he's got three tricks ~*** tiene tres bazas segurísimas; **to knock sb (out) ~*** dejar a uno sin conocimiento; **it leaves me ~** no me produce emoción alguna, me deja frío. (**b**) **~ cream** crema *f*; **~ cuts** (*US*) fiambres *mpl*; **~ duck** (*US**) vino *m* gaseado barato; **~ frame** vivero *m* de plantas; **~ front** frente *m* frío; **~ room = ~ store**; **~ selling** venta *f* en frío, venta *f* directa; **~ sore** herpes *m* labial, pupas* *fpl*; **~ start, ~ starting** (*US*) arranque *m* en frío; **~ storage** almacenaje *m* frigorífico; **to put a plan into ~ storage** archivar un proyecto, dejar un proyecto en suspenso; **~ store** cámara *f* frigorífica; **he broke into a ~ sweat** le entró un sudor frío; **~ turkey** (*Drugs*‡) mono‡ *m*, síndrome *m* de abstinencia; **~ war** guerra *f* fría; **~ wave** ola *f* de frío.
2 *n* (**a**) frío *m*; **to catch ~** coger frío; **to leave sb out in the ~** dejar a uno al margen, dejar a uno colgado.
(**b**) (*Med, also* **common ~**) resfriado *m*, catarro *m*; **to catch a ~** resfriarse, acatarrarse; **to have a ~** estar resfriado, estar acatarrado, estar constipado.
3 *adv* (*US**) (*completely*) totalmente; (*unexpectedly*) en frío; **to do sth ~** hacer algo en frío; **to know sth ~** conocer algo a fondo (*or* como la palma de la mano).
cold-blooded ['kəʊld'blʌdɪd] *adj* (*Zool*) de sangre fría, poiquilotérmico; (*fig*) insensible; (*cruel*) desalmado.
cold-bloodedly ['kəʊld'blʌdɪdlɪ] *adv* a sangre fría.
cold-hearted ['kəʊld'hɑːtɪd] *adj* insensible, cruel.
coldly ['kəʊldlɪ] *adv* fríamente (*also fig*).
coldness ['kəʊldnɪs] *n* (*lit, fig*) frialdad *f*.
cold-shoulder ['kəʊld'ʃəʊldəʳ] *vt* dar (*or* volver) la espalda a.
coleslaw ['kəʊlslɔː] *n* ensalada *f* de col.
coley ['kəʊlɪ] *n* abadejo *m*.
colic ['kɒlɪk] *n* cólico *m*.
Coliseum [ˌkɒlɪ'siːəm] *n* Coliseo *m*.
colitis [kɒ'laɪtɪs] *n* colitis *f*.
collaborate [kə'læbəreɪt] *vi* colaborar (*in, on* en; *with* con).
collaboration [kəˌlæbə'reɪʃən] *n* colaboración *f*; (*Pol: pej*) colaboracionismo *m*; **in ~** en colaboración (*with* con).
collaborative [kə'læbərətɪv] *adj*: **by a ~ effort** por un esfuerzo común, ayudándose unos a otros; **it's a ~ work** es un trabajo de colaboración.
collaborator [kə'læbəreɪtəʳ] *n* colaborador *m*, -ora *f*; (*Pol: pej*) colaboracionista *mf*.
collage [kɒ'lɑːʒ] *n* collage *m*.
collagen ['kɒlədʒən] *n* colágeno *m*.
collapse [kə'læps] **1** *n* (*Med*) colapso *m*; (*of building*) hundimiento *m*, derrumbamiento *m*, desplome *m*; (*of roadway etc*) socavón *m*; (*of plans*) fracaso *m*; (*of prices*) desplome *m*.
2 *vi* (**a**) (*Med*) sufrir un colapso; **to ~ with laughter** (*fig*) morirse de risa.
(**b**) (*building*) hundirse, derrumbarse, desplomarse; (*fig*) fracasar; **hood that ~s** capota *f* plegable; **the deal ~d** el negocio fracasó; **the company ~d** la compañía se vino abajo, la compañía se hundió.
collapsible [kə'læpsəbl] *adj* plegable; *steering-wheel* articulado.
collar ['kɒləʳ] **1** *n* cuello *m*; (*of animal, Tech*) collar *m*; (*Med*) collarín *m*; **~ size** medida *f* del cuello; **to get hot under the ~** sulfurarse.
2 *vt* prender por el cuello; (*) apropiarse, pisar.
collarbone ['kɒləbəʊn] *n* clavícula *f*.
collar-stud ['kɒləstʌd], (*US*) **collar-button** ['kɒləbʌtən] *n* botón *m* de camisa.
collate [kɒ'leɪt] *vt* cotejar.
collateral [kɒ'lætərəl] **1** *adj* colateral; **~ loan** préstamo *m* colateral, préstamo *m* pignoraticio; **~ security** garantía *f* colateral. **2** *n* (**a**) (*Fin*) seguridad *f* subsidiaria, garantía *f* subsidiaria. (**b**) (*person*) colateral *mf*.
collation [kə'leɪʃən] *n* (*meal*) colación *f*; (*of texts*) cotejo *m*.
colleague ['kɒliːg] *n* colega *m*.
collect¹ ['kɒlekt] *n* (*Eccl*) colecta *f*.
collect² [kə'lekt] **1** *vt* reunir, acumular; *people* reunir; *stamps etc* coleccionar; *fares, wages* cobrar; *taxes* recaudar; *money for charity* recaudar, colectar; (*pick up, also Brit Post*) recoger; *dust, water etc* retener; **I'll go and ~ the mail** voy por el correo; **I'll ~ you at 8** vengo a recogerte (*or* buscarte: *esp LAm*) a las 8; **I must ~ my bags from the station** tengo que recoger mi equipaje en la estación; **~ on delivery** (*US*) entrega *f* contra reembolso.
2 *vi* reunirse, acumularse; (*people*) reunirse, con-

gregarse; (*be a collector*) ser coleccionista, coleccionar; (*water*) estancarse; (*dust*) acumularse; **when do we ~?** ¿cuándo cobramos?; **to ~ for charity** hacer una colecta con fines benéficos.

3 *vr*: **to ~ o.s.** reponerse, sosegarse.

4 *adv*: **to call ~** (*US*) llamar a cobro revertido.

◆**collect up** *vt* recoger, volver a tomar.

collectable [kəˈlektəbl] *n* coleccionable *m*.

collect call [kəˈlektkɔːl] *n* (*US*) llamada *f* a cobro revertido.

collected [kəˈlektɪd] **1** *pret and ptp of* **collect**[2]. **2** *adj* (*cool*) sosegado, tranquilo; **~ works** obras *fpl* completas.

collectible [kəˈlektəbl] *n* coleccionable *m*.

collecting [kəˈlektɪŋ] *n* coleccionismo *m*, el coleccionar.

collecting-tin [kəˈlektɪŋˌtɪn] *n* bote *m* de cuestación, lata *f* petitoria.

collection [kəˈlekʃən] *n* acumulación *f*, montón *m*; (*of people*) grupo *m*; (*of pictures, stamps etc*) colección *f*; (*of fares, wages*) cobro *m*; (*of taxes*) recaudación *f*; (*Eccl*) colecta *f*; (*for charity*) colecta *f*, cuestación *f*; (*Brit Post*) recogida *f*; **to make a ~ for** hacer una colecta a beneficio de; **~ charges** (*Fin, Comm*) gastos *mpl* de cobro; **~ plate** platillo *m*.

collective [kəˈlektɪv] **1** *adj* colectivo; **~ bargaining** trato *m* colectivo, negociaciones *fpl* colectivas; **~ farm** granja *f* colectiva; **~ noun** nombre *m* colectivo; **~ ownership** propiedad *f* colectiva; **~ security** seguridad *f* colectiva; **~ unconscious** inconsciente *m* colectivo. **2** *n* colectivo *m*.

collectively [kəˈlektɪvlɪ] *adv* colectivamente.

collectivism [kəˈlektɪvɪzə] *n* colectivismo *m*.

collectivize [kəˈlektɪvaɪz] *vt* colectivizar.

collector [kəˈlektə^{r}] *n* (*of folktales etc*) recolector *m*, -ora *f*; (*of stamps etc*) coleccionista *mf*; (*tax-~*) recaudador *m*, -ora *f*; **it's a real ~'s item** es una verdadera pieza de colección (*or* para coleccionista).

colleen [ˈkɒliːn] *n* (*Ir*) muchacha *f*.

college [ˈkɒlɪdʒ] *n* colegio *m*; (*eg of Oxford*) colegio *m* mayor; (*eg of art*) escuela *f*; **C~ of Advanced Technology** (*Brit*) ≈ politécnico *m*; **C~ of Education** Escuela *f* Normal (Superior); **C~ of Further Education** ≈ Escuela *f* de Formación Profesional; **to go to ~** seguir estudios superiores.

collegiate [kəˈliːdʒɪɪt] *adj* (**a**) (*Eccl*) colegial, colegiado; **~ church** iglesia *f* colegial. (**b**) (*Univ*) que tiene colegios, organizado a base de colegios.

collide [kəˈlaɪd] *vi* chocar (*with* con; *also fig*), colisionar (*with* con).

collie [ˈkɒlɪ] *n* perro *m* pastor escocés, collie *m*, coli *m*.

collier [ˈkɒlɪə^{r}] *n* minero *m* (de carbón); (*ship*) barco *m* carbonero.

colliery [ˈkɒlɪərɪ] *n* mina *f* de carbón.

collision [kəˈlɪʒən] *n* choque *m* (*also fig*), colisión *f*; **to be on a ~ course** ir rumbo al enfrentamiento; **to come into ~ with** chocar con.

collocate [ˈkɒləˌkeɪt] *vi*: **to ~ with** colocarse con.

collocation [ˌkɒləˈkeɪʃən] *n* colocación *f* (*also Ling*).

colloquial [kəˈləʊkwɪəl] *adj* familiar, coloquial.

colloquialism [kəˈləʊkwɪəlɪzəm] *n* palabra *f* (*or* expresión *f*) familiar; (*style*) estilo *m* familiar.

colloquially [kəˈləʊkwɪəlɪ] *adv* coloquialmente.

colloquium [kəˈləʊkwɪəm] *n* coloquio *m*.

colloquy [ˈkɒləkwɪ] *n* coloquio *m*.

collude [kəˈluːd] *vi* confabularse (*with* con).

collusion [kəˈluːʒən] *n* confabulación *f*; connivencia *f*; (*Jur*) colusión *f*; **to be in ~ with** estar de connivencia con, confabularse con.

collywobbles* [ˈkɒlɪˌwɒblz] *npl* (*Anat*) ruido *m* de tripas; (*fig*) nerviosismo *m*, ataque *m* de nervios; **she had the ~** le sonaban las tripas.

Colo. (*US*) *abbr of* **Colorado**.

Cologne [kəˈləʊn] *n* Colonia *f*.

Colombia [kəˈlɒmbɪə] *n* Colombia *f*.

Colombian [kəˈlɒmbɪən] **1** *adj* colombiano. **2** *n* colombiano *m*, -a *f*.

colon[1] [ˈkəʊlən] *n* (*Anat*) colon *m*.

colon[2] [ˈkəʊlən] *n* (*Typ*) dos puntos *mpl*.

colonel [ˈkɜːnl] *n* coronel *m*.

colonial [kəˈləʊnɪəl] **1** *adj* colonial. **2** *n* colono *m*.

colonialism [kəˈləʊnɪəlɪzəm] *n* colonialismo *m*.

colonialist [kəˈləʊnɪəlɪst] *n* colonialista *mf*.

colonist [ˈkɒlənɪst] *n* colonizador *m*, -ora *f*, colono *m*.

colonization [ˌkɒlənaɪˈzeɪʃən] *n* colonización *f*.

colonize [ˈkɒlənaɪz] *vt* colonizar.

colonnade [ˌkɒləˈneɪd] *n* columnata *f*, galería *f*.

colony [ˈkɒlənɪ] *n* colonia *f*.

colophon [ˈkɒləfən] *n* colofón *m*, pie *m* de imprenta.

color [ˈkʌlə^{r}] *etc* (*US*) = **colour** *etc*; **~ line** barrera *f* de color.

Colorado [ˌkɒləˈrɑːdəʊ] *n*: **~ beetle** escarabajo *m* de la patata, dorífora *f*.

colorant [ˈkʌlərənt] *n* colorante *m*.

coloration [ˌkʌləˈreɪʃən] *n* colorido *m*, colores *mpl*, coloración *f*.

coloratura [ˌkɒlərəˈtʊərə] *n* (*passage*) coloratura *f*; (*singer*) soprano *f* de coloratura.

colorcast [ˈkʌləkɑːst] (*US*) **1** *n* programa *m* de TV en color. **2** *vt* transmitir en color.

colossal [kəˈlɒsl] *adj* colosal.

colossally [kəˈlɒsəlɪ] *adv* colosalmente, inmensamente.

colossus [kəˈlɒsəs] *n* coloso *m*.

colostomy [kəˈlɒstəmɪ] *n* colostomía *f*.

colostrum [kəˈlɒstrəm] *n* colostro *m*, calostro *m*.

colour, (*US*) **color** [ˈkʌlə^{r}] **1** *n* (**a**) color *m*; (**~s**, *combination*) colorido *m*; **~ code** código *m* de colores; **~ film** película *f* en colores; **~ photograph** fotografía *f* en color; **~ photography** fotografía *f* en colores; **~ problem** problema *m* racial; **~ slide** diapositiva *f* en color; **~ supplement** (*Brit*) suplemento *m* en color; **~ television (set)** televisor *m* en color; **~ TV** TV *f* en colores; (*US*) **people of ~** personas *fpl* de color; **it's a blue ~, it's blue in ~** es de color azul; **what ~ is it?** ¿de qué color es?; **in full ~** a todo color; **to be off ~** estar indispuesto; **to change ~** mudar de color; **to lend ~ to a story** hacer que un cuento parezca más verosímil; **let's see the ~ of your money!** ¡a ver si te retratas!, ¡a ver el dinero!; **to take all the ~ out of sth** quitar todo el colorido de algo.

(**b**) **~s** (*flag*) bandera *f*; **~ sergeant** (*Brit*) sargento *m* abanderado; **to call to the ~s** llamar a filas, llamar al servicio militar; **to come out with flying ~s** salir airoso, triunfar; **to nail one's ~s to the mast** proclamar su lealtad; mantenerse firme; **to sail under false ~s** encubrir su verdadera lealtad; **to show o.s. in one's true ~s** quitarse la máscara.

2 *vt* (*also* **to ~ in**) color(e)ar; (*paint*) pintar; (*dye*) teñir (*red* de rojo); *drawing* colorear; adornar, embellecer.

3 *vi* (*also* **to ~ up**) sonrojarse.

colour-bar [ˈkʌləbɑː^{r}] *n* (*Brit*) barrera *f* racial.

colour-blind, (*US*) **color-blind** [ˈkʌləblaɪnd] *adj* daltoniano.

colour-blindness, (*US*) **color-blindness** [ˈkʌləˌblaɪndnɪs] *n* daltonismo *m*.

colour-coded, (*US*) **color-coded** [ˈkʌləˈkəʊdɪd] *adj* con código de colores.

coloured, (*US*) **colored** [ˈkʌləd] **1** *pret and ptp of* **colour**. **2** *adj person* († *in US*), *pencil* de color; **a highly ~ tale** un cuento de los más pintorescos. **3** *n*: **~s** (*US, Brit*) personas *fpl* de color; (*in South Africa*) *personas de padres racialmente mixtos*.

-coloured, (*US*) **-colored** [ˌkʌləd] *adj*: *eg* **rust~** de color de orín, color orín.

colourfast, (*US*) **colorfast** [ˈkʌləfɑːst] *adj* no desteñible.

colour-filter, (*US*) **color-filter** [ˈkʌləˈfɪltə^{r}] *n* (*Phot*) filtro *m* de color.

colourful, (*US*) **colorful** [ˈkʌləfəl] *adj* lleno de color; *scene* vivo, animado; *person etc* pintoresco.

colouring, (*US*) **coloring** [ˈkʌlərɪŋ] *n* colorido *m*; (*substance*) colorante *m*; (*of complexion*) colores *mpl*; tez *f*; **~ (-in) book** libro *m* para colorear; **high ~** sonrojamiento *m*; **'no artificial ~'** 'sin colores artificiales'.

colourless, (*US*) **colorless** [ˈkʌləlɪs] *adj* sin color, incoloro; (*fig*) soso, insípido.

colour-scheme, (*US*) **color-scheme** [ˈkʌləˌskiːm] *n* combinación *f* de colores.

colourway [ˈkʌləweɪ] *n* (*Brit*) combinación *f* de colores.

colt [kəʊlt] *n* potro *m*, potranco *m* (*LAm*).

coltish [ˈkɒltɪʃ] *adj* juguetón, retozón.

coltsfoot [ˈkəʊltsfʊt] *n* uña *f* de caballo, fárfara *f*.

Columbia [kəˈlʌmbɪə] *n*: **(District of) ~** (*US*) Distrito *m* de Columbia; *V* **British**.

Columbine [ˈkɒləmbaɪn] *nf* Columbina.

columbine [ˈkɒləmbaɪn] *n* aguileña *f*.

Columbus [kəˈlʌmbəs] *nm* Colón; **~ Day** Día *m* de la Raza.

column [ˈkɒləm] *n* (*all senses*) columna *f*; **they gave the news only 2 ~ inches** dieron sólo 2 pulgadas de columna a la noticia; **to dodge the ~*** ponerse al socaire.

columnist [ˈkɒləmnɪst] *n* columnista *mf*, articulista *mf*.

colza [ˈkɒlzə] *n* colza *f*.

coma [ˈkəʊmə] *n* coma *m*; **to be in a ~** estar en estado de coma.

comatose [ˈkəʊmətəʊs] *adj* comatoso.

comb [kəʊm] **1** *n* (**a**) peine *m*; (*ornamental*) peineta *f*; (*for* *horse*) almohaza *f*; (*Tech*) carda; **to give one's hair a ~** peinarse (el pelo). (**b**) (*of fowl*) cresta *f*. (**c**) (*honeycomb*) panal *m*.

2 *vt* peinar; *wool* cardar; *countryside etc* peinar, registrar con minuciosidad (*for* en busca de); **to ~ one's hair** peinarse; **we've been ~ing the town for you** te hemos buscado por toda la ciudad.

◆**comb out** *vt hair* desenmarañar; **they ~ed out the useless members of the staff** se deshicieron de los miembros del personal inútiles.

combat ['kɒmbæt] **1** *n* combate *m*; **~ duty** servicio *m* de frente; **~ jacket** guerrera *f*; **~ troops** tropas *fpl* de combate; **~ zone** zona *f* de combate. **2** *vt* combatir, luchar contra.

combatant ['kɒmbətənt] *n* combatiente *mf*.

combative ['kɒmbətɪv] *adj* combativo.

combe [ku:m] *n* = **coomb**.

combination [,kɒmbɪ'neɪʃən] *n* (**a**) (*gen*) combinación *f*; **~ lock** cerradura *f* de combinación. (**b**) **~s** (*undergarment*) combinación *f*.

combinatory [,kɒmbɪ'neɪtərɪ] *adj* combinacional.

combine 1 ['kɒmbaɪn] *n* (**a**) (*Comm*) asociación *f*, (*pej*) monopolio *m*. (**b**) (*Agr*) cosechadora *f*. **2** [kəm'baɪn] *vt* combinar; *qualities etc* reunir, conjugar; **expertise ~ed with charm** la pericia combinada con la simpatía, pericia y simpatía conjuntamente. **3** [kəm'baɪn] *vi* combinarse; (*companies etc*) asociarse, fusionarse.

combined [kəm'baɪnd] **1** *pret and ptp of* **combine**. **2** *adj operation* coordinado, conjunto.

combine-harvester [kɒmbaɪn'hɑ:vɪstəʳ] *n* cosechadora *f*.

combings ['kəʊmɪŋz] *npl* peinaduras *fpl*.

combo ['kɒmbəʊ] *n* (*Mus*) grupo *m*, conjunto *m*; (*: *clothes*) conjunto *m*.

combs* [kɒmz] *npl* combinación *f*.

combustible [kəm'bʌstɪbl] **1** *adj* combustible. **2** *n* combustible *m*.

combustion [kəm'bʌstʃən] *n* combustión *f*; **~ chamber** cámara *f* de combustión.

come [kʌm] (*irr*: *pret* **came**, *ptp* **come**) *vi* (**a**) (*gen*) venir; **coming**! ¡voy!; **I'll ~ for you at 8** vengo a recogerte a las 8; **oh ~!**, **~ now!**, **~**, **~!** ¡vamos!; ¡no es para tanto!; **it ~s in 3 sizes** se hace en 3 tamaños; **to ~ and go** ir y venir; **the pain ~s and goes** el dolor es intermitente; **the picture ~s and goes** (*TV*) un momento tenemos imagen y al siguiente no; **to ~ running** llegar corriendo; **when did he ~?** ¿cuándo llegó?; **we came to a river** llegamos a un río; **then the rains came** luego llegaron las lluvias; **the time will ~ when ...** tiempo habrá que + *subj*; **it never came into my mind** no pasó siquiera por mi mente; **it came as a shock** fue un golpe, nos asombró; **when your turn ~s** cuando llegue tu turno; **when it ~s to Latin** por lo que se refiere al latín, en cuanto al latín; **when it ~s to deciding** cuando se trata de decidir.

(**b**) (*have its place*) **the harvest ~s in August** la cosecha es en agosto; **May ~s before June** mayo es antes de junio; **it ~s on the next page** está en la página siguiente; **the adjective ~s before the noun** el adjetivo precede al sustantivo.

(**c**) (*happen*) pasar; **~ what may** pase lo que pase; **recovery came slowly** la recuperación fue lenta; **no harm will ~ to him** no le pasará nada; **nothing came of it** no dio resultados; **no good will ~ of it** no dará nada bueno; no tendrá consecuencias beneficiosas; **that's what ~s of trusting him** es la consecuencia de fiarnos de él.

(**d**) **~ to** + *infin* llegar a *infin*; **I came to admire her** llegué a admirarla; **he came to admit he was wrong** por fin reconoció que se había equivocado; **now I ~ to think of it** ahora que me doy cuenta; **it came to pass that ...** (*liter*) aconteció que ....

(**e**) (******) correrse (*Sp*******), acabar (*LAm*******).

(**f**) (*phrases*) **you could see that coming** eso se veía venir; **how ~?*** ¿cómo es eso?, ¿por qué?; **how ~ you don't know?*** ¿cómo es que no lo sabes?; **~ again?*** ¿cómo?; **if it ~s to that** en cuanto a eso; si llegamos a ese punto; **it will be 2 years ~ March** en marzo hará 2 años; **a week ~ Monday** ocho diás a partir del lunes; **I like my tea just as it ~s** me gusta el té hecho de cualquier modo; **I don't know whether I'm coming or going** no sé lo que me hago, no sé si coger muchacha o ponerme a servir; **he had it coming to him** bien merecido lo tenía; **she's as pretty as they ~** más guapa no la hay; **they don't ~ any better than that** mejores no los hay; **cars like that don't ~ cheap** los coches así no son baratos; **don't ~ that game with me!*** ¡no me vengas con esos cuentos!; **that's coming it a bit strong** eso me parece algo exagerado, no es para tanto.

◆**come about** *vi* ocurrir, suceder; **it came about that ...** sucedió que ...; **how did this ~ about?** ¿cómo ha sido esto?

◆**come across 1** *vt* dar con, topar (con), encontrar(se con).

2 *vi* (**a**) (*cross*) cruzar.

(**b**) (*meaning*) ser entendido; (*message*) llegar (al público *etc*); surtir efecto; **to ~ across as** dar la impresión de ser, dar una imagen de; **it didn't ~ across like that** no lo entendimos en ese sentido, no es ésa la impresión que nos produjo.

(**c**) (*US**: *keep one's word*) cumplir la palabra.

◆**come across with*** *vt money* apoquinar*; **to ~ across with the information** soltar prenda.

◆**come along** *vi* (**a**) venir también; **are you coming along?** ¿vienes?, ¿nos acompañas?; **you'll have to ~ along with me to the station** Vd me acompaña a la comisaría.

(**b**) **~ along!** ¡vamos!, ándale (*LAm*); (*hurrying*) ¡date prisa!

(**c**) (*develop*) hacer progresos; **it's coming along nicely** va bien; **how's the book coming along?** ¿qué tal va el libro?

(**d**) (*chance etc*) presentarse.

◆**come at** *vt* (**a**) *solution* llegar a.

(**b**) (*attack*) atacar, precipitarse sobre.

◆**come away** *vi* (**a**) (*depart*) marcharse; salir de casa (*etc*).

(**b**) (*fall off*) separarse, desprenderse, soltarse.

◆**come back** *vi* (**a**) (*person*: *return*) volver, regresar (*LAm*) (*for* para); (*to mind*) volver a la memoria; **it all ~s back to money** todo viene a ser cuestión de dinero; **to ~ back to what I was saying** para volver a mi tema.

(**b**) **to ~ back with** (*reply*) replicar; responder diciendo; **when accused, he came back with a counter-accusation** cuando le acusaron, respondió con una contraacusación.

◆**come between** *vt* interponerse entre; dividir, separar; **nothing can ~ between us** no hay nada que sea capaz de separarnos.

◆**come by 1** *vt* (**a**) (*pass*) pasar.

(**b**) (*obtain*) conseguir, adquirir; **how did she ~ by that name?** ¿cómo adquirió ese nombre?

2 *vi* (**a**) (*pass*) pasar; **could I ~ by, please?** ¿me permite?

(**b**) (*visit*) visitar; entrar a ver; **next time you ~ by** la próxima vez que vengas por aquí.

◆**come down** *vi* (**a**) (*descend*) bajar (*from* de); (*rain*) caer; (*Aer*) aterrizar, (*crash*) estrellarse, (*in sea*) amarar; (*heirloom*) pasar, (*tradition*) ser transmitido; **to ~ down on sb's side** tomar partido por uno; **to ~ down against a policy** declararse en contra de una política; **if it ~s down heads** si sale cara; **so it ~s down to this** así que se reduce a esto; **to ~ down hard on sb** ser duro con uno, castigar severamente a uno.

(**b**) (*roof etc*) caerse, desplomarse, venirse abajo; (*be demolished*) ser derribado.

(**c**) (*price, temperature*) bajar.

◆**come down with** *vt* (**a**) (*become ill from*) enfermar de, caer enfermo de, contraer.

(**b**) (*: *pay out*) apoquinar.

◆**come for** *vt* venir por.

◆**come forward** *vi* (**a**) avanzar, moverse hacia adelante.

(**b**) (*present o.s.*) presentarse, ofrecerse (*to* + *infin* a + *infin*); **to ~ forward with a suggestion** ofrecer una sugerencia.

◆**come from** *vt* (**a**) (*stem from*) venir de, proceder de; resultar de.

(**b**) (*person*) ser de; **I ~ from Wigan** soy de Wigan.

(**c**) **I can't get behind where you're coming from** (*US**) no alcanzo a comprender la base de tu argumento.

◆**come in** *vi* entrar; (*train etc*) llegar; (*tide*) subir, crecer; (*Pol*) acceder al poder; (*fashion*) imponerse, ponerse de moda; **~ in!** ¡adelante!, ¡pase!; **this is where we came in** (*fig*) estamos de vuelta de todo esto; **he came in last** (*in race*) llegó el último; **he has £100 coming in each week** tiene ingresos (*or* entradas *LAm*) de 100 libras por semana; **where do I ~ in?** (*fig*) ¿qué voy a pintar yo aquí?; ¿qué papel me dais a mí?; **to ~ in on a deal** tomar parte en un negocio.

◆**come in for** *vt*: **he came in for a lot of criticism** fue blanco de muchas críticas.

◆**come into** *vt* (**a**) (*inherit*) **he came into a fortune** heredó una fortuna, le correspondió una fortuna. (**b**) (*have relevance*) **melons don't ~ into it** los melones no tienen que ver, los melones no hacen al caso.

◆**come of** *vt*: **to ~ of a good family** ser de buena familia, venir de buena familia.

◆**come off 1** *vt* (**a**) (*separate from*) desprenderse de; **the label came off the bottle** la etiqueta se desprendió de la botella; **the car came off the road** el coche salió de la carretera; **she came off her bike** se cayó de la bici.

(**b**) **~ off it!*** ¡vaya!; ¡vamos, anda!; ¡no te lo creo!; **I told him to ~ off it** le dije que dejase de hacer el tonto.

(**c**) (*give up*) dejar; **it's time you came off the pill** es hora de dejar la píldora.

2 *vi* (**a**) (*become detached*) desprenderse; soltarse; caerse; **does this lid ~ off?** ¿se puede quitar esta tapa?

(**b**) (*take place*) tener lugar, verificarse.

(**c**) (*succeed*) tener éxito, dar resultados; **to ~ off best** salir ganando; **to ~ off badly** salir malparado, salir perdiendo.

(**d**) (*cease*) **the play came off in January** la obra dejó de figurar en la cartelera en enero.

(**e**) (******) dejarlo ir******.

◆**come on 1** *vt* encontrar, descubrir.

2 *vi* (**a**) (*advance*) avanzar; (*rain etc*) empezar; (*illness*) aparecer; (*night*) acercarse; **~ on!** ¡vamos!, (*hurrying*) ¡date prisa!, (*to runner*) ¡ánimo!; **winter was coming on** entraba el invierno; **I have a cold coming on** siento que me voy a acatarrar; **I'm coming on to that next** de eso hablo en seguida.

(**b**) (*progress*) hacer progresos; (*plant*) crecer, desarrollarse; **how is the book coming on?** ¿qué tal va el libro?

(**c**) (*actor*) salir a la escena.

(**d**) (*light*) encenderse.

(**e**) (*US fig*) **he came on sincere** fingía ser sincero.

◆**come out** *vi* (*emerge*) salir (*of* de); mostrarse; (*sun*) salir; (*book*) salir (a luz); (*novelty*) aparecer, estrenarse; (*debutante*) ser presentada en sociedad, ponerse de largo; (*homosexual*) hacerse conocer, declararse; (*news*) revelarse, publicarse; (*flower*) florecer; (*photo*) salir (bien); (*stain*) salir, quitarse; **the idea came out of an experiment** la idea se originó en un experimento; (*Brit Ind*: *also* **to ~ out on strike**) ponerse en huelga; **it ~s out at £5 a head** sale a 5 libras por cabeza; **it all came out all right** todo salió bien; **to ~ out against** declararse en contra de; **to ~ out for** declararse a favor de; **she came out in spots** le salieron erupciones (en la piel); **I came out in a sweat** empecé a sudar, me cubrí de sudor; **he came out of it with credit** salió con honor.

◆**come out with** *vt remark* soltar, descolgarse con.

◆**come over 1** *vt* apoderarse de, invadir; **sleep came over her** la invadió el sueño; **what's ~ over you?** ¿qué te pasa?; **I don't know what came over me** no sé lo que me pasó.

2 *vi* (**a**) (*visit*) visitar, venir a ver.

(**b**) (*****: *be transformed*) volverse, ponerse, sentirse; **she came over quite ill** se puso bastante mala; **he came over all religious** se puso muy devoto.

(**c**) (*give impression*) **how did he ~ over?** ¿qué impresión produjo?; **the speech didn't ~ over at all well** el discurso produjo una impresión bastante mala.

◆**come round** *vi* (**a**) (*visit*) visitar, venir a ver.

(**b**) (*agree*) asentir; dejarse convencer; cambiar de idea; **he came round to our view** adoptó nuestra opinión.

(**c**) (*Med*) volver en sí.

(**d**) (*anniversary etc*) llegar.

◆**come through 1** *vt* (*survive*) sobrevivir a; *illness* recuperarse de; *test* superar.

2 *vi* (**a**) (*survive*) sobrevivir; (*illness*) recuperarse.

(**b**) (*message*) ser recibido, llegar.

◆**come through with** *vt* (*US*) = **come up with** (**b**).

◆**come to** *vi* (**a**) (*Naut*) fachear.

(**b**) (*Med*) volver en sí.

(**c**) *sum* ascender a; **how much does it ~ to?** ¿a cuánto sube?, ¿cuánto es?

(**d**) **so it ~s to this** así que viene a ser esto; **what are we coming to?** ¿adónde va a parar todo esto?

◆**come together** *vi* (**a**) (*assemble*) reunirse, juntarse; **great qualities ~ together in his work** en su obra se dan cita grandes cualidades.

(**b**) (*agree*) reconciliarse; arreglar las diferencias.

◆**come under** *vt person* ser de la competencia de, incumbir a; estar bajo la jurisdicción de; *heading* estar comprendido en, pertenecer a; **to ~ under attack** sufrir un ataque, verse atacado.

◆**come up** *vi* subir (*also fig*); (*sun*) salir; (*plant*) aparecer; (*light*) encenderse; (*difficulty*) surgir; (*in talk*) salir, surgir, ser mencionado; (*lucky number*) salir; (*Univ*) matricularse; **he came up to Oxford last year** (*Brit*) se matriculó en la universidad de Oxford el año pasado; **he has ~ up in the world** ha subido mucho en la escala social; **to ~ up before the judge** comparecer ante el juez; **his case ~s up tomorrow** su proceso se verá mañana; se presenta su pleito mañana; **to ~ up for sale** ponerse a la venta.

◆**come up against** *vt problem* tropezar con; *enemy* tener que habérselas con; *opposition* chocar con.

◆**come up to** *vt* subir a; (*reach*) llegar hasta; (*approach*) acercarse a, aproximarse a, (*in street*) abordar; (*fig*) estar a la altura de, corresponder a; *standard* llegar a, satisfacer.

◆**come up with** *vt* (**a**) *person* alcanzar, llegar a la altura de. (**b**) *proposal* presentar, proponer; *solution* ofrecer, sugerir; *surprise* salir con; **eventually he came up with the money** por fin ofreció el dinero.

◆**come upon** = **come on 1.**

comeback ['kʌmbæk] *n* (**a**) (*restoration*) restablecimiento *m*, rehabilitación *f*; esfuerzo *m* por volver a su antigua posición; **to make a ~** restablecerse, rehabilitarse; volver a resurgir; presentarse de nuevo.

(**b**) (*response*) reacción *f*; (*US*) réplica *f*; (*witty*) respuesta *f* aguda.

Comecon ['kɒmɪkɒn] *n abbr of* **Council for Mutual Economic Aid** Consejo *m* para la Mutua Ayuda Económica, COMECON *m*.

comedian [kə'miːdɪən] *n* cómico *m*.

comedienne [kə,miːdɪ'en] *n* cómica *f*.

comedown* ['kʌmdaʊn] *n* revés *m*, humillación *f*.

comedy ['kɒmɪdɪ] *n* comedia *f*; (*humour of event*) comicidad *f*; **~ of manners** comedia *f* de costumbres.

come-hither ['kʌm'hɪðəʳ] *adj look* incitante, provocativo.

comely ['kʌmlɪ] *adj* (*liter*) gentil; lindo.

come-on* [kʌm,ɒn] *n* (**a**) (*enticement*) insinuación *f*, invitación *f*; aliciente *m*; **to give sb the ~** poner ojos tiernos a uno. (**b**) (*Comm*) truco *m*, señuelo *m*.

comer ['kʌməʳ] *n*: **all ~s** todos los contendientes; **the first ~** el primero en llegar.

comestibles [kə'mestɪblz] *npl* comestibles *mpl*.

comet ['kɒmɪt] *n* cometa *m*.

comeuppance [,kʌm'ʌpəns] *n*: **to get one's ~** recibir el justo castigo.

COMEX ['kɒmeks] *n* (*US*) *abbr of* **Commodities Exchange**.

comfort ['kʌmfət] **1** *n* (**a**) (*solace*) consuelo *m*; (*from pain*) alivio *m*; **that's cold** (*or* **small**) **~, that's no ~ at all** eso no me consuela nada; **you're a great ~ to me** eres un gran consuelo; **the exam is too close for ~** el examen está demasiado cerca para que me sienta tranquilo; **to give ~ to the enemy** dar aliento al enemigo.

(**b**) (*bodily*) confort *m*, comodidad *f*; bienestar *m*; **the ~s of life** las cosas agradables de la vida diaria; **with every modern ~** con todo confort, con toda comodidad; **to live in ~** vivir cómodamente.

2 *vt* (*solace*) consolar; *pain* aliviar; (*bodily*) confortar; (*encourage*) alentar.

comfortable ['kʌmfətəbl] *adj house, chair, shoes etc* cómodo, confortable; *income* adecuado; *majority* suficiente, adecuado; *living* holgado; **to feel ~** encontrarse a gusto; **I don't feel altogether ~ about it** la cosa me trae algo preocupado; **he came closer to the truth than was ~** se acercó de manera incómoda a la verdad; **to have a ~ win over sb** vencer a uno fácilmente; **to make o.s. ~** acomodarse a su gusto; (*euph*) ir al baño; **make yourself ~!** ¡póngase cómodo!, ¡acomódese bien!

comfortably ['kʌmfətəblɪ] *adv sit etc* cómodamente; *live* holgadamente; *win* fácilmente; **to be ~ off** tener unos ingresos adecuados, vivir holgadamente.

comforter ['kʌmfətəʳ] *n* (**a**) (*scarf*) bufanda *f*; (*US*) cobertor *m* acolchado, edredón *m*. (**b**) (*baby's*) chupete *m*, chupón *m* (*LAm*).

comforting ['kʌmfətɪŋ] *adj* consolador, (re)confortante.

comfortless ['kʌmfətlɪs] *adj* incómodo, sin comodidad.

comfort station ['kʌmfət,steɪʃən] *n* (*US*) urinario *m* público, servicios *mpl*.

comfrey ['kʌmfrɪ] *n* consuelda *f*.

comfy* ['kʌmfɪ] *adj* = **comfortable.**

comic ['kɒmɪk] **1** *adj* cómico; divertido; **~ book** libro *m* de cómics; **~ opera** ópera *f* bufa, ópera *f* cómica; **~ strip** historieta *f*, tira *f* cómica, banda *f* de dibujos; **~ verses** poesías *fpl* jocosas, poesías *fpl* festivas. **2** *n* (**a**) (*person*) cómico *m*, -a *f*. (**b**) (*paper*) cómic *m*, (*child's*) tebeo *m*; **~s** (*US*) = **~ strip.**

comic(al) ['kɒmɪk(əl)] *adj* cómico; divertido, entretenido.

comically [ˈkɒmɪkəlɪ] *adv* de manera cómica; graciosamente.

coming [ˈkʌmɪŋ] **1** *adj year etc* que viene; (*future*) venidero; (*promising*) prometedor; **it's the ~ thing** es la moda del futuro.

2 *n* venida *f*, llegada *f*; (*of Christ*) advenimiento *m*; **~(s) and going(s)** ir y venir *m*, trajín *m*, ajetreo *m*.

coming-of-age [ˈkʌmɪŋəvˈeɪdʒ] *n* (llegada *f* a la) mayoría *f* de edad.

coming-out [ˈkʌmɪŋˈaʊt] *n* presentación *f* en sociedad.

Comintern [ˈkɒmɪntɜːn] *n* (*Pol*) *abbr of* **Communist International** Comintern *f*.

comma [ˈkɒmə] *n* coma *f*.

command [kəˈmɑːnd] **1** *n* (**a**) (*order*) orden *f*; mandato *m*; (*Comput*) comando *m*; **~ language** lenguaje *m* de órdenes; **~ line** orden *f*; **at the ~ of, by (the) ~ of** por orden de; **by royal ~** por real orden; **~ performance** (*Brit Theat*) representación *f* a petición del monarca; **to be at the ~ of** estar a la disposición de.

(**b**) (*control*) mando *m*, dominio *m*; **~ module** módulo *m* de mando; **~ post** puesto *m* de mando; **his ~ of English** su dominio del inglés; **~ of the seas** dominio *m* de los mares; **under the ~ of** bajo el mando de; **to be in ~ of** estar al mando de; **to be in ~ of one's faculties** seguir en control de sus facultades; **who is in ~ here?** ¿quién manda aquí?; **to have at one's ~** *men* mandar; **to have good resources at one's ~** disponer de muchos recursos; **to take ~ of** asumir el mando de.

(**c**) (*authority, Mil, Naut*) comandancia *f*; jefatura *f*; **second in ~** segundo *m*, subjefe *m*, (*Naut*) comandante *m* segundo de a bordo.

2 *vt* (**a**) (*order*) mandar, ordenar (*that* que, *to do* hacer).

(**b**) (*be in command of*) mandar, comandar.

(**c**) (*have at one's disposal*) disponer de, tener a su disposición; *attention* llamar poderosamente; *resources* tener.

(**d**) *respect etc* imponer; *sympathy* merecerse; *price* venderse a (*or* por).

(**e**) (*overlook*) *area* dominar; *view* tener, disfrutar de.

commandant [ˌkɒmənˈdænt] *n* comandante *m*.

commandeer [ˌkɒmənˈdɪəʳ] *vt stores, ship etc* requisar, expropiar; *men* reclutar por fuerza; (*) tomar, apropiarse.

commander [kəˈmɑːndəʳ] *n* (*gen*) comandante *m*, jefe *m*; (*Brit Police*) comandante *m*; (*Hist: of chivalric order*) comendador *m*; (*rank*) capitán *m* de fragata.

commander-in-chief [kəˈmɑːndərɪnˈtʃiːf] *n* jefe *m* supremo, comandante *m* en jefe.

commanding [kəˈmɑːndɪŋ] *adj position* dominante; *appearance* imponente; *lead, advantage* abrumador; **~ officer** jefe *m*, comandante *m*; **in a ~ tone** con voz de mando.

commandingly [kəˈmɑːndɪŋlɪ] *adv speak etc* con voz de mando.

commandment [kəˈmɑːndmənt] *n* mandamiento *m*; **the Ten C~s** los diez mandamientos.

commando [kəˈmɑːndəʊ] *n* (*man, group*) comando *m*.

commemorate [kəˈmeməreɪt] *vt* conmemorar.

commemoration [kəˌmeməˈreɪʃən] *n* conmemoración *f*; **in ~ of** en conmemoración de.

commemorative [kəˈmemərətɪv] **1** *adj* conmemorativo. **2** *n* (*stamp*) conmemorativo *m*.

commence [kəˈmens] **1** *vt* comenzar, empezar. **2** *vi* **to ~ to** + *infin*, **to ~** + *ger* empezar a + *infin*.

commencement [kəˈmensmənt] *n* comienzo *m*, principio *m*; (*mainly US: Univ*) ceremonia *f* de entrega de diplomas.

commend [kəˈmend] *vt* (**a**) (*praise*) alabar, elogiar; **to ~ sb for his action** alabar la acción de uno.

(**b**) (*recommend*) **I ~ him to you** se lo recomiendo; **I ~ it to your attention** creo que merece su atención; **the plan does not ~ itself to me** el proyecto no me resulta aceptable; **it has little to ~ it** poco hay que decir a su favor.

(**c**) (*entrust*) encomendar (*to* a).

commendable [kəˈmendəbl] *adj* recomendable, encomiable, loable.

commendably [kəˈmendəblɪ] *adv* de manera loable; **it was ~ short** tuvo el mérito de ser breve; **you have been ~ prompt** le felicito por la prontitud.

commendation [ˌkɒmenˈdeɪʃən] *n* (**a**) (*praise*) elogio *m*, encomio *m*; (*Mil*) felicitación *f*. (**b**) (*recommendation*) recomendación *f*.

commensurable [kəˈmenʃərəbl] *adj* conmensurable, comparable (*with* con).

commensurate [kəˈmenʃərɪt] *adj* proporcionado; **~ with** equivalente a, que corresponde a.

comment [ˈkɒment] **1** *n* comentario *m*; observación *f*; **no ~** sin comentarios, no hay comentarios; **it seems to call for ~** sobre eso convendría hacer algún comentario; **to make the ~ that ...** observar que ...

2 *vt text* comentar; **to ~ that ...** observar que ...

3 *vi* hacer comentarios, hacer una observación; **to ~ on** *text* comentar; *subject etc* hacer observaciones acerca de; **to ~ unfavourably on sth** criticar algo.

commentary [ˈkɒməntərɪ] *n* comentario *m*; reportaje *m*.

commentate [ˈkɒmenteɪt] (*Rad, TV*) **1** *vt* hacer un reportaje sobre. **2** *vi* hacer un reportaje.

commentator [ˈkɒmənteɪtəʳ] *n* comentador *m*, -ora *f*, comentarista *mf*; (*Rad, TV*) comentarista *mf*, locutor *m*, -ora *f*.

commerce [ˈkɒmɜːs] *n* comercio *m*.

commercial [kəˈmɜːʃəl] **1** *adj* comercial; **~ art** arte *m* comercial; **~ artist** artista *mf* comercial; **~ attaché** agregado *m*, -a *f* comercial; **~ bank** banco *m* comercial; **~ break** espacio *m* publicitario; **~ centre** centro *m* comercial; **~ college** escuela *f* para secretarias; **~ law** derecho *m* mercantil; **~ paper** (*esp US*) letras *fpl* comerciables; **~ property** propiedad *f* comercial; **~ radio** emisora *f* comercial; **~ television** televisión *f* comercial; **~ traveller** viajante *m*; **~ value** valor *m* comercial; **'no ~ value'** 'sin valor comercial'; **~ vehicle** vehículo *m* comercial.

2 *n* (**a**) (*Rad, TV*) anuncio *m*, emisión *f* publicitaria. (**b**) **~s** (*St Ex*) (acciones *fpl* de) empresas *fpl* comerciales.

commercialism [kəˈmɜːʃəlɪzəm] *n* mercantilismo *m*.

commercialization [kəˌmɜːʃəlaɪˈzeɪʃən] *n* comercialización *f*.

commercialize [kəˈmɜːʃəlaɪz] *vt* comercializar, convertir en comercial.

commercially [kəˈmɜːʃəlɪ] *adv* comercialmente.

commie* [ˈkɒmɪ] *adj, n* = **communist**.

commiserate [kəˈmɪzəreɪt] *vi* expresar su sentimiento; **to ~ with** compadecerse de, condolerse de.

commiseration [kəˌmɪzəˈreɪʃən] *n* conmiseración *f*.

commissar [ˈkɒmɪsɑːʳ] *n* comisario *m*.

commissariat [ˌkɒmɪˈsɛərɪət] *n* comisaría *f*.

commissary [ˈkɒmɪsərɪ] *n* (**a**) comisario *m*, -a *f*. (**b**) (*US: shop*) economato *m*.

commission [kəˈmɪʃən] **1** *n* (*order, fee*) comisión *f*; (*committee*) comisión *f*, comité *m*; (*of crime*) perpetración *f*; (*Mil*) graduación *f* de oficial, despacho *m* de oficial, (*warrant*) nombramiento *m*; **~ agent** comisionista *mf*; **on ~, on a ~ basis** a comisión; **to be out of ~** estar fuera de servicio; **to charge 10% ~** cobrar una comisión del 10 por cien; **to put out of ~** inutilizar; **to put into ~** poner en servicio activo.

2 *vt officer* nombrar (*in a regiment* a un regimiento); *ship* poner en servicio activo; *architect etc* nombrar, hacer un encargo a; *picture* comisionar, encargar; *article* encargar; **to ~ sb to do sth** encargar a uno que haga algo.

commissionaire [kəˌmɪʃəˈnɛəʳ] *n* (*Brit, Canada*) portero *m*, conserje *m*.

commissioned [kəˈmɪʃnd] *adj*: **~ officer** oficial *mf*.

commissioner [kəˈmɪʃənəʳ] *m* comisario *m*, -a *f*; **~ for oaths** notario *m* público; **~ of police** (*Brit*) jefe *m* de policía.

commit [kəˈmɪt] **1** *vt* (**a**) *crime* cometer; *error* hacer, *perjury* incurrir en; **to ~ suicide** suicidarse.

(**b**) (*involve*) *troops* enviar a la batalla; *resources* empeñar.

(**c**) (*entrust*) entregar (*to* a); (*Parl*) *bill* someter a una comisión; **to ~ sth to sb's charge** confiar algo a uno; **to ~ sth to the flames** entregar algo a las llamas; **to ~ sth to memory** aprender algo de memoria; **to ~ sb to prison** encarcelar a uno; **to ~ sb to a mental hospital** internar a uno en un manicomio; **to ~ sb for trial** remitir a uno al tribunal; **to ~ sth to paper** (*or* **writing**) poner algo por escrito.

2 *vr*: **to ~ o.s.** hacer una promesa, declararse; comprometerse; **to ~ o.s. to** comprometerse a, declararse a favor de; **without ~ing myself** sin compromiso por mi parte; **I am ~ted to help him** me he comprometido a ayudarle; **we are deeply ~ted to this policy** nos hemos declarado firmemente a favor de esta política.

commitment [kəˈmɪtmənt] *n* (**a**) (*obligation*) compromiso *m*, obligación *f*, cometido *m*. (**b**) (*quality*) entrega *f*, devoción *f*.

committal [kəˈmɪtl] *n* comisión *f*; compromiso *m*, cometido *m*; (*burial*) entierro *m*; **~ to prison** (auto *m* de) prisión *f*.

committed [kəˈmɪtɪd] *adj* comprometido.

committee [kəˈmɪtɪ] *n* comisión *f*, comité *m*; **~ of management** consejo *m* de administración; **~ meeting** reunión *f* de(l) comité; **~ member** miembro *mf* de(l) comité; **to be**

(*or* **sit**) **on a** ~ ser miembro de un comité.

commode [kə'məʊd] *n* (*with chamberpot*) sillico *m*; (*chest of drawers*) cómoda *f*.

commodious [kə'məʊdɪəs] *adj* grande, espacioso.

commodity [kə'mɒdɪtɪ] *n* artículo *m* (de consumo *or* de comercio), mercancía *f*, mercadería *f*, producto *m*; **commodities** mercancías *fpl*, géneros *mpl*; productos *mpl* de base; ~ **exchange** bolsa *f* de artículos de consumo; ~ **markets** mercados *mpl* de mercancías; ~ **trade** comercio *m* de mercancías.

commodore ['kɒmədɔːʳ] *n* comodoro *m*.

common ['kɒmən] **1** *adj* (**a**) (*belonging to many*) común (*also Math, Gram*); ~ **ground** puntos *mpl* en común; ~ **land** campo *m* común, ejido *m*; **C~ Market** Mercado *m* Común; ~ **sense** sentido *m* común; ~ **sense tells us that** ... el sentido común nos dice que ...; **surely it's** ~ **sense that** ...? ¿no es lógico que ...?; **it is** ~ **to all men** es común a todos; **A has nothing in** ~ **with B** A no tiene nada en común con B; **we have nothing in** ~ no tenemos ningún interés en común; **we have a lot in** ~ tenemos muchos intereses en común; **I, in** ~ **with everybody else** yo, al igual que todos los demás; **to work for a** ~ **aim** cooperar todos a un mismo fin; *V* **knowledge**.

(**b**) (*public*) público.

(**c**) (*frequent*) común, frecuente; **this butterfly is** ~ **in Spain** esta mariposa es común en España.

(**d**) (*usual, ordinary*) corriente, usual; *belief* vulgar; ~ **crab** cangrejo *m* común; ~ **cold** catarro *m*, resfriado *m*; ~ **law** derecho *m* consuetudinario; ~ **noun** nombre *m* común; ~ **or garden** ordinario, normal y corriente; ~ **prisoner** preso *m* común, preso *m* social; ~ **soldier** soldado *m* raso; ~ **stock** (*US*: *Fin*) acciones *fpl* ordinarias; **the** ~ **man** el hombre medio; **in** ~ **use** de uso corriente; **it is no more than** ~ **courtesy to write** no es más que una cortesía elemental escribir; **it is** ~ **to see such things now** ahora es frecuente ver tales cosas.

(**e**) (*vulgar*) ordinario, vulgar (*esp LAm*); **she's very** ~ es muy ordinaria; **as** ~ **as dirt** de lo más ordinario.

2 *n* (**a**) (*land*) campo *m* común, ejido *m*.

(**b**) ~**s** (*Pol*) estado *m* llano; **the C~s** los Comunes.

(**c**) **short** ~**s** ración *f* escasa; **to be on short** ~**s** comer mal.

(**d**) ~**s** (*US Univ*) comedor *m*.

common core ['kɒmən'kɔːʳ] *n* (*Scol*: *also* **common-core syllabus**) asignaturas *fpl* comunes, tronco *m* común.

Common Entrance ['kɒmən'entrəns] *n* (*Brit Scol*) *examen de entrada en la enseñanza privada.*

commoner ['kɒmənəʳ] *n* plebeyo *m*, -a *f*; (*Univ*) estudiante *m* que no tiene beca del colegio.

common-law ['kɒmən,lɔː] *attr*: ~ **marriage** unión *f* consensual; ~ **wife** mujer *f* en una unión consensual.

commonly ['kɒmənlɪ] *adv* comúnmente, frecuentemente; generalmente; **it is** ~ **believed that** ... se cree vulgarmente que ...

commonness ['kɒmənnɪs] *n* (**a**) (*frequency*) frecuencia *f*. (**b**) (*vulgarity*) ordinariez *f*.

commonplace ['kɒmənpleɪs] **1** *adj* vulgar, trivial; **it is** ~ **to see that** ... es frecuente ver que ...

2 *n* (**a**) (*ordinary thing*) cosa *f* común, cosa *f* corriente.

(**b**) (*Liter etc*) lugar *m* común, tópico *m*, perogrullada *f*.

common-room ['kɒmənrum] *n* salón *m* (de un colegio *etc*).

commons ['kɔmənz] *npl* (*Pol*) *V* **common 2** (**b**).

commonsense ['kɒmən,sens] *adj* racional, lógico; **the** ~ **thing to do is** ... lo lógico es ...

commonwealth ['kɒmənwelθ] *n* república *f*; **the** (**British**) **C~** la Mancomunidad (Británica); **Minister of State** (*or* **Secretary of State**) **for C~ Affairs** Ministro *m* (*or* Secretario *m*) de Estado para los Asuntos de la Commonwealth; **the C~** (*Brit Hist*) la república de Cromwell; **the C~ of Kentucky** el estado de Kentucky; **the C~ of Puerto Rico** el estado de Puerto Rico.

commotion [kə'məʊʃən] *n* tumulto *m*, confusión *f*; alboroto *m*; (*civil*) disturbio *m*, perturbación *f* del orden público; **to cause a** ~ armar un lío; **to make a** ~ (*noise*) provocar (*or* causar) un alboroto; **there was a** ~ **in the crowd** se armó un lío entre los espectadores; **what a** ~! ¡qué alboroto!

communal ['kɒmjuːnl] *adj* comunal.

communally ['kɒmjuːnəlɪ] *adv* comunalmente; **to act** ~ obrar como comunidad; **the property is held** ~ la propiedad la posee la comunidad.

commune 1 ['kɒmjuːn] *n* (*all senses*) comuna *f*.

2 [kə'mjuːn] *vi* (**a**) (*Eccl*: *esp US*) comulgar. (**b**) **to** ~ **with** conversar con, comunicarse con.

communicable [kə'mjuːnɪkəbl] *adj* comunicable; *disease* transmisible.

communicant [kə'mjuːnɪkənt] *n* comulgante *mf*.

communicate [kə'mjuːnɪkeɪt] **1** *vt* comunicar. **2** *vi* (**a**) (*Eccl*) comulgar. (**b**) (*buildings etc*) comunicarse. (**c**) (*speak*) comunicarse (*with* con).

communicating [kə'mjuːnɪkeɪtɪŋ] *adj*: ~ **rooms** cuartos *mpl* comunicados.

communication [kə,mjuːnɪ'keɪʃən] *n* comunicación *f*; ~ **breakdown** malentendido *m*; ~ **cord** (*Brit Rail*) timbre *m* de alarma; ~ **gap** falta *f* de entendimiento; ~ **problem** problema *m* de expresión; ~**s program** programa *m* de comunicación; ~ **satellite** satélite *m* de comunicaciones; ~ **science** telecomunicaciones *fpl*; ~ **skills** destrezas *fpl* comunicativas; ~**s software** paquete *m* de comunicación; ~**s technology** tecnología *f* para las comunicaciones; **to be in** ~ **with** estar en contacto con; **to get into** ~ **with** ponerse en contacto con.

communicative [kə'mjuːnɪkətɪv] *adj* comunicativo, expansivo.

communion [kə'mjuːnɪən] *n* comunión *f*; **to take** ~ comulgar; ~ **service** comunión *f*; ~ **table** mesa *f* de comunión.

communiqué [kə'mjuːnɪkeɪ] *n* comunicado *m*, parte *m*.

communism ['kɒmjʊnɪzəm] *n* comunismo *m*.

communist ['kɒmjʊnɪst] **1** *adj* comunista; **C~ Party** Partido *m* Comunista. **2** *n* comunista *mf*.

community [kə'mjuːnɪtɪ] **1** *n* comunidad *f*; (*people at large*) colectividad *f*, sociedad *f*; (*local inhabitants*) vecindario *m*; **the C~** (*EC*) la Comunidad; **the black** ~ la población negra, los habitantes negros; **the artistic** ~ el mundillo artístico; **the Ruritanian** ~ **in Rome** la colonia ruritania de Roma.

2 *attr* comunitario; ~ **bodies** organismos *mpl* comunitarios; ~ **budget** presupuesto *m* comunitario; ~ **centre** centro *m* social; ~ **charge** (*Brit formerly*) (contribución *f* de) capitación *f*, impuesto *m* municipal; ~ **chest** (*US*) fondo *m* para beneficencia social; ~ **health centre** clínica *f* comunitaria; **C~ law** derecho *m* comunitario; ~ **life** vida *f* social; ~ **medicine** medicina *f* de familia; ~ **policing** *política policial de acercamiento a la comunidad;* **C~ policy** (*EC*) política *f* comunitaria; **C~ regulations** normas *fpl* comunitarias; ~ **service** servicio *m* comunitario; ~ **singing** canto *m* colectivo; ~ **spirit** sentimiento *m* de comunidad; civismo *m*; ~ **worker** asistente *mf* social (del barrio).

communize ['kɒmjuːnaɪz] *vt* comunizar.

commutable [kə'mjuːtəbl] *adj* (*gen, Jur*) conmutable.

commutation ['kɒmjʊ'teɪʃən] *n* conmutación *f* (*also Fin*); (*US Rail etc*) uso *m* de un billete de abono; ~ **ticket** billete *m* de abono.

commute [kə'mjuːt] **1** *vt payment* conmutar (*into* en, *for* por); *sentence* conmutar (*to* en, por). **2** *vi* viajar a diario, ir y venir regularmente (*to work* al trabajo); **I work in London but I** ~ (*Brit*) trabajo en Londres pero tengo que viajar cada día.

commuter [kə'mjuːtəʳ] *n* viajero *m* diario, viajera *f* diaria (*desde los barrios exteriores etc de una ciudad al centro*); ~ **belt** (*Brit*), ~ **country** (*Brit*) zona *f* de los barrios exteriores; ~ **services** servicios *mpl* de cercanías; ~ **train** tren *m* de cercanías.

commuting [kə'mjuːtɪŋ] *n*: ~ **is very stressful** el viajar para ir al trabajo provoca mucho estrés.

compact 1 ['kɒmpækt] *n* (**a**) (*agreement*) pacto *m*, convenio *m*. (**b**) (*powder* ~) polvera *f*. (**c**) (*US Aut*) utilitario *m*.

2 [kəm'pækt] *adj* compacto; *material* apretado, sólido; *style* breve, conciso; ~ **car** (*US*) utilitario *m*; ~ **disk** disco *m* compacto.

3 [kəm'pækt] *vt material* comprimir (*into* en); condensar; **to be** ~**ed of** consistir en.

compactly [kəm'pæktlɪ] *adv* de modo compacto; apretadamente, sólidamente; brevemente, concisamente.

compactness [kəm'pæktnɪs] *n* compacidad *f*, compresión *f*; (*of style*) concisión *f*.

companion [kəm'pænɪən] **1** *n* (**a**) compañero *m*, -a *f*; (*lady's*) señora *f* de compañía; (*euph*: *lover*) compañero *m*, -a *f*. (**b**) (*Naut*) lumbrera *f*; (~*way*) escala *f* (que conduce a los camarotes). (**c**) (*handbook*) manual *m*. **2** *attr*: ~ **volume** *libro de tema relacionado.*

companionable [kəm'pænɪənəbl] *adj* sociable, simpático.

companionship [kəm'pænɪənʃɪp] *n* compañerismo *m*.

companionway [kəm'pænjənweɪ] *n* escalerilla *f*.

company ['kʌmpənɪ] *n* (**a**) (*gen*) compañía *f* (*also Mil, Theat*); (*ship's* ~) tripulación *f*; ~ **commander** capitán *m* de compañía; ~ **sergeant-major** sargento *m* mayor de una compañía; **he's good** ~ es un compañero divertido; **they**

are in good ~ están en buena compañía; **two's ~ but three's a crowd** con dos basta y sobra uno; **to do sth in ~** hacer algo en colaboración; **present ~ excepted** mejorando lo presente, salvando a los presentes; **we have ~** tenemos visita; **to join ~ with** reunirse con; **to keep sb ~** acompañar a uno, hacerle compañía a uno; **to keep ~** (*lovers*) andar en relaciones; **to keep bad ~** tener malas compañías; **a man is known by the ~ he keeps** dime con quién andas y te diré quién eres; **to part ~** separarse (*with* de), (*fig*) desprenderse, soltarse.

(**b**) (*Comm*) sociedad *f*, compañía *f*, empresa *f*; **Smith and C~** Smith y Compañía; **Wilson and ~** (*pej*) Wilson y compañía; **~ car** (*Brit*) coche *m* de la empresa; **~ director** director *m*, -ora *f* de empresa; **~ law** derecho *m* de compañías (*or* de sociedades); **~ lawyer** (*Brit Jur*) abogado *mf* empresarial; (*working within company*) abogado *mf* de la compañía; **~ man** empleado *m* que se desvive por su empresa; **~ policy** normas *fpl* de la empresa; **~ secretary** (*Brit*) apoderado *m*; **~ time** horario *m* del trabajo; **~ union** (*US*) sindicato *m* de empresa.

comparability [kɒmpərəˈbɪlɪtɪ] *n* comparabilidad *f*.

comparable [ˈkɒmpərəbl] *adj* comparable; **a ~ case** un caso análogo; **they are not ~** no se les puede comparar.

comparative [kəmˈpærətɪv] **1** *adj* relativo; (*Gram etc*) comparativo; *study* comparado, contrastado; **~ literature** literatura *f* comparada. **2** *n* comparativo *m*.

comparatively [kəmˈpærətɪvlɪ] *adv* relativamente.

compare [kəmˈpɛəʳ] **1** *n*: **beyond ~, past ~, without ~** sin comparación, impar.

2 *vt* (**a**) comparar (*to, with* con); (*put side by side: esp texts*) cotejar; **as ~d with** comparado con; **they are not to be ~d** no se les puede comparar. (**b**) (*Gram*) formar los grados de comparación de.

3 *vi* poderse comparar; **he can't ~ with you** no se le puede comparar con Vd; **it ~s favourably with the other** no pierde por comparación con el otro, supera al otro; **it ~s poorly with the other** es inferior al otro; **how do they ~ ?** ¿cuáles son sus cualidades respectivas?; **how do they ~ for speed?** ¿cuál tiene mayor velocidad?

comparison [kəmˈpærɪsn] *n* (**a**) comparación *f*; cotejo *m*; **in ~ with** en comparación con; **there's no ~** no hay comparación (posible); **this one is large in ~** comparando los dos éste es más grande; **it will bear** (*or* **stand**) **~ with the best** se puede comparar con los mejores. (**b**) (*Gram*) comparación *f*.

compartment [kəmˈpɑːtmənt] *n* compartimiento *m*; (*Rail, of case etc*) departamento *m*.

compartmentalization [ˌkɒmpɑːtˌmentəlaɪˈzeɪʃən] *n* compartimentación *f*.

compartmentalize [ˌkɒmpɑːtˈmentəlaɪz] *vt* dividir en categorías; aislar en categorías, compartimentar.

compass [ˈkʌmpəs] **1** *n* (**a**) (*Naut etc*) brújula *f*.

(**b**) (*range*) alcance *m*, extensión *f*; (*area*) ámbito *m*; **beyond my ~** fuera de mi alcance; **in a small ~** en un espacio reducido.

(**c**) (*esp US*) compás *m*.

(**d**) **~es** (*Math*) compás *m*; **a pair of ~es** un compás.

2 *vt* (*contrive*) conseguir, (*pej*) tramar; (*grasp mentally*) comprender; (*surround*) rodear; **to be ~ed about by** estar rodeado de.

compass card [ˈkʌmpəsˌkaːd] *n* (*Naut*) rosa *f* de los vientos.

compass course [ˈkʌmpəsˌkɔːs] *n* ruta *f* magnética.

compass rose [ˈkʌmpəsˈrəʊz] *n* = **compass card**.

compassion [kəmˈpæʃən] *n* compasión *f*; **to have ~ on** tener piedad de; **to move sb to ~** mover a uno a compasión.

compassionate [kəmˈpæʃənɪt] *adj* compasivo; **~ leave** baja *f* por razones familiares; **on ~ grounds** por compasión.

compassionately [kəmˈpæʃənɪtlɪ] *adv* compasivamente, con compasión.

compatibility [kəmˌpætəˈbɪlɪtɪ] *n* compatibilidad *f* (*also Comput*).

compatible [kəmˈpætɪbl] *adj* compatible (*also Comput*), conciliable.

compatriot [kəmˈpætrɪət] *n* compatriota *mf*.

compel [kəmˈpel] *vt* obligar; *admiration, respect* imponer; *surrender* exigir, hacer inevitable; **to ~ sb to do sth** forzar a uno a hacer algo; **I feel ~led to say** me veo obligado a decir.

compelling [kəmˈpelɪŋ] *adj argument etc* irresistible, apremiante, convincente; *curiosity etc* compulsivo.

compellingly [kəmˈpelɪŋlɪ] *adv* de modo convincente.

compendious [kəmˈpendɪəs] *adj* compendioso.

compendium [kəmˈpendɪəm] *n* compendio *m*.

compensate [ˈkɒmpənseɪt] **1** *vt* compensar; (*reward*) recompensar; (*for loss etc*) indemnizar, resarcir (*for* de). **2** *vi*: **to ~ for sth** compensar algo.

compensation [ˌkɒmpənˈseɪʃən] *n* compensación *f*; (*reward*) recompensa *f*; (*for loss etc*) indemnización *f*, resarcimiento *m*; **~ fund** fondo *m* de compensación.

compensatory [kɒmpənˈseɪtərɪ] *adj* compensatorio; **~ finance** financiación *f* compensatoria.

compère [ˈkɒmpɛəʳ] (*Brit*) **1** *n* presentador *m*, animador *m*. **2** *vt show* presentar. **3** *vi* actuar de presentador.

compete [kəmˈpiːt] *vi* (*as rivals*) competir, hacer competencia (*against, with* con, *for* por); (*in a race*) tomar parte (*in* en), presentarse (*in* a), concurrir (*in* a); **to ~ in a market** concurrir a un mercado.

competence [ˈkɒmpɪtəns], (*esp US*) **competency** [ˈkɒmpɪtənsɪ] *n* (**a**) aptitud *f*, capacidad *f*, competencia *f*; (*of court etc*) competencia *f*, incumbencia *f*; **that is not within my ~** eso está fuera de mi competencia. (**b**) (*Fin*) ingresos *mpl* (suficientes); **to have a modest ~** tener suficiente para vivir.

competent [ˈkɒmpɪtənt] *adj* (**a**) (*capable*) competente, capaz; **to be ~ to do sth** ser competente para hacer algo.

(**b**) (*adequate*) adecuado, suficiente; **a ~ knowledge of the language** un conocimiento suficiente del idioma.

competently [ˈkɒmpɪtəntlɪ] *adv* de modo adecuado, competentemente.

competing [kəmˈpiːtiŋ] *adj claim, product* en competencia, rival.

competition [ˌkɒmpɪˈtɪʃən] *n* (**a**) (*spirit*) competencia *f*, rivalidad *f*; **in ~ with** en competencia con; **there was keen ~ for the prize** se disputó reñidamente el premio.

(**b**) (*Comm*) competencia *f*; **unfair ~** competencia *f* desleal.

(**c**) (*contest*) concurso *m*; (*eg for Civil Service posts*) oposiciones *fpl*; **60 places to be filled by ~** 60 vacantes a cubrir por oposiciones.

competitive [kəmˈpetɪtɪv] *adj spirit* competidor, de competencia; *exam* de concurso, de 'numerus clausus'; *market, price, product* competitivo; **we must make ourselves more ~** tenemos que hacernos más competitivos; **we must improve our ~ position** tenemos que mejorar nuestras posibilidades de competir.

competitively [kəmˈpetɪtɪvlɪ] *adv do etc* con espíritu competidor; **a ~ priced product** un producto de precio competitivo.

competitiveness [kəmˈpetɪtɪvnɪs] *n* competitividad *f*.

competitor [kəmˈpetɪtəʳ] *n* (**a**) (*rival*) competidor *m*, -ora *f*, rival *mf*; (*Comm*) competidor *m*; (*Sport*) competidor *m*, -ora *f*, participante *mf*.

(**b**) (*in contest*) concursante *mf*; aspirante *mf*; (*eg for Civil Service post*) opositor *m*, -ora *f*.

compilation [ˌkɒmpɪˈleɪʃən] *n* compilación *f*, recopilación *f*.

compile [kəmˈpaɪl] *vt* compilar (*also Comput*), recopilar.

compiler [kəmˈpaɪləʳ] *n* (**a**) compilador *m*, -ora *f*, recopilador *m*, -ora *f*. (**b**) (*Comput*) compilador *m*.

complacence [kəmˈpleɪsəns] *n*, **complacency** [kəmˈpleɪsnsɪ] *n* suficiencia *f*, satisfacción *f* de sí mismo (*or* consigo); falso sentimiento *m* de seguridad.

complacent [kəmˈpleɪsənt] *adj* suficiente, satisfecho de sí mismo (*or* consigo), autosatisfecho.

complacently [kəmˈpleɪsəntlɪ] *adv* suficientemente, de modo satisfecho; **he looked at me ~** me miró complacido.

complain [kəmˈpleɪn] *vi* quejarse (*about, of* de, *that* de que, *to* a); reclamar (*about* contra, *to* ante); (*in shop etc, formally*) formular una queja; **to ~ of** (*Med*) presentar síntomas de, sufrir de; **you should ~ to the police** hay que denunciarlo a la policía; **I can't ~** yo no me quejo.

complainant [kəmˈpleɪnənt] *n* (*Jur*) demandante *mf*, querellante *mf*.

complaint [kəmˈpleɪnt] *n* (**a**) queja *f*; reclamación *f*; (*to police*) denuncia *f*; (*Jur*) querella *f*, demanda *f*; **~s department** sección *f* de reclamaciones; **~s procedure** procedimiento *m* para presentar reclamaciones; **~s book** libro *m* de reclamaciones; **to have cause for ~** tener motivo de queja; **to lodge** (*or* **make**) **a ~** formular una queja, hacer una reclamación.

(**b**) (*Med*) enfermedad *f*, mal *m*, dolencia *f*.

complaisant [kəmˈpleɪzənt] *adj* servicial, cortés; *husband* consentido.

-complected [kəmˈplektɪd] *in compounds* (*US*) = **-complexioned**.

complement 1 [ˈkɒmplɪmənt] *n* (**a**) (*gen*) complemento *m*. (**b**) (*staff*) personal *m*, dotación *f* (*also Naut*). **2** [ˈkɒmplɪment] *vt* complementar.

complementary [ˌkɒmplɪˈmentərɪ] *adj* complementario; **they**

are ~ se complementan.

complete [kəm'pliːt] **1** *adj* entero, completo; total; (*finished*) acabado; (*accomplished*) consumado; **my happiness is** ~ mi dicha es completa; **tell me the** ~ **story** cuéntamelo todo; **it is a** ~ **mistake to think that** ... es totalmente erróneo pensar que ...; **it's a** ~ **disaster** es un desastre total; **it was not a** ~ **success** (*iro*) no obtuvo un éxito rotundo que digamos; **my report is still not quite** ~ mi informe todavía no está terminado del todo; **are we** ~? ¿estamos todos?; **it comes** ~ **with instructions** se sirve con sus instrucciones correspondientes; **he arrived** ~ **with equipment** llegó con su equipo y todo.

2 *vt* completar; (*finish*) terminar, acabar, concluir; *years* cumplir; *form* rellenar, llenar; **to** ~ **my happiness** para colmo de dicha.

completely [kəm'pliːtlɪ] *adv* completamente, enteramente; totalmente; por completo; a fondo.

completeness [kəm'pliːtnɪs] *n* integridad *f*, perfección *f*; lo completo *etc*; **for the sake of** ~ para completar.

completion [kəm'pliːʃən] *n* terminación *f*, conclusión *f*; (*of contract etc*) realización *f*; **on** ~ en cuanto se termine; **to be nearing** ~ estar para terminarse; ~ **date** (*Jur*: *for work*) fecha *f* de cumplimiento; (*in house-buying*) fecha *f* de firma del contrato.

complex ['kɒmpleks] **1** *adj* complejo, complicado.

2 *n* (**a**) (*Psych*) complejo *m*; **he's got a** ~ **about it** aquello le acompleja, se siente acomplejado de (*or* con) eso.

(**b**) (*Tech*) complejo *m*; (*industrial* ~) complejo *m* industrial; **shopping** ~ complejo *m* comercial.

complexion [kəm'plekʃən] *n* tez *f*, cutis *m*; (*in terms of colour*) tez *f*, piel *f*; (*fig*) cariz *m*, aspecto *m*; **that puts a different** ~ **on it** entonces la cosa cambia de aspecto.

-complexioned [kəm'plekʃnd] *adj ending in compounds* de piel ...; **dark**~ de piel morena; **light**~ de piel blanca.

complexity [kəm'pleksɪtɪ] *n* complejidad *f*, lo complicado.

compliance [kəm'plaɪəns] *n* sumisión *f* (*with* a); (*agreement*) conformidad *f*; **in** ~ **with** de acuerdo con, obedeciendo a, conforme a.

compliant [kəm'plaɪənt] *adj* sumiso.

complicate ['kɒmplɪkeɪt] *vt* complicar.

complicated ['kɒmplɪkeɪtɪd] *adj* complicado.

complication [ˌkɒmplɪ'keɪʃən] *n* complicación *f*; lo complicado; ~**s** dificultades *fpl*; **it seems there are** ~**s** parece que han surgido dificultades.

complicity [kəm'plɪsɪtɪ] *n* complicidad *f* (*in* en).

compliment 1 ['kɒmplɪmənt] *n* (**a**) (*polite expression, of praise*) cumplido *m*; (*flirtatious*) piropo *m*; **what a nice** ~! ¡qué detalle!; **that was meant as a** ~ lo dije con buena intención; **to pay a** ~ **to** hacer cumplidos a, (*flirtatiously*) piropear a; **I take that as a** ~ agradezco la cortesía; **I take it as a** ~ **that** ... para mí es un honor que + *subj*; **they did me the** ~ **of coming along** me hicieron el honor de asistir.

(**b**) ~**s** (*greetings*) saludos *mpl*; ~**s slip** hoja *f* de cumplido; **'with** ~**s'** 'con un atento saludo'; **with the** ~**s of Mr X** con un atento saludo de X, de parte del Sr X; **with the** ~**s of the season** deseándole felices Pascuas (*etc*); **with the** ~**s of the management** obsequio *m* de la casa; **with the author's** ~**s** homenaje *m* del autor, obsequio *m* del autor; **to return the** ~ devolver el cumplido; **to send one's** ~**s to** enviar saludos a.

2 ['kɒmplɪment] *vt*: **to** ~ **sb on sth** felicitar a uno por algo.

complimentary [ˌkɒmplɪ'mentərɪ] *adj remark etc* lisonjero; favorable; *ticket* de favor; ~ **copy** ejemplar *m* obsequio; **he was very** ~ **about the play** habló en términos muy favorables de la obra.

complin(e) ['kɒmplɪn] *n* completas *fpl*.

comply [kəm'plaɪ] *vi* obedecer; acceder; **to** ~ **with** conformarse con, ajustarse a, *order* obedecer, *law* acatar.

component [kəm'pəʊnənt] **1** *adj* componente; **its** ~ **parts** las piezas que lo integran. **2** *n* componente *m*; (*Tech*) pieza *f*, componente *m*; ~**s factory** fábrica *f* de componentes.

comport [kəm'pɔːt] **1** *vi*: **to** ~ **with** concordar con. **2** *vr*: **to** ~ **o.s.** comportarse.

comportment [kəm'pɔːtmənt] *n* comportamiento *m*.

compose [kəm'pəʊz] **1** *vti* componer; **to be** ~**d of** constar de, componerse de. **2** *vr*: **to** ~ **o.s.** calmarse, tranquilizarse; **I** ~**d myself to play** me dispuse a tocar.

composed [kəm'pəʊzd] *adj* sosegado, tranquilo, sereno.

composedly [kəm'pəʊzɪdlɪ] *adv* sosegadamente.

composer [kəm'pəʊzəʳ] *n* compositor *m*, -ora *f*.

composite ['kɒmpəzɪt] **1** *adj* compuesto; ~ **motion** propuesta *f*. **2** *n* propuesta *f*.

composition [ˌkɒmpə'zɪʃən] *n* (**a**) (*gen*) composición *f*. (**b**) (*Jur*) acomodamiento *m*, arreglo *m*.

compositor [kəm'pɒzɪtəʳ] *n* cajista *m*.

compos mentis ['kɒmpɒs'mentɪs] *adj*: **to be** ~ estar en su sano (*or* entero) juicio.

compost ['kɒmpɒst] *n* abono *m* (vegetal).

compost-heap ['kɒmpɒsthiːp] *n* montón *m* de abono (vegetal).

composting ['kɒmpɒstɪŋ] *n* compostación *f*.

composure [kəm'pəʊʒəʳ] *n* serenidad *f*, calma *f*; **to recover one's** ~ serenarse.

compote ['kɒmpəʊt] *n* compota *f*.

compound 1 ['kɒmpaʊnd] *adj* compuesto; *fracture* complicado; ~ **interest** interés *m* compuesto; ~ **sentence** oración *f* compuesta. **2** ['kɒmpaʊnd] *n* (**a**) (*Chem*) compuesto *m*; (*Gram*) vocablo *m* compuesto. (**b**) (*enclosure*) recinto *m*. **3** [kəm'paʊnd] *vt* (**a**) componer, mezclar; *difficulty, offence* agravar; *debt* ajustar, componer; **to** ~ **a felony** aceptar dinero para no entablar juicio. (**b**) **it is** ~**ed of X and Z** consiste en X y Z. **4** [kəm'paʊnd] *vi*: **to** ~ **with** capitular con.

compounding ['kɑmpaʊndɪŋ] *n* composición *f*.

comprehend [ˌkɒmprɪ'hend] **1** *vt* (**a**) (*understand*) comprender, entender. (**b**) (*include*) comprender, abarcar.

2 *vi* comprender.

comprehensible [ˌkɒmprɪ'hensəbl] *adj* comprensible.

comprehensibly [ˌkɒmprɪ'hensəblɪ] *adv* comprensiblemente, de modo comprensible.

comprehension [ˌkɒmprɪ'henʃən] *n* comprensión *f*; ~ **test** test *m* de comprensión; **it is past** ~ es incomprensible; **it passes my** ~ **that** ... para mí resulta incomprensible que ...

comprehensive [ˌkɒmprɪ'hensɪv] **1** *adj* completo, exhaustivo; de gran alcance, de máximo alcance; *knowledge, study* extenso; *report* global; *account, view* de conjunto; ~ **insurance** seguro *m* a todo riesgo; ~ **school** (*Brit*) = **2**. **2** *n* (*Brit*) instituto *m* (de segunda enseñanza).

compress 1 ['kɒmpres] *n* compresa *f*. **2** [kəm'pres] *vt* comprimir (*into* en) (*also Comput*); *text etc* reducir (*into* a), condensar.

compressed [kəm'prest] *adj* comprimido; ~ **air** aire *m* comprimido; ~ **charge** (*US*) precio *m* inclusivo.

compression [kəm'preʃən] *n* compresión *f*.

compressor [kəm'presəʳ] *n* compresor *m* (*also Comput*); ~ **unit** unidad *f* de compresor.

comprise [kəm'praɪz] *vt* (*include*) comprender; (*consist of*) constar de, componerse de; *range* abarcar; **to be** ~**d within certain limits** estar incluido dentro de ciertos límites.

compromise ['kɒmprəmaɪz] **1** *n* (*spirit, art of* ~) transigencia *f*; contemporización *f*; (*agreement*) transacción *f*, avenencia *f*, arreglo *m*; concesiones *fpl* recíprocas; (*midway point*) término *m* medio; solución *f* intermedia; **we shall have to make a** ~ tendremos que hacer una concesión; **there can be no** ~ **with treason** no transigimos con la traición; **to reach a** ~ llegar a un arreglo.

2 *vt person* comprometer, *thing* poner en peligro.

3 *vi* transigir, ceder un poco para llegar a un acuerdo; contemporizar; hacerse concesiones recíprocas; llegar a un acuerdo; **I agreed to** ~ consentí en que la cosa quedase en un término medio, convine en transigir; **so we** ~**d on 7** así que convinimos en el término medio de 7; **to** ~ **with** transigir con, avenirse con.

4 *vr*: **to** ~ **o.s.** comprometerse.

compromising ['kɒmprəmaɪzɪŋ] *adj situation* comprometedor; *mind, spirit* acomodaticio.

comptometer [kɒm*p*'tɑmɪtəʳ] *n* máquina *f* de calcular; ~ **operator** operador *m*, -ora *f* de máquina de calcular.

comptroller [kən'trəʊləʳ] *n* interventor *m* -ora *f*.

compulsion [kəm'pʌlʃən] *n* obligación *f*, fuerza *f* mayor, coacción *f*; **under** ~ por fuerza; **you are under no** ~ nadie le obliga a ello.

compulsive [kəm'pʌlsɪv] *adj* compulsivo.

compulsively [kəm'pʌlsɪvlɪ] *adv* compulsivamente.

compulsorily [kəm'pʌlsərɪlɪ] *adv* por fuerza, forzosamente.

compulsory [kəm'pʌlsərɪ] *adj* obligatorio; preceptivo, de precepto; ~ **liquidation** liquidación *f* obligatoria; ~ **purchase** (*Brit*) expropiación *f*; ~ **purchase order** orden *f* de expropiación; ~ **redundancy** despido *m* forzoso.

compunction [kəm'pʌŋkʃən] *n* remordimiento *m*; compunción *f*; **without** ~ sin escrúpulo.

computation [ˌkɒmpjʊ'teɪʃən] *n* (**a**) (*gen*) cómputo *m*, cálculo *m*. (**b**) (*Comput*) computación *f*.

computational [ˌkɒmpjʊ'teɪʃənl] *adj* computacional; ~ **linguistics** lingüística *f* computacional.

compute [kəm'pjuːt] *vt* computar, calcular (*at* en).

computer [kəm'pjuːtəʳ] **1** *n* ordenador *m*, computadora *f*; **we do it by ~ now** ahora lo hacemos con el ordenador; **the records have all been put on ~** todos los registros han entrado en (el) ordenador. **2** *attr* de ordenador; informático; **~ animation** animación *f* por ordenador; **~ dating service** agencia *f* matrimonial por ordenador; **~ expert** experto *m*, -a *f* en ordenadores; **~ game** videojuego *m*; **~ graphics** gráficas *fpl* por ordenador; **~ language** lenguaje *m* de ordenador; **~ literacy** competencia *f* en la informática; **~ literate** competente en la informática; **~ model** modelo *m* informático; **~ operator** operador *m*, -ora *f* de ordenador; **~ printout** impresión *f* (de ordenador); **~ program** programa *m* de ordenador; **~ programmer** programador *m*, -ora *f* de ordenadores; **~ programming** programación *f* de ordenadores; **~ science** informática *f*, ciencias *fpl* de la computación; **~ scientist** informático *m*, -a *f*; **~ simulation** simulación *f* por ordenador; **~ skills** conocimientos *mpl* de informática; **~ studies = ~ science**; **~ time** tiempo *m* máquina; **~ typesetting** composición *f* por ordenador; **~ user** usuario *m*, -a *f* de ordenador.

computeracy [ˌkɒmpjʊ'terəsɪ] *n* competencia *f* en la informática.

computer-aided [kəm'pjuːtə'eɪdɪd] *adj*, **computer-assisted** [kəm'pjuːtəə'sɪstɪd] *adj* asistido por ordenador.

computerate [kəm'pjuːtərɪt] *adj* competente en la informática.

computer-controlled [kəm'pjuːtəkən'trəʊld] *adj* controlado por ordenador.

computerese [kəmˌpjuːtə'riːz] *n* jerga *f* informática.

computerization [kəmˌpjuːtəraɪ'zeɪʃən] *n* computerización *f*.

computerize [kəm'pjuːtəraɪz] *vt information* computerizar, informatizar; *office* instalar ordenadores en; **we're ~d now** ahora tenemos ordenador.

computing [kəm'pjuːtɪŋ] *n* informática *f*; **~ problem** problema *m* de cómputo; **~ task** tarea *f* de computar.

comrade ['kɒmrɪd] *n* camarada *mf* (*also Pol*), compañero *m*, -a *f*.

comrade-in-arms ['kɒmrɪdɪn'ɑːmz] *n* compañero *m* de armas.

comradely ['kɒmreɪdlɪ] *adj* de camarada(s); **we did it in a ~ spirit** lo hicimos como camaradas; **I gave him some ~ advice** le di unos consejos de camarada.

comradeship ['kɒmrɪdʃɪp] *n* compañerismo *m*, camaradería *f*.

COMSAT ['kɒmsæt] *n abbr of* **communications satellite** satélite *m* de comunicaciones, COMSAT *m*.

con¹ (††) [kɒn] *vt* (*also* **to ~ over**) estudiar, repasar.

con²* [kɒn] **1** *n* timo *m*, estafa *f*. **2** *vt* timar, estafar; **to ~ sb into doing sth** lograr con engaños que uno haga algo; **I was ~ned into it** me camelaron para que lo hiciera* (*or* aceptara *etc*); **he ~ned them into thinking that ...** logró con mañas que pensaran que ... **3** *attr*: **~ artist** estafador *m*, engañabobos *m*.

con³ [kɒn] *n V* **pro**.

con⁴ [kɒn] *n* (‡: *prisoner*) preso *m*, -a *f*.

Con. (*Brit*) *abbr of* **constable**.

concatenation [kɒnˌkætɪ'neɪʃən] *n* concatenación *f*.

concave ['kɒn'keɪv] *adj* cóncavo.

concavity [kɒn'kævɪtɪ] *n* concavidad *f*.

conceal [kən'siːl] *vt* ocultar (*from* a); *emotion* disimular; (*Jur*) encubrir.

concealed [kən'siːld] *adj* oculto; *emotion* disimulado; *lighting* indirecto.

concealment [kən'siːlmənt] *n* ocultación *f*; encubrimiento *m* (*also Jur*); (*of emotion*) disimulación *f*; **place of ~** escondrijo *m*.

concede [kən'siːd] *vt* conceder; *match* ceder, entregar; **I ~ that ...** confieso que ...; **to ~ victory** darse por vencido.

conceit [kən'siːt] *n* (**a**) (*pride*) presunción *f*, engreimiento *m*, vanidad *f*. (**b**) (*Liter*) concepto *m*.

conceited [kən'siːtɪd] *adj* presumido, engreído, vanidoso, creído (*LAm*); **to be ~ about** envanecerse con (*or* de, por).

conceitedly [kən'siːtɪdlɪ] *adv* vanidosamente, envanecidamente.

conceivable [kən'siːvəbl] *adj* concebible.

conceivably [kən'siːvəblɪ] *adv* posiblemente; **it cannot ~ be true** no es concebible que sea verdad; **more than one could ~ need** más de lo que se podría imaginar como necesidad.

conceive [kən'siːv] **1** *vt* (**a**) *child* concebir.

(**b**) (*imagine*) imaginar, formarse un concepto de; *idea* tener; *plan* idear; **I ~ it to be my duty** creo que es mi deber; **I cannot ~ why** no me explico por qué; **~d in plain terms** formulado en lenguaje sencillo.

(**c**) *affection, dislike etc* tomar, cobrar (*for* a).

2 *vi* concebir; **to ~ of** formarse un concepto de; **I cannot ~ of anything worse** no me puedo imaginar nada peor.

concentrate ['kɒnsəntreɪt] **1** *n* (*Chem*) concentrado *m*, sustancia *f* concentrada.

2 *vt* concentrar; *troops etc* concentrar, reunir; *hopes* cifrar (*on* en); **it ~s the mind wonderfully** hace reflexionar profundamente, da lugar a una maravillosa toma de conciencia.

3 *vi* concentrarse; (*troops etc*) concentrarse, reunirse; **to ~ on** concentrarse en, concentrar la atención en; **to ~ on doing sth** concentrarse para hacer algo; **he can't ~** no sabe concentrarse.

concentrated ['kɒnsənˌtreɪtɪd] *adj* concentrado.

concentration [ˌkɒnsən'treɪʃən] *n* concentración *f*; **~ camp** campo *m* de concentración.

concentric [kən'sentrɪk] *adj* concéntrico.

concept ['kɒnsept] *n* concepto *m*.

conception [kən'sepʃən] *n* (**a**) (*of child*) concepción *f*.

(**b**) (*idea*) idea *f*, concepto *m*; **a bold ~** un concepto grandioso; **he has not the remotest ~ of** no tiene la menor idea de.

conceptual [kən'septjʊəl] *adj* conceptual.

conceptualization [kənˌseptjʊəlaɪ'zeɪʃən] *n* conceptualización *f*.

conceptualize [kən'septjʊəlaɪz] *vt* conceptualizar.

concern [kən'sɜːn] **1** *n* (**a**) (*matter*) asunto *m*; **that's my ~** eso es asunto mío; **it's no ~ of yours** no tiene nada que ver con Vd, no le atañe a Vd; **that's your ~!** ¡allá Vd!

(**b**) (*interest*) interés *m*; **it is of some ~ to us all** nos interesa a todos; **it's of no ~** no tiene importancia.

(**c**) (*anxiety*) preocupación *f* (*for, with* por), inquietud *f*; **it is a matter for ~ that ...** es inquietante que ...; **he showed his ~** se mostró preocupado; **with growing ~** con creciente alarma.

(**d**) (*firm*) empresa *f*; **going ~** empresa *f* próspera, empresa *f* en pleno funcionamiento; **the whole ~*** el asunto entero, todo el negocio.

2 *vt* tener que ver con, interesar, concernir; **as ~s** respecto de; **that does not ~ me** eso no tiene que ver conmigo, eso no me atañe; **it ~s me closely** me toca de cerca; **the book ~s a family** el libro trata de una familia; **my question ~s money** mi pregunta se refiere al dinero; **those ~ed** los interesados; **where** (*or* **as far as**) **women are ~ed** por lo que se refiere a las mujeres; **please contact the department ~ed** sírvase contactar con la sección correspondiente; **to whom it may ~** (*reference*) a quien interese, a quien le corresponda; **as far as I am ~ed** en cuanto a mí, por lo que a mí se refiere; **to be ~ed in** tomar parte en, intervenir en; estar involucrado en; **were you ~ed in this?** ¿tú estabas metido en esto?; **to be ~ed with others in a crime** estar implicado con otros en un crimen; **I am ~ed to ...** me preocupa + *infin*, me interesa + *infin*; **we are ~ed with facts** a nosotros nos interesan los hechos.

3 *vr*: **to ~ o.s. about sb** preocuparse por uno; **to ~ o.s. with** interesarse por, ocuparse de.

concerned [kən'sɜːnd] *adj* preocupado; inquieto; **to be very ~** inquietarse mucho (*about* por); **he sounded very ~** parecía estar muy preocupado; **I am ~ about you** me traes preocupado; **I am ~ to find that ...** me inquieta descubrir que ...

concerning [kən'sɜːnɪŋ] *prep* sobre, acerca de.

concert 1 ['kɒnsət] *n* concierto *m*; **in ~ with** conjuntamente con; **to act in ~** obrar de común acuerdo; **'The Crotch' are in ~ at the Palace** el grupo 'The Crotch' aparece en persona en el Teatro Palace.

2 ['kɒnsət] *attr*: **~ grand** piano *m* de cola larga; **~ party** (*Theat*) grupo *m* de artistas de revista; (*Fin*) confabulación *f* para adquirir acciones individualmente con intención de reunirlas en bloque; **~ performance** presentación *f* (de una ópera) en concierto, versión *f* concertante; **~ performer** concertista *mf*; **~ pianist** pianista *mf* de concierto; **~ pitch** diapasón *m* normal; **~ tour** gira *f* de conciertos.

3 [kən'sɜːt] *vt* concertar; *policy* coordinar, armonizar.

concerted [kən'sɜːtɪd] *adj action etc* coordinado, conjunto; **we made a ~ effort** coordinamos los esfuerzos (*to + infin* por + *infin*).

concertgoer ['kɒnsətˌgəʊəʳ] *n* aficionado *m*, -a *f* a los conciertos; **we are regular ~s** vamos con regularidad a los conciertos; **the ~s are an odd lot** los que asisten al concierto son gente rara.

concert-hall ['kɒnsəthɔːl] *n* sala *f* de conciertos.

concertina [ˌkɒnsə'tiːnə] **1** *n* concertina *f*; **~ crash** (*Aut*) choque *m* de acordeón. **2** *vi*: **the vehicles ~ed into each other** los vehículos colisionaron en acordeón.

concertmaster ['kɒnsət,mɑːstəʳ] *n* (*US*) primer violín *m*.

concerto [kən'tʃɛətəʊ] *n* concierto *m*.

concession [kən'seʃən] *n* concesión *f*; privilegio *m*; (*of tax*) desgravación *f*, exención *f*.

concessionaire [kən,seʃə'nɛəʳ] *n* concesionario *m*, -a *f*.

concessionary [kən'seʃənərɪ] **1** *adj fare* reducido; *ticket* de favor. **2** *n* concesionario *m*, -a *f*.

conch [kɒntʃ] *n* (*shell*) concha; (*Archit*) cóclea *f*.

concierge [,kɔ̃ːnsɪ'ɛəʒ] *n* conserje *m*.

conciliate [kən'sɪlɪeɪt] *vt* conciliar.

conciliation [kən,sɪlɪ'eɪʃən] *n* conciliación *f*; **~ service** servicio *m* de conciliación (*and V* **ACAS**).

conciliator [kən'sɪlɪeɪtəʳ] *n* conciliador *m*, -ora *f*; (*Ind*) árbitro *mf*.

conciliatory [kən'sɪlɪətərɪ] *adj* conciliador, conciliatorio.

concise [kən'saɪs] *adj* conciso.

concisely [kən'saɪslɪ] *adv* concisamente, con concisión.

conciseness [kən'saɪsnɪs] *n*, **concision** [kən'sɪʒən] *n* concisión *f*.

conclave ['kɒnkleɪv] *n* cónclave *m*.

conclude [kən'kluːd] **1** *vt* (**a**) (*end*) concluir, terminar; **'to be ~d'** (*serial*) 'terminará con el próximo episodio'.

(**b**) (*arrange*) *treaty* hacer, firmar, pactar; *agreement* llegar a, concertar; *deal* cerrar.

(**c**) (*infer*) colegir, concluir; **I ~ that ...** saco la consecuencia de que ...; **what are we to ~ from that?** ¿qué consecuencia se saca de eso?; **it was ~d that ...** se concluyó que ..., se decidió que ...

(**d**) (*US*: *decide*) decidir (*to do* hacer).

2 *vi* terminar(se); **he ~d with this remark** terminó haciendo esta observación; **the judge ~d in his favour** el juez decidió a su favor.

concluding [kən'kluːdɪŋ] *adj* final.

conclusion [kən'kluːʒən] *n* (**a**) (*end*) conclusión *f*, terminación *f*; **in ~** en conclusión, para terminar; **to bring sth to a ~** concluir un asunto, llevar un asunto a su desenlace.

(**b**) (*of treaty etc*) el firmar *etc*.

(**c**) (*inference*) conclusión *f*, consecuencia *f*; **foregone ~** resultado *m* inevitable; **to come to the ~ that ...** llegar a la conclusión de que ...; **draw your own ~s** extraiga Vd las conclusiones oportunas; **to jump to ~s** sacar conclusiones precipitadas; **to try ~s with** medirse con.

conclusive [kən'kluːsɪv] *adj* concluyente, decisivo; *evidence* decisivo.

conclusively [kən'kluːsɪvlɪ] *adv* concluyentemente.

concoct [kən'kɒkt] *vt* confeccionar; *lie, story* inventar; *plot* tramar.

concoction [kən'kɒkʃən] *n* (**a**) (*act*) confección *f*; (*of story*) invención *f*. (**b**) (*substance*) mezcla *f*; (*drink*) brebaje *m*.

concomitant [kən'kɒmɪtənt] **1** *adj* concomitante. **2** *n* concomitante *m*.

concord ['kɒŋkɔːd] *n* concordia *f*, armonía *f*; (*Mus, Gram*) concordancia *f*.

concordance [kən'kɔːdəns] *n* concordancia *f*; (*index, book*) concordancias *fpl*.

concordant [kən'kɔːdənt] *adj* concordante.

concordat [kɒn'kɔːdæt] *n* concordato *m*.

Concorde ['kɒŋkɔːd] *n* Concorde *m*; **to fly by ~** volar en Concorde.

concourse ['kɒŋkɔːs] *n* (*of people*) muchedumbre *f*, concurrencia *f*; (*of rivers*) confluencia *f*; (*Comm, Rail*) explanada *f*.

concrete ['kɒnkriːt] **1** *adj* (**a**) concreto; específico; **~ music** música *f* concreta; **~ noun** nombre *m* concreto. (**b**) (*Tech*) de hormigón; **~ jungle** jungla *f* de asfalto. **2** *n* hormigón *m*, gorgón *m* (*And*). **3** *vt* revestir de hormigón.

concrete-mixer ['kɒnkriːt,mɪksəʳ] *n* hormigonera *f*, revolvedora *f* (*LAm*).

concretion [kən'kriːʃən] *n* concreción *f*.

concretize ['kɒnkrɪ'taɪz] *vt* (*US*) concretar.

concubine ['kɒŋkjʊbaɪn] *n* concubina *f*, barragana *f*, manceba *f*.

concupiscence [kən'kjuːpɪsəns] *n* concupiscencia *f*.

concupiscent [kən'kjuːpɪsənt] *adj* concupiscente.

concur [kən'kɜːʳ] *vi* (**a**) (*happen together*) concurrir, coincidir. (**b**) (*agree*) asentir; **to ~ in** convenir en; **to ~ with** estar de acuerdo con.

concurrence [kən'kʌrəns] *n* acuerdo *m*, conformidad *f*.

concurrent [kən'kʌrənt] *adj* concurrente; **~ processing** procesamiento *m* concurrente.

concurrently [kən'kʌrəntlɪ] *adv* al mismo tiempo.

concuss [kən'kʌs] *vt* producir una conmoción cerebral a.

concussion [kən'kʌʃən] *n* conmoción *f* cerebral.

condemn [kən'dem] *vt* condenar (*to* a); (*blame*) censurar; *building* declarar ruinoso; *bad food* confiscar; **~ed cell** celda *f* de los condenados a muerte; **the ~ed man** el reo de muerte; **such conduct is to be ~ed** tal conducta es censurable.

condemnation [,kɒndem'neɪʃən] *n* condena *f*, condenación *f*; (*blaming*) censura *f*.

condemnatory [,kɒndem'neɪtərɪ] *adj* condenatorio.

condensation [,kɒnden'seɪʃən] *n* condensación *f*; (*of text*) forma *f* abreviada.

condense [kən'dens] **1** *vt* condensar; *text* abreviar; **~d milk** leche *f* condensada. **2** *vi* condensarse.

condenser [kən'densəʳ] *n* condensador *m*.

condescend [,kɒndɪ'send] *vi*: **to ~ to** + *infin* dignarse + *infin*.

condescending [,kɒndɪ'sendɪŋ] *adj* superior, lleno de superioridad; desdeñoso, altivo; **he's very ~** se cree muy superior, mira por encima del hombro a los demás.

condescendingly [,kɒndɪ'sendɪŋlɪ] *adv* con aire de superioridad, con desdén.

condescension [,kɒndɪ'senʃən] *n* aire *f* de superioridad, aire *m* protector.

condiment ['kɒndɪmənt] *n* condimento *m*.

condition [kən'dɪʃən] **1** *n* (**a**) (*stipulation*) condición *f*; **on this ~** con esta condición; **on no ~** de ninguna manera; **on ~ (that)** a condición de que + *subj*.

(**b**) (*state*) condición *f*, estado *m*; **in a bad ~** en malas condiciones; **he has a heart ~** tiene una afección cardíaca; **to be in no ~ to** + *infin* no estar en condiciones de + *infin*; **to be out of ~** estar en mal estado; (*person*) no estar en forma; **to keep o.s. in ~** mantenerse en forma.

(**c**) **~s** (*circumstances*) condiciones *fpl*; **under existing ~s** en las circunstancias actuales.

(**d**) (*social*) clase *f*; **of humble ~** de clase humilde.

2 *vt* condicionar, determinar.

conditional [kən'dɪʃənl] **1** *adj* condicional; **~ offer** oferta *f* condicional; **to be ~ upon** depender de. **2** *n* potencial *m*.

conditionally [kən'dɪʃnəlɪ] *adv* condicionalmente, con reservas.

conditioned [kən'dɪʃənd] *adj* condicionado; **~ reflex** reflejo *m* condicionado.

conditioner [kən'dɪʃənəʳ] *n* (*for hair*) suavizante *m* de cabello; (*for skin*) crema *f* suavizante; (*fabric ~*) suavizante *m*.

conditioning [kən'dɪʃənɪŋ] *n* acondicionamiento *m*.

condo* ['kɒndəʊ] *n* (*US*) = **condominium**.

condole [kən'dəʊl] *vi*: **to ~ with sb** condolerse de uno; dar el pésame a uno.

condolences [kən'dəʊlənsɪz] *npl* pésame *m*; **please accept my ~** le acompaño en el sentimiento; **to send one's ~** dar el pésame.

condom ['kɒndəm] *n* condón *m*, preservativo *m*.

condominium ['kɒndə'mɪnɪəm] *n* condominio *m*; (*US*) apartamento *m*, piso *m*, condominio *m* (*LAm*) (*que es propiedad del que lo habita*); propiedad *f* horizontal.

condone [kən'dəʊn] *vt* condonar; *abuse* tolerar.

condor ['kɒndɔːʳ] *n* cóndor *m*.

conduce [kən'djuːs] *vi*: **to ~ to** conducir a.

conducive [kən'djuːsɪv] *adj*: **~ to** conducente a, propicio para, que favorece.

conduct **1** ['kɒndʌkt] *n* conducta *f*, comportamiento *m*; (*of business etc*) manejo *m*, dirección *f*, administración *f*; **~ report** (*Scol*) informe *m* de conducta.

2 [kən'dʌkt] *vt* conducir (*also Phys*); *business, negotiations, campaign etc* llevar, dirigir; *one's case* presentar; *orchestra* dirigir; **to ~ a correspondence with** estar en correspondencia con, cartearse con; **we were ~ed through a passage** nos hicieron pasar por un pasillo; **we were ~ed round by Lord X** actuó de guía Lord X.

3 [kən'dʌkt] *vi* (*Mus*) llevar la batuta.

4 [kən'dʌkt] *vr*: **to ~ o.s.** comportarse.

conducted [kən'dʌktɪd] *adj*: **~ tour** (*Brit*) (*of building*) visita *f* guiada, (*of country*) viaje *m* acompañado.

conduction [kən'dʌkʃən] *n* conducción *f*.

conductive [kən'dʌktɪv] *adj* conductivo.

conductivity [,kɒndʌk'tɪvɪtɪ] *n* conductibilidad *f*, conductividad *f*.

conductor [kən'dʌktəʳ] *n* (**a**) (*Mus*) director *m*; (*of bus*) cobrador *m*; (*US Rail*) revisor *m*. (**b**) (*lightning ~*) pararrayos *m*; (*Phys*) conductor *m*.

conductress [kən'dʌktrɪs] *n* cobradora *f*.

conduit ['kɒndɪt] *n* conducto *m*.

cone [kəʊn] *n* (*Geom*) cono *m*; (*Bot*) cono *m*, piña *f*; (*ice* *cream*) cucurucho *m*, pirucho *m* (*CAm*), cambucho *m* (*SC*).

◆**cone off** *vt road* cerrar con conos, cortar con conos.

coney ['kəʊnɪ] *n* (*US*) conejo *m*.

confab* ['kɒnfæb] *n* = **confabulation**.

confabulate [kən'fæbjʊleɪt] *vi* conferenciar.

confabulation [kən,fæbjʊ'leɪʃən] *n* conferencia *f*.

confection [kən'fekʃən] *n* (**a**) confección *f*, hechura *f*. (**b**) (*Culin*) dulce *m*, confite *m*.

confectioner [kən'fekʃənəʳ] *n* pastelero *m*, -a *f*, repostero *m*, -a *f*; **~'s (shop)** pastelería *f*, repostería *f*, confitería *f*, dulcería *f* (*LAm*); **~'s sugar** (*US*) azúcar *m* glas(eado).

confectionery [kən'fekʃənərɪ] *n* (*Brit*) pasteles *mpl*; (*sweets*) dulces *mpl*, confites *mpl*, golosinas *fpl* (*LAm*), confitería *f*.

confederacy [kən'fedərəsɪ] *n* confederación *f*; (*plot*) complot *m*; **the C~** (*US*) los Estados Confederados.

confederate 1 [kən'fedərɪt] *adj* confederado. **2** [kən'fedərɪt] *n* confederado *m*; (*Jur*) cómplice *m*; (*US Hist*) confederado *m*, -a *f*. **3** [kən'fedəreɪt] *vt* confederar. **4** [kən'fedəreɪt] *vi* confederarse.

confederation [kən,fedə'reɪʃən] *n* confederación *f*.

confer [kən'fɜːʳ] **1** *vt* conceder, otorgar (*on* a). **2** *vi* conferenciar (*about* sobre, *with* con).

conferee [,kɒnfɜː'riː] *n* (*US*) congresista *mf*.

conference ['kɒnfərəns] *n* (*assembly*) congreso *m*, conferencia *f*; (*business meeting*) conferencia *f*, reunión *f*; **~ call** conferencia *f*; **~ centre** (*town*) ciudad *f* de congresos; (*building*) palacio *m* de congresos; (*in institution*) centro *m* de conferencias; **~ member** congresista *mf*; **~ room** sala *f* de conferencias; **~ table** mesa *f* negociadora; **he's in ~ right now** precisamente ahora está conferenciando.

conferencing ['kɒnfərensɪŋ] *n* (*Comput*) conferencia *f*; **~ system** sistema *m* de conferencias.

conferment [kən'fɜːmənt], **conferral** [kən'fɜːrəl] *n* concesión *f*, otorgamiento *m* (*on* a).

confess [kən'fes] **1** *vt* confesar.

2 *vi* (*Eccl*) confesarse; **to ~ to a crime** confesarse culpable de un crimen; **to ~ to a liking for** confesar tener afición a; **I was wrong, I ~** me equivoqué, lo confieso.

3 *vr*: **I ~ myself wholly ignorant** confieso que no sé nada en absoluto de eso.

confessed [kən'fest] *adj* declarado.

confession [kən'feʃən] *n* confesión *f*; **~ of faith** profesión *f* de fe, credo *m*; **to go to ~** confesarse; **to hear sb's ~** confesar a uno; **to make a full ~** confesarlo todo, confesar de plano.

confessional [kən'feʃənl] *n* confesonario *m*.

confessor [kən'fesəʳ] *n* confesor *m*.

confetti [kən'fetiː] *n* confeti *m*.

confidant [,kɒnfɪ'dænt] *n* confidente *m*.

confidante [,kɒnfɪ'dænt] *n* confidenta *f*.

confide [kən'faɪd] **1** *vt* confiar (*to* a, en).

2 *vi*: **to ~ in** confiar en, fiarse de; **please ~ in me** puedes fiarte de mí; **to ~ to** hacer confidencias a; **he ~d to me that ...** me dijo en confianza que ....

confidence ['kɒnfɪdəns] *n* (**a**) (*gen*) confianza *f* (*in* en, *that* en que); (*secrecy*) confidencialidad *f*, reserva *f*; **in ~** en confianza; **'(write) in strict ~'** 'absoluta reserva'; **'please apply in strict ~ to ...'** 'las solicitudes bajo reserva absoluta a ...'; **to be in sb's ~, to enjoy sb's ~** disfrutar de la intimidad de uno; **to gain ~** adquirir confianza; **to give sb ~** infundir confianza a uno; **we have every ~ in you** tenemos entera confianza en Vd; **I have every ~ that ...** estoy totalmente seguro de que ...; **to put one's ~ in** confiar en; **to take sb into one's ~** revelar un secreto a uno, hacer confidencias a uno.

(**b**) (*revelation*) confidencia *f*.

confidence man ['kɒnfɪdənsmæn] *n*, *pl* **confidence men** [kɒnfɪdənsmen] timador *m*, estafador *m*.

confidence trick ['kɒnfɪdənstrɪk] *n*, (*US*) **confidence game** ['kɒnfɪdənsgeɪm] *n* timo *m*, estafa *f*.

confidence trickster ['kɒnfɪdəns,trɪkstəʳ] *n* timador *m*, estafador *m*.

confident ['kɒnfɪdənt] *adj* seguro de sí mismo, lleno de confianza; (*over~*) confiado; **to be ~ about, to be ~ of** estar seguro de; **to be ~ that ...** estar seguro de que ....

confidential [,kɒnfɪ'denʃəl] *adj information, letter, report etc* confidencial; *secretary, tone* de confianza.

confidentiality [,kɒnfɪ,denʃɪ'ælɪtɪ] *n* confidencialidad *f*.

confidentially [,kɒnfɪ'denʃəlɪ] *adv* en confianza.

confidently ['kɒnfɪdəntlɪ] *adv*: **he said ~** dijo lleno de confianza; **we ~ expect that ...** creemos con toda confianza que ...

confiding [kən'faɪdɪŋ] *adj*: **(too) ~** confiado; crédulo; **in a ~ tone** en tono de confianza.

configuration [kən,fɪgjʊ'reɪʃən] *n* configuración *f* (*also Comput*).

confine [kən'faɪn] **1** *vt* (*enclose*) encerrar (*to* en), confinar; (*fig*) limitar (*to* a); **to be ~d** (*woman*) estar de parto; **to be ~d to** limitarse a; **the damage is ~d to this part** el daño afecta únicamente esta parte; **this bird is ~d to Spain** esta ave existe únicamente en España; **to be ~d to bed** tener que guardar cama; **to be ~d to one's room** no poder dejar su cuarto.

2 *vr*: **to ~ o.s. to** limitarse a; **please ~ yourself to the facts** le ruego se limite a exponer los hechos.

confined [kən'faɪnd] *adj* reducido.

confinement [kən'faɪnmənt] *n* (*enclosure*) encierro *m* (*to* en); confinamiento *m*, confinación *f*; (*imprisonment*) prisión *f*, reclusión *f*; (*Med*) parto *m*, sobreparto *m*; **~ to barracks** arresto *m* en cuartel.

confines ['kɒnfaɪnz] *npl* confines *mpl*.

confirm [kən'fɜːm] *vt* confirmar; *treaty* ratificar; (*Eccl*) confirmar.

confirmation [,kɒnfə'meɪʃən] *n* confirmación *f*; ratificación *f*; (*Eccl*) confirmación *f*.

confirmed [kən'fɜːmd] *adj* inveterado.

confiscate ['kɒnfɪskeɪt] *vt* confiscar, incautarse de, requisar (*esp LAm*).

confiscation [,kɒnfɪs'keɪʃən] *n* confiscación *f*, incautación *f*, requisa *f* (*esp LAm*).

conflagration [,kɒnflə'greɪʃən] *n* conflagración *f*, incendio *m*.

conflate [kən'fleɪt] *vt* combinar.

conflation [kən'fleɪʃn] *n* combinación *f*.

conflict 1 ['kɒnflɪkt] *n* conflicto *m*; **~ of evidence** contradicción *f* de testimonios; **~ of interests** incompatibilidad *f*; **the theories are in ~** las teorías están reñidas; **to be in ~ with** estar en pugna con, estar reñido con; **to come into ~ with** chocar con.

2 [kən'flɪkt] *vi* estar en pugna (*with* con), estar reñido (*with* con).

conflicting [kən'flɪktɪŋ] *adj report* contradictorio; *interest* opuesto.

confluence ['kɒnfluəns] *n* confluencia *f*.

conform [kən'fɔːm] *vi* conformarse; **to ~ to, to ~ with** ajustarse a, estar de acuerdo con, cuadrar con.

conformism [kən'fɔːmɪzəm] *n* conformismo *m*.

conformist [kən'fɔːmɪst] **1** *adj* conformista. **2** *n* conformista *mf*.

conformity [kən'fɔːmɪtɪ] *n* conformidad *f*; **in ~ with** conforme a (*or* con).

confound [kən'faʊnd] *vt* confundir; **~ it!** ¡demonio!; **~ the man!** ¡maldito sea éste!

confounded [kən'faʊndɪd] *adj* condenado.

confront [kən'frʌnt] *vt* (*face squarely*) hacer frente a, encararse con; (*face defiantly*) enfrentarse con; *texts* confrontar; **the problems which ~ us** los problemas que se nos plantean; **we were ~ed by the river** estaba delante el río; **to ~ sb with sth** confrontar a uno con algo; **to ~ the accused with witnesses** confrontar al acusado con los testigos, carear a los testigos con el acusado; **to ~ sb with the facts** exponer delante de uno los hechos.

confrontation [,kɒnfrən'teɪʃən] *n* confrontación *f*; careo *m*.

Confucian [kən'fjuːʃən] **1** *adj* de Confucio. **2** *n* confuciano *m*, -a *f*.

Confucianism [kən'fjuːʃənɪzəm] *n* confucionismo *m*.

Confucius [kən'fjuːʃəs] *nm* Confucio.

confuse [kən'fjuːz] *vt* (**a**) (*mix up*) confundir (*with* con); *issue etc* complicar, embarullar, (*deliberately*) embrollar, entenebrecer; **to ~ A and B** confundir A con B.

(**b**) (*perplex*) desconcertar, dejar confuso a, aturdir; **to get ~d** desorientarse, aturrullarse, desconcertarse.

confused [kən'fjuːzd] *adj situation etc* confuso; *person* perplejo, despistado; **my mind is ~** tengo la cabeza trastornada.

confusedly [kən'fjuːzɪdlɪ] *adv* confusamente.

confusing [kən'fjuːzɪŋ] *adj* confuso, desconcertante; **it's all very ~** todo ello es muy difícil de comprender.

confusingly [kən'fjuːzɪŋlɪ] *adv* (**a**) confusamente; de manera confusa. (**b**) **~, two of them had the same name** para despistar a la gente, dos de ellos tenían el mismo nombre.

confusion [kən'fjuːʒən] *n* (**a**) (*disorder*) confusión *f*, desorden *m*; **to be in ~** estar en desorden; **to retire in ~** retirarse en desorden.

(**b**) (*perplexity*) confusión *f*, perplejidad *f*, desorientación *f*, despiste *m*; (*embarrassment*) confusión *f*, humillación *f*; **to be in ~** estar desorientado; **to be covered in ~** estar

avergonzado.
confute [kən'fjuːt] *vt* refutar.
congeal [kən'dʒiːl] **1** *vt* congelar, cuajar, coagular; **2** *vi* congelarse, cuajarse, coagularse.
congenial [kən'dʒiːnɪəl] *adj* simpático, agradable, compatible.
congenital [kən'dʒenɪtl] *adj* congénito.
congenitally [kən'dʒenɪtlɪ] *adv* congénitamente.
conger (eel) ['kɒŋgər'(iːl)] *n* congrio *m*.
congested [kən'dʒestɪd] *adj area* congestionado, superpoblado; *building etc* lleno, de bote en bote; **to get ~ with** llenarse de, atestarse de; **it's getting very ~ in here** esto se nos está poniendo muy apretado.
congestion [kən'dʒestʃən] *n* congestión *f* (*also Med*), aglomeración *f*.
conglomerate **1** [kən'glɒmərɪt] *n* conglomerado *m*. **2** [kən'glɒməreɪt] *vt* conglomerar, aglomerar. **3** [kən'glɒməreɪt] *vi* conglomerarse, aglomerarse.
conglomeration [kən,glɒmə'reɪʃən] *n* conglomeración *f*.
Congo ['kɒŋgəʊ] *n*: **the ~** el Congo; **Republic of the ~** República *f* del Congo.
Congolese [,kɒŋgəʊ'liːz] **1** *adj* congoleño. **2** *n* congoleño *m*, -a *f*.
congratulate [kən'grætjuleɪt] *vt* felicitar, dar la enhorabuena a (*on* por).
congratulations [kən,grætjʊ'leɪʃənz] *npl* felicitaciones *fpl*; **~!** ¡enhorabuena!, ¡felicidades!
congratulatory [kən'grætjʊlətərɪ] *adj* de felicitación.
congregate ['kɒŋgrɪgeɪt] *vi* congregarse.
congregation [,kɒŋgrɪ'geɪʃən] *n* (*assembly*) reunión *f*; (*Eccl: present in church*) fieles *mpl*, (*parishioners*) feligreses *mpl*; (*society of religious*) congregación *f*.
congregational [,kɒŋgrɪ'geɪʃnl] *adj* congregacionalista.
congregationalist [,kɒŋgrɪ'geɪʃənəlɪst] *n* congregacionalista *mf*.
congress ['kɒŋgres] *n* congreso *m*; **C~** (*US*) Congreso *m*; **~ member** miembro *mf* del congreso, congresista *mf*.
congressional [kɒŋ'greʃənl] *adj* del congreso.
congressman ['kɒŋgresmən] *n*, *pl* **congressmen** ['kɒŋgresmən] (*US*) diputado *m*, miembro *m* del Congreso.
congresswoman ['kɒŋgres,wʊmən] *n*, *pl* **congresswomen** ['kɒŋgreswɪmɪn] (*US*) diputada *f*, miembro *f* del Congreso.
congruence ['kɒŋgrʊəns] *n*, **congruency** ['kɒŋgrʊənsɪ] *n* congruencia *f*.
congruent ['kɒŋgrʊənt] *adj* congruente.
congruity [kɒŋ'gruːɪtɪ] *n* congruencia *f* (*with* con).
congruous ['kɒŋgrʊəs] *adj* congruo (*with* con).
conic(al) ['kɒnɪk(əl)] *adj* cónico; **conic section** sección *f* cónica.
conifer ['kɒnɪfə^r] *n* conífera *f*.
coniferous [kə'nɪfərəs] *adj* conífero.
conjectural [kən'dʒektʃərəl] *adj* conjetural.
conjecture [kən'dʒektʃə^r] **1** *n* conjetura *f*. **2** *vt* conjeturar (*from* de, por, *that* que).
conjointly ['kɒn'dʒɔɪntlɪ] *adv* conjuntamente.
conjugal ['kɒndʒʊgəl] *adj* conyugal.
conjugate ['kɒndʒʊgeɪt] *vt* conjugar.
conjugation [,kɒndʒʊ'geɪʃən] *n* conjugación *f*.
conjunction [kən'dʒʌŋkʃən] *n* conjunción *f*; **in ~ with** conjuntamente con; **in ~ with this** (*as adv*) con relación a esto, con respecto a esto.
conjunctive [kən'dʒʌŋktɪv] *adj* conjuntivo.
conjunctivitis [kən,dʒʌŋktɪ'vaɪtɪs] *n* conjuntivitis *f*.
conjuncture [kən'dʒʌŋktʃə^r] *n* coyuntura *f*.
conjure¹ [kən'dʒʊə^r] *vt* suplicar (*to do sth* hacer algo).
conjure² ['kʌndʒə^r] *vi* hacer juegos de manos; **he ~s with handkerchiefs** hace un truco con pañuelos; **a name to ~ with** un nombre prestigioso.
◆**conjure away** *vt* conjurar, hacer desaparecer.
◆**conjure up** *vt* hacer aparecer; (*fig*) evocar, hacer pensar en.
conjurer ['kʌndʒərə^r] *n* prestidigitador *m*, mago* *m*.
conjuring ['kʌndʒərɪŋ] *n* juegos *mpl* de manos, ilusionismo *m*, prestidigitación *f*.
conjuring trick ['kʌndʒərɪŋ,trɪk] *n* juego *m* de manos.
conjuror ['kʌndʒərə^r] *n* = **conjurer**.
conk¹‡ [kɒŋk] *n* (**a**) (*Brit: nose*) narigón *m*, napias‡ *fpl*. (**b**) (*blow*) golpe *m*. (**c**) (*US: head*) cholla‡ *f*, coco‡ *m*.
conk²‡ [kɒŋk] *vi*: **to ~ out*** escoñarse‡, fallar, averiarse; pararse.
conker* ['kɒŋkə^r] *n* (*Brit*) castaña *f* de Indias; **~s** (*game*) juego *m* de las castañas.
con man* ['kɒnmæn] *n*, *pl* **con men** ['kɒnmen] timador *m*, estafador *m*.
Conn. (*US*) *abbr* = **Connecticut**.
connect [kə'nekt] **1** *vt* (*join*) juntar, unir (*to* con); (*Elec*) conectar (*to* con); (*relate*) relacionar, asociar (*with* con); **to ~ sb with** poner a uno al habla con; **I'm trying to ~ you** (*Telec*) trato de ponerle, trato de comunicarle (*LAm*); **are these matters ~ed?** ¿tienen alguna relación entre sí estas cuestiones?; **to be well ~ed** estar bien relacionado; **the Jones are ~ed with the Smiths** los Jones están emparentados con los Smith; **what firm are you ~ed with?** ¿con qué empresa trabajas?; **I never ~ed you with that** nunca creía que tuvieras que ver con eso.
2 *vi* (*join*) unirse, (*Elec*) conectarse; **to ~ with** (*Rail etc*) enlazar con.
connected [kə'nektɪd] *adj languages* relacionado; (*Bot, Jur*) conexo; (*fig*) *argument etc* conexo; **~ speech** discurso *m* conexo.
connecting [kə'nektɪŋ] *adj rooms etc* comunicado; *part, wire* conectable; **~ flight** vuelo *m* de enlace; **bedroom with ~ bathroom** habitación *f* comunicada con el baño.
connecting-rod [kə'nektɪŋrɒd] *n* biela *f*.
connection, connexion [kə'nekʃən] *n* (**a**) (*joint*) juntura *f*, unión *f*; (*Mech, Elec*) conexión *f*; (*Rail etc*) enlace *m*, correspondencia *f* (*with* con); **our ~s with the town are poor** son malas nuestras comunicaciones con la ciudad; **'we've got a bad ~'** (*Telec*) 'no se oye bien la línea'.
(**b**) (*fig*) relación *f* (*between* entre, *with* con); nexo *m*, enlace *m*; **we have ~s everywhere** tenemos relaciones con todas partes; **you have to have ~s** hay que tener buenas relaciones; **no ~ with any other firm** ésta es una firma independiente; **in ~ with** a propósito de; **in this ~** con respecto a esto.
connective [kə'nektɪv] **1** *adj* conjuntivo; **~ tissue** tejido *m* conjuntivo. **2** *n* conjunción *f*.
connectivity [,kɒnek'tɪvɪtɪ] *n* conectividad *f*.
conning-tower ['kɒnɪŋ,taʊə^r] *n* (*submarine*) torrecilla *f*, (*other warship*) torre *f* de mando.
connivance [kə'naɪvəns] *n* connivencia *f*; (*agreement*) consentimiento *m*.
connive [kə'naɪv] *vi*: **to ~ at** hacer la vista gorda a; **to ~ with sb to do sth** confabularse con uno para hacer algo.
conniving [kə'naɪvɪŋ] *adj* muy dado a intrigas; mañoso, tramposo.
connoisseur [,kɒnə'sɜː^r] *n* entendido *m*, -a *f* (*of* en), conocedor *m*, -ora *f* (*of* de), experto *m*, -a *f* (*of* en).
connotation [,kɒnəʊ'teɪʃən] *n* connotación *f*.
connotative ['kɒnə,teɪtɪv] *adj* connotativo.
connote [kɒ'nəʊt] *vt* connotar.
connubial [kə'njuːbɪəl] *adj* conyugal, connubial.
conquer ['kɒŋkə^r] **1** *vt territory* conquistar; *enemy, habit etc* vencer. **2** *vi* triunfar.
conquering ['kɒŋkərɪŋ] *adj* victorioso, triunfador.
conqueror ['kɒŋkərə^r] *n* conquistador *m*; vencedor *m*.
conquest ['kɒŋkwest] *n* conquista *f*.
Cons. *abbr of* **Conservative** conservador *m*, -ora *f*.
consanguinity [,kɒnsæŋ'gwɪnɪtɪ] *n* consanguinidad *f*.
conscience ['kɒnʃəns] *n* conciencia *f*; **bad ~** mala conciencia *f*; **in all ~** en verdad; **with a clear ~** con la conciencia tranquila; **I have a clear ~ about it** no creo tener culpa alguna por ello; **I have a guilty ~ about it, I have it on my ~** me está remordiendo la conciencia por ello; **I would not have the ~ to** + *infin* no me atrevería a + *infin*; **I could not in ~ say that** en conciencia no podría decir eso.
conscience money ['kɒnʃəns,mʌnɪ] *n dinero que se paga para descargar la conciencia* (*p. ej., atrasos de impuestos*).
conscience-raising ['kɒnʃəns,reɪzɪŋ] *n* concienciación *f*.
conscience-stricken ['kɒnʃəns,strɪkən] *adj* lleno de remordimientos.
conscientious [,kɒnʃɪ'enʃəs] *adj* concienzudo; **~ objector** objetor *m* de conciencia.
conscientiously [,kɒnʃɪ'enʃəslɪ] *adv* concienzudamente.
conscientiousness [,kɒnʃɪ'enʃəsnɪs] *n* diligencia *f*, escrupulosidad *f*.
conscious ['kɒnʃəs] **1** *adj* (**a**) (*aware*) **to be ~ of** ser consciente de, saber, hacerse cargo de; **to be ~ that ...** saber (perfectamente) que ...; **to become ~ of** darse cuenta de; **to become ~ that ...** darse cuenta de que ....
(**b**) (*deliberate*) intencional, expreso.
(**c**) (*Med*) **to be ~** tener conocimiento, estar consciente; **to become ~** volver en sí.
2 *n*: **the ~** el consciente.
-conscious [-,kɒnʃəs] *in compounds*: *eg* **security~** consciente de los problemas relativos a la seguridad.
consciously ['kɒnʃəslɪ] *adv* conscientemente, a sabiendas.

consciousness ['kɒnʃəsnɪs] *n* (**a**) consciencia *f*. (**b**) (*Med*) conocimiento *m*; **to lose ~** perder el conocimiento; **to regain ~** recobrar el conocimiento, volver en sí.
consciousness-raising ['kɒnʃəsnɪs,reɪzɪŋ] *n* concienciación *f*.
conscript 1 ['kɒnskrɪpt] *n* recluta *m*, quinto *m*, conscripto *m*, -a *f* (*LAm*). **2** [kən'skrɪpt] *vt* (*Mil*) llamar al servicio militar; *labourer etc* reclutar a la fuerza.
conscripted [kən'skrɪptɪd] *adj labourer etc* reclutado a la fuerza, forzado.
conscription [kən'skrɪpʃən] *n* servicio *m* militar obligatorio; (*act*) llamada *f* al servicio militar, conscripción *f* (*LAm*).
consecrate ['kɒnsɪkreɪt] *vt* consagrar.
consecration [,kɒnsɪ'kreɪʃən] *n* consagración *f*.
consecutive [kən'sekjʊtɪv] *adj* sucesivo, seguido; (*Gram etc*) consecutivo; **on 3 ~ days** 3 días seguidos.
consecutively [kən'sekjʊtɪvlɪ] *adv* sucesivamente.
consensus [kən'sensəs] *n* consenso *m*.
consent [kən'sent] **1** *n* consentimiento *m* (*to* a); **by common ~** según la opinión general, de común acuerdo; **by mutual ~** de común acuerdo; **divorce by mutual ~** divorcio *m* por acuerdo mutuo.
2 *vi* consentir (*to* en, *to + infin* en + *infin*).
consenting [kən'sentɪŋ] *adj*: **~ party** parte *f* que da su consentimiento; **between ~ adults** entre personas de edad para consentir.
consequence ['kɒnsɪkwəns] *n* consecuencia *f*; resultado *m*; **in ~** por consiguiente; **in ~ of** de resultas de; **it is of no ~** no tiene importancia; **to put up with** (*or* **take**) **the ~s** aceptar las consecuencias.
consequent ['kɒnsɪkwənt] *adj* consiguiente.
consequential [,kɒnsɪ'kwenʃəl] *adj* (**a**) (*resulting*) consiguiente, resultante; **the moves ~ upon this decision** las medidas que resultan de esta decisión.
(**b**) (*important*) importante, con consecuencias importantes.
consequently ['kɒnsɪkwəntlɪ] *adv* por consiguiente.
conservancy [kən'sɜːvənsɪ] *n* conservación *f*; *V* **nature 2**.
conservation [,kɒnsə'veɪʃən] *n* conservación *f* (*esp* de recursos naturales), preservación *f*; **~ area** (*Brit*) zona *f* perteneciente al patrimonio artístico.
conservationism [,kɒnsə,veɪʃənɪzəm] *n* conservacionismo *m*.
conservationist [,kɒnsə'veɪʃənɪst] *n* conservacionista *mf*.
conservatism [kən'sɜːvətɪzəm] *n* conservadurismo *m*.
conservative [kən'sɜːvətɪv] **1** *adj* (**a**) (*Pol*) conservador; **C~ Party** (*Brit*) Partido *m* Conservador. (**b**) *estimate etc* prudente, cauteloso, moderado. **2** *n* conservador *m*, -ora *f*.
conservatoire [kən'sɜːvətwɑːʳ] *n* conservatorio *m*.
conservatory [kən'sɜːvətrɪ] *n* invernadero *m*.
conserve [kən'sɜːv] **1** *n* conserva *f*. **2** *vt* conservar; **to ~ one's strength** reservarse.
consider [kən'sɪdəʳ] **1** *vt* (**a**) (*deem*) considerar; **I ~ that ...** considero que ...; **I ~ it an honour** lo tengo a mucha honra; **I ~ him to be clever** le considero inteligente, creo que es inteligente; **I ~ the matter closed** para mí el asunto está concluido; **he is ~ed to be the best** se le considera el mejor.
(**b**) (*realize*) **when one ~s that ...** cuando uno se da cuenta de que ...
(**c**) (*think over*) considerar, pensar, meditar; **~ how much you owe him** considera cuánto le debes; **all things ~ed** considerándolo bien, todo bien mirado; **my ~ed opinion is that ...** estoy convencido de que ....
(**d**) (*study*) estudiar, examinar; **we are ~ing the matter** estamos estudiando el asunto; **he is being ~ed for the post** le están considerando para el puesto.
(**e**) (*entertain*) **have you ever ~ed going by train?** ¿has pensado alguna vez en ir en tren?; **would you ~ buying it?** ¿te interesa comprarlo?; **I wouldn't ~ it for a moment** no quiero pensarlo siquiera; **he refused even to ~ it** se negó a pensarlo siquiera.
(**f**) (*take into account*) tomar en cuenta; **you must ~ others' feelings** hay que tomar en cuenta los sentimientos de los demás.
2 *vr*: **I ~ myself happy** me considero feliz; **~ yourself lucky** puedes considerarte afortunado; **~ yourself dismissed** considérese despedido.
considerable [kən'sɪdərəbl] *adj* importante, apreciable, cuantioso; *sum etc* importante; *loss* sensible; **we had ~ difficulty** tuvimos bastante dificultad.
considerably [kən'sɪdərəblɪ] *adv* bastante, mucho, considerablemente.
considerate [kən'sɪdərɪt] *adj* considerado, atento, comedido; **it's most ~ of you** es muy amable de su parte.
considerately [kən'sɪdərɪtlɪ] *adv* con consideración.
consideration [kən,sɪdə'reɪʃən] *n* (**a**) (*thoughtfulness*) consideración *f*; **as a mark of my ~** en señal de mi consideración; **in ~ of** en consideración a; **out of ~ for** por respeto a; **without due ~** sin reflexión; **that is a ~** eso hay que tenerlo en cuenta; **it is under ~** lo estamos estudiando; **we are giving the matter our ~** estamos estudiando la cuestión; **to take into ~** tener en cuenta.
(**b**) (*payment*) retribución *f*; **for a ~** previo pago, mediante pago.
(**c**) (*importance*) importancia *f*, consideración *f*; **to be of no** (*or* **little**) **~** no tener importancia.
considering [kən'sɪdərɪŋ] **1** *adv* (*) teniendo en cuenta todas las circunstancias, a pesar de todo. **2** *prep* en consideración a, teniendo en cuenta ...
consign [kən'saɪn] *vt* consignar (*also Comm*); enviar; (*entrust*) confiar (*to* a); **to ~ to oblivion** sepultar en el olvido.
consignee [,kɒnsaɪ'niː] *n* consignatorio *m*, -a *f*.
consigner, consignor [kən'saɪnəʳ] *n* consignador *m*, -ora *f*.
consignment [kən'saɪnmənt] *n* consignación *f*; envío *m*, remesa *f*; **~ note** (*Brit*) talón *m* de expedición; **goods on ~** mercancías *fpl* en consignación.
consist [kən'sɪst] *vi*: **to ~ of** consistir en, constar de, componerse de.
consistency [kən'sɪstənsɪ] *n* (*of person, action*) consecuencia *f*, lógica *f*; coherencia *f*; (*density*) consistencia *f*.
consistent [kən'sɪstənt] *adj person, action, argument* consecuente, lógico; coherente; *pupil, results* constante; (*dense*) consistente; **to be ~ with** ser consecuente con, estar de acuerdo con, ser compatible con.
consistently [kən'sɪstəntlɪ] *adv* (*logically*) consecuentemente; (*all the time*) constantemente; **to act ~** obrar con consecuencia.
consolation [,kɒnsə'leɪʃən] *n* consuelo *m*; (*act*) consolación *f*; **~ goal** tanto *m* del honor; **~ prize** premio *m* de consolación, (*academic etc*) accésit *m*; **it is some ~ to know that ...** me reconforta saber que ...; **if it's any ~ to you** si te consuela de algún modo.
consolatory [kən'sɒlətərɪ] *adj* consolador.
console[1] [kən'səʊl] *vt* consolar.
console[2] ['kɒnsəʊl] *n* (*Mus, Tech etc*) consola *f*.
consolidate [kən'sɒlɪdeɪt] **1** *vt* consolidar; concentrar; fortalecer. **2** *vi* consolidarse.
consolidated [kən'sɒlɪdeɪtɪd] *adj* consolidado; **~ accounts** cuentas *fpl* consolidadas; **~ balance sheet** hoja *f* de balance consolidado; **~ fund** fondo *m* consolidado.
consolidation [kən,sɒlɪ'deɪʃən] *n* consolidación *f*; concentración *f*; fortalecimiento *m*.
consoling [kən'səʊlɪŋ] *adj* consolador, reconfortante.
consols ['kɒnsɒlz] *npl* valores *mpl* consolidados.
consommé [kən'sɒmeɪ] *n* consomé *m*, caldo *m*.
consonance ['kɒnsənəns] *n* consonancia *f*.
consonant ['kɒnsənənt] **1** *adj* consonante; **~ with** de acuerdo con, conforme a. **2** *n* consonante *f*.
consonantal [,kɒnsə'næntl] *adj* consonántico.
consort 1 ['kɒnsɔːt] *n* consorte *mf*; **prince ~** príncipe *m* consorte *m*. **2** [kən'sɔːt] *vi*: **to ~ with** ir con, asociarse con; (*agree*) concordar con.
consortium [kən'sɔːtɪəm] *n* consorcio *m*.
conspectus [kən'spektəs] *n* vista *f* general, ojeada *f* general; resumen *m*.
conspicuous [kən'spɪkjʊəs] *adj* visible, llamativo, que sobresale; (*fig*) destacado, sobresaliente; notable; **~ consumption** consumo *m* ostentoso; **to be ~** destacar(se); **to make o.s. ~** llamar la atención; singularizarse; *V* **absence**.
conspicuously [kən'spɪkjʊəslɪ] *adv* visiblemente, claramente; de modo que llama la atención; (*fig*) notablemente.
conspiracy [kən'spɪrəsɪ] *n* conspiración *f*, conjuración *f*, complot *m*; **~ of silence** conspiración *f* de silencio.
conspirator [kən'spɪrətəʳ] *n* conspirador *m*, -ora *f*.
conspiratorial [kən,spɪrə'tɔːrɪəl] *adj* de conspirador.
conspire [kən'spaɪəʳ] *vi* conspirar (*against* contra, *with* con, *to + infin* para + *infin*).
constable ['kʌnstəbl] *n* (*Brit*) policía *m*, guardia *m*.
constabulary [kən'stæbjʊlərɪ] *n* (*Brit*) policía *f*.
Constance ['kɒnstəns] *nf* Constanza.
constancy ['kɒnstənsɪ] *n* constancia *f*; fidelidad *f*.
constant ['kɒnstənt] **1** *adj* (**a**) (*unending*) constante, continuo, incesante. (**b**) (*faithful*) constante; fiel, leal; *reader etc* asiduo.
2 *n* constante *f*.
Constantine ['kɒnstəntaɪn] *nm* Constantine.
Constantinople [,kɒnstæntɪ'nəʊpl] *n* Constantinopla *f*.

constantly ['kɒnstəntlɪ] *adv* constantemente.
constellation [ˌkɒnstə'leɪʃən] *n* constelación *f*.
consternation [ˌkɒnstə'neɪʃən] *n* consternación *f*; **in** ~ consternado; **there was general** ~ se consternaron todos.
constipate ['kɒnstɪpeɪt] *vt* estreñir; **to be** ~**d** estar estreñido.
constipation [ˌkɒnstɪ'peɪʃən] *n* estreñimiento *m*.
constituency [kən'stɪtjʊənsɪ] *n* distrito *m* electoral, circunscripción *f*.
constituent [kən'stɪtjʊənt] **1** *adj* constitutivo, integrante; ~ **assembly** cortes *fpl* constituyentes. **2** *n* constitutivo *m*, componente *m*; (*Pol*) elector *m*, -ora *f*.
constitute ['kɒnstɪtjuːt] **1** *vt* constituir; (*make up*) componer, integrar. **2** *vr*: **to** ~ **o.s. a judge** constituirse en juez.
constitution [ˌkɒnstɪ'tjuːʃən] *n* constitución *f*.
constitutional [ˌkɒnstɪ'tjuːʃənl] **1** *adj* constitucional; ~ **law** derecho *m* político. **2** *n* paseo *m*.
constitutionally [ˌkɒnstɪ'tjuːʃənəlɪ] *adv* según la constitución.
constrain [kən'streɪn] *vt*: **to** ~ **sb to do sth** obligar a uno a hacer algo; **to feel** ~**ed to do sth** verse en la necesidad de hacer algo.
constraint [kən'streɪnt] *n* (*compulsion*) fuerza *f*; (*confinement*) encierro *m*; (*restraint*) reserva *f*, (*of atmosphere*) frialdad *f*; **budgetary** ~**s** restricciones *fpl* presupuestarias; **under** ~ obligado (a ello); **to feel a certain** ~ sentirse algo cohibido.
constrict [kən'strɪkt] *vt* apretar, estrechar.
constricted [kən'strɪktɪd] *adj space* limitado, reducido; *freedom, movement* restringido; (*Phon*) constrictivo; **to feel** ~ (*by clothes etc*) sentirse constreñido; **I feel** ~ **by these regulations** me siento constreñido por estas reglas.
constricting [kən'strɪktɪŋ] *adj dress, ideology* estrecho.
constriction [kən'strɪkʃən] *n* constricción *f*.
construct **1** [kən'strʌkt] *vt* construir. **2** ['kɒnstrʌkt] *n* construcción *f*.
construction [kən'strʌkʃən] *n* **(a)** (*act*) construcción *f*; (*building*) construcción *f*, edificio *m*; ~ **company** compañía *f* constructora; ~ **engineer** ingeniero *m* de construcción; ~ **industry** industria *f* de la construcción; **in course of** ~, **under** ~ en construcción. **(b)** (*interpretation*) interpretación *f*; **to put a wrong** ~ **on sth** interpretar algo mal; **it depends what** ~ **one places on his words** depende de cómo se interpreten sus palabras. **(c)** (*Gram*) construcción *f*.
constructional [kən'strʌkʃənl] *adj* estructural; ~ **toy** juguete *m* con que se construyen modelos.
constructive [kən'strʌktɪv] *adj* constructivo; positivo.
constructively [kən'strʌktɪvlɪ] *adv* constructivamente.
constructor [kən'strʌktəʳ] *n* constructor *m*.
construe [kən'struː] *vt* interpretar; (*Gram*) construir; analizar.
consul ['kɒnsəl] *n* cónsul *mf*; ~ **general** cónsul *mf* general.
consular ['kɒnsjʊləʳ] *adj* consular.
consulate ['kɒnsjʊlɪt] *n* consulado *m*.
consulship ['kɒnsəlʃɪp] *n* consulado *m*.
consult [kən'sʌlt] **1** *vt* consultar; *one's interests* tener en cuenta. **2** *vi*: **people should** ~ **more** la gente debiera consultar más entre sí; **to** ~ **together** (*US*) consultar entre sí; **to** ~ **with** (*US*) consultar con, aconsejarse con.
consultancy [kən'sʌltənsɪ] *n* (*Comm*) consultoría *f*, asesoría *f*; (*Med*) puesto *m* de especialista; ~ **fees** (*Comm*) derechos *mpl* de asesoría; (*Med*) derechos *mpl* de consulta.
consultant [kən'sʌltənt] *n* consultor *m*, -ora *f*; asesor *m*, -ora *f*; (*Tech*) consejero *m* técnico, consejera *f* técnica; (*Brit Med*) especialista *mf*; **to act as** ~ asesorar; ~ **engineer** ingeniero *m* consejero; ~ **physician** médico *mf* especialista; ~ **psychiatrist** psiquiatra *mf* especialista.
consultation [ˌkɒnsəl'teɪʃən] *n* (*act*) consulta *f*; (*meeting*) consulta *f*, consultación *f*.
consultative [kən'sʌltətɪv] *adj* consultivo; ~ **document** documento *m* consultivo; **I was there in a** ~ **capacity** yo estuve en calidad de asesor.
consulting-hours [kən'sʌltɪŋˌaʊəz] *npl* (*Brit*) horas *fpl* de consulta.
consulting-room [kən'sʌltɪŋrʊm] *n* (*Brit*) consultorio *m*, consulta *f*.
consumables [kən'sjuːməblz] *npl* artículos *mpl* de consumo.
consume [kən'sjuːm] *vt* (*eat*) comer(se), (*drink*) beber(se); (*use*) consumir, utilizar; (*by fire etc*) consumir; **the house was** ~**d by fire** la casa quedó arrasada por el fuego; **to be** ~**d with** *envy etc* estar muerto de.
consumer [kən'sjuːməʳ] **1** *n* consumidor *m*, -ora *f*. **2** *attr* consumista; ~ **behavior** (*US*), ~ **behaviour** comportamiento *m* del consumidor; ~ **choice** libertad *f* del consumidor para elegir; ~ **credit** crédito *m* al consumidor; ~ **demand** demanda *f* de consumo; ~ **durables** artículos *mpl* de equipo; ~ **goods** bienes *mpl* de consumo; ~ **price index** índice *m* de precios al consumo, IPC *m*; ~ **product** producto *m* al consumidor; ~ **protection** protección *f* al consumidor; ~ **research** estudio *m* de mercado; ~ **resistance** resistencia *f* por parte del consumidor; ~ **rights** derechos *mpl* del consumidor; ~ **sampling** muestreo *m* del consumidor; ~ **sector** sector *m* consumista; ~ **society** sociedad *f* de consumo; ~ **survey** encuesta *f* sobre consumidores.
consumerism [kən'sjuːmərɪzəm] *n* consumismo *m*; defensa *f* del consumidor.
consuming [kən'sjuːmɪŋ] *adj* arrollador, apasionado; *passion* dominante, avasallador.
consummate **1** [kən'sʌmɪt] *adj* consumado, completo; *skill* sumo. **2** ['kɒnsʌmeɪt] *vt* consumar.
consummation [ˌkɒnsʌ'meɪʃən] *n* consumación *f*.
consumption [kən'sʌmpʃən] *n* **(a)** consumo *m*. **(b)** (*Med*) tisis *f*.
consumptive [kən'sʌmptɪv] **1** *adj* tísico. **2** *n* tísico *m*, -a *f*.
cont. *abbr of* **continued** continuación *f*, sigue.
contact ['kɒntækt] **1** *n* contacto *m*; **business** ~**s** relaciones *fpl* comerciales; **he rang up one of his business** ~**s** llamó a uno de sus colegas comerciales; **he has a lot of** ~**s** tiene muchas relaciones, (*pej*) tiene muchos enchufes, tiene buenas aldabas; **you have to have a** ~ **in the business** hay que tener un buen enchufe en el negocio; **to come into** ~ **with** tocar, (*violently*) chocar con, (*fig*) tener que ver con, tratar; **to get into** ~ **with** ponerse en contacto con; **to lose** ~ **with sb** perder el contacto con uno; **to make** ~ **with sb** lograr contactar con uno; **I seem to make no** ~ **with him** me resulta imposible comunicar con él.
2 *vt* contactar (con), ponerse en contacto con, comunicar con.
contact-breaker ['kɒntækt,breɪkəʳ] *n* (*Elec*) interruptor *m*.
contact-lens ['kɒntækt,lenz] *n* lente *f* de contacto, (micro)lentilla *f*.
contact-man ['kɒntæktmæn] *n*, *pl* **contact-men** ['kɒntæktmen] intermediario *m*.
contact-print ['kɒntæktprɪnt] *n* contact *m*.
contagion [kən'teɪdʒən] *n* contagio *m*.
contagious [kən'teɪdʒəs] *adj* contagioso.
contain [kən'teɪn] **1** *vt* contener; (*Math*) ser exactamente divisible por. **2** *vr*: **to** ~ **o.s.** contenerse, contener la risa (*etc*).
container [kən'teɪnəʳ] *n* **(a)** recipiente *m*, receptáculo *m*; (*box*) caja *f*; (*wrapper etc*) envase *m*. **(b)** (*Naut, Rail etc*) contenedor *m*, contáiner *m*; ~ **depot**, ~ **terminal** terminal *f* para portacontenedores; ~ **ship** buque *m* contenedor, portacontenedores *m*; ~ **train** tren *m* de contenedores; ~ **transport** transporte *m* por contenedor.
containerization [kən,teɪnəraɪ'zeɪʃən] *n* contenerización *f*.
containerize [kən'teɪnəraɪz] *vt* contenerizar, transportar en contenedores.
containment [kən'teɪnmənt] *n* (*Pol*) contención *f*.
contaminant [kən'tæmɪnənt] *n* contaminante *m*.
contaminate [kən'tæmɪneɪt] *vt* contaminar; **to be** ~**d by** contaminarse con (*or* de).
contamination [kən,tæmɪ'neɪʃən] *n* contaminación *f*.
contango [kən'tæŋgəʊ] *n* (*St Ex*) aplazamiento *m* de pago hasta el próximo día de ajuste de cuentas.
contd *abbr of* **continued** continuación *f*, sigue.
contemplate ['kɒntempleɪt] *vt* **(a)** (*gaze on*) contemplar; **I** ~ **the future with misgiving** el futuro lo veo dudoso.
(b) (*expect*) contar con.
(c) (*intend*) pensar, intentar, proyectar; **he** ~**d suicide** pensó suicidarse; **we** ~ **a holiday in Spain** proyectamos unas vacaciones en España; **when do you** ~ **doing it?** ¿cuándo se propone hacerlo?, ¿cuándo tiene intención de hacerlo?
contemplation [ˌkɒntem'pleɪʃən] *n* contemplación *f*.
contemplative [kən'templətɪv] *adj* contemplativo.
contemporaneous [kən,tempə'reɪnɪəs] *adj* contemporáneo.
contemporaneously [kən,tempə'reɪnɪəslɪ] *adv* contemporáneamente.
contemporary [kən'tempərərɪ] **1** *adj* contemporáneo, coetáneo. **2** *n* contemporáneo *m*, -a *f*, coetáneo *m*, -a *f*.
contempt [kən'tempt] *n* desprecio *m*; ~ **of court** desacato *m* al juez (*or* al tribunal), rebeldía *f*; **beneath** ~ despreciable; **to bring into** ~ desprestigiar, envilecer; **to hold in** ~ despreciar, (*Jur*) declarar en rebeldía.
contemptible [kən'temptəbl] *adj* despreciable, vil.
contemptuous [kən'temptjʊəs] *adj* desdeñoso, despectivo;

to be ~ of desdeñar, menospreciar.

contemptuously [kən'temptjʊəslɪ] *adv* desdeñosamente, con desprecio.

contend [kən'tend] **1** *vt* afirmar, sostener (*that* que).
2 *vi* contender, luchar; **to ~ with sb for sth** contender con uno sobre algo; **we have many problems to ~ with** se nos plantean muchos problemas.

contender [kən'tendər] *n* contendiente *mf*.

contending [kən'tendɪŋ] *adj* rival, opuesto.

content[1] [kən'tent] **1** *adj* contento (*with* con), satisfecho (*with* de); **to be ~** estar contento; **he was ~ to stay there** estaba contento de seguir allí.
2 *n* contento *m*, satisfacción *f*; **to one's heart's ~** a gusto, a más no poder, hasta quedarse satisfecho.
3 *vt* contentar, satisfacer.
4 *vr*: **to ~ o.s.** contentarse (*with sth* con algo, *with saying* con decir).

content[2] ['kɒntent] *n* contenido *m*; **~s** contenido *m*; (*of book*: *heading*) índice *m* de materias.

contented [kən'tentɪd] *adj* satisfecho, contento.

contentedly [kən'tentɪdlɪ] *adv* con satisfacción, contentamente.

contentedness [kən'tentɪdnɪs] *n* contento *m*.

contention [kən'tenʃən] *n* (**a**) (*strife*) contienda *f*; **teams in ~** equipos *mpl* rivales. (**b**) (*point*) argumento *m*, aseveración *f*, pretensión *f*; **it is our ~ that ...** pretendemos que ..., sostenemos que ....

contentious [kən'tenʃəs] *adj* contencioso, conflictivo, discutible.

contentment [kən'tentmənt] *n* contento *m*.

contest 1 ['kɒntest] *n* (*struggle*) contienda *f*, lucha *f*; (*competition*) concurso *m*, prueba *f*.
2 [kən'test] *vt* (*dispute*) impugnar, atacar; *legal suit* defender; *election* ser candidato en; *seat* disputar, presentarse como candidato a; **I ~ your right to do that** niego que Vd tenga el derecho de hacer eso; **the seat was not ~ed** en las elecciones se presentó un solo candidato.
3 [kən'test] *vi*: **to ~ against** contender con; **they are ~ing for a big prize** se disputan un premio importante.

contestant [kən'testənt] *n* contendiente *mf*, contrincante *m*; (*Sport, competition etc*) concursante *mf*, aspirante *mf*.

context ['kɒntekst] *n* contexto *m*; **to put sth in ~** explicar el contexto de algo; **we must see this in ~** tenemos que ver esto en su contexto; **it was taken out of ~** fue arrancado de su contexto.

contextual [kɒn'tekstjʊəl] *adj* contextual.

contiguous [kən'tɪgjʊəs] *adj* contiguo (*to* a).

continence ['kɒntɪnəns] *n* continencia *f*.

continent ['kɒntɪnənt] **1** *adj* continente. **2** *n* continente *m*; **the C~** (*Brit*) el continente europeo; **on the C~** (*Brit*) en Europa (continental).

continental [ˌkɒntɪ'nentl] **1** *adj* continental; **~ breakfast** desayuno *m* continental; **~ climate** clima *m* continental; **~ drift** deriva *f* continental; **~ quilt** edredón *m*; **~ shelf** plataforma *f* continental. **2** *n* (*Brit*) europeo *m*, -a *f* (continental).

contingency [kən'tɪndʒənsɪ] *n* contingencia *f*; **~ fund** fondo *m* para imprevistos; **~ planning** planificación *f* para una eventual emergencia; **~ plans** medidas *fpl* de prevención; **should the ~ arise** por si acaso; **to provide for every ~** tener en cuenta todas las posibilidades; **£50 for contingencies** 50 libras para gastos imprevistos.

contingent [kən'tɪndʒənt] **1** *adj* contingente, eventual; **to be ~ upon** depender de. **2** *n* contingente *m*.

continual [kən'tɪnjʊəl] *adj* continuo, constante.

continually [kən'tɪnjʊəlɪ] *adv* constantemente.

continuance [kən'tɪnjʊəns] *n* continuación *f* (*also St Ex*); (*stay*) permanencia *f*.

continuation [kənˌtɪnjʊ'eɪʃən] *n* continuación *f*; (*lengthening*) prolongación *f*.

continue [kən'tɪnjuː] **1** *vt* continuar; seguir; *story etc* proseguir; (*retain*) mantener (*in a post* en un puesto); (*lengthen*) prolongar; **~d on page 10** sigue en la página 10; **'to be ~d'** (*serial*) 'continuará', 'seguirá'.
2 *vi* continuar; seguir; (*extend*) prolongarse; **to ~ talking, to ~ to talk** seguir hablando; **to ~ on one's way** seguir su camino; **to ~ in office** seguir en su puesto; **to ~ in a place** seguir en un sitio.

continuing [kən'tɪnjʊɪŋ] *adj* *argument* irresoluto; *correspondence* continuado; **~ education** *cursos de enseñanza para adultos*.

continuity [ˌkɒntɪ'njuːɪtɪ] *n* continuidad *f* (*also Cine*); **~ girl, ~ man** secretaria *f*, -o *m* de continuidad.

continuo [kən'tɪnjʊəʊ] *n* continuo *m*.

continuous [kən'tɪnjʊəs] *adj* continuo; **~ assessment** evaluación *f* continua; **~ inventory** inventario *m* continuo; **~ (feed) paper, ~ stationery** papel *m* continuo.

continuously [kən'tɪnjʊəslɪ] *adj* continuamente.

continuum [kən'tɪnjʊəm] *n* continuo *m*.

contort [kən'tɔːt] *vt* retorcer, deformar.

contortion [kən'tɔːʃən] *n* contorsión *f*.

contortionist [kən'tɔːʃənɪst] *n* contorsionista *mf*.

contour ['kɒntʊər] *n* contorno *m*; **~ flying** vuelo *m* rasante; **~ line** isohipsa *f*, curva *f* de nivel; **~ map** mapa *m* hipsométrico, plano *m* acotado.

contra... ['kɒntrə] *pref* contra...

contraband ['kɒntrəbænd] **1** *n* contrabando *m*. **2** *attr* de contrabando.

contrabass [ˌkɒntrə'beɪs] *n* contrabajo *m*.

contrabassoon [ˌkɒntrəbə'suːn] *n* contrafagot *m*.

contraception [ˌkɒntrə'sepʃən] *n* contracepción *f*.

contraceptive [ˌkɒntrə'septɪv] **1** *adj* anticonceptivo, anticoncepcional, contraceptivo; **~ pill** píldora *f* anticonceptiva. **2** *n* anticonceptivo *m*, contraceptivo *m*.

contract 1 ['kɒntrækt] *n* contrato *m* (*for* de); (*for public works, Theat, etc*) contrata *f*; **~ bridge** bridge-contrato *m*; **~ of employment** contrato *m* de trabajo; **~ killer** asesino *m* contratado, asesino *m* a sueldo; **~ price** precio *m* contractual; **~ work** trabajo *m* bajo contrato; **they are under ~ to X** tienen contrato con X, tienen obligaciones contractuales con X; **to enter into a ~** hacer un contrato (*with* con); **to place a ~ with** dar un contrato a; **to put work out to ~** ofrecer trabajo bajo contrato fuera de la empresa; **there's a ~ out for him*** le han puesto precio a su cabeza.
2 [kən'trækt] *vt* contraer.
3 [kən'trækt] *vi* (**a**) (*become smaller*) contraerse, encogerse. (**b**) **to ~ to do sth** comprometerse por contrato a hacer algo; **to ~ for** contratar.

◆**contract in** *vi* optar por tomar parte.

◆**contract out 1** *vt*: **this work is ~ed out** este trabajo se hace fuera de la empresa bajo contrato. **2** *vi* optar por no tomar parte (*of* en).

contracting [kən'træktɪŋ] *adj*: **~ party** contratante *mf*.

contraction [kən'trækʃən] *n* contracción *f* (*in, of* de).

contractor [kən'træktər] *n* contratista *mf*.

contractual [kən'træktʃʊəl] *adj* contractual; **~ liability** responsabilidad *f* contractual; **~ obligation** obligación *f* contractual.

contractually [kən'træktʃʊəlɪ] *adv* contractualmente, por contrato; **a ~ binding agreement** un acuerdo vinculante según contrato; **we are ~ bound to finish it** estamos obligados por contrato a terminarlo.

contradict [ˌkɒntrə'dɪkt] *vt* contradecir; (*deny*) desmentir; **don't ~ me!** ¡no repliques!

contradiction [ˌkɒntrə'dɪkʃən] *n* contradicción *f*; **~ in terms** contradicción *f* en los términos.

contradictory [ˌkɒntrə'dɪktərɪ] *adj* contradictorio.

contradistinction [ˌkɒntrədɪs'tɪŋkʃən] *n*: **in ~ to** a diferencia de.

contraflow ['kɒntrəfləʊ] *n*: **~ system** sistema *m* de contracorriente.

contraindication [ˌkɒntrəˌɪndɪ'keɪʃən] *n* contraindicación *f*.

contralto [kən'træltəʊ] **1** *n* (*person*) contralto *f*; (*voice*) contralto *m*. **2** *adj* de contralto.

contraption [kən'træpʃən] *n* dispositivo *m*, ingenio *m*, artilugio *m*; (*vehicle*) armatoste *m*.

contrapuntal [ˌkɒntrə'pʌntl] *adj* de contrapunto.

contrarily [kən'treərɪlɪ] *adv* tercamente.

contrariness [kən'treərɪnɪs] *n* terquedad *f*.

contrariwise [kən'treərɪwaɪz] *adv* al contrario; por otra parte; a la inversa.

contrary[1] ['kɒntrərɪ] **1** *adj* contrario (*to* a); **in a ~ direction** en dirección contraria.
2 *adv*: **~ to** contrario a; **~ to what we had thought** al contrario de lo que habíamos pensado.
3 *n* contrario *m*; **the ~ seems to be the case** parece que es al revés; **he holds the ~** él sostiene lo contrario; **quite the ~** muy al contrario; **on the ~** al contrario; **I know nothing to the ~** yo no sé nada en contrario; **unless we hear to the ~** a no ser que nos digan lo contrario.

contrary[2] [kən'treərɪ] *adj* terco, que siempre lleva la contraria.

contrast 1 ['kɒntrɑːst] *n* contraste *m* (*between* entre, *to, with* con); **in ~** por contraste; **in ~ to** por contraste con, a diferencia de; **to form a ~ to** (*or* **with**) contrastar con.
2 [kən'trɑːst] *vt* poner en contraste (*with* con), comparar.
3 [kən'trɑːst] *vi* contrastar (*with* con), hacer contraste (*with* con).

contrasting [kən'trɑːstɪŋ] *adj* opuesto.
contravene [ˌkɒntrə'viːn] *vt law* contravenir a; (*dispute*) oponerse a.
contravention [ˌkɒntrə'venʃən] *n* contravención *f*.
contretemps ['kɔ̃ːntrətɑ̃ːŋ] *n* contratiempo *m*, revés *m*.
contribute [kən'trɪbjuːt] **1** *vt* contribuir, aportar (*esp LAm*) (*to* a); *article* escribir (*to* para); *aid* prestar; *facts, information etc* aportar.
2 *vi* contribuir (*to, towards* a); **to ~ to** + *ger* contribuir + *infin*; **to ~ to a journal** colaborar en una revista; **to ~ to a discussion** intervenir en una discusión; **it all ~d to the muddle** todo sirvió para aumentar la confusión.
contribution [ˌkɒntrɪ'bjuːʃən] *n* contribución *f*; (*money*) donativo *m*, cuota *f*; (*salary deduction*) cotización *f*; (*to journal*) artículo *m*, colaboración *f*; (*to discussion*) intervención *f*; (*of information etc*) aportación *f*.
contributor [kən'trɪbjʊtə^r] *n* donante *mf*; (*to journal*) colaborador *m*, -ora *f* (*to* en).
contributory [kən'trɪbjʊtərɪ] *adj* contributivo; *factor, negligence* que contribuye; **~ pension** pensión *f* contributiva; **~ pension scheme** plan *m* cotizable de jubilación.
contrite ['kɒntraɪt] *adj* arrepentido, contrito.
contritely ['kɒntraɪtlɪ] *adv say etc* en tono arrepentido.
contrition [kən'trɪʃən] *n* arrepentimiento *m*.
contrivance [kən'traɪvəns] *n* (*scheme*) treta *f*, estratagema *f*; (*invention*) invención *f*; (*Mech*) aparato *m*, invento *m*, dispositivo *m*, artilugio *m*.
contrive [kən'traɪv] **1** *vt* (*invent*) inventar, idear; (*bring about*) efectuar; (*plot*) tramar. **2** *vi*: **to ~ to** + *infin* lograr que + *subj*, ingeniárselas a + *infin* (*or* para + *infin*).
contrived [kən'traɪvd] *adj* artificial; efectista.
control [kən'trəʊl] **1** *n* (**a**) (*command*) control *m*, mando *m*, gobierno *m*, dirección *f*; (*of car etc*) control *m*, conducción *f*; **~ of the seas** dominio *m* de los mares; **for reasons beyond** (*or* **outside**) **our ~** por causas ajenas a nuestra voluntad; **to be in ~** mandar, tener el mando; **to be out of ~** estar fuera de control; **to be under ~** estar bajo control; **to be under private ~** estar en manos de particulares; **to get out of ~** desmandarse; **to get under ~** conseguir dominar; **she has no ~ over the children** no tiene autoridad sobre los niños; **causes over which the vendor has no ~** causas respecto a las cuales nada puede el vendedor, causas ajenas a la voluntad del vendedor; **to lose ~ of** perder el control de; **to lose ~ of o.s.** perder el control, perder los estribos.
(**b**) (*Mech*) control *m*; **~s** (*Aer etc*) mando *m*, aparatos *mpl* de mando; **the Prince is at the ~s** el Príncipe está a los mandos.
(**c**) (*check*) freno *m* (*on* para).
(**d**) (*self-restraint*) dominio *m* de (*or* sobre) sí mismo.
(**e**) (*in experiment*) grupo *m* (de) control, norma *f* de comprobación.
2 *attr*: **~ column** palanca *f* de mando; **~ engineering** ingeniería *f* de control; **~ group** grupo *m* (de) control; **~ key** tecla *f* de control; **~ knob** botón *m* de mando; **~ panel** tablero *m* de mando; **~ point** punto *m* de control; **~ room** sala *f* de control, sala *f* de mando; **~ system** sistema *m* de control; **~ tower** torre *f* de control; **~ unit** unidad *f* de control.
3 *vt* (*command*) controlar, mandar, gobernar; *traffic, business* dirigir; *price* controlar; (*Mech*) regular, controlar; *car etc* manejar; *immigration* regular; *outbreak of disease, fire* dominar; *animal* hacerse obedecer por, imponer su autoridad a; *emotion* contener; *temper* dominar, refrenar.
4 *vr*: **to ~ o.s.** dominarse, sobreponerse; **~ yourself!** ¡domínese!, ¡cálmese!
controlled [kən'trəʊld] *adj emotion* contenido; *voice* sereno, que no revela la emoción; **~ economy** economía *f* controlada; **~ explosion** explosión *f* controlada.
-controlled [kən'trəʊld] *adj*: *eg* **a Labour~ council** un ayuntamiento laborista; **a government~ organization** una organización bajo control gubernamental; **computer~ equipment** equipo *m* computerizado.
controller [kən'trəʊlə^r] *n* director *m*, -ora *f*; inspector *m*, -ora *f*; (*Comm*) interventor *m*, -ora *f*; (*Aer*) controlador *m*, -ora *f*.
controlling [kən'trəʊlɪŋ] *adj interest* controlador, mayoritario.
controversial [ˌkɒntrə'vɜːʃəl] *adj* discutido, debatido, polémico, controvertido, conflictivo.
controversy [kɒn'trɒvəsɪ] *n* controversia *f*.
controvert ['kɒntrəvɜːt] *vt* contradecir.
contumacious [ˌkɒntjʊ'meɪʃəs] *adj* contumaz.
contumaciously [ˌkɒntjʊ'meɪʃəslɪ] *adv* contumazmente.
contumacy ['kɒntjʊməsɪ] *n* contumacia *f*.
contumely ['kɒntjʊmɪlɪ] *n* contumelia *f*.
contusion [kən'tjuːʒən] *n* contusión *f*.
conundrum [kə'nʌndrəm] *n* acertijo *m*, adivinanza *f*; (*fig*) problema *m*; enigma *m*.
conurbation [ˌkɒnɜː'beɪʃən] *n* conurbación *f*.
convalesce [ˌkɒnvə'les] *vi* convalecer.
convalescence [ˌkɒnvə'lesəns] *n* convalecencia *f*.
convalescent [ˌkɒnvə'lesənt] **1** *adj* convaleciente. **2** *n* convaleciente *mf*; **~ home** clínica *f* de reposo.
convection [kən'vekʃən] *n* convección *f*.
convector [kən'vektə^r] *n* (*also* **~ heater**) convector *m*, calentador *m* de convección.
convene [kən'viːn] **1** *vt* convocar. **2** *vi* reunirse.
convener, convenor [kən'viːnə^r] *n* (*of meeting*) organizador *m*, -ora *f*; (*of committee*) presidente *mf* (de comisión); (*of shop stewards*) jefe *mf*, presidente *mf*.
convenience [kən'viːnɪəns] *n* (**a**) comodidad *f*; conveniencia *f*; (*advantage*) ventaja *f*; **~ foods** platos *mpl* preparados; comidas *fpl* en el acto; **at your ~** cuando te venga bien; **at your earliest ~** con la mayor brevedad, tan pronto como le sea posible; **for your ~ an envelope is enclosed** para facilitar su contestación adjuntamos un sobre; **it is a great ~ to be so close** resulta muy práctico estar tan cerca; **to make a ~ of** abusar de (la amabilidad de).
(**b**) (*Brit*) (**public**) **~**(**s**) aseos *mpl* públicos; **a house with all modern ~s** una casa con todas las comodidades; **'all mod. cons'** 'todo confort'.
convenient [kən'viːnɪənt] *adj* (**a**) cómodo; *tool etc* práctico, útil; *place* accesible, céntrico; **it is ~ to live here** resulta práctico vivir aquí; **her death was certainly ~ for him** es cierto que su muerte fue oportuna para él; **we looked for a ~ place to stop** buscamos un sitio apropiado para parar; **he put it on a ~ chair** lo puso en una silla que estaba a mano.
(**b**) (*of time*) oportuno; **at a ~ moment** en un momento oportuno; **when it is ~ for you** cuando te venga bien; **would tomorrow be ~?** ¿te conviene mañana?
conveniently [kən'viːnɪəntlɪ] *adv* con comodidad, cómodamente; oportunamente; **the house is ~ situated** la casa está en un sitio muy práctico; **it fell ~ close** cayó muy cerca; **when you ~ can do so** cuando puedas hacerlo sin inconveniente.
convenor [kən'viːnə^r] *n* = **convener**.
convent ['kɒnvənt] *n* convento *m* (de monjas); **~ school** ≃ escuela *f* de monjas.
convention [kən'venʃən] *n* (*agreement*) convenio *m*, convención *f*; (*meeting*) asamblea *f*, congreso *m*.
conventional [kən'venʃənl] *adj* convencional.
conventionalism [kən'venʃənəlɪzəm] *n* convencionalismo *m*.
converge [kən'vɜːdʒ] *vi* convergir (*on* en); **to ~ on** (*persons*) dirigirse todos a.
convergence [kən'vɜːdʒəns] *n* convergencia *f*.
convergent [kən'vɜːdʒənt] *adj*, **converging** [kən'vɜːdʒɪŋ] *adj* convergente.
conversant [kən'vɜːsənt] *adj*: **~ with** versado en, enterado de; **to become ~ with** familiarizarse con, informarse sobre.
conversation [ˌkɒnvə'seɪʃən] *n* conversación *f*; **~ piece** (*Art*) cuadro *m* de conversación; (*Liter*) conversación *f*, diálogo *m*; **I said it just to make ~** lo dije sólo por decir algo; **that was a ~ stopper*** aquello dejó a todos sin habla*.
conversational [ˌkɒnvə'seɪʃənl] *adj tone* conversacional, familiar; *person* locuaz, hablador; **he's not very ~** no es amigo de la conversación; **~ mode** modo *m* de conversación.
conversationalist [ˌkɒnvə'seɪʃnəlɪst] *n*: **to be a good ~** brillar en la conversación, resultar simpático charlando; **he's not much of a ~** tiene poco que decir, no le gusta hablar mucho en las conversaciones.
conversationally [ˌkɒnvə'seɪʃnəlɪ] *adv* en tono familiar.
converse¹ ['kɒnvɜːs] **1** *adj* contrario, inverso; (*Logic*) recíproco. **2** *n* (*Math*) inversa *f*; (*Logic*) teorema *m* recíproco; **but the ~ is true** pero la verdad es al revés.
converse² [kən'vɜːs] *vi* conversar, hablar (*with* con); **to ~ by signs** hablar por señas.
conversely [kɒn'vɜːslɪ] *adv* a la inversa.
conversion [kən'vɜːʃən] *n* conversión *f* (*into* en, *to* a); (*industrial*) reconversión *f*; (*Jur*) apropiación *f* ilícita; (*Rugby*) transformación *f*; **~ kit** equipo *m* de conversión; **~ (loan) stock** obligaciones *fpl* convertibles; **~ table** tabla *f* de equivalencias.

convert **1** ['kɒnvɜːt] *n* converso *m*, -a *f*; **to become a ~** convertirse.

2 [kən'vɜːt] *vt* convertir (*also Eccl, Fin*; *into* a, en, *to* a), transformar (*into* en); *industry* reconvertir; *house* reformar, modificar; (*Jur*) apropiarse ilícitamente (*to one's own use* para uso propio); (*Sport*) *penalty, try* transformar.

3 [kən'vɜːt] *vi* convertirse (*to* a).

converter [kən'vɜːtəʳ] *n* (*Elec, Metal*) convertidor *m*.

convertibility [kən,vɜːtə'bɪlɪtɪ] *n* convertibilidad *f*.

convertible [kən'vɜːtəbl] **1** *adj* convertible; *car* descapotable; **~ debenture** obligación *f* convertible; **~ loan stock** obligaciones *fpl* convertibles. **2** *n* (*US*) descapotable *m*.

convex ['kɒn'veks] *adj* convexo.

convexity [kɒn'veksɪtɪ] *n* convexidad *f*.

convey [kən'veɪ] *vt goods* transportar, llevar; *person* llevar; *sound, smell* llevar; *current* transmitir; *news* comunicar; (*Jur*) traspasar, transferir; *meaning* tener, expresar (*to* para); **I am trying to ~ that ...** quiero dar a entender que ..., quiero sugerir que ...; **the name ~s nothing to me** el nombre no me dice nada; **what does this music ~ to you?** ¿qué es lo que esta música evoca para ti?

conveyance [kən'veɪəns] *n* (**a**) (*act*) transporte *m*; transmisión *f* (*etc*); (*Jur*) compra *f* y venta.

(**b**) (*Jur*: *deed*) compra *f* y venta.

(**c**) (*vehicle*) vehículo *m*, medio *m* de transporte; **public ~** vehículo *m* de servicio público.

conveyancing [kən'veɪənsɪŋ] *n* (*Jur*) redacción *f* de escrituras de compra y venta.

conveyor [kən'veɪəʳ] *n* portador *m*, transportador *m*; (*belt*) cinta *f* transportadora.

conveyor-belt [kən'veɪəbelt] *n* cinta *f* transportadora.

convict **1** ['kɒnvɪkt] *n* presidiario *m*, recluso *m*; **~ settlement** colonia *f* de presidiarios.

2 [kən'vɪkt] *vt* condenar; **a ~ed murderer** un asesino convicto como tal; **to ~ sb of a crime** declarar a uno culpable de un crimen; **he was ~ed of drunken driving** fue condenado por conducir en estado de embriaguez; **to ~ sb of an error** coger a uno en una falta.

conviction [kən'vɪkʃən] *n* (**a**) (*Jur*) condena *f*; **there were 12 ~s for theft** hubo 12 condenas por robo; **to have no previous ~s** no tener antecedentes penales.

(**b**) (*belief*) creencia *f*, convicción *f*, artículo *m* de fe; convencimiento *m*; **it is my ~ that ...** tengo el convencimiento de que ...; **he said with ~** dijo con convicción.

(**c**) **I am open to ~** estoy dispuesto a dejarme convencer; **it carries ~** convence, es convincente.

convince [kən'vɪns] *vt* convencer (*of* de, *that* de que); **I am not ~d** no estoy convencido, no me convenzo.

convinced [kən'vɪnst] *adj Christian etc* convencido, fiel, firme.

convincing [kən'vɪnsɪŋ] *adj* convincente.

convincingly [kən'vɪnsɪŋlɪ] *adv* convincentemente; **to prove sth ~** probar algo de modo concluyente.

convivial [kən'vɪvɪəl] *adj person* sociable; *evening* alegre, festivo, *atmosphere* alegre.

conviviality [kən,vɪvɪ'ælɪtɪ] *n* alegría *f*, buen humor *m*; compañerismo *m* alegre; **there was a certain amount of ~** nos divertimos bastante, (*pej*) se bebió una barbaridad.

convocation [,kɒnvə'keɪʃən] *n* (*act*) convocación *f*; (*meeting*) asamblea *f*.

convoke [kən'vəʊk] *vt* convocar.

convoluted ['kɒnvə,luːtɪd] *adj route* serpentino, lleno de recovecos; *argument* complicado.

convolution [,kɒnvə'luːʃən] *n* circunvolución *f*.

convolvulus [kən'vɒlvjʊləs] *n* convólvulo *m*.

convoy ['kɒnvɔɪ] **1** *n* convoy *m*; escolta *f*. **2** *vt* convoyar; escoltar.

convulse [kən'vʌls] *vt* (*fig*) convulsionar, sacudir; (*joke etc*) hacer morir de risa; **his face was ~d with pain** el dolor le crispó la cara; **to be ~d with laughter** desternillarse de risa.

convulsion [kən'vʌlʃən] *n* convulsión *f*; **~s of laughter** paroxismo *m* de risa.

convulsive [kən'vʌlsɪv] *adj* convulsivo.

cony ['kəʊnɪ] *n* (*US*) conejo *m*.

coo[1] [kuː] *vi* arrullar.

coo[2]* [kuː] *interj* (*Brit*) ¡toma!, ¡vaya!

co-occur [,kəʊə'kɜːʳ] *vi* coocurrir.

co-occurrence [,kəʊə'kʌrəns] *n* coocurrencia *f*.

cooing ['kuːɪŋ] *n* arrullos *mpl*.

cook [kʊk] **1** *n* cocinero *m*, -a *f*; **too many ~s spoil the broth** demasiadas cocineras estropean el caldo. **2** *vt* (**a**) (*Culin*) guisar, cocer, cocinar; *meal* preparar. (**b**) *accounts* (*Brit**) falsificar. **3** *vi* (*food*) cocer; (*person*) cocinar; **what's ~ing?*** ¿qué pasa?

◆**cook up** *vt* (*Culin*) preparar; (*) *excuse* inventar; *plan* tramar.

cookbook ['kʊkbʊk] *n* (*US*) libro *m* de cocina.

cooked [kʊkt] *adj meats etc* preparado.

cooker ['kʊkəʳ] *n* (**a**) (*Brit*: *stove*) cocina *f*; (*US*) olla *f* para cocinar. (**b**) (*fruit*) fruta *f* para cocer.

cookery ['kʊkərɪ] *n* cocina *f*, arte *m* de cocinar; gastronomía *f*; **French ~** la cocina francesa; **~ course** curso *m* de cocina; **her ~ is a delight** sus platos son un encanto; **I'm no good at ~** yo no sé nada de cocina.

cookery-book ['kʊkərɪbʊk] *n* libro *m* de cocina.

cookhouse ['kʊkhaʊs] *n*, *pl* **cookhouses** ['kʊk,haʊzɪz] cocina *f*; (*Mil*) cocina *f* móvil de campaña.

cookie ['kʊkɪ] *n* (*US*) (**a**) (*biscuit*) galleta *f*, bizcocho *m* (*LAm*); **that's the way the ~ crumbles** (*US**) así es la vida; **to wait to see which way the ~ crumbles*** esperar a ver por dónde van los tiros.

(**b**) (‡) tipo* *m*, tío* *m*, tía* *f*; **she's a smart ~** es una chica lista; **a tough ~** un tío duro*.

cooking ['kʊkɪŋ] **1** *n* (**a**) (*art*) cocina *f*, arte *m* culinario; **typical Galician ~** la típica cocina gallega. (**b**) (*act*) cocción *f*. **2** *attr*: **~ apple** manzana *f* para cocer; **~ foil** papel *m* de aluminio; **~ salt** sal *f* de cocina; **~ time** tiempo *m* de cocción.

cookout ['kʊkaʊt] *n* (*US*) barbacoa *f*, comida *f* al aire libre.

cool [kuːl] **1** *adj* (**a**) (*rather cold*) fresco; (*~ enough to drink etc*) tibio, bastante frío; **it is ~** (*weather*) hace fresco, (*object*) está fresco; **to get ~(er)** refrescarse; **'to be kept in a ~ place'** 'guárdese en un sitio fresco'.

(**b**) (*calm*) tranquilo, imperturbable; **as ~ as a cucumber** más fresco que una lechuga; **to keep ~** tomarlo con la calma; **keep ~!** ¡no se alarme!

(**c**) (*lacking zeal*) frío, indiferente; **to be ~ towards a plan** acoger un proyecto con poco entusiasmo; **to be ~ towards sb** tratar a uno con frialdad.

(**d**) (*calmly audacious*) fresco, descarado; **he's a ~ customer** es un caradura; **he answered me as ~ as you please** me contestó tan fresco.

(**e**) **a ~ £100*** nada menos que 100 libras, la bonita suma de 100 libras.

(**f**) (‡) fabuloso*, de aúpa*; **it was real ~, man** fue fenómeno, tío*.

2 *adv*: **to play it ~** no dejarse emocionar, no exagerar.

3 *n* (**a**) fresco *m*; **in the ~ of the evening** en el aire fresco de la tarde. (**b**) (‡) **to keep one's ~** no dejarse emocionar; **to lose one's ~** ponerse nervioso; perder los estribos.

4 *vt* (*also* **to ~ down**) enfriar; refrescar; *engine* refrigerar; (*fig*) calmar, moderar el entusiasmo (*etc*) de; **~ it!*** ¡tranqui!*

5 *vi* (*also* **to ~ down**) enfriarse; (*weather etc*) refrescarse; (*person*) tener menos calor; (*fig*) calmarse.

◆**cool down** **1** *vt V* **cool 4**. **2** *vi* (**a**) *V* **cool 5**. (**b**) (*fig*) calmarse; **~ down!** ¡cálmese!

◆**cool off** *vi* (*fig*) perder su entusiasmo, entibiarse; (*relations*) enfriarse.

coolant ['kuːlənt] *n* refrigerante *m*.

cooler ['kuːləʳ] *n* (**a**) (*US*) nevera *f* portátil. (**b**) (‡) trena‡ *f*.

cool-headed ['kuːl,hedɪd] *adj* imperturbable.

coolie ['kuːlɪ] *n* cooli *m*, culi *m*.

cooling ['kuːlɪŋ] **1** *adj* refrescante; (*Tech*) refrigerante. **2** *n* refrigeración *f*.

cooling-fan ['kuːlɪŋ,fæn] *n* ventilador *m*.

cooling-off [,kuːlɪŋ'ɒf] *attr*: **~ period** plazo *m* para que se entablen negociaciones.

cooling-tower ['kuːlɪŋtaʊəʳ] *n* torre *f* de refrigeración.

coolly ['kuːlɪ] *adv* (*calmly*) con tranquilidad; (*unenthusiastically*) con poco entusiasmo; (*boldly*) descaradamente.

coolness ['kuːlnɪs] *n* (**a**) (*coldness*) frescura *f*, lo fresco.

(**b**) (*calmness*) tranquilidad *f*, imperturbabilidad *f*; (*in battle etc*) sangre *f* fría.

(**c**) (*lack of zeal*) tibieza *f*, falta *f* de entusiasmo; (*of welcome, between persons*) frialdad *f*.

(**d**) (*audacity*) frescura *f*.

coomb [kuːm] *n* garganta *f*, desfiladero *m*.

coon‡ [kuːn] *n* (*esp US*) negro *m*, -a *f*.

coop [kuːp] *n* gallinero *m*.

◆**coop up** *vt* encerrar, enjaular.

co-op* ['kəʊ'ɒp] *n* (*Brit*) *abbr of* **cooperative society** cooperativa *f*.

cooper ['kuːpəʳ] *n* tonelero *m*.

cooperate [kəʊ'ɒpəreɪt] *vi* cooperar, colaborar (*in* en, *with* con, *to + infin* para + *infin*).
cooperation [kəʊ,ɒpə'reɪʃən] *n* cooperación *f*, colaboración *f*.
cooperative [kəʊ'ɒpərətɪv] **1** *adj* cooperativo; *person* servicial, dispuesto a ayudar; ~ **society** cooperativa *f*. **2** *n* cooperativa *f*.
cooperatively [kəʊ'ɒpərətɪvlɪ] *adv* (*jointly*) en cooperación, en colaboración, conjuntamente; (*obligingly*) servicialmente.
coopt [kəʊ'ɒpt] *vt* nombrar por cooptación, cooptar (*on to* a).
cooption [kəʊ'ɒpʃən] *n* cooptación *f*.
coordinate 1 [kəʊ'ɔːdnɪt] *n* coordenada *f*. **2** [kəʊ'ɔːdɪneɪt] *vt* coordinar.
coordinating [kəʊ'ɔːdɪneɪtɪŋ] *adj*: ~ **committee** comité *m* coordinador.
coordination [kəʊ,ɔːdɪ'neɪʃən] *n* coordinación *f*.
coordinator [kəʊ'ɔːdɪneɪtə^r] *n* coordinador *m*.
coot [kuːt] *n* (*Orn*) focha *f* (común), fúlica *f*; (*) bobo *m*, -a *f*.
coowner [,kəʊ'əʊnə^r] *n* copropietario *m*, -a *f*.
coownership [,kəʊ'əʊnəʃɪp] *n* copropiedad *f*.
cop* [kɒp] **1** *n* (**a**) (*policeman*) poli* *m* (*Sp*), guindilla‡ *m* (*Sp*); guarura‡ *m* (*Méx*), cana‡ *m* (*SC*), tira‡ *m* (*LAm*); **the ~s** la pasma‡ (*Sp*), la bofia‡ (*Sp*), la jara‡ (*Mex*), la cana‡ (*SC*); **~s and robbers** (*game*) justicias y ladrones; ~ **shop** (*Brit*‡) comisaría *f*.
(**b**) (*Brit*) **it's a fair ~!** ¡está bien!; **it's not much ~** es poca cosa, no vale gran cosa.
2 *vt* (**a**) (*Brit*: *capture*) coger, prender.
(**b**) **he ~ped 6 months** se cargó 6 meses; **you'll ~ it!** (*Brit*) ¡las vas a pagar!; **I ~ped it from the head** el director me puso como un trapo; ~ **this!** ¡hay que ver esto!; ~ **hold of this** coge esto, toma esto.
(**c**) (*US*) *drugs* comprar.
◆**cop out**‡ *vi* resbalarse‡, escabullirse, rajarse*.
copartner ['kəʊ'pɑːtnə^r] *n* consocio *mf*, copartícipe *mf*.
copartnership ['kəʊ'pɑːtnəʃɪp] *n* asociación *f*, cogestión *f*, coparticipación *f*.
cope[1] [kəʊp] *n* (*Eccl*) capa *f* pluvial.
cope[2] [kəʊp] *vi* (**a**) arreglárselas; **he's coping pretty well** se las está arreglando bastante bien; **we shall be able to ~ better next year** podremos arreglarnos mejor el año que viene; **can you ~ ?** ¿tú puedes con esto?; **how are you coping?** ¿cómo te va esto?; **he can't ~ any more** ya no aguanta más, ya no puede más.
(**b**) **to ~ with** poder con; *problem* hacer frente a; *difficulty* contender con; *situation* enfrentarse con.
Copenhagen [,kəʊpn'heɪgən] *n* Copenhague *m*.
Copernicus [kə'pɜːnɪkəs] *nm* Copérnico.
copestone ['kəʊpstəʊn] *n* (piedra *f* de) albardilla *f*.
copier ['kɒpɪə^r] *n* copiadora *f*.
co-pilot ['kəʊ'paɪlət] *n* copiloto *mf*.
coping ['kəʊpɪŋ] *n* albardilla *f*, mojinete *m*; **~stone** = **copestone**.
copious ['kəʊpɪəs] *adj* copioso, abundante.
copiously ['kəʊpɪəslɪ] *adv* copiosamente, en abundancia.
cop-out‡ ['kɒpaʊt] *n* evasión *f* de responsabilidad.
copper ['kɒpə^r] **1** *n* (**a**) (*material*) cobre *m*.
(**b**) (*utensil*) caldera *f* de lavar.
(**c**) (*money*) calderilla *f*, monedas *fpl* de poco valor; **it costs a few ~s** vale unos peniques.
(**d**) (*: *policeman*) poli* *m* (*Sp*), guindilla‡ *m* (*Sp*); *V also* **cop**.
2 *adj, attr* de cobre, cobreño; (*colour*) cobrizo; ~ **sulphate** sulfato *m* de cobre.
copper-beech ['kɒpə'biːtʃ] *n* haya *f* roja, haya *f* de sangre.
copper-bottomed [,kɒpə'bɒtəmd] *adj* con fondo de cobre; (*fig*) totalmente fiable, de máxima seguridad.
copper-coloured, (*US*) **copper-colored** ['kɒpə,kʌləd] *adj* cobrizo.
copperhead ['kɒpəhed] *n* víbora *f* cobriza.
copperplate ['kɒpəpleɪt] *attr*: ~ **writing** letra *f* caligrafiada, caligrafía *f*.
coppersmith ['kɒpəsmɪθ] *n* cobrero *m*.
coppery ['kɒpərɪ] *adj* cobreño; (*colour*) cobrizo.
coppice ['kɒpɪs] *n* soto *m*, bosquecillo *m*.
copra ['kɒprə] *n* copra *f*.
coprocessor ['kəʊ'prəʊsesə^r] *n* coprocesador *m*; **graphics ~** coprocesador *m* de gráficos.
copse [kɒps] *n* soto *m*, bosquecillo *m*.
Copt [kɒpt] *n* copto *m*, -a *f*.
'copter*, copter* ['kɒptə^r] *n abbr of* **helicopter** helicóptero *m*.
Coptic ['kɒptɪk] *adj* copto; **the ~ Church** la Iglesia Copta.
copula ['kɒpjʊlə] *n* cópula *f*.
copulate ['kɒpjʊleɪt] *vi* copularse (*with* con).
copulation [,kɒpjʊ'leɪʃən] *n* cópula *f*.
copulative ['kɒpjʊlətɪv] *adj* copulativo.
copy ['kɒpɪ] **1** *n* (**a**) (*reproduction*) copia *f*.
(**b**) (*book*) ejemplar *m*; (*journal*) número *m*.
(**c**) (*Typ*) material *m*, original *m*; **there's plenty of ~ here** tenemos aquí un material abundante; **a murder is always good ~** un asesinato es siempre un buen tema.
2 *attr*: ~ **typist** mecanógrafo *m*, -a *f*.
3 *vt* (**a**) (*also* **to ~ down, to ~ out**) copiar; imitar; **to ~ from** copiar de.
(**b**) (*send a copy to*) enviar una copia a.
copybook ['kɒpɪbʊk] **1** *n* cuaderno *m* de escritura; **to blot one's ~** tirarse una plancha*, manchar la reputación. **2** *adj* perfecto; **the pilot made a ~ landing** el piloto aterrizó perfectamente.
copy-boy ['kɒpɪ,bɔɪ] *n* chico *m* de los recados de la redacción.
copycat* ['kɒpɪkæt] *n* imitador *m*, -ora *f*, copión *m*, -ona *f*; ~ **crime** crimen *m* de imitación.
copy-edit ['kɒpɪ'edɪt] *vt* editar y corregir.
copy-editor ['kɒpɪ'edɪtə^r] *n* editor *m*, -ora *f* corrector *m*, -ora *f* de manuscritos (*or* de material *etc*).
copying-ink ['kɒpɪɪŋ,ɪŋk] *n* tinta *f* de copiar.
copying-machine ['kɒpɪɪŋmə,ʃiːn] *n* copiadora *f*.
copyist ['kɒpɪɪst] *n* copista *mf*.
copy-machine ['kɒpɪmə,ʃiːn] *n* fotocopiadora *f*.
copyreader ['kɒpɪ,riːdə^r] *n* corrector *m*, -ora *f*.
copyright ['kɒpɪraɪt] **1** *adj* protegido por los derechos de(l) autor.
2 *n* derechos *mpl* de(l) autor, copyright *m*, propiedad *f* literaria; (derechos *mpl* de) propiedad *f* intelectual; **'~ reserved'** 'es propiedad', 'reservados todos los derechos', 'copyright'; **the book is still in ~** siguen vigentes los derechos del autor de este libro; **it will be out of ~ in 2020** los derechos del autor terminarán en 2020.
3 *vt* registrar como propiedad literaria.
copywriter ['kɒpɪ,raɪtə^r] *n* escritor *m*, -ora *f* de material publicitario.
coquetry ['kɒkɪtrɪ] *n* coquetería *f*.
coquette [kə'ket] *n* coqueta *f*.
coquettish [kə'ketɪʃ] *adj* coqueta.
coquettishly [kə'ketɪʃlɪ] *adv* con aire (*or* tono *etc*) coqueta.
cor‡ [kɔː^r] *interj* (*Brit*) ¡caramba!; ~ **blimey!** ¡coño!‡
coracle ['kɒrəkl] *n* barquilla *f* de cuero.
coral ['kɒrəl] **1** *n* coral *m*. **2** *adj* coralino, de coral; ~ **island** isla *f* coralina; ~ **reef** barrera *f* coralina, arrecife *m* de coral; **C~ Sea** Mar *m* del Coral.
cor anglais ['kɔːr'ɔ̃ŋgleɪ] *n* corno *m* inglés.
corbel ['kɔːbəl] *n* ménsula *f*, repisa *f*.
cord [kɔːd] **1** *n* (**a**) cuerda *f*; (*US Elec*) cordón *m*; (**umbilical**) ~ cordón *m* umbilical. (**b**) (*cloth*) pana *f*; **~s** pantalones *mpl* de pana. **2** *vt* encordar, atar con cuerdas.
cordage ['kɔːdɪdʒ] *n* cordaje *m*, cordería *f*.
cordial ['kɔːdɪəl] **1** *adj* cordial, afectuoso. **2** *n* cordial *m*.
cordiality [,kɔːdɪ'ælɪtɪ] *n* cordialidad *f*, afecto *m*.
cordially ['kɔːdɪəlɪ] *adv* cordialmente, afectuosamente; **I ~ detest him** le odio cordialmente.
cordite ['kɔːdaɪt] *n* cordita *f*.
cordless ['kɔːdlɪs] *adj*: ~ **telephone** teléfono *m* móvil, teléfono *m* sin hilos.
cordon ['kɔːdn] **1** *n* cordón *m*. **2** *vt*: **to ~ off** acordonar.
cordon bleu [,kɔːdɔ̃n'blɜː] **1** *n* cordón *m* azul; (*Culin*) cocinero *m*, -a *f* de primera clase. **2** *adj, attr* de primera clase.
Cordova ['kɔːdəvə] *n* Córdoba *f*.
Cordovan ['kɔːdəvən] **1** *adj* cordobés. **2** *n* cordobés *m*, -esa *f*; (*leather*) cordobán *m*.
corduroy ['kɔːdərɔɪ] *n* pana *f*; **~s** pantalones *mpl* de pana; ~ **road** (*US*) camino *m* de troncos.
CORE [kɔː^r] *n* (*US*) *abbr of* **Congress of Racial Equality**.
core [kɔː^r] **1** *n* centro *m*, núcleo *m*; (*of fruit*) corazón *m*; (*of cable*) alma *f*; (*of group etc*) centro *m*; elementos *mpl* centrales; (*fig, of problem etc*) lo esencial, esencia *f*; **a hard ~ of resistance** un foco de dura resistencia; **the hard ~ of unemployment** el núcleo duro del paro; **English to the ~** inglés hasta los tuétanos; **rotten to the ~** (*fig*) corrompido hasta la médula; **shocked to the ~** profundamente afectado.
2 *attr*: ~ **curriculum** (programa *m* de) estudios *mpl* troncales, asignaturas *fpl* comunes; ~ **memory** memoria *f* de núcleos; ~ **subject** asignatura *f* común; ~ **time** período

m nuclear.
3 *vt apple* quitar el corazón de.
co-religionist ['kəʊrɪ'lɪdʒənɪst] *n* correligionario *m*, -a *f*.
corer ['kɔːrəʳ] *n* (*Culin*) despepitadora *f*.
co-respondent ['kəʊrɪs'pɒndənt] *n* codemandado *m*, -a *f* (en casos de divorcio).
Corfu [kɔː'fuː] *n* Corfú *m*.
corgi ['kɔːgɪ] *n* perro *m* galés.
coriander [ˌkɒrɪ'ændəʳ] *n* culantro *m*.
Corinth ['kɒrɪnθ] *n* Corinto *m*.
Corinthian [kə'rɪnθɪən] *adj* corintio.
cork [kɔːk] **1** *n* corcho *m*. **2** *attr* de corcho. **3** *vt* (*also* **to ~ up**) tapar con corcho, taponar; **the wine is ~ed** el vino sabe a corcho.
corkage ['kɔːkɪdʒ] *n* precio *m* que se cobra en un restaurante por una botella traída de fuera.
corked [kɔːkt] *adj wine* que sabe a corcho.
corker‡ ['kɔːkəʳ] *n* (*lie*) bola* *f*, trola* *f*; (*story*) historia *f* absurda; (*Sport*: *shot, stroke*) golpe *m* de primera; (*player*) crac* *m*; (*girl*) tía *f* buena*; **that's a ~!** ¡es cutre!‡
cork-oak [ˌkɔːk'əʊk] *n* = **cork-tree**.
corkscrew ['kɔːkskruː] **1** *n* sacacorchos *m*. **2** *attr movement* en espiral. **3** *vi* subir en espiral.
cork-tree ['kɔːktriː] *n* alcornoque *m*.
corm [kɔːm] *n* (*Bot*) bulbo *m*.
cormorant ['kɔːmərənt] *n* cormorán *m* (grande).
corn[1] [kɔːn] *n* (**a**) (*Bot*) granos *mpl*, cereales *mpl*; (*Brit*: *wheat*) trigo *m*; (*US, also* **Indian ~**) maíz *m*; **~ bread** (*US*) pan *m* de maíz; **~ meal** (*US*) harina *f* de maíz; **~ on the cob** mazorca *f*. (**b**) (*) cosas *fpl* rancias, historia *f* (*etc*) vieja; sentimentalismo *m*, sensiblería *f*.
corn[2] [kɔːn] *n* (*Med*) callo *m*; **to tread on sb's ~s** (*Brit*) herir los sentimientos de uno.
cornball* ['kɔːnbɔːl] *n* (*US*) paleto* *m*, -a *f*.
corncob ['kɔːnkɒb] *n* (*US*) mazorca *f* de maíz.
corncrake ['kɔːnkreɪk] *n* guión *m* de codornices.
cornea ['kɔːnɪə] *n* córnea *f*.
corneal ['kɔːnɪəl] *adj* corneal.
corned ['kɔːnd] *adj*: **~ beef** (*Brit*) carne *f* de vaca acecinada (enlatada).
cornelian [kɔː'niːlɪən] *n* cornalina *f*.
corner ['kɔːnəʳ] **1** *n* ángulo *m*; (*outside* ~) esquina *f*, (*inside* ~) rincón *m*; (*bend in road*) curva *f*, recodo *m*; (*Sport*) córner *m*, esquina *f*; (*kick*) córner *m*, saque *m* de esquina; (*Comm*) monopolio *m* (*in* de); **~ house** casa *f* en una esquina, casa *f* esquinera; **~ shop** tienda *f* de esquina; **a picturesque ~ of Soria** un rincón pintoresco de Soria; **the four ~s of the earth** las cinco partes del mundo; **out of the ~ of one's eye** con el rabillo del ojo; **it's round the ~** está a la vuelta de la esquina; **prosperity is just around the ~** la prosperidad está precisamente a la vuelta de la esquina; **to be in a tight ~** estar en un aprieto; **to cut ~s** atajar; **to drive sb into a ~** (*fig*) arrinconar a uno, acorralar a uno, poner a uno entre la espada y la pared; **to go round the ~** doblar la esquina; **he made a ~ in peanuts** se hizo con el monopolio de cacahuetes, acaparó el mercado de cacahuetes; **to paint o.s. into a ~** verse acorralado; **to turn the ~** doblar la esquina, (*fig*) ir saliendo del apuro.
2 *vt* acorralar, arrinconar; *person* abordar, detener; *fugitive* cazar; *market* acaparar.
3 *vi* (*Aut*) tomar una curva.
corner-flag ['kɔːnəflæg] *n* banderola *f* de esquina.
cornering ['kɔːnərɪŋ] *n*: **the new suspension allows much safer ~** (*Aut*) la nueva suspensión proporciona un mayor agarre en las curvas.
corner-kick ['kɔːnəkɪk] *n* córner *m*, saque *m* de esquina.
corner-seat ['kɔːnəsiːt] *n* asiento *m* del rincón, rinconera *f*.
cornerstone ['kɔːnəstəʊn] *n* piedra *f* angular (*also fig*).
cornet ['kɔːnɪt] *n* (**a**) (*Mus*) corneta *f*. (**b**) (*Brit*: *ice cream*) cucurucho *m*.
corn exchange ['kɔːnɪks'tʃeɪndʒ] *n* bolsa *f* de granos.
cornfield ['kɔːnfiːld] *n* (*Brit*) trigal *m*, campo *m* de trigo; (*US*) maizal *m*, milpa *f*.
cornflakes ['kɔːnfleɪks] *npl* copos *mpl* de maíz (tostado), (*loosely*) cereales *mpl*.
cornflour ['kɔːnflaʊəʳ] *n* (*Brit*) harina *f* de maíz.
cornflower ['kɔːnflaʊəʳ] *n* aciano *m*, azulina *f*; **~ blue** azul aciano.
cornice ['kɔːnɪs] *n*, **corniche** ['kɔːnɪʃ] *n* cornisa *f*.
Cornish ['kɔːnɪʃ] **1** *adj* de Cornualles; **~ pasty** empanada *f* de Cornualles. **2** *n* córnico *m*.
corn-oil ['kɔːnɔɪl] *n* aceite *m* de maíz.
corn-poppy ['kɔːnˌpɒpɪ] *n* amapola *f*.
cornstarch ['kɔːnstɑːtʃ] *n* (*US*) almidón *m* de maíz, maicena *f*.
cornucopia [ˌkɔːnjʊ'kəʊpɪə] *n* cuerno *m* de la abundancia.
Cornwall ['kɔːnwəl] *n* Cornualles *m*.
corny* ['kɔːnɪ] *adj* viejo, gastado, rancio; sentimental, sensiblero.
corolla [kə'rɒlə] *n* corola *f*.
corollary [kə'rɒlərɪ] *n* corolario *m*.
corona [kə'rəʊnə] *n* (*Anat, Astron*) corona *f*; (*Elec*) descarga *f* de corona; (*Archit*) corona *f*, alero *m*.
coronary ['kɒrənərɪ] **1** *adj* coronario; **~ thrombosis** = **2**. **2** *n* infarto *m* de miocardio, trombosis *f* coronaria.
coronation [ˌkɒrə'neɪʃən] *n* coronación *f*.
coroner ['kɒrənəʳ] *n* (*approx*) juez *m* de primera instancia e instrucción (*que establece las causas de defunción*).
coronet ['kɒrənɪt] *n* corona *f* (de marqués *etc*); (*lady's*) diadema *f*.
Corp. (**a**) (*Comm, Fin*) *abbr of* **Corporation** sociedad *f* anónima, S.A. (**b**) (*Pol*) *abbr of* **Corporation** ayuntamiento *m*, municipio *m*. (**c**) (*Mil*) *abbr of* **Corporal** cabo *m*.
corpora ['kɔːpərə] *npl of* **corpus**.
corporal ['kɔːpərəl] **1** *adj* corporal; **~ punishment** castigo *m* corporal. **2** *n* cabo *m*.
corporate ['kɔːpərɪt] *adj* corporativo, colectivo; **~ car** (*US*) coche *m* de la compañía; **~ growth** crecimiento *m* corporativo; **~ identity** identidad *f* corporativa; **~ image** imagen *f* corporativa; **~ name** nombre *m* social; **~ planning** planificación *f* corporativa; **~ strategy** estrategia *f* de la compañía.
corporation [ˌkɔːpə'reɪʃən] **1** *n* (**a**) (*Comm, Fin*) corporación *f*; (*esp US Comm*) sociedad *f* anónima. (**b**) (*Brit*: *of city*) ayuntamiento *m*. (**c**) (*Brit**) panza *f*. **2** *attr*: **~ tax** (*Brit*) impuesto *m* sobre sociedades.
corporatism ['kɔːpərətɪzəm] *n* corporacionismo *m*.
corporeal [kɔː'pɔːrɪəl] *adj* corpóreo.
corps [kɔːʳ] *n*, *pl* **corps** [kɔːz] cuerpo *m*; **~ de ballet** cuerpo *m* de baile; **~ diplomatique** cuerpo *m* diplomático.
corpse [kɔːps] *n* cadáver *m*.
corpulence ['kɔːpjʊləns] *n* gordura *f*.
corpulent ['kɔːpjʊlənt] *adj* gordo.
corpus ['kɔːpəs] *n* cuerpo *m*; **~ delicti** cuerpo *m* del delito; **C~ Christi** Corpus *m*.
corpuscle ['kɔːpʌsl] *n* glóbulo *m*, corpúsculo *m*.
corral [kə'rɑːl] (*US*) **1** *n* corral *m*. **2** *vt* acorralar.
correct [kə'rekt] **1** *adj* (**a**) (*accurate*) correcto, exacto, justo; **~!** ¡exacto!; **you are perfectly ~** tienes toda la razón, estás en lo cierto; **am I ~ in saying that ...?** ¿me equivoco al decir que ...?, ¿no es cierto que ...?
(**b**) (*proper*) correcto.
2 *vt* corregir; rectificar, enmendar; *exam* corregir, calificar; **~ me if I'm wrong** me dirás si tengo razón o no; **I stand ~ed** confieso que me equivoqué.
correcting [kə'rektɪŋ] *adj*: **~ fluid** corrector *m*.
correction [kə'rekʃən] *n* corrección *f*; rectificación *f*; (*erasure*) tachadura *f*; **I speak under ~** puede que me equivoque.
corrective [kə'rektɪv] **1** *adj* correctivo; **~ glasses** gafas *fpl* correctoras. **2** *n* correctivo *m*.
correctly [kə'rektlɪ] *adv* correctamente.
correctness [kə'rektnɪs] *n* (*accuracy*) exactitud *f*; (*properness*) corrección *f*.
correlate ['kɒrɪleɪt] **1** *vt* correlacionar. **2** *vi* tener correlación.
correlation [ˌkɒrɪ'leɪʃən] *n* correlación *f*.
correlative [kɒ'relətɪv] **1** *adj* correlativo. **2** *n* correlativo *m*.
correspond [ˌkɒrɪs'pɒnd] *vi* (**a**) (*agree*) corresponder (*to, with* a). (**b**) (*by letter*) escribirse; **to ~ with** estar en correspondencia con, cartearse con.
correspondence [ˌkɒrɪs'pɒndəns] **1** *n* (**a**) (*agreement*) correspondencia *f*.
(**b**) (*by letter*) correspondencia *f*; **to be in ~ with sb** estar en correspondencia con uno.
(**c**) (*collected letters*) epistolario *m*.
2 *attr*: **~ college** escuela *f* de enseñanza por correspondencia; **~ column** sección *f* de cartas; **~ course** curso *m* por correspondencia.
correspondent [ˌkɒrɪs'pɒndənt] *n* correspondiente *mf*; (*of paper*) corresponsal *mf*.
corresponding [ˌkɒrɪs'pɒndɪŋ] *adj* correspondiente.
correspondingly [ˌkɒrɪs'pɒndɪŋlɪ] *adv* igualmente, equivalentemente.
corridor ['kɒrɪdɔːʳ] *n* pasillo *m* (*also Rail*), corredor *m* (*also Pol*); **~s of power** pasillos *mpl* del poder.
corroborate [kə'rɒbəreɪt] *vt* corroborar, confirmar.
corroboration [kəˌrɒbə'reɪʃən] *n* corroboración *f*,

confirmación *f*.
corroborative [kə'rɒbərətɪv] *adj* corroborativo, confirmatorio.
corrode [kə'rəʊd] **1** *vt* corroer. **2** *vi* corroerse.
corroded [kə'rəʊdɪd] *adj* corroído.
corrosion [kə'rəʊʒən] *n* corrosión *f*.
corrosive [kə'rəʊzɪv] *adj* corrosivo.
corrugated ['kɒrəgeɪtɪd] *adj* ondulado, corrugado; ~ **cardboard** cartón *m* ondulado; ~ **iron** hierro *m* ondulado, calamina *f* (*LAm*); ~ **paper** papel *m* ondulado.
corrupt [kə'rʌpt] **1** *adj* corrompido; *text* viciado; *taste* depravado, estragado; *person* venal; ~ **practices** corrupción *f*. **2** *vt* corromper; (*bribe*) sobornar; (*Comput*) *data* degradar.
corruption [kə'rʌpʃən] *n* corrupción *f*.
corsage [kɔː'sɑːʒ] *n* (*of dress*) cuerpo *m*; (*flowers*) ramillete *m* (para el pecho).
corsair ['kɔːsɛəʳ] *n* corsario *m*.
corset ['kɔːsɪt] *n* faja *f*, (*old-style*) corsé *m*.
Corsica ['kɔːsɪkə] *n* Córcega *f*.
Corsican ['kɔːsɪkən] **1** *adj* corso. **2** *n* corso *m*, -a *f*.
cortège [kɔː'teɪʒ] *n* (*procession*) cortejo *m*, comitiva *f*; (*train*) séquito *m*; (*funeral* ~) cortejo *m* fúnebre.
cortex ['kɔːteks] *n*, *pl* **cortices** ['kɔːtɪsiːz] córtex *m*, corteza *f*.
corticoids ['kɔːtɪkɔɪdz] *npl*, **corticosteroids** ['kɔːtɪkəʊ'stɪərɔɪdz] *npl* corticoides *mpl*, corticosteroides *mpl*.
cortisone ['kɔːtɪzəʊn] *n* cortisona *f*.
Corunna [kə'rʌnə] *n* La Coruña.
coruscating ['kɒrəskeɪtɪŋ] *adj humour* chispeante.
corvette [kɔː'vet] *n* corbeta *f*.
COS (*Comm*) *abbr of* **cash on shipment** pago *m* al embarcar; *V* **cash 1**.
cos [kɒs] *abbr of* **cosine** coseno *m*.
'cos* [kɒs] *conj* = **because**.
cosh [kɒʃ] (*Brit*) **1** *n* cachiporra *f*. **2** *vt* golpear con una cachiporra.
cosignatory ['kəʊ'sɪgnətərɪ] *n* cosignatario *m*, -a *f*.
cosily ['kəʊzɪlɪ] *adv* (*V adj*) cómodamente, agradablemente; amistosamente; íntimamente.
cosine ['kəʊsaɪn] *n* coseno *m*.
cosiness ['kəʊzɪnɪs] *n* comodidad *f*; lo acogedor.
cos lettuce ['kɒs'letɪs] *n* (*Brit*) lechuga *f* romana.
cosmetic [kɒz'metɪk] **1** *adj* cosmético; ~ **surgery** cirugía *f* estética; **the changes are merely** ~ los cambios son puramente cosméticos. **2** *n* cosmético *m*.
cosmetician [kɒzmɪ'tɪʃən] *n* cosmetólogo *m*, -a *f*.
cosmic ['kɒzmɪk] *adj* cósmico; ~ **rays** rayos *mpl* cósmicos.
cosmogony [kɒz'mɒgənɪ] *n* cosmogonía *f*.
cosmographer [kɒz'mɒgrəfəʳ] *n* cosmógrafo *m*, -a *f*.
cosmography [kɒz'mɒgrəfɪ] *n* cosmografía *f*.
cosmology [kɒz'mɒlədʒɪ] *n* cosmología *f*.
cosmonaut ['kɒzmənɔːt] *n* cosmonauta *mf*.
cosmopolitan [ˌkɒzmə'pɒlɪtən] **1** *adj* cosmopolita. **2** *n* cosmopolita *mf*.
cosmos ['kɒzmɒs] *n* cosmos *m*.
Cossack ['kɒsæk] **1** *adj* cosaco *m*. **2** *n* cosaco *m*, -a *f*.
cosset ['kɒsɪt] *vt* mimar.
cost [kɒst] **1** *n* (**a**) precio *m*; coste *m*, costo *m*, costa *f*; **~s** (*in industry etc*) costes *mpl*; ~ **analysis** análisis *m* de costos; ~ **centre** centro *m* de costos; ~ **control** control *m* de costos; ~ **of living** coste *m* de vida; **~-of-living allowance** subsidio *m* por coste de vida; **~-of-living bonus** plus *m* de carestía de vida, prima *f* por coste de vida; **~-of-living increase** incremento *m* según el coste de vida; **~-of-living index** índice *m* de coste de vida; ~ **of sales** coste *m* de la campaña de ventas; **at** ~ a (precio de) costa; **at the** ~ **of his health** a costa de su salud; **at the** ~ **of his life** pagó con la vida; **at all ~s, at any** ~ a todo trance, a toda costa; **at great** ~ tras grandes esfuerzos, tras grandes pérdidas; **at little** ~ **to himself** con poco riesgo para sí mismo; **to my** ~ a mis expensas; **without counting the** ~ sin pensar en los riesgos; **whatever the** ~ cueste lo que cueste;
(**b**) (*Jur*) **~s** costas *fpl*, litisexpensas *fpl*; **he was ordered to pay ~s** se le condenó con costas.
2 *vt* (**a**) (*Comm*) calcular el coste de, preparar el presupuesto de; **the job was ~ed at £5000** se calculó el coste del trabajo en 5000 libras; **it has not been properly ~ed** no se ha calculado detalladamente el coste de esto.
(**b**) (*irr*: *pret and ptp* **cost**) (*gen*) costar, valer; **it** ~ **£2** costó 2 libras; **how much does this ~?** ¿cuánto vale esto?, ¿cuánto es?; **what does it** ~ **to go?** ¿cuánto cuesta el viaje?; **it'll** ~ **you*** te costará algo caro; ~ **what it may** cueste lo que cueste; **it** ~ **him his life** le costó la vida; **it** ~ **him a lot of trouble** le causó muchas molestias.
◆**cost out** *vt* presupuestar.
cost accountant ['kɒstəˌkaʊntənt] *n* contable *mf* de costos.
cost accounting ['kɒstəˌkaʊntɪŋ] *n* contabilidad *f* de costos.
co-star ['kəʊstɑːʳ] **1** *n* coestrella *f*. **2** *vt*: **the film ~s A and B** le película presenta como coestrellas A y B. **3** *vi*: **to** ~ **with sb** hacer de coestrella con uno.
Costa Rica ['kɒstə'riːkə] *n* Costa *f* Rica.
Costa Rican ['kɒstə'riːkən] **1** *adj* costarricense. **2** *n* costarricense *mf*.
cost-benefit analysis [ˌkɒstˌbenəfɪtə'næləsɪs] *n* análisis *m* costes-ventajas (*or* de costos-beneficios).
cost-conscious ['kɒstˌkɒnʃəs] *adj* consciente de (los) costos.
cost-cutting ['kɒstˌkʌtɪŋ] *n* recorte *m* de costos.
cost-effective [ˌkɒstɪ'fektɪv] *adj* rentable, beneficioso.
cost-effectiveness [ˌkɒstɪ'fektɪvnɪs] *n* rentabilidad *f*, relación *f* costo-eficacia (*or* costo-rendimiento).
coster ['kɒstəʳ] *n*, **costermonger** ['kɒstəˌmʌŋgəʳ] *n* (*Brit*) vendedor *m* ambulante.
costing ['kɒstɪŋ] *n* cálculo *m* del coste; fijación *f* del precio.
costive ['kɒstɪv] *adj* estreñido.
costliness ['kɒstlɪnɪs] *n* (*dearness*) alto precio *m*; lo caro; (*great value*) suntuosidad *f*.
costly ['kɒstlɪ] *adj* (*dear*) costoso; caro; (*valuable*) suntuoso.
cost-plus [ˌkɒst'plʌs] *n* precio *m* de coste más beneficio; **on a** ~ **basis** a base de precio de coste más beneficio.
cost-price ['kɒst'praɪs] (*Brit*) **1** *n* precio *m* de coste; **at** ~ = **2** *adv* al precio de coste.
costume ['kɒstjuːm] *n* traje *m*; (*fancy-dress*) disfraz *m*; ~ **ball** baile *m* de trajes; ~ **designer** (*Cine, TV*) encargado *m*, -a *f* de vestuario; figurinista *mf*; ~ **jewelry** (*US*), ~ **jewellery** joyas *fpl* de fantasía, bisutería *f*; ~ **party** (*US*) baile *m* de disfraces; ~ **piece,** ~ **play** obra *f* de época.
costumier [kɒs'tjuːmɪəʳ] *n*, (*esp US*) **costumer** [kɒs'tjuːmə] *n* sastre *m* de teatro.
cosy, (*US*) **cozy** ['kəʊzɪ] **1** *adj* cómodo, agradable; *atmosphere* acogedor, amistoso; *chat* íntimo, amistoso; *life* holgado. **2** *n* cubierta *f* para tetera.
cot [kɒt] *n* (*Brit*) cuna *f*, camita *f* de niño; (*US*) cama *f* plegable; ~ **death** muerte *f* en la cuna.
coterie ['kəʊtərɪ] *n* grupo *m*; tertulia *f*; (*clique*) peña *f*, camarilla *f*.
cottage ['kɒtɪdʒ] *n* casita *f* de campo; (*US*) vivienda *f* campestre, quinta *f*; (*labourer's etc*) choza *f*, barraca *f*; ~ **cheese** requesón *m*; ~ **hospital** (*Brit*) pequeño hospital *m* local; ~ **industry** industria *f* artesanal, industria *f* casera; ~ **loaf** (*Brit*) ≃ pan *m* de payés.
cottager ['kɒtɪdʒəʳ] *n* (*Brit*) aldeano *m*, -a *f*; (*US*) veraneante *mf* (que vive en una casita de campo).
cotter ['kɒtəʳ] *n* chaveta *f*.
cotton ['kɒtn] **1** *n* algodón *m*; (*plant*) algodonero *m*; (*Brit*: *sewing thread*) hilo *m* de coser; (*US Med*) algodón *m* hidrófilo (en rama).
2 *attr* de algodón; algodonero; ~ **belt** (*US*) zona *f* algodonera; ~ **bud,** ~ **swab** (*US*) bastoncillo *m* de algodón; ~ **candy** (*US*) algodón *m* azucarado; **the** ~ **industry** la industria algodonera; ~ **waste** borra *f* de algodón.
◆**cotton on*** *vi* caer en la cuenta; **to** ~ **on to** entender, caer en la cuenta de.
cottongrass ['kɒtngrɑːs] *n* algodonosa *f*, algodoncillo *m* (silvestre).
cotton-mill ['kɒtnmɪl] *n* fábrica *f* de algodón.
cotton-picking* ['kɒtnˌpɪkɪŋ] *adj* (*US*) condenado.
cottonseed-oil ['kɒtnsiːdɔɪl] *n* aceite *m* de algodón.
cottontail ['kɒtnteɪl] *n* (*US*) conejo *m* (de cola blanca).
cottonwood ['kɒtnwʊd] *n* (*US*) álamo *m* de Virginia.
cotton-wool ['kɒtn'wʊl] *n* (*Brit*) algodón *m* hidrófilo (en rama).
cotyledon [ˌkɒtɪ'liːdən] *n* cotiledón *m*.
couch [kaʊtʃ] **1** *n* canapé *m*, sofá *m*; (*psychiatrist's*) diván *m*; ~ **potato*** haragán *m*, -ana *f* del sofá; **to be on the** ~ (*US*) ir al psicoanalista. **2** *vt* (*liter*) expresar; **~ed in jargon** redactado en jerigonza.
couchette [kuː'ʃet] *n* (*Rail*) litera *f*.
couch-grass ['kaʊtʃgrɑːs] *n* hierba *f* rastrera, grana *f* del norte, agropiro *m*.
cougar ['kuːgəʳ] *n* puma *f*.
cough [kɒf] **1** *n* tos *f*. **2** *vi* toser; (‡) cantar.
◆**cough up 1** *vt* (**a**) (*lit*) escupir, arrojar.
(**b**) (**fig*) *money* desembolsar, pagar.
2 *vi* (*) desdinerarse*, pagar.
cough-drop ['kɒfdrɒp] *n* pastilla *f* para la tos.

coughing ['kɒfɪŋ] *n* toser *m*, toses *fpl*; **fit of ~** acceso *m* de tos; **you couldn't hear the symphony for ~** el público tosía tanto que apenas se oía la sinfonía.
cough-lozenge ['kɒf,lɒzɪndʒ] *n* pastilla *f* para la tos.
cough-mixture ['kɒf,mɪkstʃəʳ] *n*, **cough-syrup** ['kɒf,sɪrəp] *n* jarabe *m* para la tos.
could [kʊd] *pret and conditional of* **can¹**.
couldn't ['kʊdnt] = **could not**.
council ['kaʊnsl] *n* (**a**) (*meeting, body*) consejo *m*, junta *f*; (*Eccl*) concilio *m*; **C~ of Europe** Consejo *m* de Europa; **~ of war** consejo *m* de guerra.
(**b**) (*town* ~) concejo *m*; (*loosely*) municipio *m*, ayuntamiento *m*; **~ flat** (*Brit*) ≈ piso *m* de protección oficial; **~ house** (*Brit*) vivienda *f* protegida (alquilada del municipio); **~ housing** (*Brit*) viviendas *fpl* de protección oficial; **~ housing estate** zona *f* urbanística de viviendas de protección oficial; **~ tenant** inquilino *m*, -a *f* de una vivienda protegida; **you should write to the ~ about it** deberás escribir al Ayuntamiento acerca de eso; **the ~ should move the rubbish** les cumple a los servicios municipales recoger la basura.
councillor, (*US*) **councilor** ['kaʊnsɪləʳ] *n* (*also* **town ~**) concejal *m*, -ala *f*.
councilman ['kaʊnsɪlmən] *n*, *pl* **councilmen** ['kaʊnsɪlmən] (*US*) concejal *m*.
counsel ['kaʊnsəl] *n* (**a**) consejo *m*; **a ~ of perfection** un ideal imposible; **to keep one's own ~** guardar silencio; **to take ~ with** aconsejarse con.
(**b**) (*Jur*) abogado *mf*; **~ for the defence** (*Brit*) abogado *m* defensor, abogado *f* defensora; **~ for the prosecution** (*Brit*) fiscal *mf*.
2 *vt person* aconsejar; (*Med etc*) orientar; *prudence etc* recomendar; **to ~ sb to do sth** aconsejar a uno hacer algo.
counselling, (*US*) **counseling** ['kaʊnsəlɪŋ] **1** *n* (*gen*: *advice*) asesoramiento *m*; (*Psych*) asistencia *f* sociopsicológica; (*Brit Scol*) ayuda *f* psicopedagógica.
2 *attr*: **~ service** servicio *m* de orientación; (*Univ*) servicio *m* de orientación universitaria.
counsellor, (*US*) **counselor** ['kaʊnsələʳ] *n* (*gen*) asesor *m*, -ora *f*, consejero *m*, -a *f*; (*Psych*) consejero *m*, -a *f*; (*US Scol*) consejero *m*, -a *f*, asesor *m*, -ora *f*; (*Ireland, US Jur*: *also* **~-at-law**) abogado *mf*.
count¹ [kaʊnt] **1** *n* (**a**) (*act of counting*) cuenta *f*, cálculo *m*; (*of words etc*) recuento *m*; (*of votes*) recuento *m*, escrutinio *m*; (*Boxing*) cuenta *f*; **at the last ~** la última vez que los (*etc*) contamos; **to be out for the ~** estar K.O.; **to keep ~ of** contar; **to lose ~ of** perder la cuenta de.
(**b**) (*total*) suma *f*, total *m*.
(**c**) (*Jur*) cargo *m*, acusación *f*.
2 *vt* (**a**) (*Math*) contar; calcular.
(**b**) (*include*) incluir; **not ~ing** sin contar, además de, con exclusión de.
(**c**) (*deem*) creer, considerar; **I don't ~ him among my friends** no le considero como amigo; **I ~ it an honour** lo considero un honor; **will you ~ it against me if ...?** ¿vas a pensar mal de mí si ...?
3 *vi* (**a**) (*Math*) contar; **to ~ on one's fingers** contar con los dedos; **he ~s as 2** él cuenta por 2.
(**b**) **that doesn't ~** (*be valid*) eso no vale, (*in games*) eso no puntúa.
(**c**) (*be important*) **every second ~s** cada segundo es importante; **he doesn't ~** él no vale para esto; **he doesn't ~ for much** él apenas si vale, pinta poco; **ability ~s for little here** aquí la aptitud sirve para muy poco.
4 *vr*: **I ~ myself fortunate** me considero feliz.
◆**count down** *vi* contar atrás, contar al revés.
◆**count in** *vt* incluir; **~ me in** cuenta conmigo.
◆**count on** *vt* contar con; **to ~ on** + *ger* contar con + *infin*; **he is not to be ~ed on** no podemos confiar en él.
◆**count out** *vt* (**a**) *money etc* ir contando.
(**b**) (*Boxing*) declarar vencido.
(**c**) excluir; **~ me out** no cuentes conmigo.
◆**count towards** *vt* contar para, ser válido para.
◆**count up** *vt* contar.
count² [kaʊnt] *n* (*noble*) conde *m*.
countable ['kaʊntəbl] *adj* contable.
countdown ['kaʊntdaʊn] *n* cuenta *f* atrás, cuenta *f* al revés.
countenance ['kaʊntɪnəns] **1** *n* semblante *m*, rostro *m*; **to be out of ~** estar desconcertado; **to give** (*or* **lend**) **~ to** *news* acreditar; **to keep one's ~** contener la risa; **to lose ~** desconcertarse; **to put sb out of ~** desconcertar a uno.
2 *vt* aprobar, tolerar, sancionar.
counter¹ ['kaʊntəʳ] *n* (**a**) (*of shop*) mostrador *m*; **~ staff** personal *m* de ventas, cajeras *fpl*; **to pay over the ~** pagar al contado; **over the ~ purchases** compras *fpl* al contado; **over the ~ market** (*St Ex*) mercado *m* de acciones no cotizadas en la bolsa; **you can buy it over the ~** (*Med*) esto se compra sin receta obligatoria; **under the ~** por la trastienda. (**b**) (*in games*) ficha *f*. (**c**) (*Tech*) contador *m*.
counter² ['kaʊntəʳ] **1** *adj* contrario, de sentido opuesto (*to* a). **2** *adv*: **to run ~ to** oponerse a, ser contrario a. **3** *vt* contrarrestar; *blow* parar; devolver; *attack* contestar a. **4** *vi*: **to ~ with** contestar con.
counter... ['kaʊntəʳ] *pref* contra...
counteract [,kaʊntə'rækt] *vt* contrarrestar; neutralizar.
counter-argument ['kaʊntər,ɑːgjʊmənt] *n* contraargumento *m*.
counter-attack ['kaʊntərə,tæk] **1** *n* contraataque *m*. **2** *vt* contraatacar.
counter-attraction ['kaʊntərə,trækʃən] *n* atracción *f* rival.
counterbalance ['kaʊntə,bæləns] **1** *n* contrapeso *m*; compensación *f*. **2** *vt* contrapesar; compensar.
counterblast ['kaʊntəblɑːst] *n* respuesta *f* vigorosa (*to* a).
countercharge ['kaʊntətʃɑːdʒ] *n* recriminación *f*; contraataque *m*.
countercheck ['kaʊntətʃek] **1** *n* segunda comprobación *f*. **2** *vt* comprobar por segunda vez.
counterclaim ['kaʊntəkleɪm] *n* reconvención *f*.
counter-clockwise ['kaʊntə'klɒkwaɪz] *adv* en sentido contrario al de las agujas del reloj, sinistrórsum.
counter-culture ['kaʊntə,kʌltʃəʳ] *n* contracultura *f*.
counter-espionage ['kaʊntə'respɪənɑːʒ] *n* contraespionaje *m*.
counterfeit ['kaʊntəfiːt] **1** *adj* falso, falsificado, contrahecho. **2** *n* falsificación *f*; (*coin*) moneda *f* falsa, (*note*) billete *m* falso. **3** *vt* falsificar, contrahacer.
counterfoil ['kaʊntəfɔɪl] *n* (*Brit*) talón *m*, matriz *f*.
counterhand ['kaʊntə,hænd] *n* (*in shop*) dependiente *m*, -a *f*; (*in snack bar*) camarero *m*, -a *f*.
counter-indication ['kaʊntər,ɪndɪ'keɪʃən] *n* contraindicación *f*.
counter insurgency ['kaʊntərɪn'sɜːdʒənsɪ] *n* medidas *fpl* antiinsurrectivas.
counterinsurgent ['kaʊntərɪn'sɜːdʒənt] *n* contrainsurgente *mf*.
counterintelligence ['kaʊntərɪn,telɪdʒəns] *n* contraespionaje *m*.
countermand ['kaʊntəmɑːnd] *vt* revocar, cancelar.
counter-measure ['kaʊntəmeʒəʳ] *n* contramedida *f*.
counter-move ['kaʊntəmuːv] *n* contrajugada *f*; (*fig*) contraataque *m*; contramaniobra *f*.
counter-offensive ['kaʊntərə'fensɪv] *n* contraofensiva *f*.
counter-order ['kaʊntər,ɔːdəʳ] *n* contraorden *f*.
counterpane ['kaʊntəpeɪn] *n* sobrecama *m*, colcha *f*, cobertor *m*.
counterpart ['kaʊntəpɑːt] *n* (*person*) homólogo *m*, -a *f*; (*thing*) equivalente *m*.
counterpoint ['kaʊntəpɔɪnt] *n* contrapunto *m*.
counterpoise ['kaʊntəpɔɪz] **1** *n* contrapeso *m*; compensación *f*. **2** *vt* contrapesar; compensar.
counter-productive [,kaʊntəprə'dʌktɪv] *adj* contraproducente.
counter-proposal ['kaʊntəprə,pəʊzəl] *n* contrapropuesta *f*.
Counter-Reformation ['kaʊntə,refə'meɪʃən] *n* Contrarreforma *f*.
counter-revolution ['kaʊntərevə'luːʃən] *n* contrarrevolución *f*.
counter-revolutionary ['kaʊntərevə'luːʃənrɪ] **1** *adj* contrarrevolucionario. **2** *n* contrarrevolucionario *m*, -a *f*.
countersign ['kaʊntəsaɪn] **1** *n* (*Mil*) contraseña *f*. **2** *vt* refrendar.
countersink ['kaʊntəsɪŋk] *vt* avellanar.
counter-stroke ['kaʊntəstrəʊk] *n* contragolpe *m*.
countertenor ['kaʊntə,tenəʳ] *n* contratenor *m*; **~ voice** voz *f* de contratenor.
countervailing ['kaʊntə,veɪlɪŋ] *adj* compensatorio; **~ duties** aranceles *mpl* compensatorios.
counterweigh [,kaʊntə'weɪ] *vt* contrapesar; compensar.
counterweight ['kaʊntəweɪt] *n* contrapeso *m*.
countess ['kaʊntɪs] *n* condesa *f*.
counting ['kaʊntɪŋ] *n* cálculo *m*.
countless ['kaʊntlɪs] *adj* incontable, innumerable; **~ times** infinitas veces.
count-noun ['kaʊntnaʊn] *n* sustantivo *m* contable.
countrified ['kʌntrɪfaɪd] *adj* rústico.
country ['kʌntrɪ] **1** *n* (*political*) país *m*; (*regarded more sentimentally*) patria *f*; (*countryside*) campo *m*; (*region*)

región *f*, tierra *f*; **love of ~** amor *m* a la patria; **there's some good ~ to the north** hacia el norte hay buena tierra; **this is good fishing ~** ésta es buena tierra para la pesca; **we had to leave the road and go across ~** tuvimos que dejar la carretera e ir a través del campo; **to go to the ~** (*Brit Pol*) apelar al país, convocar elecciones generales; **to live off the ~** vivir del país.

2 *attr*: **~ bumpkin** patán *m*; **~ club** club *m* campestre; **~ cousin** pariente *m* pueblerino, parienta *f* pueblerina; **~ cottage** casita *f* (en el campo); **~ dance** contradanza *f*; baile *m* regional, baile *m* campestre; **~ dancing** baile *m* folklórico; **~ dweller** persona *f* que vive en el campo; **~ folk** gente *f* del campo; **~ gentleman** hacendado *m*; **~ house** quinta *f*, finca *f*; **~ life** vida *f* del campo, vida *f* campestre; **~ music, ~ and western** (*US Mus*) música *f* country; **~ park** parque *m*; **~ people** gente *f* del campo; **~ road** camino *m* vecinal; **~ seat** finca *f*; casa *f* solariega.

country-born [ˌkʌntrɪˈbɔːn] *adj* nacido en el campo.

country-bred [ˌkʌntrɪˈbred] *adj* criado en el campo.

countryman [ˈkʌntrɪmən] *n, pl* **countrymen** [ˈkʌntrɪmən] campesino *m*; (*fellow ~*) compatriota *m*.

countryside [ˈkʌntrɪsaɪd] *n* campo *m*.

country-wide [ˌkʌntrɪˈwaɪd] *adj* por todo el país, a escala nacional, de todo el país.

countrywoman [ˈkʌntrɪˌwʊmən] *n, pl* **countrywomen** [ˈkʌntrɪˌwɪmɪn] campesina *f*.

county [ˈkaʊntɪ] **1** *n* condado *m*. **2** *adj, attr*: **~ clerk's office** (*US*) registro *m* civil; **~ commission** (*US*), **~ council** (*Brit*) ≃ diputación *f* provincial; **~ court** (*Brit*) juzgado *m* municipal; **~ cricket** (*Brit*) *partidos de cricket entre los condados*; **~ family** (*Brit*) familia *f* aristocrática rural; **~ recorder's office** (*US*) ≃ registro *m* de la propiedad; **~ road** (*US*) ≃ carretera *f* secundaria; **~ seat** (*US*) cabeza *f* de partido; **~ town** (*esp Brit*) capital *f* de condado.

coup [kuː] *n* golpe *m*; **~ d'état** golpe *m* de estado; **~ de grâce** golpe *m* de gracia; **~ de théâtre** golpe *m* de teatro, golpe *m* de efecto; **to bring off a ~** obtener un éxito inesperado.

coupé [ˈkuːpeɪ] *n* cupé *m*.

couple [ˈkʌpl] **1** *n* (*of things*) par *m*; (*of persons*) pareja *f*; (*married ~*) matrimonio *m*; **young ~** matrimonio *m* joven; **just a ~ of minutes** dos minutos nada más; **we had a ~ in a bar*** tomamos algo en un bar; **when he's had a ~ he starts to shout*** cuando ha bebido más de la cuenta se pone a gritar.

2 *vt names etc* unir, juntar; *ideas* asociar; (*Mech*) acoplar, enganchar.

3 *vi* (*Zool*) copularse.

coupler [ˈkʌplə^{r}] *n* (*Comput*) acoplador *m*; (*US Rail*) enganche *m*; **acoustic ~** acoplador *m* acústico.

couplet [ˈkʌplɪt] *n* pareado *m*.

coupling [ˈkʌplɪŋ] *n* (*Mech*) acoplamiento *m*; (*Rail, Aut*) enganche *m*.

coupon [ˈkuːpɒn] *n* cupón *m*; vale *m*; (*Fin*) cupón *m*; (*football-pool ~*) boleto *m*.

courage [ˈkʌrɪdʒ] *n* valor *m*, valentía *f*; **~!** ¡ánimo!; **to have the ~ of one's convictions** tener el valor de sus convicciones; **to pluck up one's ~** hacer de tripas corazón; **to screw up one's ~ to** + *infin* cobrar bastante ánimo como para + *infin*; **we may take ~ from the fact that ...** es alentador el hecho de que ...; **take ~!** ¡ánimo!; **to take one's ~ in both hands** armarse de valor.

courageous [kəˈreɪdʒəs] *adj* valiente, valeroso.

courageously [kəˈreɪdʒəslɪ] *adv* valientemente.

courgette [kʊəˈʒet] *n* (*Brit*) calabacín *m*, calabacita *f*.

courier [ˈkʊrɪə^{r}] *n* estafeta *f*, mensajero *m*; correo *m* diplomático; (*travel ~*) guía *mf* de turismo.

course [kɔːs] **1** *n* **(a)** (*movement, direction*) dirección *f*, ruta *f*; (*of bullet etc*) trayectoria *f*; (*of road*) dirección *f*; (*of river, star*) curso *m*; (*of illness*) desarrollo *m*; (*Naut*) rumbo *m*, derrota *f*, (*marked on chart*) derrotero *m*; **we are on ~** vamos por buen camino, esta ruta es la buena; **we are on ~ for victory** nos encaminamos al triunfo; **to change ~** cambiar de rumbo (*also fig*); **to set ~ for** hacer rumbo a; **to steer a ~ for** ir rumbo a.

(b) (*mode of action*) proceder *m*, camino *m*; **~ of action** línea *f* de conducta, línea *f* de acción, proceder *m*; **~ of conduct** línea *f* de conducta; **~ of events** marcha *f* de los acontecimientos; **in the ordinary ~ of events** normalmente; **the ~ of true love** el camino del verdadero amor; **your best ~ is to say nothing** lo mejor es no decir nada; **there was no ~ open to me but to go** no tuve más remedio que ir; **what ~ do you suggest?** ¿qué es lo que me aconsejas?; **the affair has run its ~** el asunto ha terminado; **we will let things take their ~** dejaremos que las cosas sigan su curso normal, dejaremos correr los acontecimientos; **to take a middle ~** evitar los extremos.

(c) (*Golf*) campo *m*, cancha *f* (*LAm*); (*for races*) pista *f*, (*for horse-races*) hipódromo *m*; **to stay the ~** no cejar, continuar hasta el fin.

(d) (*in meal*) plato *m*.

(e) (*Archit*) hilada *f*.

(f) (*series*) curso *m*; (*of injections*) serie *f*; (*Univ etc*) curso *m*, asignatura *f*; **I failed the chemistry ~** me suspendieron en química; **what ~ do you take?** ¿qué asignatura haces?; **a French ~** un curso de francés; **I bought a French grammar ~** compré una gramática francesa; **a ~ of lectures** un ciclo de conferencias; **~ of treatment** tratamiento *m*, cura *f*; **to take a ~ with** seguir un curso con.

(g) (*phrases*) **in the ~ of** durante, en el curso de; durante el desarrollo de; **in ~ of construction** en vías de construcción; **it is in ~ of being applied** está en trance de ser aplicado; **in (the) ~ of time, in due ~** andando el tiempo, a su debido tiempo; **we shall inform you in due ~** se lo comunicaremos en su momento; **of ~** desde luego, naturalmente; **of ~!** ¡por supuesto!, ¡naturalmente!, ¡claro!; **of ~ it's not true** claro que no es cierto; **it is of ~ true that ...** bien es verdad que ...; **he takes it all as a matter of ~** para él todo esto no tiene nada de especial; **he took it as a matter of ~ that ...** para él era de cajón que ....

2 *vt hares* cazar (con perros).

3 *vi* (*Sport*) correr; **it sent the blood coursing through my veins** me hizo hervir la sangre.

coursing [ˈkɔːsɪŋ] *n* caza *f* con perros.

court [kɔːt] **1** *n* **(a)** (*Archit*) patio *m*.

(b) (*Sport*) pista *f*, cancha *f*.

(c) (*royal*) corte *f*; **at ~** en la corte; **~ circular** noticiario *m* de la corte; **~ shoe** (*Brit*) escarpín *m*; **to hold ~** dar audiencia, recibir en audiencia.

(d) **to pay ~ to** hacer la corte a.

(e) (*Jur*) tribunal *m*, juzgado *m*; **~ of appeal** (*Brit*) tribunal *m* de casación; **~ of inquiry** comisión *f* de investigación; **~ of justice, ~ of law** tribunal *m* de justicia; **C~ of Session** (*Scot*) Tribunal *m* Supremo de Escocia; **~ order** (*Jur*) mandato *m* judicial; **in open ~** en pleno tribunal; **to laugh sth out of ~** rechazar algo poniéndolo en ridículo; **to rule sth out of ~** desestimar algo; **to settle out of ~** negociar una solución al margen de los tribunales, arreglar una disputa de modo privado; **to take sb to ~** demandar a uno; recurrir a la vía judicial, llevar a uno ante los tribunales.

2 *vt woman* cortejar, hacer la corte a, (*less formally*) tener relaciones con; *favour* solicitar; *danger, trouble* buscar; *disaster* correr hacia.

3 *vi* estar en relaciones, ser novios; **they've been ~ing 3 years** llevan 3 años de relaciones; **are you ~ing?** ¿tienes novio?; **~ing couple** pareja *f* de novios.

court card [ˈkɔːtkɑːd] *n* (*esp Brit*) figura *f*.

courteous [ˈkɜːtɪəs] *adj* cortés, fino, correcto.

courteously [ˈkɜːtɪəslɪ] *adv* cortésmente.

courtesan [ˌkɔːtɪˈzæn] *n* cortesana *f*.

courtesy [ˈkɜːtɪsɪ] **1** *n* cortesía *f*; atención *f*; gentileza *f*; **by ~ of** con permiso de; gracias a; **to exchange courtesies** cambiar cumplidos (de etiqueta); **I'll do it out of ~** lo haré por cortesía; **you might have had the ~ to tell me** el no decírmelo fue una falta de educación; **he did me the ~ of reading it** tuvo la gentileza de leérmelo.

2 *attr*: **~ bus** autobús *m* de cortesía; **~ call, ~ visit** visita *f* de cumplido; **~ car** coche *m* de cortesía; **~ card** (*US*) tarjeta *f* (de visita); **~ coach** (*Brit*) autocar *m* de cortesía al aeropuerto; **~ light** (*Aut*) luz *f* interior; **~ title** título *m* de cortesía.

courthouse [ˈkɔːthaʊs] *n, pl* **courthouses** [ˈkɔːtˌhaʊzɪz] palacio *m* de justicia.

courtier [ˈkɔːtɪə^{r}] *n* cortesano *m*.

courtly [ˈkɔːtlɪ] *adj* cortés, elegante, fino; **~ love** amor *m* cortés.

court-martial [ˈkɔːtˈmɑːʃəl], *pl* **courts-martial** **1** *n* consejo *m* de guerra, tribunal *m* militar. **2** *vt* someter a consejo de guerra.

courtroom [ˈkɔːtrʊm] *n* sala *f* de justicia, sala *f* de tribunal.

courtship [ˈkɔːtʃɪp] *n* (*act*) cortejo *m*; (*period*) noviazgo *m*.

courtyard [ˈkɔːtjɑːd] *n* patio *m*.

cousin [ˈkʌzn] *n* primo *m*, -a *f*; **first ~** primo *m* carnal, prima *f* carnal; **second ~** primo *m* segundo, prima *f* segunda.

couth [ku:θ] *n* (*US*) buenos modales *mpl*.
couturier [ku:'tʊərɪ,eɪ] *n* modisto *m*.
cove¹ [kəʊv] *n* (*Geog*) cala *f*, ensenada *f*; (*US: valley*) valle *m*.
cove²*† [kəʊv] *n* tío* *m*.
coven ['kʌvən] *n* aquelarre *m*, asamblea *f* de brujas.
covenant ['kʌvɪnənt] **1** *n* pacto *m*, convenio *m*; (*Bible*) **C~** Alianza *f*; (**tax**) ~ (*Brit*) sistema *m* de contribuciones caritativas con beneficios fiscales para el recipiente.
2 *vi*: **to ~ with sb for sth** pactar algo con uno; **to ~ £500** contribuir 500 libras bajo 'covenant'.
Coventry ['kɒvəntrɪ] *n*: (*Brit*) **to send sb to ~** hacer el vacío a uno.
cover ['kʌvə^r] **1** *n* (**a**) (*gen*) cubierta *f*; (*lid*) tapa *f*, tapadura *f*; (*on bed*) cobertor *m*, colcha *f*; (*of chair, typewriter*) funda *f*; **~s** (*bedclothes*) ropa *f* de cama, mantas *fpl*.
(**b**) (*envelope*) sobre *m*; **first-day ~** sobre *m* de primer día; **under separate ~** por (envío) separado.
(**c**) (*of book*) forro *m*, cubierta *f*; (*of magazine*) portada *f*; **to read a book from ~ to ~** leer un libro desde el principio hasta el fin.
(**d**) (*at table*) cubierto *m*.
(**e**) (*fig*) protección *f*; (*shelter*) abrigo *m*; (*Brit: insurance*) cobertura *f*; (*pretext*) pretexto *m*; (*Fin*) cobertura *f*; (*of spy*) cobertura *f*, tapadera *f*; **under ~** al abrigo, (*indoors*) bajo techo; **under ~ of** al abrigo de, bajo, (*fig*) so capa de; **under the ~ of night** al amparo de la noche; **to break ~** salir a campo raso; **to take ~** abrigarse, ponerse al abrigo, (*Mil*) refugiarse (*from* de).
2 *vt* (**a**) (*gen*) cubrir (*with* de); revestir (*with* de); (*with lid*) tapar (*with* con); *book* forrar; (*shelter*) cubrir, proteger, abrigar; *eyes, face* tapar; **to be ~ed in confusion** estar lleno de confusión; **to be ~ed in glory** estar cubierto de gloria.
(**b**) (*protect*) proteger; *advance, retreat* cubrir, proteger.
(**c**) (*with gun*) apuntar; **I've got you ~ed** te tengo apuntado.
(**d**) (*Sport*) cubrir.
(**e**) (*distance*) cubrir, recorrir, salvar.
(**f**) (*include*) incluir, abarcar, comprender; (*be enough for*) cubrir; *problem* abarcar; *points in discussion* tratar, discutir; (*in speech*) tratar, exponer; dar razón de; *costs, insurance risk* cubrir; **to ~ all possibilities** abarcar todas las posibilidades; **to ~ one's expenses** cubrir los gastos; **to ~ a loss** cubrir una pérdida; **£50 will ~ everything** 50 libras lo cubrirá todo.
(**g**) *story* cubrir, hacer un reportaje sobre, escribir una crónica de; *news item* informar acerca de.
3 *vr*: **to ~ o.s.** protegerse a sí mismo; **to ~ o.s. with glory** cubrirse de gloria.
◆**cover in** *vt* cubrir; (*roof*) poner un techo a, techar.
◆**cover over** *vt* cubrir, revestir (*with* de).
◆**cover up 1** *vt object* cubrir completamente, tapar; *truth, facts* correr un velo sobre, ocultar, encubrir; *emotion* disimular.
2 *vi* (**a**) **to ~ up for sb** encubrir a uno.
(**b**) (*with clothes*) abrigarse, taparse bien; (*in bed*) taparse.
coverage ['kʌvərɪdʒ] *n* (**a**) alcance *m*; espacio *m* cubierto, cantidad *f* cubierta; (*of news*) cobertura *f*, reportaje *m*. (**b**) (*Fin*) cobertura *f*, conjunto *m* de los riesgos que cubre una póliza de seguros.
coveralls ['kʌvərɔ:lz] *npl* (*US*) = **overalls**.
cover-charge ['kʌvətʃɑ:dʒ] *n* precio *m* del cubierto.
covered wagon [,kʌvəd'wægən] *n* carreta *f* entoldada.
covergirl ['kʌvəgɜ:l] *n* modelo *f* de portada.
covering ['kʌvərɪŋ] **1** *n* (*wrapping*) cubierta *f*, envoltura *f*; (*dress etc*) abrigo *m*; (*Sport*) cobertura *f*; **a ~ of snow** una capa de nieve. **2** *adj*: **~ letter** carta *f* adjunta.
coverlet ['kʌvəlɪt] *n* sobrecama *m*, colcha *f*, cobertor *m*.
cover-letter ['kʌvə,letə^r] *n* carta *f* (adjunta) de explicación.
cover-note ['kʌvə,nəʊt] *n* (*Brit*) ≈ seguro *m* provisional.
cover-story ['kʌvə,stɔ:rɪ] *n* (*Press*) noticia *f* de primera página; (*in espionage etc*) tapadera *f*; **our ~ this week** nuestra noticia de primera página de esta semana.
covert ['kʌvət] **1** *adj* secreto, disimulado. **2** *n* soto *m*, matorral *m*.
cover-up ['kʌvərʌp] *n* encubrimiento *m*; **there's been a ~** están tratando de encubrir el escándalo (*etc*).
covet ['kʌvɪt] *vt* codiciar.
covetous ['kʌvɪtəs] *adj* codicioso.
covetousness ['kʌvɪtəsnɪs] *n* codicia *f*.
covey ['kʌvɪ] *n* (*Orn*) nidada *f* (de perdices); (*fig*) grupo *m*.
cow¹ [kaʊ] *n* (**a**) vaca *f*; (*of elephant etc*) hembra *f*; **till the ~s come home** hasta que la rana críe pelo. (**b**) (*: *also* **old ~**) bruja* *f*.
cow² [kaʊ] *vt* intimidar, acobardar.
coward ['kaʊəd] *n* cobarde *m*.
cowardice ['kaʊədɪs] *n*, **cowardliness** ['kaʊədlɪnɪs] *n* cobardía *f*.
cowardly ['kaʊədlɪ] *adj* cobarde.
cowbell ['kaʊbel] *n* cencerro *m*.
cowboy ['kaʊbɔɪ] *n* vaquero *m*; (*Cine etc*) cowboy *m*; **~s and Indians** (*game*) cowboys y pieles rojas; **the ~s of the building trade** los piratas de la construcción.
cowboy boots ['kaʊbɔɪ,bu:ts] *npl* botas *fpl* camperas.
cowboy hat ['kaʊbɔɪ,hæt,] *n* sombrero *m* de cowboy.
cowcatcher ['kaʊ,kætʃə^r] *n* rastrillo *m* delantero, quitapiedras *m*.
cower ['kaʊə^r] *vi* encogerse (de miedo), empequeñecerse (preso del terror); **the servants were ~ing in a corner** los criados se habían refugiado medrosos en un rincón.
cowgirl ['kaʊgɜ:l] *n* vaquera *f*.
cowherd ['kaʊhɜ:d] *n* pastor *m*, -ora *f* de ganado, vaquero *m* -a *f*.
cowhide ['kaʊhaɪd] *n* cuero *m*.
cow-house ['kaʊhaʊs] *n*, *pl* **cow-houses** ['kaʊhaʊzɪz] establo *m*.
cowl [kaʊl] *n* (*hood*) capucha *f*; (*garment*) cogulla *f*; (*of chimney*) sombrerete *m*.
cowlick ['kaʊlɪk] *n* (*US*) chavito *m*, mechón *m*.
cowling ['kaʊlɪŋ] *n* cubierta *f*.
cowman ['kaʊmən] *n*, *pl* **cowmen** ['kaʊmən] (*Brit*) pastor *m* de ganado, vaquero *m*; (*US*) ganadero *m*.
co-worker ['kəʊ'wɜ:kə^r] *n* colaborador *m*, -ora *f*.
cow-parsley [,kaʊ'pɑ:slɪ] *n* perejil *m* de monte.
cowpat ['kaʊpæt] *n* cagada *f* de vaca, boñiga *f*.
cowpoke* ['kaʊpəʊk] *n* (*US*) vaquero *m*.
cowpox ['kaʊpɒks] *n* vacuna *f*.
cowrie ['kaʊrɪ] *n* cauri *m*.
cowshed ['kaʊʃed] *n* establo *m*.
cowslip ['kaʊslɪp] *n* primavera *f*, prímula *f*.
cow town* ['kaʊtaʊn] *n* (*US*) pueblucho *m* de mala muerte.
cox [kɒks] **1** *n* timonel *m*. **2** *vt* gobernar. **3** *vi* hacer (*or* actuar) de timonel.
coxcomb ['kɒkskəʊm] *n* cresta *f* de gallo.
coxswain ['kɒksn] *n* timonel *m*.
Coy (*Mil*) *abbr of* **company**.
coy [kɔɪ] *adj* tímido; evasivo, reservado; (*roguish*) coquetón.
coyly ['kɔɪlɪ] *adv* tímidamente; con coquetería.
coyness ['kɔɪnɪs] *n* timidez *f*; coquetería *f*.
coyote [kɔɪ'əʊtɪ] *n* coyote *m*.
coziness ['kəʊzɪnɪs] *n* (*US*) = **cosiness**.
cozy ['kəʊzɪ] *adj* (*US*) = **cosy**.
CP (**a**) *n* (*Pol*) *abbr of* **Communist Party** Partido *m* Comunista, PC *m*. (**b**) (*Comm*) *abbr of* **carriage paid** porte *m* pagado, P.P.
c/p *abbr of* **carriage paid** porte pagado, P.P.
cp. *abbr of* **compare** compárese, comp.
CPA *n* (**a**) (*US*) *abbr of* **Certified Public Accountant**. (**b**) *abbr of* **critical path analysis**.
CPI *n* (*US*) *abbr of* **Consumer Price Index** Indice *m* de precios al consumo, IPC.
Cpl *abbr of* **Corporal** cabo *m*.
CP/M *n abbr of* **Central Program for Microprocessors**, CP/M *m*.
cps *npl abbr of* **characters per second** caracteres *mpl* por segundo, cps.
CPSA *n abbr of* **Civil and Public Services Association** *sindicato de funcionarios*.
CPU *n abbr of* **central processing unit** unidad *f* central de proceso, UPC *f*.
Cr (**a**) (*Comm*) *abbr of* **credit** haber *m*. (**b**) (*Comm*) *abbr of* **creditor** acreedor *m*. (**c**) (*Pol*) *abbr of* **councillor** concejal *m*, -ala *f*.
crab [kræb] **1** *n* (**a**) cangrejo *m*; **C~** (*Astron*) Cáncer *m*; **to catch a ~** (*fig*) fallar con el remo, dar una calada. (**b**) **~s** (*Med*) ladillas *fpl*. **2** *vi*: **to ~ (about)*** quejarse (acerca de).
crabapple ['kræb,æpl] *n* (*fruit*) manzana *f* silvestre; (*tree*) manzano *m* silvestre.
crabbed ['kræbd] *adj writing* apretado, indescifrable; *temperament* de miras estrechas; *mood* malhumorado, hosco.
crabby ['kræbɪ] *adj* malhumorado, hosco, gruñón.
crab grass ['kræbgrɑ:s] *n* garranchuelo *m*.
crab louse ['kræblaʊs] *n*, *pl* **crab lice** ['kræblaɪs] ladilla *f*.

crabwise ['kræb,waɪz] **1** *adj movement* como de cangrejo, lateral. **2** *adv move* como cangrejo, lateralmente.
crack [kræk] **1** *n* (**a**) (*noise*) crujido *m*; (*of whip*) chasquido *m*; (*shot*) estallido *m*; **to get a fair ~ of the whip** recibir un trato equitativo, ser tratado lo mismo que otros.
(**b**) (*blow*) golpe *m* (*on* en).
(**c**) (*fissure*) grieta *f*, hendedura *f*; (*slit*) rendija *f*; **at the ~ of dawn** al romper el alba; **to open the window a ~** abrir la ventana un poquito; **to paper over the ~s** disimular las grietas (*also fig*).
(**d**) (*: *joke*) chiste *m*, chanza *f*, cuchufleta *f*; **to make ~s about** *person* tomar el pelo a, burlarse de, *thing* poner en ridículo.
(**e**) (*: *attempt*) **to have a ~ at sth** intentar algo, probar algo.
(**f**) (*: *drug*) crack *m*, cocaína *f* dura.
2 *adj team etc* de primera categoría; **~ driver, shot** *etc* as *m*.
3 *vt* (**a**) (*cause to sound*) *whip, fingers* chasquear; *knuckles etc* crujir.
(**b**) (*break*) agrietar, hender, romper; *nut* cascar; *safe* forzar; (*) *bottle* abrir (*with* para festejar a); *oil* craquear; **to ~ one's head on the wall** dar con la cabeza contra la pared; **to ~ one's skull** fracturarse el cráneo; **to ~ sb over the head** golpear a uno en la cabeza.
(**c**) (*) *joke* contar.
(**d**) *code* descifrar; *case, mystery* resolver, aclarar; **I think we've ~ed the problem** creo que hemos resuelto el problema.
4 *vi* (**a**) (*make noise*) chasquear; crujir; (*shot*) estallar.
(**b**) (*break*) agrietarse, henderse, rajarse, romperse; (*burst*) reventar; (*voice*) cascarse; (*resistance etc*) desplomarse; **to ~ under the strain** romperse bajo el peso, (*person*) sufrir un colapso bajo la presión.
(**c**) **to get ~ing** (*Brit**) ponerse a trabajar (*etc*), poner manos a la obra; **let's get ~ing!** ¡a ello!, ¡manos a la obra!
◆**crack down on** *vt* castigar severamente; tomar medidas enérgicas contra; suprimir.
◆**crack up 1** *vt* dar bombo a; **it's not all it's ~ed up to be** no es tan bueno como la gente dice. **2** *vi* (*esp US*: *plane*) estrellarse; (*car etc*) averiarse; (*business etc*) derrumbarse, venirse abajo; fallar; no poder soportarlo más; (*Med*) sufrir un colapso nervioso; (*get angry*) enfadarse, ponerse furioso.
crackajack ['krækədʒæk] *n, adj* (*US*) = **crackerjack**.
crack-brained ['krækbreɪnd] *adj* loco.
crackdown ['krækdaʊn] *n* campaña *f* (*on* contra); medidas *fpl* enérgicas (*on* contra); supresión *f* (*on* de); período *m* de aplastamiento.
cracked [krækt] *adj* (**a**) *voice* cascado. (**b**) (*mad*) chiflado, tarado (*LAm*).
cracker ['krækəʳ] *n* (**a**) (*firework*) buscapiés *m*; (*Brit*: *Christmas* ~) sorpresa *f*. (**b**) (*biscuit*) galleta *f* de soda, galleta *f* para queso; (*US*) galleta *f*. (**c**) **a ~ of a game*** un partido fenomenal*.
crackerjack, (*US*) **crackajack** ['krækədʒæk] **1** *n* (*person*) as* *m*; (*thing*) bomba* *f*. **2** *adj* bomba*, súper*.
crackers‡ ['krækəz] *adj* (*Brit*) lelo, chiflado.
crackhead* ['kræk,hed] *n* adicto *m*, -a *f* al crack.
cracking ['krækɪŋ] **1** *n* (*petroleum*) cracking *m*; (*cracks*) grietas *fpl*, agrietamiento *m*. **2** *adj* (*Brit*) cutre*; **at a ~ speed** (*or* **pace**) a toda pastilla*. **3** *adv* (*Brit**) tope*.
crackle ['krækl] **1** *n* (*of wood, bacon*) crepitación *f*, chisporroteo *m*; (*of dry leaves*) crujido *m*; (*of shots*) traqueteo *m*. **2** *vi* crepitar, chisporrotear; crujir; traquetear.
crackling ['kræklɪŋ] *n* (**a**) (*Culin*) chicharrón *m*. (**b**) (*sound*) *V* **crackle**.
crackpot ['krækpɒt] **1** *adj* tonto, estrafalario, excéntrico. **2** *n* chiflado *m*, -a *f*, excéntrico *m*, -a *f*.
crack-up ['krækʌp] *n* crisis *f* nerviosa; (*Fin etc*) derrumbamiento *m*, quiebra *f*; (*Med*) colapso *m* nervioso.
cradle ['kreɪdl] **1** *n* cuna *f* (*also fig*); (*for house-painting etc*) plataforma *f* colgante; **from the ~ to the grave** de la cuna a la tumba; **she's a ~ snatcher*** siempre va detrás de jovencitos; **to rob the ~** (*US**) casarse con una persona mucho más joven.
2 *vt*: **to ~ a child in one's arms** mecer un niño en los brazos.
cradlesong ['kreɪdlsɒŋ] *n* canción *f* de cuna.
craft [krɑːft] **1** *n* (**a**) (*skill in general*) destreza *f*, habilidad *f*; (*craftiness*) astucia *f*. (**b**) (*special skill*) arte *m*; (*trade*) oficio *m*; **~ union** sindicato *m* de obreros especializados; **~ work** artesanía *f*.
(**c**) (*Naut*) barco *m*, embarcación *f*.
2 *vt* hacer (a mano); **~ed products** productos *mpl* de artesanía.
craftily ['krɑːftɪlɪ] *adv* astutamente.
craftiness ['krɑːftɪnɪs] *n* astucia *f*.
craftsman ['krɑːftsmən] *n, pl* **craftsmen** ['krɑːftsmən] artesano *m*; artífice *m*.
craftsmanship ['krɑːftsmənʃɪp] *n* artesanía *f*.
crafty ['krɑːftɪ] *adj* (**a**) *person, move etc* astuto. (**b**) (*) *gadget etc* ingenioso.
crag [kræg] *n* peñasco *m*, risco *m*.
craggy ['krægɪ] *adj* peñascoso, escarpado; *face* de facciones marcadas.
cram [kræm] **1** *vt* (**a**) *hen* cebar; *subject* empollar, aprender apresuradamente; *pupil* preparar apresuradamente para un examen.
(**b**) **to ~ food into one's mouth** llenarse la boca de comida; **to ~ things into a case** ir metiendo cosas apretadamente en una maleta; **we can't ~ any more in** es imposible meter más.
(**c**) **to ~ sth with** llenar algo de, henchir algo de; **the hall is ~med** la sala está de bote en bote; **the room is ~med with furniture** el cuarto está atestado de muebles; **he had his head ~med with odd ideas** tenía la cabeza cargada de ideas raras.
2 *vi* (**a**) **to ~ in, come ~ming in** entrar en masa, amontonarse; **7 of us ~med into the Mini** los 7 logramos encajarnos en el Mini; **can I ~ in here?** ¿quepo yo aquí?
(**b**) (*for exam*) empollar.
(**c**) = **3**.
3 *vr*: **to ~ o.s. with food** darse un atracón; **to ~ o.s. with cakes** atracarse de pastas.
cram-full ['kræm'fʊl] *adj* atestado (*of* de), de bote en bote.
crammer ['kræməʳ] *n* (*Scol*: *pupil*) empollón *m*, -ona *f*; (*teacher*) profesor *m*, -ora *f* que prepara rapidísimamente a sus alumnos para los exámenes.
cramp¹ [kræmp] *n* (*Med*) calambre *m*.
cramp² [kræmp] **1** *n* (*Tech*) grapa *f*; (*Archit*) pieza *f* de unión, abrazadera *f*. **2** *vt* (*hamper*) estorbar, restringir; **to ~ sb's style** cortar los vuelos a uno, cohibir a uno.
cramped [kræmpt] *adj room etc* estrecho; *writing* menudo, apretado; *position* nada cómodo; **we are very ~ for space here** estamos muy estrechos aquí.
crampon ['kræmpən] *n* garfio *m*; (*Mountaineering*) crampón *m*.
cramponning ['kræmpənɪŋ] *n* uso *m* de crampones.
cranberry ['krænbərɪ] *n* arándano *m* (agrio).
crane [kreɪn] **1** *n* (*Orn*) grulla *f*; (*Tech*) grúa *f*. **2** *vt* (*also* **to ~ up**) levantar con grúa; **to ~ one's neck** estirar el cuello.
◆**crane forward** *vi* inclinarse estirando el cuello; **to ~ forward to look at sth** estirar el cuello para mirar algo.
crane-driver ['kreɪn,draɪvəʳ] *n* gruista *mf*.
cranefly ['kreɪnflaɪ] *n* típula *f*.
crane operator ['kreɪn,ɒpəreɪtəʳ] *n* = **crane-driver**.
cranial ['kreɪnɪəl] *adj* craneal.
cranium ['kreɪnɪəm] *n, pl* **crania** ['kreɪnɪə] cráneo *m*.
crank¹ [kræŋk] **1** *n* manivela *f*, manubrio *m*; cigüeñal *m*. **2** *vt engine* (*also* **to ~ up**) dar vuelta a, hacer arrancar con la manivela.
◆**crank out*** *vt* (*US*) producir penosamente.
crank²* [kræŋk] *n* (*Brit*: *person*) maniático *m*, -a, *f*, chiflado *m*, -a *f*, excéntrico *m*, -a *f*; (*US*: *person*) gruñón *m*, -ona *f*.
crankcase ['kræŋkkeɪs] *n* cárter *m* (del cigüeñal).
crankshaft ['kræŋkʃɑːft] *n* (eje *m* del) cigüeñal *m*, árbol *m* del cigüeñal.
cranky* ['kræŋkɪ] *adj person* maniático, chiflado, excéntrico; *idea* raro, estrafalario.
cranny ['krænɪ] *n* grieta *f*.
crap** [kræp] **1** *n* (*lit, fig*) mierda** *f*. **2** *vi* cagar**.
◆**crap out**‡ *vi* (*US*) (**a**) (*back down*) rajarse*. (**b**) (*fail*) fracasar.
crape [kreɪp] *n* crespón *m*.
crappy** ['kræpɪ] *adj* (*esp US*) asqueroso.
craps [kræps] *npl* (*US*) dados *mpl*; **to shoot ~** jugar a los dados.
crash [kræʃ] **1** *n* (**a**) (*noise*) estruendo *m*, estrépito *m*; (*explosion*) estallido *m*.
(**b**) (*collision*) accidente *m*, colisión *f*; choque *m*, encontronazo *m*; (*Aer*) accidente *m* de aviación.
(**c**) (*ruin*) fracaso *m*, ruina *f*; (*Comm*) quiebra *f*; crac *m*; **the 1929 ~** la crisis económica de 1929.
(**d**) (*: *drug*) mono‡ *m*, síndrome *m* de abstinencia.
2 *vt car, aircraft* estrellar (*into* contra); estropear; **he ~ed the plate to the ground** echó el plato por tierra; **he**

~ed the plate into her face le dio con el plato en la cara; **to ~ a party*** colarse, entrar de rondón*.

3 *vi* (**a**) (*fall noisily*: *also* **to ~ down, to come ~ing down**) caer con estrépito; (*shatter*) romperse, hacerse añicos.

(**b**) (*have accident*) tener un accidente; (*2 cars etc*) colisionar, chocar; (*Aer*) estrellarse, caer a tierra; **to ~ into** chocar con, estrellarse contra.

(**c**) (*fail*) fracasar, hundirse; derrumbarse; (*Comm*) quebrar; **when the stock market ~ed** cuando la bolsa se derrumbó.

(**d**) (‡) dormir, pasar la noche.

4 *adv*: **he went ~ into a tree** dio de lleno consigo contra un árbol.

5 *interj* ¡zas!, ¡pum!

6 *adj*: **~ course** curso *m* acelerado, curso *m* concentrado; **~ programme** programa *m* de urgencia.

◆crash out‡ 1 *vt*: **to be ~ed out** estar hecho polvo. **2** *vi* caer redondo, dormirse, apalancar‡.

crash-barrier ['kræʃ,bærɪəʳ] *n* (*Brit*) valla *f* protectora.

crash-helmet ['kræʃ,helmɪt] *n* casco *m* protector.

crashing ['kræʃɪŋ] *adj*: **a ~ bore** una paliza*, un muermo*.

crash-land ['kræʃlænd] **1** *vt aircraft* poner forzosamente en tierra. **2** *vi* aterrizar forzosamente.

crash-landing ['kræʃ,lændɪŋ] *n* aterrizaje *m* forzado.

crash-pad‡ ['kræʃ,pæd] *n* guarida *f*, lugar *m* donde dormir.

crass [kræs] *adj* craso, estúpido.

crassly ['kræslɪ] *adv* estúpidamente, tontamente.

crassness ['kræsnɪs] *n* estupidez *f*.

crate [kreɪt] **1** *n* (**a**) cajón *m* de embalaje, jaula *f*. (**b**) (*: *car etc*) armatoste *m*, cacharro* *m*. **2** *vt* (*also* **to ~ up**) embalar (en cajones).

crater ['kreɪtəʳ] *n* cráter *m*.

cravat(e) [krə'væt] *n* corbata *f* de fantasía, fular *m*, foulard *m*.

crave [kreɪv] **1** *vt* suplicar, implorar; *attention* reclamar. **2** *vi*: **to ~ for** ansiar, anhelar.

craven ['kreɪvən] *adj* (*liter*) cobarde.

cravenly ['kreɪvənlɪ] *adv* de manera cobarde, con cobardía.

cravenness ['kreɪvənnɪs] *n* (*liter*) cobardía *f*.

craving ['kreɪvɪŋ] *n* deseo *m* vehemente, ansia *f*, sed *f* (*for* de); (*during pregnancy*) antojo *m*; **to get a ~ for sth** encapricharse por algo.

crawfish ['krɔːfɪʃ] *n* (*US*: *freshwater*) cangrejo *m* de río; (*saltwater*) cigala *f*.

crawl [krɔːl] **1** *n* (*action*) arrastramiento *m*; (*journey*) camino *m* a gatas; (*Swimming*) crol *m*; **the traffic went at a ~** la circulación avanzaba a paso de tortuga; **the ~ to the coast** el viaje a una lentitud desesperante hacia la costa.

2 *vi* (**a**) (*drag o.s.*) arrastrarse; avanzar a rastras; (*child*) andar a gatas, gatear; **to ~ in** entrar a gatas; **the fly ~ed up the window** la mosca subió despacito el cristal; **the cars were ~ing along** los coches avanzaban a paso de tortuga.

(**b**) **to ~ to sb** humillarse ante uno, ir humildemente a pedir perdón a uno.

(**c**) **to ~ with, to be ~ing with** estar cuajado de, estar plagado de, hervir en (*or* de).

crawler ['krɔːləʳ] *n* (*Mech*) tractor *m* de oruga; **~ lane** (*Brit Aut*) carril *m* (de autopista) para vehículos lentos.

crayfish ['kreɪfɪʃ] *n* (*freshwater*) cangrejo *m* de río; (*saltwater*) cigala *f*.

crayon ['kreɪən] **1** *n* (*Art*) pastel *m*, lápiz *m* de tiza; (*child's*) lápiz *m* de color. **2** *vt* dibujar al pastel (*etc*).

craze [kreɪz] *n* manía *f* (*for* por); (*fashion*) moda *f* (*for* de); **to be the ~** estar en boga.

crazed [kreɪzd] *adj* loco (*with* de), demente.

crazily ['kreɪzɪlɪ] *adv* locamente; *lean etc* de modo peligroso.

craziness ['kreɪzɪnɪs] *n* locura *f*, chifladura *f*.

crazy ['kreɪzɪ] *adj* (**a**) *person* loco, chiflado, tarado (*LAm*), zafado (*LAm*); *idea* disparatado, estrafalario; **to be ~ about** *person* estar chiflado por, *thing* andar loco por; **to be ~ with worry** estar loco de inquietud; **to drive sb ~** volver loco a uno; **it's enough to drive you ~** es para volverse loco; **to go ~** volverse loco; **everyone shouted like ~** todos gritaron como locos; **~ house** (*US**) casa *f* de locos*.

(**b**) *building* destartalado; **to lean at a ~ angle** inclinarse de modo peligroso.

(**c**) **~ paving** enlosado *m* (de diseño) irregular.

(**d**) (*US‡*) tope*.

crazy-bone ['kreɪzɪ,bəʊn] *n* (*US*) hueso *m* de la alegría.

CRC *n* (*US*) *abbr of* **Civil Rights Commission**.

creak [kriːk] **1** *n* (*of wood, shoe etc*) crujido *m*; (*of hinge etc*) chirrido *m*, rechinamiento *m*. **2** *vi* crujir; chirriar, rechinar.

creaky ['kriːkɪ] *adj* rechinador; (*fig*) poco sólido, inestable, nada firme.

cream [kriːm] **1** *n* (**a**) (*on milk*) nata *f*; **single ~** (*Brit*) crema *f* de leche; **double ~** (*Brit*) nata *f*.

(**b**) (*gen*) crema *f*; **~ of tartar** crémor *m* tártaro; **~ of wheat** (*US*) sémola *f*.

(**c**) (*fig*) flor *f* y nata, crema *f*, lo mejor y más selecto; **the ~ of society** la crema de la sociedad; **the ~ of the joke was that** lo más gracioso fue que.

2 *adj* color de crema.

3 *attr*: **~ cake** pastel *m* de nata; **~ cheese** requesón *m*, queso *m* de nata; **~ cracker** galleta *f* de soda, galleta *f* para queso; **~ puff** petisú *m*; **~ of tomato soup** crema *f* de sopa de tomate.

4 *vt* (**a**) *milk* desnatar; *butter* batir. (**b**) (*US**) arrollar, aplastar.

◆cream off *vt* (*fig*) quitar lo mejor de, tomarse lo mejor de.

creaminess ['kriːmɪnɪs] *n* cremosidad *f*.

creamy ['kriːmɪ] *adj* cremoso.

crease [kriːs] **1** *n* (*fold*) pliegue *m*; (*in trousers*) raya *f*; (*wrinkle*) arruga *f*. **2** *vt paper* plegar, doblar; *clothes* arrugar; **to ~ one's trousers** (*press ~ in*) hacer la raya a los pantalones. **3** *vi* plegarse, doblarse; arrugarse.

◆crease up* *vt* hacer morirse de risa.

creaseless ['kriːslɪs] *adj*, **crease-resisting** ['kriːsrɪ,zɪstɪŋ] *adj* inarrugable.

create [kriː'eɪt] **1** *vt* crear (*also Comput*); (*produce*) producir, motivar; *character* inventar; *rôle* encarnar; (*appoint*) nombrar. **2** *vi* (*Brit**) protestar, armar un lío*.

creation [kriː'eɪʃən] *n* creación *f*; (*appointment*) nombramiento *m*; (*dress etc*) modelo *m*.

creationism [kriː'eɪʃənɪzəm] *n* creacionismo *m*.

creationist [kriː'eɪʃənɪst] *n* creacionista *mf*.

creative [kriː'eɪtɪv] *adj* creativo; *work* original; **~ accounting** contabilidad *f* creativa; **~ writing** creación *f* literaria.

creatively [kriː'eɪtɪvlɪ] *adv* de manera original, con originalidad.

creativity [,kriːeɪ'tɪvɪtɪ] *n* creatividad *f*.

creator [krɪ'eɪtəʳ] *n* creador *m*, -ora *f*; **the C~** el Criador.

creature ['kriːtʃəʳ] *n* (**a**) (*animal*) criatura *f*; animal *m*, bicho *m*; **poor ~!** ¡pobre animal!, (*to human*) ¡pobrecito!; **~ comforts** bienestar *m* material.

(**b**) (*person*) **to be sb's ~** ser la criatura de uno; **wretched ~!** ¡desgraciado!; **he's a poor ~** es un infeliz; **pay no attention to that ~** no hagas caso de esa individua.

crèche [kreɪʃ] *n* (*Brit*) guardería *f* infantil.

cred* [kred] *n* = **credibility**.

credence ['kriːdəns] *n*: **to give ~ to** prestar fe a.

credentials [krɪ'denʃəlz] *npl* documentos *mpl* (de identidad *etc*); referencias *fpl*; (*of diplomat*) cartas *fpl* credenciales; **what are his ~ for the post?** ¿qué méritos alega para el puesto?

credibility [,kredə'bɪlətɪ] *n* credibilidad *f*; **~ gap** margen *m* de credibilidad; **~ rating** índice *m* de credibilidad.

credible ['kredɪbl] *adj* creíble, fidedigno, verosímil.

credibly ['kredɪblɪ] *adv* creíblemente, verosímilmente.

credit ['kredɪt] **1** *n* (**a**) (*belief*) crédito *m*; **to give ~ to** creer.

(**b**) (*reputation*) buena fama *f*, reputación *f*.

(**c**) (*honour*) honor *m*, mérito *m*; **to his ~ he confessed** dicho sea a su honor confesó la verdad; **he is a great ~ to the family** le hace mucho honor a la familia; **to come out of sth with ~** salir airoso de algo; **the only people to emerge with any ~** los únicos que salen con honor; **to pass a test with ~** salir bien de una prueba; **it does you ~** puedes enorgullecerte de ello; **he did himself great ~** se honró mucho; **to take the ~** atribuirse el mérito (*for* de); **to give ~ to** (*US*: *in film, book*) reconocer.

(**d**) (*Comm*) crédito *m*; (*side of account*) haber *m*; **'~ terms available'** 'ventas a plazos'; **to be in ~** (*account, person*) tener saldo acreedor, estar en números negros; **on ~** a crédito, al fiado; **on the ~ side** en el haber; (*fig*) en el aspecto positivo; **you have £10 to your ~** tiene 10 libras en el haber; **to give sb ~** abrir crédito a uno; **I gave you ~ for more sense** te creía con (*or* de) más inteligencia.

(**e**) **~s** (*Cine, TV*) títulos *mpl* de crédito, rótulos *mpl* de crédito.

(**f**) (*US*: *Scol etc*) unidad *f* de crédito.

2 *attr* crediticio; **~ account** cuenta *f* a crédito, credicuenta *f*; **~ agency** agencia *f* de créditos; **~ arrangements** facilidades *fpl* de pago; **~ balance** saldo *m* positivo, saldo *m* acreedor; ~ **charges** interés *m* de crédito; ~ **control** control *m* de créditos; ~ **entry** abono *m*, asiento *m* al haber; ~ **facilities** facilidades *fpl* crediticias; ~ **freeze** congelación *f* de crédito; ~ **limit** límite *m* de crédito; ~ **line** línea *f* de crédito; ~ **note** (*Brit*) nota *f* de crédito; ~ **rating** valoración *f* crediticia; ~ **regulations** (*US*), ~ **restrictions**, ~ **squeeze** restricciones *fpl* de crédito; ~ **sales** ventas *fpl* a crédito; ~ **side** haber *m* (*also fig*); ~ **transfer** transferencia *f* bancaria.

3 *vt* (**a**) (*believe*) creer, prestar fe a; **would you ~ it?** (*iro*) ¿te parece posible?; **you wouldn't ~ it** parece mentira.

(**b**) (*Comm*) **to ~ sb with £5, to ~ £5 to sb** abonar 5 libras en cuenta a uno; **please ~ this to my account** abone (*or* cargue) esto en mi cuenta.

(**c**) (*attribute*) **I ~ed you with more sense** le creía con (*or* de) más inteligencia; **we must ~ him with charm at least** por lo menos hay que reconocer que tiene gran atractivo personal; **to be ~ed with having done sth** pasar por haber hecho algo; **he ~ed them with the victory** les atribuyó (el mérito de) la victoria; **they had less drawing power than they were ~ed with** no tenían tanta fuerza atractiva como se les suponía.

creditable ['kredɪtəbl] *adj* loable, estimable.
creditably ['kredɪtəblɪ] *adv* de modo loable.
credit-card ['kredɪtkɑːd] *n* tarjeta *f* de crédito.
creditor ['kredɪtə^r] *n* acreedor *m*, -ora *f*.
credit-worthiness ['kredɪt,wɜːðɪnɪs] *n* solvencia *f*.
credit-worthy ['kredɪt,wɜːðɪ] *adj* solvente.
credo ['kreɪdəʊ] *n* credo *m*.
credulity [krɪ'djuːlɪtɪ] *n* credulidad *f*.
credulous ['kredjʊləs] *adj* crédulo.
creed [kriːd] *n* credo *m*; **the C~** el Credo.
creek [kriːk] *n* (*esp Brit: inlet*) cala *f*, ensenada *f*; (*US: stream*) riachuelo *m*; **to be up the ~ (without a paddle)**‡ estar en un apuro, estar jodido‡.
creel [kriːl] *n* nasa *f*, cesta *f* (de pescador).
creep [kriːp] **1** *n* (**a**) (*) (*toady*) cobista* *mf*, pelotillero* *m*, -a *f*; (*rotter*) canalla *m*.

(**b**) **it gives me the ~s** me horripila, me da escalofríos.

2 (*irr: pret and ptp* **crept**) *vi* (**a**) (*animal etc*) arrastrarse, reptar, deslizarse, moverse muy despacio por el suelo.

(**b**) (*person etc*) arrastrarse, andar a gatas; (*stealthily*) ir cautelosamente; (*slowly*) ir despacito, ir a paso de tortuga; **to ~ about on tiptoe** andar a (*or* de) puntillas; **to ~ along** (*traffic*) avanzar a paso de tortuga; **to ~ in** entrar sin ser sentido; **to ~ out** salir silenciosamente; **to ~ up on sb** acercarse sigilosamente a uno.

(**c**) (*fig*) **it's enough to make your flesh ~** es para poner carne de gallina; **doubts began to ~ in** las dudas empezaron a insinuarse; **an error crept in** se deslizó un error; **old age is ~ing on** se está acercando la vejez; **fear crept over him** le invadió el terror; **to ~ to s.o.*** hacer la pelotilla a uno*, dar jabón a uno*.

creeper ['kriːpə^r] *n* (*Bot*) enredadera *f*; **~s** (*US: shoes*) zapatillas *fpl* de goma; (*US: babywear*) pelele *m*.
creeping ['kriːpɪŋ] *adj* (*Med etc*) progresivo; *barrage* móvil; ~ **inflation** inflación *f* progresiva.
creepy ['kriːpɪ] *adj* horripilante, escalofriante.
creepy-crawly* ['kriːpɪ'krɔːlɪ] *n* (*Brit*) bicho *m*.
cremate [krɪ'meɪt] *vt* incinerar.
cremation [krɪ'meɪʃən] *n* incineración *f* (de cadáveres), cremación *f*.
crematorium [,kremə'tɔːrɪəm] *n*, *pl* **crematoria** [,kremə'tɔːrɪə], (*US*) **crematory** ['kremətərɪ] *n* horno *m* crematorio.
crenellated ['krenɪleɪtɪd] *adj* almenado.
crenellations [,krenɪ'leɪʃənz] *npl* almenas *fpl*.
Creole ['kriːəʊl] **1** *adj* criollo. **2** *n* criollo *m*, -a *f*.
creosote ['krɪəsəʊt] **1** *n* creosota *f*, chapote *m* (*Mex*). **2** *vt* pintar con creosota; dar un baño de creosota a.
crepe, crêpe [kreɪp] *n* crespón *m*; (*rubber*) crep *m*, crepé *m*; ~ **bandage** envoltura *f* de crepé (*or* crep); ~ **paper** papel *m* crep; **~-soled shoes** zapatos *mpl* de suela de crepé.
crept [krept] *pret and ptp of* **creep**.
crescendo [krɪ'ʃendəʊ] *n* crescendo *m*.
crescent ['kresnt] **1** *adj* creciente; ~ **moon** media luna *f*. **2** *n* (*shape*) media luna *f*; (*street*) calle *f* en forma de arco, medialuna *f*.
cress [kres] *n* mastuerzo *m*, berro *m*.
crest [krest] **1** *n* (*of bird, wave*) cresta *f*; (*of turkey*) moco *m*; (*on helmet*) cimera *f* (*also Her*); (*of hill*) cima *f*, cumbre *f*, cresta *f*; (*Her*) blasón *m*.

2 *vi* (*US*) llegar al máximo, alcanzar su punto más alto; **the flood ~ed at 2 meters** las aguas llegaron a 2 metros sobre su nivel normal.

crested ['krestɪd] *adj bird etc* crestado, con cresta; *notepaper* con escudo.
crestfallen ['krest,fɔːlən] *adj* alicaído, cabizbajo.
cretaceous [krɪ'teɪʃəs] *adj* cretáceo.
Cretan ['kriːtən] **1** *adj* cretense. **2** *n* cretense *mf*.
Crete [kriːt] *n* Creta *f*.
cretin ['kretɪn] *n* cretino *m*, -a *f*.
cretinous ['kretɪnəs] *adj* cretino; (*fig*) imbécil.
cretonne [kre'tɒn] *n* cretona *f*.
crevasse [krɪ'væs] *n* grieta *f* de glaciar.
crevice ['krevɪs] *n* grieta *f*, hendedura *f*.
crew [kruː] **1** *n* (*Naut, Aer*) tripulación *f*; (*Mil, number of ~, ~ members*) dotación *f*; personal *m*, equipo *m*; (*gang*) banda *f*, pandilla *f*; **three ~ were drowned** perecieron ahogados tres tripulantes; **they looked a sorry ~** daba lástima verlos. **2** *vt* tripular.
crew-cut ['kruːkʌt] *n* corte *m* de pelo al rape.
crewman ['kruːmən] *n*, *pl* **crewmen** ['kruːmen] (*Naut*) tripulante *m*; (*TV etc*) miembro *m* del equipo (de cámara *etc*).
crew-neck ['kruːnek] *n* cuello *m* de barco; ~ **sweater** suéter *m* con cuello de barco.
crib [krɪb] **1** *n* (**a**) (*Brit: for infant*) pesebre *m*; (*US: for toddler*) cuna *f*; ~ **death** (*US*) muerte *f* en la cuna; **portable ~** (*US*) cuna *f* portátil. (**b**) (*) (*translation*) traducción *f*; (*thing copied*) plagio *m*; (*in exam*) chuleta* *f*. **2** *vt* (*Brit**) plagiar, tomar (*from* de). **3** *vi* (*) usar una chuleta.
cribbage ['krɪbɪdʒ] *n juego de cartas que se juega utilizando un tablero de puntuación.*
crick [krɪk] **1** *n*: ~ **in the neck** tortícolis *f*. **2** *vt*: **to ~ one's neck** darse una tortícolis.
cricket[1] ['krɪkɪt] *n* (*Zool*) grillo *m*.
cricket[2] ['krɪkɪt] **1** *n* críquet *m*, cricket *m*; **that's not ~** eso no es jugar limpio. **2** *attr*: ~ **ball** pelota *f* de críquet; ~ **bat** bate *m* de críquet; ~ **match** partido *m* de críquet; ~ **pavilion** caseta *f* de críquet; ~ **pitch** terreno *m* de juego de críquet.
cricketer ['krɪkɪtə^r] *n* criquetero *m*, -a *f*, jugador *m*, -ora *f* de críquet.
crier ['kraɪə^r] *n*: **town ~** pregonero *m* público.
crikey‡ ['kraɪkɪ] *interj* (*Brit*) ¡caramba!
crime [kraɪm] *n* crimen *m*, delito *m*; **it's the ~ capital of Slobodia** es la capital del crimen de Eslobodia; ~ **prevention** prevención *f* del crimen; **C~ Squad** ≃ Brigada *f* de Investigación Criminal; ~ **statistics** estadísticas *fpl* del crimen; ~ **wave** ola *f* delictiva; ~ **writer** autor *m*, -ora *f* de novelas policíacas.
Crimea [kraɪ'mɪə] *n* Crimea *f*.
Crimean War [kraɪ'mɪən'wɔː^r] *n* Guerra *f* de Crimea.
criminal ['krɪmɪnl] **1** *adj* criminal; *act, intent* delictivo; *code, law* penal; **it would be ~ to let her go out** sería un crimen dejarla salir; **C~ Investigation Department** (*Brit*) ≃ Brigada *f* de Investigación Criminal; ~ **law** derecho *m* penal; ~ **lawyer** abogado *m*, -a *f* criminalista; ~ **negligence** imprudencia *f* criminal; ~ **record** antecedentes *mpl* delictivos.

2 *n* criminal *mf*, delincuente *mf*.

criminality [,krɪmɪ'nælɪtɪ] *n* criminalidad *f*.
criminalization [,krɪmɪnəlaɪ'zeɪʃən] *n* criminalización *f*.
criminalize ['krɪmɪnəlaɪz] *vt* criminalizar.
criminally ['krɪmɪnəlɪ] *adv* de manera criminal; ~ **insane** incapacitado legal; **the pay was ~ poor** el sueldo era tan pobre que era un crimen.
criminologist [,krɪmɪ'nɒlədʒɪst] *n* criminalista *mf*.
criminology [,krɪmɪ'nɒlədʒɪ] *n* criminología *f*.
crimp [krɪmp] *vt* rizar, encrespar.
crimped [krɪmpt] *adj* rizado, con rizos, encrespado.
crimson ['krɪmzn] **1** *adj* carmesí. **2** *n* carmesí *m*.
cringe [krɪndʒ] *vi* agacharse, encogerse; (*fig*) reptar; **to ~ with fear** encogerse de miedo.
cringing ['krɪndʒɪŋ] *adj* servil, rastrero.
crinkle ['krɪŋkl] **1** *n* arruga *f*. **2** *vt* arrugar. **3** *vi* arrugarse.
crinkly ['krɪŋklɪ] **1** *adj* arrugado; *hair* rizado, crespo. **2** *n* (*) viejo *m*, -a *f*.
crinoline ['krɪnəliːn] *n* miriñaque *m*, crinolina *f*.
cripes‡ [kraɪps] *interj* ¡coño!‡.
cripple ['krɪpl] **1** *n* lisiado *m*, -a *f*, mutilado *m*, -a *f*, cojo *m*, -a *f*; (*from birth*) minusválido *m*, -a *f*. **2** *vt* lisiar, tullir, mutilar; *ship* inutilizar; (*fig*) paralizar, estropear.

crippled ['krɪpld] **1** *adj person* tullido, lisiado; (*from birth*) minusválido; (*fig*) *plane, vehicle* averiado; (*after bomb etc*) *factory* paralizado; ~ **with rheumatism** paralizado por reumatismo. **2** *npl*: **the** ~ los tullidos; los minusválidos.

crippling ['krɪplɪŋ] *adj disease* que conduce a la parálisis; *blow, defect* muy grave, muy severo; *taxes, debts* abrumador, agobiante, demoledor.

crisis ['kraɪsɪs] *n, pl* **crises** ['kraɪsi:z] crisis *f*; ~ **management** manejo *m* de crisis.

crisis centre, (*US*) **crisis center** ['kraɪsɪs,sentəʳ] *n* (*for disaster*) ≃ centro *m* coordinador de rescate; (*for personal help*) ≃ teléfono *m* de la esperanza; (*for battered women*) centro *m* de ayuda a las mujeres maltratadas.

crisp [krɪsp] **1** *adj* duro pero quebradizo; (*after cooking*) crujiente, tostado; *hair* crespo; *air* vivificante, vigorizante; *manner, tone* resuelto, seco; *style* conciso, nervioso.

2 ~**s** *npl* (*Brit*) patatas *fpl* (*LAm*: papas *fpl*) fritas (a la inglesa).

crispbread ['krɪspbred] *n* pan *m* tostado (escandinavo).

crisply ['krɪsplɪ] *adv say etc* secamente.

crispness ['krɪspnɪs] *n* (*V adj*) naturaleza *f* dura pero quebradiza; lo crujiente; lo vivificante, lo vigorizante; resolución *f*, sequedad *f*; concisión *f*, nerviosidad *f*.

crispy ['krɪspɪ] *adj food* crujiente.

crisscross ['krɪskrɒs] **1** *adj* entrecruzado. **2** *n*: **a** ~ **of paths** veredas *fpl* entrecruzadas. **3** *vi* entrecruzarse.

criss-crossed ['krɪskrɒst] *adj* entrelazado; ~ **by** surcado de.

crit* [krɪt] *n* crítica *f*.

criterion [kraɪ'tɪərɪən] *n, pl* **criteria** [kraɪ'tɪərɪə] criterio *m*.

critic ['krɪtɪk] *n* crítico *mf* (*also* -a *f*).

critical ['krɪtɪkəl] *adj* (**a**) (*grave*) crítico, grave; *illness, injury* muy grave, de gravedad; ~ **juncture,** ~ **moment** coyuntura *f* crítica; ~ **mass** masa *f* crítica; ~ **path analysis** análisis *m* del camino crítico; **to go** ~ llegar a la coyuntura crítica.

(**b**) (*faultfinding*) crítico; severo; (*hyper*~) criticón; **to be** ~ **of** criticar.

(**c**) (*Art, Liter etc*) crítico; ~ **edition** edición *f* critica; ~ **essays** ensayos *mpl* de crítica.

critically ['krɪtɪkəlɪ] *adv* críticamente; **to be** ~ **ill** estar gravemente enfermo.

criticism ['krɪtɪsɪzəm] *n* crítica *f*.

criticize ['krɪtɪsaɪz] *vt* criticar; censurar.

critique [krɪ'ti:k] **1** *n* crítica *f*. **2** *vt*: **to** ~ **a paper** evaluar una ponencia.

croak [krəʊk] **1** *n* (*of raven*) graznido *m*; (*of frog*) canto *m*; (*of person*) gruñido *m*. **2** *vi* (**a**) (*raven*) graznar; (*frog*) croar; (*person*) gruñir, refunfuñar. (**b**) (‡) espicharla‡.

Croat ['krəʊæt] *n* croata *mf*.

Croatia [krəʊ'eɪʃɪə] *n* Croacia *f*.

Croatian [krəʊ'eɪʃɪən] **1** *adj* croata. **2** *n* croata *mf*.

crochet ['krəʊʃeɪ] **1** *n* croché *m*, labor *f* de ganchillo. **2** *vt* hacer en croché, hacer de ganchillo. **3** *vi* hacer croché, hacer labor de ganchillo.

crochet-hook ['krəʊʃɪhʊk] *n* ganchillo *m*.

crock [krɒk] **1** *n* vasija *f* de barro; **old** ~ (*person*) carcamal *m*; (*esp Brit*: *car etc*) cacharro *m*; **old** ~**s' race** rallye *m* de coches clásicos. **2** *vt* lisiar, incapacitar.

crockery ['krɒkərɪ] *n* loza *f*, vajilla *f*, los platos.

crocodile ['krɒkədaɪl] *n* cocodrilo *m*; (*Brit Scol*) doble fila *f*; **to walk in a** ~ andar en doble fila; ~ **tears** lágrimas *fpl* de cocodrilo.

crocus ['krəʊkəs] *n* azafrán *m*.

Croesus ['kri:səs] *nm* Creso.

croft [krɒft] *n* (*Scot*) granja *f* pequeña, parcela *f*.

crofter ['krɒftəʳ] *n* (*Scot*) arrendatario *m* de una granja pequeña.

croissant [krwʌsɑ̃:ŋ] *n* croissant *m*, cruasán *m*, medialuna *f*.

crone [krəʊn] *n* vieja *f*, arpía *f*, bruja *f*.

crony ['krəʊnɪ] *n* compinche *mf*, amigote *m*.

cronyism ['krəʊnɪɪzəm] *n* amiguismo *m*.

crook [krʊk] **1** *n* (**a**) (*staff*) cayado *m*; (*Eccl*) báculo *m*.

(**b**) (*bend*) curva *f*; ~ **of the arm** pliegue *m* del codo.

(**c**) (*: *person*) criminal *m*, estafador *m*, ladrón *m*, maleante *mf*; **you** ~! (*hum*) ¡animal!

2 *vt* encorvar.

3 *vi* encorvarse.

crooked ['krʊkɪd] *adj* (**a**) curvo, encorvado, torcido; *path* tortuoso; *smile* torcido. (**b**) (*) *deal, means* poco limpio; *person* criminal, nada honrado.

crookedly ['krʊkɪdlɪ] *adv smile* de manera torcida.

crookedness ['krʊkɪdnɪs] *n* (*lit*) sinuosidad *f*; (*fig*) criminalidad *f*.

croon [kru:n] *vt* canturrear, cantar en voz baja.

crooner ['kru:nəʳ] *n* vocalista *mf* (sentimental), canzonetista *mf*.

crooning ['kru:nɪŋ] *n* canturreo *m*, tarareo *m*.

crop [krɒp] **1** *n* (**a**) (*Agr*) (*species grown*) cultivo *m*; (*produce*) cosecha *f*; ~ **rotation** rotación *f* de cultivos.

(**b**) (*Orn*) buche *m*.

(**c**) (*whip*) látigo *m* (mocho), fusta *f*.

(**d**) (*hair-style*) corte *m* a lo garçon.

2 *vt* (*cut*) cortar; (*trim*) recortar; *animal's ears* desorejar, *tail* cortar; (*graze*) pacer.

3 *vi*: **a tree which** ~**s well** un árbol que rinde bien.

◆**crop out** *vi* (*Geol*) aflorar.

◆**crop up** *vi* (**a**) (*Geol*) aflorar.

(**b**) (*fig*) surgir, producirse inesperadamente; **sth must have** ~**ped up** habrán tenido alguna dificultad; **now another problem has** ~**ped up** ahora se ha planteado otro problema.

crop-dusting ['krɒp,dʌstɪŋ] *n*, **crop-spraying** ['krɒp,spreɪɪŋ] *n* fumigación *f* aérea, aerofumigación *f* (de las cosechas).

cropper* ['krɒpəʳ] *n*: **to come a** ~ coger una liebre*; (*fig*) fracasar; tirarse una plancha*.

crop-sprayer ['krɒp,spreɪəʳ] *n* (*device*) sulfatadora *f*; (*plane*) avión *m* fumigador.

croquet ['krəʊkeɪ] *n* croquet *m*.

croquette [krəʊ'ket] *n* croqueta *f*.

crosier ['krəʊʒəʳ] *n* báculo *m* (pastoral).

cross [krɒs] **1** *adj* (**a**) (*crossed*) cruzado; (*diagonal etc*) transversal, oblicuo.

(**b**) (*fig*) malhumorado; **to be** ~ estar de mal humor; **to be** ~ **with sb** estar enfadado con uno, estar enojado con uno (*LAm*); **don't be** ~ **with me** no te vayas a enfadar (*or* enojar *LAm*) conmigo; **to get** ~ enfadarse, enojarse (*about* de, por, *with* con).

2 *n* (**a**) (*mark, emblem*: *also fig*) cruz *f*; **the C**~ la Cruz; **to make the sign of the C**~ hacer la señal de la Cruz (*over* sobre).

(**b**) (*Bio*) cruce *m*; (*hybrid*) cruce *m*, híbrido *m*; (*fig*) mezcla *f*; **it's a** ~ **between A and B** es una mezcla de A y B, tiene algo de A y algo de B.

(**c**) **to cut sth on the** ~ (*Sew etc*) cortar algo al sesgo.

3 *vt* (**a**) (*place crosswise*) cruzar; **to** ~ **one's arms** cruzarse de brazos; **to** ~ **sb's hand with silver** dar una moneda de plata a uno; **the lines are** ~**ed** (*Brit Telec*) hay un cruce en las líneas, la conferencia está atravesada.

(**b**) (*draw line across*) *cheque* cruzar, rayar; ~**ed cheque** (*Brit*) cheque *m* cruzado.

(**c**) (*go across*) cruzar, pasar, atravesar; *river* (*as obstacle*) salvar.

(**d**) (*meet and pass*) cruzarse.

(**e**) (*Bio*) cruzar.

(**f**) (*thwart*) contrariar, ir contra; **to be** ~**ed in love** sufrir un fracaso sentimental.

4 *vi* (**a**) cruzar, ir al otro lado.

(**b**) (*letters*) cruzarse.

5 *vr*: **to** ~ **o.s.** santiguarse.

◆**cross off** *vt* tachar.

◆**cross out** *vt* tachar; '~ **out what does not apply**' 'táchese lo que no proceda'.

◆**cross over** *vi* = **cross 4**.

crossbar ['krɒsbɑ:ʳ] *n* travesaño *m*; (*Sport*) larguero *m*, travesaño *m*.

crossbeam ['krɒsbi:m] *n* viga *f* transversal.

crossbencher ['krɒs'bentʃəʳ] *n* diputado *m*, -a *f* independiente.

crossbill ['krɒsbɪl] *n* piquituerto *m* común.

crossbones ['krɒsbəʊnz] *npl* tibias *fpl* cruzadas; *V* **skull**.

cross-border ['krɒs'bɔ:dəʳ] *attr* transfronterizo; ~ **security** seguridad *f* a través de la frontera; ~ **travel** viajes *mpl* a través de la frontera.

crossbow ['krɒsbəʊ] *n* ballesta *f*.

crossbred ['krɒsbred] *adj* cruzado, híbrido.

crossbreed ['krɒsbri:d] **1** *n* cruce *m*, híbrido *m*, -a *f*. **2** *vt* (*irr V* **breed**) cruzar.

cross-Channel ['krɒs,tʃænl] *adj*: ~ **services** servicios *mpl* a través del Canal (de la Mancha); ~ **steamer** barco *m* que hace la travesía del Canal (de la Mancha).

cross-check ['krɒstʃek] **1** *n* comprobación *f* hecha al revés, comprobación *f* adicional; verificación *f* mediante un cotejo con otras fuentes.

2 *vt* comprobar al revés; comprobar una vez más (*or* por otro sistema); verificar cotejando con otras fuentes.

cross-compiler ['krɒskəm'paɪləʳ] *n* compilador *m* cruzado.

cross-country ['krɒs'kʌntrɪ] *adj route, walk* a campo traviesa; ~ **race** cross *m*, campo *m* a través; ~ **running**

cross *m*; ~ **skiing** esquí *m* nórdico.
cross-cultural ['krɒs'kʌltʃərəl] *adj* transcultural.
cross-current ['krɒs'kʌrənt] *n* contracorriente *f*.
cross-disciplinary [ˌkrɒs'dɪsɪplɪnərɪ] *adj* multidisciplinario.
cross-examination ['krɒsɪgˌzæmɪ'neɪʃən] *n* (*Jur*) segunda pregunta *f*, repregunta *f*; (*fig*) interrogatorio *m* severo.
cross-examine ['krɒsɪg'zæmɪn] *vt* (*Jur*) repreguntar; (*fig*) interrogar severamente.
cross-eyed ['krɒsaɪd] *adj* bizco.
cross-fertilize ['krɒs'fɜːtɪlaɪz] *vt* fecundar por fertilización cruzada.
crossfire ['krɒsfaɪəʳ] *n* fuego *m* cruzado; **we were caught in the** ~ estábamos inmovilizados en el fuego cruzado; (*fig*) nos veíamos atacados por ambos lados.
cross-grained ['krɒsgreɪnd] *adj* de fibras cruzadas.
crossing ['krɒsɪŋ] *n* (**a**) (*intersection*) cruce *m*; (*Rail*) paso *m* a nivel; (*on road*) paso *m* para peatones; (*journey*) travesía *f*; ~ **guard** (*US*) *persona encargada de ayudar a los niños a cruzar la calle.* (**b**) (*Bio*) cruce *m*.
cross-legged ['krɒs'legd] *adj* con las piernas cruzadas.
crossly ['krɒslɪ] *adv* con mal humor.
crossover ['krɒsəʊvəʳ] *n* (*Aut etc*) paso *m*.
cross-party ['krɒs'pɑːtɪ] *adj*: ~ **support** apoyo *m* multilateral.
crosspatch ['krɒspætʃ] *n* cascarrabias *mf*, gruñón *m*, -ona *f*.
crosspiece ['krɒspiːs] *n* travesaño *m*.
cross-ply ['krɒsplaɪ] *adj* (*Aut*) a carcasa diagonal.
cross-pollination ['krɒsˌpɒlɪ'neɪʃən] *n* polinización *f* cruzada.
cross-purposes ['krɒs'pɜːpəsɪz] *npl*: **to be at** ~ no comprenderse uno a otro; **we're at** ~ aquí hay un malentendido, hay un error de interpretación.
cross-question ['krɒs'kwestʃən] *vt* (*Jur*) repreguntar; (*fig*) interrogar.
cross-questioning ['krɒs'kwestʃənɪŋ] *n* (*Jur*) repregunta *f*, segunda pregunta *f*; (*fig*) interrogación *f*.
cross-refer [ˌkrɒsrɪ'fɜːʳ] *vt* remitir (*to* a), reenviar (*to* a).
cross-reference ['krɒs'refərəns] **1** *n* reenvío *m*, referencia *f* cruzada, remisión *f* (*to* a). **2** *vt* poner referencia cruzada a; **to** ~ **A to Q** poner en A una nota que remite al usuario (*etc*) a Q.
crossroads ['krɒsrəʊdz] *n* (*Brit*) cruce *m*, encrucijada *f*; (*fig*) encrucijada *f*; **to be at a** ~ (*fig*) estar en una encrucijada.
cross-section ['krɒs'sekʃən] *n* corte *m* transversal, sección *f* transversal, perfil *m*; (*fig*) sección *f* representativa, selección *f* característica.
cross-stitch ['krɒsstɪtʃ] **1** *n* punto *m* de cruz. **2** *vt* coser en punto de cruz.
crosstalk ['krɒstɔːk] *n* (*Brit*) réplicas *fpl* agudas; ~ **act** (*Theat*) diálogo *m* ágil salpicado de humor.
cross-tie ['krɒsˌtaɪ] *n* (*US*) durmiente *m*, traviesa *f*.
cross-vote [ˌkrɒs'vəʊt] *vi* votar en contra del partido.
crosswalk ['krɒsˌwɔːk] *n* (*US*) paso *m* de peatones.
crosswind ['krɒswɪnd] *n* viento *m* de costado.
crosswise ['krɒswaɪz] *adv* al través; en cruz.
crossword ['krɒswɜːd] *n* (*also* ~ **puzzle**) crucigrama *m*.
crotch [krɒtʃ] *n* (*Anat*) horcajadura *f*; (*of dress*) entrepiernas *fpl*.
crotchet ['krɒtʃɪt] *n* (*Brit*) negra *f*, capricho *m*.
crotchety ['krɒtʃɪtɪ] *adj* áspero, arisco, antojadizo.
crouch [kraʊtʃ] *vi* agacharse, acurrucarse, ponerse en cuclillas; **men** ~**ing in trenches** hombres agazapados en trincheras.
croup¹ [kruːp] *n* (*Med*) crup *m*, garrotillo *m*.
croup² [kruːp] *n* (*of horse*) grupa *f*.
croupier ['kruːpɪeɪ] *n* crupier *m*, crupié *m*.
croûton ['kruːtɔ̃n] *n* cuscurro *m*.
crow [krəʊ] **1** *n* (**a**) (*Orn*) cuervo *m*, grajo *m*, corneja *f*; **as the** ~ **flies** en línea recta; **stone the** ~**s!**‡ ¡coño!‡. (**b**) (*cry*) canto *m*, cacareo *m*.
2 *vi* (*cock*) cantar, cacarear; (*child*) gorjearse; (*fig*) jactarse, exultar; pavonearse; **it's nothing to** ~ **about** no hay motivo para sentirse satisfecho.
◆**crow over** *vt*: **to** ~ **over sth** jactarse de algo, felicitarse por algo.
crowbar ['krəʊbɑːʳ] *n* palanca *f*.
crowd [kraʊd] **1** *n* multitud *f*; muchedumbre *f*, gentío *m*; agolpamiento *m*; (*esp disorderly*) tropel *m*; (*Sport etc*) público *m*, espectadores *mpl*; (*Theat*: *on stage*) comparsa *f*; (*) grupo *m*, peña *f*; **the** ~ (*common herd*) el vulgo; **a (whole)** ~ **of,** ~**s of** una multitud de; **there was quite a** ~ había bastante gente; **how big was the** ~**?** ¿cuántas personas había?; ~ **control** control *m* de muchedumbres; ~ **scene** escena *f* con muchas comparsas; **in a** ~ en tropel, todos juntos; **to follow the** ~ dejarse llevar por los demás; **to rise above the** ~ destacar(se).
2 *vt* (**a**) (*collect*) amontonar; apretar unos contra otros.
(**b**) (*US**: *jostle*) codear; **to** ~ **the streets** llenar las calles; **to** ~ **a place with** llenar un sitio de; **to** ~ **things in** ir metiendo cosas apretadamente; **to** ~ **on sail** hacer fuerza de vela; **he was** ~**ed off the pavement** había tanta gente que tuvo que bajar de la acera.
3 *vi* reunirse, congregarse (*into* en); **to** ~ **around, to** ~ **together** agolparse, apiñarse; **to** ~ **round sb** apiñarse (*or* agruparse) en torno de uno; **to** ~ **in** entrar en tropel; **to** ~ **into a car** entrar todos apretadamente en un coche; **memories** ~**ed in upon me** me inundaron muchísimos recuerdos.
◆**crowd out** *vt* excluir; dejar fuera.
crowded ['kraʊdɪd] *adj* lleno, atestado (*with* de); *meeting, event etc* muy concurrido; **it's very** ~ **here** aquí hay muchísima gente; **the place was** ~ **out** el local estaba de bote en bote; **the houses are** ~ **together** las casas están apretadas unas contra otras; **one** ~ **hour** una sola hora llena de actividad; **it's a very** ~ **profession** es una profesión en la que sobra gente.
crowd-puller ['kraʊdˌpʊləʳ] *n* (*show*) gran atracción *f*; función *f* (*etc*) muy taquillera; (*person*) orador *m*, -ora *f* muy popular.
crowfoot ['krəʊfʊt] *n* ranúnculo *m*.
crowing ['krəʊɪŋ] *n* (*of cock*) canto *m*, cacareo *m*; (*of child*) gorjeo *m*; (*fig*) cacareo *m*.
crown [kraʊn] **1** *n* corona *f*; (*of hat*) copa *f*; (*of hill*) cumbre *f*; (*of head*) coronilla *f*; **the** ~ **of the road** el centro de la calzada; **C**~ (*Brit Jur, witness, evidence*) Estado *m*; **the C**~ (*monarch*) la Corona.
2 *attr*: ~ **colony** (*Brit*) colonia *f*; ~ **court** tribunal *m* criminal regional; ~ **jewels** joyas *fpl* reales; ~ **lands** propiedad *f* de la corona; ~ **prince** príncipe *m* heredero; ~ **princess** princesa *f* heredera.
3 *vt* (**a**) coronar; (*fig*) completar, rematar; **to** ~ **it all** para completarlo todo, (*misfortune*) para colmo de desgracias; **to** ~ **sth with success** coronar algo con éxito.
(**b**) (*) golpear en la cabeza.
crowning ['kraʊnɪŋ] **1** *adj* supremo. **2** *n* coronación *f*.
crow's-foot ['krəʊzfʊt] *n* (*eye*) pata *f* de gallo.
crow's-nest ['krəʊznest] *n* cofa *f* de vigía de tope.
CRT *n abbr of* **cathode ray tube** tubo *m* de rayos catódicos, TRC *m*.
crucial ['kruːʃəl] *adj* decisivo, crítico, crucial; (‡) guay*, de vicio*.
crucially ['kruːʃəlɪ] *adv*: ~ **important** de importancia crucial.
crucible ['kruːsɪbl] *n* crisol *m* (*also fig*).
crucifix ['kruːsɪfɪks] *n* crucifijo *m*.
crucifixion [ˌkruːsɪ'fɪkʃən] *n* crucifixión *f*.
cruciform ['kruːsɪfɔːm] *adj* cruciforme.
crucify ['kruːsɪfaɪ] *vt* crucificar (*also fig*).
crud* [krʌd] *n* (*esp US*) porquería *f*.
cruddy* ['krʌdɪ] *adj* asqueroso.
crude [kruːd] **1** *adj oil etc* crudo, *steel etc* bruto; *object, workmanship* tosco; (*vulgar*) ordinario. **2** *n* crudo *m*.
crudely ['kruːdlɪ] *adv* toscamente; ordinariamente.
crudeness ['kruːdnɪs] *n*, **crudity** ['kruːdɪtɪ] *n* tosquedad *f*; ordinariez *f*.
cruel ['krʊəl] *adj* cruel.
cruelly ['krʊəlɪ] *adv* cruelmente.
cruelty ['krʊəltɪ] *n* crueldad *f*; **society for the prevention of** ~ **to animals** sociedad *f* protectora de los animales.
cruet ['kruːɪt] *n* (*one vessel*) vinagrera *f*, salvilla *f* (*SC*); (*set*) vinagreras *fpl*; vinajeras *fpl*; (*stand*) angarillas *fpl*.
cruise [kruːz] **1** *n* crucero *m*, viaje *m* por mar; ~ **control** control *m* de crucero; ~ **missile** misil *m* de crucero. **2** *vi* (**a**) cruzar, navegar. (**b**) (*fig*) ir, andar; (*Aut etc*) ir a velocidad de crucero, llanear.
◆**cruise around** *vi* (*US*) pasear en coche.
cruiser ['kruːzəʳ] *n* crucero *m*.
cruiser-weight ['kruːzəweɪt] *n* peso *m* semipesado.
cruising speed ['kruːzɪŋspiːd] *n* velocidad *f* de crucero.
cruller ['krʌləʳ] *n* (*US*) buñuelo *m*.
crumb [krʌm] *n* migaja *f*; (*not crust*) miga *f*; **a** ~ **of comfort** una migaja de consolación.
crumble ['krʌmbl] **1** *vt* desmenuzar, desmigajar. **2** *vi* (*material*) desmenuzarse, desmigajarse; (*building etc*) desmoronarse, derrumbarse.
crumbly ['krʌmblɪ] *adj* desmenuzable; (*US*) *pastry* sobado.
crummy‡ ['krʌmɪ] *adj* (*bad*) ínfimo, de mala muerte, miserable; (*unwell*) fatal.

crumpet ['krʌmpɪt] *n* (**a**) bollo *m* blando (para tostar). (**b**) (‡) (*girl*) jai‡ *f*; (*girls*) las jais‡ (*colectivamente*); (*sex*) vida *f* sexual, actividad *f* sexual; **a bit of ~** (*Brit*) una jai‡.
crumple ['krʌmpl] **1** *vt* deshacer; *paper* estrujar; (*wrinkle*) arrugar. **2** *vi* deshacerse; arrugarse; plegarse; (*fig, also* **to ~ up**) hundirse, derrumbarse; (*person*) desplomarse.
crunch [krʌntʃ] **1** *n* crujido *m*; (*fig*) crisis *f*, punto *m* decisivo; **when the ~ comes, when it comes to the ~** en el momento de la verdad. **2** *vt* (*with teeth*) mascar, ronzar; *ground etc* hacer crujir; *numbers* devorar. **3** *vi* crujir.
crunchy ['krʌntʃɪ] *adj* crujiente, que cruje.
crupper ['krʌpəʳ] *n* (*of horse*) anca *f*, grupa *f*; (*part of harness*) baticola *f*.
crusade [kru:'seɪd] **1** *n* cruzada *f*. **2** *vi* participar en una cruzada; **to ~ for** hacer campaña en pro de.
crusader [kru:'seɪdəʳ] *n* cruzado *m*.
crush [krʌʃ] **1** *n* (**a**) (*of people*) agolpamiento *m*; aglomeración *f*; (*of cars etc*) masa *f*; **there was an awful ~** hubo la mar de gente; **there's always a ~ in the tube** el metro va siempre atestado de gente; **I lost my handbag in the ~** perdí el bolso en la aglomeración; **two died in the ~** dos murieron aplastados.
(**b**) (*) amartelamiento *m*; **to have a ~ on sb** andar amartelado por una, perder la chaveta por uno*.
(**c**) **orange ~** (*Brit*) naranjada *f*.
2 *vt* (**a**) aplastar; *paper etc* estrujar; *stones* triturar, moler; *grapes etc* prensar, exprimir; **to ~ sth into a case** meter algo a la fuerza en una maleta.
(**b**) (*fig*) *country* aplastar; *enemy, opposition* aniquilar, destruir; *person in argument* confundir, aplastar.
◆**crush in** *vi* meterse apretadamente en; **can we all ~ in?** ¿cabemos todos?
crush-barrier ['krʌʃ,bærɪəʳ] *n* (*Brit*) barrera *f* de seguridad.
crushing ['krʌʃɪŋ] *adj blow, defeat, reply* aplastante; *grief etc* abrumador; *argument* decisivo; *burden* agobiador.
crush-resistant [,krʌʃrɪ'zɪstənt] *adj* inarrugable.
crust [krʌst] **1** *n* (*of bread, Geol*) corteza *f*; (*old bread*) mendrugo *m*; (*Med*) costra *f*; (*of wine*) depósito *m*, poso *m*. **2** *vt*: **~ed with** con una costra de; con un depósito de.
crustacean [krʌs'teɪʃɪən] *n* crustáceo *m*.
crusty ['krʌstɪ] *adj* (**a**) *bread* con corteza (apetitosa). (**b**) (*fig*) malhumorado, irritable.
crutch [krʌtʃ] *n* (**a**) muleta *f*. (**b**) (*Anat*) = **crotch**.
crux [krʌks] *n*: **the ~ of the matter** lo esencial del caso, el quid, el punto capital.
cry [kraɪ] **1** *n* (**a**) grito *m*; (*of peddler, town crier*) pregón *m*; **it's a far ~ from that** esto tiene poco que ver con aquello; **the hounds were in full ~** los perros seguían de cerca la presa; **the crowd was in full ~ after him** la multitud le perseguía con gritos.
(**b**) (*watchword*) lema *m*, slogan *m*.
(**c**) (*weep*) lloro *m*, llanto *m*; **to have a good ~** dejarse llorar, aliviarse llorando.
2 *vt* (*also* **to ~ out**) gritar; *wares* pregonar; *V* **eye** *etc.*
3 *vi* (**a**) (*call*) gritar; **to ~ for** clamar por; **to ~ for help** pedir socorro a voces.
(**b**) (*weep*) llorar (*for, with* de).
4 *vr*: **to ~ o.s. to sleep** dormirse llorando.
◆**cry down** *vt* despreciar, desacreditar.
◆**cry off** *vi* retirarse, rajarse.
◆**cry out** *vi* gritar; **it's ~ing out for reform** (*fig*) pide la reforma a gritos, necesita urgentemente reformarse; **for ~ing out loud!*** ¡por Dios!; **to ~ out against** protestar contra, poner el grito en el cielo por.
◆**cry over** *vt* lamentarse de (*or* por), llorar.
crybaby ['kraɪ,beɪbɪ] *n* llorón *m*, -ona *f*.
crying ['kraɪɪŋ] **1** *adj* atroz, enorme; **it's a ~ shame*** es una verdadera vergüenza. **2** *n* lloro *m*, llanto *m*.
cryosurgery [,kraɪəʊ'sɜːdʒərɪ] *n* criocirugía *f*.
crypt [krɪpt] *n* cripta *f*.
cryptic ['krɪptɪk] *adj* misterioso, secreto, enigmático.
cryptically ['krɪptɪkəlɪ] *adv* misteriosamente.
crypto- ['krɪptəʊ] *pref* cripto-.
crypto-communist ['krɪptəʊ'kɒmjʊnɪst] *n* criptocomunista *mf*.
cryptogram ['krɪptəʊgræm] *n* criptograma *m*.
cryptographer [krɪp'tɒgrəfəʳ] *n* criptógrafo *m*, -a *f*.
cryptographic(al) [,krɪptəʊ'græfɪk(əl)] *adj* criptográfico.
cryptography [krɪp'tɒgrəfɪ] *n* criptografía *f*.
crystal ['krɪstl] **1** *n* cristal *m*. **2** *adj* cristalino; **~ ball** bola *f* de cristal; **~ set** (*Rad*) receptor *m* de cristal.
crystal-clear ['krɪstl'klɪəʳ] *adj* transparente como el cristal; (*fig*) evidente, más claro que el agua.
crystal-gazing ['krɪstl,geɪzɪŋ] *n* (*fig*) adivinación *f* del futuro en la bola de cristal.
crystalline ['krɪstəlaɪn] *adj* cristalino.
crystallize ['krɪstəlaɪz] **1** *vt* cristalizar. **2** *vi* cristalizarse; (*fig*) cuajarse, resolverse.
crystallized ['krɪstəlaɪzd] *adj fruit* escarchado.
crystallographer [,krɪstə'lɒgrəfəʳ] *n* cristalógrafo *m*, -a *f*.
crystallography [,krɪstə'lɒgrəfɪ] *n* cristalografía *f*.
CSA *n* (*US*) *abbr of* **Confederate States of America**.
CSC *n abbr of* **Civil Service Commission**.
CSE *n* (*Brit Scol*) *abbr of* **Certificate of Secondary Education** ≈ BUP *m*.
CSEU *n* (*Brit*) *abbr of* **Confederation of Shipbuilding and Engineering Unions** *sindicato de trabajadores de construcción naval*.
CS gas [,si:,es'gæs] *n* (*Brit*) gas *m* lacrimógeno.
CST *n* (*US*) *abbr of* **Central Standard Time** *hora central estándar*.
CSU *n* (*Brit*) *abbr of* **Civil Service Union** *sindicato de funcionarios*.
CT (**a**) (*Fin*) *abbr of* **cable transfer**. (**b**) (*US Post*) *abbr of* **Connecticut**.
Ct. (*US*) *abbr of* **Connecticut**.
ct *abbr of* **carat** quilate *m*.
CTC *n abbr of* **City Technology College**.
CTT *n abbr of* **Capital Transfer Tax**.
cu. *abbr of* **cubic** cúbico.
cub [kʌb] *n* cachorro *m*; (*boy; also* **~ scout**) niño *m* explorador; **~ reporter** periodista *m* novato.
Cuba ['kju:bə] *n* Cuba *f*.
Cuban ['kju:bən] **1** *adj* cubano. **2** *n* cubano *m*, -a *f*.
cubbyhole ['kʌbɪhəʊl] *n* chiribitil *m*.
cube [kju:b] **1** *n* cubo *m*; (*of sugar*) terrón *m*; **~ root** (*Math*) raíz *f* cúbica. **2** *vt* cubicar.
cubic ['kju:bɪk] *adj* cúbico; **~ measure** medida *f* cúbica; **~ metre** metro *m* cúbico.
cubicle ['kju:bɪkəl] *n* cubículo *m*; (*at swimming pool etc*) caseta *f*.
cubism ['kju:bɪzəm] *n* cubismo *m*.
cubist ['kju:bɪst] **1** *adj* cubista. **2** *n* cubista *mf*.
cuckold ['kʌkəld] **1** *n* cornudo *m*. **2** *vt* poner los cuernos a.
cuckoo ['kʊku:] **1** *n* cuco *m*, cuclillo *m*. **2** *adj* (*) lelo.
cuckoo-clock ['kʊku:klɒk] *n* reloj *m* de cuclillo.
cuckoopint [,kʊku:'paɪnt] *n* aro *m*.
cucumber ['kju:kʌmbəʳ] *n* pepino *m*.
cud [kʌd] *n*: **to chew the ~** (*lit, fig*) rumiar.
cuddle ['kʌdl] **1** *n* abrazo *m* (amoroso). **2** *vt* abrazar (amorosamente). **3** *vi* (*2 persons*) abrazarse, estar abrazados.
◆**cuddle down** *vi* (*child in bed*) acurrucarse (en la cama); **~ down now!** ¡a dormir!
◆**cuddle up** *vi*: **to ~ up to sb** arrimarse (amorosamente) a uno.
cuddly ['kʌdlɪ] *adj* mimoso; *toy* blando.
cudgel ['kʌdʒəl] **1** *n* porra *f*; **to take up the ~s for sb** salir en defensa de uno, sacar la cara por uno. **2** *vt* aporrear.
cue [kju:] *n* (**a**) (*Billiards*) taco *m*. (**b**) (*Theat*) pie *m*, apunte *m*, entrada *f*; **that gave me my ~** eso me sirvió de indicación; **to take one's ~ from** seguir el ejemplo de; **to come in on ~** entrar en el momento justo.
◆**cue in** *vt* (*Rad, TV*) dar la entrada a; **to ~ sb in on sth** (*US**) poner a uno al tanto (*or* al corriente) de algo.
cuff¹ [kʌf] **1** *n* bofetada *f*. **2** *vt* abofetear.
cuff² [kʌf] *n* (*of shirt*) puño *m*; (*US*) vuelta *f* (de pantalón); **~s*** esposas *fpl*; **to say sth off the ~** decir algo sin pensarlo, decir algo de improviso, sacar algo de la manga.
cufflinks ['kʌflɪŋks] *npl* gemelos *mpl*, broches *mpl* (*LAm*), mellizos *mpl* (*LAm*).
cu.ft *abbr of* **cubic foot, cubic feet** pie *m* cúbico, pies *mpl* cúbicos.
cu.in *abbr of* **cubic inch(es)** pulgada *f* cúbica, pulgadas *fpl* cúbicas.
cuisine [kwɪ'zi:n] *n* cocina *f*.
cul-de-sac ['kʌldə'sæk] *n* (*esp Brit*) callejón *m* sin salida.
culinary ['kʌlɪnərɪ] *adj* culinario.
cull [kʌl] **1** *n* (*of deer, seals*) matanza *f* (selectiva). **2** *vt flowers* coger; (*select*) entresacar; *deer, seals* matar (selectivamente).
culminate ['kʌlmɪneɪt] *vi* culminar (*in* en).
culminating ['kʌlmɪneɪtɪŋ] *adj* culminante.
culmination [,kʌlmɪ'neɪʃən] *n* (*fig*) culminación *f*, punto *m* culminante, colmo *m*; **it is the ~ of much effort** es la culminación de grandes esfuerzos.
culotte(s) [kjʊ:'lɒt(s)] *n*(*pl*) falda-pantalón *f*.

culpability [ˌkʌlpəˈbɪlɪtɪ] *n* culpabilidad *f*.
culpable [ˈkʌlpəbl] *adj* culpable; ~ **homicide** homicidio *m* sin premeditación.
culprit [ˈkʌlprɪt] *n* persona *f* culpable, culpado *m*, -a *f*, delincuente *mf*; (*of accident etc*) causa *f*, elemento *m* responsable.
cult [kʌlt] *n* culto *m* (*of* a).
cult figure [ˈkʌlt,fɪgəʳ] *n* figura *f* de culto.
cultivable [ˈkʌltɪvəbl] *adj* cultivable.
cultivar [ˈkʌltɪvɑːʳ] *n* (*Bot*) variedad *f* cultivada; planta *f*, cosecha *f*.
cultivate [ˈkʌltɪveɪt] *vt* cultivar (*also fig*).
cultivated [ˈkʌltɪveɪtɪd] *adj* (*fig*) culto; ~ **land** tierras *fpl* cultivadas.
cultivation [ˌkʌltɪˈveɪʃən] *n* (*Agr*) cultivo *m*; (*fig*) cultura *f*.
cultivator [ˈkʌltɪveitəʳ] *n* (**a**) (*person*) cultivador *m*, -ora *f*. (**b**) (*machine*) cultivador *m*.
cultural [ˈkʌltʃərəl] *adj* cultural; ~ **attaché** agregado *m*, -a *f* cultural.
culture [ˈkʌltʃəʳ] **1** *n* (*Agr, Bio*) cultivo *m*; (*fig*) cultura *f*; ~ **clash** choque *m* de culturas; ~ **shock** choque *m* cultural. **2** *vt tissue etc* cultivar.
cultured [ˈkʌltʃəd] *adj* culto; ~ **pearl** perla *f* cultivada.
culture fluid [ˈkʌltʃə,fluːɪd] *n* caldo *m* de cultivo.
culture gap [ˈkʌltʃə,gæp] *n* vacío *m* cultural.
culture medium [ˈkʌltʃə,miːdɪəm] *n*, *pl* **culture media** [ˈkʌltʃə,miːdɪə] caldo *m* de cultivo.
culture-vulture [ˈkʌltʃə,vʌltʃəʳ] *n* (*hum**) *persona excesivamente ávida de cultura.*
culvert [ˈkʌlvət] *n* alcantarilla *f* (debajo de una carretera).
cum [kʌm] *prep* con; **it's a sort of kitchen-~-library** es algo así como cocina y biblioteca combinadas; **I was butler-~-gardener to Lady Z** yo fui mayordomo y jardinero a la vez en el servicio de Lady Z.
cumbersome [ˈkʌmbəsəm] *adj*, **cumbrous** [ˈkʌmbrəs] *adj* molesto, incómodo, engorroso, de mucho bulto.
cumin [ˈkʌmɪn] *n* comino *m*.
cum laude [kʊmˈlaʊdeɪ] *adj* (*Univ*) cum laude.
cummerbund [ˈkʌməbʌnd] *n* faja *f*.
cumulative [ˈkjuːmjʊlətɪv] *adj* cumulativo.
cumulonimbus [ˌkjuːmjʊləʊˈnɪmbəs] *n*, *pl* **cumulonimbi** [ˌkjuːmjʊləʊˈnɪmbaɪ] cumulonimbo *m*.
cumulus [ˈkjuːmələs] *n*, *pl* **cumuli** [ˈkjuːmjʊlaɪ] cúmulo *m*.
cuneiform [ˈkjuːnɪfɔːm] *adj* cuneiforme.
cunning [ˈkʌnɪŋ] **1** *adj* (**a**) (*clever*) astuto, (*sly*) taimado. (**b**) (*skilfully made*) artificioso, ingenioso. (**c**) (*US**) precioso, mono.
2 *n* astucia *f*.
cunt** [kʌnt] *n* (**a**) coño** *m*, concha** *f* (*LAm*). (**b**) (*person*) mierda *m***; **you ~!** ¡coño!**.
CUP *n abbr of* **Cambridge University Press.**
cup [kʌp] **1** *n* taza *f*; (*Eccl, Bot*) cáliz *m*; (*Brit*: *trophy*) copa *f*; (*in ground*) hoyo *m*, hondonada *f*; (*of bra*) copa *f*; **to be in one's ~s** estar borracho; **his ~ of sorrow was full** le agobiaba el dolor; **it's not quite my ~ of tea** no es plato de mi gusto; **he's not my ~ of tea** no es de mi agrado, no es santo de mi devoción; **how's your ~?** ¿quieres más té?
2 *vt*: **to ~ one's hands** (*for shouting*) formar bocina con las manos; (*for drinking*) ahuecar las manos.
cup-bearer [ˈkʌp,bɜərəʳ] *n* copero *m*.
cupboard [ˈkʌbəd] *n* (*esp Brit*) armario *m*; (*on wall*) alacena *f*: ~ **love** (*Brit*) amor *m* interesado.
cup final [ˈkʌpfaɪnl] *n* (*Brit*) final *f* de copa.
cupful [ˈkʌpfʊl] *n* taza *f*, contenido *m* de una taza; **two ~s of milk** dos tazas de leche.
Cupid [ˈkjuːpɪd] *nm* Cupido.
cupidity [kjuːˈpɪdɪtɪ] *n* codicia *f*.
cupola [ˈkjuːpələ] *n* cúpula *f*.
cuppa* [ˈkʌpə] *n* (*Brit*) taza *f* (de té).
cup-tie [ˈkʌptaɪ] *n* (*Brit*) partido *m* de copa.
cur [kɜːʳ] *n* perro *m* de mala raza; (*person*) canalla *m*.
curable [ˈkjʊərəbl] *adj* curable.
curacy [ˈkjʊərəsɪ] *n* curato *m*; coadjutoría *f*.
curate [ˈkjʊərɪt] *n* (*parish priest*) cura *m*; (*assistant*) coadjutor *m*; **it's like the ~'s egg** (*Brit*) tiene su lado bueno y su lado malo.
curative [ˈkjʊərətɪv] *adj* curativo.
curator [kjʊəˈreɪtəʳ] *n* (*of museum*) director *m*, -ora *f*, conservador *m*, -ora *f*.
curb [kɜːb] **1** *n* (*fig*) freno *m*, estorbo *m* (*on* para); (*US*) bordillo *m*; **to put a ~ on** refrenar; = **kerb. 2** *vt* (*fig*) refrenar, reprimir, limitar; *expenditure* restringir; *temper* dominar.
curb service [ˈkɜːb,sɜːvɪs] *n* (*US*) servicio *m* drive-in.
curbstone [ˈkɜːbstəʊn] *n* (*US*) = **kerbstone.**
curd [kɜːd] *n* (*freq pl*) cuajada *f*, requesón *m*.
curdle [ˈkɜːdl] **1** *vt* cuajar; **to ~ one's blood** helar la sangre de uno. **2** *vi* cuajarse.
cure [kjʊəʳ] **1** *n* (**a**) (*Med*: *process*) cura *f*, curación *f*; (*remedy*) remedio *m*; **there is no known ~** no existe remedio. (**b**) (*Eccl*: *also* ~ **of souls**) curato *m*, cura *f* de almas. **2** *vt* curar (*of* de).
cure-all [ˈkjʊərɔːl] *n* panacea *f*, sanalotodo *m*.
curfew [ˈkɜːfjuː] *n* (toque *m* de) queda *f*.
curie [ˈkjʊərɪ] *n* curie *m*.
curing [ˈkjʊərɪŋ] *n* curación *f*; *V* **cure 2.**
curio [ˈkjʊərɪəʊ] *n* curiosidad *f*.
curiosity [ˌkjʊərɪˈɒsɪtɪ] *n* curiosidad *f*.
curious [ˈkjʊərɪəs] *adj* curioso; **I am ~ to see Granada** tengo ganas de ver Granada.
curiously [ˈkjʊərɪəslɪ] *adv* curiosamente; ~ **made** ingenioso, artificioso; ~ **enough** aunque parece mentira.
curl [kɜːl] **1** *n* (*of hair*) rizo *m*, bucle *m*; (*of smoke etc*) penacho *m*, espiral *f*.
2 *vt hair* rizar, ensortijar; *paper etc* arrollar; *lip* fruncir.
3 *vi* (*hair*) rizarse, ensortijarse, formar bucles; (*paper etc*) arrollarse; (*leaf*) abarquillarse; (*waves*) encresparse.
◆**curl up** *vi* arrollarse; (*smoke*) subir en espiral; (*animal*) apelotonarse; (*person*) hacerse un ovillo; (*) morirse de risa; **to ~ up in an armchair** hacerse un ovillo en una butaca; **to ~ up into a ball** hacerse un ovillo; **to ~ up with a book** acurrucarse con un libro.
curler [ˈkɜːləʳ] *n* (*for hair*) bigudí *m*, chicho *m*, rulo *m*.
curlew [ˈkɜːluː] *n* zarapito *m*.
curling [ˈkɜːlɪŋ] *n* (*Sport*) *deporte que se juega sobre hielo.*
curling-iron [ˈkɜːlɪŋ,aɪən] *n*, **curling-tongs** [ˈkɜːlɪŋtɒŋz] *npl* tenacillas *fpl* de rizar.
curl-paper [ˈkɜːl,peɪpəʳ] *n* papillote *m*.
curly [ˈkɜːlɪ] *adj* rizado, ensortijado.
curly-haired [ˌkɜːlɪˈhɛəd] *adj*, **curly-headed** [kɜːlɪˈhedɪd] *adj* de pelo rizado.
currant [ˈkʌrənt] *n* (*dried*) pasa *f* de Corinto; *V* **black** *etc.*
currency [ˈkʌrənsɪ] **1** *n* (**a**) (*money*) moneda *f*.
(**b**) (*fig*) uso *m*; **it had a certain ~** se usó bastante.
2 *attr*: ~ **market** mercado *m* monetario; ~ **note** pagaré *m* fiscal (*or* de tesorería); ~ **restrictions** restricciones *fpl* monetarias; ~ **snake** serpiente *f* monetaria; ~ **unit** unidad *f* monetaria.
current [ˈkʌr] **1** *adj* corriente, actual; *price, account etc* corriente; ~ **account** (*Brit*) cuenta *f* corriente; ~ **assets** activo *m* corriente; ~ **liabilities** pasivo *m* corriente; **the ~ month** el mes que corre; **the ~ year** el año presente; **the ~ number of a magazine** el último número de una revista; **the ~ opinion is that** ... se cree actualmente que ...; **it is still quite ~** se usa bastante todavía; **to be in ~ use** estar en uso corriente.
2 *n* (*most senses*) corriente *f*; (*Elec*) flúido *m*, corriente *f*.
currently [ˈkʌrəntlɪ] *adv* actualmente, en la actualidad.
curriculum [kəˈrɪkjʊləm] *n*, *pl* **curricula** [kəˈrɪkjʊlə] plan *m* de estudios, programa *m* de estudios, currículo *m*; ~ **vitae** curriculum *m* (vitae), historial *m* (profesional).
curried [ˈkʌrɪd] *adj* (preparado) con curry.
curry[1] [ˈkʌrɪ] (*Culin*) **1** *n* curry *m*. **2** *vt* preparar con curry.
curry[2] [ˈkʌrɪ] *vt horse* almohazar; *V* **favour.**
currycomb [ˈkʌrɪkəʊm] *n* almohaza *f*.
curry-powder [ˈkʌrɪ,paʊdəʳ] *n* polvo *m* de curry.
curse [kɜːs] **1** *n* (**a**) maldición *f*; **~s!** ¡maldición!; **a ~ on it!** ¡maldito sea!
(**b**) (*oath*) palabrota *f*, taco *m*.
(**c**) (*bane*) calamidad *f*; azote *m*; **the ~ (of Eve)** el período, la regla, la cuenta*; **the dampness is a ~ here** aquí la humedad es una calamidad; **drought is the ~ of Spain** la sequía es el azote de España; **it's been the ~ of my life** me ha amargado la vida, siempre me ha afligido; **the ~ of it is that** ... lo peor es que ...
2 *vt* maldecir; echar pestes de; **to ~ sb with** castigar a uno con; **to be ~d with** padecer de, tener que aguantar, sufrir la aflicción de; ~ **it!** ¡maldito sea!
3 *vi* blasfemar, echar pestes, soltar palabrotas; **to ~ and swear** echar sapos y culebras, echar tacos.
4 *vr*: **to ~ o.s.** maldecirse (*for being a fool* por tonto).
cursed [ˈkɜːsɪd] *adj* maldito.
cursive [ˈkɜːsɪv] *adj* cursivo.
cursor [ˈkɜːsəʳ] *n* cursor *m*; ~ **key** tecla *f* del cursor.
cursorily [ˈkɜːsərɪlɪ] *adv* rápidamente, de modo superficial.
cursory [ˈkɜːsərɪ] *adj* rápido, superficial.
curt [kɜːt] *adj* brusco, seco, lacónico.

curtail [kɜːˈteɪl] *vt* acortar, abreviar; restringir.
curtailment [kɜːˈteɪlmənt] *n* acortamiento *m*, abreviación *f*; restricción *f*.
curtain [ˈkɜːtn] **1** *n* cortina *f* (*also Mil*); (*small*) visillo *m*; (*Theat*) telón *m*; ~ **wall** paneles *mpl*; **when the final ~ came down** cuando el telón bajó por última vez; **it was ~s for him*** para él fue el fin. **2** *vt* proveer de cortina.
◆**curtain off** *vt* separar con cortinas.
curtain-call [ˈkɜːtnkɔːl] *n* llamada *f* a escena.
curtained [ˈkɜːtənd] *adj door etc* con cortina(s).
curtain-hook [ˈkɜːtn,hʊk] *n* gancho *m* de cortina.
curtain-pole [ˈkɜːtn,pəʊl] *n*, **curtain-rail** [ˈkɜːtn,reɪl] *n* palo *m* de las cortinas.
curtain-raiser [ˈkɜːtn,reɪzəʳ] *n* pieza *f* preliminar.
curtain-ring [ˈkɜːtnrɪŋ] *n* anilla *f*.
curtain-rod [ˈkɜːtnrɒd] *n* barra *f* de cortina.
curtly [ˈkɜːtlɪ] *adv* bruscamente, secamente.
curtness [ˈkɜːtnɪs] *n* brusquedad *f*, laconismo *m*.
curtsy [ˈkɜːtsɪ] **1** *n* reverencia *f*; **to drop a ~** = **2**. **2** *vi* hacer una reverencia (*to* a).
curvaceous* [kɜːˈveɪʃəs] *adj girl* de buen tipo, curvilínea.
curvature [ˈkɜːvətʃəʳ] *n* curvatura *f*; ~ **of the spine** escoliosis *f*.
curve [kɜːv] **1** *n* curva *f*; combadura *f*. **2** *vt* encorvar, torcer; combar. **3** *vi* encorvarse, torcerse; combarse; (*road etc*) torcerse, hacer una curva; (*through air*) volar en curva.
curved [kɜːvd] *adj* curvo, encorvado.
curvy [ˈkɜːvɪ] *adj* curvo, encorvado; *road etc* serpentino, con muchas curvas.
cushion [ˈkʊʃən] **1** *n* cojín *m*; (*Billiards*) banda *f*; (*fig*) colchón *m*. **2** *vt blow etc* amortiguar.
cushy‡ [ˈkʊʃɪ] *adj* (*Brit*) fácil, agradable; ~ **job** chollo‡ *m*.
cusp [kʌsp] *n* (*Bot, Astron*) cúspide *f*; (*tooth*) corona *f*; (*moon*) cuerno *m*.
cuspidor [ˈkʌspɪdɔːʳ] *n* (*US*) escupidera *f*.
cuss* [kʌs] **1** *n* (*US*) tipo* *m*, tío* *m*. **2** *vt etc V* **curse**.
cussed* [ˈkʌsɪd] *adj* (**a**) terco, cabezón. (**b**) = **cursed**.
cussedness* [ˈkʌsɪdnɪs] *n* terquedad *f*; **out of sheer ~** de puro terco.
custard [ˈkʌstəd] **1** *n* natillas *fpl*; crema *f* instantánea (en polvo). **2** *attr*: ~ **apple** (*Bot*) chirimoya *f*; ~ **pie** (*missile*) torta *f* de crema; ~ **powder** polvos *mpl* de natillas; ~ **tart** pastel *m* de crema.
custodial [kʌsˈtəʊdɪəl] *adj* (**a**) ~ **sentence** condena *f* de prisión. (**b**) ~ **staff** (*museum etc*) personal *m* de vigilancia.
custodian [kʌsˈtəʊdɪən] *n* custodio *m*, guardián *m*; (*museum*) conservador *m*, -ora *f*.
custody [ˈkʌstədɪ] *n* custodia *f*; **in safe ~** en buenas manos; **to be in ~** estar detenido; **to take sb into ~** detener a uno.
custom [ˈkʌstəm] **1** *n* (**a**) costumbre *f*.
(**b**) (*Brit Comm*) clientela *f*, parroquia *f*; (*total sales*) caja *f*, ventas *fpl*; **to attract ~** atraer clientela; **we've not had much ~ today** hoy hemos tenido pocos clientes.
(**c**) **~s** aduana *f*; (*duty*) derechos *mpl* de aduana; **C~s and Excise** (*Brit*) Aduanas *fpl* y Arbitrios; **to go through the ~s** pasar por la aduana.
2 *attr* (**a**) = **custom-built, custom-made**. (**b**) **~s** aduanero, aduanal, de aduana; ~ **clearance** despacho *m* aduanal; ~ **declaration** declaración *f* aduanera; ~ **duty** derechos *mpl* de aduana; ~ **inspection** revisión *f* aduanera; ~ **inspector** aduanero *m*, -a *f*; ~ **invoice** factura *f* de aduana; ~ **service** aduana *f*, servicio *m* aduanero; ~ **union** unión *f* aduanera; ~ **warehouse** depósito *m* aduanero.
customarily [ˈkʌstəmərɪlɪ] *adv* por regla general, normalmente.
customary [ˈkʌstəmərɪ] *adj* acostumbrado, de costumbre; normal; **it is ~ to** + *infin* es costumbre + *infin*, se suele + *infin*.
custom-built [ˈkʌstəm,bɪlt] *adj* hecho de encargo.
customer [ˈkʌstəməʳ] *n* (**a**) cliente *m*, -a *f*; ~ **liaison**, ~ **relations** relaciones *fpl* con los clientes; ~ **profile** perfil *m* de la clientela; ~ **service** servicio *m* de asistencia posventa; ~ **services** servicios *mpl* para los clientes. (**b**) (*) tipo* *m*.
customize [ˈkʌstəmaɪz] *vt* hacer al gusto del consumidor, adaptar en razón de un cliente particular, personalizar.
customized [ˈkʌstəmaɪzd] *adj* hecho de encargo; ~ **software** software *m* a medida del usuario.
custom-made [ˈkʌstəmˈmeɪd] *adj* (*US*) hecho a la medida, hecho para un cliente específico; fuera de serie.
customs-house [ˈkʌstəmzhaʊs] *n*, *pl* **customs-houses** [ˈkʌstəmz,haʊzɪz] aduana *f*.
customs-officer [ˈkʌstəmz,ɒfɪsəʳ] *n* aduanero *m*, -a *f*.
customs-post [ˈkʌstəmzpəʊst] *n* puesto *m* aduanero.

cut [kʌt] **1** *adj* cortado; ~ **flowers** flores *fpl* cortadas; ~ **glass** vidrio *m* tallado; ~ **prices** precios *mpl* reducidos; ~ **and dried** rutinario; seguro; preparado de antemano; convenido de antemano; ~ **off** aislado (*from* de).
2 *n* (**a**) (*incision*) corte *m*; (*in skin*) cortadura *f*.
(**b**) (*slash with sword*) tajo *m*, (*with knife*) cuchillada *f*, (*with whip*) latigazo *m*; (*insult, offence*) corte *m*; **the ~ and thrust of politics** la esgrima política; **the unkindest ~ of all** el golpe más duro; **whose ~ is it?** (*Cards*) ¿quién corta?
(**c**) (*deletion*) corte *m*, trozo *m* suprimido.
(**d**) **short ~** atajo *m*; **there is no short ~ to success** no se alcanza el éxito por ningún camino fácil; **to take a short ~** atajar, ir por el atajo, (*fig*) echar por el atajo.
(**e**) (*of clothes, diamond*) corte *m*; **to be a ~ above the rest** ser algo superior a los demás.
(**f**) (*woodcut*) grabado *m*; (*US*) foto *f*, diagrama *m*, dibujo *m*.
(**g**) (*kind of meat*) clase *f* de carne; (*slice*) tajada *f*; (*share*) parte *f*, tajada *f*.
(**h**) (*reduction*) reducción *f*, rebaja *f* (*in* de); corte *m*, recorte *m*; (*Elec*) apagón *m*; **to take a ~ in salary** sufrir una reducción de sueldo.
(**i**) (*share*) parte *f*; tajada* *f*; **the manager gets a ~ of 5%** el gerente recibe su parte de 5 por ciento.
3 (*irr*: *pret and ptp* **cut**) *vt* (**a**) (*gen*) cortar; *cards, communications, hair, hedge, drug etc* cortar; *corn* segar; *meat* trinchar; (*of wind*) cortar; *engine* parar; (*divide*) cortar, partir, dividir (*into 2* en 2); **to ~ one's finger** cortarse el dedo; **to get one's hair ~** cortarse el pelo; **to ~ sb free** cortar las cuerdas que lían a uno.
(**b**) (*shape*) *glass, stone* tallar; *disc* grabar; *hole* practicar, hacer.
(**c**) (*ignore*) no hacer caso a; fingir no ver; negar el saludo a; *class etc* ausentarse de, no asistir a.
(**d**) (*intersect*) cruzar, cortar.
(**e**) (*Aut*) *corner* tomar muy cerrado.
(**f**) (*reduce*) recortar, rebajar, reducir; *price* reducir (*by 5%* en un 5 por cien); *staff* recortar; (*delete*) cortar, suprimir; **she ~ 2 seconds off the record** mejoró la marca en 2 segundos.
(**g**) **he's ~ting a tooth** le está saliendo un diente.
4 *vi* (**a**) (*gen*) cortar; (*material*) cortarse; **this ~s both ways** esto tiene doble fila; **to ~ and run** largarse*; rajarse*; claudicar.
(**b**) (*Math etc*: *lines*) cortarse.
(**c**) (*Cine, TV*) ~! ¡corten!; **they ~ from the palace to the castle scene** pasan (*or* cambian) desde el palacio a la escena del castillo.
(**d**) (*Cards*) cortar; **to ~ for deal** cortar para determinar el repartidor.
◆**cut across** *vt* (**a**) **to ~ wood across** cortar una madera a través; cortar una madera completamente.
(**b**) atajar, tomar un atajo; **to ~ across a field** atajar por un campo, atravesar un campo.
(**c**) **this ~s across the usual categories** (*fig*) esto rebasa (*pej*: no respeta) las categorías establecidas.
◆**cut along** *vi* irse de prisa.
◆**cut away** *vt* cortar, separar cortando.
◆**cut back** **1** *vt* acortar, recortar, reducir; *expenditure, production* recortar, reducir; *staff etc* recortar.
2 *vi* (**a**) volver (*to* a).
(**b**) = **cut down 2**.
(**c**) **to ~ back on** = **cut back 1**.
◆**cut down** **1** *vt* (**a**) *tree etc* talar, derribar, cortar; *enemy* matar.
(**b**) *price* rebajar; *costs* reducir (*by 5%* en un 5 por cien); *size, majority* reducir (*by* en).
2 *vi* economizar; **to ~ down on** economizar con, reducir el consumo de.
◆**cut in** **1** *vt*: **to ~ sb in on a deal** permitir que uno participe en un negocio (*esp* poco limpio).
2 *vi* (**a**) (*Aut*) pasar peligrosamente, meterse delante (de modo peligroso).
(**b**) (*in conversation*) interrumpir, cortar; **to ~ in on a conversation** interrumpir una conversación.
◆**cut into** *vt*: **to ~ into one's holiday** interrumpir sus vacaciones; **this will ~ into our holiday** esto quitará una parte de las vacaciones; **we shall have to ~ into savings** tendremos que usar una parte de los ahorros.
◆**cut off** *vt* (**a**) cortar; (*Elec, Telec etc*) cortar, interrumpir; desconectar; *limb* amputar; **we were ~ off** nos desconectaron; **to ~ sb's life off in its prime** tronchar una vida joven.
(**b**) *troops* cercar, copar; *retreat* cortar, impedir; (*of*

flood, snow) aislar; dejar incomunicado; bloquear; **we were ~ off by the snow** quedamos bloqueados por la nieve.

(**c**) (*disinherit*) desheredar.

◆**cut out 1** *vt* (**a**) recortar; *hole etc* practicar, hacer; *diseased part* extirpar.

(**b**) (*exclude*) excluir, dejar fuera; *opposition* eliminar; *harmful substance* dejar (de tomar), suprimir (el uso de); **he ~ his nephew out of his will** borró de su testamento la mención del sobrino; **~ it out!** ¡basta ya!, ¡déjalo!; **~ out the singing!** ¡basta ya de cantar!; **you can ~ that out for a start** en primer lugar puedes olvidar eso.

(**c**) (*delete*) suprimir, tachar, cortar.

(**d**) **he's not ~ out to be a poet** no tiene madera de poeta, no tiene talento de poeta.

(**e**) **he had his work ~ out to finish it** tuvo que trabajar duro para terminarlo; **you'll have your work ~ out to manage it** vas a sudar la gota gorda para lograrlo.

2 *vi* (**a**) (*engine*) pararse; (*Elec*) cortarse, interrumpirse.

(**b**) (*US**: *leave*) pirarla*.

◆**cut through** *vi* abrirse camino, abrirse paso (a la fuerza).

◆**cut up 1** *vt* (**a**) cortar (en pedazos); desmenuzar; dividir; *meat* picar; (*wound*) herir, acuchillar.

(**b**) (*Brit**) **to be ~ up** afligirse (*about* por); **he's very ~ up** está muy deshinchado; **he was very ~ up by the death of his son** estaba muy afectado por la muerte de su hijo.

2 *vi* (**a**) **he'll ~ up for several millions*** dejará varios millones.

(**b**) **to ~ up rough** (*Brit**) cabrearse*.

(**c**) (*US*) (*clown around*) hacer tonterías, hacer el bobo.

cutaneous [kjuː'teɪnɪəs] *adj* cutáneo.

cutback ['kʌtbæk] *n* recorte *m*, corte *m*, reducción *f*; economía *f*.

cute [kjuːt] *adj* (**a**) (*nice*) mono, lindo; (*shrewd*) cuco, astuto, listo. (**b**) (*esp US*: *affecting prettiness etc*) presumido.

cut-glass ['kʌt'glɑːs] *adj* de vidrio tallado.

cuticle ['kjuːtɪkl] *n* cutícula *f*.

cutie* ['kjuːtɪ] *n* (*US*) chica *f*.

cutlass ['kʌtləs] *n* alfanje *m*, chafarote *m*.

cutler ['kʌtləʳ] *n* cuchillero *m*.

cutlery ['kʌtlərɪ] *n* cubiertos *mpl*, cuchillería *f*; **~ cabinet** caja *f* de cuchillería.

cutlet ['kʌtlɪt] *n* chuleta *f*.

cut-off ['kʌtɒf] *n* (*Mech*) cierre *m*, corte *m*; (*Elec*) desconectador *m*; (*US*) atajo *m*; **~ point** punto *m* de corte.

cutoffs* ['kʌtɔfs] *npl* tejanos *mpl* cortados.

cut-out ['kʌtaʊt] *n* (**a**) (*child's*) recorte *m*, diseño *m* para recortar, recortable *m*. (**b**) (*Elec*) cortacircuito *m*, disyuntor *m*; (*Mech*) válvula *f* de escape.

cut-price ['kʌtpraɪs] *adj* (*Brit*) a precio reducido; **~ shop, ~ store** tienda *f* de saldos.

cut-rate [ˌkʌt'reɪt] *adj* barato.

cutter ['kʌtəʳ] *n* (**a**) (*Sew etc*) cortador *m*, -ora *f*. (**b**) (*Mech*) cortadora *f*; **~s** (*for wire etc*) cizallas *fpl*, cortaalambres *m*. (**c**) (*Naut*) cúter *m*; patrullero *m*, guardacostas *m*.

cut-throat ['kʌtθrəʊt] **1** *adj competition* encarnizado, despiadado, intenso; **~ razor** (*Brit*) navaja *f* (de afeitar). **2** *n* asesino *m*.

cutting ['kʌtɪŋ] **1** *adj* cortante; *remark* mordaz; **~ board** plancha *f* para cortar; **~ edge** filo *m*, (*fig*) vanguardia *f*; **~ room** (*Cine*) sala *f* de montaje. **2** *n* (**a**) (*from paper*) recorte *m*. (**b**) (*Rail*) desmonte *m*, trinchera *f*. (**c**) (*Bot*) esqueje *m*.

cuttlefish ['kʌtlfɪʃ] *n* jibia *f*, sepia *f*.

cut-up* [ˌkʌt'ʌp] *adj* (**a**) (*Brit*) *V* **cut up**. (**b**) (*US*) gracioso.

CV *n abbr of* **curriculum vitae** curriculum *m* vitae.

CW *n* (**a**) *abbr of* **chemical weapons**. (**b**) *abbr of* **chemical warfare**.

c.w.o. *abbr of* **cash with order** pago *m* al contado.

cwt *abbr of* **hundredweight(s)**.

cyanide ['saɪənaɪd] *n* cianuro *m*; **~ of potassium** cianuro *m* de potasio.

cybernetic [ˌsaɪbə'netɪk] *adj* cibernético.

cybernetics [ˌsaɪbə'netɪks] *n sing and pl* cibernética *f*.

cyclamate ['sɪkləmeɪt] *n* ciclamato *m*.

cyclamen ['sɪkləmən] *n* ciclamen *m*, ciclamino *m*.

cycle ['saɪkl] **1** *n* (**a**) ciclo *m*; **life ~** ciclo *m* vital; **menstrual ~** ciclo *m* menstrual. (**b**) (*bicycle*) bicicleta *f*. **2** *vi* ir (*or* montar) en bicicleta; **we ~d to the coast** fuimos en bicicleta a la costa.

cycle-bell ['saɪklˌbel] *n* timbre *m* de bicicleta.

cycle-clip ['saɪklˌklɪp] *n* pinza *f* para ir en bicicleta.

cycle-lane ['saɪklˌleɪn] *n* pista *f* para ciclistas.

cycle-path ['saɪklˌpɑːθ] *n* carril *m* de bicicleta.

cycler ['saɪkləʳ] *n* (*US*) ciclista *mf*.

cycle-rack ['saɪklˌræk] *n* soporte *m* para bicicletas; (*on car roof*) baca *f* para transportar bicicletas.

cycle-shed ['saɪklˌʃed] *n* cobertizo *m* para bicicletas.

cycle-track ['saɪklˌtræk] *n* (*Sport*) pista *f* de ciclismo.

cycleway ['saɪklweɪ] *n* carril *m* de bicicleta.

cyclic(al) ['saɪklɪk(əl)] *adj* cíclico.

cycling ['saɪklɪŋ] **1** *n* ciclismo *m*. **2** *attr*: **~ holiday** vacaciones *fpl* en bicicleta; **~ tour** vuelta *f* ciclista; **~ track** velódromo *m*.

cyclist ['saɪklɪst] *n* ciclista *mf*.

cyclone ['saɪkləʊn] *n* ciclón *m*.

Cyclops ['saɪklɒps] *n* cíclope *m*.

cyclostyle ['saɪkləʊstaɪl] **1** *n* ciclostil(o) *m*. **2** *vt* ciclostilar, reproducir en ciclostil(o).

cyclostyled ['saɪkləstaɪld] *adj* en ciclostil(o).

cyclotron ['saɪklətrɒn] *n* ciclotrón *m*.

cygnet ['sɪgnɪt] *n* pollo *m* de cisne, cisnecito *m*.

cylinder ['sɪlɪndəʳ] *n* cilindro *m*.

cylinder-block ['sɪlɪndəblɒk] *n* bloque *m* de cilindros.

cylinder capacity ['sɪlɪndəkə'pæsɪtɪ] *n* cilindrada *f*.

cylinder-head ['sɪlɪndəhed] *n* culata *f* de cilindro; **~ gasket** junta *f* de culata.

cylindrical [sɪ'lɪndrɪkəl] *adj* cilíndrico.

cymbal ['sɪmbəl] *n* (*freq pl*) platillo *m*, címbalo *m*.

cynic ['sɪnɪk] *n* cínico *m*, -a *f*.

cynical ['sɪnɪkəl] *adj* cínico; despreciativo, desengañado.

cynically ['sɪnɪklɪ] *adv* con cinismo.

cynicism ['sɪnɪsɪzəm] *n* cinismo *m*; desprecio *m*, desengaño *m*.

cynosure ['saɪnəʃʊəʳ] *n*: **~ of every eye** blanco *m* de todas las miradas.

CYO *n* (*US*) *abbr of* **Catholic Youth Organization**.

cypher ['saɪfəʳ] = **cipher**.

cypress ['saɪprɪs] *n* ciprés *m*.

Cypriot ['sɪprɪət] **1** *adj* chipriota. **2** *n* chipriota *mf*.

Cyprus ['saɪprəs] *n* Chipre *f*.

Cyrillic [sɪ'rɪlɪk] **1** *adj* cirílico. **2** *n* cirílico *m*.

cyst [sɪst] *n* quiste *m*.

cystic ['sɪstɪk] *adj* cístico; **~ fibrosis** fibrosis *f* cística.

cystitis [sɪs'taɪtɪs] *n* cistitis *f*.

cytology [saɪ'tɒlədʒɪ] *n* citología *f*.

cytotoxic [ˌsaɪtəʊ'tɒksɪk] *adj* citotóxico.

CZ (*US*) *abbr of* **Canal Zone**.

czar [zɑːʳ] *n* zar *m*; (*person in authority, chief*) jefe *m*.

czarina [zɑː'riːnə] *n* zarina *f*.

Czech [tʃek] **1** *adj* checo. **2** *n* (**a**) checo *m*, -a *f*. (**b**) (*Ling*) checo *m*.

Czechoslovak ['tʃekəʊ'sləʊvæk] **1** *adj* checoslovaco. **2** *n* checoslovaco *m*, -a *f*.

Czechoslovakia ['tʃekəʊslə'vækɪə] *n* Checoslovaquia *f*.

Czechoslovakian ['tʃekəʊslə'vækɪən] **1** *adj* checoslovaco. **2** *n* checoslovaco *m*, -a *f*.

D

D, d [diː] *n* (**a**) (*letter*) D, d *f*; **D for David, D for Dog** (*US*) D de Dolores. (**b**) **D** (*Mus*) re *m*; **D major** re mayor.
D (**a**) *n* (*Scol*: *mark around 50%*) aprobado *m*, suficiente *m*. (**b**) (*US Pol*) *abbr of* **Democrat**(**ic**).
d. *n* (**a**) *abbr of* **date** fecha *f*. (**b**) *abbr of* **daughter** hija *f*. (**c**) *abbr of* **died** murió, m. (**d**) (*Rail etc*) *abbr of* **depart**(**s**) sale. (**e**) († *Brit*) *abbr of* **penny** penique *m*.
DA *n* (*US*) *abbr of* **District Attorney**.
D/A *abbr of* **deposit account**.
dab[1] [dæb] **1** *n* (*blow*) golpe *m* ligero; (*small amount*) pequeña cantidad *f*; (*of paint*) brochazo *m*; (*of liquid*) gota *f*; **~s** (*esp Brit*‡: *hands*) manos *fpl*; (*fingerprints*) huellas *fpl* dactilares.
2 *vt* (*strike*) golpear ligeramente, tocar ligeramente; (*with sponge etc*) tocar; frotar suavemente; (*moisten*) mojar ligeramente; **to ~ a stain off** quitar una mancha mojándola ligeramente; **to ~ paint on a wall** embadurnar una pared de pintura.
3 *vi*: **to ~ at one's eyes with a handkerchief** llevar repetidas veces un pañuelo a los ojos.
dab[2] [dæb] *n* (*Fish*) lenguado *m*.
dab[3]* [dæb] **1** *adj*: **to be a ~ hand at** (*Brit*) tener buena mano para, ser un hacha en. **2** *n* as* *m*, hacha *m* (*at* en). **3** *adv*: **~ in the middle** (*US*) en el mismo centro.
dabble ['dæbl] **1** *vt* salpicar, mojar; **to ~ one's feet** chapotear los pies.
2 *vi*: **to ~ in sth** interesarse en algo por pasatiempo, ser ligeramente aficionado a algo, trabajar superficialmente en algo; **I only ~ in it** para mí es un pasatiempo nada más; **to ~ in politics** jugar a la política; **to ~ in shares** jugar a la bolsa.
dabbler ['dæbləʳ] *n* (*pej*) aficionado *m*, -a *f* (*in* a), diletante *mf*; **he's just a ~** es un simple aficionado, para él es un pasatiempo nada más.
dabchick ['dæbtʃɪk] *n* somorgujo *m* menor.
Dacca ['dækə] *n* Dacca *f*.
dace [deɪs] *n* albur *m*.
dachshund ['dækshʊnd] *n* perro *m* tejonero.
dactyl ['dæktɪl] *n* dáctilo *m*.
dactylic [dæk'tɪlɪk] *adj* dactílico.
dad* [dæd] *n*, **daddy*** ['dædɪ] *n* papá *m*, papaíto *m*.
Dada ['dɑːdɑː] **1** *n* dada *m*, dadaísmo *m*. **2** *attr movement* dadaísta.
dadaism ['dɑːdɑːɪzəm] *n* dadaísmo *m*.
dadaist ['dɑːdɑːɪst] **1** *adj* dadaísta. **2** *n* dadaísta *mf*.
daddy-long-legs ['dædɪ'lɒŋlegz] *n* (*Brit*) típula *f*.
dado ['deɪdəʊ] *n* dado *m*; friso *m*.
daffodil ['dæfədɪl] *n* narciso *m* (trompón).
daffy‡ ['dæfɪ] *adj* (*US*) chiflado*.
daft [dɑːft] *adj* bobo, tonto.
dagger ['dægəʳ] *n* puñal *m*, daga *f*; (*Typ*) cruz *f*, obelisco *m*; **to be at ~s drawn** odiarse a muerte; **to look ~s at** apuñalar con la mirada, fulminar (con la mirada).
dago ['deɪgəʊ] *n término peyorativo aplicado a españoles, portugueses e italianos*.
daguerrotype [də'gerəʊ,taɪp] *n* daguerrotipo *m*.
dahlia ['deɪlɪə] *n* dalia *f*.
daily ['deɪlɪ] **1** *adj* diario, cotidiano; **our ~ bread** el pan nuestro de cada día; **~ dozen** ejercicios *mpl* matinales; **~ paper** diario *m*; **the ~ round** la rutina cotidiana.
2 *adv* a diario, cada día.
3 *n* (**a**) (*paper*) diario *m*.
(**b**) (*Brit**: *also* **~ help**, **~ woman**) asistenta *f*, chacha* *f*.
daintily ['deɪntɪlɪ] *adv* delicadamente; elegantemente, primorosamente; melindrosamente.
daintiness ['deɪntɪnɪs] *n* (**a**) delicadeza *f*; elegancia *f*, primor *m*. (**b**) melindres *mpl*.
dainty ['deɪntɪ] **1** *adj* (**a**) (*delicate*) delicado, fino; (*tasteful*) elegante, primoroso, precioso. (**b**) (*fastidious*) delicado, melindroso. **2** *n* bocado *m* exquisito, golosina *f*.
daiquiri ['daɪkɪrɪ] *n* daiquiri *m*.
dairy ['dɛərɪ] **1** *n* (*shop*) lechería *f*; (*on farm*) quesería *f*, vaquería *f*.
2 *attr* lechero; lácteo; **~ butter** mantequilla *f* de granja; **~ cattle** vacas *fpl* lecheras; **~ farm** granja *f* especializada en producción de leche; **~ farming** industria *f* lechera; **~ herd** ganado *m* lechero; **~ ice cream** helado *m* hecho con leche; **~ produce** productos *mpl* lácteos.
dairymaid ['dɛərɪmeɪd] *n* lechera *f*.
dairyman ['dɛərɪmən] *n*, *pl* **dairymen** ['dɛərɪmen] lechero *m*.
dais ['deɪɪs] *n* estrado *m*.
daisy ['deɪzɪ] *n* maya *f*, margarita *f*; **to be pushing up the daisies*** criar malvas*.
daisy-chain ['deɪzɪ,tʃeɪn] *n* (*US fig*) serie *f*.
daisy-wheel ['deɪzɪ,wiːl] *n* margarita *f*; **~ printer** impresora *f* de margarita.
Dakar ['dækəʳ] *n* Dakar *m*.
dale [deɪl] *n* (*N Eng*) valle *m*; **the** (**Yorkshire**) **D~s** los valles de Yorkshire.
dalliance ['dælɪəns] *n* (*play*) juegos *mpl*, diversiones *fpl*; (*time-wasting*) frivolidad *f*; **amorous ~** coquetería *f*, flirteo *m*.
dally ['dælɪ] *vi* (*delay*) tardar, perder el tiempo; (*amuse o.s.*) divertirse; **to ~ with** *lover* coquetear con, entretenerse en amores con; *idea* entretenerse con.
Dalmatia [dæl'meɪʃə] n Dalmacia *f*.
dalmatian [dæl'meɪʃən] *n* (*dog*) perro *m* dálmata.
daltonism ['dɔːltənɪzəm] *n* daltonismo *m*.
dam[1] [dæm] **1** *n* presa *f*; (*small*) dique *m*. **2** *vt* represar; construir una presa sobre.
◆**dam up** *vt* cerrar, tapar; *overflowing water* contener con un dique.
dam[2]* [dæm] *adj* = **damn 3, damned.**
dam[3] [dæm] *n* (*Zool*) madre *f*.
damage ['dæmɪdʒ] **1** *n* (**a**) daño *m*, perjuicio *m*; (*Mech*) avería *f*; (*visible, eg on car*) desperfectos *mpl*; **~ limitation exercise** campaña *f* para contener los daños; **what's the ~?*** ¿cuánto te debo?
(**b**) **~s** (*Jur*) daños *mpl* y perjuicios, indemnización *f*.
2 *vt* dañar, perjudicar; (*Mech*) averiar, estropear; *chances, reputation* perjudicar; **to be ~d in a collision** sufrir daños en un choque.
damaging ['dæmɪdʒɪŋ] *adj* perjudicial.
damascene ['dæməsiːn] **1** *adj* damasquinado, damasquino. **2** *vt* damasquinar.
Damascus [də'mɑːskəs] *n* Damasco *m*.
damask ['dæməsk] **1** *adj cloth* adamascado; *steel* damasquino. **2** *n* (*cloth*) damasco *m*; (*steel*) acero *m* damasquino. **3** *vt cloth* adamascar; *steel* damasquinar.
dame [deɪm] *n* (**a**) (*esp Brit*) dama *f*, señora *f*; (*Brit Theat*) vieja dama *f*. (**b**) **D~** (*Brit*: *in titles*) *título que lleva una mujer condecorada con una orden de caballería*. (**c**) (*esp US**) tía* *f*, chica *f*.
damfool* ['dæm'fuːl] *adj* (*Brit*) estúpido, tonto; **some ~ driver** algún imbécil de conductor; **that's a ~ thing to say!** ¡qué tontería!
dammit* ['dæmɪt] *excl* (*Brit*) ¡córcholis!*; **as near as ~** casi; por un pelo.
damn [dæm] **1** *vt* condenar (*also Eccl*); maldecir; **~!**, **~ it!** ¡condenación!; **~ this car!** ¡al diablo con este coche!; **the effort was ~ed from the start** desde el principio el esfuerzo estaba condenado a fracasar; **his arrogance ~ed him** su arrogancia le perdió; **the critics ~ed the book** los críticos dieron una paliza al libro; **well I'm ~ed!** ¡mecachis!; **I'll see him ~ed first** antes le veré colgado; **I'll be ~ed if ...**

que me cuelguen si ...
2 *n*: **I don't give a ~** maldito lo que me importa.
3 *adj* (*) maldito; **~ Yankee** (*US*‡) sucio yanqui *m*.
damnable ['dæmnəbl] *adj* detestable.
damnably ['dæmnəblɪ] *adv* terriblemente.
damn-all‡ ['dæm'ɔːl] **1** *adj*: **it's ~ use** no sirve para nada en absoluto. **2** *n*: **he does ~** no hace absolutamente nada; **I know ~ about it** (*Brit*) no sé absolutamente nada de eso.
damnation [dæm'neɪʃən] *n* condenación *f*; perdición *f*; **~!** ¡condenación!; **to go down to ~** ir a la perdición.
damned [dæmd] **1** *adj* (**a**) *soul* condenado, maldito. (**b**) (*damnable*) detestable, abominable; **that ~ book** ese maldito libro; **to do one's ~est to** + *infin* hacer lo imposible para + *infin*; **it's a ~ shame** es una terrible vergüenza.
2 *adv* muy, extraordinariamente; **it's ~ awkward** es terriblemente difícil; **it's ~ hot** hace un calor terrible.
3 *n*: **the ~** las almas en pena.
damning ['dæmɪŋ] *adj evidence* irrecusable.
Damocles ['dæməkliːz] *nm* Damocles.
damp [dæmp] **1** *adj* húmedo; mojado; **that was a ~ squib** (*Brit**) resultó ser un rollo*.
2 *n* humedad *f*; (*Min*) mofeta *f*.
3 *vt* (*also* **dampen** ['dæmpən]) (**a**) (*wet*) mojar, humedecer.
(**b**) (*fig*) *person* desalentar; *hopes* ahogar; *excitement* calmar; *zeal* enfriar, moderar.
◆**damp down** *vt* amortiguar; *fire* cubrir; *demand* reducir.
dampcourse ['dæmpkɔːs] *n* (*Brit*) cortahumedades *m*, aislante *m* hidrófugo.
damper ['dæmpəʳ] *n* (*Mus*) apagador *m*, sordina *f*; (*of fire*) regulador *m* de tiro; **to put a ~ on** (*fig*) acabar con, parar; disminuir; verter un jarro de agua fría sobre.
dampish ['dæmpɪʃ] *adj* algo húmedo.
dampness ['dæmpnɪs] *n* humedad *f*.
damp-proof ['dæmppruːf] *adj* a prueba de humedad.
damsel ['dæmzəl] *n* damisela *f*, doncella *f*.
damson ['dæmzən] *n* (*fruit*) ciruela *f* damascena; (*tree*) ciruelo *m* damasceno.
Dan [dæn] *nm familiar form of* **Daniel**.
dan [dæn] *n* (*Sport*) dan *m*.
dance [dɑːns] **1** *n* baile *m*; **~ of death** danza *f* de la muerte; **to lead sb a ~** (*Brit*) traerle a uno al retortero.
2 *vt* bailar.
3 *vi* bailar; (*artistically*) danzar; (*fig*) danzar, saltar, brincar; **to ~ for joy** brincar de alegría; **shall we ~?** ¿quieres bailar?
dance-band ['dɑːnsbænd] *n* orquesta *f* de baile.
dance-floor ['dɑːnsflɔːʳ] *n* pista *f* de baile.
dance-hall ['dɑːnshɔːl] *n* salón *m* de baile, sala *f* de fiestas.
dance-music ['dɑːns,mjuːzɪk] *n* música *f* de baile.
dancer ['dɑːnsəʳ] *n* bailador *m*, -ora *f*; (*professional*) bailarín *m*, -ina *f*.
dancing ['dɑːnsɪŋ] **1** *n* baile *m*. **2** *attr* de baile.
dancing-girl ['dɑːnsɪŋgɜːl] *n* bailarina *f*.
dancing-partner ['dɑːnsɪŋ,pɑːtnəʳ] *n* pareja *f* de baile.
dancing-shoes ['dɑːnsɪŋ,ʃuːz] *npl* zapatillas *fpl*.
dandelion ['dændɪlaɪən] *n* diente *m* de león.
dander ['dændəʳ] *n*: **to get sb's ~ up** sacar a uno de sus casillas.
dandified ['dændɪfaɪd] *adj* guapo, acicalado.
dandle ['dændl] *vt* hacer saltar sobre las rodillas.
dandruff ['dændrəf] *n* caspa *f*; **~ shampoo** champú *m* anticaspa.
dandy ['dændɪ] **1** *n* dandy *m*, dandi *m*, currutaco *m*. **2** *adj* (*esp US**) mono, de primera.
Dane [deɪn] *n* danés *m*, -esa *f*.
danger ['deɪndʒəʳ] *n* peligro *m*; riesgo *m*; **'~!'** (*sign*) '¡peligro!'; **there is a ~ of** hay riesgo de; **to be in ~** estar en peligro, peligrar; **to be in ~ of** + *ger* correr riesgo de + *infin*; **to be out of ~** estar fuera de peligro.
danger-area ['deɪndʒər,ɛərɪə] *n* zona *f* de peligro.
danger-list ['deɪndʒəlɪst] *n*: **to be on the ~** estar de cuidado.
danger-money ['deɪndʒə,mʌnɪ] *n* prima *f* por trabajos peligrosos, plus *m* de peligrosidad.
dangerous ['deɪndʒrəs] *adj* peligroso, arriesgado; *animal* peligroso; *substance* nocivo; **convicted of ~ driving** culpable de conducir con imprudencia temeraria.
dangerously ['deɪndʒrəslɪ] *adv* peligrosamente; arriesgadamente; **to come ~ close to** acercarse de modo peligroso a; **he likes to live ~** le gusta arriesgar la vida.
danger-point ['deɪndʒə,pɔɪnt] *n* punto *m* crítico.
danger-signal ['deɪndʒə,sɪgnl] *n* señal *f* de peligro.
danger-zone ['deɪndʒə,zəʊn] *n* zona *f* de peligro.
dangle ['dæŋgl] **1** *vt* colgar, dejar colgado; **to ~ the prospect of sth before sb** ofrecer a uno la posibilidad de algo.
2 *vi* estar colgado, pender; bambolearse; **to ~ after** ir tras de; **she kept him dangling for 3 months** ella le tuvo suspenso durante 3 meses.
Daniel ['dænjəl] *nm* Daniel.
Danish ['deɪnɪʃ] **1** *adj* danés, dinamarqués; **~ blue cheese** queso *m* mohoso danés; **~ pastry** *pasta rellena de manzana, pasta de almendras etc*. **2** *n* (**a**) **the ~** los daneses. (**b**) (*Ling*) danés *m*. (**c**) (*US*: *cake*) = **~ pastry**.
dank [dæŋk] *adj* húmedo y malsano.
Dante ['dæntɪ] *nm* Dante.
Danube ['dænjuːb] *n* Danubio *m*.
Daphne ['dæfnɪ] *nf* Dafne.
dapper ['dæpəʳ] *adj* apuesto, pulcro.
dapple ['dæpl] *vt* motear a colores.
dappled ['dæpld] *adj* moteado, salpicado de manchas; *horse* rodado.
Darby and Joan ['dɑːbɪən'dʒəʊn] *npl el matrimonio ideal, de ancianos que siguen viviendo en la mayor felicidad*; **~ club** (*Brit*) club *m* para personas de la tercera edad.
Dardanelles [,dɑːdə'nelz] *npl* Dardanelos *mpl*.
dare [dɛəʳ] **1** *n*: **to do sth for a ~** hacer algo en desafío.
2 *vt* (**a**) (*attempt*) arriesgar; *sb's anger* hacer frente a.
(**b**) **to ~ sb to do sth** desafiar a uno a hacer algo, provocar a uno a hacer algo; **I ~ you!** ¡a que no eres capaz!, ¡a ver si te atreves!; **to ~ (to) do sth** atreverse a hacer algo, osar hacer algo.
(**c**) **I ~ say** quizá; (*iro*) es muy posible; **I ~ say that ...** no me sorprendería que + *subj*; **I ~ say you're tired** sin duda estás cansado.
3 *vi*: **how ~ you!** ¡cómo te atreves!, ¡qué fresco!; **just you ~ !, you wouldn't ~!** ¡ya te guardarás de hacerlo!
daredevil ['dɛə,devl] **1** *adj* temerario. **2** *n* temerario *m*, -a *f*, atrevido *m*, -a *f*.
daren't [dɛəːnt] = **dare not**.
Dar-es-Salaam [,dɑːressə'lɑːm] *n* Dar-es-Salaam *m*.
daring ['dɛərɪŋ] **1** *adj* atrevido, osado. **2** *n* atrevimiento *m*, osadía *f*.
daringly ['dɛərɪŋlɪ] *adv* atrevidamente, osadamente.
Darius [də'raɪəs] *nm* Darío.
dark [dɑːk] **1** *adj* (**a**) (*unilluminated*) oscuro; tenebroso; **to get ~** hacerse de noche, anochecer; **as ~ as a dungeon** oscuro como boca de lobo.
(**b**) (*in colour*) oscuro; **~ glasses** gafas *fpl* negras; **~ horse** incógnita *f*, figura *f* misteriosa; (*in race*) contendiente *m* desconocido; (*US*: *in election*) candidato *m* poco conocido; (*winner*) vencedor *m* inesperado.
(**c**) *complexion, hair* moreno.
(**d**) (*cheerless*) triste, sombrío; **~ days** días *mpl* funestos, días *mpl* negros.
(**e**) (*secret*) secreto, escondido; *doings* misterioso, sospechoso; **the D~ Continent** el Continente Negro; **to keep sth ~** tener algo secreto; **keep it ~!** ¡de esto no digas ni pío!
(**f**) (*unenlightened*) ignorante; **D~ Ages** Edades *fpl* bárbaras, primera parte *f* de la Edad Media.
2 *n* oscuridad *f*; tinieblas *fpl*; **after ~** después del anochecer; **to grope about in the ~** ir buscando algo a oscuras; **we are all in the ~ about it** no sabemos nada en absoluto de ello; **to keep sb in the ~** ocultar algo a uno, no revelar a uno cierta noticia; **to be left in the ~** quedar sin saber nada de algo.
darken ['dɑːkən] **1** *vt* oscurecer; (*colour*) hacer más oscuro; **in a ~ed room** en un cuarto oscuro. **2** *vi* oscurecerse; (*sky*) anublarse.
dark-eyed [,dɑːk'aɪd] *adj* de ojos oscuros.
darkie‡ ['dɑːkɪ] *n* negro *m*, -a *f*.
darkish ['dɑːkɪʃ] *adj* algo oscuro; *hair etc* algo moreno.
darkly ['dɑːklɪ] *adv* misteriosamente.
darkness ['dɑːknɪs] *n* oscuridad *f*; tinieblas *fpl*; **the house was in ~** la casa estaba a oscuras; **to cast sb into outer ~** condenar a uno a las penas infernales.
darkroom ['dɑːkrum] *n* cuarto *m* oscuro.
dark-skinned [,dɑːk'skɪnd] *adj* de piel morena.
darling ['dɑːlɪŋ] **1** *n* querido *m*, -a *f*; (*in direct address*) querido, querida, mi vida, mi cielo; **the ~ of the muses** el querido de las musas; **yes ~** sí querida; **she's a little ~** (*child*) es un encanto.
2 *adj* muy querido; **a ~ little hat*** un sombrerito que es un encanto; **a ~ little house*** una casita adorable.
darn¹* [dɑːn] *excl*: **~!, ~ it!** ¡condenación!
darn² [dɑːn] **1** *n* zurcido *m*, zurcidura *f*. **2** *vt* zurcir.
darned* [dɑːnd] *adj* condenado, maldito.
darning ['dɑːnɪŋ] *n* (*act*) zurcidura *f*; (*garments*) cosas *fpl*

por zurcir.

darning-needle [ˈdɑːnɪŋˌniːdl] *n* aguja *f* de zurcir.

darning-wool [ˈdɑːnɪŋˌwʊl] *n* hilo *m* de zurcir.

dart [dɑːt] **1** *n* (**a**) (*Mil*) dardo *m*, saeta *f*.

(**b**) (*in game*) rehilete *m*, dardo *m*, flecha *f*; **to play ~s** jugar a los dardos.

(**c**) (*Sew*) sisa *f*.

(**d**) (*movement*) movimiento *m* rápido; **to make a ~ for** precipitarse hacia.

2 *vt look* lanzar.

3 *vi* lanzarse, precipitarse (*for, to* hacia).

◆dart away, dart off *vi* salir disparado.

dartboard [ˈdɑːtbɔːd] *n* diana *f*, blanco *m* (en el juego de dardos).

Darwinian [dɑːˈwɪnɪən] *adj* darwiniano.

Darwinism [ˈdɑːwɪnɪzəm] *n* darwinismo *m*.

Darwinist [ˈdɑːwɪnɪst] **1** *adj* darwinista. **2** *n* darwinista *mf*.

dash [dæʃ] **1** *n* (**a**) (*small quantity*) pequeña cantidad *f*, poquito *m*; **a ~ of colour** una nota de color; **with a ~ of soda** con dos gotitas de sifón.

(**b**) (*with pen*) rasgo *m*, plumada *f*; (*Morse, Typ*) raya *f*.

(**c**) (*rush*) carrera *f*; **to make a ~ for** precipitarse hacia; **to make a ~ for it** huir precipitadamente; **we shall have to make a ~ for it** tendremos que correr.

(**d**) brío *m*; **to cut a ~** hacer gran papel, destacar.

(**e**) (*Aut*) = **dashboard.**

2 *vt* (**a**) (*shatter*) romper, estrellar (*against* contra); **to ~ sth to pieces** hacer algo pedazos; **to ~ sth to the ground** tirar algo al suelo.

(**b**) *hopes* defraudar, acabar con.

3 *vi* ir de prisa, precipitarse; **we shall have to ~** tendremos que correr; **I must ~** tengo que marcharme; **the waves are ~ing against the rock** las olas se rompen contra la roca.

4 *excl* (*****: *euph*): **~!, ~ it!** ¡porras!*

◆dash away = **dash off 1.**

◆dash in *vi* entrar precipitadamente.

◆dash off 1 *vt letter* escribir de prisa; *sketch* dibujar rápidamente.

2 *vi* salir corriendo, marcharse apresuradamente.

◆dash out *vi* salir precipitadamente.

◆dash past *vi* pasar como un rayo.

◆dash up *vi* (*person*) llegar corriendo; (*car*) llegar a toda velocidad.

dashboard [ˈdæʃbɔːd] *n* cuadro *m* de mandos, tablero *m* de instrumentos.

dashed* [dæʃt] *adj* (*euph*) = **damned.**

dashing [ˈdæʃɪŋ] *adj* bizarro, gallardo, arrojado; elegante.

dashingly [ˈdæʃɪŋlɪ] *adv behave* gallardamente, arrojadamente; *dress* garbosamente.

dastardly [ˈdæstədlɪ] *adj* ruin, vil, miserable; cobarde.

DAT *n abbr of* **digital audio tape.**

data [ˈdeɪtə] *npl* (**a**) datos *mpl*. (**b**) (*Comput*) datos *mpl*; **~ capture** formulación *f* de datos; **~ dictionary, ~ directory** guía *f* de datos; **~ entry** entrada *f* de datos; **~ management** gestión *f* de datos; **~ preparation** preparación *f* de datos; **~ processing** proceso *m* de datos; **~ processor** procesador *m* de datos; **~ protection** protección *f* de datos; **~ transmission** transmisión *f* de datos, telemática *f*.

databank [ˈdeɪtəbæŋk] *n* banco *m* de datos.

database [ˈdeɪtəbeɪs] *n* base *f* de datos.

datable [ˈdeɪtəbl] *adj* datable, fechable (*to* en).

datafile [ˈdeɪtəˌfaɪl] *n* archivo *m* de datos.

datalink [ˈdeɪtəlɪŋk] *n* medio *m* de transmisión de datos.

dataphone [ˈdeɪtəfəʊn] *n* datáfono *m*.

Datapost [ˈdeɪtəpəʊst] ® *n* (*Brit*) correo *m* urgente.

date¹ [deɪt] **1** *n* (**a**) fecha *f*; **~ of birth** fecha *f* de nacimiento; **~ of issue** fecha *f* de emisión; **what's the ~?, what ~ is it today?** ¿qué día es hoy?; **closing ~, last ~** fecha *f* tope; **at a later ~** en una fecha posterior; **at some future ~** en alguna fecha futura; **at an early ~** en fecha próxima; dentro de poco; **out of ~** anticuado, (*person*) atrasado de noticias; (*expired*) caducado; **to go out of ~** quedar anticuado; **to ~** hasta la fecha; **up to ~** (*adv*) hasta la fecha; **to be up to ~** (*building etc*) tener aspecto moderno; **to be up to ~ in one's thinking** tener ideas modernas; **to be up to ~ in one's studies** estar al día en los estudios; **to bring sth up to ~** modernizar algo, poner algo al día, actualizar algo; **to bring sb up to ~** poner a uno al corriente.

(**b**) (*Fin*) plazo *m*.

(**c**) (*with girl, boy*) cita *f*; (*with friend*) compromiso *m*; **to have a ~ with sb** tener cita con uno; **have you got a ~ tonight?** ¿tienes compromiso para esta noche?; **to make a ~ with sb** citar a uno; **they made a ~ for 8 o'clock** se citaron para las 8.

(**d**) (*esp US*) pareja *f*, acompañante *mf*, novio *m*, -a *f*.

2 *vt* (**a**) (*put ~ on*) fechar, poner la fecha en.

(**b**) (*assign ~ to*) fechar (*to* en), asignar una fecha a; situar en una época.

(**c**) (*esp US**) citar; salir con.

3 *vi* (**a**) (*become old-fashioned*) ir quedando anticuado, pasar de moda.

(**b**) **to ~ back to** remontarse a; **to ~ from** datar de, ser de la época de.

date² [deɪt] *n* (*fruit*) dátil *m*; (*tree*) palmera *f* datilera.

dated [ˈdeɪtɪd] *adj* anticuado, pasado de moda.

dateline [ˈdeɪtlaɪn] *n* línea *f* de cambio de fecha.

date-palm [ˈdeɪtpɑːm] *n* palmera *f* datilera.

date-stamp [ˈdeɪtstæmp] **1** *n* fechador *m*. **2** *vt* estampar la fecha en.

dating agency [ˈdeɪtɪŋˌeɪdʒənsɪ] *n* agencia *f* de contactos.

dating service [ˈdeɪtɪŋˌsɜːvɪs] *n* servicio *m* de contactos.

dative [ˈdeɪtɪv] **1** *adj* dativo; **~ case** = **2. 2** *n* dativo *m*.

datum [ˈdeɪtəm] *n, pl* **data** dato *m*; *V* **data.**

daub [dɔːb] **1** *n* (*smear*) mancha *f*; (*bad painting*) pintarrajo *m*. **2** *vt* (*smear*) manchar (*with* de); untar (*with* de); **to ~ a wall with paint, to ~ paint on to a wall** embadurnar una pared de pintura. **3** *vi* pintarrajear.

dauber [ˈdɔːbəʳ] *n*, **daubster** [ˈdɔːbstəʳ] *n* pintor *m* de brocha gorda, mal pintor *m*.

daughter [ˈdɔːtəʳ] *n* hija *f*.

daughterboard [ˈdɔːtəˌbɔːd] *n* placa *f* hija.

daughter-in-law [ˈdɔːtərɪnlɔː] *n, pl* **daughters-in-law** nuera *f*, hija *f* política.

daunt [dɔːnt] *vt* acobardar, intimidar, desalentar; **nothing ~ed** sin inmutarse.

daunting [ˈdɔːntɪŋ] *adj* desalentador, amedrentador.

dauntless [ˈdɔːntlɪs] *adj* impávido, intrépido.

dauntlessly [ˈdɔːntlɪslɪ] *adv* impávidamente; **to carry on ~** continuar impávido.

Dave [deɪv] *nm familiar form of* **David.**

davenport [ˈdævnpɔːt] *n* (*Brit: desk*) escritorio *m* pequeño; (*US*) sofá *m*, sofá-cama *m*.

David [ˈdeɪvɪd] *nm* David.

davit [ˈdævɪt] *n* pescante *m*.

Davy Jones [ˈdeɪvɪˈdʒəʊnz] *n*: **~' locker** el fondo del mar (*tumba de los marineros ahogados*).

dawdle [ˈdɔːdl] **1** *vt*: **to ~ away** malgastar. **2** *vi* perder el tiempo, holgazanear; (*in walking etc*) andar muy despacio, ir muy despacio.

dawdler [ˈdɔːdləʳ] *n* holgazán *m*, -ana *f*, ocioso *m*, -a *f*; persona *f* que anda despacio, rezagado *m*, -a *f*.

dawdling [ˈdɔːdlɪŋ] **1** *adj* que pierde el tiempo, que holgazanea. **2** *n* pérdida *f* de tiempo.

dawn [dɔːn] **1** *n* alba *f*, amanecer *m*; (*fig*) aurora *f*, nacimiento *m*; **~ chorus** coro *m* del alba; **at ~** al alba; **from ~ to dusk** de sol a sol; **to get up with the ~** madrugar.

2 *vi* (**a**) amanecer, alborear, romper el día; **a new epoch has ~ed** ha nacido una época nueva.

(**b**) **it ~ed on me that ...** caí en la cuenta de que ..., empecé a comprender que ...

dawning [ˈdɔːnɪŋ] **1** *adj hope etc* naciente. **2** *n* = **dawn 1.**

day [deɪ] *n* (**a**) día *m*; (*working period etc*) jornada *f*; **an 8-hour ~** una jornada de 8 horas.

(**b**) (*with prep etc*) **~ after ~, ~ in ~ out** día a día, día tras día; **~ and night** día y noche; **the ~ after** el día siguiente, al día siguiente; **the ~ after tomorrow** pasado mañana; **the ~ before** el día anterior; **the ~ before yesterday** anteayer; **two ~s before this** dos días antes de esto; **the ~ before the coronation** la víspera de la coronación; **~ off** día *m* libre; **~ by ~** día por día, de día a día (*LAm*); **by ~** de día; **by the ~** diariamente, día a día, cada día, al día; **every other ~** un día sí y otro no; **from ~ to ~** de día en día; **in this ~ and age** en estos tiempos nuestros; **in my ~** en mis tiempos; **in the ~s of Queen Elizabeth, in Queen Elizabeth's ~** en tiempos de la reina Isabel; **on the ~ everything will be all right** para el día en cuestión todo estará en orden; **these ~s** estos días; **to this ~** hasta el día de hoy; **it's a year to the ~ since she died** murió precisamente hoy hace un año; **this ~ week** de hoy en ocho días.

(**c**) (*with adj etc*) **D~ of Judgement** día *m* del Juicio Final; **~ of reckoning** (*fig*) día *m* de ajustar cuentas; **it was a black ~ for the country** fue un día negro (*or* aciago) para el país; **it's early ~s yet** todavía es pronto; **one ~, some ~** algún día; **one fine ~, one of these ~s** el día menos pensado; **good ~!** ¡buenos días!; **the good old ~s** los buenos tiempos pasados; **any old ~** el mejor día; **until my dying ~** hasta la muerte.

(**d**) (*with verb*) **that'll be the ~** me gustaría verlo, habría que verlo; **she's 40 if she's a ~** tiene a lo menos 40 años; **to call it a ~** dejar de trabajar (*etc*), suspender el trabajo (*etc*); darlo por acabado; **let's call it a ~** terminemos ya; **to carry the ~** ganar la victoria; **to give sb his ~ in court** (*US**) darle a uno la oportunidad de explicarse; **it has had its ~** ha dejado ya de ser útil, ya pasó aquello; **you don't look a ~ older** no pasan por ti los días, no pareces un día más viejo; **it made my ~** hizo que el día fuese feliz para mí; **it has seen better ~s** ya no vale lo que antes; **to take a ~ off** darse un día libre, no presentarse en el trabajo (*etc*).

day-bed ['deɪbed] *n* (*US*) meridiana *f*.

day-boarder ['deɪ'bɔːdəʳ] *n* (*Scol*) alumno *m*, -a *f* de media pensión.

daybook ['deɪbʊk] *n* diario *m*; (*US*) agenda *f*.

dayboy ['deɪbɔɪ] *n* (*Brit Scol*) externo *m*.

daybreak ['deɪbreɪk] *n* amanecer *m*; **at ~** al amanecer.

day-care ['deɪkɛəʳ] *attr*: **~ centre** guardería *f*; **~ services** (*Brit*) servicios *mpl* de guardería.

day-centre ['deɪˌsentəʳ] *n* (*Brit*) centro *m* de día.

daydream ['deɪdriːm] **1** *n* ensueño *m*, ilusión *f*. **2** *vi* soñar despierto.

daygirl ['deɪgɜːl] *n* (*Brit Scol*) externa *f*.

day-labourer, (*US*) **day-laborer** ['deɪ'leɪbərəʳ] *n* jornalero *m*.

daylight ['deɪlaɪt] *n* luz *f*, luz *f* del día; **it's ~ robbery*** es una extorsión; **to beat** (*or* **knock**) **the living ~s out of sb*** dar una tremenda paliza a uno; **to scare the ~(s) out of sb*** dar un susto de muerte a uno; **to see ~** empezar a ver el final de un trabajo (*etc*).

daylight-saving ['deɪlaɪtˌseɪvɪŋ] *n* cambio *m* de hora; **~ time** hora *f* de verano.

daylong ['deɪˌlɒŋ] (*liter*) **1** *adj* que dura todo el día. **2** *adv* todo el día.

day-nurse ['deɪˌnɜːs] *n* enfermera *f* diurna.

day-nursery ['deɪˌnɜːsərɪ] *n* guardería *f* infantil.

day-old ['deɪ'əʊld] *adj chick* de un día.

day-release course [ˌdeɪrɪ'liːsˌkɔːs] *n* (*Brit*: *Comm, Ind*) curso *m* no recuperable.

day-return ['deɪrɪ'tɜːn] *n* (*Brit*: *also* **~ ticket**) billete *m* barato de ida y vuelta en un día.

day-school ['deɪˌskuːl] *n*: **to go to ~** (*Scol*) ir a un colegio sin internado.

day-shift ['deɪʃɪft] *n* turno *m* de día.

daytime ['deɪtaɪm] *n* día *m*; **in the ~** de día.

day-to-day ['deɪtə'deɪ] *adj* cotidiano, rutinario; **on a ~ basis** día por día.

day-trip ['deɪtrɪp] *n* excursión *f* de ida y vuelta en un día.

day-tripper ['deɪˌtrɪpəʳ] *n* excursionista *mf*.

daze [deɪz] **1** *n*: **to be in a ~** estar aturdido. **2** *vt* aturdir; (*dazzle*) deslumbrar.

dazed [deɪzd] *adj* aturdido.

dazzle ['dæzl] **1** *n* lo brillante, brillo *m*. **2** *vt* deslumbrar (*also fig*); **to be ~d by** (*fig*) quedar deslumbrado por.

dazzling ['dæzlɪŋ] *adj* deslumbrante, deslumbrador.

dazzlingly ['dæzlɪŋlɪ] *adv shine* deslumbradoramente; **~ beautiful** deslumbrantemente hermoso.

DB *abbr of* **database**.

dB *abbr of* **decibel** decibelio *m*, db *m*.

DBMS *n abbr of* **database management system** sistema *m* de manejo de base de datos.

DBS *n abbr of* **direct broadcasting by satellite**.

DC *n* (**a**) (*Elec*) *abbr of* **direct current**. (**b**) (*US*) *abbr of* **District of Columbia**.

DCF *n abbr of* **discounted cash-flow**.

D.D. *n* (**a**) (*Univ*) *abbr of* **Doctor of Divinity** Doctor *m* en Teología. (**b**) (*US Mil*) *abbr of* **dishonorable discharge** licencia *f* deshonrosa.

D-day ['diːdeɪ] *n* día *m* de la invasión aliada de Normandía (*6 junio 1944*); (*fig*) día *m* 'D'.

DDS *n* (*US*) *abbr of* **Doctor of Dental Science** (*or* **Surgery**).

DDT *n abbr of* **dichlorodiphenyltrichloroethane** diclorodifeniltricloroetano *m*, DDT.

DE (**a**) (*US*) *abbr of* **Delaware**. (**b**) (*Brit*) *abbr of* **Department of Employment**.

de... [diː] *pref* de...

DEA *n* (*US*) *abbr of* **Drug Enforcement Administration** *departamento para la lucha contra la droga*.

deacon ['diːkən] *n* diácono *m*.

deaconess ['diːkənes] *n* diaconisa *f*.

deactivate [diː'æktɪveɪt] *vt* desactivar.

dead [ded] **1** *adj* (**a**) muerto; **~ man** muerto *m*; (*****) botella *f* vacía; **~ march** marcha *f* fúnebre; **the ~ king** el difunto rey; **as ~ as the dodo, as ~ as a doornail, as ~ as mutton** más muerto que mi abuela; **to be ~** estar muerto; **he has been ~ 3 years** hace 3 años que murió; **to be ~ on arrival** (**in hospital**) ingresar cadáver; **to drop ~** caer muerto, morir de repente; **drop ~!*** ¡vete al cuerno!*; **to flog** (*Brit*) *or* **beat** (*US*) **a ~ horse** machacar en hierro frío; **I wouldn't be seen ~ in a hat like that!** ¡ese sombrero, ni para un apuro!; **~ men tell no tales** los muertos no hablan; *V* **set 1** (**f**).

(**b**) (*inactive etc*) *limb* sin sentido; *town* muerto, desierto; *language* muerto; *leaf* marchito, seco; *ball* parado, fuera de juego; *colour, fire* apagado; *wire* sin corriente; **~ matter** materia *f* inanimada; **~ season** estación *f* muerta.

(**c**) (*obsolete*) anticuado; **~ letter** letra *f* muerta; **all that stuff's pretty ~ now** todo eso ya no tiene interés.

(**d**) (*absolute, exact*) *silence* profundo; *stop* en seco, repentino; **~ calm** calma *f* chicha; **~ centre** el mismo centro; (*Mech*) punto *m* muerto; **~ certainty** seguridad *f* completa; **~ level** superficie *f* completamente plana; **a ~ ringer for** el doble de, la viva imagen de.

(**e**) **to cut sb ~** hacer el vacío a uno, no hacer caso alguno a uno.

2 *adv* (*Brit*) completamente, totalmente; **~ drunk** borracho como una cuba; **~ easy** facilón, chupado‡; **~ level** completamente plano; **~ slow** muy despacio; **~ straight** completamente recto; **~ tired** hecho polvo, muerto de cansancio; **~ between the eyes** justo entre los ojos; **~ on the target** exactamente en el blanco, en el mismo blanco; **we got there ~ on time** llegamos a la hora exacta, llegamos con toda puntualidad; **to be ~ against sth** estar totalmente opuesto a algo; **to be ~ certain** estar completamente seguro; **to be ~ set on doing sth** estar decidido a hacer algo; **to stop ~** parar(se) en seco.

3 *n* (**a**) **the ~** los muertos.

(**b**) **at ~ of night, in the ~ of night** en plena noche, en las altas horas; **in the ~ of winter** en lo más recio del invierno.

dead-and-alive ['dedənə'laɪv] *adj* aburrido, monótono.

dead-beat 1 ['ded'biːt] *adj* rendido; **to be ~** estar hecho polvo. **2** ['dedbiːt] *n* (*US**) gorrón *m*, vagabundo *m*.

deadbolt ['dedbəʊlt] *n* (*US*) cerrojo *m* de seguridad.

deaden ['dedn] *vt noise etc* amortiguar; *pain* aliviar.

dead end ['ded'end] *n* callejón *m* sin salida; **to reach a ~** (*fig*) llegar a un punto muerto; **~ job** trabajo *m* sin futuro; **~ kids** (*US*) chicos *mpl* de la calle.

deadening ['dednɪŋ] *adj boredom etc* de mala muerte.

dead heat ['ded'hiːt] **1** *n* empate *m*. **2** *vi* empatar (*with* con).

deadline ['dedlaɪn] *n* fecha *f* tope, fecha *f* límite, plazo *m*; hora *f* de cierre; **we cannot meet the government's ~** no podemos terminarlo (*etc*) antes de la fecha señalada por el gobierno.

deadliness ['dedlɪnɪs] *n* (*of poison*) letalidad *f*; (*of aim*) certeza *f*; (*boredom*) tedio *m*, esplín *m*.

deadlock ['dedlɒk] **1** *n* parálisis *f*; callejón *m* sin salida; **the ~ is complete** la parálisis es total, no se ve salida alguna; **to reach ~** llegar a un punto muerto. **2** *vt*: **to be ~ed** estar en un punto muerto.

deadly ['dedlɪ] **1** *adj* (**a**) mortal (*also fig*); *aim* exacto, certero; *criticism* devastador; **~ sin** pecado *m* capital; **with ~ accuracy** con la más absoluta exactitud.

(**b**) (*****) fatal*, malísimo.

2 *adv*: **~ dull** terriblemente aburrido, aburridísimo.

deadness ['dednɪs] *n* inercia *f*, falta *f* de vida.

deadnettle ['dedˌnetl] *n* ortiga *f* muerta.

deadpan ['dedˌpæn] *adj* sin expresión, inexpresivo.

dead reckoning ['ded'reknɪŋ] *n* estima *f*.

Dead Sea ['ded'siː] *n* Mar *m* Muerto; **the ~ Scrolls** los manuscritos del Mar Muerto.

deadstock [ˌded'stɒk] *n* aperos *mpl*.

dead weight [ˌded'weɪt] *n* peso *m* muerto; (*of vehicle*) tara *f*; (*fig*) lastre *m*, carga *f* inútil.

deadwood ['ded'wʊd] *n* (*fig*) persona *f* inútil, gente *f* inútil, cosas *fpl* inútiles.

deaf [def] **1** *adj* sordo (*to* a); **as ~ as a post** sordo como una tapia; **~ to all appeals** sordo a todos los ruegos; **the plea fell on ~ ears** escucharon el ruego como quien oye llover; **to turn a ~ ear to** hacer oídos sordos a.

2 *n*: **the ~** los sordos *mpl*.

deaf-aid ['defeɪd] *n* aparato *m* del oído, audífono *m*.

deaf-and-dumb ['defən'dʌm] *adj* sordomudo; **~ alphabet**

alfabeto *m* de los sordomudos.
deafen ['defn] *vt* ensordecer, asordar.
deafening ['defnɪŋ] *adj* ensordecedor.
deaf-mute ['def'mju:t] *n* sordomudo *m*, -a *f*.
deafness ['defnɪs] *n* sordera *f*.
deal¹ [di:l] *n* (**a**) (*wood*) madera *f* de pino (*or* abeto) (**b**) (*plank*) tablón *m*; (*beam*) viga *f*.
deal² [di:l] **1** *n* (**a**) (*Comm*) transacción *f*, negocio *m*, trato *m*; **big ~** negocio *m* importante; **big ~!*** (*iro*) ¡gran cosa!; **don't make such a big ~ out of it!*** ¡no hagas una montaña de un grano de arena!
(**b**) (*agreement*) pacto *m*, convenio *m*; (*secret*) pacto *m* secreto; **it's a ~!** ¡trato hecho!; **to do a ~ with** hacer un trato con; **we might do a ~** podríamos llegar a un acuerdo; **we fear A might do a ~ with B** tememos que A pudiera hacer una componenda con B.
(**c**) (*arrangement, treatment*) trato *m*; **New D~** (*US*) Nueva Política *f*, Nuevo Programa *m*, Nuevo Trato *m*; **a new ~ for the miners** un nuevo arreglo de salarios para los mineros; **he got a very bad ~** recibió un trato muy injusto, le trataron muy injustamente; **we're looking for a better ~** buscamos un arreglo más equitativo.
(**d**) (*Cards*) reparto *m*; **whose ~ is it?** ¿a quién le toca dar?
(**e**) (*amount*) **a good ~** bastante, mucho; **a great ~** muchísimo; **a great ~ of** gran cantidad de; **to make a great ~ of** *person* estimar mucho a, *thing* dar importancia a.
2 (*irr*: *pret and ptp* **dealt**) *vt* (**a**) *cards* dar.
(**b**) *blow* dar, descargar; **to ~ a blow to** (*fig*) destruir de un golpe; **to ~ a blow for freedom** librar una batalla en pro de la libertad.
3 *vi* (**a**) (*Comm etc*) comerciar; comprar y vender; cerrar un trato. (**b**) (*Cards*) ser mano.
◆**deal in** *vi* tratar en, comerciar en.
◆**deal out** *vt* repartir.
◆**deal with** *vt* (**a**) *person* tratar con, tener relaciones con; **he dealt very fairly with me** se portó muy bien conmigo; **he dealt cleverly with the ambassador** se las arregló inteligentemente con el embajador; **I'll ~ with him** yo me ocuparé de él; **he is used to ~ing with criminals** está acostumbrado a tratar con criminales.
(**b**) *problem* ocuparse de; hacer frente a; **how should we ~ with this problem?** ¿qué hemos de hacer con este problema?; **the matter has been dealt with** el asunto está concluido; **how will the government ~ with coal?** ¿qué política tiene el gobierno para el carbón?
(**c**) *subject in book etc* tratar de, versar sobre, tener por tema; **he dealt with Africa in his speech** en su discurso se ocupó de África; **the book ~s with war** el libro versa sobre la guerra.
(**d**) (*punish*) castigar; **the offenders will be dealt with** se castigará a los delincuentes; **they were dealt with severely** se les castigó de modo ejemplar.
(**e**) (*finish off*) *work* terminar, concluir; *person* despachar.
(**f**) (*in shop*) **which shop do you ~ with?** ¿en qué tienda compras tus cosas?
dealer ['di:ləʳ] *n* comerciante *m*, tratante *m* (*in* en); concesionario *m*, -a *f*; (*in drugs*) traficante *mf*; (*retail*) distribuidor *m* (*in* de), proveedor *m*; (*Cards*) repartidor *m*, -ora *f*, dador *m*, -ora *f*.
dealership ['di:ləʃɪp] *n* (*US*) representación *f*, concesión *f*.
dealing ['di:lɪŋ] *n* (**a**) (*also* **~ out**) reparto *m*, distribución *f*; (*Cards*) reparto *m*. (**b**) (*St Ex*) comercio *m*; *V* **wheel**.
dealings ['di:lɪŋz] *npl* (**a**) (*Fin*) transacciones *fpl*. (**b**) (*relations*) trato *m*, relaciones *fpl*; **to have ~ with** tratar con, tener relaciones con; **I wish to have no ~ with him** no quiero tener nada que ver con él.
dealt [delt] *pret and ptp of* **deal²**.
dean [di:n] *n* (*Eccl*) deán *m*; (*Brit Univ etc*) decano *m*.
dear [dɪəʳ] **1** *adj* (**a**) *person etc* querido; **a very ~ friend of mine** un amigo mío muy querido; **my ~est friend** mi más íntimo amigo; **he was very ~ to all of us** fue querido de todos nosotros; **because your country is very ~ to me** por el mucho amor que le tengo a vuestra patria.
(**b**) (*in letters*) **D~ John, D~ Mr White** mi querido amigo; **D~ Dr Green** (*from colleague*) mi querido amigo y colega; (*Comm etc*) **D~ Sir** muy señor mío, **D~ Sirs** muy señores míos; **D~ Miss Brown** estimada Señorita; **D~ Mrs Black** estimada Señora de Black; **D~ Madam** estimada Señora; **D~ Sir or Madam** estimado Señor, estimada Señora; **D~ John letter** carta *f* de ruptura.
(**c**) (*expensive*) caro, costoso; *shop* carero.
2 *n* (*direct address*) **my ~** querido, querida; **come along, ~** (*to child*) ven, pequeño; **be a ~ and pass the salt** ¿me das la sal, querido?; **be a ~ and phone him** sé amable y llámale; **he's a ~** es simpatiquísimo; **he's a little ~** es un niño precioso.
3 *excl*: **oh ~!, ~ me!** (*dismay*) ¡ay!, ¡Dios mío!; (*pity*) ¡qué lastima!, ¡qué pena! (*LAm*).
4 *adv sell etc* caro.
dearie* ['dɪərɪ] *n* queridito* *m*, -a *f*; **yes ~** sí, cariño; **~ me!** ¡ay!
dearly ['dɪəlɪ] *adv* (**a**) tiernamente; **to love sb ~** querer muchísimo a uno; **I would ~ like to know why** quisiera muchísimo saber por qué.
(**b**) **to pay ~ for sth** (*fig*) pagar algo caro; **it cost him ~** le costó caro.
dearness ['dɪənɪs] *n* alto precio *m*, carestía *f*.
dearth [dɜ:θ] *n* escasez *f*; falta *f*, ausencia *f*.
death [deθ] **1** *n* muerte *f*; (*euph*) fallecimiento *m*, defunción *f*; **~ to traitors!** ¡mueran los traidores!; **it will be the ~ of me** acabará conmigo, me matará; **this is ~ to our hopes** esto acaba con nuestras esperanzas; **it was ~ to the company** arruinó la sociedad; **to be in at the ~** ver el final de la caza (*etc*); **to be at ~'s door** estar a la muerte, estar in extremis; **to catch one's ~ (of cold)** coger un catarro de muerte; **to do** (*or* **put**) **to ~** matar, dar muerte a, (*Jur*) ajusticiar; **to fight to the ~** luchar a muerte; **it frightens me to ~** me da un miedo espantoso; **to hold on like grim ~** estar firmemente agarrado, (*fig*) resistir con la mayor firmeza; **he's working himself to ~** trabaja tanto que se está estropeando la salud; **he works his men to ~** a sus hombres los mata trabajando; **it worries me to ~** me preocupa muchísimo.
2 *attr*: **~ benefit** (*Insurance*) indemnización *f* (*or* beneficio *m*) por muerte; **~ blow** golpe *m* mortal; **~ cell** celda *f* de los condenados a muerte; **~ certificate** partida *f* de defunción; **~ duties** (*Brit*) derechos *mpl* de herencia, derechos *mpl* reales; **~ house** (*US*) pabellón *m* de los condenados a muerte; **~ march** marcha *f* fúnebre; **~ mask** mascarilla *f*; **~ penalty** pena *f* de muerte; **~ rate** mortalidad *f*; **~ rattle** estertor *m*; **~ ray** rayo *m* mortal; **~ roll** número *m* de víctimas, lista *f* de víctimas; **~ row** (*US*) celdas *fpl* de los condenados a muerte, corredor *m* de la muerte; **~ sentence** (condena *f* a la) pena *f* de muerte; **~ squad** escuadrón *m* de la muerte; **~ threat** amenaza *f* de muerte; **~ throes** agonía *f*; **~ toll** número *m* de víctimas; **~ warrant** sentencia *f* de muerte; **~ wish** deseo *m* de muerte.
deathbed ['deθbed] *n* lecho *m* de muerte; **~ confession** confesión *f* en el lecho de muerte; **~ conversion** conversión *f* a última hora; **~ repentance** arrepentimiento *m* de última hora.
death knell ['deθnel] *n* toque *m* de difuntos, doble *m*; **it sounded the ~ of the empire** anunció el fin del imperio, presagió la caída del imperio.
deathless ['deθlɪs] *adj* inmortal.
deathlike ['deθlaɪk] *adj* como de muerto, cadavérico.
deathly ['deθlɪ] **1** *adj* mortal; de muerte; *silence* profundo.
2 *adv* como la muerte; **~ pale** pálido como la muerte.
death's-head ['deθshed] *n* calavera *f*; **~ moth** mariposa *f* de la muerte.
deathtrap ['deθtræp] *n* sitio *m* muy peligroso.
deathwatch ['deθwɒtʃ] *attr*: **~ beetle** reloj *m* de la muerte.
deb* [deb] *n* = **débutante.**
débâcle [deɪ'bɑ:kl] *n* debacle *f*, fracaso *m*; (*Mil*) derrota *f*.
debag ['di:'bæg] *vt* (*Brit hum*) quitar (violentamente) los pantalones a.
debar [dɪ'bɑ:ʳ] *vt* excluir (*from* de); **to ~ sb from doing sth** prohibir a uno hacer algo.
debark [dɪ'bɑ:k] *vi* (*US*) desembarcar.
debarkation [di:bɑ:'keɪʃən] *n* (*US*) desembarco *m*.
debase [dɪ'beɪs] *vt* degradar, envilecer; *coinage* alterar, falsificar.
debasement [dɪ'beɪsmənt] *n* degradación *f*, envilecimiento *m*; alteración *f*, falsificación *f*.
debatable [dɪ'beɪtəbl] *adj* discutible.
debate [dɪ'beɪt] **1** *n* discusión *f*; (*Parl etc*) debate *m*; **that is in ~, that is open to ~** ése es un tema discutido. **2** *vt* discutir, debatir. **3** *vi* discutir (*with* con); **to ~ with o.s.** pensar, deliberar; **I am debating whether to do it** estoy dudando si hacerlo o no.
debater [dɪ'beɪtəʳ] *n* persona *f* que toma parte en un debate; polemista *mf*; **he was a brilliant ~** brillaba en los debates.
debating [dɪ'beɪtɪŋ] *n*: **~ is a difficult skill to learn** el saber debatir es una habilidad difícil de adquirir; **~ society** sociedad *f* de debates.

debauch [dɪ'bɔːtʃ] *vt youth* corromper; *woman* seducir.
debauched [dɪ'bɔːtʃt] *adj* vicioso.
debaucher [dɪ'bɔːtʃəʳ] *n* (*of person, taste, morals*) corruptor *m*, (*of woman*) seductor *m*.
debauchery [dɪ'bɔːtʃərɪ] *n* libertinaje *m*, corrupción *f*.
debenture [dɪ'bentʃəʳ] *n* vale *m*, bono *m*, obligación *f*.
debenture bond [dɪ'bentʃə,bɒnd] *n* obligación *f*.
debenture holder [dɪ'bentʃə,həʊldəʳ] *n* obligacionista *mf*.
debenture stock [dɪ'bentʃə,stɒk] *n* obligaciones *fpl*.
debilitate [dɪ'bɪlɪteɪt] *vt* debilitar.
debilitating [dɪ'bɪlɪteɪtɪŋ] *adj* debilitante, que debilita.
debility [dɪ'bɪlɪtɪ] *n* debilidad *f*.
debit ['debɪt] **1** *n* debe *m*; ~ **balance** saldo *m* deudor, saldo *m* negativo; ~ **card** tarjeta *f* de cobro automático; ~ **entry** débito *m*; ~ **note** nota *f* de cargo; ~ **side** debe *m*; **on the ~ side** en el lado deudor (*also fig*). **2** *vt*: **to ~ sth to sb, to ~ sb's account** cargar algo en cuenta a uno; **to ~ an account directly** domiciliar una cuenta.
debonair [,debə'neəʳ] *adj* elegante, gallardo.
Deborah ['debərə] *nf* Débora.
Debrett [də'bret] *n libro de referencia de la aristocracia del Reino Unido*, (*loosely*) anuario *m* de la nobleza.
debrief [,diː'briːf] *vt* tomar informes de (al terminarse una operación *etc*).
debriefing [,diː'briːfɪŋ] *n* informe *m* sobre una operación (*etc*).
debris ['debriː] *n* escombros *mpl*; (*Geol*) rocalla *f*.
debt [det] *n* deuda *f*; **bad ~** deuda *f* incobrable, droga *f* (*LAm*); ~ **collection** cobro *m* de morosos; ~ **collector** cobrador *m*, -ora *f* de deudas; ~ **of honour** deuda *f* de honor; ~ **ratio** razón *f* de deudas; ~ **service** (*US*), ~ **servicing** servicio *m* de la deuda; **to be in ~** tener deudas (*to* con); **to be £5 in ~** deber 5 libras (*to* a); **to be in sb's ~** (*fig*) sentirse bajo una obligación a uno; **to be out of ~** estar libre de deudas, no tener deudas; **to get into ~, to run into ~, to run up ~s** contraer deudas.
debtor ['detəʳ] *n* deudor *m*, -ora *f*; ~ **nation** nación *f* deudora.
debt-ridden ['det,rɪdn] *adj* agobiado por las deudas.
debug [,diː'bʌg] *vt* (*Tech*) resolver los problemas de, superar (*or* suprimir) las pegas de; (*remove mikes from*) quitar los micrófonos escondidos de; (*Comput*) depurar, quitar el duende de.
debugger [,diː'bʌgəʳ] *n* programa *m* de depuración.
debugging [,diː'bʌgɪŋ] *n* (*Comput*) depuración *f*.
debunk ['diː'bʌŋk] *vt* quitar lo falso y legendario de; desacreditar, demoler; *person* desenmascarar.
début ['deɪbuː] *n* debú *m*, presentación *f*; **to make one's ~** (*Theat*) hacer su presentación, estrenarse; (*in society*) presentarse en la sociedad, ponerse de largo.
débutante ['debjuːtɑ̃ːnt] *n* joven *f* que se presenta en la sociedad, debutante *f*.
Dec. *abbr of* **December** diciembre *m*, dic.
dec. *abbr of* **deceased**.
decade ['dekeɪd] *n* década *f*, decenio *m*.
decadence ['dekədəns] *n* decadencia *f*.
decadent ['dekədənt] *adj* decadente.
decaffeinated [,diː'kæfɪneɪtɪd] *adj* descafeinado.
decagram(me) ['dekəgræm] *n* decagramo *m*.
decal [dɪ'kæl] *n* (*US*) pegatina *f*.
decalcification ['diː,kælsɪfɪ'keɪʃən] *n* descalcificación *f*.
decalcify [,diː'kælsɪfaɪ] *vt* descalcificar.
decalitre, (*US*) **decaliter** ['dekə,liːtəʳ] *n* decalitro *m*.
decametre, (*US*) **decameter** ['dekə,miːtəʳ] *n* decámetro *m*.
decamp [dɪ'kæmp] *vi* (*Mil*) decampar; (*fig*) largarse, fugarse, rajarse (*LAm*).
decant [dɪ'kænt] *vt* decantar.
decanter [dɪ'kæntəʳ] *n* jarra *f*.
decapitate [dɪ'kæpɪteɪt] *vt* decapitar, degollar, descabezar.
decapitation [dɪ,kæpɪ'teɪʃən] *n* decapitación *f*, degollación *f*.
decarbonization ['diː,kɑːbənaɪ'zeɪʃən] *n* (*Aut*) descarburación *f*; (*of steel*) descarbonación *f*.
decarbonize [diː'kɑːbənaɪz] *vt* descarburar; descarbonar.
decasyllable ['dekəsɪləbl] *n* decasílabo *m*.
decathlon [dɪ'kæθlən] *n* decatlón *m*.
decay [dɪ'keɪ] **1** *n* decadencia *f*, decaimiento *m*; (*rotting*) pudrición *f*; (*of teeth*) caries *f*; (*of building*) desmoronamiento *m*.
2 *vt* deteriorar, pudrir.
3 *vi* decaer, desmoronarse; (*rot*) pudrirse; (*teeth*) cariarse; (*building*) desmoronarse, arruinarse.
decayed [dɪ'keɪd] *adj wood etc* podrido; *teeth* cariado; *family* venido a menos.
decaying [dɪ'keɪɪŋ] *adj food* en estado de putrefacción; *vegetation etc* podrido, pútrido; *flesh* en descomposición; *tooth* cariado; *building* deteriorado, en ruinas; *stone* que se descompone; *civilization* decadente.
decease [dɪ'siːs] **1** *n* fallecimiento *m*. **2** *vi* fallecer.
deceased [dɪ'siːst] **1** *adj* difunto. **2** *n*: **the ~** el difunto, la difunta.
deceit [dɪ'siːt] *n* engaño *m*, fraude *m*; (*lying*) mentira *f*.
deceitful [dɪ'siːtfʊl] *adj* engañoso, falso, fraudulento; (*lying*) mentiroso.
deceitfully [dɪ'siːtfəlɪ] *adv* engañosamente; falsamente.
deceitfulness [dɪ'siːtfʊlnɪs] *n* falsedad *f*.
deceive [dɪ'siːv] **1** *vt* engañar; *hopes* defraudar; **if my memory does not ~ me** si mal no recuerdo; **I was ~d into buying it** me engañaron para que lo comprara; **I was ~d into thinking it was new** me engañé al pensar que era nuevo; **let nobody be ~d by this** que nadie padezca engaño en este asunto.
2 *vr*: **to ~ o.s.** engañarse, equivocarse.
deceiver [dɪ'siːvəʳ] *n* impostor *m*, -ora *f*, embustero *m*, -a *f*; (*of woman*) seductor *m*.
decelerate [diː'seləreɪt] *vt* aminorar la marcha de, desacelerar, decelerar.
deceleration ['diː,selə'reɪʃən] *n* desaceleración *f*, deceleración *f*, disminución *f* de velocidad.
December [dɪ'sembəʳ] *n* diciembre *m*.
decency ['diːsənsɪ] *n* (**a**) decencia *f*; **offence against ~** atentado *m* contra el pudor; **it is no more than common ~ to** + *infin* la más mínima educación exige que + *subj*.
(**b**) **decencies** buenas costumbres *fpl*.
(**c**) (*kindness*) bondad *f*, amabilidad *f*.
decent ['diːsənt] *adj* (**a**) (*seemly*) decente; **are you ~?** (*hum*) ¿estás visible?
(**b**) (*kind*) simpático, amable, bueno; **he's a ~ sort** es buena persona; **he was very ~ to me** fue muy amable conmigo.
(**c**) (*passable*) bastante bueno; (*US**: *great*) cutre*; **a ~ sum** una cantidad considerable.
decently ['diːsəntlɪ] *adv* (**a**) decentemente. (**b**) amablemente, con amabilidad; **he very ~ offered it to me** muy amablemente me lo ofreció.
decentralization [diː,sentrəlaɪ'zeɪʃən] *n* descentralización *f*.
decentralize [diː'sentrəlaɪz] *vt* descentralizar.
decentre, (*US*) **decenter** [diː'sentəʳ] *vt* descentrar.
deception [dɪ'sepʃən] *n* engaño *m*, fraude *m*.
deceptive [dɪ'septɪv] *adj* engañoso.
deceptively [dɪ'septɪvlɪ] *adv*: **the village looks ~ near** el pueblo parece engañosamente cerca; **he was ~ obedient/still** *etc* estaba engañosamente obediente/quieto *etc*.
deceptiveness [dɪ'septɪvnɪs] *n* carácter *m* engañoso.
decibel ['desɪbel] *n* decibel(io) *m*.
decide [dɪ'saɪd] **1** *vt* decidir, determinar; **that ~d me** eso me decidió.
2 *vi* decidir, resolver; **to ~ to do sth** decidir hacer algo, decidirse a hacer algo, resolverse a hacer algo; **to ~ against sth** optar por no hacer (*etc*) algo; **to ~ in favour of sb** decidir a favor de uno.
◆**decide on** *vt*: **to ~ on sth** decidir por algo, optar por algo, quedar en algo.
decided [dɪ'saɪdɪd] *adj person* decidido, resuelto; *difference etc* marcado, acusado; (*unquestionable*) indudable.
decidedly [dɪ'saɪdɪdlɪ] *adv* decididamente; **he said ~** dijo con resolución; **it is ~ difficult** indudablemente es difícil.
decider [dɪ'saɪdəʳ] *n* (*Sport*) (partido *m* de) desempate *m*; partido *m* decisivo; gol *m* (*etc*) decisivo.
deciding [dɪ'saɪdɪŋ] *adj factor etc* decisivo, concluyente; *vote* de calidad, decisivo.
deciduous [dɪ'sɪdjʊəs] *adj* de hoja caduca.
decile ['desɪl] *n* decil *m*.
decilitre, (*US*) **deciliter** ['desɪ,liːtəʳ] *n* decilitro *m*.
decimal ['desɪməl] **1** *adj* decimal; ~ **currency** moneda *f* decimal; ~ **fraction** fracción *f* decimal; ~ **point** coma *f* decimal, coma *f* de decimales; ~ **system** sistema *m* métrico; **I've worked it out to two ~ places** lo he calculado hasta centésimas. **2** *n* decimal *m*.
decimalization [,desɪməlaɪ'zeɪʃən] *n* decimalización *f*.
decimalize ['desɪməlaɪz] *vt* decimalizar.
decimate ['desɪmeɪt] *vt* diezmar (*also fig*).
decimation [,desɪ'meɪʃən] *n* diezmamiento *m*.
decimetre, (*US*) **decimeter** ['desɪ,miːtəʳ] *n* decímetro *m*.
decipher [dɪ'saɪfəʳ] *vt* descifrar.
decipherable [dɪ'saɪfərəbl] *adj* descifrable.
decision [dɪ'sɪʒən] *n* (**a**) (*a resolve*) decisión *f*; (*Jur*) fallo *m*; ~ **table** (*Comput*) tabla *f* de decisiones; **to make** (*or* **come to, take**) **a ~** tomar una decisión. (**b**) (*resoluteness*)

resolución *f*, firmeza *f*.

decision-maker [dɪ'sɪʒən,meɪkəʳ] *n* persona *f* que toma decisiones.

decision-making [dɪ'sɪʒən,meɪkɪŋ] **1** *attr*: ~ **process** proceso *m* decisorio; ~ **unit** unidad *f* de adopción de decisiones. **2** *n*: **he's good at** ~ es bueno tomando decisiones.

decisive [dɪ'saɪsɪv] *adj* (**a**) *factor etc* decisivo, concluyente.
(**b**) (*conclusive*) terminante; *manner* tajante, categórico, firme.

decisively [dɪ'saɪsɪvlɪ] *adv* con decisión, con resolución; **to be** ~ **beaten** ser derrotado de modo decisivo.

decisiveness [dɪ'saɪsɪvnɪs] *n* carácter *m* tajante; firmeza *f*.

deck [dek] **1** *n* (**a**) cubierta *f*; (*of bus*) piso *m*; (*) suelo *m*, superficie *f*; (*US*‡: *drugs*) saquito *m* de heroina; ~ **cargo** carga *f* de cubierta; **top** ~, **upper** ~ (*of bus*) piso *m* de arriba; **to clear the** ~**s** (*fig*) despejar la mesa (*etc*); **he hit the** ~* cayó al suelo.
(**b**) (*esp US*: *of cards*) baraja *f*.
(**c**) (*of record player*) platina *f*.
2 *vt* (**a**) (*also* **to** ~ **out**) engalanar, adornar (*with* de); **all** ~**ed out** muy ataviado, de punta en blanco.
(**b**) (*US*‡) derribar de un golpe.

deck cabin ['dek,kæbɪn] *n* cabina *f* de cubierta.

deckchair ['dek,tʃɛəʳ] *n* tumbona *f*, perezosa *f* (*LAm*).

-decker ['dekəʳ] *n ending in compounds*: **single**~ (*bus*) autobús *m* de un piso; **three**~ (*Naut*) barco *m* de tres cubiertas; *V* **double-decker**.

deckhand ['dekhænd] *n* marinero *m* de cubierta.

deckhouse ['dekhaus] *n*, *pl* **deckhouses** ['dek,hauzɪz] camareta *f* alta.

declaim [dɪ'kleɪm] *vt* declamar.

declamation [,deklə'meɪʃən] *n* declamación *f*.

declamatory [dɪ'klæmətərɪ] *adj* declamatorio.

declaration [,deklə'reɪʃən] *n* declaración *f*.

declare [dɪ'klɛəʳ] **1** *vt* declarar, afirmar; *dividend* anunciar; *war* declarar; **to** ~ **sth to the customs** declarar algo en la aduana; **have you anything to** ~? ¿tiene algo que declarar?; **to** ~ **sb to be a traitor** dar a uno por traidor.
2 *vi*: **to** ~ **for, to** ~ **in favour of** pronunciarse a favor de; **well I** ~! ¡vaya por Dios!
3 *vr*: **to** ~ **o.s.** declararse; **to** ~ **o.s. surprised** confesar su sorpresa; **he** ~**d himself beaten** se dio por vencido; **to** ~ **o.s. against** afirmar su oposición a, pronunciarse en contra de.

declared [dɪ'klɛəd] *adj* declarado, abierto.

declarer [dɪ'klɛərəʳ] *n* (*Bridge*) declarante *mf*.

déclassé [deɪ'klæseɪ] *adj* desprestigiado, empobrecido; que ha perdido su categoría social.

declassify [di:'klæsɪfaɪ] *vt information* levantar el secreto de.

declension [dɪ'klenʃən] *n* declinación *f*.

declinable [dɪ'klaɪnəbl] *adj* declinable.

decline [dɪ'klaɪn] **1** *n* (*lessening*) declinación *f*, descenso *m*, disminución *f* (*in* de); (*in price*) baja *f*; (*decay*) decaimiento *m*, decadencia *f*; (*of sun, empire*) ocaso *m*; (*Med*) debilitación *f*; **to be on the** ~ ir disminuyendo; **to go into a** ~ ir debilitándose.
2 *vt* (**a**) rehusar, negarse a aceptar.
(**b**) (*Gram*) declinar.
3 *vi* (**a**) (*go down*) declinar, disminuir; (*in price*) bajar; (*decay*) decaer; (*Med*) debilitarse; **to** ~ **in importance** ir perdiendo importancia.
(**b**) (*refuse*) rehusar; **to** ~ **to do sth** rehusar hacer algo, negarse a hacer algo.

declining [dɪ'klaɪnɪŋ] *adj*: ~ **industry** industria *f* en decadencia; ~ **interest** pérdida *f* de interés; **in my** ~ **years** en mis últimos años.

declivity [dɪ'klɪvɪtɪ] *n* declive *m*.

declutch ['di:'klʌtʃ] *vi* desembragar.

decoction [dɪ'kɒkʃən] *n* decocción *f*.

decode ['di:'kəud] *vt* descifrar; (*Ling, TV*) descodificar.

decoder [di:'kəudəʳ] *n* (*Comput, TV*) descodificador *m*.

decoding [di:'kəudɪŋ] *n* (*Comput*) descodificación *f*.

decoke (*Brit Aut*) **1** ['di:kəuk] *n* descarburación *f*. **2** [di:'kəuk] *vt* descarburar.

decollate [,di:kə'leɪt] *vt* separar, alzar.

décolletage [deɪ'kɒlətɑ:ʒ] *n* escote *m*.

décolleté(e) [deɪ'kɒlteɪ] *adj dress* escotado; *woman* en traje escotado.

decolonization [di:,kɒlənaɪ'zeɪʃən] *n* descolonización *f*.

decolonize [di:'kɒlənaɪz] *vt* descolonizar.

decompose [,di:kəm'pəuz] **1** *vt* descomponer. **2** *vi* descomponerse.

decomposition [,di:kɒmpə'zɪʃən] *n* descomposición *f*.

decompression [,di:kəm'preʃən] *n* descompresión *f*; ~ **chamber** cámara *f* de descompresión; ~ **sickness** enfermedad *f* de la descompresión.

decongestion [,di:kən'dʒestʃən] *n* descongestión *f*.

deconstruction [,di:kən'strʌkʃən] *n* deconstrucción *f*.

decontaminate [,di:kən'tæmɪneɪt] *vt* descontaminar.

decontamination ['di:kən,tæmɪ'neɪʃən] *n* descontaminación *f*.

decontrol [,di:kən'trəul] **1** *n* descontrol *m*, supresión *f* del control; liberalización *f*. **2** *vt* suprimir el control de; liberalizar.

décor ['deɪkɔ:ʳ] *n* decoración *f*; (*Theat*) decorado *m*, decoración *f*.

decorate ['dekəreɪt] *vt* (**a**) adornar, decorar (*with* de); *room* empapelar, pintar; *house* pintar. (**b**) (*Mil etc*) condecorar.

decorating ['dekəreɪtɪŋ] *n*: **interior** ~ decoración *f* del hogar.

decoration [,dekə'reɪʃən] *n* (**a**) adorno *m*, ornato *m*; (*act*) decoración *f*. (**b**) (*Mil etc*) condecoración *f*.

decorative ['dekərətɪv] *adj* (*in function*) de adorno, decorativo; (*pleasant*) hermoso, elegante; ~ **arts** artes *fpl* decorativas.

decorator ['dekəreɪtəʳ] *n* (*esp Brit*) decorador *m*; pintor *m* decorador.

decorous ['dekərəs] *adj* decoroso, correcto.

decorously ['dekərəslɪ] *adv* decorosamente, correctamente.

decorum [dɪ'kɔ:rəm] *n* decoro *m*, corrección *f*.

decoy ['di:kɔɪ] **1** *n* señuelo *m*; (*bird*) cimbel *m*, reclamo *m*; (*person*) entruchón *m*; (*fig*) señuelo *m*, trampa *f*; ~ **duck** pato *m* de reclamo.
2 *vt* atraer (*or* apartar) con señuelo (*or* mediante una estratagema), entruchar; **to** ~ **sb away** lograr mediante una estratagema que uno se aparte de un sitio.

decrease [di:'kri:s] **1** *n* disminución *f* (*in* de); **to be on the** ~ ir disminuyendo. **2** *vt* disminuir, reducir. **3** *vi* disminuirse, reducirse.

decreasing [di:'kri:sɪŋ] *adj* decreciente.

decreasingly [di:'kri:sɪŋlɪ] *adv* decrecientemente.

decree [dɪ'kri:] **1** *n* decreto *m*; ~ **absolute** fallo *m* absoluto (de divorcio); ~ **nisi** fallo *m* provisional (de divorcio). **2** *vt* decretar.

decrepit [dɪ'krepɪt] *adj* decrépito.

decrepitude [dɪ'krepɪtju:d] *n* decrepitud *f*.

decriminalization [,di:'krɪmɪnəlaɪ'zeɪʃən] *n* despenalización *f*.

decriminalize [di:'krɪmɪnəlaɪz] *vt* despenalizar.

decry [dɪ'kraɪ] *vt* desacreditar, rebajar, censurar.

dedicate ['dedɪkeɪt] **1** *vt* dedicar, consagrar; (*US*) *official building* inaugurar oficialmente. **2** *vr*: **to** ~ **o.s. to** dedicarse a.

dedicated ['dedɪkeɪtɪd] *adj* totalmente entregado, de mucha entrega, dedicado; (*Comput*) dedicado, especializado.

dedication [,dedɪ'keɪʃən] *n* (**a**) dedicación *f*. (**b**) (*in book*) dedicatoria *f*. (**c**) (*quality*) dedicación *f*, entrega *f*, devoción *f*.

deduce [dɪ'dju:s] *vt* deducir; **I** ~ **that** ... me imagino que ..., supongo que ...; **what do you** ~ **from that?** ¿qué conclusión sacas de eso?; **as can be** ~**d from** según se colige de, según se desprende de.

deducible [dɪ'dju:sɪbl] *adj* deducible (*from* de).

deduct [dɪ'dʌkt] *vt* restar (*also Math*; *from* de), descontar, rebajar; *tax etc* deducir (*from* de).

deductible [dɪ'dʌktəbl] *adj* deducible, descontable.

deduction [dɪ'dʌkʃən] *n* (**a**) (*inference*) deducción *f*, conclusión *f*; **what are your** ~**s?** ¿cuáles son sus conclusiones? (**b**) (*amount*) descuento *m*, rebaja *f*; retención *f*.

deductive [dɪ'dʌktɪv] *adj* deductivo.

deed [di:d] **1** *n* (**a**) (*act*) hecho *m*, acto *m*, acción *f*; (*brave etc*) hazaña *f*. (**b**) (*Jur*) escritura *f*; ~ **of covenant** escritura *f* de 'covenant'; ~ **of partnership** contrato *m* de sociedad; ~ **of transfer** escritura *f* de traspaso. **2** *vt* (*US Jur*) *property* transferir por acto notarial.

deed-poll ['di:d,pəul] *n*: **to change one's name by** ~ cambiar su apellido por escritura legal.

deejay* ['di:dʒeɪ] *n* pinchadiscos* *mf*.

deem [di:m] *vt* juzgar, creer; **I** ~ **it a mistake** creo que es un error; **I** ~ **him a fool** considero que es tonto; **I** ~ **it to be my duty** considero que es mi deber.

deep [di:p] **1** *adj* (**a**) (*far down*) profundo, hondo; **to be 6 metres** ~ tener una profundidad de 6 metros, tener 6 metros de hondo; ~ **end** parte *f* honda; **to go off the** ~ **end*** subirse por las paredes*; **I was thrown in at the** ~ **end** (*fig*) de entrada me enfrenté con graves problemas; desde el principio tuve que trabajar (*etc*) muy en serio; no me dieron tiempo para aprender el oficio; **the streets were half a metre** ~ **in snow** las calles tenían medio metro de nieve; **to be ~ in debt** estar lleno de deudas; **to be ~ in thought** estar absorto en la meditación; **he's pretty ~ in it** está muy metido en el asunto; **to be in ~ trouble** estar en grandes apuros; **these are ~ waters, Watson** querido Watson, aquí hay honduras.

(**b**) (*far back*) ancho; **a plot 30 m ~** un terreno de 30 m de fondo; **the ~ South** (*US*) *los estados de más al sur.*

(**c**) (*Mus*) bajo, grave.

(**d**) *colour* intenso, subido, (*and dark*) oscuro; *tan* intenso.

(**e**) (*fig*) profundo; *emotion* profundo, hondo; *mystery* profundo; *breath* profundo, a pleno pulmón; *mind* penetrante; *mourning* riguroso; *person* (*reserved*) muy reservado, insondable; (*pej*) astuto, taimado; **~ grammar** gramática *f* profunda; **~ structure** estructura *f* profunda; **he's a ~ one** la procesión le va por dentro; **it's too ~ for me** no lo entiendo, no alcanzo a entenderlo.

2 *adv*: **don't go in too ~** no te metas en la parte profunda; **the miners are ~ underground** los mineros están a una gran profundidad; **the snow lay ~** había una profunda capa de nieve; **~ in his heart** en lo más hondo del corazón; **he thrust his hand ~ into his pocket** metió la mano hasta el fondo del bolsillo; **~ into the night** hasta las altas horas de la noche; **to form up 6 ~** formarse de 6 en fondo.

3 *n*: **the ~** (*liter*) el piélago.

deep-breathing ['di:p'bri:ðɪŋ] *n* gimnasia *f* respiratoria, ejercicios *mpl* respiratorios.

deep-chested ['di:p'tʃestɪd] *adj* ancho de pecho.

deepen ['di:pən] **1** *vt hole etc* ahondar, profundizar, hacer más profundo; *voice* ahuecar; *colour, emotion* intensificar; *study* ahondar en.

2 *vi* (*water etc*) hacerse más profundo; (*colour, emotion*) intensificarse; (*gloom*) aumentarse.

deepening ['di:pənɪŋ] *adj* (**a**) que se hace más profundo.

(**b**) *meaning, mystery etc* que se vuelve más oscuro.

deep-felt ['di:p'felt] *adj* hondamente sentido.

deep-freeze ['di:p'fri:z] **1** *n* (ultra)congelador *m.* **2** *vt* (ultra)congelar.

deep-freezing [,di:p'fri:zɪŋ] *n* ultracongelación *f.*

deep-frozen [,di:p'frəuzn] *adj* ultracongelado.

deep-fry ['di:p'fraɪ] *vt* freír en aceite abundante.

deep-laid ['di:p'leɪd] *adj plan* bien preparado.

deeply ['di:plɪ] *adv* profundamente, hondamente; intensamente; **to breathe ~** respirar a pleno pulmón.

deep-rooted ['di:p'ru:tɪd] *adj* muy arraigado.

deep-sea ['di:p'si:] *adj* de altura, de alta mar; **~ diving** buceo *m* de altura; **~ fishing** pesca *f* de gran altura; **~ tug** remolcador *m* de altura.

deep-seated ['di:p'si:tɪd] *adj* profundamente arraigado.

deep-set ['di:p'set] *eyes* hundido.

deep-six‡ [,di:p'sɪks] *vt* (*US*) (*throw out*) tirar; (*kill*) cargarse*.

deer [dɪəʳ] *n* ciervo *m,* venado *m.*

deerhound ['dɪəhaʊnd] *n* galgo *m* (para cazar venados); galgo *m* escocés (de pelo lanoso).

deerskin ['dɪəskɪn] *n* piel *f* de ciervo, gamuza *f.*

deerstalker ['dɪə,stɔ:kəʳ] *n* (**a**) (*person*) cazador *m* de ciervos al acecho. (**b**) (*hat*) gorro *m* de cazador (de ciervos).

deerstalking ['dɪə,stɔ:kɪŋ] *n* caza *f* de venado.

de-escalate [,di:'eskəleɪt] *vt* desescalar.

de-escalation [di:,eskə'leɪʃən] *n* (*Mil, Pol*) desescalada *f;* (*in industrial relations*) descrispación *f.*

def* [def] *adj* fantástico*, súper*.

deface [dɪ'feɪs] *vt* desfigurar, mutilar.

de facto [deɪ'fæktəu] *adj, adv* de facto.

defalcation [,di:fæl'keɪʃən] *n* desfalco *m.*

defamation [,defə'meɪʃən] *n* difamación *f.*

defamatory [dɪ'fæmətərɪ] *adj* difamatorio.

defame [dɪ'feɪm] *vt* difamar, calumniar.

default [dɪ'fɔ:lt] **1** *n*: (**a**) **in ~ of** a falta de, en ausencia de; **judgement by ~** juicio *m* en rebeldía; **he won by ~** ganó en ausencia de su adversario; **we must not let it go by ~** no debemos permitir que lo perdamos por descuido (*or* sin hacer nada). (**b**) (*Comput*) **~ options** opciones *fpl* por defecto; **~ values** valores *mpl* por defecto.

2 *vi* (**a**) (*not pay*) no pagar, ponerse en mora; **to ~ on one's payments** no pagar los plazos (*etc*).

(**b**) (*Sport*) perder por incomparecencia.

(**c**) (*Comput*) **it always ~s to drive C** siempre va a la unidad de disco C por exclusión.

defaulter [dɪ'fɔ:ltəʳ] *n* (*on payments*) moroso *m,* -a *f;* (*Mil*) delincuente *m.*

defaulting [dɪ'fɔ:ltɪŋ] *adj* (**a**) (*Stock Exchange*) moroso. (**b**) (*Jur*) en rebeldía.

defeat [dɪ'fi:t] **1** *n* derrota *f;* **eventually he admitted ~** por fin reconoció que había sido vencido. **2** *vt* vencer, derrotar; *plan* estorbar, frustrar; *hopes* defraudar; (*Parl*) *bill etc* rechazar; **this will ~ its own ends** esto será contraproducente; **the problem ~s me** el problema me trae perplejo; **it ~ed all our efforts** burló todos nuestros esfuerzos.

defeated [dɪ'fi:tɪd] *adj army, team, player* derrotado.

defeatism [dɪ'fi:tɪzəm] *n* derrotismo *m.*

defeatist [dɪ'fi:tɪst] **1** *adj* derrotista. **2** *n* derrotista *mf.*

defecate ['defəkeɪt] *vti* defecar.

defecation [,defə'keɪʃən] *n* defecación *f.*

defect 1 ['di:fekt] *n* defecto *m.* **2** [dɪ'fekt] *vi* desertar (*from* de, *to* a).

defection [dɪ'fekʃən] *n* deserción *f,* defección *f.*

defective [dɪ'fektɪv] **1** *adj* defectuoso; (*Gram*) defectivo; *child* anormal, retrasado. **2** *n* persona *f* anormal, retrasado *m,* -a *f* mental; (*Gram*) defectivo *m.*

defector [dɪ'fektəʳ] *n* desertor *m,* -ora *f,* tránsfuga *mf.*

defence, (*US*) **defense** [dɪ'fens] **1** *n* (*all senses*) defensa *f;* **Secretary (of State) for** (*or* **Minister of**) **D~** (*Brit*), **Secretary of Defense** (*US*) Secretario *m* (de Estado) (*or* Ministro *m*) de Defensa; **Department** (*or* **Ministry**) **of D~** (*Brit*), **Department of Defense** (*US*) Departamento *m* (*or* Ministerio *m*) de Defensa; **to come out in ~ of** salir en defensa de; **what have you to say in your own ~?** ¿qué tiene Vd que decir en defensa propia?

2 *attr*: **~ counsel** abogado *mf* defensor; **~ forces** fuerzas *fpl* defensivas; **~ mechanism** mecanismo *m* de defensa; **~ spending** presupuesto *m* de las fuerzas armadas, gastos *mpl* de defensa.

defenceless, (*US*) **defenseless** [dɪ'fenslɪs] *adj* indefenso; (*fig*) inocente, inofensivo.

defencelessness, (*US*) **defenselessness** [dɪ'fenslɪsnɪs] *n* indefensión *f.*

defend [dɪ'fend] *vt* defender (*against* contra, *from* de).

defendant [dɪ'fendənt] *n* (*civil*) demandado *m,* -a *f;* (*criminal*) acusado *m,* -a *f.*

defender [dɪ'fendəʳ] *n* defensor *m,* -ora *f;* (*Sport*) defensa *mf.*

defending [dɪ'fendɪŋ] *adj champion* titular; **~ counsel** (*Jur*) abogado *mf* defensor.

defense [dɪ'fens] *n* (*US*) = **defence.**

defensible [dɪ'fensɪbl] *adj* defendible; *action etc* justificable.

defensive [dɪ'fensɪv] **1** *adj* defensivo; **~ works** fortificaciones *fpl.* **2** *n* defensiva *f;* **to be on the ~** estar a la defensiva.

defensively [dɪ'fensɪvlɪ] *adv say etc* en tono defensivo.

defensiveness [dɪ'fensɪvnɪs] *n* tono *m* (*etc*) defensivo, actitud *f* defensiva.

defer¹ [dɪ'fɜ:ʳ] *vt* aplazar, diferir, postergar (*LAm*); *conscript* dar una prórroga a.

defer² [dɪ'fɜ:ʳ] *vi*: **to ~ to sb, to ~ to sb's opinion** acatar la opinión de uno, someterse al punto de vista de uno; **in this I gladly ~ to you** en esto acepto gustoso su opinión.

deference ['defərəns] *n* deferencia *f,* respeto *m;* **in ~ to, out of ~ to** por deferencia hacia.

deferential [,defə'renʃəl] *adj* respetuoso.

deferentially [,defə'renʃəlɪ] *adv* deferentemente, respetuosamente.

deferment [dɪ'fɜ:mənt] *n,* **deferral** [dɪ'fɜ:rəl] *n* aplazamiento *m;* (*Mil*) prórroga *f.*

deferred [dɪ'fɜ:d] *adj*: **~ annuity** cuota *f* de pensión; **~ credit** crédito *m* diferido; **~ liabilities** pasivo *m* diferido; **~ payment** pago *m* a plazos.

defiance [dɪ'faɪəns] *n* desafío *m* (*of* a); oposición *f* terca (*of* a); **in ~ of** en contra de, con infracción de; **to bid ~ to** desafiar a.

defiant [dɪ'faɪənt] *adj* provocativo, insolente; *tone* desafiante, retador.

defiantly [dɪ'faɪəntlɪ] *adv* de modo provocativo, insolentemente; en tono retador, en son de reto.

defibrillator [dɪ'faɪbrɪ,leɪtəʳ] *n* desfibrilador *m.*

deficiency [dɪ'fɪʃənsɪ] *n* (*lack*) falta *f;* (*defect*) defecto *m,* deficiencia *f;* (*Comm*) déficit *m,* descubierto *m;* **~ disease** mal *m* carencial.

deficient [dɪ'fɪʃənt] *adj* deficiente; (*in quantity*) insuficiente; (*incomplete*) incompleto; (*defective*) defectuoso; (*mentally*) retrasado, anormal; **to be ~ in** carecer de, estar falto de.

deficit ['defɪsɪt] *n* déficit *m;* **to be in ~** estar en déficit, tener déficit.

defile¹ ['di:faɪl] *n* desfiladero *m.*

defile² [dɪ'faɪl] *vt* manchar, deshonrar; *flag* ultrajar; *sacred*

thing profanar.
defilement [dɪ'faɪlmənt] *n* deshonra *f*; ensuciamiento *m*, corrupción *f*; profanación *f*.
definable [dɪ'faɪnəbl] *adj* definible.
define [dɪ'faɪn] *vt* definir (*also Comput*), determinar.
definite ['defɪnɪt] *adj* claro, categórico; positivo; concreto; *date etc* determinado; (*Gram*) definido; **he was very ~ about it** nos lo dijo sin dejar lugar a dudas; **we have no ~ record of it** no nos consta de manera clara; **the plan is not yet ~** todavía el proyecto no se ha aprobado de modo definitivo.
definitely ['defɪnɪtlɪ] *adv* claramente, categóricamente; **oh, ~!, yes, ~!** sí, desde luego; **did he say so ~?** ¿lo dijo claramente?; **we are ~ not going** es seguro que no vamos; **it is ~ impossible** es francamente imposible; **the plan is not yet ~ fixed** todavía el proyecto no se ha aprobado de modo definitivo.
definition [ˌdefɪ'nɪʃən] *n* (**a**) definición *f*; **by ~** por definición. (**b**) (*Phot*) nitidez *f*, claridad *f*.
definitive [dɪ'fɪnɪtɪv] *adj* definitivo.
definitively [dɪ'fɪnɪtɪvlɪ] *adv* en definitiva, con toda seguridad, definitivamente.
deflate [diː'fleɪt] *vt* desinflar; *person* quitar los humos a; quitar los ánimos (*or* esperanzas) a; *reputation* rebajar, desacreditar; (*Fin*) causar (la) deflación en; **at this news he felt very ~d** con esta noticia se desanimó por completo.
deflation [diː'fleɪʃən] *n* desinflamiento *m*; (*Fin*) deflación *f*.
deflationary [diː'fleɪʃənərɪ] *adj* (*Fin*) deflacionista, deflacionario.
deflect [dɪ'flekt] *vt* desviar (*from* de).
deflection [dɪ'flekʃən] *n* desviación *f*.
deflector [dɪ'flektəʳ] *n* deflector *m*.
defloration [ˌdiːflɔː'reɪʃən] *n* desfloración *f*.
deflower [diː'flaʊəʳ] *vt* desflorar.
defog [diː'fɒg] *vt* desempañar.
defogger [diː'fɒgəʳ] *n* (*US*) dispositivo *m* antivaho.
defoliant [diː'fəʊlɪənt] *n* defoliante *m*.
defoliate [diː'fəʊlɪeɪt] *vt* defoliar.
defoliation [ˌdiːfəʊlɪ'eɪʃən] *n* defoliación *f*.
deforest [diː'fɒrɪst] *vt* deforestar, despoblar de árboles.
deforestation [diːˌfɒrə'steɪʃən] *n* deforestación *f*, despoblación *f* forestal.
deform [dɪ'fɔːm] *vt* deformar.
deformation [ˌdiːfɔː'meɪʃən] *n* deformación *f*.
deformed [dɪ'fɔːmd] *adj* deforme, mutilado.
deformity [dɪ'fɔːmɪtɪ] *n* deformidad *f*.
defraud [dɪ'frɔːd] *vt* defraudar (*of* de); estafar; **to ~ sb of sth** estafar algo a uno.
defray [dɪ'freɪ] *vt* sufragar, pagar, costear; **to ~ sb's expenses** sufragar los gastos de uno.
defrayal [dɪ'freɪəl] *n*, **defrayment** [dɪ'freɪmənt] *n* pago *m*.
defreeze [diː'friːz] *vt* descongelar.
defrock [diː'frɒk] *vt* apartar del sacerdocio.
defrost [diː'frɒst] *vt* deshelar, descongelar.
defroster [diː'frɒstəʳ] *n* (*US*) dispositivo *m* antivaho; (*Aut*) esprai *m* antihielo.
deft [deft] *adj* diestro, hábil.
deftly ['deftlɪ] *adv* diestramente, hábilmente.
deftness ['deftnɪs] *n* destreza *f*, habilidad *f*.
defunct [dɪ'fʌŋkt] *adj* difunto; *company etc* que ya no existe; *idea, theory* que ya no tiene validez; *scheme* que no se realizó nunca.
defuse [diː'fjuːz] *vt bomb* desactivar; *tensions* calmar, apaciguar; *situation* reducir la tensión de.
defy [dɪ'faɪ] *vt* (**a**) (*challenge*) desafiar; **to ~ sb to do sth** desafiar a uno a hacer algo.
(**b**) (*resist*) oponerse tercamente a; *order* contravenir a; *bad weather* resistir a; **it defies definition** se escapa a la definición; **it defies description** resulta imposible describirlo.
degeneracy [dɪ'dʒenərəsɪ] *n* degeneración *f*, depravación *f*.
degenerate 1 [dɪ'dʒenərɪt] *adj* degenerado.
2 [dɪ'dʒenərɪt] *n* degenerado *m*, -a *f*.
3 [dɪ'dʒenəreɪt] *vi* degenerar (*into* en); **to ~ into** (*end up being*) degenerar en, terminar siendo, terminar en; **the essay ~d into jottings** el ensayo terminó siendo meros apuntes.
degeneration [dɪˌdʒenə'reɪʃən] *n* degeneración *f*.
degenerative [dɪ'dʒenərətɪv] *adj disease etc* degenerativo.
deglamourize [diː'glæməˌraɪz] *vt* quitar el atractivo de.
degradable [dɪ'greɪdəbl] *adj* degradable; **biologically ~** biodegradable.
degradation [ˌdegrə'deɪʃən] *n* degradación *f*, envilecimiento *m*.
degrade [dɪ'greɪd] **1** *vt* degradar, envilecer. **2** *vr*: **to ~ o.s.** degradarse, aplebeyarse.
degrading [dɪ'greɪdɪŋ] *adj* degradante, envilecedor.
degree [dɪ'griː] *n* (**a**) (*Math, Astron, Gram etc*) grado *m*; **10 ~s below freezing** 10 grados bajo cero.
(**b**) (*stage in process*) etapa *f*, punto *m*; **things have reached such a ~ that ...** las cosas han llegado a tal extremo que ...; **by ~s** poco a poco, gradualmente, progresivamente; **in no ~** de ninguna manera; **in some ~, to a certain ~** hasta cierto punto; **to the highest ~** en sumo grado; **he is superstitious to a ~** (*esp Brit*) es sumamente supersticioso.
(**c**) (*Univ*) título *m*; licenciatura *f*; **~ day** día *m* de concesión de títulos; **to get a ~** sacar un título; **to take one's ~** graduarse, licenciarse, recibir un título; **to take a ~ in** licenciarse en; **to do a ~ course** (*Brit Univ*) hacer una licenciatura.
(**d**) (*social*) rango *m*, condición *f* social; **people of ~** personas *fpl* de cierto rango social.
(**e**) **third ~** interrogación *f* brutal; **to give sb the third ~** interrogar a uno brutalmente, sacudir a uno*.
dehumanize [diː'hjuːmənaɪz] *vt* deshumanizar.
dehumidifier [ˌdiːhjuː'mɪdɪfaɪəʳ] *n* (*US*) deshumedecedor *m*.
dehumidify [ˌdiːhjuː'mɪdɪfaɪ] *vt* (*US*) deshumedecer.
dehydrate [diː'haɪdreɪt] *vt* deshidratar.
dehydrated [ˌdiːhaɪ'dreɪtɪd] *adj* deshidratado.
dehydration [ˌdiːhaɪ'dreɪʃən] *n* deshidratación *f*.
de-ice [diː'aɪs] *vt* deshelar, descongelar.
de-icer ['diː'aɪsəʳ] *n* deshelador *m*, descongelador *m*.
de-icing [diː'aɪsɪŋ] *n* descongelación *f*.
deictic ['daɪktɪk] *n* deíctico *m*.
deification [ˌdiːɪfɪ'keɪʃən] *n* deificación *f*.
deify ['diːɪfaɪ] *vt* deificar.
deign [deɪn] *vi*: **to ~ to** + *infin* dignarse + *infin*.
deism ['diːɪzəm] *n* deísmo *m*.
deist ['diːɪst] *n* deísta *mf*.
deity ['diːɪtɪ] *n* deidad *f*; divinidad *f*; **the D~** Dios *m*.
deixis ['daɪksɪs] *n* deixis *f*.
dejected [dɪ'dʒektɪd] *adj* abatido, desanimado.
dejectedly [dɪ'dʒektɪdlɪ] *adv say* con tono de abatimiento.
dejection [dɪ'dʒekʃən] *n* abatimiento *m*, desaliento *m*.
dekko‡ ['dekəʊ] *n* (*Brit*) vistazo *m*; **let's have a ~** déjame verlo.
Del. (*US*) *abbr of* **Delaware**.
del. *abbr of* **delete**.
delay [dɪ'leɪ] **1** *n* (*gen*) dilación *f*; (*a ~*) retraso *m*, demora *f*; **without ~** sin demora, sin dilación.
2 *vt* (**a**) (*postpone*) aplazar, demorar; **~ed broadcast** (*US*) transmisión *f* diferida; **~ed effect** efecto *m* retardado.
(**b**) (*person*) entretener; (*obstruct*) impedir; (*make slow, eg train*) retrasar, retardar; **what ~ed you?** ¿por qué has tardado tanto?; **the train was ~ed by fog** el tren se retrasó por la niebla.
3 *vi* tardar, demorarse; **don't ~!** (*in doing sth*) ¡date prisa!, ¡cuanto antes mejor!; (*on the way*) ¡no te entretengas!, ¡no tardes!
delayed-action [dɪ'leɪd'ækʃən] *adj* de acción retardada.
delaying [dɪ'leɪɪŋ] *adj*: **~ tactics** tácticas *fpl* retardatorias.
delectable [dɪ'lektəbl] *adj* delicioso, deleitable.
delectation [ˌdiːlek'teɪʃən] *n* deleite *m*, deleitación *f*.
delegate 1 ['delɪgɪt] *n* delegado *m*, -a *f*, diputado *m*, -a *f* (*to* a).
2 ['delɪgeɪt] *vt* delegar, diputar; **I was ~d to do it** me dieron autoridad para hacerlo, me nombraron para hacerlo; **that task cannot be ~d** ese cometido no se puede delegar a otro.
delegation [ˌdelɪ'geɪʃən] *n* (**a**) (*act*) delegación *f*. (**b**) (*body*) delegación *f*, diputación *f*.
delete [dɪ'liːt] *vt* suprimir, tachar; (*Comput*) cancelar; **~ key** tecla *f* de borrado.
deleterious [ˌdelɪ'tɪərɪəs] *adj* nocivo, perjudicial.
deletion [dɪ'liːʃən] *n* supresión *f*, tachadura *f*; (*Comput*) cancelación *f*.
delft [delft] *n* porcelana *f* de Delft.
Delhi ['delɪ] *n* Delhi *m*.
deli* ['delɪ] *n* = **delicatessen**.
deliberate 1 [dɪ'lɪbərɪt] *adj* (**a**) (*intentional*) intencionado, premeditado.
(**b**) (*cautious*) prudente; (*unhurried*) pausado, lento.
2 [dɪ'lɪbəreɪt] *vt* meditar; **I ~d what to do** medité lo que debiera hacer.
3 [dɪ'lɪbəreɪt] *vi* deliberar (*on* sobre); **I ~d whether to do it** dudaba si hacerlo o no.

deliberately [dɪˈlɪbərɪtlɪ] *adv* (**a**) (*intentionally*) adrede, con intención, de propósito. (**b**) (*cautiously*) prudentemente; (*slowly*) pausadamente.
deliberation [dɪˌlɪbəˈreɪʃən] *n* (**a**) (*consideration*) deliberación *f*, reflexión *f*; **after due** ~ después de meditarlo bien. (**b**) (*discussion: freq* **~s**) debates *mpl*, discusiones *fpl*. (**c**) (*slowness*) lentitud *f*; (*caution*) prudencia *f*; **to proceed with due** ~ proceder con la debida prudencia.
deliberative [dɪˈɪbərətɪv] *adj* deliberativo.
delicacy [ˈdelɪkəsɪ] *n* (**a**) delicadeza *f*; fragilidad *f*. (**b**) (*titbit*) manjar *m* exquisito, golosina *f*.
delicate [ˈdelɪkɪt] *adj* (**a**) delicado; *workmanship* fino, exquisito; escrupuloso; (*fragile*) frágil; *flavour, food* exquisito; *situation* difícil. (**b**) (*Med*) algo débil, enfermizo.
delicately [ˈdelɪkɪtlɪ] *adv* delicadamente; finamente, exquisitamente; frágilmente.
delicatessen [ˌdelɪkəˈtesn] *n* delicatessen *m*.
delicious [dɪˈlɪʃəs] *adj* delicioso, exquisito, rico.
deliciously [dɪˈlɪʃəslɪ] *adv* deliciosamente, exquisitamente, ricamente.
delight [dɪˈlaɪt] **1** *n* (*feeling*) placer *m*, deleite *m*; (*pleasurable thing*) encanto *m*, delicia *f*; **a** ~ **to the eye** un gozo para los ojos, un placer para la vista; **one of the ~s of Majorca** uno de los encantos de Mallorca; **it has been the** ~ **of many children** ha hecho las delicias de muchos niños; **the book is sheer** ~ el libro es un verdadero encanto; **to take** ~ **in sth** deleitarse con algo; **much to her** ~ con gran regocijo de su parte; **to take** ~ **in** + *ger* deleitarse en + *infin*, (*pej*) gozarse en + *infin*.
2 *vt* encantar, deleitar; **~ed!** ¡encantado!; **the play ~ed everyone** la obra encantó a todos; **we are ~ed with it** estamos encantados con él; (**I'm**) **~ed to meet you** (estoy) encantado de conocerle, mucho gusto de conocerle (*LAm*); **we shall be ~ed to come** tendremos muchísimo gusto en venir.
3 *vi*: **to** ~ **in sth** deleitarse con algo; **to** ~ **in** + *ger* deleitarse en + *infin*, (*pej*) gozarse en + *infin*.
delightedly [dɪˈlaɪtɪdlɪ] *adv* alegremente, con alegría; **she smiled** ~ sonrió encantada, sonrió contentísima.
delightful [dɪˈlaɪtfʊl] *adj* encantador, delicioso, precioso.
delightfully [dɪˈlaɪtfəlɪ] *adv* deliciosamente; **to be** ~ **vague** tener un despiste delicioso.
Delilah [dɪˈlaɪlə] *nf* Dalila.
delimit [diːˈlɪmɪt] *vt* delimitar.
delimitation [ˌdiːlɪmɪˈteɪʃən] *n* delimitación *f*.
delineate [dɪˈlɪnɪeɪt] *vt* delinear; (*portray*) bosquejar, pintar; (*delimit*) definir.
delineation [dɪˌlɪnɪˈeɪʃən] *n* delineación *f*.
delinquency [dɪˈlɪŋkwənsɪ] *n* delincuencia *f*; (*guilt*) culpa *f*.
delinquent [dɪˈlɪŋkwənt] **1** *adj* delincuente. **2** *n* delincuente *mf*.
delirious [dɪˈlɪrɪəs] *adj* delirante; **to be** ~ delirar, desvariar; **to be** ~ **with joy** estar loco de contento, estar delirante de alegría.
deliriously [dɪˈlɪrɪəslɪ] *adv* con delirio; **to be** ~ **happy** estar loco de contento.
delirium [dɪˈlɪrɪəm] *n* delirio *m*; ~ **tremens** delírium *m* tremens.
deliver [dɪˈlɪvəʳ] **1** *vt* (**a**) (*distribute*) repartir, entregar; (*Comm*) entregar; *mail* repartir; **'we** ~**'** (*Comm*) 'servicio a domicilio'.
(**b**) (*hand over: also* **to** ~ **over, to** ~ **up**) entregar (*to* a).
(**c**) *message* llevar, comunicar; *sermon, speech, judgement* pronunciar; *lecture* dar; *ball, missile* lanzar; *blow* dar.
(**d**) (*save*) librar (*from* de); ~ **us from evil** líbranos del mal.
(**e**) (*Med*) **she was ~ed of a child** dio a luz un niño; **to** ~ **a woman** asistir a un parto; **the doctor ~ed her of twins** el médico la asistió en el nacimiento de gemelos.
2 *vi* (*****) cumplir lo prometido, hacer lo pactado.
3 *vr* (**a**) **to** ~ **o.s. of** *speech* pronunciar, *remark* hacer (con solemnidad), *opinion* expresar.
(**b**) **to** ~ **o.s. up** entregarse (*to* a).
deliverance [dɪˈlɪvərəns] *n* liberación *f*, rescate *m* (*from* de).
deliverer [dɪˈlɪvərəʳ] *n* (*saviour*) libertador *m*, -ora *f*, salvador *m*, -ora *f*.
delivery [dɪˈlɪvərɪ] *n* (**a**) (*distribution*) distribución *f*, entrega *f*, repartido *m*; (*Comm*) entrega *f*; (*of mail*) reparto *m*; ~ **charge** gastos *mpl* de entrega; ~ **date** fecha *f* de entrega; ~ **man** repartidor *m*; ~ **note** nota *f* de entrega; ~ **order** orden *f* de entrega; ~ **service** servicio *m* de entrega; (*to home*) servicio *m* a domicilio; ~ **time** plazo *m* de entrega; ~ **truck** (*US*), ~ **van** (*Brit*) camioneta *f* de reparto.
(**b**) (*handing over*) entrega *f*.
(**c**) (*of speech*) pronunciación *f*; (*manner of speaking etc*) declamación *f*; presentación *f*, estilo *m*.
(**d**) (*saving*) liberación *f*, rescate *m* (*from* de).
(**e**) (*Med*) parto *m*, alumbramiento *m*; ~ **room** sala *f* de alumbramiento.
dell [del] *n* vallecito *m*.
delouse [ˈdiːˈlaʊs] *vt* despiojar, espulgar.
Delphi [ˈdelfaɪ] *n* Delfos *m*.
Delphic [ˈdelfɪk] *adj* délfico.
delphinium [delˈfɪnɪəm] *n* espuela *f* de caballero.
delta [ˈdeltə] *n* (*Geog*) delta *m*; (*letter*) delta *f*.
delta-winged [ˈdeltaˈwɪŋgd] *adj* con alas en delta.
deltoid [ˈdeltɔɪd] **1** *adj* deltoideo. **2** *n* deltoides *m*.
delude [dɪˈluːd] **1** *vt* engañar. **2** *vr*: **to** ~ **o.s.** engañarse.
deluded [dɪˈluːdɪd] *adj* iluso, engañado.
deluge [ˈdeljuːdʒ] **1** *n* diluvio *m*; (*fig*) diluvio *m*, inundación *f*; **a** ~ **of protests** un torrente de protestas.
2 *vt* inundar (*with* de); **he was ~d with gifts** quedó inundado de regalos, le llovieron los regalos encima; **we are ~d with work** tenemos trabajo hasta encima de las cabezas.
delusion [dɪˈluːʒən] *n* engaño *m*, error *m*, ilusión *f*; **~s of grandeur** ilusiones *fpl* de grandeza; **to labour under a** ~ estar equivocado.
delusive [dɪˈluːsɪv] *adj* engañoso, ilusorio.
de luxe [dɪˈlʌks] *adj* de lujo.
delve [delv] **1** *vt* cavar. **2** *vi* cavar; (*fig*) **to** ~ **into** investigar, ahondar en; **we must** ~ **deeper** tenemos que ahondar todavía más.
Dem. (*US Pol*) **1** *n abbr of* **Democrat**. **2** *adj abbr of* **Democratic**.
demagnetize [diːˈmægnɪtaɪz] *vt* desimantar.
demagogic [ˌdeməˈgɒgɪk] *adj* demagógico.
demagogue, (*US sometimes*) **demagog** [ˈdeməgɒg] *n* demagogo *m*.
demagoguery [deməˈgɒgərɪ] *n* (*US*) demagogia *f*.
demagogy [ˈdeməgɒgɪ] *n* demagogia *f*.
demand [dɪˈmɑːnd] **1** *n* (**a**) (*request*) petición *f*, solicitud *f* (*for* de); **by popular** ~ a petición del público; **on** ~ a solicitud; **abortion on** ~ aborto *m* a petición (de la interesada).
(**b**) (*urgent claim*) exigencia *f*; requerimiento *m*; (*for payment*) reclamación *f*, aviso *m*, intimación *f*; (*Pol, Ind*) reivindicación *f*; **the ~s of duty** las exigencias del deber; **there is a pressing** ~ **for** hay una urgente necesidad de; **I have many ~s on my time** mis asuntos me tienen ocupadísimo; **it makes great ~s on my resources** exige mucho dinero; **he resisted the pressing ~s made on him** resistió a los apremiantes requerimientos que se le habían dirigido.
(**c**) (*Comm*) demanda *f* (*for* de); ~ **bill,** ~ **draft** letra *f* a la vista; ~ **curve** curva *f* de la demanda; ~ **management** control *m* de la demanda; ~ **note** solicitud *f* de pago; **there is a** ~ **for** existe demanda de; **to be in** ~ tener demanda, (*fig*) ser muy solicitado, ser muy popular.
2 *vt* (**a**) exigir (*from, of* a), reclamar, solicitar perentoriamente; **I** ~ **my rights** yo reclamo mis derechos; **the job ~s care** el trabajo exige cuidado.
(**b**) **I ~ed to know why** insistí en saber por qué.
demanding [dɪˈmɑːndɪŋ] *adj* (*person*) exigente; (*task*) absorbente; **physically** ~ duro, agotador.
demarcate [ˈdiːmɑːkeɪt] *vt* demarcar.
demarcation [ˌdiːmɑːˈkeɪʃən] *n* demarcación *f*; ~ **dispute** conflicto *m* de demarcación; ~ **line** línea *f* de demarcación.
démarche [ˈdeɪmɑːʃ] *n* gestión *f*, diligencia *f*.
demean [dɪˈmiːn] *vr*: **to** ~ **o.s.** degradarse.
demeaning [dɪˈmiːnɪŋ] *adj* degradante.
demeanour, (*US*) **demeanor** [dɪˈmiːnəʳ] *n* porte *m*, conducta *f*.
demented [dɪˈmentɪd] *adj* demente; (*fig*) loco.
dementedly [dɪˈmentɪdlɪ] *adv* (*fig*) como un loco.
dementia [dɪˈmenʃɪə] *n* demencia *f*.
demerara [ˌdeməˈrɛərə] *n* (*Brit*: *also* ~ **sugar**) azúcar *m* terciado.
demerit [diːˈmerɪt] *n* demérito *m*, desmerecimiento *m*.
demesne [dɪˈmeɪn] *n* heredad *f*; tierras *fpl* solariegas.
demi... [ˈdemɪ] *pref* semi..., medio...
demigod [ˈdemɪgɒd] *n* semidiós *m*.
demijohn [ˈdemɪdʒɒn] *n* damajuana *f*.
demilitarization [ˈdiːmɪlɪtəraɪˈzeɪʃən] *n* desmilitarización *f*.
demilitarize [ˈdiːˈmɪlɪtəraɪz] *vt* desmilitarizar.
demimonde [ˌdemɪˈmɒːnd] *n* mujeres *fpl* mundanas.
demise [dɪˈmaɪz] *n* fallecimiento *m*.

demisemiquaver ['demɪsemɪˌkweɪvəʳ] *n* (*Brit*) fusa *f*.
demist [diːˈmɪst] *vt* eliminar el vaho de, desempañar.
demister [diːˈmɪstəʳ] *n* (*Brit Aut*) desempañador *m*.
demisting [diːˈmɪstɪŋ] *n* eliminación *f* del vaho.
demitasse ['demɪtæs] *n* (*US*) taza *f* pequeña, tacita *f*.
demo* ['deməʊ] *n* (**a**) (*Brit Pol*) mani* *f*, manifestación *f*, protesta *f* callejera. (**b**) (*Comm*) modelo *m* de demostración; ~ **disk** disquete *m* de demostración; ~ **tape** maqueta *f*.
demob* ['diːˈmɒb] (*Brit*) *abbr of* **demobilization, demobilize**.
demobilization ['diːˌməʊbɪlaɪˈzeɪʃən] *n* desmovilización *f*.
demobilize [diːˈməʊbɪlaɪz] *vt* desmovilizar.
democracy [dɪˈmɒkrəsɪ] *n* democracia *f*.
democrat ['deməkræt] *n* demócrata *mf*.
democratic [ˌdeməˈkrætɪk] *adj* democrático.
democratically [ˌdeməˈkrætɪklɪ] *adv* democráticamente.
democratization [dɪˌmɒkrətaɪˈzeɪʃən] *n* democratización *f*.
democratize [dɪˈmɒkrətaɪz] *vt* democratizar.
démodé [deɪˈmɒdeɪ] *adj* pasado de moda.
demographer [dɪˈmɒgrəfəʳ] *n* demógrafo *m*, -a *f*.
demographic [ˌdeməˈgræfɪk] *adj* demográfico.
demography [dɪˈmɒgrəfɪ] *n* demografía *f*.
demolish [dɪˈmɒlɪʃ] *vt* derribar, demoler; *argument* destruir; *food* devorar, zamparse.
demolisher [dɪˈmɒlɪʃəʳ] *n* (*lit, fig*) demoledor *m*, -ora *f*.
demolition [ˌdeməˈlɪʃən] *n* derribo *m*, demolición *f*; ~ **area**, ~ **zone** zona *f* de demolición; ~ **squad** pelotón *m* de demolición.
demon ['diːmən] **1** *n* demonio *m*. **2** *adj* (**a**) **the** ~ **drink** la bebida infernal, el alcohol del demonio. (**b**) (*) **he's a** ~ **squash-player** es un as en el squash*, jugando al squash es fabuloso*.
demoniacal [ˌdiːməˈnaɪəkəl] *adj* demoniaco, demoníaco.
demonology [ˌdiːməˈnɒlədʒɪ] *n* demonología *f*.
demonstrable ['demənstrəbl] *adj* demostrable.
demonstrably ['demənstrəblɪ] *adv* manifiestamente, obviamente; **a** ~ **false statement** una afirmación manifiestamente falsa.
demonstrate ['demənstreɪt] **1** *vt* demostrar. **2** *vi* manifestarse, hacer una manifestación (*against* para protestar contra, *in favour of* a favor de).
demonstration [ˌdemənˈstreɪʃən] *n* (**a**) demostración *f*, prueba *f*; manifestación *f*; ~ **model** modelo *m* de demostración. (**b**) (*Pol*) manifestación *f*.
demonstrative [dɪˈmɒnstrətɪv] **1** *adj* (**a**) (*Gram*) demostrativo. (**b**) *person* exagerado, exaltado; **not very** ~ más bien reservado. **2** *n* demostrativo *m*.
demonstrator ['demənstreɪtəʳ] *n* (*Pol*) manifestante *mf*; (*Univ etc*) ayudante *mf* (en un laboratorio).
demoralization [dɪˌmɒrəlaɪˈzeɪʃən] *n* desmoralización *f*.
demoralize [dɪˈmɒrəlaɪz] *vt* desmoralizar.
demoralizing [dɪˈmɒrəlaɪzɪŋ] *adj* desmoralizador.
Demosthenes [dɪˈmɒsθəniːz] *nm* Demóstenes.
demote [dɪˈməʊt] *vt* degradar.
demotic [dɪˈmɒtɪk] *adj* demótico.
demotion [dɪˈməʊʃən] *n* degradación *f*.
demur [dɪˈmɜːʳ] **1** *n*: **without** ~ sin reparo, sin poner reparos. **2** *vi* objetar, poner reparos.
demure [dɪˈmjʊəʳ] *adj* grave, solemne; (*modest*) recatado; (*coy*) modoso, de una coquetería disimulada; **in a** ~ **little voice** en tono dulce y algo coqueta.
demurely [dɪˈmjʊəlɪ] *adv* gravemente, solemnemente; recatadamente; con una coquetería disimulada; en tono dulce y algo coqueta.
demureness [dɪˈmjʊənɪs] *n* gravedad *f*, solemnidad *f*; recato *m*; modosidad *f*.
demurrage [dɪˈmʌrɪdʒ] *n* (*Naut*) estadía *f*.
demystification [diːˌmɪstɪfɪˈkeɪʃən] *n* desmistificación *f*.
demystify [diːˈmɪstɪfaɪ] *vt* desmistificar.
demythologize [ˌdiːmɪˈθɒlədʒaɪz] *vt* desmitificar.
den [den] *n* (*animal's*) madriguera *f*, guarida *f*; (*private room*) estudio *m*, gabinete *m*; ~ **of iniquity**, ~ **of vice** templo *m* del vicio; ~ **of thieves** ladronera *f*.
denationalization ['diːˌnæʃnəlaɪˈzeɪʃən] *n* desnacionalización *f*.
denationalize [diːˈnæʃnəlaɪz] *vt* desnacionalizar.
denatured [diːˈneɪtʃəd] *adj*: ~ **alcohol** (*US*) alcohol *m* desnaturalizado.
dendrochronology [ˌdendrəʊkrəˈnɒlədʒɪ] *n* dendrocronología *f*.
denial [dɪˈnaɪəl] *n* (*of request*) denegación *f*, negativa *f*; (*of report etc*) desmentido *m*, desmentimiento *m*; (*self*~) abnegación *f*.
denier ['denɪəʳ] *n* (**a**) (*weight*) denier *m*; **25** ~ **stockings** medias *fpl* de 25 denier. (**b**) (*coin*) denario *m*.
denigrate ['denɪgreɪt] *vt* denigrar.
denigration [ˌdenɪˈgreɪʃən] *n* denigración *f*.
denigratory [ˌdenɪˈgreɪtərɪ] *adj* denigratorio.
denim ['denɪm] *n* dril *m* (de algodón); tela *f* vaquera; ~ **jacket** chaqueta *f* vaquera, saco *m* vaquero (*LAm*); ~**s** pantalón *m* de dril, vaqueros *mpl*.
denizen ['denɪzn] *n* habitante *mf*; vecino *m*, -a *f*, morador *m*, -ora *f*.
Denmark ['denmɑːk] *n* Dinamarca *f*.
denominate [dɪˈnɒmɪneɪt] *vt* denominar.
denomination [dɪˌnɒmɪˈneɪʃən] *n* (**a**) (*name*) denominación *f*. (**b**) (*class*) clase *f*, categoría *f*; (*of coin etc*) valor *m*; (*of measure, weight*) unidad *f*; (*Eccl*) secta *f*, confesión *f*.
denominational [dɪˌnɒmɪˈneɪʃənl] *adj* (*Eccl*) sectario; (*US*) *school* confesional.
denominator [dɪˈnɒmɪneɪtəʳ] *n*: (**lowest**) **common** ~ (mínimo) denominador *m* común.
denotation [ˌdiːnəʊˈteɪʃən] *n* (**a**) (*gen, also Ling, Philos*) denotación *f*; (*meaning*) sentido *m*. (**b**) (*symbol*) símbolo *m*, señal *f*.
denotative [dɪˈnəʊtətɪv] *adj* (*Ling*) denotativo.
denote [dɪˈnəʊt] *vt* denotar; indicar, significar; (*Ling, Philos*) denotar; **what does this** ~? ¿qué quiere decir esto?
dénouement [deɪˈnuːmɒn] *n* desenlace *m*.
denounce [dɪˈnaʊns] *vt* (*to police etc*) denunciar; *treaty* denunciar, abrogar; (*inveigh against*) censurar.
dense [dens] *adj* (**a**) denso; espeso, compacto, tupido. (**b**) (*) *person* duro de mollera.
densely ['denslɪ] *adv* densamente; espesamente; ~ **populated** con gran densidad de población.
denseness ['densnɪs] *n*, **density** ['densɪtɪ] *n* densidad *f*; lo espeso, lo compacto, lo tupido.
dent [dent] **1** *n* abolladura *f*; (*in edge*) mella *f*; **to make a** ~ **in*** afectar malamente, hacer estragos en. **2** *vt* abollar; mellar; **his reputation was somewhat** ~**ed** su reputación quedaba algo deslustrada.
dental ['dentl] **1** *adj* dental; ~ **nurse** enfermero *m*, -a *f* dental; ~ **science** odontología *f*; ~ **surgeon** dentista *mf*, odontólogo *m*, -a *f*. **2** *n* dental *f*.
dental floss ['dentlˌflɒs] *n* hilo *m* de higiene dental.
dented ['dentɪd] *adj* abollado, con abolladuras.
dentifrice ['dentɪfrɪs] *n* dentífrico *m*.
dentine ['dentiːn] *n* dentina *f*, esmalte *m* dental.
dentist ['dentɪst] *n* dentista *mf*, odontólogo *m*, -a *f*; ~**'s surgery**, ~**'s office** (*US*) consultorio *m* dental.
dentistry ['dentɪstrɪ] *n* odontología *f*, dentistería *f*.
dentition [denˈtɪʃən] *n* dentición *f*.
denture ['denʃəʳ] *n* dentadura *f*; (*false teeth, also* ~**s**) dentadura *f* postiza.
denuclearize [diːˈnjuːklɪəraɪz] *vt* desnuclearizar.
denude [dɪˈnjuːd] *vt* (*Geol etc*) denudar; (*strip*) despojar (*of* de).
denuded [dɪˈnjuːdɪd] *adj terrain* denudado; ~ **of** despojado de.
denunciation [dɪˌnʌnsɪˈeɪʃən] *n* denuncia *f*, denunciación *f*; (*inveighing*) censura *f*.
Denver ['denvəʳ] *attr*: ~ **boot**, ~ **clamp** cepo *m*.
deny [dɪˈnaɪ] **1** *vt possibility, truth of statement etc* negar; *request* denegar; *charge* rechazar; *report* desmentir; *faith* renegar de; **he denies me his help** me niega su ayuda; **he denies that he said it, he denies having said it** niega haberlo dicho; **I don't** ~ **it** no lo niego; **there's no** ~**ing it** es innegable; **he was not to be denied** no se conformaba con la negativa; no iba a quedar en menos; **he was not going to be denied his revenge** nada iba a impedir su venganza.

2 *vr*: **to** ~ **o.s.** privarse; **to** ~ **o.s. sth** privarse de algo, no permitirse algo.
deodorant [diːˈəʊdərənt] *n* desodorante *m*.
deodorize [diːˈəʊdəraɪz] *vt* desodorizar.
deoxidize [diːˈɒksɪdaɪz] *vt* desoxidar.
deoxyribonucleic [dɪˈɒksɪˌraɪbəʊnjuːˈkleɪɪk] *adj*: ~ **acid** ácido *m* desoxirribonucleico.
dep. (*Rail etc*) *abbr of* **departs** sale.
depart [dɪˈpɑːt] **1** *vt*: **to** ~ **this life** partir de esta vida. **2** *vi* partir, irse, marcharse (*from* de); (*train etc*) salir (*at* a, *for* para, *from* de); **to** ~ **from** *custom, truth etc* apartarse de, desviarse de.
departed [dɪˈpɑːtɪd] *n*: **the** ~ el difunto, la difunta.
department [dɪˈpɑːtmənt] **1** *n* departamento *m*; (*of business*) sección *f*; (*of learning, activity*) ramo *m*, especialidad *f*; (*US Pol*) ministerio *m*; **D**~ **of State** (*US*) Ministerio *m* de Asuntos Exteriores; **in that** ~ **of the game** en ese

aspecto del juego. **2** *attr*: ~ **store** (grandes) almacenes *mpl*, tienda *f* por departamento (*Carib*).

departmental [ˌdiːpɑːtˈmentl] *adj* departamental; ~ **policy** política *f* del departamento; ~ **head** jefe *m* de sección.

departure [dɪˈpɑːtʃəʳ] **1** *n* (**a**) partida *f*, ida *f*; (*of train etc*) salida *f*; **'D~s'** (*Aer*) 'Salidas'; **to take one's** ~ marcharse.

(**b**) (*fig*) desviación *f* (*from* de); **new** ~ rumbo *m* nuevo, nueva orientación *f*; novedad *f*; **this is a ~ from the norm** esto se aparta de lo normal; **this is a ~ from the truth** esto no representa la verdad.

2 *attr*: ~ **board** (*Aer, Rail*) tablón *m* de salidas; ~ **gate** (*Aer*) puerta *f* de embarque; ~ **language** (*Ling*) lengua *f* de origen; ~ **lounge** (*Aer*) sala *f* de embarque; ~ **platform** andén *m* de salida; ~ **time** hora *f* de salida.

depend [dɪˈpend] *vi*: **it ~s** eso depende, según; **it ~s what you mean** depende de lo que Vd quiera decir.

◆**depend on** *vt circumstances, result etc* depender de; (*rely on*) contar con, confiar en; **can we ~ on you?** ¿podemos contar contigo?; **can we ~ on you to do it?** ¿podemos contar contigo para hacerlo?, ¿podemos confiar en que tú lo hagas?; **she ~s on her own resources** ella cuenta con sus propios recursos; **he has to ~ on his pen** tiene que vivir de su pluma; **you may ~ (up)on it** es cosa segurísima; **~ing on the weather, we can go either way** según el tiempo que haga, podemos ir por una ruta o por la otra; **~ing on the individual, there may be problems** según el individuo, puede haber problemas.

dependability [dɪˌpendəˈbɪlɪtɪ] *n* seguridad *f*; seriedad *f*, formalidad *f*.

dependable [dɪˈpendəbl] *adj thing* seguro; *person* serio, formal.

dependant [dɪˈpendənt] *n* familiar *mf* dependiente; **have you any ~s?** ¿tiene personas a su cargo?

dependence [dɪˈpendəns] *n* (*depending*) dependencia *f* (*on* de); (*reliance*) confianza *f* (*on* en); (*subordination*) subordinación *f* (*on* a); ~ **on drugs** drogodependencia *f*.

dependency [dɪˈpendənsɪ] *n* (**a**) (*Pol*) posesión *f*. (**b**) (*Ling*) dependencia *f*.

dependent [dɪˈpendənt] **1** *adj* dependiente (*on* de); (*subordinate*: *also Gram*) subordinado (*on* a); **to be ~ on** depender de. **2** *n* familiar *mf* dependiente.

depersonalize [diːˈpɜːsənəlaɪz] *vt* despersonalizar.

depict [dɪˈpɪkt] *vt* representar, pintar.

depiction [dɪˈpɪkʃən] *n* representación *f*.

depilatory [dɪˈpɪlətərɪ] **1** *adj* depilatorio. **2** *n* (*also* ~ **cream**) depilatorio *m*.

deplane [diːˈpleɪn] *vi* (*US*) salir del avión, desembarcar.

deplenish [dɪˈplenɪʃ] *vt* (*reduce*) reducir; (*empty*) vaciar.

deplete [dɪˈpliːt] *vt* agotar; mermar, reducir.

depletion [dɪˈpliːʃən] *n* agotamiento *m*; merma *f*, reducción *f*.

deplorable [dɪˈplɔːrəbl] *adj* lamentable, deplorable; **it would be ~ if** sería lamentable que + *subj*.

deplorably [dɪˈplɔːrəblɪ] *adv* lamentablemente, deplorablemente; **in ~ bad taste** de un mal gusto lamentable; **it has been ~ exaggerated** ha sido exagerado de un modo lamentable.

deplore [dɪˈplɔːʳ] *vt* lamentar, deplorar; **it is to be ~d** es de lamentar, es deplorable.

deploy [dɪˈplɔɪ] **1** *vt* desplegar. **2** *vi* desplegarse.

deployment [dɪˈplɔɪmənt] *n* despliegue *m*.

depoliticize [ˌdiːpəˈlɪtɪsaɪz] *vt* despolitizar.

depopulate [diːˈpɒpjʊleɪt] *vt* despoblar, desertizar.

depopulation [ˈdiːˌpɒpjʊˈleɪʃən] *n* despoblación *f*.

deport [dɪˈpɔːt] **1** *vt* deportar. **2** *vr*: **to ~ o.s.** comportarse.

deportation [ˌdiːpɔːˈteɪʃən] *n* deportación *f*.

deportment [dɪˈpɔːtmənt] *n* conducta *f*, comportamiento *m*; (*carriage*) porte *m*, modo *m* de andar.

depose [dɪˈpəʊz] **1** *vt* deponer; destituir. **2** *vi* declarar, deponer.

deposit [dɪˈpɒzɪt] **1** *n* (**a**) (*Geol*) depósito *m*, yacimiento *m*; (*Chem, dregs*) poso *m*, sedimento *m*.

(**b**) (*Fin etc*) depósito *m*; entrada *f*; fianza *f*; (*pledge*) señal *f*; (*act of ~ing money in account*) imposición *f*, ingreso *m*; (*on hire purchase, car*) depósito *m*, abono *m* (*LAm*); (*on house*) desembolso *m* inicial; **to have £50 on ~** tener 50 libras en cuenta de ahorros; **to leave £50 ~** hacer un desembolso inicial de 50 libras; **to lose one's ~** (*Brit Pol*) perder el depósito.

2 *vt* (**a**) (*place, lay*) depositar; *eggs* poner.

(**b**) (*entrust etc*) depositar (*in* en).

(**c**) (*leave*) depositar (*with* en), dejar (*with* con).

(**d**) (*Geol, Chem*) depositar, sedimentar.

(**e**) (*Fin*) depositar; (*pledge*) dar para señal; (*money in account*) depositar, ingresar (*in* en), (*esp savings account*) imponer (*in* en); **to ~ £X on a house** hacer un desembolso inicial de X libras para una casa, dar una entrada de X libras por una casa.

3 *attr*: (*Brit*) ~ **account** cuenta *f* de depósitos a plazo, cuenta *f* a plazo fijo; ~ **slip** hoja *f* de ingreso.

deposition [ˌdiːpəˈzɪʃən] *n* (**a**) deposición *f*. (**b**) (*Jur*) declaración *f*, deposición *f*.

depositor [dɪˈpɒzɪtəʳ] *n* depositante *mf*, impositor *m*, -ora *f*, imponente *mf*; cuentacorrentista *mf*.

depository [dɪˈpɒzɪtərɪ] *n* depositaría *f*, almacén *m*; (*fig*) pozo *m*; ~ **library** (*US*) biblioteca *f* de depósito.

depot [ˈdepəʊ] *n* (*storehouse*) depósito *m*, almacén *m*; (*Mil HQ*) depósito *m*; (*Brit*: *for vehicles*) parque *m*, cochera *f*; (*buses, US Rail*) estación *f*.

depot ship [ˈdepəʊˈʃɪp] *n* buque *m* nodriza.

depravation [ˌdeprəˈveɪʃən] *n* depravación *f*.

deprave [dɪˈpreɪv] *vt* depravar.

depraved [dɪˈpreɪvd] *adj* depravado, perverso, vicioso.

depravity [dɪˈprævɪtɪ] *n* depravación *f*, perversión *f*.

deprecate [ˈdeprɪkeɪt] *vt* desaprobar, lamentar.

deprecating [ˈdeprkeɪtɪŋ] *adj tone etc* de desaprobación.

deprecatingly [ˈdeprɪkeɪtɪŋlɪ] *adv* con desaprobación.

deprecatory [ˈdeprɪkətərɪ] *adj* de desaprobación.

depreciate [dɪˈpriːʃɪeɪt] **1** *vt* depreciar; (*fig*) desestimar. **2** *vi* depreciarse, perder valor, bajar de precio.

depreciation [dɪˌpriːʃɪˈeɪʃən] *n* depreciación *f*; (*of value*) amortización *f*; ~ **account** cuenta *f* de amortización; ~ **allowance** reservas *fpl* para depreciaciones.

depredations [ˌdeprɪˈdeɪʃənz] *npl* estragos *mpl*.

depress [dɪˈpres] *vt* (*push down*) presionar, deprimir; *status* rebajar; *trade* paralizar; *price* hacer bajar; (*dispirit*) deprimir, abatir, desalentar.

depressant [dɪˈpresnt] **1** *adj* (*Med*) deprimente, sedante. **2** *n* (*Med*) deprimente *m*, sedante *m*.

depressed [dɪˈprest] *adj area* deprimido, de elevado paro obrero; *person* abatido, desalentado, pesimista; *market* deprimido; *period* de depresión; **to feel ~ about** sentirse pesimista por.

depressing [dɪˈpresɪŋ] *adj* triste, deprimente.

depressingly [dɪˈpresɪŋlɪ] *adv* tristemente, en tono pesimista; **it was a ~ familiar story** era la triste historia de siempre.

depression [dɪˈpreʃən] *n* (*Fin, Met etc*) depresión *f*; (*slump*) crisis *f* económica, depresión *f*, bache *m*; (*in ground, road*) bache *m*, hoyo *m*; (*dejection*) depresión *f*, desaliento *m*, abatimiento *m*.

depressive [dɪˈpresɪv] **1** *adj* depresivo. **2** *n* depresivo *m*, -a *f*.

depressurization [dɪˌpreʃəraɪˈzeɪʃən] *n* descompresión *f*.

depressurize [diːˈpreʃəˌraɪz] *vt* despresurizar.

deprivation [ˌdeprɪˈveɪʃən] *n* privación *f*; **a great ~** una gran pérdida.

deprive [dɪˈpraɪv] **1** *vt*: **to ~ sb of sth** privar a uno de algo. **2** *vr*: **to ~ o.s. of sth** privarse de algo; **don't ~ yourself!** ¡no te vayas a quedar sin nada!

deprived [dɪˈpraɪvd] *adj child* desventajado, desvalido.

deprogramme, (*US, also freq Comput*) **deprogram** [diːˈprəʊgræm] *vt* desprogramar.

dept *abbr of* **department** departamento *m*.

depth [depθ] *n* (**a**) profundidad *f* (*also fig*); (*of room*) fondo *m*; (*width*) ancho *m*; (*of colour, feeling*) intensidad *f*; ~ **of field** (*Phot*) profundidad *f* del campo; **defence in ~** defensa *f* en profundidad; **investigation in ~** investigación *f* en profundidad; **to be 5 metres in ~** tener una profundidad de 5 metros; **to study a subject in ~** estudiar un tema a fondo; **he was out of his ~** (*lit*) le cubría el agua; **I'm out of my ~ with physics** (*fig*) no entiendo nada de física; **to get out of one's ~** (*lit*) meterse donde le cubre a uno, perder pie; (*fig*) meterse en honduras, salirse de su terreno.

(**b**) **~s**: **in the ~s of the sea** en los abismos del mar; **from the ~s of the mine** desde lo más hondo de la mina; **the ~s of degradation** (*fig*) la mayor degradación; **the ~s of despair** la mayor desesperación; **in the ~s of one's heart** en lo más hondo del corazón; **in the ~s of winter** en lo más crudo del invierno.

depth charge [ˈdepθtʃɑːdʒ] *n* carga *f* de profundidad.

deputation [ˌdepjʊˈteɪʃən] *n* diputación *f*, delegación *f*.

depute [dɪˈpjuːt] *vt* diputar, delegar; **to ~ sb to do sth** diputar a uno para que haga algo.

deputize [ˈdepjʊtaɪz] *vi*: **to ~ for sb** sustituir a uno, desempeñar las funciones de uno.

deputy [ˈdepjʊtɪ] **1** *adj* suplente; ~ **chairman** vicepresidente *m*, -a *f*; ~ **director** vicerrector *m*, -ora *f*; ~ **head,** ~

manager subdirector *m*, -ora *f*; ~ **minister** viceministro *m*, -a *f*. **2** *n* sustituto *m*, -a *f*; suplente *mf*; (*Pol*) diputado *m*, -a *f*; (*agent*) representante *mf*.

derail [dɪˈreɪl] *vt* hacer descarrilar.

derailment [dɪˈreɪlmənt] *n* descarrilamiento *m*.

derange [dɪˈreɪndʒ] *vt* desarreglar, descomponer; *person* volver loco, desquiciar; **to be ~d** estar desquiciado, padecer un trastorno mental.

derangement [dɪˈreɪndʒmənt] *n* desarreglo *m*; (*Med*) trastorno *m* mental.

Derby, derby[1] [ˈdɑːbɪ] *n* (*Brit Sport*) (**a**) Derby *m* (*importante carrera de caballos en Inglaterra*). (**b**) **local d~** derby *m*, encuentro *m* entre dos equipos locales.

derby[2] [ˈdɑːbɪ] *n* (*US*: *also* ~ **hat**) hongo *m* (*sombrero*).

deregulate [diːˈregjʊleɪt] *vt* desregular.

deregulation [diːˌregjʊˈleɪʃən] *n* desregulación *f*.

derelict [ˈderɪlɪkt] **1** *adj* abandonado. **2** *n* derrelicto *m*.

dereliction [ˌderɪˈlɪkʃən] *n* abandono *m*; ~ **of duty** negligencia *f*.

deride [dɪˈraɪd] *vt* ridiculizar, mofarse de.

de rigueur [dərɪˈgɜːʳ] *adv* de rigor.

derision [dɪˈrɪʒən] *n* irrisión *f*, mofas *fpl*; **this was greeted with** ~ en esto hubo risas.

derisive [dɪˈraɪsɪv] *adj* burlón, mofador, irónico.

derisively [dɪˈraɪsɪvlɪ] *adv* burlonamente.

derisory [dɪˈraɪsərɪ] *adj quantity etc* irrisorio, ridículo.

derivation [ˌderɪˈveɪʃən] *n* derivación *f*.

derivative [dɪˈrɪvətɪv] **1** *adj* (*gen, Ling*) derivado; *work* poco original. **2** *n* derivado *m*.

derive [dɪˈraɪv] **1** *vt* derivar (*from* de); *profit, advantage* sacar, obtener (*from* de); **~d demand** demanda *f* derivada. **2** *vi* derivar(se) (*from* de); **to ~ from, to be ~d from** (*fig*) proceder de, provenir de.

dermatitis [ˌdɜːməˈtaɪtɪs] *n* dermatitis *f*.

dermatologist [ˌdɜːməˈtɒlədʒɪst] *n* dermatólogo *m*, -a *f*.

dermatology [ˌdɜːməˈtɒlədʒɪ] *n* dermatología *f*.

derogatory [dɪˈrɒgətərɪ] *adj* despectivo.

derrick [ˈderɪk] *n* grúa *f*; (*of oil well*) derrick *m*, torre *f* de perforación.

derv [dɜːv] *n* (*Brit*) gas-oil *m*.

dervish [ˈdɜːvɪʃ] *n* derviche *m*; (*fig*) salvaje *m*.

DES *n* (*Brit*) *abbr of* **Department of Education and Science**.

desalinate [diːˈsælɪneɪt] *vt* desalinar.

desalination [diːˌsælɪˈneɪʃən] *n* desalinación *f*; ~ **plant** planta *f* potabilizadora (de agua de mar).

descale [diːˈskeɪl] *vt* desincrustar; **descaling agent** agente *m* desincrustante; **descaling product** producto *m* desincrustante.

descant [ˈdeskænt] **1** *n* discante *m*. **2** *vi*: **to ~ on** disertar largamente sobre.

descend [dɪˈsend] **1** *vt* descender, bajar.

2 *vi* descender, bajar (*from* de); **to ~ from** *ancestors etc* descender de; **to ~ on** caer sobre; (*as visitors*) invadir; **to ~ to** (*as inheritance*) pasar a; (*lower o.s.*) rebajarse a; **to ~ to** + *ger* rebajarse a + *infin*.

descendant [dɪˈsendənt] *n* descendiente *mf*; **to leave no ~s** no dejar descendencia.

descending [dɪˈsendɪŋ] *adj* descendente; **in ~ order** en orden descendente.

descent [dɪˈsent] *n* (**a**) (*Geog*) pendiente *f*, declive *m*; (*coming down*) descendimiento *m* (*also Rel*), bajada *f*; (*fall*) descenso *m* (*in* de).

(**b**) (*raid*) ataque *m* (*on* sobre), incursión *f*.

(**c**) (*origin*) origen *m*, familia *f*; **of Italian ~** de ascendencia italiana.

descramble [ˈdiːˈskræmbl] *vt* (*TV*) descodificar.

descrambler [ˈdiːˈskræmbləʳ] *n* (*TV*) descodificador *m*.

describe [dɪsˈkraɪb] *vt* describir (*also Geom*); **to ~ sb as** calificar a uno de.

description [dɪsˈkrɪpʃən] *n* (**a**) descripción *f*; **it was beyond** (*or* **past**) ~ superaba toda descripción. (**b**) (*sort*) clase *f*, género *m*.

descriptive [dɪsˈkrɪptɪv] *adj* descriptivo.

descriptivism [dɪsˈkrɪptɪvɪzəm] *n* descriptivismo *m*.

descriptivist [dɪsˈkrɪptɪvɪst] *n* descriptivista *mf*.

descry [dɪsˈkraɪ] *vt* divisar.

Desdemona [ˌdezdɪˈməʊnə] *nf* Desdémona.

desecrate [ˈdesɪkreɪt] *vt* profanar.

desecration [ˌdesɪˈkreɪʃən] *n* profanación *f*.

deseed [ˌdiːˈsiːd] *vt fruit* despepitar.

desegregate [diːˈsegrəgeɪt] *vt* desegregar.

desegregation [ˈdiːˌsegrəˈgeɪʃən] *n* desegregación *f*.

deselect [ˌdiːsɪˈlekt] *vt* no renovar la candidatura de, revocar el nombramiento de.

deselection [diːsɪˈlekʃən] *n* no renovación *f* de la candidatura, revocación *f* del nombramiento.

desensitize [diːˈsensɪtaɪz] *vt* desensibilizar, insensibilizar; (*Phot*) hacer insensible a la luz.

desert[1] [ˈdezət] **1** *adj* desierto; ~ **island** isla *f* desierta; ~ **rat** rata *f* del desierto. **2** *n* desierto *m*.

desert[2] [dɪˈzɜːt] **1** *vt* (*Mil, Jur etc*) desertar de; *person* abandonar, desamparar, dejar; **his luck ~ed him** la suerte le abandonó. **2** *vi* (*Mil*) desertar (*from* de, *to* a).

deserted [dɪˈzɜːtɪd] *adj road, place* desierto; *wife etc* abandonado.

deserter [dɪˈzɜːtəʳ] *n* (*Mil*) desertor *m*; (*Pol*) tránsfuga *mf*.

desertification [ˌdezɜːtɪfɪˈkeɪʃən] *n* desertización *f*.

desertify [deˈzɜːtɪfaɪ] *vt* desertizar.

desertion [dɪˈzɜːʃən] *n* deserción *f* (*also Mil*), abandono *m*.

deserts [dɪˈzɜːts] *npl* lo merecido; **to get one's** (**just**) ~ llevar su merecido.

deserve [dɪˈzɜːv] **1** *vt* merecer, ser digno de; **he got what he ~d** llevó su merecido. **2** *vi*: **to ~ well of** merecer ser bien tratado por; **to ~ to** + *infin* merecer + *infin*.

deservedly [dɪˈzɜːvɪdlɪ] *adv* merecidamente.

deserving [dɪˈzɜːvɪŋ] *adj* meritorio; **to be ~ of** merecer, ser digno de.

déshabillé [ˌdeɪzæˈbiːeɪ] *n* desabillé *m*.

desiccate [ˈdesɪkeɪt] *vt* desecar.

desiccation [ˌdesɪˈkeɪʃən] *n* desecación *f*.

desideratum [dɪˌzɪdəˈrɑːtəm] *n*, *pl* **desiderata** [dɪˌzɪdəˈrɑːtə] desiderátum *m*.

design [dɪˈzaɪn] **1** *n* (**a**) (*Tech etc*) diseño *m*; (*pattern of cloth, wallpaper etc*) dibujo *m*; (*of car etc*) diseño *m*; estilo *m*, líneas *fpl*; (*preliminary sketch*) bosquejo *m*; proyecto *m*; (*Theat, Cine*) boceto *m*; (*of building etc*) estilo *m*; (*ground plan*) distribución *f*; (*art of* ~) dibujo *m*; ~ **department** sección *f* de proyectos; ~ **studio** estudio *m* de diseños.

(**b**) (*aim*) intención *f*, propósito *m*; (*plan*) plan *m*, proyecto *m*; **~s** (*pej*) malas intenciones *fpl* (*on* con respecto a); **grand ~** plan *m* general, (*Mil*) estrategia *f* general; **by ~** adrede, intencionalmente; **to have** (**one's**) **~s on** tener sus proyectos sobre, tener la mira puesta en.

2 *vt* (*contrive*) idear; (*plan*) proyectar; (*Tech*) diseñar, proyectar; *pattern* dibujar; (*sketch*) bosquejar; **a well ~ed house** una casa bien distribuida; **a well ~ed programme** un programa bien concebido; **to be ~ed to** + *infin* estar diseñado para + *infin*, estar proyectado para + *infin*; (*fig*) tener la intención de + *infin*, ir encaminado a + *infin*; **it was not ~ed for that** no fue proyectado con esa finalidad.

3 *vi*: **to ~ to** + *infin* proponerse + *infin*.

designate 1 [ˈdezɪgnɪt] *adj* designado, nombrado. **2** [ˈdezɪgneɪt] *vt* (*name*) denominar; (*appoint*) nombrar (*to* + *infin* para que + *subj*); (*point to*) señalar; (*destine*) designar.

designation [ˌdezɪgˈneɪʃən] *n* (*name*) denominación *f*; (*appointment*) nombramiento *m*, designación *f*.

designedly [dɪˈzaɪnɪdlɪ] *adv* de propósito.

designer [dɪˈzaɪnəʳ] **1** *n* (*Tech*) diseñador *m*, proyectista *mf*; (*draughtsman*) delineante *m*; (*Art*) dibujante *mf*; (*dress* ~) modisto *m*, -a *f*; (*Theat*) escenógrafo *m*, -a *f*; (*TV*) diseñador *m*, -ora *f*. **2** *attr*: ~ **clothes** ropa *f* de diseño; ~ **drug** droga *f* de laboratorio; ~ **jeans** vaqueros *mpl* de marca; ~ **stubble** barba *f* con 'look' de tres días.

designing [dɪˈzaɪnɪŋ] **1** *adj* intrigante. **2** *n* diseño *m*, el diseñar.

desirability [dɪˌzaɪərəˈbɪlɪtɪ] *n* lo apetecible, lo atractivo, carácter *m* atractivo; deseabilidad *f*, conveniencia *f*; **the ~ of the plan is not in question** que el proyecto en sí es deseable nadie lo duda.

desirable [dɪˈzaɪərəbl] *adj* (*arousing desire*) apetecible, atractivo; (*proper*) deseable, conveniente; **oh ~ creature!** ¡oh prenda de mi corazón!; **I don't think it ~ to** + *infin* no creo que sea conveniente + *infin*.

desire [dɪˈzaɪəʳ] **1** *n* deseo *m* (*for* de, *to* + *infin* de + *infin*); **I haven't the least ~ to go** no tengo el menor deseo de ir; **to meet sb's ~s** satisfacer los deseos de uno.

2 *vt* (**a**) (*want*) desear; querer tener; **to ~ to do** desear hacer; **what does madam ~?** ¿qué manda la señora?; **it leaves much to be ~d** deja mucho que desear.

(**b**) **to ~ sb to do sth** (*wish*) rogar a uno hacer algo; (*order*) mandar a uno hacer algo.

desirous [dɪˈzaɪərəs] *adj*: ~ **of** deseoso de; **to be ~ that** querer que + *subj*; **to be ~ to** + *infin* desear + *infin*.

desist [dɪˈzɪst] *vi*: **to ~ from sth** desistir de algo; **to ~ from** + *ger* dejar de + *infin*; **we begged him to ~** le rogamos dejarlo, le rogamos no continuar.

desk [desk] **1** *n* (*in office, study etc*) mesa *f* de trabajo; (*Scol*) pupitre *m*; (*bureau*) escritorio *m*; (*of ministry, newspaper*) sección *f*; (*Brit: in shop, restaurant*) caja *f*.

2 *attr*: ~ **clerk** (*US*) recepcionista *mf*; ~ **diary** agenda *f* de mesa, diario *m* de escritorio; ~ **job** trabajo *m* de escritorio; ~ **lamp** lámpara *f* de escritorio; ~ **pad** bloc *m* de notas; ~ **study** estudio *m* sobre el papel.

desk-bound ['deskbaʊnd] *adj* sedentario.

desktop ['desktɒp] *attr* de sobremesa, de oficina, de escritorio; ~ **publishing** autoedición *f*.

desolate 1 ['desəlɪt] *adj* (*lonely*) solitario; (*deserted*) desierto, deshabitado; (*ruinous*) arruinado; (*barren*) desolado, yermo, desierto; (*dreary*) triste; *person* triste, afligido. **2** ['desəleɪt] *vt* asolar, arrasar; *person* afligir; **we were utterly ~d** quedamos profundamente afligidos.

desolately ['desəlɪtlɪ] *adv say etc* tristemente.

desolation [,desə'leɪʃən] *n* (**a**) (*act*) arrasamiento *m*. (**b**) (*state*) desolación *f*, lo desierto *etc*; soledad *f*; (*of person*) aflicción *f*.

despair [dɪs'pɛə^{r}] **1** *n* (**a**) desesperación *f*; **to be in ~** estar desesperado.

(**b**) **he is the ~ of his parents** les trae locos a sus padres.

2 *vi* perder la esperanza, desesperar(se) (*of* de); **his life is ~ed of** se desespera de su vida; **don't ~!** ¡ánimo!

despairing [dɪs'pɛərɪŋ] *adj* desesperado.

despairingly [dɪs'pɛərɪŋlɪ] *adv* desesperadamente.

despatch [dɪs'pætʃ] = **dispatch**.

desperado [,despə'rɑːdəʊ] *n* criminal *m*, bandido *m*.

desperate ['despərɪt] *adj* (**a**) (*hopeless*) desesperado; *plight, situation* desesperado, muy grave; *urgency* apremiante; *need* extremo; *measure* arriesgado; *resistance* heroico; *effort* furioso, violento; (*reckless from despair*) dispuesto a arriesgarlo todo; capaz de hacer cualquier locura; **he was ~ for money** necesitaba dinero con urgencia; **we are getting ~** empezamos a perder la esperanza; **he's a ~ man** es un hombre sumamente peligroso; **I was ~ to see her** quería a toda costa verla, moría por verla.

(**b**) (*) atroz, fatal*.

desperately ['despərɪtlɪ] *adv* desesperadamente; *fight etc* furiosamente, heroicamente; **we ~ need it** lo necesitamos urgentemente; ~ **bad** terriblemente malo; ~ **ill** gravemente enfermo.

desperation [,despə'reɪʃən] *n* desesperación *f*; **in ~** desesperado.

despicable [dɪs'pɪkəbl] *adj* vil, despreciable.

despicably [dɪs'pɪkəblɪ] *adv* despreciablemente.

despise [dɪs'paɪz] *vt* despreciar, desdeñar.

despite [dɪs'paɪt] *prep* a pesar de.

despoil [dɪs'pɔɪl] *vt* despojar (*of* de).

despondence [dɪs'pɒndəns] *n*, **despondency** [dɪs'pɒndənsɪ] *n* abatimiento *m*, desaliento *m*, pesimismo *m*.

despondent [dɪs'pɒndənt] *adj* abatido, deprimido; *letter etc* de tono triste, pesimista; **he was very ~ about our chances** habló en términos pesimistas de nuestras posibilidades.

despot ['despɒt] *n* déspota *m*.

despotic [des'pɒtɪk] *adj* despótico.

despotically [des'pɒtɪkəlɪ] *adv* despóticamente.

despotism ['despətɪzəm] *n* despotismo *m*.

des. res.* ['dez'rez] *n* = **desirable residence**.

dessert [dɪ'zɜːt] *n* postre *m*; **what is there for ~?** ¿qué hay de postre?

dessert apple [dɪ'zɜːt,æpl] *n* manzana *f* para repostería.

dessert plate [dɪ'zɜːt,pleɪt] *n* plato *m* de postre.

dessertspoon [dɪ'zɜːtspuːn] *n* (*Brit*) cuchara *f* de postre.

destabilization [diː,steɪbɪlaɪ'zeɪʃən] *n* desestabilización *f*.

destabilize [diː'steɪbɪlaɪz] *vt* desestabilizar.

destination [,destɪ'neɪʃən] *n* destino *m* (*also Rail etc*).

destine ['destɪn] *vt* destinar (*for, to* para); **to be ~d to** + *infin* estar llamado a + *infin*; **it was ~d to fail** estuvo condenado a fracasar; **it was ~d to happen this way** forzosamente tuvo que ocurrir así.

destiny ['destɪnɪ] *n* destino *m*.

destitute ['destɪtjuːt] *adj* (**a**) (*poverty-stricken*) indigente, desamparado; necesitado; **to be ~** estar en la miseria.

(**b**) **~ of** desprovisto de.

destitution [,destɪ'tjuːʃən] *n* indigencia *f*, miseria *f*.

destroy [dɪs'trɔɪ] *vt* destruir; (*kill*) matar; *pet* sacrificar; *vermin* exterminar; (*finish*) aniquilar, acabar con, anular.

destroyer [dɪs'trɔɪə^{r}] *n* destructor *m*.

destruct [dɪ'strʌkt] **1** *vt* destruir. **2** *vi* destruirse. **3** *attr*: ~ **button** botón *m* de destrucción; ~ **mechanism** mecanismo *m* de destrucción.

destructible [dɪs'trʌktəbl] *adj* destructible.

destruction [dɪs'trʌkʃən] *n* destrucción *f*; (*fig*) ruina *f*, perdición *f*; **to test a machine to ~** someter una máquina a pruebas límite.

destructive [dɪs'trʌktɪv] *adj* destructivo, destructor; *animal* dañino; **to be ~ of** ser nocivo a, ser peligroso para, ser perjudicial para.

destructively [dɪs'trʌktɪvlɪ] *adv* destructivamente.

destructiveness [dɪ'strʌktɪvnɪs] *n* destructividad *f*.

destructor [dɪs'trʌktə^{r}] *n* (*Brit: also* **refuse ~**) incinerador *m* (*or* quemador *m*) de basuras.

desuetude [dɪ'sjʊɪtjuːd] *n* desuso *m*; **to fall into ~** caer en desuso.

desulphurization [,diːsʌlfəraɪ'zeɪʃən] *n* desulfurización *f*.

desultory ['desəltərɪ] *adj way of working etc* poco metódico; esporádico; *fire etc* intermitente, irregular; (*disconnected*) inconexo.

det. (**a**) *abbr of* **detached**. (**b**) *abbr of* **detective**.

detach [dɪ'tætʃ] *vt* separar (*from* de); desvincular (*from* de); (*unstick*) despegar; (*Mil*) destacar.

detachable [dɪ'tætʃəbl] *adj* separable; (*Tech*) desprendible; desmontable.

detached [dɪ'tætʃt] *adj* (**a**) separado, suelto; *collar* postizo; *house* independiente; (*Brit*) **~ house** casa *f* independiente, hotelito *m*, chalet *m*; **~ retina** desprendimiento *m* de la retina; **to become ~** separarse, desprenderse; **they live ~ from everything** viven desligados de todo.

(**b**) (*unbiased*) imparcial, objetivo; indiferente, desinteresado; **to take a ~ view of** considerar objetivamente.

detachment [dɪ'tætʃmənt] *n* (**a**) (*act*) separación *f*. (**b**) (*Mil*) destacamento *m*. (**c**) (*fig*) imparcialidad *f*, objetividad *f*.

detail ['diːteɪl] **1** *n* (**a**) detalle *m*, pormenor *m*; **in ~** en detalle, detalladamente; **to go into ~s** entrar en detalles, pormenorizar; **they planned it down to the last ~** lo planearon todo hasta en los menores detalles.

(**b**) (*Mil*) destacamento *m*.

2 *vt* (**a**) detallar, referir con sus pormenores.

(**b**) (*Mil*) destacar (*to* + *infin* para + *infin*).

detailed ['diːteɪld] *adj* detallado, pormenorizado.

detain [dɪ'teɪn] *vt* (**a**) (*arrest*) detener. (**b**) (*keep waiting*) retener; **I was ~ed at the office** me demoré en la oficina; **I was ~ed by fog** el retraso se debe a la niebla.

detainee [,diːteɪ'niː] *n* detenido *m*, -a *f*.

detect [dɪ'tekt] *vt* descubrir; (*perceive*) percibir; *crime* resolver, *criminal* identificar; (*Tech, by radar etc*) detectar.

detectable [dɪ'tektəbl] *adj* perceptible, detectable.

detection [dɪ'tekʃən] *n* descubrimiento *m*; percepción *f*; resolución *f*, identificación *f*; detección *f*.

detective [dɪ'tektɪv] **1** *n* detective *mf*.

2 *adj attr* detectivesco; ~ **chief inspector** (*Brit*) ≃ comisario *m*; ~ **chief superintendent** (*Brit*) ≃ superintendente *m* general; ~ **constable** (*Brit*) ≃ agente *m*; ~ **inspector** (*Brit*) ≃ inspector *m*; ~ **sergeant** (*Brit*) ≃ cabo *m*; ~ **superintendent** (*Brit*) ≃ comisario *m* jefe; ~ **story** novela *f* policíaca; ~ **work** (*fig*) trabajo *m* detectivesco, trabajo *m* de investigación.

detector [dɪ'tektə^{r}] *n* detector *m*; ~ **van** (*Brit*) camioneta *f* detectora.

détente ['deɪtɑ̃ːnt] *n* distensión *f*.

detention [dɪ'tenʃən] **1** *n* detención *f*, arresto *m*. **2** *attr*: ~ **centre** (*Brit*) centro *m* de detención; ~ **home** (*US*) centro *m* de rehabilitación.

deter [dɪ'tɜː^{r}] *vt* (*discourage*) desalentar; (*dissuade*) disuadir (*from* + *ger* de + *infin*); (*prevent*) impedir (*from doing* hacer); *enemy etc* refrenar; **I was ~red by the cost** el precio me hizo abandonar la idea; **a weapon which ~s nobody** un arma que no refrena a nadie, un arma sin fuerza disuasoria; **don't let the weather ~ you** no dejes de hacerlo por el mal tiempo.

detergent [dɪ'tɜːdʒənt] **1** *adj* detergente. **2** *n* detergente *m*.

deteriorate [dɪ'tɪərɪəreɪt] *vi* empeorar, deteriorarse, degradarse.

deterioration [dɪ,tɪərɪə'reɪʃən] *n* deterioro *m*, empeoramiento *m* (*in* de), degradación *f*.

determinable [dɪ'tɜːmɪnəbl] *adj* determinable.

determinant [dɪ'tɜːmɪnənt] **1** *adj* determinante. **2** *n* determinante *m*.

determination [dɪ,tɜːmɪ'neɪʃən] *n* (**a**) (*act*) determinación *f*.

(**b**) (*resolve*) resolución *f*; **he set off with great ~** partió muy resuelto; **in his ~ to do it** estando resuelto a hacerlo.

determinative [dɪ'tɜːmɪnətɪv] **1** *adj* determinativo. **2** *n* determinativo *m*.

determine [dɪ'tɜːmɪn] **1** *vt* (**a**) (*ascertain, define*) determinar; *date etc* señalar, fijar; *scope, limits, boundary*

definir; *future course, person's fate* decidir; *dispute* determinar, resolver; (*be the deciding factor in*) determinar; **to ~ what is to be done** decidir lo que hay que hacer; **to ~ whether sth is true** decidir si algo es verdad; **we couldn't ~ who it was** no podíamos decidir quién era; **demand ~s supply** la demanda determina la oferta; **to be ~d by** depender de.
(**b**) (*impel*) **this ~d him to go** esto le determinó a ir.
(**c**) (*resolve*) **to ~ to do sth** decidir hacer algo, resolverse a hacer algo.
2 *vi*: **to ~ on** optar por.

determined [dɪ'tɜːmɪnd] *adj person* resuelto; *effort* resuelto, enérgico; **he's very ~ about it** está muy empeñado en ello; **to be ~ to do sth** estar resuelto a hacer algo.

determiner [dɪ'tɜːmɪnəʳ] *n* determinador *m*.

determining [dɪ'tɜːmɪnɪŋ] *adj* decisivo, determinante; **~ factor** factor *m* determinante.

determinism [dɪ'tɜːmɪnɪzəm] *n* determinismo *m*.

determinist [dɪ'tɜːmɪnɪst] **1** *adj* determinista. **2** *n* determinista *mf*.

deterministic [dɪˌtɜːmɪ'nɪstɪk] *adj* determinista.

deterrence [dɪ'terəns] *n* disuasión *f*.

deterrent [dɪ'terənt] **1** *adj* disuasivo, disuasorio.
2 *n* freno *m*, impedimento *m* (*on, to* para); medida *f* represiva; (*Mil*) fuerza *f* disuasiva, fuerza *f* disuasoria, contraamenaza *f*; (**nuclear**) ~ fuerza *f* disuasiva (nuclear); **to act as a ~ to** servir como un freno para, ser una amenaza a, refrenar.

detest [dɪ'test] *vt* detestar, aborrecer.

detestable [dɪ'testəbl] *adj* detestable, aborrecible, odioso.

detestation [ˌdiːtes'teɪʃən] *n* detestación *f*, aborrecimiento *m*; **to hold in ~** aborrecer, odiar.

dethrone [diː'θrəʊn] *vt* destronar.

dethronement [diː'θrəʊnmənt] *n* destronamiento *m*.

detonate ['detəneɪt] **1** *vt* hacer detonar. **2** *vi* detonar, estallar.

detonation [ˌdetə'neɪʃən] *n* detonación *f*.

detonator ['detəneɪtəʳ] *n* detonador *m*, cápsula *f* fulminante.

detour ['diːtʊəʳ] **1** *n* rodeo *m*, vuelta *f*; desviación *f*; (*Aut*) desvío *m*; **to make a ~** desviarse, hacer un rodeo. **2** *vt* (*US*) desviar. **3** *vi* (*US*) desviarse, hacer un rodeo.

detox* ['diː'tɒks] *abbr of* **detoxicate, detoxication, detoxification, detoxify**.

detoxicate [diː'tɒksɪkeɪt] *vt*, **detoxify** [diː'tɒksɪfaɪ] *vt* desintoxicar.

detoxication [diːˌtɒksɪ'keɪʃən] *n*, **detoxification** [diːˌtɒksɪfɪ'keɪʃən] *n* desintoxicación *f*.

detract [dɪ'trækt] *vi*: **to ~ from** quitar mérito (*or* atractivo *etc*) a, desvirtuar, restar valor a.

detraction [dɪ'trækʃən] *n* detracción *f*.

detractor [dɪ'træktəʳ] *n* detractor *m*, -ora *f*.

detriment ['detrɪmənt] *n* perjuicio *m*; **to the ~ of** en perjuicio de, en detrimento de; **without ~ to** sin perjuicio de, sin perjudicar (a).

detrimental [ˌdetrɪ'mentl] *adj* perjudicial (*to* a, para).

detritus [dɪ'traɪtəs] *n* detrito *m*, detritos *mpl*.

de trop [də'trəʊ] *adv*: **to be ~** estar de más, sobrar.

deuce¹ [djuːs] *adv* (*Tennis*) deuce, cuarenta iguales.

deuce² [djuːs] *n*: **a ~ of a row** un tremendo jaleo; **a ~ of a mess** una terrible confusión; **the ~ it is!** ¡qué demonio!; **what the ...?** ¿qué demonios ...?; **where the ~ ...?** ¿dónde demonios ...?; **to play the ~ with** estropear, echar a perder; *V also* **devil**.

deuced [djuːst] **1** *adj* maldito. **2** *adv* diabólicamente, terriblemente.

Deuteronomy [ˌdjuːtə'rɒnəmɪ] *n* Deuteronomio *m*.

deuterium [djuː'tɪərɪəm] *n* deuterio *m*; **~ oxide** óxido *m* deutérico.

devaluate [diː'væljʊeɪt] *vt* desvalorizar, desvalorar.

devaluation [ˌdɪvæljʊ'eɪʃən] *n* desvalorización *f*, devaluación *f*.

devalue ['diː'væljuː] *vt* desvalorizar, devaluar.

devastate ['devəsteɪt] *vt* devastar, asolar; *person* hundir en la tristeza; **we were simply ~d** nos quedamos anonadados con la noticia.

devastating ['devəsteɪtɪŋ] *adj* devastador; (*fig*) *argument etc* arrollador; *news* pasmoso; *defeat* contundente; *wit* muy agudo; *charm* irresistible.

devastatingly ['devəsteɪtɪŋlɪ] *adj beautiful, funny* devastadoramente; arrolladoramente.

devastation [ˌdevə'steɪʃən] *n* (**a**) (*act*) devastación *f*. (**b**) (*state*) devastación *f*, ruinas *fpl*.

develop [dɪ'veləp] **1** *vt* desarrollar (*also Math*); idear, crear; desenvolver; (*encourage*) fomentar; *process* perfeccionar; *plan* elaborar; *land* urbanizar; *resources, mine etc* explotar; *site* ampliar; (*Phot*) revelar; *engine trouble* empezar a tener; *disease* coger, empezar a sufrir de, mostrar los síntomas de; *tendency* coger, dar en; *liking* mostrar, acusar; *power* producir, desarrollar.
2 *vi* (**a**) desarrollarse; progresar, avanzar; evolucionar; **how is the book ~ing?** ¿qué tal te va el libro?; **to ~ into** transformarse en.
(**b**) (*symptoms etc*) aparecer, mostrarse.

developer [dɪ'veləpəʳ] *n* (**a**) (*also* **property ~**) promotor *m* inmobiliario, promotora *f* inmobiliaria, promotor *m*, -ora *f* de construcciones. (**b**) (*Phot*) revelador *m*.

developing [dɪ'veləpɪŋ] **1** *adj country* en (vías de) desarrollo. **2** *attr*: **~ bath** baño *m* de revelado.

development [dɪ'veləpmənt] **1** *n* (**a**) (*gen*) desarrollo *m*; progreso *m*; evolución *f*; (*encouragement*) promoción *f*, fomento *m*; (*of resources*) explotación *f*. (**b**) (*of land*) urbanización *f*; ensanche *m*, ampliación *f*; (*as housing*) colonia *f*. (**c**) (*Phot*) revelado *m*. (**d**) (*also* **new ~**) hecho *m* nuevo, nueva situación *f*; cambio *m*; novedad *f*; adelanto *m*, avance *m*; **what is the latest ~?** ¿hay alguna novedad?; **there are no new ~s to report** no hay cambios que registrar.
2 *attr*: **~ agency** agencia *f* de promoción; **~ area** polo *m* de promoción; **~ bank** banco *m* de desarrollo; **~ company** compañía *f* de explotación; **~ corporation** (*of new town*) corporación *f* de desarrollo, corporación *f* de promoción; **~ officer** director *m*, -ora *f* de promoción; **~ plan** plan *m* de desarrollo.

developmental [dɪˌveləp'məntl] *adj* relativo al desarrollo; **~ economics** ciencias *fpl* económicas relativas a los países en desarrollo.

deviance ['diːvɪəns] *n*, **deviancy** ['diːvɪənsɪ] (*gen, also Psych*) desviación *f*; (*sexual*) perversión *f*.

deviant ['diːvɪənt] **1** *adj* desviado; pervertido; (*Ling*) desviado. **2** *n* pervertido *m*, -a *f*.

deviate ['diːvɪeɪt] *vi* desviarse (*from* de).

deviation [ˌdiːvɪ'eɪʃən] *n* desviación *f* (*also Med*).

deviationism [ˌdiːvɪ'eɪʃənɪzəm] *n* desviacionismo *m*.

deviationist [ˌdiːvɪ'eɪʃənɪst] **1** *adj* desviacionista. **2** *n* desviacionista *mf*.

device [dɪ'vaɪs] *n* (**a**) (*Mech*) aparato *m*, mecanismo *m*, dispositivo *m*; (*explosive*) artefacto *m*; **nuclear ~** ingenio *m* nuclear.
(**b**) (*scheme*) estratagema *f*, recurso *m*.
(**c**) (*emblem*) emblema *m*; (*motto*) lema *m*.
(**d**) **to leave sb to his own ~s** dejar a uno hacer lo que le dé la gana; dejar que uno se las arregle por sí solo.

devil ['devl] **1** *n* (**a**) diablo *m*, demonio *m*; **little ~** diablillo *m*; **a poor ~** un pobre diablo; **you ~!** ¡eres el demonio!; **be a ~ and drink it** a ver si te atreves a beberlo; **~'s advocate** abogado *m* del diablo.
(**b**) (*Jur*) aprendiz *m* (de abogado); (*Typ*) aprendiz *m* de imprenta.
(**c**) (*intensifier*) **a ~ of a mess** una terrible confusión; **a ~ of a noise** un ruido de todos los demonios; **we had the ~ of a job, we had the ~'s own job** nos costó un ojo de la cara (*to get* obtener); **it's a ~ of a problem** es un problema diabólico; **why the ~ didn't you say so?** ¿por qué demonios no me lo has dicho?
(**d**) (*phrases*) **the ~!** ¡demonio!; **the ~ it is!** ¡qué demonio!; **what the ~?** ¿qué demonios ...?; **like the ~** como el demonio; **the ~ take it!** ¡que se lo lleve el diablo!; **go to the ~!** ¡vete al diablo!; **he's going to the ~** se está arruinando; **to be between the ~ and the deep blue sea** estar entre la espada y la pared; **better the ~ we know** vale más lo malo conocido que lo bueno por conocer; **the ~ finds work for idle hands** cuando el diablo no tiene que hacer con el rabo mata moscas; **to give the ~ his due** para ser justo hasta con el diablo; **there'll be the ~ to pay** esto nos va a costar muy caro, ahí será el diablo; **to play the ~ with** arruinar, estropear; **to raise the ~** armar la gorda; **talk of the ~!** ¡hablando del ruin de Roma por la puerta asoma!
(**e**) (*fire etc*) arrojo *m*, energía *f*.
2 *vt* (**a**) *meat* asar con mucho picante.
(**b**) (*US**) fastidiar.
3 *vi*: **to ~ for** (*Jur*) trabajar de aprendiz para.

devilfish ['devlfɪʃ] *n* raya *f*, manta *f*.

devilish ['devlɪʃ] **1** *adj* diabólico. **2** *adv* la mar de; **~ cunning** la mar de ingenioso.

devilishly ['devlɪʃlɪ] *adv behave* endemoniadamente.

devil-may-care ['devlmeɪ'kɛəʳ] *adj* despreocupado; (*rash*) temerario, arriesgado.

devilment ['devlmənt] *n* diablura *f*; = **devilry.**
devilry ['devlrɪ] *n* (*wickedness*) maldad *f*, crueldad *f*; (*mischief*) diablura *f*, travesura *f*, pillería *f*.
devious ['diːvɪəs] *adj path* tortuoso, sinuoso; *means, method, plan* intrincado, enrevesado; *person* taimado.
deviously ['diːvɪəslɪ] *adv act, behave* taimadamente.
deviousness ['diːvɪəsnɪs] *n* carácter *m* taimado.
devise [dɪ'vaɪz] *vt* idear, inventar, imaginar.
deviser [dɪ'vaɪzəʳ] *n* (*of scheme, plan*) inventor *m*, -ora *f*, maquinador *m*, -ora *f*.
devitalize [diː'vaɪtəlaɪz] *vt* debilitar, privar de vitalidad, desvitalizar.
devoid [dɪ'vɔɪd] *adj*: ~ **of** desprovisto de.
devolution [ˌdiːvə'luːʃən] *n* delegación *f* (de poderes).
devolve [dɪ'vɒlv] **1** *vt* delegar. **2** *vi*: **to** ~ **upon** incumbir a, corresponder a; **it ~s upon me to** + *infin* me toca a mí + *infin*.
Devonian [de'vəʊnɪən] *adj* (*Geol*) devónico.
devote [dɪ'vəʊt] **1** *vt* dedicar (*to* a; *to* + *ger* a + *infin*); **he is ~d to her** la quiere con verdadera devoción; **this room is ~d to Goya** esta sala está dedicada a Goya; **this chapter is ~d to politics** este capítulo trata de la política.
2 *vr*: **to** ~ **o.s. to** dedicarse a.
devoted [dɪ'vəʊtɪd] *adj* leal, fiel, dedicado.
devotedly [dɪ'vəʊtɪdlɪ] *adv* con devoción.
devotee [ˌdevəʊ'tiː] *n* devoto *m*, -a *f* (*of* de); partidario *m*, -a *f* (*of* de).
devotion [dɪ'vəʊʃən] *n* (**a**) devoción *f* (*to* a); (*to studies etc*) dedicación *f* (*to* a); entrega *f*; (*of friend etc*) lealtad *f*. (**b**) **~s** (*Rel*) oraciones *fpl*.
devotional [dɪ'vəʊʃənl] *adj* piadoso, devoto.
devour [dɪ'vaʊəʳ] *vt* devorar (*also fig*), comerse; **to be ~ed with curiosity** no caber en sí de curiosidad; **to be ~ed with envy** morirse de envidia.
devouring [dɪ'vaʊərɪŋ] *adj* (*fig*) absorbente.
devout [dɪ'vaʊt] *adj* devoto, piadoso.
devoutly [dɪ'vaʊtlɪ] *adv* con devoción, piadosamente.
dew [djuː] *n* rocío *m*.
dewdrop ['djuːdrɒp] *n* gota *f* de rocío.
dewlap ['djuːlæp] *n* papada *f*.
dewpond ['djuːpɒnd] *n* charca *f* formada por el rocío.
dewy ['djuːɪ] *adj* rociado; lleno de rocío; *eyes* húmedo.
dewy-eyed ['djuːɪ'aɪd] *adj* ingenuo.
dexterity [deks'terɪtɪ] *n* destreza *f*.
dexterous ['dekstrəs] *adj*, **dextrous** ['dekstrəs] *adj* diestro; **by the ~ use of** por el diestro uso de.
dexterously ['dekstrəslɪ] *adv*, **dextrously** ['dekstrəslɪ] *adv* diestramente, hábilmente.
dextrose ['dekstrəʊs] *n* dextrosa *f*.
DG *n abbr of* **Director General.**
dg *abbr of* **decigram(s)** decigramo(s) *m(pl)*.
DH *n* (*Brit*) *abbr of* **Department of Health.**
DHSS *n* (*Brit, formerly*) *abbr of* **Department of Health and Social Security.**
DI *n abbr of* **Donor Insemination.**
Di [daɪ] *nf familiar form of* **Diana.**
di... [daɪ] *pref* di....
diabetes [ˌdaɪə'biːtiːz] *n* diabetes *f*.
diabetic [ˌdaɪə'betɪk] **1** *adj* diabético. **2** *n* diabético *m*, -a *f*.
diabolic(al) [ˌdaɪə'bɒlɪk(əl)] *adj* diabólico.
diabolically [ˌdaɪə'bɒlɪkəlɪ] *adv behave etc* diabólicamente, endemoniadamente; ~ **difficult** endemoniadamente difícil; **it was ~ hot** hacía un calor de infierno.
diachronic [ˌdaɪə'krɒnɪk] *adj* diacrónico.
diacritic [ˌdaɪə'krɪtɪk] **1** *adj* (*also* **~al**) diacrítico. **2** *nm* signo *m* diacrítico.
diadem ['daɪədem] *n* diadema *f*.
diaeresis, (*US*) **dieresis** [daɪ'erɪsɪs] *n* diéresis *f*.
diagnose ['daɪəgnəʊz] *vt* diagnosticar.
diagnosis [ˌdaɪəg'nəʊsɪs] *n*, *pl* **diagnoses** [ˌdaɪəgˌnəʊsiːz] (*of patient*) diagnóstico *m*; (*science*) diagnosis *f*.
diagnostic [ˌdaɪəg'nɒstɪk] *adj* diagnóstico.
diagnostics [ˌdaɪəg'nɒstɪks] *n* diagnóstica *f*.
diagonal [daɪ'ægənl] **1** *adj* diagonal. **2** *n* diagonal *f*.
diagonally [daɪ'ægənəlɪ] *adv* diagonalmente.
diagram ['daɪəgræm] *n* esquema *m*, diagrama *m*, gráfico *m*.
diagrammatic [ˌdaɪəgrə'mætɪk] *adj* esquemático.
dial ['daɪəl] **1** *n* esfera *f*, cuadrante *m*, cara *f* (*LAm*); (*Aut: on dashboard*) reloj *m*; (*Telec*) disco *m*; (‡) jeta* *f*, cara *f*; ~ **code** (*US*) prefijo *m*; ~ **tone** (*US Telec*) tono *m* de marcar. **2** *vt* marcar.
dialect ['daɪəlekt] **1** *n* dialecto *m*. **2** *attr* dialectal; ~ **atlas** atlas *m* lingüístico; ~ **survey** estudio *m* de geografía lingüística.
dialectal [ˌdaɪə'lektl] *adj* dialectal.
dialectic [ˌdaɪə'lektɪk] *adj* dialéctico.
dialectical [ˌdaɪə'lektɪkəl] *adj* dialéctico.
dialectic(s) [ˌdaɪə'lektɪk(s)] *n* dialéctica *f*.
dialectology [ˌdaɪəlek'tɒlədʒɪ] *n* dialectología *f*.
dialling, (*US*) **dialing** ['daɪəlɪŋ] *n* marcación *f*, discado *m*; ~ **code** prefijo *m*; ~ **tone** (*Brit*) tono *m* de marcar.
dialogue, (*US*) **dialog** ['daɪəlɒg] **1** *n* diálogo *m*. **2** *vi* dialogar.
dial-up service ['daɪəlˌʌp'sɜːvɪs] *n* servicio *m* de enlace entre cuadrantes.
dialysis [daɪ'æləsɪs] *n* diálisis *f*.
diameter [daɪ'æmɪtəʳ] *n* diámetro *m*.
diametrical [ˌdaɪə'metrɪkəl] *adj* diametral.
diametrically [ˌdaɪə'metrɪkəlɪ] *adv*: ~ **opposed to** diametralmente opuesto a.
diamond ['daɪəmənd] *n* diamante *m*; (*Archit etc, Baseball*) losange *m*; **~s** (*Cards*) diamantes *mpl*, (*in Spanish pack*) oros *mpl*; ~ **cut** ~ tal para cual; ~ **jubilee** sexagésimo aniversario *m*; ~ **merchant** tratante *mf* en diamantes; ~ **necklace** collar *m* de diamantes; ~ **wedding** bodas *fpl* de diamante.
diamond-cutter ['daɪəmənd,kʌtəʳ] *n* diamantista *m*.
diamond-shaped ['daɪəmənd,ʃeɪpt] *adj* de forma de losange (*or* rombo), romboidal.
diamorphine [ˌdaɪə'mɔːfiːn] *n* diamorfina *f*.
Diana [daɪ'ænə] *nf* Diana.
diaper ['daɪəpəʳ] *n* (*US*) pañal *m*; ~ **pin** imperdible *m*, seguro *m* (*LAm*); ~ **service** servicio *m* de pañales a domicilio.
diaphanous [daɪ'æfənəs] *adj* diáfano.
diaphragm ['daɪəfræm] *n* diafragma *m*.
diarist ['daɪərɪst] *n* diarista *mf*.
diarrhoea, (*US*) **diarrhea** [ˌdaɪə'riːə] *n* diarrea *f*.
diary ['daɪərɪ] *n* diario *m*; (*engagement* ~) agenda *f*, diario *m*, calendario *m* (*US*).
diaspora [daɪ'æspərə] *n* diáspora *f*.
diatonic [ˌdaɪə'tɒnɪk] *adj* diatónico; ~ **scale** escala *f* diatónica.
diatribe ['daɪətraɪb] *n* diatriba *f*.
dibble ['dɪbl] **1** *n* plantador *m*. **2** *vt* (*also* **to** ~ **in**) plantar con plantador.
dibs [dɪbz] *n* (**a**) (*Brit*‡†) parné‡ *m*. (**b**) (*US**) **to have ~ on sth** tener derechos sobre algo; ~ **on the cookies!** ¡las galletas pa' mí!
dice [daɪs] **1** *n* dado *m*; (*as pl*) dados *mpl*; (*shapes*) cubitos *mpl*, cuadritos *mpl*; **no ~!*** (*US*) ¡ni hablar!, nada de eso.
2 *vt vegetables* cortar en cubitos; hacer macedonia de; **~d vegetables** macedonia *f* de legumbres.
3 *vi* jugar a los dados; **to ~ with death** jugar con la muerte.
dicey* ['daɪsɪ] *adj* (*Brit*) incierto, dudoso; peligroso; difícil, problemático.
dichotomy [dɪ'kɒtəmɪ] *n* dicotomía *f*.
Dick [dɪk] *nm familiar form of* **Richard.**
dick [dɪk] *n* (*US*) (**a**) (**‡**) polla**‡** *f*. (**b**) (*US*‡) detective *m*.
dickens ['dɪkɪnz] (*euph*) *en muchas frases* = **devil.**
Dickensian [dɪ'kenzɪən] *adj* dickensiano.
dicker ['dɪkəʳ] *vi* (**a**) vacilar, titubear. (**b**) (*US Comm*) regatear, cambalachear.
dickey*, dicky¹* ['dɪkɪ] *n* (**a**) (*baby talk*; *also* **dicky bird**) pajarito *m*. (**b**) (*shirt front*) pechera *f* postiza. (**c**) (*Brit*: *also* ~ **seat**) spider *m*.
dickhead‡ ['dɪkhed] *n* bobo *m*.
dicky²* ['dɪkɪ] *adj* (*Brit*) poco firme, inestable; (*Med*) **to feel** ~ sentirse algo indispuesto; **to have a ~ heart** tener una debilidad cardíaca.
dicta ['dɪktə] *npl of* **dictum.**
Dictaphone ['dɪktəfəʊn] ® *n* dictáfono ® *m*.
dictate 1 ['dɪkteɪt] *n* mandato *m*; **~s** dictados *mpl*, preceptos *mpl*.
2 [dɪk'teɪt] *vt* (**a**) (*say aloud*) dictar; (*order*) mandar, disponer; *terms* imponer.
(**b**) **I will not be ~d to** yo no estoy a las órdenes de nadie, a mí no me manda nadie.
3 [dɪk'teɪt] *vi*: **to ~ to one's secretary** dictar a su secretaria.
dictation [dɪk'teɪʃən] *n* (**a**) dictado *m*; **at ~ speed** a velocidad de dictado; **to take ~** tomar dictado; **to write at the ~ of** escribir al dictado de. (**b**) (*order*) mandato *m*.
dictator [dɪk'teɪtəʳ] *n* dictador *m*, -ora *f*.
dictatorial [ˌdɪktə'tɔːrɪəl] *adj* dictatorio; *manner etc* dictatorial, imperioso.
dictatorially [dɪktə'tɔːrɪəlɪ] *adv* dictatorialmente.

dictatorship [dɪk'teɪtəʃɪp] *n* dictadura *f*.
diction ['dɪkʃən] *n* dicción *f*; lengua *f*, lenguaje *m*.
dictionary ['dɪkʃənrɪ] *n* diccionario *m*.
dictum ['dɪktəm] *n, pl* **dicta** ['dɪktə] sentencia *f*, aforismo *m*; (*Jur*) dictamen *m*.
did [dɪd] *pret of* **do**¹.
didactic [daɪ'dæktɪk] *adj* didáctico.
didactically [dɪ'dæktɪkəlɪ] *adv* didácticamente.
diddle* ['dɪdl] *vt* (*Brit*) estafar, embaucar; **to ~ sb out of sth** estafar algo a uno.
didn't ['dɪdənt] = **did not**.
Dido [daɪdəʊ] *nf* Dido.
die¹ [daɪ] *vi* morir (*from, of* de; *for* por); (*wither*) marchitarse; (*disappear*) desvanecerse, desaparecer; (*light*) palidecer, extinguirse; **to ~ like flies** morir como chinches; **we nearly died!*** (*laughter*) era para morirse de risa, (*embarrassment*) ¡cómo nos sofocamos!, ¡qué bochorno!; (*fear*) ¡qué susto!; **never say ~!** ¡ánimo!, ¡mientras hay vida hay esperanza!; **he died a hero** murió como héroe; **the secret died with her** llevó el secreto a la tumba; **the custom dies hard** la costumbre tarda bastante en desaparecer; **to be dying for sth** morirse por algo, perecerse por algo; **to be dying to** + *infin* morirse por + *infin*; **to ~ a violent death** tener una muerte violenta, morir de manera violenta.
◆**die away** *vi* apagarse gradualmente; disminuir; desaparecer; desvanecerse; (*sound*) dejar poco a poco de oírse, alejarse hasta perderse.
◆**die back** *vi* (*Bot*) secarse.
◆**die down** *vi* (*fire*) apagarse; (*wind*) perder su fuerza, amainar; (*battle etc*) hacerse menos violento; (*discontent, excitement, protests*) calmarse, sosegarse.
◆**die off** *vi* morirse, (*family, race*) irse extinguiendo.
◆**die out** *vi* extinguirse, desaparecer; (*custom*) caer en desuso; (*of showers etc*) desaparecer.
die² [daɪ] *n* (**a**) (*pl* **dice** [daɪs]) dado *m*; **the ~ is cast** la suerte está echada. (**b**) (*pl* **dies** [daɪz]) cuño *m*, troquel *m*; matriz *f*.
die-casting ['daɪ'kɑːstɪŋ] *n* pieza *f* fundida a troquel.
diectic [daɪ'ektɪk] *n* diéctico *m*.
diehard ['daɪhɑːd] **1** *adj* intransigente, empedernido, acérrimo. **2** *n* incondicional *mf*, intransigente *mf*.
dieldrin ['diːldrɪn] *n* dieldrina *f*.
dielectric [ˌdaɪə'lektrɪk] **1** *adj* dieléctrico. **2** *n* dieléctrico *m*.
diesel ['diːzəl] **1** *n* (**a**) diesel *m*. (**b**) (‡) té *m*. **2** *attr*: **~ engine** motor *m* diesel; **~ fuel, ~ oil** gasóleo *m*, gas-oil *m*; **~ train** tren *m* diesel.
diesel-electric ['diːzəlɪ'lektrɪk] *adj* dieseleléctrico.
die-sinker ['daɪˌsɪŋkə^r] *n* grabador *m* de troqueles.
die-stamp ['daɪˌstæmp] *vt* grabar.
diet¹ ['daɪət] **1** *n* régimen *m*, dieta *f*; **to be on a ~** estar a régimen; **to go on a ~** ponerse a régimen; **to put sb on a ~** poner a uno a régimen. **2** *vi* estar a régimen.
diet² ['daɪət] *n* (*Pol*) dieta *f*.
dietary ['daɪətərɪ] *adj* dietético; **~ fibre** fibra *f* dietética.
dietetic [ˌdaɪɪ'tetɪk] **1** *adj* dietético. **2 ~s** *n* dietética *f*.
dietician [ˌdaɪɪ'tɪʃən] *n* dietético *m*, -a *f*.
differ ['dɪfə^r] *vi* (**a**) **they ~** (*things*) son distintos, (*persons*) no están de acuerdo; **the texts ~** los textos discrepan.
(**b**) **to ~ from** ser distinto de, diferenciarse de, discrepar de; **how does this ~ from that?** ¿en qué se diferencia éste de aquél?
(**c**) (*personal subject*) **I beg to ~** siento tener que disentir; **we ~ed about it** no estábamos de acuerdo sobre ello; **I ~ from you** no estoy de acuerdo contigo; **I ~ from your opinion** discrepo de tu opinión, no comparto tu opinión.
difference ['dɪfrəns] *n* diferencia *f*; **~ of opinion** desacuerdo *m*, (*euph*) controversia *f*, (*euph*: *quarrel*) riña *f*; **a novel with a ~** una novela que tiene algo distintivo; **it makes no ~** lo mismo da; **as near as makes no ~** con tan poca diferencia que no se nota; **it makes a lot of ~** importa mucho; **what ~ does it make?** ¿qué más da?; **it will make no ~ to us** no nos afectará en lo más mínimo; **that makes all the ~** eso cambia totalmente la cosa; **I'll pay the ~** yo pago la diferencia; **I see no ~ between them** no les veo diferencia alguna; **to split the ~** partir la diferencia.
different ['dɪfrənt] *adj* diferente, distinto (*from* de); **to be as ~ as chalk from cheese** parecerse como día y noche.
differential [ˌdɪfə'renʃəl] **1** *adj* diferencial; **~ calculus** cálculo *m* diferencial. **2** *n* (*Math, Aut*) diferencial *m*.
differentiate [ˌdɪfə'renʃɪeɪt] **1** *vt* diferenciar, distinguir (*from* de). **2** *vi* diferenciarse (*also Bio*); **to ~ between two things** distinguir entre dos cosas.
differentiation [ˌdɪfərenʃɪ'eɪʃən] *n* diferenciación *f*.
differently ['dɪfrəntlɪ] *adv* de modo distinto, de otro modo.
difficult ['dɪfɪkəlt] *adj* difícil; **to make life ~ for sb** hacer la vida imposible a uno.
difficulty ['dɪfɪkəltɪ] *n* dificultad *f*; (*jam*) apuro *m*, aprieto *m*; **to get into difficulties** hacerse un lío, meterse en apuros, (*eg while swimming*) encontrarse sin fuerzas para continuar, (*ship*) encontrarse en peligro; **to have ~ in breathing** tener la respiración penosa; **he's having difficulties with his wife** tiene problemas con su mujer; **we have ~ in getting enough staff** es difícil encontrar bastante personal; **I find ~ in walking** encuentro difícil el andar; **to make difficulties for sb** poner estorbos a uno; **I see no ~ in admitting that ...** no hay dificultad para reconocer que...
diffidence ['dɪfɪdəns] *n* timidez *f*, falta *f* de confianza en sí mismo.
diffident ['dɪfɪdənt] *adj* tímido, falto de confianza en sí mismo.
diffidently ['dɪfɪdəntlɪ] *adv* tímidamente, con timidez.
diffract [dɪ'frækt] *vt* difractar.
diffraction [dɪ'frækʃən] *n* difracción *f*.
diffuse 1 [dɪ'fjuːs] *adj* difuso; (*long-winded*) prolijo. **2** [dɪ'fjuːz] *vt* difundir. **3** [dɪ'fjuːz] *vi* difundirse.
diffused [dɪ'fjuːzd] *adj* difuso.
diffuseness [dɪ'fjuːsnɪs] *n* prolijidad *f*.
diffusion [dɪ'fjuːʒən] *n* difusión *f*.
dig [dɪg] **1** *n* (**a**) (*archaeological etc*) excavación *f*.
(**b**) (*prod*) empujón *m*; (*with elbow*) codazo *m*.
(**c**) (*: *remark*) indirecta *f*, zumba *f*; **to have a ~ at** aludir irónicamente a, tomar el pelo a.
2 (*irr*: *pret and ptp* **dug**) *vt* (**a**) cavar, excavar; (*of animals*) escarbar; *garden* cultivar, *patch of earth* remover con laya; *coal* extraer, sacar; *teeth, nails* hincar (*into* en).
(**b**) (*prod*) empujar, dar un codazo a; **to ~ sb in the ribs** dar a uno un codazo en las costillas.
(**c**) (‡) **I don't ~ jazz** no me gusta el jazz, el jazz no me dice nada; **I really ~ that** eso me chifla*; **~ this!** ¡mira esto!
3 *vi* cavar; **to ~ deeper into a subject** ahondar en un tema; **to ~ for gold** cavar en busca de oro.
◆**dig in 1** *vt manure* añadir al suelo.
2 *vi* (**a**) (*Mil*) atrincherarse; hacerse fuerte.
(**b**) (*) empezar a comer, hincar el diente; **~ in!** ¡a comer!
◆**dig into** *vt reserves etc* consumir, usar; **he dug into his pocket** metió la mano en el bolsillo, buscó en el bolsillo; **to ~ into a meal*** empezar a zamparse una comida.
◆**dig out** *vt hole* excavar; *buried object* sacar cavando, extraer; (*from rubble*) desescombrar; *thorn in flesh* extraer; (*fig*) sacar, extraer.
◆**dig over** *vt earth* voltear; *garden* recavar.
◆**dig up** *vt* desenterrar (*also fig*), descubrir; *flowerbed* remover la tierra de; *potatoes* sacar; *plant* desarraigar; *roadway etc* levantar.
digest 1 ['daɪdʒest] *n* resumen *m*; (*Jur*) digesto *m*. **2** [daɪ'dʒest] *vt food* digerir; (*think over*) meditar, digerir; *knowledge, territory* asimilar; *insult* tragarse; *opinion* aceptar.
digestible [dɪ'dʒestəbl] *adj* digerible; **easily ~** fácil de digerir.
digestion [dɪ'dʒestʃən] *n* digestión *f*.
digestive [dɪ'dʒestɪv] *adj* digestivo; **~ juices** jugos *mpl* digestivos; **~ system** aparato *m* digestivo; **~ tract** canal *m* digestivo.
digger ['dɪgə^r] *n* (**a**) cavador *m*, -ora *f*; (*archaeological*) excavador *m*, -ora *f*; (*Mech*) excavadora *f*. (**b**) (*) australiano *m*, -a *f*.
digging ['dɪgɪŋ] *n* (**a**) (*with spade, of hole etc*) cava *f*; (*Min*) excavación *f*. (**b**) **~s** (*Min*) material *m* excavado; (*Archaeology*) excavaciones *fpl*.
digit ['dɪdʒɪt] *n* cifra *f*, número *m*, dígito *m*.
digital ['dɪdʒɪtəl] *adj* digital; **~ clock, ~ watch** reloj *m* digital; **~ computer** ordenador *m* digital; **~ mapping** cartografía *f* digital; **~ recording** grabación *f* digital.
digitalis [ˌdɪdʒɪ'teɪlɪs] *n* digital *f*.
digitalize ['dɪdʒɪtəˌlaɪz] *vt*, **digitize** ['dɪdʒɪtaɪz] *vt* digitalizar.
digitizer ['dɪdʒɪtaɪzə^r] *n* digitalizador *m*.
diglossia [daɪ'glɒsɪə] *n* diglosia *f*.
dignified ['dɪgnɪfaɪd] *adj* grave, solemne; *gait etc* majestuoso; *action, ceremony* decoroso; **it's not ~ to** + *infin* no es elegante + *infin*.
dignify ['dɪgnɪfaɪ] *vt* dignificar; dar un título altisonante a.
dignitary ['dɪgnɪtərɪ] *n* dignatario *m*, dignidad *f*.
dignity ['dɪgnɪtɪ] *n* dignidad *f*; **it would be beneath my ~ to**

+ *infin* desmerecería de mi dignidad + *infin*; **to stand on one's ~** ponerse en su lugar, ponerse tan alto.

digress [daɪ'gres] *vi* hacer una digresión; (*pej*) divagar; **to ~ from** apartarse de; **but I ~** pero vamos al grano.

digression [daɪ'greʃən] *n* digresión *f*.

digs [dɪgz] *npl* (*Brit**) pensión *f*, alojamiento *m*.

dike¹ [daɪk] *n* (*embankment*: *also fig*) dique *m*; (*ditch*) canal *m*, acequia *f*.

dike²‡ [daɪk] *n* lesbiana *f*, tortillera‡ *f*.

dilapidated [dɪ'læpɪdeɪtɪd] *adj building etc* desmoronado, ruinoso; *vehicle etc* desvencijado.

dilapidation [dɪ,læpɪ'deɪʃən] *n* estado *m* ruinoso; lo desvencijado.

dilate [daɪ'leɪt] **1** *vt* dilatar. **2** *vi* dilatarse; extenderse; **to ~ upon** dilatarse sobre.

dilation [daɪ'leɪʃən] *n* dilatación *f*.

dilatoriness ['dɪlətərɪnɪs] *n* tardanza *f*, lentitud *f*.

dilatory ['dɪlətərɪ] *adj* tardo, lento; **to be ~ in replying** tardar mucho en contestar.

dildo ['dɪldəʊ] *n* consolador *m*.

dilemma [daɪ'lemə] *n* dilema *m*; **to be in a ~** estar en un dilema.

dilettante [,dɪlɪ'tæntɪ] *n*, *pl* **dilettanti** [,dɪlɪ'tæntɪ] diletante *mf*.

diligence ['dɪlɪdʒəns] *n* diligencia *f*.

diligent ['dɪlɪdʒənt] *adj* diligente.

diligently ['dɪlɪdʒəntlɪ] *adv* diligentemente.

dill [dɪl] *n* eneldo *m*.

dilly* ['dɪlɪ] *n* (*US*): **she's a ~** (*girl*) está muy bien*; **it's a ~** (*problem*) es un rompecabezas.

dilly-dally ['dɪlɪdælɪ] *vi* vacilar; titubear; (*loiter*) perder el tiempo.

dilly-dallying ['dɪlɪdælɪɪŋ] *n* vacilación *f*; titubeo *m*; pérdida *f* de tiempo.

dilute [daɪ'lu:t] **1** *adj* diluido. **2** *vt* diluir; (*fig*) adulterar.

dilution [daɪ'lu:ʃən] *n* dilución *f*; (*fig*) adulteración *f*.

dim [dɪm] **1** *adj* (**a**) *light* débil; *sight* turbio; *room etc* oscuro, sombrío; *object, outline* indistinto, confuso; **in the ~ and distant past** en un pasado remoto.

(**b**) (*) *opinion* poco favorable; **to take a ~ view of sth** ver algo con malos ojos, desaprobar algo.

(**c**) (*Brit**) *person* lerdo.

2 *vt light* reducir la intensidad de; *headlamps* bajar; (*fig*) *splendour* ofuscar, oscurecer; *memory* borrar; **to ~ one's lights** (*US Aut*) poner luces de cruce.

3 *vi* (*colour, light*) apagarse; (*memory*) difuminarse; (*glory*) empañarse.

dime [daɪm] *n* (*Canada, US*) *moneda de 10 centavos*; (*Drugs sl*: *also* **~ bag**) saquito *m* de marijuana de diez dólares; **~ novel** (*US*) novela *f* de cinco duros, novelucha *f*; **~ store** tienda *f* que vende mercadería barata; **a ~ a dozen** muy barato, (*fig*) a montones.

dimension [dɪ'menʃən] *n* dimensión *f*.

-dimensional [daɪ'menʃənl] *adj ending in compounds*: **two~** bidimensional.

diminish [dɪ'mɪnɪʃ] **1** *vt* disminuir. **2** *vi* disminuir(se).

diminished [dɪ'mɪnɪʃt] *adj numbers, speed, strength* reducido; *character, reputation* oscurecido; *value* (*Mus*) disminuido; **a ~ staff** una plantilla reducida; **~ responsibility** (*Jur*) responsabilidad *f* reducida.

diminishing [dɪ'mɪnɪʃɪŋ] *adj* menguante; **law of ~ returns** ley *f* de rendimiento decreciente.

diminuendo [dɪ,mɪnjʊ'endəʊ] **1** *n* (*Mus*) diminuendo *m*. **2** *vi* hacer un diminuendo.

diminution [,dɪmɪ'nju:ʃən] *n* disminución *f*.

diminutive [dɪ'mɪnjʊtɪv] **1** *adj* diminuto; (*Gram*) diminutivo. **2** *n* diminutivo *m*.

dimly ['dɪmlɪ] *adv shine etc* débilmente; *see* confusamente; **one could ~ make out forms** se veían indistintamente unos bultos.

dimmer ['dɪməʳ] *n* regulador *m* de intensidad; (*US Aut*) interruptor *m*; **~ switch** botón *m* de regulación de la intensidad.

dimming ['dɪmɪŋ] *n* (*of light*) oscurecimiento *m*; (*of mirror, reputation*) empañamiento *m*; (*of headlights*) cambio *m* a cortas.

dimness ['dɪmnɪs] *n* (*V adj*) debilidad *f*; lo turbio; oscuridad *f*, semioscuridad *f*, lo sombrío; lo indistinto, lo confuso; lo lerdo.

dimple ['dɪmpl] **1** *n* hoyuelo *m*. **2** *vt* formar hoyuelos en; *water* rizar. **3** *vi* formarse hoyuelos; (*water*) rizarse.

dimpled ['dɪmpld] *adj cheek, chin* con hoyuelo; *hand, arm* con hoyuelos.

dimwit* ['dɪmwɪt] *n* imbécil *mf*.

dim-witted* ['dɪm'wɪtɪd] *adj* lerdo, imbécil.

din [dɪn] **1** *n* estruendo *m*, estrépito *m*.

2 *vt*: **to ~ sth into sb** meter algo a la fuerza en la cabeza de uno; **I had it ~ned into me as a child** lo aprendí de niño a fuerza de repeticiones.

3 *vi*: **it ~s in my ears** me taladra el oído.

dine [daɪn] **1** *vt* dar de cenar (*or* comer) a; **they ~d me very well** me dieron muy bien de cenar. **2** *vi* cenar.

◆dine off *vt* cenar.

◆dine on *vt* cenar.

◆dine out *vi* cenar fuera; **he ~d out on the story** le invitaron por el cuento.

diner ['daɪnəʳ] *n* (**a**) (*person*) comensal *m*. (**b**) (*Rail*) coche-comedor *m*; (*US*) restaurante *m* económico; (*US Aut*) cafetería *f* de carretera.

dinero* [dɪ'nɛərəʊ] *n* (*US*) plata *f*.

dinette [dɪ'net] *n* comedor *m* pequeño, comedorcito *m*.

ding-a-ling [,dɪŋə'lɪŋ] *n* (**a**) (*of bell, telephone*) tilín *m*. (**b**) (*US‡*) bobo *m*.

dingbat‡ ['dɪŋbæt] *n* gilipollas‡ *m*.

ding-dong ['dɪŋ'dɒŋ] **1** *n*: **~!** ¡din dan!, ¡din don! **2** *adj battle* furioso, muy reñido.

dinghy ['dɪŋgɪ] *n* dingui *m*, bote *m*; (*rubber* ~) lancha *f* neumática.

dinginess ['dɪndʒɪnɪs] *n* lo deslustrado, deslucimiento *m*; color *m* oscuro; lo sombrío, oscuridad *f*; lo sucio.

dingo ['dɪŋgəʊ] *n*, *pl* **dingoes** ['dɪŋgəʊz] dingo *m*.

dingy ['dɪndʒɪ] *adj* (*dull*) deslustrado, deslucido; (*dark in colour*) de color oscuro; *room etc* sombrío, oscuro; (*dirty*) sucio.

dining-car ['daɪnɪŋkɑ:ʳ] *n* (*Brit*) coche-comedor *m*, vagón *m* restaurante.

dining-hall ['daɪnɪŋ,hɔ:l] *n* comedor *m*, refectorio *m*.

dining-room ['daɪnɪŋrʊm] *n* comedor *m*.

dining-table ['daɪnɪŋ,teɪbl] *n* mesa *f* de comedor.

dink‡ [dɪŋk] *n* (*US*) tontorrón* *m*, -ona *f*.

dinkie ['dɪŋkɪ] = **dinky 2**.

dinky* ['dɪŋkɪ] **1** *adj* (*Brit*) (*small*) pequeñito; (*nice*) mono, precioso. **2** *n abbr of* **double** (*or* **dual**) **income no kids**.

dinner ['dɪnəʳ] *n* (*evening meal*) cena *f*, (*in some regions*) comida *f*; (*lunch*) comida *f*, (*in some regions*) almuerzo *m*; (*public feast*) cena *f*, banquete *m*; (*to mark retirement etc*) cena *f* homenaje; **we were at ~ with the minister** estábamos cenando con el ministro; **can you come to ~?** ¿puedes venir a cenar?; **to have ~** cenar, comer; **when he retired they gave him a ~** cuando se jubiló le obsequiaron con una cena; **we sat down to ~ at 10.30** nos sentamos a cenar a las 10.30.

dinner-bell ['dɪnə,bel] *n* campana *f* de la cena.

dinner-dance ['dɪnə,dɑ:ns] *n* cena *f* seguida de baile.

dinner-duty ['dɪnə,djʊtɪ] *n* (*Scol*) supervisión *f* de comedor.

dinner-jacket ['dɪnə,dʒækɪt] *n* (*Brit*) smoking *m*, esmoquin *m*.

dinner-knife ['dɪnə,naɪf] *n*, *pl* **dinner-knives** ['dɪnə,naɪvz] cuchillo *m* grande.

dinner-lady ['dɪnə,leɪdɪ] *n* ayudanta *f* (*en el servicio de comidas en las escuelas*).

dinner-party ['dɪnə,pɑ:tɪ] *n* cena *f*.

dinner-plate ['dɪnə,pleɪt] *n* plato *m* grande.

dinner-roll ['dɪnə,rəʊl] *n* panecillo *m*.

dinner-service ['dɪnə,sɜ:vɪs] *n* vajilla *f*, servicio *m* de mesa.

dinner-table ['dɪnə,teɪbl] *n* mesa *f* de comedor.

dinner-time ['dɪnətaɪm] *n* hora *f* de cenar (*or* comer).

dinner-trolley ['dɪnə,trɒlɪ] *n*, **dinner-wagon** ['dɪnə,wægən] *n* carrito *m* de la comida.

dinosaur ['daɪnəsɔ:ʳ] *n* dinosaurio *m*.

dint¹ [dɪnt] *n*: **by ~ of** a fuerza de.

dint² [dɪnt] = **dent**.

diocesan [daɪ'ɒsɪsən] *adj* diocesano.

diocese ['daɪəsɪs] *n* diócesis *f*.

diode ['daɪəʊd] *n* diodo *m*.

Dionysian [,daɪə'nɪzɪən] *adj* dionisiaco.

Dionysius [,daɪə'nɪsɪəs] *nm* Dionisio.

dioxide [daɪ'ɒksaɪd] *n* dióxido *m*.

dioxin [daɪ'ɒksɪn] *n* dioxina *f*.

dip [dɪp] **1** *n* (**a**) (*bath, bathe*) baño *m*; **to go for a ~, to have a ~** darse un chapuzón, darse un remojón, ir a bañarse.

(**b**) (*Geol*) buzamiento *m*; (*of horizon*) depresión *f*; (*slope*) pendiente *f*; inclinación *f*; (*to one side*) ladeo *m*.

(**c**) *V* **lucky**.

(**d**) (*) **~s** luces *fpl* cortas, luces *fpl* de cruce.

2 *vt* (**a**) (*put into liquid*) bañar, mojar (*in, into* en); *pen* mojar; *ladle, scoop etc* meter; (*Agr*) *sheep* lavar; **she ~ped**

her hand into her pocket metió la mano en el bolsillo.
(**b**) **to ~ water out with a bucket** sacar agua con un cubo.
(**c**) *flag* bajar, saludar con; (*Aer*) *wings* saludar con; **to ~ one's lights** (*Brit Aut*) bajar los faros, poner las luces cortas, poner luces de cruce.
3 *vi* (**a**) (*slope down*) inclinarse hacia abajo; (*Geol*) buzar; **the road ~s into the valley** la carretera baja hacia el valle.
(**b**) (*move down*: *bird, plane*) bajar de picada; **the sun ~ped below the hill** el sol desapareció tras la colina.
(**c**) **to ~ into one's pocket** meter la mano en el bolsillo; **to ~ into a book** hojear un libro, leer distraídamente un libro.
Dip. *abbr of* **Diploma.**
diphtheria [dɪf'θɪərɪə] *n* difteria *f*.
diphthong ['dɪfθɒŋ] *n* diptongo *m*.
diphthongize ['dɪfθɒŋaɪz] **1** *vt* diptongar. **2** *vi* diptongarse.
diploma [dɪ'pləʊmə] *n* diploma *m*.
diplomacy [dɪ'pləʊməsɪ] *n* diplomacia *f*.
diplomat ['dɪpləmæt] *n* diplomático *m*, -a *f*.
diplomatic [ˌdɪplə'mætɪk] **1** *adj* diplomático; **~ bag, ~ pouch** (*US*) valija *f* diplomática; **~ corps, ~ service** cuerpo *m* diplomático; **~ immunity** inmunidad *f* diplomática. **2** *n*: **the D~*** el cuerpo diplomático.
diplomatically [ˌdɪplə'mætɪkəlɪ] *adv* diplomáticamente.
diplomatist [dɪ'pləʊmətɪst] *n* diplomático *m*, -a *f*.
dipole ['daɪˌpəʊl] *n* bipolo *m*.
dipped [dɪpt] *adj*: **~ headlights** luces *fpl* cortas, luces *fpl* de cruce.
dipper[1] ['dɪpəʳ] *n* (*Orn*) mirlo *m* acuático.
dipper[2] ['dɪpəʳ] *n*: **big ~** montaña *f* rusa; **Big D~** (*US Astron*) Osa *f* Mayor.
dipper[3] ['dɪpəʳ] *n* (*Culin*) cazo *m*, cucharón *m*.
dipping ['dɪpɪŋ] *n* (*Agr*) lavado *m*.
dippy* ['dɪpɪ] *adj* chiflado*.
dipso* ['dɪpsəʊ] = **dipsomaniac.**
dipsomania [ˌdɪpsəʊ'meɪnɪə] *n* dipsomanía *f*.
dipsomaniac [ˌdɪpsəʊ'meɪnɪæk] *n* dipsomaníaco *m*, -a *f*, dipsómano *m*, -a *f*.
dipstick ['dɪpstɪk] *n* (**a**) (*Aut*) varilla *f* (para comprobar el nivel del aceite), cala *f*. (**b**) (**‡**) gili**‡** *mf*.
dipswitch ['dɪpswɪtʃ] *n* (*Brit Aut*) interruptor *m*.
diptych ['dɪptɪk] *n* díptico *m*.
dir. *abbr of* **director.**
dire [daɪəʳ] *adj* (**a**) *event* horrendo, calamitoso. (**b**) (*: *film, book etc*) horrible, fatal*.
direct [daɪ'rekt] **1** *adj* directo; *current* continuo; *answer* claro, inequívoco; *manner, character* abierto, franco; **~ access** (*Comput*) acceso *m* directo; **~ action** acción *f* directa; **~ advertising** publicidad *f* directa; **~ cost** costo *m* directo; **~ current** corriente *f* continua; **~ debit** pago *m* a la orden; **~ debiting** domiciliación *f*; **~ dialling** servicio *m* (telefónico) automático; **~ free kick** golpe *m* libre directo; **~ grant school** (*Brit* †) escuela *f* subvencionada; **~ method** método *m* directo; **~ object** complemento *m* directo; **~ rule** gobierno *m* directo; **~ selling** ventas *fpl* directas; **~ speech** oración *f* directa; **~ tax** impuesto *m* directo; **~ taxation** tributación *f* directa.
2 *adv* (*in a ~ manner*) directamente; (*straight*) derecho, en línea recta.
3 *vt* (**a**) *letter, remark, gaze, attention, film etc* dirigir (*at, to* a).
(**b**) **can you ~ me to the shop?** ¿me hace el favor de decirme dónde está la tienda?, ¿podría indicarme la dirección de la tienda?
(**c**) (*control*) dirigir, gobernar, controlar.
(**d**) (*order*) mandar; **to ~ that ...** mandar que ...; **to ~ sb to do sth** mandar a uno hacer algo.
direction [dɪ'rekʃən] *n* (**a**) (*act of managing, also Theat etc*) dirección *f*.
(**b**) (*course*) dirección *f*; **~ finder** radiogoniómetro *m*; **~ indicator** (*Aut*) intermitente *m*; **in the ~ of** en dirección a, en la dirección de, hacia; **in the opposite ~** en sentido contrario; **in all ~s** por todos lados; **they ran off in different ~s** salieron corriendo cada uno por su lado.
(**c**) **~s** órdenes *fpl*, instrucciones *fpl*; **~s for use** modo *m* de empleo.
directional [dɪ'rekʃənl] *adj* direccional; **~ aerial** antena *f* dirigida; **~ light** (*Aut*) intermitente *m*.
directive [dɪ'rektɪv] *n* directiva *f*, directriz *f*.
directly [dɪ'rektlɪ] **1** *adv* (*in a direct manner*) directamente; (*in a straight line*) derecho, en línea recta; (*Brit*: *at once*) en seguida; **~ opposite** exactamente enfrente (de).
2 *conj*: **~ you hear it** (*esp Brit*) en cuanto lo oigas.
directness [daɪ'rektnɪs] *n* franqueza *f*.
director [dɪ'rektəʳ] *n* director *m* -ora *f*; **~ general** director *m*, -ora *f* general; **D~ of Education** (*Brit*) ≈ Jefe *m* de la Delegación del Ministerio de Educación; **D~ of Public Prosecutions** (*Brit Jur*) ≈ Fiscal *m* General del Estado.
directorate [daɪ'rektərɪt] *n* (**a**) (*post*) dirección *f*, cargo *m* de director. (**b**) (*body*) junta *f* directiva, consejo *m* de administración.
directorial [daɪrek'tɔːrɪəl] *adj* directivo, directorial; **~ responsibilities** obligaciones *fpl* directivas; responsabilidades *fpl* de administración.
directorship [dɪ'rektəʃɪp] *n* cargo *m* de director.
directory [dɪ'rektərɪ] *n* (*Telec*) guía *f* telefónica; (*of streets*) guía *f* de calles; (*Comput*) directorio *m*; **~ inquiries** (*Brit*), **~ assistance** (*US*) información *f*.
dirge [dɜːdʒ] *n* endecha *f*, canto *m* fúnebre.
dirigible ['dɪrɪdʒəbl] **1** *adj* dirigible. **2** *n* dirigible *m*.
dirk [dɜːk] *n* (*Scot*) puñal *m*.
dirndl ['dɜːndl] *n* falda *f* acampanada.
dirt [dɜːt] *n* (*unclean matter*) suciedad *f*, mugre *f*, (*litter*) basura *f*; (*earth*) tierra *f*; (*mud*) lodo *m*; (*obscenity*) suciedad *f*, inmundicia *f*; (*worthless stuff*) porquería *f*; **~ farmer** (*US**) pequeño granjero *m* (sin obreros); **the book is just ~** el libro es una inmundicia nada más; **to treat sb like ~** tratar a uno como una basura; **to do sb ~*, to do the ~ on sb*** (*US*) hacerle una putada a uno**‡**.
dirt-cheap ['dɜːt'tʃiːp] *adj* tirado, regalado, muy barato.
dirtily ['dɜːtɪlɪ] *adv eat, live* míseramente; (*fig*) *act, behave* bajamente; *play, fight* suciamente.
dirtiness ['dɜːtɪnɪs] *n* suciedad *f*.
dirt road ['dɜːtrəʊd] *n* (*US*) camino *m* sin firme, camino *m* de tierra.
dirt track ['dɜːttræk] *n* pista *f* de ceniza.
dirty ['dɜːtɪ] **1** *adj* sucio; (*grubby*) mugriento; (*stained*) manchado; *trick, play etc* sucio; *novel, story, joke* verde, indecente, sucio; *weather* horrible, feo; **~ old man** viejo *m* verde; **~ tricks department** sección *f* de trampas; **~ war** guerra *f* sucia; **~ word** palabra *f* fea, palabrota *f*; **to do sb's ~ work for him** hacer los trabajos sucios de uno; **there's been ~ work** (**at the crossroads**) ha habido trampa, aquí no han jugado limpio.
2 *adv* (*) *play etc* sucio*.
3 *n*: **to do the ~ on sb** (*Brit*) hacer una mala pasada a uno.
4 *vt* ensuciar; (*stain*) manchar.
dirty-minded [ˌdɜːtɪ'maɪndɪd] *adj* de mente sucia, de imaginación malsana.
disability [ˌdɪsə'bɪlɪtɪ] *n* (**a**) (*state*) incapacidad *f*; (*physical*) invalidez *f*, minusvalidez *f*, discapacidad *f*; **~ allowance, ~ benefit** subsidio *m* por incapacidad; **~ pension** pensión *f* por incapacidad laboral. (**b**) (*feature*) impedimento *m*, estorbo *m*, desventaja *f*.
disable [dɪs'eɪbl] *vt* (*cripple*) estropear, mutilar; *ship etc* inutilizar; (*disqualify etc*) incapacitar, inhabilitar (*for* para).
disabled [dɪs'eɪbld] *adj person* minusválido, discapaz.
disablement [dɪs'eɪblmənt] *n* inhabilitación *f*; (*Med*) minusvalidez *f*; *V also* **disability.**
disabuse [ˌdɪsə'bjuːz] *vt* desengañar (*of* de).
disadvantage [ˌdɪsəd'vɑːntɪdʒ] **1** *n* desventaja *f*, inconveniente *m*; **to the ~ of** con detrimento de; **to be at a ~** estar en una situación desventajosa; **this put him at a ~** esto le dejó en situación desventajosa; **to be taken at a ~** encontrarse en una situación violenta. **2** *vt* perjudicar.
disadvantaged [ˌdɪsəd'vɑːntɪdʒd] **1** *adj* desventajado; no privilegiado, marginado; perjudicado. **2** *npl*: **the ~** los no privilegiados, los marginados.
disadvantageous [ˌdɪsædvɑːn'teɪdʒəs] *adj* desventajoso.
disaffected [ˌdɪsə'fektɪd] *adj* desafecto (*towards* hacia).
disaffection [ˌdɪsə'fekʃən] *n* descontento *m*, desafección *f*.
disaffiliate [ˌdɪsə'fɪlɪˌeɪt] *vi* desafiliarse (*from* de).
disagree ['dɪsə'griː] *vi* (**a**) no estar de acuerdo (*about, on* sobre, *with* con), discrepar (*with* de); **I ~ with you** no estoy de acuerdo contigo, discrepo de ti, no comparto esa opinión; **I ~ with bullfighting** yo no apruebo el toreo, no me gustan los toros; **their findings ~** discrepan sus conclusiones.
(**b**) **to ~ with** (*of food etc*) sentar mal a, hacer daño a.
disagreeable [ˌdɪsə'griːəbl] *adj experience, task* desagradable; (*bad-tempered*) displicente, de mal genio; antipático; *tone of voice etc* malhumorado, áspero; **he was very ~ to me** me trató con bastante aspereza; **I'm rather ~ in the mornings** por la mañana estoy de bastante mal humor.

disagreeableness [ˌdɪsəˈgriːəblnɪs] *n* (*of work, experience*) desagrado *m*; (*of person*) antipatía *f*.
disagreeably [ˌdɪsəˈgriːəblɪ] *adv* con desagrado.
disagreement [ˌdɪsəˈgriːmənt] *n* (**a**) desacuerdo *m*, disconformidad *f* (*with* con); discrepancia *f* (*with* de); **so we were in ~** así que discrepamos. (**b**) (*quarrel*) riña *f*, altercado *m*.
disallow [ˈdɪsəˈlaʊ] *vt* no aceptar, no sancionar, rechazar; *goal* anular.
disambiguate [ˌdɪsæmˈbɪgjʊeɪt] *vt term etc* despejar la ambigüedad de.
disappear [ˌdɪsəˈpɪəʳ] **1** *vt* (*) hacer desaparecer. **2** *vi* desaparecer.
disappearance [ˌdɪsəˈpɪərəns] *n* desaparición *f*.
disappoint [ˌdɪsəˈpɔɪnt] *vt* decepcionar, desilusionar; *hopes* defraudar; **we were ~ed with the book** el libro nos decepcionó; **we shall be ~ed if you don't come** sentiremos mucho que no vengas; **her daughter ~ed her** su hija la defraudó.
disappointing [ˌdɪsəˈpɔɪntɪŋ] *adj* decepcionante, desilusionante; **it is ~ that ...** es triste que + *subj*.
disappointingly [ˌdɪsəˈpɔɪntɪŋlɪ] *adv* de manera decepcionante; **it was ~ brief** fue tan breve que decepcionó; **~, nothing happened** a nuestro pesar no pasó nada.
disappointment [ˌdɪsəˈpɔɪntmənt] *n* (**a**) decepción *f*, desilusión *f*; **to our ~** a nuestro pesar. (**b**) (*event*) contratiempo *m*; decepción *f*; **~ in love** fracaso *m* sentimental; **he is a big ~ to us** nos ha decepcionado muchísimo.
disapproval [ˌdɪsəˈpruːvəl] *n* desaprobación *f*.
disapprove [ˌdɪsəˈpruːv] *vi*: **to ~ of** desaprobar; **he ~s of gambling** no le gusta el juego, está en contra del juego; **I think he ~s of me** creo que me tiene poca simpatía; **I strongly ~** yo estoy firmemente en contra; **but father ~d** pero papá no quiso permitirlo; **your mother would ~** tu madre estaría en contra.
disapproving [ˌdɪsəˈpruːvɪŋ] *adj look etc* de desaprobación.
disapprovingly [ˌdɪsəˈpruːvɪŋlɪ] *adv* con desaprobación.
disarm [dɪsˈɑːm] **1** *vt* desarmar; *bomb* desactivar. **2** *vi* desarmarse.
disarmament [dɪsˈɑːməmənt] *n* desarme *m*.
disarmer [dɪsˈɑːməʳ] *n* partidario *m*, -a *f* del desarme.
disarming [dɪsˈɑːmɪŋ] *adj smile etc* encantador; *speech* conciliador.
disarmingly [dɪsˈɑːmɪŋlɪ] *adv* encantadoramente.
disarrange [ˌdɪsəˈreɪndʒ] *vt* desarreglar, descomponer.
disarranged [ˌdɪsəˈreɪndʒd] *adj bed* deshecho; *hair, clothes* desarreglado.
disarray [ˌdɪsəˈreɪ] *n* desorden *m*, confusión *f*; desarreglo *m*; (*of dress*) desaliño *m*; **in ~** desordenado, en confusión; **the plan was thrown into ~ by the storm** la tormenta dio al traste con el proyecto.
disassemble [ˌdɪsəˈsembl] *vt* desmontar.
disassociate [ˌdɪsəˈsəʊʃɪˌeɪt] *vt* separar, desligar (*from* de).
disaster [dɪˈzɑːstəʳ] *n* desastre *m*; **~ area** región *f* devastada; **~ fund** fondo *m* de ayuda para casos de desastres; **to court ~** correr al desastre.
disastrous [dɪˈzɑːstrəs] *adj* catastrófico, desastroso, funesto, nefasto.
disastrously [dɪˈzɑːstrəslɪ] *adv* catastróficamente.
disavow [ˈdɪsəˈvaʊ] *vt* desconocer, rechazar.
disavowal [ˌdɪsəˈvaʊəl] *n* negativa *f*, rechazo *m*.
disband [dɪsˈbænd] **1** *vt army* licenciar; *organization* desmantelar, disolver. **2** *vi* desbandarse; disolverse.
disbar [ˌdɪsˈbɑːʳ] *vt barrister* excluir del ejercicio de la abogacía, prohibir ejercer; **he was ~red** le prohibieron ejercer la abogacía.
disbelief [ˈdɪsbəˈliːf] *n* incredulidad *f*.
disbelieve [ˈdɪsbəˈliːv] **1** *vt* no creer, desconfiar de. **2** *vi* no creer (*in* en).
disbeliever [ˈdɪsbəˈliːvəʳ] *n* incrédulo *m*, -a *f*; (*Eccl*) descreído *m*, -a *f*.
disbelieving [ˈdɪsbɪˈliːvɪŋ] *adj* incrédulo; desconfiado.
disburden [dɪsˈbɜːdn] **1** *vt* descargar. **2** *vr*: **to ~ o.s. of** descargarse de.
disburse [dɪsˈbɜːs] *vt* desembolsar.
disbursement [dɪsˈbɜːsmənt] *n* desembolso *m*.
disc [dɪsk] *n* disco *m*; (*Med*) vértebra *f*; (*Comput*) = **disk**.
discard 1 [ˈdɪskɑːd] *n* descarte *m* (*also Cards*), desecho *m*.
2 [dɪsˈkɑːd] *vt* descartar; (*Cards*) descartarse de; rechazar, desechar; *clothing* dejar de llevar; *unwanted thing* tirar; *habit* renunciar a.
3 [dɪsˈkɑːd] *vi* descartar(se).
disc brakes [ˈdɪskbreɪks] *npl* (*Brit*) frenos *mpl* de disco.
discern [dɪˈsɜːn] *vt* percibir, discernir.
discernible [dɪˈsɜːnəbl] *adj* perceptible.
discernibly [dɪˈsɜːnəblɪ] *adv* sensiblemente, visiblemente.
discerning [dɪˈsɜːnɪŋ] *adj* perspicaz.
discernment [dɪˈsɜːnmənt] *n* perspicacia *f*, discernimiento *m*.
discharge 1 [ˈdɪstʃɑːdʒ] *n* (**a**) (*of weapon, Elec*: *unloading*) descarga *f*; (*of debt*) pago *m*, descargo *m*; (*of duty*) desempeño *m*, ejecución *f*; (*Mil*) licenciamiento *m*; (*of worker*) despedida *f*; (*of bankrupt*) rehabilitación *f*.
(**b**) (*Med*) pus *m*.
2 [dɪsˈtʃɑːdʒ] *vt* (**a**) *weapon, current, cargo, ship* descargar; *shot, arrow* disparar.
(**b**) *debt* pagar, descargar; *duty* desempeñar, cumplir; *task* ejecutar.
(**c**) *troops* licenciar; *worker* despedir; *person from duty* dispensar, exonerar (*from* de); *prisoner* poner en libertad; *patient* dar de alta; *bankrupt* rehabilitar; **to be ~d from the army** ser licenciado del ejército; **they ~d him from hospital on Monday** le dieron de alta el lunes.
3 [dɪsˈtʃɑːdʒ] *vi* (*river, Elec*) descargar (*into* en); (*Med*) supurar.
disciple [dɪˈsaɪpl] *n* discípulo *m*, -a *f*.
disciplinarian [ˌdɪsɪplɪˈnɛərɪən] *n* ordenancista *mf*.
disciplinary [ˈdɪsɪplɪnərɪ] *adj* disciplinario; **~ action, ~ measure** medida *f* de disciplina.
discipline [ˈdɪsɪplɪn] **1** *n* disciplina *f*. **2** *vt* disciplinar.
disc-jockey [ˈdɪskˌdʒɒkɪ] *n* pinchadiscos *mf*.
disclaim [dɪsˈkleɪm] *vt* negar, rechazar; desconocer; (*Jur*) renunciar a; **he ~ed all knowledge of it** dijo que no sabía nada en absoluto de ello.
disclaimer [dɪsˈkleɪməʳ] *n* negación *f*; (*Jur*) renuncia *f*; **to put in a ~** negarlo, rechazarlo.
disclose [dɪsˈkləʊz] *vt* revelar.
disclosure [dɪsˈkləʊʒəʳ] *n* revelación *f*.
disco* [ˈdɪskəʊ] *n* disco(teca) *f*.
disco-dancing [ˈdɪskəʊˌdɑːnsɪŋ] *n* baile *m* disco.
discolour, (*US*) discolor [dɪsˈkʌləʳ] **1** *vt* de(s)colorar. **2** *vi* de(s)colorarse.
discolouration, (*US*) discoloration [dɪsˌkʌləˈreɪʃən] *n* de(s)coloramiento *m*.
discoloured, (*US*) discolored [dɪsˈkʌləd] *adj* de(s)colorado.
discomfit [dɪsˈkʌmfɪt] *vt* desconcertar.
discomfiture [dɪsˈkʌmfɪtʃəʳ] *n* desconcierto *m*, confusión *f*.
discomfort [dɪsˈkʌmfət] *n* (*lack of comfort*) incomodidad *f*, falta *f* de comodidades; (*physical*) malestar *m*; (*uneasiness*) inquietud *f*.
discomposure [ˌdɪskəmˈpəʊʒəʳ] *n* desconcierto *m*, confusión *f*.
disconcert [ˌdɪskənˈsɜːt] *vt* desconcertar.
disconcerting [ˌdɪskənˈsɜːtɪŋ] *adj* desconcertante.
disconcertingly [ˌdɪskənˈsɜːtɪŋlɪ] *adv* de modo desconcertante; **he spoke in a ~ frank way** desconcertó a todos hablando con tanta franqueza.
disconnect [ˈdɪskəˈnekt] *vt* separar, desacoplar; (*Elec*) desconectar.
disconnected [ˈdɪskəˈnektɪd] *adj* (*fig*) inconexo.
disconsolate [dɪsˈkɒnsəlɪt] *adj* inconsolable.
disconsolately [dɪsˈkɒnsəlɪtlɪ] *adv* inconsolablemente.
discontent [ˈdɪskənˈtent] *n* descontento *m*.
discontented [ˈdɪskənˈtentɪd] *adj* descontento, disgustado.
discontentment [ˈdɪskənˈtentmənt] *n* descontento *m*.
discontinuance [ˌdɪskɒnˈtɪnjʊəns] *n*, **discontinuation** [ˌdɪskənˌtɪnjʊˈeɪʃən] *n* (*of production etc*) cesación *f*, interrupción *f*.
discontinue [ˈdɪskənˈtɪnjuː] *vt* suspender, descontinuar, interrumpir, terminar; *payment* suspender; *newspaper etc* anular el abono de; **'D~d'** (*Comm*) 'Fin de serie'.
discontinuity [ˌdɪskɒntɪˈnjuːɪtɪ] *n* discontinuidad *f*; interrupción *f*.
discontinuous [ˈdɪskənˈtɪnjʊəs] *adj* discontinuo; interrumpido.
discord [ˈdɪskɔːd] *n* discordia *f*; (*Mus*) disonancia *f*; **to sow ~ among** sembrar la discordia entre, sembrar cizaña entre.
discordant [dɪsˈkɔːdənt] *adj* discorde; (*Mus*) disonante.
discothèque [ˈdɪskəʊtek] *n* discoteca *f*.
discount 1 [ˈdɪskaʊnt] *n* descuento *m*, rebaja *f*; **~ house** (*US*) tienda *f* de rebajas; **~ rate** tasa *f* de descuento; **~ store** (*US*) economato *m*; **to be at a ~** (*fig*) no valorarse en su justo precio; **to give a ~ of 10%** dar un descuento del 10 por cien; **to sell at a ~** vender con descuento, vender a precio reducido.

2 [dɪsˈkaʊnt] *vt* (**a**) descontar, rebajar; **~ed cash-flow** cashflow *m* actualizado.
(**b**) (*leave out of account*) dejar a un lado, descartar, desechar; *report etc* considerar exagerado.
discourage [dɪsˈkʌrɪdʒ] *vt* (**a**) (*dishearten*) desalentar, desanimar.
(**b**) (*advise against*) *development etc* oponerse a, desaprobar; *offer, advances* rechazar; *tendency* resistir; **to ~ sb from doing sth** disuadir a uno de hacer algo; **smoking is ~d** se recomienda no fumar.
discouragement [dɪsˈkʌrɪdʒmənt] *n* (**a**) (*depression*) desaliento *m*. (**b**) (*act*) oposición *f*; desaprobación *f*; disuasión *f*; (*obstacle*) estorbo *m*; **it's a real ~ to progress** es un verdadero estorbo para el progreso.
discouraging [dɪsˈkʌrɪdʒɪŋ] *adj* desalentador; **he was ~ about it** habló de ello en tono pesimista.
discourse 1 [ˈdɪskɔːs] *n* discurso *m*; (*talk*) plática *f*; (*essay*) tratado *m*; **~ analysis** análisis *m* del discurso. **2** [dɪsˈkɔːs] *vi*: **to ~ upon** (*converse*) platicar sobre, (*make a speech*) disertar sobre.
discourteous [dɪsˈkɜːtɪəs] *adj* descortés, desatento.
discourteously [dɪsˈkɜːtɪəslɪ] *adv* descortésmente.
discourtesy [dɪsˈkɜːtɪsɪ] *n* descortesía *f*.
discover [dɪsˈkʌvəʳ] *vt* descubrir.
discoverer [dɪsˈkʌvərəʳ] *n* descubridor *m*, -ora *f*.
discovery [dɪsˈkʌvərɪ] *n* descubrimiento *m*.
discredit [dɪsˈkredɪt] **1** *n* descrédito *m*; **it was to the general's ~ that ...** fue un descrédito para el general que .... **2** *vt* desacreditar, deshonrar; (*disbelieve*) poner en duda; **that theory is now ~ed** esa teoría ya está desacreditada; **all his evidence is thus ~ed** por lo tanto se pone en duda todo su testimonio.
discreditable [dɪsˈkredɪtəbl] *adj* deshonroso, vergonzoso.
discreet [dɪsˈkriːt] *adj* discreto, circunspecto, prudente.
discrepancy [dɪsˈkrepənsɪ] *n* discrepancia *f*, diferencia *f*.
discrete [dɪsˈkriːt] *adj* discreto.
discretion [dɪsˈkreʃən] *n* discreción *f*, circunspección *f*, prudencia *f*; **at one's ~** a discreción; **at the chairman's ~ the meeting may ...** le incumbe al presidente decidir si la junta ...; **he may at his ~ allow ...** puede discrecionalmente permitir ...; **it is within his ~ to +** *infin* es de su competencia + *infin*; **to use one's own ~** juzgar una cosa por sí mismo, obrar como mejor le parezca a uno; **~ is the better part of valour** una retirada a tiempo es una victoria; **to reach years of ~** llegar a la edad del discernimiento.
discretionary [dɪsˈkreʃənərɪ] *adj* discrecional.
discriminate [dɪsˈkrɪmɪneɪt] **1** *vt* distinguir (*from* de). **2** *vi*: **to ~ against** discriminar a (*or* contra), hacer una distinción en perjuicio de; **to ~ between** distinguir entre.
discriminating [dɪsˈkrɪmɪneɪtɪŋ] *adj* perspicaz, discernidor; *taste etc* fino.
discrimination [dɪsˌkrɪmɪˈneɪʃən] *n* (**a**) (*discernment*) discernimiento *m*, perspicacia *f*; (*good taste*) buen gusto *m*, finura *f*. (**b**) (*distinction*) distinción *f* (*between* entre); (*partiality*) parcialidad *f*, discriminación *f* (*against* a, contra); **racial ~** discriminación *f* racial.
discriminatory [dɪsˈkrɪmɪnətərɪ] *adj duty etc* discriminatorio.
discursive [dɪsˈkɜːsɪv] *adj* divagador, prolijo; (*Ling*) discursivo.
discus [ˈdɪskəs] *n* disco *m*.
discuss [dɪsˈkʌs] *vt* discutir, hablar de, tratar de, estudiar, comentar; *theme* tratar.
discussant [dɪsˈkʌsənt] *n* (*US*) miembro *mf* de la mesa (de la sección de un congreso).
discussion [dɪsˈkʌʃən] *n* discusión *f*; **it is under ~** lo están estudiando; **to come up for ~** someterse a discusión.
disdain [dɪsˈdeɪn] **1** *n* desdén *m*. **2** *vt* desdeñar. **3** *vi*: **to ~ to +** *infin* no dignarse + *infin*.
disdainful [dɪsˈdeɪnfʊl] *adj* desdeñoso.
disdainfully [dɪsˈdeɪnfəlɪ] *adv* desdeñosamente.
disease [dɪˈziːz] *n* enfermedad *f*; (*liter*) morbo *m*; dolencia *f*; (*fig*) mal *m*.
diseased [dɪˈziːzd] *adj person* enfermo; *tissue* contagiado; *mind* enfermo, morboso.
disembark [ˌdɪsɪmˈbɑːk] *vti* desembarcar.
disembarkation [ˌdɪsembɑːˈkeɪʃən] *n* (*of goods*) desembarque *m*; (*by person*) desembarco *m*.
disembodied [ˈdɪsɪmˈbɒdɪd] *adj* incorpóreo.
disembowel [ˌdɪsɪmˈbaʊəl] *vt* desentrañar, destripar.
disenchanted [ˈdɪsɪnˈtʃɑːntɪd] *adj*: **to be ~ with sb** quedar desencantado (*or* desengañado) con uno; **to be ~ with Slobodia** quedar desencantado (*or* desengañado) de Eslobodia.
disenchantment [ˌdɪsɪnˈtʃɑːntmənt] *n* desencanto *m*.
disenfranchise [ˈdɪsɪnˈfræntʃaɪz] *vt* = **disfranchise**.
disengage [ˌdɪsɪnˈgeɪdʒ] **1** *vt* (*free*) soltar, desasir; (*Mech*) desacoplar, desenganchar; *clutch* desembragar. **2** *vi* (*Mil*) retirarse, romper el contacto.
disengaged [ˌdɪsɪnˈgeɪdʒd] *adj* libre, desocupado.
disengagement [ˌdɪsɪnˈgeɪdʒmənt] *n* retirada *f*, rompimiento *m* de contacto.
disentangle [ˈdɪsɪnˈtæŋgl] **1** *vt* desenredar, desenmarañar (*also fig*; *from* de). **2** *vr*: **to ~ o.s.** desenredarse (*from* de), librarse (*from* de).
disestablish [ˈdɪsɪsˈtæblɪʃ] *vt* (*Eccl*) separar del Estado.
disestablishment [ˌdɪsɪsˈtæblɪʃmənt] *n* (*Eccl*) separación *f* del Estado.
disfavour, (*US*) **disfavor** [dɪsˈfeɪvəʳ] *n* desaprobación *f*; **to fall into ~** (*custom*) dejar de usarse, caer en desuso, (*person*) caer en desgracia; **to look with ~ on sth** desaprobar algo.
disfigure [dɪsˈfɪgəʳ] *vt* desfigurar; afear.
disfigured [dɪsˈfɪgəd] *adj* desfigurado.
disfigurement [dɪsˈfɪgəmənt] *n* desfiguración *f*; afeamiento *m*.
disfranchise [ˈdɪsˈfræntʃaɪz] *vt* privar de los derechos civiles, (*esp*) privar del derecho de votar.
disgorge [dɪsˈgɔːdʒ] *vt* vomitar, arrojar; (*bird*) desembuchar; (*fig*) devolver, restituir.
disgrace [dɪsˈgreɪs] **1** *n* (**a**) (*state of shame*) ignominia *f*, deshonra *f*; **there is no ~ in being poor** no es vergonzoso ser pobre; **to be in ~** estar desacreditado, (*pet, child*) estar castigado; **to bring ~ on** deshonrar; **to fall into ~** caer en desgracia.
(**b**) (*downfall*) caída *f*.
(**c**) (*shameful thing*) vergüenza *f*; escándalo *m*; **it's a ~** es una vergüenza; **what a ~!** ¡qué vergüenza!; **she's a ~ to her family** es la vergüenza de su familia.
2 *vt* deshonrar, desacreditar; **he was ~d and banished** le destituyeron de sus cargos y le desterraron.
3 *vr*: **to ~ o.s.** deshonrarse.
disgraceful [dɪsˈgreɪsfʊl] *adj* vergonzoso, deshonroso; *behaviour* escandaloso; **~!** ¡qué vergüenza!
disgracefully [dɪsˈgreɪsfəlɪ] *adv* vergonzosamente; escandalosamente.
disgruntled [dɪsˈgrʌntld] *adj* disgustado (*at, with* de), contrariado, malhumorado; **to look ~** poner mala cara.
disguise [dɪsˈgaɪz] **1** *n* disfraz *m*; **to be in ~** estar disfrazado. **2** *vt* disfrazar (*as* de). **3** *vr*: **to ~ o.s. as** disfrazarse de.
disgust [dɪsˈgʌst] **1** *n* repugnancia *f*, aversión *f*; **it fills me with ~** me da asco.
2 *vt* repugnar, inspirar aversión a, dar asco a; (*disappointment etc*) disgustar; **the thought ~s me** el pensamiento me repugna; **you ~ me** me das asco; **he was ~ed by his failure** se enfureció contra sí mismo por su fracaso; **I am ~ed with you** me das vergüenza; **I was ~ed with the referee** el árbitro me dio asco.
disgusted [dɪsˈgʌstɪd] *adj* asqueado, lleno de asco; **in a ~ voice** en tono disgustado.
disgustedly [dɪsˈgʌstɪdlɪ] *adv* asqueadamente, con asco; **... he said ~** ... dijo con asco.
disgusting [dɪsˈgʌstɪŋ] *adj* repugnante, asqueroso; **~!** ¡qué asco!
disgustingly [dɪsˈgʌstɪŋlɪ] *adv* asquerosamente; **they are ~ rich** son tan ricos que da asco.
dish [dɪʃ] **1** *n* (**a**) plato *m*; (*large, for serving etc*) fuente *f*; (*food*) plato *m*; platillo *m* (*Mex*); **a typical Spanish ~** un plato típico español; **to wash the ~es** fregar los platos.
(**b**) (*Astron*) reflector *m*; (*TV*) antena *f* parabólica.
(**c**) (*****: *girl, boy*) bombón* *m*; **this is not my ~*** esto no me gusta; yo no sé nada de esto.
2 *vt hopes, chances* confundir, burlar.
◆**dish out** *vt* (*fig*) (*gen*) distribuir; repartir; *criticism* difundir.
◆**dish up** *vt* (*fig*) servir; ofrecer, producir; sacar; **he ~ed up the same old arguments** repitió los argumentos de siempre.
dishabille [ˌdɪsæˈbiːl] *n* desabillé *m*.
dish aerial [ˈdɪʃɛərɪəl] *n*, (*US*) **dish antenna** [ˈdɪʃænˈtenə] *n* antena *f* parabólica.
disharmony [ˈdɪsˈhɑːmənɪ] *n* discordia *f*; (*Mus*) disonancia *f*.
dishcloth [ˈdɪʃklɒθ] *n*, *pl* **dishcloths** [ˈdɪʃklɒðz] trapo *m* (de fregar), paño *m* de cocina, bayeta *f*.
dishearten [dɪsˈhɑːtn] *vt* desalentar, desanimar; **don't be ~ed!** ¡ánimo!

disheartening [dɪs'hɑːtnɪŋ] *adj* desalentador.

dishevelled, (*US*) **disheveled** [dɪ'ʃevəld] *adj* despeinado, desmelenado.

dishmop ['dɪʃmɒp] *n* fregona *f* para lavar los platos.

dishonest [dɪs'ɒnɪst] *adj person* nada honrado, falso, tramposo; *means* fraudulento.

dishonestly [dɪs'ɒnɪstlɪ] *adv* fraudulentamente; **to act ~** obrar con poca honradez.

dishonesty [dɪs'ɒnɪstɪ] *n* falta *f* de honradez, falsedad *f*; (*of means*) fraude *m*.

dishonour, (*US*) **dishonor** [dɪs'ɒnə^r] **1** *n* deshonra *f*, deshonor *m*. **2** *vt* deshonrar; *cheque etc* negarse a aceptar, no pagar; *promise* faltar a, no cumplir.

dishonourable, (*US*) **dishonorable** [dɪs'ɒnərəbl] *adj* deshonroso.

dishonourably, (*US*) **dishonorably** [dɪs'ɒnərəblɪ] *adv* deshonrosamente; **to be ~ discharged** ser licenciado con deshonor.

dishrack ['dɪʃræk] *n* escurridera *f* de platos.

dishrag ['dɪʃræg] *n* trapo *m* para fregar los platos.

dish soap ['dɪʃsəʊp] *n* (*US*) lavavajillas *m*.

dishtowel ['dɪʃtaʊəl] *n* trapo *m* de secar los platos.

dishware ['dɪʃweə^r] *n* (*US*) loza *f*, vajilla *f*.

dishwasher ['dɪʃ,wɒʃə^r] *n* (*person*) friegaplatos *mf*; (*machine*) (máquina *f*) lavaplatos *m*, lavavajillas *m*.

dishwashing liquid ['dɪʃ,wɒʃɪŋ,lɪkwɪd] *n* (*US*) lavavajillas *m*.

dishwater ['dɪʃwɔːtə^r] *n* agua *f* de lavar platos; (*fig*) agua *f* sucia.

dishy* ['dɪʃɪ] *adj* (*Brit*) mono, apetitoso.

disillusion [,dɪsɪ'luːʒən] **1** *n* desilusión *f*, desengaño *m*. **2** *vt* desilusionar, desengañar; **to be ~ed with sb** quedar desilusionado con uno; **to be ~ed with Paris** quedar desilusionado de París.

disillusionment [,dɪsɪ'luːʒənmənt] *n* desilusión *f*.

disincentive [,dɪsɪn'sentɪv] *n* desincentivo *m*.

disinclination [,dɪsɪnklɪ'neɪʃən] *n* aversión *f* (*for* a, hacia, por).

disinclined ['dɪsɪn'klaɪnd] *adj*: **to be ~ to do sth** estar poco dispuesto a hacer algo, tener pocas ganas de hacer algo; **I feel very ~** no me siento con ganas.

disinfect [,dɪsɪn'fekt] *vt* desinfectar.

disinfectant [,dɪsɪn'fektənt] *n* desinfectante *m*.

disinfection [,dɪsɪn'fekʃən] *n* desinfección *f*.

disinflation [,dɪsɪn'fleɪʃən] *n* desinflación *f*.

disinflationary [,dɪsɪn'fleɪʃənərɪ] *adj* desinflacionista.

disinformation [,dɪsɪnfə'meɪʃən] *n* desinformación *f*.

disingenuous [,dɪsɪn'dʒenjʊəs] *adj* doble, poco sincero.

disingenuousness [,dɪsɪn'dʒenjʊəsnɪs] *n* falsedad *f*, insinceridad *f*.

disinherit ['dɪsɪn'herɪt] *vt* desheredar.

disintegrate [dɪs'ɪntɪgreɪt] *vi* disgregarse, desagregarse, desintegrarse.

disintegration [dɪs,ɪntɪ'greɪʃən] *n* disgregación *f*, desagregación *f*, desintegración *f*.

disinter ['dɪsɪn'tɜː^r] *vt* desenterrar.

disinterested [dɪs'ɪntrɪstɪd] *adj* desinteresado.

disinterestedly [dɪs'ɪntrɪstɪdlɪ] *adv act etc* de manera desinteresada.

disinterment [,dɪsɪn'tɜːmənt] *n* exhumación *f*, desenterramiento *m*.

disinvest [,dɪsɪn'vest] *vt* desinvertir.

disinvestment [,dɪsɪn'vestmənt] *n* desinversión *f*.

disjointed [dɪs'dʒɔɪntɪd] *adj* (*fig*) inconexo, descosido, desarticulado.

disjunctive [dɪs'dʒʌŋktɪv] *adj* disyuntivo.

disk [dɪsk] *n* (*esp US*) = **disc**; (*Comput*) disco *m*; **~ drive** unidad *f* de disco, disk drive *m*; **~ operating system** sistema *m* operativo de discos; **~ pack** paquete *m* de discos; **~ unit** unidad *f* de disco.

diskette [dɪs'ket] *n* disquete *m*, diskette *m*, disco *m* flexible.

diskless ['dɪsklɪs] *adj* sin disco(s).

dislike [dɪs'laɪk] **1** *n* aversión *f*, antipatía *f* (*for, of* a, hacia); **to take a ~ to** coger (*LAm*: agarrar) antipatía a, tomar hincha a.

2 *vt* (**a**) (*object: person*) tener aversión a, tener antipatía a; **I ~ him** me resulta antipático; **it's not that I ~ him** no es que yo le tenga aversión.

(**b**) (*object: thing*) **I ~ that** eso no me gusta, eso me desagrada; **I ~ flying** no me gusta ir en avión.

dislocate ['dɪsləʊkeɪt] *vt bone* dislocarse, descoyuntar; *traffic* interceptar, interrumpir; *plans* trastornar, dar al traste con.

dislocation [,dɪsləʊ'keɪʃən] *n* dislocación *f*; interceptación *f*; trastorno *m*; confusión *f*.

dislodge [dɪs'lɒdʒ] *vt enemy etc* desalojar (*from* de); *object etc* desprender; hacer caer.

disloyal ['dɪs'lɔɪəl] *adj* desleal.

disloyalty ['dɪs'lɔɪəltɪ] *n* deslealtad *f*.

dismal ['dɪzməl] *adj* (*dark*) sombrío, tenebroso; (*depressing*) triste, tétrico; (*depressed*) abatido; *tone* lúgubre; *failure* catastrófico; (*very bad*) malísimo, fatal.

dismally ['dɪzməlɪ] *adv* (*sadly*) tristemente; **to fail ~** tener un fracaso catastrófico; **the play was ~ bad** la obra fue fatal.

dismantle [dɪs'mæntl] *vt machine* desmontar, desarmar; *fort, ship* desmantelar.

dismast [dɪs'mɑːst] *vt* desarbolar.

dismay [dɪs'meɪ] **1** *n* consternación *f*; **there was general ~** se consternaron todos; **in ~** consternado; **to my ~** para mi consternación; **to fill sb with ~** consternar a uno.

2 *vt* consternar; **I am ~ed to hear that ...** me da pena saber que ...; **don't look so ~ed!** ¡no te aflijas!

dismember [dɪs'membə^r] *vt* desmembrar.

dismemberment [dɪs'membəmənt] *n* desmembramiento *m*, desmembración *f*.

dismiss [dɪs'mɪs] **1** *vt* (**a**) (*discharge*) *worker* despedir, *official* destituir (*from* de), (*Mil*) licenciar; (*send away*) mandar ir; dar permiso para irse a; *assembly* disolver; **to be ~ed from the service** ser separado del servicio.

(**b**) *thought* rechazar, apartar de sí; *request* rechazar; *possibility* descartar, desechar; **to ~ a subject briefly** hablar brevemente de un asunto; **with that he ~ed the matter** con eso dio por concluido el asunto.

(**c**) (*Jur*) *appeal* rechazar; **the case was ~ed** el tribunal absolvió al acusado.

2 *vi* (*Mil*) romper filas; **~!** ¡rompan filas!

dismissal [dɪs'mɪsəl] *n* despedida *f*; destitución *f*.

dismissive [dɪs'mɪsɪv] *adj*: **he said in a ~ tone** dijo como quien no quería tomar la cosa en serio; **he was very ~ about it** parecía no tomar la cosa en serio.

dismount [dɪs'maʊnt] **1** *vt* desmontar. **2** *vi* desmontarse, apearse, bajar (*from* de).

Disneyland ['dɪznɪ,lænd] *n* Disneylandia *f* (*also fig*).

disobedience [,dɪsə'biːdɪəns] *n* desobediencia *f*.

disobedient [,dɪsə'biːdɪənt] *adj* desobediente.

disobey ['dɪsə'beɪ] *vti* desobedecer.

disobliging ['dɪsə'blaɪdʒɪŋ] *adj* poco servicial.

disorder [dɪs'ɔːdə^r] **1** *n* (**a**) (*confusion*) desorden *m*; desarreglo *m*; **to be in ~** estar en desorden; **to retreat in ~** retirarse a la desbandada.

(**b**) (*commotion*) disturbio *m*, tumulto *m*; **there were ~s in the streets** hubo disturbios en las calles.

(**c**) (*Med*) (*upset*) trastorno *m*; (*illness*) enfermedad *f*; **mental ~** trastorno *m* mental.

2 *vt* desordenar; (*Med*) trastornar.

disordered [dɪs'ɔːdəd] *adj* desordenado; desarreglado; (*Med*) trastornado.

disorderly [dɪs'ɔːdəlɪ] *adj* (**a**) (*untidy*) desordenado; *person* poco metódico.

(**b**) (*unruly*) turbulento, indisciplinado; *youth* revoltoso; *meeting* alborotado; **the meeting became ~** la reunión se alborotó.

(**c**) *conduct* escandaloso; **~ house** (*euph*) burdel *m*.

disorganization [dɪs,ɔːgənaɪ'zeɪʃən] *n* desorganización *f*; confusión *f*, falta *f* de organización.

disorganize [dɪs'ɔːgənaɪz] *vt* desorganizar; *communications etc* interrumpir.

disorganized [dɪs'ɔːgənaɪzd] *adj person* poco metódico.

disorient [dɪs'ɔːrɪənt], **disorientate** [dɪs'ɔːrɪənteɪt] *vt* desorientar.

disown [dɪs'əʊn] *vt* rechazar, desconocer; *belief etc* renegar de, repudiar.

disparage [dɪs'pærɪdʒ] *vt* menospreciar, denigrar, hablar mal de.

disparagement [dɪs'pærɪdʒmənt] *n* denigración *f*.

disparaging [dɪs'pærɪdʒɪŋ] *adj person* despreciativo; *remark etc* despectivo.

disparagingly [dɪs'pærɪdʒɪŋlɪ] *adv*: **to speak ~ of** hablar en términos despreciativos de.

disparate ['dɪspərɪt] *adj* dispar.

disparity [dɪs'pærɪtɪ] *n* disparidad *f*.

dispassionate [dɪs'pæʃnɪt] *adj* desapasionado, imparcial.

dispassionately [dɪs'pæʃnɪtlɪ] *adv* de modo desapasionado.

dispatch [dɪs'pætʃ] **1** *n* (**a**) (*act of sending*) (*of person*) envío *m*, (*of goods*) consignación *f*, envío *m*; (*killing*) ejecución *f*, muerte *f*; **~ documents** documentos *mpl* de envío; **~ note** aviso *m* de envío.

(**b**) (*speed*) prontitud *f*.

(**c**) (*message*) mensaje *m*, despacho *m*, informe *m*; (*Mil*) parte *m*, comunicado *m*.

2 *vt* (**a**) (*send*) *person* enviar, *goods* consignar, enviar, remitir.

(**b**) (*kill*) despachar.

(**c**) (*transact*) despachar.

(**d**) *food* despachar, despabilar.

dispatch-box [dɪs'pætʃbɒks] *n* (*Brit*) cartera *f*.

dispatch-case [dɪs'pætʃ,keɪs] *n* portafolios *m*.

dispatcher [dɪs'pætʃəʳ] *n* transportista *m*.

dispatch-rider [dɪs'pætʃ,raɪdəʳ] *n* correo *m*; (*Mil*) correo *m* militar.

dispel [dɪs'pel] *vt* disipar, dispersar; *doubts* disipar, barrer; (*fig*) desvanecer.

dispensable [dɪs'pensəbl] *adj* prescindible, innecesario.

dispensary [dɪs'pensərɪ] *n* (*Brit*) dispensario *m*, farmacia *f*.

dispensation [,dɪspen'seɪʃən] *n* (*distribution, exemption*) dispensación *f*; (*of justice*) administración *f*; (*Eccl*) dispensa *f*; (*ruling*) decreto *m*; **~ of Providence** designio *m* divino.

dispense [dɪs'pens] *vt* (**a**) (*issue*) dispensar, repartir; (*Pharm*) preparar; *justice* administrar. (**b**) **to ~ sb from** dispensar a uno de, eximir a uno de.

◆**dispense with** *vt* prescindir de; deshacerse de.

dispenser [dɪs'pensəʳ] *n* (*Brit*) (**a**) (*person*) farmacéutico *m*, -a *f*. (**b**) (*device*) dosificador *m*; distribuidor *m* automático, máquina *f* expendedora.

dispensing [dɪs'pensɪŋ] *attr*: **~ chemist** farmacéutico *m*, -a *f*.

dispersal [dɪs'pɜːsəl] *n* dispersión *f*; (*of light*) descomposición *f*.

disperse [dɪs'pɜːs] **1** *vt* dispersar; *light* descomponer. **2** *vi* dispersarse; **they ~d to their homes** fue cada uno a su casa.

dispersion [dɪs'pɜːʃən] *n* dispersión *f*.

dispirit [dɪs'pɪrɪt] *vt* desalentar, desanimar.

dispirited [dɪs'pɪrɪtɪd] *adj* abatido, deprimido, desanimado.

dispiritedly [dɪs'pɪrɪtɪdlɪ] *adv* desalentadamente, desanimadamente.

dispiriting [dɪs'pɪrɪtɪŋ] *adj* deprimente, desalentador.

displace [dɪs'pleɪs] *vt* (**a**) (*shift*) desplazar, sacar de su sitio. (**b**) (*remove from office*) destituir; (*oust*) quitar el puesto a, reemplazar. (**c**) (*Phys, Naut*) desplazar; (*Chem*) reemplazar.

displaced [dɪs'pleɪst] *adj*: **~ person** desplazado *m*, -a *f*.

displacement [dɪs'pleɪsmənt] *n* (**a**) (*shift*) cambio *m* de sitio. (**b**) (*removal from office*) destitución *f*; (*ousting*) reemplazo *m*. (**c**) (*Phys, Naut*) desplazamiento *m*; (*Chem*) reemplazo *m*. (**d**) **~ activity** (*Psych*) actividad *f* de sustitución.

display [dɪs'pleɪ] **1** *n* (**a**) (*act of ~ing*) exhibición *f*; (*showing*) exposición *f*; (*Comput*) visualización *f*, despliegue *m*; (*of goods for sale*) exposición *f*, presentación *f*; (*of emotion*) manifestación *f*, demostración *f*; (*of energy, quality*) despliegue *m*; (*Mil*) alarde *m*, demostración *f* militar; **to make a ~ of** hacer alarde de; **to be on ~** estar expuesto.

(**b**) (*showiness*) aparato *m*, pompa *f*, ostentación *f*.

2 *vt* (*put on view*) exponer, presentar; (*Comput*) desplegar; *emotion etc* acusar, manifestar, demostrar; *quality, energy* desplegar; (*show ostentatiously*) ostentar, hacer ostentación de, lucir.

display advertising [dɪs'pleɪ,ædvətaɪzɪŋ] *n* (*Press*) pancartas *fpl* publicitarias, publicidad *f* gráfica.

display unit [dɪs'pleɪjuːnɪt] *n* (*Comput*) monitor *m*.

display window [dɪs'pleɪ,wɪndəʊ] *n* escaparate *m*.

displease [dɪs'pliːz] *vt* (*be disagreeable to*) desagradar; (*offend*) ofender; (*annoy*) enojar, enfadar; **to be ~d at** (*or* **with**) estar disgustado con (*or* de).

displeasing [dɪs'pliːzɪŋ] *adj* desagradable.

displeasure [dɪs'pleʒəʳ] *n* desagrado *m*, enojo *m*, indignación *f*, disgusto *m*; **to incur sb's ~** ofender a uno.

disport [dɪs'pɔːt] *vr*: **to ~ o.s.** retozar, jugar; divertirse.

disposable [dɪs'pəʊzəbl] *adj* (**a**) *napkin etc* de usar y tirar, desechable; **~ goods** productos *mpl* no reutilizables. (**b**) (*available*) disponible; **~ income** renta *f* disponible.

disposal [dɪs'pəʊzəl] *n* (**a**) (*placing, arrangement*) disposición *f*, colocación *f*, orden *m*.

(**b**) (*sale*) venta *f*; (*of house etc*) traspaso *m*; (*of rights*) enajenación *f*; (*rubbish ~*) recogida *f* de basuras.

(**c**) **to have at one's ~** disponer de, tener a su disposición; **I am at your ~** estoy a su disposición.

dispose [dɪs'pəʊz] *vt* (**a**) (*place, arrange*) disponer, colocar, poner en orden.

(**b**) (*determine*) determinar, decidir.

(**c**) (*persuade*) inclinar, mover; **to ~ sb to help** mover a uno a ayudar; **to be ~d to do sth** estar dispuesto a hacer algo; **to be well ~d towards sth** estar bien dispuesto hacia algo.

◆**dispose of** *vt* (**a**) (*have at one's command*) disponer de.

(**b**) (*get rid of*) deshacerse de; eliminar; *rubbish* tirar, botar (*LAm*); depositar; *rights* enajenar, ceder; (*sell*) vender; *house etc* traspasar; (*give away*) regalar; *food* comerse, despachar; (*finish*) terminar, concluir; *problem* resolver; *argument* echar por tierra; *business* despachar; (*kill*) matar, despachar.

disposer [dɪs'pəʊzəʳ] *n* (*also* **waste ~**) equipo *m* de destrucción de basuras.

disposition [,dɪspə'zɪʃən] *n* (**a**) (*placing*) disposición *f*, colocación *f*; orden *m*.

(**b**) **~s** preparativos *mpl*; plan *m*; **to make one's ~s** hacer preparativos.

(**c**) **to be at the ~ of** estar a la disposición de.

(**d**) (*temperament*) natural *m*, temperamento *m*.

(**e**) (*inclination*) propensión *f* (*to* a); **I have no ~ to help him** no estoy dispuesto a ayudarle.

dispossess ['dɪspə'zes] *vt tenant* desahuciar; **to ~ sb of** desposeer a uno de, privar a uno de.

disproportion [,dɪsprə'pɔːʃən] *n* desproporción *f*.

disproportionate [,dɪsprə'pɔːʃnɪt] *adj* desproporcionado.

disproportionately [,dɪsprə'pɔːʃnɪtlɪ] *adv* desproporcionadamente.

disprove [dɪs'pruːv] *vt* refutar, confutar.

disputable [dɪs'pjuːtəbl] *adj* discutible.

disputation [,dɪspjuː'teɪʃən] *n* disputa *f*.

disputatious [,dɪspjuː'teɪʃəs] *adj* discutidor, disputador.

dispute [dɪs'pjuːt] **1** *n* disputa *f*; (*spoken*) discusión *f*, altercado *m*; (*labour ~*) conflicto *m* laboral; (*Jur*) contencioso *m*; **beyond ~** indiscutible, incuestionable; **it is beyond ~ that ...** es indudable que ...; **territory in ~** territorio *m* en litigio.

2 *vt* disputar; cuestionar, expresar dudas acerca de; protestar de; **I ~ that** lo dudo; **I do not ~ the fact that ...** no niego que ...; **to ~ possession of a house with sb** contender con uno sobre la posesión de una casa; **the final will be ~d between A and B** se disputarán la final A y B.

3 *vi* discutir (*about, over* sobre, *whether* si).

disputed [dɪs'pjuːtɪd] *adj* discutible; *territory etc* en litigio; **a ~ matter** un asunto contencioso, un asunto en litigio; **a ~ decision** una decisión discutida.

disqualification [dɪs,kwɒlɪfɪ'keɪʃən] *n* (*act, effect*) inhabilitación *f*; (*Sport*) descalificación *f*; (*thing that disqualifies*) impedimento *m*, desventaja *f*.

disqualify [dɪs'kwɒlɪfaɪ] *vt* inhabilitar, incapacitar (*for* para); (*Sport*) descalificar.

disquiet [dɪs'kwaɪət] **1** *n* inquietud *f*, desasosiego *m*. **2** *vt* inquietar.

disquieting [dɪs'kwaɪətɪŋ] *adj* inquietante.

disquisition [,dɪskwɪ'zɪʃən] *n* disquisición *f*.

disregard ['dɪsrɪ'gɑːd] **1** *n* indiferencia *f* (*for* a); (*neglect*) descuido *m* (*of* de); despreocupación *f*; **with complete ~ for** sin atender en lo más mínimo a; **with complete ~ for his own safety** sin considerar un momento su propia salvación.

2 *vt* desatender, descuidar; (*ignore*) no hacer caso de, hacer caso omiso de, pasar por alto.

disrepair ['dɪsrɪ'pɛəʳ] *n* mal estado *m*; **to fall into ~** (*house*) desmoronarse; (*machinery etc*) deteriorarse, descomponerse.

disreputable [dɪs'repjʊtəbl] *adj* de mala fama; (*shameful*) vergonzoso, escandaloso; *clothing etc* horrible, asqueroso.

disreputably [dɪs'repjʊtəblɪ] *adv* vergonzosamente.

disrepute ['dɪsrɪ'pjuːt] *n*: **to bring into ~** desacreditar, desprestigiar.

disrespect ['dɪsrɪs'pekt] *n* falta *f* de respeto, desacato *m*; **I meant no ~** no quería ofenderle.

disrespectful [,dɪsrɪs'pektfʊl] *adj* irrespetuoso.

disrobe ['dɪs'rəʊb] **1** *vt* desnudar, desvestir. **2** *vi* desnudarse.

disrupt [dɪs'rʌpt] *vt* romper; (*fig*) *communications etc* desorganizar, interrumpir; *plans* desbaratar, dar al traste con, trastornar.

disruption [dɪs'rʌpʃən] *n* rompimiento *m*; (*fig*) desorganización *f*, interrupción *f*; desbaratamiento *m*.

disruptive [dɪs'rʌptɪv] *adj* que tiende a romper la unidad; destructivo, subversivo, perjudicial.

dissatisfaction ['dɪs,sætɪs'fækʃən] *n* descontento *m*, insatisfacción *f*; disgusto *m*.

dissatisfied ['dɪs'sætɪsfaɪd] *adj* descontento, insatisfecho; **everyone was ~ with the result** el resultado no gustó a

nadie, el resultado dejó insatisfechos a todos.
dissect [dɪ'sekt] *vt* hacer la disección de; anatomizar, seccionar; (*fig*) analizar minuciosamente.
dissection [dɪ'sekʃən] *n* disección *f*; (*fig*) análisis *m* minucioso.
dissemble [dɪ'sembl] **1** *vt* disimular, encubrir. **2** *vi* fingir, ser hipócrita.
disseminate [dɪ'semɪneɪt] *vt* diseminar, difundir, divulgar.
dissemination [dɪˌsemɪ'neɪʃən] *n* diseminación *f*, difusión *f*.
dissension [dɪ'senʃən] *n* disensión *f*, discordia *f*.
dissent [dɪ'sent] **1** *n* disentimiento *m*; (*Eccl*) disidencia *f*. **2** *vi* disentir (*from* de); (*Eccl*) disidir.
dissenter [dɪ'sentəʳ] *n* (*Eccl*) disidente *mf*.
dissentient [dɪ'senʃɪənt] **1** *adj* (*also* **dissenting**) disidente, desconforme, discrepante; **there was one ~ voice** hubo una voz en contra. **2** *n* disidente *mf*.
dissertation [ˌdɪsə'teɪʃən] *n* disertación *f*; (*US Univ*) tesis *f*; (*Brit Univ*) tesina *f*.
disservice ['dɪs'sɜːvɪs] *n* deservicio *m*; **to do a ~ to** perjudicar a.
dissidence ['dɪsɪdəns] *n* disidencia *f*.
dissident ['dɪsɪdənt] **1** *adj* disidente. **2** *n* disidente *mf*.
dissimilar ['dɪ'sɪmɪləʳ] *adj* distinto, diferente (*to* de)
dissimilarity [ˌdɪsɪmɪ'lærɪtɪ] *n* desemejanza *f*, disimilitud *f*.
dissimulate [dɪ'sɪmjʊleɪt] *vt* disimular.
dissimulation [dɪˌsɪmjʊ'leɪʃən] *n* disimulación *f*.
dissipate ['dɪsɪpeɪt] *vt* disipar; *fear, doubt etc* desvanecer; (*waste*) derrochar, desperdiciar.
dissipated ['dɪsɪpeɪtɪd] *adj* disoluto.
dissipation [ˌdɪsɪ'peɪʃən] *n* (*act*) disipación *f*; (*waste*) derroche *m*, desperdicio *m*; (*moral*) disipación *f*, disolución *f*, libertinaje *m*, vicio *m*.
dissociate [dɪ'səʊʃɪeɪt] **1** *vt* separar, desligar (*from* de). **2** *vr*: **to ~ o.s. from** hacerse insolidario de, separarse de, desligarse de.
dissociation [dɪˌsəʊsɪ'eɪʃən] *n* disociación *f*.
dissoluble [dɪ'sɒljʊbl] *adj* disoluble.
dissolute ['dɪsəluːt] *adj* disoluto.
dissolution [ˌdɪsə'luːʃən] *n* disolución *f* (*also Pol*).
dissolvable [dɪ'zɒlvəbl] *adj* soluble.
dissolve [dɪ'zɒlv] **1** *vt* disolver (*also fig, Pol etc*), desleír. **2** *vi* disolverse; desleírse; (*fade*) desvanecerse; **to ~ into tears** deshacerse en lágrimas.
dissonance ['dɪsənəns] *n* disonancia *f*.
dissonant ['dɪsənənt] *adj* disonante.
dissuade [dɪ'sweɪd] *vt* disuadir (*from* de); **to ~ sb from doing sth** disuadir a uno de hacer algo.
dissuasion [dɪ'sweɪʒən] *n* disuasión *f*.
dissuasive [dɪ'sweɪsɪv] *adj* (*gen*) *voice, person* disuasivo; *powers* disuasorio.
distaff ['dɪstɑːf] *n* rueca *f*; **the ~ side** la rama femenina; **on the ~ side** por parte de la madre.
distance ['dɪstəns] **1** *n* distancia *f* (*also fig*); (*difference*) diferencia *f*; **it's a good ~** está bastante lejos, (*journey*) es mucho camino; **what ~ is it to London?** ¿cuánto hay de aquí a Londres?; **~ learning** enseñanza *f* a distancia, enseñanza *f* por correspondencia; **~ race** carrera *f* de larga distancia; **within speaking ~** al alcance de la voz; **within easy ~** a poca distancia, no muy lejos (*of* de); **to be within striking ~ of** estar al alcance de; **at a ~** a distancia; **at a ~ of 60 km** a una distancia de 60 km; **at this ~** a esta distancia; **at this ~ of time** después de tanto tiempo; **from a ~** desde lejos; **in the ~** a lo lejos; **in the middle ~** en segundo término; **to keep one's ~** mantenerse a distancia, (*fig*) guardar las distancias; **to keep sb at a ~** guardar las distancias con uno.
2 *vr*: **to ~ o.s. from** distanciarse de.
distancing ['dɪstənsɪŋ] *n*: **~ o.s. from others is sometimes necessary** a veces es necesario guardar las distancias con los demás.
distant ['dɪstənt] *adj* (**a**) distante, lejano, remoto (*from* de); **it is 12 km ~** dista 12 km, está a 12 km; **is it very ~?** ¿dista mucho?, ¿está muy lejos?; **in some far ~ land** en algún país lejano; **we had a ~ view of the sea** vimos el mar a lo lejos; **in some ~ future** en un futuro remoto.
(**b**) *relation, resemblance* lejano.
(**c**) (*fig*) reservado, frío; **to be ~ with sb** tratar a uno con frialdad.
distantly ['dɪstəntlɪ] *adv* (**a**) **we are ~ related** somos parientes lejanos; **it ~ resembles the one we had before** tiene una ligera semejanza con el que teníamos antes. (**b**) **he treated me ~** (*fig*) me trató con frialdad.
distaste ['dɪs'teɪst] *n* aversión *f*, repugnancia *f* (*for* por).
distasteful [dɪs'teɪstfʊl] *adj* desagradable, repugnante; *task* nada grato; **it is ~ to me to have to** + *infin* me es poco grato tener que + *infin*.
Dist. Atty. (*US*) *abbr of* **District Attorney**.
distemper¹ [dɪs'tempəʳ] **1** *n* pintura *f* al temple. **2** *vt* pintar al temple.
distemper² [dɪs'tempəʳ] *n* (*Vet*) moquillo *m*; (*fig*) mal *m*, destemplanza *f*.
distend [dɪs'tend] **1** *vt* dilatar, hinchar. **2** *vi* dilatarse, hincharse.
distension [dɪs'tenʃən] *n* distensión *f*, dilatación *f*, hinchazón *f*.
distich ['dɪstɪk] *n* dístico *m*.
distil, (*US*) **distill** [dɪs'tɪl] *vt* destilar; **distilled water** agua *f* destilada.
distillation [ˌdɪstɪ'leɪʃən] *n* destilación *f*.
distiller [dɪs'tɪləʳ] *n* destilador *m*.
distillery [dɪs'tɪlərɪ] *n* destilería *f*.
distinct [dɪs'tɪŋkt] *adj* (**a**) (*different*) distinto (*from* de); **~ as ~ from** a diferencia de. (**b**) (*clearly perceptible*) claro, inconfundible, visible; (*unmistakable*) inequívoco; **a ~ French accent** un marcado acento francés; **there is a ~ chance that** ... existe una clara posibilidad de que + *subj*.
distinction [dɪs'tɪŋkʃən] *n* (**a**) (*difference*) distinción *f*; **to draw a ~ between** hacer una distinción entre.
(**b**) (*eminence*) distinción *f*; **a man of ~** un hombre distinguido; **an artist of ~** un artista destacado; **to gain** (*or* **win**) **~** distinguirse (*as* como); **you have the ~ of being the first** a Vd le corresponde el honor de ser el primero.
(**c**) (*Univ etc*) sobresaliente *m*.
distinctive [dɪs'tɪŋktɪv] *adj* distintivo, característico.
distinctly [dɪs'tɪŋktlɪ] *adv* claramente; inconfundiblemente; **it is ~ possible** bien podría ser (*that* que + *subj*); **it is ~ awkward** es sumamente difícil.
distinguish [dɪs'tɪŋgwɪʃ] **1** *vt* distinguir (*from* de). **2** *vi*: **to ~ between** distinguir entre. **3** *vr*: **to ~ o.s.** distinguirse (*as* como); (*iro*) señalarse, lucirse.
distinguishable [dɪs'tɪŋgwɪʃəbl] *adj* distinguible.
distinguished [dɪs'tɪŋgwɪʃt] *adj* distinguido (*for* por), eminente, destacado.
distinguishing [dɪs'tɪŋgwɪʃɪŋ] *adj* distintivo.
distort [dɪs'tɔːt] *vt* deformar; (*fig*) deformar, torcer, tergiversar; distorsionar.
distorted [dɪs'tɔːtɪd] *adj* (*lit, fig*) distorsionado; **he gave us a ~ version of the events** nos dio una versión distorsionada de los hechos.
distortion [dɪs'tɔːʃən] *n* deformación *f*; (*of sound*) distorsión *f*; (*fig*) deformación *f*, torcimiento *m*, tergiversación *f*; distorsión *f*.
distr. *abbr of* **distribution**; **distributor**.
distract [dɪs'trækt] *vt* distraer; *attention* distraer, apartar (*from* de); (*bewilder*) aturdir, confundir.
distracted [dɪs'træktɪd] *adj* alocado, aturdido; **like one ~** como un loco; **she is easily ~** se distrae fácilmente; **to be ~ with anxiety** estar loco de inquietud.
distractedly [dɪs'træktɪdlɪ] *adv* locamente, como un loco.
distracting [dɪs'træktɪŋ] *adj* que distrae la atención, molesto.
distraction [dɪs'trækʃən] *n* (**a**) (*being distracted*) distracción *f*. (**b**) (*bewilderment*) aturdimiento *m*, confusión *f*; **to drive sb to ~** volver loco a uno. (**c**) (*amusement*) diversión *f*.
distrain [dɪs'treɪn] *vi*: **to ~ upon** secuestrar, embargar.
distraint [dɪs'treɪnt] *n* secuestro *m*, embargo *m*.
distrait [dɪs'treɪ] *adj* distraído.
distraught [dɪs'trɔːt] *adj* muy turbado, loco de inquietud (*etc*); **in a ~ voice** en una voz embargada por la emoción.
distress [dɪs'tres] **1** *n* (*pain*) dolor *m*; (*mental anguish*) angustia *f*, pena *f*, aflicción *f*; (*misfortune*) desgracia *f*; (*want*) miseria *f*; (*danger*) peligro *m*; (*Med*) agotamiento *m*; **to be in ~** estar en un apuro, (*Med*) estar con dolor, (*ship etc*) estar en peligro; **to be in financial ~** pasar apuros.
2 *vt* (*pain*) doler; (*cause anguish to*) apenar, afligir; (*Med*) agotar, fatigar; **I am ~ed to hear that** ... me da pena saber que ...; **I am very ~ed at the news** estoy afligidísimo por la noticia.
distressed [dɪs'trest] *adj* afligido, angustiado.
distressing [dɪs'tresɪŋ] *adj* doloroso, penoso, que da pena.
distressingly [dɪs'tresɪŋlɪ] *adv* dolorosamente, penosamente; **a ~ bad picture** un cuadro tan malo que daba pena.
distress-rocket [dɪs'tresˌrɒkɪt] *n* cohete *m* de señales.
distress-signal [dɪs'tresˌsɪgnəl] *n* señal *f* de socorro.
distribute [dɪs'trɪbjuːt] *vt* distribuir, repartir.
distribution [ˌdɪstrɪ'bjuːʃən] *n* distribución *f*, reparto *m*, repartimiento *m*; (*Ling*) distribución *f*; **~ network** red *f* de

distribución; ~ **rights** derechos *mpl* de distribución.

distributional [ˌdɪstrɪˈbjuːʃənəl] *adj* distribucional.

distributive [dɪsˈtrɪbjʊtɪv] **1** *adj* distributivo; ~ **trade** comercio *m* de repartimiento. **2** *n* (*Ling*) adjetivo *m* distributivo.

distributor [dɪsˈtrɪbjʊtəʳ] *n* (**a**) repartidor *m*, -ora *f*, distribuidor *m*, -ora *f*; (*Comm*) concesionario *m*, -a *f*, distribuidor *m*; (*firm*) (compañía *f*) distribuidora *f*; (*Cine*) distribuidor *m*. (**b**) (*Elec, Mech*) distribuidor *m*; (*Aut*) delco ® *m*.

distributorship [dɪsˈtrɪbjʊtəʃɪp] *n* distribución *f* (en) exclusiva.

district [ˈdɪstrɪkt] **1** *n* zona *f*, región *f*; (*of town*) barrio *m*; (*of country*) comarca *f*; (*US Pol*) distrito *m*; (*postal* ~) distrito *m* postal.

2 *attr*: ~ **attorney** (*US*) fiscal *m* de un distrito judicial; ~ **commissioner** (*Brit*) jefe *m* de policía de distrito; ~ **council** (*Brit*) ≃ ayuntamiento *m*; ~ **manager** gerente *mf* regional; ~ **nurse** *enfermera de la Seguridad Social encargada de una zona determinada.*

distrust [dɪsˈtrʌst] **1** *n* desconfianza *f*, recelo *m*. **2** *vt* desconfiar de, recelar.

distrustful [dɪsˈtrʌstfʊl] *adj* desconfiado, receloso.

disturb [dɪsˈtɜːb] *vt peace, order, meeting etc* perturbar, alterar; *process, course* interrumpir; (*Psych*) *balance of mind* trastornar; (*disarrange*) desordenar; *person* (*disquiet*) perturbar, inquietar, (*bother*) molestar; **don't ~ yourself!** ¡no se moleste!; **do not ~!** por favor no molestar; **sorry to ~ you!** ¡perdone la molestia!; **I am seriously ~ed** estoy muy preocupado.

disturbance [dɪsˈtɜːbəns] *n* (*act, state*) perturbación *f*; alteración *f*; (*outbreak of violence*) tumulto *m*, alboroto *m*; (*to service*) interrupción *f* (*to* de); (*Pol*) disturbio *m*; (*of mind*) trastorno *m*; ~ **of the peace** alteración *f* del orden público; **there was a ~ in the crowd** se alborotaron algunos de los espectadores; **the ~s in Slobodia** los disturbios en Eslobodia.

disturbed [dɪsˈtɜːbd] *adj state* alborotado, nada tranquilo; (*Psych*) trastornado; **to have a ~ night** dormir mal.

disturbing [dɪsˈtɜːbɪŋ] *adj influence, thought* perturbador; *event* inquietante, preocupante; **it is ~ that ...** es inquietante que ...

disturbingly [dɪsˈtɜːbɪŋlɪ] *adv* de manera inquietante; **a ~ large number** un número tan grande que resulta inquietante; **the bomb fell ~ close** la bomba cayó tan cerca que causó inquietud.

disunited [ˈdɪsjʊˈnaɪtɪd] *adj* desunido.

disunity [ˌdɪsˈjuːnɪtɪ] *n* desunión *f*.

disuse [ˈdɪsˈjuːs] *n* desuso *m*; **to fall into ~** caer en desuso.

disused [ˈdɪsˈjuːzd] *adj* abandonado.

disyllabic [ˌdɪsɪˈlæbɪk] *adj* disílabo.

ditch [dɪtʃ] **1** *n* zanja *f*; (*at roadside*) cuneta *f*, arroyo *m*; (*irrigation channel*) acequia *f*; (*defensive*) foso *m*; **to die in the last ~** luchar hasta quemar el último cartucho.

2 *vt* (*) (*get rid of*) deshacerse de, zafarse de, sacudirse a; *car etc* abandonar; **to ~ a plane** hacer un amaraje forzoso.

ditching [ˈdɪtʃɪŋ] *n* (**a**) abertura *f* de zanjas; **hedging and ~** mantenimiento *m* de setos y zanjas. (**b**) (*Aer*) amaraje *m*.

dither [ˈdɪðəʳ] (*esp Brit*) **1** *n*: **to be all of a ~, to be in a ~** (*fig*) = **2**. **2** *vi* estar nerviosísimo; (*be undecided*) no saber qué hacer, vacilar.

dithery [ˈdɪðərɪ] *adj* (*fig*) nervioso; indeciso, vacilante; (*from old age*) chocho.

ditto [ˈdɪtəʊ] *adj* ídem, lo mismo; ~ **marks**, ~ **sign** comillas *fpl*; **I say ~** yo digo lo mismo; **'~', he said** dijo 'yo también'.

ditty [ˈdɪtɪ] *n* cancioneta *f*.

diuretic [ˌdaɪjʊəˈretɪk] **1** *adj* diurético. **2** *n* diurético *m*.

diurnal [daɪˈɜːnl] *adj* diurno.

diva [ˈdiːvə] *n*, *pl* **~s** *or* **dive** [ˈdiːve] diva *f*.

divan [dɪˈvæn] *n* diván *m*, cama *f* turca.

dive [daɪv] **1** *n* (**a**) zambullida *f*; (*artistic, from board etc*) salto *m*; (*by professional diver, of submarine*) inmersión *f*; (*Aer*) picado *m*, picada *f* (*LAm*); **his reputation has taken a ~*** su reputación ha caído en picado.

(**b**) (‡) tasca *f*.

2 *vi* (*US*: *irr*: *pret* **dove**, *pp* **dived**) (**a**) (*duck etc*) zambullirse; (*from bank etc*: *also* **to ~ in**) tirarse al agua, saltar al agua, zambullirse; (*artistically*) saltar; (*professional diver*) bucear, sumergirse; (*submarine*) sumergirse; **the kids were diving for coins** los niños se tiraban al agua para recoger monedas; **to ~ for pearls** pescar perlas; **to ~ into the water** tirarse al agua.

(**b**) (*Aer*) picar.

(**c**) **to ~ for cover** (*fig*) meterse precipitadamente en un abrigo, buscar cobijo precipitadamente; **the goalkeeper ~d for the ball** el portero se lanzó a parar el balón; **to ~ into the undergrowth** meterse en la maleza; **to ~ into one's pocket** meter la mano en el bolsillo; **to ~ into a bar** entrar de prisa en un bar; **I ~d into the shop for a paper*** pasé corriendo por la tienda a por un periódico.

(**d**) (*prices etc*) bajar de golpe, caer en picado.

dive-bomb [ˈdaɪvbɒm] *vt* bombardear en picado.

dive-bomber [ˈdaɪvˌbɒməʳ] *n* bombardero *m* en picado.

dive-bombing [ˈdaɪvˌbɒmɪŋ] *n* bombardeo *m* en picado.

diver [ˈdaɪvəʳ] *n* (**a**) (*professional*) buzo *m*, buceador *m*; (*sporting*) saltador *m*, -ora *f*. (**b**) (*Orn*) colimbo *m*.

diverge [daɪˈvɜːdʒ] *vi* divergir (*from* de); **to ~ from** apartarse de.

divergence [daɪˈvɜːdʒəns] *n* divergencia *f*.

divergent [daɪˈvɜːdʒənt] *adj* divergente.

divers [ˈdaɪvɜːz] *adj pl* (*liter*) diversos, varios.

diverse [daɪˈvɜːs] *adj* diverso, variado.

diversification [daɪˌvɜːsɪfɪˈkeɪʃən] *n* diversificación *f*.

diversify [daɪˈvɜːsɪfaɪ] **1** *vt* diversificar **2** *vi* diversificarse.

diversion [daɪˈvɜːʃən] *n* (*pastime, Mil*) diversión *f*; (*Brit*: *of route*) desviación *f*, desvío *m*; **'D~'** (*road sign*) 'Desvío'.

diversionary [daɪˈvɜːʃnərɪ] *adj* de diversión.

diversity [daɪˈvɜːsɪtɪ] *n* diversidad *f*.

divert [daɪˈvɜːt] *vt* (*amuse*) divertir; (*turn aside*) desviar; (*Brit*) *traffic* desviar.

diverting [daɪˈvɜːtɪŋ] *adj* divertido.

divest[1] [daɪˈvest] **1** *vt*: **to ~ sb of sth** despojar a uno de algo. **2** *vr*: **to ~ o.s. of one's rights** renunciar a sus derechos; **he ~ed himself of his coat** se quitó el abrigo.

divest[2] [daɪˈvest] *vti* (*US Fin*) desinvertir.

divestment [daɪˈvestmənt] *n* (*US Fin*) desinversión *f*.

divide [dɪˈvaɪd] **1** *n* (*Geog*: *esp US*) divisoria *f*.

2 *vt* dividir (*by* por, *from* de, *into* en); partir; separar; **to ~ the House** (*Brit Parl*) hacer que la Cámara proceda a la votación.

3 *vi* dividirse (*into* en); separarse; (*road etc*) bifurcarse; ~ **and rule** divide y vencerás; **the House ~d** (*Brit Parl*) la Cámara procedió a la votación.

◆**divide off 1** *vt* dividir.

2 *vi* dividirse.

◆**divide out** *vt* repartir.

◆**divide up** *vt* dividir, partir.

divided [dɪˈvaɪdɪd] *adj* dividido; ~ **highway** (*US*) carretera *f* de doble calzada.

dividend [ˈdɪvɪdend] *n* dividendo *m*; (*fig*) beneficio *m*; ~ **warrant** cédula *f* de dividendo; **this should pay handsome ~s** (*fig*) esto ha de proporcionar grandes beneficios.

dividers [dɪˈvaɪdəz] *npl* compás *m* de puntas.

dividing-line [dɪˈvaɪdɪŋlaɪn] *n* línea *f* divisoria.

divination [ˌdɪvɪˈneɪʃən] *n* adivinación *f*.

divine[1] [dɪˈvaɪn] **1** *adj* divino; (*fig*) sublime; (*) estupendo*, maravilloso; ~ **right** derecho *m* divino; ~ **service** culto *m*, oficio *m* divino. **2** *n* teólogo *m*.

divine[2] [dɪˈvaɪn] *vt* adivinar.

divinely [dɪˈvaɪnlɪ] *adv* divinamente; (*fig*) sublimemente; (*) divinamente, maravillosamente.

diviner [dɪˈvaɪnəʳ] *n* adivinador *m*, -ora *f*; (*water* ~) zahorí *m*.

diving [ˈdaɪvɪŋ] *n* (*professional*) el bucear, buceo *m*; (*sporting*) salto *m*.

diving-bell [ˈdaɪvɪŋbel] *n* campana *f* de buzo.

diving-board [ˈdaɪvɪŋbɔːd] *n* trampolín *m*.

diving-suit [ˈdaɪvɪŋsuːt] *n* escafandra *f*, traje *m* de buceo.

divining rod [dɪˈvaɪnɪŋrɒd] *n* varilla *f* de zahorí.

divinity [dɪˈvɪnɪtɪ] *n* (**a**) (*deity*) divinidad *f*. (**b**) (*as study*) teología *f*.

divisible [dɪˈvɪzəbl] *adj* divisible.

division [dɪˈvɪʒən] *n* división *f* (*also Math, Mil, Brit Police*); separación *f*; (*sharing out*) repartimiento *m*; (*within company etc*) sección *f*; (*disagreement*) discordia *f*; (*Brit Parl*) votación *f*; **approved without a ~** aprobado por unanimidad; **there is a ~ of opinion about this** sobre esto hay diversos pareceres; **upper-~ student** (*US*) estudiante *mf* de tercer (*or* cuarto) año; ~ **of labour** repartimiento *m* del trabajo; ~ **sign** signo *m* de división.

divisional [dɪˈvɪʒənl] *adj* de división, divisional.

divisive [dɪˈvaɪsɪv] *adj* divisivo, divisionista.

divisor [dɪˈvaɪzəʳ] *n* divisor *m*.

divorce [dɪˈvɔːs] **1** *n* divorcio *m*; (*fig*) separación *f* (*from* de); ~ **court** tribunal *m* de pleitos matrimoniales; ~ **proceedings** pleito *m* de divorcio; **to get a ~** divorciarse (*from* de).

2 *vt* divorciarse de; (*fig*) divorciar, separar (*from* de).
3 *vi* divorciarse.
divorced [dɪ'vɔːst] *adj* divorciado.
divorcee [dɪˌvɔː'siː] *n* divorciado *m*, -a *f*.
divot ['dɪvɪt] *n* terrón *m*; (*Golf*) chuleta *f*.
divulge [daɪ'vʌldʒ] *vt* divulgar, revelar.
divvy ['dɪvɪ] **1** *n* (*Brit**) *abbr of* **dividend** dividendo *m*. **2** *vt* (*US*‡: *also* **to ~ up**) dividir.
Dixie ['dɪksɪ] *n el sur de los Estados Unidos.*
dixie ['dɪksɪ] *n* (*Brit Mil*) olla *f*, marmita *f*.
DIY *abbr of* **do-it-yourself** bricolaje *m*.
dizzily ['dɪzɪlɪ] *adv* vertiginosamente.
dizziness ['dɪzɪnɪs] *n* vértigo *m*, vértigos *mpl*.
dizzy ['dɪzɪ] *adj* (**a**) *speed* vertiginoso; *height* que produce vértigo.
(**b**) *feeling* de vértigo; (*dazed*) mareado, aturdido; **to feel ~, to get ~** marearse, estar mareado, tener vértigos; **I'm feeling rather ~** me está dando vueltas la cabeza.
(**c**) (*esp US**) alelado, cascabelero, casquivano.
DJ *n* (**a**) *abbr of* **disc-jockey** pinchadiscos *m*. (**b**) *abbr of* **dinner-jacket** smoking *m*.
Djakarta [dʒə'kɑːtə] *n* Yakarta *f*.
djellabah ['dʒeləbə] *n* chilaba *f*.
DJIA *n* (*US St Ex*) *abbr of* **Dow Jones Industrial Average**.
Djibouti [dʒɪ'buːtɪ] *n* Yibuti *m*.
dl *abbr of* **decilitre(s)** decilitro(s) *m(pl)*, dl.
D Lit(t) [ˌdiː'lɪt] *n* (**a**) *abbr of* **Doctor of Letters**. (**b**) *abbr of* **Doctor of Literature**.
DM *abbr of* **Deutschmark** marco *m* alemán.
dm *abbr of* **decimetre(s)** decímetro(s) *m(pl)*, dm.
DMU *n abbr of* **decision-making unit**.
D Mus [ˌdiː'mʌz] *n abbr of* **Doctor of Music** Doctor *m*, -ora *f* en Música.
DMZ *n abbr of* **demilitarized zone**.
DNA *n abbr of* **deoxyribonucleic acid** ácido *m* desoxirribonucleico, ADN.
DNB *n abbr of* **Dictionary of National Biography**.
do. *abbr of* **ditto** lo mismo, ídem, íd.
do¹ [duː] (*irr: pret* **did**, *ptp* **done**) **1** *vt* hacer; (*Culin*) guisar, preparar; (*Theat*) *play* representar, poner, *rôle* hacer, *personage* hacer de, hacer el papel de; *duty* cumplir, hacer; *homage* rendir, tributar (*to* a); *problem* resolver; *dishes* lavar; *room* limpiar; *hair* peinar, (*wash and set*) arreglar; (*Univ etc*) *subject* estudiar, cursar; *distance* cubrir, recorrer, salvar; *speed* alcanzar, ir a; (*) *town etc* hacer la visita de, recorrer los monumentos de; (*) *country* visitar, recorrer, viajar por; (*Brit*‡: *cheat*) estafar, timar; **they ~ you very well in this hotel** en este hotel la comida es muy buena; **what's to ~?*** ¿qué pasa?; **that does it!** ¡no aguanto más!; ¡es el colmo!; **now what can I ~ for you?** ¿en qué puedo ayudarle?; **there's nothing to be done about it** no hay nada que hacer; **to have one's hair done** arreglarse el pelo; **he was done for speeding**‡ le multaron por exceso de velocidad; **she was done for pilfering**‡ la procesaron por ladrona; **to ~ again** rehacer, repetir, volver a hacer.
2 *vi* (**a**) (*act, proceed*) hacer; obrar, actuar, proceder; **you did well** hiciste muy bien; **you would ~ well to draw with him** sería muy honroso lograr un empate con él; **to ~ better** mejorar, hacer progresos; **you can ~ better than that** eres capaz de hacerlo mejor; **you would ~ better to accept** sería aconsejable aceptar; **~ as you are told!** ¡haz lo que te digo!; **~ as you think best** haga lo que mejor le parezca; **~ as you would be done by** trata como quieres ser tratado.
(**b**) (*fare*) **how is he ~ing?** ¿qué tal le va esto?; **how did you ~ at school?** ¿qué tal te fue en el colegio?; **how do you ~?** tengo mucho gusto en conocerle, (*less formally*) encantado, mucho gusto; **to ~ badly** sufrir reveses, ir perdiendo, fracasar, (*in exam*) salir mal; **you didn't ~ so badly** no has hecho del todo mal; **to ~ well** tener éxito, prosperar, (*in exam*) salir bien; **her son's ~ing well** su hijo tiene una buena posición; **business is ~ing well** los negocios van bien; **the crops are ~ing well** la cosecha se muestra buena.
(**c**) (*cook*) cocer.
(**d**) (*answer purpose*) servir; (*be suitable*) convenir, venir al caso, ser a propósito; **this one will ~** me quedo con éste; **will this ~?** ¿qué te parece éste?; (*suffice*) bastar; **will that ~?** ¿te basta eso?; **that will ~** con eso basta; está bien así; **that will have to ~** tendremos que conformarnos con eso; **that will ~!** ¡basta ya!, ¡cállate!, ¡déjate de eso!; **that won't ~** eso no vale; eso no se hace; **that will never ~** eso no resultará, eso no saldrá bien; eso no puede ser, eso no se puede consentir; **it would never ~ to** + *infin* sería inconcebible + *infin*, sería intolerable que + *subj*; **to make ~** arreglárselas por su cuenta; **to make ~ with** contentarse con, conformarse con.
3 *v aux* (**a**) (*emphatic*) **DO tell me** dígamelo, por favor; **I DO feel better** ciertamente me encuentro mejor; **I DO hope so** así lo espero; **I DO so wish I could** ¡ojalá pudiera!; **but I DID ~ it** pero yo sí lo hice.
(**b**) (*with inversion*) **rarely does it happen that...** rara vez ocurre que ...
(**c**) (*in questions*) **~ you know him?** ¿le conoces?
(**d**) (*negation with* not) **you ~ not earn enough** Vd no gana bastante.
4 *verb substitute*: **I spoke before you did** yo hablé antes que tú; **he talks to servants as others ~ to their dogs** habla a los criados como otros a sus perros; **~ as I ~** haz tú como yo; **so ~ I** yo también, yo hago lo mismo; **did you see him? ... I did** ¿le viste? ... yo sí; **but I didn't** pero yo no; **you didn't see him but I did** tú no le viste pero yo sí; **he spoke as he often did** habló como lo había hecho muchas veces.
5 *vr*: **to ~ o.s. proud** (*or* **well**) darse buena vida, vivir a cuerpo de rey.
6 *n* (*) (**a**) (*gathering*) reunión *f*; (*Brit: ceremony*) ceremonia *f*, acto *m*; (*Brit: party*) fiesta *f*, guateque *m*.
(**b**) (*trouble*) lío *m*; **that was quite a ~** eso sí que fue un lío; **he had a ~ with the police** tuvo un lío con la policía.
(**c**) **~s and don'ts** reglas *fpl*; **he gave us a series of ~s and don'ts** nos dio una serie de cosas que hacer y que evitar hacer.
(**d**) (*phrases*) **it's a poor ~ when ...** mala cosa cuando ...; **fair ~s!** ¡seamos justos!; **fair ~s all round** la parte justa para cada uno.
◆**do away with** *vt* suprimir, eliminar; acabar con; abolir; *pet* sacrificar.
◆**do down*** *vt* (**a**) (*Brit: cheat*) timar, estafar; (*play false*) hacer una mala pasada a.
(**b**) (*denigrate*) hablar mal de, denigrar; dejar en mal lugar.
◆**do for** *vt* (**a**) (‡) acabar con.
(**b**) (*: *as servant*) ser asistenta de, hacer la limpieza (en casa) de; llevar la casa a.
◆**do in**‡ *vt* apiolar‡, cargarse a‡.
◆**do into** *vt*: **to ~ a book into English** (*Liter*) traducir un libro al inglés.
◆**do out** *vt* (**a**) *room* (*decorate*) renovar, pintar, decorar; (*clean*) limpiar.
(**b**) **to ~ sb out of sth** estafar algo a uno; **they did me out of my big chance** me pisaron mi gran oportunidad; **nobody can ~ you out of that** nadie puede hacer que pierdas eso.
◆**do over** *vt* (**a**) (*repeat*) rehacer, volver a hacer.
(**b**) (‡) dar una paliza a.
◆**do up** *vt* (*tie*) liar, atar; *buttons* abotonar, *clasp* abrochar, *fastener etc* cerrar; *parcel* envolver.
(**b**) *room* renovar, decorar.
◆**do with** *vt* (**a**) (*need etc*) **I could really ~ with a beer** no me iría mal una cerveza; **I could ~ with another** necesito otro además; **we could ~ with more money** no nos vendría mal más dinero; **we could have done with you there** nos hacías gran falta.
(**b**) (*concern*) **it's nothing to ~ with me** no tiene que ver conmigo; **she won't have anything to ~ with him** no quiere tener nada que ver con él; **we have nothing to ~ with the neighbours** no tenemos contacto alguno con los vecinos.
(**c**) **I can't be ~ing with pop**‡ no aguanto la música pop.
◆**do without** *vt* pasarse sin, prescindir de; **one can't ~ without money** es imprescindible tener dinero.
do² [dəʊ] *n* (*Mus*) do *m*.
DOA *adj abbr of* **dead on arrival** ingresó cadáver.
d.o.b. *n abbr of* **date of birth** fecha *f* de nacimiento.
Doberman ['dəʊbəmən] *n* (*also* **~ pinscher**) dóberman *m*.
doc* [dɒk] *n* (*US*) = **doctor**; (*in direct address*) doctor.
docile ['dəʊsaɪl] *adj* dócil.
docility [dəʊ'sɪlɪtɪ] *n* docilidad *f*.
dock¹ [dɒk] *n* (*Bot*) acedera *f*, romaza *f*.
dock² [dɒk] *vt animal* descolar; *hair, tail* recortar; (*Brit*) *pay etc* reducir, rebajar; **I've been ~ed £1** me han rebajado la paga en una libra.
dock³ [dɒk] **1** *n* (*Naut*) dársena *f*, muelle *m*; (*with gates*) dique *m*; **~s** muelles *mpl*, puerto *m*; **~ warrant** conocimiento *m* de almacén; resguardo *m* de entrega; **to be in ~** (*Brit**: *car*) estar en el taller.
2 *vt ship* poner en dique, hacer entrar en dique; *space-*

craft atracar, acoplar.

3 *vi* (**a**) (*Naut*) entrar en dique, atracar al muelle, (*loosely*) llegar; **we ~ed at 5** llegamos a las 5, entramos en el puerto a las 5; **when we ~ed at Vigo** cuando llegamos a Vigo.

(**b**) (*spacecraft*) atracar (*with* con), acoplarse (*with* a).

dock[4] [dɒk] *n* (*Brit Jur*) banquillo *m* (de los acusados).

docker [ˈdɒkəʳ] *n* trabajador *m* portuario, estibador *m*.

docket [ˈdɒkɪt] *n* (*Brit*) certificado *m*; (*label*) etiqueta *f*, marbete *m*; (*bill*) factura *f*.

docking [ˈdɒkɪŋ] *n* (*spacecraft*) atraque *m*, acoplamiento *m*; **~ manoeuvre** maniobra *f* de atraque.

dock labourer [ˈdɒk,leɪbərəʳ] *n*, **dock worker** [ˈdɒk,wɜːkəʳ] *n*, (*US*) **dock walloper*** [ˈdɒk,wɒləpəʳ] *n* trabajador *m* portuario.

dockland(s) [ˈdɒklænd(z)] *n*(*pl*) zona *f* del puerto, zona *f* portuaria.

dockyard [ˈdɒkjɑːd] *n* astillero *m*, (*naval*) arsenal *m*.

doctor [ˈdɒktəʳ] **1** *n* (**a**) (*Med*) médico *m*, -a *f*; **to be under the ~** estar bajo tratamiento médico; **to go to the ~'s** ir al médico; **it was just what the ~ ordered*** fue mano de santo; **~'s line, ~'s note** (*Brit*), **~'s excuse** (*US*) baja *f*.

(**b**) (*Univ*) doctor *m*, -ora *f* (*of* en); **~'s degree** doctorado *m*.

2 *vt* (**a**) (*Med*) medicinar, tratar, curar.

(**b**) (*Brit*) *cat etc* castrar.

(**c**) *drink, food* adulterar; *text* ajustar, manipular.

(**d**) **to ~ up** *machine etc* remendar, arreglar de cualquier modo.

3 *vr*: **to ~ o.s.** tomar medicinas, curarse.

doctoral [ˈdɒktərəl] *adj* doctoral; **~ thesis** (*Brit*), **~ dissertation** (*US*) tesis *f* doctoral.

doctorate [ˈdɒktərɪt] *n* doctorado *m*.

doctrinaire [,dɒktrɪˈnɛəʳ] **1** *adj* doctrinario. **2** *n* doctrinario *m*, -a *f*.

doctrinal [dɒkˈtraɪnl] *adj* doctrinal.

doctrine [ˈdɒktrɪn] *n* doctrina *f*.

docudrama [ˈdɒkjʊ,drɑːmə] *n* docudrama *m*.

document 1 [ˈdɒkjʊmənt] *n* documento *m*. **2** [ˈdɒkjʊment] *vt* documentar.

documentary [,dɒkjʊˈmentərɪ] **1** *adj* documental; (*Comm, Fin*) documentario; **~ bill of exchange** letra *f* de cambio documentaria; **~ (letter of) credit** crédito *m* documentario; **~ evidence** prueba *f* documental. **2** *n* documental *m*.

documentation [,dɒkjʊmenˈteɪʃən] *n* documentación *f*.

document case [ˈdɒkjʊmənt,keɪs] *n* portadocumentos *m*.

document reader [ˈdɒkjʊmənt,riːdəʳ] *n* (*Comput*) lector *m* de documentos.

DOD *n* (*US*) *abbr of* **Department of Defense** Ministerio *m* de Defensa.

do-dad* [ˈduːdæd] *n* (*US*) = **doodad**.

dodder [ˈdɒdəʳ] *vi* chochear.

dodderer [ˈdɒdərəʳ] *n* chocho *m*.

doddering [ˈdɒdərɪŋ] *adj*, **doddery** [ˈdɒdərɪ] *adj* chocho.

doddle‡ [ˈdɒdl] *n*: **it's a ~** (*Brit*) es un chollo‡.

dodecaphonic [,dəʊdekəˈfɒnɪk] *adj* dodecafónico.

dodge [dɒdʒ] **1** *n* (**a**) (*of body*) regate *m*, esguince *m*, evasión *f*.

(**b**) (*) truco *m*; maniobra *f*; (*Mech*) dispositivo *m*.

2 *vt* (*elude*) evadir, *blow* esquivar, *pursuer* dar esquinazo a; **to ~ the issue** esquivar la cuestión; andar con rodeos; **to ~ work** gandulear.

3 *vi* hurtar el cuerpo, dar un esguince; (*fig*) escurrir el bulto; **to ~ into a shop** entrar de repente en una tienda; **to ~ round a corner** doblar una esquina (y desaparecer); **to ~ behind a tree** ocultarse tras un árbol.

◆**dodge about** *vi* ir de aquí para allá.

dodgem [ˈdɒdʒəm] *n* (*Brit*) coche *m* de choque, chocón *m*.

dodger [ˈdɒdʒəʳ] *n* gandul *mf*; **artful ~** trampista *mf*, tunante *m*.

dodgy* [ˈdɒdʒɪ] *adj* (*Brit*) = **dicey**.

dodo [ˈdəʊdəʊ] *n* (**a**) dodó *m*. (**b**) (*US**) bobo *m*.

DOE *n* (**a**) (*Brit*) *abbr of* **Department of the Environment** Departamento *m* del Medio Ambiente. (**b**) (*US*) *abbr of* **Department of Energy** Departamento *m* de Energía.

doe [dəʊ] *n* (*deer*) gama *f*; (*rabbit*) coneja *f*; (*hare*) liebre *f*.

doer [ˈduːəʳ] *n* (**a**) (*author of deed*) hacedor *m*, -ora *f*; agente *m*; **he's a great ~ of crosswords** adora los crucigramas. (**b**) (*active person*) persona *f* enérgica, persona *f* dinámica.

does [dʌz] *V* **do**[1].

doeskin [ˈdəʊskɪn] *n* ante *m*, piel *f* de ante.

doesn't [ˈdʌznt] = **does not**.

doff [dɒf] *vt* (*liter*) quitarse.

dog [dɒg] **1** *n* (**a**) perro *m*; (*fox*) zorro *m*; **the ~s** (*Brit*: *greyhounds*) carreras *fpl* de galgos, canódromo *m*.

(**b**) (*term of abuse etc*) tunante *m*, bribón *m*; (‡: *unattractive girl*) callo‡ *m*; **~'s breakfast*** revoltijo *m*; **you ~!** ¡canalla!, (*hum*) ¡tunante!; **dirty ~*** tío *m* sucio*, tipo *m* asqueroso*; **gay ~*** tío *m* alegre*; **you lucky ~!*** ¡qué suerte tienes!; **he's a lucky ~*** es un tío suertudo.

(**c**) (*Telec*‡) teléfono *m*; **~s‡** (*feet*) tachines‡ *mpl*.

(**d**) (*phrases*) **to be a ~ in the manger** ser el perro del hortelano; **to be top ~** ser el gallo del lugar, triunfar; **she was dressed up like a ~'s dinner*** estaba hecha un adefesio; **~ eats ~ in this place** aquí los perros se comen unos a otros; **to go to the ~s** echarse a perder, arruinarse; **you haven't a ~'s chance** no tienes la más remota posibilidad, no tienes ni esperanza; **to lead a ~'s life** llevar una vida de perros; **let sleeping ~s lie** vale más no meneallo; **to put on the ~*** (*US*) vestirse de punta en blanco.

2 *vt* seguir los pasos de, seguir la pista de; **he was ~ged by ill luck** le persiguió la mala suerte.

dog-basket [ˈdɒg,bɑːskɪt] *n* cesto *m* del perro.

dog-biscuit [ˈdɒg,bɪskɪt] *n* galleta *f* de perro.

dog-breeder [ˈdɒg,briːdəʳ] *n* criador *m*, -ora *f* de perros.

dogcart [ˈdɒgkɑːt] *n* dócar *m*.

dog-collar [ˈdɒg,kɒləʳ] *n* collar *m* de perro; (*Eccl*: *hum*) gola *f*, alzacuello(s) *m*, cuello *m* de cura.

dog-days [ˈdɒgdeɪz] *npl* canícula *f*, caniculares *mpl*.

doge [dəʊdʒ] *n* dux *m*.

dog-eared [ˈdɒgɪəd] *adj* sobado, muy manoseado.

dog-end‡ [ˈdɒgend] *n* colilla *f*, toba‡ *f*.

dog-fancier [ˈdɒg,fænsɪəʳ] *n* (*connoisseur*) entendido *m*, -a *f* en perros; (*breeder*) criador *m*, -ora *f* de perros.

dogfight [ˈdɒgfaɪt] *n* (*Aer*) combate *m* aéreo (reñido y confuso); (*fig*) batalla *f* muy reñida.

dogfish [ˈdɒgfɪʃ] *n* perro *m* marino, cazón *m*.

dog fox [ˈdɒg,fɒks] *n* zorro *m* macho.

dogged [ˈdɒgɪd] *adj* tenaz, obstinado.

doggedly [ˈdɒgɪdlɪ] *adv* tenazmente.

doggedness [ˈdɒgɪdnɪs] *n* tenacidad *f*.

doggerel [ˈdɒgərəl] *n* versos *mpl* ramplones, malos versos *mpl*, coplas *fpl* de ciego.

doggie [ˈdɒgɪ] *n* = **doggy**.

doggo* [ˈdɒgəʊ] *adv*: **to lie ~** (*Brit*) no bullir; estar escondido.

doggone* [,dɒgˈgɒn] (*US*) **1** *excl* ¡maldición! **2** *adj* condenado, maldito.

dog-guard [ˈdɒg,gɑːd] *n* (*Aut*) reja *f* separadora.

doggy [ˈdɒgɪ] *n* perrito *m*; **~ bag** bolsita *f* para el perro.

dog-handler [ˈdɒg,hændləʳ] *n* (*Police etc*) entrenador *m* de perros.

doghouse [ˈdɒghaʊs] *n*, *pl* **doghouses** [ˈdɒg,haʊzɪz] (*US*) perrera *f*; **to be in the ~** estar en desgracia.

dog Latin [ˈdɒgˈlætɪn] *n* latín *m* macarrónico, latinajo *m*.

dogleg [ˈdɒgleg] *n* (*in road etc*) codo *m*, ángulo *m* abrupto.

dog-licence [ˈdɒg,laɪsəns] *n* permiso *m* para perro.

doglike [ˈdɒglaɪk] *adj* canino; de perro.

dogma [ˈdɒgmə] *n* dogma *m*.

dogmatic [dɒgˈmætɪk] *adj* dogmático.

dogmatically [dɒgˈmætɪkəlɪ] *adv* dogmáticamente.

dogmatism [ˈdɒgmətɪzəm] *n* dogmatismo *m*.

dogmatize [ˈdɒgmətaɪz] *vi* dogmatizar.

do-gooder* [ˈduːˈgʊdəʳ] *n persona bien intencionada*; (*pej*) *bienhechor candoroso y entrometido*.

dog-paddle [ˈdɒg,pædl] **1** *n* braza *f* de perro. **2** *vi* nadar como los perros.

dog-rose [ˈdɒgrəʊz] *n* escaramujo *m*, rosal *m* silvestre.

dogsbody* [ˈdɒgzbɒdɪ] *n*: **to be a ~** hacer de todo; **to be the general ~** ser el burro de carga para todos.

dogshow [ˈdɒgʃəʊ] *n* exposición *f* canina.

Dog Star [ˈdɒg,stɑːʳ] *n* Sirio *m*.

dog tag [ˈdɒgtæg] *n* (*US*) placa *f* de identidad (*or* de identificación).

dog-tired [ˈdɒgˈtaɪəd] *adj*: **to be ~** estar rendido.

dogtrack [ˈdɒgtræk] *n* canódromo *m*.

dogtrot [ˈdɒgtrɒt] *n* trote *m* lento.

dog-watch [ˈdɒgwɒtʃ] *n* (*Naut*) guardia *f* de cuartillo.

doily [ˈdɔɪlɪ] *n* pañito *m* de adorno.

doing [ˈduːɪŋ] **1** *pres part of* **do**; **there's not much ~** hay poca animación; **nothing ~!** ¡de ninguna manera!, ¡ni hablar!; **this is your ~** eres tú quien ha hecho esto; **it was none of my ~** no he tenido que ver; **it takes some ~** no es nada fácil, exige bastante esfuerzo (*or* fuerza *etc*).

2 *n* (**a**) **~s** (*deeds*) hechos *mpl*; acciones *fpl*; (*conduct*) conducta *f*, actuación *f*; (*happenings*) sucesos *mpl*; **there**

were great ~s in the house hubo muchísima actividad en la casa.

(**b**) (*: *Mech etc*) **~s** chisme *m*; **that ~s with two knobs** (*Brit*) aquel chisme con dos botones.

do-it-yourself ['du:ɪtjə'self] *attr* hágalo Vd mismo; (*as n*) bricolaje *m*; **~ enthusiast, ~ expert** bricolador *m*, -ora *f*, bricolero *m*, -a *f*, aficionado *m*, -a *f* al bricolaje; **~ kit** juego *m* de montar; **~ shop** tienda *f* de bricolaje.

do-it-yourselfer [ˌdu:ɪtjə'selfəʳ] *n* aficionado *m*, -a *f* al bricolaje.

doldrums ['dɒldrəmz] *npl* (*Naut*) zona *f* de las calmas ecuatoriales; **to be in the ~** (*fig: person*) estar abatido, (*business*) estar encalmado, (*St Ex*) estar en calma.

dole [dəʊl] *n* limosna *f*; (*of unemployed*) subsidio *m* de paro; **~ queue** cola *f* de los parados; **to be on the ~** (*Brit*) estar parado; **love on the ~** el amor en la miseria.

◆dole out *vt* repartir (parcamente), distribuir (con parsimonia).

doleful ['dəʊlfʊl] *adj* triste, lúgubre, lastimero.

dolefully ['dəʊlfəlɪ] *adv* tristemente.

doll [dɒl] *n* muñeca *f*; (*esp US*‡) gachí‡ *f*, jai‡ *f*.

◆doll up* **1** *vt* adornar, ataviar. **2** *vi* = **3**. **3** *vr*: **to ~ o.s. up** emperejilarse, ataviarse.

dollar ['dɒləʳ] *n* dólar *m*; **you can bet your bottom ~ that ...** es completamente seguro que ...; **it's ~s to doughnuts that ...*** es tan cierto como hay Dios que ...*.

dollar area ['dɒlərˌɛərɪə] *n* zona *f* en que se emplea el dólar.

dollar bill [dɒlə'bɪl] *n* billete *m* de un dólar.

dollar diplomacy ['dɒlədɪ'pləʊməsɪ] *n* diplomacia *f* a golpe de dólar.

dollar rate ['dɒləreɪt] *n* cambio *m* del dólar.

dollar sign ['dɒləˌsaɪn] *n* signo *m* del dólar.

dollop ['dɒləp] *n* porción *f*, masa *f*.

doll's house ['dɒlzhaus] *n*, *pl* **doll's houses** ['dɒlzhaʊzɪz] casa *f* de muñecas.

Dolly ['dɒlɪ] *nf familiar form of* **Dorothy**.

dolly ['dɒlɪ] *n* (**a**) (*doll*) muñequita *f*. (**b**) (*: *girl*) chica *f*, jovencita *f*; **you're a ~ to help me*** eres un ángel por ayudarme. (**c**) (*US*) carretilla *f*. (**d**) (*Cine, TV*) travelín *m*, plataforma *f* rodante.

dolly bird‡ ['dɒlɪbɜ:d] *n* (*Brit*) niña *f* mona*.

dolomite ['dɒləmaɪt] *n* dolomía *f*, dolomita *f*.

Dolomites ['dɒləmaɪts] *npl* Dolomitas *fpl*, Alpes *mpl* Dolomíticos.

dolphin ['dɒlfɪn] *n* delfín *m*.

dolphinarium [ˌdɒlfɪ'nɛərɪəm] *n* delfinario *m*.

dolt [dəʊlt] *n* imbécil *m*, mastuerzo *m*; **you ~!** ¡bobalicón!

domain [dəʊ'meɪn] *n* (*lands*) heredad *f*, propiedad *f*; (*empire*) dominio *m*; (*sphere*) campo *m*, competencia *f*; **the matter is now in the public ~** el asunto es ya del dominio público.

dome [dəʊm] *n* cúpula *f*; bóveda *f* (*also fig*); (*Geog*) colina *f* redonda.

domed [dəʊmd] *adj forehead, building* abovedado.

domestic [də'mestɪk] **1** *adj* doméstico; *appliance* de uso doméstico; *industry, product* nacional; *trade* interior; *strife* interno, intestino; (*home-loving*) casero, hogareño: **~ flight** vuelo *m* nacional; **~ market** mercado *m* nacional, mercado *m* interior; **~ science** (*esp Brit*) ciencia *f* del hogar; **~ staff** personal *m* de servicio; criados *mpl*, servidumbre *f*; **~ trade** comercio *m* interior; **~ work** trabajo *m* de casa, labor *f* doméstica.

2 *n* doméstico *m*.

domestically [dəʊ'mestɪkəlɪ] *adv*: **a ~ produced article** un artículo producido en el país; **she is not ~ inclined** no tiene inclinación doméstica.

domesticate [də'mestɪkeɪt] *vt* domesticar.

domesticated [də'mestɪkeɪtɪd] *adj* domesticado; *person* casero, hogareño.

domestication [dəʊˌmestɪ'keɪʃən] *n* domesticación *f*.

domesticity [ˌdəʊmes'tɪsɪtɪ] *n* domesticidad *f*.

domicile ['dɒmɪsaɪl] (*Brit*) **1** *n* domicilio *m*. **2** *vt*: **to be ~d in** domiciliarse en.

domiciliary [ˌdɒmɪ'sɪlɪərɪ] *adj* domiciliario.

dominance ['dɒmɪnəns] *n* dominación *f*.

dominant ['dɒmɪnənt] *adj* dominante.

dominate ['dɒmɪneɪt] *vti* dominar.

dominating ['dɒmɪneɪtɪŋ] *adj* dominante, dominador.

domination [ˌdɒmɪ'neɪʃən] *n* dominación *f*.

domineer [ˌdɒmɪ'nɪəʳ] *vi* dominar, tiranizar (*over sb* a alguien).

domineering [ˌdɒmɪ'nɪərɪŋ] *adj* dominante, dominador, tiránico.

Dominic ['dɒmɪnɪk] *nm* Domingo.

Dominica [ˌdɒmɪ'ni:kə] *n* Dominica *f*.

Dominican [də'mɪnɪkən] **1** *adj* dominicano. **2** *n* (*Pol*) dominicano *m*, -a *f*; (*Eccl*) dominico *m*, dominicano *m*.

Dominican Republic [də'mɪnɪkənrɪ'pʌblɪk] *n* República *f* Dominicana.

dominion [də'mɪnɪən] *n* dominio *m*; (*Brit Pol*) dominio *m*.

domino ['dɒmɪnəʊ] *n*, *pl* **dominoes** ['dɒmɪnəʊz] (*dress*) dominó *m*; (*in game*) ficha *f* de dominó; **~ effect** (*Pol*) reacción *f* en cadena; **~ theory** (*Pol*) teoría *f* de la reacción en cadena.

dominoes ['dɒmɪnəʊz] *npl* dominó *m*.

Domitian [də'mɪʃɪən] *nm* Domiciano.

don[1] [dɒn] *vt* ponerse.

don[2] [dɒn] *n* (*Brit Univ*) profesor *m*, -ora *f* (*esp en Oxford y Cambridge*).

donate [dəʊ'neɪt] *vt* donar.

donation [dəʊ'neɪʃən] *n* donativo *m*.

done [dʌn] **1** *ptp of* **do**[1].

2 *adj* (**a**) **~!** ¡trato hecho!; **well ~!** ¡muy bien!, ¡bravo!

(**b**) (*Culin*) **I like my meat well ~** me gusta la carne muy hecha; **is it ~ yet?** ¿está hecho ya?

(**c**) **it's not ~** no se hace, es mal visto; **it's not ~ to yawn** no es elegante bostezar, es de mal gusto bostezar.

(**d**) **have you ~?** ¿has terminado?; **I've ~ with travelling** he terminado de viajar, he renunciado a los viajes; **I've ~ with him** he roto con él.

(**e**) **I'm ~ for** (*tired*) estoy rendido; **if we don't leave now we shall be ~ for** si no nos vamos ahora estamos perdidos; **the car is ~ for** el coche está estropeado del todo; **as a musician he's ~ for** ya no vale para músico.

(**f**) **to feel ~ in*, to be ~ up*** estar rendido.

donkey ['dɒŋkɪ] *n* burro *m*, burra *f*; **it went on for ~'s years*** (*Brit*) continuó durante muchísimos años; **I haven't seen him for ~'s years*** (*Brit*) hace siglos que no le he visto.

donkey-engine ['dɒŋkɪˌendʒɪn] *n* pequeña máquina *f* de vapor, motor *m* auxiliar.

donkey-jacket ['dɒŋkɪˌdʒækɪt] *n* chaqueta *f* de lanilla de trabajo.

donkey-work ['dɒŋkɪˌwɜ:k] *n* trabajo *m* duro y aburrido.

donnish ['dɒnɪʃ] *adj* de erudito, de profesor; de aspecto erudito; (*pej*) profesoril; pedantesco; **he looks very ~** tiene aspecto de muy erudito.

donor ['dəʊnəʳ] *n* donante *mf*.

Don Quixote [dɒn'kwɪksət] *nm* Don Quijote.

don't [dəʊnt] **1** = **do not**. **2** *n* prohibición *f*, consejo *m* negativo.

don't knows [ˌdəʊnt'nəʊz] *npl V* **know 3 (b)**.

donut ['dəʊnʌt] *n* (*US*) buñuelo *m*, rosquilla *f*.

doodad* ['du:dæd] *n* (*US*) artilugio *m*.

doodah* ['du:dɑ:] *n* (**a**) (*Brit: gadget*) = **doodad***. (**b**) **to go all of a ~** ponerse a temblar; ponerse muy nervioso.

doodle ['du:dl] **1** *n* garabatos *mpl* (*or* dibujos *etc*) que hace uno para distraerse. **2** *vi* garrapatear, borronear, borrajear (para distraerse).

doodlebug ['du:dlbʌg] *n* (*Brit*) bomba *f* volante.

doohickey* [ˌdu:'hɪkɪ] *n* trasto *m*.

doom [du:m] **1** *n* (*fate*) suerte *f*, hado *m*; (*death*) perdición *f*, muerte *f*; (*Rel*) juicio *m* final; **a sense of ~** una sensación de desastre; **it's all ~ and gloom here** aquí reina el catastrofismo.

2 *vt* condenar (a muerte *etc*); predestinar (a la perdición *etc*); **to be ~ed to die** estar sentenciado a muerte; **the plan was ~ed to fail** el proyecto tenía fatalmente que fracasar, el proyecto estaba llamado a fracasar; **the ~ed ship** el buque fatalmente siniestrado.

doomsday ['du:mzdeɪ] *n* día *m* del juicio final; **the ~ scenario** los resultados más catastróficos.

doomwatcher ['du:mˌwɒtʃəʳ] *n* cataclismista *mf*, catastrofista *mf*.

doomwatching ['du:mˌwɒtʃɪŋ] *n* cataclismismo *m*, catastrofismo *m*.

door [dɔ:ʳ] *n* puerta *f*; entrada *f*; (*of vehicle*) portezuela *f*; **3 ~s up from us** 3 puertas arriba de nosotros; **behind closed ~s** a puerta cerrada; **from ~ to ~** de puerta en puerta; **next ~** en la casa de al lado; **at the table next ~*** en la mesa de al lado; **my next ~ neighbour** mi vecino de (la casa de) al lado; **this is next ~ to lunacy** esto raya en la locura; **he was on the ~ at the club** hacía de portero (*or* echador *etc*) en el club; **she was on the ~ at the theatre** hacía de acomodadora en el teatro; **to be out of ~s** estar al aire libre; **to be at death's ~** estar a la muerte; **to bang the ~** dar un portazo; **it closed the ~ on negotiations** cerró la puerta de las negociaciones; **never darken my ~ again**

no vuelva nunca por aquí; **to lay the blame** (*or* **sth**) **at sb's ~** echar a uno la culpa; **to leave the ~ open for** (*fig*) dejar la puerta abierta para; **a name like that opens ~s** un apellido así abre muchas puertas; **this opened the ~ to further progress** esto facilitó los progresos ulteriores; **to pay at the ~** pagar a la entrada; **to show sb to the ~** acompañar a uno a la puerta; **to show sb the ~** enseñar la puerta a uno; **to shut the ~ on a proposal** negarse a considerar una propuesta; **to slam the ~** dar un portazo; **to slam the ~ in sb's face** dar con la puerta en las narices de uno; **to slam the ~ on negotiations** terminar de modo concluyente las negociaciones.

doorbell ['dɔːbel] *n* timbre *m* (de llamada).

doorchain ['dɔːtʃeɪn] *n* cadena *f* de la puerta.

doorframe ['dɔːfreɪm] *n* marco *m* de la puerta.

door-handle ['dɔː,hændl] *n* tirador *m* (de puerta), puño *m*; (*of car*) manija *f*.

door-jamb ['dɔːdʒæm] *n* jamba *f* de la puerta.

doorkeeper ['dɔː,kiːpəʳ] *n* conserje *m*, portero *m*.

doorknob ['dɔːnɒb] *n* pomo *m* (de puerta), tirador *m* (de puerta).

door-knocker ['dɔː,nɒkəʳ] *n* aldaba *f*, llamador *m*.

doorman ['dɔːmən] *n*, *pl* **doormen** ['dɔːmən] portero *m*.

doormat ['dɔːmæt] *n* felpudo *m*, estera *f*, alfombrilla *f*.

doornail ['dɔːneɪl] *n* *V* **dead**.

doorpost ['dɔːpəʊst] *n* jamba *f* (de puerta).

doorstep ['dɔːstep] *n* umbral *m*, peldaño *m* de la puerta; **we don't want an airport on our ~** no queremos un aeropuerto aquí tan cerca.

doorstop ['dɔːstɒp] *n* tope *m* (de puerta).

door-to-door ['dɔːtədɔːʳ] *adj*: **~ salesman** vendedor *m* de puerta en puerta, vendedor *m* a domicilio; **~ selling** ventas *fpl* a domicilio.

doorway ['dɔːweɪ] *n* puerta *f*, entrada *f*; portal *m*.

dope [dəʊp] **1** *n* (**a**) (*varnish*) barniz *m*.
(**b**) (*Drugs‡*) droga *f*, narcótico *m*; **to do ~** (*US**) doparse, drogarse.
(**c**) (‡: *information*) informes *mpl*, información *f*; **give me the ~** dime, desembucha*; **what's the ~ on him?** ¿qué es lo que se sabe de él?
(**d**) (*: *person*) mastuerzo* *m*, idiota *mf*; **you ~!** ¡bobo!
2 *attr* (**a**) (*Drugs‡*) **~ fiend** drogata‡ *mf*; **~ peddler, ~ pusher** camello* *m*; **~ test** prueba *f* contra drogas.
(**b**) **~ sheet*** periódico *m* de carreras de caballos.
3 *vt* narcotizar, drogar.

dopehead* ['dəʊphed] *n* porrero* *m*, -a *f*.

dopey* ['dəʊpɪ] *adj* (*dazed*) aturdido, mareado; (*silly*) imbécil.

doping ['dəʊpɪŋ] *n* drogado *m*, doping *m*.

Dordogne [dɔr'dɔɲ] *n* (*region*) Dordoña *f*; (*river*) Dordoña *m*.

dorf‡ [dɔːf] *n* (*US*) borde* *mf*.

Doric ['dɒrɪk] *adj* (*Archit*) dórico.

dorm* [dɔːm] *n* = **dormitory**.

dormant ['dɔːmənt] *adj* (**a**) inactivo; **to be ~, to lie ~** dormir. (**b**) (*fig*) inactivo, latente, en estado latente.

dormer ['dɔːməʳ] *n* (*also* **~ window**) buhardilla *f*.

dormice ['dɔːmaɪs] *npl* of **dormouse**.

dormitory ['dɔːmɪtrɪ] *n* (*Brit*) dormitorio *m*; (*US Univ*) colegio *m* mayor; **~ suburb** (*esp Brit*) barrio *m* dormitorio; **~ town** (*esp Brit*) pueblo *m* dormitorio.

Dormobile ['dɔːməbiːl] ® *n* (*Brit*) combi *m*.

dormouse ['dɔːmaʊs] *n*, *pl* **dormice** ['dɔːmaɪs] lirón *m*.

Dorothy ['dɒrəθɪ] *nf* Dorotea.

dorsal ['dɔːsl] *adj* dorsal.

dory[1] ['dɔːrɪ] *n* (*Fish*) gallo *m*, pez *m* de San Pedro.

dory[2] ['dɔːrɪ] *n* (*boat*) arenera *f*.

DOS [dɒs] *n abbr of* **disk operating system** sistema *m* operativo de discos.

dosage ['dəʊsɪdʒ] *n* dosificación *f*, dosis *f*.

dose [dəʊs] **1** *n* dosis *f*. **2** *vt* (*also* **to ~ up**) administrar una dosis a; medicinar; *wine* adulterar. **3** *vr*: **to ~ o.s.** (*also* **to ~ o.s. up**) medicinarse (*with* de).

dosh‡ [dɒʃ] *n* guita‡ *f*, dinero *m*.

doss‡ [dɒs] *vi* (**a**) (*sleep*) dormir; **to ~ down** echarse. (**b**) **to ~ around** gandulear, no hacer nada.

dosser‡ ['dɒsəʳ] *n* (*Brit*) gandul* *m*, vago *m*; *persona que vive en pensiones de mala muerte*.

dosshouse* ['dɒshaʊs] *n*, *pl* **dosshouses** ['dɒs,haʊzɪz] refugio *m* nocturno para pobres.

dossier ['dɒsɪeɪ] *n* expediente *m*, do(s)sier *m*.

DOT *n* (*US*) *abbr of* **Department of Transportation**.

Dot [dɒt] *nf familiar form of* **Dorothy**.

dot [dɒt] **1** *n* punto *m*; **three ~s** (*Typ*) puntos *mpl* suspensivos; **~s and dashes** puntos *mpl* y rayas; **at 7 o'clock on the ~** a las 7 en punto; **to pay on the ~** pagar puntualmente; **in the year ~** (*Brit*) en tiempos de Maricastaña; **~ command** orden *f* con punto (inicial); **~ prompt** indicación *f* de punto.
2 *vt* (**a**) *letter* poner el punto sobre; **to ~ the i's and cross the t's** (*fig*) poner los puntos sobre las íes.
(**b**) (*speckle*) puntear, motear, salpicar de puntos.
(**c**) (*scatter*; *also* **to ~ about**) esparcir, desparramar; **to be ~ted with** estar salpicado de; **they are ~ted about the country** se encuentran esparcidos por el país.
(**d**) (*) **to ~ sb a blow** dar un golpe a uno; **he ~ted him one** le pegó, le pegó un porrazo.

dotage ['dəʊtɪdʒ] *n* chochez *f*; **to be in one's ~** chochear.

dote [dəʊt] *vi*: **to ~ on** adorar, idolatrar.

doting ['dəʊtɪŋ] *adj* chocho, tontamente cariñoso; **her ~ parents** sus padres que la adoran, sus complacientes padres.

dot-matrix printer [,dɒt,meɪtrɪks'prɪntəʳ] *n* impresora *f* matricial (*or* de matriz) de puntos.

dotted ['dɒtɪd] *adj*: **~ line** línea *f* de puntos; **to sign on the ~ line** (*fig*) aprobar algo maquinalmente.

dotty* ['dɒtɪ] *adj* (*Brit*) chiflado*, disparatado; *idea, scheme* estrafalario, tonto; **you must be ~!** ¿estás loco o qué?; **it's driving me ~** esto me trae loco.

double ['dʌbl] **1** *adj* doble; *sense* doble, ambiguo; **the ~ 6** el 6 doble; **~ 9** (*Telec*) nueve nueve; **the word has ~ 'm'** la palabra se escribe con dos 'm'(emes); **~ the sum, a ~ sum** el doble, una cantidad doble; **it is ~ what it was** es el doble de lo que era; **my income is ~ that of my neighbour** gano dos veces más que mi vecino; **he's ~ your age** te dobla la edad; **to be bent ~** estar encorvado; **~ act** (*Theat*) número *m* doble; **~ bed** cama *f* de matrimonio; **~ bend** (*Brit Aut*) curva *f* en S; **~ bluff** engaño *m* doble; **~ bogey** más dos *m*; **~ chin** papada *f*; **~ density disk** disco *m* de doble densidad; **~ Dutch*** (*Brit*) galimatías *m*; **it's ~ Dutch to me*** (*Brit*) para mí es chino; **to talk ~ Dutch*** (*Brit*) hablar chino; **in ~ figures** 10 o más; **~ helix** hélice *f* doble; **~ pay** paga *f* doble; **it's ~ pay on Sundays** los domingos se paga el doble; **~ room** habitación *f* doble; **to do a ~ take** quedarse quedado (*or* atónito); **~ time** *V* **~ pay**; **in ~ time** (*Mil*) a paso ligero; **~ track** (*Rail*) vía *f* doble; **a ~ whisky** un whisky doble.
2 *adv*: **~ or quits** doble o nada; **to cost ~** costar el doble; **to fold sth ~** doblar algo; **to pay ~** pagar el doble; **to see ~** ver doble.
3 *n* (**a**) (*quantity*) doble *m*; (*person*) doble *mf*.
(**b**) **~s** (*Tennis*) juego *m* de dobles.
(**c**) (*Bridge*) doble *m*, contra *f*.
(**d**) **at the ~** corriendo, (*Mil*) a paso ligero.
(**e**) (*drink*) doble *m*.
4 *vt* doblar; *money, quantity etc* doblar, duplicar; *efforts* redoblar; (*Theat, Bridge*) doblar.
5 *vi* doblarse; (*quantity etc*) doblarse, duplicarse.

◆**double back** *vi* volver sobre sus pasos.

◆**double for** *vt* sustituir, hacer las veces de (*also Theat*).

◆**double over** *vt* doblar.

◆**double up 1** *vt*: **to be ~d up with laughter** troncharse de risa; **to be ~d up with pain** doblarse de dolor.
2 *vi* (*lodgers*) compartir la misma habitación.

double-acting [,dʌbl'æktɪŋ] *adj* de doble acción.

double agent ['dʌbl'eɪdʒənt] *n* agente *m* doble.

double bar [,dʌbl'bɑːʳ] *n* (*Mus*) barra *f* doble.

double-barrelled ['dʌbl,bærəld] *adj* de dos cañones; (*Brit**) *name* de dos apellidos (unidos con guión).

double bass ['dʌbl'beɪs] *n* contrabajo *m*.

double bassoon [,dʌblbə'suːn] *n* contrafagot *m*.

double bill [,dʌbl'bɪl] *n* (*Cine*) programa *m* doble.

double bind* [,dʌbl'baɪnd] *n* callejón *m* sin salida*.

double-blind ['dʌbl,blaɪnd] *adj*: **~ experiment** *experimento en el que ni el analizador ni el sujeto conoce las características*; **~ method** *método según el cual ni el analizador ni el sujeto conoce las características del producto*.

double boiler [,dʌbl'bɔɪləʳ] *n* (*US*) baño *m* de María.

double-book [,dʌbl'bʊk] *vt*: **we were ~ed** habíamos hecho dos citas distintas; (*in hotel*) **we found we were ~ed** encontramos que habían reservado la habitación para dos parejas distintas.

double booking [,dʌbl'bʊkɪŋ] *n* doble reserva *f*.

double-breasted ['dʌbl'brestɪd] *adj* cruzado, con botonadura doble.

double-check ['dʌbl'tʃek] **1** *vti* verificar dos veces. **2** *n* doble verificación *f*.

double cream [,dʌbl'kriːm] *n* (*Brit*) nata *f* enriquecida.

double-cross ['dʌbl'krɒs] **1** *n* engaño *m*, trampa *f*, traición

f. **2** *vt* engañar, traicionar.
double-date [ˌdʌbl'deɪt] **1** *vt* engañar con otro/otra. **2** *vi* (*US*) salir dos parejas.
double dealer [ˌdʌbl'diːlər] *n* traidor *m*, -ora *f*.
double-dealing ['dʌbl'diːlɪŋ] *n* trato *m* doble, juego *m* doble, duplicidad *f*.
double-decker ['dʌbl'dekər] *n* (*Aut*) autobús *m* de dos pisos; (*Culin*) sándwich *m* doble.
double declutch [ˌdʌbldiː'klʌtʃ] *vi* hacer un doble desembragaje.
double-digit [ˌdʌbl'dɪdʒɪt] *adj* de dos dígitos.
double door [ˌdʌbl'dɔːr] *n* puerta *f* partida.
double eagle [ˌdʌbl'iːgl] *n* doble eagle *m*.
double-edged ['dʌbl'edʒd] *adj* de doble filo.
double entendre ['duːblɑ̃ːn'tɑ̃ːndr] *n* equívoco *m*, frase *f* ambigua.
double entry ['dʌbl'entrɪ] *n* partida *f* doble; ~ **book-keeping** contabilidad *f* por partida doble.
double exposure [ˌdʌblɪks'pəʊʒər] *n* doble exposición *f*.
double-faced [ˌdʌbl'feɪst] *adj material* reversible; (*pej*) *person* de dos caras.
double fault [ˌdʌbl'fɔːlt] **1** *n* falta *f* doble. **2** *vi* cometer doble falta.
double feature [ˌdʌbl'fiːtʃər] *n* (*Cine*) sesión *f* doble, programa *m* doble.
double-figure [ˌdʌbl'fɪgər] *adj* = **double-digit**.
double flat [ˌdʌbl'flæt] *n* doble bemol *m*.
double-glaze [ˌdʌbl'gleɪz] *vt*: **to ~ a window** termoaislar una ventana.
double-glazed [ˌdʌbl'gleɪzd] *adj* con doble acristalamiento.
double glazing [ˌdʌbl'gleɪzɪŋ] *n* (*Brit*) doble acristalamiento *m*.
double indemnity [ˌdʌblɪn'demnɪtɪ] *n* doble indemnización *f*; ~ **coverage** seguro *m* de doble indemnización.
double jeopardy [ˌdʌbl'dʒepədɪ] *n* (*esp US*) procesamiento *m* por segunda vez.
double-jointed ['dʌbl'dʒɔɪntɪd] *adj* con articulaciones muy flexibles.
double knit(ting) ['dʌbl'nɪt(ɪŋ)] **1** *n* (*wool*) lana *f* gruesa. **2** *adj* de lana gruesa.
double knot ['dʌblnɒt] *n* doble lazo *m*.
double lock [ˌdʌbl'lɒk] **1** *vt* cerrar con dos vueltas. **2** *n* cerradura *f* doble.
double marking [ˌdʌbl'mɑːkɪŋ] *n* doble corrección *f*.
double negative [ˌdʌbl'negətɪv] *n* doble negación *f*.
double-park [ˌdʌbl'pɑːk] *vti* aparcar en doble fila.
double-parking [ˌdʌbl'pɑːkɪŋ] *n* aparcamiento *m* en doble fila.
double pneumonia ['dʌblnjuː'məʊnɪə] *n* pulmonía *f* doble.
double-quick ['dʌbl'kwɪk] *adv* rapidísimamente, con toda prontitud, (*Mil*) a paso ligero.
double sharp [ˌdʌbl'ʃɑːp] *n* doble sostenido *m*.
double-sided disk [ˌdʌblˌsaɪdɪd'dɪsk] *n* disco *m* de dos caras.
double-space [ˌdʌbl'speɪs] *vt* escribir a doble espacio.
double-spaced ['dʌbl'speɪst] *adv* a doble espacio.
double spacing [ˌdʌbl'speɪsɪŋ] *n*: **in ~** a doble espacio.
double standards [ˌdʌbl'stændədz] *npl*: **to have ~** medir a dos raseros.
double star [ˌdʌbl'stɑːr] *n* estrella *f* binaria.
double stopping [ˌdʌbl'stɒpɪŋ] *n* doble cuerda *f*.
doublet ['dʌblɪt] *n* (**a**) (††) jubón *m*. (**b**) (*Ling*) doblete *m*.
double-talk ['dʌblˌtɔːk] *n* palabras *fpl* insinceras.
double-think ['dʌblθɪŋk] *n*: **a piece of ~** pasaje *m* (*etc*) lleno de contradicciones, ejemplo *m* (*etc*) de hipocresía.
doubleton ['dʌbltən] *n* dubletón *m*.
double windows [ˌdʌbl'wɪndəʊz] *npl* doble acristalado *m*.
doubling ['dʌblɪŋ] *n* (*number*) multiplicación *f* por dos; (*letter*) duplicación *f*.
doubly ['dʌblɪ] *adv* doblemente.
doubt [daʊt] **1** *n* (*a* ~) duda *f*; (*state*) duda *f*, incertidumbre *f*; **no ~!** ¡sin duda!; **beyond ~, past all ~, without** (**a**) ~ fuera de toda duda, indudablemente; **beyond all reasonable ~** más allá de toda duda; **when in ~** en caso de duda; **the matter is still in some ~** el caso sigue dudoso; **she was in ~ whether to ...** dudaba si ...; **there is some ~ about it** sobre esto existen dudas; **there is no ~ that ...** es indudable que ..., no cabe duda de que ...; **I have no ~ that it is true** no dudo que es verdad; **to begin to have one's ~s** empezar a dudar; **to clear up sb's ~s** sacar a uno de dudas; **to cast** (*or* **throw**) **~ on** poner en duda; **let there be no ~ about it** que nadie dude de esto; **the marks left no ~ about how he died** las señales no dejaban lugar a dudas sobre cómo murió.

2 *vt* dudar; (*distrust*) dudar de; **I ~ it** lo dudo; **to ~ sb's loyalty** dudar de la lealtad de uno; **she ~ed whether to go** dudaba si iría; **I greatly ~ whether he will accept** dudo mucho que acepte; **I never ~ed you** nunca tuve dudas acerca de ti.

3 *vi* dudar; **~ing Thomas** Tomás el incrédulo.
doubter ['daʊtər] *n* escéptico *m*, -a *f*.
doubtful ['daʊtfʊl] *adj* dudoso, incierto; *character, place* sospechoso; **I am ~ whether ...** dudo si ...; **he remained ~ about it** tenía todavía sus dudas sobre ello; **of ~ efficacy** de eficacia incierta.
doubtfully ['daʊtfəlɪ] *adv* inciertamente; **he said ~** dijo nada convencido.
doubtfulness ['daʊtfʊlnɪs] *n* (*hesitation*) vacilación *f*, duda *f*; (*uncertainty*) incertidumbre *f*; (*suspicious quality*) carácter *m* sospechoso.
doubtless ['daʊtlɪs] *adv* sin duda; a no dudar(lo), a buen seguro.
douche [duːʃ] **1** *n* ducha *f*; (*Med*) jeringa *f*. **2** *vt* duchar. **3** *vi* ducharse.
dough [dəʊ] *n* masa *f*, pasta *f*; (*) pasta *f*.
doughboy* ['dəʊbɔɪ] *n* (*US*) soldado *m* de infantería; (*Hist*) *soldado de la Primera Guerra Mundial*.
doughnut ['dəʊnʌt] *n* (*Brit*) buñuelo *m*, rosquilla *f*.
doughty ['daʊtɪ] *adj person* valiente, esforzado; *deed* hazañoso.
doughy ['dəʊɪ] *adj* pastoso.
dour ['dʊər] *adj* (*grim*) austero, severo; (*obstinate*) terco; **a ~ Scot** un escocés cerrado; **a ~ struggle** una batalla muy reñida.
Douro ['dʊərəʊ] *n* Duero *m*.
douse [daʊs] *vt fire, light* apagar; (*with water*) mojar, lavar (*with* de).
dove¹ [dʌv] *n* paloma *f* (*also Pol*).
dove² [dəʊv] (*US*) *pret of* **dive**.
dovecote ['dʌvkɒt] *n* palomar *m*.
dove-grey [ˌdʌv'greɪ] *adj* gris paloma.
Dover ['dəʊvər] *n* Dover *m*.
dovetail ['dʌvteɪl] **1** *n* cola *f* de milano. **2** *vt* ensamblar a cola de milano. **3** *vi* (*fig*) encajar (con), ajustarse; **to ~ in with** encajar perfectamente con.
dovish ['dʌvɪʃ] *adj* (*Pol etc*) blando.
dowager ['daʊədʒər] *n* viuda *f* de un título; **~ duchess** duquesa *f* viuda.
dowdiness ['daʊdɪnɪs] *n* falta *f* de elegancia.
dowdy ['daʊdɪ] *adj* poco elegante, poco atractivo.
dowel ['daʊəl] *n* clavija *f*.
Dow-Jones average [ˌdaʊˌdʒəʊnz'ævərɪdʒ] *n* (*US Fin*: *also* **Dow-Jones index**) índice *m* Dow-Jones.
down¹ [daʊn] *n* (*Orn*) plumón *m*, flojel *m*; (*fluff*) pelusa *f*; (*on face*) bozo *m*; (*on body*) vello *m*; (*on fruit*) pelusilla *f*; (*Bot*) vilano *m*.
down² [daʊn] *n* (*Geog*) colina *f*; **the D~s** (*Brit*) las Downs (*colinas del sur de Inglaterra*).
down³ [daʊn] **1** *adv* (**a**) (*downwards*) abajo, hacia abajo, para abajo; (*to the ground*) por tierra, en tierra; (*to the south*) hacia el sur; **to fall ~** caerse; **I ran all the way ~** bajé toda la distancia corriendo; **there was snow all the way ~** estaba nevando durante todo el recorrido.

(**b**) **~ below** allá abajo; **~ by the river** abajo en la ribera; **~ on the shore** abajo en la playa; **~ to** hasta; **~ under** en Australia (*or* en Nueva Zelanda); **to go ~ under** ir a Australia *etc*.

(**c**) **to be ~** (*price, temperature, etc*) haber bajado; (*Aer*) haber aterrizado, estar en tierra; (*person*) haber caído, estar en tierra; **you're ~ for Tuesday** te hemos apuntado para el martes; **she's ~ with the flu** está en cama con gripe; **the computer is ~** el ordenador no funciona, el ordenador tiene una avería; **to be ~ from college** haber terminado el curso universitario; **he's not ~ yet** (*eg for breakfast*) todavía no ha bajado, sigue en cama; **to be ~ and out** no tener donde caerse muerto, estar sin un cuarto; **to be 3 goals ~** tener 3 goles menos; **one ~, five to go** uno en el bote y quedan cinco; tenemos uno y faltan cinco; **I'm £20 ~** he perdido 20 libras, me faltan 20 libras; **to be ~ on sb** (*esp US*) tener inquina a uno; **I'm ~ to my last cigarette** me queda un cigarrillo nada más; **it's ~ to him** le toca a él, le incumbe a él; **it's all ~ to us now** ahora nosotros somos los únicos responsables.

(**d**) (*Fin*) **to pay £50 ~** pagar un depósito de 50 libras, hacer un desembolso inicial de 50 libras.

2 *prep*: **~ the hill** cuesta abajo; **~ river** río abajo (*from* de); **to walk ~ the street** bajar la calle, ir por la calle; **the rain was running ~ the trunk** la lluvia corría por el tronco.

3 *interj*: ~! ¡abajo!; ~!, ~ **boy!** (*to dog*) ¡quieto!; ~ **with the tyrant!** ¡abajo el tirano!, ¡muera el tirano!
4 *adj* (**a**) (*Brit*) *train, stroke* descendente.
(**b**) **to feel** ~ estar triste, estar deprimido.
5 *vt food* devorar; *drink* beberse (de un trago), tragarse; *person* derribar, echar por los suelos; *plane* derribar, abatir; *V* **tool.**
6 *n*: **to have a ~ on sb*** (*Brit*) tener inquina a uno; *V* **up.**

down-and-out ['daʊnən,aʊt] **1** *adj* derrotado, pobrísimo. **2** *n* pobre *mf*, vagabundo *m*.
down-at-heel(s) ['daʊnət'hiːl(z)] *adj* decaído, venido a menos; *appearance* desastrado.
downbeat* ['daʊn,biːt] *adj* (*gloomy*) pesimista, deprimido; (*unemphatic*) apático, callado; de tono menor.
down-bow ['daʊn,bəʊ] *n* descenso *m* de arco.
downcast ['daʊnkɑːst] *adj* abatido, alicaído.
down-cycle ['daʊn,saɪkl] *n* ciclo *m* de caída.
downer‡ ['daʊnəʳ] *n* (*tranquilizer*) tranquilizante *m*; (*depressing experience*) experiencia *f* deprimente; (*fig*) jarro *m* de agua fría.
downfall ['daʊnfɔːl] *n* caída *f*, ruina *f*; **it will be his ~** será su perdición.
downgrade 1 ['daʊngreɪd] *n*: **to be on the ~** ir cuesta abajo, estar en plena decadencia. **2** [daʊn'greɪd] *vt* degradar, asignar a un grado más bajo.
downhearted ['daʊn'hɑːtɪd] *adj* desanimado; **don't be ~** no te dejes desanimar.
downhill ['daʊn'hɪl] **1** *adv* cuesta abajo; **to go ~** ir cuesta abajo, (*fig*) ir de capa caída; estar en franca decadencia.
2 *adj* en declive.
down-home* [,daʊn'həʊm] (*US*) *adj* (*from the South*) del sur; (*narrow-minded*) cerrado de miras.
down-in-the-mouth ['daʊnɪnðə'maʊθ] *adj* decaído, deprimido.
download [,daʊn'ləʊd] *vt* (*Comput*) descargar.
downloading [,daʊn'ləʊdɪŋ] *n* descarga *f*.
down-market [,daʊn'mɑːkɪt] **1** *adj product* inferior, para la sección popular del mercado (*or* de la clientela). **2** *adv*: **to go ~** buscar clientela en la sección popular.
down payment ['daʊn,peɪmənt] *n* (*Fin*) entrada *f*, pago *m* al contado; (*deposit*) desembolso *m* inicial.
downplay* ['daʊn'pleɪ] *vt* (*US*) minimizar la importancia de, quitar importancia a.
downpour ['daʊnpɔːʳ] *n* aguacero *m*, chaparrón *m*.
downright ['daʊnraɪt] **1** *adj person* franco; *lie* abierto, patente, manifiesto; (*obvious*) notorio, evidente; (*out-and-out*) abierto, declarado. **2** *adv* completamente, rotundamente.
down-river ['daʊn'rɪvəʳ] *adv* = **downstream.**
down side ['daʊn,saɪd] *n* lo malo (*of* de), pega *f*, desventaja *f*.
Down's syndrome ['daʊnz,sɪndrəʊm] **1** *n* mongolismo *m*. **2** *attr*: **a ~ baby** un niño mongólico.
downstairs ['daʊn'steəz] **1** *adv* abajo; (*in lower flat*) en el piso de abajo; **to fall ~** caer escaleras abajo; **he went slowly ~** bajó despacio la escalera. **2** *adj* de abajo; **a ~ window** una ventana de la planta baja. **3** *n*: **the ~** el piso inferior, la parte de abajo.
downstream ['daʊn'striːm] *adv* aguas abajo, río abajo (*from* de); **to go ~** ir río abajo; **to swim ~** nadar con la corriente; **a town ~ from Soria** una ciudad más abajo de Soria; **about 5 km ~ from Zamora** unos 5 km más abajo de Zamora.
downstroke ['daʊnstrəʊk] *n* (*with pen*) pierna *f*; (*by child when learning*) palote *m*; (*Mech*) carrera *f* descendente.
downswept ['daʊnswept] *adj wings* con caída posterior.
downswing ['daʊnswɪŋ] *n* (*fig*) recesión *f*, caída *f*.
downtime ['daʊn,taɪm] *n* tiempo *m* de inactividad, tiempo *m* muerto.
down-to-earth ['daʊntʊ'ɜːθ] *adj* práctico, realista.
downtown ['daʊn'taʊn] **1** *adv go* hacia el centro (de la ciudad), *be* en el centro (de la ciudad). **2** *adj* del centro (de la ciudad), céntrico; **~ Bognor** el centro de Bognor.
downtrodden ['daʊn,trɒdn] *adj* oprimido, pisoteado.
downturn ['daʊntɜːn] *n* descenso *m*, bajada *f*, disminución *f*.
downward ['daʊnwəd] *adj curve, movement etc* descendente; *slope* en declive; *tendency* a la baja.
downward(s) ['daʊnwəd(z)] *adv* hacia abajo.
downwind ['daʊn,wɪnd] *adv* a favor del viento.
downy ['daʊnɪ] *adj* velloso; (*and soft*) blando, suave.
dowry ['daʊrɪ] *n* dote *f*.
dowse [daʊz] *vt* = **douse.**
dowser ['daʊzəʳ] *n* zahorí *m*.
doyen ['dɔɪən] *n* decano *m*.
doyenne ['dɔɪen] *n* decana *f*.
doz. *n abbr of* **dozen** docena *f*.
doze [dəʊz] **1** *n* sueño *m* ligero; sueño *m* breve; **to have a ~** (*after meal*) echar una siestecita. **2** *vi* dormitar; **to ~ off** quedarse medio dormido, dormirse.
dozen ['dʌzn] *n* docena *f*; **three ~ oranges** tres docenas de naranjas; **they arrived in (their) ~s, they arrived by the ~** llegaron a docenas.
dozy* ['dəʊzɪ] *adj* amodorrado; soñoliento.
DP *n abbr of* **data processing.**
D.Ph., D. Phil. [,diː'fɪl] *n abbr of* **Doctor of Philosophy.**
DPM *n abbr of* **Diploma in Psychological Medicine.**
DPP *n* (*Brit*) *abbr of* **Director of Public Prosecutions.**
DPT *n abbr of* **diphtheria, pertussis, tetanus** vacuna *f* trivalente.
dpt *abbr of* **department** departmento *m*, dto.
DPW *n* (*US*) *abbr of* **Department of Public Works** ≃ Ministerio *m* de obras Públicas y Urbanismo.
Dr (**a**) (*Med*) *abbr of* **Doctor** doctor *m*, Dr. (**b**) (*Fin*) *abbr of* **debtor** deudor *m*. (**c**) (*street*) *abbr of* **Drive.**
dr (*Fin*) *abbr of* **debtor** deudor *m*.
drab [dræb] *adj* (*fig*) gris, monótono, triste.
drabness ['dræbnɪs] *n* monotonía *f*, tristeza *f*.
drachm [dræm] *n* (**a**) (*measure, Pharm*) dracma *f*. (**b**) = **drachma.**
drachma ['drækmə] *n* dracma *m* (*sometimes f*).
draconian [drə'kəʊnɪən] *adj* draconiano, severo, riguroso.
draft [drɑːft] **1** *n* (**a**) (*Comm*) giro *m*, letra *f* de cambio; orden *f* de pago.
(**b**) (*Mil*) destacamento *m*; (*reinforcements*) refuerzos *mpl*; (*conscription*) quinta *f*; (*US*) llamada *f* a filas, leva *f* (*LAm*).
(**c**) (*preliminary study*: *also* **first ~, rough ~**) borrador *m*; **third ~** tercera versión *f*; *V* **draught.**
(**d**) (*Comput*) borrador *m*, impresión *f* tenue de puntos.
2 *attr* (**a**) (*US Mil*) **~ board** junta *f* de reclutamiento; **~ card** cartilla *f* militar; **~ dodger** prófugo *m*.
(**b**) **~ agreement** proyecto *m* de (un) acuerdo; **~ bill, ~ law** anteproyecto *m* de estatuto; **~ letter** borrador *m* de carta, (*more formal*) proyecto *m* de carta; **~ version** versión *f* preliminar.
3 *vt* (**a**) *document* redactar; *scheme* preparar; (*rough out*) hacer un borrador de, preparar una versión de.
(**b**) (*Mil*) destacar, (*send*) mandar (*to* a); (*US*: *conscript*) quintar, llamar al servicio militar; (*fig*) forzar, obligar.
draftee [drɑːf'tiː] *n* (*US*) recluta *mf*.
draftsman ['drɑːftsmən] *etc* (*US*) = **draughtsman** *etc*.
drag [dræg] **1** *n* (**a**) (*net etc*) rastra *f*, red *f* barredera; (*sledge*) narria *f*.
(**b**) (*Aer etc*) resistencia *f* al avance.
(**c**) (*fig*) obstáculo *m*, estorbo *m* (*on* a, para); (*boring thing*) cosa *f* pesada, lata *f*.
(**d**) (*: *on cigarette*) chupada *f*, fumada *f*, calada* *f*.
(**e**) (*: *Theat etc*) travesti *m*; **in ~** en travesti.
(**f**) **to have a ~** (*US**) tener un enchufe*.
(**g**) **the main ~** (*US**) la calle mayor.
2 *vt object* arrastrar, llevar arrastrado; *sea bed, river etc* dragar, rastrear, efectuar obras de dragado en; **to ~ the anchor** garrar; **to ~ a secret out of sb** arrancar un secreto a uno.
3 *vi* arrastrarse por el suelo; (*go very slowly*) moverse muy despacio; (*time*) pasar lentamente; **the book begins to ~** el libro empieza a cansar; **how that afternoon ~ged!** ¡cómo nos aburrimos aquella tarde!; **to ~ for** rastrear en busca de.
◆**drag about 1** *vt* arrastrar de un lado a otro.
2 *vi* arrastrarse de un lado a otro.
3 *vr*: **to ~ o.s. about (in pain** *etc*) arrastrarse (de dolor *etc*).
◆**drag along 1** *vt*: **to ~ sth along** arrastrar algo tras sí, arrastrar algo con mucha dificultad.
2 *vr*: **to ~ o.s. along** arrastrarse.
◆**drag apart** *vt* separar por la fuerza.
◆**drag away** *vt* arrancar; **she ~ged him away from the television** le arrancó de la televisión.
◆**drag down** *vt* arrastrar hacia abajo; **to ~ sb down to one's level** (*fig*) hacer bajar a uno al nivel de uno; **his illness is ~ging him down** su enfermedad le está debilitando mucho.
◆**drag in** *vt reference* traer por los pelos, hacer entrar a la fuerza; *person* implicar, involucrar.
◆**drag on** *vi*: **to ~ on and on** continuar como si nunca

fuera a acabarse; ser interminable, ir para largo.
◆drag out 1 *vt story etc* ir alargando, hacer interminable. **2** *vi* = **drag on.**
◆drag up *vt* sacar a luz, sacar a relucir.
draglift ['dræglɪft] *n* (*Ski*) arrastre *m*.
dragnet ['drægnet] *n* (**a**) rastra *f*, red *f* barredera; (*fig*) emboscada *f*. (**b**) (*US Pol*) dragadora *f*.
dragon ['drægən] *n* dragón *m*; (*woman*) fiera *f*.
dragonfly ['drægənflaɪ] *n* libélula *f*, caballito *m* del diablo.
dragoon [drə'guːn] **1** *n* dragón *m*. **2** *vt* tiranizar; **to ~ sb into doing sth** obligar a uno (por intimidación) a hacer algo, forzar a uno a hacer algo.
drag queen* ['drægkwiːn] *n* travestí *m*.
drag race ['drægreɪs] *n* (*US Aut*) carrera *f* de coches trucados de salida parada.
drag show* ['drægʃəʊ] *n* espectáculo *m* de travestismo *m*.
dragster ['drægstəʳ] *n* coche *m* trucado.
drain [dreɪn] **1** *n* (**a**) (*outlet*) desaguadero *m*; (*in street*) boca *f* de alcantarilla, sumidero *m*; (*Agr*) zanja *f* de drenaje; **the ~s** (*sewage system*) las alcantarillas, el alcantarillado; **it's money down the ~*** es dinero tirado, eso es tirar el dinero; **to go down the ~*** perderse, echarse a perder.
(**b**) (*fig*) (*source of loss*) desaguadero *m*, sumidero *m*, desagüe *m*; (*loss*) pérdida *f*, disminución *f*; **to be a ~ on** *energies, resources* consumir, agotar; **they are a great ~ on our reserves** constituyen el gran sumidero de nuestras reservas.
(**c**) **there's just a ~ left** quedan unas gotitas.
2 *vt* (**a**) desaguar; (*Agr, Med*) drenar; (*Mech*) purgar, drenar; *glass* apurar; *last drops* apurar, beberse, tragarse; *lake* desangrar, desecar.
(**b**) (*fig*) agotar, consumir; **the country is being ~ed of wealth** el país está siendo empobrecido; **to feel ~ed of energy** estar agotado, sentirse sin fuerzas.
3 *vi* (*washed dishes*) escurrirse.
◆drain away 1 *vt* vaciar. **2** *vi* (*water etc*) irse.
◆drain into *vt river etc* desaguar en.
◆drain off *vt* desangrar; vaciar.
drainage ['dreɪnɪdʒ] *n* (*act*) desagüe *m*; (*Agr, Med*) drenaje *m*; (*of marsh*) desecación *f*; (*sewage system*) alcantarillado *m*.
drainage area ['dreɪnɪdʒ,ɛərɪə] *n*, **drainage basin** ['dreɪnɪdʒ,beɪsn] *n* (*Geol*) cuenca *f* hidrográfica.
drainage channel ['dreɪnɪdʒ,tʃænl] *n* zanja *f* de drenaje.
drainage tube ['dreɪnɪdʒ,tjuːb] *n* (*Med*) tubo *m* de drenaje.
draining-board ['dreɪnɪŋ,bɔːd] *n*, (*US*) **drainboard** ['dreɪnbɔːd] *n* escurreplatos *m*, escurridera *f*, escurridor *m*.
drainpipe ['dreɪnpaɪp] **1** *n* tubo *m* de desagüe. **2** *attr*: **~ trousers** (*Brit*) pantalones *mpl* pitillo.
Drake [dreɪk] *nm* Draque.
drake [dreɪk] *n* pato *m* (macho).
dram [dræm] *n* (*Brit*) (*Pharm*) dracma *f*; (*of drink*) trago *m*.
drama ['drɑːmə] **1** *n* drama *m*. **2** *attr*: **~ critic** crítico *mf* de teatro.
dramatic [drə'mætɪk] *adj* dramático; espectacular, sensacional; *example* elocuente; *décor etc* de gran efecto.
dramatically [drə'mætɪkəlɪ] *adv* dramáticamente; de manera espectacular *etc*.
dramatics [drə'mætɪks] *npl* (*Theat*) arte *m* dramático; (*****) teatro *m*; *V* **amateur.**
dramatis personae ['dræmətɪspɜː'səʊnaɪ] *n* personajes *mpl* (del drama *etc*).
dramatist ['dræmətɪst] *n* dramaturgo *mf* (*also* -a *f*).
dramatization [,dræmətaɪ'zeɪʃən] *n* dramatización *f*.
dramatize ['dræmətaɪz] *vt* (**a**) (*Theat*) adaptar al teatro, escenificar, dramatizar; **X ~d by Y** X en versión dramática de Y.
(**b**) (*show quality of*) poner de manifiesto, demostrar palpablemente. (**c**) (*exaggerate*) exagerar.
drank [dræŋk] *pret of* **drink.**
drape [dreɪp] **1** *n* colgadura *f*; (*Brit*: *hangings*) cortinas *fpl*; **~s** (*US*) cortinas *fpl*.
2 *vt object* adornar con colgaduras, cubrir (*in, with* de), vestir (*with* de); *cloth, clothing* arreglar los pliegues de; **~ this round your shoulders** ponte esto sobre las espaldas; **he ~d a towel about himself** se cubrió con una toalla; **he ~d an arm about my shoulders** me ciñó el hombro con su brazo.
draper ['dreɪpəʳ] *n* (*Brit*) pañero *m*, mercero *m* (*LAm*), (*linen*) lencero *m*.
drapery ['dreɪpərɪ] *n* (**a**) (*hangings*) colgaduras *fpl*, ropaje *m*; (*as merchandise*) pañería *f*, mercería *f* (*LAm*), bonetería *f* (*Mex*). (**b**) (*Brit*: *also* **draper's shop**) pañería *f*, tienda *f* de paños, mercería *f* (*LAm*), bonetería *f* (*Mex*).
drastic ['dræstɪk] *adj* drástico; enérgico, fuerte; *measure* draconiano, severo; *reduction etc* importante; *change* radical.
drastically ['dræstɪkəlɪ] *adv* drásticamente; enérgicamente; severamente; **to be ~ reduced** sufrir una reducción importante; **he ~ revised his ideas** cambió radicalmente de ideas.
drat* [dræt] *vt*: **~!, ~ it!** ¡maldición!
dratted* ['drætɪd] *adj* maldito.
draught, (*US*) **draft** [drɑːft] **1** *n* (**a**) (*drink*) trago *m*; (*Med*) dosis *f*; **at one ~** de un trago.
(**b**) (*Naut*) calado *m*.
(**c**) (*of air*) corriente *f* de aire; (*breeze*) viento *m*, brisa *f*; **to feel the ~** (*fig*) tener dificultades, sufrir las consecuencias, resentirse de los efectos.
(**d**) **~s** (*Brit*: *game*) juego *m* de damas.
2 *attr horse* de tiro; **~ beer** cerveza *f* al grifo, cerveza *f* de barril; *V also* **draft.**
draughtboard ['drɑːftbɔːd] *n* (*Brit*) tablero *m* de damas.
draught excluder, (*US*) **draft excluder** ['drɑːftɪks'kluːdəʳ] *n* burlete *m*.
draught horse, (*US*) **draft horse** ['drɑːfthɔːs] *n* caballo *m* de tiro.
draughtiness, (*US*) **draftiness** ['drɑːftɪnɪs] *n* corriente *f* de aire.
draught-proof, (*US*) **draft-proof** ['drɑːftpruːf] *adj* a prueba de corrientes de aire.
draught-proofing, (*US*) **draft-proofing** ['drɑːft,pruːfɪŋ] *n* burlete *m*.
draughtsman, (*US*) **draftsman** ['drɑːftsmən] *n*, *pl* **draughtsmen,** (*US*) **draftsmen** ['drɑːftsmən] (**a**) delineante *m*, proyectista *m*. (**b**) (*Brit*: *in game*) dama *f*, pieza *f*.
draughtsmanship, (*US*) **draftsmanship** ['drɑːftsmənʃɪp] *n* (*skill*) arte *m* del delineante; (*quality*) habilidad *f* para el dibujo.
draughty, (*US*) **drafty** ['drɑːftɪ] *adj room* que tiene corrientes de aire, lleno de corrientes de aire; *day, place* de mucho viento.
draw [drɔː] **1** *n* (**a**) (*Sport*) empate *m*, (*Chess*) tablas *fpl*.
(**b**) (*lottery*) sorteo *m* (*for* de); **it's the luck of the ~** así es la suerte.
(**c**) (*attraction*) atracción *f*; (*Theat*) función *f* taquillera, obra *f* de mucho éxito.
(**d**) **to beat sb to the ~** (*lit*) desenfundar más rápido que uno; (*fig*) adelantarse a uno; **to be quick on the ~** ser rápido en sacar la pistola; (*fig*) ser muy listo.
(**e**) (*of chimney*) tiro *m*.
2 (*irr*: *pret* **drew,** *ptp* **drawn**) *vt* (**a**) (*pull along*) tirar; arrastrar; (*pull at*) tirar de; *bow* tender; *curtains* correr; **to ~ one's hand over one's eyes** pasar la mano por los ojos; **to ~ one's hat over one's eyes** bajar el sombrero sobre los ojos; **I drew her to me** tiré de ella hacia mí; **I drew her to the window** la llevé a la ventana; **his shouts ~ me to the place** sus gritos me llevaron al lugar, fui al lugar siguiendo sus gritos; **we ~ him into the plan** le persuadimos a que participara en el proyecto.
(**b**) (*extract*) sacar, extraer; *cork, gun, sword, confession, tooth* sacar; (*pluck out*) arrancar; *card* robar; *trumps* arrastrar; (*Med*) *boil* hacer reventar; *money* retirar; *lots* echar; *number, prize* sacarse; *wages* cobrar; *salary* ganar, percibir, cobrar; *cheque* girar (*on* a cargo de, *for* por); *blood* hacer manar, derramar; *breath* tomar, respirar; *inspiration etc* sacar.
(**c**) (*attract, cause*) atraer; provocar; *attention* llamar (*to* sobre); *laughter* causar, provocar; *applause* despertar, motivar; *criticism* provocar; **it drew no reply** no hubo contestación a esto; **he refuses to be ~n** se niega a hablar de ello, se guarda de hacer comentario alguno; **to feel ~n to** sentirse atraído por, sentir la atracción de; *person* tener simpatía por.
(**d**) (*Art etc*) *drawing, scene* dibujar; *line* trazar, tirar; (*Liter*) *character* trazar.
(**e**) (*formulate*) *conclusion* sacar; *comparison, distinction* hacer.
(**f**) **the boat ~s 2 metres** el barco tiene un calado de 2 metros.
(**g**) **to ~ a game** (*Sport*) lograr el empate, empatar (*with* con); (*Chess*) entablar.
(**h**) (*Culin*) *fowl* destripar.
(**i**) (*Tech*) *wire* estirar.
3 *vi* (**a**) (*move*) **to ~ to one side** moverse a un lado, apartarse; **the train drew into the station** el tren entró en

la estación; **the car drew into the kerb** el coche paró junto a la acera; **we could ~ in here** podríamos parar aquí; *V* **ahead, level, near.**
(**b**) (*chimney*) tirar (bien).
(**c**) (*Art*) dibujar.
(**d**) (*Sport*) empatar; (*Chess*) entablar.
(**e**) (*tea*) prepararse.

◆draw aside 1 *vt covering* apartar; *curtain* descorrer; *person* apartar, llamar aparte, llevar aparte.
2 *vi* ir aparte, apartarse.

◆draw away 1 *vt* apartar, llevar aparte.
2 *vi* irse, apartarse, retirarse; alejarse; (*in race*) adelantarse (a los otros), dejar atrás a los otros.

◆draw back 1 *vt* retirar; *curtain* descorrer.
2 *vi* retroceder; dar un paso hacia atrás; (*fig*) volverse atrás, cejar; **to ~ back from doing sth** no atreverse a hacer algo.

◆draw down *vt blind* bajar; (*fig*) *blame, ridicule* atraer.

◆draw forth *vt comment etc* motivar, provocar, dar lugar a.

◆draw in 1 *vt* tirar hacia dentro, retirar; *breath* tomar, aspirar; (*attract*) atraer.
2 *vi* (**a**) (*train etc*) llegar, entrar.
(**b**) (*days*) acortarse, hacerse más cortos.

◆draw off *vt* (**a**) *gloves* quitarse.
(**b**) *liquid* vaciar, trasegar.
(**c**) *pursuers* apartar, desviar.

◆draw on 1 *vt* (**a**) *gloves* ponerse.
(**b**) **to ~ sb on** engatusar a uno.
(**c**) = **draw upon.**
2 *vi* (*night etc*) acercarse.

◆draw out 1 *vt* (**a**) (*take out*) sacar.
(**b**) (*lengthen*) alargar, estirar; *wire* tirar.
(**c**) *person* hacer hablar, hacer menos reservado; (*pej*) sonsacar.
2 *vi* (**a**) (*train etc*) arrancar, ponerse en marcha, salir de la estación.
(**b**) (*days*) hacerse más largos.

◆draw together 1 *vt* reunir, juntar.
2 *vi* reunirse, juntarse; (*fig*) hacerse más unidos.

◆draw up 1 *vt* (**a**) (*raise*) levantar, alzar; *water from well* sacar.
(**b**) (*move*) *chair* acercar.
(**c**) (*form up*) *men* formar; *army* ordenar para el combate.
(**d**) *report etc* redactar, preparar.
2 *vi* pararse, acercarse y parar.
3 *vr*: **to ~ o.s. up** erguirse, estirarse.

◆draw (up)on *vt source* inspirarse en; *text* poner a contribución; *resources* usar, hacer uso de, explotar, recurrir a; *experience* beneficiarse de, aprovechar; *bank account* retirar dinero de.

drawback [ˈdrɔːbæk] *n* inconveniente *m*, desventaja *f* (*of, to* de).
drawbridge [ˈdrɔːbrɪdʒ] *n* puente *m* levadizo.
drawee [drɔːˈiː] *n* girado *m*, librado *m*.
drawer¹ [ˈdrɔːəʳ] *n* (*Comm*) girador *m*.
drawer² [drɔːʳ] *n* cajón *m*; gaveta *f*; **out of the top ~** de primera calidad, de categoría superior; bien nacido.
drawers [drɔːz] *npl* (*man's*) calzoncillos *mpl*, (*woman's*) bragas *fpl*.
drawing¹ [ˈdrɔːɪŋ] *n* (*Art*) dibujo *m*.
drawing² [ˈdrɔːɪŋ] *attr* (*Fin*): **~ account** cuenta *f* de anticipos; fondo *m* para gastos; **~ rights** derechos *mpl* de giro.
drawing-board [ˈdrɔːɪŋbɔːd] *n* tablero *m* de delineante; (*Art*) tablero *m* de dibujo; **back to the ~!** ¡a recomenzar!
drawing-office [ˈdrɔːɪŋˌɒfɪs] *n* sección *f* de delineantes.
drawing-paper [ˈdrɔːɪŋˌpeɪpəʳ] *n* papel *m* de dibujo.
drawing-pen [ˈdrɔːɪŋˌpen] *n* tiralíneas *m*.
drawing-pin [ˈdrɔːɪŋpɪn] *n* (*Brit*) chinche *f*.
drawing power [ˈdrɔːɪŋˌpaʊəʳ] *n* fuerza *f* de atracción, poder *m* de convocatoria, capacidad *f* de arrastre.
drawing-room [ˈdrɔːɪŋrʊm] *n* salón *m*, sala *f* (*LAm*).
drawl [drɔːl] **1** *n* habla *f* lenta y pesada. **2** *vt* pronunciar lenta y pesadamente, arrastrar. **3** *vi* hablar lenta y pesadamente.
drawn [drɔːn] **1** *ptp of* **draw. 2** *adj* (**a**) *game* empatado. (**b**) *face* cansado, ojeroso. (**c**) **long ~ out** larguísimo, interminable. (**d**) **with ~ sword** con la espada en la mano. (**e**) **~ butter** (*US*) mantequilla *f* derretida.
drawstring [ˈdrɔːstrɪŋ] *n* cordón *m*.
dray [dreɪ] *n* carro *m* pesado.
dread [dred] **1** *n* pavor *m*, terror *m*; **to go in ~ of** tener pavor a; **to fill sb with ~** infundir terror a uno.
2 *adj* espantoso.
3 *vt* tener miedo a, temer; **I ~ what may happen when he comes** me horroriza lo que pueda pasar cuando venga; **I ~ to think of it** el pensamiento me horroriza.
dreadful [ˈdredfʊl] *adj* terrible, espantoso; (*fig*) horrible, fatal, malísimo; **how ~!** ¡qué barbaridad!, qué horror!; **I feel ~** me siento muy mal; **I feel ~ about it** la cosa me da vergüenza, me da muchísima pena.
dreadfully [ˈdredfəlɪ] *adv* terriblemente; (*fig*) malísimamente; **I'm ~ sorry** lo siento muchísimo; **it's ~ difficult** es terriblemente difícil.
dreadnought [ˈdrednɔːt] *n* (*Hist*) acorazado *m*.
dream [driːm] **1** *n* sueño *m*; (*daydream*) ensueño *m*; (*ideal*) ideal *m*; (*fond hope*) ilusión *f*; **bad ~** pesadilla *f*; **sweet ~s!** ¡duerme bien!; **the house of my ~s** mi casa ideal, la casa soñada, la casa de mis ilusiones; **isn't it a ~?*** es un sueño, ¿verdad?; **to see sth in a ~** ver algo en sueños; **she goes about in a ~** parece que está soñando; **my fondest ~ is to ~** + *infin* el sueño de mi vida es + *infin*, mi mayor ilusión es + *infin*; **to be rich beyond one's ~s** ser más rico de lo que jamás se soñara; **to succeed beyond one's wildest ~s** tener muchísimo más éxito de lo que se esperaba; **it went like a ~** fue a las mil maravillas.
2 *attr* ideal; **~ boat*** sueño* *m*; **it's/he's a ~ boat*** es un sueño*; **my ~ house** mi casa ideal; **~ ticket** (*Pol*) lista *f* de candidatos ideal; **~ world** mundo *m* de ensueño; **to live in a ~ world** vivir en un mundo de sueños, vivir de pura fantasía.
3 (*pret and ptp* **dreamed** *or* **dreamt**) *vti* soñar (*of* con, *that* que); **you must have ~ed it** lo habrás imaginado; **I wouldn't ~ of it!** ¡ni hablar!; **I wouldn't ~ of going** no iría ni soñando, ¿ir? ¡ni soñarlo!

◆dream away *vt*: **to ~ away the day** pasar el día soñando.

◆dream up *vt* inventar, idear; **who ~ed this one up?** ¿a quién debemos esta idea?

dreamer [ˈdriːməʳ] *n* soñador *m*, -ora *f*, fantaseador *m*, -ora *f*; visionario *m*, -a *f*.
dreamily [ˈdriːmɪlɪ] *adv* distraídamente, como si estuviera soñando.
dreamland [ˈdriːmlænd] *n* reino *m* del ensueño, país *m* de los sueños; utopia *f*.
dreamless [ˈdriːmlɪs] *adj* sin sueños.
dreamlike [ˈdriːmlaɪk] *adj* de ensueño, como de sueño.
dreamt [dremt] *pret and ptp of* **dream.**
dreamy [ˈdriːmɪ] *adj* (**a**) *character* soñador, distraído, muy en las nubes. (**b**) *tone etc* del que fantasea, distraído; *music* soñador, de sueño. (**c**) (*) precioso, maravilloso.
dreariness [ˈdrɪərɪnɪs] *n* tristeza *f*, monotonía *f*; lo aburrido.
dreary [ˈdrɪərɪ] *adj* triste, monótono; *book etc* aburrido.
dredge¹ [dredʒ] **1** *n* draga *f*, rastra *f*. **2** *vt channel* dragar, limpiar (*etc*) con draga; *mud etc* dragar; **to ~ up** pescar; (*fig*) sacar a luz.
dredge² [dredʒ] *n* (*Culin*) espolvoreador *m*.
dredger¹ [ˈdredʒəʳ] *n* draga *f*.
dredger² [ˈdredʒəʳ] *n* (*Culin*) espolvoreador *m*.
dredging¹ [ˈdredʒɪŋ] *n* dragado *m*, obras *fpl* de dragado.
dredging² [ˈdredʒɪŋ] *n* (*Culin*) espolvoreado *m*.
dregs [dregz] *npl* heces *fpl*, sedimento *m*; (*fig*) hez *f*; **the ~ of society** la hez de la sociedad; **to drain a glass to the ~** apurar un vaso hasta las heces.
drench [drentʃ] **1** *n* (*Vet*) poción *f*. **2** *vt* mojar (*in, with* de), empapar (*in, with* en); **to get ~ed** mojarse hasta los huesos.
drenching [ˈdrentʃɪŋ] **1** *adj rain* torrencial. **2** *n*: **to get a ~** mojarse hasta los huesos.
Dresden [ˈdrezdən] *n* Dresde *m*; **~ china** loza *f* de Dresde.
dress [dres] **1** *n* (*in general*) vestido *m*, indumentaria *f*; (*clothing*) ropa *f*; (*frock*) vestido *m*.
2 *attr*: **~ shirt** camisa *f* de frac; **~ shop** casa *f* de modas; **~ suit** traje *m* de etiqueta.
3 *vt* (**a**) (*clothe*) vestir (*in* de, *in green* de verde); **to be ~ed in** vestir, llevar, ir vestido de; **to get ~ed** vestirse; *V also* **dressed.**
(**b**) (*Theat*) *play* hacer los trajes para.
(**c**) (*decorate*) *hair* peinar; *shop window* poner, decorar; *Christmas tree* arreglar, adornar.
(**d**) (*Culin*) aderezar, aliñar.
(**e**) (*Agr*) abonar (*with* de).
(**f**) *skins* adobar, curtir; *stone* labrar; *wood* desbastar.
(**g**) (*Mil*) *troops* formar.
(**h**) *wound* curar, vendar.
4 *vi* (**a**) vestirse; **to ~ for dinner** (*man*) ponerse smoking; (*woman*) ponerse traje de noche.

(**b**) (*Mil*) formar, alinearse.
◆**dress down*** *vt* (*Brit*) poner como un trapo.
◆**dress up 1** *vt* ataviar, engalanar (*in* de); **to ~ sb up as** disfrazar a uno de; **they ~ed the setback up as a triumph** hicieron creer que el revés era un triunfo.
2 *vi* ataviarse, engalanarse (*in* de); (*formally*) vestirse de etiqueta; **to ~ up as** disfrazarse de.
dress circle ['dres'sɜːkl] *n* (piso *m*) principal *m*.
dress coat ['dres'kəʊt] *n* frac *m*.
dress designer ['dresdɪ'zaɪnəʳ] *n* modisto *m*, -a *f*.
dressed [drest] *adj* vestido; **well-~** bien vestido; **to be ~ for the country** (*or* **town** *or* **tennis**) ir vestido para ir al campo (*or* a la ciudad *or* al tenis); **~ as a man** vestido de hombre; **~ in black** vestido de negro.
dresser ['dresəʳ] *n* (**a**) (*furniture*) aparador *m* (con estantes), rinconera *f*; (*US*) cómoda *f* con espejo. (**b**) (*Theat*) camarero *m*, -a *f*; (*Cine, TV*) tocadorista *mf*. (**c**) **he's an elegant ~** se viste elegantemente.
dressing ['dresɪŋ] *n* (**a**) (*act*) el vestir(se). (**b**) (*Med*) vendaje *m*. (**c**) (*Culin*) salsa *f*, aliño *m*. (**d**) (*Agr*) abono *m*.
dressing-case ['dresɪŋkeɪs] *n* neceser *m*.
dressing-down* ['dresɪŋ'daʊn] *n* rapapolvo* *m*; **to give sb a ~** echar un rapapolvo a uno*.
dressing-gown ['dresɪŋgaʊn] *n* (*Brit*) (*woman's*) bata *f*, salto *m* de cama; (*man's*) batín *m*.
dressing-room ['dresɪŋrʊm] *n* vestidor *m*; (*Theat*) camarín *m*, camerino *m*.
dressing-station ['dresɪŋ,steɪʃən] *n* puesto *m* de socorro.
dressing-table ['dresɪŋ,teɪbl] *n* tocador *m*.
dress length ['dres,leŋθ] *n* (*material*) largo *m* de vestido.
dressmaker ['dresmeɪkəʳ] *n* costurera *f*, modista *f*.
dressmaking ['dresmeɪkɪŋ] *n* costura *f*, corte *m* y confección.
dress parade ['drespə'reɪd] *n* desfile *m* de gala.
dress rehearsal ['dresrɪ'hɜːsəl] *n* ensayo *m* general.
dress uniform ['dres'juːnɪfɔːm] *n* uniforme *m* de gala.
dressy ['dresɪ] *adj person, clothing* elegante.
drew [druː] *pret of* **draw**.
dribble ['drɪbl] **1** *n* (**a**) (*water etc*) gotitas *fpl*.
(**b**) (*Sport*) regate *m*.
2 *vt* (**a**) dejar caer gota a gota.
(**b**) (*Sport*) regatear, driblar.
3 *vi* (**a**) gotear, caer gota a gota (*down* por); (*from mouth*) babear.
(**b**) (*Sport*) regatear, driblar (*past* a).
dribbler ['drɪbləʳ] *n* (*Sport*) driblador *m*.
driblet ['drɪblɪt] *n* adarme *m*; **in ~s** por adarmes.
dribs [drɪbz] *npl*: **~ and drabs** cantidades *fpl* pequeñísimas; **in ~ and drabs** gota a gota; **the money came in in ~ and drabs** el dinero llegó por adarmes (*or* por gotas).
dried [draɪd] *adj* seco; *fruit* desecado, paso.
dried out [,draɪd'aʊt] *adj alcoholic* seco.
drier ['draɪəʳ] *n* = **dryer**.
drift [drɪft] **1** *n* (**a**) (*Naut*) impulso *m* de la corriente, velocidad *f* de la corriente; (*amount off course*) deriva *f*; (*fig*) tendencia *f*, movimiento *m*; (*Ling*) evolución *f*; **the ~ of events** la tendencia de los acontecimientos; **the ~ from the land** la despoblación del campo, el éxodo rural; **the ~ to the city** el movimiento hacia la ciudad.
(**b**) (*fig: lack of drive*) inacción *f*.
(**c**) (*of sand, snow*) montón *m*; (*of clouds, leaves*) banco *m*; (*Geol*) terrenos *mpl* de acarreo.
(**d**) (*fig*) (*sense*) significado *m*; (*purpose*) intención *f*, propósito *m*; **to catch sb's ~** caer en la cuenta de lo que uno quiere decir; **I don't get your ~** no te entiendo.
2 *vt* (*carry*) impeler, llevar; (*pile up*) amontonar.
3 *vi* (**a**) (*Naut*) ir a la deriva, decaer; (*on water, in air etc*) flotar, dejarse llevar por la corriente (*or* el viento); (*be off course*) derivar; (*snow*) amontonarse.
(**b**) (*fig*) vivir sin rumbo, no tener propósito fijo; **to ~ into war** dejarse llevar a la guerra; **to ~ from job to job** cambiar a menudo de trabajo sin propósito fijo; **he just lets things ~** deja que sus cosas vayan a la deriva.
◆**drift apart** *vi* irse separando poco a poco, irse separando sin quererlo.
◆**drift away** *vi* dejarse llevar por la corriente.
◆**drift off** *vi* = **drift away**; (*doze off*) dormirse, quedarse medio dormido.
drifter ['drɪftəʳ] *n* (**a**) (*Naut*) trainera *f*. (**b**) (*person*) vago *m*.
drift-ice ['drɪftaɪs] *n* hielo *m* flotante.
drift-net ['drɪfnet] *n* traína *f*.
driftwood ['drɪftwʊd] *n* madera *f* de deriva, madera *f* de playa.
drill¹ [drɪl] **1** *n* (**a**) (*Mech*) taladro *m*; (*part of brace and bit*) broca *f*; (*bench machine*) fresadora *f*; (*dentist's*) fresa *f*; (*in mining*) perforadora *f*, barrena *f*; (*in roadmending*: *also* **pneumatic ~**) martillo *m* picador, taladradora *f*.
(**b**) (*Mil etc*) instrucción *f*; (*Scol*) ejercicios *mpl*, educación *f* física; (*for fire*) simulacro *m* de incendio; **you all know the ~*** todos sabéis lo que habéis de hacer; **what's the ~?*** ¿qué es lo que tenemos que hacer?
2 *vt* (**a**) *metal etc* perforar, taladrar, barrenar; *hole* practicar; **to ~ sb full of holes*** agujerear a uno como a un colador*.
(**b**) (*Mil*) enseñar instrucción a; (*Sport etc*) entrenar, adiestrar; **to ~ a class in French verbs** hacer ejercicios de los verbos franceses con una clase; **to ~ sb to do sth** enseñar metódicamente a uno a hacer algo; **I had it ~ed into me as a boy** me lo hicieron comprender a la fuerza siendo chico.
3 *vi* (**a**) perforar (*for* en busca de).
(**b**) (*Mil*) hacer instrucción; (*Sport etc*) entrenarse, adiestrarse.
drill² [drɪl] **1** *n* (*Agr*) (**a**) (*machine*) sembradora *f*. (**b**) (*row*) hilera *f*, surco *m*. **2** *vt* (*Agr*) sembrar con sembradora.
drill³ [drɪl] *n* (*cloth*) dril *m*.
drilling¹ ['drɪlɪŋ] *n* (*for oil etc*) perforación *f*; **~ platform** plataforma *f* de perforación; **~ rig** torre *f* de perforación, cabria *f* de perforación.
drilling² ['drɪlɪŋ] *n* (*Mil*) instrucción *f*.
drily, dryly ['draɪlɪ] *adv* secamente; **he said ~** dijo guasón, dijo con su humorismo peculiar.
drink [drɪŋk] **1** *n* (*gen, alcohol*) bebida *f*; (*a draught*) trago *m*; **the ~‡** el mar, el agua; **~s cupboard** mueble-bar *m*; **~s trolley** carrito *m* de bebidas; **I need a ~ of water** necesito un trago de agua; **could I have a ~ of water?** ¿puedes darme un poco de agua?; **to have a ~** tomar algo; **will you have a ~?** ¿quieres tomar algo?; **we had a ~ or two** tomamos unas copas (*LAm*: unos tragos); **to take to ~** darse a la bebida; **she has a ~ problem** tiene problema alcohólico; **to ask friends round for ~s** invitar a los amigos a tomar algo en casa; **he's a long ~ of water** (*US*: *tall*) es más alto que un espárrago.
2 (*irr*: *pret* **drank**, *ptp* **drunk**) *vt* beber; tomar; **what will you ~ ?, what are you ~ing?** ¿qué quieres tomar?; **to ~ sb under the table** beber hasta tumbar a uno.
3 *vi* (*ie ~ alcohol*) beber; **thanks, I don't ~** gracias, yo no bebo; **to ~ like a fish** beber como una esponja; **to ~ to sb** brindar por uno, beber a la salud de uno; **to ~ to the success of** brindar por el éxito de.
4 *vr*: **to ~ o.s. to death** morir alcoholizado; **to ~ o.s. silly** beber hasta emborracharse.
◆**drink down** *vt* beber de un trago.
◆**drink in** *vt* (*fig*) beber, embeberse en; *words* estar pendiente de.
◆**drink off** *vt* beber de un trago.
◆**drink out of** *vt* beber de.
◆**drink up 1** *vt* beberse, terminar de beber. **2** *vi* terminar de beber; **~ up, we're going** termina ya, que nos vamos.
drinkable ['drɪŋkəbl] *adj water* potable; *coffee, wine etc* bebible; **it's quite a ~ wine** es un vino nada malo.
drink-driving ['drɪŋk'draɪvɪŋ] *attr*: **~ campaign** campaña *f* contra el alcohol en carretera; **~ offence** delito *m* de conducir en estado de embriaguez.
drinker ['drɪŋkəʳ] *n* bebedor *m*, -ora *f*.
drinking ['drɪŋkɪŋ] *n* el beber; (*drunkenness*) bebida *f*; **~ too much alcohol can be dangerous** beber demasiado alcohol es peligroso; **eating and ~** comer y beber; **he wasn't used to ~** no estaba acostumbrado a beber; **there was a lot of heavy ~** se bebía mucho; **his problem was ~** la bebida era su problema; **his ~ caused his marriage to break up** la bebida fue la causa de la ruptura de su matrimonio; **I don't object to ~ in moderation** no me opongo a que se beba con moderación; **~ by the under-18s must be stopped** se ha de impedir que los menores de 18 años beban.
drinking-bout ['drɪŋkɪŋbaʊt] *n* juerga *f* de borrachera.
drinking chocolate ['drɪŋkɪŋ,tʃɒklɪt] *n* chocolate *m* (*bebida*).
drinking companion ['drɪŋkɪŋkəm,pænjən] *n* compañero *m*, -a *f* de bar.
drinking fountain ['drɪŋkɪŋ,faʊntɪn] *n* fuente *f* (de agua potable).
drinking session ['drɪŋkɪŋ,seʃən] *n* juerga *f* de borrachera; **they went out for a ~** se fueron de copas.
drinking-song ['drɪŋkɪŋsɒŋ] *n* canción *f* de taberna.
drinking-trough ['drɪŋkɪŋtrɒf] *n* abrevadero *m*, camellón *m*.
drinking-up ['drɪŋkɪŋʌp] *attr*: **~ time** tiempo *m* permitido para terminar de beber (en el pub).
drinking-water ['drɪŋkɪŋ,wɔːtəʳ] *n* agua *f* potable.

drip [drɪp] **1** *n* (**a**) (*act*) goteo *m*, el gotear. (**b**) (*one drop*) gota *f*; (*from roof, inside house*) gotera *f*. (**c**) (*Med: also* ~ **feed**) gota a gota *m*. (**d**) (‡) pelmazo* *m*. **2** *vt* dejar caer gota a gota. **3** *vi* gotear, caer gota a gota (*down* por).

drip-dry ['drɪp'draɪ] *adj* de lava y pon.

drip-feed‡ ['drɪp,fi:d] **1** *n* (alimentación *f*) gota a gota *m*; **to be on a** ~ recibir alimentación gota a gota. **2** *vt* (*irr*: *V* **feed**) alimentar gota a gota.

dripmat ['drɪpmæt] *n* posavasos *m*.

dripping ['drɪpɪŋ] **1** *adj tap etc* que gotea; *clothes* chorreantes, que chorrean agua; **to be** ~ **wet** estar calado. **2** *n* pringue *m*, grasa *f*.

drive [draɪv] **1** *n* (**a**) (*outing*) paseo *m* (en coche *etc*); (*journey*) viaje *m* (en coche *etc*); **to go for a** ~ dar un paseo (*or* una vuelta) en coche; **to take sb for a** ~ llevar a uno de paseo en coche; **it's a long** ~ es un trayecto largo.

(**b**) (*Hunting*) batida *f*; (*Mil*) ataque *m*, avance *m*; (*fig*) campaña *f* (*against, on* contra, para suprimir).

(**c**) (*stroke*) golpe *m* fuerte, golpe *m* directo; (*Golf, Tennis*) drive *m*.

(**d**) (*energy*) energía *f*, vigor *m*; dinamismo *m*; (*driving force*) impulso *m*; **the** ~ **to power** el empuje hacia el poder; **the sex** ~ el instinto sexual, la libido; **the strongest of man's** ~**s** el más fuerte de los instintos humanos.

(**e**) (*carriageway*) calzada *f*, avenida *f*.

(**f**) (*Mech*) mecanismo *m* de transmisión; (*Comput*) unidad *f* de disco.

2 (*irr*: *pret* **drove**, *ptp* **driven**) *vt* (**b**) (*urge in a direction*) empujar, impeler, *game* batir; *cattle* guiar, llevar.

(**b**) (*urge on*) hacer trabajar, hacer sudar; **he drove us to victory** él nos condujo a la victoria.

(**c**) (*steer*) *car, carriage etc* conducir, manejar (*LAm*); *plough* manejar; **he** ~**s a taxi** es taxista; **Pepe** ~**s a Shark** Pepe tiene un Tiburón.

(**d**) (*power*) mover, actuar; *vehicle etc* impulsar; (*Comput*) controlar, accionar; **the wind** ~**s the boat along** el viento empuja el barco; **a car** ~**n by steam** un coche impulsado por vapor, un coche que funciona con vapor.

(**e**) *ball etc* golpear con fuerza; *furrow* hacer; *hole* perforar, practicar; *tunnel* abrir, construir; *road* construir; *nail* clavar (*into* en); *teeth etc* hincar (*into* en); *object* introducir a la fuerza (*into* en); (*fig*) *bargain* hacer; **to** ~ **a post into the ground** hincar un poste en el suelo a martillazos (*etc*); **to** ~ **a way through** abrirse paso por; *V* **home 3 (b)**.

(**f**) (*carry*) *passenger* llevar en coche; **I'll** ~ **you home** te llevo (a casa).

(**g**) (*force*) **to** ~ **sb to do** (*or* **into doing**) **sth**, forzar a uno a hacer algo; **to** ~ **sb mad** volver a uno loco; **to** ~ **sb to despair** hacer desesperar a uno; **to** ~ **people to revolt** provocar a la gente a que se subleve.

3 *vi* (**a**) (*steer*) conducir, manejar (*LAm*); '~ **slowly**' 'marcha moderada'; **to** ~ **on the left** circular por la izquierda.

(**b**) (*go etc*) pasearse en coche, dar un paseo en coche; **to** ~ **to London** ir en coche a Londres; **he drove alone** hizo el viaje solo; **he drove 50 miles in an hour** recorrió 50 millas en una hora; **he had been driving all day** había pasado todo el día al volante; **she drove into the garage** entró en el garaje; **he drove into a wall** chocó con un muro; **next time we'll** ~ **here** la próxima vez vamos en coche.

(**c**) **the rain is driving down** está lloviendo a chuzos.

(**d**) **to let** ~ **at** asestar un golpe a; (*fig*) denunciar, atacar.

◆**drive along 1** *vt* (*wind, current*) empujar.

2 *vi* (*vehicle*) circular; (*person*) conducir.

◆**drive at** *vt* insinuar, querer decir; **what are you driving at?** ¿qué quieres decir?, ¿qué pretendes?

◆**drive away 1** *vt* (**a**) (*chase away*) ahuyentar; *person* alejar; *cares* alejar, quitarse de encima.

(**b**) (*in car*) llevarse (en coche).

2 *vi* = **drive off 2.**

◆**drive back 1** *vt* rechazar; *defenders* obligar a ceder terreno; *crowd* obligar a retroceder.

2 *vi* volver (en coche).

◆**drive in 1** *vt nail* clavar.

2 *vi* entrar (en coche).

◆**drive off 1** *vt* = **drive away 1.**

2 *vi* irse, marcharse (en coche) partir; (*car*) arrancar y partir.

◆**drive on 1** *vt* empujar, llevar adelante.

2 *vi* seguir adelante; ~ **on!** ¡adelante!

◆**drive on to** *vt ferry* embarcar en.

◆**drive out 1** *vt* expulsar; obligar a salir (*of* de).

2 *vi* dar un paseo en coche.

◆**drive over 1** *vt* (**a**) (*convey*) llevar en coche.

(**b**) (*crush*) aplastar.

2 *vi* venir (*or* ir) en coche; **we drove over in 2 hours** vinimos en 2 horas; **we drove over to see them** fuimos a verlos (en coche).

◆**drive up 1** *vt price etc* hacer subir.

2 *vi* llegar (en coche); acercarse; **to** ~ **up to town** ir (en coche) a la ciudad.

drive-in ['draɪv,ɪn] (*US*) **1** *n* restaurante *m* donde se sirve al cliente en su automóvil; (*cinema*) autocine *m*. **2** *attr bank etc* dispuesto para el uso del automovilista en su coche; ~ **cinema** autocine *m*.

drivel ['drɪvl] **1** *n* tonterías *fpl*. **2** *vi* decir tonterías.

driven ['drɪvn] *ptp of* **drive**.

-driven ['drɪvn] *adj ending in compounds* que funciona con, accionado por; **electricity**~ que funciona con electricidad, accionado por electricidad; **steam**~ impulsado por vapor, a vapor.

driver ['draɪvə^r] *n* (*Aut*) conductor *m*, -ora *f*; chófer *mf*, chofer *mf* (*LAm*); (*Brit Rail*) maquinista *m*; (*of coach*) cochero *m*; ~**'s licence,** (*US*) ~**'s license** carnet *m* de conducir; *V* **racing 2.**

driveshaft ['drɑɪvʃɑ:ft] *n* árbol *m* motor.

drive-up window [draɪvʌp'wɪndəʊ] *n* (*US*) taquilla *f* para automovilistas.

driveway ['draɪvweɪ] *n* camino *m* de entrada, avenida *f*.

drive-yourself ['draɪvjɔ:'self] *attr*: ~ **service** servicio *m* de alquiler sin chófer.

driving ['draɪvɪŋ] **1** *adj rain* torrencial. **2** *attr power* motor; (*fig*) impulsor; (*Aut*) de conducción, para conductor *etc*. **3** *n* conducción *f*, el conducir, el manejar (*LAm*).

driving belt ['draɪvɪŋbelt] *n* correa *f* de transmisión.

driving instructor ['draɪvɪŋɪn'strʌktə^r] *n* instructor *m*, -ora *f* de conducción.

driving lesson ['draɪvɪŋ,lesn] *n* clase *f* de conducción.

driving licence (*Brit*), (*US*) **driver's license** ['draɪvərs,laɪsəns] *n* carnet *m* de conducir.

driving mirror ['draɪvɪŋ,mɪrə^r] *n* retrovisor *m*.

driving school ['draɪvɪŋsku:l] *n* autoescuela *f*, escuela *f* automovilista, academia *f* de conductores.

driving seat ['draɪvɪŋ,si:t] *n* asiento *m* del conductor; **he's in the** ~ **now** (*fig*) ahora él es quien manda, ahora él es el jefe.

driving test ['draɪvɪŋtest] *n* examen *m* de conducción.

driving wheel ['draɪvɪŋ,wi:l] *n* rueda *f* motriz.

drizzle ['drɪzl] **1** *n* llovizna *f*, garúa *f* (*LAm*). **2** *vi* lloviznar.

drizzly ['drɪzlɪ] *adj* lloviznoso.

droll [drəʊl] *adj* (*funny*) divertido, gracioso; (*odd*) raro.

dromedary ['drɒmɪdərɪ] *n* dromedario *m*.

drone [drəʊn] **1** *n* (**a**) (*Ent, fig*) zángano *m*. (**b**) (*noise*) zumbido *m*; (*of voice*) tono *m* monótono. **2** *vi* zumbar; (*voice*) hablar monótonamente; **he** ~**d on and on** hablaba interminablemente en tono monótono.

drool [dru:l] *vi* babear; **to** ~ **over** (*fig*) caérsele a uno la baba por.

droop [dru:p] **1** *vt* inclinar; dejar caer (*over* por). **2** *vi* (*slope*) inclinarse; (*fall*) caer, colgar; (*flower*) marchitarse; (*fig: spirit*) decaer, (*person*) desanimarse.

drooping ['dru:pɪŋ] *adj* caído; *flower* marchito; *ears* gacho; *movement* lánguido, desmayado.

drop [drɒp] **1** *n* (**a**) (*of liquid*) gota *f* (*also Med*); (*sweet*) pastilla *f*; **just a** ~ dos gotitas nada más; sólo una pizca; **there's just a** ~ **left** quedan unas gotas; **with a** ~ **of soda** con un poquitín de sifón; **I haven't touched a** ~ no he probado una sola gota; **in 3 weeks we didn't have a** ~ **of rain** no cayó ni una gota en 3 semanas; **it's a** ~ **in the ocean** es una gota de agua en el mar; **he's had a** ~ **too much** lleva una copa de más.

(**b**) (*fall*) caída *f*; (*by parachute*) lanzamiento *m*; (*in price*) baja *f*; (*of temperature etc*) descenso *m*; (*in number, demand*) disminución *f*, reducción *f* (*in* de); ~ **shipment** remesa *f* directa; **at the** ~ **of a hat** con cualquier pretexto; en seguida.

(**c**) (*slope*) bajada *f*, declive *m*, pendiente *f*; (*cliff*) precipicio *m*; (*for secret mail etc*) escondrijo *m* (para correo secreto); **there's a** ~ **of 6 metres** está a una altura de 6 metros sobre el suelo; **to have the** ~ **on sb** (*US**) llevar la delantera a uno, tener ventaja sobre uno.

(**d**) (*Theat*) telón *m* de boca.

2 *vt* (**a**) (*let fall*) (*deliberately*) dejar caer; (*accidentally*) caérsele a uno; (*let go of*) soltar; *bomb, parachutist* lanzar; *anchor* echar; *letter in pillar box* echar; *note* poner (*to* a); *curtsy* hacer; *hint* soltar; *passenger* dejar (*at* en); *eyes*,

voice bajar; *price* reducir; *charge* retirar; (*allow to drip*) verter a gotas.

(**b**) *game, enemy* derribar, tumbar.

(**c**) (*lose*) perder; **Bivar ~ped a point at home** Bivar empató en casa; **they say he ~ped a packet*** dicen que perdió un dineral.

(**d**) (*Sew*) *hem* alargar, extender hacia abajo.

(**e**) (*omit*) omitir; *letter H* no pronunciar; *syllable* comerse.

(**f**) (*abandon*) *claim, plan* renunciar a, abandonar; *condition etc* suprimir; *habit* dejar; *subject* dejar, cambiar de; *friend* romper con; **~ that!** ¡déjese de eso!; **we had to ~ what we were doing** tuvimos que dejar lo que estábamos haciendo; **they ~ped him like a hot brick** le abandonaron como a perro sarnoso; **I've been ~ped from the team** ya no formo parte del equipo.

(**g**) **to ~ acid** (*Drugs*‡) tomar ácido.

3 *vi* (**a**) (*fall*) caer; caer a tierra; (*terrain*) bajar; (*drip*) gotear; (*crouch*) agacharse; **to ~ with fatigue** caer rendido; **I feel ready to ~** estoy que no me tengo; **he let it ~ that ...** reveló que ...; dio a entender que ...; **so we let the matter ~** así que dejamos el asunto.

(**b**) (*decrease*) (*wind*) calmarse, amainar; (*price, temperature*) bajar; (*demand, number*) disminuir.

◆**drop across*** *vi*: **we ~ped across to see him** nos dejamos caer por su casa*; **he ~ped across to see us** se dejó caer por casa*.

◆**drop away** *vi* (*attendance etc*) disminuir.

◆**drop back, drop behind** *vi* quedarse atrás, rezagarse; (*rate etc*) bajar.

◆**drop by** *vi* = **drop in.**

◆**drop down** *vi* caer; (*crouch*) agacharse; **we ~ped down to the coast** bajamos hacia la costa.

◆**drop in** *vi* entrar un momento; entrar de paso, entrar de sopetón; **to ~ in on** visitar inesperadamente; **do ~ in any time** ven a vernos cuando quieras (sin ceremonia).

◆**drop off 1** *vt passenger* dejar.

2 *vi* (**a**) (*part*) desprenderse, separarse.

(**b**) (*decrease*) bajar, disminuir.

(**c**) (*sleep*) quedarse dormido.

(**d**) (*passenger*) apearse, bajar.

◆**drop out** *vi* (**a**) (*part*) desprenderse, separarse.

(**b**) (*person*) darse de baja; retirarse; (*Univ etc*) abandonar los estudios, ahorcarse los libros; (*socially*) marginarse; **to ~ out of** *course etc* dejar de asistir a, *team* dejar de ser miembro de, *race* abandonar; **he ~ped out of my life** no volví a saber nada de él.

◆**drop round 1** *vt*: **I'll ~ it round to you** pasaré por casa para dártelo.

2 *vi* = **drop in.**

drop goal [ˈdrɒpˌgəʊl] *n* (*Rugby*) drop *m*.

drop handlebars [ˈdrɒpˌhændlbɑːz] *npl* manillar *m* de (bicicleta de) carreras.

drop-kick [ˈdrɒpkɪk] *n* puntapié *m* de botepronto.

drop-leaf table [drɒpliːfˈteɪbl] *n* mesa *f* de ala abatible.

droplet [ˈdrɒplɪt] *n* gotita *f*.

drop-off [ˈdrɒpɒf] *n* disminución *f*.

drop-out [ˈdrɒpaʊt] *n* (**a**) automarginado *m*, -a *f*; (*Univ etc*) persona *f* que ha abandonado los estudios (*etc*). (**b**) (*Rugby*) puntapié *m* de saque.

dropper [ˈdrɒpəʳ] *n* (*Med etc*) cuentagotas *m*.

dropping-out [ˌdrɒpɪŋˈaʊt] *n* automarginación *f*; (*Univ*) abandono *m* de los estudios.

droppings [ˈdrɒpɪŋz] *npl* excremento *m* (de animales).

dropshot [ˈdrɒpˌʃɒt] *n* dejada *f*.

dropsical [ˈdrɒpsɪkəl] *adj* hidrópico.

dropsy [ˈdrɒpsɪ] *n* hidropesía *f*.

dross [drɒs] *n* (*Brit*) escoria *f* (*also fig*).

drought [draʊt] *n* sequía *f*.

drove [drəʊv] **1** *pret of* **drive. 2** *n* (*Agr*) rebaño *m*, manada *f*; (*of people*) multitud *f*; **people came in ~s** la gente acudió en tropel.

drover [ˈdrəʊvəʳ] *n* boyero *m*, pastor *m*.

drown [draʊn] **1** *vt* (*kill*) anegar; *kittens etc* ahogar; (*inundate*) anegar, inundar; *sound* apagar; *cry* ahogar; *sorrows* olvidar emborrachándose; **his cries were ~ed by the noise of the waves** sus gritos se perdieron en el estruendo de las olas; **he came in like a ~ed rat** entró mojado hasta los huesos.

2 *vi* (*also* **to be ~ed**) perecer ahogado, ahogarse.

3 *vr*: **to ~ o.s.** ahogarse.

◆**drown out** *vt sound* ahogar.

drowning [ˈdraʊnɪŋ] *n* ahogo *m*.

drowse [draʊz] *vi* dormitar, quedar medio dormido; **to ~ off** adormecerse.

drowsily [ˈdraʊzɪlɪ] *adv* soñolientamente, soporíferamente.

drowsiness [ˈdraʊzɪnɪs] *n* somnolencia *f*; (*sluggishness*) modorra *f*.

drowsy [ˈdraʊzɪ] *adj* (*sleepy*) soñoliento; (*sluggish*) amodorrado; (*lulling*) soporífero; **to be ~, to feel ~** tener sueño.

drub [drʌb] *vt* apalear, vapulear; (*fig*) derrotar, cascar.

drubbing [ˈdrʌbɪŋ] *n* paliza *f*; (*fig*) paliza *f*, derrota *f*.

drudge [drʌdʒ] **1** *n* esclavo *m* del trabajo; (*in home*) esclava *f* de la cocina. **2** *vi* trabajar como un esclavo.

drudgery [ˈdrʌdʒərɪ] *n* trabajo *m* penoso, faena *f* monótona; **to take the ~ out of work** hacer el trabajo menos penoso.

drug [drʌg] **1** *n* (*Med*) droga *f*, medicamento *m*, fármaco *m*; (*eg heroin*) droga *f*, estupefaciente *m*; **to be a ~ on the market** ser invendible.

2 *vt person* drogar, administrar narcóticos a; narcotizar; *wine etc* echar un narcótico a; **to be ~ged with sleep** estar muerto de sueño.

3 *vr*: **to ~ o.s.** drogarse.

drug abuse [ˈdrʌgəˈbjuːs] *n* toxicomanía *f*.

drug-addict [ˈdrʌgˈædɪkt] *n* drogadicto *m*, -a *f*, toxicómano *m*, -a *f*.

drug-addiction [ˈdrʌgəˈdɪkʃən] drogadicción *f*, drogodependencia *f*, toxicomanía *f*.

drug-check [ˈdrʌgtʃek] *n* prueba *f* anti-doping.

druggist [ˈdrʌgɪst] *n* farmacéutico *m*; **~'s** (**shop**) farmacia *f*.

druggy‡ [ˈdrʌgɪ] *n*, **drugster**‡ [ˈdrʌgstəʳ] *n* drogata‡ *mf*, drogota‡ *mf*.

drug-habit [ˈdrʌgˌhæbɪt] *n* adicción *f* (a las drogas).

drug-peddler [ˈdrʌgˌpedləʳ] *n*, **drug-pusher** [ˈdrʌgˌpʊʃəʳ] *n* droguero *m*, traficante *mf* en drogas, camello* *mf*.

drug-related [ˈdrʌgrɪˌleɪtɪd] *adj* relacionado con la droga; **~ crime** drogodelincuencia *f*.

drug-runner [ˈdrʌgˌrʌnəʳ] *n* narcotraficante *mf*.

drug-squad [ˈdrʌgskwɒd] *n* brigada *f* antidrogas, grupo *m* de estupefacientes.

drugstore [ˈdrʌgstɔːʳ] *n* (*US*) farmacia *f* (*donde se venden comestibles, revistas, etc*).

drug-taker [ˈdrʌgˌteɪkəʳ] *n* consumidor *m*, -ora *f* de drogas, el (*or* la) que se droga.

drug-taking [ˈdrʌgˌteɪkɪŋ] *n* consumo *m* de drogas.

drug-traffic [ˈdrʌgˈtræfɪk] *n* narcotráfico *m*, tráfico *m* de narcóticos.

drug-user [ˈdrʌgˌjuːzəʳ] *n* consumidor *m*, -ora *f* de drogas, drogadicto *m*, -a *f*.

druid [ˈdruːɪd] *n* druida *m*.

drum [drʌm] **1** *n* (*Mus*) tambor *m*, (*large*) timbal *m*, bombo *m*; (*Mech*) tambor *m*; (*for oil*) bidón *m*; (*of gas*) bombona *f*; (*of ear*) tímpano *m*; **~s** (*in band*) batería *f*; **to beat a ~ for a product** (*US*) hacer publicidad de un producto.

2 *vt*: **to ~ one's fingers on the table** tabalear, tamborilear con los dedos en la mesa; **to ~ sth into sb** hacer que uno aprenda algo a fuerza de repetírselo.

3 *vi* (*Mus*) tocar el tambor; (*with fingers*) tabalear, tamborilear, teclear; (*with heels*) zapatear; **the noise is ~ming in my ears** el ruido me está taladrando los oídos; **his words ~med in my mind** sus palabras se repetían incansablemente en mi cabeza.

◆**drum into** *vt*: **I had that ~med into me years ago** hace años que me hicieron comprender eso a la fuerza (*or* a fuerza de repetírmelo).

◆**drum out** *vt*: **to ~ sb out** expulsar a uno.

◆**drum up** *vt support* tratar de conseguir; reunir, organizar; *trade* fomentar.

drumbeat [ˈdrʌmˌbiːt] *n* redoble *m*.

drum brake [ˈdrʌmbreɪk] *n* (*Aut*) freno *m* de tambor.

drumhead [ˈdrʌmhed] *n* parche *m* de tambor; **~ court-martial** consejo *m* de guerra sumarísimo.

drumkit [ˈdrʌmkɪt] *n* batería *f*.

drum-machine [ˈdrʌmməˈʃiːn] *n* caja *f* de ritmos.

drum-major [ˌdrʌmˈmeɪdʒəʳ] *n* (*Brit*) tambor *m* mayor.

drum-majorette [ˌdrʌmmeɪdʒəˈret] *n* (*esp US*) batonista *f*.

drummer [ˈdrʌməʳ] *n* tambor *m*; (*in pop group*) batería *m*.

drumming [ˈdrʌmɪŋ] *n* tamborileo *m*.

drumroll [ˈdrʌmˌrəʊl] *n* redoble *m*.

drumstick [ˈdrʌmstɪk] *n* palillo *m*, baqueta *f*; (*Culin*) pierna *f* de pavo (*etc*).

drunk [drʌŋk] **1** *ptp of* **drink.**

2 *adj*: **to be ~** estar borracho; **to get ~** emborracharse (*on* con); **to get sb ~** emborrachar a uno; **as ~ as a lord** (*or* **sailor** *US*) más borracho que una cuba; **to be ~ with joy** estar ebrio de alegría; **he was charged with being ~ and disorderly** se le acusó de estar borracho y alterar el

orden público.

3 *n* (*) borracho *m*, -a *f*.

drunkard ['drʌŋkəd] *n* borracho *m*, -a *f*.

drunken ['drʌŋkən] *adj* borracho; **a ~ brawl** una reyerta de borrachos; **in a ~ voice** en una voz de borracho; **charged with ~ driving** acusado de conducir en estado de embriaguez.

drunkenly ['drʌŋkənlɪ] *adv quarrel* embriagadamente; *sing* con voz de borracho; *walk* con pasos de borracho.

drunkenness ['drʌŋkənnɪs] *n* embriaguez *f*.

drupe [dru:p] *n* drupa *f*.

druthers* ['drʌðəz] *n* (*US*): **if I had my ~** si por mí fuera.

dry [draɪ] **1** *adj* (**a**) (*gen*) seco; *climate* árido, seco; *weather* seco, sin lluvia; *bread* sin mantequilla, (*stale*) viejo; **as ~ as a bone** completamente seco; **I'm very ~** tengo mucha sed; **the river ran ~** se secó el río; **to wipe sth ~** secar algo (con un paño *etc*); **~ dock** dique *m* seco; **~ fly** (*Fishing*) mosca *f* seca; **~ goods, ~ goods store** (*US*) mercería *f*; **~ ice** nieve *f* carbónica; **~ land** (*Agr*) tierras *fpl* de secano; (*not sea*) tierra *f* firme; **~ measure** medida *f* para áridos; **~ rot** podredumbre *f* seca; **~ run** viaje *m* (*etc*) de ensayo, prueba *f*; **~ shampoo** champú *m* en polvo; **~ ski-slope** pista *f* de esquí artificial; **~ stone wall** muro *m* seco.

(**b**) *wine etc* seco.

(**c**) *state* seco, prohibicionista.

(**d**) *humour* agudo; lacónico.

(**e**) (*dull*) aburrido, pesado; **as ~ as dust** de lo más aburrido.

2 *n*: **to be in the ~** estar bajo techo.

3 *vt* secar; (*wipe*) enjugar, secar; *tears* enjugarse.

4 *vi* secarse.

◆dry off 1 *vt* secar.

2 *vi* secarse.

◆dry out 1 *vt* (**a**) secar.

(**b**) *alcoholic* desalcoholizar.

2 *vi* (**a**) secarse.

(**b**) (*alcoholic*) desalcoholizarse.

◆dry up 1 *vt* secar.

2 *vi* (**a**) (*spring etc*) secarse, agotarse; (*supply*) agotarse.

(**b**) (*Met*) dejar de llover.

(**c**) (*dry the dishes*) secar los platos.

(**d**) (*: *be silent*) callarse; (*in speech etc*) cortarse, atascarse, enmudecer; **oh do ~ up!** ¡cállate por Dios!

dry-as-dust ['draɪəz'dʌst] *adj* de lo más seco, de lo más aburrido.

dry-clean ['draɪ'kli:n] *vt* limpiar en seco.

dry cleaner's ['draɪ'kli:nəz] *n* tintorería *f*.

dry cleaning ['draɪ'kli:nɪŋ] *n* limpieza *f* en seco.

dryer ['draɪə^r] *n* (*for hair*) secador *m*.

dry-eyed ['draɪ'aɪd] *adj* sin lágrimas.

drying ['draɪɪŋ] *adj wind* secante; **~ cupboard** armario *m* de tender; **~ room** habitación *f* de tender.

drying-up ['draɪɪŋ'ʌp] *n* secamiento *m*; deshidratación *f*.

dryly ['draɪlɪ] = **drily**.

dryness ['draɪnɪs] *n* sequedad *f*, lo seco; (*of climate*) aridez *f*; (*of wit*) agudeza *f*; laconismo *m*.

dry-shod ['draɪ'ʃɒd] *adv* a pie enjuto.

D/s *abbr of* **days after sight** a ... días vista.

D.Sc. *abbr of* **Doctor of Science.**

DSS *n* (*Brit*) *abbr of* **Department of Social Security.**

DST *n* (*US*) *abbr of* **Daylight Saving Time.**

DT *n* (*Comput*) *abbr of* **data transmission** transmisión *f* de datos.

DTI *n* (*Brit*) *abbr of* **Department of Trade and Industry.**

DTP *n abbr of* **desktop publishing.**

DTs *npl abbr of* **delirium tremens** delírium *m* tremens.

dual ['djʊəl] *adj* doble; (*Gram*) dual; **~ carriageway** (*Brit*) autovía *f*; **~ control** doble mando *m*; **~ nationality** nacionalidad *f* doble; **~ ownership** condominio *m*; **~ personality** conciencia *f* doble.

dualism ['djʊəlɪzəm] *n* dualismo *m*.

dualist ['djʊəlɪst] **1** *adj* dualista. **2** *n* dualista *mf*.

duality [djʊ'ælɪtɪ] *n* dualidad *f*.

dual-purpose ['djʊəl'pɜ:pəs] *adj* que sirve para dos cosas, de doble finalidad, de doble uso.

dub¹ [dʌb] *vt knight* armar caballero a; (*with name*) apodar.

dub² [dʌb] *vt film* doblar.

Dubai [du:'baɪ] *n* Dubai *m*.

dubbin ['dʌbɪn] *n* adobo *m* impermeable, cera *f*.

dubbing ['dʌbɪŋ] *n* (*Cine*) doblaje *m*; **~ mixer** mezclador *m*, -ora *f* de sonido.

dubiety [dju:'baɪətɪ] *n* incertidumbre *f*.

dubious ['dju:bɪəs] *adj* dudoso; *compliment* equívoco; *character* sospechoso; **to be ~ about** tener dudas sobre; **I am ~ whether ...** dudo si ...

dubiously ['dju:bɪəslɪ] *adv look etc* con duda; *act* de manera sospechosa.

Dublin ['dʌblɪn] **1** *n* Dublín *m*. **2** *attr*: **~ Bay prawn** langostina *f*.

Dubliner ['dʌblɪnə^r] *n* dublinés *m*, -esa *f*.

ducal ['dju:kəl] *adj* ducal.

ducat ['dʌkɪt] *n* ducado *m* (*moneda*).

duchess ['dʌtʃɪs] *n* duquesa *f*.

duchy ['dʌtʃɪ] *n* ducado *m* (*territorio*).

duck¹ [dʌk] *n* (*Orn*) pato *m*, -a *f*; ánade *m*; (*domestic*) pato *m*; (*Cricket*) cero *m*; **yes, ~(s)** (*Brit**) sí, cariño; **like water off a ~'s back** sin producir efecto alguno; **he's a dead ~** está quemado; **that issue is a dead ~** esa cuestión ya no tiene interés; **to play ~s and drakes** hacer saltar una piedra plana sobre el agua; **to play ~s and drakes with** despilfarrar; **to take to sth like a ~ to water** encontrarse en seguida en su elemento; **to make a ~, to be out for a ~** (*Brit Cricket*) ser eliminado a cero.

duck² [dʌk] **1** *n* (**a**) (*under water*) chapuz *m*.

(**b**) (*to escape*) agachada *f*, (*Boxing*) esquiva *f*.

2 *vt* (**a**) (*in water*) chapuzar.

(**b**) (*to escape*) agachar (la cabeza *etc*), bajar.

(**c**) *problem* eludir, esquivar; *question* esquivar.

3 *vi* (**a**) (*in water*) chapuzarse, sumergirse.

(**b**) (*to escape*) agachar la cabeza, agacharse, hurtar el cuerpo.

◆duck out of *vt* (*fig*) eludir, esquivar.

duck³ [dʌk] *n* (*US*) dril *m*.

duckbill ['dʌkbɪl] *n*, **duck-billed platypus** ['dʌkbɪld'plætɪpəs] *n* ornitorrinco *m*.

duckie* ['dʌkɪ] *n*: **~!** (*Brit*) ¡cariño!

ducking ['dʌkɪŋ] *n* chapuz *m*, inmersión *f*; **to give sb a ~** meter la cabeza en el agua a uno.

duckling ['dʌklɪŋ] *n* patito *m*, anadón *m*.

duckpond ['dʌkpɒnd] *n* estanque *m* de patos.

duck soup* [ˌdʌk'su:p] *n* (*US*: *fig*): **it's just ~** es cosa de coser y cantar.

duckweed ['dʌkwi:d] *n* lenteja *f* de agua.

ducky* ['dʌkɪ] **1** *n*: **~!** ¡cariño! **2** *adj* (*US*) muy mono.

duct [dʌkt] *n* conducto *m*, canal *m*.

ductile ['dʌktaɪl] *adj* dúctil.

ductless ['dʌktlɪs] *adj* endocrino; **~ gland** glándula *f* endocrina.

dud* [dʌd] **1** *adj coin etc* falso; *shell* que no estalla; *merchandise* invendible; *cheque* sin fondos. **2** *n* (*coin*) moneda *f* falsa; (*shell*) obús *m* que no estalla; (*machine*) filfa *f*; (*person*) persona *f* inútil.

dude* [dju:d] *n* (*US*) petimetre *m*, gomoso *m*; tió* *m*, individuo *m*; **~ ranch** rancho *m* para turistas.

dudgeon ['dʌdʒən] *n*: **in high ~** enojadísimo.

duds [dʌdz] *npl* (*US**) prendas *fpl* de vestir, trapos* *mpl*; pertenencias *fpl*.

due [dju:] **1** *adj* (**a**) (*owing*) debido; **to be ~** (*Fin*) ser pagadero; **I have £50 ~ to me** me deben 50 libras; **our thanks are ~ to her** le estamos muy agradecidos; **to fall ~** (*Fin*) vencer; **he's ~ a salary raise** (*US*) le corresponde un aumento de sueldo; **I'm ~ for a holiday next week** en principio voy de vacaciones la semana que viene.

(**b**) (*proper*) conveniente, oportuno; debido; **with all ~ care** con todo el debido cuidado.

(**c**) (*of timing etc*) **~ date** fecha *f* de vencimiento; fecha *f* de pago; **the train is ~ at 6** el tren debe llegar a las 6; **when is the plane ~ (in)?** ¿cuándo debe aterrizar el avión?; **I'm ~ in Chicago tomorrow** mañana me esperan en Chicago; **it was ~ to happen yesterday** se esperaba para ayer; **when is it ~ to happen?** ¿para cuándo se prevé?; **it is ~ to be demolished** se proyecta su demolición.

(**d**) **~ to** debido a, por causa de; **it is all ~ to** todo se debe a; **what is this ~ to?** ¿a qué se debe esto?

2 *adv*: **to go ~ east** ir derecho hacia el este; **~ east of the town** exactamente al este del pueblo.

3 *n* (**a**) (*debt*) deuda *f*; (*desert*) lo que merece uno; **to get one's ~** recibir lo que merece uno, (*in bad sense*) llevar su merecido; **to give him his ~** hay que reconocer la razón (*or* las cualidades *etc*) que tiene; **to give him his ~, I ...** para ser justo con él, yo ...

(**b**) **~s** (*fees*) derechos *mpl*.

duel ['djʊəl] **1** *n* duelo *m*; **to fight a ~** = **2**. **2** *vi* batirse en duelo.

duellist, (*US*) **duelist** ['djʊəlɪst] *n* duelista *m*.

duet [dju:'et] *n* dúo *m*.

duff¹* [dʌf] *adj* (*Brit*) (*poor quality*) soso, insípido, sin valor;

(*useless*) inútil.
duff²‡ [dʌf] *vt*: **to ~ sb up** dar una paliza a uno.
duff³ [dʌf] *n* (*Culin*) budín *m*, pudín *m*.
duff⁴‡ [dʌf] *n* culo‡ *m*; **he just sits on his ~ all day** pasa el día sin hacer nada; **get off your ~!** ¡no te quedes ahí sentado y haz algo!
duffel-bag, duffle-bag ['dʌfəlbæg] *n* (*Mil*) talego *m* para efectos de uso personal; bolsa *f* de lona.
duffel-coat, duffle-coat ['dʌfəlkəʊt] *n* comando *m*, abrigo *m* tres cuartos.
duffer ['dʌfəʳ] *n* zoquete *m*.
dug¹ [dʌg] *n* (*Zool*) teta *f*, ubre *f*.
dug² [dʌg] *pret and ptp of* **dig**.
dugout ['dʌgaʊt] *n* (*Mil*) refugio *m* subterráneo.
duke [dju:k] *n* duque *m*.
dukedom ['dju:kdəm] *n* ducado *m* (*título*).
dukes‡ [dju:ks] *npl* puños *mpl*.
dulcet ['dʌlsɪt] *adj* dulce, suave.
dulcimer ['dʌlsɪməʳ] *n* dulcémele *m*.
dull [dʌl] **1** *adj colour, gleam* apagado; *light* sombrío, pálido; *surface* deslustrado, mate; *sound, pain* sordo; *edge* embotado; *day, weather* gris; *stock market* inactivo, flojo; *person* (*slow*) lerdo, torpe; (*uninteresting*) soso, insípido, pesado; **as ~ as ditchwater** de lo más aburrido; **I feel ~ today** hoy me siento desanimado, hoy me encuentro sin fuerzas.
2 *vt edge* embotar; *surface* deslustrar; *pain* aliviar; *person* entorpecer; *enthusiasm etc* enfriar.
dullard ['dʌləd] *n* zoquete *m*.
dullness ['dʌlnɪs] *n* lo deslustrado; lo sombrío; inactividad *f*, flojedad *f*; torpeza *f*; lo soso, insipidez *f*.
dullsville* ['dʌlzvɪl] *n* (*US*): **it's ~ here** esto es un muermo*.
dully ['dʌllɪ] *adv* de modo apagado, con brillo apagado; pálidamente; sordamente, con ruido sordo.
duly ['dju:lɪ] *adv* (*properly*) debidamente; (*punctually*) a su debido tiempo; **he ~ arrived at 3** llegó en efecto a las 3; **he ~ protested** protestó de la manera que se había previsto; **everybody was ~ shocked** se escandalizaron todos según era de esperar.
dumb [dʌm] *adj* (**a**) mudo; **the ~ millions** los millones que no tienen voz; **~ animal** bruto *m*; **~ show** pantomima *f*, espectáculo *m* de mímica; **in ~ show** por señas; **to become ~** quedar mudo; **to strike sb ~** dejar a uno sin habla.
(**b**) (*) estúpido; soso; **as ~ as an ox** más bruto que un adoquín; **~ blonde** rubia *f* boba; **to act ~** hacerse el sueco*.
dumb-ass‡ ['dʌmæs] (*US*) **1** *adj* burro. **2** *n* burro *m*, -a *f*.
dumbbell ['dʌmbel] *n* (**a**) (*Sport*) pesa *f*. (**b**) (*US**) bobo *m*, -a *f*.
dumbcluck* ['dʌmklʌk] *n* borde* *mf*.
dumbfound [dʌm'faʊnd] *vt* dejar sin habla, pasmar; **we were ~ed** quedamos mudos de asombro.
dumbness ['dʌmnɪs] *n* mudez *f*; (*) estupidez *f*.
dumbo* ['dʌmbəʊ] *n* (*US*) imbécil *m*.
dumbstruck ['dʌmstrʌk] *adj*: **we were ~** quedamos mudos de asombro.
dumbwaiter ['dʌm'weɪtəʳ] *n* (*Brit*) estante *m* giratorio; (*US*) montaplatos *m*.
dum-dum ['dʌmdʌm] *adj*: **~ bullet** bala *f* dum-dum.
dummy ['dʌmɪ] **1** *adj* falso, postizo; **~ company** empresa *f* fantasma; **~ number** (*Press*) número *m* cero; **~ run** ensayo *m*, prueba *f*. **2** *n* (*life-size figure*) muñeco *m*; (*tailor's*) maniquí *m*; (*packet*) envase *m* vacío; (*Brit*: *baby's*) chupete *m*; (*Bridge*) muerto *m*; (*Fin*) persona *f* ficticia; hombre *m* de paja.
dump [dʌmp] **1** *n* (*heap*) montón *m*; (*rubbish tip*) vertedero *m*, basurero *m*, vaciadero *m*, botadero *m* (*LAm*); (*Mil*) depósito *m*; (*: *hovel*) tugurio *m*, casucha *f*; (*: *town*) pueblucho *m*, poblachón *m*; (*Comput*) vuelco *m* de memoria; **to be down in the ~s*** tener murria.
2 *vt rubbish etc* descargar, verter, vaciar; (*get rid of*) deshacerse de, dejar; *goods* inundar el mercado de; (*Comput*) volcar; **to ~ sth down*** poner algo (con mucho ruido); **can I ~ this here?*** ¿puedo dejar esto aquí?
dumper ['dʌmpəʳ] *n* (*also* **~ truck**) dúmper *m*.
dumping ['dʌmpɪŋ] *n* (*Comm*) dúmping *m*.
dumping-ground ['dʌmpɪŋ,graʊnd] *n* vertedero *m*.
dumpling ['dʌmplɪŋ] *n* pelota *f*, bola *f* de masa hervida.
dumptruck ['dʌmptrʌk] *n* (*US*) dúmper *m*.
dumpy ['dʌmpɪ] *adj* regordete, culibajo.
dun¹ [dʌn] *adj* pardo.
dun² [dʌn] *vt*: **to ~ sb** apremiar a uno para que pague lo que debe; (*fig*) dar la lata a uno.
dunce [dʌns] *n* burro *m*, -a *f*, zopenco *m*, -a *f*.
dunderhead ['dʌndəhed] *n* zoquete *m*.
dune [dju:n] *n* duna *f*.
dung [dʌŋ] *n* excremento *m*; (*as manure*) estiércol *m*.
dungarees [,dʌŋgə'ri:z] *npl* mono *m*; (*Brit*: *of child, woman*) peto *m*.
dung beetle ['dʌŋ,bi:tl] *n* escarabajo *m* pelotero.
dungeon ['dʌndʒən] *n* mazmorra *f*, calabozo *m*.
dunghill ['dʌŋhɪl] *n* estercolero *m*.
dunk [dʌŋk] *vt* (*US*) (**a**) *bread etc* mojar, remojar. (**b**) (*Basketball*: *also* **slam ~**) machacar.
Dunkirk [dʌn'kɜ:k] *n* Dunquerque *m*.
dunnock ['dʌnək] *n* acentor *m* (común).
duo ['dju:əʊ] *n* dúo *m*.
duodecimal [,dju:əʊ'desɪməl] *adj* duodecimal.
duodenal [,dju:əʊ'di:nl] *adj* duodenal; **~ ulcer** úlcera *f* duodenal.
duodenum [,dju:əʊ'di:nəm] *n* duodeno *m*.
dupe [dju:p] **1** *n* primo *m*, inocentón *m*; **to be the ~ of** ser víctima de. **2** *vt* engañar, embaucar; (*swindle*) timar.
duple ['dju:pl] *adj* (*gen*) doble; (*Mus*) de dos tiempos; **~ time** (*Mus*) tiempo *m* doble.
duplex ['dju:pleks] **1** *adj* doble. **2** *n* (*US house*: *also* **~ house**) casa *f* semiseparada, casa *f* para dos familias; (*US apartment*: *also* **~ apartment**) dúplex *m*.
duplicate 1 ['dju:plɪkɪt] *adj* duplicado; **~ key** duplicado *m* de una llave. **2** ['dju:plɪkɪt] *n* duplicado *m*; (*copy of letter etc*) copia *f*, doble *m*; **in ~** por duplicado. **3** ['dju:plɪkeɪt] *vt* duplicar; repetir; imitar; *text* hacer a multicopista.
duplicating machine ['dju:plɪkeɪtɪŋmə'ʃi:n] *n* multicopista *f*.
duplication [,dju:plɪ'keɪʃən] *n* duplicación *f*; repetición *f* (incómoda); pluralidad *f* (innecesaria).
duplicator ['dju:plɪkeɪtəʳ] *n* multicopista *m*.
duplicitous [dju:'plɪsɪtəs] *adj* (*liter*) tramposo.
duplicity [dju:'plɪsɪtɪ] *n* duplicidad *f*, doblez *f*.
durability [,djʊərə'bɪlɪtɪ] *n* lo duradero, durabilidad *f*.
durable ['djʊərəbl] **1** *adj* duradero; **~ goods** (*US*) bienes *mpl* de consumo duraderos. **2 ~s** *npl* bienes *mpl* duraderos; **consumer ~s** artículos *mpl* de equipo.
duration [djʊə'reɪʃən] *n* duración *f*; **for the ~*** mientras dure la guerra.
Dürer ['djʊərəʳ] *nm* Durero.
duress [djʊə'res] *n* compulsión *f*; **under ~** por coacción.
Durex ['djʊəreks] ® *n* preservativo *m*.
during ['djʊərɪŋ] *prep* durante.
durst†† [dɜ:st] *pret of* **dare**.
dusk [dʌsk] *n* crepúsculo *m*, anochecer *m*; **at ~** al atardecer; **in the gathering ~** en la creciente oscuridad.
dusky ['dʌskɪ] *adj* oscuro; *complexion* moreno.
dust [dʌst] **1** *n* polvo *m*; (*sweepings*) barreduras *fpl*; (*rubbish*) basura *f*; (*of coal*) cisco *m*; **to bite the ~** morder el polvo; **to kick up the ~** levantar una polvareda; **to raise a ~** armarla; **to shake the ~ of a place off one's feet** salir muy ofendido de un lugar; **when the ~ has settled** (*fig*) cuando se aclare la atmósfera; **to throw ~ in sb's eyes** engañar a uno.
2 *vt* (**a**) quitar el polvo a, desempolvar, (*by beating*) sacudir el polvo a; (*clean*) limpiar.
(**b**) **to ~ sth with** salpicar algo de; (*Culin etc*) espolvorear algo de; **~ the insecticide on the surface** espolvoree el insecticida sobre la superficie.
◆**dust down** *vt* quitar el polvo a, desempolvar.
◆**dust off** *vt* = **dust down**.
◆**dust out** *vt box, cupboard* quitar el polvo de.
dustbag ['dʌstbæg] *n* bolsa *f* de aspiradora.
dustbin ['dʌstbɪn] *n* (*Brit*) cubo *m* de (la) basura; balde *m* (*LAm*); **~ liner** bolsa *f* de basura.
dustbowl ['dʌstbəʊl] *n* terreno *m* inutilizado por la erosión, zona *f* desértica.
dustcart ['dʌstkɑ:t] *n* (*Brit*) camión *m* de la basura.
dustcloud ['dʌstklaʊd] *n* polvareda *f*.
dust-cover ['dʌst,kʌvəʳ] *n* guardapolvo *m*; (*of book*) forro *m*, sobrecubierta *f*, camisa *f*.
duster ['dʌstəʳ] *n* (**a**) (*Brit*) (*cloth*) paño *m*, trapo *m*, sacudidor *m*, bayeta *f*; (*of feathers*) plumero *m*; (*for blackboard*) borrador *m*. (**b**) (*US*) guardapolvo *m*.
dustheap ['dʌsthi:p] *n* basurero *m*.
dusting ['dʌstɪŋ] *n* (**a**) limpieza *f*. (**b**) (*) paliza *f*.
dusting powder ['dʌstɪŋ,paʊdəʳ] *n* polvos *mpl* secantes.
dust-jacket ['dʌst,dʒækɪt] *n* forro *m*, sobrecubierta *f*, camisa *f*.
dustman ['dʌstmən] *n*, *pl* **dustmen** ['dʌstmən] (*Brit*) basurero *m*, recogedor *m* de basura.
dustpan ['dʌstpæn] *n* cogedor *m*.

dust-proof ['dʌstpru:f] *adj* a prueba de polvo.
dust-sheet ['dʌsʃi:t] *n* guardapolvo *m*.
dust-storm ['dʌsstɔ:m] *n* vendaval *m* de polvo.
dust-up* ['dʌstʌp] *n* (*Brit*) pelea *f*, reyerta *f*, riña *f*; **to have a ~ with** pelearse con.
dusty ['dʌstɪ] *adj* polvoriento, empolvado; **to get ~** cubrirse de polvo; **not so ~** nada malo; **to give sb a ~ answer** dar a uno una respuesta equívoca.
Dutch [dʌtʃ] **1** *adj* holandés; **~ auction** subasta *f* a la baja; **~ barn** *granero de acero con techo curvo*; **~ cap** diafragma *m*; **~ cheese** queso *m* de bola; **~ courage** envalentonamiento *m* (del que ha bebido), valentía *f* de botella; **~ elm disease** enfermedad *f* holandesa del olmo, grafiosis *f*; **~ oven** olla *f*; **~ school** (*Art*) escuela *f* holandesa; **~ treat** *comida* (*etc*) *en la que cada uno paga lo suyo*; **to talk to sb like a ~ uncle** decirle cuatro verdades a uno; **to be in ~ with sb** (*US**) estar en la lista negra de uno.
2 *n* (**a**) **the ~** los holandeses.
(**b**) (*Ling*) holandés *m*.
3 (*) *as adv*: **to go ~** pagar cada uno su cuota, ir a escote.
Dutchman ['dʌtʃmən] *n*, *pl* **Dutchmen** ['dʌtʃmən] holandés *m*; **it's him or I'm a ~** que me maten si no es él.
Dutchwoman ['dʌtʃ,wʊmən] *n*, *pl* **Dutchwomen** ['dʌtʃ,wɪmɪn] holandesa *f*.
dutiable ['dju:tɪəbl] *adj* sujeto a derechos de aduana.
dutiful ['dju:tɪfʊl] *adj* obediente, sumiso.
dutifully ['dju:tɪfəlɪ] *adv* obedientemente, sumisamente.
duty ['dju:tɪ] **1** (**a**) (*gen*) deber *m*, obligación *f*; **out of a sense of ~** por compromiso, cumpliendo con su deber; **it is my ~ to** + *infin* me incumbe + *infin*, me corresponde + *infin*; **to be in ~ bound to** + *infin* estar obligado a + *infin*; **it is no part of my ~ to** + *infin* no me corresponde + *infin*; **I feel it to be my ~** creo que es mi deber; **to do one's ~ by** cumplir con; **to fail in one's ~** faltar a su deber; **to make it one's ~ to** + *infin* encargarse de + *infin*.
(**b**) **duties** (*of post*) funciones *fpl*; responsabilidad *f*; **to neglect one's duties** no cumplir sus funciones; **to take up one's duties** entrar en funciones.
(**c**) (*Med, Mil etc*) servicio *m*; **an off ~ policeman** un policía franco de servicio; **to be off ~** estar libre, (*Mil*) estar libre (*or* franco) de servicio; **to be on ~** estar de servicio; **to do ~ as** servir de; **to do ~ for** servir en lugar de; **to go on ~** entrar de servicio.
(**d**) (*Fin*) derechos *mpl* (de aduana); aranceles *mpl*; **to pay ~ on** pagar derechos de aduana por.
2 *attr*: **~ call** visita *f* de cumplido.
duty-free ['dju:tɪ'fri:] *adj* libre de impuestos; **~ shop** tienda *f* libre de impuestos.
duty officer ['dju:tɪ,ɒfɪsəʳ] *n* oficial *m* de guardia.
duty-paid [,dju:tɪ'peɪd] *adj* con aranceles pagados.
duty roster ['dju:tɪ,rɒstəʳ] *n*, **duty rota** ['dju:tɪ,rəʊtə] *n* lista *f* de guardias.
duvet ['du:veɪ] *n* (*Brit*) edredón *m*.
DV *abbr of* **Deo volente,** *God willing* Dios mediante.
DVM *n* (*US*) *abbr of* **Doctor of Veterinary Medicine**.
dwarf [dwɔ:f] **1** *adj* enano; diminuto, pequeñito; **~ bean** judía *f* enana, fríjol *m*. **2** *n* enano *m*, -a *f*. **3** *vt* achicar, empequeñecer, hacer que parezca pequeño; (*stunt*) impedir el crecimiento de.
dwell [dwel] (*irr*: *pret and ptp* **dwelt**) *vi* morar; **to ~ on** *subject* explicar largamente, explayarse en; insistir en; hacer hincapié en; *thought* meditar; *note, syllable* dar énfasis a, alargar.
dweller ['dweləʳ] *n* morador *m*, -ora *f*; **~ in** habitante *mf* de; inquilino *m*, -a *f* de.
dwelling ['dwelɪŋ] *n* morada *f*, vivienda *f*.
dwelling house ['dwelɪŋhaʊs] *n*, *pl* **dwelling houses** ['dwelɪŋ,haʊzɪz] casa *f*.
dwelt [dwelt] *pret and ptp of* **dwell**.
dwindle ['dwɪndl] *vi* (*also* **to ~ away**) disminuir, menguar; ir desapareciendo, ir acabándose; **to ~ to** quedar reducido a.
dwindling ['dwɪndlɪŋ] **1** *adj* que va disminuyendo, menguante. **2** *n* disminución *f*.
dye [daɪ] **1** *n* tinte *m*, colorante *m*; (*hue*) matiz *m*, color *m*; **of (the) deepest ~** de lo más vil, de la peor calaña. **2** *vt* teñir (*green* de verde).
dyed-in-the-wool ['daɪdɪnðə'wʊl] *adj* (*fig*) testarudo.
dyeing ['daɪɪŋ] *n* tinte *m*, tintura *f*.
dyer ['daɪəʳ] *n* tintorero *m*; **~'s** tintorería *f*.
dyestuff ['daɪstʌf] *n* tinte *m*, colorante *m*.
dyeworks ['daɪwɜ:ks] *npl* tintorería *f*.
dying ['daɪɪŋ] **1** *present participle of* **die**. **2** *adj* *man* moribundo, agonizante; *moments* final; *words* último. **3** *n*: **the ~** los moribundos.
dyke [daɪk] *n* = **dike**[1] and **dike**[2].
dynamic [daɪ'næmɪk] **1** *adj* dinámico. **2** *n* dinámica *f*.
dynamics [daɪ'næmɪks] *n* dinámica *f*.
dynamism ['daɪnəmɪzəm] *n* dinamismo *m*.
dynamite ['daɪnəmaɪt] **1** *n* dinamita *f*; **that issue is ~** ese asunto es dinamita; **the book is ~** el libro es explosivo. **2** *vt* dinamitar, volar con dinamita.
dynamo ['daɪnəməʊ] *n* (*esp Brit*) dinamo *f*, dínamo *f* (*also m in LAm*).
dynastic [daɪ'næstɪk] *adj* dinástico.
dynasty ['dɪnəstɪ] *n* dinastía *f*.
d'you ['dju:] = **do you**.
dysentery ['dɪsntrɪ] *n* disentería *f*.
dysfunction [dɪs'fʌŋkʃən] *n* disfunción *f*.
dysfunctional [dɪs'fʌŋkʃənəl] *adj* disfuncional.
dyslexia [dɪs'leksɪə] *n* dislexia *f*.
dyslexic [dɪs'leksɪk] **1** *adj* disléxico. **2** *n* disléxico *m*, -a *f*.
dysmenorrhoea, (*US*) **dysmenorrhea** [,dɪsmenə'rɪə] *n* dismenorrea *f*.
dyspepsia [dɪs'pepsɪə] *n* dispepsia *f*.
dyspeptic [dɪs'peptɪk] *adj* dispéptico.
dysphasia [dɪs'feɪzɪə] *n* disfasia *f*.
dystrophy ['dɪstrəfɪ] *n* distrofia *f*; **muscular ~** distrofia *f* muscular.

E

E, e [iː] *n* (*letter*) E, e *f*; **E** (*Mus*) mi *m*; **E major** mi *m* mayor; **E for Edward, E for Easy** (*US*) E de Enrique; **E number** número *m* E.

E *abbr of* **east** este, E.

E&OE *abbr of* **errors and omissions excepted** salvo error u omisión, s.e.u.o.

E.A. (*US*) *abbr of* **educational age.**

ea. *abbr of* **each** cada uno, c/u.

each [iːtʃ] **1** *adj* cada (*invariable*); (~ *and every, any*) todo; ~ **one of them** cada uno de ellos; ~ **and every child** todos los niños sin excepción.

2 *pron* cada uno; **they help** ~ **other** (*2 persons*) se ayudan (mutuamente), se ayudan uno a otro, se ayudan el uno al otro, (*more than 2 persons*) se ayudan unos a otros; ~ **of us** cada uno de nosotros; ~ **of the countries** cada uno de los países; **a bit of ~, please** un poco de cada cosa.

3 *adv* (*apiece*) **two sweets** ~ dos dulces por persona, dos dulces para cada uno; **we paid £5** ~ pagamos 5 libras cada uno.

eager ['iːgər] *adj* impaciente; *desire etc* apremiante, vehemente; (*hopeful*) ilusionado; (*ambitious*) ambicioso; **to be** ~ **for** ansiar, anhelar, tener vivo deseo de; **to be** ~ **to** + *infin* ansiar + *infin*, impacientarse por + *infin*; **don't be so ~!** ¡ten paciencia!, ¡no te afanes!; ~ **beaver** entusiasta *mf*.

eagerly ['iːgəlɪ] *adv* con impaciencia, con ansia; con ilusión.

eagerness ['iːgənɪs] *n* impaciencia *f*; afán *m*, ansia *f*, deseo *m* (*for* de); (*hopefulness*) ilusión *f*; **in his** ~ **to get there first** en su ansia por llegar el primero.

EAGGF *n abbr of* **European Agricultural Guidance and Guarantee Fund** Fondo *m* Europeo de Orientación y de Garantía Agrícola, FEOGA *m*.

eagle ['iːgl] *n* águila *f*; (*Golf*) eagle *m*, menos dos *m*; **with** ~ **eye** con ojos de lince.

eagle-eyed ['iːgl'aɪd] *adj* de ojos de lince.

eaglet ['iːglɪt] *n* aguilucho *m*.

ear[1] [ɪər] *n* (*Anat*) oreja *f*; (*sense, Mus*) oído *m*; **to bend sb's** ~ (*US**) hinchar la cabeza a uno; **a word in your** ~ una palabra en confianza; **to be all ~s** ser todo oídos; **he's up to his ~s in debt** tiene deudas hasta encima de la coronilla; **he could not believe his ~s** no daba crédito a sus oídos; **to give** (*or* **lend**) ~ **to** prestar oído a; **to give sb a thick ~*** darle un cachete a uno; **it goes in one** ~ **and out the other** por un oído le entra y por el otro le sale; **to have a good** ~ tener buen oído; **she has an** ~ **for music** tiene buen oído para la música; **to have one's** ~ **to the ground** (*fig*) mantenerse al corriente; **to have the minister's** ~ poder contar con el interés del ministro; **to play by** ~ tocar de oído; **we're playing it by** ~ (*fig*) obramos por instinto, vamos improvisando; **to prick up one's ~s** aguzar el oído; **he set them by the ~s** sembró la discordia entre ellos, causó desavenencias entre ellos; *V* **deaf, inner** *etc.*

ear[2] [ɪər] *n* (*Bot*) espiga *f*; **to come into** ~ espigar.

earache ['ɪəreɪk] *n* dolor *m* de oídos.

eardrops ['ɪədrɒps] *npl* (*Med*) gotas *fpl* para el oído.

eardrum ['ɪədrʌm] *n* tímpano *m*.

earflap ['ɪəflæp] *n* orejera *f*.

earful* ['ɪəfʊl] *n* (**a**) **I got an** ~ **of Wagner** me llenaron los oídos de Wagner; **get an** ~ **of this** (*Brit*) escucha esto. (**b**) **to give sb an** ~ regañar a uno; **she gave me an** ~ **of her complaints** me soltó el rollo de sus quejas*.

earl [ɜːl] *n* conde *m*.

earldom ['ɜːldəm] *n* condado *m*.

early ['ɜːlɪ] **1** *adj* temprano (*also Bot*); (*first*) primero, primitivo; *age* tierno; *death* prematuro, temprano; *reply* pronto; *retirement* anticipado, prematuro; *diagnosis* precoz; *book, work etc* juvenil, de primera época; **an** ~ **Victorian table** una mesa victoriana de primera época; ~ **Christian art** arte *m* cristiano primitivo; ~ **bird** (*fig*) madrugador *m*, -ora *f*; ~ **closing is on Mondays** las tiendas se cierran temprano los lunes; ~ **frosts** heladas *fpl* tempranas; ~ **fruits** frutas *fpl* tempranas; ~ **man** el hombre primitivo; ~ **retirement** jubilación *f* anticipada; ~ **stages** (*of insect*) estados *mpl* inmaduros; **an** ~ **summer** un verano precoz; ~ **warning system** sistema *m* de alarma anticipada, sistema *m* de alerta previa; **it's** ~ **in the day** (*or* **it's** ~ **days**) **to say that** (*Brit*) es demasiado pronto para decir eso; **we need two seats on an** ~ **flight** necesitamos dos plazas en el primer vuelo en que las haya; **to be in one's** ~ **forties** tener poco más de 40 años; *V* **date, life** *etc.*

2 *adv* (**a**) (*gen*) temprano; **as** ~ **as possible** lo más pronto posible, cuanto antes; **as** ~ **as 1978** ya en 1978; **a month earlier** un mes antes; **earlier on** antes; ~ **in the morning** muy de mañana, de madrugada; ~ **in the afternoon** a primera hora de la tarde, en las primeras horas de la tarde; ~ **in the week** en los primeros días de la semana; ~ **last century** a principios del siglo pasado; ~ **in his life** en su juventud; ~ **in the twenties** al comienzo de los años veinte, al principio de los años veinte; ~ **in the book** en las primeras páginas del libro; **the earliest I can do it is next Tuesday** lo más pronto que lo podré hacer será el martes que viene.

(**b**) (*in good time*) con tiempo, con anticipación; **to book** ~ reservar con mucha anticipación; **to come an hour** ~ llegar con una hora de anticipación; **he took his summer holiday** ~ anticipó el veraneo, salió en fecha temprana para veranear.

earmark ['ɪəmɑːk] *vt* (*fig*) reservar (*for* para), destinar (*for* a); **an ~ed grant** una subvención destinada a fines especiales.

earmuff ['ɪəmʌf] *n* orejera *f*.

earn [ɜːn] *vt salary etc* ganar(se), percibir; *interest* devengar; (*win for o.s.*) merecer(se); adquirir, obtener; **~ed income** ingresos *mpl* devengados, renta *f* devengada; **it ~ed him the nickname of X** le valió el apodo de X.

earner ['ɜːnər] *n* persona *f* que gana un sueldo; asalariado *m*, -a *f*; **there are 3 ~s in the family** en la familia hay 3 que ganan un sueldo; **the shop is a nice little** ~ la tienda es una buena fuente de ingresos, la tienda es rentable.

earnest[1] ['ɜːnɪst] *adj person, character etc* serio, formal; *wish etc* fervoroso; **it is my** ~ **wish that ...** deseo con fervor que + *subj*; **to be in** ~ hablar con la mayor seriedad; **are you in ~?** ¿esto va de veras?, ¿me lo dices en serio?

earnest[2] ['ɜːnɪst] *n* prenda *f*, señal *f*; ~ **money** fianza *f*; **as an** ~ **of** en señal de.

earnestly ['ɜːnɪstlɪ] *adv speak etc* con la mayor seriedad; **I** ~ **entreat you** se lo suplico de todo corazón.

earnestness ['ɜːnɪstnɪs] *n* seriedad *f*, formalidad *f*.

earning ['ɜːnɪŋ] **1** *attr*: ~ **potential** potencial *m* ganador; ~ **power** poder *m* adquisitivo. **2** **~s** *npl* (*of individual*) sueldo *m*, ingresos *mpl*; (*of company etc*) ganancias *fpl*, beneficios *mpl*, utilidades *fpl*; **~s related benefits** beneficios *mpl* relacionados con los ingresos.

ear, nose and throat [ˌɪəˌnəʊzən'θrəʊt] *attr* (*Med*): ~ **department** departamento *m* de otorrinolaringología; ~ **specialist** otorrinolaringólogo *m*, -a *f*.

earphone ['ɪəfəʊn] *n* (*US*) auricular *m*.

earphones ['ɪəfəʊnz] *npl* auriculares *mpl*, cascos *mpl*, audífono *m* (*LAm*).

earpiece ['ɪəpiːs] *n* auricular *m*.

ear-piercing ['ɪəˌpɪəsɪŋ] *adj* penetrante, que taladra el oído.

ear-plug ['ɪəplʌg] *n* tapón *m* para el oído.

earring ['ɪərɪŋ] *n* (*long*) pendiente *m*; (*round*) arete *m*, zarcillo *m*.

earshot ['ɪəʃɒt] *n*: **to be within** ~ estar al alcance del oído; **to be out of** ~ estar fuera del alcance del oído.

ear-splitting ['ɪəˌsplɪtɪŋ] *adj* que rompe el tímpano, que taladra el oído, ensordecedor.

earth [ɜːθ] **1** *n* (**a**) (*world*) tierra *f*; ~ **sciences** ciencias *fpl* concernientes a la Tierra; geología *f*; **here on** ~ en este mundo; **to come down to** ~, **to get back to** ~ volver a la realidad; **it must have cost the** ~ habrá costado un potosí; **to promise the** ~ prometer el oro y el moro; **nothing on** ~ **will stop me now** no lo dejo ahora por nada del mundo; **it tasted like nothing on** ~ (*good*) tenía un sabor como nada de este mundo, (*bad*) sabía a algo inmundo; **what on** ~...? ¿qué demonios ...?; **why on** ~ **do it now?** ¿por qué demonios hacerlo ahora?

(**b**) (*soil*) tierra *f*.

(**c**) (*Zool*) madriguera *f*; **to go to** ~ (*fox*) meterse en su madriguera, (*person*) esconderse, refugiarse; **to run to** ~ encontrar finalmente.

(**d**) (*Brit Elec*) tierra *f*; ~ **cable**, ~ **lead** cable *m* de toma de tierra.

2 *vt* (*Elec*) conectar a tierra.

◆**earth up** *vt* (*Agr*) acollar.

earthbound ['ɜːθbaʊnd] *adj* terrestre; (*fig*) prosaico.

earthen ['ɜːθən] *adj* de tierra; *pot* de barro.

earthenware ['ɜːθənwɛəʳ] **1** *n* loza *f* de barro. **2** *attr* de barro.

earthly ['ɜːθlɪ] *adj* (**a**) (*lit*) terrenal, mundano; ~ **paradise** paraíso *m* terrenal.

(**b**) (*fig*) **to be of no** ~ **use** no servir para nada en absoluto; **there is no** ~ **reason why not** no hay la más pequeña razón en contra; **he hasn't an** ~ (*Brit*) no tiene posibilidad alguna, no tiene ni esperanza.

earthquake ['ɜːθkweɪk] *n* terremoto *m*, seísmo *m*, temblor *m* (de tierra) (*LAm*).

earthscape ['ɜːθskeɪp] *n vista de la tierra desde una nave espacial.*

earth-shaking ['ɜːθˌʃeɪkɪŋ] *adj*, **earth-shattering** ['ɜːθˌʃætərɪŋ] *adj* trascendental.

earthward(s) ['ɜːθwəd(z)] *adv* hacia la tierra.

earthwork ['ɜːθwɜːk] *n* terraplén *m*.

earthworm ['ɜːθwɜːm] *n* lombriz *f*.

earthy ['ɜːθɪ] *adj* terroso; *flavour* terrero; *character* práctico; nada espiritual; (*coarse*) grosero.

eartrumpet ['ɪəˌtrʌmpɪt] *n* trompetilla *f* acústica.

earwax ['ɪəwæks] *n* cerumen *m*, cera *f* de los oídos.

earwig ['ɪəwɪg] *n* tijereta *f*, cortaplumas *m*.

ease [iːz] **1** *n* (**a**) (*easiness*) facilidad *f*; **with** ~ con facilidad, fácilmente.

(**b**) (*relief from pain*) alivio *m*.

(**c**) (*freedom from worry*) tranquilidad *f*; alivio *m*; **a life of** ~ una vida desahogada; **to live a life of** ~ vivir con desahogo.

(**d**) (*relaxed state*) comodidad *f*; **to be at (one's)** ~ sentirse cómodo, encontrarse a gusto; **to be ill at** ~ sentirse molesto; **to put sb at his** ~ lograr que uno se sienta cómodo; **to set sb's mind at** ~ tranquilizar el ánimo a uno; **stand at** ~! en su lugar ¡descanso!; **to take one's** ~ descansar.

(**e**) (*of manner*) naturalidad *f*.

2 *vt* (**a**) *task* facilitar.

(**b**) *pain* aliviar; *mind* tranquilizar, aliviar; (*slacken*) aflojar; *pressure* aflojar; *weight* aligerar; *impact* suavizar, mitigar.

3 *vi* (*wind*) amainar, calmarse; (*rain*) moderarse; **prices have** ~**d** han bajado ligeramente los precios.

4 *vr*: **to** ~ **o.s. of a burden** quitarse un peso de encima.

◆**ease along** *vt*: **to** ~ **a table along** mover una mesa con cuidado.

◆**ease off** **1** *vt*: **to** ~ **a lid off** levantar una tapa poco a poco.

2 *vi* suavizarse, aligerarse; (*at work*) trabajar menos; (*pain*) aliviarse; (*tension*) decrecer.

◆**ease up** **1** *vt*: **to** ~ **a weight up** levantar un peso con cuidado.

2 *vi* (**a**) = **ease off 2**.

(**b**) **to** ~ **up on sb** tratar a uno con menos rigor.

easel ['iːzl] *n* caballete *m*.

easily ['iːzɪlɪ] *adv* fácilmente, con facilidad; **to win** ~ ganar fácilmente; **it could** ~ **be** bien podría ser; **the engine is running** ~ el motor funciona bien; **it holds 4 litres** ~ caben 4 litros largos; **it's** ~ **the best** es con mucho el mejor, seguramente es el mejor; **to take life** ~ no preocuparse por nada.

easiness ['iːzɪnɪs] *n* facilidad *f*.

east [iːst] **1** *n* este *m*, oriente *m*; (*of Spain*) Levante *m*; **the E**~ el Oriente.

2 *adj* del este, oriental; *wind* del este; **E**~ **Africa** África *f* Oriental; **E**~ **Berlin** (*Hist*) Berlín Este; **E**~ **Berliner** (*Hist*) berlinés *m*, -esa *f* oriental (*or* del Este); **the E**~ **End** (*of London*) *la zona del Este de Londres*; **E**~ **German** (*Hist*: *n*) alemán *m*, -ana *f* oriental, (*adj*) germanooriental; **E**~ **Germany** (*Hist*) Alemania *f* Oriental; **the E**~ **Side** (*of New York*) *la zona del Este de Nueva York.*

3 *adv* al este, hacia el este.

eastbound ['iːstbaʊnd] *adj traffic* que va hacia el este; *carriageway* dirección este.

Easter ['iːstəʳ] **1** *n* Pascua *f* de Resurrección; (*period, loosely*) Semana *f* Santa.

2 *attr*: ~ **bonnet** sombrero *m* de primavera; ~ **Day**, ~ **Sunday** Domingo *m* de Resurrección; ~ **egg** huevo *m* de Pascua; ~ **Island** Isla *f* de Pascua; ~ **Monday** lunes *m* de Pascua de Resurrección; ~ **parade** desfile *m* de Pascua; ~ **week** Semana *f* Santa.

easterly ['iːstəlɪ] *adj* este, oriental; *wind* del este.

eastern ['iːstən] *adj* del este, oriental.

easterner ['iːstənəʳ] *n* (*esp US*) habitante *mf* del este.

easternmost ['iːstənməʊst] *adj* (el) más oriental, situado más al este.

Eastertide ['iːstətaɪd] *n* = **Easter**.

east-facing ['iːstˌfeɪsɪŋ] *adj* con cara al este, orientado hacia el este; ~ **slope** vertiente *f* este.

East Indies ['iːst'ɪndɪz] *npl* Indias *fpl* Orientales.

east-south-east [ˌiːstsaʊθ'iːst] *n* estesudeste *m*.

eastward ['iːstwəd] **1** *adj advance etc* hacia el este, en dirección este. **2** *adv* (*also* ~**s**) hacia el este, en dirección este.

easy ['iːzɪ] **1** *adj* (**a**) (*simple*) fácil; sencillo; **it's** ~ **to see why** es fácil comprender por qué; **he's** ~ **to get on with** es muy simpático; **I'm** ~* me es igual; **an** ~ **house** una casa de fácil manejo; **to come in an** ~ **first** llegar fácilmente el primero; **it's as** ~ **as pie** (*or* **ABC** *etc*) es facilísimo, más fácil no puede ser; **they made it very** ~ **for us** nos lo pusieron muy fácil; **'Slobodian made** ~**'** 'Eslóbode por etapas fáciles'.

(**b**) (*relaxed, comfortable*) **to feel** ~ **in one's mind** estar tranquilo; **you can rest** ~ puedes dormir tranquilo.

(**c**) *life, conditions* holgado, cómodo; ~ **chair** butaca *f*, sillón *m*; **to be on** ~ **street*** vivir en el lujo.

(**d**) *manners* natural, sin afectación; *style* llano, corriente; *movement* suelto.

(**e**) *money, credit* abundante; ~ **money** dinero *m* fácil; **by** ~ **payments** con facilidades de pago; **steel is easier** el acero tiene menos demanda; **prices are easier** los precios han bajado ligeramente.

(**f**) *pace* lento, pausado.

(**g**) *woman* fácil; **of** ~ **virtue** de moral relajada; **she's an** ~ **lay** (*US*: **make**‡) es un coño caliente‡, es una tía fácil*.

2 *adv* (*) fácilmente; ~ **there!** ¡despacio!; ~ **come** ~ **go** así se viene y así se va; ~ **does it!** ¡con calma!; ¡despacito!, ¡no hay prisa!; **to go** ~ **on sb** tratar a uno con menos rigor; **to go** ~ **with** moderar; emplear más cuidado con; economizar en; **go** ~ **with the sugar!** ¡cuidado con el azúcar!; **stand** ~! en su lugar ¡descanso!; **he's got it** ~* lo tiene fácil*; **to take it** ~ (*rest*) descansar; (*go slow*) ir despacio; **take it** ~! ¡cálmese!, ¡no se ponga nervioso!

easy-going ['iːzɪ'gəʊɪŋ] *adj* acomodadizo, nada severo; (*morally*) de manga ancha; (*lazy*) indolente.

eat [iːt] (*irr*: *pret* **ate**, *ptp* **eaten**) **1** *vt* comer; *meal* tomar; (*with envy etc*) consumir, devorar; **to** ~ **one's way through the menu** pedir todos los platos en la lista; **I thought he was going to** ~ **me** creía que iba a comerme vivo; **what's** ~**ing you?*** ¿qué mosca te ha picado?

2 *vi* comer; **he always** ~**s well** siempre tiene buen apetito; **this fish** ~**s well** este pescado es muy sabroso; **he had them** ~**ing out of his hand** los tenía totalmente dominados.

3 ~**s*** *npl* (*Brit*) comida *f*, comestibles *mpl*; **let's get some** ~**s** vamos a comer algo.

◆**eat away** *vt* corroer; desgastar.

◆**eat in** *vi* comer en casa.

◆**eat into** *vt metal* corroer; *surface etc* desgastar; *reserves etc* mermar; *leisure time etc* reducir.

◆**eat out** *vi* comer fuera, comer en un restaurante.

◆**eat up** *vt* comerse, acabar; **to** ~ **up the miles** tragar los kilómetros; **this fire** ~**s up coal** esta chimenea devora el carbón; **to be** ~**en up with envy** consumirse de envidia.

eatable ['iːtəbl] **1** *adj* comestible; **2** ~**s** *npl* comestibles *mpl*.

eaten ['iːtn] *ptp of* **eat**.

eater ['iːtəʳ] *n* (**a**) (*person*) **to be a big** ~ tener siempre buen apetito, ser comilón; **I'm not a big ~** yo como bastante poco. (**b**) (*apple etc*) manzana *f* (*etc*) de boca.

eatery ['iːtərɪ] *n* (*US*) restaurante *m*.

eating ['iːtɪŋ] **1** *n* (**a**) (*act*) el comer. (**b**) **to be good ~** ser sabroso. **2** *attr*: **~ apple** manzana *f* de mesa; **~ olives** aceitunas *fpl* de boca.

eating-house ['iːtɪŋhaʊs] *n, pl* **eating-houses** ['iːtɪŋ,haʊzɪz] restaurante *m*.

eau de Cologne ['əʊdəkə'ləʊn] *n* agua *f* de colonia, colonia *f*.

eaves ['iːvz] *npl* alero *m*.

eavesdrop ['iːvzdrɒp] *vi* escuchar a escondidas, orejear (*LAm*) (*on a conversation* una conversación).

eavesdropper ['iːvz,drɒpəʳ] *n* escuchador *m* escondido.

ebb [eb] **1** *n* reflujo *m*; **the ~ and flow** el flujo y reflujo; **to be at a low ~** estar decaído; **at a low ~ in his fortunes** en un punto bien bajo de su vida.

2 *attr*: **~ tide** marea *f* menguante.

3 *vi* bajar; menguar; (*fig*) decaer; **to ~ and flow** fluir y refluir; **life is ~ing from him** le están abandonando sus últimas fuerzas.

◆**ebb away** *vi* (*fig*) menguar, disminuir.

ebonite ['ebənaɪt] *n* ebonita *f*.

ebony ['ebənɪ] **1** *n* ébano *m*. **2** *attr* de ébano.

EBU *n abbr of* **European Broadcasting Union** Unión *f* Europea de Radiodifusión, UER *f*.

ebullience [ɪ'bʌlɪəns] *n* exaltación *f*, entusiasmo *m*, exuberancia *f*, animación *f*.

ebullient [ɪ'bʌlɪənt] *adj* exaltado, entusiasta, exuberante, animado.

EC *n abbr of* **European Community** Comunidad *f* Europea, CE *f*.

eccentric [ɪk'sentrɪk] **1** *adj* excéntrico. **2** *n* excéntrico *m*, -a *f*.

eccentrically [ɪk'sentrɪkəlɪ] *adv* de manera excéntrica.

eccentricity [,eksən'trɪsɪtɪ] *n* excentricidad *f*.

Ecclesiastes [ɪ,kliːzɪ'æstiːz] *n* (*Bible*): **the Book of ~** el Libro de Eclesiastés.

ecclesiastic [ɪ,kliːzɪ'æstɪk] *n* eclesiástico *m*.

ecclesiastical [ɪ,kliːzɪ'æstɪkəl] *adj* eclesiástico.

ECG *n abbr of* **electrocardiogram** electrocardiograma *m*.

ECGD *n abbr of* **Export Credits Guarantee Department** Departamento *m* de Garantía de Crédito a la Exportación.

echelon ['eʃəlɒn] **1** *n* escalón *m*. **2** *vt* escalonar.

echo ['ekəʊ] **1** *n* (*pl* **echoes** ['ekəʊz]) eco *m*; **to cheer sb to the ~** aplaudir a uno repetidas veces, ovacionar a uno.

2 *vt sound* repetir; (*imitate*) imitar; *opinion etc* hacerse eco de; **his opinion is ~ed by ...** su opinión es coreada por ...

3 *vi* resonar, hacer eco; **the valley ~ed with shouts** resonaban los gritos por el valle.

echo-chamber ['ekəʊ,tʃeɪmbəʳ] *n* (*Rad, TV*) cámara *f* de eco.

echo-sounder ['ekəʊ,saʊndəʳ] *n* sonda *f* acústica.

éclair ['eɪkleəʳ] *n* relámpago *m* de chocolate.

éclat ['eɪklɑː] *n* brillo *m*; (*success*) éxito *m* brillante; **with great ~** brillantemente.

eclectic [ɪ'klektɪk] **1** *adj* ecléctico. **2** *n* ecléctico *m*, -a *f*.

eclecticism [ɪ'klektɪsɪzəm] *n* eclecticismo *m*.

eclipse [ɪ'klɪps] **1** *n* eclipse *m*. **2** *vt* eclipsar.

eclogue ['eklɒg] *n* égloga *f*.

ECM *n* (**a**) *abbr of* **electronic counter-measure** contramedida *f* electrónica. (**b**) (*US*) *abbr of* **European Common Market** Mercado *m* Común Europeo, MCE *m*.

eco... ['iːkəʊ] *pref* eco...

ecobalance ['iːkəʊ,bæləns] *n* ecoequilibrio *m*.

ecoclimatic [,iːkəʊklaɪ'mætɪk] *adj* ecoclimático.

eco-friendly ['iːkəʊ'frendlɪ] *adj* amigo de la ecología, ecológicamente puro.

eco-labelling, (*US*) **eco-labeling** [,iːkəʊ'leɪbəlɪŋ] *n* etiquetado *m* ecologista.

ecological [,iːkəʊ'lɒdʒɪkəl] *adj* ecológico.

ecologically [,iːkəʊ'lɒdʒɪkəlɪ] *adv* ecológicamente; **an ~ sound scheme** un plan ecológicamente razonable.

ecologist [ɪ'kɒlədʒɪst] *n* ecólogo *m*, -a *f*; (*Pol*) ecologista *mf*.

ecology [ɪ'kɒlədʒɪ] **1** *n* ecología *f*. **2** *attr*: **~ movement** movimiento *m* ecologista.

econometric [ɪ,kɒnə'metrɪk] *adj* econométrico.

econometrics [ɪ,kɒnə'metrɪks] *n* econometría *f*.

economic(al) [,iːkə'nɒmɪk(əl)] *adj* económico; *rent* equitativo; (*~ to operate, to run*) rentable; **~ aid** ayuda *f* económica; **~ expansion** expansión *f* económica; **~ forecast** previsiones *fpl* económicas; **~ growth** crecimiento *m* económico; **~ indicator** indicador *m* económico; **~ policy** política *f* económica; **~ sanctions** sanciones *fpl* económicas; **~ warfare** guerra *f* económica.

economically [,iːkə'nɒmɪkəlɪ] *adj* económicamente; de modo rentable.

economics [,iːkə'nɒmɪks] *npl* economía *f* política; (*Univ*) ciencias *fpl* económicas; **home ~** (*US*) economía *f* doméstica.

economist [ɪ'kɒnəmɪst] *n* economista *mf*.

economize [ɪ'kɒnəmaɪz] **1** *vt* economizar, ahorrar. **2** *vi* economizar (*on* en).

economy [ɪ'kɒnəmɪ] **1** *n* (**a**) (*saving*) economía *f*; **~ of scale** economía *f* de escala; **to make economies, to practise ~** economizar; **he writes with great ~** escribe con gran economía.

(**b**) (*system*) economía *f*.

2 *attr*: **~ class** (*Aer*) clase *f* económica, clase *f* turista; **~ drive** campaña *f* de economías (presupuestarias); **~ size** tamaño *m* económico, tamaño *m* familiar.

ecosensitive ['iːkəʊ'sensɪtɪv] *adj* ecosensible.

ecosphere ['iːkəʊ,sfɪəʳ] *n* ecosfera *f*.

ecosystem ['iːkəʊ,sɪstɪm] *n* ecosistema *m*, sistema *m* ecológico.

ecotype ['iːkə,taɪp] *n* ecotipo *m*.

ECS *n abbr of* **extended character set** conjunto *m* de caracteres extendido.

ECSC *n abbr of* **European Coal and Steel Community** Comunidad *f* Europea del Carbón y del Acero, CECA *f*.

ecstasy ['ekstəsɪ] *n* (**a**) éxtasis *m*; **in an ~ of passion** en un arrebato de amor, arrebatado por el amor; **to be in ecstasies** estar en éxtasis; **to go into ecstasies over sth** extasiarse ante algo. (**b**) (‡: *drug*) éxtasis* *m*, metanfetamina *f*.

ecstatic [eks'tætɪk] *adj* extático.

ecstatically [eks'tætɪkəlɪ] *adv* con éxtasis.

ECT *n abbr of* **electroconvulsive therapy** terapia *f* de electroshock; *V* **electroconvulsive.**

ectomorph ['ektəʊ,mɔːf] *n* ectomorfo *m*.

ectopic [ek'tɒpɪk] *adj* ectópico; **~ pregnancy** embarazo *m* ectópico.

ectoplasm ['ektəʊplæzəm] *n* ectoplasma *m*.

ECU ['eɪkjuː] *n abbr of* **European Currency Unit** Unidad *f* de Cuenta Europea, UCE *f*.

ecu ['eɪkjuː] *n* ecu *m*.

Ecuador [,ekwə'dɔːʳ] *n* El Ecuador.

Ecuador(i)an [,ekwə'dɔːr(ɪ)ən] **1** *adj* ecuatoriano. **2** *n* ecuatoriano *m*, -a *f*.

ecumenical [,iːkjʊ'menɪkəl] *adj* ecuménico; **~ council** concejo *m* ecuménico; **~ movement** movimiento *m* ecuménico.

ecumenism [iː'kjuːmənɪzəm] *n* ecumenismo *m*.

eczema ['eksɪmə] *n* eccema *m*, eczema *m*.

Ed [ed], **Eddie** ['edɪ] *nm familiar forms of* **Edward.**

ed. [ed] (**a**) *n abbr of* **edition** edición *f*, ed. (**b**) *n abbr of* **editor.** (**c**) *abbr of* **edited by** en edición de.

Edam ['iːdæm] *n* (*also* **~ cheese**) queso *m* de Edam, queso *m* de bola.

eddy ['edɪ] **1** *n* remolino *m*. **2** *vi* arremolinarse.

edelweiss ['eɪdlvaɪs] *n* edelweiss *m*.

edema [ɪ'diːmə] *n* (*esp US*) edema *m*.

Eden ['iːdn] *n* Edén *m*.

EDF *n abbr of* **European Development Fund** Fondo *m* Europeo de Desarrollo, FED *m*.

edge [edʒ] **1** *n* (*cutting*) filo *m*, corte *m*; (*border*: *of chair, cliff, wood etc*) borde *m*; (*of page, sheet*) margen *m*; (*of coin, table etc*) canto *m*; (*of town*) afueras *fpl*; (*of lake etc*) margen *f*, orilla *f*; (*end*) extremidad *f*; **to be on ~** estar de canto, (*fig*) tener los nervios de punta; **my nerves are on ~** tengo los nervios de punta; **to be on the ~ of disaster** estar al borde del desastre; **to have the** (*or* **an**) **~ on** (*or* **over**) **sb** llevar ventaja a; ganar a uno por los pelos; **to put an ~ on** afilar; **to set sb's teeth on ~** dar dentera a uno; **to smooth the rough ~s** limar las asperezas (*also fig*); **to take the ~ off** embotar; **to take the ~ off one's appetite** engañar el hambre; **to take the ~ off an argument** quitar fuerza a un argumento.

2 *vt* (**a**) (*Sew*) ribetear, orlar (*with* de); *path etc* poner un borde a; **~d in, ~d with** ribeteado de; bordeado de.

(**b**) **to ~ one's way into a room** introducirse con dificultad en un cuarto (atestado de gente).

◆**edge along 1** *vt* mover algo de canto (poco a poco). **2** *vi* avanzar de lado poco a poco.

◆**edge away** *vi* alejarse poco a poco.

◆**edge in 1** *vt* introducir de canto.

2 *vi* abrirse paso poco a poco; colarse.

◆**edge out** 1 *vt* (*defeat*) derrotar por muy poco; (*ostracize*) apartar. 2 *vi* asomarse con precaución.
◆**edge up** *vi* (**a**) (*price etc*) subir poco a poco, aumentar lentamente.
(**b**) **to ~ up to sb** acercarse con cautela a uno.
edgeways [ˈedʒweɪz] *adv* de lado, de canto; *V* **word.**
edgewise [ˈedʒwaɪz] *adv* de canto.
edginess [ˈedʒɪnɪs] *n* tirantez *f*, irritabilidad *f*.
edging [ˈedʒɪŋ] *n* (*Sew*) ribete *m*, orla *f*; (*of path etc*) borde *m*.
edgy [ˈedʒɪ] *adj* nervioso, inquieto.
edibility [ˌedɪˈbɪlətɪ] *n* comestibilidad *f*.
edible [ˈedɪbl] *adj* comestible.
edict [ˈiːdɪkt] *n* edicto *m*.
edification [ˌedɪfɪˈkeɪʃən] *n* edificación *f*.
edifice [ˈedɪfɪs] *n* edificio *m* (*esp* grande, imponente).
edify [ˈedɪfaɪ] *vt* edificar.
edifying [ˈedɪfaɪɪŋ] *adj* edificante.
Edinburgh [ˈedɪnbərə] *n* Edimburgo *m*.
edit [ˈedɪt] *vt newspaper, magazine, series* dirigir, ser director de; *text, book* preparar una edición de; *script* preparar para la imprenta, (*correct*) corregir; (*Comput*) editar; **~ed by** (*newspaper etc*) bajo la dirección de, (*text, book*) prólogo y notas de, a cargo de, (en) edición de; **~ key** tecla *f* de edición; **to ~ a phrase out** eliminar una frase.
◆**edit out** *vt*: **to ~ words out** eliminar unas palabras, suprimir unas palabras.
editing [ˈedɪtɪŋ] *n* (*of magazine*) redacción *f*; (*of newspaper, dictionary*) dirección *f*; (*of article, series of texts, tape*) edición *f*; (*of film*) montaje *m*; (*Comput*) edición *f*; (*video*) editaje *m*.
edition [ɪˈdɪʃən] *n* edición *f*; (*Typ*: *no of copies*) tirada *f*.
editor [ˈedɪtəʳ] *n* (*of newspaper, magazine, series*) director *m*, -ora *f*; (*staff ~*) redactor-jefe *m*, redactora-jefa *f*; (*of a book*) autor *m*, -ora *f* de la edición; (*TV, Comput, also of critical text*) editor *m*, -ora *f*; **~'s note** nota *f* de la redacción.
editorial [ˌedɪˈtɔːrɪəl] 1 *adj* editorial; de la dirección; **~ board** consejo *m* de redacción; **~ corrections** ajustes *mpl* de estilo, ajustes *mpl* de redacción; **~ staff** redacción *f*. 2 *n* editorial *m*, artículo *m* de fondo.
editorialist [ˌedɪˈtɔːrɪəlɪst] *n* (*US*) editorialista *mf*.
editor-in-chief [ˈedɪtərɪnˈtʃiːf] *n* jefe *m*, -a *f* de redacción.
editorship [ˈedɪtəʃɪp] *n* dirección *f*; **under the ~ of** bajo la dirección de.
Edmund [ˈedmənd] *nm* Edmundo.
EDP *n abbr of* **electronic data processing** proceso *m* electrónico de datos, PED *m*.
EDT *n* (*US*) *abbr of* **Eastern Daylight Time.**
educability [ˌedjʊkəˈbɪlɪtɪ] *n* educabilidad *f*.
educable [ˈedjʊkəbl] *adj* educable.
educate [ˈedjʊkeɪt] *vt* educar; formar; instruir; **where were you ~d?** ¿dónde cursó sus estudios?; **the prince is being privately ~d** el príncipe tiene un preceptor particular.
educated [ˈedjʊkeɪtɪd] *adj* culto.
education [ˌedjʊˈkeɪʃən] 1 *n* educación *f*; enseñanza *f*; instrucción *f*; formación *f* cultural, cultura *f*; (*as Univ department etc*) pedagogía *f*; **I never had much ~** pasé poco tiempo en la escuela; **they paid for his ~** le pagaron los estudios; **Department of E~ and Science** (*Brit*) ≃ Dirección *f* General de Educación y Ciencia; **Minister of E~** (*Brit*) Ministro *m*, -a *f* de Educación y Ciencia; *V* **primary** *etc*.
2 *attr*: **~ authority** (*Brit*) ≃ delegación *f* de educación; **~ department** (*Brit*: *of local authority*) ≃ departamento *m* de educación; **E~ Department** (*Ministry*) Ministerio *m* de Educación.
educational [ˌedjʊˈkeɪʃənl] *adj policy etc* educacional, relativo a la educación; *function etc, centre* docente; *film etc* instructivo, educativo; **~ television** televisión *f* escolar.
education(al)ist [ˌedjʊˈkeɪʃn(əl)ɪst] *n* educacionista *mf*.
educationally [ˌedjʊˈkeɪʃnəlɪ] *adv* (*as regards teaching methods*) pedagógicamente; (*as regards education, schooling*) educativamente; **~ subnormal** de inteligencia inferior a la normal.
educative [ˈedjʊkətɪv] *adj* educativo.
educator [ˈedjʊkeɪtəʳ] *n* educador *m*, -ora *f*.
educe [ɪˈdjuːs] *vt* educir, sacar.
Edward [ˈedwəd] *nm* Eduardo; **~ the Confessor** Eduardo el Confesor.
Edwardian [edˈwɔːdɪən] (*Brit*) 1 *adj* eduardiano. 2 *n* eduardiano *m*, -a *f*.
EE *abbr of* **electrical engineer.**
EEC *n abbr of* **European Economic Community** Comunidad *f* Económica Europea, CEE.
EEG *n abbr of* **electroencephalogram** electroencefalograma *m*.
eel [iːl] *n* anguila *f*.
e'en [iːn] (*liter*) = **even.**
EENT *n* (*US*) *abbr of* **eye, ear, nose and throat.**
EEOC *n* (*US*) *abbr of* **Equal Employment Opportunities Commission** *comisión que investiga la discriminación racial o sexual en el empleo.*
e'er [ɛəʳ] (*liter*) = **ever.**
eerie [ˈɪərɪ] *adj* misterioso; *sound, experience* extraño, fantástico, horripilante.
EET *n abbr of* **Eastern European Time.**
eff⁑ [ef] *vi*: **he was ~ing all over the place** soltaba palabrotas por todas partes.
efface [ɪˈfeɪs] 1 *vt* borrar. 2 *vr*: **to ~ o.s.** retirarse modestamente, lograr pasar inadvertido.
effect [ɪˈfekt] 1 *n* (*result*) efecto *m*, consecuencia *f*, resultado *m*; (*impression*) efecto *m*, impresión *f*; **~s** efectos *mpl*; **pleasing ~** impresión *f* agradable; **striving after ~** efectismo *m*; **just for ~** sólo por impresionar; **in ~** en realidad; **to be in ~** (*Jur*) estar vigente; **to come into ~** entrar en vigor; **of no ~** inútil; **to be of no ~** no tener efecto, no hacer mella; (*Jur*) no tener fuerza legal; **to no ~** inútilmente; **a message to the ~ that ...** un mensaje en el sentido de que ...; **to the same ~** del mismo tenor, a este tenor, en el mismo sentido; **to this ~** con este propósito; **or words to that ~** o algo parecido; **to good ~** con éxito, con buenos resultados; **an increase with immediate ~** un aumento a partir de hoy; **with ~ from April** a partir de abril; **to feel the ~(s) of** sentir los efectos de, estar resentido de; **to give ~ to** poner en efecto, hacer efectivo; **to have an ~** dejarse sentir, surtir efecto (*on* en); **to put into ~** poner en vigor; **to take ~** (*remedy*) surtir efecto, (*law*) entrar en vigor (*from* a partir de).
2 *vt* efectuar, llevar a cabo; *sale* efectuar; *saving* hacer.
effective [ɪˈfektɪv] 1 *adj* eficaz; (*striking*) impresionante, llamativo, logrado; (*real*) efectivo, verdadero; (*Mil*) útil para todos los servicios; **~ capacity** (*Tech*) capacidad *f* útil; **~ date** fecha *f* de vigencia; **~ power** (*Tech*) potencia *f* real; **~ from** en vigor a partir de; **to become ~** entrar en vigor (*from, on* a partir de).
2 **~s** *npl* efectivos *mpl*.
effectively [ɪˈfektɪvlɪ] *adv* eficazmente; (*strikingly*) de manera impresionante; acertadamente; (*in fact*) en efecto, realmente.
effectiveness [ɪˈfektɪvnɪs] *n* eficacia *f*, efectividad *f*.
effectual [ɪˈfektjʊəl] *adj* eficaz.
effectuate [ɪˈfektjʊeɪt] *vt* efectuar, lograr.
effeminacy [ɪˈfemɪnəsɪ] *n* afeminación *f*, afeminamiento *m*.
effeminate [ɪˈfemɪnɪt] *adj* afeminado.
effervesce [ˌefəˈves] *vi* estar en efervescencia, (*begin to ~*) entrar en efervescencia; bullir, hervir; (*fig*) ser muy alegre, ser muy vivo.
effervescence [ˌefəˈvesns] *n* efervescencia *f*.
effervescent [ˌefəˈvesnt] *adj* efervescente (*also fig*).
effete [ɪˈfiːt] *adj* decadente; agotado, cansado.
effeteness [ɪˈfiːtnɪs] *n* decadencia *f*, cansancio *m*.
efficacious [ˌefɪˈkeɪʃəs] *adj* eficaz.
efficacy [ˈefɪkəsɪ] *n* eficacia *f*.
efficiency [ɪˈfɪʃənsɪ] *n* eficiencia *f*, eficacia *f*; buena marcha *f*; (*Mech*) rendimiento *m*.
efficient [ɪˈfɪʃənt] *adj* eficiente; *remedy, product* eficaz; (*Mech*) de buen rendimiento; *person* eficiente, eficaz, competente, capaz.
efficiently [ɪˈfɪʃəntlɪ] *adv* eficientemente, eficazmente.
effigy [ˈefɪdʒɪ] *n* efigie *f*.
effing⁑ [ˈefɔŋ] *adj* (*euph*) = **fucking.**
efflorescent [ˌeflɔːˈresnt] *adj* eflorescente.
effluent [ˈeflʊənt] *n* efluente *m*, aguas *fpl* residuales.
effluvium [eˈfluːvɪəm] *n*, *pl* **effluvia** [eˈfluːvɪə] efluvio *m*, emanación *f*, tufo *m*.
effort [ˈefət] *n* (**a**) esfuerzo *m*; **all his ~ was directed to** todos sus esfuerzos iban dirigidos a; **to make an ~ to** + *infin* esforzarse por + *infin*, hacer un esfuerzo por + *infin*; **to make every ~ to** + *infin*, **to spare no ~ to** + *infin* no regatear medio para + *infin*.
(**b**) (*) resultado *m*, producto *m*; obra *f*; tentativa *f*; **good ~!** ¡bien hecho!; **it was a pretty poor ~** fue una exhibición pobre; **what did you think of his latest ~?** ¿qué opinas de su nueva obra?; **it's not bad for a first ~** siendo su primer intento no es nada malo; **it wasn't worth the ~** no valía la pena.
effortless [ˈefətlɪs] *adj* sin esfuerzo alguno, fácil.
effortlessly [ˈefətlɪslɪ] *adv* sin esfuerzo alguno, fácilmente.

effrontery [ɪˈfrʌntərɪ] *n* descaro *m*; **what ~!** ¡qué frescura!; **he had the ~ to say** llegó su cinismo hasta decir.
effusion [ɪˈfjuːʒən] *n* efusión *f*.
effusive [ɪˈfjuːsɪv] *adj* efusivo.
effusively [ɪˈfjuːsɪvlɪ] *adv* con efusión.
effusiveness [ɪˈfjuːsɪvnɪs] *n* efusividad *f*.
EFL *n abbr of* **English as a Foreign Language**; *V* **English**.
EFT *n abbr of* **electronic funds transfer** transferencia *f* electrónica de fondos.
eft [eft] *n* tritón *m*.
EFTA [ˈeftə] *n abbr of* **European Free Trade Association** Asociación *f* Europea para el Libre Comercio, AELC *f*.
e.g. *adv abbr of* **exempli gratia** por ejemplo, p.ej.
egalitarian [ɪˌgælɪˈtɛərɪən] *adj* igualitario.
egalitarianism [ɪˌgælɪˈtɛərɪənɪzəm] *n* igualitarismo *m*.
egg[1] [eg] *n* (**a**) huevo *m*; **~s** (*of some insects*) carrocha *f*; **to lay an ~*** (*esp US*) fracasar totalmente; **as sure as ~s (is ~s)** sin ningún género de dudas; **don't put all your ~s in one basket** no pongas toda la carne en el asador; **we all had ~ on our faces*** todos hemos quedado en ridículo.
(**b**) (*) tío* *m*; **bad ~** sinvergüenza *m*.
egg[2] [eg] *vt*: **to ~ sb on** animar a uno, incitar a uno; **to ~ sb on to do sth** incitar a uno a hacer algo.
eggbeater [ˈegˌbiːtəʳ] *n* batidor *m* de huevos; (*US**) helicóptero *m*.
eggcup [ˈegkʌp] *n* huevera *f*.
egg custard [ˌegˈkʌstəd] *n* ≃ natillas *fpl* de huevo.
egg flip [ˈegˈflɪp] *n* yema *f* mejida.
egghead* [ˈeghed] *n* intelectual *mf*.
eggnog [ˈegˈnɒg] *n* yema *f* mejida, ponche *m* de huevo.
eggplant [ˈegplɑːnt] *n* berenjena *f*.
egg roll [ˌegˈrəʊl] *n paté a base de huevo con carne de cerdo y legumbres.*
egg-shaped [ˈegʃeɪpt] *adj* oviforme.
eggshell [ˈegʃel] *n* cáscara *f* de huevo.
egg timer [ˈegˌtaɪməʳ] *n* cronómetro *m* para huevos.
egg whisk [ˈegwɪsk] *n* batidor *m* de huevos.
egg white [ˈegwaɪt] *n* clara *f* (de huevo).
egg yolk [ˈegjəʊk] *n* yema *f* (de huevo).
eglantine [ˈegləntaɪn] *n* eglantina *f*.
EGM *n abbr of* **extraordinary general meeting**.
ego [ˈiːgəʊ] **1** *n* ego *m*, el yo; amor *m* propio; **to boost one's ~*** halagar el yo. **2** *attr*: **~ trip*** autobombada *f*.
egocentric(al) [ˌegəʊˈsentrɪk(əl)] *adj* egocéntrico.
egoism [ˈegəʊɪzəm] *n* egoísmo *m*.
egoist [ˈegəʊɪst] *n* egoísta *mf*.
egoistical [ˌegəʊˈɪstɪkəl] *adj* egoísta.
egomania [ˌiːgəʊˈmeɪnɪə] *n* egomanía *f*.
egotism [ˈegəʊtɪzəm] *n* egotismo *m*.
egotist [ˈegəʊtɪst] *n* egotista *mf*.
egotistic(al) [ˌegəʊˈtɪstɪk(əl)] *adj* egotista.
egregious [ɪˈgriːdʒəs] *adj* atroz, enorme; *liar etc* notorio.
egress [ˈiːgres] *n* salida *f*.
egret [ˈiːgret] *n* garceta *f*.
Egypt [ˈiːdʒɪpt] *n* Egipto *m*.
Egyptian [ɪˈdʒɪpʃən] **1** *adj* egipcio. **2** *n* egipcio *m*, -a *f*.
Egyptology [ˌiːdʒɪpˈtɒlədʒɪ] *n* egiptología *f*.
eh [eɪ] *interj* (*please repeat*) ¿cómo?, ¿qué?; (*inviting assent*) ¿no?, ¿verdad?, ¿no es así?
EIB *n abbr of* **European Investment Bank** Banco *m* Europeo de Inversiones, BEI *m*.
eider [ˈaɪdəʳ] *n*, **eider duck** [ˈaɪdəˈdʌk] *n* eider *m*, pato *m* de flojel.
eiderdown [ˈaɪdədaʊn] *n* edredón *m*.
eight [eɪt] **1** *adj* ocho. **2** *n* ocho *m*; (*Rowing*) bote *m* de a ocho; **to have had one over the ~** llevar una copa de más.
eighteen [ˈeɪˈtiːn] *adj* dieciocho.
eighteenth [ˈeɪˈtiːnθ] *adj* decimoctavo.
eighth [eɪtθ] **1** *adj* octavo; (*US Mus*) **~ note** corchea *f*. **2** *n* octavo *m*, octava parte *f*.
eightieth [ˈeɪtɪɪθ] *adj* octogésimo; ochenta; **the ~ anniversary** el ochenta aniversario.
eighty [ˈeɪtɪ] *adj* ochenta; **the eighties** (*eg* 1980*s*) los años ochenta; **to be in one's eighties** tener más de ochenta años, ser ochentón.
Eire [ˈɛərə] *n* Eire *m*.
EIS *n abbr of* **Educational Institute of Scotland** *sindicato de profesores.*
Eisteddfod [aɪsˈteðvɒd] *n festival galés en el que se celebran concursos de música y poesía.*
either [ˈaɪðəʳ] **1** *adj* (**a**) (*one or other*) cualquier ... de los dos; **you can do it ~ way** puedes hacerlo de este modo o del otro; (*neg sense*) **I don't like ~ book** no me gusta ninguno de los dos libros, no me gusta ni uno ni otro.
(**b**) (*each*) cada; **on ~ side of the street** en cada lado de la calle, en ambos lados de la calle.
2 *pron* cualquiera de los dos, uno u otro; **~ of us** cualquiera de nosotros; (*neg sense*) **I don't want ~ of them** no quiero ninguno de los dos, no quiero ni uno ni otro.
3 *conj*: **~ come in or stay out** o entras o quedas fuera.
4 *adv* tampoco; **I won't go ~** yo no voy tampoco.
ejaculate [ɪˈdʒækjʊleɪt] *vt* (**a**) (*cry out*) exclamar; proferir (de repente), lanzar. (**b**) (*Physiol*) eyacular.
ejaculation [ɪˌdʒækjʊˈleɪʃən] *n* (**a**) (*cry*) exclamación *f*. (**b**) (*Physiol*) eyaculación *f*.
eject [ɪˈdʒekt] **1** *vt* expulsar, echar; *tenant* desahuciar. **2** *vi* (*Aer*) eyectarse.
ejection [ɪˈdʒekʃən] *n* expulsión *f*; desahucio *m*.
ejector [ɪˈdʒektəʳ] *n* expulsor *m*; **~ seat** asiento *m* expulsable, asiento *m* de eyección, asiento *m* eyectable.
eke [iːk] *vt*: **to ~ out** suplir las deficiencias de; *money etc* hacer que llegue; **to ~ out a livelihood** ganarse la vida a duras penas.
EKG *n* (*US*) *abbr of* **electrocardiogram**.
el* [el] *n* (*US*) *abbr of* **elevated railroad**.
elaborate 1 [ɪˈlæbərɪt] *adj* complicado; detallado; *meal* de muchos platos; *work of art* primoroso, rebuscado; *courtesy* exquisito, estudiado.
2 [ɪˈlæbəreɪt] *vt* elaborar.
3 [ɪˈlæbəreɪt] *vi* explicarse con muchos detalles; **to ~ on** ampliar, dar más explicaciones acerca de; **he refused to ~** se negó a dar más detalles, se negó a ampliar la referencia.
elaborately [ɪˈlæbərɪtlɪ] *adv* de manera complicada; con muchos detalles; primorosamente.
elaboration [ɪˌlæbəˈreɪʃən] *n* elaboración *f*.
elapse [ɪˈlæps] *vi* pasar, transcurrir.
elastic [ɪˈlæstɪk] **1** *adj* elástico; (*fig*) elástico, flexible; **~ band** (*Brit*) goma *f* elástica, gomita *f*. **2** *n* elástico *m*; (*Sew*) goma *f*.
elasticity [ˌiːlæsˈtɪsɪtɪ] *n* elasticidad *f*; **~ of demand** elasticidad *f* de la demanda.
elate [ɪˈleɪt] *vt* regocijar.
elated [ɪˈleɪtɪd] *adj*: **to be ~** alegrarse (*at, with* de), estar eufórico.
elation [ɪˈleɪʃən] *n* alegría *f*, euforia *f*, júbilo *m*.
Elba [ˈelbə] *n* Elba *f*.
elbow [ˈelbəʊ] **1** *n* codo *m*; (*of road etc*) recodo *m*; **at one's ~** a la mano, muy cerca; **out at the ~(s)** raído, descosido.
2 *vt* empujar con el codo; **to ~ sb aside** apartar a uno a codazos; **to ~ one's way through** abrirse paso codeando (por).
elbow grease* [ˈelbəʊgriːs] *n* trabajo *m* duro; energía *f*; **it's a matter of ~** es a base de puños.
elbow joint [ˈelbəʊˌdʒɔɪnt] *n* articulación *f* del codo.
elbow-rest [ˈelbəʊˌrest] *n* (*of a chair*) brazo *m*.
elbow-room [ˈelbəʊrʊm] *n* espacio *m* (suficiente); espacio *m* para moverse; libertad *f* de acción.
elder[1] [ˈeldəʳ] **1** *adj* mayor; **~ statesman** estadista *m* veterano; figura *f* muy respetada; **Pliny the E~** Plinio el Viejo. **2** *n* (*Eccl*) anciano *m*; **my ~s** mis mayores; **the ~s of the tribe** los jefes de la tribu.
elder[2] [ˈeldəʳ] *n* (*Bot*) saúco *m*.
elderberry [ˈeldəˌberɪ] *n* baya *f* del saúco; **~ wine** vino *m* de saúco.
elderly [ˈeldəlɪ] *adj* de edad, mayor; **to be getting ~** ir para viejo.
eldest [ˈeldɪst] *adj* (el, la) mayor; primogénito *m*, -a *f*; **my ~ son** mi hijo mayor; **the ~ of the four** el mayor de los cuatro.
Eleanor [ˈelɪnəʳ] *nf* Leonor.
elec. *abbr of* **electric, electricity**.
elect [ɪˈlekt] **1** *vt* elegir; **to ~ sb a member** elegir a uno socio; **to ~ to** + *infin* optar por + *infin*, decidir + *infin*. **2** *adj* electo; **president ~** presidente *m* electo. **3** *n*: **the ~** los elegidos, los predestinados.
elected [ɪˈlektɪd] *adj* elegido; **~ government** gobierno *m* elegido.
election [ɪˈlekʃən] **1** *n* elección *f* (*for* a); **general ~** elecciones *fpl* generales.
2 *attr*: **~ agent** secretario *m*, -a *f* electoral; **~ campaign** campaña *f* electoral; **~ college** colegio *m* electoral; **~ expenses** gastos *mpl* de la campaña electoral; **~ machine** aparato *m* electoral.
electioneer [ɪˌlekʃəˈnɪəʳ] *vi* hacer su campaña electoral; (*pej*) hacer propaganda electoral.
electioneering [ɪˌlekʃəˈnɪərɪŋ] *n* campaña *f* electoral; (*pej*) maniobras *fpl* electorales.

elective [ɪ'lektɪv] **1** *adj* electivo; (*US*: *Univ*) facultativo, optativo. **2** *n* (*also* ~ **subject**) asignatura *f* facultativa (*or* discrecional).

elector [ɪ'lektəʳ] *n* elector *m*, -ora *f*.

electoral [ɪ'lektərəl] *adj* electoral; ~ **college** (*US*) colegio *m* electoral; ~ **register,** ~ **roll** censo *m*, lista *f* electoral.

electorally [ɪ'lektərəlɪ] *adv*: **an** ~ **damaging incident** un incidente con malas consecuencias electorales; **this was not** ~ **popular** esto no gustó a los votantes.

electorate [ɪ'lektərɪt] *n* electorado *m*; número *m* de votantes; censo *m*.

electric [ɪ'lektrɪk] **1** *adj* eléctrico; **the atmosphere was** ~ la atmósfera estaba cargada de electricidad; ~ **blanket** manta *f* eléctrica; ~ **blue** azul *m* eléctrico; ~ **chair** silla *f* eléctrica; ~ **charge** carga *f* eléctrica; ~ **clock** reloj *m* eléctrico; ~ **cooker** cocina *f* eléctrica; ~ **current** corriente *f* eléctrica; ~ **eel** anguila *f* eléctrica; ~ **eye** célula *f* fotoeléctrica; ~ **fence** cercado *m* electrificado; ~ **field** campo *m* eléctrico; ~ **fire** (*Brit*) estufa *f* eléctrica, calentador *m* eléctrico; ~ **guitar** guitarra *f* eléctrica; ~ **heater** = ~ **fire**; ~ **light** luz *f* eléctrica; ~ **organ** órgano *m* eléctrico; ~ **ray** (*Zool*) torpedo *m*, tembladera *f*, temblón *m*; ~ **shock** electrochoque *m*; ~ **shock treatment** tratamiento *m* por electrochoque; ~ **windows** (*Aut*) elevalunas *m* eléctrico.
2 *npl*: **the** ~**s*** (*Brit*) el sistema eléctrico.

electrical [ɪ'lektrɪkəl] *adj* eléctrico; ~ **engineer** perito *m*, -a *f* electricista, ingeniero *m*, -a *f* electricista; ~ **engineering** electrotecnia *f*; ~ **fittings** accesorios *mpl* eléctricos; ~ **storm** tronada *f*, tormenta *f* eléctrica.

electrically [ɪ'lektrɪkəlɪ] *adv* por electricidad.

electrician [ɪlek'trɪʃən] *n* electricista *mf*; (*Cine, TV*) iluminista *mf*.

electricity [ɪlek'trɪsɪtɪ] **1** *n* electricidad *f*. **2** *attr*: **E~ Board** (*Brit*) compañía *f* eléctrica estatal; ~ **dispute** conflicto *m* del sector eléctrico.

electrification [ɪ'lektrɪfɪ'keɪʃən] *n* electrificación *f*.

electrify [ɪ'lektrɪfaɪ] *vt* electrificar; (*fig*) electrizar; **electrified fence** cercado *m* eléctrico.

electrifying [ɪ'lektrɪfaɪɪŋ] *adj* electrizante.

electro... [ɪ'lektrəʊ] *pref* electro...

electrocardiogram [ɪ'lektrəʊ'kɑːdɪəgræm] *n* electrocardiograma *m*.

electrocardiograph [ɪ,lektrəʊ'kɑːdɪəgræf] *n* electrocardiógrafo *m*.

electroconvulsive [ɪ,lektrəkən'vʌlsɪv] *adj* electroconvulsivo; ~ **therapy** terapia *f* electroconvulsiva, electroterapia *f*.

electrocute [ɪ'lektrəʊkjuːt] *vt* electrocutar.

electrocution [ɪ,lektrəʊ'kjʊʃːən] *n* electrocución *f*.

electrode [ɪ'lektrəʊd] *n* electrodo *m*.

electrodynamics [ɪ'lektrəʊdaɪ'næmɪks] *n* electrodinámica *f*.

electroencephalogram [ɪ,lektrəuen'sefələ,græm] *n* electroencefalograma *m*.

electrolyse [ɪ'lektrəʊ,laɪz] *vt* electrolizar.

electrolysis [ɪlek'trɒlɪsɪs] *n* electrólisis *f*.

electrolyte [ɪ'lektrəʊ,laɪt] *n* electrolito *m*.

electromagnet [ɪ'lektrəʊ'mægnɪt] *n* electroimán *m*.

electromagnetic [ɪ'lektrəʊmæg'netɪk] *adj* electromagnético.

electromagnetism [ɪ,lektrəʊ'mægnɪtɪzəm] *n* electromagnetismo *m*.

electron [ɪ'lektrɒn] **1** *n* electrón *m*. **2** *attr*: ~ **camera** cámara *f* electrónica; ~ **gun** pistola *f* de electrones; ~ **microscope** microscopio *m* electrónico.

electronic [ɪlek'trɒnɪk] *adj* electrónico; ~ **banking** banco *m* informatizado; ~ **data processing** proceso *m* electrónico de datos; ~ **fund transfer** transferencia *f* electrónica de fondos; ~ **keyboard** teclado *m* electrónico; ~ **mail** correo *m* electrónico; ~ **mailbox** buzón *m* electrónico; ~ **publishing** autoedición *f* electrónica; ~ **shopping** compra *f* computerizada; ~ **spreadsheet** hoja *f* electrónica; ~ **surveillance** vigilancia *f* electrónica; ~ **tag** etiqueta *f* electrónica de control.

electronically [ɪlek'trɒnɪklɪ] *adv* electrónicamente.

electronics [ɪlek'trɒnɪks] *n* electrónica *f*.

electroplate [ɪ'lektrəʊpleɪt] *vt* galvanizar, electrochapar.

electroplated [ɪ'lektrəʊpleɪtɪd] *adj* galvanizado, electrochapado.

electroshock [ɪ'lektrəʊ,ʃɒk] *attr*: ~ **treatment** electrochoque *m*; ~ **therapy** terapia *f* de electrochoque.

electrostatic [ɪ,lektrəʊ'stætɪk] *adj* electrostático.

electrostatics [ɪ,lektrəʊ'stætɪks] *n* electrostática *f*.

electrotherapy [ɪ,lektrəʊ'θerəpɪ] *n* electroterapia *f*.

elegance ['elɪgəns] *n* elegancia *f*.

elegant ['elɪgənt] *adj* elegante.

elegantly ['elɪgəntlɪ] *adv* elegantemente.

elegiac [,elɪ'dʒaɪək] *adj* elegíaco.

elegy ['elɪdʒɪ] *n* elegía *f*.

element ['elɪmənt] *n* elemento *m* (*also Chem, Elec etc*); ~**s** (*rudiments*) elementos *mpl*, primeras nociones *fpl*; **to be in one's** ~ estar en su elemento; **to be out of one's** ~ estar fuera de su elemento, estar como pez fuera del agua; **to brave the** ~**s** arrostrar la tempestad, (*go out*) salir a la intemperie; **it's the personal** ~ **that counts** es el factor personal el que cuenta; **it has an** ~ **of truth about it** tiene su poquito de verdad.

elemental [,elɪ'mentl] *adj* elemental.

elementary [,elɪ'mentərɪ] *adj* elemental; (*primitive*) rudimentario; ~ **school** escuela *f* primaria; ~ **schooling** primera enseñanza *f*; ~, **my dear Watson** elemental, querido Watson.

elephant ['elɪfənt] *n* elefante *m*, -a *f*.

elephantiasis [,elɪfən'taɪəsɪs] *n* elefantiasis *f*.

elephantine [,elɪ'fæntaɪn] *adj* (*fig*) elefantino, mastodóntico.

elevate ['elɪveɪt] *vt* elevar; (*Eccl*) alzar; *person* exaltar; (*in rank*) ascender (*to* a).

elevated ['elɪveɪtɪd] *adj* elevado, sublime; ~ **railway,** ~ **railroad** (*US*) ferrocarril *m* urbano elevado.

elevating ['elɪveɪtɪŋ] *adj reading* enriquecedor.

elevation [,elɪ'veɪʃən] *n* (*act*) elevación *f*; (*of person*) exaltación *f*; (*in rank*) ascenso *m*; (*of style*) sublimidad *f*; (*hill*) altura *f*; (*Aer etc*) altitud *f*; (*Archit*) alzado *m*.

elevator ['elɪveɪtəʳ] **1** *n* (**a**) (*Agr*) almacén *m* de granos, elevador *m* de granos; (*Aer*) timón *m* de profundidad; (*US*) ascensor *m*, (*for goods*) montacargas *m*. (**b**) (*US*: *also* ~ **shoe**) zapato *m* de tacón alto. **2** *attr*: ~ **car** (*US*) caja *f* de ascensor; ~ **shaft** (*US*) hueco *m* del ascensor.

eleven [ɪ'levn] **1** *adj* once. **2** *n* once *m* (*also Sport*); **the** ~ **plus** (*Brit† Scol*) *examen selectivo realizado por niños mayores de 11 anos*.

elevenses* [ɪ'levnzɪz] *npl* (*Brit*): **to have** ~ tomar las once(s)*.

eleventh [ɪ'levnθ] *adj* undécimo, onceno; **at the** ~ **hour** a última hora.

elf [elf] *n*, *pl* **elves** [elvz] duende *m*; (*Nordic Myth*) elfo *m*.

elfin ['elfɪn] *adj* de duende(s), mágico; de elfo(s).

elicit [ɪ'lɪsɪt] *vt* sacar, (lograr) obtener, provocar.

elide [ɪ'laɪd] *vt* elidir.

eligibility [,elɪdʒə'bɪlɪtɪ] *n* elegibilidad *f*.

eligible ['elɪdʒəbl] *adj* elegible; (*desirable*) deseable, atractivo; *bachelor* de partido; **he's the most** ~ **bachelor in town** es el soltero más cotizado de la ciudad; **to be** ~ **for** llenar los requisitos para, tener derecho a.

Elijah [ɪ'laɪdʒə] *nm* Elías.

eliminate [ɪ'lɪmɪneɪt] *vt* eliminar; suprimir; *suspect, possibility etc* descartar; *person* (*in purge*) eliminar.

elimination [ɪ,lɪmɪ'neɪʃən] **1** *n* eliminación *f*; supresión *f*. **2** *attr*: ~ **round** eliminatoria *f*.

Elishah [ɪ'laɪʃə] *nm* Elíseo.

elision [ɪ'lɪʒən] *n* elisión *f*.

élite [eɪ'liːt] *n* élite *f*, elite *f*, minoría *f* selecta.

elitism [ɪ'liːtɪzəm] *n* elitismo *m*.

elitist [ɪ'liːtɪst] **1** *adj* elitista. **2** *n* elitista *mf*.

elixir [ɪ'lɪksəʳ] *n* elixir *m*.

Elizabeth [ɪ'lɪzəbəθ] *nf* Isabel.

Elizabethan [ɪ,lɪzə'biːθən] **1** *adj* isabelino. **2** *n* isabelino *m*, -a *f*.

elk [elk] *n* alce *m*, anta *m*.

ellipse [ɪ'lɪps] *n* elipse *f*.

ellipsis [ɪ'lɪpsɪs] *n*, *pl* **ellipses** [ɪ'lɪpsiːz] (*omission*) elipsis *f*; (*dots*) puntos *mpl* suspensivos.

elliptic(al) [ɪ'lɪptɪk(əl)] *adj* elíptico.

elliptically [ɪ'lɪptɪkəlɪ] *adv* de manera elíptica.

elm [elm] *n* (*also* ~ **tree**) olmo *m*.

elocution [,elə'kjuːʃən] *n* elocución *f*.

elocutionist [,elə'kjuːʃənɪst] *n* profesor *m*, -ora *f* de elocución; recitador *m*, -ora *f*.

elongate ['iːlɒŋgeɪt] *vt* alargar, extender.

elongated ['iːlɒŋgeɪtɪd] *adj* alargado, estirado, extendido.

elongation [,iːlɒŋ'geɪʃən] *n* alargamiento *m*, estiramiento *m*.

elope [ɪ'ləʊp] *vi* (*1 person*) fugarse con su amante, (*2 persons*) fugarse para casarse; **to** ~ **with** fugarse con.

elopement [ɪ'ləʊpmənt] *n* fuga *f*.

eloquence ['eləkwəns] *n* elocuencia *f*.

eloquent ['eləkwənt] *adj* elocuente.

eloquently ['eləkwəntlɪ] *adv* elocuentemente.

El Salvador [el'sælvədɔːʳ] *n* El Salvador.

else [els] *adv* (**a**) (*after pron*) **all** ~, **everything** ~ todo lo demás; **everyone** ~ todos los demás; **anyone** ~ **would do it**

cualquier otra persona lo haría; **anything ~ is impossible** cualquier otra cosa es imposible; **have you anything ~ to tell me?** ¿tiene algo más que decirme?; **anything ~, madam?** (*in shop*) ¿algo más, señora?, ¿alguna cosita más, señora?; **that was sb ~** fue otra persona; **there's sb ~, isn't there?** hay alguien más, ¿verdad?; **somewhere ~** en otra parte; **it's** (*or* **she's**) **something ~**! ¡es fuera de serie!

(**b**) (*after pron, neg*) **I don't know anyone ~ here** aquí no conozco a nadie más; **nobody ~ knows** no lo sabe ningún otro; **there's nothing ~ I can do** no hay nada más que pueda hacer; **nothing ~, thanks** nada más, gracias.

(**c**) (*adv of quantity*) **there was little ~ to do** apenas quedaba otra cosa que hacer; **and much ~ besides** y mucho más también.

(**d**) (*after interrog*) **how ~?** ¿de qué otra manera?; **what ~?** ¿qué más?; **where ~?**¿en qué otro sitio?; **where ~ can he have gone?** ¿a qué otro sitio habrá podido ir?; **who ~?** ¿quién más?; **who ~ could do it as well as you?** ¿qué otra persona podría hacerlo tan bien como Vd?

(**e**) (*standing alone*) **how could I have done it ~?** ¿de qué otro modo hubiera podido hacerlo?; **red or ~ black** rojo o bien negro; **or ~ I'll do it** si no, lo hago yo; **do this, or ~...** haga esto, pues de otro modo ...

elsewhere ['els'wɛəʳ] *adv be* en otra parte; *go* a otra parte.

ELT *n abbr of* **English Language Teaching** enseñanza *f* del inglés; *V* **English.**

elucidate [ɪ'luːsɪdeɪt] *vt* aclarar, elucidar, esclarecer.

elucidation [ɪ,luːsɪ'deɪʃən] *n* aclaración *f*, elucidación *f*.

elude [ɪ'luːd] *vt blow etc* eludir, esquivar, evitar; *grasp* escapar de; *pursuer* escaparse de, burlar, zafarse de; *obligation* zafarse de; **the name ~s me** se me escapa el nombre; **the answer has so far ~d us** hasta ahora no hemos encontrado la solución.

elusive [ɪ'luːsɪv] *adj* (**a**) difícil de encontrar. (**b**) (*fig*) esquivo; inaprensible, escurridizo.

elusiveness [ɪ'luːsɪvnɪs] *n* carácter *m* esquivo.

elver ['elvəʳ] *n* angula *f*.

elves [elvz] *npl of* **elf.**

Elysium [ɪ'lɪzɪəm] *n* Elíseo *m*.

EM *abbr of* **Engineer of Mines.**

emaciated [ɪ'meɪsɪeɪtɪd] *adj* demacrado; **to become ~** demacrarse.

emaciation [ɪ,meɪsɪ'eɪʃən] *n* demacración *f*.

email, e-mail ['iːmeɪl] *n* correo *m* electrónico.

emanate ['eməneɪt] *vi* emanar, proceder (*from* de).

emanation [,emə'neɪʃən] *n* emanación *f*.

emancipate [ɪ'mænsɪpeɪt] *vt* emancipar; *slave* manumitir.

emancipated [ɪ'mænsɪpeɪtɪd] *adj* emancipado; *slave* manumitido; (*fig*) libre.

emancipation [ɪ,mænsɪ'peɪʃən] *n* emancipación *f*; manumisión *f*; (*fig*) libertad *f*.

emasculate [ɪ'mæskjʊleɪt] *vt* castrar, emascular; (*fig*) mutilar, estropear.

emasculated [ɪ'mæskjʊleɪtɪd] *adj* castrado, emasculado; (*fig*) mutilado, estropeado; *style* empobrecido.

embalm [ɪm'bɑːm] *vt* embalsamar.

embalmer [ɪm'bɑːməʳ] *n* embalsamador *m*.

embalming [ɪm'bɑːmɪŋ] **1** *n* embalsamamiento *m*. **2** *attr*: **~ fluid** líquido *m* embalsador.

embankment [ɪm'bæŋkmənt] *n* terraplén *m*.

embargo [ɪm'bɑːgəʊ] **1** *n* prohibición *f* (*on* de); (*Jur*) embargo *m*; **to be under an ~** estar prohibido; **there is an ~ on arms** está prohibido comerciar en armas, hay embargo sobre el comercio de armas; **there is an ~ on that subject** está prohibido discutir ese asunto; **to lift an ~** levantar una prohibición; **to put an ~ on sth** prohibir el comercio de algo, (*fig*) prohibir el uso de algo.

2 *vt* prohibir; (*Jur*) embargar.

embark [ɪm'bɑːk] **1** *vt* embarcar. **2** *vi* embarcarse (*for* con rumbo a, *on* en); **to ~ upon** emprender, lanzarse a.

embarkation [,embɑː'keɪʃən] *n* embarco *m*, embarque *m*.

embarrass [ɪm'bærəs] *vt* desconcertar, turbar, azorar, apenar (*LAm*); (*deliberately*) poner en un aprieto; (*financially*) crear dificultades económicas a; **to be ~ed** sentirse violento, sentirse molesto, estar azorado; **to be financially ~ed** tener dificultades económicas, andar mal de dinero; **I was ~ed by the question** la pregunta me desconcertó; **I feel ~ed about it** me siento algo avergonzado por eso.

embarrassed [ɪm'bærəst] *adj*: **he said with an ~ laugh** dijo riéndose pero evidentemente molesto (*or* incómodo).

embarrassing [ɪm'bærəsɪŋ] *adj experience etc* embarazoso, desconcertante; *moment, situation* violento.

embarrassingly [ɪm'bærəsɪŋlɪ] *adv* de manera desconcertante; violentamente; **there were ~ few people** había tan pocas personas que resultaba desconcertante.

embarrassment [ɪm'bærəsmənt] *n* (**a**) (*state*) desconcierto *m*, turbación *f*, azoramiento *m*, pena *f* (*LAm*); **financial ~** apuros *mpl*, dificultades *fpl* económicas; **I am in a state of some ~** mi situación es algo delicada.

(**b**) (*object*) estorbo *m*; **you are an ~ to us all** eres un estorbo para todos nosotros.

embassy ['embəsɪ] *n* embajada *f*; **the Spanish E~** la embajada de España.

embattled [ɪm'bætld] *adj army* en orden de batalla; *city* sitiado.

embed [ɪm'bed] **1** *vt* empotrar; *weapon, teeth etc* clavar, hincar (*in* en); (*Ling*) incrustar. **2** *vr*: **to ~ itself in** empotrarse en.

embedding [ɪm'bedɪŋ] *n* (*gen, Ling*) incrustación *f*.

embellish [ɪm'belɪʃ] *vt* embellecer; (*fig, story etc*) adornar (*with* de).

embellishment [ɪm'belɪʃmənt] *n* embellecimiento *m*; (*fig*) adorno *m*.

embers ['embəz] *npl* rescoldo *m*, ascuas *fpl*.

embezzle [ɪm'bezl] *vt* malversar, desfalcar.

embezzlement [ɪm'bezlmənt] *n* malversación *f*, desfalco *m*.

embezzler [ɪm'bezləʳ] *n* malversador *m*, -ora *f*, desfalcador *m*, -ora *f*.

embitter [ɪm'bɪtəʳ] *vt* amargar; *relations etc* envenenar, amargar.

embittered [ɪm'bɪtəd] *adj* resentido, rencoroso; **to be very ~** estar muy amargado, estar muy resentido (*about* por, *against* contra).

embittering [ɪm'bɪtərɪŋ] *adj experience etc* amargo; que causa resentimiento.

emblazon [ɪm'bleɪzən] *vt* engalanar (*or* esmaltar) con colores brillantes; (*fig*) escribir de modo llamativo, adornar de modo llamativo; ensalzar.

emblem ['embləm] *n* emblema *m*.

emblematic [,emblɪ'mætɪk] *adj* emblemático.

embodiment [ɪm'bɒdɪmənt] *n* encarnación *f*, personificación *f*; **to be the very ~ of virtue** ser la misma virtud, ser la misma personificación de la virtud.

embody [ɪm'bɒdɪ] *vt* (**a**) *spirit, quality* encarnar, personificar; *idea etc* expresar. (**b**) (*include*) incorporar.

embolden [ɪm'bəʊldən] *vt* animar (*to* + *infin* a + *infin*), envalentonar (*to* + *infin* para que + *subj*).

embolism ['embəlɪzəm] *n* embolia *f*.

emboss [ɪm'bɒs] *vt* realzar; estampar en relieve; **~ed paper** papel *m* con nombre (*etc*) en relieve; **~ed with the royal arms** con el escudo real en relieve.

embouchure [,ɒmbʊ'ʃʊəʳ] *n* (*Mus*) boquilla *f*.

embrace [ɪm'breɪs] **1** *n* abrazo *m*.

2 *vt* (**a**) (*clasp*) abrazar, dar un abrazo a.

(**b**) (*include*) abarcar.

(**c**) *offer* aceptar; *opportunity* aprovechar; *course of action* adoptar; *doctrine, party* adherirse a; *profession* dedicarse a; *religion* convertirse a.

3 *vi* abrazarse.

embrasure [ɪm'breɪʒəʳ] *n* (*Archit*) alféizar *m*; (*Mil*) tronera *f*, aspillera *f*.

embrocation [,embrəʊ'keɪʃən] *n* embrocación *f*.

embroider [ɪm'brɔɪdəʳ] *vt* bordar, recamar; (*fig*) adornar con detalles ficticios.

embroidery [ɪm'brɔɪdərɪ] **1** *n* bordado *m*. **2** *attr*: **~ silk** seda *f* de bordar; **~ thread** hilo *m* de bordar.

embroil [ɪm'brɔɪl] *vt* embrollar, enredar; **to ~ sb with** indisponer a uno con; **to ~ A with B** mezclar a A con B; **to get ~ed in sth** enredarse en algo, hacerse un lío con algo.

embroilment [ɪm'brɔɪlmənt] *n* embrollo *m*.

embryo ['embrɪəʊ] **1** *n* embrión *m*; (*fig*) embrión *m*, germen *m*; **in ~** en embrión.

2 *attr* embrionario.

embryologist [,embrɪ'ɒledʒɪst] *n* embriólogo *m*, -a *f*.

embryology [,embrɪ'ɒlədʒɪ] *n* embriología *f*.

embryonic [,embrɪ'ɒnɪk] *adj* embrionario.

emcee* ['em'siː] (*US*) **1** *n* presentador *m*, animador *m*. **2** *vt* presentar; **to ~ a show** animar un espectáculo.

EMCF *n abbr of* **European Monetary Cooperation Fund** Fondo *m* Europeo de Cooperación Monetaria, FECOM *m*.

emend [ɪ'mend] *vt* enmendar.

emendation [,iːmen'deɪʃən] *n* enmienda *f*.

emerald ['emərəld] **1** *n* esmeralda *f*. **2** *adj* de color esmeralda, esmeraldino; **~ green** verde esmeralda; **the E~ Isle** la verde Irlanda.

emerge [ɪ'mɜːdʒ] *vi* salir (*from* de; *also fig*), aparecer, dejarse ver; (*problem etc*) surgir; **it ~s that ...** resulta que

...; **what has ~d from this inquiry?** ¿qué se saca de esta investigación?

emergence [ɪ'mɜːdʒəns] *n* salida *f*, aparición *f*.

emergency [ɪ'mɜːdʒənsɪ] **1** *n* emergencia *f*; crisis *f*; necesidad *f* urgente, necesidad *f* apremiante; estado *m* de excepción; situación *f* imprevista; **there is a national ~** existe una crisis nacional; **in an ~, in case of ~** en caso de urgencia; **to provide for emergencies** prevenirse contra toda eventualidad (*or* contingencia).

2 *attr* de urgencia, de emergencia; **~ blinkers** intermitentes *mpl* de emergencia; **~ brake** freno *m* de mano, freno *m* de auxilio; **~ case** caso *m* de emergencia; **~ centre** centro *m* de emergencia; **~ exit** salida *f* de urgencia, salida *f* de emergencia; **~ flasher** (*US Aut*) señales *fpl* de emergencia; **~ landing** aterrizaje *m* forzoso (*or* forzado); **~ lane** (*US*) andén *m*, arcén *m*; **~ measure** medida *f* de urgencia; **~ meeting** reunión *f* extraordinaria; **~ powers** poderes *mpl* extraordinarios; **~ ration** ración *f* de reserva; **~ service** (*Med*) urgencias *fpl*; **~ services** servicios *mpl* de emergencia; **~ stop** (*Aut*) parada *f* en seco; **~ supply** provisión *f* de reserva; **~ ward** sala *f* para casos de urgencia.

emergent [ɪ'mɜːdʒənt] *adj*, **emerging** [ɪ'mɜːdʒɪŋ] *adj* emergente.

emeritus [iː'merɪtəs] *adj* emeritus, jubilado.

emery ['emərɪ] **1** *n* esmeril *m*. **2** *attr*: **~ board** tabla *f* de esmeril; **~ cloth** tela *f* de esmeril; **~ paper** papel *m* de esmeril.

emetic [ɪ'metɪk] **1** *adj* emético, vomitivo. **2** *n* emético *m*, vomitivo *m*.

emigrant ['emɪgrənt] **1** *adj* emigrante. **2** *n* emigrante *mf*.

emigrate ['emɪgreɪt] *vi* emigrar.

emigration [,emɪ'greɪʃən] *n* emigración *f*.

émigré(e) ['emɪgreɪ] *n* emigrado *m*, -a *f*.

Emily ['emɪlɪ] *nf* Emilia.

eminence ['emɪnəns] *n* eminencia *f*; **His E~** Su Eminencia; **Your E~** Vuestra Eminencia.

eminent ['emɪnənt] *adj* eminente.

eminently ['emɪnəntlɪ] *adj* sumamente.

emir [e'mɪə^{r}] *n* emir *m*.

emirate [e'mɪərɪt] *n* emirato *m*.

emissary ['emɪsərɪ] *n* emisario *m*.

emission [ɪ'mɪʃən] *n* emisión *f*; **~ controls** controles *mpl* de emisiones.

emit [ɪ'mɪt] *vt light, signals etc* emitir; *smoke etc* arrojar; *smell* despedir; *cry* dar; *sound* producir.

emitter [ɪ'mɪtə^{r}] *n* (*Electronics*) emisor *m*.

Emmanuel [ɪ'mænjʊəl] *nm* Manuel.

Emmy ['emɪ] *n* (*US TV*) Emmy *m*.

emollient [ɪ'mɒlɪənt] **1** *adj* emoliente. **2** *n* emoliente *m*.

emolument [ɪ'mɒljʊmənt] *n* emolumento *m*.

emote* [ɪ'məʊt] *vi* actuar de una manera muy emocionada.

emotion [ɪ'məʊʃən] *n* emoción *f*.

emotional [ɪ'məʊʃənl] *adj* emocional; afectivo; emotivo; *moment* de honda emoción, muy emotivo; *person* (*warm-hearted*) sentimental, (*taking things too hard*) demasiado sensible, (*showing excessive emotion*) exaltado, exagerado; **~ tension** tensión *f* emocional; **an ~ farewell** una despedida emotiva; **to get ~** emocionarse.

emotionalism [ɪ'məʊʃnəlɪzəm] *n* emoción *f*, emotividad *f*; sentimentalismo *m*; (*in newspaper etc*) sensacionalismo *m*.

emotionally [ɪ'məʊʃnəlɪ] *adv* con emoción; **~ unstable** emocionalmente inestable.

emotionless [ɪ'məʊʃənlɪs] *adj* sin emoción.

emotive [ɪ'məʊtɪv] *adj* emotivo.

empanel [ɪm'pænl] *vt jury* seleccionar; **to ~ sb for a jury** inscribir a uno para jurado.

empathize ['empəθaɪz] *vi* sentir empatía (*with* con), empatizar(se) (*with* con).

empathy ['empəθɪ] *n* empatía *f*.

emperor ['empərə^{r}] *n* emperador *m*.

emphasis ['emfəsɪs] *n* énfasis *m*; **to lay** (*or* **put**) **~ on** subrayar; **the ~ is on sport** se le concede mucha importancia al deporte; **this year the ~ is on femininity** este año las modas hacen resaltar la feminidad.

emphasize ['emfəsaɪz] *vt* (*Gram*) acentuar; (*fig*) dar importancia a, subrayar, recalcar, enfatizar (*LAm*); **I must ~ that** ... tengo que subrayar que ...

emphatic [ɪm'fætɪk] *adj* enfático; *speech, condemnation etc* categórico, enérgico; *person* decidido; **he was most ~ that** ... dijo categóricamente que ...

emphatically [ɪm'fætɪkəlɪ] *adv* con énfasis; **yes, ~** sí, sin ningún género de dudas; **the answer is ~ no** bajo ningún concepto.

emphysema [emfɪ'siːmə] *n* enfisema *m*.

Empire ['empaɪə^{r}] *adj costume, furniture* estilo Imperio; **the ~ State** (*US*) el estado de Nueva York.

empire ['empaɪə^{r}] *n* imperio *m*.

empire-builder ['empaɪə,bɪldə^{r}] *n* (*fig*) constructor *m* de imperios.

empire-building ['empaɪə,bɪldɪŋ] *n* (*fig*) construcción *f* de imperios.

empiric(al) [em'pɪrɪk(əl)] *adj* empírico.

empiricism [em'pɪrɪsɪzəm] *n* empirismo *m*.

empiricist [em'pɪrɪsɪst] *n* empírico *m*.

emplacement [ɪm'pleɪsmənt] *n* (*Mil*) emplazamiento *m*.

emplane [ɪm'pleɪn] *vi* (*US*) subir al avión; embarcar (en avión).

employ [ɪm'plɔɪ] **1** *n*: **to be in the ~ of** trabajar por, (*as servant etc*) estar al servicio de. **2** *vt person* emplear; *thing* emplear, usar; *time* ocupar; **to be ~ed in** emplearse en.

employable [ɪm'plɔɪəbl] *adj person* que se puede emplear; *skill* útil, utilizable.

employee [,emplɔɪ'iː] *n* empleado *m*, -a *f*, dependiente *m*, -a *f*.

employer [ɪm'plɔɪə^{r}] *n* empresario *m*, -a *f*; patrón *m*, -ona *f*; **~s' organization** organización *f* patronal; **my ~** mi amo, mi jefe.

employment [ɪm'plɔɪmənt] *n* (**a**) (*act*) empleo *m*; uso *m*.

(**b**) (*job*) empleo *m*, colocación *f*, puesto *m*; ocupación *f*; **to be in ~** tener trabajo; **to give ~ to** emplear a; **to look for ~** buscar empleo, buscar colocación; **conditions of ~** condiciones *fpl* de empleo; **her ~ prospects are poor** tiene pocas posibilidades de colocarse; **~ agency** agencia *f* de colocaciones; **~ exchange** (*Brit*), **~ office** (*US*) bolsa *f* de trabajo.

(**c**) (*jobs collectively*) empleo *m*; **full ~** pleno empleo *m*; **a high level of ~** un alto nivel de trabajo; **Secretary** (**of State**) **for** (*or* **Minister of**) **E~** (*Brit*), **Secretary for E~** (*US*) Ministro *m* de Trabajo; **Department of E~** (*Brit*) Ministerio *m* de Trabajo; **~ statistics** estadística *f* del empleo.

emporium [em'pɔːrɪəm] *n* emporio *m*.

empower [ɪm'paʊə^{r}] *vt*: **to ~ sb to do sth** autorizar a uno a hacer algo.

empress ['emprɪs] *n* emperatriz *f*.

emptiness ['emptɪnɪs] *n* vacío *m*, lo vacío; (*of person's life*) vaciedad *f*, vacuidad *f*; **its ~ of moral content** su carencia de todo contenido moral.

empty ['emptɪ] **1** *adj* vacío; *house* desocupado; *place* desierto; *vehicle* vacío, sin carga; *post* vacante; *threat, words* vano, inútil; *phrase* hueco, sin significado real; **I'm ~** tengo hambre.

2 *n* (*gen pl*) envase *m*, botella *f* (*etc*) vacía; casco *m*; **V returnable.**

3 *vt contents* vaciar, verter; *container* vaciar, descargar; *place, room* dejar vacío; desocupar, desalojar.

4 *vi* vaciarse; (*vehicle*) quedar vacío; (*room etc*) quedar desocupado; (*place*) quedar desierto; **to ~ into** (*river*) desembocar en.

empty-handed ['emptɪ'hændɪd] *adj*: **to return ~** volver con las manos vacías, volver manivacío.

empty-headed ['emptɪ'hedɪd] *adj* casquivano.

EMS *n abbr of* **European Monetary System** Sistema *m* Monetario Europeo, SME *m*.

EMT *n abbr of* **emergency medical technician**.

emu ['iːmjuː] *n* dromeo *m*, emú *m*.

emulate ['emjʊleɪt] *vt* emular (*also Comput*).

emulator ['emjʊ,leɪtə^{r}] *n* (*Comput*) emulador *m*.

emulation [,emjʊ'leɪʃən] *n* emulación *f* (*also Comput*).

emulsifier [ɪ'mʌlsɪ,faɪə^{r}] *n* agente *m* emulsionador, emulsionante *m*.

emulsify [ɪ'mʌlsɪfaɪ] *vt* emulsionar.

emulsion [ɪ'mʌlʃən] *n* emulsión *f*; **~ (paint)** pintura *f* emulsionada.

enable [ɪ'neɪbl] *vt*: **to ~ sb to do sth** permitir a uno hacer algo, capacitar a uno para hacer algo, poner a uno en condiciones para hacer algo; **I am now ~d to go** ahora puedo ir.

enact [ɪ'nækt] *vt* (**a**) (*Jur*) decretar (*that* que); *law* promulgar. (**b**) (*perform*) *play, scene* representar; *part* hacer.

enactment [ɪ'næktmənt] *n* (**a**) promulgación *f*. (**b**) representación *f*.

enamel [ɪ'næməl] **1** *n* esmalte *m*. **2** *attr*: **~ paint** pintura *f* esmaltada. **3** *vt* esmaltar, pintar al esmalte.

enamelled, (*US*) **enameled** [ɪ'næməld] *adj* esmaltado.

enamelling, (*US*) **enameling** [ɪ'næməlɪŋ] *n* esmaltado *m*.

enamelware [ɪ'næməlwεə^r] *n* utensilios *mpl* de hierro esmaltado.
enamour, (*US*) **enamor** [ɪ'næmə^r] *vt*: **to be ~ed of** *person* estar enamorado de, *thing* estar entusiasmado con.
enc. *abbr of* **enclosure(s), enclosed** adjunto.
encamp [ɪn'kæmp] *vi* acamparse.
encampment [ɪn'kæmpmənt] *n* campamento *m*.
encapsulate [ɪn'kæpsjʊleɪt] *vt* (*fig*) resumir, encerrar, encapsular.
encase [ɪn'keɪs] *vt* encerrar; (*Tech*) revestir; **to be ~d in** estar revestido de.
encash [ɪn'kæʃ] *vt* cobrar, hacer efectivo.
encashment [ɪn'kæʃmənt] *n* cobro *m*.
encephalitis [,ensefə'laɪtɪs] *n* encefalitis *f*.
encephalogram [ɪn'sefələgræm] *n* encefalograma *m*.
enchain [ɪn'tʃeɪn] *vt* encadenar.
enchant [ɪn'tʃɑːnt] *vt* encantar (*also fig*); **we were ~ed with the place** el sitio nos encantó.
enchanter [ɪn'tʃɑːntə^r] *n* hechicero *m*.
enchanting [ɪn'tʃɑːntɪŋ] *adj* encantador.
enchantingly [ɪn'tʃɑːntɪŋlɪ] *adv* de manera encantadora, deliciosamente.
enchantment [ɪn'tʃɑːntmənt] *n* (*act*) encantamiento *m*; (*charm*) encanto *m*; **it lent ~ to the scene** aumentó el encanto de la escena.
enchantress [ɪn'tʃɑːntrɪs] *n* hechicera *f*.
encircle [ɪn'sɜːkl] *vt* rodear (*with* de); (*Mil*) envolver; *waist, shoulders etc* ceñir; **it is ~d by a wall** está rodeado de una tapia.
encirclement [ɪn'sɜːklmənt] *n* (*Mil*) envolvimiento *m*.
encircling [ɪn'sɜːklɪŋ] *adj movement* envolvente.
encl. *abbr of* **enclosure(s), enclosed** adjunto.
enclave ['enkleɪv] *n* enclave *m*.
enclitic [ɪn'klɪtɪk] *adj* enclítico.
enclose [ɪn'kləʊz] *vt* (**a**) *land, garden* cercar (*with* de); (*put in a receptacle*) meter, encerrar; (*include*) encerrar.
(**b**) (*with letter*) remitir adjunto, adjuntar, acompañar; **~d herewith please find ...** le mandamos adjunto ...; **the ~d letter** la carta adjunta.
enclosure [ɪn'kləʊʒə^r] *n* (**a**) (*act*) cercamiento *m*; (*place*) cercado *m*, recinto *m*. (**b**) (*in letter*) carta *f* adjunta, carta *f* inclusa.
encode [ɪn'kəʊd] *vt* codificar; (*Ling*) cifrar.
encoder [ɪn'kəʊdə^r] *n* (*Comput*) codificador *m*.
encoding [ɪn'kəʊdɪŋ] *n* (*Comput, Ling*) codificación *f*.
encomium [ɪn'kəʊmɪəm] *n* elogio *m*, encomio *m*.
encompass [ɪn'kʌmpəs] *vt* (**a**) (*surround*) cercar, rodear (*with* de). (**b**) (*include*) abarcar. (**c**) (*bring about*) lograr; (*pej*) lograr, efectuar.
encore [ɒŋ'kɔː^r] **1** *interj* ¡otra!, ¡bis!
2 *n* bis *m*, repetición *f*; **to call for an ~** pedir una repetición; **to give an ~** repetir algo a petición del público, dar un bis; **to sing a song as an ~** bisar una canción.
3 *vt song* pedir la repetición de, *person* pedir una repetición a.
encounter [ɪn'kaʊntə^r] **1** *n* encuentro *m*; **~ group** grupo *m* de encuentro. **2** *vt* encontrar, encontrarse con; *difficulty etc* tropezar con.
encourage [ɪn'kʌrɪdʒ] *vt person* animar, alentar, dar aliento a; *industry* fomentar, estimular; *growth* estimular; (*in a belief*) fortalecer, reforzar; **to ~ sb to do sth** animar a uno a hacer algo.
encouragement [ɪn'kʌrɪdʒmənt] *n* (*act*) estímulo *m*, (*of industry*) fomento *m*; (*support*) aliento *m*, ánimo(s) *m(pl)*, aprobación *f*; **to give ~ to** infundir ánimo(s) a, dar aliento a; **to give ~ to the enemy** dar aliento al enemigo.
encouraging [ɪn'kʌrɪdʒɪŋ] *adj* alentador, esperanzador; favorable, halagüeño; **it is not an ~ prospect** es una perspectiva nada halagüeña; **he was always very ~** siempre me daba aliento.
encouragingly [ɪn'kʌrɪdʒɪŋlɪ] *adv* favorablemente; *speak etc* en tono alentador.
encroach [ɪn'krəʊtʃ] *vi* avanzar; **to ~ on** *rights* usurpar; *land* (*of neighbour*) invadir, pasar los límites de; *land* (*by sea*) hurtar, invadir; *person's subject* invadir; *time* ocupar, quitar, llevar (una parte cada vez mayor de).
encroachment [ɪn'krəʊtʃmənt] *n* usurpación *f* (*on* de); invasión *f* (*on* de); abuso *m* (*on* de); **this new ~ on our liberty** esta nueva usurpación de nuestra libertad.
encrust [ɪn'krʌst] *vt* incrustar (*with* de).
encrustation [,ɪnkrʌs'teɪʃn] *n* incrustación *f*.
encrusted [ɪn'krʌstɪd] *adj*: **~ with** incrustado de.
encrypt [ɪn'krɪpt] *vt* codificar.
encryption [ɪn'krɪpʃən] *n* codificación *f*.
encumber [ɪn'kʌmbə^r] *vt person, movement* estorbar; (*with debts*) gravar, cargar; *place* llenar (*with* de); **to be ~ed with** tener que cargar con, (*debts*) estar gravado de.
encumbrance [ɪn'kʌmbrəns] *n* estorbo *m*; (*of debt*) carga *f*, gravamen *m*; **without ~** sin familia.
encyclical [en'sɪklɪkəl] *n* encíclica *f*.
encyclopaedia, encyclopedia [en,saɪkləʊ'piːdɪə] *n* enciclopedia *f*.
encyclopaedic, encyclopedic [en,saɪkləʊ'piːdɪk] *adj* enciclopédico.
end [end] **1** *n* (**a**) (*in physical sense*) (*of street etc*) final *m*; (*of line, table etc*) extremo *m*; (*of rope etc*) cabo *m*; (*point*) punta *f*; (*of estate etc*) límite *m*; (*Sport*) lado *m*; (*of town*) parte *f*, zona *f*, barrio *m*; **the ~s of the earth** los confines del mundo; **at the ~ of** al cabo de, en el extremo de; al final de; **from one ~ to the other, from ~ to ~** de un extremo a otro; **on ~** de punta, de cabeza, de canto; **~ to ~** juntando los dos extremos; **to be at the ~ of one's tether** estar casi completamente agotado; no poder más; **to change ~s** (*Sport*) cambiar de lado; **to get hold of the wrong ~ of the stick** tomar el rábano por las hojas; **to keep one's ~ up** defenderse bien; **to make both ~s meet** hacer llegar el dinero; poder llegar a fin de mes; **to read a book to the very ~** leer un libro hasta el mismo final; **to stand on ~** (*hair*) erizarse, *object* poner de punta; **to start at the wrong ~** empezar por el fin.
(**b**) (*of time, process, resources*) fin *m*, final *m*; término *m*, conclusión *f*; límite *m*; (*of book etc*) desenlace *m*, conclusión *f*; **the ~ of the empire** el fin del imperio; **that was the ~ of him** así terminó él; **it's not the ~ of the world** no es ningún desastre; **at the ~ of the day** (*fig*) a la larga; al fin y al cabo; **at the ~ of 3 months** al cabo de 3 meses; **at the ~ of the century** a fines del siglo; **in the ~** al fin, por fin, finalmente; **no ~ of*** la mar de*; **no ~ of an expert** sumamente experto, más experto que nadie; **it caused no ~ of trouble** causó la mar de problemas; **3 days on ~** 3 días seguidos; **for days on ~** día tras día, durante una infinidad de días; **towards the ~ of** hacia el final de, *century etc* hacia fines de; **to be at an ~** estar terminando, (*be all over*) haber terminado ya; **to be at the ~ of one's resources** haber agotado los recursos; **there's no ~ to it all** esto no tiene fin, esto es inacabable; **to bring to an ~** terminar; clausurar; **to come** (*or* **draw**) **to an ~** terminarse; **to come to a bad ~** tener mal fin, ir a acabar mal; **that's the ~ of the matter, that's an ~ to the matter** asunto concluido; **you'll never hear the ~ of it** esto no se olvidará pronto, esto no es fácil que se olvide; **to make an ~ of, to put an ~ to** acabar con, poner fin a; **to meet one's ~** encontrar la muerte; **we see no ~ to it** no entrevemos posibilidad alguna de que termine; **to think no ~ of sb** tener un muy alto concepto de uno; **that movie is the ~!*** (*US*) esa película es el no va más.
(**c**) (*remnant*) cabo *m*; resto *m*; pedazo *m*.
(**d**) (*aim*) fin *m*, objeto *m*, propósito *m*, intención *f*; **to this ~, with this ~ in view** con este propósito; **to the ~ that ...** a fin de que + *subj*; **with what ~?** ¿para qué?; **the ~ justifies the means** el fin justifica los medios; **to gain one's ~s** salirse con la suya.
2 *adj* final; **~-all** *V* **be-all**; **~ game** (*Chess*) fase *f* final; **the ~ house** la última casa; **~ line** (*Basketball*) línea *f* de fondo; **~ note** nota *f* final; **~ product** producto *m* final; **~ result** resultado *m* final.
3 *vt* terminar, acabar; *abuse etc* acabar con; *book* concluir; **to ~ it all** terminarlo del todo; (*kill o.s.*) suicidarse.
4 *vi* terminar, acabar; **to ~ by saying** terminar diciendo; **to ~ in** terminar en; **to ~ with** terminar con.
◆**end off** *vt* poner fin a.
◆**end up** *vi* terminar, acabar; **to ~ up at** parar en.
endanger [ɪn'deɪndʒə^r] *vt* poner en peligro; arriesgar; exponer, aventurar; **~ed species** especie *f* en peligro (de extinción).
endear [ɪn'dɪə^r] **1** *vt*: **this did not ~ him to the public** esto no le granjeó las simpatías del público. **2** *vr*: **to ~ o.s. to** hacerse querer de (*or* por).
endearing [ɪn'dɪərɪŋ] *adj* simpático, entrañable.
endearingly [ɪn'dɪərɪŋlɪ] *adv* encantadoramente.
endearment [ɪn'dɪəmənt] *n* palabra *f* cariñosa, ternura *f*.
endeavour, (*US*) **endeavor** [ɪn'devə^r] **1** *n* (*attempt*) esfuerzo *m* (*to do* por hacer), tentativa *f* (*to do* de hacer); (*striving*) empeño *m*, esfuerzos *mpl*; **in spite of my best ~s** a pesar de todos mis esfuerzos; **to use every ~ to** + *infin* no regatear esfuerzo para + *infin*.
2 *vi*: **to ~ to do** esforzarse por hacer, procurar hacer.
endemic [en'demɪk] *adj* endémico.

ending ['endɪŋ] *n* (**a**) (*gen*) fin *m*, conclusión *f*; (*of book etc*) desenlace *m*; **the tale has a happy ~** el cuento tiene un desenlace feliz. (**b**) (*Ling*) terminación *f*, desinencia *f*.
endive ['endaɪv] *n* escarola *f*, endibia *f*.
endless ['endlɪs] *adj* interminable, inacabable; *screw etc* sin fin.
endlessly ['endlɪslɪ] *adv* interminablemente, sin parar.
endocrine ['endəʊkraɪn] **1** *adj* endocrino; **~ gland** glándula *f* endocrina. **2** *n* endocrina *f*.
endocrinologist [,endəʊkraɪ'nɒlədʒɪst] *n* endocrinólogo *m*, -a *f*.
endodontics [,endəʊ'dɒntɪks] *n sing* endodoncia *f*.
endogenous [,en'dɒdʒɪnəs] *adj* endógeno.
endomorf ['endəʊ,mɔːf] *n* endomorfo *m*.
endorse [ɪn'dɔːs] *vt* endosar; (*Brit*) *licence* poner nota de una sanción en, dejar constancia de sanción en; (*fig*) aprobar, confirmar, ratificar.
endorsee [ɪn,dɔː'siː] *n* endosatorio *m*, -a *f*.
endorsement [ɪn'dɔːsmənt] *n* endoso *m*; (*Brit*: *in licence*) nota *f* de sanción; (*fig*) aprobación *f*, confirmación *f*.
endorser [ɪn'dɔːsə^r] *n* endosante *mf*.
endow [ɪn'daʊ] *vt* dotar (*with* con, (*fig*) de); *institution* fundar, crear; **to be ~ed with** (*fig*) estar dotado de.
endowment [ɪn'daʊmənt] **1** *n* (**a**) (*act*) dotación *f*; (*creation*) fundación *f*, creación *f*. (**b**) (*amount*) dotación *f*. (**c**) (*fig*) dote *f*, cualidad *f*, talento *m*. **2** *attr*: **~ assurance, ~ insurance** (*US*) seguro *m* dotal; **~ mortgage** hipoteca *f* dotal; **~ policy** seguro *m* mixto.
endpaper ['endpeɪpə^r] *n* guarda *f*.
endue [ɪn'djuː] *vt* dotar (*with* de).
endurable [ɪn'djʊərəbl] *adj* aguantable, tolerable, soportable.
endurance [ɪn'djʊərəns] *n* resistencia *f*, aguante *m*; **beyond ~, past ~** intolerable; **to have great powers of ~** tener gran resistencia; **~ race** carrera *f* de resistencia; **~ test** prueba *f* de resistencia.
endure [ɪn'djʊə^r] **1** *vt* aguantar, soportar, tolerar; resistir; **I can't ~ him** no le aguanto, no le puedo ver; **I can't ~ it a moment longer** no lo aguanto un momento más; **I can't ~ being corrected** no tolero que me corrijan; **I can't ~ being too hot** no resisto el calor excesivo.
2 *vi* (*last*) durar, perdurar; (*not give in*) aguantar, resistir, sufrir sin rendirse.
enduring [ɪn'djʊərɪŋ] *adj* permanente, perdurable.
end-user ['end'juːzə^r] *n* usuario *m*, -a *f* final.
endways ['endweɪz] *adv* de punta; de lado, de canto.
ENE *abbr of* **east-north-east** estenordeste, ENE.
enema ['enɪmə] *n* enema *f*.
enemy ['enɪmɪ] **1** *adj* enemigo; **~ alien** extranjero *m* enemigo, extranjera *f* enemiga. **2** *n* enemigo *m*, -a *f*; **the ~ within** el enemigo interior; **to be one's own worst ~** ser enemigo de sí mismo.
enemy-occupied [,enəmɪ'ɒkjʊpaɪd] *adj*: **~ territory** territorio *m* ocupado por el enemigo.
energetic [,enə'dʒetɪk] *adj* enérgico; *person etc* enérgico, activo; *protest* vigoroso.
energetically [,enə'dʒetɪkəlɪ] *adv* enérgicamente; activamente; vigorosamente.
energize ['enədʒaɪz] *vt* activar, energizar, dar energía a.
energizing ['enədʒaɪzɪŋ] *adj food* energético.
energy ['enədʒɪ] **1** *n* energía *f*; vigor *m*; **Secretary (of State) for** (*cr* **Minister of**) **E~** (*Brit*) Secretario *m* (de Estado) (*or* Ministro *m*) de Energía.
2 *attr* energético; **~ conservation** conservación *f* de la energía, ahorro *m* energético; **~ crisis** crisis *f* energética; **~-giving** *food etc* energético; **~-intensive industry** industria *f* consumidora de gran cantidad de energía; **~ level** nivel *m* energético; **~ needs** necesidades *fpl* energéticas, requisitos *mpl* energéticos; **~ policy** política *f* de energía; **~ resources** recursos *mpl* energéticos.
energy-saving ['enədʒɪ,seɪvɪŋ] **1** *n* ahorro *m* de energía. **2** *attr device* que ahorra energía; *policy* para ahorrar energía.
enervate ['enɜːveɪt] *vt* enervar, debilitar.
enervating ['enɜːveɪtɪŋ] *adj* enervador; deprimente.
enfeeble [ɪn'fiːbl] *vt* debilitar.
enfeeblement [ɪn'fiːblmənt] *n* debilitación *f*.
enfilade [,enfɪ'leɪd] *vt* enfilar.
enfold [ɪn'fəʊld] *vt* envolver; (*in arms*) abrazar, estrechar (en los brazos).
enforce [ɪn'fɔːs] *vt law* hacer cumplir, (*from a date*) aplicar, poner en vigor; *claim* hacer valer; *rights* hacer respetar; *demand* insistir en; *sentence* ejecutar; *obedience, will* imponer (*on* a).
enforceable [ɪn'fɔːsəbl] *adj laws, rules* ejecutable, que se puede hacer cumplir.
enforced [ɪn'fɔːst] *adj* inevitable; forzoso, forzado.
enforcement [ɪn'fɔːsmənt] *n* aplicación *f*; ejecución *f*.
enfranchise [ɪn'frænʃaɪz] *vt* (*free*) emancipar; *slave* manumitir; *voter* conceder el derecho de votar a.
enfranchisement [ɪn'frænʃɪzmənt] *n* emancipación *f* (*of* de); concesión *f* del derecho de votar (*of* a).
Eng. (**a**) *abbr of* **England** Inglaterra *f*. (**b**) *abbr of* **English** inglés *m and adj*.
engage [ɪn'geɪdʒ] **1** *vt attention* llamar, atraer; ocupar; *taxi etc* alquilar; *servant* tomar a su servicio; *person in conversation* abordar (entablando conversación con), (*and delay*) entretener; *workmen* apalabrar, ajustar; *lawyer etc* requerir los servicios de; *enemy* atacar, trabar batalla con; (*Mech*) *cog etc* engranar con, *coupling* acoplar, *gear* meter; **to ~ to do sth** comprometerse a hacer algo.
2 *vi* (*Mech*) engranar.
3 *vr*: **to ~ o.s. to do sth** comprometerse a hacer algo.
◆**engage in** *vt* dedicarse a, ocuparse en; *sport etc* tomar parte en.
◆**engage with** *vt* (*Mech*) engranar con.
engagé [ɑ̃ːŋgæ'ʒeɪ] *adj writer etc* comprometido.
engaged [ɪn'geɪdʒd] *adj* (**a**) **to be ~** (*seat*) estar ocupado; (*person*) estar ocupado; tener compromiso; no estar libre; (*Brit*: *toilet*) estar ocupado.
(**b**) (*Brit Telec*) **to be ~** estar comunicando, estar ocupado (*LAm*); **~ signal, ~ tone** señal *f* de estar comunicando.
(**c**) **to be ~ in** estar ocupado en, dedicarse a; **what are you ~ in?** ¿a qué se dedica Vd?
(**d**) **to be ~** (**to be married**) estar prometido; (*2 persons*) estar prometidos, ser novios, tener relaciones formales; **they've been ~ for 2 years** llevan 2 años de relaciones formales; **to get ~** prometerse (*to* con); **the ~ couple** los novios.
(**e**) *writer etc* comprometido.
engagement [ɪn'geɪdʒmənt] **1** *n* (**a**) (*contract*) contrato *m*; obligación *f*; **to enter into an ~ to** + *infin* comprometerse a + *infin*.
(**b**) (*appointment*) compromiso *m*, cita *f*; **have you an ~ tonight?** ¿tienes compromiso para esta noche?; **I have an ~ at 10** tengo una cita a las 10; **owing to a previous ~** por tener compromiso anterior.
(**c**) (*Mil*) combate *m*, acción *f*.
(**d**) (*to marry*) compromiso *m*; (*period etc*) noviazgo *m*; **they have announced their ~** han anunciado su compromiso, se han dado palabra de casamiento; **the ~ is announced of Miss A to Mr B** los señores de A tienen el placer de comunicar que por los señores de B ha sido pedida la mano de su encantadora hija Isabel para su hijo Juan.
2 *attr*: **~ book, ~ diary** dietario *m*; agenda *f* de trabajo; **~ party** fiesta *f* de compromiso; **~ ring** anillo *m* de prometida, anillo *m* de compromiso (*note*: *Spanish equivalent is usually a bracelet*, pulsera *f* de pedido).
engaging [ɪn'geɪdʒɪŋ] *adj* atractivo, simpático; *enthusiasm etc* contagioso.
engender [ɪn'dʒendə^r] *vt* engendrar; (*fig*) engendrar, suscitar, motivar.
engine ['endʒɪn] **1** *n* (**a**) (*gen*) motor *m*. (**b**) (*Rail*) máquina *f*, locomotora *f*; **back to the ~** de espaldas a la máquina; **facing the ~** de frente a la máquina. **2** *attr*: **~ failure, ~ trouble** avería *f* del motor.
engine-block ['endʒɪn,blɒk] *n* (*Aut*) bloque *m* del motor.
-engined ['endʒɪnd] *adj eg* **four~** de cuatro motores, cuatrimotor, tetramotor; **petrol~** propulsado por gasolina.
engine-driver ['endʒɪn,draɪvə^r] *n* (*Brit*) maquinista *m*.
engineer [,endʒɪ'nɪə^r] **1** *n* ingeniero *m*, -a *f*; mecánico *mf*; (*US Rail*) maquinista *m*; *V* **civil** *etc*. **2** *vt* (*pej*) tramar, gestionar, lograr.
engineering [,endʒɪ'nɪərɪŋ] **1** *n* ingeniería *f*. **2** *attr*: **~ factory** fábrica *f* de maquinaria; **~ industry** industria *f* de ingeniería; **~ works** taller *m* de ingeniería.
engine-room ['endʒɪnrʊm] *n* sala *f* de máquinas.
engine-shed ['endʒɪn,ʃed] *n* (*Brit Rail*) cochera *f* de tren.
England ['ɪŋglənd] *n* Inglaterra *f*.
English ['ɪŋglɪʃ] **1** *adj* inglés; **~ breakfast** desayuno *m* inglés, desayuno *m* a la inglesa; **~ horn** corno *m* inglés.
2 *n* (**a**) **the ~** los ingleses.
(**b**) (*Ling*) inglés *m*; **Old ~** inglés *m* antiguo; **King's ~, Queen's ~** inglés *m* correcto; **~ speaker** anglófono *m*, -a *f*, anglohablante *mf*; **in plain ~** sin rodeos, en buen romance; **~ as a Foreign Language** inglés *m* para extranjeros; **~ as a**

Second Language inglés *m* como segunda lengua; ~ **for Special Purposes** inglés *m* para fines específicos; ~ **Language Teaching** enseñanza *f* del inglés.

English Channel ['ɪŋglɪʃ'tʃænl] *n* Canal *m* de la Mancha.

Englishman ['ɪŋglɪʃmən] *n, pl* **Englishmen** ['ɪŋglɪʃmən] inglés *m*.

English-speaking ['ɪŋglɪʃ,spiːkɪŋ] *adj* anglófono, anglohablante, de habla inglesa.

Englishwoman ['ɪŋglɪʃ,wʊmən] *n, pl* **Englishwomen** ['ɪŋglɪʃ,wɪmɪn] inglesa *f*.

engrave [ɪn'greɪv] *vt* grabar (*also fig*: *on* en); burilar.

engraver [ɪn'greɪvə^{r}] *n* grabador *m*.

engraving [ɪn'greɪvɪŋ] *n* grabado *m*.

engross [ɪn'grəʊs] *vt* (**a**) *attention, person* absorber; **to be ~ed in** estar entregado a, estar absorto en; **to become ~ed in** dedicarse por completo a. (**b**) (*Jur*) copiar.

engrossing [ɪn'grəʊsɪŋ] *adj* absorbente.

engulf [ɪn'gʌlf] *vt* tragar; sumergir, hundir; **to be ~ed by** quedar sumergido bajo.

enhance [ɪn'hɑːns] *vt* realzar, intensificar, aumentar; *price etc* aumentar.

enhancement [ɪn'hɑːnsmənt] *n* realce *m*, intensificación *f*; aumento *m*, incremento *m*.

enigma [ɪ'nɪgmə] *n* enigma *m*.

enigmatic [,enɪg'mætɪk] *adj* enigmático.

enigmatically [,enɪg'mætɪkəlɪ] *adv* enigmáticamente.

enjambement [ɪn'dʒæmmənt] *n* encabalgamiento *m*.

enjoin [ɪn'dʒɔɪn] *vt*: **to ~ sth on sb** imponer algo a uno; **to ~ sb to do sth** ordenar a uno hacer algo; **to ~ sb from doing sth** (*US*) prohibir a uno hacer algo.

enjoy [ɪn'dʒɔɪ] **1** *vt* (**a**) (*have use of*) *health, possession etc* disfrutar de, gozar de; *income, sb's confidence* tener; *advantage* poseer.

(**b**) (*take delight in*) *meal* comer con gusto; *pipe* fumar con fruición; **~ your meal!** ¡que aproveche!; **I ~ed the book** me gustó el libro; **did you ~ the game?** ¿te gustó el partido?, ¿qué tal el partido?; **I ~ reading** me gusta leer, me gusta la lectura; **I hope you ~ your holiday** que lo pases muy bien en las vacaciones; que te diviertas mucho en las vacaciones; **the author did not mean his book to be ~ed exactly** el autor no quería que su libro resultase meramente divertido.

2 *vr*: **to ~ o.s.** pasarlo bien, divertirse; **~ yourselves!** ¡que lo paséis bien!; **we ~ed ourselves tremendously** lo pasamos en grande, nos divertimos la mar de bien; **he ~ed himself chasing the girls** se divirtió persiguiendo a las chicas.

enjoyable [ɪn'dʒɔɪəbl] *adj* agradable; (*amusing*) divertido.

enjoyment [ɪn'dʒɔɪmənt] *n* (**a**) (*use*) disfrute *m*; posesión *f*. (**b**) (*delight*) placer *m*, fruición *f*; **he listened with real ~** escuchó con verdadero placer.

enlarge [ɪn'lɑːdʒ] **1** *vt* extender, aumentar, ensanchar; (*Phot*) ampliar; (*Med*) dilatar; *business* extender, ampliar; **~d heart** dilatación *f* del corazón; **~d edition** edición *f* aumentada.

2 *vi* extenderse, aumentarse; **to ~ upon** extenderse sobre, ampliar la referencia a, explicar con más detalles.

enlargement [ɪn'lɑːdʒmənt] *n* extensión *f*, aumento *m*, ensanche *m*; (*Phot*) ampliación *f*.

enlarger [ɪn'lɑːdʒə^{r}] *n* (*Phot*) ampliadora *f*.

enlighten [ɪn'laɪtn] *vt* (**a**) (*inform*) informar, instruir; **can you ~ me?** ¿puede ayudarme?; **I was able to ~ him about it** pude darle informes sobre este asunto. (**b**) (*civilize*) ilustrar, iluminar.

enlightened [ɪn'laɪtnd] *adj* ilustrado, culto; bien informado; *despot* ilustrado; *attitude etc* comprensivo, inteligente.

enlightening [ɪn'laɪtnɪŋ] *adj* informativo, lleno de datos útiles; *experience etc* instructivo.

enlightenment [ɪn'laɪtnmənt] *n* ilustración *f*; aclaración *f*; *V* **age**.

enlist [ɪn'lɪst] **1** *vt* (*Mil*) alistar, reclutar; *support etc* conseguir; **~ed man** (*US*) soldado *m* (*etc*) que no es oficial, soldado *m* raso. **2** *vi* alistarse (*in* en).

enlistment [ɪn'lɪstmənt] *n* alistamiento *m*.

enliven [ɪn'laɪvn] *vt* avivar, animar.

en masse [ɑ̃ːŋ'mæs] *adv* en masa.

enmesh [ɪn'meʃ] *vt* coger en una red; **to get ~ed in** enredarse en.

enmity ['enmɪtɪ] *n* enemistad *f*.

ennoble [ɪ'nəʊbl] *vt* ennoblecer.

ennui [ɑ̃ː'nwiː] *n* tedio *m*, aburrimiento *m*.

enology [iː'nɒlədʒɪ] *etc* (*US*) = **oenology** *etc*.

enormity [ɪ'nɔːmɪtɪ] *n* enormidad *f*.

enormous [ɪ'nɔːməs] *adj* enorme.

enormously [ɪ'nɔːməslɪ] *adv* enormemente.

enough [ɪ'nʌf] **1** *adv* bastante, suficientemente; **not big ~** no suficientemente grande; **she sings well ~** canta bastante bien; *V* **good, sure** *etc*.

2 *adj* bastante, suficiente; **I hadn't ~ money to buy it** no tuve bastante dinero para comprarlo.

3 *n*: **that's ~, thanks** con eso basta, gracias; ya está bien, gracias; **that's ~ now!** ¡basta ya!; **it is ~ for us to know that ...** nos basta saber que ...; **there's more than ~ for all** hay más que suficiente para todos; **~ is ~** bueno está lo bueno, basta y sobra; **~ is as good as a feast** rogar a Dios por santos mas no por tantos; **it was ~ to drive you mad** era para volverse loco; **as if that weren't ~** por si fuera poco; **we have ~ to live on** tenemos lo suficiente para vivir, tenemos con qué vivir; **one can never have ~ of his music** es imposible escuchar demasiado su música; **I've had ~ of him** estoy harto de él; **tell me when you've had ~** dime en cuanto te empieces a cansar; **I had ~ to do to find one** me costó trabajo encontrar uno.

4 *interj*: **~ of this!** ¡basta ya!, ¡concluyamos de una vez!

enquire [ɪn'kwaɪə^{r}] *etc* = **inquire**.

enrage [ɪn'reɪdʒ] *vt* enfurecer, hacer rabiar; **to be ~d with pain** rabiar de dolor.

enrapture [ɪn'ræptʃə^{r}] *vt* embelesar, arrebatar, extasiar.

enrich [ɪn'rɪtʃ] *vt* enriquecer; *soil* fertilizar.

enriched [ɪn'rɪtʃt] *adj food etc* enriquecido.

enrichment [ɪn'rɪtʃmənt] *n* enriquecimiento *m*; fertilización *f*.

enrol, (*US*) **enroll** [ɪn'rəʊl] **1** *vt member* registrar, inscribir; *student* matricular; (*Mil*) alistar. **2** *vi* inscribirse; matricularse; alistarse; **to ~ for a course** matricularse para un curso.

enrolment, (*US*) **enrollment** [ɪn'rəʊlmənt] *n* inscripción *f*; matrícula *f*; alistamiento *m*.

en route [ɑ̃ː*n*'ruːt] *adv* en el camino; **to be ~ for** ir camino de, ir con rumbo a, dirigirse a; **it was stolen ~** lo robaron durante el viaje.

ensconce [ɪn'skɒns] *vr*: **to ~ o.s.** instalarse cómodamente, acomodarse; **to be ~d in** estar cómodamente instalado en.

ensemble [ɑ̃ː*n*sɑ̃ː*m*bl] *n* (*whole*) conjunto *m*; (*general effect*) impresión *f* de conjunto; (*dress*) conjunto *m*; (*Mus*) conjunto *m* (musical), agrupación *f*.

enshrine [ɪn'ʃraɪn] *vt* (*fig*) encerrar, englobar.

ensign ['ensaɪn] *n* (**a**) (*flag*) bandera *f*; **Red E~** (*Brit*) Enseña *f* Roja (*bandera de la marina mercante británica*); **White E~** (*Brit*) Enseña *f* Blanca (*bandera de la marina de guerra británica*). (**b**) (*rank*) alférez *m*.

enslave [ɪn'sleɪv] *vt* esclavizar; (*fig*) dominar.

enslavement [ɪn'sleɪvmənt] *n* esclavitud *f*.

ensnare [ɪn'snɛə^{r}] *vt* entrampar, coger en una trampa (*also fig*).

ensue [ɪn'sjuː] *vi* (*follow*) seguirse; (*happen*) sobrevenir; (*result*) resultar (*from* de).

ensuing [ɪn'sjuːɪŋ] *adj* consiguiente, subsiguiente, resultante.

en suite [ɑ̃'swiːt] *adj*: **with bathroom ~, with an ~ bathroom** con baño adjunto.

ensure [ɪn'ʃʊə^{r}] *vt* asegurar.

ENT *n* (*Med*) *abbr of* **ear, nose and throat** otorrinolaringología *f*.

entail [ɪn'teɪl] **1** *n* vínculo *m*.

2 *vt* (**a**) (*necessitate*) imponer; (*imply*) suponer; (*bring in its train*) acarrear; **it ~s a lot of work** supone mucho trabajo para nosotros; **it ~ed buying a new car** nos obligó a comprar un nuevo coche; **what does the job ~?** ¿cuáles son las funciones del puesto?

(**b**) (*Jur*) vincular.

entangle [ɪn'tæŋgl] *vt* enredar, enmarañar; **to get ~d in an affair** quedar enredado en un asunto; **to get ~d with sb** meterse en un lío con uno.

entanglement [ɪn'tæŋglmənt] *n* enredo *m*, embrollo *m*; (*love affair*) aventura *f* amorosa; (*Mil*) alambrada *f*; **to keep out of ~s** no meterse en líos.

entente [ɑ̃ː*n*'tɑ̃ː*n*t] *n* (*Pol*) entente *f*, trato *m* secreto.

enter ['entə^{r}] **1** *vt* (**a**) (*go into*) entrar en; penetrar en; *hospital* ingresar en; **it never ~ed my head** jamás se me pasó por la cabeza.

(**b**) (*fig*) *society* ingresar en, hacerse socio de; *army* alistarse en; *college, school* matricularse en.

(**c**) (*write down*) *note* anotar, apuntar; *name etc* escribir; *member* inscribir, matricular; *record* asentar, anotar, dar entrada a, registrar; *data* (*Comput*) introducir; *claim, request* presentar, formular; *order* (*Comm*) asentar; *protest* formular; **to ~ a horse for a race** inscribir un caballo para una carrera; **to ~ one's son for Eton** apuntar (*or* inscribir) a su hijo para Eton (como futuro alumno); **to ~ a dog for a show** inscribir un perro en un concurso canino.

2 *vi* (**a**) entrar; (*Theat*) entrar en escena; **~ Macbeth** sale Macbeth; **'Do not ~'** (*US*) 'se prohíbe la entrada', (*Aut*) 'dirección prohibida'.

(**b**) **to ~ for** *competition, race* participar en, tomar parte en, presentarse para; *post* presentarse como candidato a, oponerse a.

◆**enter into** *vt* (**a**) *agreement* llegar a, firmar; *bargain* cerrar; *contract* hacer, firmar; *obligation* contraer; *explanation* dar; *argument* meterse en, tomar parte en; *conversation* entablar; *negotiations* iniciar; *relations* establecer (*with* con); *marriage* contraer (*with* con).

(**b**) *calculations, plans* formar parte de; **that doesn't ~ into it at all** eso no figura aquí para nada, eso no afecta la cosa en lo más mínimo; **her feelings don't ~ into it** sus sentimientos no tienen que ver; **to ~ into the spirit of the game** tomar parte en el juego con entusiasmo.

◆**enter up** *vt entry* asentar; *ledger* hacer, llevar; *diary* poner al día.

◆**enter (up)on** *vt career* emprender; *office* tomar posesión de; *term of office* empezar; *one's 20th year* empezar.

enteric [en'terɪk] *adj* entérico; **~ fever** fiebre *f* entérica.

enteritis [ˌentə'raɪtɪs] *n* enteritis *f*.

enterprise ['entəpraɪz] **1** *n* (**a**) (*firm, undertaking*) empresa *f*. (**b**) (*spirit*) iniciativa *f*; espíritu *m* emprendedor, empuje *m*; *V* **free** *etc.* **2** *attr*: **the ~ culture** la cultura empresarial; **~ zone** zona *f* de empresas.

enterprising ['entəpraɪzɪŋ] *adj person, spirit* emprendedor; **an ~ thing to do** una cosa que muestra mucha iniciativa; **that was ~ of you** en eso has mostrado mucha iniciativa.

enterprisingly ['entəpraɪzɪŋlɪ] *adv* de modo emprendedor, con mucha iniciativa.

entertain [ˌentə'teɪn] **1** *vt* (**a**) (*amuse*) divertir, entretener.

(**b**) *guest* (*at home*) recibir, recibir en casa, alojar consigo; (*make a fuss of*) festejar, agasajar; **they ~ a good deal** reciben mucho; **they ~ed him with a dinner** le invitaron a cenar; (*formally*) le obsequiaron con una cena.

(**c**) *idea, hope* abrigar, acariciar; *proposal* estudiar, considerar; **I wouldn't ~ it for a moment** tal idea es totalmente inconcebible para mí.

2 *vi* (*at home*) recibir en casa.

entertainer [ˌentə'teɪnəʳ] *n* artista *mf*, actor *m*, actriz *f*, músico *m* (*etc*).

entertaining [ˌentə'teɪnɪŋ] *adj* divertido, entretenido.

entertainingly [ˌentə'teɪnɪŋlɪ] *adv* de manera divertida, graciosamente.

entertainment [ˌentə'teɪnmənt] **1** *n* (**a**) (*amusement*) diversión *f*; **for your ~** para divertiros.

(**b**) (*show*) función *f*, espectáculo *m*, fiesta *f*; (*musical ~*) concierto *m*; **to put on an ~** organizar un espectáculo.

2 *attr*: **~ allowance** extra *m* de visita, gastos *mpl* de representación; **~ business** mundo *m* de los espectáculos; **~ expenses = ~ allowance**; **~ guide** guía *f* del ocio; **~ tax** impuesto *m* sobre los espectáculos.

enthrall, (*US*) **enthral** [ɪn'θrɔːl] *vt* (*fig*) embelesar, extasiar; captar la atención de; **we listened ~ed** escuchamos embelesados.

enthralling [ɪn'θrɔːlɪŋ] *adj* embelesador, cautivador.

enthrone [ɪn'θrəʊn] *vt* entronizar.

enthuse [ɪn'θuːz] *vi*: **to ~ over** entusiasmarse muchísimo por, extasiarse ante.

enthusiasm [ɪn'θuːzɪæzəm] *n* entusiasmo *m* (*for* por).

enthusiast [ɪn'θuːzɪæst] *n* entusiasta *mf* (*for* por).

enthusiastic [ɪnˌθuːzɪ'æstɪk] *adj person* entusiasta; *cry etc* entusiástico; **to be ~ about** entusiasmarse por, estar lleno de entusiasmo por.

enthusiastically [ɪnˌθuːzɪ'æstɪkəlɪ] *adv* con entusiasmo; **he shouted ~** gritó entusiasmado.

entice [ɪn'taɪs] *vt* tentar, atraer (con maña); (*in bad sense*) seducir; **to ~ sb away from sb** inducir mañosamente a uno a dejar a una persona; **to ~ sb away from a place** inducir mañosamente a uno a abandonar un sitio; **to ~ sb into a room** inducir mañosamente a uno a entrar en un cuarto; **to ~ sb to do sth** tentar a uno a hacer algo.

enticement [ɪn'taɪsmənt] *n* (**a**) (*act*) tentación *f*, atracción *f*; seducción *f*; persuasión *f* (mañosa). (**b**) (*bait*) atractivo *m*, aliciente *m*, cebo *m*.

enticing [ɪn'taɪsɪŋ] *adj* atractivo, tentador, seductor.

enticingly [ɪn'taɪsɪŋlɪ] *adv* atractivamente, seductoramente.

entire [ɪn'taɪəʳ] *adj* entero, completo; total; todo; **the ~ world** el mundo entero; **the ~ trip** todo el viaje; **the ~ stock** todas las existencias.

entirely [ɪn'taɪəlɪ] *adv* enteramente, totalmente; **that is not ~ true** eso no es del todo verdad.

entirety [ɪn'taɪərətɪ] *n*: **in its ~** en su totalidad, enteramente.

entitle [ɪn'taɪtl] *vt* (**a**) *book etc* titular; **the book is ~d X** el libro se titula X.

(**b**) **to ~ sb to do sth** autorizar a uno para hacer algo; **to be ~d to do sth** tener derecho a hacer algo; **to ~ sb to sth** dar a uno derecho a algo; **I think I am ~d to some respect** creo que se me debe cierto respeto.

entitlement [ɪn'taɪtlmənt] *n* derecho *m*; autorización *f*; **holiday ~** derecho *m* a vacaciones.

entity ['entɪtɪ] *n* entidad *f*, ente *m*; **legal ~** persona *f* jurídica.

entomb [ɪn'tuːm] *vt* sepultar.

entomologist [ˌentə'mɒlədʒɪst] *n* entomólogo *m*, -a *f*.

entomology [ˌentə'mɒlədʒɪ] *n* entomología *f*.

entourage [ˌɒntʊ'rɑːʒ] *n* séquito *m*.

entr'acte ['ɒntrækt] *n* descanso *m*, intermedio *m*, entreacto *m*.

entrails ['entreɪlz] *npl* entrañas *fpl*, tripas *fpl*; (*US*) asadura *f*, menudos *mpl*.

entrain [ɪn'treɪn] *vi* (*esp Mil*) tomar el tren (*for* a).

entrance[1] ['entrəns] **1** *n* (**a**) (*place*) entrada *f*.

(**b**) (*act*) entrada *f* (*into* en); (*into profession etc*) ingreso *m*; (*Theat*) entrada *f* en escena; **to make one's ~** hacer su entrada.

2 *attr*: **~ card** pase *m*; **~ examination** examen *m* de ingreso; **~ fee** (*Brit*) cuota *f* (de entrada); **~ permit** pase *m*; **~ qualifications, ~ requirements** requisitos *mpl* de entrada.

entrance[2] [ɪn'trɑːns] *vt* encantar, hechizar; **we listened ~d** escuchamos extasiados.

entrance hall ['entrənsˌhɔːl] *n* hall *m* de entrada.

entrance ramp ['entrənsˌræmp] *n* (*US*) rampa *f* de acceso.

entrancing [ɪn'trɑːnsɪŋ] *adj* encantador, cautivador, delicioso.

entrancingly [ɪn'trɑːnsɪŋlɪ] *adv play etc* maravillosamente, deliciosamente; **it was ~ beautiful** contemplamos extasiados aquella belleza.

entrant ['entrənt] *n* participante *mf*, concurrente *mf*, concursante *mf*.

entrap [ɪn'træp] *vt* coger en una trampa; (*fig*) entrampar.

entrapment [ɪn'træpmənt] *n* acción *f* de entrampar; **he complained of ~** se quejó de que le habían entrampado.

entreat [ɪn'triːt] *vt* rogar, suplicar; **to ~ sb to do sth** suplicar a uno hacer algo.

entreating [ɪn'triːtɪŋ] **1** *adj* suplicante. **2** *n* súplica *f*, suplicación *f*.

entreatingly [ɪn'triːtɪŋlɪ] *adv* de modo suplicante.

entreaty [ɪn'triːtɪ] *n* ruego *m*, súplica *f*.

entrée ['ɒntreɪ] *n* entrada *f*; (*US*) plato *m* fuerte, plato *m* principal.

entrench [ɪn'trentʃ] **1** *vt* atrincherar; **to be ~ed** (*also fig*) estar atrincherado; (*Pol*: *clause*) ser artículo inalterable. **2** *vr*: **to ~ o.s.** atrincherarse.

entrenched [ɪn'trentʃt] *adj* (*Mil*) atrincherado; (*fig*) *person* de ideas fijas; *attitude* inamovible; *clause* inalterable; **~ interests** intereses *mpl* creados.

entrenchment [ɪn'trentʃmənt] *n* trinchera *f*.

entrepôt ['ɒntrəpəʊ] *n* centro *m* comercial, centro *m* de distribución; almacén *m*, depósito *m*.

entrepreneur [ˌɒntrəprə'nɜːʳ] *n* (*Comm*) empresario *m*, patrón *m*; contratista *m*; (*Fin*) capitalista *m*.

entrepreneurial [ˌɒntrəprə'nɜːrɪəl] *adj* empresarial.

entropy ['entrəpɪ] *n* entropía *f*.

entrust [ɪn'trʌst] *vt*: **to ~ sth to sb, to ~ sb with sth** confiar algo a uno.

entry ['entrɪ] **1** *n* (**a**) (*place*) entrada *f*; (*passage*) callejuela *f*; (*of street*) bocacalle *f*; **'no ~'** 'se prohíbe la entrada', (*Aut*) 'dirección prohibida'.

(**b**) (*act*) entrada *f* (*into* en); acceso *m* (*into* a); (*into profession etc*) ingreso *m* (*into* en); (*into office*) toma *f* de posesión (*into, on* de); **~ into the hall had been forbidden** se había prohibido el acceso a la sala; **to make one's ~** hacer su entrada.

(**c**) (*Sport etc*) (*total*) participación *f*, participantes *mpl*; (*competitor*) participante *mf*, concurrente *mf*.

(**d**) (*in reference book*) artículo *m*; entrada *f*; (*in diary*) apunte *m*; (*in account*) partida *f*, rubro *m* (*LAm*); (*in record*) apunte *m*, apuntación *f*, entrada *f*.

2 *attr*: **~ fee** cuota *f* (de entrada); **~ form** boleto *m* de inscripción; **~ permit** permiso *m* de entrada; **~ phone** portero *m* automático; **~ qualifications, ~ requirements** requisitos *mpl* de entrada.

entwine [ɪn'twaɪn] *vt* entrelazar, entretejer.

enumerate [ɪ'nju:məreɪt] *vt* enumerar.
enumeration [ɪ,nju:mə'reɪʃən] *n* enumeración *f*.
enunciate [ɪ'nʌnsɪeɪt] *vt words* pronunciar, articular; *principle* enunciar.
enunciation [ɪ,nʌnsɪ'eɪʃən] *n* pronunciación *f*, articulación *f*; enunciación *f*.
enuresis [,enjʊə'ri:sɪs] *n* enuresis *f*.
envelop [ɪn'veləp] *vt* envolver (*in* en).
envelop(e) ['envələʊp] *n* sobre *m*; (*Aer*) envoltura *f*.
enveloping [ɪn'veləpɪŋ] *adj movement* envolvente.
envelopment [ɪn'veləpmənt] *n* envolvimiento *m*.
envenom [ɪn'venəm] *vt* envenenar.
enviable ['envɪəbl] *adj* envidiable.
envious ['envɪəs] *adj* envidioso; *look etc* de envidia; **to be ~ of** tener envidia de, envidiar; **it makes me ~** me da envidia; **I am ~ of your good luck** te envidio tu suerte.
enviously ['envɪəslɪ] *adv* con envidia.
environment [ɪn'vaɪərənmənt] *n* medio *m* ambiente, ambiente *m*, entorno *m*; (*Comput*) entorno *m*; **Department of the E~** (*Brit*) Ministerio *m* del Medio Ambiente; **Secretary (of State) for** (*or* **Minister of**) **the E~** (*Brit*) Secretario *m* (de Estado) (*or* Ministro *m*) del Medio Ambiente.
environmental [ɪn,vaɪərən'mentl] *adj* ambiental, medioambiental; **~ concern** preocupación *f* ambiental; **~ pollution** contaminación *f* ambiental.
environmentalism [ɪn,vaɪrən'mentəlɪzəm] *n* ambientalismo *m*.
environmentalist [ɪn,vaɪrən'mentəlɪst] **1** *adj* ambiental; ecologista. **2** *n* ambientalista *mf*, ecologista *mf*.
environmentally [ɪn,vaɪərən'mentlɪ] *adv*: **an ~ acceptable product** un producto aceptable en lo que concierne al medio ambiente; **it is not ~ safe** ofrece un peligro ambiental.
environment-friendly [ɪn'vaɪrənment'frendlɪ] *adj* que no daña al medio ambiente, ecológico.
environs [ɪn'vaɪərənz] *npl* alrededores *mpl*, inmediaciones *fpl*.
envisage [ɪn'vɪzɪdʒ] *vt* (**a**) (*foresee*) prever; **it is ~d that ...** se prevé que ...; **an increase is ~d next year** está previsto que se aumentará el año que viene.
(**b**) (*imagine*) concebir, formarse una idea de, representarse; **it is hard to ~ such a situation** es difícil formarse una idea de tal situación.
envision [ɪn'vɪʒən] *vt* (*US*) (**a**) (*imagine*) imaginar. (**b**) (*foresee*) prever.
envoy ['envɔɪ] *n* enviado *m*.
envy ['envɪ] **1** *n* envidia *f*; **it was the ~ of all the neighbours** nos lo envidiaban todos los vecinos. **2** *vt* envidiar, tener envidia a; **to ~ sb sth** envidiar algo a uno.
enzyme ['enzaɪm] *n* enzima *f*.
EOC *n abbr of* **Equal Opportunities Commission**.
Eocene ['i:əʊsi:n] *adj* (*Geol*) eoceno.
eolithic [,i:əʊ'lɪθɪk] *adj* eolítico.
eon ['i:ən, 'i:ɒn] *n* (*US*) eón *m*; (*loosely*) eternidad *f*.
EP *n abbr of* **extended play** duración *f* ampliada.
EPA *n* (*US*) *abbr of* **Environmental Protection Agency** Agencia *f* para la Protección del Medio Ambiente.
epaulette ['epɔ:let] *n* charretera *f*.
ephedrine ['efɪdrɪn] *n* efedrina *f*.
ephemeral [ɪ'femərəl] *adj* efímero.
Ephesians [ɪ'fi:ʒjənz] *npl* efesios *mpl*.
epic ['epɪk] **1** *adj* épico. **2** *n* épica *f*, epopeya *f*.
epicene ['epɪsi:n] *adj* epiceno.
epicentre, (*US*) **epicenter** ['epɪsentə^r] *n* epicentro *m*.
epicure ['epɪkjʊə^r] *n* epicúreo *m*, gastrónomo *m*.
epicurean [,epɪkjʊ'ri:ən] **1** *adj* epicúreo. **2** *n* epicúreo *m*.
epicureanism [,epɪkjʊə'rɪənɪzəm] *n* epicureísmo *m*.
epidemic [,epɪ'demɪk] **1** *adj* epidémico. **2** *n* epidemia *f*.
epidermis [,epɪ'dɜ:mɪs] *n* epidermis *f*.
epidural [,epɪ'djʊərəl] **1** *adj*: **~ (anaesthetic)** raquianestesis *f*. **2** *n* = **1**.
epiglottis [,epɪ'glɒtɪs] *n* epiglotis *f*.
epigram ['epɪgræm] *n* epigrama *m*.
epigrammatic(al) [,epɪgrə'mætɪk(əl)] *adj* epigramático.
epigraph ['epɪgrɑ:f] *n* epígrafe *m*.
epigraphy [ɪ'pɪgrəfɪ] *n* epigrafía *f*.
epilepsy ['epɪlepsɪ] *n* epilepsia *f*, alferecía *f*.
epileptic [,epɪ'leptɪk] **1** *adj* epiléptico; **~ fit** acceso *m* epiléptico. **2** *n* epiléptico *m*, -a *f*.
epilogue ['epɪlɒg] *n* epílogo *m*.
Epiphany [ɪ'pɪfənɪ] *n* Epifanía *f*.
episcopacy [ɪ'pɪskəpəsɪ] *n* episcopado *m*.
episcopal [ɪ'pɪskəpəl] *adj* episcopal.
episcopalian [ɪ,pɪskə'peɪlɪən] **1** *adj* episcopalista. **2** *n* episcopalista *mf*.
episcopate [ɪ'pɪskəʊpət] *n* episcopado *m*.
episode ['epɪsəʊd] *n* episodio *m*; (*TV*) capítulo *m* (televisivo), entrega *f* (televisiva).
episodic [,epɪ'sɒdɪk] *adj* episódico.
epistemological [ɪ,pɪstɪmə'lɒdʒɪkəl] *adj* epistemológico.
epistemology [ɪ,pɪstə'mɒlədʒɪ] *n* epistemología *f*.
epistle [ɪ'pɪsl] *n* epístola *f*.
epistolary [ɪ'pɪstələrɪ] *adj* epistolar.
epitaph ['epɪtɑ:f] *n* epitafio *m*.
epithet ['epɪθet] *n* epíteto *m*.
epitome [ɪ'pɪtəmɪ] *n* epítome *m*, compendio *m*, resumen *m*; (*fig*) representación *f* en miniatura; **to be the ~ of virtue** ser la misma virtud, ser la virtud en persona.
epitomize [ɪ'pɪtəmaɪz] *vt* epitomar, compendiar, resumir; (*fig*) personificar; representar en miniatura; **he ~d resistance to the enemy** se cifraba en él la resistencia al enemigo; **he ~d virtue** era la misma virtud, era la virtud en persona.
epoch ['i:pɒk] *n* época *f*; **to mark an ~** hacer época.
epoch-making ['i:pɒk,meɪkɪŋ] *adj* que hace época.
eponymous [ɪ'pɒnɪməs] *adj* epónimo.
EPOS ['i:pɒs] *n abbr of* **electronic point of sale**.
Epsom salts ['epsɒm,sɔ:lts] *npl* epsomita *f*, sal *f* de La Higuera.
EPW *n* (*US*) *abbr of* **enemy prisoner of war**.
equable ['ekwəbl] *adj climate etc* uniforme, igual; *person*, ecuánime; *tone* tranquilo, afable.
equal ['i:kwəl] **1** *adj* igual (*to* a); *treatment* equitativo; **~ in value** de igual valor; **with ~ ease** con la misma facilidad; **E~ Opportunities Commission** (*Brit*) Comisión *f* para la Igualdad de Oportunidades; **~ opportunities** (*or* **opportunity**) **employer** empresario *m* no discriminatorio; **~ rights campaign** campaña *f* en pro de la igualdad de derechos; **~ time** (*US Rad, TV*) derecho *m* de respuesta; **~(s) sign** (*Math*) signo *m* de igualdad; **other things being ~** en igualdad de circunstancias, si todo sigue igual; **to be ~ to** *task* tener fuerzas para, *situation* estar a la altura de; **I don't feel ~ to it** no me siento con fuerzas para ello; **he is ~ to every demand made upon him** hace bien cuanto se le pide; **to be ~ to doing sth** tener fuerzas para hacer algo.
2 *n* igual *mf*; **without ~** sin igual, sin par; **it has no ~ in modern times** no hay nada parecido en los tiempos modernos; **to treat sb as an ~** tratar a uno de igual a igual.
3 *vt* ser igual a; **6 + 4 ~s 10** 6 más 4 son 10.
equality [ɪ'kwɒlɪtɪ] *n* igualdad *f*; **~ of opportunity** igualdad *f* de oportunidades.
equalization [,i:kwəlaɪ'zeɪʃən] *n* igualización *f*; nivelación *f*; (*Fin*) compensación *f*; **~ account** cuenta *f* de compensación; **~ fund** fondo *m* de compensación.
equalize ['i:kwəlaɪz] **1** *vt* igualar; nivelar. **2** *vi* (*Sport*) lograr el empate, lograr la igualada, igualar.
equalizer ['i:kwəlaɪzə^r] *n* (**a**) (*Sport*) igualada *f*, tanto *m* del empate. (**b**) (*US*) pipa‡ *f*, revólver *m*.
equally ['i:kwəlɪ] *adv* igualmente; *share etc* por igual; *treat etc* equitativamente.
equanimity [,ekwə'nɪmɪtɪ] *n* ecuanimidad *f*.
equate [ɪ'kweɪt] *vt* igualar; equiparar (*to, with* con); considerar equivalente (*to, with* a), comparar (*to, with* con).
equation [ɪ'kweɪʒən] *n* ecuación *f*.
equator [ɪ'kweɪtə^r] *n* ecuador *m*.
equatorial [,ekwə'tɔ:rɪəl] *adj* ecuatorial.
Equatorial Guinea [,ekwə'tɔ:rɪəl'gɪnɪ] *n* Guinea *f* Ecuatorial.
equerry ['ekwərɪ] *n* caballerizo *m* del rey.
equestrian [ɪ'kwestrɪən] **1** *adj* ecuestre. **2** *n* jinete *m*, -a *f*.
equi... ['i:kwɪ] *pref* equi...
equidistant ['i:kwɪ'dɪstənt] *adj* equidistante.
equilateral ['i:kwɪ'lætərəl] *adj* equilátero.
equilibrium [,i:kwɪ'lɪbrɪəm] *n* equilibrio *m*.
equine ['ekwaɪn] *adj* equino.
equinoctial [,i:kwɪ'nɒkʃəl] *adj* equinoccial.
equinox ['i:kwɪnɒks] *n* equinoccio *m*.
equip [ɪ'kwɪp] *vt* equipar (*with* de); *person* proveer (*with* de); **to be ~ped with** (*person*) estar provisto de, (*machine etc*) estar dotado de; **to be well ~ped to** + *infin* estar bien dotado para + *infin*.
equipment [ɪ'kwɪpmənt] *n* equipo *m*, material *m*; (*tools*) avíos *mpl*; (*mental*) aptitud *f*, dotes *fpl*.
equitable ['ekwɪtəbl] *adj* equitativo.
equitably ['ekwɪtəblɪ] *adv* equitativamente.
equity ['ekwɪtɪ] *n* (**a**) equidad *f*. (**b**) (*Fin*: *also* **~ capital**)

capital *m* propio, patrimonio *m* neto; **equities** acciones *fpl*. (**c**) **E~** (*Brit*) *sindicato de actores*.
equivalence [ɪ'kwɪvələns] *n* equivalencia *f*.
equivalent [ɪ'kwɪvələnt] **1** *adj* equivalente (*to* a); **to be ~ to** equivaler a. **2** *n* equivalente *m*.
equivocal [ɪ'kwɪvəkəl] *adj* equívoco, ambiguo.
equivocate [ɪ'kwɪvəkeɪt] *vi* usar equívocos, no dar una respuesta clara, soslayar el problema.
equivocation [ɪˌkwɪvə'keɪʃən] *n* equívoco *m*; evasión *f*, ambigüedad *f*.
E.R. *abbr of* **Elizabeth Regina** la reina Isabel.
ERA *n* (*US Pol*) *abbr of* **Equal Rights Amendment**.
era ['ɪərə] *n* época *f*, era *f*; **to mark an ~** hacer época.
eradicate [ɪ'rædɪkeɪt] *vt* desarraigar, extirpar.
eradication [ɪˌrædɪ'keɪʃən] *n* desarraigo *m*, extirpación *f*.
erase [ɪ'reɪz] *vt* (**a**) borrar (*also Comput, fig*). (**b**) (*US**) liquidar*.
erase head [ɪ'reɪzˌhed] *n* cabezal *m* borrador.
eraser [ɪ'reɪzə^r] *n* goma *f* de borrar, borrador *m*.
Erasmism [ɪ'ræzmɪzəm] *n* erasmismo *m*.
Erasmist [ɪ'ræzmɪst] **1** *adj* erasmista. **2** *n* erasmista *mf*.
Erasmus [ɪ'ræzməs] *nm* Erasmo.
erasure [ɪ'reɪʒə^r] *n* borradura *f*, raspadura *f*; (*Comput*) borrado *m*.
ERDF *n abbr of* **European Regional Development Fund** Fondo *m* Europeo de Desarrollo Regional, FEDER *m*.
ere [ɛə^r] (††) **1** *prep* antes de; **~ long** dentro de poco. **2** *conj* antes de que.
erect [ɪ'rekt] **1** *adj* erguido, derecho; vertical. **2** *vt* (*build*) erigir, construir, levantar; (*assemble*) montar; **to ~ sth into a principle** constituir algo en principio.
erectile [ɪ'rektaɪl] *adj* eréctil.
erection [ɪ'rekʃən] *n* (**a**) (*act*) erección *f*, construcción *f*; (*assembly*) montaje *m*. (**b**) (*structure*) edificio *m*, construcción *f*. (**c**) (*Physiol*) erección *f*.
erectly [ɪ'rektlɪ] *adv* de manera erguida; verticalmente.
erector [ɪ'rektə^r] *attr*: **~ set** (*US*) juego *m* de construcciones.
erg [ɜːg] *n* ergio *m*, erg *m*.
ergonomic [ˌɜːgəʊ'nɒmɪk] *adj* ergonómico.
ergonomics [ˌɜːgəʊ'nɒmɪks] *n* ergonomía *f*.
ergot ['ɜːgət] *n* cornezuelo *m* (del centeno).
Eric ['erɪk] *nm* Erico.
Erie ['ɪərɪ] *n*: **Lake ~** Lago *m* Erie.
Erin ['ɪərɪn] *n* Erín *m* (*nombre antiguo y sentimental de Irlanda*).
ERISA [ə'rɪsə] *n* (*US*) *abbr of* **Employee Retirement Income Security Act** *ley que regula pensiones de jubilados*.
ERM *n abbr of* **Exchange Rate Mechanism**.
ermine ['ɜːmɪn] *n* armiño *m*.
Ernest ['ɜːnɪst] *nm* Ernesto.
ERNIE ['ɜːnɪ] *n* (*Brit*) *abbr of* **Electronic Random Number Indicator Equipment** *computadora que elige al azar los números ganadores de los bonos del Estado*.
erode [ɪ'rəʊd] *vt* (*Geol*) causar erosión en, erosionar; *metal* corroer, desgastar; (*fig*) erosionar, mermar, perjudicar.
erogenous [ɪ'rɒdʒənəs] *adj* erógeno; **~ zone** zona *f* erógena.
Eros ['ɪərɒs] *nm* Eros.
erosion [ɪ'rəʊʒən] *n* (*Geol*) erosión *f*; (*of metal*) desgaste *m*.
erosive [ɪ'rəʊzɪv] *adj* erosivo, erosionante.
erotic [ɪ'rɒtɪk] *adj* erótico; erotómano.
erotica [ɪ'rɒtɪkə] *npl* literatura *f* erótica.
eroticism [ɪ'rɒtɪsɪzəm] *n* erotismo *m*; erotomanía *f*.
eroticize [ɪ'rɒtɪsaɪz] *vt* erotizar.
err [ɜː^r] *vi* errar, equivocarse; (*sin*) pecar; **to ~ is human** de los hombres es errar; **to ~ on the side of** pecar de, pecar por exceso de.
errand ['erənd] *n* recado *m*, mandado *m*; misión *f*; **~ of mercy** misión *f* de caridad; **what ~ brings you here?** ¿qué te trae por aquí?; **to run an ~** llevar un recado, hacer un mandado.
errand-boy ['erəndbɔɪ] *n* recadero *m*, mandadero *m*.
errant ['erənt] *adj* errante; *knight* andante.
errata [e'rɑːtə] *npl of* **erratum**.
erratic [ɪ'rætɪk] *adj* (*uncertain*) irregular, poco constante; *conduct* excéntrico; *person* voluble; *record, results etc* desigual, poco uniforme; (*Geol, Med*) errático.
erratically [ɪ'rætɪkəlɪ] *adv* de modo irregular (*etc*).
erratum [e'rɑːtəm] *n, pl* **errata** [e'rɑːtə] errata *f*.
erroneous [ɪ'rəʊnɪəs] *adj* erróneo.
erroneously [ɪ'rəʊnɪəslɪ] *adv* equivocadamente.
error ['erə^r] *n* error *m*, equivocación *f*; **~ message** mensaje *m* de error; **by ~** por equivocación; **~s and omissions excepted** salvo error u omisión; **by some human ~** por algún fallo humano; **to be in ~** estar equivocado; **to see the ~ of one's ways** reconocer las faltas en que uno ha incurrido.
ersatz ['ɛəzæts] **1** *adj* sucedáneo, sustituto. **2** *n* sucedáneo *m*, sustituto *m*.
erstwhile ['ɜːstwaɪl] *adj* (*liter*) antiguo.
erudite ['erʊdaɪt] *adj* erudito.
eruditely ['erʊdaɪtlɪ] *adv* eruditamente.
erudition [ˌerʊ'dɪʃən] *n* erudición *f*.
erupt [ɪ'rʌpt] *vi* (*volcano*) estar en erupción; (*begin to ~*) entrar en erupción; (*Med*) hacer erupción; (*anger, war etc*) estallar; **to ~ into a room** irrumpir en un cuarto.
eruption [ɪ'rʌpʃən] *n* (*Geol, Med*) erupción *f*; (*fig*) explosión *f*.
erysipelas [ˌerɪ'sɪpɪləs] *n* erisipela *f*.
erythrocyte [ɪ'rɪθrəʊˌsaɪt] *n* eritrocito *m*.
ESA *n abbr of* **European Space Agency** Agencia *f* Europea del Espacio, AEE *f*.
Esau ['iːsɔː] *nm* Esaú.
escalate ['eskəleɪt] **1** *vt* extender, intensificar, escalar. **2** *vi* extenderse, intensificarse, escalarse.
escalation [ˌeskə'leɪʃən] *n* extensión *f*, intensificación *f*, escalamiento *m*, escalada *f*; **~ clause** cláusula *f* de precio escalonado.
escalator ['eskəleɪtə^r] **1** *n* escalera *f* mecánica. **2** *attr*: **~ clause** (*Fin*) cláusula *f* de precio escalonado.
escalope ['eskə'lɒp] *n* escalope *f*.
escapade [ˌeskə'peɪd] *n* aventura *f*, travesura *f*.
escape [ɪs'keɪp] **1** *n* escape *m*; fuga *f*, huida *f*, evasión *f*; (*leak*) fuga *f*; (*from duties etc*) escapatoria *f*; **it was a lucky ~ for him** tuvo suerte al poderse escapar; **to have a narrow ~** escapar por los pelos; **to make one's ~** escapar; **to make good one's ~** escapar y desaparecer.

2 *attr*: **~ chute** rampa *f* de emergencia; **~ clause** cláusula *f* de excepción; **~ hatch** escotilla *f* de escape (*or* de salvamento); **~ key** (*Comput*) tecla *f* de escape; **~ mechanism** mecanismo *m* de escape; **~ pipe** tubo *m* de escape; **~ route** ruta *f* de escape; **~ valve** válvula *f* de escape; **~ velocity** (*Space*) velocidad *f* de escape.

3 *vt* (*avoid*) evitar, eludir; *consequences, death* escapar a; *vigilance* burlar; **the meaning ~s me** se me escapa el significado; **the fact had ~d me for the moment** por el momento el hecho se me escapó; **a cry ~d him** no pudo contener un grito; *V* **notice**.

4 *vi* escapar(se); evadirse, huir; (*leak*) fugarse; **to ~ from** *person* escaparse a, *prison* escaparse de, *clutches* librarse de; **to ~ to France** huir a Francia, refugiarse en Francia; **to ~ with a fright** escapar llevándose un susto; **he just ~d being run over** por poco murió atropellado.
escaped [ɪs'keɪpt] *adj prisoner* fugado.
escapee [ɪskeɪ'piː] *n* (*from prison*) fugado *m*, -a *f*.
escapement [ɪs'keɪpmənt] *n* (*of watch*) escape *m*.
escapism [ɪs'keɪpɪzəm] *n* escapismo *m*, evasión *f*, evasionismo *m*.
escapist [ɪs'keɪpɪst] **1** *adj* escapista, evasionista; **~ literature** literatura *f* de evasión. **2** *n* escapista *mf*, evasionista *mf*.
escapologist [ˌeskəɪ'pɒlədʒɪst] *n* rey *m* de la evasión, evasionista *mf*.
escarpment [ɪs'kɑːpmənt] *n* escarpa *f*.
eschatological [ˌeskətə'lɒdʒɪkəl] *adj* (*Rel*) escatológico.
eschatology [ˌeskə'tɒlədʒɪ] *n* (*Rel*) escatología *f*.
eschew [ɪs'tʃuː] *vt* evitar, renunciar a, abstenerse de.
escort 1 ['eskɔːt] *n* (**a**) (*entourage*) acompañamiento *m*; (*lady's*) acompañante *m*; (*girl supplied by agency*) azafata *f*, señorita *f* de compañía.

(**b**) (*Mil*) escolta *f*; (*Naut*) convoy *m*, buque *m* de escolta.

2 ['eskɔːt] *attr*: **~ agency** agencia *f* de azafatas; **~ vessel** buque *m* (de) escolta.

3 [ɪs'kɔːt] *vt* acompañar; (*Mil*) escoltar; (*Naut*) convoyar, escoltar; **to ~ sb home** acompañar a uno a su casa.
escrow ['eskrəʊ] *n* garantía *f*; depósito *m* en fideicomiso; **in ~** en depósito; **~ account** cuenta *f* de plica.
escutcheon [ɪs'kʌtʃən] *n* escudo *m* de armas, blasón *m*; (*fig*) honor *m*.
ESE *abbr of* **east-south-east** estesudeste, ESE.
-ese ['iːz] *suffix*: *eg* **biotechese** lenguaje *m* de la biotecnología, (*pej*) jerga *f* biotecnológica.
ESF *n abbr of* **European Social Fund** Fondo *m* Social Europeo, FSE *m*.
Eskimo ['eskɪməʊ] **1** *adj* esquimal. **2** *n* (**a**) esquimal *mf*. (**b**) (*Ling*) esquimal *m*.
ESL *n abbr of* **English as a Second Language** inglés *m* como

segunda lengua.

ESN *adj abbr of* **educationally subnormal** de inteligencia inferior a la normal.

esophagus [ɪ'sɒfəgəs] *n* (*US*) = **oesophagus.**

esoteric [,esəʊ'terɪk] *adj* esotérico.

ESP *n abbr of* **extrasensory perception** percepción *f* extrasensorial.

esp. *abbr of* **especially.**

espadrille [,espə'drɪl] *n* alpargata *f.*

espalier [ɪ'spæljəʳ] *n* espaldar *m.*

esparto [e'spɑːtəʊ] *n* esparto *m.*

especial [ɪs'peʃəl] *adj* especial, particular.

especially [ɪs'peʃəlɪ] *adv* especialmente; sobre todo, ante todo; en particular; **it is ~ awkward** es especialmente difícil; **you ~ ought to know** tú debieras saberlo más que nadie; **why me ~?** ¿por qué yo y no otro?; **~ when it rains** sobre todo cuando llueve.

Esperantist [,espə'ræntɪst] *n* esperantista *mf.*

Esperanto [,espə'ræntəʊ] *n* esperanto *m.*

espionage [,espɪə'nɑːʒ] *n* espionaje *m.*

esplanade [,esplə'neɪd] *n* paseo *m*; (*by sea*) paseo *m* marítimo; (*Mil*) explanada *f.*

espousal [ɪ'spaʊzl] *n* adherencia *f* (*of* a); adopción *f* (*of* de).

espouse [ɪs'paʊz] *vt cause* adherirse a; *plan* adoptar.

espresso [es'presəʊ] *adj*: **~ bar** café *m* donde se sirve café exprés; **~ coffee** café *m* exprés.

esprit de corps ['espriːdə'kɔːʳ] *n* espíritu *m* de cuerpo.

espy [ɪs'paɪ] *vt* divisar.

Esq. (*Brit*) *abbr of* **esquire** Don, D.

Esquire [ɪs'kwaɪəʳ] *n*: **Henry Crun ~** (*on envelope*) Sr D. Henry Crun.

essay 1 ['eseɪ] *n* ensayo *m*; (*Scol*) composición *f.* **2** [e'seɪ] *vt* probar, ensayar; *task* intentar; **to ~ to +** *infin* intentar + *infin.*

essayist ['eseɪɪst] *n* ensayista *mf*; tratadista *mf.*

essence ['esəns] *n* esencia *f*; **the ~ of the matter is** lo esencial es; **in ~ the book is not about religion** fundamentalmente el libro no tiene que ver con la religión; **speed is of the ~** es esencial hacerlo con la mayor prontitud.

essential [ɪ'senʃəl] **1** *adj* esencial; indispensable, fundamental, imprescindible; **it is ~ to +** *infin* es imprescindible + *infin*; **it is ~ that ...** es necesario que + *subj.* **2** *n* elemento *m* necesario, factor *m* imprescindible; **we have all the ~s** tenemos todo lo necesario; **in all ~s** fundamentalmente.

essentially [ɪ'senʃəlɪ] *adv* esencialmente, en su esencia.

EST *n* (**a**) (*US*) *abbr of* **Eastern Standard Time.** (**b**) *abbr of* **electric shock treatment** terapia *f* de electroshock.

est. (**a**) *abbr of* **estimated.** (**b**) *abbr of* **established**; **~ 1888** se fundó en 1888.

establish [ɪs'tæblɪʃ] **1** *vt* establecer, fundar, crear; *assembly etc* constituir, crear; *date* determinar; *facts* verificar; *proof* demostrar, probar; *relations* entablar; *precedent* crear; **to ~ that ...** comprobar que ..., constatar que ...; **his father ~ed him in business** su padre compró el negocio para él; **he ~ed her in a flat** la instaló en un piso; **the book ~ed him as a writer** el libro le consagró como escritor.

2 *vr*: **to ~ o.s.** crearse una reputación, hacerse un negocio sólido; **to ~ itself** establecerse, consolidarse, (*custom*) arraigar.

established [ɪs'tæblɪʃt] *adj person, business* de buena reputación, sólido; *custom* arraigado; *fact* conocido, admitido; *church* oficial, del Estado; *staff* fijo, de plantilla.

establishment [ɪs'tæblɪʃmənt] *n* (**a**) (*act, body*) establecimiento *m*, fundación *f*; (*business house*) establecimiento *m*, casa *f.*

(**b**) (*Mil*) fuerzas *fpl*, efectivos *mpl*; (*servants*) casa *f*, servidumbre *f*; (*staff of company etc*) plantel *m*, personal *m*; **to be on the ~** ser de plantilla; **they have a smaller ~ nowadays** ahora mantienen una casa más modesta, tienen menos servicio ahora.

(**c**) **the E~** (*Brit Pol*) el sistema (*la clase dirigente, los que mandan*).

estate [ɪs'teɪt] *n* (**a**) (*land*) finca *f*, hacienda *f.*

(**b**) (*property, assets*) propiedad *f*; (*real ~*) bienes *mpl* raíces, inmuebles *mpl* (*LAm*).

(**c**) (*inheritance*) bienes *mpl* relictos; herencia *f*, heredad *f*; testamentaría *f*; **he left a large ~** dejó una inmensa fortuna.

(**d**) (*Pol*) estado *m*; **third ~** estado *m* llano; **fourth ~** (*hum*) la prensa.

estate agency [ɪs'teɪt,eɪdʒənsɪ] *n* (*esp Brit*) agencia *f* inmobiliaria.

estate agent [ɪs'teɪt,eɪdʒənt] *n* (*esp Brit*) corredor *m*, -ora *f* de fincas, agente *m* inmobiliario, agente *f* inmobiliaria.

estate car [ɪs'teɪtkɑːʳ] *n* (*Brit*) furgoneta *f*, rubia *f*, camioneta *f* (*LAm*).

estate duty [ɪs'teɪt,djuːtɪ] *n* (*Brit*) impuesto *m* de sucesión, impuesto *m* sobre los bienes heredados.

esteem [ɪs'tiːm] **1** *n* estima *f*, estimación *f*; consideración *f*; **to hold sb in high ~** estimar en mucho a uno, tener un alto concepto de uno; **to hold sb in low ~** estimar en poco a uno; **to rise in sb's ~** merecer que uno le estime más.

2 *vt* estimar, apreciar; **I would ~ it a privilege** lo consideraría un privilegio; **my ~ed colleague** mi estimado colega.

Esther ['estəʳ] *nf* Ester.

esthete ['iːsθiːt] *n* (*US*) *etc* = **aesthete** *etc.*

Esthonia [es'təʊnɪə] = **Estonia.**

Esthonian [es'təʊnɪən] = **Estonian.**

estimable ['estɪməbl] *adj* estimable.

estimate 1 ['estɪmɪt] *n* (*judgement*) estimación *f*, apreciación *f*; (*approximate assessment*) estimación *f*; tasa *f*, cálculo *m*; (*for work etc*) presupuesto *m* previo; **E~s** (*Parl*) presupuesto *m*; **at a rough ~** aproximadamente.

2 ['estɪmeɪt] *vt* (*judge*) estimar, apreciar; (*assess*) calcular, computar, tasar (*at* en); **to ~ that ...** calcular que ...

3 ['estɪmeɪt] *vi*: **to ~ for** *building work etc* presupuestar, hacer un presupuesto de.

estimation [,estɪ'meɪʃən] *n* (**a**) (*judgement*) opinión *f*; juicio *m*; **in my ~** a mi juicio; **what is your ~ of him?** ¿qué concepto tienes de él? (**b**) (*esteem*) estima *f*, aprecio *m.*

estimator ['estɪmeɪtəʳ] *n* asesor *m*, -ora *f.*

Estonia [e'stəʊnɪə] *n* Estonia *f.*

Estonian [e'stəʊnɪən] **1** *adj* estonio. **2** *n* (**a**) estonio *m*, -a *f.* (**b**) (*Ling*) estonio *m.*

estrange [ɪs'treɪndʒ] *vt* enajenar, apartar (*from* de); **his ~d wife** su mujer que vive separada de él; **to become ~d** enemistarse (*from* con).

estrangement [ɪs'treɪndʒmənt] *n* enajenación *f*; alejamiento *m*, distanciamiento *m*; separación *f.*

estrogen ['iːstrəʊdʒən] *n* (*US*) = **oestrogen.**

estrus ['iːstrəs] (*US*) = **oestrus.**

estuary ['estjʊərɪ] *n* estuario *m*, ría *f.*

ET *n* (**a**) (*Brit*) *abbr of* **Employment Training.** (**b**) (*US*) *abbr of* **Eastern Time.**

ETA *n abbr of* **estimated time of arrival.**

et al [et'æl] *abbr of* **et alii** y otros.

etc. *abbr of* **etcetera** etcétera, etc.

etcetera [ɪt'setrə] **1** *as adv* etcétera. **2 ~s** *npl* extras *mpl*, adornos *mpl.*

etch [etʃ] *vt* grabar al aguafuerte.

etching ['etʃɪŋ] *n* aguafuerte *f*; **he invited her in to see his ~s** la invitó a entrar a ver su colección de sellos.

ETD *n abbr of* **estimated time of departure.**

eternal [ɪ'tɜːnl] *adj* eterno; sempiterno; de siempre.

eternally [ɪ'tɜːnəlɪ] *adv* eternamente; sempiternamente; siempre.

eternity [ɪ'tɜːnɪtɪ] *n* eternidad *f*; **it seemed like an ~** parecía un siglo, parecía que no iba a acabar (*etc*) nunca.

ethane ['iːθeɪn] *n* etano *m.*

ethanol ['eθənɒl] *n* etanol *m.*

ether ['iːθəʳ] *n* éter *m.*

ethereal [ɪ'θɪərɪəl] *adj* etéreo (*also fig*).

ethic ['eθɪk] *n* ética *f*; *V* **work.**

ethical ['eθɪkəl] *adj* ético; (*honourable*) honrado.

ethics ['eθɪks] *n* ética *f*; (*honourableness*) moralidad *f.*

Ethiopia [,iːθɪ'əʊpɪə] *n* Etiopía *f.*

Ethiopian [,iːθɪ'əʊpɪən] **1** *adj* etíope. **2** *n* etíope *mf.*

ethnic ['eθnɪk] *adj* étnico; **~ minority** minoría *f* étnica.

ethnicity [eθ'nɪsɪtɪ] *n* etnicidad *f.*

ethnocentric [,eθnəʊ'sentrɪk] *adj* etnocéntrico.

ethnocentrism [,eθnəʊ'sentrɪzəm] *n* etnocentrismo *m.*

ethnographer [eθ'nɒgrəfəʳ] *n* etnógrafo *m*, -a *f.*

ethnographic [,eθnəʊ'græfɪk] *adj* etnográfico.

ethnography [eθ'nɒgrəfɪ] *n* etnografía *f.*

ethnological [,eθnəʊ'lɒdʒɪkl] *adj* etnológico.

ethnologist [eθ'nɒlədʒɪst] *n* etnólogo *m*, -a *f.*

ethnology [eθ'nɒlədʒɪ] *n* etnología *f.*

ethnomusicology [,eθnəʊmjuːzɪ'kɒlədʒɪ] *n* etnomusicología *f.*

ethos ['iːθɒs] *n* genio *m*, carácter *m* (nacional), actitud *f* vital.

ethyl ['iːθaɪl] *n* etilo *m.*

ethylene ['eθɪliːn] *n* etileno *m.*

etiology [,iːtɪ'ɒlədʒɪ] *n* etiología *f.*

etiquette ['etɪket] *n* etiqueta *f*; (*of profession*) honor *m* profesional; **it is not ~ to** + *infin* no es elegante + *infin*, está mal visto + *infin*.
Eton crop ['i:tn'krɒp] *n* corte *m* a lo garçon.
Etruscan [ɪ'trʌskən] **1** *adj* etrusco. **2** *n* (**a**) etrusco *m*, -a *f*. (**b**) (*Ling*) etrusco *m*.
et seq. *abbr of* **et sequentia** y siguientes, y sigs.
ETU *n* (*Brit*) *abbr of* **Electrical Trades Union** *sindicato de electricistas*.
ETV *n* (*US*) *abbr of* **Educational Television**.
etymological [ˌetɪmə'lɒdʒɪkəl] *adj* etimológico.
etymologically [ˌetɪmə'lɒdʒɪkəlɪ] *adv* etimológicamente.
etymology [ˌetɪ'mɒlədʒɪ] *n* etimología *f*.
etymon ['etɪmɒn] *n*, *pl* **etymons** ['etɪmɒnz] *or* **etyma** ['etɪmə] étimo *m*.
eucalyptus [ˌju:kə'lɪptəs] *n* eucalipto *m*.
Eucharist ['ju:kərɪst] *n* Eucaristía *f*.
Euclid ['ju:klɪd] *nm* Euclides.
Euclidean [ju:'klɪdɪən] *adj* euclidiano.
Eugene [ju:'ʒeɪn] *nm* Eugenio.
eugenic [ju:'dʒenɪk] *adj* eugenésico.
eugenics [ju:'dʒenɪks] *n* eugenismo *m*, eugenesia *f*.
eulogize ['ju:lədʒaɪz] *vt* elogiar, encomiar.
eulogy ['ju:lədʒɪ] *n* elogio *m*, encomio *m*.
eunuch ['ju:nək] *n* eunuco *m*.
euphemism ['ju:fɪmɪzəm] *n* eufemismo *m*.
euphemistic [ˌju:fɪ'mɪstɪk] *adj* eufemístico.
euphonic [ju:'fɒnɪk] *adj*, **euphonious** [ju:'fəʊnɪəs] *adj* eufónico.
euphony ['ju:fənɪ] *n* eufonía *f*.
euphoria [ju:'fɔ:rɪə] *n* euforia *f*.
euphoric [ju:'fɒrɪk] *adj* eufórico.
Euphrates [ju:'freɪti:z] *n* Eufrates *m*.
Eurasia [jʊə'reɪʃə] *n* Eurasia *f*.
Eurasian [jʊə'reɪʃn] **1** *adj* eurasiático. **2** *n* eurasiático *m*, -a *f*.
Euratom [jʊər'ætəm] *n abbr of* **European Atomic Energy Commission** Comisión *f* Europea de Energía Atómica.
eureka [jʊə'ri:kə] *interj* ¡eureka!
eurhythmics [ju:'rɪðmɪks] *n* euritmia *f*.
Euripides [jʊ'rɪpɪdi:z] *nm* Eurípides.
Euro..., **euro...** ['jʊərəʊ] *pref* euro...
Eurobonds ['jʊərəʊbɒndz] *npl* eurobonos *mpl*.
Eurocheque ['jʊərəʊtʃek] **1** *n* eurocheque *m*. **2** *attr*: **~ card** tarjeta *f* de eurocheque.
Eurocommunism ['jʊərəʊˌkɒmjʊnɪzəm] *n* eurocomunismo *m*.
Eurocommunist ['jʊərəʊˌkɒmjʊnɪst] **1** *adj* eurocomunista. **2** *n* eurocomunista *mf*.
Eurocrat ['jʊərəʊkræt] *n* (*hum*) eurócrata *mf*.
Eurocredit ['jʊərəʊˌkredɪt] *n* Eurocrédito *m*.
Eurocurrency ['jʊərəʊˌkʌrənsɪ] *n* eurodivisa *f*.
Eurodollar ['jʊərəʊˌdɒlər] *n* eurodólar *m*.
Euromarket ['jʊərəʊˌmɑ:kɪt] *n*, **Euromart** ['jʊərəʊˌmɑ:t] *n* euromercado *m*, Mercado *m* Común.
Euro-MP ['jʊərəʊˌemˌpi:] *n abbr of* **Member of the European Parliament** eurodiputado *m*, -a *f*.
Europe ['jʊərəp] *n* Europa *f*; **to go into ~, to join ~** (*Brit Pol*) entrar en Europa.
European [ˌjʊərə'pi:ən] **1** *adj* europeo; **~ (Economic) Community** Comunidad *f* (Económica) Europea; **~ Commission** Comisión *f* Europea; **~ Court of Justice** Tribunal *m* de Justicia Europeo; **~ Monetary System** Sistema *m* Monetario Europeo; **~ Parliament** Parlamento *m* Europeo; **~ plan** (*US*) habitación *f* (de hotel) con servicios (pero sin comidas). **2** *n* europeo *m*, -a *f*.
europeanization [ˌjʊərəˌpɪənaɪ'zeɪʃən] *n* europeización *f*.
europeanize [ˌjʊərə'pɪənaɪz] *vt* europeizar.
Europhile ['jʊərəʊfaɪl] *n* eurófilo *m*, -a *f*.
Europhobe ['jʊərəʊfəʊb] *n* eurófobo *m*, -a *f*.
Euro-size ['jʊərəʊˌsaɪz] *n*: **~ 1** (*Comm*) talla *f* europea 1.
Eurospeak ['jʊərəʊspi:k] *n* (*hum*) jerga *f* burocrática de la CE.
Eurovision ['jʊərəvɪʒən] *n* Eurovisión *f*.
Eurydice [jʊ'rɪdɪsi:] *nf* Eurídice.
Eustachian [ju:'steɪʃən] *adj*: **~ tube** trompa *f* de Eustaquio.
euthanasia [ˌju:θə'neɪzɪə] *n* eutanasia *f*.
evacuate [ɪ'vækjʊeɪt] *vt* evacuar; *building etc* desocupar.
evacuation [ɪˌvækjʊ'eɪʃən] *n* evacuación *f*.
evacuee [ɪˌvækjʊ'i:] *n* evacuado *m*, -a *f*.
evade [ɪ'veɪd] *vt* evadir, eludir; *grasp* escaparse de; **to ~ taxes** defraudar impuestos; *V* **issue**.
evaluate [ɪ'væljʊeɪt] *vt* evaluar, calcular (el valor de); tasar.
evaluation [ɪˌvæljʊ'eɪʃən] *n* evaluación *f*, cálculo *m*.
evanescent [ˌi:və'nesnt] *adj* efímero, evanescente, fugaz.
evangelic(al) [ˌi:væn'dʒelɪk(əl)] *adj* evangélico.
evangelism [ɪ'vændʒəˌlɪzəm] *n* evangelismo *m*.
evangelist [ɪ'vændʒəlɪst] *n* evangelista *mf*; evangelizador *m*, -ora *f*, misionero *m*, -a *f*; **St John the E~** San Juan Evangelista.
evangelize [ɪ'vændʒɪlaɪz] *vt* evangelizar.
evaporate [ɪ'væpəreɪt] **1** *vt* evaporar; **~d milk** leche *f* evaporada. **2** *vi* evaporarse; (*fig*) desvanecerse, esfumarse.
evaporation [ɪˌvæpə'reɪʃən] *n* evaporación *f*.
evasion [ɪ'veɪʒən] *n* evasiva *f*, evasión *f*.
evasive [ɪ'veɪzɪv] *adj* evasivo; **he was very ~** contestó de manera evasiva.
evasively [ɪ'veɪzɪvlɪ] *adv* de manera evasiva.
evasiveness [ɪ'veɪzɪvnɪs] *n* carácter *m* evasivo.
Eve [i:v] *nf* Eva.
eve[1] [i:v] *n* víspera *f*; **on the ~ of** la víspera de, (*fig*) en vísperas de.
eve[2] [i:v] *n* (*liter*: *evening*) tarde *f*.
even ['i:vən] **1** *adj* (**a**) (*level*) llano; (*smooth*) liso, igual, uniforme; (*on same level*) a nivel.
(**b**) (*regular*) *speed* uniforme; *temperature etc* uniforme, constante; *treatment* equitativo; *temper* ecuánime, apacible; *tone* imperturbable.
(**c**) (*equal*) *score, teams, match etc* igual; **now we're ~** ahora vamos iguales; **the chances are about ~** las posibilidades son más o menos iguales; **to be ~ with** (*at game*) andar igual con, (*fig*) estar en paz con; **to break ~** salir sin ganar ni perder; **to get ~ with** ajustar cuentas con, desquitarse con; **I'll get ~ with you yet!** ¡me las pagarás!; **that makes us ~** (*at game*) eso iguala el tanteo, (*fig*) tal para cual.
(**d**) *number* par.
2 *adv* (**a**) **~ the priest was there** hasta el cura estuvo allí; **pick them all, ~ the little ones** cógelos todos incluso los pequeños; **~ on Sundays** incluso los domingos; **and he ~ sings** e incluso canta.
(**b**) (+ *comp adj or adv*) **~ more curious** aun más curioso, más curioso aun; **~ faster** aun más rápidamente.
(**c**) (*phrases*) **~ I** yo también; **~ as you tricked me** del mismo modo que Vd me engañó; **~ as I went in** en el mismo momento en que yo entraba; **~ if, ~ though** aunque + *subj*, aun cuando + *subj*, si bien + *indic*; **~ so** aun así; sin embargo.
(**d**) (+ *neg*) **not ~** ni siquiera; **not ~ a look** ni una mirada siquiera; **he didn't ~ kiss me** ni me besó siquiera; **without ~ reading it** sin leerlo siquiera.
3 *vt surface* allanar, nivelar.
◆**even out** *vt inequalities* igualar, allanar; *distribution* hacer uniforme; *thing distributed* repartir equitativamente.
◆**even up 1** *vt* (**a**) = **even out**.
(**b**) *score etc* igualar, nivelar.
2 *vi*: **to ~ up with sb** ajustar cuentas con uno.
even-handed ['i:vən'hændɪd] *adj* imparcial; equitativo.
even-handedly ['i:vən'hændɪdlɪ] *adv* imparcialmente; equitativamente.
evening ['i:vnɪŋ] **1** *n* (*early*) tarde *f*, (*at sunset*) atardecer *m*, (*after dark*) noche *f*; **~ was coming on** atardecía, anochecía; **good ~!** ¡buenas tardes!, ¡buenas noches!
2 *attr*: **~ class** clase *f* nocturna; **~ dress** (*man's*) traje *m* de etiqueta, (*woman's*) traje *m* de noche; **~ fixture** partido *m* nocturno; **~ institute** escuela *f* nocturna; **~ match = ~ fixture**; **~ paper** periódico *m* de la tarde, vespertino *m*; **~ performance** función *f* de noche; **~ prayers** oraciones *fpl* de la tarde; **~ service** (*Rel*) misa *f* vespertina; **~ star** estrella *f* vespertina, lucero *m* de la tarde.
evenly ['i:vənlɪ] *adv* (*smoothly*) lisamente; (*uniformly*) de modo uniforme; *distribute etc* igualmente, equitativamente; *speak etc* en el mismo tono, apaciblemente; *look etc* sin alterarse.
evenness ['i:vənnɪs] *n* lisura *f*; uniformidad *f*; igualdad *f*; (*of treatment*) imparcialidad *f*; (*of temper*) serenidad *f*, ecuanimidad *f*.
evensong ['i:vənsɒŋ] *n* vísperas *fpl*.
even-stevens* [ˌi:vən'sti:vənz] *adv*: **to be ~ with sb** estar en paz con uno; ir parejo con uno; **they're pretty well ~** están más o menos igualados.
event [ɪ'vent] *n* suceso *m*, acontecimiento *m*; evento *m*; (*in a programme*) número *m*; (*Sport*) prueba *f*; (*ceremony*) acto *m*; **programme of ~s** (*civic*) programa *m* de actos, (*shows*) programa *m* de atracciones; **coming ~s** sucesos *mpl* venideros, (*shows etc*) atracciones *fpl* venideras; **current ~s** actualidades *fpl*; **this is quite an ~!** ¡esto sí es

un acontecimiento!; **the ~ will show** ya lo veremos, ello dirá, veremos qué consecuencias tendrá esto; **at all ~s, in any ~** en todo caso; **in either ~** en cualquiera de los dos casos; **in the ~** tal como resultó después; **in the ~ of** en caso de; **in the ~ of his dying** en caso de que muriese; **in the ~ that ...** caso (de) que + *subj*; **to be expecting a happy ~** estar en estado de buena esperanza; **to be wise after the ~** mostrar sabiduría cuando ya no hay remedio.

even-tempered ['iːvən'tempəd] *adj* ecuánime, apacible.

eventful [ɪ'ventfʊl] *adj life, journey etc* accidentado, azaroso; *match etc* lleno de incidentes, lleno de emoción, memorable.

eventide home ['iːvəntaɪd,həʊm] *n* hogar *m* de ancianos.

eventing [ɪ'ventɪŋ] *n* concurso *m* hípico (de tres días).

eventual [ɪ'ventʃʊəl] *adj* final, definitivo; consiguiente.

eventuality [ɪ,ventʃʊ'ælɪtɪ] *n* eventualidad *f*; **in that ~** en esa eventualidad; **in the ~ of** en la eventualidad de; **to be ready for any ~** estar dispuesto a aguantar cualquier posibilidad.

eventually [ɪ'ventʃʊəlɪ] *adv* (*at last*) finalmente, al fin y al cabo, al final (*LAm*); (*given time*) con el tiempo, a la larga; en su día.

eventuate [ɪ'ventjʊeɪt] *vi*: **to ~ in** (*US*) resultar en.

ever ['evəʳ] *adv* (**a**) (*always*) siempre; **~ after, ~ since** desde entonces, (*conj*) después de que; **as ~** como siempre; **as ~, yours ~** (*ending letter*) recibe un abrazo de tu amigo ...; **for ~** para siempre; **for ~ and ~, for ~ and a day** por siempre jamás.

(**b**) (+ *neg*: *at no time*) nunca, jamás; **hardly ~** casi nunca; **better than ~** mejor que nunca; **more than ~** más que nunca; **nothing ~ happens** no pasa nunca nada; **all she ~ does is make jam** lo único que hace en la vida es hacer mermelada; **not often if ~** rara vez si nunca.

(**c**) (*at any time*) **if you ~ go there** si acaso vas allí alguna vez; **did you ~ find it?** ¿lo encontraste por fin?; **did you ~ meet him?** ¿llegó a conocerle?; **did you ~?*** ¿se vio jamás tal cosa?; **a nice man, if ~ I saw one** hombre simpático si los hay.

(**d**) (*emphasizing question*) **what ~ did he want?** ¿qué demonios quería?; **why ~ did you do it?** ¿por qué demonios lo hiciste?

(**e**) (*intensive*) **he's ~ so nice** es simpatiquísimo; **it's ~ so cold** hace un frío terrible; **we're ~ so grateful** le estamos profundamente agradecidos; **~ so much** muchísimo; **~ so little** muy poco; **~ so many things** tantísimas cosas, la mar de cosas; **as quickly as ~ you can** lo más pronto posible; **before ~ you were born** antes de que nacieras.

(**f**) (*after superl*) **the best ~** el mejor que se ha visto jamás; **the coldest night ~** la noche más fría que nunca hemos tenido; **as soon as ~ I can** en cuanto pueda.

ever-changing [evə'tʃeɪndʒɪŋ] *adj* siempre variable, infinitamente mudable.

Everest ['evərɪst] *n*: (**Mount**) **~** monte *m* Everest, Everest *m*.

everglade ['evəgleɪd] *n* (*US*) *tierra baja pantanosa cubierta de altas hierbas*.

evergreen ['evəgriːn] **1** *adj* (**a**) *trees, shrubs* de hoja perenne; siempreverde; **~ oak** encina *f*. (**b**) (*fig*) *memory* imperecedero; *song etc* de popularidad perenne. **2** *n* árbol *m* (*etc*) de hoja perenne.

ever-growing ['evə'grəʊɪŋ] *adj* que va en continuo aumento.

everlasting [,evə'lɑːstɪŋ] *adj* eterno, perdurable, perpetuo; (*pej*) interminable.

everlastingly [,evə'lɑːstɪŋlɪ] *adv* eternamente; (*pej*) interminablemente.

evermore ['evə'mɔːʳ] *adv* eternamente; **for ~** por (*or* para) siempre jamás.

every ['evrɪ] *adj* cada (*invariable*); (*each and every, any*) todo; **~ man** cada hombre, todo hombre, todos los hombres; **~ man Jack** todo ser viviente; **~ one** cada uno; **~ one of them** todos ellos; **his ~ effort** todos sus esfuerzos; **I gave you ~ assistance** te ayudé en lo que podía; **she had ~ chance** se le dieron todas las posibilidades; **we wish you ~ success** te deseamos todo el éxito posible; **I have ~ reason to think that ...** tengo sólidas razones para pensar que ...; **~ day** cada día; **~ other month** un mes sí y otro no, cada dos meses; **~ other person has a car** de cada dos personas una tiene coche; **~ 5 years** cada 5 años; **~ now and then, ~ now and again** de vez en cuando; **~ so often** cada cierto tiempo; *V* **bit** *etc*.

everybody ['evrɪbɒdɪ] *pron* todos, todo el mundo.

everyday ['evrɪdeɪ] *adj* (*occurring daily*) diario, cotidiano, de todos los días; (*usual*) corriente, acostumbrado; (*commonplace*) vulgar; (*routine*) rutinario; **for ~ (use)** de diario; **in ~ use** de uso corriente; **~ clothes** ropa *f* para todos los días; **it's an ~ event** es un suceso ordinario.

everyone ['evrɪwʌn] *pron* = **everybody**.

everyplace ['evrɪpleɪs] *adv* (*US*) = **everywhere**.

everything ['evrɪθɪŋ] *pron* (**a**) (*as subject etc*) todo; **~ is ready** todo está dispuesto; **~ nice had been sold** se había vendido todo lo deseable; **time is ~** el tiempo lo es todo; **money isn't ~** el dinero no lo es todo en la vida; **I've argued with him and ~, but he won't listen** he razonado y todo eso con él, pero no quiere escuchar.

(**b**) (*as object*) **he sold ~** lo vendió todo.

everywhere ['evrɪwɛəʳ] *adv be* en todas partes, *go* a todas partes, por todas partes; **I looked ~** busqué por todas partes; **~ in Spain** en todas partes de España; **~ you go you'll find the same** en todas partes encontrarás lo mismo.

evict [ɪ'vɪkt] *vt* desahuciar, desalojar, expulsar.

eviction [ɪ'vɪkʃən] **1** *n* desahucio *m*, desalojo *m*, expulsión *f*. **2** *attr*: **~ notice** orden *f* de desahucio (desalojo *LAm*).

evidence ['evɪdəns] **1** *n* (**a**) (*obviousness*) evidencia *f*; **in ~** bien visible, manifiesto.

(**b**) (*sign*) prueba *f*, indicios *mpl*; (*testimony*) testimonio *m*; (*facts*) hechos *mpl*, datos *mpl*; **there is ~ to show that ...** hay indicios que demuestran que ...; **what ~ is there for this belief?** ¿qué hechos se alegan a favor de tal creencia?

(**c**) (*Jur*) testimonio *m*, declaración *f*, deposición *f*; **there is no ~ against him** no hay evidencia en contra suya; **to call sb in ~** llamar a uno como testigo; **to give ~** prestar declaración, (*more formally*) deponer, dar testimonio; **to hold sth in ~** citar algo como prueba; **to turn Queen's** (*or* **King's**) **~** (*Brit*), **to turn state's ~** (*US*) delatar a los cómplices.

2 *vt* (*make evident*) patentizar; (*prove*) probar; *emotion* dar muestras de; **as is ~d by the fact that ...** según lo demuestra el hecho de que ....

evident ['evɪdənt] *adj* evidente, manifiesto, claro; **it is ~ that ...** es evidente que ..., se ve que ...; **to be ~ in** manifestarse en; **as is all too ~** como queda bien patente; **as is ~ from her novel** como queda bien claro de su novela.

evidently ['evɪdəntlɪ] *adv*: **~!** ¡naturalmente!; **it is ~ difficult** por lo visto es difícil; **~ he cannot come** por lo visto no puede venir.

evil ['iːvl] **1** *adj* malo, pernicioso; *person* malo, malvado, perverso; (*unlucky*) aciago; *influence* funesto; *smell* horrible; **~ eye** aojo *m*, mal *m* de ojo; **~ spirit** espíritu *m* maligno; **he had his ~ way with her** se la llevó al huerto, la sedujo.

2 *n* mal *m*, maldad *f*; **the lesser of two ~s** el menor de dos males; **to do ~** hacer mal; **to speak ~ of** hablar mal de.

evildoer ['iːvlduːəʳ] *n* malhechor *m*, -ora *f*.

evilly ['iːvɪlɪ] *adv* malvadamente, perversamente; aciagamente; diabólicamente.

evil-minded ['iːvl'maɪndɪd] *adj* malintencionado, mal pensado.

evil-smelling ['iːvl'smelɪŋ] *adj* fétido, maloliente, hediondo.

evince [ɪ'vɪns] *vt* dar señales de, mostrar.

eviscerate [ɪ'vɪsəreɪt] *vt* destripar.

evocation [,evə'keɪʃən] *n* evocación *f*.

evocative [ɪ'vɒkətɪv] *adj* sugestivo, evocador, sugerente.

evoke [ɪ'vəʊk] *vt* evocar.

evolution [,iːvə'luːʃən] *n* evolución *f* (*also Bio*); desarrollo *m*.

evolutionary [,iːvə'luːʃnərɪ] *adj* evolutivo.

evolve [ɪ'vɒlv] **1** *vt* desarrollar, producir; *gas, heat etc* desprender. **2** *vi* evolucionar, desarrollarse.

ewe [juː] *n* oveja *f*.

ewer ['juːəʳ] *n* aguamanil *m*.

ex [eks] **1** *prep*: **~ dividend** sin dividendo; **price ~ factory** precio *m* en fábrica; *V* **~ officio**.

2 *n*: **my ~*** mi antiguo marido, mi ex mujer, mi ex novio *etc*.

ex- [eks] *pref* (*former*) ex, antiguo: **~ambassador in Moscow** ex embajador en Moscú; **~leader of** antiguo jefe de; **~minister** ex ministro; *V* **ex-husband, ex-serviceman** *etc*.

exacerbate [eks'æsəbeɪt] *vt* exacerbar.

exact [ɪg'zækt] **1** *adj* exacto; **99, to be ~** concretamente 99, en concreto 99. **2** *vt* exigir (*from* a); *obedience etc* imponer (*from* a).

exacting [ɪg'zæktɪŋ] *adj* exigente; *conditions* severo, arduo.

exaction [ɪg'zækʃən] *n* exacción *f*.

exactitude [ɪg'zæktɪtjuːd] *n* exactitud *f*.

exactly [ɪg'zæktlɪ] *adv* exactamente; (*of time*) en punto; **~!**

¡exacto!; **what did you tell him ~?** ¿qué le dijiste, en concreto?; **he is not ~ an actor** no es un actor que digamos; **and I'm not ~ a dwarf** y yo tampoco soy un enano precisamente.
exactness [ɪg'zæktnɪs] *n* exactitud *f*.
exaggerate [ɪg'zædʒəreɪt] *vt* exagerar.
exaggerated [ɪg'zædʒəreɪtɪd] *adj* exagerado.
exaggeration [ɪg'zædʒəreɪʃən] *n* exageración *f*.
exalt [ɪg'zɔːlt] *vt* (*elevate*) exaltar, elevar; (*praise*) ensalzar.
exaltation [,egzɔːl'teɪʃən] *n* exaltación *f*, elevación *f*; ensalzamiento *m*.
exalted [ɪg'zɔːltɪd] *adj* exaltado, elevado.
exam* [ɪg'zæm] *n* = **examination.**
examination [ɪg,zæmɪ'neɪʃən] *n* (*Scol*) examen *m*; (*Jur*) interrogación *f*; (*inquiry*) investigación *f* (*into* de); (*by Customs etc*) registro *m*; (*of account*) revisión *f*; (*Med*) reconocimiento *m*; **our chemistry ~** nuestro examen de química; **the matter is under ~** el asunto está bajo estudio; **to enter** (*or* **go in for, sit**) **an ~** presentarse a un examen; **to take an ~ in** examinarse en.
examine [ɪg'zæmɪn] *vt* examinar; inspeccionar, escudriñar; (*Jur*) interrogar; *baggage etc* registrar; (*Med*) examinar, hacer un reconocimiento médico de; **we are examining whether ...** estamos pensando si ...; **we are examining the question** estamos estudiando la cuestión; **I was ~d in maths** me examinaron de matemáticas.
examinee [ɪg,zæmɪ'niː] *n* examinando *m*, -a *f*; **to be a bad ~** hacer siempre mal los exámenes.
examiner [ɪg'zæmɪnəʳ] *n* examinador *m*, -ora *f*; inspector *m*, -ora *f*.
example [ɪg'zɑːmpl] *n* ejemplo *m*; (*copy, specimen*) ejemplar *m*; (*Math*) problema *m*; **for ~** por ejemplo; **following the ~ of** siguiendo el ejemplo de; **to make an ~ of sb** castigar a uno de modo ejemplar; **to set an ~** dar ejemplo.
exasperate [ɪg'zɑːspəreɪt] *vt* exasperar, irritar, sacar de quicio; **to get ~d** irritarse.
exasperating [ɪg'zɑːspəreɪtɪŋ] *adj* irritante, que le saca a uno de quicio; **it's so ~!** es para volverse loco; **you're an ~ person** eres un hombre imposible.
exasperatingly [ɪg'zɑːspəreɪtɪŋlɪ] *adv*: **~ slow/stupid** tan lento/estúpido que le saca a uno de quicio.
exasperation [ɪg,zɑːspə'reɪʃən] *n* exasperación *f*, irritación *f*.
excavate ['ekskəveɪt] *vt* excavar.
excavation [,ekskə'veɪʃən] *n* excavación *f*.
excavator ['ekskəveɪtəʳ] *n* (*person*) excavador *m*, -ora *f*; (*machine*) excavadora *f*.
exceed [ɪk'siːd] *vt* exceder (*by* en); *number* pasar de, exceder de; *limit* rebasar; *speed limit* sobrepasar; *rights* ir más allá de, abusar de; *powers, instructions* excederse en; *hopes, expectations* superar; **a fine not ~ing £50** una multa que no pase de 50 libras.
exceedingly [ɪk'siːdɪŋlɪ] *adv* sumamente, sobremanera.
excel [ɪk'sel] **1** *vt* aventajar, superar. **2** *vi* sobresalir (*at, in* en). **3** *vr*: **to ~ o.s.** (*often iro*) lucirse, pasarse (*LAm*).
excellence ['eksələns] *n* excelencia *f*.
Excellency ['eksələnsɪ] *n* Excelencia *f*; **His ~** su Excelencia; **yes, Your ~** sí, Excelencia.
excellent ['eksələnt] *adj* excelente.
excellently ['eksələntlɪ] *adv* excelentemente, muy bien; **to do sth ~** hacer algo muy bien.
excelsior [ek'selsɪɔːʳ] *n* (*US*) virutas *fpl* de embalaje.
except [ɪk'sept] **1** *vt* exceptuar, excluir. **2** *prep* (*also* **~ for**) excepto, con excepción de, salvo; sin contar; menos; dejando aparte; **all ~ me** todos menos yo; **~ (that) ...** salvo que ...
excepting [ɪk'septɪŋ] *prep* = **except.**
exception [ɪk'sepʃən] *n* excepción *f*; **with the ~ of** a excepción de; **without ~** sin excepción; **to be an ~ to the rule** ser excepción de la regla; **the ~ proves the rule** la excepción confirma la regla; **to make an ~** hacer una excepción; **to take ~ to** desaprobar, (*feel offended*) ofenderse por, molestarse por.
exceptional [ɪk'sepʃənl] *adj* excepcional.
exceptionally [ɪk'sepʃənəlɪ] *adv*: **~ good** excepcionalmente bueno; **it happens ~ that ...** ocurre en casos excepcionales que ...
excerpt ['eksɜːpt] *n* extracto *m*.
excess [ɪk'ses] **1** *n* (**a**) exceso *m*; (*Comm*) excedente *m*; **in ~** de sobra; **in ~ of** superior a; **to carry to ~** llevar al exceso; **to drink to ~** beber en exceso.
(**b**) (*fig*) exceso *m*, desmán *m*, desafuero *m*.
2 *attr* excedente, sobrante; **~ demand** exceso *m* de demanda; **~ fare** suplemento *m*; **~ luggage, ~ baggage** exceso *m* de equipaje; **~ profits tax** impuesto *m* sobre las ganancias excesivas; **~ supply** exceso *m* de oferta; **~ weight** exceso *m* de peso.
excessive [ɪk'sesɪv] *adj* excesivo; **with ~ courtesy** con exagerada cortesía.
excessively [ɪk'sesɪvlɪ] *adv* excesivamente; exageradamente; **you are ~ kind** es Vd amable en exceso.
exchange [ɪks'tʃeɪndʒ] **1** *n* (**a**) (*act*) cambio *m*; (*of prisoners, publications, stamps etc*) canje *m*; (*of ideas, information*) intercambio *m*; **~ of contracts** intercambio *m* de escrituras; **~ of shots** tiroteo *m*; **~ of views** cambio *m* de impresiones; **~ of words** diálogo *m*; **in ~ for** a cambio de.
(**b**) **foreign ~** (*Fin*) divisas *fpl*.
(**c**) (*building*) (*of corn, cotton etc*) lonja *f*; (*labour ~*) bolsa *f* de trabajo; (*stock ~*) bolsa *f*; (*Telec*) central *f* telefónica.
2 *attr*: **~ control** (*Fin*) control *m* de divisas; **~ rate** (*Fin*) tipo *m* de cambio; **~ restrictions** (*Fin*) restricciones *fpl* monetarias; **~ value** contravalor *m*; **~ visit** visita *f* de intercambio.
3 *vt* cambiar (*for* por); *prisoners, publications, stamps etc* canjear (*for* por, *with* con); *greetings, shots* cambiar; *courtesies* hacerse; *blows* darse; **we ~d glances** nos miramos el uno al otro, cruzamos una mirada.
exchangeable [ɪks'tʃeɪndʒəbl] *adj* cambiable; canjeable.
exchequer [ɪks'tʃekəʳ] *n* hacienda *f*, tesoro *m*, erario *m*; **the E~** (*Brit*) la Hacienda *f* del Fisco.
excisable [ek'saɪzəbl] *adj* tasable.
excise 1 ['eksaɪz] *n* impuestos *mpl* interiores; **the E~** (*Brit*) *organismo recaudador de derechos de aduana y de importación.*
2 ['eksaɪz] *attr*: **~ duties** (*Brit*) impuestos *mpl* sobre consumos o ventas.
3 [ek'saɪz] *vt* (*cut*) cortar, quitar; (*fig*) suprimir, eliminar.
excision [ek'sɪʒən] *n* corte *m*; supresión *f*; (*Med*) excisión *f*.
excitability [ɪk'saɪtə'bɪlɪtɪ] *n* excitabilidad *f*; exaltación *f*, nerviosismo *m*.
excitable [ɪk'saɪtəbl] *adj* excitable; exaltado, nervioso.
excite [ɪk'saɪt] *vt* (*move to emotion*) emocionar, llenar de emoción, entusiasmar; (*stimulate*) excitar, estimular; provocar; *revolt* instigar; *interest* despertar, suscitar; **to ~ sb to action** provocar a uno a la acción.
excited [ɪk'saɪtɪd] *adj* emocionado, entusiasmado, ilusionado; *voice etc* lleno de emoción; **to be ~** estar muy emocionado, (*and upset*) estar agitado; **I'm so ~ about the new house** la nueva casa me da mucha ilusión; **to get ~** emocionarse, entusiasmarse (*about, over* por); (*crowd etc*) alborotarse; (*discussion*) acalorarse; (*get upset*) agitarse; **don't get so ~!** ¡no te emociones tanto!
excitedly [ɪk'saɪtɪdlɪ] *adv* con emoción, con entusiasmo; **he said ~** dijo entusiasmadísimo, dijo excitadísimo.
excitement [ɪk'saɪtmənt] *n* emoción *f*, entusiasmo *m*; excitación *f*; ilusión *f*; agitación *f*; alboroto *m*; **his arrival caused great ~** su llegada produjo una enorme emoción; **why all the ~?, what's all the ~ about?** ¿a qué se debe tanta conmoción?
exciting [ɪk'saɪtɪŋ] *adj* emocionante, apasionante; excitante; **how ~!** ¡qué ilusión!, ¡qué emocionante!; **it's a most ~ film** es una película llena de emoción.
excl. *abbr of* **excluding, exclusive (of)** con exclusión de.
exclaim [ɪks'kleɪm] *vi* exclamar.
exclamation [,eksklə'meɪʃən] *n* exclamación *f*; **~ mark, ~ point** (*US*) signo *m* de admiración.
exclamatory [eks'klæmətərɪ] *adj* exclamatorio.
exclude [ɪks'kluːd] *vt* excluir; exceptuar; *possibility of error etc* evitar.
excluding [ɪks'kluːdɪŋ] *as prep* excepto, con exclusión de; sin contar; **everything ~ the piano** todo excepto el piano.
exclusion [ɪks'kluːʒən] **1** *n* exclusión *f*; **to the ~ of** con exclusión de. **2** *attr*: **total ~ zone** zona *f* de exclusión total; **~ clause** cláusula *f* de exclusión.
exclusive [ɪks'kluːsɪv] **1** *adj* (**a**) (*owned by one*) exclusivo; único; **~ agency** agencia *f* exclusiva; **~ policy** política *f* exclusivista; **~ rights** exclusiva *f*, derechos *mpl* exclusivos; **~ story** reportaje *m* exclusivo; **~ to** privativo de; **they are mutually ~** se excluyen mutuamente.
(**b**) (*select*) *area, club, gathering* selecto; *offer* de privilegio.
2 *adv* (*not including*) **from 13 to 20 ~** del 13 al 20 exclusive; **till 9 January ~** hasta el 9 de enero exclusive; **~ of** excepto, con exclusión de; sin contar.
3 *n* (*story*) reportaje *m* exclusivo, exclusiva *f*, pisotón *m*.
exclusively [ɪks'kluːsɪvlɪ] *adv* exclusivamente.

exclusiveness [ɪks'kluːsɪvnɪs] *n* exclusividad *f*.
excommunicate [ˌekskə'mjuːnɪkeɪt] *vt* excomulgar.
excommunication ['ekskəˌmjuːnɪ'keɪʃən] *n* excomunión *f*.
ex-con* [ˌeks'kɒn] *n* ex convicto *m*.
excrement ['ekskrɪmənt] *n* excremento *m*.
excrescence [ɪks'kresns] *n* excrecencia *f*.
excreta [eks'kriːtə] *npl* excremento *m*.
excrete [eks'kriːt] *vt* excretar.
excretion [eks'kriːʃən] *n* excreción *f*.
excretory [eks'kriːtərɪ] *adj* excretorio.
excruciating [ɪks'kruːʃɪeɪtɪŋ] *adj pain* agudísimo, atroz; (*very bad*) horrible, fatal.
excruciatingly [ɪks'kruːʃɪeɪtɪŋlɪ] *adv* atrozmente; (*very badly*) horriblemente, fatal; **it was ~ funny** era para morirse de risa.
exculpate ['ekskʌlpeɪt] *vt* exculpar.
excursion [ɪks'kɜːʃən] **1** *n* excursión *f*. **2** *attr*: **~ ticket** billete *m* de excursión; **~ train** tren *m* de excursión, tren *m* de recreo.
excursionist [ɪk'skɜːʃənɪst] *n* excursionista *mf*.
excursus [ek'skɜːsɪz] *n* excursus *m*.
excusable [ɪks'kjuːzəbl] *adj* perdonable, disculpable, excusable.
excuse 1 [ɪks'kjuːs] *n* disculpa *f*, excusa *f*; razón *f*, defensa *f*, justificación *f*; (*insincere*) pretexto *m*; **there's no ~ for this** esto no admite disculpa; **it's only an ~** es un pretexto nada más; **to make ~s for sb** presentar excusas de uno; **he's only making ~s** está buscando pretextos; **he gives poverty as his ~** alega su pobreza; **what's your ~ this time?** ¿qué razón me das esta vez?

2 [ɪks'kjuːz] *vt* disculpar, perdonar; **to ~ sb sth** perdonar algo a uno; **to ~ sb from doing sth** dispensar a uno de hacer algo, eximir a uno de hacer algo; **that does not ~ your conduct** eso no justifica su conducta; **~ me!** (*in passing sb*) ¡perdón!, por favor, con (su) permiso; (*on interrupting sb*) perdone Vd; (*on leaving table*) ¡con permiso!; **if you will ~ me I must go** con permiso de Vds tengo que marcharme; **I must ask to be ~d this time** esta vez les ruego dispensarme; **may I be ~d for a moment?** ¿puedo salir un momento?

3 [ɪks'kjuːz] *vr*: **to ~ o.s. from doing sth** dispensarse de hacer algo; **after 10 minutes he ~d himself** después de 10 minutos pidió permiso y se fue.
ex-directory [ˌeksdɪ'rektərɪ] *adj*: **the number is ~** el número no figura en la guía (*por razones de seguridad etc*); **they are ~** su número no figura en la guía; **he had to go ~** tuvo que pedir que su número no figurara en la guía.
ex dividend [ˌeks'dɪvɪdend] *adj* sin dividendo.
execrable ['eksɪkrəbl] *adj* execrable, abominable; *manners* detestable.
execrably ['eksɪkrəblɪ] *adv* execrablemente.
execrate ['eksɪkreɪt] *vt* execrar, abominar (de).
execration [ˌeksɪ'kreɪʃən] *n* execración *f*, abominación *f*.
executant [ɪg'zekjʊtənt] *n* ejecutante *mf*.
execute ['eksɪkjuːt] *vt* (**a**) ejecutar (*also Art, Mus, Comput*); *order* cumplir; *scheme* llevar a cabo, realizar; *document* otorgar. (**b**) *man* ejecutar, ajusticiar.
execution [ˌeksɪ'kjuːʃən] *n* (**a**) ejecución *f*; cumplimiento *m*; realización *f*; otorgamiento *m*; (*of act, crime*) comisión *f*; **in the ~ of his duties** en el desempeño de sus obligaciones. (**b**) (*killing*) ejecución *f*.
executioner [ˌeksɪ'kjuːʃnəʳ] *n* verdugo *m*.
executive [ɪg'zekjʊtɪv] **1** *adj* ejecutivo; **~ assistant** ayudante *m* ejecutivo, ayudante *f* ejecutiva; **~ car** coche *m* de ejecutivo; **~ committee** junta *f* directiva; **~ director** (*Brit*) director *m* ejecutivo, directora *f* ejecutiva; **~ jet** reactor *m* ejecutivo; **~ officer** oficial *m* ejecutivo; **~ power** poder *m* ejecutivo; **~ privilege** (*US Pol*) inmunidad *f* del ejecutivo; **~ producer** (*TV*) productor *m* ejecutivo, productora *f* ejecutiva; **~ vice-president** vicepresidente *m* ejecutivo, vicepresidenta *f* ejecutiva.

2 *n* (**a**) (*power*) poder *m* ejecutivo, autoridad *f* suprema. (**b**) (*person*) ejecutivo *m*, gerente *mf*, directivo *m*, director *m*, -ora *f*.
executor [ɪg'zekjʊtəʳ] *n* albacea *m*, testamentario *m*.
executrix [ɪg'zekjʊtrɪks] *n* albacea *f*, ejecutora *f* testamentaria.
exegesis [ˌeksɪ'dʒiːsɪs] *n* exégesis *f*.
exemplary [ɪg'zemplərɪ] *adj* ejemplar.
exemplify [ɪg'zemplɪfaɪ] *vt* ejemplificar; ilustrar, demostrar; **as exemplified by X** según lo demuestra X.
exempt [ɪg'zem*p*t] **1** *adj* exento, libre (*from* de); **to be ~ from paying** estar dispensado de pagar. **2** *vt* exentar, eximir, dispensar (*from* de).
exemption [ɪg'zem*p*ʃən] *n* exención *f* (*from* de); inmunidad *f* (*from* de).
exercise ['eksəsaɪz] **1** *n* (**a**) ejercicio *m*; **to do (physical) ~s** hacer gimnasia; **to take ~** hacer ejercicio; **in the ~ of my duties** en el ejercicio de mi cargo.

(**b**) **~s** (*US*: *ceremony*) ceremonias *fpl*.

2 *attr*: **~ bicycle, ~ bike*** bicicleta *f* de ejercicio, bicicleta *f* estática; **~ book** cuaderno *m*.

3 *vt* (**a**) (*use*) *authority, influence, option, power* ejercer; *patience, restraint* usar de, emplear; *right* valerse de; **to ~ care** tomar cuidado de, proceder con cautela; tomar precaución.

(**b**) *mind* preocupar; **I am much ~d about it** esto me tiene preocupadísimo.

(**c**) *horse, team* entrenar; *dog* llevar de paseo; *muscle* ejercitar, hacer ejercicios con.

4 *vi* ejercitarse, hacer ejercicios.
exert [ɪg'zɜːt] **1** *vt* ejercer, emplear. **2** *vr*: **to ~ o.s.** esforzarse, afanarse (*to do* por hacer); (*overdo things*) trabajar demasiado; **he doesn't ~ himself at all** no hace el más mínimo esfuerzo.
exertion [ɪg'zɜːʃən] *n* esfuerzo *m*; (*overdoing things*) esfuerzo *m* excesivo, trabajo *m* excesivo.
exeunt ['eksɪʌnt] *vi* (*Theat*) salen, vánse.
ex gratia [ˌeks'greɪʃə] *adj payment* ex-gratia, a título gracioso.
exhalation [ˌeks*h*ə'leɪʃən] *n* exhalación *f*.
exhale [eks'heɪl] **1** *vt air* espirar, exhalar; *fumes* despedir. **2** *vi* espirar.
exhaust [ɪg'zɔːst] **1** *n* (*fumes*) gases *mpl* de escape; (*Aut etc*) escape *m*; (*Aut*: *also* **~ pipe**) tubo *m* de escape. **2** *attr* de escape. **3** *vt* (*all senses*) agotar; **to be ~ed** estar agotado.
exhaustible [ɪg'zɔːstəbl] *adj resource* que se puede agotar, limitado.
exhausting [ɪg'zɔːstɪŋ] *adj* agotador.
exhaustion [ɪg'zɔːstʃən] *n* agotamiento *m*; (*nervous*) postración *f* nerviosa.
exhaustive [ɪg'zɔːstɪv] *adj* exhaustivo.
exhaustively [ɪg'zɔːstɪvlɪ] *adv* de modo exhaustivo.
exhaustiveness [ɪg'zɔːstɪvnɪs] *n* exhaustividad *f*.
exhibit [ɪg'zɪbɪt] **1** *n* objeto *m* expuesto; pieza *f* de museo; (*painting etc*) obra *f* expuesta; (*Jur*) documento *m*; **to be on ~** estar expuesto.

2 *vt signs etc* mostrar, manifestar; *emotion* acusar; *exhibit* exponer, presentar al público; *film* presentar.

3 *vi* (*painter etc*) exponer, hacer una exposición.
exhibition [ˌeksɪ'bɪʃən] **1** *n* demostración *f*, manifestación *f*; (*by painter, sport etc*) exposición *f*; (*Brit Univ*) beca *f*; **an ~ of bad temper** una demostración de mal genio; **to be on ~** estar expuesto; **to make an ~ of o.s.** ponerse en ridículo.

2 *attr*: **~ game, ~ match** partido *m* de exhibición.
exhibitionism [ˌeksɪ'bɪʃənɪzəm] *n* exhibicionismo *m*.
exhibitionist [ˌeksɪ'bɪʃənɪst] **1** *adj* exhibicionista. **2** *n* exhibicionista *mf*.
exhibitor [ɪg'zɪbɪtəʳ] *n* expositor *m*, -ora *f*.
exhilarate [ɪg'zɪləreɪt] *vt* levantar el ánimo de, estimular, vigorizar; arrebatar; **to feel ~d** sentirse muy estimulado, estar alegre.
exhilarating [ɪg'zɪləreɪtɪŋ] *adj* tónico, vigorizador, estimulador.
exhilaration [ɪgˌzɪlə'reɪʃən] *n* (*effect*) efecto *m* tónico, efecto *m* vigorizador; (*mood*) euforia *f*, júbilo *m*, alegría *f*; **the ~ of speed** lo emocionante de la velocidad.
exhort [ɪg'zɔːt] *vt* exhortar (*to do* a hacer).
exhortation [ˌegzɔː'teɪʃən] *n* exhortación *f*.
exhumation [ˌeks*h*juː'meɪʃən] *n* exhumación *f*.
exhume [eks'hjuːm] *vt* exhumar, desenterrar.
ex-husband [ˌeks'hʌzbənd] *n* ex marido *m*.
exigence ['eksɪdʒəns] *n*, **exigency** [ɪg'zɪdʒənsɪ] *n* (*need*) exigencia *f*, necesidad *f*; (*emergency*) caso *m* de urgencia.
exigent ['eksɪdʒənt] *adj* exigente; urgente.
exiguous [eg'zɪgjʊəs] *adj* exiguo.
exile ['eksaɪl] **1** *n* (**a**) (*state*) destierro *m*, exilio *m*; **government in ~** gobierno *m* en el exilio. (**b**) (*person*) exilado *m*, -a *f*, exiliado *m*, -a *f*, desterrado *m*, -a *f*. **2** *vt* desterrar, poner en el exilio, exilar, exiliar.
exiled ['eksaɪld] *adj* exiliado.
exist [ɪg'zɪst] *vi* existir; vivir.
existence [ɪg'zɪstəns] *n* existencia *f*; vida *f*; **to be in ~** existir; **to come into ~** formarse, nacer, fundarse, empezar a tener existencia.
existent [ɪg'zɪstənt] *adj* existente, actual.

existential [ˌegzɪsˈtenʃəl] *adj* existencial.
existentialism [ˌegzɪsˈtenʃəlɪzəm] *n* existencialismo *m*.
existentialist [ˌegzɪsˈtenʃəlɪst] **1** *adj* existencialista. **2** *n* existencialista *mf*.
existing [ɪgˈzɪstɪŋ] *adj* existente, actual.
exit [ˈeksɪt] **1** *n* salida *f*; (*Theat*) mutis *m*; **to make one's ~** salir, marcharse. **2** *attr*: **~ permit** permiso *m* de salida; **~ poll** encuesta *f* de votantes al salir del centro electoral; **~ ramp** (*US*) vía *f* de acceso; **~ visa** visado *m* de salida. **3** *vt* (*Comput*) salir de; **if we have to ~ the plane** (*US*) si tenemos que abandonar (*or* salir de) el avión. **4** *vi* (*Theat*) hacer mutis; (*Comput*) salir (del sistema); **~ Hamlet** váse Hamlet.
exodus [ˈeksədəs] *n* éxodo *m*; **there was a general ~** salieron todos.
ex officio [ˌeksəˈfɪʃɪəʊ] **1** *adv act* ex officio, oficialmente. **2** *adj member* nato, ex officio.
exonerate [ɪgˈzɒnəreɪt] *vt* exculpar, disculpar (*from* de).
exoneration [ɪgˌzɒnəˈreɪʃən] *n* exculpación *f*.
exorbitance [ɪgˈzɔːbɪtəns] *n* exorbitancia *f*.
exorbitant [ɪgˈzɔːbɪtənt] *adj* excesivo, exorbitante.
exorbitantly [ɪgˈzɔːbɪtəntlɪ] *adv* excesivamente.
exorcise [ˈeksɔːsaɪz] *vt* exorcizar, conjurar.
exorcism [ˈeksɔːsɪzəm] *n* exorcismo *m*.
exorcist [ˈeksɔːsɪst] *n* exorcista *mf*.
exotic [ɪgˈzɒtɪk] **1** *adj* exótico. **2** *n* planta *f* exótica.
exotica [ɪgˈzɒtɪkə] *npl* objetos *mpl* exóticos.
exoticism [ɪgˈzɒtɪsɪzəm] *n* exotismo *m*.
exp. *abbr of* **expenses**; **expired**; **export**; **express**.
expand [ɪksˈpænd] **1** *vt* extender; ensanchar; dilatar; *number* aumentar; *chest* expandir; *market, operations etc* expandir, expansionar; *wings* abrir, desplegar; (*Math*) desarrollar.
2 *vi* extenderse; ensancharse; dilatarse; (*number*) aumentarse; (*market etc*) expandirse; (*person*) ponerse más expansivo.
◆**expand (up)on** *vt theme* tratar más extensamente, explayarse en el análisis de.
expanded [ɪksˈpændɪd] *adj* (*Metal, Tech*) dilatado; **~ polystyrene** poliestireno *m* dilatado.
expander [ɪksˈpændəʳ] *n* ejercitador *m* pectoral; = **chest expander**.
expanding [ɪksˈpændɪŋ] *adj metal etc* dilatable; *bracelet* expandible; *market, industry, profession* en expansión; **the ~ universe** el universo en expansión; **~ file** carpeta *f* de acordeón; **a job with ~ opportunities** un empleo con perspectivas de futuro; **a rapidly ~ industry** una industria en rápida expansión.
expanse [ɪksˈpæns] *n* extensión *f*; (*of wings*) envergadura *f*.
expansion [ɪksˈpænʃən] *n* extensión *f*; dilatación *f*; (*of town etc*) ensanche *m*; (*of economy, trade etc*) expansión *f*; (*of number*) aumento *m*; (*Math etc*) desarrollo *m*; **~ board** placa *f* de expansión; **~ bottle** (*or* **tank**) (*Aut*) depósito *m* del agua; **~ bus** bus *m* de expansión; **~ card** tarjeta *f* de expansión; **~ slot** ranura *f* para tarjetas de expansión.
expansionism [ɪksˈpænʃənɪzəm] *n* expansionismo *m*.
expansionist [ɪksˈpænʃənɪst] *adj* expansionista.
expansive [ɪksˈpænsɪv] *adj* expansivo (*also fig*).
expansively [ɪksˈpænsɪvlɪ] *adv* (*in detail*) *relate* extensamente, en extensión, ampliamente; (*warmly*) *welcome, say* cálidamente; **to gesture ~** hacer ademanes extravagantes.
expansiveness [ɪkˈspænsɪvnɪs] *n* expansividad *f*.
expat* = **expatriate**.
expatiate [eksˈpeɪʃɪeɪt] *vi*: **to ~ on** extenderse en un análisis de, extenderse en alabanzas (*etc*) de.
expatriate [eksˈpætrɪeɪt] **1** *adj* expatriado. **2** *n* expatriado *m*, -a *f*. **3** *vt* desterrar. **4** *vr*: **to ~ o.s.** expatriarse.
expect [ɪksˈpekt] **1** *vt* (**a**) (*with n*) *storm, defeat, baby etc* esperar; *fun, good time* prometerse; contar con; **it's not what I ~ed** no es lo que yo esperaba; **I ~ed as much, just what I ~ed** ya me lo figuraba; **difficulties are only to be ~ed** es natural que haya dificultades; **as might have been ~ed, as one might ~, as was to be ~ed** como era de esperar, como podía esperarse; **we ~ your help** contamos con su ayuda; **I ~ed nothing less of you** no esperaba menos de ti; **it was not so tough as I ~ed (it to be)** era menos severo de lo que yo esperaba; **when least ~ed** el día menos pensado, a lo mejor; **we ~ you tomorrow** le esperamos mañana; **he is ~ed in Madrid** le esperan en Madrid; **is he ~ing you?** ¿tiene Vd cita con él?, ¿está Vd citado?; **don't ~ me till you see me** no contéis conmigo hasta verme llegar; **you know what to ~** ya sabes a qué atenerte.
(**b**) (*with verb*) **I ~ to see him** espero verle; **we ~ he will come** contamos con que venga; **I ~ you to be punctual** cuento con que seas puntual; **so you ~ me to pay?** ¿así que esperas que pague yo?; **what do you ~ me to do about it?** ¿qué pretendes que haga yo?; **how do you ~ me to go out like this?** ¿cómo pretendes que salga así?; **she can't be ~ed to know that** no está obligada a saber eso; **it is ~ed that ...** se espera que + *subj*; se prevé que + *indic*; **it is hardly to be ~ed that ...** apenas cabe esperar que + *subj*.
(**c**) (*think, suppose*) imaginarse; suponer; figurarse; **I ~ so** supongo que sí; **I ~ he's there by now** me imagino que ya habrá llegado.
2 *vi*: **to be ~ing** estar encinta, estar en estado (interesante).
expectancy [ɪksˈpektənsɪ] *n* (*state*) expectación *f*; (*hope, chance*) expectativa *f* (*of* de); (*life* ~) esperanza *f* de vida, vida *f* media, índice *m* vital.
expectant [ɪksˈpektənt] *adj* expectante; (*hopeful*) ilusionado; **~ mother** mujer *f* encinta, futura madre *f*.
expectantly [ɪksˈpektəntlɪ] *adv* con expectación; **to wait ~** esperar a ver qué sale.
expectation [ˌekspekˈteɪʃən] *n* (**a**) (*state*) expectación *f*; **in ~ of** en expectación de, esperando.
(**b**) (*hope*) esperanza *f*, expectativa *f*; **~s** (*in will*) esperanzas *fpl* de heredar; **~ of life** esperanza *f* de vida, vida *f* media, índice *m* vital; **our ~ is that ...** esperamos que ...; **contrary to ~s** en contra de lo que se esperaba; **it is beyond our ~s** es mejor de lo que esperábamos; **to come up to one's ~s** resultar tan bueno como se esperaba; **to exceed one's ~s** sobrepasar lo que se esperaba; **to fall below one's ~s** no llegar a lo que se esperaba.
expectorate [eksˈpektəreɪt] *vt* expectorar.
expedience [ɪksˈpiːdɪəns] *n*, **expediency** [ɪksˈpiːdɪənsɪ] *n* conveniencia *f*, oportunidad *f*.
expedient [ɪksˈpiːdɪənt] **1** *adj* conveniente, oportuno. **2** *n* expediente *m*, recurso *m*.
expedite [ˈekspɪdaɪt] *vt* (*speed up*) acelerar; *business* despachar (con prontitud); *progress* facilitar.
expedition [ˌekspɪˈdɪʃən] *n* expedición *f*.
expeditionary [ˌekspɪˈdɪʃənrɪ] *adj* expedicionario; **~ force** fuerza *f* expedicionaria.
expeditious [ˌekspɪˈdɪʃəs] *adj* rápido, pronto.
expeditiously [ˌekspɪˈdɪʃəslɪ] *adv* con toda prontitud.
expel [ɪksˈpel] *vt* arrojar, expeler; *person* expulsar.
expend [ɪksˈpend] *vt money* expender, gastar; *ammunition* usar; *resources* consumir, agotar; *time* pasar; *effort* dedicar (*on* a); *care* poner (*on* en).
expendability [ɪksˌpendəˈbɪlətɪ] *n* prescindibilidad *f*.
expendable [ɪksˈpendəbl] **1** *adj* que se puede sacrificar, que no es insustituible; reemplazable, sustituible. **2** **~s** *npl* géneros *mpl* (*or* elementos *mpl etc*) reemplazables.
expenditure [ɪksˈpendɪtʃəʳ] *n* (*of money etc*) gasto *m*, desembolso *m*; (*of effort, energy*) despliegue *m*; **after a great ~ of time on it** después de dedicarle mucho tiempo.
expense [ɪksˈpens] *n* gasto *m*, gastos *mpl*; costa *f*; **~s** gastos *mpl*; **at great ~** gastándose muchísimo dinero; **at my ~** a mi costa, corriendo yo con los gastos; **at the ~ of** (*fig*) a costa de, a expensas de; **regardless of ~** sin parar en gastos, sin escatimar gastos; **with all ~s paid** con todos los gastos pagados; **to be a great ~ to sb** costar a uno mucho dinero; **to go to ~** meterse en gastos (*over* por); **to pay sb's ~s** pagar los gastos a uno; **to put sb to ~** hacer que uno gaste dinero; *V* **business** *etc*.
2 *attr*: **~ account** cuenta *f* de gastos (de representación).
expensive [ɪksˈpensɪv] *adj* caro, costoso; *shop etc* carero.
expensively [ɪksˈpensɪvlɪ] *adv* costosamente; (*sparing no expense*) sin pararse en gastos.
expensiveness [ɪksˈpensɪvnɪs] *n* carestía *f*.
experience [ɪksˈpɪərɪəns] **1** *n* experiencia *f*; **to know from bitter ~ that ...** saber por amargas experiencias personales que ...; **to learn by ~, to profit from ~** aprender por la experiencia.
2 *vt* experimentar; *fate, loss* sufrir; *difficulty* tener, tropezar con.
experienced [ɪksˈpɪərɪənst] *adj* experimentado, perito, experto (*in* en).
experiment [ɪksˈperɪmənt] **1** *n* experimento *m*; experiencia *f*; prueba *f*, ensayo *m*; **as an ~, by way of ~** como experimento. **2** *vi* experimentar, hacer experimentos (*on* en, *with* con).
experimental [eksˌperɪˈmentl] *adj* experimental; **the process is still at the ~ stage** el proceso está todavía en prueba.

experimentally [eks,perɪ'mentəlɪ] *adv* experimentalmente, como experimento.
experimentation [eks,perɪmen'teɪʃən] *n* experimentación *f*.
experimenter [ɪks'perɪmentəʳ] *n* investigador *m*, -ora *f*.
expert ['ekspɜ:t] **1** *adj* experto, perito (*at, in* en); *touch etc* hábil; *witness, evidence* pericial; ~ **system** sistema *m* experto; ~ **valuation** tasación *f* pericial. **2** *n* experto *m*, -a *f* (*at, in* en); técnico *m*; especialista *mf*.
expertise [,ekspə'ti:z] *n* pericia *f*; conocimientos *mpl* técnicos; (*of touch etc*) habilidad *f*.
expertly ['ekspɜ:tlɪ] *adv* expertamente.
expertness ['ekspɜ:tnɪs] *n* pericia *f*; habilidad *f*.
expiate ['ekspɪeɪt] *vt* expiar.
expiation [,ekspɪ'eɪʃən] *n* expiación *f*.
expiatory ['ekspɪətərɪ] *adj* expiatorio.
expiration [,ekspaɪə'reɪʃən] *n* (**a**) (*ending*) terminación *f*; expiración *f*; (*Comm*) vencimiento *m*, caducidad *f*. (**b**) (*of breath*) espiración *f*.
expire [ɪks'paɪəʳ] *vi* (**a**) (*end*) terminar; (*die*) expirar; (*reach its term*) expirar, cumplirse, (*Comm*) vencer, (*ticket*) caducar, vencerse. (**b**) (*breathe out*) espirar.
expiry [ɪks'paɪərɪ] *n*: ~ **date** fecha *f* de caducidad; = **expiration.**
explain [ɪks'pleɪn] **1** *vt* explicar; *plan* exponer; *mystery* aclarar; *conduct* explicar; justificar; **that ~s it** con eso todo queda aclarado.
2 *vr*: **to ~ o.s.** (*clearly*) hablar más claro, explicarse con más detalles; (*morally*) justificar su conducta; **kindly ~ yourself!** ¡explíquese Vd!
◆**explain away** *vt*: **to ~ sth away** justificar algo hábilmente, dar razones convincentes de algo, *difficulty* salvar hábilmente; **just you ~ that away!** ¡a ver si logras justificar eso!
explainable [ɪks'pleɪnəbl] *adj* explicable.
explanation [,eksplə'neɪʃən] *n* explicación *f*; aclaración *f*; **what is the ~ of this?** ¿cómo se explica esto?; **there must be some ~** ha de haber alguna razón.
explanatory [ɪks'plænətərɪ] *adj* explicativo; aclaratorio.
expletive [eks'pli:tɪv] **1** *n* (*Gram*) palabra *f* expletiva; (*oath*) palabrota *f*, taco *m*; **'~ deleted'** 'se suprime palabrota'. **2** *adj* (*Gram*) expletivo.
explicable [eks'plɪkəbl] *adj* explicable.
explicit [ɪks'plɪsɪt] *adj* explícito.
explicitly [ɪks'plɪsɪtlɪ] *adv* explícitamente.
explicitness [ɪk'splɪsɪtnɪs] *n* carácter *m* explícito, lo explícito, claridad *f*.
explode [ɪks'pləʊd] **1** *vt* volar, hacer saltar, explotar, explosionar; *rumour, myth, belief, theory* desacreditar, refutar.
2 *vi* estallar, hacer explosión, explotar, explosionar; (*with anger etc*) reventar (*with* de); **the town ~d in revolt** estalló la rebelión en la ciudad; **when I said that he ~d** cuando dije eso se puso furioso.
exploit 1 ['eksplɔɪt] *n* hazaña *f*, proeza *f*. **2** [ɪks'plɔɪt] *vt* explotar.
exploitable [eks'plɔɪtəbl] *adj* explotable.
exploitation [,eksplɔɪ'teɪʃən] *n* explotación *f*.
exploitative [eks'plɔɪtətɪv] *adj* explotador.
exploiter [eks'plɔɪtəʳ] *n* explotador *m*, -ora *f*.
exploration [,eksplɔ:'reɪʃən] *n* exploración *f*.
exploratory [eks'plɒrətərɪ] *adj* exploratorio, preparatorio, de sondaje.
explore [ɪks'plɔ:ʳ] *vt* explorar; (*fig*) examinar, sondar, investigar.
explorer [ɪks'plɔ:rəʳ] *n* explorador *m*, -ora *f*.
explosion [ɪks'pləʊʒən] *n* explosión *f* (*also fig*).
explosive [ɪks'pləʊzɪv] **1** *adj* explosivo (*also fig*). **2** *n* explosivo *m*. **3** *attr*: **~s expert** artificiero *m*.
explosiveness [ik'spləʊzɪvnɪs] *n* carácter *m* explosivo.
exponent [eks'pəʊnənt] *n* exponente *mf*, partidario *m*, -a *f* (*of* de), intérprete *mf* (*of* de); (*Gram*) exponente *m*.
exponential [,ekspəʊ'nenʃəl] *adj* exponencial.
exponentially [,ekspəʊ'nenʃlɪ] *adv* de manera exponencial.
export 1 ['ekspɔ:t] *n* exportación *f*, artículo *m* de exportación.
2 ['ekspɔ:t] *attr*: ~ **agent** agente *mf* de exportación; ~ **credit** crédito *m* a la exportación; ~ **duty** derechos *mpl* de exportación; ~ **earnings** ganancias *fpl* por exportación; ~ **invoice** factura *f* de exportación; ~ **licence, ~ license** (*US*) permiso *m* de exportación; ~ **manager** director *m*, -ora *f* de exportación; **~-orientated** (*Brit*), **~-oriented** (*esp US*) dedicado a la exportación; ~ **sales** ventas *fpl* de exportación; ~ **subsidy** subsidio *m* de exportación; ~ **trade** comercio *m* de exportación.
3 [eks'pɔ:t] *vt* exportar.
exportable [eks'pɔ:təbl] *adj* exportable.
exportation [,ekspɔ:'teɪʃən] *n* exportación *f*.
exporter [eks'pɔ:təʳ] *n* exportador *m*, -ora *f*.
exporting [ek'spɔ:tɪŋ] *adj* exportador; ~ **company** empresa *f* exportadora; ~ **country** país *m* exportador.
expose [ɪks'pəʊz] **1** *vt* exponer (*also Phot*); *weakness* descubrir; *falsity* demostrar; *ignorance, weakness* revelar, descubrir; *fake, plot, imposter* desenmascarar; **to ~ sb to ridicule** exponer a uno al ridículo.
2 *vr* (**a**) **to ~ o.s. to** *risk, danger* exponerse a.
(**b**) **to ~ o.s.** (*sexually*) practicar el exhibicionismo.
exposé [ek'spəʊzeɪ] *n* exposición *f*, revelación *f*.
exposed [ɪks'pəʊzd] *adj* expuesto; *land, house* desprotegido; (*Elec*) *wire* al aire; *pipe, beam* al descubierto; **to be ~** (*thing normally hidden*) estar al descubierto; **to be ~ to** estar expuesto a.
exposition [,ekspə'zɪʃən] *n* exposición *f*, explicación *f*.
expostulate [ɪks'pɒstjʊleɪt] *vi* protestar; **to ~ with** reconvenir a, discutir con, tratar de convencer a.
expostulation [ɪks,pɒstjʊ'leɪʃən] *n* protesta *f*, reconvención *f*.
exposure [ɪks'pəʊʒəʳ] *n* exposición *f* (*also Phot*); revelación *f*; desenmascaramiento *m*; (*sexual*) exhibición *f*, acto *m* de exhibicionismo; **a house with a southerly ~** una casa orientada hacia el sur; **to die from ~** morir de frío, morir por estar a la intemperie; **he's getting a lot of ~** se le dedica mucha atención (pública, en la prensa *etc*); **to threaten sb with ~** amenazar con desenmascarar a uno.
exposure-meter [ɪks'pəʊʒə,mi:təʳ] *n* fotómetro *m*.
expound [ɪks'paʊnd] *vt* exponer, explicar; *text* comentar.
ex-president [,eks'prezɪdənt] *n* ex presidente *m*, -a *f*.
express [ɪks'pres] **1** *adj* (**a**) (*clear*) expreso, explícito, categórico; ~ **warranty** garantía *f* escrita.
(**b**) (*Brit*) *letter* urgente; *service etc* rápido; ~ **coach** autobús *m* rápido; ~ **delivery** (*Brit*) entrega *f* urgente; ~ **train** rápido *m*.
2 *n* rápido *m*.
3 *adv*: **to send sth ~** enviar algo por carta urgente (*etc*).
4 *vt* (**a**) (*make known*) expresar.
(**b**) (*squeeze out*) *juice* exprimir.
5 *vr*: **to ~ o.s.** expresarse.
expression [ɪks'preʃən] *n* expresión *f*; **as an ~ of thanks** en señal de agradecimiento; **if you'll pardon the ~** hablando con perdón, perdonen la palabra.
expressionism [eks'preʃənɪzəm] *n* expresionismo *m*.
expressionist [eks'preʃənɪst] **1** *adj* expresionista. **2** *n* expresionista *mf*.
expressionless [ɪks'preʃənlɪs] *adj* sin expresión, inexpresivo.
expressive [ɪks'presɪv] *adj* expresivo.
expressively [ɪks'presɪvlɪ] *adv* expresivamente.
expressiveness [ɪks'presɪvnɪs] *n* expresividad *f*.
expressly [ɪks'preslɪ] *adv* expresamente; *deny, prohibit etc* terminantemente.
expresso [ɪk'spresəʊ] = **espresso.**
expressway [ɪks'presweɪ] *n* (*US*) autopista *f*.
expropriate [eks'prəʊprɪeɪt] *vt* expropiar.
expropriation [eks,prəʊprɪ'eɪʃən] *n* expropiación *f*.
expulsion [ɪks'pʌlʃən] *n* expulsión *f*.
expunge [ɪks'pʌndʒ] *vt* borrar, tachar.
expurgate ['ekspɜ:geɪt] *vt* expurgar.
exquisite [eks'kwɪzɪt] **1** *adj* exquisito, primoroso; *pain etc* intenso. **2** *n* (††) petimetre *m*, figurín *m*.
exquisitely [eks'kwɪzɪtlɪ] *adv* primorosamente, con primor.
ex-serviceman ['eks'sɜ:vɪsmən] *n*, *pl* **ex-servicemen** ['eks'sɜ:vɪsmen] excombatiente *m*.
ex-smoker ['eks'sməʊkəʳ] *n* (*US*) persona *f* que ha dejado de fumar.
ext. (*Telec*) *abbr of* **extension** extensión *f*.
extant [eks'tænt] *adj* existente.
extemporary [ɪks'tempərərɪ] *adj* improvisado, hecho sin preparación.
extempore [eks'tempərɪ] **1** *adv* de improviso, sin preparación. **2** *adj* improvisado, hecho sin preparación.
extemporize [ɪks'tempəraɪz] *vti* improvisar.
extend [ɪks'tend] **1** *vt* (**a**) extender; *hand* tender, alargar; *building etc* ensanchar, ampliar; *road etc* prolongar; (*increase*) aumentar; *term, stay* prolongar, prorrogar.
(**b**) *thanks, welcome* dar, ofrecer; *invitation* enviar.
(**c**) *athlete* pedir el máximo esfuerzo a; **the staff is fully ~ed** el personal trabaja al máximum; el personal rinde todo lo que puede; **that child is not sufficiently ~ed** a ese niño no se le exige bastante esfuerzo.

2 *vi* extenderse; prolongarse; **to ~ over** abarcar, incluir; **to ~ to** extenderse a, llegar hasta, (*fig*) abarcar, incluir; **does that ~ to me?** ¿eso me incluye a mí?

3 *vr*: **to ~ o.s.** trabajar (*etc*) al máximum, esforzarse.

extendable [ɪk'stendɪbl] *adj* extensible.

extended [ɪk'stendɪd] *adj* extendido; ampliado; **during our ~ stay** durante nuestra estancia prolongada; **~ area network** red *f* de área extendida; **~ family** familia *f* extendida; **~ forecast** (*US*) pronóstico *m* a largo plazo, pronóstico *m* para varios días; **to grant sb ~ credit** conceder a uno un crédito ilimitado; **he has been granted ~ leave** se le ha permitido prolongar su permiso.

extensible [ɪks'tensɪbl] *adj* extensible.

extension [ɪks'tenʃən] **1** *n* extensión *f*; (*of building etc*) ensanche *m*, ampliación *f*; anejo *m*; (*of road*) prolongación *f*; (*of term, stay*) prolongación *f*, prórroga *f*; (*Comm*) prórroga *f*; (*increase*) aumento *m*; (*Telec*) extensión *f*, supletorio *m* (*LAm*), interno *m* (*SC*); **by ~** por extensión.

2 *attr*: **~ cable, ~ cord** (*Elec*) prolongación *f* eléctrica; **~ course(s)** *cursos nocturnos organizados por una universidad*; **~ ladder** escalera *f* extensible; **~ lead** (*Elec*) extensión *f* de cable.

extensive [ɪks'tensɪv] *adj* extenso; vasto, ancho, dilatado; *use etc* frecuente, general, común.

extensively [ɪks'tensɪvlɪ] *adv* extensamente; **to travel ~** viajar por muchos países; **he travelled ~ in Mexico** viajó por muchas partes de Méjico; **it is used ~** se usa comúnmente.

extent [ɪks'tent] *n* (*space*) extensión *f*; (*scope*) alcance *m*; **the ~ of the problem** el alcance del problema; **to the ~ of** + *ger* hasta el punto de + *infin*; **to a certain ~, to some ~** hasta cierto punto; **to the full ~** en toda su extensión; (*fig*) completamente; **to a great** (*or* **large**) **~** en gran parte, en alto grado; **to a lesser ~** en menor grado; **to such an ~ that** hasta tal punto que; **to that ~** hasta ahí; **to what ~?** ¿hasta qué punto?

extenuate [eks'tenjʊeɪt] *vt* atenuar, mitigar, disminuir (la gravedad de).

extenuating [eks'tenjʊeɪtɪŋ] *adj circumstance* atenuante.

exterior [eks'tɪərɪər] **1** *adj* exterior, externo. **2** *n* exterior *m*; (*appearance*) aspecto *m*.

exteriorize [eks'tɪərɪəraɪz] *vt* exteriorizar.

exterminate [eks'tɜːmɪneɪt] *vt* exterminar.

extermination [eks,tɜːmɪ'neɪʃən] *n* exterminio *m*.

exterminator [eks'tɜːmɪneɪtər] *n* (*US*) exterminador *m* de plagas.

extern ['ekstɜːn] *n* (*US*) externo *m*, -a *f*.

external [eks'tɜːnl] **1** *adj* externo, exterior; **~ account** cuenta *f* con el exterior; **~ audit** auditoría *f* externa; **~ trade** comercio *m* exterior; **for ~ use** para uso externo. **2** **~s** *npl* exterioridad *f*, aspecto *m* exterior.

externally [eks'tɜːnəlɪ] *adv* externamente, exteriormente; por fuera.

extinct [ɪks'tɪŋkt] *adj volcano* extinto, apagado, extinguido; *animal* extinto, desaparecido.

extinction [ɪks'tɪŋkʃən] *n* extinción *f*.

extinguish [ɪks'tɪŋgwɪʃ] *vt* extinguir, apagar; *title etc* suprimir.

extinguisher [ɪks'tɪŋgwɪʃər] *n* (*for fire*) extintor *m*; (*for candle*) apagador *m*, apagavelas *m*.

extirpate ['ekstɜːpeɪt] *vt* extirpar.

extirpation [,ekstə'peɪʃən] *n* extirpación *f*.

extn (*Telec*) *abbr of* **extension** extensión *f*.

extol, (*US*) **extoll** [ɪks'tɒl] *vt* ensalzar, alabar.

extort [ɪks'tɔːt] *vt* obtener por fuerza (*from* de), exigir por amenazas (*from* a).

extortion [ɪks'tɔːʃən] *n* exacción *f*; (*by public official*) concusión *f*.

extortionate [ɪks'tɔːʃənɪt] *adj price etc* excesivo, exorbitante.

extortioner [ɪks'tɔːʃənər] *n* desollador *m*; (*official*) concusionario *m*.

extra ['ekstrə] **1** *adj* adicional; de más, de sobra; *charge, pay etc* extraordinario; *part* de repuesto; **we need 2 ~ chairs** necesitamos 2 sillas más; **we seem to have 2 ~ men** parece que tenemos 2 hombres de sobra; **~ charge** recargo *m*; suplemento *m*; **~ pay** sobresueldo *m*; **~ time** (*Sport*) prórroga *f*; **postage ~** gastos de franqueo no incluidos; **postage and packing ~** gastos de envío no incluidos; **5 tons ~ to requirements** un excedente de 5 toneladas; **to take ~ care** ir con especial cuidado; **for ~ security** para mayor seguridad; **you must make an ~ effort** tienes que hacer un esfuerzo excepcional; **service is ~** el servicio no está incluido; **the wine is ~** el vino no está incluido (en el precio).

2 *adv* (**a**) (*with adj, adv, verb*) especialmente, extraordinariamente; **~ big** más grande que lo normal; **~ smart** más elegante que de costumbre; **with ~ special care** con especial cuidado; **of ~ special quality** de calidad superior; **this is ~ difficult** esto es extraordinariamente difícil; **to sing ~ loud** cantar extraordinariamente fuerte.

(**b**) (*after verb*) **we shall have to work ~** tendremos que trabajar más; **to pay ~** pagar más; pagar un suplemento.

3 *n* (**a**) (*on bill*) extra *m*, suplemento *m*; (*Theat*) extra *mf*, comparsa *mf*; (*of paper*) edición *f* extraordinaria; (*spare part, US*) repuesto *m*; **~s** (*Aut*: *also* **optional ~s**) accesorios *mpl*, extras *mpl*.

(**b**) **what shall we do with the ~?** ¿qué hacemos con el exceso?, ¿qué hacemos con lo que sobra?

extra... ['ekstrə] *pref* extra...

extract 1 ['ekstrækt] *n* (*Liter*) cita *f*, trozo *m*; (*Pharm*) extracto *m*; (*of beef etc*) extracto *m*, concentrado *m*; **~s from 'Don Quijote'** (*as book*) selecciones *fpl* del 'Quijote'.

2 [ɪks'trækt] *vt* sacar (*from* de); extraer (*also Math*); *confession etc* arrancar, sacar, obtener.

extraction [ɪks'trækʃən] *n* extracción *f*; obtención *f*.

extractor [ɪks'træktər] **1** *n* extractor *m*. **2** *attr*: **~ fan** (*Brit*) extractor *m* de olores.

extracurricular [,ekstrəkə'rɪkjʊlər] *adj* extracurricular.

extraditable ['ekstrədaɪtəbl] *adj* sujeto a extradición.

extradite ['ekstrədaɪt] *vt* extraditar.

extradition [,ekstrə'dɪʃən] *n* extradición *f*.

extramarital [,ekstre'mærɪtəl] *adj* extramarital, fuera del matrimonio.

extramural ['ekstrə'mjʊərəl] *adj jurisdiction etc* (de) extramuros; *activities* de carácter privado; (*esp Brit*) *course* para externos; **an ~ chapel** una capilla extramuros; **Department of E~ Studies** (*Brit Univ*) Departamento *m* de cursos para externos.

extraneous [eks'treɪnɪəs] *adj* extraño; **~ to** ajeno a.

extraordinarily [ɪks'trɔːdnrɪlɪ] *adv* extraordinariamente.

extraordinary [ɪks'trɔːdnrɪ] *adj* extraordinario; (*exceptional*) excepcional, poco común, insólito; (*odd*) raro; (*incredible*) increíble; **how ~!** ¡qué raro!; **~ general meeting** junta *f* general extraordinaria; **~ meeting of shareholders** (*Brit*) junta *f* extraordinaria de accionistas; **~ reserve** (*Fin*) reserva *f* extraordinaria; **it is ~ that** ... es increíble que + *subj*.

extrapolate [ɪks'træpəleɪt] *vt* extrapolar.

extrapolation [ɪks,træpə'leɪʃən] *n* extrapolación *f*.

extrasensory ['ekstrə'sensərɪ] *adj*: **~ perception** percepción *f* extrasensorial.

extraspecial [,ekstrə'speʃəl] *adj* muy especial; **to take ~ care over sth** tomar extremadas precauciones en algo.

extraterrestrial [,ekstrətə'restrɪəl] *adj* extraterrestre.

extraterritorial ['ekstrə,terɪ'tɔːrɪəl] *adj* extraterritorial.

extravagance [ɪks'trævəgəns] *n* (**a**) prodigalidad *f*; derroche *m*; despilfarro *m*; lujo *m* desmedido. (**b**) exorbitancia *f*; lo excesivo; rareza *f*.

extravagant [ɪks'trævəgənt] *adj* (**a**) (*lavish*) pródigo; (*wasteful*) derrochador, despilfarrador; (*luxurious*) muy lujoso. (**b**) *price* exorbitante; *praise, claim etc* exagerado, excesivo; (*odd*) raro, estrafalario.

extravagantly [ɪks'trævəgəntlɪ] *adv spend etc* profusamente, con gran despilfarro; (*luxuriously*) muy lujosamente; *praise* excesivamente; *behave* de modo raro.

extravaganza [eks,trævə'gænzə] *n* obra *f* extravagante y fantástica.

extravehicular [,ekstrəvɪ'hɪkjʊlər] *adj* fuera de la nave.

extreme [ɪks'triːm] **1** *adj* extremo; *care, poverty etc* extremado; *case* excepcional.

2 *n* extremo *m*, extremidad *f*; **~s of temperature** temperaturas *fpl* extremas; **in the ~** en sumo grado; **to go from one ~ to the other** pasar de un extremo a otro; **to go to ~s** ir muy lejos, tomar medidas extremas.

extremely [ɪks'triːmlɪ] *adv* sumamente, extremadamente; sobremanera; **it is ~ difficult** es sumamente difícil, es dificilísimo; **we are ~ glad** nos alegramos muchísimo.

extremism [ɪks'triːmɪzəm] *n* extremismo *m*.

extremist [ɪks'triːmɪst] **1** *adj* extremista. **2** *n* extremista *mf*, ultra *mf*.

extremity [ɪks'tremɪtɪ] *n* (**a**) (*end*) extremidad *f*, punta *f*. (**b**) (*want*) apuro *m*, necesidad *f*; **in this ~** en tal apuro; **to be driven to ~** estar muy apurado. (**c**) **extremities** (*Anat*) extremidades *fpl*; (*measures*) medidas *fpl* extremas.

extricate ['ekstrɪkeɪt] **1** *vt* (*disentangle*) desenredar, soltar; (*fig*) librar, sacar (*from* de). **2** *vr*: **to ~ o.s. from** (*fig*) lograr sacarse de.

extrinsic [eks'trɪnsɪk] *adj* extrínseco.
extrovert ['ekstrəʊvɜːrt] **1** *adj* extrovertido, extravertido. **2** *n* extrovertido *m*, -a *f*, extravertido *m*, -a *f*.
extrude [eks'truːd] *vt* sacar; (*force out*) expulsar; (*Tech*) estirar.
extrusion [eks'truːʒən] *n* extrusión *f*, estirado *m*.
exuberance [ɪg'zuːbərəns] *n* euforia *f*; exuberancia *f*.
exuberant [ɪg'zuːbərənt] *adj person, spirit etc* eufórico; *growth, style etc* exuberante.
exuberantly [ɪg'zuːbərəntlɪ] *adv* eufóricamente; exuberantemente.
exude [ɪg'zjuːd] **1** *vt* exudar; rezumar, destilar, sudar. **2** *vi* rezumarse.
exult [ɪg'zʌlt] *vi* exultar; **to ~ in, to ~ at** regocijarse por; **to ~ over** triunfar sobre; **to ~ to find** regocijarse al encontrar.
exultant [ɪg'zʌltənt] *adj* regocijado, jubiloso.
exultantly [ɪg'zʌltəntlɪ] *adv* jubilosamente, exultantemente.
exultation [,egzʌl'teɪʃən] *n* exultación *f*, júbilo *m*.
ex-wife [,eks'waɪf] *n* ex mujer *f*.
ex-works [,eks'wɜːks] *adj* (*Brit*) *price* franco fábrica, en fábrica.
eye [aɪ] **1** *n* ojo *m* (*also of needle*); (*Bot*) yema *f*; **~s right!** ¡vista a la derecha!; **an ~ for an ~ (and a tooth for a tooth)** ojo por ojo (y diente por diente); **as far as the ~ can see** hasta donde alcanza la vista; **it happened before my very ~s** ocurrió delante de mis propios ojos; **the grass grows before your very ~s** crece la hierba a ojos vistas; **in the ~s of** a los ojos de; **with an ~ to the future** cara al futuro; **with an ~ to a possible job** con miras a un empleo eventual; **with an ~ to** + *infin* con la intención de + *infin*; **with the naked ~** a simple vista; **it's all my ~!*** ¡es puro cuento!; **to be all ~s** ser todo ojos; **that's one in the ~ for him!** ese golpe va dirigido a él; **there wasn't a dry ~ in the house** no había ojos sin lágrimas en todo el teatro; **to be up to one's ~s** (*in work*) estar hasta los ojos de trabajo; **to catch the ~** llamar la atención; atraer las miradas; **to catch sb's ~** atraer la atención de uno; **to catch the Speaker's ~** hacer uso de la palabra (con permiso del presidente); **to clap ~s on** clavar la vista en; **to close one's ~s to** (*fig*) hacer la vista gorda a; **to cock one's ~ at** mirar con intención a; **to cry one's ~s out** llorar a moco tendido; **he did** (*or* **went into**) **it with his ~s open** lo hizo con los ojos abiertos; **to feast one's ~s on sth** recrear la vista mirando algo, mirar algo con fruición; **to give sb the glad ~** lanzar una mirada incitante a uno; **to have an ~ for sth** tener afición a algo, saber apreciar algo; saber elegir; **to have an ~ to sth** tener algo en cuenta; obrar (*or* actuar *etc*) con miras a algo; **to have good ~s** tener buena vista; **to have one's ~s on** (*watch*) vigilar, echar una mirada a; (*covet*) echar el ojo a; **she had ~s only for me** no dejaba de mirarme a mí; **it hits you in the ~** salta a la vista; **to keep an ~ on sth** (*watch*) vigilar; (*bear in mind*) tener algo en cuenta; (*follow*) no perder algo de vista; **he couldn't keep his ~s off the girl** se le fueron los ojos tras la chica; **to keep one's ~s peeled** estar alerta; **keep your ~s open for bag-snatchers!** ¡mucho ojo con los del tirón!; **keep an ~ out for snakes** cuidado por si hay culebras; **to make ~s at sb** lanzar una mirada incitante a uno; **there's more in this than meets the ~** esto tiene su miga; **to open sb's ~s to sth** abrir los ojos de uno a algo; **to rub one's ~s** restregarse los ojos; **to run one's ~ over sth** recorrer algo con la vista; echar un vistazo a; **I don't see ~ to ~ with him over that** en eso no estoy completamente de acuerdo con él; **when I first set ~s on him** la primera vez que le puse los ojos encima; **it's 5 years since I set ~s on him** hace 5 años que no le veo; **to shut one's ~s to sth** cerrar los ojos a algo, hacer la vista gorda a (*or* ante) algo; **we must not shut our ~s to this** importa que nos demos cuenta de esto; **he couldn't take his ~s off the girl** se le fueron los ojos tras la joven; **to turn a blind ~ to sth** fingir no ver algo, hacer la vista gorda a (*or* ante) algo.
2 *vt* ojear, mirar (detenidamente, sospechosamente *etc*).
◆**eye up** *vt*: **he was ~ing the girl up** se comía a la joven con los ojos.
eyeball ['aɪbɔːl] *n* globo *m* del ojo.
eyebath ['aɪbɑːθ] *n*, *pl* **eyebaths** ['aɪbɑːðz] (*esp Brit*) ojera *f*, lavaojos *m*.
eyebrow ['aɪbraʊ] **1** *n* ceja *f*; **to raise one's ~s** levantar las cejas; **he never raised an ~ at it** no se sorprendió en lo más mínimo; **2** *attr*: **~ pencil** lápiz *m* de cejas; **~ tweezers** pinzas *fpl* para las cejas.
eye-catcher ['aɪ,kætʃər] *n* cosa *f* que llama la atención.
eye-catching ['aɪ,kætʃɪŋ] *adj* llamativo, vistoso.
eye-contact ['aɪ,kɒntækt] *n* contacto *m* ocular.
eye-cup ['aɪ,kʌp] *n* = **eyebath**.
-eyed [aɪd] *adj* de ojos ...; **green~** de ojos verdes; **two~** de dos ojos.
eye doctor ['aɪ,dɒktər] *n* (*US*) oculista *mf*.
eye-dropper ['aɪ,drɒpər] *n* cuentagotas *m*.
eye-drops ['aɪdrɒps] *npl* gotas *fpl* para los ojos.
eyeful* ['aɪfʊl] *n*: **he got an ~ of mud** el lodo le dio de lleno en el ojo; **get an ~ of this!** ¡echa un vistazo a esto!, ¡mírame esto!; **she's quite an ~!** ¡está buenísima!*
eyeglass ['aɪglɑːs] *n* lente *m*; (*worn in the eye*) monóculo *m*; **~es** (*esp US*) gafas *fpl*.
eyelash ['aɪlæʃ] *n* pestaña *f*.
eyelet ['aɪlɪt] *n* (*Sew*) ojete *m*.
eye-level ['aɪ,levl] *n* altura *f* del ojo.
eyelid ['aɪlɪd] *n* párpado *m*.
eyeliner ['aɪ,laɪnər] *n* lápiz *m* de ojos, delineador *m* de ojos.
eye-opener* ['aɪ,əʊpnər] *n* (**a**) revelación *f*, sorpresa *f* grande; **it was an ~ to me** fue una revelación para mí. (**b**) (*US*) copa *f* para despertarse.
eye-patch ['aɪ,pætʃ] *n* parche *m*.
eye-pencil ['aɪ,pensl] *n* lápiz *m* de ojos.
eyepiece ['aɪpiːs] *n* ocular *m*.
eyeshade ['aɪʃeɪd] *n* visera *f*.
eyeshadow ['aɪ,ʃædəʊ] *n* sombreador *m* de ojos, sombra *f* de ojos.
eyesight ['aɪsaɪt] *n* vista *f*; (*extent of* ~) alcance *m* de la vista.
eye-socket ['aɪsɒkɪt] *n* cuenca *f* del ojo.
eyesore ['aɪsɔːr] *n* monstruosidad *f*, cosa *f* antiestética.
eyestrain ['aɪstreɪn] *n* vista *f* fatigada; **to get ~** cansar los ojos, cansar la vista; **to suffer from ~** padecer de los ojos.
eye test ['aɪ,test] *n* test *m* visual, test *m* de visión; examen *m* de los ojos.
eye-tooth ['aɪtuːθ] *n*, *pl* **eye-teeth** ['aɪtiːθ] colmillo *m*; **I'd give my eye-teeth to see it** daría todo lo que tengo por verlo.
eyewash ['aɪwɒʃ] *n* (*Med*) colirio *m*; (*****) música *f* celestial; **it's a lot of ~!** ¡es puro cuento!
eyewitness ['aɪ,wɪtnɪs] *n* testigo *mf* presencial, testigo *mf* ocular.
eyrie ['aɪərɪ] *n* aguilera *f*.
Ezekiel [ɪ'ziːkɪəl] *nm* Ezequiel.

F

F, f [ef] *n* (**a**) (*letter*) F, f *f*; **F for Frederick, F for Fox** (*US*) F de Francia. (**b**) F (*Mus*) fa *m*; **F major** fa *m* mayor.

F. (**a**) *abbr of* **Fahrenheit** termómetro *m* Fahrenheit. (**b**) (*Eccl*) *abbr of* **Father** Padre *m*, P^e^.

f. (**a**) (*Math*) *abbr of* **foot, feet.** (**b**) *abbr of* **following** siguiente, sig. (**c**) (*Biol*) *abbr of* **female** hembra *f*.

FA *n* (**a**) (*Brit Sport*) *abbr of* **Football Association** ≃ Asociación *f* Futbolística Española, AFE *f*; ~ **Cup** Copa *f* de la FA. (**b**) (*) *abbr of* (**sweet**) **Fanny Adams.**

fa [fɑː] *n* (*Mus*) fa *m*.

FAA *n* (*US*) *abbr of* **Federal Aviation Administration.**

fab‡ [fæb] *adj* (*Brit*) = **fabulous.**

Fabian ['feɪbɪən] **1** *adj* fabianista; ~ **Society** Sociedad *f* Fabiana. **2** *n* fabianista *mf*.

fable ['feɪbl] *n* fábula *f*.

fabled ['feɪbld] *adj* fabuloso, legendario.

fabric ['fæbrɪk] **1** *n* (**a**) (*cloth*) tejido *m*, tela *f*. (**b**) (*Archit*) fábrica *f*; **the upkeep of the** ~ la manutención de los edificios; **the** ~ **of society** la estructura de la sociedad; **the** ~ **of Church and State** (*freq hum*) los fundamentos de la Iglesia y del Estado. **2** *attr*: ~ **ribbon** cinta *f* de tela.

fabricate ['fæbrɪkeɪt] *vt goods etc* fabricar; (*fig*) inventar; *document, evidence* falsificar.

fabrication [ˌfæbrɪ'keɪʃən] *n* invención *f*, ficción *f*; **the whole thing is a** ~ todo es mentira, todo es un cuento.

fabulous ['fæbjʊləs] *adj* fabuloso; (*) fabuloso*, estupendo*.

fabulously ['fæbjʊləslɪ] *adv* fabulosamente; ~ **rich** fabulosamente rico; **it was** ~ **successful** tuvo un éxito fabuloso.

façade [fə'sɑːd] *n* fachada *f* (*also fig*).

face [feɪs] **1** *n* (**a**) (*Anat etc*) cara *f*, rostro *m*, semblante *m*; (*of dial, watch*) esfera *f*, cara *f* (*LAm*); (*of sundial*) cuadrante *m*; (*surface*) superficie *f*; (*Min*) cara *f* de trabajo; (*of building*) frente *f*, fachada *f*; ~ **of the earth** faz *f* de la tierra; ~ **downwards** boca abajo; ~ **upwards** boca arriba; **to bring A** ~ **to** ~ **with B** confrontar A con B; **to bring two people** ~ **to** ~ poner a dos personas cara a cara; **in the** ~ **of** ante, en presencia de, en vista de; **in the** ~ **of this threat** ante esta amenaza; **in the** ~ **of such difficulties** vistas tantas dificultades; **courage in the** ~ **of the enemy** valor frente al enemigo; **the wind was blowing in our** ~**s** el viento nos daba de cara.

(**b**) (*phrases*) **to fly in the** ~ **of reason** oponerse abiertamente a la razón; **they laughed in his** ~ se le rieron en la cara; **he'll laugh on the other side of his** ~ pasará de la risa al llanto; **he didn't dare to look me in the** ~ no osaba mirarme a la cara; **I could never look him in the** ~ **again** yo no tendría valor para mirarle a la cara; **to look sb square in the** ~ mirar directamente a los ojos de uno; **to tell sb sth to his** ~ decirle algo a uno en su cara; **to say sth to sb's** ~ decir algo en la cara de uno; **to set one's** ~ **against sth** oponerse resueltamente a algo; **to show one's** ~ asomar la cara, dejarse ver; **shut your** ~**!*** ¡cállate ya!, ¡calla la boca!; **to struggle to keep a straight** ~ esforzarse por contener la risa.

(**c**) (*expression*) (**wry** ~) mueca *f*; **to go about with a long** ~ andar cariacontecido; **to make** ~**s, to pull** ~**s** hacer muecas (*at* a); **to pull a** (**wry**) ~ poner cara de desagrado.

(**d**) (*effrontery*) cara *f*, cara *f* dura, descaro *m*; **to have the** ~ **to** + *infin* ser bastante descarado para + *infin*.

(**e**) (*dignity*) prestigio *m*; **to lose** ~ desprestigiarse, perder prestigio; quedar mal; **to save** (**one's**) ~ salvar las apariencias.

(**f**) (*outward show*) **on the** ~ **of it** a primera vista, según las apariencias; **to put a brave** ~ **on sth** hacer buena cara a algo.

2 *vt* (**a**) (*look towards*: *of person, object*) estar de cara a; ponerse de cara a; volver la cara hacia; ~ **the wall!** ¡póngase de cara a la pared!; **turn it to** ~ **the fire** gírelo para que esté de cara a la lumbre; **they sat facing each other** estaban sentados uno frente al otro; **to sit facing the engine** estar sentado de frente a la máquina.

(**b**) (*of building*) mirar hacia, estar enfrente de, dar a; **the flat** ~**s the Town Hall** el piso está enfrente del Ayuntamiento; **the house** ~**s the sea** la casa está frente al mar; **the house** ~**s the south** la casa está orientada hacia el sur.

(**c**) (*fig*) *person, enemy, electorate* encararse con, enfrentarse con; *consequences, danger* arrostrar, hacer cara a; *facts* reconocer; *situation* hacer frente a; *problem* afrontar; **we** ~ **grave problems** afrontamos unos problemas graves; **we are** ~**d with grave problems** se nos plantean graves problemas; **he** ~**s a fine of £100** se arriesga a una multa de 100 libras; **we will** ~ **him with the facts** le expondremos los hechos; **let's** ~ **it!** ¡seamos realistas!; **we're poor, let's** ~ **it!** ¡reconozcamos que somos pobres!

(**d**) (*Tech*) revestir, forrar (*with* de).

3 *vi*: **to** ~ **in a direction** estar orientado en una dirección; **which way does it** ~**?** ¿en qué dirección está orientado?; ~ **this way!** ¡vuélvase hacia aquí!

◆**face about** *vi* (*Mil*) dar media vuelta; (*fig*) cambiar de actitud, cambiar de postura.

◆**face down** *vt* (*US*) intimidar con la mirada.

◆**face on to** *vt* mirar hacia, dar a.

◆**face out** *vt*: **to** ~ **it out** insistir descaradamente en ello.

◆**face up to** *vt*: **to** ~ **up to sth** reconocer la realidad de algo, hacer frente a algo, arrostrar algo; **she** ~**d up to it bravely** lo aguantó con mucha resolución.

face card ['feɪskɑːd] *n* (*US*) figura *f*.

facecloth ['feɪsklɒθ] *n* (*Brit*) manopla *f*, paño *m*.

facecream ['feɪskriːm] *n* crema *f* (de belleza).

-faced [feɪst] *adj ending in compounds* de cara ..., *eg* **brown**~ de cara morena, **long**~ de cara larga.

face-flannel ['feɪsˌflænl] *n* (*Brit*) manopla *f*, paño *m*.

faceless ['feɪslɪs] *adj* sin cara, sin rostro.

facelift ['feɪslɪft] *n* (**a**) estirado *m* de piel, estiramiento *m* facial. (**b**) (*fig*) reforma *f* (superficial), modernización *f* (ligera); **to give a** ~ **to** remozar; mejorar de aspecto.

face-off ['feɪsɒf] *n* (*US*) confrontación *f*.

facepack ['feɪspæk] *n* tratamiento *m* facial.

face-powder ['feɪsˌpaʊdə^r^] *n* polvos *mpl*.

facer* ['feɪsə^r^] *n* (*Brit*) problema *m* desconcertante; **that's a** ~**!** ¡vaya problemazo!*

face-saver ['feɪsˌseɪvə^r^] *n* maniobra *f* para salvar las apariencias.

face-saving ['feɪsˌseɪvɪŋ] **1** *adj*: ~ **operation** maniobra *f* para salvar las apariencias.

2 *n*: ~ **is important** importa salvar las apariencias; **this is a piece of blatant** ~ esto es una maniobra transparente para salvar las apariencias.

facet ['fæsɪt] *n* faceta *f* (*also fig*).

facetious [fə'siːʃəs] *adj person* chistoso; *remark* festivo, gracioso; *speech* divertido, lleno de chistes.

facetiously [fə'siːʃəslɪ] *adv* chistosamente; **he said** ~ dijo guasón.

facetiousness [fə'siːʃəsnɪs] *n* carácter *m* festivo (*etc*); chistes *mpl*.

face-to-face [ˌfeɪstə'feɪs] **1** *adj* cara a cara. **2** *adv* cara a cara.

face-value ['feɪs'væljuː] *n* valor *m* nominal; (*of stamp, coin etc*) valor *m* facial; (*fig*) valor *m* aparente, significado *m* literal; **you can't take it at its** ~ no se deje engañar por las apariencias; **I took his statement at its** ~ tomé lo que dijo en sentido literal.

facial ['feɪʃəl] **1** *adj* de la cara, facial. **2** *n* tratamiento *m* facial, masaje *m* facial; limpieza *f*.

facile ['fæsaɪl] *adj* fácil, superficial, ligero.

facilitate [fə'sɪlɪteɪt] *vt* facilitar.

facility [fə'sɪlɪtɪ] *n* facilidad *f*; **facilities** (*most senses*) facilidades *fpl*; (*US euph*) servicios *mpl*; **recreational facilities** instalaciones *fpl* recreativas.

facing ['feɪsɪŋ] **1** *prep* de cara a, frente a.
2 *as adj* opuesto, de enfrente; **the houses** ~ las casas de enfrente; **on a** ~ **page** en una página de enfrente.
3 *n* (*Tech*) revestimiento *m*; (*Sew*) vuelta *f*, guarnición *f*; **~s** (*Sew*) vueltas *fpl*.

-facing ['feɪsɪŋ] *adj ending in compounds*: **south~** con orientación sur, orientado hacia el sur.

facsimile [fæk'sɪmɪlɪ] **1** *adj* facsímil. **2** *n* facsímil *m*. **3** *attr*: ~ **machine** teleproductor *m* de imágenes; ~ **transmission** telefacsímil *m*.

fact [fækt] *n* hecho *m*; (*real world*) realidad *f*; ~ **and fiction** lo real y lo ficticio; **~s and figures** hechos *mpl* y números; ~ **sheet** hoja *f* informativa; **the ~s of life** los hechos (*or* las realidades) de la vida, (*esp*) las cosas de la vida, los detalles de la reproducción humana; **hard ~s** hechos *mpl* innegables; **a film based on** ~ una película basada en hechos verídicos; **it has no basis in** ~ carece de base real; **as a matter of ~, in ~, in point of** ~ a decir verdad, de hecho; en realidad; **the** ~ **of the matter is** la pura verdad es; **the** ~ **is that** ... el hecho es que ..., ello es que ...; **it is a** ~ **that** ... se ha comprobado que ...; **the** ~ **that I am here** el hecho de que estoy aquí; **is that a** ~? ¿(lo dices) en serio?; **to bow to the ~s** reconocer que las cosas son así, doblegarse ante los hechos; **I don't dispute your ~s** yo no niego los hechos que alega; **to know for a** ~ **that** ... saber a ciencia cierta que ...; **to stick to the ~s** atenerse a los hechos; *V* **accessory**.

fact-finding ['fækt,faɪndɪŋ] *adj mission, visit* de investigación, de indagación, de reconocimiento.

faction ['fækʃən] *n* facción *f*.

factious ['fækʃəs] *adj* faccioso.

factitious [fæk'tɪʃəs] *adj* facticio.

factitive ['fæktɪtɪv] *adj* factivo, causativo.

factor ['fæktəʳ] *n* (**a**) (*fact*) factor *m*, hecho *m*, elemento *m*; **the Falklands** ~ el factor Malvinas.
(**b**) (*Math*) factor *m*; **highest common** ~ máximo común divisor *m*.
(**c**) (*Comm*) agente *m*.

factorial [fæk'tɔːrɪəl] *adj, n* factorial *m*.

factoring ['fæktərɪŋ] *n* factorización *f*.

factory ['fæktərɪ] **1** *n* (**a**) fábrica *f*, factoría *f*.
(**b**) (‡) comisaría *f*.
2 *attr*: ~ **farming** agricultura *f* industrializada, cría *f* intensiva; ~ **floor opinion** opinión *f* de las bases sindicales, opinión *f* de los obreros; ~ **inspector** inspector *m*, -ora *f* de fábricas; ~ **ship** buque *m* factoría; ~ **work** trabajo *m* de fábrica; ~ **worker** obrero *m*, -a *f* de fábrica.

factotum [fæk'təʊtəm] *n* factótum *m*.

factual ['fæktjʊəl] *adj* objetivo, que consta de hechos, basado en datos; de carácter expositivo; ~ **error** error *m* de hecho.

factually ['fæktjʊəlɪ] *adv* objetivamente; ~ **speaking, I would say** ... limitándome a los hechos, diría que ...

faculty ['fækəltɪ] *n* (**a**) facultad *f*. (**b**) (*Univ*) facultad *f*. (**c**) (*esp US*: *Univ*) profesorado *m*.

fad [fæd] *n* manía *f*; novedad *f*; **it's just a** ~ es una novedad nada más, es una moda pasajera; **he has his ~s** tiene sus caprichos; **the** ~ **for Italian clothes** la manía de los trajes italianos.

faddish ['fædɪʃ], **faddy** ['fædɪ] *adj person* caprichoso, dengoso, que tiene sus manías, difícil de contentar; *distaste, desire* idiosincrático.

fade [feɪd] **1** *vt colour, dress* descolorar, desteñir; *flower* marchitar.
2 *vi* (**a**) (*colour, dress*) descolorarse, desteñirse, perder su color; (*flower*) marchitarse; **guaranteed not to** ~ no se descolora.
(**b**) (*light*) apagarse gradualmente; (*sound*) desvanecerse; (*memory etc*) desvanecerse; **the daylight was fading fast** anochecía rápidamente; **he saw his chances fading** veía como se estaban acabando sus posibilidades.
◆**fade away** *vi* (*sight*) desdibujarse, desvanecerse; (*sound*) apagarse, dejar poco a poco de oírse; **she was fading away** (*dying*) se consumía lentamente, (*slimming*) adelgazaba muchísimo; **this season the team has just ~d away** en esta temporada el equipo casi ha dejado de figurar.
◆**fade in** *vt* (*Cine*) hacer aparecer gradualmente.
◆**fade out** *vi* = **fade away**.
◆**fade to** *vi* (*Cine*) fundir a.
◆**fade up** *vt* = **fade in**.

faded ['feɪdɪd] *adj plant* marchito, seco; *colour, dress* descolorido; *glory* marchito.

fade-in ['feɪdɪn] *n* (*Cine, TV*) fundido *m*.

fade-out ['feɪdaʊt] *n* (*Cine*) fundido *m* (de cierre); **to do a** ~* (*US*) desaparecer.

faeces, (*US*) **feces** ['fiːsiːz] *npl* excrementos *mpl*.

faff* [fæf] *vi*: **to** ~ **about** perder el tiempo, ocuparse en bagatelas; **stop ~fing about!** ¡déjate de tonterías!

fag [fæg] **1** *n* (**a**) (*Brit**: *job*) faena *f*, lata *f* (*LAm*), trabajo *m* penoso; **what a** ~! ¡qué faena!; **it's just too much** ~ la verdad, es mucho trabajo.
(**b**) (*Brit Scol*) alumno *m* joven que trabaja por otro mayor.
(**c**) (*Brit*‡: *cigarette*) pitillo *m*, cigarro *m* (*LAm*), pucho *m* (*SC*).
(**d**) (*esp US*‡) maricón *m*.
2 *vt* (*Brit*) fatigar, cansar; **to be ~ged out** estar rendido.
3 *vi* trabajar como un negro; **to** ~ **for** (*Brit Scol*) trabajar por.

fag-end‡ ['fægend] *n* colilla *f*; (*fig*) cabo *m*; desperdicios *mpl*.

faggot, (*mainly US*) **fagot** ['fægət] *n* (**a**) haz *m* de leña, astillas *fpl*. (**b**) (*esp US*‡) maricón‡ *m*.

fah [fɑː] *n* (*Mus*) fa *m*.

Fahrenheit ['færənhaɪt] *attr*: ~ **thermometer** termómetro *m* de Fahrenheit (*grados Fahrenheit menos 32 × 5/9 = grados centígrados*).

fail [feɪl] **1** *n* (**a**) (*Univ*) suspenso *m* (*in* en).
(**b**) **without** ~ sin falta.
2 *vt* (**a**) *person* faltar a, faltar en sus obligaciones a; decepcionar; **his strength ~ed him** se sintió desfallecer, le abandonaron sus fuerzas; **his heart ~ed him** se encontró sin ánimo; **words** ~ **me** no encuentro palabras para expresarme; **you have ~ed me** me has decepcionado.
(**b**) (*Univ*) *exam* no aprobar, salir mal en; *candidate* suspender.
3 *vi* (**a**) (*run short*: *supply, strength*) acabarse; (*engine*) fallar; (*voice*) irse, debilitarse, desfallecer; (*eyes*) debilitarse; (*light*) acabarse; (*crop*) fallar; perderse; (*electricity supply etc*) cortarse, interrumpirse; (*mechanism*) tener una avería, averiarse; (*patient*) debilitarse, hacerse más débil; **the light was ~ing** iba anocheciendo.
(**b**) (*neglect*) **to** ~ **to do sth** dejar de hacer algo; **he ~ed to appear** no se presentó, dejó de presentarse; **don't** ~ **to visit her** no dejes de visitarla; **to** ~ **to keep one's word** faltar a su palabra.
(**c**) (*be unable*) **I** ~ **to see how** no veo cómo; **I** ~ **to understand why** no puedo comprender por qué; **but she ~ed to come** pero no vino.
(**d**) (*not succeed*) fracasar, no tener éxito; (*remedy*) no surtir efecto; (*hopes*) frustrarse, malograrse; (*Fin*) quebrar; (*Univ etc*) ser suspendido (*in* en); **a ~ed painter** un pintor fracasado; **to** ~ **to be elected** no lograr ser elegido; **to** ~ **to win a prize** no obtener un premio; **to** ~ **by 5 votes** perder por 5 votos.
(**e**) **to** ~ **in one's duty to sb** faltar a uno, faltar en sus obligaciones a uno.

failing ['feɪlɪŋ] **1** *prep* a falta de; ~ **that** si eso no es posible.
2 *n* falta *f*, defecto *m*; flaqueza *f*; **the plan has numerous ~s** el plan tiene muchos defectos; **it is his only** ~ es su único punto débil.
3 *adj*: **he was in** ~ **health** su salud era cada vez más débil, iba desfalleciendo; **we reached the top in** ~ **light** anochecía cuando llegamos a la cumbre; **life in a** ~ **marriage** la vida en un matrimonio que anda mal.

failsafe ['feɪlseɪf] *attr*: ~ **device** mecanismo *m* de seguridad, mecanismo *m* a prueba de fallo.

failure ['feɪljəʳ] **1** *n* (**a**) (*lack of success*) fracaso *m*; (*of hopes*) malogro *m*; (*failed thing*) fracaso *m*, (*person*) fracasado *m*, -a *f*; (*Mech*) fallo *m*, avería *f*; (*Elec*) corte *m*, interrupción *f*, apagón *m* (*LAm*); (*of crop*) fallo *m*; pérdida *f*; (*Fin*) quiebra *f*; **the crop was a total** ~ el cultivo se perdió por completo.
(**b**) **your** ~ **to come** el hecho de que no viniste, el dejar de venir (tú); ~ **to pay** incumplimiento *m* en el pago, impago *m*.
(**c**) (*Univ*) suspenso *m* (*in* en).
2 *attr*: ~ **rate** (*in exams*) porcentaje *m* de suspensos; (*of machine*) porcentaje *m* de averías.

fain†† [feɪn] *adv* (*used only with 'would'*) de buena gana.

faint [feɪnt] **1** *adj* débil; *colour* pálido; *line* tenue; *outline* borroso, indistinto; *trace* apenas perceptible; *sound* casi imperceptible, débil; *voice* débil; *smell* tenue; *hope* nada firme; *idea, memory* vago; *resemblance* ligero; *heart* medroso; **to feel ~** estar mareado, tener vahídos; **I haven't the ~est (idea)** no tengo la más remota idea.

2 *n* desmayo *m*; **to be in a ~** estar desmayado, estar sin conocimiento; **to fall down in a ~** desmayarse.

3 *vi* (*also* **to ~ away**) desmayarse, perder conocimiento; **to be ~ing with tiredness** estar rendido; **to be ~ing with hunger** estar muerto de hambre.

fainthearted [ˈfeɪntˈhɑːtɪd] *adj* medroso, pusilánime, apocado.

faintheartedness [ˌfeɪntˈhɑːtɪdnɪs] *n* pusilanimidad *f*; cobardía *f*.

fainting fit [ˈfeɪntɪŋ,fɪt] *n*, **fainting spell** [ˈfeɪntɪŋ,spel] *n* síncope *m*, desvanecimiento *m*.

faintly [ˈfeɪntlɪ] *adv call, say* débilmente; *breathe, shine* débilmente, ligeramente; *write, mark, scratch* vagamente, débilmente; (*slightly*) ligeramente; **this is ~ reminiscent of ...** esto me recuerda vagamente ...

faintness [ˈfeɪntnɪs] *n* debilidad *f*; tenuidad *f*; lo indistinto; (*Med*) desmayo *m*, desfallecimiento *m*.

fair[1] [fɛəʳ] **1** *adj* **(a)** (*beautiful*) bello, hermoso; **the ~ sex** el bello sexo.

(b) (*blond*) *hair* rubio; *skin* blanco.

(c) (*clean*) *name* honrado; *reputation* bueno; **~ copy** copia *f* en limpio.

(d) (*just*) justo, equitativo; *hearing, report, summary* imparcial; *comment* acertado; *means* recto; *play* limpio; *competition* leal; *chance, price, warning* razonable; **~ enough!** ¡vale!, ¡muy bien!; **as is only ~** como es justo; **but to be ~** pero en honor a la verdad; **it's not ~!** ¡no hay derecho!; **it's not ~ on the old** afecta injustamente a los viejos; **~ deal** trato *m* equitativo, politica *f* equitativa; **~ game** caza *f* legal; (*fig*) objeto *m* legítimo; **it is ~ game for criticism** es un objeto legítimo de la crítica; **to give sb a ~ share*** tratar justamente a uno; **~ trade** comercio *m* legítimo; **~ trade agreement** (*US*) acuerdo *m* por el cual el vendedor promete no vender un producto a un precio inferior al fijado por el fabricante; **~ wage** salario *m* justo; **~ wear and tear** desgaste *m* por uso justo.

(e) (*middling*) regular, mediano.

(f) (*promising*) prometedor, favorable, bastante bueno.

(g) (*Met*) *sky* sereno, despejado; *day, weather* bueno; **if it's ~ tomorrow** si hace buen tiempo mañana.

2 *adv* **(a) to play ~** jugar limpio.

(b) it hit the target ~ and square dio en el centro del blanco; **so he told me ~ and square** así que me lo dijo sin rodeos.

(c) (*: *fairly*) **we were ~ terrified** nos asustamos bastante; **then it ~ rained** entonces sí que llovió.

fair[2] [fɛəʳ] *n* **(a)** (*Comm etc*) feria *f*.

(b) (*Brit*: *funfair*) parque *m* de atracciones; verbena *f*.

fairground [ˈfɛəgraʊnd] *n* real *m* (de la feria); parque *m* de atracciones.

fair-haired [ˈfɛəˈhɛəd] *adj*, **fair-headed** [ˈfɛəˈhedɪd] *adj* rubio, pelirrubio.

fairly [ˈfɛəlɪ] *adv* **(a)** justamente, equitativamente, con imparcialidad; rectamente; limpio, limpiamente. **(b) ~ good** bastante bueno. **(c)** (*utterly*) completamente.

fair-minded [ˈfɛəˈmaɪndɪd] *adj* imparcial, equitativo.

fair-mindedness [ˌfɛəˈmaɪndɪdnɪs] *n* imparcialidad *f*.

fairness [ˈfɛənɪs] *n* (*V* **fair**[1]) **(a)** hermosura *f*. **(b)** lo rubio; blancura *f*. **(c)** justicia *f*, imparcialidad *f*; **in all ~** para ser justo (*to him* con él).

fair-sized [ˈfɛəsaɪzd] *adj* bastante grande.

fair-skinned [ˌfɛəˈskɪnd] *adj* de tez blanca.

fairway [ˈfɛəweɪ] *n* (*Naut*) canalizo *m*; (*Golf*) calle *f*, fairway *m*.

fair-weather [ˈfɛə,weðəʳ] *adj*: **~ friend** amigo *m*, -a *f* en la prosperidad, amigo *m*, -a *f* del buen viento.

fairy [ˈfɛərɪ] **1** *n* **(a)** hada *f*. **(b)** (‡) maricón‡ *m*. **2** *attr* feérico, mágico; **~ footsteps** pasos *mpl* ligeros; **~ godmother** hada *f* madrina; **~ queen** reina *f* de las hadas.

fairy cycle [ˈfɛərɪ,saɪkl] *n* bicicleta *f* de niño.

fairyland [ˈfɛərɪlænd] *n* tierra *f* de (las) hadas; (*fig*) país *m* de ensueño; **he must be living in ~** vive en la luna.

fairy-lights [ˈfɛərɪlaɪts] *npl* bombillas *fpl* de colorines.

fairy-story [ˈfɛərɪ,stɔːrɪ], **fairy-tale** [ˈfɛərɪteɪl] **1** *n* cuento *m* de hadas; (*fig*) cuento *m*, patraña *f*. **2** *adj* fantástico, de ensueño.

fait accompli [ˌfeɪtəˈkɒmplɪ] *n* hecho *m* consumado.

faith [feɪθ] *n* fe *f* (*also Eccl*); (*trust*) confianza *f* (*in* en); (*doctrine*) creencia *f*; (*sect, confession*) religión *f*; **bad ~** mala fe *f*; **in good ~** de buena fe; **what ~ does he belong to?** ¿qué religión tiene?; **to break ~** faltar a su palabra (*with* dada a); **to have ~ in** tener fe en; **to keep ~** cumplir la palabra (*with* dada a); **to pin one's ~ to** cifrar sus esperanzas en.

faithful [ˈfeɪθfʊl] **1** *adj* fiel (*also Eccl*); *friend, servant* leal; *translation* fiel; *account* exacto. **2** *npl*: **the ~** los fieles.

faithfully [ˈfeɪθfəlɪ] *adv* fielmente; lealmente; con exactitud; **yours ~** (*Brit*) le saluda atentamente.

faithfulness [ˈfeɪθfʊlnɪs] *n* fidelidad *f*; lealtad *f*; exactitud *f*.

faith-healer [ˈfeɪθ,hiːləʳ] *n* curador *m*, -ora *f* por fe.

faith-healing [ˈfeɪθ,hiːlɪŋ] *n* curación *f* por fe.

faithless [ˈfeɪθlɪs] *adj* desleal, pérfido, infiel.

faithlessness [ˈfeɪθlɪsnɪs] *n* infidelidad *f*, deslealtad *f*, perfidia *f*.

fake [feɪk] **1** *n* (*thing*) falsificación *f*, impostura *f*; imitación *f*; (*person*) impostor *m*, -ora *f*, embustero *m*, -a *f*, (*as term of abuse*) farsante *mf*.

2 *adj* falso, fingido, contrahecho.

3 *vt* contrahacer, falsificar, fingir; (*improvise*) improvisar; **to ~ an illness** fingirse enfermo.

4 *vi* fingir.

◆fake up *vt* = **fake 3**.

fakir [ˈfɑːkɪəʳ] *n* faquir *m*.

falcon [ˈfɔːlkən] *n* halcón *m*.

falconer [ˈfɔːlkənəʳ] *n* halconero *m*.

falconry [ˈfɔːlkənrɪ] *n* halconería *f*, cetrería *f*.

Falkland Islands [ˈfɔːlklənd,aɪləndz] *npl* Islas *fpl* Malvinas.

fall [fɔːl] **1** *n* caída *f*; (*Fin*) baja *f*; (*decrease*) disminución *f*; (*in price, demand, temperature*) descenso *m* (*in* de); (*Mil*) caída *f*, toma *f*, rendición *f*; (*of ground*) declive *m*, desnivel *m*; (*of water*; *also* **~s**) salto *m* de agua, catarata *f*, cascada *f*; (*US*) otoño *m*; **the F~** la Caída; **~ of earth** corrimiento *m* de tierras; **~ of rocks** derrumbamiento *m* de piedras; **~ of snow** nevada *f*; **to have a ~** sufrir una caída; **to be riding for a ~** presumir demasiado.

2 (*irr*: *pret* **fell**, *ptp* **fallen**) *vi* caer; caerse; (*fig*: *empire, government, night, hair, drapery*; *morally etc*) caer; (*decrease*) disminuir; (*price, level, demand, temperature etc*) bajar, descender; (*Mil*) caer, rendirse; (*ground*) estar en declive; (*wind*) amainar; **his face fell** se inmutó; **night was ~ing** anochecía, se hacía de noche; **at a time of ~ing interest rates** en un período cuando bajan los tipos de interés; **to ~ among thieves** ir a parar entre ladrones.

◆fall about* *vi* (*laugh*) desternillarse (de risa)*.

◆fall apart *vi* (*object*) romperse, deshacerse; (*empire*) desmoronarse; (*scheme, marriage*) fracasar.

◆fall away *vi* **(a)** (*ground*) descender, estar en declive (*to* hacia).

(b) (*plaster etc*) desconcharse; (*cliff*) desmoronarse; (*stage of rocket, part*) desprenderse.

(c) (*numbers etc*) bajar, disminuir; (*zeal*) enfriarse; (*trade etc*) decaer.

(d) (*morally*) abandonar sus principios; (*Rel*) apostatar; perder la fe; (*in quality*) empeorar.

◆fall back *vi* **(a)** retroceder; (*Mil*) replegarse (*on* sobre), retirarse.

(b) it fell back into the sea volvió a caer al mar.

(c) (*price etc*) bajar.

(d) to ~ back on *remedy etc* recurrir a, echar mano a.

◆fall backwards *vi* caer de espaldas.

◆fall behind *vi* quedarse atrás, rezagarse; **to ~ behind with one's payments** atrasarse en los pagos.

◆fall down *vi* **(a)** (*fall*) caer, caerse; (*person*) caerse; dar consigo en el suelo; (*building*) hundirse, derrumbarse; venirse abajo; **to ~ down the stairs** caer rodando por la escalera; **to ~ down and worship sb** arrodillarse ante uno; **the rain was ~ing down** llovía a cántaros.

(b) (*fail*) fracasar; ser frustrado; **that is where you fell down** ésta es la causa de tu fracaso; *V* **job**.

◆fall for *vt* **(a)** *person* enamorarse de; *thing* aficionarse a, tomar afición a; *place* apreciar los encantos de.

(b) *trick* dejarse engañar por; **he fell for it** picó, se la tragó.

◆fall in *vi* **(a)** (*roof*) desplomarse, hundirse.

(b) (*Mil*) alinearse, formar filas; **~ in!** ¡en filas!

(c) (*Comm*) vencer; expirar.

(d) to ~ in with (*meet*) encontrarse con, juntarse con.

(e) to ~ in with (*agree to*) convenir en, aprobar; aceptar; *opinion* adherirse a.

◆fall into *vt* **(a)** (*river*) desembocar en.

(b) *error* incurrir en; *conversation* entablar; *habit* adquirir.

(c) it ~s into 4 parts se divide en 4 partes; **it ~s into**

this category está incluido en esta categoría; se puede clasificar en este apartado.
◆**fall off** *vi* = **fall away** (**b**) (**c**) (**d**).
◆**fall on** *vt* (**a**) (*tax etc*) incidir en.
(**b**) (*accent*) cargar sobre, caer sobre.
(**c**) (*Mil*) caer sobre.
(**d**) **to ~ on one's food** caer sobre la comida, atacar las viandas; **people were ~ing on each other in delight** todos se abrazaban de puro contentos.
(**e**) (*birthday etc*) caer en.
(**f**) (*find*) tropezar con, dar con; **to ~ on a way of doing sth** topar por casualidad con la forma de hacer algo.
(**g**) (*duty*) = **fall to**.
(**h**) **my gaze fell on certain details** quedé mirando ciertos detalles, empecé a estudiar ciertos detalles.
◆**fall out** *vi* (**a**) caer; desprenderse.
(**b**) (*quarrel*) reñir, pelearse, tener un disgusto (*with* con).
(**c**) (*Mil*) romper filas.
(**d**) (*come to pass*) **it fell out that ...** resultó que ...; **it fell out as we had expected** pasó como lo habíamos esperado.
◆**fall over 1** *vt object* tropezar con.
2 *vi* (**a**) (*person, object*) caer, caerse.
(**b**) (*fig*) **to ~ over backwards to help sb** desvivirse por ayudar a uno; **they were ~ing over each other to buy them** se estaban pegando por comprarlos.
◆**fall through** *vi* (*plans etc*) fracasar.
◆**fall to** *vi* (**a**) ponerse a trabajar (*etc*); empezar a comer; **~ to!** ¡a ello!, ¡vamos!; **to ~ to** + *ger* empezar a + *infin*, ponerse a + *infin*.
(**b**) **to ~ to temptation** sucumbir a la tentación.
(**c**) (*duty*) corresponder a, incumbir a, tocar a.
◆**fall upon** *V* **fall on**.
fallacious [fə'leɪʃəs] *adj* erróneo, engañoso, falaz.
fallacy ['fæləsɪ] *n* error *m*; sofisma *m*; mentira *f*; falacia *f*.
fall-back ['fɔːlbæk] *attr*: **~ position** segunda línea *f* de defensa; posición *f* de repliegue.
fallen ['fɔːlən] **1** *ptp of* **fall; the ~** los caídos. **2** *adj* (*morally*) perdido.
fall guy* ['fɔːlgaɪ] *n* (*US*) cabeza *f* de turco; víctima *f* (de un truco), víctima *f* predestinada.
fallibility [,fælɪ'bɪlɪtɪ] *n* falibilidad *f*.
fallible ['fæləbl] *adj* falible.
falling ['fɔːlɪŋ] *adj market etc* descendente, decreciente.
falling-off ['fɔːlɪŋ'ɒf] *n* (*in quantity*) disminución *f*; (*of price etc*) baja *f*, descenso *m*; (*in quality*) empeoramiento *m*.
falling star ['fɔːlɪŋ'stɑːʳ] *n* estrella *f* fugaz.
Fallopian [fə'ləʊpɪən] *adj*: **~ tube** trompa *f* de Falopio.
fallout ['fɔːlaʊt] **1** *n* (**a**) polvillo *m* radiactivo, lluvia *f* radiactiva. (**b**) (*fig*) consecuencias *fpl*, repercusiones *fpl*; beneficios *mpl* secundarios. **2** *attr*: **~ shelter** refugio *m* antiatómico.
fallow ['fæləʊ] **1** *adj* barbecho; **to lie ~** estar en barbecho; (*fig*) quedar sin emplear, no ser utilizado. **2** *n* barbecho *m*.
fallow deer ['fæləʊ'dɪəʳ] *n* gamo *m*.
false [fɔːls] *adj* (**a**) (*mistaken*) falso; erróneo; **~ alarm** falsa alarma *f*; **~ friend** falso amigo *m*; **~ move** paso *m* en falso; **~ note** nota *f* falsa; **~ start** (*race*) salida *f* nula; (*fig*) falso comienzo *m*; **~ step** paso *m* en falso.
(**b**) (*deceitful*) falso, engañoso; *person* desleal, pérfido; **by** (*or* **under, with**) **~ pretences** con fraude, mediante fraude, con engaño; **~ promises** promesas *fpl* falsas; **~ witness** falso testimonio *m*; **to bear ~ witness** jurar en falso, perjurarse; **under ~ colours** bajo pabellón falso; **to be ~ to sb, to play sb ~** traicionar a uno; **his words rang ~** sus palabras sonaban falsas (*or* a falso).
(**c**) (*counterfeit*) falso; *hair, jewel, teeth* postizo; **~ bottom** doble fondo *m*; **~ door** puerta *f* falsa.
falsehood ['fɔːlshʊd] *n* (*falseness*) falsedad *f*; (*lie*) mentira *f*.
falsely ['fɔːlslɪ] *adv* falsamente.
falseness ['fɔːlsnɪs] *n* falsedad *f*; (*of person*) perfidia *f*.
falsetto [fɔːl'setəʊ] **1** *adj voice* de falsete. **2** *adv sing* con voz de falsete. **3** *n* falsete *m*.
falsies* ['fɔːlsɪz] *npl* rellenos *mpl*.
falsification [,fɔːlsɪfɪ'keɪʃən] *n* falsificación *f*.
falsify ['fɔːlsɪfaɪ] *vt* falsificar.
falsity ['fɔːlsɪtɪ] *n* falsedad *f*.
falter ['fɔːltəʳ] **1** *vt* decir titubeando **2** *vi* (*waver*) vacilar, titubear; (*voice*) desfallecer, empañarse (por emoción); **without ~ing** sin vacilar.
faltering ['fɔːltərɪŋ] *adj step* vacilante; *voice* entrecortado.
falteringly ['fɔːltərɪŋlɪ] *adv say* en voz entrecortada.
fame [feɪm] *n* fama *f*; **Bader, of 1940 ~** Bader, famoso por lo que hizo en 1940.
famed [feɪmd] *adj* famoso.
familiar [fə'mɪlɪəʳ] *adj* (**a**) (*known, usual*) familiar; (*well-known*) conocido, consabido; (*common*) corriente, común; **it's a ~ feeling** es un sentimiento común, es un sentimiento que conocemos todos; **his voice sounds ~** me parece que conozco su voz; **it doesn't sound ~** no me suena.
(**b**) (*conversant*) **to be ~ with** estar familiarizado con, conocer; estar enterado de; **to make o.s. ~ with** familiarizarse con.
(**c**) (*intimate*) íntimo; de confianza; (*pej*) fresco; que presume de amigo; *language etc* familiar; **to be on ~ terms with** tener confianza con; **he got too ~** se tomó demasiadas confianzas.
familiarity [fə,mɪlɪ'ærɪtɪ] *n* (**a**) familiaridad *f*; (*knowledge*) conocimiento *m* (*with* de); **~ breeds contempt** lo conocido no se estima. (**b**) (*of tone*) intimidad *f*; confianza *f*; (*pej*) frescura *f*; **familiarities** familiaridades *fpl*, confianzas *fpl*.
familiarize [fə'mɪlɪəraɪz] **1** *vt* familiarizar (*with* con). **2** *vr*: **to ~ o.s. with** familiarizarse con.
familiarly [fə'mɪlɪəlɪ] *adv* con demasiada confianza.
family ['fæmɪlɪ] **1** *n* familia *f*; **to be one of the ~** ser como de la familia; **to be in the ~ way** estar en estado de buena esperanza; **to get** (*or* **put**) **a girl in the ~ way** dejar encinta a una joven; **to run in the ~** venir de familia.
2 *attr gathering etc* familiar; **~ allowance** (*Brit*) subsidio *m* familiar; **~ business** negocio *m* de la familia; **~ butcher** carnicero *m* doméstico; **~ credit** (*Brit*) ≈ suplemento *m* familiar, puntos* *mpl*; **~ doctor** médico *m*, -a *f* de cabecera; **~ friend** amigo *m*, -a *f* de la familia; **~ hotel** hotel *m* familiar; **~ income** ingresos *mpl* familiares; **~ life** vida *f* doméstica; **~ man** (*having family*) padre *m* de familia, (*home-loving*) hombre *m* casero; **~ name** nombre *m* de familia, apellido *m*; **~ pet** animal *m* doméstico; **~ planning** planificación *f* familiar; **~ planning clinic** clínica *f* de planificación familiar; **~-size(d) packet** paquete *m* familiar; **~ tree** árbol *m* genealógico.
famine ['fæmɪn] *n* hambre *f* (general y grave), hambruna *f*; (*of goods*) escasez *f*, carestía *f*.
famished ['fæmɪʃt] *adj* hambriento, famélico; **I'm simply ~** tengo un hambre canina.
famous ['feɪməs] *adj* famoso, célebre (*for* por).
famously ['feɪməslɪ] *adv* (*fig*) estupendamente bien, a las mil maravillas.
fan¹ [fæn] **1** *n* abanico *m* (*also fig*); (*Agr*) aventador *m*; (*machine, Aut*) ventilador *m*; (*electric*) abanico *m* eléctrico, ventilador *m*; **when the shit hits the ~*⁎** cuando se arma la gorda*.
2 *vt face* abanicar; (*mechanically*) ventilar; (*Agr*) aventar; *fire* soplar; (*fig*) excitar, atizar.
3 *vr*: **to ~ o.s.** abanicarse, hacerse aire.
◆**fan out 1** *vt cards etc* exponer (*or* ordenar) en abanico.
2 *vi* (*Mil etc*) desparramarse (en abanico), avanzar en abanico; diseminarse, dispersarse.
fan² [fæn] *n* aficionado *m*, -a *f*, admirador *m*, -ora *f*, entusiasta *mf*, (*Sport*) hincha *mf*; (*of pop music*) fan *mf*; **I am not one of his ~s** no soy de sus admiradores, yo no soy de los que le admiran.
fanatic [fə'nætɪk] *n* fanático *m*, -a *f*.
fanatic(al) [fə'nætɪk(əl)] *adj* fanático.
fanaticism [fə'nætɪsɪzəm] *n* fanatismo *m*.
fanbelt ['fænbelt] *n* correa *f* de ventilador.
fanciable* ['fænsɪəbl] *adj* (*Brit*) guapo, bueno*.
fancied ['fænsɪd] *adj* (*imaginary*) imaginario; (*preferred*) favorito; selecto; **a much ~ possibility** una posibilidad en que muchos creen; **a little ~ team** un equipo que se cree con pocas posibilidades.
fanciful ['fænsɪfʊl] *adj temperament* caprichoso; *construction, explanation etc* fantástico; (*unreal*) imaginario.
fan-club ['fænklʌb] *n* club *m* de admiradores; (*Mus*) club *m* de fans.
fancy ['fænsɪ] **1** *n* (**a**) (*delusion*) quimera *f*, suposición *f* arbitraria; **it's just your ~** lo habrás soñado; **it's one of her fancies** son cosas de ella.
(**b**) (*imaginative capacity*) fantasía *f*, imaginación *f*; **in the realm of ~** en el mundo de la fantasía.
(**c**) (*whim*) capricho *m*, antojo *m*; **to have a ~ for sth** antojarse algo a uno; **as the ~ takes her** según su capricho.
(**d**) (*taste*) afición *f*, gusto *m*; **to take a ~ to sth** tomar afición a algo, encapricharse por algo; **to take a ~ to sb** tomar cariño a uno, (*amorously*) prendarse de uno; **to take**

(or tickle) sb's ~ atraer a uno, cautivar a uno, (*amuse*) caer en gracia a uno.

2 *adj* (a) (*ornamental*) de adorno, de lujo; *jewels etc* de fantasía; ~ dress disfraz *m*; ~ dress ball baile *m* de disfraces; baile *m* de trajes; ~ footwork (*fig*) filigranas *fpl*; ~ goods géneros *mpl* de fantasía; ~ work (*Sew*) labor *f*.

(b) (*pej*) *idea* fantástico, estrafalario; *price* excesivo; her ~ man* su amante; his ~ woman* su querida.

3 *vt* (a) (*picture to o.s.*) imaginarse, figurarse; (*rather think*) creer, suponer; I ~ he is away creo (*LAm*: se me hace) que está fuera; he fancies he knows it all se cree un pozo de sabiduría; ~!, ~ that!, just ~! ¡fíjate!, (*doubting*) ¡parece mentira!; ¡lo que son las cosas!; ~ meeting you! ¡qué casualidad encontrarle a Vd!; ~ him winning! ¡qué raro que lo ganara él!

(b) (*want, like*) aficionarse a, encapricharse por; I don't ~ the idea no me gusta la idea; what do you ~? ¿qué quieres tomar?; do you ~ a stroll? ¿te apetece (*LAm*: ¿se te antoja) dar un paseo?; he fancies her* (*Brit*) ella le gusta, se siente atraído por ella.

(c) (*have high opinion of*) tener un alto concepto de; he fancies his game cree tener muchísima habilidad; I don't ~ his chances of winning no le doy mucha esperanza de ganar.

4 *vr*: to ~ o.s. (a) (*imagine o.s.*) creerse, soñar que uno es *etc*; he fancied himself in Spain soñó que estaba en España.

(b) (*Brit*) presumir; you ~ yourself! ¡eres un presumido!; he fancies himself as a footballer las echa de futbolista.

fancydan* [ˌfænsɪˈdæn] *n* (*US*) chulo *m*.

fancy-free [ˈfænsɪˈfriː] *adj* sin compromiso.

fanfare [ˈfænfɛəʳ] *n* toque *m* de trompeta, fanfarria *f*.

fanfold paper [ˈfænfəʊld,peɪpəʳ] *n* papel *m* plegado en abanico (*or* en acordeón).

fang [fæŋ] *n* colmillo *m*.

fan-heater [ˈfæn,hiːtəʳ] *n* (*Brit*) calefactor *m*, calentador *m* de aire.

fanlight [ˈfænlaɪt] *n* (montante *m* de) abanico *m*.

fanmail [ˈfænmeɪl] *n* cartas *fpl* escritas por admiradores.

Fanny [ˈfænɪ] *nf* (a) *familiar form of* Frances. (b) sweet ~ Adams‡ (*Brit*) absolutamente nada, nada de nada, na' de na'‡.

fanny* [ˈfænɪ] *n* (*esp US*: *buttocks*) culo** *m*; (*Brit***: *vagina*) coño** *m*.

fan-shaped [ˈfæn,ʃeɪpt] *adj* de (*or* en) abanico.

fantasia [fænˈteɪzɪə] *n* (*Liter, Mus*) fantasía *f*.

fantasize [ˈfæntəsaɪz] *vi* fantasear.

fantastic [fænˈtæstɪk] *adj* (*gen*) fantástico; (*: *excellent*) estupendo*, bárbaro* (*LAm*).

fantastically [fænˈtæstɪkəlɪ] *adv* fantásticamente; ~ learned enormemente erudito.

fantasy [ˈfæntəzɪ] *n* fantasía *f*.

fan-vaulting [ˈfæn,vɔːltɪŋ] *n* bóveda *f* de abanico.

fanzine [ˈfænziːn] *n* fanzine *m*.

FAO *n abbr of* Food and Agriculture Organization Organización *f* para la Alimentación y la Agricultura, OAA *f*.

faq *abbr of* of fair average quality de calidad estándar.

far [fɑːʳ] 1 *adv* (a) (*distance*: *lit*) lejos, a lo lejos (*also* ~ away, ~ off); not ~ from Dover no muy lejos de Dover; is it ~? ¿está lejos?, ¿dista mucho?; how ~ is it to Irún? ¿cuánto hay de aquí a Irún?; ~ and near, ~ and wide por todas partes; as ~ as hasta; so ~ hasta aquí; a bridge too ~ un puente de más; to walk ~ into the hills penetrar profundamente en los montes.

(b) (*distance*: *fig*) how ~ ...? ¿hasta qué punto ...?; how ~ have you gone in your work? ¿a qué punto han llegado tus trabajos?; ~ into the night hasta las altas horas de la noche; he's not ~ off 70 tiene casi 70 años, frisa en los 70 años; she was not ~ off tears estaba al borde de las lágrimas; as ~ back as we can recall hasta donde alcanza la memoria; so ~ hasta aquí, (*in time*) hasta ahora; so ~ this year en lo que va del año; so ~ so good hasta aquí, bien; so ~ and no further hasta aquí pero ni un paso más.

(c) (*phrases*) as ~ as I know, as ~ as I can tell que yo sepa; I will help you as ~ as I can te ayudaré en lo que pueda; as ~ as I am concerned en cuanto a mí, por lo que a mí se refiere; in so ~ as ... en la medida en que ..., en cuanto ...; ~ from approving it, I ... lejos de aprobarlo, yo ...; ~ from it! ¡nada de eso!; ~ be it from me to + *infin* no permita Dios que yo + *subj*.

(d) (*with adj or adv*) ~ better mucho mejor; it is ~ better not to go más vale no ir; ~ and away the best, the best by ~ con mucho el mejor; ~ superior to muy superior a; ~ faster than mucho más rápidamente que.

(e) (*with* go) to go ~ (*plan etc*) ir lejos; that young man will go ~ ese joven irá lejos, ese joven tiene un brillante porvenir; it doesn't go ~ enough no va bastante lejos, no tiene todo el alcance que quisiéramos; to go too ~ ir demasiado lejos; pasarse, propasarse, excederse; the theory is good as ~ as it goes la teoría es buena dentro de sus límites; he was pretty ~ gone (*dying*) se acercaba a la muerte, (*drunk*) estaba muy borracho; for a white wine you won't go ~ wrong with this si buscas un vino blanco éste ofrece bastante garantía; he wasn't ~ wrong (*or* off, out) casi acertaba, casi estaba en lo justo; he's gone too ~ to back out now ha ido demasiado lejos para retirarse ahora; to go ~ to + *infin* contribuir mucho a + *infin*; to go so ~ as to + *infin* llegar a + *infin*.

2 *adj* lejano, remoto; at the ~ end en el otro extremo, (*of room*) en el fondo; at the ~ side en el lado opuesto; the ~ north el extremo norte.

farad [ˈfærəd] *n* faradio *m*.

faraway [ˈfɑːrəweɪ] *adj* remoto; *look* preocupado, distraído.

farce [fɑːs] *n* (*Theat*) farsa *f*; (*fig*) farsa *f*, absurdo *m*, tontería *f*; this is a ~ esto es absurdo; what a ~ this is! ¡qué follón!; the trial was a ~ el proceso fue una parodia de la justicia.

farcical [ˈfɑːsɪkəl] *adj* absurdo, ridículo.

far-distant [ˈfɑːˈdɪstənt] *adj* lejano, remoto.

fare [fɛəʳ] 1 *n* (a) (*cost*) precio *m* (del viaje, del billete); (*ticket*) billete *m*, boleto *m* (*LAm*); (*Naut*) pasaje *m*; ~ stage, ~ zone (*US*) zona *f* (del recorrido del autobús); ~s please! ¡billetes, por favor!

(b) (*person*) pasajero *m*, -a *f*.

(c) (*food*) comida *f*.

2 *vi*: to ~ badly pasarlo mal, irle mal a uno; to ~ well pasarlo bien, irle bien a uno; how did you ~? ¿qué tal le fue?; to ~ alike correr la misma suerte.

Far East [ˈfɑːrˈiːst] *n* Extremo Oriente *m*, Lejano Oriente *m*.

Far Eastern [ˈfɑːrˈiːstən] *adj* del Extremo Oriente.

farewell [fɛəˈwel] 1 *interj* ¡adiós!; it's ~ to all that ya se acabó todo eso; you can say ~ to your wallet puedes considerar tu cartera como perdida.

2 *n* adiós *m*; (*ceremony*) despedida *f*; to bid ~ to despedirse de.

3 *attr* de despedida.

far-fetched [ˈfɑːˈfetʃt] *adj* inverosímil, poco probable; *comparison* traído por los pelos.

far-flung [ˈfɑːflʌŋ] *adj* extenso.

farinaceous [ˌfærɪˈneɪʃəs] *adj* farináceo.

farm [fɑːm] 1 *n* granja *f*; cortijo *m*, quinta *f*, estancia *f* (*LAm*); (*of mink, oysters etc*) criadero *m*; (*house*) cortijo *m*, alquería *f*, casa *f* de labranza.

2 *attr* agrícola; ~ produce productos *mpl* agrícolas; ~ tractor tractor *m* agrícola.

3 *vt* (*till*) cultivar, labrar; he ~s 300 acres tiene una finca de 300 acres.

4 *vi* (*till*) cultivar la tierra; (*as profession*) ser agricultor; he ~s in Devon tiene una finca (*or* tierras) en Devon.

◆**farm out** *vt* arrendar, dar en arriendo; *work* dar fuera, confiar a terceros.

farmer [ˈfɑːməʳ] *n* agricultor *m*, cultivador *m*, hacendado *m* (*LAm*), granjero *m*; (*peasant* ~) labrador *m*; estanciero *m* (*LAm*).

farmhand [ˈfɑːmhænd] *n* labriego *m*, mozo *m* de labranza, peón *m*.

farmhouse [ˈfɑːmhaʊs] *n*, *pl* **farmhouses** [ˈfɑːm,haʊzɪz] cortijo *m*, alquería *f*, casa *f* de labranza, casa *f* de hacienda (*LAm*).

farming [ˈfɑːmɪŋ] 1 *n* (*tilling*) cultivo *m*, labranza *f*; (*in general*) agricultura *f*. 2 *attr* agrícola; the ~ community los agricultores; good ~ practice técnicas *fpl* agrícolas reconocidas.

farm labourer, (*US*) **farm laborer** [ˈfɑːm,leɪbərəʳ] *n* trabajador *m* agrícola.

farmland [ˈfɑːmlænd] *n* tierras *fpl* de labrantío.

farmstead [ˈfɑːmsted] *n* alquería *f*.

farm worker [ˈfɑːm,wɜːkəʳ] *n* trabajador *m*, -ora *f* agrícola.

farmyard [ˈfɑːmjɑːd] *n* corral *m*.

Faroes [ˈfɛərəʊz] *npl*, **Faroe Islands** [ˈfɛərəʊ,aɪləndz] *npl* Islas *fpl* Feroe.

far-off [ˈfɑːrˈɒf] *adj* lejano, remoto.

far-out* [ˌfɑːrˈaʊt] *adj* (a) (*odd*) raro, extraño; estrafalario. (b) (*modern*) muy moderno, de vanguardia. (c) (*superb*) guai*, fenomenal*, tremendo*. (**d**) (*Pol etc*) extremista.

farrago [fəˈrɑːgəʊ] *n* fárrago *m*.

far-reaching [ˈfɑːˈriːtʃɪŋ] *adj* trascendental, de gran alcance, de ancha repercusión.

farrier [ˈfærɪəʳ] *n* (*esp Brit*) herrador *m*.

farrow [ˈfærəʊ] **1** *n* lechigada *f* de puercos. **2** *vt* parir. **3** *vi* parir (la cerda).

far-seeing [ˈfɑːˈsiːɪŋ] *adj* clarividente, previsor.

far-sighted [ˈfɑːˈsaɪtɪd] *adj* présbita; (*fig*) clarividente, previsor.

far-sightedly [ˈfɑːˈsaɪtɪdlɪ] *adv* de modo clarividente, con previsión.

far-sightedness [ˈfɑːˈsaɪtɪdnɪs] *n* clarividencia *f*, previsión *f*.

fart** [fɑːt] **1** *n* (**a**) pedo** *m*. (**b**) **he's a boring old ~** es un tío terriblemente pesado*, es un carrozón*. **2** *vi* pederse**, tirarse un pedo**.

◆fart about, fart around**** *vi* = **mess about**.

farther [ˈfɑːðəʳ] *comp of* **far**; = **further**.

farthest [ˈfɑːðɪst] *superl of* **far**; = **furthest**.

farthing [ˈfɑːðɪŋ] *n* cuarto *m* de penique.

FAS *abbr of* **free alongside ship** libre al costado del barco.

fascia [ˈfeɪʃə] *n* (*on building*) faja *f*; (*Brit Aut*) tablero *m*.

fascicle [ˈfæsɪkl] *n*, **fascicule** [ˈfæsɪkjuːl] *n* fascículo *m*.

fascinate [ˈfæsɪneɪt] *vt* fascinar, encantar.

fascinating [ˈfæsɪneɪtɪŋ] *adj* fascinador, encantador, sugestivo.

fascination [ˌfæsɪˈneɪʃən] *n* fascinación *f*, encanto *m*, sugestión *f*; **his former ~ with the cinema** la atracción que tuvo para él el cine.

fascism [ˈfæʃɪzəm] *n* fascismo *m*.

fascist [ˈfæʃɪst] **1** *adj* fascista. **2** *n* fascista *mf*.

fashion [ˈfæʃən] **1** *n* (**a**) (*usage, manner*) uso *m*, manera *f*, estilo *m*; **it is not my ~ to pretend** yo no acostumbro fingir; **after a ~** en cierto modo; medianamente; no muy bien; **I play after a ~** toco algo; **after the ~ of** a la manera de; **in the French ~** a la francesa, a lo francés, al estilo francés; **in one's own ~** a su propio modo.

(**b**) (*vogue*) moda *f*; **it's all the ~ now** ahora está muy de moda; **it's the ~ to say that ...** es un tópico decir que ...; **to be in ~** estar de moda; **to be out of ~** haber pasado de moda; **to come into ~** empezar a estar de moda; **to dress in the latest ~** vestirse a la última moda; **to go out of ~** pasar de moda; **to set the ~** imponer la moda (*for* de), dictar la moda (*for* de).

(**c**) (*good taste*) buen tono *m*, buen gusto *m*; **what ~ demands** lo que impone el buen gusto; **a man of ~** un hombre elegante.

2 *attr*: **~ designer** modisto *m*, -a *f*; **~ editor** director *m*, -ora *f* de modas; **~ house** casa *f* de modas; **~ magazine** revista *f* de modas; **~ model** modelo *mf*; **~ page** sección *f* de modas; **~ paper** revista *f* de modas; **~ parade** desfile *m* de modelos, presentación *f* de modelos; **~ plate** figurín *m* de moda; **~ show** presentación *f* de modelos.

3 *vt* formar, labrar, forjar (*on* sobre).

fashionable [ˈfæʃnəbl] *adj dress etc* de moda, elegante; *place, restaurant* de buen tono, elegante; **~ people** gente *f* elegante, gente *f* bien*; **in ~ society** en la buena sociedad; **it is ~ to** + *infin* está de moda + *infin*; **he is hardly a ~ painter now** es un pintor que no está ahora muy de moda.

fashionably [ˈfæʃnəblɪ] *adv*: **to be ~ dressed** estar vestido muy elegantemente, ir vestido de acuerdo con la moda actual.

fast¹ [fɑːst] **1** *adj* (**a**) (*speedy*) rápido, veloz; ligero; (*Sport*) *pitch* seco y firme; *court* rápido; *train* rápido, expreso; **~ lane** (*Aut*) carril *m* de adelantamiento; (*Brit*) carril *m* de la derecha, (*most countries*) carril *m* de la izquierda; **he lives life in the ~ lane** vive deprisa; **he was too ~ for me** corrió más que yo; **to pull a ~ one on sb** jugar una mala pasada a uno, embaucar a uno; **he's a ~ talker*** es un pretencioso.

(**b**) (*clock*) **to be ~** estar adelantado; **my watch is 5 minutes ~** mi reloj está 5 minutos adelantado.

(**c**) *woman* cachonda, fresca; *life, set* entregado a los placeres, hedonista; disoluto.

(**d**) (*firm*) fijo, firme; *friend* leal; *colour* sólido, inalterable; *film* rápido.

2 *adv* (**a**) (*speedily*) rápidamente; de prisa; **~er!** ¡más!; **how ~ can you type?** ¿cuántas palabras haces por minuto?; **I ran as ~ as I could** corrí cuanto pude; **don't speak so ~** habla más despacio; **not so ~!** ¡más despacio!, (*interrupting*) ¡un momento!; **as ~ as I finished them he wrapped them up** a medida que yo los terminaba él los envolvía.

(**b**) **to play ~ and loose with** jugar con.

(**c**) (*firmly*) firmemente; **~ asleep** profundamente dormido; **to hold ~** agarrarse bien, (*fig*) mantenerse firme; **hold ~!** ¡agarraos!, (*stop*) ¡para!; **to make sth ~** sujetar algo; **to make a rope ~** atar firmemente una cuerda; **to make a boat ~** amarrar una barca; **to stand ~** mantenerse firme; **to stick ~** quedar bien pegado; **to be stuck ~ in the mud** quedar atascado en el lodo; **to be stuck ~ in a doorway** estar metido por una puerta sin poderse mover.

fast² [fɑːst] **1** *n* ayuno *m*. **2** *vi* ayunar.

fast day [ˈfɑːstdeɪ] *n* día *m* de ayuno.

fasten [ˈfɑːsn] **1** *vt* (**a**) asegurar, sujetar, fijar; (*with rope*) atar; (*with paste*) pegar; *box, door, window* cerrar; (*with bolt*) echar el cerrojo a; *belt, dress* abrochar; **to ~ two things together** pegar dos cosas.

(**b**) (*fig*) **to ~ the blame on sb** echar (*or* achacar) la culpa a uno; **to ~ the responsibility on sb** atribuir a uno la responsabilidad; **they're trying to ~ the crime on me** tratan de demostrar que yo fui autor del crimen.

2 *vi* (*box etc*) cerrarse.

◆fasten down *vt blind, flap* cerrar.

◆fasten on to *vt* agarrarse de, pegarse a, (*fig*) fijarse en; **he ~ed on to me at once** se fijó en mí en seguida, (*as companion*) se me pegó a mí en seguida; **to ~ on to a pretext** echar mano (*or* valerse) de un pretexto.

◆fasten up 1 *vt dress, coat* abotonar, abrochar. **2** *vi*: **it ~s up in front** se abrocha por delante.

◆fasten (up)on *vt gaze* fijar en, dirigir a; **to ~ (up)on an excuse** aferrarse a una excusa; **to ~ (up)on the idea of doing** aferrarse a la idea de hacer.

fastener [ˈfɑːsnəʳ] *n*, **fastening** [ˈfɑːsnɪŋ] *n* (*of door etc*) cerrojo *m*, pestillo *m*; (*on box*) cierre *m*; (*on dress*) broche *m*, corchete *m*; (*for papers*) grapa *f*; (*zip-~*) cremallera *f*.

fast food [ˈfɑːstˈfuːd] *n* (**a**) (*snack*) comida *f* rápida, platos *mpl* preparados. (**b**) (*place*: *also* **~ restaurant**) restaurante *m* fast-food, hamburguesería *f*; fast-food *m*.

fast forward [ˈfɑːstˈfɔːwəd] **1** *n* (*also* **~ button**) botón *m* de avance rápido. **2** *vt* hacer avanzar rápidamente. **3** *vi* avanzar rápidamente.

fastidious [fæsˈtɪdɪəs] *adj* delicado, quisquilloso; (*about cleanliness etc*) exigente; *taste* fino; *mind* refinado.

fastidiously [fæsˈtɪdɪəslɪ] *adv examine, clean, check* meticulosamente, quisquillosamente.

fastidiousness [fæsˈtɪdɪəsnɪs] *n* meticulosidad *f*, exigencia *f*.

fast-moving [ˌfɑːstˈmuːvɪŋ] *adj* rápido, veloz; *target* que cambia rápidamente de posición; *goods* de venta rápida, que se venden rápidamente; *plot* muy movido, lleno de acciones, que se desarrolla rápidamente.

fastness [ˈfɑːstnɪs] *n* (*Mil*) fortaleza *f*; (*of mountain etc*) lo más intrincado; **in their Cuban mountain ~** en las espesuras serranas de Cuba.

fat [fæt] **1** *adj* (**a**) *person* gordo; (*thick*) grueso; **~ cat*** (*esp US*) pez *m* gordo*, potentado *m*; **~ farm** (*US**) clínica *f* de adelgazamiento; **to get ~** engordar.

(**b**) *meat* poco magro, que tiene mucha grasa; (*greasy*) grasiento, graso.

(**c**) *land* fértil; *living* lujoso; *profit* pingüe; *salary* muy grande; **the ~ years** los años de las vacas gordas.

(**d**) (*) **a ~ lot he knows!** ¡maldito lo que él sabe!; **a ~ chance he's got** no tiene ni chance*; **a ~ lot of good you did us!** ¡menudo provecho que nos has traído!; **a ~ lot of good that is!** y eso ¿para qué sirve?

2 *n* (*on person*) carnes *fpl*; (*of meat*) grasa *f*; (*for cooking*) manteca *f* (de cerdo); (*lard*) lardo *m*; **to live on the ~ of the land** vivir a cuerpo de rey, nadar en la abundancia; comer opíparamente; **now the ~ is in the fire** aquí se va a armar la gorda.

fatal [ˈfeɪtl] *adj* fatal (*also Comput*); *consequences* funesto (*to* para); *accident, injury* mortal; **that was ~** eso fue el colmo; **it's ~ to say that** es peligrosísimo decir eso.

fatalism [ˈfeɪtəlɪzəm] *n* fatalismo *m*.

fatalist [ˈfeɪtəlɪst] *n* fatalista *mf*.

fatalistic [ˌfeɪtəˈlɪstɪk] *adj* fatalista.

fatality [fəˈtælɪtɪ] *n* calamidad *f*, desgracia *f*; fatalidad *f*; (*victim*) víctima *f*, muerto *m*; **luckily there were no fatalities** por fortuna no hubo víctimas.

fatally [ˈfeɪtəlɪ] *adv* fatalmente; *injure etc* mortalmente, a muerte.

fate [feɪt] *n* (**a**) (*force*) hado *m*, destino *m*, sino *m*; **the F~s** las Parcas; **what ~ has in store for us** lo que la suerte nos va a deparar.

(**b**) (*person's lot*) suerte *f*; **to leave sb to his ~** dejar a uno a su suerte; **to meet one's ~** encontrar la muerte; **this sealed his ~** esto acabó de perderle.

fated ['feɪtɪd] *adj friendship, person* predestinado, condenado; **to be ~ to do** estar predestinado a hacer, tener fatalmente que hacer.

fateful ['feɪtfʊl] *adj* fatal, fatídico; decisivo.

fat-free ['fætfri:] *adj diet* sin grasa.

fathead* ['fæthed] *n* imbécil *mf*; **you ~!** ¡imbécil!

fat-headed* ['fæt,hedɪd] *adj* imbécil.

father ['fɑ:ðəʳ] **1** *n* padre *m*; **F~s of the Church** Santos Padres *mpl*; **Our F~** Padre nuestro; **to say three Our F~s** rezar tres padrenuestros; **F~ Brown** (*Rel*) (el) padre Brown; **~ confessor** padre *m* confesor, director *m* espiritual; **F~ Christmas** (*Brit*) Papá *m* Noel; **Old F~ Time** el Tiempo; **F~'s Day** Día *m* del Padre; **city ~s** prohombres *mpl* de la ciudad; **my ~ and mother** mis padres; **like ~ like son** de tal palo tal astilla; **a ~ and mother of a row*** una bronca fenomenal*; **the ~ of English poetry** el padre de la poesía inglesa; **to talk to sb like a ~** hablar a uno en tono paternal.

2 *vt child* engendrar; (*fig*) inventar, producir; **to ~ sth on sb** atribuir algo a uno.

father-figure ['fɑ:ðə,fɪgəʳ] *n* figura *f* que sirve de padre, persona *f* que se finge (*or* cree *etc*) dotada de las cualidades paternales.

fatherhood ['fɑ:ðəhʊd] *n* paternidad *f*.

father-in-law ['fɑ:ðərɪnlɔ:] *n, pl* **fathers-in-law** suegro *m*, padre *m* político.

fatherland ['fɑ:ðəlænd] *n* patria *f*.

fatherless ['fɑ:ðəlɪs] *adj* huérfano de padre.

fatherly ['fɑ:ðəlɪ] *adj* paternal.

fathom ['fæðəm] **1** *n* braza *f*; **5 ~s deep** de (*or* a *etc*) una profundidad de 5 brazas.

2 *vt* (*Naut*) sond(e)ar; (*fig*) profundizar, penetrar; *mystery* desentrañar; **we couldn't ~ it out** no logramos sacar nada en claro; **I can't ~ why** no comprendo por qué.

fathomless ['fæðəmlɪs] *adj* insondable.

fatigue [fə'ti:g] **1** *n* (**a**) fatiga *f*, cansancio *m*; (*Tech*) fatiga *f*.

(**b**) (*Mil*) faena *f*.

(**c**) (*Mil*: *also* **~s**) uniforme *m* (or traje *m*) de faena (*or* de cuartel), mono *m*.

2 *attr* (*Mil*) **~ dress = 1 c**; **~ duty** servicio *m* de fajina; **~ party** destacamento *m* de fajina.

3 *vt* fatigar, cansar.

fatigued [fə'ti:gd] *adj* fatigado.

fatiguing [fə'ti:gɪŋ] *adj* fatigoso.

fatless ['fætlɪs] *adj food* sin grasa.

fatness ['fætnɪs] *n* gordura *f*.

fatso‡ ['fætsəʊ] *n* (*pej*) gordo *m*, -a *f*.

fatstock ['fætstɒk] *n* (*Agr*) animales *mpl* de engorde.

fatten ['fætn] **1** *vt animal* engordar, cebar. **2** *vi* engordar.

fattening ['fætnɪŋ] **1** *adj food* que hace engordar. **2** *nm* (*Agr*) engorde *m*.

fatty ['fætɪ] **1** *adj* graso; *tissue, degeneration etc* grasoso; **~ acid** ácido *m* graso. **2** *n* (*) gordinflón* *m*, -ona *f*; **~!** ¡gordo!

fatuity [fə'tju:ɪtɪ] *n* fatuidad *f*, necedad *f*.

fatuous ['fætjʊəs] *adj* fatuo, necio.

fatuously ['fætjʊəslɪ] *adv* neciamente.

faucet ['fɔ:sɪt] *n* (*US*) grifo *m*, llave *f* (*LAm*).

faugh [fɔ:] *interj* ¡fu!

fault [fɔ:lt] **1** *n* (**a**) (*defect*: *in character*) defecto *m*; (*in manufacture*) desperfecto *m*, imperfección *f*; (*in supply, machine*) avería *f*; **with all his ~s** con todos sus defectos; **her ~ is excessive shyness** peca de demasiado reservada; **generous to a ~** excesivamente generoso, generoso hasta el exceso; **to find ~ with** criticar, poner peros a.

(**b**) (*Geol*) falla *f*.

(**c**) (*blame*) culpa *f*; **it's all your ~** tienes toda la culpa; **it's not my ~** yo no tengo la culpa; **whose ~ is it if ...?** ¿quién tiene la culpa si ...?; **you were not at ~** tú no tuviste la culpa; **you were at ~ in not telling me** hiciste mal en no decírmelo; **your memory is at ~** recuerdas mal.

(**d**) (*mistake*) falta *f* (*also Tennis etc*); **through no ~ of his own** sin falta alguna de su parte.

2 *vt* tachar, encontrar defectos en; **it cannot be ~ed** es intachable; **you cannot ~ him on spelling** no le encontrarás falta alguna en la escritura.

faultfinder ['fɔ:lt,faɪndəʳ] *n* criticón *m*, -ona *f*.

faultfinding ['fɔ:lt,faɪndɪŋ] **1** *adj* criticón, reparón. **2** *n* manía *f* de criticar.

faultless ['fɔ:ltlɪs] *adj* impecable, intachable, sin defecto.

faultlessly ['fɔ:ltlɪslɪ] *adv* impecablemente.

faulty ['fɔ:ltɪ] *adj* defectuoso, imperfecto.

faun [fɔ:n] *n* fauno *m*.

fauna ['fɔ:nə] *n* fauna *f*.

Faust [faʊst] *nm* Fausto.

faux pas ['fəʊ'pɑ:] *n* (*false move*) paso *m* en falso; (*gaffe*) plancha *f*, metedura *f* (*LAm*: metida *f*) de pata.

favour, (*US*) **favor** ['feɪvəʳ] **1** *n* (**a**) (*approval, regard*) favor *m*; aprobación *f*; (*protection*) amparo *m*; **to be in ~** (*thing*) tener mucha aceptación, (*dress etc*) estar de moda; **to be in ~ with** (*person*) tener el apoyo de, (*at court etc*) gozar de favor cerca de; **to be out of ~** (*thing*) no estimarse, (*dress etc*) estar fuera de moda; **to curry ~** buscar favores; **to curry ~ with sb** tratar de congraciarse con uno; **to find ~ with sb** caer en gracia a uno; **to look with ~ on** favorecer; **to stand high in sb's ~** ser tenido en mucho por uno.

(**b**) (*kindness*) favor *m*; **~s** (*of woman*) favores *mpl*; **to ask a ~ of** pedir un favor a; **to do sb a ~** hacer un favor a uno; **please do me the ~ of** + *ger* haga el favor de + *infin*; **do me a ~!‡** (*as answer*) ¡nada de eso!; ¿crees que soy tan tonto?; **do me a ~ and clear off!*** ¡por Dios, lárgate!*

(**c**) **your ~ of the 5th inst** (*Comm*) su atenta del 5 del corriente.

(**d**) (*partiality*) parcialidad *f*; **by your ~** con permiso de Vd; **to show ~ to sb** favorecer a uno.

(**e**) (*aid, support*) apoyo *m*; **in ~ of** a favor de; **balance in your ~** saldo *m* a su favor; **that's a point in his ~** es un punto a su favor; **to be in ~ of** *person* apoyar, estar por; *thing* aprobar, ser partidario de; **to be in ~ of** + *ger* apoyar la idea de + *infin*, ser partidario de + *infin*.

(**f**) (*token*) prenda *f*.

2 *vt person* favorecer, (*unjustly*) mostrar parcialidad hacia; *idea, scheme* aprobar, ser partidario de; *party* apoyar; (*choose to wear*) elegir; *progress* ser propicio a, ayudar; *team, horse* preferir; **fortune ~s the brave** la fortuna ayuda a los valientes; **he eventually ~ed us with a visit** por fin nos honró con su visita, por fin se dignó visitarnos; **most ~ed nation treatment** trato *m* de nación más favorecida.

favourable, (*US*) **favorable** ['feɪvərəbl] *adj* favorable; *conditions etc* propicio.

favourably, (*US*) **favorably** ['feɪvərəblɪ] *adv* favorablemente.

favoured, (*US*) **favored** ['feɪvəd] *adj* favorecido; (*favourite*) predilecto; **~ by nature** dotado por la naturaleza (*with* de); **one of the ~ few** uno de los pocos afortunados.

favourite, (*US*) **favorite** ['feɪvərɪt] **1** *adj* favorito, predilecto; **~ son** (*US Pol*) hijo *m* predilecto. **2** *n* favorito *m*, -a *f* (*also Sport*); (*at court*) valido *m*, privado *m*; (*mistress*) querida *f*.

favouritism, (*US*) **favoritism** ['feɪvərɪtɪzəm] *n* favoritismo *m*.

fawn¹ [fɔ:n] **1** *n* (**a**) (*Zool*) cervato *m*. (**b**) (*colour*) beige. **2** *adj* beige.

fawn² [fɔ:n] *vi*: **to ~ on** (*animal*) acariciar; (*fig*) adular, lisonjear; congraciarse con.

fawning ['fɔ:nɪŋ] *adj* adulador, servil.

fax [fæks] **1** *n* fax *m*. **2** *attr*: **~ message** fax *m*; **~ number** número *m* de (tele)fax. **3** *vt* faxear.

faze* [feɪz] *vt* (*esp US*) perturbar; molestar; marear.

fazed* [feɪzd] *adj* (*US*) pasmado*.

FBA *abbr of* **Fellow of the British Academy.**

FBI *n* (*US*) *abbr of* **Federal Bureau of Investigation** ≃ Brigada *f* de Investigación Criminal, BIC *f*.

FC *n abbr of* **football club** club *m* de fútbol, C.F. *m*.

FCA *n* (**a**) *abbr of* **Fellow of the Institute of Chartered Accountants.** (**b**) (*US*) *abbr of* **Farm Credit Administration.**

FCC *n* (*US*) *abbr of* **Federal Communications Commission.**

FCO *n* (*Brit*) *abbr of* **Foreign and Commonwealth Office** ≃ Ministerio *m* de Asuntos Exteriores, Min. de AA EE.

F.D. (*US*) *abbr of* **Fire Department.**

FDA *n* (*US*) *abbr of* **Food and Drug Administration.**

FDIC *n* (*US*) *abbr of* **Federal Deposit Insurance Corporation.**

FDR *initials of* **Franklin Delano Roosevelt.**

fealty ['fi:əltɪ] *n* (*Hist*) lealtad *f* (feudal).

fear [fɪəʳ] **1** *n* miedo *m* (*of* a, de), temor *m*; aprensión *f*; **for ~ of** temiendo, por miedo de; **for ~ that ...** por miedo de que + *subj*; **no ~!** ¡ni hablar!; **there's no ~ of that happening** no hay peligro de que ocurra eso; **without ~ or favour** imparcialmente, sin temor ni favor; **to go in ~ of one's life** temer por su vida; **to put the ~ of God into sb** dar un susto mortal a uno.

2 *vt* temer; *person* tener miedo a, *thing* tener miedo de.

3 *vi*: **to ~ for** temer por; **to ~ to** + *infin* tener miedo de + *infin*; **never ~!** ¡no hay cuidado!, ¡no temas!

fearful ['fɪəfʊl] *adj* (**a**) (*frightened*) temeroso (*of* de);

aprensivo; (*cowardly*) tímido. (**b**) (*frightening*) pavoroso, horrendo. (**c**) (*****) tremendo*****, terrible.

fearfully ['fɪəfəlɪ] *adv cower etc* con miedo; *say* tímidamente; (*****) terriblemente.

fearfulness ['fɪəfʊlnɪs] *n* (*fear*) medrosidad *f*; (*shyness*) timidez *f*.

fearless ['fɪəlɪs] *adj* intrépido, audaz; ~ **of** sin temor a.

fearlessly ['fɪəlɪslɪ] *adv* intrépidamente, audazmente; **he went on** ~ siguió impertérrito.

fearlessness ['fɪəlɪsnɪs] *n* intrepidez *f*, audacia *f*.

fearsome ['fɪəsəm] *adj* temible, espantoso.

fearsomely ['fɪəsəmlɪ] *adv* espantosamente.

feasibility [ˌfiːzə'bɪlɪtɪ] **1** *n* factibilidad *f*, viabilidad *f*; **to doubt the** ~ **of a scheme** dudar si un proyecto es factible. **2** *attr*: ~ **analysis** análisis *m* de viabilidad; ~ **study** estudio *m* de factibilidad.

feasible ['fiːzəbl] *adj* factible, hacedero, posible; **to make sth** ~ posibilitar algo.

feast [fiːst] **1** *n* (**a**) (*meal*) banquete *m*, festín *m*. (**b**) (*Eccl*) fiesta *f*. **2** *vt* banquetear; agasajar, festejar. **3** *vi* banquetear; **to** ~ **on** regalarse con.

feast-day ['fiːstdeɪ] *n* fiesta *f*.

feat [fiːt] *n* hazaña *f*, proeza *f*.

feather ['feðəʳ] **1** *n* pluma *f*; **in fine** ~ de excelente humor; **that is a** ~ **in his cap** es un triunfo para él; se ha apuntado un tanto; **you could have knocked me down with a** ~ casi me caigo patas arriba; **to show the white** ~ mostrarse cobarde. **2** *vt* (**a**) emplumar. (**b**) *oar* volver horizontal.

feather-bed ['feðə'bed] **1** *n* plumón *m*. **2** *vt* subvencionar (demasiado), dar primas (excesivas) a.

featherbedding ['feðəˌbedɪŋ] *n* subvencionismo *m*.

featherbrain ['feðəbreɪn] *n* cabeza *f* de chorlito.

featherbrained ['feðəbreɪnd] *adj* cascabelero.

feather duster ['feðə'dʌstəʳ] *n* plumero *m*.

featherweight ['feðəweɪt] *n* peso *m* pluma.

feathery ['feðərɪ] *adj texture* plumoso; (*light*) ligero como pluma.

feature ['fiːtʃəʳ] **1** *n* (**a**) rasgo *m* distintivo, característica *f*; (*Ling*: *also* **distinctive** ~) rasgo *m* distintivo.

(**b**) (*of face*) facción *f*; ~**s** facciones *fpl*, rostro *m*.

(**c**) (*Theat*) número *m*, (*Cine*) largometraje *m*, película *f* principal.

(**d**) (*in paper*) artículo *m*, crónica *f*.

2 *attr*: ~ **article** crónica *f* especial, reportaje *m* especial; ~ **film** largometraje *m*, película *f* principal.

3 *vt* (*portray*) delinear, representar; (*in paper etc*) presentar, ofrecer (como atracción principal); *actor* presentar; **a film featuring Garbo as ...** una película que presenta a Garbo en el papel de ...

4 *vi* existir, constar, figurar.

featureless ['fiːtʃəlɪs] *adj* sin rasgos distintivos, monótono.

feature-writer ['fiːtʃəˌraɪtəʳ] *n* articulista *mf*, cronista *mf*.

Feb. *abbr of* **February** febrero *m*, feb.

febrile ['fiːbraɪl] *adj* febril.

February ['februərɪ] *n* febrero *m*.

feces ['fiːsiːz] *npl* (*US*) = **faeces.**

feckless ['feklɪs] *adj* irreflexivo; casquivano.

fecund ['fiːkənd] *adj* fecundo.

fecundity [fɪ'kʌndɪtɪ] *n* fecundidad *f*.

Fed [fed] (**a**) (*US****) *n abbr of* **federal officer** federal***** *mf*. (**b**) (*US Banking*) *n abbr of* **Federal Reserve Board.** (**c**) (*esp US*) *abbr of* **federal, federated, federation.**

fed [fed] **1** *pret and ptp of* **feed. 2** *adj*: **to be** ~ **up*** estar harto (*with* de).

federal ['fedərəl] **1** *adj* federal; **F**~ **Reserve Bank** (*US*) Banco *m* de Reserva Federal; ~ **tax** impuesto *m* federal. **2** *nm* (*US Hist*) federal *m*.

federalism ['fedərəlɪzəm] *n* federalismo *m*.

federalist ['fedərəlɪst] *n* federalista *mf*.

federalize ['fedərəlaɪz] *vt* federar, federalizar.

federate ['fedəreɪt] **1** *vt* federar. **2** *vi* federarse.

federation [ˌfedə'reɪʃən] *n* federación *f*.

fedora [fə'dɔːrə] *n* (*US*) sombrero *m* flexible, sombrero *m* tirolés.

fee [fiː] *n* (*professional*) derechos *mpl*, honorarios *mpl*; (*to club etc*) cuota *f*; (*for admission*) precio *m* (de entrada); (*for doctor's visit*) precio *m* de visita; ~**s** (*Univ etc*) (gastos *mpl* de) matrícula *f*; **for a small** ~ pagando un poco, por un pequeño reconocimiento.

feeble ['fiːbl] *adj* débil (*also Med*); flojo; *light, sound* tenue; *effort* irresoluto, débil; *argument* poco convincente.

feeble-minded ['fiːbl'maɪndɪd] *adj* imbécil; irresoluto.

feeble-mindedness [ˌfiːbl'maɪndɪdnɪs] *n* debilidad *f* mental; irresolución *f*.

feebleness ['fiːblnɪs] *n* debilidad *f* (*also Med*); flojedad *f*; tenuidad *f*; irresolución *f*.

feebly ['fiːblɪ] *adv* débilmente; flojamente.

feed [fiːd] **1** *n* (**a**) (*food*) comida *f*; (*Agr*) pienso *m*; **to be off one's** ~ no tener apetito, estar desganado.

(**b**) (*****) cuchipanda***** *f*, comilona***** *f*; **to have a good** ~ darse un atracón*****.

(**c**) (*Mech*) tubo *m* de alimentación.

2 (*irr*: *pret and ptp* **fed**) *vt* (*nourish*) alimentar, nutrir; (*give meal to*) dar de comer a; (*Brit*) *baby* dar el pecho a, dar de mamar a, (*with bottle*) dar el biberón a; *fire* cebar; (*fig*) alimentar; **they fed us well at the hotel** nos dieron bien de comer en el hotel; **to** ~ **sth into a machine** ir metiendo algo en una máquina; **to** ~ **data into the computer** suministrar datos al ordenador, hacer entrar datos en el ordenador; **to** ~ **sb on sth** dar algo de comer a uno.

3 *vi* comer; (*Agr*) pacer; **to** ~ **on** comer, alimentarse de (*also fig*).

◆**feed back** *vt information, results* proporcionar, facilitar.

◆**feed in** *vt tape, wire* alimentar; *facts, information* introducir.

◆**feed up** *vt* (**a**) *animal* cebar. (**b**) (*****) **it really** ~**s me up** me saca totalmente de quicio.

feedback ['fiːdbæk] *n* (**a**) (*Rad*) realimentación *f*. (**b**) (*information etc*) feedback *m*, transmisión *f* en dirección inversa; (*reaction*) efecto *m* recíproco, retroacción *f*, reacción *f*; **we're not getting much** ~ casi no se nota reacción alguna.

feeder ['fiːdəʳ] **1** *n* (**a**) (*Mech*) alimentador *m*, tubo *m* de alimentación. (**b**) (*Geog*) afluente *m*; (*Rail*) ramal *m* tributario. (**c**) (*device*: *for birds etc*) comedero *m*. (**d**) (*Brit*: *bib*) babero *m*. **2** *attr*: ~ **primary** (**school**) (*Scol*) escuela *f* primaria que provee de alumnos a una secundaria; ~ **service** (*US*) servicio *m* secundario (de transportes).

feeding ['fiːdɪŋ] *n* alimentación *f*; (*meals collectively*) comida *f*, comidas *fpl*.

feeding-bottle ['fiːdɪŋˌbɒtl] *n* (*esp Brit*) biberón *m*.

feeding-ground ['fiːdɪŋˌgraʊnd] *n* terreno *m* de pasto.

feeding-stuffs ['fiːdɪŋˌstʌfs] *npl* piensos *mpl*.

feedpipe ['fiːdpaɪp] *n* tubo *m* de alimentación.

feedstuffs ['fiːdstʌfs] *npl* piensos *mpl*.

feel [fiːl] **1** *n* (*sense of touch*) tacto *m*; (*sensation*) sensación *f*; **at the** ~ **of his skin** al contacto con su piel; **to be rough to the** ~ ser áspero al tacto; **to know silk by its** ~ conocer la seda al tocarla; **to get the** ~ **of** acostumbrarse a, (*knack*) coger el tino a.

2 (*irr*: *pret and ptp* **felt**) *vt* (**a**) (*explore*) tocar, palpar, tentar; *pulse* tomar; (*caress*) acariciar, palpar.

(**b**) (*perceive*) *blow, pain, heat, need* sentir; experimentar; **I felt it move** lo sentí moverse, sentí que se movió; **I felt it getting hot** sentí como se estaba calentando.

(**c**) (*be conscious of*) estar consciente de, darse cuenta de; **I** ~ **my position very much** me doy plenamente cuenta de mi situación.

(**d**) (*experience*) sentir, experimentar; (*be affected by*) resentirse de; **I** ~ **no interest in it** no me interesa; **we are beginning to** ~ **the effects** empezamos a resentirnos de los efectos; **the consequences will be felt next year** se sufrirán las consecuencias el año que viene.

(**e**) (*think, believe*) **I** ~ **that ...** creo que ..., siento que (+ *indic*), me parece que ...; **I** ~ **strongly that ...** estoy convencido de que ....

3 *vi* (**a**) (*explore*) **to** ~ **about in the dark** buscar a tientas en la oscuridad; **to** ~ **(around) in one's pocket for a key** buscar una llave en el bolsillo; **I can't see but I'll** ~ **for it** no veo nada pero lo buscaré tanteando.

(**b**) (*be*) sentirse; **to** ~ **bad, to** ~ **ill** sentirse mal; **to** ~ **old** sentirse viejo; **to** ~ **cold** (*person*) tener frío; **to** ~ **hungry** tener hambre; **how do you** ~**?** ¿qué tal te encuentras?; **she's not** ~**ing quite herself** no se encuentra del todo bien; **to** ~ **all the better for sth** sentirse mucho mejor después de algo; **I don't** ~ **up to it** no me siento con fuerzas para ello.

(**c**) (*think*) **how do you** ~ **about this?** ¿qué opinas de esto?; **how does it** ~ **to go hungry?** ¿cómo le gusta pasar hambre?

(**d**) (*give impression of*) **it** ~**s rough** es áspero al tacto; **it** ~**s like silk** es como la seda al tacto, parece ser seda; **it** ~**s cold** está frío (al tacto); **it** ~**s colder out here** aquí fuera hace más frío; **it** ~**s like rain** parece que va a llover; **how does it** ~**?** ¿qué impresión te hace?

(**e**) (*sympathize*) **I ~ for you** lo siento en el alma, te compadezco; **we ~ for you (in your loss)** te acompañamos en el sentimiento.

(**f**) **to ~ like doing sth** tener ganas de hacer algo; **I ~ like an apple** me apetece una manzana; **do you ~ like a walk?** ¿quieres dar un paseo?, ¿te apetece dar un paseo?; **I go out whenever I ~ like it** salgo siempre cuando quiero; **right now I don't ~ like it** ahora mismo no quiero.

◆**feel out*** *vt* (*US*) *person* sondear la opinión de; **to ~ out the ground** tantear el terreno, reconocer el terreno.

◆**feel up**‡ *vt*: **to ~ sb up** meter mano a una*.

feeler ['fi:lə^r] *n* (**a**) (*Zool*) antena *f*; tentáculo *m*. (**b**) (*Pol etc*) sondeo *m*, tentativa *f*; **to put out a ~** hacer un sondeo.

feeling ['fi:lɪŋ] *n* (**a**) (*sensation*) sensación *f*; **a cold ~** una sensación de frío; **to have no ~ in one's arm** no tener sensibilidad en un brazo.

(**b**) (*emotion*) sentimiento *m*, emoción *f*; (*tenderness*) ternura *f*; **bad ~** rencor *m*, envidia *f*, hostilidad *f*; **a man of ~** un hombre sensible; **to speak with ~** hablar con convicción, (*angrily*) hablar con pasión; **~s** sentimientos *mpl*; **you can imagine my ~s** puedes suponer cuáles serían mis sentimientos; **to appeal to sb's finer ~s** apelar a los sentimientos nobles de uno; **to hurt sb's ~s** herir los sentimientos de uno; **to relieve one's ~s** desahogarse; **to spare sb's ~s** no herir los sentimientos de uno.

(**c**) (*appreciation*) **he has no ~ for music** no sabe apreciar la música.

(**d**) (*opinion*) opinión *f*, parecer *m*; **our ~s do not matter** nuestras opiniones no valen para nada; **my ~ is that ...** creo que ...; **what is your ~?** ¿qué opina Vd?; **the general ~ was that ...** en general se creía que ....

(**e**) (*foreboding*) presentimiento *m*; **I have a ~ that ...** presiento que ..., se me antoja que ..., me barrunto que ....

feelingly ['fi:lɪŋlɪ] *adv* con honda emoción.

fee-paying ['fi:,peɪɪŋ] *adj pupil* que paga pensión; *school* privado.

feet [fi:t] *npl of* **foot.**

feign [feɪn] *vt* fingir, aparentar; *excuse etc* inventar; **to ~ mad(ness)** fingirse loco; **to ~ sleep** fingirse dormido; **to ~ dead** fingirse muerto; **to ~ not to know** fingir no saber.

feigned [feɪnd] *adj* fingido.

feint [feɪnt] **1** *n* treta *f*, estratagema *f*; (*Fencing*) finta *f*. **2** *vi* hacer una finta.

feisty* ['faɪstɪ] *adj* (*US*) (*lively*) animado; (*quarrelsome*) pendenciero.

feldspar ['feldspɑ:^r] *n* feldespato *m*.

felicitate [fɪ'lɪsɪteɪt] *vt* felicitar, congratular.

felicitations [fɪlɪsɪ'teɪʃənz] *npl* felicitaciones *fpl*.

felicitous [fɪ'lɪsɪtəs] *adj* feliz, oportuno.

felicity [fɪ'lɪsɪtɪ] *n* felicidad *f*; (*phrase*) ocurrencia *f* oportuna.

feline ['fi:laɪn] **1** *adj* felino. **2** *n* felino *m*.

fell[1] [fel] *pret of* **fall.**

fell[2] [fel] *vt* derribar (*with a blow* de un golpe); *tree* talar, cortar; *cattle* acogotar.

fell[3] [fel] *n* (*Brit Geog*) (*hill*) montaña *f*; (*moor*) brezal *m*, páramo *m*.

fell[4] [fel] *adj* (*liter*) cruel, feroz; (*fatal*) funesto; **at one ~ swoop** de un solo golpe.

fell[5] [fel] *n* (*hide, pelt*) piel *f*.

fellatio [fɪ'leɪʃɪəʊ] *n*, **fellation** [fɪ'leɪʃən] *n* felación *f*.

fellow ['feləʊ] *n* (**a**) (*comrade*) compañero *m*, -a *f*; (*~-being*) prójimo *m*; **one's ~ animals** sus prójimos los animales; **our ~ Ruritanians** nuestros compatriotas; **'my ~ Americans ...'** (*in speech*) 'queridos compatriotas ...'

(**b**) (*other half*) pareja *f*; (*equal*) igual *mf*; **it has no ~** no tiene par.

(**c**) (*Brit Univ etc*) *miembro de la junta de gobierno de un colegio*; (*of society*) socio *mf*, miembro *mf*.

(**d**) (*chap*) tipo* *m*, sujeto* *m*, tío* *m*; **he's an odd ~** es un tipo raro; **well, this journalist ~** bueno, el tal periodista; **those journalist ~s** los periodistas esos; **a ~ gets no peace** no le dejan a uno en paz; **my dear ~!** ¡hombre!; **nice ~** buen chico *m*, buena persona *f*; **old ~** viejo *m*; **look here, old ~** mira, amigo; **poor ~!** ¡pobrecito!; **some poor ~** algún pobre diablo; **young ~** chico *m*; **I say, young ~** oye, joven.

fellow-being ['feləʊ'bi:ɪŋ] *n* prójimo *m*.

fellow-citizen ['feləʊ'sɪtɪzn] *n* conciudadano *m*, -a *f*.

fellow-countryman ['feləʊ'kʌntrɪmən] *n*, *pl* **fellow-countrymen** ['feləʊ'kʌntrɪmən] compatriota *m*; paisano *m*; **'my fellow-countrymen ...'** (*in speech*) 'queridos compatriotas ...'

fellow-countrywoman ['feləʊ'kʌntrɪwʊmən] *n*, *pl* **fellow-countrywomen** ['feləʊ'kʌntrɪwɪmɪn] compatriota *f*, paisana *f*.

fellow-creature ['feləʊ'kri:tʃə^r] *n* prójimo *m*.

fellow-feeling ['feləʊ'fi:lɪŋ] *n* simpatía *f*, afinidad *f*.

fellow-member ['feləʊ'membə^r] *n* consocio *mf*.

fellow-men ['feləʊ'men] *npl* prójimos *mpl*.

fellow-passenger ['feləʊ'pæsɪndʒə^r] *n* compañero *m*, -a *f* de viaje.

fellowship ['feləʊʃɪp] *n* (**a**) (*companionship*) compañerismo *m*. (**b**) (*society*) asociación *f*. (**c**) (*Brit Univ*) dignidad *f* del **fellow.** (**d**) (*US*: *grant*) beca *f*.

fellow-sufferer [,feləʊ'sʌfərə^r] *n* persona *f* que tiene la misma enfermedad que uno; compañero *m*, -a *f* en la desgracia.

fellow-traveller, (*US*) **fellow-traveler** ['feləʊ'trævlə^r] *n* compañero *m*, -a *f* de viaje; (*Pol*) filocomunista *mf*, comunizante *mf*.

fellow-worker ['feləʊ'wɜ:kə^r] *n* compañero *m*, -a *f* de trabajo, colega *m*.

felon ['felən] *n* criminal *m*, delincuente *mf* (de mayor cuantía).

felonious [fɪ'ləʊnɪəs] *adj* criminal, delincuente.

felony ['felənɪ] *n* crimen *m*, delito *m* mayor, delito *m* grave.

felspar ['felspɑ:^r] *n* feldespato *m*.

felt[1] [felt] *pret and ptp of* **feel.**

felt[2] [felt] **1** *n* fieltro *m*. **2** *attr*: **~ hat** sombrero *m* de fieltro; **~ tip pen** rotulador *m*.

female ['fi:meɪl] **1** *adj animal, plant* hembra; *slave, subject* del sexo femenino; **a ~ voice** una voz de mujer; **the ~ hippopotamus** el hipopótamo hembra; **a ~ friend** una amiga; **the ~ sex** el sexo femenino; **~ labour** trabajo *m* de mujeres, trabajo *m* femenino; **~ suffrage** derecho *m* de las mujeres a votar. **2** *n* hembra *f*.

feminine ['femɪnɪn] **1** *adj* femenino (*also Gram*). **2** *n* femenino *m*; **in the ~** en femenino.

femininity [,femɪ'nɪnɪtɪ] *n* feminidad *f*.

feminism ['femɪnɪzəm] *n* feminismo *m*.

feminist ['femɪnɪst] **1** *adj* feminista. **2** *n* feminista *mf*.

femme fatale ['femfə'tæl] *n* mujer *f* fatal.

femoral ['femərəl] *adj* femoral.

femur ['fi:mə^r] *n* fémur *m*.

fen [fen] *n* (*Brit*) pantano *m*.

fence [fens] **1** *n* (**a**) cerca *f*, cercado *m*, valla *f*; **to mend one's ~s** restablecer la reputación; mejorar las relaciones; **to sit on the ~** ver los toros desde la barrera; no resolverse, estar a ver venir.

(**b**) (*) perista* *mf*.

2 *vt* cercar; *machinery etc* cubrir, proteger.

3 *vi* (*Sport*) esgrimir; (*fig*) defenderse con evasivas.

◆**fence in** *vt* encerrar con cerca.

◆**fence off** *vt* separar con cerca.

fenced [fenst] *adj*: **~ area** zona *f* cercada con valla.

fencer ['fensə^r] *n* esgrimidor *m*, -ora *f*.

fencing ['fensɪŋ] **1** *n* (**a**) (*Sport*) esgrima *f*. (**b**) (*for making fences*) materiales *mpl* para cercas. **2** *attr*: **~ master** maestro *m* de esgrima.

fend [fend] *vi*: **to ~ for o.s.** arreglárselas.

◆**fend off** *vt attack* defenderse de, rechazar; *blow* apartar; *trouble etc* mantener a raya.

fender ['fendə^r] *n* (*round fire*) guardafuego *m*; (*US Aut*) parachoques *m*; guardafango *m*; (*US Rail*) trompa *f*; (*Naut*) defensa *f*.

fenestration [,fenɪs'treɪʃən] *n* ventanaje *m*.

fenland ['fenlənd] *n* terreno *m* pantanoso, marisma *f*.

fennel ['fenl] *n* hinojo *m*.

FEPC *n* (*US*) *abbr of* **Fair Employment Practices Committee.**

FERC *n* (*US*) *abbr of* **Federal Energy Regulatory Commission.**

Ferdinand ['fɜ:dɪnænd] *nm* Fernando.

ferment 1 ['fɜ:ment] *n* (*leaven*) fermento *m*; (*process*) fermentación *f*; (*fig*) agitación *f*, conmoción *f*; **to be in a ~** estar en conmoción, estar en ebullición. **2** [fə'ment] *vt* hacer fermentar. **3** [fə'ment] *vi* fermentar.

fermentation [,fɜ:men'teɪʃən] *n* fermentación *f*.

fermium ['fɜ:mɪəm] *n* fermio *m*.

fern [fɜ:n] *n* helecho *m*.

ferocious [fə'rəʊʃəs] *adj* feroz, fiero; (*fig*) violento.

ferociously [fə'rəʊʃəslɪ] *adv* ferozmente.

ferociousness [fə'rəʊʃəsnɪs] *n* ferocidad *f*.

ferocity [fə'rɒsɪtɪ] *n* ferocidad *f*.

ferret ['ferɪt] **1** *n* hurón *m*. **2** *vi* (**a**) cazar con hurones. (**b**) **to ~ about** buscar revolviéndolo todo.

◆**ferret out** *vt person* encontrar por fin; *secret* descubrir, lograr saber.

Ferris wheel ['ferɪswi:l] *n* (*US*) noria *f*.
ferrite ['feraɪt] *n* ferrito *m*, ferrita *f*.
ferro- ['ferəʊ] *pref* ferro-.
ferro-alloy ['ferəʊ'ælɔɪ] *n* ferroaleación *f*.
ferrous ['ferəs] *adj* ferroso.
ferrule ['feru:l] *n* regatón *m*, contera *f*.
ferry ['ferɪ] **1** *n* (*small boat*) balsa *f*, barca *f* (de pasaje), embarcadero *m* (*LAm*); (*large, for cars, trains etc*) ferry *m*, transbordador *m*.
2 *vt*: **to ~ sb across** llevar a uno a la otra orilla; **to ~ sth across** transportar (*or* pasar) algo a través del río (*etc*).
ferryboat ['ferɪbəʊt] *n* = **ferry**.
ferryman ['ferɪmən] *n*, *pl* **ferrymen** ['ferɪmən] balsero *m*, barquero *m*.
fertile ['fɜ:taɪl] *adj* (*Agr*) fértil (*of, in* en; *also fig*); (*Bio*) fecundo.
fertility [fə'tɪlɪtɪ] **1** *n* fertilidad *f*; fecundidad *f*. **2** *attr*: **~ drug** (*Med*) droga *f* de fecundidad, medicamento *m* contra la infertilidad.
fertilization [ˌfɜ:tɪlaɪ'zeɪʃən] *n* fecundación *f*, fertilización *f*.
fertilize ['fɜ:tɪlaɪz] *vt* fecundar, fertilizar; (*Agr*) abonar.
fertilizer ['fɜ:tɪlaɪzəʳ] *n* fertilizante *m*, abono *m*.
fervent ['fɜ:vənt] *adj*, **fervid** ['fɜ:vɪd] *adj* fervoroso, ardiente, apasionado.
fervently ['fɜ:vəntlɪ] *adv* fervorosamente, ardientemente; **we ~ wish that ...** deseamos con fervor que ...
fervour, (*US*) **fervor** ['fɜ:vəʳ] *n* fervor *m*, ardor *m*, pasión *f*.
fester ['festəʳ] *vi* ulcerarse, enconarse; (*fig*) amargarse.
festival ['festɪvəl] *n* fiesta *f*; (*Mus etc*) festival *m*.
festive ['festɪv] *adj* festivo, regocijado; **the ~ season** las Navidades; **to be in a ~ mood** estar muy alegre.
festivity [fes'tɪvɪtɪ] *n* (*celebration*) fiesta *f*, festividad *f*; (*joy*) regocijo *m*; **festivities** regocijos *mpl*, festejos *mpl*, fiestas *fpl*.
festoon [fes'tu:n] **1** *n* guirnalda *f*, festón *m*; (*Sew*) festón *m*.
2 *vt* adornar, engalanar, enguirnaldar, festonear (*with* de); **to be ~ed with** estar adornado de.
FET *n* (*US*) *abbr of* **Federal Excise Tax**.
fetal ['fi:tl] *adj* (*US*) = **foetal**.
fetch [fetʃ] **1** *vt* (**a**) (*bring*) traer; ir por, ir a buscar; (*) atraer; **I'll go and ~ it for you** te lo voy a buscar; **please ~ my coat** ¿me trae el abrigo?; **they're ~ing the doctor** han ido por el médico; **please ~ the doctor** llama al médico; **they ~ed him all that way** le hicieron venir desde tan lejos; **to ~ sb back from Spain** hacer que uno vuelva de España.
(**b**) *blow, sigh* dar.
(**c**) *price* venderse por, venderse a; **how much did it ~?** ¿cuánto dieron por él?
2 *vi*: **to ~ and carry** ir de acá para allá, trajinar; ocuparse en oficios humildes; **to ~ and carry for sb** ser como el esclavo de uno.
◆**fetch in** *vt person* hacer entrar; *thing* entrar.
◆**fetch out** *vt* sacar.
◆**fetch up 1** *vt* (*Brit**) arrojar, vomitar. **2** *vi* ir a parar.
fetching ['fetʃɪŋ] *adj* atractivo.
fête [feɪt] **1** *n* (*Brit*) fiesta *f*; **to be en ~** estar de fiesta. **2** *vt* festejar.
fetid ['fetɪd] *adj* hediondo, fétido.
fetish ['fetɪʃ] *n* fetiche *m*.
fetishism ['fetɪʃɪzəm] *n* fetichismo *m*.
fetishist ['fetɪʃɪst] *n* fetichista *mf*.
fetlock ['fetlɒk] *n* (*joint*) espolón *m*; (*hair*) cernejas *fpl*.
fetter ['fetəʳ] *vt* poner grillos a, encadenar; trabar; (*fig*) estorbar.
fetters ['fetəz] *npl* grillos *mpl*; (*fig*) trabas *fpl*.
fettle ['fetl] *n*: **in fine ~** en buenas condiciones; (*of mood*) de excelente humor.
fetus ['fi:təs] *n* (*US*) = **foetus**.
feud [fju:d] **1** *n* enemistad *f* heredada (entre dos familias *etc*), odio *m* de sangre; disputa *f*. **2** *vi* reñir, pelear.
feudal ['fju:dl] *adj* feudal; **~ system** feudalismo *m*.
feudalism ['fju:dəlɪzəm] *n* feudalismo *m*.
fever ['fi:vəʳ] *n* (*disease*) fiebre *f*; (*high temperature*) fiebre *f*, calentura *f*; **a ~ of excitement** una emoción febril; **the gambling ~** la fiebre del juego; **the excitement was at ~ pitch** la emoción estaba al rojo vivo; **she's in a ~ about the party** está muy agitada por la fiesta.
fevered ['fi:vəd] *adj* = **feverish**.
feverish ['fi:vərɪʃ] *adj* (**a**) (*Med*) febril, calenturiento; **to be ~** tener fiebre. (**b**) (*fig*) febril.
feverishly ['fi:vərɪʃlɪ] *adv* febrilmente.
feverishness ['fi:vərɪʃnɪs] *n* (*Med, fig*) febrilidad *f*.
few [fju:] *adj* pocos; algunos, unos; **a ~, some ~** unos pocos, unos cuantos; **a ~ of us** algunos de nosotros; **quite a ~, not a ~** no pocos, algunos; **a good ~** un buen número (de); **he had had a ~*** llevaba ya una copa de más; **every ~ minutes** cada pocos minutos; **in the next ~ days** un día de éstos que vienen; **the ~** los pocos, la minoría; **the lucky ~** los afortunados (que son pocos); **such men are ~** hay pocos hombres así; **they are ~ and far between** son poquísimos, son contadísimos.
fewer ['fju:əʳ] *adj comp* menos; **~ than 10** menos de 10; **they have ~ than I** tienen menos que yo; **no ~ than 8 goals** nada menos que 8 goles; **the ~ the better** cuantos menos mejor.
fewest ['fju:ɪst] *adj superl* los menos, las menos, el menor número (de).
fewness ['fju:nɪs] *n* corto número *m*.
fey [feɪ] *adj* vidente.
fez [fez] *n* fez *m*.
ff *abbr of* **following** siguientes, sigs.
FFA *n* (*US*) *abbr of* **Future Farmers of America**.
FH *abbr of* **fire hydrant**.
FHA *n* (*US*) *abbr of* **Federal Housing Association**.
fiancé [fɪ'ɑ̃:nseɪ] *n* novio *m*, prometido *m*.
fiancée [fɪ'ɑ̃:nseɪ] *n* novia *f*, prometida *f*.
fiasco [fɪ'æskəʊ] *n* fiasco *m*.
fiat ['faɪæt] *n* fíat *m*, autorización *f*.
fib [fɪb] **1** *n* mentirilla *f*, bola *f*. **2** *vi* decir mentirillas.
fibber ['fɪbəʳ] *n* mentirosillo *m*, -a *f*.
fibre, (*US*) **fiber** ['faɪbəʳ] *n* (**a**) fibra *f*. (**b**) (*fig*) nervio *m*, carácter *m*.
fibreboard, (*US*) **fiberboard** ['faɪbəbɔ:d] *n* panel *m* de madera conglomerada, fibra *f* vulcanizada.
fibre-glass, (*US*) **fiberglass** ['faɪbəglɑ:s] *n* fibra *f* de vidrio, fibravidrio *m*.
fibre-optic, (*US*) **fiber-optic** [ˌfaɪbər'ɒptɪk] *adj*: **~ cable** cable *m* de fibra óptica.
fibre-optics, (*US*) **fiber-optics** [ˌfaɪbər'ɒptɪks] *n* transmisión *f* por fibra óptica.
fibre-tip (pen) ['faɪbətɪp('pen)] *n* (*Brit*) rotulador *m* de punta de fibra.
fibroid ['faɪbrɔɪd] *n* fibroma *m*.
fibrositis [ˌfaɪbrə'saɪtɪs] *n* fibrositis *f*.
fibrous ['faɪbrəs] *adj* fibroso.
fibula ['fɪbjʊlə] *n* peroné *m*.
FIC *n* (*US*) *abbr of* **Federal Information Centers**.
FICA *n* (*US*) *abbr of* **Federal Insurance Contributions Act**.
fickle ['fɪkl] *adj* inconstante, veleidoso, voluble.
fickleness ['fɪklnɪs] *n* inconstancia *f*, veleidad *f*, volubilidad *f*.
fiction ['fɪkʃən] *n* (**a**) (*invention*) ficción *f*, invención *f*. (**b**) (*Liter*) ficción *f*, novelística *f*, género *m* novelístico.
fictional ['fɪkʃənl] *adj* novelesco; relativo a la novela (*etc*).
fictionalize ['fɪkʃənəlaɪz] *vt* novelar.
fictionalized ['fɪkʃənəlaɪzd] *adj* novelado.
fictitious [fɪk'tɪʃəs] *adj* ficticio.
fiddle ['fɪdl] **1** *n* (**a**) (*Mus*) violín *m*; **to play second ~** desempeñar un papel secundario (*to* después de).
(**b**) (*esp Brit**) trampa *f*, superchería *f*; **tax ~** defraudación *f* fiscal, evasión *f* fiscal; **it's a ~** aquí hay trampa, son unos tramposos; **to be on the ~** trampear, trapichear*.
2 *vt* (*esp Brit**) *results* falsificar; *accounts* manipular, falsificar; *extra money, privilege* agenciarse; *job etc* agenciarse, obtener por enchufe*; **to ~ one's income-tax** defraudar impuestos.
3 *vi* (**a**) (*Mus*) tocar el violín.
(**b**) (*esp Brit**) hacer trampas; **to ~ with** jugar nerviosamente con, manosear; **sb's been fiddling with it** alguno lo ha estropeado.
◆**fiddle about, fiddle around** *vi* perder el tiempo.
fiddler ['fɪdləʳ] *n* (**a**) (*Mus*) violinista *mf*. (**b**) (*esp Brit**) tramposo *m*, -a *f*.
fiddlesticks ['fɪdlstɪks] *interj* ¡tonterías!
fiddling ['fɪdlɪŋ] **1** *adj* trivial, insignificante. **2** *n* (*) trampas *fpl*, trapicheos* *mpl*.
fiddly ['fɪdlɪ] *adj task* difícil, complicado; *object* complicado (*or* difícil) de manejar.
fidelity [fɪ'delɪtɪ] *n* fidelidad *f*; **high ~** (*abbr*: **hi-fi**) alta fidelidad *f*.
fidget ['fɪdʒɪt] **1** *n* (**a**) persona *f* inquieta, azogado *m*, -a *f*.
(**b**) **~s** agitación *f* nerviosa; **to have the ~s** ser un azogue, no poder estar quieto.
2 *vt* poner nervioso.
3 *vi* ser un azogue, agitarse nerviosamente; **don't ~!**,

stop ~ing! ¡estáte quieto!; **to ~ about** revolverse nerviosamente; **to ~ with** jugar con.

fidgety ['fɪdʒɪtɪ] *adj* azogado, nervioso; **to be ~** tener azogue, no poder tenerse quieto.

fiduciary [fɪ'dju:ʃɪərɪ] *adj* fiduciario.

fief [fi:f] *n* feudo *m.*

field [fi:ld] **1** *n* (**a**) (*Agr, Elec, Her, Mil*) campo *m*; (*meadow*) prado *m*; (*Sport*) campo *m*, cancha *f* (*LAm*); (*Geol*) yacimiento *m*; (*Comput*) campo *m*, sector *m*; **~ of battle** campo *m* de batalla; **~ of vision** campo *m* visual; **a scientist working in the ~** un científico que trabaja en el terreno; **to be the first in the ~** ser el primero en inventar algo (*etc*); **to take the ~** salir a campaña (*against* contra); (*fig*) salir a (la) palestra.

(**b**) (*fig*) esfera *f*; especialidad *f*; **~ of activity** esfera *f* de actividades, ámbito *m* de acción; **in the ~ of painting** en la esfera de la pintura, en la pintura; **what's your ~?** ¿qué especialidad tiene Vd?; **it's not my ~** no es de mi competencia.

(**c**) (*in race etc*) competidores *mpl*, (*in competition*) concurrentes *mpl*, (*for post*) opositores *mpl*, candidatos *mpl*; **is there a strong ~?** ¿se ha presentado gente buena?; **to lead the ~** ir en cabeza, llevar la delantera; **to play the ~*** (*US*) alternar con cualquiera.

2 *attr*: **~ event** prueba *f* de atletismo; **~ hand** (*US*) jornalero *m*; **~ hospital** hospital *m* de campaña; **~ study** estudio *m* de campo; **~ test, ~ trial** (*Agr*) prueba *f* de campo.

3 *vt ball* parar, recoger; *team* presentar.

field day ['fi:lddeɪ] *n* (*Mil*) día *m* de maniobras; **to have a ~** (*fig*) obtener un gran éxito, triunfar; divertirse muchísimo.

fielder ['fi:ldəʳ] *n* jugador *m* del equipo que defiende.

fieldfare ['fi:ldfɛəʳ] *n* zorzal *m* real.

fieldglasses ['fi:ld,glɑ:sɪz] *npl* gemelos *mpl* (de campo), prismáticos *mpl.*

fieldgun ['fi:ldgʌn] *n* cañón *m* de campaña.

field-kitchen ['fi:ld'kɪtʃɪn] *n* cocina *f* de campaña.

field-marshal ['fi:l*d*'mɑ:ʃəl] *n* (*Brit*) mariscal *m* de campo; (*Spain*) capitán *m* general del ejército.

fieldmouse ['fi:ldmaʊs] *n, pl* **fieldmice** ['fi:ldmaɪs] ratón *m* de campo.

field-officer ['fi:ld,ɒfɪsəʳ] *n* oficial *m* superior.

fieldsman ['fi:ldzmən] *n* = **fielder.**

field-sports ['fi:ldspɔ:ts] *npl* caza *f.*

field-test ['fi:ld,test] *vt* probar sobre el terreno.

field-trip ['fi:l*d*trɪp] *n* salida *f* (*or* excursión *f*) de estudios.

fieldwork ['fi:ldwɜ:k] *n* labor *f* de campo, trabajo *m* en el terreno.

field-worker ['fi:ld,wɜ:kəʳ] *n* investigador *m*, -ora *f* que trabaja en el terreno.

fiend [fi:nd] *n* (**a**) demonio *m*, diablo *m*; (*fig*) desalmado *m*. (**b**) (*for hobby etc*) fanático *m*, -a *f*, entusiasta *mf* (*for* de).

fiendish ['fi:ndɪʃ] *adj* diabólico.

fiendishly ['fi:ndɪʃlɪ] *adv* diabólicamente; **~ difficult** terriblemente difícil; **~ expensive** carísimo.

fierce [fɪəs] *adj animal etc* feroz, salvaje; cruel; *look* feroz; *attack* furioso; *wind* violento; *heat, competition* intenso; *supporter* acérrimo.

fiercely ['fɪəslɪ] *adv* ferozmente; furiosamente; intensamente.

fierceness ['fɪəsnɪs] *n* ferocidad *f*; furia *f*; intensidad *f.*

fiery ['faɪərɪ] *adj* (*burning*) ardiente; (*red*) rojo; *taste* muy picante, picaro (*LAm*); *temperament, speech* apasionado, vehemente; *horse* fogoso; *liquor* ardiente, muy fuerte.

FIFA ['fi:fə] *n abbr of* **Fédération Internationale de Football Association** FIFA *f.*

fife [faɪf] *n* pífano *m.*

FIFO ['faɪfəʊ] *abbr of* **first in first out** primero en entrar, primero en salir.

fifteen [fɪf'ti:n] **1** *adj* quince. **2** *n* quince *m.*

fifteenth [fɪf'ti:nθ] *adj* decimoquinto.

fifth [fɪfθ] **1** *adj* quinto; **~ column** quinta columna *f.* **2** *n* quinto *m*, quinta parte *f*; (*Mus*) quinta *f*; *V also* **amendment.**

fifth columnist [,fɪfθ'kɒləmnɪst] *n* quintacolumnista *mf.*

fiftieth ['fɪftɪɪθ] *adj* quincuagésimo; cincuenta; **the ~ anniversary** el cincuenta aniversario.

fifty ['fɪftɪ] *adj* cincuenta; **the fifties** (*eg 1950s*) los años cincuenta; **to be in one's fifties** tener más de cincuenta años, ser cincuentón.

fifty-fifty ['fɪftɪ'fɪftɪ] **1** *adv*: **to go ~** ir a medias, ir mitad y mitad. **2** *adj*: **there is a ~ chance** hay un cincuenta por cien de posibilidades; **it's a ~ deal** es un acuerdo para repartir los beneficios mitad y mitad; **we'll do it on a ~ basis** lo haremos a base de mitad y mitad, iremos por partes iguales.

fiftyish ['fɪftɪɪʃ] *adj* de unos cincuenta años.

fig [fɪg] *n* higo *m*; (*early*) breva *f*; (*tree*) higuera *f*; (**I don't give**) **a ~ for J.B!** ¡me importa un comino J.B!

fight [faɪt] **1** *n* (**a**) (*Mil*) combate *m*; (*between 2 persons*) pelea *f*; (*struggle, campaign*) lucha *f* (*for* por); **in fair ~** en buena lid; **to make a ~ of it** no dejarse vencer fácilmente; **to put up a good ~** defenderse bien, dar buena cuenta de sí.

(**b**) (*argument*) disputa *f* (*over* sobre); (*quarrel, esp US*) riña *f*, pelea *f*; **to have a ~ with sb** tener una pelea con uno; **to pick a ~ with sb** meterse con uno.

(**c**) (*fighting spirit*) combatividad *f*, ánimo *m* (de pelear), brío *m*; **to show ~** enseñar los dientes, mostrarse dispuesto a resistir; **there was no ~ left in him** no le quedaba ningún ánimo de luchar más.

2 (*irr*: *pret and ptp* **fought**) *vt* (*Mil*) *enemy* batirse con, luchar con (*or* contra); *battle* dar, librar; *bull* lidiar; *fire* luchar por sofocar, combatir; *proposal, urge, tendency* combatir, resistir, luchar contra; **to ~ a case** negar una acusación; **we shall ~ this case all the way** seguiremos luchando por cambiar esta decisión, no nos conformaremos nunca con esta decisión; **to ~ one's way out** lograr salir luchando; **to ~ one's way to the sea** abrirse paso luchando hacia el mar.

3 *vi* pelear, luchar (*against* contra, *for* por, *with* con); batirse; **did you ~ in the war?** ¿fue Vd soldado cuando la guerra?, ¿desempeñó algún papel en la guerra?; **they were ~ing over it** lo estaban disputando a golpes; **we shall have to ~** tendremos que luchar; **to go down ~ing** seguir luchando hasta el fin.

◆**fight back 1** *vt*: **to ~ back one's tears** andar a puñetazos con las lágrimas. **2** *vi* defenderse, resistir; contraatacar.

◆**fight down** *vt* reprimir.

◆**fight off** *vt attack* rechazar; *sleep* sacudirse; *illness etc* luchar por no sucumbir ante.

◆**fight on** *vi* seguir luchando.

◆**fight out** *vt*: **to ~ it out** decidirlo luchando; **they fought it out** siguieron luchando hasta que uno cedió; **leave them to ~ it out** deja que se arreglen entre ellos.

fightback ['faɪtbæk] *n* remontada *f*; resistencia *f*, defensa *f*; contraataque *m.*

fighter ['faɪtəʳ] **1** *n* (**a**) combatiente *mf*; luchador *m*, -ora *f* (*for* por); (*warrior*) guerrero *m*, soldado *m*; (*boxer*) boxeador *m*; **a bonny ~** un valiente guerrero. (**b**) (*Aer*) caza *m*. **2** *attr*: **~ command** jefatura *f* de cazas.

fighter-bomber ['faɪtə'bɒməʳ] *n* caza-bombardero *m.*

fighter pilot ['faɪtə'paɪlət] *n* piloto *m* de caza.

fighting ['faɪtɪŋ] **1** *n* (*in general*) el luchar, el pelear; (*battle*) combate *m*; **the street ~ lasted all day** se luchó todo el día en las calles; **there has been ~ in the colony** ha estallado la guerra en la colonia, ha habido disturbios sangrientos en la colonia; **we want no ~ here** aquí nada de pendencias; **the Slobodians are fond of ~** a los eslobodios les gusta pelearse.

2 *attr*: **~ bull** toro *m* de lidia; **~ chance** buena posibilidad *f*; **~ cock** gallo *m* de pelea; **~ forces** fuerzas *fpl* militares; **~ line** frente *m* de combate; **~ man** guerrero *m*, soldado *m*; **~ spirit** espíritu *m* de lucha, combatividad *f*; **~ strength** número *m* de soldados (listos para el combate); **~ talk** palabras *fpl* que provocan a pelea.

figleaf ['fɪgli:f] *n, pl* **figleaves** ['fɪgli:vz] (*fig*) hoja *f* de parra.

figment ['fɪgmənt] *n*: **~ of the imagination** quimera *f*, producto *m* de la imaginación.

fig tree ['fɪgtri:] *n* higuera *f.*

figurative ['fɪgərətɪv] *adj sense etc* figurado; (*Art*) figurativo.

figuratively ['fɪgərətɪvlɪ] *adv* figuradamente, en sentido figurado; **he was speaking ~** hablaba en metáfora; **you should understand this ~** hay que entender esto en sentido figurado.

figure ['fɪgəʳ] **1** *n* (**a**) (*statue*) figura *f*, estatua *f.*

(**b**) (*form of body*) tipo *m*, línea *f*, talle *m*, silueta *f*; **a fine ~ of a man** un hombre de físico imponente; **a fine ~ of a woman** una real hembra; **she's got a nice ~** tiene buen tipo, tiene buen físico (*LAm*); **to keep one's ~** guardar la línea; **to lose one's ~** perder la línea; **to be ~-conscious** ser cuidadoso con la línea.

(**c**) (*person*) figura *f*; **the central ~ in the crisis** la figura más importante de la crisis; **to cut a ~** hacer papel; **to cut a sorry ~** parecer ridículo, salir desairado.

(**d**) (*diagram*) figura *f*, dibujo *m.*

(**e**) (*Math*) (*numeral*) cifra *f*, número *m*, guarismo *m*;

(*quantity*) cifra *f*, cantidad *f*; (*price*) precio *m*; (*sum*) suma *f*; ~ **of eight,** ~ **eight** (*US*) (*in dance etc*) figura *f* de ocho; **in round ~s** en números redondos; **to be good at ~s** ser fuerte en aritmética; **to have a six-~ income** ganar más de 100.000 libras al año; **to reach double ~s** llegar a 10; **to reach 3 ~s** ascender a 100; **we want inflation brought down to single ~s** queremos que la inflación baje a menos de 10 por cien.

(**f**) (*Geom, Dancing, Skating*) figura *f*.

(**g**) ~ **of speech** figura *f*, tropo *m*.

2 *vt* (*in diagram*) representar; (*picture mentally*) representarse, figurarse; (*esp US*) imaginar; **I ~ it like this** (*US*) yo lo veo del modo siguiente.

3 *vi* (**a**) (*appear*) figurar (*among* entre, *as* como); constar.

(**b**) (*esp US*) **it doesn't ~** no tiene sentido; **that ~s** es natural; es comprensible.

◆**figure in*** *vt* (*US*) contar a.

◆**figure on** *vt* (*US*) contar con; proyectar; esperar.

◆**figure out 1** *vt person* entender; *problem* resolver; *writing* descifrar; *sum* calcular; *means etc* inventar, imaginar; **I can't ~ it out at all** no me lo explico, no lo comprendo. **2** *vi*: **to ~ out at** venir a ser.

◆**figure up** *vt* (*US*) calcular.

-figure ['fɪgəʳ] *adj*: **a four~ sum** una suma superior a mil (libras *etc*); **a seven~ number** un número de siete cifras.

figurehead ['fɪgəhed] *n* mascarón *m* de proa, figurón *m* de proa; (*fig: esp pej*) figura *f* decorativa.

figure-skate ['fɪgə,skeɪt] *vi* hacer patinaje artístico (sobre hielo).

figure-skating ['fɪgə,skeɪtɪŋ] *n* patinaje *m* de figuras, patinaje *m* artístico.

figurine [fɪgə'riːn] *n* figurilla *f*, estatuilla *f*.

Fiji ['fiːdʒiː] *n* (*also* **the ~ Islands**) las (Islas *fpl*) Fiji; **in ~** en las Fiji.

filament ['fɪləmənt] *n* filamento *m*.

filbert ['fɪlbət] *n* avellana *f*.

filch [fɪltʃ] *vt* sisar, ratear.

file¹ [faɪl] **1** *n* (*tool*) lima *f*. **2** *vt* (*also* **to ~ away, to ~ down, to ~ off**) limar.

file² [faɪl] **1** *n* (*folder*) carpeta *f*; (*dossier*) expediente *m*; (*eg loose-leaf* ~) archivador *m*, clasificador *m*; (*bundle of papers*) legajo *m*; (*cabinet*) fichero *m*, archivo *m*; (*Comput*) fichero *m*; **the ~s** los archivos; **the Lucan ~** el expediente Lucan; **police ~s** archivos *mpl* policíacos; **to close the ~s** cerrar la carpeta; **to have sth on ~** tener algo archivado.

2 *vt* (**a**) (*also* **to ~ away**) archivar; clasificar; registrar.

(**b**) (*Jur*) *suit* entablar, presentar; **to ~ a claim** presentar una reclamación; **to ~ a petition for divorce** entablar pleito de divorcio.

file³ [faɪl] **1** *n* (*row*) fila *f*, hilera *f*; **in single ~** en fila de a uno. **2** *vi*: **to ~ past** desfilar; **they ~d past the general** desfilaron ante el general.

◆**file in** *vi* entrar en fila.

◆**file out** *vi* salir en fila.

file server ['faɪl,sɜːvəʳ] *n* servidor *m* de archivos.

filial ['fɪlɪəl] *adj* filial.

filiation [,fɪlɪ'eɪʃən] *n* filiación *f*.

filibuster ['fɪlɪbʌstəʳ] (*US*) **1** *n* (*person*) obstruccionista *mf*, filibustero *m*; (*act*) maniobra *f* obstruccionista, filibusterismo *m*. **2** *vi* usar de maniobras obstruccionistas.

filigree ['fɪlɪgriː] *n* filigrana *f*.

filing ['faɪlɪŋ] *n* (*of documents*) clasificación *f*; (*of claim etc*) formulación *f*, presentación *f*; **to do the ~** archivar documentos.

filing-cabinet ['faɪlɪŋ,kæbɪnɪt] *n* fichero *m*, archivador *m*.

filing-clerk ['faɪlɪŋ,klɑːk] *n* (*Brit*) archivero *m*, -a *f*.

filings ['faɪlɪŋz] *npl* limaduras *fpl*.

Filipino [fɪlɪ'piːnəʊ] **1** *adj* filipino. **2** *n* (**a**) (*person*) filipino *m*, -a *f*. (**b**) (*Ling*) tagalo *m*.

fill [fɪl] **1** *vt* llenar (*with* de); (*stuff*) rellenar; (*charge, fuel, load*) cargar; *space* llenar completamente, ocupar completamente; *tooth* empastar, obturar; *tyre* inflar; *sail* hinchar; *post, chair* ocupar; *vacancy* cubrir; *requirement* llenar; *order* despachar; **he ~ed the post very well** desempeñó muy bien el cargo.

2 *vi* (*also* **to ~ up**) llenarse (*with* de); (*sail*) hincharse.

3 *n*: **to eat one's ~** hartarse de comer; **to have a ~ of tobacco** cargar la pipa; **I've had my ~ of that** estoy harto ya de eso.

◆**fill in 1** *vt* (**a**) llenar; *depression* terraplenar; *form* llenar; *details* añadir; *outline* completar; *time* ocupar. (**b**) (*) **to ~ sb in** informar a uno, poner a uno en antecedentes; **~ me in on what happened** dime lo que pasó.

2 *vi*: **to ~ in for sb** hacer las veces de uno, sustituir a uno, suplir a uno.

◆**fill out 1** *vt* (*fatten*) engordar; *form* rellenar, llenar.

2 *vi* echar carnes; (*face*) redondearse.

◆**fill up 1** *vt* llenar (hasta el borde), colmar; (*Brit*) *form* rellenar, llenar.

2 *vi* (**a**) = **fill 2**.

(**b**) **to ~ up with fuel** repostar combustible.

3 *vr*: **to ~ o.s. up with** darse un atracón de, llenarse el estómago de.

filler ['fɪləʳ] *n* (**a**) (*utensil, of bottle*) rellenador *m*; (*funnel*) embudo *m*. (**b**) (*for cracks in wood etc*) masilla *f*; (*Press*) relleno *m*.

filler-cap ['fɪləkæp] *n* (*Aut*) tapa *f* del depósito de gasolina, trampilla *f*.

fillet ['fɪlɪt] **1** *n* (*all senses*) filete *m*. **2** *vt fish* quitar la raspa de, desespinar; cortar en filetes.

fill-in ['fɪlɪn] *n* sustituto *m*, suplente *mf*.

filling ['fɪlɪŋ] **1** *adj food* sólido, que llena el estómago. **2** *n* relleno *m*; (*Mech*) empaquetadura *f*; (*of tooth*) obturación *f*, empaste *m*.

filling-station ['fɪlɪŋ,steɪʃən] *n* gasolinera *f*, estación *f* de servicio.

fillip ['fɪlɪp] *n* estímulo *m*; **to give a ~ to** estimular.

filly ['fɪlɪ] *n* potra *f*.

film [fɪlm] **1** *n* (**a**) (*thin skin*) película *f*; (*of dust*) capa *f*; (*fig*) velo *m*.

(**b**) (*Phot, Cine*) película *f*, film *m*, filme *m*; **the ~s** el cine; **to make a ~ of** *book* hacer una película de, *event* filmar.

2 *attr*: **~ buff** cineasta *mf*, cinéfilo *m*, -a *f*; **~ camera** cámara *f* cinematográfica; **~ festival** festival *m* de cine (*or* cinematográfico); **~ library** cinemateca *f*; **~ premiere** estreno *m* oficial, premier *f*; **~ rights** derechos *mpl* cinematográficos; **~ script** guión *m*; **~ sequence** secuencia *f*; **~ set** plató *m*; **~ studio** estudio *m* (de cine); **~ test** prueba *f* cinematográfica.

3 *vt book* hacer una película de, *event* filmar; *scene* rodar (*at, in* en).

◆**film over** *vi* empañarse, cubrirse con película.

film-fan ['fɪlmfæn] *n* aficionado *m*, -a *f* al cine, cineasta *mf*.

filmic ['fɪlmɪk] *adj* fílmico.

filming ['fɪlmɪŋ] *n* filmación *f*.

film-maker ['fɪlmmeɪkəʳ] *n* cineasta *mf*.

film-making ['fɪlmmeɪkɪŋ] *n* cinematografía *f*.

filmsetting ['fɪlmsetɪŋ] *n* fotocomposición *f*.

filmstar ['fɪlmstɑːʳ] *n* astro *m*, estrella *f* (de cine).

filmstrip ['fɪlmstrɪp] *n* tira *f* (*or* cinta *f*) de película, tira *f* proyectable.

filmy ['fɪlmɪ] *adj* transparente, diáfano.

Filofax ['faɪləʊ,fæks] ® *n* filofax ® *m*.

filter ['fɪltəʳ] **1** *n* (**a**) filtro *m*. (**b**) (*Brit Aut*) semáforo *m* de flecha verde de desvío. **2** *attr*: **~ coffee** café *m* (molido) para filtrar; (*Aut*) **~ lane** ≃ carril *m* de giro; **~ light** semáforo *m* de flecha de desvío. **3** *vt* filtrar. **4** *vi* filtrarse.

◆**filter in** *vi* infiltrarse; (*person etc*) introducirse.

◆**filter out 1** *vt impurities* quitar filtrando. **2** *vi* (*news*) trascender, llegar a saberse.

◆**filter through** *vi* = **filter in.**

filter paper ['fɪltə,peɪpəʳ] *n* papel *m* de filtro.

filter-tip [,fɪltə'tɪp] *n* filtro *m*; **~ cigarette** cigarrillo *m* con filtro.

filter-tipped ['fɪltə,tɪpt] *adj* con filtro.

filth [fɪlθ] *n* inmundicia *f*, suciedad *f*, porquería *f*; (*fig*) inmundicias *fpl*.

filthy ['fɪlθɪ] **1** *adj* inmundo, sucio, puerco; (*fig*) inmundo, obsceno. **2** (*) *adv*: **they're ~ rich** son tan ricos que dan asco.

filtration [fɪl'treɪʃən] *n* filtración *f*.

fin [fɪn] *n* (*all senses*) aleta *f*.

fin. *abbr of* **finance.**

final ['faɪnl] **1** *adj* (**a**) (*last*) último, final; *exam* de fin de curso; **~ demand** demanda *f* final; **~ dividend** dividendo *m* final; **~ instalment** plazo *m* final, último plazo *m*. (**b**) (*conclusive*) terminante, decisivo, definitivo; **and that's ~** y no hay más que decir, y sanseacabó; **the judges' decisions will be ~** las decisiones de los jueces serán inapelables. **2** *n* (*Sport*) final *f*; **~s** (*Univ*) examen *m* de fin de curso; **the World Cup ~s** las finales de la Copa Mundial.

finale [fɪ'nɑːlɪ] *n* (*Mus*) final *m*; **grand ~** (*Theat*) gran escena *f* final; (*fig*) final *m* impresionante, final *m* triunfal.

finalist ['faɪnəlɪst] *n* (*Sport*) finalista *mf*.

finality [faɪ'nælɪtɪ] *n* finalidad *f*; (*decision*) resolución *f*; **he said with ~** dijo de modo terminante.

finalization [ˌfaɪnəlaɪ'zeɪʃən] *n* ultimación *f*, conclusión *f*.
finalize ['faɪnəlaɪz] *vt* ultimar, completar, concluir, aprobar de modo definitivo; *date etc* decidir, acordar.
finally ['faɪnəlɪ] *adv* (**a**) (*lastly*) por último, finalmente; (*eventually*) por fin. (**b**) (*irrevocably*) de modo definitivo, definitivamente.
finance [faɪ'næns] **1** *n* (*in general*) finanzas *fpl*, asuntos *mpl* financieros; (*funds*) finanzas *fpl*, fondos *mpl* (*also* **~s**); **~ company** sociedad *f* financiera; **~ director** director *m*, -ora *f* de finanzas; **the country's ~s** la situación económica del país; **Minister of F~** Ministro *m*, -a *f* de Hacienda.
2 *vt* financiar, proveer fondos para.
financial [faɪ'nænʃəl] *adj* financiero; *policy, resources* económico; **~ accounting** contabilidad *f* financiera; **~ adviser** asesor *m* financiero, asesora *f* financiera; **~ analysis** análisis *m* financiero; **~ backing** respaldo *m* financiero, apoyo *m* económico; **~ director** director *m*, -ora *f* de finanzas; **~ management** administración *f* financiera; **~ statement** estado *m* financiero, balance *m*; **F~ Times Index** índice *m* bursátil del Financial Times; **~ year** (*Brit*) año *m* económico, año *m* fiscal, ejercicio *m*.
financially [faɪ'nænʃəlɪ] *adv*: **~ independent** independiente en el aspecto económico; **~ sound** económicamente sólido; **a ~ successful scheme** un plan económicamente satisfactorio; **this is not ~ possible** esto no es posible por razones financieras.
financier [faɪ'nænsɪəʳ] *n* financiero *m*, -a *f*.
financing [faɪ'nænsɪŋ] *n* financiación *f*.
finch [fɪntʃ] *n* pinzón *m*.
find [faɪnd] (*irr*: *pret and ptp* **found**) **1** *vt* (**a**) (*gen*) encontrar, hallar; descubrir; (*stumble on*) dar con, tropezar con; **where did you ~ it?** ¿dónde lo encontraste?; **how did you ~ him?** (*in health*) ¿qué tal le encontraste?; **it's found all over Spain** se encuentra (*or* existe) en todas partes de España; **it's not to be found** no se encuentra; **I now ~ it is not so** ahora descubro que no es así; **it has been found that ...** se ha comprobado que ...
(**b**) (*supply, obtain*) facilitar, proporcionar, proveer; **we found him a car** le facilitamos un coche; **if you can ~ the time** si tienes el tiempo; **can you ~ the money?** ¿podrás reunir el dinero?; **they found half the cost** lograron hacerse con la mitad del precio; **all found** todo incluido.
(**c**) (*with adj*) **you will not ~ it easy** no le será fácil (*to do* hacer); **I found it impossible** me fue imposible (*to go* ir); **I ~ the house small** la casa me resulta pequeña.
(**d**) (*Jur*) declarar; **V guilty**.
2 *vi*: **to ~ for the defendant** (*Jur*) fallar a favor del demandado.
3 *vr*: **to ~ o.s.** encontrarse; verse; **I found myself alone** me encontré solo; **I ~ myself at a loss** me encuentro perplejo; **he found himself** descubrió su verdadera vocación (*or* identidad *etc*).
4 *n* hallazgo *m*.
◆find out 1 *vt* (*realize*) darse cuenta de; (*discover*) averiguar, (llegar a) saber; **to ~ sb out** conocer el juego de uno, calar a uno; **his pride found him out** su orgullo le traicionó.
2 *vi*: **to ~ out about** informarse sobre, buscar detalles acerca de; **we didn't ~ out about it in time** no nos enteramos a tiempo.
finder ['faɪndəʳ] *n* descubridor *m*, -ora *f*, el (la) que encuentra algo.
finding ['faɪndɪŋ] *n* (**a**) descubrimiento *m*. (**b**) **~s** (*Jur etc*) fallo *m*; (*of report etc*) recomendaciones *fpl*.
fine¹ [faɪn] **1** *adj* (**a**) (*delicate, small*) *thread* fino, sutil; *particle, print* menudo; *line* tenue; *pencil, nib* delgado; *edge* muy afilado; *distinction* delicado, sutil; **the ~r points of the argument** los puntos más sutiles del argumento.
(**b**) (*good*) bueno; (*beautiful*) bello, hermoso; (*exquisitely made*) fino, delicado, primoroso; *dress* elegante; (*showy*) vistoso; (*imposing*) magnífico, imponente; (*selected*) escogido; (*pure*) refinado, puro; *ideal* bello; *feeling* elevado, noble; *person* admirable; (*accomplished*) excelente, experto; **~!** ¡magnífico!, ¡estupendo!; **~ arts** bellas artes *fpl*; **eleven of England's ~st** (*hum*) once de los mejores de Inglaterra; **that's ~ by me** por mí, bien; de acuerdo; **it's a ~ thing to** + *infin* es admirable + *infin*.
(**c**) (*iro*) bueno, lindo, valiente; **that's all very ~, but ...** todo eso está muy bien, pero ...; **a ~ friend you are!** ¡valiente amigo!, ¡menudo amigo!; **you're a ~ one!** ¡estás tú bueno!, ¡qué tío!
(**d**) (*weather*) *day etc* bueno; **to be ~** hacer buen tiempo.
2 *adv* (**a**) muy bien; **~ and dandy** (*US*) requetebién; **you're doing ~** lo estás haciendo la mar de bien; **to feel ~** estar como un reloj.
(**b**) **to chop sth up ~** cortar algo en trozos menudos; **to cut** (*or* **run**) **it ~** llegar con muy poco tiempo, llegar justo a tiempo, dejarse muy poco tiempo.
◆fine down *vti* adelgazar.
fine² [faɪn] **1** *n* multa *f*, boleta *f* (*Carib*). **2** *vt* multar.
fine-drawn ['faɪn'drɔːn] *adj* estirado en un hilo muy delgado; *wire* muy delgado; *distinction etc* sutil, fino.
fine-grained ['faɪn'greɪnd] *adj* de grano fino.
finely ['faɪnlɪ] *adv* (**a**) sutilmente; menudamente. (**b**) hermosamente; primorosamente; elegantemente; vistosamente. (**c**) (*iro*) lindamente.
fineness ['faɪnnɪs] *n* (**a**) fineza *f*. (**b**) (*Metal*) pureza *f*.
finery ['faɪnərɪ] *n* galas *fpl*, adornos *mpl*, trajes *mpl* vistosos; **spring in all its ~** la primavera con todo su esplendor.
fine-spun ['faɪnspʌn] *adj* *yarn etc* fino; (*fig*: *hair*) fino, sedoso.
finesse [fɪ'nes] **1** *n* (**a**) (*in judgement*) discriminación *f* sutil, discernimiento *m*; (*in action*) diplomacia *f*, tino *m*, sutileza *f*; (*cunning*) astucia *f*. (**b**) (*Cards*) impase *m*. **2** *vt* hacer el impase a.
fine-tooth comb [ˌfaɪn,tuːθ'kəʊm] *n* peine *m* espeso; **to go over** (*or* **through**) **sth with a ~** revisar (*or* examinar) algo a fondo.
fine-tune [ˌfaɪn'tjuːn] *vt* poner a punto; (*fig*) hacer más preciso, matizar; poner a punto.
fine-tuning [ˌfaɪn'tjuːnɪŋ] *n* matización *f*; puesta *f* a punto.
finger ['fɪŋgəʳ] **1** *n* (**a**) dedo *m*; **first ~, index ~** dedo *m* índice; **little ~** dedo *m* meñique; **middle ~** dedo *m* del corazón; **his ~s are all thumbs** es terriblemente desmañado; **to burn one's ~s, to get one's ~s burned** (*fig*) cogerse los dedos, pillarse los dedos; **to get** (*or* **pull**) **one's ~ out‡** espabilarse; **get your ~ out!‡** ¡espabílate!; **to have green ~s** tener mucha habilidad en jardinería; **to have a ~ in the pie** meter su cucharada; **to keep one's ~s crossed** tocar madera, esperar que todo salga bien; **and please keep your ~s crossed for me** y te ruego tocar madera; **they never laid a ~ on her** no la tocaron en absoluto; **he didn't lift a ~ to help** no movió un dedo para ayudarnos; **to point the ~ of scorn at sb** señalar a uno con el dedo; **to put one's ~ on** (*fig*) concretar, señalar acertadamente; **to put one's ~ on it** (*or* **on the spot**) poner el dedo en la llaga; **there was nothing you could put your ~ on** no había nada concreto; **he slipped through their ~s** se les escapó entre los dedos; **to snap one's ~s at sb** (*fig*) tratar a uno con desprecio; **to twist sb round one's little ~** hacer que uno baile al son que le tocan; **to put two ~s up at sb*** (*Brit*), **to give sb the ~‡** (*US*) hacer un corte de mangas a uno.
(**b**) (*Aer*) corredor *m* de carga y descarga, brazo *m*.
2 *attr*: **~ exercises** (*for piano etc*) ejercicios *mpl* de dedos.
3 *vt* (**a**) (*touch*) manosear, tocar; (*Mus*) tocar (distraídamente).
(**b**) (*esp US‡*) (*identify*) señalar; identificar; (*betray*) traicionar, delatar.
fingerboard ['fɪŋgə,bɔːd] *n* (*Mus*) diapasón *m*.
fingerbowl ['fɪŋgə,bəʊl] *n* lavafrutas *m*.
finger food ['fɪŋgə,fuːd] *n* (*US*) tapas *fpl*.
fingering ['fɪŋgərɪŋ] *n* (*Mus*) digitación *f*.
fingermark ['fɪŋgəmɑːk] *n* huella *f*.
fingernail ['fɪŋgəneɪl] *n* uña *f*.
fingerprint ['fɪŋgəprɪnt] **1** *n* huella *f* dactilar, huella *f* digital. **2** *vt* tomar las huellas dactilares a; (*Med*) identificar genéticamente.
fingerstall ['fɪŋgəstɔːl] *n* dedil *m*.
fingertip ['fɪŋgətɪp] *n* punta *f* (*or* yema *f*) del dedo; **to have sth at one's ~s** tener algo a mano, (*fig*) saber(se) algo al dedillo.
finicky ['fɪnɪkɪ] *adj* delicado, melindroso, superferolítico*.
finish ['fɪnɪʃ] **1** *n* (**a**) (*end*) fin *m*, final *m*, conclusión *f*; remate *m*; (*Sport*) poste *m* de llegada; **to be in at the ~** estar presente en la conclusión; **to fight to a ~** seguir luchando hasta decidir la victoria.
(**b**) (*of manufactured article*) acabado *m*; **gloss(y) ~** acabado *m* brillo; **to have a rough ~** estar sin pulir.
2 *vt* (**a**) (*also* **to ~ off, to ~ up**) terminar, acabar, concluir; completar, llevar a cabo, rematar; dar la última mano a; *person* (*destroy*) quemar, acabar con; **that last kilometre nearly ~ed me** el kilómetro final casi acabó conmigo; **I'm ~ed** (*tired*) estoy rendido; **he's ~ed** (*fig*) está quemado; **as a film star she's ~ed** como estrella está quemada.
(**b**) (*Tech*) acabar.

3 *vi* (**a**) terminar, acabar; **to ~ doing sth** terminar de hacer algo; **to ~ by saying that** ... terminar diciendo que ...; **to ~ with** terminar con; **she ~ed with him** rompió con él; **wait till I've ~ed with him!** ¡a ver lo que le voy a hacer!, ¡ya verás cómo le dejo!

(**b**) (*Sport*) llegar; **to ~ third** llegar el tercero.

◆**finish off** *vt* (**a**) *V* **finish 2 (a)**. (**b**) (*kill*) despachar; (*destroy*) acabar con.

◆**finish up 1** *vt food* terminar, acabar; *V* **finish 2 (a)**. **2** *vi*: **to ~ up at** ir a parar a.

finished ['fɪnɪʃt] *adj* acabado, terminado; **~ goods** productos *mpl* acabados; **~ product** producto *m* acabado.

finishing-line ['fɪnɪʃɪŋ,laɪn] *n* línea *f* de meta.

finishing-school ['fɪnɪʃɪŋ,sku:l] *n* escuela *f* de educación social para señoritas.

finite ['faɪnaɪt] *adj* (**a**) finito, que tiene fin. (**b**) (*Gram*) *mood, verb* conjugado; **~ verb** verbo *m* finito.

fink* [fɪŋk] *n* (*US*) (*informer*) soplón* *m*; (*strikebreaker*) esquirol *m*.

◆**fink out*** *vi* acobardarse.

Finland ['fɪnlənd] *n* Finlandia *f*.

Finn [fɪn] *n* finlandés *m*, -esa *f*.

Finnish ['fɪnɪʃ] **1** *adj* finlandés. **2** *n* finlandés *m*.

Finno-Ugrian ['fɪnəʊ'u:grɪən], **Finno-Ugric** ['fɪnəʊ'u:grɪk] **1** *adj* fino-húngaro. **2** *n* (*Ling*) fino-húngaro *m*.

fiord [fjɔ:d] *n* fiordo *m*.

fir [fɜ:ʳ] *n* abeto *m*.

fircone ['fɜ:kəʊn] *n* piña *f* (de abeto).

fire [faɪəʳ] **1** *n* (**a**) (*gen*) fuego *m*; (*accidental, damaging*) incendio *m*; (*in grate*) fuego *m*, lumbre *f*; (*electric ~*) estufa *f* eléctrica; **to be on ~** estar ardiendo, estar en llamas; **to catch ~** encenderse, prenderse; **to cook sth on a slow ~** cocer algo a fuego lento; **to hang ~** demorarse, estar en suspenso; **to make up a ~** echar carbón a la lumbre; **to play with ~** jugar con fuego; **to set on ~, to set ~ to** pegar (*or* prender) fuego a, incendiar; **to sit by** (*or* **round**) **the ~** estar sentado al lado de la chimenea, estar sentado al amor de la lumbre; **to take ~** encenderse.

(**b**) (*Mil*) **to hold one's ~** no disparar; **to open ~** abrir fuego, romper el fuego; **to be under ~** (*fig*) ser criticado.

(**c**) (*fig*) ardor *m*, pasión *f*; entusiasmo *m*; **the ~ of youth** el ardor de la juventud; **men with ~ in their bellies** hombres llenos de celo idealista.

2 *attr*: **it's a ~ hazard, it's a ~ risk** es un peligro de incendio.

3 *vt* (**a**) (*set ~ to*) encender, incendiar, pegar fuego a, quemar; *bricks, pottery* cocer.

(**b**) *gun, shot, salute* disparar; *torpedo, rocket* lanzar; **to ~ a question at sb** disparar una pregunta inesperada a uno.

(**c**) (*fig*) *imagination* excitar, enardecer, exaltar; *interest* despertar; (*inspire*) inspirar.

(**d**) (*) *person* despedir, echar (*LAm*), rajar* (*SC*); **you're ~d!** ¡queda Vd despedido!

4 *vi* (**a**) (*catch ~*) encenderse.

(**b**) (*Mil*) hacer fuego; **to ~ at, to ~ on** hacer fuego sobre, tirar a; **they were firing at each other all day** se estaban tiroteando todo el día; **~!** ¡fuego!; **~ away!** (*fig*) ¡adelante!, ¡siga no más! (*LAm*).

(**c**) (*Aut*) encenderse; dar explosiones; **the engine is not firing on one cylinder** uno de los cilindros del motor no se enciende (*LAm*: no prende).

◆**fire off** *vt* = **fire 3 (b)**.

◆**fire on** *vt* = **fire at**.

◆**fire up*** *vi* (*fig*) ponerse furioso.

fire-alarm ['faɪərə,lɑ:m] *n* alarma *f* de incendios.

firearm ['faɪərɑ:m] *n* arma *f* de fuego.

fireball ['faɪəbɔ:l] *n* bola *f* de fuego.

Firebird ['faɪəbɜ:d] *n*: **the ~** (*Mus*) el Pájaro de fuego.

firebomb ['faɪəbɒm] **1** *n* bomba *f* incendiaria. **2** *vt* colocar una bomba incendiaria en; (*Aer*) bombardear con bombas incendiarias.

firebrand ['faɪəbrænd] *n* (**a**) tea *f*. (**b**) (*fig*) partidario *m* violento, partidaria *f* violenta, revoltoso *m*, -a *f*.

firebreak ['faɪəbreɪk] *n* (línea *f*) cortafuegos *m*.

firebrick ['faɪəbrɪk] *n* ladrillo *m* refractario.

fire-brigade ['faɪəbrɪ,geɪd] *n* (*Brit*) cuerpo *m* de bomberos.

firebug ['faɪəbʌg] *n* (*US*) incendiario *m*, -a *f*, pirómano *m*, -a *f*.

fire chief ['faɪətʃi:f] *n* (*US*) jefe *mf* del cuerpo de bomberos.

fireclay ['faɪəkleɪ] *n* (*Brit*) arcilla *f* refractaria.

firecracker ['faɪə,krækəʳ] *n* (*US*) petardo *m*.

fire-curtain ['faɪə,kɜ:tn] *n* telón *m* metálico, telón *m* a prueba de incendios.

firedamp ['faɪədæmp] *n* grisú *m*.

fire-department ['faɪədɪ,pɑ:tmənt] *n* = **fire-brigade**.

fire-door ['faɪədɔ:ʳ] *n* puerta *f* contra incendios.

fire-drill ['faɪə'drɪl] *n* (ejercicio *m* de) simulacro *m* de incendio.

fire-eater ['faɪər,i:təʳ] *n* tragafuegos *mf*; (*fig*) matamoros *m*.

fire-engine ['faɪər,endʒɪn] *n* bomba *f* de incendios, coche *m* de bomberos.

fire-escape ['faɪərɪs,keɪp] *n* escalera *f* de incendios.

fire-exit ['faɪər,egzɪt] *n* salida *f* de incendios (*or* de emergencia).

fire-extinguisher ['faɪərɪks'tɪŋgwɪʃəʳ] *n* extintor *m*.

fire-fighter ['faɪə,faɪtəʳ] *n* bombero *m*.

fire-fighting ['faɪə,faɪtɪŋ] *n* lucha *f* por apagar incendios; **~ equipment** equipo *m* contra incendios.

firefly ['faɪəflaɪ] *n* luciérnaga *f*.

fireguard ['faɪəgɑ:d] *n* alambrera *f*, guardafuego *m*.

firehouse ['faɪəhaʊs] *n*, *pl* **firehouses** ['faɪəhaʊzɪz] (*US*) parque *m* de bomberos.

fire-hydrant ['faɪə,haɪdrənt] *n* boca *f* de incendios.

fire insurance ['faɪərɪn,ʃʊərəns] *n* seguro *m* contra incendios.

fire-irons ['faɪər,aɪənz] *npl* útiles *mpl* de chimenea.

fire-lane ['faɪəleɪn] *n* (*US*) (línea *f*) cortafuegos *m*.

firelight ['faɪəlaɪt] *n* lumbre *f*.

firelighter ['faɪə,laɪtəʳ] *n* astillas *fpl* (para encender el fuego), tea *f*.

fireman ['faɪəmən] *n*, *pl* **firemen** ['faɪəmən] (*of fire service*) bombero *m*; (*Rail*) fogonero *m*.

fireplace ['faɪəpleɪs] *n* chimenea *f*; (*hearth*) hogar *m*.

fireplug ['faɪəplʌg] *n* (*US*) boca *f* de incendios.

firepower ['faɪə,paʊəʳ] *n* (*Mil*) potencia *f* de fuego.

fire prevention ['faɪəprɪ'venʃən] *n* prevención *f* de incendios.

fireproof ['faɪəpru:f] **1** *adj* incombustible, a prueba de fuego; *dish* refractario; *material* ignífugo, ininflamable, incombustible. **2** *vt* ignifugar.

fire-raiser ['faɪə,reɪzəʳ] *n* (*Brit*) incendiario *m*, -a *f*, pirómano *m*, -a *f*.

fire-raising ['faɪə,reɪzɪŋ] *n* (*Brit*) (delito *m* de) incendiar *m*, piromanía *f*.

fire regulations ['faɪə,regjʊ'leɪʃənz] *npl* normas *fpl* para la prevención de incendios.

fire-resistant ['faɪərɪ,zɪstənt] *adj* ignífugo.

fire-screen ['faɪəskri:n] *n* pantalla *f* refractaria.

fire-service ['faɪə,sɜ:vɪs] *n* cuerpo *m* de bomberos, servicio *m* de extinción de incendios.

fireside ['faɪəsaɪd] **1** *n* hogar *m*. **2** *attr* hogareño, doméstico, familiar; **~ chair** butaca *f* cerca de la lumbre; **~ chat** charla *f* íntima.

fire-station ['faɪə,steɪʃən] *n* parque *m* de bomberos.

fire-tender ['faɪə,tendəʳ] *n*, **firetruck** ['faɪətrʌk] *n* (*US*) coche *m* de bomberos.

firetower ['faɪə,taʊəʳ] *n* (*US*) torre *f* de vigilancia contra incendios.

firetrap ['faɪətræp] *n* lugar *m* (*or* edificio *m etc*) con peligro de incendio; **this house is a ~** en caso de incendio esta casa es una trampa.

firewater* ['faɪə,wɔ:təʳ] *n* (*US*) licor *m*, aguardiente *m*.

firewood ['faɪəwʊd] *n* leña *f*, astillas *fpl*.

firework ['faɪəwɜ:k] *n* fuego *m* artificial; petardo *m*; **~s** (*fig*) explosión *f* (de cólera *etc*); **there will be ~s at the meeting** (*fig*) en la reunión se va a armar la gorda.

firing ['faɪərɪŋ] *n* (**a**) (*Mil*) disparo *m*, (*continuous*) tiroteo *m*, cañoneo *m*. (**b**) (*Aut*) encendido *m*. (**c**) (*of bricks etc*) cocción *f*. (**d**) (*esp US**) despido *m*.

firing-hammer ['faɪərɪŋ,hæməʳ] *n* martillo *m*.

firing-line ['faɪərɪŋlaɪn] *n* línea *f* de fuego.

firing-pin ['faɪərɪŋ,pɪn] *n* = **firing-hammer**.

firing-squad ['faɪərɪŋskwɒd] *n* pelotón *m* de ejecución.

firm[1] [fɜ:m] **1** *adj* firme; (*Comm*) *offer, order* en firme; **as ~ as a rock** tan firme como una roca; **he was very ~ about it** se mostró muy decidido, lo dijo de modo terminante; **these prices are ~** estos precios son invariables; **to stand ~** mantenerse firme. **2** *adv*: **to buy ~** comprar firme.

◆**firm up 1** *vt* fortalecer, reforzar; *proposal etc* redondear. **2** *vi* fortalecerse, reforzarse.

firm[2] [fɜ:m] *n* firma *f*, empresa *f*, casa *f* de comercio; **the old ~** (*hum*) la vieja firma.

firmament ['fɜ:məmənt] *n* firmamento *m*.

firmly ['fɜ:mlɪ] *adv* firmemente; con firmeza.

firmness ['fɜ:mnɪs] *n* firmeza *f*.

firmware ['fɜ:mwεəʳ] *n* soporte *m* lógico inalterable, software *m* de ROM.

first [fɜ:st] **1** *adj* primero; primitivo, original; **~ base** (*Base-*

ball) primera base *f*; *V* **cousin**; (*Univ*) ~ **degree** licenciatura *f*; ~ **edition** primera edición *f*; (*of early or rare book*) edición *f* príncipe; ~ **floor** (*Brit*) primer piso *m*; (*US*) planta *f* baja; ~ **form** (*Brit Scol*) ≃ primer curso *m* de secundaria; ~ **fruits** primicias *fpl*; ~ **gear** primera *f* (velocidad *f*); ~ **lady** (*US*) primera dama *f*; **the ~ lady of jazz** la primera dama del jazz; ~ **language** (*mother tongue*) lengua *f* materna; (*in state etc*) lengua *f* principal; ~ **lieutenant** (*US Aer*) teniente *m*; (*Brit Naut*) teniente *m* de navío; ~ **mate** primer oficial *m*; ~ **name** nombre *m* de pila; **to be on ~ name terms with sb** tutear a uno; ~ **night** (*Theat*) estreno *m*; ~ **offender** persona *f* que comete un delito por primera vez, persona *f* sin antecedentes penales; ~ **officer** primer oficial *m*; **~-past-the-post system** sistema *m* mayoritario; ~ **performance** estreno *m*; ~ **person** primera persona *f*; ~ **school** escuela *f* primaria; ~ **strike** primer golpe *m*; ~ **strike weapon** arma *f* de primer golpe; ~ **string** (*n*: *Sport*) crack *mf*; **~-string** (*adj*) de primera; ~ **violin** primer violín *m*; **he hadn't the ~ idea how to do it** no tenía la más mínima idea de cómo hacerlo; *V* **thing (c)**.

2 *adv* primero; (*firstly*) en primer lugar; (*for the first time*) por primera vez; ~ **of all,** ~ **and foremost** ante todo; **head** ~ de cabeza; **stern** ~ la popa por delante; **ladies** ~ las señoras pasan primero; **women and children ~!** ¡primero las mujeres y los niños!; **to come** ~ (*in race*) ganar, llegar el primero; (*in league*) ir en cabeza, ocupar el primer puesto; (*have priority*) venir primero, tener la prioridad; **it was done on a ~ come ~ served basis** lo hicieron por riguroso orden de llegada; **to get in** ~ (*fig*) madrugar; **to go** ~ entrar (*etc*) el primero, (*Rail*) viajar en primera; **you go ~!** ¡Vd primero!, ¡pase Vd!

3 *n* primero *m*, -a *f*; (*Brit Univ*) primera clase *f*, sobresaliente *m*; **at** ~ al principio; **I didn't see them at** ~ no les vi de momento; **from the** ~ desde el principio; **from ~ to last** desde el principio hasta el fin; **it was a ~ for Pérez** fue el primer triunfo de Pérez; **to be the ~ to do sth** ser el primero en hacer algo; **he came in an easy** ~ llegó con mucho el primero, ganó fácilmente.

first aid ['fɜːst'eɪd] **1** *n* primera curación *f*, primeros auxilios *mpl*. **2** *attr*: ~ **box,** ~ **kit** botiquín *m*; ~ **post** puesto *m* de socorro; ~ **station** caseta *f* de primeros auxilios.

first-born ['fɜːstbɔːn] *n* primogénito *m*, -a *f*.

first-class ['fɜːstklɑːs] **1** *adj* de primera clase; ~ **mail,** ~ **post** correo *m* de primera clase; ~ **ticket** billete *m* de primera clase. **2** *adv*: **to send a letter** ~ enviar una carta por correo de primera clase; **to travel** ~ viajar en primera.

first-degree ['fɜːstdɪ'griː] *attr*: ~ **burns** quemaduras *fpl* de primer grado.

first-ever ['fɜːst,evəʳ] *adj* primerísimo.

first-footing [,fɜːst'fʊtɪŋ] *n*: **to go** ~ (*Scot*) ser la primera visita durante la noche de Año Nuevo.

first-generation ['fɜːst,dʒenə'reɪʃən] *adj*: **he's a ~ American** es americano de primera generación.

first-hand ['fɜːst'hænd] *adj* de primera mano; directo, personal; **at** ~ directamente.

firstly ['fɜːstlɪ] *adv* en primer lugar.

first-named [,fɜːst'neɪmd] *adj*: **the** ~ el primero, la primera.

first-nighter ['fɜːst'naɪtəʳ] *n* estrenista *mf*.

first-rate ['fɜːst'reɪt] *adj* de primera clase; magnífico, estupendo; **she is ~ at her work** su trabajo es de primera clase; **~!** ¡magnífico!

first-time ['fɜːst'taɪm] *adj*: ~ **buyer** persona *f* que compra su primera vivienda.

firth [fɜːθ] *n* (*gen Scot*) estuario *m*, ría *f*.

fir-tree ['fɜːtriː] *n* abeto *m*.

fiscal ['fɪskəl] *adj* fiscal; monetario; *policy* fiscal, financiero, económico; ~ **year** año *m* económico.

fish [fɪʃ] **1** *n*, *pl* **fish (a)** pez *m*, (*as food*) pescado *m*; ~ **and chips** (*esp Brit*) pescado *m* frito con patatas fritas; **to be like a ~ out of water** estar como pez fuera del agua; **there are other ~ in the sea** hay otros peces en el mar; **to have other ~ to fry** tener cosas más importantes que hacer.

(b) (*) tío *m**; **big** ~ pez *m* gordo; **odd** ~ tío *m* raro*; **he's a (bit of a) cold** ~ es un tipo frío*; **he's a poor** ~ es un pobre hombre.

2 *attr*: **~-and-chip shop** (*esp Brit*) *tienda donde se vende pescado rebozado junto con patatas fritas*; ~ **course** pescado *m*; ~ **merchant** (*US*) pescadero *m*, -a *f*; ~ **soup** sopa *f* de pescado.

3 *vt river* pescar en.

4 *vi* pescar; (*trawler etc*) faenar; **to ~ for** (tratar de) pescar; *compliment etc* andar a la pesca de; **he ~ed in his pocket for it** lo buscó en el bolsillo; **to ~ in troubled waters** (*fig*) pescar en río revuelto; **to go ~ing** ir de pesca.

◆**fish out** *vt* **(a)** sacar. **(b) this lake has been ~ed out** en este lago se ha pescado tanto que ya no quedan peces.

◆**fish up** *vt* sacar.

fishbone ['fɪʃbəʊn] *n* espina *f* (de pez), raspa *f*.

fishbowl ['fɪʃbəʊl] *n* pecera *f*.

fishcake ['fɪʃkeɪk] *n* croqueta *f* de pescado.

fisherman ['fɪʃəmən] *n*, *pl* **fishermen** ['fɪʃəmən] pescador *m*; **~'s tale** (*Brit fig*) cuento *m* de pescador.

fishery ['fɪʃərɪ] **1** *n* pesquería *f*, pesquera *f*. **2** *attr*: ~ **policy** política *f* pesquera; ~ **protection** protección *f* pesquera.

fish-eye ['fɪʃaɪ] **1** *n* (*in door*) mirilla *f*. **2** *attr*: ~ **lens** (*Phot*) objetivo *m* de ojo de pez.

fish factory ['fɪʃ,fæktərɪ] *n* fábrica *f* de elaboración de pescado.

fish-farm ['fɪʃfɑːm] *n* criadero *m* de peces, piscifactoría *f*.

fish-farmer ['fɪʃ,fɑːməʳ] *n* acuicultor *m*, -ora *f*.

fish-farming ['fɪʃ,fɑːmɪŋ] *n* cría *f* de peces, piscicultura *f*, acuicultura *f*.

fish-finger [,fɪʃ'fɪŋgəʳ] *n* (*Brit*) filete *m* de pescado empanado.

fish-glue ['fɪʃgluː] *n* cola *f* de pescado.

fish-hook ['fɪʃhʊk] *n* anzuelo *m*.

fishing ['fɪʃɪŋ] **1** *n* pesca *f*. **2** *attr* pesquero; de pesca; ~ **fleet** flota *f* pesquera; ~ **industry** industria *f* pesquera; ~ **licence,** ~ **permit** licencia *f* para pescar; ~ **port** puerto *m* pesquero; **to go on a ~ expedition** ir de pesca.

fishing-boat ['fɪʃɪŋbəʊt] *n* barca *f* pesquera.

fishing-grounds ['fɪʃɪŋgraʊndz] *npl* pesquería *f*.

fishing-line ['fɪʃɪŋlaɪn] *n* sedal *m*.

fishing-net ['fɪʃɪŋnet] *n* red *f* de pesca.

fishing-rod ['fɪʃɪŋrɒd] *n* caña *f* de pescar.

fishing-tackle ['fɪʃɪŋ,tækl] *n* aparejo *m* de pescar.

fish-knife ['fɪʃnaɪf] *n*, *pl* **fish-knives** ['fɪʃnaɪvz] cuchillo *m* de pescado.

fish-manure ['fɪʃmə,njʊəʳ] *n* abono *m* de pescado.

fish-market ['fɪʃmɑːkɪt] *n* mercado *m* de pescado, pescadería *f*.

fishmeal ['fɪʃmiːl] *n* harina *f* de pescado.

fishmonger ['fɪʃmʌŋgəʳ] *n* pescadero *m*; **~'s (shop)** pescadería *f*.

fishnet ['fɪʃnet] *attr*: ~ **stockings** medias *fpl* de red, medias *fpl* de rejilla; ~ **tights** leotardo *m* de red.

fish-paste ['fɪʃpeɪst] *n* pasta *f* de pescado.

fishplate ['fɪʃpleɪt] *n* (*Rail*) eclisa *f*.

fishpond ['fɪʃpɒnd] *n* piscina *f*, vivero *m*.

fish-shop ['fɪʃʃɒp] *n* pescadería *f*.

fish-slice ['fɪʃslaɪs] *n* (*Brit*) pala *f* para el pescado.

fish stick ['fɪʃstɪk] *n* (*US*) croqueta *f* de pescado.

fishstore ['fɪʃstɔːʳ] *n* (*US*) pescadería *f*.

fishtank ['fɪʃtæŋk] *n* acuario *m*.

fishwife ['fɪʃwaɪf] *n*, *pl* **fishwives** ['fɪʃwaɪvz] pescadera *f*; (*pej*) verdulera *f*.

fishy ['fɪʃɪ] *adj* **(a)** *eye* como de pez; (*of taste*) que sabe a pescado, (*of smell*) que huele a pescado. **(b)** (*) sospechoso; **it's** ~ me huele a camelo; **there's sth ~ going on here** aquí hay gato encerrado, me huele a chamusquina.

fissile ['fɪsaɪl] *adj* físil.

fission ['fɪʃən] *n* (*Phys*) fisión *f*; (*Bio*) escisión *f*.

fissionable ['fɪʃnəbl] *adj* fisionable.

fissure ['fɪʃəʳ] *n* grieta *f*, hendedura *f*; (*Anat, Geol, Metal*) fisura *f*.

fissured ['fɪʃəd] *adj* agrietado.

fist [fɪst] *n* **(a)** puño *m*; **to shake one's ~ at sb** amenazar a uno con el puño; **to make a poor ~ of sth** hacer algo mal. **(b)** (*) escritura *f*.

fistfight ['fɪst,faɪt] *n* lucha *f* a puñetazos.

fistful ['fɪstfʊl] *n* puñado *m*.

fisticuffs ['fɪstɪkʌfs] *npl* puñetazos *mpl*.

fit¹ [fɪt] **1** *adj* **(a)** (*suitable*) adecuado, conveniente, apto, a propósito, apropiado (*for* para); hábil, capaz; **the ~test** (*Bio*) los mejor dotados; ~ **for duty** apto para servicio; **a meal ~ for a king** una comida digna de un rey; **to be ~ for** ser adecuado para; **he's not ~ for the job** no es adecuado para el puesto, no merece que se le dé el puesto; **he's not ~ to teach** no tiene madera de profesor; **he is not ~ to drive** no es apto para conducir; ~ **to eat** bueno de comer; **it's not ~ to eat** no se puede comer, es incomible; **it's not ~ to be seen** es indigno de que lo vean las gentes; **is this ~ to wear?** ¿puedo ponerme esto?; **I felt ~ to drop** tuve ganas de caerme rendido; **to see** (*or* **think**) ~ **to** + *infin* estimar conveniente + *infin*; **he saw ~ to** + *infin* se vio en el caso de + *infin*; **do as you think ~** haga lo que mejor le parezca.

(**b**) (*Med*) sano, bien de salud; en buen estado físico; (*Sport*) en forma; **3 players are not ~** 3 jugadores están lesionados; **come when you're ~ again** ven cuando te hayas repuesto del todo; **to be as ~ as a fiddle** andar como un reloj; **are you ~?*** ¿estás listo?, ¿vamos?; **to get ~** (*Sport*) entrenarse, (*Med*) reponerse; **to keep ~** mantenerse en forma, mantenerse en buen estado físico.

2 *adv*: **to laugh ~ to burst*** desternillarse de risa*.

3 *vt* (**a**) (*make suitable*) ajustar, acomodar, adaptar (*to* a); **to ~ sb for a post** capacitar a uno para un puesto.

(**b**) (*suit*) *description, facts* cuadrar con, corresponder con, estar de acuerdo con; *colour scheme etc* hacer juego con; (*of dress etc*) sentar bien a, ir bien a.

(**c**) (*try on*) *clothes* probar (*on* a).

(**d**) (*fill up, exactly correspond to*) encajar en; **it ~s the space perfectly** encaja perfectamente en el espacio; **the key does not ~ the lock** la llave no entra en la cerradura.

(**e**) (*put*) **to ~ two things together** unir dos cosas; **I ~ted A into B** encajé A en B; **you ~ it in here** se encaja aquí, se coloca aquí; **to ~ the key into the lock** introducir la llave en la cerradura.

(**f**) (*supply*) **to ~ sth with** proveer algo de; **~ted with a heater** provisto de un calentador, dotado de un calentador; **I'm having a new door ~ted** me van a colocar una nueva portezuela; *V also* **fitted**.

4 *vi* (**a**) (*correspond*) corresponder, estar de acuerdo; **the facts don't ~** los datos no tienen sentido; **it all ~s** todo hace un conjunto lógico.

(**b**) (*of clothes etc*) entallar; **the suit ~s well** el traje le sienta bien.

(**c**) (*of space*) encajarse; caber; **it ~s in here, it ~s on here** se encaja aquí; **do they ~?** ¿se encajan uno en otro?; **does it ~?** ¿cabe?; **it won't ~ in here** aquí no cabe; **the key doesn't ~** la llave no sirve; **the key ~s into the lock** la llave encaja en la cerradura.

5 *n* ajuste *m*, corte *m*; correspondencia *f*; **it's a good ~** le sienta bien; **the suit is a tight ~** el traje me viene bastante estrecho; **it's not a good ~** no se ajusta bien; **there is no ~ between A and B** no hay correspondencia entre A y B.

◆**fit in 1** *vt*: **can you ~ me in?** ¿puedes incluirme?, ¿tienes un hueco para mí?; **I'll see if the director can ~ you in** voy a ver si el director tiene tiempo para verle; **I ~ted in a trip to Ávila** logré hacer una excursión a Ávila. **2** *vi* (*of person*) **he ~s in well here** aquí se lleva bien con todos; **I don't ~ in here** aquí no estoy bien.

◆**fit on** *vi*: **this bottle top won't ~ on any more** este tapón ya no cabe; **it should ~ on this end somewhere** tendría que ir por esta parte.

◆**fit out** *vt expedition, person* equipar; *ship* armar; **to ~ sb out with** proveer a uno de, equipar a uno con.

◆**fit up** *vt* (**a**) equipar, montar, instalar; **to ~ sb up with** proveer a uno de, equipar a uno con; **they have ~ted their house up with all modern conveniences** han equipado su casa con todas las comodidades modernas.

(**b**) (‡) incriminar dolosamente.

fit² [fɪt] *n* (*Med*) acceso *m*, ataque *m*; **~ of anger** arranque *m* de cólera; **~ of coughing** acceso *m* de tos; **by ~s and starts** a rachas, a empujones; **we were in ~s (of laughter)** moríamos de risa; **he'd have a ~ if he knew** le daría un ataque si lo supiera.

fitful ['fɪtfʊl] *adj* espasmódico, irregular, intermitente.

fitfully ['fɪtfəlɪ] *adv* espasmódicamente, a rachas, por intervalos.

fitment ['fɪtmənt] *n* (*Brit*) mueble *m*.

fitness ['fɪtnɪs] *n* (**a**) (*suitability*) conveniencia *f*, oportunidad *f*; (*for post etc*) idoneidad *f*, capacidad *f*. (**b**) (*Med*) (buena) salud *f*, (buen) estado *m* físico; **~ activity** (*US*) ejercicios *mpl* para mantenerse en forma; **~ classes** clases *fpl* de gimnasia; **~ fanatic** fanático *m*, -a *f* de la buena salud.

fitted ['fɪtɪd] *adj* (**a**) *suit, carpet* hecho a medida; *cupboard* empotrado. (**b**) **to be ~ for sth** tener talento para algo, ser idóneo para algo, ser apto para algo.

fitter ['fɪtəʳ] *n* (*Mech*) (mecánico *m*) ajustador *m*.

fitting ['fɪtɪŋ] **1** *adj* (*suitable*) conveniente, adecuado; (*worthy*) digno; **it is ~ that ...** es propio que + *subj*, es justo que + *subj*; **it is not ~ that ...** no está bien que + *subj*.

2 *n* (**a**) (*of dress*) prueba *f*; (*size*) medida *f*.

(**b**) **~s** (*Brit*) guarniciones *fpl*; (*for bathroom*) aparatos *mpl* sanitarios; (*electrical*) accesorios *mpl* eléctricos.

3 *attr*: **~ room** probador *m*, vestidor *m* (*LAm*).

fittingly ['fɪtɪŋlɪ] *adv* convenientemente, adecuadamente; dignamente; **~, it was he who ...** según cabía razonablemente esperar, era él quien ...

five [faɪv] **1** *adj* cinco. **2** *n* cinco *m*; **give me ~!‡** ¡choquen esos cinco!‡.

five-and-ten-cent store [ˌfaɪvən'tensent'stɔːʳ] *n*, **five-and-dime** [ˌfaɪvən'daɪm] *n*, **five-and-ten** [ˌfaɪvən'ten] *n* (*US*) almacén *m* de baratillo.

five-fold ['faɪvˌfəʊld] **1** *adj* quintuplo. **2** *adv* cinco veces.

five-o'-clock shadow ['faɪvəklɒk'ʃædəʊ] *n* barba *f* crecida.

fiver* ['faɪvəʳ] *n* (*Brit*) billete *m* de 5 libras.

five spot* ['faɪvspɒt] *n* (*US*) billete *m* de cinco dólares.

five-star ['faɪvstɑːʳ] *attr*: **~ hotel** hotel *m* de cinco estrellas; **~ restaurant** ≈ restaurante *m* de cinco estrellas.

five-year ['faɪv'jɪəʳ] *adj*: **~ plan** plan *m* quinquenal.

fix [fɪks] **1** *vt* (**a**) (*secure*) fijar, asegurar, sujetar; *bayonet* calar; (*Phot*) fijar; **to ~ sth in one's memory** grabar algo en la memoria.

(**b**) (*direct*) *attention* fijar (*on* en); *eyes* clavar (*on* en); *hopes* poner (*on* en); *blame* echar (*on* a).

(**c**) **to ~ sb with one's eyes** fijar los ojos en uno.

(**d**) (*place*) fijar (*at* en).

(**e**) (*determine position of*) fijar, precisar.

(**f**) (*determine*) *author, date etc* fijar, señalar; *price* fijar, determinar.

(**g**) (*arrange, prepare*: *also* **to ~ up**) arreglar; decidir; organizar, preparar; **it's all ~ed up** todo está arreglado; **there is nothing ~ed yet** todavía no se ha decidido nada; **he ~ed it with the police** se los arregló con la policía; **I'll soon ~ him!*** ¡me lo cargaré!*; **that ought to ~ him*** eso ha de acabar con él, que se apañe con esto.

(**h**) (*esp US*) dar, servir, preparar; **can I ~ you a drink?** ¿te preparo algo de beber?; **I'll ~ you some supper** te prepararé algo para cenar.

(**i**) (*repair*) componer, arreglar.

(**j**) (*Sport etc*) *game, jury* amañar; **it's been ~ed!** ¡hay tongo!

(**k**) **how are we ~ed for time?** ¿cómo vamos de tiempo?; **how are we ~ed for money?** ¿qué tal andamos de dinero?

2 *n* (**a**) (*Aer etc*) posición *f*.

(**b**) (*) aprieto *m*; **to be in a ~** estar en un aprieto.

(**c**) (‡) (*of drug*) dosis *f*; (*shot*) pinchazo‡ *m*; **to give o.s. a ~** pincharse‡.

◆**fix on** *vt* escoger; *date etc* fijar, señalar.

◆**fix up 1** *vt* (**a**) = **fix 1 (g)**. (**b**) (*provide*) **to ~ sb up with sth** proveer a uno de algo; **to ~ sb up with a job** conseguir un puesto para uno. **2** *vi*: **to ~ up with sb** arreglarlo con uno; **to ~ up with sb to** + *infin* convenir con uno en + *infin*.

fixated [fɪk'seɪtɪd] *adj*: **mother ~** con fijación en la madre, con fijación materna.

fixation [fɪk'seɪʃən] *n* fijación *f*.

fixative ['fɪksətɪv] *n* fijativo *m*.

fixed [fɪkst] *adj* (*all senses*) fijo; **~ assets** activo *m* fijo; **~ capital** capital *m* fijo; **~ charge** gasto *m* fijo; **~ costs** costos *mpl* fijos; **~ debt** deuda *f* consolidada; **~ format** formato *m* fijo; **~ investment** inversión *f* fija; **~ link** enlace *m* fijo; **~ price** precio *m* fijo; **~ star** estrella *f* fija; **~ wheel** piñón *m* fijo, rueda *f* fija; **~ yield securities** valores *mpl* de renta fija.

fixedly ['fɪksɪdlɪ] *adv* fijamente.

fixer* ['fɪksəʳ] *n* apañador *m*, -ora* *f*, amañador *m*, -ora* *f*.

fixings ['fɪksɪŋz] *npl* (*US*) accesorios *mpl*, guarniciones *fpl*.

Fixit* ['fɪksɪt] *n*: **Mr ~** Señor *m* Arreglalotodo*.

fixture ['fɪkstʃəʳ] *n* (**a**) cosa *f* fija; (*furniture etc*) mueble *m* fijo, instalación *f* fija; **the house was sold with ~s and fittings** (*Brit*) la casa se vendió acondicionada. (**b**) (*Brit Sport*) partido *m*, encuentro *m*. (**c**) (*person*) cliente *m* fijo.

fixture-list ['fɪkstʃəˌlɪst] *n* lista *f* de encuentros.

fizz [fɪz] **1** *n* (**a**) efervescencia *f*; (*noise*) ruido *m* sibilante. (**b**) (*) champán *m*; (*US*: *soft drink*) gaseosa *f*. **2** *vi* estar (*or* entrar) en efervescencia; hacer un ruido sibilante.

fizzle ['fɪzl] = **fizz**.

◆**fizzle out** *vi* apagarse; (*fig*) no dar resultado, fracasar.

fizzy ['fɪzɪ] *adj* gaseoso, espumoso, efervescente.

fjord [fjɔːd] *n* = **fiord**.

FL (*US Post*) *abbr of* **Florida**.

Fla. (*US*) *abbr of* **Florida**.

flab* [flæb] *n* grasa *f*, michelín* *m*.

flabbergast ['flæbəgɑːst] *vt* pasmar, dejar sin habla; **I was ~ed by the news** la noticia me causó estupor.

flabby ['flæbɪ] *adj* flojo, fofo, blanducho; (*fat*) gordo; (*fig*)

débil, soso.
flaccid ['flæksɪd] *adj* fláccido.
flaccidity [flæk'sɪdɪtɪ] *n* flaccidez *f*.
flag[1] [flæg] *n* (*Bot*) falso ácoro *m*, lirio *m*.
flag[2] [flæg] *n* (*stone*) losa *f*.
flag[3] [flæg] **1** *n* bandera *f*, pabellón *m*; (*small, charity etc*) banderita *f*; (*small, as souvenir, also Sport*) banderín *m*; (*Comput*) señalizador *m*, bandera *f*; **~ of convenience** pabellón *m* de conveniencia; **~ of truce** bandera *f* de parlamento; **to keep the ~ flying** seguir defendiéndose, resistir, no rendir la bandera; **to show the ~** hacer acto de presencia.
2 *vt* (**a**) (*signal*) hacer señales con una bandera a. (**b**) *path etc* señalar con banderitas; *item, reference* señalar, marcar; indicar de manera especial.
◆**flag down** *vt*: **to ~ sb down** hacer señales a uno para que se detenga.
flag[4] [flæg] *vi* (*strength*) acabarse, flaquear, decaer; (*enthusiasm etc*) enfriarse; (*conversation*) languidecer.
flag day ['flægdeɪ] *n* (*Brit*) día *m* de la banderita, cuestación *f*; **F~ Day** (*US*) día *m* de la Bandera (*14 junio*).
flagellate ['flædʒəleɪt] *vt* flagelar.
flagellation [ˌflædʒə'leɪʃən] *n* flagelación *f*.
flagging ['flægɪŋ] *adj* que flaquea; que se enfría; que languidece.
flag officer ['flægˌɒfɪsər] *n* (*Naut*) oficial *m* superior de la marina.
flagon ['flægən] *n* (*approx*) jarro *m*; (*as measure*) *botella de unos 2 litros*.
flagpole ['flægpəʊl] *n* asta *f* de bandera.
flagrant ['fleɪgrənt] *adj* notorio, escandaloso.
flagrantly ['fleɪgrəntlɪ] *adv* notoriamente, escandalosamente; **~ unfair** notoriamente injusto.
flagship ['flægʃɪp] *n* buque *m* insignia, buque *m* escuadra, (††) capitana *f*.
flagstaff ['flægstɑːf] *n* asta *f* de bandera.
flagstone ['flægstəʊn] *n* losa *f*.
flag stop ['flægstɒp] *n* (*US*) parada *f* a petición.
flag-waving ['flægˌweɪvɪŋ] *n* (*fig*) patriotismo *m* de banderita.
flail [fleɪl] **1** *n* mayal *m*. **2** *vt* (*Agr*) desgranar; (*fig*) golpear, azotar. **3** *vi* (*arms etc*: *also* **to ~ about**) debatirse.
flair [flɛər] *n* instinto *m*, aptitud *f* especial, don *m* (*for* para).
flak [flæk] *n* (**a**) fuego *m* antiaéreo. (**b**) (*) críticas *fpl*, comentarios *mpl* adversos; **to get a lot of ~** ser muy criticado.
flake [fleɪk] **1** *n* escama *f*, hojuela *f*; (*of snow*) copo *m*.
2 *vt* separar en escamas.
3 *vi* (*also* **to ~ away, to ~ off**) desprenderse en escamas.
◆**flake off** *vi* (**a**) *V* **flake 3**. (**b**) **~ off!**‡ (*US*) ¡lárgate!*, ¡pírala!*
◆**flake out*** **1** *vt*: **to be ~d out** (*Brit*) estar rendido. **2** *vi* (*Brit*) caer rendido.
flak-jacket ['flækˌdʒækɪt] *n* chaleco *m* antibala.
flaky ['fleɪkɪ] *adj* (**a**) escamoso; desmenuzable; **~ pastry** hojaldre *m*. (**b**) (*US*‡) chiflado*.
flambé ['flɑːmbeɪ] *adj* flameado.
flamboyant [flæm'bɔɪənt] *adj dress etc* vistoso, llamativo; *character, speech* extravagante; *style* rimbombante.
flame [fleɪm] **1** *n* (**a**) llama *f*; **to be in ~s** arder en llamas; **to burst into ~s** estallar en llamas; **to commit sth to the ~s** entregar algo a las llamas; **to fan the ~s** soplar el fuego; **we watched the house go up in ~s** mirábamos cómo la casa ardía en llamas.
(**b**) (*) amante *mf*; **old ~** amante *mf* de otros tiempos.
2 *vi* (*burn*) llamear; (*shine*) brillar.
◆**flame up** *vi* (*fig*) estallar, (*person*) inflamarse.
flame-coloured, (*US*) **flame-colored** ['fleɪmˌkʌləd] *adj* de un amarillo intenso.
flame-proof ['fleɪmpruːf] *adj* a prueba de fuego.
flamethrower ['fleɪmˌθrəʊər] *n* lanzallamas *m*.
flaming ['fleɪmɪŋ] *adj* (**a**) llameante, en llamas. (**b**) (‡) condenado*.
flamingo [flə'mɪŋgəʊ] *n* flamenco *m*.
flammable ['flæməbl] *adj* inflamable.
flan [flæn] *n* (*Brit*) tarta *f* de fruta, tarteleta *f* de fruta.
Flanders ['flɑːndəz] *n* Flandes *m*.
flange [flændʒ] *n* pestaña *f*, reborde *m*, resalte *m*, brida *f*.
flanged [flændʒd] *adj* con pestaña.
flank [flæŋk] **1** *n* (*of person*) costado *m*; (*of animal*) ijada *f*; (*of hill*) lado *m*, falda *f*; (*Mil*) flanco *m*.
2 *attr*: **~ attack** ataque *m* de flanco.
3 *vt* lindar con, estar contiguo a; (*Mil etc*) flanquear; **it is ~ed by hills** tiene unas colinas a su lado; **he was ~ed by two policemen** iba escoltado por dos guardias.
flannel ['flænl] **1** *n* (**a**) (*cloth*) franela *f*; (*Brit*: *face ~*) manopla *f*, paño *m*; **~s** (*Brit*) (*trousers*) pantalones *mpl* de franela; (*underclothes*) ropa *f* interior de lana.
(**b**) (*) (*soft soap*) jabón* *m*, coba* *f*; (*Brit*: *waffle*) paja *f*.
2 *adj* de franela.
3 *vt* (*Brit**) dar coba a*.
4 *vi* (*Brit**) llenar muchos renglones (*etc*) sin decir nada de valor.
flannelette [ˌflænə'let] *n* muletón *m*.
flap [flæp] **1** *n* (**a**) (*on dress*) faldilla *f*; (*of pocket*) cartera *f*; (*of envelope*) solapa *f*; (*of table*) hoja *f* plegadiza; (*of counter*) trampa *f*; (*of skin*) colgajo *m*; (*Aer*) flap *m*.
(**b**) (*of wing*) aletazo *m*, movimiento *m*.
(**c**) (*Brit**) (*crisis*) crisis *f*; (*row*) lío* *m*; **there's a big ~ on** hay una crisis; se ha armado un lío imponente*; **to get into a ~** ponerse nervioso, azorarse.
2 *vt wings* batir; (*shake*) sacudir; *arms* agitar.
3 *vi* (**a**) (*wings*) aletear; (*sail*) sacudirse; (*flag etc*) ondear, agitarse.
(**b**) (*Brit**) ponerse nervioso, azorarse; **don't ~!** ¡con calma!
flapdoodle* ['flæpˌduːdl] *n* chorrada* *f*.
flapjack ['flæpdʒæk] *n* torta *f* de avena, hojuela *f*, panqueque *m* (*LAm*).
flapper* ['flæpər] *n* (*Hist*) joven *f* a la moda (*de los 1920*).
flare [flɛər] **1** *n* (**a**) (*blaze*) llamarada *f*; (*signal*) cohete *m* de señales, (*Mil*) bengala *f*, proyectil *m* de iluminación; (*solar*) erupción *f* solar.
(**b**) (*Sew*) vuelo *m*.
2 *vt* (*Sew*) abocinar, acampanar.
3 *vi* (**a**) (*blaze*) llamear, resplandecer, fulgurar; (*shine*) brillar.
(**b**) (*skirt*) acampanarse.
◆**flare up** *vi* (**a**) llamear, encenderse. (**b**) (*fig*: *person*) encolerizarse; ponerse hecho una fiera (*at* con); (*revolt etc*) estallar; (*epidemic*) declararse.
flared [flɛəd] *adj skirt* de vuelo amplio; *trousers* de perneras amplias, acampanado.
flarepath ['flɛəpɑːθ] *n* pista *f* iluminada con balizas.
flare-up ['flɛər'ʌp] *n* (*fig*) explosión *f*; (*of anger*) arranque *m* de cólera; (*quarrel*) riña *f*; (*of trouble*) manifestación *f* súbita, estallido *m*.
flash [flæʃ] **1** *n* (**a**) (*of light*) relámpago *m*; destello *m*, ráfaga *f*; (*of gun*) fogonazo *m*; **~ of lightning** relámpago *m*; **like a ~** como un relámpago.
(**b**) (*moment*) instante *m*; **in a ~** en un instante.
(**c**) **~ of inspiration** ráfaga *f* de inspiración; **~ of wit** rasgo *m* de ingenio; **~ in the pan** esfuerzo *m* abortado, éxito *m* único; chiripa *f*; **it was just a ~ in the pan** eso fue por chiripa.
(**d**) (*news ~*) flash *m*, noticia *f* de última hora; mensaje *m* urgente.
(**e**) (*Phot*) flash *m*, magnesio *m*.
2 (*) *adj*: **a really ~ car** un coche realmente fabuloso*.
3 *vt* (**a**) *light* despedir, lanzar; *look* dirigir, lanzar (rápidamente); *message* transmitir por heliógrafo, transmitir por radio, (*fig*) transmitir rápidamente.
(**b**) *torch* encender; **~ it this way** proyéctala por aquí; **he ~ed the light in my eyes** hizo brillar la luz en mis ojos, dio con la luz en mis ojos.
(**c**) **to ~ sth about** sacar algo a relucir, hacer ostentación de algo.
4 *vi* (**a**) relampaguear, destellar; (*window, reflection*) brillar; **to ~ on and off** encenderse y apagarse.
(**b**) **to ~ past** pasar como un rayo.
(**c**) **to ~ back to** (*Cine*) volver atrás a.
(**d**) (*) exhibirse, desenfundar*.
flashback ['flæʃbæk] *n* escena *f* retrospectiva, vuelta *f* atrás (*to* a).
flash bulb ['flæʃbʌlb] *n* flash *m*, bombilla *f* fusible.
flash card ['flæʃkɑːd] *n* tarjeta *f*, carta *f*.
flash cube ['flæʃkjuːb] *n* flash *m* de cubo.
flasher* ['flæʃər] *n* (*Brit*) exhibicionista *m*.
flash flood ['flæʃflʌd] *n* riada *f*.
flash gun ['flæʃgʌn] *n* disparador *m* de flash.
flashily ['flæʃɪlɪ] *adv*: **to dress ~** vestirse a lo chulo.
flashing ['flæʃɪŋ] *n* (*) exhibicionismo *m*.
flashlight ['flæʃlaɪt] *n* (*Phot*) flash *m*; (*torch*) linterna *f* eléctrica.
flashpoint ['flæʃpɔɪnt] *n* (**a**) punto *m* de inflamación. (**b**) (*fig*) punto *m* de explosión.

flashy ['flæʃɪ] *adj jewel etc* de relumbrón; *car etc* ostentoso; *person* charro, chulo.
flask [flɑːsk] *n* frasco *m*; redoma *f*; (*vacuum* ~) termo *m*, termos *m*; (*Chem*) matraz *m*.
flat [flæt] **1** *adj* (**a**) (*level*) *countryside etc* llano; *object* plano; horizontal; (*smooth*) liso, igual; *tyre* desinflado; *foot* plano; *painted surface* mate, sin brillo; *rate* uniforme, igual; **400 metres** ~ 400 metros lisos; ~ **nose** nariz *f* chata; ~ **race** carrera *f* lisa; ~ **rate** tipo *m* fijo, tipo *m* estándar; ~ **roof** azotea *f*; ~ **screen** pantalla *f* plana; **as** ~ **as a pancake** *countryside* totalmente llano, (*after bombing*) desnudo como la palma de la mano; **the town was just** ~ la ciudad quedó totalmente arrasada.
(**b**) (*downright*) terminante, categórico; **and that's** ~ no hay más que decir.
(**c**) (*Mus*) *voice, instrument* desafinado; *key* bemol; **E** ~ **major** mi bemol mayor.
(**d**) (*dull, lifeless*) *taste, style* insípido, soso; *drink* muerto; *battery* descargado; *tone* monótono; *lecture etc* aburrido, pesado; *business* flojo; *feeling* de abatimiento; **to be** ~* (*US*) no tener ni un céntimo; **to be feeling rather** ~ sentirse algo deprimido.
2 *adv* (**a**) **to fall** ~ (**on one's face**) caer de bruces, caer de boca; **to fall** ~ (*joke*) caer mal, no hacer gracia a uno, (*suggestion*) caer en el vacío; **to be lying down** ~ estar tendido; **to put sth** ~ **on the table** extender algo sobre la mesa.
(**b**) (*Mus*) **to sing** ~, **to play** ~ desafinar.
(**c**) **to be** ~ **broke*** (*Brit*) no tener ni un céntimo; **to go** ~ **out** ir a máxima velocidad; (*Aut*) ir con el acelerador pisado a fondo; **to go** ~ **out for sth** tratar de conseguir algo por todos los medios; **to turn sth down** ~ rechazar algo de plano.
3 *n* (**a**) (*Brit: rooms*) piso *m*, apartamento *m*, departamento *m* (*SC*).
(**b**) superficie *f* plana, superficie *f* lisa; (*of hand*) palma *f*; (*of sword*) plano *m*; **racing on the** ~ carreras *fpl* (de caballos) sin obstáculos; **this car can do 160 km/h. on the** ~ este coche puede correr a 160 km/h. en superficie plana.
(**c**) (*Mus*) bemol *m*.
(**d**) (*Aut, esp US*) pinchazo *m*, neumático *m* pinchado.
(**e**) (*Geog*) ~**s** (*mud* ~) marisma *f*; (*salt* ~) salinas *fpl*.
flat-bottomed ['flæt'bɒtəmd] *adj boat* de fondo plano.
flat-chested ['flæt'tʃestɪd] *adj* de pecho plano.
flatfish ['flætfɪʃ] *n, pl* **flatfish** pez *m* pleuronecto (*p.ej. platija, lenguado*).
flatfooted ['flæt'fʊtɪd] *adj* de pies planos; (*Brit**) torpe, desmañado.
flatiron ['flæt,aɪən] *n* plancha *f*.
flatlet ['flætlɪt] *n* (*Brit*) piso *m* pequeño, pisito *m*, apartamentito *m*.
flatly ['flætlɪ] *adv refuse etc* de plano; *deny* terminantemente; **we are** ~ **opposed to** quedamos totalmente opuestos a.
flatmate ['flætmeɪt] *n* compañero *m*, -a *f* de piso.
flatness ['flætnɪs] *n* llanura *f*, lo llano; (*fig*) insipidez *f*, monotonía *f*, aburrimiento *m*.
flat-racing ['flæt,reɪsɪŋ] *n* carreras *fpl* de caballos sin obstáculos.
flatten ['flætn] **1** *vt* (**a**) (*also* **to** ~ **out**) allanar, aplanar; (*smoothe*) alisar; *map etc* extender. (**b**) *house, city* aplastar. (**c**) (*fig*) desconcertar, aplastar. **2** *vr*: **to** ~ **o.s. against a wall** aplanarse contra una pared.
◆**flatten out** **1** *vt* = **flatten 1 (a)**. **2** *vi* (*Aer*) enderezarse; (*road, countryside*) nivelarse, allanarse.
flatter ['flætəʳ] **1** *vt* adular, lisonjear, halagar; (*photo, clothes etc*) favorecer. **2** *vr*: **to** ~ **o.s.** felicitarse, congratularse (*on* de, *that* de que); **you** ~ **yourself!** ¡presumido!
flatterer ['flætərəʳ] *n* adulador *m*, -ora *f*.
flattering ['flætərɪŋ] *adj* lisonjero; halagüeño; *photo, clothes etc* que favorece.
flatteringly ['flætərɪŋlɪ] *adv speak etc* en términos lisonjeros.
flattery ['flætərɪ] *n* adulación *f*, lisonjas *fpl*, halago(s) *m*(*pl*).
flatulence ['flætjʊləns] *n* flatulencia *f*; (*fig*) hinchazón *f*.
flatulent ['flætjʊlənt] *adj* flatulento; (*fig*) hinchado.
flatworm ['flætwɜːm] *n* platelminto *m*.
flaunt [flɔːnt] **1** *vt* ostentar, lucir; hacer gala de. **2** *vr*: **to** ~ **o.s.** pavonearse.
flautist ['flɔːtɪst] *n* (*Brit*) flautista *mf*, flauta *m*.
flavin ['fleɪvɪn] *n* flavina *f*.
flavour, (*US*) **flavor** ['fleɪvəʳ] **1** *n* sabor *m* (*of* a), gusto *m*; (*flavouring*) condimento *m*; **with a banana** ~ con sabor a plátano. **2** *vt* sazonar, condimentar (*with* con); (*fig*) dar un sabor característico a; ~**ed with** con sabor a.
flavouring, (*US*) **flavoring** ['fleɪvərɪŋ] *n* condimento *m*.
flavourless, (*US*) **flavorless** ['fleɪvəlɪs] *adj* insípido, soso.
flaw [flɔː] *n* desperfecto *m*, imperfección *f*; (*crack*) grieta *f*; (*in character, scheme, case etc*) defecto *m*.
flawed [flɔːd] *adj* imperfecto, defectuoso.
flawless ['flɔːlɪs] *adj* intachable, impecable.
flax [flæks] *n* lino *m*.
flaxen ['flæksən] *adj hair* muy rubio.
flay [fleɪ] *vt* (**a**) desollar. (**b**) (*fig: beat*) azotar; (*defeat*) cascar; (*criticize*) despellejar.
flea [fliː] **1** *n* pulga *f*; **to send sb away with a** ~ **in his ear** echar a uno la pulga detrás de la oreja. **2** *attr*: ~ **collar** collar *m* antipulgas.
fleabag‡ ['fliːbæg] *n* (*Brit: person*) guarro *m*, -a *f*; (*US: hotel*) hotelucho *m* de mala muerte*.
fleabite ['fliːbaɪt] *n* picadura *f* de pulga; (*fig*) pérdida *f* (*etc*) insignificante, nada *f*.
fleabitten ['fliːbɪtn] *adj* infestado de pulgas; (*fig*) miserable.
flea-market ['fliː,mɑːkɪt] *n* mercado *m* de baratijas y cosas usadas.
fleapit* ['fliːpɪt] *n* (*Brit*) cine *m* de bajísima categoría.
fleck [flek] **1** *n* punto *m*, mancha *f*. **2** *vt* puntear, salpicar (*with* de).
fled [fled] *pret and ptp of* **flee**.
fledged [fledʒd] *adj* plumado.
fledg(e)ling ['fledʒlɪŋ] **1** *n* (**a**) volantón *m*, pajarito *m*. (**b**) (*fig*) novato *m*, -a *f*. **2** *adj* en ciernes; nuevo, joven, que acaba de establecerse; ~ **poet** poeta *mf* en ciernes.
flee [fliː] (*irr: pret and ptp* **fled**) **1** *vt* (*escape from*) huir de, abandonar; (*shun*) evitar. **2** *vi* huir (*from* de), darse a la fuga, fugarse (*to* a); (*vanish*) desaparecer.
fleece [fliːs] **1** *n* vellón *m*; lana *f*. **2** *vt* esquilar; (*fig*) pelar, mondar.
fleece-lined [,fliːs'laɪnd] *adj* forrado de muletón.
fleecy ['fliːsɪ] *adj* lanudo; *cloud* aborregado.
fleet¹ [fliːt] *n* (*Naut, Aer*) flota *f*; (*of cars*) parque *m*; **the British** ~ la armada inglesa; **F~ Air Arm** (*Brit*) Fuerzas *fpl* Aéreas de la Armada.
fleet² [fliːt] *adj*, **fleet-footed** ['fliːt'fʊtɪd] *adj* (*also* ~ **of foot**) veloz, ligero, rápido.
fleeting ['fliːtɪŋ] *adj* fugaz, momentáneo, efímero, pasajero; *moment, visit* breve.
fleetingly ['fliːtɪŋlɪ] *adv* fugazmente, momentáneamente.
Fleming ['flemɪŋ] *n* flamenco *m*, -a *f*.
Flemish ['flemɪʃ] **1** *adj* flamenco. **2** *n* flamenco *m*.
flesh [fleʃ] *n* carne *f* (*also fig*); (*of fruit*) pulpa *f*; **in the** ~ en persona; **of** ~ **and blood** de carne y hueso; **my own** ~ **and blood** mi familia, mis parientes, los de mi sangre; **it was more than** ~ **and blood could stand** era inaguantable, rebasaba el límite de lo soportable; **to go the way of all** ~ pagar tributo a la muerte; **to press sb's** ~ estrechar la mano a uno; **to put on** ~ echar carnes; *V* **creep**.
◆**flesh out** *vt* (*fig*) desarrollar.
flesh colour, (*US*) **flesh color** ['fleʃ,kʌləʳ] *n* (*gen, Art*) color *m* carne.
flesh-coloured, (*US*) **flesh-colored** ['fleʃ,kʌləd] *adj* de color del cutis.
fleshpots ['fleʃpɒts] *npl* (*fig*) vida *f* de lujo; **to remember the** ~**s of Egypt** recordar los ollas de Egipto.
flesh wound ['fleʃwuːnd] *n* herida *f* superficial.
fleshy ['fleʃɪ] *adj* (*fat*) gordo; (*Bot etc*) carnoso.
flew [fluː] *pret of* **fly**.
flex [fleks] **1** *n* (*Brit*) cable *m*, flexible *m*, hilo *m*, cordón *m* (de la luz); prolongación *f* eléctrica. **2** *vt* doblar; *muscle* flexionar. **3** *vi* doblarse; flexionarse.
flexibility [,fleksɪ'bɪlɪtɪ] *n* flexibilidad *f* (*also fig*).
flexible ['fleksəbl] *adj* flexible (*also fig*); ~ **working hours** horas *fpl* de trabajo flexibles; **we have to be** ~ **about this** hay que mostrarse flexibles en este asunto.
flexion ['flekʃən] *n* flexión *f*.
flexitime ['fleksɪ,taɪm] *n* horario *m* flexible.
flexor ['fleksəʳ] **1** *n* flexor *m*, músculo *m* flexor. **2** *adj* flexor.
flibbertigibbet ['flɪbətɪ'dʒɪbɪt] *n* casquivana *f*.
flick [flɪk] **1** *n* (**a**) (*blow*) golpecito *m* rápido; (*with finger*) capirotazo *m*; (*of whip*) chasquido *m*; **with a** ~ **of the wrist** con un movimiento rápido de la muñeca.
(**b**) (*Brit**) película *f*; **the** ~**s** el cine.
2 *vt* (*strike*) dar un golpecito a; (*touch in passing*) rozar levemente; (*with finger*) dar un capirotazo a; *whip* chasquear; **to** ~ **sth with a whip** dar algo ligeramente con el látigo; **to** ~ **sth away** quitar algo con un movimiento rápido; **to** ~ **over the pages** hojear rápidamente las páginas.
◆**flick off** *vt* (**a**) *dust, ash* tirar con el dedo. (**b**) *light etc*

apagar.
◆**flick on** *vt light etc* encender.
◆**flick out 1** *vt* (**a**) **the snake ~ed its tongue out** la serpiente lengueteaba. (**b**) *light etc* apagar. **2** *vi* **the snake's tongue ~ed out** la serpiente lengueteaba.
◆**flick through** *vt pages* hojear rápidamente.
flicker ['flɪkəʳ] **1** *n* parpadeo *m*; **without a ~ of** sin la menor señal de. **2** *vi* (*light*) parpadear, (*on going out*) brillar con luz mortecina; (*flame*) vacilar; (*snake's tongue etc*) vibrar; **the candle ~ed out** la vela parpadeó y se apagó.
flickknife ['flɪknaɪf] *n, pl* **flickknives** ['flɪknaɪvz] (*Brit*) navaja *f* de muelle, navaja *f* de resorte.
flier ['flaɪəʳ] *n* (**a**) aviador *m*, -ora *f*. (**b**) (*US*) prospecto *m*, folleto *m*.
flight [flaɪt] *n* (**a**) (*flying*) vuelo *m*; (*of bullet*) trayectoria *f*; (*distance flown*) recorrido *m*; **~ of fancy** sueño *m*, ilusión *f*; **to be in the first ~** ser de primera categoría; **to take ~** alzar el vuelo.
(**b**) (*escape*) huida *f*, fuga *f*; **~ of capital** evasión *f* de capitales; **to be in full ~** huir en desorden; **to put to ~** ahuyentar, (*Mil*) poner en fuga; **to take to ~** darse a la fuga.
(**c**) **~ of steps** tramo *m*, escalera *f*; **we live 3 ~s up** vivimos en el tercer piso.
(**d**) (*group of birds*) bandada *f*; (*Aer: unit*) escuadrilla *f*.
flight attendant ['flaɪtə'tendənt] *n* auxiliar *mf* de vuelo.
flightbag ['flaɪtbæg] *n* bolso *m* de bandolera.
flight-crew ['flaɪtkruː] *n* tripulación *f*.
flightdeck ['flaɪtdek] *n* cubierta *f* de vuelo.
flightless ['flaɪtlɪs] *adj bird* incapaz de volar.
flight-lieutenant ['flaɪtlef'tenənt] *n* (*Brit*) teniente *m* de aviación.
flight-log ['flaɪtlɒg] *n* (*Aer*) diario *m* de vuelo.
flightpath ['flaɪtpɑːθ] *n* trayectoria *f* de vuelo.
flightplan ['flaɪtplæn] *n* plan *m* de vuelo, carta *f* de vuelo.
flight-recorder ['flaɪtrɪˌkɔːdəʳ] *n* registrador *m* de vuelo.
flight-sergeant ['flaɪt'sɑːdʒənt] *n* (*Brit*) sargento *m* de aviación.
flight-simulator ['flaɪtˌsɪmjʊleɪtəʳ] *n* simulador *m* de vuelo.
flight-test ['flaɪttest] *vt* probar en vuelo.
flighty ['flaɪtɪ] *adj* frívolo, poco serio; caprichoso, inconstante; travieso; coqueta.
flimsily ['flɪmzɪlɪ] *adv* débilmente; muy delgadamente, muy ligeramente; de modo diáfano; **~ covered** ligeramente cubierto.
flimsiness ['flɪmzɪnɪs] *n* debilidad *f*, endeblez *f*; delgadez *f*, ligereza *f*; diafanidad *f*; lo baladí.
flimsy ['flɪmzɪ] **1** *adj* (*weak*) débil, endeble; (*thin*) muy delgado, muy ligero; *cloth* diáfano; *excuse* baladí. **2** *nm* (*Brit*) papel *m* de copiar; copia *f*.
flinch [flɪntʃ] *vi* acobardarse, arredrarse, retroceder (*from* ante), encogerse de miedo; **without ~ing** sin cejar, sin vacilar.
fling [flɪŋ] **1** *n* (**a**) **to go on a ~** echar una cana al aire; **to have one's ~** correrla; **youth will have its ~** los jóvenes han de correrla; **to have a ~ at sth** intentar algo; **he had a final ~** tuvo una juerga de despedida.
(**b**) (*) aventura *f* amorosa.
(**c**) **highland ~** *cierto baile escocés*.
2 (*irr: pret and ptp* **flung**) *vt* arrojar, tirar, lanzar; *rider* tirar al suelo; **to ~ sb into jail** echar a uno en la cárcel, encarcelar a uno; **to ~ one's arms round sb** echar los brazos encima a uno; **to ~ open** abrir de golpe.
3 *vr*: **to ~ o.s.** arrojarse, precipitarse; **to ~ o.s. over a cliff** despeñarse por un precipicio.
◆**fling down 1** *vt* tirar.
2 *vr*: **to ~ o.s. down** tirarse al suelo.
◆**fling off** *vt clothes* quitarse (de prisa).
◆**fling on 1** *vt clothes* ponerse (de prisa).
2 *vr*: **to ~ o.s. on sb** echarse sobre uno.
◆**fling out 1** *vt rubbish* tirar; *remark* lanzar; *person* expulsar.
2 *vi*: **she flung out of the room** salió indignada del cuarto.
flint [flɪnt] **1** *n* (*material*) sílex *m*; (*one ~*) pedernal *m*; (*of lighter*) piedra *f*. **2** *attr*: **~ axe** hacha *f* de sílex.
flinty ['flɪntɪ] *adj* (**a**) *material* de sílex; *soil* que tiene muchas piedras, pedregoso. (**b**) (*fig*) empedernido, de piedra.
flip¹ [flɪp] **1** *n* capirotazo *m*; (*Aer**) vuelo *m*.
2 *attr*: **~ side** cara *f* secundaria, cara *f* B.
3 *vt* (*with fingers*) echar de un capirotazo; (*jerk*) mover de un tirón; *coin* echar a cara o cruz; **to ~ open** abrir de golpe.
4 *vi* (*) enloquecer, perder la chaveta*.
◆**flip off** *vt cigarette ash* quitar de un golpe de dedo (*or* de un capirotazo).
◆**flip out*** *vi* enloquecer; *V also* **flip¹ 3**.
◆**flip over** *vi* (*esp US Aut etc*) capotar, dar una vuelta de campana.
◆**flip through** *vt*: **to ~ through a book** hojear un libro.
flip²* [flɪp] *adj* = **flippant**.
flip³* [flɪp] *excl* ¡porras!
flip-flop ['flɪpflɒp] **1** *n* (**a**) **~s** (*sandals*) chancletas *fpl*. (**b**) (*Comput*) circuito *m* basculante (*or* biestable), flip-flop *m*. (**c**) (*fig: esp US*) cambio *m* de chaquetas, golpe *m* de timón. **2** *vi* (*US fig*) cambiar de opinión, cambiarse de chaqueta, dar un golpe de timón.
flippancy ['flɪpənsɪ] *n* falta *f* de seriedad, ligereza *f*.
flippant ['flɪpənt] *adj* poco serio, ligero.
flippantly ['flɪpəntlɪ] *adv* con poca seriedad, ligeramente.
flipper ['flɪpəʳ] *n* aleta *f* (*also**).
flipping* ['flɪpɪŋ] *adj* (*Brit*) condenado*.
flirt [flɜːt] **1** *n* mariposón *m*, coqueta *f*; **she's a great ~** es terriblemente coqueta.
2 *vi* flirtear, coquetear (*with* con), mariposear; **to ~ with** (*fig*) jugar con, entretenerse con; **to ~ with death** jugar con la muerte; **to ~ with an idea** acariciar una idea.
flirtation [flɜː'teɪʃən] *n* flirteo *m*.
flirtatious [flɜː'teɪʃəs] *adj man* mariposón, *woman* coqueta; *glance etc* coqueta.
flit [flɪt] **1** *vi* (**a**) revolotear, volar con vuelo cortado; (*before eyes etc*) pasar rápidamente. (**b**) (*Brit**) mudarse a la chita callando. (**c**) (*person*) **to ~ in, ~ out** *etc* (*Brit: lightly*) entrar, salir *etc* con ligereza; (*US: affectedly*) entrar/salir a pasitos amanerados. **2** *n*: **to do a** (**moonlight**) **~*** (*Brit*) mudarse a la chita callando.
flitch [flɪtʃ] *n*: **~ of bacon** hoja *f* de tocino.
Flo [fləʊ] *nf familiar form of* **Florence**.
float [fləʊt] **1** *n* (**a**) (*Fishing*) corcho *m*; (*of seaplane etc*) pontón *m*, flotador *m*.
(**b**) (*in procession*) carroza *f*, paso *m*.
(**c**) (*Fin: loan*) préstamo *m*; (*in shop*) dinero *m* en caja antes de empezar las ventas del día (para cambios *etc*).
2 *vt* (**a**) hacer flotar; (*refloat*) poner a flote.
(**b**) *company* lanzar, fundar; *share issue, loan* emitir.
(**c**) **to ~ an idea** sugerir una idea.
(**d**) **to ~ the pound** (hacer) flotar la libra esterlina.
3 *vi* (**a**) flotar; (*bather*) hacer la plancha; (*flag, hair*) ondear; **it ~ed to the surface** salió a la superficie.
(**b**) **we shall let the pound ~** dejaremos flotar la libra esterlina.
◆**float (a)round*** *vi* (*rumour, news*) circular, correr.
◆**float away** *vi* irse a la deriva.
◆**float off** *vi* (*wreck etc*) irse a la deriva.
floating ['fləʊtɪŋ] *adj object, population etc* flotante; **~ assets** activo *m* flotante; **~ currency** moneda *f* flotante; **~ debt** deuda *f* flotante; **~ dock** dique *m* flotante; **~ exchange** tipo *m* de cambio flotante; **~ rib** costilla *f* flotante; **~ vote** voto *m* de los indecisos; **~ voter** votante *m* indeciso, votante *f* indecisa.
flock¹ [flɒk] **1** *n* (*Agr etc*) rebaño *m*; (*of birds*) bandada *f*; (*Eccl*) grey *f*; (*of people*) multitud *f*, tropel *m*; **they came in ~s** acudieron en tropel.
2 *vi* (*also* **to ~ together**) congregarse, reunirse; **to ~ about sb** reunirse en torno de uno; **to ~ to** acudir en tropel a.
flock² [flɒk] *n* (*wool*) borra *f*.
floe [fləʊ] *n* (*also* **ice ~**) témpano *m* de hielo.
flog [flɒg] *vt* (**a**) azotar. (**b**) (*Brit‡*) vender.
flogger ['flɒgəʳ] *n* partidario *m*, -a *f* del restablecimiento de la pena de azotes.
flogging ['flɒgɪŋ] *n* azotaina *f*, paliza *f*.
flood [flʌd] **1** *n* inundación *f*; (*in river*) avenida *f*; (*tide*) pleamar *f*, flujo *m*; (*fig*) torrente *m*, diluvio *m*; **the F~** el Diluvio; **a ~ of letters** una riada de cartas; **a ~ of light** un torrente de luz; **to be in ~** estar crecido; **to weep ~s of tears** llorar a mares.
2 *vt* inundar, anegar; **to ~ the market with sth** inundar (*or* saturar) el mercado de algo; **we are ~ed with applications** tenemos montones de solicitudes.
3 *vi* desbordar.
◆**flood in** *vi*: **to come ~ing in** (*people*) entrar a raudales, (*applications*) llegar a montones.
◆**flood out** *vt*: **ten families were ~ed out** diez familias tuvieron que abandonar sus casas debido a la inundación.
flood-control ['flʌdkəntrəʊl] *n* medidas *fpl* para controlar las inundaciones.
floodgate ['flʌdgeɪt] *n* compuerta *f*, esclusa *f*.

flooding ['flʌdɪŋ] *n* inundación *f*.
floodlight ['flʌdlaɪt] **1** *n* foco *m*. **2** (*irr*: *V* **light**) *vt* iluminar con focos.
floodlighting ['flʌdlaɪtɪŋ] *n* iluminación *f* con focos.
floodplain ['flʌdpleɪn] *n* llanura *f* sujeta a inundaciones (de un río).
flood-tide ['flʌdtaɪd] *n* pleamar *f*, marea *f* creciente.
floor [flɔːʳ] **1** *n* (**a**) (*gen*) suelo *m*; (*of sea etc*) fondo *m*; (*dance* ~) pista *f*; (*Cine, TV*) plató *m*; **the F~** (*St Ex*) el parqué; **to cross the ~** (**of the House**) atravesar la sala; **to have the ~** tener la palabra; **to hold the ~** tener a los asistentes (*etc*) pendientes de su palabra; **to take the ~** salir a bailar, (*fig*) salir a palestra; **to wipe the ~ with*** cascar*.
(**b**) (*storey*) piso *m*; *V* **first** *etc*.
2 *attr*: ~ **lamp** (*US*) lámpara *f* de pie.
3 *vt* (**a**) *room* solar, entarimar (*with* de).
(**b**) *person* derribar; (*fig*) anonadar, apabullar.
(**c**) (*US Aut*) *accelerator* pisar.
floor area ['flɔːrɛərɪə] *n* área *f* total.
floorboard ['flɔːbɔːd] *n* tabla *f* (del suelo).
floorcloth ['flɔːklɒθ] *n* bayeta *f*.
floor-covering ['flɔːˌkʌvərɪŋ] *n* recubrimiento *m* de piso.
flooring ['flɔːrɪŋ] *n* suelo *m*; (*material*) solería *f*.
floor-manager ['flɔːˌmænɪdʒəʳ] *n* jefe *mf* de plató.
floorplan ['flɔːplæn] *n* planta *f*.
floorpolish ['flɔːˌpɒlɪʃ] *n* cera *f* (para suelos).
floor-polisher ['flɔːˌpɒlɪʃəʳ] *n* encerador *m* de piso.
floorshow ['flɔːʃəʊ] *n* (espectáculo *m* de) cabaret *m*, atracciones *fpl* (en la pista de baile).
floorspace ['flɔːspeɪs] *n* espacio *m* útil.
floorwalker ['flɔːˌwɔːkəʳ] *n* (*US*) jefe *mf* de sección (de unos grandes almacenes), vigilante *mf*.
floosie‡, floozie‡ ['fluːzɪ] *n* putilla *f*‡.
flop [flɒp] **1** (*) *n* fracaso *m*. **2** *vi* (**a**) (*drop etc*) dejarse caer pesadamente (*into* en). (**b**) (*: *fail*) fracasar.
flophouse ['flɒphaʊs] *n*, *pl* **flophouses** ['flɒpˌhaʊzɪz] (*US*) pensión *f* de mala muerte, fonducha *f*.
floppy ['flɒpɪ] **1** *adj* flojo, colgante; ~ **disk** disco *m* flexible, disquete *m*, diskette *m*, floppy *m*. **2** *n* = ~ **disk**.
flora ['flɔːrə] *n* flora *f*.
floral ['flɔːrəl] *adj* floral; *tribute etc* de flores, floral.
Florence ['flɒrəns] (**a**) *nf* Florencia. (**b**) *n* (*Geog*) Florencia *f*.
Florentine ['flɒrəntaɪn] **1** *adj* florentino. **2** *n* florentino *m*, -a *f*.
florescence [flə'resns] *n* florescencia *f*.
florid ['flɒrɪd] *adj* florido (*also Liter etc*); *complexion* rojizo, subido de color.
Florida ['flɒrɪdə] *n* Florida *f*.
florin ['flɒrɪn] *n* florín *m*; (*Brit* ††) florín *m* (*moneda de 2 chelines*).
florist ['flɒrɪst] *n* florista *mf*; **~'s (shop)** floristería *f*, florería *f*.
floss [flɒs] *n* (*also* ~ **silk**) cadarzo *m*; seda *f* floja.
Flossie ['flɒsɪ] *nf familiar form of* **Florence**.
flotation [fləʊ'teɪʃən] *n* (*lit*: *of boat etc*) flotación *f*; (*Fin*) (*of shares, loan etc*) emisión *f*; (*of company*) lanzamiento *m*; ~ **tank** tanque *m* de flotación.
flotilla [flə'tɪlə] *n* flotilla *f*.
flotsam ['flɒtsəm] *n* pecio(s) *m*(*pl*), restos *mpl* flotantes; ~ **and jetsam** (*fig*) restos *mpl*, desechos *mpl*.
flounce[1] [flaʊns] *n* (*Sew*) volante *m*.
flounce[2] [flaʊns] *vi*: **to ~ about** moverse violentamente; **to ~ away, to ~ off** alejarse exagerando los movimientos del cuerpo; **to ~ in** entrar con gesto exagerado; **to ~ out** salir enfadado.
flounced [flaʊnst] *adj dress* guarnecido con volantes.
flounder[1] ['flaʊndəʳ] *n* (*Fish*) (*especie de*) platija *f*.
flounder[2] ['flaʊndəʳ] *vi* quedar indeciso, no saber qué hacer (*etc*); estar confuso; (*in a speech etc*) tropezar, perder el hilo, no saber qué decir.
◆**flounder about** *vi* revolcarse, debatirse, forcejear; (*fig*) quedar indeciso.
flour ['flaʊəʳ] *n* harina *f*.
flour-bin ['flaʊəbɪn] *n* harinero *m*.
flourish ['flʌrɪʃ] **1** *n* (**a**) (*with pen*) rasgo *m*, plumada *f*; (*on signature*) rúbrica *f*; (*of hand*) movimiento *m*, ademán *m*; **to do sth with a ~** hacer algo con un ademán triunfal; **we like to do things with a ~** nos gusta hacer las cosas con estilo.
(**b**) (*Mus*: *on guitar*) floreo *m*, (*fanfare*) toque *m* de trompeta.
2 *vt weapon etc* blandir; *stick etc* agitar, menear; (*fig*) hacer gala de, mostrar orgullosamente.
3 *vi* florecer, prosperar; (*plant etc*) crecer rápidamente.
flourishing ['flʌrɪʃɪŋ] *adj* floreciente, próspero; (*Bot*) lozano; (*healthy*) como un reloj.
flour-mill ['flaʊəmɪl] *n* molino *m* de harina.
floury ['flaʊərɪ] *adj* harinoso.
flout [flaʊt] *vt* mofarse de, no hacer caso de; *law* incumplir.
flow [fləʊ] **1** *n* (*stream*) corriente *f*; (*jet*) chorro *m*; (*movement*) flujo *m*, movimiento *m*; (*quantity flowing*) caudal *m*, cantidad *f*; (*direction of* ~) curso *m*; (*of words etc*) torrente *m*; (*of dress etc*) movimiento *m* suave, movimiento *m* elegante; (*of music*) lo suave; **to have a ready ~ of words** hablar con soltura; **to maintain a steady ~** mantener un movimiento constante.
2 *vi* fluir, correr (*along, down* por); (*tide*) subir, crecer; (*hair*) ondear (*in the wind* al viento); (*blood, being shed*) derramarse, (*from wound*) manar, correr; **tears were ~ing down her cheeks** le corrían las lágrimas por las mejillas; **to ~ from** (*fig*) provenir de; **to ~ past** pasar (delante de); **to ~ with** abundar en.
◆**flow away** *vi* irse.
◆**flow back** *vi* refluir.
◆**flow in** *vi* entrar; **money is ~ing in** entra el dinero en grandes cantidades; **people are ~ing in** entra la gente a raudales.
◆**flow into** *vt river* desaguar en, desembocar en.
◆**flow over** *vi* desbordarse.
flowchart ['fləʊtʃɑːt] *n* flujograma *m*, organigrama *m*; (*Comput*) = **flowsheet**.
flow diagram ['fləʊˌdaɪəgræm] *n* = **flowsheet**.
flower ['flaʊəʳ] **1** *n* flor *f*; (*fig*) flor *f*, flor *f* y nata; **in ~** en flor. **2** *attr*: ~ **arrangement** arreglo *m* floral; ~ **children** hijos *mpl* de la flor; ~ **people** gente *f* de la flor, hippies *mpl*; ~ **power** filosofía *f* de la flor; ~ **stall** floristería *f*, florería *f*. **3** *vi* florecer.
flowerbed ['flaʊəbed] *n* cuadro *m*, macizo *m*, reata *f* (*Mex*).
flowered ['flaʊəd] *adj cloth, shirt etc* floreado, de flores.
flower-garden ['flaʊəˌgɑːdn] *n* jardín *m* (de flores).
flowerhead ['flaʊəˌhed] *n* cabezuela *f*.
flowering ['flaʊərɪŋ] **1** *adj* floreciente, en flor. **2** *n* floración *f*.
flowerpot ['flaʊəpɒt] *n* tiesto *m*, maceta *f*.
flower-seller ['flaʊəˌseləʳ] *n* floristo *m*, -a *f*, vendedor *m*, -ora *f* de flores.
flower-shop ['flaʊəʃɒp] *n* floristería *f*, florería *f*.
flower-show ['flaʊəʃəʊ] *n* exposición *f* de flores.
flowery ['flaʊərɪ] *adj* florido (*also fig*); *design* floreado.
flowing ['fləʊɪŋ] *adj movement, stream* corriente; *hair* suelto; *style* fluido, corriente.
flown [fləʊn] *ptp of* **fly**.
flowsheet ['fləʊˌʃiːt] *n* (*Comput*) diagrama *m* de flujo, organigrama *m*, ordinograma *m*; (*Administration*) organigrama *m*.
fl. oz. *abbr of* **fluid ounce**.
F/Lt *abbr of* **Flight Lieutenant** teniente *m* de aviación.
flu [fluː] **1** *n* gripe *f*, trancazo* *m*. **2** *attr*: ~ **vaccine** vacuna *f* antigripal.
fluctuate ['flʌktjʊeɪt] *vi* fluctuar; variar.
fluctuation [ˌflʌktjʊ'eɪʃən] *n* fluctuación *f*; variación *f*.
flue [fluː] *n* humero *m*, cañón *m* de chimenea; (*of lamp, boiler*) tubo *m*.
fluency ['fluːənsɪ] *n* fluidez *f*; elocuencia *f*, facundia *f*; facilidad *f* de lengua; competencia *f*, soltura *f*, dominio *m*; **his ~ in Russian** su dominio del ruso.
fluent ['fluːənt] *adj style* fluido, corriente; *speaker* elocuente, facundo; de lengua fácil; (*in foreign language*) competente, que habla con soltura; **he is ~ in Russian, his Russian is ~** domina el ruso, habla ruso con soltura.
fluently ['fluːəntlɪ] *adv* con fluidez, corrientemente; elocuentemente; **he speaks Russian ~** domina el ruso.
fluff [flʌf] **1** *n* pelusa *f*, lanilla *f*. **2** *vt* (**a**) (*also* **to ~ out**) *feathers* encrespar. (**b**) *shot* errar; (*Theat*) *lines* decir mal.
fluffy ['flʌfɪ] *adj* velloso, lanudo; *hair* encrespado; (*feathered*) plumoso; *surface* que tiene mucha pelusa.
fluid ['fluːɪd] **1** *adj* fluido, líquido; *situation* inestable; *plan* flexible; ~ **ounce** onza *f* líquida. **2** *n* fluido *m*, líquido *m*.
fluidity [fluː'ɪdɪtɪ] *n* fluidez *f*; inestabilidad *f*.
fluke[1] [fluːk] *n* (*Zool*) trematodo *m*; (*Fish*) (especie *f* de) platija *f*.
fluke[2] [fluːk] *n* chiripa *f*, racha *f* de suerte; **to win by a ~** ganar por chiripa.
fluky ['fluːkɪ] *adj* afortunado.
flummox ['flʌməks] *vt* (*disconcert*) desconcertar, confundir; (*startle*) asombrar; **I was completely ~ed** quedé totalmente

despistado.

flung [flʌŋ] *pret and ptp of* **fling.**

flunk* [flʌŋk] (*US*) **1** *vt student* suspender; *course* perder; *exam* no aprobar, salir mal en.

2 *vi* ser suspendido; **I ~ed** me suspendieron.

◆**flunk out*** *vi* salir del colegio (*etc*) sin recibir un título.

flunk(e)y ['flʌŋkɪ] *n* lacayo *m* (*also fig*); adulador *m*, -a *f*.

fluorescence [flʊə'resns] *n* fluorescencia *f*.

fluorescent [flʊə'resnt] *adj* fluorescente; **~ lamp** lámpara *f* fluorescente.

fluoridate ['flʊərɪ,deɪt] *vt* fluorizar.

fluoridation [,flʊərɪ'deɪʃən] *n* fluoración *f*, fluorización *f*.

fluoride ['flʊəraɪd] *n* fluoruro *m*.

fluorine ['flʊəriːn] *n* flúor *m*.

flurry ['flʌrɪ] **1** *n* (**a**) (*nervous haste*) agitación *f*, estado *m* nervioso; **a ~ of activity** un frenesí de actividad; **to be in a ~** estar agitado, estar nervioso.

(**b**) (*of snow etc*) ráfaga *f*.

2 *vt* agitar, hacer nervioso; **to get flurried** ponerse nervioso.

flush¹ [flʌʃ] *vt game* levantar.

◆**flush out** *vt criminal* poner al descubierto; **to ~ sb out** hacer que uno salga, hacer salir a uno.

flush² [flʌʃ] **1** *vt* (*also* **to ~ out**) limpiar con un chorro de agua; *WC* hacer funcionar. **2** *vi* (*WC*) funcionar.

◆**flush away** *vt* (*down sink*) tirar por el fregadero; (*down lavatory*) tirar al retrete; (*down drain*) tirar por la alcantarilla.

flush³ [flʌʃ] **1** *n* (*on face*) rubor *m*; (*in sky*) arrebol *m*; (*of fever*) calor *m* súbito; **in the first ~ of success** en el momento emocionado del triunfo; **in the first ~ of youth** en la primera juventud; **no longer in the first ~ of youth** ya algo entrado en años.

2 *vt*: **to be ~ed with success** estar muy emocionado con el triunfo; **a face ~ed with drink** una cara encendida por el [...]cohol.

[...]*vi* ruborizarse, sonrojarse; (*with anger*) sofocarse, [...]se rojo de ira.

[...] [flʌʃ] *adj* (**a**) (*Tech*) nivelado, igual, parejo, a ras; **to** [...]**ke two things ~** nivelar dos cosas. (**b**) **to be ~‡** tener dinero.

flush⁵ [flʌʃ] *n* (*Cards*) flux *m*.

Flushing ['flʌʃɪŋ] *n* Flesinga *m*.

fluster ['flʌstəʳ] **1** *n* confusión *f*, aturdimiento *m*; conmoción *f*; **to be in a ~** estar azacaneado.

2 *vt* aturdir, poner nervioso, aturrullar; **to get ~ed** aturrullarse.

flute [fluːt] *n* flauta *f*.

fluted ['fluːtɪd] *adj* (*Archit*) estriado, acanalado.

flutist ['fluːtɪst] *n* (*US*) flautista *mf*.

flutter ['flʌtəʳ] **1** *n* (**a**) (*of wings*) revoloteo *m*, aleteo *m*, movimiento *m*; (*of eyelashes*) pestañeo *m*.

(**b**) (*excitement*) emoción *f*, agitación *f*, conmoción *f*; **to cause a ~** agitar los espíritus, causar un revuelo; **to be in a ~** estar muy agitado.

(**c**) (*Brit**) apuesta *f*; **to have a ~ on a race** apostar a un caballo.

2 *vt* agitar, menear, mover ligeramente; (*fig*) agitar.

3 *vi* (*bird etc*) revolotear, aletear; (*butterfly*) mover ligeramente las alas; (*flag*) ondear; (*heart*) palpitar; **a leaf came ~ing down** cayó balanceándose una hoja.

fluty ['fluːtɪ] *adj tone* aflautado.

fluvial ['fluːvɪəl] *adj* fluvial.

flux [flʌks] *n* (*flow*) flujo *m*; **to be in a state of ~** estar continuamente cambiando.

fly¹ [flaɪ] **1** *n* (**a**) mosca *f*; **there's a ~ in the ointment** existe una dificultad; **he's the ~ in the ointment** es la única pega, él es el estorbo; **there are no flies on him** no se chupa el dedo, no tiene ni pelo de tonto; **people were dropping like flies** las personas caían como moscas; **to fish with a ~** pescar a mosca; **he wouldn't hurt a ~** serío incapaz de matar una mosca.

(**b**) (*on trousers*: *also* **flies**) bragueta *f*.

(**c**) **flies** (*Theat*) peine *m*, telar *m*.

(**d**) (*carriage*) calesa *f*.

2 (*irr*: *pret* **flew**, *ptp* **flown**) *vt* (**a**) hacer volar; *plane* pilotar, pilotear (*LAm*), dirigir; *passengers, goods etc* transportar (en avión); *ocean etc* atravesar (en avión); *distance* recorrer (en avión); *flag* enarbolar, llevar, tener izado.

(**b**) *danger* huir (de); *country* abandonar, salir de.

3 *vi* (**a**) volar; (*travel by air*) ir en avión; (*fly a plane*) pilotar un avión; (*flag*) estar izado, ondear; **do you ~ often?** ¿viajas mucho por avión?; **we ~ (with) Iberia** vamos con Iberia; **to send sth ~ing** echar algo a rodar; **to ~ into pieces** hacerse pedazos; **to ~ open** abrirse de repente; **to let ~** (*shoot*) tirar, disparar, hacer fuego; (*emotionally*) desahogarse; (*verbally*) empezar a proferir insultos (*etc*); **to let ~ at** (*shoot*) tirar sobre, disparar contra, (*emotionally*) desahogarse criticando, (*verbally*) empezar a llenar de injurias.

(**b**) (*rush*) lanzarse, precipitarse; **I must ~** tengo que correr; **to ~ at sb** lanzarse sobre uno, arremeter contra uno, (*fig*) ponerse furioso con uno; **to ~ into a rage** encolerizarse; **to ~ to sb's help** ir volando a socorrer a uno; **to ~ to sb's side** volar hacia el lado de uno.

(**c**) (*escape*) evadirse, huir (*from* de); (*vanish*) desaparecer; **to ~ for one's life** salvar la vida huyendo.

◆**fly away** *vi* irse volando.

◆**fly back** *vi* regresar (en avión).

◆**fly in** *vi* llegar (en avión).

◆**fly into** *vt*: **to ~ into London Airport** llegar (en avión) al aeropuerto de Londres.

◆**fly off** *vi* (**a**) (*bird, insect*) alejarse volando; (*in plane*) partir (en avión).

(**b**) (*part*) desprenderse, separarse.

◆**fly out** **1** *vt*: **we shall ~ supplies out to them** les enviaremos provisiones por avión; **the hostages have been flown out** los rehenes han partido en avión.

2 *vi* irse, partir (en avión).

◆**fly over** *vt* sobrevolar.

fly² [flaɪ] *adj* (*esp Brit*) avispado, espabilado.

fly³* [flaɪ] *n*: **on the ~** a hurtadillas; disimuladamente, sigilosamente.

flyaway ['flaɪəweɪ] *adj hair* suelto, lacio; (*frivolous*) frívolo.

fly-blown ['flaɪbləʊn] *adj* lleno de cresas; (*fig*) viejo, gastado.

flybutton ['flaɪ,bʌtn] *n* botón *m* de bragueta.

flyby ['flaɪ,baɪ] *n* (*US*) desfile *m* aéreo.

fly-by-night ['flaɪbaɪnaɪt] **1** *adj* informal, [...] poca confianza, nada confiable. **2** *n* persona *f* informa[...]squivano *m*, -a *f*; persona *f* nada confiable.

flycatcher ['flaɪ,kætʃəʳ] *n* (*Orn*) papamo[...]

fly-fishing ['flaɪ,fɪʃɪŋ] *n* pesca *f* a (*or* c[...]

fly-half ['flaɪ,hɑːf] *n* apertura *m*.

flying ['flaɪɪŋ] **1** *adj* volante, volad[...]o, veloz; **~ bomb** bomba *f* volante; **~ bu**[...]e *m*; **to come out with ~ colours** salir airoso, [...] **doctor** médico *m* rural aerotransportado; **the F~ Du**[...]**man** el holandés errante; **~ fish** pez *m* volante; **~ fortress** fortaleza *f* volante; **~ fox** zorro *m* volador; **~ jump** salto *m* vigoroso; **~ officer** subteniente *m* de aviación; **~ picket** piquete *m* volante (*or* móvil); **~ saucer** platillo *m* volante; **~ squad** brigada *f* móvil, equipo *m* volante; **~ start** salida *f* lanzada; **to get off to a ~ start** entrar con buen pie; **~ suit** traje *m* de vuelo; **~ trapeze** trapecio *m* volador; **~ visit** visita *f* relámpago.

2 *n* el volar, el ir en avión; (*as profession, hobby*) aviación *f*.

flying-boat ['flaɪɪŋbəʊt] *n* hidroavión *m*.

flying-machine ['flaɪɪŋmə,ʃiːn] *n* avión *m*, máquina *f* de volar.

flying time ['flaɪɪŋ'taɪm] *n* horas *fpl* de vuelo, duración *f* del vuelo.

flyleaf ['flaɪliːf] *n*, *pl* **flyleaves** ['flaɪliːvz] hoja *f* de guarda.

flyover ['flaɪ,əʊvəʳ] *n* (**a**) (*Brit*) paso *m* superior, paso *m* elevado, paso *m* a desnivel (*LAm*). (**b**) (*US*) = **flypast**.

flypaper ['flaɪ,peɪpəʳ] *n* papel *m* matamoscas.

flypast ['flaɪpɑːst] *n* (*Brit*) desfile *m* aéreo.

fly-posting [,flaɪ'pəʊstɪŋ] *n* pegada *f* (ilegal) de carteles.

flysheet ['flaɪʃiːt] *n* (*Brit*) hoja *f* volante.

flyspray ['flaɪspreɪ] *n* rociador *m* de moscas.

fly-swat(ter) ['flaɪswɒt(əʳ)] *n* matamoscas *m*.

fly-tipping [,flaɪ'tɪpɪŋ] *n* descarga *f* (ilegal) de basura *etc*.

flyweight ['flaɪweɪt] *n* peso *m* mosca; **light ~** peso *m* mosca ligero.

flywheel ['flaɪwiːl] *n* volante *m* (de motor).

FM *n* (**a**) (*Brit Mil*) *abbr of* **Field Marshal.** (**b**) (*Rad*) *abbr of* **frequency modulation** frecuencia *f* modulada.

FMB *n* (*US*) *abbr of* **Federal Maritime Board.**

FMCS *n* (*US*) *abbr of* **Federal Mediation and Conciliation Services.**

FO (**a**) (*Brit Pol*) *n abbr of* **Foreign Office** Ministerio *m* de Asuntos Exteriores, Min. de AA.EE. (**b**) (*Aer*) *abbr of* **Flying Officer** subteniente *m* de aviación.

fo. *abbr of* **folio** folio *m*.

foal [fəʊl] **1** *n* potro *m*, -a *f*. **2** *vi* parir (*la yegua*).

foam [fəʊm] **1** *n* espuma *f*. **2** *vi* espumar, echar espuma; **to ~ at the mouth** espumajear (de rabia).

foambath ['fəumbɑːθ] *n, pl* **foambaths** ['fəumbɑːðz] baño *m* de espuma.

foam-extinguisher [ˌfəumɪk'stɪŋgwɪʃəʳ] *n* lanzaespumas *m*, extintor *m* de espuma.

foam-rubber ['fəum'rʌbəʳ] *n* espuma *f* de caucho, goma *f* esponjosa, caucho *m* alveolar.

foamy ['fəumɪ] *adj* espumoso.

FOB, f.o.b. *abbr of* **free on board** franco a bordo, f.a.b.

fob [fɒb] **1** *vt*: **to ~ sb off** apartar a uno de un propósito con excusas; **to ~ sb off with sth** persuadir a uno a aceptar algo (de modo fraudulento).

2 *n* (††) faltriquera *f* de reloj.

FOC *abbr of* **free of charge** libre de cargos.

focal ['fəukəl] *adj* focal; **~ distance** distancia *f* focal; **~ plane** plano *m* focal; **~ point** punto *m* focal; (*fig*) centro *m* de atención.

focus ['fəukəs] **1** *n* foco *m*; (*of attention etc*) centro *m*; **to be in ~** estar enfocado; **to be out of ~** estar desenfocado.

2 *vt* enfocar (*on* a); *attention etc* fijar, concentrar (*on* en); **all eyes were ~sed on him** todos le miraban fijamente.

3 *vi* enfocar(se).

◆**focus on** *vt* enfocar a.

fodder ['fɒdəʳ] *n* pienso *m*, forraje *m*; **~ grain** cereales *mpl* forrajeros, cereal-pienso *m*.

FOE *n* (**a**) (*Brit*: *also* **FoE**) *abbr of* **Friends of the Earth**. (**b**) (*US*) *abbr of* **Fraternal Order of Eagles** *sociedad benéfica*.

foe [fəu] *n* (*liter*) enemigo *m*.

foetal, (*US*) **fetal** ['fiːtl] *adj* fetal.

foetus, (*US*) **fetus** ['fiːtəs] *n* feto *m*.

fog [fɒg] **1** *n* niebla *f*; (*fig*) confusión *f*. **2** *vt* (*fig*) *matter* entenebrecer; *person* ofuscar; (*Phot*) velar; *spectacles, window* (*also* **to ~ up**) empañar. **3** *vi* (*fig*: *also* **to ~ up**) empañarse.

fogbank ['fɒgbæŋk] *n* banco *m* de niebla.

fogbound ['fɒgbaund] *adj* inmovilizado por la niebla.

fogey* ['fəugɪ] *n*: **old ~** persona *f* de ideas anticuadas, persona *f* chapada a la antigua, carroza* *m*.

foggy ['fɒgɪ] *adj* nebuloso, brumoso; *day* de niebla; (*Phot*) velado; **it is ~** hay niebla; **I haven't the foggiest** (**idea**) no tengo la más remota idea.

foghorn ['fɒghɔːn] *n* sirena *f* (de niebla).

foglamp ['fɒglæmp] *n* (*Brit*), **foglight** ['fɒglaɪt] *n* (*US*) (*Aut*) faro *m* antiniebla.

fog-signal ['fɒgˌsɪgnl] *n* aviso *m* de niebla.

foible ['fɔɪbl] *n* flaco *m*; manía *f*; debilidad *f*.

foil[1] [fɔɪl] *n* (**a**) (*metal*) hoja *f*, hojuela *f*; (*Culin*) aluminio *m* doméstico. (**b**) (*fig*) contraste *m* (*to* con); **to act as a ~ to sth** servir de contraste con algo, hacer resaltar algo.

foil[2] [fɔɪl] *vt* frustrar.

foil[3] [fɔɪl] *n* (*Fencing*) florete *m*.

foist [fɔɪst] **1** *vt*: **to ~ sth off on sb** encajar algo a uno, lograr con engaño que uno acepte algo; **the job was ~ed on to me** lograron mañosamente que yo me encargara de ello.

2 *vr*: **to ~ o.s. on sb** insistir en acompañar a uno, pegarse a uno.

fol. *abbr of* **folio** folio *m*.

fold[1] [fəuld] *n* (*Agr*) redil *m*, aprisco *m*; **to return to the ~** (*Eccl*) volver al redil de la Iglesia.

fold[2] [fəuld] **1** *n* pliegue *m*, doblez *m*, arruga *f*; (*Geol*) pliegue *m*.

2 *vt* plegar, doblar; *wings* recoger; **to ~ one's arms** cruzar los brazos; **to ~ sb in one's arms** abrazar a uno tiernamente, estrechar a uno contra el pecho; **to ~ sth in a wrapper** envolver algo en una envoltura.

3 *vi* (**a**) plegarse, doblarse.

(**b**) (*fig*) fracasar, terminar; (*Comm*) quebrar, entrar en liquidación; (*Theat*) cerrar.

◆**fold away 1** *vt clothes, newspaper* doblar (*or* plegar) para guardar. **2** *vi* (*table, bed*) plegarse.

◆**fold back** *vt* doblar (hacia abajo), plegar.

◆**fold down 1** *vt* = **fold back**. **2** *vi*: **it ~s down at night** de noche se dobla hacia abajo.

◆**fold in** *vt* (*Culin*) *flour, sugar* mezclar.

◆**fold over** *vt paper* plegar; *blanket* hacer el embozo con.

◆**fold up 1** *vt* doblar, *chair etc* plegar.

2 *vi* (**a**) doblarse, plegarse; **to ~ up** (**with laughter**)* troncharse de risa*. (**b**) (*fig*) = **fold 3** (**b**).

-fold [fəuld] *suf*: *eg* **thirty~** (*adj*) de treinta veces, (*adv*) treinta veces.

fold-away ['fəuldəweɪ] *attr* plegable, plegadizo.

folder ['fəuldəʳ] *n* (*file*) carpeta *f*; (*binder*) carpeta *f* de anillas; (*brochure*) folleto *m*, desplegable *m*; (*of matches*) carterita *f*.

folding ['fəuldɪŋ] *adj* plegable, plegadizo; de tijera; **~ chair** silla *f* de tijera; **~ doors** puertas *fpl* plegadizas; **~ money, ~ stuff*** billetes *mpl* (de banco); **~ rule(r)** metro *m* plegable; **~ seat** asiento *m* plegadizo; **~ table** mesa *f* plegable.

fold-up ['fəuldʌp] *attr* plegable, plegadizo.

foliage ['fəulɪɪdʒ] *n* hojas *fpl*, follaje *m*.

foliation [ˌfəulɪ'eɪʃən] *n* foliación *f*.

folio ['fəulɪəu] *n* folio *m*; (*book*) infolio *m*, libro *m* en folio.

folk [fəuk] **1** *n* (**a**) (*tribe*) nación *f*, tribu *f*, pueblo *m*.

(**b**) (*people in general*; *also* **~s**) gente *f*; **my ~s** mi familia, mis parientes; **the old ~s** los viejos; **hullo ~s!** ¡hola, amigos!; **they're strange ~ here** aquí la gente es algo rara.

2 *adj* folk(lórico), tradicional.

folk-art ['fəukɑːt] *n* arte *m* folklórico.

folkdance ['fəukdɑːns] *n* baile *m* popular, danza *f* tradicional.

folkdancing ['fəukˌdɑːnsɪŋ] *n* baile *m* folklórico.

folklore ['fəuklɔːʳ] *n* folklore *m*, foklor *m*.

folkloric ['fəukˌlɔːrɪk] *adj* folklórico, folclórico.

folkmusic ['fəukˌmjuːzɪk] *n* música *f* folklórica, música *f* popular típica.

folkrock [ˌfəuk'rɒk] *n* folk rock *m*.

folksinger ['fəukˌsɪŋəʳ] *n* cantante *mf* folklorista, cantante *m* típico, cantante *f* típica.

folksong ['fəuksɒŋ] *n* canción *f* popular, canción *f* tradicional.

folksy* ['fəuksɪ] *adj* afectadamente folklorista; que finge ser popular (*or* tradicional *etc*), que se esfuerza por parecer que es del pueblo.

folktale ['fəukteɪl] *n* cuento *m* popular.

folk wisdom ['fəuk'wɪzdəm] *n* saber *m* popular.

foll. *abbr of* **following** siguiente(s), sig., sigs.

follicle ['fɒlɪkl] *n* folículo *m*.

follow ['fɒləu] **1** *vt* (**a**) (*gen*) seguir; *suspect* vigilar, se[illegible] la pista a; (*pursue*) perseguir; **there's sb ~ing us** [illegible] nos viene siguiendo; **the road ~s the coast** la carre[illegible] por la costa; **to ~ sb into a room** entrar en una hab[illegible] detrás de uno; **they ~ed this with threats** tras [illegible] empezaron a amenazarnos.

(**b**) *advice, example* seguir; *person* imitar el ejemplo de; *instructions* seguir; *news* estar al corriente de, estar enterado de; **do you ~ football?** ¿te interesa el fútbol?; **we ~ Borchester** somos hinchas del Borchester.

(**c**) *profession* ejercer.

(**d**) (*understand*) *person* comprender, *argument* seguir el hilo de.

2 *vi* (**a**) (*come behind*) seguir.

(**b**) (*result*) seguirse; resultar; **as ~s** como sigue, a saber; **it ~s that ...** síguese que ..., resulta que ...; **it doesn't ~ at all that ...** no es lógico que ... + *subj*.

(**c**) (*understand*) comprender; **I don't quite ~** no te comprendo del todo.

◆**follow about, follow around** *vt* seguir a todas partes.

◆**follow on** *vi* (**a**) **we'll ~ on behind** nosotros seguiremos, vendremos después. (**b**) **it ~s on from what I said** es la consecuencia lógica de lo que dije.

◆**follow out** *vt idea, plan* llevar a cabo; *order* ejecutar, cumplir; *instructions* seguir.

◆**follow through** *vt shot* terminar, completar; *plan* llevar hasta el fin; *clue* investigar; *matter* perseguir, obtener más detalles sobre; *suggestion* adoptar.

◆**follow up** *vt* = **follow through**; *offer* reiterar; *visit etc* repetir, pasar a la segunda etapa de.

follower ['fɒləuəʳ] *n* (*Pol etc*) partidario *m*, -a *f*, adherente *mf*; (*Sport*) seguidor *m*, -ora *f*, hincha *mf*; (*pej*) secuaz *mf*; (*Philos etc*) discípulo *m*; (*imitator*) imitador *m*, -ora *f*; **~s** (*of prince etc*) séquito *m*; **all the ~s of football** todos los que se interesan por el fútbol; **the ~s of fashion** los que siguen la moda.

following ['fɒləuɪŋ] **1** *adj* siguiente; *wind* en popa; **the ~** lo siguiente.

2 *n* (*Pol etc*) partidarios *mpl*, (*pej*) secuaces *mpl*; (*of prince etc*) séquito *m*; **football has no ~ here** aquí nadie se interesa por el fútbol.

follow-my-leader ['fɒləumaɪ'liːdəʳ] *n juego en el que los participantes hacen lo que alguien manda*.

follow-through ['fɒləu'θruː] *n* continuación *f*.

follow-up ['fɒləu'ʌp] **1** *n* seguimiento *m*; (*Comm etc*) continuación *f*, reiteración *f*. **2** *adj*: (*Telec*) **~ call** llamada *f* de reiteración; **~ interview** entrevista *f* complementaria; **~ letter** carta *f* recordativa; **~ survey** investigación *f* complementaria; **~ visit** visita *f* de reiteración, visita *f* com-

plementaria.
folly ['fɒlɪ] *n* (**a**) locura *f*. (**b**) (*Archit*) disparate *m*.
foment [fəʊ'ment] *vt* fomentar (*also Med*); *revolt etc* provocar, instigar.
fomentation [ˌfəʊmen'teɪʃən] *n* fomentación *f*; fomento *m*.
fond [fɒnd] *adj* (*loving*) cariñoso, afectuoso; (*doting*) demasiado indulgente; *hope* fervoroso; **to be ~ of** *thing* ser aficionado a, tener afición a; *person* tener mucho cariño a; **to be ~ of** + *ger* ser aficionado a + *infin*; **to become** (*or* **grow**) **~ of** *thing* aficionarse a, *person* tomar cariño a.
fondant ['fɒndənt] **1** *adj* delicado; **~ blue** azul *m* pastel. **2** *n* glaseado *m*.
fondle ['fɒndl] *vt* acariciar.
fondly ['fɒndlɪ] *adv* con cariño, afectuosamente; *hope* fervorosamente; *imagine* inocentemente.
fondness ['fɒndnɪs] *n* cariño *m*; afición *f* (*for* a).
font [fɒnt] *n* pila *f* (bautismal); (*Typ*) fundición *f*; (*Comput*) fuente *f*, tipo *m* de letra.
fontanel(le) [ˌfɒntə'nel] *n* fontanela *f*.
food [fuːd] **1** *n* alimento *m*, comida *f*; (*edible matter*) comestible *m*; (*for animals*) pasto *m*, pienso *m*; **to buy ~** comprar víveres, comprar provisiones; **the ~ is good here** aquí se come bien; **the cost of ~** el coste de la alimentación; **she gave him ~** le dio de comer; **he likes plain ~** le gustan las comidas sencillas; **to send ~ and clothing** enviar comestibles y ropa; **to be off one's ~** no tener apetito, estar desganado; **to give sb ~ for thought** dar a uno en qué pensar, dar motivo de reflexión.
2 *attr*: **~ additive** aditivo *m* alimenticio; **~ chain** cadena *f* de alimentación; **~ crop** cosecha *f* de alimentos; **~ mixer** mezcladora *f*, batidora *f*; **~ parcel** paquete *m* de comestibles; **~ prices** precios *mpl* alimenticios; **~ processing** preparación *f* de alimentos; **~ processor** robot *m* de cocina; **~ rationing** racionamiento *m* de víveres; **~ science** ciencia *f* de la alimentación; **~ subsidy** subvención *f* alimenticia; **~ supply** suministro *m* de alimentos; **~ supplies** víveres *mpl*; **~ technology** tecnología *f* de la alimentación.
foodie* ['fuːdɪ] *n* persona *f* que se interesa con entusiasmo en la preparación y consumo de los alimentos; entusiasta *mf* de la comida saludable.
food poisoning ['fuːdˌpɔɪznɪŋ] *n* botulismo *m*, intoxicación *f* alimenticia, toxinfección *f* alimentaria.
foodstuffs ['fuːdstʌfs] *npl* comestibles *mpl*, artículos *mpl* alimenticios.
food-value ['fuːdˌvæljuː] *n* valor *m* alimenticio.
fool[1] [fuːl] **1** *n* (**a**) tonto *m*, -a *f*, imbécil *mf*, zonzo *m*, -a *f* (*LAm*); **you ~!** ¡imbécil!; **some ~ of a minister** algún ministro imbécil; **he's nobody's ~** no le toma el pelo nadie; **to be ~ enough to** + *infin* ser bastante tonto como para + *infin*; **don't be a ~!** ¡no seas tonto!, ¡déjate de tonterías!; **there's no ~ like an old ~** la cabeza blanca y el seso por venir; **to act** (*or* **play**) **the ~** hacer el tonto; **to live in a ~'s paradise** vivir en un mundo de sueños, imaginarse una novela, hacerse ilusiones; **to make a ~ of sb** poner a uno en ridículo, engañar a uno; **to make a ~ of o.s.** ponerse en ridículo; **to send sb on a ~'s errand** enviar a uno a una misión inútil.
(**b**) (*Hist*) bufón *m*.
2 *adj* (*****) tonto.
3 *vt* (*deceive*) engañar, embaucar; (*puzzle*) confundir, dejar perplejo; **you can't ~ me** a mí no me engaña nadie; **you could have ~ed me!** casi lo creí; **you had me properly ~ed there** eso sí que me despistó; **that ~ed nobody** no se dejó engañar nadie por eso; **that ~ed him!** ¡aquello coló!, ¡se lo tragó!
4 *vi* chancear, bromear; **no ~ing** en serio; **no ~?** ¿en serio?, ¿sin bromas?; **I was only ~ing** lo dije en broma; **quit ~ing!** ¡déjate de tonterías!
◆**fool about, fool around** *vi* divertirse, juguetear; hacer el tonto; perder el tiempo neciamente; **to ~ about with** jugar con, (*and damage*) estropear.
◆**fool away** *vt time* perder ociosamente; *money* despilfarrar.
fool[2] [fuːl] *n* (*Brit Culin*: *also* **fruit ~**) puré *m* de frutas con nata (*or* natillas); **gooseberry ~** ≃ puré *m* de grosella con nata (*or* natillas).
foolery ['fuːlərɪ] *n* bufonadas *fpl*; (*nonsense*) tonterías *fpl*.
foolhardiness ['fuːlˌhɑːdɪnɪs] *n* temeridad *f*.
foolhardy ['fuːlˌhɑːdɪ] *adj* temerario.
foolish ['fuːlɪʃ] *adj* tonto, necio; imbécil; ridículo; absurdo; estúpido; imprudente; **~ thing** tontería *f*; **don't be ~** no seas tonto; **that was very ~ of you** en eso fuiste muy imprudente; **I felt very ~** creí haberme puesto en ridículo; **to make sb look ~** hacer que uno parezca ridículo, ridiculizar a uno.
foolishly ['fuːlɪʃlɪ] *adv* tontamente, neciamente; **~, I agreed** como un tonto consentí.
foolishness ['fuːlɪʃnɪs] *n* tontería *f*, necedad *f*; imbecilidad *f*; ridiculez *f*; estupidez *f*; imprudencia *f*.
foolproof ['fuːlpruːf] *adj device* seguro; a toda prueba, a prueba de impericia; *plan etc* infalible, que no tiene fallo, a prueba de tontos.
foolscap ['fuːlskæp] **1** *n* (*approx*) papel *m* tamaño folio. **2** *attr*: **~ envelope** ≃ sobre *m* tamaño folio; **~ sheet** ≃ folio *m*.
foot [fʊt] **1** *n*, *pl* **feet** [fiːt] pie *m*; (*of animal, furniture*) pata *f*; (*of hill, page, stairs etc*) pie *m*; **... my ~!*** ... y un cuerno*, ... y un jamón*; **lady, my ~!*** ¡dama, ni hablar!; **at the ~ of the hill** al pie de la colina; **he's on his feet all day long** está trajinando todo el santo día, no descansa en todo el día; **he's on his feet again** ha vuelto a levantarse y a salir; **it's wet under ~** el suelo está mojado; **to come** (*or* **go**) **on ~** venir (*or* ir) a pie, venir (*or* ir) andando *or* caminando (*LAm*); **to drag one's feet** (*fig*) echarse atrás, hacerse el roncero; **to fall on one's feet** tener suerte, caer de pie; **to find one's feet** acostumbrarse al ambiente; **to get cold feet** perder su entusiasmo (*or* interés *etc*), desanimarse; empezar a tener dudas; **to get one's ~ in the door** abrirse una brecha; **to have one ~ in the grave** estar con un pie en la sepultura; **to have one's feet on the ground** (*fig*) ser realista, ser práctico; **to keep one's feet** mantenerse en pie; **to put one's ~ down** (*Aut*) acelerar, (*fig*) oponerse enérgicamente, adoptar una actitud firme; **to put one's feet up** (*fig*) descansar; **she never put a ~ wrong** lo hizo perfectamente, lo hizo impecablemente; **to put one's ~ in it** meter la pata; **to put one's best ~ forward** animarse a continuar; hacer lo posible por hacer una buena impresión; **to rise to one's feet** ponerse de pie, levantarse; **to set ~ inside sb's door** poner los pies en la casa de uno, pasar el umbral de uno; **to set sth on ~** promover algo, poner algo en marcha; **to set ~ on dry land** poner el pie en tierra firme; **to shoot o.s. in the ~** (*fig*) pegarse un tiro en el pie; **to sit at sb's feet** ser discípulo de uno; **to stand on one's own two feet** volar con sus propias alas; **to start off on the right ~** entrar con buen pie; **it all started off on the wrong ~** todo empezó mal; **to sweep a girl off her feet** enamorar perdidamente a una chica; **to trample sth under ~** pisotear algo; **the children are always under my feet** siempre tengo los niños pegados.
2 (*****) *vt* (**a**) *bill* pagar.
(**b**) **to ~ it*** (*walk*) ir andando, (*dance*) bailar.
footage ['fʊtɪdʒ] *n* (**a**) distancia *f*, extensión *f* (medida en pies). (**b**) (*Cine*) cantidad *f*, extensión *f*; imágenes *fpl*; secuencias *fpl* filmadas.
foot-and-mouth (disease) ['fʊtən'maʊθ(dɪ'ziːz)] *n* fiebre *f* aftosa, glosopeda *f*.
football ['fʊtbɔːl] **1** *n* (*Brit*: *game*) fútbol *m*; (*ball*) balón *m*.
2 *attr*: **~ coupon** (*Brit*) boleto *m* de quinielas; **~ hooligan** (*Brit*) espectador *m* de fútbol violento; **~ hooliganism** (*Brit*) violencia *f* en las gradas; **~ league** (*Brit*) liga *f* de fútbol; **~ player** futbolista *mf*; **~ season** temporada *f* de fútbol.
footballer ['fʊtbɔːlər] *n* futbolista *mf*.
football-pool ['fʊtbɔːlˌpuːl] *n* quinielas *fpl*.
footboard ['fʊtbɔːd] *n* estribo *m*.
footbrake ['fʊtbreɪk] *n* pedal *m* del freno; freno *m* de pie.
footbridge ['fʊtbrɪdʒ] *n* puente *m* peatonal, pasarela *f*.
-footed ['fʊtɪd] *adj* de ... patas; **four~** de cuatro patas; **light~** ligero (de pies).
footer ['fʊtər] (**a**) (*Brit**) fútbol *m*. (**b**) (*Typ, Comput*) pie *m* de página.
-footer ['fʊtər] *n ending in compounds*: **he's a six~** mide 6 pies.
footfall ['fʊtfɔːl] *n* paso *m*, pisada *f*.
foot-fault ['fʊtˌfɔːlt] *n* (*Tennis*) falta *f* de saque.
footgear ['fʊtgɪər] *n* calzado *m*.
foothills ['fʊthɪlz] *npl* estribaciones *fpl*.
foothold ['fʊthəʊld] *n* pie *m* firme, asidero *m* para el pie; **to gain a ~** ganar pie, lograr establecerse.
footing ['fʊtɪŋ] *n* (**a**) (*lit*) pie *m*; **to lose** (*or* **miss**) **one's ~** perder el pie.
(**b**) (*fig*) pie *m*, posición *f*; **on an equal ~** en un mismo pie de igualdad (*with* con); **on a friendly ~** en relaciones amistosas; **on a war ~** en pie de guerra; **to gain a ~** ganar pie, lograr establecerse; **to put a company on a sound financial ~** poner una compañía en un pie financiero firme.

footle ['fu:tl] **1** *vt*: **to ~ away** malgastar. **2** *vi* perder el tiempo, hacer el tonto.

footlights ['fʊtlaɪts] *npl* candilejas *fpl*.

footling ['fu:tlɪŋ] *adj* trivial, insignificante.

footloose ['fʊtlu:s] *adj* libre; (*wandering*) andariego; **~ and fancy-free** libre como el aire.

footman ['fʊtmən] *n, pl* **footmen** ['fʊtmən] *n* lacayo *m*.

footmark ['fʊtmɑ:k] *n* huella *f*, pisada *f*.

footnote ['fʊtnəʊt] *n* nota *f* (al pie de la página).

foot passengers ['fʊt,pæsəndʒəz] *npl* pasajeros *mpl* de a pie.

footpath ['fʊtpɑ:θ] *n, pl* **footpaths** ['fʊtpɑ:ðz] senda *f*, sendero *m*; (*Brit*: *pavement*) acera *f*, vereda *f* (*SC*), banqueta *f* (*Mex*).

footplate ['fʊtpleɪt] *n* (*esp Brit*) plataforma *f* del maquinista.

footprint ['fʊtprɪnt] *n* huella *f*, pisada *f*.

footpump ['fʊtpʌmp] *n* bomba *f* de pie.

footrest ['fʊtrest] *n* apoyapié *m*, reposapiés *m*.

footrot ['fʊtrɒt] *n* uñero *m*.

Footsie* ['fʊtsɪ] *n* = **Financial Times Stock Exchange 100 Index.**

footsie* ['fʊtsɪ] *n*: **to play ~ with** hacer del pie con, acariciar con el pie.

footslog‡ ['fʊtslɒg] *vi* andar, marchar.

footslogger* ['fʊtslɒgə^r] *n* peatón *m*; (*Mil*) soldado *m* de infantería.

foot-soldier ['fʊt,səʊldʒə^r] *n* soldado *m* de infantería.

footsore ['fʊtsɔ:^r] *adj*: **to be ~** tener los pies cansados (*or* doloridos).

footstep ['fʊtstep] *n* paso *m*, pisada *f*; **to follow in sb's ~s** seguir los pasos de uno.

footstool ['fʊtstu:l] *n* escabel *m*, banquillo *m*.

footway ['fʊt,weɪ] *n* acera *f*.

footwear ['fʊtwɛə^r] *n* calzado *m*.

footwork ['fʊtwɜ:k] *n* (*Sport*) juego *m* de piernas.

fop [fɒp] *n* petimetre *m*, currutaco *m*.

foppish ['fɒpɪʃ] *adj* petimetre, litri*.

FOR *abbr of* **free on rail** franco en ferrocarril.

for [fɔ:^r] **1** *prep* (**a**) (*destined for*) para; **hats ~ women** sombreros para mujeres; **is this ~ me?** ¿es esto para mí?; **a job ~ next week** un trabajo para la semana que viene; **we went to Tossa ~ our holidays** fuimos a pasar nuestras vacaciones a Tossa, las vacaciones las pasamos en Tossa; **it's time ~ dinner** es hora de comer; **'Groucho ~ Mayor'** (*slogan*) 'Groucho Alcalde'; **anyone ~ tennis?** ¿hay quien quiera jugar al tenis?; **to write ~ the papers** escribir en los periódicos; **I have news ~ you** tengo que darte una noticia; **it was ~ your good** era para (*or* por) tu bien.

(**b**) (*as, representing*) por; **member ~ Hove** diputado por Hove; **M ~ Madrid** M de Madrid; **a cheque ~ £500** un cheque por valor de 500 libras; **agent ~ Ford cars** distribuidor de automóviles Ford; **will you write ~ me?** ¿quieres escribir en mi nombre?; **I'll go ~ you** yo iré en tu lugar; **if not the government will do it ~ them** si no el gobierno lo hará en su lugar; **they shot him ~ a traitor** le fusilaron por traidor.

(**c**) (*in exchange for*) por; **I'll give you this ~ that** te doy éste por ése; **I sold it ~ £5** lo vendí por 5 libras; **she sold the house ~ several millions** vendió la casa en varios millones; **to exchange one's hat ~ another** cambiar el sombrero por otro; **word ~ word** palabra por palabra; **1 dead ~ every 5 injured** 1 muerto por cada 5 lisiados; **what's the German ~ 'hill'?** ¿cómo se dice en alemán 'colina'?

(**d**) (*in favour of*) **I'm ~ the government** yo estoy a favor del gobierno; **a collection ~ the poor** una colecta a beneficio de los pobres; **the campaign ~ education** la campaña pro (*or* en pro de la) enseñanza; **I'm all ~ it** lo apruebo sin reserva.

(**e**) (*because of*) por, a causa de, con motivo de, debido a; **~ this reason** por esta razón; **famous ~ its church** famoso por su iglesia; **the reason ~ not doing it** la razón por no hacerlo; **we chose it ~ its climate** lo escogimos por su clima; **if it were not ~ him** si no fuera por él; **to shout ~ joy** gritar de alegría.

(**f**) (*purpose*) **what ~?** ¿para qué?, ¿por qué?; **what's this ~?** ¿para qué es esto?, ¿para qué sirve esto?

(**g**) (*bound for*) **he left ~ Ohio** partió para Ohio; **the ship left ~ Vigo** el buque partió (con) rumbo a Vigo; **the train ~ Madrid** el tren de Madrid; **where are you ~ ?** ¿adónde se dirige Vd?

(**h**) (*considering*) **tall ~ his age** alto para su edad.

(**i**) (*in spite of*) **he's nice ~ a policeman** para policía es muy simpático, a pesar de ser policía es muy simpático; **~ all that** pese a todo; *V also* **all.**

(**j**) **oh ~ a horse!** ¡quién tuviera un caballo!

(**k**) (*distance*) **there was nothing to be seen ~ miles** no había nada que ver en muchos kilómetros; **the trail led on ~ many kilometres** el camino siguió por muchos kilómetros.

(**l**) (*time*: *past*) **he was away ~ 2 years** estuvo ausente (durante) 2 años; **was he away ~ long?** ¿estuvo fuera mucho tiempo?; **it has not rained ~ 3 weeks** hace 3 semanas que no llueve, desde hace 3 semanas no llueve; **we went to the seaside ~ the day** fuimos a pasar el día en la playa; (*future*) **I'm going ~ 3 weeks** voy por 3 semanas; **will it be ~ long?** ¿será mucho tiempo?

(**m**) **now ~ it!** ¡ahora!; ¡ya viene!; **he'll be ~ it!** ¡le va a tocar la gorda!; **there's nothing ~ it** no hay más remedio; *V* **but.**

(**n**) (*with verb clause*) **it is ~ you to decide** te toca a ti decidir; **it is best ~ you to go** más vale que vayas; **it is right ~ you to go** es justo que vayas; **it's bad ~ you to smoke so much** te hace daño fumar tanto; **~ this to be possible** para que esto sea posible; **~ him to fail now would be disastrous** sería terrible que fracasara ahora; **he gave orders ~ it to be done** mandó que se hiciera, dio instrucciones para que se hiciera.

2 *conj* pues, ya que.

forage ['fɒrɪdʒ] **1** *n* forraje *m*. **2** *vi* forrajear; **to ~ for** buscar.

foray ['fɒreɪ] *n* correría *f*, incursión *f* (*into* en).

forbad(e) [fə'bæd] *pret of* **forbid.**

forbear [fɔ:'bɛə^r] (*irr*: *V* **bear**) *vi* contenerse; tener paciencia; **to ~ to** + *infin* abstenerse de + *infin*.

forbearance [fɔ:'bɛərəns] *n* paciencia *f*, dominio *m* sobre sí mismo.

forbearing [fɔ:'bɛərɪŋ] *adj* indulgente.

forbears ['fɔ:bɛəz] *npl* antepasados *mpl*.

forbid [fə'bɪd] (*irr*: *pret* **forbad(e)**, *ptp* **forbidden**) *vt* prohibir; **to ~ sth to sb, to ~ sb sth** prohibir algo a uno; **to ~ sb to do sth** prohibir a uno hacer algo; **that's ~den** eso está prohibido; **'smoking ~den'** 'prohibido fumar'; *V* **God.**

forbidden [fə'bɪdn] **1** *ptp of* **forbid. 2** *adj* prohibido.

forbidding [fə'bɪdɪŋ] *adj appearance etc* formidable; imponente; (*dismal*) lúgubre; *person's manner* severo.

forbore [fɔ:'bɔ:^r] *pret of* **forbear.**

forborne [fɔ:'bɔ:n] *ptp of* **forbear.**

force [fɔ:s] **1** *n* (**a**) (*gen*) fuerza *f*; **~ of gravity** fuerza *f* de gravedad; **I can see the ~ of that** comprendo la fuerza de ese argumento; **to resort to ~** recurrir a la fuerza; **to yield to ~** rendirse a la fuerza; **by ~** a la fuerza; **by ~ of** a fuerza de; **by ~ of circumstances** debido a las circunstancias; **by ~ of habit** por costumbre; **by sheer ~** por fuerza mayor; a viva fuerza; **to be in ~** (*Jur*) ser vigente, estar en vigor, (*price*) regir, imperar; **to come in ~** venir en gran número.

(**b**) (*persons*) personal *m*; (*Mil*) cuerpo *m*, fuerza *f*, ejército *m*; **the ~** la policía; **a strong ~ of police** un numeroso cuerpo de policía; **~s** (*Brit Mil*) fuerzas *fpl* armadas; **representatives of the three ~s** (*Mil*) representantes de los tres ejércitos; **to join ~s** coligarse, juntar meriendas.

2 *vt* (**a**) (*compel*) forzar, obligar; *door* forzar, violentar, descerrajar; *pace* apresurar; *plant* hacer madurar temprano; (*cause*) hacer; **to ~ a smile** sonreír forzadamente; **to ~ a country into war** empujar a un país a que declare la guerra; **to ~ sb into a corner** arrinconar a uno, hacer que uno quede arrinconado; **to ~ a car off the road** hacer que un coche salga de la calzada; **to ~ sb into bankruptcy** hacer que uno quiebre.

(**b**) **to ~ sb to do sth** forzar a uno a hacer algo; **I am ~d to say** me veo obligado a decir.

(**c**) **to ~ sth on sb** imponer algo a uno, forzar a uno a aceptar algo; **the decision was ~d on him** se le impuso la decisión; **to ~ open** forzar, abrir por fuerza; **we ~d the secret out of him** logramos por fuerza que nos dijera el secreto; **to ~ a bill through parliament** emplear todos los medios para hacer aprobar por el parlamento un proyecto de ley.

3 *vr*: **to ~ o.s. to** + *infin* hacer un esfuerzo por + *infin*.

◆**force back** *vt* hacer retroceder.

◆**force down** *vt* (**a**) (*gen*) hacer bajar. (**b**) (*Aer*) obligar a aterrizar. (**c**) *food* tragar por fuerza; **can you ~ a bit more down?** ¿cabe todavía un poco más?

◆**force in** *vt* introducir por fuerza.

◆**force out** *vt* (**a**) (*gen*) hacer salir; empujar hacia fuera; **he was ~d out of office** le obligaron a dimitir el cargo. (**b**) *words* pronunciar con dificultad.

forced [fɔːst] *adj smile, laughter* forzado; *landing* forzoso; *march, sale, loan* forzado; *entry* violento, a la fuerza; *error* forzado; ~ **saving** ahorros *mpl* forzados.

force-feed ['fɔːsfiːd] *vt* alimentar a la fuerza.

force-feeding ['fɔːs,fiːdɪŋ] *n* alimentación *f* a la fuerza.

forceful ['fɔːsfʊl] *adj* enérgico, vigoroso.

forcefully ['fɔːsfʊlɪ] *adv* enérgicamente, vigorosamente.

forcefulness ['fɔːsfʊlnɪs] *n* energía *f*, vigor *m*.

force majeure ['fɔːsmə'ʒɜːʳ] *n* fuerza *f* mayor.

forcemeat ['fɔːsmiːt] *n* relleno *m* (de carne picada), picadillo *m* de relleno.

forceps ['fɔːseps] *n sing and pl* fórceps *m*; pinzas *fpl*, tenacillas *fpl*.

forcible ['fɔːsəbl] *adj* (**a**) (*done by force*) a la fuerza, a viva fuerza, por fuerza. (**b**) (*telling*) enérgico, vigoroso.

forcibly ['fɔːsəblɪ] *adv* a la fuerza; enérgicamente.

forcing-house ['fɔːsɪŋ,haʊs] *n, pl* **forcing-houses** ['fɔːsɪŋ,haʊzɪz] (*Agr etc*) maduradero *m*; (*fig*) *instituto etc donde se llevan a cabo cursos intensivos*.

ford [fɔːd] **1** *n* vado *m*, botadero *m* (*Mex*). **2** *vt* vadear.

fordable ['fɔːdəbl] *adj* vadeable.

fore [fɔːʳ] **1** *adv*: ~ **and aft** de popa a proa, por todas partes.

2 *adj* anterior, delantero; (*Naut*) de proa.

3 *n*: **to be at the** ~ ir delante; **to come to the** ~ empezar a destacar.

4 *interj* (*Golf*) ¡atención!

forearm ['fɔːrɑːm] *n* antebrazo *m*.

forebears ['fɔːbɛəz] *npl* = **forbears**.

forebode [fɔː'bəʊd] *vt* presagiar, anunciar.

foreboding [fɔː'bəʊdɪŋ] *n* presagio *m*; presentimiento *m*; **to have a** ~ **that** ... presentir que ...; **to have** ~**s** tener una corazonada.

forecast ['fɔːkɑːst] **1** *n* pronóstico *m*; previsión *f*; **according to all the** ~**s** según todas las previsiones; **what is the** ~ **for the weather?** ¿qué pronóstico hacen del tiempo?

2 (*irr*: *V* **cast**) *vt* pronosticar, prever.

forecaster ['fɔːkɑːstəʳ] *n* (*Econ, Pol, Sport*) pronosticador *m*, -ora *f*; (*Met*) meteorólogo *m*, -a *f*.

forecastle ['fəʊksl] *n* camarote *m* de la tripulación; (*Hist*) castillo *m* de proa.

foreclose [fɔː'kləʊz] *vti* extinguir el derecho de redimir (una hipoteca).

foreclosure [fɔː'kləʊʒəʳ] *n* extinción *f* del derecho de redimir (una hipoteca).

forecourt ['fɔːkɔːt] *n* atrio *m*, antepatio *m*; (*of garage*) patio *m*.

foredoomed [fɔː'duːmd] *adj*: **to be** ~ **to** + *infin* estar condenado de antemano a + *infin*.

forefathers ['fɔː,fɑːðəz] *npl* antepasados *mpl*.

forefinger ['fɔː,fɪŋgəʳ] *n* (dedo *m*) índice *m*.

forefoot ['fɔːfʊt] *n, pl* **forefeet** ['fɔːfiːt] mano *f*, pie *m* delantero, pata *f* delantera.

forefront ['fɔːfrʌnt] *n*: **to be in the** ~ estar en la vanguardia (*of* de); estar en primer plano.

foregather [fɔː'gæðəʳ] *vi* reunirse.

forego [fɔː'gəʊ] (*irr*: *pret* **forewent**, *ptp* **foregone**) *vt* pasarse sin, privarse de, renunciar a.

foregoing ['fɔːgəʊɪŋ] *adj* anterior, precedente.

foregone ['fɔːgɒn] *adj*: ~ **conclusion** resultado *m* inevitable.

foreground ['fɔːgraʊnd] **1** *n* primer plano *m*, primer término *m*; **in the** ~ en primer término. **2** *vt* traer al primer plano; destacar, subrayar.

forehand ['fɔːhænd] **1** *n* directo *m*, derechazo *m*. **2** *attr* directo.

forehead ['fɒrɪd] *n* frente *f*.

foreign ['fɒrɪn] *adj* (**a**) extranjero; *relations, trade etc* exterior; ~ **agent** agente *m* extranjero, agente *f* extranjera; ~ **aid** ayuda *f* exterior; ~ **bill** letra *f* sobre el exterior; ~ **currency** moneda *f* extranjera, divisas *fpl*; ~ **debt** deuda *f* externa; ~ **exchange** divisas *fpl*; ~ **exchange dealer** tratante *m* de divisas; ~ **exchange market** mercado *m* de divisas; ~ **investment** inversión *f* extranjera; inversión *f* en el extranjero; **F**~ **Legion** Legión *f* Extranjera; **F**~ **Minister, F**~ **Secretary** Ministro *m*, -a *f* de Asuntos Exteriores; **F**~ **Ministry, F**~ **Office** (*Brit*) Ministerio *m* de Asuntos Exteriores; ~ **policy** política exterior; **F**~ **Service** Servicio *m* Exterior (*Sp*); ~ **trade** comercio *m* exterior.

(**b**) *body* extraño; (*belonging to sb else*) ajeno (*to* a); **deceit is** ~ **to his nature** no cabe en él el engaño, el engaño es ajeno a su modo de ser.

foreigner ['fɒrɪnəʳ] *n* extranjero *m*, -a *f*.

foreknowledge ['fɔː'nɒlɪdʒ] *n* presciencia *f*; **to have** ~ **of sth** saber algo de antemano.

foreland ['fɔːlənd] *n* cabo *m*, promontorio *m*.

foreleg ['fɔːleg] *n* pata *f* delantera, brazo *m*.

forelock ['fɔːlɒk] *n* guedeja *f*; **to take time by the** ~ tomar la ocasión por los pelos.

foreman ['fɔːmən] *n, pl* **foremen** ['fɔːmən] (*of workers*) capataz *m*, caporal *m* (*Mex*); mayoral *m*; (*Jur*) presidente *m* (del jurado).

foremast ['fɔːmɑːst] *n* (palo *m*) trinquete *m*.

foremost ['fɔːməʊst] *adj* primero, delantero; (*outstanding*) primero, principal.

forename ['fɔːneɪm] *n* nombre *m*, nombre *m* de pila.

forenoon ['fɔːnuːn] *n* mañana *f*.

forensic [fə'rensɪk] *adj* forense; *medicine* legal, forense.

foreplay ['fɔːpleɪ] *n* caricias *fpl* estimulantes, excitación *f* preliminar.

forequarters ['fɔː,kwɔːtəz] *npl* cuartos *mpl* delanteros.

forerunner ['fɔː,rʌnəʳ] *n* precursor *m*, -ora *f*.

foresail ['fɔːseɪl] *n* trinquete *m*.

foresee [fɔː'siː] (*irr*: *V* **see**) *vt* prever.

foreseeable [fɔː'siːəbl] *adj* previsible; **in the** ~ **future** hasta donde se pueda ver.

foreseeably [fɔː'siːəblɪ] *adv* previsiblemente.

foreshadow [fɔː'ʃædəʊ] *vt* prefigurar, anunciar; presagiar; (*person*) prever.

foreshore ['fɔːʃɔːʳ] *n* playa *f* (entre los límites de pleamar y bajamar).

foreshorten [fɔː'ʃɔːtn] *vt* escorzar.

foreshortening [fɔː'ʃɔːtnɪŋ] *n* escorzo *m*.

foresight ['fɔːsaɪt] *n* previsión *f*; **lack of** ~ imprevisión *f*, falta *f* de precaución.

foreskin ['fɔːskɪn] *n* prepucio *m*.

forest ['fɒrɪst] **1** *n* bosque *m*; (*large, dense*) selva *f*. **2** *attr* forestal, del bosque; ~ **fire** incendio *m* forestal, incendio *m* de bosque; ~ **ranger** = **forester**; ~ **track**, ~ **trail** camino *m* forestal.

forestall [fɔː'stɔːl] *vt* anticiparse a, adelantarse a (e impedir).

forester ['fɒrɪstəʳ] *n* (*expert*) ingeniero *m* de montes; (*keeper*) guardabosques *m*.

forestry ['fɒrɪstrɪ] **1** *n* silvicultura *f*; (*as Univ course*) ciencias *fpl* forestales.

2 *attr*: **F**~ **Commission** (*Brit*) ≈ Comisión *f* del Patrimonio Forestal.

foretaste ['fɔːteɪst] *n* anticipo *m*, muestra *f*.

foretell [fɔː'tel] (*irr*: *V* **tell**) *vt* (*predict*) predecir, pronosticar; (*presage*) presagiar.

forethought ['fɔːθɔːt] *n* prevención *f*, previsión *f*; (*pej*) premeditación *f*.

forever [fər'evəʳ] *adv* (**a**) (*incessantly*) constantemente, sin cesar. (**b**) (*for always*) para siempre.

forewarn [fɔː'wɔːn] *vt* prevenir; **to be** ~**ed** estar prevenido, precaverse; ~**ed is forearmed** hombre prevenido vale por dos.

foreword ['fɔːwɜːd] *n* prefacio *m*.

forfeit ['fɔːfɪt] **1** *n* (*loss*) pérdida *f*; (*fine*) multa *f*; (*penalty*) pena *f*; (*in games*) prenda *f*; ~**s** juego *m* de prendas. **2** *vt* perder (el derecho a).

forfeiture ['fɔːfɪtʃəʳ] *n* pérdida *f*.

forgather [fɔː'gæðəʳ] *vi* reunirse.

forgave [fə'geɪv] *pret of* **forgive**.

forge[1] [fɔːdʒ] **1** *n* (*fire*) fragua *f*; (*smithy*) herrería *f*; (*ironworks*) fundición *f*, fundidora *f* (*LAm*).

2 *vt* (**a**) *metal* forjar, fraguar; *friendship, plan, unity etc* fraguar. (**b**) (*falsify*) falsificar, falsear, contrahacer.

forge[2] [fɔːdʒ] *vi*: **to** ~ **ahead** avanzar constantemente; adelantarse muchísimo (*of* a).

forger ['fɔːdʒəʳ] *n* falsificador *m*, -ora *f*, falsario *m*, -a *f*.

forgery ['fɔːdʒərɪ] *n* falsificación *f*.

forget [fə'get] (*irr*: *pret* **forgot**, *ptp* **forgotten**) **1** *vt* olvidar, olvidarse de; **I forgot my umbrella in a train** dejé el paraguas en un tren; ~ **it!** ¡no se preocupe!; ¡no importa!; **and don't you** ~ **it!** ¡y que no se te olvide esto!; **never to be forgotten** inolvidable; **to** ~ **to do sth** olvidarse de hacer algo; **I forgot all about it** se me olvidó por completo; **I forgot to tell you why** se me olvidó decirte por qué; **if there's no money, you can** ~ **(about) the new car** si no hay dinero, puedes olvidarte del nuevo coche.

2 *vi* olvidarse; **I** ~ no recuerdo, me he olvidado; **but I forgot** pero se me olvidó.

3 *vr*: **to** ~ **o.s.** propasarse, olvidar los buenos modales, pasarse (*LAm*); **you** ~ **yourself, sir!** ¡prudencia, caballero!

◆**forget about** *vt* olvidarse de; **let's** ~ **about it!** ¡pelillos a

la mar!
forgetful [fə'getfʊl] *adj character* olvidadizo, desmemoriado; descuidado; ~ **of all else** olvidando todo lo demás, sin hacer caso de todo lo demás; **he's terribly** ~ tiene un tremendo despiste, tiene pésima memoria.
forgetfulness [fə'getfʊlnɪs] *n* olvido *m*, falta *f* de memoria; descuido *m*; (*absentmindedness*) despiste *m*.
forget-me-not [fə'getmɪnɒt] *n* nomeolvides *f*.
forgettable [fə'getəbl] *adj* olvidable; digno de ser olvidado.
forgivable [fə'gɪvəbl] *adj* perdonable.
forgive [fə'gɪv] (*irr*: *V* **give**) *vt* perdonar, disculpar (*LAm*); **to** ~ **sb** (**for**) **sth** perdonar algo a uno, perdonar a uno por algo.
forgiven [fə'gɪvn] *ptp of* **forgive.**
forgiveness [fə'gɪvnɪs] *n* (*pardon*) perdón *m*; (*compassion*) misericordia *f*.
forgiving [fə'gɪvɪŋ] *adj* perdonador, misericordioso; **to feel** ~ estar dispuesto a perdonar.
forgo [fɔː'gəʊ] (*irr*: *V* **go**) *vt* = **forego.**
forgot [fə'gɒt] *pret of* **forget.**
forgotten [fə'gɒtn] *ptp of* **forget.**
fork [fɔːk] **1** *n* (*at table*) tenedor *m*; (*Agr*) horca *f*, horquilla *f*; (*Mech etc*) horquilla *f*; (*of cycle*) tijera *f*; (*in road*) bifurcación *f*, empalme *m* (*LAm*); (*Anat*) horcajadura *f*, entrepierna *f*; (*in river*) horcajo *m*; (*of tree*) horcadura *f*.
2 *vt* cultivar con horquilla.
3 *vi* (*road*) bifurcarse, hacer empalme (*LAm*); ~ **right for Oxford** tuerza a la derecha para ir a Oxford.
◆**fork out*** **1** *vt* desembolsar (de mala gana).
2 *vi* aflojar la pasta* (*for* para comprar).
◆**fork over** = **fork 2.**
◆**fork up** *vt* (**a**) *soil* remover con la horquilla. (**b**) = **fork out 1.**
forked [fɔːkt] *adj* ahorquillado, bifurcado; *lightning* en zigzag; *tail* hendido; *tongue* bífido.
fork-lift ['fɔːklɪft] *attr*: ~ **truck** carretilla *f* elevadora, carretilla *f* de horquilla.
forlorn [fə'lɔːn] *adj* abandonado, desamparado; *appearance* de abandono; **to look** ~ (*person*) tener aspecto triste; **why so** ~? ¿por qué tan triste?; ~ **hope** empresa *f* desesperada; esperanza *f* que tiene poca probabilidad de verse realizada.
forlornly [fə'lɔːnlɪ] *adv* tristemente; con aire de abandono.
form [fɔːm] **1** *n* (**a**) (*shape, style, type, method etc*; *also Liter, Gram*) forma *f*; **a new** ~ **of government** un nuevo sistema de gobierno; **the same thing in a new** ~ la misma cosa bajo una nueva forma; **choose another** ~ **of words** busque otra expresión; **it took the** ~ **of a cash prize** consistió en un premio en metálico; **what** ~ **will the ceremony take?** ¿en qué consistirá la ceremonia?
(**b**) (*shape vaguely seen*) figura *f*, bulto *m*.
(**c**) (*Brit Scol*) clase *f*.
(**d**) (*Brit*: *bench*) banco *m*.
(**e**) (*document*) hoja *f*, formulario *m*; **to fill up a** ~ llenar una hoja; **has he got any** ~?* ¿tiene antecedentes penales?; *V* **application.**
(**f**) (*customary method*) forma *f*; **in due** ~ en la debida forma, en la forma reglamentaria; **that is common** ~ eso es muy corriente; **what's the** ~? ¿qué es lo que hemos de hacer?
(**g**) (*formality*) **for** ~**'s sake** por pura fórmula, para salvar las apariencias.
(**h**) (*behaviour*) **it's bad** ~ **to** + *infin* es de mal gusto + *infin*, es de mala educación + *infin*.
(**i**) (*condition*) estado *m* físico; **to be in good** ~, **to be on** ~ (*Sport*) estar en forma, (*be witty*) estar de vena; **to be out of** ~ estar desentrenado.
(**j**) **to study** (**the**) ~ (*Brit Racing*) estudiar resultados anteriores.
2 *vt* formar; *habit* adquirir; *body* formar, integrar, formar parte de; *company* fundar, establecer; *plan* concebir; *idea* hacerse; *impression, opinion* formarse; *queue* hacer; **to** ~ **the plural** formar el plural; **to** ~ **a government** formar gobierno; **those who** ~ **the group** los que integran el grupo.
3 *vi* formarse; **an idea** ~**ed in his mind** una idea tomó forma en su mente; **how do ideas** ~? ¿cómo se forman las ideas?
◆**form up** **1** *vt troops* formar. **2** *vi* alinearse, (*Mil*) formar.
formal ['fɔːməl] *adj* formal; *person's manner* ceremonioso, protocolario, estirado; *person's character* etiquetero; *greeting* ceremonioso; *visit* de cumplido, oficial; *education etc* convencional, regular; *proposal* formal, oficial; *function* protocolario; *dance, dress* de etiqueta; (*relating to form*) formal; ~ **acceptance** aceptación *f* formal; ~ **denial** negación *f* formal; **don't be so** ~! ¡no te andes con tantos cumplidos!; **there was no** ~ **agreement** no hubo contrato en forma.
formaldehyde [fɔː'mældɪhaɪd] *n* formaldehido *m*.
formalin(e) ['fɔːməlɪn] *n* formalina *f*.
formalism ['fɔːməlɪzəm] *n* formalismo *m*.
formalist ['fɔːməlɪst] **1** *adj* formalista. **2** *n* formalista *mf*.
formality [fɔː'mælɪtɪ] *n* (**a**) (*of occasion*) ceremonia *f*, lo ceremonioso; (*of person*) lo etiquetero; (*of dress etc*) etiqueta *f*; **with all due** ~ en la debida forma; **it's a mere** ~ es pura fórmula.
(**b**) **formalities** ceremonias *fpl*; formalidades *fpl*; requisitos *mpl*; **first there are certain formalities** primero hay ciertos requisitos; **let's do without the formalities** prescindamos de los trámites de costumbre.
formalize ['fɔːməlaɪz] *vt* formalizar.
formally ['fɔːməlɪ] *adv greet etc* ceremoniosamente; *open, visit* oficialmente; *agree etc* en forma.
format ['fɔːmæt] **1** *n* formato *m*. **2** *attr*: ~ **line** línea *f* de formato. **3** *vt* formatear.
formation [fɔː'meɪʃən] **1** *n* formación *f*; **in battle** ~ en orden de batalla. **2** *attr*: ~ **flying** vuelo *m* en formación.
formative ['fɔːmətɪv] **1** *adj* formativo. **2** *n* formativo *m*.
formatting ['fɔːmætɪŋ] *n* formateado *m*, formateo *m*, formación *f*.
former ['fɔːməʳ] **1** *adj* (**a**) (*of two*) primero, anterior; **your** ~ **idea** su primera idea.
(**b**) (*earlier*) antiguo; **a** ~ **seat of government** una antigua sede del gobierno.
(**c**) (*of person*) ex, que fue; ~ **president** ex presidente *m*; **a** ~ **ambassador in Lima** embajador que fue en Lima.
2 *pron*: **the** ~ (... **the latter**) aquél *etc* (... éste *etc*).
formerly ['fɔːməlɪ] *adv* antes, antiguamente.
form feed ['fɔːm,fiːd] *n* salto *m* de página.
formic ['fɔːmɪk] *adj*: ~ **acid** ácido *m* fórmico.
Formica [fɔː'maɪkə] ® *n* formica ® *f*.
formidable ['fɔːmɪdəbl] *adj* formidable.
formless ['fɔːmlɪs] *adj* informe.
formula ['fɔːmjʊlə] *n*, *pl* ~**s** *or* **formulae** ['fɔːmjʊliː] fórmula *f*.
formulaic [,fɔːmjʊ'leɪɪk] *adj* formulaico, formulario.
formulate ['fɔːmjʊleɪt] *vt* formular.
formulation [,fɔːmjʊ'leɪʃən] *n* formulación *f*.
fornicate ['fɔːnɪkeɪt] *vi* fornicar.
fornication [,fɔːnɪ'keɪʃən] *n* fornicación *f*.
forsake [fə'seɪk] (*irr*: *pret* **forsook**, *ptp* **forsaken**) *vt person etc* abandonar, dejar, desamparar; *plan* renunciar a; *belief* renegar de; **he forsook Seville for Madrid** abandonó Sevilla y se fue a vivir a Madrid.
forsaken [fə'seɪkən] *ptp of* **forsake.**
forsook [fə'sʊk] *pret of* **forsake.**
forsooth [fə'suːθ] *adv* (†† *or hum*) en verdad; (*excl*) ~! ¡caramba!
forswear [fɔː'swɛəʳ] (*irr*: *V* **swear**) **1** *vt* abjurar de, renunciar a. **2** *vr*: **to** ~ **o.s.** perjurarse.
forsythia [fɔː'saɪθɪə] *n* forsitia *f*.
fort [fɔːt] *n* fuerte *m*, fortín *m*; **to hold the** ~ (*fig*) defenderse, seguir en su puesto, encargarse del trabajo (temporalmente); **hold the** ~ **till I get back** hazte cargo hasta que yo regrese.
forte ['fɔːtɪ, (*US*) fɔːt] *n* fuerte *m*; (*Mus*) forte *m*.
forth [fɔːθ] *adv*: **and so** ~ etcétera; y así sucesivamente; **from this day** ~ de aquí en adelante; *V* **back** *etc*.
forthcoming [fɔːθ'kʌmɪŋ] *adj* (**a**) (*approaching*) venidero, próximo; *book etc* de próxima aparición, en preparación.
(**b**) (*available*) disponible; **if help is** ~ si nos mandan socorros, si nos ayudan; **if funds are** ~ si nos facilitan fondos; **no answer was** ~ no hubo respuesta.
(**c**) *character* afable, comunicativo; **he's not very** ~ no dice mucho; **he's not** ~ **with strangers** tiene poca confianza con los desconocidos.
forthright ['fɔːθraɪt] *adj person* directo, franco; enérgico; *answer etc* terminante; *refusal* rotundo.
forthwith ['fɔːθ'wɪθ] *adv* (*then and there*) en el acto; (*without delay*) sin dilación.
fortieth ['fɔːtɪɪθ] *adj* cuadragésimo; cuarenta; **the** ~ **anniversary** el cuarenta aniversario.
fortification [,fɔːtɪfɪ'keɪʃən] *n* fortificación *f*.
fortified ['fɔːtɪfaɪd] *adj wine* encabezado.
fortify ['fɔːtɪfaɪ] **1** *vt* (*Mil*) fortificar; (*strengthen*) fortalecer; *wine* encabezar; *person* vigorizar, fortalecer; **to** ~ **sb in a belief** confirmar la opinión que tiene uno.
2 *vr*: **to** ~ **o.s.** (*fig*) fortalecerse.

fortitude ['fɔːtɪtjuːd] *n* fortaleza *f*, entereza *f*, valor *m*.
fortnight ['fɔːtnaɪt] *n* (*esp Brit*) quince días *mpl*, quincena *f*; **today ~** de hoy en quince días.
fortnightly ['fɔːtnaɪtlɪ] (*esp Brit*) **1** *adj* que sale (*etc*) cada quince días, quincenal. **2** *adv* cada quince días, quincenalmente.
FORTRAN, Fortran ['fɔːtræn] *n* (*Comput*) *abbr of* **formula translator** FORTRAN *m*, Fortran *m*.
fortress ['fɔːtrɪs] *n* fortaleza *f*, plaza *f* fuerte, alcázar *m*.
fortuitous [fɔː'tjuːɪtəs] *adj* fortuito, casual.
fortuitously [fɔː'tjuːɪtəslɪ] *adv* fortuitamente, por casualidad.
fortunate ['fɔːtʃənɪt] *adj* afortunado; (*happy*) dichoso, feliz; **to be ~** (*person*) tener suerte; **that was ~ for you** en eso tuviste suerte.
fortunately ['fɔːtʃənɪtlɪ] *adv* afortunadamente.
fortune ['fɔːtʃən] *n* (**a**) (*luck, fate*) fortuna *f*, suerte *f*; **by good ~** por fortuna; **the ~s of war** las vicisitudes de la guerra, las peripecias de la guerra; **we had the good ~ to find him** tuvimos la suerte de encontrarle; **he restored the company's ~s** restableció la prosperidad de la empresa, devolvió el éxito a la compañía; **to tell sb's ~** decir a uno la buenaventura; **to try one's ~** probar fortuna.
(**b**) (*money*) fortuna *f*, caudal *m*; **to come into a ~** heredar una fortuna; **to cost a ~** valer un dineral; **to make a ~** enriquecerse, hacer su pacotilla; **to marry a ~** casarse con una mujer acaudalada.
fortune-hunter ['fɔːtʃən,hʌntəʳ] *n* (*man*) cazador *m* de dotes, cazadotes *m*; (*woman*) mujer *f* que busca un marido rico.
fortune-teller ['fɔːtʃən,teləʳ] *n* adivina *f*.
fortune-telling ['fɔːtʃən,telɪŋ] *n* adivinación *f*.
forty ['fɔːtɪ] *adj* cuarenta; **the forties** (*eg 1940s*) los años cuarenta; **to be in one's forties** tener más de cuarenta años, ser cuarentón.
fortyish ['fɔːtɪɪʃ] *adj* de unos cuarenta años.
forum ['fɔːrəm] *n* foro *m*; (*fig*) tribunal *m*, foro *m*.
forward ['fɔːwəd] **1** *adj* (**a**) (*front*) delantero; *position* (*Mil etc*) avanzado; (*Naut*) de proa; *movement* progresivo, de avance; *gears* de avance; **~ line** línea *f* delantera; **~ pass** pase *m* adelantado.
(**b**) *season, crop* adelantado; precoz.
(**c**) *person* atrevido, fresco, descarado.
(**d**) (*Comm*) **~ buying** compra *f* a término, compras *fpl* para el futuro; **~ delivery** entrega *f* en fecha futura; **~ market** mercado *m* de futuros, mercado *m* forward; **~ planning** planificación *f*; **~ sales** ventas *fpl* que deben efectuarse en fecha posterior.
2 *n* (*Sport*) delantero *m*, -a *f*.
3 *vt* (**a**) (*send*) enviar; (*re-address*) hacer seguir; **'to be ~ed', 'please ~'** 'se ruega hacer seguir'; **~ing address** dirección *f* a la que han de hacerse seguir las cartas; **she left no ~ing address** no dejó dirección; **~ing agent** agente *mf* de tránsito, agente *mf* de transporte.
(**b**) (*promote*) promover, avanzar; favorecer.
forward-looking ['fɔːwəd,lʊkɪŋ] *adj* (**a**) *plan etc* con miras al futuro. (**b**) *person* previsor; consciente de las posibilidades futuras; (*Pol*) progresista.
forward(s) ['fɔːwəd(z)] *adv* adelante, hacia adelante; (*Naut*) hacia la proa; **~!** ¡adelante!; **~ march!** de frente ¡mar!; **the lever is placed well ~** la palanca está colocada bastante hacia adelante; **from that day ~** desde ese día en adelante, a partir de entonces; **to go ~** ir hacia adelante, avanzar; (*fig*) progresar, hacer progresos.
forwardness ['fɔːwədnɪs] *n* (**a**) (*of crop etc*) precocidad *f*. (**b**) (*pertness*) frescura *f*, descaro *m*.
forwent [fɔː'went] *pret of* **forgo**.
fossil ['fɒsl] **1** *adj* fósil; **~ fuel** combustible *m* fósil. **2** *n* fósil *m*.
fossilized ['fɒsɪlaɪzd] *adj* fosilizado.
foster ['fɒstəʳ] *vt* (**a**) (*encourage*) fomentar, promover; (*aid*) favorecer; *hope* alentar. (**b**) *child* criar, acoger en una familia.
fosterage ['fɒstərɪdʒ] *n* (*US*), **fostering** ['fɒstərɪŋ] *n* acogimiento *m* familiar.
foster-brother ['fɒstə,brʌðəʳ] *n* hermano *m* de leche.
foster-home ['fɒstəhəʊm] *n* casa *f* cuna, familia *f* adoptiva.
foster-mother ['fɒstə,mʌðəʳ] *n* madre *f* adoptiva; (*wet-nurse*) ama *f* de leche.
fought [fɔːt] *pret and ptp of* **fight**.
foul [faʊl] **1** *adj* (*dirty*) sucio, puerco; (*disgusting*) asqueroso; (*of bad quality*) horrible; (*morally vile*) vil, horrible; *air* viciado; *blow, language* sucio; *breath* fétido; *calumny* vil; *smell* insoportable; *weather* feo, horrible; **to fall ~ of** *person* indisponerse con, ponerse a malas con, *rule* infringir; **to fall ~ of the law** tener un lío con la justicia; **someone is sure to cry '~'** es seguro que alguien dirá que no hemos jugado limpio.
2 *n* (*Sport*) falta *f* (*on* contra).
3 *vt* (**a**) (*dirty*) ensuciar; *good name, one's nest* manchar. (**b**) (*block*) atascar, obstruir; (*catch up in*) enredarse en; (*hit*) chocar contra.
(**c**) (*Sport*) cometer una falta contra.
4 *vi* (**a**) (*Sport*) cometer falta. (**b**) (*rope etc*) enredarse.
◆**foul up*** *vt* armar un lío con*, liar*, embrollar; joder‡; *relationship* estropear.
foulmouthed ['faʊl'maʊðd] *adj* malhablado.
foul play ['faʊl,pleɪ] *n* (*Sport*) mala jugada *f*, jugada *f* sucia; (*Jur*) muerte *f* violenta; intervención *f* siniestra.
foul-smelling ['faʊl'smelɪŋ] *adj* hediondo.
foul-tempered ['faʊl'tempəd] *adj*: **to be ~** (*habitually*) ser un cascarrabias; (*on one occasion*) estar malhumorado.
foul-up* ['faʊlʌp] *n* (*US*) lío* *m*, embrollo *m*, follón* *m*.
found[1] [faʊnd] *pret and ptp of* **find**.
found[2] [faʊnd] *vt* fundar, establecer; *fortune* crear; **a statement ~ed on fact** una declaración basada en hechos.
found[3] [faʊnd] *vt* (*Tech*) fundir.
foundation [faʊn'deɪʃən] **1** *n* (**a**) (*act*) fundación *f*, establecimiento *m*; creación *f*.
(**b**) (*basis*) base *f*, fundamento *m*; **statement devoid of ~** declaración *f* que carece de base.
(**c**) (*make-up*) maquillaje *m* de fondo, base *f*.
(**d**) **~s** (*Archit*) cimientos *mpl*; **to lay the ~s** echar los cimientos (*of* de; *also fig*).
2 *attr*: **~ course** curso *m* de base; **~ cream** crema *f* base; **~ garment** corsé *m*; **~ stone** (*Brit*) primera piedra *f*; (*fig*) piedra *f* angular.
founder[1] ['faʊndəʳ] *n* fundador *m*, -ora *f*; **~ member** (*Brit*) miembro *m* fundador, miembro *f* fundadora.
founder[2] ['faʊndəʳ] *vi* irse a pique, hundirse; (*fig*) fracasar (*on* debido a).
founding ['faʊndɪŋ] **1** *adj*: **F~ Fathers** (*US*) Padres *mpl* Fundadores. **2** *n* fundación *f*.
foundling ['faʊndlɪŋ] *n* niño *m* expósito, niña *f* expósita, inclusero *m*, -a *f*; **~ hospital** inclusa *f*.
foundry ['faʊndrɪ] *n* fundición *f*, fundidora *f* (*LAm*).
fount [faʊnt] *n* (**a**) (*liter: spring*) fuente *f*, manantial *m*; **~ of justice** (*fig*) fuente *f* de justicia. (**b**) (*Brit Typ*) fundición *f*, familia *f* (de la letra).
fountain ['faʊntɪn] *n* (*natural*) fuente *f*, manantial *m* (*also fig*); (*artificial*) fuente *f*, surtidor *m*; (*jet*) chorro *m*.
fountainhead ['faʊntɪnhed] *n* fuente *f*, origen *m*; **to go to the ~** acudir a la propia fuente.
fountain-pen ['faʊntɪnpen] *n* estilográfica *f*, plumafuente *f* (*LAm*).
four [fɔːʳ] **1** *adj* cuatro. **2** *n* cuatro *m*; **to be on all ~s with** (*thing*) concordar con, estar en completa armonía con; **to go on all ~s** ir a gatas; **to form ~s** formar a cuatro; **to make up a ~ for bridge** completar los cuatro para bridge; **~-figure debt** deuda *f* de 1000 libras o más; **~-~ time** compás *m* de cuatro por cuatro; **~-minute mile** milla *f* que se corre en cuatro minutos.
four-colour, (*US*) **four-color** ['fɔː,kʌləʳ] *attr*: **~ (printing) process** cuatricromía *f*.
four-cycle ['fɔː,saɪkl] *adj* (*US*) = **four-stroke**.
four-door ['fɔː'dɔːʳ] *adj car* de cuatro puertas.
four-engined ['fɔːr'endʒɪnd] *adj* cuatrimotor, tetramotor.
four-eyes* ['fɔːraɪz] *n* cuatrojos* *mf*.
fourflusher* ['fɔː'flʌʃəʳ] *n* (*US*) embustero *m*.
fourfold ['fɔːfəʊld] **1** *adj* cuádruple. **2** *adv* cuatro veces.
fourfooted ['fɔː'fʊtɪd] *adj* cuadrúpedo.
four-handed ['fɔː'hændɪd] *adj* de cuatro jugadores.
four-letter ['fɔː,letəʳ] *adj*: **~ word** (*lit*) que tiene cuatro letras; (*fig*) taco *m*, palabrota *f*.
four-part ['fɔːpɑːt] *adj song* para cuatro voces.
four-ply ['fɔːplaɪ] *adj wood* de cuatro capas; *wool* de cuatro hebras.
fourposter ['fɔː,pəʊstəʳ] *n* (*also* **~ bed**) cama *f* de columnas.
fourscore†† ['fɔː'skɔːʳ] *adj* ochenta.
four-seater [,fɔː'siːtəʳ] *n* coche *m* (*etc*) con cuatro asientos.
foursome ['fɔːsəm] *n* grupo *m* de cuatro personas.
foursquare ['fɔːskweəʳ] **1** *adj* firme; franco, sincero. **2** *adv*: **to stand ~ with sb** estar en completa armonía con uno, apoyar a uno incondicionalmente.
four-star ['fɔːstɑːʳ] *attr*: **~ hotel** hotel *m* de cuatro estrellas; **~ petrol** (*Brit*) ≃ gasolina *f* súper.
four-stroke ['fɔːstrəʊk] *adj* (*Aut*) de cuatro tiempos.
fourteen ['fɔː'tiːn] *adj* catorce.
fourteenth ['fɔː'tiːnθ] *adj* decimocuarto.

fourth [fɔːθ] **1** *adj* cuarto; **the F~ of July** (*US*) el cuatro de julio; ~ **dimension** cuarta dimensión *f*; ~ **estate** (*hum*) la prensa; ~ **gear** cuarta *f* (velocidad *f*); ~ **note** (*US Mus*) cuarta *f*. **2** *n* cuarto *m*, cuarta parte *f*; (*Mus*) cuarta *f*; **to make a** ~ (*Cards*) unirse a otras tres personas (para que se pueda jugar).
fourthly [ˈfɔːθlɪ] *adv* en cuarto lugar.
fourth-rate [ˈfɔːθˈreɪt] *adj* (*fig*) de cuarta categoría.
four-wheel [ˈfɔːwiːl] *attr*: ~ **drive** tracción *f* de 4 por 4, tracción *f* a las cuatro ruedas.
fowl [faʊl] *n* (*bird in general*) ave *f*; (*chicken*) ave *f* de corral, gallina *f*; (*served as food*) pollo *m*; **the ~s of the air** las aves.
fowling-piece [ˈfaʊlɪŋ,piːs] *n* escopeta *f*.
fowl pest [ˈfaʊlpest] *n* peste *f* aviar.
fox [fɒks] **1** *n* zorra *f*, (*dog-~*) zorro *m*; (*fig*) zorro *m*; **he's an old** ~ es un viejo zorro.
2 *vt* confundir, dejar perplejo; **this will ~ them** esto les ha de despistar; **you had me properly ~ed there** eso me tuvo completamente despistado.
3 *vi* disimular, fingir.
foxcub [ˈfɒkskʌb] *n* cachorro *m* (de zorro).
foxed [fɒkst] *adj book* manchado.
fox-fur [ˈfɒksfɜːʳ] *n* piel *f* de zorro.
foxglove [ˈfɒksglʌv] *n* dedalera *f*.
foxhole [ˈfɒkshəʊl] *n* madriguera *f* de zorro; (*Mil*) hoyo *m* de protección.
foxhound [ˈfɒkshaʊnd] *n* perro *m* raposero.
foxhunt [ˈfɒkshʌnt] *n* cacería *f* de zorras.
foxhunting [ˈfɒks,hʌntɪŋ] *n* caza *f* de zorras; **to go** ~ ir de caza de zorros.
fox-terrier [ˈfɒksˈterɪəʳ] *n* foxterrier *m*, perro *m* raposero, perro *m* zorrero.
foxtrot [ˈfɒkstrɒt] *n* fox *m*.
foxy [ˈfɒksɪ] *adj* taimado, astuto.
foyer [ˈfɔɪeɪ] *n* hall *m*, vestíbulo *m*; (*Theat*) foyer *m*.
FP (**a**) (*US*) *abbr of* **fireplug** boca *f* de incendio. (**b**) *n* (*Brit*) *abbr of* **former pupil**.
FPA *n* (*Brit*) *abbr of* **Family Planning Association** Asociación *f* de Planificación Familiar.
Fr (*Rel*) (**a**) *abbr of* **Father** Padre *m*, P., P^{e}. (**b**) *abbr of* **Friar** fray *m*, Fr.
fr. *abbr of* **franc(s)** franco(s) *m(pl)*, f.
fracas [ˈfrækɑː] *n* gresca *f*, riña *f*.
fraction [ˈfrækʃən] *n* (*Math*) fracción *f*, quebrado *m*; (*fig*) pequeña porción *f*, parte *f* muy pequeña; **for a ~ of a second** por un instante.
fractional [ˈfrækʃənl] *adj* fraccionario; (*fig*) muy pequeño.
fractionally [ˈfrækʃnəlɪ] *adv* ligeramente.
fractious [ˈfrækʃəs] *adj* (*character*) díscolo, displicente; *horse* rebelón; (*mood*) malhumorado.
fracture [ˈfræktʃəʳ] **1** *n* fractura *f*. **2** *vt* fracturar. **3** *vi* fracturarse.
fragile [ˈfrædʒaɪl] *adj* frágil, quebradizo; *person* delicado.
fragility [frəˈdʒɪlɪtɪ] *n* fragilidad *f*.
fragment 1 [ˈfrægmənt] *n* fragmento *m*; trozo *m*; **to smash sth to ~s** hacer algo añicos. **2** [frægˈment] *vt* fragmentar. **3** [frægˈment] *vi* fragmentarse.
fragmentary [frægˈmentərɪ] *adj* fragmentario.
fragmentation [,frægmenˈteɪʃən] *n* fragmentación *f*; ~ **grenade** granada *f* de fragmentación.
fragmented [frægˈmentɪd] *adj* fragmentado.
fragrance [ˈfreɪgrəns] *n* fragancia *f*.
fragrant [ˈfreɪgrənt] *adj* fragante, oloroso; *memory* dulce.
frail [freɪl] *adj* frágil, quebradizo; delicado; (*Med*) débil; (*morally*) flaco, endeble.
frailty [ˈfreɪltɪ] *n* fragilidad *f*; (*Med*) debilidad *f*; (*moral*) flaqueza *f*.
frame [freɪm] **1** *n* (**a**) (*framework*) estructura *f*, esqueleto *m*; (*Tech*) armazón *f*, bastidor *m*; (*Sew*) tambor *m*, bastidor *m* para bordar; (*of spectacles*) montura *f*, armadura *f*; (*of bicycle*) cuadro *m*; (*of picture, door, window*) marco *m*; (*Video*) cuadro *m*; ~ **of reference** sistema *m* de referencias, sistema *m* de coordenadas; perspectiva *f* intelectual, marco *m* ideológico; **to put sb in the ~*** acusar a uno, delatar a uno.
(**b**) (*body*) figura *f*, talle *m*; **his large** ~ su cuerpo fornido; **her whole ~ was shaken by sobs** los sollozos sacudían su cuerpo entero.
(**c**) ~ **of mind** estado *m* de ánimo; **when you're in a better ~ of mind** cuando estés de mejor humor.
2 *vt* (**a**) (*construct*) construir; (*arrange*) disponer, arreglar; (*contrive*) idear; *sound* articular; *question etc* formular, expresar.
(**b**) *picture* poner un marco a, enmarcar; (*fig*) servir de marco a; **he appeared ~d in the doorway** apareció en el marco de la puerta; **she was ~d against the sunset** el ocaso le servía de marco.
(**c**) (*: *also* **to ~ up**) encasquetar, incriminar dolosamente; **I've been ~d!** ¡me han hecho trampa!
3 *vi* (**a**) **how is it framing?** ¿qué tal se está desarrollando?; **he's framing well** hace buenos progresos, promete.
(**b**) **to ~ up to sb** ponerse en actitud para defenderse contra uno.
frame house [ˈfreɪm,haʊs] *n* (*US*), *pl* **frame houses** [ˈfreɪm,haʊzɪz] casa *f* de madera.
framer [ˈfreɪməʳ] *n* (*also* **picture** ~) fabricante *mf* de marcos.
frame-up* [ˈfreɪmʌp] *n* estratagema *f* para incriminar a uno; **it's a** ~ aquí hay trampa.
framework [ˈfreɪmwɜːk] *n* (*Tech*) armazón *f*, esqueleto *m*; (*fig*) estructura *f*, sistema *m*, organización *f*, marco *m*; **within the ~ of the constitution** dentro del marco de la constitución.
framing [ˈfreɪmɪŋ] *n* (**a**) (*also* **picture** ~) enmarcado *m*. (**b**) (*Art, Phot*) encuadrado *m*.
Fran [fræn] *nf familiar form of* **Frances.**
franc [fræŋk] *n* franco *m*.
France [frɑːns] *n* Francia *f*.
Frances [ˈfrɑːnsɪs] *nf* Francisca.
franchise [ˈfræntʃaɪz] *n* (**a**) (*Pol*) derecho *m* de votar, sufragio *m*. (**b**) (*Comm*) franquicia *f*; ~ **holder** franquiciado *m*, -a *f*.
franchisee [,fræntʃaɪˈziː] *n* franquiciado *m*, -a *f*, concesionario *m*, -a *f*.
franchising [ˈfræntʃaɪzɪŋ] *n* franquiciamiento *m*.
franchisor [,fræntʃaɪˈzɔːʳ] *n* franquiciador *m*, -ora *f*, (compañía *f*) concesionaria *f*.
Francis [ˈfrɑːnsɪs] *nm* Francisco.
Franciscan [frænˈsɪskən] **1** *adj* franciscano. **2** *n* franciscano *m*.
francium [ˈfrænsɪəm] *n* francio *m*.
franco [ˈfræŋkəʊ] *adj*: ~ **invoice** factura *f* franca.
Franco... [ˈfræŋkəʊ] *prefix* franco-; **~-British** franco-británico.
francophile [ˈfræŋkəʊfaɪl] *n* francófilo *m*, -a *f*.
francophobe [ˈfræŋkəʊfəʊb] *n* francófobo *m*, -a *f*.
frangipane [ˈfrændʒɪpeɪn] *n*, **frangipani** [,frændʒɪˈpɑːnɪ] *n* (*perfume, pastry*) frangipani *m*; (*shrub*) flor *f* de cebo, frangipani *m* blanco, jazmín *m* de las Antillas.
franglais [frɑ̃ˈglɛ] *n* (*hum*) franglés *m*.
Frank[1] [fræŋk] *n* (*Hist*) franco *m*.
Frank[2] [fræŋk] *nm familiar form of* **Francis.**
frank[1] [fræŋk] *adj* franco.
frank[2] [fræŋk] *vt letter* franquear.
Frankenstein [ˈfræŋkənstaɪn] *nm* Frankenstein.
frankfurter [ˈfræŋk,fɜːtəʳ] *n* salchicha *f*.
frankincense [ˈfræŋkɪnsens] *n* incienso *m*.
franking machine [ˈfræŋkɪŋməˈʃiːn] *n* (máquina *f*) franqueadora *f*.
Frankish [ˈfræŋkɪʃ] **1** *adj* fráncico. **2** *n* fráncico *m*.
frankly [ˈfræŋklɪ] *adv* francamente.
frankness [ˈfræŋknɪs] *n* franqueza *f*.
frantic [ˈfræntɪk] *adj* frenético, furioso; **to be ~ with worry** andar como loco de inquietud; **to drive sb** ~ sacar a uno de quicio.
frantically [ˈfræntɪkəlɪ] *adv* frenéticamente, con frenesí.
fraternal [frəˈtɜːnl] *adj* fraternal, fraterno.
fraternity [frəˈtɜːnɪtɪ] *n* fraternidad *f*; (*guild*) cofradía *f*; (*US*) club *m* de estudiantes.
fraternization [,frætənaɪˈzeɪʃən] *n* fraternización *f*.
fraternize [ˈfrætənaɪz] *vi* confraternizar (*with* con), fraternizar (*with* con).
fratricide [ˈfrætrɪsaɪd] *n* (**a**) (*act*) fratricidio *m*. (**b**) (*person*) fratricida *m*.
fraud [frɔːd] **1** *n* (**a**) fraude *m*; estafa *f*, trampa *f*. (**b**) (*person*) impostor *m*, -ora *f*, farsante *m*.
2 *attr*: ~ **squad** grupo *m* de estafas, brigada *f* de delitos monetarios.
fraudster* [ˈfrɔːdstəʳ] *n* defraudador *m*, -ora *f*.
fraudulence [ˈfrɔːdjʊləns] *n* fraudulencia *f*, fraude *m*.
fraudulent [ˈfrɔːdjʊlənt] *adj* fraudulento; ~ **conversion** apropiación *f* ilícita.
fraught [frɔːt] *adj* (**a**) tenso, lleno de tensión; difícil; **things got a bit** ~ la situación se puso difícil. (**b**) ~ **with** cargado de, lleno de.
fray[1] [freɪ] *n* combate *m*, lucha *f*; refriega *f*; **to be ready for the** ~ tener ganas de pelear; **to gird o.s. for the** ~ aprestarse para la lucha.

fray² [freɪ] **1** *vt* desgastar, raer; *nerves* destrozar, crispar. **2** *vi* deshilacharse; **to ~ against, to ~ on** ludir con, rozar.
frayed [freɪd] *adj* raído, dishilachado; *nerves* crispado, de punta; **tempers were getting ~** todos estaban a punto de perder la paciencia.
frazzle* ['fræzl] **1** *n*: **to beat sb to a ~** (*Sport*) cascar a uno*, derrotar a uno por completo; **it was burned to a ~** quedó carbonizado; **to be worn to a ~** estar hecho un trapo*. **2** *vt* (*US*) agotar, rendir; reventar*.
FRB *n* (*US*) *abbr of* **Federal Reserve Bank** Banco *m* de Reserva Federal.
FRCM *n* (*Brit*) *abbr of* **Fellow of the Royal College of Music.**
FRCO *n* (*Brit*) *abbr of* **Fellow of the Royal College of Organists.**
FRCP *n* (*Brit*) *abbr of* **Fellow of the Royal College of Physicians.**
FRCS *n* (*Brit*) *abbr of* **Fellow of the Royal College of Surgeons.**
freak [fri:k] **1** *n* (**a**) (*abnormal specimen*) monstruo *m*, monstruosidad *f*; curiosidad *f*, rareza *f*; ejemplar *m* anormal; (*Bio*) mutación *f*; **the result was a ~** el resultado fue totalmente imprevisible, el resultado se debió a una chiripa.
(**b**) (*whim*) capricho *m*.
(**c**) (*) (*person*) fenómeno *m*; (*mad*) chalado* *m*, -a *f*, chiflado* *m*, -a *f*; (*oddly dressed*) adefesio *m*; **peace ~*** fanático *m*, -a *f* de la paz; *V* **Jesus.**
2 *adj* = **freakish.**
◆**freak out‡** **1** *vt* afectar mucho; impresionar de mala manera, dejar frío. **2** *vi* desmadrarse; marginarse, abandonarlo todo; (*on drugs*) ir de viaje‡, hacer el viaje‡.
freakish ['fri:kɪʃ] *adj* (**a**) *specimen* anormal, monstruoso; *result* inesperado, imprevisible, fortuito. (**b**) *person* caprichoso.
freak-out‡ ['fri:kaʊt] *n* desmadre *m*; (*party*) fiesta *f* loca*; (*on drug*) viaje‡ *m*.
freaky* ['fri:kɪ] *adj* raro, estrafalario.
freckle ['frekl] *n* peca *f*.
freckled ['frekld] *adj*, **freckly** ['freklɪ] *adj* pecoso, lleno de pecas.
Fred [fred], **Freddie, Freddy** ['fredɪ] *nm familiar forms of* **Frederick.**
Frederick ['fredrɪk] *nm* Federico.
free [fri:] **1** *adj* (**a**) (*at liberty etc*) libre (*from, of* de); (*not fixed*) suelto, libre; (*untied*) libre, desatado; *account, choice, translation, verse* libre; *port* franco; **~ agent** persona *f* independiente; **to be a ~ agent** poder actuar libremente; **F~ Church** (*Brit*) Iglesia *f* libre, Iglesia *f* independiente; **~ collective bargaining** = negociación *f* colectiva entre sindicatos y patronal; **~ composition** ejercicio *m* (de expresión escrita) de carácter libre; **~ enterprise** libre empresa *f*, libertad *f* de empresa; **~-enterprise economy** economía *f* de libre empresa; **~ fall** (*Space*) caída *f* libre; **~ fight** sarracina *f*, riña *f* general; **~ flight** vuelo *m* a motor parado; **~ format** formato *m* libre; **~ hit** tiro *m* (*or* lanzamiento *m*) directo; **~ kick** golpe *m* franco, golpe *m* libre; **~ labour** trabajadores *mpl* no sindicados; **~ love** amor *m* libre; **~ market** mercado *m* libre (*in* de); **~ pass** permiso *m* para entrada gratuita; **~ period** (*Educ*) hora *f* libre; **~ port** puerto *m* franco; **~ post** correo *m* libre de franqueo; **~ school** escuela *f* libre; **~ speech** libertad *f* de palabra, libertad *f* de expresión; **~ trade** libre cambio *m*; **~ trader** librecambista *mf*; **~-trade zone** zona *f* franca; **~ of duty** libre de derechos de aduana; **a surface ~ from dust** una superficie libre de polvo; **the fishing is ~** la pesca está autorizada; **the area is ~ of malaria** no hay paludismo en la región; **to be ~ to** + *infin* poder libremente + *infin*, ser libre de + *infin*; **he is not ~ to act** tiene las manos atadas; **we are ~ of him at last** por fin nos hemos librado de él; **to break ~** soltarse; **to let sb go ~** poner en libertad a uno; **to set ~** *person* poner en libertad, libertar, librar; *slave* manumitir, emancipar; *animal* soltar.
(**b**) (*not occupied*) libre; *post* vacante; *premises* desocupado; **is this table ~?** ¿está libre esta mesa?; **are you ~ tomorrow?** ¿estás libre mañana?
(**c**) (*improper*) *language etc* libre, desvergonzado; (*insolent*) descarado; **~ and easy** despreocupado, poco ceremonioso.
(**d**) (*generous*) **to be ~ with** ser liberal con, no regatear; dar en abundancia; **to be ~ with one's money** gastar libremente, no reparar en gastos; **he's very ~ in blaming others** echa libremente la culpa a otros; **he's too ~ with his remarks** es demasiado libre en sus comentarios; **to be ~ with one's hands** (*stealing*) ser largo de manos, (*amorously*) ser tocotón; **to make ~ of** (*or* **with**) usar como si fuera cosa propia.
(**e**) (*for nothing*) gratuito; *ticket* de favor; **~ of charge** gratis; (*Comm*) gratuito, libre de cargo; **admission ~** entrada gratis; **catalogue ~ on request** el catálogo se envía gratis a petición; **~ on board** (*Comm*) franco a bordo; **to get sth for ~*** obtener algo gratis.
2 *adv* gratis.
3 *vt* (*set free*) poner en libertad, libertar; *slave* manumitir; *animal* soltar; (*untie*) desatar, soltar; *knot, tangle* desenredar; *place, surface etc* despejar, desembarazar (*of* de); (*rescue*) librar, salvar (*from* de), rescatar; (*from burden, tax etc*) eximir, exentar (*from* de).
4 *vr*: **to ~ o.s.** desatarse, soltarse.
-free [fri:] *adj*: *e.g.* **additive~** sin aditivos; **duty~** libre de impuestos; **lead~** sin plomo.
freebie* ['fri:bɪ] **1** *adj* gratuito. **2** *n* comida *f* (*or* bebida *f etc*) gratuita, ganga *f*; **it's a ~** es gratis.
freebooter ['fri:bu:tə^r] *n* filibustero *m*.
freedom ['fri:dəm] **1** *n* libertad *f*; exención *f* (*from* de), inmunidad *f* (*from* contra); (*ease*) facilidad *f*, soltura *f*; **~ of a city** ciudadanía *f* de honor; **~ of action** libertad *f* de acción; **~ of association** libertad *f* de asociación; **~ of the press** libertad *f* de prensa; **~ of speech** libertad *f* de palabra, libertad *f* de expresión; **~ of worship** libertad *f* de cultos.
2 *attr*: **~ fighter** luchador *m*, -ora *f* por la libertad.
free-floating ['fri:'fləʊtɪŋ] *adj* libre, que flota libremente.
freefone ['fri:fəʊn] *n* = **Freephone.**
free-for-all ['fri:fə'rɔ:l] *n* sarracina *f*, riña *f* general, refriega *f*, barullo *m*.
freehand ['fri:hænd] *adj* hecho a pulso.
freehold ['fri:həʊld] (*Brit*) **1** *adj*: **~ property** = **2**. **2** *n* feudo *m* franco, alodio *m*, propiedad *f* absoluta.
freeholder ['fri:,həʊldə^r] *n* (*Brit*) poseedor *m*, -ora de feudo franco.
freeing ['fri:ɪŋ] *n* puesta *f* en libertad.
freelance ['fri:lɑ:ns] **1** *adj* independiente, autónomo, de libre dedicación. **2** *n* periodista *mf* (*etc*) independiente; persona *f* de libre dedicación, informador *m*, -ora *f* (*etc*) por libre, francotirador *m*, -ora *f*. **3** *vi* ir por libre, trabajar por libre, trabajar por cuenta propia.
freeloader* ['fri:ləʊdə^r] *n* (*US*) gorrón *m*, invitadizo *m*.
freely ['fri:lɪ] *adv* libremente; (*generously*) liberalmente; *confess, speak etc* francamente; **you may come and go ~** Vd puede ir y venir con toda libertad.
freeman ['fri:mən] *n, pl* **freemen** ['fri:mən] (*Hist*) hombre *m* libre; (*of city*) ciudadano *m* de honor.
freemason ['fri:,meɪsn] *n* masón *m*, francmasón *m*.
freemasonry ['fri:,meɪsnrɪ] *n* masonería *f*, francmasonería *f*; (*fig*) compañerismo *m*, camaradería *f*.
Freephone ['fri:fəʊn] ® *n* (*Brit Telec*) = llamada *f* telefónica sin cargo al usuario.
free-range ['fri:reɪndʒ] *attr*: **~ eggs** huevos *mpl* de granja, huevos *mpl* de corral; **~ poultry** aves *fpl* de granja.
free-ranging ['fri:'reɪndʒɪŋ] *adj discussion* sobre temas muy diversos; sin conclusiones preconcebidas; *role* libre, amplio.
freesia ['fri:zɪə] *n* fresia *f*.
free-standing ['fri:'stændɪŋ] *adj* independiente.
freestyle ['fri:staɪl] *adj*: **200 metres ~** 200 metros libres; **~ race** carrera *f* de estilo libre; **~ wrestling** lucha *f* libre.
freethinker ['fri:'θɪŋkə^r] *n* librepensador *m*, -ora *f*.
freethinking ['fri:'θɪŋkɪŋ] **1** *adj* librepensador. **2** *n* librepensamiento *m*.
freeway ['fri:weɪ] *n* (*US*) autopista *f*.
freewheel ['fri:'wi:l] (*Brit*) **1** *n* rueda *f* libre. **2** *vi* (*cyclist*) andar a rueda libre, (*Aut*) ir en punto muerto.
freewheeling ['fri:,wi:lɪŋ] *adj discussion* desenvuelto; (*free*) libre, espontáneo; (*careless*) irresponsable.
freewill ['fri:'wɪl] *n* libre albedrío *m*.
freeze [fri:z] (*irr*: *pret* **froze**, *ptp* **frozen**) **1** *vt* helar; *food, prices, wages etc, video* congelar; **we're simply frozen** estamos francamente helados.
2 *vi* helarse; congelarse; (*fig*) quedar helado (de miedo *etc*); (*remain motionless*) quedarse rígido, permanecer enteramente inmóvil; **I'm freezing** estoy helado; **it's freezing** hay helada, hiela; (*fig*) hace un frío glacial; **to ~ to death** morir de frío; **the smile froze on his lips** se le heló la sonrisa en los labios; **it will ~ tonight** esta noche habrá helada.
3 *n* helada *f*; ola *f* de frío; (*of prices, wages etc*) congelación *f*.

◆**freeze out** *vt competitor* deshacerse de (quitándole la clientela).
◆**freeze over** *vi* helarse; congelarse; **the lake has frozen over** el lago está helado.
◆**freeze up 1** *vt* helar; **we're frozen up at home** en casa las cañerías están heladas.
2 *vi* = **freeze over.**
freeze-dried [ˌfriːzˈdraɪd] *adj* deshidratado por congelación, liofilizado.
freeze-dry [ˌfriːzˈdraɪ] *vt* deshidratar por congelación, liofilizar.
freezer [ˈfriːzəʳ] *n* congelador *m*, (ultra)congelador *m*, congeladora *f* (*LAm*).
freeze-up [ˈfriːzʌp] *n* helada *f*, ola *f* de frío.
freezing [ˈfriːzɪŋ] **1** *adj* glacial (*also fig*), helado; ~ **mixture** mezcla *f* refrigerante. **2** *adv*: **it's ~ cold** hace un frío glacial. **3** *n* (**a**) (*deep* ~) (ultra)congelación *f*; (*of rents etc*) congelación *f*. (**b**) = **freezing-point.**
freezing-point [ˈfriːzɪŋpɔɪnt] *n* punto *m* de congelación; **5 degrees below ~** 5 grados bajo cero.
freight [freɪt] **1** *n* flete *m*; (*load*) carga *f*; (*goods*) mercancías *fpl*; (*esp Brit*: *ship's cargo*) flete *m*; **to send sth (by) ~** enviar algo por flete. **2** (*as adv*) ~ **collect** (*US*), ~ **forward** flete *m* por cobrar, porte *m* por cobrar; ~ **free** franco de porte; ~ **inward** flete *m* sobre compras; ~ **paid** porte *m* pagado. **3** *vt* enviar por flete.
freightage [ˈfreɪtɪdʒ] *n* flete *m*.
freight-car [ˈfreɪtkɑːʳ] *n* (*US*) vagón *m* de mercancías.
freight charges [ˈfreɪtˌtʃɑːdʒɪz] *npl* gastos *mpl* de transporte.
freighter [ˈfreɪtəʳ] *n* (**a**) (*Naut*) buque *m* de carga, nave *f* de mercancías. (**b**) (*person*: *carrier*) transportista *m*; (*agent*) fletador *m*.
freight forwarder [ˈfreɪtˌfɔːwədəʳ] *n* agente *m* expedidor.
freightliner [ˈfreɪtˌlaɪnəʳ] *n* tren *m* de mercancías de contenedores.
freight-plane [ˈfreɪtˌpleɪn] *n* avión *m* de transporte de mercancías.
freight terminal [ˈfreɪtˌtɜːmɪnl] *n* terminal *f* de mercancías, (*Aer*) terminal *f* de carga.
freight-train [ˈfreɪttreɪn] *n* (*US*) (tren *m*) mercancías *m*.
freight-yard [ˈfreɪtˌjɑːd] *n* área *f* de carga.
French [frentʃ] **1** *adj* francés; ~ **bean** judía *f* enana, fríjol *m*; ~ **bread** pan *m* francés; ~ **chalk** jaboncillo *m* de sastre, esteatita *f*; ~ **door** (*US*) puertaventana *f*; ~ **dressing** vinagreta *f*; ~ **fried potatoes,** ~ **fries** (*US*) patatas *fpl* (*LAm*: papas *fpl*) fritas; ~ **horn** trompa *f* de llaves; ~ **kiss** beso *m* de tornillo; ~ **leave** despedida *f* a la francesa; ~ **letter** condón *m*; ~ **loaf** barra *f* de pan francés; ~ **pastry** pastelito *m* relleno de nata (*or* frutas); ~ **polish** laca *f*; ~ **toast** (*Brit*: *toast*) tostada *f tostada sólo por un lado*; (*bread fried in egg*) torrija *f*; ~ **windows** puertaventanas *fpl*.
2 *n* (**a**) **the** ~ los franceses. (**b**) (*Ling*) francés *m*; **pardon my ~*** perdona la palabra.
French-Canadian [ˈfrentʃkəˈneɪdɪən] **1** *adj* francocanadiense. **2** *n* (**a**) francocanadiense *mf*. (**b**) (*Ling*) francés *m* canadiense.
French Guiana [ˌfrentʃgaɪˈænə] *n* Guayana *f* Francesa.
Frenchified [ˈfrentʃɪfaɪd] *adj* afrancesado.
Frenchman [ˈfrentʃmən] *n*, *pl* **Frenchmen** [ˈfrentʃmən] francés *m*.
French-polish [ˌfrentʃˈpɒlɪʃ] *vt* (*Brit*) laquear.
French Riviera [ˈfrentʃˌrɪvɪˈɛərə] *n* la Riviera.
French-speaking [ˈfrentʃˌspiːkɪŋ] *adj* francófono, francohablante, de habla francesa.
Frenchwoman [ˈfrentʃˌwʊmən] *n*, *pl* **Frenchwomen** [ˈfrentʃˌwɪmɪn] francesa *f*.
Frenchy* [ˈfrentʃɪ] *n* gabacho* *m*, -a *f*, francés *m*, -esa *f*.
frenetic [frɪˈnetɪk] *adj* frenético.
frenzied [ˈfrenzɪd] *adj effort etc* frenético; *crowd etc* enloquecido.
frenzy [ˈfrenzɪ] *n* frenesí *m*, delirio *m*.
frequency [ˈfriːkwənsɪ] **1** *n* frecuencia *f* (*also Elec*); **high ~** alta frecuencia *f*; **low ~** baja frecuencia *f*. **2** *attr*: ~ **band** banda *f* de frecuencia; ~ **distribution** distribución *f* de frecuencia; ~ **modulation** frecuencia *f* modulada; ~ **sweeper** barredor *m* de frecuencia.
frequent 1 [ˈfriːkwənt] *adj* frecuente. **2** [frɪˈkwent] *vt* frecuentar.
frequentative [frɪˈkwentətɪv] **1** *adj* frecuentativo. **2** *n* frecuentativo *m*.
frequenter [frɪˈkwentəʳ] *n* frecuentador *m*, -ora *f* (*of* de).
frequently [ˈfriːkwəntlɪ] *adv* frecuentemente, con frecuencia, a menudo.
fresco [ˈfreskəʊ] *n*, *pl* **fresco(e)s** [ˈfreskəʊz] fresco *m*.
fresh [freʃ] *adj* (**a**) (*new*) nuevo; ~ **paint** (*US*) recién pintado; **to start a ~ life** comenzar una vida nueva; **he has had a ~ attack** ha sufrido un nuevo ataque; **it is ~ in my memory** se conserva muy fresco en mi memoria; **to put ~ courage into sb** reanimar a uno.
(**b**) (*newly come*) ~ **from Spain** recién llegado (*or* importado *etc*) de España; ~ **from the oven** acabadito de salir del horno.
(**c**) (*inexperienced*) nuevo.
(**d**) (*not stale*) *fruit etc* fresco; *bread* nuevo, tierno; *vegetable* natural; *air* fresco, puro (*and V* **air**); *water* dulce; **as ~ as a daisy** tan fresco como una rosa; **to feel perfectly ~** estar lleno de vigor.
(**e**) (*: *cheeky*) fresco*, descocado*; **to get ~ with sb** ponerse fresco con uno*.
(**f**) (*cool*) fresco.
(**g**) *wind* recio.
(**h**) *face, complexion* de buen color.
fresh-air fiend* [ˌfreʃˈɛəˌfiːnd] *n*: **he's a ~** siempre quiere estar al aire libre.
freshen [ˈfreʃn] **1** *vt* refrescar. **2** *vi* (*temperature*) refrescarse; (*wind*) soplar más recio; (*person*) lavarse, arreglarse.
◆**freshen up 1** *vt* = **freshen 1.**
2 *vi* (*person*) lavarse, arreglarse.
freshener [ˈfreʃnəʳ] *n*: **air ~** ambientador *m*; **skin ~** tónico *m* para la piel.
fresher* [ˈfreʃəʳ] *n* (*Brit*) = **freshman.**
freshly [ˈfreʃlɪ] *adv* nuevamente; recientemente; ~ **made** nuevo, recién hecho, acabado de hacer.
freshman [ˈfreʃmən] *n*, *pl* **freshmen** [ˈfreʃmən] (*Univ*) estudiante *m* de primer año, novato *m*.
freshness [ˈfreʃnɪs] *n* frescura *f*; lozanía *f*; (*newness*) novedad *f*; vigor *m*.
freshwater [ˈfreʃˌwɔːtəʳ] *adj* de agua dulce; ~ **fish** pez *m* de agua dulce.
fret[1] [fret] **1** *vt* (**a**) (*wear away*) corroer, raer, desgastar.
(**b**) *person* irritar, molestar.
(**c**) **to ~ the hours away** pasar las horas consumiéndose de inquietud.
2 *vi* inquietarse, apurarse; impacientarse (*at* por); **it's ~ting for its mother** se está apurando por la ausencia de su madre; **don't ~!** ¡no te apures!
3 *n*: **to be in a ~** estar muy inquieto, apurarse.
fret[2] [fret] *n* (*for guitar*) traste *m*.
fretful [ˈfretfʊl] *adj* displicente, quejoso; impaciente; inquieto.
fretfully [ˈfretfəlɪ] *adv* impacientemente; inquietamente.
fretfulness [ˈfretfʊlnɪs] *n* displicencia *f*; impaciencia *f*; inquietud *f*.
fretsaw [ˈfretsɔː] *n* sierra *f* de calados.
fretwork [ˈfretwɜːk] *n* calado *m*.
Freudian [ˈfrɔɪdɪən] *adj* freudiano; ~ **slip** desliz *m* freudiano.
Fri. *abbr of* **Friday** viernes *m*, vier.
friable [ˈfraɪəbl] *adj* friable, desmenuzable.
friar [ˈfraɪəʳ] *n* (**a**) fraile *m*; **black ~** dominico *m*; **grey ~** franciscano *m*; **white ~** carmelita *m*. (**b**) (*before name*) fray.
fribie* [ˈfriːbɪ] *n* (*US*) = **freebie.**
fricassee [ˈfrɪkəsiː] *n* fricandó *m*, fricasé *m*.
fricative [ˈfrɪkətɪv] **1** *adj* fricativo. **2** *n* fricativa *f*.
friction [ˈfrɪkʃən] **1** *n* (**a**) (*Tech*) fricción *f*, rozamiento *m*; (*Med etc*) frote *m*, frotamiento *m*. (**b**) (*fig*) tirantez *f*, desavenencia *f* (*about, over* con motivo de). **2** *attr*: ~ **feed** alimentación *f* por fricción, avance *m* por fricción.
Friday [ˈfraɪdɪ] *n* viernes *m*; **Good ~** Viernes *m* Santo.
fridge* [frɪdʒ] *n* (*Brit*) frigo *m*, nevera *f*, heladera *f* (*SC*), refrigeradora *f* (*LAm*).
fridge-freezer [ˈfrɪdʒˈfriːzəʳ] *n* frigorífico-congelador *m*.
fried [fraɪd] *adj* frito; ~ **egg** huevo *m* frito, huevo *m* estrellado (*LAm*).
friend [frend] *n* amigo *m*, -a *f*; **F~** (*Rel*) cuáquero *m*, -a *f*; **~s** amigos *mpl*, amistades *fpl*; **~!** (*Mil*) ¡gente de paz!; **a ~ of mine** un amigo mío; **he's no ~ of mine** no es uno de mis amigos; **he is no ~ to violence** no es partidario de la violencia; **we're the best of ~s** somos muy amigos; **to be ~s with sb** ser amigo de uno; **to have a ~ at court** tener el padre alcalde, tener enchufe; **to make ~s with sb** hacerse amigo de uno, trabar amistad con uno; **he makes ~s easily** hace amigos con facilidad.
friendless [ˈfrendlɪs] *adj* sin amigos.
friendliness [ˈfrendlɪnɪs] *n* simpatía *f*; amabilidad *f*; cordialidad *f*; lo acogedor.

friendly ['frendlɪ] **1** *adj* (**a**) *person* simpático; amable; **people here are very ~** aquí la gente es muy simpática; **he's a ~ soul** es simpatiquísimo; **your ~ neighbourhood policeman** el simpático guardia urbano que vigila su barrio; **to be ~ with** ser amigo de; **to get ~** hacerse amigos.
(**b**) *relationship, greeting, tone* amistoso, cordial; *shout* jovial; *atmosphere, place* acogedor; *match* amistoso; *nation* amigo; **~ fire** fuego *m* amigo; **~ society** (*Brit*) mutualidad *f*, sociedad *f* de socorro mutuo, montepío *m*; **that wasn't a very ~ thing to do** eso no fue la acción de un amigo.
2 *n* (*Sport*) partido *m* amistoso.

-friendly ['frendlɪ] *suf* que no daña, que no perjudica, que no afecta a, *eg* **environment~** que no daña al medio ambiente, ecológico; *V* **user~** *etc*.

friendship ['frendʃɪp] *n* amistad *f*; (*US*) compañerismo *m*.

Friesland ['fri:zlənd] *n* Frisia *f*.

frieze [fri:z] *n* friso *m*.

frigate ['frɪgɪt] *n* fragata *f*.

fright [fraɪt] *n* (**a**) (*sudden fear*) susto *m*, sobresalto *m*; (*state of alarm*) terror *m*; **what a ~ you gave me!** ¡qué susto me diste!; **to have a ~** tener un susto, llevarse un susto; **to take ~** asustarse (*at* de).
(**b**) (*: *person*) espantajo *m*; **doesn't she look a ~?** ¡qué adefesio de mujer!

frighten ['fraɪtn] *vt* asustar, espantar, sobresaltar; alarmar; **to be ~ed** tener miedo (*of* a); **don't be ~ed!** ¡no te asustes!; **she is easily ~ed** es asustadiza; **to ~ sb into doing sth** obligar a uno a hacer algo infundiéndole miedo, amenazar a uno para que haga algo.

◆**frighten away, frighten off** *vt* ahuyentar, espantar.

frighteners‡ ['fraɪtnəz] *npl*: **to put the ~ on sb** meterle a uno el ombligo para dentro*.

frightening ['fraɪtnɪŋ] *adj* espantoso, aterrador.

frighteningly ['fraɪtnɪŋlɪ] *adv thin* alarmantemente; *ugly* espantosamente; *expensive, uncertain* terriblemente.

frightful ['fraɪtfʊl] *adj* espantoso, horrible, horroroso; (*very bad*) horrible, malísimo.

frightfully ['fraɪtfəlɪ] *adv* (*fig*) terriblemente, tremendamente; **it's ~ hard** es terriblemente difícil; **it's ~ good** es la mar de bueno; **I'm ~ sorry** lo siento muchísimo, lo siento en el alma.

frightfulness ['fraɪtfʊlnɪs] *n* horror *m*.

frigid ['frɪdʒɪd] *adj* frío; (*Med*) frígido; *atmosphere, look etc* glacial.

frigidity [frɪ'dʒɪdɪtɪ] *n* frialdad *f*; (*Med*) frigidez *f*.

frill [frɪl] *n* lechuga *f*, volante *m*; **~s** (*fig*) adornos *mpl*; **~s and furbelows** encajes *mpl* y puntillas *fpl*; **a package holiday without ~s** unas vacaciones de paquete sin adornos.

frilly ['frɪlɪ] *adj* con volantes, con adornos.

fringe [frɪndʒ] **1** *n* (**a**) (*Sew*) franja *f*, orla *f*, borde *m*; (*Brit*: *hair*) flequillo *m*.
(**b**) (*edge*) margen *m*; **the outer ~s of the city** las periferias, las partes exteriores de la ciudad; **on the ~s of the lake** en los bordes del lago; **to live on the ~ of society** vivir al margen de la sociedad.
(**c**) (*social*) elementos *mpl* periféricos, elementos *mpl* marginados.
2 *attr*: **~ benefits** beneficios *mpl* complementarios, complementos *mpl*; **~ group** grupo *m* marginal; **~ organization** organización *f* marginal, organización *f* no oficial; **~ theatre** (*Brit*) teatro *m* periférico, teatro *m* experimental.

frippery ['frɪpərɪ] *n* perifollos *mpl*, perejiles *mpl*.

Frisbee ['frɪzbɪ] ® *n* disco *m* volador.

Frisian ['frɪʒən] **1** *adj* frisio; **~ Islands** Islas *fpl* Frisias.
2 *n* (**a**) frisio *m*, -a *f*.
(**b**) (*Ling*) frisio *m*.

frisk [frɪsk] **1** *vt* cachear, registrar. **2** *vi* (*also* **to ~ about**) retozar, juguetear, brincar.

friskiness ['frɪskɪnɪs] *n* vivacidad *f*.

frisky ['frɪskɪ] *adj* retozón, juguetón; *horse* fogoso; **he's pretty ~ still** sigue bastante activo.

fritter[1] ['frɪtə^r] *n* fruta *f* de sartén, buñuelo *m*.

fritter[2] ['frɪtə^r] *vt* (*also* **to ~ away**) desperdiciar, disipar.

frivolity [frɪ'vɒlɪtɪ] *n* frivolidad *f*, informalidad *f*, ligereza *f*.

frivolous ['frɪvələs] *adj* frívolo, poco formal, ligero.

frizz [frɪz], **frizzle** ['frɪzl] **1** *n* rizos *mpl* pequeños y muy apretados. **2** *vt* rizar con rizos pequeños y muy apretados.

frizz(l)y ['frɪz(l)ɪ] *adj* muy ensortijado, crespo, frito*.

fro [frəʊ] *adv*: **to and ~** de un lado a otro, de aquí para allá; **to and ~ movement** vaivén *m*.

frock [frɒk] *n* vestido *m*.

frock-coat ['frɒk'kəʊt] *n* levita *f*.

Frog* [frɒg] *n*, **Froggy*** ['frɒgɪ] *n* gabacho* *m*, -a *f*, francés *m*, -esa *f*.

frog [frɒg] *n* rana *f*; **to have a ~ in one's throat** padecer carraspera.

frogman ['frɒgmən] *n*, *pl* **frogmen** ['frɒgmən] hombre-rana *m*, submarinista *m*.

frog-march ['frɒgmɑ:tʃ] *vt* llevar codo con codo, llevar a la fuerza (cogidos los brazos).

frogspawn ['frɒgspɔ:n] *n* huevas *fpl* de rana.

frolic ['frɒlɪk] **1** *n* juego *m* alegre; (*party*) fiesta *f*, holgorio *m*; (*prank*) travesura *f*. **2** *vi* juguetear, retozar; divertirse (*with* con).

frolicsome ['frɒlɪksəm] *adj* retozón, juguetón; (*mischievous*) travieso.

from [frɒm] *prep* (**a**) de; **~ A to Z** de A a Z, desde A hasta Z; **~ door to door** de puerta en puerta; **~ £2 upwards** desde 2 libras en adelante; **he had gone ~ home** se había ido de su casa; **to pick sb ~ the crowd** escoger a uno de la multitud.
(**b**) (*time*) **~ Friday** a partir del viernes; **~ a child** desde niño; **~ that time** desde aquel momento.
(**c**) (*deprivation*) **to take sth ~ sb** quitar algo a uno; **he stole the book ~ me** me robó el libro; **I'll buy it ~ you** te lo compraré.
(**d**) (*against*) **to shelter ~ the rain** abrigarse de la lluvia.
(**e**) (*distinguishing*) **to know good ~ bad** saber distinguir entre el bien y el mal, saber distinguir el bien del mal.
(**f**) (*originating*) **the train ~ Madrid** el tren de Madrid, el tren procedente de Madrid; **he comes ~ Segovia** es de Segovia; **where are you ~?** ¿de dónde es Vd?; **a message ~ him** un mensaje de parte de él; **tell him that ~ me** dile eso de parte mía; **one of the best performances we have seen ~ him** uno de los mejores papeles que le hayamos visto; **to drink ~ a cup** beber de una taza; **we learned it ~ him** lo aprendimos de él; **we learned it ~ a book** lo aprendimos en un libro.
(**g**) (*because of*) **~ what he says** por lo que dice, según lo que dice; **to act ~ conviction** obrar por convicción; **~ sheer necessity** por pura necesidad; **to die ~ a fever** morir de una fiebre; **he is tired ~ overwork** está cansado por exceso de trabajo.
(**h**) **~ above** desde encima; **~ afar** desde lejos; **~ among** de entre.

frond [frɒnd] *n* fronda *f*.

front [frʌnt] **1** *adj* (**a**) (*gen*) delantero, anterior; (*first*) primero; **~ bench(es)** (*Brit Parl*) escaños *mpl* de los ministros (y del gobierno fantasma); **~ desk** (*US*) recepción *f* de un hotel; **~ door** puerta *f* principal, puerta *f* de entrada; **~ garden** jardín *m* delante de la casa; **~ line** primera línea *f*; **~ matter** preliminares *mpl*; **~ money** capital *m* inicial; **~ page** primera página *f*, (*of newspaper*) primera plana *f*; **~ room** (*lit*) cuarto *m* que da a la calle, (*freq*) salón *m*; **~ row** primera fila *f*; **~ runner** corredor *m*, -ora *f* que va en cabeza; (*candidate*) favorito *m*, -a *f*; **~ seat** asiento *m* delantero; **~ tooth** incisivo *m*; **~ vowel** vocal *f* frontal; **~ wheel** rueda *f* delantera.
(**b**) **~ elevation** alzado *m* frontal; **~ view** vista *f* de frente.
2 *n* (**a**) frente *m* (*also Mil, Pol, Met*); (*forepart*) parte *f* delantera, parte *f* anterior; (*of house*) fachada *f*; (*of book, start*) principio *m*; (*of shirt etc*) pechera *f*; (*Theat*) auditorio *m*; (*Brit*: *beach*) playa *f*, (*promenade*) paseo *m* marítimo; **on Brighton ~** en la playa de Brighton; **cold ~** frente *m* frío; **popular ~** frente *m* popular; **at** (*or* **in**) **the ~ of the book** al principio del libro; **in ~** delante; **in ~ of** delante de; **to be in ~** ir primero, ir delante, (*in race*) ir en cabeza; **to come to the ~** empezar a destacar; **to push one's way to the ~** abrirse camino a empujones hasta la primera fila (*etc*); **to send sb on in ~** enviar a uno por delante; *V also* **up-~**.
(**b**) (*fig*) apariencias *fpl*; **it's all just ~ with him** con él no son más que apariencias; **to put on a bold ~** hacer de tripas corazón.
(**c**) (*Pol etc*) fachada *f*; tapadera *f* (*for* de); **~ organization** organización *f* fachada; **it's merely a ~ organization** sólo es una tapadera; **~ for subversion** tapadera *f* de la subversión.
3 *adv*: **eyes ~!** (*Mil*) ¡ojos al frente!
4 *vt* (*TV etc*) *programme* presentar; *organization* liderar; *illegal body* servir de fachada (*or* tapadera) a; *band* ser el vocalista principal en.
5 *vi* (**a**) **to ~ for** *illegal body* servir de fachada (*or* tapadera) a. (**b**) **to ~ on** (**to**) dar a, estar enfrente de.

frontage ['frʌntɪdʒ] *n* fachada *f*.

frontal ['frʌntl] *adj* frontal; *attack* de frente.

frontbencher ['frʌnt'bentʃə^r] *n* (*Brit Parl*) (*government*)

figura f eminente del Gobierno; (opposition) figura f eminente de la Oposición.
front-end ['frʌnt,end] attr: ~ costs gastos mpl iniciales; ~ processor procesador m frontal.
frontier ['frʌntɪəʳ] 1 n frontera f; to push back the ~s of knowledge ampliar los conocimientos (científicos etc), ensanchar el horizonte del conocimiento. 2 attr fronterizo; ~ dispute conflicto m fronterizo; ~ post puesto m de frontera.
frontiersman [frʌn'tɪəzmən] n, pl frontiersmen [frʌn'tɪəzmən] hombre m de la frontera.
frontispiece ['frʌntɪspiːs] n frontispicio m.
front-line ['frʌntlaɪn] adj troops, news de primera línea; countries, areas fronterizo a una zona en guerra.
front-loader [,frʌnt'ləʊdəʳ] n (also front-loading washing machine) lavadora f de carga frontal.
front-loading ['frʌnt'ləʊdɪŋ] attr de carga frontal.
frontman ['frʌntmæn] n, pl frontmen ['frʌntmen] (TV etc) presentador m.
front-page ['frʌnt'peɪdʒ] adj de primera página, de primera plana; ~ news noticias fpl de primera plana.
frontwards ['frʌntwədz] adv de frente, con la parte delantera primero.
front-wheel ['frʌntwiːl] attr: ~ drive tracción f delantera.
frost [frɒst] 1 n helada f; (visible, also hoar ~, white ~) escarcha f; 4 degrees of ~ (Brit) 4 grados bajo cero.
2 vt (a) cubrir de escarcha; the grass was ~ed over el césped apareció cubierto de escarcha.
(b) plant quemar.
(c) (US Culin) alcorzar, escarchar.
3 vi: to ~ over, to ~ up cubrirse de escarcha, escarcharse.
frostbite ['frɒstbaɪt] n congelación f.
frostbitten ['frɒst,bɪtn] adj congelado.
frostbound ['frɒstbaʊnd] adj helado; bloqueado por la helada.
frosted ['frɒstɪd] adj glass deslustrado; (US Culin) alcorzado, escarchado.
frostily ['frɒstɪlɪ] adv (fig) glacialmente.
frosting ['frɒstɪŋ] n (US Culin) azúcar m glaseado.
frosty ['frɒstɪ] adj (a) (Met) in ~ weather en época de hielo; on a ~ morning una mañana de helada; it was ~ last night anoche heló.
(b) surface escarchado, cubierto de escarcha.
(c) (fig) glacial.
froth [frɒθ] 1 n espuma f; (fig) bachillerías fpl. 2 vi espumar, echar espuma; to ~ at the mouth espumajear.
frothy ['frɒθɪ] adj (a) espumoso. (b) (fig) frivolón, superficial, de poca sustancia, vacío.
frown [fraʊn] 1 n ceño m; he said with a ~ dijo frunciendo el entrecejo. 2 vi fruncir el entrecejo; to ~ at mirar con ceño.
◆frown (up)on vt desaprobar.
frowning ['fraʊnɪŋ] adj (fig) ceñudo, amenazador, severo.
frowsy, frowzy ['fraʊzɪ] adj (dirty) sucio; (untidy) desaliñado; (smelly) fétido, maloliente; (neglected) descuidado.
froze [frəʊz] pret of freeze.
frozen ['frəʊzn] 1 ptp of freeze. 2 adj food congelado; ~ assets activo m congelado.
FRS n (a) (Brit) abbr of Fellow of the Royal Society. (b) (US) abbr of Federal Reserve System banco m central de los EE.UU.
fructify ['frʌktɪfaɪ] vi fructificar.
frugal ['fruːgəl] adj frugal.
frugality [fruː'gælɪtɪ] n frugalidad f.
frugally ['fruːgəlɪ] adv give out en pequeñas cantidades; live económicamente, sencillamente.
fruit [fruːt] 1 n sing and pl (on the tree etc) fruto m (also Bio, fig); (served as food) fruta f, frutas fpl; to bear ~ (fig) dar resultado, dar fruto, fructificar.
2 vi frutar, dar fruto.
fruit-basket ['fruːt,bɑːskɪt] n frutero m, canasto m de la fruta.
fruit-cake ['fruːtkeɪk] n tarta f de frutas.
fruit cocktail ['fruːt'kɒkteɪl] n cóctel m de frutas.
fruit-cup ['fruːtkʌp] n ≈ sangría f.
fruit-dish ['fruːtdɪʃ] n frutero m.
fruit-drop [,fruːt'drɒp] n bombón m de fruta.
fruiterer ['fruːtərəʳ] n (Brit) frutero m; ~'s (shop) frutería f.
fruit-farm ['fruːtfɑːm] n granja f frutera.
fruit-farmer ['fruːt,fɑːməʳ] n fruticultor m, -ora f, granjero m frutícola.
fruit-farming ['fruːt,fɑːmɪŋ] n fruticultura f.
fruitfly ['fruːtflaɪ] n mosca f de la fruta.
fruitful ['fruːtfʊl] adj (fig) fructuoso, provechoso.
fruitfully ['fruːtfəlɪ] adv (fig) fructuosamente, fructíferamente, provechosamente.
fruitfulness ['fruːtfʊlnɪs] n (of soil) fertilidad f, fecundidad f, productividad f; (of plant) fertilidad f, fecundidad; (of discussion etc) utilidad f.
fruit-grower ['fruːt,grəʊəʳ] n fruticultor m, -ora f, granjero m frutícola.
fruit-growing ['fruːt,grəʊɪŋ] n fruticultura f.
fruit-gum ['fruːtgʌm] n (Brit) caramelo m de goma.
fruition [fruː'ɪʃən] n cumplimiento m; (of plan etc) realización f; to bring to ~ realizar; to come to ~ llegar a la madurez, (plan etc) verse logrado, realizarse, (hope) cumplirse.
fruit juice ['fruːt,dʒuːs] n zumo m de fruta, jugo m de fruta (LAm).
fruit-knife ['fruːtnaɪf] n, pl fruit-knives ['fruːtnaɪvz] cuchillo m de la fruta.
fruitless ['fruːtlɪs] adj infructuoso, inútil.
fruit-machine ['fruːtmə,ʃiːn] n (Brit) (máquina f) tragaperras m.
fruit-salad [,fruːt'sæləd] n macedonia f de frutas, ensalada f de frutas (LAm).
fruit-salts ['fruːtsɒlts] npl sal f de fruta(s).
fruit-tree ['fruːttriː] n (árbol m) frutal m.
fruity ['fruːtɪ] adj (a) que sabe a fruta; wine afrutado. (b) voice pastoso. (c) joke etc verde; style de fuerte sabor.
frump [frʌmp] n espantajo m, adefesio m, mujer f desaliñada.
frumpish ['frʌmpɪʃ] adj desaliñado.
frustrate [frʌs'treɪt] vt frustrar; to feel ~d sentirse frustrado.
frustrating [frʌs'treɪtɪŋ] adj frustrante.
frustration [frʌs'treɪʃən] n frustración f.
fry¹ [fraɪ] n (Fish) pececillos mpl; small ~ gente f de poca monta, gente f menuda.
fry² [fraɪ] 1 n fritada f. 2 vt freír; fried fish pescado m frito. 3 vi freírse.
frying ['fraɪɪŋ] n: there was a smell of ~ olía a frito.
frying-pan ['fraɪɪŋ,pæn], (US) frypan ['fraɪpæn] n sartén f; to jump out of the ~ into the fire escaparse del trueno para dar en el relámpago, salir de Guatemala y dar en Guatepeor.
fry-up ['fraɪʌp] n (Brit) fritura f.
FSLIC n (US) abbr of Federal Savings and Loan Insurance Corporation.
F/T (US) abbr of full-time.
F.T. n (Brit) abbr of Financial Times; V financial.
ft abbr of foot, feet pie m, pies mpl.
FTC n (US) abbr of Federal Trade Commission.
FTSE 100 Index n abbr of Financial Times Stock Exchange 100 Index.
fuchsia ['fjuːʃə] n fucsia f.
fuck** [fʌk] 1 n polvo** m; to have a ~ echar un polvo**, joder**; like ~ he will! ¡si es por los cojones!**
2 vt joder** (Sp), coger** (LAm); ~ it! ¡joder!**, ¡carajo!** (LAm).
3 vi joder** (Sp), coger** (LAm); ~! ¡joder!**, ¡carajo!** (LAm).
◆fuck about**, fuck around** vi joder**; to ~ about (or around) with manosear; estropear.
◆fuck off** vi: ~ off! ¡vete a la mierda!**
◆fuck up** vt joder**.
fuck-all** [,fʌk'ɔːl] (Brit) 1 adj: it's ~ use no sirve para nada en absoluto. 2 n: I know ~ about it no sé nada en absoluto de eso; he's done ~ today hoy no ha hecho nada en absoluto.
fucker** ['fʌkəʳ] n hijoputa** m, cabronazo** m.
fucking** ['fʌkɪŋ] 1 adj maldito, condenado*; jodido**. 2 adv: a ~ awful film una película endiabladamente mala; it's ~ cold hace un frío de demonios. 3 n joder** m, jodienda** f.
fuck-up** ['fʌkʌp] n lío* m, follón* m.
fuddled ['fʌdld] adj (drunk) borracho; (confused) aturdido; to get ~ emborracharse.
fuddy-duddy* ['fʌdɪ,dʌdɪ] 1 adj viejo; chapado a la antigua. 2 n persona f chapada a la antigua, vejestorio m.
fudge [fʌdʒ] 1 n dulce m de azúcar. 2 vt issue, problem esquivar, rehuir, dejar sin concretar, dejar en estado confuso. 3 vi quedar indeciso, no resolverse.
fuel [fjʊəl] 1 n combustible m, carburante m; (specifically coal) carbón m, (wood) leña f; (fig) pábulo m; to add ~ to the flames echar leña al fuego.
2 attr energético; ~ crisis crisis f energética; ~ needs

necesidades *fpl* energéticas; ~ **policy** política *f* energética.

3 *vt* (**a**) aprovisionar de combustible. (**b**) (*fig*) *speculation etc* estimular, provocar; *dispute* avivar, acalorar.

4 *vi* aprovisionarse de combustible.

fuel-cap ['fjʊəlkæp] *n* (*Aut*) tapa *f* del depósito de gasolina, trampilla *f*.

fuel injection ['fjʊəlɪn'dʒekʃən] *attr* de inyección; ~ **engine** motor *m* de inyección.

fuel-oil ['fjʊəlɔɪl] *n* aceite *m* combustible, fuel-oil *m*, mazut *m*.

fuel-pump ['fjʊəlpʌmp] *n* bomba *f* de combustible.

fuel-saving ['fjʊəl,seɪvɪŋ] *adj* que ahorra combustible.

fuel-tank ['fjʊəltæŋk] *n* depósito *m* de combustible.

fug [fʌg] *n* (*esp Brit*) aire *m* viciado (*or* confinado, cargado), tufo *m*; **what a** ~! ¡qué olor!; **there's a** ~ **in here** aquí huele a encerrado.

fuggy ['fʌgɪ] *adj* (*esp Brit*) *air* viciado, cargado; *room* que huele a encerrado.

fugitive ['fju:dʒɪtɪv] **1** *adj* fugitivo. **2** *n* fugitivo *m*, -a *f*; (*refugee*) refugiado *m*, -a *f*; ~ **from justice** prófugo *m*, -a *f*.

fugue [fju:g] *n* fuga *f*.

fulcrum ['fʌlkrəm] *n* fulcro *m*.

fulfil, (*US*) **fulfill** [fʊl'fɪl] **1** *vt duty, promise* cumplir con; *ambition, norm, plan* realizar; *condition* satisfacer, llenar; *order* ejecutar. **2** *vr*: **to** ~ **o.s.** realizarse (plenamente).

fulfilling [fʊl'fɪlɪŋ] *adj work etc* que realiza a uno.

fulfilment, (*US*) **fulfillment** [fʊl'fɪlmənt] *n* cumplimiento *m*; realización *f*; satisfacción *f*; ejecución *f*; (*satisfied feeling*) contento *m*, satisfacción *f*.

full [fʊl] **1** *adj* (**a**) (*filled*) lleno; *vehicle etc* completo (*also* ~ **up**); ~ **of cares** lleno de cuidados; ~ **of hope** lleno de esperanza, ilusionado; ~ **to bursting** lleno de bote en bote; ~ **to overflowing** lleno hasta los bordes; ~ **house** (*Theat*) lleno *m*; '~ **house**' 'no hay localidades'; ~ **measure** medida *f* completa, cantidad *f* completa; **to be** ~ **of** estar lleno de; **I'm** ~ **(up)** (*of food*) no puedo más; **we are** ~ **up for July** no tenemos nada libre para julio; **I've had a** ~ **day** he estado ocupado todo el día; **he's had a** ~ **life** ha tenido una vida llena de actividades; **he was very** ~ **of himself*** estaba la mar de engreído; no paró de hablar de sus cosas.

(**b**) (*fig*) *session* pleno, plenario; *member* de número; *authority, employment, power* pleno.

(**c**) (*complete*) completo; *account* detallado, extenso; *meal* completo; *fare, pay, price* íntegro; sin descuento; *speed, strength* máximo; *text* íntegro; *dress* de etiqueta, *uniform* de gala; **in** ~ **colour** a todo color; ~ **cost** coste *m* total; ~ **employment** pleno empleo *m*; ~ **house** (*Cards*) full *m*; ~ **marks** puntuación *f* máxima; ~ **member** socio *mf* numerario; ~ **moon** luna *f* llena, plenilunio *m*; ~ **name** nombre *m* y apellidos; **he was suspended on** ~ **pay** se le suspendió sin reducción de sueldo; ~ **professor** (*US*) profesor *m*, -ora *f* titular; **with** ~ **particulars** con todos los detalles; **until we have** ~ **information** hasta que tengamos todos los datos; **in the** ~ **sense of the word** en el sentido más amplio de la palabra; **a** ~ **hour** una hora entera, una hora larga; **a** ~ **3 miles** 3 millas largas.

(**d**) *face* redondo; *figure* llenito; holgado; *bosom* abultado, (*euph*) importante; *lips* grueso; *skirt* amplio; *V* **speed** *etc*.

2 *adv* (**a**) ~ **well** perfectamente, muy bien, sobradamente; **to know** ~ **well that** ... saber perfectamente que ...; **he understands** ~ **well that** ... se da cuenta cabal de que ...

(**b**) **it hit him** ~ **in the face** le dio de lleno en la cara.

3 *n*: **in** ~ sin abreviar, por extenso, sin quitar nada; **name in** ~ nombre *m* y apellidos; **text in** ~ texto *m* íntegro; **to pay in** ~ pagar la deuda entera; **to the** ~ completamente, al máximum.

fullback ['fʊlbæk] *n* defensa *mf*; (*Rugby*) zaguero *m*.

full-beam ['fʊl'bi:m] *attr*: ~ **headlights** luces *fpl* largas, luces *fpl* de carretera.

full-blast ['fʊl'blɑ:st] *adv work* a máxima capacidad; *travel* a toda velocidad; *play etc* al máximo volumen, a toda potencia.

full-blooded ['fʊl'blʌdɪd] *adj character* viril, vigoroso; *attack* vigoroso; *animal* de raza.

full-blown ['fʊl'bləʊn] *adj* (*fig*) hecho y derecho.

full-bodied ['fʊl'bɒdɪd] *adj cry* fuerte; *wine* de mucho cuerpo.

full-cream ['fʊl'kri:m] *adj*: ~ **milk** leche *f* cremosa, leche *f* sin desnatar.

full-dress ['fʊl'dres] **1** *adj function* de etiqueta, de gala. **2** *n* traje *m* de etiqueta.

fuller ['fʊləʳ] *n*: ~**'s earth** tierra *f* de batán.

full-face [,fʊl'feɪs] *adj portrait* de rostro entero.

full-fledged ['fʊl'fledʒd] *adj* (*US*) = **fully-fledged.**

full-frontal ['fʊl'frʌntl] *adj* (*unrestrained*) desenfrenado; ~ **nude** desnudo *m* visto de frente.

full-grown ['fʊl'grəʊn] *adj* crecido, maduro.

full-length ['fʊl'leŋθ] **1** *adj picture* de cuerpo entero; *novel, study* completo, extenso; *pool etc* de tamaño normal; ~ **film** cinta *f* de largo metraje, largometraje *m*. **2** *adv*: **he was lying** ~ estaba tumbado todo lo largo que era.

fullness ['fʊlnɪs] *n* plenitud *f*; amplitud *f*; **in the** ~ **of time** a su debido tiempo.

full-page [,fʊl'peɪdʒ] *adj advert etc* de plana entera, de página entera.

full-scale ['fʊl'skeɪl] *adj study* amplio, extenso; *investigation* de gran alcance; *attack* en gran escala; *plan, model* de tamaño natural.

full-sized ['fʊl'saɪzd] *adj* de tamaño normal.

full stop ['fʊl'stɒp] *n* (*Brit*) punto *m*; **you failed,** ~ te suspendieron, y punto; **to come to a** ~ (*fig*) pararse, paralizarse, quedar detenido en un punto muerto.

full-throated ['fʊl'θrəʊtɪd] *adj cry etc* fuerte, a pleno pulmón.

full-time ['fʊl'taɪm] **1** *adj professional* en plena dedicación, *worker* que trabaja una jornada completa, que trabaja a pleno tiempo; ~ **course** curso *m* a dedicación plena; ~ **employment,** ~ **work** trabajo *m* de jornada completa; **a** ~ **job** un puesto de plena dedicación.

2 *adv*: **to work** ~ trabajar en régimen de dedicación exclusiva, trabajar una jornada entera.

3 *n* (*Sport*) fin *m* del partido.

fully ['fʊlɪ] *adv* (**a**) (*completely*) completamente, enteramente; ~ **dressed** completamente vestido; **I'm not** ~ **convinced** no me convenzo del todo; **I don't** ~ **understand** no lo acabo de comprender. (**b**) (*at least*) **he earns** ~ **as much as I do** gana sin duda tanto como yo; **it is** ~ **3 miles** son lo menos 3 millas; **we waited** ~ **3 hours** esperamos 3 horas largas.

fully-fashioned ['fʊlɪ'fæʃnd] *adj stocking* menguado, de costura francesa.

fully-fledged ['fʊlɪ'fledʒd] *adj* (*Brit*) *bird* adulto; en edad de volar, capaz de volar; (*fig*) hecho y derecho, con pleno derecho.

fully-paid ['fʊlɪ'peɪd] *adj*: ~ **share** acción *f* liberada.

fulminate ['fʊlmɪneɪt] *vi*: **to** ~ **against** tronar contra.

fulsome ['fʊlsəm] *adj* exagerado, excesivo; *person* servil, obsequioso.

fumble ['fʌmbl] **1** *vt* manosear, revolver (*etc*) torpemente; *ball* dejar caer; **to** ~ **one's way along** ir a tientas.

2 *vi*: **to** ~ **for sth** buscar algo con las manos; **to** ~ **for a word** titubear buscando una palabra; **to** ~ **in one's pockets** revolver en los bolsillos; **to** ~ **with sth** manejar (*etc*) algo torpemente; **to** ~ **with a door** tratar torpemente de abrir una puerta.

fume [fju:m] *vi* (**a**) humear. (**b**) (*be furious*) estar furioso, rabiar, echar humo; echar pestes (*at thing* contra, *at person* de).

fumes [fju:mz] *npl* humo *m*, gas *m*, vapor *m*.

fumigate ['fju:mɪgeɪt] *vt* fumigar.

fumigation [,fju:mɪ'geɪʃən] *n* fumigación *f*.

fun [fʌn] **1** *n* (*amusement*) diversión *f*; (*merriment*) alegría *f*; (*joke*) broma *f*; **for** ~, **in** ~ en broma; **it's great** ~ es muy divertido; **he's great** ~ es una persona divertidísima; **it's not much** ~ **for us** no nos divertimos en absoluto; **it's only his** ~ está bromeando, te está tomando el pelo; **to do sth for the** ~ **of it** hacer algo para divertirse, hacer algo sin propósito serio; **to have** ~ divertirse; **have** ~! ¡que os divirtáis!, ¡que lo paséis bien!; **what** ~ **we had!** ¡cómo nos divertimos!; **we had** ~ **with the passports** nos armamos un lío con los pasaportes; **they had lots of** ~ **and games at the party** se divirtieron una barbaridad en la fiesta; **he's having** ~ **and games with the nurse** se entiende con la enfermera; **she's been having** ~ **and games with the washing-machine** ha tenido muchos líos con la lavadora; **to make** ~ **of, to poke** ~ **at** burlarse de, ridiculizar; **to spoil the** ~ aguar la fiesta.

2 *adj*: **it's a** ~ **thing** es para divertirse; **she's a** ~ **person** es una persona divertida; es una persona a quien le gustan las diversiones.

function ['fʌŋkʃən] **1** *n* función *f*; **it is no part of my** ~ **to** + *infin* no corresponde a mi cargo + *infin*, no me compete a mí + *infin*; **to exceed one's** ~**s** excederse en sus funciones.

2 *vi* funcionar.

functional ['fʌŋkʃnəl] *adj* funcional; ~ **analysis** análisis *m*

funcional.
functionalism ['fʌŋkʃnəlɪzəm] *n* funcionalismo *m*.
functionary ['fʌŋkʃənərɪ] *n* funcionario *m*.
function key ['fʌŋkʃənkiː] *n* tecla *f* de función.
function word ['fʌŋkʃənwɜːd] *n* palabra *f* funcional.
fund [fʌnd] **1** *n* fondo *m*; **~s** fondos *mpl*; **to be in ~s** estar en fondos; **to have a ~ of stories** saber un montón de chistes.
2 *vt* (**a**) (*Fin*) financiar; proveer fondos a; *debt* consolidar. (**b**) *campaign etc* pagar, costear, financiar.
fundamental [ˌfʌndə'mentl] **1** *adj* fundamental; **to be ~ to** ser esencial para. **2** *n*: **~s** fundamentos *mpl*.
fundamentalism [ˌfʌndə'mentəlɪzəm] *n* fundamentalismo *m*, integrismo *m*.
fundamentalist [ˌfʌndə'mentəlɪst] **1** *adj* fundamentalista, integrista. **2** *n* fundamentalista *mf*, integrista *mf*.
fundamentally [ˌfʌndə'mentəlɪ] *adv* fundamentalmente, esencialmente.
funding ['fʌndɪŋ] *n* (**a**) (*funds*) fondos *mpl*, finanzas *fpl*; (*act of ~*) financiación *f*, provisión *f* de fondos. (**b**) (*of debt*) consolidación *f*.
fund-raiser ['fʌnd,reɪzə^r] *n* recogedor *m*, -ora *f* de fondos.
fund-raising ['fʌnd,reɪzɪŋ] *n* recolección *f* de fondos, recaudación *f* de fondos.
funeral ['fjuːnərəl] **1** *adj and attr march etc* fúnebre; *pyre* funerario; *service* de difuntos; **~ cortège** cortejo *m* fúnebre, comitiva *f* fúnebre; **~ director** director *m* de funeraria; **~ march** marcha *f* fúnebre; **~ oration** oración *f* fúnebre; **~ parlour** funeraria *f*; **~ procession = ~ cortège**; **~ service** exequias *fpl*.
2 *n* entierro *m*, funerales *mpl*; **that's your ~!*** ¡allá te las compongas!, ¡allá tú!, ¡con tu pan te lo comas!
funereal [fjuː'nɪərɪəl] *adj* fúnebre, funéreo.
funfair ['fʌnfɛə^r] *n* parque *m* de atracciones.
fungi ['fʌŋgaɪ] *npl of* **fungus**.
fungicide ['fʌŋgɪsaɪd] *n* fungicida *m*.
fungoid ['fʌŋgɔɪd] *adj* parecido a un hongo, como un hongo; (*Med*) fungoide.
fungous ['fʌŋgəs] *adj* fungoso.
fungus ['fʌŋgəs] *n*, *pl* **fungi** ['fʌŋgaɪ] hongo *m*.
funicular [fjuː'nɪkjʊlə^r] *n* (*also* **railway**) (ferrocarril *m*) funicular *m*.
funk* [fʌŋk] **1** *n* (**a**) (*Brit*: *state*) canguelo* *m*, jindama* *f*, mieditis* *f*; **to be in a (blue) ~** estar muerto de miedo.
(**b**) (*person*) gallina* *mf*, mandria *mf*.
2 *vt*: **to ~ it** rajarse, dejar de hacer algo por miedo, retirarse por miedo; **to ~ doing something** dejar de hacer algo por miedo.
funky* ['fʌŋkɪ] *adj* cobarde, miedoso; **you're ~!** ¡cobarde!
fun-loving ['fʌn,lʌvɪŋ] *adj* amigo de diversiones, amigo de pasarlo bien.
funnel ['fʌnl] **1** *n* embudo *m*; (*Brit Naut, Rail etc*) chimenea *f*. **2** *vt traffic etc* acanalar, canalizar (*through* por); *aid, finance* encauzar, dirigir (*through* por).
funnily ['fʌnɪlɪ] *adv* de un modo divertido; **~ enough ...** cosa curiosa ..., cosa más rara ...
funny ['fʌnɪ] **1** *adj* (**a**) (*amusing*) divertido, gracioso, cómico; (*full of jokes*) chistoso; **~ money*** una millonada; **~ story** chiste *m*; **I thought the film very ~** la película me hizo mucha gracia; **that's not ~** eso no tiene gracia; **I find it ~ that ..., it strikes me as ~ that ...** me hace mucha gracia que ...; **he's trying to be ~** quiere hacerse el gracioso; **don't try to be ~** no se haga el gracioso.
(**b**) (*odd*) raro, curioso; **a ~ feeling** una sensación rara; **I find it ~ that ..., it strikes me as ~ that ...** me extraña que + *subj*, se me hace extraño que + *subj*; **the ~ thing about it is that ...** lo curioso es que ...; **he's ~ that way** tiene esa manía.
2 *n*: **funnies** (*US*) sección *f* de historietas gráficas (del periódico).
funnybone ['fʌnɪbəʊn] *n* hueso *m* de la alegría.
fun-run ['fʌnrʌn] *n* maratón *m* (corto, de ciudad, para los no atletas).
fur [fɜː^r] **1** *n* piel *f*; (*on tongue*) saburra *f*; (*in kettle*) sarro *m*; **~ coat** abrigo *m* de pieles. **2** *vi* (*kettle etc*: *also* **to ~ up**) cubrirse de sarro, formar sarro.
furbish ['fɜːbɪʃ] *vt*: **to ~ up** renovar, restaurar.
furious ['fjʊərɪəs] *adj* furioso; *effort etc* frenético, violento; *pace* vertiginoso; **to be ~ with sb** estar muy enfadado con uno; **to get ~** ponerse furioso.
furiously ['fjʊərɪəslɪ] *adv* con furia.
furl [fɜːl] *vt* (*Naut*) aferrar; *wings* recoger.
furlong ['fɜːlɒŋ] *n* estadio *m* (*octava parte de una milla*).
furlough ['fɜːləʊ] *n* (*Mil etc*) licencia *f*, permiso *m*.
furnace ['fɜːnɪs] *n* horno *m*; **the town was like a ~** la ciudad era un horno.
furnish ['fɜːnɪʃ] *vt* (**a**) (*provide*) proveer, suministrar, proporcionar (*sb with sth* algo a uno); *opportunity* dar, proporcionar, deparar; *proof* aducir; *information* facilitar; **we are ~ed with all that is necessary** estamos equipados con todo lo necesario.
(**b**) *room* amueblar (*with* de); **~ed flat** (*Brit*) piso *m* amueblado.
furnishings ['fɜːnɪʃɪŋz] *npl* muebles *mpl*, mobiliario *m*.
furniture ['fɜːnɪtʃə^r] *n* muebles *mpl*, mobiliario *m*, mueblaje *m*; (*piece of ~*) mueble *m*.
furniture mover ['fɜːnɪtʃə,muːvə^r] *n* (*US*), **furniture remover** ['fɜːnɪtʃərɪ,muːvə^r] *n* compañía *f* de mudanzas.
furniture polish ['fɜːnɪtʃə,pɒlɪʃ] *n* cera *f* para muebles.
furniture shop ['fɜːnɪtʃə,ʃɒp] *n* tienda *f* de muebles.
furniture van ['fɜːnɪtʃə,væn] *n* camión *m* de mudanzas.
furore [fjʊə'rɔːrɪ] *n*, (*US*) **furor** ['fjʊərɔː^r] *n* ola *f* de protestas; escándalo *m*; ola *f* de entusiasmo.
furrier ['fʌrɪə^r] *n* peletero *m*.
furrow ['fʌrəʊ] **1** *n* surco *m*; (*on face*) arruga *f*; **to plough a lonely ~** ser el único en estudiar (*etc*) algo.
2 *vt* surcar; arrugar.
3 *vi* arrugarse; **his brow ~ed** frunció el ceño.
furrowed ['fʌrəʊd] *adj*: **with ~ brow** con ceño fruncido.
furry ['fɜːrɪ] *adj* peludo; **~ toy** juguete *m* de felpa.
further ['fɜːðə^r] *comp of* **far**: **1** *adv* (**a**) (*place*) más lejos, más allá; **move it ~ away** apártalo un poco más; **~ back** más atrás; **~ off** más lejos; **~ on** más adelante; **how much ~ is it?** ¿cuánto camino nos queda?; **have you much ~ to go?** ¿le queda mucho camino por hacer?; **I got no ~ with him** no pude adelantar más con él, no pude hacer más progresos con él; **nothing is ~ from my thoughts** nada más lejos de mi intención.
(**b**) (*more*) además; **and I ~ believe that ...** y creo además que ...
(**c**) **to go ~ into a matter** estudiar una cosa más a fondo; **they questioned us ~** nos hicieron más preguntas; **he heard nothing ~** no le volvieron a decir nada; **don't trouble yourself any ~** no se moleste más.
(**d**) **~ to that** además de eso; **~ to my letter of the 7th** con relación a mi carta del 7.
2 *adj* (**a**) (*place*) más lejano, más remoto, de más allá; *end, side* opuesto; **at the ~ end** en el otro extremo.
(**b**) (*additional*) nuevo, adicional; complementario, supletorio; *education* superior; **~ education** educación *f* postescolar; **~ facts** nuevos datos *mpl*, más datos *mpl*; **after ~ consideration** después de considerarlo más detenidamente; **until ~ notice** hasta nuevo aviso; **till ~ orders** hasta nueva orden; **without ~ loss of time** sin más pérdida de tiempo.
3 *vt* promover, fomentar, adelantar.
furtherance ['fɜːðərəns] *n* promoción *f*, fomento *m*.
furthermore ['fɜːðɜː'mɔː^r] *adv* además.
furthermost ['fɜːðəməʊst] *adj* más lejano.
furthest ['fɜːðɪst] *superl of* **far**: **1** *adv* más lejos; **that's the ~ that anyone has gone** es el punto extremo a que han llegado, nadie ha ido más allá.
2 *adj* más lejano; extremo.
furtive ['fɜːtɪv] *adj* furtivo.
furtively ['fɜːtɪvlɪ] *adv* furtivamente.
fury ['fjʊərɪ] *n* furor *m*, furia *f*; violencia *f*; frenesí *m*; **the Furies** las Furias; **like ~** a toda furia, (*of person*) hecho una furia; **to be in a ~** estar furioso; **to work o.s. up into a ~** montar en cólera.
furze [fɜːz] *n* aulaga *f*, tojo *m*.
fuse, (US) fuze [fjuːz] **1** *n* (*Elec*) plomo *m*, fusible *m*; (*Mil*) mecha *f*, espoleta *f*; **he's on a very short ~*** tiene mucho genio.
2 *vt* (**a**) (*Brit Elec*) fundir. (**b**) (*fig*) fusionar.
3 *vi* (**a**) (*Elec*) fundirse; **the lights ~d** se fundieron los plomos. (**b**) (*fig*) fusionarse.
fuse-box ['fjuːzbɒks] *n* caja *f* de fusibles.
fused [fjuːzd] *adj* (*Elec*) con fusible; **~ plug** enchufe *m* con fusible.
fuselage ['fjuːzəlɑːʒ] *n* fuselaje *m*.
fuse-wire ['fjuːzwaɪə^r] *n* alambre *m* de fusible.
fusilier [ˌfjuːzɪ'lɪə^r] *n* (*Brit*) fusilero *m*.
fusillade [ˌfjuːzɪ'leɪd] *n* descarga *f* cerrada (*also fig*).
fusion ['fjuːʒən] *n* fusión *f* (*also fig*), fundición *f*.
fuss [fʌs] **1** *n* (**a**) (*noise, bustle*) conmoción *f*, bulla *f*, alharacas *fpl*.
(**b**) (*dispute*) lío *m*; protesta *f*; **that ~ about the money** ese lío con el dinero; **to kick up (or make) a ~** dar cuatro

voces, armar un lío; **I think you were quite right to make a ~** creo que hiciste bien en protestar.

(**c**) (*excessive display*) aspaviento *m*, hazañería *f*; **it's a lot of ~ about nothing** mucho ruido y pocas nueces; **there's no need to make such a ~** no es para tanto; **to make a ~ of** hacer mimos a, hacer fiestas a.

(**d**) (*formalities*) ceremonias *fpl*; trámites *mpl*; **such a ~ to get a passport!** ¡tanta lata para conseguir un pasaporte!

2 *vt person* molestar, fastidiar; **don't ~ me!** ¡no fastidies!

3 *vi* agitarse, preocuparse (por bagatelas); **to ~ over sb** mimar con exceso a uno.

◆**fuss about, fuss around** *vi* andar azacaneado, andar de acá para allá; preocuparse de menudencias.

fussily ['fʌsɪlɪ] *adv* (*V adj*) exigentemente, puntillosamente.

fusspot* ['fʌspɒt] *n* quisquilloso *m*, -a *f*.

fussy ['fʌsɪ] *adj* (**a**) *person* (*demanding*) exigente; quisquilloso; (*nervous*) nervioso. (**b**) *details* nimio; *dress* con muchos ringorrangos; *decoration* con muchos adornos.

fusty ['fʌstɪ] *adj* mohoso, rancio; *air, room* que huele a cerrado.

futile ['fju:taɪl] *adj* inútil, vano, infructuoso.

futility [fju:'tɪlɪtɪ] *n* inutilidad *f*, lo inútil.

future ['fju:tʃəʳ] **1** *adj* futuro; venidero; **in ~ years** en los años venideros.

2 *n* (**a**) futuro *m*, porvenir *m*; **in (the) ~** en el futuro, en lo sucesivo; **in the near ~** en fecha próxima; **there's no ~ in it** esto no tiene porvenir; **what does the ~ hold for us?** ¿qué nos tiene reservado el destino?

(**b**) **~s** (*Comm*) futuros *mpl*; **~s market** mercado *m* de futuros.

futurism ['fju:tʃərɪzəm] *n* futurismo *m*.

futurist ['fju:tʃərɪst] *n* (*futurologist*) futurólogo *m*, -a *f*; (*Art*) futurista *mf*.

futuristic [,fju:tʃə'rɪstɪk] *adj* futurístico.

futurologist [,fju:tʃər'ɒlədʒɪst] *n* futurólogo *m*, -a *f*.

futurology [,fju:tʃər'ɒlədʒɪ] *n* futurología *f*.

fuze [fju:z] *n* (*US*) = **fuse**.

fuzz [fʌz] *n* (**a**) tamo *m*, pelusa *f*; (*on face*) vello *m*. (**b**) **the ~** (‡) la pasma‡, la bofia‡ (*Sp*), la jara‡ (*Mex*), la cana‡ (*SC*).

fuzzily ['fʌzɪlɪ] *adv* (**a**) borrosamente. (**b**) confusamente.

fuzzy ['fʌzɪ] *adj* (**a**) (*hairy*) velloso; *hair* muy rizado. (**b**) (*blurred*) borroso. (**c**) *reasoning* confuso, nada claro.

fwd (*esp Comm*) *abbr of* **forward**.

fwy (*US*) *abbr of* **freeway**.

FY *abbr of* **fiscal year**.

FYI *abbr of* **for your information**.

G

G, g [dʒiː] *n* (**a**) (*letter*) G, g *f*; **G for George** G de Gerona. (**b**) **G** (*Mus*) sol *m*, **G major** sol *m* mayor; **G-string** (*Mus*) cuerda *f* de sol; (*hum*) tanga *f*, taparrabo *m*. (**c**) (*Scol*: *mark*) *abbr of* **Good** Notable, N. (**d**) (*US Cine*) *abbr of* **general audience** todos los públicos. (**e**) (‡) *abbr of* **grand** (*Brit*) mil libras *fpl*, (*US*) mil dólares *mpl*.

g. (**a**) *abbr of* **gram(s)**, **gramme(s)** gramo(s) *m(pl)*, gr. (**b**) *n abbr of* **gravity** gravedad *f*, g.; **G-force** fuerza *f* de la gravedad.

GA (*US Post*) *abbr of* **Georgia**.

g.a. *abbr of* **general average**.

GAB *n abbr of* **General Arrangements to Borrow**.

gab* [gæb] **1** *n* (*chatter*) cháchara *f*; (*chat*) charla *f*; **to have the gift of (the)** ~ tener mucha labia, tener un pico de oro. **2** *vi* parlotear, charlar, cotorrear.

gabardine [ˌgæbəˈdiːn] *n* gabardina *f*.

gabble [ˈgæbl] **1** *n* torrente *m* de palabras ininteligibles.
2 *vt* decir (*or* leer *etc*) atropelladamente, pronunciar de modo ininteligible.
3 *vi* hablar atropelladamente; parlotear, cotorrear.

◆gabble away *vi*: **they were gabbling away in French** hablaban atropelladamente en francés, parlaban francés.

gabby* [ˈgæbɪ] *adj* (*esp US*) hablador, locuaz.

gaberdine [ˌgæbəˈdiːn] *n* gabardina *f*.

gable [ˈgeɪbl] **1** *n* aguilón *m*.
2 *attr*: ~ **end** hastial *m*; ~ **roof** tejado *m* de dos aguas, tejado *m* de caballete.

Gabon [gəˈbɒn] *n* Gabón *m*.

Gabriel [ˈgeɪbrɪəl] *nm* Gabriel.

gad[1] [gæd] *vi*: **to ~ about** salir mucho, viajar mucho, callejear.

gad[2] [gæd] *interj* ¡cáspita!

gadabout [ˈgædəbaʊt] *n* azotacalles *mf*, pindonga *f*.

gadfly [ˈgædflaɪ] *n* tábano *m*.

gadget [ˈgædʒɪt] *n* artilugio *m*, chisme *m*, aparato *m*.

gadgetry [ˈgædʒɪtrɪ] *n* chismes *mpl*, aparatos *mpl*.

gadolinium [ˌgædəˈlɪnɪəm] *n* gadolinio *m*.

gadwall [ˈgædwɔːl] *n* ánade *m* friso.

Gael [geɪl] *n* gaélico *m*, -a *f*.

Gaelic [ˈgeɪlɪk] **1** *adj* gaélico. **2** *n* (*Ling*) gaélico *m*.

gaff[1] [gæf] **1** *n* arpón *m*, garfio *m*. **2** *vt* arponear, enganchar.

gaff[2]‡ [gæf] *n*: **to blow the ~** descubrir el pastel.

gaffe [gæf] *n* plancha *f*, patinazo *m*, metedura *f* de pata; **to make a ~** tirarse una plancha.

gaffer [ˈgæfəʳ] *n* (**a**) (*old man*) vejete *m*, tío *m*. (**b**) (*Brit*: *foreman*) capataz *m*; (*boss*) jefe *m*; (*Cine, TV*) iluminista *mf*.

gag [gæg] **1** *n* (**a**) mordaza *f*; (*Parl*) clausura *f*. (**b**) (*Theat*) morcilla *f*; (*joke*) chiste *m*; (*hoax*) broma *f*; (*gimmick*) truco *m* publicitario; **is this a ~?** ¿es una broma esto?; **it's a ~ to raise funds** es un truco para reunir fondos.
2 *vt* amordazar; (*fig*) amordazar, hacer callar; (*Parl*) clausurar; *discussion* impedir, estorbar.
3 *vi* (*Theat*) meter morcillas; (*joke*) contar chistes, chunguearse; **I was only ~ging** lo dije en broma.

gaga* [ˈgɑːˈgɑː] *adj* gagá*, lelo, chocho; **to be going ~** chochear; **to go ~** (*senile*) chochear; (*ecstatic*) caérsele a uno la baba.

gage [geɪdʒ] *n* (*US*) = **gauge**.

gaggle [ˈgægl] *n* manada *f*.

gaiety [ˈgeɪɪtɪ] *n* alegría *f*, regocijo *m*; (*of gathering etc*) animación *f*; **gaieties** diversiones *fpl* alegres; **it contributes to the ~ of nations** alegra al mundo entero.

gaily [ˈgeɪlɪ] *adv* alegremente.

gain [geɪn] **1** *n* (*increase*) aumento *m* (*in, of* de); (*profit, earning*) ganancia *f*, beneficio *m*; **his loss is our ~** pierde él y ganamos nosotros; **there have been ~s of up to 3 points** ha habido alzas de hasta 3 enteros; **I lost all my ~s** perdí todas mis ganancias.
2 *vt* ganar; *objective* conseguir; *possession, territory etc* adquirir; *approval, respect* merecer, captar, conquistar; (*reach*) llegar a, alcanzar, ganar; *time* ganar; **my watch has ~ed 5 minutes** mi reloj se ha adelantado 5 minutos; **I've ~ed 3 kilos** he engordado 3 kilos; **the shares have ~ed 4 points** las acciones han subido 4 enteros; **what have you ~ed by it?** ¿qué has ganado con esto?; **what do you hope to ~?** ¿qué provecho vas a sacar?
3 *vi* (*shares etc*) aumentar en valor, subir; (*Med*) mejorar; (*in weight*) engordar, poner carnes; (*in advantage*) ganar terreno; **to ~ in popularity** resultar más popular, adquirir mayor popularidad; **it ~s in contrast with the other picture** gana al compararse con el otro cuadro.

◆gain (up)on *vt*: **to ~ (up)on sb** ir ganando terreno a uno, ir alcanzando a uno; (*and outstrip*) ir dejando atrás a uno.

gainer [ˈgeɪnəʳ] *n*: **to be the ~** salir ganando.

gainful [ˈgeɪnfʊl] *adj employment* remunerado, retribuido.

gainfully [ˈgeɪnfəlɪ] *adv*: **to be ~ employed** tener un trabajo retribuido; **there was nothing that could ~ be said** no había nada provechoso que se pudiese decir.

gainsay [ˌgeɪnˈseɪ] (*irr*: *V* **say**) *vt* (*liter*) contradecir, negar; **it cannot be gainsaid** es innegable.

gait [geɪt] *n* modo *m* de andar, paso *m*.

gaiter [ˈgeɪtəʳ] *n* polaina *f*.

gal* [gæl] *n* = **girl**.

gal. *abbr of* **gallon(s)**.

gala [ˈgɑːlə] **1** *n* fiesta *f*; (*Sport*) certamen *m*, concurso *m*. **2** *attr*: ~ **day** día *m* de gala.

galactic [gəˈlæktɪk] *adj* (*Med*) lácteo; (*Astron*) galáctico.

Galapagos Islands [gəˈlæpəgəsˌaɪləndz] *npl* Islas *fpl* (de los) Galápagos.

Galatians [gəˈleɪʃənz] *npl* Galateos *mpl*.

galaxy [ˈgæləksɪ] *n* galaxia *f*; (*fig*) grupo *m* brillante, constelación *f*, pléyade *f*.

gale [geɪl] *n* ventarrón *m*, vendaval *m*; (*storm*) tormenta *f*, tempestad *f*; **to blow a ~** soplar una galerna, soplar una tempestad.

gale-force [ˈgeɪlfɔːs] *attr*: ~ **10** vendaval *m* de fuerza 10; ~ **winds** vientos *mpl* de tormenta.

Galen [ˈgeɪlən] *nm* Galeno.

gale-warning [ˈgeɪlˌwɔːnɪŋ] *n* aviso *m* de tormenta.

Galicia [gəˈlɪʃɪə] *n* (**a**) (*Central Europe*) Galitzia *f*. (**b**) (*Spain*) Galicia *f*.

Galician [gəˈlɪʃɪən] **1** *adj* gallego. **2** *n* (**a**) gallego *m*, -a *f*. (**b**) (*Ling*) gallego *m*.

Galilean [ˌgælɪˈliːən] **1** *adj* (*Bible, Geog*) galileo; (*Astron*) galileico. **2** *n* galileo *m*, -a *f*; **the ~** (*Bible*) el Galileo.

Galilee [ˈgælɪliː] *n* Galilea *f*.

gall[1] [gɔːl] **1** *n* (**a**) (*Anat*) bilis *f*, hiel *f*. (**b**) (*fig*) hiel *f*; bilis *f*; (*) descaro *m*; **she had the ~ to say that** tuvo el descaro de decir eso. **2** *vt* mortificar.

gall[2] [gɔːl] *n* (*Bot*) agalla *f*; (*on animal*) matadura *f*.

gallant **1** *adj* (**a**) [ˈgælənt] (*brave*) valiente, valeroso, bizarro; (*showy*) lucido, gallardo; (*stately*) imponente; **the ~ captain** el intrépido capitán.
(**b**) [gəˈlænt] (*attentive to women*) galante; cortés, atento.
2 [gəˈlænt] *n* galán *m*.

gallantly [ˈgæləntlɪ] *adv* (**a**) valientemente. (**b**) galantemente; cortésmente.

gallantry [ˈgæləntrɪ] (**a**) (*bravery*) valentía *f*, valor *m*, heroísmo *m*, bizarría *f*. (**b**) (*courtesy*) galantería *f*, cortesía *f*; **gallantries** galanterías *fpl*.

gall-bladder [ˈgɔːlˌblædəʳ] *n* vesícula *f* biliar.

galleon [ˈgælɪən] *n* galeón *m*.

gallery ['gælərɪ] *n* galería *f* (*also Min, Theat*); (*for spectators*) tribuna *f*; (**art**) ~ museo *m* (de bellas artes); **to play to the ~** actuar para la galería.
galley ['gælɪ] *n* (**a**) (*ship*) galera *f*. (**b**) (*kitchen*) cocina *f*, fogón *m*. (**c**) (*Typ*) galerada *f*, galera *f*.
galley-proof ['gælɪpruːf] *n* galerada *f*.
galley-slave ['gælɪsleɪv] *n* galeote *m*.
Gallic ['gælɪk] *adj* gálico, galo, galicano.
gallicism ['gælɪsɪzəm] *n* galicismo *m*.
galling ['gɔːlɪŋ] *adj* mortificante.
gallium ['gælɪəm] *n* galio *m*.
gallivant [ˌgælɪ'vænt] *vi* = **gad**[1].
gallon ['gælən] *n* galón *m* (= 4,546 *litros*, *US* = 3,785 *litros*).
gallop ['gæləp] **1** *n* galope *m*; (*distance covered*) galopada *f*; **at a ~** a galope; **at full ~** a galope tendido; **to break into a ~** echar a galopar.
2 *vt* hacer galopar.
3 *vi* galopar; **to ~ past** desfilar a galope.
◆**gallop off** *vi* alejarse a galope.
◆**gallop up** *vi* llegar a galope.
galloping ['gæləpɪŋ] *adj* (*Med and fig*) galopante.
gallows ['gæləʊz] **1** *n sing* horca *f*. **2** *attr*: ~ **humour** (*fig*) humor *m* negro *or* macabro.
gallstone ['gɔːlstəʊn] *n* cálculo *m* biliario.
Gallup poll ['gæləpˌpəʊl] *n* sondeo *m* Gallup, encuesta *f* Gallup.
galore [gə'lɔːʳ] *adv* en abundancia, a porrillo.
galosh [gə'lɒʃ] *n* chanclo *m* (de goma).
galumph [gə'lʌmf] *vi* (*hum*) brincar alegre pero torpemente, brincar como un elefante contento.
galvanic [gæl'vænɪk] *adj* galvánico.
galvanism ['gælvənɪzəm] *n* galvanismo *m*.
galvanize ['gælvənaɪz] *vt* (**a**) galvanizar. (**b**) (*fig*) galvanizar; **to ~ sb into life** sacudir a uno de su abstracción; **to ~ sb into doing sth** sacudir a uno para que haga algo.
galvanized ['gælvənaɪzd] *adj* galvanizado.
galvanometer [ˌgælvə'nɒmɪtəʳ] *n* galvanómetro *m*.
Gambia ['gæmbɪə] *n*: (**The**) ~ Gambia *f*.
Gambian ['gæmbɪən] **1** *adj* gambiano. **2** *n* gambiano *m*, -a *f*.
gambit ['gæmbɪt] *n* gambito *m*; (*fig*) táctica *f*; **opening ~** estrategia *f* inicial.
gamble ['gæmbl] **1** *n* jugada *f* (de resultado imprevisible); empresa *f* arriesgada; **life's a ~** la vida es una lotería; **I did it as a pure ~** lo hice para probar suerte nada más; **the ~ came off** la tentativa tuvo éxito, la jugada nos salió bien; **to have a ~ on** *horse* jugar dinero a, apostar a, *company shares* especular en.
2 *vt* jugar, aventurar en el juego; **to ~ one's future** jugarse el porvenir.
3 *vi* jugar; (*Fin*) especular; **to ~ on the Stock Exchange** jugar a la bolsa; **he ~d on my being there** confiaba en que yo estuviera; **to ~ with others' money** especular con el dinero ajeno.
◆**gamble away** *vt* perder en el juego.
gambler ['gæmbləʳ] *n* jugador *m*, -ora *f*.
gambling ['gæmblɪŋ] **1** *n* juego *m*; **~ on the Stock Exchange** especulación *f* en la bolsa. **2** *attr*: ~ **debts** deudas *fpl* de juego; ~ **losses** pérdidas *fpl* de juego; **I'm not a ~ man** yo no juego.
gambling-den ['gæmblɪŋden] *n* garito *m*, casa *f* de juego.
gambol ['gæmbəl] *vi* brincar, retozar, juguetear.
game[1] [geɪm] **1** *n* (**a**) (*gen*) juego *m*; deporte *m*; (*match: with ball etc*) partido *m*, (*of cards, chess, snooker etc*) partida *f*; (*at bridge*) manga *f*; **~s** (*eg Olympic*) juegos *mpl*; **~, set and match** juego, set y partido; **~ of chance** juego *m* de azar; **~ theory** teoría *f* de los juegos; **it's only a ~** es un juego nada más; **this isn't a ~** esto no es ninguna broma, esto va de veras; **the ~ is not worth the candle** la cosa no vale la pena; **I was no good at ~s at school** en el colegio no tenía talento para los deportes; **to be off one's ~** no estar en forma, estar desentrenado; **to go to ~** (*Bridge*) ir a manga; **to have a ~ of chess** echar una partida de ajedrez; **to have a ~ with** (*tease*) tomar el pelo a, hacer una broma a; **to play the ~** (*fig*) jugar limpio; **he plays a good ~ of football** juega bien al fútbol, es buen futbolista; **two can play at that ~** donde las dan las toman; **to play a double ~** jugar doble; **to play a waiting ~** estar a ver venir, esperar hasta ver qué pasa; **to put sb off his ~** hacer fallar a uno; **that's what the ~'s all about** es lo más esencial, es lo más importante.
(**b**) (*deception*) **the ~ is up** todo se acabó; **they saw the ~ was up** comprendieron que ya no había nada que hacer; **what's the ~?** ¿qué hacéis ahí?, ¿qué pretendéis con eso?; **to give the ~ away** tirar de la manta; **we know his little ~** le conocemos el juego, le hemos calado; **I wonder what his ~ is?** ¿qué estará tramando?
(**c**) (*: *trouble*) lío* *m*; **I had such a ~ getting here** me hice un lío al venir aquí*; **what a ~ this is!** ¡qué faena!*
(**d**) (*business*) **how long have you been in this ~?** ¿cuánto tiempo llevas dedicado a esto?; **what's your ~?** ¿a qué te dedicas?
(**e**) (*) prostitución *f*; **to be on the ~** ser prostituta, hacer la calle*.
(**f**) (*Hunting*) caza *f*; *V* **big 1**.
2 *attr*: ~ **bird** ave *f* de caza; ~ **fish** salmón *m or* trucha *f*; ~ **fishing** pesca *f* de salmón *or* de trucha; ~ **laws** leyes *fpl* relativas a la caza; **~s master** profesor *m* de educación física; **~s mistress** profesora *f* de educación física; ~ **park** parque *m* natural, reserva *f* natural; ~ **plan** (*US: fig*) táctica *f*; ~ **reserve** coto *m* de caza; ~ **show** programa *m* concurso; ~ **warden** guarda *m* de caza, guardamonte *m*.
3 *adj* animoso, valiente; **are you ~?** ¿quieres?, ¿te animas?; **I'm ~** me apunto, cuenta conmigo; **to be ~ for anything** atreverse a todo.
4 *vi* jugar (por dinero).
game[2] [geɪm] *adj* (*lame*): **a ~ leg** una pierna coja.
gamebag ['geɪmbæg] *n* morral *m*.
gamecock ['geɪmkɒk] *n* gallo *m* de pelea.
gamekeeper ['geɪmˌkiːpəʳ] *n* guardabosque *m*.
gamely ['geɪmlɪ] *adv* bravamente.
gamesman ['geɪmzmən] *n*, *pl* **gamesmen** ['geɪmzmən] jugador *m* astuto.
gamesmanship ['geɪmzmənʃɪp] *n* arte *m* de ganar astutamente; habilidad *f*; **piece of ~** truco *m* para ganar.
gamester ['geɪmstəʳ] *n* jugador *m*, tahur *m*.
gamete ['gæmiːt] *n* gameto *m*.
gamin ['gæmɛ̃] *n* golfillo *m*.
gamine [gæ'miːn] **1** *n* chica *f* provocativa, joven *f* picaruela. **2** *attr*: ~ **haircut** corte *m* a lo garçon.
gaming ['geɪmɪŋ] **1** *n* juego *m*. **2** *attr*: ~ **laws** leyes *fpl* reguladoras del juego.
gaming-house ['geɪmɪŋhaʊs] *n*, *pl* **gaming-houses** ['geɪmɪŋhaʊzɪz] casa *f* de juego.
gamma ['gæmə] **1** *n* gama *f*. **2** *attr*: ~ **rays** rayos *mpl* gama.
gammon ['gæmən] *n* (*Brit*) jamón *m*.
gammy* ['gæmɪ] *adj* (*Brit*) tullido, lisiado.
gamp* [gæmp] *n* (*Brit*) paraguas *m*.
gamut ['gæmət] *n* gama *f*; **to run the whole ~ of ...** recorrer toda la gama de ...
gamy ['geɪmɪ] *adj meat* faisandé.
gander ['gændəʳ] *n* (**a**) ganso *m* (macho). (**b**) **to take a ~**‡ echar un vistazo (*at* a).
gang [gæŋ] *n* pandilla *f*, cuadrilla *f*, grupo *m*; (*of workmen*) brigada *f*; (*criminal*) pandilla *f*; **G~ Of Four** (*Pol*) Banda *f* de los Cuatro; **he's one of the ~ now** ya es uno de los nuestros.
◆**gang together** *vi* formar un grupo (*or* una pandilla), agruparse.
◆**gang up** *vi* conspirar, confabularse, obrar de concierto (*against, on* contra).
gang-bang‡ ['gæŋbæŋ] **1** *n* violación *f* múltiple, violación *f* colectiva; sexo *m* tribal‡. **2** *vt* violar colectivamente.
ganger ['gæŋəʳ] *n* (*Brit*) capataz *m*.
Ganges ['gændʒiːz] *n* Ganges *m*.
gangland ['gæŋlænd] *n* mundillo *m* del crimen; ~ **murder** asesinato *m* en el mundillo del crimen, asesinato *m* por ajuste de cuentas entre criminales.
gangling ['gæŋglɪŋ] *adj* larguirucho, desgarbado.
ganglion ['gæŋglɪən] *n*, *pl* **ganglia** ['gæŋglɪə] ganglio *m*.
gangplank ['gæŋplæŋk] *n* (*Naut*) plancha *f*.
gangrene ['gæŋgriːn] *n* gangrena *f*.
gangrenous ['gæŋgrɪnəs] *adj* gangrenoso.
gangster ['gæŋstəʳ] *n* pistolero *m*, pandillero *m*, gán(g)ster *m*.
gangsterism ['gæŋstərɪzəm] *n* gan(g)sterismo *m*.
gangway ['gæŋweɪ] *n* pasillo *m*, pasadizo *m*; (*Naut: on ship*) escalerilla *f*, pasarela *f*; (*from ship to shore*) plancha *f*, pasadera *f*; (*between seats*) pasillo *m*; **~!** ¡abran paso!
gannet ['gænɪt] *n* alcatraz *m*.
gantlet ['gæntlɪt] *n* (*US Rail*) vía *f* traslapada, vía *f* de garganta.
gantry ['gæntrɪ] *n* caballete *m*; (*on crane, railway signal*) pórtico *m*; (*for rocket*) torre *f* de lanzamiento.
GAO *n* (*US*) *abbr of* **General Accounting Office** *oficina general de contabilidad gubernamental*.
gaol [dʒeɪl] *n*, *vt* (*Brit*) = **jail**.
gap [gæp] *n* (*natural*) vacío *m*, hueco *m*; (*man-made*) aber-

tura *f*, brecha *f*; (*in wall etc*) boquete *m*; (*between bars etc*) distancia *f*, separación *f*; (*in mountains*) desfiladero *m*; (*in writing*) espacio *m*; (*in text*) laguna *f*; omisión *f*; (*of time*) intervalo *m*, brecha *f*; (*in process*) solución *f* de continuidad; (*in quality*) disparidad *f*; (*maladjustment*) desfase *m*, desajuste *m*; (*in traffic, trees*) claro *m*; (*crack*) hendedura *f*, resquicio *m*; **there is a ~ in the balance of payments** hay un desequilibrio en la balanza de pagos; **we discerned a ~ in the market** vimos una abertura en el mercado; **to close the ~** cerrar la brecha; **he left a ~ which it will be hard to fill** dejó un hueco difícil de llenar; **leave a ~ for the name** deje un espacio para poner el nombre; **without a ~** sin solución de continuidad.

gape [geɪp] *vi* (**a**) abrirse (mucho), estar muy abierto; **the chasm ~d before him** se abría delante de él la sima.

(**b**) (*person*) estar boquiabierto; pensar en las musarañas; **to ~ at** mirar boquiabierto, embobarse con.

gaping [ˈgeɪpɪŋ] *adj* (**a**) abierto. (**b**) *person* boquiabierto, embobado.

gap-toothed [ˈgæpˈtuːθt] *adj* que ha perdido un diente (*or* varios dientes).

garage [ˈgærɑːʒ] **1** *n* (*of house*) garaje *m*, cochera *f*; (*for repairs*) taller *m*; (*petrol station*) gasolinera *f*, estación *f* de servicio. **2** *attr*: **~ mechanic** mecánico *m*; **~ proprietor** propietario *m*, -a *f* de un taller de reparaciones; **~ sale** venta *f* de objetos usados (*en una casa particular*). **3** *vt* dejar en garaje.

garageman [ˈgærɑːʒ,mæn] *n*, *pl* **garagemen** [ˈgærɑːʒmen] garajista *m*.

garaging [ˈgærɑːʒɪŋ] *n* plazas *fpl* de garaje.

garb [gɑːb] **1** *n* traje *m*, vestido *m*; (*of profession etc*) vestido *m* típico; (*iro*) ropaje *m* (*also fig*). **2** *vt* vestir (*in* de).

garbage [ˈgɑːbɪdʒ] **1** *n* basuras *fpl*, desperdicios *mpl*; (*fig*) basura *f*; (*Comput*) **~ in, ~ out** basura entra, basura sale. **2** *attr*: **~ bag** (*US*) bolsa *f* de la basura; **~ can** (*US*) cubo *m* de la basura; **~ collector** (*US*), **~ man** (*US*) basurero *m*; **~ disposal unit** triturador *m* de basuras; **~ dump** (*US*) vertedero *m*; **~ truck** (*US*) camión *m* de la basura.

garble [ˈgɑːbl] *vt* mutilar, falsear (por selección).

garbled [ˈgɑːbld] *adj* mutilado, confuso.

Garda [ˈgɑːdə] *n* Policía *f* irlandesa.

garden [ˈgɑːdn] **1** *n* jardín *m*; **G~ of Eden** Edén *m*; **everything in the ~ is lovely** todo está a las mil maravillas.

2 *attr* de jardín; **~ center** (*US*), **~ centre** centro *m* de jardinería; **~ city** (*Brit*) ciudad *f* jardín; **~ flat** piso *m* con jardín en planta baja; **~ furniture** muebles *mpl* de jardín, muebles *mpl* de exterior; **~ hose** manguera *f* de jardín; **to lead sb up the ~ path** embaucar a uno; **~ produce** productos *mpl* de jardín; **~ seat** banco *m* de jardín; **~ shears** tijeras *fpl* de jardín; **~ tools** útiles *mpl* de jardinería; **he lives just over the ~ wall from us** vive justo al otro lado de la valla.

3 *vi* cultivar un huerto, trabajar en el jardín (*or* huerto).

gardener [ˈgɑːdnəʳ] *n* jardinero *m*, -a *f*; (*market*) hortelano *m*; **I'm no ~** no entiendo de jardinería.

gardenia [gɑːˈdiːnɪə] *n* gardenia *f*.

gardening [ˈgɑːdnɪŋ] *n* jardinería *f*, horticultura *f*.

garden-party [ˈgɑːdn,pɑːtɪ] *n* garden-party *m*, recepción *f* (al aire libre).

garfish [ˈgɑː,fɪʃ] *n* aguja *f*.

gargantuan [gɑːˈgæntjʊən] *adj* gargantuesco, colosal, gigantesco.

gargle [ˈgɑːgl] **1** *n* (*act*) gárgaras *fpl*; (*liquid*) gargarismo *m*. **2** *vi* gargarizar, hacer gárgaras, gargarear (*LAm*).

gargoyle [ˈgɑːgɔɪl] *n* gárgola *f*.

garish [ˈgɛərɪʃ] *adj* chillón, llamativo, charro.

garland [ˈgɑːlənd] **1** *n* guirnalda *f*. **2** *vt* enguirnaldar (*with* de).

garlic [ˈgɑːlɪk] **1** *n* ajo *m*. **2** *attr*: **~ press** aparato *m* para machacar ajos; **~ salt** sal *f* de ajo; **~ sausage** salchicha *f* de ajo.

garlicky [ˈgɑːlɪkɪ] *adj food* con ajo; *breath* con olor a ajo.

garment [ˈgɑːmənt] *n* prenda *f* (de vestir).

garner [ˈgɑːnəʳ] **1** *n* (*liter*) troj *f*, granero *m*; (*fig*) acopio *m*, abundancia *f*; provisión *f*. **2** *vt* entrojar; (*fig*) recoger, acumular.

garnet [ˈgɑːnɪt] *n* granate *m*.

garnish [ˈgɑːnɪʃ] **1** *n* (*Culin*) aderezo *m*. **2** *vt* adornar (*with* de); (*Culin*) aderezar (*with* de).

garnishing [ˈgɑːnɪʃɪŋ] *n* (*Culin*) aderezo *m*.

Garonne [gəˈrɒn] *n* Garona *m*.

garret [ˈgærɪt] *n* guardilla *f*, desván *m*.

garrison [ˈgærɪsən] **1** *n* guarnición *f*. **2** *attr*: **~ town** ciudad *f* con guarnición; **~ troops** tropas *fpl* de guarnición. **3** *vt* guarnecer.

garrotte [gəˈrɒt] **1** *n* garrote *m*. **2** *vt* agarrotar.

garrulity [gəˈruːlɪtɪ] *n* garrulidad *f*.

garrulous [ˈgærʊləs] *adj* gárrulo.

garter [ˈgɑːtəʳ] *n* liga *f*; **Order of the G~** Orden *f* de la Jarretera; **Knight of the G~** Caballero *m* de la Orden de la Jarretera.

garter belt [ˈgɑːtəbelt] *n* (*US*) portaligas *m*, liguero *m*.

gas [gæs] **1** *n* (**a**) gas *m*. (**b**) (*US*: *gasoline*) gasolina *f*; = **gasoline**; **to step on the ~*** tumbar la aguja*, acelerar la marcha. (**c**) (‡: *fun*) **what a ~!** ¡qué estupendo!*; **he's a ~!** ¡es un tío divertidísimo!* **2** *vt* asfixiar con gas, gasear. **3** *vi* (*) charlar, parlotear.

gasbag [ˈgæsbæg] *n* (*Aer*) bolsa *f* de gas; (*) charlatán *m*, -ana *f*.

gas-bracket [ˈgæs,brækɪt] *n* brazo *m* de lámpara de gas.

gas-burner [ˈgæs,bɜːnəʳ] *n* mechero *m* de gas.

gas can [ˈgæs,kæn] *n* (*US*) bidón *m* de gasolina.

gas-canister [ˈgæs,kænɪstəʳ] *n* bombona *f* de gas.

gas-chamber [ˈgæs,tʃeɪmbəʳ] *n* cámara *f* de gas.

Gascon [ˈgæskən] **1** *adj* gascón. **2** *n* (**a**) gascón *m*, -ona *f*. (**b**) (*Ling*) gascón *m*.

Gascony [ˈgæskənɪ] *n* Gascuña *f*.

gas-cooker [ˈgæsˈkʊkəʳ] *n* cocina *f* de (*or* a) gas.

gas-cooled [ˈgæskuːld] *adj*: **~ reactor** reactor *m* enfriado por gas.

gas-cylinder [ˈgæs,sɪlɪndəʳ] *n* bombona *f* de gas.

gaseous [ˈgæsɪəs] *adj* gaseoso.

gas fire [ˈgæsˈfaɪəʳ] *n* estufa *f* de gas.

gas-fired [ˈgæs,faɪəd] *adj* de gas, alimentado por gas.

gas-fitter [ˈgæs,fɪtəʳ] *n* gasista *m*, empleado *m* del gas.

gas-fittings [ˈgæs,fɪtɪŋz] *npl* instalación *f* de gas.

gas-guzzler* [ˈgæsˈgʌzləʳ] *n* chupagasolina* *m*.

gash [gæʃ] **1** *n* raja *f*, hendedura *f*; (*wound*) cuchillada *f*. **2** *vt* rajar, hender; (*wound*) acuchillar. **3** *adj* (*Brit*‡) (*spare*) de sobra; (*free*) gratuito.

gas-heater [ˈgæs,hiːtəʳ] *n* estufa *f* de gas.

gasholder [ˈgæs,həʊldəʳ] *n* gasómetro *m*.

gasification [,gæsɪfɪˈkeɪʃən] *n* gasificación *f*.

gas-jet [ˈgæsdʒet] *n* llama *f* de mechero de gas.

gasket [ˈgæskɪt] *n* junta *f*.

gaslight [ˈgæslaɪt] *n* luz *f* de gas, alumbrado *m* de gas.

gas lighter [ˈgæs,laɪtəʳ] *n* mechero *m* de gas.

gas lighting [ˈgæs,laɪtɪŋ] *n* alumbrado *m* de gas.

gaslit [ˈgæslɪt] *adj* con alumbrado de gas.

gas-main [ˈgæsmeɪn] *n* cañería *f* maestra de gas.

gasman [ˈgæsmæn] *n*, *pl* **gasmen** [ˈgæsmen] gasista *m*, empleado *m* del gas.

gas-mantle [ˈgæs,mæntl] *n* manguito *m* incandescente.

gasmask [ˈgæsmɑːsk] *n* careta *f* antigás.

gas-meter [ˈgæs,miːtəʳ] *n* contador *m* (*LAm*: medidor *m*) de gas.

gasohol [ˈgæsəʊhɒl] *n* (*US*) gasohol *m*.

gas-oil [ˈgæsɔɪl] *n* gasóleo *m*.

gasoline [ˈgæsəliːn] *n* (*US*) gasolina *f*, nafta *f* (*SC*), bencina *f* (*SC*).

gasometer [gæˈsɒmɪtəʳ] *n* (*Brit*) gasómetro *m*.

gas-oven [ˈgæs,ʌvn] *n* cocina *f* de (*or* a) gas.

gasp [gɑːsp] **1** *n* boqueada *f*; (*cry*) grito *m* sofocado; **last ~** boqueada *f*; **to be at one's last ~** estar dando las boqueadas; **with a ~ of astonishment** con un grito sofocado de asombro.

2 *vi* boquear, anhelar, respirar con dificultad; (*pant*) jadear; **to ~ for air** (*or* **breath**) luchar por respirar; **I was ~ing for a smoke** tenía unas tremendas ganas de fumar; **to ~ with astonishment** dar un grito sofocado de asombro.

◆**gasp out** *vt* decir con voz entrecortada.

gas pedal [ˈgæs,pedəl] *n* (*esp US*) acelerador *m*.

gasper‡ [ˈgɑːspəʳ] *n* (*Brit*) pito* *m*, pitillo* *m*.

gas-pipe [ˈgæspaɪp] *n* tubo *m* de gas.

gas pipeline [,gæsˈpaɪplaɪn] *n* gasoducto *m*.

gas pump [ˈgæs,pʌmp] *n* (*US*) (*in car*) bomba *f* de gasolina; (*in gas station*) surtidor *m* de gasolina.

gas-ring [ˈgæsrɪŋ] *n* hornillo *m* de gas.

gassed‡ [gæst] *adj* (*US*) bebido, enmonado*.

gas station [ˈgæs,steɪʃən] *n* (*US*) gasolinera *f*.

gas-stove [ˈgæsˈstəʊv] *n* cocina *f* de (*or* a) gas.

gassy [ˈgæsɪ] *adj* gaseoso.

gastank [ˈgæstæŋk] *n* (*US*) depósito *m* de gasolina.

gas-tap [ˈgæstæp] *n* llave *f* del gas.

gastric [ˈgæstrɪk] *adj* gástrico; **~ flu** gripe *f* gastrointestinal; **~ juice** jugos *mpl* gástricos; **~ ulcer** úlcera *f* gástrica.

gastritis [gæs'traɪtɪs] *n* gastritis *f.*
gastro... ['gæstrəʊ] *pref* gastro...
gastroenteritis [,gæstrəʊ,entə'raɪtɪs] *n* gastroenteritis *f.*
gastronome ['gæstrənəʊm] *n*, **gastronomist** [,gæs'trɒnəmɪst] *n* gastrónomo *m*, -a *f.*
gastronomic [,gæstrə'nɒmɪk] *adj* gastronómico.
gastronomy [gæs'trɒnəmɪ] *n* gastronomía *f.*
gastropod ['gæstrəpɒd] *n* gastrópodo *m.*
gas turbine [,gæs'tɜːbaɪn] *n* turbina *f* de gas.
gas worker ['gæs,wɜːkəʳ] *n* trabajador *m*, -ora *f* de la compañía de gas.
gasworks ['gæswɜːks] *n* fábrica *f* de gas.
gat‡ [gæt] *n* (*US*) revólver *m*, quitapenas‡ *m.*
gate [geɪt] *n* (**a**) puerta *f* (*also of town*); (*iron*) verja *f*; (*Rail*) barrera *f*; (*of sluice*) compuerta *f.* (**b**) (*Sport*) entrada *f*, taquillaje *m*, recaudación *f.*
gâteau ['gætəʊ], *pl* **gâteaux** ['gætəʊz] *n* (*Brit*) tarta *f.*
gatecrash ['geɪtkræʃ] **1** *vt* colarse (de gorra) en, asistir sin ser invitado a. **2** *vi* colarse (de gorra), asistir sin ser invitado.
gatecrasher ['geɪt,kræʃəʳ] *n* intruso *m*, -a *f*, colado *m*, -a *f.*
gatehouse ['geɪthaʊs] *n*, *pl* **gatehouses** ['geɪt,haʊzɪz] casa *f* del guarda (*or* del portero *etc*).
gatekeeper ['geɪt,kiːpəʳ] *n* portero *m*; (*Rail*) guardabarrera *m.*
gate-legged ['geɪtlegd] *adj*: ~ **table** mesa *f* de alas abatibles.
gate-money ['geɪt,mʌnɪ] *n* ingresos *mpl* de entrada, recaudación *f.*
gatepost ['geɪtpəʊst] *n* poste *m* (de una puerta de cercado); **between you, me, and the** ~ en confianza, entre nosotros.
gateway ['geɪtweɪ] *n* (**a**) = **gate.** (**b**) (*fig*) puerta *f*, pórtico *m* (*to* de).
gather ['gæðəʳ] **1** *vt* (**a**) (*assemble*) reunir, recoger; acumular, acopiar; (*harvest*) recolectar; *flowers, wood* coger (*Sp*), recoger (*LAm*); (*Sew*) fruncir.
(**b**) (*collect*) **to ~ dust** empolvarse; **to ~ speed** ganar velocidad, ir cada vez más rápidamente; **to ~ strength** cobrar fuerzas.
(**c**) (*infer*) **to ~ that ...** colegir que, sacar la consecuencia que ...; **I ~ from him that ...** según lo que él me dice; **what are we to ~ from this?** ¿qué consecuencia sacamos de esto?; **as you will have ~ed** según habrás comprendido; **as one ~s from these reports** según se desprende de estos informes.
2 *vi* reunirse, juntarse, congregarse; (*clouds*) amontonarse; (*Med*) formar pus; **the ~ing storm** la tormenta que amenaza.
3 *n* (*Sew*) frunce *m.*
◆gather in *vt* recoger; *taxes etc* recaudar.
◆gather round 1 *vt*: **to ~ round sb** agruparse en torno a uno. **2** *vi*: **~ round!** ¡acercaos!
◆gather together 1 *vt* reunir, juntar. **2** *vi* reunirse, juntarse, congregarse.
◆gather up *vt* recoger.
gathered ['gæðəd] *adj* (*Sew*) fruncido.
gathering ['gæðərɪŋ] *n* (**a**) (*meeting*) reunión *f*, asamblea *f*; (*persons present*) concurrencia *f.* (**b**) (*Med*) absceso *m.* (**c**) (*Typ*) alzado *m.*
GATT [gæt] *n abbr of* **General Agreement on Tariffs and Trade** Acuerdo *m* General Sobre Aranceles Aduaneros y Comercio, GATT *m.*
gauche [gəʊʃ] *adj* torpe, desmañado; (*socially*) falto de confianza, poco seguro de sí mismo.
gaudy ['gɔːdɪ] *adj colour, cloth* chillón, llamativo; *building etc* vulgar y hortera.
gauge [geɪdʒ] **1** *n* (*standard measure*) norma *f* de medida; (*of gun etc*) calibre *m*; (*test*) indicación *f*, prueba *f*; (*instrument*) calibrador *m*; indicador *m*, manómetro *m*; (*Rail*) ancho *m*, entrevía *f*, trocha *f* (*LAm*).
2 *vt* medir; calibrar; (*fig*) juzgar, estimar; **to ~ the distance with one's eye** medir la distancia con el ojo; **to ~ the right moment** elegir el momento propicio.
Gaul [gɔːl] *n* (**a**) Galia *f.* (**b**) (*person*) galo *m*, -a *f.*
Gaullist ['gəʊlɪst] **1** *adj* gaulista, golista. **2** *n* gaulista *mf*, golista *mf.*
gaunt [gɔːnt] *adj* flaco, desvaído, chupado; (*fig*) severo, adusto.
gauntlet ['gɔːntlɪt] *n* guante *m*; (*armour*) guantelete *m*; **to run the** ~ (*Mil Hist*) correr baquetas; **to run the ~ of** (*fig*) pasar por los peligros de; salir ileso de; **to throw down the** ~ arrojar el guante.
gauze [gɔːz] *n* gasa *f.*
gave [geɪv] *pret of* **give.**
gavel ['gævl] *n* martillo *m* (*de presidente o subastador*).
gavotte [gə'vɒt] *n* gavota *f.*
Gawd‡ [gɔːd] *excl* (*Brit* = **God**) ¡Dios mío!
gawk [gɔːk] **1** *n* papamoscas *mf.* **2** *vi* papar moscas.
gawky ['gɔːkɪ] *adj* desgarbado, torpe.
gawp* [gɔːp] *vi* papar moscas; **to ~ at** mirar boquiabierto.
gay [geɪ] **1** *adj* (**a**) (*US†: cheerful*) alegre; *appearance* brillante, vistoso; *colour* vivo, brillante; *life* lleno de placeres.
(**b**) (*homosexual*) gay, homosexual; ~ **club** club *m* para gays; ~ **lib(eration)** campaña *f* pro derechos de los homosexuales; ~ **movement** movimiento *m* homosexual; ~ **rights** derechos *mpl* de los homosexuales. **2** *n* gay *mf*, homosexual *mf.*
gayness ['geɪnɪs] *n* homosexualidad *f.*
Gaza Strip ['gɑːzə'strɪp] *n* Franja *f* de Gaza.
gaze [geɪz] **1** *n* mirada *f* (fija); **his ~ met mine** cruzamos una mirada. **2** *vi* (*also* **to ~ at, to ~ upon**) mirar (con fijeza), contemplar.
gazelle [gə'zel] *n* gacela *f.*
gazette [gə'zet] *n* gaceta *f.*
gazetteer [,gæzɪ'tɪəʳ] *n* diccionario *m* geográfico.
gazump* [gə'zʌmp] (*Brit*) **1** *vt person* ofrecer un precio más alto que; **we were ~ed** ofrecieron más que nosotros. **2** *vi* faltar a una promesa de vender (*esp* una casa) para aceptar un precio más alto ofrecido por otro.
gazumping* [gə'zʌmpɪŋ] *n la subida del precio de una casa una vez que ya ha sido apalabrado.*
gazunder* [gə'zʌndəʳ] (*Brit*) **1** *vt person* ofrecer un precio más bajo a; **we were ~ed** nos ofrecieron menos de lo antes convenido. **2** *vi* ofrecer un precio más bajo de lo antes convenido. **3** *n la baja en la oferta para comprar una casa una vez que ya ha sido apalabrada.*
GB *n abbr of* **Great Britain** Gran Bretaña *f.*
GBH *n* (*Brit Jur*) *abbr of* **grievous bodily harm** graves daños *mpl* corporales.
GC *n* (*Brit*) *abbr of* **George Cross** *medalla del valor civil.*
GCA *n abbr of* **ground-controlled approach** aproximación *f* controlada desde tierra.
GCE *n* (*Brit*) *abbr of* **General Certificate of Education** ≃ bachillerato *m* elemental y superior.
GCHQ *n* (*Brit*) *abbr of* **Government Communications Headquarters** *entidad gubernamental que recoge datos mediante escuchas electrónicas.*
GCSE *n* (*Brit*) *abbr of* **General Certificate of Secondary Education** ≃ bachillerato *m* elemental y superior.
gdn *abbr of* **garden** jardín *m.*
Gdns *abbr of* **Gardens** jardines *mpl.*
GDP *n abbr of* **gross domestic product** producto *m* interno bruto, PIB *m.*
GDR *n* (*Hist*) *abbr of* **German Democratic Republic** República *f* Democrática Alemana, RDA *f.*
gear [gɪəʳ] **1** *n* (**a**) (*equipment*) equipo *m*, herramientas *fpl*, pertrechos *mpl*; (*fishing*) aparejo *m*; (*possessions*) cosas *fpl*, bártulos *mpl*; (*Brit: clothing*) ropa *f*, traje *m.*
(**b**) (*apparatus*) aparato *m*, mecanismo *m.*
(**c**) (*Mech*) engranaje *m*, rueda *f* dentada; **in ~** en juego, engranado; **to be in ~ with** engranar con; **to throw out of ~** desengranar, (*fig*) dislocar.
(**d**) (*Aut etc: speed*) marcha *f*, velocidad *f*, cambio *m*; **there are 5 forward ~s** hay 5 marchas adelante; **high ~** (*US*) (*fourth*) cuarta velocidad *f*, directa *f*; (*fifth*) quinta velocidad *f*, superdirecta *f*; **to change ~** (*Brit*), **to shift ~** (*US*) cambiar de marcha.
2 *attr*: ~ **ratio** (*of cycle*) proporción *f* entre plato y piñón.
3 *vt* (*Mech*) engranar (*into, with* con); **the programme is ~ed in with** (*or* **to**) **the plan** el programa forma parte integral del plan.
4 *vi* engranar (*into, with* con); **it ~s in with the plan** concuerda con el plan, se desarrolla al ritmo del plan.
◆gear down *vt* (*Mech*) desmultiplicar; (*fig*) reducir, rebajar.
◆gear up 1 *vt* (*Mech*) multiplicar; (*fig*) aumentar; intensificar. **2** *vi* hacer preparativos, prepararse; **they are ~ing up to fight** se están disponiendo para luchar.
gearbox ['gɪəbɒks] *n* (*Brit Aut*) caja *f* de cambios; (*Mech*) caja *f* de engranajes.
gear-lever ['gɪə,liːvəʳ], **gear-change** ['gɪə,tʃeɪndʒ] *n* (*Brit*), (*US*) **gearshift** ['gɪə,ʃɪft] *n*, **gearstick*** ['gɪə,stɪk] *n* (*Brit*) palanca *f* de cambios.
gearwheel ['gɪəwiːl] *n* rueda *f* dentada.
gecko ['gekəʊ] *n* geco *m*, dragón *m.*
GED *n* (*US*) *abbr of* **general educational development.**
geddid* ['gedɪd] = **get it?** (¿entiendes?).

gee¹* [dʒiː] *interj* (*esp US*) ¡caramba!; ~ **whiz!*** ¡corcholis!*; ~ **up!** ¡arre!
gee²* [dʒiː] *n* (*also* ~-~: *baby talk*) caballito *m*, tatán *m*.
geese [giːs] *npl of* **goose**.
geezer* ['giːzəʳ] *n* (*Brit*) vejancón* *m*, tío* *m*.
Geiger counter ['gaɪgə,kaʊntəʳ] *n* contador *m* Geiger.
geisha ['geɪʃə] *n* geisha *f*.
gel [dʒel] **1** *n* gel *m*. **2** *vi* aglutinarse; (*fig*) cuajar.
gelatin(e) ['dʒelətiːn] *n* gelatina *f*.
gelatinous [dʒɪ'lætɪnəs] *adj* gelatinoso.
geld [geld] *vt* castrar, capar.
gelding ['geldɪŋ] *n* caballo *m* castrado.
gelignite ['dʒelɪgnaɪt] *n* gelignita *f*.
gelt* [gelt] *n* (*US*) pasta* *f*.
gem [dʒem] *n* joya *f* (*also fig*), piedra *f* preciosa, gema *f*.
Gemini ['dʒemɪniː] *npl* (*Zodiac*) Géminis *m*, Gemelos *mpl*.
Gen. (*Mil*) *abbr of* **General** General *m*, Gen., Gral.
gen. *abbr of* **general, generally**.
gen* [dʒen] (*Brit*) *n* información *f*; **to give sb the ~ on sth** poner a uno al corriente de algo.
◆gen up* (*Brit*) **1** *vt*: **to ~ sb up** informar a uno; **I'm thoroughly ~ned up now** ahora estoy bien enterado, ahora estoy completamente al tanto. **2** *vi*: **to ~ up on sth** informarse acerca de algo.
gendarme ['ʒɑ̃ːndɑːm] *n* gendarme *m*.
gender ['dʒendəʳ] *n* género *m*.
gene [dʒiːn] *n* gene *m*, gen *m*.
genealogical [,dʒiːnɪə'lɒdʒɪkəl] *adj* genealógico.
genealogist [,dʒiːnɪ'ælədʒɪst] *n* genealogista *mf*.
genealogy [,dʒiːnɪ'ælədʒɪ] *n* genealogía *f*.
genera ['dʒenərə] *npl of* **genus**.
general ['dʒenərəl] **1** *adj* general; (*common*) corriente, usual; ~ **anaesthetic**, ~ **anesthetic** (*US*) anestesia *f* general; ~ **assembly** asamblea *f* general; ~ **average** media *f* general; (*Comm*) avería *f* general; ~ **audit** auditoría *f* general; ~ **cargo** mercancías *fpl* (de) general, cargamento *m* mixto; ~ **delivery** (*US, Canada*) lista *f* de correos; ~ **expenses** gastos *mpl* generales; ~ **knowledge** conocimientos *mpl* generales; ~ **manager** director *m*, -ora *f* general; ~ **partnership** sociedad *f* regular colectiva; ~ **practice** (*Med*) medicina *f* general; ~ **practitioner** médico *m*, -a *f* de medicina general; ~ **reserve** reserva *f* general; ~ **staff** estado *m* mayor general; ~ **store** tienda *f* (de pueblo) que vende de todo; ~ **strike** huelga *f* general.
2 *n* (*Mil*) general *m*, -ala *f*; (*servant*) chica *f* para todo; **in** ~ en general, por lo general.
generalissimo [,dʒenərə'lɪsɪməʊ] *n* generalísimo *m*.
generality [,dʒenə'rælɪtɪ] *n* generalidad *f*.
generalization [,dʒenərəlaɪ'zeɪʃən] *n* generalización *f*.
generalize ['dʒenərəlaɪz] *vi* generalizar.
generally ['dʒenərəlɪ] *adv* generalmente, en general, por lo común; ~ **speaking** en términos generales.
general-purpose [,dʒenərəl'pɜːpəs] *adj tool, dictionary* de uso general.
generalship ['dʒenərəlʃɪp] *n* estrategia *f*, táctica *f*; (*leadership*) dirección *f*, don *m* de mando.
generate ['dʒenəreɪt] *vt* (*Elec etc*) generar; (*fig*) producir.
generating ['dʒenəreɪtɪŋ] *attr*: ~ **set** grupo *m* electrógeno; ~ **station** central *f* generadora.
generation [,dʒenə'reɪʃən] **1** *n* (*gen, Ling*) generación *f*. **2** *attr*: ~ **gap** desnivel *m* generacional, barrera *f* generacional.
generative ['dʒenərətɪv] *adj* generativo; ~ **grammar** gramática *f* generativa.
generator ['dʒenəreɪtəʳ] *n* grupo *m* electrógeno, generador *m*.
generic [dʒɪ'nerɪk] *adj* genérico.
generosity [,dʒenə'rɒsɪtɪ] *n* generosidad *f*.
generous ['dʒenərəs] *adj* generoso; espléndido, dadivoso; *supply, quantity* abundante, amplio, liberal.
generously ['dʒenərəslɪ] *adv* generosamente; abundantemente.
genesis ['dʒenɪsɪs] *n* (**a**) génesis *f*. (**b**) **G~** Génesis *m*.
genet ['dʒenɪt] *n* jineta *mf*.
genetic [dʒɪ'netɪk] *adj* genético, genésico; ~ **code** código *m* genético; ~ **engineering** ingeniería *f* genética; ~ **fingerprint(ing)** huella *f* genética.
genetically [dʒɪ'netɪkəlɪ] *adv* (*gen*) genéticamente; ~ **engineered** manipulado genéticamente.
geneticist [dʒɪ'netɪsɪst] *n* geneticista *mf*; (*Med*) genetista *mf*.
genetics [dʒɪ'netɪks] *npl* genética *f*.
Geneva [dʒɪ'niːvə] *n* Ginebra *f*; ~ **Convention** Convención *f* de Ginebra.
genial ['dʒiːnɪəl] *adj* simpático, afable.
geniality [,dʒiːnɪ'ælɪtɪ] *n* simpatía *f*, afabilidad *f*.
genially ['dʒiːnɪəlɪ] *adv* afablemente.
genie ['dʒiːnɪ] *n* genio *m*.
genital ['dʒenɪtl] **1** *adj* genital; ~ **herpes** herpes *m* genital. **2** *npl*: ~**s** genitales *mpl*.
genitalia [,dʒenɪ'teɪlɪə] *npl* genitales *mpl*.
genitive ['dʒenɪtɪv] **1** *adj* genitivo; ~ **case** = **2**. **2** *n* genitivo *m*.
genius ['dʒiːnɪəs] *n* genio *m*; genialidad *f*; **man of ~** hombre *m* genial; **he's a ~** es un genio, es genial; **you're a ~!** (*iro*) ¡eres un hacha!; **he has a ~ for propaganda** es un genio para la propaganda; **you have a ~ for forgetting things** tienes un don especial para olvidar las cosas.
Genoa ['dʒenəʊə] *n* Génova *f*.
genocide ['dʒenəʊsaɪd] *n* genocidio *m*.
Genoese [,dʒenəʊ'iːz] **1** *adj* genovés. **2** *n* genovés *m*, -esa *f*.
genotype ['dʒenəʊtaɪp] *n* genotipo *m*.
genre [ʒɑ̃ːnr] *n* género *m*.
gent* [dʒent] *n abbr of* **gentleman** caballero *m*; **~s'*** wáter *m* (de caballeros); **what will you have, ~s?** (*hum*) ¿qué vais a tomar, caballeros?
genteel [dʒen'tiːl] *adj* (*iro*) fino, elegante; (*pej*) cursi; *accent etc* refinado, de buen tono, señorito*.
gentian ['dʒenʃɪən] *n* genciana *f*; ~ **violet** violeta *f* de genciana.
gentile ['dʒentaɪl] **1** *adj* no judío; (*pagan*) gentil. **2** *n* no judío *m*, -a *f*; (*pagan*) gentil *mf*.
gentility [dʒen'tɪlɪtɪ] *n* (*iro*) finura *f*, elegancia *f*; buen tono *m*.
gentle ['dʒentl] *adj person's character* benévolo, amable; apacible; *breeze, heat, stop, progress, transition etc* suave; *rule* blando; *sound, voice* dulce; *push, touch* ligero; (*slow*) lento, pausado; *hint, reminder* discreto; *animal etc* manso, dócil, apacible; (*tender*) dulce, tierno; **of ~ birth** bien nacido; ~ **reader** amado lector; **the ~ sex** el sexo débil.
gentleman ['dʒentlmən] **1** *n, pl* **gentlemen** ['dʒentlmən] (*man*) señor *m*; (*having gentlemanly qualities*) caballero *m*; (*at court*) gentilhombre *m*; **~'s ~** ayuda *m* de cámara; **gentlemen's agreement** pacto *m* de caballeros; **young ~** señorito *m*; **there's a ~ waiting to see you** le espera un señor; **to be a perfect ~** ser un cumplido caballero; **he's no ~** poco caballero es él; **'gentlemen'** (*lavatory*) 'caballeros'.
2 *attr*: ~ **farmer** terrateniente *m*.
gentlemanly ['dʒentlmənlɪ] *adj* caballeroso; cortés, fino.
gentleness ['dʒentlnɪs] *n* amabilidad *f*; suavidad *f*; dulzura *f*; mansedumbre *f*; docilidad *f*; ternura *f*.
gentlewoman ['dʒentl,wʊmən] *n, pl* **gentlewomen** ['dʒentl,wɪmɪn] dama *f*, señora *f* de buena familia.
gently ['dʒentlɪ] *adv* suavemente; dulcemente; (*slowly*) despacio, pausadamente, poco a poco; apaciblemente; tiernamente; **~!**, **~ now!**, **~ there!** ¡más despacio!, ¡con cuidado!
gentrification [,dʒentrɪfɪ'keɪʃən] *n* aburguesamiento *m*.
gentrify ['dʒentrɪfaɪ] *vt* aburguesar.
gentry ['dʒentrɪ] *n* (*Brit*) alta burguesía *f*, pequeña aristocracia *f*; (*pej*) familias *fpl* bien, gente *f* bien; (*set of people*) gente *f*.
genuflect ['dʒenjʊflekt] *vi* doblar la rodilla.
genuflexion, (*US*) **genuflection** [,dʒenjʊ'flekʃən] *n* genuflexión *f*.
genuine ['dʒenjʊɪn] *adj* auténtico, legítimo, genuino; *person* sincero; **this dancer is the ~ article** esta bailarina es un ejemplar auténtico.
genuinely ['dʒenjʊɪnlɪ] *adv prove, originate* auténticamente; *feel, think* sinceramente; *sorry, surprised, unable* verdaderamente.
genuineness ['dʒenjʊɪnnɪs] *n* autenticidad *f*; sinceridad *f*.
genus ['dʒenəs] *n, pl* **genera** ['dʒenərə] género *m*.
geo... ['dʒiːəʊ] *pref* geo...
geodesic [,dʒɪ(ː)əʊ'desɪk] *adj* geodésico.
geodesy [dʒiː'ɒdɪsɪ] *n* geodesia *f*.
Geoffrey ['dʒefrɪ] *nm* Geofredo, Godofredo.
geographer [dʒɪ'ɒgrəfəʳ] *n* geógrafo *m*, -a *f*.
geographical [dʒɪə'græfɪkəl] *adj* geográfico.
geography [dʒɪ'ɒgrəfɪ] *n* geografía *f*; **let me show you the ~ of the house** (*euph*) te voy a mostrar dónde están los servicios.
geological [dʒɪəʊ'lɒdʒɪkəl] *adj* geológico.
geologist [dʒɪ'ɒlədʒɪst] *n* geólogo *m*, -a *f*.
geology [dʒɪ'ɒlədʒɪ] *n* geología *f*.
geomagnetic [,dʒiːəʊmæg'netɪk] *adj* geomagnético.
geometric(al) [dʒɪə'metrɪk(əl)] *adj* geométrico; ~ **progres-**

sion progresión *f* geométrica.

geometrically [dʒɪə'metrɪkəlɪ] *adv* geométricamente.

geometry [dʒɪ'ɒmɪtrɪ] *n* geometría *f*.

geomorphology [ˌdʒiːəʊmɔː'fɒlədʒɪ] *n* geomorfología *f*.

geophysical [ˌdʒiːəʊ'fɪzɪkəl] *adj* geofísico.

geophysicist [ˌdʒiːəʊ'fɪzɪsɪst] *n* geofísico *m*, -a *f*.

geophysics [dʒɪəʊ'fɪzɪks] *n sing* geofísica *f*.

geopolitical [ˌdʒiːəʊpə'lɪtɪkəl] *adj* geopolítico.

geopolitics ['dʒiːəʊ'pɒlɪtɪks] *n sing* geopolítica *f*.

Geordie* ['dʒɔːdɪ] *n* (*Brit*) habitante *mf* de Tyneside en el NE de Inglaterra.

George [dʒɔːdʒ] *nm* Jorge.

Georgia ['dʒɔːdʒɪə] *n* (*US and USSR*) Georgia *f*.

Georgian ['dʒɔːdʒɪən] *adj* (*Brit*) georgiano.

geostationary [ˌdʒiːəʊ'steɪʃənərɪ] *adj* geostacionario.

geostrategic [ˌdʒiːəʊstrə'tiːdʒɪk] *adj* geoestratégico.

geostrategy [ˌdʒiːəʊ'strætədʒɪ] *n* geoestrategia *f*.

geothermal [ˌdʒiːəʊ'θɜːməl] *adj* geotérmico.

geranium [dʒɪ'reɪnɪəm] *n* geranio *m*.

gerbil ['dʒɜːbɪl] *n* gerbo *m*, jerbo *m*.

geriatric [ˌdʒerɪ'ætrɪk] **1** *adj* geriátrico. **2** *n* geriátrico *m*, -a *f*.

geriatrics [ˌdʒerɪ'ætrɪks] *n sing* geriatría *f*.

germ [dʒɜːm] *n* germen *m*; (*Med*) microbio *m*, bacilo *m*, bacteria *f*; (*Bio, also fig*) germen *m*; **the ~ of an idea** el germen de una idea.

German ['dʒɜːmən] **1** *adj* alemán; **~ Democratic Republic** (*Hist*) República *f* Democrática Alemana; **~ measles** rubeola *f*, rubéola *f*; **~ shepherd** (**dog**) (*US*) pastor *m* alemán, perro *m* lobo. **2** *n* (**a**) alemán *m*, -ana *f*. (**b**) (*Ling*) alemán *m*.

germane [dʒɜː'meɪn] *adj* relacionado (*to* con); **not ~ to the issue** inoportuno.

Germanic [dʒɜː'mænɪk] *adj* germánico.

germanium [dʒɜː'meɪnɪəm] *n* germanio *m*.

germanophile [dʒɜː'mænəfaɪl] *n* germanófilo *m*, -a *f*.

germanophobe [dʒɜː'mænəfəʊb] *n* germanófobo *m*, -a *f*.

German-speaking ['dʒɜːmənˌspiːkɪŋ] *adj* de habla alemana.

Germany ['dʒɜːmənɪ] *n* Alemania *f*; **East ~** (*Hist*) Alemania *f* Oriental; **West ~** (*Hist*) Alemania *f* Occidental.

germ carrier ['dʒɜːmˌkærɪəʳ] *n* portador *m*, -ora *f* de microbios (*or* bacterias).

germ cell ['dʒɜːm'sel] *n* célula *f* germen.

germ-free [ˌdʒɜːm'friː] *adj* esterilizado.

germicidal [ˌdʒɜːmɪ'saɪdl] *adj* germicida, microbicida, bactericida.

germicide ['dʒɜːmɪsaɪd] *n* germicida *m*, bactericida *m*.

germinate ['dʒɜːmɪneɪt] *vi* germinar.

germination [ˌdʒɜːmɪ'neɪʃən] *n* germinación *f*.

germ-killer ['dʒɜːmˌkɪləʳ] *n* germicida *m*, bactericida *m*.

germ plasm ['dʒɜːm'plæzəm] *n* germen *m* plasma.

germproof ['dʒɜːmpruːf] *adj* a prueba de microbios (*or* bacterias).

germ warfare [ˌgɜːm'wɔːfɛəʳ] *n* guerra *f* bacteriana.

gerontocracy [ˌdʒerɒn'tɒkrəsɪ] *n* gerontocracia *f*.

gerontologist [ˌdʒerɒn'tɒlədʒɪst] *n* gerontólogo *m*, -a *f*.

gerontology [ˌdʒerɒn'tɒlədʒɪ] *n* gerontología *f*.

Gerry ['dʒerɪ] *nm familiar form of* **Gerald, Gerard**.

gerrymander ['dʒerɪmændəʳ] *vi* falsificar elecciones.

gerrymandering ['dʒerɪmændərɪŋ] *n* fraude *m* electoral, pucherazo* *m*.

gerund ['dʒerənd] *n* (*Latin*) gerundio *m*; (*English*) sustantivo *m* verbal.

gerundive [dʒə'rʌndɪv] **1** *adj* gerundivo. **2** *n* gerundio *m*.

gestalt [gə'ʃtɑːlt] **1** *n* gestalt *m*. **2** *attr*: **~ psychology** psicología *f* gestalt.

Gestapo [ges'tɑːpəʊ] *n* Gestapo *f*.

gestate [dʒes'teɪt] *vt* (**a**) (*Bio*) llevar en el útero. (**b**) (*fig*) *idea* meditar.

gestation [dʒes'teɪʃən] *n* gestación *f*.

gesticulate [dʒes'tɪkjʊleɪt] *vi* accionar, gesticular, manotear.

gesticulation [dʒesˌtɪkjʊ'leɪʃən] *n* gesticulación *f*, manoteo *m*.

gestural ['dʒestʃərəl] *adj language* gestual.

gesture ['dʒestʃəʳ] **1** *n* (**a**) (*lit*) ademán *m*, gesto *m*.

(**b**) (*fig*) demostración *f*; (*small token*) muestra *f*, detalle *m*; **as a ~ of friendship** en señal de amistad; **as a ~ of support** para demostrar nuestro apoyo; **empty ~** pura formalidad *f*; **what a nice ~!** ¡qué detalle!

2 *vi* hacer un ademán; **he ~d towards the door** con la mano indicó la puerta.

3 *vt* expresar con un ademán.

get [get] (*irr*: *pret* **got**, *ptp* **got**, *US* **gotten**) **1** *vt* (**a**) (*obtain*) obtener, adquirir, (*after effort*) lograr, conseguir; (*buy*) comprar; (*find*) encontrar; (*gain*) ganar; *prize* ganar, llevarse; *reputation* granjearse, hacerse; *credit, glory* atribuirse; (*receive*) recibir; *radio station* captar, sintonizar; *wage* cobrar; *benefit, profit* sacar; *goals, points* marcar; **he got it for me** él me lo procuró; **he got me a job** me consiguió un puesto; **that's what got him the rise** eso fue lo que le valió el aumento; **I never got an answer** no me contestaron; **~ me Mr X, please** (*Telec*) póngame (*LAm*: comuníqueme) con el Sr X, por favor; **he got 6 months** le condenaron a 6 meses de prisión; **I don't ~ much from his lectures** saco poco provecho de sus clases; **we shan't ~ anything out of him** no lograremos sacarle nada, no nos dirá nada; **what are you ~ting out of it?** ¿qué vas a sacar de ello?, ¿qué vas a sacar en beneficio propio?; **you may ~ some fun out of it** puede que te resulte divertido; **we got him on the subject of drugs** logramos que hablase de las drogas.

(**b**) (*arrest*) prender, detener; (*capture, kill*) cazar; **got you at last!** ¡por fin te he cazado!; **I'll ~ him one day!** ¡algún día me lo cargaré!; **I'll ~ you yet!** ¡me las pagarás!; **he got it from the teacher** el profesor le echó un rapapolvo; **they're out to ~ him** andan tras él, se proponen cargárselo.

(**c**) *disease* coger (*Sp*), agarrar (*LAm*); **to ~ religion** darse a la religión; *V* **bad 2**.

(**d**) (*: *irritate*) **that's what ~s me!** ¡eso es lo que más me fastidia!

(**e**) (*: *attract*) **this tune ~s me** esta melodía me chifla*, esta melodía me apasiona.

(**f**) (*strike*) dar en; **it got him on the head** le dio en la cabeza; **it ~s me in the throat** me afecta la garganta.

(**g**) (*: *understand*) comprender; (**do you**) **~ it?** ¿ya caes?*, ¿me entiendes?

(**h**) (*move*) trasladar, pasar; **we can't ~ it through the door** no lo podemos pasar por la puerta; **to ~ sth past the customs** conseguir pasar algo por la aduana; **how can we ~ it home?** ¿cómo podemos llevarlo a casa?

(**i**) (*fetch*) buscar, traer, ir a buscar; *person* llamar, ir por; **I'll go and ~ it for you** te lo voy a buscar; **please ~ the doctor** por favor llame al médico; **can I ~ you a drink?** ¿quieres tomar algo?, ¿te traigo algo de beber?

(**j**) *meal* preparar, hacer.

(**k**) **to have got** tener, poseer; **what have you got there?** ¿qué tienes ahí?; **there you've got me** eso no te lo puedo decir, no sé nada de eso.

(**l**) **to have got to** + *infin* tener que + *infin*.

(**m**) **to ~ sb to do sth** (*persuading*) conseguir que uno haga algo, persuadir a uno a hacer algo; (*ordering*) encargar a uno que haga algo.

(**n**) **to get** + *ptp or adj*: **to ~ sth done** mandar hacer algo; **to ~ one's hair cut** hacerse cortar el pelo, cortarse el pelo; **to ~ one's feet wet** mojarse los pies; (*often translated by a simple verb, eg*) **to ~ sth ready** preparar algo; **to ~ sb drunk** emborrachar a uno.

(**o**) **to ~ sth going** poner algo en marcha, hacer que algo empiece a funcionar; **to ~ a plan moving** hacer que se empiece a realizar un proyecto.

2 *vi* (**a**) (*become*) ponerse, volverse, hacerse (*for usage, V* **become 2 (c)**; to ~ + *ptp or adj is often translated by passive, vi or vr*) **to ~ beaten** ser vencido; **to ~ run over** ser atropellado; **to ~ angry** enfadarse, enojarse (*LAm*); **to ~ dark** hacerse de noche, anochecer; **to ~ drunk** emborracharse; **to ~ excited** emocionarse; **to ~ hurt** hacerse daño; **to ~ married** casarse; **to ~ old** envejecer(se); **to ~ wet** mojarse.

(**b**) (*reach*) **to ~ from A to B** ir de A a B, trasladarse de A a B; **to ~ to a place** llegar a un lugar; **how did it ~ here?** ¿cómo vino a parar aquí?; **he got there late** llegó tarde; **now we're ~ting somewhere** ahora empezamos a hacer progresos; **the whisky has got to him*** el whisky le ha afectado.

(**c**) (‡: *go*) largarse*; **~!** ¡lárgate!*

(**d**) **to ~** + *ger* empezar a + *infin*; **we got talking** empezamos a charlar; **to ~ going, to ~ moving** ponerse en marcha; **~ going!** ¡menearse!; ¡andando!; **the idea never got going** la idea nunca tuvo consecuencias prácticas.

(**e**) (+ *infin*) **to ~ to do sth** llegar (con el tiempo) a hacer algo; **to ~ to like sth** tomar afición a algo; **we never got to see him** no logramos verle; **eventually I got to be an expert at it** por fin llegué a hacerlo bastante bien.

3 *vr*: **to ~ o.s. arrested** hacerse detener; **to ~ o.s. drunk** emborracharse; **to ~ o.s. lost** extraviarse.

◆**get about** *vi* (**a**) (*person*) salir mucho, viajar mucho, ir a muchos sitios; (*after illness*) levantarse y salir. (**b**) (*re-

port) saberse, divulgarse.

◆**get above** *vr*: **to ~ above o.s.** engreírse.

◆**get across 1** *vt* (**a**) *load etc* pasar, hacer pasar. (**b**) *message etc* hacer entender, lograr comunicar. (**c**) **he got across the manager*** se indispuso con el jefe. **2** *vi* (**a**) (*person*) lograr cruzar. (**b**) (*message etc*) surtir efecto; (*meaning*) ser comprendido; **to ~ across to** lograr comunicar con, hacerse entender por.

◆**get after** *vt* perseguir, dar caza a.

◆**get along 1** *vt*: **we'll try to ~ him along** trataremos de hacerle venir. **2** *vi* (**a**) seguir andando; (*depart*) irse; **we must be ~ting along** es hora de irnos ya; **~ along now!** ¡vete ya!; **~ along with you!*** (*Brit*) ¡no digas bobadas! (**b**) (*manage*) **we ~ along (somehow)** vamos tirando; **to ~ along without sth** pasarse sin algo. (**c**) (*be on good terms*) *V* **~ on.** (**d**) (*progress*) *V* **~ on.**

◆**get around** *vi* (**a**) = **~ about** (**a**). (**b**) **to ~ around to sth** llegar por fin a algo; empezar a estudiar (*etc*) algo; **I never seem to ~ around to it** parece que nunca tengo tiempo para eso.

◆**get at** *vt* (**a**) (*reach*) llegar a; **a place hard to ~ at** un lugar de difícil acceso; **as soon as he ~s at the drink** en cuanto se pone a beber; **he's not easy to ~ at** es difícil ponerse en contacto con él; **let me ~ at him!** ¡que me dejen llegar a él!

(**b**) (*ascertain*) descubrir, averiguar.

(**c**) (*suggest*) apuntar a; **what are you ~ting at?** ¿qué quieres decir con eso?

(**d**) (*attack*) atacar; (*spoil*) estropear; (*tease*) tomar el pelo a, (*unpleasantly*) meterse con; **are you ~ting at me?** ¿lo dices por mí?

(**e**) (*: *bribe*) sobornar; (*intimidate*) intimidar; **he's been got at** le han sobornado; le han intimidado.

◆**get away 1** *vt* (*remove*) quitar, quitar de en medio; separar; **to ~ sth away from sb** quitar algo a uno; **to get sb away** ayudar a uno a escapar.

2 *vi* (*leave*) conseguir marcharse; salir, ir fuera; ir de vacaciones; (*escape*) escaparse, evadirse; (*at start of race*) escapar; **~ away!*** ¡no digas bobadas!; **to ~ away from** *place, person* escaparse de; **to ~ away from it all** evadirse del bullicio; dejar atrás los problemas; **to ~ away with** (*steal*) llevarse, alzarse con; **to ~ away with it** (*go unpunished*) salir impune, quedar sin castigo; **you shan't ~ away with it!** ¡me las pagarás!; **there's no ~ting away from it** los hechos son hechos, hay que reconocer la verdad.

◆**get back 1** *vt* recobrar, recuperar. **2** *vi* (**a**) (*return*) volver, regresar; **to ~ back to sb** (*Telec*) llamar a uno; **~ back!** ¡atrás! (**b**) **to ~ back at sb** desquitarse con uno.

◆**get behind** *vi* quedarse atrás.

◆**get by 1** *vt* (*pass*) pasar, lograr pasar; *person* (*fig*) eludir, burlar la vigilancia de.

2 *vi* (**a**) (*pass*) pasar, lograr pasar. (**b**) (*manage*) arreglárselas; **we'll ~ by** nos las arreglaremos, nos las apañaremos; **I can ~ by in Dutch** me defiendo en holandés.

◆**get down 1** *vt* (**a**) (*lift down*) bajar; descolgar; (*swallow*) tragar.

(**b**) (*note*) apuntar; (*put in writing*) poner por escrito.

(**c**) (*depress*) deprimir; desanimar; **this is ~ting me down** no puedo con esto, apenas aguanto esto; **don't let it ~ you down** no te dejes desanimar.

2 *vi* (**a**) bajar; **to ~ down to** llegar a.

(**b**) **to ~ down to a problem** abordar un problema, empezar a estudiar un problema; **to ~ down to work** ponerse (seriamente) a trabajar; **~ down to it!** ¡a ello!, ¡manos a la obra!

◆**get in 1** *vt person etc* hacer entrar; *plants etc* plantar; *harvest* recoger; *money* recaudar; *word* decir, lograr decir; *supplies* obtener; *blow* lograr dar.

2 *vi* (**a**) (*enter*) (lograr) entrar (en); (*arrive home*) llegar a casa, regresar; (*train etc*) llegar.

(**b**) (*Pol*) ser elegido.

(**c**) **to ~ in with sb** (*gain favour*) congraciarse con uno; llegar a tener influencia con uno.

(**d**) **she got in with a bad crowd** formó unas amistades peligrosas, alternó con gente de mala fama.

(**e**) **to ~ in on** lograr introducirse en, lograr tomar parte en; *V* **act 1 (d)**.

◆**get into** *vt house etc* lograr entrar en; *vehicle* subir a; *club* ingresar en, hacerse miembro de; *clothes* ponerse; *difficulty* meterse en; *habit* adquirir; **I can't ~ into this dress** no logro encajarme en este vestido, este vestido me está pequeño; **what's got into you?** ¿qué mosca te ha picado?

◆**get off 1** *vt* (**a**) *burden* quitarse de encima; *clothes* quitarse; *stain* sacar, quitar.

(**b**) *letter* escribir; mandar, despachar (*to* a); *work* despachar, terminar.

(**c**) (*learn*) aprender.

(**d**) **to ~ an accused person off** lograr que se absuelva a un acusado.

(**e**) (*Naut*) *boat* sacar a flote; *persons* desembarcar.

(**f**) **let's ~ off this subject** cambiemos de tema; **we've rather got off the subject** nos hemos alejado bastante del tema; **she got off washing up** se zafó del deber de lavar los platos.

2 *vi* (**a**) (*from vehicle*) apearse (de), bajar (de); **to tell sb where he ~s off*** cantar a uno los cuarenta.

(**b**) (*depart*) irse, marcharse; (*escape*) escapar; **~ off!** ¡suelta!; **but he got off** pero se libró (del castigo); **he got off with a fine** se libró con una multa; **he got off unharmed** salió indemne; *V also* **~ away.**

(**c**) (*sleep*) conciliar el sueño, dormirse.

(**d**) **to ~ off with sb*** liarse con uno*, ligar con uno*.

◆**get on 1** *vt* poner; *clothes* ponerse.

2 *vi* (**a**) (*mount*) subir (a), ponerse encima (de).

(**b**) (*progress, succeed*) hacer progresos; tener éxito; **how did you ~ on?** ¿qué tal te fue?; **how are you ~ting on with him?** ¿cómo te avienes con él?; **I can't ~ on with this child** no hago carrera con este niño; **I can't ~ on with maths** no me entran las matemáticas; **he's keen to ~ on** quiere ir adelante, es ambicioso.

(**c**) (*with numerals etc*) **he's ~ting on for 70** anda cerca de los 70; **he's ~ting on now** va para viejo; **it's ~ting on for 9** son casi las 9; **there were ~ting on for 50 people** había unas cincuenta personas.

(**d**) (*continue*) seguir; **time is ~ting on, it's ~ting on** se hace tarde; **~ on, man!** ¡sigue!, ¡adelante!; **let's ~ on with it** vamos; prosigamos; **this will do to be ~ting on with** esto basta por ahora.

(**e**) (*agree*) **to ~ on with sb** llevarse bien con uno, congeniar con uno; **they ~ on well together** se llevan bien.

◆**get on to** *vt* (**a**) (*find, recognize*) *facts, truth* descubrir; encontrar, localizar; (*identify*) identificar; **the police got on to him at once** la policía se puso sobre su pista en seguida.

(**b**) (*contact*) ponerse en contacto con, contactar con, comunicar con; (*Telec*) llamar; **I'll ~ on to him** hablaré con él.

(**c**) **she's always ~ting on to me** siempre me está regañando.

◆**get out 1** *vt* (**a**) hacer salir; (*take out*) sacar; *stain* sacar, quitar; *book* (*from library*) sacar.

(**b**) *book* (*publish*) publicar.

(**c**) *problem* resolver.

(**d**) (*prepare*) *plan etc* preparar, hacer.

2 *vi* (**a**) (*leave*) salir; irse; **to ~ out of the bus** bajar del autobús; **~ out!** ¡vete!, ¡fuera de aquí!

(**b**) (*escape*) escaparse; **to ~ out of** *duty* librarse de, zafarse de; *habit* perder; *difficulty* salir de; **there's no ~ting out of it** no hay más remedio.

(**c**) (*news*) saberse, divulgarse, hacerse público.

◆**get over 1** *vt* (**a**) (*lift over*) hacer pasar por encima de.

(**b**) (*put across*) comunicar, hacer comprender.

(**c**) (*finish*) terminar; **let's ~ it over (with)!** ¡vamos a concluir de una vez!

(**d**) *difficulty* vencer, superar; salir de; *illness* reponerse de; *fright* sobreponerse a; *grief* dominar; *surprise* volverse de; *resentment* olvidar.

2 *vi* (*cross*) pasar, cruzar.

◆**get round** *vt* (**a**) *difficulty* soslayar; *corner etc* dar la vuelta a. (**b**) *person* persuadir, engatusar; *V also* **~ around.**

◆**get round to** *vt*: **to ~ round to doing sth** encontrar tiempo para hacer algo; **I never got round to going to see her** no tuve tiempo de ir a verla; **I shan't ~ round to that before next week** no lo podré hacer antes de la semana próxima.

◆**get through 1** *vt* (**a**) conseguir pasar por.

(**b**) (*Parl*) *bill* hacer aprobar.

(**c**) *message etc* = **get across 1** (**b**), **get over 1** (**b**).

(**d**) *exam* aprobar.

(**e**) *time* pasar; *period, work* llegar al final de, terminar; *money* gastar; *food etc* consumir.

2 *vi* (**a**) **to ~ through (to)** (*Telec*) (lograr) comunicar con; (*fig*) hacerse comprender por, llegar a.

(**b**) (*be accepted*) pasar, ser aceptado, ser aprobado.

◆**get together 1** *vt* reunir, juntar. **2** *vi* reunirse; verse; (*for celebration*) organizar una fiesta.

◆**get under** **1** *vt* (**a**) **to ~ under a fence/rope** *etc* pasar por debajo de una cerca/cuerda *etc.* (**b**) (*lit*) hacer pasar por debajo; (*fig: control*) *fire, revolt* controlar. **2** *vi* (*pass underneath*) pasar por debajo.

◆**get up** **1** *vt* (**a**) (*lift*) levantar, alzar; (*take up*) subir.
(**b**) (*from bed*) hacer levantarse; (*wake*) despertar.
(**c**) *speed etc* aumentar.
(**d**) (*learn*) aprender; (*revise*) repasar.
(**e**) (*organize*) organizar, preparar.
(**f**) (*dress*) ataviar (*in* de); (*disguise*) disfrazar (*as* de).
2 *vi* (**a**) (*stand*) levantarse, ponerse de pie; (*from bed*) levantarse; (*bird etc*) alzar el vuelo; (*rise*) subir; **~ up!** ¡levántate!, (*to horse*) ¡arre!
(**b**) (*wind*) empezar a soplar recio; (*fire*) avivarse; (*sea*) embravecerse.
(**c**) (*be involved in, do*) **to ~ up to** llegar a; **to ~ up to mischief** andar en diabluras; **what did you ~ up to in London?** ¿qué diabluras hiciste en Londres?; **you never know what he'll ~ up to next** nunca se sabe qué bobadas hará.
3 *vr*: **to ~ o.s. up as** disfrazarse de, vestir de.

get-at-able [getˈætəbl] *adj* accesible.

getaway [ˈgetəweɪ] **1** *n* escape *m*, huida *f*, fuga *f*; **to make one's ~** escaparse. **2** *attr*: **the thieves' ~ car** el coche en que los ladrones habían huido.

Gethsemane [geθˈsemənɪ] *n* Getsemaní *m*.

get-rich-quick* [ˌgetˌrɪtʃˈkwɪk] *adj*: **~ scheme** plan *m* para hacer una rápida fortuna.

get-together [ˈgettəˌgeðəʳ] *n* (*meeting*) reunión *f*; (*regular social gathering*) tertulia *f*; (*party*) guateque *m*.

getup [ˈgetʌp] *n* atavío *m*, traje *m*.

get-up-and-go* [ˌgetʌpəndˈgəʊ] *n*: **he's got lots of ~** tiene mucho empuje.

get-well card [ˌgetˈwelˌkɑːd] *n* tarjeta *f* que se envía a uno que está enfermo deseándole que se mejore.

geyser [ˈgiːzəʳ] *n* (*Geog*) géiser *m*; (*Brit: heater*) calentador *m* de agua.

G-Force *n abbr of* **force of gravity**.

Ghana [ˈgɑːnə] *n* Ghana *f*.

Ghanaian [gɑːˈneɪən] **1** *adj* ghanés. **2** *n* ghanés *m*, -esa *f*.

ghastly [ˈgɑːstlɪ] *adj* (**a**) horrible; (*pale*) pálido; (*corpselike*) cadavérico. (**b**) (*) horrible, fatal, malísimo; *person* pesado; **how ~!** ¡qué horror!; **it must be ~ for her** debe ser horrible para ella.

Ghent [gent] *n* Gante *m*.

gherkin [ˈgɜːkɪn] *n* pepinillo *m*.

ghetto [ˈgetəʊ] *n* gueto *m*; (*Hist*) judería *f*.

ghetto-blaster [ˈgetəʊˌblɑːstəʳ] *n* cassette *m* portátil con altavoz incorporado.

ghost [gəʊst] **1** *n* fantasma *m*, espectro *m*; (*TV*) imagen *f* fantasma; **without the ~ of a smile** sin la más leve sonrisa; **he hasn't the ~ of a chance** no tiene la más remota posibilidad; **to give up the ~** entregar el alma, (*fig*) perder toda esperanza; **the car finally gave up the ~** por fin el coche se averió definitivamente.
2 *attr*: **~ edition** edición *f* inexistente; **~ image** (*Cine, TV*) imagen *f* fantasma; **~ story** cuento *m* de fantasmas; **~ town** ciudad *f* muerta, pueblo *m* fantasma; **~ word** palabra *f* inexistente; **~ writer** negro *m*, -a *f*.
3 *vt book* escribir por otro; **an autobiography ~ed by X** una autobiografía escrita por el negro X.

ghostly [ˈgəʊstlɪ] *adj* espectral, fantasmal.

ghost-write [ˈgəʊstˌraɪt] (*irr: V* **write**) *vt V* **ghost 3**.

ghoul [guːl] *n* demonio *m* necrófago; (*fig*) persona *f* de gustos inhumanos.

ghoulish [ˈguːlɪʃ] *adj* espantosamente cruel; sádico; macabro.

GHQ *n abbr of* **General Headquarters** cuartel *m* general.

G.I. *n* (*US*) (**a**) *abbr of* **Government Issue** propiedad *f* del Estado. (**b**) *abbr of* soldado *m* (raso) americano; **~ bride** novia *f* (*or* esposa *f*) de un soldado americano; **~ Joe** ≃ el recluta Pérez.

giant [ˈdʒaɪənt] **1** *n* gigante *m*; **XYZ, the computer ~** XYZ, líder en ordenadores; **he was a ~ among actors** como actor fue un coloso. **2** *adj* gigantesco, gigante.

giant-killer [ˈdʒaɪəntˌkɪləʳ] *n* matagigantes *m*.

Gib* [dʒɪb] *n* = **Gibraltar**.

gibber [ˈdʒɪbəʳ] *vi* farfullar, hablar atropelladamente, hablar de una manera ininteligible.

gibbering [ˈdʒɪbərɪŋ] *adj* farfullador; **I sounded like a ~ idiot** daba la impresión de desvariar.

gibberish [ˈdʒɪbərɪʃ] *n* galimatías *m*, guirigay *m*.

gibbet [ˈdʒɪbɪt] *n* horca *f*.

gibbon [ˈgɪbən] *n* gibón *m*.

gibe [dʒaɪb] **1** *n* pulla *f*, dicterio *m*. **2** *vi* mofarse (*at* de).

giblets [ˈdʒɪblɪts] *npl* menudillos *mpl*.

Gibraltar [dʒɪˈbrɔːltəʳ] *n* Gibraltar *m*.

Gibraltarian [ˌdʒɪbrɔːlˈtɛərɪən] **1** *adj* gibraltareño. **2** *n* gibraltareño *m*, -a *f*.

giddily [ˈgɪdɪlɪ] *adv* (*light-heartedly*) frívolamente; (*heedlessly*) despreocupadamente, a la ligera.

giddiness [ˈgɪdɪnɪs] *n* vértigo *m*.

giddy [ˈgɪdɪ] *adj speed* vertiginoso; *character* atolondrado, ligero de cascos; (*dizzy*) mareado; **to feel ~** sentirse mareado; **it makes me ~** me marea, me da vértigo.

GIFT [gɪft] *n abbr of* **Gamete In** (*or* **Intra**) **Fallopian Transfer**.

gift [gɪft] **1** *n* (**a**) (*present*) regalo *m*; obsequio *m*; (*Eccl*) ofrenda *f*; (*Jur*) donación *f*; (*bargain*) ganga *f*; **~ tax** impuesto *m* sobre donaciones; **the office is in the ~ of** la dignidad está en manos de; **it's a ~!*** ¡está tirado!*; **I wouldn't have it as a ~** no lo quiero ni regalado; **don't look a ~ horse in the mouth** a caballo regalado no le mires el dentado.
(**b**) (*faculty, talent*) don *m*, talento *m*, prenda *f*; **~ of tongues** don *m* de las lenguas; **he has a ~ for administration** tiene talento para la administración; **he has artistic ~s** tiene dotes artísticas.
2 *vt* dar, donar.

gift certificate [ˈgɪftˌsəˈtɪfɪkɪt] *n* (*US*) vale-regalo *m*.

gift-coupon [ˈgɪftˌkuːpɒn] *n* cupón *m* de regalo.

gifted [ˈgɪftɪd] *adj* talentoso.

gift-shop [ˈgɪftˌʃɒp] *n*, **gift-store** [ˈgɪftˌstɔːʳ] *n* (*US*) tienda *f* de regalos; (*in signs*) 'artículos *mpl* de regalo'.

gift-token [ˈgɪftˌtəʊkən] *n*, **gift-voucher** [ˈgɪftˌvaʊtʃəʳ] *n* vale-regalo *m*.

giftwrap [ˈgɪftˌræp] *vt* envolver en papel de regalo.

giftwrapped [ˈgɪftˌræpt] *adj* envuelto para regalo.

giftwrapping [ˈgɪftˌræpɪŋ] *n* envoltorio *m* de regalo, papel *m* de colores para regalo.

gig [gɪg] *n* (**a**) (*vehicle*) calesín *m*. (**b**) (*Naut*) lancha *f*, canoa *f*. (**c**) (*Mus*) actuación *f*; concierto *m*. (**d**) (*US: job*) trabajo *m* temporal.

gigabyte [ˈdʒɪgəˌbaɪt] *n* gigabyte *m*.

gigantic [dʒaɪˈgæntɪk] *adj* gigantesco.

gigawatt [ˈdʒɪgəˌwɒt] *n* gigavatio *m*.

giggle [ˈgɪgl] **1** *n* risilla *f* sofocada, risilla *f* tonta; **she got the ~s** le dio la risa tonta; **they did it for a ~** (*Brit*) lo hicieron para reírse. **2** *vi* reírse con una risilla sofocada (*or* tonta).

giggly [ˈgɪglɪ] *adj* dado a la risa tonta.

GIGO [ˈgaɪgəʊ] (*Comput*) *abbr of* **garbage in, garbage out** basura entra, basura sale, BEBS.

gigolo [ˈʒɪgələʊ] *n* gigoló *m*.

gild [gɪld] (*irr: pret* **gilded**, *ptp* **gilded** *or* **gilt**) *vt* dorar; *metal* dorar, sobredorar; (*fig*) embellecer, adornar; *pill* dorar.

gilded [ˈgɪldɪd] *adj* dorado.

gilding [ˈgɪldɪŋ] *n* doradura *f*, dorado *m*.

Giles [dʒaɪlz] *nm* Gil.

gill[1] [dʒɪl] *n* (*Brit*) *cuarta parte de una pinta* (= *approx* ⅛ *litro*).

gill[2] [gɪl] *n* (*Fish*) agalla *f*, branquia *f*; **to look green about the ~s** tener mala cara.

gillie [ˈgɪlɪ] *n* (*Scot*) ayudante *m* de cazador (*or* pescador); (*Scot*) criado *m*.

gilt [gɪlt] **1** *ptp of* **gild**. **2** *adj* dorado. **3** *n* (**a**) dorado *m*; (*fig*) atractivo *m*. (**b**) (*Fin*) **~s** papel *m* del Estado.

gilt-edged [ˈgɪltˈedʒd] *adj*: **~ securities** (*Brit*) papel *m* del Estado, valores *mpl* de máxima confianza.

gimbal(s) [ˈdʒɪmbəl(z)] *n* (*Aut, Naut*) cardán *m*.

gimcrack [ˈdʒɪmkræk] *adj furniture* de mala calidad.

gimlet [ˈgɪmlɪt] *n* barrena *f* de mano.

gimmick [ˈgɪmɪk] *n* (*Theat*) truco *m* característico; (*Comm*) truco *m* publicitario; **it's just a sales ~** es un truco para vender más.

gimmickry [ˈgɪmɪkrɪ] *n* truquería *f*.

gimmicky [ˈgɪmɪkɪ] *adj* truquero.

gimp* [gɪmp] *n* (*US*) cojo *m*, -a *f*.

gin[1] [dʒɪn] *n* (*drink*) ginebra *f*; **~ and it** (*Brit*) vermú *m* con ginebra; **~ and tonic** gin-tonic *m*.

gin[2] [dʒɪn] *n* (*trap*) trampa *f*; (*Mech*) desmotadera *f* de algodón.

ginger [ˈdʒɪndʒəʳ] **1** *n* (**a**) jengibre *m*. (**b**) (*fig*) energía *f*, empuje *m*. **2** *adj hair* rojo, bermejo; *cat* de color melado, barcino, amarillento.

◆**ginger up** *vt* (*Brit*) espabilar, estimular.

ginger-ale [ˈdʒɪndʒərˈeɪl] *n*, **ginger-beer** [ˈdʒɪndʒəˈbɪəʳ] *n* gaseosa *f* de jengibre.

gingerbread [ˈdʒɪndʒəbred] *n* pan *m* de jengibre.

ginger-group [ˈdʒɪndʒəgruːp] *n* (*Brit*) grupo *m* de activistas, grupo *m* de presión.

gingerly ['dʒɪndʒəlɪ] **1** *adj* cauteloso. **2** *adv* con tiento, con pies de plomo.

gingery ['dʒɪndʒərɪ] *adj hair* rojo, bermejo.

gingham ['gɪŋəm] *n* guinga *f*, guingán *m*.

gingivitis [ˌdʒɪndʒɪ'vaɪtɪs] *n* gingivitis *f*.

Ginny ['dʒɪnɪ] *nf familiar form of* **Virginia**.

ginormous* [dʒaɪ'nɔːməs] *adj* (*hum*) enorme de grande.

gipsy ['dʒɪpsɪ] **1** *n* gitano *m*, -a *f*. **2** *attr* gitano, cíngaro; ~ **moth** lagarta *f*.

giraffe [dʒɪ'rɑːf] *n* jirafa *f*.

gird [gɜːd] (*irr*: *pret and ptp* **girded** *or* **girt**) **1** *vt* ceñir; rodear (*with* de). **2** *vr*: **to ~ o.s. for the fight** (*or* **fray**) aprestarse para la lucha.

◆**gird on** *vt*: **to ~ on one's sword** ceñirse la espada.

◆**gird up** *vt*: **to ~ up one's loins** aprestarse para la lucha.

girder ['gɜːdəʳ] *n* viga *f*.

girdle ['gɜːdl] **1** *n* cinto *m*, ceñidor *m*; (*belt, also fig*) cinturón *m*; (*woman's*) faja *f*. **2** *vt* ceñir, rodear (*also fig*; *with* de).

girl [gɜːl] **1** *n* chica *f*, muchacha *f*; (*small*) niña *f*; (*young woman*) chica *f*, joven *f*; (*servant*) criada *f*, chica *f*; (*girlfriend*) amiguita *f*; **best ~** novia *f*; **old ~** (*Brit*: *of school*) antigua alumna *f*; (*) vieja *f*.

2 *attr*: ~ **Friday** empleada *f* de confianza; ~ **guide** (*Brit*), ~ **scout** (*US*) exploradora *f*, muchacha-guía *f*.

girlfriend ['gɜːlfrend] *n* amiga *f*, amiguita *f*; compañera *f*.

girlhood ['gɜːlhʊd] *n* juventud *f*, mocedad *f*.

girlie ['gɜːlɪ] **1** *n* (*US**) nena *f*, chiquilla *f*. **2** *attr*: ~ **magazine** revista *f* de desnudos, revista *f* de destape.

girlish ['gɜːlɪʃ] *adj* de niña; juvenil; (*pej*) afeminado.

giro ['dʒaɪrəʊ] (*Brit*) **1** *n*: **National G~** Giro *m* postal. **2** *attr*: **bank ~ system** sistema *m* de giro bancario; **by ~ transfer** mediante giro; ~ **cheque** cheque *m* de giro.

Gironde [dʒɪ'rɒnd] *n* Gironda *m*.

girt [gɜːt] *pret and ptp of* **gird**.

girth [gɜːθ] *n* (**a**) (*strap*) cincha *f*. (**b**) (*measure*) circunferencia *f*; (*stoutness*) gordura *f*, obesidad *f*; **because of its great ~** por su gran tamaño, por lo abultado.

gist [dʒɪst] *n* esencia *f*, lo esencial, quid *m*; **to get the ~ of a matter** entender lo esencial de una cuestión.

git‡ [gɪt] *n* (*Brit*) bobo *m*, -a *f*.

give [gɪv] (*irr*: *pret* **gave**, *ptp* **given**) **1** *vt* (**a**) (*bestow free*) dar; (*as present*) regalar; (*hand over*) entregar; *aid* prestar; *life* dar, sacrificar; *party* ofrecer, organizar (*for* en honor de); **to ~ sth to sb, to ~ sb sth** dar algo a uno; **I wouldn't want it if you gave it to me** eso no lo quiero ni regalado; (**God**) **~ me strength!** ¡Dios me dé paciencia!; **~ me the old songs!** ¡para mí las canciones viejas!

(**b**) (*deliver*) entregar; *regards etc* dar; *one's word* dar, empeñar; *promise* hacer; **to ~ sth into sb's hands** entregar (*or* confiar) algo a uno; **to ~ sb sth to eat** dar de comer a uno.

(**c**) (*pay*) pagar, dar; **what did you ~ for it?** ¿cuánto pagaste por él?; **I would ~ a lot to know** daría un dineral por saberlo.

(**d**) (*dedicate*) *energy, time etc* dedicar, consagrar; **he gave his life to it** consagró su vida a ello.

(**e**) *cry etc* lanzar, proferir, dar; **to ~ a smile** sonreir (*to* a); **to ~ a start** sobresaltarse.

(**f**) (*state, present, utter*) *particulars* hacer constar; *example* citar; *details etc* dar; *recitation etc* ofrecer; *play* representar, poner; *lecture* dar; *speech* pronunciar; *decision* comunicar, (*by judge etc*) dictar; **he ~s no references** no cita referencias; **it gave no sign of life** no dio señal alguna de vida; **~ us a song!** ¡cántanos algo!; **I ~ you the Queen** brindemos por la Reina.

(**g**) (*impart*) comunicar; (*pass on*) transmitir; *disease* contagiar con; **to ~ sb to understand that ...** dar a uno a entender que ...; **I was given to believe that ...** me hicieron creer que ...

(**h**) (*allot, grant, assign*) dar; conceder, otorgar; *contract, job* dar; *task* imponer; *name* dar, poner, (*formally*) imponer; *punishment* condenar a, castigar con; **in A.D. 500 ~ or take a few years** en el año 500 después de J.C. quitando o poniendo alguno.

(**i**) (*produce*) *result* dar por resultado, producir, arrojar; **it ~s a total of 80** arroja un total de 80, suman 80; **it ~s 6% a year** rinde un 6 por cien al año; **it ~s an average of 4** da un promedio de 4.

(**j**) (*cause*) ocasionar, causar; **you gave me much pain** me causaste mucha pena.

(**k**) (*allow*) permitir; **I gave myself 10 minutes to do it** me permití 10 minutos para hacerlo; **he can ~ you 5 years** él tiene la ventaja de ser 5 años más joven que tú; **how long would you ~ that marriage?** ¿cuánto tiempo crees que durará ese matrimonio?

(**l**) (*) **to ~ it to sb** (*beat*) dar una paliza a uno; (*verbally*) poner a uno como un trapo*; **I gave him what for** le dije cuatro verdades; **I'll ~ him what for!** ¡me las pagará!; **holidays? I'll ~ you holidays!** ¡ni vacaciones ni pollos en vinagre!*

2 *vi* (**a**) (*bestow*) dar; **to ~ and take** hacer concesiones mutuas; **to ~ as good as one gets** devolver golpe por golpe.

(**b**) (*stretch*) dar de sí; (*break*) romperse; (*door etc*) ceder; (*floor, roof etc*) hundirse.

(**c**) **what ~s?** (*esp US**) ¿qué pasa?, ¿qué se cuece por ahí?*

3 *n* elasticidad *f*.

◆**give away 1** *vt* (**a**) (*give free*) regalar, obsequiar (*esp LAm*); (*get rid of*) deshacerse de; (*sell cheap*) regalar, malvender; (*Sport*) *ball* regalar; *bride* conducir al altar. (**b**) (*disclose*) revelar, descubrir; (*betray*) traicionar. **2** *vr*: **to ~ o.s. away** venderse, traicionarse.

◆**give back** *vt* devolver.

◆**give in 1** *vt* entregar, dar; *name* poner, dar. **2** *vi* ceder; rendirse, darse por vencido; (*agree*) consentir; **I ~ in!** ¡me rindo!; **to ~ in to** *person* condescender con, ceder a las súplicas de; *threats* rendirse ante, sucumbir ante; **she always ~s in to him** ella hace siempre lo que él quiere.

◆**give off** *vt* emitir, despedir, arrojar.

◆**give on to** *vt* dar a.

◆**give out 1** *vt* (**a**) (*hand out*) distribuir, repartir. (**b**) (*announce*) anunciar; (*reveal*) revelar, divulgar; **to ~ it out that ...** anunciar que ..., (*falsely*) hacer creer que ... (**c**) *smoke etc* emitir, arrojar. **2** *vi* (*supply*) agotarse, acabarse; (*patience*) acabarse; (*engine etc*) fallar.

◆**give over 1** *vt* (**a**) entregar; (*transfer*) traspasar; (*devote*) dedicar. (**b**) (*: *stop*) dejar; **~ over arguing!** ¡deja de discutir! **2** *vi* (*) cesar; **~ over!** ¡basta ya! **3** *vr*: **to ~ o.s. over to** entregarse a, darse a.

◆**give up 1** *vt* (**a**) (*devote*) dedicar; **to ~ up one's life to music** dedicar su vida a la música.

(**b**) (*renounce*) ceder; renunciar a; (*sacrifice*) sacrificar; *habit* dejar; *idea, interest* abandonar, renunciar a; *seat, place* ceder; *post* dimitir de, renunciar a; **to ~ up smoking** dejar de fumar; **eventually she gave him up** por fin ella rompió con él.

(**c**) (*hand over, deliver*) entregar; *authority etc* ceder, traspasar.

(**d**) (*abandon hope for*) *patient* desahuciar; *visitor* no esperar más tiempo; (*for lost*) dar por perdido; *problem* renunciar a resolver; **we'd given you up** creíamos que no ibas a venir; **they gave him up for dead** le dieron por muerto.

2 *vi* (**a**) darse por vencido, rendirse; perder la esperanza, desanimarse; **I ~ up!** ¡me rindo!; **don't ~ up yet!** ¡anímate!

(**b**) (*Mech*) averiarse, fallar, estropearse; **the car gave up on us** nos falló el coche.

3 *vr*: **to ~ o.s. up** entregarse (a la policía *etc*); **to ~ o.s. up to** *vice etc* entregarse a, darse a.

give-and-take ['gɪvən'teɪk] *n* toma y daca *m*, concesiones *fpl* mutuas.

giveaway ['gɪvəweɪ] **1** *adj*: ~ **price** precio *m* obsequio, precio *m* de ruina; ~ **terms** condiciones *fpl* excesivamente generosas. **2** *n* (*gift*) regalo *m*; ganga *f*; (*revelation*) revelación *f* involuntaria; **the exam was a ~** el examen estaba tirado.

given ['gɪvn] **1** *ptp of* **give**.

2 (**a**) **~ money one can do anything** con dinero todo es posible.

(**b**) **on a ~ day** un día determinado; **in a ~ time** en un tiempo dado; **~ that ...** dado que ...

(**c**) **to be ~ to** ser dado a, ser adicto a; **to be ~ to** + *ger* ser propenso a + *infin*.

(**d**) **~ name** (*Scot, US*) nombre *m* de pila.

3 *npl*: **~s** (*US*) hechos *mpl* reconocidos; datos *mpl*, bases *fpl*.

giver ['gɪvəʳ] *n* donante *mf*, donador *m*, -ora *f*.

gizmo‡ ['gɪzməʊ] *n* (*US*) artilugio *m*, chisme *m*.

gizzard ['gɪzəd] *n* molleja *f*; **it sticks in my ~** no lo puedo tragar.

glacé ['glæseɪ] *adj fruit* escarchado; ~ **icing** azúcar *m* escarchado.

glacial ['gleɪsɪəl] *adj* glacial.

glaciation [ˌgleɪsɪ'eɪʃən] *n* glaciación *f*.

glacier ['glæsɪəʳ] *n* glaciar *m.*
glad [glæd] *adj* alegre; *news etc* bueno; ~ **rags*** ropa *f* dominguera; **to be ~ about** alegrarse de; **I'm very ~ for you** me alegro mucho por ti; **to be ~ that** ... alegrarse de que + *subj*; **I am ~ to hear it** me alegro de saberlo; **I shall be ~ to come** tendré mucho gusto en venir; **he seemed ~** se mostró satisfecho.
gladden ['glædn] *vt* alegrar, regocijar.
glade [gleɪd] *n* claro *m.*
glad-hand* ['glædhænd] *vt* (*hum*) estrechar (con entusiasmo fingido) la mano de.
gladiator ['glædɪeɪtəʳ] *n* gladiador *m.*
gladiolus [ˌglædɪ'əʊləs] *n, pl* **gladioli** [ˌglædɪ'əʊlaɪ] estoque *m,* gladíolo *m.*
gladly ['glædlɪ] *adv* alegremente, con satisfacción; **yes, ~** sí, con mucho gusto.
gladness ['glædnɪs] *n* alegría *f*; satisfacción *f.*
glam‡ [glæm] **1** *vt*: **to ~ up** embellecer, adornar; mejorar el aspecto de. **2** *adj V* **glamorous. 3** *n V* **glamour.**
glamorize ['glæməraɪz] *vt* embellecer; hacer más atractivo; **this programme ~s crime** este programa presenta el crimen bajo una luz favorable.
glamorous ['glæmərəs] *adj* encantador, atractivo, hechicero.
glamour, (*US*) **glamor** ['glæməʳ] *n* encanto *m,* atractivo *m,* glamour *m.*
glamour-girl, (*US*) **glamor-girl** ['glæməgɜːl] *n* belleza *f,* guapa *f.*
glance [glɑːns] **1** *n* ojeada *f,* vistazo *m*; mirada *f*; **at a ~** de un vistazo; **at first ~** a primera vista; **with many a backward ~ at** (*fig*) pensando con mucha nostalgia en.
2 *vi* (*look*) mirar; **she ~d in my direction** miró hacia donde yo estaba; **to ~ at** *person etc* lanzar una mirada a, *object* echar un vistazo a, ojear; **to ~ at, to ~ over, to ~ through** *book etc* hojear, examinar por encima, examinar de paso.
◆**glance away** *vi* apartar los ojos.
◆**glance down** *vi* echar un vistazo hacia abajo.
◆**glance off** *vt*: **to ~ off sth** chocar con algo y rebotar, desviarse al chocar con algo.
◆**glance round** *vi* (*round about*) echar un vistazo alrededor; (*behind*) echar un vistazo atrás.
◆**glance up** *vi* (*raise eyes*) elevar la mirada; (*look upwards*) mirar hacia arriba.
glancing ['glɑːnsɪŋ] *adj blow* oblicuo.
gland [glænd] *n* (*Bio*) glándula *f*; (*Mech*) prensaestopas *m.*
glandular ['glændjʊləʳ] *adj* glandular; ~ **fever** mononucleosis *f* infecciosa.
glans [glænz] *n*: ~ **(penis)** glande *m.*
glare [glɛəʳ] **1** *n* **(a)** (*of light*) luz *f* deslumbradora, reverbero *m,* brillo *m,* luminosidad *f*; (*dazzle*) deslumbramiento *m*; **because of the ~ of the light in Spain** debido a lo fuerte de la luz en España; **in the full ~ of publicity** bajo los focos de la publicidad.
(b) (*look*) mirada *f* feroz.
2 *vi* **(a)** (*light*) relumbrar, deslumbrar.
(b) (*person*) mirar ferozmente (*at* a), echar fuego por los ojos.
glaring ['glɛərɪŋ] *adj* **(a)** (*dazzling*) deslumbrador, fuerte.
(b) *colour* chillón; *mistake* manifiesto, notorio.
glaringly ['glɛərɪŋlɪ] *adv*: ~ **obvious** totalmente obvio, meridianamente claro.
glass [glɑːs] **1** *n* **(a)** (*material*) vidrio *m,* cristal *m*; (*glassware*) artículos *mpl* de vidrio, cristalería *f*; (*Met*) barómetro *m*; (*spyglass*) catalejo *m*; (*mirror*) espejo *m*; **under ~** (*exhibit*) bajo vidrio, en una vitrina, (*plant*) en invernáculo; **to look at o.s. in the ~** mirarse en el espejo.
(b) (*tumbler, also for wine*) vaso *m*; (*for beer*) caña *f*; (*stemmed*; *for sherry, champagne etc*) copa *f*; (*for liqueur, brandy*) copita *f.*
(c) **~es** (*spectacles*) gafas *fpl,* lentes *mpl*; anteojos *mpl* (*LAm*); (*binoculars*) gemelos *mpl.*
2 *attr* de vidrio, de cristal; ~ **case** vitrina *f*; ~ **door** puerta *f* vidriera, puerta *f* de cristales; ~ **eye** ojo *m* de cristal; ~ **fiber** (*US*), ~ **fibre** (*n*) fibra *f* de vidrio; (*attr*) de fibra de vidrio; ~ **industry** industria *f* vidriera; ~ **slipper** zapatilla *f* de cristal; ~ **wool** lana *f* de vidrio.
glassblower ['glɑːsˌbləʊəʳ] *n* soplador *m* de vidrio.
glassblowing ['glɑːsˌbləʊɪŋ] *n* soplado *m* de vidrio.
glasscutter ['glɑːsˌkʌtəʳ] *n* (*person*) cortador *m* de vidrio.
glassful ['glɑːsfʊl] *n* vaso *m.*
glasshouse ['glɑːshaʊs] *n, pl* **glasshouses** ['glɑːsˌhaʊzɪz] (*Brit Hort*) invernáculo *m,* invernadero *m*; (*Brit‡*) cárcel *f* (militar).
glasspaper ['glɑːsˌpeɪpəʳ] *n* (*Brit*) papel *m* de vidrio.
glassware ['glɑːswɛəʳ] *n* artículos *mpl* de vidrio, cristalería *f.*
glassworks ['glɑːswɜːks] *n* fábrica *f* de vidrio.
glassy ['glɑːsɪ] *adj substance* vítreo; *surface* liso; *water* espejado; *eye* vidrioso.
glassy-eyed [ˌglɑːsɪ'aɪd] *adj* de mirada vidriosa; (*from drugs, drink*) de mirada perdida; (*from displeasure*) de mirada glacial.
Glaswegian [glæz'wiːdʒən] **1** *adj* de Glasgow. **2** *n* nativo *m,* -a *f* (*or* habitante *mf*) de Glasgow.
glaucoma [glɔː'kəʊmə] *n* glaucoma *m.*
glaze [gleɪz] **1** *n* vidriado *m,* barniz *m,* lustre *m.* **2** *vt* **(a)** (*Brit: put glass in*) poner vidrios a, vidriar. **(b)** *pottery* vidriar; (*Culin*) glasear; (*fig*) lustrar. **3** *vi*: **to ~ over** (*eyes*) velarse.
glazed [gleɪzd] *adj* **(a)** *surface* vidriado; *paper* satinado; *eye* vidrioso; (*Culin*) glaseado. **(b)** (*Brit*) *door, window etc* con cristal; *picture* barnizado. **(c)** (*US**) achispado*.
glazier ['gleɪzɪəʳ] *n* (*Brit*) vidriero *m.*
GLC *n* (*formerly*) *abbr of* **Greater London Council** Corporación *f* Metropolitana de Londres.
gleam [gliːm] **1** *n* (*of light*) rayo *m,* destello *m*; (*of colour*) viso *m*; (*in one's eye*) chispa *f*; (*fig*) vislumbre *f*; **there is a ~ of hope** hay un rayo de esperanza.
2 *vi* brillar (*in the sun* al sol; *with* de), relucir, destellar.
gleaming ['gliːmɪŋ] *adj* reluciente.
glean [gliːn] **1** *vt* espigar; (*fig*) espigar, recoger; **to ~ information about** rebuscar datos sobre; **from what I have been able to ~** de lo que yo he podido saber. **2** *vi* espigar.
gleaner ['gliːnəʳ] *n* espigador *m,* -ora *f.*
gleanings ['gliːnɪŋz] *npl* (*fig*) fragmentos *mpl* recogidos.
glebe [gliːb] *n* terreno *m* beneficial.
glee [gliː] *n* alegría *f,* júbilo *m,* regocijo *m.*
glee club ['gliːklʌb] *n* orfeón *m,* sociedad *f* coral.
gleeful ['gliːfəl] *adj* alegre, regocijado.
gleefully ['gliːfəlɪ] *adv* con júbilo.
glen [glen] *n* cañada *f,* valle *m* estrecho.
glib [glɪb] *adj person* de mucha labia, poco sincero; *speech* elocuente pero insincero; *explanation* fácil.
glibly ['glɪblɪ] *adv* con poca sinceridad; elocuentemente pero con poca sinceridad; con una facilidad sospechosa.
glibness ['glɪbnɪs] *n* labia *f*; falta *f* de sinceridad; facilidad *f.*
glide [glaɪd] **1** *n* deslizamiento *m*; (*Aer*) planeo *m*; (*Mus*) ligadura *f.*
2 *vi* **(a)** deslizarse; **to ~ away, to ~ off** escurrirse, irse silenciosamente; **she ~s to the door** se desliza hacia la puerta.
(b) (*Aer*) planear.
glider ['glaɪdəʳ] *n* planeador *m,* velero *m*; (*towed*) avión *m* remolcado; (*US: swing*) columpio *m.*
gliding ['glaɪdɪŋ] *n* planeo *m.*
glimmer ['glɪməʳ] **1** *n* luz *f* trémula, luz *f* tenue, vislumbre *f*; **without a ~ of understanding** sin dar el menor indicio de haber comprendido; **there is a ~ of hope** hay un rayo de esperanza.
2 *vi* brillar con luz trémula (*or* tenue).
glimpse [glɪmps] **1** *n* vislumbre *f*; vista *f* momentánea; **to catch a ~ of** vislumbrar. **2** *vt* vislumbrar, entrever, ver por un instante.
glint [glɪnt] **1** *n* destello *m,* centelleo *m*; fulgor *m*; (*in one's eye*) chispa *f.* **2** *vi* destellar, centellear.
glissando [glɪ'sændəʊ] *adv* glisando.
glisten ['glɪsn] *vi* relucir, brillar.
glitch* [glɪtʃ] *n* (*US*) fallo *m* técnico, fallo *m* en un sistema electrónico.
glitter ['glɪtəʳ] **1** *n* brillo *m,* resplandor *m.* **2** *vi* relucir, brillar, rutilar; **all that ~s is not gold** no es oro todo lo que reluce.
glitterati* [ˌglɪtə'rɑːtiː] *npl* (*hum*) celebridades *fpl* del mundillo literario y artístico.
glittering ['glɪtərɪŋ] *adj*, **glittery** ['glɪtərɪ] *adj* reluciente, brillante (*also fig*); ~ **prize** premio *m* de oro.
glitz* [glɪts] *n* ostentación *f,* relumbrón *m,* atractivo *m* ostentoso.
glitzy* ['glɪtsɪ] *adj* ostentoso, de relumbrón, ostentosamente atractivo.
gloaming ['gləʊmɪŋ] *n* crepúsculo *m*; **in the ~** al anochecer.
gloat [gləʊt] *vi* relamerse; **to ~ over** *money etc* recrearse contemplando, *sight* saborear, *news* refocilarse con, *victory* manifestar satisfacción maligna por, *beaten enemy* triunfar jactanciosamente de.
gloating ['gləʊtɪŋ] *adj*: **with a ~ smile** sonriendo satisfecho, con una sonrisa satisfecha.

glob [glɒb] *n* (*US*) gotita *f*, glóbulo *m*; masa *f* redonda, masa *f* pequeña; grumo *m*.

global ['gləʊbl] *adj* (*world-wide*) mundial; *sum etc* global; **~ village** pueblo *m* global; **~ warming** recalentamiento *m* global.

globally ['gləʊbəlɪ] *adv* mundialmente; globalmente.

globe [gləʊb] *n* globo *m*, esfera *f*; (*spherical map*) esfera *f* terrestre, globo *m* terráqueo.

globe artichoke ['gləʊb'ɑːtɪtʃəʊk] *n* alcachofa *f*.

globe-trotter ['gləʊb,trɒtə^r] *n* trotamundos *mf*.

globe-trotting ['gləʊb,trɒtɪŋ] *n* viajar *m* alrededor del mundo.

globular ['glɒbjʊlə^r] *adj* globular.

globule ['glɒbjuːl] *n* glóbulo *m*.

gloom [gluːm] *n*, **gloominess** ['gluːmɪnɪs] *n* oscuridad *f*, semioscuridad *f*, penumbra *f*, tenebrosidad *f*; (*fig*) pesimismo *m*; melancolía *f*, tristeza *f*; **it's not all gloom and doom here** aquí no todo son pronósticos de desastre.

gloomily ['gluːmɪlɪ] *adv* oscuramente, lóbregamente; de modo pesimista, con pesimismo; melancólicamente, tristemente.

gloomy ['gluːmɪ] *adj* oscuro, lóbrego, tenebroso; *atmosphere, character, forecast* pesimista; *outlook* nada prometedor; *day, tone* melancólico, triste.

glorification [,glɔːrɪfɪ'keɪʃən] *n* glorificación *f*.

glorify ['glɔːrɪfaɪ] *vt* glorificar; (*praise*) alabar, ensalzar; **it was nothing but a glorified cottage** resultó ser solamente una casita con pretensiones de palacio.

glorious ['glɔːrɪəs] *adj* glorioso; *day, view, stroke etc* magnífico; **it was a ~ muddle** la confusión era mayúscula, resultó un lío colosal.

gloriously ['glɔːrɪəslɪ] *adv* gloriosamente; magníficamente; **it was ~ sunny** hacía un sol magnífico.

glory ['glɔːrɪ] **1** *n* gloria *f*; (*fig*) esplendor *m*; **~ be!** ¡gracias a Dios!; **to be in one's ~** estar en sus glorias; **to go to ~** subir a los cielos.

2 *vi*: **to ~ in** gloriarse de; **I ~ in the name of Ruritanian** me enorgullezco de ser ruritanio; **the café glories in the name of El Dorado** el café tiene el magnífico nombre de El Dorado.

glory-hole* ['glɔːrɪhəʊl] *n* cuarto *m* (*or* cajón *etc*) en desorden, leonera* *f*.

gloss[1] [glɒs] (*note*) **1** *n* glosa *f*. **2** *vt* glosar, comentar.

◆**gloss over** *vt* (*excuse*) disculpar; (*play down*) paliar, colorear, restar importancia a; (*cover up*) pasar por alto, encubrir.

gloss[2] [glɒs] **1** *n* (*shine*) lustre *m*, brillo *m*.

2 *attr*: **~ finish** acabado *m* brillo; **~ paint** pintura *f* esmalte; **~ paper** papel *m* satinado.

3 *vt* lustrar, pulir.

glossary ['glɒsərɪ] *n* glosario *m*.

glossily ['glɒsɪlɪ] *adv* brillantemente; **~ illustrated** elegantemente ilustrado, ilustrado con lujo.

glossy ['glɒsɪ] **1** *adj surface* lustroso, brillante; *hair* liso; *cloth, paper* satinado; *magazine etc* impreso en papel satinado; de lujo, elegante. **2** *n*: **the glossies*** las revistas elegantes.

glottal ['glɒtl] *adj* glotal; **~ stop** oclusión *f* glotal.

glottis ['glɒtɪs] *n* glotis *f*.

Gloucs. *abbr of* **Gloucestershire**.

glove [glʌv] **1** *n* guante *m*; **to fit sb like a ~** sentar a uno como el anillo al dedo. **2** *attr*: **~ compartment** guantera *f*; **~ puppet** títere *m* de guante.

gloved [glʌvd] *adj hand* enguantado.

glove-maker ['glʌv,meɪkə^r] *n*, **glover** ['glʌvə^r] *n* guantero *m*, -a *f*.

glow [gləʊ] **1** *n* (*of lamp, sun etc*) luz *f* (difusa); (*of jewel*) brillo *m*; (*of fire*) calor *m* vivo; (*bright colour*) color *m* vivo; (*in sky*) arrebol *m*; (*Tech*) incandescencia *f*; (*warm feeling*) sensación *f* de bienestar; (*of satisfaction etc*) sensación *f* grata, sentimiento *m* de vivo placer.

2 *vi* (*lamp, sun, jewel etc*) brillar (con luz difusa); (*fire*) arder vivamente; (*Tech*) estar candente; **to ~ with pleasure** experimentar una sensación de bienestar; **to ~ with health** rebosar de salud.

glower ['glaʊə^r] *vi*: **to ~ at** mirar con ceño.

glowering ['glaʊərɪŋ] *adj person, sky* ceñudo.

glowing ['gləʊɪŋ] *adj* candente, incandescente; *light* brillante; *fire* vivo; *cheek etc* encendido; *colour* intenso; *report etc* entusiasta.

glow-worm ['gləʊwɜːm] *n* (*Brit*) luciérnaga *f*.

gloxinia [glɒk'sɪnɪə] *n* gloxínea *f*.

glucose ['gluːkəʊs] *n* glucosa *f*.

glue [gluː] **1** *n* cola *f*, goma *f* (de pegar); (*as drug*) pegamento *m*. **2** *vt* (*also* **to ~ on, to ~ together**) encolar, pegar; **her face was ~d to the window** tenía la cara pegada a la ventana.

glue-sniffer ['gluː,snɪfə^r] *n* esnifador *m*, -ora *f* de pegamento, persona *f* que inhala (*or* esnifa) pegamento.

glue-sniffing ['gluː,snɪfɪŋ] *n* inhalación *f* de colas, esnife *m* pegamentoso.

gluey ['gluːɪ] *adj* pegajoso, viscoso.

glum [glʌm] *adj* (*by nature*) taciturno, melancólico; *mood* triste, abatido; *tone* melancólico, sombrío.

glumly ['glʌmlɪ] *adv walk, shake one's head* sombríamente; *answer* tristemente, sombríamente; *look, inspect* taciturnamente, tristemente.

glut [glʌt] **1** *n* superabundancia *f*, exceso *m*; exceso *m* de oferta; **to be a ~ on the market** abarrotar el mercado.

2 *vt person* hartar, saciar; *market* abarrotar, inundar; **to be ~ted with fruit** (*person*) haberse atracado de frutas.

3 *vr*: **to ~ o.s.** atracarse (*with* de).

gluten ['gluːtən] *n* gluten *m*; **~-free** sin gluten, libre de gluten.

glutenous ['gluːtənəs] *adj* glutenoso.

gluteus [glʊ'tiːəs] *n*, *pl* **glutei** [glʊ'tiːaɪ] glúteo *m*.

glutinous ['gluːtɪnəs] *adj* glutinoso.

glutton ['glʌtn] *n* glotón *m*, -ona *f*; **to be a ~ for work** trabajar incansablemente.

gluttonous ['glʌtənəs] *adj* glotón, goloso.

gluttony ['glʌtənɪ] *n* glotonería *f*, gula *f*.

glycerin(e) [,glɪsə'riːn] *n* glicerina *f*.

glycerol ['glɪsərɒl] *n* glicerol *m*.

glycogen ['glaɪkəʊdʒen] *n* glicógeno *m*.

glycol ['glaɪkɒl] *n* glicol *m*.

GM *n* (**a**) *abbr of* **general manager** director *m*, -ora *f* general. (**b**) (*Brit*) *abbr of* **George Medal** *medalla del valor civil*. (**c**) (*US*) *abbr of* **General Motors**.

gm, gms *abbr of* **gram(s), gramme(s)** gramo(s) *m(pl)*, g., gr.

G-man ['dʒiːmæn] *n*, *pl* **G-men** ['dʒiːmen] (*US*) agente *m* del FBI.

GMAT *n* (*US*) *abbr of* **Graduate Management Admissions Test**.

GMT *n abbr of* **Greenwich Mean Time** hora *f* media de Greenwich.

GMWU *n* (*Brit*) *abbr of* **General and Municipal Workers' Union** *sindicato de trabajadores autónomos y municipales*.

gnarled [nɑːld] *adj* nudoso, torcido.

gnash [næʃ] *vt teeth* rechinar.

gnat [næt] *n* mosquito *m*, jején *m* (*LAm*).

gnaw [nɔː] **1** *vt* roer; **~ed by doubts** asaltado por dudas; **~ed by hunger** atormentado por el hambre. **2** *vi* roer; **to ~ at** roer.

◆**gnaw away, gnaw off** *vt* roer.

gnawing ['nɔːɪŋ] *adj sound* mordisqueante; (*fig*) *remorse, anxiety etc* corrosivo; *hunger* con retortijones; *pain* punzante; **I had a ~ feeling that something had been forgotten** tenía el mal presentimiento de que se había olvidado algo.

gneiss [naɪs] *n* gneis *m*.

gnome [nəʊm] *n* gnomo *m*; **the G~s of Zurich** (*hum*) los banqueros suizos.

gnomic ['nəʊmɪk] *adj* gnómico.

gnostic ['nɒstɪk] **1** *adj* gnóstico. **2** *n* gnóstico *m*, -a *f*.

GNP *n abbr of* **gross national product** producto *m* nacional bruto, PNB *m*.

gnu [nuː] *n* ñu *m*.

go [gəʊ] (*irr*: *pret* **went**, *ptp* **gone**) **1** *vi* (**a**) (*gen*) ir; viajar; andar; **to ~ to London** ir a Londres; **to ~ to England** ir a Inglaterra; **all roads ~ to Rome** todos los caminos van a Roma; **to ~ the shortest way** tomar el camino más corto; **to ~ (at) 90 k.p.h.** ir a 90 k.p.h.; **the numbers that ~ from 6 to 12** los números que van de 6 a 12; **to ~ to sb for sth** acudir a uno a pedir (*or* buscar) algo; **there he ~es!** ¡ahí va!; **here ~es!** ¡vamos a ver!, ¡a ello!; **who ~es there?** ¿quién va?, ¿quién vive?; **what ~es?** (*US**) ¿qué hay de nuevo?; **there you ~ again!** ¡has vuelto a la misma canción!; **there ~es the bell** suena el timbre; **what shall I ~ in?** ¿qué traje me pongo?; **where do we ~ from here?** ¿adónde vamos desde aquí?; **it ~es by seasons** esto va por temporadas; **it ~es by age** varía según la edad, depende de la edad; **promotion ~es by seniority** los ascensos se hacen por orden de antigüedad.

(**b**) (*progress*) ir, andar; **business is ~ing well** los negocios van (*or* andan) bien; **everything went well** todo salió bien, todo resultó perfecto; **how's it ~ing?, how ~es it?** ¿qué tal?, ¿cómo anda esto?, ¿cómo te va esto?; **how** did the exam ~? ¿qué tal el examen?; **we'll see how things ~** veremos cómo va; **she had so much ~ing for her** tenía tantas cosas a su favor; **to make the party ~** animar la fiesta; *V* **get, keep** *etc.*

(c) (*purpose etc*) **to ~ and see sb, to ~ to see sb** ir a ver a uno; **he went and bought it** lo compró, por fin se decidió a comprarlo; (*near future*) **I am ~ing to see him** voy a verle.

(d) (*function*) funcionar, marchar, andar; **it won't ~** no funciona; **it ~es on petrol** funciona con gasolina; **it ~es on wheels** marcha sobre ruedas; **to make sth ~** hacer funcionar algo; **to set a machine ~ing** poner en marcha una máquina.

(e) (*depart*) irse, marcharse, salir, partir; (*train etc*) salir, partir; **let's ~!** ¡vamos!, ¡vámonos!; **don't ~ yet** no te vayas tan pronto, quédate un poco más; **be gone!, get you gone!** ¡váyase!; **~!** (*starting race*) ¡ya!; **from the word ~** desde el principio; **when does the train ~?** ¿a qué hora sale el tren?; **200 hamburgers, to ~** (*US*) 200 hamburguesas para llevar.

(f) (*disappear etc*) **my hat has gone** ha desaparecido mi sombrero; **my money is all gone** ya no me queda dinero; **the coffee is all gone** se acabó el café; **he'll have to ~** (*be dismissed*) tendremos que deshacernos de él, tendremos que echarle; **luxuries will have to ~** tendremos que prescindir de las cosas de lujo; **the trees have been gone for years** hace años que se quitaron los árboles; **his mind is ~ing** está perdiendo la cabeza; **all my teeth have gone** he perdido todos mis dientes.

(g) (*be sold*) venderse; **it went next day** se vendió al día siguiente; **it went for £5** se vendió por 5 libras; **~ing, ~ing, gone!** (*auction*) ¡a la una ... a las dos ... a las tres!

(h) (*time*) pasar; **the day went slowly** el día pasó lentamente; **how is the time ~ing?** ¿cuánto tiempo ha pasado ya?; ¿cómo va la hora?

(i) (*of the hour*) **it has gone 3** ya dieron las 3, son las 3 y pico; **it has gone 8 already** son las 8 dadas.

(j) (*pass by descent etc*) pasar; **his books went to the college** sus libros pasaron al colegio; **the silver medal went to Slobodia** la medalla de plata fue para Eslobodia.

(k) (*extend*) **the garden ~es down to the lake** el jardín se extiende hasta el lago; **it's good as far as it ~es** dentro de sus límites es bueno.

(l) (*be available*) estar disponible; **are there any houses ~ing?** ¿hay casas en venta?; **are there any jobs ~ing?** ¿están ofreciendo empleos?; **anything that's ~ing** lo que haya.

(m) (*exist*) **as prices ~ that's not dear** considerando los precios que corren eso no es caro; **he's quite nice as professors ~** para profesor, es buena persona.

(n) (*text*) decir, rezar; **the text ~es ...** reza el texto así ...; **as the saying ~es** como dice el refrán; **how does the song ~?** ¿cómo es la canción?

(o) (*be acceptable*) **anything ~es with him** se allana a todo; se amolda a todo; hace las cosas de cualquier modo; **what I say ~es** aquí mando yo; **that ~es for me too** yo de acuerdo, yo contigo, yo también; **anything ~es these days** todo se permite hoy; **these colours don't ~ at all** estos colores no se combinan en absoluto; **white ~es with anything** el blanco va con todo.

(p) (*fit*) **it ~es under the table** cabe debajo de la mesa; **where does this book ~?** ¿dónde pongo este libro?; **this part ~es here** esta pieza se coloca aquí; **3 into 12 ~es 4** 12 entre 3 son 4.

(q) (*break etc*) romperse, estropearse; (*give way*) ceder, hundirse; (*fall*) caer; **a fuse went** se quemó un plomo; **it went at the seams** se deshizo por las juntas; **there ~es another button!** ¡ahí va otro botón!

(r) (*help, contribute*) **the qualities that ~ to make a king** las cualidades que hacen a un rey; **it ~es to show that** sirve para demostrar que; **the money ~es to help the poor** el dinero se destina a ayudar a los pobres; **the money will ~ towards a deposit on the flat** el dinero aumentará lo que tenemos ahorrado para el depósito del piso.

(s) (*+ ger*) **to ~ fishing** ir de pesca; **to ~ hunting** ir de caza; **to ~ riding** montar a caballo.

(t) (*become*) hacerse, volverse, ponerse; (*ie ~ bad*) pasarse; (*milk*) cortarse; **to ~ black** ponerse negro; **to ~ mad** volverse loco; **to ~ communist** hacerse comunista; **the country went socialist** el país pasó al socialismo; **to ~ pale** palidecer, ponerse pálido; **suddenly she went all patriotic** de repente se volvió muy patriótica, de golpe le dio el patriotismo; **my tyre's gone flat** se ha pinchado mi neumático.

(u) (*let ~*) **let me ~!** ¡suelta!, ¡déjame!; **to let an animal ~** soltar un animal, poner un animal en libertad; **to let ~ of sth** soltar algo; **to let o.s. ~** (*emotionally*) desahogarse, (*angrily*) perder los estribos, (*on a subject*) entusiasmarse; (*physically*) abandonarse, dejar de cuidarse; (*relax*) relajarse; **they've let the house ~** han dejado de cuidar la casa; **we'll let it ~ at that** dejémoslo ahí.

(v) (*make a noise*) **he went 'psst'** dijo 'psst'; **the balloon went bang** el globo estalló; **the hooter ~es at 5** la sirena suena a las 5; **cats ~ 'miaow'** los gatos hacen 'miau'.

(w) (*remain*) **eight down and two to ~** ocho tenemos y faltan dos, ocho hechos y dos por hacer.

(x) (*to go and ...*) **I'll ~ and see** voy a ver; **he went and shut the door** cerró la puerta, fue a cerrar la puerta; **now you've gone and done it!*** ¡ahora sí la has hecho buena!

(y) (*going to + infin*) **I'm ~ing to tell him** voy a decírselo; **I'm not ~ing to put up with that** no voy a aguantar eso.

2 *vt*: **to ~ it** (*speed*) ir a toda velocidad; (*work hard*) obrar enérgicamente; (*live it up*) correrla; **~ it!** ¡a ello!, ¡ánimo!; **to ~ it alone** hacerlo solo, hacerlo sin ayuda de nadie; **to ~ one better** hacer mejor todavía (*than* que); **to ~ 3 hearts** marcar 3 corazones.

3 *n* **(a)** (*energy*) energía *f*, empuje *m*; **there's no ~ about him** le falta energía; **it's all ~ here** aquí todo es actividad frenética.

(b) **to be on the ~** trajinar, moverse, estar trabajando, estar viajando; **to have two novels on the ~** tener dos novelas entre manos; **to keep sb on the ~** hacer que uno siga trabajando, no dejar descansar a uno.

(c) (*attempt*) **at one ~, in one ~** de un solo golpe, de un tirón; **to have a ~** (*Brit*) intentar, probar suerte; **have a ~!** ¡a ver!; **to have a ~ at sth** intentar algo; **to have a ~ at + *ger*** intentar + *infin*.

(d) (*attack etc*) **to have a ~ at sb** atacar a uno; criticar a uno; emprenderla con uno, tomarla con uno.

(e) (*turn*) **it's your ~** te toca a ti; **whose ~ is it?** ¿a quién le toca?

(f) (*success*) **it's all the ~** hace furor; **it's no ~** es inútil, es imposible; **to make a ~ of sth** tener éxito en algo.

(g) (*bargain*) **it's a ~!** ¡trato hecho!; **is it a ~?** ¿hace?, ¿estamos de acuerdo?

(h) **the lights were at ~** la luz estaba en verde, se mostraba luz verde; **all systems are ~** todo está listo; todo funciona perfectamente; **all systems ~!** ¡todo listo!

◆**go about, go around 1** *vt*: **to ~ about one's business** ocuparse de sus asuntos; **to ~ about a task** emprender un trabajo; **he knows how to ~ about it** sabe lo que hay que hacer, sabe cómo hacerlo. **2** *vi* **(a)** (*move about*) andar (de un sitio para otro); **to ~ around barefoot** andar descalzo; **to ~ around stirring up trouble** andar metiendo cizaña; **to ~ about together** ir juntos, salir juntos; **to ~ about with** salir con, alternar con. **(b)** (*Naut*) virar. **(c)** (*rumour*) correr.

◆**go across 1** *vt river, road* atravesar, cruzar. **2** *vi* (*cross*) cruzar; **she went across to Mrs Smith's** cruzó para ir a casa de la Sra de Smith.

◆**go after** *vt girl* andar tras; (*follow*) seguir; (*seek*) buscar; (*persecute*) cazar, perseguir.

◆**go against** *vt* **(a)** (*oppose*) *principle* ir en contra de, oponerse a; *person* oponerse a. **(b)** (*prove hostile to*) ser desfavorable a; **luck went against him** la suerte le fue contraria.

◆**go ahead** *vi* (*also* **go on ahead**) ir adelante; **~ ahead!** (*fig*) ¡sigue!, ¡adelante!; *V* **ahead 1 (a)**.

◆**go along** *vi* **(a)** ir; (*go away*) marcharse; **to ~ along with** ir con, acompañar a; **I'll tell you as we ~ along** te lo diré de camino; **I'm learning as I ~ along** aprendo mientras lo hago, aprendo poco a poco. **(b)** (*fig*) **to ~ along with a plan** aprobar un proyecto; **we don't ~ along with that** no estamos de acuerdo con eso.

◆**go at** *vt* (*undertake*) emprender; (*attack*) lanzarse sobre, acometer.

◆**go away** *vi* (*depart*) irse, marcharse; (*vanish*) desaparecer; **don't ~ away with the idea that ...** no vayas a pensar que ...

◆**go back** *vi* **(a)** (*return*) volver, regresar; (*retreat*) retroceder. **(b)** (*in time*) **it ~es back to Elizabeth I** se remonta a Isabel I; **it ~es back a long way** esto tiene mucha historia, esto es muy antiguo. **(c)** (*extend*) extenderse; **the path ~es back to the river** la senda se extiende hasta el río; **the cave ~es back 300 metres** la caverna tiene 300 metros de fondo. **(d)** (*revert*) **I sold the car and went back to**

a bicycle vendí el coche y volví a la bicicleta; **he went back to his old habits** volvió a sus antiguas costumbres.

◆**go back on** *vt*: **to ~ back on one's word** faltar a su palabra.

◆**go before 1** *vt*: **the matter has gone before a grand jury** (*US*) el asunto se ha sometido a un gran jurado. **2** *vi* ir primero; (*in order*) anteceder, preceder; **all that has gone before** todo lo que ha pasado (*etc*) antes.

◆**go below** *vi* (*Naut*) bajar.

◆**go by 1** *vt* (**a**) *place* pasar, pasar delante de, pasar cerca de, pasar junto a. (**b**) (*be guided by*) atenerse a, guiarse por; (*base o.s. on*) basarse en, fundarse en; **to ~ by appearances** juzgar por las apariencias; **that's nothing to ~ by** eso no es criterio seguro, eso no es nada; **the only thing to ~ by is** ... el único criterio que vale es ... **2** *vi* (*person*) pasar; (*time*) pasar, transcurrir; **in days gone by** en tiempos pasados, antaño; **to let a chance ~ by** perder una oportunidad.

◆**go down 1** *vt* bajar, descender; **to ~ down a slope** bajar (por) una pendiente; **to ~ down a mine** bajar a una mina.

2 *vi* (**a**) (*descent*) bajar; descender.

(**b**) (*fall*) caer, caerse; (*temperature etc*) bajar, descender; (*tide*) bajar.

(**c**) (*sink*) hundirse.

(**d**) (*Brit Univ*) salir de la universidad; marcharse; terminar el curso.

(**e**) (*sun, moon*) ponerse.

(**f**) (*be swallowed*) tragarse; (*fig*) ser aceptable; poderse aguantar; **that omelette went down a treat*** esa tortilla era sabrosísima; **that will ~ down well with him** eso le va a gustar; **his speech didn't ~ down at all well** su discurso fue recibido muy mal; **how will this series ~ down in Slobodia?** ¿qué van a pensar de esta serie en Eslobodia?

(**g**) (*lose*) ser derrotado (*to* por), perder (*to* frente a); **Jaca went down 2-0 to Huesca** el Jaca perdió 2-0 frente al Huesca.

(**h**) (*tyre*) desinflarse.

(**i**) (*be remembered*) ser recordado; **he went down to posterity as** ... pasó a la posteridad como ...; **it will ~ down as a failure** será recordado como un fracaso.

(**j**) **to ~ down with flu** coger una gripe.

◆**go for** *vt* (**a**) (*fetch*) ir por, ir a buscar. (**b**) *price* venderse por. (**c**) (*attack*) atacar, acometer; (*verbally*) meterse con; **~ for him!** (*to dog*) ¡a él!; **~ for it!** ¡a ello!; (**d**) (*: *like, admire*) entusiasmarse por; **I really ~ for that film** esa película me chifla de verdad*; **I don't ~ for him at all** me resulta la mar de antipático*. (**e**) (*strive for*) dedicarse a obtener, esforzarse por ganar (*etc*); (*choose*) escoger, optar por.

◆**go forward** *vi* (*person, vehicle*) avanzar; **they let the suggestion ~ forward that** ... (*fig*) dieron a entender que ...

◆**go in** *vi* (**a**) (*enter*) entrar (en); (*fit*) caber (en), poderse colocar (en); (*have a place*) ponerse en, deber colocarse en; (*Sport*) entrar a batear; (*Mil*) atacar. (**b**) (*sun, moon*) esconderse, cubrirse.

◆**go in for** *vt* (**a**) (*compete in*) presentarse a; *exam* tomar, presentarse para; *post* solicitar, ser candidato para, presentarse para. (**b**) *hobby* dedicarse a; (*collect*) coleccionar; (*buy*) comprar, adquirir; *style etc* adoptar, seguir; *activity* tomar parte en; **we don't ~ in for such things here** aquí esas cosas no se hacen.

◆**go into** *vt* (**a**) (*enter*) entrar en; caber en; **to ~ into politics** entrar en la política, dedicarse a la política; **to ~ into first gear** meter primera velocidad; **he went into a long explanation** se engolfó en una larga explicación; **let's not ~ into all that now** dejamos todo eso por ahora. (**b**) (*investigate*) examinar, investigar.

◆**go in with** *vt* asociarse con, unirse con; **she went in with her sister to buy the present** entre ella y su hermana compraron el regalo.

◆**go off 1** *vt* (*Brit*) perder el gusto por; **I've gone off him lately*** ahora no me chifla tanto*.

2 *vi* (**a**) (*leave*) irse, marcharse; **he went off with the au pair** se marchó con la chica au pair.

(**b**) (*gun*) dispararse; (*explosive*) estallar, explosionar.

(**c**) (*Brit*) (*go bad*) pasarse, deteriorarse; (*lose quality*) perder su calidad, bajar de calidad; (*Sport*) perder forma; (*lose the knack*) perder el tino.

(**d**) (*go to sleep*) dormirse, quedar dormido.

(**e**) (*happen*) pasar; **how did it ~ off?** ¿qué tal resultó?, ¿qué tal te fue?; **it all went off well** todo salió perfecto.

◆**go on 1** *vt* (**a**) (*be guided by*) guiarse por; basarse en; **there's nothing to ~ on** no hay pista que podamos seguir; **that's nothing to ~ on** no se puede juzgar por eso; **what are you ~ing on?** ¿en qué te basas?

(**b**) **I don't ~ much on that*** eso no me gusta.

2 *vi* (**a**) (*fit*) **the lid won't ~ on** la tapa no se puede poner; **these shoes won't ~ on** mis pies no caben en estos zapatos.

(**b**) (*proceed on one's way*) seguir adelante, seguir su camino; (*progress*) avanzar, ir adelante; **everything is ~ing on normally** todo sigue normal, todo avanza normalmente.

(**c**) (*continue*) seguir, continuar; **to ~ on** + *ger* seguir + *ger*, continuar + *ger*; **~ on!** ¡vamos!, (*with narrative*) ¡adelante!, (*surprise*) ¡anda!; **~ on with you!** ¡no digas bobadas!; **that'll do to be ~ing on with** eso basta por ahora.

(**d**) (*talk*) **he does ~ on so** habla más que siete, no para de hablar; **don't ~ on so!** ¡no machaques!; **she's always ~ing on about it** siempre está con la misma cantilena; **he's always ~ing on about the government** siempre está echando pestes contra el gobierno; **if you ~ on like that** si sigues en ese plan; **don't ~ on like that!** ¡no te pongas así!; **to ~ on at sb** reñir a uno.

(**e**) (*proceed*) **to ~ on to** pasar a; **she went on to learn Arabic** pasó a aprender el árabe; **he went on to say that** ... dijo a continuación que ...

(**f**) (*occur*) pasar; **what's ~ing on?** ¿qué pasa?; **it had been ~ing on in her absence** había pasado en su ausencia; **how long will this ~ on for?** ¿cuánto tiempo durará esto?

(**g**) (*behave*) conducirse, comportarse; **what a way to ~ on!** ¡qué manera de comportarse!

(**h**) (*Theat*) salir (a escena); **to ~ on as substitute** (*Sport*) jugar como suplente.

(**i**) (*light*) encenderse, prenderse (*LAm*).

◆**go on for** *vt* (*with numbers*) **it's ~ing on for 8** son casi las 8; **he's ~ing on for 70** va para los 70.

◆**go out** *vi* (**a**) (*depart*) salir; **to ~ out for a meal** ir a comer fuera; **she went out with him for 2 years** salió con él durante 2 años; **the mail has gone out** ha salido el correo; **to ~ out to work** ir al trabajo; **she ~es out to work** trabaja, tiene un trabajo; **my heart went out to him** le compadecí mucho, sentí una gran compasión por él.

(**b**) (*fire, light*) apagarse; (*fashion*) pasar de moda, quedar anticuado; (*custom*) dejar de usarse.

(**c**) (*tide*) retirarse.

(**d**) (*end: year etc*) terminar, acabar.

◆**go over 1** *vt* (**a**) (*examine*) examinar, escudriñar; (*check*) revisar, repasar; (*rehearse*) repasar; **to ~ over a house** visitar una casa, examinar una casa; **to ~ over the ground** estudiar el terreno, reconocer el terreno.

(**b**) (*cross*) pasar por encima (de); *terrain* recorrer, atravesar.

(**c**) (*touch up*) retocar.

2 *vi* (**a**) **how did it ~ over?** ¿qué tal lo recibió el público? (*etc*).

(**b**) **to ~ over to** (*change party etc*) pasarse a.

(**c**) (*overturn*) volcar.

◆**go round 1** *vt obstacle etc* dar la vuelta a, hacer un rodeo para evitar.

2 *vi* (**a**) (*turn*) girar; dar vueltas; **the idea was ~ing round in my head** la idea daba vueltas en mi cabeza.

(**b**) (*make a detour*) hacer un rodeo, dar una vuelta.

(**c**) **to ~ round to John's house** ir a casa de Juan.

(**d**) (*circulate*) circular, correr; **the word is ~ing round that** ... se dice que ..., corre la voz de que ...

(**e**) (*suffice*) ser bastante, alcanzar para todos; **there's enough to ~ round** hay bastante (para todos); **to make the money ~ round** arreglárselas en cuanto al dinero.

◆**go through 1** *vt* (**a**) (*pass*) pasar (por), pasar a través (de); penetrar; **the book went through 8 editions** el libro tuvo 8 ediciones.

(**b**) (*undergo*) sufrir, experimentar.

(**c**) (*examine*) examinar, estudiar; (*revise*) repasar; **to ~ through sb's pockets** registrar los bolsillos de uno.

(**d**) (*use up*) *money* gastar; *supply* usar, gastar.

2 *vi* (**a**) (*pass, be approved*) ser aprobado, ser aceptado; (*deal*) concluirse, hacerse; (*motion*) votarse, aprobarse; **it all went through safely** todo se aprobó sin problema.

(**b**) **the bullet went right through** la bala pasó de parte a parte.

◆**go through with** *vt*: **to ~ through with a plan** llevar un proyecto a cabo; **I can't ~ through with it!** ¡no puedo seguir con esto!

◆**go to** *vt*: **~ to it!** ¡adelante!, ¡empieza!

◆**go together** *vi* ir juntos; (*colours etc*) hacer juego, armonizar; (*ideas etc*) complementarse.

◆**go under 1** *vt*: **he now ~es under the name of Moriarty** ahora se conoce por Moriarty. **2** *vi* (*ship*) hundirse; (*person*) desaparecer debajo del agua; (*fig*) hundirse, fracasar.

◆**go up** *vi* (**a**) (*travel*) subir; **to ~ up to London** ir a Londres; **to ~ up to sb** acercarse a uno, abordar a uno.

(**b**) (*level, price etc*) subir; **the total ~es up to ...** el total asciende a ...

(**c**) (*Brit Univ*) entrar en la universidad; volver a la universidad.

(**d**) (*explode*) estallar; explotar; *V* **smoke.**

◆**go with** *vt* (**a**) (*accompany*) ir con, acompañar a; (*lovers*) salir con. (**b**) (*match*) armonizar con, hacer juego con.

◆**go without 1** *vt* pasarse sin. **2** *vi* pasárselas.

goad [gəʊd] **1** *n* aguijada *f*, aguijón *m*; (*fig*) estímulo *m*.

2 *vt* aguijonear, picar; (*fig*) incitar, provocar, (*anger*) irritar, (*taunt*) provocar con insultos; **to ~ sb into fury** provocar a uno hasta la furia; **to ~ sb into doing sth, to ~ sb to do sth** incitar porfiadamente a uno a hacer algo.

◆**goad on** *vt* pinchar, provocar; **to ~ sb on to doing sth** provocar a uno para que haga algo.

go-ahead [ˈgəʊəhed] **1** *adj* emprendedor, enérgico. **2** *n* luz *f* verde; **to give the ~** dar luz verde (*for, to* a); **to get the ~** recibir luz verde.

goal [gəʊl] *n* (**a**) (*purpose*) fin *m*, objeto *m*, meta *f*; (*ambition*) ambición *f*; **to reach one's ~** llegar a la meta, realizar una ambición.

(**b**) (*~posts*) meta *f*, portería *f*; **to keep ~, to play in ~** ser portero.

(**c**) (*score*) gol *m*, tanto *m*; **~!** ¡gol!; **to score a ~** marcar un gol.

goal-area [ˈgəʊl,ɛərɪə] *n* área *f* de meta.

goal average [ˈgəʊl,ævərɪdʒ] *n* promedio *m* de goles, golaverage *m*.

goalie* [ˈgəʊlɪ] *n* = **goalkeeper.**

goalkeeper [ˈgəʊl,kiːpəʳ] *n* guardameta *mf*, portero *m*, -a *f*.

goal-kick [ˈgəʊlˈkɪk] *n* saque *m* de portería.

goal-line [ˈgəʊllaɪn] *n* línea *f* de portería.

goalmouth [ˈgəʊlmaʊθ] *n* portería *f*.

goalpost [ˈgəʊlpəʊst] *n* poste *m* de la portería; **to move the ~s** (*fig*) mover los postes, cambiar las reglas del juego.

goal-scorer [ˈgəʊl,skɔːrəʳ] *n* goleador *m*, -ora *f*.

goat [gəʊt] *n* cabra *f*, macho *m* cabrío; **to get sb's ~*** sacar a uno de quicio.

goatee [gəʊˈtiː] *n* barbas *fpl* de chivo.

goatherd [ˈgəʊthɜːd] *n* cabrero *m*.

goatskin [ˈgəʊtskɪn] *n* piel *f* de cabra.

gob⁑ [gɒb] **1** *n* (**a**) (*spit*) salivazo *m*. (**b**) (*esp Brit: mouth*) boca *f*. **2** *vti* escupir.

gobbet [ˈgɒbɪt] *n* (*of food etc*) trocito *m*, pequeña porción *f*; **~s of information** pequeños elementos *mpl* de información.

gobble [ˈgɒbl] **1** *n* gluglú *m*. **2** *vt* engullir; **to ~ up** tragarse, engullirse ávidamente. **3** *vi* (*turkey*) gluglutear.

gobbledygook* [ˈgɒbldɪguːk] *n* jerga *f* burocrática, prosa *f* administrativa (enrevesada).

go-between [ˈgəʊbɪ,twiːn] *n* medianero *m*, -a *f*, intermediario *m*, -a *f*, tercero *m*, -a *f*; (*pimp*) alcahuete *m*, -a *f*.

Gobi Desert [ˈgəʊbɪˈdezət] *n* desierto *m* del Gobi.

goblet [ˈgɒblɪt] *n* copa *f*.

goblin [ˈgɒblɪn] *n* duende *m*, trasgo *m*.

gobsmacked⁑ [ˈgɒbsmækt] *adj*: **I was ~** quedé parado*.

gob-stopper* [ˈgɒb,stɒpəʳ] *n* (*Brit*) *caramelo grande y redondo.*

go-by* [ˈgəʊbaɪ] *n*: **to give sth the ~** pasar algo por alto, omitir algo; **to give a place the ~** dejar de visitar un sitio; **to give sb the ~** desairar a uno (no haciendo caso de él), no hacer caso de uno.

GOC *n abbr of* **General Officer Commanding** general *m*, jefe *m*.

go-cart [ˈgəʊkɑːt] *n* cochecito *m* de niño.

god [gɒd] *n* dios *m*; **G~** Dios *m*; **~s** (*Theat*) paraíso *m*, gallinero *m*; **for G~'s sake!** ¡por Dios!; **good G~!, my G~!** ¡Dios mio!, ¡santo Dios!; **G~ forbid!** ¡no lo permita Dios!; **please G~!** ¡plegue a Dios!; **G~ willing** si Dios quiere, Dios mediante; **G~-speed!** †† buena suerte, ande Vd con Dios; **G~ (only) knows** sólo Dios sabe; **I hope to ~ she'll be happy** Dios quiera que sea feliz; **G~ helps those who help themselves** a quien madruga Dios le ayuda; **G~ help them if that's what they think** Dios se la depare buena si piensan así; **he thinks he's G~'s gift to women*** se cree creado para ser la felicidad de las mujeres; **what in G~'s name is he doing?** ¿qué demonios está haciendo?

god-awful⁑ [ˈgɒdˈɔːfʊl] *adj* horrible, fatal*.

godchild [ˈgɒdtʃaɪld] *n, pl* **godchildren** [ˈgɒdtʃɪldrən] ahijado *m*, -a *f*.

goddam⁑ [ˈgɒdˈdæm] (*US*) **1** *adj* (*also* **goddamn(ed)**) maldito, puñetero⁑. **2** *excl* (*also* **goddammit**) ¡maldición!

goddaughter [ˈgɒd,dɔːtəʳ] *n* ahijada *f*.

goddess [ˈgɒdɪs] *n* diosa *f*.

godfather [ˈgɒd,fɑːðəʳ] *n* padrino *m* (*to* de).

god-fearing [ˈgɒd,fɪərɪŋ] *adj* temeroso de Dios, timorato.

godforsaken [ˈgɒdfə,seɪkn] *adj person* dejado de la mano de Dios; *place* triste, remoto, desierto.

Godfrey [ˈgɒdfrɪ] *nm* Godofredo.

godhead [ˈgɒdhed] *n* divinidad *f*.

godless [ˈgɒdlɪs] *adj* impío, descreído.

godlike [ˈgɒdlaɪk] *adj* divino.

godly [ˈgɒdlɪ] *adj* piadoso.

godmother [ˈgɒd,mʌðəʳ] *n* madrina *f* (*to* de).

godparents [ˈgɒd,pɛərənts] *npl* padrinos *mpl*.

godsend [ˈgɒdsend] *n* cosa *f* llovida del cielo; **it was a ~ to us** fue un regalo celestial para nosotros.

godson [ˈgɒdsʌn] *n* ahijado *m*.

-goer [ˈgəʊəʳ] *n ending in compounds*: **cinema~** asiduo *m*, -a *f* del cine; *V* **opera, theatre** *etc*.

goes [gəʊz] *V* **go.**

gofer [ˈgəʊfeʳ] *n* (*US*) recadero *m*, -a *f*.

go-getter* [ˈgəʊgetəʳ] *n* (*esp US*) (**a**) persona *f* dinámica, persona *f* emprendedora. (**b**) (*pej*) arribista *mf*, egoísta *mf*.

goggle [ˈgɒgl] *vi* salírsele a uno los ojos de las órbitas; **to ~ at** mirar con ojos desorbitados, mirar sin comprender.

goggle-box* [ˈgɒgl,bɒks] *n* (*Brit TV*) caja *f* boba*.

goggle-eyed [ˈgɒgl,aɪd] *adj* con ojos desorbitados.

goggles [ˈgɒglz] *npl* (*Aut etc*) anteojos *mpl*; (*of skin-diver*) gafas *fpl* submarinas; (*) gafas *fpl*.

go-go [ˈgəʊgəʊ] *adj* (**a**) *dancer, dancing* gogó. (**b**) (*US*) *market, stocks* especulativo. (**c**) (*US*) *team etc* dinámico.

going [ˈgəʊɪŋ] **1** *n* (**a**) (*departure*) ida *f*, salida *f*, partida *f*.

(**b**) (*pace*) **good ~!** ¡bien hecho!; **that was good ~** eso fue muy rápido; **it was slow ~** el avance fue lento.

(**c**) (*state of surface etc*) estado *m* del camino, (*Sport*) estado *m* de la pista; (*Racing*) terreno *m*; **the path is hard ~** el camino está muy malo; **let's cross while the ~ is good** crucemos mientras podamos; **we made money all the while the ~ was good** mientras las condiciones eran favorables ganábamos dinero; **the book was heavy ~** la lectura del libro resultó pesada; **it's heavy ~ talking to her** exige mucho esfuerzo conversar con ella.

2 *adj concern* próspero, en pleno funcionamiento; *price, rate, salary etc* actual, existente, corriente.

going-over [ˈgəʊɪŋˈəʊvəʳ] *n* (**a**) (*check*) inspección *f*; **we gave the house a thorough ~** registramos la casa de arriba abajo.

(**b**) (*fig: beating*) paliza *f*; **they gave him a ~** le dieron una paliza.

goings-on [ˈgəʊɪŋzˈɒn] *npl* actividades *fpl* (sospechosas); conducta *f* (sospechosa); tejemaneje *m*.

goitre, (*US*) **goiter** [ˈgɔɪtəʳ] *n* bocio *m*.

go-kart [ˈgəʊkɑːt] *n* kart *m*.

go-karting [ˈgəʊ,kɑːtɪŋ] *n* karting *m*.

Golan Heights [ˈgəʊlænˈhaɪts] *npl*: **the ~** los Altos del Golán.

gold [gəʊld] **1** *n* oro *m*. **2** *attr* de oro; **~ bar** barra *f* de oro; **~ braid** galón *m*; **~ disc** (*Mus*) disco *m* de oro; **~ dust** oro *m* en polvo; **Biros are like ~ dust in this office** los bolígrafos parece que se los lleva el viento de esta oficina; **~ fever** fiebre *f* del oro; **~ leaf** pan *m* de oro; **~ medal** medalla *f* de oro; **~ medallist** medallero *m*, -a *f* de oro; **~ miner** minero *m* de oro; **~ mining** minería *f* de oro; **~ plate** vajilla *f* de oro; **~ reserves** reservas *fpl* de oro; **~ standard** patrón *m* oro.

goldbrick* [ˈgəʊldˈbrɪk] (*US*) **1** *n* (**a**) (*swindle*) estafa *f*. (**b**) (*person*) gandul *m*. **2** *vi* escurrir el bulto.

Gold Coast [ˈgəʊldˈkəʊst] *n* (*Hist*) Costa *f* de Oro.

goldcrest [ˈgəʊldkrest] *n* reyezuelo *m* (sencillo).

gold-digger [ˈgəʊld,dɪgəʳ] *n* aventurera *f*.

golden [ˈgəʊldən] *adj* de oro; dorado; áureo; *deed* meritorio; *hours* dorado; *opportunity* excelente; **~ age** (*Myth*) edad *f* dorada, edad *f* de oro; **G~ Age** (*Sp*) Siglo *m* de Oro; **the ~ boy of boxing** el joven ídolo del boxeo, el niño bonito del boxeo; **~ eagle** águila *f* real; **G~ Fleece** Vellocino *m* de oro, Toisón *m* de oro; **~ handcuffs** prima *f* de lealtad; **~ handshake** pago *m* cuantioso por baja incentivada; **~ hello** prima *f* de ingreso, prima *f* de contratación; **~ jubilee** quincuagésimo aniversario *m*; **~ mean**

justo medio *m*; ~ **oldie*** melodía *f* del ayer, vieja canción *f*; ~ **rule** regla *f* de oro; ~ **share** accionariado *m* mayoritario; **the ~ sixties** (*Mus etc*) los dorados sesenta; ~ **wedding** bodas *fpl* de oro.

goldenrod ['gəʊldən'rɒd] *n* vara *f* de oro.

goldfield ['gəʊldfiːld] *n* campo *m* aurífero.

gold-filled ['gəʊld,fɪld] *adj* lleno de oro; (*Tech*) revestido de oro, enchapado en oro; *tooth* empastado de oro.

goldfinch ['gəʊldfɪntʃ] *n* jilguero *m*.

goldfish ['gəʊldfɪʃ] *n* pez *m* de colores.

goldfish bowl ['gəʊldfɪʃ,bəʊl] *n* pecera *f*.

Goldilocks ['gəʊldɪlɒks] *nf* Rubiales.

gold-mine ['gəʊldmaɪn] *n* mina *f* de oro; (*fig*) río *m* de oro, potosí *m*.

gold-plated [,gəʊld'pleɪtɪd] *adj* chapado en oro; (*fig**) *deal, contract* de oro.

gold-rimmed [,gəʊld'rɪmd] *adj spectacles* con montura de oro.

gold-rush ['gəʊldrʌʃ] *n* rebatiña *f* del oro.

goldsmith ['gəʊldsmɪθ] *n* orfebre *m*; **~'s shop** tienda *f* de orfebre.

golf [gɒlf] **1** *n* golf *m*. **2** *vi* jugar al golf.

golfball ['gɒlfbɔːl] *n* (**a**) pelota *f* de golf. (**b**) (*Typ*) cabeza *f* de escritura, esfera *f* impresora, bola *f*.

golf-buggy ['gɒlfbʌgɪ] *n* cochecito *m* de golf.

golf-club ['gɒlfklʌb] *n* (**a**) (*society*) club *m* de golf. (**b**) (*stick*) palo *m* (de golf).

golf-course ['gɒlfkɔːs] *n* campo *m* (*LAm*: cancha *f*) de golf.

golfer ['gɒlfər] *n* golfista *mf*.

golfing ['gɒlfɪŋ] *n* golf *m*, golfismo *m*.

golf-links ['gɒlflɪŋks] *npl* campo *m* de golf.

Golgotha ['gɒlgəθə] *n* Gólgota *m*.

Goliath [gə'laɪəθ] *nm* Goliat.

golliwog ['gɒlɪwɒg] *n* (*Brit*) negrito *m*, muñeco *m* negrito.

golly[1]* ['gɒlɪ] *n* (*Brit*) = **golliwog**.

golly[2]* ['gɒlɪ] *interj* (*Brit*) ¡caramba!

golosh [gə'lɒʃ] *n* chanclo *m*, galocha *f*.

Gomorrah [gə'mɒrə] *n* Gomorra *f*.

gonad ['gɒnæd] *n* gónada *f*.

gondola ['gɒndələ] *n* góndola *f*; (*Aer*) barquilla *f*; ~ **car** (*US Rail*) vagón *m* descubierto, batea *f*.

gondolier [,gɒndə'lɪər] *n* gondolero *m*.

gone [gɒn] *ptp of* **go**.

goner‡ ['gɒnər] *n*: **he's a ~** está muerto, está desahuciado.

gong [gɒŋ] *n* (**a**) gong *m*, gongo *m*. (**b**) (*Brit**) medalla *f*, condecoración *f*; (*in civil service*) cinta* *f*, cintajo* *m*.

gonna* ['gɒnə] (*esp US*) = **going to**; *V* **go 1 (y)**.

gonorrhoea, (*US*) **gonorrhea** [,gɒnə'rɪə] *n* gonorrea *f*.

goo* [guː] *n* (**a**) cosa *f* muy pegajosa, sustancia *f* viscosa.
(**b**) (*sentimentality*) lenguaje *m* sentimental, sentimentalismo *m*.

good [gʊd] **1** *adj* (*comp* **better**, *superl* **best**) (**a**) (*gen, also of ~ quality, right, morally sound, favourable etc*) bueno, (*before m sing n* buen) **a ~ book** un buen libro; **the G~ Book** la Biblia; **G~ Friday** Viernes *m* Santo; **~!** ¡bueno!, ¡muy bien!; **~ one!** ¡muy bien!; **~ for you!** ¡muy bien tú!; **~ old Peter!** ¡bravo Pedro!

(**b**) (*sufficient*) **~ enough!** ¡muy bien!; **that's ~ enough for me** eso me basta; **it's just not ~ enough!** ¡esto no se puede consentir!

(**c**) (*pleasant*) **it's ~ to see you** me alegro de verte; **how ~ it is to know that ...!** ¡cuánto me alegro de saber que ...!; **it's ~ to be here** da gusto estar aquí; **it's as ~ as a holiday to me** esto me vale tanto como unas vacaciones.

(**d**) (*beneficial*) bueno, provechoso; (*advantageous*) ventajoso; (*wholesome*) sano, saludable; **~ to eat** bueno de comer; **it's ~ for you** es cosa muy sana; **it's ~ for you to swim** la natación es cosa sana; **oil is ~ for burns** el aceite es bueno para las quemaduras; **spirits are not ~ for me** los licores no me sientan bien; **he eats more than is ~ for him** come más de lo que le conviene.

(**e**) (*useful*) bueno, útil, servible; **the only ~ chair** la única silla servible (*or* sana); **to be ~ for** servir para; **he's ~ for nothing** es completamente inútil; **he's ~ for 10 years yet** tiene todavía por delante 10 años de vida; **he's ~ for £5** seguramente tendrá 5 libras para contribuir; **I'm ~ for another mile** tengo fuerzas para ir otra milla más; **it'll be ~ for some years** durará todavía algunos años; **a ticket ~ for 3 months** un billete valedero para 3 meses.

(**f**) (*clever*) **to be ~ at** ser hábil en, tener aptitud para, ser fuerte en; **she's ~ with cats** entiende de gatos; **she's ~ at maths** es buena para matemáticas, se le dan muy bien las matemáticas.

(**g**) (*kind*) bueno, amable; **he's a ~ sort** es buena persona; **he was ~ to me** fue muy amable conmigo; **he was so ~ as to** + *infin* tuvo la amabilidad de + *infin*; **please be so ~ as to** + *infin* ¿me hace el favor de + *infin*?, (*more formally*) tenga la bondad de + *infin*; **that's very ~ of you** es Vd muy amable.

(**h**) (*well-behaved*) de buenos modales, educado; **the child has been as ~ as gold** el niño se ha portado como un ángel, el niño ha sido más bueno que el pan; **be ~!** (*morally*) ¡sé bueno!, (*in behaviour*) ¡pórtate bien!, (*at this moment*) ¡estáte formal!

(**i**) (*at least*) **a ~ 3 hours** 3 horas largas; **a ~ 4 miles** 4 millas largas; **a ~ £10** lo menos 10 libras.

(**j**) (*practically*) **it's as ~ as new** está como nuevo; **it's as ~ as done** está casi terminado; **it's as ~ as lost** puede darse por perdido; **they're as ~ as beaten** pueden darse por vencidos; **it was as ~ as a holiday** nos ha valido tanto como unas vacaciones; **she as ~ as told me so** casi me lo dijo.

(**k**) **to make ~** *promise* cumplir, *accusation* hacer bueno, probar, *claim* justificar; *loss* compensar, reparar; *damage* reparar; pagar; **to make a chair ~** reparar una silla.

2 *adv* (**a**) bien; **a ~ strong stick** un bastón bien sólido; **a ~ long walk** un paseo bien largo; **to come ~*** empezar a dar de sí, dar buenos resultados; justificarse; alcanzar su plenitud; **to look ~** tener buen aspecto; **it's looking ~** promete, parece muy bien; **you're looking ~!** ¡qué guapa estás!; **to feel ~** estar satisfecho, creer haber hecho algo meritorio, (*in health*) estar como un reloj; **to give as ~ as one gets** devolver golpe por golpe; **you never had it so ~** nunca habéis estado mejor; **to hold ~** ser valedero, seguir verdadero (*of* con respecto a); **to make ~** salir bien, tener éxito, demostrar tener capacidad.

(**b**) **~ and*** bien; **~ and hot** bien caliente; **~ and strong** bien fuerte; **they were cheated ~ and proper** fueron timados por las buenas; **they were beaten ~ and proper** fueron vencidos rotundamente.

3 *n* (**a**) bien *m*, provecho *m*, utilidad *f*; **the ~** (*abstract*) lo bueno, (*people*) los buenos; **~ and evil** el bien y el mal; **there is much ~ in him** tiene buenas cualidades; **there is some ~ in him** no es del todo malo; **for ~** definitivamente, para siempre; **he's gone for ~** se ha ido para no volver; **for the ~ of** en bien de, a beneficio de; **it's for your own ~** es por su propio bien; **it's no ~** es inútil, no sirve para nada; **it's no ~ complaining** de nada sirve quejarse, no vale la pena de quejarse; **what's the ~ of it?** ¿para qué sirve?; **I'm no ~ at such things** yo no sirvo para tales cosas; **he's no ~** (*morally*) es un perdido; **he's up to no ~** está tramando algo malo; **he'll come to no ~** acabará mal, tendrá mal fin; **we're £2 to the ~** hemos ganado 2 libras; **we're a spoon to the ~** tenemos una cuchara de sobra; **to do ~** hacer bien; **he never did any ~** nunca hizo nada bueno; **it can't do any ~** es imposible que sea útil; **it will do him no ~ at all** no le aprovechará en lo más mínimo; **this medicine will do you ~** esta medicina le sentará bien; **much ~ may it do him!** ¡buen provecho le haga!

(**b**) **~s** bienes *mpl*, efectos *mpl*; (*Comm*) géneros *mpl*, artículos *mpl*, mercancías *fpl*; **~ and chattels** (*Jur*) bienes *mpl* muebles; (*loosely*) cosas *fpl*, enseres *mpl*; **to deliver the ~s*** cumplir lo prometido.

4 *attr*: **~s siding** apartadero *m* de mercancías; **~s station** estación *f* de mercancías; **~s train** (tren *m*) mercancías *m*; **~s vehicle** vehículo *m* de transporte, camión *m*; **~s wagon** vagón *m* de mercancías; **~s yard** estación *f* de mercancías.

goodbye ['gʊd'baɪ] **1** *interj* ¡adiós! **2** *n* adiós *m*; **to say ~ to** despedirse de; (*fig*) dar por perdido; **you can say ~ to your wallet** ya no volverás a ver la cartera.

good-for-nothing ['gʊdfə'nʌθɪŋ] **1** *adj* inútil. **2** *n* perdido *m*, pelafustán *m*.

good-hearted [,gʊd'hɑːtɪd] *adj* de buen corazón.

good-humoured, (*US*) **good-humored** ['gʊd'hjuːməd] *adj person* afable, jovial; (*in mood*) de buen humor; *remark etc* jovial; *discussion* de tono amistoso.

good-humouredly, (*US*) **good-humoredly** [,gʊd'hjuːmədlɪ] *adv* afablemente; jovialmente; amistosamente.

good-looker* [,gʊd'lʊkər] *n* (*man*) hombre *m* guapo, tío* *m* bueno; (*woman*) mujer *f* guapa, tía* *f* buena; (*horse etc*) caballo *m etc* de buena estampa.

good-looking ['gʊd'lʊkɪŋ] *adj* bien parecido, guapo.

goodly ['gʊdlɪ] *adj* (*fine*) agradable, excelente; (*handsome*) hermoso, bien parecido; *sum etc* importante; *number* crecido.

good-natured ['gʊd'neɪtʃəd] *adj person* afable, bonachón; *discussion* de tono amistoso.

goodness ['gʊdnɪs] *n* (*virtue, kindness*) bondad *f*; (*good quality*) buena calidad *f*; (*essence*) sustancia *f*, lo mejor; **~!, ~ gracious!, ~ me!** ¡Dios mío!; **for ~' sake!** ¡por Dios!; **~ only knows!** ¡quién sabe!; **thank ~!** ¡gracias a Dios!

good-tempered ['gʊd'tempəd] *adj* afable, ecuánime, de natural apacible; *tone* afable, amistoso; *discussion* sereno, sin pasión.

good-time ['gʊd'taɪm] *adj*: **~ girl** chica *f* alegre.

goodwill ['gʊd'wɪl] *n* (**a**) buena voluntad *f*; **~ mission** misión *f* de buena voluntad. (**b**) (*Comm*) clientela *f*; fondo *m* de comercio.

goody* ['gʊdɪ] (*esp US*) **1** *adj* beatuco*, santurrón. **2** *interj* (*also* ~ ~) ¡qué bien!, ¡qué estupendo!* **3** *n* (**a**) (*Culin*) golosina *f*. (**b**) (*Cine*) bueno *m*; **the goodies** los buenos.

goody-goody* [ˌgʊdɪ'gʊdɪ] **1** *adj* virtuosillo*, beato. **2** *n* pequeño santo *m*, pequeña santa *f*, angelito* *m*.

gooey* ['gu:ɪ] *adj* pegajoso, viscoso; *sweet* empalagoso.

goof‡ [gu:f] **1** *n* bobo *m*, -a *f*. **2** *vi* (**a**) (*err*) tirarse una plancha. (**b**) (*US*: *also* **to ~ off**) gandulear.

◆**goof around*** *vi* (*US*) hacer el tonto.

goofy‡ ['gu:fɪ] *adj* bobo.

gook‡ [gu:k] *n* (*US*: *pej*) asiático *m*, -a *f*.

goolies*‡ ['gu:lɪz] *npl* cataplines*‡ *mpl*.

goon [gu:n] *n* (**a**) imbécil *mf*, idiota *mf*. (**b**) (*US*: *Hist*) *gorila contratado para sembrar el terror entre los obreros*. (**c**) (*US*) guardaespaldas *m*, esbirro *m*.

goose [gu:s] **1** *n*, *pl* **geese** [gi:s] (*domestic*) ganso *m*, -a *f*, oca *f*; (*wild*) ánsar *m*; **to cook sb's ~** hacer la santísima a uno; **to kill the ~ that lays the golden eggs** matar la gallina de los huevos de oro. **2** *vt* (*) *girl* palpar, meter mano a.

gooseberry ['gʊzbərɪ] *n* grosella *f* espinosa; **to play ~** hacer de carabina; **I don't want to play ~** (*Brit*) no quiero estar de más, no quiero llevar la cesta.

gooseberry-bush ['gʊzbərɪˌbʊʃ] *n* grosellero *m* espinoso.

goosebumps ['gu:sbʌmps] *npl* (*US*), **gooseflesh** ['gu:sfleʃ] *n*, **goosepimples** ['gu:sˌpɪmplz] *npl* carne *f* de gallina.

goose-step ['gu:sstep] **1** *n* paso *m* de ganso, paso *m* de la oca. **2** *vi* marchar a paso de ganso (*or* de la oca).

GOP *n* (*US Pol*) *abbr of* **Grand Old Party** Partido *m* Republicano.

gopher ['gəʊfər] *n* ardillón *m*, ardilla *f* de tierra.

gorblimey‡ [ˌgɔ:'blaɪmɪ] *excl* (*Brit*) ¡puñetas!‡

Gordian ['gɔ:dɪən] *adj*: **to cut the ~ knot** cortar el nudo gordiano.

gore[1] [gɔ:r] *n* sangre *f* (derramada).

gore[2] [gɔ:r] *vt* cornear.

gorge [gɔ:dʒ] **1** *n* (**a**) (*Geog*) cañón *m*, barranco *m*, garganta *f*. (**b**) (*Anat*) garganta *f*; **my ~ rises at it** me da asco.

2 *vt* engullir.

3 *vi* (*also vr*: **to ~ o.s.**) hartarse, atracarse (*on* de).

gorgeous ['gɔ:dʒəs] *adj* magnífico, brillante, vistoso; (*) maravilloso; **hullo ~!*** ¿qué hay, ricura?*

gorilla [gə'rɪlə] *n* gorila *m*.

gormandize ['gɔ:məndaɪz] *vi* glotonear.

gormless* ['gɔ:mlɪs] *adj* (*Brit*) bobo, idiota; torpe.

gorse [gɔ:s] *n* aulaga *f*, tojo *m*.

gory ['gɔ:rɪ] *adj* ensangrentado; *details, story* sangriento.

gosh* [gɒʃ] *interj* ¡cielos!; **~ darn!** (*US*) ¡caramba!

goshawk ['gɒshɔ:k] *n* azor *m*.

gosling ['gɒzlɪŋ] *n* ansarino *m*.

go-slow ['gəʊ'sləʊ] (*Brit*) **1** *n* huelga *f* de celo. **2** *vi* hacer huelga de celo, (*strictly*) trabajar con arreglo a las bases.

gospel ['gɒspəl] **1** *n* evangelio *m*; **the G~ according to St Mark** el Evangelio según San Marcos; **as though it were ~ truth** como si fuese el evangelio. **2** *attr*: **~ music** música *f* de espiritual negro; **~ song** espiritual *m* negro.

gossamer ['gɒsəmər] *n* hilos *mpl* de telaraña; (*fabric*) gasa *f* sutil; **~ thin** muy delgado.

gossip ['gɒsɪp] **1** *n* (**a**) (*person*: *great talker*) hablador *m*, -ora *f*; (*pej*) chismoso *m*, -a *f*, murmurador *m*, -ora *f*, comadre *f*, mala lengua *f*.

(**b**) (*conversation*) charla *f*; **we had a good old ~** charlamos un buen rato, echamos un buen párrafo.

(**c**) (*scandal*) chismes *mpl*, chismorreo *m*, comadreo *m*, habladurías *fpl*, murmuración *f*; **piece of ~** chisme *m*, hablilla *f*.

2 *vi* (*talk*) charlar, echar un párrafo; (*talk scandal*) cotillear, contar chismes.

gossip column ['gɒsɪpˌkɒləm] *n* gacetilla *f*, crónica *f* de sociedad.

gossiping ['gɒsɪpɪŋ] **1** *adj* chismoso. **2** *n* chismorreo *m*.

gossip writer ['gɒsɪpˌraɪtər] *n* cronista *mf* de sociedad.

gossipy ['gɒsɪpɪ] *adj* chismoso; *style* familiar, anecdótico.

got [gɒt] *pret and ptp of* **get**.

Goth [gɒθ] *n* godo *m*, -a *f*.

Gothic ['gɒθɪk] **1** *adj race* godo; (*Archit, Typ*) gótico; *novel etc* horripilante, terrorífico. **2** *n* (*Archit, Ling etc*) gótico *m*.

gotta* ['gɒtə] (*esp US*) = **got to**; *V* **get 1 (l)**.

gotten ['gɒtn] (*US*) *ptp of* **get**.

gouache [gʊ'ɑ:ʃ] *n* guache *m*, gouache *f*.

gouge [gaʊdʒ] **1** *n* gubia *f*. **2** *vt* excavar con gubia; (*fig*) excavar.

◆**gouge out** *vt*: **to ~ sb's eyes out** sacar los ojos a uno.

goulash ['gu:læʃ] *n* puchero *m* húngaro.

gourd [gʊəd] *n* calabaza *f*.

gourmand ['gʊəmənd] *n* glotón *m*.

gourmet ['gʊəmeɪ] *n* gastrónomo *m*, -a *f*.

gout [gaʊt] *n* gota *f*.

gouty ['gaʊtɪ] *adj* gotoso.

gov‡ [gʌv] *n abbr of* **governor** (**d**) jefe *m*, patrón *m*; **yes ~!** ¡sí, jefe!

govern ['gʌvən] *vt* gobernar; dominar; (*guide*) guiar, regir; (*Gram*) regir; **to ~ one's temper** contenerse, dominarse.

governess ['gʌvənɪs] *n* institutriz *f*, gobernanta *f*.

governing ['gʌvənɪŋ] *adj*: **~ board** (*Brit Scol*) consejo *m* directivo de escuela; **~ body** junta *f* directiva; junta *f* de gobierno, consejo *m* rector; **~ principle** principio *m* rector.

government ['gʌvnmənt] **1** *n* gobierno *m*; administración *f*; Estado *m*; (*Gram etc*) régimen *m*.

2 *attr* estatal, del Estado; gubernamental, del gobierno; oficial; **~ body** ente *m* gubernamental, ente *m* oficial; **~ bonds** títulos *mpl* del Estado; **~ department** ministerio *m*; **~ expenditure** gasto *m* público; **~ grant** subvención *f* gubernamental; **~ house** (*Brit*) palacio *m* del gobernador; **~ issue** propiedad *f* del Estado; **~-owned corporation** empresa *f* pública, empresa *f* del Estado; **~ policy** política *f* del gobierno; **~ securities** deuda *f* pública del Estado; **~ spending** gastos *mpl* gubernamentales; **~ stock** papel *m* de Estado; **~ subsidy** subvención *f* gubernamental.

governmental [ˌgʌvən'mentl] *adj* gubernamental, gubernativo.

governor ['gʌvənər] *n* (**a**) gobernador *m*, -ora *f*; (*esp Brit*: *of prison*) director *m*, -ora *f*, alcalde *m*. (**b**) (*Brit Scol*) miembro *mf* del consejo. (**c**) (*Mech*) regulador *m*. (**d**) (*Brit‡*) (*boss*) jefe *m*, patrón *m*; (*father*) viejo* *m*; **thanks, ~!** ¡gracias, jefe!

governor-general ['gʌvənə'dʒenərəl] *n* (*Brit*) gobernador *m*, -ora *f* general.

governorship ['gʌvənəʃɪp] *n* gobierno *m*, cargo *m* de gobernador(a).

Govt *abbr of* **government** gobierno *m*, gob.^{no}.

gown [gaʊn] *n* (*dress*) vestido *m*, traje *m*; (*Jur, Univ*) toga *f*.

GP *n abbr of* **general practitioner** médico *m*, -a *f* general.

GPO *n* (**a**) (*Brit*) *abbr of* **General Post Office** Administración *f* General de Correos.

(**b**) (*US*) *abbr of* **Government Printing Office**.

gr. (**a**) *abbr of* **gross 2** gruesa *f*. (**b**) (*Comm*) *abbr of* **gross 1** (**d**) bruto, bto.

grab [græb] **1** *n* (**a**) (*snatch*) arrebatiña *f*, agarro *m*; (*) robo *m*; **it's all up for ~s*** todo se ofrece a quien lo quiera, está a disposición de cualquiera; **to make a ~ at sth** tratar de arrebatar algo.

(**b**) (*esp Brit Mech*) cubeta *f* (draga), cuchara *f* (de dos mandíbulas).

2 *vt* (**a**) asir, coger, arrebatar; (*fig*) arrebatarse, apropiarse.

(**b**) (‡) chiflar*; **how does that ~ you?** ¿qué te parece?; **that really ~bed me** aquello me entusiasmó de verdad; **it doesn't ~ me** no me va*.

3 *vi*: **to ~ at** (*snatch*) tratar de arrebatar; (*in falling*) tratar de asir.

grace [greɪs] **1** *n* (**a**) (*Rel*) gracia *f*, gracia *f* divina.

(**b**) (*gracefulness*) finura *f*, elegancia *f*; (*of shape*) armonía *f*; (*of movement*) garbo *m*, donaire *m*; (*of style*) elegancia *f*, amenidad *f*.

(**c**) **with a good ~** de buen talante; **with a bad ~** a regañadientes; **he had the ~ to apologize** tuvo la cortesía de pedir perdón.

(**d**) **to get into sb's good ~s** congraciarse con uno.

(**e**) (*delay*) demora *f*; **days of ~** (*Brit Jur*) días *mpl* de gracia; **3 days' ~** un plazo de 3 días.

(**f**) (*blessing*) bendición *f* de la mesa; **to say ~** bendecir la mesa.

(**g**) (*in title*: *dukes*) **His G~ the Duke** su Excelencia; **yes,**

Your G~ sí, Excelencia.

(**h**) (*in title*: *Eccl*) **His G~ Archbishop X** su Ilustrísima Monseñor X; **yes, your G~** sí, Ilustrísima.

2 *attr*: **~ period** período *m* de gracia.

3 *vt* adornar (*with* de), embellecer; **he ~d the meeting with his presence** honró a los asistentes con su presencia.

graceful ['greɪsfʊl] *adj* gracioso, agraciado; *movement* airoso, elegante, garboso; *compliment* elegante; *lines* grácil.

gracefully ['greɪsfəlɪ] *adv* elegantemente, con garbo.

graceless ['greɪslɪs] *adj* desgarbado, torpe; (*impolite*) descortés, grosero.

grace-note ['greɪsnəʊt] *n* apoyadura *f*.

gracious ['greɪʃəs] *adj* (*merciful*) clemente; (*urbane*) cortés, afable; *monarch* gracioso; **~** (**me**)! ¡Dios mío!; **~ living** vida *f* elegante; **he was very ~ to me** estuvo muy amable conmigo.

graciously ['greɪʃəslɪ] *adv wave, smile* graciosamente; (*with good grace*) *agree etc* de buena gana; *live* indulgentemente; (*frm*) *consent, allow* graciosamente; (*Rel*) misericordiosamente, con misericordia.

graciousness ['greɪʃəsnɪs] *n* (*of person*) amabilidad *f*; (*of action, style*) gracia *f*; (*of house, room, gardens*) elegancia *f*; (*of wave, smile*) bondad *f*; (*of God*) misericordia *f*.

gradate [grə'deɪt] **1** *vt* degradar. **2** *vi* degradarse.

gradation [grə'deɪʃən] *n* gradación *f*.

grade [greɪd] **1** *n* (**a**) (*degree*) grado *m*; (*quality*) clase *f*, calidad *f*; (*in hierarchy, staff etc*) categoría *f*, rango *m*; (*mark*) nota *f*, clase *f*; **to make the ~** alcanzar el nivel deseado, tener éxito, ser satisfactorio; **to be promoted to a higher ~** ser ascendido a una categoría superior.

(**b**) (*US Scol*) curso *m*, año *m*; clase *f*.

(**c**) (*US*: *slope*) pendiente *f*.

2 *attr*: **~ crossing** (*US*) paso *m* a nivel; **~ school** (*US*) escuela *f* primaria.

3 *vt* (**a**) clasificar, graduar.

(**b**) (*Scol, Univ*) calificar, dar nota a.

◆**grade down** *vt* degradar de categoría.

◆**grade up** *vt* subir de categoría.

graded ['greɪdɪd] *adj* graduado.

grader ['greɪdəʳ] *n* (*US Scol*) examinador *m*, -ora *f*.

gradient ['greɪdɪənt] *n* (*Brit*) pendiente *f*.

grading ['greɪdɪŋ] *n* (*gen*) graduación *f*; (*by size*) gradación *f*; (*Scol etc*) calificación *f*.

gradual ['grædjʊəl] *adj* gradual; paulatino; progresivo.

gradually ['grædjʊəlɪ] *adv* gradualmente; poco a poco; paulatinamente; progresivamente.

graduate 1 ['grædjʊɪt] *n* graduado *m*, -a *f*, licenciado *m*, -a *f* (*in* en); universitario *m*, -a *f*; (*US*) bachiller *mf*.

2 ['grædjʊɪt] *attr*: **~ course** curso *m* para graduados; **~ school** (*esp US*) departamento *m* de graduados; **~ student** (*US*) graduado *m*, -a *f*.

3 ['grædjʊeɪt] *vt* graduar.

4 ['grædjʊeɪt] *vi* (*Univ*) obtener el título (*in* en); **to ~ as** recibirse de.

graduated ['grædjʊeɪtɪd] *adj tube, flask, tax etc* graduado; **in ~ stages** en pasos escalonados; **~ pension scheme** plan *m* de pensiones graduado.

graduation [,grædjʊ'eɪʃən] *n* graduación *f*; (*US*) entrega *f* del bachillerato.

graffito [græ'fi:təʊ] *n, pl* **graffiti** [grə'fi:tɪ] pintada *f*, grafiti *m*.

graft¹ [grɑ:ft] (*Hort, Med*) **1** *n* injerto *m*. **2** *vt* injertar (*in, into, on to* en).

graft²* [grɑ:ft] **1** *n* corrupción *f*, chanchullos *mpl*; **hard ~** (*Brit*) trabajo *m* muy duro. **2** *vi* (**a**) (*work*) currar‡. (**b**) (*swindle*) trampear.

grafter* ['grɑ:ftəʳ] *n* (**a**) (*swindler etc*) timador *m*, estafador *m*. (**b**) (*Brit*: *hard worker*) fajador *m*, -ora *f*.

graham flour ['greɪəm,flaʊəʳ] *n* (*US*) harina *f* de trigo sin cerner.

Grail [greɪl] *n*: **the ~** el Grial.

grain [greɪn] *n* (**a**) (*single seed*) grano *m*; (*corn*) granos *mpl*, cereales *mpl*; (*US*) trigo *m*.

(**b**) (*fig*) **with a ~ of salt** con un grano de sal; **there's not a ~ of truth in it** eso no tiene ni pizca de verdad.

(**c**) (*in wood*) fibra *f*, hebra *f*; (*in stone*) vena *f*, veta *f*; (*in leather*) flor *f*; (*in cloth*) granilla *f*; **it goes against the ~ with me to** + *infin* se me hace cuesta arriba + *infin*; **to saw with the ~** aserrar a hebra.

(**d**) (*Pharm*) grano *m*.

grainy ['greɪnɪ] *adj* (*Phot*) granulado, con grano; *substance* granulado.

gram [græm] *n* gramo *m*.

grammar ['græməʳ] **1** *n* gramática *f*. **2** *attr*: **~ school** (*Brit*) (*state*) instituto *m*, (*private, religious*) colegio *m* de segunda enseñanza.

grammarian [grə'mɛərɪən] *n* gramático *m*, -a *f*.

grammatical [grə'mætɪkəl] *adj* gramatical; **in ~ English** en inglés correcto; **that's not ~** eso no es correcto.

grammaticality [grə,mætɪ'kælətɪ] *n* gramaticalidad *f*.

grammatically [grə'mætɪkəlɪ] *adv* bien, correctamente.

grammaticalness [grə'mætɪkəlnɪs] *n* gramaticalidad *f*.

gram(me) [græm] *n* gramo *m*.

gramophone ['græməfəʊn] **1** *n* (*esp Brit*) gramófono *m*. **2** *attr*: **~ needle** aguja *f* de gramófono; **~ record** disco *m* de gramófono.

Grampian ['græmpɪən] *n*: **the ~ Mountains, the G~s** los Montes Grampianos.

grampus ['græmpəs] *n* orca *f*.

gran* [græn] *n* (*Brit*) = **grandmother**.

Granada [grə'nɑ:də] *n* Granada *f*.

granary ['grænərɪ] *n* granero *m*, troj *f*; **~ loaf** ® pan *m* con granos enteros.

grand [grænd] **1** *adj* (**a**) (*fine, splendid*) magnífico, imponente, grandioso; *person* distinguido, augusto; *style* elevado, sublime; *staircase etc* principal; **~ jury** (*US*) jurado *m* de acusación; **~ master** (*Chess, Mus etc*) gran maestro *m*; **~ opera** ópera *f*; **~ piano** piano *m* de cola; **G~ Prix** grand prix *m*, gran premio *m*; **~ slam** (*Bridge*) bola *f*; **~ total** importe *m* total; **G~ Tour** gran gira *f* europea; (*fig*) visita *f* extensa.

(**b**) (*) magnífico, bárbaro*, estupendo*; **a ~ game** un magnífico partido; **we had a ~ time** lo pasamos estupendamente*.

2 *n* (**a**) (*piano*) piano *m* de cola.

(**b**) (*Brit*‡) mil libras *fpl*, (*US*‡) mil dólares *mpl*.

grandchild ['græntʃaɪld] *n, pl* **grandchildren** ['græn,tʃɪldrən] nieto *m*, -a *f*; **grandchildren** nietos *mpl*.

grand(d)ad* ['grændæd] *n* abuelito* *m*; **yes, ~** sí, abuelo.

grand(d)addy* ['grændædɪ] *n* (*US*) = **grandfather**.

granddaughter ['græn,dɔ:təʳ] *n* nieta *f*.

grandee [,græn'di:] *n* grande *m* de España.

grandeur ['grændjəʳ] *n* magnificencia *f*, grandiosidad *f*, sublimidad *f*.

grandfather ['grænd,fɑ:ðəʳ] **1** *n* abuelo *m*. **2** *attr*: **~ clock** reloj *m* de pie, reloj *m* de caja.

grandiloquence [græn'dɪləkwəns] *n* altisonancia *f*, grandilocuencia *f*.

grandiloquent [græn'dɪləkwənt] *adj* altisonante, grandilocuente.

grandiose ['grændɪəʊz] *adj* grandioso; (*pej*) *building etc* ostentoso, hecho para impresionar; *scheme, plan* vasto, ambicioso; *style* exagerado, pomposo.

grandma* ['grænmɑ:] *n*, **grandmama*** ['grænmə,mɑ:] *n* abuelita* *f*; **yes, ~** sí, abuela.

grandmother ['græn,mʌðəʳ] *n* abuela *f*.

grandpa* ['grænpɑ:] *n*, **grandpapa*** ['grænpə,pɑ:] abuelito* *m*; **yes, ~** sí, abuelo.

grandparents ['græn,pɛərənts] *npl* abuelos *mpl*.

grandson ['grænsʌn] *n* nieto *m*.

grandstand ['grændstænd] **1** *n* tribuna *f*. **2** *attr*: **to have a ~ view of** abarcar todo el panorama de.

grange [greɪndʒ] *n* (*US Agr*) cortijo *m*, alquería *f*; (*Brit*) casa *f* solariega, casa *f* de señor.

granite ['grænɪt] *n* granito *m*.

granny* ['grænɪ] *n* abuelita* *f*, nana *f*; **yes, ~** sí, abuela.

granny flat* ['grænɪ,flæt] *n* pisito *m* para la abuela.

grant [grɑ:nt] **1** *n* (**a**) (*act*) otorgamiento *m*, concesión *f*; (*thing granted*) concesión *f*; (*Jur*) cesión *f*; (*gift*) donación *f*. (**b**) (*Brit*: *scholarship*) beca *f*; (*subsidy*) subvención *f*.

2 *vt* (*bestow, concede*) otorgar, conceder; (*Jur*) ceder; (*give*) donar; *proposition* asentir a; **~ed, he's rather old** de acuerdo, es bastante viejo; **~ed that** ... dado que ..., supuesto que ...; **~ing this** (**to**) **be so** dado que así sea; **to take sth for ~ed** dar algo por sentado, suponer algo; **we may take that for ~ed** eso es indudable; **he takes her for ~ed** no le aprecia a ella como es debido, no le hace caso alguno a ella.

grant-aided ['grɑ:nt,eɪdɪd] *adj* subvencionado.

grantee [grɑ:n'ti:] *n* cesionario *m*, -a *f*.

grant-in-aid ['grɑ:ntɪn'eɪd] *n* subvención *f*.

grantor [grɑ:n'tɔ:ʳ, 'grɑ:ntəʳ] *n* cedente *mf*.

granular ['grænjʊləʳ] *adj* granular.

granulated ['grænjʊleɪtɪd] *adj* granulado.

granule ['grænju:l] *n* gránulo *m*.

grape [greɪp] *n* uva *f*; **sour ~s!** ¡están verdes!; **it's just sour ~s with him** es un envidioso.

grapefruit ['greɪpfru:t] *n* toronja *f*, pomelo *m*.

grape harvest ['greɪp,hɑːvɪst] *n* vendimia *f*.
grape hyacinth [,greɪp'haɪəsɪnθ] *n* jacinto *m* de penacho.
grape-juice ['greɪpdʒuːs] *n* mosto *m*; zumo *m* de uva, jugo *m* de uva (*LAm*).
grapeshot ['greɪpʃɒt] *n* metralla *f*.
grapevine ['greɪpvaɪn] *n* vid *f*; (*trained against wall etc*) parra *f*; (*) teléfono *m* árabe, medio *m* de comunicación clandestina; **I hear on the ~ that** ... por rumores que corren sé que ..., me ha dicho alguno que ...
graph [grɑːf] *n* gráfica *f*, gráfico *m*.
grapheme ['græfiːm] *n* grafema *m*.
graphic ['græfɪk] *adj* gráfico; **~ artist** grafista *mf*; **~ arts** artes *fpl* gráficas; **~ design** diseño *m* gráfico; **~ designer** (*TV*) grafista *mf*.
graphical ['græfɪkəl] *adj* (*gen, also Math*) gráfico; **~ display unit** unidad *f* de demostración gráfica.
graphically ['græfɪkəlɪ] *adv* gráficamente.
graphics ['græfɪks] *n* (**a**) (*art of drawing*) artes *fpl* gráficas; (*Math etc*: *use of graphs*) gráficas *fpl*. (**b**) (*Comput*) gráficos *mpl*; **~ environment** entorno *m* gráfico; **~ pad** tablero *m* de gráficos. (**c**) (*TV*) dibujos *mpl*.
graphite ['græfaɪt] *n* grafito *m*.
graphologist [græ'fɒlədʒɪst] *n* grafólogo *m*, -a *f*.
graphology [græ'fɒlədʒɪ] *n* grafología *f*.
graph paper ['grɑːf,peɪpəʳ] *n* papel *m* cuadriculado.
grapnel ['græpnəl] *n* rezón *m*, arpeo *m*.
grapple ['græpl] **1** *vt* asir, agarrar; (*Naut*) aferrar.
2 *vi* (*wrestlers etc*) agarrarse; **to ~ with sb** agarrar a uno, luchar a brazo partido con uno; **to ~ with a problem** esforzarse por resolver un problema, tratar de vencer un problema.
grappling iron ['græplɪŋ,aɪən] *n* arpeo *m*, garfio *m*.
grasp [grɑːsp] **1** *n* (**a**) agarro *m*, asimiento *m*; (*handclasp*) apretón *m*; **to be within sb's ~** estar al alcance de la mano; **he has a strong ~** agarra muy fuerte; **he lost his ~ and fell** no pudo agarrarse más y cayó.
(**b**) (*fig*) (*power*) garras *fpl*, control *m*; (*range*) alcance *m*; (*mental hold*) comprensión *f*, capacidad *f* intelectual; **it's within everyone's ~** está al alcance de todos; **to have a good ~ of** dominar, conocer a fondo.
2 *vt* (**a**) (*hold firmly*) asir, agarrar; *hand* estrechar, apretar; *weapon etc* empuñar; *chance* asir; *power, territory* apoderarse de.
(**b**) (*get mental hold of*) comprender.
3 *vi*: **to ~ at** hacer por asir, tratar de asir.
grasping ['grɑːspɪŋ] *adj* avaro, codicioso.
grass [grɑːs] **1** *n* (**a**) hierba *f*; (*lawn*) césped *m*; (*grazing*) pasto *m*; **'keep off the ~'** 'se prohíbe pisar la hierba'; **to let the ~ grow under one's feet** dejar crecer la hierba; **he doesn't let the ~ grow under his feet** no cría moho; **to put a horse out to ~** echar un caballo al pasto.
(**b**) (‡) hierba* *f*, marijuana *f*.
(**c**) (*Brit*‡: *person*) soplón* *m*.
2 *attr*: **~ court** pista *f* de césped; **~ cutter** cortacésped *m*.
3 *vt* (*also* **to ~ over**) cubrir de hierba.
4 *vi* (*Brit*‡) soplar*, dar el chivatazo‡; **to ~ on** delatar a.
grass-green ['grɑːs,griːn] *adj* verde hierba.
grasshopper ['grɑːs,hɒpəʳ] *n* saltamontes *m*, chapulín *m* (*CAm, Mex*).
grassland ['grɑːslænd] *n* pradera *f*, dehesa *f*; pasto *m*.
grass-roots ['grɑːs'ruːts] **1** *n* (*Pol etc*) base *f* popular. **2** *attr* básico; popular; **~ opinion** opinión *f* de las bases populares; **~ politics** política *f* donde se trata de los problemas corrientes de la gente.
grass-snake ['grɑːssneɪk] *n* culebra *f* nadadora.
grass widow ['grɑːs'wɪdəʊ] *n* (*Brit*) mujer *f* cuyo marido está ausente.
grass widower ['grɑːs'wɪdəʊəʳ] *n* (*Brit*) marido *m* cuya mujer está ausente; ≈ Rodríguez *m*.
grassy ['grɑːsɪ] *adj* herboso, cubierto de hierba.
grate[1] [greɪt] *n* hogar *m*; (*strictly*) parrilla *f* de hogar, emparrillado *m*.
grate[2] [greɪt] **1** *vt* (**a**) *food* rallar; **~d cheese** queso *m* rallado.
(**b**) *teeth* hacer rechinar.
2 *vi* (*make a noise*) rechinar; (*rub on*) rozar; **to ~ on** rozar con, (*fig*) molestar; **to ~ on the ear** herir el oído; **to ~ on one's nerves** destrozar los nervios a uno.
grateful ['greɪtfʊl] *adj* agradecido, reconocido; **with ~ thanks** con mis más efusivas gracias; **I am ~ for your letter** agradezco su carta; **I am most ~ to you** te lo agradezco muchísimo; **I should be ~ if** ... agradecería que + *subj*.
gratefully ['greɪtfəlɪ] *adv* agradecidamente, con agradecimiento; **she looked at me ~** me miró agradecida.
grater ['greɪtəʳ] *n* rallador *m*.
gratification [,grætɪfɪ'keɪʃən] *n* (**a**) (*reward*) gratificación *f*, recompensa *f*; (*tip*) propina *f*.
(**b**) (*pleasure*) placer *m*, satisfacción *f*; **to my great ~** con gran satisfacción mía.
gratified ['grætɪfaɪd] *adj* contento, satisfecho.
gratify ['grætɪfaɪ] *vt person* complacer; *whim etc* satisfacer; **I was gratified to hear that** ... me alegré de saber que ...; **he was much gratified** estuvo muy contento.
gratifying ['grætɪfaɪɪŋ] *adj* gratificante, satisfactorio, grato; **with ~ speed** con loable prontitud; **it is ~ to know that** ... me es grato saber que ...
grating[1] ['greɪtɪŋ] *n* reja *f*, enrejado *m*, emparrillado *m*.
grating[2] ['greɪtɪŋ] *adj tone etc* áspero.
gratis ['grɑːtɪs] *adv* gratis.
gratitude ['grætɪtjuːd] *n* agradecimiento *m*, reconocimiento *m*, gratitud *f*.
gratuitous [grə'tjuːɪtəs] *adj* gratuito, innecesario.
gratuitously [grə'tjuːɪtəslɪ] *adv* gratuitamente, de manera gratuita.
gratuity [grə'tjuːɪtɪ] *n* gratificación *f*, propina *f*.
grave[1] [greɪv] *adj* grave; serio; (*anxious*) preocupado; solemne.
grave[2] [greɪv] *n* sepultura *f*; (*with monument*) tumba *f*, sepulcro *m*; **common ~** fosa *f* común.
grave[3] [grɑːv] *adj*: **~ accent** acento *m* grave.
gravedigger ['greɪv,dɪgəʳ] *n* sepulturero *m*.
gravel ['grævəl] **1** *n* grava *f*, cascajo *m*, recebo *m*. **2** *attr*: **~ path** camino *m* de grava.
gravel bed ['grævl,bed] *n* gravera *f*.
gravelled, (*US*) **graveled** ['grævəld] *adj* engravado, cubierto con grava.
gravelly ['grævəlɪ] *adj* (**a**) arenisco, cascajoso. (**b**) *voice* áspero.
gravel pit ['grævl,pɪt] *n* gravera *f*.
gravely ['greɪvlɪ] *adj* gravemente; seriamente; **~ wounded** gravemente herido, herido de gravedad; **he is ~ ill** está grave; **he spoke ~** habló en tono preocupado.
graven ['greɪvən] *adj*: **~ image** ídolo *m*; **it is ~ on my memory** lo tengo grabado en la memoria.
graveness ['greɪvnɪs] *n* gravedad *f*.
gravestone ['greɪvstəʊn] *n* lápida *f* (sepulcral).
graveyard ['greɪvjɑːd] *n* cementerio *m* (*also fig*), camposanto *m*.
graving dock ['greɪvɪŋdɒk] *n* dique *m* de carena.
gravitate ['grævɪteɪt] *vi* gravitar; **to ~ towards** (*fig*) dejarse atraer por, tender hacia.
gravitation [,grævɪ'teɪʃən] *n* gravitación *f*; (*fig*) tendencia *f* (*towards* hacia).
gravitational [,grævɪ'teɪʃənl] *adj* gravitatorio, gravitacional.
gravity ['grævɪtɪ] **1** *n* (**a**) (*Phys*) gravedad *f*.
(**b**) (*seriousness*) gravedad *f*, seriedad *f*; solemnidad *f*; **the ~ of the situation** lo grave de la situación, los peligros de la situación; **he spoke with the utmost ~** habló con la mayor solemnidad.
2 *attr*: **~ feed** alimentación *f* por gravedad.
gravy ['greɪvɪ] **1** *n* (**a**) salsa *f*. (**b**) (*US*‡) ganga *f*. **2** *attr*: **to get on the ~ train‡** coger un chollo‡.
gravy-boat ['greɪvɪ,bəʊt] *n* salsera *f*.
gray [greɪ] *etc* (*esp US*) = **grey** *etc*.
graze[1] [greɪz] (*Agr*) **1** *vt grass* pacer; *cattle* apacentar, pastar. **2** *vi* pacer, pastar.
graze[2] [greɪz] **1** *n* roce *m*, abrasión *f*, desolladura *f*. **2** *vt* (*touch*) rozar al pasar; (*scrape*) raspar, raer.
grazing ['greɪzɪŋ] *n* (**a**) (*land*) pasto *m*. (**b**) (*act*) apacentamiento *m*, pastoreo *m*.
grease [griːs] **1** *n* grasa *f*; (*dirt*) mugre *f*; (*of candle*) sebo *m*. **2** *vt* engrasar, lubricar.
grease-gun ['griːsgʌn] *n* pistola *f* engrasadora, engrasadora *f* a presión.
grease monkey ['griːs,mʌŋkɪ] *n* (*US*) mecánico *m*, -a *f*, maquinista *mf*.
grease-nipple ['griːs,nɪpl] *n* engrasador *m*.
greasepaint ['griːspeɪnt] *n* maquillaje *m*.
greaseproof ['griːspruːf] *adj* (*Brit*) a prueba de grasa, impermeable a la grasa; *paper* apergaminado.
greaser‡ ['griːsəʳ] *n* (**a**) (*mechanic*) mecánico *m*. (**b**) (*motorcyclist*) motociclista *m*. (**c**) (*pej*: *ingratiating person*) pelota* *mf*, cepillo *mf* (*LAm*), lameculos‡ *mf*. (**d**) (*US pej*: *Latin American*) sudacaca‡ *m*.
grease remover ['griːsrɪ,muːvəʳ] *n* quitagrasas *m*.

greasiness ['gri:sɪnɪs] *n* lo grasiento; lo resbaladizo; mugre *f*.
greasy ['gri:sɪ] *adj* (**a**) *substance, surface* grasiento; *road etc* resbaladizo; *hair* graso; (*grubby*) mugriento; **~ pole** cucaña *f*, palo *m* ensebado. (**b**) *person* adulón, cobista, zalamero.
great [greɪt] **1** *adj* (**a**) (*large*) grande, vasto, enorme; *sum* importante; *care etc* especial; *age* avanzado; *time* largo; **the G~ Barrier Reef** la Gran Barrera de Coral; **G~ Bear** Osa *f* Mayor; **G~ Dane** (perro *m*) danés *m*; **G~ Powers** Grandes Potencias *fpl*; **G~ Seal** sello *m* real; **the G~ Wall of China** la Gran Muralla China; **of ~ power** de gran potencia; **to my ~ surprise** con gran sorpresa mía; **what a ~ (big) dog!** ¡qué perro más grande!; **to be ~ friends** ser muy amigos; **it was a ~ joke** fue divertidísimo; **to have no ~ opinion of** no tener mayor concepto de.
(**b**) (*important*) grande, importante, principal; **the ~ thing is that ...** lo importante es que ...
(**c**) (*outstanding*) grande, famoso, destacado; **a ~ man** un gran hombre; **he has a ~ future** tiene un brillante porvenir.
(**d**) (*clever*) **to be ~ at, to be ~ on** ser fuerte en, ser bueno para, entender mucho de.
(**e**) (*keen*) **he's a ~ angler** tiene gran afición a la pesca; **he's a ~ arguer** tiene la manía de discutir; **he's a ~ eater** tiene buen apetito, es muy comilón.
(**f**) (*) magnífico, estupendo*, bárbaro* (*LAm*); **~!** ¡magnífico!; **it's ~!** ¡es fabuloso!*; **you were ~!** ¡estuviste magnífico!; **he's a ~ guy** es un tío (*LAm*: tipo) estupendo*.
2 *adv* (‡): **the lads done ~** los chicos han jugado fenómeno*.
3 *npl*: **the ~** los grandes; **the ~ and the good** (*hum*) los grandes y los buenos.
great-aunt ['greɪt'ɑ:nt] *n* tía *f* abuela.
Great Britain ['greɪt'brɪtn] *n* Gran Bretaña *f*.
greatcoat ['greɪtkəʊt] *n* gabán *m*, (*Mil etc*) sobretodo *m*.
greater ['greɪtə^r] *adj* (*comp of* **great**) mayor; **G~ London** gran Londres.
greatest ['greɪtɪst] *adj* (*superl of* **great**) (**a**) el mayor, la mayor; **with the ~ difficulty** con la mayor dificultad; **the ~ writer of his age** el mayor escritor de su época; **when the heat is at its ~** cuando más aprieta el calor; **~ common factor, ~ common divisor** máximo común divisor *m*.
(**b**) (*) **it's the ~!** ¡es el colmo!, ¡es el delirio!*; **he's the ~!** ¡es fabuloso!*
great-grandchild ['greɪt'grænt∫aɪld] *n*, *pl* **great-grandchildren** ['greɪt'græn,t∫ɪldrən] bisnieto *m*, -a *f*.
great-granddaughter [,greɪt'grænd,dɔ:tə^r] *n* bisnieta *f*.
great-grandfather ['greɪt'grænd,fɑ:ðə^r] *n* bisabuelo *m*.
great-grandmother ['greɪt'græn,mʌðə^r] *n* bisabuela *f*.
great-grandson [,greɪt'grændsʌn] *n* bisnieto *m*.
great-great-grandfather ['greɪt'greɪt'grænd,fɑ:ðə^r] *n* tatarabuelo *m*.
great-great-grandson ['greɪt'greɪt'grænsʌn] *n* tataranieto *m*.
great-hearted ['greɪt'hɑ:tɪd] *adj* valiente.
Great Lakes ['greɪt'leɪks] *npl* Grandes Lagos *mpl*.
greatly ['greɪtlɪ] *adv* grandemente, mucho, muy, sumamente; **~ superior** muy superior; **we were ~ amused** nos divirtió muchísimo; **it is ~ to be regretted** es muy de lamentar; **not ~ expensive** no muy caro.
great-nephew ['greɪt,nefju:] *n* sobrinonieto *m*.
greatness ['greɪtnɪs] *n* grandeza *f*.
great-niece ['greɪt,ni:s] *n* sobrinanieta *f*.
great tit ['greɪttɪt] *n* (*Orn*) carbonero *m* común.
great-uncle ['greɪt,ʌŋkl] *n* tío *m* abuelo.
Great War ['greɪt'wɔ:^r] *n* Primera Guerra *f* Mundial (*1914-18*).
grebe [gri:b] *n* zampullín *m*, somormujo *m*.
Grecian ['gri:∫ən] *adj* griego.
Greece [gri:s] *n* Grecia *f*.
greed [gri:d] *n*, **greediness** ['gri:dɪnɪs] *n* codicia *f*, avaricia *f*; avidez *f* (*for* de); (*for food*) gula *f*, glotonería *f*; (*as a sin*) avaricia *f*.
greedily ['gri:dɪlɪ] *adv* con avidez; *eat* vorazmente.
greedy ['gri:dɪ] *adj* codicioso, avaro; ávido (*for* de); (*for food*) goloso, glotón; **don't be so ~!** ¡no seas glotón!
Greek [gri:k] **1** *adj* griego; **~ Orthodox Church** Iglesia *f* Ortodoxa griega. **2** *n* (**a**) griego *m*, -a *f*. (**b**) (*Ling*) griego *m*; **ancient ~** griego *m* antiguo; **it's ~ to me** para mí es chino, no entiendo ni palabra.
Greek-Cypriot ['gri:k'sɪprɪət] **1** *adj* grecochipriota. **2** *n* grecochipriota *mf*.
green [gri:n] **1** *adj* (**a**) verde; (*fresh*) fresco; (*unripe, unseasoned*) verde; (*raw*) crudo; *complexion* pálido; **~ algae** algas *fpl* verdes; **~ beans** judías *fpl* verdes, ejotes *mpl* (*Mex*), chauchas *fpl* (*SC*); **~ belt** (*Brit*) zona *f* verde; **the G~ Berets** los boinas verdes *mpl*; **~ card** (*Brit Aut, US Admin*) tarjeta *f* verde; **G~ Cross Code** (*Brit*) código *m* de seguridad vial; **~ fingers** (*Brit*), **~ thumb** (*US*) habilidad *f* para la jardinería; **~ light** luz *f* verde; **to give the ~ light to** dar luz verde a; **G~ Paper** (*Brit Pol*) libro *m* verde; **~ peas** guisantes *mpl*; **~ pepper** (*spice*) pimienta *f* verde; (*vegetable*) pimiento *m* verde, pimentón *m* verde; **~ pound** libra *f* verde; **~ revolution** revolución *f* verde; **~ room** camerino *m*; **~ salad** ensalada *f* (a base de lechuga); **~ vegetables** verdura *f*; **~ wellie brigade*** señoritos *mpl* del campo; **she was ~ with envy** quedaba muda de envidia; le comía la envidia; **to grow ~, to look ~** verdear.
(**b**) (*inexperienced*) nuevo, novato; (*naïve*) crédulo.
(**c**) (*Pol*) verde; **~ issues** temas *mpl* verdes; **G~ Party** Partido *m* Verde; **~ policies** programas *mpl* verdes; **~ politics** política *f* verde; **the ~ vote** el voto verde.
2 *n* (**a**) (*colour*) verde *m*.
(**b**) (*lawn*) césped *m*; (*field*) prado *m*; (*for bowls etc*) pista *f*; (*Golf*) green *m*; (*of village*) césped *m* comunal.
(**c**) **~s** (*Brit*) verduras *fpl*.
(**d**) (*Pol*) **the G~s** los verdes; **I'm a G~ now** ahora yo soy Verde.
greenback ['gri:nbæk] *n* (*US*) billete *m* (de banco).
greenery ['gri:nərɪ] *n* verdura *f*.
green-eyed ['gri:naɪd] *adj* de ojos verdes; **the ~ monster** (*fig*) la envidia.
greenfield ['gri:n,fi:ld] *n* (*also* **~ site**) solar *m* sin edificar, terreno *m* sin edificar.
greenfinch ['gri:nfɪnt∫] *n* verderón *m*.
greenfly ['gri:nflaɪ] *n* pulgón *m*.
greengage ['gri:ngeɪdʒ] *n* (*Brit*) (ciruela *f*) claudia *f*.
greengrocer ['gri:n,grəʊsə^r] *n* (*Brit*) verdulero *m*, -a *f*; **~'s (shop)** verdulería *f*, verdurería *f* (*Carib*).
greenhorn ['gri:nhɔ:n] *n* bisoño *m*, novato *m*.
greenhouse ['gri:nhaʊs] **1** *n*, *pl* **greenhouses** ['gri:n,haʊzɪz] invernáculo *m*, invernadero *m*. **2** *attr*: **~ effect** efecto *m* invernadero; **~ gas** gas *m* invernadero.
greenish ['gri:nɪ∫] *adj* verdoso.
Greenland ['gri:nlənd] *n* Groenlandia *f*.
Greenlander ['gri:nləndə^r] *n* groenlandés *m*, -esa *f*.
greenness ['gri:nnɪs] *n* (**a**) verdor *m*, lo verde. (**b**) (*fig*) inexperiencia *f*; credulidad *f*.
greenstuff ['gri:nstʌf] *n* verduras *fpl*, legumbres *fpl*.
greensward ['gri:nswɔ:d] *n* césped *m*.
Greenwich ['grɪnɪdʒ] *attr*: **~ mean time** hora *f* media de Greenwich.
greet [gri:t] *vt* (*in general*) recibir; (*with words etc*) saludar; (*welcome*) dar la bienvenida a; (*meet one's eyes*) presentarse a; **this was ~ed with relief by everybody** todos sintieron un gran alivio al saber la noticia; **the statement was ~ed with laughter** se recibió la declaración con risas.
greeting ['gri:tɪŋ] **1** *n* (*with words etc*) saludo *m*, salutación *f*; (*welcome*) bienvenida *f*; **~s!** ¡bienvenido!; **~s** (*in letter*) recuerdos *mpl*. **2** *attr*: **~(s) card** tarjeta *f* de saludo; tarjeta *f* de felicitación.
Greg [greg] *nm familiar form of* **Gregory**.
gregarious [grɪ'gɛərɪəs] *adj* gregario.
Gregorian [grɪ'gɔ:rɪən] *adj* gregoriano; **~ chant** canto *m* gregoriano.
Gregory ['gregərɪ] *nm* Gregorio.
gremlin* ['gremlɪn] *n* duendecillo *m*, diablillo *m*.
Grenada [gre'neɪdə] *n* Granada *f*.
grenade [grɪ'neɪd] *n* granada *f*; (*hand* **~**) granada *f* de mano.
grenade-launcher [grɪ'neɪd,lɔ:nt∫ə^r] *n* lanzagranadas *m*.
Grenadian [gre'neɪdɪən] **1** *adj* granadino. **2** *n* granadino *m*, -a *f*.
grenadier [,grenə'dɪə^r] *n* granadero *m*.
grenadine ['grenədi:n] *n* granadina *f*.
grew [gru:] *pret of* **grow**.
grey [greɪ] **1** *adj* gris; *horse etc* rucio; **~ area** zona *f* en penumbra; (*fig*) zona *f* gris; **~ matter** materia *f* gris, seso *m*; **~ mullet** lisa *f* dorada, mújol *m* dorado; **~ squirrel** ardilla *f* gris; **to go ~, turn ~** (*hair*) encanecer. **2** *n* (**a**) gris *m*. (**b**) (*horse*) rucio *m*. **3** *vi* (*hair*) encanecer.
greybeard ['greɪbɪəd] *n* anciano *m*, viejo *m*.
grey-haired ['greɪ'hɛəd] *adj* canoso.
greyhound ['greɪhaʊnd] **1** *n* galgo *m*, lebrel *m*. **2** *attr*: **~ track** canódromo *m*.
greying ['greɪɪŋ] *adj hair* grisáceo, que encanece.
greyish ['greɪɪ∫] *adj* grisáceo; *hair* entrecano.

grid [grɪd] *n* (*with bars*) reja *f*; (*Culin etc*) parrilla *f*; (*Brit Elec*) red *f*; (*Aut*) portaequipajes *m*, portamaletas *m* (sobre el techo) *etc*; (*of cycle*) parrilla *f*; (*on map*) cuadrícula *f*; (*Aut**) cacharro* *m*; (*US Sport*) = **gridiron**; ~ **map** mapa *m* cuadriculado.

griddle ['grɪdl] **1** *n* plancha *f*. **2** *vt* asar a la plancha.

gridiron ['grɪd,aɪən] *n* (**a**) (*Culin etc*) parrilla *f*. (**b**) (*US*) campo *m* de fútbol (americano).

gridlock ['grɪdlɒk] *n* (*US Aut*) atasco *m*, retención *f*, bloqueo *m*.

grief [gri:f] *n* dolor *m*, pesar *m*, aflicción *f*; **good** ~! ¡demonio!; **to come to** ~ sufrir un percance; fracasar, fallar.

grief-stricken ['gri:f,strɪkən] *adj* apesadumbrado.

grievance ['gri:vəns] *n* queja *f*, motivo *m* de queja; reivindicación *f*; agravio *m*, injusticia *f*; ~ **procedure** sistema *m* de trámite de quejas; **to have a** ~ **against sb** tener queja de (*or* contra) uno.

grieve [gri:v] **1** *vt* dar pena a; **you** ~ **me** me das pena; **it** ~**s one to see ...** da pena ver ...

2 *vi* afligirse, acongojarse (*about, at* de, por); **to** ~ **for** llorar, llorar la pérdida (*etc*) de.

grieved [gri:vd] *adj tone etc* lastimoso, apenado.

grievous ['gri:vəs] *adj loss etc* cruel, doloroso, penoso; *blow* severo; *pain* fuerte; *crime, offence* grave; *error* lamentable, craso; *task* penoso; ~ **bodily harm** graves daños *mpl* corporales.

grievously ['gri:vəslɪ] *adv hurt, offend* gravemente; *err, be mistaken* lamentablemente; ~ **wounded** gravemente herido.

griffin ['grɪfɪn] *n* grifo *m*.

griffon ['grɪfən] *n* (*dog*) grifón *m*.

grifter ['grɪftəʳ] *n* (*US*) (**a**) propietario *m* de una caseta de feria (*etc*); garitero *m*. (**b**) (‡) fullero *m*; estafador *m*, timador *m*.

grill [grɪl] **1** *n* (*aparatus*) parrilla *f*, grill *m*; (*meat*) asado *m* a la parrilla; *V also* **grille**. **2** *vt* (**a**) asar a la parrilla. (**b**) (*) interrogar (sin piedad).

grille [grɪl] *n* rejilla *f*; (*of window*) reja *f*; (*screen*) verja *f*.

grilled [grɪld] *adj* (asado) a la parrilla.

grilling ['grɪlɪŋ] *n* (*fig*) interrogatorio *m* intenso; **to give sb a** ~ interrogar a uno intensamente.

grillroom ['grɪlrʊm] *n* parrilla *f*, grill *m*.

grilse [grɪls] *n* salmón *m* joven (*que sólo ha estado una vez en el mar*).

grim [grɪm] *adj* (**a**) (*stern*) severo; (*frowning*) ceñudo; (*unrelenting*) inexorable, inflexible; *battle* porfiado, muy reñido, encarnizado; *humour* macabro; (*frightful*) horrible; *outlook, situation* grave; **with a** ~ **smile** sonriendo inexorable; **the** ~ **truth** la verdad lisa y llana; **the** ~ **facts** los hechos inexorables.

(**b**) (*) horrible, malísimo.

grimace [grɪ'meɪs] **1** *n* mueca *f*, visaje *m*. **2** *vi* hacer una mueca, hacer muecas.

grime [graɪm] *n* mugre *f*, suciedad *f*.

grimly ['grɪmlɪ] *adv* severamente; inexorablemente; encarnizadamente; **he smiled** ~ sonrió inexorable; **to hang on** ~ resistir sin cejar.

grimness ['grɪmnɪs] *n* (*V adj*) severidad *f*; inflexibilidad *f*; lo porfiado, lo encarnizado; lo macabro; gravedad *f*.

grimy ['graɪmɪ] *adj* mugriento, sucio.

grin [grɪn] **1** *n* sonrisa *f* (abierta, bonachona, burlona *etc*); (*grimace*) mueca *f*.

2 *vi* sonreír (mostrando los dientes, bonachón, burlón *etc*; *at* a); **to** ~ **and bear it** sonreír y resignarse, poner al mal tiempo buena cara.

grind [graɪnd] **1** *n* trabajo *m* pesado; rutina *f*; (*boredom*) lo pesado; **the daily** ~ la rutina diaria; **the work was such a** ~ el trabajo era tan pesado.

2 *vt* (*irr*: *pret and ptp* **ground**) *corn etc* moler; *stone* pulverizar; *teeth* hacer rechinar; (*sharpen*) amolar, afilar; (*oppress*) agobiar, oprimir; (*US Culin*) picar; **to** ~ **into powder** reducir a polvo.

3 *vi* (*machine etc*) rechinar, funcionar con dificultad; **to** ~ **against** ludir ruidosamente con; **to** ~ **to a halt** (*or* **standstill**) pararse con gran estruendo de frenos.

◆**grind away*** *vi* trabajar como un esclavo; (*Mus*) tocar laboriosamente; **to** ~ **away at grammar** empollar la gramática*, machacar la gramática*.

◆**grind down** *vt* pulverizar, (*wear away*) desgastar; (*oppress*) agobiar, oprimir; **to** ~ **down to powder** reducir a polvo.

◆**grind on** *vi*: **the case went** ~**ing on for months** el pleito se desarrollaba penosamente durante varios meses.

◆**grind out** *vt* reproducir mecánicamente (*or* laboriosamente *etc*).

◆**grind up** *vt* pulverizar.

grinder ['graɪndəʳ] *n* (**a**) (*person*) molendero *m*; (*Tech*) amolador *m*; esmerilador *m*.

(**b**) (*machine*) amoladora *f*; esmeriladora *f*; (*for coffee etc*) molinillo *m*; (*US*: *for meat*) picadora *f* de carne.

(**c**) ~**s** (*Anat*) muelas *fpl*.

grinding ['graɪndɪŋ] **1** *adj*: ~ **sound** rechinamiento *m*; ~ **poverty** miseria *f* absoluta, pura miseria *f*. **2** *n* molienda *f*; pulverización *f*; afilado *m*.

grindingly ['graɪndɪŋlɪ] *adv*: **a** ~ **familiar routine** una rutina tremendamente monótona; ~ **poor** pobrísimo.

grindstone ['graɪndstəʊn] *n* muela *f*; **to keep one's nose to the** ~ batir el yunque.

gringo ['grɪŋgəʊ] *n* (*US*) gringo *m*, -a *f*.

grip [grɪp] **1** *n* (**a**) (*grasp*) agarre *m*, asimiento *m*; (*handclasp*) apretón *m*; **to come to** ~**s with** luchar a brazo partido con; **to get to** ~**s with a problem** enfrentarse con un problema, esforzarse por resolver un problema.

(**b**) (*handle*) asidero *m*, agarradero *m*; (*of weapon*) empuñadura *f*.

(**c**) (*bag*) maletín *m*, saco *m* de mano (con cremallera), bolsa *f*.

(**d**) (*fig*: *power*) garras *fpl*; control *m*, dominio *m*; **in the** ~ **of winter** paralizado por el invierno; **in the** ~ **of a strike** paralizado por una huelga; **to lose one's** ~ perder las fuerzas, decaer; **get a** ~ **on yourself!** ¡cálmese!, ¡domínese!

2 *vt* (**a**) (*hold firmly*) agarrar, asir; *weapon* empuñar; *hand* apretar; **the wheels** ~ **the road** las ruedas se agarran a la carretera.

(**b**) (*fig*) (*interest*) absorber la atención de, tener suspenso a; (*fear*) apoderarse de, agarrar.

3 *vi* (*wheel*) agarrarse.

gripe [graɪp] **1** *n* (**a**) (*Med*: *also* ~**s**) retortijón *m* de tripas. (**b**) (*) queja *f*. **2** *vt* dar cólico a. **3** *vi* (*) quejarse.

griping ['graɪpɪŋ] **1** *adj pain* retortijante. **2** *n* (*) quejadumbre *f*.

gripping ['grɪpɪŋ] *adj* absorbente, muy emocionante.

grisly ['grɪzlɪ] *adj* horripilante, espeluznante; repugnante, asqueroso.

grist [grɪst] *n*: **it's all** ~ **to his mill** saca agua de las piedras, saca provecho de todo.

gristle ['grɪsl] *n* cartílago *m*, ternilla *f*.

gristly ['grɪslɪ] *adj* cartilaginoso, ternilloso.

grit [grɪt] **1** *n* (**a**) arena *f*, cascajo *m*; (*dust*) polvo *m*.

(**b**) ~**s** (*US*) maíz *m* a medio moler.

(**c**) (*fig*: *courage*) valor *m*; (*firmness of character*) firmeza *f*; (*endurance*) aguante *m*.

2 *vt* (**a**) *teeth* hacer rechinar; **to** ~ **one's teeth** (**and bear it**) apretar los dientes.

(**b**) *road* cubrir de arena (*or* grava *etc*), enarenar.

gritty ['grɪtɪ] *adj* arenisco, arenoso.

grizzle ['grɪzl] *vi* (*Brit*) gimotear.

grizzled ['grɪzld] *adj* gris, canoso.

grizzly ['grɪzlɪ] **1** *adj* gris, canoso; ~ **bear** = **2**. **2** *n* oso *m* pardo.

groan [grəʊn] **1** *n* gemido *m*, quejido *m*. **2** *vt* decir gimiendo; **'yes', he** ~**ed** 'sí', dijo gimiendo. **3** *vi* gemir, quejarse; (*creak*) crujirse; **to** ~ **under** sufrir bajo, (*weight*) crujir bajo.

groats [grəʊts] *npl* avena *f* a medio moler.

grocer ['grəʊsəʳ] *n* (*esp Brit*) tendero *m* (de ultramarinos), mantequero *m*, abacero *m*, almacenero *m* (*SC*), bodeguero *m* (*CAm, Carib*), abarrotero *m* (*esp LAm*); ~**'s** (**shop**) tienda *f* de ultramarinos, tienda *f* de comestibles, mantequería *f*, abacería *f*, almacén *m* (*SC*), bodega *f* (*CAm, Carib*); tienda *f* de abarrotes (*esp LAm*).

groceries ['grəʊsərɪz] *npl* comestibles *mpl*, provisiones *fpl*.

grocery ['grəʊsərɪ] *n* (*esp Brit*) tienda *f* de ultramarinos, tienda *f* de comestibles, mantequería *f*, abacería *f*; *V also* **grocer**.

grog [grɒg] *n* (*Brit*) grog *m*.

groggy ['grɒgɪ] *adj* (*unsteady*) inseguro, vacilante; (*after blow*) aturdido, turulato; (*Boxing*) groggy, grogui; **I feel a bit** ~ no me siento del todo bien.

groin [grɔɪn] *n* ingle *f*.

groom [gru:m] **1** *n* groom *m*, mozo *m* de caballos; (*bridegroom*) novio *m*.

2 *vt horse* almohazar, cuidar; *dog* cepillar; **to be well** ~**ed** (*person*) estar muy acicalado; **she's always well** ~**ed** siempre está muy elegante; **to** ~ **sb for a post** preparar a uno para un puesto.

grooming ['gru:mɪŋ] *n* (**a**) (*gen, also well-groomedness*) acicalamiento *m*. (**b**) (*of horse*) almohazamiento *m*; (*of dog*) cepillado *m*.

groove [gru:v] **1** *n* ranura *f*, estría *f*, acanaladura *f*; (*of record*) surco *m*; **to be in a ~** estar metido en una rutina; **to be in the ~‡** estar en forma; estar de moda, ser lo último*.

2 *vt* (*put ~ in*) estriar, acanalar.

grooved [gru:vd] *adj* estriado, acanalado.

groovy‡ ['gru:vɪ] *adj* (*marvellous*) estupendo*, guay‡, total*, tope*; (*up-to-date*) moderno, nuevo.

grope [grəʊp] **1** *vt* (**a**) **to ~ one's way** ir a tientas; **to ~ one's way towards** (*fig*) avanzar a tientas hacia. (**b**) (*) *woman* sobar. **2** *vi* ir a tientas; **to ~ for** buscar a tientas (*also fig*).

◆grope about, grope around *vi* andar a tientas; **to ~ about for sth** buscar algo a tientas.

grosgrain ['grəʊgreɪn] *n* grogrén *m*, cordellate *m*.

gross [grəʊs] **1** *adj* (**a**) (*large*) grueso, enorme; (*fat*) muy gordo.

(**b**) (*flagrant*) *abuse* grave; *injustice* grave, intolerable.

(**c**) *error* craso; (*vulgar*) grosero.

(**d**) (*Comm etc*) bruto; **~ income** renta *f* bruta; **~ margin** margen *m* bruto; **~ national product** producto *m* nacional bruto; **~ output** producción *f* bruta; **~ payment** (pago *m*) íntegro *m*; **~ profit** ganancia *f* bruta; **~ sales** ventas *fpl* brutas; **~ wage** salario *m* bruto; **~ weight** peso *m* bruto; **~ yield** rendimiento *m* bruto.

(**e**) (*US*: *disgusting*) asqueroso.

2 *adv*: **she earns £50,000 a year ~** gana en total 50,000 libras al año.

3 *n* gruesa *f*; **by the ~** en gruesas; **in (the) ~** en grueso.

4 *vt*: **he ~es £40,000 a year** gana en total 40,000 libras al año.

◆gross out* *vt* (*US*) asquear, dar asco a.

◆gross up* *vt* (*US*) *salary etc* recaudar en bruto.

grossly ['grəʊslɪ] *adv* groseramente; **~ exaggerated** enormemente exagerado; **~ fat** tan gordo que da asco.

grossness ['grəʊsnɪs] *n* gordura *f*; grosería *f*.

grotesque [grəʊ'tesk] *adj* grotesco.

grotto ['grɒtəʊ] *n* gruta *f*.

grotty* ['grɒtɪ] *adj* (*Brit*) sucio; asqueroso, horrible; **I feel a bit ~** no me siento bien.

grouch* [graʊtʃ] **1** *vi* refunfuñar, quejarse. **2** *n* (**a**) (*person*) refunfuñón *m*, -ona *f*, cascarrabias *mf*. (**b**) (*complaint*) queja *f*.

grouchy* ['graʊtʃɪ] *adj* malhumorado.

ground¹ [graʊnd] **1** *n* (**a**) (*soil*) suelo *m*, tierra *f*; (*US Elec*; *also* **~ wire**) tierra *f*.

(**b**) (*surface*) suelo *m*, tierra *f*; (*terrain*) terreno *m*; **above ~** sobre la tierra, (*fig*) vivo, con vida; **on the ~** sobre el terreno; **to break new ~** (*fig*) hacer algo nuevo; **to cover a lot of ~** recorrer una gran distancia, (*fig*) tocar muchos puntos; **to cut the ~ from under sb's feet** minar el terreno a uno; **to fall to the ~** caer al suelo, (*fig*) venirse al suelo, caer por su base; **to get off the ~** (*Aer*) despegar, (*fig*) realizarse, resultar factible; **to go to ~** (*fox*) meterse en su madriguera, (*person*) esconderse, refugiarse; **to prepare the ~ for sth** preparar el terreno para algo; **to raze sth to the ~** arrasar algo; **to run sb to ~** localizar (por fin) a uno, averiguar el paradero de uno; **it suits you down to the ~** (*Brit*: *dress*) te sienta perfectamente; **it suits me down to the ~** (*fig*) me conviene perfectamente, me viene de perilla.

(**c**) (*surface, fig*) terreno *m*; **to be on dangerous ~** pisar un terreno peligroso; **to be on firm** (*or* **sure**) **~** hablar con conocimiento de causa; **to be on one's home ~** tratar materia que uno conoce a fondo; **to gain ~** ganar terreno; **to give** (*or* **lose**) **~** perder terreno; **to hold** (*or* **stand**) **one's ~** mantenerse firme, mantenerse en sus trece; **to shift one's ~** cambiar de postura.

(**d**) (*pitch*) terreno *m*, campo *m*; **they won on their own ~** ganaron en su propio terreno.

(**e**) (*estate, property*) tierras *fpl*.

(**f**) **~s** (*gardens*) jardines *mpl*, parque *m*.

(**g**) **~s** (*sediment*) poso *m*, sedimento *m*.

(**h**) (*Art*) fondo *m*; primera capa *f*; **on a blue ~** sobre un fondo azul.

(**i**) (*reason*) causa *f*, motivo *m*, razón *f*; (*basis*) fundamento *m*; **~(s) for complaint** motivo *m* de queja; **on the ~(s) of** con motivo de, por causa de, debido a; **on the ~(s) that ...** porque, por + *infin*, (*pej*) pretextando que; **on good ~s** con razón; **what ~(s) have you for saying so?** ¿en qué se basa para decir eso?

2 *attr*: **~ attack** ataque *m* de tierra; (*Aer*) ataque *m* a superficie; **~ bass** bajo *m* rítmico; **~ floor** (*Brit*) planta *f* baja, primer piso *m* (*LAm*); **he got in on the ~ floor** (*fig*) empezó por abajo; **~ floor flat** (*Brit*) piso *m* de planta baja (*LAm*: de primer piso); **~ forces** fuerzas *fpl* de tierra; **~ frost** helada *f*, escarcha *f*; **~ ivy** hiedra *f* terrestre; **~ level** nivel *m* del suelo; **~ pollution** contaminación *f* del suelo; **~ rent** (*esp Brit*) alquiler *m* del terreno; **~ rules** reglas *fpl* básicas; **we can't change the ~ rules at this stage** a estas alturas ya no se pueden cambiar las reglas; **~ wire** (*US*) cable *m* de toma de tierra.

3 *vt* (**a**) *ship* varar.

(**b**) (*US Elec*) conectar a tierra.

(**c**) (*Aer*) hacer permanecer en tierra; **he ordered the planes to be ~ed** ordenó que permaneciesen los aviones en tierra; **to be ~ed by bad weather** no poder despegar por el mal tiempo.

(**d**) (*teach*) **to ~ sb in maths** enseñar a uno los rudimentos de las matemáticas; **to be well ~ed in** tener un buen conocimiento de, estar versado en.

(**e**) (*US*) *student* encerrar, no dejar salir.

4 *vi* (*Naut*) varar, encallar; (*lightly*) tocar (*on* en).

ground² [graʊnd] **1** *pret and ptp of* **grind**. **2** *adj glass* deslustrado; *coffee* molido; (*US*) *meat* picado; **~ beef** (*US*) picadillo *m*.

groundbait ['graʊnd,beɪt] *n* cebo *m* de fondo.

groundcloth ['graʊndklɒθ] *n* (*US*) tela *f* impermeable.

ground-colour ['graʊnd,kʌləʳ] *n* primera capa *f*; fondo *m*.

ground-control ['graʊndkən,trəʊl] *n* (*Aer*) control *m* de(sde) tierra.

ground-crew ['graʊndkru:] *n* personal *m* de tierra.

groundhog ['graʊndhɒg] *n* (*US*) marmota *f* de América.

grounding ['graʊndɪŋ] *n* (**a**) (*Naut*) varada *f*. (**b**) (*in education*) instrucción *f* en los rudimentos (*in* de); **to give sb a ~ in** enseñar a uno los rudimentos de.

groundkeeper ['graʊnd,ki:pəʳ] *n* cuidador *m* del terreno de juego, encargado *m* de la pista de deportes.

groundless ['graʊndlɪs] *adj* infundado.

groundnut ['graʊndnʌt] **1** *n* (*Brit*) cacahuete *m*, maní *m* (*LAm*). **2** *attr*: **~ oil** aceite *m* de cacahuete.

groundplan ['graʊndplæn] *n* planta *f*, distribución *f*.

groundsel ['graʊnsl] *n* hierba *f* cana.

groundsheet ['graʊndʃi:t] *n* tela *f* impermeable.

groundskeeper ['graʊndz,ki:pəʳ] *n* (*US*) = **groundkeeper**.

groundsman ['graʊndzmən] *n*, *pl* **groundsmen** ['graʊndzmən] encargado *m* de campo, cuidador *m* de campo.

groundspeed ['graʊnd,spi:d] *n* (*Aer*) velocidad *f* respecto a la tierra.

groundstaff ['graʊndstɑ:f] *n* (*Aer*) personal *m* de tierra.

groundswell ['graʊndswel] *n* mar *m* de fondo; (*fig*) marejada *f*.

ground-to-air ['graʊndtʊ'ɛəʳ] *adj*: **~ missile** misil *m* tierra-aire.

ground-to-ground ['graʊndtə'graʊnd] *adj*: **~ missile** misil *m* tierra-tierra.

groundwater ['graʊndwɔ:təʳ] *n* agua *f* subterránea.

groundwork ['graʊndwɜ:k] *n* trabajo *m* preliminar, trabajo *m* preparatorio; **to do the ~ for** echar las bases de.

group [gru:p] **1** *n* grupo *m*, agrupación *f*; (*Mus*) conjunto *m* musical.

2 *attr* colectivo; *discussion* en grupo; *photo* de conjunto; **~ booking** reserva *f* por grupos; **~ captain** (*Brit*) jefe *m* de escuadrilla; **~ dynamics** dinámica *f* de grupo; **~ practice** práctica *f* colectiva; **~ sex** cama *f* redonda, sexo *m* en grupo, fornicación *f* colectiva; **~ therapy** terapia *f* de grupo, terapia *f* grupal.

3 *vt* (*also* **to ~ together**) agrupar.

grouper ['gru:pəʳ] *n* (*Fish*) mero *m*.

groupie* ['gru:pɪ] *n* groupie* *f*, chica *f* que asedia a las figuras de la música pop.

grouping ['gru:pɪŋ] *n* agrupamiento *m*.

grouse¹ [graʊs] *n*: **black ~** gallo *m* lira; **red ~** lagópodo *m* escocés.

grouse²* [graʊs] **1** *n* queja *f*; motivo *m* de queja. **2** *vi* quejarse.

grout [graʊt] **1** *n* lechada *f*. **2** *vt* enlechar.

grove [grəʊv] *n* arboleda *f*, bosquecillo *m*; **~ of pines** pineda *f*; **~ of poplars** alameda *f*.

grovel ['grɒvl] *vi* arrastrarse; (*fig*) humillarse (*to* ante).

grovelling, (*US*) **groveling** ['grɒvlɪŋ] *adj* rastrero, servil.

grow [grəʊ] (*irr*: *pret* **grew**, *ptp* **grown**) **1** *vt* (**a**) (*Agr*) cultivar; *beard etc* dejar crecer; **to be ~n over with** estar cubierto de.

(**b**) **the lizard grew a new tail** al lagarto le salió una cola nueva, al lagarto se le reprodujo la cola.

2 *vi* (**a**) crecer; (*be cultivated*) cultivarse; (*increase*) aumentar; (*industry, market*) extenderse, desarrollarse, expandirse; **that plant does not ~ in England** esa planta no se da en Inglaterra; **will it ~ here?** ¿se puede cultivar aquí?

(**b**) **to ~ to** + *infin* (*fig*) llegar a + *infin*.

(**c**) (*with adj: become*) volverse, ponerse; (*often translated by vi or vr*) **to ~ angry** enfadarse; **to ~ cold** (*thing*) enfriarse, (*person*) empezar a tener frío, (*weather*) empezar a hacer frío; **to ~ dark** ponerse oscuro, oscurecerse, (*at dusk*) anochecer; **to ~ old** envejecer(se).

◆**grow apart** *vi* (*friends*) irse separando, ir perdiendo el contacto.

◆**grow away from** *vt* irse separando de, ir perdiendo el contacto con.

◆**grow in** *vi* (*nail*) crecer hacia adentro; (*hair*) crecer de nuevo.

◆**grow into** *vt* hacerse, llegar a ser; **to ~ into a job** acostumbrarse a un trabajo.

◆**grow on** *vt*: **the book ~s on one** el libro gusta cada vez más, el libro llega a gustar con el tiempo; **the habit grew on him** la costumbre arraigó en él.

◆**grow out of** *vt* (**a**) **she grew out of her clothes** se le hizo pequeña la ropa; **to ~ out of a habit** perder una costumbre (con el tiempo). (**b**) **to ~ out of** (*originate in*) resultar de, originarse de.

◆**grow up** *vi* (*person*) crecer (mucho), (*become adult*) hacerse hombre, hacerse mujer; (*custom etc*) arraigar, imponerse; **~ up!** ¡no seas niño!; **hatred grew up between them** nació el odio entre ellos; **she grew up into a lovely woman** con el tiempo se transformó en una mujer hermosa.

growbag ['grəʊbæg] *n* bolsa *f* de cultivo.

grower ['grəʊəʳ] *n* cultivador *m*, -ora *f*.

growing ['grəʊɪŋ] *adj* (**a**) *crop etc* que crece, que se desarrolla; **~ season** época *f* de cultivos; época *f* del desarrollo (de las plantas). (**b**) (*increasing*) creciente. (**c**) *child* que está creciendo; **~ pains** (*fig*) problemas *mpl* inherentes al crecimiento.

growl [graʊl] **1** *n* gruñido *m*. **2** *vi* gruñir; rezongar; (*thunder*) reverberar. **3** *vt*: **'yes', he ~ed** 'sí', dijo refunfuñando.

grown [grəʊn] **1** *ptp of* **grow**. **2** *adj* crecido, adulto.

grown-up ['grəʊn'ʌp] **1** *adj* adulto; propio de persona mayor. **2** *n* persona *f* mayor.

growth [grəʊθ] **1** *n* (**a**) crecimiento *m*; aumento *m*; desarrollo *m*, expansión *f*; **to reach full ~** llegar a la madurez, (*fig*) alcanzar su plenitud.

(**b**) (*Bot*) vegetación *f*; **with 3 days' ~ on his face** con barba de 3 días.

(**c**) (*Med*) tumor *m*.

2 *attr*: **~ area** polo *m* de desarrollo; **~ hormone** hormona *f* del crecimiento; **~ industry** industria *f* en desarrollo; **~ point** punto *m* de desarrollo; **~ potential** potencial *m* de crecimiento; **~ rate** (*Econ etc*) tasa *f* de crecimiento, tasa *f* de desarrollo; **~ shares** (*US*), **~ stock** acciones *fpl* con perspectivas de valorización; **~ town** ciudad *f* en vías de desarrollo.

groyne [grɔɪn] *n* (*esp Brit*) rompeolas *m*, espigón *m*.

GRSM *n abbr of* **Graduate of the Royal Schools of Music**.

GRT *n abbr of* **gross register tons** toneladas *fpl* de registro bruto, TRB *fpl*.

grub [grʌb] **1** *n* (**a**) (*larva*) gusano *m*.

(**b**) (*) comida *f*; **~ up!** ¡la comida está servida!, ¡a comer!

2 *vi*: **to ~ about in the earth for sth** remover la tierra buscando algo.

◆**grub up** *vt* arrancar, desarraigar; (*discover*) desenterrar.

grubbiness ['grʌbɪnɪs] *n* suciedad *f*.

grubby ['grʌbɪ] *adj* sucio, mugriento.

grudge [grʌdʒ] **1** *n* (motivo *m* de) rencor *m*; **to bear sb a ~, to have a ~ against sb** tener inquina a uno, guardar rencor a uno.

2 *vt* (**a**) (*give unwillingly*) escatimar, dar de mala gana.

(**b**) (*envy*) envidiar; **I don't ~ you your success** no te envidio tu éxito; **he ~s us our pleasures** mira con malos ojos nuestros placeres.

grudging ['grʌdʒɪŋ] *adj praise etc* poco generoso; **with ~ admiration** admirándolo a pesar de sí.

grudgingly ['grʌdʒɪŋlɪ] *adv* de mala gana.

gruel [grʊəl] *n* gachas *fpl*.

gruelling, (*US*) **grueling** ['grʊəlɪŋ] *adj* duro, penoso; *match etc* muy reñido.

gruesome ['gru:səm] *adj* horrible, horripilante.

gruff [grʌf] *adj voice* bronco; *manner* brusco, malhumorado.

gruffly ['grʌflɪ] *adv* bruscamente.

grumble ['grʌmbl] **1** *n* queja *f*; (*noise*) ruido *m* sordo, estruendo *m* lejano.

2 *vi* refunfuñar, quejarse; (*thunder etc*) retumbar a lo lejos; **to ~ about, to ~ at** quejarse de, murmurar de, protestar de.

grumbling ['grʌmblɪŋ] **1** *n*: **I couldn't stand his constant ~** no podía soportar su constante regruñir. **2** *adj person* gruñón, refunfuñón; **~ sound** gruñido *m*; **~ appendix** falsa apendicitis *f*.

grumpily* ['grʌmpɪlɪ] *adv* gruñonamente, malhumoradamente.

grumpiness* ['grʌmpɪnɪs] *n* mal humor *m*.

grumpy* ['grʌmpɪ] *adj* gruñón, malhumorado.

grunt [grʌnt] **1** *n* gruñido *m*. **2** *vt reply etc* decir gruñendo. **3** *vi* gruñir.

gruppetto [gru:'petəʊ] *n* grupeto *m*.

gr. wt. *abbr of* **gross weight** peso *m* bruto.

gryphon ['grɪfən] *n* = **griffin**.

GSA *n* (*US*) *abbr of* **General Services Administration**.

GSUSA *n* (*US*) *abbr of* **Girl Scouts of the United States of America**.

GT *n abbr of* **gran turismo** GT.

GU (*US Post*) *abbr of* **Guam**.

Guadeloupe [,gwɑ:də'lu:p] *n* Guadalupe *f*.

guano ['gwɑ:nəʊ] *n* guano *m*.

guarantee [,gærən'ti:] **1** *n* garantía *f*; **there is no ~ that ...** no es seguro que + *subj*; **it is under ~** está bajo garantía; **I give you my ~** se lo aseguro.

2 *vt* garantizar (*against* contra, *for 3 months* por 3 meses); (*ensure*) asegurar; (*make o.s. responsible for*) responder de; **I ~ that ...** les aseguro que ..., les prometo que ...; **I can't ~ good weather** no puedo garantizar el buen tiempo.

guaranteed [,gærən'ti:d] *adj* garantizado; asegurado, seguro; **~ bonus** bonificación *f* garantizada; **~ loan** préstamo *m* garantizado; **~ prices** precios *mpl* garantizados.

guarantor [,gærən'tɔ:ʳ] *n* garante *mf*, fiador *m*, -ora *f*; **to act** (*or* **stand**) **as ~ for sb** actuar de fiador para uno.

guaranty ['gærəntɪ] *n* (*Fin*) garantía *f*, caución *f*; (*agreement*) garantía *f*.

guard [gɑ:d] **1** *n* (**a**) (*Mil duty, Fencing*) guardia *f*; (*safeguard*) resguardo *m*; **to be on ~** estar de guardia; **on ~!** ¡en guardia!; **to be on one's ~** estar alerta, estar sobre aviso, estar prevenido (*against* contra); **to be off one's ~** estar desprevenido; **to catch sb off his ~** coger (*LAm*: agarrar) a uno desprevenido; **to be under ~** estar bajo guardia; **to drop** (*or* **lower**) **one's ~** bajar la guardia, descuidarse; **to keep ~** vigilar; **to mount ~** montar (la) guardia; **to put sb on his ~** poner a uno en guardia, prevenir a uno (*against* contra); **to stand ~ over sth** montar la guardia sobre algo.

(**b**) (*of sword*) guarda *f*, guarnición *f*.

(**c**) (*regiment, squad of men*) guardia *f*; **he's one of the old ~** es uno de los viejos; **to change ~** relevar la guardia.

(**d**) (*person*) (*soldier*) guardia *m*; (*sentry*) centinela *m*; (*escort*) escolta *f*; (*security ~*) guarda *m* jurado; (*Brit Rail*) jefe *m* de tren.

2 *attr*: **~ duty** guardia *f* de turno.

3 *vt place etc* guardar, proteger, defender (*against, from* de); *person* vigilar, (*while travelling*) escoltar.

◆**guard against** *vt* guardarse de, precaverse de (*or* contra); (*prevent*) impedir, estorbar, evitar; **in order to ~ against this** para evitar esto.

guard dog ['gɑ:d,dɒg] *n* perro *m* guardián.

guarded ['gɑ:dɪd] *adj* cauteloso, circunspecto.

guardedly ['gɑ:dɪdlɪ] *adv* cautelosamente, con circunspección.

guardhouse ['gɑ:dhaʊs] *n*, *pl* **guardhouses** ['gɑ:d,haʊzɪz] cuartel *m* de la guardia; cárcel *f* militar.

guardian ['gɑ:dɪən] **1** *n* (**a**) protector *m*, -ora *f*, guardián *m*, -ana *f*. (**b**) (*Jur*) tutor *m*, -ora *f*. **2** *attr*: **~ angel** ángel *m* custodio, ángel *m* de la guarda.

guardrail ['gɑ:dreɪl] *n* pretil *m*.

guardroom ['gɑ:drʊm] *n* cuarto *m* de guardia.

guardsman ['gɑ:dzmən] *n*, *pl* **guardsmen** ['gɑ:dzmən] (*Brit*) soldado *m* de la guardia real; (*US*) guardia *m* (nacional).

guard's-van ['gɑ:dzvæn] *n* (*Brit*) furgón *m*.

Guatemala [,gwɑ:tɪ'mɑ:lə] *n* Guatemala *f*.

Guatemalan [,gwɑ:tɪ'mɑ:lən] **1** *adj* guatemalteco. **2** *n* guatemalteco *m*, -a *f*.

guava ['gwɑːvə] *n* guayaba *f*.
Guayana [gaɪ'ɑːnə] *n* Guayana *f*.
gubbins* ['gʌbɪnz] *n* (*Brit*) (**a**) (*thing*) chisme *m*, cacharro* *m*. (**b**) (*silly person*) bobo *m*, -a *f*.
gubernatorial [ˌguːbənə'tɔːrɪəl] *adj* (*esp US*) de(l) gobernador; ~ **election** elección *f* de gobernador.
gudgeon¹ ['gʌdʒən] *n* (*Fish*) gobio *m*.
gudgeon² ['gʌdʒən] *n* (*Tech*) gorrón *m*; cuello *m* de eje.
Guernsey ['gɜːnzɪ] *n* Guernesey *m*.
guerrilla [gə'rɪlə] **1** *n* guerrillero *m*, -a *f*. **2** *attr*: ~ **band** guerrilla *f*; ~ **warfare** guerra *f* de guerrilleros.
guess [ges] **1** *n* conjetura *f*, suposición *f*; estimación *f* aproximada; **at a** ~ a poco más o menos; **my** ~ **is that ...** yo conjeturo que ..., imagino que ...; **it's anybody's** ~ **whether** cualquiera sabe si; **your** ~ **is as good as mine!** ¡vaya Vd a saber!, lo mismo me lo pregunto yo; **have a** ~, **I'll give you 3** ~**es** a ver si lo adivinas.
2 *vti* (**a**) adivinar, conjeturar, suponer; **to** ~ **right** acertar; ~ **what!** ¿sabes lo que pasa?; ~ **who!** ¡a ver si adivinas quién soy!, ¿me conoces?; **you'll never** ~ no lo adivinarás nunca; **you've** ~**ed it!** has acertado, estás en lo cierto; **I** ~**ed as much** ya lo suponía; **I** ~**ed him to be about 20** le daba unos 20 años; **all that time we never** ~**ed** en todo el tiempo no lo sospechábamos; **I never** ~**ed it was so big** no lo suponía nunca tan grande; **to keep sb** ~**ing** tener a uno en suspenso; **to** ~ **at** conjeturar, (tratar de) estimar aproximadamente.
(**b**) (*esp US*) creer, imaginar, suponer; **I** ~ **we'll buy it** me imagino que lo compraremos; **I** ~ **so** creo que sí; así será sin duda.
guessing game ['gesɪŋˌgeɪm] *n* acertijo *m*, adivinanza *f*.
guesstimate* ['gestɪmɪt] *n* estimación *f* aproximada.
guesswork ['geswɜːk] *n* conjeturas *fpl*; **it's all** ~ son meras conjeturas.
guest [gest] **1** *n* convidado *m*, -a *f*, invitado *m*, -a *f*; (*at hotel etc, lodger*) huésped *m*, -eda *f*; ~ **of honour** agasajado *m*, -a *f*; invitado *m*, -a *f* de honor; **be my** ~ (*have a drink etc*) invito yo, ¡te invito!; (*please use it*) está a tu disposición; **we were their** ~**s last summer** pasamos un rato en casa de ellos el verano pasado.
2 *attr*: ~ **artist(e)** = **guest-star**; ~ **book** libro *m* de los huéspedes; ~ **speaker** orador *m* invitado, oradora *f* invitada.
3 *vi* (*US*) aparecer como invitado.
guest-house ['gesthaʊs] *n*, *pl* **guest-houses** ['gestˌhaʊzɪz] casa *f* de huéspedes.
guest-room ['gestrʊm] *n* cuarto *m* de huéspedes.
guest-star ['geststɑːʳ] *n* estrella *f* invitada.
guff‡ [gʌf] *n* música *f* celestial.
guffaw [gʌ'fɔː] **1** *n* risotada *f*, carcajada *f*. **2** *vi* reírse a carcajadas.
Guiana [gaɪ'ɑːnə] *n* Guayana *f*.
guidance ['gaɪdəns] *n* (*control*) dirección *f*, gobierno *m*; (*advice*) consejos *mpl*; orientación *f*; **under the** ~ **of** bajo la dirección de; **I tell you this for your** ~ te lo digo para tu gobierno.
guide [gaɪd] **1** *n* (**a**) (*person*) guía *mf*; (*girl* ~) exploradora *f*, muchacha-guía *f*. (**b**) (*book, Mech, fig*) guía *f*. **2** *vt* guiar; orientar; conducir; (*govern*) dirigir, gobernar.
guidebook ['gaɪdbʊk] *n* guía *f* (del turista *etc*).
guided ['gaɪdɪd] *adj*: ~ **missile** misil *m* teledirigido; ~ **tour** excursión *f* con guía.
guide-dog ['gaɪdˌdɒg] *n* perro-guía *m*.
guideline ['gaɪdlaɪn] *n* línea *f* directriz, pauta *f*; (*for writing*) falsilla *f*.
guidepost ['gaɪdpəʊst] *n* poste *m* indicador.
guiding ['gaɪdɪŋ] *adj*: ~ **principle** principio *m* director; ~ **star** estrella *f* de guía.
guild [gɪld] *n* gremio *m*, cofradía *f*, asociación *f* benéfica.
guilder ['gɪldəʳ] *n* florín *m* (holandés).
guildhall ['gɪldˌhɔːl] *n* ayuntamiento *m*, casa *f* consistorial.
guile [gaɪl] *n* astucia *f*, maña *f*.
guileful ['gaɪlfʊl] *adj* astuto, mañoso.
guileless ['gaɪllɪs] *adj* inocente, candoroso.
guillemot ['gɪlɪmɒt] *n* arao *m*.
guillotine [ˌgɪlə'tiːn] **1** *n* guillotina *f*. **2** *vt* guillotinar.
guilt [gɪlt] *n* culpa *f*, culpabilidad *f*; ~ **complex** complejo *m* de culpabilidad; **to admit one's** ~ confesarse culpable.
guiltily ['gɪltɪlɪ] *adv*: **he said** ~ dijo como confesándose culpable; **he looked round** ~ volvió la cabeza como si fuera culpable.
guiltless ['gɪltlɪs] *adj* inocente, libre de culpa (*of* de).
guilty ['gɪltɪ] *adj* (**a**) (*Jur etc*) culpable (*of* de); **verdict of** ~ sentencia *f* de culpabilidad; **to find sb** ~ declarar culpable a uno; **to find sb not** ~ declarar inocente a uno; **to plead** ~ confesarse culpable; **to plead not** ~ negar la acusación; **'not** ~**', he replied** 'soy inocente', contestó.
(**b**) *look* lleno de confusión; *conscience* lleno de remordimiento; *thought* pecaminoso, criminal.
Guinea ['gɪnɪ] *n* Guinea *f*.
guinea ['gɪnɪ] *n* (*Brit*) guinea *f* (= *21 chelines*).
Guinea-Bissau ['gɪnɪbɪ'saʊ] *n* Guinea-Bissau *f*.
guinea-fowl ['gɪnɪfaʊl] *n* gallina *f* de Guinea, pintada *f*.
guinea-pig ['gɪnɪpɪg] *n* cobayo *m*, conejillo *m* de Indias; (*fig*) cobayo *m*.
Guinevere ['gwɪnɪvɪəʳ] *nf* Ginebra.
guise [gaɪz] *n*: **in that** ~ de esa manera; **under the** ~ **of** bajo el disfraz de; so capa de.
guitar [gɪ'tɑːʳ] *n* guitarra *f*.
guitarist [gɪ'tɑːrɪst] *n* guitarrista *mf*; (*electric* ~) guitarrero *m*, -a *f*.
gulch [gʌlʃ] *n* (*US*) barranco *m*.
gulf [gʌlf] **1** *n* golfo *m*; (*also fig*) abismo *m*, sima *f*; **the G**~ el Golfo (Pérsico); **G**~ **of Suez** Golfo *m* de Suez. **2** *attr*: **G**~ **States** Estados *mpl* del Golfo (Pérsico); **G**~ **Stream** Corriente *f* del Golfo.
gull [gʌl] **1** *n* gaviota *f*. **2** *vt* estafar, timar.
gullet ['gʌlɪt] *n* esófago *m*; garganta *f*, gaznate *m*.
gullibility [ˌgʌlɪ'bɪlɪtɪ] *n* credulidad *f*, simpleza *f*.
gullible ['gʌlɪbl] *adj* crédulo, simplón.
gully ['gʌlɪ] *n* barranco *m*, torrentera *f*.
gulp [gʌlp] **1** *n* trago *m*, sorbo *m*; **at one** ~ de un trago; **'yes', he said with a** ~ 'sí', dijo tragando saliva.
2 *vt* (*also* **to** ~ **down**) tragarse, engullir.
3 *vi* tragar saliva.
gum¹ [gʌm] *n* (*Anat*) encía *f*.
gum² [gʌm] **1** *n* (*in general*) goma *f*; (*Brit*: *adhesive*) goma *f*, cola *f*, pegamento *m*, cemento *m* (*LAm*); (*chewing*) chicle *m*; ~ **arabic** goma *f* arábiga.
2 *vt* engomar, pegar con goma.
◆**gum up** *vt* (*fig*) estropear, paralizar, parar, inutilizar; **to** ~ **up the works** paralizar el mecanismo, (*fig*) estropearlo todo.
gum³ [gʌm] *interj*: **by** ~**!** ¡caramba!
gumboil ['gʌmbɔɪl] *n* flemón *m*.
gumboots ['gʌmbuːts] *npl* (*Brit*) botas *fpl* de agua.
gumdrop ['gʌmdrɒp] *n* pastilla *f* de goma.
gummed [gʌmd] *adj* engomado; ~ **envelope** sobre *m* engomado; ~ **label** etiqueta *f* engomada.
gummy ['gʌmɪ] *adj* gomoso.
gump* [gʌmp] *n* (**a**) (*sense*) sentido *m* común. (**b**) (*fool*) tonto *m*, imbécil *mf*.
gumption* ['gʌmpʃən] *n* (*Brit*) seso *m*, sentido *m* común.
gumshoe ['gʌmʃuː] *n* (*US*) (**a**) zapato *m* de goma. (**b**) (*) detective *m*.
gum-tree ['gʌmtriː] *n* árbol *m* gomero; eucalipto *m*; **to be up a** ~* (*Brit*) estar en un aprieto.
gun [gʌn] **1** *n* (**a**) (*gen*) arma *f* de fuego; (*artillery piece*) cañón *m*; (*shot*~) escopeta *f*; (*rifle*) fusil *m*; (*pistol*) revólver *m*, pistola *f*; **a 21** ~ **salute** una salva de 21 cañonazos; **the** ~**s** (*Mil*) la artillería; **big** ~* pez *m* gordo, espadón *m*; **to be going great** ~**s** hacer grandes progresos, ir a las mil maravillas; **to jump the** ~ salir antes de tiempo; (*fig*) obrar con anticipación, madrugar; **to stick to one's** ~**s** mantenerse en sus trece.
(**b**) (*Brit*: *person*) cazador *m*; escopeta *f*.
2 *vt* disparar sobre, atacar.
◆**gun down** *vt* abatir a tiros, abalear (*LAm*).
◆**gun for** *vt* andar a la caza de, perseguir; **it's really the boss they're** ~**ning for** en realidad esto va contra el jefe.
gun-battle ['gʌnˌbætl] *n* tiroteo *m*.
gunboat ['gʌnbəʊt] **1** *n* (*seagoing*) cañonero *m*; (*small*) lancha *f* cañonera. **2** *attr*: ~ **diplomacy** diplomacia *f* cañonera.
gun-carriage ['gʌnˌkærɪdʒ] *n* cureña *f*; (*at funeral*) armón *m* de artillería.
gun-cotton ['gʌnˌkɒtn] *n* algodón *m* pólvora.
gun-crew ['gʌnkruː] *n* dotación *f* de un cañón.
gun-dog ['gʌnˌdɒg] *n* perro *m* de caza.
gunfight ['gʌnfaɪt] *n* tiroteo *m*.
gunfire ['gʌnfaɪəʳ] *n* cañoneo *m*, fuego *m*; tiros *mpl*, tiroteo *m*.
gunge* [gʌndʒ] **1** *n* porquería *f* (viscosa). **2** *vt*: **to** ~ **up** atascar, obstruir.
gung-ho ['gʌŋ'həʊ] *adj* (**a**) (*over-enthusiastic*) (tontamente) optimista; (locamente) entusiasta; (ingenuamente) emprendedor. (**b**) (*jingoistic*) militarista; patriotero (con exceso); jingoísta.

gunk* [gʌŋk] *n* = **gunge**.
gun law [ˈgʌn,lɔː] *n* (**a**) (*rule by the gun*) ley *f* del terror, pistolerismo *m*. (**b**) (*Jur*) ley *f* que rige la tenencia y uso de armas de fuego.
gun licence [ˈgʌn,laɪsns] *n* licencia *f* de armas.
gun-maker [ˈgʌn,meɪkəʳ] *n* armero *m*.
gunman [ˈgʌnmən] *n*, *pl* **gunmen** [ˈgʌnmən] pistolero *m*, gángster *m*.
gunmetal [ˈgʌn,metl] *n* bronce *m* de cañón.
gunner [ˈgʌnəʳ] *n* artillero *m*.
gunnery [ˈgʌnərɪ] **1** *n* (**a**) (*art, skill, science*) tiro *m*, puntería *f*. (**b**) (*guns*) artillería *f*. **2** *attr*: ~ **officer** oficial *m* de artillería.
gunny [ˈgʌnɪ] *n* arpillera *f*; (*also* ~ **bag**, ~ **sack**) saco *m* de yute.
gunpoint [ˈgʌnpɔɪnt] *n*: **to hold sb at** ~ tener a uno cautivo a punta de pistola.
gunpowder [ˈgʌn,paʊdəʳ] **1** *n* pólvora *f*. **2** *attr*: **G~ Plot** (*Brit*) Conspiración *f* de la Pólvora.
gunroom [ˈgʌn,rʊm] *n* (*in house*) sala *f* de armas; (*Brit Naut*) sala *f* de suboficiales.
gunrunner [ˈgʌn,rʌnəʳ] *n* contrabandista *m* de armas, traficante *m* de armas.
gunrunning [ˈgʌn,rʌnɪŋ] *n* contrabando *m* de armas.
gunship [ˈgʌnʃɪp] *n* helicóptero *m* de combate, helicóptero *m* artillado.
gunshot [ˈgʌnʃɒt] *n* cañonazo *m*; tiro *m*, disparo *m*; escopetazo *m*; ~ **wound** escopetazo *m*; **within** ~ a tiro de fusil.
gunsmith [ˈgʌnsmɪθ] *n* armero *m*.
gun-turret [ˈgʌn,tʌrɪt] *n* torreta *f*.
gunwale [ˈgʌnl] *n* borde *m*, regala *f*.
gurgle [ˈgɜːgl] **1** *n* (*of liquid*) gorgoteo *m*, gluglú *m*; (*baby's*) gorjeo *m*. **2** *vi* gorgotear, hacer gluglú; gorjear.
guru [ˈgʊruː] *n* guru *m*.
Gus [gʌs] *nm familiar form of* **Angus, Augustus**.
gush [gʌʃ] **1** *n* (**a**) (*of liquid*) chorro *m*, borbotón *m*; (*of words*) torrente *m*.
(**b**) (*fig*) efusión *f*; sentimentalismo *m*; afectación *f*.
2 *vt blood etc* chorrear, derramar a borbollones.
3 *vi* (**a**) (*liquid*) chorrear, borbotar, salir a borbollones (*from* de).
(**b**) (*person*) hacer extremos.
◆**gush over** *vt* hablar con efusión de, extasiarse ante.
gusher [ˈgʌʃəʳ] *n* (**a**) (*oilwell*) pozo *m* surtido. (**b**) **to be a** ~ (*person*) ser muy efusivo.
gushing [ˈgʌʃɪŋ] *adj* efusivo.
gusset [ˈgʌsɪt] *n* escudete *m*.
gust [gʌst] **1** *n* ráfaga *f*, racha *f*. **2** *vi* soplar racheado; **the wind ~ed up to 120 k.p.h.** hubo rachas de hasta 120 km/h.
gusto [ˈgʌstəʊ] *n* entusiasmo *m*; **with** ~ con entusiasmo.
gusty [ˈgʌstɪ] *adj* borrascoso; *wind* racheado.
gut [gʌt] **1** *n* (**a**) (*Anat*) intestino *m*, tripa *f*; (*string*) cuerda *f* de tripa; **to bust a** ~‡ echar los bofes; **I'll have his ~s for garters!**‡ ¡le despachurro las narices!; **I hate his ~s**‡ no lo puedo ver ni en pintura; **to spill one's ~s**‡ contar la propia vida y milagros; **to work one's ~s out** echar los bofes.
(**b**) **~s** (*Anat*) tripas *fpl*; (*fig*) (*content*) meollo *m*, sustancia *f*; (*pluck*) valor *m*; (*staying power*) aguante *m*, resistencia *f*; (*moral strength*) carácter *m*; **to have ~s** tener agallas*.
(**c**) (*Naut*) estrecho *m*.
2 *adj*: ~ **feeling** instinto *m* visceral; ~ **reaction** reacción *f* visceral.
3 *vt animal* destripar; (*of fire etc*) destruir el interior de.
gutless* [ˈgʌtlɪs] *adj* cobarde; debilucho, sin carácter.
gutsy* [ˈgʌtsɪ] *adj* valiente; atrevido; vigoroso.
gutta-percha [ˈgʌtəˈpɜːtʃə] *n* gutapercha *f*.
gutter¹ [ˈgʌtəʳ] *n* (*in street*) arroyo *m*, cuneta *f*, desagüe *m* (*CAm*); (*on roof*) canal *m*, canalón *m*, gotera *f*; **the** ~ (*fig*) los barrios bajos, (*criminal*) el hampa; **he rose from the** ~ (*fig*) salió de la nada.
gutter² [ˈgʌtəʳ] *vi* (*candle*) irse consumiendo.
guttering [ˈgʌtərɪŋ] *n* canales *mpl*, canalones *mpl*.
gutter-press [ˈgʌtəˈpres] *n* prensa *f* sensacionalista, prensa *f* amarilla.
guttersnipe [ˈgʌtəsnaɪp] *n* golfillo *m*.
guttural [ˈgʌtərəl] *adj* gutural.
guv [gʌv] *n* (= **governor**): **thanks, ~!** ¡gracias, jefe!
Guy [gaɪ] *nm* Guido; ~ **Fawkes Day** (*Brit*) *5 de noviembre, aniversario de la Conspiración de la Pólvora.*
guy¹ [gaɪ] **1** *n* mamarracho *m*; (*esp US**) tío* *m*, individuo *m*, tipo* *m*; **he's a nice** ~ es un buen chico; **hey, (you) ~s!** ¡eh, amigos!; **are you ~s ready to go?** ¿están todos listos para salir?
2 *vt* ridiculizar; (*Theat etc*) parodiar.
guy² [gaɪ] *n*, **guy-rope** [ˈgaɪrəʊp] *n* viento *m*, cuerda *f*.
Guyana [gaɪˈænə] *n* Guayana *f*.
Guyanese [,gaɪəˈniːz] **1** *adj* guyanés. **2** *n* guyanés *m*, -esa *f*.
guzzle [ˈgʌzl] *vt* tragarse, engullir.
guzzler [ˈgʌzləʳ] *n* trágon *m*, -ona *f*, comilón *m*, -ona *f*; *V* **gas**.
gym* [dʒɪm] *n* gimnasio *m*.
gymkhana [dʒɪmˈkɑːnə] *n* (*esp Brit*) gincana *f*.
gymnasium [dʒɪmˈneɪzɪəm] *n*, *pl* **gimnasia** [dʒɪmˈneɪzɪə] gimnasio *m*.
gymnast [ˈdʒɪmnæst] *n* gimnasta *mf*.
gymnastic [dʒɪmˈnæstɪk] *adj* gimnástico.
gymnastics [dʒɪmˈnæstɪks] *n sing and pl* gimnasia *f*.
gymshoes [ˈdʒɪmʃuːz] *npl* zapatillas *fpl* deportivas.
gymslip [ˈdʒɪmslɪp] *n* (*Brit*) túnica *f* de gimnasia.
gynaecological, (*US*) **gynecological** [,gaɪnɪkəˈlɒdʒɪkəl] *adj* ginecológico.
gynaecologist, (*US*) **gynecologist** [,gaɪnɪˈkɒlədʒɪst] *n* ginecólogo *m*, -a *f*.
gynaecology, (*US*) **gynecology** [,gaɪnɪˈkɒlədʒɪ] *n* ginecología *f*.
gyp¹‡ [dʒɪp] (*US*) **1** *n* (**a**) estafa *f*, timo *m*. (**b**) (*person*) estafador *m*, timador *m*. **2** *vt* estafar, timar.
gyp²‡ [dʒɪp] *n* (*Brit*): **to give sb** ~ echar un rapapolvo de aúpa a uno; poner a uno como un trapo; **it's giving me** ~ me duele una barbaridad.
gypsum [ˈdʒɪpsəm] *n* yeso *m*.
gypsy [ˈdʒɪpsɪ] *n* (*esp US*) = **gipsy**.
gyrate [dʒaɪˈreɪt] *vi* girar.
gyration [,dʒaɪˈreɪʃən] *n* giro *m*, vuelta *f*.
gyratory [,dʒaɪˈreɪtərɪ] *adj* giratorio.
gyro... [ˈdʒaɪrəʊ] *pref* giro...
gyrocompass [ˈdʒaɪrəʊˈkʌmpəs] *n* girocompás *m*.
gyroscope [ˈdʒaɪrəskəʊp] *n* giróscopo *m*.

H

H, h [eɪtʃ] *n* (*letter*) H, h *f*; **H for Harry, H for How** (*US*) H de Historia.
H⁑ [eɪtʃ] *n* caballo⁑ *m*, heroína *f*.
h. *abbr of* **hour(s)** hora(s) *f*(*pl*), h.
h. & c. *abbr of* **hot and cold water** con agua corriente caliente y fría.
ha [hɑː] *interj* ¡ah!
habeas corpus [ˈheɪbɪəsˈkɔːpəs] *n* hábeas corpus *m*.
haberdasher [ˈhæbədæʃə(r)] *n* (*Brit*) mercero *m*, -a *f*, (*US*) camisero *m*, -a *f*; **~'s (shop)** mercería *f*, (*US*) camisería *f*.
haberdashery [ˌhæbəˈdæʃərɪ] *n* (*Brit*) mercería *f*, (*US*) prendas *fpl* de caballero.
habit [ˈhæbɪt] *n* (**a**) (*custom*) costumbre *f*, hábito *m*; **bad ~** vicio *m*, mala costumbre *f*; **from ~, out of sheer ~** por costumbre; **to be in the ~ of** + *ger* acostumbrar + *infin*, soler + *infin*; **to get into the ~ of** + *ger* acostumbrarse a + *infin*; **to get out of the ~ of** + *ger* perder la costumbre de + *infin*; dejar de + *infin*; **to have a ~*** (*drugs*) drogarse habitualmente; **to make a ~ of sth** aficionarse a algo; **let's hope he doesn't make a ~ of it** esperamos que no siga haciéndolo; **to make a ~ of** + *ger* adquirir la costumbre de + *infin*. (**b**) (*dress*) hábito *m*.
habitable [ˈhæbɪtəbl] *adj* habitable.
habitat [ˈhæbɪtæt] *n* hábitat *m*, habitación *f*.
habitation [ˌhæbɪˈteɪʃən] *n* habitación *f*.
habit-forming [ˈhæbɪtˌfɔːmɪŋ] *adj* que conduce al hábito morboso.
habitual [həˈbɪtjʊəl] *adj* habitual, acostumbrado, usual; *drunkard, liar etc* inveterado, empedernido.
habitually [həˈbɪtjʊəlɪ] *adv* por costumbre; constantemente.
habituate [həˈbɪtjʊeɪt] *vt* acostumbrar, habituar (*to* a).
habitué(e) [həˈbɪtjʊeɪ] *n* asiduo *m*, -a *f*, parroquiano *m*, -a *f*.
hacienda [ˌhæsɪˈendə] *n* (*US*) hacienda *f*.
hack[1] [hæk] **1** *n* (*blow, cut*) corte *m*, hachazo *m*, tajo *m*; (*kick*) puntapié *m* (en la espinilla); (*dent*) mella *f*.
2 *vt* (**a**) (*with knife etc*) cortar, acuchillar, tajar; (*dent*) mellar; **to ~ sb on the shin** dar a uno un puntapié en la espinilla; **to ~ sth to pieces** cortar algo en pedazos (violentamente, despiadadamente *etc*); **to ~ an army to pieces** destrozar un ejército; **to ~ one's way through sth** abrirse paso por algo a fuerza de tajos.
(**b**) **I can't ~ it** (*US*) no puedo hacerlo.
3 *vi* (**a**) **to ~ at** tirar tajos a. (**b**) (*Comput*) **to ~ into a system** piratear un sistema.
◆**hack around*** *vi* (*US*) gandulear, vaguear.
◆**hack down** *vt* derribar a hachazos *etc*.
hack[2] [hæk] **1** *n* (**a**) (*Brit*) (*hired horse*) caballo *m* de alquiler; (*bad horse*) rocín *m*. (**b**) (*writer*) escritorzuelo *m*, -a *f*, plumífero *m*, -a *f*; (*journalist*) periodista *mf*, gacetillero *m*, -a *f*. (**c**) (*US**) taxi *m*.
2 *attr*: **to be a ~ reporter** ser un reportero del tres al cuatro; **~ writer** = **1** (**b**).
3 *adj* = **hackneyed.**
4 *vi* montar (a caballo).
hackberry [ˈhækberɪ] *n* almez *m*.
hacker [ˈhækə(r)] *n* (*Comput*) (*enthusiast*) computomaníaco *m*, -a *f*; (*pirate*) pirata *m* informático, pirata *f* informática, intruso *m* informático, intrusa *f* informática.
hackery* [ˈhækərɪ] *n* (**a**) = **hackwork.** (**b**) = **hacking[3]**.
hackette* [hæˈket] *n* periodista *f*.
hacking[1] [ˈhækɪŋ] *adj cough* seco.
hacking[2] [ˈhækɪŋ] *adj*: **~ jacket** (*Brit*) chaqueta *f* de montar.
hacking[3] [ˈhækɪŋ] *n*: **computer ~** piratería *f* informática, intrusión *f* informática.
hackle [ˈhækl] *n*: **with his ~s up** encolerizado; dispuesto a luchar; **to make sb's ~s rise** encolerizar a uno, provocar a uno, poner los pelos de punta a uno.
hackney cab [ˈhæknɪˈkæb] *n*, **hackney carriage** [ˈhæknɪˈkærɪdʒ] *n* coche *m* de alquiler.
hackneyed [ˈhæknɪd] *adj* trillado, gastado.
hacksaw [ˈhæksɔː] *n* sierra *f* para metales.
hackwork [ˈhækwɜːk] *n* trabajo *m* de rutina; trabajo *m* de poca originalidad; (*iro*) periodismo *m*.
had [hæd] *pret and ptp of* **have.**
haddock [ˈhædək] *n* eglefino *m*, merlango *m*.
Hades [ˈheɪdiːz] *n* infierno *m*.
hadn't [ˈhædnt] = **had not.**
Hadrian [ˈheɪdrɪən] *nm* Adriano; **~'s Wall** Muralla *f* de Adriano.
haematological, (*US*) **hematological** [ˌhiːmətəˈlɒdʒɪkəl] *adj* hematológico.
haematologist, (*US*) **hematologist** [ˌhiːməˈtɒlədʒɪst] *n* hematólogo *m*, -a *f*.
haematology, (*US*) **hematology** [ˌhiːməˈtɒlədʒɪ] *n* hematología *f*.
haemoglobin, (*US*) **hemoglobin** [ˌhiːməʊˈgləʊbɪn] *n* hemoglobina *f*.
haemophilia, (*US*) **hemophilia** [ˌhiːməʊˈfɪlɪə] *n* hemofilia *f*.
haemophiliac, (*US*) **hemophiliac** [ˌhiːməʊˈfɪlɪæk] **1** *adj* hemofílico. **2** *n* hemofílico *m*, -a *f*.
haemorrhage, (*US*) **hemorrhage** [ˈhemərɪdʒ] **1** *n* hemorragia *f*. **2** *vi* sangrar.
haemorrhoids, (*US*) **hemorrhoids** [ˈhemərɔɪdz] *npl* hemorroides *fpl*.
hafnium [ˈhæfnɪəm] *n* hafnio *m*.
haft [hɑːft] *n* mango *m*, puño *m*.
hag [hæg] *n* bruja *f*.
haggard [ˈhægəd] *adj* ojeroso, trasnochado.
haggis [ˈhægɪs] *n* (*Scot*) *estómago de cordero relleno con el hígado, el corazón y la lengua del animal, avena etc* (*plato escocés*).
haggish [ˈhægɪʃ] *adj* como de bruja, brujeril.
haggle [ˈhægl] *vi* (**a**) (*discuss*) discutir, disputar; **don't ~!** ¡no discutas! (**b**) (*in selling*) regatear; **to ~ about** (*or* **over**) **the price** regatear, regatear el precio.
haggling [ˈhæglɪŋ] *n* (**a**) (*discussion*) discusión *f*, disputa *f*. (**b**) (*over price*) regateo *m*.
hagiographer [ˌhægɪˈɒgrəfə(r)] *n* hagiógrafo *m*, -a *f*.
hagiography [ˌhægɪˈɒgrəfɪ] *n* hagiografía *f*.
hag-ridden [ˈhægrɪdn] *adj* atormentado por una pesadilla; (*) dominado por una mujer.
Hague [heɪg] *n*: **The ~** La Haya.
ha-ha [ˈhɑːˈhɑː] *interj* ¡ja, ja!
hail[1] [heɪl] (*Met*) **1** *n* granizo *m*, pedrisco *m*; **a ~ of bullets** una lluvia de balas. **2** *vi* granizar.
◆**hail down** *vt* (*fig*) llover.
hail[2] [heɪl] **1** *n* (*shout*) grito *m*; (*greeting*) saludo *m*; **~!** ¡hola!, (*poet*) ¡salve!; **H~ Mary** Ave María *f*; Dios te salve, María; **to be within ~** estar al alcance de la voz.
2 *vt* (**a**) (*call to*) llamar a, gritar a; (*greet*) saludar; **within ~ing distance** al habla, al alcance de la voz.
(**b**) (*acknowledge*) aclamar (*as king* rey).
3 *vi*: **to ~ from** ser natural de, ser de.
hail-fellow-well-met [ˈheɪlˌfeləʊˈwelˈmet] *adj* (demasiado) efusivo, campechano.
hailstone [ˈheɪlstəʊn] *n* granizo *m*, piedra *f* (de granizo).
hailstorm [ˈheɪlstɔːm] *n* granizada *f*, granizal *m* (*And*).
hair [hɛə(r)] **1** *n* (**a**) (*one ~*) pelo *m*, cabello *m*; **~'s breadth** (ancho *m* de un) pelo *m*; **to escape by a ~'s breadth** escapar por un pelo; **to be within a ~'s breadth of** estar a dos dedos de; **to split ~s** pararse en cosas nimias, hilar muy delgado; **he didn't turn a ~** no se inmutó, ni siquiera pestañeó.
(**b**) (*head of ~*) pelo *m*, cabello *m*, cabellera *f*; (*on legs etc*) vello *m*; **grey ~, white ~** canas *fpl*; **long ~** melena *f*; **to comb one's ~** peinarse; **to do one's ~, to have one's ~**

done arreglarse el pelo; **keep your ~ on!*** (*Brit*) ¡cálmate!; **to let one's ~ down** (*fig*) (*celebrate*) echar una cana al aire, (*talk freely*) sincerarse, entrar en el terreno de las confidencias; **to part one's ~** hacerse la raya; **this will put ~s on your chest!*** ¡esto te hará la mar de bien!*; **it was enough to make your ~ stand on end** era espeluznante; **to tear one's ~** mesarse el pelo, (*fig*) rasgarse las vestiduras.

2 *attr*: **to have/make a ~ appointment** tener/pedir hora en la peluquería; **~ follicle** folículo *m* capilar; **~ implant** implante *m* capilar; **~ transplant** trasplante *m* capilar.

hairband ['hɛəbænd] *n* cinta *f*.

hairbrush ['hɛəbrʌʃ] *n* cepillo *m* para el pelo.

hair-clip ['hɛəklɪp] *n* horquilla *f*, clipe *m*.

hair-clippers ['hɛə,klɪpəz] *npl* maquinilla *f* para cortar el pelo.

hair-conditioner ['hɛəkən,dɪʃənəʳ] *n* suavizante *m* de cabello.

haircream ['hɛəkriːm] *n* brillantina *f*; fijador *m*, laca *f*.

hair-curler ['hɛə,kɜːləʳ] *n* chicho *m*, rulo *m*, bigudí *m*.

haircut ['hɛəkʌt] *n* corte *m* de pelo; **to get** (*or* **have**) **a ~** hacerse cortar el pelo.

hairdo ['hɛəduː] *n* peinado *m*.

hairdresser ['hɛə,dresəʳ] *n* peluquero *m*, -a *f*; **~'s** (**shop** *or* **salon**) peluquería *f*.

hairdressing ['hɛədresɪŋ] **1** *n* peluquería *f*. **2** *attr*: **~ salon** salón *m* de peluquería.

hair-drier, hair-dryer ['hɛədraɪəʳ] *n* secador *m* de pelo.

-haired [hɛəd] *adj* de pelo ..., *eg* **fair~** pelirrubio; **long~** de pelo largo, melenudo.

hair-grip ['hɛəgrɪp] *n* (*Brit*) horquilla *f*, clipe *m*.

hairless ['hɛəlɪs] *adj* sin pelo, pelón, calvo; (*beardless*) lampiño.

hairline ['hɛəlaɪn] **1** *n* límite *m* del pelo; (*in writing*) rayita *f*; (*Tech*) estría *f* muy delgada; **with a receding ~** con acusadas entradas capilares.

2 *attr*: **~ crack, ~ fracture** grieta *f* muy fina, grieta *f* casi imperceptible.

hairnet ['hɛənet] *n* redecilla *f*.

hair-oil ['hɛərɔɪl] *n* brillantina *f*.

hairpiece ['hɛəpiːs] *n* postizo *m*, tupé *m*; trenza *f* postiza.

hairpin ['hɛəpɪn] **1** *n* horquilla *f*. **2** *attr*: **~ bend** (*Brit*), **~ curve** curva *f* en horquilla.

hair-raising ['hɛə,reɪzɪŋ] *adj* espeluznante.

hair-remover ['hɛərɪ,muːvəʳ] *n* depilatorio *m*.

hair-restorer ['hɛərɪ,stɔːrəʳ] *n* regenerador *m* del pelo, loción *f* capilar.

hair shirt [,hɛə'ʃɜːt] *n* cilicio *m*.

hair-slide ['hɛəslaɪd] *n* (*Brit*) pasador *m*.

hair specialist ['hɛə,speʃəlɪst] *n* especialista *mf* capilar.

hair-splitting ['hɛə,splɪtɪŋ] **1** *adj* nimio; *discussion* sobre detalles nimios.

2 *n* sofismas *mpl*, sofistería *f*.

hairspray ['hɛəspreɪ] *n* laca *f* (para el pelo).

hairspring ['hɛəsprɪŋ] *n* muelle *m* espiral muy fino (de un reloj).

hair style ['hɛəstaɪl] *n* peinado *m*.

hair stylist ['hɛə,staɪlɪst] *n* peluquero *m*, -a *f* estilista.

hairy ['hɛərɪ] *adj* (**a**) peludo, velloso. (**b**) (*) *experience* horripilante, espeluznante; *problem* peliagudo.

Haiti ['heɪtɪ] *n* Haití *m*.

Haitian ['heɪʃɪən] **1** *adj* haitiano. **2** *n* haitiano *m*, -a *f*.

hake [heɪk] *n* (*Brit*) merluza *f*.

halcyon ['hælsɪən] *adj*: **~ days** días *mpl* felices.

hale [heɪl] *adj* sano, robusto; **~ and hearty** sano y fuerte.

half [hɑːf] *n*, *pl* **halves** [hɑːvz] **1** *n* (**a**) (*quantity*) mitad *f*; (*Brit*: **~ pint**) media pinta *f*; **~ and ~** mitad y mitad; **my better ~, my other ~** mi cara mitad, la media naranja; **by ~** (*fig*) con mucho; **better by ~** con mucho el mejor; **to be too clever by ~** pasarse de listo; **it has increased by ~** ha aumentado en la mitad; **to do sth by halves** hacer algo a medias; **to go halves with sb** ir a medias con uno; **to cut sth in ~** cortar algo en dos mitades; **they don't know the ~ of it** no saben de la misa la media; **we have a problem and a ~** tenemos un problema mayúsculo, vaya problemazo que tenemos.

(**b**) (*Sport*: *person*) medio *m*, -a *f*.

(**c**) (*Sport*: *period*) tiempo *m*; **first/second ~** primer/segundo tiempo *m*.

2 *adj* medio; **~ an orange** media naranja; **a pound and a ~, one and a ~ pounds** libra *f* y media; **3 and a ~ hours, 3 hours and a ~** 3 horas y media; **~ past 4** las 4 y media; **come at ~ 3*** ven a las 3 y media; **~ a moment!, ~ a second!** ¡un momento!

3 *adv* (**a**) medio, a medias, semi ...; casi; **~ asleep** medio dormido, dormido a medias, semidormido; **~ done** a medio hacer; **~ laughing, ~ crying** medio riendo, medio llorando; **I only ~ read it** lo leí sólo a medias; **he ~ got up** se levantó a medias; **it cost only ~ as much** costó la mitad nada más; **there were only ~ as many people as before** había solamente la mitad de los que había antes; **they paid ~ as much again** pagaron la mitad más.

(**b**) (*Brit*: *with* **not**) **it was not ~ as bad as I had thought** no era ni con mucho tan malo como me lo había imaginado; **he didn't ~ run*** corrió muchísimo; **it didn't ~ rain!*** ¡había que ver cómo llovía!; **it wasn't ~ dear*** nos resultó sumamente caro; **not ~!*** ¡y cómo!, ¡ya lo creo!

half-adder ['hɑːf'ædəʳ] *n* semisumador *m*.

half-a-dollar [,hɑːfə'dɒləʳ] *n* (*value*) medio dólar *m*.

half-a-dozen [,hɑːfə'dʌzən] *n* media docena *f*.

half-and-half [,hɑːfənd'hɑːf] *adv* mitad y mitad.

half-an-hour [,hɑːfən'aʊəʳ] *n* media hora *f*.

half-back ['hɑːfbæk] *n* medio *m*, -a *f*.

half-baked ['hɑːf'beɪkt] *adj* a medio cocer; (*fig*) *plan, idea* a medio cocer, mal concebido, mal pensado; *person* soso.

half-board [,hɑːf'bɔːd] *n* (*in hotel*) media pensión *f*.

half-bred ['hɑːfbred] *adj* mestizo.

half-breed ['hɑːfbriːd] *n* mestizo *m*, -a *f*.

half-brother ['hɑːf,brʌðəʳ] *n* medio hermano *m*, hermanastro *m*.

half-caste ['hɑːfkɑːst] **1** *adj* mestizo. **2** *n* mestizo *m*, -a *f*.

half-circle ['hɑːf'sɜːkl] *n* semicírculo *m*.

half-closed [,hɑːf'kləʊzd] *adj* entreabierto.

half-cock ['hɑːf'kɒk] *n* posición *f* de medio amartillado (de la escopeta *etc*); **to go off at ~** (*fig*) obrar precipitadamente, obrar antes del momento propicio; (*of plan*) ponerse en efecto sin la debida preparación, fracasar por falta de preparación, fallar por prematuro.

half-cocked [,hɑːf'kɒkt] *adj gun* con el seguro echado; *plan, scheme* mal elaborado.

half-crown ['hɑːf'kraʊn] *n* (††) media corona *f*.

half-cup ['hɑːf,kʌp] *attr*: **~ brassiere** sostén *m* de media copa.

half-day [,hɑːf'deɪ] *n* medio día *m*, media jornada *f*; **~ holiday** fiesta *f* de media jornada; **~ closing is on Mondays** los lunes se cierra por la tarde.

half-dead ['hɑːf'ded] *adj* medio muerto, más muerto que vivo.

half-dozen ['hɑːf'dʌzn] *n* media docena *f*.

half-dressed [,hɑːf'drest] *adj* a medio vestir.

half-educated [,hɑːf'edjʊkeɪtɪd] *adj*: **he is ~** tiene poca cultura.

half-empty ['hɑːf'emptɪ] *adj* medio vacío; *hall etc* semidesierto.

half fare [,hɑːf'fɛəʳ] **1** *n* medio pasaje *m*.

2 *adv*: **to travel ~** viajar pagando medio pasaje.

half-forgotten [,hɑːffə'gɒtn] *adj* medio olvidado.

half-frozen [,hɑːf'frəʊzən] *adj* medio helado.

half-full ['hɑːf'fʊl] *adj* a medio llenar, mediado.

half-hearted ['hɑːf'hɑːtɪd] *adj* poco entusiasta, indiferente; *effort* débil.

half-heartedly ['hɑːf'hɑːtɪdlɪ] *adv* con poco entusiasmo.

half-heartedness [,hɑːf'hɑːtɪdnɪs] *n* carencia *f* de entusiasmo.

half-holiday ['hɑːf'hɒlɪdɪ] *n* (*Brit*) (*Scol*) medio asueto *m*, fiesta *f* de media jornada; (*in shop*) descanso *m*.

half-hour ['hɑːf'aʊəʳ] *n* media hora *f*.

half-hourly [,hɑːf'aʊəlɪ] **1** *adv* cada media hora. **2** *adj*: **at ~ intervals** cada media hora.

half-inch [,hɑːf'ɪntʃ] **1** *n* media pulgada *f*. **2** *vt* (‡) apañar*.

half-length ['hɑːf'leŋθ] *adj* de medio cuerpo.

half-life ['hɑːflaɪf] *n* (*Phys*) media vida *f*.

half-light ['hɑːflaɪt] *n* media luz *f*.

half-mast ['hɑːf'mɑːst] *n*: **at ~** (*Brit*) a media asta.

half-measures ['hɑːf'meʒəz] *npl* medidas *fpl* poco eficaces, medias tintas *fpl*; **we don't want any ~** no queremos paños calientes.

half-monthly [,hɑːf'mʌnθlɪ] *adj* quincenal.

half-moon ['hɑːf'muːn] *n* media luna *f*.

half-naked ['hɑːf'neɪkɪd] *adj* semidesnudo.

half note ['hɑːf'nəʊt] *n* (*US Mus*) blanca *f*.

half-open [,hɑːf'əʊpən] *adj* medio abierto.

half-panelled, (*US*) **half-paneled** [,hɑːf'pænəld] *adj* chapado hasta media altura.

half-pay ['hɑːf'peɪ] **1** *n* media paga *f*; **to retire on ~** jubilarse con media paga. **2** *attr*: **a ~ officer** un militar retirado.

halfpenny ['heɪpnɪ] *n* medio penique *m*.

half-pint [ˌhɑːfˈpaɪnt] *n* media pinta *f*; (*) enano *m*, -a *f*.
half-price [ˈhɑːfˈpraɪs] **1** *adv* a mitad de precio. **2** *adj ticket etc* a mitad de precio.
half-seas over [ˈhɑːfsiːzˈəʊvəʳ] *adv*: **to be ~** estar entre dos velas.
half-serious [ˌhɑːfˈsɪərɪəs] *adj* entre serio y en broma.
half-sister [ˈhɑːfˌsɪstəʳ] *n* media hermana *f*, hermanastra *f*.
half-size [ˈhɑːfˌsaɪz] *n* (*in shoes*) media talla *f*.
half-size(d) [ˌhɑːfˈsaɪz(d)] *adj* medio, de tamaño medio.
half-term [ˈhɑːfˈtɜːm] *n* (*Brit*) vacación *f* a mediados del trimestre.
half-timbered [ˌhɑːfˈtɪmbəd] *adj* con entramado de madera.
half-time [ˈhɑːfˈtaɪm] **1** *n* (*Sport*) descanso *m*. **2** *attr*: **~ work** trabajo *m* de media jornada. **3** *adv*: **to work ~** trabajar media jornada.
half-tone [ˈhɑːftəʊn] **1** *adj*: **~ illustration** fotograbado *m* a media tinta. **2** *n* (*US*) semitono *m*.
half-track [ˈhɑːfˈtræk] *n* camión *m* semi-oruga.
half-truth [ˈhɑːfˈtruːθ] *n*, *pl* **half-truths** [ˈhɑːfˈtruːðz] verdad *f* a medias.
half-volley [ˈhɑːfˈvɒlɪ] *n* media volea *f*.
halfway [ˈhɑːfˈweɪ] **1** *adv* a medio camino; **we're ~ there** estamos a medio camino; **~ through the film** hacia la mitad de la película; **to meet sb ~** partir el camino con uno, (*fig*) hacer concesiones mutuas.
2 *adj* intermedio; **~ house** (*fig*) punto *m* intermediario, término *m* medio.
halfwit [ˈhɑːfwɪt] *n* bobo *m*, -a *f*.
half-witted [ˈhɑːfˈwɪtɪd] *adj* imbécil, bobo.
half-year [ˌhɑːfˈjɪəʳ] *n* medio año *m*, semestre *m*; **results for the ~** resultados *mpl* para el semestre, resultados *mpl* semestrales.
half-yearly [ˈhɑːfˈjɪəlɪ] (*esp Brit*) **1** *adv* semestralmente. **2** *adj* semestral; **~ results** resultados *mpl* semestrales.
halibut [ˈhælɪbət] *n* halibut *m*, hipogloso *m*.
halitosis [ˌhælɪˈtəʊsɪs] *n* halitosis *f*.
hall [hɔːl] *n* (*entrance-~*) vestíbulo *m*, hall *m*; (*for concerts etc*) sala *f*; (*dining-room*) comedor *m*; (*Brit Univ*: *central ~*) paraninfo *m*; (*hostel*: *also* **~ of residence**) residencia *f*, colegio *m* mayor; (*large house*) casa *f* solariega.
hallelujah [ˌhælɪˈluːjə] *n* aleluya *f*.
hallmark [ˈhɔːlmɑːk] *n* (marca *f* del) contraste *m*; (*fig*) sello *m*; **the outrage has all the ~s of the CLF** el atentado lleva el auténtico sello del CLF.
hallo [hʌˈləʊ] = **hullo**.
halloo [həˈluː] **1** *interj* ¡sus!, ¡hala! **2** *n* grito *m*. **3** *vi* gritar.
hallow [ˈhæləʊ] *vt* santificar.
hallowed [ˈhæləʊd] *adj ground etc* sagrado, santificado.
Hallowe'en [ˈhæləʊˈiːn] *n* (*Scot, US*) víspera *f* de Todos los Santos.
hall-porter [ˌhɔːlˈpɔːtəʳ] *n* (*Brit*) portero *m*, conserje *m*.
hallstand [ˈhɔːlstænd] *n* perchero *m*.
hallucinate [həˈluːsɪneɪt] *vi* alucinar, tener alucinaciones.
hallucination [həˌluːsɪˈneɪʃən] *n* alucinación *f*; ilusión *f*, fantasma *m*.
hallucinatory [həˈluːsɪnətərɪ] *adj* alucinante.
hallucinogen [həˈluːsɪnəˌdʒen] *n* alucinógeno *m*.
hallucinogenic [həˌluːsɪnəʊˈdʒenɪk] **1** *adj* alucinógeno. **2** *n* alucinógeno *m*.
hallucinosis [həˌluːsɪˈnəʊsɪs] *n* alucinosis *f*.
hallway [ˈhɔːlweɪ] *n* vestíbulo *m*, hall *m*.
halo [ˈheɪləʊ] *n* halo *m*, aureola *f*, nimbo *m*.
halogen [ˈheɪləʊdʒɪn] *n* halógeno *m*; **~ lamp** lámpara *f* halógena.
halogenous [həˈlɒdʒɪnəs] *adj* halógeno.
halt [hɔːlt] **1** *n* (**a**) alto *m*, parada *f*; interrupción *f*; **10 minutes' ~** parada *f* de 10 minutos; **to call a ~** mandar hacer alto, parar; **to call a ~ to** parar, atajar; **to come to a ~** pararse, (*process etc*) interrumpirse.
(**b**) (*Brit Rail*) apeadero *m*.
2 *attr*: **~ sign** señal *f* de stop.
3 *vt* parar, detener; interrumpir.
4 *vi* hacer alto; pararse; (*process etc*) interrumpirse; **~!** ¡alto!
halter [ˈhɔːltəʳ] *n* cabestro *m*, ronzal *m*; (*noose*) dogal *m*.
halting [ˈhɔːltɪŋ] *adj* vacilante, titubeante.
haltingly [ˈhɔːltɪŋlɪ] *adv* vacilantemente, titubeantemente; con vacilación.
halve [hɑːv] **1** *vt object* partir por mitad; *quantity* reducir en la mitad; **to ~ a game** empatar. **2** *vi* reducirse en la mitad.
halves [hɑːvz] *npl of* **half**.
halyard [ˈhæljəd] *n* driza *f*.

ham [hæm] **1** *n* (**a**) jamón *m*; pernil *m*; **~s** (*Anat*) nalgas *fpl*. (**b**) (*) maleta* *m*; (*Theat*: *also* **~ actor**) comicastro *m*, racionista *mf*. (**c**) (*Rad**) radioaficionado *m*, -a *f*. **2** *vt*: **to ~ it up*** = **3**. **3** *vi* (*Theat**) actuar de una manera exagerada (*or* paródica, melodramática).
Hamburg [ˈhæmbɜːg] *n* Hamburgo.
hamburger [ˈhæmˌbɜːgəʳ] *n* hamburguesa *f*; (*US*: *also* **~ meat**) carne *f* picada.
ham-fisted [ˈhæmˈfɪstɪd] *adj*, **ham-handed** [ˈhæmˈhændɪd] *adj* torpe, desmañado.
Hamitic [hæˈmɪtɪk] *adj* camítico.
hamlet [ˈhæmlɪt] *n* aldehuela *f*, caserío *m*.
hammer [ˈhæməʳ] **1** *n* martillo *m*; (*Mus*) macillo *m*; (*of firearm*) percusor *m*; **~ and sickle** hoz *f* y martillo; **to come under the ~** ser subastado; **to go at it ~ and tongs** luchar (*etc*) a brazo partido.
2 *vt* (**a**) martillar; batir; **to ~ a post into the ground** hincar un poste en el suelo a martillazos; **to ~ a point home** subrayar repetidas veces un argumento; **to ~ some sense into sb** hacer que uno vaya comprendiendo algo a fuerza de repetírselo; **to ~ sth into shape** formar algo a martillo.
(**b**) (*: *Sport etc*) cascar*, dar una paliza a.
(**c**) (*Fin*) declarar insolvente.
3 *vi*: **to ~ at** (*or* **on**) **a door** dar golpes en una puerta; **to ~ away at** *subject* insistir con ahinco en, machacar en, *work* trabajar asiduamente en; **to ~ away on the piano** tocar estrepitosamente el piano.
◆**hammer down** *vt lid* asegurar con clavos.
◆**hammer in** *vt*: **to ~ sth in** clavar algo con martillo.
◆**hammer out** *vt dent* quitar a martillo, extender bajo el martillo; (*fig*) *settlement etc* elaborar trabajosamente.
◆**hammer together** *vt pieces of wood etc* clavar.
hammerhead [ˈhæməhed] *n* (*shark*) pez *m* martillo.
hammering [ˈhæmərɪŋ] *n* (**a**) martilleo *m*. (**b**) (*) paliza* *f*; **to give sb a ~** dar una paliza a uno; **to get** (*or* **take**) **a ~** recibir una paliza.
hammertoe [ˈhæmətəʊ] *n* dedo *m* (en) martillo.
hammock [ˈhæmək] *n* hamaca *f*, (*Naut*) coy *m*.
hammy* [ˈhæmɪ] *adj actor* exagerado, melodramático.
hamper[1] [ˈhæmpəʳ] *n* cesto *m*, canasta *f*.
hamper[2] [ˈhæmpəʳ] *vt* estorbar, impedir.
hamster [ˈhæmstəʳ] *n* hámster *m*.
hamstring [ˈhæmstrɪŋ] **1** *n* tendón *m* de la corva; **~ injury** lesión *f* del tendón de la corva. **2** *vt* (*irr*: *V* **string**) desjarretar; (*fig*) paralizar.
hand [hænd] **1** *n* (**a**) (*gen*) mano *f*; **~s off!** ¡no tocar!; ¡fuera las manos!; **~s off Ruritania!** ¡manos fuera de Ruritania!; **~s up!** ¡arriba las manos!; **to be clever with one's ~s** tener mucha destreza manual; **to go on one's ~s and knees** ir a gatas.
(**b**) (*phrases with verb*) **A is ~ in glove with B** A y B son uña y carne, están conchabados A y B; **his ~ was everywhere** se notaba su influencia por todas partes; **to bear a ~** arrimar el hombro; **to change ~s** cambiar de dueño; **to clutch at an offer with both ~s** agarrar una oferta con las dos manos; **he never does a ~'s turn** no da golpe; **to force sb's ~** forzar la mano a uno; **to get one's ~ in** adquirir práctica, irse acostumbrando; **to give sb a ~** echarle una mano a uno; **to have a ~ in** tomar parte en, intervenir en; **he had no ~ in it** no tuvo arte ni parte en ello; **to hold ~s** (*children*) ir cogidos (*LAm*: tomados) de la mano, (*lovers*) hacer manitas; **to join ~s** darse las manos; **to keep one's ~ in** conservar la práctica (*at* de), mantenerse en forma; **to keep one's ~s off sth** no tocar algo; **to lay ~s on** echar mano a, (*obtain*) conseguir, (*Eccl*) imponer las manos a; **to lend a ~** arrimar el hombro; **to lend sb a ~** echarle una mano a uno; **lend a ~!** ¡manos a la obra!; **to make money ~ over fist** amasar una fortuna muy rápidamente; **to put one's ~ to sth** emprender algo; **to shake ~s** estrecharse la mano, darse las manos; **to shake ~s with sb** estrechar la mano a uno; **we shook ~s on it** nos dimos las manos para confirmar el acuerdo; **to show one's ~** revelar su intención; **to sit on one's ~s** (*US**) (*audience*) aplaudir con desgana; (*committee etc*) no hacer nada, no dar golpe; **to take a ~** tomar parte, intervenir (*at, in* en); **to throw up one's ~s (in horror)** escandalizarse; **I could do it with one ~ tied behind my back** lo podría hacer con una mano atada a la espalda; **to try one's ~ at sth** probar algo, ensayar algo; **to turn one's ~ to** dedicarse a; **he can turn his ~ to anything** vale tanto para un barrido como para un fregado; **to wash one's ~s of** desentenderse de; **to win ~s down** ganar fácilmente.
(**c**) (*phrases with adj*) **to rule with a firm ~** gobernar con

firmeza; **they gave him a big ~*** le aplaudieron calurosamente; **let's give X a big ~!*** ¡muchos aplausos para X!; **to give sb a free ~** dar carta blanca a uno; **to have a free ~** tener carta blanca; **to have one's ~s full** estar ocupado; **with a heavy ~** con mano dura; **with a high ~** despóticamente; **to give sb a helping ~** echar una mano a uno; **to get** (*or* **gain**) **the upper ~** empezar a dominar; **to have the upper ~** tener la ventaja; **many ~s make light work** muchas manos facilitan el trabajo.

(**d**) (*phrases with prep before n*) (*at*) **at ~** a mano; **to be near** (*or* **close**) **at ~** estar a la mano; estar cerca; **winter was at ~** se acercaba el invierno; **at first ~** de primera mano, directamente; de buena tinta; **I heard it only at second ~** lo supe sólo de modo indirecto; **to suffer at the ~s of** sufrir a manos de; (*by*) **by ~** *make* a mano, *raise etc* a fuerza de brazos; **'by ~'** (*on envelope*) 'en su mano'; **to send a letter by ~** enviar una carta en mano; **to take sb by the ~** llevar a uno de la mano; (*from*) **to live from ~ to mouth** vivir al día, vivir de la mano a la boca; (*in*) **gun in ~** el revólver en la mano, empuñando el revólver; **to be in sb's ~s** estar en manos de uno; **they were going along ~ in ~** iban cogidos de la mano; **these matters go ~ in ~** estos asuntos están estrechamente relacionados; **to have sth in ~** tener algo entre manos; **to have a matter in ~** estar estudiando un asunto; **the situation is in ~** se ha conseguido dominar la situación; **he has them well in ~** los domina perfectamente; **to put sth in ~** emprender algo; **to take sb in ~** enseñar a uno, entrenar a uno; imponer disciplina a uno; **to take sth in ~** hacerse cargo de algo; **I like to have sth in ~** me gusta tener algo en reserva; **money in ~** dinero *m* disponible; **how much have we in ~?** ¿cuánto tenemos en el haber?, ¿cuánto tenemos en efectivo?; (*into*) **to fall into enemy ~s** caer en manos del enemigo; **to play into sb's ~s** ceder la ventaja a un contrario; **to put sth into a lawyer's ~s** poner un asunto en manos de un abogado; **to take justice into one's own ~s** tomar la justicia por su mano; (*off*) **to get sth off one's ~s** deshacerse de algo; terminar de hacer algo; (*on*) **on the left ~** a la izquierda, **on the right ~** a la derecha; **on every ~, on all ~s** por todas partes; **on the one ~** por una parte; **on the other ~** por otra parte; **to be on ~** estar a la mano; **he's on my ~s all day** está conmigo todo el día; **to have work on ~** tener trabajo entre manos; **the goods were left on his ~s** los géneros resultaron ser invendibles; (*out*) **to condemn sb out of ~** condenar a uno sin más; **to shoot sb out of ~** fusilar a uno sin más; **to get out of ~** desmandarse; (*matter*) desorbitarse, salirse de los límites; (*to*) **to come to ~** llegar; aparecer; **your letter of the 3rd is to ~** he recibido su carta del 3.

(**e**) (*of instrument*) aguja *f*; (*of clock*) manecilla *f*.

(**f**) (*measure*) palmo *m*.

(**g**) (*Cards*) mano *f*; **to have a ~ of bridge** echar una partida de bridge.

(**h**) (*writing*) escritura *f*, letra *f*; **in one's own ~** de puño y letra de uno; **he writes a good ~** tiene buena letra; **to put one's ~ to sth** firmar algo.

(**i**) (*in marriage*) **to ask for sb's ~** pedir la mano de una; **she gave him her ~** se casó con él.

(**j**) (*person*) operario *m*, -a *f*; (*Agr etc*) peón *m*; **~s** (*Naut*) tripulación *f*; **all ~s on deck!** ¡todos a la cubierta!; **to be lost with all ~s** desaparecer con toda la tripulación; **to be a good ~ at** tener buena mano para, ser hábil en; **to be an old ~** ser perro viejo.

2 *vt* dar, entregar, poner en manos de; alargar; pasar; **you've got to ~ it to him** hay que reconocer que lo hace (*etc*) muy bien.

◆**hand around** *vt* = **hand round**.
◆**hand back** *vt* devolver.
◆**hand down** *vt* bajar, pasar; *heirloom* pasar, dejar en herencia; *tradition* transmitir; (*US*) *judgement* dictar, imponer; *person* ayudar a bajar.
◆**hand in** *vt* entregar; *resignation* presentar; *person* ayudar a subir.
◆**hand off** *vt* (*Rugby*) rechazar.
◆**hand on** *vt tradition* transmitir; *news* comunicar; *object* pasar.
◆**hand out** *vt* repartir, distribuir.
◆**hand over 1** *vt* entregar. **2** *vi*: **to ~ over to** ceder su puesto a, entregar sus funciones a.
◆**hand round** *vt* pasar de mano en mano; (*distribute*) repartir; *chocolates etc* ofrecer.
◆**hand up** *vt* subir.

handbag ['hænd*b*æg] **1** *n* bolso *m*, cartera *f* (*LAm*). **2** *vt* (*) poner fuera de combate a golpe de bolso, eliminar a bolsazos.

handball ['hænd*b*ɔːl] **1** *n* (*Sport*) balonmano *m*; (*offence in football*) mano *f*. **2** *vt* (*) pasar en cadena humana.

handbasin ['hænd,beɪsn] *n* lavabo *m*.

handbell ['hænd*b*el] *n* campanilla *f*.

handbill ['hænd*b*ɪl] *n* prospecto *m*, folleto *m*.

handbook ['hænd*b*ʊk] *n* manual *m*; (*guide*) guía *f*.

handbrake ['hænd*b*reɪk] *n* (*Brit*) freno *m* de mano.

handcart ['hænd*k*ɑːt] *n* carretilla *f*, carretón *m*.

handclap ['hænd*k*læp] *n* palmada *f*; **to give a player the slow ~** batir palmas a ritmo lento (para que un jugador se esfuerce más o se dé prisa).

handclasp ['hænd*k*lɑːsp] *n* apretón *m* de manos.

hand controls ['hændkən,trəʊlz] *npl* controles *mpl* manuales.

handcraft ['hænd*k*rɑːft] *vt* (*US*) hacer a mano; **~ed products** productos *mpl* hechos a mano, productos *mpl* artesanales.

handcream ['hænd*k*riːm] *n* crema *f* para las manos.

handcuff ['hænd*k*ʌf] *vt* poner las esposas a, esposar.

handcuffs ['hænd*k*ʌfs] *npl* esposas *fpl*.

hand-drier, hand-dryer ['hænd,draɪəʳ] *n* secamanos *m* automático.

-handed ['hændɪd] *adj* de...mano(s); de mano(s) ...; **four~ game** juego *m* para cuatro personas.

handful ['hænd*f*ʊl] *n* puñado *m*, manojo *m*; **a ~ of people** un puñado de gente; **he's a real ~** tiene el diablo en el cuerpo.

hand-grenade ['hænd*g*rɪ,neɪd] *n* granada *f* (de mano).

handgrip ['hænd*g*rɪp] *n* = **handle**; = **grip**.

handgun ['hænd*g*ʌn] *n* (*esp US*) revólver *m*, pistola *f*.

hand-held ['hændheld] *adj* portátil.

handicap ['hændɪkæp] **1** *n* desventaja *f*, estorbo *m*, obstáculo *m*; (*Med*) minusvalía *f*, discapacidad *f*; (*Sport*) hándicap *m*.

2 *vt* perjudicar, estorbar; (*Sport*) handicapar; **he has always been ~ped by his accent** su acento siempre ha sido una desventaja para él.

handicapped ['hændɪkæpt] **1** *adj*: **mentally ~** minusválido mental; **physically ~** mutilado, tullido, minusválido, discapacitado. **2** *n*: **the ~** los minusválidos.

handicraft ['hændɪkrɑːft] **1** *n* artesanía *f*; (*skill*) destreza *f* manual. **2** *attr*: **~ teacher** profesor *m*, -ora *f* de oficios manuales.

handily ['hændɪlɪ] *adv* (**a**) *positioned etc* cómodamente, convenientemente.

(**b**) (*US*) *win etc* fácilmente.

handiness ['hændɪnɪs] *n* (**a**) (*nearness*) proximidad *f*, lo cercano; **because of the ~ of the library** debido a que la biblioteca está tan cerca, porque resulta tan cómodo ir a la biblioteca.

(**b**) (*convenience*) conveniencia *f*, comodidad *f*; carácter *m* manuable, facilidad *f* en el manejo.

(**c**) (*skill*) habilidad *f*, destreza *f*; **his ~ with a gun** su destreza con un fusil.

hand-in-hand ['hændɪn'hænd] *adv*: **to go ~** ir cogidos de la mano; **it goes ~ with** está estrechamente relacionado con; **these plans should go ~** estos proyectos deben realizarse al mismo ritmo.

handiwork ['hændɪwɜːk] *n* obra *f*.

handkerchief ['hæŋkətʃɪf] *n* pañuelo *m*.

hand-knitted [,hænd'nɪtɪd] *adj* tricotado a mano.

handle ['hændl] **1** *n* (*haft*) mango *m*; puño *m*; (*lever*) palanca *f*; (*crank*) manivela *f*; (*for winding*) manubrio *m*; (*of basket, jug etc*) asa *f*, asidero *m*; (*of door, drawer etc*) tirador *m*, manija *f*, puño *m*; (*fig*) pretexto *m*, asidero *m*; (*) título *m*; **to have a ~ to one's name*** tener título de nobleza; **to fly off the ~*** salirse de sus casillas, perder los estribos.

2 *vt* (**a**) (*touch*) tocar, (*improperly*) manosear; (*Sport*) tocar con la mano; (*delicately*) manejar, manipular; **'~ with care'** 'manéjese con cuidado'; **don't ~ the fruit** no manosees la fruta; **the police ~d him roughly** la policía le trató severamente.

(**b**) (*fig*) *situation, theme, resources etc* manejar; *car* conducir, *ship* gobernar; *unruly element* saber dominar; **I'll ~ this** yo me encargo de esto; **do you ~ tax matters?** ¿tiene Vd que ver con las contribuciones?; **we ~ 2000 travellers a day** por aquí pasan 2000 viajeros cada día; **can the port ~ big ships?** ¿el puerto tiene capacidad para los buques grandes?

(**c**) (*Comm*) *product* tratar en, comerciar en.

3 *vi* (*horse, car*) comportarse.

handlebar ['hændlbɑːʳ] **1** *n* manillar *m*, manubrio *m*. **2** *attr*: **~ moustache** bigote *m* Dalí, bigote *m* daliniano.

-handled ['hændld] *adj ending in compounds* con mango de ...; **a wooden~ spade** una pala con mango de madera.

handler [ˈhændləʳ] *n* (*Comm*) tratante *m*, comerciante *m*; (*Sport*) entrenador *m*, -ora *f*; (*of dog*) amo *m*, -a *f*.

handling [ˈhændlɪŋ] **1** *n* manejo *m*, manejar *m*; manipulación *f*; manoseo *m*; (*of car*) conducción *f*; (*of ship*) gobierno *m*; (*Aer*) asistencia *f* en tierra; servicio *m* de equipajes; **rough ~** malos tratos *mpl*; **his ~ of the matter** su manejo del asunto, su modo de manejar el asunto.

2 *attr*: **~ charge** gastos *mpl* de tramitación.

hand lotion [ˈhænd,ləʊʃən] *n* loción *f* para las manos.

hand-luggage [ˈhænd,lʌgɪdʒ] *n* equipaje *m* de mano, bultos *mpl* de mano.

handmade [ˈhændmeɪd] *adj* hecho a mano; de artesanía; **~ paper** papel *m* de tina, papel *m* de mano.

handmaid(en) [ˈhændmeɪd(ən)] *n* (*Hist*) criada *f*; azafata *f*.

hand-me-down* [ˈhændmɪdaʊn] *n* (*US*) prenda *f* usada.

handout [ˈhændaʊt] *n* (**a**) (*act*) distribución *f*, repartimiento *m*. (**b**) (*charity*) limosna *f*, caridad *f*. (**c**) (*press ~*) nota *f* de prensa; (*leaflet*) folleto *m*; impreso *m*, octavilla *f*; (*at lecture*) jandote *m*.

handover [ˈhændəʊvəʳ] *n* entrega *f*.

hand-picked [ˈhændˈpɪkt] *adj* seleccionado a mano, muy escogido, seleccionado cuidadosamente.

hand print [ˈhændprɪnt] *n* manotada *f*.

hand puppet [ˈhænd,pʌpɪt] *n* títere *m*.

handrail [ˈhændreɪl] *n* pasamano *m*.

handset [ˈhændset] *n* (*Telec*) aparato *m*, auricular *m*.

hands-free [,hændzˈfriː] *adj*: **~ car phone** teléfono *m* (móvil) manos libres.

handshake [ˈhændʃeɪk] *n* apretón *m* de manos; (*Comput*) coloquio *m*, (*as data signal*) 'acuse de recibo'.

hands-off [,hændzˈɒf] *adj policy etc* de no intervención.

handsome [ˈhænsəm] *adj* (**a**) (*beautiful*) hermoso, bello; elegante; *man* guapo, bien parecido, distinguido. (**b**) *gesture, salary, treatment etc* generoso; *fortune, profit* considerable; *victory* fácil, agobiador.

handsomely [ˈhænsəmlɪ] *adv* (**a**) elegantemente; generosamente. (**b**) *win* fácilmente.

hands-on [,hændzˈɒn] *adj* práctico; inmediato; personal; **~ experience** experiencia *f* práctica.

handspring [ˈhændsprɪŋ] *n* voltereta *f* sobre las manos, salto *m* de paloma.

handstand [ˈhændstænd] *n* posición *f* de manos, pino *m*; **to do a ~** hacer el pino.

hand-stitched [,hændˈstɪtʃt] *adj* cosido a mano.

hand-to-hand [ˈhændtəˈhænd] *adv, adj* cuerpo a cuerpo.

hand-to-mouth [ˈhændtəˈmaʊθ] **1** *adj existence* precario. **2** *adv*: **to live ~** vivir precariamente.

hand towel [ˈhænd,taʊəl] *n* toalla *f* de manos.

hand-woven [,hændˈwəʊvən] *adj* tejido a mano.

handwriting [ˈhænd,raɪtɪŋ] *n* escritura *f*, letra *f*.

handwritten [ˈhændˈrɪtn] *adj* escrito a mano.

handy [ˈhændɪ] *adj* (**a**) (*near*) a mano; próximo, cercano; **the shop is ~** la tienda está cerca; **to keep sth ~** tener algo listo para usar.

(**b**) (*convenient*) cómodo, práctico; *machine etc* manuable, fácil de manejar; **a ~ little car** un coche práctico; **it's ~ living here** resulta muy práctico vivir aquí; **it's ~ for the shops** está muy cerca de las tiendas; **to come in ~** venir bien, servir.

(**c**) (*skilful*) hábil, diestro; **to be ~ with one's fists** saber defenderse con los puños; **to be ~ with a gun** saber manejar una pistola; **I'm not at all ~** no soy nada manitas.

handyman [ˈhændɪmən] *n, pl* **handymen** [ˈhændɪmən] factótum *m*; hombre *m* que tiene dotes prácticas (para hacer trabajos de carpintería en casa *etc*).

hang [hæŋ] (*irr*: *pret and ptp* **hung,** (*Jur*) *pret and ptp* **hanged**) **1** *vt* (**a**) (*suspend*) colgar, suspender; *wallpaper* pegar; *meat* manir.

(**b**) *head* bajar, inclinar.

(**c**) (*decorate*) ornar, decorar; **to ~ a room with tapestries** entapizar un cuarto, adornar un cuarto con tapicerías; **balconies hung with flags** balcones *mpl* engalanados con banderas; **trees hung with lights** árboles *mpl* llenos de farolillos; **a wall hung with ivy** un muro cubierto de hiedra.

(**d**) *criminal* ahorcar; **~ the fellow!** ¡qué tío!, ¡qué tipo! (*LAm*); **~ it (all)!** ¡por Dios!; ¡demonio!; **~ the expense!** ¡que no se hable de los gastos!; **I'll be ~ed if I know** que me maten si lo sé.

(**e**) (*US**: *turn*) **'~ a right here, buddy'** 'oye, tira a la derecha aquí'.

2 *vi* colgar, pender, estar suspendido (*from* de, *on* en); (*garment, hair*) caer; **a picture ~ing on the wall** un cuadro colgado en la pared; **the hawk hung motionless in the sky** el halcón se mantenía inmóvil en el cielo; **he'll ~ for it** por este crimen le ahorcarán.

3 *vr*: **to ~ o.s.** ahorcarse.

4 *n* (**a**) (*of garment*) caída *f*.

(**b**) **to get the ~ of it** coger el tino; **to get the ~ of sth** lograr entender algo; **I can't get the ~ of this machine** no entiendo el modo de manejar esta máquina.

◆**hang about, hang around 1** *vt place* frecuentar; (*haunt*) rondar, merodear; **to ~ about a woman** andar rondando a una mujer, andar detrás de una mujer; **the clouds hung about the summit** las nubes se pegaban a la cumbre. **2** *vi* (*idle*) no hacer nada, haraganear; (*wait*) esperar; **to keep sb ~ing about** hacer esperar a uno.

◆**hang back** *vi* quedarse atrás, resistirse a pasar adelante; (*fig*) vacilar, no resolverse.

◆**hang down 1** *vt*: **her hair ~s down her back** el pelo le cae por la espalda. **2** *vi* colgar, pender.

◆**hang in*** *vi*: **~ in there!** (*US*) ¡mantente firme!

◆**hang on 1** *vt*: **to ~ on sb's words** escuchar atentamente lo que dice uno; **everything ~s on his decision** todo depende de su decisión; **we are all ~ing on his decision** todos estamos pendientes de su decisión; **time ~s heavy on him** se le hacen las horas siglos, para él no corre el tiempo.

2 *vi* (**a**) (*: *wait*) esperar; **~ on!** ¡espera (un momento)!

(**b**) (*hold out*) resistir; **they're still ~ing on** siguen resistiendo; **to ~ on like grim death** resistir con la mayor tenacidad, aguantarlo sin cejar.

(**c**) **to ~ on to** *object* agarrarse a; *principle* aferrarse a; (*: *keep*) guardar, quedarse con; conservar; **~ on to it till I see you** guárdalo hasta que nos veamos.

◆**hang out 1** *vt washing, banner* tender; *streamer etc* colgar.

2 *vi* (**a**) (*hang*) colgar (fuera); **to ~ out of the window** asomarse por la ventana.

(**b**) (*) (*live*) vivir; (*spend time*) pasar el rato.

(**c**) (*: *hold out*) resistir, aguantar; **they're ~ing out for more** siguen firmes en pedir más.

(**d**) **to let it all ~ out*** (*US*) contarlo todo, revelarlo todo; abrir su pecho; soltarse el pelo.

◆**hang over** *vt* (**a**) **to be hung over*** tener resaca*.

(**b**) (*hang*) colgar por el borde; sobresalir; **he hung over the table** se inclinó sobre la mesa.

(**c**) (*fig*) cernerse sobre; **a heavy silence hung over the town** se cernía sobre la ciudad un profundo silencio; **the threat ~ing over us** la amenaza que se cierne sobre nosotros.

◆**hang together** *vi* (**a**) (*persons*) mantenerse unidos.

(**b**) (*argument etc*) ser consistente, ser lógico.

◆**hang up 1** *vt* (**a**) colgar, suspender; (*Telec*) colgar.

(**b**) (*delay*) causar un retraso a; **we were hung up in the fog** sufrimos un retraso debido a la niebla; **he's hung up with a visitor** se retrasa por una visita; **we are hung up for a lack of bricks** no podemos ir adelante por falta de ladrillos.

(**c**) (*) **to be hung up** (*tense*) estar acomplejado (*about* por); **to be hung up on sth** estar obsesionado por algo.

2 *vi* (*Telec*) colgar.

hangar [ˈhæŋəʳ] *n* hangar *m*.

hangdog [ˈhæŋdɒg] *adj* avergonzado; **he had a ~ look** tenía cara de pocos amigos.

hanger [ˈhæŋəʳ] *n* (**a**) (*for clothes*) percha *f*, colgadero *m*. (**b**) (*Jur*) partidario *m*, -a *f* del restablecimiento de la pena de muerte.

hanger-on [ˈhæŋərˈɒn] *n* parásito *m*, pegote *m*.

hang-glide [ˈhæŋ,glaɪd] *vi* hacer vuelo con ala delta.

hang-glider [ˈhæŋ,glaɪdəʳ] *n* ala *f* delta, cometa *f* delta.

hang-gliding [ˈhæŋ,glaɪdɪŋ] *n* vuelo *m* libre, vuelo *m* con cometa delta.

hanging [ˈhæŋɪŋ] **1** *adj* pendiente, colgante; *lamp* de techo; *garden* colgante, pensil; **~ committee** junta *f* seleccionadora (de una exposición); **~ judge** (*Hist*) juez *m* muy severo, juez *m* amigo de la horca; **it's not a ~ matter** no es cosa de vida o de muerte.

2 *n* (**a**) (*execution*) ahorcadura *f*, ejecución *f* (en la horca). (**b**) (*curtains etc*) **~s** colgaduras *fpl*, tapices *mpl*.

hangman [ˈhæŋmən] *n, pl* **hangmen** [ˈhæŋmən] verdugo *m*.

hangnail [ˈhæŋneɪl] *n* padrastro *m*.

hang-out* [ˈhæŋaʊt] *n* guarida *f*, nidal *m*.

hangover [ˈhæŋ,əʊvəʳ] *n* (**a**) (*after drinking*) resaca *f*, cruda *f* (*LAm*). (**b**) (*left-over*) restos *mpl*, vestigio *m*; asunto *m* sin resolver; **it's a ~ from pre-war days** es de la preguerra.

hang-up* ['hæŋʌp] *n* (**a**) (*problem*) problema *m*, lío* *m*; (*delay*) retraso *m*. (**b**) (*complex*) complejo *m*; (*obsession*) obsesión *f*.
hank [hæŋk] *n* madeja *f*.
hanker ['hæŋkəʳ] *vi*: **to ~ after** añorar; **to ~ for** anhelar, suspirar por.
hankering ['hæŋkərɪŋ] *n* (*feeling*) añoranza *f*; (*wish*) anhelo *m*; **to have a ~ for** anhelar, suspirar por.
hankie*, hanky* ['hæŋkɪ] *n* pañuelo *m*.
hanky-panky* ['hæŋkɪ'pæŋkɪ] *n* trucos *mpl*, trampas *fpl*, supercherías *fpl*; (*sexual*) relaciones *fpl* sospechosas; **there's some ~ going on** esto huele a camelo, aquí hay trampa; **we want no ~ with the girls** aquí nadie se meta en líos con las chicas*.
Hannibal ['hænɪbəl] *nm* Aníbal.
Hanover ['hænəvəʳ] *n* Hanovre *m*.
Hanoverian [ˌhænəʊ'vɪərɪən] **1** *adj* hanoveriano. **2** *n* hanoveriano *m*, -a *f*.
Hansard ['hænsɑːd] *n* Actas *fpl* oficiales de los debates del parlamento británico.
hansom ['hænsəm] *n* cabriolé *m*.
Hants [hænts] *n abbr of* **Hampshire**.
ha'penny* ['heɪpnɪ] *n* = **halfpenny**.
haphazard ['hæp'hæzəd] **1** *adj* fortuito. **2** *adv* de cualquier modo, a la buena de Dios.
haphazardly [ˌhæp'hæzədlɪ] *adv arrange* de cualquier modo; *select* al azar.
hapless ['hæplɪs] *adj* desventurado.
happen ['hæpən] *vi* (**a**) (*occur*) pasar, suceder, ocurrir, acontecer, acaecer; producirse; (*take place*) tener lugar, verificarse; **what ~ed?** ¿qué pasó?; **how did it ~?** ¿cómo fue esto?; **an explosion ~ed** se produjo una explosión; **these things ~** son cosas que pasan; **whatever ~s** suceda lo que suceda; **see it doesn't ~ again** y que no vuelva a ocurrir; **as it ~s, it (so) ~s that** ... da la casualidad que ...; lo que pasa es que ...; **as if nothing had ~ed** como si tal cosa; **how does it ~ that ...?** ¿cómo es posible que ... + *subj*?; **a funny thing ~ed to me** me pasó algo raro; **if anything should ~ to him** si le sobreviniera algo malo; **what ~ed to him?** ¿qué fue de él?
(**b**) (*chance*) **I ~ed to be there** me encontraba allí por casualidad; **if anyone should ~ to see you** si acaso te ven; **do you ~ to know him?** ¿le conoces por ventura?; **I ~ to know that** ... pues me consta que ...; **it ~s to be true** a pesar de todo es verdad, da la casualidad que es verdad.
◆**happen (up)on** *vt*: **to ~ (up)on sth** tropezar con algo; **to ~ (up)on the solution** dar con la solución.
happening ['hæpnɪŋ] **1** *n* suceso *m*, acontecimiento *m*; (*Theat etc*) happening *m*, acontecimiento *m*; **there will be a '~' in the park** habrá un 'acontecimiento' en el parque.
2 *attr* (*) que es lo último*, de lo último.
happenstance ['hæpənstæns] *n* (*US*) azar *m*, casualidad *f*; **by ~** por casualidad.
happily ['hæpɪlɪ] *adv* (**a**) (*fortunately*) por fortuna, afortunadamente. (**b**) (*merrily*) alegremente; **now they are living ~ in Seville** ahora viven muy contentos en Sevilla; **they lived ~ ever after** vivieron felices. (**c**) (*aptly*) felizmente.
happiness ['hæpɪnɪs] *n* (*contentment*) felicidad *f*, dicha *f*, contento *m*; (*merriment*) alegría *f*.
happy ['hæpɪ] *adj* (**a**) (*fortunate*) feliz, dichoso, afortunado; **that ~ age** aquella época tan feliz; **we ~ few** nosotros tan pocos y tan afortunados.
(**b**) (*contented*) contento, satisfecho; **~ hour** hora *f* de la felicidad; **~ birthday!** ¡feliz cumpleaños!; **are you ~?** ¿estás contento?; **are you ~ with him?** ¿eres feliz con él?; **we are not entirely ~ about the plan** no estamos del todo contentos con el proyecto, no nos satisface del todo el proyecto; **your success makes us all ~** su éxito nos alegra a todos; **he tried to make her ~** se esforzó por hacerla feliz; **this should keep everyone ~** esto deberá tenerles a todos contentos; **we're very ~ for you** nos alegramos mucho por ti; **we were ~ to hear it** nos alegramos de saberlo; **I am ~ to inform you that ...** tengo mucho gusto en comunicarle que ...
(**c**) (*merry, cheerful*) alegre; (*) entre dos velas*; *ending of book etc* feliz; **to be as ~ as a lark** (*or* **sand-boy**) estar como unas pascuas.
(**d**) (*apt*) feliz, oportuno; **~ mean, ~ medium** justo *m* medio, término *m* medio; **it seems to be a ~ solution** parece ser una solución satisfactoria.
happy-go-lucky ['hæpɪgəʊ'lʌkɪ] *adj* despreocupado.
Hapsburg ['hæpsbɜːg] *n* Habsburgo.
hara-kiri ['hærə'kɪrɪ] *n* haraquiri *m*.
harangue [hə'ræŋ] **1** *n* arenga *f*. **2** *vt* arengar.
harass ['hærəs] *vt* acosar, hostigar; (*Mil*) hostilizar, picar; *person* (*with worries etc*) atormentar, perseguir; **to be ~ed by doubts** ser atormentado por las dudas.
harassed ['hærəst] *adj look* preocupado.
harassment ['hærəsmənt] *n* acoso *m*, hostigamiento *m*; (*sexual*) importunación *f*, acoso *m*.
harbinger ['hɑːbɪndʒəʳ] *n* heraldo *m*, nuncio *m*; precursor *m*; presagio *m*; **~ of doom** presagio *m* del desastre; **the swallow is a ~ of spring** la golondrina anuncia la venida de la primavera.
harbour, (*US*) **harbor** ['hɑːbəʳ] **1** *n* puerto *m*; **outer ~** rada *f*.
2 *attr* portuario; **~ dues, ~ fees** derechos *mpl* portuarios.
3 *vt fear, hope etc* abrigar; (*lodge*) hospedar; (*conceal*) esconder; **that corner ~s the dust** en ese rincón se amontona el polvo.
harbour master, (*US*) **harbor master** ['hɑːbəˌmɑːstəʳ] *n* capitán *m* de puerto.
hard [hɑːd] **1** *adj* (**a**) (*unyielding, also fig*) duro; sólido, firme; *mud, snow* endurecido; *muscle* firme; *line, outline* sólido, firme, claro; *court, currency, water* duro; *drink* alcohólico; *liquor* espiritoso; *decision* (*final*) definitivo, irrevocable; *look* fijo; **he's as ~ as nails** tiene muchísima resistencia; **~ ass** (*US***) bestia* *mf*, duro *m*, -a *f* de pelar; **~ cash** dinero *m* contante y sonante; **~ center** (*US*), **~ centre** relleno *m* duro; **~ copy** copia *f* impresa; **~ court** cancha *f* (de tenis) de cemento; **~ currency** moneda *f* dura, divisa *f* fuerte; **~ disk** disco *m* duro (*or* rígido); **~ drug** droga *f* dura; **~ goods** artículos *mpl* de equipo; **~ hat** (*of construction worker etc*) casco *m*; (*riding hat*) sombrero *m* de montar; (*fig: construction worker*) albañil *m*; (*adj: fig*) conservador; **~ landing** aterrizaje *m* duro; **~ liquor** licor *m* espiritoso; **~ news** noticias *fpl* fidedignas, información *f* sólida; **~ palate** paladar *m*; **~ porn*** pornografía *f* dura; (*attr*) porno duro; **~ rock** rock *m* duro; **~ sell** venta *f* (con propaganda) agresiva; publicidad *f* agresiva; venta *f* difícil; **~ sell tactics** (*or* **techniques**) táctica *f* (*or* técnicas *fpl*) de promoción agresiva; **~ shoulder** (*Brit*) arcén *m*; **~ stuff*** (*alcohol*) bebidas *fpl* fuertes; (*drugs*) droga *f* dura; (*Aut*) **~ top** techo *m* duro; **~ top car** coche *m* de techo duro.
(**b**) (*harsh, tough*) *work* arduo, penoso, agotador; *blow* duro, (*fig*) cruel, rudo; *frost* fuerte; *weather, winter* severo; *climate* áspero; *light* duro; *fight, match* muy reñido; *rule* severo; *decision* injusto; *fact* concreto; sólido; *word* nada amistoso; *luck, times* malo; **~ lines!, ~ luck!** (*Brit*) ¡mala suerte!
(**c**) (*person*) severo, inflexible; (*Pol*) **the ~ left** la izquierda dura; **you're a ~ man** eres cruel; **to be ~ on sb** ser muy duro con uno; **to be ~ on one's clothes** destrozar la ropa.
(**d**) (*difficult*) difícil; **to be ~ to beat** ser difícil de vencer; **I find it ~ to believe that** ... se me hace cuesta arriba creer que ...; **to be ~ to please** ser exigente, ser quisquilloso; **he's ~ of hearing** es duro de oído; **we shall have to do it the ~ way** tendremos que hacerlo a pulso.
2 *adv* (**a**) (*strenuously*) mucho; de firme; **to pull a rope ~** tirar fuertemente de una cuerda; **he threw it ~ down** lo arrojó violentamente; **to hit sb ~** dar un golpe recio a uno, (*fig*) ser un golpe cruel para uno; **to be ~ at it** trabajar (*etc*) con ahinco; **to work ~** trabajar mucho; **to rain ~** llover mucho; **to beg ~ for sth** pedir algo con insistencia; **to think ~** pensar mucho, meditar profundamente; **to look ~** mirar fijamente; **to drink ~** beber con exceso; **hold ~!** ¡para el carro!; ¡un momento!, ¡despacito!; **to try one's ~est to** + *infin* esforzarse mucho por + *infin*.
(**b**) **to be ~ up*** estar a la cuarta pregunta*; **to be ~ up for books*** no tener casi libros, estar muy falto de libros; **I was ~ put to it** estuve en un aprieto; **to be ~ put to it to decide** encontrar difícil decidir; **to be ~ done by** (*Brit*) ser tratado injustamente; **he took it pretty ~** fue un golpe bastante rudo para él.
(**c**) **~ by** (*adv*) muy cerca; (*prep*) muy cerca de; **A followed ~ upon B** A siguió de cerca a B.
hard-and-fast ['hɑːdən'fɑːst] *adj rule* rígido; *decision* definitivo, irrevocable.
hardback ['hɑːdbæk] **1** *adj* empastado, de tapa dura; **~ book** = **2**. **2** *n* libro *m* empastado, libro *m* de tapa dura.
hard-bitten ['hɑːd'bɪtn] *adj* de carácter duro.
hardboard ['hɑːdbɔːd] *n* chapa *f* de madera dura.
hard-boiled ['hɑːd'bɔɪld] *adj egg* cocido, duro; *person* de carácter duro, severo.

hard-core ['hɑːdkɔːr] *adj*: ~ **pornography** pornografía *f* dura; ~ **resistance** resistencia *f* empedernida, resistencia *f* incondicional.
hard-cover ['hɑːd,kʌvər] *adj*: ~ **book** libro *m* encuadernado.
hard-drinking ['hɑːd'drɪŋkɪŋ] *adj* bebedor.
hard-earned ['hɑːd'ɜːnd] *adj* ganado con el sudor de la frente.
harden ['hɑːdn] **1** *vt* endurecer (*also Comm*), solidificar; **to ~ sb to adversity** acostumbrar a uno a la adversidad; **to ~ sb to war** aguerrir a uno; **he ~ed his heart** se mostró más inflexible.
2 *vi* endurecerse (*also Comm*), solidificarse; **his voice ~ed** adoptó un tono más áspero.
hardened ['hɑːdnd] *adj criminal* habitual.
hardening ['hɑːdnɪŋ] *n* endurecimiento *m* (*also Comm*); ~ **of the arteries** endurecimiento *m* de las arterias, arteriosclerosis *f*.
hard-faced ['hɑːdfeɪst] *adj* severo, inflexible.
hard-fought ['hɑːd'fɔːt] *adj* muy reñido.
hard-headed ['hɑːd'hedɪd] *adj* práctico, realista, poco sentimental.
hard-hearted ['hɑːd'hɑːtɪd] *adj* duro de corazón, insensible.
hard-hitting ['hɑːd,hɪtɪŋ] *adj speech etc* contundente.
hardiness ['hɑːdɪnɪs] *n* robustez *f*; resistencia *f*.
hard-liner [,hɑːd'laɪnər] *n* duro *m*, -a *f*; partidario *m*, -a *f*, político *m* (*etc*) de línea dura.
hard-luck ['hɑːdlʌk] *attr*: **he pitched me a ~ story** me contó sus infortunios, me contó su historia tan trágica.
hardly ['hɑːdlɪ] *adv* (**a**) (*in a hard manner*) duramente; difícilmente; (*badly*) mal.
(**b**) (*scarcely*) apenas; **he can ~ read** apenas sabe leer; **that can ~ be true** eso difícilmente puede ser verdad; ~ **anyone** casi nadie; ~ **ever** casi nunca; ~! ¡nada de eso!
hardness ['hɑːdnɪs] *n* dureza *f*; dificultad *f*; rigor *m*; severidad *f*; ~ **of hearing** dureza *f* de oído; ~ **of heart** insensibilidad *f*.
hard-nosed [,hɑːd'nəʊzd] *adj* (*fig*) duro.
hard-on** ['hɑːdɒn] *n* empalme** *m*, erección *f*.
hard-pressed ['hɑːdprest] *adj*: **to be ~** estar en apuros; **our ~ economy** nuestra economía erizada de problemas.
hardship ['hɑːdʃɪp] **1** *n* trabajos *mpl*, penas *fpl*; infortunio *m*; prueba *f*; (*economic etc*) apuro *m*, privación *f*; **to suffer ~(s)** pasar apuros; **it is no ~ to him (to give up smoking)** no le cuesta nada (dejar de fumar).
2 *attr*: ~ **clause** (*Jur*) cláusula *f* de salvaguarda.
hardtack ['hɑːdtæk] *n* (*Naut*) galleta *f*.
hardware ['hɑːdwɛər] **1** *n* ferretería *f*, quincalla *f*; (*Mil*) armas *fpl*, armamento *m*; (*Comput*) hardware *m*, equipos *mpl*, material *m* informático, soporte *m* físico.
2 *attr*: ~ **dealer** ferretero *m*; ~ **shop**, ~ **store** ferretería *f*, quincallería *f*; ~ **specialist** (*Comput*) especialista *mf* en hardware.
hard-wearing ['hɑːd'wɛərɪŋ] *adj* resistente, duradero.
hard-won ['hɑːd'wʌn] *adj* ganado a duras penas.
hardwood ['hɑːdwʊd] *n* madera *f* dura; ~ **tree** árbol *m* de hojas caducas.
hard-working ['hɑːd'wɜːkɪŋ] *adj* trabajador.
hardy ['hɑːdɪ] *adj* fuerte, robusto; (*Bot*) resistente.
hare [hɛər] **1** *n* liebre *f*; **first catch your ~** no hay que empezar por el tejado. **2** *vi* (*) correr, ir rápidamente; **he went haring past** pasó como un rayo; **to ~ in, out, through** *etc* (*Brit*) entrar, salir, pasar *etc* a toda pastilla*.
harebell ['hɛəbel] *n* campánula *f*.
hare-brained ['hɛəbreɪnd] *adj* casquivano.
harelip ['hɛə'lɪp] *n* labio *m* leporino.
harelipped [,hɛə'lɪpt] *adj* de labio leporino, labihendido.
harem [hɑː'riːm] *n* harén *m*.
haricot ['hærɪkəʊ] *n* (*Brit*: *also* ~ **bean**) alubia *f*, judía *f*.
hark [hɑːk] *vi*: ~! ¡escucha!; ~ **at this!** ¡oye!; ~ **at him!** ¡qué cosas dice!, ¡quién fue a hablar!; ~ **at him singing!** ¡cómo canta el tío!; **to ~ to** escuchar.
◆**hark back** *vi*: **to ~ back to** *matter* volver a, *earlier occasion* recordar; **he's always ~ing back to that** siempre está con la misma canción.
Harlequin ['hɑːlɪkwɪn] *nm* Arlequín.
harlot ['hɑːlət] *n* ramera *f*.
harm [hɑːm] **1** *n* daño *m*, mal *m*; perjuicio *m*; **to be out of ~'s way** estar a salvo; **to keep out of ~'s way** evitar el peligro, permanecer (*or* mantenerse) lejos del sitio peligroso; **there's no ~ in** + *ger* no hay ningún mal en + *infin*; **I see no ~ in that** no veo nada en contra de eso; **to do sb ~** hacer daño a uno, (*fig*) perjudicar a uno; **it does more ~ than good** es peor el remedio que la enfermedad; **the ~ is done now** el mal ya está hecho; **he means no ~** tiene buenas intenciones.
2 *vt person* hacer daño a, hacer mal a; *crops etc* dañar, estropear; *interests etc* perjudicar.
3 *vi* sufrir daños; **will it ~ in the rain?** ¿lo estropeará la lluvia?; **it won't ~ for that** eso no le hará daño.
harmful ['hɑːmfʊl] *adj* perjudicial (*to* para), dañoso, nocivo; *pest, tobacco etc* dañino.
harmless ['hɑːmlɪs] *adj* inocuo, inofensivo; **to make a bomb ~** desactivar una bomba.
harmlessly ['hɑːmlɪslɪ] *adv* inocuamente, inofensivamente; sin causar daños.
harmonic [hɑː'mɒnɪk] *adj* armónico.
harmonica [hɑː'mɒnɪkə] *n* armónica *f*.
harmonics [hɑː'mɒnɪks] *n* armonía *f*.
harmonious [hɑː'məʊnɪəs] *adj* armonioso.
harmoniously [hɑː'məʊnɪəslɪ] *adv* armoniosamente.
harmonium [hɑː'məʊnɪəm] *n* armonio *m*.
harmonize ['hɑːmənaɪz] *vti* armonizar (*with* con).
harmony ['hɑːmənɪ] *n* armonía *f*; **close ~** armonía *f* cerrada.
harness ['hɑːnɪs] **1** *n* guarniciones *fpl*, arreos *mpl*; ~ **race** carrera *f* de trotones; **to die in ~** morir con las botas puestas; **to get back in ~** volver al trabajo, volver a su puesto.
2 *vt* (**a**) *horse* poner guarniciones a, enjaezar; **to ~ a horse to a cart** enganchar un caballo a un carro.
(**b**) *resources etc* hacer trabajar, utilizar, aprovechar.
harp [hɑːp] **1** *n* arpa *f*. **2** *vi*: **to ~ on** hablar constantemente de; **stop ~ing on it!** ¡no machaques!
harpist ['hɑːpɪst] *n* arpista *mf*.
harpoon [hɑː'puːn] **1** *n* arpón *m*. **2** *vt* arponear.
harpsichord ['hɑːpsɪkɔːd] *n* clavicordio *m*, clavicémbalo *m*.
harpy ['hɑːpɪ] *n* arpía *f*.
harquebus ['hɑːkwɪbəs] *n* (*Hist*) arcabuz *m*.
harridan ['hærɪdən] *n* bruja *f*.
harried ['hærɪd] *adj expression etc* preocupado.
harrier ['hærɪər] *n* (**a**) (*dog*) perro *m* de caza. (**b**) **~s** (*cross-country runners*) corredores *mpl* de cross. (**c**) (*Orn*) aguilucho *m*.
Harris ['hærɪs] *adj*: ~ **Tweed** ® tweed *m* producido en la isla de Harris.
harrow ['hærəʊ] **1** *n* grada *f*. **2** *vt* (**a**) (*Agr*) gradar. (**b**) (*fig*) torturar, destrozar.
harrowing ['hærəʊɪŋ] *adj* horrendo, horroroso, angustioso.
Harry ['hærɪ] *nm* Enrique; **to play old ~ with*** endiablar, estropear.
harry ['hærɪ] *vt* (*devastate*) asolar; (*Mil*) hostilizar; *person etc* hostigar, acosar.
harsh [hɑːʃ] *adj person, decision etc* severo, duro, cruel; *voice, cloth etc* áspero; *contrast* violento; *weather* severo; *colour* chillón; *taste* acerbo; *words* nada amistoso.
harshly ['hɑːʃlɪ] *adv* severamente, duramente; ásperamente.
harshness ['hɑːʃnɪs] *n* severidad *f*, dureza *f*, rigor *m*; aspereza *f*.
hart [hɑːt] *n* ciervo *m*.
harum-scarum ['hɛərəm'skɛərəm] **1** *adj* tarambana, atolondrado. **2** *n* tarambana *mf*.
harvest ['hɑːvɪst] **1** *n* cosecha *f*, recolección *f*; (*time of year*) siega *f*; (*of grape*) vendimia *f*; (*fig*) cosecha *f*.
2 *attr*: ~ **festival** fiesta *f* de la cosecha.
3 *vt* cosechar (*also fig*), recoger, recolectar.
4 *vi* cosechar, segar.
harvester ['hɑːvɪstər] *n* (*person*) segador *m*, -ora *f*; (*machine*) cosechadora *f*, segadora-trilladora *f*.
harvest home [,hɑːvɪst'həʊm] *n* (*festival*) ≈ fiesta *f* de la cosecha; (*season*) cosecha *f*.
harvesting ['hɑːvɪstɪŋ] *n* cosecha *f*, cosechado *m*.
harvest time ['hɑːvɪst,taɪm] *n* siega *f*.
has [hæz] *V* **have**.
has-been* ['hæzbiːn] *n* celebridad *f* del pasado; persona *f* quemada; vieja gloria *f*.
hash[1] [hæʃ] *n* picadillo *m*; (*) embrollo *m*, lío* *m*; **to make a ~ of sth** armarse un lío con algo*, estropear algo, hacer algo muy mal; **to settle sb's ~*** cargarse a uno*, acabar con uno.
◆**hash up** *vt*: **to ~ sth up** rehacer algo (y presentarlo como nuevo).
hash[2]**‡** [hæʃ] *n* hachís *m*, chocolate‡ *m*.
hashish ['hæʃɪʃ] *n* hachís *m*.
hasn't ['hæznt] = **has not**.
hasp [hɑːsp] *n* pasador *m*, sujetador *m*.
hassle* ['hæsl] **1** *n* (*squabble*) pelea *f*, riña *f*; (*difficulty*) lío* *m*, problema *m*; (*bustle*) bullicio *m*; **no ~!** ¡no hay pro-

blema!; **it's not worth the ~** no vale la pena.

2 *vt* molestar, fastidiar, dar la lata a*.

hassock ['hæsək] *n* (*Eccl*) cojín *m*.

haste [heɪst] *n* prisa *f*, precipitación *f*; **more ~ less speed, make ~ slowly** vísteme despacio que tengo prisa; **to do sth in ~** hacer algo de prisa; hacer algo precipitadamente; **to make ~** darse prisa; **make ~!** ¡date prisa!; **to make ~ to** + *infin* apresurarse a + *infin*.

hasten ['heɪsn] **1** *vt* acelerar; **to ~ one's steps** apretar el paso.

2 *vi* darse prisa, apresurarse; **to ~ to** + *infin* apresurarse a + *infin*.

◆**hasten away** *vi* marcharse precipitadamente (*from* de).

◆**hasten back** *vi* volver con toda prisa, darse prisa para volver.

◆**hasten off** *vi* = **hasten away**.

◆**hasten on** *vi* seguir adelante con toda prisa.

◆**hasten up** *vi* llegar apresuradamente, acudir rápidamente.

hastily ['heɪstɪlɪ] *adv* (*hurriedly*) de prisa, precipitadamente; *speak* sin reflexión, con impaciencia; *judge* a la ligera; **I ~ suggested that ...** me apresuré a sugerir que ...

hasty ['heɪstɪ] *adj* (*hurried*) apresurado, precipitado; (*rash*) irreflexivo, inconsiderado, imprudente; (*quick-tempered*) impaciente, que tiene genio; (*superficial*) ligero; **don't be so ~** hay que tomar las cosas con más calma.

hat [hæt] *n* sombrero *m*; **my ~!** ¡caramba!; **that's old ~** eso es de lo más anticuado; eso lo tenemos archisabido; **I'll eat my ~ if ...** que me maten si ...; **to hang one's ~ up** (*fig*) jubilarse; **keep it under your ~** de esto no digas ni pío; **to pass the ~ round** pasar el platillo; **to raise** (*or* **take off**) **one's ~** descubrirse; **to take one's ~ off to** (*fig*) descubrirse ante; saludar con respeto; **~s off to Joe!** ¡muy bien Paco!; **to wear two ~s** (*fig*) ostentar dos representaciones; **to talk through one's ~** decir tonterías; **now wearing my other ~** (*fig*) hablando ahora en mi otra calidad de ...

hatband ['hætbænd] *n* cinta *f* de sombrero.

hatbox ['hætbɒks] *n* sombrerera *f*.

hatch[1] [hætʃ] *n* (**a**) (*Naut*) escotilla *f*; (*Aut*) portón *m*. (**b**) (*Brit*) (**service** *or* **serving**) **~** ventanilla *f* para servir.

hatch[2] [hætʃ] **1** *vt* (**a**) *chick* empollar, incubar; sacar del cascarón. (**b**) (*fig*: *also* **to ~ up**) idear; *plot* tramar.

2 *vi* (*bird*) salir del huevo; (*insect*) eclosionar; **the egg ~ed** el pollo rompió el cascarón y salió; **those eggs never ~ed** esos huevos resultaron ser hueros.

hatch[3] [hætʃ] *vt* (*Art*) sombrear.

hatchback ['hætʃbæk] *n* (*door*) puerta *f* trasera, portón *m*; (*vehicle*) coche *m* con portón trasero.

hat-check ['hæt,tʃek] *attr*: **~ girl** (*US*) encargada *f* del guardarropa.

hatchery ['hætʃərɪ] *n* criadero *m*, vivero *m*.

hatchet ['hætʃɪt] **1** *n* hacha *f* (pequeña), machado *m*; **to bury the ~** echar pelillos a la mar, envainar la espada.

2 *attr*: **~ job*** golpe *m* cruel pero eficaz; faena *f* desagradable pero necesaria; **~ man*** (*US*) asesino *m* a sueldo; ejecutor *m* de faenas desagradables por cuenta de otro.

hatchet-faced ['hætʃɪt,feɪst] *adj* de cara de cuchillo.

hatching[1] ['hætʃɪŋ] *n* incubación *f*; salida *f* del huevo; eclosión *f*; (*fig*) ideación *f*; preparación *f*, maquinación *f*.

hatching[2] ['hætʃɪŋ] *n* (*Art*) sombreado *m*.

hatchway ['hætʃweɪ] *n* escotilla *f*.

hate [heɪt] **1** *n* (**a**) odio *m*; **~ mail** cartas *fpl* en las que se expresa odio al destinatario.

(**b**) **one of my pet ~s** uno de mis hinchas, una de las cosas que más detesto.

2 *vt* (**a**) odiar, detestar, aborrecer; **to ~ sb like poison** odiar a uno a muerte.

(**b**) **I ~ to see that** me da asco ver aquello; **I ~ to say so** lamento tener que decirlo; **I ~ having to do it** me repugna hacerlo; **I ~ to trouble you** siento muchísimo molestarle; **I should ~ to have to sell it** lamentaría tener que venderlo; **he ~s to be corrected** detesta que le corrijan.

hateful ['heɪtfʊl] *adj* odioso, repugnante.

hatless ['hætlɪs] *adj* sin sombrero, descubierto.

hatpin ['hætpɪn] *n* agujón *m*.

hatrack ['hætræk] *n* percha *f* para sombreros.

hatred ['heɪtrɪd] *n* odio *m* (*for* a), aborrecimiento *m* (*for* de).

hat shop ['hætʃɒp] *n* sombrerería *f*.

hatstand ['hætstænd] *n* percha *f* para sombreros, sombrerera *f* (*Carib*).

hatter ['hætə[r]] *n* sombrerero *m*.

hat tree ['hættriː] *n* (*US*) percha *f* para sombreros.

hat-trick ['hættrɪk] *n* (*fig*) tres tantos *mpl* (*or* triunfos *mpl*) en un partido; serie *f* de tres victorias (*etc*); **to do the ~, to get** (*or* **score**) **a ~** marcar tres tantos en un partido.

haughtily ['hɔːtɪlɪ] *adv* arrogantemente.

haughtiness ['hɔːtɪnɪs] *n* altanería *f*, arrogancia *f*, altivez *f*.

haughty ['hɔːtɪ] *adj* altanero, arrogante, altivo.

haul [hɔːl] **1** *n* (**a**) (*act of pulling*) tirón *m*, estirón *m* (*on* de).

(**b**) (*distance*) recorrido *m*, trayecto *m*; **it's a good** (*or* **long**) **~** es mucho camino.

(**c**) (*amount of fish*) redada *f*; (*financial*) ganancia *f*; (*stolen*) botín *m*; (*arms ~, drugs ~*) alijo *m*; **the thieves made a good ~** los ladrones obtuvieron un cuantioso botín.

2 *vt* (*drag*) tirar, arrastrar; (*transport*) acarrear, transportar; **he was ~ed before the manager** tuvo que presentarse al gerente.

3 *vi*: **to ~ on, to ~ at** tirar de; (*Naut*) halar.

◆**haul down** *vt flag* arriar.

◆**haul in** *vt net etc* ir recogiendo.

◆**haul up** *vt* (**a**) ir levantando. (**b**) **he was ~ed up in court** fue llevado ante el tribunal.

haulage ['hɔːlɪdʒ] *n* (*act*) acarreo *m*, transporte *m*; (*cost*) gastos *mpl* de acarreo; **~ company** compañía *f* de transportes (por carretera); **~ contractor** contratista *m* de transportes, transportista *m*.

hauler ['hɔːlə[r]] (*US*), **haulier** ['hɔːlɪə[r]] *n* contratista *m* de transportes, transportista *m*.

haunch [hɔːntʃ] *n* anca *f*; (*of meat*) pierna *f*; **to sit on one's ~es** sentarse en cuclillas.

haunt [hɔːnt] **1** *n* (*animal's*) nidal *m*, guarida *f*, querencia *f*; **I know his ~s** conozco sus sitios favoritos, sé dónde suele estar; **it's a ~ of artists** es lugar predilecto de los artistas.

2 *vt* (**a**) (*frequent*) frecuentar, rondar; **he ~s the theatres** aparece constantemente en los teatros.

(**b**) (*of ghost*) aparecer en, andar por; **the house is ~ed** en la casa andan fantasmas, la casa está embrujada; **~ed house** casa *f* de fantasmas, casa *f* encantada.

(**c**) *person* perseguir; obsesionar; **he is ~ed by memories** le persiguen sus recuerdos, le atormentan sus recuerdos; **he is ~ed by the thought that ...** le obsesiona el pensamiento de que ...

haunted ['hɔːntɪd] *adj look etc* obsesionado.

haunting ['hɔːntɪŋ] *adj* obsesionante; *melody* inolvidable.

hauntingly ['hɔːntɪŋlɪ] *adv*: **a ~ lovely scene** una escena de una belleza inolvidable.

haute couture [otkutyr] *n* alta costura *f*.

haute cuisine [otkwizin] *n* alta cocina *f*.

Havana [hə'vænə] *n* La Habana.

have [hæv] (*irr*: *3rd sing present* **has**, *pret and ptp* **had**) **1** *vt* (**a**) (*possess*) tener; poseer; **all I ~** todo lo que tengo; **~ you any bananas?** (*in shop*) ¿hay plátanos?; **I ~ no words to express ...** no encuentro palabras para expresar ...; **I ~ no German** no sé alemán; **I ~ it!** ¡ya!; **... and what ~ you ...** y qué sé yo qué más; etcétera, etcétera; **the dog had him by the throat** el perro le tenía agarrado por la garganta; **I never guessed he had it in him** no le suponía nunca capaz de eso; **you must give it all you ~, you must put everything you ~ into it** tienes que emplearte a fondo.

(**b**) (*bear, carry*) tener, llevar; **the book has no name on it** el libro no lleva el nombre del dueño; **to ~ a hat on** llevar un sombrero (puesto); **do you ~ a pound about you?** ¿llevas encima una libra?

(**c**) *baby* parir, dar a luz; **she's going to ~ a baby** va a tener un niño.

(**d**) (*obtain, acquire, hand over*) **to ~ a letter from sb** recibir una carta de uno; **to ~ no news** no tener noticias; **I ~ it on good authority that ...** sé de buena tinta que ...; **it is to be had at the chemist's** se vende en la farmacia; **it's not to be had anywhere** no se consigue en ninguna parte; **I must ~ £5 at once** necesito 5 libras en seguida; **you can ~ it for £2** te lo vendo por 2 libras; **let me ~ your pen** ¿me prestas la pluma?; **he let me ~ some money** me facilitó dinero; **I will let you ~ my reply tomorrow** les daré mi respuesta mañana.

(**e**) (*strike*) dar, pegar; **let him ~ it!** ¡dale!; **then they let him ~ it** luego empezaron a pegarle, (*fig*: *scold*) luego le dijeron cuatro verdades.

(**f**) (*eat, drink etc*) tomar; **I don't ~ anything at night** por la noche no tomo nada; **to ~ tea with sb** tomar el té con uno, merendar con uno; **he's having his dinner** está comiendo; **what did you ~ at the dinner?** ¿qué te dieron de comer en el banquete?; **will you ~ a drink?** ¿quieres tomar algo?; **will you ~ some more?** ¿quieres más?; **to ~ a cigarette** fumar un pitillo.

(**g**) (*n phrases*; *V also n*) **to ~ a game** echar una

partida; **to ~ a bath** tomar un baño; **to ~ a lesson** tomar lección; **to ~ measles** tener sarampión; **to ~ a good time** pasarlo bien; **did you ~ any trouble?** ¿tuviste alguna dificultad?; **I had a strange adventure** me pasó algo raro; **I never seem to ~ anything happen to me** parece que no me pasa nunca nada.

(**h**) (*wish*) **which will you ~?** ¿cuál quieres?; **what more would you ~?** ¿qué más quieres?; **as ill-luck would ~ it** desgraciadamente, como quiso la suerte; **I would ~ you know that ...** sepa Vd que ...

(**i**) (*permit*) permitir, tolerar; **I won't ~ such behaviour** no tolero esta conducta; **I'm not having that** no puedo consentir en que se haga (*or* diga *etc*) eso; **we can't ~ that** eso no se puede consentir; **we don't ~ children here** aquí no recibimos a los matrimonios que traigan hijos, aquí no se reciben niños.

(**j**) (*insist, say*) **he will ~ it that ...** sostiene que ...; **he will not ~ it that ...** no quiere reconocer que ...; **as rumour has it** según se dice; **as Keats has it** según (dice) Keats.

(**k**) (*: *deceive*) **you've been had** te han engañado; **I'm not to be had that way** no se me engaña así; **there you ~ me** de eso no sé nada en absoluto.

(**l**) (*obligation*) **to ~ to do sth** tener que hacer algo; **it has to be done this way** ha de hacerse de este modo; **does it ~ to be ironed?** ¿hay que plancharlo?

(**m**) (*causative*) **to ~ sth done** hacer hacer algo; **to ~ a suit made** mandar confeccionar un traje; **please ~ it repaired** por favor mándelo componer; **he had his watch stolen** le robaron el reloj; **he had his arm broken** se rompió el brazo; **I won't ~ her insulted** no permito que se le insulte; **to ~ sb do sth** hacer que uno haga algo; **he would ~ me do it** insistió en que yo lo hiciera; **what else would you ~ me do?** ¿qué más queréis que haga?; **there was a general desire to ~ it over with** todos estaban deseando que se concluyese de una vez.

(**n**) **I ~ letters to write** tengo cartas que escribir; **~n't you anything to do?** ¿no tienes nada que hacer?

(**o**) (*auxiliary*) haber; **he has gone** ha ido; **he had spoken** había hablado; **it has been raining for 3 days** llueve desde hace 3 días; **I ~n't seen him for 2 years** hace 2 años que no le veo; **never having seen it before, I ...** como no lo había visto antes, yo ...; **'I ~ 2 cars' ... 'so ~ I'** 'tengo 2 coches' ... 'yo también'; **'it's gone!' ... 'so it has!'** '¡ha desaparecido!' ... '¡es verdad!'

(**p**) **I had better, sooner** *etc*: *V* **better, sooner** *etc*.

(**q**) **you've had it!*** ¡estás listo!*; **we must run or we've had it*** tenemos que correr o estamos listos*; **I've had it*** estoy hasta las narices (*or* el último pelo)*.

(**r**) (*have sex with*) poseer, dormir con.

2 *n*: **the ~s and the ~-nots** los ricos y los pobres.

◆**have down** *vt*: **we are having the Smiths down for a few days** hemos invitado a los Smith a pasar unos días con nosotros.

◆**have in** *vt* (**a**) *person* hacer entrar; *doctor etc* llamar; **let's ~ him in!** ¡que pase!, ¡que entre!; **to ~ sb in to supper** invitar a uno a cenar; **we're having people in** tenemos invitados.

(**b**) **to ~ it in for sb*** tener manía a uno, tenérsela jurada a uno.

◆**have off** *vt*: **to ~ it off**** (*Brit*) echar un polvo**; **to ~ it off with sb**** tirarse con una**.

◆**have on** *vt* (**a**) *clothes* llevar, tener puesto; **he had nothing on** estaba desnudo.

(**b**) (*Brit: be busy*) **I ~ a lot on this week** tengo muchos compromisos esta semana, esta semana estoy muy ocupado; **do you ~ anything on tonight?** ¿tienes compromiso para esta noche?

(**c**) (*Brit*) (*tease*) tomar el pelo a; (*deceive*) embaucar; **they're having you on** te están tomando el pelo.

◆**have out** *vt* (**a**) *tooth* hacer sacar.

(**b**) **to ~ it out with sb** resolver un problema hablando con uno; (*unfriendly*) ajustar cuentas con uno; **I'm going to ~ it out with him** voy a poner las cosas en claro con él.

◆**have up** *vt* (**a**) *guest* hacer venir, invitar.

(**b**) (*: *charge*) **to ~ sb up** llevar a uno ante los tribunales (*for* acusándole de); **he was had up for larceny** le procesaron por ladrón.

haven ['heɪvn] *n* puerto *m*; (*fig*) refugio *m*, asilo *m*.

have-nots ['hævnɒts] *npl*: **the ~** los pobres, los desposeídos.

haven't ['hævnt] = **have not**.

haversack ['hævəsæk] *n* mochila *f*.

havoc ['hævək] *n* estragos *mpl*, destrucción *f*; **to make ~ of, to play ~ with** hacer estragos en, arruinar, estropear.

haw¹ [hɔː] *n* baya *f* del espino.

haw² [hɔː] *vi*: **to hem and ~, to hum and ~** vacilar.

Hawaii [hə'waɪiː] *n* (Islas *fpl*) Hawai *m*.

Hawaiian [hə'waɪjən] **1** *adj* hawaiano. **2** *n* hawaiano *m*, -a *f*.

hawfinch ['hɔːfɪntʃ] *n* picogordo *m*.

hawk¹ [hɔːk] *n* (*Orn*) halcón *m*, gavilán *m*; (*Pol*) halcón *m*; **he was watching me like a ~** me vigilaba estrechamente, no me quitaba ojo.

hawk² [hɔːk] *vt* pregonar, vender por las calles.

hawk³ [hɔːk] *vi* carraspear.

◆**hawk up** *vt* arrojar tosiendo.

hawker ['hɔːkə^r] *n* vendedor *m* ambulante.

hawk-eyed [ˌhɔːk'aɪd] *adj* con ojos de lince.

hawkish ['hɔːkɪʃ] *adj* (*Pol etc*) duro.

hawser ['hɔːzə^r] *n* guindaleza *f*, calabrote *m*, maroma *f*.

hawthorn ['hɔːθɔːn] *n* espino *m*, oxiacanta *f*.

hay [heɪ] *n* heno *m*; **to hit the ~*** acostarse; **to make ~ of*** *enemy* desbaratar; *team* cascar*; *argument* destruir; **to make ~ while the sun shines** hacer su agosto; **that ain't ~** (*US**) no es moco de pavo*, es una pasta gansa*.

haycock ['heɪkɒk] *n* montón *m* de heno.

hay fever ['heɪˌfiːvə^r] *n* fiebre *f* del heno, catarro *m* del heno.

hayfork ['heɪfɔːk] *n* bieldo *m*.

hayloft ['heɪlɒft] *n* henil *m*, henal *m*.

haymaker ['heɪmeɪkə^r] *n* heneador *m*, -ora *f*, labrador *m*, -ora *f* que trabaja en la siega (*or* la recolección) del heno.

haymaking ['heɪmeɪkɪŋ] *n* henificación *f*; época *f* del heno; siega *f* del heno, recolección *f* del heno.

hayseed* ['heɪsiːd] *n* (*US*) palurdo *m*, paleto* *m*.

haystack ['heɪstæk] *n* almiar *m*.

haywire* ['heɪwaɪə^r] *adj* (*confused*) en desorden; descompuesto; (*mad*) loco; **to go ~** (*person*) destornillarse*; (*scheme etc*) embrollarse, embarrullarse; **it's all gone ~** en eso existe la mayor confusión, todo está en desorden.

hazard ['hæzəd] **1** *n* riesgo *m*. **2** *attr*: **~ warning lights** señales *fpl* de emergencia. **3** *vt* (**a**) arriesgar, poner en peligro. (**b**) *guess, remark* atreverse a hacer, aventurar.

hazardous ['hæzədəs] *adj* arriesgado, peligroso; **~ pay** (*US*) prima *f* por trabajos peligrosos.

haze¹ [heɪz] *n* calina *f*, neblina *f*; (*fig*) confusión *f*; **a ~ of tobacco smoke filled the room** el cuarto estaba lleno de humo de tabaco.

haze² [heɪz] *vt* (*US*) gastar novatadas a.

hazel ['heɪzl] **1** *n* avellano *m*. **2** *adj eyes* garzo.

hazelnut ['heɪzlnʌt] *n* avellana *f*.

hazelwood ['heɪzl,wʊd] *n* madera *f* de avellano.

haziness ['heɪzɪnɪs] *n* (**a**) lo calinoso, lo brumoso. (**b**) (*fig*) confusión *f*, vaguedad *f*.

hazing ['heɪzɪŋ] *n* (*US*) novatadas *fpl*.

hazy ['heɪzɪ] *adj* (**a**) calinoso, brumoso. (**b**) (*fig*) confuso, vago; **he's ~ about dates** no recuerda exactamente las fechas; **I'm ~ about maths** tengo solamente una idea vaga de las matemáticas; **he seemed very ~** parecía no tener ninguna idea clara.

H-bomb ['eɪtʃbɒm] *m* bomba *f* H.

HCF *n abbr of* **highest common factor** máximo común divisor *m*.

HE (**a**) *abbr of* **high explosive**. (**b**) *abbr of* **His** *or* **Her Excellency** Su Excelencia, S.E. (**c**) (*Eccl*) *abbr of* **His Eminence** Su Eminencia, S.Emª.

he [hiː] **1** *pron* él; **~ who** el que, quien. **2** *n* macho *m*, varón *m*; **to play ~** (*children's game*) dar la despedida. **3** *attr* macho.

head [hed] **1** *n* (**a**) (*Anat*) cabeza *f*; **~ of hair** cabellera *f*; **~ first, ~ foremost** de cabeza; **to go ~ over heels** caer patas arriba; **to fall ~ over heels in love with sb** enamorarse perdidamente de uno; **from ~ to foot** de pies a cabeza; **we are banging our ~s against a brick wall** estamos machacando en hierro frío; **to bite sb's ~ off** echar un rapapolvo a uno; **to give a horse its ~** dar rienda suelta a un caballo; **to give sb his ~** dar rienda suelta a uno; **she has her ~ in the clouds** está en las nubes; **to hide one's ~ in the sand** meter la cabeza debajo del ala; **now he can hold his ~ up again** ahora ha recuperado la propia estimación; **to keep one's ~ above water** (*fig*) ir tirando; **to laugh one's ~ off*** desternillarse de risa*; **to nod one's ~** asentir con la cabeza, mover la cabeza afirmativamente; **to shake one's ~** negar algo con la cabeza, mover la cabeza negativamente; **he stands ~ and shoulders above the rest** los demás no le llegan a la suela del zapato; **I could do it standing on my ~** lo podría hacer sin mirar; **to talk one's ~ off** hablar por los codos; **to turn one's ~ the other way** (*fig*) hacer la vista gorda; **he is taller than his brother by a ~** le saca la cabeza a su hermano; **to win by**

a (short) ~ ganar por una cabeza (escasa); **on his own ~ be it** sea bajo su propia responsabilidad; **to put a price on sb's ~** poner precio a la cabeza de uno; **to stand on one's ~** hacer el pino; **to stand an argument on its ~** demostrar la falsedad de un argumento; **to give orders over sb's ~** dar órdenes sin consultar a uno; **they went over my ~ to the mayor** hablaron con el alcalde sin hacer caso de mí; **to sell a house over sb's ~** vender una casa sin decir nada a uno; **the wine goes to my ~** el vino se me sube a la cabeza; **success has gone to his ~** el éxito le ha subido a la cabeza.

(b) (*intellect, mind*) cabeza *f*, inteligencia *f*; talento *m*; **two ~s are better than one** cuatro ojos ven más que dos; **don't bother your ~ about it** no te preocupes, no te canses tratando de explicarlo (*etc*); **it never entered my ~** jamás se me pasó por la cabeza; **to have a bad ~** tener dolor de cabeza; **to have a swelled** (*or* **swollen**) **~** ser vanidoso; **to have a ~ for business** tener talento para los negocios; **to have a ~ for languages** tener aptitud para los idiomas; **to have no ~ for heights** no tener cabeza para las alturas; **he has a good ~ on him** es inteligente, tiene cabeza, tiene talento; **to keep one's ~** no perder la cabeza; **to lose one's ~** perder la cabeza; **so we put our ~s together** así que tratamos los dos de resolverlo; **to turn sb's ~** (*make mad*) trastornar el juicio de uno, (*make vain*) envanecer a uno.

(c) (*phrases with prep*) **it was above their ~s** estaba fuera de su alcance, no eran lo bastante inteligentes para comprenderlo; **to do a sum in one's ~** hacer un cálculo mental; **to be soft** (*or* **weak**) **in the ~** ser un poco tocado, andar mal de la cabeza; **to get sth into sb's ~** meter a uno algo en la cabeza; **he has got it into his ~ that ...** cree firmemente que ...; **get it into your ~ that ...** date cuenta de que ...; **I can't get that tune out of my ~** me obsesiona esa melodía; **what put that into your ~?** ¿de dónde sacas eso?; **to take it into one's ~ to** + *infin* ocurrirse a uno + *infin*; **to be off one's ~** estar loco; **you must be off your ~!** ¿estás loco?; **this will bring matters to a ~** con esto las cosas llegarán a la crisis, con esto llegamos al momento de la verdad.

(d) (*person*) (*leader*) jefe *m*, cabeza *m*; (*of school*) director *m*, -ora *f*; **~ of a department** jefe *m*, -a *f* de departamento; **~ of state** jefe *m*, -a *f* de estado; **crowned ~** testa *f* coronada; **£5 a ~** 5 libras por persona (*or* por cabeza).

(e) (*on coin*) cara *f*; **to toss ~s or tails** echar a cara o cruz; **~s I win, tails you lose** cara, yo gano, cruz, tu pierdes; **I couldn't make ~ or tail of it** no logré sacar nada en claro, no tiene pies ni cabeza.

(f) 20 ~ of cattle 20 reses *fpl*; **20 ~ of sheep** 20 ovejas *fpl*.

(g) (*of objects etc*) (*of bed*) cabecera *f*; (*of table, bridge, nail etc*) cabeza *f*; (*of arrow etc*) punta *f*; (*of stick*) puño *m*; (*of cylinder*) culata *f*; (*Comput*) cabeza *f* (grabadora), cabezal *m*; (*Naut*) proa *f*; (*Geog*) punta *f*; (*of water*) altura *f* de caída; (*on beer*) espuma *f*; (*Bot*) flor *f*, cabezuela *f*; (*of tree*) copa *f*; (*of corn*) espigas *fpl*; **at the ~ of the valley** al final del valle; **to bring sth to a ~** hacer que algo llegue a su punto decisivo; **to come to a ~** (*abscess*) supurar, (*fig*) llegar a la crisis.

(h) (*heading*) título *m*, encabezamiento *m*; (*section*) sección *f*, apartado *m*; **under this ~** en este apartado.

(i) (*front place*) cabeza *f*; **~ of the family** cabeza *mf* de la familia; **to be at the ~ of the list** encabezar la lista; **to be at the ~ of the league** ir en cabeza de la liga.

(j) acid ~‡ aficionado *m*, -a *f* al ácido.

(k) (*US***) cagadero** *m*.

2 *attr* **(a)** principal, primero; **~ boy** (*Brit Scol*) alumno *m* principal; **~ buyer** comprador *m*, -ora *f* principal; **~ clerk** encargado *m*, -a *f*; **~ cook** primer cocinero *m*, primera cocinera *f*, jefe *m*, -a *f* de cocina; **~ girl** (*Brit Scol*) alumna *f* principal; **~ man** (*hum*) jefe *m*; **~ office** oficina *f* central; **~ salesman** vendedor *m* en jefe; **to have a ~ start** (*fig*) empezar con gran ventaja (*over* con respecto a); **~ teacher** director *m*, -ora *f*; **~ waiter** jefe *m* de comedor.

(b) *part* delantero, de frente.

3 *vt* **(a)** *list etc* encabezar, estar a la cabeza de; *league* ir en cabeza de; *poll* ganar; *rebellion* acaudillar; *company* dirigir; *team* capitanear.

(b) *football* cabecear; *goal* cabecear, rematar con la cabeza.

(c) he ~ed the boat for the shore dirigió la barca hacia la costa; **to be ~ed for** ir con rumbo a.

4 *vi*: **to ~ for, to ~ towards** dirigirse a (*or* hacia); encaminarse a; **to be ~ing for** ir con rumbo a; **where are you ~ing for?** ¿adónde se dirige?; **we are ~ing for ruin** vamos camino de la ruina.

◆**head off** *vt* interceptar, atajar; desviar; (*fig*) distraer, apartar.

headache ['hedeɪk] *n* dolor *m* de cabeza; (*sick*) jaqueca *f*; (*fig*) quebradero *m* de cabeza, dolor *m* de cabeza; **that's his ~** allá él, eso a él.

headband ['hedbænd] *n* cinta *f* (para la cabeza), venda *f* (para la cabeza).

headboard ['hed,bɔːd] *n* cabecera *f*.

headcheese ['hed,tʃiːz] *n* (*US*) carne *f* en gelatina.

head cold ['hedkəʊld] *n* resfriado *m* de cabeza.

headcount ['hedkaʊnt] *n* recuento *m* de la asistencia.

head-dress ['heddres] *n* toca *f*, tocado *m*.

headed ['hedɪd] *adj notepaper* membretado, con membrete.

-headed ['hedɪd] *adj* con cabeza ..., de cabeza ..., *eg* **small~** de cabeza pequeña; **fair~** pelirrubio.

header ['hedəʳ] *n* (*fall*) caída *f* de cabeza; (*dive*) salto *m* de cabeza; (*Sport*) cabezazo *m*; (*Typ, Comput*) encabezamiento *m*.

header-block ['hedə,blɒk] *n* bloque *m* de encabezamiento, encabezamiento *m*.

head-first [,hed'fɜːst] *adv* de cabeza.

headgear ['hedgɪəʳ] *n* sombrero *m*; (*woman's*) tocado *m*.

headguard ['hedgɑːd] *n* casco *m* protector; protector *m* facial.

headhunt ['hed,hʌnt] *vt* cazar; **he was ~ed by a bank** fue cazado por un banco.

headhunter ['hed,hʌntəʳ] *n* cazador *m* de cabezas; (*fig*) cazatalentos *mf*, cazaejecutivos *mf*, cazador *m*, -ora *f* de cabezas.

headhunting ['hed,hʌntɪŋ] **1** *n* (*fig*) caza *f* de cabezas; (*fig*) caza *f* de talentos, caza *f* de cerebros. **2** *attr*: **~ agency** agencia *f* de caza de talentos.

heading ['hedɪŋ] *n* (*title*) encabezamiento *m*, título *m*; (*letterhead*) membrete *m*; (*section*) sección *f*, apartado *m*; **to come under the ~ of** clasificarse bajo, estar incluido en.

headlamp ['hedlæmp] *n* (*Brit*) faro *m*.

headland ['hedlənd] *n* promontorio *m*.

headless ['hedlɪs] *adj* sin cabeza; acéfalo.

headlight ['hedlaɪt] *n* faro *m*.

headline ['hedlaɪn] **1** *n* encabezamiento *m*, cabeza *f*; **~s** titulares *mpl*; **this will hit the ~s** saldrá en primera plana, esto es sensacional. **2** *vt* anunciar con titulares.

headlong ['hedlɒŋ] **1** *adj fall* de cabeza, de bruces; *rush etc* precipitado. **2** *adv* de cabeza, de bruces; precipitadamente.

headman ['hedmæn] *n, pl* **headmen** ['hedmen] cacique *m*.

headmaster ['hed'mɑːstəʳ] *n* (*Brit*) director *m* (de colegio *etc*).

headmistress ['hed'mɪstrɪs] *n* (*Brit*) directora *f* (de colegio *etc*).

head-on ['hed'ɒn] **1** *adj collision* de frente, frontal. **2** *adv* de frente; **he crashed ~ with a truck** colisionó frontalmente con un camión.

headphone(s) ['hedfəʊn(z)] *n*(*pl*) auricular(es) *m*(*pl*), audífono(s) *m*(*pl*).

headquarter ['hedkwɔːtəʳ] *vt* (*US*): **the company is ~ed in Reno** la compañía tiene su sede en Reno.

headquarters ['hed'kwɔːtəz] **1** *npl* (*Mil*) cuartel *m* general; (*of party, organization*) sede *f*; (*Comm*) oficina *f* central, central *f*; (*of revolt etc*) centro *m*, foco *m*. **2** *attr*: **~ staff** plantilla *f* de la oficina central.

headrest ['hedrest] *n* reposacabezas *m*, apoyacabezas *m*.

head restraint ['hedrɪs'treɪnt] *n* (*Aut*) apoyacabezas *m*.

headroom ['hedrʊm] *n* espacio *m* para la cabeza; espacio *m* para estar (derecho) de pie; (*under bridge etc*) luz *f*, altura *f* libre; **'2 m ~'** '2 m. de altura libre'.

headscarf ['hedskɑːf] *n, pl* **~s** *or* **headscarves** ['hedskɑːvz] pañuelo *m*.

headset ['hedset] *n* auriculares *mpl*, audífonos *mpl*.

headship ['hedʃɪp] *n* jefatura *f*; dirección *f*; (*of school*) puesto *m* de director(a).

head-shrinker* ['hed,ʃrɪŋkəʳ] *n* psiquíatra *mf*.

headsman ['hedzmən] *n, pl* **headsmen** ['hedzmən] verdugo *m*.

headsquare ['hedskwɛəʳ] *n* pañuelo *m* de cabeza.

headstand ['hedstænd] *n* posición *f* de cabeza.

headstone ['hedstəʊn] *n* lápida *f* (mortuoria).

headstrong ['hedstrɒŋ] *adj* voluntarioso, impetuoso, testarudo.

headwaters ['hed,wɔːtəz] *npl* cabecera *f* (de un río).

headway ['hedweɪ] *n* progreso *m*; **to make ~** avanzar, (*fig*) hacer progresos; **we could make no ~ against the current** no logramos avanzar contra la corriente, la corriente nos impidió avanzar; **I didn't make much ~ with him** no he conseguido hacer carrera con él.

headwind ['hedwɪnd] *n* viento *m* contrario, viento *m* de proa.

headword ['hedwɜːd] *n* (palabra *f* que encabeza un) artículo *m*.

heady ['hedɪ] *adj wine* fuerte, lleno, cabezudo; (*fig*) embriagador.

heal [hiːl] **1** *vt* curar, sanar (*of* de); (*fig*) curar, remediar. **2** *vi* (*also* **to ~ up**) cicatrizarse.

healer ['hiːləʳ] *n* curador *m*, -ora *f*.

healing ['hiːlɪŋ] **1** *adj* curativo, sanativo. **2** *n* curación *f*.

health [helθ] **1** *n* (**a**) (*of person*) salud *f*; (*public* ~) sanidad *f*, higiene *f*; (*Brit*) **Department of/Secretary of State for H~ and Social Security**, (*US*) **Department/Secretary of H~ and Human Services** Ministerio *m* de/Secretario *m* de Estado de Sanidad y Seguridad Social; **Minister/Ministry of H~** (*Brit*) Ministro *m*/Ministerio *m* de Sanidad, Dirección *f* General de Sanidad (*Spain*); **to be in good** (*or* **bad**) **~** estar bien (*o* mal) de salud; **to restore sb to ~** devolver la salud a uno.

(**b**) (*toast*) brindis *m*; **good ~!** ¡salud!; **here's a ~ to X!** ¡vaya por X!; **to drink** (**to**) **sb's ~** beber a la salud de uno, brindar por uno.

2 *attr*: **H~ Authority** (*Brit*) autoridades *fpl* sanitarias; **~ benefit** (*US*) subsidio *m* de enfermedad; **~ care** asistencia *f* sanitaria; **~ center** (*US*), **~ centre** centro *m* médico, ambulatorio *m*; **~ education** educación *f* sanitaria; **~ farm** centro *m* de salud; **~ foods** alimentos *mpl* naturales; **~ hazard** riesgo *m* para la salud; **~ insurance** seguro *m* de enfermedad; **~ problem** (*personal*) problema *m* de salud, (*public*) problema *m* sanitario; **~ resort** (*watering place*) balneario *m*; (*in mountains*) sanatorio *m*; **National H~ Service** Seguro *m* de Enfermedad (*Sp*); **H~ Service doctor** médico *m* de la Seguridad Social; **~ visitor** auxiliar *m* sanitario, auxiliar *f* sanitaria.

healthful ['helθfʊl] *adj*, **health-giving** ['helθ,gɪvɪŋ] *adj* sano, saludable.

healthily ['helθɪlɪ] *adv live etc* sanamente; **~ sceptical about ...** sanamente escéptico acerca de ...

healthy ['helθɪ] *adj* (**a**) (*healthful*) sano, saludable; *place etc* salubre. (**b**) *person* sano, con buena salud; **to be ~** tener buena salud.

heap [hiːp] **1** *n* montón *m*, pila *f*, rimero *m*; (*fig**) montón* *m*; **a whole ~ of trouble** un montón de disgustos*; **a whole ~ of people** muchísimas personas; **~s of times** muchísimas veces; **we have ~s** tenemos montones*; **we have ~s of time** nos sobra tiempo, tenemos tiempo de sobra; **the news struck him all of a ~** la noticia le tumbó.

2 *vt* (*also* **to ~ up**) amontonar, apilar; *plate, spoon etc* colmar (*with* de); **to ~ together** juntar en un montón; **to ~ favours on sb** colmar a uno de favores.

3 *adv* (*) **~s** muchísimo; **~s better** muchísimo mejor.

hear [hɪəʳ] (*irr*: *pret and ptp* **heard**) **1** *vt* oír; (*perceive*) sentir; (*listen to*) escuchar; *lecture* asistir a; *piece of news* saber; (*Jur*) *case* ver; **do you ~ me?** ¿me oyes?; **I ~ bad reports of him** me dan malos informes sobre él; **I never ~d such rubbish!** ¡en mi vida he oído tantos disparates!; **I have ~d it said that ...** he oído decir que ...; **to ~ sb speak** oír hablar a uno; **I could hardly make myself ~d** apenas pude hacerme oír; **to ~ that ...** oír decir que ...; **when I ~d that ...** cuando supe que ...

2 *vi* oír; **~ ~!** ¡muy bien!; **to ~ about, to ~ of** oír hablar de, oír mentar (*LAm*), saber, enterarse de; **when I ~d of it** cuando lo supe; **I've never ~d of him** no le conozco en absoluto; **he won't ~ of it** no lo permite, no quiere autorizarlo; **I won't ~ of it!** ¡ni hablar!; **to ~ from** tener noticias de, recibir carta de; **you'll be ~ing from me** le escribiré; **you will ~ from my solicitor** Vd recibirá una comunicación de mi abogado; **let's ~ from you soon!** ¡no dejes de escribirnos pronto!, ¡mándanos noticias tuyas!

◆**hear out** *vt*: **to ~ sb out** escuchar a uno hasta el fin; **let us ~ him out** que diga todo lo que quiera.

heard [hɜːd] *pret and ptp of* **hear**.

hearer ['hɪərəʳ] *n* oyente *mf*.

hearing ['hɪərɪŋ] *n* (**a**) (*sense of* ~) oído *m*; **~ defect** defecto *m* auditivo; **in my ~** en mi presencia, estando yo delante; **to be out of ~** estar fuera del alcance del oído; **to be within ~** estar al alcance del oído. (**b**) (*act*) audición *f*; (*Jur*) vista *f*; **to condemn sb without a ~** condenar a uno sin escuchar su defensa; **he never got a fair ~** en ningún momento se le permitió explicar su punto de vista; (*Jur*) no se le juzgó imparcialmente.

hearing-aid ['hɪərɪŋeɪd] *n* aparato *m* del oído, audífono *m*.

hearing-assisted ['hɪərɪŋə'sɪstɪd] *adj* (*US*): **~ telephone** teléfono *m* con sonido aumentado.

hearken ['hɑːkən] *vi*: **to ~ to** (††, *liter*) escuchar.

hearsay ['hɪəseɪ] **1** *n* rumores *mpl*, hablillas *fpl*; **it's just ~** son rumores; **by ~** de oídas. **2** *attr*: **~ evidence** testimonio *m* basado en lo que ha dicho otro.

hearse [hɜːs] *n* coche *m* fúnebre, coche *m* mortuorio.

heart [hɑːt] **1** *n* (**a**) (*Anat*) corazón *m*; **she spoke with beating ~** le palpitaba el corazón al decirlo; **to clasp sb to one's ~** abrazar a uno estrechamente; **to have a weak ~** ser cardíaco.

(**b**) (*fig*) (*Cards*) corazones *mpl*; (*in Spanish pack*) copas *fpl*; (*of lettuce*) cogollo *m*; (*of place, earth etc*) corazón *m*, seno *m*, centro *m*; **in the ~ of the country** en lo más retirado del campo; **in the ~ of the wood** en el centro del bosque; **the ~ of the matter** lo esencial, el quid del asunto, el grano.

(**c**) (*symbol of love*) corazón *m*; **with all one's ~** de todo corazón, con toda el alma; **affair of the ~** aventura *f* sentimental; **to break sb's ~** (*in love*) partir el corazón a uno, (*by behaviour etc*) matar a uno a disgustos; **to break one's ~ over** partirse el corazón por; **to die of a broken ~** morir de pena; **to lose one's ~ to** enamorarse de; **to wear one's ~ on one's sleeve** llevar el corazón en la mano; **to win sb's ~** enamorar a uno.

(**d**) (*seat of feeling, sympathy etc*) corazón *m*, alma *f*; **he's a man after my own ~** es un hombre como me gustan; **at ~** en el fondo; **to have sb's interests at ~** tener presente el interés de uno; **to be sick at ~** estar muy deprimido, sentirlo en el alma; **from the ~** con toda sinceridad; **his words came from the ~** sus palabras salieron del corazón; **in his ~ of ~s** en lo más íntimo de su corazón; **the plan is dear** (*or* **close**) **to my ~** con este proyecto se asocian mis sentimientos más íntimos; **with a heavy ~** con dolor, sintiéndolo; **his ~ is in the right place** es buena persona, tiene buen corazón; **to cut sb to the ~** herir a uno en lo vivo; **to cry one's ~ out** llorar a mares; **it would have done your ~ good** te habría alegrado el corazón; **to eat one's ~ out** estar muriéndose de pena; sufrir en silencio; **to have no ~** no tener entrañas; **have a ~!** ¡ten un poco de piedad!; **he has a ~ of gold** es buenísima persona, tiene buenísimo corazón; **to open one's ~ to sb** abrir su pecho con uno; **to set sb's ~ at rest** tranquilizar a uno; **to take sth to ~** tomar algo a pecho.

(**e**) (*seat of desire, intention*) **his ~ was not in it** no tenía fe en lo que estaba haciendo; **to set one's ~ on** poner el corazón en; **to throw o.s. ~ and soul into an enterprise** lanzarse de todo corazón a una empresa; *V* **content** *etc*.

(**f**) (*symbol of courage*) **to be in good ~** estar lleno de confianza, (*soil*) estar en buen estado; **I could not find it in my ~ to** + *infin*, **I did not have the ~ to** + *infin* no tuve valor para + *infin*; **to have one's ~ in one's mouth** tener el alma en un hilo, tener el corazón en un puño; **to lose ~** descorazonarse; **to put new ~ into sb** infundir ánimo a uno; **my ~ sank** se me cayeron las alas del corazón; **to take ~** cobrar ánimo; **we may take ~ from the fact that ...** que nos aliente el hecho de que ...

(**g**) **by ~** de memoria.

2 *attr*: **he's a ~ case, he has a ~ condition** sufre de una condición cardíaca; **~ complaint, ~ disease** enfermedad *f* cardíaca; **~ murmur** soplo *m* del corazón; **~ surgeon** cirujano *m* cardiólogo; **~ surgery** cirugía *f* cardíaca; **~ transplant** trasplante *m* del corazón; **~ trouble** enfermedad *f* cardíaca.

heartache ['hɑːteɪk] *n* angustia *f*, pena *f*.

heart-attack ['hɑːtətæk] *n* ataque *m* cardíaco.

heartbeat ['hɑːtbiːt] *n* latido *m* del corazón.

heartbreak ['hɑːtbreɪk] *n* angustia *f*, congoja *f*.

heartbreaking ['hɑːt,breɪkɪŋ] *adj* angustioso, desgarrador, que parte el corazón.

heartbroken ['hɑːt,brəʊkən] *adj* angustiado, acongojado; **she was ~ about it** esto le partió el corazón.

heartburn ['hɑːtbɜːn] *n* acedía *f*.

heartburning ['hɑːt,bɜːnɪŋ] *n* (*bad feeling*) envidia *f*, rencor *m*; (*regret*) sentimiento *m*.

-hearted ['hɑːtɪd] *adj* de corazón ...; **faint~** medroso, pusilánime, apocado.

hearten ['hɑːtn] *vt* animar, alentar, infundir ánimo a.

heartening ['hɑːtnɪŋ] *adj* alentador.

heart failure ['hɑːt,feɪljəʳ] *n* fallo *m* de corazón, colapso *m* cardíaco.

heartfelt ['hɑːtfelt] *adj* cordial, sincero; *sympathy* más sentido; *thanks* más efusivo.

hearth [hɑːθ] *n* (*lit, fig*) hogar *m*, chimenea *f*.
hearth-rug [ˈhɑːθrʌg] *n* alfombrilla *f*.
heartily [ˈhɑːtɪlɪ] *adv* sinceramente, cordialmente; enérgicamente; fuertemente; *laugh* a carcajadas; *eat* con buen apetito; *thank* con efusión; *sing* con entusiasmo; **to be ~ glad** alegrarse sinceramente; **to be ~ sick of** estar completamente harto de.
heartland [ˈhɑːtlænd] *n* corazón *m*; zona *f* central, zona *f* interior.
heartless [ˈhɑːtlɪs] *adj* cruel, inhumano.
heartlessly [ˈhɑːtlɪslɪ] *adv* cruelmente, despiadadamente.
heartlessness [ˈhɑːtlɪsnɪs] *n* crueldad *f*, inhumanidad *f*.
heart-lung machine [ˌhɑːtˈlʌŋməˌʃiːn] *n* máquina *f* de circulación extracorpórea.
heartrending [ˈhɑːtˌrendɪŋ] *adj* angustioso, desgarrador; **it was ~ to see them** se me (*etc*) partía el corazón al verlos.
heart-searching [ˈhɑːtˌsɜːtʃɪŋ] *n* examen *m* de conciencia.
heart-shaped [ˈhɑːtʃeɪpt] *adj* acorazonado, en forma de corazón.
heartstrings [ˈhɑːtstrɪŋz] *npl* fibras *fpl* del corazón; **to pull at** (*or* **touch**) **sb's ~** tocar la fibra sensible de uno.
heart-throb* [ˈhɑːtθrɒb] *n* persona *f* idolatrada; **Bogart was my mother's ~** mi madre idolatraba a Bogart; **he's the ~ of the teenagers** es el ídolo de las quinceañeras; **we met her latest ~** conocimos a su amiguito del momento.
heart-to-heart [ˈhɑːttəˈhɑːt] **1** *adj* íntimo, franco; **~ talk** = **2**. **2** *n* conversación *f* íntima.
heart-warming [ˈhɑːtˌwɔːmɪŋ] *adj* reconfortante, grato.
hearty [ˈhɑːtɪ] **1** *adj person* campechano, francote; *feelings* sincero, cordial; *effort* enérgico; *kick, slap etc* fuerte; *laugh* sano, franco; *appetite* bueno; *meal* abundante; *thanks* efusivo; **to be a ~ eater** tener buen diente. **2** *n* (*****) tipo *m* campechano*.
heat [hiːt] **1** *n* (**a**) (*warmth*) calor *m*; (*heating system*) calefacción *f*; **in the ~ of the day** en las horas de más calor.

(**b**) (*fig*) calor *m*, ardor *m*, vehemencia *f*, pasión *f*; tensión *f*; **in the ~ of the moment** en el calor del momento; **when the ~ is on** cuando se aplican las presiones; **he replied with some ~** contestó bastante indignado; **it'll take the ~ off us** esto nos dará un respiro; **to take the ~ out of a situation** reducir la tensión de una situación; **to turn on the ~** empezar a ejercer presiones, (*Pol*) crear un ambiente de crisis.

(**c**) (*Sport*) (prueba *f*) eliminatoria *f*, prueba *f* clasificatoria.

(**d**) (*Zool*) celo *m*; **to be on ~** (*Brit*) estar en celo.

(**e**) (*US*‡: *police*) bofia‡ *f*.

(**f**) (*US*‡: *criticism*) **he took a lot of ~ for that mistake** le abucharon por ese error‡.

2 *attr*: **~ exhaustion** agotamiento *m* por calor, debilidad *f* por calor; **~ loss** pérdida *f* de calor.

3 *vt* (*also* **to ~ up**) calentar; (*fig*) acalorar.

4 *vi* (*also* **to ~ up**) calentarse; (*fig*) calentarse, acalorarse.
heated [ˈhiːtɪd] *adj* (**a**) calentado; **~ pool** piscina *f* de agua calentada; **~ rear window** luneta *f* trasera térmica. (**b**) (*fig*) *discussion etc* acalorado; **to become ~** acalorarse.
heatedly [ˈhiːtɪdlɪ] *adv* con vehemencia, con pasión; **he replied ~** contestó indignado.
heater [ˈhiːtəʳ] *n* calentador *m*.
heath [hiːθ] *n* (*place*) brezal *m*; (*plant*) brezo *m*; **native ~** patria *f* chica.
heat haze [ˈhiːtheɪz] *n* neblina *f* de calor.
heathen [ˈhiːðən] **1** *adj* pagano. **2** *n* pagano *m*, -a *f*; (*fig*) bárbaro *m*, -a *f*.
heathenish [ˈhiːðənɪʃ] *adj* pagano, gentílico.
heathenism [ˈhiːðənɪzəm] *n* paganismo *m*.
heather [ˈheðəʳ] *n* brezo *m*.
heating [ˈhiːtɪŋ] **1** *n* calefacción *f*.

2 *attr*: **~ engineer** técnico *m* en calefacciones; **~ plant** = **~ system**; **~ power** poder *m* calorífico; **~ system** sistema *m* de calefacción.
heatproof [ˈhiːtpruːf] *adj*, **heat-resistant** [ˈhiːtrɪˌzɪstənt] *adj* termorresistente, a prueba de calor; *ovenware* refractario.
heat rash [ˈhiːtræʃ] *n* sarpullido *m*.
heat-seeking [ˈhiːtˌsiːkɪŋ] *adj*: **~ missile** misil *m* buscador del calor.
heat-sensitive [ˈhiːtˈsensɪtɪv] *adj* sensible al calor.
heat-shield [ˈhiːtʃiːld] *n* escudo *m* contra el calor.
heatstroke [ˈhiːtstrəʊk] *n* insolación *f*, golpe *m* de calor.
heat treatment [ˈhiːtˌtriːtmənt] *n* tratamiento *m* de calor.
heatwave [ˈhiːtweɪv] *n* ola *f* de calor.
heave [hiːv] **1** *n* (*lift*) esfuerzo *m* para levantar; (*pull*) tirón *m* (*on* de); (*push*) empujón *m*; (*throw*) echada *f*, tirada *f*; **with a ~ of his shoulders** con un fuerte movimiento de hombros; **one more ~ and they're out** un empujón más y los echamos fuera a todos.

2 *vt* (*irr: pret and ptp* **heaved**, (*Naut*) *pret and ptp* **hove**) (*pull*) tirar de; (*push*) empujar; (*lift*) levantar; (*drag*) arrastrar; (*carry*) llevar; (*throw*) tirar, lanzar; *sigh* exhalar.

3 *vi* (**a**) (*water etc*) subir y bajar, agitarse; (*surface*) palpitar, ondular; (*feel sick*) basquear, tener náuseas; **it makes me ~** me da asco; **to ~ at, to ~ on** tirar de; (*Naut*) jalar. (**b**) **to ~ in**(**to**) **sight** aparecer.
◆**heave to** *vi* ponerse al pairo.
◆**heave up** *vt* (*vomit*) devolver, arrojar.
heave-ho [ˈhiːvˈhəʊ] *interj* ¡ahora!, (*Naut*) ¡iza!; **to give sb the ~*** dar el pasaporte a uno*.
heaven [ˈhevn] *n* (**a**) cielo *m*; **~s** cielos *mpl*; (**good**) **~s!** ¡cielos!; **thank ~!** ¡gracias a Dios!; **~ forbid!** ¡no lo quiera Dios!; **~ forbid that I ...** Dios me libre de + *infin*; **for ~'s sake!** ¡por Dios!; **seventh ~** paraíso *m*; **to be in seventh ~** estar en el séptimo cielo; **an injustice that cries out to ~** una injusticia que clama al cielo; **~ help them if they do** que Dios les ayude si lo hacen; **~ knows why** Dios sabe por qué; **~ knows I tried enough** Dios sabe lo mucho que me esforcé; **what in ~'s name does that mean?** ¿qué demonios quieres decir con eso?; **to move ~ and earth** remover cielo y tierra, remover Roma con Santiago (*to* + *infin* para + *infin*); **to stink to high ~** heder a perro muerto.

(**b**) (*fig*) paraíso *m*; **the trip was ~** el viaje fue una maravilla; **this place is just ~** este lugar es el paraíso; **isn't he ~?** ¡qué hombre más estupendo!
heavenly [ˈhevnlɪ] *adj* (**a**) celestial; (*Astron*) celeste; **~ body** cuerpo *m* celeste; **H~ Father** Padre *m* celestial. (**b**) (*fig*) maravilloso, estupendo.
heaven-sent [ˈhevnˈsent] *adj* milagroso, como llovido del cielo.
heavenward(s) [ˈhevnwəd(z)] *adv* hacia el cielo.
heavily [ˈhevɪlɪ] *adv fall, move, tread* pesadamente; *rain* fuertemente, mucho; *concentrate* densamente; *sigh, sleep* profundamente; *drink* con exceso; **~ underlined** subrayado con línea gruesa; **to be ~ in debt** estar muy endeudado; **your account is ~ overdrawn** su cuenta tiene un grave saldo deudor; **to lean ~ on** apoyarse mucho en; **to lose ~** (*team*) sufrir una grave derrota, (*gambler*) tener pérdidas cuantiosas; **it weighs ~ on him** pesa mucho sobre él; **she's ~ into spiritualism*** (*esp Brit*) está profundamente metida en el espiritismo, se dedica con pasión al espiritismo.
heavily-built [ˈhevɪlɪˈbɪlt] *adj* corpulento.
heavily-laden [ˌhevɪlɪˈleɪdən] *adj* muy cargado.
heaviness [ˈhevɪnɪs] *n* peso *m*; pesadez *f* (*also fig*); lo fuerte, fuerza *f*; densidad *f*; gravedad *f*; (*drowsiness*) letargo *m*, modorra *f*; **~ of heart** tristeza *f*.
heavy [ˈhevɪ] **1** *adj* (**a**) pesado; **to be ~** ser pesado, pesar mucho; **is it ~?** ¿pesa mucho?; **how ~ are you?** ¿cuánto pesas?

(**b**) (*fig*) *cruiser, fall, industry, tread* pesado; *cloth, features, line, sea, type* grueso; *emphasis, expense, meal, rain, scent, shower* fuerte; *concentration, population, traffic* denso; (*boring*) pesado; *book, film* pesado; *atmosphere* pesado, opresivo; *blow* fuerte, duro; *build of person* corpulento; *burden* (*fig*) grave, oneroso; *crop* abundante; *defeat* grave; *feeling* aletargado; *fire* (*Mil*) intenso; *food* indigesto; *heart* triste; *humour* laborioso; *liquid* espeso, viscoso; *loss* considerable, cuantioso; *movement* lento, torpe, pesado; *part* (*Theat*) serio, trágico; *responsibility* grave; *sigh, silence, sleep* profundo; *sky* encapotado; *soil* arcilloso; *surface* difícil; *task* duro, penoso; **~ artillery** artillería *f* pesada; **~ cream** (*US*) nata *f* enriquecida; **~ goods** géneros *mpl* de bulto; **~ goods vehicle** vehículo *m* pesado; **~ industry** industria *f* pesada; **~ smoker** gran fumador *m*; **~ type** negrita *f*; **~ user** usuario *m*, -a *f* de gran cantidad; **we are ~ users of paper** usamos mucho papel, somos grandes consumidores de papel; **~ water** agua *f* pesada; **~ wine** vino *m* fuerte; **the mayor's ~ mob*** los forzudos del alcalde, los esbirros del alcalde; **eyes ~ with sleep** ojos de sueño; **the air was ~ with scent** el aire estaba cargado de perfumes; **I've had a ~ day** he tenido un día muy cargado; **to be a ~ drinker** (*etc*) beber (*etc*) mucho, beber (*etc*) con exceso; **to be a ~ sleeper** tener el sueño profundo; **the book has a lot of ~ symbolism** el libro tiene gran densidad de simbolismo, el libro tiene mucho simbolismo concentrado.

2 *n* (*****) forzudo *m*, gorila* *m*, matón *m*.

heavy-duty [ˌhevɪˈdjuːtɪ] *attr* para cargas pesadas.

heavy-handed [ˌhevɪˈhændɪd] *adj* (*harsh*) de mano dura; (*clumsy*) torpe, desmañado.

heavy-hearted [ˌhevɪˈhɑːtɪd] *adj* afligido, apesadumbrado.

heavy-laden [ˌhevɪˈleɪdn] *adj* lastrado.

heavy-set [ˈhevɪˈset] *adj* (*US*) corpulento, fornido.

heavyweight [ˈhevɪweɪt] **1** *adj* pesado, de mucho peso. **2** *n* (*Boxing*) peso *m* pesado; (*important person*) pez *m* gordo*.

Hebe⁑ [ˈhiːbɪ] *n* (*US pej*) judío *m*, -a *f*.

he-bear [ˈhiːbɛəʳ] *n* oso *m* macho.

Hebraist [ˈhiːbreɪɪst] *n* hebraísta *mf*.

Hebrew [ˈhiːbruː] **1** *adj* hebreo. **2** *n* (**a**) hebreo *m*, -a *f*. (**b**) (*Ling*) hebreo *m*.

Hebrides [ˈhebrɪdiːz] *npl* Hébridas *fpl*.

heck [hek] *interj* (*euph*) = **hell**.

heckle [ˈhekl] *vti* interrumpir, molestar con preguntas.

heckler [ˈheklәʳ] *n* el (la) que interrumpe (*or* molesta) a un orador.

heckling [ˈheklɪŋ] *n* interrupciones *fpl*, gritos *mpl* de protesta.

hectare [ˈhektɑːʳ] *n* hectárea *f*.

hectic [ˈhektɪk] *adj* (*fig*) febril; *speed* loco; **we had 3 ~ days** tuvimos 3 días llenos de frenética actividad, tuvimos 3 días llenos de confusión (*or* incertidumbre *etc*); **he has a ~ life** tiene una vida muy agitada; **things are pretty ~ here** aquí es la monda; **the journey was pretty ~** el viaje era para volverse loco.

hectogram(me) [ˈhektәʊgræm] *n* hectogramo *m*.

hectolitre, (*US*) **hectoliter** [ˈhektәʊˌliːtәʳ] *n* hectolitro *m*.

Hector [ˈhektәʳ] *nm* Héctor.

hector [ˈhektәʳ] **1** *vt* intimidar con bravatas. **2** *vi* echar bravatas.

hectoring [ˈhektәrɪŋ] *adj person* lleno de bravatas; *tone, remark* amedrentador.

he'd [hiːd] = **he would; he had.**

hedge [hedʒ] **1** *n* (**a**) seto *m* vivo. (**b**) (*fig*) defensa *f*, protección *f*; (*Fin*) cobertura *f*; **as a ~ against inflation** para protegerse contra la inflación.

2 *vt* (**a**) cercar con un seto.

(**b**) (*fig*) **to ~ sth about, to ~ sth in** rodear algo, encerrar algo; **to be ~d about with** estar erizado de.

(**c**) **to ~ a bet** hacer apuestas compensatorias.

3 *vi* (**a**) contestar con evasivas, no querer comprometerse a nada; **stop ~ing!, don't ~ with me!** ¡dímelo sin sofismas!

(**b**) (*Fin*) **to ~ against inflation** cubrirse contra la inflación.

◆**hedge off** *vt* separar con un seto.

hedge clippers [ˈhedʒˌklɪpәz] *npl* tijeras *fpl* de podar.

hedgehog [ˈhedʒhɒg] *n* erizo *m*.

hedgehop [ˈhedʒhɒp] *vi* volar a ras de tierra.

hedgerow [ˈhedʒrәʊ] *n* seto *m* vivo.

hedgesparrow [ˈhedʒˌspærәʊ] *n* acentor *m* (común).

hedging [ˈhedʒɪŋ] *n* (**a**) (*Bot*) seto *m* vivo; **~ plant** planta *f* para seto vivo. (**b**) (*fig: evasions*) evasivas *fpl*; sofismas *mpl*. (**c**) (*Fin etc*) cobertura *f*.

hedonism [ˈhiːdәnɪzәm] *n* hedonismo *m*.

hedonist [ˈhiːdәnɪst] *n* hedonista *mf*.

hedonistic [ˌhiːdәˈnɪstɪk] *adj* hedonista.

heebie-jeebies* [ˌhiːbɪˈdʒiːbɪz] *npl*: **to have the ~** (*shaking*) tener un tembleque*; (*fright, nerves*) estar hecho un flan*, estar que no se cabe dentro de la camisa*; **it gives me the ~** (*revulsion*) me da asco; (*fright, apprehension*) me da escalofríos.

heed [hiːd] **1** *n* atención *f*; **to give** (*or* **pay**) **~ to** prestar atención a, hacer caso de; **to take no ~ of sth** no hacer caso de algo, hacer caso omiso de algo, no tener algo en cuenta; **to take ~ to** + *infin* poner atención en + *infin*; **take ~!** ¡ten cuidado!; ¡atención!

2 *vt* prestar atención a, hacer caso de; tener en cuenta.

heedless [ˈhiːdlɪs] *adj* desatento, descuidado; **to be ~ of** no hacer caso de.

heedlessly [ˈhiːdlɪslɪ] *adv* sin hacer caso.

heehaw [ˈhiːhɔː] **1** *n* rebuzno *m*. **2** *vi* rebuznar.

heel[1] [hiːl] **1** *n* (**a**) (*Anat*) talón *m*, calcañar *m*; (*of shoe*) tacón *m*; **to be at** (*or* **on**) **sb's ~s** pisar los talones a uno; **to be down at ~** ir mal vestido, estar desaseado; **to be under the ~ of** estar bajo los talones de; **to bring sb to ~** sobreponerse a uno, meter a uno en cintura; **to cool one's ~s** hacer antesala, tener que esperar; **to dig one's ~s in** mantenerse en sus trece; **to drag one's ~** arrastrar los pies; **to follow hard on sb's ~s** seguir a uno muy de cerca; **to be hot on sb's ~s, to tread hard on sb's ~s** pisar los talones de uno; **to keep to ~** (*dog*) obedecer, seguir de cerca al dueño (*etc*); **to kick one's ~s** no tener nada que hacer; **to show sb a clean pair of ~s, to take to one's ~s** poner pies en polvorosa; **to turn on one's ~** dar media vuelta.

(**b**) (*) canalla *m*.

2 *vt* (**a**) *shoe* poner tacón a; **to be well ~ed*** ser un ricacho.

(**b**) *ball* talonear.

heel[2] [hiːl] *vi*: **to ~ over** ladearse, (*Naut*) zozobrar, escorar.

heel bar [ˈhiːlbɑːʳ] *n* rápido *m*, (tienda *f* de) reparación *f* de calzado al momento.

heft* [heft] **1** *n* (*US*) peso *m*; (*fig*) influencia *f*; **the ~ of** la mayor parte de. **2** *vt* levantar; sopesar.

hefty* [ˈheftɪ] *adj object* pesado; *person* fuerte, fornido; *dose etc* grande, mayúsculo; *book, file etc* abultado.

hegemony [hɪˈgemәnɪ] *n* hegemonía *f*.

hegira [heˈdʒaɪәrә] *n* hégira *f*.

he-goat [ˈhiːgәʊt] *n* macho *m* cabrío.

heifer [ˈhefәʳ] *n* novilla *f*, vaquilla *f*.

heigh [heɪ] *interj* ¡oye!, ¡eh!

heigh-ho [ˈheɪˈhәʊ] *interj* ¡ay!

height [haɪt] *n* (**a**) (*altitude*) altura *f*, elevación *f*, altitud *f*; **~ above sea level** altura *f* sobre el nivel del mar; **at a ~ of 2000 m** a una altura de 2000 m; **to be 20 m in ~** medir (*LAm*: tener) 20 m de alto, tener una altura de 20 m; **to gain ~** ganar altura; **to lose ~** perder altura.

(**b**) (*of person*) talla *f*, estatura *f*; **of average ~** de mediana estatura, de talla mediana; **he drew himself up to his full ~** se irguió; **what ~ are you?** ¿cuánto mides de alto?

(**c**) (*hill*) colina *f*, cerro *m*; **the ~s** las cumbres.

(**d**) (*fig*) (*of fever*) crisis *f*; **the ~ of absurdity** el colmo de lo absurdo; **it's the ~ of fashion** está muy de moda; **at the ~ of summer** en los días más calurosos del verano; **at the ~ of the battle** en los momentos más críticos de la batalla; **his performance never reached the ~s** su actuación nunca llegó a las alturas.

heighten [ˈhaɪtn] *vt* (*raise*) elevar, hacer más alto; (*increase*) aumentar; (*enhance*) realzar, intensificar.

heinous [ˈheɪnәs] *adj* atroz, nefando.

heir [ɛәʳ] *n* heredero *m*, -a *f*; **~ apparent, ~ at law** heredero *m* forzoso, heredera *f* forzosa; **~ to the throne** heredero *m*, -a *f* del trono; **he is ~ to a fortune** ha de heredar una fortuna.

heiress [ˈɛәres] *n* heredera *f*; (*) soltera *f* adinerada.

heirloom [ˈɛәluːm] *n* reliquia *f* de familia.

heist⁑ [haɪst] (*US*) **1** *n* robo *m* a mano armada. **2** *vt* robar a mano armada.

held [held] *pret and ptp of* **hold**.

Helen [ˈhelɪn] *nf* Elena, Helena.

helical [ˈhelɪkәl] *adj* helicoidal.

helicopter [ˈhelɪkɒptәʳ] **1** *n* helicóptero *m*. **2** *attr*: **~ gunship** helicóptero *m* de combate, helicóptero *m* artillado; **~ pad** = **helipad**; **~ station** helipuerto *m*. **3** *vt*: **to ~ troops in** transportar tropas por helicóptero, helitransportar tropas.

heliograph [ˈhiːlɪәʊgrɑːf] *n* heliógrafo *m*.

heliotrope [ˈhiːlɪәtrәʊp] *n* heliotropo *m*.

helipad [ˈhelɪpæd] *n* plataforma *f* de helicóptero, pista *f* de helicóptero.

heliport [ˈhelɪpɔːt] *n* helipuerto *m*.

helium [ˈhiːlɪәm] *n* helio *m*.

helix [ˈhiːlɪks] *n*, *pl* **helices** [ˈhelɪsiːz] hélice *f*.

hell [hel] *n* infierno *m*; **~!, oh ~!** ¡demonio!; **all ~ was let loose** se desencadenó un ruido infernal; fue la monda; **a ~ of a lot** muchísimos, la mar de, una barbaridad de; **a ~ of a noise** un ruido de todos los diablos; **we had a ~ of a time** (*bad*) pasamos un rato malísimo, (*good*) lo pasamos en grande; **they did it just for the ~ of it** lo hicieron sólo por el gusto de hacerlo, lo hicieron porque sí; **who the ~ are you?** ¿quién demonios es Vd?; **what the ~!** ¡qué diantre!; **what the ~ do you want?** ¿qué demonios quieres?; **like ~!** ¡ni hablar!; **to run like ~** correr a todo correr; **to work like ~** trabajar como un demonio; **it was as hot as ~** hacía un calor del infierno; **come ~ or high water** contra viento y marea; **get the ~ out of here!** ¡vete al diablo!; **let's get the ~ out of here!** ¡vámonos!; **to give sb ~** poner a uno como un trapo; **to go ~ for leather** ir como el demonio; **go to ~!** ¡vete al diablo!; **till ~ freezes over** hasta cuando la rana críe pelo; **I hope to ~ that ...!** ¡ojalá ...!; **to make sb's life ~** amargar la vida a uno; **there'll be (all) ~ to pay** esto sí que nos va a costar carísimo; **to raise ~** armar la gorda.

he'll [hiːl] = **he will; he shall.**

hellacious* [heˈleɪʃәs] *adj* (*US*) infernal.

hellbent ['hel'bent] *adj* (**a**) (*determined*) totalmente resuelto; **to be ~ on doing sth** estar totalmente resuelto a hacer algo. (**b**) (*fast*) rapidísimo, velocísimo.
hellcat ['helkæt] *n* harpía *f*, bruja *f*.
hellebore ['helɪbɔːʳ] *n* eléboro *m*.
Hellene ['heliːn] *n* heleno *m*, -a *f*.
Hellenic [he'liːnɪk] *adj* helénico.
Hellespont ['helɪspɒnt] *n* Helesponto *m*.
hellfire ['hel'faɪəʳ] *n* llamas *fpl* del infierno.
hellhole ['helhəʊl] *n* infierno *m*.
hellish ['helɪʃ] **1** *adj* infernal, diabólico; (*) horrible. **2** *adv* (‡) muy, terriblemente.
hellishly* ['helɪʃlɪ] *adv* endemoniadamente.
hello [hʌ'ləʊ] = **hullo**.
hell's angel [ˌhelz'eɪndʒəl] *n* ángel *m* del infierno.
helluva‡ ['heləvə] = **hell of a**; *V* **hell**.
helm [helm] *n* timón *m*; **to be at the ~** (*fig*) gobernar, estar en el mando.
helmet ['helmɪt] *n* casco *m*.
helmsman ['helmzmən] *n*, *pl* **helmsmen** ['helmzmən] timonel *m*.
help [help] **1** *n* (**a**) ayuda *f*; auxilio *m*, socorro *m*; favor *m*, protección *f*; **~!** ¡socorro!; **by** (*or* **with**) **the ~ of** con la ayuda de; **without ~** sin ayuda de nadie; **to call for ~** pedir socorro; **to come to sb's ~** acudir en auxilio de uno; **there's no ~ for it** no hay más remedio; **to be past ~** estar desahuciado.
(**b**) (*person*: *servant*) criada *f*; (*in shop etc*) empleado *m*; **daily ~** asistenta *f*; **mother's ~** niñera *f*; **she has no ~ in the house** no tiene criada; **we're short of ~ in the shop** nos falta personal en la tienda; **'~ wanted'** (*US*) 'ofertas *fpl* de trabajo'; **he's a great ~** me ayuda muchísimo; **you're a great ~!** (*iro*) ¡valiente ayuda!
2 *vt* (**a**) ayudar; (*esp in distress*) auxiliar, socorrer; *scheme etc* promover; *progress* facilitar; *pain* aliviar; **so ~ me God!** bien lo sabe Dios; (*as oath*) ¡así Dios me salve!; **to ~ sb to do sth** ayudar a uno a hacer algo; **this will ~ to save it** esto contribuirá a salvarlo; **to ~ sb down** ayudar a uno a bajar; **to ~ sb on with a dress** ayudar a uno a ponerse un vestido; **to ~ sb out of a jam** ayudar a uno a salir de un apuro; **to ~ sb up** ayudar a uno a subir.
(**b**) (*at table*) servir; **to ~ sb to soup** servir la sopa a uno.
(**c**) (*avoid*) **he can't ~ coughing** no puede dejar de toser; **I couldn't ~ (doing) it** no pude menos de hacerlo; **he's a chap you couldn't ~ but admire** es un tío que no se puede menos de admirar; **it can't be ~ed** no hay más remedio, no queda otra (*LAm*); **he won't if I can ~ it** no lo hará si yo puedo evitarlo; **can I ~ it if it rains?** ¿es que yo puedo impedir que llueva?; **don't spend more than you can ~** no gastes más de lo necesario.
3 *vi* ayudar.
4 *vr*: **to ~ o.s.** ayudarse a sí mismo; (*at table*) servirse; **~ yourself!** (*to food*) ¡sírvete!, (*to other things*) está a tu disposición, toma cuanto quieras; **to ~ o.s. to** *food* servirse, (*steal*) alzarse con, llevarse, robar.
◆**help along** *vt person* ayudar; *scheme etc* promover, fomentar.
◆**help out 1** *vt*: **to ~ sb out** ayudar a uno; (*of a vehicle*) ayudar a uno a bajar. **2** *vi* ayudar.
helper ['helpəʳ] *n* ayudante *mf*, asistente *mf*; auxiliar *mf*; (*co-worker*) colaborador *m*, -ora *f*.
helpful ['helpfʊl] *adj* útil, provechoso; *attitude, remark* positivo; *person* servicial, atento; **he was very ~ to me** me ayudó mucho; **you have been most ~** Vd ha sido muy amable; **it would be ~ if you could come** sería bueno que pudieras venir; **would it be ~ if ...?** ¿sería conveniente que ...?
helpfully ['helpfəlɪ] *adv* amablemente.
helpfulness ['helpfʊlnɪs] *n* utilidad *f*; (*of person*) amabilidad *f*.
helping ['helpɪŋ] **1** *adj*: **to give sb a ~ hand** echar una mano a uno. **2** *n* porción *f*, ración *f*; **will you have a second ~?** ¿quieres servirte más?
helpless ['helplɪs] *adj* (*forsaken*) desamparado; (*destitute*) desvalido; (*powerless*) impotente; (*of weak character*) débil, incapaz, inútil; *creature* indefenso; *invalid* imposibilitado; **we were ~ to do anything about it** nos veíamos imposibilitados para remediarlo; **to feel ~** sentirse perplejo, estar indeciso.
helplessly ['helplɪslɪ] *adv struggle* en vano; **he said ~** dijo indeciso.
helplessness ['helplɪsnɪs] *n* desamparo *m*; impotencia *f*; incapacidad *f*, inutilidad *f*; irresolución *f*.
helpline ['helplaɪn] *n* teléfono *m* de la esperanza.
helpmate ['helpmeɪt] *n* buen compañero *m*, buena compañera *f*; (*spouse*) esposo *m*, -a *f*.
Helsinki ['helsɪŋkɪ] *n* Helsinki *m*.
helter-skelter ['heltə'skeltəʳ] **1** *adv* atropelladamente. **2** *n* (**a**) (*rush*) desbandada *f* general. (**b**) (*Brit*: *at fair*) tobogán *m*.
hem [hem] *n* dobladillo *m*; (*edge*) orilla *f*.
◆**hem in** *vt* encerrar, cercar (*also Mil*).
he-man* ['hiːmæn] *n*, *pl* **he-men** ['hiːmen] machote *m*.
hematology [ˌhiːmə'tɒlədʒɪ] *n* (*US*) = **haematology**.
hemiplegia [hemɪ'pliːdʒɪə] *n* hemiplejía *f*.
hemiplegic [ˌhemɪ'pliːdʒɪk] **1** *adj* hemipléjico. **2** *n* hemipléjico *m*, -a *f*.
hemisphere ['hemɪsfɪəʳ] *n* hemisferio *m*.
hemistich ['hemɪstɪk] *n* hemistiquio *m*.
hemline ['hemlaɪn] *n* bajo *m* (del vestido).
hemlock ['hemlɒk] *n* cicuta *f*.
hemo... ['hiːməʊ] *etc* (*US*) = **haemo...** *etc*.
hemp [hemp] *n* cáñamo *m*; (*Indian* ~) hachís *m*.
hemstitch ['hemstɪtʃ] *n* vainica *f*.
hen [hen] **1** *n* gallina *f*; (*female bird*) hembra *f*. **2** *adj* (**a**) (*Orn*) **the ~ bird** el pájaro hembra. (**b**) de mujeres, para mujeres; femenino; **~ party** reunión *f* de mujeres; **Tuesday is ~ night in this pub** la noche del martes en este bar es para mujeres (solas).
henbane ['henbeɪn] *n* beleño *m*.
hence [hens] *adv* (**a**) (*place*) de aquí, desde aquí; (*poet*) ~! ¡fuera de aquí!
(**b**) (*time*) desde ahora; **5 years ~** de aquí a 5 años.
(**c**) (*therefore*) por lo tanto, por eso; **~ my letter** de aquí que le escribiera; **~ the fact that ...** de aquí que ...
henceforth ['hens'fɔːθ] *adv*, **henceforward** ['hens'fɔːwəd] *adv* de hoy en adelante, (*of past time*) en lo sucesivo.
henchman ['hentʃmən] *n*, *pl* **henchmen** ['hentʃmən] (*follower*) secuaz *m*, partidario *m*; (*guard*) guardaespaldas *m*.
hen-coop ['hen,kuːp] *n* gallinero *m*.
hendecasyllabic ['hendekəsɪ'læbɪk] *adj* endecasílabo.
hendecasyllable ['hendekə,sɪləbl] *n* endecasílabo *m*.
henhouse ['hen'haʊs] *n*, *pl* **henhouses** ['hen,haʊzɪz] gallinero *m*.
henna ['henə] *n* alheña *f*.
hennaed ['henəd] *adj hair* alheñado.
henpecked ['henpekt] *adj* dominado por su mujer; **~ husband** calzonazos* *m*.
Henry ['henrɪ] *nm* Enrique.
hepatitis [ˌhepə'taɪtɪs] *n* hepatitis *f*.
heptagon ['heptəgən] *n* heptágono *m*.
heptagonal [hep'tægənəl] *adj* heptagonal.
heptameter [hep'tæmɪtəʳ] *n* heptámetro *m*.
heptathlon [hep'tæθlən] *n* heptatlón *m*.
her [hɜːʳ] **1** *pron* (**a**) (*direct*) la; **I see ~** la veo; **I have never seen HER** a ella no la he visto nunca; **H~ Indoors*, H~ Inside*** la parienta*. (**b**) (*indirect*) le; **I gave ~ the book** le di el libro; **I'm speaking to ~** le estoy hablando. (**c**) (*after prep*) ella; **he thought of ~** pensó en ella; **without ~** sin ella; **if I were ~** yo que ella; **it's ~** es ella; **younger than ~** más joven (*or* menor) que ella. **2** *poss adj* su, sus; **~ book/table** su libro/mesa; **~ friends** sus amigos.
herald ['herəld] **1** *n* heraldo *m*; (*fig*) precursor *m*, anunciador *m*. **2** *vt* anunciar, proclamar.
heraldic [he'rældɪk] *adj* heráldico.
heraldry ['herəldrɪ] *n* heráldica *f*.
herb [hɜːb, *US* ɜːrb] *n* hierba *f* (fina); **~ tea** infusión *f* de hierbas.
herbaceous [hɜː'beɪʃəs] *adj* herbáceo.
herbage ['hɜːbɪdʒ] *n* herbaje *m*, vegetación *f*, plantas *fpl*.
herbal ['hɜːbəl] *adj* herbario; **~ tea** infusión *f* de hierbas.
herbalist ['hɜːbəlɪst] *n* herbolario *m*, -a *f*.
herbarium [hɜː'bɛərɪəm] *n* herbario *m*.
herbert* ['hɜːbət] *n* tipo* *m*, tío* *m*; **some ~** algún tío*.
herb-garden ['hɜːb,gɑːdn] *n* jardín *m* de hierbas finas.
herbicide ['hɜːbɪsaɪd] *n* herbicida *m*.
herbivore ['hɜːbɪ,vɔːʳ] *n* herbívoro *m*.
herbivorous [hɜː'bɪvərəs] *adj* herbívoro.
Herculean [ˌhɜːkju'liːən] *adj* hercúleo; **~ task** obra *f* de romanos.
Hercules ['hɜːkjuliːz] *nm* Hércules.
herd [hɜːd] **1** *n* rebaño *m*, hato *m*, manada *f*; (*of pigs*) piara *f*; (*of people etc*) multitud *f*, tropel *m*; **the common ~** el vulgo; **~ instinct** instinto *m* gregario.
2 *vt* (*tend*) guardar; (*gather*) reunir en manada (*etc*); (*move*) llevar en manada.
◆**herd together** *vi* reunirse en manada, (*in confusion*)

apiñarse unos contra otros; (*people*) reunirse, ir juntos.
herd-book ['hɜːdbʊk] *n* libro *m* genealógico.
herdsman ['hɜːdzmən] *n, pl* **herdsmen** ['hɜːdzmən] (*of cattle*) vaquero *m*; (*of sheep etc*) pastor *m*.
here [hɪəʳ] **1** *adv* (*place where*) aquí; (*motion to*) acá; **~!** (*at roll call*) ¡presente!, (*offering sth*) ¡toma!, (*interj*) ¡oye!, ¡eh!; **~ and now** ahora mismo; **~ and there** aquí y allá; **~, there and everywhere** en todas partes; **~ below** aquí abajo; **in ~, please** por aquí, por favor; **up to ~** hasta aquí; **my mate ~ will do it** este compañero mío lo hará; **and ~ he laughed** y en este punto se rió; **~ is, ~ are** he aquí; **~ it is** aquí lo tienes; **that's neither ~ nor there** eso no viene al caso; **spring is ~** ha llegado la primavera; **he's ~ at last** por fin ha llegado; **~'s to X!** ¡vaya por X!; **come ~!** ¡ven acá!; **~ he comes** ya viene.
2 *n*: **the ~ and now** la situación actual; el mundo tal como es; el presente.
hereabouts ['hɪərə,baʊts] *adv* por aquí (cerca).
hereafter [hɪər'ɑːftəʳ] **1** *adv* en el futuro; **Central Bank, ~ CB** Banco Central, en lo sucesivo BC. **2** *n* futuro *m*; **the ~** la otra vida, el más allá.
hereby ['hɪə'baɪ] *adv* por este medio; (*with reference to document*) por la presente.
hereditaments [,herɪ'dɪtəmənts] *npl* herencia *f*, bienes *mpl* por heredar.
hereditary [hɪ'redɪtərɪ] *adj* hereditario; **~ disease** enfermedad *f* hereditaria.
heredity [hɪ'redɪtɪ] *n* herencia *f*.
herein [,hɪər'ɪn] *adv* (*liter*) en esto; (*in letter*) en ésta.
hereinafter [,hɪərɪn'ɑːftəʳ] *adv* (*Jur*) más adelante, más abajo, a continuación; (*frm*) de ahora en adelante.
hereof [,hɪər'ɒv] *adv* (*liter*) de esto.
heresiarch [he'riːzɪɑːk] *n* heresiarca *mf*.
heresy ['herəsɪ] *n* herejía *f*.
heretic ['herətɪk] *n* hereje *mf*.
heretical [hɪ'retɪkəl] *adj* herético.
hereto [,hɪə'tuː] *adv* a esto; **the parties ~** las partes abajo firmantes.
heretofore [,hɪətʊ'fɔːʳ] *adv* (*liter*) hasta ahora; hasta este momento.
hereupon ['hɪərə'pɒn] *adv* en seguida.
herewith ['hɪə'wɪð] *adv* junto con esto; **I send you ~ ...** le mando adjunto ...
heritable ['herɪtəbl] *adj objects, property etc* heredable, hereditable; *person* que puede heredar.
heritage ['herɪtɪdʒ] *n* herencia *f*; (*fig*) patrimonio *m*.
hermaphrodite [hɜː'mæfrədaɪt] **1** *adj* hermafrodita.
2 *n* hermafrodita *m*.
hermetic [hɜː'metɪk] *adj* hermético.
hermetically [hɜː'metɪkəlɪ] *adv* herméticamente; **~ sealed** cerrado herméticamente.
hermeticism [hɜː'metɪsɪzəm] *n* hermetismo *m*.
hermit ['hɜːmɪt] *n* ermitaño *m*; **~ crab** ermitaño *m*.
hermitage ['hɜːmɪtɪdʒ] *n* ermita *f*.
hernia ['hɜːnɪə] *n* hernia *f*.
hero ['hɪərəʊ] *n, pl* **heroes** ['hɪərəʊz] héroe *m*; (*Liter etc*) protagonista *m*, personaje *m* principal.
Herod ['herəd] *nm* Herodes.
heroic [hɪ'rəʊɪk] *adj* heroico.
heroically [hɪ'rəʊɪkəlɪ] *adv* heroicamente.
heroics [hɪ'rəʊɪks] *n* (*slightly pej*: *language*) lenguaje *m* altisonante; (*deeds*) acciones *fpl* heroicas, acciones *fpl* extravagantes; (*behaviour*) comportamiento *m* atrevido.
heroin ['herəʊɪn] **1** *n* heroína *f*. **2** *attr*: **~ addict** heroinómano *m*, -a *f*; **~ addiction** heroinomanía *f*; **~ user** heroinómano *m*, -a *f*.
heroine ['herəʊɪn] *n* heroína *f*; (*Liter etc*) protagonista *f*, personaje *m* principal.
heroism ['herəʊɪzəm] *n* heroísmo *m*.
heron ['herən] *n* garza *f* (real).
hero-worship ['hɪərəʊ,wɜːʃɪp] *n* culto *m* a los héroes; **he was the object of real ~** fue el objeto de un verdadero culto.
herpes ['hɜːpiːz] *n* herpes *m or fpl*.
herring ['herɪŋ] *n* arenque *m*; *V* **red**.
herringbone ['herɪŋbəʊn] *attr*: **~ pattern** (*Sew*) muestra *f* espiga; (*of floor*) espinapez *m*; **~ stitch** punto *m* de escapulario.
herring-gull ['herɪŋ,gʌl] *n* gaviota *f* argéntea.
herring-pond ['herɪŋpɒnd] *n*: **to cross the ~** (*hum*) cruzar el charco (*el Atlántico*).
hers [hɜːz] *poss pron* (el/la) suyo/a, (los/las) suyos/as, de ella; **this car is ~** este coche es suyo (*or* de ella); **a friend of ~** un amigo suyo; **is this poem ~?** ¿es de ella este poema?; **the one I like best is ~** el que más me gusta es el suyo.
herself [hɜː'self] *pron* (*reflexive*) se; (*emphatic*) ella misma; (*after prep*) sí (misma); **she washed ~** se lavó; **she said to ~** dijo entre (*or* para) sí; **she did it ~** lo hizo ella misma; **she went ~** fue ella misma, fue en persona; **she did it by ~** lo hizo ella sola.
Herts [hɑːts] *n abbr of* **Hertfordshire.**
hertz [hɜːts] *n* hercio *m*, hertzio *m*, hertz *m*.
he's [hiːz] = **he is; he has.**
hesitancy ['hezɪtənsɪ] *n* = **hesitation.**
hesitant ['hezɪtənt] *adj* vacilante, irresoluto, indeciso; **I am somewhat ~ about accepting it** no me resuelvo a aceptarlo.
hesitantly ['hezɪtəntlɪ] *adv* irresolutamente, indecisamente; *speak, suggest* con indecisión.
hesitate ['hezɪteɪt] *vi* vacilar, mostrarse indeciso; (*in speech*) titubear; **to ~ about, to ~ over** no tomar una resolución sobre; **he ~d over his reply** tardó en dar su respuesta; **to ~ to** + *infin* vacilar en + *infin*; **I ~ to condemn him outright** no me puedo persuadir a condenarlo del todo, no me decido todavía a condenarlo del todo; **don't ~ to ask me** no vaciles en pedírmelo.
hesitation [,hezɪ'teɪʃən] *n* vacilación *f*, irresolución *f*, indecisión *f*; **without the slightest ~** sin vacilar un momento; **I feel a certain ~ about it** tengo algunas dudas acerca de ello.
hessian ['hesɪən] **1** *n* arpillera *m*. **2** *attr* (*made of* ~) de arpillera.
het* [het] *adj*: **to get ~ up** acalorarse, emocionarse (*about, over* por); **don't get so ~ up!** ¡tranquilízate!
hetero* ['hetərəʊ] = **heterosexual.**
heterodox ['hetərədɒks] *adj* heterodoxo.
heterodoxy ['hetərədɒksɪ] *n* heterodoxia *f*.
heterogeneous ['hetərəʊ'dʒiːnɪəs] *adj* heterogéneo.
heterosexual ['hetərəʊ'seksjʊəl] **1** *adj* heterosexual.
2 *n* heterosexual *mf*.
heterosexuality ['hetərəʊ,seksjʊ'ælɪtɪ] *n* heterosexualidad *f*.
heuristic [hjʊə'rɪstɪk] *adj* heurístico; **~ search** investigación *f* heurística.
hew [hjuː] *vt* (*irr*: *pret* **hewed,** *ptp* **hewed** *or* **hewn**) cortar, tajar; (*shape*) labrar, tallar.
◆**hew down** *vt* talar.
◆**hew out** *vt* excavar; **a figure ~n out of the rock** una figura tallada en la roca; **to ~ out a career** hacerse una carrera, abrirse paso en su profesión.
hewn [hjuːn] *ptp of* **hew.**
hex¹* [heks] (*US*) **1** *n* (**a**) (*spell*) maleficio *m*, mal *m* de ojo, aojo *m*. (**b**) (*witch*) bruja *f*. **2** *vt* embrujar.
hex² [heks] *adj* (*Comput*) hexadecimal; **~ code** código *m* hexadecimal.
hexadecimal [,heksə'desɪməl] *adj* hexadecimal; **~ notation** notación *f* hexadecimal.
hexagon ['heksəgən] *n* hexágono *m*.
hexagonal [hek'sægənəl] *adj* hexagonal.
hexameter [hek'sæmɪtəʳ] *n* hexámetro *m*.
hey [heɪ] *interj* ¡oye!, ¡eh!
heyday ['heɪdeɪ] *n* auge *m*, apogeo *m*, buenos tiempos *mpl*; **in the ~ of the theatre** en el apogeo del teatro.
H.F. *n abbr of* **high frequency** alta frecuencia *f*.
HGV *n abbr of* **heavy goods vehicle** camión *m* de gran capacidad.
H.H. (**a**) *abbr of* **His** (*or* **Her**) **Highness** Su Alteza, S.A. (**b**) (*Eccl*) *abbr of* **His Holiness** Su Santidad, S.S.
HI (*US Post*) *abbr of* **Hawaii.**
hi [haɪ] *interj* ¡oye!, ¡eh!; (*hullo*) ¡hola!, ¡buenas!
hiatus [haɪ'eɪtəs] *n* (*Gram*) hiato *m*; (*fig*) vacío *m*, laguna *f*, interrupción *f*; solución *f* de continuidad.
hibernate ['haɪbəneɪt] *vi* invernar, hibernar.
hibernation [,haɪbə'neɪʃən] *n* hibernación *f*.
hibiscus [hɪ'bɪskəs] *n* hibisco *m*.
hiccough ['hɪkʌp], **hiccup** ['hɪkʌp] **1** *n* (**a**) hipo *m*; **it gives me ~s** me da hipo, me hace hipar; **to have ~s** tener hipo. (**b**) **a slight ~ in the proceedings** (*fig*) una pequeña dificultad (*or* interrupción) en los actos. **2** *vt* decir hipando; **'yes', he ~ed** 'sí', dijo hipando. **3** *vi* hipar.
hick [hɪk] (*US*) **1** *adj* rústico, de aldea. **2** *n* palurdo *m*, paleto *m*.
hickory ['hɪkərɪ] *n* nuez *f* dura, nogal *m* americano.
hid [hɪd] *pret of* **hide.**
hidden ['hɪdn] **1** *ptp of* **hide. 2** *adj* escondido; (*fig*) oculto, secreto; **~ assets** activo *m* oculto; **~ reserves** reservas *fpl* ocultas.
hide¹ [haɪd] *n* (*skin*) piel *f*, pellejo *m*; (*tanned*) cuero *m*; (*of*

person) pellejo *m*.

hide² [haɪd] **1** *n* (*Brit Hunting*) paranza *f*, puesto *m*, trepa *f*; (*Orn*) observatorio *m*; escondite *m*, aguardado *m*.

2 *vt* (*irr*: *pret* **hid**, *ptp* **hidden**) esconder (*from* de); ocultar (*from* a, de); *feeling etc* ocultar, encubrir, disimular; **I have nothing to ~** no tengo nada que ocultar.

3 *vi* esconderse, ocultarse (*from* de); **he's hiding behind his chief** se está buscando la protección de su jefe.

◆**hide away 1** *vt* esconder, ocultar. **2** *vi* esconderse.

◆**hide out, hide up** *vi* quedar ocultado, ocultarse (por mucho tiempo).

hide-and-seek ['haɪdən'siːk] *n* escondite *m*; **to play ~ with** jugar al escondite con (*also fig*).

hideaway ['haɪdəweɪ] *n* escondrijo *m*, escondite *m*.

hidebound ['haɪdbaʊnd] *adj* rígido, aferrado a la tradición.

hideous ['hɪdɪəs] *adj* horrible.

hideously ['hɪdɪəslɪ] *adv* horriblemente; **~ ugly** feísimo.

hideout ['haɪdaʊt] *n* escondrijo *m*, guarida *f*.

hiding¹* ['haɪdɪŋ] *n* (*beating*) paliza *f*; **to be on a ~ to nothing** tener todas las de perder, no tener posibilidad alguna de ganar.

hiding² ['haɪdɪŋ] *n*: **to be in ~** estar escondido; **he is in ~ in France** se ha refugiado en Francia; **to go into ~** ocultarse, refugiarse; (*Pol*) pasar a la clandestinidad.

hiding place ['haɪdɪŋpleɪs] *n* escondrijo *m*.

hie [haɪ] (*arch or hum*) **1** *vt* apresurar. **2** *vi* ir, ir volando, correr. **3** *vr*: **to ~ o.s. home** apresurarse a volver a casa.

hierarchic(al) [,haɪə'rɑːkɪk(əl)] *adj* jerárquico.

hierarchy ['haɪərɑːkɪ] *n* jerarquía *f*.

hieroglyph ['haɪərəglɪf] *n* jeroglífico *m*.

hieroglyphic [,haɪərə'glɪfɪk] **1** *adj* jeroglífico. **2** *n* jeroglífico *m*.

hi-fi ['haɪ'faɪ] (*abbr of* **high fidelity**) **1** *adj* de alta fidelidad; **~ equipment** equipo *m* de alta fidelidad; **~ set** equipo *m* de hi-fi (*or* de alta fidelidad); **~ system** sistema *m* de alta fidelidad. **2** *n* alta fidelidad *f*.

higgledy-piggledy* ['hɪgldɪ'pɪgldɪ] **1** *adv be etc* en desorden; *do etc* de cualquier modo, de trochemoche, a la buena de Dios. **2** *adj* revuelto, desordenado.

high [haɪ] **1** *adj* (**a**) alto; **it's 20 m ~** tiene 20 m de alto; **how ~ is that tree?** ¿qué altura tiene ese árbol?, ¿cuánto mide ese árbol de alto?; **I knew him when he was so ~** le conocí tamañito, le conocí de niño; **~ altar** altar *m* mayor; **~ chair** silla *f* alta; **~ heels** tacones *mpl* altos; (*shoes*) zapatos *mpl* de tacón alto; *V* **tide**; **~ wire** cuerda *f* floja.

(**b**) (*fig*) *frequency, tension, temperature, treason etc* alto; *number, speed* grande; *price, rent, stake* elevado; *post* importante; *street* mayor; *quality* superior, bueno; *opinion* bueno; *note* agudo; *sea* tempestuoso; *wind* recio, fuerte; *polish* brillante; (*Culin*) pasado, manido; (*rotten*) pasado; **to play for ~ stakes** arriesgarse, jugarse el todo por el todo; **~ and dry** en seco; **to leave sb ~ and dry** dejar a uno plantado, dar plantón a uno (*LAm*); **~ and mighty** engreído; **~ beam** (*Aut*) luces *fpl* largas, luces *fpl* de carretera; **H~ Church** *sector de la Iglesia Anglicana de tendencia conservadora*; **~ color** (*US*), **~ colour** color *m* subido; **~ comedy** alta comedia *f*; **~ command** alto mando *m*; **~ commission** alta comisión *f*; **~ commissioner** alto comisario *m*; **~ court** tribunal *m* supremo; **~ finance** altas finanzas *fpl*; **H~ German** alto alemán *m*; **~ hurdles** vallas *fpl* altas; **to have ~ jinks** pasárselo pipa; **~ life** vida *f* de la buena sociedad; **~ living** vida *f* regalada; **~ mass** misa *f* mayor, misa *f* solemne; *V* **noon**; **~ official** alto funcionario *m*; **~ point** (*of show, evening*) clímax *m*, punto *m* climático; (*of visit, holiday*) momento *m* más interesante; **~ priest** sumo sacerdote *m*; **~ priestess** suma sacerdotisa *f*; **~ school** (*Scot, US*) instituto *m*; **~ seas** alta mar *f*; **~ season** temporada *f* alta; **~ season prices** precios *mpl* de temporada alta; **~ society** buena sociedad *f*; *V* **spirit**; **~ spot** = **~ point**; **~ summer** parte *f* más calurosa del verano, estío *m*; **~ tech(nology)** alta tecnología *f*.

(**c**) **to be ~ (on drugs)‡** estar iluminado‡, estar colocado‡.

2 *adv* (**a**) *fly etc* a gran altura; **~ above my head** muy por encima de mi cabeza; **it rose ~ in the air** se elevó por los aires; **it sailed ~ over the house** voló por los aires muy por encima de la casa.

(**b**) **to aim ~** picar muy alto; **to blow ~** soplar recio; **the numbers go as ~ as 20** los números llegan hasta 20; **I had to go as ~ as £8 for it** tuve que pagar 8 libras nada menos por él; **the bidding went as ~ as £50** se ofrecieron hasta 50 libras; **it went for as ~ as £60** se vendió por 60 libras nada menos; **to live ~ on the hog** (*US**) vivir como un rajá; **to hunt ~ and low for sb** buscar a uno por todas partes; **to run ~** (*sea*) embravecerse, (*river*) estar crecido; (*feelings*) encenderse, exaltarse; **feelings were running ~** la gente estaba muy acalorada.

3 *n* (*Met*) zona *f* de alta presión; (*Met*: *esp US*) temperatura *f* máxima; (*Fin*) máximo *m*; **on ~** en las alturas, en el cielo; **exports have reached a new ~** las exportaciones han alcanzado cifras nunca conocidas antes; **to be on a ~*** estar a las mil maravillas.

highball ['haɪbɔːl] *n* (*US*) jáibol *m*, whisky *m* soda.

highborn ['haɪbɔːn] *adj* linajudo, de ilustre cuna.

highboy ['haɪbɔɪ] *n* (*US*) cómoda *f* alta.

highbrow ['haɪbraʊ] (*freq pej*) **1** *adj* intelectual, culto, esotérico. **2** *n* intelectual *mf*, persona *f* culta.

high-class ['haɪ'klɑːs] *adj* de clase superior.

high-density [,haɪ'densɪtɪ] *attr*: **~ housing** alta densidad *f* de inquilinos.

high-diving ['haɪ,daɪvɪŋ] *n* salto *m* de palanca.

high-energy [,haɪ'enədʒɪ] *attr*: **~ particle** partícula *f* de alta energía; **~ physics** física *f* de altas energías.

higher ['haɪəʳ] **1** *adj comp of* **high**; más alto; *form, study etc* superior; *price* más elevado; *number, speed* mayor; **~ education** educación *f* (*or* enseñanza *f*) superior; **~ rate tax** impuesto *m* en la banda superior; **any number ~ than 6** cualquier número superior a 6.

2 *adv comp of* **high**; **to fly ~ than the clouds** volar encima de las nubes; **to fly ~ still** volar a mayor altura todavía; **~ up the hill** más arriba en la colina; **~ up the road** más hacia el final de la calle.

3 *n* (*Scot Scol*) = **Higher Grade**; *V* **4**.

4 *attr*: **H~ Grade** (*Scot Scol*) *examen de estado que se realiza a la edad de 16 años*; ≈ (*Sp*) Curso *m* de Orientación Universitaria (COU); **H~ National Certificate** (*Brit*) Certificado *m* Nacional de Estudios Superiores; **H~ National Diploma** (*Brit*) Diploma *m* Nacional de Estudios Superiores.

high-explosive ['haɪɪks'pləʊsɪv] **1** *n* explosivo *m* fuerte, explosivo *m* rompedor.

2 *adj*: **~ shell** obús *m* de alto explosivo.

highfalutin(g) ['haɪfə'luːtɪn] *adj* presuntuoso, pomposo.

high-fibre, (*US*) **high-fiber** ['haɪ'faɪbəʳ] *adj*: **~ diet** dieta *f* rica en fibra.

high-fidelity [,haɪfɪ'delɪtɪ] *adj* de alta fidelidad.

high-flier [,haɪ'flaɪəʳ] *n* (*fig*) persona *f* de mucho talento, persona *f* de grandes dotes; ambicioso *m*, -a *f*.

high-flown ['haɪfləʊn] *adj* exagerado, altisonante.

high-flying ['haɪ'flaɪɪŋ] *adj* de gran altura; (*fig*) *aim, ambition* de altos vuelos; *person* superdotado.

high-frequency [,haɪ'friːkwənsɪ] *adj* de alta frecuencia.

high-grade ['haɪ'greɪd] *adj* de calidad superior.

high-handed ['haɪ'hændɪd] *adj* arbitrario, despótico.

high-handedly [,haɪ'hændɪdlɪ] *adv* arbitrariamente, despóticamente.

high-hat* ['haɪ'hæt] **1** *adj* encopetado, esnob*. **2** *n* sombrero *m* de copa, cilindro* *m*.

high-heeled ['haɪhiːld] *adj shoes* de tacones altos.

high-intensity [,haɪɪn'tensɪtɪ] *adj*: **~ lights** (*Aut*) faros *mpl* halógenos.

highjack ['haɪdʒæk] *etc* = **hijack** *etc*.

high jump ['haɪdʒʌmp] *n* salto *m* de altura; **he's for the ~*** (*Brit*) (*reprimand*) le van a dar una buena bronca; (*going to be sacked*) le van a despedir.

highland ['haɪlənd] **1** *n* tierras *fpl* altas, montañas *fpl*; **the H~s** (*Brit*) las tierras altas de Escocia. **2** *attr people* montañés, de montaña; *region* montañoso; **H~ fling** *cierto baile escocés*; **H~ Games** juegos *mpl* escoceses.

highlander ['haɪləndəʳ] *n* montañés *m*, -esa *f*; **H~** (*Brit*) habitante *mf* de las tierras altas de Escocia.

high-level ['haɪ'levl] *adj* de alto nivel; **~ nuclear waste** desechos *mpl* nucleares de alta radiactividad; **~ language** lenguaje *m* de alto nivel.

highlight ['haɪlaɪt] **1** *n* (*Art*) claro *m*, realce *m*, toque *m* de luz; (*fig*) aspecto *m* notable, aspecto *m* interesante; momento *m* culminante; **~s** (*in hair*) vetas *fpl*, reflejos *mpl*. **2** *vt* subrayar, destacar; *hair* vetear, poner reflejos en.

highlighter ['haɪlaɪtəʳ] *n* (*pen*) marcador *m*.

highly ['haɪlɪ] *adv* (**a**) muy, muy bien, sumamente; **~ amusing** divertidísimo; **~ coloured** (*fig*) exagerado; **~ paid** muy bien pagado, muy bien retribuido; **~ placed official** oficial *m* de categoría, funcionario *m* importante; **~ regarded** muy estimado, muy bien reputado; **~ seasoned** muy picante; **~ strung** (*Brit*) muy excitable, (muy) nervioso, hipertenso.

(**b**) **to praise sb ~** alabar mucho a uno; **to speak ~ of** decir mil bienes de; **to think ~ of sb** tener en mucho a uno.

high-minded ['haɪ'maɪndɪd] *adj person* de nobles pensamientos, magnánimo; *act* noble, altruista.

high-mindedness [,haɪ'maɪndɪdnɪs] *n* nobleza *f* de pensamientos, magnanimidad *f*; altruismo *m*.

high-necked [,haɪ'nekt] *adj* de cuello alto.

highness ['haɪnɪs] *n* altura *f*; **H~** (*as title*) Alteza *f*; **His** (*or* **Her**) **Royal H~** Su Alteza Real.

high-octane ['haɪ,ɒkteɪn] *attr*: **~ petrol** gasolina *f* de alto octanaje, supercarburante *m*.

high performance [,haɪpə'fɔːməns] *adj* de gran rendimiento.

high-pitched ['haɪ'pɪtʃt] *adj* de tono alto, agudo; *voice* aflautado.

high-powered ['haɪ'pauəd] *adj* de gran potencia; *person* enérgico, dinámico.

high-pressure ['haɪ'preʃəʳ] *adj* de alta presión; (*fig*) enérgico, dinámico, apremiante; **~ salesman** vendedor *m* enérgico; **~ selling** venta *f* (con propaganda) agresiva.

high-priced [,haɪ'praɪst] *adj* muy caro.

high-profile ['haɪ'prəʊfaɪl] *attr*: **~ activity** actividad *f* que quiere llamar la atención, actividad *f* que trata de darse publicidad.

high-protein [,haɪ'prəutiːn] *adj* rico en proteínas.

high-quality ['haɪ'kwɒlɪtɪ] *adj* de gran calidad, de calidad superior.

high-ranking ['haɪ'ræŋkɪŋ] *adj* de categoría; *official* de alto rango, de alto grado; (*Mil*) de alta graduación.

high-rise ['haɪraɪz] *attr*: **~ building** edificio *m* elevado, torre *f*.

high-risk [,haɪ'rɪsk] *attr investment, policy* de alto riesgo.

highroad ['haɪrəʊd] *n* (*esp Brit*) carretera *f*; (*fig*) camino *m* real (*to* de).

high-sounding ['haɪ'saʊndɪŋ] *adj* altisonante.

high-speed ['haɪ'spiːd] *adj vehicle etc* de alta velocidad; *test etc* rápido; **~ train** tren *m* de alta velocidad.

high-spending ['haɪ'spendɪŋ] *adj* que gasta mucho; (*pej*) derrochador, pródigo.

high-spirited ['haɪ'spɪrɪtɪd] *adj* brioso, animoso; *horse* fogoso; (*merry*) alegre.

high street ['haɪstriːt] *n* (*Brit*) calle *f* mayor; **~ banks** bancos *mpl* de la calle mayor (que aceptan depósitos de clientes individuales).

high-strung ['haɪ,strʌŋ] *adj* (*US*) muy excitable, (muy) nervioso, hipertenso.

high tea [,haɪ'tiː] *n* (*Brit*) merienda-cena *f*.

high-tech* [,haɪ'tek] *attr* al-tec*, de alta tecnología.

high-tension ['haɪ'tenʃən] *adj* de alta tensión.

high-test ['haɪ'test] *adj*: **~ fuel** supercarburante *m*.

high-up* ['haɪ'ʌp] **1** *adj* de categoría, importante.
2 *n* oficial *m* importante, alto cargo *m*, pez *m* gordo*.

high water ['haɪ'wɔːtəʳ] **1** *n* pleamar *f*, marea *f* alta. **2** *attr*: **~ mark** línea *f* de pleamar.

highway ['haɪweɪ] **1** *n* carretera *f*; autopista *f*; **~s department** administración *f* de carreteras. **2** *attr*: **~ code** (*Brit*) código *m* de la circulación; **~ robbery** salteamiento *m*, atraco *m* (en la carretera).

highwayman ['haɪweɪmən] *n*, *pl* **highwaymen** ['haɪweɪmən] salteador *m* de caminos.

hijack ['haɪdʒæk] **1** *n* = **hijacking. 2** *vt* piratear, secuestrar (*esp* en el aire).

hijacker ['haɪdʒækəʳ] *n* pirata *m* (aéreo), secuestrador *m* (aéreo).

hijacking ['haɪdʒækɪŋ] *n* piratería *f* (aérea), secuestro *m* (aéreo).

hike¹ [haɪk] **1** *n* caminata *f*, excursión *f* a pie; **to go on a ~** dar una caminata; **take a ~!*** ¡lárgate!*
2 *vt*: **to ~ it** ir a pie.
3 *vi* dar una caminata, ir de excursión (a pie); ir a pie, ir andando.

hike² [haɪk] (*US*) **1** *n* aumento *m*. **2** *vt* aumentar, subir.

◆**hike up** *vt* (**a**) *skirt, socks* subirse. (**b**) *prices, amounts* subir de golpe, aumentar.

hiker ['haɪkəʳ] *n* excursionista *mf* (a pie), caminador *m*, -ora *f*.

hiking ['haɪkɪŋ] *n* excursionismo *m* (a pie).

hilarious [hɪ'lɛərɪəs] *adj scene etc* divertido, regocijante; *laughter* alegre.

hilarity [hɪ'lærɪtɪ] *n* regocijo *m*, alegría *f*; **there was some ~ at this** en esto hubo algunas risas; **it caused ~ in the audience** provocó las carcajadas del público.

hill [hɪl] *n* colina *f*, cerro *m*, otero *m*; (*high*) montaña *f*; (*slope*) cuesta *f*; **to be over the ~*** estar en la pendiente vital, ser demasiado viejo; no servir ya; **to chase sb up ~ and down dale** perseguir a uno por todas partes; **to curse sb up ~ and down dale** echar mil pestes de uno; **to take to the ~s** echarse al monte.

hillbilly ['hɪl'bɪlɪ] (*US*) **1** *n* rústico *m* montañés; (*pej*) palurdo *m*, -a *f*. **2** *attr*: **~ music** música *f* country.

hill climb ['hɪlklaɪm] *n* (*Sport*) ascensión *f* de montaña.

hill-farmer ['hɪl,fɑːməʳ] *n* agricultor *m*, -ora *f* de montaña.

hill-farming ['hɪl,fɑːmɪŋ] *n* agricultura *f* de montaña.

hillfort ['hɪl'fɔːt] *n* castro *m*.

hilliness ['hɪlɪnɪs] *n* montañosidad *f*.

hillock ['hɪlək] *n* montículo *m*, altozano *m*.

hillside ['hɪlsaɪd] *n* ladera *f*.

hilltop ['hɪltɒp] *n* cumbre *f*.

hill-walker ['hɪl,wɔːkəʳ] *n* montañero *m*, -a *f*.

hill-walking ['hɪl,wɔːkɪŋ] *n* caminatas *fpl* de montaña.

hilly ['hɪlɪ] *adj* montuoso, montañoso, accidentado; *road* de fuertes pendientes.

hilt [hɪlt] *n* puño *m*, empuñadura *f*; **up to the ~** hasta las cachas; **he's in debt (right) up to the ~** está agobiado de deudas; **to back sb up to the ~** apoyar a uno incondicionalmente; **to prove sth up to the ~** probar algo completamente, demostrar algo hasta la saciedad.

him [hɪm] *pron* (**a**) (*direct*) le, lo (*esp LAm*); **I see ~** le (*or* lo) veo; **I have never seen HIM** a él no le (*or* lo) he visto nunca. (**b**) (*indirect*) le; **I gave ~ the book** le di el libro; **I'm speaking to ~** le estoy hablando. (**c**) (*after prep*) él; **she thought of ~** pensó en él; **without ~** sin él; **if I were ~** yo que él; **it's ~** es él; **younger than ~** más joven (*or* menor) que él.

Himalayas [,hɪmə'leɪəz] *npl* los montes Himalaya, el Himalaya.

himself [hɪm'self] *pron* (*reflexive*) se; (*emphatic*) él mismo; (*after prep*) sí (mismo); **he washed ~** se lavó; **he said to ~** dijo entre (*or* para) sí; **he did it ~** lo hizo él mismo; **he went ~** fue él mismo, fue en persona; **he did it by ~** lo hizo él solo.

hind¹ [haɪnd] *n* cierva *f*.

hind² [haɪnd] *adj* trasero, posterior.

hinder¹ ['hɪndəʳ] *vt person* estorbar, impedir, *progress etc* estorbar, dificultar; *trade, traffic* entorpecer; **to ~ sb from doing sth** impedir a uno hacer algo.

hinder² ['haɪndəʳ] *adj part* trasero.

Hindi ['hɪndiː] *n* hindi *m*.

hindmost ['haɪndməʊst] *adj* postrero, último.

hindquarters ['haɪnd,kwɔːtəz] *npl* cuartos *mpl* traseros.

hindrance ['hɪndrəns] *n* estorbo *m*, obstáculo *m* (*to* para).

hindsight ['haɪndsaɪt] *n* percepción *f* retrospectiva, comprensión *f* a posteriori; **with the benefit of ~** como vemos en retrospectiva, con la perspectiva del tiempo transcurrido.

Hindu ['hɪn'duː] **1** *adj* hindú. **2** *n* hindú *mf*.

Hinduism ['hɪnduːɪzəm] *n* hinduismo *m*.

Hindustan [,hɪndʊ'stɑːn] *n* Indostán *m*.

Hindustani ['hɪndʊ'stɑːnɪ] *n* (*Ling*) indostánico *m*, indostani *m*.

hinge [hɪndʒ] **1** *n* gozne *m*, bisagra *f*; charnela *f* (*also Zool*); (*for stamps*) fijasellos *m*; (*fig*) eje *m*.
2 *vt* engoznar.
3 *vi* moverse sobre goznes; **to ~ on** moverse sobre, girar sobre; (*fig*) depender de.

hinged [hɪndʒd] *adj* con goznes, de bisagra.

hint [hɪnt] **1** *n* (**a**) (*suggestion*) indirecta *f*, indicación *f*, insinuación *f*; (*advice*) consejo *m*; **broad ~** indicación *f* inconfundible; **~s for purchasers** aviso *m* a los compradores; **~s on maintenance** instrucciones *fpl* para la manutención; **to drop** (*or* **let fall, throw out**) **a ~** soltar una indirecta; **to drop a ~ that ...** insinuar que ...; **take a ~ from me** permite que te dé un consejo; **to take the ~** aprovechar la indicación; darse por aludido.
(**b**) (*trace*) señal *f*, indicio *m*; **without the least ~ of** sin la menor señal de; **with just a ~ of garlic** con un ligerísimo sabor a ajo; **with a ~ of irony** con un dejo de ironía.
2 *vt*: **to ~ that ...** insinuar que ...
3 *vi* soltar indirectas; **to ~ at** hacer alusión a; **what are you ~ing (at)?** ¿qué pretendes insinuar?

hinterland ['hɪntəlænd] *n* hinterland *m*, interior *m*, traspaís *m*.

hip¹ [hɪp] **1** *n* (*Anat*) cadera *f*; **to shoot from the ~** (sacar el revólver y) disparar sin apuntar. **2** *attr*: **~ replacement (operation)** operación *f* de trasplante de cadera; **~ size** talla *f* de cadera.

hip² [hɪp] *n* (*Bot*) escaramujo *m*.

hip[3] [hɪp] *interj*: ~ ~ **hurray!** ¡viva!
hip[4]***** [hɪp] *adj*: **to be** ~ (*up-to-date*) estar al día; (*well-informed*) estar al tanto (de lo que pasa), estar enterado.
hip-bath ['hɪpbɑːθ] *n, pl* **hip-baths** ['hɪpbɑːðz] baño *m* de asiento, polibán *m*.
hipbone ['hɪpbəʊn] *n* hueso *m* de la cadera.
hip-flask ['hɪpflɑːsk] *n* frasco *m* de bolsillo.
hip-joint ['hɪp,dʒɔɪnt] *n* articulación *f* de la cadera.
hipped[1] [hɪpt] *adj* (*Archit*) a cuatro aguas.
hipped[2]***** [hɪpt] *adj* (*US*) triste; enojado, resentido; ~ **on** obsesionado por.
hippie* ['hɪpɪ] **1** *n* hippie* *mf*, hippy* *mf*. **2** *adj* hippy*, hippie*.
hippo* ['hɪpəʊ] *n* hipopótamo *m*.
hip-pocket ['hɪp'pɒkɪt] *n* bolsillo *m* trasero.
Hippocrates [hɪ'pɒkrətiːz] *nm* Hipócrates.
Hippocratic [,hɪpəʊ'krætɪk] *adj*: ~ **oath** juramento *m* hipocrático.
hippodrome ['hɪpədrəʊm] *n* (*Hist*) hipódromo *m*.
hippopotamus [,hɪpə'pɒtəməs] *n, pl* **hippopotamuses** [,hɪpə'pɒtəməsɪz] *or* **hippopotami** [,hɪpə'pɒtəmaɪ] hipopótamo *m*.
hippy* ['hɪpɪ] = **hippie***.
hipster ['hɪpstə^r] **1** *n* (**a**) ~**s** (*Brit*) *pantalón que se lleva a la altura de la cadera*. (**b**) (*US**) entusiasta *mf* del jazz.
2 *attr*: ~ **skirt** (*Brit*) falda *f* abrochada en la cadera.
hire ['haɪə^r] **1** *n* alquiler *m*; (*of person*) salario *m*, jornal *m*; **'for ~'** 'se alquila'; **to be on** ~ estar de alquiler.
2 *attr*: ~ **car** (*Brit*) coche *m* de alquiler; ~ **charges** tarifa *f* de alquiler.
3 *vt thing*, (*Brit*) *car* alquilar; *person* contratar, emplear.
◆**hire out** *vt car, tools* alquilar.
hired ['haɪəd] *adj*: ~ **car** coche *m* alquilado, coche *m* de alquiler; ~ **killer** asesino *m* a sueldo.
hireling ['haɪəlɪŋ] *n* mercenario *m*.
hire purchase ['haɪə'pɜːtʃɪs] **1** *n* (*Brit*) compra *f* a plazos; **to buy sth on** ~ comprar algo a plazos. **2** *attr*: ~ **agreement** acuerdo *m* de compra a plazos; ~ **finance company** compañía *f* de crédito comercial.
hirsute ['hɜːsjuːt] *adj* hirsuto.
his [hɪz] **1** *poss adj* su, sus; ~ **book/table** su libro/mesa; ~ **friends** sus amigos. **2** *poss pron* (el/la) suyo/a, (los/las) suyos/as, de él; **this book is** ~ este libro es suyo (*or* de él); **a friend of** ~ un amigo suyo; **is this painting** ~? ¿es de él este cuadro?; **the one I like best is** ~ el que más me gusta es el suyo.
Hispanic [hɪs'pænɪk] **1** *adj* hispánico; (*within US*) hispano. **2** *n* (*within US*) hispano *m*, -a *f*.
hispanicism [hɪs'pænɪsɪzəm] *n* hispanismo *m*.
hispanicize [hɪs'pænɪsaɪz] *vt* españolizar, hispanizar.
Hispanism ['hɪspənɪzəm] *n* hispanismo *m*.
hispanist ['hɪspənɪst] *n* hispanista *mf*.
Hispano... [hɪ'spænəʊ] *pref* hispano...
hispanophile [hɪs'pænəʊfaɪl] *n* hispanófilo *m*, -a *f*.
hispanophobe [hɪs'pænəʊfəʊb] *n* hispanófobo *m*, -a *f*.
hiss [hɪs] **1** *n* silbido *m*, siseo *m*; (*of protest*) silbido *m*.
2 *vt* silbar; **to ~ an actor off the stage** abuchear a un actor (hasta que abandone la escena).
3 *vi* silbar, sisear; (*in protest*) silbar.
histogram ['hɪstəgræm] *n* histograma *m*.
histology [hɪs'tɒlədʒɪ] *n* histología *f*.
historian [hɪs'tɔːrɪən] *n* historiador *m*, -ora *f*.
historic(al) [hɪs'tɒrɪk(əl)] *adj* histórico.
historically [hɪs'tɒrɪkəlɪ] *adv* históricamente.
historicism [hɪ'stɒrɪsɪzəm] *n* historicismo *m*.
historicist [hɪ'stɒrɪsɪst] *adj* historicista.
historiographer [,hɪstɒrɪ'ɒgrəfə^r] *n* historiógrafo *m*, -a *f*.
historiography [,hɪstɒrɪ'ɒgrəfɪ] *n* historiografía *f*.
history ['hɪstərɪ] *n* historia *f*; **that's ancient** ~ ésa es cosa vieja; **to go down in** ~ pasar a la historia (*as* como); **to know the inner ~ of an affair** conocer el secreto de un asunto; **to make** ~ hacer época, marcar un hito.
histrionic [,hɪstrɪ'ɒnɪk] *adj* histriónico.
histrionics [,hɪstrɪ'ɒnɪks] *npl* histrionismo *m*; **I'm tired of his** ~ estoy harto de sus payasadas.
hit [hɪt] **1** *n* (**a**) (*blow*) golpe *m*; (*shot*) tiro *m* certero; (*Baseball*) jit *m*; (*with shell etc*) impacto *m*; (*good guess*) acierto *m*; **direct** ~ impacto *m* directo; **we made 3 ~s on the target** dimos 3 veces en el blanco; **that's a ~ at you** lo dijo por ti; **he made a ~ at the government** hizo un ataque contra el gobierno.
(**b**) (*Mus, Theat etc*) éxito *m*, sensación *f*; (*in pop music*) impacto *m*, hit *m*; **to be a** ~ obtener un éxito, ser un triunfo; **the song was a big** ~ la canción tuvo un exitazo; **to make a ~ with sb** caer en gracia a uno, chiflar a uno*.
2 *attr* (*) sensacional; ~ **show** espectáculo *m* de éxito; ~ **song** canción *f* éxito.
3 (*irr*: *pret and ptp* **hit**) *vt* (**a**) (*strike*) *person* golpear, pegar; (*wound*) herir; *target* alcanzar, hacer blanco en, acertar, dar en; **to ~ sb a blow** dar un golpe a uno; **to ~ one's head against a wall** dar con la cabeza contra una pared; **the president was ~ by 3 bullets** el presidente fue alcanzado por 3 balas; **the house was ~ by a bomb** la casa fue blanco de una bomba; **I realized my plane had been** ~ me di cuenta de que mi avión había sido tocado; **his father used to ~ him** su padre le pegaba; **then it ~ me** (*fig*) aquello fue el flechazo; en seguida me di cuenta; **a lot of what he said ~ home** gran parte de lo que dijo dio en el blanco (*or* hizo mella); **to ~ the road*** ponerse en camino, largarse*.
(**b**) (*collide with*) chocar con, dar contra.
(**c**) (*damage*) hacer daño a, afectar; **the crops were ~ by the rain** las lluvias dañaron los cultivos; **the news ~ him hard** la noticia le afectó mucho; **the company has been hard** ~ la compañía ha sido afectada de mala manera, la compañía ha sufrido un rudo golpe; **to ~ the bottle*** beber mucho.
(**d**) (*find, reach*) llegar a, alcanzar; *problem* tropezar con; **when we ~ the main road** cuando lleguemos a la carretera.
(**e**) (*) **he ~ me for 10 bucks** (*US*) me dio un sablazo de 10 dólares*; **how much can we ~ them for?** ¿qué cantidad podremos sacarles?
4 *vi* (*collide*) chocar; **to ~ against** chocar con, dar contra; **to ~ at** asestar un golpe a, (*fig*) atacar, apuntar a, satirizar; **to do sth ~ or miss** hacer algo a la buena de Dios; **to ~ and run** atacar y retirarse.
◆**hit back** *vi* devolver golpe por golpe, defenderse.
◆**hit off** *vt* (**a**) (*imitate*) imitar, remedar; *resemblance* coger; (*describe*) describir con gran acierto. (**b**) **to ~ it off with sb** hacer buenas migas con uno; **they don't ~ it off** no se llevan bien.
◆**hit out** *vi* lanzar un ataque, (*wildly*) repartir golpes; **to ~ out at sb** asestar un golpe a uno, (*fig*) atacar a uno.
◆**hit (up)on** *vt* dar con, tropezar con; **I ~ (up)on the idea** se me ocurrió la idea.
hit-and-miss [,hɪtən'mɪs] *adj* al azar; **it's all rather** ~ todo es a la buena de Dios.
hit-and-run ['hɪtən'rʌn] *adj*: ~ **accident** *accidente de carretera en el que el conductor se da a la fuga*; ~ **driver** conductor *m* que atropella y huye; ~ **raid** ataque *m* relámpago.
hitch [hɪtʃ] **1** *n* (**a**) (*tug*) tirón *m*.
(**b**) (*knot*) cote *m*, vuelta *f* de cabo.
(**c**) (*fig*) obstáculo *m*, dificultad *f*, interrupción *f*; **without a** ~ a pedir de boca; **there was a ~ of 15 minutes** hubo un retraso de 15 minutos; **there's been a** ~ ha surgido una dificultad.
2 *vt* (**a**) (*shift*) mover de un tirón; **he ~ed a chair over** acercó una silla a tirones.
(**b**) (*fasten*) atar, amarrar (*to* a); **to ~ a horse to a wagon** enganchar un caballo a un carro.
(**c**) **to ~ lifts** hacer autostop, hacer dedo (*SC*), pedir aventón (*Mex*); **to ~ a lift to Rome** llegar a Roma en autostop.
(**d**) **to get ~ed*** casarse.
3 *vi* (*) = **hitch-hike**.
◆**hitch up** *vt* alzar.
hitch-hike ['hɪtʃhaɪk] *vi* hacer autostop, hacer dedo (*SC*), pedir aventón (*Mex*).
hitch-hiker ['hɪtʃhaɪkə^r] *n* autostopista *mf*.
hitch-hiking ['hɪtʃhaɪkɪŋ] *n* autostop *m*, autostopismo *m*.
hi-tech* ['haɪ'tek] *attr* al-tec*, de alta tecnología.
hither ['hɪðə^r] *adv* (*liter*) acá; ~ **and thither** acá y acullá.
hitherto ['hɪðə'tuː] *adv* hasta ahora.
Hitlerian [hɪt'lɪərɪən] *adj* hitleriano.
hitlist ['hɪtlɪst] *n* lista *f* de los 'sentenciados a muerte'.
hitman ['hɪtmæn] *n, pl* **hitmen** ['hɪtmen] pistolero *m*, asesino *m* (a sueldo), hombre *m* del gatillo.
hit-or-miss ['hɪtɔː'mɪs] *adj*: ~ **shot** disparo *m* hecho sin apuntar; **with his ~ attitude** con su actitud despreocupada; **he operates on a ~ basis** funciona a la buena de Dios.
hit parade ['hɪtpəreɪd] *n* relación *f* de discos más populares, escala *f* de éxitos.
hit-squad ['hɪtskwɒd] *n* escuadrón *m* de la muerte.
Hittite ['hɪtaɪt] **1** *adj* heteo, hitita. **2** *n* (**a**) heteo *m*, -a *f*, hitita *mf*. (**b**) (*Ling*) hitita *m*.

HIV *n abbr of* **human immunodeficiency virus** virus *m* de la inmunodeficiencia humana, VIH *m*; ~ **negative** VIH negativo; ~ **positive** VIH positivo.
hive [haɪv] *n* colmena *f*; **a ~ of industry** un centro de industria, un lugar donde se trabaja muchísimo.
◆**hive off** *vt* separar; (*Fin*) vender (por separado); (*privatize*) privatizar.
hives [haɪvz] *npl* (*Med*) urticaria *f*.
hiya* ['haɪjə] *excl* ¡hola!
HK *abbr of* **Hong Kong**.
hl *abbr of* **hectolitre(s)** hectolitro(s), *m(pl)*, hl.
HM *abbr of* **Her** (*or* **His**) **Majesty** Su Majestad, S.M.
HMG *n* (*Brit*) *abbr of* **Her** (*or* **His**) **Majesty's Government** el Gobierno de Su Majestad; *V* **majesty**.
HMI *n* (*Brit*) *abbr of* **Her** (*or* **His**) **Majesty's Inspector**.
HMO *n* (*US*) *abbr of* **health maintenance organization** seguro *m* médico global.
HMS *n* (*Brit*) *abbr of* **Her** (*or* **His**) **Majesty's Ship** *buque de guerra británico*.
HMSO *n* (*Brit*) *abbr of* **Her** (*or* **His**) **Majesty's Stationery Office** *imprenta del gobierno*.
HNC *n* (*Brit Scol*) *abbr of* **Higher National Certificate** Certificado *m* Nacional de Estudios Superiores; *V* **higher**.
HND *n* (*Brit Scol*) *abbr of* **Higher National Diploma** Diploma *m* Nacional de Estudios Superiores; *V* **higher**.
HO (**a**) (*Comm etc*) *abbr of* **head office**. (**b**) (*Brit Pol*) *abbr of* **Home Office**.
hoard [hɔːd] **1** *n* acumulación *f*; provisión *f*; (*money*) tesoro *m* escondido; (*arms*) alijo *m*.
2 *vt* (*also* **to ~ up**) acumular, amontonar (en secreto); *money* atesorar; *goods in short supply* retener, acaparar.
hoarder ['hɔːdəʳ] *n*: **to be a ~** ser un acaparador.
hoarding¹ ['hɔːdɪŋ] *n* (*act*) acumulación *f*, retención *f*; acaparamiento *m*.
hoarding² ['hɔːdɪŋ] *n* (*Brit*) (*fence*) valla *f* de construcción; (*for posters*) valla *f* publicitaria, cartelera *f*.
hoarfrost ['hɔː'frɒst] *n* escarcha *f*.
hoarse [hɔːs] *adj* ronco; **to be ~** tener la voz ronca; **in a ~ voice** con voz ronca; **to shout o.s. ~** enronquecer a fuerza de gritar.
hoarsely ['hɔːslɪ] *adv* en voz ronca.
hoarseness ['hɔːsnɪs] *n* (*Med*) ronquera *f*; (*hoarse quality*) ronquedad *f*.
hoary ['hɔːrɪ] *adj* cano; *joke etc* viejo.
hoax [həʊks] **1** *n* trampa *f*, truco *m*, mistificación *f*.
2 *vt* engañar, burlar, mistificar.
hoaxer ['həʊksəʳ] *n* trampista *mf*.
hob [hɒb] *n* quemador *m*.
hobble ['hɒbl] **1** *n* (*lameness*) cojera *f*; (*rope*) maniota *f*; **to walk with a ~** cojear.
2 *vt horse* manear.
3 *vi* (*also* **to ~ along**) cojear, andar cojeando; **to ~ to the door** ir cojeando a la puerta.
hobbledehoy ['hɒbldɪ'hɒɪ] *n* gamberro *m*.
hobby ['hɒbɪ] *n* hobby *m*, pasatiempo *m*, afición *f*; **it's just a ~** es sólo un pasatiempo; **he began to paint as a ~** empezó a pintar como distracción.
hobby-horse ['hɒbɪhɔːs] *n* caballito *m* (de niño), caballo *m* mecedor; (*fig*) caballo *m* de batalla, tema *f*, manía *f*; **he's riding his ~ again** ha vuelto a la misma canción.
hobgoblin ['hɒb,gɒblɪn] *n* duende *m*, trasgo *m*.
hobnail ['hɒbneɪl] *n* clavo *m* (de botas).
hobnailed ['hɒbneɪld] *adj boots* con clavos.
hobnob ['hɒbnɒb] *vi* tratarse con familiaridad; **to ~ with** codearse con, alternar con.
hobo ['həʊbəʊ] *n* (*US*) vagabundo *m*; obrero *m* temporero, obrero *m* migratorio.
Hobson's choice ['hɒbsənz'tʃɔɪs] *n* (*Brit*) opción *f* única; **it's ~** o lo tomas o lo dejas.
hock¹ [hɒk] *n* (*Anat*) corvejón *m*.
hock² [hɒk] *n* (*Brit*: *wine*) vino *m* del Rin.
hock³* [hɒk] **1** *vt* empeñar. **2** *n*: **in ~** *person* empeñado, endeudado; *object* empeñado.
hockey ['hɒkɪ] **1** *n* hockey *m*; (*Brit*: *also US* **field ~**) hockey *m* sobre hierba; (*US*: *also Brit* **ice ~**) hockey *m* sobre hielo.
2 *attr*: **~ player** jugador *m*, -ora *f* de hockey; **~ stick** palo *m* de hockey.
hocus-pocus ['həʊkəs'pəʊkəs] *n* (*jugglery*) abracadabra *m*, pasapasa *m*; (*deception*) trampa *f*, mistificación *f*.
hod [hɒd] *n* capacho *m*.
hodgepodge ['hɒdʒpɒdʒ] *n* = **hotchpotch**.
hoe [həʊ] **1** *n* azada *f*, azadón *m*, sacho *m*. **2** *vt earth* azadonar; *crop* sachar.
hog [hɒg] **1** *n* (**a**) (*lit, fig*) cerdo *m*, puerco *m*, chancho *m* (*LAm*); **to go the whole ~** liarse la manta a la cabeza, echar el todo por el todo. (**b**) (*US**) (*car*) cochazo* *m*, coche *m* grande; (*motorbike*) moto *f* grande.
2 *vt food* devorar; (*take for o.s.*) acaparar, tragarse lo mejor de; **to ~ all the credit** acapararse todo el mérito.
Hogmanay ['hɒgmənei] *n* (*Scot*) noche *f* vieja.
hogshead ['hɒgzhed] *n medida de capacidad esp del vino* (= 52,5 *galones* = (*approx*) 225 *litros*), pipa *f*.
hogwash ['hɒgwɒʃ] *n* (*US*) bazofia *f*; (*fig*) cuentos *mpl*, bazofia *f*.
hoi polloi [,hɔɪpə'lɔɪ] *n*: **the ~** las masas; la plebe, el vulgo.
hoist [hɔɪst] **1** *n* (*lift*) montacargas *m*; (*crane*) grúa *f*; **to give sb a ~** (**up**) ayudar a uno a subir.
2 *vt* (*also* **to ~ up**) alzar, levantar; *flag* enarbolar, (*Naut*) izar.
hoity-toity ['hɔɪtɪ'tɔɪtɪ] **1** *adj* presumido, repipi*. **2** *interj* ¡tate!
hokum* ['həʊkəm] *n* (*US*) tonterías *fpl* (sentimentales).
hold [həʊld] **1** *n* (**a**) (*grasp*) agarro *m*, asimiento *m*; (*Wrestling*) presa *f*; **with no ~s barred** (*fig*) sin restricción, permitiéndose todo; sin cuartel; **to catch** (*or* **get, lay, seize, take**) **~ of** agarrar, asirse de, coger (*Sp*); **catch ~!** ¡toma!; **to get ~ of** (*fig*) (*take over*) adquirir, apoderarse de, (*obtain*) procurarse, conseguir; **where did you get ~ of that?** ¿dónde has adquirido eso?; **we're trying to get ~ of him** tratamos de ponernos en contacto con él; **where did you get ~ of that idea?** ¿de dónde te salió esa idea?; **you get ~ of some odd ideas** te formas unas ideas muy raras; **to have ~ of** estar agarrado a; **to keep ~ of** seguir agarrado a; (*fig*) guardar para sí; **to relax one's ~** desasirse (*on* de).
(**b**) (*place to grip*) asidero *m*.
(**c**) (*fig*) influencia *f*, dominio *m* (*over* sobre); arraigo *m*; **this broke the dictator's ~** esto acabó con el dominio del dictador; **to gain a firm ~ over sb** llegar a dominar a uno; **drink has a ~ on him** la bebida está muy arraigada en él; **to have a ~ over** (*person*) dominar a uno, ejercer gran influencia sobre uno.
(**d**) (*Naut*) bodega *f*; (*Aer*) compartimento *m* de carga, bodega *f* de carga.
(**e**) **to put a plan on ~** suspender temporalmente la ejecución de un plan; (*Telec*) **to put sb on ~** poner al comunicante en espera; **to be on ~** estar en espera.
2 (*irr*: *pret and ptp* **held**) *vt* (**a**) (*gen*) tener; (*take ~ of*) agarrar, coger (*Sp*); (*bear weight of*) soportar; *attention* mantener; *belief* tener; *note* sostener; *road* agarrarse a; **~ him or he'll fall** sóstenle que va a caer; **he held my arm** me tuvo por el brazo; **~ this for a moment** coge esto un momento; **to ~ sth tight** agarrar algo fuertemente; **to ~ sb tight** abrazar a uno estrechamente; **to ~ sth in place** sujetar algo en un lugar; **to ~ sb to his promise** hacer que uno cumpla su promesa; **he ~s the key to the mystery** él tiene la clave del misterio; **he held us spellbound** nos tuvo embelesados; **can he ~ an audience?** ¿sabe mantener el interés de un público?
(**b**) (*keep back*) retener, guardar; **I will ~ the money for you** guardaré el dinero para ti; **'~ for arrival'** (*US*: *on letters*) 'no reexpedir', 'reténgase'; **the police held him for 3 days** le detuvo la policia durante 3 días; **we are ~ing it pending inquiries** lo guardamos mientras se hagan indagaciones.
(**c**) (*check, restrain*) *enemy, breath* contener; **~ it!** ¡para!, para el carro!; **~ everything!** ¡que se pare todo!; **there was no ~ing him** no había manera de detenerle.
(**d**) (*possess*) *post, town, lands* ocupar; *shares, title* tener; *reserves* tener en reserva, tener guardado; *record* ostentar, estar en posesión de.
(**e**) (*contain*) contener, tener capacidad (*or* cabida) para; **this ~s the money** esto contiene el dinero; **this bag won't ~ them all** en este saco no caben todos; **a car that ~s 6** un coche de 6 plazas; **what the future ~s for us** lo que el futuro guarda para nosotros.
(**f**) *interview, meeting, election* celebrar; *conversation* tener, (*formally*) celebrar; **the meeting will be held on Monday** se celebrará la reunión el lunes, la reunión tendrá lugar el lunes.
(**g**) (*consider*) **to ~ that** ... creer que ..., sostener que ...; **I ~ that** ... tengo para mí que ...; **it is held by some that** ... hay quien cree que ...; **to ~ sth to be true** creer que algo es verdad; **to ~ sb guilty** juzgar a uno culpable; **to ~ sb responsible** hacer a uno responsable (*for* de); **to ~ sb in respect** tener respeto a uno; **to ~ sb dear** tener cariño a uno.

3 *vi* (**a**) (*stick*) pegarse; (*not give way*) mantenerse firme, resistir; (*weather*) continuar, seguir bueno; **the ceasefire seems to be ~ing** el cese de fuego parece que se mantiene.

(**b**) (*be true*) valer, ser valedero; **the objection does not ~** la objeción no vale.

4 *vr*: **to ~ o.s. ready** (*or* **in readiness**) estar listo (*for* para); **to ~ o.s. upright** mantenerse erguido.

◆**hold against** *vt*: **they held his origins against him** creían que sus orígenes eran deshonrosos para él; **you won't ~ this against me, will you?** ¿verdad que no vas a pensar mal de mí por esto?

◆**hold back 1** *vt* (*keep*) guardar, retener; (*stop*) *water etc* retener; *progress* refrenar; *information* ocultar, no revelar; *names etc* no comunicar; *emotion, tears* contener; **are you ~ing sth back from me?** ¿me estás ocultando algo?

2 *vi* refrenarse; mantenerse a distancia; (*in doubt*) vacilar; **I could hardly ~ back from** + *ger* apenas pude abstenerme de + *infin*.

3 *vr*: **to ~ o.s. back** contenerse, refrenarse.

◆**hold down** *vt* (**a**) *object* sujetar.

(**b**) (*oppress*) oprimir, subyugar.

(**c**) **to ~ down a job** (*retain*) mantenerse en su puesto; (*be equal to*) estar a la altura de su cargo.

◆**hold forth** *vi* hablar largamente (*about, on* de); disertar pomposamente.

◆**hold in** *vt emotion* contener.

◆**hold off 1** *vt attack, enemy* rechazar; tener a raya; *threat* apartar; *person* defenderse contra.

2 *vi* (**a**) mantenerse a distancia; no tomar parte; (*wait*) esperar.

(**b**) **if the rain ~s off** si no llueve.

◆**hold on** *vi* (**a**) (*grip*) agarrarse bien.

(**b**) (*not give way*) aguantar, resistir; defenderse; **~ on!** ¡ánimo!; **can you ~ on?** ¿te animas a continuar?

(**c**) (*wait*) esperar, seguir esperando; **~ on!** ¡tente!, ¡espera!, (*Telec*) ¡no cuelgue!

◆**hold on to** *vt* (**a**) (*grip*) agarrarse bien a.

(**b**) (*retain*) guardar, quedarse con; *post* retener.

◆**hold out 1** *vt hand* tender, alargar; *arm* extender; *object* ofrecer, alargar; *possibility* ofrecer; *hope* dar.

2 *vi* (**a**) (*resist*) resistir (*against* a), aguantar; **to ~ out for sth** resistir hasta conseguir algo, insistir en algo.

(**b**) (*last*) durar.

(**c**) **to ~ out on sb** no acceder a los deseos de uno; ocultar algo a uno.

◆**hold over** *vt* aplazar, posponer.

◆**hold to** *vt* atenerse a.

◆**hold together 1** *vt persons* mantener unidos; *company, group* mantener la unidad de.

2 *vi* (**a**) (*persons*) mantenerse unidos.

(**b**) (*argument*) ser sólido, ser lógico; (*deal etc*) mantenerse.

◆**hold up 1** *vt* (**a**) (*support*) apoyar, sostener.

(**b**) (*raise*) *hand* levantar, alzar; *head* mantener erguido; **to ~ sth up to the light** acercar algo a la luz.

(**c**) (*display*) mostrar, enseñar; **to ~ sth up as a model** presentar algo como modelo.

(**d**) (*delay*) atrasar; (*stop*) detener, parar; *work* interrumpir; *delivery, payment* suspender; **we were held up for 3 hours** no nos pudimos mover durante 3 horas; **the train was held up** el tren sufrió un retraso; **the train was held up by fog** el tren venía con retraso debido a la niebla; **we are held up for** (*or* **by lack of**) **bricks** la escasez de ladrillos entorpece el trabajo.

(**e**) (*rob*) atracar, asaltar.

2 *vi* (**a**) (*weather*) seguir bueno.

(**b**) **to ~ up under the strain** soportar bien la presión.

(**c**) (*remain strong*) durar; mantenerse bien, seguir en pie.

◆**hold with** *vt* estar de acuerdo con, aprobar.

holdall ['həʊldɔːl] *n* (*Brit*) funda *f*, neceser *m*, bolsa *f* de viaje.

holder ['həʊldəʳ] *n* (**a**) (*person*) tenedor *m*, -ora *f*, poseedor *m*, -ora *f*; (*of bonds*) tenedor *m*, -ora *f*; (*of title, credit card, office, passport*) titular *mf*; (*of record*) poseedor *m*, -ora *f*, detentor *m*, -ora *f*.

(**b**) (*support*) soporte *m*; (*handle*) asidero *m*; (*haft*) mango *m*; (*vessel*) receptáculo *m*; (*for cigarette*) boquilla *f*; (*in compounds*) porta ..., *eg* **lamp-~** portalámparas *m*.

holding ['həʊldɪŋ] **1** *n* (**a**) (*act*) tenencia *f*.

(**b**) (*thing*) posesión *f*, propiedad *f*.

(**c**) (*Comm*) participación *f*; **~s** valores *mpl* en cartera.

2 *attr*: **~ company** (compañía *f*) holding *m*, compañía *f* tenedora; **~ operation** operación *f* de contención.

holdup ['həʊldʌp] *n* (**a**) (*robbery*) atraco *m*; **~ man** atracador *m*. (**b**) (*Brit*) (*stoppage*) parada *f*, interrupción *f*, suspensión *f*; (*delay*) retraso *m*; (*of traffic*) embotellamiento *m*, retención *f*.

hole [həʊl] **1** *n* (**a**) agujero *m*; (*in ground*) hoyo *m*; (*Golf*) hoyo *m*, cazoleta *f*; (*hollow*) cavidad *f*, hueco *m*; (*in road*) bache *m*; (*in wall*) boquete *m*; (*in defences, dam*) brecha *f*; (*burrow*) madriguera *f*; (*in clothes*) roto *m*; **through a ~ in the clouds** a través de un agujero de las nubes; **to bore** (*or* **make**) **a ~ in** hacer un agujero en.

(**b**) (*fig*: *defect*) defecto *m*, fallo *m*; **this will make a ~ in my salary** esto dejará temblando mi sueldo; **his injury leaves a ~ in the team** su lesión deja un vacío en el equipo; **to pick ~s in** encontrar defectos en.

(**c**) (*fig*: *jam*) apuro *m*, aprieto *m*; **to be in a ~** estar en un aprieto; **to get sb out of a ~** sacar a uno de un aprieto.

(**d**) (*) (*room*) cuchitril *m*; (*house*) casucha *f*; (*town*) poblacho *m*, pueblo *m* muerto.

2 *vt* (**a**) (*pierce*) agujerear, perforar; *ship etc* abrir una brecha en, causar desperfectos a.

(**b**) *ball* (*Golf*) embocar; (*Snooker*) meter en la tronera.

3 *vi*: **to ~ in one** hacer un hoyo de un golpe; **to ~ out** embocar; **to ~ out in 7** terminar en 7 golpes.

◆**hole up** *vi* (*animal*) ocultarse (en la querencia), retirarse (a la madriguera *etc*); (*wanted man*) esconderse, refugiarse.

hole-and-corner ['həʊlən'kɔːnəʳ] *adj* furtivo; **to do sth in a ~ way** hacer algo de tapadillo.

hole-in-the-heart ['həʊlɪnðə'hɑːt] *n* soplo *m* cardíaco.

holey* ['həʊlɪ] *adj* lleno de rotos; agujereado.

holiday ['hɒlədɪ] **1** *n* (*day*) (día *m* de) fiesta *f*, día *m* festivo, (día *m*) feriado *m* (*LAm*); (*period*) vacaciones *fpl*; **~s with pay** vacaciones *fpl* retribuidas; **tomorrow is a ~** mañana es fiesta; **to be on** (**one's**) **~**(**s**) estar de vacaciones; **to declare a day a ~** declarar un día festivo; **to take a ~** tomarse unas vacaciones; **it was no ~** (**I can tell you**) no era ningún lecho de rosas (te lo aseguro).

2 *attr town* de veraneo; *mood etc* alegre, festivo; **~ clothes** ropa *f* de veraneo, traje *m* de sport; **~ home** casa *f* (*or* piso *m etc*) para ocupar durante las vacaciones; **~ pay** sueldo *m* de vacaciones; **~ resort** punto *m* de veraneo; centro *m* turístico; **~ season** (*Brit*) temporada *f* de vacaciones; (*US*) Navidades *fpl*; **~ spirit** espíritu *m* festivo; **~ traffic** tráfico *m* de coches que van de vacaciones.

3 *vi* (*Brit*) pasar las vacaciones, (*esp*) veranear.

holiday-camp ['hɒlədɪkæmp] *n* (*Brit*) colonia *f* veraniega.

holiday-maker ['hɒlədɪˌmeɪkəʳ] *n* (*esp Brit*) veraneante *mf*, excursionista *mf*, turista *mf*.

holier-than-thou ['həʊlɪəðən'ðaʊ] *adj* fariseo; **he's always so ~** es un doña perfecta.

holiness ['həʊlɪnɪs] *n* santidad *f*; **His H~** Su Santidad.

holistic [həʊ'lɪstɪk] *adj* holístico.

Holland ['hɒlənd] *n* Holanda *f*.

hollandaise [ˌhɒlən'deɪz] *adj*: **~ sauce** salsa *f* holandesa.

holler* ['hɒləʳ] *vti* (*also* **to ~ out**) gritar, vocear.

hollow ['hɒləʊ] **1** *adj* (**a**) hueco, ahuecado; *cheeks, eyes* hundido.

(**b**) (*fig*) *sound* sordo; *voice* sepulcral, cavernoso; *laughter* irónico; *doctrine etc* vacío, falso; *victory* más aparente que real, pírrico; *promise* sin efecto práctico, falso.

2 *adv* (**a**) **to sound ~** sonar a hueco; (*fig*) sonar a falso.

(**b**) **to beat sb ~*** cascar a uno*, vencer a uno fácilmente.

3 *n* hueco *m*; concavidad *f*; (*in ground*) hoyo *m*, depresión *f*; (*small valley*) hondonada *f*; **in the ~ of one's back** en los riñones; **in the ~ of one's hand** en el hueco de la mano.

4 *vt* (*also* **to ~ out**) ahuecar, excavar, vaciar.

hollow-cheeked [ˌhɒləʊ'tʃiːkt] *adj* de mejillas hundidas.

hollow-eyed ['hɒləʊ'aɪd] *adj* de ojos hundidos; (*with fatigue etc*) ojeroso.

hollowly ['hɒləʊlɪ] *adv*: **to laugh ~** reír huecamente.

hollowness ['hɒləʊnɪs] *n* (**a**) oquedad *f*, lo hueco. (**b**) (*fig*) vaciedad *f*; falsedad *f*.

holly ['hɒlɪ] **1** *n* (*also* **~ tree**) acebo *m*. **2** *attr*: **~ berry** baya *f* de acebo.

hollyhock ['hɒlɪhɒk] *n* malva *f* loca.

holmium ['hɒlmɪəm] *n* holmio *m*.

holm oak ['həʊm'əʊk] *n* encina *f*.

holocaust ['hɒləkɔːst] *n* holocausto *m* (*also fig*).

hologram ['hɒləgræm] *n* holograma *m*.

holograph ['hɒləgrɑːf] **1** *adj* ológrafo. **2** *n* ológrafo *m*.

holography [hɒˈlɒgrəfɪ] *n* holografía *f*.

hols* [hɒlz] *npl* = **holidays**.

holster [ˈhəʊlstəʳ] *n* pistolera *f*, funda *f* (de pistola).

holy [ˈhəʊlɪ] **1** *adj* santo; sagrado; **H~ Bible** Santa Biblia *f*; **H~ Communion** Sagrada Comunión *f*; **H~ Family** Sagrada Familia *f*; **the H~ Father** el Santo Padre; **H~ Ghost** Espíritu *m* Santo; **H~ Land** Tierra *f* Santa; **H~ Office** Santo Oficio *m*; **~ orders** órdenes *fpl* sagradas; **to take ~ orders** ordenarse (de sacerdote); **H~ See** Santa Sede *f*; **H~ Spirit** Espíritu *m* Santo; **H~ Trinity** Santa Trinidad *f*; **~ water** agua *f* bendita; **H~ Week** Semana *f* Santa; **H~ Writ** Sagrada Escritura *f*; **by all that's ~** por todo lo más sagrado; **~ cow!***, **~ smoke!*** (*etc*) ¡santo cielo!; **he's a ~ terror*** (*child*) tiene el diablo en el cuerpo; (*master*) es un amo de lo más feroz. **2** *n*: **the ~ of holies** el sanctum sanctorum.

homage [ˈhɒmɪdʒ] *n* homenaje *m*; **~ volume** tomo-homenaje *m*; **to do** (*or* **pay**) **~ to** rendir homenaje a.

homburg [ˈhɒmbɜːg] *n* sombrero *m* de fieltro.

home [həʊm] **1** *n* (**a**) casa *f*; (*more officially*) domicilio *m*; (*more sentimentally*) hogar *m*; (*town*) ciudad *f* natal, (*region, native land*) patria *f*; (*Bio*) habitat *m*, (*environment*) ambiente *m* natural; (*Sport*) meta *f*; (*in children's games*) la madre; (*for the elderly*) residencia *f*; (*institution*) asilo *m*; **~ for the aged** asilo *m* de ancianos; **we live in Madrid but my ~ is in Jaén** vivimos en Madrid pero nací en Jaén; **for some years he made his ~ in France** durante algunos años vivió en Francia; **refugees who made their ~ in Britain** los refugiados que se establecieron en Gran Bretaña; **Scotland is the ~ of whisky** Escocia es la patria del whisky; **for us it's a ~ from ~** (*Brit*) aquí estamos como en casa; **an Englishman's ~ is his castle** para el inglés su casa es como su castillo; **there's no place like ~** no hay nada como la propia casa; **that remark came near ~** esa observación le hirió en lo vivo; **he comes from a good ~** es de buena familia; **to have a ~ of one's own** tener casa propia; **to give sb a ~** recibir a uno en casa; **he leaves ~ at 8** sale de casa a las 8; **'good ~ wanted for puppy'** 'búscase buen hogar para perrito'; **the puppy went to a good ~** el perrito fue a vivir con una buena familia; **this tool has no ~** esta herramienta no tiene lugar propio.

(**b**) (*Comput*) punto *m* inicial, punto *m* de partida.

(**c**) (*phrases with at*) **at ~** en casa; **at ~ and abroad** dentro y fuera del país; **is Mr Pérez at ~?** ¿está (en casa) el Sr Pérez?; **the duchess is at ~ on Fridays** la duquesa recibe los viernes; **Lady Rebecca is not at ~ to anyone** Lady Rebecca no recibe a nadie; **he's at ~ on any subject** sabe de cualquier materia; **I'm not at ~ in Japanese** apenas me defiendo en japonés, sé muy poco de japonés; **to feel at ~** sentirse como en casa; **make yourself at ~!** ¡estás en tu casa!; **to make sb feel at ~** hacer que uno se sienta como en casa; **he immediately made himself at ~ in the new job** en seguida se familiarizó con el nuevo trabajo.

(**d**) (*Sport*) **to play at ~** jugar en casa, jugar en el propio terreno, jugar en campo propio; **Villasanta are at ~ to Castroforte** Villasanta recibe en casa a Castroforte; **they lost nine games at ~** perdieron nueve partidos en casa.

2 *attr* (**a**) casero, de casa, doméstico; **~ address** (*on form etc*) domicilio *m*; **my ~ address** mi dirección particular, las señas de mi casa; **~ banking** banco *m* en casa; **~ brew** cerveza *f* casera; **~ comforts** comodidades *fpl* domésticas; **~ computer** ordenador *m* doméstico; **~ computing** informática *f* doméstica; **~ cooking** cocina *f* doméstica; **~ economics** (*Scol*) ciencia *f* del hogar; **~ fries** (*US*) *carne picada frita con patatas y col*; **to be on ~ ground** (*or* **territory**) (*fig*) estar en su terreno (*or* lugar); **~ help** (*act*) atención *f* domiciliaria, ayuda *f* a domicilio; (*Brit*: *person*) asistenta *f*; **~ improvements** reformas *fpl* en casa; **~ journey** viaje *m* a casa, viaje *m* de vuelta; **~ leave** permiso *m* para irse a casa; **~ life** vida *f* doméstica, vida *f* de familia; **~ owners** propietarios *mpl* de viviendas; **~ ownership** propiedad *f* de viviendas; **~ run** (*of ship, truck*) viaje *m* de vuelta; **~ truths** verdades *fpl* bien claras; **to tell sb a few ~ truths** decir a uno cuatro verdades; **~ video** vídeo *m* doméstico; **~ visit** visita *f* a domicilio.

(**b**) (*Sport*) **to play at one's ~ ground** jugar en casa; **~ match** partido *m* de (*or* en) casa; **~ run** (*Baseball*) carrera *f* completa, home run *m*, jonrón *m* (*LAm*); **the ~ side** el equipo de casa, el equipo local; **~ victory** victoria *f* local.

(**c**) (*Racing*) **~ straight**, (*US*) **~ stretch** recta *f* final, recta *f* de llegada; **we're on the ~ stretch** (*fig*) ésta es la última etapa.

(**d**) (*native*) natal; **~ area** región *f* natal; **~ port** puerto *m* de origen; **~ town** ciudad *f* natal.

(**e**) *defence, industry, product, flight* nacional; *population* metropolitano; *news* del país, nacional, doméstico; *policy* doméstico; *trade* interior; **H~ Counties** *los condados alrededor de Londres*; **~ country** patria *f*, país *m* de origen; **on the ~ front** (*Mil, Pol etc*) en el país; (*hum**: *at home*) en casa; **H~ Guard** (*Brit*) cuerpo *m* de voluntarios para la defensa nacional (*1940-45*); **~ market** mercado *m* nacional, mercado *m* interior; **~ news** (*gen*) noticias *fpl* de casa; (*Pol*) información *f* nacional; **H~ Office** (*Brit*) Ministerio *m* del Interior; **~ rule** autonomía *f*, autogobierno *m*; **~ sales** ventas *fpl* nacionales; **H~ Secretary** (*Brit*) Ministro *m*, -a *f* del Interior; **~ waters** aguas *fpl* territoriales.

3 *adv* (**a**) **to be ~** estar en casa; (*return*) estar de vuelta; **to be ~ and dry** lograr ponerse a salvo, llegar a buen puerto; **to come ~** volver a casa, (*from abroad*) volver a la patria; **to get ~** llegar a casa; **to go ~, to return ~** ir a casa, (*from abroad*) volver a la patria; **to see sb ~** acompañar a uno a su casa; **to send sb ~** enviar a uno a su casa; **to stay ~** quedarse en casa; **to write ~** escribir a la familia; **it's nothing to write ~ about*** no tiene nada de particular; **as we say back ~** como dicen en mi tierra; **the first ~ gets the cup** el primero que llegue se lleva la copa; **it's a long journey ~** hay mucho camino para llegar a casa.

(**b**) (*right in etc*) **to bring sth ~ to sb** hacer que uno se dé cuenta cabal de algo; **it came ~ to me that ...** me di cuenta cabal de que ...; **to drive a nail ~** hacer que un clavo entre a fondo; **to press an advantage ~** aprovecharse todo lo posible de una ventaja; **to drive a point ~** subrayar un punto; **to strike ~** (*shell etc*) hacer blanco, (*argument etc*) herir en lo vivo.

4 *vi* volver a casa; (*animal*) buscar la querencia.

◆**home in on** *vt*: **to ~ in on the target** buscar el blanco; **they ~d in on the pub** fueron derechito a la taberna.

home-baked [ˈhəʊmˈbeɪkt] *adj bread etc* casero.

homebody [ˈhəʊmbɒdɪ] *n* (*US*) persona *f* hogareña.

homebound [ˈhəʊmbaʊnd] *adj*: **the ~ traveller** el viajero que vuelve a (*or* se dirige a) casa.

home-brewed [ˈhəʊmˈbruːd] *adj* hecho en casa.

home buying [ˈhəʊmˌbaɪɪŋ] *n* compra *f* de vivienda.

homecoming [ˈhəʊmkʌmɪŋ] *n* regreso *m* (al hogar).

home-grown [ˈhəʊmˈgrəʊn] *adj* de cosecha propia (*also fig*).

homeland [ˈhəʊmlænd] *n* (**a**) tierra *f* natal, patria *f*. (**b**) (*S. Africa*) bantustán *m*, territorio *m* nativo.

homeless [ˈhəʊmlɪs] **1** *adj* sin hogar, sin techo; **the storm left a hundred ~** la tormenta dejó sin hogar a cien personas. **2** *npl*: **the ~** los sin hogar.

homelessness [ˈhəʊmlɪsnɪs] *n* el estar sin hogar; **the increase in ~** el aumento de la cifra de los que no tienen hogar.

homeliness [ˈhəʊmlɪnɪs] *n* llaneza *f*, sencillez *f*.

home loan [ˈhəʊmˈləʊn] *n* hipoteca *f*.

home-lover [ˈhəʊmˌlʌvəʳ] *n* persona *f* hogareña.

home-loving [ˈhəʊmˌlʌvɪŋ] *adj* hogareño, casero, apegado al hogar.

homely [ˈhəʊmlɪ] *adj* (**a**) casero, doméstico, familiar; (*unpretentious*) llano, sencillo; *atmosphere* acogedor; **it's very ~ here** aquí se está como en casa. (**b**) (*US*) feo, poco atractivo.

home-made [ˈhəʊmˈmeɪd] *adj* casero, de fabricación casera.

home-maker [ˈhəʊmˌmeɪkəʳ] *n* (*US*) ama *f* de casa.

homeopath [ˈhəʊmɪəʊpæθ] *etc* (*US*) = **homoeopath** *etc*.

Homer [ˈhəʊməʳ] *nm* Homero.

homer* [ˈhəʊməʳ] *n* (*Brit*) trabajo *m* fuera de hora, chollo‡ *m*.

Homeric [həʊˈmerɪk] *adj* homérico.

homesick [ˈhəʊmsɪk] *adj* nostálgico; **to be ~** sentir nostalgia, tener morriña.

homesickness [ˈhəʊmsɪknɪs] *n* nostalgia *f*, morriña *f*.

homespun [ˈhəʊmspʌn] *adj* tejido en casa, hecho en casa; (*fig*) llano, llanote.

homestead [ˈhəʊmsted] *n* (*US*) casa *f*, caserío *m*; (*farm*) granja *f*.

homeward [ˈhəʊmwəd] *adj*: **~ journey** viaje *m* hacia casa, viaje *m* de regreso.

homeward(s) [ˈhəʊmwəd(z)] *adv* hacia casa; (*from abroad*) hacia la patria; **~ bound** (*Naut*) con rumbo al puerto de origen.

homework [ˈhəʊmwɜːk] *n* deberes *mpl*, tarea(s) *f(pl)*; **to do one's ~** (*fig*) documentarse, prepararse, hacer el trabajo preparatorio; **~ exercise** deberes *mpl*.

homeworker [ˈhəʊmwɜːkəʳ] *n* asalariado *m*, -a *f* que trabaja

desde casa.
homeworking ['həʊmwɜːkɪŋ] *n* trabajo *m* desde casa.
homey* ['həʊmɪ] *adj* (*US*) íntimo, cómodo.
homicidal [ˌhɒmɪ'saɪdl] *adj* homicida; **to feel ~** (*fig*) sentirse capaz de matar, tener ganas de matar.
homicide ['hɒmɪsaɪd] *n* (*act*) homicidio *m*; (*person*) homicida *mf*.
homily ['hɒmɪlɪ] *n* homilía *f*; (*fig*) sermón *m*.
homing ['həʊmɪŋ] *adj*: **~ device** dispositivo *m* buscador de blancos; **~ instinct** instinto *m* de buscar la querencia; **~ pigeon** paloma *f* mensajera, paloma *f* buscadora de blancos.
hominid ['hɒmɪnɪd] *n* homínido *m*.
hominy ['hɒmɪnɪ] *n* (*US*) maíz *m* molido.
homo‡ ['həʊməʊ] *n* (*pej*) *abbr of* **homosexual** marica‡ *m*.
homoeopath, (*US*) **homeopath** ['həʊmɪəʊpæθ] *n* homeópata *mf*.
homoeopathic, (*US*) **homeopathic** [ˌhəʊmɪəʊ'pæθɪk] *adj* homeopático.
homoeopathy, (*US*) **homeopathy** ['həʊmɪ'ɒpəθɪ] *n* homeopatía *f*.
homogeneity ['hɒməʊdʒə'niːɪtɪ] *n* homogeneidad *f*.
homogeneous [ˌhɒmə'dʒiːnɪəs] *adj* homogéneo.
homogenize [hə'mɒdʒənaɪz] *vt* homogenizar.
homograph ['hɒməʊgrɑːf] *n* homógrafo *m*.
homonym ['hɒmənɪm] *n* homónimo *m*.
homophobia ['hɒməʊ'fəʊbɪə] *n* homofobia *f*.
homophobic ['hɒməʊ'fəʊbɪk] *adj* homofóbico.
homophone ['hɒməfəʊn] *n* homófono *m*.
homosexual ['hɒməʊ'seksjʊəl] **1** *adj* homosexual. **2** *n* homosexual *mf*.
homosexuality ['hɒməʊseksjʊ'ælɪtɪ] *n* homosexualidad *f*.
Hon. *abbr of* **Honorary** *or* **Honourable** (*in titles*).
Honduran [hɒn'djʊərən] **1** *adj* hondureño. **2** *n* hondureño *m*, -a *f*.
Honduras [hɒn'djʊərəs] *n* Honduras *f*.
hone [həʊn] **1** *n* piedra *f* de afilar. **2** *vt* afilar.
honest ['ɒnɪst] *adj* (*upright*) honrado, recto; (*speaking openly*) franco, sincero; **by ~ means** por medios legales; **the ~ truth is** la pura verdad es; **what is your ~ opinion?** ¿qué piensas francamente de esto?; **be ~!** ¡di la verdad!; **to be perfectly ~ with you, ...** para decirlo con toda franqueza ...; **you were not entirely ~ with me** no fuiste completamente franco conmigo.
honestly ['ɒnɪstlɪ] *adv* honradamente; francamente; **I don't ~ know, ~ I don't know** francamente no lo sé; **~?** ¿de veras?
honest-to-God ['ɒnɪstə'gɒd] *adj*, **honest-to-goodness** ['ɒnɪstə'gʊdnɪs] *adj* cien por cien.
honesty ['ɒnɪstɪ] *n* honradez *f*, rectitud *f*; franqueza *f*; **in all ~** con toda franqueza; **~ is the best policy** la honradez es el mejor capital.
honey ['hʌnɪ] *n* (**a**) miel *f*. (**b**) (*) **yes, ~** sí, querida; **hullo ~!** ¡oye, guapa!; **she's a ~** es un encanto, ¡qué guapa!, ¡qué linda! (*LAm*).
honeybee ['hʌnɪbiː] *n* abeja *f* (obrera).
honey blonde [ˌhʌnɪ'blɒnd] **1** *adj* rubio miel. **2** *n* rubia *f* miel.
honeycomb ['hʌnɪkəʊm] **1** *n* panal *m*. **2** *vt*: **the building is ~ed with passages** hay un sinfín de pasillos en el edificio; **the hill is ~ed with galleries** una multitud de galerías penetran por la colina.
honeydew melon ['hʌnɪdjuː'melən] *n* melón *m* dulce.
honeyed ['hʌnɪd] *adj* meloso, melifluo.
honeyfuggle* ['hʌnɪˌfʌgəl] *vt* (*US*) obtener mediante un truco.
honeymoon ['hʌnɪmuːn] **1** *n* luna *f* de miel, viaje *f* de novios. **2** *attr*: **the ~ couple** la pareja de recién casados; **~ period** (*Pol etc*) período *m* de gracia, cien días *mpl*. **3** *vi* pasar la luna de miel.
honeypot ['hʌnɪpɒt] *n* mielera *f*.
honeysuckle ['hʌnɪˌsʌkl] *n* madreselva *f*.
Hong Kong [ˌhɒŋ'kɒŋ] *n* Hong Kong *m*.
honk [hɒŋk] **1** *n* (*Orn*) graznido *m*; (*Aut*) bocinazo *m*.
2 *vi* graznar; tocar la bocina, bocinar.
honky‡ ['hɒŋkɪ] *n* (*US pej*) blanco *m*, blancucho* *m*.
honky-tonk* ['hɒŋkɪˌtɒŋk] *n* (**a**) (*US: club*) garito *m*. (**b**) (*Mus*) honky-tonk* *m*.
Honolulu [ˌhɒnə'luːluː] *n* Honolulú *m*.
honor ['ɒnəʳ] (*US*) = **honour**.
honorable ['ɒnərəbl] (*US*) = **honourable**.
honorably ['ɒnərəblɪ] (*US*) = **honourably**.
honorarium [ˌɒnə'rɛərɪəm] *n* honorarios *mpl*.
honorary ['ɒnərərɪ] *adj* honorario; *president, member* de honor; (*unpaid*) no remunerado; **~ degree** doctorado *m* honoris causa; **~ secretary** secretario *m* honorario, secretaria *f* honoraria.
honour, (*US*) **honor** ['ɒnəʳ] **1** *n* (**a**) honor *m*; (*good name*) honra *f*; (*uprightness*) honradez *f*; **in ~ of** en honor de; **on my ~!** ¡palabra de honor!; **it's a great ~ for him** es un gran honor para él; **to be on one's ~ to** + *infin*, **to be** (**in**) **~ bound to** + *infin* estar moralmente obligado a + *infin*; **I consider it an ~ to** + *infin* tengo a mucha honra + *infin*; **I had the ~ to** + *infin* (*or* **of** + *ger*) tuve el honor de + *infin*; **to hold sb in high ~** tener un altísimo concepto de uno.
(**b**) **Your H~** (*title*) Señor Juez.
(**c**) (*Brit: medal etc*) condecoración *f*.
(**d**) **~s** honores *mpl*; **last ~s** honras *fpl* fúnebres; **the ~s are even** se ha logrado un empate; **to bury sb with full military ~s** sepultar a uno con todos los honores militares; **to do the ~s of the house** hacer los honores de la casa.
(**e**) **to take ~s in chemistry** (*Brit Univ*) graduarse en química con honores.
(**f**) (*Bridge*) **~s** honores *mpl*; **3 ~s tricks** 3 bazas *fpl* de honores.
2 *attr*: **~s course** (*Brit Univ*) licenciatura *f*; **~s degree** (*Brit Univ*) título *m* con honores; **H~s List** (*Brit*) lista *f* de condecoraciones.
3 *vt* honrar; *pledge, signature* hacer honor a; *cheque* aceptar, pagar; (*respect*) respetar, reverenciar; **I ~ you for it** te respeto más por esto; **to ~ sb with one's confidence** honrar a uno con su confianza; **I am deeply ~ed** lo tengo a mucha honra; **I should be ~ed if ...** estimaría que + *subj*.
honourable, (*US*) **honorable** ['ɒnərəbl] *adj* (*worthy*) honorable; (*upright*) honrado; *title, deed etc* honroso; *mention* honorífico; **the ~ member for Woodford** el señor diputado de Woodford.
honourably, (*US*) **honorably** ['ɒnərəblɪ] *adv* honradamente.
Hons. (*Univ*) *abbr of* **Honours**.
Hon. Sec. *abbr of* **Honorary Secretary**.
hooch* [huːtʃ] *n* (*US*) licor *m* (*esp* ilícito).
hood¹ [hʊd] *n* (*of cloak, raincoat, Eccl*) capucha *f*; (*Univ*) muceta *f* (con capucha); (*of penitent, hawk*) capirote *m*; (*Brit Aut*) capota *f*, toldo *m* (*Mex*); (*US Aut*) capó *m*.
hood²‡ [hʊd] (*US*) *n* = **hoodlum**.
hooded ['hʊdɪd] *adj* encapuchado; encapirotado.
hoodlum* ['huːdləm] *n* (*US*) gorila* *m*, matón *m*.
hoodoo ['huːduː] *n* vudú *m*; gafe *m*, gafancia *f*, mala suerte *f*; **there's a ~ on it** tiene gafe.
hoodwink ['hʊdwɪŋk] *vt* burlar, engañar.
hooey* ['huːɪ] *n* música *f* celestial*; **~!** ¡tonterías!
hoof [huːf] **1** *n, pl* **hoofs** *or* **hooves** [huːvz] casco *m*, pezuña *f*; (*foot*) pata *f*; **cattle on the ~** ganado *m* en pie; **~ and mouth disease** (*US*) fiebre *f* aftosa, glosopeda *f*. **2** *vt* (*): **to ~ it** (*walk*) ir a pie, (*depart*) liar el petate.
hoofed [huːft] *adj* ungulado.
hoo-ha* ['huːˌhɑː] *n* (*fuss*) lío* *m*, follón* *m*; (*noise*) estrépito *m*; (*of publicity etc*) bombo* *m*; **there was a great ~ about it** se armó un tremendo follón*.
hook [hʊk] **1** *n* (**a**) gancho *m*; garfio *m*; (*Fishing*) anzuelo *m*; (*hanger*) colgadero *m*; **~s and eyes** corchetes *mpl*; **to swallow sth ~, line and sinker** tragar algo completamente; **by ~ or by crook** como sea, por las buenas o por las malas; **to get sb off the ~** sacar a uno del atolladero; **to let sb off the ~** dejar escapar a uno, permitir que uno se salve; **to sling one's ~‡** (*depart*) largarse*; (*stop work*) suspender el trabajo; **to take the phone off the ~** descolgar el teléfono.
(**b**) (*Boxing*) gancho *m*, crochet *m*.
(**c**) (*Golf*) golpe *m* con efecto a la izquierda.
(**d**) **~s‡** manos *fpl*.
2 *vt* (**a**) (*attach*) enganchar; (*Fishing*) pescar, coger, enganchar; **to ~ sth to a rope** enganchar algo a una cuerda; **to ~ a rope round a nail** atar una cuerda a un clavo; **she finally ~ed him*** ella por fin le pescó; **to ~ it*** largarse*.
(**b**) (*curve*) encorvar.
(**c**) (*) **to be ~ed on** estar adicto a, entregarse a; (*pej*) enviciarse con; **to be ~ed on drugs** quedar enganchado a la droga*, quedar colgado*.
3 *vi* (**a**) engancharse (*on to* a).
(**b**) encorvarse.
(**c**) (*US**) trabajar como prostituta.
◆**hook up** *vt* enganchar, *dress* abrochar.
hookah ['hʊkɑː] *n* narguile *m*.
hooked [hʊkt] *adj* ganchudo.
hooker ['hʊkəʳ] *n* (**a**) (*Sport*) talonador *m*. (**b**) (*US‡*) puta *f*.

hook(e)y ['hʊkɪ] *n*: **to play ~** (*esp US*) hacer novillos.
hook-nosed [,hʊk'nəʊzd] *adj* de nariz ganchuda.
hookup ['hʊkʌp] *n* (*Elec*) acoplamiento *m*; (*Rad*) transmisión *f* en circuito; **a ~ with Eurovision** una emisión conjunta con Eurovisión.
hookworm ['hʊkwɜːm] *n* anquilostoma *m*.
hooligan ['huːlɪgən] *n* gamberro *m*.
hooliganism ['huːlɪgənɪzəm] *n* gamberrismo *m*.
hoop [huːp] *n* aro *m*; (*in croquet*) arco *m*, aro *m*.
hoopoe ['huːpuː] *n* abubilla *f*.
hooray [hʊ'reɪ] = **hurrah**.
Hooray Henry [,huːreɪ'henrɪ] *n* (*Brit pej*) señorito *m*.
hoot [huːt] **1** *n* (**a**) (*of owl*) grito *m*, ululato *m*; (*of horn*) bocinazo *m*; (*of ship, factory*) toque *m* de sirena.
(**b**) (*laugh*) risotada *f*; **it was a ~!*** (*Brit*) ¡era para morirse de risa!
2 *vt* (*also* **to ~ off**) silbar, abuchear; **to ~ sb off the stage** abuchear a uno hasta que abandone la escena.
3 *vi* (*owl*) ulular, gritar; (*person*) silbar; (*Aut: person*) tocar la bocina, (*car*) dar un bocinazo; (*ship*) dar un toque de sirena; **to ~ with laughter** morirse de risa.
hooter ['huːtəʳ] *n* (**a**) (*of ship, factory*) sirena *f*; (*Brit Aut*) bocina *f*, claxon *m*. (**b**) (*Brit*‡) nariz *f*, napias‡ *fpl*.
Hoover ['huːvəʳ] ® **1** *n* aspirador *m*. **2** *vti* limpiar con aspirador, pasar la aspiradora por.
hooves [huːvz] *npl of* **hoof**.
hop¹ [hɒp] *n* (*Bot: also* **~s**) lúpulo *m*.
hop² [hɒp] **1** *n* (**a**) salto *m*, saltito *m*, brinco *m*; (*Aer*) salto *m*, etapa *f* de un vuelo; **~, skip and jump** triple salto *m*; **in one ~** de un salto, (*Aer*) sin hacer escala; **to catch sb on the ~** coger a uno desprevenido; **the uncertainty should keep them on the ~** la incertidumbre deberá mantenerles en estado de alerta.
(**b**) (*: *dance*) baile *m*.
2 *vt* cruzar de un salto; **to ~ it*** escabullirse, largarse*; **~ it!** ¡lárgate!*
3 *vi* saltar, brincar; saltar con un pie; saltar a la pata coja; (*limp*) cojear; **to be ~ping mad*** echar chispas*.
◆**hop along** *vi* avanzar a saltos.
◆**hop off** **1** *vt* bajar de. **2** *vi* (**a**) bajar.
(**b**) (*) largarse; **~ off!** ¡lárgate!
◆**hop on** **1** *vt* subir a. **2** *vi* subir; **~ on!** ¡sube!
◆**hop out** *vi* salir de un salto; **to ~ out of bed** saltar de la cama.
hope [həʊp] **1** *n* esperanza *f*; (*trust*) confianza *f*; (*hopefulness*) ilusión *f*; (*chance*) posibilidad *f*; **some ~s!, not a ~!** ¡ni esperanza!, ¡ni peligro!, ¡de eso ni hablar!; **my ~ is that ...** yo espero que ...; **there is no ~ of that** no hay posibilidad alguna de eso; **you are my last ~** tú eres mi única salvación; **he's the bright ~ of the team** es la esperanza dorada del equipo; **to be full of ~** estar lleno de ilusión, estar muy ilusionado; **to build up ~s** hacerse ilusiones; **to conceive the ~ that ...** hacerse la ilusión de + *infin*; **you haven't got a ~ in hell of that** no tienes la más remota posibilidad de lograrlo; **he held out the ~ that ...** ofreció la esperanza de que ...; **to live in ~ of sth** vivir con (*or* en) la esperanza de algo; **to lose ~** perder la esperanza, desesperarse; **to place ~ in sth** poner esperanzas en algo; **to raise sb's ~s** hacer que uno conciba esperanzas.
2 *attr*: **~ chest** (*US*) ajuar *m* (de novia).
3 *vt*: **to ~ that ...** esperar que + *subj*; **I ~ he comes soon** ojalá venga pronto; **I ~ you don't think I'm going to do it!** ¡no pensarás que lo haga yo!; **I should ~ so!** ¡ya era hora!; **to ~ to** + *infin* esperar + *infin*; **hoping to hear from you** en espera de tus gratas noticias; **what do you ~ to gain from that?** ¿qué pretendes ganar con eso?
4 *vi* esperar; **to ~ for sth** esperar algo; **we'll just have to ~ for the best** tendremos que mantener el optimismo a pesar de todo; **to ~ against ~** esperar desesperando; **to ~ in** confiar en.
hopeful ['həʊpfʊl] **1** *adj person* lleno de esperanzas, optimista, (*falsely*) ilusionado; *prospect etc* esperanzador, prometedor; **he wasn't very ~** no se mostró muy optimista; **I'm not very ~ that ...** no me hago muchas ilusiones de que + *subj*; **it looks ~** promete mucho. **2** *n* aspirante *mf*; candidato *m*, -a *f*; **young ~** joven *m* ilusionado, joven *f* ilusionada.
hopefully ['həʊpfəlɪ] *adv* (**a**) con optimismo; con ilusión. (**b**) (*one hopes*) **~!** ¡ojalá!; **~ I shan't need it** en el mejor de los casos no lo voy a necesitar; **~ they won't come** es de esperar que no vengan.
hopeless ['həʊplɪs] *adj* (**a**) *person* (*without hope*) desesperado, sin esperanza.
(**b**) (*impossible, useless*) *situation* desesperado, irremediable; *task* imposible; (*Med*) *case* desahuciado; *drunkard etc* incurable; **to give sth up as ~** renunciar a algo por imposible; **the boss is ~** el jefe es un caso perdido; **I'm ~ at it** yo soy inútil para eso; **it's ~** todo es inútil, no tiene remedio; **it's ~ trying to** + *infin* es inútil tratar de + *infin*.
hopelessly ['həʊplɪslɪ] *adv live etc* sin esperanza; **she looked at me ~** me miró desesperada; **I'm ~ confused** estoy totalmente despistado; **it's ~ dear for us** es excesivamente caro para nosotros.
hopelessness ['həʊplɪsnɪs] *n* desesperación *f*; lo irremediable; imposibilidad *f*.
hop field ['hɒpfiːld] *n* campo *m* de lúpulo.
hopper ['hɒpəʳ] *n* (*Agr etc*) tolva *f*; (*Rail*) vagón *m* tolva.
hop-picking ['hɒp,pɪkɪŋ] *n* recolección *f* del lúpulo.
hopscotch ['hɒpskɒtʃ] *n*: **to play ~** jugar a la pata coja, jugar a la reina mora.
Horace ['hɒrɪs] *nm* Horacio.
Horatian [hɒ'reɪʃən] *adj* horaciano.
horde [hɔːd] *n* horda *f*; (*fig*) multitud *f*, muchedumbre *f*.
horizon [hə'raɪzn] *n* horizonte *m*; **there are new schemes on the ~** hay nuevos planes en perspectiva; **that's over the ~ now** eso queda ya a la espalda.
horizontal [,hɒrɪ'zɒntl] *adj* horizontal; **~ integration** integración *f* horizontal.
horizontally [,hɒrɪ'zɒntəlɪ] *adv* horizontalmente.
hormonal [hɔː'məʊnəl] *adj* hormonal.
hormone ['hɔːməʊn] **1** *n* hormona *f*. **2** *attr*: **~ treatment** tratamiento *m* de hormonas.
horn [hɔːn] *n* (**a**) (*of bull etc*) cuerno *m*; (*of deer*) asta *f*; (*of insect*) antena *f*; (*of snail*) tentáculo *m*; (*material*) cuerno *m*; **H~ of Africa** Cuerno *m* de Africa; **~ of plenty** cuerno *m* de la abundancia, cornucopia *f*; **to be on the ~s of a dilemma** estar entre la espada y la pared; **to draw in one's ~s** recoger velas, (*with money*) hacer economías.
(**b**) (*Mus*) cuerno *m*, trompa *f*; (*Aut*) bocina *f*, claxon *m*; **to blow** (*or* **sound**) **one's ~** tocar la bocina, tocar el claxon.
(**c**) (*US*‡) teléfono *m*; **to get on the ~ to sb** telefonear a uno.
◆**horn in*** *vi* (*esp US*) entrometerse (*on* en).
hornbeam ['hɔːnbiːm] *n* carpe *m*.
hornbill ['hɔːnbɪl] *n* búcero *m*.
horned [hɔːnd] *adj* con cuernos, enastado; (*in compounds*) de cuernos ...
hornet ['hɔːnɪt] *n* avispón *m*; **~'s nest** (*fig*) avispero *m*.
hornless ['hɔːnlɪs] *adj* sin cuernos, mocho.
hornpipe ['hɔːnpaɪp] *n* (**a**) (*Mus*) chirimía *f*. (**b**) (*Naut*) *cierto baile de marineros*.
horn-rimmed ['hɔːnrɪmd] *adj spectacles* de concha, de carey (*LAm*).
horny ['hɔːnɪ] *adj* (**a**) *material* córneo; *hand* calloso. (**b**) (*esp US*‡) cachondo, caliente.
horoscope ['hɒrəskəʊp] *n* horóscopo *m*; **to cast a ~** sacar un horóscopo.
horrendous [hɒ'rendəs] *adj* horrendo; (*hum*) horroroso.
horrible ['hɒrɪbl] *adj* horrible.
horribly ['hɒrɪblɪ] *adv* horriblemente; **it's ~ difficult** es terriblemente difícil; **he swore most ~** soltó unos tacos espantosos.
horrid ['hɒrɪd] *adj* horrible, horroroso; (*) horrible; *person etc* de lo más antipático, inaguantable; **you ~ thing!** ¡qué ofensivo!, ¡qué antipático!; **to be ~ to sb** tratar a uno muy mal, portarse muy mal con uno; **don't be ~!** ¡no fastidies!
horrific [hɒ'rɪfɪk] *adj* horrendo.
horrifically [hɒ'rɪfɪklɪ] *adv* espantosamente, terriblemente; **~ injured** con heridas espantosas.
horrify ['hɒrɪfaɪ] *vt* horrorizar; (*shock*) escandalizar, pasmar; **they were all horrified** se escandalizaron todos; **I was horrified to discover that ...** me horrorizó descubrir que ...
horrifying ['hɒrɪfaɪɪŋ] *adj* horroroso, horripilante.
horrifyingly ['hɒrɪ,faɪɪŋlɪ] *adv* horrorosamente, de manera horripilante.
horror ['hɒrəʳ] **1** *n* horror *m*; **to have a ~ of** tener horror a; **I found to my ~ that ...** me horroricé al descubrir que ...; **then to my ~ it moved** luego — ¡qué susto! — se movió; **it gives me the ~s** me da horror; **~s!** ¡qué horror!; **you ~!** ¡bestia! **2** *attr*: **~ film** película *f* de miedo.
horror-stricken ['hɒrə,strɪkən] *adj*, **horror-struck** ['hɒrə,strʌk] *adj* horrorizado.
hors d'oeuvres [ɔː'dɜːvr] *npl* entremeses *mpl*.
horse [hɔːs] **1** *n* (**a**) (*Zool*) caballo *m*; (*in gymnastics*) potro

m; (*Tech*) caballete *m*; (*cavalry*) caballería *f*; **that's a ~ of a different colour** eso es harina de otro costal; **it's straight from the ~'s mouth** lo sé de buena tinta, me lo dijo el mismo interesado; **to change ~s in midstream** cambiar de política (*or* personal *etc*) a mitad de camino; **to eat like a ~** comer como una vaca; **to get on one's high ~** darse ínfulas, adoptar una actitud altanera; **hold your ~s!** ¡para el carro!, ¡despacito!

(**b**) (‡) caballo‡ *m*, heroína *f*.

2 *attr*: **H~ Guards** (*Brit*) Guardia *f* Montada.

◆**horse about***, **horse around*** *vi* hacer el borde*, hacer el animal*, tontear.

horse-artillery [ˈhɔːsɑːˈtɪlərɪ] *n* artillería *f* montada.

horseback [ˈhɔːsbæk] **1** *n*: **on ~** a caballo. **2** *attr*: **~ riding** (*US*) equitación *f*.

horse-box [ˈhɔːsbɒks] *n* remolque *m* para caballerías, (*Rail*) vagón *m* para caballerías.

horse brass [ˈhɔːsbrɑːs] *n* jaez *m*.

horse-breaker [ˈhɔːsˌbreɪkəʳ] *n* domador *m*, -ora *f* de caballos.

horse-breeder [ˈhɔːsˌbriːdəʳ] *n* criador *m*, -ora *f* de caballos.

horse chestnut [ˈhɔːsˈtʃesnʌt] *n* (*fruit*) castaña *f* de Indias; (*tree*) castaño *m* de Indias.

horse-collar [ˈhɔːsˌkɒləʳ] *n* collera *f*.

horse-dealer [ˈhɔːsˌdiːləʳ] *n* chalán *m*.

horse-doctor [ˈhɔːsˌdɒktəʳ] *n* veterinario *m*, -a *f*.

horse-drawn [ˈhɔːsdrɔːn] *adj* de tracción de sangre, de tracción animal, traído por caballo(s).

horseflesh [ˈhɔːsfleʃ] *n* (**a**) (*meat*) carne *f* de caballo. (**b**) (*horses*) caballos *mpl*.

horsefly [ˈhɔːsflaɪ] *n* tábano *m*.

horsehair [ˈhɔːshɛəʳ] *n* crin *m*.

horsehide [ˈhɔːshaɪd] *n* cuero *m* de caballo.

horse-laugh [ˈhɔːslɑːf] *n* risotada *f*, carcajada *f*.

horse mackerel [ˈhɔːsˈmækrəl] *n* jurel *m*.

horseman [ˈhɔːsmən] *n*, *pl* **horsemen** [ˈhɔːsmən] (*rider*) jinete *m*, charro *m* (*Mex*); (*expert*) caballista *m*.

horsemanship [ˈhɔːsmənʃɪp] *n* equitación *f*, manejo *m* (del caballo).

horse-manure [ˈhɔːsməˌnjʊəʳ] *n* abono *m* de caballo.

horsemeat [ˈhɔːsmiːt] *n* (*Culin*) carne *f* de caballo.

horse opera [ˈhɔːsˌɒpərə] *n* (*US*) película *f* del Oeste.

horseplay [ˈhɔːspleɪ] *n* payasadas *fpl*, pelea *f* amistosa.

horsepower [ˈhɔːsˌpaʊəʳ] **1** *n* caballo *m* (de fuerza), caballaje *m*; potencia *f* en caballos; **what is the ~ of this car?** ¿qué potencia tiene este coche?

2 *attr*: **a 20 ~ engine** un motor de 20 caballos.

horse-race [ˈhɔːsreɪs] *n* carrera *f* de caballos.

horse-racing [ˈhɔːsˌreɪsɪŋ] *n* carreras *fpl* de caballos, hipismo *m*.

horseradish [ˈhɔːsˌrædɪʃ] *n* rábano *m* picante.

horse-riding [ˈhɔːsˌraɪdɪŋ] *n* (*Brit*) equitación *f*.

horse-sense [ˈhɔːssens] *n* sentido *m* común.

horseshit** [ˈhɔːsʃɪt] *n* (*lit*) caca** *f* de caballo; (*fig*) gilipollada‡ *f*.

horseshoe [ˈhɔːsʃuː] **1** *n* herradura *f*. **2** *attr*: **~ arch** arco *m* de herradura.

horse show [ˈhɔːsʃəʊ] *n* concurso *m* hípico.

horse-trading [ˈhɔːsˌtreɪdɪŋ] *n* (*Pol etc*) toma y daca *m*, intercambio *m* de favores, chalaneo *m*.

horse trailer [ˈhɔːsˌtreɪləʳ] *n* (*US*) remolque *m* para caballerías.

horse trials [ˈhɔːstraɪəlz] *npl* concurso *m* hípico.

horsewhip [ˈhɔːswɪp] **1** *n* látigo *m*. **2** *vt* zurriagar.

horsewoman [ˈhɔːsˌwʊmən] *n*, *pl* **horsewomen** [ˈhɔːswɪmɪn] amazona *f*, caballista *f*, charra *f* (*Mex*).

hors(e)y [ˈhɔːsɪ] *adj* (*fond of horses*) aficionado a los caballos; (*fond of racing*) aficionado a las carreras de caballos, carrerista; *appearance* caballuno.

horticultural [ˌhɔːtɪˈkʌltʃərəl] *adj* hortícola; **~ show** exposición *f* de horticultura.

horticulture [ˈhɔːtɪkʌltʃəʳ] *n* horticultura *f*.

horticulturist [ˌhɔːtɪˈkʌltʃərɪst] *n* horticultor *m*, -ora *f*.

hose [həʊz] **1** *n* (**a**) (*stockings*) medias *fpl*; (*socks*) calcetines *mpl*; (††) calzas *fpl*.

(**b**) (*Brit*: *hosepipe*) manga *f*, manguera *f*.

2 *vt* (*also* **to ~ down**) regar (*or* limpiar *etc*) con manga.

◆**hose out** *vt* regar con manguera.

hosepipe [ˈhəʊzpaɪp] *n* manga *f*, manguera *f*.

hosier [ˈhəʊʒɪəʳ] *n* calcetero *m*, -a *f*.

hosiery [ˈhəʊʒɪərɪ] *n* calcetería *f*.

hospice [ˈhɒspɪs] *n* hospicio *m*.

hospitable [hɒsˈpɪtəbl] *adj* hospitalario; *atmosphere etc* acogedor.

hospitably [hɒsˈpɪtəblɪ] *adv* de modo hospitalario.

hospital [ˈhɒspɪtl] **1** *n* hospital *m*. **2** *attr*: **~ administration** administración *f* de hospital; **~ administrator** (*Brit*) administrador *m*, -ora *f* de hospital; (*US*) director *m*, -ora *f* de hospital; **~ doctor** interno *m*, -a *f*; **~ facilities** instalaciones *fpl* hospitalarias; **~ management** (*act*) gestión *f* hospitalaria, (*persons*) dirección *f* de hospital; **~ nurse** enfermera *f* de hospital; **~ ship** buque *m* hospital; **90% of ~ cases are released within 3 weeks** el 90% de los casos clínicos son dados de alta en tres semanas.

hospitality [ˌhɒspɪˈtælɪtɪ] *n* hospitalidad *f*.

hospitalization [ˌhɒspɪtəlaɪˈzeɪʃən] *n* hospitalización *f*.

hospitalize [ˈhɒspɪtəlaɪz] *vt* hospitalizar.

host¹ [həʊst] *n* (**a**) (*crowd*) multitud *f*; **I have a ~ of problems** tengo un montón de problemas; **for a whole ~ of reasons** por muchísimas razones; **they came in ~s** acudieron a millares.

(**b**) (††) hueste *f*, ejército *m*.

host² [həʊst] **1** *n* (*to guest*) huésped *m*, -eda *f*; (*Bio*) huésped *m*, hospedador *m*; (*at meal*) anfitrión *m*, -ona *f*; (*of inn*) patrón *m*, mesonero *m*; **I thanked my ~s** di las gracias a los que me habían invitado; **we were ~s for a week to a Spanish boy** recibimos en casa durante una semana a un joven español. **2** *attr*: **~ country** (*for conference, games etc*) país *m* anfitrión. **3** *vt congress* organizar; (*TV*) *show* presentar.

host³ [həʊst] *n* (*Eccl*) hostia *f*.

hostage [ˈhɒstɪdʒ] *n* rehén *m*; **to take sb ~** tomar a uno como rehén.

hostel [ˈhɒstəl] *n* parador *m*; (*youth ~*) albergue *m* para jóvenes; (*Univ*) residencia *f* (de estudiantes).

hosteller, (*US*) **hosteler** [ˈhɒstələʳ] *n* persona que va de albergues para jóvenes.

hostelling, (*US*) **hosteling** [ˈhɒstəlɪŋ] *n* vacaciones *fpl* a base de albergues; **~ is very popular among the young** ir de albergues es popular entre la gente joven.

hostelry [ˈhɒstəlrɪ] *n* mesón *m*.

hostess [ˈhəʊstes] *n* huéspeda *f*; anfitriona *f* (*V* **host²**); (*Aer*) azafata *f*; (*in night club*) cabaretera *f*.

hostile [ˈhɒstaɪl] *adj* (*enemy*) enemigo, hostil; *manner, voice etc* nada amistoso; *circumstances etc* adverso, desfavorable; **they were ~ to the plan** se opusieron al proyecto.

hostility [hɒsˈtɪlɪtɪ] *n* hostilidad *f* (*to, towards* hacia), enemistad *f*, antagonismo *m*; **hostilities** hostilidades *fpl*; **to start hostilities** romper las hostilidades; **to call for an end to hostilities** abogar por un cese de hostilidades.

hostler [ˈɒsləʳ] *n* (††) mozo *m* de cuadra.

hot [hɒt] **1** *adj* (**a**) caliente; *climate* cálido; *day, summer* caluroso, de calor; *sun* abrasador; *spring* termal; **with running ~ and cold (water)** con agua corriente caliente y fría; **to be ~** (*person*) tener calor, (*thing*) estar caliente, (*weather*) hacer calor; (*in children's games*) estar caliente; **to be very ~** (*person*) tener mucho calor, (*thing*) estar muy caliente, (*weather*) hacer mucho calor; **to get ~** (*thing*) calentarse, (*weather*) empezar a hacer calor; **it made me go ~ and cold** me dio escalofríos; **it was a very ~ day** fue un día de mucho calor; **it was a ~ and tiring walk** fue una caminata que nos hizo sudar y nos cansó mucho; **to get ~ and bothered** sofocarse.

(**b**) (*fig*) *taste* picante; *contest* muy reñido; *dispute* acalorado; *temper* vivo; *temperament* apasionado, ardiente, vehemente; *situation* caliente, muy difícil, apurado, *pursuit* enérgico; *supporter* acérrimo; (*: *sexually*) *animal* en celo; *person* cachondo; (*: *stolen*) robado; **~ air*** (*empty talk*) palabras *fpl* huecas; (*nonsense*) música *f* celestial*; **to blow ~ air*** fanfarronear; **~ flush** sofoco *m* de calor; **~ line** teléfono *m* rojo; teléfono *m* de emergencia; **~ money** dinero *m* caliente; **she's a ~ piece‡** está muy buena*; **~ potato** (*fig*) carbón *m* ardiente; **~ pursuit** persecución *f* en caliente, persecución *f* armada (a través de una frontera *etc*); **~ seat** (*US*: *electric chair*) silla *f* eléctrica; **to be in the ~ seat** (*fig*) ser quien sufre las consecuencias, estar en primera fila; **~ spot*** (*for amusement*) lugar *m* de diversión; (*night club*) sala *f* de fiestas; (*Brit*: *trouble area*) punto *m* (*or* lugar *m*) caliente; **~ war** guerra *f* a tiros; **that's ~** (*esp US**) qué bueno, qué estupendo; *V* **stuff 1** (**e**), **temper 1** (**a**).

(**c**) **news ~ from the press** una noticia que acaba de publicarse en la prensa; **to be ~ on sb's trail** seguir enérgicamente la pista de uno; **he's pretty ~ at maths** es un hacha para las matemáticas, es muy fuerte en matemáticas; **he's a pretty ~ player** es un jugador experto; **to make a place too ~ for sb** hacer que uno abandone un lugar; **to make things ~ for sb** amargar la vida a uno, hacer insoportable la vida a uno.

2 *adv*: **to blow ~ and cold** ser veleta, mudar a todos los vientos; **to give it to sb ~ and strong** no morderse la lengua con uno; **to go at it ~ and strong** pelearse (*etc*) violentamente.

3 *n*: **he's got the ~s for her‡** ella le pone cachondo.

◆**hot up*** **1** *vt food* (re)calentar; *engine* aumentar la potencia de; *pace* forzar, aumentar.

2 *vi* (*dispute*) acalorarse; (*tension*) intensificarse; (*party*) animarse.

hot-air [ˌhɒt'ɛəʳ] *attr*: ~ **balloon** globo *m* de aire caliente.

hotbed ['hɒtbed] *n* (*fig*) semillero *m*.

hot-blooded ['hɒt'blʌdɪd] *adj* apasionado, impetuoso.

hotchpotch ['hɒtʃpɒtʃ] *n* mezcolanza *f*, baturrillo *m*.

hot cross bun [ˌhɒtˌkrɒs'bʌn] *n bollo a base de especias y pasas marcado con una cruz y que se come en Viernes Santo.*

hot dog ['hɒtdɒg] *n* (*Culin*) perrito *m* caliente.

hotel [həʊ'tel] **1** *n* hotel *m*. **2** *attr*: ~ **industry** comercio *m* hotelero; ~ **manager** director *m*, -ora *f* de hotel; ~ **receptionist** recepcionista *mf* de hotel; ~ **room** habitación *f* de hotel; ~ **staff** plantilla *f* de hotel; ~ **work** trabajo *m* de hostelería; ~ **workers** trabajadores *mpl*, -oras *fpl* de hostelería.

hotelier [həʊ'telɪəʳ] *n*, **hotelkeeper** [həʊ'telˌkiːpəʳ] *n* hotelero *m*.

hotfoot ['hɒt'fʊt] **1** *adv* a toda prisa. **2** *vt*: **to ~ it*** ir volando.

hothead ['hɒthed] *n* exaltado *m*, -a *f*, fanático *m*, -a *f*, extremista *mf*.

hotheaded ['hɒt'hedɪd] *adj* (*extreme*) exaltado, fanático, extremista; (*rash*) impetuoso.

hothouse ['hɒthaʊs] *n*, *pl* **hothouses** ['hɒthaʊzɪz] invernáculo *m*.

hotly ['hɒtlɪ] *adv* con pasión, con vehemencia.

hotpants ['hɒtpænts] *npl* shorts *mpl*.

hotplate ['hɒtpleɪt] *n* calentador *m*, placa *f* calentadora *f*, calientaplatos *m*.

hotpot ['hɒtpɒt] *n* (*esp Brit*) estofado *m*.

hotrod‡ ['hɒtrɒd] *n* (*US Aut*) bólido *m*.

hotshot‡ ['hɒtʃɒt] (*US*) **1** *adj* de primera, de aúpa*. **2** *n* personaje *m*, pez *m* gordo*.

hot-tempered [ˌhɒt'tempəd] *adj* irascible.

Hottentot ['hɒtəntɒt] **1** *adj* hotentote. **2** *n* (**a**) hotentote *mf*. (**b**) (*Ling*) hotentote *m*.

hot tub ['hɒt'tʌb] *n* jacuzzi *m*.

hot-water bottle [hɒt'wɔːtəˌbɒtl] *n* bolsa *f* de agua caliente.

hound [haʊnd] **1** *n* (**a**) perro *m* (de caza), podenco *m*, sabueso *m*.

(**b**) (*fig*) canalla *m*

2 *vt* acosar, perseguir; **they ~ed him for the money** le persiguieron para que pagase el dinero; **I will not be ~ed into a decision** no tolero que me presionen para decidirme.

◆**hound down** *vt*: **to ~ sb down** perseguir a uno hasta encontrarle.

◆**hound on** *vt*: **to ~ sb on** incitar a uno (*to + infin* a + *infin*).

◆**hound out** *vt*: **to ~ sb out** hacer que uno abandone su puesto (*etc*) a fuerza de darle guerra.

hour [aʊəʳ] *n* hora *f*; **30 miles an ~** 30 millas por hora; **after ~s** (*Brit*) fuera de horas; **at all ~s of the day and night** a todas las horas del día y de la noche; **by the ~** por horas; **~ by ~** hora tras hora, cada hora; **on the ~** a la hora en punto; **out of ~s** fuera de horas; **she's out till all ~s** se queda fuera hasta muy tarde, vuelve a casa a las tantas; **to keep late ~s** trasnochar, acostarse a altas horas de la noche; **to strike the ~** dar la hora; **it takes ~s** es cosa de muchas horas; **we waited ~s** esperamos horas y horas; **to work long ~s** trabajar largas horas.

hourglass ['aʊəglɑːs] *n* reloj *m* de arena.

hourhand ['aʊəhænd] *n* horario *m*.

hourly ['aʊəlɪ] **1** *adj* de cada hora; **the ~ rate** el sueldo por hora; **~ wage** sueldo *m* por hora; **there's an ~ bus** hay un autobús cada hora.

2 *adv* cada hora; **we expected him ~** le esperábamos de un momento a otro.

hourly-paid [ˌaʊəlɪ'peɪd] *adj* pagado por hora.

house [haʊs] *n*, *pl* **houses** ['haʊzɪz] **1** *n* casa *f*; (*Comm*) casa *f*, firma *f*; (*Theat*: *auditorium*) sala *f*, (*audience*) público *m*, (*Parl*) cámara *f*; (*Brit Scol*) *subdivisión de un colegio de internado*; (*Univ*) colegio *m*, (*part of college or school*) pabellón *m*; (*lineage*) casa *f*, familia *f*; **'~ full'** 'no hay localidades'; **~ and home** hogar *m*; **~ of cards** castillo *m* de naipes; **H~ of Commons** Cámara *f* de los Comunes; **~ of God** templo *m*, iglesia *f*; **H~ of Lords** Cámara *f* de los Lores; **H~s of Parliament** Parlamento *m*, Cámara *f* de los Lores y la de los Comunes; **H~ of Representatives** (*US*) Cámara *f* de Representantes; **training in ~** formación *f* en la empresa; **it's on the ~** la casa invita, es cortesía de la casa, está pagado (por el dueño); **to bring the ~ down** (*Theat*) hacer venirse abajo el teatro, (*speech*) obtener un exitazo, ser muy aplaudido, (*joke*) hacer morir de risa a todos; **to get on like a ~ on fire** (*progress*) avanzar rapidísimamente, (*2 persons*) llevarse la mar de bien, avenirse maravillosamente; **to keep ~** llevar la casa (*for* a, para); **to keep open ~** recibir a todo el mundo, ser muy hospitalario; (*US*) recibir en casa las visitas; **to move ~** mudarse; **to put one's ~ in order** arreglar los asuntos personales; reformar la propia vida; **to set up ~** poner casa, establecerse.

2 *attr*: ~ **contents insurance** seguro *m* del contenido de una casa; ~ **dog** perro *m* de casa; ~ **guest** invitado *m*, -a *f*; ~ **journal**, ~ **magazine** revista *f* de la empresa (*de circulación interna*); ~ (**music**) música *f* acid*; ~ **prices** precios *mpl* de la propiedad inmobiliaria; ~ **sale** venta *f* de una casa; ~ **wine** vino *m* de la casa.

3 [haʊz] *vt person* alojar, hospedar; *population* proveer viviendas para; (*store*) guardar, almacenar; (*Mech*) encajar; **the building will not ~ them all** no cabrán todos en el edificio.

house-agent ['haʊsˌeɪdʒənt] *n* (*Brit*) agente *m* inmobiliario, agente *f* inmobiliaria.

house arrest ['haʊsəˌrest] *n* arresto *m* domiciliario.

houseboat ['haʊsbəʊt] *n* casa *f* flotante, bote-vivienda *m*.

housebound ['haʊsbaʊnd] *adj* que no puede salir de casa.

houseboy ['haʊsbɔɪ] *n* muchacho *m* de casa.

housebreaker ['haʊsˌbreɪkəʳ] *n* ladrón *m* de casas.

housebreaking ['haʊsˌbreɪkɪŋ] *n* robo *m* en una casa.

housebroken ['haʊsˌbrəʊkən] *adj* (*US*) domesticado.

housecleaning ['haʊs'kliːnɪŋ] *n* limpieza *f* de la casa.

housecoat ['haʊskəʊt] *n* bata *f*.

housedress ['haʊsdres] *n* vestido *m* de casa, vestido *m* sencillo.

housefather ['haʊsˌfɑːðəʳ] *n* hombre *m* encargado de una residencia de niños.

housefly ['haʊsflaɪ] *n* mosca *f* doméstica.

houseful ['haʊsfʊl] *n*: **there was a ~ of people** la casa estaba llena de gente.

household ['haʊshəʊld] **1** *n* casa *f*, familia *f*.

2 *attr* doméstico, de (la) casa; ~ **accounts** cuentas *fpl* de la casa; **H~ Cavalry** (*Brit*) Caballería *f* de la Guardia Real; ~ **chores** quehaceres *mpl* domésticos; ~ **gods** penates *mpl*; ~ **goods** enseres *mpl* domésticos; ~ **linen** ropa *f* de casa; ~ **refuse** basura *f* doméstica; ~ **soap** jabón *m* familiar; ~ **troops** (*Brit*) guardia *f* real; **he's a ~ name** es una persona conocidísima; **it's a ~ word** es un nombre conocidísimo.

householder ['haʊsˌhəʊldəʳ] *n* amo *m*, -a *f* (de casa); cabeza *f* de familia; dueño *m*, -a *f* de una casa, arrendatario *m*, -a *f*, inquilino *m*, -a *f*; (*as electoral qualification*) propietario *m*, -a *f* de vivienda.

house-hunt ['haʊshʌnt] *vi* (*Brit*) buscar casa.

house-hunting ['haʊsˌhʌntɪŋ] *n* búsqueda *f* de vivienda.

house-husband ['haʊsˌhʌzbənd] *n marido que trabaja en la casa.*

housekeeper ['haʊsˌkiːpəʳ] *n* (*in house*) ama *f* de casa, ama *f* de llaves; (*in hotel*) gobernanta *f*.

housekeeping ['haʊsˌkiːpɪŋ] *n* gobierno *m* de la casa, faenas *fpl* domésticas, (*Comput*) gestión *f* interna; ~ (**money**) dinero *m* para gastos domésticos.

houselights ['haʊslaɪts] *npl* (*Theat*) luces *fpl* de la sala.

housemaid ['haʊsmeɪd] *n* criada *f*, mucama *f* (*LAm*); **~'s knee** (*Med*) higroma *m*, hidrartrosis *f*.

houseman ['haʊsmən] *n*, *pl* **housemen** ['haʊsmən] (*Brit*: *in hospital*) interno *m*.

house manager ['haʊs'mænɪdʒəʳ] *n* empresario *m* teatral.

housemartin ['haʊsˌmɑːtɪn] *n* avión *m* común.

housemaster ['haʊsˌmɑːstəʳ] *n*, **housemistress** ['haʊsˌmɪstrɪs] *n* (*Brit Scol*) *profesor/profesora a cargo de la subdivisión de un colegio de internado.*

housemother ['haʊsˌmʌðəʳ] *n* mujer *f* encargada de una residencia de niños.

house-owner ['haʊsˌəʊnəʳ] *n* propietario *m*, -a *f* de una casa.

house painter ['haʊsˌpeɪntəʳ] *n* pintor *m* (de brocha gorda).

house party ['haʊsˌpɑːtɪ] *n* grupo *m* de invitados (que pasan varios días en una casa de campo).

house physician ['haʊsfɪˌzɪʃən] *n* (*Brit*) médico *m* interno, médica *f* interna.

house plant ['haʊsplɑːnt] *n* planta *f* de interior.
house-proud ['haʊspraʊd] *adj*: **she's very ~** tiene la casa como una plata.
houseroom ['haʊsrʊm] *n* capacidad *f* de una casa; **to give sth ~** guardar algo en su casa; **I wouldn't give it ~** no lo admitiría en mi casa.
house-sit ['haʊssɪt] *vt* (*irr*: *V* **sit**): **I'm ~ting for the Sinclairs** vivo en la casa de los Sinclair para vigilarla en ausencia de los dueños.
house-sparrow ['haʊs,spærəʊ] *n* gorrión *m* común.
house surgeon ['haʊs,sɜːdʒən] *n* (*Brit*) cirujano *m* interno, cirujana *f* interna, médico *m* interno, médica *f* interna (en el hospital).
house-to-house ['haʊstə'haʊs] *adj and adv* de casa en casa.
housetop ['haʊstɒp] *n* tejado *m*; **to shout sth from the ~s** pregonar algo a los cuatro vientos.
house-trained ['haʊstreɪnd] *adj* (*Brit*) *pet* bien enseñado, limpio, domesticado.
housewares ['haʊswɛəz] *npl* (*US*) artículos *mpl* de uso doméstico, utensilios *mpl* domésticos.
house-warming ['haʊs,wɔːmɪŋ] *n* fiesta *f* de estreno de una casa.
housewife ['haʊswaɪf] *n*, *pl* **housewives** ['haʊswaɪvz] ama *f* de casa; madre *f* de familia.
housewifely ['haʊswaɪflɪ] *adj* doméstico.
housewifery ['haʊswɪfərɪ] *n* gobierno *m* de la casa, faenas *fpl* domésticas.
housework ['haʊswɜːk] *n* quehaceres *mpl* domésticos.
housing ['haʊzɪŋ] **1** *n* (**a**) (*act*) alojamiento *m*; provisión *f* de vivienda.
(**b**) (*houses*) casas *fpl*, viviendas *fpl*; **there's a lot of new ~** hay muchas casas nuevas.
(**c**) (*Mech*) caja *f*, cubierta *f*, tapa *f*.
2 *attr*: **~ association** asociación *f* de la vivienda; **~ benefit** subsidio *m* de vivienda; **~ cooperative** cooperativa *f* de la vivienda; **~ development** (*US*), **~ estate** (*Brit*), **~ scheme** (*Brit*) urbanización *f*, reparto *m* (*Mex*); **~ market** mercado *m* de la vivienda; **~ policy** política *f* de la vivienda; **~ project** proyecto *m* para la construcción de viviendas; **~ shortage** crisis *f* de la vivienda; **~ stock** total *m* de viviendas; **~ subsidy** subsidio *m* por vivienda.
hove [həʊv] *pret and ptp of* **heave** (*Naut*).
hovel ['hɒvəl] *n* casucha *f*, tugurio *m*.
hover ['hɒvəʳ] *vi* permanecer inmóvil (en el aire), estar suspendido, flotar (en el aire); (*hawk etc*) cernerse; **to ~ round sb** rondar a uno, girar en torno a uno.
hovercraft ['hɒvəkrɑːft] *n* hidrodeslizador *m*, aerodeslizador *m*.
hoverport ['hɒvə,pɔːt] *n* terminal *f* de hidrodeslizador.
how [haʊ] *adv* (**a**) (*in what way*) cómo; **~ did you do it?** ¿cómo lo hiciste?; **I know ~ you did it** yo sé cómo lo hiciste; **~ is it that ...?** ¿cómo resulta que ...?, ¿por qué ...? ¿cómo es posible que ... + *subj*?; **~ can that be?** ¿cómo puede ser eso?; **I see ~ it is** comprendo la situación; **~ was the play?** ¿qué tal la comedia?; **~ do you like your steak?** ¿cómo le gusta que se le sirva el biftec?; **~ do you like the steak?** ¿qué tal te parece el biftec?; **~'s that for cheek?** ¿qué opinas de eso como ejemplo de cara dura?; **to know ~ to do sth** saber hacer algo; **to learn ~ to do sth** aprender a hacer algo, aprender cómo se hace algo, aprender el modo de hacer algo; **and ~!** ¡y cómo!; **I like it, but ~ about you?** a mí me gusta, pero ¿y tú?; *V* **about 2 (c)**.
(**b**) (*health*) **~ are you?** ¿cómo está Vd?, ¿qué tal estás?
(**c**) (*with adj or adv etc*) **~ beautiful!** ¡qué hermoso!; **~ big it is!** ¡qué grande es!; **I know ~ hard it is** yo sé lo difícil que esto es; **~ kind of you!** es Vd muy amable; **~ fast?** ¿a qué velocidad?; **~ big is it?** ¿cómo es de grande?, ¿de qué tamaño es?; **~ wide is this room?** ¿cuánto tiene este cuarto de ancho?; **~ wide shall I make it?** ¿de qué ancho lo hago?; **~ old are you?** ¿cuántos años tienes?; **~ glad I am to see you!** ¡cuánto me alegro de verte!; **~ sorry I am for you!** ¡cuánto te compadezco!; **~ she's changed!** ¡cuánto ha cambiado!; *V* **about, else, much** *etc*.
howdy* ['haʊdɪ] *excl* (*US*) ¡hola!
how-d'ye-do ['haʊdjə'duː] *n* lío *m*; **this is a fine ~!** ¡en buen berenjenal nos hemos metido!, ¡vaya problemazo!
however [haʊ'evəʳ] **1** *adv* (**a**) (*with verb*) **~ I do it** como quiera que lo haga; **~ he may want to do it** de cualquier modo que quiera hacerlo; **~ that may be** sea como sea.
(**b**) (*with adj or adv*) por (muy) ... que + *subj*; **~ rough it is** por (muy) tosco que sea; **~ fast he runs** por rápido que corra; **~ hot it is** por mucho calor que haga; *V* **many, much**.
2 *conj* sin embargo, no obstante.
howitzer ['haʊɪtsəʳ] *n* obús *m*.
howl [haʊl] **1** *n* aullido *m*, chillido *m*, grito *m*, alarido *m*; berrido *m*; bramido *m*; **with a ~ of rage** dando un alarido de furia; **to set up a ~** (*fig*) poner el grito en el cielo.
2 *vi* (*animal etc*) aullar, chillar; (*person*) gritar, dar alaridos; (*child*) berrear; (*with laughter*) reírse a carcajadas; (*wind*) bramar; **to ~ with rage** bramar de furia, bramar furioso.
◆**howl down** *vt*: **to ~ sb down** hacer callar a uno a gritos.
howler ['haʊləʳ] *n* plancha *f*, planchazo *m*, falta *f* garrafal.
howling ['haʊlɪŋ] *adj success* clamoroso.
hoy [hɔɪ] *interj* ¡eh!, ¡hola!
hoyden ['hɔɪdn] *n* marimacho *f*.
HP *n* (*Brit*) *abbr of* **hire purchase** compra *f* a plazos.
h.p. *n abbr of* **horsepower** caballos *mpl* de vapor, C.V.
HQ *n abbr of* **headquarters** cuartel *m* general, Estado *m* Mayor, E.M.
HR *n* (*US*) *abbr of* **House of Representatives.**
hr(s) *abbr of* **hour(s)** hora(s) *f*(*pl*), h.
H.R.H. *abbr of* **Her (His) Royal Highness** Su Alteza Real, S.A.R.
HRT *n abbr of* **hormone replacement therapy.**
H.S. (*US*) *abbr of* **high school.**
HST *n* (*US*) *abbr of* **Hawaiian Standard Time.**
HT *n abbr of* **high tension** alta tensión *f*.
ht *abbr of* **height** altura *f*, alt.
hub [hʌb] *n* cubo *m*; (*fig*) centro *m*, eje.
hubbub ['hʌbʌb] *n* barahúnda *f*, batahóla *f*; **a ~ of voices** un ruido confuso de voces.
hubby* ['hʌbɪ] *n* marido *m*.
hubcap ['hʌbkæp] *n* tapacubos *m*.
hubris ['hjuːbrɪs] *n* orgullo *m* (desmesurado).
huckster ['hʌkstəʳ] *n* (*US*) vendedor *m* ambulante, mercachifle *m*, buhonero *m*.
HUD *n* (*US*) *abbr of* **Department of Housing and Urban Development.**
huddle ['hʌdl] **1** *n* (*of things*) montón *m*, grupo *m*; (*of persons*) grupo *m*, corrillo *m*; **to go into a ~** ir aparte para conferenciar.
2 *vt* amontonar, poner muy juntos.
3 *vi* amontonarse, apretarse (unos contra otros); acurrucarse; **the chairs were ~d in a corner** las sillas estaban amontonadas en un rincón; **we ~d round the fire** nos arrimamos al fuego, nos apiñábamos junto a la lumbre.
◆**huddle down** *vi* (*crouch*) agacharse; (*snuggle*) acurrucarse, apretarse.
◆**huddle together 1** *vt* = **huddle 2.**
2 *vi* amontonarse, apretarse (unos contra unos); acurrucarse; **they were huddling together for warmth** estaban acurrucados para darse calor.
◆**huddle up** *vi* amontonarse, apretarse (unos contra unos); acurrucarse.
hue[1] [hjuː] *n* (*colour*) color *m*; (*shade*) matiz *m*, tono *m*; (*of opinion*) matiz *m*; **people of every political ~** gente *f* de todos los matices políticos.
hue[2] [hjuː] *n*: **~ and cry** alarma *f*; (*of protest*) clamor *m*, griterío *f*; **they set up a great ~ and cry** protestaron clamorosamente; **there was a ~ and cry after him** se le persiguió enérgicamente.
huff [hʌf] **1** *n* rabieta *f*; **to go off in a ~** irse amostazado; **to get into a ~** amostazarse, picarse. **2** *vi*: **to ~ and puff** (*out of breath*) jadear, resollar; **he ~ed and puffed a lot and then said yes** resopló mucho y luego dijo que bueno.
huffed* [hʌft] *adj* enojado.
huffily ['hʌfɪlɪ] *adv* malhumoradamente; **he said ~** dijo malhumorado.
huffiness ['hʌfɪnɪs] *n* mal humor *m*.
huffy ['hʌfɪ] *adj* (*of character*) enojadizo; (*in mood*) malhumorado, ofendido, **he was a bit ~ about it** se ofendió un tanto por ello.
hug [hʌg] **1** *n* abrazo *m*; **give me a ~** dame un abrazo.
2 *vt* (*lovingly*) abrazar; (*of bear etc*) apretar con los brazos, apretujar; *coast* no apartarse de; *prejudice etc* acariciar; *idea* aferrarse a; *belief* afirmarse en.
3 *vr*: **to ~ o.s.** felicitarse (*on* por).
huge [hjuːdʒ] *adj* enorme, vasto, inmenso; (*over-large*) descomunal.
hugely ['hjuːdʒlɪ] *adv* enormemente; **we enjoyed ourselves ~** nos divertimos una barbaridad; **he laughed ~** se rio una barbaridad.
hugeness ['hjuːdʒnɪs] *n* inmensidad *f*.
hugger-mugger ['hʌgə,mʌgəʳ] **1** *n* confusión *f*; **a ~ of**

books un montón de libros en desorden.
2 *adv* desordenadamente.

Hugh [hjuː] *nm* Hugo, Ugo.

Huguenot ['hjuːgənəʊ] **1** *adj* hugonote. **2** *n* hugonote *m*, -a *f*.

huh [hʌ] *excl* ¡eh!

hulk [hʌlk] *n* (*wreck*) barco *m* viejo; (*hull*) casco *m* (arrumbado); (*large, unwieldy vessel*) carcamán *m*; (*mass*) bulto *m*, mole *f*.

hulking ['hʌlkɪŋ] *adj* grueso, pesado; ~ **great brute** hombracho *m*, hombretón *m*.

hull [hʌl] **1** *n* casco *m*. **2** *vt fruit* descascarar.

hullabaloo* [ˌhʌləbə'luː] *n* (*noise*) vocería *f*, tumulto *m*; (*fuss*) lío* *m*, bronca *f*; **a great ~ broke out** estalló un ruido espantoso; **that ~ about the money** ese lío que se armó por el dinero*.

hullo [hʌ'ləʊ] *interj* (*greeting*) ¡hola!; (*surprise*) ¡caramba!; (*Telec*: *calling*) ¡oiga!, (*answering*) ¡diga!, ¡bueno! (*Mex*), ¡hola! (*SC*), ¡aló! (*And*); **~, what's all this!** ¡vamos a ver!

hum [hʌm] **1** *n* zumbido *m*; tarareo *m*; (*of voices etc*) ruido *m* confuso, murmullo *m*.
2 *vt tune* tararear, canturrear.
3 *vi* (**a**) (*insect, wire etc*) zumbar; (*person*) canturrear, tararear una canción; **to ~ with activity** bullir de actividad; **to make things ~** desplegar gran actividad; avivarlo, estimular la actividad; **then things began to ~** entonces sí empezaron a pasar cosas, hubo luego una actividad frenética.
(**b**) (*) oler mal.
(**c**) **to ~ and haw** vacilar, no resolverse.

human ['hjuːmən] **1** *adj* humano; **~ being** ser *m* humano; **~ factor** factor *m* humano; **~ nature** naturaleza *f* humana; **it's ~ nature to be jealous** es cosa natural tener celos; **~ race** género *m* humano; **~ relations** relaciones *fpl* humanas; **~ remains** restos *mpl* humanos; **~ resources** recursos *mpl* humanos; **~ rights** derechos *mpl* humanos; **~ shield** escudo *m* humano. **2** *n* humano *m*, -a *f*.

humane [hjuː'meɪn] *adj* (**a**) (*compassionate*) humano, humanitario. (**b**) **~ studies** ciencias *fpl* humanas, humanidades *fpl*.

humanely [hjuː'meɪnlɪ] *adv* humanamente.

humanism ['hjuːmənɪzəm] *n* humanismo *m*.

humanist ['hjuːmənɪst] *n* humanista *mf*.

humanistic [ˌhjuːmə'nɪstɪk] *adj* humanístico.

humanitarian [hjuːˌmænɪ'tɛərɪən] **1** *adj* humanitario. **2** *n* humanitario *m*, -a *f*.

humanitarianism [hjuːˌmænɪ'tɛərɪənɪzəm] *n* humanitarismo *m*.

humanity [hjuː'mænɪtɪ] *n* humanidad *f*; **the humanities** las humanidades.

humanize ['hjuːmənaɪz] *vt* humanizar.

humankind ['hjuːmən'kaɪnd] *n* género *m* humano.

humanly ['hjuːmənlɪ] *adv* humanamente; **all that is ~ possible** todo lo que pueda hacer un hombre, todo lo que cabe dentro de las posibilidades humanas.

humanoid ['hjuːmənɔɪd] **1** *adj* humanoide. **2** *n* humanoide *mf*.

humble ['hʌmbl] **1** *adj* humilde. **2** *vt* humillar. **3** *vr*: **to ~ o.s.** humillarse.

humble-bee ['hʌmblbiː] *n* abejorro *m*.

humbleness ['hʌmblnɪs] *n* humildad *f*.

humbly ['hʌmblɪ] *adv* humildemente, con humildad.

humbug ['hʌmbʌg] *n* (**a**) (*nonsense*) bola *f*, embustes *mpl*, disparates *mpl*; **~!** ¡bobadas!
(**b**) (*Brit*: *sweet*) caramelo *m* de menta.
(**c**) (*person*) farsante *mf*, charlatán *m*, -ana *f*; **he's an old ~** es un farsante.

humdinger* ['hʌmdɪŋə^r] *n*: **it's a ~!** ¡es una auténtica maravilla!; **a real ~ of a car** un coche maravilloso.

humdrum ['hʌmdrʌm] *adj* monótono, aburrido; tedioso; vulgar, ordinario; rutinario; mediocre, sin interés.

humerus ['hjuːmərəs] *n*, *pl* **humeri** ['hjuːməraɪ] húmero *m*.

humid ['hjuːmɪd] *adj* húmedo.

humidifier [hjuː'mɪdɪfaɪə^r] *n* humectador *m*, humedecedor *m*.

humidify [hjuː'mɪdɪfaɪ] *vt* humedecer.

humidity [hjuː'mɪdɪtɪ] *n* humedad *f*.

humiliate [hjuː'mɪlɪeɪt] *vt* humillar.

humiliating [hjuː'mɪlɪeɪtɪŋ] *adj* vergonzoso, humillante.

humiliatingly [hjuː'mɪlɪeɪtɪŋlɪ] *adv* vergonzosamente, de manera humillante; **we were ~ defeated** sufrimos una derrota vergonzosa.

humiliation [hjuːmɪlɪ'eɪʃən] *n* humillación *f*.

humility [hjuː'mɪlɪtɪ] *n* humildad *f*.

humming ['hʌmɪŋ] *n* zumbido *m*; tarareo *m*, canturreo *m*.

hummingbird ['hʌmɪŋbɜːd] *n* colibrí *m*, picaflor *m*.

humming-top ['hʌmɪŋtɒp] *n* trompa *f*.

hummock ['hʌmək] *n* montecillo *m*, morón *m*.

humor ['hjuːmə^r] *etc* (*US*) = **humour** *etc*.

humorist ['hjuːmərɪst] *n* persona *f* chistosa; bromista *mf*; (*writer*) humorista *mf*; **what a ~ you are!** ¡qué gracioso eres!

humorless ['hjuːməlɪs] (*US*) = **humourless.**

humorous ['hjuːmərəs] *adj person* gracioso, chistoso, divertido; *writer, genre* festivo, cómico; *joke, event, book* divertido; *tone* festivo.

humorously ['hjuːmərəslɪ] *adv* graciosamente, de manera divertida; en tono festivo.

humour, (*US*) **humor** ['hjuːmə^r] **1** *n* (**a**) (*amusingness*) humorismo *m*; (*sense of ~*) sentido *m* del humor; (*creative talent*) vis *f* cómica; (*of joke, event*) gracia *f*; (*of situation*) comicidad *f*; **he has no ~** no tiene sentido del humor; **I see no ~ in that** eso no me hace gracia alguna; **this is no time for ~** no es tiempo para chistes; **I don't like the ~ in 'Macbeth'** no me gustan las escenas cómicas de 'Macbeth'.
(**b**) (*mood*) humor *m*; **to be in good ~** estar de buen humor; **to be in high good ~** estar de excelente humor; **they were in no ~ for fighting** no estaban de humor para pelear; **to be out of ~** estar de mal humor.
(**c**) (*whim*) capricho *m*.
(**d**) (*Med* ††) humor *m*.
2 *vt* complacer, seguir el humor a; (*indulge*) mimar.

-humoured, (*US*) **-humored** ['hjuːməd] *adj* de humor ...

humourless, (*US*) **humorless** ['hjuːməlɪs] *adj person* sin sentido del humor; *joke* sin gracia.

hump [hʌmp] **1** *n* (*Anat*) joroba *f*, corcova *f*, giba *f*; (*camel's*) giba *f*; (*in ground*) montecillo *m*; **to give sb the ~** (*Brit*) jorobar a uno, fastidiar a uno; **to have the ~** (*Brit*) estar de mal humor; **to be over the ~*** estar en la pendiente vital, ser demasiado viejo; no servir ya; **we're over the ~ now** ya hemos vencido la cuesta.
2 *vt* (**a**) **to ~ one's back** encorvarse, corcovarse.
(**b**) (*: *carry*) llevar, llevar al hombro.
(**c**) (******) joder****** (*Sp*), coger****** (*LAm*).

humpback ['hʌmpbæk] *n* (**a**) (*person*) jorobado *m*, -a *f*; (*whale*: *also* **~ whale**) rorcual *m*; **to have a ~** ser jorobado.

humpbacked ['hʌmpbækt] *adj* corcovado, jorobado; (*Brit*) *bridge* de fuerte pendiente.

humph [mm] *interj* ¡bah!; ¡veremos!

humpy ['hʌmpɪ] *adj* desigual.

humus ['hjuːməs] *n* humus *m*.

Hun [hʌn] *n* (*Hist*) huno *m*; (*pej*) tudesco *m*, alemán *m*; **a ~** un alemán, **the ~** los alemanes.

hunch [hʌntʃ] **1** *n* (**a**) (*Anat*) *V* **hump.**
(**b**) (*premonition*) corazanada *f*, pálpito *m*; sospecha *f*; **it's only a ~** no es más que una sospecha que tengo; **I have a ~ that** ... me da el pálpito que ...; **the detective had one of his ~es** el detective tuvo uno de sus pálpitos; **~es sometimes pay off** a veces los presentimientos se cumplen.
2 *vt* (*also* **to ~ up**) encorvar; **to ~ one's back** encorvarse; **to sit ~ed up** estar sentado con el cuerpo doblado.

hunchback ['hʌntʃbæk] *n* jorobado *m*, -a *f*, corcovado *m*, -a *f*.

hunchbacked ['hʌntʃbækt] *adj* jorobado, corcovado.

hundred ['hʌndrɪd] **1** *adj* ciento, (*before n*) cien; **a ~ and one** ciento uno; **I've got a ~ and one things to do** tengo la mar de cosas que hacer; **a ~ and ten** ciento diez; **a ~ thousand** cien mil; **a ~ per cent** (*fig*) cien por cien; **H~ Years' War** Guerra *f* de los Cien Años.
2 *n* ciento *m*, (*less exactly*) centenar *m*, centena *f*; **~s of people** centenares *mpl* de personas; **in ~s, by the ~** a centenares; **for ~s of thousands of years** durante centenares de miles de años; **I've told you ~s of times** te lo he dicho cientos de veces.

hundredfold ['hʌndrɪdfəʊld] **1** *adj* céntuplo. **2** *adv* cien veces.

hundredth ['hʌndrɪdθ] **1** *adj* centésimo. **2** *n* centésimo *m*, centésima parte *f*.

hundredweight ['hʌndrɪdweɪt] *n* (*Brit, Canada*: = 112 *libras* = 50,8 *kilogramos*) *approx* quintal *m*, (*US*: = 100 *libras* = 45,3 *kilogramos*).

hung [hʌŋ] *pret and ptp of* **hang**; **~ jury** jurado *m* cuyos miembros no se pueden poner de acuerdo.

Hungarian [hʌŋ'gɛərɪən] **1** *adj* húngaro. **2** *n* (**a**) húngaro *m*, -a *f*. (**b**) (*Ling*) húngaro *m*.

Hungary ['hʌŋgərɪ] *n* Hungría *f*.

hunger ['hʌŋgə^r] **1** *n* hambre *f* (*also fig*: *for* de). **2** *vi* tener hambre, estar hambriento; **to ~ after, to ~ for** tener hambre de, ansiar, anhelar.

hunger march ['hʌŋgə,mɑːtʃ] *n* (*Brit*) marcha *f* del hambre.

hunger strike ['hʌŋgəstraɪk] *n* huelga *f* de hambre.

hungrily ['hʌŋgrɪlɪ] *adv eat etc* ansiosamente, ávidamente; **to look ~ at sth** mirar algo con ganas de comerlo.

hungry ['hʌŋgrɪ] *adj* hambriento; *land* pobre, estéril; **to be ~** tener hambre (*for* de); **to be very ~** tener mucha hambre; **to go ~** pasar hambre; **to make sb ~** hambrear a uno, hacer pasar hambre a uno.

hunk [hʌŋk] *n* (**a**) (*chunk*) pedazo *m* (grande), (buen) trozo *m*. (**b**) (*: *man*) tío *m* bueno*, cachas* *m*.

hunker* ['hʌŋkə^r] *vi*: **to ~ down** agacharse.

hunky* ['hʌŋkɪ] *adj* (**a**) (*strong*) fornido, fuerte, macizo. (**b**) (*: *attractive*) bueno*.

hunky-dory* [,hʌŋkɪ'dɔːrɪ] *adj* (*esp US*) guay*; **it's all ~** es guay del Paraguay*.

hunt [hʌnt] **1** *n* caza *f*, cacería *f* (*for* de); (*party*) partida *f* de caza; grupo *m* de cazadores; (*search*) busca *f*, búsqueda *f* (*for* de); (*pursuit*) persecución *f*; **the ~ for the murderer** la persecución del asesino; **to be on the ~ for** ir a la caza de; **the ~ is on, the ~ is up** ha comenzado la búsqueda; **we joined in the ~ for the missing key** ayudamos a buscar la llave perdida.

2 *vt animal* cazar; (*search for*) buscar; (*pursue*) perseguir; *hounds etc* emplear en la caza; *country* recorrer de caza, cazar en.

3 *vi* cazar; dedicarse a la caza; **to ~ for** buscar; **to ~ about for** buscar por todas partes; **he ~ed for it in his pocket** lo buscó en el bolsillo; **to go ~ing** ir de caza.

◆**hunt down** *vt person* perseguir (y encontrar); *thing* buscar hasta dar con.

◆**hunt out, hunt up** *vt* (*look for*) buscar; (*find*) encontrar.

hunter ['hʌntə^r] *n* (**a**) cazador *m*, -ora *f*. (**b**) (*horse*) caballo *m* de caza.

hunter-gatherer ['hʌntə'gæðərə^r] *n* cazador-recolector *m*.

hunting ['hʌntɪŋ] **1** *n* caza *f*, montería *f*. **2** *attr* de caza; **the ~ fraternity** los aficionados a la caza; **~ lodge** pabellón *m* de caza; **~ pink** levitín *m* rojo de caza; **~ season** época *f* de caza.

hunting-box ['hʌntɪŋbɒks] *n* pabellón *m* de caza.

hunting-ground ['hʌntɪŋgraʊnd] *n* cazadero *m*; **a happy ~ for** un buen terreno para.

hunting-horn ['hʌntɪŋ,hɔːn] *n* cuerno *m* de caza.

huntress ['hʌntrɪs] *n* cazadora *f*.

Hunts [hʌnts] *n abbr of* **Huntingdonshire**.

huntsman ['hʌntsmən] *n*, *pl* **huntsmen** ['hʌntsmən] cazador *m*, montero *m*.

hurdle ['hɜːdl] *n* zarzo *m*, valla *f*; (*Sport*) valla *f*; (*fig*) obstáculo *m*.

hurdler ['hɜːdlə^r] *n* vallista *mf*.

hurdle race ['hɜːdlreɪs] *n* carrera *f* de vallas.

hurdling ['hɜːdlɪŋ] *n* salto *m* de vallas.

hurdy-gurdy ['hɜːdɪ,gɜːdɪ] *n* organillo *m*.

hurl [hɜːl] **1** *vt* lanzar, arrojar; **to ~ back** *enemy* rechazar; **to ~ insults at sb** llenar a uno de improperios.

2 *vr*: **to ~ o.s. at** (*or* **upon**) **sb** abalanzarse sobre uno; **to ~ o.s. into the fray** lanzarse a la batalla; **to ~ o.s. over a cliff** arrojarse por un precipicio.

hurly-burly ['hɜːlɪ'bɜːlɪ] *n* tumulto *m*; **the ~ of politics** la vida alborotada de la política.

hurrah [hʊ'rɑː], **hurray** [hʊ'reɪ] **1** *interj* ¡viva!, ¡vítor!; **~ for Brown!** ¡viva Brown! **2** *n* vítor *m*.

hurricane ['hʌrɪkən] **1** *n* huracán *m*.

2 *attr*: **~ lamp** lámpara *f* a prueba de viento.

hurried ['hʌrɪd] *adj* apresurado, hecho de prisa; *reading etc* superficial; **he had a ~ meal** comió de prisa.

hurriedly ['hʌrɪdlɪ] *adv* con prisa, apresuradamente; *study etc* superficialmente; *write etc* a vuela pluma; **I left ~** me apresuré a salir.

hurry ['hʌrɪ] **1** *n* prisa, tener apuro *m* (*LAm*); **to be in a ~** tener prisa, tener apuro (*LAm*) (*to do* por hacer), estar de prisa; **I'm in no ~, I'm not in any ~** no tengo prisa; **they were in no ~ to pay us** no se dieron prisa por pagarnos; **to do sth in a ~** hacer algo de prisa; **are you in a ~ for this?** ¿corre prisa esto?; **is there any ~?** ¿corre prisa?; **what's all the ~?, what's your ~?** ¿por qué tanta prisa?, ¿por qué tanto apuro? (*LAm*); **there's no (great) ~** no hay prisa; **I shan't come back here in a ~** aquí no pongo los pies nunca más; **he won't do that again in a ~** no volverá a hacer eso si puede evitarlo.

2 *vt work etc* (*also* **to ~ along, to ~ on, to ~ up**) apresurar, dar prisa a, apurar, acelerar; **they hurried him to a doctor** le llevaron con toda prisa a un médico; **troops were hurried to the spot** se enviaron tropas al lugar con toda prisa; **this is a plan that cannot be hurried** éste es proyecto que no admite prisa; **to ~ the work along** acelerar el ritmo del trabajo; **to ~ sb away, to ~ sb off** hacer marchar a uno de prisa; **the policeman hurried him away** el policía se le llevó apresuradamente; **to ~ sb out** dar prisa a uno para que salga.

3 *vi* apresurarse (*to do* a hacer), darse prisa (*to do* para hacer), apurarse (*LAm*) (*to do* para hacer); **~!** ¡dése prisa!; **don't ~!** ¡no hay prisa!; **I must ~** tengo prisa, tengo que correr; **she hurried home** se dio prisa para llegar a casa; **to ~ after sb** correr detrás de uno; **to ~ along** correr, ir de prisa; **to ~ away, to ~ off** marcharse de prisa; **to ~ back** darse prisa para volver, volver de prisa; **to ~ in** entrar de prisa, entrar corriendo; **to ~ out** salir de prisa, salir corriendo; **to ~ over** *place* cruzar rápidamente; *work* concluir aprisa, hacer con precipitación.

◆**hurry up 1** *vt*: **to ~ sb up** hacer que uno se dé prisa. **2** *vi* darse prisa; **~ up!** ¡date prisa!

hurt [hɜːt] **1** *n* (*wound etc*) herida *f*, lesión *f*; (*harm*) daño *m*, mal *m*, perjuicio *m*.

2 (*irr*: *pret and ptp* **hurt**) *vt* (*injure, bodily*) herir, hacer mal a, hacer daño a, lastimar; (*cause pain to*) doler; (*damage*) dañar; *business, interests etc* perjudicar, afectar; *feelings* herir, ofender; (*be bad for*) hacer daño a; **he ~ his foot** se lastimó el pie; **where does it ~ you?** ¿dónde le duele?; **to get ~** hacerse daño; **in such affairs sb's bound to get ~** en estos asuntos siempre sale alguno perjudicado; **wine never ~ anybody** el vino no hizo nunca daño a nadie; **she's feeling rather ~ about it** se ha ofendido bastante por ello.

3 *vi* (*feel pain*) doler; (*take harm*) sufrir daño, estropearse, echarse a perder; **does it ~ much?** ¿duele mucho?; **it won't ~ for being left another week** no se va a estropear si lo dejamos una semana más.

4 *vr*: **to ~ o.s.** hacerse daño, lastimarse.

5 *adj foot etc* lastimado, lisiado; *feelings* ofendido; **with a ~ look** con cara de ofendido; **in a ~ tone** quejoso, ofendido; **~ books** (*US*) libros *mpl* deteriorados (en tienda).

hurtful ['hɜːtfʊl] *adj* dañoso, perjudicial; *remark etc* hiriente.

hurtle ['hɜːtl] **1** *vt* arrojar (violentamente).

2 *vi*: **to ~ along, to ~ past** (*adv*) ir como un rayo; **to ~ down** caer con violencia; **the car ~d past us** el coche cruzó como un rayo delante de nosotros; **the rock ~d over the cliff** la roca cayó estrepitosamente por el precipicio.

husband ['hʌzbənd] **1** *n* marido *m*; esposo *m*; **now they're ~ and wife** ahora son marido y mujer. **2** *vt* economizar, ahorrar, manejar prudentemente.

husbandry ['hʌzbəndrɪ] *n* (**a**) (*Agr*) agricultura *f*, labranza *f*. (**b**) (*fig*: *also* **good ~**) buen gobierno *m*, manejo *m* prudente.

hush [hʌʃ] **1** *n* silencio *m*; **a ~ fell** se hizo un silencio.

2 *vi* hacer callar, acallar, imponer silencio a.

3 *vi* callar(se); **~!** ¡chitón!; ¡cállate!

◆**hush up** *vt affair* encubrir, echar tierra a; *person* tapar la boca a.

hushed [hʌʃt] *adj tone* callado, muy bajo; *silence* profundo; **all were ~** se callaron todos.

hush-hush* ['hʌʃ'hʌʃ] *adj* muy secreto.

hush-money* ['hʌʃ,mʌnɪ] *n* mamela* *f*, precio *m* del silencio, dinero *m* por callar.

husk [hʌsk] **1** *n* cáscara *f*, vaina *f*; hollejo *m*, (*of corn*) cascabillo *m*. **2** *vt* descascarar, desvainar.

huskily ['hʌskɪlɪ] *adv* roncamente, en voz ronca.

huskiness ['hʌskɪnɪs] *n* ronquedad *f*.

husky[1] ['hʌskɪ] *adj* (**a**) *voice, person* ronco. (**b**) (*tough*) fornido.

husky[2] ['hʌskɪ] *n* perro *m* esquimal.

hussar [hə'zɑː^r] *n* húsar *m*.

hussy ['hʌsɪ] *n* pícara *f*, desvergonzada *f*; **you ~!** ¡lagarta!; **she's a little ~** es una fresca.

hustings ['hʌstɪŋz] *npl* (*esp Brit*) elecciones *fpl*; campaña *f* electoral.

hustle ['hʌsl] **1** *n* (**a**) actividad *f* febril, bullicio *m*; (*pushfulness*) empuje *m*; **~ and bustle** ajetreo *m*, actividad *f* bulliciosa; **to get a ~ on*** darse prisa. (**b**) (*US**) timo *m*, chanchullo* *m*.

2 *vt* (**a**) (*jostle*) empujar, codear; (*hurry up*) *person* dar prisa a, *thing* acelerar; **I refuse to be ~d** no tolero que me den prisa; **I won't be ~d into anything** yo no resuelvo las cosas de prisa; **they ~d him into a car** le metieron en un coche a empellones, le hicieron entrar sin ceremonia en un coche; **to ~ sb out of a room** echar a uno de un cuarto a empellones.

(**b**) (*US*‡) solicitar (mediante presiones ilícitas), (*less vigorously*) enrollarse con.

3 *vi* (**a**) darse prisa, menearse.

(**b**) (*US*) (*: *work*) currelar‡, currar*; (‡: *prostitute o.s.*) prostituirse.

◆**hustle in 1** *vt*: **to ~ sb in** hacer entrar a empellones, hacer entrar sin ceremonia. **2** *vi* entrar de prisa.

◆**hustle out 1** *vt*: **they ~d him out** le echaron a empellones, le hicieron salir sin ceremonia. **2** *vi* salir de prisa.

hustler ['hʌsləʳ] *n* (*go-getter*) persona *f* dinámica; (*swindler*) estafador *m*, timador *m*; (*prostitute*) puta *f*, ramera *f*.

hut [hʌt] *n* casilla *f*; (*shed*) cobertizo *m*; (*hovel*) barraca *f*, cabaña *f*; choza *f*, (*mountain ~*) albergue *m* de montaña.

hutch [hʌtʃ] *n* conejera *f*.

HV, h.v. *n abbr of* **high voltage** alto voltaje *m*.

HVT *n abbr of* **high-velocity train** tren *m* de alta velocidad, TAV *m*.

hyacinth ['haɪəsɪnθ] *n* (*Bot, Min*) jacinto *m*.

hyaena [haɪ'iːnə] *n* hiena *f*.

hybrid ['haɪbrɪd] **1** *adj* híbrido. **2** *n* híbrido *m*, -a *f*.

hybridism ['haɪbrɪdɪzəm] *n* hibridismo *m*.

hybridization [,haɪbrɪdaɪ'zeɪʃən] *n* hibridación *f*.

hybridize ['haɪbrɪdaɪz] *vti* hibridar.

hydra ['haɪdrə] *n* hidra *f*; **H~** (*Myth*) Hidra *f*.

hydrangea [haɪ'dreɪndʒə] *n* hortensia *f*.

hydrant ['haɪdrənt] *n* boca *f* de riego; (*fire ~*) boca *f* de incendios.

hydrate ['haɪdreɪt] **1** *n* hidrato *m*. **2** *vt* hidratar.

hydraulic [haɪ'drɒlɪk] *adj* hidráulico; **~ brake** freno *m* hidráulico; **~ press** prensa *f* hidráulica; **~ suspension** suspensión *f* hidráulica.

hydraulics [haɪ'drɒlɪks] *n* hidráulica *f*.

hydro... ['haɪdrəʊ] *pref* hidro...

hydro ['haɪdrəʊ] *n* (*Brit*) balneario *m*.

hydrocarbon ['haɪdrəʊ'kɑːbən] *n* hidrocarburo *m*.

hydrochloric ['haɪdrə'klɒrɪk] *adj*: **~ acid** ácido *m* clorhídrico.

hydrocyanic ['haɪdrəsaɪ'ænɪk] *adj*: **~ acid** ácido *m* cianhídrico.

hydrodynamics ['haɪdrəʊdaɪ'næmɪks] *n* hidrodinámica *f*.

hydroelectric ['haɪdrəʊɪ'lektrɪk] *adj* hidroeléctrico; **~ power station, ~ power plant** central *f* hidroeléctrica.

hydroelectricity [,haɪdrəʊɪlek'trɪsɪtɪ] *n* hidroelectricidad *f*.

hydrofoil ['haɪdrəʊfɔɪl] *n* hidroala *f*.

hydrogen ['haɪdrɪdʒən] **1** *n* hidrógeno *m*. **2** *attr*: **~ bomb** bomba *f* de hidrógeno; **~ chloride** cloruro *m* de hidrógeno; **~ peroxide** peróxido *m* de hidrógeno.

hydrography [haɪ'drɒgrəfɪ] *n* hidrografía *f*.

hydrolysis [haɪ'drɒlɪsɪs] *n* hidrólisis *f*.

hydrolyze ['haɪdrəʊlaɪz] **1** *vt* hidrolizar. **2** *vi* hidrolizarse.

hydrometer [haɪ'drɒmɪtəʳ] *n* aerómetro *m*.

hydrophobia [,haɪdrə'fəʊbɪə] *n* hidrofobia *f*.

hydrophobic [,haɪdrə'fəʊbɪk] *adj* hidrofóbico.

hydroplane ['haɪdrəʊpleɪn] *n* hidroavión *m*.

hydroponic [,haɪdrəʊ'pɒnɪk] *adj* hidropónico.

hydroponics [,haɪdrəʊ'pɒnɪks] *n sing* hidroponia *f*.

hydropower ['haɪdrəʊ,paʊəʳ] *n* hidrofuerza *f*.

hydrotherapy [,haɪdrəʊ'θerəpɪ] *n* hidroterapia *f*.

hydroxide [haɪ'drɒksaɪd] *n* hidróxido *m*.

hyena [haɪ'iːnə] *n* hiena *f*.

hygiene ['haɪdʒiːn] *n* higiene *f*.

hygienic [haɪ'dʒiːnɪk] *adj* higiénico.

hymen ['haɪmen] *n* himen *m*.

hymn [hɪm] *n* himno *m*.

hymnal ['hɪmnəl] *n*, **hymn book** ['hɪmbʊk] *n* himnario *m*.

hype* [haɪp] **1** *n* exageraciones *fpl*, cuentos *mpl*; supercheria *f*; propaganda *f*; (*Comm*) bombo *m* publicitario*, promoción *f* de lanzamiento. **2** *vt* (*Comm*) dar bombo publicitario a*.

◆**hype up* 1** *vt* exagerar, dar bombo a*; *person* excitar; *numbers* aumentar. **2** *vi* pincharse*, picarse*.

hyper... ['haɪpəʳ] *pref* hiper...

hyper ['haɪpəʳ] *adj* hiperactivo, histérico.

hyperacidity ['haɪpərə'sɪdɪtɪ] *n* hiperacidez *f*.

hyperactive [,haɪpər'æktɪv] *adj* hiperactivo, hipercenético.

hyperactivity [,haɪpəræk'tɪvɪtɪ] *n* hiperactividad *f*.

hyperbola [haɪ'pɜːbələ] *n* hipérbola *f*.

hyperbole [haɪ'pɜːbəlɪ] *n* hipérbole *f*.

hyperbolic(al) [,haɪpə'bɒlɪk(əl)] *adj* hiperbólico.

hypercorrection [,haɪpəkə'rekʃən] *n* hipercorrección *f*, ultracorrección *f*.

hypercritical ['haɪpə'krɪtɪkəl] *adj* hipercrítico.

hyperinflation ['haɪpəɪn'fleɪʃən] *n* hiperinflación *f*.

hypermarket ['haɪpə,mɑːkɪt] *n* (*Brit*) hipermercado *m*.

hyperopia ['haɪpər'əʊpɪə] *n* hipermetropía *f*.

hypersensitive ['haɪpə'sensɪtɪv] *adj* hipersensible.

hypertension ['haɪpə'tenʃən] *n* hipertensión *f*.

hypertrophy [haɪ'pɜːtrəfɪ] *n* hipertrofía *f*.

hyphen ['haɪfən] *n* guión *m*.

hyphenate ['haɪfəneɪt] *vt* escribir (*or* unir, separar) con guión.

hypnosis [hɪp'nəʊsɪs] *n* hipnosis *f*.

hypnotherapy [,hɪpnəʊ'θerəpɪ] *n* hipnoterapia *f*.

hypnotic [hɪp'nɒtɪk] **1** *adj* hipnótico. **2** *n* hipnótico *m*.

hypnotism ['hɪpnətɪzəm] *n* hipnotismo *m*.

hypnotist ['hɪpnətɪst] *n* hipnotista *mf*.

hypnotize ['hɪpnətaɪz] *vt* hipnotizar.

hypo ['haɪpəʊ] *n* hiposulfito *m* sódico.

hypoallergenic [,haɪpəʊ,ælə'dʒenɪk] *adj* hipoalérgeno.

hypochondria [,haɪpəʊ'kɒndrɪə] *n* hipocondría *f*.

hypochondriac [,haɪpəʊ'kɒndrɪæk] **1** *adj* hipocondríaco. **2** *n* hipocondríaco *m*, -a *f*.

hypocrisy [hɪ'pɒkrɪsɪ] *n* hipocresía *f*.

hypocrite ['hɪpəkrɪt] *n* hipócrita *mf*.

hypocritical [,hɪpə'krɪtɪkəl] *adj* hipócrita.

hypocritically [,hɪpə'krɪtɪkəlɪ] *adv* hipócritamente.

hypodermic [,haɪpə'dɜːmɪk] *n* (*also* **~ needle**) aguja *f* hipodérmica.

hypotenuse [haɪ'pɒtɪnjuːz] *n* hipotenusa *f*.

hypothalamus [,haɪpə'θæləməs] *n*, *pl* **hypothalami** [,haɪpə'θæləmaɪ] hipotálamo *m*.

hypothermia [,haɪpəʊ'θɜːmɪə] *n* hipotermia *f*.

hypothesis [haɪ'pɒθɪsɪs] *n*, *pl* **hypotheses** [haɪ'pɒθɪsiːz] hipótesis *f*.

hypothesize [haɪ'pɒθɪsaɪz] *vi* hipotetizar.

hypothetic(al) [,haɪpəʊ'θetɪk(əl)] *adj* hipotético.

hypothetically [,haɪpəʊ'θetɪkəlɪ] *adv* hipotéticamente.

hysterectomy [,hɪstə'rektəmɪ] *n* histerectomía *f*.

hysteria [hɪs'tɪərɪə] *n* histerismo *m*, histeria *f*.

hysterical [hɪs'terɪkəl] *adj* histérico; **~ laughter** risa *f* histérica; **to get ~** ponerse histérico, excitarse locamente.

hysterically [hɪs'terɪkəlɪ] *adv* histéricamente; **to weep ~** llorar histéricamente; **to laugh ~** reír histéricamente; **'come here', she shouted ~** 'ven acá', gritó histérica.

hysterics [hɪs'terɪks] *npl* histerismo *m*, paroxismo *m* histérico; **to go into ~** ponerse histérico; **we were in ~ about it** casi nos morimos de risa.

Hz (*Rad etc*) *abbr of* **hertz** hertzio *m*, Hz.

I

I, i [aɪ] *n* (*letter*) I, i *f*; **I for Isaac, I for Item** (*US*) I de Inés, I de Isabel; **to dot the i's and cross the t's** poner los puntos sobre las íes.

I [aɪ] *pron* yo.

I. (*Geog*) *abbr of* **Island, Isle** isla *f*.

i. *abbr of* **interest** interés *m*.

IA (*US Post*) *abbr of* **Iowa**.

IAEA *n abbr of* **International Atomic Energy Agency** Organización *f* Internacional de Energía Atómica, OIEA *f*.

iambic [aɪ'æmbɪk] **1** *adj* yámbico; ~ **pentameter** pentámetro *m* yámbico. **2** *n* yambo *m*, verso *m* yámbico.

IATA [aɪ'ɑːtə] *n abbr of* **International Air Transport Association** Asociación *f* Internacional del Transporte Aéreo, IATA *f*, AITA *f*.

IBA *n* (*Brit*) *abbr of* **Independent Broadcasting Authority** *entidad que controla los medios privados de televisión y radio.*

Iberia [aɪ'bɪərɪə] *n* Iberia *f*.

Iberian [aɪ'bɪərɪən] **1** *adj* ibero, ibérico. **2** *n* ibero *m*, -a *f*.

Iberian Peninsula [aɪ'bɪərɪənpə'nɪnsjʊlə] *n* Península *f* Ibérica.

IBEW *n* (*US*) *abbr of* **International Brotherhood of Electrical Workers**.

ibex ['aɪbeks] *n* cabra *f* montés, íbice *m*.

ib(id) *adv abbr of* **ibidem** ibídem.

ibis ['aɪbɪs] *n* ibis *f*.

IBM *n abbr of* **International Business Machines**.

IBRD *n abbr of* **International Bank of Reconstruction and Development** Banco *m* Internacional para la Reconstrucción y el Desarrollo, BIRD *m*.

i/c. *abbr of* **in charge (of)** encargado (de).

ICA *n* (*Brit*) (**a**) *abbr of* **Institute of Contemporary Arts**. (**b**) *abbr of* **Institute of Chartered Accountants**.

ICAO *n abbr of* **International Civil Aviation Organization** Organización *f* de Aviación Civil Internacional, OACI *f*.

ICBM *n abbr of* **intercontinental ballistic missile** misil *m* balístico intercontinental.

ICC *n* (**a**) *abbr of* **International Chamber of Commerce** Cámara *f* de Comercio Internacional, CCI *f*. (**b**) (*US*) *abbr of* **Interstate Commerce Commission**.

ice [aɪs] **1** *n* (**a**) hielo *m*; **my feet are like** ~ tengo los pies helados; **to break the** ~ (*fig*) romper el hielo; **he cuts no** ~ ni pincha ni corta, no pinta nada; **it cuts no** ~ **with me** no me convence; **to keep sth on** ~ conservar algo en frigorífico, (*fig*) tener algo en reserva; **to put a plan on** ~ posponer un proyecto; **to skate on thin** ~ pisar terreno peligroso.

(**b**) (*Brit*: *ice cream*) helado *m*.

2 *vt* (**a**) helar; *drink* enfriar, echar cubos de hielo a.

(**b**) *cake* alcorzar, escarchar, garapiñar.

3 *vi* (*also* **to ~ over, to ~ up**) helarse.

ice-age ['aɪseɪdʒ] **1** *n* época *f* glacial. **2** *adj* de la época glacial.

ice-axe, (*US*) **ice-ax** ['aɪsæks] *n* piolet *m*, piqueta *f*.

iceberg ['aɪsbɜːg] *n* iceberg *m*; ~ **lettuce** lechuga *f* repollo.

ice-blue [,aɪs'bluː] *adj* azul claro, azul pálido.

icebound ['aɪsbaʊnd] *adj road* helado, bloqueado por el hielo; *ship* preso entre los hielos.

icebox ['aɪsbɒks] *n* (**a**) (*Brit*: *part of refrigerator*) congelador *m*; **this room is like an** ~ este cuarto es como un congelador.

(**b**) (*US*: *refrigerator*) nevera *f*, frigo *m*, refrigeradora *f* (*LAm*), heladera *f* (*SC*).

icebreaker ['aɪs,breɪkəʳ] *n* rompehielos *m*.

ice-bucket ['aɪs,bʌkɪt] *n* cubito *m* para hielo.

icecap ['aɪskæp] *n* casquete *m* de hielo.

ice-cold ['aɪs'kəʊld] *adj* más frío que el hielo; *drink* helado.

ice-cream ['aɪs'kriːm] *n* helado *m*.

ice-cube ['aɪskjuːb] *n* cubito *m* de hielo, cubeta *f* de hielo.

iced [aɪst] *adj cake* escarchado; *drink* con hielo.

ice dance ['aɪsdɑːns] *n* baile *m* sobre hielo.

icefield ['aɪsfiːld] *n* campo *m* de hielo, banquisa *f*.

icefloe ['aɪsfləʊ] *n* témpano *m* de hielo.

ice-hockey ['aɪs'hɒkɪ] *n* hockey *m* sobre hielo.

icehouse ['aɪshaʊs] *n*, *pl* **icehouses** ['aɪshaʊzɪz] (**a**) (*US*) nevera *f*. (**b**) (*of Eskimo*) iglú *m*.

Iceland ['aɪslənd] **1** *n* Islandia *f*. **2** *attr*: ~ **spar** espato *m* de Islandia.

Icelander ['aɪsləndəʳ] *n* islandés *m*, -esa *f*.

Icelandic [aɪs'lændɪk] **1** *adj* islandés. **2** *n* islandés *m*.

ice-lolly [,aɪs'lɒlɪ] *n* (*Brit*) polo *m*, paleta *f* (*LAm*).

iceman ['aɪsmæn] *n*, *pl* **icemen** ['aɪsmen] (*US*) vendedor *m* de hielo, repartidor *m* de hielo.

icepack ['aɪspæk] *n* compresa *f* de hielo.

ice-pick ['aɪspɪk] *n* piolet *m*, piqueta *f*.

ice-rink ['aɪsrɪŋk] *n* pista *f* de hielo, pista *f* de patinaje.

ice-skate ['aɪsskeɪt] **1** *n* patín *m* de hielo, patín *m* de cuchilla. **2** *vi* patinar sobre hielo.

ice-skating ['aɪsskeɪtɪŋ] *n* patinaje *m* sobre hielo.

ichthyology [,ɪkθɪ'ɒlədʒɪ] *n* ictiología *f*.

icicle ['aɪsɪkl] *n* carámbano *m*.

icily ['aɪsɪlɪ] *adv* glacialmente (*also fig*).

iciness ['aɪsɪnɪs] *n* (*fig*) lo glacial.

icing ['aɪsɪŋ] *n* formación *f* de hielo; (*on cake*) alcorza *f*, garapiña *f*; (*bonus*) prima *f* imprevista; **this is the ~ on the cake** (*fig*) ésta es la guinda que corona la tarta.

icing-sugar ['aɪsɪŋ'ʃʊgəʳ] *n* (*Brit*) azúcar *m* de alcorza, azúcar *m* glas, azúcar *m* flor (*SC*).

ICJ *n abbr of* **International Court of Justice** Corte *f* Internacional de Justicia, CJI *f*.

icky‡ ['ɪkɪ] *adj* (*US*) (*messy*) desordenado; (*fig*: *horrible*) asqueroso.

icon ['aɪkɒn] *n* icono *m*; (*Comput*) símbolo *m* gráfico.

iconoclasm [aɪ'kɒnə,klæzəm] *n* iconoclastia *f*.

iconoclast [aɪ'kɒnəklæst] *n* iconoclasta *mf*.

iconoclastic [aɪ,kɒnə'klæstɪk] *adj* iconoclasta.

iconographic [aɪ,kɒnə'græfɪk] *adj* iconográfico.

iconography [,aɪkɒ'nɒgrəfɪ] *n* iconografía *f*.

ICR *n* (*US*) *abbr of* **Institute for Cancer Research**.

ICU *n abbr of* **intensive care unit** unidad *f* de vigilancia intensiva, UVI *f*.

icy ['aɪsɪ] *adj* helado, glacial; (*fig*) glacial; **it's ~ cold** hace un frío glacial.

ID (**a**) (*US Post*) *abbr of* **Idaho**. (**b**) *n abbr of* **identification, identity**; *V* **identification, identity**.

id [ɪd] *n* id *m*.

I'd [aɪd] = **I would; I had.**

IDA *n abbr of* **International Development Association** Asociación *f* Internacional de Fomento, AIF *f*.

Ida. (*US*) *abbr of* **Idaho**.

ID card [,aɪ'diː,kɑːd] *n abbr of* **identity card** carnet *m* de identidad, C.I. *m*.

IDD *n abbr of* **international direct dialling** marcado *m* directo internacional.

idea [aɪ'dɪə] *n* idea *f*; concepto *m*; ocurrencia *f*; **good ~!** ¡buena idea!; **what an ~!, the very ~!** ¡ni hablar!, ¡qué cosas dices!; **the ~ is to sell it** nos proponemos venderlo; **whose ~ was it to come this way?** ¿a quién se le ocurrió venir por aquí?; **it would not be a bad ~ to paint it** no le vendría mal una mano de pintura; **that's the ~!** ¡eso es!; **what's the big ~?** ¿qué haces ahí?, ¿qué pretendes con esto?; ¿a santo de qué ...?; **you'll have to buck up your ~s** tendrás que menearte; **to get an ~ of sth** hacerse una idea de algo; **to get an ~ for a novel** encontrar la inspiración para hacer una novela; **you're getting the ~** (*plan etc*) estás empezando a comprender, (*knack*) estás cogiendo el tino; **to get an ~ into one's head** metérsele a uno una idea en la cabeza; **don't go getting ~s** no te hagas ilusiones; no se te ocurra pensar que ...; **where did you get that ~?** ¿de dónde sacas eso?; **he has some ~ of French** tiene algunas nociones de francés; **I've no ~!** ¡ni idea!; **I haven't the foggiest** (*or* **remotest** *etc*) ~ no tengo la más remota idea; **I had no ~ that ...** no tenía la menor idea de que ...; **it was awful, you've no ~** fue horrible, te lo aseguro; **he hit on the ~ of** +. *ger* se le ocurrió + *infin*; **to put ~s into sb's head** sugerir ideas a uno.

ideal [aɪ'dɪəl] **1** *adj* ideal; perfecto; soñado. **2** *n* ideal *m*.

idealism [aɪ'dɪəlɪzəm] *n* idealismo *m*.

idealist [aɪ'dɪəlɪst] *n* idealista *mf*.

idealistic [aɪˌdɪə'lɪstɪk] *adj* idealista.

idealize [aɪ'dɪəlaɪz] *vt* idealizar.

ideally [aɪ'dɪəlɪ] *adv* idealmente; perfectamente; **they are ~ suited to each other** hacen una pareja ideal, están hechos idealmente el uno para la otra; **~, we should all go** en el mejor de los casos, debemos ir todos.

idée fixe ['iːdeɪ'fiːks] *n* idea *f* fija.

identical [aɪ'dentɪkəl] *adj* idéntico; **~ twins** gemelos *mpl* idénticos, gemelas *fpl* idénticas.

identically [aɪ'dentɪkəlɪ] *adv* idénticamente.

identifiable [aɪˌdentɪ'faɪəbl] *adj* identificable.

identifier [aɪ'dentɪfaɪə^r] *n* identificador *m*.

identification [aɪˌdentɪfɪ'keɪʃən] **1** *n* identificación *f*. **2** *attr*: **~ mark** señal *f* de identificación; **~ papers** documentos *mpl* de identidad, papeles *mpl*; **~ parade** (*Brit*) = **identity parade**; **~ tag** (*US*) chapa *f* de identificación.

identify [aɪ'dentɪfaɪ] **1** *vt* identificar; acertar. **2** *vi*: **to ~ with** identificarse con. **3** *vr*: **to ~ o.s.** identificarse, establecer su identidad; **to ~ o.s. with** identificarse con.

identikit [aɪ'dentɪkɪt] *n*: **~ picture** retrato-robot *m*.

identity [aɪ'dentɪtɪ] **1** *n* identidad *f*; **to withhold sb's ~** silenciar el nombre de uno. **2** *attr*: **~ card** cédula *f* personal, carnet *m* de identidad; **~ crisis** crisis *f* de identidad; **~ disc** chapa *f* de identidad; **~ papers** documentación *f* personal, carnet *m* de identidad; **~ parade** (*Brit*) careo *m* de sospechosos, rueda *f* de reconocimiento.

ideogram ['ɪdɪəgræm] *n* ideograma *m*.

ideological [ˌaɪdɪə'lɒdʒɪkəl] *adj* ideológico.

ideologically [ˌaɪdɪə'lɒdʒɪkəlɪ] *adv* ideológicamente.

ideologist [ˌaɪdɪ'ɒlədʒɪst] *n* ideólogo *m*, -a *f*.

ideologue ['ɪdɪəlɒg] *n* ideólogo *m*, -a *f*.

ideology [ˌaɪdɪ'ɒlədʒɪ] *n* ideología *f*.

ides [aɪdz] *npl* idus *mpl*.

idiocy ['ɪdɪəsɪ] *n* imbecilidad *f*; estupidez *f*.

idiom ['ɪdɪəm] *n* (**a**) (*phrase*) idiotismo *m*, modismo *m*, locución *f*. (**b**) (*style of expression*) lenguaje *m*.

idiomatic [ˌɪdɪə'mætɪk] *adj* idiomático.

idiomatically [ˌɪdɪə'mætɪkəlɪ] *adv* idiomáticamente.

idiosyncrasy [ˌɪdɪə'sɪŋkrəsɪ] *n* idiosincrasia *f*.

idiosyncratic [ˌɪdɪəsɪŋˌkrætɪk] *adj* idiosincrásico.

idiot ['ɪdɪət] *n* idiota *mf*, imbécil *mf*, tonto *m*, -a *f*; **you ~!** ¡imbécil!; **~ board*** (*TV*) chuleta* *f*, autocue *m*.

idiotic [ˌɪdɪ'ɒtɪk] *adj* idiota, imbécil, tonto, estúpido; *laughter* tonto; **that was ~ of you** has hecho el tonto.

idiotically [ˌɪdɪ'ɒtɪkəlɪ] *adv* tontamente, estúpidamente; **to laugh ~** reírse como un tonto.

idle ['aɪdl] **1** *adj* (**a**) ocioso; (*lazy*) holgazán, flojo (*LAm*); (*work-shy*) vago; *student etc* gandul; (*without work*) desocupado; *moment* de ocio, libre; **the machine is never ~** la máquina no está parada jamás; **the strike made 100 workers ~** la huelga dejó sin trabajo a 100 obreros; **the machine stood ~ for hours** la máquina estaba parada durante horas enteras.

(**b**) (*Comm*) **~ capacity** capacidad *f* sin utilizar; **~ money** capital *m* improductivo; **~ time** tiempo *m* de paro.

(**c**) (*vain*) *fear* vano, infundado; ocioso, inútil; *question* ocioso; **~ chatter, ~ talk** charla *f* insustancial.

2 *vi* haraganear, gandulear; (*Mech*) marchar en vacío; **we spent a few days idling in Paris** pasamos unos días ociosos en París; **we ~d over our meal** no nos dimos prisa para terminar la comida.

◆**idle away** *vt time* perder, malgastar.

idleness ['aɪdlnɪs] *n* (*V adj*) (**a**) ociosidad *f*; holgazanería *f*; flojera *f* (*LAm*); gandulería *f*; desocupación *f*; **to live in ~** vivir en el ocio. (**b**) inutilidad *f*; frivolidad *f*.

idler ['aɪdlə^r] *n* ocioso *m*, -a *f*, holgazán *m*, -ana *f*, vago *m*, -a *f*; (*student etc*) gandul *m*.

idling ['aɪdlɪŋ] *adj*: **~ speed** velocidad *f* de marcha en vacío.

idly ['aɪdlɪ] *adv* ociosamente; vanamente, inútilmente; **he glanced ~ out of the window** miró distraído por la ventana.

idol ['aɪdl] *n* ídolo *m*.

idolater [aɪ'dɒlətə^r] *n* idólatra *mf*.

idolatrous [aɪ'dɒlətrəs] *adj* idólatra, idolátrico.

idolatry [aɪ'dɒlətrɪ] *n* idolatría *f*.

idolize ['aɪdəlaɪz] *vt* idolatrar.

IDP *n abbr of* **integrated data processing** proceso *m* integrado de datos, PID *m*.

idyll ['ɪdɪl] *n* idilio *m*.

idyllic [ɪ'dɪlɪk] *adj* idílico.

i.e. *abbr of* **id est, that is, namely** esto es, a saber.

if [ɪf] **1** *conj* (**a**) si; (*open condition*) **~ he comes I'll go** si él viene yo iré; (*past: habit*) **~ it was fine we went out** si hacía buen tiempo dábamos un paseo; (*past: unfulfilled*) **~ you were to say that you would be wrong** si dijeses eso te equivocarías; **~ you had said that you would have been wrong** si hubieras dicho eso te habrías equivocado; **~ I had known I would have told you** de haberlo sabido te lo habría dicho, si lo sé te lo digo*; **~ I were you** yo en tu lugar, yo que tú; **~ and when she comes** si (en efecto) viene, en el caso de que venga.

(**b**) (*although*) **I couldn't eat it ~ I tried** no lo podría comer ni que me lo propusiera; **a nice film ~ rather long** una buena película si bien es algo larga.

(**c**) (*whether*) si; **I don't know ~ he's here** no sé si está aquí.

(**d**) **~ anything this one is better** hasta creo que éste es mejor; éste es mejor si cabe; **~ not** si no; **~ so** si es así; **~ it isn't old Bludnok!** ¡qué sorpresa ver al amigo Bludnok!

(**e**) **~ only to see him** aunque sea sólo para verle; **~ only for a few hours** aunque sea sólo por unas pocas horas; **~ only I could!** ¡ojalá pudiera!, ¡si solamente pudiera!; **~ only I had known!** ¡si lo hubiese sabido!; **~ only we had a car!** ¡quién tuviera coche!; *V* **as, even** *etc*.

2 *n* hipótesis *f*; duda *f*; **there are a lot of ~s and buts** hay muchas dudas no resueltas; **it's a big ~** es una duda importante, es sumamente dudoso.

IFAD *n abbr of* **International Fund for Agricultural Development** Fondo *m* Internacional de Desarrollo Agrícola, FIDA *m*.

IFC *n abbr of* **International Finance Corporation**.

iffy* ['ɪfɪ] *adj* dudoso, incierto.

IFTO *n abbr of* **International Federation of Tour Operators** Federación *f* Internacional de Touroperadores.

IG *n* (*US*) *abbr of* **Inspector General**.

igloo ['ɪgluː] *n* iglú *m*.

Ignatius [ɪg'neɪʃəs] *nm* Ignacio, Íñigo.

igneous ['ɪgnɪəs] *adj* ígneo.

ignite [ɪg'naɪt] **1** *vt* encender, incendiar, pegar (*LAm*: prender) fuego a. **2** *vi* encenderse, incendiarse.

ignition [ɪg'nɪʃən] **1** *n* ignición *f*; (*Aut*) encendido *m*. **2** *attr*: (*Aut*) **~ coil** bobina *f* de encendido; **~ key** llave *f* de contacto; **~ switch** interruptor *m* de encendido.

ignoble [ɪg'nəʊbl] *adj* innoble, vil.

ignominious [ˌɪgnə'mɪnɪəs] *adj* ignominioso, oprobioso; *defeat* vergonzoso.

ignominiously [ˌɪgnə'mɪnɪəslɪ] *adv* ignominiosamente; **to be ~ defeated** sufrir una derrota vergonzosa.

ignominy ['ɪgnəmɪnɪ] *n* ignominia *f*, oprobio *m*, vergüenza *f*.

ignoramus [ˌɪgnə'reɪməs] *n* ignorante *mf*.

ignorance ['ɪgnərəns] *n* ignorancia *f*; **to be in ~ of sth** ignorar algo, desconocer algo.

ignorant ['ɪgnərənt] *adj* ignorante; **to be ~ of** ignorar, no saber, desconocer.

ignorantly ['ɪgnərəntlɪ] *adv* neciamente; **we ~ went to the next house** por ignorancia fuimos a la casa de al lado.

ignore [ɪg'nɔː^r] *vt* (**a**) no hacer caso de, desatender; (*omit*) hacer caso omiso de; pasar por alto; *awkward fact* cerrar los ojos ante; **we can safely ~ that** eso lo podemos dejar a un lado. (**b**) *person* no hacer el menor caso de; **I smiled but she ~d me** le sonreí pero ella hizo como si no me viera; **just ~ him** haz como si no existiera.

iguana [ɪ'gwɑːnə] *n* iguana *f*.

ikon ['aɪkɒn] *n* icono *m*.

IL (*US Post*) *abbr of* **Illinois**.

ILA *n* (*US*) *abbr of* **International Longshoremen's Association**.

ILEA ['ɪlɪə] (*formerly*) *n abbr of* **Inner London Education Authority**.

ilex ['aɪleks] *n* encina *f*.

ILGWU *n* (*US*) *abbr of* **International Ladies' Garment Workers Union**.

Iliad ['ɪlɪæd] *n* Ilíada *f*.

ilk [ɪlk] *n*: **and others of that ~** y otros de ese jaez.

Ill. (*US*) *abbr of* **Illinois**.

ill [ɪl] **1** *adj* (**a**) (*Med*) enfermo, malo; **to be ~** estar enfermo; **to fall** (*or* **take, be taken**) ~ ponerse enfermo, enfermar; **to feel** ~ sentirse mal; **it made me quite** ~ me hizo sentirme mal.

(**b**) *fame, temper, turn etc* malo; *V* **ease 1 (d).**

2 *adv* mal; **we can** ~ **afford to lose him** mal podemos permitir que se vaya; **to speak** ~ **of sb** hablar mal de uno, criticar a uno; **he took it very** ~ se ofendió bastante; **don't take it** ~ no lo tomes a mal.

3 *n* (*Med*) mal *m*; (*fig*) infortunio *m*, desgracia *f*; **the ~s of the economy** la dolencia de la economía.

I'll [aɪl] = **I will, I shall.**

ill-advised ['ɪləd'vaɪzd] *adj* inconsiderado, imprudente; **an** ~ **plan** un proyecto nada recomendable; **you were very** ~ en eso no anduvo muy acertado; **you would be** ~ **to** + *infin* sería poco aconsejable que + *subj*.

ill-assorted ['ɪlə'sɔːtɪd] *adj* mal avenido.

ill-at-ease ['ɪlət'iːz] *adj* molesto; inquieto, intranquilo.

ill-bred ['ɪl'bred] *adj* mal educado, mal criado.

ill-breeding [ˌɪl'briːdɪŋ] *n* mala educación *f*.

ill-considered ['ɪlkən'sɪdəd] *adj plan* nada recomendable; *act* irreflexivo.

ill-disposed ['ɪldɪs'pəʊzd] *adj* malintencionado; **to be** ~ **towards sb** estar maldispuesto hacia uno; **he is** ~ **towards the idea** la idea no le hace gracia.

ill-effects ['ɪlɪ'fekts] *npl* efectos *mpl* adversos.

illegal [ɪ'liːgəl] *adj* ilegal, ilícito.

illegality [ˌɪliː'gælɪtɪ] *n* ilegalidad *f*.

illegally [ɪ'liːgəlɪ] *adv* ilegalmente, ilícitamente.

illegible [ɪ'ledʒəbl] *adj* ilegible.

illegibly [ɪ'ledʒəblɪ] *adv* de un modo ilegible.

illegitimacy [ˌɪlɪ'dʒɪtɪməsɪ] *n* ilegitimidad *f*.

illegitimate [ˌɪlɪ'dʒɪtɪmɪt] *adj* ilegítimo.

illegitimately [ˌɪlɪ'dʒɪtɪmɪtlɪ] *adv* ilegítimamente.

ill-equipped ['ɪlɪ'kwɪpt] *adj expedition etc* defectuosamente equipado; **he was** ~ **for the task** no tenía talento para el cometido, no reunía las cualidades para la tarea.

ill-fated ['ɪl'feɪtɪd] *adj* malogrado, malhadado, funesto.

ill-favoured, (*US*) **ill-favored** ['ɪl'feɪvəd] *adj* feo, mal parecido.

ill-feeling ['ɪl'fiːlɪŋ] *n* hostilidad *f*, rencor *m*.

ill-formed [ˌɪl'fɔːmd] *adj* mal formado.

ill-founded ['ɪl'faʊndɪd] *adj claim etc* mal fundado, infundado.

ill-gotten ['ɪl'gɒtn] *adj* mal adquirido, malhabido.

ill health ['ɪl'helθ] *n* mala salud *f*; **to be in** ~ no estar bien de salud.

ill humour, (*US*) **ill humor** ['ɪl'hjuːmə^r] *n* mal humor *m*.

ill-humoured, (*US*) **ill-humored** ['ɪl'hjuːməd] *adj* malhumorado.

illiberal [ɪ'lɪbərəl] *adj* iliberal; intolerante.

illicit [ɪ'lɪsɪt] *adj* ilícito.

illicitly [ɪ'lɪsɪtlɪ] *adv* ilícitamente.

illimitable [ɪ'lɪmɪtəbl] *adj* ilimitado, sin límites.

ill-informed ['ɪlɪn'fɔːmd] *adj* mal informado, poco enterado, ignorante.

illiquid [ɪ'lɪkwɪd] *adj*: ~ **assets** activos *mpl* no realizables (a corto plazo).

illiteracy [ɪ'lɪtərəsɪ] *n* analfabetismo *m*.

illiterate [ɪ'lɪtərɪt] **1** *adj* analfabeto; (*fig*) sin instrucción, poco instruido; iletrado; *style etc* inculto. **2** *n* analfabeto *m*, -a *f*.

ill-judged ['ɪl'dʒʌdʒd] *adj* imprudente.

ill-kempt ['ɪl'kempt] *adj* desaliñado, desaseado.

ill luck ['ɪl'lʌk] *n* mala suerte *f*; **as** ~ **would have it** desgraciadamente, como quiso la suerte.

ill-mannered ['ɪl'mænəd] *adj* mal educado, sin educación.

ill-natured ['ɪl'neɪtʃəd] *adj* malévolo, malicioso.

illness ['ɪlnɪs] *n* enfermedad *f*, mal *m*, dolencia *f*; indisposición *f*.

ill-nourished [ˌɪl'nʌrɪʃt] *adj* malnutrido.

illogic [ɪ'lɒdʒɪk] *n* falta *f* de lógica.

illogical [ɪ'lɒdʒɪkəl] *adj* falto de lógica, ilógico.

illogicality [ɪˌlɒdʒɪ'kælɪtɪ] *n* falta *f* de lógica, contrasentido.

illogically [ɪ'lɒdʒɪkəlɪ] *adv* ilógicamente.

ill-omened ['ɪl'əʊmənd] *adj* de mal agüero; nefasto.

ill-prepared [ˌɪlprɪ'pɛəd] *adj* mal preparado.

ill-starred ['ɪl'stɑːd] *adj* malhadado, malogrado.

ill-suited ['ɪl'suːtɪd] *adj* impropio; mal avenido; **they are** ~ no se convienen uno a otro; **he is** ~ **to the job** no conviene al puesto.

ill-tempered ['ɪl'tempəd] *adj person* de mal genio; *remark, tone etc* malhumorado.

ill-timed ['ɪl'taɪmd] *adj* inoportuno, intempestivo.

ill-treat ['ɪl'triːt] *vt* maltratar, tratar mal.

ill-treatment ['ɪl'triːtmənt] *n* maltratamiento *m*, maltrato *m*, malos tratos *mpl*.

illuminate [ɪ'luːmɪneɪt] *vt* iluminar (*also Art*); (*decorate with lights*) poner luminarias en; *subject* aclarar; **the castle is ~d in summer** en el verano el castillo está iluminado.

illuminated [ɪ'luːmɪneɪtɪd] *adj sign etc* luminoso; *manuscript* iluminado.

illuminating [ɪ'luːmɪneɪtɪŋ] *adj* aclaratorio; *book, speech etc* instructivo; *remark etc* revelador, significativo.

illumination [ɪˌluːmɪ'neɪʃən] *n* iluminación *f* (*also Art*), alumbrado *m*; (*Brit: for special effect*) iluminación *f*; **~s** (*festive etc*) luminarias *fpl*, luces *fpl*.

illuminator [ɪ'luːmɪneɪtə^r] *n* iluminador *m*, -ora *f*.

illumine [ɪ'luːmɪn] *vt* = **illuminate.**

ill-use ['ɪl'juːz] *vt* maltratar, tratar mal.

illusion [ɪ'luːʒən] *n* apariencia *f*; espejismo *m*; imaginaciones *fpl*; (*optical* ~) ilusión *f* de óptica; **to be under an** ~ estar equivocado; **I am under no ~s on that score** sobre ese punto no tengo ilusiones; **he cherishes the** ~ **that ...** abriga la esperanza de que + *subj*; **it gives an** ~ **of space** crea una impresión de espacio.

illusionist [ɪ'luːʒənɪst] *n* prestidigitador *m*, -ora *f*, ilusionista *mf*.

illusive [ɪ'luːsɪv] *adj*, **illusory** [ɪ'luːsərɪ] *adj* ilusorio.

illustrate ['ɪləstreɪt] *vt* (**a**) (*exemplify*) ilustrar; *subject* aclarar; *point* ejemplificar, demostrar; **I can best ~ this in the following way** esto quedará más claro si se explica del modo siguiente. (**b**) *book* ilustrar; **a book ~d by X** un libro con grabados (*etc*) de X.

illustrated ['ɪləstreɪtɪd] *adj*: ~ **paper** revista *f* gráfica.

illustration [ˌɪləs'treɪʃən] *n* (*example*) ejemplo *m*; (*explanation*) explicación *f*, aclaración *f*; (*in book*) grabado *m*, lámina *f*, ilustración *f*; **by way of** ~ como ejemplo, a modo de ejemplo.

illustrative ['ɪləstrətɪv] *adj* ilustrativo, ilustrador, aclaratorio; **to be** ~ **of sth** ejemplificar algo.

illustrator ['ɪləstreɪtə^r] *n* ilustrador *m*, -ora *f*.

illustrious [ɪ'lʌstrɪəs] *adj* ilustre.

illustriously [ɪ'lʌstrɪəslɪ] *adv* ilustremente.

ill-will ['ɪl'wɪl] *n* mala voluntad *f*; (*spite*) rencor *m*, encono *m*; **I bear you no** ~ **for that** no le guardo rencor por eso.

ILO *n abbr of* **International Labour Organization** Organización *f* Internacional del Trabajo, OIT *f*.

ILT *n abbr of* **Instrument Landing System.**

ILWU *n* (*US*) *abbr of* **International Longshoremen's and Warehousemen's Union.**

I'm [aɪm] = **I am.**

image ['ɪmɪdʒ] *n* (**a**) imagen *f* (*also Liter, Eccl*); ~ **processing** proceso *m* de imágenes; **to be the very** (*or* **spitting**) ~ **of** ser el vivo retrato (*or* la viva imagen) de; **to make sb in one's own** ~ hacer a uno a su imagen.

(**b**) (*public face*) imagen *f*; reputación *f*, opinión *f*; **the company's** ~ la reputación de la compañía; **we must improve our** ~ tenemos que mejorar nuestra imagen.

imagery ['ɪmɪdʒərɪ] *n* (*Liter*) imágenes *fpl*, metáforas *fpl*.

imaginable [ɪ'mædʒɪnəbl] *adj* imaginable; **the biggest surprise** ~ la mayor sorpresa que se puede imaginar.

imaginary [ɪ'mædʒɪnərɪ] *adj* imaginario.

imagination [ɪˌmædʒɪ'neɪʃən] *n* imaginación *f*; (*capacity for* ~) imaginativa *f*; (*inventiveness*) inventiva *f*; **it's all ~!** ¡es pura fantasía!, ¡lo has soñado!; **she lets her** ~ **run away with her** se deja llevar por la imaginación.

imaginative [ɪ'mædʒɪnətɪv] *adj* imaginativo.

imaginatively [ɪ'mædʒɪnətɪvlɪ] *adv* imaginativamente.

imaginativeness [ɪ'mædʒɪnətɪvnɪs] *n* imaginativa *f*.

imagine [ɪ'mædʒɪn] *vt* imaginar, imaginarse, figurarse; (**just**) **~!** ¡imagínate!, ¡fíjate!; **you can** ~ **how I felt!** ¡puedes suponer lo que yo sufría!; **don't** ~ **that ...** no te vayas a pensar que yo + *subj*; **to fondly** ~ **that ...** hacerse la ilusión de que ..., creer inocentemente que ...

imam [ɪ'mɑːm] *n* imán *m*.

imbalance [ɪm'bæləns] *n* desequilibrio *m*, falta *f* de equilibrio.

imbecile ['ɪmbəsiːl] **1** *adj* imbécil. **2** *n* imbécil *mf*; **you ~!** ¡imbécil!

imbecility [ˌɪmbɪ'sɪlɪtɪ] *n* imbecilidad *f*.

imbibe [ɪm'baɪb] **1** *vt* (*drink*) beber; (*absorb*) embeber; (*fig*) embeberse de (*or* en), empaparse de. **2** *vi* beber.

imbroglio [ɪm'brəʊlɪəʊ] *n* embrollo *m*, lío *m*.

imbue [ɪm'bjuː] *vt*: **to** ~ **sth with** imbuir algo de (*or* en), empapar algo de; **to be ~d with** estar empapado de.

IMF *n abbr of* **International Monetary Fund** Fondo *m* Monetario Internacional, FMI *m*.

imitable ['ɪmɪtəbl] *adj* imitable.

imitate [ˈɪmɪteɪt] *vt* imitar; (*pej*) remedar; (*make another copy of*) copiar, reproducir.

imitation [ˌɪmɪˈteɪʃən] **1** *n* imitación *f*; (*pej*) remedo *m*; **in ~ of** a imitación de; **beware of ~s** desconfíe de las imitaciones.
2 *attr*: **~ gold** oro *m* de imitación; **~ jewels, ~ jewellery** bisutería *f*, joyas *fpl* de imitación; **~ leather** imitación *f* a piel; **~ marble** mármol *m* artificial.

imitative [ˈɪmɪtətɪv] *adj* imitativo; imitador; **a style ~ of Joyce's** un estilo que imita el de Joyce.

imitator [ˈɪmɪteɪtəʳ] *n* imitador *m*, -ora *f*.

immaculate [ɪmækjʊlɪt] *adj* (*spotless*) limpísimo, perfectamente limpio, inmaculado; *style etc* perfecto; (*Eccl*) inmaculado, purísimo; **I~ Conception** Inmaculada Concepción *f*.

immaculately [ɪˈmækjʊlɪtlɪ] *adv* (*clean*) perfectamente; (*behave*) impecablemente, perfectamente, intachablemente; (*dressed*) impecablemente.

immanent [ˈɪmənənt] *adj* inmanente.

Immanuel [ɪˈmænjʊəl] *nm* Emanuel.

immaterial [ˌɪməˈtɪərɪəl] *adj* inmaterial, incorpóreo; **it is ~ whether ...** no importa si ...; **that is quite ~** eso no hace al caso; **that is ~ to me** eso me es indiferente.

immature [ˌɪməˈtjʊəʳ] *adj* inmaturo, no maduro; *specimen* joven; *fruit* verde; *work* juvenil.

immaturity [ˌɪməˈtjʊərɪtɪ] *n* inmadurez *f*, falta *f* de madurez; juventud *f*.

immeasurable [ɪˈmeʒərəbl] *adj* inmensurable, inconmensurable.

immeasurably [ɪˈmeʒərəblɪ] *adv* enormemente.

immediacy [ɪˈmiːdɪəsɪ] *n* inmediatez *f*; urgencia *f*.

immediate [ɪˈmiːdɪət] *adj* inmediato; (*pressing*) urgente, apremiante; *danger* inminente; (*prime*) primero, principal; **~ access** (*Comput*) entrada *f* inmediata; **the ~ area** las inmediaciones; **for ~ delivery** para entrega inmediata; **my ~ object** mi primer propósito; **we must take ~ action** hay que obrar inmediatamente.

immediately [ɪˈmiːdɪətlɪ] **1** *adv* **(a)** (*of time*) inmediatamente, enseguida, en seguida; sin demora; en el acto; **~ following the dinner** inmediatamente después de la cena; **~ following this discussion** a raíz de esta discusión.
(b) (*of place*) **~ next to the wall** muy junto a la pared.
2 *conj* (*Brit*) así que, luego que, al instante que; **let me know ~ he comes** avíseme en cuanto venga.

immemorial [ˌɪmɪˈmɔːrɪəl] *adj* inmemorial, inmemorable; **from time ~** desde tiempo inmemorial.

immense [ɪˈmens] *adj* inmenso, enorme.

immensely [ɪˈmenslɪ] *adv* enormemente; **we were ~ cheered** nos alegramos enormemente; **did you enjoy yourselves? yes, ~** ¿qué tal lo pasasteis? estupendamente; **it is ~ difficult** es enormemente difícil.

immensity [ɪˈmensɪtɪ] *n* inmensidad *f*.

immerse [ɪˈmɜːs] **1** *vt* sumergir, sumir, hundir; **to be ~d in** (*fig*) estar absorto en. **2** *vr*: **to ~ o.s. in** (*fig*) sumergirse en.

immersion [ɪˈmɜːʃən] **1** *n* inmersión *f*, sumersión *f*. **2** *attr*: **~ course** curso *m* de inmersión; **~ heater** (*Brit*) calentador *m* de inmersión.

immigrant [ˈɪmɪgrənt] **1** *adj* inmigrante; **~ community** comunidad *f* de inmigrantes; **~ worker** trabajador *m*, -ora *f* inmigrante. **2** *n* inmigrante *mf*.

immigrate [ˈɪmɪgreɪt] *vi* inmigrar.

immigration [ˌɪmɪˈgreɪʃən] *n* inmigración *f*; **~ authorities** autoridades *fpl* de inmigración; **~ control** control *m* de inmigración; **I~ (Department)** (Departamento *m* de) Inmigración *f*; **~ quota** cuota *f* de inmigración.

imminence [ˈɪmɪnəns] *n* inminencia *f*.

imminent [ˈɪmɪnənt] *adj* inminente.

immobile [ɪˈməʊbaɪl] *adj* inmóvil, inmoble.

immobility [ˌɪməʊˈbɪlɪtɪ] *n* inmovilidad *f*.

immobilize [ɪˈməʊbɪlaɪz] *vt* inmovilizar.

immoderate [ɪˈmɒdərɪt] *adj* excesivo, inmoderado.

immoderately [ɪˈmɒdərɪtlɪ] *adv* excesivamente; **to drink ~** beber en exceso.

immodest [ɪˈmɒdɪst] *adj* (*indecent*) deshonesto, impúdico; (*impudent*) descarado.

immodestly [ɪˈmɒdɪstlɪ] *adv* impúdicamente; descaradamente.

immodesty [ɪˈmɒdɪstɪ] *n* deshonestidad *f*, impudicia *f*; descaro *m*.

immolate [ˈɪməʊleɪt] *vt* inmolar.

immoral [ɪˈmɒrəl] *adj* inmoral; *earnings* ilícito.

immorality [ˌɪməˈrælɪtɪ] *n* inmoralidad *f*.

immortal [ɪˈmɔːtl] **1** *adj* inmortal; *fame etc* imperecedero. **2** *n* inmortal *mf*.

immortality [ˌɪmɔːˈtælɪtɪ] *n* inmortalidad *f*.

immortalize [ɪˈmɔːtəlaɪz] *vt* inmortalizar.

immovable [ɪˈmuːvəbl] **1** *adj* inmoble, inmóvil; que no se puede mover; *feast etc* fijo; (*fig*) inalterable, inconmovible; **he was quite ~** estuvo inflexible. **2 ~s** *npl* inmuebles *mpl*.

immune [ɪˈmjuːn] *adj* inmune (*also Med*; *from, to* a, contra); **~ system** sistema *m* inmunológico; **to be ~ from taxes** estar exento de impuestos.

immunity [ɪˈmjuːnɪtɪ] *n* inmunidad *f* (*also Med*; *from, to* contra); exención *f* (*from* de); **diplomatic ~** inmunidad *f* diplomática.

immunization [ˌɪmjʊnaɪˈzeɪʃən] *n* inmunización *f*.

immunize [ˈɪmjʊnaɪz] *vt* inmunizar.

immunodeficiency [ɪˌmjuːnəʊdɪˈfɪʃənsɪ] *n* inmunodeficiencia *f*.

immunological [ɪˌmjuːnəˈlɒdʒɪkəl] *adj* inmunológico; **~ defences** defensas *fpl* inmunológicas.

immunologist [ɪmjʊˈnɒlədʒɪst] *n* inmunólogo *m*, -a *f*.

immunology [ˌɪmjʊˈnɒlədʒɪ] *n* inmunología *f*.

immunosuppressant [ɪˈmjuːnəʊsəˈpresənt] **1** *adj* inmunosupresivo. **2** *n* inmunosupresivo *m*, inmunosupresor *m*.

immunosuppressive [ɪˈmjʊːnəʊsəˈpresɪv] *adj* inmunosupresivo, inmunosupresor.

immunotherapy [ˌɪmjʊnəʊˈθerəpɪ] *n* inmunoterapia *f*.

immure [ɪˈmjʊəʳ] *vt* emparedar; (*fig*) encerrar; **to be ~d in** estar encerrado en.

immutability [ɪˌmjuːtəˈbɪlɪtɪ] *n* inmutabilidad *f*, inalterabilidad *f*.

immutable [ɪˈmjuːtəbl] *adj* inmutable, inalterable.

immutably [ɪˈmjuːtəblɪ] *adv* inmutablemente; inalterablemente.

imp [ɪmp] *n* diablillo *m*; (*fig*) diablillo *m*, pícaro *m*, pillín *m*.

imp. *abbr of* **imperial**.

impact [ˈɪmpækt] **1** *n* impacto *m*, choque *m*; (*fig*) impacto *m*, efecto *m*, consecuencias *fpl*; **the book had a great ~ on its readers** el libro conmovió profundamente a sus lectores; **the speech made no ~** el discurso no hizo mella.
2 *attr*: **~ printer** impresora *f* de impacto. **3** [ɪmˈpækt] *vt* (*US*) impactar, afectar (a), tener un efecto en (*or* sobre).

impacted [ɪmˈpæktɪd] *adj tooth* impactado; **~ area** (*US*) zona *f* superpoblada.

impair [ɪmˈpɛəʳ] *vt* perjudicar, dañar, deteriorar, debilitar.

impaired [ɪmˈpɛəd] *adj* dañado, deteriorado; **~ capital** capital *m* disminuido.

impala [ɪmˈpɑːlə] *n* impala *m*.

impale [ɪmˈpeɪl] **1** *vt* (*as punishment*) empalar; (*on sword etc*) espetar, atravesar. **2** *vr*: **to ~ o.s. on** atravesarse en.

impalpable [ɪmˈpælpəbl] *adj* impalpable; (*fig*) intangible, inaprensible.

imparity [ɪmˈpærɪtɪ] *n* disparidad *f*.

impart [ɪmˈpɑːt] *vt* comunicar, impartir, hacer saber.

impartial [ɪmˈpɑːʃəl] *adj* imparcial.

impartiality [ɪmˌpɑːʃɪˈælɪtɪ] *n* imparcialidad *f*.

impartially [ɪmˈpɑːʃəlɪ] *adv* imparcialmente.

impassable [ɪmˈpɑːsəbl] *adj* intransitable; *river etc* invadeable; *barrier* infranqueable.

impasse [æmˈpɑːs] *n* callejón *m* sin salida; cerrazón *f*; parálisis *f*, situación *f* sin solución; **the ~ lasted 3 months** la parálisis duró 3 meses; **the ~ is complete** la parálisis es total; **negotiations have reached an ~** las negociaciones han llegado a un punto muerto, las negociaciones están en un callejón sin salida.

impassioned [ɪmˈpæʃnd] *adj* apasionado, exaltado.

impassive [ɪmˈpæsɪv] *adj* impasible, imperturbable.

impassively [ɪmˈpæsɪvlɪ] *adv* imperturbablemente; **he listened ~** escuchó impasible.

impatience [ɪmˈpeɪʃəns] *n* impaciencia *f*.

impatiens [ɪmˈpeɪʃɪˌenz] *n* impatiens *f*.

impatient [ɪmˈpeɪʃənt] *adj* impaciente; intolerante; **to be ~ to** + *infin* impacientarse por + *infin*; **to be ~ of sth** no sufrir algo con paciencia, no aguantar algo; **to get** (*or* **become, grow**) **~ about sth** impacientarse ante algo, impacientarse por algo; **to get ~ with sb** perder la paciencia con uno; **to make sb ~** impacientar a uno.

impatiently [ɪmˈpeɪʃəntlɪ] *adv* con impaciencia, impacientemente.

impeach [ɪmˈpiːtʃ] *vt* **(a)** (*accuse*) acusar (*esp* de alta traición); (*try*) procesar; (*US*) someter a un proceso de incapacitación (presidencial). **(b)** (*criticize*) censurar; tachar.

impeachable [ɪmˈpiːtʃəbl] *adj* sujeto a acusación (de alta traición); (*US*) sujeto a proceso de incapacitación (presidencial).

impeachment [ɪm'piːtʃmənt] *n* denuncia *f*, acusación *f* (*esp* de alta traición); proceso *m*; (*US*) proceso *m* de incapacitación (presidencial).

impeccable [ɪm'pekəbl] *adj* impecable, intachable.

impeccably [ɪm'pekəblɪ] *adv clean* impecablemente; *behave* impecablemente; intachablemente; *dress* impecablemente.

impecunious [,ɪmpɪ'kjuːnɪəs] *adj* inope, indigente, falto de dinero.

impede [ɪm'piːd] *vt person* estorbar; (*fig*) dificultar, estorbar, impedir.

impediment [ɪm'pedɪmənt] *n* obstáculo *m*, estorbo *m* (*to* para); (*Jur*) impedimento *m*; (*in speech*) defecto *m* del habla, impedimento *m*.

impedimenta [ɪm,pedɪ'mentə] *npl* equipaje *m*; (*Mil*) impedimenta *f*.

impel [ɪm'pel] *vt* impulsar, mover (*to* + *infin* a + *infin*); **I feel ~led to say** ... me veo obligado a decir ...

impend [ɪm'pend] *vi* amenazar, ser inminente, cernerse.

impending [ɪm'pendɪŋ] *adj* inminente; (*near*) próximo; **his ~ fate** el hado que le amenaza; **his ~ retirement** su jubilación que va a realizarse en breve; **our ~ removal** nuestra mudanza en fecha próxima.

impenetrability [ɪm,penɪtrə'bɪlɪtɪ] *n* impenetrabilidad *f*.

impenetrable [ɪm'penɪtrəbl] *adj* impenetrable (*to* a); *mind etc* insondable, enigmático.

impenitence [ɪm'penɪtəns] *n* impenitencia *f*.

impenitent [ɪm'penɪtənt] *adj* impenitente.

impenitently [ɪm'penɪtəntlɪ] *adv* impenitentemente, incorregiblemente.

imperative [ɪm'perətɪv] **1** *adj* (**a**) *tone* imperioso, perentorio; (*necessary*) esencial, indispensable; (*pressing*) urgente, apremiante; **it is ~ that** ... es imprescindible que + *subj*.

(**b**) (*Gram*) imperativo; **~ mood** modo *m* imperativo.

2 *n* imperativo *m* (*also Gram*).

imperatively [ɪm'perətɪvlɪ] *adv* (*speak*) imperiosamente; perentoriamente.

imperceptible [,ɪmpə'septəbl] *adj* imperceptible, insensible.

imperceptibly [,ɪmpə'septəblɪ] *adv* imperceptiblemente, insensiblemente.

imperfect [ɪm'pɜːfɪkt] **1** *adj* imperfecto (*also Gram*), defectuoso; **~ competition** competición *f* imperfecta. **2** *n* imperfecto *m*.

imperfection [,ɪmpə'fekʃən] *n* (*state*) imperfección *f*; (*blemish*) desperfecto *m*, tacha *f*.

imperfectly [ɪm'pɜːfɪktlɪ] *adv* defectuosamente.

imperial [ɪm'pɪərɪəl] *adj* imperial; **~ gallon** (*Brit*) galón *m* inglés.

imperialism [ɪm'pɪərɪəlɪzəm] *n* imperialismo *m*.

imperialist [ɪm'pɪərɪəlɪst] *n* imperialista *mf*.

imperialistic [ɪm,pɪərɪə'lɪstɪk] *adj* imperialista.

imperil [ɪm'perɪl] *vt* poner en peligro, arriesgar.

imperious [ɪm'pɪərɪəs] *adj* imperioso, arrogante; *need* apremiante.

imperiously [ɪm'pɪərɪəslɪ] *adv* imperiosamente.

imperishable [ɪm'perɪʃəbl] *adj* imperecedero.

impermanent [ɪm'pɜːmənənt] *adj* impermanente.

impermeable [ɪm'pɜːmɪəbl] *adj* impermeable (*to* a).

impersonal [ɪm'pɜːsnl] *adj* impersonal.

impersonality [ɪm,pɜːsə'nælɪtɪ] *n* impersonalidad *f*.

impersonally [ɪm'pɜːsnəlɪ] *adv* impersonalmente.

impersonate [ɪm'pɜːsəneɪt] *vt* hacerse pasar por; (*Theat*) imitar, personificar.

impersonation [ɪm,pɜːsə'neɪʃən] *n* (*Theat*) imitación *f*.

impersonator [ɪm'pɜːsəneɪtə^r] *n* (*Theat*) imitador *m*, -ora *f*.

impertinence [ɪm'pɜːtɪnəns] *n* impertinencia *f*, insolencia *f*, descaro *m*; **an ~, a piece of ~** una impertinencia; **it would be an ~ to** + *infin* sería improcedente + *infin*; **what ~!, the ~ of it!** ¡qué frescura!

impertinent [ɪm'pɜːtɪnənt] *adj* impertinente, insolente, descarado; **to be ~ to sb** decir impertinencias a uno; **don't be ~!** ¡no seas fresco!

impertinently [ɪm'pɜːtɪnəntlɪ] *adv* impertinentemente, descaradamente.

imperturbable [,ɪmpə'tɜːbəbl] *adj* imperturbable.

impervious [ɪm'pɜːvɪəs] *adj* impermeable, impenetrable (*to* a); (*fig*) insensible (*to* a).

impetigo [,ɪmpɪ'taɪgəʊ] *n* impétigo *m*.

impetuosity [ɪm,petjʊ'ɒsɪtɪ] *n* impetuosidad *f*, irreflexión *f*.

impetuous [ɪm'petjʊəs] *adj* impetuoso, irreflexivo.

impetuously [ɪm'petjʊəslɪ] *adv* impetuosamente, irreflexivamente.

impetus ['ɪmpɪtəs] *n* ímpetu *m*; (*fig*) impulso *m*, incentivo *m*; **to give an ~ to sales** impulsar las ventas, incentivar las ventas.

impiety [ɪm'paɪətɪ] *n* impiedad *f*.

impinge [ɪm'pɪndʒ] *vi*: **to ~ on** afectar a.

impingement [ɪm'pɪndʒmənt] *n* intrusión *f*, usurpación *f*.

impious ['ɪmpɪəs] *adj* impío.

impiously ['ɪmpɪəslɪ] *adv* impíamente.

impish ['ɪmpɪʃ] *adj* travieso, endiablado.

implacable [ɪm'plækəbl] *adj* implacable.

implacably [ɪm'plækəblɪ] *adv* implacablemente.

implant 1 ['ɪmplɑːnt] *n* implante *m*. **2** [ɪm'plɑːnt] *vt* implantar.

implausible [ɪm'plɔːzəbl] *adj* inverosímil; poco convincente.

implausibly [ɪm'plɔːzəblɪ] *adv* inverosímilmente, poco convincentemente.

implement 1 ['ɪmplɪmənt] *n* herramienta *f*, instrumento *m*; (*Agr*) apero *m*; **~s** aperos *mpl*, implementos *mpl*.

2 ['ɪmplɪment] *vt* poner por obra, llevar a cabo, hacer efectivo; realizar, ejecutar.

implementation [,ɪmplɪmen'teɪʃən] *n* realización *f*, ejecución *f*.

implicate ['ɪmplɪkeɪt] *vt* comprometer; implicar, involucrar; enredar; **he ~d 3 others** acusó a 3 más (de haber tomado parte en el delito); delató a 3 cómplices suyos; **with 2 others ~d in the crime** con otros 2 implicados en el delito; **are you ~d in this?** ¿andas metido en esto?

implication [,ɪmplɪ'keɪʃən] *n* (**a**) (*act*) comprometimiento *m*.

(**b**) (*in crime*) complicidad *f*, implicación *f*.

(**c**) (*consequence etc*) consecuencia *f*, inferencia *f*; implicación *f*; **~s** consecuencias *fpl*, trascendencia *f*; **by ~, then** ... de ahí se deduce, pues, ...; **he did not realize the full ~s of his words** no se dio cuenta de la trascendencia de sus palabras; **we shall have to study all the ~s** tendremos que estudiar todas las consecuencias.

implicit [ɪm'plɪsɪt] *adj* implícito; *faith etc* incondicional, absoluto.

implicitly [ɪm'plɪsɪtlɪ] *adv* implícitamente; sin reservas, incondicionalmente.

implied [ɪm'plaɪd] *adj* implícito, tácito; **~ contract** contrato *m* tácito; **~ warranty** garantía *f* implícita; **it is not stated but it is ~** no se declara abiertamente pero se sobreentiende.

implode [ɪm'pləʊd] **1** *vt* (**a**) implosionar. (**b**) (*Phon*) pronunciar implosivamente. **2** *vi* implosionar.

implore [ɪm'plɔː^r] *vt thing* implorar, suplicar; *person* suplicar; **I ~ you!** ¡se lo suplico!; **to ~ sb to do sth** suplicar a uno hacer algo.

imploring [ɪm'plɔːrɪŋ] *adj* suplicante; *look etc* lleno de suplicación.

imploringly [ɪm'plɔːrɪŋlɪ] *adv* de modo suplicante.

implosion [ɪm'pləʊʒən] *n* implosión *f* (*also Phon*).

imply [ɪm'plaɪ] *vt* (*involve*) implicar, suponer, presuponer; (*mean*) querer decir, significar; (*state indirectly*) dar a entender; (*hint*) insinuar; **that implies some intelligence** eso supone cierta inteligencia; **are you ~ing that ...?** ¿quieres decir que ...?; **what do you ~ by that?** ¿qué quieres insinuar con eso?; **he implied he would do it** dio a entender que lo haría; **it implies a lot of work for him** supone mucho trabajo para él, representa mucho trabajo para él.

impolite [,ɪmpə'laɪt] *adj* descortés, mal educado.

impolitely [,ɪmpə'laɪtlɪ] *adv* con descortesía.

impoliteness [,ɪmpə'laɪtnɪs] *n* mala educación *f*, descortesía *f*.

impolitic [ɪm'pɒlɪtɪk] *adj* impolítico.

imponderable [ɪm'pɒndərəbl] **1** *adj* imponderable. **2 ~s** *npl* (elementos *mpl*) imponderables *mpl*.

import 1 ['ɪmpɔːt] *n* (**a**) (*Comm*) importación *f*, artículo *m* importado.

(**b**) (*meaning*) significado *m*, sentido *m*; importancia *f*; **of general ~** de significado general.

2 ['ɪmpɔːt] *attr*: **~ duty** derechos *mpl* de entrada; **~ levy** impuesto *m* sobre importaciones; **~ licence, ~ license** (*US*), **~ permit** permiso *m* de importación; **~ quota** cupo *m* de importación; **~ surcharge** sobrecarga *f* de importación; **~ trade** comercio *m* importador.

3 [ɪm'pɔːt] *vt* (**a**) (*Comm*) importar (*from* de, *into* en).

(**b**) (*mean*) significar, querer decir.

importance [ɪm'pɔːtəns] *n* importancia *f*; **of some ~** de cierta importancia, importante; **a fact of the first ~** un hecho primordial; **to attach great ~ to sth** conceder mucha importancia a algo; **to be of ~** tener importancia; **that's of no ~** eso no importa; **to be full of one's own ~** darse ínfulas.

important [ɪm'pɔːtənt] *adj* importante; de categoría; *news etc* destacado, trascendente; *personage* destacado; **it's not** ~ no importa, no tiene importancia; **to become** ~ cobrar importancia; **to try to look** ~ tratar de hacer figura.
importantly [ɪm'pɔːtəntlɪ] *adv say etc* en tono rimbombante.
importation [,ɪmpɔː'teɪʃən] *n* importación *f.*
imported [ɪm'pɔːtɪd] *adj article* de importación.
importer [ɪm'pɔːtəʳ] *n* importador *m,* -ora *f.*
import-export trade [,ɪmpɔːt'ekspɔːt,treɪd] *n* comercio *m* de importación y exportación.
importing [ɪm'pɔːtɪŋ] *adj*: ~ **company** empresa *f* importadora, empresa *f* de importación; ~ **country** país *m* importador.
importunate [ɪm'pɔːtjʊnɪt] *adj demand etc* importuno; *person* molesto, pesado.
importune [,ɪmpɔː'tjuːn] *vt* importunar, perseguir, fastidiar; (*prostitute*) abordar con fines inmorales.
importunity [,ɪmpɔː'tjuːnɪtɪ] *n* importunidad *f*; pesadez *f.*
impose [ɪm'pəʊz] **1** *vt* imponer (*on* a); (*palm off*) hacer aceptar (*on a*).
2 *vi*: **to** ~ **upon** (*deceive*) embaucar; (*take advantage of*) *kindness etc* abusar de, *person* abusar de la amabilidad de; **I don't wish to** ~ **upon you** no quiero abusar, no quiero molestarle.
imposing [ɪm'pəʊzɪŋ] *adj* imponente, impresionante; majestuoso.
imposition [,ɪmpə'zɪʃən] *n* (*act*) imposición *f*; (*burden*) carga *f,* molestia *f*; abuso *m*; (*tax*) impuesto *m*; **it's a bit of an** ~ me resulta algo molesto; **I fear it's rather an** ~ **for you** me temo que le vaya a molestar bastante.
impossibility [ɪm,pɒsə'bɪlɪtɪ] *n* imposibilidad *f.*
impossible [ɪm'pɒsəbl] **1** *adj* imposible; *person* inaguantable, insufrible; **you're** ~! ¡eres imposible!, ¡no puedo contigo!; **to make it** ~ **for sb to do sth** quitar a uno la posibilidad de hacer algo, imposibilitar algo a uno. **2** *n*: **to do the** ~ hacer lo imposible.
impossibly [ɪm'pɒsəblɪ] *adv* imposiblemente; ~ **difficult** de lo más difícil, tan difícil que resulta imposible.
impost ['ɪmpəʊst] *n* impuesto *m.*
impostor [ɪm'pɒstəʳ] *n* impostor *m,* -ora *f,* embustero *m,* -a *f.*
imposture [ɪm'pɒstʃəʳ] *n* impostura *f,* engaño *m,* fraude *m.*
impotence ['ɪmpətəns] *n* impotencia *f.*
impotent ['ɪmpətənt] *adj* impotente.
impound [ɪm'paʊnd] *vt goods* embargar, confiscar.
impoverish [ɪm'pɒvərɪʃ] *vt* empobrecer, reducir a la miseria; *land* agotar.
impoverished [ɪm'pɒvərɪʃt] *adj* empobrecido, necesitado, indigente; *land* agotado.
impoverishment [ɪm'pɒvərɪʃmənt] *n* empobrecimiento *m*; agotamiento *m.*
impracticability [ɪm,præktɪkə'bɪlɪtɪ] *n* impracticabilidad *f,* imposibilidad *f.*
impracticable [ɪm'præktɪkəbl] *adj* impracticable, no factible, imposible de realizar.
impractical [ɪm'præktɪkəl] *adj* falto de sentido práctico, poco práctico; (*awkward*) desmañado.
impracticality [ɪm,præktɪ'kælɪtɪ] *n* falta *f* de sentido práctico.
imprecation [,ɪmprɪ'keɪʃən] *n* imprecación *f.*
imprecise [,ɪmprɪ'saɪs] *adj* impreciso.
imprecision [,ɪmprɪ'sɪʒən] *n* imprecisión *f.*
impregnable [ɪm'pregnəbl] *adj* inexpugnable.
impregnate ['ɪmpregneɪt] *vt* impregnar, empapar (*with* de); (*Bio*) fecundar; **to become ~d with** impregnarse de.
impregnation [,ɪmpreg'neɪʃən] *n* impregnación *f*; (*Bio*) fecundación *f.*
impresario [,ɪmpre'sɑːrɪəʊ] *n* empresario *m.*
impress 1 ['ɪmpres] *n* impresión *f,* señal *f*; (*fig*) sello *m,* huella *f.*
2 [ɪm'pres] *vt* (**a**) (*mark, stamp*) estampar; (*fig*) grabar, inculcar; **I must** ~ **upon you that** ... tengo que subrayar que ...; **it ~ed itself upon my mind** quedó grabado en mi memoria; **I tried to** ~ **the importance of the job on him** traté de convencerle de la importancia del puesto.
(**b**) (*affect*) impresionar; **he does it just to** ~ **people** lo hace sólo para impresionar a la gente; **he is not easily ~ed** no se deja impresionar fácilmente; **I was not ~ed** no me hizo buena impresión; **he ~ed me quite favourably** me hizo una impresión bastante buena; **how did it** ~ **you?** ¿qué impresión te produjo?; **the play deeply ~ed everyone** la obra causó honda impresión en todos.
3 [ɪm'pres] *vi* hacer buena impresión.
impression [ɪm'preʃən] *n* (**a**) (*effect*) impresión *f*; **to make an** ~ impresionar; **she's out to make an** ~ se dedica a impresionar, quiere causar una sensación; **to make an** ~ **on sb** impresionar a uno; **what** ~ **did it make on you?** ¿qué impresión le produjo?; **all our arguments seemed to make no** ~ **on him** todos nuestros argumentos al parecer no tuvieron efecto alguno en él; **he could make no** ~ **on his opponent's majority** no logró rebajar la mayoría de su rival.
(**b**) (*vague idea*) impresión *f*; **to be under the** ~ **that** ..., **to have the** ~ **that** ... tener la impresión de que ...; **my ~s of Ruritania** mis impresiones de Ruritania.
(**c**) (*imprint*) impresión *f*; huella *f,* señal *f.*
(**d**) (*esp Brit Typ*) edición *f,* tirada *f.*
(**e**) (*Theat*) imitación *f.*
impressionable [ɪm'preʃnəbl] *adj* impresionable; influenciable; sensible; **at an** ~ **age** en una edad impresionable.
impressionism [ɪm'preʃənɪzəm] *n* impresionismo *m.*
impressionist [ɪm'preʃənɪst] **1** *adj* impresionista. **2** *n* (**a**) (*Art*) impresionista *mf.* (**b**) (*Theat*) imitador *m,* -ora *f.*
impressionistic [ɪm,preʃə'nɪstɪk] *adj* impresionista.
impressive [ɪm'presɪv] *adj* impresionante.
impressively [ɪm'presɪvlɪ] *adv* de modo impresionante.
imprest [ɪm'prest] *attr*: ~ **system** sistema *m* de fondo fijo.
imprimatur [ɪmprɪ'meɪtəʳ] *n* imprimátur *m.*
imprint 1 ['ɪmprɪnt] *n* impresión *f,* huella *f,* señal *f*; (*Typ*) pie *m* de imprenta; **under the HarperCollins** ~ publicado por HarperCollins.
2 [ɪm'prɪnt] *vt* imprimir, estampar (*on* en); (*fig*) grabar (*on the mind* en la memoria); (*Bio, Psych*) imprimir (*on* a).
imprinting [ɪm'prɪntɪŋ] *n* (*Bio, Psych*) impresión *f.*
imprison [ɪm'prɪzn] *vt* encarcelar, poner en la cárcel; **the judge ~ed him for 10 years** el juez le condenó a 10 años de prisión.
imprisonment [ɪm'prɪznmənt] *n* encarcelamiento *m,* detención *f,* prisión *f*; ~ **without trial** detención *f* sin procesamiento; **the judge sentenced him to 10 years'** ~ el juez le condenó a 10 años de prisión; **to escape from** ~ escapar de la cárcel.
improbability [ɪm,prɒbə'bɪlɪtɪ] *n* improbabilidad *f*; inverosimilitud *f.*
improbable [ɪm'prɒbəbl] *adj* improbable; inverosímil; **it is** ~ **that it will happen** no es probable que ocurra, es poco probable que ocurra.
impromptu [ɪm'prɒmptjuː] **1** *adj performance* improvisado, no preparado de antemano; *utterance* espontáneo, impremeditado.
2 *adv perform* de improviso, sin preparación; *say etc* de repente.
3 *n* improvisación *f.*
improper [ɪm'prɒpəʳ] *adj* impropio, incorrecto, indebido; (*Comput*) incorrecto; (*unseemly*) indecoroso; (*indecent*) indecente, deshonesto.
improperly [ɪm'prɒpəlɪ] *adv* impropiamente, incorrectamente, indebidamente; indecorosamente; indecentemente, deshonestamente.
impropriety [,ɪmprə'praɪətɪ] *n* inconveniencia *f*; incorrección *f*; falta *f* de decoro; indecencia *f,* deshonestidad *f*; (*of language*) impropiedad *f.*
improve [ɪm'pruːv] **1** *vt* mejorar; perfeccionar; reformar; (*beautify*) embellecer; *land* abonar, bonificar; *property* aumentar el valor de; *production, yield* aumentar; *mind* ilustrar, edificar; *opportunity* aprovechar.
2 *vi* mejorar(se); perfeccionarse; (*production, yield*) aumentar(se); (*price*) subir; (*weather*) mejorar, componerse; (*in skill, studies etc*) hacer progresos; **the patient is improving** el enfermo está mejor; **he is in ~d health** está mejor de salud; **in these ~d circumstances** en mejores circunstancias.
3 *vr*: **to** ~ **o.s.** (*in mind*) instruirse; (*in wealth etc*) mejorar su situación.
◆**improve on** *vt* mejorar, perfeccionar; **to** ~ **on sb's offer** ofrecer más que otro; **it cannot be ~d on** es inmejorable.
improvement [ɪm'pruːvmənt] **1** *n* mejora *f,* mejoramiento *m*; perfeccionamiento *m*; reforma *f*; embellecimiento *m*; aumento *m,* subida *f* (*in* de); progreso *m,* adelantamiento *m*; (*Med*) mejoría *f*; enmienda *f*; **there has been some** ~ **in the patient's condition** el enfermo está algo mejor; **it's an** ~ **on the old one** es mejor que el antiguo; **to make ~s in a text** enmendar un texto; **to make ~s to a property** hacer reformas en un inmueble.
2 *attr*: ~ **grant** subvención *f* para modernizar (una casa *etc*).
improvidence [ɪm'prɒvɪdəns] *n* imprevisión *f.*
improvident [ɪm'prɒvɪdənt] *adj* impróvido, imprevisor.
improvidently [ɪm'prɒvɪdəntlɪ] *adv* impróvidamente.

improving [ɪm'pruːvɪŋ] *adj* edificante, instructivo.
improvisation [ˌɪmprəvaɪ'zeɪʃən] *n* improvisación *f.*
improvise ['ɪmprəvaɪz] *vti* improvisar, repentizar.
imprudence [ɪm'pruːdəns] *n* imprudencia *f.*
imprudent [ɪm'pruːdənt] *adj* imprudente.
imprudently [ɪm'pruːdəntlɪ] *adv* imprudentemente.
impudence ['ɪmpjʊdəns] *n* descaro *m,* insolencia *f,* atrevimiento *m*; **what ~!** ¡qué frescura!; **he had the ~ to say that ...** tuvo la cara (dura) de decir que ...
impudent ['ɪmpjʊdənt] *adj* descarado, insolente, atrevido.
impudently ['ɪmpjʊdəntlɪ] *adv* descaradamente, insolentemente.
impugn [ɪm'pjuːn] *vt* impugnar.
impulse ['ɪmpʌls] **1** *n* (*Mech etc*) impulso *m*; (*fig*) impulso *m,* impulsión *f,* estímulo *m*; incitación *f*; **to act on ~** obrar por capricho, obrar sin reflexión; **my first ~ was to** + *infin* mi primer impulso fue de + *infin,* primero intenté + *infin*; **to yield to a sudden ~** dejarse llevar por un impulso.
2 *attr*: **~ buy(ing), ~ purchase** compra *f* impulsiva; **~ goods** mercancías *fpl* expuestas para la compra impulsiva; **~ sales** ventas *fpl* impulsivas.
impulsion [ɪm'pʌlʃən] *n* impulsión *f.*
impulsive [ɪm'pʌlsɪv] *adj person* irreflexivo, que no reflexiona, impulsivo; *act* irreflexivo.
impulsively [ɪm'pʌlsɪvlɪ] *adv* por impulso; sin reflexión, sin pensar.
impulsiveness [ɪm'pʌlsɪvnɪs] *n,* **impulsivity** [ɪmpʌl'sɪvɪtɪ] *n* (*US*) irreflexión *f*; carácter *m* impulsivo.
impunity [ɪm'pjuːnɪtɪ] *n* impunidad *f*; **with ~** impunemente.
impure [ɪm'pjʊəʳ] *adj* impuro; adulterado, mezclado; (*morally*) deshonesto.
impurity [ɪm'pjʊərɪtɪ] *n* impureza *f*; deshonestidad *f.*
imputation [ˌɪmpjʊ'teɪʃən] *n* imputación *f*; acusación *f.*
impute [ɪm'pjuːt] *vt* imputar, achacar, atribuir (*to* a); acusar.
IN (*US Post*) *abbr of* **Indiana.**
in [ɪn] **1** *adv* **(a)** dentro, adentro; **~ here** aquí dentro; **~ there** allí dentro; **day ~, day out** día tras día; **£200 a week all ~** 200 libras por semana todo incluido.
(b) to be ~ (*person*) estar, estar en casa, estar en la oficina (*etc*); **is Mr Eccles ~?** ¿está el Sr Eccles?; **the train is ~** ha llegado el tren; **when the Tories were ~** cuando los conservadores estaban en el poder; **when the sun is ~** cuando el sol está escondido; **the harvest is ~** ha terminado la recolección; **strawberries are ~** es la temporada de las fresas, las fresas están en sazón; **short skirts were ~** la falda corta estaba de moda.
(c) to be ~ for a post ser candidato a un puesto, solicitar un puesto; **to be ~ for a competition** concurrir a un certamen, tomar parte en un concurso; **to be ~ for an exam** presentarse a un examen; **we're ~ for it now** aquí se va a armar la gorda; **you don't know what you're ~ for** no sabes lo que te pescas; **we're ~ for a hard time** vamos a pasar un mal rato; **he's ~ for a surprise** le espera una sorpresa.
(d) to be ~ on the secret estar en el secreto; **to be ~ on a plan** estar enterado de un proyecto.
(e) to be well ~ with sb estar muy metido con uno, tener mucha confianza con uno.
(f) to be all ~, to feel all ~ estar rendido, no poder más.
(g) (*: *in prison*) **he's ~ for larceny** está preso por ladrón; **he's ~ for 5 years** cumple una condena de 5 años; **what's he ~ for?** ¿de qué delito se le acusa?
2 *prep* **(a)** (*place*) en; dentro de; **~ the house** en la casa; **~ one's hand** en la mano; **~ Rome** en Roma; **~ Italy** en Italia; **~ prison** en la cárcel; **~ school** en la escuela; **~ the distance** a lo lejos; **~ everybody's eyes** a los ojos de todos; **it is not ~ him to do that** no es capaz de hacer eso, no cabe en él hacer eso; **he has it ~ him to succeed** es capaz de triunfar; **our colleagues ~ Madrid** nuestros colegas de Madrid; **we find it ~ Galdós** lo encontramos en Galdós; **~ him we have a great leader** en él tenemos un gran caudillo.
(b) (*in respect of*) **better ~ health** mejor de salud; **strong ~ maths** fuerte en matemáticas; **a change ~ policy** un cambio de política; **a rise ~ prices** una subida de los precios; **3 metres ~ length** 3 metros de largo; **long ~ the leg** de piernas largas; **diseased ~ mind** de mentalidad anormal; **deaf ~ one ear** sordo de un oído.
(c) (*ratio*) **1 ~ 7** 1 sobre 7, 1 de cada 7; **15 pence ~ the pound** 15 peniques de cada libra.
(d) (*time*) **~ 1972** en 1972; **~ the 20th century** en el siglo XX; **~ May** en mayo; **~ summer** en el verano; **~ the past** en el pasado; **~ these times** en estos tiempos; **~ the reign of** bajo el reinado de; **it was built ~ a week** fue construido en una semana; **I'll bring it back ~ a week** lo devolveré dentro de una semana, lo devolveré de aquí a ocho días; **~ a week he was back** al cabo de una semana volvió; **~ the morning** por la mañana; **at 8 ~ the morning** a las 8 de la mañana; **~ the daytime** de día, durante el día; **I haven't seen him ~ years** hace años que no le veo.
(e) (*state, fig*) **~ tears** llorando; **~ despair** desesperado; **~ good health** en buen estado de salud; **~ ruins** en ruinas; **any man ~ his senses** cualquier hombre sensato.
(f) (*clothed in*) **the girl ~ green** la chica vestida de verde; **he went out ~ his new raincoat** al salir se puso el impermeable nuevo; **she looks nice ~ that hat** con ese sombrero está guapísima.
(g) (*weather*) **~ the rain** bajo la lluvia; **~ the July sun** bajo el sol de julio.
(h) (*concerned with*) **he's ~ the tyre business** se dedica al comercio de neumáticos, tiene un negocio de neumáticos; **those ~ teaching** los profesores, los que se dedican a enseñar; **he travels ~ soap** es viajante en jabones; **she has shares ~ oil** tiene acciones de compañías de petróleo; **he's something ~ advertising** tiene un puesto (importante) en la publicidad; **the latest thing ~ hats** lo más nuevo en sombreros.
(i) (*manner*) **~ this way** de este modo; **~ the American fashion** a la americana; **~ alphabetical order** por orden alfabético; **cut ~ half** cortado por el medio; **~ French** en francés; **written ~ pencil** escrito con (*or* a) lápiz; **painted ~ black** pintado de negro; **packed ~ dozens** envasados por docenas; **~ hundreds** a cientos, a centenares; **~ cash** en metálico; **~ mourning** de luto; **~ his shirt** en camisa; **~ writing** por escrito; **~ anger** con enojo.
(j) (*after superlative*) **the best pupil ~ the class** el mejor alumno de la clase; **the biggest ~ Europe** el mayor de Europa.
(k) (*with verb*) **~ saying this** al decir esto; **~ making a fortune he lost his wife** mientras se ganaba una fortuna, perdió a su mujer.
3 *n*: **~s and outs** recovecos *mpl*; (*fig*) detalles *mpl* nimios; interioridades *fpl.*
4 *adj* (*) **an ~ joke** un chiste para iniciados; **it's the ~ thing** está de moda; **it's the ~ place to eat** es el restaurante que está de moda; **she wore a very ~ dress** llevaba un vestido de lo más 'in'*.
in. *abbr of* **inch** pulgada *f.*
in... [ɪn] *pref* in...
-in [ɪn] *n ending in compounds*: *eg* **love~** reunión *f* de fraternidad colectiva; **sit~** sentada *f*; **teach~** reunión *f* de autoenseñanza colectiva.
inability [ˌɪnə'bɪlɪtɪ] *n* incapacidad *f,* falta *f* de aptitud; **my ~ to come** el que yo no pueda venir.
inaccessibility ['ɪnækˌsesə'bɪlɪtɪ] *n* inaccesibilidad *f.*
inaccessible [ˌɪnæk'sesəbl] *adj* inaccesible.
inaccuracy [ɪn'ækjʊrəsɪ] *n* inexactitud *f,* incorrección *f.*
inaccurate [ɪn'ækjʊrɪt] *adj* inexacto, incorrecto, erróneo.
inaccurately [ɪn'ækjʊrɪtlɪ] *adv* erróneamente.
inaction [ɪn'ækʃən] *n* inacción *f.*
inactive [ɪn'æktɪv] *adj* inactivo.
inactivity [ˌɪnæk'tɪvɪtɪ] *n* inactividad *f.*
inadequacy [ɪn'ædɪkwəsɪ] *n* insuficiencia *f*; (*of person*) incapacidad *f.*
inadequate [ɪn'ædɪkwɪt] *adj* insuficiente, inadecuado; defectuoso; *person* incapaz.
inadequately [ɪn'ædɪkwɪtlɪ] *adv* de modo inadecuado.
inadmissible [ˌɪnəd'mɪsəbl] *adj* inadmisible.
inadvertence [ˌɪnəd'vɜːtəns] *n* inadvertencia *f*; **by ~** por inadvertencia, por equivocación, por descuido.
inadvertent [ˌɪnəd'vɜːtənt] *adj* inadvertido; accidental.
inadvertently [ˌɪnəd'vɜːtəntlɪ] *adv* por equivocación, por descuido.
inadvisability ['ɪnədˌvaɪzə'bɪlɪtɪ] *n* imprudencia *f,* inconveniencia *f.*
inadvisable [ˌɪnəd'vaɪzəbl] *adj* no aconsejable, desaconsejable, imprudente, inconveniente.
inalienable [ɪn'eɪlɪənəbl] *adj* inalienable.
inamorata [ɪnˌæmə'rɑːtə] *n* amada *f,* querida *f.*
inane [ɪ'neɪn] *adj* necio, fatuo, sonso (*LAm*).
inanimate [ɪn'ænɪmɪt] *adj* inanimado.
inanition [ˌɪnə'nɪʃən] *n* inanición *f.*
inanity [ɪ'nænɪtɪ] *n* necedad *f,* fatuidad *f,* inutilidad *f*; **inanities** estupideces *fpl,* necedades *fpl.*
inapplicable [ɪn'æplɪkəbl] *adj* inaplicable.
inappropriate [ˌɪnə'prəʊprɪɪt] *adj* inoportuno, inconveniente,

impropio, poco apropiado.
inappropriately [ˌɪnə'prəʊprɪɪtlɪ] *adv* inoportunamente.
inappropriateness [ˌɪnə'prəʊprɪɪtnɪs] *n* impropiedad *f.*
inapt [ɪn'æpt] *adj* impropio; (*lacking skill*) inhábil.
inaptitude [ɪn'æptɪtjuːd] *n* impropiedad *f*; inhabilidad *f.*
inarticulate [ˌɪnɑː'tɪkjʊlɪt] *adj* (*of character*) incapaz de expresarse, que habla poco y mal; **an ~ speech** un discurso mal pronunciado; **he was ~ with rage** la rabia le embargó la voz.
inarticulately [ˌɪnɑː'tɪkjʊlɪtlɪ] *adv*: **he speaks ~** habla poco y mal; **he was mumbling ~** hablaba entre dientes y apenas se le entendía.
inartistic [ɪnɑː'tɪstɪk] *adj work* poco artístico, antiestético, burdo, mal hecho; *person* falto de talento artístico.
inasmuch [ɪnəz'mʌtʃ]: **~ as** *conj* puesto que, ya que, por cuanto que.
inattention [ˌɪnə'tenʃən] *n* inatención *f*, desatención *f*, distracción *f.*
inattentive [ˌɪnə'tentɪv] *adj* desatento, distraído.
inattentively [ˌɪnə'tentɪvlɪ] *adv* distraídamente.
inaudible [ɪn'ɔːdəbl] *adj* inaudible, que no se puede oír; **he was almost ~** apenas se le podía oír.
inaudibly [ɪn'ɔːdəblɪ] *adv* de modo inaudible; **he spoke almost ~** habló tan bajo que apenas se le podía oír.
inaugural [ɪ'nɔːgjʊrəl] *adj* inaugural; *speech* de apertura.
inaugurate [ɪ'nɔːgjʊreɪt] *vt* inaugurar.
inauguration [ɪˌnɔːgjʊ'reɪʃən] *n* inauguración *f*; ceremonia *f* de apertura; (*US Pol*) toma *f* de posesión (*de su cargo por el presidente*).
inauspicious [ˌɪnɔːs'pɪʃəs] *adj* poco propicio, desfavorable.
inauspiciously [ˌɪnɔːs'pɪʃəslɪ] *adv* de modo poco propicio, en condiciones desfavorables.
in-between ['ɪnbɪ'twiːn] *adj* intermedio; de en medio; **it's rather ~** ocupa una posición más bien intermedia, no es ni lo uno ni lo otro.
inboard ['ɪnbɔːd] *adj engine* interior.
inborn ['ɪn'bɔːn] *adj* innato, ingénito; instintivo.
inbound ['ɪnˌbaʊnd] (*US*) **1** *adv* hacia el interior. **2** *adj* que va hacia el interior; *flight* entrante.
inbred ['ɪn'bred] *adj tendency etc* innato, ingénito; instintivo; (*of race*) engendrado por endogamia; **people there are very ~** allí la endogamia ha debilitado a la gente.
inbreeding ['ɪn'briːdɪŋ] *n* endogamia *f.*
inbuilt ['ɪnbɪlt] *adj feeling etc* innato, inherente.
Inc. (*US*) *abbr of* **Incorporated** sociedad *f* anónima, S.A.
inc. *abbr of* **including, inclusive.**
Inca ['ɪŋkə] **1** *n* inca *mf.* **2** *attr* incaico, incásico.
incalculable [ɪn'kælkjʊləbl] *adj* incalculable; *person etc* voluble, veleidoso.
Incan ['ɪŋkən] *adj* inca, incaico, de los incas.
incandescence [ˌɪnkæn'desns] *n* incandescencia *f.*
incandescent [ˌɪnkæn'desnt] *adj* incandescente; **she was ~ (with rage)** estaba que trinaba.
incantation [ˌɪnkæn'teɪʃən] *n* conjuro *m*, ensalmo *m.*
incapability [ɪnˌkeɪpə'bɪlɪtɪ] *n* incapacidad *f.*
incapable [ɪn'keɪpəbl] *adj* incapaz (**of** de); incompetente; (*physically*) imposibilitado; **to be ~ of speech** no poder hablar; **she is ~ of shame** no tiene vergüenza; **he was drunk and ~** estaba totalmente borracho.
incapacitate [ˌɪnkə'pæsɪteɪt] *vt* incapacitar, inhabilitar; descalificar; (*physically*) imposibilitar.
incapacity [ˌɪnkə'pæsɪtɪ] *n* incapacidad *f*; insuficiencia *f.*
incarcerate [ɪn'kɑːsəreɪt] *vt* encarcelar.
incarceration [ɪnˌkaːsə'reɪʃən] *n* encarcelamiento *m*, encarcelación *f.*
in-car entertainment ['ɪnˌkaːrˌentə'teɪnmənt] *n* radiocassette *f* de coche.
incarnate 1 [ɪn'kɑːnɪt] *adj*: **the devil ~** el mismo diablo, el diablo en persona; **to become ~** encarnar. **2** ['ɪnkɑːneɪt] *vt* encarnar.
incarnation [ˌɪnkɑː'neɪʃən] *n* encarnación *f*; **to be the ~ of vice** ser el mismo vicio.
incautious [ɪn'kɔːʃəs] *adj* incauto, imprudente.
incautiously [ɪn'kɔːʃəslɪ] *adv* incautamente.
incendiary [ɪn'sendɪərɪ] **1** *adj* incendiario; **~ bomb** bomba *f* incendiaria. **2** *n* (**a**) (*person*) incendiario *m*, pirómano *m*, -a *f*. (**b**) (*bomb*) bomba *f* incendiaria.
incense[1] ['ɪnsens] *n* incienso *m.*
incense[2] [ɪn'sens] *vt* indignar, encolerizar.
incensed [ɪn'senst] *adj* furioso, encolerizado.
incentive [ɪn'sentɪv] **1** *n* incentivo *m*, estímulo *m*; **an ~ to harder work** un incentivo para que se trabaje más. **2** *attr*: **~ bonus** prima *f* de incentiva; **~ scheme** sistema *m* de primas de incentiva, plan *m* de incentivos; **~ wage** salario *m* incentivo.
inception [ɪn'sepʃən] *n* comienzo *m*, principio *m*; **from its ~** desde los comienzos.
incertitude [ɪn'sɜːtɪtjuːd] *n* incertidumbre *f.*
incessant [ɪn'sesnt] *adj* incesante, constante, continuo.
incessantly [ɪn'sesntlɪ] *adv* constantemente, sin cesar.
incest ['ɪnsest] *n* incesto *m.*
incestuous [ɪn'sestjʊəs] *adj* incestuoso.
inch [ɪntʃ] **1** *n* pulgada *f* (= *2,54 cm*); **~es** (*of person*: *height*) estatura *f*, (*of waist*) cintura *f*; **not an ~ from my face** a dos centímetros de mi cara; **~ by ~, by ~es** palmo a palmo; **not an ~ of territory** ni un palmo de territorio; **we searched every ~ of the room** registramos minuciosamente el cuarto; **every ~ of soil is used** se aprovecha la tierra hasta el último centímetro; **he's every ~ a man** es todo un hombre; **he's every ~ a soldier** es lo que se llama un soldado; **to be within an ~ of** estar a dos dedos de; **he didn't give an ~** no nos ofreció la menor concesión; **give him an ~ and he'll take a yard** dale un dedo y se toma hasta el codo.
2 *vt*: **to ~ forward** mover poco a poco hacia adelante.
3 *vi*: **to ~ (one's way) forward** avanzar palmo a palmo; **prices are ~ing up** los precios suben paulatinamente.
◆**inch out 1** *vt* derrotar por la mínima.
2 *vi* avanzar muy despacio.
inchoate ['ɪnkəʊeɪt] *adj* rudimentario, incompleto, todavía no formado.
inch tape ['ɪntʃteɪp] *n* cinta *f* en pulgadas para medir.
incidence ['ɪnsɪdəns] *n* frecuencia *f*; extensión *f*; intensidad *f*; distribución *f*; **the ~ of measles in children** la frecuencia del sarampión en los niños; **the ~ of taxation** el peso de las contribuciones.
incident ['ɪnsɪdənt] *n* incidente *m*, episodio *m*, suceso *m*; **~ room** centro *m* de coordinación; **the Agadir ~** el episodio de Agadir; **to provoke a diplomatic ~** provocar un incidente diplomático; **a life full of ~** una vida azarosa, una vida llena de acontecimientos; **to arrive without ~** llegar sin novedad.
incidental [ˌɪnsɪ'dentl] **1** *adj* incidental, (*casual*) fortuito; (*inessential*) no esencial, accesorio, de importancia secundaria; **~ expenses** (gastos *mpl*) imprevistos *mpl*, gastos *mpl* accesorios; **~ music** música *f* de fondo; **the troubles ~ to any journey** las dificultades que acarrea cualquier viaje; **but that is ~ to my purpose** pero eso queda al margen de mi propósito.
2 *n* (**a**) (*event etc*) cosa *f* fortuita; cosa *f* accesoria, cosa *f* sin importancia.
(**b**) **~s** (*Comm etc*) imprevistos *mpl.*
incidentally [ˌɪnsɪ'dentəlɪ] *adv* por cierto; de paso, de pasada; incidentemente; **and ~ ...** y a propósito ...; **it was interesting only ~** tenía un interés solamente incidental.
incinerate [ɪn'sɪnəreɪt] *vt* incinerar, quemar.
incineration [ɪnˌsɪnə'reɪʃən] *n* incineración *f.*
incinerator [ɪn'sɪnəreɪtə^r] *n* incinerador *m.*
incipient [ɪn'sɪpɪənt] *adj* incipiente, naciente.
incise [ɪn'saɪz] *vt* cortar; (*Art*) grabar, tallar; (*Med*) incidir, hacer una incisión en.
incision [ɪn'sɪʒən] *n* incisión *f*, corte *m.*
incisive [ɪn'saɪsɪv] *adj mind* penetrante; *tone* mordaz; *words, criticism, speech* tajante, incisivo.
incisively [ɪn'saɪsɪvlɪ] *adv* con penetración; mordazmente; de modo tajante.
incisiveness [ɪn'saɪsɪvnɪs] *n* penetración *f*; mordacidad *f*; lo tajante.
incisor [ɪn'saɪzə^r] *n* incisivo *m.*
incite [ɪn'saɪt] *vt* incitar, estimular, provocar; **to ~ sb to do sth** incitar a uno a hacer algo.
incitement [ɪn'saɪtmənt] *n* incitación *f*, instigación *f* (**to** de).
incivility [ˌɪnsɪ'vɪlɪtɪ] *n* descortesía *f*, incivilidad *f.*
incl. *abbr of* **included, including, inclusive (of).**
inclemency [ɪn'klemənsɪ] *n* inclemencia *f*; (*of weather*) intemperie *f.*
inclement [ɪn'klemənt] *adj* inclemente, riguroso; *weather* malo, feo.
inclination [ˌɪnklɪ'neɪʃən] *n* (**a**) (*slope*) inclinación *f.*
(**b**) (*tendency*) inclinación *f*, propensión *f*; **my ~ is to** + *infin* yo prefiero la idea de + *infin*; **what are his natural ~s?** ¿cuáles son sus propensiones naturales?; **to have an ~ to meanness** tener tendencia a ser tacaño; **I have no ~ to help him** no estoy dispuesto a ayudarle, tengo pocas ganas de ayudarle; **to follow one's ~** seguir su capricho, hacer lo que le dé la gana.
incline 1 ['ɪnklaɪn] *n* cuesta *f*, pendiente *f.*
2 [ɪn'klaɪn] *vt* (**a**) (*slope*) inclinar, ladear, poner

oblicuamente; **he ~d his head** inclinó la cabeza, bajó la cabeza.
(**b**) (*fig*) **to ~ sb to adopt a plan** inducir a uno a adoptar un plan.
(**c**) **to be ~d to** + *infin* (*tendency*) inclinarse a + *infin*, tener tendencia a + *infin*, ser propenso a + *infin*; (*person's volition*) estar dispuesto a + *infin*, estar por + *infin*; **it's ~d to break** tiende a romperse; **I'm ~d to believe you** estoy dispuesto a creerte; **the child is ~d to be left-handed** el niño tiene tendencias de zurdo; **he's that way ~d** él es así; **if you feel so ~d** si quieres.
3 [ɪn'klaɪn] *vi* (**a**) (*slope, act*) inclinarse, ladearse, (*state*) estar inclinado, estar ladeado.
(**b**) (*fig*) **I ~ to the belief that** ... yo prefiero creer que ..., yo creo más lógica la opinión de que ...; **yellow inclining to red** amarillo que tira a rojo.

inclined [ɪn'klaɪnd] *adj plane* inclinado.

inclose [ɪn'kləʊz] *vt* = **enclose**.

include [ɪn'klu:d] *vt* incluir; comprender, contener, encerrar; (*with letter*) adjuntar, enviar adjunto; **your name is not ~d in the list** su nombre no figura en la lista; **does that remark ~ me?** ¿se refiere esa observación también a mí?; **he is not ~d in the team** no forma parte del equipo; **he sold the lot, books ~d** lo vendió todo, incluso los libros; **everything ~d** (*hotel etc*) todo incluido; **all the team members, myself ~d** todos los miembros del equipo, yo entre ellos.

◆**include out** *vt* (*hum*) excluir, dejar fuera; **~ me out** no contéis conmigo.

including [ɪn'klu:dɪŋ] *as prep* incluso, inclusive, con inclusión de; **seven ~ this one** siete con (inclusión de) éste; **everyone came, ~ the priest** vinieron todos, incluso (*or* hasta) el cura; **terms £80, not ~ service** precio 80 libras, servicio no incluido; **up to and ~ Chapter 7** hasta el capítulo 7 inclusive; **$20 ~ post and packing** $20 incluido gastos de envío.

inclusion [ɪn'klu:ʒən] *n* inclusión *f*.

inclusive [ɪn'klu:sɪv] **1** *adj* inclusivo, completo; **~ terms** todo incluido; **to be ~ of** incluir.
2 *adv* inclusive; **from the 10th to the 15th ~** del 10 al 15 ambos inclusive.

inclusively [ɪn'klu:sɪvlɪ] *adv* = **inclusive 2**.

incognito [ɪn'kɒgnɪtəʊ] **1** *adv travel etc* de incógnito. **2** *n* incógnito *m*.

incoherence [,ɪnkəʊ'hɪərəns] *n* incoherencia *f*; ininteligibilidad *f*.

incoherent [,ɪnkəʊ'hɪərənt] *adj* incoherente, inconexo; ininteligible; *argument etc* sin pies ni cabeza; **his speech became ~** empezó a hablar de modo ininteligible; **he was ~ with rage** no podía hablar de rabia.

incoherently [,ɪnkəʊ'hɪərəntlɪ] *adv* de modo incoherente; de modo ininteligible.

incombustible [,ɪnkəm'bʌstəbl] *adj* incombustible.

income ['ɪnkʌm] **1** *n* ingresos *mpl*, renta *f*, entrada *f*; (*profit*) rédito *m* (*from* de); **to live up to one's ~** gastarse toda la renta; **to live beyond one's ~** gastar más de lo que se gana; **to live within one's ~** vivir con arreglo a los ingresos; **I can't live on my ~** no puedo vivir con lo que gano.
2 *attr*: **~ and expenditure account** cuenta *f* de gastos e ingresos; **~ band, ~ bracket, ~ group** categoría *f* económica; **the lower ~ groups** los económicamente débiles; **~s policy** política *f* de rentas; **~ support** (*Brit*) ≃ ayuda *f* compensatoria.

incomer ['ɪn,kʌmər] *n* recién llegado *m*, recién llegada *f*; persona *f* nueva (en una sociedad *etc*); inmigrante *mf*.

income-tax ['ɪnkʌmtæks] **1** *n* impuesto *m* sobre la renta. **2** *attr*: **~ inspector** recaudador *m*, -ora *f* de impuestos; **~ return** declaración *f* de ingresos.

incoming ['ɪn,kʌmɪŋ] *adj* entrante, nuevo; *tide* ascendente; **~ call** llamada *f* que se recibe; **~ flight** vuelo *m* entrante; **~ mail** correo *m* entrante.

incomings ['ɪn,kʌmɪŋz] *npl* ingresos *mpl*.

incommensurable [,ɪnkə'menʃərəbl] *adj* inconmensurable.

incommensurate [,ɪnkə'menʃərɪt] *adj* desproporcionado; **to be ~ with** no guardar relación con.

incommode [,ɪnkə'məʊd] *vt* incomodar, molestar.

incommodious [,ɪnkə'məʊdɪəs] *adj* estrecho, nada espacioso; incómodo.

incommunicado [,ɪnkəmjʊnɪ'kɑ:dəʊ] *adj* incomunicado.

in-company ['ɪnkʌmpənɪ] *adj*: **~ training** formación *f* en la empresa.

incomparable [ɪn'kɒmpərəbl] *adj* incomparable, sin par.

incomparably [ɪn'kɒmpərəblɪ] *adv* incomparablemente; **this one is ~ better** éste es mejor sin ningún género de dudas.

incompatibility ['ɪnkəm,pætə'bɪlɪtɪ] *n* incompatibilidad *f*.

incompatible [,ɪnkəm'pætəbl] *adj* incompatible (*with* con).

incompetence [ɪn'kɒmpɪtəns] *n* incompetencia *f*, inhabilidad *f*, incapacidad *f*.

incompetent [ɪn'kɒmpɪtənt] *adj* incompetente, inhábil, incapaz.

incomplete [,ɪnkəm'pli:t] *adj* incompleto, defectuoso; (*unfinished*) sin terminar, inacabado.

incompletely [,ɪnkəm'pli:tlɪ] *adv* incompletamente.

incompleteness [,ɪnkəm'pli:tnɪs] *n* lo incompleto, estado *m* incompleto; **because of its ~** debido a que no está terminado.

incomprehensible [ɪn,kɒmprɪ'hensəbl] *adj* incomprensible.

incomprehensibly [ɪn,kɒmprɪ'hensəblɪ] *adv* de modo incomprensible.

incomprehension [,ɪnkɒmprɪ'henʃən] *n* incomprensión *f*.

inconceivable [,ɪnkən'si:vəbl] *adj* inconcebible.

inconceivably [,ɪnkən'si:vəblɪ] *adj* inconcebiblemente.

inconclusive [,ɪnkən'klu:sɪv] *adj reasoning etc* poco concluyente, poco convincente, cuestionable; *interview, investigation* que no da resultados definitivos.

inconclusively [,ɪnkən'klu:sɪvlɪ] *adv* de modo inconcluyente, de modo poco convincente; **it ended ~** terminó sin resultados definitivos.

incongruity [,ɪnkɒŋ'gru:ɪtɪ] *n* incongruencia *f*; desacuerdo *m*, falta *f* de lógica; lo absurdo.

incongruous [ɪn'kɒŋgruəs] *adj* incongruo; disonante, que no concuerda, nada lógico; *appearance etc* estrafalario, absurdo; **it seems ~ that** parece extraño que.

inconsequent [ɪn'kɒnsɪkwənt] *adj* inconsecuente.

inconsequential [ɪn,kɒnsɪ'kwenʃəl] *adj* inconsecuente; (*unimportant*) sin trascendencia.

inconsequentially [,ɪnkɒnsɪ'kwenʃəlɪ] *adv talk etc* sin sustancia, sin propósito serio.

inconsiderable [,ɪnkən'sɪdərəbl] *adj* insignificante.

inconsiderate [,ɪnkən'sɪdərɪt] *adj* desconsiderado; **it was most ~ of you** has obrado con poca formalidad.

inconsistency [,ɪnkən'sɪstənsɪ] *n* inconsecuencia *f*; incongruencia *f*; anomalía *f*; **I see an ~ here** aquí veo una contradicción.

inconsistent [,ɪnkən'sɪstənt] *adj* inconsecuente; incongruo; anómalo; **this is ~ with what you told me** esto no concuerda con lo que me dijiste.

inconsolable [,ɪnkən'səʊləbl] *adj* inconsolable.

inconsolably [,ɪnkən'səʊləblɪ] *adv* inconsolablemente.

inconspicuous [,ɪnkən'spɪkjuəs] *adj* apenas visible, discreto, que no llama la atención; (*fig*) poco llamativo, modesto; **try to be as ~ as possible** procure no llamar la atención.

inconspicuously [,ɪnkən'spɪkjuəslɪ] *adv* de modo apenas visible, discretamente, sin llamar la atención; de modo poco llamativo, modestamente.

inconstancy [ɪn'kɒnstənsɪ] *n* inconstancia *f*, veleidad *f*.

inconstant [ɪn'kɒnstənt] *adj* inconstante, mudable, veleidoso.

incontestable [,ɪnkən'testəbl] *adj* incontestable.

incontinence [ɪn'kɒntɪnəns] *n* incontinencia *f* (*also Med*).

incontinent [ɪn'kɒntɪnənt] *adj* incontinente.

incontrovertible [ɪn,kɒntrə'vɜ:təbl] *adj* incontrovertible.

incontrovertibly [ɪn,kɒntrə'vɜ:tɪblɪ] *adv* de manera incontrovertible; **this is ~ true** ésta es una verdad incontrovertible.

inconvenience [,ɪnkən'vi:nɪəns] **1** *n* incomodidad *f*, molestia *f*, inconvenientes *mpl*; **the ~ of living at a distance** los inconvenientes de vivir lejos; **you caused a lot of ~** nos creó muchas dificultades; **to put sb to ~** molestar a uno.
2 *vt* incomodar, molestar, causar inconvenientes a.

inconvenient [,ɪnkən'vi:nɪənt] *adj house, journey etc* incómodo, poco práctico, molesto; *time* malo, inoportuno; **it is ~ for me to have no car** me es incómodo no tener coche; **it's all very ~** es muy difícil.

inconveniently [,ɪnkən'vi:nɪəntlɪ] *adv* incómodamente, de modo poco práctico; a deshora, inoportunamente, en un momento inoportuno; **to come ~ early** venir tan temprano que crea dificultades.

inconvertibility ['ɪnkən,vɜ:tɪ'bɪlɪtɪ] *n* inconvertibilidad *f*.

inconvertible [,ɪnkən'vɜ:təbl] *adj* inconvertible.

incorporate [ɪn'kɔ:pəreɪt] *vt* incorporar (*in, into* a); incluir; comprender, contener; (*add*) agregar, añadir; **a product incorporating vitamin Q** un producto que contiene vitamina Q; **to ~ a company** constituir una compañía en sociedad (anónima).

incorporated [ɪn'kɔ:pəreɪtɪd] *adj* (*US Comm*): **Jones & Lloyd I~** Jones y Lloyd Sociedad Anónima (*abbr* S.A.).

incorporation [ɪn,kɔːpəˈreɪʃən] *n* incorporación *f*; inclusión *f*, adición *f*; (*Comm*) constitución *f* en sociedad anónima.
incorrect [ˌɪnkəˈrekt] *adj* incorrecto, erróneo, inexacto.
incorrectly [ˌɪnkəˈrektlɪ] *adv* incorrectamente, erróneamente; **a letter ~ addressed** una carta con las señas mal puestas.
incorrigible [ɪnˈkɒrɪdʒəbl] *adj* incorregible; **an ~ smoker** un fumador impenitente; **you're ~!** ¡eres un perdido!
incorrigibly [ɪnˈkɒrɪdʒəblɪ] *adv* de manera incorregible.
incorruptible [ˌɪnkəˈrʌptəbl] *adj* incorruptible; (*not open to bribery*) insobornable.
increase 1 [ˈɪnkriːs] *n* aumento *m*, incremento *m* (*in* de); crecimiento *m*; (*in price*) subida *f*, alza *f*; **an ~ in pay** un aumento de sueldo; **to be on the ~** ir en aumento.
2 [ɪnˈkriːs] *vt* aumentar, acrecentar, incrementar.
3 [ɪnˈkriːs] *vi* aumentar(se), acrecentarse, tomar incremento; crecer, ir creciendo; (*price*) subir; **to ~ from 8% to 10%** pasar de 8 a 10 por cien.
increasing [ɪnˈkriːsɪŋ] *adj* creciente.
increasingly [ɪnˈkriːsɪŋlɪ] *adv* cada vez más, más y más, de más en más; crecientemente; **it becomes ~ difficult** se hace más y más difícil; **our ~ difficult task** nuestra labor cada vez más difícil.
incredible [ɪnˈkredəbl] *adj* increíble.
incredibly [ɪnˈkredəblɪ] *adv* increíblemente.
incredulity [ˌɪnkrɪˈdjuːlɪtɪ] *n* incredulidad *f*.
incredulous [ɪnˈkredjʊləs] *adj* incrédulo.
incredulously [ɪnˈkredjʊləslɪ] *adv* con incredulidad.
increment [ˈɪnkrɪmənt] *n* aumento *m*, incremento *m* (*in* de); **an ~ in salary** un aumento de sueldo.
incremental [ɪnkrɪˈmentəl] *adj* incremental; **~ compiler** compilador *m* incremental.
incriminate [ɪnˈkrɪmɪneɪt] *vt* acriminar, incriminar.
incriminating [ɪnˈkrɪmɪneɪtɪŋ] *adj*, **incriminatory** [ɪnˈkrɪmɪnətərɪ] *adj* acriminador, incriminatorio.
incrimination [ɪn,krɪmɪˈneɪʃən] *n* acriminación *f*, incriminación *f*.
incrust [ɪnˈkrʌst] *vt* incrustar (*with* de).
incrustation [ˌɪnkrʌsˈteɪʃən] *n* incrustación *f*; costra *f*.
incubate [ˈɪnkjʊbeɪt] **1** *vt egg* empollar, incubar; (*Med*) incubar. **2** *vi* incubarse.
incubation [ˌɪnkjʊˈbeɪʃən] *n* incubación *f*; **~ period** período *m* de incubación.
incubator [ˈɪnkjʊbeɪtəʳ] *n* incubadora *f*.
incubus [ˈɪŋkjʊbəs] *n* íncubo *m*.
inculcate [ˈɪnkʌlkeɪt] *vt* inculcar (*in* en).
inculcation [ˌɪnkʌlˈkeɪʃən] *n* inculcación *f*.
incumbency [ɪnˈkʌmbənsɪ] *n* incumbencia *f*.
incumbent [ɪnˈkʌmbənt] **1** *adj*: **to be ~ on sb** incumbir a uno (*to do* hacer).
2 *n* titular *mf*, poseedor *m*, -ora *f* (de un cargo o dignidad); (*Eccl*) beneficiado *m*.
incunabula [ˌɪnkjʊˈnæbjʊlə] *npl* incunables *mpl*.
incur [ɪnˈkɜːʳ] *vt* incurrir en; *debt, obligation* contraer; *expenditure* hacer; *loss* sufrir; *expenses, charges* incurrir en.
incurable [ɪnˈkjʊərəbl] **1** *adj* incurable; (*fig*) irremediable. **2** *n* incurable *mf*.
incurably [ɪnˈkjʊərəblɪ] *adv* (*fig*) irremediablemente; **to be ~ optimistic** tener un optimismo indestructible.
incurious [ɪnˈkjʊərɪəs] *adj* poco curioso.
incuriously [ɪnˈkjʊərɪəslɪ] *adv look etc* sin curiosidad, sin interés.
incursion [ɪnˈkɜːʃən] *n* incursión *f*, invasión *f*.
Ind. (*US*) *abbr of* **Indiana**.
indebted [ɪnˈdetɪd] *adj* endeudado; (*fig*): **to be ~ to sb** estar en deuda con uno; **I am ~ to you for your help** agradezco su ayuda.
indebtedness [ɪnˈdetɪdnɪs] *n* (**a**) (*Fin*) endeudamiento *m*, deuda *f*. (**b**) (*fig*) deuda *f* (*to* con); agradecimiento *m*.
indecency [ɪnˈdiːsnsɪ] *n* indecencia *f*.
indecent [ɪnˈdiːsnt] *adj* indecente; *haste* nada decoroso; **~ assault** atentado *m* contra el pudor; **~ exposure** exhibicionismo *m* (sexual).
indecently [ɪnˈdiːsntlɪ] *adv* indecentemente.
indecipherable [ˌɪndɪˈsaɪfərəbl] *adj* indescifrable.
indecision [ˌɪndɪˈsɪʒən] *n* irresolución *f*, indecisión *f*.
indecisive [ˌɪndɪˈsaɪsɪv] *adj* (**a**) *person* irresoluto, indeciso, vacilante. (**b**) *result etc* poco decisivo, que no resuelve nada.
indecisively [ˌɪndɪˈsaɪsɪvlɪ] *adv* (**a**) con irresolución, indecisamente, de modo vacilante. (**b**) **it ended ~** terminó sin resultados definitivos.
indecisiveness [ˌɪndɪˈsaɪsɪvnɪs] *n* (**a**) irresolución *f*, indecisión *f*. (**b**) lo poco decisivo.
indeclinable [ˌɪndɪˈklaɪnəbl] *adj* indeclinable.
indecorous [ɪnˈdekərəs] *adj* indecoroso.
indecorously [ɪnˈdekərəslɪ] *adv* indecorosamente.
indecorum [ˌɪndɪˈkɔːrəm] *n* indecoro *m*, falta *f* de decoro.
indeed [ɪnˈdiːd] *adv* (**a**) (*really, in fact*) en efecto; **and ~ he did** y en efecto lo hizo; **it is ~ true that ...** es en efecto verdad que ...; **~ you may** claro que puedes; **it is ~ difficult** es verdaderamente difícil, es difícil de verdad; **it is ~ a big house** es en efecto una casa grande, es una casa realmente grande; **I may ~ be wrong** es posible en efecto que me equivoque.
(**b**) (*intensifies*) **~!**, **~ yes!**, **yes ~!** ¡claro que sí!, ¡ya lo creo!; **that is praise ~** eso sí es una alabanza; **I'm very glad ~** me alegro muchísimo; **they're very bad ~** son malísimos; **onions ~!** ¡ nada de cebollas!, ¡cebollas, ni hablar!
(**c**) (*showing interest etc*) **~?**, **is it ~?**, **did you ~?** ¿de veras?
indefatigable [ˌɪndɪˈfætɪgəbl] *adj* incansable.
indefatigably [ˌɪndɪˈfætɪgəblɪ] *adv* incansablemente.
indefensible [ˌɪndɪˈfensəbl] *adj* indefendible; *theory etc* insostenible; **your conduct has been ~** su conducta no tiene excusa, su conducta no admite disculpa.
indefensibly [ˌɪndɪˈfensəblɪ] *adv* indefendiblemente.
indefinable [ˌɪndɪˈfaɪnəbl] *adj* indefinible.
indefinably [ˌɪndɪˈfaɪnəblɪ] *adv* indefiniblemente.
indefinite [ɪnˈdefɪnɪt] *adj* (**a**) impreciso, indefinido; incierto, poco seguro; **he was very ~ about it all** mostró no tener ninguna idea clara sobre el asunto; **our plans are somewhat ~ as yet** todavía no tenemos plan concreto; **to be on ~ leave** estar de permiso indefinido. (**b**) (*Gram*) indefinido; **~ article** artículo *m* indefinido.
indefinitely [ɪnˈdefɪnɪtlɪ] *adv* (**a**) indefinidamente; **it extends ~ into space** se prolonga indefinidamente en el espacio.
(**b**) **we can carry on ~** podemos continuar hasta cuando sea (*or* por tiempo indefinido).
indelible [ɪnˈdeləbl] *adj* indeleble, imborrable (*also fig*); **~ pencil** lápiz *m* tinta.
indelibly [ɪnˈdeləblɪ] *adv* indeleblemente, imborrablemente.
indelicacy [ɪnˈdelɪkəsɪ] *n* indecoro *m*, falta *f* de decoro; inoportunidad *f*.
indelicate [ɪnˈdelɪkɪt] *adj* indecoroso, inoportuno.
indemnification [ɪn,demnɪfɪˈkeɪʃən] *n* indemnización *f*.
indemnify [ɪnˈdemnɪfaɪ] *vt* indemnizar, resarcir (*against, for* de).
indemnity [ɪnˈdemnɪtɪ] *n* (*security*) indemnidad *f*; (*compensation*) indemnización *f*, reparación *f*.
indent 1 [ˈɪndent] *n* (*Brit Comm*) pedido *m*; (*Mil etc*) requisición *f*.
2 [ɪnˈdent] *vt* (*cut into*) endentar, mellar; (*Typ, Comput*) sangrar.
3 [ɪnˈdent] *vi*: **to ~ for** pedir, requisar; **to ~ on sb for sth** (*Brit*) pedir algo a uno, requisar algo a uno.
indentation [ˌɪndenˈteɪʃən] *n* mella *f*, muesca *f*; (*Typ*) sangría *f*.
indenture [ɪnˈdentʃəʳ] *n* (*Comm*) escritura *f*, instrumento *m*; carta *f* partida (por ABC); (*freq pl*) contrato *m* de aprendizaje.
independence [ˌɪndɪˈpendəns] **1** *n* independencia *f*.
2 *attr*: **~ day** día *m* de la independencia; **I~ Day** (*US*) Día *m* de la Independencia (*4 julio*).
independent [ˌɪndɪˈpendənt] **1** *adj* independiente (*of* de); **~ school** (*Brit*) escuela *f* privada; **of ~ means** acomodado; **to become ~** independizarse (*of* de). **2** *n* (*Pol*) diputado *m* independiente, diputada *f* independiente.
independently [ˌɪndɪˈpendəntlɪ] *adv* independientemente; **~ of what he may decide** sin tomar en cuenta lo que él decida.
in-depth [ˈɪn,depθ] *adj study etc* a fondo, exhaustivo; **~ investigation** investigación *f* en profundidad.
indescribable [ˌɪndɪsˈkraɪbəbl] *adj* indescriptible; (*pej*) indecible, incalificable.
indescribably [ˌɪndɪsˈkraɪbəblɪ] *adv* indescriptiblemente; (*pej*) indeciblemente, de modo incalificable; **~ bad** tan malo que resulta incalificable.
indestructibility [ˌɪndɪstrʌktəˈbɪlɪtɪ] *n* indestructibilidad *f*.
indestructible [ˌɪndɪsˈtrʌktəbl] *adj* indestructible.
indeterminable [ˌɪndɪˈtɜːmɪnəbl] *adj* indeterminable.
indeterminacy [ˌɪndɪˈtɜːmɪnəsɪ] *n* carácter *m* indeterminado.
indeterminate [ˌɪndɪˈtɜːmɪnɪt] *adj* indeterminado.
indeterminately [ˌɪndɪˈtɜːmɪnɪtlɪ] *adv* de modo indeterminado.
index [ˈɪndeks] **1** *n, pl* **indexes** *or* **indices** [ˈɪndɪsiːz] (*finger, of book, Econ*) índice *m*; (*Math*) exponente *m*; (*fig*)

indicación *f* (*to* de); (*Eccl*) **I~** índice *m* expurgatorio.

2 *attr*: ~ **card** ficha *f*; ~ **finger** (dedo *m*) índice *m*; ~ **number** índice *m*, indicador *m*.

3 *vt book* poner índice a; *book* (*for catalogue*) indizar; *entry* poner en un índice; **it is ~ed under Smith** está clasificado bajo Smith, está clasificado en el artículo Smith.

indexation [ˌɪndek'seɪʃən] *n*, **indexing** ['ɪndeksɪŋ] *n* indexación *f*, indización *f*, indiciación *f*.

indexed ['ɪndekst] *adj*, **index-linked** [ɪndeks'lɪŋkt] *adj* indexado, indiciado.

index-linking [ˌɪndeks'lɪŋkɪŋ] *n* indexación *f*, indiciación *f*.

India ['ɪndɪə] **1** *n* la India.

2 *attr*: ~ **paper** papel *m* de China, papel *m* biblia.

Indian ['ɪndɪən] **1** *adj* indio; (*American Indian*) indio, indígena; ~ **club** maza *f* de gimnasia; ~ **elephant** elefante *m* asiático; ~ **file** fila *f* india; ~ **hemp** cáñamo *m* índico; ~ **ink** tinta *f* china; ~ **summer** veranillo *m* de San Martín; ~ **tea** té *m* indio; ~ **tonic** (**water**) agua *f* tónica.

2 *n* indio *m*, -a *f*; (*American Indian*) indio *m*, -a *f*, indígena *mf*.

Indian Ocean ['ɪndɪən'əʊʃən] *n* Océano *m* Índico.

indiarubber ['ɪndɪə'rʌbəʳ] *n* caucho *m*; (*eraser*) goma *f* de borrar.

indicate ['ɪndɪkeɪt] *vt* indicar.

indication [ˌɪndɪ'keɪʃən] *n* indicación *f*, indicio *m*, señal *f*.

indicative [ɪn'dɪkətɪv] **1** *adj* indicativo (*also Gram*); **to be ~ of** indicar. **2** *n* indicativo *m*.

indicator ['ɪndɪkeɪtəʳ] *n* indicador *m* (*also Econ etc*); (*Brit Aut*) indicador *m* de dirección, (*light*) intermitente *m*.

indices ['ɪndɪsiːz] *npl of* **index**.

indict [ɪn'daɪt] *vt* (**a**) acusar (*for, on a charge of* de), encausar, procesar. (**b**) (*fig*) condenar, criticar severamente, enjuiciar duramente.

indictable [ɪn'daɪtəbl] *adj* procesable, denunciable.

indictment [ɪn'daɪtmənt] *n* (**a**) (*charge*) acusación *f*, sumaria *f*; (*act*) procesamiento *m*. (**b**) (*fig*) condenación *f*, crítica *f* severa, enjuiciamiento *m* duro; **the report is an ~ of our whole system** el informe critica duramente todo nuestro sistema.

Indies ['ɪndɪz] *npl* las Indias; *V* **East** ~ *etc*.

indifference [ɪn'dɪfrəns] *n* indiferencia *f* (*to* ante); ~ **analysis** análisis *m* de indiferencia; ~ **curve** curva *f* de indiferencia; **it is a matter of supreme ~ to me** no me importa en lo más mínimo.

indifferent [ɪn'dɪfrənt] *adj* (**a**) indiferente; desinteresado, imparcial; **it is ~ to me** me es igual, me es indiferente.

(**b**) (*mediocre*) ordinario, regular.

indifferently [ɪn'dɪfrəntlɪ] *adv* (**a**) indiferentemente; **they go ~ to one or the other** van sin distinción al uno o al otro. (**b**) (*pej*) regularmente; **she performed ~** su actuación fue regular nada más.

indigence ['ɪndɪdʒəns] *n* indigencia *f*.

indigenous [ɪn'dɪdʒɪnəs] *adj* indígena (*to* de).

indigent ['ɪndɪdʒənt] *adj* indigente.

indigestible [ˌɪndɪ'dʒestəbl] *adj* indigesto; indigerible, indigestible.

indigestion [ˌɪndɪ'dʒestʃən] *n* indigestión *f*, empacho *m*.

indignant [ɪn'dɪgnənt] *adj* indignado; **to be ~ about sth** indignarse por algo; **to get ~ with sb** indignarse con uno; **it's no good getting ~** de nada sirve perder la paciencia; **to make sb ~** indignar a uno.

indignantly [ɪn'dɪgnəntlɪ] *adv* con indignación, indignado.

indignation [ˌɪndɪg'neɪʃən] *n* indignación *f*; ~ **meeting** mitin *m* de protesta.

indignity [ɪn'dɪgnɪtɪ] *n* indignidad *f*; ultraje *m*, afrenta *f*; **to suffer the ~ of** + *ger* sufrir la indignidad de + *infin*.

indigo ['ɪndɪgəʊ] **1** *n* añil *m*. **2** *adj* añil (*invar*), color de añil.

indirect [ˌɪndɪ'rekt] *adj* indirecto; ~ **exporting** exportación *f* indirecta; ~ **free kick** golpe *m* libre indirecto; ~ **labour** (*workers*) mano *f* de obra indirecta, (*work*) trabajo *m* indirecto; ~ **speech** oración *f* indirecta; ~ **tax** contribución *f* indirecta.

indirectly [ˌɪndɪ'rektlɪ] *adv* indirectamente.

indirectness [ˌɪndɪ'rektnɪs] *n* oblicuidad *f*, tortuosidad *f*.

indiscernible [ˌɪndɪ'sɜːnəbl] *adj* imperceptible.

indiscipline [ɪn'dɪsɪplɪn] *n* indisciplina *f*.

indiscreet [ˌɪndɪs'kriːt] *adj* indiscreto, imprudente.

indiscreetly [ˌɪndɪs'kriːtlɪ] *adv* indiscretamente.

indiscretion [ˌɪndɪs'kreʃən] *n* indiscreción *f*, imprudencia *f*.

indiscriminate [ˌɪndɪs'krɪmɪnɪt] *adj* indistinto, sin distinción; *bombing, terrorism* indiscriminado; *person* falto de discernimiento; *admirer* ciego.

indiscriminately [ˌɪndɪs'krɪmɪnɪtlɪ] *adv* indistintamente, sin distinción; indiscriminadamente; *admire* ciegamente.

indispensable [ˌɪndɪs'pensəbl] *adj* indispensable, imprescindible.

indisposed [ˌɪndɪs'pəʊzd] *adj*: **to be ~** estar indispuesto.

indisposition [ˌɪndɪspə'zɪʃən] *n* indisposición *f*, enfermedad *f*.

indisputable [ˌɪndɪs'pjuːtəbl] *adj* incontestable, incuestionable, indiscutible.

indisputably [ˌɪndɪs'pjuːtəblɪ] *adv* incontestablemente; **it is ~ the best** es el mejor sin ningún género de dudas; **oh, ~** claro que sí.

indissoluble [ˌɪndɪ'sɒljʊbl] *adj* indisoluble; *link* irrompible.

indissolubly [ˌɪndɪ'sɒljʊblɪ] *adv* indisolublemente; **to be ~ linked** tener vínculos irrompibles.

indistinct [ˌɪndɪs'tɪŋkt] *adj* indistinto; confuso.

indistinctly [ˌɪndɪs'tɪŋktlɪ] *adv* indistintamente; confusamente.

indistinguishable [ˌɪndɪs'tɪŋgwɪʃəbl] *adv* indistinguible (*from* de).

indite [ɪn'daɪt] *vt* (*liter*) *letter* endilgar.

individual [ˌɪndɪ'vɪdjʊəl] **1** *adj* individual; personal; (*for one person alone*) particular, propio; ~ **bargaining** negociación *f* individual; **we do not sell the ~ volumes** no vendemos los tomos sueltos; **he has a very ~ style** tiene un estilo muy personal (*or* muy suyo). **2** *n* individuo *m*.

individualism [ˌɪndɪ'vɪdjʊəlɪzəm] *n* individualismo *m*.

individualist [ˌɪndɪ'vɪdjʊəlɪst] *n* individualista *mf*.

individualistic ['ɪndɪˌvɪdjʊə'lɪstɪk] *adj* individualista.

individuality [ˌɪndɪˌvɪdjʊ'ælɪtɪ] *n* individualidad *f*, personalidad *f*.

individualize [ˌɪndɪ'vɪdjʊəlaɪz] *vt* individuar, individualizar.

individually [ˌɪndɪ'vɪdjʊəlɪ] *adv* individualmente; particularmente; **they're all right ~** cada uno de por sí es buena persona.

indivisibility [ˌɪndɪˌvɪzə'bɪlətɪ] *n* indivisibilidad *f*.

indivisible [ˌɪndɪ'vɪzəbl] *adj* indivisible.

Indo... ['ɪndəʊ] *pref* indo...

Indo-China ['ɪndəʊ'tʃaɪnə] *n* la Indochina.

indoctrinate [ɪn'dɒktrɪneɪt] *vt* adoctrinar (*with* en).

indoctrination [ɪnˌdɒktrɪ'neɪʃən] *n* adoctrinamiento *m*, adoctrinación *f*.

Indo-European ['ɪndəʊˌjʊərə'piːən] **1** *adj* indoeuropeo. **2** *n* (**a**) indoeuropeo *m*, -a *f*. (**b**) (*Ling*) indoeuropeo *m*.

indolence ['ɪndələns] *n* indolencia *f*, pereza *f*.

indolent ['ɪndələnt] *adj* indolente, perezoso.

indolently ['ɪndələntlɪ] *adv* perezosamente.

indomitable [ɪn'dɒmɪtəbl] *adj* indómito, indomable.

indomitably [ɪn'dɒmɪtəblɪ] *adv* indómitamente, indomablemente.

Indonesia [ˌɪndəʊ'niːzɪə] *n* Indonesia *f*.

Indonesian [ˌɪndəʊ'niːzɪən] **1** *adj* indonesio. **2** *n* indonesio *m*, -a *f*.

indoor ['ɪndɔːʳ] *adj* interior; de casa; de puertas adentro; ~ **aerial** antena *f* interior; ~ **athletics** atletismo *m* en sala, atletismo *m* en pista cubierta; ~ **football** fútbol *m* (en) sala; ~ **games** juegos *mpl* de salón; ~ **plant** planta *f* de interior; ~ **pool** piscina *f* cubierta.

indoors [ɪn'dɔːz] *adv* en casa; dentro; bajo techado; **Her I~*** (*hum*) la parienta*; **to go ~** entrar (en la casa); **he had to spend a week ~** tuvo que estar una semana en casa; **I like the outside but what's it like ~?** me gusta lo de fuera, pero ¿qué tal está por dentro?

indrawn [ˌɪn'drɔːn] *adj*: **we watched with ~ breath** mirábamos casi sin respirar.

indubitable [ɪn'djuːbɪtəbl] *adj* indudable.

indubitably [ɪn'djuːbɪtəblɪ] *adv* indudablemente, sin duda.

induce [ɪn'djuːs] *vt* inducir; producir, ocasionar; *sleep etc* provocar; (*Elec*) inducir; **to ~ sb to do sth** inducir a uno a hacer algo, persuadir a uno a hacer algo; **nothing would ~ me to go** nada me persuadiría a ir.

inducement [ɪn'djuːsmənt] *n* incentivo *m*, aliciente *m*, estímulo *m*; **to hold out sth to sb as an ~** ofrecer algo a uno como aliciente; **it offers no ~ to harder work** no ofrece estímulo para trabajar más; **as an added ~ it has ...** tiene además el atractivo de ...

induct [ɪn'dʌkt] *vt* (*Eccl*) instalar; *new member etc* iniciar (*into* en); (*US Mil*) quintar.

induction [ɪn'dʌkʃən] **1** *n* (*Eccl*) instalación *f*; (*of member*) iniciación *f*; (*US Mil*) quinta *f*; (*Elec, Philos*) inducción *f*.

2 *attr*: ~ **coil** carrete *m* de inducción; ~ **course** curso *m* (*or* cursillo *m*) introductorio.

inductive [ɪn'dʌktɪv] *adj* inductivo.

indulge [ɪn'dʌldʒ] **1** *vt desire etc* satisfacer, dar rienda suelta a; *whim* condescender con; *person* complacer, dar gusto a; *child etc* consentir, mimar.

2 *vi* (*: *drink*) beber (con exceso); **to ~ in** darse el lujo de, permitirse; (*viciously*) darse a, abandonarse a.

3 *vr*: **to ~ o.s.** darse gusto, permitirse un lujo.

indulgence [ɪn'dʌldʒəns] *n* (**a**) (*of desire etc*) satisfacción *f*, gratificación *f*; (*vicious*) abandono *m* (*in* a), desenfreno *m*; (*tolerance*) tolerancia *f*, complacencia *f*. (**b**) (*Eccl*) indulgencia *f*.

indulgent [ɪn'dʌldʒənt] *adj* indulgente (*towards* con).

indulgently [ɪn'dʌldʒəntlɪ] *adv* indulgentemente.

industrial [ɪn'dʌstrɪəl] **1** *adj* industrial; laboral, de trabajo; **~ accident** accidente *m* laboral, accidente *m* de trabajo; **~ action** huelga *f*; **~ archaeology** arqueología *f* industrial; **~ belt, ~ estate** (*Brit*), **~ park, ~ zone** (*US*) zona *f* industrial; **~ correspondent** (*Brit*) corresponsal *mf* de información laboral; **~ court** = **~ tribunal**; **~ design** diseño *m* industrial; **~ diamond** diamante *m* natural, diamante *m* industrial; **~ dispute** (*Brit*) conflicto *m* laboral; **~ espionage** espionaje *m* industrial; **~ goods** bienes *mpl* de producción; **~ hygiene** higiene *f* industrial; **~ injury** accidente *m* laboral, accidente *m* de trabajo; **~ injury benefit** subsidio *m* por accidente laboral; **~ potential** potencial *m* industrial; **~ relations** relaciones *fpl* empresariales; **I~ Revolution** Revolución *f* Industrial; **~ safety** seguridad *f* industrial; **~ tribunal** magistratura *f* del trabajo, tribunal *m* laboral; **~ union** sindicato *m* industrial; **~ unrest** conflictividad *f* laboral; **~ waste** (*Brit*) residuos *mpl* (*or* vertidos *mpl*) industriales. **2** **~s** *npl* acciones *fpl* industriales.

industrialism [ɪn'dʌstrɪəlɪzəm] *n* industrialismo *m*.

industrialist [ɪn'dʌstrɪəlɪst] *n* industrial *m*.

industrialization [ɪn,dʌstrɪəlaɪ'zeɪʃən] *n* industrialización *f*.

industrialize [ɪn'dʌstrɪəlaɪz] *vt* industrializar.

industrious [ɪn'dʌstrɪəs] *adj* trabajador, laborioso; *student* aplicado, diligente.

industriously [ɪn'dʌstrɪəslɪ] *adv* laboriosamente; con aplicación, diligentemente.

industriousness [ɪn'dʌstrɪəsnɪs] *n* laboriosidad *f*; aplicación *f*, diligencia *f*.

industry ['ɪndəstrɪ] *n* (**a**) (*Tech*) industria *f*; **the hotel ~** el comercio hotelero; **the tourist ~** el turismo.

(**b**) (*industriousness*) laboriosidad *f*, aplicación *f*, diligencia *f*.

inebriate 1 [ɪ'niːbrɪɪt] *n* borracho *m*, -a *f*. **2** [ɪ'niːbrɪeɪt] *vt* embriagar, emborrachar.

inebriated [ɪ'niːbrɪeɪtɪd] *adj* ebrio, borracho.

inebriation [ɪ,niːbrɪ'eɪʃən] *n* embriaguez *f*.

inedible [ɪn'edɪbl] *adj* incomible, no comestible.

ineducable [ɪn'edjʊkəbl] *adj* ineducable.

ineffable [ɪn'efəbl] *adj* inefable.

ineffaceable [,ɪnɪ'feɪsəbl] *adj* imborrable.

ineffective [,ɪnɪ'fektɪv] *adj*, **ineffectual** [,ɪnɪ'fektjʊəl] *adj remedy etc* ineficaz, inútil; *person* incapaz, inútil; **he's wholly ~** es un cero a la izquierda; **the plan proved ~** el proyecto no surtió efecto.

ineffectively [,ɪnɪ'fektɪvlɪ] *adv* ineficazmente, inútilmente.

ineffectual [,ɪnɪ'fektjʊəl] *adj* ineficaz, inútil.

ineffectually [,ɪnɪ'fektjʊəlɪ] *adv* ineficazmente, inútilmente.

inefficacious [,ɪnefɪ'keɪʃəs] *adj* ineficaz.

inefficacy [ɪn'efɪkəsɪ] *n* ineficacia *f*.

inefficiency [,ɪnɪ'fɪʃənsɪ] *n* ineficacia *f*; incapacidad *f*, incompetencia *f*.

inefficient [,ɪnɪ'fɪʃənt] *adj* ineficaz, ineficiente; *person* incapaz, incompetente.

inefficiently [,ɪnɪ'fɪʃəntlɪ] *adv* ineficazmente; de modo incompetente.

inelastic [,ɪnɪ'læstɪk] *adj* inelástico; (*fig*) rígido, poco flexible; **~ demand** demanda *f* inelástica; **~ supply** suministro *m* inelástico.

inelegant [ɪn'elɪgənt] *adj* inelegante, poco elegante.

inelegantly [ɪn'elɪgəntlɪ] *adv* inelegantemente.

ineligible [ɪn'elɪdʒəbl] *adj* inelegible; **to be ~ to vote** no tener derecho a votar.

ineluctable [,ɪnɪ'lʌktəbl] *adj* ineludible.

inept [ɪ'nept] *adj* inepto; *person* incompetente, incapaz.

ineptitude [ɪ'neptɪtjuːd] *n*, **ineptness** [ɪ'neptnɪs] *n* inepcia *f*, ineptitud *f*; incompetencia *f*, incapacidad *f*.

inequality [,ɪnɪ'kwɒlɪtɪ] *n* desigualdad *f*.

inequitable [ɪn'ekwɪtəbl] *adj* injusto.

inequity [ɪn'ekwɪtɪ] *n* injusticia *f*.

ineradicable [,ɪnɪ'rædɪkəbl] *adj* inextirpable.

inert [ɪ'nɜːt] *adj* inerte, inactivo; (*motionless*) inmóvil; **he lay ~ on the floor** estuvo tumbado sin moverse en el suelo.

inertia [ɪ'nɜːʃə] *n* inercia *f* (*also Phys*), inacción *f*; pereza *f*; **~ selling** venta *f* por inercia.

inertia-reel [ɪ'nɜːʃə,riːl] *attr*: **~ seat-belt** cinturón *m* de seguridad retráctil.

inescapable [,ɪnɪs'keɪpəbl] *adj* ineludible.

inessential ['ɪnɪ'senʃəl] **1** *adj* no esencial. **2** *n* cosa *f* no esencial.

inestimable [ɪn'estɪməbl] *adj* inapreciable, inestimable.

inevitability [ɪn,evɪtə'bɪlɪtɪ] *n* inevitabilidad *f*.

inevitable [ɪn'evɪtəbl] *adj* inevitable, ineludible; forzoso; **it was ~ it should happen** tuvo forzosamente (*or* fatalmente) que ocurrir.

inevitably [ɪn'evɪtəblɪ] *adv* inevitablemente, forzosamente.

inexact [,ɪnɪg'zækt] *adj* inexacto.

inexactitude [,ɪnɪg'zæktɪtjuːd) *n* inexactitud *f*.

inexactly [,ɪnɪg'zæktlɪ] *adv* de modo inexacto.

inexcusable [,ɪnɪks'kjuːzəbl] *adj* imperdonable.

inexcusably [,ɪnɪks'kjuːzəblɪ] *adv* imperdonablemente.

inexhaustible [,ɪnɪg'zɔːstəbl] *adj* inagotable.

inexorable [ɪn'eksərəbl] *adj* inexorable, implacable.

inexorably [ɪn'eksərəblɪ] *adv* inexorablemente, implacablemente.

inexpedient [,ɪnɪks'piːdɪənt] *adj* inoportuno, inconveniente, imprudente.

inexpensive [,ɪnɪks'pensɪv] *adj* económico, barato.

inexpensively [,ɪnɪks'pensɪvlɪ] *adv* económicamente.

inexperience [,ɪnɪks'pɪərɪəns] *n* inexperiencia *f*, falta *f* de experiencia.

inexperienced [,ɪnɪks'pɪərɪənst] *adj* inexperto, falto de experiencia.

inexpert [ɪn'ekspɜːt] *adj* imperito, inexperto, inhábil.

inexpertly [ɪn'ekspɜːtlɪ] *adv* sin habilidad, desmañadamente.

inexplicable [,ɪnɪks'plɪkəbl] *adj* inexplicable.

inexplicably [,ɪnɪks'plɪkəblɪ] *adv* inexplicablemente, misteriosamente.

inexpressible [,ɪnɪks'presəbl] *adj* inefable.

inexpressive [,ɪnɪks'presɪv] *adj style etc* inexpresivo; *person* reservado, callado.

inextinguishable [,ɪnɪks'tɪŋgwɪʃəbl] *adj* inextinguible, inapagable.

inextricable [,ɪnɪks'trɪkəbl] *adj* inextricable, inseparable, imposible de desenredar (*etc*).

inextricably [,ɪnɪks'trɪkəblɪ] *adv*: **~ entwined** entrelazados de modo inextricable.

infallibility [ɪn,fælə'bɪlɪtɪ] *n* infalibilidad *f*.

infallible [ɪn'fæləbl] *adj* infalible; indefectible.

infallibly [ɪn'fæləblɪ] *adv* infaliblemente; indefectiblemente.

infamous ['ɪnfəməs] *adj* infame.

infamy ['ɪnfəmɪ] *n* infamia *f*.

infancy ['ɪnfənsɪ] *n* infancia *f*; (*Jur*) menor edad *f*; **from ~** desde niño; **it is still in its ~** está todavía en mantillas.

infant ['ɪnfənt] **1** *adj mortality etc* infantil; *class, school* de párvulos; *industry etc* naciente; **~ mortality** mortandad *f* infantil, mortalidad *f* infantil; **~ school** (*Brit*) parvulario *m*; **~ welfare clinic** clínica *f* pediátrica.

2 *n* criatura *f*, niño *m*, -a *f*; (*Jur*) menor *mf*; **the ~ Jesus** el niño Jesús.

infanta [ɪn'fæntə] *n* infanta *f*.

infante [ɪn'fæntɪ] *n* infante *m*.

infanticide [ɪn'fæntɪsaɪd] *n* (**a**) (*act*) infanticidio *m*. (**b**) (*person*) infanticida *mf*.

infantile ['ɪnfəntaɪl] *adj* infantil (*also Med*); **~ paralysis** parálisis *f* infantil; **don't be so ~!** ¡no seas niño!

infantilism [ɪn'fæntɪ,lɪzəm] *n* infantilismo *m*.

infantry ['ɪnfəntrɪ] *n* infantería *f*.

infantryman ['ɪnfəntrɪmən] *n*, *pl* **infantrymen** ['ɪnfəntrɪmən] soldado *m* de infantería; (*Hist*) infante *m*, peón *m*.

infatuated [ɪn'fætjʊeɪtɪd] *adj*: **to be ~ with** *idea etc* encapricharse por; *person* estar chiflado por.

infatuation [ɪn,fætjʊ'eɪʃən] *n* encaprichamiento *m*; chifladura *f*.

infect [ɪn'fekt] *vt air, well, wound etc* infectar, inficionar; *person* contagiar (*with* con); (*fig*) contagiar, comunicar; (*pej*) corromper, inficionar; **to be ~ed with** (*act*) contagiarse de, (*state*) estar contagiado de; **he ~s everybody with his enthusiasm** contagia a todos con su entusiasmo.

infected [ɪn'fektɪd] *adj* infectado.

infection [ɪn'fekʃən] *n* (*Med*) infección *f*, contagio *m*; (*fig*) contagio *m*; **she has a slight ~** está ligeramente indispuesta.

infectious [ɪn'fekʃəs] *adj* contagioso (*also fig*), infeccioso.

infectiousness [ɪn'fekʃəsnɪs] *n* contagiosidad *f*.

infelicitous [,ɪnfɪ'lɪsɪtəs] *adj* poco feliz, inoportuno, impropio.

invigorating [ɪn'vɪgəreɪtɪŋ] *adj* vigorizante, vigorizador.

invincibility [ɪn,vɪnsɪ'bɪlɪtɪ] *n* invencibilidad *f*.

invincible [ɪn'vɪnsəbl] *adj* invencible.

invincibly [ɪn'vɪnsəblɪ] *adv* de manera invencible; ~ **ignorant** irremediablemente ignorante; ~ **right** irrebatiblemente correcto.

inviolability [ɪn,vaɪələ'bɪlɪtɪ] *n* inviolabilidad *f*.

inviolable [ɪn'vaɪələbl] *adj* inviolable.

inviolate [ɪn'vaɪəlɪt] *adj* inviolado.

invisibility [ɪn,vɪzə'bɪlɪtɪ] *n* invisibilidad *f*.

invisible [ɪn'vɪzəbl] **1** *adj* invisible; ~ **assets** activo *m* invisible; ~ **balance** balance *m* invisible; ~ **earnings** ingresos *mpl* invisibles; ~ **exports** exportaciones *fpl* invisibles; ~ **imports** importaciones *fpl* invisibles; ~ **ink** tinta *f* simpática; ~ **mending** puntada *f* invisible. **2** ~**s** *npl* (*Comm*) ingresos *mpl* invisibles.

invisibly [ɪn'vɪzɪblɪ] *adv* invisiblemente.

invitation [,ɪnvɪ'teɪʃən] **1** *n* invitación *f*; convite *m*. **2** *attr*: ~ **card** tarjeta *f* de invitación.

invite 1 [ɪn'vaɪt] *vt* (**a**) (*gen*) invitar, (*esp to food and drink*) convidar; **to** ~ **sb to supper** invitar a uno a cenar; **to** ~ **sb to do sth** invitar a uno a hacer algo; **to** ~ **sb to have a drink** convidar a uno a tomar algo.

(**b**) (*request*) pedir, rogar; **he** ~**s our opinions** pide nuestras opiniones.

(**c**) *trouble etc* correr a, buscarse; **it's just inviting trouble** esto es crear dificultades para sí; **to do so is to** ~ **defeat** hacer esto es procurar la propia derrota.

(**d**) (*induce*) inducir a, sugerir; **A** ~**s comparison with B** A nos induce a compararlo con B, se impone la comparación de A con B; **she seems to** ~ **stares** según parece le gusta que la mire la gente.

2 ['ɪnvaɪt] *n* (*) invitación *f*.

◆**invite in** *vt* invitar a entrar.

◆**invite out** *vt* invitar, convidar (*a un restaurante, al cine etc*).

◆**invite over** *vt* convidar, invitar (a casa).

inviting [ɪn'vaɪtɪŋ] *adj* atractivo, atrayente, tentador; *look* incitante, provocativo; *food* apetitoso.

invitingly [ɪn'vaɪtɪŋlɪ] *adv* de modo atractivo (*etc*); de modo incitante; apetitosamente.

in vitro [ɪn'vi:trəʊ] *adj, adv* in vitro; ~ **fertilization** fecundación *f* in vitro.

invocation [,ɪnvəʊ'keɪʃən] *n* invocación *f*.

invoice ['ɪnvɔɪs] **1** *n* factura *f*; **as per** ~ según factura; **to send an** ~ pasar factura, presentar factura. **2** *attr*: ~ **clerk** facturador *m*, -ora *f*. **3** *vt* facturar; ~**d value** valor *m* según facturación.

invoicing ['ɪnvɔɪsɪŋ] *n* facturación *f*.

invoke [ɪn'vəʊk] *vt* invocar; *aid* suplicar, implorar; *law* recurrir a, acogerse a; *spirit* conjurar.

involuntarily [ɪn'vɒləntərɪlɪ] *adv* involuntariamente, sin querer.

involuntary [ɪn'vɒləntərɪ] *adj* involuntario.

involve [ɪn'vɒlv] **1** *vt* (**a**) (*physically*) enredar, enmarañar; *matter* complicar, entenebrecer.

(**b**) (*implicate etc*) implicar, involucrar, comprometer; **to** ~ **sb in a quarrel** mezclar a uno en una disputa; **the persons** ~**d** los interesados; **the forces** ~**d** las fuerzas en juego; **a question of principle is** ~**d** aquí está en juego un principio; **to be** ~**d in** estar implicado en, estar metido en, andar envuelto en; **to be** ~**d in a plot** estar implicado en un complot; **was he** ~**d in it?** ¿anduvo él metido en ello?, ¿tuvo él que ver con el asunto?; **how did you come to be** ~**d?** ¿cómo llegaste a estar envuelto en esto?; **to get** (*or* **become**) ~**d in** meterse en, enredarse en, embrollarse en; **he got** ~**d with a girl** tuvo un lío con una joven; **I don't want to get** ~**d** no quiero dejarme ir demasiado lejos, allí no entro yo.

(**c**) (*imply*) suponer, implicar, traer consigo, acarrear, ocasionar; **it** ~**s moving house** ello supone que tendremos que mudar de casa; **it** ~**d a lot of expense** nos acarreó muchos gastos; **does it** ~ **much trouble?** ¿esto supone mucho trabajo para Vd?

2 *vr*: **to** ~ **o.s. in** interesarse en; tomar parte en, participar en; (*pej*) involucrarse en.

involved [ɪn'vɒlvd] *adj* complicado; *style* enrevesado, laberíntico; **to become** ~, **to get** ~ complicarse.

involvement [ɪn'vɒlvmənt] *n* enredo *m*; compromiso *m*; (*difficulty*) apuro *m*, dificultad *f*; **we don't know the extent of his** ~ no sabemos hasta qué punto se había comprometido; **his** ~ **in the plot** su participación en el complot; **we must keep out of** ~**s** hay que evitar los compromisos.

invulnerability [ɪn,vʌlnərə'bɪlɪtɪ] *n* invulnerabilidad *f*.

invulnerable [ɪn'vʌlnərəbl] *adj* invulnerable.

inward ['ɪnwəd] *adj* interior, interno; íntimo; espiritual.

inward-looking ['ɪnwəd,lʊkɪŋ] *adj* introvertido.

inwardly ['ɪnwədlɪ] *adv* interiormente; *laugh etc* para sí, entre sí, para sus adentros.

inward(s)[1] ['ɪnwəd(z)] *adv* hacia dentro, para dentro.

inwards[2]* ['ɪnədz] *npl* tripas *fpl*.

I/O *n* (*Comput*) *abbr of* **input/output** entrada/salida, E/S; ~ **error** error *m* de E/S.

IOC *n abbr of* **International Olympic Committee** Comité *m* Olímpico Internacional, COI *m*.

iodine ['aɪədi:n] *n* yodo *m*.

iodoform [aɪ'ɒdəfɔ:m] *n* yodoformo *m*.

IOM (*Brit*) *abbr of* **Isle of Man**.

ion ['aɪən] *n* ion *m*.

Ionian [aɪ'əʊnɪən] *adj* jonio, jónico.

Ionian Sea [aɪ,əʊnɪən'si:] *n* Mar *m* Jónico.

Ionic [aɪ'ɒnɪk] *adj* jónico.

ionic [aɪ'ɒnɪk] *adj* (*Chem*) iónico.

ionize ['aɪənaɪz] *vt* ionizar.

ionosphere [aɪ'ɒnəsfɪəʳ] *n* ionosfera *f*.

iota [aɪ'əʊtə] *n* (*letter*) iota *f*; (*fig*) jota *f*, ápice *m*; **there's not one** ~ **of truth in it** eso no tiene ni pizca de verdad; **if he had an** ~ **of sense** si tuviera un poquito de inteligencia.

IOU *n abbr of* **I owe you** pagaré *m*.

IOW (*Brit*) *abbr of* **Isle of Wight**.

IPA *n abbr of* **International Phonetic Alphabet**.

ipecacuanha [,ɪpɪkækjʊ'ænə] *n* ipecacuana *f*.

IQ *n abbr of* **intelligence quotient** cociente *m* intelectual, C.I. *m*.

IR *abbr of* **Inland Revenue**.

IRA *n* (**a**) (*Pol*) *abbr of* **Irish Republican Army** IRA *m*. (**b**) (*US*) *abbr of* **individual retirement account** cuenta *f* individual para la jubilación.

Irak [ɪ'rɑ:k] *n* Irak *m*, Iraq *m*.

Iraki [ɪ'rɑ:kɪ] **1** *adj* iraquí. **2** *n* iraquí *mf*.

Iran [ɪ'rɑ:n] *n* Irán *m*.

Iranian [ɪ'reɪnɪən] **1** *adj* iranio, iraní. **2** *n* (*ancient*) iranio *m*, -a *f*, (*modern*) iraní *mf*.

Iraq [ɪ'rɑ:k] *n* Irak *m*, Iraq *m*.

Iraqi [ɪ'rɑ:kɪ] **1** *adj* iraquí. **2** *n* iraquí *mf*.

irascibility [ɪ,ræsɪ'bɪlɪtɪ] *n* irascibilidad *f*.

irascible [ɪ'ræsɪbl] *adj* irascible, de prontos enojos.

irascibly [ɪ'ræsɪblɪ] *adv*: **he said** ~ dijo colérico.

irate [aɪ'reɪt] *adj* colérico, enojado, indignado; **he got very** ~ se encolerizó mucho.

IRBM *n abbr of* **intermediate range ballistic missile** misil *m* balístico de alcance medio.

ire [aɪəʳ] *n* (*liter*) ira *f*, cólera *f*, iracundia *f*; **to rouse sb's** ~ provocar la ira de uno; **that always rouses his** ~ eso siempre le saca de quicio.

Ireland ['aɪələnd] *n* Irlanda *f*; **Northern** ~ Irlanda *f* del Norte; **Republic of** ~ República *f* de Irlanda.

iridescence [,ɪrɪ'desns] *n* irisación *f*.

iridescent [,ɪrɪ'desnt] *adj* iridiscente, irisado, tornasolado.

iridium [ɪ'rɪdɪəm] *n* iridio *m*.

iris ['aɪərɪs] *n* (*Anat*) iris *m*; (*Bot*) lirio *m*.

Irish ['aɪərɪʃ] **1** *adj* irlandés; ~ **coffee** café *m* irlandés; ~ **stew** estofado *m* irlandés. **2** *n* (**a**) **the** ~ los irlandeses. (**b**) (*Ling*) irlandés *m*.

Irish Free State ['aɪərɪʃ'fri:'steɪt] *n* Estado *m* Libre de Irlanda.

Irishman ['aɪərɪʃmən] *n, pl* **Irishmen** ['aɪərɪʃmən] irlandés *m*.

Irish Sea ['aɪərɪʃ'si:] *n* Mar *m* de Irlanda.

Irishwoman ['aɪərɪʃ,wʊmən] *n, pl* **Irishwomen** ['aɪrɪʃ,wɪmɪn] irlandesa *f*.

irk [ɜ:k] *vt* fastidiar, molestar.

irksome ['ɜ:ksəm] *adj* molesto, pesado, fastidioso.

IRN *n* (*Brit*) *abbr of* **Independent Radio News** *servicio de noticias en las cadenas de radio privadas*.

IRO *n* (**a**) (*Brit*) *abbr of* **Inland Revenue Office**. (**b**) (*US*) *abbr of* **International Refugee Organization**.

iron ['aɪən] **1** *n* (**a**) (*Min*) hierro *m*, fierro *m* (*Méx*); (*fig*) hierro *m*, acero *m*; **man of** ~ hombre *m* de acero; **old** ~ chatarra *f*, hierro *m* viejo; **to strike while the** ~ **is hot** a hierro candente batir de repente.

(**b**) ~**s** (*fetters*) hierros *mpl*, grillos *mpl*; (*) (*at table*) cuchillo *m* y tenedor *m*; (*guns*) pistolas *fpl*; **to have too many** ~**s in the fire** tener demasiados asuntos entre manos; **to put sb in** ~**s** aherrojar a uno, echar grillos a uno.

(**c**) (*Golf*) hierro *m*.

(**d**) (*flat* ~) plancha *f*, planchador *m*.

infelicity [ˌɪnfɪˈlɪsɪtɪ] *n* inoportunidad *f*, impropiedad *f*.
infer [ɪnˈfɜːʳ] *vt* deducir, colegir, inferir (*from* de).
inference [ˈɪnfərəns] *n* deducción *f*, inferencia *f*, conclusión *f*.
inferential [ˌɪnfəˈrenʃəl] *adj* ilativo, deductivo.
inferentially [ˌɪnfəˈrenʃəlɪ] *adv* por inferencia, por deducción.
inferior [ɪnˈfɪərɪəʳ] **1** *adj* inferior (*to* a). **2** *n* inferior *mf*.
inferiority [ɪnˌfɪərɪˈɒrɪtɪ] **1** *n* inferioridad *f*. **2** *attr*: ~ **complex** complejo *m* de inferioridad.
infernal [ɪnˈfɜːnl] *adj* infernal; (*fig*) maldito, infernal.
infernally [ɪnˈfɜːnəlɪ] *adv*: **it's ~ awkward** es terriblemente difícil.
inferno [ɪnˈfɜːnəʊ] *n* infierno *m*; **it's like an ~ in there** allí dentro hace un calor insufrible; **in a few minutes the house was a blazing ~** en pocos minutos la casa estaba hecha una hoguera.
infertile [ɪnˈfɜːtaɪl] *adj* estéril, infecundo.
infertility [ˌɪnfɜːˈtɪlɪtɪ] *adj* esterilidad *f*, infecundidad *f*.
infest [ɪnˈfest] *vt* infestar; **to be ~ed with** estar plagado de.
infestation [ˌɪnfesˈteɪʃən] *n* infestación *f*, plaga *f*.
infidel [ˈɪnfɪdəl] **1** *adj* infiel, pagano, descreído. **2** *n* infiel *mf*, pagano *m*, -a *f*, descreído *m*, -a *f*; **the I~** los descreídos, la gente descreída.
infidelity [ˌɪnfɪˈdelɪtɪ] *n* infidelidad *f* (*to* para con); **marital ~** infidelidad *f* conyugal.
in-fighting [ˈɪnfaɪtɪŋ] *n* lucha *f* cuerpo a cuerpo; (*fig*) riñas *fpl*, disputas *fpl*; dimes *mpl* y diretes; **political ~** riñas *fpl* políticas.
infiltrate [ˈɪnfɪltreɪt] **1** *vt* infiltrarse en. **2** *vi* infiltrarse.
infiltration [ˌɪnfɪlˈtreɪʃən] *n* infiltración *f*.
infiltrator [ˈɪnfɪltreɪtəʳ] *n* agente *mf*; persona *f* que se infiltra en una organización (*or* a través de una frontera *etc*).
infinite [ˈɪnfɪnɪt] **1** *adj* infinito; (*fig*) infinito, inmenso, enorme; **we had ~ trouble finding it** nos costó la mar de trabajo encontrarlo; **he took ~ pains over it** lo hizo con el mayor esmero.
2 *n*: **the ~** el infinito.
infinitely [ˈɪnfɪnɪtlɪ] *adv* infinitamente; **this is ~ harder** esto es muchísimo más difícil, esto es mil veces más difícil.
infiniteness [ˈɪnfɪnɪtnɪs] *n* infinidad *f*.
infinitesimal [ˌɪnfɪnɪˈtesɪməl] *adj* infinitesimal.
infinitive [ɪnˈfɪnɪtɪv] **1** *adj* infinitivo. **2** *n* infinitivo *m*.
infinitude [ɪnˈfɪnɪtjuːd] *n* infinitud *f*.
infinity [ɪnˈfɪnɪtɪ] *n* (*Math*) infinito *m*; (*fig*) infinidad *f*; **an ~ of** infinidad de, un sinfín de.
infirm [ɪnˈfɜːm] *adj* enfermizo, achacoso, débil; **~ of purpose** irresoluto; **the old and ~** los ancianos y enfermos.
infirmary [ɪnˈfɜːmərɪ] *n* hospital *m*; (*at bullring etc*) enfermería *f*.
infirmity [ɪnˈfɜːmɪtɪ] *n* (*state*) debilidad *f*; (*illness*) enfermedad *f*, achaque *m*, dolencia *f*; (*moral*) flaqueza *f*.
infix [ˈɪnfɪks] *n* infijo *m*.
in flagrante delicto [ɪnfləˈgræntɪdɪˈlɪktəʊ] *adv* en flagrante.
inflame [ɪnˈfleɪm] *vt* inflamar (*also Med*); **to be ~d with** arder de, inflamarse de.
inflammable [ɪnˈflæməbl] *adj* inflamable; (*situation etc*) explosivo, de gran tirantez.
inflammation [ˌɪnfləˈmeɪʃən] *n* inflamación *f*.
inflammatory [ɪnˈflæmətərɪ] *adj* inflamatorio; *propaganda, speech* incendiario.
inflatable [ɪnˈfleɪtəbl] *adj* inflable, hinchable.
inflate [ɪnˈfleɪt] *vt* hinchar, inflar (*with* de); (*fig*) hinchar (*with* de); *report etc* exagerar; *price* inflar, aumentar de modo excesivo; *currency* provocar la inflación de.
inflated [ɪnˈfleɪtɪd] *adj report* exagerado; *price* excesivo.
inflation [ɪnˈfleɪʃən] *n* inflación *f* (*also Fin*); **~ accounting** contabilidad *f* de inflación.
inflationary [ɪnˈfleɪʃnərɪ] *adj* inflacionista, inflacionario; **~ gap** desequilibrio *m* inflacionario.
inflationism [ɪnˈfleɪʃənɪzəm] *n* inflacionismo *m*.
inflation-proof [ɪnˈfleɪʃənˌpruːf] *adj* resistente a la inflación.
inflect [ɪnˈflekt] *vt* (**a**) torcer, doblar; *voice* modular. (**b**) (*Gram*) *noun etc* declinar; *verb* conjugar.
inflected [ɪnˈflektɪd] *adj language* flexional.
inflection [ɪnˈflekʃən] *n* inflexión *f*.
inflectional [ɪnˈflekʃənl] *adj* con inflexión.
inflexibility [ɪnˌfleksɪˈbɪlɪtɪ] *n* inflexibilidad *f*; (*fig*) rigidez *f*.
inflexible [ɪnˈfleksəbl] *adj* inflexible.
inflexion [ɪnˈflekʃən] *n* inflexión *f*.
inflict [ɪnˈflɪkt] **1** *vt wound etc* infligir, inferir (*on* a); *penalty, tax etc* imponer (*on* a); *grief, damage etc* causar (*on* a).
2 *vr*: **to ~ o.s. on sb** molestar a uno acompañándole (*or* visitándole *etc*).
infliction [ɪnˈflɪkʃən] *n* (*act*) imposición *f*; (*penalty etc*) pena *f*, castigo *m*.
in-flight [ˈɪnflaɪt] *attr*: **~ meal** comida *f* servida durante el vuelo; **~ movie** película *f* proyectada durante el vuelo; **~ services** servicios *mpl* de a bordo.
inflow [ˈɪnfləʊ] **1** *n* afluencia *f*. **2** *attr*: **~ pipe** tubo *m* de entrada.
influence [ˈɪnflʊəns] **1** *n* influencia *f*, influjo *m* (*on* sobre); ascendiente *m* (*over* sobre); valimiento *m* (*with* cerca de); **a man of ~** un hombre influyente; **to be under the ~ (of drink)** estar borracho; **to be under the ~ of drugs** estar bajo los efectos de las drogas; **to drive under the ~** conducir en estado de embriaguez; **to bring every ~ to bear on sb** ejercer todas las presiones posibles sobre uno; **to have ~** (*person*) tener el padre alcalde, tener buenas aldabas; **you've got to have ~ to get a job** para conseguir un puesto hay que tener un buen enchufe; **to have ~ over sb** tener ascendiente sobre uno.
2 *vt person etc* influir en, influenciar; sugestionar; *decision etc* influir en, afectar; **the novelist has been ~d by Torrente** el novelista ha sufrido la influencia de Torrente, el novelista está influido por Torrente; **what factors ~d your decision?** ¿qué factores influyeron en tu decisión?; **don't let him ~ you** no te dejes convencer por él; **to be easily ~d** ser sugestionable.
influential [ˌɪnflʊˈenʃəl] *adj* influyente, prestigioso.
influenza [ˌɪnflʊˈenzə] *n* gripe *f*.
influx [ˈɪnflʌks] *n* afluencia *f*; (*Mech etc*) aflujo *m*, entrada *f*.
info* [ˈɪnfəʊ] *n* = **information.**
inform [ɪnˈfɔːm] **1** *vt* informar (*about* sobre, *of* de); avisar; comunicar, participar; **I am happy to ~ you that ...** tengo el gusto de comunicarle que ...; **well ~ed** enterado, instruido; **to be ~ed about sth** estar enterado de algo, estar al corriente de algo; **why was I not ~ed?** ¿por qué no me avisaron?; **I should like to be ~ed as soon as he comes** que me avisen en cuanto llegue; **to keep sb ~ed about sth** tener a uno al corriente de algo.
2 *vi* soplar; **to ~ against** (*or* **on**) **sb** delatar a uno, denunciar a uno.
3 *vr*: **to ~ o.s. about sth** informarse sobre algo.
informal [ɪnˈfɔːməl] *adj person* desenvuelto, afable, poco ceremonioso; *occasion* informal, sin ceremonia, sin protocolo; *dance* sin etiqueta; *visit, gathering* de confianza, íntimo; *tone, manner* familiar; llano, sencillo; (*unofficial*) extraoficial, oficioso.
informality [ˌɪnfɔːˈmælɪtɪ] *n* afabilidad *f*; informalidad *f*; falta *f* de ceremonia; intimidad *f*; familiaridad *f*; llaneza *f*, sencillez *f*; **we liked the ~ of the occasion** nos gustó la función por su ausencia de ceremonia.
informally [ɪnˈfɔːməlɪ] *adv*: **it was organized very ~** se organizó sin ceremonia; **the president spoke ~ to the journalists** el presidente habló en tono de confianza con los periodistas; **I have been told ~ that ...** me han dicho de modo extraoficial que ..., me han dicho oficiosamente que ...
informant [ɪnˈfɔːmənt] *n* informante *mf*; **my ~** el que me lo dijo; **who was your ~?** ¿quién te lo dijo?.
informatics [ˌɪnfɔːˈmætɪks] *n* informática *f*.
information [ˌɪnfəˈmeɪʃən] **1** *n* (**a**) (*gen*) información *f*, informes *mpl*, datos *mpl*; (*news*) noticias *fpl*; **a piece of ~** una información, un dato, una noticia; '~' 'informaciones'; **to ask for ~** pedir informes; **to gather ~ about sth** tomar informes sobre algo, informarse sobre algo, reunir datos acerca de algo; **we have no ~ on that point** no tenemos información sobre ese particular.
(**b**) (*knowledge*) conocimientos *mpl*; **he writes well but is short of ~** escribe bien pero tiene escasos conocimientos; **for your ~** para su gobierno; para sacarle de duda.
(**c**) (*Jur*) denuncia *f*, delatación *f*; **to lay ~ about a crime** denunciar un crimen; **to lay ~ against sb** delatar a uno.
2 *attr*: **~ bureau, ~ office** centro *m* (*or* oficina *f*) de informaciones; **~ line** línea *f* de información; **~ network** red *f* informativa; **~ processing** proceso *m* de información; **~ retrieval** recuperación *f* de informaciones (*or* de la información); **~ room** centro *m* de información; **~ service** servicio *m* de información; **~ technology** informática *f*; **~ theory** teoría *f* de la información.
informative [ɪnˈfɔːmətɪv] *adj* informativo.
informativity [ɪnˌfɔːməˈtɪvɪtɪ] *n* informatividad *f*.
informed [ɪnˈfɔːmd] *adj* informado.
informer [ɪnˈfɔːməʳ] *n* (*Jur*) denunciante *mf*, delator *m*, -ora *f*; (*police* ~) informador *m*, -ora *f*, soplón *m*, -ona* *f*, oreja* *mf* (*LAm*).
infra... [ˈɪnfrə] *pref* infra...

infraction [ɪn'frækʃən] *n* infracción *f*, violación *f*.
infra dig* ['ɪnfrə'dɪg] *adj* deshonroso, indecoroso; **he thinks it ~ to explain** considera el explicarse un menoscabo de su dignidad.
infra-red ['ɪnfrə'red] *adj* infrarrojo.
infrasonic ['ɪnfrə,sɒnɪk] *adj* infrasónico.
infrasound ['ɪnfrə,saʊnd] *n* infrasonido *m*.
infrastructure ['ɪnfrə,strʌtʃər] *n* infraestructura *f*.
infrequency [ɪn'fri:kwənsɪ] *n* infrecuencia *f*, rareza *f*.
infrequent [ɪn'fri:kwənt] *adj* poco frecuente, infrecuente, raro.
infrequently [ɪn'fri:kwəntlɪ] *adv* rara vez, pocas veces.
infringe [ɪn'frɪndʒ] **1** *vt* infringir, vulnerar, violar. **2** *vi*: **to ~ on** invadir, usurpar.
infringement [ɪn'frɪndʒmənt] *n* infracción *f*, vulneración *f*, violación *f*; (*of rights etc*) invasión *f*, abuso *m*; (*Sport*) falta *f*.
infuriate [ɪn'fjʊərɪeɪt] *vt* enfurecer, poner rabioso; **to be ~d** estar furioso; **this kind of thing ~s me** estas cosas me hacen rabiar; **at times you ~ me** hay veces que me sacas de quicio.
infuriating [ɪn'fjʊərɪeɪtɪŋ] *adj* enloquecedor; **it's simply ~** es para volverse loco.
infuriatingly [ɪn'fjʊərɪeɪtɪŋlɪ] *adv* enloquecedoramente.
infuse [ɪn'fju:z] *vt* (**a**) infundir (*into* a); **to ~ courage into sb** infundir ánimo a uno; **they were ~d with a new hope** se les infundió una nueva esperanza. (**b**) *tea etc* preparar, hacer una infusión de.
infusion [ɪn'fju:ʒən] *n* infusión *f*; **~ of tea** infusión *f* de té.
ingenious [ɪn'dʒi:nɪəs] *adj* ingenioso, inventivo, hábil; *machine etc* ingenioso; *scheme etc* genial.
ingeniously [ɪn'dʒi:nɪəslɪ] *adv* ingeniosamente, hábilmente; con genialidad.
ingénue [,ɛ:nʒeɪ'nju:] *n* ingenua *f*, muchacha *f* candorosa.
ingenuity [,ɪndʒɪ'nju:ɪtɪ] *n* ingeniosidad *f*, inventiva *f*, habilidad *f*; genialidad *f*.
ingenuous [ɪn'dʒenjʊəs] *adj* ingenuo, candoroso.
ingenuously [ɪn'dʒenjʊəslɪ] *adv* ingenuamente, cándidamente.
ingenuousness [ɪn'dʒenjʊəsnɪs] *n* ingenuidad *f*, candidez *f*.
ingest [ɪn'dʒest] *vt* ingerir.
ingestion [ɪn'dʒestʃən] *n* ingestión *f*.
inglenook ['ɪŋglnʊk] *n* rincón *m* de la chimenea.
inglorious [ɪn'glɔ:rɪəs] *adj* ignominioso, vergonzoso.
in-going ['ɪngəʊɪŋ] *adj* entrante.
ingot ['ɪŋgət] *n* lingote *m*, barra *f*; **~ steel** acero *m* en lingotes.
ingrained ['ɪn'greɪnd] *adj* (profundamente) arraigado.
ingratiate [ɪn'greɪʃɪeɪt] *vr*: **to ~ o.s. with sb** congraciarse con uno, hacerse simpático a uno, insinuarse en el favor de uno.
ingratiating [ɪn'greɪʃɪeɪtɪŋ] *adj smile etc* insinuante, lleno de insinuación; *person* congraciador, zalamero.
ingratitude [ɪn'grætɪtju:d] *n* ingratitud *f*, desagradecimiento *m*.
ingredient [ɪn'gri:dɪənt] *n* ingrediente *m*, componente *m*.
ingress ['ɪngres] *n* ingreso *m*, entrada *f*.
in-group ['ɪn,gru:p] *n* grupo *m* exclusivista (*or* excluyente).
ingrowing ['ɪn,grəʊɪŋ] *adj*: **~ (toe)nail** uñero *m*, uña *f* encarnada.
inguinal ['ɪŋgwɪnl] *adj* inguinal.
inhabit [ɪn'hæbɪt] *vt* habitar; vivir en; ocupar.
inhabitable [ɪn'hæbɪtəbl] *adj* habitable.
inhabitant [ɪn'hæbɪtənt] *n* habitante *m*.
inhabited [ɪn'hæbɪtɪd] *adj* habitado, poblado.
inhalant [ɪn'heɪlənt] *n* inhalante *m*.
inhalation [,ɪnhə'leɪʃən] *n* aspiración *f*; (*Med*) inhalación *f*.
inhalator ['ɪnhəleɪtər] *n* inhalador *m*.
inhale [ɪn'heɪl] **1** *vt* aspirar; (*Med*) inhalar. **2** *vi* (*smoker*) aspirar el humo.
inhaler [ɪn'heɪlər] *n* inhalador *m*.
inharmonious [,ɪnhɑ:'məʊnɪəs] *adj* inarmónico, disonante; (*fig*) discorde, poco armonioso.
inhere [ɪn'hɪər] *vi* ser inherente (*in* a).
inherent [ɪn'hɪərənt] *adj* inherente, innato, inmanente, intrínseco; **~ vice** vicio *m* inherente; **~ in** inherente a; **with all the ~ difficulties** con todas las dificultades inevitables.
inherently [ɪn'hɪərəntlɪ] *adv* intrínsecamente.
inherit [ɪn'herɪt] *vt* heredar.
inheritance [ɪn'herɪtəns] *n* herencia *f*; (*fig*) patrimonio *m*, legado *m*; **~ law** ley *f* de herencia; **~ tax** impuesto *m* de sucesión; **our national ~** nuestro patrimonio nacional; **it's an ~ from the last government** es un legado del gobierno anterior.
inheritor [ɪn'herɪtər] *n* heredero *m*, -a *f*.
inhibit [ɪn'hɪbɪt] *vt* inhibir, impedir, imposibilitar; **to ~ sb from doing sth** impedir a uno hacer algo; **don't let my presence ~ the discussion** no quiero que mi presencia impida la discusión; **we cannot ~ change** no podemos detener los cambios.
inhibited [ɪn'hɪbɪtɪd] *adj* cohibido; **to feel rather ~** sentirse algo cohibido.
inhibition [,ɪnhɪ'bɪʃən] *n* inhibición *f*.
inhibitory [ɪn'hɪbɪtərɪ] *adj* inhibitorio.
inhospitable [,ɪnhɒs'pɪtəbl] *adj* inhospitalario; *place, country* inhóspito; *attitude, remark* poco amistoso.
inhospitably [,ɪnhɒs'pɪtəblɪ] *adv* de modo inhospitalario.
inhospitality ['ɪn,hɒspɪ'tælɪtɪ] *n* inhospitalidad *f*.
in-house ['ɪn'haʊs] **1** *adv* dentro de la empresa. **2** *adj* interno, en casa; **~ training** formación *f* en la empresa.
inhuman [ɪn'hju:mən] *adj* inhumano.
inhumane [,ɪnhjʊ(:)'meɪn] *adj* inhumano.
inhumanity [,ɪnhju:'mænɪtɪ] *n* inhumanidad *f*.
inhumation [,ɪnhju:'meɪʃən] *n* inhumación *f*.
inimical [ɪ'nɪmɪkəl] *adj*: **~ to** opuesto a, contrario a, perjudicial para.
inimitable [ɪ'nɪmɪtəbl] *adj* inimitable.
inimitably [ɪ'nɪmɪtəblɪ] *adv* inimitablemente.
iniquitous [ɪ'nɪkwɪtəs] *adj* inicuo; enorme; monstruoso; diabólico.
iniquitously [ɪ'nɪkwɪtəslɪ] *adv* inicuamente; enormemente; monstruosamente; diabólicamente.
iniquity [ɪ'nɪkwɪtɪ] *n* iniquidad *f*; perversidad *f*; injusticia *f*; enormidad *f*; **iniquities** (*of system*) injusticias *fpl*, (*of person*) excesos *mpl*, desmanes *mpl*.
initial [ɪ'nɪʃəl] **1** *adj* inicial; primero; **~ expenses** gastos *mpl* iniciales; **in the ~ stages** al principio, en las primeras etapas; **my ~ reaction was to ...** mi primera reacción era de ...
2 *n* inicial *f*, letra *f* inicial (*also* **~ letter**); **~s** (*of person etc*) iniciales *fpl*, (*used as abbreviation*) sigla *f*.
3 *vt* marcar (*or* firmar *etc*) con sus iniciales.
initialize [ɪ'nɪʃəlaɪz] *vt* inicializar.
initially [ɪ'nɪʃəlɪ] *adv* al principio, en un principio.
initiate 1 [ɪ'nɪʃɪɪt] *n* iniciado *m*, -a *f*.
2 [ɪ'nɪʃɪeɪt] *vt* (**a**) (*begin*) iniciar, empezar, dar comienzo a, dar origen a; *reform etc* promover; *fashion* introducir; (*Jur*) *proceedings* entablar.
(**b**) **to ~ sb into a secret** iniciar a uno en un secreto; **to ~ sb into a society** admitir a uno a una sociedad.
initiation [ɪ,nɪʃɪ'eɪʃən] *n* iniciación *f*; principio *m*, comienzo *m*; admisión *f*; **~ rite** ceremonia *f* de iniciación.
initiative [ɪ'nɪʃətɪv] *n* iniciativa *f*; **on one's own ~** por iniciativa propia, motu proprio; **to take the ~** tomar la iniciativa; **to use one's own ~** obrar por cuenta propia.
initiator [ɪ'nɪʃɪeɪtər] *n* iniciador *m*, -ora *f*.
inject [ɪn'dʒekt] *vt* (*Med etc*) inyectar (*into* en); (*fig*) injertar, introducir (*into* en), infundir (*into* a); **to ~ sb with sth** inyectar algo en uno; **to ~ new life into a club** infundir un espíritu nuevo a un club.
injection [ɪn'dʒekʃən] *n* inyección *f*.
injudicious [,ɪndʒʊ'dɪʃəs] *adj* imprudente, indiscreto.
injudiciously [,ɪndʒʊ'dɪʃəslɪ] *adv* imprudentemente, indiscretamente.
injunction [ɪn'dʒʌŋkʃən] *n* mandato *m*; (*Jur*) entredicho *m*; interdicto *m*.
injure ['ɪndʒər] **1** *vt* (**a**) (*physically*) herir, hacer daño a, lastimar, lesionar, (*permanently*) lisiar; **he ~d his arm** se lesionó el brazo.
(**b**) *chances, reputation, trade etc* perjudicar; (*offend*) ofender, agraviar; *feelings* herir.
2 *vr*: **to ~ o.s.** hacerse daño, lesionarse.
injured ['ɪndʒəd] **1** *adj person* herido; lesionado; **with an ~ arm** con un brazo lesionado; **an ~ player** un jugador lesionado; **there were 4 ~** hubo 4 heridos; **in an ~ tone** en tono ofendido; **the ~ party** la persona ofendida, la persona perjudicada. **2** *npl*: **the ~** los heridos.
injurious [ɪn'dʒʊərɪəs] *adj* (*harmful*) nocivo, dañoso, perjudicial (*to* para); (*insulting*) injurioso, ofensivo; **~ to health** perjudicial para la salud.
injury ['ɪndʒərɪ] *n* (**a**) (*physical*) herida *f*, lesión *f*; **~ benefit** subsidio *m* por daño; **~ time** tiempo *m* de descuento; **3 players have injuries** 3 jugadores están lesionados; **to do sb an ~** herir a uno; **to do o.s. an ~** hacerse daño, lesionarse.
(**b**) (*fig*) perjuicio *m*, daño *m*; **our reputation has suffered ~** nuestra reputación ha sido perjudicada.
injustice [ɪn'dʒʌstɪs] *n* injusticia *f*; **you do me an ~** me juzgas mal, eres injusto conmigo.

ink [ɪŋk] **1** *n* tinta *f*; **in ~** con tinta. **2** *vt* (**a**) (*Typ*) entintar. (**b**) (*US**) firmar.
◆**ink in** *vt* entintar.
◆**ink out** *vt* tachar con tinta.
◆**ink over** *vt* volver a escribir con tinta.
ink blot ['ɪŋkblɒt] *n* borrón *m* de tinta.
ink-jet printer ['ɪŋkdʒet'prɪntəʳ] *n* impresora *f* de chorro de tinta.
inkling ['ɪŋklɪŋ] *n* (*hint*) indicio *m*; (*suspicion*) sospecha *f*; (*vague idea*) atisbo *m*; idea *f* vaga; **I had no ~ that ...** no se me ocurrió que ..., no tuve la menor idea de que ...; **we had some ~ of it** nos habíamos formado alguna idea de ello; **there was no ~ of the disaster to come** no había indicio alguno del desastre que había de sobrevenir.
inkpad ['ɪŋkpæd] *n* almohadilla *f*, tampón *m* (de entintar).
inkpot ['ɪŋkpɒt] *n* tintero *m*.
inkstain ['ɪŋksteɪn] *n* mancha *f* de tinta.
inkstand ['ɪŋkstænd] *n* escribanía *f*.
inkwell ['ɪŋkwel] *n* tintero *m*.
inky ['ɪŋkɪ] *adj* (*stained*) manchado de tinta; (*black*) negro como la tinta.
INLA ['ɪnlə] *n* (*Brit*) *abbr of* **Irish National Liberation Army**.
inlaid ['ɪn'leɪd] **1** *pret and ptp of* **inlay**. **2** *adj*: **~ floor** entarimado *m*; **~ work** taracea *f*.
inland 1 ['ɪnlənd] *adj* interior; del interior; **I~ Revenue** Fisco *m*, Hacienda *f*; **~ revenue stamp** timbre *m* fiscal; **~ sea** mar *m* interior; **~ town** ciudad *f* del interior; **~ waterway** canal *m*.
2 ['ɪn,lænd) *adv* tierra adentro, hacia el interior.
3 ['ɪn,lænd] *n* interior *m* (del país).
in-laws ['ɪn,lɔːz] *npl* parientes *mpl* políticos, suegros *mpl*.
inlay 1 ['ɪnleɪ] *n* taracea *f*; incrustación *f*. **2** ['ɪn'leɪ] *vt* (*irr*: *V* **lay**) taracear, embutir, incrustar; **a sword inlaid with jewels** una espada incrustada de joyas.
inlet ['ɪnlet] **1** *n* (**a**) (*Geog*) ensenada *f*, cala *f*, entrante *m*. (**b**) (*Mech*) admisión *f*, entrada *f*. **2** *attr* (*Mech*): **~ pipe** tubo *m* de entrada; **~ valve** válvula *f* de entrada, válvula *f* de admisión.
inmate ['ɪnmeɪt] *n* habitante *mf*, ocupante *mf*, residente *mf*; inquilino *m*, -a *f*; (*of hospital*) enfermo *m*, -a *f*, (*of asylum*) internado *m*, -a *f*; (*of prison*) preso *m*, -a *f*, presidiario *m*, -a *f*.
inmost ['ɪnməust] *adj* = **innermost**.
inn [ɪn] **1** *n* posada *f*, hostería *f*, mesón *m*; (*poor, wayside*) venta *f*; (*large, wayside*) fonda *f*; (*pub*) taberna *f*; **I~s of Court** (*London*) Colegio *m* de Abogados. **2** *attr*: **~ sign** letrero *m* de mesón.
innards* ['ɪnədz] *npl* tripas *fpl*.
innate [ɪ'neɪt] *adj* innato.
innately [ɪ'neɪtlɪ] *adv* de manera innata; **it is not ~ evil** no es malo de por sí.
inner ['ɪnəʳ] *adj* interior, interno; *thoughts etc* íntimo, secreto; **~ cabinet** consejillo *m*; **~ city** barrios *mpl* céntricos de la ciudad; **~ city problems** problemas *mpl* de los barrios céntricos; **~ ear** oído *m* interno; **the ~ life** la vida interior; **the ~ man** el estómago; **~ ring-road** carretera *f* de circunvalación interior; **~ rooms** habitaciones *fpl* interiores; **~ tube** cámara *f* de aire, llanta *f* (*LAm*).
innermost ['ɪnəməust] *adj* (más) interior, más central; *thoughts etc* más íntimo, más secreto.
innerspring ['ɪnə,sprɪŋ] *attr*: **~ mattress** (*US*) colchón *m* de muelles interiores.
inning ['ɪnɪŋ] *n* (*US*: *Baseball*) inning *m*; **~s** *sing and pl* (*Cricket*) turno *m*, entrada *f*; (*fig*) turno *m*, oportunidad *f*; **he's had a good ~s** ha tenido una vida (*or* carrera *etc*) larga.
innkeeper ['ɪnkiːpəʳ] *n* posadero *m*, -a *f*, mesonero *m* -a *f*; ventero *m*, -a *f*; fondista *mf*; tabernero *m*, -a *f* (*V* **inn**).
innocence ['ɪnəsns] *n* inocencia *f*; **in all ~** inocentemente; sin segunda intención, sin malicia.
Innocent ['ɪnəsnt] *nm* (*pope*) Inocencio.
innocent ['ɪnəsnt] **1** *adj* inocente (*of* de); *amusement etc* honesto. **2** *n* inocente *mf*.
innocently ['ɪnəsntlɪ] *adv* inocentemente.
innocuous [ɪ'nɒkjuəs] *adj* innocuo, inofensivo.
innovate ['ɪnəuveɪt] *vi* introducir novedades.
innovation [,ɪnəu'veɪʃən] *n* innovación *f*, novedad *f*.
innovative ['ɪnəu,veɪtɪv] *adj* innovativo.
innovator ['ɪnəuveɪtəʳ] *n* innovador *m*, -ora *f*.
innovatory ['ɪnəu,veɪtərɪ] *adj* innovador.
innuendo [,ɪnju'endəu] *n*, *pl* **~es** indirecta *f*, insinuación *f*.
innumerable [ɪ'njuːmərəbl] *adj* innumerable; **there are ~ reasons** hay infinidad de razones; **I've told you ~ times** te lo he dicho mil veces.
innumeracy [ɪ'njuːmərəsɪ] *n* incompetencia *f* en el cálculo, incompetencia *f* en matemáticas.
innumerate [ɪ'njuːmərɪt] *adj* incompetente en el cálculo, incompetente en matemáticas.
inoculate [ɪ'nɒkjuleɪt] *vt* inocular (*against* contra, *with* de).
inoculation [ɪ,nɒkju'leɪʃən] *n* inoculación *f*.
inoffensive [,ɪnə'fensɪv] *adj* inofensivo.
inoperable [ɪn'ɒpərəbl] *adj* inoperable.
inoperative [ɪn'ɒpərətɪv] *adj* inoperante.
inopportune [ɪn'ɒpətjuːn] *adj* inoportuno.
inopportunely [ɪn'ɒpətjuːnlɪ] *adv* inoportunamente, a deshora.
inordinate [ɪ'nɔːdɪnɪt] *adj* desmesurado, excesivo, desmedido.
inordinately [ɪ'nɔːdɪnɪtlɪ] *adv* desmesuradamente, excesivamente.
inorganic [,ɪnɔː'gænɪk] *adj* inorgánico; **~ chemistry** química *f* inorgánica.
in-patient ['ɪn,peɪʃənt] *n* paciente *m* interno, paciente *f* interna.
input ['ɪnpʊt] **1** *n* (*contribution*) contribución *f*, aportación *f*; (*of effort, time*) inversión *f*; (*Elec, Mech*) entrada *f*, potencia *f* de entrada; (*Fin*) dinero *m* invertido, inversión *f*; (*Comput*) entrada *f*, introducción *f*, input *m*.
2 *vt* introducir, entrar.
input-output device [,ɪnpʊt'aʊtpʊtdɪ'vaɪs] *n* dispositivo *m* de entrada y salida.
inquest ['ɪnkwest] *n* (**a**) (*Jur*) investigación *f*, pesquisa *f* judicial; (*coroner's*) **~** encuesta *f* judicial, encuesta *f* postmortem.
(**b**) (*fig*) indagación *f*, encuesta *f*; **an ~ was held on the defeat** la derrota fue objeto de amplio análisis; **he likes to hold an ~ on every game** le gusta discutir cada partido hasta la saciedad.
inquire [ɪn'kwaɪəʳ] **1** *vt* preguntar; informarse de, pedir informes sobre; **to ~ sth of sb** preguntar algo a uno; **he ~d the price** preguntó cuánto costaba.
2 *vi* preguntar; **to ~ about, to ~ after, to ~ for** preguntar por, pedir informes sobre; **to ~ into** investigar, examinar, indagar; **to ~ into the truth of sth** averiguar la verdad de un suceso; **to ~ of sb** preguntar a uno; **'~ at No. 14'** 'razón: núm. 14'; **'~ within'** 'se dan informaciones'; **I was only inquiring** era una simple pregunta.
inquirer [ɪn'kwaɪərəʳ] *n* (*asker*) el (*or* la *etc*) que pregunta; (*researcher*) investigador *m*, -ora *f* (*into* de).
inquiring [ɪn'kwaɪərɪŋ] *adj mind* activo, penetrante, curioso; *look etc* interrogativo, de interrogación.
inquiringly [ɪn'kwaɪərɪŋlɪ] *adv look etc* interrogativamente.
inquiry [ɪn'kwaɪərɪ] **1** *n* (**a**) (*question*) pregunta *f*; petición *f* de informes; (*Comput*) interrogación *f*; **'Inquiries'** (*sign etc*) 'Informaciones'; **'inquiries at No. 14'** 'razón: núm. 14'; **'all inquiries to the secretary'** 'dirigirse al secretario'; **on ~** al preguntar; **have you an ~?** ¿quiere Vd preguntar algo?; **to make inquiries** pedir informes, tomar informes (*about, on* sobre; *of* a).
(**b**) **a look of ~** una mirada interrogativa.
(**c**) (*Jur etc*) investigación *f*, pesquisa *f*, indagación *f*, examen *m*, encuesta *f*; **there will have to be an ~** esto tendrá que ser investigado; **to hold an ~ into sth** investigar algo, examinar algo; **the police are making inquiries** la policía está investigando el asunto.
(**d**) (*commission etc*) comisión *f* de investigación, comisión *f* investigadora; **to set up an ~ into the disaster** nombrar una comisión para investigar el desastre.
2 *attr*: **~ agent** investigador *m* privado, investigadora *f* privada; **~ desk** mesa *f* de informaciones; **~ office** oficina *f* de informaciones.
inquisition [,ɪnkwɪ'zɪʃən] *n* investigación *f*, inquisición *f*; **the I~** la Inquisición, el Santo Oficio.
inquisitive [ɪn'kwɪzɪtɪv] *adj mind etc* inquiridor, activo, curioso; (*pej*) preguntón, fisgón, curioso.
inquisitively [ɪn'kwɪzɪtɪvlɪ] *adv* con curiosidad *f*.
inquisitiveness [ɪn'kwɪzɪtɪvnɪs] *n* curiosidad *f*.
inquisitor [ɪn'kwɪzɪtəʳ] *n* inquisidor *m*.
inquisitorial [ɪn,kwɪzɪ'tɔːrɪəl] *adj* inquisitorial.
inroad ['ɪnrəud] *n* incursión *f*, irrupción *f* (*into* en); (*fig*) invasión *f*, usurpación *f* (*into* de); **to make ~s into one's savings** mermar los ahorros de uno.
inrush ['ɪnrʌʃ] *n* irrupción *f*; (*of tourists etc*) afluencia *f*.
INS *n* (*US*) *abbr of* **Immigration and Naturalization Service**.
ins. (**a**) *abbr of* **insurance** seguro *m*. (**b**) *abbr of* **inches** pulgadas *fpl*.
insalubrious [,ɪnsə'luːbrɪəs] *adj* insalubre, malsano.
insane [ɪn'seɪn] *adj person* loco, demente; *act etc* insensato;

you must be ~! ¿estás loco?; **to become ~** volverse loco; **to drive sb ~** volver loco a uno.

insanely [ɪn'seɪnlɪ] *adv*: **to laugh ~** reírse como un loco; **to be ~ jealous** ser terriblemente celoso.

insanitary [ɪn'sænɪtərɪ] *adj* insalubre, antihigiénico.

insanity [ɪn'sænɪtɪ] *n* locura *f*, demencia *f*; (*of act etc*) insensatez *f*; **to drive sb to ~** volver loco a uno.

insatiable [ɪn'seɪʃəbl] *adj* insaciable.

inscribe [ɪn'skraɪb] *vt* inscribir; *book* dedicar; **~d stock** acciones *fpl* registradas.

inscription [ɪn'skrɪpʃən] *n* inscripción *f*; (*in book*) dedicatoria *f*; (*label*) rótulo *m*, letrero *m*.

inscrutability [ɪn,skru:tə'bɪlɪtɪ] *n* inescrutabilidad *f*.

inscrutable [ɪn'skru:təbl] *adj* inescrutable, enigmático, insondable.

inseam ['ɪnsi:m] *attr* (*US*): **~ measurement** medida *f* de pernera.

insect ['ɪnsekt] **1** *n* insecto *m*.

2 *attr*: **~ bite** picadura *f* de insecto; **~ powder** insecticida *m* en polvo; **~ repellent** repelente *m* de insectos; **~ spray** insecticida *m* en aerosol.

insecticide [ɪn'sektɪsaɪd] *n* insecticida *m*.

insectivorous [,ɪnsek'tɪvərəs] *adj* insectívoro.

insecure [,ɪnsɪ'kjʊʳ] *adj* inseguro.

insecurity [,ɪnsɪ'kjʊərɪtɪ] *n* inseguridad *f*.

inseminate [ɪn'semɪneɪt] *vt* inseminar.

insemination [ɪn,semɪ'neɪʃən] *n* inseminación *f*, fecundación *f*.

insensate [ɪn'senseɪt] *adj* insensato.

insensibility [ɪn,sensə'bɪlɪtɪ] *n* (**a**) insensibilidad *f* (*to* a), impasibilidad *f*; inconsciencia *f* (*of* de).

(**b**) (*Med*) estupor *m*, desmayo *m*, pérdida *f* de conocimiento.

insensible [ɪn'sensəbl] *adj* (**a**) (*insensitive*) insensible (*to* a), impasible, inconmovible; (*unaware*) inconsciente (*of* de).

(**b**) (*Med*) sin conocimiento; **he fell down ~** cayó sin conocimiento; **the blow knocked him ~** el golpe le hizo perder el conocimiento; **to drink o.s. ~** beber hasta perder el conocimiento.

insensitive [ɪn'sensɪtɪv] *adj* insensible (*to* a).

insensitivity [ɪn,sensɪ'tɪvɪtɪ] *n* insensibilidad *f*.

inseparable [ɪn'sepərəbl] *adj* inseparable, indisoluble; **the two questions are ~** los dos asuntos no se pueden considerar por separado.

inseparably [ɪn'sepərəblɪ] *adv* inseparablemente, indisolublemente.

insert 1 ['ɪnsɜ:t] *n* cosa *f* insertada; (*page*) hoja *f* suelta; (*section*) sección *f* añadida, materia *f* adicional.

2 [ɪn'sɜ:t] *vt* insertar, intercalar; *object, finger etc* introducir, meter dentro; (*in newspaper*) publicar; *advert* poner; (*Comput*) insertar.

insertion [ɪn'sɜ:ʃən] *n* inserción *f*; introducción *f*; publicación *f*; (*new section*) sección *f* añadida, materia *f* adicional.

in-service ['ɪn'sɜ:vɪs] *adj*: **~ benefits** beneficios *mpl* en funcionamiento; **~ course** cursillo *m* en funcionamiento; **~ training** formación *f* en funcionamiento.

inset ['ɪnset] **1** *n* (*Typ*) grabado *m* (*or* mapa, dibujo *etc*) que se imprime en un ángulo de otro mayor; recuadro *m*, encarte *m*. **2** *vt* (*irr*: *V* **set**) insertar; (*Typ*) imprimir como recuadro (*or* encarte); (*indent*) sangrar.

inshore ['ɪn'ʃɔ:ʳ] **1** *adv be, fish* cerca de la orilla; *blow, flow, go* hacia la orilla. **2** *adj* costero, cercano a la orilla; **~ fishing** pesca *f* de bajura.

inside ['ɪn'saɪd] **1** *adv* (**a**) dentro; hacia dentro; por dentro; (*on bus*) en el piso inferior, abajo; **he wouldn't come ~** no quiso entrar; **please step ~** pase Vd; **to pass the ball ~** pasar el balón hacia dentro.

(**b**) (‡) **to be ~** estar a la sombra‡; **he's gone ~ for 5 years** le han metido a la sombra por 5 años‡; **they put him ~** le metieron a la sombra‡.

2 *prep* (*also* **~ of**) (**a**) (*place*) dentro de; en el interior de.

(**b**) (*time*) **~ 4 hours** en menos de 4 horas; **~ the record** en tiempo inferior a la marca; **his time was 5 seconds ~ the record** superó el récord en 5 segundos.

3 *adj* (**a**) interior; interno.

(**b**) (*Brit Aut*) **~ lane** carril *m* de la izquierda, (*most countries*) carril *m* de la derecha.

(**c**) *information* secreto, confidencial; **the ~ story** la historia (hasta ahora) secreta; **it must be an ~ job*** tiene que ser obra de un empleado de la casa.

4 *n* (**a**) interior *m*, parte *f* interior; (*lining*) forro *m*; **to know the ~ of an affair** conocer el secreto de un asunto; **to see a firm from the ~** estudiar una empresa por dentro; **on the ~** por dentro; **ladies walk on the ~ of the pavement** las señoras van en la parte de la acera más alejada de la calzada; **to overtake on the ~** (*Brit*) adelantar por la izquierda, (*most countries*) adelantar por la derecha.

(**b**) **to be ~ out** estar al revés; **to put a dress on ~ out** ponerse un vestido al revés; **to turn sth ~ out** volver algo al revés; **they turned the whole place ~ out** lo revolvieron todo, lo registraron todo de arriba abajo; **to know a subject ~ out** conocer un tema de cabo a rabo.

(**c**) (*Anat**: *also* **~s**) estómago *m*, tripas *fpl*; **I have a pain in my ~** me duele el estómago.

inside-forward ['ɪnsaɪd'fɔ:wəd] *n* delantero *m*, -a *f* interior.

inside-left ['ɪnsaɪd'left] *n* interior *m* izquierdo, interior *f* izquierda.

inside-leg ['ɪnsaɪd'leg] *n* (*also* **~ measurement**) medida *f* de pernera.

insider [ɪn'saɪdəʳ] *n* persona *f* enterada; persona *f* que es de la casa (*etc*), empleado *m*, -a *f* de la casa; **~ dealing, ~ trading** operaciones *fpl* de iniciados, abuso *m* de información privilegiada.

inside-right ['ɪnsaɪd'raɪt] *n* interior *m* derecho, interior *f* derecha.

insidious [ɪn'sɪdɪəs] *adj* insidioso; pernicioso; maligno; *agitation etc* clandestino, subversivo.

insidiously [ɪn'sɪdɪəslɪ] *adv* insidiosamente; perniciosamente; clandestinamente.

insight ['ɪnsaɪt] *n* penetración *f* (psicológica), perspicacia *f*, intuición *f*; nueva percepción *f*, revelación *f*; **the visit gave us an ~ into their way of life** la visita fue para nosotros una revelación de su manera de vivir; **to gain** (*or* **get** *etc*) **an ~ into sth** adquirir una nueva percepción de algo, comprender algo mejor.

insightful ['ɪn,saɪtful] *adj* (*US*) penetrante.

insignia [ɪn'sɪgnɪə] *npl* insignias *fpl*.

insignificance [,ɪnsɪg'nɪfɪkəns] *n* insignificancia *f*; **A pales into ~ beside B** A pierde toda su importancia al compararse con B.

insignificant [,ɪnsɪg'nɪfɪkənt] *adj* insignificante.

insincere [,ɪnsɪn'sɪəʳ] *adj* poco sincero, insincero, nada franco, doble.

insincerity [,ɪnsɪn'serɪtɪ] *n* falta *f* de sinceridad, insinceridad *f*, doblez *f*.

insinuate [ɪn'sɪnjʊeɪt] **1** *vt* (**a**) *object* insinuar, introducir (*into* en).

(**b**) (*hint*) insinuar; **what are you insinuating?** ¿qué quieres insinuar?; **to ~ that ...** insinuar que ..., dar a entender que ...

2 *vr*: **to ~ o.s. into** insinuarse en, introducirse en.

insinuating [ɪn'sɪnjʊeɪtɪŋ] *adj* insinuador; *remark* malintencionado, con segunda intención.

insinuation [ɪn,sɪnjʊ'eɪʃən] *n* (**a**) (*act*) insinuación *f*, introducción *f*. (**b**) (*hint*) insinuación *f*; indirecta *f*, sugestión *f*; **it carries the ~ that ...** lleva implícita la noción de que ...; **he made certain ~s** soltó ciertas indirectas.

insipid [ɪn'sɪpɪd] *adj* insípido, soso, insulso.

insipidity [,ɪnsɪ'pɪdɪtɪ] *n* insipidez *f*, sosería *f*, insulsez *f*.

insist [ɪn'sɪst] **1** *vt*: **to ~ that sth is so** insistir en que algo es así; **to ~ that sth be done** insistir en que algo se haga. **2** *vi* insistir; (*obstinately*) porfiar, empeñarse, persistir; **if you ~** si Vd insiste; **to ~ on sth** insistir en algo, exigir algo; **to ~ on doing sth** insistir en hacer algo, empeñarse en hacer algo, obstinarse en hacer algo.

insistence [ɪn'sɪstəns] *n* insistencia *f* (*on* en); empeño *m* (*on* en); porfía *f*; **I did it at his ~** lo hice ante su insistencia, lo hice cediendo a sus ruegos.

insistent [ɪn'sɪstənt] *adj* insistente; porfiado, persistente; urgente; **he was most ~ about it** se empeñó mucho en ello; **he said in ~ tones** dijo en tono apremiante.

insistently [ɪn'sɪstəntlɪ] *adv* con insistencia; porfiadamente; urgentemente.

in situ [ɪn'sɪtju:] *adv* in situ, en el sitio.

insofar [ɪnsə'fɑ:ʳ] *conj*: **~ as** en tanto que + *subj*.

insole ['ɪnsəʊl] *n* plantilla *f*.

insolence ['ɪnsələns] *n* insolencia *f*, descaro *m*, atrevimiento *m*.

insolent ['ɪnsələnt] *adj* insolente, descarado, atrevido; **don't be ~!** ¡qué frescura!

insolently ['ɪnsələntlɪ] *adv* insolentemente, descaradamente.

insolubility [ɪn,sɒljʊ'bɪlətɪ] *n* insolubilidad *f*.

insoluble [ɪn'sɒljʊbl] *adj* insoluble.

insolvable [ɪn'sɒlvəbl] *adj* irresoluble.

insolvency [ɪn'sɒlvənsɪ] *n* insolvencia *f*.

insolvent [ɪn'sɒlvənt] *adj* insolvente; **to declare sb ~** declarar a uno insolvente.

insomnia [ɪn'sɒmnɪə] *n* insomnio *m*.

insomniac [ɪn'sɒmnɪæk] **1** *adj* insomne. **2** *n* insomne *mf*.

insomuch [,ɪnsəʊ'mʌtʃ] *adv*: ~ **as** puesto que, ya que, por cuanto que; ~ **that** ... hasta tal punto que ...

insouciance [ɪn'su:sɪəns] *n* despreocupación *f*.

insouciant [ɪn'su:sɪənt] *adj* despreocupado.

Insp. *abbr of* **inspector**.

inspect [ɪn'spekt] *vt* inspeccionar, examinar; (*officially*) registrar, reconocer; *troops* pasar revista a; (*Brit*: *ticket*) revisar.

inspection [ɪn'spekʃən] **1** *n* inspección *f*, examen *m*; registro *m*, reconocimiento *m*; (*Mil*) revista *f*. **2** *attr*: ~ **pit** (*Aut*) foso *m* de reconocimiento.

inspector [ɪn'spektəʳ] *n* inspector *m*, -ora *f*; (*Brit Rail, on bus etc*) revisor *m*, -ora *f*, controlador *m*, -ora *f* (*LAm*); ~ **of schools** (*Brit*) inspector *m*, -ora *f* de enseñanza; ~ **of taxes** inspector *m*, -ora *f* de Hacienda.

inspectorate [ɪn'spektərɪt] *n* inspectorado *m*.

inspiration [,ɪnspə'reɪʃən] *n* inspiración *f*; **to find** ~ **in** inspirarse en; **you have been an** ~ **to us all** nos ha inspirado a todos.

inspirational [,ɪnspɪ'reɪʃənl] *adj* inspirador.

inspire [ɪn'spaɪəʳ] *vt* inspirar; **to** ~ **sth in sb, to** ~ **sb with sth** inspirar algo a uno, infundir algo a uno, llenar a uno de algo; **to** ~ **sb to do sth** mover a uno a hacer algo.

inspired [ɪn'spaɪəd] *adj move, work etc* genial; **in an** ~ **moment** en un momento de inspiración.

inspiring [ɪn'spaɪərɪŋ] *adj* inspirador.

Inst. *abbr of* **Institute** Instituto *m*.

inst. *abbr of* **instant, of the present month** corriente, de los corrientes, cte..

instability [,ɪnstə'bɪlɪtɪ] *n* inestabilidad *f*.

instal(l) [ɪn'stɔ:l] **1** *vt* instalar; **to be ~ed in office** tomar posesión de su cargo. **2** *vr*: **to** ~ **o.s.** instalarse.

installation [,ɪnstə'leɪʃən] *n* instalación *f*.

instalment, (*US*) **installment** [ɪn'stɔ:lmənt] **1** *n* (*of story etc*) entrega *f*; (*Comm*) plazo *m*; **payment by ~s** pago *m* a plazos; **to pay in ~s** pagar a plazos.

2 *attr*: ~ **plan** (*US*) pago *m* a plazos, compra *f* a plazos.

instance ['ɪnstəns] **1** *n* (**a**) (*example*) ejemplo *m*; caso *m*; **for** ~ por ejemplo; **in that** ~ en ese caso; **in many ~s** en muchos casos; **in the present** ~ en el caso presente; **in the first** ~ primero, en primer lugar; **let's take an actual** ~ tomemos un caso concreto.

(**b**) **at the** ~ **of** (*Jur*) a instancia de, a petición de.

2 *vt* poner por caso, citar como ejemplo.

instant ['ɪnstənt] **1** *adj* inmediato, instantáneo; ~ **coffee** café *m* instantáneo; ~ **replay** repetición *f* de jugada; **the 3rd** ~ el 3 del (mes) corriente.

2 *n* instante *m*, momento *m*; **in an** ~**, on the** ~**, this** ~ al instante, en seguida.

3 *as conj*: **tell me the** ~ **he comes** avíseme en cuanto venga, avíseme en seguida que venga; **the** ~ **I heard it** en el momento en que lo supe.

instantaneous [,ɪnstən'teɪnɪəs] *adj* instantáneo.

instantaneously [,ɪnstən'teɪnɪəslɪ] *adv* instantáneamente.

instantly ['ɪnstəntlɪ] *adv* al instante, inmediatamente, en seguida.

instead [ɪn'sted] *adv* en cambio, en lugar de eso; ~ **of** en lugar de, en vez de; **he went** ~ **of me** fue en mi lugar; **this is** ~ **of a Christmas present** esto hace las veces de un regalo de Reyes.

instep ['ɪnstep] *n* empeine *m*.

instigate ['ɪnstɪgeɪt] *vt* instigar.

instigation [,ɪnstɪ'geɪʃən] *n* instigación *f*; **at the** ~ **of** a instigación de.

instigator ['ɪnstɪgeɪtəʳ] *n* instigador *m*, -ora *f*.

instil, (*US*) **instill** [ɪn'stɪl] *vt* infundir, inculcar; **to** ~ **sth into sb** infundir algo a uno, inculcar algo en uno.

instinct 1 [ɪn'stɪŋkt] *adj*: ~ **with** lleno de, imbuido de.

2 ['ɪnstɪŋkt] *n* instinto *m*; **by** ~ por instinto.

instinctive [ɪn'stɪŋktɪv] *adj* instintivo.

instinctively [ɪn'stɪŋktɪvlɪ] *adv* instintivamente, por instinto.

instinctual [ɪn'stɪŋktjʊəl] *adj* instintivo.

institute ['ɪnstɪtju:t] **1** *n* instituto *m*; (*for professional training*) escuela *f*; (*of professional body*) colegio *m*, asociación *f*; (*US*: *course*) curso *m*, cursillo *m*.

2 *vt* (*found*) instituir, establecer, fundar; *inquiry etc* iniciar, empezar; *proceedings* entablar.

institution [,ɪnstɪ'tju:ʃən] *n* (**a**) (*act*) institución *f*, establecimiento *m*, fundación *f*; iniciación *f*; entablación *f*.

(**b**) (*organization*) instituto *m*, asociación *f*.

(**c**) (*workhouse etc*) asilo *m*; (*madhouse*) manicomio *m*; (*Med*) hospital *m*.

(**d**) (*custom etc*) institución *f*, costumbre *f*, tradición *f*; (*person etc*) persona *f* conocidísima; **it is too much of an** ~ **to abolish** es una costumbre demasiado arraigada para poder suprimirla; **tea is a British** ~ el té es una institución en Gran Bretaña.

institutional [,ɪnstɪ'tju:ʃənl] *adj* institucional; ~ **investor** inversionista *mf* institucional.

institutionalize [,ɪnstɪ'tju:ʃnəlaɪz] *vt* (**a**) reglamentar; institucionalizar. (**b**) *person* meter en un asilo.

institutionalized [,ɪnstɪ'tju:ʃənə,laɪzd] *adj* institucionalizado.

instruct [ɪn'strʌkt] *vt* (**a**) (*teach*) instruir (*about, in* de, en, sobre); **to** ~ **sb in maths** enseñar matemáticas a uno.

(**b**) (*order*) **to** ~ **sb to do sth** mandar a uno hacer algo.

(**c**) (*Brit*) *solicitor* dar instrucciones a, instruir; *barrister* constituir.

instruction [ɪn'strʌkʃən] **1** *n* (**a**) (*teaching*) instrucción *f*, enseñanza *f*; **to give sb** ~ **in fencing** enseñar esgrima a uno.

(**b**) (*order*) orden *f*, mandato *m*; (*Comput*) instrucción *f*; ~**s** instrucciones *fpl*; órdenes *fpl*; **'~ for use'** (*on packet etc*) 'modo de empleo' *m*; **operating ~s** (*of pilot etc*) órdenes *fpl*, consigna *f*; **on the ~s of** por orden de; **we have given ~s for the transfer of** ... hemos cursado órdenes para la transferencia de ...

2 *attr*: ~ **book** manual *m* de instrucciones; ~ **cycle** ciclo *m* de instrucción.

instructive [ɪn'strʌktɪv] *adj* instructivo, informativo, aleccionador.

instructor [ɪn'strʌktəʳ] *n* instructor *m*, -ora *f*, profesor *m*, -ora *f*; (*US Univ*) profesor *m* -ora *f* auxiliar; (*ski* ~) monitor *m*, -ora *f*.

instructress [ɪn'strʌktrɪs] *n* instructora *f*; profesora *f*.

instrument ['ɪnstrʊmənt] **1** *n* (*all senses*) instrumento *m*.

2 *attr*: ~ **board** (*Aut, Aer*) tablero *m* (*or* cuadro *m*) de instrumentos (*or* de mandos); ~ **panel** (*US Aut*) salpicadero *m*; (*Aer*) tablero *m* de instrumentos; **set of ~s** instrumental *m*; **to fly on ~s** volar por instrumentos.

instrumental [,ɪnstrʊ'mentl] *adj* (**a**) (*Mus*) instrumental; ~ **music** músic *f* instrumental; ~ **performer** instrumentista *mf*. (**b**) **to be** ~ **in** + *ger* contribuir materialmente a + *infin*, ser instrumento eficaz para + *infin*.

instrumentalist [,ɪnstrʊ'mentəlɪst] *n* instrumentista *mf*.

instrumentality [,ɪnstrʊmen'tælɪtɪ] *n* mediación *f*, agencia *f*; **by** (*or* **through**) **the** ~ **of** por medio de, gracias a.

instrumentation [,ɪnstrʊmen'teɪʃən] *n* instrumentación *f*.

insubordinate [,ɪnsə'bɔ:dənɪt] *adj* insubordinado, desobediente, rebelde.

insubordination ['ɪnsə,bɔ:dɪ'neɪʃən] *n* insubordinación *f*, desobediencia *f*, rebeldía *f*.

insubstantial [,ɪnsəb'stænʃəl] *adj* insustancial.

insufferable [ɪn'sʌfərəbl] *adj* insufrible, inaguantable.

insufferably [ɪn'sʌfərəblɪ] *adv* de modo insufrible; ~ **rude** de lo más grosero.

insufficiency [,ɪnsə'fɪʃənsɪ] *n* insuficiencia *f*.

insufficient [,ɪnsə'fɪʃənt] *adj* insuficiente.

insufficiently [,ɪnsə'fɪʃəntlɪ] *adv* insuficientemente.

insular ['ɪnsjələʳ] *adj* insular; (*fig*) de miras estrechas.

insularity [,ɪnsjʊ'lærɪtɪ] *n* insularidad *f*; (*fig*) estrechez *f* de miras.

insulate ['ɪnsjʊleɪt] *vt* aislar (*from* de).

insulating tape ['ɪnsjʊleɪtɪŋ,teɪp] *n* (*Brit*) cinta *f* aislante, cinta *f* aisladora.

insulation [,ɪnsjʊ'leɪʃən] **1** *n* aislamiento *m*. **2** *attr*: ~ **material** material *m* aislante.

insulator ['ɪnsjʊleɪtəʳ] *n* aislante *m*, aislador *m*.

insulin ['ɪnsjʊlɪn] *n* insulina *f*.

insult 1 ['ɪnsʌlt] *n* insulto *m*, injuria *f*, ultraje *m*, ofensa *f*; **they are an** ~ **to the profession** son un insulto para la profesión; **and to add** ~ **to injury** ... y por si esto fuera poco ..., para más inri, y encima ...

2 [ɪn'sʌlt] *vt* insultar, injuriar; ofender; **he felt ~ed by this offer** creyó que tal oferta era deshonrosa para él; **now don't feel ~ed** pues no te vayas a ofender.

insulting [ɪn'sʌltɪŋ] *adj* insultante, injurioso; ofensivo; deshonroso.

insultingly [ɪn'sʌltɪŋlɪ] *adv* injuriosamente, ofensivamente.

insuperable [ɪn'su:pərəbl] *adj* insuperable.

insuperably [ɪn'su:pərəblɪ] *adv*: ~ **difficult** dificilísimo; **A is** ~ **better than B** A es con mucho mejor que B.

insupportable [,ɪnsə'pɔ:təbl] *adj* insoportable.

insurable [ɪn'ʃʊərəbl] *adj* asegurable.

insurance [ɪn'ʃʊərəns] **1** *n* (*Comm*) seguro *m*.

2 *attr*: ~ **agent** agente *mf* de seguros; ~ **broker** corredor *m*, -ora *f* de seguros, agente *mf* de seguros; ~ **certificate** certificado *m* de seguro; ~ **claim** demanda *f* de seguro; ~ **company** compañía *f* de seguros; ~ **office** oficina *f* aseguradora, oficina *f* de seguros; ~ **policy** póliza *f* (de seguros); ~ **premium** prima *f* de seguros; ~ **rates** tipo *m* de seguro; ~ **scheme** plan *m* de seguro; ~ **stamp** sello *m* de pago de la Seguridad Social; ~ **surveyor** tasador *m*, -ora *f* de seguros.

insure [ɪn'ʃʊə^{r}] **1** *vt* asegurar (*against* contra). **2** *vi* asegurarse (*against* contra).

insured [ɪn'ʃʊəd] *n*: **the** ~ el asegurado, la asegurada.

insurer [ɪn'ʃʊərə^{r}] *n* asegurador *m*, -ora *f*.

insurgent [ɪn'sɜːdʒənt] **1** *adj* insurrecto, insurgente. **2** *n* insurrecto *m*, -a *f*, insurgente *mf*.

insurmountable [ˌɪnsə'maʊntəbl] *adj* insuperable.

insurrection [ˌɪnsə'rekʃən] *n* sublevación *f*, insurrección *f*.

insurrectionary [ˌɪnsə'rekʃnərɪ] *adj* rebelde, insurreccional.

Int. *abbr of* **International** Internacional.

int. *abbr of* **interest** interés *m*.

intact [ɪn'tækt] *adj* intacto; íntegro; ileso, entero, sano; **not a window was left** ~ no quedaba cristal sano (*or* sin romper).

intake ['ɪnteɪk] **1** *n* (**a**) (*Mech*) admisión *f*, toma *f*, entrada *f*; tubo *m* de admisión, válvula *f* de admisión.

(**b**) (*quantity*) cantidad *f* admitida, número *m* admitido; **what is your student** ~? ¿cuántos alumnos se matriculan (cada año)?

(**c**) (*of food*) consumo *m*.

2 *attr*: ~ **valve** válvula *f* de admisión.

intangible [ɪn'tændʒəbl] *adj* intangible; ~ **assets** activo *m* intangible.

integer ['ɪntɪdʒə^{r}] *n* (número *m*) entero *m*.

integral ['ɪntɪgrəl] **1** *adj* (*whole*) íntegro; *part, component* integrante; (*Math*) integral; **it is an** ~ **part of the plan** es parte integrante (*or* esencial) del proyecto.

2 *n* (*Math*) integral *f*.

integrate ['ɪntɪgreɪt] **1** *vt* integrar (*also Math*); combinar en un todo, formar un conjunto con. **2** *vi* integrarse (*into* en).

integrated ['ɪntɪgreɪtɪd] *adj plan* de conjunto, que forma un conjunto; *personality* armonioso, estable, sano; *population, school* integrado, sin separación racial; ~ **circuit** circuito *m* integrado.

integration [ˌɪntɪ'greɪʃən] *n* integración *f*.

integrator ['ɪntɪgreɪtə^{r}] *n* integrador *m*.

integrity [ɪn'tegrɪtɪ] *n* integridad *f*, honradez *f*, rectitud *f*; (*Comput*) integridad *f*.

integument [ɪn'tegjʊmənt] *n* integumento *m*.

intellect ['ɪntɪlekt] *n* intelecto *m*.

intellectual [ˌɪntɪ'lektjʊəl] **1** *adj* intelectual. **2** *n* intelectual *mf*.

intellectually [ˌɪntɪ'lektjʊəlɪ] *adv* intelectualmente.

intelligence [ɪn'telɪdʒəns] **1** *n* (**a**) (*understanding*) inteligencia *f*.

(**b**) (*information*) información *f*, informes *mpl*, noticias *fpl*; **shipping** ~ noticias *fpl* navieras; **according to our latest** ~ según las últimas noticias.

2 *attr*: ~ **agent** agente *mf* de inteligencia, agente *m* secreto; **I~ Corps** (*Brit*) Cuerpo *m* de Informaciones; ~ **officer** oficial *m* de informaciones; ~ **quotient** cociente *m* intelectual; ~ **service** servicio *m* de información; ~ **test** test *m* de inteligencia; **I~ work** trabajo *m* de inteligencia.

intelligent [ɪn'telɪdʒənt] *adj* inteligente.

intelligently [ɪn'telɪdʒəntlɪ] *adv* inteligentemente.

intelligentsia [ɪnˌtelɪ'dʒentsɪə] *n* intelectualidad *f*.

intelligibility [ɪnˌtelɪdʒə'bɪlɪtɪ] *n* inteligibilidad *f*.

intelligible [ɪn'telɪdʒəbl] *adj* inteligible, comprensible; **it is scarcely** ~ **that ...** apenas es creíble que ...

intelligibly [ɪn'telɪdʒəblɪ] *adv* inteligiblemente, de modo inteligible.

INTELSAT ['ɪntelˌsæt] *n abbr of* **International Telecommunications Satellite Organization** Organización *f* Internacional de Telecomunicaciones por Satélite.

intemperance [ɪn'tempərəns] *n* intemperancia *f*, inmoderación *f*; (*drunkenness*) exceso *m* en la bebida.

intemperate [ɪn'tempərɪt] *adj* intemperante, inmoderado; (*drunken*) dado a la bebida, que bebe con exceso.

intend [ɪn'tend] *vt* (**a**) (*n object*) **what does he** ~ **by that?** ¿qué quiere decir con eso?; **I** ~ **it as a present** pienso darlo como regalo; **it is ~ed for John** está destinado a Juan, es para Juan; **no offence was ~ed, he ~ed no offence** no tenía la intención de ofender a nadie; **I** ~ **no disrespect** no quiero faltarle al respeto; **that remark was ~ed for you** esa observación iba dirigida a ti, eso lo dijo por ti.

(**b**) (*with verb*) **to** ~ **to** + *infin*, **to** ~ + *ger* pensar + *infin*, proponerse + *infin*; **what do you** ~ **to do about it?** ¿qué piensas hacer?; **this scheme is ~ed to help** este proyecto tiene la finalidad de ayudar; **I** ~ **that he should see it** pretendo que él lo vea, quiero que él lo vea; **I fully** ~ **to punish him** tengo la firme intención de castigarle.

intended [ɪn'tendɪd] **1** *adj* deseado. **2** *n* († *or hum*) prometido *m*, -a *f*.

intense [ɪn'tens] *adj* intenso; *interest etc* muy grande, sumo, enorme; *person* exagerado, nervioso; *look* penetrante; ardiente.

intensely [ɪn'tenslɪ] *adv* intensamente; ~ **difficult** sumamente difícil, terriblemente difícil, dificilísimo; **she speaks so** ~ habla en tono tan exagerado.

intensification [ɪnˌtensɪfɪ'keɪʃən] *n* intensificación *f*.

intensifier [ɪn'tensɪˌfaɪə^{r}] *n* intensificador *m*.

intensify [ɪn'tensɪfaɪ] **1** *vt* intensificar; aumentar, reforzar. **2** *vi* intensificarse; aumentar(se), reforzarse.

intensity [ɪn'tensɪtɪ] *n* intensidad *f*; (*of interest etc*) fuerza *f*; (*of person*) exageración *f*, nerviosismo *m*, hipertensión *f*.

intensive [ɪn'tensɪv] *adj* intensivo; *course* intensivo, concentrado; *study* profundo, detenido; ~ **care** asistencia *f* intensiva, vigilancia *f* intensiva; ~ **care unit** unidad *f* de vigilancia intensiva.

intensively [ɪn'tensɪvlɪ] *adv* intensivamente; profundamente, detenidamente.

intent [ɪn'tent] **1** *adj* (*absorbed*) absorto (*on* en), atento; **to be** ~ **on doing sth** estar resuelto a hacer algo.

2 *n* intento *m*, propósito *m*; **with** ~ **to** + *infin* con el propósito de + *infin*; **to all ~s and purposes** prácticamente, en realidad, en efecto.

intention [ɪn'tenʃən] *n* intención *f*; intento *m*, propósito *m*; proyecto *m*; **my** ~ **is to** + *infin* me propongo + *infin*, intento + *infin*; **I have no** ~ **of** + *ger* no es mi propósito + *infin*; **with the best ~s** con buena voluntad; **what are your ~s?** ¿qué piensas hacer?, ¿qué proyectos tienes?; **his ~s towards the girl were strictly honourable** pensaba casarse honradamente con la joven.

intentional [ɪn'tenʃənl] *adj* intencional, deliberado.

intentionally [ɪn'tenʃnəlɪ] *adv* intencionalmente, de propósito, adrede.

intently [ɪn'tentlɪ] *adv* atentamente, fijamente.

inter [ɪn'tɜː^{r}] *vt* enterrar, sepultar.

inter... ['ɪntə^{r}] *prefix* inter..., entre...

interact [ˌɪntər'ækt] *vi* obrar recíprocamente (*on* en); (*Comput*) interactuar, interaccionar (*with* con).

interaction [ˌɪntər'ækʃən] *n* interacción *f*, acción *f* recíproca, influencia *f* mutua; (*Comput*) interactuación *f*, interacción *f*.

interactive [ˌɪntər'æktɪv] *adj* interactivo; ~ **computing** computación *f* interactiva; ~ **processing** procesamiento *m* interactivo; ~ **video** vídeo *m* interactivo.

interactively [ˌɪntər'æktɪvlɪ] *adv* interactivamente.

inter alia [ˌɪntər'ælɪə] *adv* entre otros.

inter-bank ['ɪntəˌbæŋk] *adj* interbancario; ~ **loan** préstamo *m* entre bancos; ~ **rate** tasa *f* de descuento entre bancos.

interbreed ['ɪntə'briːd] (*irr*: *V* **breed**) **1** *vt* cruzar. **2** *vi* cruzarse.

intercalate [ɪn'tɜːkəleɪt] *vt* intercalar.

intercalation [ɪnˌtɜːkə'leɪʃən] *n* intercalación *f*.

intercede [ˌɪntə'siːd] *vi* interceder (*for* por, *with* con).

intercept [ˌɪntə'sept] *vt* interceptar; detener; (*Math*) cortar; (*cut off*) atajar.

interception [ˌɪntə'sepʃən] *n* interceptación *f*, detención *f*; atajo *m*.

interceptor [ˌɪntə'septə^{r}] *n* interceptor *m*.

intercession [ˌɪntə'seʃən] *n* intercesión *f*, mediación *f*.

interchange 1 ['ɪntə'tʃeɪndʒ] *n* (**a**) intercambio *m*, cambio *m*; canje *m*; alternación *f*.

(**b**) (*Aut*) cruce *m*.

2 [ˌɪntə'tʃeɪndʒ] *vt* intercambiar, cambiar; *prisoners, publications etc* canjear; (*alternate*) alternar.

interchangeable [ˌɪntə'tʃeɪndʒəbl] *adj* intercambiable.

interchangeably [ˌɪntə'tʃeɪndʒəblɪ] *adv* de manera intercambiable, intercambiando los dos (*etc*).

inter-city ['ɪntə'sɪtɪ] **1** *n* (*Brit Rail*: *also* ~ **train**) tren *m* de largo recorrido, tren *m* intercity. **2** *adj* de largo recorrido, intercity.

intercollegiate ['ɪntəkə'liːdʒɪɪt] *adj* interuniversitario.

intercom* ['ɪntəkɒm] *n* intercomunicador *m*, interfono *m*.

intercommunicate [ˌɪntəkə'mjuːnɪkeɪt] *vi* comunicarse.

intercommunication ['ɪntəkəˌmjuːnɪ'keɪʃən] *n* intercomunicación *f*.

intercommunion [ˌɪntəkə'mjuːnɪən] *n* intercomunión *f*.

inter-company [ˌɪntəˈkʌmpənɪ] *adj*: ~ **relations** relaciones *fpl* entre compañías.
interconnect [ˌɪntəkəˈnekt] *vt* interconectar.
interconnecting [ˌɪntəkəˈnektɪŋ] *adj rooms* comunicados; *trains* con correspondencia.
intercontinental [ˈɪntəˌkɒntɪˈnentl] *adj* intercontinental.
intercostal [ˌɪntəˈkɒstl] *adj* intercostal.
intercourse [ˈɪntəkɔːs] *n* (**a**) (*social*) trato *m*, relaciones *fpl*, comercio *m*. (**b**) (*sexual*) comercio *m* sexual, trato *m* sexual, coito *m*; **to have (sexual) ~ with** tener comercio sexual con.
interdenominational [ˈɪntədɪˌnɒmɪˈneɪʃənl] *adj* interconfesional.
interdepartmental [ˈɪntəˌdiːpɑːtˈmentl] *adj* interdepartamental.
interdependence [ˌɪntədɪˈpendəns] *n* interdependencia *f*.
interdependent [ˌɪntədɪˈpendənt] *adj* interdependiente.
interdict [ˈɪntədɪkt] *n* entredicho *m*, interdicto *m*.
interdiction [ˌɪntəˈdɪkʃən] *n* interdicción *f*.
interdisciplinary [ˌɪntəˈdɪsɪplɪnərɪ] *adj* interdisciplinario.
interest [ˈɪntrɪst] **1** *n* (**a**) (*curiosity*) interés *m*; **of great ~** de gran interés; **questions of public ~** asuntos *mpl* de interés público; **to be of ~** interesar; **it is of no ~ to us** no nos interesa; **what are your ~s?** ¿qué cosas te interesan?; ¿qué pasatiempos tienes?; **to do sth just for ~** hacer algo como pasatiempo nada más; **to have an ~ in** estar interesado en, interesarse en (*or* por); **to show ~** mostrar interés (*in* en, por); **to take an ~ in sth** interesarse en (*or* por) algo; **to take no further ~ in sth** dejar de interesarse en algo; no participar más en algo.

(**b**) (*profit, advantage*) ventaja *f*, provecho *m*, beneficio *m*; **in one's own ~(s)** en beneficio propio; **it is in your own ~ to confess** hay que confesarlo en beneficio propio; **in the ~s of hygiene** en interés de la higiene; **to act in sb's ~s** obrar en beneficio de uno; **to declare an ~** declarar su interés (*in* en); **to promote sb's ~s** fomentar los intereses de uno; **it is not in Ruritania's ~ to leave the base** le perjudicará a Ruritania abandonar la base.

(**c**) (*Comm: share, stake*) participación *f*, interés *m*; **~s** intereses *mpl*; **the coal ~** la industria hullera, los propietarios de las minas de carbón; **the conservative ~** los conservadores, el partido conservador; **the landed ~** los terratenientes; **business ~s** los negocios, el mundo de los negocios, los empresarios; **Switzerland is looking after British ~s** Suiza se encarga de los intereses británicos; **to have a financial ~ in a company** tener acciones en una compañía, ser accionista de una compañía.

(**d**) (*Comm: on loan, shares etc*) interés *m*; rédito *m*; **at an ~ of 5%** con interés de 5 por ciento; **to bear ~** devengar intereses; **to bear ~ at 5%** producir un 5 por ciento de interés; **to lend at ~** dar a interés; **to put out at ~** poner a interés; **to repay with ~** (*iro*) devolver con creces; **shares that yield a high ~** acciones *fpl* que rinden bien.

2 *attr*: **~ rate** tipo *m* de interés; **~ warrant** cupón *m* de interés.

3 *vt* interesar; **to be ~ed in** (*financially*) estar interesado en, (*from curiosity*) interesarse en (*or* por); **the company is ~ed in acquiring 200** la compañía está interesada en adquirir 200; **I'm not ~ed in football** no me interesa el fútbol.

4 *vr*: **to ~ o.s. in** interesarse en (*or* por).
interest-bearing [ˈɪntrɪstˌbɛərɪŋ] *adj* con interés.
interested [ˈɪntrɪstɪd] *adj*: **~ party, ~ person** interesado *m*, -a *f*.
interest-free [ˌɪntrɪstˈfriː] *adj* libre de interés.
interesting [ˈɪntrɪstɪŋ] *adj* interesante.
interestingly [ˈɪntrɪstɪŋlɪ] *adv* interesantemente.
interface [ˈɪntəfeɪs] **1** *n* interfaz *f*, interface *m* (*also Comput*). **2** *vi*: **to ~ with** conectar con.
interfacing [ˈɪntəfeɪsɪŋ] *n* acoplamiento *m*.
interfere [ˌɪntəˈfɪəʳ] *vi* intervenir, entrometerse, mezclarse (*in* en); **to ~ with** (*hinder*) estorbar, dificultar, impedir; (*damage*) manosear, estropear; (*Rad etc*) interferir; **who told you to ~?** ¿quién te mete a ti en esto?
interference [ˌɪntəˈfɪərəns] *n* intervención *f*, intromisión *f*, entrometimiento *m*; interposición *f*; (*Rad etc*) interferencia *f*.
interfering [ˌɪntəˈfɪərɪŋ] *adj* entrometido.
interferon [ˌɪntəˈfɪərɒn] *n* interferón *m*.
intergovernmental *adj* [ˌɪntəˌgʌvnˈmentl] *adj* intergubernamental.
interim [ˈɪntərɪm] **1** *n* ínterin *m*, intermedio *m*; **in the ~** entretanto, en el ínterin, interinamente. **2** *attr* interino, provisional; **~ dividend** dividendo *m* a cuenta, dividendo *m* parcial.
interior [ɪnˈtɪərɪəʳ] **1** *adj* interior, interno; **~ decorating** decoración *f* del hogar; decoración *f* de interiores; **~ decorator, ~ designer** decorador *m*, -ora *f* de interiores, diseñador *m*, -ora *f* de interiores; **~ sprung mattress** colchón *m* de muelles. **2** *n* interior *m*; **Ministry** (*or* **Department** *etc*) **of the I~** Ministerio *m* del Interior.
interject [ˌɪntəˈdʒekt] *vt* interponer.
interjection [ˌɪntəˈdʒekʃən] *n* interposición *f*; (*word*) interjección *f*, exclamación *f*.
interlace [ˌɪntəˈleɪs] **1** *vt* entrelazar. **2** *vi* entrelazarse.
interlard [ˌɪntəˈlɑːd] *vt*: **to ~ with** salpicar de, entreverar de.
interleave [ˌɪntəˈliːv] *vt* interfoliar; (*Comput*) intercalar.
interleaving [ˌɪntəˈliːvɪŋ] *n* interfoliación *f*; (*Comput*) intercalación *f*.
inter-library [ˌɪntəˈlaɪbrərɪ] *attr*: **~ loan** préstamo *m* interbibliotecario.
interline [ˌɪntəˈlaɪn] *vt* (**a**) (*Typ*) interlinear. (**b**) (*Sew*) entretelar.
interlinear [ˌɪntəˈlɪnɪəʳ] *adj* interlineal.
interlink [ˌɪntəˈlɪŋk] *vt* vincular, enlazar.
interlinked [ˌɪntəˈlɪŋkt] *adj* vinculados (entre sí).
interlock [ˌɪntəˈlɒk] **1** *vt* trabar, unir, entrelazar; *wheels* endentar, engranar.

2 *vi* trabarse, unirse, entrelazarse; (*wheels etc*) endentarse, engranar; **the parts of the plan ~** las partes del plan tienen una fuerte trabazón.
interlocutor [ˌɪntəˈlɒkjʊtəʳ] *n* interlocutor *m*, -ora *f*.
interloper [ˈɪntələʊpəʳ] *n* intruso *m*, -a *f*; (*Comm*) intérlope *m*, comerciante *m* (*etc*) no autorizado.
interlude [ˈɪntəluːd] *n* intervalo *m*, intermedio *m*; (*rest*) descanso *m*; (*Theat: playlet, interval*) intermedio *m*; (*Mus*) interludio *m*.
intermarriage [ˌɪntəˈmærɪdʒ] *n* matrimonio *m* mixto; matrimonio *m* entre parientes.
intermarry [ˈɪntəˈmærɪ] *vi* casarse (parientes *or* personas de distintas razas, religiones *etc*); **in this village they have intermarried for centuries** en este pueblo se vienen casando los parientes desde hace siglos.
intermediary [ˌɪntəˈmiːdɪərɪ] **1** *adj* intermediario. **2** *n* intermediario *m*, -a *f*.
intermediate [ˌɪntəˈmiːdɪət] **1** *adj* intermedio, medio; intermediario; **~ goods** productos *mpl* intermedios; **~ range ballistic missile** misil *m* balístico de alcance medio; **~ range weapon** arma *f* de medio alcance; **~ stop** escala *f*.

2 *n* (*US*) (*person*) intermediario *m*, -a *f*; (*Aut*) coche *m* de tamaño mediano.
interment [ɪnˈtɜːmənt] *n* entierro *m*.
intermezzo [ˌɪntəˈmetsəʊ] *n* intermezzo *m*.
interminable [ɪnˈtɜːmɪnəbl] *adj* inacabable, interminable.
interminably [ɪnˈtɜːmɪnəblɪ] *adv*: **he spoke ~** habló como si nunca fuera a acabar.
intermingle [ˌɪntəˈmɪŋgl] **1** *vt* entremezclar. **2** *vi* entremezclarse.
intermission [ˌɪntəˈmɪʃən] *n* intermisión *f*, interrupción *f*, intervalo *m*; (*Theat*) descanso *m*; **it went on without ~** continuó sin interrupción.
intermittent [ˌɪntəˈmɪtənt] *adj* intermitente.
intermittently [ˌɪntəˈmɪtəntlɪ] *adv* a intervalos, a ratos.
intern 1 [ɪnˈtɜːn] *vt* internar, recluir, encerrar.

2 [ˈɪntɜːn] *n* (*US Med*) interno *m*, -a *f* de hospital.
internal [ɪnˈtɜːnl] *adj* interno, interior; **~ audit** auditoría *f* interna; **~ combustion engine** motor *m* de explosión; **as we know from ~ evidence** como sabemos por indicios internos.
internalize [ɪnˈtɜːnəlaɪz] *vt* interiorizar.
internally [ɪnˈtɜːnəlɪ] *adv* interiormente; **not to be taken ~** (*Med*) sólo para uso externo.
international [ˌɪntəˈnæʃnəl] **1** *adj* internacional; **I~ Atomic Energy Authority** Organización *f* Internacional de Energía Atómica; **I~ Brigade** (*1936*) Brigadas *fpl* Internacionales; **I~ Chamber of Commerce** Cámara *f* de Comercio Internacional; **I~ Court of Justice** Corte *f* Internacional de Justicia; **~ date line** línea *f* de cambio de fecha; **I~ Labour Organization** Organización *f* Internacional del Trabajo; **~ law** derecho *m* internacional, derecho *m* de gentes; **I~ Monetary Fund** Fondo *m* Monetario Internacional; **~ money order** giro *m* postal internacional; **I~ Standards Organization** Organización *f* Internacional de Normalización.

2 *n* (**a**) (*Sport: game*) partido *m* internacional, (*player*) jugador *m*, -ora *f* internacional. (**b**) **I~** (*Pol*) Internacional *f*.

Internationale [ˌɪntəˌnæʃə'nɑːl] *n* Internacional *f.*
internationalism [ɪntə'næʃnəlɪzəm] *n* internacionalismo *m.*
internationalize [ˌɪntə'næʃnəlaɪz] *vt* internacionalizar.
internationally [ɪntə'næʃnəlɪ] *adv* internacionalmente.
internecine [ˌɪntə'niːsaɪn] *adj*: ~ **war** guerra *f* de aniquilación mutua.
internee [ˌɪntɜː'niː] *n* internado *m*, -a *f.*
internment [ɪn'tɜːnmənt] **1** *n* internamiento *m;* internación *f.*
2 *attr*: ~ **camp** campo *m* de internamiento.
interpersonal [ˌɪntə'pɜːsənl] *adj* entre personas, interpersonal.
interphone ['ɪntəˌfəʊn] *n* interfono *m.*
interplanetary [ˌɪntə'plænɪtərɪ] *adj* interplanetario.
interplay ['ɪntəpleɪ] *n* interacción *f.*
Interpol ['ɪntəˌpɒl] *n abbr of* **International Criminal Police Organization** Interpol *f.*
interpolate [ɪn'tɜːpəleɪt] *vt* interpolar.
interpolation [ɪnˌtɜːpə'leɪʃən] *n* interpolación *f.*
interpose [ˌɪntə'pəʊz] *vt* interponer; *remark* introducir, hacer de paso; **'never!', ~d John** '¡jamás!', cortó Juan.
interpret [ɪn'tɜːprɪt] **1** *vt* interpretar; (*translate*) interpretar, traducir; (*understand*) entender, explicar; **how are we to ~ that remark?** ¿cómo hemos de entender esa observación?; **if I ~ your wishes correctly** si entiendo bien sus deseos; **that is not how I ~ it** yo lo entiendo de otro modo. **2** *vi* interpretar; servir de intérprete (*for* para).
interpretation [ɪnˌtɜːprɪ'teɪʃən] *n* interpretación *f*; traducción *f*; (*meaning*) significado *m*; **what ~ am I to place on your conduct?** ¿cómo he de entender tu conducta?; **the words bear another ~** las palabras tienen otro significado, las palabras pueden entenderse de otro modo.
interpretative [ɪn'tɜːprɪtətɪv] *adj* interpretativo, aclaratorio, explicativo.
interpreter [ɪn'tɜːprɪtə^r] *n* intérprete *mf.*
interregnum [ˌɪntə'regnəm] *n* interregno *m.*
interrelate [ˌɪntərɪ'leɪt] *vt* interrelacionar.
interrelated [ˌɪntərɪ'leɪtɪd] *adj* interrelacionado.
interrelation [ˌɪntərɪ'leɪʃən] *n* interrelación *f.*
interrelationship [ˌɪntərɪ'leɪʃənʃɪp] *n* interrelación *f.*
interrogate [ɪn'terəgeɪt] *vt* interrogar (*also Comput*).
interrogation [ɪnˌterə'geɪʃən] **1** *n* interrogación *f.* **2** *attr*: ~ **mark, ~ point** signo *m* (*or* punto *m*) de interrogación.
interrogative [ˌɪntə'rɒgətɪv] **1** *adj* interrogativo. **2** *n* interrogativo *m.*
interrogatively [ˌɪntəˌrɒgətɪvlɪ] *adv* interrogativamente.
interrogator [ɪn'terəgeɪtə^r] *n* interrogador *m*, -ora *f.*
interrogatory [ˌɪntə'rɒgətərɪ] *adj* interrogante.
interrupt [ˌɪntə'rʌpt] *vti* interrumpir.
interruption [ɪntə'rʌpʃən] *n* interrupción *f.*
intersect [ˌɪntə'sekt] **1** *vt* cruzar, cortar. **2** *vi* (*Geom*) intersecarse; (*roads etc*) cruzarse.
intersection [ˌɪntə'sekʃən] *n* intersección *f*; cruce *m.*
intersperse [ˌɪntə'spɜːs] *vt* esparcir, entremezclar; **dashes ~d with dots** rayas con puntos a intervalos (*or* a ratos); **a speech ~d with jokes** un discurso salpicado de chistes.
interstate [ˌɪntə'steɪt] *adj* (*esp US*) interestatal; ~ **highway** autopista *f.*
interstellar [ˌɪntə'stelə^r] *adj* interestelar.
interstice [ɪn'tɜːstɪs] *n* intersticio *m.*
intertwine [ˌɪntə'twaɪn] **1** *vt* entrelazar, entretejer. **2** *vi* entrelazarse, entretejerse.
interurban [ˌɪntɜː'ɜːbən] *adj* interurbano.
interval ['ɪntəvəl] *n* intervalo *m*; (*Theat*) descanso *m*, intermedio *m*; (*more formally*) entreacto *m*; (*TV*) intermedio *m;* (*Sport etc*) descanso *m*; **at ~s** de vez en cuando, de trecho a trecho, a ratos, a intervalos; **at rare ~s** muy de tarde en tarde; **at regular ~s** con regularidad; **the work went on without an ~** el trabajo continuó sin interrupción; **there was an ~ for meditation** se hizo una pausa para la meditación.
intervene [ˌɪntə'viːn] *vi* (**a**) (*person*) intervenir (*in* en); tomar parte, participar (*in* en). (**b**) (*occur*) surgir, interponerse, sobrevenir; **if nothing ~s to prevent it** si no surge nada que lo impida.
intervening [ˌɪntə'viːnɪŋ] *adj* intermedio.
intervention [ˌɪntə'venʃən] **1** *n* intervención *f.* **2** *attr*: ~ **price** precio *m* de intervención.
interventionism [ˌɪntə'venʃənɪzəm] *n* dirigismo *m.*
interventionist [ˌɪntə'venʃənɪst] **1** *adj* dirigista. **2** *n* dirigista *mf.*
interview ['ɪntəvjuː] **1** *n* entrevista *f*, (*for press, TV etc*) interviú *f*; **to have an ~ with sb** entrevistarse con uno.
2 *vt* entrevistarse con, (*for press, TV etc*) hacer una interviú a, interviuvar; **3% of those ~ed did not know that ...** un 3 por cien de los entrevistados ignoraban que ...
interviewee ['ɪntəˌvjuː'iː] *n* persona *f* entrevistada.
interviewer ['ɪntəvjuːə^r] *n* interviuvador *m*, -ora *f*; (*Press*) reportero *m*, periodista *mf.*
inter-war [ˌɪntə'wɔː^r] *adj*: **the ~ years** el período de entreguerras, los años entre las guerras.
interweave [ˌɪntə'wiːv] (*irr*: *V* **weave**) *vt* entretejer.
intestate [ɪn'testɪt] *adj* intestado.
intestinal [ˌɪntes'taɪnl] *adj* intestinal.
intestine [ɪn'testɪn] *n* intestino *m*; **large ~** intestino *m* grueso; **small ~** intestino *m* delgado.
intimacy ['ɪntɪməsɪ] *n* intimidad *f*; (*euph*) relaciones *fpl* íntimas; **intimacies** familiaridades *fpl.*
intimate 1 ['ɪntɪmeɪt] *vt* dar a entender, indicar, intimar.
2 ['ɪntɪmɪt] *adj* íntimo; *friendship etc* estrecho; *knowledge* profundo, detallado; *detail etc* personal, privado; **they are ~ friends** son íntimos amigos; **they are very ~** son muy amigos; **he was ~ with her** (*euph*) tuvo relaciones íntimas con ella; **they became ~** se intimaron; **A became ~ with B** A se intimó con B.
3 ['ɪntɪmɪt] *n* amigo *m*, -a *f* de confianza; (*pej*) compinche *m.*
intimately ['ɪntɪmɪtlɪ] *adv* íntimamente; a fondo, profundamente.
intimation [ˌɪntɪ'meɪʃən] *n* (*news*) indicación *f*, intimación *f*; (*hint*) insinuación *f*, indirecta *f*; **it was the first ~ we had had of it** fue la primera indicación que habíamos tenido de ello.
intimidate [ɪn'tɪmɪdeɪt] *vt* intimidar, acobardar, amedrentar.
intimidating [ˌɪn'tɪmɪdeɪtɪŋ] *adj* amedrentador.
intimidation [ɪnˌtɪmɪ'deɪʃən] *n* intimidación *f.*
into ['ɪntʊ] *prep* en; a; dentro de; hacia el interior de; **to put sth ~ a box** poner algo en una caja; **to go ~ the wood** penetrar en el bosque; **to go off ~ the desert** ir hacia el interior del desierto; **to go ~ town** ir a la ciudad; **it got ~ the cage** entró en la jaula; **they got ~ the plane** subieron al avión; **it fell ~ the lake** cayó al lago, cayó en el lago; **to change sth ~ sth else** convertir algo en otra cosa; **to translate a text ~ Latin** traducir un texto al latín; **to grow ~ a man** hacerse hombre; **she's ~ spiritualism*** se le ha dado la manía del espiritismo, le ha dado por el espiritismo; **what are you ~ now?*** ¿a qué te dedicas ahora?
intolerable [ɪn'tɒlərəbl] *adj* intolerable, inaguantable, insufrible; **it is ~ that ...** no se puede consentir que + *subj.*
intolerably [ɪn'tɒlərəblɪ] *adv* insufriblemente; **he is ~ vain** es tremendamente vanidoso.
intolerance [ɪn'tɒlərəns] *n* intolerancia *f*, intransigencia *f.*
intolerant [ɪn'tɒlərənt] *adj* intolerante (*of* con, para), intransigente.
intonation [ˌɪntəʊ'neɪʃən] *n* entonación *f.*
intone [ɪn'təʊn] *vt* entonar; (*Eccl etc*) salmodiar.
intoxicant [ɪn'tɒksɪkənt] **1** *adj* embriagador. **2** *n* bebida *f* alcohólica.
intoxicate [ɪn'tɒksɪkeɪt] *vt* embriagar (*also fig*); (*Med*) intoxicar.
intoxicated [ɪn'tɒksɪkeɪtɪd] *adj* ebrio, borracho; **to be ~ with** (*fig*) estar ebrio de.
intoxicating [ɪn'tɒksɪkeɪtɪŋ] *adj* embriagador; ~ **drink** bebida *f* alcohólica.
intoxication [ɪnˌtɒksɪ'keɪʃən] *n* embriaguez *f* (*also fig*); (*Med*) intoxicación *f.*
intra... ['ɪntrə] *prefix* intra...
intractability [ɪnˌtræktə'bɪlətɪ] *n* (*of person*) indocilidad *f*, intratabilidad *f*; (*problem*) insolubilidad *f*; (*situation*) dificultad *f*; (*Med, disease*) incurabilidad *f.*
intractable [ɪn'træktəbl] *adj person* intratable; *material* difícil de trabajar; *problem* insoluble, espinoso.
intramural [ˌɪntrə'mjʊərəl] *adj* entre muros.
intramuscular [ˌɪntrə'mʌskjʊlə^r] *adj* intramuscular.
intransigence [ɪn'trænsɪdʒəns] *n* intransigencia *f.*
intransigent [ɪn'trænsɪdʒənt] *adj* intransigente.
intransitive [ɪn'trænsɪtɪv] *adj* intransitivo, neutro.
intrauterine [ˌɪntrəˌjuːtəraɪn] *adj* intrauterino; ~ **coil, ~ device** dispositivo *m* intrauterino, espiral *f.*
intravenous [ˌɪntrə'viːnəs] *adj* intravenoso.
intravenously [ˌɪntrə'viːnəslɪ] *adv* por vía intravenosa.
in-tray ['ɪnˌtreɪ] *n* bandeja *f* de entrada.
intrepid [ɪn'trepɪd] *adj* intrépido.
intrepidity [ˌɪntrɪ'pɪdɪtɪ] *n* intrepidez *f.*
intrepidly [ɪn'trepɪdlɪ] *adv* intrépidamente.
intricacy ['ɪntrɪkəsɪ] *n* lo intrincado; complejidad *f.*

intricate ['ɪntrɪkɪt] *adj* intrincado; complejo.
intricately ['ɪntrɪkɪtlɪ] *adv* intrincadamente, de modo intrincado.
intrigue [ɪn'triːg] **1** *n* intriga *f*; (*amorous*) amoríos *mpl*, lío *m*.
2 *vt* intrigar, interesar, fascinar, despertar la curiosidad de; **she ~s me** ella me fascina; **I am ~d to know whether** me interesa saber si; **I am much ~d by your news** me interesa muchísimo esa noticia; **we were ~d by a sign** nos llamó la atención un letrero, un letrero despertó nuestra curiosidad.
3 *vi* intrigar, andar en intrigas, meterse en líos.
intriguer [ɪn'triːgə^r] *n* intrigante *mf*.
intriguing [ɪn'triːgɪŋ] *adj* (**a**) (*scheming*) enredador.
(**b**) (*fascinating*) intrigante, fascinador, curioso, interesante; seductor; misterioso; **a most ~ problem** un problema interesantísimo; **an ~ gadget** un chisme de los más curiosos; **how very ~!** ¡qué raro!, ¡muy interesante!
intrinsic [ɪn'trɪnsɪk] *adj* intrínseco; **~ value** valor *m* intrínseco.
intrinsically [ɪn'trɪnsɪklɪ] *adv* intrínsecamente.
intro... ['ɪntrəʊ, 'ɪntrə] *prefix* intro...
introduce [ˌɪntrə'djuːs] *vt* (**a**) (*insert*) introducir, meter, insertar (*into* en).
(**b**) (*put forward*) *new thing, reform etc* introducir; *new fashion* introducir, poner de moda, lanzar; *new product, bill* presentar; *newcomer* presentar, dar a conocer; *book* (*preface*) prologar; *subject into conversation* mencionar, sacar a colación; **be careful how you ~ the subject** hay que abordar el tema con mucho cuidado; **I was ~d into a dark room** me hicieron entrar en un cuarto oscuro; **I was ~d into his presence** me llevaron ante él; **I was ~d to chess at 8** empecé a jugar al ajedrez a los 8 años; **I was ~d to Milton too young** me hicieron leer a Milton demasiado temprano.
(**c**) *person* presentar; **may I ~ Mr X?** permítame presentarle al Sr X; **I don't think we've been ~d** creo que no nos han presentado.
introduction [ˌɪntrə'dʌkʃən] *n* introducción *f*, inserción *f*; (*of persons*) presentación *f*; (*to book*) prólogo *m*, introducción *f*; **my ~ to life in Cadiz** mi primera experiencia de la vida en Cádiz; **my ~ to maths** el comienzo de mis estudios matemáticos; **to give sb an ~ to a person** dar a uno una carta de recomendación para una persona; **will you make the ~s?** ¿quieres presentarnos?
introductory [ˌɪntrə'dʌktərɪ] *adj* preliminar; **~ offer** oferta *f* preliminar.
introit ['ɪntrɔɪt] *n* introito *m*.
introspection [ˌɪntrəʊ'spekʃən] *n* introspección *f*.
introspective [ˌɪntrəʊ'spektɪv] *adj* introspectivo.
introspectiveness [ˌɪntrəʊ'spektɪvnɪs] *n* introspección *f*.
introversion [ˌɪntrəʊ'vɜːʃən] *n* introversión *f*.
introvert ['ɪntrəʊvɜːt] **1** *adj* introvertido. **2** *n* introvertido *m*, -a *f*.
introverted [ˌɪntrəʊ'vɜːtɪd] *adj* introvertido.
intrude [ɪn'truːd] **1** *vt* introducir (sin derecho), meter (*in* en); imponer (*upon* a).
2 *vi* entrometerse, encajarse (*upon* en); estorbar, molestar; **am I intruding?** ¿te molesto?, (*esp LAm*) ¿te estorbo?; **to ~ on sb's privacy** molestar a uno cuando quiere estar a solas; ; **sometimes sentimentality ~s** a veces se asoma el sentimentalismo; **he lets no feelings of pity ~** no deja lugar a la compasión.
intruder [ɪn'truːdə^r] *n* intruso *m*, -a *f*.
intrusion [ɪn'truːʒən] *n* intrusión *f*; invasión *f*; **the ~ of sentimentality** la aparición del sentimentalismo; **please pardon the ~** siento tener que molestarle.
intrusive [ɪn'truːsɪv] *adj* intruso.
intuit [ɪn'tjʊɪt] *vt* (*esp US*) intuir.
intuition [ˌɪntjuː'ɪʃən] *n* intuición *f*.
intuitive [ɪn'tjuːɪtɪv] *adj* intuitivo.
intuitively [ɪn'tjuːɪtɪvlɪ] *adv* intuitivamente, por intuición.
inundate ['ɪnʌndeɪt] *vt* inundar (*also fig*).
inundation [ˌɪnʌn'deɪʃən] *n* inundación *f*.
inure [ɪn'jʊə^r] *vt* acostumbrar, habituar (*to* a), endurecer; **to be ~d to** estar habituado a.
inv. *abbr of* **invoice**.
invade [ɪn'veɪd] *vt* invadir.
invader [ɪn'veɪdə^r] *n* invasor *m*, -ora *f*.
invading [ɪn'veɪdɪŋ] *adj* invasor.
invalid¹ [ɪn'vælɪd] *adj* inválido, nulo; **to become ~** caducar.
invalid² ['ɪnvəlɪd] **1** *adj* inválido, enfermo, minusválido. **2** *n* inválido *m*, -a *f*, minusválido *m*, -a *f*. **3** *attr*: **~ car, ~ carriage** (*Brit*) coche *m* de inválido. **4** *vt*: **to ~ sb out of the army** (*esp Brit*) licenciar a uno por invalidez.
invalidate [ɪn'vælɪdeɪt] *vt* invalidar, anular, quitar valor a; *argument* destruir.
invalidity [ˌɪnvə'lɪdɪtɪ] *n* invalidez *f*; nulidad *f*.
invaluable [ɪn'væljʊəbl] *adj* inestimable, inapreciable.
invariable [ɪn'vɛərɪəbl] *adj* invariable, inalterable.
invariably [ɪn'vɛərɪəblɪ] *adv* invariablemente; **it ~ happens that ...** ocurre siempre que ...; **he is ~ late** siempre llega tarde.
invasion [ɪn'veɪʒən] *n* invasión *f*.
invasive [ɪn'veɪsɪv] *adj* invasor.
invective [ɪn'vektɪv] *n* invectiva *f*; palabras *fpl* fuertes, improperios *mpl*.
inveigh [ɪn'veɪ] *vi*: **to ~ against** vituperar, hablar en contra de, condenar.
inveigle [ɪn'viːgl] *vt*: **she ~d him up to her room** le indujo mañosamente a subir a su habitación; **he was ~d into the duke's service** fue persuadido a entrar a servir al duque; **to ~ sb into sth** inducir (engañosamente) a uno a algo; **to ~ sb into doing sth** persuadir (mañosamente) a uno a hacer algo; **he let himself be ~d into it** se dejó engatusar para que lo hiciera.
invent [ɪn'vent] *vt* inventar; idear.
invention [ɪn'venʃən] *n* (**a**) (*gadget etc*) invención *f*, invento *m*. (**b**) (*inventiveness*) inventiva *f*. (**c**) (*falsehood*) ficción *f*, mentira *f*; **it's sheer ~ on her part** son cosas que ella ha soñado, son cosas de ella; **it's ~ from start to finish** es mentira desde el principio hasta el fin.
inventive [ɪn'ventɪv] *adj* inventivo, ingenioso.
inventiveness [ɪn'ventɪvnɪs] *n* inventiva *f*, ingenio *m*.
inventor [ɪn'ventə^r] *n* inventor *m*, -ora *f*.
inventory ['ɪnvəntrɪ] **1** *n* inventario *m*. **2** *attr*: **~ control** control *m* de existencias (*or* del inventario). **3** *vt* inventariar.
inverse ['ɪn'vɜːs] **1** *adj* inverso. **2** *n*: **the ~** lo inverso, lo contrario.
inversely [ɪn'vɜːslɪ] *adv* a la inversa.
inversion [ɪn'vɜːʃən] *n* inversión *f*.
invert [ɪn'vɜːt] *vt* invertir, volver al revés, trastrocar.
invertebrate [ɪn'vɜːtɪbrɪt] **1** *adj* invertebrado. **2** *n* invertebrado *m*.
inverted [ɪn'vɜːtɪd] *adj*: **~ commas** (*Brit*) comillas *fpl*; **in ~ commas** entre comillas; **~ snob** esnob *mf* a la inversa; **~ snobbery** esnobismo *m* a la inversa.
invert sugar ['ɪnvɜːt'ʃʊgə^r] *n* azúcar *m* invertido.
invest [ɪn'vest] **1** *vt* (**a**) *money* invertir (*in* en); **~ed capital** capital *m* invertido.
(**b**) (*Mil*) sitiar, cercar.
(**c**) **to ~ sb with sth** investir a uno de (*or* con) algo; **to be ~ed with a dignity** revestirse con una dignidad; **he ~ed it with a certain mystery** lo revistió con cierto misterio; **he seems to ~ it with some importance** parece que da cierta importancia a la cosa.
2 *vi*: **to ~ in** *company etc* invertir dinero en; (*buy*) comprar, adquirir; (*support*) apoyar, demostrar tener confianza en; **to ~ with** invertir dinero en.
investigate [ɪn'vestɪgeɪt] *vt* investigar; examinar, estudiar.
investigation [ɪnˌvestɪ'geɪʃən] *n* investigación *f*; pesquisa *f*; examen *m*, estudio *m* (*into* de).
investigative [ɪn'vestɪˌgeɪtɪv] *adj* investigador; **~ journalism** periodismo *m* de investigación.
investigator [ɪn'vestɪgeɪtə^r] *n* investigador *m*, -ora *f*.
investiture [ɪn'vestɪtʃə^r] *n* investidura *f*.
investment [ɪn'vestmənt] **1** *n* (**a**) (*Comm*) inversión *f*; **~s** inversiones *fpl*, fondos *mpl* invertidos, (*shares*) valores *mpl* en cartera.
(**b**) (*Mil*) sitio *m*, cerco *m*.
(**c**) (*investiture*) investidura *f*.
2 *attr*: **~ analyst** analista *mf* financiero; **~ bank** (*US*) banco *m* de inversión; **~ company** compañía *f* de inversiones; **~ goods** bienes *mpl* de inversión; **~ grant** subvención *f* para la inversión; **~ income** ingresos *mpl* procedentes de inversiones; **~ policy** política *f* inversionista; **~ portfolio** cartera *f* de inversiones; **~ trust** compañía *f* inversionista, sociedad *f* de cartera.
investor [ɪn'vestə^r] *n* inversionista *mf*.
inveterate [ɪn'vetərɪt] *adj* inveterado, empedernido, habitual, incurable.
invidious [ɪn'vɪdɪəs] *adj* odioso, injusto.
invigilate [ɪn'vɪdʒɪleɪt] (*Brit*) **1** *vt examination* vigilar. **2** *vi* vigilar (durante los exámenes).
invigilator [ɪn'vɪdʒɪleɪtə^r] *n* (*Brit*) celador *m*, -ora *f*.
invigorate [ɪn'vɪgəreɪt] *vt* vigorizar; *campaign etc* avivar, estimular.

2 *attr* de hierro; **I~ Age** Edad *f* de(l) Hierro; **~ constitution** constitución *f* de hierro; **I~ Curtain** telón *m* de acero; **I~ Curtain Countries** (*Hist*) países *mpl* más allá del telón de acero; **the I~ Duke** el Duque de Wellington; **with an ~ hand** (*or* **fist**) con mano de hierro; **the ~ fist in the velvet glove** la mano de hierro en guante de terciopelo; (*Brit Pol*) **the I~ Lady** la Dama de hierro; **~ lung** pulmón *m* de acero, pulmotor *m*; **~ oxide** óxido *m* de hierro; **~ pyrites** pirita *f* ferruginosa; **~ rations** ración *f* de reserva, víveres *mpl* de reserva; **~ and steel industry** (industria *f*) siderúrgica *f*; **~ will** voluntad *f* férrea.

3 *vt clothes* planchar.

◆iron out *vt unevenness* allanar; *crease* quitar; *difficulties* allanar, suprimir; *problems* suavizar; *differences* nivelar.

ironclad ['aɪənklæd] **1** *adj* acorazado; (*fig*) *guarantee* firme, a toda prueba. **2** *n* acorazado *m*.

iron-foundry ['aɪən,faʊndrɪ] *n* fundición *f* de hierro, fundidora *f* (*LAm*).

ironic(al) [aɪ'rɒnɪk(əl)] *adj* irónico.

ironically [aɪ'rɒnɪkəlɪ] *adv* irónicamente; *say etc* con ironía; **~ enough** paradójicamente, como quiso la suerte.

ironing ['aɪənɪŋ] *n* (*act*) planchado *m*; (*clothes*) ropa *f* por planchar, ropa *f* planchada; **to give a dress an ~** planchar un vestido.

ironing-board ['aɪənɪŋbɔːd] *n* tabla *f* de planchar.

ironmonger ['aɪən,mʌŋgəʳ] *n* (*Brit*) ferretero *m*, quincallero *m*; **~'s (shop)** ferretería *f*, quincallería *f*.

ironmongery ['aɪən,mʌŋgərɪ] *n* (*Brit*) quincalla *f*, ferretería *f* (*also fig*).

iron ore ['aɪənɔːʳ] *n* mineral *m* de hierro.

ironstone ['aɪən,stəʊn] *n* (*china*) porcelana *f* resistente.

ironwork ['aɪənwɜːk] *n* herraje *m*; obra *f* de hierro.

ironworks ['aɪənwɜːks] *n sing and pl* herrería *f*, fundición *f*, fábrica *f* de hierro.

irony ['aɪərənɪ] *n* ironía *f*; **the ~ of fate** lo irónico del destino; **the ~ of it is that** ... lo irónico es que ...

Iroquois ['ɪrəkwɔɪ] **1** *adj* iroqués. **2** *n* (**a**) iroqués *m*, -esa *f*. (**b**) (*Ling*) iroqués *m*.

irradiate [ɪ'reɪdɪeɪt] *vt* irradiar.

irradiation [ɪ,reɪdɪ'eɪʃən] *n* irradiación *f*.

irrational [ɪ'ræʃənl] *adj* irracional.

irrationality [ɪ,ræʃə'nælɪtɪ] *n* irracionalidad *f*.

irrationally [ɪ'ræʃnəlɪ] *adv* irracionalmente.

irreconcilable [ɪ,rekən'saɪləbl] *adj* irreconciliable, inconciliable.

irrecoverable [,ɪrɪ'kʌvərəbl] *adj* irrecuperable, incobrable.

irredeemable [,ɪrɪ'diːməbl] *adj* irredimible; (*Comm*) perpetuo, no amortizable.

irreducible [,ɪrɪ'djuːsəbl] *adj* irreducible.

irrefutable [,ɪrɪ'fjuːtəbl] *adj* irrefutable, irrebatible.

irregardless [ɪrɪ'gɑːdlɪs] *adv* (*US*) de cualquier modo; a pesar de todo.

irregular [ɪ'regjʊləʳ] **1** *adj* irregular; anormal; *surface* desigual; (*unlawful*) ilegal, no conforme con la ley; **this is really most ~** realmente esto no se debiera permitir.

2 *n* guerrillero *m*.

irregularity [ɪ,regjʊ'lærɪtɪ] *n* irregularidad *f*; anormalidad *f*; desigualdad *f*.

irregularly [ɪ'regjʊləlɪ] *adv* de manera irregular.

irrelevance [ɪ'reləvəns] *n* impertinencia *f*, inoportunidad *f*, inaplicabilidad *f*.

irrelevant [ɪ'reləvənt] *adj* impertinente, inoportuno, inaplicable, fuera de propósito; **that's ~** eso no hace al caso.

irrelevantly [ɪ'reləvəntlɪ] *adv* impertinentemente, inoportunamente.

irreligious [,ɪrɪ'lɪdʒəs] *adj* irreligioso.

irremediable [,ɪrɪ'miːdɪəbl] *adj* irremediable.

irremediably [,ɪrɪ'miːdɪəblɪ] *adv* irremediablemente.

irremovable [,ɪrɪ'muːvəbl] *adj* inamovible.

irreparable [ɪ'repərəbl] *adj* irreparable.

irreparably [ɪ'repərəblɪ] *adv* irreparablemente.

irreplaceable [,ɪrɪ'pleɪsəbl] *adj* insustituible, irreemplazable.

irrepressible [,ɪrɪ'presəbl] *adj* incontrolable, irrefrenable.

irreproachable [,ɪrɪ'prəʊtʃəbl] *adj* irreprochable, intachable.

irresistible [,ɪrɪ'zɪstəbl] *adj* irresistible.

irresistibly [,ɪrɪ'zɪstəblɪ] *adv* irresistiblemente.

irresolute [ɪ'rezəluːt] *adj* irresoluto, indeciso.

irresolutely [ɪ'rezəluːtlɪ] *adv* irresolutamente, indecisamente.

irresoluteness [ɪ'rezəluːtnɪs] *n* irresolución *f*, indecisión *f*.

irrespective [,ɪrɪ'spektɪv]: **~ of** *prep* aparte de, sin consideración a, con independencia de.

irresponsibility ['ɪrɪs,pɒnsə'bɪlɪtɪ] *n* irresponsabilidad *f*, falta *f* de seriedad.

irresponsible [,ɪrɪs'pɒnsəbl] *adj* irresponsable, poco serio.

irresponsibly [,ɪrɪs'pɒnsəblɪ] *adv* irresponsablemente, poco seriamente.

irretrievable [,ɪrɪ'triːvəbl] *adj* irrecuperable; *error* irreparable.

irretrievably [,ɪrɪ'triːvəblɪ] *adv*: **~ lost** totalmente perdido, perdido sin remedio.

irreverence [ɪ'revərəns] *n* irreverencia *f*; falta *f* de respeto.

irreverent [ɪ'revərənt] *adj* irreverente, irrespetuoso.

irreverently [ɪ'revərəntlɪ] *adv* de modo irreverente, irrespetuosamente.

irreversible [,ɪrɪ'vɜːsəbl] *adj process* irreversible; *decision* irrevocable.

irrevocable [ɪ'revəkəbl] *adj* irrevocable.

irrevocably [ɪ'revəkəblɪ] *adv* irrevocablemente.

irrigable ['ɪrɪgəbl] *adj* regable.

irrigate ['ɪrɪgeɪt] *vt* (*Agr*) regar; (*Med*) irrigar.

irrigated ['ɪrɪgeɪtɪd] *adj* regado; **~ land** tierra *f* de regadío.

irrigation ['ɪrɪ'geɪʃən] **1** *n* (*Agr*) riego *m*; (*Med*) irrigación *f*.

2 *attr*: **~ channel** canal *m* de riego, acequia *f*.

irritability [,ɪrɪtə'bɪlɪtɪ] *n* irritabilidad *f*.

irritable ['ɪrɪtəbl] *adj* (*temperament*) irritable, de prontos enojos; (*mood*) de mal humor; **to get ~** ponerse nervioso.

irritably ['ɪrɪtəblɪ] *adv*: **he said ~** dijo malhumorado.

irritant ['ɪrɪtənt] *n* irritante *m*.

irritate ['ɪrɪteɪt] *vt* (**a**) irritar, sacar de quicio, impacientar, molestar; **to get ~d** irritarse, enfadarse. (**b**) (*Med*) irritar.

irritating ['ɪrɪteɪtɪŋ] *adj person etc* molesto, pesado, enojoso; *thing* molesto, fastidioso; **it's really most ~** es para sacar a uno de quicio.

irritatingly ['ɪrɪteɪtɪŋlɪ] *adv* pesadamente, enojosamente; fastidiosamente.

irritation [,ɪrɪ'teɪʃən] *n* (**a**) irritación *f*, enojo *m*. (**b**) (*Med*) picazón *f*, picor *m*.

irruption [ɪ'rʌpʃən] *n* irrupción *f*.

IRS *n* (*US*) *abbr of* **Internal Revenue Service**.

is [ɪz] *V* **be**.

Is. *abbr of* **Isle(s)**, **Island(s)** Isla(s) *f(pl)*.

Isaac ['aɪzək] *nm* Isaac.

Isabel ['ɪzəbel] *nf* Isabel.

Isaiah [aɪ'zaɪə] *nm* Isaías.

ISBN *n abbr of* **International Standard Book Number** Numeración *f* Internacional Normalizada de Libros, ISBN *f*.

-ish [ɪʃ] *suffix* (**a**) **black~** negruzco; **dear~** algo caro; **small~** más bien pequeño; **cold~** un poco frío. (**b**) **at four~** a eso de las 4; **she must be forty~** tendrá alrededor de 40 años.

isinglass ['aɪzɪŋglɑːs] *n* cola *f* de pescado.

Islam ['ɪzlɑːm] *n* Islam *m*.

Islamic [ɪz'læmɪk] *adj* islámico; **~ law** derecho *m* islámico; **~ revolution** revolución *f* islámica.

island ['aɪlənd] **1** *n* isla *f*; (*in street*) refugio *m*. **2** *attr* isleño.

islander ['aɪləndəʳ] *n* isleño *m*, -a *f*.

isle [aɪl] *n* isla *f*.

islet ['aɪlɪt] *n* isleta *f*, islote *m*.

ism ['ɪzəm] *n* (*pej*) ismo *m*.

isn't ['ɪznt] = **is not**.

ISO *n abbr of* **International Standards Organization** Organización *f* Internacional de Normalización, OIN *f*.

iso... ['aɪsəʊ] *pref* iso...

isobar ['aɪsəʊbɑːʳ] *n* isobara *f*.

isolate ['aɪsəʊleɪt] *vt* aislar.

isolated ['aɪsəʊleɪtɪd] *adj place etc* aislado, apartado; *case* único; **to feel ~** sentirse aislado.

isolation [,aɪsəʊ'leɪʃən] **1** *n* aislamiento *m*; **we cannot discuss this in ~** no podemos discutir esto como tema independiente; **things like this don't happen in ~** estas cosas no ocurren aisladas; **she's being kept in ~** (*Med*) está en una sala de aislamiento. **2** *attr*: **~ hospital** hospital *m* de contagiosos; **~ ward** sala *f* de aislamiento.

isolationism [,aɪsəʊ'leɪʃənɪzəm] *n* aislacionismo *m*.

isolationist [aɪsəʊ'leɪʃənɪst] **1** *adj* aislacionista. **2** *n* aislacionista *mf*.

Isolde [ɪ'zɒldə] *nf* Iseo, Isolda.

isometric [,aɪsəʊ'metrɪk] **1** *adj* isométrico; **~ exercises** ejercicios *mpl* isométricos. **2** **~s** *npl* isométrica *f*.

isosceles [aɪ'sɒsɪliːz] *adj*: **~ triangle** triángulo *m* isósceles.

isotherm ['aɪsəʊθɜːm] *n* isoterma *f*.

isothermal [,aɪsəʊ'θɜːməl] *adj* isotérmico.

isotope ['aɪsəʊtəʊp] *n* isótopo *m*.

Israel ['ɪzreɪl] *n* Israel *m*.

Israeli [ɪz'reɪlɪ] **1** *adj* israelí. **2** *n* israelí *mf*.

Israelite ['ɪzrɪəlaɪt] **1** *adj* israelita. **2** *n* israelita *mf*.
iss. *abbr of* **issue.**
issue ['ɪʃuː] **1** *n* (**a**) (*outcome*) resultado *m*, consecuencia *f*; **in the ~** en fin; **until the ~ is decided** hasta que se sepa el resultado; **to await the ~** esperar el resultado.
(**b**) (*matter*) cuestión *f*, asunto *m*, problema *m*, punto *m*; **an ~ of fact** una cuestión de hechos; **side ~** cuestión *f* secundaria; **the point at ~** el punto en cuestión, el asunto en litigio; **the ~ is whether ...** se trata de decidir si ...; **it's not a political ~** no es una cuestión política; **to cloud** (*or* **confuse**) **the ~** entenebrecer el asunto; **to evade the ~** evadir el tema, esquivar la pregunta; soslayar el problema; **to face the ~** afrontar la situación; **to force the ~** forzar una decisión; **to join** (*or* **take**) **~ with sb** llevar la contraria a uno, oponerse a uno; **I think we should make an ~ of this** creo que éste es un punto clave, creo que esto vale como tema de discusión (*or* protesta *etc*); **do you want to make an ~ of it?** ¿quieres que esto llegue a ser un asunto conflictivo?; **I feel I must take ~ with you over that** permítaseme disentir de esa opinión.
(**c**) (*of shares, stamps etc*) emisión *f*; (*of rations*) distribución *f*, repartimiento *m*.
(**d**) (*of book*: *size of ~*) edición *f*, tirada *f*; (*copy*) número *m*.
(**e**) (*offspring*) sucesión *f*, descendencia *f*; **to die without ~** morir sin dejar descendencia.
(**f**) (*Med*) flujo *m*.
2 *attr* (*Mil etc*) reglamentario; (*Fin*) **~ price** precio *m* de emisión.
3 *vt shares, stamps etc* emitir; poner en circulación; *rations etc* distribuir, repartir; *book* publicar; *book* (*in library*) servir; *order* dar; *decree* promulgar; *certificate, passport etc* expedir; *cheque* extender; *licence* facilitar; **'when ~d'** (*St Ex*) 'cuando se emita'; **a warrant has been ~d for the arrest of X** se ha ordenado la detención de X; **to ~ a rifle to each man, to ~ each man with a rifle** dar un fusil a cada hombre; **we were ~d with 10 rounds each** nos dieron a cada uno 10 cartuchos.
4 *vi* salir (*from* de); **to ~ from** (*fig*) provenir de; **to ~ in** dar por resultado.
issued ['ɪʃuːd] *adj*: **~ capital** capital *m* emitido.
Istanbul ['ɪstæn'buːl] *n* Estambul *m*.
isthmus ['ɪsməs] *n* istmo *m*.
IT *n* (**a**) (*Comput*) *abbr of* **information technology** informática *f*. (**b**) (*Fin*) *abbr of* **income-tax** impuesto *m* sobre la renta.
it[1] [ɪt] *pron* (**a**) (*nom*) el, ella, ello; (*acc*) lo, la; (*dat*) le; (*after prep*) él, ella, ello.
(**b**) (*nom pron referring to a specific noun, freq not translated*) **~'s on the table** está en la mesa; **where is ~?** ¿dónde está?
(**c**) (*pron referring to 'this affair', 'that whole business'*) ello, eso, *eg* **~ is difficult** es difícil, ello es difícil; **I have no money for ~** no tengo dinero para ello; **he won't agree to ~** no quiere consentir en eso; **he's dropped us in ~*** nos la ha hecho buena*.
(**d**) (*never translated in such cases as*) **~ is true that ...** es verdad que ...; **~ was raining** llovía; **~ is 4 o'clock** son las 4; **~ is not in him to do it** no es capaz de hacer eso; **~ is said that ...** se dice que ...; **I have heard ~ said that ...** he oído decir que ...; **I do not think ~ (is) wise to go** creo que es más prudente no ir; **~ is I, ~'s me** soy yo; **~'s Jack** soy Juanito; **~ was he who brought them** fue él quien los trajo.
(**e**) (*special uses with* to be) **this is ~** ya llegó la hora; ahí viene; (*before action*) ¡vamos!, ¡a ello!; **that's ~** (*agreeing*) eso es; (*adjusting machine etc*) ya está, está bien; (*on finishing sth*) eso es todo, hemos terminado, está hecho, nada más; **that's ~ then!** ¡muy bien!; **that's just ~!** ¡ahí está la dificultad!; **the worst of ~ is that ...** lo peor del caso es que ...; **how is ~ that ...?** ¿cómo resulta que ...? (*and V* **how** (**a**)).
(**f**) (*predicative*) **you're ~!** (*children's games*) ¡tú te quedas!; **she thinks she's just ~*** se da mucho tono, se cree la mar de elegante*.
(**g**) (*) (*sexual attraction*) aquél* *m*, atracción *f* sexual; **she's got ~** tiene aquél*, tiene tilín*; **he's got ~** (*talent*) tiene talento, reúne las cualidades necesarias; **he hasn't quite got ~** no alcanza el nivel deseado; queda algo corto.
it[2]* [ɪt] *n* vermú *m* italiano.
ITA *n* (*Brit*) *abbr of* **initial teaching alphabet** *alfabeto parcialmente fonético, para enseñar lectura.*
Italian [ɪ'tæliən] **1** *adj* italiano. **2** *n* (**a**) italiano *m*, -a *f*. (**b**) (*Ling*) italiano *m*.
italic [ɪ'tælɪk] *adj* (*Typ*) en bastardilla; (*of Italy*) itálico.
italicize [ɪ'tælɪsaɪz] *vt* poner en bastardilla, subrayar.
italics [ɪ'tælɪks] *npl* (letra) bastardilla *f*, cursiva *f*; **in ~** en bastardilla, en cursiva; **my ~** lo subrayado es mío.
Italy ['ɪtəlɪ] *n* Italia *f*.
ITC *n* (*Brit*) *abbr of* **Independent Television Commission.**
itch [ɪtʃ] **1** *n* (**a**) (*Med*) (*an ~*) picazón *f*, comezón *f*; (*the ~*) sarna *f*.
(**b**) (*fig*) prurito *m*, deseo *m* vehemente; **to have the ~ to do sth** tener el prurito de hacer algo, rabiar por hacer algo.
2 *vi* (**a**) picar, sentir comezón; **my leg ~es** me pica la pierna, siento comezón en la pierna.
(**b**) **to ~ to do sth** tener el prurito de hacer algo, rabiar por hacer algo.
itching ['ɪtʃɪŋ] *n* picazón *f*, comezón *f*.
itching powder ['ɪtʃɪŋ,paʊdə^r] *n* polvos *mpl* de pica-pica.
itchy ['ɪtʃɪ] *adj*: **to feel ~** sentir comezón; **to have ~ feet** (*fig*) tener mal asiento, no querer estar quieto; **to have an ~ leg** sentir comezón en la pierna.
it'd ['ɪtd] = **it would; it had.**
item ['aɪtəm] *n* artículo *m*; (*detail*) detalle *m*; (*Comm*) partida *f*; (*in programme*) número *m*; (*on agenda*) asunto *m* a tratar; (*in newspaper*) noticia *f*, información *f*, suelto *m*; **~ of clothing** prenda *f* (de vestir); **what's the next ~?** ¿qué viene después?; **it's an important ~ in our policy** es un punto importante de nuestra política; **they're something of an ~** son una pareja inseparable.
itemize ['aɪtəmaɪz] *vt* detallar, particularizar, especificar; **~d bill** (*of customer*) cuenta *f* detallada, (*Comm*) factura *f* detallada.
iterative ['ɪtərətɪv] *adj* iterativo; **~ statement** (*Comput*) sentencia *f* iterativa.
itinerant [ɪ'tɪnərənt] *adj* ambulante.
itinerary [aɪ'tɪnərərɪ] *n* ruta *f*, itinerario *m*; (*book, map*) guía *f*.
it'll ['ɪtl] = **it will; it shall.**
ITN *n* (*Brit*) *abbr of* **Independent Television News** *servicio de noticias en las cadenas privadas de televisión.*
ITO *n abbr of* **International Trade Organization** Organización *f* Internacional de Comercio, OIC *f*.
its [ɪts] **1** *poss adj* su(s). **2** *poss pron* (el) suyo, (la) suya *etc*.
it's [ɪts] = **it is, it has.**
itself [ɪt'self] *pron* (*nom*) él mismo, ella misma, ello mismo; (*acc, dat*) se; (*after prep*) sí mismo, sí misma; **he is always politeness ~** siempre es la misma cortesía, siempre es la cortesía en persona; **that was an achievement in ~** eso fue un triunfo de por sí; *V* **oneself.**
ITU *n abbr of* **International Telecommunications Union** Unión *f* Internacional para las Telecomunicaciones, UIT *f*.
ITV *n* (*Brit*) *abbr of* **Independent Television** *cadenas privadas de televisión.*
IUD *n abbr of* **intrauterine device** dispositivo *m* intrauterino, DIU *m*.
I.V. *n* (*US*) gota a gota *m*.
i.v. *abbr of* **invoice value** valor *m* total de factura.
I've [aɪv] = **I have.**
IVF *n abbr of* **in vitro fertilization.**
ivory ['aɪvərɪ] **1** *n* marfil *m*; **ivories*** (*teeth*) dientes *mpl*, (*Mus*) teclas *fpl*, (*Billiards*) bolas *fpl;* **to tickle the ivories*** tocar el piano. **2** *attr* de marfil; **~ tower** torre *f* de marfil.
Ivory Coast ['aɪvərɪ'kəʊst] *n* Costa *f* de Marfil.
ivy ['aɪvɪ] **1** *n* hiedra *f*. **2** *attr*: **I~ League** (*US*) *grupo de ocho universidades privadas de Nueva Inglaterra* (*de gran prestigio*).

J

J, j [dʒeɪ] *n* (*letter*) J, j *f*; **J for Jack, J for Jig** (*US*) J de José.

JA *n abbr of* **judge advocate**.

J/A *abbr of* **joint account** cuenta *f* conjunta.

jab [dʒæb] **1** *n* (*poke*) pinchazo *m*; (*with elbow*) codazo *m*; (*blow*) golpe *m*; (*Boxing*) gancho *m*; (*prick*) pinchazo *m*; (*Med**) inyección *f*; (‡: *of drug*) chut‡ *m*.

2 *vt* hurgonear; dar un codazo a; golpear, dar un golpe rápido a; pinchar; **he ~bed a gun in my back** me puso un revólver en los riñones; **I ~bed the knife in my arm** me pinché el brazo con el cuchillo; **he ~bed the knife into the table** clavó el cuchillo en la mesa; **he ~bed a finger at the map** dio con el dedo en el mapa.

3 *vi*: **to ~ at sb with a knife** tratar de acuchillar a uno; **he ~bed at the map with a finger** dio con el dedo en el mapa.

jabber ['dʒæbəʳ] **1** *n* (*also* **jabbering** ['dʒæbərɪŋ]) torrente *m* de palabras ininteligibles; farfulla *f*; (*of monkeys*) chillidos *mpl*; **a ~ of French** un torrente de francés; **a ~ of voices** un ruido confuso de voces.

2 *vt* decir atropelladamente.

3 *vi* hablar atropelladamente, hablar de modo ininteligible; farfullar; (*monkeys*) chillar; **they were ~ing away in Russian** hablaban atropelladamente en ruso.

jabbering ['dʒæbərɪŋ] = **jabber 1**.

jacaranda [ˌdʒækə'rændə] *n* jacarandá *f*.

jack [dʒæk] *n* (*Mech*) gato *m*, gata *f* (*And, SC*); (*boot~*) sacabotas *m*; (*Bowls*) boliche *m*; (*Cards*) valet *m*, criado *m*, (*in Spanish pack*) sota *f*; (*Naut*) marinero *m*; (*Fish*) lucio *m* joven.

◆**jack in**‡ *vt* dejar, abandonar.

◆**jack off**** *vi* (*US*) masturbar, hacerse una paja**.

◆**jack up** *vt* (*Mech*) alzar con gato; *price, production etc* aumentar.

Jack [dʒæk] *nm familiar form of* **John** (Juanito); **I'm all right, ~!** ¡a mí nada!; **~ Frost** *personificación del hielo*; **~ Ketch** *el verdugo*; **before you can say ~ Robinson** en un decir Jesús; **~ Tar** *el marinero*.

jackal ['dʒækɔːl] *n* chacal *m*; (*fig*) paniaguado *m*, secuaz *m*.

jackanapes ['dʒækəneɪps] *n* mequetrefe *m*.

jackass ['dʒækæs] *n* burro *m* (*also fig*).

jackboot ['dʒækbuːt] *n* bota *f* de montar, bota *f* militar; **under the ~ of the Nazis** bajo el azote de los nazis.

jackdaw ['dʒækdɔː] *n* grajilla *f*, grajo *m*.

jacket ['dʒækɪt] **1** *n* chaqueta *f*, americana *f*, saco *m* (*LAm*); (*of boiler etc*) camisa *f*, envoltura *f*; (*of book*) sobrecubierta *f*, camisa *f*; (*US: of record*) funda *f*.

2 *attr*: **~ potatoes, potatoes baked in their ~s** (*Brit*) patatas *fpl* enteras, patatas *fpl* con su piel.

jackhammer ['dʒækˌhæməʳ] *n* (*esp US*) taladradora *f*, martillo *m* picador.

jack-in-the-box ['dʒækɪnðəbɒks] *n* caja *f* sorpresa, caja *f* de resorte.

jack-knife ['dʒæknaɪf] **1** *n*, *pl* **jack-knives** ['dʒæknaɪvz] navaja *f*.

2 *attr*: **~ dive** salto *m* de carpa.

3 *vi*: **the lorry ~d** el remolque del camión quedó atravesado.

jack-of-all-trades ['dʒækəv'ɔːltreɪdz] *n* factótum *m*, chico *m* para todo, manitas *m*; aprendiz *m* de todo, maestro de nada.

jack-o'-lantern ['dʒækəʊ'læntən] *n* fuego *m* fatuo; (*US*) linterna *f* hecha con una calabaza vaciada.

jack plane ['dʒækpleɪn] *n* garlopa *f*.

jack plug ['dʒækplʌg] *n* enchufe *m* de clavija.

jackpot ['dʒækpɒt] *n* bote *m*; (*fig*) premio *m* gordo; **he hit the ~** sacó el premio gordo (*LAm*: la gorda), (*fig*) acertó, se puso las botas, dio en el blanco.

jack rabbit ['dʒækˌræbɪt] *n* (*US*) liebre *f* grande.

jacks [dʒæks] *n sing* (*game*) cantillos *mpl*.

jackstraw ['dʒækstrɔː] *n* (*US*) pajita *f*.

Jacob ['dʒeɪkəb] *nm* Jacob.

Jacobean [ˌdʒækə'biːən] *adj* de la época de Jacobo I (de Inglaterra).

Jacobin ['dʒækəbɪn] **1** *adj* jacobino. **2** *n* jacobino *m*, -a *f*.

Jacobite ['dʒækəbaɪt] **1** *adj* jacobita. **2** *n* jacobita *mf*.

Jacuzzi [dʒə'kuːzɪ] ® *n* jacuzzi ® *m*, baño *m* de burbujas, hidromasaje *m*.

jade1 [dʒeɪd] *n* (*horse*) rocín *m*; (†: *woman*) mujerzuela *f*; **you ~!** ¡picarona!, ¡lagarta!

jade2 [dʒeɪd] **1** *n* (*Min*) jade *m*. **2** *adj* verde jade (*invar*).

jaded ['dʒeɪdɪd] *adj* cansado, (*fed up*) hastiado; **to feel ~** estar cansado; **to get ~** cansarse, perder el entusiasmo.

jade-green ['dʒeɪd'griːn] *adj* verde jade (*invar*).

jag1 [dʒæg] *n* punta *f*, púa *f*.

jag2* [dʒæg] *n*: **to go on a ~** ir de juerga.

jagged ['dʒægɪd] *adj* dentado, mellado, desigual.

jaguar ['dʒægjʊəʳ] *n* jaguar *m*.

jail [dʒeɪl] **1** *n* cárcel *f*; **2 years' ~** 2 años de prisión, condena *f* de 2 años. **2** *vt* encarcelar.

jailbird ['dʒeɪlbɜːd] *n* presidiario *m*.

jailbreak ['dʒeɪlbreɪk] *n* fuga *f* (de la cárcel).

jailbreaker ['dʒeɪlˌbreɪkəʳ] *n* evadido *m*, -a *f*, fugado *m*, -a *f*.

jailer ['dʒeɪləʳ] *n* carcelero *m*.

jakes‡ [dʒeɪks] *nm* meadero‡ *m*.

jalop(p)y [dʒə'lɒpɪ] *n* cacharro *m*, armatoste *m*.

jalousie ['ʒælʊ(ː)ziː] *n* celosía *f*.

jam1 [dʒæm] **1** *n* (**a**) (*food*) mermelada *f*.

(**b**) (*: *the best*) lo mejor, la parte más rica; **you want ~ on it!** (*Brit*) ¡y un jamón con chorreras!*; **the ~ is spread very thin** hay cosas buenas pero forman una capa muy delgada. (**c**) (‡: *luck*) chorra‡ *f*; **look at that for ~!** ¡qué chorra tiene el tío!‡

2 *vt* hacer mermelada de.

jam2 [dʒæm] **1** *n* (**a**) (*blockage*) atasco *m*, obstrucción *f*; (*of people*) agolpamiento *m*; (*Aut*) embotellamiento *m*, aglomeración *f*; colapso *m*; caravana *f*, tapón *m* (*Carib*); **there's a ~ in the pipe** se ha atascado el tubo, está atascado el tubo; **there was a ~ in the doorway** se había agolpado la gente en la puerta; **you never saw such a ~!** ¡había que ver cómo se agolpaba la gente!; **a 5-km ~ of cars** una cola de coches que se extiende hasta 5 km; **there are always ~s here** aquí siempre se embotella el tráfico.

(**b**) (*: *difficulty*) apuro *m*, aprieto *m*; **to be in a ~** estar en un aprieto; **to get into a ~** meterse en un apuro; **to get into a ~ with a problem** armarse un lío con un problema; **to get sb out of a ~** ayudar a uno a salir del paso.

2 *vt pipe etc* atascar, obstruir; *wheel* trabar; *exit, road* cerrar, obstruir; colapsar; (*Rad*) interferir, embrollar; **it's got ~med** se ha atascado, no se puede mover (*or* quitar, retirar *etc*); **people ~med all the exits** la gente se agolpaba en todas las salidas; **the room was ~med with people** el cuarto estaba atestado de gente; **to ~ one's fingers in the door** cogerse los dedos en la puerta; **to ~ sth into a box** meter algo apretadamente en una caja.

3 *vi* (**a**) (*pipe etc*) atascarse, obstruirse; (*nut, part, wheel etc*) trabarse; (*gun*) encasquillarse; **this part has ~med** no se puede mover esta pieza.

(**b**) (*Mus**) improvisar.

◆**jam in** *vt*: **if we can ~ 2 more books in** si podemos introducir a la fuerza 2 libros más; **there were 15 people ~med in one room** había 15 personas apretadas unas contra otras en un cuarto.

◆**jam on** *vt* (**a**) **to ~ a hat on one's head** encasquetarse un sombrero; **with his hat ~med on his head** con la cabeza encasquetada en un sombrero. (**b**) **to ~ one's brakes on**

echar los frenos con violencia, frenar de repente.
Jamaica [dʒə'meɪkə] *n* Jamaica *f*.
Jamaican [dʒə'meɪkən] **1** *adj* jamaiquino. **2** *n* jamaiquino *m*, -a *f*.
jamb [dʒæm] *n* jamba *f*.
jamboree [ˌdʒæmbə'riː] *n* (*of Scouts*) congreso *m* de exploradores; (*) francachela *f*, juerga *f*.
James [dʒeɪmz] *nm* Jaime, Diego; (*Saint*) Santiago; (*British kings*) Jacobo.
jam-full ['dʒæm'fʊl] *adv* de bote en bote.
jamjar ['dʒæmdʒɑːʳ] *n* pote *m* para (*or* de) mermelada.
jamming ['dʒæmɪŋ] *n* (*Rad*) interferencia *f*.
jammy‡ ['dʒæmɪ] *adj* chorrero‡.
jam-packed ['dʒæm'pækt] *adj* atestado, lleno a rebosar.
jam-pot ['dʒæmpɒt] *n* pote *m* para (*or* de) mermelada.
jam roll [ˌdʒæm'rəʊl] *n* brazo *m* de gitano con mermelada.
jam session* ['dʒæmˌseʃən] *n* sesión *f* de improvisación de jazz (*or* de rock).
Jan. *abbr of* **January** enero *m*, ene, en.º.
Jane [dʒeɪn] *nf* Juana.
jangle ['dʒæŋgl] **1** *n* sonido *m* discordante (metálico), cencerreo *m*.
  2 *vt* chocar, hacer sonar de manera discordante.
  3 *vi* sonar de manera discordante, cencerrear.
jangling ['dʒæŋglɪŋ] **1** *adj* discordante, desapacible, ruidoso. **2** *n* cencerreo *m*.
janitor ['dʒænɪtəʳ] *n* portero *m*, conserje *m*; (*Scol*) bedel *m*.
January ['dʒænjʊərɪ] *n* enero *m*.
Janus ['dʒeɪnəs] *nm* Jano.
Jap* [dʒæp] (*US*‡) = **Japanese.**
Japan [dʒə'pæn] *n* el Japón.
japan [dʒə'pæn] **1** *n* laca *f* japonesa. **2** *vt* charolar con laca japonesa.
Japanese [ˌdʒæpə'niːz] **1** *adj* japonés. **2** *n* (**a**) japonés *m*, -esa *f*; **the ~** (*pl*) los japoneses. (**b**) (*Ling*) japonés *m*.
jape [dʒeɪp] *n* burla *f*, broma *f*.
japonica [dʒə'pɒnɪkə] *n* rosal *m* de China, rosal *m* japonés.
jar[1] [dʒɑːʳ] *n* (*small*) tarro *m*, pote *m*; frasco *m*; (*with handles*) jarra *f*; (*large*) tinaja *f*; **to have a ~*** tomar un trago.
jar[2] [dʒɑːʳ] **1** *n* (**a**) (*jolt*) sacudida *f*, choque *m*; vibración *f*. (**b**) (*fig*) sacudida *f*, sorpresa *f* desagradable; **it gave me a bit of a ~** me chocó bastante.
  2 *vt* (*jog*) tocar; mover; (*shake*) sacudir, hacer vibrar; **he must have ~red the camera** ha debido mover ligeramente la máquina; **sb ~red my elbow** alguien me hizo mover el codo.
  3 *vi* (*grate*) chirriar; (*shake*) vibrar; (*sounds*) ser discorde, sonar mal; (*colours*) chillar; **to ~ on sb** poner a uno los nervios de punta, crispar los nervios a uno.
jar[3] [dʒɑːʳ] *n*: **on the ~** *V* **ajar.**
jargon ['dʒɑːgən] *n* (*incomprehensible*) jerigonza *f*; (*specialist*) jerga *f*.
jarring ['dʒɑːrɪŋ] *adj sound* discorde, desapacible; *colour* chillón; (*fig*) opuesto, adverso, discorde.
Jas. *abbr of* **James.**
jasmin(e) ['dʒæzmɪn] *n* jazmín *m*.
jasper ['dʒæspəʳ] *n* jaspe *m*.
jaundice ['dʒɔːndɪs] *n* ictericia *f*.
jaundiced ['dʒɔːndɪst] *adj* (*fig: envious, sour*) envidioso, avinagrado, agrio; (*disillusioned*) desilusionado, decepcionado.
jaunt [dʒɔːnt] *n* excursión *f* (corta) (*also fig*); viajecito *m*.
jauntily ['dʒɔːntɪlɪ] *adv* con garbo, airosamente; con confianza; **he replied ~** contestó satisfecho.
jauntiness ['dʒɔːntɪnɪs] *n* garbo *m*; confianza *f*, satisfacción *f*.
jaunting car ['dʒɔːntɪŋˌkɑːʳ] *n* tílburi *m* (irlandés).
jaunty ['dʒɔːntɪ] *adj* garboso, airoso; alegre; desenvuelto; confiado, satisfecho.
Java ['dʒɑːvə] *n* Java *f*.
Javanese [ˌdʒɑːvə'niːz] **1** *adj* javanés. **2** *n* javanés *m*, -esa *f*.
javelin ['dʒævlɪn] **1** *n* jabalina *f*; **to throw the ~** lanzar la jabalina.
  2 *attr*: **~ thrower** lanzador *m*, -ora *f* de jabalina; **~ throwing** lanzamiento *m* de jabalina.
jaw [dʒɔː] **1** *n* (**a**) (*Anat*) mandíbula *f*; (*of horse etc*) quijada *f*; (*Mech*) mordaza *f*, mandíbula *f*.
  (**b**) **~s** (*Anat*) boca *f*; (*fig: swallowing*) boca *f*, fauces *fpl*; (*holding*) garras *fpl*; **they rode into the very ~s of death** entraron en la misma boca del infierno.
  (**c**) (*) cháchara *f*; palabrería *f*; **we had a good old ~** charlamos largo rato; **it's just a lot of ~** mucho ruido y pocas nueces; **hold your ~!** ¡cállate la boca!
  2 *vt* (‡) soltar el rollo a*.
  3 *vi* (*) charlar; hablar por los codos, hablar interminablemente.
jawbone ['dʒɔːbəʊn] **1** *n* mandíbula *f*, maxilar *m*. **2** *vt* (*US**) presionar, ejercer presión sobre.
jawbreaker* ['dʒɔːˌbreɪkəʳ] *n* (*US*) trabalenguas *m*, palabra *f* kilométrica, terminacho *m*.
jawline ['dʒɔːlaɪn] *n* mandíbula *f*.
jay [dʒeɪ] *n* arrendajo *m*.
jaywalk ['dʒeɪwɔːk] *vi* cruzar la calle descuidadamente; ir a pie por la calzada.
jaywalker ['dʒeɪˌwɔːkəʳ] *n* peatón *m* imprudente.
jaywalking ['dʒeɪˌwɔːkɪŋ] *n* imprudencia *f* al cruzar la calle.
jazz [dʒæz] **1** *n* (**a**) jazz *m*. (**b**) (*) palabrería *f*, disparates *mpl*; rollo* *m*; **and all that ~** y todo el rollo ése*; **don't give me that ~!** ¡no me vengas con cuentos! **2** *attr* de jazz. **3** *vt* (**a**) (*also* **to ~ up**) sincopar; (*fig*) animar, avivar. (**b**) (*US**) exagerar.
jazz band ['dʒæzbænd] *n* orquesta *f* de jazz.
jazzy ['dʒæzɪ] *adj* (*Mus*) sincopado; *dress etc* de colores llamativos, de colores chillones.
JCB ['dʒeɪ'siː'biː] ® *n* excavadora *f*.
JCC *n* (*US*) *abbr of* **Junior Chamber of Commerce.**
JCS *n* (*US*) *abbr of* **Joint Chiefs of Staff.**
jct. (*Rail*) *abbr of* **junction.**
J.D. *n* (*US*) (**a**) *abbr of* **Doctor of Laws** *título universitario*. (**b**) *abbr of* **Justice Department.**
jealous ['dʒeləs] *adj* celoso; envidioso; **~ husband** marido *m* celoso; **with ~ care** con el mayor celo; **to be ~** tener celos (*of sb* de uno); **to make sb ~** dar celos a uno.
jealously ['dʒeləslɪ] *adv* celosamente; envidiosamente.
jealousy ['dʒeləsɪ] *n* celos *mpl*; envidia *f*.
jeans [dʒiːnz] *npl* (pantalones *mpl*) vaqueros *mpl*, tejanos *mpl*.
jeep [dʒiːp] *n* jeep *m*, yip *m*.
jeer [dʒɪəʳ] **1** *n* (*shout*) mofa *f*, befa *f*, grito *m* de sarcasmo, grito *m* de protesta; (*insult*) insulto *m*, dicterio *m*; (*boo*) abucheo *m*.
  2 *vt* mofarse de; llenar de insultos; abuchear.
  3 *vi* mofarse (*at* de), befar; gritar con sarcasmo (*etc*; *at* a), prorrumpir en befas (*or* gritos sarcásticos *etc*).
jeering ['dʒɪərɪŋ] **1** *adj* mofador, sarcástico; **he was led through a ~ crowd** le hicieron pasar por una multitud que le llenó de insultos.
  2 *n* mofas *fpl*, befas *fpl*, gritos *mpl* de sarcasmo, protestas *fpl*; insultos *mpl*; abucheo *m*.
Jeez‡ [dʒiːz] *interj* ¡Santo Dios!
jehad [dʒɪ'hæd] *n* yihad *m*.
Jehovah [dʒɪ'həʊvə] *nm* Jehová; **~'s Witnesses** Testigos *mpl* de Jehová.
jejune [dʒɪ'dʒuːn] *adj* árido; insípido, sin sustancia.
jell [dʒel] *vi* convertirse en jalea, cuajar; (*fig*) cuajar.
jellabah ['dʒeləbə] *n* chilaba *f*.
jello ['dʒeləʊ] *n* (*US*) = **jelly[1]**.
jelly[1] ['dʒelɪ] *n* jalea *f*, gelatina *f*; **my legs turned to ~** las piernas no me sostenían.
jelly[2]‡ ['dʒelɪ] *n* = **gelignite.**
jelly baby [ˌdʒelɪ'beɪbɪ] *n* caramelo *m* de goma (*en forma de niño*).
jelly bean [ˌdʒelɪ'biːn] *n* caramelo *m* de goma (*en forma de judía*).
jellyfish ['dʒelɪfɪʃ] *n* medusa *f*, aguamala *f*.
jemmy ['dʒemɪ] *n* (*Brit*) pie *m* de cabra, palanqueta *f*.
Jenny, Jennie ['dʒenɪ] *nf familiar form of* **Jennifer.**
jeopardize ['dʒepədaɪz] *vt* arriesgar, poner en peligro, comprometer.
jeopardy ['dʒepədɪ] *n*: **to be in ~** estar en peligro, correr riesgo; **to put sth in ~** poner algo en peligro, hacer peligrar algo.
jeremiad [ˌdʒerɪ'maɪəd] *n* jeremiada *f*.
Jeremiah [ˌdʒerɪ'maɪə] *nm*, **Jeremy** ['dʒerəmɪ] *nm* Jeremías.
Jericho ['dʒerɪkəʊ] *n* Jericó *m*.
jerk [dʒɜːk] **1** *n* (**a**) (*push, pull, twist etc*) tirón *m*, sacudida *f*; (*Med*) espasmo *m* muscular; **physical ~s** (*Brit*) ejercicios *mpl* físicos, gimnasia *f*; **by ~s** a sacudidas; **he sat up with a ~** se incorporó de repente, se incorporó con un movimiento brusco; **to put a ~ in it*** menearse.
  (**b**) (‡) pelmazo* *m*, memo *m*; **what a ~!‡** ¡qué pesado!
  2 *vt* (*shake etc*) sacudir, dar una sacudida a; (*pull*) tirar bruscamente de; (*throw*) arrojar con un movimiento rápido; *meat* (*US*) atasajar; **to ~ sth along** mover algo a tirones; **to ~ sth away from sb** quitar algo a uno de un tirón.
  3 *vi* sacudirse, dar una sacudida; **to ~ along** moverse a

sacudidas, avanzar a tirones.

4 *vr*: **to ~ o.s. free** librarse con un movimiento brusco; **to ~ o.s. along** moverse a sacudidas, avanzar a tirones.

◆**jerk off**‡ *vi* hacerse una paja‡.

◆**jerk out** *vt words* decir con voz entrecortada.

jerkily ['dʒɜːkɪlɪ] *adv move etc* a tirones, a sacudidas; *play, write etc* de modo desigual, nerviosamente.

jerkin ['dʒɜːkɪn] *n* justillo *m*.

jerkwater* ['dʒɜːk,wɔːtə^r] *adj* (*US*) de poca monta; **a ~ town** un pueblucho*.

jerky ['dʒɜːkɪ] *adj movement* espasmódico, nervioso; (*uneven*) desigual, nervioso.

Jeroboam [,dʒerə'bəʊəm] *nm* Jeroboam.

Jerome [dʒə'rəʊm] *nm* Jerónimo.

Jerry[1] ['dʒerɪ] *nm familiar form of* **Gerald, Gerard.**

Jerry[2]* ['dʒerɪ] *n* (*Brit Mil*): **a ~** un alemán; **~** los alemanes.

jerry* ['dʒerɪ] *n* (*Brit*) orinal *m*.

jerry-builder ['dʒerɪ,bɪldə^r] *n* mal constructor *m*, tapagujeros *m*.

jerry-building ['dʒerɪ,bɪldɪŋ] *n* mala construcción *f*, construcción *f* defectuosa.

jerry-built ['dʒerɪbɪlt] *adj* mal construido, de pacotilla, chapucero.

jerry-can ['dʒerɪkæn] *n* bidón *m*.

Jersey ['dʒɜːzɪ] *n* (**a**) (*Geog*) (Isla *f* de) Jersey *m*. (**b**) (*Zool*) vaca *f* de Jersey.

jersey ['dʒɜːzɪ] *n* jersey *m*.

Jerusalem [dʒə'ruːsələm] **1** *n* Jerusalén *m*. **2** *attr*: **~ artichoke** aguaturma *f*, pataca *f*, tupinambo *m*.

jessamine ['dʒesəmɪn] *n* jazmín *m*.

jest [dʒest] **1** *n* chanza *f*, broma *f*; (*verbal*) chiste *m*; **in ~** en broma, de guasa. **2** *vi* bromear, chancearse; **he was only ~ing** lo dijo en broma nada más.

jester ['dʒestə^r] *n* bufón *m*.

jesting ['dʒestɪŋ] **1** *adj person* chistoso, guasón; *tone* guasón; *reference* burlón, en broma. **2** *n* chanzas *fpl*, bromas *fpl*; chistes *mpl*.

Jesuit ['dʒezjʊɪt] **1** *adj* jesuita. **2** *n* jesuita *m*.

Jesuitical [,dʒezjʊ'ɪtɪkəl] *adj* jesuítico.

Jesus ['dʒiːzəs] **1** *nm* Jesús; **~ Christ** Jesucristo; **~ Christ!*** ¡Santo Dios!

2 *attr*: **~ freak*** sectario *m* fanático de Jesús; **~ sandals** (*Brit*) sandalias *fpl* nazarenas.

jet[1] [dʒet] *n* (*Min*) azabache *m*.

jet[2] [dʒet] **1** *n* (**a**) (*of liquid*) chorro *m*, surtidor *m*; (*gas burner*) mechero *m*; **a ~ of flame** una llama.

(**b**) (*Aer*) jet *m*, avión *m* a reacción.

2 *attr* (*Aer*) a reacción, a chorro; **the ~ age** la época de los jet; **~ engine** motor *m* a reacción, reactor *m*; **~ fighter** avión *m* de caza a reacción, caza *m* a reacción; **~ plane** = **1** (**b**); **~ propulsion** propulsión *f* por reacción, propulsión *f* a chorro.

3 *vt* lanzar en chorro, echar en chorro.

4 *vi* chorrear, salir a chorro.

jet-black ['dʒet'blæk] *adj* de azabache, negro como el azabache.

jet-lag ['dʒet,læg] **1** *n* jet-lag *m*, desfase *m* horario, desfase *m* debido a un largo viaje en avión. **2** *vt*: **to be ~ged** tener jet-lag, estar desfasado por el viaje (en avión).

jet-powered ['dʒet'paʊəd] *adj*, **jet-propelled** ['dʒetprə'peld] *adj* a reacción, a chorro.

jetsam ['dʒetsəm] *n* echazón *f*, cosas *fpl* desechadas.

jet-set ['dʒetset] *n* alta sociedad *f* internacional, jet-set *f*, jet *f*.

jet-setter ['dʒet,setə^r] *n* miembro *mf* de la jet-set.

jet-stream ['dʒetstriːm] *n* corriente *f* en chorro.

jettison ['dʒetɪsn] *vt* (*Naut etc*) echar al mar, echar por la borda; (*Aer*) vaciar; (*fig*) desechar, abandonar, librarse de; **we can safely ~ that** bien podemos prescindir de eso.

jetty ['dʒetɪ] *n* malecón *m*, muelle *m*, embarcadero *m*.

Jew [dʒuː] *n* judío *m*, -a *f*.

jewel ['dʒuːəl] *n* joya *f* (*also fig*), alhaja *f*; (*of watch*) rubí *m*.

jewel-case ['dʒuːəlkeɪs] *n* joyero *m*, estuche *m* de joyas, guardajoyas *m*.

jewelled, (*esp US*) **jeweled** ['dʒuːəld] *adj* adornado con piedras preciosas, enjoyado; *watch* con rubíes.

jeweller, (*esp US*) **jeweler** ['dʒuːələ^r] *n* joyero *m*; **~'s (shop)** joyería *f*.

jewellery, (*esp US*) **jewelry** ['dʒuːəlrɪ] *n* joyas *fpl*, alhajas *fpl*; **~ box = jewel-case**; **jewelry store** (*US*) joyería *f*.

Jewess ['dʒuːɪs] *n* judía *f*.

Jewish ['dʒuːɪʃ] *adj* judío.

Jewishness ['dʒuːɪʃnɪs] *n* carácter *m* judaico.

Jewry ['dʒʊərɪ] *n* judería *f*, los judíos.

Jew's-harp ['dʒuːz'hɑːp] *n* birimbao *m*.

Jezebel ['dʒezəbel] *nf* Jezabel.

JFK *n* (*US*) *abbr of* **John Fitzgerald Kennedy International Airport.**

jib[1] [dʒɪb] **1** *n* (*Naut*) foque *m*; (*Mech*) aguilón *m*, brazo *m*. **2** *attr*: **~ boom** botalón *m* de foque.

jib[2] [dʒɪb] *vi* (*horse*) plantarse, rehusar; (*person*) rehusar; **I ~ at that** no puedo consentir en eso; **he ~bed at it** se negó a aprobarlo (*etc*), no quiso permitirlo, se opuso a ello.

jibe [dʒaɪb] **1** *n* pulla *f*, dicterio *m*. **2** *vi* mofarse (*at* de).

jiffy* ['dʒɪfɪ] *n* instante *m*, momento *m*; **I'll be with you in a ~** un momento y estoy con vosotros; **to do sth in a ~** hacer algo en un decir Jesús, hacer algo en un santiamén.

jig[1] [dʒɪg] **1** *n* (*dance*) giga *f*.

2 *vi* (*dance*) bailar (la giga); **to ~ along, to ~ up and down** vibrarse, sacudirse, (*person*) moverse a saltitos; **to keep ~ging up and down** no poder estarse quieto.

jig[2] [dʒɪg] *n* (*Mech*) plantilla *f* (de guía); (*Rail*) gálibo *m*.

jigger[1] ['dʒɪgə^r] *n* (*Min*) criba *f*; (*Mech*) aparato *m* vibratorio.

jigger[2]* ['dʒɪgə^r] *n* (*US*) medida *f* (de whisky *etc*); (*thingummy*) chisme *m*.

jiggered* ['dʒɪgəd] *adj* (*Brit*): **well I'm ~!** ¡caramba!; **I'm ~ if I will** que me cuelguen si lo hago.

jiggery-pokery* ['dʒɪgərɪ'pəʊkərɪ] *n* (*Brit*) trampas *fpl*, embustes *mpl*, maniobras *fpl* poco limpias; **there's some ~ going on** hay trampa; están maquinando algo.

jiggle ['dʒɪgl] **1** *n* zangoloteo *m*. **2** *vt* zangolotear. **3** *vi* zangolotearse.

jigsaw ['dʒɪgsɔː] *n* (**a**) sierra *f* de vaivén. (**b**) (*also* **~ puzzle**) rompecabezas *m*, puzzle *m*.

jilt [dʒɪlt] *vt* dar calabazas a, dejar plantado a; **her ~ed lover** su amante abandonado.

Jim [dʒɪm] *nm familiar form of* **James.**

jimdandy* ['dʒɪm'dændɪ] *adj* (*US*) estupendo*, fenomenal*.

jimjams‡ ['dʒɪmdʒæmz] *npl* delírium *m* tremens; **it gives me the ~** me horripila, me da grima.

Jimmy ['dʒɪmɪ] *nm familiar form of* **James**; **to have a ~ (Riddle)**‡ mear‡.

jimmy ['dʒɪmɪ] *n* (*US*) = **jemmy.**

jingle ['dʒɪŋgl] **1** *n* (**a**) (*sound*) tintineo *m*, retintín *m*, ruido *m* (de campanita, monedas *etc*); cascabeleo *m*. (**b**) (*Liter*) verso *m*, poemita *m* popular, rima *f* infantil; (*TV etc*) anuncio *m* cantado, anuncio *m* rimado; (*Pol*: *slogan*) pareado *m*.

2 *vt* hacer sonar.

3 *vi* tintinear, retiñir, cascabelear.

jingo ['dʒɪŋgəʊ] *n* patriotero *m*, -a *f*, jingoísta *mf*; **by ~!** ¡caramba!

jingoism ['dʒɪŋgəʊɪzəm] *n* patriotería *f*, jingoísmo *m*.

jingoist(ic) [,dʒɪŋgəʊ'ɪst(ɪk)] *adj* patriotero, jingoísta.

jinks [dʒɪŋks] *npl*: **high ~** jolgorio *m*; fiesta *f* animadísima; **we had high ~ last night** anoche nos lo pasamos pipa.

jinx* [dʒɪŋks] **1** *n* cenizo* *m*, gafe* *m*; (*gremlin*) duendecillo *m*; **there's a ~ on it** esto está como encantado, esto está que da rabia. **2** *vt* traer mala suerte a; gafar*.

jitney* ['dʒɪtniː] *n* (*US*) (**a**) autobús *m* pequeño, colectivo *m* (*LAm*). (**b**) *moneda de 5 centavos.*

jitterbug ['dʒɪtəbʌg] **1** *n* (*dance*) *baile acrobático al ritmo de jazz o bugui-bugie*; (*person*) persona *f* aficionada a bailar el jitterbug. **2** *vi* bailar (el jazz).

jitters* ['dʒɪtəz] *npl* inquietud *f*, nerviosismo *m*; mieditis* *f*; **to get the ~** ponerse nervioso; **to have the ~** estar nervioso; **to give sb the ~** poner nervioso a uno.

jittery* ['dʒɪtərɪ] *adj* muy inquieto, nervioso; **to get ~** inquietarse, ponerse nervioso.

jiujitsu [dʒuː'dʒɪtsuː] *n* jiu-jitsu *m*.

jive [dʒaɪv] **1** *n* (**a**) (*music, dancing*) swing *m*, jazz *m*.

(**b**) (*US*‡) (*big talk*) alardes *mpl*, jactancias *fpl*; (*nonsense*) chorradas‡ *fpl*; (*of blacks etc*; *also* **~ talk**) jerga *f*; **don't give me all that ~** deja de decir chorradas‡.

2 *vi* (**a**) (*dance*) bailar el swing, bailar el jazz.

(**b**) (‡: *be kidding*) bromear.

Jly *abbr of* **July** julio, jul.

Jnr (*US*) *abbr of* **junior** junior, jr.

Jo [dʒəʊ] *nf familiar form of* **Josephine.**

Joan [dʒəʊn] *nf* Juana; **~ of Arc** Juana de Arco.

job [dʒɒb] **1** *n* (**a**) (*piece of work*) trabajo *m*, tarea *f*; (*Comput*) trabajo *m*; **the man for the ~** el más apropiado, el hombre ideal; **the ~ in hand** el trabajo que tenemos entre manos; **to be on the ~** estar trabajando; **she's doing a good ~** trabaja bien; **he has done a good ~ with the book** el libro le ha salido bien; **he never did a ~ in his life** no ha trabajado nunca; **to fall down on the ~** fracasar, demostrar no tener capacidad; **she had a nose ~ done*** tuvo cirugía estética para mejorar la nariz; **he knows his ~** sabe su oficio; **to make a good ~ of sth** hacer algo bien; *V* **odd.**

(**b**) (*: *crime*) golpe* *m*, robo *m*; **that warehouse ~** ese robo en el almacén.

(**c**) (*piecework*) destajo *m*; **by the ~** a destajo.

(**d**) (*duty*) deber *m*, cometido *m*; **my ~ is to sell them** mi deber es venderlos, yo estoy encargado de venderlos; **that's not his ~** eso no le incumbe a él; **he does his ~** cumple con su deber; **I had the ~ of telling him** a mí me tocó decírselo.

(**e**) (*post, employment*) empleo *m*, puesto *m*, trabajo *m*; **we shall create 1000 new ~s** vamos a crear 1000 puestos de trabajo más; **~s for the boys*** amiguismo* *m*, enchufismo* *m*; **to be in a ~** tener trabajo; **to be out of a ~** estar sin trabajo, estar desocupado; **to lie down on the ~** echarse en el surco; **to look for a ~** buscar un empleo; **to lose one's ~** perder su empleo, ser despedido; **automation has put them out of a ~** la automatización les ha quitado el trabajo, han sido despedidos debido a la automatización.

(**f**) (*state of affairs*) **it's a bad ~** es una situación difícil; es lamentable, es terrible; **she gave him up as a bad ~** por imposible rompió con él; **to make the best of a bad ~** poner a mal tiempo buena cara; sacar el máximo partido de una situación (adversa); **that's a good ~!, and a good ~ too!** ¡menos mal!; **it's a good ~ that ...** menos mal que ...

(**g**) (*difficulty*) **we had quite a ~ getting here** nos costó trabajo venir aquí; **he has a ~ to express himself** le cuesta expresarse.

(**h**) (*) **it's just the ~!** ¡estupendo!*; **a holiday in Majorca would be just the ~** sería estupendo pasar unas vacaciones en Mallorca*; **this machine is just the ~** esta máquina nos viene perfecto.

2 *attr* (**a**) **~ analysis** análisis *m* del trabajo, análisis *m* ocupacional; **~ centre** (*Brit*) agencia *f* de colocaciones; **~ classification** clasificación *f* de trabajos; **~ club** grupo *m* de asesoramiento para desempleados; **~ control language** lenguaje *m* de control de trabajo; **~ creation** creación *f* de empleo; **~ creation scheme** plan *m* de creación de nuevos empleos; **~ description** descripción *f* del trabajo; **~ evaluation, ~ grading** evaluación *f* de empleos; **~ hunting** búsqueda *f* de trabajo; **500 ~ losses** pérdida *f* de 500 puestos de trabajo; **~ number** número *m* del trabajo; **~ opportunity** oportunidad *f* de trabajo; **~ queue** (*Comput*) cola *f* de trabajos; (*persons*) cola *f* de los que buscan trabajo; **~ satisfaction** satisfacción *f* profesional, satisfacción *f* laboral; **~ security** seguridad *f* en el trabajo, garantía *f* de trabajo; **~ seeker** persona *f* que busca trabajo; **~ share** (*or* **sharing**) **scheme** plan *m* para compartir empleos; **~ specification** especificación *f* del trabajo, profesionagrama *m*; **~ study** estudio *m* del trabajo.

(**b**) **~ lot** lote *m* suelto de mercancías, saldo *m*.

Job [dʒəʊb] *nm* Job; **~'s comforter** *el que, bajo pretexto de animar a otro, le desconsuela todavía más.*

jobber [ˈdʒɒbəʳ] *n* (*Brit St Ex*) agiotista *mf*; (*agent*) corredor *m*, -ora *f*; (*middleman*) intermediario *m*, -a *f*.

jobbery [ˈdʒɒbərɪ] *n* (*Brit*) intrigas *fpl*, chanchullos *mpl*; **piece of ~** intriga *f*, chanchullo *m*; **by a piece of ~** por enchufe.

jobbing [ˈdʒɒbɪŋ] **1** *adj* que trabaja a destajo; **~ printer** impresor *m* de circulares, folletos *etc.* **2** *n* agiotaje *m*; comercio *m* de intermediario.

jobholder [ˈdʒɒb,həʊldəʳ] *n* empleado *m*, -a *f*.

jobless [ˈdʒɒblɪs] **1** *adj* sin trabajo. **2** *npl*: **the ~** los desocupados, los parados; **the ~ figures** las cifras de personas sin trabajo.

joblessness [ˈdʒɒblɪsnɪs] *n* carencia *f* de trabajo.

Jock* [dʒɒk] *nm el escocés típico*; **the ~s** los escoceses.

jock [dʒɒk] *n* (**a**) = **jockstrap.** (**b**) (*US*) deportista *m*.

jockey [ˈdʒɒkɪ] **1** *n* jockey *m*, yoquei *m*; **~ shorts** calzoncillos *mpl* de jockey.

2 *vt*: **to ~ sb into doing sth** persuadir mañosamente a uno a hacer algo; **to ~ sb out of doing sth** disuadir mañosamente a uno de hacer algo; **to ~ sb out of a post** lograr mañosamente que uno renuncie a un puesto.

3 *vi*: **to ~ for a position** maniobrar para conseguir una posición.

jockstrap [ˈdʒɒkstræp] *n* suspensorio *m*.

jocose [dʒəˈkəʊs] *adj*, **jocular** [ˈdʒɒkjʊləʳ] *adj* (*merry*) alegre, de buen humor; (*humorous*) guasón, zumbón, jocoso.

jocularity [,dʒɒkjʊˈlærətɪ] *n* jocosidad *f*.

jodhpurs [ˈdʒɒdpɜːz] *npl* pantalones *mpl* de montar.

Joe [dʒəʊ] *nm familiar form of* **Joseph** (Pepe); (*US**) tipo* *m*, tío* *m*; **the average ~** el hombre de la calle; **a good ~** un buen chico; **~ Bloggs*, ~ Public*** (*Brit*) *ciudadano de a pie británico*; **~ College** (*US*) *típico estudiante norteamericano*; **~ Soap*** fulano *m*.

jog [dʒɒg] **1** *n* (**a**) (*push etc*) empujoncito *m*, sacudida *f* (ligera), codazo *m*; (*encouragement*) estímulo *m*; **to give sb's memory a ~** refrescar la memoria de uno.

(**b**) (*pace*) trote *m* corto; **to go at a steady ~** andar a trote corto.

(**c**) **to go for a ~** hacer footing.

2 *vt* (*push etc*) empujar (ligeramente), sacudir (levemente); (*encourage*) estimular; *memory* refrescar; **he ~ged my arm** me dio ligeramente con el codo; **to ~ sb's memory** refrescar la memoria de uno.

3 *vi* (**a**) (*also* **to ~ along**) andar a trote corto, avanzar despacio; (*fig*) hacer algunos progresos, avanzar pero sin prisa; **we keep ~ging along** vamos tirando.

(**b**) (*Sport*) hacer footing.

jogger [ˈdʒɒgəʳ] *n* persona *f* que hace footing.

jogging [ˈdʒɒgɪŋ] **1** *n* footing *m*, futing *m*, jogging *m*. **2** *attr*: **~ shoes** zapatillas *fpl* de jogging; **~ suit** chandal *m*.

joggle [ˈdʒɒgl] **1** *n* traqueo *m*. **2** *vt* traquetear. **3** *vi* traquetear.

jog-trot [ˈdʒɒgˈtrɒt] *n*: **at a ~** a trote corto.

John [dʒɒn] *nm* Juan; **~ the Baptist** San Juan Bautista; **~ Bull** *personificación del pueblo inglés*; **~ Doe** (*US*) fulano *m*; *el norteamericano medio*; **~ Dory** ceo *m*; **~ Hancock*, ~ Henry*** firma *f*, rúbrica *f*; **~ Q Public*** (*US*) *el hombre de la calle, el público*; **St ~ the Evangelist** San Juan Evangelista; **St ~ of the Cross** San Juan de la Cruz; **Pope ~ Paul II** el Papa Juan Pablo II.

john[1]‡ [dʒɒn] *n* (*US*) wáter *m*, meadero‡ *m*.

john[2]‡ [dʒɒn] *n* (*US*) cliente *m* de prostituta.

Johnny [ˈdʒɒnɪ] *nm* Juanito.

johnny* [ˈdʒɒnɪ] *n* tío* *m*, sujeto *m*.

joie de vivre [ˈʒwɑːdəˈviːvr] *n* goce *m* del vivir, alegría *f* vital.

join [dʒɔɪn] **1** *n* juntura *f*; (*Sew*) costura *f*.

2 *vt* (**a**) *two things* unir, juntar, poner juntos; (*Tech*) unir, acoplar, ensamblar; **everybody ~ed hands** se cogieron (*LAm*: se tomaron) todos de la mano; **to his genius he ~s humanity** a su genialidad une la humanidad.

(**b**) *society* ingresar en; *club* hacerse socio de; *party* afiliarse a, hacerse miembro de; *company* entrar en, tomar un puesto en; llegar a formar parte de; (*Mil*) alistarse en; **to ~ one's regiment** incorporarse a su regimiento; **to ~ one's ship** volver a su buque; **where the track ~s the road** donde el camino empalma con la carretera.

(**c**) *person* reunirse con, unirse a, juntarse con; **may I ~ you?** ¿se permite?; **will you ~ me in a drink?** ¿quieres tomar algo conmigo?; **they ~ed us last Friday** vinieron a estar con nosotros el viernes pasado; **they will ~ us for the holidays** vendrán a pasar las vacaciones con nosotros; **to ~ sb in doing sth** acompañar a uno en hacer algo, hacer algo juntamente con uno; **they ~ed us in protesting** se hicieron eco de nuestras protestas.

(**d**) (*river*) desembocar en, confluir con; (*road*) empalmar con, unirse a.

3 *vi* (**a**) unirse, juntarse; (*lines*) empalmar; (*rivers*) confluir; **where the paths ~** donde empalman los caminos.

(**b**) **to ~ with sb in sth** acompañar a uno en algo, participar juntamente con uno en algo; **we ~ with you in that feeling** compartimos esa opinión, nos hacemos eco de eso; **we ~ with you in hoping that ...** lo mismo que Vds esperamos que ...

(**c**) (*Pol etc*) hacerse miembro.

◆**join in 1** *vt*: **she ~ed in the discussion** intervino en el debate. **2** *vi* tomar parte (en), participar (en); **he doesn't ~ in much** apenas participa en nuestras actividades; **they all ~ed in singing the last song** todos cantaron la última canción.

◆**join on 1** *vt* unir; añadir. **2** *vi*: **he ~ed on to the queue** se unió a la cola; **it ~s on here** se coloca aquí.

◆**join together 1** *vt* unir. **2** *vi* unirse (to + *infin* para + *infin*).

◆**join up 1** *vt* (**a**) unir; **~ed up writing** escritura *f* cursiva. (**b**) = **join 2** (**a**). **2** *vi* (**a**) unirse; **to ~ up with sb** reunirse con uno. (**b**) (*Mil*) alistarse.

joiner [ˈdʒɔɪnəʳ] *n* (*Brit*) carpintero *m* (de blanco), ensamblador *m*.

joinery [ˈdʒɔɪnərɪ] *n* (*Brit*) carpintería *f*.

joint [dʒɔɪnt] **1** *adj* (en) común; combinado; *action, effort, product etc* conjunto, colectivo; *agreement* mutuo; *declaration etc* conjunto; *responsibility* solidario, que comparten todos; *committee etc* mixto; (*in compounds*) co ...; ~ **account** cuenta *f* indistinta, cuenta *f* conjunta; ~ **author** coautor *m*, -ora *f*; ~ **communiqué** comunicado *m* conjunto; ~ **consultations** consultas *fpl* bilaterales; ~ **heir** coheredero *m*, -a *f*; ~ **interest** (*Comm*) coparticipación *f*; ~ **liability** responsabilidad *f* solidaria; obligación *f* mancomunada; ~ **owners** copropietarios *mpl*; ~ **ownership** copropiedad *f*; ~ **partner** copartícipe *mf*; ~ **stock** fondo *m* social; **~-stock bank** banco *m* por acciones; ~ **stock company** sociedad *f* anónima; ~ **venture** (*Fin*) empresa *f* (*or* sociedad *f*) conjunta; acuerdo *m* de riesgos compartidos.

2 *n* (**a**) (*Tech*: *metal*) junta *f*, juntura *f*, unión *f*; (*wood*) ensambladura *f*; (*hinge*) bisagra *f*; (*Anat*) articulación *f*, coyuntura *f*; (*knuckle*) nudillo *m*; (*Bot*) nudo *m*; (*Brit*: *of meat*) cuarto *m*; **to be out of ~** (*bone*) estar descoyuntado, estar dislocado; (*fig*) estar fuera de quicio; **to put a bone out of ~** dislocarse un hueso; **to put sb's nose out of ~** desconcertar a uno (adelantándose a él); **to throw sb's plans out of ~** estropear los planes de uno.

(**b**) (‡: *place*) antro *m*, tugurio *m*, garito *m*.

(**c**) (‡: *drugs*) porro‡ *m*, cigarrillo *m* de marijuana.

3 *vt* articular; *parts* juntar, unir; *wood etc* ensamblar; (*Brit Culin*) cortar.

jointed [ˈdʒɔɪntɪd] *adj* articulado; (*folding*) plegadizo, plegable.

jointly [ˈdʒɔɪntlɪ] *adv* en común; colectivamente; mutuamente; conjuntamente.

joist [dʒɔɪst] *n* viga *f*, vigueta *f*.

joke [dʒəʊk] **1** *n* (*hoax etc*) broma *f*, burla *f*; (*witticism, story*) chiste *m*; (*person*) hazmerreír *m*; **he's a standing ~** es un pobre hombre, es un hombre que da risa; **it's a standing ~ here** aquí eso siempre provoca a risa; **it's no ~** no es cosa de risa, no es para reírse; **it's no ~ having to +** *infin* no tiene nada de divertido + *infin*; **the ~ is that** lo gracioso es que; **the ~ is on you** tu eres el aludido, eso lo dicen por ti; **it's beyond a ~** esto es el colmo, esto pasa de castaño oscuro; **what sort of a ~ is this?** ¿qué broma es ésta?; **is that your idea of a ~?** ¿es que eso tiene gracia?; **to crack** (*or* **make**) **a ~** hacer un chiste; **to crack ~s with sb** contar chistes con uno; **they spent an evening cracking ~s together** pasaron una tarde contándose chistes; **he will have his little ~** siempre está con sus bromas, le gusta tomar el pelo; **he made a ~ of the disaster** tomó el desastre en chunga; **to play a ~ on sb** gastar una broma a uno; **I can take a ~** tengo mucho aguante; **he can't take a ~** no le gusta que se le tome el pelo; **to tell a ~** contar un chiste; **why do you have to turn everything into a ~?** ¿eres incapaz de tomar nada en serio?

2 *vi* bromear, chancearse, chunguearse; hablar en broma; (*tell ~s*) contar chistes; **I was only joking** lo dije en broma; **I'm not joking** esto lo digo en serio; **you must be joking!** pero ¿lo dices en serio?; **to ~ about sth** tomar algo en chunga.

jokebook [ˈdʒəʊk,bʊk] *n* libro *m* de chistes.

joker [ˈdʒəʊkəʳ] *n* (**a**) (*wit*) chistoso *m*, -a *f*, guasón *m*, -ona *f*; (*practical ~*) bromista *mf*. (**b**) (*Cards*) comodín *m*; **he's the ~ in the pack** (*fig*) es el elemento desconocido. (**c**) (*) **some ~** algún gracioso.

jokey [ˈdʒəʊkɪ] *adj person* chistoso, guasón; *reference etc* humorístico; *mood, tone* guasón.

joking [ˈdʒəʊkɪŋ] **1** *adj reference etc* humorístico; *tone* guasón; **I'm not in a ~ mood** no estoy para bromas.

2 *n* bromas *fpl*; chistes *mpl*; **but ~ apart, ...** pero bromas aparte, ...

jokingly [ˈdʒəʊkɪŋlɪ] *adv* humorísticamente; **he said ~** dijo en broma, dijo guasón.

jollification [,dʒɒlɪfɪˈkeɪʃən] *n* (*merriment*) regocijo *m*, festividades *fpl*; (*party*) fiesta *f*, guateque *m*.

jolliness [ˈdʒɒlɪnɪs] *n* jovialidad *f*.

jollity [ˈdʒɒlɪtɪ] *n* alegría *f*, regocijo *m*.

jolly [ˈdʒɒlɪ] **1** *adj* alegre; divertido; *character* alegre, jovial; **J~ Roger** pabellón *m* negro (de los piratas); **it was all very ~** todo ha sido muy agradable; **to get ~*** achisparse*; **we had a ~ time** lo pasamos muy bien, nos divertimos mucho; **it wasn't very ~ for the rest of us** los demás no nos divertimos nada.

2 (*Brit**) *adv* muy, terriblemente; **it's ~ hard** es terriblemente difícil; **we were ~ glad** nos alegramos muchísimo; **you did ~ well** lo hiciste la mar de bien*; **you've ~ well got to** no tienes más remedio en absoluto; **~ good!** ¡estupendo!*

3 *vt*: **to ~ sb along** engatusar a uno, seguir el humor a uno; **to ~ sb into doing sth** engatusar a uno para que haga algo.

jollyboat [ˈdʒɒlɪbəʊt] *n* esquife *m*.

jolt [dʒəʊlt] **1** *n* sacudida *f*, choque *m*; **to give sb a ~** (*fig*) dar una sacudida a uno; **it gave me a bit of a ~** me dio un susto, con eso me pegué un susto.

2 *vt* sacudir; *elbow etc* empujar (ligeramente), sacudir (levemente); **to ~ sb into doing sth** dar una sacudida a uno para animarle a hacer algo; **to ~ sb out of his complacency** hacer que uno se dé cuenta de la necesidad de hacer algo, destruir el optimismo de uno.

3 *vi* (*vehicle*) traquetear, dar saltos.

jolting [ˈdʒəʊltɪŋ] *n* (*of vehicle*) traqueteo *m*.

jolty [ˈdʒəʊltɪ] *adj vehicle* que traquetea, que da saltos.

Jonah [ˈdʒəʊnə] *nm* Jonás.

Jonathan [ˈdʒɒnəθən] *nm* Jonatás.

jonquil [ˈdʒɒŋkwɪl] *n* junquillo *m*.

Jordan [ˈdʒɔːdn] *n* (**a**) (*river*) Jordán *m*. (**b**) (*country*) Jordania *f*.

Jordanian [dʒɔːˈdeɪnɪən] **1** *adj* jordano. **2** *n* jordano *m*, -a *f*.

Joseph [ˈdʒəʊzɪf] *nm* José.

Josephine [ˈdʒəʊzɪfiːn] *nf* Josefina.

josh‡ [dʒɒʃ] *vt* (*US*) tomar el pelo a.

Joshua [ˈdʒɒʃwə] *nm* Josué.

josser‡ [ˈdʒɒsəʳ] *n* tío *m*, individuo *m*.

joss-stick [ˈdʒɒsstɪk] *n* pebete *m*.

jostle [ˈdʒɒsl] **1** *n* empujón *m*, empellón *m*, codazo *m*.

2 *vt* empujar, zarandear.

3 *vi* empujar(se), dar(se) empellones, codear(se); **they were all jostling for a place** todos se estaban empujando para asegurarse un sitio.

jot [dʒɒt] **1** *n* jota *f*, pizca *f*; **there's not a ~ of truth in it** eso no tiene ni pizca de verdad; *V* **care**. **2** *vt*: **to ~ down** apuntar.

jotter [ˈdʒɒtəʳ] *n* (*Brit*) cuaderno *m*, bloc *m*, taco *m* para notas.

jottings [ˈdʒɒtɪŋz] *npl* apuntes *mpl*.

joule [dʒuːl] *n* julio *m*, joule *m*.

journal [ˈdʒɜːnl] *n* (**a**) (*newspaper*) periódico *m*; (*review, magazine*) revista *f*; (*diary*) diario *m*; (*Naut*) diario *m* de navegación. (**b**) (*Mech*) gorrón *m*, muñón *m*.

journal bearing [ˈdʒɜːnlˈbɛərɪŋ] *n* cojinete *m*.

journalese [ˈdʒɜːnəˈliːz] *n* lenguaje *m* (*or* estilo *m*) periodístico.

journalism [ˈdʒɜːnəlɪzəm] *n* periodismo *m*.

journalist [ˈdʒɜːnəlɪst] *n* periodista *mf*.

journalistic [,dʒɜːnəˈlɪstɪk] *adj* periodístico.

journey [ˈdʒɜːnɪ] **1** *n* viaje *m*; trayecto *m*; camino *m*; **Scott's ~ to the Pole** la expedición de Scott al Polo; **the capsule's ~ through space** el trayecto de la cápsula por el espacio; **pleasant ~!** ¡buen viaje!; **at ~'s end** al fin del viaje; **to be on a ~** estar de viaje; **have you much ~ left?** ¿le queda mucho camino?

2 *vi* viajar.

journeyman [ˈdʒɜːnɪmən] *n*, *pl* **journeymen** [ˈdʒɜːnɪmən] oficial *m*.

joust [dʒaʊst] **1** *n* justa *f*, torneo *m*. **2** *vi* justar.

Jove [dʒəʊv] *nm* Júpiter; **by ~!** ¡caramba!, ¡por Dios!

jovial [ˈdʒəʊvɪəl] *adj* jovial.

joviality [,dʒəʊvɪˈælɪtɪ] *n* jovialidad *f*.

jowl [dʒaʊl] *n* (*Anat*: *jaw*) quijada *f*; (*chin*) barba *f*; (*cheek*) carrillo *m*; (*Zool*) papada *f*.

joy [dʒɔɪ] *n* (*gladness*) alegría *f*, júbilo *m*, regocijo *m*, gozo *m*; (*pleasant quality*) deleite *m*, encanto *m*; **the ~s of opera** los encantos de la ópera; **it's a ~ to hear him** da gozo escucharle; **to be a ~ to the eye** ser un gozo para los ojos; **to be beside o.s. with ~** no caber en sí de gozo; **to jump for ~** saltar de alegría; **I wish you ~!** ¡enhorabuena! (*also iro*); **no ~!*** ¡nada!; **we got no ~ out of it** no logramos nada, no nos sirvió de nada, no nos dio resultado alguno.

joyful [ˈdʒɔɪfʊl] *adj* alegre; jubiloso, regocijado; **to be ~ about** alegrarse de.

joyfully [ˈdʒɔɪfəlɪ] *adv* alegremente; con júbilo, regocijadamente.

joyfulness [ˈdʒɔɪfʊlnɪs] *n* alegría *f*; júbilo *m*, regocijo *m*.

joyless [ˈdʒɔɪlɪs] *adj* sin alegría, triste.

joyous [ˈdʒɔɪəs] *adj* alegre.

joyride [ˈdʒɔɪraɪd] **1** *n* paseo *m* en coche (*etc*) (sin permiso del dueño), excursión *f* en coche (*etc*). **2** *vi* pasearse en coche (*etc*) (sin permiso del dueño).

joystick [ˈdʒɔɪstɪk] *n* (*Aer*) palanca *f* de mando; (*Comput*) palanca *f* de control, bastoncillo *m* de mando.

JP *n* (*Brit*) *abbr of* **Justice of the Peace** juez *m* de paz.
Jr *abbr of* **junior** junior, jr.
JTPA *n* (*US*) *abbr of* **Job Training Partnership Act** programa *m* gubernamental de formación profesional.
jubilant [ˈdʒuːbɪlənt] *adj* jubiloso.
jubilation [ˌdʒuːbɪˈleɪʃən] *n* júbilo *m*.
jubilee [ˈdʒuːbɪliː] *n* (*Hist, Eccl*) jubileo *m*; (*anniversary: strictly*) quincuagésimo aniversario *m*; *V* **silver** *etc*.
Judaea [dʒuːˈdɪə] *n* Judea *f*.
Judah [ˈdʒuːdə] *n* Judá *f*.
Judaic [dʒuːˈdeɪɪk] *adj* judaico.
Judaism [ˈdʒuːdeɪɪzəm] *n* judaísmo *m*.
Judaize [ˈdʒuːdeɪaɪz] *vi* judaizar.
Judaizer [ˈdʒuːdeɪˌaɪzəʳ] *n* judaizante *mf*.
Judas [ˈdʒuːdəs] *nm* Judas.
judder [ˈdʒʌdəʳ] (*Brit*) **1** *n* vibración *f*. **2** *vi* vibrar.
Judeo-Spanish [ˈdʒuːdeɪəʊˈspænɪʃ] **1** *adj* judeoespañol, sefardí. **2** *n* (*Ling*) judeoespañol *m*, ladino *m*.
judge [dʒʌdʒ] **1** *n* (*Jur*) juez *mf* (*also* -a *f*); (*Sport*) árbitro *m*, (*in races*) juez *m*; (*connoisseur*) conocedor *m*, -ora *f* (*of* de), (*expert*) perito *m* (*of* en); **Book of J~s** (Libro *m* de los) Jueces *mpl*; **~ of appeal** juez *m* de alzadas, juez *m* de apelaciones; **the ~'s rules** (*Brit*) los derechos del detenido; **he's a fine ~ of horses** es un excelente conocedor de caballos; **I'm no ~ of wines** yo no entiendo de vinos; **I'll be the ~ of that** yo decidiré aquello, lo juzgaré yo mismo.
2 *vt person, case* juzgar; *question* decidir, resolver; (*Sport*) arbitrar; (*consider*) juzgar, considerar; **I ~ it to be right** lo considero acertado; **I ~ him a fool** considero que es tonto; **as far as can be ~d** a mi modo de ver, según mi juicio; **one has to ~ the distance** hay que calcular la distancia; **he ~d the moment well** acertó escogiendo tal momento; **who can ~ this question?** ¿quién puede resolver esta cuestión?
3 *vi* juzgar; opinar, expresar una opinión; **to ~ by, judging by** a juzgar por; **to ~ of** juzgar de, opinar sobre; **who am I to ~?** ¿es que yo soy capaz de juzgar? **only an expert can ~** sólo lo puede decidir un experto; **to ~ for o.s.** formar su propia opinión.
judge-advocate [ˈdʒʌdʒˈædvəkɪt] *n* (*Mil*) auditor *m* de guerra.
judg(e)ment [ˈdʒʌdʒmənt] *n* (**a**) (*Jur*) juicio *m*; sentencia *f*, fallo *m*; **Last J~** Juicio *m* Final; **J~ Day** día *m* del Juicio Final; **~ seat** tribunal *m*; **it's a ~ on you for lying** es un castigo por haber mentido; **to pass** (*or* **pronounce**) **~** (*Jur*) pronunciar sentencia (*on* en, sobre), (*fig*) emitir un juicio crítico sobre, dictaminar sobre.
(**b**) (*opinion*) opinión *f*, parecer *m*; juicio *m*; **a critical ~ of Auden** un juicio crítico de Auden.
(**c**) (*understanding*) juicio *m*; criterio *m*; entendimiento *m*, discernimiento *m*; buen sentido *m*; **against my better ~** en contra de lo que me aconsejaba mi juicio; **in my ~** en mi opinión; **to the best of my ~** según mi leal saber y entender; **to have good** (*or* **sound**) **~** tener buen juicio, tener buen criterio.
judg(e)mental [dʒʌdʒˈmentl] *adj* crítico.
judicature [ˈdʒuːdɪkətʃəʳ] *n* judicatura *f*.
judicial [dʒuːˈdɪʃəl] *adj* judicial; imparcial; *murder, separation etc* legal; **~ inquiry** investigación *f* judicial.
judicially [dʒuːˈdɪʃəlɪ] *adv* judicialmente; legalmente.
judiciary [dʒuːˈdɪʃɪərɪ] **1** *adj* judicial. **2** *n* judicatura *f*.
judicious [dʒuːˈdɪʃəs] *adj* juicioso; prudente, sensato, acertado.
judiciously [dʒuːˈdɪʃəslɪ] *adv* juiciosamente; prudentemente, acertadamente.
Judith [ˈdʒuːdɪθ] *nf* Judit.
judo [ˈdʒuːdəʊ] *n* judo *m*, yudo *m*.
Judy [ˈdʒuːdɪ] *nf familiar form of* **Judith**.
jug [dʒʌg] **1** *n* (**a**) jarro *m*. (**b**) (‡: *jail*) chirona‡ *f*. (**c**) **~s** (*US*‡) tetas* *fpl*. **2** *vt* (**a**) **~ged hare** liebre *f* en estofado. (**b**) (‡) meter a la sombra‡.
juggernaut [ˈdʒʌgənɔːt] *n* monstruo *m* destructor de los hombres; (*Aut*) camión *m* grande, camionazo *m*.
juggins‡ [ˈdʒʌgɪnz] *n* bobo *m*, -a *f*.
juggle [ˈdʒʌgl] **1** *vi* hacer juegos malabares, hacer juegos de manos (*with* con); **to ~ with** (*fig*) = **2**. **2** *vt* arreglar de otro modo; (*pej*) falsear, falsificar, hacer trampa con.
juggler [ˈdʒʌgləʳ] *n* malabarista *mf*.
jugglery [ˈdʒʌglərɪ] *n*, **juggling** [ˈdʒʌglɪŋ] *n* juegos *mpl* malabares, malabarismo *m*, juegos *mpl* de manos; (*pej*) trampas *fpl*, fraude *m*.
Jugoslav [ˈjuːgəʊˈslɑːv] **1** *adj* yugoslavo. **2** *n* yugoslavo *m*, -a *f*.
Jugoslavia [ˈjuːgəʊˈslɑːvɪə] *n* Yugoslavia *f*.
jugular [ˈdʒʌgjʊləʳ] **1** *adj*: **~ vein** vena *f* yugular. **2** *n* vena *f* yugular.
juice [dʒuːs] *n* (**a**) (*fruit* ~) jugo *m*, zumo *m*. (**b**) (*Brit Aut**) gasolina *f*. (**c**) (*Elec**) fluido *m*, fuerza *f*, corriente *f*.
juicer [ˈdʒuːsəʳ] *n* (*US*) licuadora *f*.
juiciness [ˈdʒuːsɪnɪs] *n* (**a**) jugosidad *f*. (**b**) (*) lo picante, lo sabroso.
juicy [ˈdʒuːsɪ] *adj* (**a**) jugoso, zumoso. (**b**) (*) *story etc* picante, sabroso; *contract etc* sustancioso, ganancioso.
jujube [ˈdʒuːdʒuːb] *n* pastilla *f*.
jujutsu [dʒuːˈdʒɪtsʊ] *n* jiu-jitsu *m*.
jukebox [ˈdʒuːkbɒks] *n* tocadiscos *m* automático, tocadiscos *m* tragaperras, gramola *f*.
Jul. *abbr of* **July** julio *m*, jul.
julep [ˈdʒuːlep] *n* julepe *m*.
Julian [ˈdʒuːlɪən] *nm* Juliano, Julián.
Juliet [ˈdʒuːlɪet] *nf* Julieta.
Julius [ˈdʒuːlɪəs] *nm* Julio; **~ Caesar** Julio César.
July [dʒuːˈlaɪ] *n* julio *m*.
jumble [ˈdʒʌmbl] **1** *n* (**a**) revoltijo *m*, confusión *f*; **a ~ of furniture** un montón de muebles revueltos; **a ~ of sounds** unos ruidos confusos. (**b**) (*at sale*) objetos *mpl* usados, (*esp*) ropa *f* usada.
2 *vt* (*also* **to ~ together, to ~ up**) mezclar, emburujar; **papers ~d up together** papeles *mpl* revueltos; **they were just ~d together anyhow** estaban amontonados sin orden.
jumble-sale [ˈdʒʌmblseɪl] *n* (*Brit*) venta *f* de objetos usados (con fines benéficos), bazar *m* benéfico, rastrillo* *m* (benéfico).
jumbo [ˈdʒʌmbəʊ] **1** *n* (**a**) elefante *m*.
(**b**) (*Aer*: *also* **~ jet**) jumbo *m*.
2 *adj* colosal, enorme; (*Comm*: *also* **~ sized**) de tamaño extra.
jump [dʒʌmp] **1** *n* salto *m*, brinco *m*; (*Sport*) salto *m*; (*Comput*) salto *m*; (*fig*) ascenso *m*, aumento *m*; **to give a ~** dar un saltito; **to give sb a ~** dar un susto a uno; **you gave me quite a ~!** ¡ay qué susto me diste!; **to have the ~ on sb*** llevar ventaja a uno; **the temperature took a ~** subió rápidamente la temperatura; **there has been a big ~ in the reserves** las reservas han subido de golpe; **to keep one ~ ahead** mantener la delantera (*of sb* con respecto a uno); **in one ~ he went from novice to master** en limpio salto pasó de novicio a maestro.
2 *vt* (**a**) *ditch etc* saltar, saltar por encima de, salvar; **to ~ the lights*** (*Aut*) saltarse un semáforo en rojo; *V* **gun, rail** *etc*.
(**b**) *horse* hacer saltar; presentar en un concurso hípico.
(**c**) (*omit*) pasar por alto, omitir.
3 *vi* (**a**) (*leap*) saltar, brincar, dar saltos; (*Sport*) saltar; (*Aer*) lanzarse (en paracaídas); (*Comput*) saltar.
(**b**) (*fig*: *start*) asustarse, sobresaltarse, pegar un bote; **to make sb ~** dar un susto a uno; **you did make me ~!** ¡ay qué susto me diste!
(**c**) (*fig*: *emotion*) **to ~ for joy** saltar de alegría, no caber en sí de gozo; **everyone was ~ing up and down** (*angry*) todos estaban que brincaban, (*excited*) todos brincaban de emoción.
◆**jump about, jump around** *vi* dar saltos, brincar; moverse de un lado para otro.
◆**jump across** *vt*: **to ~ across a stream** cruzar un arroyo de un salto, saltar por encima de un arroyo.
◆**jump at** *vt*: **to ~ at a chance** apresurarse a aprovechar una oportunidad; **to ~ at an offer** aceptar una oferta con entusiasmo, agarrarse a una oferta.
◆**jump down** *vi* bajar de un salto, saltar a tierra.
◆**jump in** *vi*: **~ in!** ¡sube!, ¡vamos!; **to ~ into a car** entrar de prisa en un coche.
◆**jump off** *vi* (*Showjumping*) participar en un desempate.
◆**jump on** *vt* (**a**) **to ~ on** (**to**) **a chair** ponerse encima de una silla de un salto; **we ~ed on** (**to**) **the train** subimos de prisa al tren.
(**b**) (*) **to ~ on sb** poner verde a uno*; **we must ~ on this abuse** tenemos que acabar con este abuso.
◆**jump out** *vi*: **to ~ out of bed** saltar de la cama; **I nearly ~ed out of my skin!** ¡vaya susto que me pegué!; **he ~ed out from behind a tree** salió de repente de detrás de un árbol; **it ~s out at you** (*fig*) salta a la vista.
◆**jump over** *vt* saltar, saltar por (encima de), salvar.
◆**jump to** *vt*: **~ to it!** ¡apúrate!, ¡volando!
◆**jump up** *vi* ponerse de pie de un salto.
jumped-up [ˈdʒʌmptˈʌp] *adj* arribista, presuntuoso.
jumper [ˈdʒʌmpəʳ] *n* (**a**) (*person*) *n* saltador *m*, -ora *f*. (**b**) (*Brit*: *pullover*) suéter *m*, jersey *m*; (*US*: *pinafore dress*)

mandil *m*.

jumper cables ['dʒʌmpəʳˌkeɪbəlz] *npl* (*US*) = **jump leads**.

jumping ['dʒʌmpɪŋ] *n* (*Sport*) pruebas *fpl* de salto.

jumping bean ['dʒʌmpɪŋˌbiːn] *n* judía *f* saltadora, fríjol *m* saltador.

jumping-off ['dʒʌmpɪŋ'ɒf] *attr*: ~ **place** punto *m* de partida; base *f* avanzada.

jump-jet ['dʒʌmpdʒet] *n* avión *m* (a chorro) de despegue vertical.

jump leads ['dʒʌmpˌliːdz] *npl* (*Brit Aut*) cables *mpl* puente de batería, cables *mpl* de emergencia.

jump-off ['dʒʌmpɒf] *n* (*Showjumping*) prueba *f* (*or* saltos *mpl*) de desempate.

jump-rope ['dʒʌmprəʊp] *n* (*US*) comba *f*, cuerda *f* de saltar.

jump-seat ['dʒʌmpsiːt] *n* asiento *m* plegable.

jump-start ['dʒʌmpstɑːt] **1** *n* arranque *m* en segunda. **2** *vt* arrancar en segunda.

jumpsuit ['dʒʌmpsuːt] *n* (*US*) mono *m*.

jumpy ['dʒʌmpɪ] *adj* nervioso, asustadizo.

Jun. *abbr of* **June** junio, jun.

junction ['dʒʌŋkʃən] *n* juntura *f*, unión *f*; (*Brit*: *of roads*) cruce *m*, entronque *m* (*Méx*), crucero *m* (*LAm*); (*Brit Rail*) empalme *m*; (*Brit*: *of rivers*) confluencia *f*.

junction box ['dʒʌŋkʃənbɒks] *n* caja *f* de empalmes.

juncture ['dʒʌŋktʃəʳ] *n* coyuntura *f*; **at this** ~ en este momento, en esta coyuntura; a estas alturas.

June [dʒuːn] *n* junio *m*.

jungle ['dʒʌŋgl] **1** *n* selva *f*, jungla *f*; (*fig*) maraña *f*, selva *f*. **2** *attr*: ~ **bunny** (*US*‡) negrito* *m*, -a* *f*; ~ **warfare** guerra *f* de la selva.

junior ['dʒuːnɪəʳ] **1** *adj* (*in age*) menor, más joven; (*on a staff*) más nuevo; *position, rank* subalterno; *section* (*in competition etc*) juvenil, para menores; **Roy Smith, J~** Roy Smith, hijo; ~ **college** (*US*) colegio *m* que comprende los dos primeros años universitarios; ~ **executive** joven ejecutivo *m*, -a *f*, ejecutivo *m* subalterno, ejecutiva *f* subalterna; ~ **high school** (*US*) instituto *m* de enseñanza media; ~ **minister** subsecretario *m*, -a *f*; ~ **partner** socio *mf* menos antiguo; ~ **school** (*Brit*) escuela *f* primaria.

2 *n* menor *mf*, joven *mf*; (*US**) hijo *m*, niño *m*; (*Brit Scol*) alumno *m* (*or* alumna *f*) de 8 a 11 años; (*US Univ*) estudiante *mf* de tercer año; (*office* ~) recadero *m*; **he is my ~ by 3 years, he is 3 years my** ~ tiene 3 años menos que yo, le llevo 3 años.

juniper ['dʒuːnɪpəʳ] *n* enebro *m*.

junk[1] [dʒʌŋk] *n* (*Naut*) junco *m*.

junk[2] [dʒʌŋk] **1** *n* (*lumber*) trastos *mpl* viejos; (*rubbish*) basura *f*, desperdicios *mpl*; (*iron*) chatarra *f*, hierro *m* viejo; (*cheap goods*) baratijas *fpl*; **the play is a lot of** ~ la obra es una porquería; **he talks a lot of** ~ no habla más que tonterías.

2 *vt* (*esp US*) echar a la basura, tirar, desechar.

junk-bonds ['dʒʌŋkbɒndz] *npl* obligaciones *fpl* basura.

junket ['dʒʌŋkɪt] **1** *n* (**a**) dulce *m* de leche cuajada. (**b**) (*) fiesta *f*, juerga* *f*, jira *f*, excursión *f*. **2** *vi* ir de juerga*, estar de fiesta; ir de jira.

junketing ['dʒʌŋkɪtɪŋ] *n* (*also* ~**s**) festividades *fpl*, fiestas *fpl*.

junk-food ['dʒʌŋkfuːd] *n* comida *f* basura.

junkheap ['dʒʌŋkhiːp] *n*: **to end up on the** ~ terminar en el cubo de la basura.

junkie‡ ['dʒʌŋkɪ] *n* drogadicto *m*, -a *f*, yonqui‡ *mf*; **chocolate** ~ adicto *m*, -a *f* al chocolate.

junkmail ['dʒʌŋkmeɪl] *n* propaganda *f* de buzón, materiales *mpl* publicitarios enviados por correo.

junkman ['dʒʌŋkmæn] *n*, *pl* **junkmen** ['dʒʌŋkmen] chatarrero *m*.

junkshop ['dʒʌnkʃɒp] *n* tienda *f* de trastos viejos.

junkyard ['dʒʌŋkjɑːd] *n* depósito *m* de chatarra, chatarrería *f*.

Juno ['dʒuːnəʊ] *nf* Juno.

Junoesque [ˌdʒuːnəʊ'esk] *adj figure* imponente, majestuoso; *woman* de belleza majestuosa.

Jun(r). *abbr of* **junior** junior, jr.

junta ['dʒʌntə] *n* junta *f*.

Jupiter ['dʒuːpɪtəʳ] *nm* Júpiter.

Jurassic [dʒʊ'ræsɪk] *adj* jurásico.

juridical [dʒʊə'rɪdɪkəl] *adj* jurídico.

jurisdiction [ˌdʒʊərɪs'dɪkʃən] *n* jurisdicción *f*; competencia *f*; **to come within sb's** ~ ser de la competencia de uno.

jurisprudence [ˌdʒʊərɪs'pruːdəns] *n* jurisprudencia *f*; **medical** ~ medicina *f* legal.

jurist ['dʒʊərɪst] *n* jurista *m*.

juror ['dʒʊərəʳ] *n* jurado *m* (*persona*).

jury ['dʒʊərɪ] *n* jurado *m* (*conjunto de jurados*); **to be on the** ~ ser miembro del jurado.

jury-box ['dʒʊərɪbɒks] *n* tribuna *f* del jurado.

jury duty ['dʒʊərɪˌdjuːtɪ] *n*: **to do** ~ actuar como jurado.

juryman ['dʒʊərɪmən] *n*, *pl* **jurymen** ['dʒʊərɪmən] (miembro *m* del) jurado *m*.

jury-mast ['dʒʊərɪmɑːst] *n* bandola *f*.

jury-rig ['dʒʊərɪrɪg] *n* aparejo *m* provisional.

jury-rigging ['dʒʊərɪˌrɪgɪŋ] *n* amaño *m* de un jurado.

just[1] [dʒʌst] *adj* (*upright*) justo, recto, imparcial; (*accurate*) exacto, correcto; (*deserved*) merecido, apropiado; (*well grounded*) justificado, lógico; **as is only** ~ como es justo, como es de razón; **the** ~ los justos.

just[2] *adv* (**a**) (*exactly*) exactamente, precisamente; justo, justamente; ~ **at that moment** en aquel mismo momento; ~ **here** aquí mismo; ~ **by the church** al lado mismo de la iglesia, justo al lado de la iglesia, muy cerca de la iglesia; ~ **beyond the pub** justo después de la tasca, un poco más allá de la tasca; **it's ~ (on) 4 o'clock** son las 4 en punto; ~ **so!** ¡eso es!, ¡perfectamente!, ¡precisamente!; **that's ~ it!** ¡ahí está la dificultad!; **it's ~ the same** es exactamente igual; ~ **like that** así nada más; **it's ~ what I needed** es precisamente lo que necesitaba, es justamente lo que me hacía falta; **they were ~ like two brothers** eran (en todo) como dos hermanos; **we were ~ talking about it** precisamente estábamos hablando de eso; ~ **when he started to sing** precisamente cuando empezaba a cantar; **I was ~ going** estaba a punto de marcharme; **now ~ what did he say?** ¿qué es lo que dijo, en concreto?; ~ **how many we don't know** no sabemos exactamente cuántos; **a policeman? that's ~ what I am** ¿un policía? justamente yo lo soy.

(**b**) (*with* as) **you sing ~ as well as I do** cantas tan bien como yo; ~ **as you wish** como quieras; ~ **as it started to rain** justo cuando empezó a llover, en el momento en que empezó a llover; **we left everything ~ as it was** lo dejamos todo exactamente como estaba; **it's ~ as well it's insured** menos mal que está asegurado; **it would be ~ as well if he went** más vale que se vaya él.

(**c**) (*only*) solamente, sólo, tan sólo; ~ **as a joke** en broma nada más; ~ **for a laugh** sólo para hacer reír; ~ **once** una vez nada más, solamente una vez, una vez solamente; ~ **the two of us** nosotros dos solamente; **we're ~ good friends** somos amigos nada más; ~ **a little bit** un poquito; ~ **a few** unos pocos; **he's ~ a lad** no es más que un chico; ~ **let me get at him!** ¡que me dejen llegar a él!

(**d**) (*merely*) **I ~ told him to go away** le dije que se fuera, nada más; **it's ~ that I don't like it** es que no me gusta; **we're ~ amateurs** somos simples aficionados; ~ **wait a moment!** ¡espere un momento!; ~ **imagine!** ¡imagínese!; ~ **listen!** ¡escucha un poco!; ~ **look!** ¡mira!, ¡fíjate!; ~ **a tick!** ¡un momentito!

(**e**) (*positively*) **it's ~ fine!** ¡es francamente maravilloso!, ¡es sencillamente maravilloso!; **it's ~ perfect!** ¡qué maravilla!

(**f**) (*barely*) **I ~ managed to catch it** por poco lo perdí; **he was only ~ saved from drowning** poco faltó para que muriese ahogado; **you're ~ in time** llegas justamente con tiempo; ~ **before it rained** momentos antes de que lloviese.

(**g**) (*with* have *etc*) **I have ~ seen him** acabo de verle; **I had ~ seen him** acababa de verle; **the book is ~ out** el libro acaba de publicarse; ~ **appointed** recién nombrado; ~ **received** acabado de recibir; ~ **cooked** recién hecho, recién salido del horno.

(**h**) (*emphatic*) **don't I ~ !*** ¡ya lo creo!; ¡y cómo!; *V* **now, yet** *etc*.

justice ['dʒʌstɪs] *n* (**a**) justicia *f*; **to bring sb to** ~ llevar a uno ante el tribunal, hacer que uno sea procesado; **to do sb** ~ hacer justicia a uno, tratar debidamente a uno; **to do o.s.** ~ quedar bien; **to do a meal** ~ hacer los debidos honores a una comida; **this work does not do your talents** ~ este ensayo no está a la altura de su talento.

(**b**) (*Brit*: *person*) juez *m*, juez *m* municipal; ~ **of the peace** (*approx*) juez *m* de paz; **(Lord) Chief J~** Presidente *m* del Tribunal Supremo.

justifiable ['dʒʌstɪfaɪəbl] *adj* justificable; justificado.

justifiably ['dʒʌstɪfaɪəblɪ] *adv* justificadamente; **and ~ so** y con razón; ~ **proud** orgulloso y con razón.

justification [ˌdʒʌstɪfɪ'keɪʃən] *n* justificación *f*.

justified ['dʒʌstɪfaɪd] *adj* (**a**) justificado; ~ **homicide** homicidio *m* justificado. (**b**) (*Typ*) *margin* justificado; **right** ~ justificado a la derecha.

justify ['dʒʌstɪfaɪ] *vt* (**a**) justificar, vindicar; dar motivo para; (*excuse*) disculpar; **the future does not ~ the slightest optimism** el futuro no autoriza el más leve optimismo;

to be justified in + *ger* tener motivo para + *infin*, tener plenamente razón al + *infin*; **you were not justified in that** en eso no tuviste razón; **am I justified in thinking that ...?** ¿hay motivo para creer que ...? (**b**) (*Typ, Comput*) alinear, justificar.

justly ['dʒʌstlı] *adv* justamente, con justicia; con derecho; debidamente; con razón; **it has been ~ said that ...** con razón se ha dicho que ...

justness ['dʒʌstnıs] *n* justicia *f*; rectitud *f*.

jut [dʒʌt] *vi* (*also* **to ~ out**) sobresalir.

Jute [dʒu:t] *n* juto *m*, -a *f*.

jute [dʒu:t] *n* yute *m*.

juvenile ['dʒu:vənaıl] **1** *adj* juvenil; de (*or* para) menores; (*pej*) infantil; **~ court** tribunal *m* tutelar de menores; **~ delinquency** delincuencia *f* juvenil; **~ delinquent** delincuente *mf* juvenil. **2** *n* joven *mf*.

juxtapose ['dʒʌkstəpəuz] *vt* yuxtaponer.

juxtaposition [ˌdʒʌkstəpə'zıʃən] *n* yuxtaposición *f*.

K

K, k [keɪ] *n* (*letter*) K, k *f*; **K for King** K de Kilo.
K (**a**) *abbr of* **kilo-** kilo-.
(**b**) *n abbr of* **a thousand**; **£100K** 100.000 libras.
(**c**) (*Brit*) *abbr of* **Knight** *caballero de una orden.*
(**d**) *n* (*Comput*) *abbr of* **kilobyte.**
Kaffir [ˈkæfəʳ] *n* cafre *mf.*
Kafkaesque [ˌkæfkəˈesk] *adj* kafkiano.
kaftan [ˈkæftæn] *n* caftán *m.*
Kaiser [ˈkaɪzəʳ] *n* emperador *m.*
Kalahari Desert [ˌkæləˈhɑːrɪˈdezət] *n* desierto *m* de Kalahari.
kale [keɪl] *n* (**a**) (*cabbage*) col *f* rizada. (**b**) (*US**) pasta* *f.*
kaleidoscope [kəˈlaɪdəskəʊp] *n* calidoscopio *m.*
kaleidoscopic [kəˌlaɪdəˈskɒpɪk] *adj* calidoscópico.
kamikaze [ˌkæmɪˈkɑːzɪ] *n* kamikaze *m.*
Kampala [kæmˈpɑːlə] *n* Kampala *f.*
Kampuchea [ˌkæmpʊˈtʃɪə] *n* Kampuchea *f.*
Kampuchean [ˌkæmpʊˈtʃɪən] **1** *adj* kampucheano. **2** *n* kampucheano *m,* -a *f.*
kanga‡ [ˈkæŋgə] *n* boca‡ *m.*
kangaroo [ˌkæŋgəˈruː] **1** *n* canguro *m.* **2** *attr:* ~ **court** tribunal *m* desautorizado.
Kans. (*US*) *abbr of* **Kansas.**
kaolin [ˈkeɪəlɪn] *n* caolín *m.*
kapok [ˈkeɪpɒk] *n* capoc *m.*
kaput* [kəˈpʊt] *adj*: **it's** ~ está kaput*, está roto, está estropeado; se acabó; **it went** ~ hizo kaput*, se rompió, se estropeó.
karat [ˈkærət] *n* = **carat.**
karate [kəˈrɑːtɪ] *n* karate *m.*
kart [kɑːt] **1** *n* kart *m.* **2** *vi* conducir un kart.
karting [ˈkɑːtɪŋ] *n* carrera *f* de karts, kárting *m.*
kasbah [ˈkæzbɑː] *n* casba(h) *f.*
Kashmir [kæʃˈmɪəʳ] *n* Cachemira *f.*
Kate [keɪt] *nf familiar form of* **Catherine** *etc.*
Katharine, Katherine [ˈkæθərɪn], **Kathleen** [ˈkæθliːn] *nf* Catalina.
kayak [ˈkaɪæk] *n* kayac *m.*
kazoo [kəˈzuː] *n* kazoo *m,* chiflato *m.*
KB *n abbr of* **kilobyte.**
KC *n* (*Brit*) *abbr of* **King's Counsel** abogado *mf* (*de categoría superior*).
kd (*US*) *abbr of* **knocked down** desmontado.
kebab [kəˈbæb] *n* kebab *m,* pincho *m* (moruno), broqueta *f* (*LAm*), brocheta *f* (*LAm*).
kedge [kedʒ] *n* anclote *m.*
kedgeree [ˌkedʒəˈriː] *n* (*Brit*) *plato de pescado desmenuzado, huevos y arroz.*
keel [kiːl] **1** *n* quilla *f*; **on an even** ~ (*Naut*) en iguales calados, (*fig*) en equilibrio, equilibrado; **to keep sth on an even** ~ mantener el equilibrio de algo.
2 *vi*: **to** ~ **over** (*Naut*) zozobrar, dar de quilla, (*fig*) volcar(se), (*person*) desplomarse.
keelhaul [ˈkiːlhɔːl] *vt* pasar por debajo de la quilla (*como castigo*).
keen[1] [kiːn] *adj* (**a**) *edge* afilado; *wind* penetrante, glacial; *eyesight, hearing* agudo; *mind* agudo, penetrante, perspicaz; *look* fijo, penetrante; (*Brit*) *price* bajo, competitivo, económico; *competition* intenso; *interest* grande; *emotion* intenso, vivo, hondo; *appetite* bueno; **to have a** ~ **sense of history** tener un profundo sentido de la historia.
(**b**) (*Brit*: *of person*) entusiasta; celoso; **he's a** ~ **footballer** es muy aficionado a jugar al fútbol; **he's a** ~ **socialist** es un socialista acérrimo; **try not to seem too** ~ procura no mostrar demasiado entusiasmo; **to be as** ~ **as mustard** ser extraordinariamente entusiasta; **I'm terribly** ~ **about the new play** la nueva obra me hace muchísima ilusión; **he's very** ~ **about the programme** tiene mucho entusiasmo por el programa; **to be** ~ **on sth** ser aficionado a algo; **are you** ~ **on opera?** ¿te gusta la ópera?; **I'm not all that** ~ **on grapes** no me gustan mucho las uvas; **I'm not** ~ **on the idea** no me hace gracia la idea; **he's** ~ **on her** ella le interesa bastante; **I'm not very** ~ **on him** no es santo de mi devoción; **to be** ~ **to** + *infin* tener vivo deseo de + *infin,* tener muchas ganas de + *infin,* ansiar + *infin*; **I'm not** ~ **to do it** no tengo ganas de hacerlo.
keen[2] [kiːn] *n* (*Ir Mus*) lamento *m* fúnebre por la muerte de una persona.
keenly [ˈkiːnlɪ] *adv* (**a**) de modo penetrante; agudamente; (*intensely*) intensamente, (*acutely*) vivamente; **he felt her death** ~ su muerte le afectó profundamente; **he looked at me** ~ me miró fijamente.
(**b**) *work etc* con entusiasmo.
keenness [ˈkiːnnɪs] *n* (**a**) (*of edge, wind, hearing etc*) penetración *f,* agudeza *f*; intensidad *f,* viveza *f.*
(**b**) (*of person*) entusiasmo *m,* ilusión *f*; interés *m,* afición *f.*
keep [kiːp] (*irr: pret and ptp* **kept**) **1** *vt* (**a**) (*observe, fulfil*) *promise* cumplir; *rule* observar, atenerse a; *appointment* acudir a; *festivity* observar, celebrar.
(**b**) (*impose*) *order* mantener, imponer.
(**c**) (*possess etc*) *dog, servant* tener; *chicken, sheep etc* criar, dedicarse a criar, ocuparse en la cría de; *family* mantener; *shop* tener; *business, hotel etc* ser propietario de, dirigir; *diary* escribir; *account, record, house* llevar; **he ~s a good cellar** mantiene una buena bodega; **he doesn't** ~ **his garden neat** no mantiene en buen estado su jardín; **he ~s his 3 daughters in clothes** les paga los vestidos a sus 3 hijas; **he has his parents to** ~ tiene que mantener a sus padres.
(**d**) (*detain*) detener; (*in conversation etc*) entretener; **they kept him in prison for 6 months** le tuvieron 6 meses en la cárcel; **illness kept her at home** se quedó en casa debido a la enfermedad, la enfermedad no le permitió salir de casa; **what kept you?** ¿por qué vienes tarde?, ¿a qué se debe este retraso?; **I musn't** ~ **you** no te entretengo más.
(**e**) (*prevent*) **to** ~ **sb from doing sth** impedir a uno hacer algo, no dejar a uno hacer algo.
(**f**) (*save*) poner aparte, tener guardado, reservar; **I was ~ing it for you** lo guardaba para ti.
(**g**) (*retain*) guardar, retener; reservar; *secret, figure etc* guardar; *job* retener, mantenerse en; (*not give back*) quedarse con; (*in museum etc*) conservar, custodiar; ~ **the change** quédese con la vuelta; **to** ~ **one's seat** permanecer sentado, (*Parl*) retener su escaño; **to** ~ **money by one** guardar algún dinero para un apuro.
(**h**) (*with adj, verb etc*) **to** ~ **sth clean** conservar algo limpio; **'K~ Spain Clean'** 'Mantenga limpia España'; **she always ~s the house very clean** tiene la casa siempre muy limpia; **to** ~ **sth safe** tener algo seguro; **to** ~ **sth warm** tener algo caliente, mantener el calor de algo; **to** ~ **sb talking** entretener a uno en conversación; **to** ~ **sb waiting** hacer que uno espere, hacer esperar a uno; **to** ~ **one's eyes fixed on sth** tener los ojos puestos en algo; **to** ~ **sb at it** obligar a uno a seguir trabajando (*etc*).
2 *vi* (**a**) (*remain*) quedar(se), permanecer; seguir, continuar; **to** ~ **quiet** no hacer ruido; no decir nada, quedar callado, callarse; ~ **still!** ¡estáte quieto!; **to** ~ **clear of** evitar cualquier contacto con; seguir libre de; **how are you ~ing?** ¿cómo sigue Vd?; **to** ~ **well** estar bien de salud.
(**b**) (*with ger*) **to** ~ + *ger* seguir + *ger,* continuar + *ger*; no dejar de + *infin*; **she ~s talking** sigue hablando; no deja de hablar; **she ~s asking me for it** me lo está pidiendo constantemente; **to** ~ **smiling** seguir con la sonrisa en los labios; **to** ~ **standing** seguir en pie; **to** ~ **going** seguir ade-

lante, no cejar; **we ~ going somehow** vamos tirando; nos arreglamos para continuar; **I can ~ going in French** me defiendo en francés.

(**c**) (*continue*) seguir, continuar; **to ~ at work** seguir trabajando, mantenerse en su puesto; **~ straight on for Madrid** para ir a Madrid vaya Vd todo seguido; **to ~ to the left** circular por la izquierda.

(**d**) (*of food*) conservarse fresco, conservarse en buen estado; **an apple that ~s** una manzana que dura; **the news will ~ till I see you** no pierdes nada si me guardo la noticia hasta que nos veamos.

3 *vr*: **he ~s himself now** ahora se mantiene a sí mismo; **to ~ o.s. clean** mantenerse limpio, cuidar su limpieza personal; **they ~ themselves to themselves** evitan tener contacto con otros, permanecen aislados.

4 *n* (**a**) comida *f*, subsistencia *f*; **to earn one's ~** trabajar por la comida, pagar la comida trabajando; (*fig*) producir (*etc*) bastante; **I pay £50 a week for my ~** la pensión me cuesta 50 libras a la semana; **he isn't worth his ~** no trabaja como debe, no merece que sigamos empleándole.

(**b**) (*Hist*) torreón *m*, torre *f* del homenaje.

(**c**) **for ~s*** para siempre jamás, permanentemente, para guardar.

◆**keep at** *vt*: **to ~ at sth** trabajar sin descansar en algo, no cejar en algo, perseverar en algo; **~ at it!** ¡dale!

◆**keep away 1** *vt*: **to ~ sb away** mantener a uno a distancia, alejar a uno (*from* de), no dejar a uno acercarse (*from* a); **they kept him away from school** no le dejaron ir a la escuela; **it ~s rats away** aleja las ratas; **one should ~ guns away from children** hay que guardar las armas de fuego fuera del alcance de los niños.

2 *vi* mantenerse alejado (*from* de), mantenerse a distancia; (*not attend*) no venir, no acudir; no dejarse ver; **to ~ away from sb** evitar a uno, evitar cualquier contacto con uno; no meterse en líos con uno; **you ~ away from my daughter!** ¡no venga más a ver a mi hija!; **he can't ~ away from the subject** siempre vuelve al mismo tema.

◆**keep back 1** *vt* (**a**) (*retain*) guardar, retener.

(**b**) (*conceal*) *information* ocultar, guardar secreto; *emotion* contener, reprimir; *names of victims* no comunicar.

(**c**) *enemy* no dejar avanzar, tener a raya; *progress* estorbar, cortar el paso a.

2 *vi* mantenerse atrás; no acercarse; hacerse a un lado; **~ back, please!** ¡más atrás, por favor!

◆**keep down 1** *vt* (**a**) (*hold down*) sujetar; no dejar subir.

(**b**) *price, temperature* mantener bajo; *growth, spending* restringir, limitar.

(**c**) (*oppress*) oprimir; dominar; **you can't ~ a good man down** a la larga los realmente buenos salen a flote.

(**d**) **she can't ~ any food down** vomita toda la comida.

2 *vi* seguir acurrucado (*or* tumbado *etc*); no levantar la cabeza; **~ down!** ¡abajo!

◆**keep from 1** *vt* (**a**) **to ~ sth from sb** ocultar algo a uno, no decir algo a uno.

(**b**) **to ~ from** + *gen* abstenerse de + *infin*, guardarse de + *infin*; **I can't ~ from wishing that ...** no puedo dejar de desear que ...

2 *vr*: **to ~ o.s. from** + *ger* = **1** (**b**).

◆**keep in 1** *vt* (**a**) *fire* mantener encendido.

(**b**) *feelings* contener.

(**c**) *person, pet* no dejar salir, tener encerrado; (*in school*) hacer quedar en la escuela (como castigo).

2 *vi*: **to ~ in with sb** mantener buenas relaciones con uno, cultivar la amistad de uno; (*pej*) asegurarse de la protección de uno.

◆**keep off 1** *vt* (**a**) tener a raya, cerrar el paso a; no dejar entrar; alejar; **~ the dog off!** ¡que no se acerque más el perro!; **to ~ off the grass** no pisar la hierba.

(**b**) **to ~ sb off a subject** procurar que uno no toque un tema, convencer a uno para que no discuta un asunto; **to ~ off a subject** no tocar un tema.

2 *vi* mantenerse a distancia; **'~ off'** 'no acercarse', 'prohibida la entrada'; **if the rain ~s off** si no llueve.

◆**keep on 1** *vt* (**a**) **to ~ one's hat on** no quitarse el sombrero, seguir con el sombrero puesto.

(**b**) **to ~ the light on** tener la luz puesta (*LAm*: prendida).

(**c**) **to ~ sb on in a job** mantener a uno en un puesto; **they kept him on for years** siguieron empleándole durante muchos años.

2 *vi* (**a**) continuar; seguir avanzando, ir adelante; **to ~ on with sth** continuar con algo; **to ~ on** + *ger* seguir + *ger*, continuar + *ger*; **he ~s on hoping** no renuncia a esperar, no pierde la esperanza.

(**b**) **she does ~ on** machaca mucho, es muy machacona; **don't ~ on (so)!** (*Brit*) ¡no machaques!; **to ~ on at sb about sth** (*Brit*) insistir en algo con uno.

◆**keep out 1** *vt* no dejar entrar, excluir.

2 *vi* permanecer fuera; **'~ out'** 'no acercarse', 'prohibida la entrada'; **to ~ out of** *place, organization* no entrar en, *affair* no meterse en, *trouble* evitar; **you ~ out of this!** ¡no te metas en esto!

◆**keep to** *vt* (**a**) **to ~ sth to o.s.** guardar algo para sí; guardar algo en secreto; **but he kept the news to himself** pero no comunicó la noticia a nadie.

(**b**) **to ~ sb to his promise** obligar a uno a cumplir su promesa.

◆**keep together 1** *vt* mantener unido(s); no separar, no dispersar.

2 *vi* mantenerse unidos; no separarse, no dispersarse.

◆**keep under** *vt*: **to ~ sb under** tener a uno subyugado.

◆**keep up 1** *vt* (**a**) (*maintain*) mantener; conservar; *correspondence, study etc* continuar; *custom* mantener.

(**b**) (*hold up*) sostener.

(**c**) **to ~ sb up at night** hacer trasnochar a uno, tener a uno en vela; **I don't want to ~ you up** no quiero entretenerte más.

(**d**) **to ~ it up** mantener el nivel, seguir como antes; no cejar; **~ it up!** ¡ánimo!, ¡dale!

2 *vi* no rezagarse; **to ~ up with** (*in pace*) ir al paso de, *friends* mantener contacto con, seguir en contacto con, *rival* emular, mantenerse a la altura de; **to ~ up with the Joneses** procurar no quedar en menos con respecto a los vecinos; **to ~ up with one's work** hacer su trabajo al ritmo apropiado, mantenerse al día en su trabajo; **to ~ up with the times** ir con los tiempos, mantenerse al día.

keeper ['ki:pəʳ] *n* (*game~*) guardabosque *m*; (*in art gallery, museum, library*: *expert*) conservador *m*, -ora *f*, (*attendant*) vigilante *mf*, cuidadero *m*, -a *f*; (*in record office*) archivero *m*, -a *f*; (*in zoo*) guardián *m*; (*in park*) guarda *m*; **am I my brother's ~?** ¿soy yo guarda de mi hermano?

keep-fit [ˌki:p'fɪt] **1** *n* ejercicios *mpl* para mantenerse en forma (*or* de mantenimiento). **2** *attr*: **~ classes** clases *fpl* de mantenimiento (*or* para mantenerse en forma).

keeping ['ki:pɪŋ] *n* (**a**) **to be in ~ with** estar de acuerdo con, estar en armonía con; **to be out of ~ with** estar en desacuerdo con.

(**b**) **to be in the ~ of X** estar en manos de X, estar bajo la custodia de X; **to be in safe ~** estar en un lugar seguro, estar en buenas manos; **to give sth to sb for safe ~** dar algo a uno para mayor seguridad.

keepsake ['ki:pseɪk] *n* recuerdo *m*.

keester* ['ki:stəʳ] *n* (*US*) trasero* *m*.

keg [keg] **1** *n* barrilete *m*, cuñete *m*. **2** *attr*: **~ beer** cerveza *f* de barril.

kelp [kelp] *n* quelpo *m* (de Patagonia).

Kelper* ['kelpəʳ] *n* nativo *m*, -a *f* (*or* habitante *mf*) de las Malvinas.

Ken [ken] *nm familiar form of* **Kenneth**.

Ken. (*US*) *abbr of* **Kentucky**.

ken [ken] **1** *n*: **to be beyond sb's ~** ser incomprensible para uno; **to be within sb's ~** ser comprensible para uno.

2 *vt* (*Scot*) *person etc* conocer, *fact* saber; (*recognize*) reconocer.

kennel ['kenl] **1** *n* (*doghouse*) perrera *f*, caseta *f* de perro; (*pack*) jauría *f*; **~s** (*dogs' home*) residencia *f* canina. **2** *attr*: **~ maid** chica *f* que trabaja en una residencia canina.

Kenya ['kenjə] *n* Kenia *f*.

Kenyan ['kenjən] **1** *adj* keniano. **2** *n* keniano *m*, -a *f*.

kepi ['keɪpɪ] *n* quepis *m*.

kept [kept] **1** *pret and ptp of* **keep**. **2** *adj*: **~ woman** querida *f*, amante *f*.

kerb [kɜ:b] *n*, **kerbstone** ['kɜ:bstəʊn] *n* (*Brit*) bordillo *m*, encintado *m*, cordón *m* (*SC*), cuneta *f* (*CAm*); **~ broker** corredor *m*, -ora *f* que no es miembro de la Bolsa; **~ market** mercado *m* no oficial (que funciona después del cierre de la Bolsa).

kerb-crawler ['kɜ:bˌkrɔ:ləʳ] *n* conductor *m* que busca prostitutas desde su coche.

kerb-crawling ['kɜ:bˌkrɔ:lɪŋ] *n* busca *f* de prostitutas desde el coche.

kerb drill ['kɜ:bdrɪl] *n* enseñanza *f* (a niños) de la disciplina del peatón; prácticas *fpl* de cruce.

kerchief ['kɜ:tʃɪf] *n* pañuelo *m*, pañoleta *f*.

kerfuffle* [kə'fʌfl] *n* (*Brit*) lío* *m*, follón* *m*.

kernel ['kɜ:nl] *n* almendra *f*; (*fig*) núcleo *m*, meollo *m*; **a ~ of truth** un grano de verdad.

kerosene ['kerəsi:n] *n* keroseno *m*, queroseno *m*, querosén *m* (*LAm*); ~ **lamp** lámpara *f* de petróleo.
kestrel ['kestrəl] *n* cernícalo *m* (vulgar).
ketch [ketʃ] *n* queche *m*.
ketchup ['ketʃəp] *n* salsa *f* de tomate, catsup *m*.
kettle ['ketl] *n* (*approx*) hervidor *m*, olla *f* en forma de cafetera (*or* tetera), pava *f*; **this is a pretty ~ of fish!** ¡en buen berenjenal nos hemos metido!; **that's another** (*or* **a different**) **~ of fish** eso es harina de otro costal.
kettledrum ['ketldrʌm] *n* timbal *m*.
key [ki:] **1** *n* (**a**) (*door~ etc*) llave *f*; (*Comput, of typewriter, piano etc*) tecla *f*; (*of wind instrument*) llave *f*, pistón *m*; (*Telec*) manipulador *m*; (*Tech*) chaveta *f*, cuña *f*; (*Elec*) llave *f*, interruptor *m*; (*Archit*) clave *f*.
(**b**) (*Mus*) tono *m*; **major ~** tono *m* mayor; **minor ~** tono *m* menor; **change of ~** cambio *m* de tonalidad; **to be in ~** estar a tono, estar templado; **to play off ~** desafinar, tocar desafinadamente; **to make a speech in a low ~** pronunciar un discurso en un tono bajo.
(**c**) (*fig: to problem, also Bio, Chess*) clave *f* (*to* de); **the ~ to the mystery** la clave del misterio.
2 *attr* clave; **~ industry** industria *f* clave; **~ man** hombre *m* clave; **~ move** movida *f* clave; **~ question** cuestión *f* principal, cuestión *f* madre; **~ signature** (*Mus*) armadura *f*.
3 *vt* (*Tech*) enchavetar, acuñar; (*Mus*) templar, afinar; (*Comput, Typ*) teclear, meter.
◆**key in** *vt* (*Comput, Typ*) picar, teclear.
◆**key up** *vt* (**a**) emocionar; **to be all ~ed up** estar emocionadísimo, tener los nervios en punta. (**b**) (*Comput*) teclear, meter (en el ordenador).
keyboard ['ki:bɔ:d] **1** *n* teclado *m*; **~s** (*Mus*) teclados *mpl*. **2** *attr*: **~ instruments** instrumentos *mpl* de teclado; **~ player** teclista *mf*. **3** *vt* (*Comput*) *text* teclear.
keyboarder ['ki:,bɔ:dəʳ] *n*, **keyboard operator** ['ki:bɔ:d,ɒpəreɪtəʳ] *n* teclista *mf*.
keyhole ['ki:həʊl] *n* ojo *m* de la cerradura.
keying ['ki:ɪŋ] *n* (*Comput*) introducción *f* de datos.
key-money ['ki:,mʌnɪ] *n* entrada *f*.
Keynesian ['ki:nzɪən] **1** *adj* keynesiano. **2** *n* keynesiano *m*, -a *f*.
keynote ['ki:nəʊt] *n* tónica *f*; (*fig*) tónica *f*, piedra *f* clave, idea *f* fundamental; **~ speech** discurso *m* de apertura, discurso *m* en que se sientan las bases de una política (*or* programa).
keypad ['ki:pæd] *n* teclado *m* numérico.
key-puncher ['ki:,pʌntʃəʳ] *n* teclista *mf*.
key-ring ['ki:rɪŋ] *n* llavero *m*.
keystone ['ki:stəʊn] *n* piedra *f* clave; (*fig*) piedra *f* angular.
keystroke ['ki:strəʊk] *n* pulsación *f* (de una tecla).
keyword ['ki:wɜ:d] *n* palabra *f* clave.
kg *abbr of* **kilogram(me)(s)** kilogramo(s) *mpl*, kg.
khaki ['kɑ:kɪ] **1** *n* caqui *m*. **2** *adj* caqui.
kharja ['χɑ:ʒə] *n* jarcha *f*.
Khartoum [kɑ:'tu:m] *n* Jartum *m*.
Khmer [kmeəʳ] **1** *n* jemer *mf*; **the ~ Rouge** los jemeres rojos. **2** *adj* jemer.
KHz *abbr of* **kilohertz**.
kibbutz [kɪ'bʊts] *n*, *pl* **kibbutzim** [kɪ'bʊtsɪm] kibbutz *m*.
kibitzer ['kɪbɪtsəʳ] *n* (*US*) mirón *m*, -ona *f*.
kibosh‡ ['kaɪbɒʃ] *n*: **to put the ~ on sth** desbaratar algo, acabar con algo definitivamente.
kick [kɪk] **1** *n* (**a**) patada *f*, puntapié *m*; (*Sport*) puntapié *m*, golpe *m*, tiro *m*; (*of animal*) coz *f*; **a ~ at goal** un tiro a gol; **I got a ~ on the leg** recibí un golpe en la pierna; **I gave him a ~ in the pants*** le di una patada en el trasero*; **what he needs is a good ~ in the pants*** hay que empujarle a patadas; **it was like a ~ in the teeth*** me sentó como una patada en la barriga*; **to take a ~ at** dirigir un puntapié a.
(**b**) (*of firearm*) culatazo *m*.
(**c**) (*: *of drink etc*) fuerza *f*; **a drink with a ~ to it** una bebida muy fuerte.
(**d**) (*: *thrill*) **to do sth for ~s** hacer algo sólo para disfrutar de la emoción que ello produce, hacer algo sólo para divertirse; **I get a ~ out of it** me entusiasma, encuentro placer en esto, lo hago porque me gusta.
(**e**) **he's on a fishing ~ now** (*) ahora le ha dado por la pesca; **she's on this liberation ~** está metida en el tinglado de la liberación.
2 *vt* (**a**) *ball etc* dar un puntapié a; golpear (con el pie); *goal* marcar; *person* dar una patada a; (*animal*) dar de coces a; **to ~ sb's bottom** dar a uno una patada en el trasero; **to ~ a man when he's down** dar a moro muerto gran lanzada; **to ~ sb downstairs** echar a uno escaleras abajo a patadas; **to ~ sb upstairs*** deshacerse de uno ascendiéndole; (*Brit Parl*) hacer que un miembro de los Comunes pase a serlo de los Lores; **to ~ a door shut** cerrar una puerta violentamente con el pie; **to ~ one's legs in the air** agitar las piernas.
(**b**) (*) **to ~ it** dejarlo, abandonarlo; **to ~ a habit** deshacerse de un vicio; **I've ~ed smoking** ya no fumo.
3 *vi* (**a**) dar coces, cocear; dar patadas.
(**b**) (*gun*) dar un culetazo, recular.
(**c**) (*) protestar, quejarse; respingar, reaccionar.
4 *vr*: **I could have ~ed myself** me mordía las manos, me dio rabia por tonto yo.
◆**kick about 1** *vt* (**a**) **to ~ a ball about** divertirse con un balón; **he's been ~ed about a lot** ha sufrido muchos malos tratos, le han maltratado mucho.
(**b**) (*) **he's ~ed about the world** ha viajado mucho, ha visto mucho mundo.
2 *vi* (*) **it's ~ing about here somewhere** andará por ahí; **I ~ed about in London for two years** durante 2 años viví a la buena de Dios en Londres.
◆**kick against** *vt* protestar contra; reaccionar contra.
◆**kick around 1** *vt*: **to ~ an idea around** dar vueltas a una idea; **to ~ sb around** (*fig*) tratar a uno a patadas. **2** *vi*: **they just ~ around all day** se pasan el día sin hacer nada (*or* sin dar golpe).
◆**kick away** *vt* apartar con el pie.
◆**kick back** *vi* (*gun*) dar un culetazo, recular.
◆**kick down** *vt* derribar.
◆**kick in** *vt* (**a**) romper a patadas. (**b**) (*US‡*) sacudir*, apoquinar.
◆**kick off** *vi* (*Sport*) hacer el saque inicial; (*loosely*) comenzar; (*fig*) comenzar, empezar.
◆**kick out 1** *vt*: **to ~ sb out** echar a uno a puntapiés, (*fig*) poner a uno de patitas en la calle, expulsar a uno.
2 *vi* repartir coces; **~ out against** *V* **~ against**.
◆**kick up*** *vt fuss, row etc* armar.
kickback ['kɪkbæk] *n* (**a**) (*Mil*) culatazo *m*. (**b**) (*fig*) reacción *f*, resaca *f*, contragolpe *m*. (**c**) (*) soborno *m*, bocado* *m*, mordida* *f*.
kicker ['kɪkəʳ] *n* (*Rugby*) pateador *m*.
kick-off ['kɪkɒf] *n* saque *m* inicial.
kick-start ['kɪk'stɑ:t] **1** *n* arranque *m* por pedal. **2** *vt* arrancar con el pedal.
kick-starter ['kɪk,stɑ:təʳ] *n* pedal *m* de arranque.
kick turn ['kɪk,tɜ:n] *n* (*Ski*) cambio *m* brusco de marcha.
kid [kɪd] **1** *n* (**a**) (*Zool*) cabrito *m*, -a *f*, chivo *m*, -a *f*; (*meat*) carne *f* de cabrito; (*skin*) cabritilla *f*.
(**b**) (*) (*child*) chiquillo *m*, -a *f*, chaval* *m*, -ala *f*, pibe* *m*, -a *f* (*And, SC*), escuincle* *mf* (*Mex*); (*US: form of address*) chico *m*, -a *f*; **when I was a ~** cuando yo era chaval*; **that's ~'s stuff** eso es para chicos, son chiquilladas.
2 *attr*: **~ brother*** hermano *m* menor; **~ gloves** guantes *mpl* de cabritilla; (*fig*) trato *m* de guante blanco.
3 *vt* (*) tomar el pelo a*; **you can't ~ me** no se me engaña así; **I ~ you not** no bromeo, sin bromas.
4 *vi* (*) bromearse, chunguearse*; **I was only ~ding** lo decía en broma; **no ~ding!** ¡en serio!; **are you ~ding?** ¿lo dices en serio?; **are you ~ding!** ¡ni hablar!; **you must be ~ding!** ¡me estás tomando el pelo!*, ¡no es posible!
5 *vr* (*) **to ~ o.s.** engañarse a sí mismo, hacerse ilusiones; **he ~s himself that ...** se hace creer que ...; **it's time we stopped ~ding ourselves** es hora ya de desengañarnos, es hora ya de despertar a la realidad.
◆**kid on* 1** *vt*: **he's ~ding you on*** te está tomando el pelo*. **2** *vi* bromear.
kiddy* ['kɪdɪ] *n* chiquillo *m*, -a *f*.
kidnap ['kɪdnæp] *vt* secuestrar, raptar.
kidnapper, (*US*) **kidnaper** ['kɪdnæpəʳ] *n* secuestrador *m*, -ora *f*, raptor *m*, -ora *f*.
kidnapping, (*US*) **kidnaping** ['kɪdnæpɪŋ] *n* secuestro *m*, rapto *m*.
kidney ['kɪdnɪ] **1** *n* riñón *m*; (*fig*) índole *f*, especie *f*. **2** *attr*: **~ disease** enfermedad *f* renal; **~ failure** fracaso *m* renal; **~ machine** riñon *m* artificial; **~ stone** cálculo *m* renal; **~ transplant** trasplante *m* de riñon (*or* renal).
kidney bean ['kɪdnɪ,bi:n] *n* judía *f* enana, frijol *m*, poroto *m* (*SC*).
kidney dish ['kɪdnɪ,dɪʃ] *n* batea *f*.
kidney-shaped ['kɪdnɪ,ʃeɪpt] *adj* ariñonado, con forma de riñon.
kike‡ [kaɪk] *n* (*US*) judío *m*, -a *f*.
kill [kɪl] **1** *vt* (**a**) matar; dar muerte a; asesinar; destruir;

he was ~ed by savages le mataron los salvajes, fue muerto por los salvajes; **I'll ~ you for this!** (*hum*) ¡te voy a matar!; **thou shalt not ~** no matarás.

(**b**) (*fig*) *rumour, threat* acabar con; *feeling, hope etc* destruir; *flavour, taste* quitar; *lights* apagar; (*Parl*) *bill* ahogar; (*) hacer morir de risa; (*) hacer una impresión irresistible en; **this heat is ~ing me** este calor acabará conmigo; **I'll do it if it ~s me** lo haré aunque me vaya en ello la vida; **the pace is ~ing him** se está matando trabajando (*etc*) a tal ritmo; **my feet are ~ing me!*** ¡los pies me están matando!*; **this will ~ you*** vas a morir de risa*; **to be dressed to ~** ir pero muy acicalada, estar de punto en blanco.

2 *vr*: **to ~ o.s.** matarse; suicidarse; **to ~ o.s. with work** matarse trabajando; **to ~ o.s. laughing*** morir de risa*.

3 *n* (**a**) (*Hunting*) pieza *f*, animal *m* matado, (*collectively*) piezas *fpl*, animales *mpl* matados.

(**b**) (*act of ~ing*) matanza *f*; **to go in for the ~** entrar a matar.

◆**kill off** *vt* exterminar; acabar de matar, rematar.

killer ['kɪləʳ] **1** *n* (**a**) matador *m*, -ora *f*; (*murderer*) asesino *m*, -a *f*; **diphtheria used to be a ~** antes la difteria mataba a sus víctimas.

(**b**) (*fig*) **it's a ~** (*joke*) es de morirse de risa; (*task*) es agotador; (*question*) es muy difícil; (*very impressive*) es muy impresionante.

2 *attr*: **~ disease** enfermedad *f* mortal; **the ~ instinct** el instinto de matar; **~ punch** puñetazo *m* mortal.

killer bee ['kɪləbiː] *n* abeja *f* asesina.

killer whale ['kɪləweɪl] *n* orca *f*.

killing ['kɪlɪŋ] **1** *adj* (**a**) *disease etc* que mata, mortal.

(**b**) (*fig*) *journey, work* agotador, durísimo; *burden* abrumador.

(**c**) (*ravishing*) irresistible; (*funny*) divertidísimo, muy cómico; **it was ~** fue para morirse de risa.

2 *n* (**a**) matanza *f*; (*murder*) asesinato *m*.

(**b**) (*Fin*) éxito *m* financiero; **to make a ~** tener un gran éxito financiero, hacer su agosto.

killingly ['kɪlɪŋlɪ] *adv*: **~ funny** divertidísimo; **it was ~ funny** fue para morirse de risa.

killjoy ['kɪldʒɔɪ] *n* aguafiestas *mf*; **don't be such a ~!** ¡no vayas a aguar la fiesta!

kiln [kɪln] *n* horno *m*.

kilo ['kiːləʊ] *n* kilo *m*.

kilobyte ['kɪləʊ,baɪt] *n* kilobyte *m*, kilooctet o *m*.

kilocycle ['kɪləʊ,saɪkl] *n* kilociclo *m*.

kilogram(me) ['kɪləʊgræm] *n* kilo(gramo) *m*.

kilohertz ['kɪləʊ,hɜːts] *n* kilohercio *m*.

kilolitre, (*US*) **kiloliter** ['kɪləʊ,liːtəʳ] *n* kilolitro *m*.

kilometre, (*US*) **kilometer** ['kɪləʊmiːtəʳ] *n* kilómetro *m*.

kilometric [,kɪləʊ'metrɪk] *adj* kilométrico.

kiloton ['kɪləʊ,tʌn] *n* kilotón *m*.

kilowatt ['kɪləʊwɒt] *n* kilovatio *m*.

kilowatt-hour ['kɪləʊwɒt,aʊə] *npl* kilovatio-hora *m*; **200 ~s** 200 kilovatios-hora.

kilt [kɪlt] *n* falda *f* escocesa.

kilter ['kɪltəʳ] *n*: **to be out of ~** (*esp US*) estar descentrado; estar desfasado; quedar desbaratado.

kimono [kɪ'məʊnəʊ] *n* quimono *m*, kimono *m*.

kin [kɪn] *n* familia *f*, parientes *mpl*, parentela *f*; **next of ~** pariente *m* más próximo, parientes *mpl* más proximos.

kind [kaɪnd] **1** *adj* (**a**) *person* bondadoso, amable, bueno; **you're very ~, you're too ~** eres muy amable; **to be ~ to sb** ser amable con uno; **please be so ~ as to** + *infin* tenga la bondad de + *infin*; **would you be so ~ as to** + *infin*? ¿me hace el favor de + *infin*?; **he was ~ enough to** + *infin* tuvo la amabilidad de + *infin*; **they were not ~ to the play in New York** trataron la obra algo duramente en Nueva York; **we must be ~ to animals** hay que tratar bien a los animales.

(**b**) *act* bueno; *climate* bueno, benigno; *criticism, remark, word* elogioso, comprensivo, favorable; *tone of voice* cariñoso, tierno; *treatment* bueno, blando; **it's very ~ of you** eres muy amable; **that wasn't very ~ of you** eso me ha parecido algo injusto, en eso fuiste demasiado duro.

2 *n* (**a**) clase *f*, género *m*, especie *f*; **but not that ~** pero no de ese tipo, pero no como eso; **he's the ~ who'll cheat you** es de los que te engañarán; **to pay in ~** pagar en especie, (*fig*) pagar en la misma moneda.

(**b**) (*a ~ of*) **a ~ of** uno a modo de; **he's a ~ of agent** es algo así como un agente; **I'm not that ~ of girl** yo no soy de ésas; **he's not that ~ of person** no es capaz de hacer eso, no es de los que hacen tales cosas; **I felt a ~ of pity** sentí algo parecido a la compasión, en cierto modo sentí compasión; **and all that ~ of thing** y otras cosas por el estilo; **it's not my ~ of thing** es una cosa que no me gusta; yo no sé nada de eso; **that's the ~ of thing I mean** eso es precisamente lo que quiero decir; **I don't like that ~ of talk** no me gusta ese modo de hablar; **what ~ of book?** ¿qué clase de libro?; **what ~ of man is he?** ¿qué clase de hombre es?; **it takes all ~s (of people)** cada loco con su tema.

(**c**) (*of a ~*) **three of a ~** tres de la misma especie; (*pej*) tres del mismo jaez; **one of a ~** modelo *m* exclusivo, modelo *m* único; **he's one of a ~** es un fuera de serie; **books of all ~s** toda clase de libros, libros de toda clase; **it's tea of a ~** es té pero apenas, es lo que apenas se puede llamar té; **perfect of its ~** perfecto en su línea; **sth of the ~** algo por el estilo; **nothing of the ~!** ¡nada de eso!, ¡ni hablar!

3 *adv* (*: **~ of**) **it's ~ of awkward** es bastante difícil; **it's ~ of blue** es más bien azul; **it's ~ of hot in here** hace bastante calor aquí; **it's ~ of finished** está más o menos terminado; **aren't you pleased? ~ of** ¿no te alegras? en cierto modo.

kindergarten ['kɪndə,gɑːtn] *n* jardín *m* de infancia, kindergarten *m*, kinder* *m*.

kind-hearted ['kaɪnd'hɑːtɪd] *adj* bondadoso, de buen corazón.

kind-heartedness ['kaɪnd'hɑːtɪdnɪs] *n* bondad *f*.

kindle ['kɪndl] **1** *vt* encender (*also fig*). **2** *vi* encenderse (*also fig*).

kindliness ['kaɪndlɪnɪs] *n* bondad *f*, benevolencia *f*.

kindling ['kɪndlɪŋ] *n* leña *f* menuda, astillas *fpl*.

kindly ['kaɪndlɪ] **1** *adj* bondadoso, benévolo; *climate etc* bueno, benigno; *remark etc* elogioso, comprensivo, favorable; *tone of voice* cariñoso, tierno; *treatment* bueno, blando.

2 *adv* (**a**) bondadosamente, amablemente; **he very ~ helped me** muy amablemente me ayudó; **to take ~ to sth** aceptar algo de buen grado; **to think ~ of sb** tener un buen concepto de uno; **he would take it ~ if you did so** te agradecería que lo hicieses.

(**b**) **~ pass the salt** ¿me haces el favor de pasar la sal?; **~ wait a moment** haga el favor de esperar un momento; **'~ pay here'** 'se ruega pagar aquí'.

kindness ['kaɪndnɪs] *n* (**a**) bondad *f*, amabilidad *f*, benevolencia *f*; atención *f*, consideración *f*; **they treated him with every ~** le trataron con todo género de consideraciones; **to show ~ to sb** mostrarse bondadoso con uno.

(**b**) (*a ~*) favor *m*; **to do sb a ~** hacer un favor a uno; **it would be a ~ to tell him** decírselo sería un favor.

kindred ['kɪndrɪd] **1** *adj* (*related by blood*) emparentado; (*fig*) afín, semejante, análogo; **~ spirits** espíritus *mpl* afines.

2 *n* (*relationship*) parentesco *m*; (*relations*) familia *f*, parientes *mpl*.

kinescope ['kɪnəskəʊp] *n* (*US*) tubo *m* de rayos catódicos, cinescopio *m*.

kinetic [kɪ'netɪk] *adj* cinético; **~ energy** energía *f* cinética.

kinetics [kɪ'netiks] *npl* cinética *f*.

king [kɪŋ] **1** *n* (**a**) rey *m*; (*fig, Chess, Cards*) rey *m*; (*Draughts*) dama *f*; **an oil ~** un magnate del petróleo; **the ~ and queen** los reyes; **the Three K~s** los Reyes, los Reyes Magos; **to live like a ~** vivir a cuerpo de rey.

(**b**) (*Brit Jur*) **K~'s Bench** departamento *m* del Tribunal Supremo; **K~'s Counsel** abogado *mf* (*de categoría superior*); **to turn K~'s evidence** delatar a los cómplices.

2 *attr*: **~ penguin** pingüino *m* real.

kingcup ['kɪŋkʌp] *n* botón *m* de oro.

kingdom ['kɪŋdəm] *n* reino *m*; **till K~ come*** hasta el día del Juicio.

kingfisher ['kɪŋfɪʃəʳ] *n* martín *m* pescador.

kingly ['kɪŋlɪ] *adj* real, regio; digno de un rey.

kingmaker ['kɪŋ,meɪkəʳ] *n* persona *f* muy influyente.

kingpin ['kɪŋpɪn] *n* (*Tech*) perno *m* real, perno *m* pinzote; (*fig*) piedra *f* angular, cosa *f* fundamental, persona *f* principal.

kingship ['kɪŋʃɪp] *n* dignidad *f* real, monarquía *f*; **they offered him the ~** le ofrecieron el trono (*or* la corona).

king-size(d) ['kɪŋsaɪz(d)] *adj* de tamaño extra, extra largo; **~ bed** cama *f* de gran tamaño.

kink [kɪŋk] **1** *n* (**a**) (*in rope etc*) coca *f*, enroscadura *f*; (*in hair*) rizo *m*; (*in paper etc*) arruga *f*, pliegue *m*. (**b**) (*fig*) peculiaridad *f*, manía *f*, (*sexual*) perversión *f*.

2 *vi* formar cocas (*etc*).

kinky ['kɪŋkɪ] *adj* (**a**) enroscado; rizado, ensortijado; arrugado. (**b**) (*fig*) peculiar; torcido, (*esp*) de gustos

sexuales pervertidos; *dress etc* excéntrico.
kinsfolk ['kɪnzfəʊk] *npl* familia *f*, parientes *mpl*.
kinship ['kɪnʃɪp] *n* (*of family*) parentesco *m*; (*fig*) afinidad *f*, relación *f*.
kinsman ['kɪnzmən] *n*, *pl* **kinsmen** ['kɪnzmən] pariente *m*.
kinswoman ['kɪnz,wʊmən] *n*, *pl* **kinswomen** ['kɪnz,wɪmɪn] parienta *f*.
kiosk ['kiːɒsk] *n* (*Brit*) quiosco *m*, kiosco *m*; (*Brit Telec*) cabina *f*.
kip‡ [kɪp] (*Brit*) **1** *n* (*lodging*) alojamiento *m*; (*bed*) pulguero‡ *m*; (*sleep*) sueño *m*; **to have a ~** dormir un rato.
2 *vi* dormir; **to ~ down** echarse a dormir.
kipper ['kɪpəʳ] *n* (*Brit*) arenque *m* ahumado.
kirby grip ['kɜːbɪ,grɪp] *n* horquilla *f*.
kirk [kɜːk] *n* (*Scot*) iglesia *f*; **the K~** la Iglesia (Presbiteriana) de Escocia.
kiss [kɪs] **1** *n* beso *m*; (*light touch*) roce *m*; **~ of death** beso *m* de la muerte; **~ of life** beso *m* de la vida, respiración *f* boca a boca; **to blow sb a ~** tirar un beso a uno, dar un beso volado a uno.
2 *vt* besar; **to ~ sb good-bye** besar a uno y decirle adios; **he ~ed her goodnight** le dio un beso de despedida.
3 *vi*: **they ~ed** se besaron, se dieron un beso; **to ~ and be friends** hacer las paces; **to ~ and tell** (*fig*) dar un beso y confesarlo todo (vendiendo una historia escandalosa a un periódico).
◆**kiss away** *vt* curar con un beso.
kiss-curl ['kɪskɜːl] *n* (*Brit*) caracol *m*.
kisser‡ ['kɪsəʳ] *n* (*face*) jeta‡ *f*; (*mouth*) morrera‡ *f*.
kiss-off* ['kɪsɒf] *n* (*US*): **to give sth the ~** tirar algo, despedirse de algo; **to give sb the ~** (*employee*) poner a uno de patitas en la calle*, despedir a uno; (*boyfriend*) plantar a uno*, dejar a uno.
kissogram ['kɪsə,græm] *n* besograma *m*.
kissproof ['kɪspruːf] *adj* indeleble.
Kit [kɪt] *nmf familiar form of* **Catherine** *etc*, **Christopher**.
kit [kɪt] *n* (*gear in general*) avíos *mpl*; (*baggage*) equipaje *m*; (*tools*) herramientas *fpl*, herramental *m*; (*first-aid*) botiquín *m*; (*Mil*) equipo *m*; **the whole ~ and caboodle** toda la pesca.
◆**kit out, kit up** *vt*: **to ~ sb out** (*or* **up**) equipar a uno (*with* de).
kitbag ['kɪtbæg] *n* saco *m* de viaje; (*Mil*) mochila *f*.
kitchen ['kɪtʃɪn] **1** *n* cocina *f*. **2** *attr*: **~ cabinet** consejillo *m*; **~ garden** huerto *m*; **~ knife** cuchillo *m* de cocina; **~ paper** toallitas *fpl* de papel; **~ range** cocina *f* económica; **~ roll** rollo *m* de cocina; **~ salt** sal *f* de cocina; **~ sink** fregadero *m*; **they had everything with them except the ~ sink** lo tenían todo consigo menos la abuela; **~ sink play** obra *f* ultrarrealista, obra *f* que tiene por tema la vida doméstica cruda; **~ unit** módulo *m* de cocina.
kitchenette [,kɪtʃɪ'net] *n* cocina *f* pequeña.
kitchenmaid ['kɪtʃɪn,meɪd] *n* ayudanta *f* de cocina.
kitchenware ['kɪtʃɪnwɛəʳ] *n* batería *f* de cocina.
kite [kaɪt] **1** *n* **(a)** (*Orn*) milano *m* real. **(b)** (*toy*) cometa *f*; **~ mark** señal *f* de aprobación (de la BSI); **to fly a ~** (*fig*) lanzar una idea para sondear la opinión, (*pej*) soltar una especie; **go fly a ~!*** (*US*) ¡vete al cuerno!* **(c)** (*Fin‡*) cheque *m* sin valor. **2** *vi* (‡) estafar un banco.
kith [kɪθ] *n*: **~ and kin** parientes *mpl* y amigos.
kitsch [kɪtʃ] **1** *adj* kitsch; cursi. **2** *n* kitsch *m*; cursilería *f*.
kitten ['kɪtn] *n* gatito *m*, -a *f*, minino *m*, -a *f*; **I was having ~s*** (*Brit*), **I nearly had ~s*** (*Brit*) me llevé un tremendo susto*.
kittenish ['kɪtənɪʃ] *adj* (*fig*) picaruelo, coquetón, retozón.
kittiwake ['kɪtɪweɪk] *n* gaviota *f* tridáctila, gavina *f*.
Kitty ['kɪtɪ] *nf familiar form of* **Catherine** *etc*.
kitty ['kɪtɪ] *n* (*collection*) colecta *f*, fondo *m*; (*Cards*) puesta *f*, bote *m*, polla *f*; **how much have we in the ~?** ¿cuánto tenemos en el bote?
kiwi ['kiːwiː] *n* (*Orn*) kiwi *m*; (*: *New Zealander*) neozelandés *m*, -esa *f*; **~ fruit** kiwi *m*.
KKK *n* (*US*) *abbr of* **Ku Klux Klan**.
Klansman ['klænzmən] *n*, *pl* **Klansmen** ['klænzmen] (*US*) miembro *m* del Ku Klux Klan.
klaxon ['klæksn] *n* claxon *m*.
kleptomania [,kleptəʊ'meɪnɪə] *n* cleptomanía *f*.
kleptomaniac [,kleptəʊ'meɪnɪæk] *n* cleptómano *m*, -a *f*.
klutz‡ [klʌts] *n* (*US*) gilipollas‡ *mf*, persona *f* torpe, persona *f* atontada.
km *abbr of* **kilometre(s)** kilómetro(s) *m(pl)*, km.
km/h *abbr of* **kilometre(s) per hour** kilómetros *mpl* por hora, km/h.
knack [næk] *n* tino *m*; maña *f*, destreza *f*, tranquillo *m*, truco *m*; **it's just a ~** es un truco que se aprende; **to get the ~ of doing sth** aprender el modo de hacer algo; **to have the ~ of doing sth** tener el don de hacer algo; **he has a happy ~ of saying the right thing** siempre acierta al escoger la palabra exacta.
knacker ['nækəʳ] (*Brit*) **1** *n* matarife *m* de caballos. **2** *vt* (*) agotar, reventar; **I'm ~ed** estoy agotado, no puedo más.
knapsack ['næpsæk] *n* mochila *f*.
knave [neɪv] *n* bellaco *m*, bribón *m*; (*Cards*) valet *m*, (*in Spanish pack*) sota *f*.
knavery ['neɪvərɪ] *n* bellaquería *f*.
knavish ['neɪvɪʃ] *adj* bellaco, bribón, vil.
knead [niːd] *vt* amasar, sobar; (*fig*) formar.
knee [niː] **1** *n* rodilla *f*; **on bended ~, on one's ~s** de rodillas; **to bow the ~ to** humillarse ante, someterse a; **to bring sb to his ~s** someter a uno, humillar a uno; **to fall on one's ~s, to go down on one's ~s** arrodillarse, caer de rodillas; **to go down on one's ~s to sb** implorar a uno de rodillas.
2 *vt* dar un rodillazo a.
kneebend ['niːbend] *n* flexión *f* de piernas.
knee-breeches ['niː,brɪtʃɪz] *npl* calzón *m* corto.
kneecap ['niːkæp] **1** *n* rótula *f*, choquezuela *f*. **2** *vt*: **to ~ sb** destrozar a tiros la rótula de uno.
kneecapping ['niː,kæpɪŋ] *n* destrozo *m* a tiros de la rótula de uno.
knee-deep ['niː'diːp] *adv*: **to be ~ in** estar metido hasta las rodillas en; **the place was ~ in paper** había montones de papeles por todos lados; **to go into the water ~** avanzar hasta que el agua llegue a las rodillas.
knee-high ['niː'haɪ] **1** *adv* hasta las rodillas; al nivel de las rodillas. **2** *adj*: **~ grass** hierba *f* que crece hasta la altura de las rodillas.
knee-jerk ['niːdʒɜːk] *n* reflejo *m* rotular; (*fig*) reacción *f* instintiva, reacción *f* automática; **he's a ~ conservative** es de derechas hasta la médula.
knee-joint ['niːdʒɔɪnt] *n* articulación *f* de la rodilla.
kneel [niːl] (*irr*: *pret and ptp* **knelt**) *vi* (*also* **to ~ down**) (*act*) arrodillarse, ponerse de rodillas, hincarse de rodillas; (*state*) estar de rodillas; **to ~ to** (*fig*) hincar la rodilla ante.
knee-length ['niːleŋθ] *attr*: **~ sock** calcetín *m* de media.
knee-level ['niː,levl] *n* altura *f* de la rodilla.
kneeling ['niːlɪŋ] *adj figure* arrodillado, de rodillas.
kneepad ['niːpæd] *n* rodillera *f*.
kneeroom ['niːrʊm] *n* espacio *m* para las piernas.
knees-up* ['niːzʌp] *n* (*Brit hum*) baile *m*.
knell [nel] *n* toque *m* de difuntos, doble *m*; *V* **deathknell**.
knelt [nelt] *pret and ptp of* **kneel**.
knew [njuː] *pret of* **know**.
knickerbockers ['nɪkəbɒkəz] *npl* pantalones *mpl* cortos; (*US*) pantalones *mpl* de golf, pantalones *mpl* holgados.
knickers ['nɪkəz] *npl* **(a)** (*Brit*) bragas *fpl*; (*old-fashioned*) pantalones *mpl* de señora; **~!‡** ¡narices!*; **to get one's ~ in a twist*** armarse un lío*. **(b)** (††) = **knickerbockers**.
knick-knack ['nɪknæk] *n* chuchería *f*, bujería *f*, baratija *f*.
knife [naɪf] **1** *n*, *pl* **knives** [naɪvz] cuchillo *m*; (*folding*) navaja *f*; (*Mech*) cuchilla *f*; **~ and fork** (*at table*) cubierto *m*; **war to the ~** guerra *f* a muerte; **to have one's ~ into sb** tener inquina a uno; **before you can say ~** en un decir Jesús; **to turn the ~ in the wound** remover el cuchillo en la llaga.
2 *vt* acuchillar.
knifebox ['naɪfbɒks] *n* portacubiertos *m*.
knife-edge ['naɪfedʒ] *n* filo *m* (de cuchillo); **to be balanced on a ~** (*fig*) estar pendiente de un hilo.
knife-grinder ['naɪf,graɪndəʳ] *n* amolador *m*, afilador *m*.
knife-point ['naɪfpɔɪnt] *n*: **at ~** a punta de navaja.
knifing ['naɪfɪŋ] *n* cuchillazo *m*, navajazo *m*; herida *f* (*or* muerte *f*) con cuchillo.
knight [naɪt] **1** *n* caballero *m*; (*Chess*) caballo *m*; **~ in shining armour** príncipe *m* azul; **K~ (of the Order) of the Garter** (*Brit*) caballero *m* de la orden de la Jarretera. **2** *vt* (*Hist*) armar caballero; (*modern British*) dar el título de *Sir* a.
knight-errant ['naɪt'erənt] *n* caballero *m* andante.
knight-errantry ['naɪt'erəntrɪ] *n* caballería *f* andante.
knighthood ['naɪthʊd] *n* **(a)** (*order*) caballería *f*. **(b)** (*title*) título *m* de caballero; (*modern British*) título *m* de *Sir*.
knightly ['naɪtlɪ] *adj* caballeroso, caballeresco.
Knight Templar ['naɪt'templəʳ] *n* caballero *m* templario, templario *m*.
knit [nɪt] **1** *vt dress* hacer a punto de aguja, tricotar, tejer

(*LAm*); *brows* fruncir.
2 *vi* hacer calceta, hacer media, hacer punto, tricotar, tejer (*LAm*); (*bone*) soldarse; (*fig*) unirse.
◆**knit together** *vt* (*fig*) juntar, unir.
◆**knit up 1** *vt* montar. **2** *vi* (*wound*) cerrarse, curarse.
knit stitch ['nɪt,stɪtʃ] *n* punto *m* de media.
knitted ['nɪtɪd] *adj* de punto; ~ **goods** géneros *mpl* de punto.
knitting ['nɪtɪŋ] *n* labor *f* de punto; **she was doing her** ~ estaba haciendo calceta.
knitting-machine ['nɪtɪŋmə,ʃiːn] *n* máquina *f* de tricotar, tricotosa *f*, tejedora *f*.
knitting-needle ['nɪtɪŋ,niːdl] *n*, **knitting-pin** ['nɪtɪŋ,pɪn] *n* aguja *f* de hacer calceta (*or* punto).
knitting-wool ['nɪtɪŋ,wʊl] *n* lana *f* para labores.
knitwear ['nɪtwɛəʳ] *n* géneros *mpl* de punto.
knives [naɪvz] *npl of* **knife**.
knob [nɒb] *n* (*natural*) protuberancia *f*, bulto *m*; (*Mech etc*) botón *m*; (*of door*) tirador *m*; (*of stick*) puño *m*; ~ **of sugar** terrón *m* de azúcar.
knobbly ['nɒblɪ] *adj*, **knobby** ['nɒbɪ] *adj* nudoso.
knock [nɒk] **1** *n* (**a**) (*blow*) golpe *m*; (*in collision*) choque *m*; (*on door*) llamada *f*; (*Aut*) golpeteo *m*; **there was a** ~ **on the door** se llamó a la puerta; **he got a** ~ **on the head** recibió un golpe en la cabeza; **to get the** ~‡ mosquearse, ofenderse; ponerse negro*.
(**b**) (*fig*) golpe *m*; **the team took a hard** ~ **yesterday** ayer el equipo recibió un rudo golpe; **he can take plenty of hard** ~**s** sabe aguantar todos los reveses.
2 *vt* (**a**) (*strike*) golpear; (*collide with*) chocar contra; **to** ~ **a hole in sth** abrir a la fuerza un agujero en algo; **to** ~ **the bottom out of a box** desfondar una caja; **to** ~ **the smile off sb's face** hacer que uno deje de sonreír a fuerza de golpes; **to** ~ **sb on the head** golpear a uno en la cabeza; **to** ~ **one's head on a beam** dar con la cabeza contra una viga; **to** ~ **sth to the floor** dar con algo en el suelo.
(**b**) (*: *criticize*) criticar, denigrar, hablar mal de; (*Comm*) hacer publicidad en contra de.
3 *vi* golpear; (*at door*) llamar a la puerta; (*Aut*) golpear, martillear.
◆**knock about 1** *vt person* pegar, maltratar, (*beat up*) aporrear; **the place was badly** ~**ed about** el lugar sufrió grandes estragos; **the car was rather** ~**ed about** el coche sufrió algunos desperfectos.
2 *vi* vagabundear, andar vagando, rodar; **I've** ~**ed about a bit** he visto mucho mundo; **he's** ~**ing about somewhere** andará por ahí, estará rodando por ahí; **he** ~**s about with some strange friends** anda con unas amistades rarísimas.
◆**knock against** *vt* chocar contra, dar contra.
◆**knock around 1** *vt*: **to** ~ **an idea around** dar vueltas a una idea. **2** *vi* holgazanear, no hacer nada; *V* ~ **about**.
◆**knock back*** *vt* (**a**) *drink* beberse (de un trago); **he can certainly** ~ **them back** él sí sabe beber.
(**b**) **it** ~**ed us back £500** nos costó 500 libras.
(**c**) (*shock*) asombrar, pasmar; **the smell** ~**s you back** el olor le echa a uno para atrás*.
◆**knock down** *vt* (**a**) (*demolish*) *building* derribar, demoler, echar por tierra; *person* derribar; *pedestrian* atropellar; *argument etc* destruir.
(**b**) *price* rebajar.
(**c**) (*at auction*) **to** ~ **sth down to sb for £50** rematar algo a uno en 50 libras; **it was** ~**ed down to X** se adjudicó a X.
(**d**) **completely** ~**ed down** sin montar, a montar por el comprador (y a su coste).
◆**knock in** *vt* hacer entrar a golpes; *nail* clavar; *container* abrir a golpes.
◆**knock into** *vt* chocar contra, dar con; (*) *person* topar.
◆**knock off 1** *vt* (**a**) (*remove*) quitar (de un golpe); (*make fall*) hacer caer.
(**b**) (*Brit*‡: *steal*) birlar*, limpiar‡.
(**c**) (‡) (*arrest*) detener; (*kill*) despenar‡, cargarse*.
(**d**) (**‡) *woman* tirarse a**‡.
(**e**) (*: *finish*) *task* ejecutar prontamente, despachar; *work* terminar, suspender; **to** ~ **off smoking** dejar de fumar; **so we had to** ~ **it off** así que tuvimos que dejarlo; ~ **it off, will you?** ¡déjalo, por Dios!
(**f**) (*discount*) **to** ~ **£20 off the price** rebajar el precio en 20 libras, descontar 20 libras del precio; **to** ~ **3 seconds off the record** mejorar la marca en 3 segundos.
2 *vi* (*) suspender el trabajo, terminar; salir del trabajo; **he** ~**s off at 5** sale del trabajo a las 5.
◆**knock on** *vi*: **he's** ~**ing on** es bastante viejo; **he's** ~**ing on 60** va para los 60.
◆**knock out** *vt* (**a**) (*stun*) dejar sin sentido, hacer perder el conocimiento; (*Boxing*) poner fuera de combate, dejar K.O.
(**b**) (*remove*) *teeth* romper; *passage in text* suprimir, quitar; (*from competition*) eliminar.
(**c**) *product* producir, fabricar; hacer.
(**d**) (*shock*) pasmar, aturdir; (*exhaust*) agotar, dejar para el arrastre.
(**e**) (*stop*) estropear, dejar fuera de servicio.
◆**knock over** *vt* volcar; *pedestrian* atropellar.
◆**knock together 1** *vt* construir (*or* componer *etc*) de prisa.
2 *vi* (*knees*) entrechocarse.
◆**knock up 1** *vt* (**a**) (*build*) construir de prisa; construir toscamente; *meal* preparar de prisa.
(**b**) (*Brit**: *wake*) despertar, llamar.
(**c**) (*Brit**) (*tire*) agotar; (*make ill*) dejar enfermo; **he was** ~**ed up for a month** el agotamiento le duró un mes.
(**d**) (‡: *make pregnant*) dejar encinta.
2 *vi* (*Tennis etc*) pelotear.
◆**knock up against** *vt difficulties, people* tropezarse con.
knockabout ['nɒkəbaʊt] *adj* bullicioso, tumultuoso, confuso; ~ **comedy** farsa *f* bulliciosa, (*fig*) payasadas *fpl*.
knock-back* ['nɒkbæk] *n* rechazo *m*, feo *m*; **to get the** ~ sufrir un feo.
knockdown ['nɒkdaʊn] *adj*: ~ **price** (*Brit*) precio *m* obsequio, precio *m* de saldo.
knocker ['nɒkəʳ] *n* (**a**) (*on door*) aldaba *f*. (**b**) (*: *critic*) detractor *m*, -ora *f*, crítico *m*, -ora *f*. (**c**) ~**s**‡ tetas *fpl*.
knocker-up ['nɒkə'rʌp] *n* (*Brit*) despertador *m*.
knock-for-knock ['nɒkfə'nɒk] *attr*: ~ **agreement** acuerdo *m* de pago respectivo.
knocking ['nɒkɪŋ] **1** *adj*: ~ **copy** anuncio *m* destinado a denigrar el producto de otro, contrapublicidad *f*. **2** *n* golpes *mpl*, golpeo *m*; (*at door*) llamada *f*; (*Aut*) golpeteo *m*.
knocking-off time* [,nɒkɪŋ'ɒf,taɪm] *n* hora *f* de salir del trabajo.
knocking-shop‡ ['nɒkɪŋʃɒp] *n* casa *f* de putas.
knock-kneed ['nɒk'niːd] *adj* patizambo; (*fig*) débil, irresoluto.
knock-on ['nɒk'ɒn] **1** *attr*: ~ **effect** repercusiones *fpl*, consecuencias *fpl*, reacción *f* en cadena. **2** *n* (*Rugby*) autopase *m*.
knockout ['nɒkaʊt] **1** *adj*: ~ **agreement** acuerdo *m* secreto para no hacerse competencia; ~ **blow** golpe *m* aplastante, (*Boxing*) K.O. *m*, queo *m*; ~ **competition** concurso *m* eliminatorio, eliminatoria *f*.
2 *n* (**a**) (*Boxing*) knock-out *m*, K.O. *m*, queo *m*. (**b**) (*competition*) concurso *m* eliminatorio, eliminatoria *f*. (**c**) (*) **he's a** ~**!** ¡es la monda!*; **she's a** ~ es una chica estupenda; **it was a real** ~ fue una noticia (*etc*) sorprendente, la noticia nos pasmó.
knock-up ['nɒkʌp] *n* (*Tennis*) peloteo *m*.
knoll [nəʊl] *n* otero *m*, montículo *m*.
knot [nɒt] **1** *n* nudo *m* (*also Naut, in wood*); (*bow*) lazo *m*; (*of people*) grupo *m*, corrillo *m*; **to tie the** ~ (*fig*) prometerse, casarse; **to get tied up in** ~**s** anudarse, enmarañarse, (*fig*) armarse un lío, crearse confusiones; **to tie a** ~ hacer un nudo.
2 *vt* anudar, atar; **get** ~**ted!**‡ ¡fastídiate!*
3 *vi* anudarse.
◆**knot together** *vt* atar, anudar.
knot-hole ['nɒthəʊl] *n* agujero *m* (que deja un nudo en la madera).
knotted ['nɒtid] *adj rope etc* anudado, con nudos.
knotty ['nɒtɪ] *adj* nudoso; (*fig*) difícil, complicado, espinoso.
knout [naʊt] *n* knut *m*.
know [nəʊ] (*irr*: *pret* **knew**, *ptp* **known**) **1** *vt* (**a**) (*gen*) *fact etc* saber; **to** ~ **Japanese** saber japonés; **what do you** ~**?*** ¿qué hay de nuevo?; **well, what do you** ~**!** ¡caramba!, ¡qué cosa más rara!; **don't I** ~ **it!** ¡y tú que me lo dices!, ¡si lo sabré yo!; **not if I** ~ **it** no será, si puedo evitarlo; **you** ~ **what you can do with it!**‡ ¡métetelo por donde te quepa!‡; **to** ~ **what's what** saber cuántas son cinco; **it was big, (you)** ~ **what I mean?** era grande, ¿sabes?; **you don't** ~ **how glad I am to see you** no sabes cuánto me alegro de verte; **to get to** ~ **sth** (llegar a) saber algo, enterarse de algo.
(**b**) (*be acquainted with*) *person, book, subject etc* conocer; **do you** ~ **him?** ¿le conoces?; **if I** ~ **him he'll say no** estoy seguro que dirá que no; **do you** ~ **Spain?** ¿conoces España?; **to come to** ~ **sb, to get to** ~ **sb** (llegar a) conocer a uno.

(**c**) (*recognize*) conocer, reconocer; **to ~ sb by sight** conocer a uno de vista; **to ~ sb by** (*or* **from**) **his walk** conocer a uno por su modo de andar; **I knew him at once** le reconocí en seguida.

2 *vi* (**a**) (*gen*) saber **I ~!** ¡ya sé!; **who ~s?** ¿quién sabe?; **one never ~s, you never ~** nunca se sabe; **I don't ~, I wouldn't ~** no sé; **how should I ~?** ¿yo qué sé?; **it's not easy, you ~** mire, esto no es fácil; **it was big, you ~** era grande, sabes; **we'll let you ~** le avisaremos; **why didn't you let me ~?** ¿por qué no me has avisado?; **afterwards they just don't want to ~** después 'si te vi no me acuerdo'; **it's been there for as long as I've ~n** está allí desde siempre.

(**b**) **to ~ about, to ~ of** saber de, tener conocimiento de, estar enterado de; **I don't ~ about you, but I ...** por ti no sé, pero yo ...; **I didn't ~ about that** no sabía nada de eso, lo ignoraba; **oh, I don't ~ about that** pues eso no es cierto; ¡hombre, no tanto!; **she ~s about cats** ella entiende de gatos; **did you ~ about John?** ¿has oído lo de Juan?; **I don't ~ about you!** (*despairing*) ¿qué le vamos a hacer?; **not that I ~ of** que yo sepa, no.

(**c**) **to ~ how to** + *infin* saber + *infin*.

3 *n* (**a**) **to be in the ~** estar enterado, estar en el ajo; **those not in the ~** los no avisados.

(**b**) **there were 7% don't ~s** hubo un 7 por ciento que 'no sabe, no contesta'.

knowable ['nəʊəbl] *adj* conocible.

know-all ['nəʊɔːl] *n* sabelotodo *mf*.

know-how ['nəʊhaʊ] *n* saber hacer *m*, know-how *m*; habilidad *f*, destreza *f*; experiencia *f*; (*expertise*) pericia *f*; **a certain amount of technical ~** algunos conocimientos *mpl* técnicos.

knowing ['nəʊɪŋ] **1** *adj* (*sharp*) astuto, avispado; *look etc* de complicidad, malicioso; **worth ~** digno de saberse.

2 *n*: **there's no ~** no hay modo de saberlo; **there's no ~ what he'll do** es imposible adivinar lo que hará.

knowingly ['nəʊɪŋlɪ] *adv* (**a**) (*intentionally*) a sabiendas, adrede. (**b**) *look etc* maliciosamente, con malicia.

know-it-all ['nəʊɪtɔːl] *n* (*US*) sabelotodo *mf*.

knowledge ['nɒlɪdʒ] *n* (*knowing*) conocimiento *m*; (*person's range of information*) conocimientos *mpl*, saber *m*; (*learning*) erudición *f*, ciencia *f*; **the advance of ~** el progreso de la ciencia; **his ~ will die with him** morirá su erudición con él; **to my ~, to the best of my ~** según mi leal entender y saber, que yo sepa; **not to my ~** que yo sepa; **without my ~** sin saberlo yo; **that is common ~** eso lo sabe todo el mundo; **his failure is common ~** su fracaso es ya del dominio público; **it is common ~ that ...** se sabe perfectamente que ..., es notorio que ...; **it has come to my ~ that** he llegado a saber que; **to have a ~ of Welsh** saber algo de galés; **to have a working ~ of** dominar los principios esenciales de; **to have a thorough ~ of** conocer a fondo.

knowledgeable ['nɒlɪdʒəbl] *adj person* entendido, erudito (*about* en); *remark* informado.

knowledgeably ['nɒlɪdʒəblɪ] *adv* de manera erudita, con conocimiento de causa.

known [nəʊn] **1** *ptp of* **know; X, ~ as Y** X, conocido por el nombre de Y; **a product ~ everywhere** un producto conocido en todas partes; **he is ~ everywhere** se le conoce en todas partes; **to become ~** (*fact*) llegar a saberse, (*person*) llegar a ser conocido; **it became ~ that ...** se supo que ...; **he let it be ~ that ...** dio a entender que ..., informó que ...; **to make o.s. ~** darse a conocer (*to* a); **to make sth ~ to sb** anunciar algo a uno, hacer que uno se entere de algo; **to make one's wishes ~** hacer que se sepa lo que uno desea.

2 *adj*: **a ~ thief** un ladrón conocido; **a ~ expert** un experto reconocido como tal; **he is a ~ quantity** es alguien que por lo menos conocemos, es de sobra conocido; **the ~ facts** los hechos establecidos, los hechos ciertos.

knuckle ['nʌkl] *n* nudillo *m*; **it was a bit near the ~** rayaba en la indecencia; **to rap sb's ~s, to rap sb over the ~s** echar un rapapolvo a uno.

◆**knuckle down** *vi*: **to ~ down to sth** ponerse a hacer algo con ahinco, dedicarse a algo en serio.

◆**knuckle under** *vi* darse por vencido, someterse; **to ~ under to threats** someterse ante las amenazas.

knucklebone ['nʌkl,bəʊn] *n* nudillo *m*.

knuckleduster ['nʌkl,dʌstəʳ] *n* puño *m* de hierro.

knucklehead‡ ['nʌkl,hed] *n* cabezahueca *m*.

knurl [nɜːl] **1** *n* nudo *m*, protuberancia *f*; (*of coin*) cordón *m*. **2** *vt coin* acordonar.

knurled [nɜːld] *adj* nudoso; *coin* moleteado.

K.O. *abbr of* **knockout**.

koala [kəʊ'ɑːlə] *n* coala *f*.

kohlrabi [kəʊl'rɑːbɪ] *n* colinabo *m*.

kook* [kuːk] *n* (*US*) majareta* *mf*, excéntrico *m*, -a *f*.

kookie‡, kooky‡ ['kuːkɪ] *adj* (*US*) loco, chiflado*.

Koran [kɒ'rɑːn] *n* Corán *m*, Alcorán *m*.

Koranic [kɒ'rænɪk] *adj* coránico, alcoránico.

Korea [kə'rɪə] *n* Corea *f*; **North ~** Corea *f* del Norte; **South ~** Corea *f* del Sur.

Korean [kə'rɪən] **1** *adj* coreano. **2** *n* coreano *m*, -a *f*.

kosher ['kəʊʃəʳ] *adj* autorizado por la ley judía, kosher, cosher.

kowtow ['kaʊ'taʊ] *vi* (*bow*) saludar humildemente; **to ~ to sb** humillarse ante uno, doblegarse servilmente ante uno.

kph *abbr of* **kilometres per hour** kilómetros *mpl* por hora, kph.

Kraut‡ [kraʊt] **1** *adj* alemán. **2** *n* alemán *m*, -ana *f*.

Kremlinologist [,kremlɪ'nɒlədʒɪst] *n* kremlinólogo *m*, -a *f*.

Kremlinology [,kremlɪ'nɒlədʒɪ] *n* kremlinología *f*.

krum(m)horn ['krʌmhɔːn] *n* cuerno *m*.

Kruschev [kruːs'tʃɒf] *nm* Jruschov.

krypton [krɪptɒn] *n* criptón *m*.

KS (*US Post*) *abbr of* **Kansas**.

Kt (*Brit*) *abbr of* **Knight** *caballero de una orden*.

Kuala Lumpur ['kwɑːlə'lʊmpʊəʳ] *n* Kuala Lumpur *m*.

kudos* ['kjuːdɒs] *n* prestigio *m*, gloria *f*.

kummel ['kʊməl] *n* cúmel *m*, kummel *m*.

kumquat ['kʌmkwɒt] *n* naranja *f* china.

kung fu ['kʌŋ'fuː] *n* kung fu *m*.

Kurd [kɜːd] *n* kurdo *m*, -a *f*.

Kurdish ['kɜːdɪʃ] **1** *adj* kurdo. **2** *n* (*Ling*) kurdo *m*.

Kurdistan [,kɜːdɪ'stæn] *n* Kurdistán *m*.

Kuwait [kʊ'weɪt] *n* Kuwait *m*, Koweit *m*, Koveit *m*.

Kuwaiti [kʊ'weɪtɪ] *adj*, *n* kuwaití *mf*, koweití *mf*, koveití *mf*.

kW. *abbr of* **kilowatt**(**s**) kilovatio(s) *mpl*, kv.

kW/h. *abbr of* **kilowatt-hours** kilovatios-hora *mpl*, kv/h.

KY (*US Post*) *abbr of* **Kentucky**.

L

L, l [el] *n* (*letter*) L, l *f*; **L for Lucy, L for Love** (*US*) L de Lorenzo.

L (**a**) (*maps etc*) *abbr of* **lake.**

(**b**) (*Aut*) *abbr of* **learner**; **L-plate** (*Brit*) placa *f* de aprendiz de conductor.

(**c**) (*garment size*) *abbr of* **large.**

(**d**) *abbr of* **left** izquierda, izq.

l. (**a**) *abbr of* **left** izquierdo, izq. (**b**) *abbr of* **litre**(**s**) litro(s) *m*(*pl*), l.

LA (**a**) (*US Post*) *abbr of* **Louisiana.** (**b**) *abbr of* **Los Angeles.**

La. (*US*) *abbr of* **Louisiana.**

lab* [læb] *n* = **laboratory.**

Lab. (**a**) [læb] *n abbr of* **Labour** laborista *mf*; *also adj*. (**b**) (*Canada*) *abbr of* **Labrador.**

label [ˈleɪbl] **1** *n* etiqueta *f*, rótulo *m*, marbete *m*; (*on specimen etc*) letrero *m*; (*on spine of book*) tejuelo *m*; (*fig*) calificación *f*, designación *f*, descripción *f*, clasificación *f*; **a record on the CCS** ~ un disco de la marca CCS.

2 *vt* (**a**) etiquetar, poner etiqueta a; rotular, poner un letrero a; **it is not clearly ~led** la etiqueta no es legible; no hay etiqueta (*etc*) que lo describa claramente; **every case must be ~led** cada maleta ha de llevar una etiqueta.

(**b**) (*fig*) calificar (*as* de), designar (*as* como), describir (*as* como); apodar; **to ~ sb as** (*fig*) tachar a uno de; **to be ~led as** estar encasillado como; **he got himself ~led a troublemaker** se hizo una reputación de turbulento.

labelling [ˈleɪbəlɪŋ] *n* etiquetado *m*, etiquetaje *m*.

labia [ˈleɪbɪə] *npl of* **labium.**

labial [ˈleɪbɪəl] **1** *adj* labial. **2** *n* labial *f*.

labiodental [ˌleɪbɪəʊˈdentəl] **1** *adj* labiodental. **2** *n* labiodental *f*.

labium [ˈleɪbɪəm] *n, pl* **labia** [ˈleɪbɪə] labio *m*.

labor [ˈleɪbəʳ] (*US*) = **labour.**

laboratory [ləˈbɒrətərɪ, *US* ˈlæbrəˌtɔːrɪ] *n* laboratorio *m*; ~ **assistant** ayudante *mf* de laboratorio; ~ **coat** bata *f* de laboratorio; ~ **test** prueba *f* de laboratorio.

laborious [ləˈbɔːrɪəs] *adj* penoso; difícil, pesado.

laboriously [ləˈbɔːrɪəslɪ] *adv* penosamente, con dificultad.

labour, (*US*) **labor** [ˈleɪbəʳ] **1** *n* (**a**) (*work in general*) trabajo *m*; **Ministry of L~** Ministerio *m* de Trabajo.

(**b**) (*task*) trabajo *m*, labor *f*, faena *f*, tarea *f*; **a ~ of love** una tarea muy grata, un trabajo agradable; **~s of Hercules** trabajos *mpl* de Hércules.

(**c**) (*toil*) pena *f*, fatiga *f*, esfuerzo *m*; **after much** ~ tras grandes esfuerzos.

(**d**) (*Jur*) **hard** ~ trabajos *mpl* forzados; **5 years' hard** ~ 5 años de trabajos forzados.

(**e**) (*persons*) obreros *mpl*, mano *f* de obra; (*as class*) clase *f* obrera; **we are short of** ~ nos falta mano de obra; **capital and** ~ la empresa y los obreros.

(**f**) (*Brit Pol*) **L~** laborismo *m*, Partido *m* Laborista; **to vote** ~ votar por un candidato laborista.

(**g**) (*Med*) parto *m*; (*also* ~ **pains**) dolores *mpl* del parto; **to be in** ~ estar de parto.

2 *attr* de trabajo; laboral; ~ **camp** campamento *m* de trabajo; ~ **cost** costo *m* de la mano de obra; **L~ Day** Día *m* del Trabajo (*1 mayo*; *en US, Canada, primer lunes de setiembre*); ~ **dispute** conflicto *m* laboral; ~ **exchange** (*Brit*†) bolsa *f* de trabajo; ~ **force** mano *f* de obra, fuerza *f* laboral; ~ **law** (*as study*) derecho *m* del trabajo, derecho *m* laboral; ~ **lawyer** abogado *mf* laboralista; ~ **market** mercado *m* del trabajo (*or* laboral); ~ **movement** movimiento *m* obrero; **L~ Party** Partido *m* Laborista; ~ **relations** relaciones *fpl* laborales; ~ **shortage** escasez *f* de mano de obra; ~ **supply** oferta *f* de mano de obra; ~ **union** (*US*) sindicato *m*; ~ **ward** (*Med*) sala *f* de partos.

3 *vt point etc* insistir en, machacar en, desarrollar con nimiedad; **I won't ~ the point** me abstengo de subrayar esto, no hace falta insistir en esto.

4 *vi* (**a**) (*work*) trabajar (*at* en); **to ~ in vain** trabajar en balde; **to ~ to do sth** afanarse por hacer algo; **to ~ under a delusion** estar equivocado.

(**b**) (*move etc*) moverse penosamente, avanzar con dificultad; **to ~ up a hill** subir penosamente una cuesta; **the engine is ~ing** el motor no funciona bien.

laboured, (*US*) **labored** [ˈleɪbəd] *adj breathing* fatigoso; *movement* torpe, lento, penoso; *style* pesado, premioso.

labourer, (*US*) **laborer** [ˈleɪbərəʳ] *n* (*on roads etc*) peón *m*; (*farm* ~) labriego *m*, bracero *m*, peón *m*, afanador *m* (*Mex*); (*day* ~) jornalero *m*; **bricklayer's** ~ peón *m* de albañil.

labouring, (*US*) **laboring** [ˈleɪbərɪŋ] *adj class* obrero.

labour-intensive, (*US*) **labor-intensive** [ˈleɪbərɪnˈtensɪv] *adj*: ~ **industry** industria *f* en que se emplea mucha mano de obra.

labourite, (*US*) **laborite** [ˈleɪbəraɪt] *n* (*pej*) laborista *mf*.

labour-saving, (*US*) **labor-saving** [ˈleɪbəˌseɪvɪŋ] *adj* que ahorra trabajo; ~ **device** máquina *f* que ahorra trabajo.

labrador [ˈlæbrədɔːr] *n* labrador *m*.

laburnum [ləˈbɜːnəm] *n* lluvia *f* de oro, codeso *m*.

labyrinth [ˈlæbərɪnθ] *n* laberinto *m*.

labyrinthine [ˌlæbəˈrɪnθaɪn] *adj* laberíntico.

lac [læk] *n* laca *f*.

lace [leɪs] **1** *n* (**a**) (*open fabric*) encaje *m*, (*as trimming*) puntilla *f*; (*of gold, silver*) galón *m*. (**b**) (*of shoe etc*) cordón *m*, agujeta *f* (*Mex*).

2 *vt* (**a**) (*Sew*) guarnecer con encajes (*etc*). (**b**) (*also* **to ~ up**) *shoe etc* atar, atar el cordón de. (**c**) *drink* echar licor a; **a drink ~d with brandy** una bebida reforzada con coñac.

◆**lace into**‡ *vt*: **to ~ into sb** dar una paliza a uno.

lace-maker [ˈleɪsˌmeɪkəʳ] *n* encajero *m*, -a *f*.

lacemaking [ˈleɪsˌmeɪkɪŋ] *n* labor *f* de encaje.

lacerate [ˈlæsəreɪt] *vt* lacerar; *feelings etc* herir.

laceration [ˌlæsəˈreɪʃən] *n* laceración *f*.

lace-ups [ˈleɪsʌps] *npl* (*also* **lace-up shoes**) zapatos *mpl* con cordones.

lachrymose [ˈlækrɪməʊs] *adj* lacrimoso, lloroso.

lack [læk] **1** *n* falta *f*, ausencia *f*, carencia *f*; escasez *f*; **for ~ of, through ~ of** por falta de; **there is a grave ~ of water** nos hace muchísima falta el agua; **there is no ~ of money** no es que falte dinero.

2 *vt* no tener; carecer de, necesitar; **we ~ time to do it** nos falta tiempo para hacerlo; **we're ~ing 3 players to make up a team** nos hacen falta 3 jugadores para completar el equipo; **he does not ~ talent** no carece de talento, es cierto que tiene talento; **what is it that you ~?** ¿qué es lo que te hace falta?; **he ~s confidence** no tiene confianza en sí mismo; **~ing men, what can we do?** a falta de hombres, ¿qué podemos hacer?

3 *vi* (**a**) (*thing*) **to be ~ing** faltar, estar ausente, no haber; **but money is ~ing** pero no hay dinero, pero falta el dinero; **nothing was ~ing to make the play succeed** no faltaba nada para que la obra obtuviera un éxito; **where decency is ~ing** donde falta la decencia.

(**b**) (*person*) **he is ~ing in confidence** no tiene confianza en sí mismo, le falta confianza en sí mismo, carece de confianza en sí mismo; **it's not that he's ~ing in good qualities** no es que le falten buenas cualidades.

lackadaisical [ˌlækəˈdeɪzɪkəl] *adj* lánguido, indiferente; (*dreamy*) ensimismado, despistado, distraído; (*slow*) perezoso, tardo; (*careless*) descuidado, informal.

lackey [ˈlækɪ] *n* lacayo *m* (*also fig*).

lacklustre, (*US*) **lackluster** [ˈlækˌlʌstəʳ] *adj surface* deslustrado, deslucido; *style etc* inexpresivo; *eyes* apagado; *person* pesado, soso.

laconic [lə'kɒnɪk] *adj* lacónico.
laconically [lə'kɒnɪkəlɪ] *adv* lacónicamente.
lacquer ['lækəʳ] **1** *n* laca *f*, maque *m*, pintura *f* al duco. **2** *vt* laquear, maquear, pintar al duco.
lacquered ['lækəd] *adj* barnizado con laca, laqueado, pintado al duco.
lacrosse [lə'krɒs] *n* lacrosse *f*.
lactate ['lækteɪt] *vi* lactar.
lactation [læk'teɪʃən] *n* lactancia *f*.
lacteal ['læktɪəl] *adj* lácteo.
lactic ['læktɪk] *adj* láctico.
lactose ['læktəʊs] *n* lactosa *f*.
lacuna [lə'kjuːnə] *n*, *pl* **lacunae** [lə'kjuːniː] laguna *f*.
lacustrine [lə'kʌstraɪn] *adj* lacustre.
lacy ['leɪsɪ] *adj* (*of lace*) de encaje; (*like lace*) parecido a encaje; (*fig*) transparente, diáfano.
lad [læd] *n* muchacho *m*, chico *m*, pibe *m* (*And, SC*), chavo *m* (*Mex*); (*country* ~) mozo *m*, zagal *m*; (*in stable etc*) mozo *m*; **young** ~ muchacho *m*, mozalbete *m*; **when I was a** ~ cuando yo era chaval; **he's only a** ~ es muy joven; **don't do that,** ~! ¡no hagas eso, joven!; **come on,** ~**s!** ¡vamos, muchachos!; **all together,** ~**s!** ¡todos juntos, muchachos!; **he's a bit of a** ~ es un chico poco formal; es un tipo muy divertido; **he's a bit of a** ~ **with the girls** les da guerra a las chicas, se bromea mucho con las chicas.
ladder ['lædəʳ] **1** *n* **(a)** escalera *f* (de mano), escala *f*; (*Brit*: *in stocking*) carrera *f*.
(b) (*fig*) camino *m*, escalón *m* (*to* de); **social** ~ escala *f* social; **it's a first step up the** ~ es el primer peldaño; **to be at the top of the** ~ estar en la cumbre de su profesión (*etc*), ocupar el rango más alto.
2 *attr*: ~ **truck** (*US*) coche-escala *m*.
3 *vt* (*Brit*) *stocking* hacer una carrera en.
4 *vi* (*Brit*: *stocking*) hacerse una carrera, desmallarse.
ladderproof ['lædəpruːf] *adj* (*Brit*) *stocking* indesmallable.
laddie* ['lædɪ] *n* (*esp Scot*) = **lad.**
lade [leɪd] (*irr*: *pret* **laded,** *ptp* **laden**) **1** *vt* cargar (*with* de). **2** *vi* tomar cargamento.
laden ['leɪdn] *ptp of* **lade**; ~ **with** cargado de.
la-di-da* ['lɑːdɪ'dɑː] **1** *adj* afectado, repipi*. **2** *adv talk etc* de manera afectada, con afectación.
lading ['leɪdɪŋ] *n* cargamento *m*, flete *m*.
ladle ['leɪdl] **1** *n* (*at table*) cucharón *m*, cacillo *m*; (*in kitchen*) cazo *m*. **2** *vt* (*also* **to** ~ **out**) servir (*or* sacar *etc*) con cucharón; (*fig*) repartir generosamente, distribuir a manos llenas.
lady ['leɪdɪ] **1** *n* señora *f*; (*aged, distinguished, noble*) dama *f*; (*Brit title*) **L~ (Gladys) Crumm** Lady (Gladys) Crumm; **'Ladies'** (*lavatory*) 'Señoras'; **'Ladies Only'** 'Sólo Damas'; **ladies and gentlemen!** ¡señoras y señores!; ~ **of the house** señora *f* de la casa; **the minister and his** ~ el ministro y su esposa; **your good** ~ su esposa; **Our L~** Nuestra Señora *f*; **young** ~ señorita *f*, joven *f*; **his young** ~ su novia *f*; **she's no** ~ esa mujer no es lo que aparenta, es una mujer que tiene historia; **shall we join the ladies?** ¿pasamos a estar con las señoras?; ~**'s cycle** bicicleta *f* de señora; **ladies' final** final *f* femenina; **ladies' man** hombre *m* de salón, Perico *m* entre ellas; **ladies' room** lavabo *m* de señoras.
2 *attr* **(a)** ~ **doctor** médica *f*; ~ **friend** amiga *f*; ~ **guest** invitada *f*; ~ **mayoress** (*Brit*) alcaldesa *f*; ~ **member** socio *f*, señora *f* socio.
(b) (*Rel*) **L~ Chapel** capilla *f* de la Virgen; **L~ Day** (*Brit*) día *m* de la Anunciación (*25 marzo*).
ladybird ['leɪdɪbɜːd] (*Brit*) *n*, (*US*) **ladybug** ['leɪdɪbʌg] *n* mariquita *f*, vaca *f* de San Antón.
lady-in-waiting ['leɪdɪɪn'weɪtɪŋ] *n* dama *f* de honor.
ladykiller ['leɪdɪ,kɪləʳ] *n* tenorio *m*, ladrón *m* de corazones.
ladylike ['leɪdɪlaɪk] *adj* elegante, fino, distinguido, bien educado; (*pej*) afeminado.
lady-love ['leɪdɪlʌv] *n* amada *f*.
lady's finger ['leɪdɪz,fɪŋgəʳ] *n* (*Bot*) quimbombó *m*.
ladyship ['leɪdɪʃɪp] *n*: **Her L~, Your L~** Su Señoría.
lady's maid ['leɪdɪz,meɪd] *n* doncella *f*.
LAFTA ['læftə] *n abbr of* **Latin-American Free Trade Association** Asociación *f* Latinoamericana de Libre Comercio, ALALC *f*.
lag[1] [læg] **1** *n* retraso *m*.
2 *vi* retrasarse; (*in pace*) rezagarse, quedarse atrás.
◆**lag behind** **1** *vi* retrasarse; (*in pace*) rezagarse, quedarse atrás; **we** ~ **behind in space exploration** nos hemos retrasado en la exploración espacial. **2** *vt*: **Ruritania** ~**s behind Slobodia** Ruritania anda a rastras detrás de Eslobodia, Ruritania no ha hecho tantos progresos como Eslobodia.
lag[2] [læg] *vt* (*Tech*) revestir, recubrir, forrar (*with* de); *boiler* calorifugar.
lag[3]‡ [læg] **1** *n* (*esp Brit*: *also* **old** ~) presidiario *m*. **2** *vt* meter a la sombra‡.
lager ['lɑːgəʳ] *n* cerveza *f* ligera dorada; ~ **lout** (*Brit**) gamberro *m* de litrona.
laggard ['lægəd] *n* (*having fallen behind*) rezagado *m*, -a *f*; (*idler*) holgazán *m*, -ana *f*.
lagging ['lægɪŋ] *n* (*Tech*) revestimiento *m*, forro *m*.
lagoon [lə'guːn] *n* laguna *f*.
Lagos ['leɪgɒs] *n* Lagos *m*.
lah [lɑː] *n* (*Mus*) la *m*.
laicize ['leɪɪsaɪz] *vt* laicizar.
laid [leɪd] *pret and ptp of* **lay**; **to be** ~ **up** (*Med*) estar enfermo, tener que guardar cama (*with* a causa de); (*car etc*) estar fuera de circulación, estar en garaje.
laid-back* [,leɪd'bæk] *adj* (*esp US*) *person* relajado, ecuánime; *party* tranquilo, pacífico.
lain [leɪn] *ptp of* **lie[2]**.
lair [lɛəʳ] *n* cubil *m*, guarida *f*.
laird [lɛəd] *n* (*Scot*) señor *m*; terrateniente *m*, propietario *m*.
laissez-faire ['leɪseɪ'fɛəʳ] *n* laissez-faire *m*.
laity ['leɪɪtɪ] *n* laicado *m*, legos *mpl*; (*fig*) legos *mpl*.
lake[1] [leɪk] *n* (*colour*) laca *f*.
lake[2] [leɪk] *n* (*Geog*) lago *m*; **the L~s** (*England*) los Lagos; ~ **Michigan** el Lago Michigan.
Lake District ['leɪk,dɪstrɪkt] *n* País *m* de los Lagos.
lake-dweller ['leɪk,dweləʳ] *n* (*Hist*) persona *f* que vive en una habitación *f* lacustre.
lake-dwelling ['leɪk,dwelɪŋ] *n* habitación *f* lacustre.
lakeside ['leɪksaɪd] *n* ribera *f* de(l) lago, orilla *f* de(l) lago.
Lallans ['lælənz] *n dialecto y lengua literaria de las Tierras Bajas* (*Lowlands*) *de Escocia*.
lam[1]‡ [læm] **1** *vt* pegar, dar una paliza a. **2** *vi*: **to** ~ **into sb** dar una paliza a uno.
lam[2]‡ [læm] *n*: **to be on the** ~ (*US*) ser fugitivo de la justicia.
lama ['lɑːmə] *n* lama *m*.
lamb [læm] **1** *n* cordero *m*, -a *f*; (*older*) borrego *m*, -a *f*; (*meat*) (carne *f* de) cordero *m*; **the L~ of God** el Cordero de Dios; **my poor** ~! ¡pobrecito!; **he took it like a** ~ recibió la noticia con la mayor tranquilidad, no se ofendió en lo más mínimo; **to go like a** ~ **to the slaughter** ir como borrego al matadero.
2 *attr*: ~ **chop** chuleta *f* de cordero.
3 *vi* parir (*la oveja*).
lambast(e) [læm'beɪst] *vt* dar una paliza a; (*fig*) poner como un trapo.
lambing ['læmɪŋ] *n* (época *f* del) parto *m* de las ovejas.
lamb-like ['læmlaɪk] *adj* manso como un cordero.
lambskin ['læmskɪn] *n* (piel *f* de) cordero *m*.
lamb's lettuce ['læmz'letɪs] *n* valeriana *f*.
lamb's wool, lambswool ['læmzwʊl] *n* lana *f* de cordero, añinos *mpl*.
lame [leɪm] **1** *adj* **(a)** *animal, person* cojo, lisiado; ~ **duck** (*St Ex*) especulador *m*, -ora *f* insolvente; (*fig*) persona *f* quemada; persona *f* completamente incapaz; ~ **duck industry** industria *f* insolvente; industria *f* en declive; ~ **duck president** (*etc*) presidente *m* (*etc*) no reelegido en los últimos meses de su mandato; **to be** ~ (*permanently*) ser cojo, (*temporarily*) estar cojo; **to be** ~ **in one foot** ser cojo de un pie, cojear de un pie; **to go** ~ estropearse un pie, lisiarse un pie, empezar a cojear.
(b) (*fig*) *excuse* débil, poco convincente; *argument* flojo; (*Liter*) *metre* defectuoso, que cojea.
2 *vt* lisiar, dejar cojo; incapacitar.
lamé ['lɑːmeɪ] *n* lamé *m*, lama *f*.
lamely ['leɪmlɪ] *adv walk etc* cojeando; *argue, say etc* sin convicción.
lameness ['leɪmnɪs] *n* cojera *f*; incapacidad *f*; (*fig*) falta *f* de convicción; flojedad *f*.
lament [lə'ment] **1** *n* lamento *m*; queja *f*; (*Liter etc*) elegía *f* (*for* por).
2 *vt* lamentar, lamentarse de; **to** ~ **sb** llorar a uno, llorar la pérdida de uno; **it is much to be** ~**ed that ...** es de lamentar que + *subj*.
3 *vi* lamentarse (*for, over* de).
lamentable ['læməntəbl] *adj* lamentable.
lamentably ['læməntəblɪ] *adv* lamentablemente.
lamentation [,læmən'teɪʃən] *n* lamentación *f*.
laminate **1** ['læmɪneɪt] *vt* laminar. **2** ['læmɪnɪt] *n* laminado *m*.
laminated ['læmɪneɪtɪd] *adj* laminado; *document* plastificado; *glass* inastillable; ~ **wood** contrachapado *m*.

lamp [læmp] *n* lámpara *f*; linterna *f*; (*in street*) farol *m*; (*Aut, Rail etc*) faro *m*; (*bulb*) bombilla *f*; (*fig*) antorcha *f*.
lampblack ['læmpblæk] *n* negro *m* de humo.
lamp-bracket ['læmp,brækɪt] *n* brazo *m* de lámpara.
lamp-chimney ['læmp,tʃɪmnɪ] *n*, **lampglass** ['læmpglɑːs] *n* tubo *m* de lámpara.
lampholder ['læmp,həʊldəʳ] *n* portalámpara *m*.
lamplight ['læmplaɪt] *n* luz *f* de (la) lámpara; **by ~, in the ~** a la luz de la lámpara.
lamplighter ['læmp,laɪtəʳ] *n* farolero *m*.
lampoon [læm'puːn] **1** *n* pasquín *m*, sátira *f*. **2** *vt* pasquinar, satirizar.
lamppost ['læmppəʊst] *n* (*Brit*) (poste *m* de) farol *m*, farola *f*.
lamprey ['læmprɪ] *n* lamprea *f*.
lampshade ['læmpʃeɪd] *n* pantalla *f* (de lámpara).
lamp-standard ['læmp,stændəd] *n* poste *m* de farola.
LAN [læn] *n abbr of* **local area network** red *f* de área local, RAL *f*.
Lancastrian [læŋ'kæstrɪən] **1** *adj* de Lancashire. **2** *n* nativo *m*, -a *f* (*or* habitante *mf*) de Lancashire.
lance [lɑːns] **1** *n* lanza *f*. **2** *vt* alancear, herir con lanza; (*Med*) abrir con lanceta.
lance-corporal ['lɑːns'kɔːpərəl] *n* (*Brit*) soldado *m* de primera, cabo *m* interino.
Lancelot ['lɑːnslət] *nm* Lanzarote.
lancer ['lɑːnsəʳ] *n* lancero *m*; **~s** (*dance*) lanceros *mpl*.
lancet ['lɑːnsɪt] *n* lanceta *f*; **~ arch** ojiva *f* aguda; **~ window** ventana *f* ojival.
Lancs. [læŋks] *n abbr of* **Lancashire.**
land [lænd] **1** *n* (*in most senses*) tierra *f*; (*nation*) país *m*; (*region*) tierra *f*, región *f*; (*soil*) tierra *f*, suelo *m*; (*as property*) tierras *fpl*, finca *f*; (*tract of* ~) terreno *m*; (*Agr, fig*) campo *m*, agricultura *f*, *eg* **the drift from the ~** la despoblación del campo, el éxodo rural; **he went on the ~** se dedicó a la agricultura; **~ of milk and honey** paraíso *m* terrenal, jauja *f*; **~ of promise, promised ~** tierra *f* de promisión; **back to the ~!** ¡a cultivar la tierra! (*campaña de tiempos de guerra*); **by ~** por tierra, por vía terrestre; **on ~** en tierra; **to live off the ~** (*army etc*) vivir sobre el país; **to see how the ~ lies** tantear el terreno, hacer un reconocimiento.
2 *attr breeze etc* de tierra; *defences, forces, route* terrestre; *law, question* agrario; **~ agent** administrador *m*, -ora *f* (de una finca); **~ forces** fuerzas *fpl* terrestres; **~ office business** (*US**) negocio *m* próspero; **~ reform** reforma *f* agraria; **~ register, ~ registry** catastro *m*, registro *m* catastral, registro *m* de la propiedad inmobiliaria.
3 *vt* (**a**) *person, goods, fish at port etc* desembarcar.
(**b**) *fish* (*on hook*) pescar, coger, sacar del agua, traer a la orilla; (*fig: obtain*) conseguir, lograr; *prize* obtener, ganar, sacar; *job* conseguir.
(**c**) *plane* poner en tierra.
(**d**) *blow* dar, asestar (*on* en).
(**e**) (*Brit: place*) **it ~ed him in debt** le hizo contraer deudas; **it ~ed him in jail** por ello acabó en la cárcel; **it ~ed me in a mess** me puso en un apuro, me creó un lío; **I got ~ed with the job** tuve que cargar con el cometido; **I got ~ed with him for 2 hours** tuve que cargar con él durante 2 horas.
4 *vi* (**a**) (*from ship*) desembarcar (*at* en).
(**b**) (*Aer*) aterrizar, tomar tierra; (*on sea*) amerizar, amarar; (*on moon*) alunizar; (*bird, insect*) posar(se).
(**c**) (*hit, strike*) dar en, hacer blanco en; **the hat ~ed in my lap** el sombrero cayó sobre mis rodillas; **it ~ed square on the target** dio de lleno en el blanco; **the bomb ~ed on the building** la bomba hizo blanco en el edificio; **the blow ~ed on his cheek** el golpe le dio en la mejilla; **to ~ on one's feet** caer de pies; **to ~ on one's head** caer de cabeza; **where did it ~?** ¿dónde fue a caer?
(**d**) (*fig*) llegar; terminar; **to ~ up at Wigan** ir a parar a Wigan; **to ~ up in a dreadful mess** terminar haciéndose un tremendo lío.
landau ['lændɔː] *n* landó *m*.
landed ['lændɪd] *adj* (**a**) *person* hacendado, que posee tierras; *property* que consiste en tierras; **~ gentry** terratenientes *mpl*, pequeña aristocracia *f* rural; **~ property** bienes *mpl* raíces. (**b**) (*Comm*) **~ cost** precio *m* más otros costes incluyendo derechos de importación.
landfall ['lændfɔːl] *n* (*Naut*) recalada *f*; aterrada *f*.
landfill ['lændfɪl] **1** *n* vertedero *m* de basuras. **2** *attr*: **~ site** vertedero *m* de basuras.
landholder ['lænd,həʊldəʳ] *n* terrateniente *mf*.
landing ['lændɪŋ] *n* (**a**) (*Naut*) desembarco *m*, desembarque *m*.
(**b**) (*Aer*) aterrizaje *m*; (*on sea*) amaraje *m*, amerizaje *m*; (*on moon*) alunizaje *m*; (*descent*) descenso *m*.
(**c**) (*of stairs*) descanso *m*, rellano *m*.
landing-card ['lændɪŋ,kɑːd] *n* tarjeta *f* de desembarque.
landing-craft ['lændɪŋkrɑːft] *n* barcaza *f* (*or* lancha *f*) de desembarco.
landing-field ['lændɪŋfiːld] *n* campo *m* de aterrizaje.
landing-gear ['lændɪŋgɪəʳ] *n* tren *m* de aterrizaje.
landing-ground ['lændɪŋgraʊnd] *n* campo *m* de aterrizaje.
landing-lights ['lændɪŋ,laɪts] *npl* luces *fpl* de aterrizaje.
landing-net ['lændɪŋnet] *n* salabardo *m*, manga *f*, cuchara *f*.
landing-party ['lændɪŋ,pɑːtɪ] *n* destacamento *m* de desembarco.
landing-run ['lændɪŋrʌn] *n* recorrido *m* de aterrizaje.
landing-stage ['lændɪŋsteɪdʒ] *n* (*Brit*) desembarcadero *m*.
landing-strip ['lændɪŋstrɪp] *n* pista *f* de aterrizaje.
landing-wheels ['lændɪŋwiːlz] *npl* ruedas *fpl* de aterrizaje.
landlady ['lænd,leɪdɪ] *n* (*owner*) dueña *f*; (*of boarding house*) patrona *f*; (*of flat*) propietaria *f*.
landless ['lændlɪs] **1** *adj peasant etc* sin tierras, que no posee tierras. **2** *npl*: **the ~** los (campesinos *etc*) sin tierra, los desposeídos, los de abajo.
landlessness ['lændlɪsnɪs] *n* situación *f* de los desposeídos (de tierra).
landlocked ['lændlɒkt] *adj* cercado de tierra, mediterráneo, sin acceso al mar.
landlord ['lændlɔːd] *n* (*of property, land*) propietario *m*, dueño *m*; (*Brit: of boarding house*) patrón *m*; (*of flat*) casero *m*; (*of inn*) posadero *m*, mesonero *m*; (*Brit: of pub*) patrón *m*.
landlubber ['lænd,lʌbəʳ] *n* contramaestre *m* de muralla.
landmark ['lændmɑːk] *n* (**a**) (*Naut*) marca *f*, señal *f* fija; (*boundary mark*) mojón *m*; (*high place*) punto *m* destacado, punto *m* (*or* edificio *etc*) prominente; (*well-known thing*) lugar *m* muy conocido.
(**b**) **to be a ~** (*fig*) hacer época, formar época, marcar un hito histórico.
landmass ['lænd,mæs] *n* masa *f* continental.
landmine ['lændmaɪn] *n* mina *f* terrestre.
landowner ['lænd,əʊnəʳ] *n* terrateniente *mf*, hacendado *m*, -a *f*.
Land Rover ['lænd,rəʊvəʳ] ® *n* (*Aut*) (vehículo *m*) todo terreno *m*.
landscape ['lænskeɪp] **1** *n* paisaje *m*. **2** *attr*: **~ gardener** jardinero *m*, -a *f* paisajista, arquitecto *m*, -a *f* de jardines; **~ gardening** arquitectura *f* de jardines, paisajismo *m*; **~ orientation** (*Inform*) formato *m* horizontal; **~ painter** paisajista *mf*. **3** *vt park etc* reformar artísticamente, *terrain* ajardinar, convertir en parque.
landscaping ['lænskeipiŋ] *n* arquitectura *f* paisajista.
landslide ['lændslaɪd] **1** *n* corrimiento *m* de tierras, desprendimiento *m* de tierras; (*Pol*) victoria *f* electoral arrolladora; **the Liberal ~ of 1906** la victoria arrolladora de los liberales en 1906.
2 *attr*: **~ majority** mayoría *f* abrumadora (*or* aplastante); **to win a ~ majority** barrer (*or* ganar) por mayoría abrumadora; **~ victory** victoria *f* abrumadora (*or* aplastante).
landslip ['lændslɪp] *V* **landslide.**
land tax ['lændtæks] *n* contribución *f* territorial.
landward ['lændwəd] *adj* de hacia tierra, de la parte de la tierra; **on the ~ side** en el lado de la tierra.
landward(s) ['lændwəd(z)] *adv* hacia tierra; **to ~** en la dirección de la tierra.
lane [leɪn] **1** *n* (*in country*) camino *m* vecinal, vereda *f*; (*in town*) callejón *m*; (*between plantations*) vereda *f*; (*Sport*) calle *f*, banda *f*; (*Aut*) carril *m*; (*Aer*) vía *f* aérea, pasillo *m* aéreo; (*Naut*) ruta *f* marítima.
2 *attr*: **~ closure** cierre *m* de carril; **~ markings** líneas *fpl* divisorias.
langlauf ['lɑːŋ,laʊf] *n* esquí *m* nórdico.
language ['læŋgwɪdʒ] **1** *n* (*faculty of speech, mode of speech*) lenguaje *m*; (*national tongue*) lengua *f*, idioma *m*; (*style*) lengua *f*, estilo *m*; redacción *f*; (*Comput*) lenguaje *m*; **bad ~** lenguaje *m* indecente; palabrotas *fpl*, tacos *mpl*; **to use bad ~** (*habitually*) ser mal hablado; **modern ~s** lenguas *fpl* modernas; **strong ~** palabras *fpl* mayores; **that's no ~ to use to your mother!** ¡así no se habla a tu madre!; **we don't talk the same ~** (*fig*) no hablamos la misma lengua.
2 *attr*: **~ barrier** barrera *f* lingüística; **~ laboratory** laboratorio *m* de idiomas.
languid ['læŋgwɪd] *adj* lánguido.
languidly ['læŋgwɪdlɪ] *adv* lánguidamente.

languidness ['læŋgwɪdnɪs] *n* languidez *f*.
languish ['læŋgwɪʃ] *vi* languidecer; (*in prison*) pudrirse; (*pine*) consumirse (*for* por); (*amorously*) ponerse sentimental.
languishing ['læŋgwɪʃɪŋ] *adj* lánguido; *look, tone etc* amoroso, sentimental.
languor ['læŋgəʳ] *n* languidez *f*.
languorous ['læŋgərəs] *adj* lánguido.
lank [læŋk] *adj person* alto y flaco; *hair* lacio; *grass* largo.
lanky ['læŋkɪ] *adj* larguirucho, desmadejado.
lanolin(e) ['lænəʊlɪn] *n* lanolina *f*.
lantern ['læntən] *n* linterna *f* (*also Archit*); (*Naut*) faro *m*, farol *m*; (*of lighthouse*) fanal *m*.
lantern-jawed ['læntən'dʒɔːd] *adj* chupado de cara.
lantern lecture ['læntən,lektʃəʳ] *n* conferencia *f* con proyecciones.
lantern slide ['læntənslaɪd] *n* diapositiva *f*.
lanyard ['lænjəd] *n* acollador *m*.
Laos [laʊs] *n* Laos *m*.
Laotian ['laʊʃɪən] **1** *adj* laosiano. **2** *n* laosiano *m*, -a *f*.
lap[1] [læp] **1** *n* (*Anat*) regazo *m*; (*knees*) rodillas *fpl*; (*skirt*) falda *f*; (*fig*) seno *m*; (*overlap*) traslapo *m*, solapa *f*; **to sit on sb's ~** (*woman's*) estar sentado en el regazo (*or* en el halda) de una, (*man's*) estar sentado en las rodillas de uno; **it's in the ~ of the gods** está en manos de los dioses; **to live in the ~ of luxury** nadar en la abundancia.
2 *vt* (*overlap*) traslapar; (*wrap*) envolver (*in* en; *also fig*); **to ~ sth about with** cercar algo de, (*fig*) envolver algo en.
3 *vi* (*overlap*) traslaparse.
lap[2] [læp] (*Sport*) **1** *n* (*round*) vuelta *f*; (*stage*) etapa *f*, fase *f*; **~ of honour** vuelta *f* de honor; **we're on the last ~ now** (*fig*) ésta es la última etapa, hemos vencido la cuesta ya.
2 *vt*: **to ~ sb** doblar a uno, aventajar a uno en una vuelta entera.
3 *vi*: **to ~ at 190 k.p.h.** hacer una vuelta a 190 k.p.h.
lap[3] [læp] **1** *n* (*lick*) lamedura *f*, lametada *f*, lengüetada *f*; (*of waves*) chapaleteo *m*.
2 *vt* **(a)** (*lick*) lamer.
(b) (*of water*) estar al nivel de, correr tan alto como.
3 *vi* (*waves*) chapalear; **to ~ against** besar, tocar, lamer.
◆**lap over** *vi* desbordarse, irse, salir fuera.
◆**lap up** *vt* beber con la lengua, tomar a lengüetadas; (*fig*) aceptar con entusiasmo, absorber, aprender con facilidad.
laparoscopy [,læpə'rɒskəpɪ] *n* laparoscopia *f*.
laparotomy [,læpə'rɒtəmɪ] *n* laparotomía *f*.
La Paz [lae'pæz] *n* La Paz.
lapdog ['læpdɒg] *n* perro *m* faldero.
lapel [lə'pel] *n* solapa *f*.
lapidary ['læpɪdərɪ] **1** *adj* lapidario. **2** *n* lapidario *m*, -a *f*.
lapis lazuli ['læpɪs'læzjʊlaɪ] *n* lapislázuli *m*.
Lapland ['læplænd] *n* Laponia *f*.
Laplander ['læplændəʳ] *n* lapón *m*, -ona *f*.
Lapp [læp] *n* **(a)** lapón *m*, -a *f*. **(b)** (*Ling*) lapón *m*.
lapping ['læpɪŋ] *n* (*of water*) chapaleteo *m*.
Lappish ['læpɪʃ] *n* (*Ling*) lapón *m*.
lapse [læps] **1** *n* **(a)** (*error*) error *m*, equivocación *f*; (*moral*) desliz *m*, falta *f*; lapso *m*; (*relapse*) recaída *f* (*into* en).
(b) (*of time*) intervalo *m*, período *m*, lapso *m*; **after a ~ of 4 months** después de un período de 4 meses, al cabo de 4 meses.
2 *vi* **(a)** (*err*) caer en el error, equivocarse; (*morally*) cometer un desliz; (*relapse*) recaer, reincidir (*into* en); **to ~ from duty** faltar a su deber; **to ~ into one's old ways** volver a las andadas, volver a las malas costumbres; **he ~d into the vernacular** recurrió a la lengua vernácula; **he ~d into silence** se calló, quedó callado, no dijo más.
(b) (*expire*) caducar; (*cease to exist*) dejar de existir, desaparecer.
(c) (*time*) pasar, transcurrir.
lapsed [læpst] *adj* (*Rel*) que no practica.
laptop ['læptɒp] *n* (*also* **~ computer**) ordenador *m* portátil plegable.
lapwing ['læpwɪŋ] *n* avefría *f*.
larboard ['lɑːbəd] **1** *adj* de babor. **2** *n* babor *m*.
larceny ['lɑːsənɪ] *n* hurto *m*, ratería *f*, latrocinio *m*; **grand ~** (*US*) robo *m* de cantidad importante; **petty ~** robo *m* de menor cuantía *f*.
larch [lɑːtʃ] *n* (*also* **~ tree**) alerce *m*.
lard [lɑːd] **1** *n* manteca *f* de cerdo. **2** *vt* lardear, mechar; (*fig*) **to ~ sth with** adornar algo de, salpicar algo de, sembrar algo de.
larder ['lɑːdəʳ] *n* despensa *f*.
lardy ['lɑːdɪ] *adj* mantecoso.
large [lɑːdʒ] **1** *adj* grande; *packet etc* abultado, voluminoso; *interests* extenso; *powers* amplio, extenso; *sum* importante; *family* numeroso; (*main, chief*) principal; **as ~ as life** así como es; en persona; **there he was as ~ as life** ahí estaba en persona; **there it was as ~ as life** allí se nos apareció de modo inconfundible; **it looked ~r than life** parecía más grande de lo que era en realidad.
2 *n*: **ambassador at ~** embajador *m* itinerante (que no está acreditado permanentemente en ningún país); **people at ~** la gente en general; **the world at ~** el mundo en general; **the prisoner is still at ~** el preso está todavía en libertad; **the virus is still at ~** el virus constituye todavía un peligro, el virus todavía no ha sido controlado.
3 *adv V* **by.**
largely ['lɑːdʒlɪ] *adv* en su mayor parte, en gran parte.
largeness ['lɑːdʒnɪs] *n* gran tamaño *m*; lo abultado (*etc*); extensión *f*; importancia *f*; lo numeroso.
larger ['lɑːdʒəʳ] *adj comp of* **large**; más grande, mayor; **to grow ~** crecer; aumentar(se); **to make ~** hacer más grande; aumentar; *premises etc* ampliar, ensanchar.
large-scale ['lɑːdʒ'skeɪl] *adj* en gran escala, de gran envergadura; **very ~ integration** integración *f* a muy gran escala.
large-size(d) ['lɑːdʒ'saɪz(d)] *adj* de gran tamaño, de tamaño extra.
largesse [lɑː'ʒes] *n* generosidad *f*, liberalidad *f*; (*gift*) dádiva *f* espléndida.
largish ['lɑːdʒɪʃ] *adj* bastante grande, más bien grande.
largo ['lɑːgəʊ] *n* (*Mus*) largo *m*.
lariat ['lærɪət] *n* lazo *m*.
lark[1] [lɑːk] *n* (*Orn*) alondra *f*; **to get up with the ~** levantarse con las gallinas, madrugar; *V* **happy.**
lark[2]* [lɑːk] **1** *n* **(a)** (*joke etc*) broma *f*, travesura *f*; **that's a ~!, what a ~!** ¡qué bien!, ¡qué risa!; **that was a ~!** ¡cómo nos reímos con aquello!; **isn't he a ~?** ¿es célebre, no?; **to do sth for a ~** hacer algo para divertirse, divertirse haciendo algo; **to hell with this for a ~!** ¡vaya lío*!, ¡qué follón!*; **to have a ~ with sb** gastar una broma a uno, tomar el pelo a uno*.
(b) (*business, affair*) **that ice-cream ~** ese asunto de los helados; **the Suez ~** la fiestecita de Suez; **this dinner-jacket ~** esta faena de ponerse smoking*.
2 *vi* (*be on a spree*) andar de jarana; (*amuse o.s.*) divertirse.
◆**lark about, lark around** *vi* hacer travesuras, gastarse bromas, divertirse tontamente; **stop ~ing about!** ¡basta de bromas!; **to ~ about with sth** (*play*) divertirse con algo, jugar con algo, (*damage*) estropear algo, manosear algo.
larkspur ['lɑːkspɜːʳ] *n* espuela *f* de caballero.
larky* ['lɑːkɪ] *adj* guasón, bromista.
Larry ['lærɪ] *nm familiar form of* **Laurence, Lawrence.**
larva ['lɑːvə] *n*, *pl* **larvae** ['lɑːviː] larva *f*.
laryngitis [,lærɪn'dʒaɪtɪs] *n* laringitis *f*.
larynx ['lærɪŋks] *n* laringe *f*.
lasagna, lasagne [lə'zænjə] *n* lasaña *f*.
lascivious [lə'sɪvɪəs] *adj* lascivo, lujurioso.
lasciviously [lə'sɪvɪəslɪ] *adv* lascivamente.
lasciviousness [lə'sɪvɪəsnɪs] *n* lascivia *f*, lujuria *f*.
laser ['leɪzəʳ] **1** *n* láser *m*. **2** *attr*: **~ beam** rayo *m* láser; **~ printer** impresora *f* (por) láser; **~ rangefinder** telémetro *m* lasérico; **~ surgery** cirugía *f* (con) láser.
lash [læʃ] **1** *n* **(a)** (*whip*) látigo *m*, (*used for punishment*) azote *m*; (*thong*) tralla *f*.
(b) (*stroke*) latigazo *m*, (*as punishment*) azote *m*; (*of tail*) coletazo *m*; **the ~ of the rain** el azote de la lluvia; **under the ~ of the Nazis** bajo el azote de los nazis.
(c) (*Anat*) pestaña *f*.
2 *vt* **(a)** (*beat etc*) azotar, dar latigazos a, fustigar; (*of hail, rain, waves*) azotar; (*fig: criticize*) fustigar, dar una paliza a, increpar; **the lion was ~ing its tail** el león daba coletazos; **he was ~ing the horse along** le daba duramente al caballo con el látigo; **the wind ~ed the trees** el viento azotaba los árboles; **the wind ~ed the sea into a fury** el viento levantaba enormes olas; **to ~ sb with one's tongue** increpar duramente a uno; **to ~ sb into a fury** provocar a uno hasta la furia.
(b) (*tie*) atar, (*Naut*) trincar, amarrar (*to* a).
3 *vr*: **to ~ o.s. into a fury** montar en cólera.
◆**lash about** *vi* gesticular violentamente.
◆**lash down** *vt* sujetar, atar firmemente.
◆**lash out 1** *vt* (*) **he had to ~ out £50** tuvo que desembolsar 50 libras; **he was ~ing out the money** gastaba pródigamente; **they were ~ing out the drink** estaban

sirviendo las bebidas en grandes cantidades.

2 *vi* (**a**) (*) desdinerarse, pagar; repartir dinero generosamente; **now we can really ~ out** ahora sí podemos gastar; **he ~ed out and bought himself a Rolls** dejó de economizar y se compró un Rolls. (**b**) (*with fists*) repartir golpes a diestro y siniestro, dar golpes furiosos sin mirar a quien; (*with feet*) tirar coces; **to ~ out at** (*or* **against**) arremeter contra.

lashing ['læʃɪŋ] *n* (**a**) (*beating*) azotamiento *m*, azotes *mpl*; **to give sb a ~** azotar a uno, (*fig*) dar una paliza a uno. (**b**) (*tie*) atadura *f*, (*Naut*) trinca *f*, amarradura *f*. (**c**) **~s*** (*esp Brit*) montones* *mpl*.

lash-up* ['læʃʌp] *n* reparación *f* improvisada; arreglo *m* provisional, improvisación *f*.

lass [læs] *n* (*esp Scot*) muchacha *f*, chica *f*, joven *f*, piba *f* (*And, SC*), chava *f* (*Mex*); (*country ~*) moza *f*, zagala *f*.

lassie* ['læsɪ] *n* (*esp Scot*) = **lass**.

lassitude ['læsɪtju:d] *n* lasitud *f*.

lasso [læ'su:] **1** *n* lazo *m*. **2** *vt* lazar, coger con el lazo.

last[1] [lɑ:st] **1** *adj* último; final; extremo; *week, month etc* pasado; **the L~ Supper** la Última Cena; **~ Monday, on Monday ~** el lunes pasado; **~ night** anoche; **the night before ~** anteanoche; **the year before ~** el año antepasado; **the ~ trick but one** la penúltima baza; **the ~ day but two of the trial** el antepenúltimo día del proceso; **the ~ trick but 3** la tercera baza antes de la última; **during the ~ 20 years** en los últimos 20 años; **he has not been seen these ~ 3 years** hace 3 años que no se le ve; **to be the ~ (one) to do sth** ser el último en hacer algo; **to be ~ but not least** ser el último pero no el menos importante; **and ~ but not least came John** y como fin de fiesta se presentó Juan; **you must pick up every ~ one** hay que recoger absolutamente todos; **that's the ~ thing to worry about** eso es lo de menos; **that was the ~ thing I expected** eso era lo que menos yo esperaba; **I'll drink it if it's the ~ thing I do** lo beberé y ¡arda Troya! (*V also* **thing** (**c**)); **they left me till ~** me atendieron (*etc*) el último, me dejaron hasta el fin; **you're the ~ person to be entrusted with it** tú eres el menos indicado para hacerse cargo de ello.

2 *n* último *m*, -a *f*, última cosa *f*, lo último; (*end*) fin *m*; **each one better than the ~** cada uno mejor que el anterior (*or* precedente); **my ~** mi última carta; **at ~** por fin; **at long ~** por fin, después de tanto tiempo (*or* esperar *etc*); **to the ~** hasta el fin; **this is the ~ of it** éste es el último de la serie (*etc*), con éste terminamos, después de éste no quedan más; **that was the ~ we saw of him** no le volvimos a ver; **I shall be glad to see the ~ of this** estoy deseando que termine esto; **to breathe one's ~** exhalar el último suspiro; **we shall never hear the ~ of it** no nos dejarán olvidarlo nunca; **you haven't heard the ~ of this** este asunto no se puede dar por concluido; **the ~ we heard of him he was in Río** según las últimas noticias estaba en Río; **to look one's ~ on sth** ver algo por última vez, despedirse de algo (antes de su desaparición).

3 *adv* por último; en último lugar; por última vez; finalmente; **to arrive ~** llegar el último; **the horse came in ~** el caballo llegó el último, el caballo ocupó el último puesto en la clasificación; **when I ~ saw him** cuando le vi por última vez.

last[2] [lɑ:st] **1** *vt* durar; **it ~ed me a lifetime** me duró toda la vida; **the car has ~ed me 8 years** el coche me ha durado 8 años.

2 *vi* durar; perdurar; permanecer, resistir; sostenerse, mantenerse; (*continue*) continuar, seguir; (*cloth etc*) ser duro, ser resistente; **it ~s 2 hours** dura 2 horas; **it can't ~** no puede seguir así; **things are too good to ~** las cosas van demasiado bien para que duren; **will this material ~?** ¿es resistente este paño?; **he won't ~ long in this job** no durará mucho tiempo en este puesto; **the previous boss ~ed only a week** el jefe anterior permaneció solamente una semana en el puesto.

◆**last out 1** *vt*: **I can ~ you out any time** de todos modos yo resisto mejor que tú; **he ~ed all his colleagues out** sobrevivió a todos sus colegas; **my money doesn't ~ out the month** el dinero no me llega para un mes entero; **can you ~ out another mile?** ¿aguantas una milla más? **2** *vi* resistir, continuar; (*money, resources*) durar, llegar, alcanzar; **I can't ~ out** no puedo más, no resisto más.

last[3] [lɑ:st] *n* horma *f*; **stick to your ~!** ¡zapatero, a tus zapatos!

last-ditch ['lɑ:st'dɪtʃ] *adj defence, stand* de lo más terco, de último recurso, que continúa hasta quemar el último cartucho; **a ~ effort** un último esfuerzo.

last-gasp ['lɑ:st'gɑ:sp] *adj* de última hora.

lasting ['lɑ:stɪŋ] *adj* duradero, perdurable, permanente; constante; *shame etc* eterno; *colour* sólido.

lastly ['lɑ:stlɪ] *adv* por último, finalmente.

last-minute ['lɑ:st'mɪnɪt] *adj decision etc* de última hora.

lat. *abbr of* **latitude** latitud *f*.

latch [lætʃ] **1** *n* picaporte *m*, pestillo *m*; **to be on the ~** estar cerrado con picaporte; **to drop the ~** echar el pestillo.

2 *vt* cerrar con picaporte; (*fig*) sujetar, asegurar.

◆**latch on*** *vi* (*understand*) comprender.

◆**latch on to** *vt* adherirse a; **to ~ on to sth** fijarse en algo; **to ~ on to sb** pegarse a uno.

latchkey ['lætʃki:] **1** *n* llavín *m*. **2** *attr*: **~ child** niño *m*, -a *f* cuya madre trabaja.

late [leɪt] **1** *adj* (**a**) (*person*) **to be ~ for sth** llegar tarde para algo; **I was too ~ for it** llegué tarde para ello; **I was ~ in getting up** tardé en levantarme; **I don't want to make you ~** no quiero entretenerle.

(**b**) (*impersonal*) **it's ~** es tarde; **it's ~ in the day to change your mind** es tarde para mudar de opinión; **it's getting ~** se está haciendo tarde.

(**c**) (*far on in day, season etc*) tardío; *hour* avanzado; *delivery* atrasado; *entry* tardío; **~ frost** helada *f* tardía; **~ potato** patata *f* tardía; **at a ~ hour** a una hora avanzada, a última hora; **we had a ~ night last night** anoche no volvimos a casa hasta muy tarde; anoche continuó la fiesta (*etc*) hasta muy tarde; **in the ~ eighties** en los últimos años ochenta; **in the ~ spring** hacia fines de la primavera; **in the ~ morning** en la última parte de la mañana; **a ~ 18th century building** un edificio de fines del siglo XVIII; **L~ Stone Age** período *m* neolítico; **L~ Latin** latín *m* tardío; **Easter is ~ this year** la Semana Santa cae tarde este año.

(**d**) (*deceased*) fallecido, difunto, finado; **the ~ king** el finado rey.

(**e**) (*former*) antiguo, ex; **~ prime minister** antiguo primer ministro *m*, ex primer ministro *m*.

2 *adv* (**a**) (*not on time*) tarde; **to come ~** llegar tarde; **to arrive too ~** llegar tarde (*for* para); **the train arrived 8 minutes ~** el tren llegó con 8 minutos de retraso; **better ~ than never** más vale tarde que nunca; **to sit up ~, to stay up ~** velar, no acostarse hasta las altas horas, trasnochar; **you've left it a bit ~** lo has dejado un poco tarde; **~ in the day** a última hora del día; **it's a bit ~ in the day to change your mind** es algo tarde para cambiar de idea; **~ at night, ~ in the night** ya muy entrada la noche; **~ into the night** hasta muy entrada la noche; **~ in the afternoon** a última hora de la tarde; **~ in the year** hacia fines del año; **~ in life** a una edad avanzada; **~ last century** hacia fines del siglo pasado; **of ~** últimamente, recientemente; **as ~ as 1900** todavía en 1900.

(**b**) **~ of No. 13** que vivió hasta hace poco en el núm. 13; **~ of the Diplomatic Service** hasta hace poco miembro del Cuerpo Diplomático, ex miembro del Cuerpo Diplomático.

latecomer ['leɪtkʌmə^r] *n* recién llegado *m*, -a *f*; el (*etc*) que llega tarde; **the firm is a ~ to the industry** la compañía es nueva en la industria, la compañía acaba de establecerse en la industria.

lateen [lə'ti:n] *n* vela *f* latina.

late-lamented ['leɪtlə'mentɪd] *adj* malogrado, fallecido.

lately ['leɪtlɪ] *adv* últimamente, recientemente; hace poco; **till ~** hasta hace poco.

latency ['leɪtənsɪ] *n* estado *m* latente.

lateness ['leɪtnɪs] *n* lo tarde; lo tardío; lo reciente; (*of hour*) lo avanzado; (*delay*) retraso *m*; **he was fined for persistent ~** le impusieron una multa por venir constantemente tarde.

late-night ['leɪt'naɪt] *adj*: **~ show, ~ performance** sesión *f* de noche; **~ opening** (*or* **shopping**) **is on Thursdays** se abre tarde los jueves; **is there a ~ bus?** ¿hay autobús a última hora de la noche?

latent ['leɪtənt] *adj* latente; **~ defect** defecto *m* latente.

later ['leɪtə^r] **1** *adj comp of* **late**; más tardío; (*in newness*) más reciente; (*in series*) posterior, ulterior; *hour* más avanzada; **his ~ symphonies** sus sinfonías más recientes, sus sinfonías posteriores; **this version is ~ than that one** esta versión es posterior a ésa; **at a ~ meeting** en una reunión celebrada después; **in his ~ years** en sus últimos años.

2 *adv comp of* **late**; más tarde; (*afterwards*) luego, después; posteriormente; **a moment ~** un momento después; **a few years ~** a los pocos años; varios años después; **yes dear, ~** (*on being interrupted*) sí querida, luego; **see you ~!**

¡hasta pronto!; **no ~ than yesterday** no más lejos que ayer, ayer sin ir más lejos; **not ~ than 1980** antes de 1980; **~ on** más tarde, después.
lateral ['lætərəl] *adj* lateral; **~ thinking** pensamiento *m* lateral.
laterally ['lætərəlɪ] *adv* lateralmente.
latest ['leɪtɪst] **1** *adj superl of* **late**; último; más reciente; *fashion, news etc* último; **his ~ painting** su último cuadro, su cuadro más reciente; **to be the ~ to do sth** ser el último en hacer algo; **what is the ~ date you can come?** ¿hasta qué fecha estás libre para venir?
2 *adv superl of* **late**; **he came ~** él vino el último.
3 *n* **(a)** **what's the ~ on ...?** ¿qué noticias hay sobre ...?; **it's the ~ in computers** es lo último en ordenadores; **have you seen John's ~?*** (*girl*) ¿has visto a la amiguita actual de Juan?; **have you heard John's ~?** (*joke*) ¿has oído el último chiste de Juan?; **did you hear about John's ~?** (*exploit*) ¿te han contado la última de Juan?, ¿has oído lo de Juan?
(b) **at the ~** a lo más tarde, a más tardar, como límite.
latex ['leɪteks] *n* látex *m*.
lath [læθ] *n, pl* **laths** [lɑːðz] listón *m*.
lathe [leɪð] *n* torno *m*.
lather ['læðəʳ] **1** *n* espuma *f* (de jabón), jabonaduras *fpl*; (*of sweat*) espuma *f*; **the horse was in a ~** el caballo estaba cubierto de espuma; **he arrived in a ~** llegó todo sudado.
2 *vt* enjabonar; (*) zurrar.
3 *vi* hacer espuma.
latifundia [ˌlætɪ'fʊndɪə] *npl* latifundios *mpl*.
Latin ['lætɪn] **1** *adj* latino; **~ lover** galán *m* latino; **~ quarter** barrio *m* latino.
2 *n* **(a)** (*person*) latino *m*, -a *f*; **the ~s** los latinos.
(b) (*Ling*) latín *m*.
Latin America ['lætɪnə'merɪkə] *n* América *f* Latina, Latinoamérica *f*, Hispanoamérica *f*.
Latin-American ['lætɪnə'merɪkən] **1** *adj* latinoamericano. **2** *n* latinoamericano *m*, -a *f*.
latinism ['lætɪnɪzəm] *n* latinismo *m*.
latinist ['lætɪnɪst] *n* latinista *mf*.
latinity [lə'tɪnɪtɪ] *n* latinidad *f*.
latinization [ˌlætɪnaɪ'zeɪʃən] *n* latinización *f*.
latinize ['lætɪnaɪz] *vti* latinizar.
latish ['leɪtɪʃ] **1** *adv* algo tarde. **2** *adj* algo tardío.
latitude ['lætɪtjuːd] *n* latitud *f*; (*fig*) libertad *f*.
latitudinal [ˌlætɪ'tjuːdɪnl] *adj* latitudinal.
Latium ['leɪʃɪəm] *n* Lacio *m*.
latrine [lə'triːn] *n* letrina *f*.
latter ['lætəʳ] *adj* **(a)** (*later*) más reciente; posterior; último; (*of two*) segundo; **the ~ part of the story** la segunda mitad del cuento; **in the ~ part of the century** hacia fines del siglo; **the ~ opinion** esta (última) opinión; **his ~ end** el final de su vida, su muerte.
(b) **the former ... the ~** aquél ... éste.
latter-day ['lætə'deɪ] *adj* moderno, reciente; **L~ Saints** los Mormones.
latterly ['lætəlɪ] *adj* últimamente, recientemente.
lattice ['lætɪs] **1** *n* enrejado *m*; (*on window*) reja *f*, celosía *f*.
2 *attr*: **~ window** ventana *f* de celosía; **~ work** enrejado *m*, celosía *f*.
latticed ['lætɪst] *adj window* con reja.
Latvia ['lætvɪə] *n* Letonia *f*, Latvia *f*.
Latvian ['lætvɪən] **1** *adj* letón, latvio. **2** *n* letón *m*, -ona *f*, latvio *m*, -a *f*.
laud [lɔːd] *vt* (*liter*) alabar, elogiar.
laudable ['lɔːdəbl] *adj* loable; plausible.
laudably ['lɔːdəblɪ] *adv* de modo loable, laudablemente.
laudanum ['lɔːdnəm] *n* láudano *m*.
laudatory ['lɔːdətərɪ] *adj* laudatorio.
laugh [lɑːf] **1** *n* risa *f*; (*loud*) carcajada *f*, risotada *f*; **what a ~!** ¡qué risa!, ¡qué bien!; **just for a ~** sólo para hacer reír; **it's a (bit of a) ~** es cosa de risa; **he's a (bit of a) ~** es un tío tonto; **he got a ~** hizo reír a la gente; **to have a good ~ over sth** reírse mucho con algo; **to have the ~ over sb** llevar ventaja a uno, quedar por encima de uno; **to have the last ~** reírse el último; **to play sth for ~s** representar algo con el propósito de hacer reír al público; **the joke didn't raise a ~** el chiste no hizo reír a nadie.
2 *vi* reír, reírse; (*loud*) reírse a carcajadas, carcajearse; **to ~ about sth, to ~ over sth** reírse con algo; **it's nothing to ~ about** no es cosa de risa (*or* reírse (*LAm*)); **to ~ at sb** reírse de uno, burlarse de uno; **we must be able to ~ at ourselves** hay que ver los aspectos ridículos de nosotros mismos; **to ~ out loud** soltar la carcajada, reírse abiertamente; **he who ~s last ~s longest** el último que ríe ríe más fuerte, al freír será el reír; **to ~ like a hyena** reírse como un loco; **don't make me ~!** (*iro*) ¡me haces reír!; **they'll be ~ing all the way to the bank** irán contentísimos al banco; **it's all right for him, he's ~ing** para él no hay problema.
◆**laugh down** *vt* ridiculizar.
◆**laugh off** *vt*: **to ~ sth off** tomar algo a risa; **he ~s everything off** no toma nada en serio; *V* **scorn**.
laughable ['lɑːfəbl] *adj* ridículo, absurdo; cómico, divertido; **it's ~ that ...** es absurdo que + *subj*.
laughing ['lɑːfɪŋ] **1** *adj* risueño, alegre; **it's no ~ matter** no es cosa de risa. **2** *n* risa *f*.
laughing-gas ['lɑːfɪŋ'gæs] *n* gas *m* hilarante.
laughingly ['lɑːfɪŋlɪ] *adv*: **he said ~** dijo riendo; **what is ~ called progress** lo que se llama irónicamente el progreso.
laughing-stock ['lɑːfɪŋstɒk] *n* hazmerreír *m*.
laughter ['lɑːftəʳ] **1** *n* risa *f*, risas *fpl*; **amid the ~ of those present** entre las risas de los asistentes; **at this there was ~** en esto hubo risas; **to burst into ~** soltar la carcajada.
2 *attr*: **~ line** (*Brit*) arruga *f* producida al reír.
Launcelot ['lɑːnslət] *nm* Lanzarote.
launch [lɔːntʃ] **1** *n* **(a)** (*act*: *Naut*) botadura *f*; (*Aer etc*) lanzamiento *m*; (*Comm etc*) lanzamiento *m*, presentación *f*. **(b)** (*vessel*) lancha *f*, falúa *f*.
2 *attr*: **~ pad** rampa *f* de lanzamiento; **~ vehicle** (*Space*) lanzadera *f*.
3 *vt* (*throw*) lanzar; *rocket etc* lanzar; *new vessel* botar; *lifeboat* echar al agua, largar; *offensive* emprender, comenzar; *company* crear, fundar, lanzar; *new product* lanzar, presentar, introducir en el mercado; *film, play* estrenar; *idea* lanzar; *plan* poner en operación; *share issue etc* emitir; **to ~ sb on his way** ayudar a uno a emprender su carrera, poner a uno en camino; **once he is ~ed on this subject we shall never stop him** en cuanto se ponga a hablar de este tema no le haremos nunca callar.
◆**launch forth** *vi* lanzarse, ponerse en marcha.
◆**launch into** *V* **~ out into**.
◆**launch out** *vi* lanzarse, ponerse en marcha; **now we can afford to ~ out a bit** ahora nos podemos permitir algunas cosas de lujo, ahora podemos extender nuestras actividades (*etc*); **to ~ out into** lanzarse a; **to ~ out into business** engolfarse en los negocios; **to ~ out into a career** emprender una carrera; **he ~ed out into a violent speech** pasó a pronunciar un discurso violento.
launcher ['lɔːntʃəʳ] *n* (*for rocket*) lanzacohetes *m*.
launching ['lɔːntʃɪŋ] **1** *n* botadura *f*; lanzamiento *m*; inauguración *f*, iniciación *f*; estreno *m*; emisión *f*. **2** *attr*: **~ ceremony** ceremonia *f* de botadura.
launching-pad ['lɔːntʃɪŋpæd] *n* rampa *f* de lanzamiento.
launching-site ['lɔːntʃɪŋsaɪt] *n* rampa *f* de lanzamiento.
launder ['lɔːndəʳ] **1** *vt* **(a)** lavar (y planchar). **(b)** (*) *money* lavar*, blanquear*. **2** *vi* resistir el lavado (bien, mal *etc*).
launderette [ˌlɔːndə'ret] *n* (*Brit*) lavandería *f* automática.
laundering ['lɔːndərɪŋ] *n* **(a)** colada *f*. **(b)** (*: *of money*) lavado* *m*, blanqueo* *m*.
laundress ['lɔːndrɪs] *n* lavandera *f*.
Laundromat ['lɔːndrəˌmæt] ® *n* (*US*) lavandería *f* automática.
laundry ['lɔːndrɪ] **1** *n* **(a)** (*establishment*) lavadero *m*, lavandería *f*. **(b)** (*clothes*: *dirty*) ropa *f* sucia, ropa *f* por lavar, (*washed*) ropa *f* lavada, colada *f*. **2** *attr*: **~ basket** cesto *m* de la ropa sucia; **~ list** lista *f* de ropa para lavar; **~ mark** marca *f* de lavandería.
laureate ['lɔːrɪɪt] *n* laureado *m*; **Poet L~** (*Brit*) Poeta *m* Laureado.
laurel ['lɒrəl] *n* laurel *m* (cerezo); **to look to one's ~s** no dormirse sobre sus laureles; **to rest on one's ~s** dormirse sobre sus laureles; **to win one's ~s** cargarse de laureles, laurearse.
laurel wreath ['lɔːrəlˌriːθ] *n* corona *f* de laurel, laureles *mpl*.
Laurence ['lɒrəns] *nm* Lorenzo.
Lausanne [ləʊ'zæn] *n* Lausana *f*.
lav* [læv] *n* = **lavatory**.
lava ['lɑːvə] **1** *n* lava *f*. **2** *attr*: **~ flow** torrente *m* de lava.
lavatorial [ˌlævə'tɔːrɪəl] *adj humour* cloacal, escatológico.
lavatory ['lævətrɪ] **1** *n* (*Brit*) wáter *m*, excusado *m*, inodoro *m*; (*room*) lavabo *m*, aseos *mpl*; **public ~** urinarios *mpl*. **2** *attr*: **~ bowl, ~ pan** taza *f* de lavabo; **~ paper** papel *m* higiénico; **~ seat** asiento *m* de retrete.
lavender ['lævɪndəʳ] **1** *n* espliego *m*, lavanda *f*, lavándula *f*.
2 *attr*: **~ blue** *adj* azul lavanda.
lavender water ['lævɪndəˌwɔːtəʳ] *n* lavanda *f*.
lavish ['lævɪʃ] **1** *adj* **(a)** (*abundant*) profuso, abundante;

(*luxurious*) lujoso.

(**b**) (*of person, prodigal*) pródigo; *expenditure* pródigo, liberal; **to be ~ of** ser pródigo de, prodigar, no escatimar; **to be ~ with one's money** gastar libremente su dinero, derrochar su dinero.

2 *vt*: **to ~ care on sth** poner la máxima atención en algo; **to ~ attentions on sb** colmar a uno de atenciones.

lavishly ['lævɪʃlɪ] *adv* profusamente, en profusión, abundantemente; lujosamente; pródigamente; **the house is ~ furnished** la casa está lujosamente amueblada; **he spends money ~** derrocha su dinero.

lavishness ['lævɪʃnɪs] *n* (**a**) (*abundance*) profusión *f*, abundancia *f*; lujo *m*. (**b**) (*of person*) prodigalidad *f*.

law [lɔː] **1** *n* (*a ~, the ~*) ley *f*; (*study, body of ~s*) derecho *m*, jurisprudencia *f*; (*Sport, games*) regla *f*; **the L~** (*Jewish*) la ley de Moisés, (*) la policía; **~ and order** orden *m* público; **~ and order in tourist areas** la seguridad ciudadana en las zonas turísticas; **the forces of ~ and order** las fuerzas del orden; **by the ~ of averages** por la estadística, estadísticamente; **~ of gravity** ley *f* de la gravedad; **~ of nature** ley *f* natural; **~ of supply and demand** ley *f* de la oferta y demanda; **according to ~, in ~** según derecho; **by ~** según la ley, de acuerdo con la ley; **in-~** político, *eg* **brother-in-~** hermano *m* político, cuñado *m*; **it's the ~** es la ley; **his word is ~** su palabra es ley; **is there a ~ against it?** ¿hay una ley que lo prohíba?; **he is above the ~** está por encima de la ley; **he is outside the ~** está fuera de la ley; **to be a ~ unto o.s.** obrar por cuenta propia, no hacer caso alguno de los demás; **to go to ~** pleitear, poner pleito (*about* sobre), recurrir a la ley; **to have the ~ on sb** denunciar a uno a la policía, llevar a uno ante el tribunal; **to keep within the ~** obrar legalmente; **to lay down the ~** hablar autoritariamente; **to practise ~** ejercer de abogado, ejercer la abogacía; **to take the ~ into one's own hands** tomarse la justicia por su mano; **to take a case to ~** recurrir a la vía judicial.

2 *attr*: **~ enforcement officer** policía *m*; **~ faculty** facultad *f* de Derecho; **L~ Lords** (*Brit Parl*) jueces *mpl* que son miembros de la Cámara de los Lores; **~ partner** compañero *m*, -a *f* de bufete; **~ reports** actas *fpl* de procesos; **~ school** (*US*) facultad *f* de Derecho; **~ student** estudiante *mf* de Derecho.

law-abiding ['lɔːə,baɪdɪŋ] *adj* observante de la ley, que vive conforme a la ley; decente.

lawbreaker ['lɔː,breɪkəʳ] *n* transgresor *m*, -ora *f*, infractor *m*, -ora *f* de la ley.

lawcourt ['lɔːkɔːt] *n* tribunal *m* (de justicia).

lawful ['lɔːfʊl] *adj* legítimo, lícito, legal; **~ money** moneda *f* legal.

lawfully ['lɔːfəlɪ] *adv* legítimamente, lícitamente.

lawgiver ['lɔː,gɪvəʳ] *n* (*Brit*) legislador *m*, -ora *f*.

lawless ['lɔːlɪs] *adj act* ilegal; *person* rebelde, violento, criminal; *country* sin leyes, ingobernable, anárquico.

lawlessness ['lɔːlɪsnɪs] *n* desorden *m*; violencia *f*; anarquía *f*; criminalidad *f*.

lawmaker ['lɔː,meɪkəʳ] *n* legislador *m*, -ora *f*.

lawn[1] [lɔːn] *n* (*grass*) césped *m*.

lawn[2] [lɔːn] *n* (*cloth*) linón *m*.

lawnmower ['lɔːn,məʊəʳ] *n* cortacésped *m*, segadora *f* (*LAm*).

lawn tennis ['lɔːn'tenɪs] *n* tenis *m*.

Lawrence ['lɒrəns] *nm* Lorenzo.

lawrencium [lɒ'rensɪəm] *n* laurencio *m*.

lawsuit ['lɔːsuːt] *n* pleito *m*, litigio *m*, proceso *m*; **to bring a ~ against sb** entablar demanda judicial contra uno.

lawyer ['lɔːjəʳ] *n* abogado *mf* (*also* -a *f*).

lax [læks] *adj* flojo; negligente, descuidado, poco exigente; indisciplinado; (*morally*) laxo; **to be ~ in** + *ger* ser negligente en + *infin*; **things are very ~ at the school** en la escuela hay poca disciplina; **he is ~ in his approach** su actitud es poco seria.

laxative ['læksətɪv] **1** *adj* laxante. **2** *n* laxante *m*.

laxity ['læksɪtɪ] *n*, **laxness** ['læksnɪs] *n* flojedad *f*; negligencia *f*, descuido *m*; falta *f* de disciplina; (*moral*) laxitud *f*, relajamiento *m*.

lay[1] [leɪ] *n* (*Mus, Liter*) trova *f*, canción *f*.

lay[2] [leɪ] *adj* (*not in orders*) laico, lego, seglar; (*not expert*) profano, no experto; **~ person** (*Rel*) lego *m*, -a *f*; (*non-specialist*) profano *m*, -a *f*.

lay[3] [leɪ] *pret of* **lie**[2].

lay[4] [leɪ] **1** *n* (**a**) (*of countryside, district etc*) disposición *f*, situación *f*; **the ~ of the land** la configuración del terreno, (*fig*) la situación actual, el estado actual de las cosas.

(**b**) **hen in ~** gallina *f* ponedora; **to come into ~** empezar a poner huevos; **to go out of ~** dejar de poner huevos.

(**c**) (‡) **she's an easy ~** es un coño caliente‡, es una tía fácil*; **she's a good ~** es una tía buena*.

(**d**) (‡‡: *act*) polvo‡‡ *m*.

2 (*irr*: *pret, ptp* **laid**) *vt* (**a**) (*prostrate, etc*) *corn* abatir, encamar; *dust* matar; *fears* aquietar, acallar; *ghost* conjurar, exorcizar; **to ~ sth flat** derribar algo, tirar algo al suelo; extender algo (sobre la mesa *etc*); **to ~ a town flat** arrasar (*or* destruir) una ciudad.

(**b**) (*place, put*) poner, colocar; dejar; *blame* echar (*on* a); *bricks* poner, colocar; *cable, mains, track* tender; *cloth, meal* poner; *carpet, lino* extender; *fire* preparar; *foundations* echar; *foundation stone* colocar; *gun* apuntar; *hand etc* poner (*on* en); *bomb, explosives* colocar; *mines* sembrar; *pipes etc* (*in building*) instalar; *plans* hacer, formar, preparar; *responsibility* atribuir (*on* a); *scene* poner, situar; *tax* imponer (*on* a); **to ~ the table** (*Brit*) poner la mesa; **to ~ a plan before sb** exponer un proyecto ante uno; **to ~ a claim before sb** presentar una reivindicación a uno.

(**c**) *egg* poner; **to ~ eggs** (*hen*) poner huevos, (*fish, insect etc*) desovar.

(**d**) *bet* hacer (*on* a); *money* apostar (*on* a); **to ~ that ...** apostar a que ...; **I ~ you a fiver on it!** ¡te apuesto 5 libras a que es así!

(**e**) *accusation, charge* hacer; *complaint* formular, presentar; *information* dar.

(**f**) (‡) tirarse a‡‡, follar‡‡.

3 *vi* (*hen*) poner, poner huevos.

4 *vr*: **to ~ o.s. open to attack** exponerse al ataque, dejarse expuesto al ataque; *V also* **charge 1(c)**, **open 1(d)**.

◆**lay about** *vi*: **to ~ about one** dar palos de ciego, repartir golpes a diestro y siniestro.

◆**lay aside** *vt* (**a**) (*save*) ahorrar, guardar.

(**b**) (*put away*) poner aparte, poner a un lado; *book, pen etc* dejar; *work* dejar, suspender.

(**c**) (*abandon*) desechar; *plan etc* arrinconar, dar carpetazo a.

◆**lay away** *vt* (*US*) = **lay aside** (**a**).

◆**lay by** *vt* = **lay aside** (**a**) (**b**).

◆**lay down 1** *vt* (**a**) (*put down*) *book, pen etc* dejar, poner a un lado; (*lay flat*) acostar, poner en tierra, extender; *burden* posar, depositar en tierra; *cards* extender sobre el tapete.

(**b**) *ship* colocar la quilla de.

(**c**) *wine* poner en bodega, guardar en cava.

(**d**) (*give up*) *arms* deponer, rendir, dejar; *life* dar, sacrificar.

(**e**) (*establish*) *condition* asentar; *policy* asentar, trazar, marcar; *precedent* sentar, establecer; *principle* afirmar; *ruling* dictar; **to ~ it down that ...** asentar que ..., dictaminar que ...

2 *vi* (*Cards*) poner sus cartas sobre el tapete; (*Bridge*: *as dummy*) tumbarse.

3 *vr*: **to ~ o.s. down** tumbarse, echarse.

◆**lay in** *vt supplies* proveerse de; (*amass*) acumular; (*buy*) comprar.

◆**lay into*** *vt* (*attack, criticize*) dar una paliza a; *food etc* lanzarse sobre, asaltar.

◆**lay off 1** *vt* (**a**) *workers* despedir (temporalmente, por falta de trabajo), suspender. (**b**) (*) **to ~ off sb** dejar a uno en paz; dejar de acosar a uno; **to ~ off cigarettes** dejar de fumar (cigarrillos).

2 *vi* (**a**) (*Naut*) virar de bordo.

(**b**) (*) **~ off, will you?** ¡déjalo!, por Dios!; **to ~ off** + *ger* dejar de + *infin*.

◆**lay on 1** *vt* (**a**) (*Brit*: *install*) instalar; conectar; **a house with water laid on** una casa con agua corriente.

(**b**) *paint etc* poner, pintar; **to ~ it on (thick)*** (*flatter*) elogiar más de la cuenta, (*exaggerate*) recargar las tintas.

(**c**) *tax etc, duty* imponer (a).

(**d**) *blows* descargar (sobre); **to ~ it on sb** dar una paliza a uno.

2 *vi* arremeter, empezar a luchar, darse golpes.

◆**lay out 1** *vt* (**a**) (*dispose*) tender, extender; disponer, arreglar; *garden, town* trazar, hacer el trazado de; *ideas* exponer, explicar; **the house is well laid out** la casa está bien distribuida; **the town is well laid out** la ciudad tiene un trazado elegante.

(**b**) *corpse* amortajar.

(**c**) *money* (*spend*) gastar; (*invest*) invertir, emplear (*on* en).

(**d**) (*) (*knock out*) derribar; poner fuera de combate; (*Boxing*) dejar K.O.; (*with drink*) hacer perder el conocimiento a; (*illness*) debilitar gravemente.

2 *vr*: **to ~ o.s. out** hacer un gran esfuerzo (*to + infin* por + *infin*); **to ~ o.s. out for sb** hacer lo posible por ayudar (*or* complacer *etc*) a uno; **to ~ o.s. out to please** volcarse por complacer a uno.

◆**lay over** *vi* (*US*) pasar la noche, descansar.

◆**lay up 1** *vt* (**a**) (*store*) guardar; almacenar; (*amass*) acumular; (*save*) ahorrar, atesorar; *trouble* crear para sí.

(**b**) (*put into reserve*) *ship* desarmar; *boat* amarrar; *car etc* encerrar en el garaje, dejar de usar temporalmente.

(**c**) (*Med*) obligar a guardar cama; **she was laid up for weeks** tuvo que guardar cama durante varias semanas.

2 *vr*: **to ~ o.s. up** agotarse, enfermar.

layabout ['leɪəbaʊt] *n* (*Brit*) gandul *m*, vago *m*, -a *f*.

lay brother ['leɪ'brʌðə^r] *n* donado *m*, lego *m*, hermano *m* lego.

layby ['leɪbaɪ] *n* (*Brit Aut*) apartadero *m*.

lay days ['leɪdeɪz] *npl* (*Comm*) días *mpl* de detención (*or* inactividad).

layer ['leɪə^r] **1** *n* (**a**) (*gen*) capa *f*; (*Geol*) estrato *m*. (**b**) (*Agr*) acodo *m*. (**c**) (*hen*) gallina *f* ponedora; **the best ~** la más ponedora. **2** *vt* (*Agr*) acodar.

layette [leɪ'et] *n* canastilla *f*, ajuar *m* (de niño).

lay figure ['leɪ'fɪgə^r] *n* maniquí *m*.

laying ['leɪɪŋ] *n* (*placing*) colocación *f*; (*of cable, track etc*) tendido *m*; (*of eggs*) puesta *f*, postura *f*; **~ on of hands** imposición *f* de manos.

layman ['leɪmən] *n*, *pl* **laymen** ['leɪmən] (*Eccl*) seglar *m*, lego *m*; (*fig*) profano *m*, persona *f* no experta, lego *m*.

lay-off ['leɪɒf] *n* paro *m* involuntario, despido *m* (temporal).

layout ['leɪaʊt] *n* plan *m*, distribución *f*, trazado *m*; disposición *f*; (*Typ etc*) composición *f*.

layover ['leɪəʊvə^r] *n* (*US*) parada *f* intermedia; (*Aer*) escala *f*.

layperson ['leɪpɜːsn] *n* (*Eccl*) seglar *mf*, lego *m*, -a *f*; (*fig*) profano *m*, -a *f*, lego *m*, -a *f*.

lay sister ['leɪ'sɪstə^r] *n* donada *f*, lega *f*.

Lazarus ['læzərəs] *nm* Lázaro.

laze [leɪz] **1** *n*: **to have a ~*** descansar.

2 *vi* (*also* **to ~ about**) no hacer nada, darse al ocio; (*pej*) holgazanear, gandulear; **we ~d in the sun for a week** durante una semana tomamos el sol y nada más.

lazily ['leɪzɪlɪ] *adv* perezosamente; lentamente.

laziness ['leɪzɪnɪs] *n* pereza *f*, holgazanería *f*, vaguedad *f*, indolencia *f*.

lazy ['leɪzɪ] *adj* perezoso, holgazán, vago; *movement etc* lento; *excuse etc* poco convincente; **we had a ~ holiday** pasamos unas vacaciones descansadas; **to have a ~ eye** tener un ojo vago.

lazybones ['leɪzɪˌbəʊnz] *n* gandul *m*, vago *m*, -a *f*.

lazy Susan [ˌleɪzɪ'suːzn] *n* (*dish*) bandeja *f* giratoria para servir la comida en la mesa.

LB (*Canada*) *abbr of* **Labrador**.

lb. *abbr of* **libra, pound** libra *f*.

LBO *n abbr of* **leveraged buy-out**.

l.b.w. (*Cricket*) *abbr of* **leg before wicket**.

L/C (*Comm*) *abbr of* **letter of credit** letra *f* de crédito.

L.C. *n* (*US*) *abbr of* **Library of Congress** Biblioteca *f* del Congreso.

l.c. (*Typ*) *abbr of* **lower case** minúscula *f*, min.

LCD *n abbr of* **liquid crystal display** visualizador *m* cristal líquido, VCL *m*.

L-Cpl *abbr of* **lance-corporal**.

Ld *abbr of* **Lord**.

LDS *n* (**a**) *abbr of* **Licentiate in Dental Surgery**. (**b**) *abbr of* **Latter-day Saints** Iglesia *f* de Jesucristo de los Santos de los últimos días.

LEA *n* (*Brit*) *abbr of* **Local Education Authority**.

lea [liː] *n* (*poet*) prado *m*.

leach [liːtʃ] **1** *vt* lixiviar. **2** *vi* lixiviarse.

lead[1] [led] **1** *n* (*metal*) plomo *m*; (*Naut*) sonda *f*, escandallo *m*; (*Typ*) regleta *f*, interlínea *f*; (*in pencil*) mina *f*; **they filled him full of ~*** le acribillaron a balazos; **to swing the ~*** fingirse enfermo, racanear*, hacer el rácano*.

2 *attr*: **~ acetate** acetato *m* de plomo; **~ oxide** óxido *m* de plomo; **~ paint** pintura *f* a base de plomo; **~ pencil** lápiz *m*; **~ pipe** tubería *f* de plomo; **~ poisoning** saturnismo *m*, plumbismo *m*, intoxicación *f* por el plomo; **~ seal** sello *m* de plomo; **~ shot** perdigonada *f*.

lead[2] [liːd] **1** *n* (**a**) (*front position*) delantera *f*, cabeza *f*; (*leading position, Sport*) liderato *m*; (*distance, time ahead*) ventaja *f*; **to be in the ~** ir en cabeza, ir primero; (*in league etc*) ocupar el primer puesto; **to take the ~** tomar la delantera, tomar el mando; (*Sport*) tomar la delantera, tomar la cabeza; **to have 2 minutes' ~ over sb** llevar a uno una ventaja de 2 minutos; **to have a ~ of half a length** tener medio cuerpo de ventaja.

(**b**) (*example*) ejemplo *m*; iniciativa *f*; **to follow sb's ~** seguir el ejemplo de uno; **to give sb a ~** guiar a uno, dar el ejemplo a uno, mostrar el camino a uno; **to take the ~** tomar la iniciativa (*in* en, *in doing* en hacer).

(**c**) (*clue*) pista *f*, indicación *f*; **the police have a ~** la policía tiene una pista; **it gave the police a ~ to the criminal** puso a la policía sobre la pista del criminal; **give me a ~** (*in guessing*) ¿me puedes dar alguna indicación?

(**d**) (*Cards*) **it's my ~** soy mano, salgo yo; **whose ~ is it?** ¿quién sale?; **if the ~ is in hearts** si la salida es a corazones.

(**e**) (*Theat*) papel *m* principal; (*in opera*) voz *f* cantante; (*person*) primer actor *m*, primera actriz *f*; **with Garbo in the ~** con la Garbo en el primer papel; **~ singer** cantante *mf*; **to play the ~** tener el papel principal; **to sing the ~** llevar la voz cantante.

(**f**) (*leash*) traílla *f*, cuerda *f*, correa *f* (*LAm*).

(**g**) (*Elec*) conductor *m*, cable *m* (eléctrico).

(**h**) (*Press*) primer párrafo *m*, entrada *f*.

2 *attr*: **~ story** reportaje *m* principal, noticia *f* más sobresaliente; **~ time** margen *m* de tiempo; tiempo *m* desde el pedido hasta la entrega.

3 (*irr*: *pret and ptp* **led**) *vt* (**a**) (*conduct*) conducir; llevar; guiar; **to ~ sb to a table** conducir a uno a una mesa; **kindly ~ me to him** haga el favor de conducirme a su presencia (*or* de llevarme donde está); **each reference led me to another** cada referencia me llevó a otra; **one thing led to another** una cosa nos (*etc*) llevó a otra; **this ~s me to an important point** esto me lleva a un punto importante; **what led you to Venice?** ¿qué te llevó a Venecia?, ¿con qué motivo fuiste a Venecia?; **to ~ the way** ir primero, (*fig*) dar el ejemplo, mostrar el camino; **he is easily led** es muy sugestionable; **they led him into the king's presence** le condujeron ante el rey; **to ~ sb into error** inducir a uno a error.

(**b**) (*be the leader of, govern*) *government* dirigir, encabezar; *party* encabezar, ser el jefe de; *expedition, regiment* mandar; *team* capitanear; *movement, revolution* encabezar, acaudillar; *orchestra* (*Brit*) ser primer violín de, (*US*) dirigir; *league, procession* ir a la cabeza de, encabezar.

(**c**) (*be first in*) ser el primero en, sobresalir en, ocupar el primer puesto en; **to ~ the field** ir el primero de todos, estar a la cabeza, ganar; **they led us by 30 seconds** nos llevaban una ventaja de 30 segundos; **A ~s B by 4 games to 1** A aventaja a B por 4 juegos a 1; **Britain led the world in textiles** en la industria textil Inglaterra superaba a los demás, en los textiles Inglaterra ocupaba el primer puesto.

(**d**) *card* salir con, salir de.

(**e**) *life* llevar; **to ~ a strange life** llevar una vida muy rara; **to ~ sb a wretched life** amargar la vida a uno, tratar a uno como una basura; *V also* **dance, life**.

(**f**) (*induce*) **to ~ sb to do sth** inducir (*or* llevar, inclinar, persuadir, mover) a uno a hacer algo; **to ~ sb to believe that ...** hacer creer a uno que ...; **I am led to the conclusion that ...** llego a la conclusión de que ...

4 *vi* (**a**) (*go in front*) llevar la delantera, ir primero; **~ on!** ¡adelante!; **to ~ by 10 metres** tener una ventaja de 10 metros; **he easily ~s** sobresale, supera fácilmente a los demás.

(**b**) (*be in command*) tener el mando, ser el jefe.

(**c**) (*Cards*) ser mano, salir; **who ~s?** ¿quién sale?; **South ~s** Sur sale.

(**d**) (*of street etc*) **to ~ to** conducir a, llevar a, salir a, desembocar en; **this street ~s to the station** esta calle conduce a la estación, por esta calle se va a la estación; **where does this corridor ~?** ¿adónde conduce este pasillo?; **it ~s into that room** comunica con ese cuarto.

(**e**) (*result in*) dar, producir; **it led to a result** dio un resultado; **it led to a change** produjo un cambio; **it led to nothing** no dio resultado, no surtió efecto, no condujo a nada; **it led to his arrest** dio lugar a su detención; **it led to war** causó la guerra.

◆**lead along** *vt* llevar (por la mano *etc*).

◆**lead away** *vt* conducir a otra parte, llevar fuera; **he was led away by the police** se lo llevó la policía; **we must not be led away from the main issue** no nos apartemos del asunto principal.

◆**lead back 1** *vt*: **to ~ sb back** hacer volver a uno, conducir a uno a donde estaba; **this road ~s you back to**

Jaca por este camino se vuelve a Jaca.

2 *vi*: **this road ~s back to Burgos** por este camino se vuelve a Burgos; **it all ~s back to the butler** todo nos lleva de nuevo al mayordomo (como sospechoso).

◆**lead in 1** *vt* hacer entrar a.

2 *vi*: **this is a way of ~ing in** ésta es una manera de introducir el argumento (*etc*).

◆**lead off 1** *vt* (**a**) = **lead away**.

(**b**) **the streets that ~ off (from) the square** las calles que salen de la plaza; **a room ~ing off (from) another** un cuarto que comunica con otro.

2 *vi* (*begin*) empezar; (*Sport*) comenzar, abrir el juego; (*Cards*) salir (*with* con).

◆**lead on 1** *vt* (*persuade*) engatusar, halagar; (*amorously*) coquetear con, ir dando esperanzas a; (*morally*) seducir; (*make talk*) hacer hablar a, tirar de la lengua a; **this led him on to say that ...** esto hizo que dijera a continuación que ...

2 *vi* ir primero, ir a la cabeza; **you ~ on** tú primero; **~ on!** ¡vamos!

◆**lead out** *vt* conducir fuera, llevar fuera; **to ~ a girl out to dance** sacar a una chica a bailar.

◆**lead up** *vi* (**a**) **to ~ up to** conducir a; preparar el terreno para; **events that led up to the war** los sucesos que condujeron a la guerra; **what's all this ~ing up to?** ¿qué propósito tiene todo esto?, ¿adónde conduce todo esto?; **he led carefully up to the proposal** preparó el terreno con cuidado antes de formular la propuesta.

(**b**) **the years that led up to the war** los años que precedieron a la guerra.

leaded ['ledɪd] *adj* (**a**) **~ lights** cristales *mpl* emplomados. (**b**) (*also n*) **~ petrol** gasolina *f* con plomo.

leaden ['ledn] *adj* (*of lead*) de plomo, plúmbeo; (*in colour*) plomizo; (*fig*) pesado, triste.

leaden-eyed [ˌledn'aɪd] *adj*: **to be ~** tener los párpados pesados.

leader ['liːdəʳ] *n* (**a**) (*person*: *gen*) jefe *mf*, líder *mf*; (*Pol*) líder *mf*; jefe *mf*, dirigente *mf*; (*esp military*) caudillo *m*; (*of gang*) cuadrillero *m*; (*of rebels*) cabecilla *mf*; (*guide*) guía *mf*, conductor *m*, -ora *f*; (*Brit Mus: of orchestra*) primer violín *m*, (*of band*) director *m*, -ora *f*; (*US Mus*: *of orchestra*) director *m*, -ora *f*; **~ of the opposition** jefe *mf* de la oposición; **~ of the party** jefe *mf* del partido; **a ~ of the masses** un conductor de masas; **our political ~s** nuestros dirigentes políticos.

(**b**) (*Sport*) (*person*) primero *m*, -a *f*; (*in league*) líder *m*; (*horse etc*) caballo *m* (*etc*) delantero, caballo *m* (*etc*) que va en primer lugar.

(**c**) (*Brit Press*) artículo *m* de fondo, editorial *m*.

(**d**) (*Comm*: *company, product*) líder *m*; (*share*) acción *f* líder; (*indicator*) índice *m*, indicador *m* (económico).

leaderene [ˌliːdə'riːn] *n* (*hum*) líder *f*.

leadership ['liːdəʃɪp] *n* (**a**) (*persons, office*) jefatura *f*, dirección *f*; mando *m*; liderato *m*, liderazgo *m*; protagonismo *m*; caudillaje *m*; **under the ~ of** bajo la jefatura de; **a crisis in the ~** una crisis de dirección, una crisis en la dirigencia; **to resign the ~** dimitir la jefatura; **to take over the ~** asumir la dirección, tomar el mando.

(**b**) (*quality*) iniciativa *f*; (*powers of* ~) dotes *fpl* de mando.

leader-writer ['liːdəˌraɪtəʳ] *n* (*Brit*) editorialista *mf*.

lead-free [ˌled'friː] *adj* sin plomo.

lead-in ['liːd'ɪn] *n* introducción *f*; entrada *f*; **a useful ~ to a discussion** una manera útil de introducir una discusión.

leading ['liːdɪŋ] *adj* (**a**) (*front*) delantero; *wheel* delantero, conductor; **~ edge** (*Aer*) borde *m* de ataque; **~ edge technology** tecnología *f* punta.

(**b**) *part, person, idea etc* principal, importante; (*outstanding*) sobresaliente, destacado; (*in race*) primero, delantero; **~ article** (*Brit*) artículo *m* de fondo, editorial *m*; **~ brand** marca *f* líder; **~ lady** primera actriz *f*; **~ light** figura *f* principal; **~ man** primer galán *m*; **~ note** sensible *f*; **~ product** producto *m* líder; **~ role** papel *m* principal; **~ supplier** proveedor *m* líder.

(**c**) **~ question** (*Jur*) pregunta *f* inductiva; **~ strings** andadores *mpl*.

leaf [liːf] **1** *n, pl* **leaves** [liːvz] hoja *f*; **~ tobacco** tabaco *m* en rama; **to come into ~** echar hojas, cubrirse de hojas; **to take a ~ out of sb's book** seguir el ejemplo de uno; **to turn over a new ~** reformarse, cambiar de modo de ser, hacer vida nueva.

2 *vi* (*Bot*) echar hojas.

◆**leaf through** *vt*: **to ~ through a book** hojear un libro, trashojar un libro.

leaf bud ['liːfbʌd] *n* yema *f*.

leafless ['liːflɪs] *adj* sin hojas, deshojado.

leaflet ['liːflɪt] **1** *n* folleto *m*, hoja *f* volante; prospecto *m*. **2** *vt*: **to ~ a constituency** (*Pol*) repartir folletos en un distrito.

leaf mould, (*US*) **leaf mold** ['liːfməʊld] *n* mantillo *m* (de hojas), abono *m* verde.

leafy ['liːfɪ] *adj* frondoso.

league¹ [liːg] *n* (*measure*) legua *f*.

league² [liːg] **1** *n* liga *f* (*also Sport*); sociedad *f*, asociación *f*, comunidad *f*; **L~ of Nations** Sociedad *f* de las Naciones; **he's not in the same ~** (*fig*) pertenece a otra clase; **to be in ~ with sb** estar de manga con uno, haberse confabulado con uno.

2 *attr*: **~ champions** campeón *m* de liga; **~ leader** líder *m* de la liga; **~ table** clasificación *f*.

leak [liːk] **1** *n* (*hole*) agujero *m*; (*Naut*) vía *f* de agua; (*of blood*) derrame *m*; (*in roof etc*) gotera *f*; (*of gas, liquid*) escape *m*, fuga *f*, pérdida *f*, salida *f*; (*of information, money*) filtración *f*; **to spring a ~** abrirse una vía de agua; **to take a ~‡** hacer aguas‡.

2 *vt* (**a**) rezumar, dejar perderse, derramar; **it's ~ing acid all over the place** se está derramando el ácido por todas partes.

(**b**) *information* filtrar (*to* a).

3 *vi* (**a**) (*ship*) hacer agua; (*receptacle*) rezumarse, tener agujeros, estar agujereado; (*pipe*) tener fugas, dejar fugarse el gas (*etc*); (*pen*) derramar tinta, derramarse.

(**b**) (*gas, liquid etc*) escaparse, fugarse, salirse, irse; (*ooze out*) rezumarse; (*drop by drop*) gotear; (*information, money*) filtrarse.

◆**leak away** *vi* irse, agotarse debido a una fuga.

◆**leak in** *vi* filtrarse, gotear.

◆**leak out** *vi* (**a**) = **leak away**. (**b**) (*news*) filtrarse, divulgarse (sin autorización), llegar a saberse, trascender; **finally it ~ed out that ...** por fin se supo que ...

leakage ['liːkɪdʒ] *n* = **leak**.

leakproof ['liːkpruːf] *adj* estanco, hermético.

leaky ['liːkɪ] *adj boat* que hace agua, que tiene vías de agua; *roof* que tiene goteras; *receptacle* agujereado, defectuoso; *organization* muy sujeto a filtraciones.

lean¹ [liːn] **1** *adj* (*thin*) flaco; magro; *face* enjuto; *meat* magro; *year* difícil, de carestía; **a ~er and fitter economy** una economía más enjuta y más dinámica; **the ~ years** los años de las vacas flacas; **to grow ~** enflaquecer.

2 *n* carne *f* magra.

lean² [liːn] **1** *n* inclinación *f*.

2 (*irr*: *pret and ptp* **leaned** *or* **leant**) *vt* ladear, inclinar, poner oblicuamente; **to ~ a ladder against a wall** poner (*or* apoyar) una escala contra una pared; **to ~ one's head on sb's shoulder** apoyar la cabeza en el hombro de uno.

3 *vi* ladearse, inclinarse, estar ladeado, estar inclinado; **to ~ against sth** apoyarse en algo; **to ~ on sth** apoyarse en algo (*also fig*); **to ~ on sb for support** contar con el apoyo de uno; **to ~ on sb*** ejercer presión sobre uno, intimidar a uno, amenazar a uno; **to ~ to the Left** inclinarse a la izquierda; **to ~ towards sb's opinion** inclinarse hacia la opinión de uno.

◆**lean back** *vi* reclinarse, echar el cuerpo atrás.

◆**lean forward** *vi* inclinarse.

◆**lean out** *vi* asomarse (*of* a).

◆**lean over 1** *vt*: **to ~ over sb** inclinarse sobre uno.

2 *vi* inclinarse; **to ~ over backwards to help sb** volcarse por ayudar a uno, desvivirse por ayudar a uno; **we have ~ed over backwards to get agreement** hemos hecho todas las concesiones posibles para llegar a un acuerdo.

Leander [liː'ændəʳ] *nm* Leandro.

leaning ['liːnɪŋ] **1** *adj* inclinado; **the L~ Tower of Pisa** la Torre Inclinada de Pisa.

2 *n* inclinación *f* (*to, towards* hacia); tendencia *f*, propensión *f* (*to* a); predilección *f* (*to, towards* por); **what are his ~s?** ¿cuál es su predilección?; **he has artistic ~s** se siente atraído por una carrera artística.

leanness ['liːnnɪs] *n* flaqueza *f*; magrez *f*; carestía *f*, pobreza *f*.

leant [lent] *pret and ptp of* **lean²**.

lean-to ['liːntuː] *n* colgadizo *m*, alpende *m*.

leap [liːp] **1** *n* salto *m*, brinco *m*; (*fig*) salto *m*; **the great ~ forward** (*China*) el gran salto hacia adelante; **~ in the dark** salto *m* en el vacío; **by ~s and bounds** a pasos agigantados; **in one ~** de un salto.

2 (*irr*: *pret and ptp* **leaped** *or* **leapt**) *vt* saltar, saltar por encima de.

3 *vi* saltar, brincar, dar un salto; (*of fish*) saltar, bañarse; **my heart ~ed** mi corazón dio un vuelco; **to ~ at a chance** agarrar (con ambas manos) una oportunidad; **to ~ at an offer** apresurarse a aceptar una oferta; **to ~ down** bajar de un salto, saltar en tierra; **to ~ for joy** saltar de alegría; **to ~ out of a car** saltar de un coche; **the answer ~t out at me** (*or* **off the page**) la solución se ofreció de golpe; **to ~ over** saltar, saltar por (encima de), salvar; **to ~ to one's feet** ponerse de pie de un salto.

◆**leap about** *vi* dar saltos, brincar.

◆**leap up** *vi* (*person*) ponerse de pie de un salto, (*flame*) subir de repente, brotar, (*figure etc*) subir de punto.

leapfrog ['li:pfrɒg] **1** *n* pídola *f*, fil *m* derecho, saltacabrilla *f*; **to play ~** jugar a la pídola. **2** *vt* saltar por encima de (*also fig*). **3** *vi* jugar a la pídola, saltar.

leapt [lept] *pret and ptp of* **leap.**

leap year ['li:pjɪəʳ] *n* año *m* bisiesto.

learn [lɜ:n] (*irr*: *pret and ptp* **learned** *or* **learnt**) *vti* (**a**) (*in general*) aprender; *news, fact etc* saber, enterarse de; (*discover, find out*) descubrir, averiguar; **he'll ~!** ¡un día aprenderá!; **to ~ to do sth** aprender a hacer algo; **to ~ how to do sth** aprender a hacer algo, aprender cómo se hace algo, aprender el modo de hacer algo; **he's ~ing the hard way** aprende por el método duro; **to ~ about sth** (*hear of*) saber algo, (*instruct o.s.*) informarse sobre algo, instruirse en algo; **to ~ from experience** aprender por experiencia; **to ~ from others' mistakes** escarmentar en cabeza ajena; **to ~ of** saber, tener noticia de.

(**b**) (‡) enseñar; **I'll ~ you!** ¡yo te enseñaré!

◆**learn off** *vt* aprender de memoria.

◆**learn up** *vt* esforzarse por aprender, repasar, empollar.

learned ['lɜ:nɪd] *adj person* docto, sabio, erudito; *remark, speech* erudito; *profession* liberal; **~ body** academia *f*; **~ society** sociedad *f* científica; **to be ~ in** ser erudito en, ser muy entendido en.

learnedly ['lɜ:nɪdlɪ] *adv* eruditamente.

learner ['lɜ:nəʳ] *n* principiante *mf*, aprendiz *m*, -iza *f* (*also Brit Aut*); (*student*) estudiante *mf*, estudioso *m*, -a *f*.

learner-driver ['lɜ:nə'draɪvəʳ] *n* (*Brit*) aprendiz *m* de conductor, aprendiza *f* de conductora.

learning ['lɜ:nɪŋ] *n* (**a**) (*act*) el aprender, aprendizaje *m*, estudio *m*; **~ difficulties** dificultades *fpl* de aprendizaje. (**b**) (*fund of ~*) saber *m*, conocimientos *mpl*; (*erudition*) saber *m*, erudición *f*; **man of ~** sabio *m*, erudito *m*; **seat of ~** centro *m* de estudios.

learnt [lɜ:nt] *pret and ptp of* **learn.**

lease [li:s] **1** *n* arriendo *m*, contrato *m* de arrendamiento; **to take a house on a 99-year ~** tomar una casa con un contrato de arriendo de 99 años; **to let sth out on ~** dar algo en arriendo; **to give sb a new ~ of life** (*Brit*) devolver la vitalidad a uno, servir de tónico a uno; sacar a uno a flote; **to take on a new ~ of life** (*person*) recobrar su vigor, (*thing*) renovarse.

2 *vt* (*take*) arrendar (*from* de), tomar en arriendo; (*give*: *also* **to ~ out**) arrendar, dar en arriendo.

◆**lease back** *vt* subarrendar.

leaseback ['li:sbæk] *n* rearrendamiento *m* al vendedor, subarriendo *m*.

leasehold ['li:shəʊld] **1** *n* (*contract*) arrendamiento *m*; (*property*) inmueble *m* arrendado.

2 *attr* arrendado, alquilado; **~ reform** reforma *f* del sistema de arriendos.

leaseholder ['li:shəʊldəʳ] *n* arrendatario *m*, -a *f*.

leash [li:ʃ] *n* traílla *f*, cuerda *f*.

leasing ['li:sɪŋ] *n* (*option to buy*) alquiler *m* con opción a compra, leasing *m*; (*renting*) arrendamiento *m*, alquiler *m*; (*Fin*) arrendamiento *m* financiero.

least [li:st] **1** *adj* menor; más pequeño; mínimo; menos importante, menos considerable; **the ~ of them** el menor de ellos; **with the ~ possible expenditure** gastándose lo menos posible; **that's the ~ of my worries** eso es lo de menos; **not the ~ of her qualities was ...** no era la menos importante de sus cualidades ...

2 *adv* menos; **the ~ expensive car** el coche menos costoso; **he deserves it ~ of all** se lo merece menos que todos los demás; **she is ~ able to afford it** ella es quien menos puede permitírselo; **~ of all would I wish to offend him** ante todo no quiero ofenderle; **nobody knew, ~ of all Jennie** nadie lo sabía, y Jennie menos que todos; **in all countries, not ~ in the USA** en todos los países, y más en EE.UU.

3 *n* lo menos; **it's the ~ one can ask** es lo menos que se puede pedir; **you gave yourself the ~** te has servido la ración más pequeña; **at ~** a lo menos, al menos, por lo menos, cuando menos; **at ~ it's fine** por lo menos hace buen tiempo; **there were 8 at ~** había a lo menos 8; **we can at ~ try** al menos podemos probarlo; **at the very ~** lo menos; **I'm not the ~ bit hungry** no tengo el más mínimo apetito; **not in the ~!** ¡en absoluto!, ¡de ninguna manera!; **he was not in the ~ upset** no se alteró en lo más mínimo; **to say the ~** para no decir más.

leastways* ['li:stweɪz] *adv* de todos modos.

leastwise ['li:stwaɪz] *adv* por lo menos.

leather ['leðəʳ] **1** *n* cuero *m*; piel *f*; (*wash ~*) gamuza *f*. **2** *attr*: **~ goods** artículos *mpl* de cuero; **~ jacket** cazadora *f* de piel (*or* de cuero), chupa‡ *f* de cuero. **3** *vt* (*) zurrar*.

leather-bound ['leðə,baʊnd] *adj* encuadernado en cuero.

leathering* ['leðərɪŋ] *n*: **to give sb a ~** dar una paliza a uno.

leathern ['leðə(:)n] *adj* de cuero.

leatherneck* ['leðənek] *n* (*US*) infante *m* de marina.

leathery ['leðərɪ] *adj* correoso; *skin* curtido.

leave [li:v] **1** *n* (**a**) (*permission*) permiso *m*; **by your ~** con permiso de Vd; **without so much as a 'by your ~'** sin pedir permiso a nadie; **to ask ~ to do sth** pedir permiso para hacer algo; **I take ~ to doubt it** me permito dudarlo.

(**b**) (*permission to be absent*) permiso *m*; (*Mil, brief*) permiso *m*, (*lengthy, compassionate etc*) licencia *f*; **~ of absence** permiso *m* para estar ausente, excedencia *f*; **to be on ~** estar de permiso, estar de licencia.

(**c**) (*departure*) **to take one's ~** despedirse (*of* de); **I must take my ~** tengo que marcharme; **to take ~ of one's senses** perder el juicio; **have you taken ~ of your senses?** ¿se te ha vuelto el juicio?

2 (*irr*: *pret and ptp* **left**) *vt* (**a**) (*allow to remain*) dejar; **to ~ 2 pages blank** dejar 2 páginas en blanco; **let's ~ it at that** dejemos las cosas así; **to ~ sth with sb** dejar algo en manos de uno; entregar algo a uno; **to ~ things lying about** dejar las cosas de cualquier modo; **to ~ one's supper** dejar la cena sin comer; **to ~ one's greens** no comer las verduras; **to ~ a good impression on sb** producir a uno una buena impresión; **it ~s much to be desired** deja mucho que desear; **take it or ~ it** lo tomas o lo dejas, una de dos, o esto o lo otro, como quieras.

(**b**) (*forget*) dejar, olvidar.

(**c**) (*person*) **I'll ~ you at the station** te dejo en la estación; **to ~ a wife and 2 children** dejar una viuda y 2 hijos; **he has left his wife** ha abandonado a su mujer; **I must ~ you** tengo que despedirme de vosotros, con permiso de vosotros me voy; **you may ~ us** Vd puede retirarse; **to ~ sb free for the afternoon** dejar a uno la tarde libre.

(**d**) (*bequeath*) dejar, legar.

(**e**) (*Math*) **3 from 10 ~s 7** de 3 a 10 van 7, 10 menos 3 son 7.

(**f**) (*remain, be over, be left*) quedar; sobrar; **all the money I have left** todo el dinero que me queda; **how many are there left?** ¿cuántos quedan?; **we were left with 4** quedamos con 4, nos quedaron 4; **nothing was left for me but to sell it** no tuve más remedio que venderlo; **there are 3 left over** sobran 3.

(**g**) (*entrust*) **I ~ it to you** le toca a Vd decidir, que lo decida Vd; **~ it to me** yo me encargo de eso; **I ~ it to you to do** lo dejo en sus manos; que lo haga Vd; **I ~ it to you to judge** júzguelo Vd.

(**h**) (*depart from, quit*) salir de, abandonar; dejar; **to ~ a place** salir de un lugar, abandonar un lugar; **when the king left Rome** cuando el rey abandonó Roma; **to ~ home** salir de su casa; **to ~ prison** salir de la cárcel; **to ~ school** salir del colegio; **to ~ the table** levantarse de la mesa; **to ~ one's post** dejar su puesto, dimitir su cargo, (*improperly*) abandonar su puesto; **to ~ the road** salir fuera de la carretera; **to ~ the rails** descarrilar.

3 *vi* irse, marcharse; salir (*for* para); (*of train etc*) salir.

4 *vr*: **he left himself with two problems** se quedó con dos problemas.

◆**leave about, leave around** *vt* dejar tirado.

◆**leave aside** *vt* dejar de lado, omitir; prescindir de; **leaving that aside, let's consider ...** dejando eso de lado, consideremos ...

◆**leave behind** *vt* (**a**) (*not take*) *person* dejar, no llevar consigo; **we have left all that behind us** todo eso ha quedado a la espalda; **he left the children behind** no llevó consigo a los niños, dejó allí a los niños.

(**b**) (*forget*) olvidar, dejar.

(**c**) (*outdistance*) dejar atrás.

◆**leave in** *vt passage, words* dejar tal como está, conservar; *plug etc* dejar puesto.

◆**leave off 1** *vt* (**a**) (*stop*) *habit* renunciar a, dejar; *work* terminar, suspender; **to ~ off smoking** dejar de fumar; **to ~ off working** dejar de trabajar; terminar de trabajar; **when it ~s off raining** cuando deje de llover.

(**b**) *lid* no poner, dejar sin poner; *clothes* quitarse, no ponerse.

(**c**) *gas etc* no poner, no encender.

2 *vi* terminar, cesar; suspender el trabajo (*etc*); **when the rain ~s off** cuando deje de llover; **~ off, will you?** ¡déjalo!

◆**leave on** *vt* (**a**) *lid etc* dejar puesto; **to ~ one's hat on** seguir con el sombrero puesto, no quitarse el sombrero.

(**b**) *gas, light* dejar puesto, dejar encendido, dejar prendido (*LAm*).

◆**leave out** *vt* (**a**) (*omit*) omitir, suprimir; prescindir de; *person* dejar fuera; **poor Jane felt left out** la pobre de Jane se sentía excluida; **nobody wanted to be left out** nadie quería quedar fuera.

(**b**) (*not put back*) dejar fuera; no devolver a su lugar; **it got left out in the rain** quedó fuera bajo la lluvia; **the cat was left out all night** el gato pasó toda la noche fuera.

◆**leave over** *vt* (**a**) (*remain*) quedar; **there's nothing left over** no queda nada.

(**b**) (*postpone*) dejar, posponer.

leaven ['levn] **1** *n* levadura *f*; (*fig*) mezcla *f*; estímulo *m*. **2** *vt* leudar; (*fig*) penetrar e influenciar, servir de estímulo a, ayudar a transformar.

leavening ['levnıŋ] *n* levadura *f*; (*fig*) mezcla *f*, estímulo *m*.

leaves [li:vz] *npl of* **leaf.**

leave-taking ['li:v,teıkıŋ] *n* despedida *f*.

leaving ['li:vıŋ] **1** *adj ceremony, present* de despedida. **2** *n* (*departure*) salida *f*.

leavings ['li:vıŋz] *npl* sobras *fpl*, restos *mpl*.

Lebanese [,lebə'ni:z] **1** *adj* libanés. **2** *n* libanés *m*, -esa *f*.

Lebanon ['lebənən] *n* Líbano *m*.

lecher ['letʃə^r] *n* libertino *m*.

lecherous ['letʃərəs] *adj* lascivo, lujurioso.

lecherously ['letʃərəslı] *adv* lascivamente.

lechery ['letʃərı] *n* lascivia *f*, lujuria *f*.

lectern ['lektə(:)n] *n* atril *m*; (*Eccl*) facistol *m*.

lector ['lektɔ:^r] *n* (*Univ*) lector *m*, -ora *f*.

lecture ['lektʃə^r] **1** *n* (*formal, by visitor etc*) conferencia *f*; (*Univ class*) clase *f*; explicación *f*; (*fig*) sermoneo *m*; **to attend ~s on** seguir un curso sobre (*or* de); **to give a ~** dar una conferencia; **to read sb a ~** sermonear a uno.

2 *attr*: **~ course** ciclo *m* de conferencias; **~ notes** apuntes *mpl* de clase.

3 *vt* (*scold*) sermonear; **he ~s us in French** nos da clases de francés.

4 *vi* dar una conferencia, dar una clase; **he ~s in Law** da clases de derecho; **to ~ on** (*Univ*) dar un curso sobre, explicar; **he ~s at 9 o'clock** da su clase a las 9; **he ~s at Princeton** es profesor en Princeton; **he's lecturing at the moment** ahora está en clase; **he ~s well** habla muy bien.

lecture-hall ['lektʃə,hɔ:l] *n* = **lecture-room.**

lecturer ['lektʃərə^r] *n* (*visitor*) conferenciante *mf*, conferencista *mf*; (*Brit Univ*) profesor *m*, -ora *f*.

lecture-room ['lektʃə,rʊm] *n*, **lecture-theater** ['lektʃə,θıətə^r] *n* (*US*) sala *f* de conferencias; (*Univ*) aula *f*.

lectureship ['lektʃəʃıp] *n* cargo *m* (*or* puesto *m*) de profesor (adjunto).

LED *n abbr of* **light-emitting diode** diodo *m* emisor de luz.

led [led] *pret and ptp of* **lead.**

ledge [ledʒ] *n* repisa *f*, reborde *m*; (*along wall*) retallo *m*; (*of window*) antepecho *m*, alféizar *m*; (*shelf*) anaquel *m*; (*on mountain*) plataforma *f*, saliente *m*, cama *f* de roca.

ledger ['ledʒə^r] *n* libro *m* mayor.

ledger line ['ledʒə,laın] *n* línea *f* suplementaria.

lee [li:] **1** *adj* a sotavento, de sotavento. **2** *n* sotavento *m*; (*shelter*) socaire *m*; **in the ~ of** al socaire de, al abrigo de.

leech [li:tʃ] *n* sanguijuela *f* (*also fig*).

leek [li:k] *n* puerro *m*.

leer [lıə^r] **1** *n* mirada *f* impúdica, mirada *f* maliciosa; sonrisa *f* impúdica; **he said with a ~** dijo sonriendo impúdico.

2 *vi* mirar impúdico, mirar malicioso (*at sb* a uno); sonreír impúdico (*at sb* a uno).

leery ['lıərı] *adj* (*US*) cauteloso; sospechoso; **to be ~ of** recelar de.

lees [li:z] *npl* heces *fpl*, poso *m*.

leeward ['li:wəd] **1** *adj* a sotavento, de sotavento.

2 *adv* a sotavento.

3 *n* sotavento *m*; **to ~** a sotavento (*of* de).

Leeward Isles ['li:wəd,aılz] *npl* Islas *fpl* de Sotavento.

leeway ['li:weı] *n* (*Naut*) deriva *f*; (*fig*: *scope*) libertad *f* de acción; (*fig*: *backlog etc*) atraso *m*, tiempo *m* (*etc*) perdido; **to make up ~** salir del atraso, recuperar el tiempo perdido.

left¹ [left] *pret and ptp of* **leave.**

left² [left] **1** *adj* (**a**) izquierdo; **~ back** defensa *m* izquierdo, defensa *f* izquierda; **~ half** medio *m* izquierda, medio *m* volante izquierda; **~ wing** (*Mil, Sport*) ala *f* izquierda.

(**b**) (*Pol*) izquierdista.

2 *adv* a la izquierda, hacia la izquierda; **we are a ~ of centre party** somos un partido del centro izquierdo; **they were coming at us ~, right, and centre** nos atacaban desde todas partes.

3 *n* (**a**) izquierda *f*; **on the ~, to the ~** a la izquierda; **to keep to the ~** (*Aut*) circular por la izquierda.

(**b**) (*Pol*) izquierda *f*, izquierdas *fpl*; **he has always been on the ~** siempre ha sido de izquierdas; **he's further to the ~ than I am** es más izquierdista que yo.

(**c**) (*Boxing*) izquierdazo *m*.

left-hand ['lefthænd] *adj*: **~ drive** conducción *f* por la izquierda; **~ page** página *f* izquierda; **~ side** izquierda *f*; **~ turn** vuelta *f* a la izquierda.

left-handed ['left'hændıd] *adj* zurdo; (*fig*) *person* torpe, desmañado; *compliment* ambiguo, de doble filo; *marriage* de la mano izquierda, morganático; *tool* para zurdo.

left-hander [,left'hændə^r] *n* zurdo *m*, -a *f*.

leftism ['leftızəm] *n* izquierdismo *m*.

leftist ['leftıst] **1** *adj* izquierdista. **2** *n* izquierdista *mf*.

left-luggage ['left'lʌgıdʒ] **1** *n* (*also* **~ office**) (*Brit*) consigna *f*. **2** *attr*: **~ locker** (*Brit*) consigna *f* automática.

left-over ['leftəʊvə^r] **1** *adj* sobrante, restante. **2** *n* (**a**) (*survivor*) superviviente *mf*; **a ~ from another age** una reliquia de otra edad. (**b**) **~s** sobras *fpl*, restos *mpl*.

leftward ['leftwəd] *adj movement etc* a (*or* hacia) la izquierda.

leftward(s) ['leftwəd(z)] *adv move etc* a (*or* hacia) la izquierda.

left-wing ['left,wıŋ] *adj* izquierdista.

left-winger ['left'wıŋə^r] *n* izquierdista *mf*.

lefty* ['leftı] *n* (*Pol*) izquierdista *mf*, rojillo *m*, -a *f*.

leg [leg] **1** *n* (**a**) (*Anat*) pierna *f*; (*of animal, bird, furniture*) pata *f*; (*support*) pie *m*; (*of trousers*) pernera *f*; (*of stocking*) caña *f*; (*of pork*) pernil *m*; (*of lamb, veal, boot*) pierna *f*; **I've been on my ~s all day** he estado trajinando todo el santo día; **to be on one's last ~s** estar en las últimas; **to give sb a ~ up** ayudar a uno a subir (*also fig*); **he hasn't a ~ to stand on** no tiene razón alguna, no hay nada que hable a su favor; **to pull sb's ~*** tomar el pelo a uno*; **to shake a ~*** bailar; **to show a ~*** despertar, levantarse; **show a ~!*** ¡a levantarse!; **to stand on one's own two ~s** (*fig*) ser independiente; **to stretch one's ~s** estirar las piernas, (*after stiffness*) desentumecerse las piernas, (*fig*) dar un paseíto; **to take to one's ~s** poner pies en polvorosa, echar a correr; **to walk sb off his ~s** dejar a uno rendido tras una larguísima caminata.

(**b**) (*of competition*) etapa *f*, fase *f*; vuelta *f*; **first ~** primera vuelta *f*.

2 *vt*: **to ~ it** ir andando, ir a pie.

legacy ['legəsı] *n* legado *m*; (*fig*) herencia *f*, patrimonio *m*.

legal ['li:gəl] *adj* (**a**) (*lawful*) lícito, legítimo. (**b**) (*relating to the law*) legal; *department, entity, inquiry* jurídico; *matter* de derecho; **~ action** demanda *f* judicial; **to take ~ action against sb** entablar una demanda judicial contra uno; **~ advice** asesoría *f* jurídica; **~ aid** asistencia *f* letrada; **~ costs** costas *fpl*; **~ holiday** (*US*) fiesta *f* oficial; **~ owner** propietario *m*, -a *f* en derecho; **~ profession** abogacía *f*; **~ tender** moneda *f* de curso legal.

legalese [,li:gə'li:z] *n* jerga *f* legal.

legalistic [,li:gə'lıstık] *adj* legalista.

legality [lı'gælıtı] *n* legalidad *f*.

legalization [,li:gəlaı'zeıʃən] *n* legalización *f*.

legalize ['li:gəlaız] *vt* legalizar; autorizar, legitimar.

legally ['li:gəlı] *adv* según la ley, según el derecho; legalmente; **~ enforceable** legalmente ejecutable; **to be ~ responsible for sth** tener responsabilidad legal por algo; *V* **binding.**

legate ['legıt] *n* legado *m*.

legatee [,legə'ti:] *n* legatario *m*, -a *f*.

legation [lı'geıʃən] *n* legación *f*.

legato [lı'gɑ:təʊ] (*Mus*) **1** *adj* ligado.

2 *adv* ligado.

3 *n* ligadura *f*.

leg-bone ['legbəʊn] *n* tibia *f*.

legend ['ledʒənd] *n* leyenda *f*.

legendary ['ledʒəndərı] *adj* legendario.

legerdemain [ˈledʒədəˈmeɪn] *n* juego *m* de manos, prestidigitación *f*; (*fig*) trapacería *f*.

-legged [ˈlegɪd] *adj* de piernas ..., *eg* **long~** de piernas largas, zancudo; **three~** de tres piernas, *stool* de tres patas.

leggings [ˈlegɪŋz] *npl* polainas *fpl*; (*baby's*) pantalones *mpl* polainas.

leggy [ˈlegɪ] *adj* zanquilargo, zancudo, patilargo; *girl* de piernas largas; de piernas atractivas.

Leghorn [ˈlegˈhɔːn] *n* Livorno *m*, (*Hist*) Liorna *f*.

legibility [ˌledʒɪˈbɪlɪtɪ] *n* legibilidad *f*.

legible [ˈledʒəbl] *adj* legible.

legibly [ˈledʒəblɪ] *adv* legiblemente.

legion [ˈliːdʒən] *n* legión *f* (*also fig*); **they are ~** son legión, son muchos.

legionary [ˈliːdʒənərɪ] **1** *adj* legionario. **2** *n* legionario *m*.

legionnaire [ˌliːdʒəˈnɛəʳ] *n* legionario *m*; **~'s disease** enfermedad *f* del legionario, legionella *f*.

leg-iron [ˈlegˌaɪən] *n* aparato *m* ortopédico.

legislate [ˈledʒɪsleɪt] **1** *vt*: **to ~ sth out of existence** matar algo con legislación.

2 *vi* legislar; **one cannot ~ for every case** es imposible legislar para todo.

legislation [ˌledʒɪsˈleɪʃən] *n* legislación *f*.

legislative [ˈledʒɪslətɪv] *adj* legislativo; **~ action** tramitación *f* legislativa; **~ body** cuerpo *m* legislativo.

legislator [ˈledʒɪsleɪtəʳ] *n* legislador *m*, -ora *f*.

legislature [ˈledʒɪslətʃəʳ] *n* cuerpo *m* legislativo, asamblea *f* legislativa.

legist [ˈliːdʒɪst] *n* legista *m*.

legit‡ [ləˈdʒɪt] *adj* = **legitimate**.

legitimacy [lɪˈdʒɪtɪməsɪ] *n* legitimidad *f*.

legitimate 1 [lɪˈdʒɪtɪmɪt] *adj* legítimo; (*proper*) admisible, justo; **the ~ theatre** el teatro teatro, el teatro propiamente dicho, el teatro verdadero.

2 [lɪˈdʒɪtɪmeɪt] *vt* legitimar.

legitimately [lɪˈdʒɪtɪmɪtlɪ] *adv* legítimamente; admisiblemente, justamente.

legitimation [lɪˌdʒɪtɪˈmeɪʃn] *n* legitimación *f*.

legitimize [lɪˈdʒɪtɪmaɪz] *vt* = **legitimate 2**.

legless [ˈleglɪs] *adj* sin piernas; sin patas; (*) borracho.

legman [ˈlegmæn] *n*, *pl* **legmen** [ˈlegmen] reportero *m*, -a *f*.

leg-pull* [ˈlegpʊl] *n* broma *f*, tomadura *f* de pelo*.

leg-puller* [ˈlegpʊləʳ] *n* bromista *mf*.

leg-pulling* [ˈlegˌpʊlɪŋ] *n* tomadura *f* de pelo*.

legroom [ˈlegrʊm] *n* espacio *m* para las piernas.

leg-show [ˈlegʃəʊ] *n* exhibición *f* de piernas, varietés *mpl*.

legume [ˈlegjuːm] *n* (*species*) legumbre *f*; (*pod*) vaina *f*.

leguminous [leˈgjuːmɪnəs] *adj* leguminoso.

legwarmers [ˈlegˌwɔːməz] *npl* calientapiernas *fpl*, calentadores *mpl* de piernas.

legwork [ˈlegwɜːk] *n* trabajo *m* callejero; **to do the ~** hacer los preparativos.

Leics. *abbr of* **Leicestershire**.

leisure [ˈleʒəʳ] **1** *n* ocio *m*, tiempo *m* libre; **people of ~** gente *f* acomodada, gente *f* con tiempo libre; **a life of ~** una vida regalada; **to be at ~** estar desocupado, no tener nada que hacer; **do it at your ~** hágalo en sus ratos libres, hágalo cuando tenga tiempo; **to have the ~ to do sth** disponer de bastante tiempo para hacer algo.

2 *attr*: **~ centre** polideportivo *m*; **~ industry** industria *f* que produce lo que pide la gente para ocupar su tiempo libre; **~ occupation** pasatiempo *m*, modo *m* de ocuparse durante los ratos libres; **in one's ~ time** en sus ratos libres, en los momentos de ocio; **~ suit** conjunto *m* tipo chandal; **~ wear** ropa *f* de sport.

leisured [ˈleʒəd] *adj pace* pausado; *class* acomodado.

leisurely [ˈleʒəlɪ] **1** *adj* pausado, lento. **2** *adv* pausadamente, despacio, con calma.

leitmotiv [ˈlaɪtməʊˌtiːf] *n* leitmotiv *m*.

lemma [ˈlemə], *pl* **~s** *or* **lemmata** [ˈlemətə] *n* lema *m*.

lemmatization [ˌlemətaɪˈzeɪʃən] *n* lematización *f*.

lemming [ˈlemɪŋ] *n* lem(m)ing *m*.

lemon [ˈlemən] **1** *n* (**a**) (*fruit*) limón *m*; (*tree*) limonero *m*. (**b**) (*drink*) limonada *f*. (**c**) (*) bobo *m*, -a *f*; **I felt a bit of a ~** aparecía como bastante tonto; **you ~!** ¡bobo! **2** *attr* de limón; limonero; (*colour*) limonado, (de) color limón, alimonado. **3** *adj* = **2**.

lemonade [ˌleməˈneɪd] *n* limonada *f*.

lemon cheese [ˌlemənˈtʃiːz] *n*, **lemon curd** [ˌlemənˈkɜːd] *n* (*Brit*) cuajado *m* de limón.

lemon-grove [ˈlemənɡrəʊv] *n* limonar *m*.

lemon-juice [ˈleməndʒuːs] *n* zumo *m* de limón.

lemon sole [ˌlemənˈsəʊl] *n* (*Brit*) platija *f*.

lemon-squash [ˈleməmˈskwɒʃ] *n* bebida *f* de limón, zumo *m* de limón.

lemon-squeezer [ˈlemənˌskwiːzəʳ] *n* exprimelimones *m*, exprimidor *m*, prensalimones *m*.

lemon tea [ˌlemənˈtiː] *n* té *m* con limón.

lemur [ˈliːməʳ] *n* lémur *m*.

Len [len] *nm familiar form of* **Leonard**.

lend [lend] (*irr*: *pret and ptp* **lent**) **1** *vt* prestar; dejar; (*fig*) prestar, dar, añadir.

2 *vi*: **to ~ at 10%** prestar dinero a 10 por ciento.

3 *vr*: **to ~ o.s. to** prestarse a; **it does not ~ itself to being filmed** no es apto para ser transformado en película.

◆lend out *vt* prestar.

lender [ˈlendəʳ] *n* prestador *m*, -ora *f*; (*professional*) prestamista *mf*.

lending [ˈlendɪŋ] *adj*: **~ library** biblioteca *f* de préstamo; **~ limit** límite *m* de préstamo; **~ policy** política *f* de préstamos; **~ rate** tipo *m* de interés.

length [leŋθ] *n* (**a**) (*gen*) largo *m*, longitud *f*; (*Naut*) eslora *f*; **along the whole ~ of the river** a lo largo de todo el río; **over the ~ and breadth of England** por toda Inglaterra, en toda la extensión de Inglaterra; **the ~ of skirts** el largo de las faldas; **the ~ of this letter** la extensión de esta carta; **to be 4 metres in ~, to have a ~ of 4 metres** tener 4 metros de largo; **what ~ is it?** ¿cuánto tiene de largo?; **what ~ do you want?** ¿cuánto quiere?; **to measure one's ~** (**on the floor**) medir el suelo; **to go to any ~(s)** no pararse en barras; ser capaz de hacer cualquier cosa; **to go to any ~(s) to** + *infin* hacer todo lo posible para + *infin*; **to go to great ~s in** extremarse en; **to go to the ~ of** + *ger* llegar al extremo de + *infin*.

(**b**) (*Sport*: *in race*) cuerpo *m*; **to win by half a ~** ganar por medio cuerpo; **to win by 4 ~s** ganar por 4 cuerpos.

(**c**) (*Sport*: *of pool*) larga *f*; **to swim 40 ~s** nadar 40 largas.

(**d**) (*section*: *of cloth*) corte *m*; (*of road, track etc*) tramo *m*.

(**e**) (*of time*) espacio *m*, extensión *f*, duración *f*; **~ of life** duración *f* de la vida; **~ of service** duración *f* del servicio; **~ of a syllable** cantidad *f* de una sílaba; **for what ~ of time?** ¿durante cuánto tiempo?; **at ~** (*finally*) por fin, finalmente; **to speak at ~** hablar largamente; **to discuss sth at ~** discutir algo detenidamente; **to explain sth at ~** explicar algo por extenso.

lengthen [ˈleŋθən] **1** *vt* alargar, prolongar, extender. **2** *vi* alargarse, prolongarse, extenderse; (*days*) crecer.

lengthily [ˈleŋθɪlɪ] *adv* largamente, extensamente.

length mark [ˈleŋθˌmɑːk] *n* (*Phon*) signo *m* de vocal larga.

lengthways [ˈleŋθweɪz], **lengthwise** [ˈleŋθwaɪz] **1** *adj* longitudinal, de largo.

2 *adv* longitudinalmente; a lo largo; **to measure sth ~** medir el largo de algo.

lengthy [ˈleŋθɪ] *adj* largo, extenso; (*pej*) larguísimo; *illness etc* de larga duración; *meeting* prolongado.

lenience [ˈliːnɪəns] *n*, **leniency** [ˈliːnɪənsɪ] *n* lenidad *f*, poca severidad *f*; indulgencia *f*.

lenient [ˈliːnɪənt] *adj* poco severo, más bien blando; indulgente.

leniently [ˈliːnɪəntlɪ] *adv* con poca severidad, con indulgencia.

Leningrad [ˈlenɪngræd] *n* Leningrado *m*.

Leninism [ˈlenɪnɪzəm] *n* leninismo *m*.

Leninist [ˈlenɪnɪst] **1** *adj* leninista. **2** *n* leninista *mf*.

lenitive [ˈlenɪtɪv] *adj* lenitivo.

lens [lenz] *n* (*Opt, Phot*) lente *f*; (*of camera*) objetivo *m*; (*hand~, for stamps etc*) lupa *f*; (*Anat*) cristalino *m*.

lens cap [ˈlenzkæp] *n* tapa *f* de objetivo.

lens hood [ˈlenshʊd] *n* parasol *m* de objetivo.

Lent [lent] *n* cuaresma *f*.

lent [lent] *pret and ptp of* **lend**.

Lenten [ˈlentən] *adj* cuaresmal.

lentil [ˈlentl] **1** *n* lenteja *f*. **2** *attr*: **~ soup** sopa *f* de lentejas.

Leo [ˈliːəʊ] *n* (*Zodiac*) Leo *m*.

Leon [ˈliːɒn] *n* León *m*.

Leonese [liːəˈniːz] **1** *adj* leonés. **2** *n* (**a**) leonés *m*, -esa *f*. (**b**) (*Ling*) leonés *m*.

leonine [ˈliːənaɪn] *adj* leonino.

leopard [ˈlepəd] *n* leopardo *m*; **the ~ cannot change its spots** genio y figura hasta la sepultura.

leopardskin [ˈlepədskɪn] *n* piel *f* de leopardo.

leotard [ˈlɪətɑːd] *n* leotardo *m*.

leper [ˈlepəʳ] **1** *n* leproso *m*, -a *f* (*also fig*). **2** *attr*: **~ colony** leprosería *f*, colonia *f* de leprosos.

lepidoptera [ˌlepɪˈdɒptərə] *npl* lepidópteros *mpl*.

lepidopterist [ˌlepɪˈdɒptərɪst] *n* lepidopterólogo *m*, -a *f*.
leprechaun [ˈleprəkɔːn] *n* (*Ir*) duende *m*.
leprosy [ˈleprəsɪ] *n* lepra *f*.
leprous [ˈleprəs] *adj* leproso.
lesbian [ˈlezbɪən] **1** *adj* lesbio. **2** *n* lesbiana *f*.
lesbianism [ˈlezbɪənɪzəm] *n* lesbianismo *m*.
lèse-majesté, lese-majesty [ˈleɪzˈmæʒəstɪ] *n* lesa majestad *f*.
lesion [ˈliːʒən] *n* lesión *f*.
Lesotho [lɪˈsuːtuː] *n* Lesoto *m*.
less [les] **1** *adj* (**a**) (*in size, degree etc*) menor, inferior; **a sum ~ than £1** una cantidad inferior a 1 libra; **A or B, whichever is the ~** la menor de las dos cantidades A o B; **it's nothing ~ than a disaster** es nada menos que un desastre; **it's nothing ~ than disgraceful** es francamente vergonzoso; **St James the L~** Santiago el Menor; **no ~ a person than the bishop** no otro que el obispo, el obispo y no otro, el mismísimo obispo; **that was told me by the minister no ~** eso me lo dijo el mismo ministro.
(**b**) (*in quantity*) menos; **now we eat ~ bread** ahora comemos menos pan; **of ~ importance** de menos importancia; **~ noise please!** ¡menos ruido por favor!; **~ of it!** ¡basta ya!; **to grow ~** menguar, decrecer, disminuir.
2 *adv* menos; **~ and ~** cada vez menos; **~ than 6** menos de 6; **in ~ than an hour** en menos de una hora; **he works ~ than I (do)** él trabaja menos que yo; **it's ~ than you think** es menos de lo que piensas; **he is ~ well known** es menos conocido; **the ~ he works the ~ he earns** cuando menos trabaja menos gana; **even ~** menos aun; **still ~** menos todavía; **none the ~** sin embargo, a pesar de todo, con todo; **there will be so much the ~ to pay** tanto menos habrá que pagar; **can't you let me have it for ~?** ¿no me lo puedes dejar en menos?; **the problem is ~ one of capital than of personnel** el problema más que de capitales es de personal.
3 *prep* menos; **the price ~ 10%** el precio menos 10 por ciento; **the price ~ VAT** el precio excluyendo el IVA; **a year ~ 4 days** un año menos 4 días.
-less [lɪs] sin, *eg* **hat~** sin sombrero, **sun~** sin sol.
lessee [leˈsiː] *n* arrendatario *m*, -a *f*, inquilino *m*, -a *f*.
lessen [ˈlesn] **1** *vt* disminuir, reducir, aminorar; *cost, stature etc* rebajar. **2** *vt* disminuir(se), reducirse, menguar.
lessening [ˈlesnɪŋ] *n* disminución *f*, reducción *f*.
lesser [ˈlesəʳ] *adj comp of* **less**; menor, más pequeño; inferior; **to a ~ extent** en menor grado; *V* **evil**.
lesson [ˈlesn] *n* lección *f*; clase *f*; **~s** clases *fpl*; **a French ~** una clase de francés; **to give a ~** dar clase; **to have a ~** tomar lección; **to learn one's ~** (*fig*) escarmentar; **let that be a ~ to you!** ¡que te sirva de lección!, ¡para que aprendas!; **to teach sb a ~** (*fig*) hacer que uno vaya aprendiendo.
lessor [leˈsɔːʳ] *n* arrendador *m*, -ora *f*.
lest [lest] *conj* para que no + *subj*, de miedo que + *subj*; **~ we forget** para que no olvidemos; **~ he catch me unprepared** para que no me coja (*LAm*: agarre) desprevenido; **I feared ~ he should fall** temía que fuera a caer; **I didn't do it ~ sb should object** no lo hice por miedo de que alguien pusiera peros.
let¹ [let] *n* (**a**) (*Tennis*) dejada *f*, let *m*. (**b**) (*Jur*) **without ~ or hindrance** sin estorbo ni obstáculo.
let² [let] (*irr: pret and ptp* **let**) **1** *vt* (**a**) (*permit*) dejar, permitir; **to ~ sb do sth** dejar a uno hacer algo, permitir a uno hacer algo, permitir que uno haga algo; **~ me help you** déjeme ayudarle.
(**b**) *blood* (*surgically*) sacar.
(**c**) (*hire out*) alquilar; **'to ~'** 'se alquila'; **we can't find a house to ~** no encontramos una casa que alquilar.
(**d**) (*v aux, gen translated by subj*) **~ us pray** oremos; **~'s go!** ¡vamos!; **~'s get out here** (*bus, train*) bajémonos aquí; **~ there be light** haya luz; **~ there be no mistake about it** entiéndase bien que ...; **~ them all come!** ¡que vengan todos!; **~ their need be never so great** por muy grande que sea su necesidad; **~ X be 6** supongamos que X equivale a 6.
2 *vi* (*be hired*) alquilarse (*at, for* en).
3 *vr*: **to ~ o.s. be seen** dejarse ver.
◆**let away** *vt*: **to ~ sb away with sth** dejar a uno salirse con la suya.
◆**let by** *vt* dejar pasar.
◆**let down 1** *vt* (**a**) (*lower*) *window etc* bajar; (*on rope*) bajar (*to* a); *hair* soltar, dejar suelto; *dress* alargar; **to ~ sb down on a rope** descolgar a uno con una cuerda.
(**b**) (*disappoint, defraud*) **to ~ sb down** faltar a uno; desilusionar a uno; defraudar la confianza (*or* las esperanzas *etc*) de uno; dejar a uno plantado; **it has never ~ us down yet** no nos ha fallado nunca; **the weather ~ us down** el tiempo nos defraudó; **we all felt ~ down** todos nos sentimos defraudados; **I was badly ~ down** me llevé un gran chasco.
(**c**) **to ~ sb down gently** ser indulgente con uno, castigar a uno con poca severidad.
(**d**) *tyre* desinflar, deshinchar.
2 *vr*: **to ~ o.s. down** no estar a la altura de su fama.
◆**let in 1** *vt* (**a**) (*allow to enter*) dejar entrar; *visitor* hacer pasar; **shoes that ~ in water** zapatos que dejan entrar el agua.
(**b**) (*commit*) **I got ~ in for £50** tuve que pagar (*or* contribuir *etc*) 50 libras; **it ~ us in for a lot of trouble** nos causó muchas molestias, nos planteó muchos problemas.
(**c**) **to ~ sb in on a secret** revelar un secreto a uno; **to ~ sb in on a deal** dejar que uno participe en un trato.
2 *vr*: **you don't know what you're ~ting yourself in for** no sabes lo que te pescas.
◆**let into** *vt* (**a**) **to ~ sb into a house** dejar a uno entrar en una casa.
(**b**) **a plaque ~ into a wall** una lápida empotrada en una pared.
◆**let off** *vt* (**a**) (*fire*) *arrow, gun* disparar; *firework* hacer estallar; *steam* dejar escapar.
(**b**) (*pardon*) perdonar, dejar libre, absolver; **to ~ sb off a duty** perdonar una obligación a uno; **they ~ him off with a warning** le dejaron salir con una amonestación; **he was ~ off with a fine** escapó con una multa.
(**c**) (*allow to leave*) dejar salir.
(**d**) (*hire*) alquilar.
◆**let on*** *vi* revelar el secreto, cantar*; **to ~ on about sth to sb** revelar algo a uno; **he's not ~ting on** no dice nada; **don't go and ~ on about this** de esto no digas ni pío; **he ~ on that ...** reveló que ...
◆**let out** *vt* (**a**) (*allow out*) *person* dejar salir; *prisoner* poner en libertad; *cattle etc* soltar, echar al pasto; **I'll ~ you out** te acompaño a la puerta; **the watchman ~ me out** el sereno me abrió la puerta; **the dog is ~ out at 8** se le deja salir al perro a las 8.
(**b**) *secret* revelar, decir.
(**c**) *fire* dejar que se apague.
(**d**) *dress* ensanchar; *belt* desabrochar.
(**e**) (*hire*) alquilar.
(**f**) (*exonerate*) **that ~s me out** eso me deja libre; **that fact ~s him out** ese hecho le disculpa.
(**g**) (*utter*) *yell* dar.
◆**let past** *vt* = **let by**.
◆**let through** *vt* = **let by**.
◆**let up** *vi* (**a**) (*cease*) terminar, cesar; **when the rain ~s up** cuando deje de llover tanto.
(**b**) (*cease to press*) dejar de presionar, moderarse (*on* en el uso de, en el consumo de); trabajar (*etc*) con menos intensidad; **to ~ up on sb** tratar a uno con menos rigor.
let-down [ˈletdaʊn] *n* decepción *f*, chasco *m*, desilusión *f*.
lethal [ˈliːθəl] *adj* (**a**) mortífero; *wound etc, dose* mortal, letal; *weapon* mortífero. (**b**) (*) fatal, atroz.
lethargic [leˈθɑːdʒɪk] *adj* aletargado, letárgico.
lethargy [ˈleθədʒɪ] *n* letargo *m*.
Lethe [ˈliːθiː] *n* Lete(o) *m*.
let-out [ˈletaʊt] *n* (*Brit*) escapatoria *f*; **~ clause** cláusula *f* que incluye una escapatoria.
Lett [let] = **Latvian**.
letter [ˈletəʳ] **1** *n* (**a**) (*of alphabet*) letra *f*; **the ~ of the law** la ley escrita; **to the ~** a la letra, al pie de la letra.
(**b**) (*missive*) carta *f*; **~ of acknowledgement** carta *f* de acuse de recibo; **~ of advice** carta *f* de aviso; **~ of allotment** carta *f* de asignación; **~ of application** carta *f* de solicitud; **~ of appointment** carta *f* de confirmación de un puesto de trabajo; **~ of attorney** poder *m*; **~s of credence** cartas *fpl* credenciales; **~ of credit** carta *f* de crédito; **documentary ~ of credit** carta *f* de crédito documentaria; **irrevocable ~ of credit** carta *f* de crédito irrevocable; **~ of intent** carta *f* de intenciones; **~ of introduction** carta *f* de recomendación (*to* para); **~ of lien** carta *f* de gravamen; **~ of reference** carta *f* de recomendación; **~s of Galdós** (*as published*) epistolario *m* de Galdós; **~s patent** patente *m* de privilegio, letra *f* de patente; **by ~** por carta, por escrito.
(**c**) **~s** (*learning*) letras *fpl*; **man of ~s** hombre *m* de letras, literato *m*.
2 *attr*: **~ quality printer** impresora *f* calidad carta.
3 *vt* rotular, inscribir, estampar con letras.

letter-bomb ['letəbɒm] *n* carta-bomba *f.*
letterbox ['letəbɒks] *n* (*esp Brit*) buzón *m.*
letter-card ['letəkɑːd] *n* (*Brit*) carta-tarjeta *f.*
lettered ['letəd] *adj person* culto; *object* rotulado, marcado con letras; ~ **in gold** marcado con letras doradas.
letterfile ['letəfaɪl] *n* carpeta *f,* guardacartas *m.*
letterhead ['letəhed] *n* membrete *m,* encabezamiento *m.*
lettering ['letərɪŋ] *n* letras *fpl,* inscripción *f,* rótulo *m.*
letter-opener ['letər,əupnə^r] *n* abrecartas *m.*
letterpress ['letəpres] *n* (*Typ*) texto *m* impreso, impresión *f* tipográfica; (*method*) prensa *f* de copiar.
letter-writer ['letə,raɪtə^r] *n* escritor *m,* -ora *f* de cartas (*or* de la carta *etc*); **I'm not much of a** ~ yo apenas escribo cartas.
letting ['letɪŋ] *n* arrendamiento *m.*
lettuce ['letɪs] *n* lechuga *f.*
let-up* ['letʌp] *n* (*break*) calma *f,* respiro *m,* tregua *f,* descanso *m*; (*reduction*) reducción *f,* disminución *f* (*in* de); **we worked 5 hours without a** ~ trabajamos 5 horas sin interrupción; **there was no** ~ no hubo ningún intervalo de calma; **if there is a** ~ **in the rain** si deja un momento de llover.
leucocyte ['luːkə,saɪt] *n* leucocito *m.*
leukaemia, (*esp US*) **leukemia** [luː'kiːmɪə] *n* leucemia *f.*
Levant [lɪ'vænt] *n* Oriente *m* Medio.
Levantine ['levəntaɪn] **1** *adj* levantino. **2** *n* levantino *m,* -a *f.*
levee[1] ['leveɪ] *n* (*reception*) besamanos *m,* recepción *f.*
levee[2] ['levɪ] *n* (*bank*) ribero *m,* dique *m.*
level ['levl] **1** *adj* llano, plano, raso; a nivel, nivelado; igual, uniforme; *spoonful* rasado; *gaze, tone* ecuánime; *judgement, mind* juicioso; **to be** ~ **with** estar a nivel con; **to be** ~ **with the ground** estar a ras de tierra; **to be** ~ **with the water** estar a flor del agua; **I'll do my** ~ **best** haré todo lo que pueda.
2 *adv* (*with ground; horizontally*) a nivel; ras con ras; **to draw** ~ **with sb** llegar a la altura de uno, alcanzar a uno, (*in league etc*) llegar a empatar con uno, colocarse en igual posición que uno.
3 *n* **(a)** (*instrument*) nivel *m.*
(b) (*altitude, degree*) nivel *m*; **at eye** ~ a la altura del ojo; **at roof** ~ a la altura de los tejados; **speed on the** ~ velocidad *f* sobre superficie llana; **on the international** ~ a nivel internacional; **it's on the** ~* es un negocio serio; es un negocio limpio; **is he on the** ~?* ¿es de fiar?, ¿es una persona honrada?; **are you telling me this on the** ~?* ¿me lo dices en serio?; **to be on a** ~ **with** estar al nivel de; **to be on a** ~ **with the ground** estar a ras de la tierra; **to be on a** ~ **with** (*fig*) estar al nivel de; ser parangonable con; **that trick is on a** ~ **with the other** esa jugada es tan vil como la otra; **to come down to sb's** ~ bajar al nivel en que está uno.
(c) (*flat place*) llano *m.*
4 *vt* **(a)** *ground etc* nivelar, allanar; *building* derribar; *site* desmontar, despejar; *quantities* igualar, nivelar; **to** ~ **sth to** (*or* **with**) **the ground** arrasar algo.
(b) *blow* asestar (*at* a); *weapon* apuntar (*at* a); *accusation* dirigir (*against, at* a), hacer (*against, at* contra).
5 *vi* (*US**): **I'll** ~ **with you** te lo voy a decir con franqueza; **you didn't** ~ **with me** no has sido franco conmigo.
◆**level down** *vt* nivelar por abajo, rebajar al mismo nivel.
◆**level off, level out** *vi* nivelarse; (*of prices etc*) estabilizarse; (*Aer*) enderezarse.
◆**level up** *vt* elevar al mismo nivel.
level-crossing ['levl'krɒsɪŋ] *n* (*Brit*) paso *m* a nivel.
leveler ['levələ^r] *n* (*US*) = **leveller.**
level-headed ['levl'hedɪd] *adj* juicioso, sensato.
leveller, (*US*) **leveler** ['levələ^r] *n persona en pro de la igualdad de derechos.*
levelling, (*US*) **leveling** ['levlɪŋ] **1** *n* nivelación *f*; aplanamiento *m.* **2** *adj*: ~ **process** proceso *m* de nivelación.
levelling-off [,levəlɪŋ'ɒf] *n* nivelación *f.*
levelly ['levəlɪ] *adv gaze etc* con compostura, con ecuanimidad, sin emocionarse.
level-peg [,levl'peg] *vi*: **they were ~ging** iban empatados.
level-pegging [,levl'pegɪŋ] *n* igualdad *f,* situación *f* de empate; **it's** ~ **now** van muy iguales, están empatados.
lever ['liːvə^r] **1** *n* palanca *f* (*also fig*). **2** *vt* apalancar.
◆**lever up** *vt*: **to** ~ **sth up** alzar algo con palanca.
leverage ['liːvərɪdʒ] **1** *n* apalancamiento *m*; (*fig*) influencia *f*; fuerza *f*; ventaja *f.* **2** *as vt*: **~d buy-out** *compra de todas las acciones de una compañía pagándolas con dinero prestado a cambio de asegurar que las acciones serán compradas.*
leveret ['levərɪt] *n* lebrato *m.*
leviathan [lɪ'vaɪəθən] *n* leviatán *m*; (*fig*) buque *m* (*etc*) enorme.
Levi's ['liːvaɪz] ® *npl* vaqueros *mpl,* levis *mpl.*
levitate ['levɪteɪt] **1** *vt* elevar por levitación.
2 *vi* elevarse por levitación.
levitation [,levɪ'teɪʃən] *n* levitación *f.*
Levite ['liːvaɪt] *n* levita *m.*
Leviticus [lɪ'vɪtɪkəs] *n* Levítico *m.*
levity ['levɪtɪ] *n* frivolidad *f,* ligereza *f,* informalidad *f*; (*mirth*) risas *fpl.*
levy ['levɪ] **1** *n* **(a)** (*act*) exacción *f* (de tributos); (*tax*) impuesto *m*; (*surcharge*) sobrecarga *f,* sobretasa *f.* **(b)** (*Mil*) leva *f.*
2 *vt* **(a)** *tax* exigir (*on* a), recaudar; *fine* imponer (*on* a). **(b)** (*Mil*) reclutar.
lewd [luːd] *adj* impúdico, obsceno; *song, story etc* verde, colorado (*LAm*).
lewdly ['luːdlɪ] *adv* impúdicamente, obscenamente.
lewdness ['luːdnɪs] *n* impudicia *f,* obscenidad *f*; lo verde.
lexeme ['leksiːm] *n* lexema *m.*
lexical ['leksɪkəl] *adj* léxico.
lexicalize ['leksɪkəlaɪz] *vt* lexicalizar.
lexicographer [,leksɪ'kɒgrəfə^r] *n* lexicógrafo *m,* -a *f.*
lexicographical [,leksɪkəʊ'græfɪkəl] *adj* lexicográfico.
lexicography [,leksɪ'kɒgrəfɪ] *n* lexicografía *f.*
lexicologist [,leksɪ'kɒlədʒɪst] *n* lexicólogo *m,* -a *f.*
lexicology [,leksɪ'kɒlədʒɪ] *n* lexicología *f.*
lexicon ['leksɪkən] *n* léxico *m.*
lexis ['leksɪs] *n* vocabulario *m.*
Leyden ['laɪdn] **1** *n* Leiden. **2** *attr*: ~ **jar** botella *f* de Leiden.
l.h. *abbr of* **left hand** izquierda *f,* izq.
LI (*US Post*) *abbr of* **Long Island.**
liability [,laɪə'bɪlɪtɪ] *n* **(a)** (*responsibility*) responsabilidad *f*; riesgo *m*; (*burden*) carga *f* onerosa, lastre *m*; desventaja *f*; ~ **insurance** seguro *m* contra responsabilidades, seguro *m* contra terceros; **one's** ~ **for tax** la cantidad que uno puede ser llamado a pagar en impuestos; **he's a real** ~ es un estorbo, es un cero a la izquierda.
(b) liabilities obligaciones *fpl,* compromisos *mpl*; (*Comm*) pasivo *m,* deudas *fpl*; **to meet one's liabilities** satisfacer sus deudas.
liable ['laɪəbl] *adj* **(a)** (*subject*) **to be** ~ ser el responsable; **to be** ~ **for** ser responsable de, responder de; **to be** ~ **for taxes** (*thing*) estar sujeto a impuestos, (*person*) tener que pagar impuestos; **the plan is** ~ **to changes** el plan bien puede sufrir cambios. **(b)** (*likely*) **to be** ~ **to** + *infin* tener tendencia a + *infin,* ser propenso a + *infin*; estar predispuesto a + *infin*; **he is** ~ **not to come** es capaz de no venir, tiene tendencia a no venir; es fácil que no venga; **the pond is** ~ **to freeze** el estanque tiene tendencia a helarse, el estanque bien puede helarse; **we are** ~ **to get shot at here** aquí corremos el riesgo de que disparen sobre nosotros, aquí estamos expuestos a los tiros.
liaise [lɪ'eɪz] *vi*: **to** ~ **with** (*Brit*) enlazar con.
liaison [lɪ'eɪzɒn] **1** *n* **(a)** (*coordination*) enlace *m,* conexión *f,* coordinación *f*; (*Mil*) enlace *m.* **(b)** (*affair*) lío *m,* relaciones *fpl* (amorosas).
2 *attr*: ~ **committee** comité *m* coordinador; ~ **officer** oficial *m* de enlace.
liana [lɪ'ɑːnə] *n* bejuco *m,* liana *f.*
liar ['laɪə^r] *n* mentiroso *m,* -a *f,* embustero *m,* -a *f*; ~! ¡mentira!
Lib. [lɪb] (*Pol*) **(a)** *n abbr of* **Liberal** liberal *mf*; *also adj.* **(b)** *n abbr of* **Liberation**: **Women's Lib.** = **Women's Liberation Movement** Movimiento *m* de Liberación de la Mujer.
libation [laɪ'beɪʃən] *n* libación *f.*
libber* ['lɪbə^r] *n* liberacionista *f,* feminista *f.*
libel ['laɪbəl] **1** *n* difamación *f,* calumnia *f* (*on* de); (*written*) libelo *m*; **it's a** ~! (*hum*) ¡es mentira!; **it's a** ~ **on all of us!** ¡esto nos calumnia a todos!
2 *attr*: ~ **laws** leyes *fpl* contra la difamación; ~ **suit** pleito *m* por difamación.
3 *vt* difamar, calumniar.
libellous, (*US*) **libelous** ['laɪbələs] *adj* difamatorio, calumnioso.
liberal ['lɪbərəl] **1** *adj* liberal (*also Pol*); *offer etc* generoso; *supply* abundante; (*in views*) tolerante; ~ **arts** artes *fpl* liberales; **L~ Democratic Party, L~ Democrats** (*Brit Pol*) partido *m* democrático liberal. **2** *n* liberal *mf.*
liberalism ['lɪbərəlɪzəm] *n* liberalismo *m.*
liberality [,lɪbə'rælɪtɪ] *n* generosidad *f,* liberalidad *f.*
liberalization [,lɪbərəlaɪ'zeɪʃən] *n* liberalización *f.*

liberalize [ˈlɪbərəlaɪz] *vt* liberalizar.

liberally [ˈlɪbərəlɪ] *adv* liberalmente; generosamente; abundantemente; con tolerancia.

liberal-minded [ˈlɪbərəlˈmaɪndɪd] *adj* tolerante, de amplias miras.

liberal-mindedness [ˈlɪbərəlˈmaɪndɪdnɪs] *n* tolerancia *f*, amplitud *f* de miras.

liberate [ˈlɪbəreɪt] *vt* (*free*) libertar, librar (*from* de); *prisoner* poner en libertad; *gas etc* dejar escapar.

liberated [ˈlɪbəreɪtɪd] *adj* liberado.

liberation [ˌlɪbəˈreɪʃən] *n* liberación *f*; ~ **theology** teología *f* de la liberación; *V also* **Lib.**

liberator [ˈlɪbəreɪtəʳ] *n* libertador *m*, -ora *f*.

Liberia [laɪˈbɪərɪə] *n* Liberia *f*.

Liberian [laɪˈbɪərɪən] **1** *adj* liberiano. **2** *n* liberiano *m*, -a *f*.

libertarian [ˌlɪbəˈtɛərɪən] **1** *adj* libertario. **2** *n* libertario *m*, -a *f*.

libertinage [ˈlɪbətɪnɪdʒ] *n* libertinaje *m*.

libertine [ˈlɪbətiːn] *n* libertino *m*.

liberty [ˈlɪbətɪ] **1** *n* libertad *f*; ~ **of conscience** libertad *f* de conciencia; ~ **of the press** libertad *f* de prensa; **it's a (dead) ~!*** ¡no hay derecho!; **taking the car without permission was a bit of a ~** tomarse el coche sin permiso era un poco fuerte; **to be at ~** estar en libertad, (*at leisure*) estar desocupado; **to be at ~ to** + *infin* tener permiso para + *infin*, tener el derecho de + *infin*, estar autorizado para + *infin*; **is he at ~ to come?** ¿está libre para venir?; **when you are at ~ to study it** cuando tengas tiempo para estudiarlo; **to restore sb to ~** devolver la libertad a uno; **to set sb at ~** poner a uno en libertad; **I have taken the ~ of giving your name** me he tomado la libertad de darles su nombre; **to take liberties with a text** tomarse libertades con un texto; **to take liberties with sb** tratar a uno con demasiada familiaridad, (*sexually*) propasarse con una. **2** *attr*: **it's ~ hall here** aquí hay un régimen de libertad total.

libidinous [lɪˈbɪdɪnəs] *adj* libidinoso.

libido [lɪˈbiːdəʊ] *n* libido *f*.

Libor *n abbr of* **London inter-bank offered rate.**

Libra [ˈliːbrə] *n* (*Zodiac*) Libra *f*.

librarian [laɪˈbrɛərɪən] *n* bibliotecario *m*, -a *f*.

librarianship [laɪˈbrɛərɪənʃɪp] *n* (**a**) (*post*) puesto *m* de bibliotecario. (**b**) (*esp Brit*: *science*) biblioteconomía *f*, bibliotecnia *f*, bibliotecología *f*.

library [ˈlaɪbrərɪ] **1** *n* biblioteca *f*; (*esp private*) librería *f*; (*Comput*) biblioteca *f*.

2 *attr*: ~ **book** libro *m* de biblioteca; ~ **card,** ~ **ticket** carnet *m* (de biblioteca); ~ **pictures** (*TV*) imágenes *fpl* de archivo; ~ **science** = **librarianship** (**b**); ~ **software** programa *m* de biblioteca.

librettist [lɪˈbretɪst] *n* libretista *mf*.

libretto [lɪˈbretəʊ] *n* libreto *m*.

Libya [ˈlɪbɪə] *n* Libia *f*.

Libyan [ˈlɪbɪən] **1** *adj* libio. **2** *n* libio *m*, -a *f*.

lice [laɪs] *npl of* **louse.**

licence, (*US*) **license**[1] [ˈlaɪsəns] *n* (**a**) (*permit*) licencia *f*, permiso *m*; autorización *f*; (*Aut etc*) carnet *m*, permiso *m*; **to manufacture sth under ~** fabricar algo bajo licencia.

(**b**) (*excess*) libertinaje *m*, desenfreno *m*; (*freedom*) libertad *f*; **you can allow some ~ in translation** puedes permitirte cierta libertad al traducirlo.

licence number [ˈlaɪsənsˌnʌmbəʳ] *n* (*Aut*) número *m* de matrícula.

license[2] [ˈlaɪsəns] **1** *vt* licenciar, autorizar, dar permiso a; *car* sacar la patente (*LAm*: la matrícula) de; **to be ~d to** + *infin* tener permiso para + *infin*, estar autorizado para + *infin*.

2 *n* (*US*) = **licence.**

licensed [ˈlaɪsənsd] *adj car* con matrícula; *dog, gun* con licencia, que tiene licencia; *dealer, restaurant* autorizado; ~ **premises** (*Brit*) establecimiento *m* autorizado para la venta de bebidas alcohólicas; ~ **trade** comercio *m* autorizado, negocio *m* autorizado; ~ **victualler** vendedor *m*, -ora *f* de bebidas alcohólicas.

licensee [ˌlaɪsənˈsiː] *n* concesionario *m*, -a *f*, licenciatario *m*, -a *f*; (*Brit*: *of bar*) patrón *m*, -ona *f*.

license plate [ˈlaɪsənsˌpleɪt] *n* (*US Aut*) placa *f* de matrícula, patente *f* (*SC*).

licensing [ˈlaɪsənsɪŋ] **1** *n* licenciación *f*; autorización *f*; (*Aut*) matrícula *f*. **2** *attr*: ~ **hours** horas *fpl* durante las cuales se permite la venta y consumo de alcohol (*en un bar etc*); ~ **laws** (*Brit*) leyes *fpl* reguladoras de la venta y consumo de alcohol.

licentiate [laɪˈsenʃɪɪt] *n* (*person*) licenciado *m*, -a *f*; (*title*) licencia *f*, licenciatura *f*.

licentious [laɪˈsenʃəs] *adj* licencioso.

lichen [ˈlaɪkən] *n* liquen *m*.

lichgate [ˈlɪtʃgeɪt] *n* entrada *f* de cementerio.

licit [ˈlɪsɪt] *adj* lícito.

lick [lɪk] **1** *n* (**a**) lamedura *f*, lengüetada *f*; **a ~ of paint** una mano de pintura; **a ~ of polish** un poquito de cera. (**b**) (*) **to go at a good ~** ir a buen tren, correr rápidamente.

2 *vt* (**a**) (*with tongue, of flames*) lamer; (*of waves*) besar. (**b**) (*: *tan, defeat*) dar una paliza a.

◆**lick off** *vt* quitar de un lametazo.

◆**lick up** *vt* beber a lengüetadas.

licking [ˈlɪkɪŋ] *n* (**a**) lamedura *f*. (**b**) (*) paliza *f*; **to give sb a ~** dar una paliza a uno.

lickspittle* [ˈlɪkspɪtl] *n* cobista* *mf*, pelotillero* *m*, -a *f*.

licorice [ˈlɪkərɪs] *n* (*US*) regaliz *m*, orozuz *m*.

lid [lɪd] *n* (**a**) (*of box, case, pot etc*) tapa *f*; (*of pan etc*) cobertera *f*; (*: *hat*) techo* *m*; **he's flipped his ~**‡ ha perdido la chaveta*; **that puts the ~ on it** se acabó, eso es el fin; **to take the ~ off a scandal** tirar de la manta para revelar un escándalo. (**b**) (*Anat*) párpado *m*.

lidded [ˈlɪdɪd] *adj* (**a**) *pot etc* con tapa, con cobertera. (**b**) **heavily ~ eyes** ojos *mpl* con párpados gruesos.

lido [ˈliːdəʊ] *n* (*bathing*) establecimiento *m* de baños; (*Brit*: *swimming*) centro *m* de natación, piscina *f*, alberca *f* (*LAm*); (*boating*) centro *m* de balandrismo.

lie[1] [laɪ] **1** *n* mentira *f*; **it's a ~!** ¡es mentira!; **to give the ~ to** *person* dar el mentís a, *report* desmentir; **to tell a ~** mentir.

2 *vt*: **to ~ one's way out of it** salir del apuro mintiendo.

3 *vi* mentir.

lie[2] [laɪ] (*irr*: *pret* **lay,** *ptp* **lain**) **1** *vi* (**a**) (*person etc*: *act*) echarse, acostarse, tenderse; (*state*) estar echado, estar tumbado, estar acostado, estar tendido; (*in grave*) yacer, estar enterrado; **here ~s** aquí yace; **he lay where he had fallen** quedaba donde había caído; **to let things ~** dejar estar las cosas como están; **don't ~ on the grass** no te eches sobre el césped; **to ~ asleep** estar dormido; **to ~ dead** yacer muerto; **to ~ in bed** estar en la cama, (*lazily*) seguir en la cama; **to ~ helpless** estar tumbado sin poder ayudarse; **to ~ resting** estar descansando; **to ~ still** quedarse inmóvil.

(**b**) (*objects etc*) estar; (*be situated*) estar, estar situado, encontrarse; (*stretch*) extenderse; **Slobodia ~s in third place** Eslobodia está en tercer lugar, Eslobodia ocupa la tercera posición; **the book lay on the table** el libro estaba en la mesa; **the book lay unopened** el libro quedaba sin abrir; **the snow lay half a metre deep** había medio metro de nieve; **the snow did not ~** la nieve se derritió; **the money is lying in the bank** el dinero sigue en el banco; **it ~s further on** cae más adelante; **our road lay along the river** nuestro camino seguía a lo largo del río; **the road ~s over the hills** el camino cruza las colinas; **the factory lay idle** la fábrica estaba parada; **obstacles ~ in the way** hay obstáculos por delante; **the plain lay before us** la llanura se extendía delante de nosotros; **how does the land ~?** ¿cuál es el estado actual de las cosas?; **where does the difficulty ~?** ¿en qué consiste la dificultad?; **the fault ~s with you** la falta es tuya, tú eres el culpable; **it ~s with you to reform it** te corresponde a ti reformarlo; **it does not ~ with me** no depende de mí, no me toca a mí.

(**c**) (*evidence etc*) ser admisible.

2 *n* (*of ball etc*) posición *f*; ~ **of the land** configuración *f* del terreno, (*fig*) estado *m* actual de las cosas.

◆**lie about, lie around** *vi* (*objects*) estar esparcidos; estar en desorden; (*person*) pasar el tiempo sin hacer nada; **we lay about on our beds** quedamos tumbados en las camas; **it must be lying about somewhere** estará por aquí, debe de andar por aquí.

◆**lie back** *vi* recostarse (*against, on* sobre); ~ **back and think of England!** ¡tranquilízate y piensa en la patria!

◆**lie behind** *vt* (*fig*) subyacer a; estar detrás de; ser la razón fundamental de; **what ~s behind his attitude?** ¿cuál es la verdadera razón de su actitud?

◆**lie down** *vi* (**a**) (*act*) echarse, acostarse; tumbarse; (*state*) estar echado, estar tumbado; estar tendido; ~ **down!** (*to dog*) ¡échate!; **to ~ down on the job** gandulear.

(**b**) (*fig*) **to ~ down under it, to take it lying down** aceptarlo sin protestar, soportarlo sin chistar, tragarlo; **he's not one to take things lying down** no es de los que aceptan mansamente las injusticias.

◆**lie in** *vi* seguir en la cama, no levantarse.

◆**lie over** *vi* quedar aplazado, quedar en suspenso.

◆**lie to** *vi* (*Naut*: *act*) ponerse a la capa, (*state*) estar a la capa.

◆**lie up** *vi* (*hide*) esconderse; (*rest*) descansar; (*Naut*) estar amarrado.

lie-abed ['laɪəbed] *n* dormilón *m*, -ona *f*.

Liechtenstein ['lɪktənstaɪn] *n* Liechtenstein *m*.

lied [li:d], *pl* **lieder** ['li:dər] *n* lied *m*.

lie-detector ['laɪdɪ,tektər] **1** *n* detector *m* de mentiras. **2** *attr*: ~ **test** prueba *f* con el detector de mentiras.

lie-down* [,laɪ'daʊn] *n* (*Brit*) breve descanso *m*, siestecita *f*.

lief [li:f] *adv*: **I'd as** ~ **not go** igual me da no ir, de igual gana no voy.

Liège [lɪ'eɪʒ] *n* Lieja *f*.

liege [li:dʒ] *n* (*lord*) señor *m* feudal; (*vassal*) vasallo *m*; **my** ~ señor.

liege lord ['li:dʒ,lɔ:d] *n* señor *m* feudal.

liegeman ['li:dʒmæn] *n, pl* **liegemen** ['li:dʒmen] vasallo *m*.

lie-in [,laɪ'ɪn] *n*: **to have a** ~ (*Brit*) seguir en la cama.

lien [lɪən] *n* derecho *m* de retención (*on* de); **banker's** ~ gravamen *m* bancario; **general** ~ gravamen *m* general; **vendor's** ~ gravamen *m* del vendedor.

lieu [lu:] *n*: **in** ~ **of** en lugar de, en vez de.

Lieut. *abbr of* **Lieutenant.**

lieutenant [lef'tenənt] *n* lugarteniente *m*; (*Brit Mil*) teniente *m*; (*Brit, US Naut*) teniente *m* de navío.

lieutenant-colonel [lef'tenənt'kɜ:nl] *n* (*Brit, US Mil*) teniente *m* coronel.

lieutenant-commander [lef'tenəntkə'mɑ:ndər] *n* capitán *m* de corbeta.

lieutenant-general [lef'tenənt'dʒenərəl] *n* (*Brit, US Mil*) teniente *m* general.

life [laɪf] *n, pl* **lives** [laɪvz] **1** *n* (**a**) (*gen*) vida *f*; ser *m*, existencia *f*; modo *m* de vivir; (*of licence etc*) vigencia *f*, validez *f*; (*of battery*) vida *f*, duración *f*; **bird** ~ los pájaros; **plant** ~ vida *f* vegetal, las plantas; **there is not much insect** ~ **here** aquí hay pocos insectos.

(**b**) (*with adj*) **early** ~ juventud *f*, años *mpl* juveniles; **in her early** ~ en su juventud; **in later** ~ más tarde, en los años posteriores; **the good** ~ una vida agradable, (*Rel*) la vida santa; **it's a good** ~ es una vida agradable; **low** ~ hampa *f*; **private** ~ vida *f* privada; **the private** ~ **of Henry VIII** la vida íntima de Enrique VIII; **Woodhouse, known in private** ~ **as Plum** Woodhouse, conocido en la intimidad como Plum; **in real** ~ en la vida real; **my** ~**!*** ¡Dios mío!; **what a** ~**!** (*bad*) ¡qué vida ésta!, (*good*) ¡vaya vida!, ¡vaya vidorra!

(**c**) (*with* to be) **is there** ~ **after death?** ¿hay vida después de la muerte?; **to be a matter of** ~ **and death** ser cosa de vida o de muerte; **to be the** ~ **and soul of the party** ser el alma de la fiesta; **such is** ~**!, that's** ~**!** ¡así es la vida!; **how's** ~**?** ¿qué tal?, ¿cómo van tus cosas?; **this is the** ~**!** ¡qué vida nos chupamos!, ¡esto es jauja!; **it's more than my** ~**'s worth** sería jugarme la vida.

(**d**) (*with prep*) **at my time of** ~ a mi edad, con los años que yo tengo; **for** ~ de por vida; **to be on trial for one's** ~ ser acusado de un crimen capital; **for one's** ~**, for dear** ~ para salvarse la vida, desesperadamente, (*all out*) a más no poder; **run for your lives!** ¡sálvese el que pueda!; **for the** ~ **of me I can't see why** que me maten si comprendo por qué; **from** ~ del natural; **never in my** ~ en mi vida; **not on your** ~**!** ¡ni hablar!; **to the** ~ al vivo; **true to** ~ conforme con la realidad, verdadero; **she brought the party to** ~ animó la fiesta; **his acting brought the character to** ~ su actuación dio vida al personaje; **to come to** ~ resucitar(se), (*fig*) empezar a animarse.

(**e**) (*with verb other than* to be) **to bear a charmed** ~ salir milagrosamente ileso de todos los peligros; **she began** ~ **as a teacher** primero se dedicó a la enseñanza; ~ **begins at 40** la vida comienza a los 40; **to depart this** ~ partir de esta vida; **you gave me the fright of my** ~**!** ¡qué susto me diste!; **to lay down one's** ~ dar su vida, entregar su vida; **to lead a quiet** ~ llevar una vida tranquila; **to lead a strange** ~ llevar una vida muy rara; **to live the** ~ **of Riley** darse buena vida; **to live one's own** ~ ser dueño de su propia vida; **how many lives were lost?** ¿cuántas víctimas hubo?; **no lives were lost** no hubo víctimas; **to make a new** ~ **for oneself, to start a new** ~ comenzar una vida nueva; **to paint from** ~ pintar del natural; **to put new** ~ **into sb** reanimar a uno, infundir nueva vida a uno; **to risk** ~ **and limb** jugarse la vida; **he can't spell to save his** ~ no sabe escribir correctamente aun si le va la vida en ello; **to see** ~ ver mundo; **to sell one's** ~ **dearly** vender muy cara la vida; **to take one's** ~ **in one's hands** jugarse la vida; **to take sb's** ~ quitar la vida a uno; **to take one's own** ~ suicidarse.

(**f**) (*****) = ~ **imprisonment**; **to do** ~ cumplir una condena de reclusión perpetua; **to get** ~ ser condenado a reclusión perpetua.

(**g**) (*liveliness*) vida *f*, vivacidad *f*, vitalidad *f*; animación *f*.

(**h**) (*Liter*) vida *f*, biografía *f*.

2 *attr*: ~ **and death struggle** lucha *f* a muerte; ~ **annuity** pensión *f* (*or* anualidad *f*) vitalicia; ~ **assurance** (*esp Brit*) seguro *m* sobre la vida; ~ **class** clase *f* de dibujo al natural; ~ **expectancy** esperanza *f* de vida; ~ **force** fuerza *f* vital; ~ **form** forma *f* de vida; ~ **imprisonment** prisión *f* a perpetuidad, condena *f* perpetua; ~ **insurance** seguro *m* sobre la vida; ~ **interest** usufructo *m* vitalicio; **to take out a** ~ **membership** inscribirse como miembro por vida; ~ **peer** (*Brit Parl*) *miembro de la Cámara de los Lores de carácter no hereditario*; ~ **president** presidente *mf* de por vida; ~ **sciences** ciencias *fpl* de la vida; ~ **sentence** condena *f* a perpetuidad; ~ **span** vida *f*; (*of product*) vida *f* útil; ~ **story** biografía *f*; historia *f* de la vida (de uno); **it was her** ~**'s work** fue el trabajo de toda su vida.

lifebelt ['laɪfbelt] *n* cinturón *m* salvavidas.

lifeblood ['laɪfblʌd] *n* sangre *f* vital; (*fig*) alma *f*, nervio *m*, sustento *m*.

lifeboat ['laɪfbəʊt] **1** *n* (*from shore*) lancha *f* de socorro; (*from ship*) bote *m* salvavidas. **2** *attr*: ~ **station** estación *f* de lancha de socorro.

lifeboatman ['laɪfbəʊtmən] *n, pl* **lifeboatmen** ['laɪfbəʊtmən] tripulante *m* de una lancha de socorro.

lifebuoy ['laɪfbɔɪ] *n* boya *f* salvavidas, guindola *f*.

life-cycle ['laɪf,saɪkl] *n* ciclo *m* vital.

life-giving ['laɪfgɪvɪŋ] *adj* que da vida, vivificante.

lifeguard ['laɪfgɑ:d] *n* (*on beach*) vigilante *m*, salvavidas *m*; (*Mil*) guardia *m* de corps.

Life Guards ['laɪf,gɑ:dz] *npl* (*Brit Mil*) *regimiento de caballería*.

life-jacket ['laɪf,dʒækɪt] *n* chaleco *m* salvavidas.

lifeless ['laɪflɪs] *adj* sin vida, muerto, exánime; (*fig*) soso, flojo.

lifelessness ['laɪflɪsnɪs] *n* (*fig*) falta *f* de vida, sosería *f*, flojedad *f*.

lifelike ['laɪflaɪk] *adj* natural, vivo.

lifeline ['laɪflaɪn] *n* cuerda *f* salvavidas; (*fig*) alma *f*, sustento *m*.

lifelong ['laɪflɒŋ] *adj* de toda la vida.

life preserver ['laɪfprɪ,zɜ:vər] *n* (**a**) (*Brit*) cachiporra *f*. (**b**) (*US*) chaleco *m* salvavidas.

lifer* ['laɪfər] *n* presidiario *m* de por vida, persona *f* condenada a reclusión perpetua.

life-raft ['laɪfrɑ:ft] *n* balsa *f* salvavidas.

life-saver ['laɪf,seɪvər] *n* salvador *m*, -ora *f*, socorrista *mf*.

life-saving ['laɪfseɪvɪŋ] **1** *n* salvamento *m*; (*training for* ~) socorrismo *m*. **2** *attr* de salvamento, salvavidas; ~ **raft** balsa *f* salvavidas.

life-size(d) ['laɪf'saɪz(d)] *adj* de tamaño natural.

life-style ['laɪfstaɪl] *n* estilo *m* de vida.

life-support ['laɪfsə,pɔ:t] *attr*: ~ **system** sistema *m* de respiración artificial (*pulmón artificial etc*).

lifetime ['laɪftaɪm] *n* (**a**) vida *f*; **the** ~ **of a horse** el término medio de vida de un caballo; **once in a** ~ una vez en la vida; **in my** ~ durante mi vida; **in the** ~ **of this parliament** en la vida de este parlamento; **she gave half away in her** ~ cedió la mitad en vida; **the chance of a** ~ una oportunidad única en la vida; **the work of a** ~ el trabajo de una vida entera.

(**b**) (*fig*) eternidad *f*, mucho tiempo *m*; **it seemed a** ~ parecía una eternidad.

lifework ['laɪf'wɜ:k] *n* trabajo *m* de toda la vida.

LIFO ['laɪfəʊ] *abbr of* **last in, first out** último en entrar, primero en salir, UEPS.

lift [lɪft] **1** *n* (**a**) (*act of* ~*ing*) alzamiento *m*, levantamiento *m*, elevación *f*; (*effort*) esfuerzo *m* para levantar; (*upward push*) empuje *m* para arriba; (*help*) ayuda *f* (para levantar); (*Aer*) sustentación *f*, fuerza *f* de sustentación; (*Mech, of valve etc*) carrera *f*, juego *m*; **give me a** ~ **with this trunk** ¿me ayudas a levantar este baúl?

(**b**) (*Brit*: *in car etc*) viaje *m* gratuito, viaje *m* en coche (*etc*) ajeno, aventón *m* (*LAm*), raid *m* (*LAm*); **to give sb a** ~ llevar a uno (gratis) en su coche, dar aventón (*or* raid) a uno (*LAm*); **I can give you a** ~ **to Burgos** le puedo llevar a Burgos; **can I give you a** ~**?** ¿quiere que le lleve?

(**c**) (*Brit*: *elevator*) ascensor *m*, elevador *m* (*LAm*); (*for goods*) montacargas *m*.

(**d**) (*boost*) estímulo *m*; **it gave us a** ~ nos alentó, nos animó.

2 *vt* (**a**) (*raise*) alzar, levantar, elevar; (*pick up*) coger (*Sp*), agarrar (*LAm*), recoger; *potatoes etc* recoger; *child etc* levantar en brazos; *hat* quitarse; (*by air*) transportar en avión, transportar por puente aéreo.

(**b**) (*fig*) *restrictions etc* levantar, suprimir.

(**c**) (*) birlar*, ratear*; (*Liter etc*) copiar, plagiar (*from* de).

(**d**) (*boost*) alentar, animar.

3 *vi* levantarse, alzarse; (*clouds*) disiparse.

◆**lift down** *vt*: **to ~ sb down** bajar a uno en brazos; **to ~ sth down carefully** bajar algo con cuidado.

◆**lift off** *vi* (*rocket*) despegar.

◆**lift out** *vt* sacar.

◆**lift up** *vt* alzar, levantar, elevar.

lift-attendant ['lɪftə,tendənt] (*Brit*) *n*, **lift-boy** ['lɪftbɔɪ] (*Brit*) *n*, **liftman** ['lɪftmæn] *n*, *pl* **liftmen** ['lɪftmen] ascensorista *m*.

lift-cage ['lɪftkeɪdʒ] *n* (*Brit*) caja *f* de ascensor.

lift-off ['lɪftɒf] *n* despegue *m*.

lift-shaft ['lɪftʃɑːft] *n* (*Brit*) hueco *m* del ascensor.

ligament ['lɪgəmənt] *n* ligamento *m*.

ligature ['lɪgətʃəʳ] *n* (*Med, Mus*) ligadura *f*; (*Typ*) ligado *m*.

light[1] [laɪt] **1** *n* (**a**) (*gen*) luz *f*; lumbre *f*; **~ and shade** luz *f* y sombra; **the ~ of day** la luz del día; **this report will never see the ~ of day** este informe no verá nunca la luz pública; **in the cold ~ of day** a la luz del día; **against the ~** a trasluz; **at first ~** al rayar el día; **by the ~ of a candle** a la luz de una vela; **in the ~ of** a la luz de; **you're in my ~** me estás quitando la luz; **in the ~ of what you say** por lo que dices; **it is ~ now** ahora es de día; **there is ~ at the end of the tunnel** se empieza a ver un rayo de esperanza, hay luz al final del túnel; **to bring to ~** sacar a luz, descubrir; **to come to ~** salir a luz, descubrirse; **to cast** (*or* **shed, throw**) **~ on** aclarar, arrojar luz sobre; **it revealed him in a strange ~** le reveló bajo una luz extraña; **to see the ~** (*be born*) nacer; (*understand*) comprender, caer en la cuenta; (*Rel*) convertirse, darse cuenta de su error; **I don't see things in that ~** yo no veo las cosas así; **to see things in a new ~** ver las cosas bajo otro aspecto, ver las cosas desde otro punto de vista; **to stand in sb's ~** quitar la luz a uno.

(**b**) (*lamp*) luz *f*, lámpara *f*; (*Aut, Naut*) faro *m*; **~s out** hora *f* de apagar las luces; toque *m* de silencio; **what time is ~s out?** ¿a qué hora se apagan las luces?; **I went out like a ~*** me quedé dormido en seguida; **to hide one's ~ under a bushel** ocultar las cualidades propias, darse de menos, retirarse modestamente; **to show sb a ~** alumbrar a uno.

(**c**) (*signal*) **the ~s** (*Aut*) el semáforo, las luces de tráfico; **green ~** (*also fig*) luz *f* verde; **to get the green ~ from sb** recibir luz verde de uno; **to give sb the green ~** dar luz verde a uno; **red ~** luz *f* roja (*also fig*).

(**d**) (*flame*) fuego *m*, lumbre *f*; **have you a ~?** ¿tienes fuego?; **to put a ~ to sth, to set ~ to sth** pegar fuego a algo, encender algo.

(**e**) (*Art*) toque *m* de luz; **~ and shade** claroscuro *m*.

(**f**) (*Archit*) cristal *m*, vidrio *m*.

(**g**) (*person*) **leading ~** figura *f* principal, figura *f* más destacada (*in* de); **shining ~** lumbrera *f*, figura *f* genial.

(**h**) **~s** (*intelligence*) luces *fpl*, conocimientos *mpl*; **according to his ~s** según Dios le da a entender.

2 *adj* (**a**) (*bright*) claro; (*illuminated*) bañado de luz, con mucha luz; **to grow ~** clarear, hacerse de día.

(**b**) *colour* claro; *hair* rubio; *skin* blanco; **a ~ green dress** un vestido verde claro.

3 (*irr*: *pret and ptp* **lit** *or* **lighted**) *vt* (**a**) (*illuminate*) alumbrar, iluminar; **she appeared at a ~ed window** se asomó a una ventana iluminada; **to ~ the way for sb** alumbrar a uno.

(**b**) *cigarette, fire etc* encender; **with a ~ed candle** con una vela encendida.

4 *vi* (**a**) (*begin to shine*) alumbrarse, iluminarse.

(**b**) (*ignite, switch on*) encenderse.

(**c**) **to ~ into sb‡** embestir a uno, empezar a pegar a uno.

◆**light out*** *vi* largarse* (*for* para).

◆**light up 1** *vt* (*illuminate*) alumbrar, iluminar; **a smile lit up her face** una sonrisa le iluminó la cara. **2** *vi* (**a**) (*begin to shine*) alumbrarse, iluminarse; **her face lit up** se iluminó su cara. (**b**) (*smoke*) encender un cigarrillo (*etc*), empezar a fumar.

light[2] [laɪt] (*irr*: *pret and ptp* **lit** *or* **lighted**) *vi*: **to ~ on** dar con, tropezar con, encontrar.

light[3] [laɪt] **1** *adj* (*in weight*) ligero; *food, gun, meal, sleep, troops, wine, work* ligero; *soil* poco denso; (*Naut*) en lastre; *lorry, train* vacío, sin carga; *breeze, punishment, tax, wound etc* leve; *task* fácil; *comedy, reading* ameno, de puro entretenimiento; (*morally*) ligero, liviano; (*cheerful*) alegre; **~ flyweight** peso *m* mosca ligero; **~ industry** industria *f* ligera; **~ opera** opereta *f*, ≃ (*Sp*) zarzuela *f*; **~ verse** poesías *fpl* festivas; **as ~ as air, as ~ as a feather** tan ligero como la pluma; **to be ~ on one's feet** ser ligero de pies, moverse con agilidad; **it was no ~ matter** era un asunto bastante grave, no era ninguna bagatela; **to make ~ of** no dar importancia a, restar importancia a.

2 *adv*: **to sleep ~** tener el sueño ligero; **to travel ~** viajar con poco equipaje.

3 *n*: **~s** (*Anat*) bofes *mpl*.

light bulb ['laɪtbʌlb] *n* bombilla *f*, foco *m* (*LAm*).

light-coloured ['laɪt'kʌləd] *adj* claro, de color claro.

light-emitting ['laɪtɪ,mɪtɪŋ] *adj*: **~ diode** diodo *m* luminoso.

lighten[1] ['laɪtn] **1** *vt* (**a**) (*light*) iluminar. (**b**) *color* hacer más claro. **2** *vi* (**a**) (*sky etc*) clarear. (**b**) (*Met*) relampaguear.

lighten[2] ['laɪtn] **1** *vt load* aligerar, hacer menos pesado; *cares* aliviar; *heart* alegrar. **2** *vi* (*load*) aligerarse, hacerse menos pesado; (*heart*) alegrarse.

lighter[1] ['laɪtəʳ] **1** *n* encendedor *m*, mechero *m*. **2** *attr*: **~ flint** piedra *f* de mechero; **~ fuel** gas *m* de encendedor.

lighter[2] ['laɪtəʳ] *n* (*Naut*) gabarra *f*, barcaza *f*.

light-fingered ['laɪt'fɪŋgəd] *adj* largo de uñas.

light fitting ['laɪt,fɪtɪŋ] *n* guarnición *f* del alumbrado.

light-footed ['laɪt'fʊtɪd] *adj* ligero (de pies).

light-haired ['laɪt'hɛəd] *adj* rubio.

light-headed ['laɪt'hedɪd] *adj* (*by temperament*) ligero de cascos, casquivano; (*dizzy*) mareado; (*with fever*) delirante; (*with excitement*) exaltado; **wine makes me ~** el vino me sube a la cabeza.

light-hearted ['laɪt'hɑːtɪd] *adj* alegre; *remark etc* poco serio, dicho en tono festivo.

light-heartedly ['laɪt'hɑːtɪdlɪ] *adv* alegremente.

lighthouse ['laɪthaʊs] *n*, *pl* **lighthouses** ['laɪthaʊzɪz] faro *m*.

lighthouse-keeper ['laɪthaʊs,kiːpəʳ] *n* torrero *m*.

lighting ['laɪtɪŋ] **1** *n* (*act*) iluminación *f*; encendimiento *m*; (*system*) alumbrado *m*; (*at pop show*) equipo *m* luminoso. **2** *attr*: **~ effects** efectos *mpl* luminosos; **~ engineer** luminotécnico *m*; **~ engineering** luminotecnia *f*; **~ fixtures** guarniciones *fpl* de alumbrado; **~ man** (*TV*) iluminista *m*.

lighting-up ['laɪtɪŋ'ʌp] *n*: **~ time** (*Brit*) hora *f* de encender las luces.

lightly ['laɪtlɪ] *adv* ligeramente; levemente; ágilmente; alegremente; *act etc* sin pensarlo bien, a la ligera; **~ clad** vistiendo ropa ligera, con muy poca ropa; **~ wounded** levemente herido; **to get off ~** escapar casi indemne; ser castigado con poca severidad; **this is not a charge to be made ~** este tipo de acusación no se hace a la ligera; **to speak ~ of sb** hablar de uno en términos despreciativos; **to speak ~ of dangers** despreciar los peligros; **to touch ~ on a matter** mencionar un asunto de paso.

light meter ['laɪt,miːtəʳ] *n* fotómetro *m*, exposímetro *m*.

lightness[1] ['laɪtnɪs] *n* (*brightness*) claridad *f*, luminosidad *f*; (*of colour*) claridad *f*.

lightness[2] ['laɪtnɪs] *n* (*in weight etc*) ligereza *f*, poco peso *m*; levedad *f*; agilidad *f*; alegría *f*.

lightning ['laɪtnɪŋ] **1** *n* relámpago *m*, (*doing damage*) rayo *m*; **as quick as ~, like (greased) ~** como un relámpago; **where the ~ struck** donde dio el rayo.

2 *attr* relámpago; **~ attack** ataque *m* relámpago; **~ strike** huelga *f* relámpago; **~ visit** visita *f* relámpago.

lightning conductor ['laɪtnɪŋkən,dʌktəʳ] *n*, (*US*) **lightning rod** [rɒd] *n* pararrayos *m*.

light pen ['laɪtpen] *n*, **light pencil** ['laɪt,pensl] *n* lápiz *m* óptico, fotoestilo *m*.

lightship ['laɪtʃɪp] *n* buque-faro *m*.

light show ['laɪtʃəʊ] *n* óptico-cinético *m*, psicodélico *m*, juego *m* de luces.

light-skinned [,laɪt'skɪnd] *adj* de piel blanca.

light wave ['laɪtweɪv] *n* onda *f* luminosa.

lightweight ['laɪtweɪt] **1** *adj* ligero, de poco peso. **2** *n* persona *f* de poco peso; (*Boxing*) peso *m* ligero; (*fig*) persona *f* de poca importancia.

light-year ['laɪtjɪəʳ] *n* año *m* luz; **3000 ~s away** a una distancia de 3000 años-luz.

ligneous ['lɪgnɪəs] *adj* leñoso.

lignite ['lɪgnaɪt] *n* lignito *m*.

lignum vitae ['lɪgnəm'viːtaɪ] *n* palo *m* santo; (*tree*) guayaco *m*.

Ligures ['lɪgjʊəz] *npl* ligures *mpl*.

Ligurian [lɪ'gjʊərɪən] **1** *adj* ligur. **2** *n* ligur *mf*.

like [laɪk] **1** *adj* parecido, semejante; igual; mismo; **in ~ cases** en casos parecidos; **on this and ~ subjects** sobre este tema y otros parecidos; **two birds of ~ genus** dos pájaros del mismo género; **the 3 divided the work into a ~ number of parts** los 3 se dividieron el trabajo en otras tantas porciones; **~ father ~ son** de tal palo tal astilla; **they are as ~ as two peas** se parecen como dos gotas de agua.

2 *prep* (**a**) (*similar to*) **to be ~ sb** parecerse a uno; **they are very ~ each other** se parecen mucho; **a house ~ mine** una casa parecida a la mía, una casa como la mía; **eyes ~ stars** ojos como estrellas; **I found one ~ it** encontré otro parecido (*or* igual); **people ~ that** las personas de esa clase; **the Russians are ~ that** los rusos son así; **he is rather ~ you** tiene bastante parecido contigo; **who(m) is he ~?** ¿a quién se parece?; **what's he ~?** ¿cómo es?, ¿qué tal es?; **what's the coat ~?** ¿cómo es el abrigo?; **she was ~ a sister to me** fue (como) una hermana para mí; **the portrait is not ~ him** el retrato no le representa bien; **the figure is more ~ 300** la cifra se acerca más bien a 300.

(**b**) (*idioms*) **it's not ~ him** no es propio de él (*to come late* venir tarde), no es característico de él; **I never saw anything ~ it** no he visto nunca nada igual; **isn't it ~ him?** ¡son cosas de él!; **that's just ~ a woman!** ¡eso es muy de mujeres!; **that's more ~ it!** ¡eso es mucho mejor!; **that hat's nothing ~ as nice as this one** ese sombrero es muy inferior a éste; **that's sth ~ a fish!** ¡eso es mucho pez!; **I was thinking of sth ~ a doll** pensaba en algo así como una muñeca, pensaba en una muñeca o algo por el estilo; *V* **feel, look** *etc*.

(**c**) (*in a similar way*) como; del mismo modo que, igual que; tal como; **~ a man** como un hombre; **~ mad** como un loco (*V also* **mad**); **~ that** así; **he thinks ~ us** opina lo mismo que nosotros; **just ~ anybody else** igual que cualquier otro; **A, ~ B, thinks that ...** A, al igual que B, considera que ...

3 *adv*: **it's nothing ~** no tiene parecido alguno, no se parece ni con mucho; **very ~, ~ enough, as ~ as not** a lo mejor; **I found this money, ~*** (*Brit*) me encontré este dinero, sabes.

4 *conj* (*: *as*) como, del mismo modo que; **~ we used to (do)** como hacíamos antes; **do it ~ I do** hazlo como yo; **it's just ~ I say** es como yo lo digo; **you look ~ you'd seen a ghost** parece que acabas de ver un fantasma; **he felt ~ he'd won the pools** estaba como si hubiera ganado el premio gordo.

5 *n* (**a**) (*equal etc*) semejante *mf*; **we shall not see his ~ again** otro como él no le veremos nunca; **did you ever see the ~?** ¿se vio jamás tal cosa?; **and the ~, and such ~** y otros por el estilo, y otros de ese jaez; **I've no time for the ~s of him*** los hombres así no los puedo ver.

(**b**) (*taste*) **~s** gustos *mpl*, simpatías *fpl*; **~s and dislikes** predilecciones *fpl* y aversiones, simpatías *fpl* y antipatías.

6 *vt* (**a**) *person* querer, tener simpatía a, tener cariño a, apreciar; **I ~ him** me es simpático; **I don't ~ him at all** me resulta totalmente antipático; **don't you ~ me a little bit?** ¿no me quieres un poquitín?; **how do you ~ him?** ¿qué tal te parece?; **he is well ~d here** aquí se le quiere mucho.

(**b**) (*find pleasure in*) gustar, *eg* **I ~ black shoes** me gustan los zapatos negros; **I ~ football** me gusta el fútbol; **I ~ dancing** me gusta bailar; **we ~ it here** nos gusta aquí; **your father won't ~ it** esto no le va a gustar a tu padre; **I ~ your nerve!** ¡qué frescura!; **well, I ~ that!** (*iro*) ¡habráse visto!; **how do you ~ Cádiz?** ¿qué te parece Cádiz?; **how do you ~ it here?** ¿estás contento aquí?; **how would you ~ a walk?** ¿te apetece (*LAm*: se te antoja) dar un paseo?

(**c**) (*wish, wish for*) querer; **I should ~ more time** quisiera tener más tiempo; **I should ~ to know why** quisiera saber por qué; **I should ~ you to do it** quiero que lo hagas; **I ~ to be obeyed** me gusta que me obedezcan; **whether he ~s it or not** quiera o no quiera, de buen o mal grado; **~ it or not, Lord Lucan lives** quieras o no, vive Lord Lucan; **he is free to act as he ~s** está libre para hacer lo que le dé la gana; **as you ~** como quieras; **if you ~** si quieres; **a cat or, if you ~, a feline** un gato, o si se prefiere, un felino; **when you ~** cuando quieras; **would you ~ a drink?** ¿quieres tomar algo?; **would you ~ to go to Seville?** ¿te gustaría ir a Sevilla?

-like [laɪk] *adj ending in compounds* parecido a, semejante a, como; **bird~** como un pájaro; **with queen~ dignity** con dignidad de reina; *V* **cat~** *etc*.

likeable ['laɪkəbl] *adj* simpático.

likeableness ['laɪkəblnɪs] *n* simpatía *f*.

likelihood ['laɪklɪhʊd] *n* probabilidad *f*; **in all ~** según todas las probabilidades; **there is no ~ of that** eso no es probable; **there is little ~ that ...** es poco probable que + *subj*.

likely ['laɪklɪ] **1** *adj* (**a**) (*probable*) probable; verosímil; **a ~ explanation** una razón verosímil, una explicación razonable; **a ~ story!** ¡puro cuento!, ¡qué cuento más inverosímil!; **the ~ outcome** el resultado más probable; **the plan most ~ to succeed** el plan con mejores probabilidades de éxito; **an incident ~ to cause trouble** un incidente que bien pudiera dar lugar a disturbios; **he is not ~ to come** no es probable que venga, es difícil que venga; **is it ~ that I did?** ¿es probable que lo hiciera yo?

(**b**) (*suitable*) apropiado; **I asked 6 ~ people** se lo pregunté a 6 personas apropiadas.

(**c**) (*promising*) prometedor; **a ~ youth** un joven prometedor, un joven que promete.

2 *adv* probablemente; **as ~ as not** a lo mejor; **very ~ they've lost it** a lo mejor lo han perdido; **not ~!** ¡ni hablar!

like-minded ['laɪk'maɪndɪd] *adj* animado por los mismos sentimientos; **they looked for others ~** buscaron otros de igual parecer.

liken ['laɪkən] *vt* comparar (*to* con), asemejar (*to* a).

likeness ['laɪknɪs] *n* (**a**) (*resemblance*) parecido *m*, semejanza *f*; **family ~** aire *m* de familia.

(**b**) (*appearance*) aspecto *m*; forma *f*; **in the ~ of** bajo el aspecto de; **to assume the ~ of** tomar la forma de, adoptar la apariencia de.

(**c**) (*portrait*) retrato *m*; **speaking ~** retrato *m* vivo.

likewise ['laɪkwaɪz] *adv* asimismo, igualmente; además; lo mismo; **~ it is true that ...** asimismo es verdad que ...; **he did ~** él hizo lo mismo.

liking ['laɪkɪŋ] *n* (**a**) (*for person*) simpatía *f* (*for* a), cariño *m* (*for* a); afición *f* (*for* a); **to have a ~ for sb** tener simpatía a uno, tener cariño a uno; **to take a ~ to sb** tomar cariño a uno, coger simpatía a uno.

(**b**) (*for thing*) gusto *m* (*for* por), afición *f* (*for* a); **it's too strong for my ~** para mí es demasiado fuerte, es fuerte para mi gusto; **to be to sb's ~** ser del gusto de uno; **to have a ~ for sth** ser aficionado a algo; **to take a ~ to sth** tomar gusto a algo, cobrar afición a algo.

lilac ['laɪlək] **1** *n* lila *f*. **2** *adj* color de lila.

Lille [li:l] *n* Lila *f*.

Lilliputian [,lɪlɪ'pju:ʃɪən] **1** *adj* liliputiense. **2** *n* liliputiense *mf*.

Lilo ['laɪləʊ] ® *n* colchón *m* inflable.

lilt [lɪlt] *n* (*sound*) ritmo *m* marcado, compases *mpl*, armonía *f*; (*song*) canción *f*; **a song with a ~ to it** una canción de agradable ritmo.

lilting ['lɪltɪŋ] *adj voice* armonioso, melodioso.

lily ['lɪlɪ] *n* lirio *m*, azucena *f*; **~ of the valley** muguete *m*, lirio *m* de los valles.

lily-livered ['lɪlɪ'lɪvəd] *adj* cobarde, pusilánime.

lily pad ['lɪlɪpæd] *n* hoja *f* de nenúfar.

lily-white ['lɪlɪwaɪt] *adj* blanco como la azucena.

Lima ['li:mə] *n* Lima *f*.

lima bean ['li:mə,bi:n] *n* (*US*) fríjol *m* de media luna, judía *f* de la peladilla.

limb [lɪm] *n* (*Anat*) miembro *m*; (*Bot*) rama *f*; **to be** (*or* **go**) **out on a ~** estar aislado; estar (*or* quedar) en (una) situación peligrosa (*or* desventajosa); **to tear sb ~ from ~** despedazar a uno, desmembrar a uno.

-limbed [lɪmd] *adj ending in compounds*: *V* **long-limbed**.

limber¹ ['lɪmbəʳ] **1** *adj* ágil; flexible.

2 *vt* hacer flexible.

◆**limber up** *vi* agilitarse; (*Sport*) entrar en calor, hacer ejercicios preparatorios; (*fig*) entrenarse, prepararse.

limber² ['lɪmbəʳ] *n* (*Mil*) armón *m* (de artillería).

limbless ['lɪmlɪs] *adj* (que está) falto de un brazo (*or* pierna).

limbo¹ ['lɪmbəʊ] *n* limbo *m*; **to be in ~** (*fig*) estar olvidado; quedar en un estado indeterminado, quedar sin resolver.

limbo² ['lɪmbəʊ] *n* (*dance*) limbo *m*.

lime¹ [laɪm] (*Geol*) **1** *n* cal *f*; (*bird~*) liga *f*. **2** *vt* (*Agr*) abonar con cal.

lime² [laɪm] *n* (*Bot*: *linden*) tilo *m*.

lime³ [laɪm] *n* (*Bot*: *citrus fruit*) lima *f*; (*tree*) limero *m*.

lime-green [,laɪm'gri:n] *adj* verde lima.

lime-juice ['laɪmdʒu:s] *n* jugo *m* de lima.

limekiln ['laɪmkɪln] *n* horno *m* de cal.

limelight ['laɪmlaɪt] *n* luz *m* de calcio; **to be in the ~** estar a la vista del público, ser el centro de atención, estar en el candelero; **he had long experience of the ~** tuvo una larga experiencia de estar a la luz de la publicidad; **to hog the**

~ chupar cámara; **he never sought the** ~ no trató nunca de llamar hacia sí la atención.

limerick ['lɪmərɪk] *n especie de quintilla jocosa.*

limestone ['laɪmstəʊn] *n* piedra *f* caliza.

lime-tree ['laɪmtriː] *n* (*linden*) tilo *m.*

limey* ['laɪmɪ] *n* (*US, Australia*) inglés *m,* -esa *f.*

limit ['lɪmɪt] **1** *n* límite *m*; **it's the** (**very**) **~!** ¡es el colmo!, ¡no faltaba más!; **he's the ~!, isn't he the ~?** ¿qué le vamos a hacer?, ¡qué tío!; **to be at the ~ of one's endurance** ya no poder más, estar completamente agotado; **I am at the ~ of my patience** ya no tengo más paciencia; **to be off ~s** (*US*) estar fuera de los límites; **he was 3 times over the ~** (*Aut*) había ingerido 3 veces más de la cantidad de alcohol permitida; **there is a ~ to what one can do** no es infinita la fuerza que tiene uno; **it is true within ~s** es verdad dentro de ciertos límites; **to go to the ~ to help sb** hacer todo lo posible para ayudar a uno, volcarse por ayudar a uno; **to know no ~s** ser infinito, no tener límites.

2 *vt* limitar, restringir (*to* a); **that plant is ~ed to Spain** esa planta se encuentra únicamente en España; **are you ~ed as to time?** ¿hay restricción de tiempo?

3 *vr*: **to ~ o.s. to a few remarks** limitarse a unas pocas observaciones; **I ~ myself to 10 cigarettes a day** me permito tan sólo 10 cigarrillos al día.

limitation [ˌlɪmɪ'teɪʃən] *n* limitación *f,* restricción *f*; (*Jur*) prescripción *f*; **he has his ~s** tiene su puntos flacos; **there is no ~ on exports** no hay restricción de artículos exportados.

limited ['lɪmɪtɪd] *adj* limitado, restringido; *edition* limitado; *intelligence* más bien mediocre; *means* escaso, reducido; *person* de cortos alcances, de miras estrechas; **L~** (*Brit*: *Comm, Jur*) sociedad *f* anónima; **~ (liability) company** sociedad *f* anónima; **~ partner** socio *mf* con responsabilidad equivalente a la cantidad invertida en la sociedad; **~ partnership** sociedad *f* en comandita, sociedad *f* limitada; **to a ~ extent** hasta cierto punto.

limiting ['lɪmɪtɪŋ] *adj* restrictivo.

limitless ['lɪmɪtlɪs] *adj* ilimitado, sin límites.

limo* ['lɪməʊ] *n* (*US*) = **limousine.**

limousine ['lɪməziːn] *n* limusina *f,* limosina *f.*

limp¹ [lɪmp] **1** *n* cojera *f*; **to walk with a ~** cojear.

2 *vi* cojear; **he ~ed off** se marchó cojeando; **he ~ed to the door** se fue cojeando a la puerta; **the ship managed to ~ to port** el buque llegó con dificultad al puerto.

limp² [lɪmp] *adj* flojo, lacio; fláccido; *cover etc* flexible; *movement etc* lánguido; **I feel ~ today** hoy me siento sin fuerzas; **she felt ~ all over** tenía un desmayo en todo el cuerpo; **he said in a ~ voice** dijo en tono desmayado; **let your body go ~** deja que el cuerpo pierda su rigidez.

limpet ['lɪmpɪt] **1** *n* lapa *f*; (*fig*) persona *f* tenaz. **2** *attr*: **~ mine** mina-ventosa *f.*

limpid ['lɪmpɪd] *adj liquid* límpido, cristalino, transparente; *air* diáfano, puro; *eyes* claro.

limply ['lɪmplɪ] *adv* flojamente; lánguidamente; **he said ~** dijo en tono desmayado.

limpness ['lɪmpnɪs] *n* flojedad *f*; languidez *f.*

limp-wristed* ['lɪmp'rɪstɪd] *adj* inútil; (*pej, gay*) de la acera de enfrente, sarasa‡.

limy ['laɪmɪ] *adj* calizo.

linchpin ['lɪntʃpɪn] *n* pezonera *f*; (*fig*) pivote *m,* eje *m.*

Lincs [lɪŋks] *abbr of* **Lincolnshire.**

linctus ['lɪŋktəs] *n* jarabe *m* para la tos.

linden ['lɪndən] *n* (*also* **~ tree**) tilo *m.*

line¹ [laɪn] **1** *n* (**a**) (*rope etc*) cuerda *f*; (*washing ~*) cuerda *f* de tender la ropa; (*fishing ~*) sedal *m.*

(**b**) (*Geom etc*) línea *f*; (*on tennis court etc*) raya *f*; (*on face, palm*) arruga *f,* (*in palmistry*) raya *f,* línea *f*; (*Mil*: *front*) frente *m*; **the L~** (*Geog*) el ecuador; **~ of command** cadena *f* de mando; **~ of fire** línea *f* de tiro; **~ of life** línea *f* de la vida; **~ of sight, ~ of vision** visual *f*; **the ~s of a ship** las formas de un buque; **all along the ~** en toda la línea, (*fig*) completamente, cien por cien; **I draw the ~ at that** yo de ahí no paso; **I draw the ~ at blasphemy** no tolero la blasfemia; **one must draw the ~ somewhere** hay que fijar ciertos límites; **to know where to draw the ~** tener sentido de la moderación, saber dónde conviene detenerse; **his job is on the ~** su puesto está en peligro, se expone a perder su puesto; **to lay it on the ~** decirlo claramente, hablar con franqueza; **to lay one's reputation on the ~** arriesgar su reputación; **to shoot a ~*** darse bombo*, tirarse un farol*.

(**c**) (*row*) fila *f,* hilera *f,* línea *f*; (*Sport*) línea *f*; (*of waiting cars etc*) cola *f,* (*of parked cars*) fila *f*; (*US*: *queue*) cola *f*; **ship of the ~** navío *m* de línea; **~ of battle** línea *f* de batalla; **~ of traffic** cola *f* de coches; **to fall** (*or* **get**) **into ~** (*abreast*) meterse en fila, (*behind one another*) formar hilera, hacer cola; **to stand in ~** (*US*) hacer cola.

(**d**) (*in factory*) línea *f.*

(**e**) (*Elec*) línea *f*; **to be on ~** estar en (pleno) funcionamiento; **to come on ~** entrar en (pleno) funcionamiento.

(**f**) (*of aircraft, liners*) línea *f.*

(**g**) (*of descent*) línea *f,* linaje *m*; **in an unbroken ~** en línea directa; **in the male ~** por el lado de los varones; **descent in the male ~** varonía *f.*

(**h**) (*Rail*: *gen*) línea *f*; (*track*) vía *f*; **down ~** vía *f* descendente; **up ~** vía *f* ascendente; **to cross the ~(s)** cruzar la vía; **to leave the ~(s)** descarrilar; **the ~ to Palencia** el ferrocarril de Palencia, la línea de Palencia.

(**i**) (*Telec*) línea *f*; (*flex*) hilo *m*; **on ~** (*Comput*) en línea; **to be on the ~ to sb** estar al habla con uno; **hold the ~!** ¡no cuelgue Vd!, ¡espere un momento!; **can you get me a ~ to Chicago?** ¿me puede poner con Chicago?

(**j**) (*of print*) renglón *m,* línea *f*; (*Poet*) verso *m*; **~s** (*Theat*) papel *m*; **below the ~ expenditure** gastos *mpl* por debajo de los costos; **in the very next ~** a renglón seguido; **to drop sb a ~** poner unas líneas a uno; **to read between the ~s** leer entre líneas.

(**k**) (*fig*: *course*) **~ of argument** argumento *m*; **~ of conduct** línea *f* de conducta; **~ of inquiry** línea *f* de investigación; pista *f*; **~ of thought** hilo *m* del pensamiento; **to be on the right ~s** ir bien, ir por buen camino; **he takes the ~ that ...** razona que ..., arguye que ...; **to take a hard ~** seguir una política de mano dura; **hard ~s!** ¡mala suerte!; **it's hard ~s on Joe** es mala suerte para Pepe; **what ~ is the government taking?** ¿cuál es la actitud del gobierno?; **this is the official ~** ésta es la versión oficial; **somewhere along the ~ we went wrong** en algún punto nos hemos equivocado; **to take a strong ~ with sb** adoptar una actitud firme con uno.

(**l**) (*fig*: *clue*) pista *f*; indicación *f*; **to give sb a ~ on sth** poner a uno sobre la pista de algo; **can you give me a ~ on it?** ¿me puedes dar algunas indicaciones acerca de ello?; **the police have a ~ on the criminal** la policía tiene una información sobre el delincuente.

(**m**) (*fig*: *notions of conformity*) **along the ~s of, on the ~s of** de acuerdo con, conforme a, a tenor de; **sth along these ~s** algo por el estilo, algo en este sentido; **it's all in the ~ of duty** es una parte normal del deber; **he did it in the ~ of duty** lo hizo cumpliendo su deber; **he's in ~ for promotion** tiene posibilidades para el ascenso; **to be in ~ with** estar de acuerdo con, ser conforme a; **to be out of ~ with** no ser conforme con; **to bring sth into ~ with** alinear algo con; **to fall into ~ with** conformarse con; **to get out of ~** salir de la fila; **to keep the party in ~** mantener la disciplina del partido; **to keep people in ~** mantener a la gente a raya; **to step out of ~** salir de la fila; **to toe the ~** conformarse, someterse, acatar lo dispuesto.

(**n**) (*fig*: *métier, speciality*) especialidad *f,* rama *f*; profesión *f*; **the best in its ~** el mejor en su línea; **what ~ are you in?** ¿a qué se dedica?; **that's not in my ~** eso no es de mi especialidad; **fishing's more in my ~** me interesa más la pesca, de pesca sí sé algo; **we have a good ~ in spring hats** tenemos un buen surtido de sombreros para primavera; **that ~ did not sell at all** ese género resultó ser invendible.

2 *attr*: **~ drawing** dibujo *m* de líneas.

3 *vt* (**a**) (*cross with ~s*) rayar; *field etc* surcar; *face etc* arrugar.

(**b**) **to ~ the streets** ocupar las aceras; **to ~ the route** alinearse a lo largo de la ruta; **the streets were ~d with cheering crowds** en las calles había a cada lado multitudes que gritaban entusiastas; **portraits ~d the walls** las paredes estaban llenas de retratos.

◆**line up 1** *vt people, objects* alinear, poner en fila; *support* alinear, organizar.

2 *vi* (*along street etc*) alinearse, (*in queue*) hacer cola, ponerse en fila, (*Mil*: *abreast*) meterse en fila, (*behind one another*) formar fila; **they ~d up in opposition to** (*or* **against**) **the chairman** se alinearon para oponerse al presidente; **they ~d up behind** (*or* **with**) **the head** se alinearon para apoyar al director; **the teams ~d up like this ...** los equipos formaron así ...

line² [laɪn] *vt clothes etc* forrar (*with* de); (*Tech*) revestir (*with* de); *brakes* guarnecer.

lineage ['lɪnɪɪdʒ] *n* linaje *m.*

lineal ['lɪnɪəl] *adj* lineal, en línea recta; *descent* en línea directa.

lineament [ˈlɪnɪəmənt] *n* lineamento *m.*
linear [ˈlɪnɪəʳ] *adj* lineal; *measure* de longitud.
lined [laɪnd] *adj face etc* arrugado; *paper* reglado; *coat* forrado, con forro; (*Tech*) revestido; **to become ~** arrugarse.
line editing [ˈlaɪnˈedɪtɪŋ] *n* corrección *f* por líneas.
line feed [ˈlaɪnˈfiːd] *n* avance *m* de línea.
line fishing [ˈlaɪn,fɪʃɪŋ] *n* pesca *f* con caña.
line judge [ˈlaɪn,dʒʌdʒ] *n* juez *mf* de fondo.
linen [ˈlɪnɪn] **1** *n* (**a**) lino *m*, hilo *m*; lienzo *m*. (**b**) (*household* ~) ropa *f* de casa; (*bed* ~) ropa *f* de cama; (*table* ~) mantelería *f*; (*personal*) ropa *f* blanca; **clean ~** ropa *f* limpia; **dirty ~** ropa *f* sucia, ropa *f* para lavar; **to wash one's dirty ~ in public** lavar los trapos sucios en público.
2 *adj* de lino.
linen-basket [ˈlɪnɪn,bɑːskɪt] *n* canasta *f* (*or* cesto *m*) de la ropa.
linen-closet [ˈlɪnɪn,klɒzɪt] *n*, **linen-cupboard** [ˈlɪnɪn,kʌbəd] *n* armario *m* para ropa blanca.
line-out [ˈlaɪnaʊt] *n* saque *m* de banda.
line-printer [ˈlaɪn,prɪntəʳ] *n* impresora *f* de línea.
liner¹ [ˈlaɪnəʳ] *n* (*Naut*) transatlántico *m*, vapor *m* de línea.
liner² [ˈlaɪnəʳ] *n* (*bin* ~) bolsa *f* (de la basura).
linesman [ˈlaɪnzmən] *n*, *pl* **linesmen** [ˈlaɪnzmən] (*Sport*) juez *m* de línea, linier *m*, rayador *m* (*SC*); (*Rail*) guardavía *m*; (*Elec*) celador *m*, recorredor *m* de la línea.
line-up [ˈlaɪnʌp] *n* (*Sport etc*) alineación *f*, formación *f*; (*US*: *suspects*) desfile *m* de sospechosos, rueda *f* de presos; (*queue*) cola *f*.
ling¹ [lɪŋ] *n* (*Fish*) *especie de* abadejo *m*.
ling² [lɪŋ] *n* (*Bot*) brezo *m*.
linger [ˈlɪŋgəʳ] *vi* (**a**) (*also* **to ~ on**; *be unwilling to go*) tardar en marcharse, permanecer por indecisión; (*in dying*) tardar en morirse; (*pain*) persistir, durar; (*of doubts etc*) persistir, quedar; **won't you ~ here a while?** ¿no puedes quedarte aquí un rato?
(**b**) (*take one's time*: *on journey etc*) quedarse atrás, retardarse; **to ~ on a subject** dilatarse en un tema; **I let my eye ~ on the scene** seguía sin apartar los ojos de la escena; **to ~ over a meal** comer despacio, no darse prisa por terminar de comer; **to ~ over a task** hacer un trabajo despacio.
lingerie [ˈlænʒəriː] *n* ropa *f* blanca, ropa *f* interior (de mujer), ropa *f* íntima (*LAm*).
lingering [ˈlɪŋgərɪŋ] *adj* lento, prolongado; *death* lento; *doubt* persistente, que no se desvanece; *look* fijo.
lingo* [ˈlɪŋgəʊ] *n* (*language*) lengua *f*, idioma *m*; (*specialist jargon*) jerga *f*.
lingua franca [ˈlɪŋgwəˈfræŋkə] *n* lengua *f* franca.
linguist [ˈlɪŋgwɪst] *n* (**a**) (*speaker of languages*) polígloto *m*, -a *f*, políglota *mf*; (*Univ etc*) estudiante *mf* de idiomas; **he's a good ~** domina varios idiomas, aprende los idiomas con facilidad; **I'm no ~** no puedo con los idiomas; **the company needs more ~s** la compañía necesita más gente que sepa idiomas.
(**b**) (*specialist in linguistics*) lingüista *mf*.
linguistic [lɪŋˈgwɪstɪk] *adj* lingüístico.
linguistician [,lɪŋgwɪsˈtɪʃən] *n* lingüista *mf*, especialista *mf* en lingüística.
linguistics [lɪŋˈgwɪstɪks] *n* lingüística *f*.
liniment [ˈlɪnɪmənt] *n* linimento *m*.
lining [ˈlaɪnɪŋ] *n* (*of clothes etc*) forro *m*; (*Anat, Tech*) revestimiento *m*; (*of brake*) guarnición *f*.
link [lɪŋk] **1** *n* (*of chain*) eslabón *m*; (*fig*: *connection*) enlace *m*, conexión *f*; (*bond*) lazo *m*, vínculo *m*; **a new rail ~ for El Toboso** nuevo enlace *m* ferroviario para El Toboso; **cultural ~s** relaciones *fpl* culturales; **the ~s of friendship** los lazos de la amistad.
2 *vt* eslabonar; *spaceships* acoplar; (*fig*) enlazar, unir, vincular; **to ~ arms** cogerse del brazo; **we are ~ed by telephone to ...** tenemos conexión telefónica con ...; **we are ~ed in friendship** nos vincula la amistad; **the two companies are now ~ed** ahora están unidas las dos compañías.
◆**link together 1** *vt* = **link**. **2** *vi* (*parts*) eslabonarse.
◆**link up 1** *vt* = **link**. **2** *vi* (*persons*) reunirse (*with* con); (*companies etc*) unirse; (*spaceships etc*) acoplarse; (*railway lines*) empalmar.
linkage [ˈlɪŋkɪdʒ] *n* (**a**) unión *f*, conexión *f*, enlace *m*. (**b**) (*Tech*) articulación *f*; acoplamiento *m*; (*Comput*) enlace *m*.
linked [lɪŋkt] *adj problems etc* relacionado, vinculado.
linking verb [ˈlɪŋkɪŋ,vɜːb] *n* verbo *m* copulativo.
linkman [ˈlɪŋkmæn] *n*, *pl* **linkmen** [ˈlɪŋkmen] (*Rad, TV*) locutor *m*, -ora *f* de continuidad.
links [lɪŋks] *npl* campo *m* de golf, cancha *f* de golf (*LAm*).
link-up [ˈlɪŋkʌp] *n* unión *f*; enlace *m*, vinculación *f*; (*of spaceships*) acoplamiento *m*, atraque *m*.
linnet [ˈlɪnɪt] *n* pardillo *m* (común).
lino [ˈlaɪnəʊ] (*Brit*) *n*, **linoleum** [lɪˈnəʊlɪəm] *n* linóleo *m*.
Linotype [ˈlaɪnəʊtaɪp] ® *n* linotipia *f*.
linseed [ˈlɪnsiːd] **1** *n* linaza *f*. **2** *attr*: **~ oil** aceite *m* de linaza.
lint [lɪnt] *n* hilas *fpl*.
lintel [ˈlɪntl] *n* dintel *m*.
lion [ˈlaɪən] *n* león *m*; (*fig*) celebridad *f*; **~'s share** parte *f* del león; **to beard the ~ in his den** entrar en el cubil de la fiera; **to put one's head in the ~'s mouth** meterse en la boca del lobo.
lion cub [ˈlaɪən,kʌb] *n* cachorro *m* de léon.
lioness [ˈlaɪənɪs] *n* leona *f*.
lion-hearted [,laɪənˈhɑːtɪd] *adj* valiente.
lionize [ˈlaɪənaɪz] *vt*: **to ~ sb** tratar a uno como una celebridad.
lion-tamer [ˈlaɪən,teɪməʳ] *n* domador *m*, -ora *f* de leones.
lip [lɪp] *n* (**a**) (*Anat and fig*) labio *m*; (*of jug*) pico *m*; (*of cup, crater*) borde *m*; **my ~s are sealed** soy como una esfinge; **to bite one's ~** (*fig*) morderse el labio; **to hang on sb's ~s** estar pendiente de las palabras de uno; **to keep a stiff upper ~** no inmutarse, aguantarlo todo sin chistar; poner a mal tiempo buena cara; **to lick** (*or* **smack**) **one's ~s** relamerse, chuparse los labios; **to read sb's ~s** leer en los labios de uno.
(**b**) (**‡**: *abuse*) injurias *fpl*; (*backchat*) insolencia *f*; **none of your ~!** ¡cállate la boca!
lip-gloss [ˈlɪpglɒs] *n* brillo *m* de labios.
lipid [ˈlaɪpɪd] *n* lípido *m*.
lipread [ˈlɪpriːd] (*irr*: *V* **read**) **1** *vt* leer los labios a. **2** *vi* leer en los labios.
lip-reading [ˈlɪp,riːdɪŋ] *n* labiolectura *f*, lectura *f* labial.
lip-salve [ˈlɪpsælv] *n* (*Brit*) manteca *f* de cacao, crema *f* protectora para labios.
lip-service [ˈlɪp,sɜːvɪs] *n* jarabe *m* de pico; **to pay ~ to an ideal** alabar un ideal pero por cumplir; **that was only ~** eso fue solamente de dientes para fuera.
lipstick [ˈlɪpstɪk] *n* lápiz *m* labial, rojo *m* de labios, barra *f* de labios.
liquefaction [,lɪkwɪˈfækʃən] *n* licuefacción *f*.
liquefy [ˈlɪkwɪfaɪ] **1** *vt* licuar, liquidar. **2** *vi* licuarse, liquidarse.
liqueur [lɪˈkjʊəʳ] **1** *n* licor *m*. **2** *attr*: **~ glass** copa *f* de licores.
liquid [ˈlɪkwɪd] **1** *adj* (**a**) líquido; *measure* para líquidos; **~ crystal display** visualizador *m* de cristal líquido; **~ waste** vertidos *mpl* líquidos. (**b**) (*fig*) *sound* claro, puro, (*in Phonetics*) líquido; *air* diáfano; **~ assets** activo *m* circulante, activo *m* líquido.
2 *n* líquido *m*; (*Phonetics*) líquida *f*.
liquidate [ˈlɪkwɪdeɪt] *vt* (*all senses*) liquidar.
liquidation [,lɪkwɪˈdeɪʃən] *n* liquidación *f*; **to go into ~** entrar en liquidación.
liquidator [ˈlɪkwɪdeɪtəʳ] *n* liquidador *m*, -ora *f*.
liquidity [lɪˈkwɪdɪtɪ] *n* liquidez *f*; **~ ratio** relación *f* de liquidez.
liquidize [ˈlɪkwɪdaɪz] **1** *vt* licuar, liquidar. **2** *vi* licuarse, liquidarse.
liquidizer [ˈlɪkwɪdaɪzəʳ] *n* licuadora *f*.
Liquid Paper [ˈlɪkwɪdˈpeɪpəʳ] ® *n* Tipp-Ex ® *m*.
liquor [ˈlɪkəʳ] **1** *n* bebidas *fpl* fuertes; **hard ~** licor *m* espiritoso; **to be in ~** estar borracho; **to be the worse for ~** haber bebido más de la cuenta, estar algo borracho. **2** *attr*: **~ cabinet** (*US*) mueble-bar *m*; **~ store** (*US*) bodega *f*, tienda *f* de bebidas alcohólicas, licorería *f* (*LAm*).
liquorice [ˈlɪkərɪs] *n* (*Brit*) regaliz *m*, orozuz *m*.
lira [ˈlɪərə] *n* lira *f*.
Lisbon [ˈlɪzbən] *n* Lisboa *f*.
lisle [laɪl] *n* hilo *m* de Escocia.
lisp [lɪsp] **1** *n* ceceo *m*; (*of child*) balbuceo *m*; **to speak with a ~** cecear. **2** *vt* decir ceceando; decir balbuceando. **3** *vi* cecear; balbucear.
lissom [ˈlɪsəm] *adj* ágil, ligero.
list¹ [lɪst] **1** *n* lista *f*; listado *m*; relación *f*; catálogo *m*; (*of officials*) escalafón *m*; (*Mil etc*) anuario *m*; **to be on the active ~** estar en activo.
2 *attr*: **~ price** precio *m* de lista, precio *m* de catálogo.
3 *vt* poner en una lista; registrar, inscribir; hacer una lista de; catalogar; (*Fin*) cotizar (*at* a); (*Comput*) listar; **he began to ~ all he had been doing** empezó a enumerar

todas las cosas que había hecho; **it is not ~ed** no consta (en la lista).

list² [lɪst] (*Naut*) **1** *n* escora *f*, inclinación *f*; **to have a bad ~** escorar de modo peligroso; **to have a ~ of 20°** escorar a un ángulo de 20°. **2** *vi* escorar (*to port* a babor), inclinarse; **to ~ badly** escorar de modo peligroso.

listed [ˈlɪstɪd] *adj*: **~ building** (*Brit*) monumento *m* histórico, edificio *m* declarado de interés histórico-artístico; **~ company** compañía *f* cotizable; **~ securities** valores *mpl* registrados en bolsa.

listen [ˈlɪsn] *vi* (*hear*) escuchar, oír (*to sth* algo, *to sb* a uno); (*heed*) escuchar, prestar atención, dar oídos, atender (*to* a); **~!** ¡escucha!; **~ to me!** ¡escúchame!; **he wouldn't ~** no quiso escuchar.

◆listen in *vi* escuchar (*also Rad*); **to ~ in to** *conversation, programme* escuchar.

◆listen out for *vt* estar a la escucha de.

listener [ˈlɪsnəʳ] *n* oyente *mf*; (*Rad*) radioescucha *mf*, radioyente *mf*; **dear ~s!** (*Rad*) ¡queridos oyentes!; **to be a good ~** tener mucha paciencia, saber escuchar.

listening [ˈlɪsnɪŋ] **1** *n*: **good ~!** ¡que gocen!; **we don't do much ~ now** ahora escuchamos muy poco la radio. **2** *attr*: **~ comprehension test** ejercicio *m* de comprensión auditiva; **~ device** aparato *m* auditivo, aparato *m* de escucha.

listening-post [ˈlɪsnɪŋpəʊst] *n* puesto *m* de escucha.

listeria [lɪsˈtiːərɪə] *n* listeria *f*.

listing [ˈlɪstɪŋ] *n* (**a**) (*gen, Comput*) listado *m*. (**b**) (*St Ex*) **they have a ~ on the Stock Exchange** cotizan en la Bolsa. (**b**) **~s** *npl* cartelera *f*, guía *f* del espectáculo.

listless [ˈlɪstlɪs] *adj* lánguido, desmayado, apático, indiferente.

listlessly [ˈlɪstlɪslɪ] *adv* lánguidamente, con apatía, con indiferencia.

listlessness [ˈlɪstlɪsnɪs] *n* languidez *f*, desmayo *m*, apatía *f*, indiferencia *f*.

lists [lɪsts] *npl* (*Hist*) liza *f*; **to enter the ~** (*fig*) salir a la palestra.

lit [lɪt] *pret and ptp of* **light**; **to be ~ up*** estar achispado*.

Lit. [lɪt] *n abbr of* **literature**.

litany [ˈlɪtənɪ] *n* letanía *f*.

liter [ˈliːtəʳ] *n* (*US*) = **litre**.

literacy [ˈlɪtərəsɪ] **1** *n* alfabetismo *m*, capacidad *f* de leer y escribir; **~ is low in Slobodia** en Eslobodia son pocos los que saben leer y escribir.

2 *attr*: **~ campaign** campaña *f* de alfabetización; **~ test** prueba *f* de saber leer y escribir.

literal [ˈlɪtərəl] **1** *adj* (**a**) literal. (**b**) (*fig*) material. **2** *nm* (*Typ*) errata *f*.

literally [ˈlɪtərəlɪ] *adv* (**a**) (*in a literal way*) literalmente. (**b**) (*fig*) materialmente, *eg* **it was ~ impossible to work there** era materialmente imposible trabajar allí; **it had ~ ceased to exist** había dejado materialmente de existir.

literal-minded [ˈlɪtərəlˈmaɪndɪd] *adj* sin imaginación, poco imaginativo.

literary [ˈlɪtərərɪ] *adj* literario; **~ agent** agente *m* literario, agente *f* literaria; **~ remains** obras *fpl* póstumas.

literate [ˈlɪtərɪt] *adj* alfabetizado, que sabe leer y escribir; **highly ~** (*fig*) muy culto; **not very ~** (*fig*) poco culto, que tiene poca cultura.

literati [ˌlɪtəˈrɑːtiː] *npl* literatos *mpl*.

literature [ˈlɪtərɪtʃəʳ] *n* (**a**) literatura *f*. (**b**) (*brochures etc*) impresos *mpl*, folletos *mpl*; información *f* impresa; (*learned studies of subject*) estudios *mpl* impresos, bibliografía *f*.

lithe [laɪð] *adj* ágil, ligero.

lithium [ˈlɪθɪəm] *n* litio *m*.

lithograph [ˈlɪθəʊgrɑːf] **1** *n* (*also* **litho**) litografía *f*. **2** *vt* litografiar.

lithographer [lɪˈθɒgrəfəʳ] *n* litógrafo *m*.

lithography [lɪˈθɒgrəfɪ] *n* litografía *f*.

Lithuania [ˌlɪθjʊˈeɪnɪə] *n* Lituania *f*.

Lithuanian [ˌlɪθjʊˈeɪnɪən] **1** *adj* lituano. **2** *n* (**a**) lituano *m*, -a *f*. (**b**) (*Ling*) lituano *m*.

litigant [ˈlɪtɪgənt] *n* litigante *mf*.

litigate [ˈlɪtɪgeɪt] *vi* litigar, pleitear.

litigation [ˌlɪtɪˈgeɪʃən] *n* litigio *m*, litigación *f*, pleitos *mpl*.

litigious [lɪˈtɪdʒəs] *adj* litigioso.

litmus [ˈlɪtməs] *n* tornasol *m*; **~ paper** papel *m* de tornasol; **~ test** prueba *f* de tornasol, (*fig*) prueba *f* de fuego.

litre, (*US*) **liter** [ˈliːtəʳ] *n* litro *m*.

litter [ˈlɪtəʳ] **1** *n* (**a**) (*vehicle*) litera *f*; (*Med*) camilla *f*.

(**b**) (*bedding*) lecho *m*, cama *f* de paja.

(**c**) (*Zool*) camada *f*, cría *f*, críos *mpl*.

(**d**) (*rubbish*) basura *f*, desperdicios *mpl*; (*papers*) papeles *mpl* (viejos); (*wrappings*) envases *mpl*; **'No ~'**, **'Take your ~ home'** 'No tirar basura'.

(**e**) (*general untidiness*) desorden *m*, confusión *f*; **in a ~** en desorden; **a ~ of books** un montón de libros en desorden, un revoltijo de libros.

2 *vt* (**a**) *animal* dar cama de paja a.

(**b**) (*give birth to*) parir.

(**c**) **to ~ papers about a room, to ~ a room with papers** esparcir papeles por un cuarto, dejar los papeles esparcidos por un cuarto; **a page ~ed with mistakes** una página plagada de errores; **a street ~ed with paper** una calle llena de papeles.

3 *vi* (*cat*) parir.

litter-basket [ˈlɪtəbɑːskɪt] *n*, **litter-bin** [ˈlɪtəbɪn] *n* papelera *f*.

litterbug [ˈlɪtəbʌg] *n*, **litter-lout** [ˈlɪtəlaʊt] persona *f* que esparce papeles usados (*or* envases *etc*) por las calles (*or* en el campo).

little [ˈlɪtl] **1** *adj* (**a**) pequeño, chico; poco; escaso; **a ~ book** un libro pequeño; **a ~ wine** un poco de vino; **her ~ brother** su hermano menor, su hermanito; **with no ~ trouble** con bastante dificultad, con no poca dificultad.

(**b**) (*~ with noun, often translated by suffix, eg*) **a ~ house** una casita; **just a ~ gift** (*as charity*) una limosnita; **a very ~ fish** un pececillo; **a ~ sip** un sorbito.

2 *adv* poco; **he reads ~** lee poco; **a ~ read book** un libro poco leído, un libro que se lee poco; **a ~ better** un poco mejor; **~ more than a month ago** hace poco más de un mes; **we were not a ~ worried** nos inquietamos bastante, quedamos muy inquietos; **~ does he know that ...** no tiene la menor idea de que ...; **I walk as ~ as possible** voy a pie lo menos posible.

3 *n* poco *m*; **he knows ~** sabe poco; **to spend ~ or nothing** gastar poco o nada; **he had ~ to say** poco fue lo que tenía que decir, apenas tenía nada que decir; **there was (but) ~ we could do** apenas había nada que hacer; **give me a ~** dame un poco; **~ by ~** poco a poco; **for a ~** un rato, por un rato, durante un rato; **in ~** en pequeño; **to make ~ of sth** sacar poco en claro de algo.

little-known [ˌlɪtlˈnəʊn] *adj* poco conocido.

littleness [ˈlɪtlnɪs] *n* pequeñez *f*; poquedad *f*; (*fig*) mezquindad *f*.

littoral [ˈlɪtərəl] **1** *adj* litoral. **2** *n* litoral *m*.

liturgical [lɪˈtɜːdʒɪkəl] *adj* litúrgico.

liturgy [ˈlɪtədʒɪ] *n* liturgia *f*.

livable [ˈlɪvəbl] *adj* llevadero, soportable.

livable-in [ˈlɪvəbl,ɪn] *adj* habitable.

livable-with [ˈlɪvəbl,wɪð] *adj* tratable, simpático.

live¹ [lɪv] **1** *vt life* llevar, tener, pasar; *experience* vivir; **to ~ a happy life** tener (*or* llevar) una vida feliz; **to ~ a part** encarnar brillantemente un papel; (*pej*) vivir como un personaje de teatro.

2 *vi* vivir; **long ~ the Queen!** ¡viva la reina!; **to ~ and learn** vivir para ver; **one ~s and learns** todos los días se aprende algo; **to ~ and let ~** vivir y dejar vivir, ser tolerante con todos; **to ~ from hand to mouth** vivir al día; **to ~ high, to ~ well** darse buena vida, nadar en la abundancia; **to ~ like a king (*or* lord)** vivir a cuerpo de rey; **as long as I ~** mientras viva; **he hasn't long to ~** no le queda mucho de vida; **to ~ again** volver a vivir; **he ~d by certain ideals** vivió con arreglo a ciertos ideales; **to ~ by one's pen** vivir de su pluma; **I ~ for the day (when) I retire** que venga pronto el día en que me jubile; **a night that will ~ in the nation's history** una noche que vivirá en la historia nacional; **her voice will ~ with me until I die** su voz vivirá siempre en mi memoria; **if you haven't been to Río you haven't ~d** si no has estado en Río no sabes qué es vivir; **they all ~d happily ever after** todos comieron perdices y fueron felices.

◆live down *vt* lograr borrar.

◆live in 1 *vt house etc* vivir en, habitar, ocupar; **a house not fit to be ~d in** una casa no habitable.

2 *vi* (*servant etc*) estar de interno, ser interno.

◆live off *vt* (**a**) vivir de; **to ~ off one's estate** vivir de las rentas de su finca; **he ~s off his uncle** vive a costa de su tío; *V* **land**.

(**b**) *food* alimentarse de, comer (únicamente).

◆live on 1 *vt* (**a**) = **live off (b)**.

(**b**) **to ~ on a private income** vivir de unas rentas particulares; **what does he ~ on?** ¿de qué vive?; **she doesn't earn enough to ~ on** no gana bastante para vivir; **to ~ on hope** nutrirse de esperanzas.

(**c**) **he ~s on his uncle** vive a costa de su tío.

2 *vi* (*go on living*) vivir, seguir viviendo; (*memory*) seguir vivo.

◆**live out 1** *vt period, reign* vivir hasta el fin de, sobrevivir a; **to ~ out one's life** pasar el resto de la vida.

2 *vi* (*servant*) vivir fuera.

◆**live through** *vt*: **to ~ through an experience** vivir una experiencia.

◆**live together** *vi* (*in amity*) convivir; (*as lovers*) vivir juntos, vivir liados.

◆**live up 1** *vt* (*) **to ~ it up** correr las grandes juergas*; **let's go and ~ it up** vamos a echar una cana al aire; **he was living it up with a Swede** lo pasaba en grande con una sueca*.

2 *vi*: **to ~ up to a standard** vivir con arreglo a (*or* en conformidad con) una norma; **to ~ up to a promise** cumplir una promesa; **to ~ up to one's reputation** estar a la altura de su fama; **it ~d up to our hopes** correspondía a nuestras esperanzas; **this will give him sth to ~ up to** esto le dará una meta que seguir.

◆**live with** *vt person* vivir con; **to ~ with the knowledge that ...** vivir sabiendo que ...; **it's a fact one has to ~ with** es un hecho que uno tiene que aceptar; **you'll learn to ~ with it** aprenderás a aguantarlo.

live[2] [laɪv] **1** *adj* **(a)** *person* vivo; **a real ~ duke** un duque en persona, un duque de carne y hueso.

(b) (*fig*) *issue etc* candente, de actualidad.

(c) (*lively*) vivo, dinámico, lleno de vida; **a very ~ class** una clase de mucha animación.

(d) **~ broadcast** transmisión *f* en directo, transmisión *f* en vivo; **~ performance, ~ show** actuación *f* en vivo.

(e) *weight* en vivo; *cartridge* con bala; **~ coal** ascua *f*, brasa *f*; **~ export** exportación *f* en pie; **~ rail** raíl *m* electrizado; **~ shell** obús *m* con carga explosiva; **~ wire** alambre *m* con corriente, alambre *m* conectado, (*fig*) persona *f* dinámica, persona *f* emprendedora.

2 *adv*: **to broadcast ~** transmitir en directo, transmitir en vivo.

lived-in [ˈlɪvd,ɪn] *adj* acogedor, familiar; reconfortante.

live-in [ˈlɪv,ɪn] *attr*: **~ lover** compañero *m*, -a *f*; **~ maid** criada *f* interna, criada *f* que duerme en la casa donde sirve.

livelihood [ˈlaɪvlɪhʊd] *n* vida *f*; sustento *m*; **rice is their ~** el arroz es su único sustento; **to earn a ~** ganarse la vida.

liveliness [ˈlaɪvlɪnɪs] *n* vida *f*, vivacidad *f*, viveza *f*; energía *f*; animación *f*; alegría *f*.

livelong [ˈlɪvlɒŋ] *adj*: **all the ~ day** todo el santo día.

lively [ˈlaɪvlɪ] *adj person, imagination, account etc* vivo; *campaign, effort, speech* enérgico; *conversation* animado; *interest* grande; *horse* brioso; *pace* rápido; *party, scene etc* bullicioso, alegre; *tune* alegre; **things are getting ~** se está animando la fiesta; esto se está complicando; **to have a ~ time of it** pasar un rato lleno de incidentes; **to look ~** estar espabilado.

liven [ˈlaɪvn] **1** *vt*: **to ~ up** animar, estimular; alegrar. **2** *vi*: **to ~ up** animarse; alegrarse.

liver[1] [ˈlɪvəʳ] *n*: **fast ~** calavera *m*; **good ~** gastrónomo *m*; persona *f* que se da buena vida.

liver[2] [ˈlɪvəʳ] **1** *n* (*Anat*) hígado *m*. **2** *attr*: **~ complaint** mal *m* de hígado, afección *f* hepática.

liveried [ˈlɪvərɪd] *adj* en librea.

liverish [ˈlɪvərɪʃ] *adj*: **to be ~, to feel ~** sentirse mal del hígado.

liver pâté [ˌlɪvəˈpæteɪ] *n* foie gras *m*, paté *m* de hígado.

Liverpudlian [ˌlɪvəˈpʌdlɪən] **1** *adj* de Liverpool. **2** *n* habitante *mf* (*or* nativo *m*, -a *f*) de Liverpool.

liver sausage [ˈlɪvə,sɒsɪdʒ] *n* salchicha *f* de hígado.

liverwort [ˈlɪvə,wɜːt] *n* hepática *f*.

liverwurst [ˈlɪvəwɜːst] *n* (*esp US*) embutido *m* de hígado.

livery [ˈlɪvərɪ] **1** *n* librea *f*; (*liter*) ropaje *m*. **2** *attr*: **~ company** (*Brit*) gremio *m* (*antiguo, de la Ciudad de Londres*); **~ stable** caballeriza *f* de alquiler.

lives [laɪvz] *npl of* **life.**

livestock [ˈlaɪvstɒk] *n* ganado *m*, ganadería *f*, hacienda *f* (*SC*).

livid [ˈlɪvɪd] *adj* **(a)** (*in colour*) lívido. **(b)** (*furious*) **he was ~** estaba furioso; **he got ~** se puso negro.

living [ˈlɪvɪŋ] **1** *adj* vivo, viviente; *image, language* vivo; **~ or dead** vivo o muerto; **'The L~ Desert'** 'El desierto viviente'; **a ~ death** una vida peor que la muerte; **a ~ skeleton** un esqueleto ambulante; **the biggest flood in ~ memory** la mayor inundación de que hay memoria (*or* que se recuerda); **the greatest ~ pianist** el (*or* la) mejor pianista que vive hoy (*or* de los que viven hoy).

2 *n* **(a)** vida *f*; **to earn** (*or* **make**) **a ~** ganarse la vida; **to make a bare ~** ganar lo justo para vivir; **he thinks the world owes him a ~** se cree con derecho a todo; **the quality of urban ~** la calidad de la vida urbana; **to work for one's ~** ganarse la vida trabajando.

(b) (*Brit Eccl*) beneficio *m*.

(c) **the ~** (*pl*: *people*) los vivos.

3 *attr* de vida; **~ conditions** condiciones *fpl* de vida; **~ expenses** gastos *mpl* de mantenimiento; **~ quarters** alojamiento *m*, residencia *f*; **~ standards** nivel *m* de vida; **~ wage** jornal *m* suficiente para vivir.

living-room [ˈlɪvɪŋrʊm] *n* cuarto *m* de estar, living *m*, estancia *f* (*LAm*).

living-space [ˈlɪvɪŋspeɪs] *n* espacio *m* vital (*also fig*).

Livy [ˈlɪvɪ] *nm* Tito Livio.

Liz [lɪz] *nf familiar form of* **Elizabeth.**

lizard [ˈlɪzəd] *n* lagarto *m*, (*small*) lagartija *f*.

ll. *abbr of* **lines** líneas *fpl*.

llama [ˈlɑːmə] *n* llama *f*.

LL.B. *n abbr of* **Bachelor of Laws** licenciado *m*, -a *f* en Derecho, Ldo, -a en Dcho.

LL.D. *n abbr of* **Doctor of Laws** Doctor *m*, -ora *f* en Derecho, Dr. (Dra.) en Dcho.

LMT *n* (*US*) *abbr of* **Local Mean Time.**

lo [ləʊ] *interj*: **~ and behold the result!** ¡he aquí el resultado!, ¡ved aquí el resultado!; **and ~ and behold there it was** y por milagro ahí estaba.

loach [ləʊtʃ] *n* locha *f*.

load [ləʊd] **1** *n* **(a)** (*thing carried*) carga *f* (*also fig*); (*weight*) peso *m*; (*quantity*: *of mail, washing etc*) cantidad *f*; (*Agr etc*: *as measure*) carretada *f*; **under full ~** en plena carga.

(b) (*Elec, Tech*) carga *f*; **to spread the ~** repartir la carga, (*fig*) repartir el trabajo, repartir la responsabilidad (*etc*).

(c) **~s of, a ~ of** gran cantidad de, montones de; **thanks, we have ~s** gracias, tenemos bastante; **it's a ~ of old rubbish*** es una basura, no vale para nada; **that's a ~ off my mind** ¡qué alivio!, ¡se me quita un peso de encima!; **get a ~ of this!*** ¡mírame esto!, ¡escucha esto un poco!

2 *vt* (*gen, Comput, Elec*) cargar (*with* con, de); (*burden, weigh down*) agobiar (*with* de); **to ~ sb with honours** llenar a uno de honores, colmar a uno de honores; **the branch was ~ed with pears** la rama estaba cargada de peras; **the whole thing is ~ed with problems** el asunto está erizado de dificultades; **we're ~ed with debts** estamos llenos de deudas.

3 *vi* **(a)** (*lorry etc*) cargar, tomar carga; **'~ing and unloading'** (*street sign*) 'permitido carga y descarga'.

(b) (*Mil*) cargar; **~!** ¡carguen armas!; **how does this gun ~?** ¿cómo se carga esta escopeta?; **to ~ again** volver a cargar.

4 *vr*: **to ~ o.s. with** cargarse de.

◆**load down** *vt* cargar, sobrecargar (*with* de); **he was ~ed down with debt** estaba cargado de deudas; **we're ~ed down with work** tenemos trabajo hasta encima de las cejas.

◆**load up** *vt* cargar (*with* de).

load-bearing [ˈləʊd,beərɪŋ] *adj beam etc* maestro.

loaded [ˈləʊdɪd] *adj* **(a)** cargado; *dice* cargado, lastrado; *gun* cargado. **(b)** *question* intencionado, que sugiere una contestación. **(c)** **to be ~‡** (*drunk*) estar trompa‡; (*rich*) estar podrido de dinero*, (*carry much money*) llevar encima mucho dinero.

loader [ˈləʊdəʳ] *n* cargador *m*.

loading [ˈləʊdɪŋ] *n* (*Comm*: *Insurance*) sobreprima *f*.

loading-bay [ˈləʊdɪŋ,beɪ] *n*, **loading-dock** [ˈləʊdɪŋ,dɒk] *n* área *f* de carga y descarga.

loadline [ˈləʊdlaɪn] *n* línea *f* de flotación (con carga), línea *f* de carga.

loadstone [ˈləʊdstəʊn] *n* piedra *f* imán.

loaf[1] [ləʊf] *n*, *pl* **loaves** [ləʊvz] pan *m*; (*large, cottage*) hogaza *f*; (*small, French*) barra *f*; (*of sugar*) pan *m*, pilón *m*; **half a ~ is better than no bread** menos da una piedra, peor es nada; **use your ~!‡** (*Brit*) ¡despabílate!

loaf[2] [ləʊf] *vi* haraganear, gandulear.

loafer [ˈləʊfəʳ] *n* vago *m*, gandul *m*; (*in street*) azotacalles *m*.

loaf sugar [ˈləʊf,ʃʊgəʳ] *n* pan *m* de azúcar.

loaf tin [ˈləʊftɪn] *n* bandeja *f* de horno.

loam [ləʊm] *n* marga *f*.

loamy [ˈləʊmɪ] *adj* margoso.

loan [ləʊn] **1** *n* (*thing lent between persons*) préstamo *m*; (*Comm, public*) empréstito *m*; **it's on ~** está prestado; **I asked for the ~ of the book** le pedí prestado el libro; **I had it on ~ from the company** me lo prestó la compañía; **she is**

on ~ to another department presta sus servicios en otra sección; **to raise a ~** (*public*) procurar un empréstito, lanzar un empréstito; **to subscribe a ~** suscribir un préstamo.

2 *attr*: **~ account** cuenta *f* de crédito; **~ agreement** acuerdo *m* de préstamo; **~ capital** empréstito *m*; **~ fund** fondo *m* de empréstitos; **~ shark** tiburón *m*, usurero *m* extorsionador.

3 *vt* (*US, also Brit**) prestar.

loan-translation [ˌləʊntrænzˈleɪʃən] *n* calco *m* lingüístico.

loanword [ˈləʊnwɜːd] *n* préstamo *m*.

loath [ləʊθ] *adj*: **nothing ~** de buena gana; **to be ~ to do sth** estar poco dispuesto a hacer algo; **to be ~ for sb to do sth** no querer en absoluto que uno haga algo.

loathe [ləʊð] *vt thing* abominar, detestar, aborrecer; *person* odiar; **I ~ doing it** me repugna hacerlo; **he ~s being corrected** abomina que se le corrija.

loathing [ˈləʊðɪŋ] *n* aversión *f* (*of* hacia, por); aborrecimiento *m* (*of* de); odio *m* (*of* hacia, por); **it fills me with ~** me da asco; **the ~ which I felt for him** el odio que sentía hacia él.

loathsome [ˈləʊðsəm] *adj thing* asqueroso, repugnante; *person* odioso.

loathsomeness [ˈləʊðsəmnɪs] *n* lo asqueroso; lo odioso.

loaves [ləʊvz] *npl of* **loaf.**

lob [lɒb] **1** *n* voleo *m* alto, lob *m*, globo *m*.

2 *vt ball* volear por alto; **to ~ sth over to sb** tirar algo a uno.

3 *vi* volear por alto.

lobby [ˈlɒbɪ] **1** *n* (**a**) (*entrance hall*) vestíbulo *m*; (*corridor*) pasillo *m*; (*anteroom*) antecámara *f*; (*waiting-room*) sala *f* de espera.

(**b**) (*Brit Parl etc*) lobby *m*, cabildo *m*; **the environmentalist ~** el lobby ambientista.

2 *attr*: **~ correspondent** (*Brit*) periodista *m* parlamentario, periodista *f* parlamentaria.

3 *vt*: **to ~ one's member of parliament** presionar para convencer a su diputado, ejercer presión sobre su diputado.

4 *vi* cabildear, ejercer presión, presionar, capitulear (*And, SC*); **to ~ for a reform** hacer lobby a favor de una reforma, presionar en pro de una reforma.

lobbying [ˈlɒbɪɪŋ] *n* cabildeo *m*.

lobbyist [ˈlɒbɪɪst] *n* cabildero *m*, -a *f*.

lobe [ləʊb] *n* lóbulo *m*.

lobelia [ləʊˈbiːlɪə] *n* lobelia *f*.

lobotomy [ləʊˈbɒtəmɪ] *n* lobotomía *f*.

lobster [ˈlɒbstəʳ] *n* langosta *f*; (*large*) bogavante *m*.

lobster-pot [ˈlɒbstəpɒt] *n* langostera *f*, nasa *f*.

local [ˈləʊkəl] **1** *adj* local; *government, colour, anaesthetic,* (*Telec*) *call* local; *radio station* comarcal, regional; *train* de cercanías; *road* vecinal; *usage, word* local, regional, restringido; (*in distribution, frequency*) poco común, localizado, que no se encuentra en todos los sitios, de distribución restringida; **he's a ~ man** es de aquí; **~ area network** red *f* de área local; **~ authority** autoridad *f* local; **the ~ doctor** el médico del pueblo, el médico del barrio; **~ time** hora *f* local; **to drink the ~ wine** beber el vino del país.

2 *n* (*) (**a**) **the ~** (*Brit*) la taberna.

(**b**) **the ~s** los vecinos, el vecindario, los de aquí; **he's one of the ~s** es de aquí.

locale [ləʊˈkɑːl] *n* lugar *m*, escenario *m*.

locality [ləʊˈkælɪtɪ] *n* localidad *f*.

localize [ˈləʊkəlaɪz] *vt* localizar.

localized [ˈləʊkəlaɪzd] *adj* localizado, local.

locally [ˈləʊkəlɪ] *adv*: **houses are dear ~** por aquí las casas cuestan bastante; **we deliver free ~** en la ciudad y sus inmediaciones la entrega a domicilio es gratuita; **the plant is common ~** la planta es común en ciertas localidades.

locate [ləʊˈkeɪt] *vt* (**a**) (*place*) colocar, establecer, ubicar (*esp LAm*); **to be ~d at** estar situado en, estar ubicado en, radicar en.

(**b**) (*find*) encontrar, localizar; **we ~d it eventually** por fin lo encontramos; por fin averiguamos su paradero.

location [ləʊˈkeɪʃən] *n* (**a**) (*place*) situación *f*, posición *f*; ubicación *f*; (*placing*) colocación *f*.

(**b**) (*finding*) localización *f*.

(**c**) (*Cine*) rodaje *m* fuera del estudio; terreno *m* para rodaje de exteriores; **to be on ~ in Mexico** estar rodando en Méjico; **to film on ~** filmar en exteriores.

locative [ˈlɒkətɪv] *n* (*also* **~ case**) locativo *m*.

loch [lɒx] *n* (*Scot*) lago *m*; (*sea ~*) ría *f*, brazo *m* de mar.

lock¹ [lɒk] *n* (*of hair*) mechón *m*, guedeja *f*; (*ringlet*) bucle *m*; **~s** cabellos *mpl*.

lock² [lɒk] **1** *n* (**a**) (*on door, box etc*) cerradura *f*; (*Mech*) retén *m*, tope *m*; (*of gun*; *also Wrestling*) llave *f*; **~, stock and barrel** por completo, del todo; **to put sth under ~ and key** encerrar algo bajo llave.

(**b**) (*on canal*) esclusa *f*; (*pressure chamber*) cámara *f* intermedia.

2 *vt door etc* cerrar con llave; (*Mech*) trabar; *steering-wheel* bloquear; (*Comput*) *screen* desactivar; **the armies were ~ed in combat** los ejércitos estaban luchando encarnizadamente; **they were ~ed in each other's arms** quedaban estrechamente abrazados.

3 *vi* cerrarse con llave; (*Mech*) trabarse.

◆**lock away** *vt*: **to ~ sth away** guardar algo bajo llave.

◆**lock in** *vt* encerrar; **to ~ sb in a room** encerrar a uno en un cuarto.

◆**lock on** *vi* seguir, perseguir; **to ~ on to** (*Mech*) acoplarse a, unirse a.

◆**lock out** *vt*: **to ~ sb out** cerrar la puerta a uno, dejar a uno en la calle; **the workers were ~ed out** los obreros quedaron sin trabajo por lock-out; **to find o.s. ~ed out** estar fuera sin llave para abrir la puerta.

◆**lock up 1** *vt* encerrar; (*in prison*) encarcelar; *capital* inmovilizar; **you ought to be ~ed up!** ¡irás a parar a la cárcel!

2 *vi* echar la llave.

locker [ˈlɒkəʳ] *n* armario *m* (particular); cajón *m* con llave; (*Rail etc*) casillero *m* (de consigna), consigna *f* automática; (*US*) cámara *f* de frío; (*of gymnasium*) cabina *f*.

locker-room [ˈlɒkəˌrʊm] *n* vestuario *m*.

locket [ˈlɒkɪt] *n* medallón *m*, guardapelo *m*.

lockgate [ˈlɒkgeɪt] *n* puerta *f* de esclusa.

lockjaw [ˈlɒkdʒɔː] *n* trismo *m*.

lock-keeper [ˈlɒkˌkiːpəʳ] *n* esclusero *m*.

locknut [ˈlɒknʌt] *n* contratuerca *f*.

lockout [ˈlɒkaʊt] *n* lock-out *m*, cierre *m* patronal.

lock-picker [ˈlɒkˌpɪkəʳ] *n* espadista *m*.

locksmith [ˈlɒksmɪθ] *n* cerrajero *m*.

lock-up [ˈlɒkʌp] **1** *n* (*prison*) cárcel *f*, jaula *f*; (*Brit*: *shop*) tienda *f* sin trastienda. **2** *attr* con cerradura; **~ (garage)** (*Brit*) garaje *m*, (*inside large garage*) jaula *f*; **~ stall** (*US*) jaula *f*, cochera *f*.

loco¹* [ˈləʊkəʊ] *n* = **locomotive.**

loco² [ˈləʊkəʊ] (*Comm*) **1** *attr*: **~ price** *precio cotizado en un lugar (aceptando el comprador todos los costos y riesgos al trasladar la mercancía a otro lugar)*. **2** *adv*: **~ Southampton** *lo mismo que* **1**, *más*: *la mercancía se halla en Southampton como lugar de origen*.

locomotion [ˌləʊkəˈməʊʃən] *n* locomoción *f*.

locomotive [ˌləʊkəˈməʊtɪv] **1** *adj* locomotor. **2** *n* locomotora *f*, máquina *f*.

locum (tenens *Brit frm*) [ˈləʊkəm(ˈtenenz)] *n* interino *m*, -a *f*.

locus [ˈlɒkəs] *n*, *pl* **loci** [ˈlɒkiː] punto *m*, sitio *m*; (*Math*) lugar *m* (geométrico).

locust [ˈləʊkəst] *n* (**a**) (*Zool*) langosta *f*, acridio *m* (*Mex, SC*).

(**b**) (*Bot*) algarroba *f*.

locust tree [ˈləʊkəstˌtriː] *n* acacia *f* falsa; algarrobo *m*.

locution [ləˈkjuːʃən] *n* locución *f*.

locutory [ˈlɒkjʊtərɪ] *n* locutorio *m*.

lode [ləʊd] *n* filón *m*, veta *f*.

lodestar [ˈləʊdstɑːʳ] *n* estrella *f* polar; (*fig*) norte *m*.

lodestone [ˈləʊdstəʊn] *n* piedra *f* imán.

lodge [lɒdʒ] **1** *n* (*in park*) casa *f* del guarda; (*porter's*) portería *f*; (*Univ, master's*) rectoría *f*; (*masonic*) logia *f*.

2 *vt person* alojar, hospedar; *object* (*place*) colocar, (*insert*) meter, introducir; *complaint* presentar (*with a*); **to ~ sth with sb** dejar algo en manos de uno, entregar algo a uno; **the bullet is ~d in the lung** la bala se ha alojado en el pulmón.

3 *vi* alojarse, hospedarse (*at, in* en; *with* con, en casa de); (*of object*: *end up*) ir a parar; (*remain*) quedarse, fijarse, quedar empotrado (*in* en); introducirse, penetrar (*in* en); **where do you ~?** ¿dónde tienes tu pensión?, ¿en qué pensión vives?; **the bullet ~d in the lung** la bala se alojó en el pulmón; **a bomb ~d in the engine-room** una bomba se incrustó en la sala de máquinas.

lodger [ˈlɒdʒəʳ] *n* (*Brit*) huésped *m*, -eda *f*; **I was a ~ there once** hace tiempo me hospedé allí; **she takes ~s** tiene una pensión.

lodging [ˈlɒdʒɪŋ] *n* alojamiento *m*, hospedaje *m*; **~s** (*in general*) alojamiento *m*, pensión *f*; (*room*) habitación *f*; **they gave me a night's ~** me recibieron en su casa esa noche;

to look for ~s buscar alojamiento, buscar una pensión; **we took ~s with Mrs P** nos hospedamos en casa de la Sra de P; **are they good ~s?** ¿es buena la pensión?
lodging-house ['lɒdʒɪŋhaʊs] *n*, *pl* **lodging-houses** ['lɒdʒɪŋ,haʊzɪz] casa *f* de huéspedes, pensión *f*.
loess ['ləʊɪs] *n* loess *m*.
loft [lɒft] **1** *n* (*of house*) desván *m*; (*straw~*) pajar *m*; (*Eccl*) galería *f*. **2** *vt pelota* liftar.
loftily ['lɒftɪlɪ] *adv* en alto, hacia lo alto; *say etc* orgullosamente, arrogantemente.
loftiness ['lɒftɪnɪs] *n* altura *f*; grandiosidad *f*; sublimidad *f*; altanería *f*, orgullo *m*.
lofty ['lɒftɪ] *adj* (*high*) alto, elevado, encumbrado; (*grandiose*) grandioso; (*noble*) noble, sublime; (*haughty*) altanero, orgulloso.
log[1] [lɒg] **1** *n* (**a**) leño *m*, tronco *m*. (**b**) (*Naut: apparatus*) corredera *f*; *V* **logbook**.
2 *attr*: ~ **cabin** cabina *f* de troncos; ~ **fire** fuego *m* de madera.
3 *vt* apuntar, anotar, registrar; **we ~ged 50 kilometres that day** ese día recorrimos (*or* cubrimos) 50 kilómetros.
4 *vi* cortar (y transportar) troncos.
◆**log in 1** *vt* meter en el sistema. **2** *vi* entrar al sistema, acceder, iniciar la sesión, tomar contacto.
◆**log off 1** *vt* sacar del sistema. **2** *vi* salir del sistema, terminar de operar, finalizar la sesión.
◆**log on** *vt, vi* = **log in.**
◆**log out** *vt, vi* = **log off.**
◆**log up** *vt* registrar.
log[2] [lɒg] **1** *n abbr of* **logarithm** logaritmo *m*, log. **2** *attr*: ~ **tables** tablas *fpl* de logaritmos.
loganberry ['ləʊgənbərɪ] *n* (*fruit*) frambuesa *f* norteamericana; (*bush*) frambueso *m* norteamericano.
logarithm ['lɒgərɪθəm] *n* logaritmo *m*.
logbook ['lɒgbʊk] *n* (*Naut*) cuaderno *m* de bitácora, diario *m* de navegación, diario *m* de a bordo; (*Aer*) libro *m* de vuelo; (*Tech*) cuaderno *m* de trabajo.
logger ['lɒgəʳ] *n* (*dealer*) maderero *m*, negociante *m* en maderas; (*woodcutter*) leñador *m*.
loggerheads ['lɒgəhedz] *npl*: **to be at** ~ estar de pique (*with* con).
logging ['lɒgɪŋ] *n* explotación *f* forestal; transporte *m* de troncos.
logic ['lɒdʒɪk] *n* lógica *f*; **in** ~ lógicamente.
logical ['lɒdʒɪkəl] *adj* lógico; ~ **circuit** circuito *m* lógico; ~ **record** registro *m* lógico.
logically ['lɒdʒɪkəlɪ] *adv* lógicamente.
logician [lɒ'dʒɪʃən] *n* lógico *mf*.
logistic [lɒ'dʒɪstɪk] *adj* logístico.
logistics [lɒ'dʒɪstɪks] *n* logística *f*.
logjam ['lɒgdʒæm] *n* (*fig*) atolladero *m*; bloqueo *m*; **to clear the** ~ desbloquear el camino, quitar los obstáculos.
logo ['ləʊgəʊ] *n* logo *m*, logotipo *m*.
log-off ['lɒg'ɒf] *n* salida *f* del sistema.
log-on ['lɒg'ɒn] *n* entrada *f* al sistema.
log-rolling ['lɒg,rəʊlɪŋ] *n* intercambio *m* de favores políticos, sistema *m* de concesiones mutuas.
logy ['ləʊgɪ] *adj* (*US*) torpe, lerdo.
loin [lɔɪn] *n* ijada *f*; (*of meat*) lomo *m*; **~s** lomos *mpl*; **to gird up one's ~s** aprestarse para la lucha.
loin chop [,lɔɪn'tʃɒp] *n* chuleta *f*.
loincloth ['lɔɪnklɒθ] *n*, *pl* **loincloths** ['lɔɪnklɒðz] taparrabo *m*.
Loire [lwɑːr] *n* Loira *m*.
loiter ['lɔɪtəʳ] *vi* (*waste time*) perder el tiempo; (*idle*) gandulear, holgazanear; (*fall behind*) rezagarse; (*on the way*) entretenerse; **don't ~ on the way!** ¡no te entretengas!; **to ~ with intent** rondar un edificio (*etc*) con fines criminales, merodear con fines criminales.
◆**loiter away** *vt*: **to ~ away the time** perder el tiempo.
loll [lɒl] *vi* (*head*) colgar, caer; **to ~ against** recostarse con indolencia contra.
◆**loll about, loll around** *vi* repantigarse.
◆**loll back** *vi*: **to ~ back on** = **loll against**; **to ~ back in a chair** repanchigarse en un asiento, estar repanchigado en un asiento.
◆**loll out** *vi*: **the dog's tongue was ~ing out** la lengua del perro colgaba hacia fuera.
lollipop ['lɒlɪpɒp] **1** *n* pirulí *m*; (*round*) chupachupa *f*, (*flat*) piruleta *f*; (*iced* ~) polo *m*. **2** *attr*: ~ **lady***, ~ **man*** (*Brit*) vigilante *mf* de paso de peatones (*que vigila a los niños cerca de las escuelas*).
lollop ['lɒləp] *vi* (*esp Brit*) moverse desgarbadamente; **to ~ along** moverse torpemente, arrastrar los pies.
lolly ['lɒlɪ] *n* (**a**) (‡: *money*) parné‡ *m*. (**b**) (*) = **lollipop.**
Lombard ['lɒmbɑːd] **1** *adj* lombardo. **2** *n* lombardo *m* -a *f*.
Lombardy ['lɒmbədɪ] **1** *n* Lombardía *f*. **2** *attr*: ~ **poplar** chopo *m* lombardo.
London ['lʌndən] **1** *n* Londres *m*. **2** *attr* londinense.
Londoner ['lʌndənəʳ] *n* londinense *mf*.
London pride [,lʌndən'praɪd] *n* (*Bot*) corona *f* de rey.
lone [ləʊn] *adj* solitario, único, aislado; ~ **ranger** llanero *m* solitario; **to play a ~ hand** actuar solo; **to be a ~ wolf** ser un solitario; *V* **lonely.**
loneliness ['ləʊnlɪnɪs] *n* soledad *f*; aislamiento *m*.
lonely ['ləʊnlɪ] *adj* solitario, solo; *place etc* aislado, remoto; (*deserted*) desierto; ~ **hearts column** sección *f* del corazón solitario; **to feel** ~ sentirse muy solo; **it's a ~ life** es una vida solitaria; **it's terribly ~ out here** aquí se siente uno terriblemente solo.
loner ['ləʊnəʳ] *n* individualista *mf*, solitario *m*, -a *f*.
lonesome ['ləʊnsəm] *adj* solitario, aislado.
long[1] [lɒŋ] **1** *adj* (**a**) (*of size*) largo; *mirror* de cuerpo entero; *division, drink, memory* largo; (*Cards*) *suit* fuerte; *person** alto; **it is 6 metres** ~ tiene 6 metros de largo; **how ~ is it?** ¿cuánto tiene de largo?; **the ~ arm of the law** el brazo de la ley; el alcance de la ley; **a list as ~ as your arm** una lista larguísima; ~ **drink** refresco *m*, bebida *f* no alcohólica; **not by a ~ chalk, not by a ~ shot** ni con mucho; **to pull a ~ face** hacer una mueca; **to be ~ in the leg** tener piernas largas; ~ **sight** presbicia *f*, hipermetropía *f*; **to have ~ sight** ser présbita; **he's a bit ~ in the tooth*** es bastante viejo ya; **the speech was ~ on rhetoric and short on details** el discurso tenía mucho retoricismo y pocos detalles.
(**b**) (*of time*) largo; prolongado; *job* de muchas horas, de muchos años (*etc*); **to be ~ in** + *ger* tardar en + *infin*; **how ~ is the lesson?** ¿cuánto tiempo dura la clase?; **the days are getting ~er** los días se están alargando; **the course is 6 months** ~ el curso es de 6 meses, el curso dura 6 meses; *V* **time** *etc*.
2 *adv* (**a**) (*a long time*) largo tiempo, mucho tiempo; largamente; **don't be ~!** ¡vuelve pronto!; **I shan't be** ~ (*in finishing*) termino pronto, en seguida concluyo; no voy a tardar; (*in returning*) vuelvo pronto; **will you be ~?** ¿vas a tardar mucho?; **how ~ is it since you saw him?** ¿cuánto tiempo hace que no le ves?; **how ~ have you been learning Spanish?** ¿desde cuándo aprendes español?; **it didn't last** ~ fue cosa de unos pocos minutos (*or* días *etc*); **we didn't stay** ~ no nos quedamos mucho tiempo; **he talked ~ about politics** habló largamente de política; **it has ~ been useless** desde hace tiempo no sirve; **I have ~ wanted to say that ...** desde hace mucho estoy deseando decir que ...; **to live** ~ ser longevo; **women live ~er than men** las mujeres son más longevas que los hombres; ~ **before** (*adv*) mucho antes, mucho tiempo antes; **you should have done it ~ before now** debiste hacerlo hace mucho tiempo ya; ~ **before** (*conj*) mucho antes de que + *subj*; **not ~ before** (*adv*) poco tiempo antes; **all night** ~ toda la noche.
(**b**) **~er** más tiempo; **we stayed ~er than you** quedamos más tiempo que vosotros; **how much ~er can you stay?** ¿hasta cuándo podéis quedaros?; **wait a little ~er** espera un poco más; **how much ~er do we have to wait?** ¿hasta cuándo tenemos que esperar?; **he no ~er comes** ya no viene.
(**c**) (*in comparisons*) **as ~ as** mientras; **as ~ as the war lasted** mientras duró la guerra; **as ~ as the war lasts** mientras dure la guerra; **stay as ~ as you like** quédate hasta cuando quieras, quédate el tiempo que quieras; **as ~ as, so ~ as** (*provided that*) con tal que + *subj*.
(**d**) **so ~!** ¡hasta luego!; *V* **ago.**
3 *n* (**a**) **the ~ and the short of it is that ...** en resumidas cuentas ...; **before** ~ en breve, dentro de poco, (*in past contexts*) poco tiempo después; **are you going for ~?** ¿vas a estar mucho tiempo?; **to take ~ to** + *infin* tardar en + *infin*.
(**b**) (*Fin*) **~s** *pl* valores *mpl* a largo plazo.
long[2] [lɒŋ] *vi*: **to ~ for sth** anhelar algo, suspirar por algo; **to ~ for sb** sentir la ausencia de uno, suspirar por uno; **to ~ to do sth** anhelar hacer algo.
long. *abbr of* **longitude** longitud *f*.
-long [lɔŋ] *adj*: *eg* **month~** que dura un mes (entero); *V* **day~** *etc*.
long-armed ['lɒŋ'ɑːmd] *adj* de brazos largos.
long-awaited ['lɒŋə'weɪtɪd] *adj* anhelado, esperado.
longboat ['lɒŋbəʊt] *n* lancha *f*.
longbow ['lɒŋbəʊ] *n* arco *m*.
long-dated ['lɒŋ'deɪtɪd] *adj* a largo plazo.

long-distance ['lɒŋ'dɪstəns] **1** *adj bus* para servicio interurbano; *race* de fondo, de larga distancia, de resistencia; *train* de largo recorrido; ~ **call** conferencia *f* (interurbana); ~ **flight** vuelo *m* de larga distancia.
2 *adv*: **to call sb ~** llamar a uno por conferencia interurbana.

long-drawn-out ['lɒŋdrɔːn'aʊt] *adj* muy prolongado, larguísimo, interminable.

long-eared ['lɒŋ'ɪəd] *adj* orejudo, de orejas largas.

longed-for ['lɒŋdfɔːʳ] *adj* ansiado, apetecido.

longevity [lɒn'dʒevɪtɪ] *n* longevidad *f*.

long-forgotten ['lɒŋfə'gɒtn] *adj* olvidado hace mucho tiempo.

long-haired ['lɒŋ'hɛəd] *adj person* de pelo largo, pelilargo, melenudo; *dog etc* de pelo largo.

longhand ['lɒŋhænd] **1** *adj* escrito a mano. **2** *n* escritura *f* normal; **in ~** en escritura normal.

long-haul ['lɒŋ,hɔːl] *adj transport* de larga distancia.

longing ['lɒŋɪŋ] **1** *adj* anhelante. **2** *n* anhelo *m*, ansia *f*, deseo *m* vehemente (*for* de); nostalgia *f* (*for* de); (*sexual*) hambre *f* sexual, instinto *m* sexual.

longingly ['lɒŋɪŋlɪ] *adv* con anhelo, con ansia.

longish ['lɒŋɪʃ] *adj* bastante largo.

longitude ['lɒŋgɪtjuːd] *n* longitud *f*.

longitudinal [,lɒŋgɪ'tjuːdɪnl] *adj* longitudinal.

longitudinally [,lɒŋgɪ'tjuːdɪnəlɪ] *adv* longitudinalmente.

longjohns* ['lɒŋdʒɒnz] *npl* calzoncillos *mpl* largos.

long-jump ['lɒŋdʒʌmp] *n* (*Brit*) salto *m* de longitud.

long-jumper ['lɒŋ,dʒʌmpəʳ] *n* saltador *m*, -ora *f* de longitud.

long-lasting ['lɒŋ'lɑːstɪŋ] *adj* largo; duro; *material, memory etc* duradero.

long-legged ['lɒŋ'legɪd] *adj* de piernas largas, zancudo.

long-life ['lɒŋ'laɪf] *adj* de larga duración.

long-limbed [,lɒŋ'lɪmd] *adj* patilargo.

long-lived ['lɒŋ'lɪvd] *adj* longevo, de larga vida, que vive hasta una edad avanzada; *rumour etc* duradero, persistente; **women are more ~ than men** las mujeres son más longevas que los hombres.

long-lost ['lɒŋ'lɒst] *adj* perdido hace mucho tiempo, desaparecido hace mucho tiempo.

long-playing ['lɒŋ'pleɪɪŋ] *adj*: ~ **record** elepé *m*.

long-range ['lɒŋ'reɪndʒ] *adj gun* de gran alcance; *aircraft* de gran autonomía, de largo radio de acción; *plan* a largo plazo; ~ **weather forecast** predicción *f* meteorológica a largo plazo.

long-run ['lɒŋrʌn] *adj* largo, de alcance largo.

long-running ['lɒŋ'rʌnɪŋ] *adj dispute etc* largo; *play* taquillero, que se mantiene mucho tiempo en la cartelera; *programme* de alcance largo.

longship ['lɒŋʃɪp] *n* (*Viking*) barco *m* vikingo.

longshoreman ['lɒŋʃɔːmən] *n*, *pl* **longshoremen** ['lɒŋʃɔːmən] (*esp US*) estibador *m*, obrero *m* portuario.

long-sighted ['lɒŋ'saɪtɪd] *adj* (*Brit Med*) présbita; (*fig*) previsor, clarividente.

long-sightedness ['lɒŋ'saɪtɪdnɪs] *n* (*Med*) presbicia *f*, hipermetropía *f*; (*fig*) previsión *f*, clarividencia *f*.

long-sleeved ['lɒŋsliːvd] *adj* de manga larga.

long-standing ['lɒŋ'stændɪŋ] *adj* de mucho tiempo, existente desde hace mucho tiempo, viejo.

long-suffering ['lɒŋ'sʌfərɪŋ] *adj* sufrido, resignado.

long-term ['lɒŋ'tɜːm] *adj* a largo plazo (*also fig*); ~ **unemployment** desempleo *m* de larga duración.

long-time ['lɒŋ'taɪm] *adj* = **long-standing**.

long-wave ['lɒŋ'weɪv] *adj* de onda larga.

longways ['lɒŋweɪz] *adv* longitudinalmente, a lo largo.

long-winded ['lɒŋ'wɪndɪd] *adj* prolijo; interminable.

long-windedly ['lɒŋ'wɪndɪdlɪ] *adv* prolijamente.

loo* [luː] *n* (*Brit*) wáter *m*.

loofah ['luːfəʳ] *n* (*Brit*) esponja *f* de lufa.

look [lʊk] **1** *n* (**a**) (*glance*) mirada *f*; vistazo *m*, ojeada *f*; **he gave me a furious ~** me miró furioso, me lanzó una mirada furiosa; **she gave me a dirty ~** me miró recelosa, me lanzó una mirada llena de recelo; **we got some very odd ~s** la gente nos miró extrañada; **to have** (*or* **take**) **a ~ at sth** echar un vistazo a algo; **have a ~ at this!** mírame esto!; ¡vean esto!; **let's have a ~** déjame verlo, a ver; **do you want a ~?** ¿quieres verlo?; **to take a good ~ at sth** mirar algo con cuidado, examinar algo detenidamente; **take a long hard ~ before deciding** antes de decidir conviene pensar muchísimo; **to have a ~ round a house** inspeccionar una casa; **shall we have a ~ round the town?** ¿visitamos la ciudad?

(**b**) (*search*) **to have a ~ for sth** buscar algo; **have another ~!** ¡vuelve a buscar!; **I've had a good ~ for it already** lo he buscado ya en todas partes.

(**c**) (*air, appearance*) aspecto *m*, apariencia *f*; aire *m*; traza *f*; **good ~s** buen parecer *m*; **by the ~ of things** según parece; **by the ~ of him** a juzgar por su aspecto; **you can't go by ~s alone** es arriesgado juzgar por las apariencias nada más; **he had the ~ of a sailor** tenía aire de marinero; **he had a sad ~** tenía un aire triste; **I don't like the ~ of him** no me hace buena impresión; **I don't like the ~ of it at all** esto tiene traza de ser peligroso (*etc*), no me fío de esto; **she has kept her ~s** sigue tan guapa como siempre; **she's losing her ~s** no es tan guapa como antes; **~s aren't everything** la belleza no lo es todo.

(**d**) (*fashion*) moda *f*, estilo *m*; **the 1999 ~** la moda de 1999; **the new ~** la nueva moda.

2 *vt* (**a**) *emotion* expresar con los ojos, expresar con la mirada.

(**b**) **to ~ sb** (**straight**) **in the eye** mirar directamente a los ojos de uno; **I would never be able to ~ him in the eye** (*or* **face**) **again** no podría resistir su mirada, siempre me avergonzaría al verle; **he ~ed me up and down** me miró de arriba abajo.

(**c**) (*heed*) ~ **where you're going!** ¡cuidado!, ¡atención!; ~ **what you've done now!** ¡mira lo que has hecho!

(**d**) *age* representar; **she's 70 but doesn't ~ it** tiene 70 años pero no los representa.

3 *vi* (**a**) (*see, glance*) mirar; ~ **here!** ¡oye!; **just ~!** ¡mira!, ¡fíjate!; ~ **before you leap** antes de que te cases mira lo que haces.

(**b**) (*search*) mirar, buscar; ~ **again!** ¡vuelve a buscar!; **you can't have ~ed far** no has mirado mucho.

(**c**) **it ~s south** (*house etc*) mira hacia el sur, está orientada hacia el sur, tiene orientación sur.

(**d**) (*seem*) parecer; tener aire de, tener traza de; mostrarse; **he ~s happy** parece contento; **it ~s all right to me** me parece que está bien; **how does it ~ to you?** ¿qué te parece?; **she was not ~ing herself** parecía otra, no parecía la misma; **he ~ed surprised** hizo un gesto de extrañeza; **she ~ed prettier than ever** estaba más guapa que nunca; **how pretty you ~!** ¡qué guapa estás!; **to ~ well** (*person*) tener buena cara; **it ~s well** parece muy bien, tiene buena apariencia; **it ~s well on you** te sienta bien, te cae bien.

(**e**) **to ~ like** parecerse a; **he ~s like his brother** se parece a su hermano; **the picture doesn't ~ like him** el retrato no se le parece, el retrato no le representa bien; **it ~s like rain** parece que va a llover; **it ~s like cheese to me** me parece que es queso; **the festival ~s like being lively** el festival se anuncia animado.

◆**look about, look around 1** *vt*: **to ~ around one** mirar a su alrededor. **2** *vi* mirar alrededor; **to ~ about for sth** andar buscando algo.

◆**look after 1** *vt* (*attend to*) ocuparse de, encargarse de; (*watch over*) vigilar; *person* cuidar de.

2 *vr*: **he can ~ after himself** sabe valerse por sí mismo; **she can't ~ after herself any more** ya no puede cuidarse de sí misma.

◆**look at** *vt* (**a**) (*observe*) mirar.

(**b**) (*consider*) considerar, examinar; *problem* enfocar; estudiar; **it depends how you ~ at it** depende de cómo se enfoca la cuestión, depende del punto de vista de uno; **whichever way you ~ at it** se mire por donde se mire.

(**c**) (*check*) examinar, escudriñar; revisar; **will you ~ at the engine?** ¿quiere revisar el motor?; **I'll ~ at it tomorrow** lo veré mañana.

(**d**) (*accept*) **I wouldn't even ~ at the job** no aceptaría el puesto por nada del mundo; **the landlady won't ~ at Ruritanians** la patrona no aguanta los ruritanios.

◆**look away** *vi* desviar los ojos, apartar la mirada (*from* de).

◆**look back** *vi* (**a**) (*look behind*) mirar hacia atrás, volver la cabeza. (**b**) (*in memory*) considerar el pasado, volverse atrás; **to ~ back on** recordar, evocar.

◆**look down** *vi* (**a**) (*lower eyes*) bajar los ojos; (*look downward*) mirar hacia abajo.

(**b**) **the castle ~s down on the town** el castillo domina la ciudad.

(**c**) **to ~ down on** (*fig*) despreciar, mirar por encima del hombro.

◆**look for** *vt* (**a**) (*seek*) buscar.

(**b**) (*expect*) esperar.

◆**look forward** *vi* (**a**) considerar el futuro; mirar hacia el futuro.

(**b**) **to ~ forward to** alegrarse de antemano de, pensar con mucha ilusión en, prometerse; **I'm so ~ing forward to**

the trip el viaje me hace mucha ilusión; **we had been ~ing forward to it for weeks** durante semanas enteras veníamos pensando en eso con mucha ilusión; **I'n not ~ing forward to it at all** no me prometo nada bueno con respecto a eso; **to ~ forward to** + *ger* tener ganas de + *infin.*

◆**look in** *vi* (**a**) (*see in*) mirar hacia dentro.

(**b**) (*visit*) hacer una breve visita (*on* a), pasar por casa, entrar por un instante, caer por casa (*LAm*); **I'll ~ in on Monday** pasaré por casa el lunes.

(**c**) (*TV*) mirar la televisión.

◆**look into** *vt* investigar.

◆**look on 1** *vt* (*consider*) considerar; **I ~ on him as a friend** le considero como amigo; **we do not ~ on it with favour** no lo enjuiciamos favorablemente.

2 *vi* (**a**) (*watch*) mirar; (*pej*) estar de mirón.

(**b**) **it ~s on to the garden** da al jardín.

◆**look out 1** *vt* (*Brit*) (*search for*) buscar; (*choose*) escoger.

2 *vi* (**a**) (*look outside*) mirar hacia fuera; **to ~ out of the window** mirar por la ventana; **it ~s out on to the garden** da al jardín.

(**b**) (*take care*) tener cuidado, tener ojo; **~ out!** ¡ojo!; ¡atención!; **to ~ out for o.s.** valerse por sí mismo; **he's only ~ing out for himself** (*pej*) sólo considera sus propios intereses; **do ~ out for pickpockets** ten ojo con los carteristas.

(**c**) **to ~ out for** (*seek*) buscar; estar a la mira de; (*expect*) estar a la expectativa de; (*await*) esperar.

◆**look over** *vt* examinar; revisar; **to ~ a place over** dar un vistazo a un sitio; **he was ~ing me over** me miraba de arriba abajo.

◆**look round** *vi* (**a**) (*look about one*) mirar a su alrededor; **to ~ round for sb** buscar a uno.

(**b**) (*look back*) volver la cabeza; mirar hacia atrás.

(**c**) (*visit*) inspeccionar, visitar; **we're just ~ing round** lo estamos viendo nada más; **do you mind if we ~ round?** ¿le importa que entremos a verlo?

◆**look through** *vt* (**a**) *window* mirar por. (**b**) *papers etc* hojear, registrar; *belongings* registrar. (**c**) **he ~ed through me** me miró sin verme, me miró cómo si fuera transparente.

◆**look to** *vt* (**a**) (*attend to*) ocuparse de, mirar por; **we must ~ to the future** tenemos que fijar la mira en el futuro.

(**b**) (*look after*) cuidar de, ocuparse de.

(**c**) (*rely on*) contar con; acudir a; tener puestas las esperanzas en; **it's no good ~ing to me for help** es inútil acudir a mí buscando ayuda; **to ~ to sb to** + *infin* esperar que uno + *subj*, contar con uno para + *infin.*

◆**look up 1** *vt* (**a**) (*visit*) ir a ver, visitar.

(**b**) (*seek out*) buscar; averiguar.

2 *vi* (**a**) (*raise eyes*) levantar los ojos; (*look upward*) mirar para arriba.

(**b**) (*improve*) mejorar, ir mejor; **things are ~ing up** las cosas van mejor.

(**c**) **to ~ up to sb** respetar a uno, admirar a uno.

◆**look upon** = **look on 1**.

look-alike ['lʊkə,laɪk] *n* parecido *m*, -a *f*.

looked-for ['lʊktfɔːʳ] *adj* esperado, deseado.

looker* ['lʊkəʳ] *n* (*US*) guapa *f*.

looker-on ['lʊkər'ɒn] *n* espectador *m*, -ora *f*; (*pej*) mirón *m*, -ona *f*.

look-in* ['lʊkɪn] *n* oportunidad *f* para tomar parte; **we never got** (*or* **had**) **a ~** no nos dejaron participar, (*of losers*) nunca tuvimos posibilidades de ganar.

-looking ['lʊkɪŋ] *adj ending in compounds*: **strange~** de aspecto raro; **mad~** que parece loco.

looking-glass ['lʊkɪŋglɑːs] *n* espejo *m*.

look-out ['lʊkaʊt] **1** *n* (**a**) (*tower etc*) atalaya *f*, puesto *m* de observación; (*viewpoint*) miradero *m*.

(**b**) (*person*) vigía *m*.

(**c**) (*act*) observación *f*, vigilancia *f*; **to be on the ~ for, to keep a ~ for** estar a la mira de; **to keep a sharp ~** estar ojo avizor.

(**d**) (*esp Brit**: *prospect*) perspectiva *f*; **it's a poor ~ for cotton** el algodón tiene un porvenir dudoso; **it's a grim ~ for us** es una perspectiva negra para nosotros, esto no nos promete nada bueno; **that's his ~!** ¡allá él!

2 *attr*: **~ post** puesto *m* de observación.

look-see* ['lʊksiː] *n* vistazo *m*.

look-up ['lʊkʌp] *n* consulta *f*; **~ table** tabla *f* de consulta.

LOOM *n* (*US*) *abbr of* **Loyal Order of Moose** *asociación benéfica*.

loom¹ [luːm] *n* telar *m*.

loom² [luːm] *vi* (*also* **to ~ up**) surgir, aparecer, asomarse; (*threaten*) amenazar; **dangers ~ ahead** se vislumbran los peligros que hay por delante; **the ship ~ed up out of the mist** el buque surgió de la niebla; **to ~ large** ser de gran importancia, presentarse muy importante.

looming ['luːmɪŋ] *adj danger etc* que amenaza, inminente.

loon [luːn] *n* bobo *m*, -a *f*.

loony* ['luːnɪ] **1** *adj* loco; **the ~ left** la izquierda tonta; **to drive sb ~** volver loco a uno; **to go ~** volverse loco. **2** *n* loco *m*, -a *f*.

loony bin* ['luːnɪbɪn] *n* manicomio *m*.

loop [luːp] **1** *n* (*knot*) lazo *m*, (*Naut*) gaza *f*; (*bend*) curva *f*, vuelta *f*, recodo *m*; (*Elec*) circuito *m* cerrado; (*Comput*) bucle *m*; (*Sew*) presilla *f*; (*Aer*) rizo *m*; **to knock sb for a ~*** (*US*) dejar a uno pasmado; **to loop the ~** hacer el rizo, rizar el rizo.

2 *vt rope etc* hacer gaza con; (*fasten*) asegurar con gaza (*or* presilla); **to ~ a rope round a post** pasar una cuerda alrededor de un poste.

3 *vi* (*rope etc*) formar lazo; (*line, road etc*) serpentear.

loophole ['luːphəʊl] *n* (*Mil*) aspillera *f*, tronera *f*; (*fig*) escapatoria *f*; pretexto *m*; (*in law*) rendija *f*; **every law has a ~** hecha la ley hecha la trampa.

loop-line ['luːplaɪn] *n* (*Rail*) desviación *f*.

loopy* ['luːpɪ] *adj* chiflado*.

loose [luːs] **1** *adj* (**a**) (*not attached, not firm*) suelto; *change, end* suelto; (*untied*) suelto, desatado; (*not tight*) flojo; (*movable*) movible, movedizo; *earth* poco firme; *bandage, button, knot, screw* flojo; *tooth* inseguro; *dress* holgado, ancho; *pulley, wheel* (*Mech*) loco, flotante; *connection* desconectado; **these trousers are too ~ round the waist** estos pantalones son demasiado holgados por la cintura; '**~ chippings**' 'gravilla suelta'; **~ cover** funda *f* que se puede quitar; **~ end** cabo *m* suelto; **to be at a ~ end** no tener nada que hacer, estar desocupado; **to tie up ~ ends** atar cabos; **~ scrum** melé *f* abierta; **~ talk** (*careless*) palabras *fpl* pronunciadas sin pensar; (*indecent*) palabras *fpl* indecentes; **to have a ~ tongue** (*talkative*) ser muy hablador, (*gossipy*) ser chismoso, ser una mala lengua, (*telling secrets*) no saber guardar un secreto; **to become** (*or* **come, get, work**) **~** (*part*) soltarse, desprenderse, (*knot*) aflojarse, desatarse; **to break ~** desatarse, escaparse, (*fig*) desencadenarse; **to cast** (*or* **let, set, turn**) **~** soltar; **to cut ~** separarse, independizarse (*from* de); **to hang ~** caer suelto; (*US**) relajarse, tomar las cosas con calma; **to tear sth ~** arrancar algo, quitar algo violentamente; **to tear o.s. ~** soltarse; quitarse violentamente las trabas.

(**b**) (*unpacked*) sin envase, a granel, suelto.

(**c**) (*not exact*) *translation* libre, aproximado, (*pej*) poco exacto; *thinking* ilógico; *style* impreciso, vago; **there is a ~ connection between them** entre ellos existe una relación no muy estrecha.

(**d**) (*morally*) relajado; *conduct, life* inmoral, disoluto; *woman* fácil.

2 *n* (*) **to be on the ~** (*free*) estar en libertad; **to be** (*or* **go**) **on the ~** ir de juerga*, echar una cana al aire.

3 *vt* (*free*) soltar; (*untie*) desatar; (*slacken*) aflojar; *storm, abuse etc* desencadenar.

◆**loose off** *vt gun* disparar (*at* sobre).

◆**loose off at** *vt* (*fire*) disparar sobre; (*verbally*) empezar a soltar injurias contra.

loose box ['luːs,bɒks] *n* (*Brit*: *for horses*) establo *m* móvil.

loose-fitting ['luːs'fɪtɪŋ] *adj* suelto.

loose-leaf ['luːs'liːf] *adj book* de hojas sueltas, de hojas cambiables; **~ binder, ~ folder** carpeta *f* de anillas.

loose-limbed ['luːs'lɪmd] *adj* de movimientos sueltos, ágil.

loose-living ['luːs'lɪvɪŋ] *adj* de vida airada, de vida inmoral.

loosely ['luːslɪ] *adv* sueltamente; flojamente; holgadamente; libremente, aproximadamente; con poca exactitud; ilógicamente; imprecisamente; disolutamente; **it is ~ translated as** se traduce aproximadamente por; **~ dressed** con vestidos holgados.

loosen ['luːsn] **1** *vt* (*free*) soltar; (*untie*) desatar; (*slacken*) aflojar; *restrictions* aflojar, liberalizar; *V* **tongue** *etc.*

2 *vi* soltarse; desatarse; aflojarse.

◆**loosen up 1** *vt muscles* desentumecer.

2 *vi* (*before game*) desentumecer los músculos, entrar en calor; **to ~ up on sb** tratar a uno con menos rigor.

looseness ['luːsnɪs] *n* (**a**) soltura *f*; flojedad *f*; holgura *f*; libertad *f*. (**b**) imprecisión *f*. (**c**) disolución *f*; relajación *f*. (**d**) (*Med*) diarrea *f*.

loot [luːt] **1** *n* botín *m*, presa *f*; (*) ganancias *fpl*, botín *m*, (*money*) pasta* *f* (*Sp*), plata *f*. **2** *vt* saquear.

looter ['luːtəʳ] *n* saqueador *m*, -ora *f*.

looting ['luːtɪŋ] *n* saqueo *m.*

lop [lɒp] *vt tree* mochar, desmochar; *branches* podar; (*esp fig*) cercenar.

◆lop away, lop off *vt* cortar.

lope [ləʊp] *vi* (*also* **to ~ along**) correr a paso largo; **to ~ off** alejarse a paso largo.

lop-eared ['lɒp,ɪəd] *adj* de orejas caídas.

lop-sided ['lɒp'saɪdɪd] *adj* desproporcionado; desequilibrado; ladeado, sesgado; (*fig*) desequilibrado, falso.

loquacious [lə'kweɪʃəs] *adj* locuaz.

loquacity [lə'kwæsɪtɪ] *n* locuacidad *f.*

lord [lɔːd] **1** *n* (**a**) señor *m*; (*Brit title*) lord *m*; **L~ (John) Smith** (*Brit*) Lord (John) Smith; **the L~s** (*Parl*) la Cámara de los Lores; **the ~s of England** (*peers*) los nobles de Inglaterra; **my ~** (*to bishop*) Ilustrísima, (*to noble*) señor, (*to judge*) señor juez; **~ of the manor** señor *m* feudal; **~ and master** dueño *m.*

(**b**) (*Rel*) **the L~** el Señor; **Our L~** Nuestro Señor; **L~'s Prayer** padrenuestro *m*; **good L~!** ¡Dios mío!; **L~ knows where ...!*** ¡Dios sabe dónde ...!

2 *attr*: **my ~ bishop of Tooting** su Ilustrísima el obispo de Tooting; **L~ Lieutenant** *representante de la Corona en un condado*; **L~ Mayor, L~ Provost** (*Scot*) alcalde *m.*

3 *vt*: **to ~ it** hacer el señor, mandar despóticamente; **to ~ it over sb** dominar a uno despóticamente, mandar a uno como señor.

lordliness ['lɔːdlɪnɪs] *n* lo señorial, carácter *m* señorial; (*pej*) altivez *f*, arrogancia *f.*

lordly ['lɔːdlɪ] *adj house, vehicle etc* señorial, señoril; *manner* altivo, arrogante; *command* imperioso.

lords-and-ladies ['lɔːdzənd'leɪdɪz] *n* (*Bot*) aro *m.*

lordship ['lɔːdʃɪp] *n* (*title*) señoría *f*; (*rule*) señorío *m*; **his ~** su señoría; **your L~** Señoría.

lore [lɔːʳ] *n* saber *m* popular; ciencia *f*, tradiciones *fpl*; **in local ~** según la tradición local; **he knows a lot about plant ~** sabe mucho de las plantas, es muy erudito en botánica.

lorgnette [lɔː'njet] *n* impertinentes *mpl.*

Lorraine [lɒ'reɪn] *n* Lorena *f.*

lorry ['lɒrɪ] *n* (*Brit*) camión *m*; **it fell off the back of a ~*** es de trapicheo*, es de segunda mano.

lorry-driver ['lɒrɪ,draɪvəʳ] *n* camionero *m*, camionista *m*, conductor *m* de camión.

lorry-load ['lɒrɪ,ləʊd] *n* carga *f* (de un camión).

lose [luːz] (*irr*: *pret and ptp* **lost**) **1** *vt* (**a**) (*gen*) perder; quedarse sin; *patient* no lograr salvar la vida de.

(**b**) (*passive with* lost) **to be lost** perderse, quedar perdido; **to be lost at sea** (*person*) perecer en el mar, morir ahogado; **the ship was lost with all hands** el buque se hundió con toda la tripulación; **all is lost!** ¡todo está perdido!, ¡se acabó todo!; **to get lost** perderse, extraviarse, errar el camino; **get lost!**⁑ ¡vete a la porra!⁑; **to be lost in thought** estar absorto en meditación; **to be lost in wonder** quedar asombrado; **to look lost** parecer confuso, parecer desorientado, tener aire perplejo; **after his death I felt lost** después de su muerte me sentía perdido; **I'm lost without my secretary** sin mi secretaria no valgo para nada, no puedo hacer nada sin mi secretaria; **to give sb up for lost** dar a uno por perdido; **the motion was lost** se rechazó la moción; **he was lost to science** se perdió para la ciencia; **he is lost to all finer feelings** es insensible a todos los sentimientos nobles; **the joke was lost on her** no comprendió el chiste; **the remark was lost on him** la observación pasó inadvertida por él; **this modern music is lost on me** no entiendo esta música moderna.

(**c**) (*outstrip etc*) dejar atrás, adelantarse a; *pursuers* zafarse de; *unwanted companion* deshacerse de.

(**d**) (*cause loss of*) hacer perder; **it lost him the job** le costó el puesto; **that lost us the war** eso nos hizo perder la guerra; **that lost us the game** eso nos costó la victoria.

2 *vi* (**a**) perder; ser vencido; **you can't ~** no tienes pérdida, tienes forzosamente que salir ganando; **the story did not ~ in the telling** el cuento no perdió en la narración.

(**b**) **the clock is losing** el reloj atrasa.

3 *vr*: **to ~ o.s.** perderse, extraviarse, errar el camino; (*in speech*) padecer una confusión, perder el hilo; **to ~ o.s. in thought** ensimismarse.

◆lose out *vi* perder, salir perdiendo.

loser ['luːzəʳ] *n* (*person*) perdedor *m*, -ora *f*; fracasado *m*, -a *f*, desgraciado *m*, -a *f*; (*Sport etc*) el que pierde, el vencido, el equipo derrotado; (*card*) carta *f* perdedora; **to be a bad ~** no saber perder, tener mal perder; **to be a good ~** saber perder, tener buen perder; **to come off the ~** salir perdiendo.

losing ['luːzɪŋ] **1** *adj team* vencido, derrotado; *trick etc* perdedor. **2** *npl* **~s** pérdidas *fpl.*

loss [lɒs] *n* (**a**) (*gen*) pérdida *f*; **~ of appetite** inapetencia *f*; **~ of earnings** pérdida *f* de sueldo; **~ of memory** amnesia *f*; **without ~ of time** sin pérdida de tiempo, sin demora; **since the ~ of his wife** desde que perdió a su mujer, desde que se murió su mujer; **there was a heavy ~ of life** hubo muchas víctimas, perecieron muchos; **the army suffered heavy ~es** el ejército sufrió pérdidas cuantiosas; **to cut one's ~es** cortar por lo sano; **the company makes a ~ on this product** la empresa pierde dinero con este producto; **the company made a ~ in 1999** la empresa tuvo un balance adverso en 1999, la compañía salió con déficit en 1999.

(**b**) **it's your ~** Vd es el que pierde; **he's no ~** no vamos a sentir su ausencia; **he's a dead ~** es una calamidad; **the book is a dead ~** el libro es absolutamente inútil, el libro no vale para nada en absoluto; **the ship is a total ~** el buque puede considerarse como totalmente perdido.

(**c**) **to be at a ~** estar perplejo, no saber qué hacer; **to be at a ~ to explain sth** no saber cómo explicarse algo; **we are at a ~ to know why** no sabemos en absoluto por qué; **to be at a ~ for words** no encontrar palabras con que expresarse; **he's never at a ~ (for words)** tiene mucha facilidad de palabra, tiene la palabra facilísima; **to sell sth at a ~** vender algo con pérdida.

loss-leader ['lɒs,liːdəʳ] *n* artículo *m* de lanzamiento.

loss-maker ['lɒs'meɪkəʳ] *n* (*business*) negocio *m* no rentable, negocio *m* deficitario; (*product*) producto *m* no rentable.

loss-making ['lɒs,meɪkɪŋ] *adj enterprise* deficitario, no rentable.

lost [lɒst] **1** *pret and ptp of* **lose**. **2** *adj* perdido; **~ days** (*at work*) días *mpl* no trabajados; **'~ property'** (*notice*) 'objetos perdidos'; **~ time** tiempo *m* perdido.

lost-and-found department ['lɒstən'faʊnddɪ,pɑːtmənt] *n* (*US*), **lost property office** ['lɒst'prɒpətɪ,ɒfɪs] *n* oficina *f* de objetos perdidos.

lot [lɒt] *n* (**a**) (*random selection*) **by ~** echando suertes; mediante sorteo; **to cast ~s, to draw ~s** echar suertes (*for sth* para decidir quién tendrá algo, *to decide sth* para decidir algo); **the ~ fell on him** él resultó elegido, la suerte le tocó a él; **to throw in one's ~ with sb** unirse a la suerte de uno.

(**b**) (*share*) porción *f*, parte *f*; (*destiny*) suerte *f*; **his ~ was different** su suerte fue otra; **it fell to my ~** me cayó en suerte, me cupo en suerte; **it falls to my ~ to** + *infin* me incumbe + *infin.*

(**c**) (*plot*) solar *m*, terreno *m*; (*Cine*) solar *m.*

(**d**) (*at auction*) lote *m*; **he's a bad ~** es un mal sujeto; **I'll send it in 3 ~s** (*Comm*) se lo mando en 3 paquetes (*or* tandas).

(**e**) (*quantity*) cantidad *f*; grupo *m*, colección *f*; **a fine ~ of students** un buen grupo de estudiantes; **a ~ of money** mucho dinero; **a ~ of books, ~s of books** muchos libros; **quite a ~ of books** bastantes libros; **such a ~ of books** tantos libros; **an awful ~ of things to do** la mar de cosas que hacer; **we have ~s of flowers (that we don't want)** nos sobran flores, tenemos flores de sobra; **that's the ~** eso es todo; **the whole ~ of them** ellos todos, todos ellos sin excepción; **he collared the ~** se los llevó todos; **big ones, little ones, the ~!** ¡los grandes, los pequeños, todos!

(**f**) (*as adv*) **I read a ~** leo bastante; **we don't go out a ~** no salimos mucho; **things have changed a ~** las cosas han cambiado mucho; **there wasn't a ~ we could do** apenas había nada que pudiéramos hacer; **he drinks an awful ~** bebe una barbaridad; **I'd give a ~ to know** me gustaría muchísimo saberlo; **I feel ~s better** me encuentro mucho mejor; **thanks a ~!** ¡muchas gracias!

loth [ləʊθ] *adj* = **loath**.

lotion ['ləʊʃən] *n* loción *f.*

lottery ['lɒtərɪ] *n* lotería *f.*

lotto ['lɒtəʊ] *n* (*game*) lotería *f.*

lotus ['ləʊtəs] *n* loto *m*; **~ position** postura *f* del loto.

loud [laʊd] **1** *adj* (**a**) *voice, tone etc* alto; *shout etc* fuerte, recio; (*noisy*) ruidoso, estrepitoso; *applause* fuerte, estrepitoso; *behaviour* ruidoso, turbulento, maleducado; (*~-mouthed*) gritón.

(**b**) *colour* chillón; (*in bad taste*) charro, cursi.

2 *adv V* **loudly**; **to say sth out ~** decir algo en voz alta.

loudhailer ['laʊd'heɪləʳ] *n* (*Brit*) megáfono *m*, bocina *f.*

loudly ['laʊdlɪ] *adv* en voz alta; fuertemente; ruidosamente, estrepitosamente.

loud-mouth* ['laʊdmaʊθ] *n* bocazas* *m.*

loud-mouthed ['laʊd'maʊðd] *adj* gritón.

loudness ['laʊdnɪs] *n* lo alto; fuerza *f*; ruido *m*; lo chillón; vulgaridad *f.*

loudspeaker ['laʊd'spiːkəʳ] *n* altavoz *m*, altoparlante *m*.
Louis ['luːɪ] *nm* Luis.
Louisiana [lʊ,iːzɪ'ænə] *n* Luisiana *f*.
lounge [laʊndʒ] **1** *n* (*esp Brit*: *in house*) salón *m*, cuarto *m* de estar, living *m*, estancia *f* (*LAm*); (*Aer*) sala *f*; (*on liner etc*) salón *m*.
2 *attr*: ~ **bar** salón-bar *m*; ~ **suit** (*Brit*) traje *m* de calle.
3 *vi* (*saunter*) pasearse despacito; (*idle*) gandulear, pasar un rato sin hacer nada; **to ~ against a wall** apoyarse distraídamente en una pared; **to ~ back in a chair** repanchigarse en un asiento; **we spent a week lounging in Naples** pasamos una semana en Nápoles sin hacer nada.
◆**lounge about, lounge around** *vi* holgazanear, gandulear, tirarse a la bartola.
lounger ['laʊndʒəʳ] *n* gandul *m*, haragán *m*, -ana *f*; azotacalles *mf*.
louse [laʊs] *n*, *pl* **lice** [laɪs] (**a**) (*insect*) piojo *m*. (**b**) (‡) canalla *m*, mierda‡ *m*.
◆**louse up‡** *vt*: **to ~ sth up** joder algo‡.
lousy ['laʊzɪ] *adj* (**a**) piojoso. (**b**) (‡) malísimo, horrible; *trick etc* vil, asqueroso; **I'm a ~ player** yo juego fatal*; **all for a few ~ quid** todo por unas jodidas libras‡; **we had a ~ time** lo pasamos fatal*. (**c**) (‡) **to be ~ with money** estar podrido de dinero*.
lout [laʊt] gamberro *m*; patán *m*.
loutish ['laʊtɪʃ] *adj* grosero, maleducado.
Louvain ['luːveɪn] *n* Lovaina.
louver, louvre ['luːvəʳ] *n* (*Archit*) lumbrera *f*; (*blind*) persiana *f*.
lovable ['lʌvəbl] *adj* amable, simpático.
love [lʌv] **1** *n* (**a**) amor *m* (*for, of, towards* a, de); cariño *m*; (*for hobby etc*) afición *f* (*for, of* a); **first ~** primer amor *m*; **~ in a cottage** contigo pan y cebolla; **~ at first sight** amor *m* a primera vista, flechazo *m*; **for ~** por amor, (*free*) gratis, (*without stakes*) sin jugarse dinero, sin apuestas; **not for ~ nor money** por nada del mundo; **for the ~ of** por el amor de; **the ~ of God** (**for man**) el amor de Dios; **the ~ of** (**man for**) **God** el amor a Dios; **for the ~ of God!** ¡por Dios!; **to marry for ~** casarse por amor; **he studies history for the ~ of it** estudia la historia por pura afición al tema; **to be in ~** estar enamorado (*with* de); **to fall in ~** enamorarse (*with* de); **to make ~** hacer el amor; **to make ~ to sb** (*court*) pretender a una, (*sexually*) hacer el amor a una, (*fig*: *butter up, work on*) hacer la pelotilla a uno; **there is no ~ lost between them** existe entre ellos una fuerte antipatía, no se pueden ver.
(**b**) (*greetings, in letters etc*) **'(with my) ~', '~ from ...'** 'besos'; **give him my ~** mándale recuerdos míos; **to send one's ~ to sb** mandar cariñosos saludos a uno.
(**c**) (*person*) amado *m*, -a *f*; **yes, ~** sí, querida; sí, cariño; **my ~** mi amor, mi vida, mi cielo; **the child's a little ~** el niño es una monada.
(**d**) (*Tennis*) **~ all** cero-cero; **15 ~** 15 a cero.
2 *attr*: **~ game** (*Tennis*) *juego en el cual el que recibe no ha marcado ningún punto.*
3 *vt person etc* amar, querer; tener cariño a; *hobby etc* ser muy aficionado a; **she ~s me, she ~s me not** me quiere, no me quiere; **I ~ Madrid** me encanta Madrid, me gusta muchísimo Madrid; **I ~ this record** me encanta este disco; **he ~s swimming, he ~s to swim** le gusta muchísimo nadar, le entusiasma la natación; **I should ~ to come** me gustaría mucho venir, me encantaría venir; **I'd ~ to!** ¡con mucho gusto!, ¡yo, encantado!; **~ me ~ my dog** quien quiere a Beltrán quiere a su can.
love-affair ['lʌvə,feəʳ] *n* amores *mpl*; aventura *f* sentimental; (*pej*) amoríos *mpl*.
lovebird ['lʌvbɜːd] *n* periquito *m*; **~s** (*fig*) palomitos *mpl*, tórtolos *mpl*.
love-bite ['lʌv,baɪt] *n* mordisco *m* amoroso.
love-child ['lʌvtʃaɪld] *n*, *pl* **love-children** ['lʌv,tʃɪldrən] hijo *m*, -a *f* de ganancia, hijo *m*, -a *f* natural.
love-hate ['lʌvheɪt] *attr*: **~ relationship** relación *f* de amor-odio.
loveless ['lʌvlɪs] *adj* sin amor.
love-letter ['lʌv,letəʳ] *n* carta *f* amorosa, carta *f* de amor.
love-life ['lʌvlaɪf] *n* vida *f* sentimental; vida *f* sexual.
loveliness ['lʌvlɪnɪs] *n* hermosura *f*, belleza *f*; encanto *m*.
lovelorn ['lʌvlɔːn] *adj* suspirando de amor, herido de amor; abandonado por su amante.
lovely ['lʌvlɪ] **1** *adj* (*beautiful*) hermoso; bello; (*delightful*) encantador, precioso, delicioso; (*pleasing, of objects etc*) mono, precioso, rico; *person* (*charming*) simpático; **isn't it ~?** ¿verdad que es precioso?; ¡qué rico!, ¡qué monada!; **we had a ~ time** lo pasamos la mar de bien; **I hope you have a ~ time!** ¡que os divirtáis!; **it's been ~ to see you** ha sido una visita encantadora; **he was a ~ man** era una bella persona.
2 *n* (*) belleza *f*, guapa *f*.
love-making ['lʌv,meɪkɪŋ] *n* (*courtship*) galanteo *m*; (*sexual*) trato *m* sexual, relaciones *fpl* sexuales.
love-match ['lʌvmætʃ] *n* matrimonio *m* por amor.
love-nest ['lʌvnest] *n* nido *m* de amor.
love-potion ['lʌv,pəʊʃən] *n* filtro *m*.
lover ['lʌvəʳ] *n* (**a**) amante *mf*; (*pej*) amante *mf*, querido *m*, -a *f*; **he became her ~** se hizo amante de ella; **we were ~s for 2 years** durante 2 años fuimos amantes; **so she took a ~** así que tomó un amante; **the ~s** los amantes, los novios.
(**b**) **a ~ of** (*hobby, wine etc*) un amigo de, una amiga de, un aficionado a, una aficionada a; **he is a great ~ of the violin** tiene muchísima afición al violín.
(**c**) (*in compounds*) *eg* **music-~** persona *f* aficionada a la música, melómano *m*, -a *f*; **football-~s everywhere** los aficionados al fútbol de todas partes.
lover-boy ['lʌvə,bɔɪ] *n* (*hum, iro*) macho *m*, macarra *m*.
loveseat ['lʌv,siːt] *n* (*US*) canapé *m*, confidente *m*.
lovesick ['lʌvsɪk] *adj* enfermo de amor, amartelado.
lovesong ['lʌvsɒŋ] *n* canción *f* de amor.
love-story ['lʌv,stɔːrɪ] *n* historia *f* de amor.
love-token ['lʌv,təʊkən] *n* prenda *f* (*or* prueba *f*) de amor.
lovey-dovey* [,lʌvɪ'dʌvɪ] *adj* tierno, sentimental.
loving ['lʌvɪŋ] *adj* amoroso; cariñoso, tierno.
-loving ['lʌvɪŋ] *adj ending in compounds*: **money~** amante del dinero, aficionado al dinero.
loving-cup ['lʌvɪŋkʌp] *n* copa *f* de la amistad (que circula en una cena *etc*, en que beben todos).
lovingly ['lʌvɪŋlɪ] *adv* amorosamente; cariñosamente, tiernamente.
low¹ [ləʊ] **1** *adj* bajo; *light, number, rate, speed, temperature, voice* bajo; *bow* profundo; *blow* sucio; *dress* escotado; *card* pequeño; *gear* primero; *price* bajo; reducido, módico; *stock* escaso; *diet* deficiente; *note, tone* grave; *health* débil, malo; *birth, rank* humilde; *manners* grosero; *character* vil; *opinion* malo; *joke, song* verde; *trick* sucio, malo; *comedian* chabacano; **~ beam headlights** (*US*) luces *fpl* de cruce; **L~ Church** *sector de la Iglesia Anglicana de tendencia más protestante*; **~ comedy** farsa *f*; **L~ Latin** bajo latín *m*; **~ mass** misa *f* rezada; **~ point** punto *m* (más) bajo; **~ salt** sal *f* dietética; **~ season** temporada *f* baja; **L~ Sunday** Domingo *m* de Cuasimodo; **~ vowel** vocal *f* grave; **5 at the ~est** 5 como mínimo; **activity is at its ~est** las actividades están en su punto más bajo; **the battery is ~** la batería se está acabando; **the temperature is in the ~ 40s** la temperatura es de 40 grados y alguno más; **to feel ~** estar por el suelo*; **stocks are getting ~** las existencias van escaseando; **to cook on a ~ heat** (*or* **oven, stove**) cocer a fuego lento; **we are getting ~ on fuel** tenemos poco combustible, se nos está agotando el combustible; *V* **tide**.
2 *adv swing etc* bajo, cerca de la tierra (*etc*); *say, sing* bajo, en voz baja; **to bow ~** hacer una profunda reverencia; **a dress cut ~ in the back** un vestido muy escotado de espalda; **to fall ~** (*morally*) envilecerse, caer muy bajo; **England never fell so ~** Inglaterra nunca cayó tan bajo; **to lay sb ~** derribar a uno, abatir a uno, poner a uno fuera de combate; **to be laid ~ with 'flu** ser postrado por la gripe; **to lie ~** estar escondido, no asomar la cabeza; **to play ~** (*Cards*) poner pequeño; **to run ~** escasear, casi agotarse; **to sink ~ = to fall ~**.
3 *n* (**a**) (*Met*) área *f* de baja presión, depresión *f*; (*US*) temperatura *f* mínima.
(**b**) (*Aut*) primera (marcha) *f*.
(**c**) (*fig*) punto *m* más bajo; **to reach a new ~** caer a su punto más bajo; **this represents a new ~ in deceit** ésta es la peor forma de vileza; no se ha visto cosa más vil; *V* **all-time**.
low² [ləʊ] **1** *n* mugido *m*. **2** *vi* mugir.
lowborn ['ləʊ'bɔːn] *adj* de humilde cuna.
lowbrow ['ləʊbraʊ] **1** *adj* nada intelectual, poco culto. **2** *n* persona *f* nada intelectual, persona *f* de poca cultura.
low-budget [,ləʊ'bʌdʒɪt] *adj* de bajo presupuesto; **~ film** película *f* de presupuesto modesto.
low-calorie [,ləʊ'kælərɪ] *adj* bajo en calorías, acalórico.
low-class ['ləʊ,klɑːs] *adj* de clase baja.
low-cost ['ləʊ'kɒst] *adj* económico.
Low Countries ['ləʊ,kʌntrɪz] *npl* Países *mpl* Bajos.
low-cut ['ləʊ'kʌt] *adj dress* escotado.
low-density [,ləʊ'densɪtɪ] *attr* de baja densidad.

low-down ['ləʊdaʊn] **1** *adj* bajo, vil. **2** *n* (*) verdad *f*; informes *mpl* confidenciales; **he gave me the ~ on it** me contó la verdad del caso; **come on, give us the ~** ven, dinos la verdad.

lower[1] ['ləʊəʳ] **1** *adj comp of* **low**; más bajo, menos alto; inferior; **~ classes** clase *f* baja; **~ middle class** clase *f* media-baja; **L~ House** (*Brit Parl*) Cámara *f* baja; **the ~ income groups** los grupos de renta baja.

2 *adv comp of* **low**; más bajo.

3 *vt* bajar; *boat* lanzar; *flag, sail* arriar; (*reduce*) reducir, disminuir; *price* rebajar; *morale, resistance* debilitar; *guard* aflojar; (*in dignity*) humillar; **to ~ one's headlights** (*US*) poner luces de cruce.

4 *vr*: **to ~ o.s.** descolgarse (*by, on, with* con); (*fig*) envilecerse; **to ~ o.s. to do sth** rebajarse a hacer algo.

lower[2] ['laʊəʳ] *vi* (*person*) fruncir el entrecejo, mirar con ceño; (*sky*) encapotarse.

lower-case ['ləʊə,keɪs] *attr* minúsculo, de letra minúscula; **~ letter** minúscula *f*.

lower-class ['ləʊə,klɑːs] *adj* de la clase baja.

lowering ['laʊərɪŋ] *adj* ceñudo; amenazador; *sky* encapotado.

low-fat ['ləʊ'fæt] *attr*: **~ foods** alimentos *mpl* bajos en grasas; **~ milk** leche *f* desnatada.

low-flying ['ləʊ,flaɪɪŋ] *adj* de baja cota.

low-grade ['ləʊ,greɪd] *adj* de baja calidad.

low-heeled ['ləʊ'hiːld] *adj shoes* de tacones bajos.

lowing ['ləʊɪŋ] *n* mugidos *mpl*.

low-key [,ləʊ'kiː] *adj speech* moderado, en un tono bajo.

lowland ['ləʊlənd] **1** *n* tierra *f* baja; **the L~s** las tierras bajas de Escocia. **2** *adj* de tierra baja.

lowlander ['ləʊləndəʳ] *n* habitante *mf* de tierra baja.

low-level ['ləʊ'levl] *adj* de bajo nivel; **~ language** lenguaje *m* de bajo nivel.

lowliness ['ləʊlɪnɪs] *n* humildad *f*.

low-loader [,ləʊ'ləʊdəʳ] *n* (*Aut*) *camión de plataforma baja para el transporte de maquinaria pesada.*

lowly ['ləʊlɪ] *adj* humilde.

low-lying ['ləʊ,laɪɪŋ] *adj* bajo.

low-minded ['ləʊ'maɪndɪd] *adj* vulgar, vil, mezquino.

low-necked ['ləʊ'nekt] *adj* escotado.

lowness ['ləʊnɪs] *n* bajeza *f*, lo bajo; escasez *f*; gravedad *f*; humildad *f*; vileza *f*; lo verde; (*of spirits*) abatimiento *m*.

low-paid [,ləʊ'peɪd] **1** *adj* mal pagado. **2** *npl*: **the ~** los mal pagados.

low-pitched ['ləʊpɪtʃt] *adj note, voice* bajo; *campaign, speech* en tono menor.

low-pressure ['ləʊ'preʃəʳ] *adj* de baja presión.

low-priced [,ləʊ'praɪst] *adj* barato, económico.

low-profile ['ləʊ'prəʊfaɪl] *attr*: **~ activity** actividad *f* discreta, actividad *f* que evita llamar la atención.

low-risk [,ləʊ'rɪsk] *attr* de bajo riesgo.

low-spirited ['ləʊ'spɪrɪtɪd] *adj* deprimido, abatido.

low-tension ['ləʊ'tenʃən] *adj* de baja tensión.

low water ['ləʊ'wɔːtəʳ] **1** *n* bajamar *f*, marea *f* baja.

2 *attr*: **~ mark** línea *f* de bajamar.

loyal ['lɔɪəl] *adj* leal, fiel (*to* a).

loyalist ['lɔɪəlɪst] *n* legitimista *mf*, gubernamental *mf*; (*Spain, 1936*) republicano *m*, -a *f*; (*eg Ulster*) lealista *mf*.

loyally ['lɔɪəlɪ] *adv* lealmente.

loyalty ['lɔɪəltɪ] *n* lealtad *f*, fidelidad *f* (*to* a); **one's loyalties** la lealtad de uno.

lozenge ['lɒzɪndʒ] *n* (**a**) (*Med*) pastilla *f*. (**b**) (*Math*) rombo *m*; (*Her*) losange *m*.

LP *n* (**a**) (*Pol*) *abbr of* **Labour Party** Partido *m* Laborista. (**b**) (*Mus*) *abbr of* **long-playing record** elepé *m*.

LPN *n* (*US*) *abbr of* **Licensed Practical Nurse** *enfermera practicante*.

LPU *n abbr of* **least publishable unit** cuanto *m* de publicación.

LRAM *n* (*Brit*) *abbr of* **Licentiate of the Royal Academy of Music** Licenciado *m*, -a *f* de la Real Academia de Música.

LSAT *n* (*US*) *abbr of* **Law School Admission Test.**

LSD *n abbr of* **lysergic acid diethylamide** dimetilamida *f* del ácido lisérgico, LSD *f*.

L.S.D. *n* (*Brit* ††) *abbr of* **librae, solidi, denarii = pounds, shillings and pence** *antigua moneda británica*; (*) pasta* *f*.

LSE *n* (*Brit*) *abbr of* **London School of Economics.**

LSI *n abbr of* **large-scale integration** integración *f* a gran escala.

LST *n* (*US*) *abbr of* **Local Standard Time.**

LT *n* (*Elec*) *abbr of* **low tension** baja tensión *f*.

Lt *abbr of* **lieutenant** teniente *m*, ten.te.

Lt.-Col. *abbr of* **lieutenant-colonel** teniente *m* coronel.

Ltd *abbr of* **limited** Sociedad *f* Anónima, S.A.

Lt.-Gen. *abbr of* **lieutenant-general** teniente *m* general.

lubricant ['luːbrɪkənt] **1** *adj* lubricante. **2** *n* lubricante *m*.

lubricate ['luːbrɪkeɪt] *vt* lubricar, engrasar.

lubricating ['luːbrɪkeɪtɪŋ] *adj* lubricante; **~ oil** aceite *m* lubricante.

lubrication [,luːbrɪ'keɪʃən] *n* lubricación *f*, engrase *m*.

lubricator ['luːbrɪkeɪtəʳ] *n* lubricador *m*.

lubricious [luː'brɪʃəs] *adj* verde, salaz, lascivo.

lubricity [luː'brɪsɪtɪ] *n* lubricidad *f*.

Lucan ['luːkən] *nm* Lucano.

lucerne [luː'sɜːn] *n* (*esp Brit*) alfalfa *f*.

lucid ['luːsɪd] *adj* claro, lúcido; **~ interval** intervalo *m* lúcido.

lucidity [luː'sɪdɪtɪ] *n* lucidez *f*.

lucidly ['luːsɪdlɪ] *adv* claramente, con claridad.

Lucifer ['luːsɪfəʳ] *nm* Lucifer.

luck [lʌk] *n* suerte *f*, fortuna *f*; azar *m*; **bad ~, hard ~** mala suerte *f*; **bad ~!** ¡mala suerte!; **good ~** suerte *f*; **best of ~!, good ~!** ¡que tengas suerte!; **beginner's ~** suerte *f* del principiante; **any ~?** ¿y qué?; **here's ~!** (*toast*) ¡salud!; **no such ~!** ¡ojalá!; **with any ~** a lo mejor; **worse ~!** ¡desgraciadamente!; **better ~ next time!** ¡a la tercera va la vencida!; **and the best of ~!** (*iro*) ¡Dios te la depare buena!; **to be in ~** estar de suerte, tener suerte; **to be out of ~, to be down on one's ~** estar de malas; **to bring sb bad ~** traer mala suerte a uno; **as ~ would have it** quiso la suerte que ...; **to have the devil's own ~, to have the ~ of the devil** tener chorra, tener buena pata; **to have the ~ to + infin** tener la suerte de + *infin*; **to keep sth for ~** guardar algo por si trae suerte; **take this for ~** toma esto por si trae suerte; **to do sth trusting to ~** hacer algo a la buena de Dios; **to try one's ~** probar fortuna.

luckily ['lʌkɪlɪ] *adv* afortunadamente, por fortuna.

luckless ['lʌklɪs] *adj* desdichado, desafortunado.

lucky ['lʌkɪ] *adj person* afortunado, feliz, que tiene suerte; *day* de buen agüero; *move, shot etc* afortunado; *charm* que trae suerte; **~ dip** (*Brit*) caja *f* de las sorpresas; **~ number** número *m* afortunado; **this is my ~ day** éste es mi día de suerte; **third time ~!** ¡a la tercera va la vencida!; **~ you!** ¡qué suerte!; **to be ~** (*person*) tener suerte; (*charm etc*) traer suerte; **you'll be ~!** (*: *iro*) ¡sería milagro!; **I should be so ~!*** ¡ojalá!; **you'll be ~ to get £50 for that old banger‡** sería un milagro si te dieran 50 libras por el cacharro ese*; **to be a ~ sort** tener buena sombra; **to be born ~** nacer de pie; **to be ~ in that ...** tener la suerte de que ...; **that was very ~ for you** en eso tuviste mucha suerte; **to believe in one's ~ star** creer en su buena estrella; **to strike (it) ~** tener suerte, estar de suerte; **you can think yourself ~ that ...** puedes considerarte afortunado que ...

lucrative ['luːkrətɪv] *adj* lucrativo, provechoso.

lucre ['luːkəʳ] *n*: **filthy ~** el vil metal.

Lucretia [luː'kriːʃə] *nf* Lucrecia.

Lucretius [luː'kriːʃəs] *nm* Lucrecio.

lucubration [,luːkjʊ'breɪʃən] *n* lucubración *f*.

Lucy ['luːsɪ] *nf* Lucía.

Luddite ['lʌdaɪt] **1** *adj* ludista. **2** *n* ludista *mf*.

ludic ['luːdɪk] *adj* lúdico.

ludicrous ['luːdɪkrəs] *adj* absurdo, ridículo.

ludicrously ['luːdɪkrəslɪ] *adv* absurdamente, ridículamente.

ludo ['luːdəʊ] *n* (*Brit*) ludo *m*.

luff [lʌf] **1** *n* orza *f*. **2** *vi* orzar.

luffa ['lʌfə] *n* (*US*) esponja *f* de lufa.

lug [lʌg] **1** *n* (**a**) oreja *f*; agarradera *f*; (*Tech*) orejeta *f*; (‡) oreja *f*.

(**b**) (*tug*) tirón *m*.

2 *vt* (*drag*) arrastrar; llevar con dificultad; (*pull*) tirar de; **to ~ sth about** (*or* **around**) **with one** llevar algo consigo (con dificultad); **to ~ sth along** arrastrar algo; **to ~ sth in** llevar algo dentro arrastrándolo, *subject* sacar a colación; **they ~ged him off to the theatre** le llevaron contra su voluntad al teatro.

luggage ['lʌgɪdʒ] *n* equipaje *m*.

luggage-boot ['lʌgɪdʒ,buːt] *n* (*Brit Aut*) maletero *m*, portaequipajes *m*.

luggage car ['lʌgɪdʒ,kɑːr] *n* (*US*) furgón *m* de equipaje.

luggage-carrier ['lʌgɪdʒ,kærɪəʳ] *n*, **luggage-grid** ['lʌgɪdʒ,grɪd] *n* portaequipajes *m*, baca *f*.

luggage checkroom ['lʌgɪdʒ,ʃekrʊm] *n* (*US*) consigna *f*.

luggage-handler ['lʌgɪdʒ,hændləʳ] *n* despachador *m* de equipaje.

luggage-label ['lʌgɪdʒ,leɪbl] *n* etiqueta *f* de equipaje.

luggage-locker ['lʌgɪdʒ,lɒkəʳ] *n* consigna *f* automática.

luggage-rack ['lʌgɪdʒ,ræk] *n* (*Rail etc*) rejilla *f*, redecilla *f*;

(*Aut*) portaequipajes *m*, baca *f*.
luggage-van ['lʌgɪdʒ,væn] *n* (*Brit*) furgón *m* (de equipajes).
lugger ['lʌgəʳ] *n* lugre *m*.
lughole‡ ['lʌgəʊl] *n* oreja *f*; oído *m*.
lugsail ['lʌgsl] *n* vela *f* al tercio.
lugubrious [luː'guːbrɪəs] *adj* lúgubre, triste.
lugubriously [luː'guːbrɪəslɪ] *adv* lúgubremente, tristemente.
lugworm ['lʌg,wɜːm] *n* lombriz *f* de mar.
Luke [luːk] *nm* Lucas.
lukewarm ['luːkwɔːm] *adj* tibio, templado; (*fig*) tibio, indiferente, poco entusiasta.
lull [lʌl] **1** *n* tregua *f*, respiro *m*, intervalo *m* de calma; (*in storm, wind*) recalmón *m*.
2 *vt person* calmar, (*to sleep*) adormecer, arrullar; *fears etc* calmar, aquietar, sosegar.
lullaby ['lʌləbaɪ] *n* nana *f*, canción *f* de cuna.
lumbago [lʌm'beɪgəʊ] *n* lumbago *m*.
lumbar ['lʌmbəʳ] *adj* lumbar.
lumber[1] ['lʌmbəʳ] **1** *n* (**a**) (*timber*) maderos *mpl*, maderas *fpl* (de sierra).
(**b**) (*junk*) trastos *mpl* viejos.
2 *vt* (**a**) *space, room* obstruir (*with* de); **to ~ things together** amontonar cosas; (*fig*) juntar cosas sin orden.
(**b**) (*Brit**) **to ~ sb with sth** hacer que uno cargue con algo; **he got ~ed with the job** tuvo que cargar con el trabajo; **I got ~ed with the girl for the evening** tuve que pasar toda la tarde con la chica.
3 *vi* cortar y aserrar árboles, explotar los bosques.
lumber[2] ['lʌmbəʳ] *vi*: **to ~ about, to ~ along** moverse pesadamente, avanzar con ruido sordo.
lumbering[1] ['lʌmbərɪŋ] *n* (*US*) explotación *f* forestal.
lumbering[2] ['lʌmbərɪŋ] *adj* pesado, torpe.
lumberjack ['lʌmbədʒæk] *n*, **lumberman** ['lʌmbəmən] *n*, *pl* **lumbermen** ['lʌmbəmən] maderero *m*, hachero *m*, leñador *m*; trabajador *m* forestal.
lumber jacket ['lʌmbə,dʒækɪt] *n* chaqueta *f* de leñador.
lumber mill ['lʌmbə,mɪl] *n* aserradero *m*.
lumber room ['lʌmbərʊm] *n* trastera *f*.
lumberyard ['lʌmbəjɑːd] *n* (*US*) almacén *m* de madera.
luminary ['luːmɪnərɪ] *n* lumbrera *f*.
luminescence [,luːmɪ'nesns] *n* luminescencia *f*.
luminosity [,luːmɪ'nɒsɪtɪ] *n* luminosidad *f*.
luminous ['luːmɪnəs] *adj* luminoso.
lumme‡ ['lʌmɪ] *interj* (*Brit*) = **lummy**.
lummox* ['lʌməks] *n* (*US*) bobo *m*.
lummy‡ ['lʌmɪ] *interj* (*Brit*) ¡caray!*
lump [lʌmp] **1** *n* (**a**) (*of earth, sugar etc*) terrón *m*; (*mass*) masa *f* informe; (*fragment*) trozo *m*, pedazo *m*; (*swelling*) bulto *m*, hinchazón *f*; (*on surface*) protuberancia *f*; (*in throat*) nudo *m*; (*person*) zoquete *m*, paquete *m* (*LAm*); **with a ~ in one's throat** con un nudo en la garganta; **I get a ~ in my throat** se me anuda la garganta.
(**b**) (*: *person*) zoquete *m*, paquete *m* (*LAm*); **ugly ~** foca* *f*.
2 *attr*: **~ sugar** azúcar *m* en terrones, azúcar *m* de cortadillo; **~ sum** suma *f* global.
3 *vt*: (*Brit**) **to ~ it** (*go*) largarse*; (*bear it*) aguantarlo; **you'll have to ~ it** tendrás que aguantarlo; **if he doesn't like it he can ~ it** si no le gusta que se fastidie*.
◆**lump together** *vt objects* amontonar; *persons, subjects* poner juntos, agrupar, mezclar.
lumpish ['lʌmpɪʃ] *adj* torpe, pesado.
lumpy ['lʌmpɪ] *adj soil* aterronado; *liquid etc* lleno de grumos, con muchos grumos; *bed etc* desigual, nada cómodo.
lunacy ['luːnəsɪ] *n* locura *f*; **it's sheer ~!** ¡es una locura!
lunar ['luːnəʳ] *adj* lunar; **~ eclipse** eclipse *m* lunar; **~ module** módulo *m* lunar; **~ month** mes *m* lunar.
lunatic ['luːnətɪk] **1** *adj* lunático, loco, demente; **~ asylum** manicomio *m*; **~ fringe** franja *f* lunática. **2** *n* loco *m*, -a *f*.
lunch [lʌntʃ] **1** *n* (*also more formally* **luncheon** ['lʌntʃən]) almuerzo *m*, comida *f*; (*snack*) bocadillo *m*; **he's out to ~*** (*US*) está en la luna; **to have ~, to take ~** almorzar, comer. **2** *vi* almorzar, comer (*on fish* pescado); tomar un bocadillo.
lunch-break ['lʌntʃ,breɪk] *n* descanso *m* de comer.
luncheon meat ['lʌntʃən,miːt] *n* carne *f* en conserva, carne *f* en lata.
luncheon voucher ['lʌntʃən,vaʊtʃəʳ] *n* (*Brit*) vale *m* de comida.
lunch-hour ['lʌntʃaʊəʳ] *n* hora *f* de comer.
lunchtime ['lʌntʃtaɪm] *n* hora *f* de comer.
lung [lʌŋ] **1** *n* pulmón *m*. **2** *attr*: **~ cancer** cáncer *m* de pulmón.
lunge [lʌndʒ] **1** *n* arremetida *f*, embestida *f*; (*Fencing*) estocada *f*.
2 *vi* arremeter (*at* contra, *with* con), embestir; dar una estocada; **to ~ at sb** abalanzarse sobre uno; **he ~d with his right** le asestó un derechazo.
lupin ['luːpɪn] *n* altramuz *m*, lupino *m*.
lurch[1] [lɜːtʃ] *n*: **to leave sb in the ~** dejar a uno en la estacada, dejar a uno plantado.
lurch[2] [lɜːtʃ] **1** *n* sacudida *f*, tumbo *m*, movimiento *m* repentino; (*Naut*) bandazo *m*; **to give a ~** dar un tumbo (*etc*).
2 *vi* (*vehicle etc*) dar sacudidas, dar tumbos, dar un tumbo; (*Naut*) dar un bandazo; (*person*) tambalearse.
◆**lurch along** *vi* (*vehicle*) ir dando tumbos; (*person*) avanzar tambaleándose.
◆**lurch in** *vi* entrar tambaleándose.
◆**lurch out** *vi* salir tambaleándose.
lure [ljʊəʳ] **1** *n* (**a**) (*bait*) cebo *m*; (*decoy*) señuelo *m*.
(**b**) (*fig*) aliciente *m*, atractivo *m*; encanto *m*; (*deceitful*) señuelo *m*.
2 *vt* atraer (con señuelo); *person* atraer, tentar; seducir; **to ~ sb into a trap** hacer que uno caiga en una trampa; **to ~ sb into a house** persuadir mañosamente a uno a entrar en una casa.
◆**lure away** *vt*: **to ~ sb away from** apartar a uno de.
◆**lure on** *vt*: **to ~ sb on to destruction** hacer que uno avance ciegamente hacia su ruina.
◆**lure out** *vt*: **to ~ sb out** persuadir mañosamente a uno a salir.
lurex ['lʊəreks] *n* lúrex *m*.
lurid ['ljʊərɪd] *adj light* misterioso, fantástico; *colour of skin* lívido, cárdeno; *dress etc* chillón; *language* fuerte, pintoresco; *account* sensacional; *detail* horripilante, espeluznante.
lurk [lɜːk] *vi* estar escondido; estar en acecho.
lurking ['lɜːkɪŋ] *adj fear etc* vago, indefinible.
luscious ['lʌʃəs] *adj* delicioso, suculento, riquísimo, exquisito; *style* empalagoso; *girl* delicioso, apetitoso.
lusciousness ['lʌʃəsnɪs] *n* suculencia *f*, riqueza *f*; exquisitez *f*; lo empalagoso.
lush [lʌʃ] **1** *adj* (**a**) *growth, vegetation* lozano, exuberante; *pasture* rico. (**b**) *fruit etc V* **luscious**. (**c**) (*opulent*) opulento, lujoso. **2** *n* (‡) alcohólico *m*, -a *f*.
lushness ['lʌʃnɪs] *n* (**a**) lozanía *f*, exuberancia *f*. (**b**) *V* **lusciousness**. (**c**) opulencia *f*, lujo *m*.
lust [lʌst] **1** *n* (*sexual*) lujuria *f*, lascivia *f*; sensualidad *f*; (*greed*) codicia *f*, deseo *m* vehemente (*for* de).
2 *vi* lujuriar.
◆**lust after, lust for** *vt* (*sexually*) apetecer contacto carnal con; *object* codiciar.
luster ['lʌstəʳ] *n* (*US*) = **lustre**.
lustful ['lʌstfʊl] *adj* lujurioso, libidinoso; *look etc* lascivo.
lustfully ['lʌstfəlɪ] *adv* lujuriosamente, libidinosamente; lascivamente.
lustfulness ['lʌstfʊlnɪs] *n* lujuria *f*, lascivia *f*; sensualidad *f*.
lustre, (*US*) **luster** ['lʌstəʳ] *n* lustre *m*, brillo *m*.
lustreless, (*US*) **lusterless** ['lʌstəlɪs] *adj* deslustrado; *eyes* apagado.
lustrous ['lʌstrəs] *adj* lustroso, brillante.
lusty ['lʌstɪ] *adj person* vigoroso, fuerte, robusto; *plant* lozano; *cry* fuerte; *effort etc* grande.
lute [luːt] *n* laúd *m*.
lutetium [lʊ'tiːʃɪəm] *n* lutecio *m*.
Luther ['luːθəʳ] *nm* Lutero.
Lutheran ['luːθərən] **1** *adj* luterano. **2** *n* luterano *m*, -a *f*.
Lutheranism ['luːθərənɪzəm] *n* luteranismo *m*.
luv* [lʌv] *n* (= **love**): **yes, ~** sí, cariño.
Luxembourg ['lʌksəmbɜːg] *n* Luxemburgo *m*.
luxuriance [lʌg'zjʊərɪəns] *n* lozanía *f*, exuberancia *f*.
luxuriant [lʌg'zjʊərɪənt] *adj* lozano, exuberante.
luxuriantly [lʌg'zjʊərɪəntlɪ] *adv* con lozanía, de manera exuberante.
luxuriate [lʌg'zjʊərɪeɪt] *vi* (*plant*) crecer con exuberancia; (*person*) disfrutar; **to ~ in** disfrutar de, deleitarse con, entregarse al lujo de.
luxurious [lʌg'zjʊərɪəs] *adj* lujoso.
luxuriously [lʌg'zjʊərɪəslɪ] *adv* lujosamente.
luxury ['lʌkʃərɪ] **1** *n* (*gen*) lujo *m*; (*article*) artículo *m* de lujo; **to live in ~** vivir en el lujo. **2** *attr* de lujo; **~ tax** impuesto *m* de lujo.
LV *abbr of* **luncheon voucher**.
LW *n* (*Rad*) *abbr of* **long wave** onda *f* larga, OL *f*.
lyceum [laɪ'siːəm] *n* liceo *m*.
lychee [,laɪ'tʃiː] *n* lychee *m*, lichi *m*.

lychgate ['lɪtʃgeɪt] *n* entrada *f* de cementerio.
Lycra ['laɪkrə] ® *n* licra *f*.
lye [laɪ] *n* lejía *f*.
lying¹ ['laɪɪŋ] **1** *adj* mentiroso, falso. **2** *n* mentiras *fpl*.
lying² ['laɪɪŋ] *V* **lie²**.
lying-in ['laɪɪŋ'ɪn] **1** *n* (*Med*) parto *m*. **2** *attr*: ~ **ward** sala *f* de maternidad.
lymph [lɪmf] **1** *n* linfa *f*. **2** *attr*: ~ **gland** ganglio *m* linfático.
lymphatic [lɪm'fætɪk] **1** *adj* linfático. **2** *n* vaso *m* linfático.
lymphocyte ['lɪmfəʊ,saɪt] *n* linfocito *m*.
lynch [lɪntʃ] *vt* linchar.
lynching ['lɪntʃɪŋ] *n* linchamiento *m*.
lynch law ['lɪntʃlɔː] *n* ley *f* del linchamiento.
lynx [lɪŋks] *n* lince *m*.
lynx-eyed ['lɪŋksaɪd] *adj* de ojos de lince.
Lyons ['laɪənz] *n* Lyón *m*.
lyre ['laɪəʳ] *n* lira *f*.
lyrebird ['laɪəbɜːd] *n* ave *f* lira.
lyric ['lɪrɪk] **1** *adj* lírico. **2** *n* (*poem*) poema *m* lírico, poesía *f* lírica; (*genre*) lírica *f*; (*words of song*) letra *f* de una canción.
lyrical ['lɪrɪkəl] *adj* lírico; (*fig*) elocuente, entusiasta; **to grow** (*or* **wax**) ~ **about sth** entusiasmarse por algo, extasiarse ante algo.
lyricism ['lɪrɪsɪzem] *n* lirismo *m*.
lyricist ['lɪrɪsɪst] *n* letrista *mf*.
lysergic [lɪ'sɜːdʒɪk] *adj*: ~ **acid** ácido *m* lisérgico.
Lysol ['laɪsɒl] ® *n* lisol ® *m*.

M

M, m [em] *n* (*letter*) M, m *f*; **M for Mary, M for Mike** (*US*) M de Madrid.
M (**a**) *abbr of* **million**(**s**). (**b**) (*garment size*) *abbr of* **medium.**
m (**a**) *abbr of* **married** se casó con. (**b**) *abbr of* **metre**(**s**) metro(s) *m(pl)*, m. (**c**) *abbr of* **mile**(**s**) milla(s) *f(pl)*. (**d**) *abbr of* **male** macho *m*. (**e**) *abbr of* **minute**(**s**) minuto(s) *m* (*pl*), m.
MA (**a**) *n* (*Univ*) *abbr of* **Master of Arts**. (**b**) (*US Post*) *abbr of* **Massachusetts.**
M.A. (*US*) *abbr of* **Military Academy.**
ma* [mɑː] *n* mamá* *f*.
ma'am [mæm] *n* = **madam.**
mac [mæk] *n* (**a**) (*Brit*) impermeable *m*. (**b**) **this way, M~!*** ¡por aquí, amigo!
macabre [məˈkɑːbr] *adj* macabro.
macadam [məˈkædəm] *n* macadán *m*.
macadamize [məˈkædəmaɪz] *vt* macadamizar.
macaroni [ˌmækəˈrəʊnɪ] *n* macarrones *mpl*.
macaronic [ˌmækəˈrɒnɪk] *adj* macarrónico.
macaroon [ˌmækəˈruːn] *n* macarrón *m* (de almendras), mostachón *m*.
macaw [məˈkɔː] *n* guacamayo *m*, avacanza *m*.
mace[1] [meɪs] *n* (*Bot*) macis *f*.
mace[2] [meɪs] *n* maza *f*.
macebearer [ˈmeɪsˌbɛərəʳ] *n* macero *m*.
macerate [ˈmæsəreɪt] **1** *vt* macerar. **2** *vi* macerar(se).
Mach [mæk] *n* mach *m*.
machete [məˈtʃeɪtɪ] *n* machete *m*.
Machiavelli [ˌmækɪəˈvelɪ] *nm* Maquiavelo.
Machiavellian [ˌmækɪəˈvelɪən] *adj* maquiavélico.
machination [ˌmækɪˈneɪʃən] *n* maquinación *f*.
machine [məˈʃiːn] **1** *n* (**a**) máquina *f* (*also fig*); aparato *m*; (*Aut*) coche *m*; (*cycle*) bicicleta *f*; (*Aer*) aparato *m*, avión *m*.
(**b**) (*Pol etc*) organización *f*, aparato *m*.
2 *attr* mecánico, (hecho) a máquina; **~ age** época *f* de la máquina; **~ code** código *m* máquina; **~ error** error *m* de la máquina; **~ intelligence** inteligencia *f* máquina; **~ language** lenguaje *m* máquina; **~ operator** maquinista *mf*; **~ time** tiempo *m* máquina; **~ translation** traducción *f* automática, traducción *f* automatizada.
3 *vt* (*Tech*) trabajar a máquina, acabar a máquina; (*Sew*) coser a máquina.
machine-gun [məˈʃiːngʌn] **1** *n* ametralladora *f*. **2** *vt* ametrallar.
machine-gunner [məˈʃiːngʌnəʳ] *n* ametrallador *m*.
machine-made [məˈʃiːnmeɪd] *adj* hecho a máquina.
machine-readable [məˈʃiːnˈriːdəbl] *adj* legible por máquina; **in ~ form** en forma legible por máquina; **~ code** código *m* legible por máquina.
machinery [məˈʃiːnərɪ] *n* (**a**) (*machines*) maquinaria *f*; (*mechanism*) mecanismo *m*. (**b**) (*fig*) mecanismo *m*, organización *f*, sistema *m*.
machine-shop [məˈʃiːnʃɒp] *n* taller *m* de máquinas.
machine-stitch [məˈʃiːnˌstɪtʃ] *vt* coser a máquina.
machine-tool [məˈʃiːntuːl] *n* máquina *f* herramienta.
machine-washable [məˈʃɪːnˈwɒʃəbl] *adj* lavable en la lavadora.
machinist [məˈʃiːnɪst] *n* (*Tech*) maquinista *mf*; operario *m* de máquina, mecánico *m*; (*Sew*) costurera *f* a máquina.
machismo [məˈtʃɪzməʊ] *n* machismo *m*.
macho [ˈmætʃəʊ] **1** *adj* macho, masculino. **2** *n* macho *m*, machista *m*, machote *m*.
mackerel [ˈmækrəl] **1** *n* caballa *f*, berdel *m*, escombro *m*. **2** *attr*: **~ sky** cielo *m* aborregado.
mackintosh [ˈmækɪntɒʃ] *n* impermeable *m*.
macramé [məˈkrɑːmɪ] *n* macramé *m*.
macro... [ˈmækrəʊ] *pref* macro...
macro [ˈmækrəʊ] *n* (*Comput*) *abbr of* **macro-instruction** macroinstrucción *f*, macro *m*.
macrobiotic [ˌmækrəʊbaɪˈɒtɪk] *adj* macrobiótico.
macrocosm [ˈmækrəʊkɒzəm] *n* macrocosmo *m*.
macroeconomic [ˌmækrəʊˌiːkəˈnɒmɪk] *adj* macroeconómico.
macroeconomics [ˌmækrəʊˌiːkəˈnɒmɪks] *n* macroeconomía *f*.
macroeconomy [ˌmækrəʊɪˈkɒnəmɪ] macroeconomía *f*.
macroscopic [ˌmækrəˈskɒpɪk] *adj* macroscópico.
mad [mæd] **1** *adj* (**a**) (*deranged*) loco; demente; *dog* rabioso; *idea* loco, insensato, disparatado; *gallop, rush etc* loco, precipitado; **~ cow disease** encefalopatía *f* espongiforme bovina; **~ as a hatter, ~ as a March hare** más loco que una cabra; **raving ~, stark (staring) ~** loco de atar; **a ~ thing (to do)** una locura; **are you ~?** ¿estás loco?; **you must be ~!** ¡qué locura!; **to be ~ with joy** estar loco de alegría; **to drive sb ~** volver loco a uno; **to go ~** volverse loco, enloquecer; **this is patriotism gone ~** esto es el patriotismo en grado ridículo; **to play** (*etc*) **like ~** tocar (*etc*) como un loco; **to rain like ~** llover muchísimo; **the plant grows like ~** la planta crece con una rapidez asombrosa.
(**b**) (**: angry*) furioso; **to be ~ about sth** estar furioso por algo; **to be ~ about** (*or* **at**) **sb** estar furioso contra uno; **to get ~** enfadarse, ponerse furioso (*with* con); **it's no good getting ~ with me** de nada sirve ponerte furioso conmigo; **it makes me ~** me saca de quicio, me da rabia; **~ as a hornet** (*US*) cabreadísimo*.
(**c**) (**: enthusiastic*) loco; **to be ~ about** (*or* **on**) estar loco por, ser muy aficionado a, entusiasmarse por; **he's ~ about her** está locamente enamorado de ella; **I'm just ~ about you** ando loco por ti; **I can't say I'm ~ about the idea** la idea no me apasiona que digamos.
2 (*) *adv*: **to be ~ keen on sth** entusiasmarse como un loco por algo; **to be ~ keen to do sth** desear con vehemencia hacer algo.
-mad [mæd] *adj ending in compounds eg* **pony~ teenagers** quinceañeras *fpl* locas por los caballitos; **soccer~ boys** chicos *mpl* con la manía del fútbol.
Madagascar [ˌmædəˈgæskəʳ] *n* Madagascar *m*.
madam [ˈmædəm] *n* señora *f*; **yes ~** sí señora; **little ~** niña *f* precoz, niña *f* repipi; *V* **dear.**
madame [ˈmædəm] *n, pl* **mesdames** [ˈmeɪdæm] (**a**) madama *f*, señora *f*; **M~ Dupont** la señora de Dupont. (**b**) (*of brothel*) ama *f*, dueña *f*.
madcap [ˈmædkæp] **1** *adj* atolondrado. **2** *n* locuelo *m*, -a *f*, tarambana *mf*.
madden [ˈmædn] *vt* volver loco; (*fig*) volver loco, enfurecer, sacar de quicio; **a ~ed bull** un toro enloquecido; **it ~s me** me saca de quicio, me da rabia.
maddening [ˈmædnɪŋ] *adj delay etc* desesperante, exasperante; **he can be ~ at times** hay veces cuando saca a todos de quicio; **isn't it ~?** ¡es para volverse loco!
maddeningly [ˈmædnɪŋlɪ] *adv* de modo desesperante; **~ slow** terriblemente lento.
made [meɪd] *pret and ptp of* **make.**
Madeira [məˈdɪərə] *n* Madera *f*; (*wine*) vino *m* de Madera.
made-to-measure [ˌmeɪdtəˈmeʒəʳ] *adj* (*Brit*) hecho a la medida.
made-to-order [ˌmeɪdtəˈɔːdəʳ] *adj* (*Brit*) hecho de encargo, (*US*) hecho a la medida.
made-up [ˈmeɪdˈʌp] *adj* hecho; compuesto, artificial; *dress* confeccionado; *story* ficticio; *face* pintado, maquillado.
Madge [maedʒ] *nf familiar form of* **Margaret.**
madhouse [ˈmædhaʊs] *n, pl* **madhouses** [ˈmædˌhaʊzɪz] manicomio *m*, casa *f* de locos; **this is a ~!** ¡esto es un guirigay!
madly [ˈmædlɪ] *adv* locamente; furiosamente, como un loco; con rabia; **it was ~ exciting** fue divertidísimo, nos

divertimos una barbaridad; **to be ~ in love with sb** estar enamorado perdidamente de uno.

madman ['mædmən] *n, pl* **madmen** ['mædmən] loco *m.*

madness ['mædnɪs] *n* locura *f*; demencia *f*; furia *f*; rabia *f*; **it's sheer ~!** ¡es una locura!; **what ~!** ¡qué locura!

Madonna [mə'dɒnə] *n* Virgen *f.*

Madrid [mə'drɪd] **1** *n* Madrid *m.* **2** *attr* madrileño, matritense.

madrigal ['mædrɪgəl] *n* madrigal *m.*

madwoman ['mædwʊmən] *n, pl* **madwomen** ['mæd,wɪmɪn] loca *f.*

maelstrom ['meɪlstrəʊm] *n* maelstrom *m*; (*fig*) vórtice *m*, remolino *m.*

maestro [mɑː'estrəʊ] *n* maestro *m.*

Mae West ['meɪ'west] *n* (*Aer*: *hum*) chaleco *m* salvavidas.

MAFF *n* (*Brit*) *abbr of* **Ministry of Agriculture, Fisheries and Food.**

mafia ['mæfɪə] *n* mafia *f.*

mafioso [,mæfɪ'əʊsəʊ] *n, pl* **mafiosi** [,mæfɪ'əʊsɪ] mafioso *m.*

mag* [mæg] *n* revista *f.*

magazine [,mægə'ziːn] *n* (**a**) (*journal*) revista *f.* (**b**) (*in rifle*) depósito *m* de cartuchos, recámara *f*; (*Typ*) almacén *m* de matrices; (*Rad etc*) depósito *m*; (*Mil*: *store*) almacén *m*, (*for powder*) polvorín *m*, (*Naut*) santabárbara *f.* (**c**) (*programme*) magazine *m*, programa *m* magazine.

Magdalen ['mægdəlɪn] *nf* Magdalena.

Magellan [mə'gelən] **1** *nm* Magallanes. **2** *attr*: **~ Straits** Estrecho *m* de Magallanes.

magenta [mə'dʒentə] **1** *n* magenta *f.* **2** *adj* color magenta.

Maggie ['mægɪ] *nf familiar form of* **Margaret.**

maggot ['mægət] *n* cresa *f*, gusano *m.*

maggoty ['mægətɪ] *adj* agusanado, lleno de gusanos.

Maghrib ['mʌgrəb] *n* Magreb *m.*

Magi ['meɪdʒaɪ] *npl*: **the ~** los Reyes Magos.

magic ['mædʒɪk] **1** *adj* (**a**) mágico; **~ carpet** alfombra *f* encantada; **~ lantern** linterna *f* mágica; **to say the ~ word** dar la fórmula mágica. (**b**) (*) fabuloso*, estupendo*. **2** *n* magia *f*; **by ~** por arte de magia; **as if by ~** como por ensalmo, como por encanto; **the ~ of that moment** la magia de ese momento; **her dance was utter ~** su baile era la más pura poesía; **Matthews is ~*** Matthews es fabuloso*.

magical ['mædʒɪkəl] *adj* mágico.

magically ['mædʒɪkəlɪ] *adv* por arte de magia; (*fig*) como por ensalmo.

magician [mədʒɪʃən] *n* mago *m*, mágico *m*, brujo *m*; (*conjuror*) mago *m*, prestidigitador *m.*

magisterial [,mædʒɪs'tɪərɪəl] *adj* magistral.

magistracy ['mædʒɪstrəsɪ] *n* magistratura *f.*

magistrate ['mædʒɪstreɪt] *n* magistrado *m*, -a *f*; juez *mf* (municipal); **~s' court** juzgado *m* de paz, juzgado *m* correccional.

magma ['mægmə] *n* magma *m.*

Magna C(h)arta ['mægnə'kɑːtə] *n* (*Brit*) Carta *f* Magna.

magnanimity [,mægnə'nɪmɪtɪ] *n* magnanimidad *f.*

magnanimous [mæg'nænɪməs] *adj* magnánimo.

magnanimously [mæg'nænɪməslɪ] *adv* magnánimamente.

magnate ['mægneɪt] *n* magnate *m*, potentado *m.*

magnesia [mæg'niːʃə] *n* magnesia *f.*

magnesium [mæg'niːzɪəm] *n* magnesio *m*; **~ sulphate** sulfato *m* magnésico.

magnet ['mægnɪt] *n* imán *m* (*also fig*).

magnetic [mæg'netɪk] *adj* magnético; (*fig*) magnético, atractivo; **~ card reader** lector *m* de tarjeta magnética; **~ disk** disco *m* magnético; **~ field** campo *m* magnético; **~ mine** mina *f* magnética; **~ needle** aguja *f* magnética; **~ north** polo *m* magnético; **~ stripe** raya *f* magnética; **~ tape** cinta *f* magnética.

magnetically [mæg'netɪkəlɪ] *adv* magnéticamente.

magnetism ['mægnɪtɪzəm] *n* magnetismo *m*; (*fig*) magnetismo *m* personal.

magnetizable [,mægnɪ'taɪzəbl] *adj* magnetizable.

magnetize ['mægnɪtaɪz] *vt* magnetizar (*also fig*), iman(t)ar.

magneto [mæg'niːtəʊ] *n* magneto *f.*

magnetometer [,mægnɪ'tɒmɪtəʳ] *n* magnetómetro *m.*

magnetosphere [mæg'niːtəʊ,sfɪəʳ] *n* magnetosfera *f.*

magnificat [mæg'nɪfɪkæt] *n* magníficat *m.*

magnification [,mægnɪfɪ'keɪʃən] *n* (**a**) (*Opt*) aumento *m*, ampliación *f*; **high ~** gran aumento *m*; **low ~** pequeño aumento *m.* (**b**) (*fig*) exageración *f.*

magnificence [mæg'nɪfɪsəns] *n* magnificencia *f.*

magnificent [mæg'nɪfɪsənt] *adj* magnífico; suntuoso; **~!** ¡magnífico!

magnificently [mæg'nɪfɪsəntlɪ] *adv* magníficamente; **you did ~** lo hiciste estupendamente bien.

magnify ['mægnɪfaɪ] *vt* (**a**) (*Opt*) aumentar; **to ~ sth 7 times** aumentar algo 7 veces; **~ing glass** lente *f* de aumento, lupa *f*; **~ing power** aumento *m.* (**b**) (*fig*) agrandar, exagerar; (*praise*) magnificar.

magnitude ['mægnɪtjuːd] *n* magnitud *f*; (*fig*) magnitud *f*, envergadura *f*; **a star of the first ~** una estrella de primera magnitud; **in operations of this ~** en operaciones de esta envergadura.

magnolia [mæg'nəʊlɪə] *n* magnolia *f.*

magnum ['mægnəm] **1** *n* botella *f* doble, botella *f* de litro y medio. **2** *adj*: **~ opus** obra *f* maestra.

magpie ['mægpaɪ] *n* urraca *f*, marica *f.*

Magyar ['mægjɑːʳ] **1** *adj* magiar. **2** *n* magiar *mf.*

maharajah [,mɑːhə'rɑːdʒə] *n* maharajá *m.*

Mahdi ['mɑːdɪ] *n* mahdi *m.*

mahjong(g) [,mɑː'dʒɒŋ] *n* dominó *m* chino.

mahogany [mə'hɒgənɪ] *n* caoba *f.*

Mahomet [mə'hɒmɪt] *nm* Mahoma.

Mahometan [mə'hɒmɪtən] **1** *adj* mahometano. **2** *n* mahometano *m*, -a *f.*

maid [meɪd] *n* (**a**) (*servant*) criada *f*, doncella *f*, sirvienta *f* (*esp LAm*); (*in hotel etc*) camarera *f*; **lady's ~** doncella *f*; **~ of honour** dama *f* de honor. (**b**) (††, *liter*) doncella *f*; (*young girl*) muchacha *f*; **old ~** solterona *f*; **she'll be an old ~** quedará para vestir santos.

maiden ['meɪdn] **1** *n* doncella *f.*

2 *adj* virginal, intacto; soltera; *flight, voyage etc* de estreno, inaugural; *speech* primero, inaugural.

3 *attr*: **~ aunt** tía *f* solterona; **~ lady** soltera *f*; **~ name** apellido *m* de soltera.

maidenhair ['meɪdnhɛəʳ] *n* (*also* **~ fern**) cabello *m* de Venus, culantrillo *m.*

maidenhead ['meɪdnhed] *n* virginidad *f*, himen *m.*

maidenhood ['meɪdnhʊd] *n* doncellez *f.*

maidenly ['meɪdnlɪ] *adj* virginal; recatado, modesto.

maid-of-all-work [,meɪdəv'ɔːl,wɜːk] *n* chica *f* para todo.

maidservant ['meɪd,sɜːvənt] *n* criada *f*, sirvienta *f.*

mail¹ [meɪl] **1** *n* (*Mil*) malla *f*, cota *f* de malla. **2** *vt*: **the ~ed fist** (*fig*) la mano dura.

mail² [meɪl] **1** *n* (*in general*) correo *m*; (*letters*) cartas *fpl*, correspondencia *f*; **is there any ~ for me?** ¿hay cartas para mí?

2 *vt* (*esp US*) (*post off*) echar al correo; (*send by ~*) enviar por correo.

mailbag ['meɪlbæg] *n* saca *f* de correos.

mailboat ['meɪlbəʊt] *n* vapor *m* correo.

mailbomb ['meɪlbɒm] *n* (*US*) paquete-bomba *m.*

mailbox ['meɪlbɒks] *n* (*US*: *in street*) buzón *m*; (*in office etc*) casilla *f*; (*Comput*) buzón *m.*

mailcar ['meɪlkɑːʳ] *n* (*US Rail*) furgón *m* postal, vagón-correo *m.*

mailcarrier ['meɪlkærɪəʳ] *n* (*US*) cartero *m*, -a *f.*

mailcoach ['meɪlkəʊtʃ] *n* (*Hist*) diligencia *f*, coche *m* correo; (*Rail*) furgón *m* postal, vagón-correo *m.*

maildrop ['meɪldrɒp] *n* (*act*) entrega *f* de correo; (*address*) dirección *f* para correo.

mailing ['meɪlɪŋ] **1** *n* envío *m.* **2** *attr*: **~ list** lista *f* de envío.

mailman ['meɪlmæn] *n, pl* **mailmen** [meɪlmen] (*US*) cartero *m.*

mail-merge ['meɪlmɜːdʒ] *n* fusión *f* del correo electrónico.

mail-order ['meɪl,ɔːdəʳ] *n* pedido *m* postal; **~ catalog** (*US*), **~ catalogue** catálogo *m* de ventas por correo; **~ firm, ~ house** casa *f* de ventas por correo.

mailshot ['meɪlʃɒt] *n* circular *f*, mailing *m.*

mailtrain ['meɪltreɪn] *n* tren-correo *m*, tren *m* postal.

mailvan ['meɪlvæn] *n* (*Brit Rail*) furgón *m* postal, vagón-correo *m.*

maim [meɪm] *vt* mutilar, lisiar, estropear; **to be ~ed for life** quedar lisiado de por vida.

main [meɪn] **1** *adj* principal, más importante; mayor; *beam, pipe etc* maestro; *floor* primero, bajo; *office* central; **the ~ objective is ...** el objetivo principal es ...; **the ~ thing is to +** *infin* lo más importante es + *infin*; **~ clause** oración *f* principal; **~ course** plato *m* principal; **~ line** (*Rail*) línea *f* principal, línea *f* troncal, (*of argument*) argumento *m* central; **~ memory** memoria *f* principal, memoria *f* central; **~ road** carretera *f*, ruta *f* principal; **~ street** calle *f* mayor.

2 *n* (**a**) (*pipe*) cañería *f* maestra, tubería *f* matriz, conducción *f*; (*Elec*: *also* **~s**) red *f* eléctrica; **~s supply** suministro *m* de la red; **it runs off the ~s** funciona con electricidad de la red.

(**b**) **the ~** (*poet*) el océano, la alta mar; **Spanish M~**

Mar *m* de las Antillas, Mar *m* Caribe.

(**c**) **in the ~** en general, en su mayoría, en su mayor parte.

mainbrace ['meɪnbreɪs] *n* braza *f* de mayor.

mainframe ['meɪnfreɪm] *n* (*also* **~ computer**) computadora *f* (*or* ordenador *m*) central.

mainland ['meɪnlənd] *n* tierra *f* firme, continente *m*.

mainline‡ ['meɪn'laɪn] *vti* chutarse‡, inyectarse.

mainly ['meɪnlɪ] *adv* principalmente; en su mayoría, en su mayor parte.

mainmast ['meɪnmɑːst] *n* palo *m* mayor.

mainsail ['meɪnsl] *n* vela *f* mayor.

mainspring ['meɪnsprɪŋ] *n* (*of watch*) muelle *m* real; (*fig*) motivo *m* principal, origen *m*.

mainstay ['meɪnsteɪ] *n* estay *m* mayor; (*fig*) sostén *m* principal, pilar *m*.

mainstream ['meɪnstriːm] (*fig*) **1** *n* corriente *f* principal, línea *f* central (de evolución *etc*); **to be in the ~ of modern philosophy** estar en la línea central de la evolución de la filosofía moderna.

2 *attr* de la corriente principal, en la línea central.

maintain [meɪn'teɪn] *vt* (**a**) (*continue*) *attitude, correspondence, order, progress, speed etc* mantener; *advantage, silence* guardar; *war* continuar, sostener; *rights* mantener, sostener, afirmar; *opposition* afirmar (*to* a); **if the improvement is ~ed** si se mantiene la mejora.

(**b**) (*support*) *family* mantener, sustentar; *student* pagar los estudios de.

(**c**) *road etc* conservar en buen estado; (*Mech*) entretener, mantener.

(**d**) (*assert*) sostener, afirmar; **to ~ that ...** sostener que ...

maintenance ['meɪntɪnəns] **1** *n* mantenimiento *m*; conservación *f*; (*Mech*) entretenimiento *m*; manutención *f*. **2** *attr*: **~ agreement, ~ contract** contrato *m* de mantenimiento; **~ allowance** pensión *f* alimenticia; **~ charges, ~ costs** gastos *mpl* de conservación; **~ crew** personal *m* de servicios; **~ grant** pensión *f* alimenticia, (*of student*) beca *f*; **~ man** reparador *m*; **~ order** obligación *f* alimenticia; **~ staff** personal *m* de servicios.

Mainz [maɪnts] *n* Maguncia *f*.

maisonette [ˌmeɪzə'net] *n* (*esp Brit*) casita *f*, dúplex *m*.

maître d'hôtel [ˌmetrədəʊ'tel] *n* (*US also* **maître d'** ['metrəˌdiː]) jefe *m* de comedor, maître *m*.

maize [meɪz] *n* (*Brit*) maíz *m*, milpa *f* (*Mex*), choclo *m* (*LAm*).

maize-field ['meɪzfiːld] *n* maizal *m*.

Maj. *abbr of* **Major** comandante *m*.

majestic [mə'dʒestɪk] *adj* majestuoso.

majestically [mə'dʒestɪkəlɪ] *adv* majestuosamente.

majesty ['mædʒɪstɪ] *n* majestad *f*; **Her M~, His M~** Su Majestad; **Your M~** (Vuestra) Majestad.

Maj.-Gen. *abbr of* **Major-General** general *m* de división.

major ['meɪdʒə^r] **1** *adj* mayor (*also Mus*), principal; **of ~ interest** de máximo interés; **of ~ importance** de la mayor importancia; **~ league** (*US*) liga *f* principal; **~ part, ~ portion** mayor parte *f*; **Smith M~** (*Brit Scol*) Smith el mayor; **~ suit** (*Cards*) palo *m* mayor.

2 *n* (**a**) (*Jur*) mayor *mf* de edad. (**b**) (*Mil*) comandante *m*. (**c**) (*US Univ*: *course*) asignatura *f* principal, especialidad *f*. (**d**) (*US Univ*) **he's a Spanish ~** estudia el español como asignatura principal.

3 *vi* (*US Univ*): **to ~ in French** estudiar el francés como asignatura principal, especializarse en francés.

Majorca [mə'jɔːkə] *n* Mallorca *f*.

Majorcan [mə'jɔːkən] **1** *adj* mallorquín. **2** *n* (**a**) mallorquín *m*, -ina *f*. (**b**) (*Ling*) mallorquín *m*.

majordomo ['meɪdʒə'dəʊməʊ] *n* mayordomo *m*.

majorette [ˌmeɪdʒə'ret] *n* batonista *f*.

major-general ['meɪdʒə'dʒenərəl] *n* general *m* de división.

majority [mə'dʒɒrɪtɪ] **1** *n* mayoría *f*; **a two-thirds ~** una mayoría de las dos terceras partes; **the great ~ of lecturers** la mayor parte de los conferenciantes; **the vast ~** la inmensa mayoría; **to attain one's ~** llegar a mayoría de edad; **such people are in a ~** tales personas son las más, predominan tales personas; **to be in a ~ of 3** formar parte de una mayoría de 3.

2 *attr* mayoritario; **by a ~ decision** por decisión de la mayoría; **~ interest** interés *m* mayoritario; **~ rule** gobierno *m* mayoritario, gobierno *m* de la mayoría; **~ (share)holding** accionado *m* mayoritario; **by a ~ verdict** por fallo mayoritario; **by a ~ vote** por la mayoría de los votos.

make [meɪk] (*irr*: *pret and ptp* **made**) **1** *vt* (**a**) (*gen*) hacer; (*manufacture*) fabricar; (*build*) construir; (*confect*) elaborar; (*form*) formar; (*create*) crear; (*put together*) componer; *bed, effort, fire, noise, peace, remark, tea, war, will* hacer; *dress* confeccionar; *meal* preparar; *speech* pronunciar; *error* cometer; *payment* efectuar; *cards* barajar; *face* poner; *sense* tener; **to ~ sb a judge** constituir a uno juez, nombrar a uno juez; **to ~ sb king** elevar a uno al trono; **they've made Eccles secretary** han nombrado secretario a Eccles; **to ~ a friend of sb** trabar amistad con uno; **he's as cunning as they ~ 'em** es de lo más astuto que hay; **to ~ A into B** convertir A en B, transformar A en B; **I'm not made for running** yo no estoy hecho para correr; **to be made of** estar hecho de, estar compuesto de, consistir en, constar de; **it's made of gold** es de oro, está hecho de oro; **to show what one is made of** demostrar las cualidades que tiene uno; **what do you ~ of this?** ¿qué te parece esto?; **what did you ~ of the film?** ¿qué impresión te produjo la película?; **what do you ~ of him?** ¿qué piensas de él?, ¿qué impresión te has formado de él?; **I can ~ nothing of it** no lo entiendo, no saco nada en claro; **I don't know what to ~ of it** no me lo explico; **they don't ~ songs** (*etc*) **like that any more** ya no hay canciones (*etc*) como las de antes.

(**b**) (*complete, constitute*) *circuit* cerrar; *trick* ganar, hacer; **2 and 2 ~ 4** 2 y 2 son 4; **that ~s 20** eso hace 20, con ése son 20; **it still doesn't ~ a set** todavía no completa un juego entero; **it doesn't ~ a full course** no equivale a una asignatura completa; **to ~ a contract** (*Cards*) cumplir un contrato; **South leads and ~s 5 tricks** Sur sale y efectúa 5 bazas; **it made a nice surprise** fue una sorpresa agradable; **partridges ~ good eating** las perdices son buenas para comer; **it ~s pleasant reading** da gusto leerlo; **he made a good husband** resultó ser un buen marido; **he'll ~ a good footballer** será buen futbolista, tiene madera de futbolista; **I made one of the party** yo era (uno) del grupo; *V* **night** *etc*.

(**c**) (*earn etc*) ganar; **he ~s £300 a week** gana 300 libras a la semana; **how much do you ~?** ¿cuánto ganas?, ¿qué sueldo cobras?; **to ~ a fortune** enriquecerse, hacer su pacotilla*; **what will you ~ by it?** ¿cuánto vas a ganar en esto?; **how much do you stand to ~?** ¿cuánto esperas ganar?

(**d**) (*assure future of*) hacer la fortuna de; asegurar el triunfo de; **it made my day** me dio un día feliz, hizo un buen día para mí; **he's got it made*** lo tiene asegurado, se lo tiene apañado*; **this film made her** esta película fue el principio de su éxito; **he was made for life** se aseguró un porvenir brillante; **to ~ or break sb** hacer la fortuna o ser la ruina de uno; **to ~ or mar sth** decidir de una vez la suerte de algo.

(**e**) (*with pred adj*) hacer; **to ~ sb happy** hacer a uno feliz; **to ~ sb angry** irritar a uno, provocar a uno, sacar a uno de quicio; **to ~ sb ashamed** dar vergüenza a uno; **to ~ sb sleepy** dar sueño a uno; **to ~ sb rich** enriquecer a uno; **to ~ sb ill** sentar a uno mal; **to ~ sth ready** preparar algo; **to ~ iron hot** calentar un trozo de hierro; **to ~ one's voice heard** hacer que se le escuche a uno.

(**f**) (*say, agree*) **let's ~ it 9 o'clock** citémonos para las 9, pongamos las 9.

(**g**) (*judge*) creer; representar, pintar; **the situation is not so bad as you ~ it** la situación es menos grave de lo que crees, la situación no es tan grave como la pintas.

(**h**) (*calculate*) calcular; **what do you ~ the time?** ¿qué hora tienes?; **I ~ it 7.30** yo tengo las 7 y media; **how many do you ~ it?** ¿cuántos dices tú?, ¿cuántos tienes en total?; **I ~ the distance 98 km** calculo que la distancia es de 98 km; **I ~ the total 17** calculo que hay 17 en total.

(**i**) (*force*) **to ~ sb do sth** forzar (*or* obligar, compeler) a uno a hacer algo; (*persuade*) inclinar (*or* inducir) a uno a hacer algo; **you can't ~ me** no puedes forzarme a hacerlo; **what ~s you do it?** ¿por qué te ves obligado a hacerlo?; **what made you say that?** ¿por qué dijiste eso?; **to ~ sb laugh** darle risa a uno, hacerle reír a uno.

(**j**) (*reach, attain*) **we made 15 knots** alcanzamos una velocidad de 15 nudos; **we shall never ~ the shore** no llegamos nunca a la playa, será imposible alcanzar la playa; **to ~ it** (*arrive*) llegar; (*achieve sth*) conseguir lo que se deseaba; (*succeed*) tener éxito, triunfar; **eventually we made it** por fin llegamos; **we just made it in time** llegamos justo a tiempo; **can you ~ it by 10?** ¿puedes llegar para las 10?; **to ~ it with sb‡** darse el lote con una‡.

2 *vi* (**a**) (*tide*) crecer, subir.

(**b**) **he made as if to** + *infin* hizo como si quisiese + *infin*, fingió que iba a + *infin*, hizo ademán de + *infin*; **he was making like he didn't have any money*** (*US*) hacía como que no tenía dinero.

(**c**) **it's ~ or break week** es la semana del triunfo o del fracaso.

3 *vr* (**a**) (*become*) **to ~ o.s. an expert in** llegar a ser experto en; **to ~ o.s. dictator** hacerse dictador, constituirse en dictador.

(**b**) (*with pred adj*) **to ~ o.s. comfortable** acomodarse a su gusto; **to ~ o.s. ill with work** enfermar por exceso de trabajo; **to ~ o.s. ridiculous** ponerse en ridículo; *V* **hear** *etc*.

(**c**) (*force*) **to ~ o.s. do sth** obligarse a hacer algo; **I have to ~ myself (do it)** tengo que hacer un esfuerzo (por hacerlo).

4 *n* (**a**) (*brand*) marca *f*; (*type etc*) tipo *m*, modelo *m*; **it's a good ~** es buena marca; **what ~ of car was it?** ¿qué marca de coche fue?; **these are my own ~** estos son según mi propia receta; **they have rifles of Belgian ~** tienen fusiles de fabricación belga.

(**b**) (*) **to be on the ~** barrer hacia dentro*; **the town is full of dealers on the ~** la ciudad está llena de comerciantes que no pierden ripio.

◆**make after** *vt* seguir a, perseguir a.

◆**make away** *vi* = **make off**.

◆**make away with** *vt* (*murder*): **to ~ away with sb** eliminar a uno; **to ~ away with o.s.** quitarse la vida, suicidarse.

◆**make for** *vi* (**a**) (*place*) dirigirse a, encaminarse a; **where are you making for?** ¿adónde se dirige Vd?

(**b**) **to ~ for sb** atacar a uno, abalanzarse sobre uno.

(**c**) *result* contribuir a, conducir a; **it ~s for optimism** ayuda a crear el optimismo, fomenta el optimismo; **it ~s for difficulties** tiende a crear dificultades.

◆**make off** *vi* largarse; huir, escaparse; **to ~ off with** llevarse, alzarse con; escaparse con.

◆**make out 1** *vt* (**a**) (*draw up*) *cheque, document, receipt* extender; *list* hacer, redactar; *form* llenar; *case* exponer, explicar; justificar; **the cheque should be made out to Pérez** el cheque será nominativo a favor de Pérez, el cheque se debe girar a favor de Pérez (*LAm*).

(**b**) (*see, distinguish*) distinguir, vislumbrar, divisar; *writing* (lograr) leer, descifrar; (*understand*) entender; **I can't ~ it out at all** no me lo explico, no lo entiendo; **I can't properly ~ him out** no le acabo de entender.

(**c**) (*claim*) representar; **you ~ him out to be better than he is** haces creer que es mejor de lo que es en realidad; **he's not as rich as people ~ out** es menos rico de lo que dice la gente; **how do you ~ that out?** ¿cómo deduces eso?, ¿cómo llegas a esa conclusión?; **he ~s out that ...** da a entender que ..., da la impresión de que ...; nos hace creer que ...; **all the time he made out he was working** todo el tiempo hacía creer que estaba trabajando; **the play ~s him out to be a fool** la obra le representa como tonto.

2 *vi* arreglárselas, salir bien; **we're making out** vamos tirando; **we made out eventually** por fin nos las arreglamos; **how are you making out?** ¿cómo te va esto?; **how did you ~ out?** ¿qué tal te fue?; **to ~ out with a girl‡** (*US*) darse el lote con una chica‡.

◆**make over** *vt* ceder, traspasar (*to* a).

◆**make up 1** *vt* (**a**) (*invent*) inventar; **you're making it up!** ¡puro cuento!

(**b**) (*put together*) hacer; fabricar; confeccionar; *medicine* preparar; *bed* hacer; *collection* formar, reunir; *parcel* empaquetar; *list* hacer, redactar; (*Typ*) componer.

(**c**) (*counterbalance, replace*) *loss* reponer, compensar; *deficit* cubrir; **to ~ up (lost) time** recuperar el tiempo perdido; **to ~ it up to sb** compensar a uno por sus pérdidas.

(**d**) (*settle*) *dispute* componer, arreglar; **to ~ up a quarrel with sb, to ~ it up with sb** hacer las paces con uno.

(**e**) *face* pintarse, maquillarse; **to ~ up an actor** maquillar a un actor.

(**f**) (*constitute*) componer, integrar; formar, constituir; **the parts which ~ it up** las partes que lo integran; **the group was made up of 8 bishops** el grupo lo integraban 8 obispos.

(**g**) (*complete*) completar, hacer.

(**h**) *fire* echar carbón (*etc*) a.

2 *vi* (**a**) (*become friends*) hacer las paces.

(**b**) (*apply cosmetics*) pintarse, maquillarse.

◆**make up for** *vt*: **to ~ up for sb's losses** compensar a uno por sus pérdidas, indemnizar a uno de sus pérdidas; **to ~ up for a lack of** suplir una falta de; **to ~ up for lost time** recuperar el tiempo perdido.

◆**make up on** *vt* alcanzar, coger.

◆**make up to*** *vt*: **to ~ up to sb** (procurar) congraciarse con uno, (procurar) ganarse la amistad de uno; halagar a uno, hacer zalamerías a uno.

make-believe ['meɪkbɪ,li:v] **1** *adj* fingido, simulado; *world etc* de ensueño, soñado.

2 *n* ficción *f*, invención *f*; imaginación *f*; **a world of ~** un mundo de ensueño; **don't worry, it's just ~** no te apures, es de mentirijillas.

3 *vi* fingir.

maker ['meɪkəʳ] *n* hacedor *m*, -ora *f*, creador *m*, -ora *f*; artífice *mf*; (*builder*) constructor *m*, -ora *f*; (*manufacturer*) fabricante *m*; **the M~** el Hacedor; **to go to meet one's M~** pasar a mejor vida.

makeshift ['meɪkʃɪft] **1** *adj* improvisado; provisional, temporal. **2** *n* improvisación *f*; expediente *m*; arreglo *m* provisional.

make-up ['meɪkʌp] **1** *n* (**a**) (*composition*) composición *f*; estructura *f*; (*of person etc*) carácter *m*, modo *m* de ser, naturaleza *f*; (*of clothes*) confección *f*; (*Typ*) ajuste *m*.

(**b**) (*for face*) maquillaje *m*, cosméticos *mpl*; (*Theat*: *for a role*) caracterización *f*.

2 *attr*: **~ artist** maquillador *m*, -ora *f*; **~ bag** bolsa *f* del maquillaje; **~ girl** maquilladora *f*; **~ man** maquillador *m*; **~ remover** desmaquillador *m*.

makeweight ['meɪkweɪt] *n* contrapeso *m*; (*fig*) suplente *m*, sustituto *m*; (*pej*) tapa(a)gujeros *m*.

making ['meɪkɪŋ] *n* (**a**) fabricación *f*; construcción *f*; elaboración *f*; formación *f*; creación *f*; confección *f*; preparación *f*; **in the ~** en vías de formarse (*or* hacerse *etc*); **it's still in the ~** está todavía en construcción, está todavía sin acabar; **while it was still in the ~** mientras se estaba haciendo; **it's a civil war in the ~** es una guerra civil en potencia; **it's history in the ~** es la historia como proceso actual, es la historia que actualmente se está escribiendo; **the mistake was not of my ~** no soy yo el responsable del error; **it was the ~ of him** fue la causa de su éxito, (*morally*) fue el motivo de su reforma moral.

(**b**) **~s** elementos *mpl* (necesarios); ingredientes *mpl*; **he has the ~s of an actor** tiene talento para ser actor, tiene madera de actor.

Malachi ['mælə,kaɪ] *nm* Malaquías *m*.

malachite ['mælə,kaɪt] *n* malaquita *f*.

maladjusted ['mælə'dʒʌstɪd] *adj* inadaptado.

maladjustment ['mælə'dʒʌstmənt] *n* inadaptación *f*, desajuste *m*.

maladministration ['mæləd,mɪnɪs'treɪʃən] *n* mala administración *f*.

maladroit ['mælə'drɔɪt] *adj* torpe.

maladroitly ['mælə'drɔɪtlɪ] *adv* torpemente.

maladroitness ['mælə'drɔɪtnɪs] *n* torpeza *f*.

malady ['mælədɪ] *n* mal *m*, enfermedad *f*.

Malagasy ['mæləgɑ:zɪ] **1** *adj* madagascarí. **2** *n* madagascarí *mf*.

malaise [mæ'leɪz] *n* malestar *m*.

malapropism ['mæləprɒpɪzəm] *n* despropósito *m* lingüístico, equivocación *f* de palabras.

malaria [mə'lɛərɪə] **1** *n* paludismo *m*, malaria *f*. **2** *attr*: **~ control** lucha *f* antimalaria.

malarial [mə'lɛərɪəl] *adj* palúdico.

Malawi [mə'lɑ:wɪ] *n* Malawi *m*, Malaui *m*.

Malawian [mə'lɑ:wɪən] **1** *adj* malawiano, malauiano. **2** *n* malawiano *m*, -a *f*, malauiano *m*, -a *f*.

Malay [mə'leɪ] **1** *adj* malayo. **2** *n* (**a**) malayo *m*, -a *f*. (**b**) (*Ling*) malayo *m*.

Malaya [mə'leɪə] *n* Malaya *f*, Malaca *f*.

Malayan [mə'leɪən] **1** *adj* malayo. **2** *n* malayo *m*, -a *f*.

Malaysia [mə'leɪzɪə] *n* Malasia *f*.

Malaysian [mə'leɪzɪən] **1** *adj* malasio. **2** *n* malasio *m*, -a *f*.

malcontent ['mælkən'tent] **1** *adj* malcontento, desafecto, revoltoso. **2** *n* malcontento *m*, -a *f*, desafecto *m*, -a *f*, revoltoso *m*, -a *f*.

Maldives ['mɔ:ldaɪvz] *npl* Maldivas *fpl*.

male [meɪl] **1** *adj* (*Bio, Mech*) macho; (*manly*) viril, masculino; *attire etc* de hombres, para hombre; **~ chauvinist pig** *V* **chauvinist**; **~ child** hijo *m* varón; **~ menopause** (*hum*) menopausia *f* masculina; **~ nurse** enfermero *m*; **~ prostitute** prostituto *m*; **~ sex** sexo *m* masculino; **~ voice choir** coro *m* de hombres.

2 *n* macho *m* (*also Bio*); varón *m*.

malediction [,mælɪ'dɪkʃən] *n* maldición *f*.

malefactor ['mælɪfæktəʳ] *n* malhechor *m*, -ora *f*.

malevolence [mə'levələns] *n* malevolencia *f*.

malevolent [mə'levələnt] *adj* malévolo.

malevolently [mə'levələntlɪ] *adv* con malevolencia.

malformation ['mælfɔː'meɪʃən] *n* malformación *f*, deformidad *f*.

malformed [ˌmæl'fɔːmd] *adj* malformado, deforme.

malfunction [mæl'fʌŋkʃən] **1** *n* funcionamiento *m* defectuoso. **2** *vi* funcionar mal.

Malgache [mæl'gætʃɪ] *n* Malgache *m*.

malice ['mælɪs] *n* malevolencia *f*, mala voluntad *f*; (*Jur*) intención *f* delictuosa; **out of ~** por malevolencia; **with ~ toward none** sin malevolencia para nadie; **to bear sb ~** guardar rencor a uno; **I bear him no ~** no le guardo rencor.

malicious [mə'lɪʃəs] *adj* malévolo, maligno; rencoroso; **~ damage** daños *mpl* intencionados; **~ slander** calumnia *f* intencionada.

maliciously [mə'lɪʃəslɪ] *adv* con malevolencia, con malignidad; rencorosamente.

malign [mə'laɪn] **1** *adj* maligno, enconoso. **2** *vt* calumniar, difamar; tratar injustamente, ser injusto con; **you ~ me** eso no es justo, ésa no era mi intención.

malignancy [mə'lɪgnənsɪ] *n* malignidad *f*.

malignant [mə'lɪgnənt] *adj* maligno (*also Med*).

malignity [mə'lɪgnɪtɪ] *n* malignidad *f*.

malinger [mə'lɪŋgər] *vi* fingirse enfermo, hacer la encorvada*.

malingerer [mə'lɪŋgərər] *n* enfermo *m* fingido, enferma *f* fingida, calandria* *mf*.

mall [mɔːl] *n* (**a**) alameda *f*, paseo *m*; (*US*: *pedestrian street*) calle *f* peatonal. (**b**) (*esp US*: *also* **shopping ~**) centro *m* comercial.

mallard ['mæləd] *n* pato *m* real, ánade *m* real.

malleability [ˌmælɪə'bɪlɪtɪ] *n* maleabilidad *f*.

malleable ['mælɪəbl] *adj* maleable.

mallet ['mælɪt] *n* mazo *m*.

mallow ['mæləʊ] *n* malva *f*.

malnourished [ˌmæl'nʌrɪʃt] *adj* desnutrido.

malnutrition ['mælnjʊ'trɪʃən] *n* desnutrición *f*.

malodorous [mæ'ləʊdərəs] *adj* maloliente, hediondo.

malpractice ['mæl'præktɪs] *n* procedimientos *mpl* ilegales (*or* inmorales); práctica *f* abusiva; abuso *m* de autoridad; mala conducta *f*; (*Med*) negligencia *f*.

malt [mɔːlt] **1** *n* malta *f*. **2** *attr*: **~ extract** extracto *m* de malta; **~ liquor** (*US*) cerveza *f*; **~ whisky** (*Brit*) whisky *m* de malta. **3** *vt barley* hacer germinar; *drink etc* preparar con malta; **~ed milk** leche *f* malteada; **~ing barley** cebada *f* cervecera.

Malta ['mɔːltə] *n* Malta *f*.

Maltese ['mɔːl'tiːz] **1** *adj* maltés; **~ Cross** cruz *f* de Malta. **2** *n* (**a**) maltés *m*, -esa *f*. (**b**) (*Ling*) maltés *m*.

maltreat [mæl'triːt] *vt* maltratar, tratar mal.

maltreatment [mæl'triːtmənt] *n* maltrato *m*, maltratamiento *m*, malos tratos *mpl*.

mam(m)a* [mə'mɑː] *n* mamá *f**.

mammal ['mæməl] *n* mamífero *m*.

mammalian [mæ'meɪlɪən] *adj* mamífero.

mammary ['mæmərɪ] **1** *adj* mamario; **~ gland** mama *f*, teta *f*. **2** *n*: **mammaries** (*hum*) pechos *mpl*.

mammography [mæ'mɒgrəfɪ] *n* mamografía *f*.

Mammon ['mæmən] *nm* Mammón.

mammoth ['mæməθ] **1** *n* mamut *m*. **2** *adj* gigantesco, colosal; (*Comm*) de tamaño extra.

mammy ['mæmɪ] *n* (**a**) (*) mamaíta* *f*. (**b**) (*US*) nodriza *f* negra.

man [mæn] **1** *n*, *pl* **men** [men] (**a**) (*gen*) hombre *m*; varón *m*; (*humanity in general*) el hombre, los hombres, el género humano; (*servant*) criado *m*; (*workman*) obrero *m*; (*Mil*) soldado *m*; (*Naut*) marinero *m*; **men's doubles** dobles *mpl* masculinos; **men's final** final *f* masculina; **men's room** (*esp US*) lavabo *m* de caballeros.

(**b**) (*with adj*) **best ~** padrino *m* de boda, testigo *m* del novio; **~ Friday** criado *m* fiel; **all good men and true** todos los que merecen llamarse hombres; **her ~** su marido; **our ~ in Slobodia** (*agent*) nuestro agente en Eslobodia, (*representative*) nuestro representante en Eslobodia, (*ambassador*) nuestro embajador en Eslobodia; **old ~** viejo *m*, anciano *m*; **my old ~*** el viejo*, el pariente*; **the grand old ~ of the party** el líder veterano del partido; **the strong ~ of the government** el hombre fuerte del gobierno; **young ~** joven *m*; **her young ~** su novio.

(**c**) (*with qualifying phrase*) **~ about town** hombre *m* mundano, joven *m* amigo de los placeres, señorito *m*; **~ and boy** desde pequeño; **~ and wife** marido y mujer; **~ in the moon** mujer *f* de la luna; **~ in the street** hombre *m* de la calle, hombre *m* medio; **~ of letters** literato *m*; **~ of means, ~ of property** hombre *m* acaudalado; **~ of parts** hombre *m* de talento; **~ of the world** hombre *m* de mundo.

(**d**) (*used as pron etc*) **men say that ...** se dice que ...; **when a ~ needs a wash** cuando uno necesita lavarse; **what else could a ~ do?** ¿es que se podía hacer otra cosa?; **one ~ one vote** un voto para cada uno; **any ~** cualquiera, cualquier hombre; **no ~** nadie; **that ~ Jones** ese Jones; **as one ~** unánimemente; como un sólo hombre, todos a uno; **~ to ~** de hombre a hombre; **they're communists to a ~** todos sin excepción son comunistas.

(**e**) (*sort, type*) **I'm not a drinking ~** no bebo; **I'm not a football ~** no soy aficionado al fútbol, no me gusta el fútbol; **he's a 4-pint ~** es de los que se beben 4 pintas; **I'm a whisky ~ myself** yo prefiero el whisky; **he's a Celtic ~** es del Celtic; **he's his own ~** es un hombre muy fiel a sí mismo; **he's a ~'s ~** es un hombre estimado entre otros hombres; **are you ~ enough to do it?** ¿tienes bastante valor para hacerlo?; **it's got to be a local ~** tiene que ser uno de aquí; **then I'm your ~** entonces yo soy el que busca Vd; **to feel (like) a new ~** sentirse como nuevo.

(**f**) (*in direct address*) **you can't do that, ~** hombre, no puedes hacer eso; **~, was I startled!** ¡vaya susto que me llevé!; **hey ~!*** ¡oye, tronco!*; **my good ~** buen hombre; **good ~!** ¡bravo!, ¡muy bien!; **look here, old ~** mira, amigo.

(**g**) (*verb phrases*) **he's not the ~ to do it** no es capaz de hacerlo; **he's not the ~ for the job** no es persona adecuada para el puesto; **to make a ~ of sb** hacer un hombre de uno; **~ proposes, God disposes** el hombre propone y Dios dispone; **to reach ~'s estate** llegar a la edad viril; **this will separate** (*or* **sort**) **the men from the boys** con esto se verá quiénes son hombres y quiénes no.

(**h**) (*Chess etc*) pieza *f*, ficha *f*, trebejo *m*.

(**i**) **the M~‡** (*US*) (*boss*) el jefe; (*police*) el policía; (*white man*) el blanco.

2 *vt ship* tripular; *fortress, watchtower* guarnecer; *guns* servir; *pumps* acudir a, hacer funcionar; **a fully ~ned ship** un buque con toda su tripulación; **the telephone is ~ned all day** el telefonista está de servicio todo el día; **~ning levels** niveles *mpl* de personal; *V also* **manned**.

manacle ['mænəkl] **1** *n* manilla *f*; **~s** esposas *fpl*, grillos *mpl*.

2 *vt* poner esposas a; **they were ~d together** iban esposados juntos; **his hands were ~d** llevaba esposas en las muñecas.

manage ['mænɪdʒ] **1** *vt* (**a**) *tool etc* manejar; manipular; *car* conducir; *ship* gobernar.

(**b**) *company* dirigir; *organization* regir, administrar; (*Comput*) *system, network* gestionar; *property* administrar; *affair* manejar; *election* (*pej*) falsificar; **~d currency** moneda *f* dirigida, moneda *f* planificada; **~d fund** fondo *m* dirigido.

(**c**) *person, child, animal* manejar; **she can't ~ children** no puede con los niños; **I can ~ him** yo sé llevarle.

(**d**) (*contrive, offer, take*) **£5 is the most I can ~** 5 libras es todo lo que puedo darte (*or* pagar *etc*); **I shall ~ it** yo sabré hacerlo; **you'll ~ it next time** lo harás la próxima vez; **can you ~ the cases?** ¿puedes llevar las maletas?; **thanks, I can ~ them** gracias, yo puedo con ellas; **can you ~ two more in the car?** ¿puedes llevar dos más en el coche?; **can you ~ 8 o'clock?** ¿puedes venir para las 8?; **can you ~ another cup?** ¿quieres otra taza?; **I can ~ another cake** me atrevo con otra pasta; **I couldn't ~ another mouthful** no podría comer ni un bocado más.

(**e**) (*with verb*) **to ~ to do sth** lograr hacer algo; arreglárselas para hacer algo, ingeniarse para hacer algo; **how did you ~ to get it?** ¿cómo lo conseguiste?; **he ~d not to get his feet wet** logró no mojarse los pies.

2 *vi* arreglárselas, ir tirando; **can you ~?** ¿tú puedes con eso?; **thanks, I can ~** gracias, yo puedo; **she ~s well enough** se las arregla bastante bien; **how do you ~?** ¿cómo te las arreglas?; **to ~ without sth** saber pasarse sin algo; **to ~ without sb** saber prescindir de uno.

manageable ['mænɪdʒəbl] *adj* manejable; *person, animal* dócil; **of ~ size** de tamaño razonable.

management ['mænɪdʒmənt] **1** *n* (**a**) (*act*) manejo *m*; gobierno *m*; dirección *f*; gerencia *f*, gerenciación *f*, administración *f*.

(**b**) (*persons*) dirección *f*; junta *f* de directores; (*as a class*) empresariado *m*, empresa *f*, clase *f* patronal; (*Theat*) empresa *f*; **~ and labour** dirección *f* y obreros; **'under new ~'** 'nueva dirección'; **almost always ~ is at fault** las más veces la empresa tiene la culpa.

2 *attr*: ~ **accounting** contabilidad *f* de gestión; ~ **audit** auditoría *f* administrativa; ~ **chart** gestionigrama *m*; ~ **committee** consejo *m* de administración, comité *m* directivo; ~ **consultancy** consultoría *f* gerencial; ~ **consultant** consultor *m*, -ora *f* en dirección de empresas; ~ **fee** honorarios *mpl* de dirección; ~ **review** revisión *f* de gestión (de la gerencia); ~ **services** servicios *mpl* de administración; ~ **trainee** aspirante *mf* a un puesto directivo.

manager ['mænɪdʒəʳ] *n* (*Comm etc*) director *m*, -ora *f*; gerente *mf*; (*of estate etc*) administrador *m*, -ora *f*; (*Sport*) mánager *m*; (*Theat*) empresario *m*; (*of farm*) mayoral *m*; **she's a good** ~ es buena administradora, es muy económica.

manageress ['mænɪdʒə'res] *n* directora *f*; administradora *f*.

managerial [,mænə'dʒɪərɪəl] *adj* directivo, directorial; gerencial; administrativo; **the** ~ **class** la clase patronal; **at** ~ **level** a nivel directivo; ~ **responsibilities** obligaciones *fpl* directivas; responsabilidades *fpl* de administración; **the** ~ **society** la sociedad patronal; ~ **staff** personal *m* dirigente; ~ **structure** estructura *f* administrativa; ~ **style** estilo *m* administrativo.

managing ['mænɪdʒɪŋ] *adj* (**a**) (*Brit pej*) mandón. (**b**) ~ **director** (*Brit*) director *m*, -ora *f* general; ~ **partner** socio *mf* gerente.

man-at-arms ['mænət'ɑːmz] *n*, *pl* **men-at-arms** ['menət'ɑːmz] hombre *m* de armas.

manatee [,mænə'tiː] *n* manatí *m*.

Manchuria [mæn'tʃʊərɪə] *n* Manchuria *f*.

Manchurian [mæn'tʃʊərɪən] **1** *adj* manchuriano. **2** *n* manchuriano *m*, -a *f*.

Mancunian [mæn'kjuːnɪən] **1** *adj* de Manchester. **2** *n* habitante *mf* (*or* nativo *m*, -a *f*) de Manchester.

mandarin ['mændərɪn] *n* (**a**) (*person*) mandarín *m* (*also fig*). (**b**) (*Ling*) **M~** mandarina *f*. (**c**) (*also* ~ **orange**) mandarina *f*.

mandate ['mændeɪt] **1** *n* mandato *m*; (*country*) territorio *m* bajo mandato. **2** *vt* (**a**) asignar como mandato (*to* a). (**b**) *delegate* encargar.

mandated ['mændeɪtɪd] *adj* (**a**) *territory* bajo mandato. (**b**) *delegate* encargado.

mandatory ['mændətərɪ] *adj* obligatorio; preceptivo; **to be** ~ **upon sb to do sth** incumbir a uno como obligación hacer algo.

man-day ['mæn'deɪ] *n*, *pl* **man-days** ['mæn'deɪz] día-hombre *m*.

mandible ['mændɪbl] *n* mandíbula *f*.

mandolin(e) ['mændəlɪn] *n* mandolina *f*, bandolina *f* (*LAm*).

mandrake ['mændreɪk] *n* mandrágora *f*.

mandrill ['mændrɪl] *n* mandril *m*.

mane [meɪn] *n* (*of lion, person*) melena *f*; (*of horse*) crin *f*, crines *fpl*.

man-eater ['mæn,iːtəʳ] *n* tigre *m* (*etc*) cebado, tigre *m* (*etc*) devorador de hombres; (*: *woman*) devoradora *f* de hombres.

man-eating ['mæn,iːtɪŋ] *adj* antropófago.

maneuver [mə'nuːvəʳ] *etc* (*US*) = **manoeuvre** *etc*.

manful ['mænfʊl] *adj* valiente, resuelto.

manfully ['mænfəlɪ] *adv* valientemente, resueltamente.

manganese [,mæŋgə'niːz] **1** *n* manganeso *m*. **2** *attr*: ~ **oxide** óxido *m* de manganeso; ~ **steel** acero *m* manganésico.

mange [meɪndʒ] *n* roña *f*, sarna *f*.

mangel(-wurzel) ['mæŋgl('wɜːzl)] *n* remolacha *f* forrajera.

manger ['meɪndʒəʳ] *n* pesebre *m*.

mangle¹ ['mæŋgl] **1** *n* exprimidor *m*. **2** *vt* pasar por el exprimidor.

mangle² ['mæŋgl] *vt* destrozar, mutilar, magullar; *text etc* mutilar, estropear.

mango ['mæŋgəʊ] *n*, *pl* **mangoes** *or* **mangos** ['mæŋgəʊz] (*fruit and tree*) mango *m*.

mangold(-wurzel) ['mæŋgəld('wɜːzl)] *n* remolacha *f* forrajera.

mangrove ['mæŋgrəʊv] **1** *n* mangle *m*. **2** *attr*: ~ **swamp** manglar *m*.

mangy ['meɪndʒɪ] *adj* roñoso, sarnoso.

manhandle ['mæn,hændl] *vt* (*esp Brit*) mover a brazo; (*fig*) maltratar.

manhole ['mænhəʊl] **1** *n* agujero *m* de hombre, registro *m* de inspección, pozo *m* de visita. **2** *attr*: ~ **cover** tapa *f* de registro, tapadera *f* de cloaca.

manhood ['mænhʊd] *n* (**a**) (*state*) virilidad *f*; (*age*) edad *f* viril; **to reach** ~ llegar a la edad viril.

(**b**) (*manliness*) hombradía *f*, masculinidad *f*.

(**c**) (*men collectively*) **English** ~, **England's** ~ todos los ingleses, todos los hombres de Inglaterra.

man-hour ['mæn'aʊəʳ] *n*, *pl* **man-hours** ['mæn'aʊəz] hora-hombre *f*.

manhunt ['mænhʌnt] *n* persecución *f* (de un criminal), caza *f* (de hombre).

mania ['meɪnɪə] *n* manía *f*; **to have a** ~ **for sth** tener la manía de algo; **to have a** ~ **for doing sth** tener la manía de hacer algo; **speed** ~ manía *f* de la velocidad.

maniac ['meɪnɪæk] **1** *adj* maníaco. **2** *n* maníaco *m*, -a *f*; (*fig*) maniático *m*, -a *f*; **these sports** ~**s** estos fanáticos del deporte; **he drives like a** ~ conduce como un loco.

maniacal [mə'naɪəkəl] *adj* maníaco.

maniacally [mə'naɪəkəlɪ] *adv laugh etc* como un maníaco.

manic ['mænɪk] *adj* maníaco.

manic-depressive ['mænɪkdɪ'presɪv] **1** *adj* maniacodepresivo. **2** *n* maniacodepresivo *m*, -a *f*.

Manichean [,mænɪ'kiːən] **1** *adj* maniqueo. **2** *n* maniqueo *m*, -a *f*.

Manicheanism [,mænɪ'kiːənɪzəm] *n* maniqueísmo *m*.

manicure ['mænɪkjʊəʳ] **1** *n* manicura *f*. **2** *attr*: ~ **case**, ~ **set** estuche *m* de manicura. **3** *vt person* hacer manicura a; *nails* limpiar, arreglar.

manicurist ['mænɪkjʊərɪst] *n* manicuro *m*, -a *f*.

manifest ['mænɪfest] **1** *adj* manifiesto, evidente, patente; **to make sth** ~ poner algo de manifiesto.

2 *n* (*Naut, Comm*) manifiesto *m*.

3 *vt* mostrar, revelar, patentizar.

manifestation [,mænɪfes'teɪʃən] *n* manifestación *f*.

manifestly ['mænɪfestlɪ] *adv* evidentemente.

manifesto [,mænɪ'festəʊ] *n*, *pl* **manifestoes** *or* **manifestos** [,mænɪ'festəʊz] proclama *f*, manifiesto *m*.

manifold ['mænɪfəʊld] **1** *adj* múltiple. **2** *n* (*Aut*) colector *m*.

manikin ['mænɪkɪn] *n* (**a**) (*dwarf*) enano *m*. (**b**) (*Art*) maniquí *m*; (*fashion model*) maniquí *f*, modelo *f*.

Manila [mə'nɪlə] *n* Manila *f*.

manil(l)a [mə'nɪlə] *adj paper, envelope* manila.

manioc ['mænɪɒk] *n* mandioca *f*, yuca *f*.

manipulate [mə'nɪpjʊleɪt] *vt* manipular, manejar.

manipulation [mə,nɪpjʊ'leɪʃən] *n* manipulación *f*, manipuleo *m*.

manipulative [mə'nɪpjʊlətɪv] *adj* manipulativo.

manipulator [mə'nɪpjʊ,leitəʳ] *n* manipulador *m*, -ora *f*.

mankind [mæn'kaɪnd] *n* humanidad *f*, género *m* humano, los hombres.

manlike ['mænlaɪk] *adj* (**a**) (*manly*) varonil. (**b**) (*like man*) parecido al hombre.

manliness ['mænlɪnɪs] *n* virilidad *f*, masculinidad *f*, hombría *f*.

manly ['mænlɪ] *adj* varonil, viril, masculino; (*courageous*) valiente; (*strong*) fuerte; **to be very** ~ ser muy hombre, ser todo un hombre.

man-made ['mæn'meɪd] *adj* artificial, sintético.

manna ['mænə] maná *m*; ~ **from heaven** maná *m* caído del cielo.

manned [mænd] *adj* tripulado; *satellite etc* pilotado.

mannequin ['mænɪkɪn] **1** *n* (*Art*) maniquí *m*; (*fashion* ~) modelo *f*. **2** *attr*: ~ **parade** desfile *m* de modelos.

manner ['mænəʳ] *n* (**a**) (*mode*) manera *f*, modo *m*; ~ **of payment** modo *m* de pago, forma *f* de pago; **after this** ~, **in this** ~ de esta manera; **after** (*or* **in**) **the** ~ **of X** a la manera de X, en el estilo de X; **in like** ~ de la misma manera; **in such a** ~ **that** ... de tal manera que ...; **a painter in the grand** ~ un pintor de cuadros grandiosos; **in a** ~ **of speaking** (*so to speak*) por así decirlo, como si dijéramos, (*up to a point*) hasta cierto punto, en cierto modo; **it's a** ~ **of speaking** es un modo de decir; **as (if) to the** ~ **born** como si estuviese acostumbrado desde la cuna.

(**b**) ~**s** (*of society*) costumbres *fpl*; **a novel of** ~**s** una novela de costumbres; ~**s maketh man** la conducta forma al hombre.

(**c**) (*behaviour etc*) conducta *f*; aire *m*, ademán *m*, porte *m*; manera *f* de ser; **his** ~ **to his parents** su modo de comportarse con sus padres; **I don't like his** ~ no me gusta su actitud; **he had the** ~ **of an old man** tenía aire de viejo; **there's sth odd about his** ~ tiene un aire algo raro.

(**d**) ~**s** (*good, bad etc*) modales *mpl*; educación *f*, crianza *f*; **bad** ~**s** mala educación *f*; **good** ~**s** educación *f*; **road** ~**s** educación *f* en la carretera, comportamiento *m* en la carretera; **it's bad** ~**s to yawn** es de mala educación bostezar; **good** ~**s demand that** ... la educación exige que ...; **to have bad** ~**s** ser mal criado, ser mal educado; **he has no** ~**s** no tiene crianza, es un mal criado; **to forget one's** ~**s** descomedirse; **to teach sb** ~**s** enseñarle a uno a portarse bien.

(**e**) (*class, type*) clase *f*, especie *f*; **all ~ of birds** toda clase de aves, aves de toda clase; **no ~ of doubt** sin ningún género de duda; **by no ~ of means** de ningún modo; **what ~ of man is he?** ¿qué tipo de hombre es?

mannered ['mænəd] *adj style* amanerado; (*in compounds*) de modales ...; *V* **bad-~** *etc.*

mannerism ['mænərɪzəm] *n* (**a**) (*Art, Liter*) manierismo *m*, (*pej*) amaneramiento *m*. (**b**) (*trick of speech, gesture*) movimiento *m* típico, peculiaridad *f*.

mannerist ['mænərɪst] **1** *adj* manierista. **2** *n* manierista *mf*.

mannerliness ['mænəlɪnɪs] *n* (buena) educación *f*, crianza *f*, cortesía *f*.

mannerly ['mænəlɪ] *adj* (bien) educado, bien criado, cortés.

mannikin ['mænɪkɪn] *n* = **manikin**.

mannish ['mænɪʃ] *adj* hombruno.

manoeuvrability, (*US*) **maneuverability** [mə,nuːvrə'bɪlɪtɪ] *n* maniobrabilidad *f*.

manoeuvrable, (*US*) **maneuverable** [mə'nuːvrəbl] *adj* maniobrable, manejable.

manoeuvre, (*US*) **maneuver** [mə'nuːvə^r] **1** *n* maniobra *f*; **this leaves us little room for ~** esto apenas nos deja espacio en que hacer cambios de posición, con esto nos quedan pocas posibilidades de hacer ajustes.

2 *vt* hacer maniobrar; manipular, manejar; **to ~ a gun into position** mover un cañón a su posición; **I was ~d into it** me embaucaron para que lo hiciera; **to ~ sb into doing sth** lograr mañosamente que uno haga algo.

3 *vi* maniobrar (*also fig*).

manoeuvring, (*US*) **maneuvering** [mə'nuːvrɪŋ] *n* el maniobrar; **political ~s** maniobras *fpl* políticas.

man-of-war ['mænəv'wɔː^r] *n, pl* **men-of-war** ['menəv'wɔː^r] *n* buque *m* de guerra.

manometer [mə'nɒmɪtə^r] *n* manómetro *m*.

manor ['mænə^r] *n* (**a**) (*feudal*) feudo *m*; señorío *m*; (*modern*) finca *f*. (**b**) (*Brit**) distrito *m*, barrio *m*; *V* **manor house**.

manor house ['mænəhaʊs] *n, pl* **manor houses** ['mænə,haʊzɪz] casa *f* señorial, casa *f* solariega.

manorial [mə'nɔːrɪəl] *adj* señorial.

manpower ['mænpaʊə^r] *n* mano *f* de obra; personal *m*; recursos *mpl* humanos, potencial *m* humano; **~ planning** planificación *f* de personal.

manqué ['mɔːŋkeɪ] *adj*: **a novelist ~** uno que hubiera podido ser novelista.

manse [mæns] *n* (*esp Scot*) casa *f* del pastor (protestante).

manservant ['mæn,sɜːvənt] *n, pl* **menservants** ['men,sɜːvənts] criado *m*.

mansion ['mænʃən] *n* palacio *m*, hotel *m*; casa *f* grande; (*of ancient family*) casa *f* solariega; **M~ House** *residencia del alcalde de Londres.*

man-sized ['mænsaɪzd] *adj* de tamaño de hombre; (*fig*) bien grande, grandote.

manslaughter ['mæn,slɔːtə^r] *n* homicidio *m* sin premeditación.

mantelpiece ['mæntlpiːs] *n*, **mantelshelf** ['mæntlʃelf] *n, pl* **mantelshelves** ['mæntlʃelvz] manto *m* (de chimenea), repisa *f* de chimenea.

mantilla [mæn'tɪlə] *n* mantilla *f*, velo *m*.

mantis ['mæntɪs] *n*: **praying ~** mantis *f* religiosa.

mantle ['mæntl] **1** *n* (**a**) (*cloak: also fig, Zool*) manto *m*, capa *f*. (**b**) (*gas ~*) manguito *m* incandescente, camisa *f* incandescente. **2** *vt* cubrir, ocultar; envolver (*in* en).

man-to-man ['mæntə'mæn] *adj, adv* de hombre a hombre.

mantra ['mæntrə] *n* mantra *m*.

mantrap ['mæntræp] *n* cepo *m*.

manual ['mænjʊəl] **1** *adj* manual; **~ training** enseñanza *f* de artes y oficios; **~ worker** trabajador *m*, -ora *f* manual. **2** *n* (**a**) (*book*) manual *m*. (**b**) (*Mus*) teclado *m*.

manually ['mænjʊəlɪ] *adv* manualmente, a mano.

manufacture [,mænjʊ'fæktʃə^r] **1** *n* (**a**) (*act*) fabricación *f*. (**b**) (*product*) manufactura *f*, producto *m*. **2** *vt* fabricar (*also fig*), manufacturar; **~d goods** artículos *mpl* manufacturados.

manufacturer [,mænjʊ'fæktʃərə^r] *n* fabricante *mf*, manufactero *m*, industrial *mf*.

manufacturing [,mænjʊ'fæktʃərɪŋ] **1** *adj* manufacturero, fabril; **~ capacity** capacidad *f* de fabricación; **~ costs** costos *mpl* de fabricación; **~ industries** industrias *fpl* manufactureras. **2** *n* fabricación *f*.

manure [mə'njʊə^r] **1** *n* estiércol *m*, abono *m*. **2** *attr*: **~ heap** estercolero *m*. **3** *vt* estercolar, abonar.

manuscript ['mænjʊskrɪpt] **1** *adj* manuscrito. **2** *n* manuscrito *m*; (*original of book, article*) original *m*.

Manx [mæŋks] **1** *adj* de la Isla de Man. **2** *n* (**a**) **the ~** los habitantes de la Isla de Man. (**b**) (*Ling*) lengua *f* (*celta*) de la Isla de Man.

Manxman ['mæŋksmən] *n, pl* **Manxmen** ['mæŋksmən] habitante *m* de la Isla de Man.

many ['menɪ] **1** *adj* muchos, muchas; **~ people** muchas personas, mucha gente, muchos; **in ~ cases** en muchos casos; **~ of them** muchos de ellos; **~ a time I have seen him act, ~'s the time I have seen him act** muchas veces le he visto representar; **he has as ~ as I have** tiene tantos como yo; **he has 3 times as ~ as I have** tiene 3 veces más que yo; **there were as ~ as 20** había hasta 20; **and as ~ more** y otros tantos; **how ~ were there?** ¿cuántos había?; **however ~ you have** por muchos que tengas; **so ~ flies** tantas moscas; **ever so ~ people** la mar de gente, tantísimas personas; **a good ~ houses, a great ~ houses** muchísimas casas, (un) buen número de casas; **too ~ difficulties** demasiadas dificultades; **there's one too ~** hay uno de más, hay uno que sobra, sobra uno.

2 *n* muchos *mpl*, muchas *fpl*; gran número *m*; **the ~** la mayoría, las masas.

many-coloured, (*US*) **many-colored** ['menɪ'kʌləd] *adj* multicolor.

many-sided ['menɪ'saɪdɪd] *adj figure* multilátero; *talent, personality* multifacético, polifacético; *problem* complicado.

Maoism ['maʊɪzəm] *n* maoísmo *m*.

Maoist ['maʊɪst] **1** *adj* maoísta. **2** *n* maoísta *mf*.

Maori ['maʊrɪ] **1** *adj* maorí. **2** *n* maorí *mf*.

Mao Tse-tung ['maʊtseɪ'tʊŋ] *nm* Mao Zedong.

map [mæp] **1** *n* mapa *m*; (*of streets, town*) plano *m*; (*chart*) carta *f*; **it's right off the ~** está muy aislado, está en el quinto infierno; **this will put Cheam on the ~** esto dará Cheam a conocer, ahora sí que se hablará de Cheam.

2 *vt* trazar el mapa (*or* plano) de, levantar el plano de.

◆**map out** *vt* proyectar; ordenar, organizar.

maple ['meɪpl] **1** *n* (*also* **~ tree**) arce *m*, maple *m* (*LAm*). **2** *attr*: **~ leaf** hoja *f* de arce; **~ sugar** azúcar *m* de arce; **~ syrup** jarabe *m* de arce.

mapmaker ['mæp,meɪkə^r] *n* cartógrafo *m*, -a *f*.

mapmaking ['mæp,meɪkɪŋ] *n*, **mapping** ['mæpɪŋ] *n* cartografía *f*; trazado *m* de mapas, levantamiento *m* de planos.

mar [mɑː^r] *vt* estropear; desfigurar; echar a perder; *happiness etc* afectar; *enjoyment* aguar.

Mar. *abbr of* **March** marzo *m*, mar.

maraschino [,mærəs'kiːnəʊ] *n* marrasquino *m*; **~ cherries** guindas *fpl* en conserva de marrasquino.

marathon ['mærəθən] **1** *n* (*also* **~ race**) maratón *m* (*sometimes f*). **2** *adj* (*fig*) larguísimo, interminable, maratón, marotoniano.

maraud [mə'rɔːd] *vi* merodear.

marauder [mə'rɔːdə^r] *n* merodeador *m*; intruso *m*.

marauding [mə'rɔːdɪŋ] **1** *adj* merodeador; intruso, indeseable. **2** *n* merodeo *m*.

marble ['mɑːbl] **1** *n* (**a**) (*material*) mármol *m*. (**b**) (*glass ball*) canica *f*, bola *f*; **to lose one's ~s**‡ perder la chaveta*; **to play ~s** jugar a las bolas. **2** *adj* marmóreo (*also fig*), de mármol; **~ quarry** cantera *f* de mármol; **~ staircase** escalera *f* de mármol.

marbled ['mɑːbld] *adj surface* jaspeado.

March [mɑːtʃ] *n* marzo *m*.

march[1] [mɑːtʃ] **1** *n* marcha *f* (*also Mus, fig*); (*fig: long walk*) caminata *f*; **an army on the ~** un ejército en marcha; **we were on the ~ to the capital** marchábamos sobre la capital; **it's a day's ~ from here** está a un día de marcha desde aquí, (*fig*) eso queda lejísimos; **to steal a ~ on sb** madrugar, ganar por la mano a uno, sacar la delantera a uno.

2 *vt* (**a**) *soldiers* hacer marchar, llevar.

(**b**) *distance* recorrer (marchando); (*fig*) llevar andado.

3 *vi* marchar; (*fig*) andar, ir a pie; (*stalk*) ir resueltamente, caminar con resolución; **forward ~!, quick ~!** de frente ¡mar!; **to ~ into a room** entrar resueltamente en un cuarto; **to ~ past** desfilar; **to ~ past sb** desfilar ante uno.

◆**march in** *vi* entrar (resueltamente *etc*).

◆**march off 1** *vt*: **they ~ed him off** se lo llevaron sin ceremonia.

2 *vi* irse (resueltamente *etc*).

◆**march on 1** *vt* marchar sobre. **2** *vi* seguir marchando.

◆**march out** *vi* salir (airado, resueltamente *etc*).

◆**march up to** *vt*: **to ~ up to sb** acercarse resueltamente a uno; abordar a uno tan fresco.

march[2] [mɑːtʃ] *n* (*Hist*) marca *f*; **the Spanish M~** la Marca Hispánica; **the Welsh ~es** la marca galesa.

marcher ['mɑːtʃə^r] *n* (*on demonstration*) marchista *mf*, manifestante *mf*.

marching ['mɑːtʃɪŋ] *adj song etc* de marcha; **to get one's ~ orders*** ser despedido; **to give sb his ~ orders*** despedir a uno.

marchioness ['mɑːʃənɪs] *n* marquesa *f*.

march-past ['mɑːtʃ,pɑːst] *n* desfile *m*.

mare [mɛəʳ] *n* yegua *f*.

mare's-nest ['mɛəznest] *n* parto *m* de los montes, hallazgo *m* ilusorio.

marg* [mɑːdʒ] *n* (*Brit*) *abbr of* **margarine.**

Margaret ['mɑːgərɪt] *nf* Margarita.

margarine [,mɑːdʒə'riːn] *n*, **marge*** [mɑːdʒ] (*Brit*) *n* margarina *f*.

Marge [mɑːdʒ] *nf familiar form of* **Margaret, Marjory.**

marge* [mɑːdʒ] = **marg*.**

margin ['mɑːdʒɪn] *n* margen *m* (*also Fin, Typ*); (*fig*) margen *m*; reserva *f*; excedente *m*, sobrante *m*; **~ of error** margen *m* de error; **~ of profit** margen *m* de beneficios; **~ of safety** margen *m* de seguridad; **to write sth in the ~** escribir algo al margen; **they live on the ~ of society** viven en el margen de la sociedad.

marginal ['mɑːdʒɪnl] *adj note, profit etc* marginal; *case etc* dudoso, incierto; *interest, matter* periférico; (*Pol*) *seat* de escasa mayoría; **of ~ importance** de dudosa importancia; **~ land** tierras *fpl* marginales.

marginally ['mɑːdʒɪnəlɪ] *adv* ligeramente.

marguerite [,mɑːgə'riːt] *n* margarita *f*.

Maria [mə'riːə] *nf* María.

Marian ['mɛərɪən] *adj* mariano.

Marie Antoinette [mə'riːæntwɑː'net] *nf* María Antonieta.

marigold ['mærɪgəʊld] *n* caléndula *f*, maravilla *f*.

marihuana, marijuana [,mærɪ'hwɑːnə] *n* marijuana *f*.

marina [mə'riːnə] *n* centro *m* de deportes acuáticos, puerto *m* deportivo.

marinade [,mærɪ'neɪd] **1** *n* escabeche *m*. **2** *vt* (*also* **marinate** ['mærɪneɪt]) escabechar, marinar.

marine [mə'riːn] **1** *adj* marino; marítimo; **M~ Corps** (*US*) Infantería *f* de Marina; **~ engineer** ingeniero *m* naval; **~ engineering** ingeniería *f* naval; **~ insurance** seguro *m* marítimo; **~ life** vida *f* marina.

2 *n* (**a**) (*fleet*) marina *f*.

(**b**) (*person*) infante *m* de marina; **~s** (*Brit*) infantería *f* de marina; **tell that to the ~s!** ¡a otro perro con ese hueso!, ¡cuéntaselo a tu abuela!

mariner ['mærɪnəʳ] *n* marinero *m*, marino *m*.

mariolatry [,mɛərɪ'ɒlətrɪ] *n* mariolatría *f*.

marionette [,mærɪə'net] *n* marioneta *f*, títere *m*.

marital ['mærɪtl] *adj* marital; matrimonial; **~ counselling** orientación *f* sobre problemas matrimoniales; **~ problems** problemas *mpl* matrimoniales, problemas *mpl* conyugales; **~ status** estado *m* civil.

maritime ['mærɪtaɪm] *adj* marítimo; **~ law** código *m* marítimo, derecho *m* marítimo.

marjoram ['mɑːdʒərəm] *n* mejorana *f*, orégano *m*.

Mark [mɑːk] *nm* Marcos; **~ Antony** Marco Antonio.

mark¹ [mɑːk] *n* (*coin*) marco *m*.

mark² [mɑːk] **1** *n* (**a**) (*written symbol on paper etc*) señal *f*, marca *f*; llamada *f*; (*sign, indication*) señal *f*, indicio *m*; (*as signature*) cruz *f*; (*trade~*) marca *f*; (*stain*) mancha *f*; (*imprint, trace*) huella *f*; **gas ~ 1** número 1 del gas; **the ~s of violence** las señales de la violencia; **he had the ~s of old age** tenía los indicios de la vejez; **he left the ring without a ~ on his body** salió del cuadrilátero sin llevar señal alguna en el cuerpo; **it's the ~ of a gentleman** así se distinguen los caballeros, es señal de caballerosidad; **as a ~ of my disapproval** en señal de mi desaprobación; **as a ~ of our gratitude** en señal de nuestro agradecimiento; **it bears the ~ of genius** tiene el sello de la genialidad; **to leave one's ~** dejar memoria de sí; **to leave one's ~ on sth** dejar sus huellas en algo; **to make one's ~** firmar con una cruz, (*fig*) señalarse, distinguirse, destacar.

(**b**) (*Sport*) raya *f*; **on your ~s, get set, go!** ¡preparados, listos, ya!; **to be quick off the ~** ser muy listo; adelantarse a los demás; **to be slow off the ~** ser lerdo; dejar que otros cojan la delantera a uno; **to be up to the ~** ser satisfactorio, estar a la altura de las circunstancias; **to come up to the ~** alcanzar el nivel que era de esperar; **to overstep the ~** propasarse.

(**c**) (*label*) etiqueta *f*.

(**d**) **of ~** de categoría, de cierta distinción.

(**e**) (*target*) blanco *m*; **to be wide of the ~** errar, no dar en el blanco, (*fig*) no acertar, ser erróneo, alejarse de la verdad; **he's on the ~** (*fig*) ha dado en el blanco, está en lo cierto; **he's way off the ~** (*fig*) no acierta ni con mucho; se aleja mucho de la verdad; **to hit the ~** dar en el blanco, (*fig*) acertar, dar en el clavo; **to reach the £1000 ~** alcanzar el total de 1000 libras.

(**f**) (*in exam; also* **~s**) puntuación *f*; calificación *f*, nota *f*; **52 ~s** 52 puntos, 52 por cien; **to get high ~s in French** sacar buena nota en francés; **you get no ~s at all as a cook** como cocinera no vales para nada; **there are no ~s for guessing** las simples conjeturas no merecen punto alguno.

(**g**) (*model, type*) serie *f*; **a Spitfire M~ 1** un Spitfire (de) primera serie.

2 *vt* (**a**) (*make a ~ on*) señalar, marcar, poner una señal en; (*stain*) manchar; desfigurar; **~ it with an asterisk** ponga un asterisco allí; **he was not ~ed at all** no mostraba señal alguna de golpe; **a bird ~ed with red** un pájaro manchado de rojo, un pájaro con manchas rojas.

(**b**) (*label*) rotular, poner un rótulo a; (*Comm*) poner una etiqueta a, indicar el precio de; **this exhibit is not ~ed** este objeto no lleva rótulo; **the chair is ~ed at £20** se indica el precio de la silla como de 20 libras.

(**c**) (*indicate*) señalar, marcar, indicar; (*characterize*) señalar, distinguir; *anniversary etc* señalar, celebrar; *birthday* festejar; *rhythm, time* (*Mus*) marcar; **stones ~ the path** unas piedras señalan el camino; **this ~s the frontier** esto marca la frontera; **it ~s a change of policy** ello indica un cambio de política; **this ~s him as a future star** esto le señala como un as futuro; **it's not ~ed on the map** no está indicado en el mapa, no consta en el mapa.

(**d**) (*note down*) apuntar; (*notice*) advertir, observar; (*heed*) prestar atención a; **did you ~ where it fell?** ¿has notado dónde cayó?; **~ you, ~ my words** entiéndase bien que ...; **~ you, he may have been right** fíjate que puede haber tenido razón; **~ what I say** escucha lo que te digo.

(**e**) *exam* puntuar, calificar; *candidate* dar nota a; **we ~ed him (as) first class** le dimos nota de sobresaliente.

(**f**) (*Sport*) marcar, doblar.

◆**mark down** *vt* (**a**) (*note*) apuntar. (**b**) (*select*) escoger. (**c**) (*Comm*) rebajar (*to* a); *student* dar nota mala a; reducir la puntuación de.

◆**mark off** *vt* (**a**) señalar; distinguir, separar (*from* de); (*by stages etc*) jalonar. (**b**) *list* marcar; *names* poner una señal a; (*cross out*) tachar.

◆**mark out** *vt* (**a**) *road etc* trazar, marcar; jalonar; **the track is ~ed out by flags** el camino está jalonado de banderas. (**b**) (*select*) escoger; señalar; (*distinguish*) distinguir, señalar; **he is ~ed out for promotion** se le ha señalado para un ascenso.

◆**mark up** *vt* (**a**) (*on board etc*) apuntar. (**b**) (*Comm*) aumentar, aumentar el precio de.

mark-down ['mɑːkdaʊn] *n* (*Comm*) reducción *f*.

marked [mɑːkt] *adj contrast, accent etc* acusado, fuerte; marcado; *improvement etc* notable, grande; **~ man** hombre *m* que ha llamado la atención; hombre *m* que se ha señalado como futura víctima; **~ price** precio *m* corriente; **it is becoming more ~** se acusa cada vez más.

markedly ['mɑːkɪdlɪ] *adv* marcadamente; fuertemente; notablemente; **it is ~ better than the other** es netamente superior al otro; **they are not ~ different** no son obviamente distintos.

marker ['mɑːkəʳ] *n* (**a**) (*Billiards etc*) marcador *m*, (*in other games*) ficha *f*. (**b**) (*in book*) registro *m*. (**c**) (*signal*) señal *f*; (*signpost*) poste *m* indicador; **to put down a ~** (*fig*) dejar una señal, marcar un lugar. (**d**) (*also* **~ pen**) rotulador *m*, marcador *m*. (**e**) (*Comput*) bandera *f*.

market ['mɑːkɪt] **1** *n* mercado *m*; (*stock exchange*) bolsa *f*; **there's no ~ for pink socks** los calcetines rosados no encuentran salida; **to be in the ~ for sth** estar dispuesto a comprar algo; **to be on the ~** estar de venta; **it's the dearest shirt on the ~** es la camisa más cara del mercado; **to bring** (*or* **put**) **a product on to the ~** lanzar un producto al mercado; **to come on to the ~** (empezar a) venderse, ponerse en venta, ofrecerse; **to corner the ~ in maize** acaparar el maíz; **to find a ready ~** venderse fácilmente, tener fácil salida; **to flood the ~ with sth** inundar el mercado de algo; **strawberries are flooding the ~** las fresas inundan el mercado; **to play the ~** jugar a la bolsa; **to rig the ~** manipular la lonja.

2 *attr*: **~ analysis** análisis *m* de mercado(s); **~ day** día *m* de mercado; **~ demand** demanda *f* de mercado; **~ economy** economía *f* de mercado; **~ forces** fuerzas *fpl* del mercado; factores *mpl* comerciales; **~ garden** (*Brit*) huerto *m*, (*large*) huerta *f*; **~ gardener** (*Brit*) hortelano *m*; **~ gardening** (*Brit*) horticultura *f*; **~ intelligence** información *f* del mercado; **~ leader** líder *m* del mercado;

~ **opportunity** oportunidad *f* comercial; ~ **penetration** penetración *f* del mercado; ~ **place** mercado *m*, plaza *f* del mercado; ~ **potential** potencial *m* comercial; ~ **price** precio *m* de mercado, precio *m* corriente; ~ **rates** precios *mpl* del mercado, (*Fin*) cotizaciones *fpl*; ~ **research** prospección *f* de mercados, análisis *m* de mercados; ~ **researcher** prospector *m*, -ora *f* de mercados; ~ **share** cuota *f* de mercado, participación *f* en el mercado; ~ **square** plaza *f* del mercado; ~ **study**, ~ **survey** estudio *m* del mercado; ~ **town** mercado *m*; ~ **trends** tendencias *fpl* de mercado; ~ **value** valor *m* en el mercado, valor *m* comercial.

3 *vt* vender, poner a la venta; *new product etc* llevar al mercado, mercadear, comercializar.

4 *vi* (*esp US*) ir de compras; hacer las compras.

marketability [ˌmɑːkɪtəˈbɪlɪtɪ] *n* comerciabilidad *f*, vendibilidad *f*.

marketable [ˈmɑːkɪtəbl] *adj* vendible, comerciable, comercializable; negociable; de valor comercial; ~ **securities** valores *mpl* comerciables, valores *mpl* realizables.

marketeer [ˌmɑːkɪˈtɪəʳ] *n* (*Brit Pol*) partidario *m*, -a *f* del Mercado Común.

marketing [ˈmɑːkɪtɪŋ] *n* márketing *m*, márquetin *m*, mercadeo *m*; mercadotecnia *f*. **2** *attr*: ~ **agreement** acuerdo *m* mercantil; ~ **department** sección *f* mercantil, sección *f* de márketing; ~ **manager** director *m*, -ora *f* comercial, director *m*, -ora *f* de márketing; ~ **plan** plan *m* de distribución de mercancías; ~ **strategy** estrategia *f* mercadológica.

market-led [ˈmɑːkɪtˈled] *adj* generado (*or* condicionado) por el mercado.

marking [ˈmɑːkɪŋ] **1** *n* (*mark*) señal *f*, marca *f*; (*on animal*) mancha *f*, pinta *f*; (*coloration*) coloración *f*; (*of exams*) puntuación *f*, calificación *f*.

2 *attr*: ~ **ink** tinta *f* de marcar, tinta *f* indeleble; ~ **pen** rotulador *m*, marcador *m*.

mark-reader [ˈmɑːkˌriːdəʳ], **mark-scanner** [ˈmɑːkˌskænəʳ] *n* lector *m* de marcas.

mark-reading [ˈmɑːkˌriːdɪŋ], **mark-scanning** [ˈmɑːkˌskænɪŋ] *n* lectura *f* de marcas.

marksman [ˈmɑːksmən] *n*, *pl* **marksmen** [ˈmɑːksmən] tirador *m*.

marksmanship [ˈmɑːksmənʃɪp] *n* puntería *f*.

mark-up [ˈmɑːkʌp] *n* margen *m* (de beneficio); valor *m* añadido; aumento *m* de precio.

marl [mɑːl] *n* marga *f*.

marlin [ˈmɑːlɪn] *n* (*Fish*) aguja *f*.

marlin(e) [ˈmɑːlɪn] *n* (*Naut*) merlín *m*, empalmadura *f*, trincafía *f*.

marlinespike [ˈmɑːlɪnspaɪk] *n* pasador *m*.

marly [ˈmɑːlɪ] *adj* margoso.

marmalade [ˈmɑːməleɪd] **1** *n* mermelada *f* (de naranjas amargas). **2** *attr*: ~ **orange** naranja *f* amarga.

marmoreal [mɑːˈmɔːrɪəl] *adj* marmóreo.

marmoset [ˈmɑːməzet] *n* tití *m*.

marmot [ˈmɑːmət] *n* marmota *f*.

maroon[1] [məˈruːn] **1** *adj* granate, corinto, rojo oscuro. **2** *n* (*colour*) marrón *m*.

maroon[2] [məˈruːn] *vt* abandonar (en una isla desierta); (*fig*) aislar, dejar aislado; dejar en un sitio peligroso; **we were ~ed by floods** quedamos aislados por las inundaciones.

maroon[3] [məˈruːn] *n* (*firework*) petardo *m*.

marquee [mɑːˈkiː] *n* (*esp Brit*) tienda *f* grande, entoldado *m*; (*US*) marquesina *f*.

marquess, marquis [ˈmɑːkwɪs] *n* marqués *m*.

marquetry [ˈmɑːkɪtrɪ] *n* marquetería *f*.

Marrakesh [ˌmærəˈkeʃ] *n* Marakech *m*.

marriage [ˈmærɪdʒ] **1** *n* (*as institution*) matrimonio *m*; (*wedding*) boda *f*, bodas *fpl*; casamiento *m*; (*fig*) unión *f*; ~ **of convenience** matrimonio *m* de conveniencia; **aunt by** ~ tía *f* política; **to be related by** ~ estar emparentados; **to become related by** ~ **to sb** emparentar con uno; **to give sb in** ~ **to** casar a una con, dar a una en matrimonio a.

2 *attr*: ~ **bed** lecho *m* nupcial, tálamo *m*; ~ **broker** casamentero *m*, -a *f*; ~ **bureau** agencia *f* matrimonial; ~ **ceremony** matrimonio *m*; ~ **certificate** partida *f* de matrimonio; ~ **counseling** (*US*), ~ **guidance** orientación *f* matrimonial; ~ **(guidance) counsel(l)or** consejero *m*, -a *f* de orientación matrimonial; ~ **licence** licencia *f* de matrimonio (*or* matrimonial); ~ **lines** (*Brit*) partida *f* de matrimonio; ~ **partner** cónyuge *mf*, consorte *mf*; ~ **rate** (índice *m*) de nupcialidad *f*; ~ **settlement** contrato *m* matrimonial; capitulaciones *fpl* matrimoniales; ~ **vows** votos *mpl* matrimoniales.

marriageable [ˈmærɪdʒəbl] *adj* casadero.

married [ˈmærɪd] *adj person* casado; *life, love, state etc* conyugal; ~ **couple** matrimonio *m*; ~ **man** casado *m*, ~ **woman** casada *f*; **the** ~ **state** el estado matrimonial; **her** ~ **name** su apellido de casada; ~ **quarters** alojamiento *m* para matrimonio.

marrow [ˈmærəʊ] *n* (**a**) (*Anat*) médula *f*, tuétano *m*, meollo *m*; (*fig*) meollo *m*; (*as food*) tuétano *m* de hueso; **a Spaniard to the** ~ español hasta los tuétanos; **to be frozen to the** ~ estar completamente helado.

(**b**) (*Brit Bot*: *also* **vegetable** ~) calabacín *m*.

marrowbone [ˈmærəʊbəʊn] *n* hueso *m* con tuétano; **~s*** (*hum*) rodillas *fpl*.

marry [ˈmærɪ] **1** *vt* (*give or join in marriage*) casar (*to* con); (*take in marriage*) casarse con, casar con; (*fig*) conjugar, unir; **he has 3 daughters to** ~ **(off)** tiene 3 hijas por casar; **he's married to his job** está casado con su trabajo; **to** ~ **money** casarse con uno (*or* una) que tiene una fortuna.

2 *vi* (*also* **to get married**) casarse; **to** ~ **again** volver a casarse, casarse en segundas nupcias; **to** ~ **beneath o.s.** casarse con uno (*or* una) de rango inferior; **to** ~ **into a family** emparentar con una familia; **to** ~ **into the peerage** casarse con un título.

◆**marry up** *vt* conjugar.

Mars [mɑːz] *nm* Marte.

Marseillaise [ˌmɑːsəˈleɪz] *n*: **the** ~ la Marsellesa.

Marseilles [mɑːˈseɪlz] *n* Marsella *f*.

marsh [mɑːʃ] **1** *n* pantano *m*, ciénaga *f*; (*salt-~*) marisma *f*. **2** *attr*: ~ **fever** paludismo *m*; ~ **gas** gas *m* de los pantanos, metano *m*; ~ **marigold** botón *m* de oro; ~ **warbler** papamoscas *m*.

marshal [ˈmɑːʃəl] **1** *n* (*Mil*) mariscal *m*; (*at ceremony*) maestro *m* de ceremonias; (*Brit: at sports meeting etc*) oficial *m*; (*US*) alguacil *m*, oficial *m* de justicia.

2 *vt facts, ideas etc* ordenar, arreglar; *evidence* presentar; *soldiers, procession* formar.

marshalling yard [ˈmɑːʃəlɪŋˌjɑːd] *n* (*Rail*) playa *f* de clasificación, estación *f* clasificadora, zona *f* de enganche.

marshland [ˈmɑːʃlænd] *n* pantanal *m*.

marshmallow [ˈmɑːʃˈmæləʊ] *n* (*Bot*) malvavisco *m*; (*sweet*) 'esponjas' *fpl*.

marshy [ˈmɑːʃɪ] *adj* pantanoso.

marsupial [mɑːˈsuːpɪəl] **1** *adj* marsupial. **2** *n* marsupial *m*.

mart [mɑːt] *n* (*trade centre*) emporio *m*; (*market*) mercado *m*; (*auction-room*) martillo *m*; (*property* ~) (*in newspaper*) bolsa *f* de la propiedad.

marten [ˈmɑːtɪn] *n* marta *f*.

Martial [ˈmɑːʃəl] *nm* Marcial.

martial [ˈmɑːʃəl] *adj* marcial; castrense; ~ **arts** artes *fpl* marciales; ~ **bearing** porte *m* militar; ~ **law** ley *f* marcial, gobierno *m* militar.

Martian [ˈmɑːʃɪən] **1** *adj* marciano. **2** *n* marciano *m*, -a *f*.

Martin [ˈmɑːtɪn] *nm* Martín.

martin [ˈmɑːtɪn] *n* avión *m*.

martinet [ˌmɑːtɪˈnet] *n* ordenancista *mf*, rigorista *mf*.

Martini [mɑːˈtiːnɪ] ® *n* vermú *m*; (*US: cocktail*) martini *m* americano (*vermú seco con ginebra*).

Martinique [ˌmɑːtɪˈniːk] *n* Martinica *f*.

Martinmas [ˈmɑːtɪnməs] *n* día *m* de San Martín (*11 noviembre*).

martyr [ˈmɑːtəʳ] **1** *n* mártir *mf*; **to be a** ~ **to arthritis** ser martirizado por la artritis, ser víctima de la artritis. **2** *vt* martirizar.

martyrdom [ˈmɑːtədəm] *n* martirio *m*.

martyrize [ˈmɑːtɪraɪz] *vt* martirizar.

marvel [ˈmɑːvəl] **1** *n* maravilla *f*; prodigio *m*; **if he gets there it will be a** ~ si llega será milagro; **it's a** ~ **to me how he does it** no llego a comprender cómo lo hace, me asombra el que lo pueda hacer.

2 *vi* maravillarse (*at* de, con).

marvellous, (*US*) **marvelous** [ˈmɑːvələs] *adj* maravilloso; **~!** ¡magnífico!; **isn't it ~?** ¡qué bien! (*also iro*).

marvellously, (*US*) **marvelously** [ˈmɑːvələslɪ] *adv* maravillosamente; a maravilla.

Marxism [ˈmɑːksɪzəm] *n* marxismo *m*.

Marxist [ˈmɑːksɪst] **1** *adj* marxista. **2** *n* marxista *mf*.

Mary [ˈmɛərɪ] *nf* María *f*; ~ **Magdalen** la Magdalena; ~ **Queen of Scots**, ~ **Stuart** María Estuardo.

marzipan [ˌmɑːzɪˈpæn] *n* mazapán *m*.

mascara [mæsˈkɑːrə] *n* rímel *m*, máscara *f*.

mascot [ˈmæskət] *n* mascota *f*.

masculine [ˈmæskjʊlɪn] **1** *adj* masculino; varonil; *woman* hombruno. **2** *n* masculino *m*.

masculinity [ˌmæskjʊˈlɪnɪtɪ] *n* masculinidad *f.*
MASH [mæʃ] *n* (*US*) *abbr of* **mobile army surgical unit** unidad *f* quirúrgica móvil del ejército.
mash [mæʃ] **1** *n* (*mixture*) mezcla *f*; (*pulp*) pasta *f*, amasijo *m*; (*Brit*: *potatoes*) puré *m* de patatas; (*in brewing*) malta *f* remojada; (*bran*) afrecho *m* remojado.
2 *vt* mezclar; amasar, despachurrar; *potatoes* hacer un puré de.
mashed [mæʃt] *adj*: ~ **potatoes** puré *m* de patatas, puré *m* de papas (*LAm*).
mashie [ˈmæʃɪ] *n* hierro *m* número 5.
mask [mɑːsk] **1** *n* máscara *f* (*also fig*); (*disguise*) disfraz *m*; (*protective*) antifaz *m*; (*Comput, Elec*) máscara *f*; (*gas ~ etc*) careta *f*; (*surgeon's, death ~*) mascarilla *f*; *V* **masque.**
2 *vt* enmascarar (*also Comput*); (*fig*) encubrir, ocultar, enmascarar; *effect of drug* enmascarar.
masked [mɑːskt] *adj* enmascarado; (*terrorist etc*) encapuchado; ~ **ball** baile *m* de máscaras.
masochism [ˈmæzəʊkɪzəm] *n* masoquismo *m.*
masochist [ˈmæzəʊkɪst] *n* masoquista *mf.*
masochistic [ˌmæzəʊˈkɪstɪk] *adj* masoquista.
mason [ˈmeɪsn] *n* (**a**) (*builder*) albañil *m*; (*in quarry*) cantero *m*; (*of tombs*) escultor *m.* (**b**) (*free~*: *also* **M~**) masón *m*, francmasón *m.*
masonic [məˈsɒnɪk] *adj* (*also* **M~**) masónico.
masonry [ˈmeɪsnrɪ] *n* (**a**) albañilería *f*; mampostería *f.* (**b**) (*free~*) masonería *f*, francmasonería *f.*
masque [mɑːsk] *n* mascarada *f.*
masquerade [ˌmæskəˈreɪd] **1** *n* baile *m* de máscaras, mascarada *f*; (*fig*) farsa *f.* **2** *vi*: **to ~ as** disfrazarse de, hacerse pasar por.
mass[1] [mæs] *n* (*Eccl, Mus*: *also* **M~**) misa *f*; **to go to ~** ir a misa, oír misa; **to hear ~** oír misa; **to say ~** decir misa.
mass[2] [mæs] **1** *n* (**a**) masa *f* (*also Phys*); (*vague shape*) bulto *m*; (*of mountains*) macizo *m.*
(**b**) (*great quantity*) montón *m*, gran cantidad *f*; (*of people*) muchedumbre *f*; **the ~es** las masas; **a great ~ of people** una gran muchedumbre; **the ~ of** la mayoría de; **the great ~ of** la inmensa mayoría de; **in the ~** en conjunto; **to gather in ~es** acudir en masa, reunirse en tropel; **we have ~es** tenemos montones; **he's a ~ of bruises** está cubierto de cardenales; **the garden is a ~ of yellow** el jardín es todo flores amarillas; **he's a ~ of nerves** es una madeja de nervios, tiene una tremenda tensión nerviosa.
2 *attr* masivo; en masa; ~ **grave** fosa *f* común; ~ **hysteria** histerismo *m* colectivo; ~ **market** mercado *m* popular; ~ **media** medios *mpl* de comunicación; ~ **meeting** mitín *m* (*or* reunión *f*) popular, manifestación *f*; ~ **murder** matanza *f*; ~ **noun** sustantivo *m* no contable; ~ **production** fabricación *f* en serie; ~ **protest** protesta *f* masiva; ~ **psychology** psicología *f* de masas; ~ **resignation(s)** dimisión *f* en masa; ~ **unemployment** paro *m* masivo.
3 *vt* juntar en masa, reunir; *troops etc* concentrar.
4 *vi* juntarse en masa, reunirse; (*Mil*) concentrarse.
Mass. (*US*) *abbr of* **Massachusetts.**
massacre [ˈmæsəkəʳ] **1** *n* matanza *f*, carnicería *f*, degollina *f*, masacre *f* (*also m*); (*fig*) masacre *f* (*also m*). **2** *vt* hacer una carnicería de, matar despiadadamente, masacrar; (*fig*) masacrar.
massage [ˈmæsɑːʒ] **1** *n* masaje *m*; **'M~'** (*euph*) 'Relax'. **2** *attr*: ~ **parlor** (*US*), ~ **parlour** sala *f* de masaje; (*euph*) sala *f* de relax. **3** *vt* masajear, dar masaje a; (*) *figures* maquillar*.
masseur [mæˈsɜːʳ] *n* masajista *m.*
masseuse [mæˈsɜːz] *n* masajista *f.*
massif [mæˈsiːf] *n* macizo *m.*
massive [ˈmæsɪv] *adj* (*solid*) macizo, sólido; *head etc* grande, abultado; (*imposing*) imponente, impresionante; *contribution, support, intervention* enérgico, fuerte, masivo, en gran escala.
massively [ˈmæsɪvlɪ] *adv* macizamente, sólidamente; de modo imponente; enérgicamente, fuertemente, masivamente.
massiveness [ˈmæsɪvnɪs] *n* macicez *f*, solidez *f*; lo grande, lo abultado; energía *f*, fuerza *f.*
mass-produce [ˈmæsprəˈdjuːs] *vt* fabricar en serie.
mast[1] [mɑːst] *n* (*Naut*) mástil *m*, palo *m*; (*Rad etc*) torre *f*, mástil *m*; **10 years before the ~** 10 años de servicio como marinero.
mast[2] [mɑːst] *n* (*Bot*: *of oak*) bellota *f*, (*of beech*) hayuco *m.*
mastectomy [mæˈstektəmɪ] *n* (*Med*) mastectomía *f.*
-masted [ˈmɑːstɪd] *adj ending in compounds* de ... palos; **three~** de tres palos.
master [ˈmɑːstəʳ] **1** *n* (*of the house etc*) señor *m*, amo *m*; (*owner*) dueño *m*; (*Naut*: *of ship*) capitán *m*, (*of boat*) patrón *m*; (*expert, musician, painter etc*) maestro *m*; (*of Mil order*) maestre *m*; (*teacher*) maestro *m*, (*in secondary school*) profesor *m*; (*Brit*: *of college*) director *m*, rector *m*; **old ~** (*man*) pintor *m* clásico, (*work*) obra *f* clásica, cuadro *m* de uno de los pintores clásicos; **the young ~** el señorito; **M~ of Arts** licenciado *m*, -a *f* (superior) en Filosofía y Letras, (*Hist*) maestro *m* en artes; **she's working for her M~'s (degree)** estudia para su licenciatura superior; **~ of ceremonies** maestro *m* de ceremonias; (*of show*) presentador *m*, animador *m*; **~ of foxhounds** cazador *m* mayor; **M~ of the Rolls** (*Brit*) juez *mf* del tribunal de apelación; **to be a past ~ at politics** ser un político consumado; **to be ~ of** poseer; **to be ~ of the situation** ser dueño de la situación, ser dueño del baile; **the ~ is not at home** el señor no está; **I am the ~ now** ahora mando yo; **to be ~ in one's own house** mandar en su propia casa; **to be one's own ~** ser independiente; trabajar por cuenta propia; **to be the ~ of one's fate** decidir su propio destino; **to make o.s. ~ of** apoderarse de; **to meet one's ~** ser derrotado por fin, tener que sucumbir por fin.
2 *attr* maestro; ~ **baker** maestro *m* panadero; ~ **bedroom** dormitorio *m* principal; ~ **builder** contratista *m* de construcciones; ~ **card** carta *f* maestra; ~ **class** clase *f* magistral; ~ **copy** original *m*; ~ **disk** disco *m* maestro; ~ **file** fichero *m* maestro; ~ **key** llave *f* maestra; ~ **mariner** capitán *m*; ~ **mason** albañil *m* maestro; ~ **plan** plan *m* maestro, plan *m* rector; ~ **sergeant** (*US*) sargento *m* mayor; ~ **spy** jefe *mf* de espías, controlador *m*, -ora *f* de espías; ~ **stroke** toque *m* magistral; golpe *m* maestro; ~ **switch** interruptor *m* principal; ~ **tape** máster *m*, cinta *f* máster, cinta *f* original.
3 *vt* (*defeat*) vencer, derrotar; *difficulty etc* vencer; *situation* dominar; *one's defects* sobreponerse a; *subject* dominar; *craft* llegar a ser maestro en.
masterful [ˈmɑːstəfʊl] *adj* imperioso, autoritario; *personality etc* dominante.
masterfully [ˈmɑːstəfəlɪ] *adv* magistralmente.
masterly [ˈmɑːstəlɪ] *adj* magistral, genial.
mastermind [ˈmɑːstəmaɪnd] **1** *n* inteligencia *f* genial, cerebro *m*; (*in crime etc*) mente *f* directora, figura *f* principal. **2** *vt operation etc* dirigir, planear.
masterpiece [ˈmɑːstəpiːs] *n* obra *f* maestra.
Mastersingers [ˈmɑːstəˌsɪŋəz] *npl*: **'The ~'** 'Los maestros cantores'.
mastery [ˈmɑːstərɪ] *n* (*sway*) dominio *m*; autoridad *f*; (*skill*) maestría *f*; (*over competitors etc*) dominio *m*, superioridad *f*; **to gain the ~ of** (*take over*) hacerse el señor de, (*dominate*) llegar a dominar.
masthead [ˈmɑːsthed] *n* (**a**) (*Naut*) tope *m.* (**b**) (*of newspaper*) mancheta *f.*
mastic [ˈmæstɪk] *n* masilla *f.*
masticate [ˈmæstɪkeɪt] *vti* masticar.
mastiff [ˈmæstɪf] *n* mastín *m*, alano *m.*
mastitis [mæsˈtaɪtɪs] *n* mastitis *f.*
mastodon [ˈmæstədən] *n* mastodonte *m.*
mastoid [ˈmæstɔɪd] **1** *adj* mastoides. **2** *n* mastoides *f.*
masturbate [ˈmæstəbeɪt] *vi* masturbarse.
masturbation [ˌmæstəˈbeɪʃən] *n* masturbación *f.*
masturbatory [ˈmæstəˈbeɪtərɪ] *adj* masturbatorio.
mat[1] [mæt] **1** *n* estera *f*, (*small*) esterilla *f*; (*round*) ruedo *m*; (*at door*) felpudo *m*; (*on table*) salvamanteles *m*; (*of lace etc*) tapetito *m*; (*of hair*) greña *f.*
2 *vt* enmarañar, entretejer.
3 *vi* enmarañarse, entretejerse.
mat[2] [mæt] *adj* mate.
matador [ˈmætədɔːʳ] *n* matador *m*, diestro *m.*
match[1] [mætʃ] *n* cerilla *f*, fósforo *m*; (*fuse*) mecha *f.*
match[2] [mætʃ] **1** *n* (**a**) (*person etc*) igual *mf*; **the two of them make a good ~** hacen una buena pareja; **the skirt is a good ~ for the jumper** la falda hace juego con el jersey; **to be a ~ for sb** poder competir (*etc*) con uno en pie de igualdad; **he's a ~ for anybody** puede dar ciento y raya al más pintado; **A is no ~ for B** A no puede con B; **A was more than a ~ for B** A venció fácilmente a B; **to meet one's match** encontrar la horma de su zapato.
(**b**) (*marriage*) casamiento *m*, matrimonio *m*; **who thought up this ~?** ¿quién ideó este matrimonio?; **she made a good ~** se casó bien; **he's a good ~** es buen partido.
(**c**) (*Sport*) partido *m*, encuentro *m*; (*race*) carrera *f*; (*Boxing*) lucha *f*; (*Fencing*) asalto *m*; (*quiz etc*) concurso

m; **they never tried to make a ~ of it** no se esforzaron en ningún momento por vencer; **let's make a ~ of it** juguemos con la intención de ganar.

2 *attr* (*Tennis*) ~ **ball** bola *f* de partido; ~ **play** partido *m* serio; ~ **point** punto *m* de match.

3 *vt* (**a**) (*pair off*) emparejar, parear; equiparar; **to ~ A against B** hacer que A compita con B; **they're well ~ed** hacen una buena pareja; **the teams are well ~ed** los equipos son muy iguales.

(**b**) (*equal*) igualar, ser igual a, valer lo que; **A doesn't quite ~ B in originality** en cuanto a originalidad A no vale lo que B; **the results did not ~ our hopes** los resultados no estaban a la altura de nuestras esperanzas.

(**c**) (*clothes, colours*) hacer juego con; **his tie ~es his socks** su corbata hace juego con los calcetines; **can you ~ this silk?** ¿tiene una seda igual que ésta?

4 *vi* hacer juego, armonizar, ser a tono; **with a skirt to ~** con una falda acompañada, con una falda a tono.

◆**match up** *vt two objects* emparejar; *more than two* agrupar.

◆**match up to** *vt* estar a la altura de; **he didn't ~ up to the situation** no estaba a la altura de las circunstancias.

matchbox ['mætʃbɒks] *n* cajita *f* de cerillas.

matching ['mætʃɪŋ] *adj* acompañado, a tono, que hace juego con; ~ **funds** (*US*) fondos *mpl* compensatorios.

matchless ['mætʃlɪs] *adj* sin par, incomparable.

matchmaker ['mætʃ,meɪkə^r] *n* casamentero *m*, -a *f*.

matchmaking ['mætʃ,meɪkɪŋ] **1** *n* actividades *fpl* de casamentero. **2** *adj* casamentero.

matchstick ['mætʃstɪk] *n* fósforo *m*.

matchwood ['mætʃwʊd] *n* astillas *fpl*; **to smash sth to ~** hacer algo añicos; **to be smashed to ~** ser convertido en un montón de astillas.

mate¹ [meɪt] **1** *n* mate *m*. **2** *vti* dar jaque mate a, matar; **white plays and ~s in 2** blanco juega y mata en 2.

mate² [meɪt] **1** *n* (*companion*) compañero *m*, camarada *m*, compinche *m* (*LAm*); (*married*) compañero *m*, -a *f*; cónyuge *mf*; (*Zool*) macho *m*, hembra *f*; (*assistant*) ayudante *m*, peón *m*; (*Brit Naut*) primer oficial *m*, piloto *m*, segundo *m* de a bordo; (*US Naut*) segundo *m* de a bordo; **John and his ~s** Juan y sus compañeros; **plumber's ~** ayudante *m* de fontanero, aprendiz *m* de fontanero; **look here ~*** mire, amigo; mire, compadre; **yes ~*** sí, hombre.

2 *vt* (*Zool*) parear, acoplar; (*fig*) unir; **they are well ~d** hacen una buena pareja.

3 *vi* (*Zool*) parearse, acoplarse; **age should not ~ with youth** no debe casarse el viejo con la joven.

material [mə'tɪərɪəl] **1** *adj* material; importante, esencial; *well-being etc* físico; *loss, damage* importante, considerable; (*Jur*) *fact etc* fundamental, pertinente.

2 *n* (*ingredient, equipment, also fig*) material *m*; (*substance*) materia *f*; (*data*) datos *mpl*, material *m*; (*cloth*) tejido *m*, tela *f*; **~s** material *m*, materiales *mpl*; **~s science** ciencias *fpl* de los materiales.

materialism [mə'tɪərɪəlɪzəm] *n* materialismo *m*.

materialist [mə'tɪərɪəlɪst] **1** *adj* materialista. **2** *n* materialista *mf*.

materialistic [mə'tɪərɪə'lɪstɪk] *adj* materialista.

materialize [mə'tɪərɪəlaɪz] **1** *vt* materializar. **2** *vi* (*spirit*) tomar forma visible; (*idea etc*) materializarse, realizarse, convertirse en hecho.

materially [mə'tɪərɪəlɪ] *adv* materialmente; **that does not ~ alter things** eso no afecta la cosa de modo sensible; **they are not ~ different** no difieren en su esencia.

materiel [mə,tɪərɪ'el] *n* (*US*) material *m* bélico.

maternal [mə'tɜːnl] *adj grandfather etc* materno; *affection etc* maternal.

maternity [mə'tɜːnɪtɪ] **1** *n* maternidad *f*. **2** *attr*: ~ **allowance** (*Brit*) subsidio *m* de natalidad; ~ **dress** vestido *m* premamá; ~ **home,** ~ **hospital** casa *f* de maternidad; ~ **leave** licencia *f* de maternidad, permiso *m* para parto; ~ **ward** sala *f* de partos.

matey* ['meɪtɪ] **1** *adj* (*Brit*) *person* afable, simpático; bonachón; *atmosphere* acogedor; *gathering* sin ceremonias, familiar, de ambiente acogedor. **2** *nm* (*Brit: in direct address*) chico, hijo.

math [mæθ] *n* (*US**) = **mathematics** mates* *fpl*.

mathematical [,mæθə'mætɪkəl] *adj* matemático; **he's a ~ genius** tiene un genio para las matemáticas, es un matemático genial; **I'm not very ~** no tengo instinto para las matemáticas, entiendo poco de matemáticas.

mathematically [,mæθə'mætɪkəlɪ] *adv* matemáticamente.

mathematician [,mæθəmə'tɪʃən] *n* matemático *m*, -a *f*.

mathematics [,mæθə'mætɪks] *n* matemáticas *fpl*.

Mat(h)ilda [mə'tɪldə] *nf* Matilde.

maths* [mæθs], (*US*) **math*** [mæθ] *n* = **mathematics** mates* *fpl*.

matinée ['mætɪneɪ] **1** *n* función *f* de tarde. **2** *attr*: ~ **idol** ídolo *m* del público.

matinee coat ['mætɪneɪ,kəʊt] *n* (*Brit*) abriguito *m* de lana.

matiness* ['meɪtɪnɪs] *n* afabilidad *f*, simpatía *f*; lo bonachón; carácter *m* familiar; ambiente *m* acogedor.

mating ['meɪtɪŋ] **1** *n* (*Zool*) apareamiento *m*, acoplamiento *m*; (*fig*) unión *f*. **2** *attr*: ~ **call** grito *m* del macho; ~ **season** época *f* del celo.

matins ['mætɪnz] *n sg or pl* maitines *mpl*.

matriarch ['meɪtrɪɑːk] *n* matriarca *f*.

matriarchal [,meɪtrɪ'ɑːkl] *adj* matriarcal.

matriarchy ['meɪtrɪɑːkɪ] *n* matriarcado *m*.

matric* [mə'trɪk] *n* (*Brit*) = **matriculation.**

matricide ['meɪtrɪsaɪd] *n* (**a**) (*act*) matricidio *m*. (**b**) (*person*) matricida *mf*.

matriculate [mə'trɪkjʊleɪt] **1** *vt* matricular. **2** *vi* matricularse.

matriculation [mə,trɪkjʊ'leɪʃən] *n* matriculación *f*; (*Brit Univ*) examen *m* de ingreso.

matrimonial [,mætrɪ'məʊnɪəl] *adj* matrimonial; conyugal.

matrimony ['mætrɪmənɪ] *n* matrimonio *m*; vida *f* conyugal.

matrix ['meɪtrɪks], *pl* **matrixes** *or* **matrices** ['meɪtrɪ,siːz] *n* matriz *f*; molde *m*.

matron ['meɪtrən] *n* (*married woman*) matrona *f*; (*in hospital*) supervisora *f*, enfermera *f* jefe (*or* jefa); (*in school*) ama *f* de llaves, ecónoma *f*; (*in hotel*) gobernanta *f*.

matronly ['meɪtrənlɪ] *adj* matronal, de matrona; *figure etc* maduro y algo corpulento.

matron-of-honour, (*US*) **matron-of-honor** ['meɪtrənəv'ɒnə^r] *n*, *pl* **matrons-of-hono(u)r** ['meɪtrənzəv'ɒnə^r] dama *f* de honor (casada).

matt [mæt] *adj* mate.

matted ['mætɪd] *adj* enmarañado, entretejido; espeso; ~ **hair** greña *f*.

matter ['mætə^r] **1** *n* (**a**) (*substance*) materia *f*; sustancia *f*; (*Typ*) material *m*.

(**b**) (*Med*) pus *m*, materia *f*.

(**c**) (*Liter etc*) materia *f*, tema *m*; **form and ~** la forma y el contenido, la forma y la materia.

(**d**) (*question, affair*) asunto *m*, cuestión *f*, cosa *f*; **for that ~, for the ~ of that** si vamos a eso, en cuanto a eso; **in this ~** en este asunto; **in the ~ of** en materia de, en asuntos de; **there's the ~ of my expenses** hay aquello de mis gastos; **it will be a ~ of a few weeks** será cosa de varias semanas; **it's a ~ of a couple of hours** es cosa de dos horas; **in a ~ of 10 minutes** en cosa de 10 minutos; **it is no great ~** es poca cosa, no importa; **that's quite another ~, that's another ~ altogether, that's a very different ~** eso es totalmente distinto, eso es harina de otro costal; **it's an easy ~ to** + *infin* es fácil + *infin*; **it will be no easy ~** no será fácil; **it's a serious ~** es cosa seria; **it's no laughing ~** no es cosa de risa; **business ~s** negocios *mpl*; **money ~s** asuntos *mpl* financieros; **the ~ in hand** el asunto de que se trata; **as ~s stand** tal como están las cosas; **the ~ is closed** el asunto está concluido; **to make ~s worse** para colmo de desgracias; **he doesn't mince ~s** no tiene pelos en la lengua; **well, not to mince ~s** bueno, para decirlo como es; **as a ~ of course** por rutina; **it's a ~ of course with us** con nosotros es cosa de cajón (*V also* **course 1** (**b**)); **as a ~ of fact ...** en realidad ..., el caso es que ...; a decir verdad; **as a ~ of fact we were just talking about you** precisamente estábamos hablando de ti; **it's a ~ of form** es pura formalidad; **it's a ~ of taste** es cuestión de gusto.

(**e**) (*importance*) **no ~, it makes no ~** no importa; **what ~?** ¿qué importa?; **no ~ how you do it** no importa cómo lo hagas; **no ~ what he says** diga lo que diga; **no ~ how big it is** por grande que sea; **no ~ how hot it is** por mucho calor que haga; **no ~ when** no importa cuándo; **no ~ who goes** quienquiera que vaya; **get one, no ~ how** procura uno, del modo que sea.

(**f**) (*difficulty, problem*) **what's the ~?** ¿qué hay?, ¿qué pasa?; **what's the ~ with you?** ¿te pasa algo?, ¿qué tienes?; **what's the ~ with John?** ¿qué le pasa a Juan?; **what's the ~ with my hat?** ¿qué tiene mi sombrero?; ¿qué le pasa a mi sombrero?; **what's the ~ with singing?** ¿es que está prohibido cantar?; **sth's the ~ with the lights** algo les pasa a las luces; **nothing's the ~** no pasa nada; **as if nothing was the ~** como si no hubiese pasado nada, como si tal cosa.

2 *vi* importar; **it doesn't ~** no importa, lo mismo da, es igual; **what does it ~?** ¿qué importa?; **does it ~ to you if I go?** ¿te importa que yo vaya?; **why should it ~ to me?** y a mí ¿qué?; **some things ~ more than others** algunas cosas son más importantes que otras.

matter-of-fact ['mætərəv'fækt] *adj* natural, normal; flemático.

Matthew ['mæθjuː] *nm* Mateo.

matting ['mætɪŋ] *n* estera *f*.

mattins ['mætɪnz] *n sg or pl* = **matins.**

mattock ['mætək] *n* azadón *m*.

mattress ['mætrɪs] *n* colchón *m*.

mature [mə'tjʊəʳ] **1** *adj* maduro; *cheese, man, wine etc* hecho; (*Comm*) vencido; **~ student** estudiante *mf* de edad superior a la normal (*p.ej.*, de 26 años o más); **of ~ years** de edad madura; **to become ~** (*Comm*) vencer. **2** *vti* madurar; (*Comm*) vencer.

maturity [mə'tjʊərɪtɪ] *n* madurez *f*; (*Comm*) vencimiento *m*.

maudlin ['mɔːdlɪn] *adj* (*sentimental*) sensiblero; (*weepy*) llorón, al punto de deshacerse en lágrimas.

maul [mɔːl] *vt* destrozar, magullar, herir; *writer, play etc* maltratar; *text* estropear; **he got badly ~ed in the press** la prensa le puso como un trapo.

maunder ['mɔːndəʳ] *vi* divagar.

Maundy ['mɔːndɪ] *attr*: **~ money** (*Brit*) *dinero que reparte el monarca a los pobres el Jueves Santo*; **~ Thursday** Jueves *m* Santo.

Maurice ['mɒrɪs] *nm* Mauricio.

Mauritania [ˌmɔːrɪ'teɪnɪə] *n* Mauritania *f*.

Mauritanian [ˌmɔːrɪ'teɪnɪən] **1** *adj* mauritano. **2** *n* mauritano *m*, -a *f*.

Mauritian [mə'rɪʃən] **1** *adj* mauriciano. **2** *n* mauriciano *m*, -a *f*.

Mauritius [mə'rɪʃəs] *n* Mauricio *m*.

mausoleum [ˌmɔːsə'liːəm] *n* mausoleo *m*.

mauve [məʊv] **1** *adj* (de) color de malva. **2** *n* color *m* de malva.

maverick ['mævərɪk] **1** *n* (*US Agr*) res *f* sin marcar; (*Pol etc*) disidente *mf*, inconformista *mf*, persona *f* independiente. **2** *adj* disidente, inconformista.

maw [mɔː] *n* (*Anat*) estómago *m*; (*of cow etc*) cuajar *m*; (*of bird*) molleja *f*, buche *m*; (*fig*) fauces *fpl*.

mawkish ['mɔːkɪʃ] *adj* empalagoso, sensiblero, insulso.

mawkishness ['mɔːkɪʃnɪs] *n* sensiblería *f*, insulsez *f*.

max. *adj, n abbr of* **maximum.**

maxi* ['mæksi] *n* (*skirt*) maxifalda *f*, maxi* *f*; (*coat*) maxi* *f*.

maxi... ['mæksi] *pref* maxi...

maxilla [mæk'sɪlə] *n* maxilar *m* superior.

maxim ['mæksɪm] *n* máxima *f*.

maximization [ˌmæksɪmaɪ'zeɪʃən] *n* maximización *f*; potenciación *f*.

maximize ['mæksɪmaɪz] *vt* maximizar, llevar al máximum; potenciar.

maximum ['mæksɪməm] **1** *adj* máximo; **~ efficiency** eficacia *f* máxima; **~ effort** esfuerzo *m* supremo; **~ expenditure** gasto *m* máximo; **~ load** carga *f* máxima; **~ price** precio *m* máximo; **~ speed** velocidad *f* máxima. **2** *n, pl* **maximums** *or* **maxima** ['mæksɪmə] máximo *m*, máximum *m*; tope *m*; **at the ~** como máximo, a lo sumo; **(up) to the ~** al máximo; **up to a ~ of £8** hasta 8 libras como máximum.

maxisingle ['mæksɪ'sɪŋgəl] *n* maxisingle *m*.

May [meɪ] **1** *n* mayo *m*. **2** *attr*: **~ Day** primero *m* de mayo; **~ Queen** reina *f* de mayo.

may¹ [meɪ] *n* (*Bot*) flor *f* del espino; (*Brit: tree*) espino *m*.

may² [meɪ] (*irr: pret* **might**) *vi* **(a)** (*of possibility*) poder, ser posible; **it ~ rain** es posible que llueva, puede llover, puede que llueva; **it ~ be that** ... puede ser que + *subj*, quizá + *subj*; **he ~ not be hungry** puede no tener hambre; **I ~ have said so** es posible que lo haya dicho, puedo haberlo dicho; **I might have said so** pudiera haberlo dicho; **yes, I ~** sí, es posible; **be that as it ~** sea como fuere; **that's as ~ be** eso puede ser; **as soon as ~ be** lo más pronto posible.

(b) (*of permission*) poder, tener permiso para; **yes, you ~** sí, puedes; **if I ~** si me lo permites; **~ I?** ¿me permite?, con permiso; **~ I see it?** ¿me permites verlo?; **~ I come in?** ¿se puede?; **~ I go now?** ¿puedo irme ya?; **you ~ smoke** se permite fumar; **you ~ not smoke** se prohíbe fumar; **if I ~ advise you** si permites que te dé un consejo.

(c) (*auxiliary*) **I hope he ~ succeed** espero que lo logre; **I hoped he might succeed this time** esperaba que lo lograra esta vez; **such a policy as might bring peace** una política que pudiera traernos la paz; **we ~ as well go** más vale irnos, bien podemos irnos; **might I suggest that ...?** me permito sugerir que ...; **mightn't it be better to** + *infin*? ¿no sería aconsejable + *infin*?; **he might have offered to help** bien pudiera habernos ofrecido su ayuda; **you might shut the door!** ¡podrías (*or* podías) cerrar la puerta!; **you might have told me!** ¡habérmelo dicho!; **you might try Smith's** quizá valga la pena de buscarlo en la tienda de Smith; **as you might expect** como era de esperar, según cabía esperar; **run as he might** por mucho que corriese.

(d) (*of wishing*) **~ you be lucky!** ¡que tengas suerte!; **~ you be forgiven!** ¡que Dios le perdone!; **long ~ he reign!** ¡que reine muchos años!; **or ~ I never eat prawns again** o que no vuelva nunca a comer gambas.

(e) (*in questions*) **who might you be?** ¿quién es Vd?; **how old might you be?** ¿cuántos años tendrá Vd?

Maya ['maɪjə], **Mayan** ['maɪjən] **1** *adj* maya. **2** *n* maya *mf*.

maybe ['meɪbiː] **1** *adv* quizá, tal vez. **2** *conj*: **~ he'll come** quizá venga.

mayday ['meɪdeɪ] *n* señal *f* de socorro, s.o.s. *m*.

mayfly ['meɪflaɪ] *n* cachipolla *f*, efímera *f*.

mayhem ['meɪhem] *n* **(a)** alboroto *m*; violencia *f* (personal). **(b)** (*US Jur*) mutilación *f* criminal.

mayn't [meɪnt] = **may not.**

mayo* ['meɪəʊ] *n* (*US*) mayonesa *f*.

mayonnaise [meɪə'neɪz] *n* mayonesa *f*.

mayor [mɛəʳ] *n* alcalde *m*, alcadesa *f*, intendente *m* (*LAm*); **Mr M~** Señor Alcalde; **Madam M~** Señora Alcaldesa.

mayoralty ['mɛərəltɪ] *n* alcaldía *f*.

mayoress ['mɛəres] *n* alcaldesa *f*.

maypole ['meɪpəʊl] *n* mayo *m*.

maze [meɪz] *n* laberinto *m*; **to be in a ~** (*fig*) estar perplejo.

MB **(a)** *n abbr of* **Bachelor of Medicine.** **(b)** *n abbr of* **megabyte.** **(c)** (*Canada*) *abbr of* **Manitoba.**

M.B.A. *n* (*US*) *abbr of* **Master of Business Administration** *título universitario*.

MBBS, MChB *n abbrs of* **Bachelor of Medicine and Surgery** *título universitario*.

M.B.E. *n* (*Brit*) *abbr of* **Member of the Order of the British Empire** *título ceremonial*.

MC *n* **(a)** *abbr of* **Master of Ceremonies** (*V* **master 1**). **(b)** (*US*) *abbr of* **Member of Congress** *diputado del Congreso de EE.UU.*

MCAT *n* (*US*) *abbr of* **Medical College Admissions Test.**

MCP *n abbr of* **male chauvinist pig** (*V* **chauvinist**).

m/cycle *abbr of* **motorcycle** motocicleta *f*.

MD **(a)** *n abbr of* **Doctor of Medicine.**

(b) *n abbr of* **managing director** director *m*, -ora *f* gerente.

(c) *abbr of* **mentally deficient** de inteligencia inferior a la normal.

(d) (*US Post*) *abbr of* **Maryland.**

MDT *n* (*US*) *abbr of* **Mountain Daylight Time.**

ME **(a)** *n abbr of* **myalgic encephalomyelitis.** **(b)** *n* (*US*) *abbr of* **medical examiner.** **(c)** (*US Post*) *abbr of* **Maine.**

me¹ [miː] *pron* me; (*after prep*) mí; **like ~** como yo; **what, ~?** ¿cómo, yo?; **with ~** conmigo; **dear ~!** ¡vaya!; **it's ~** soy yo; **it's ~, Paul** (*identifying self*) soy Pablo.

me² [miː] *n* (*Mus*) mi *m*.

mead [miːd] *n* aguamiel *f*, hidromiel *m*.

meadow ['medəʊ] *n* prado *m*, pradera *f*; (*esp water ~*) vega *f*.

meadowsweet ['medəʊswiːt] *n* reina *f* de los prados.

meagre, (*US*) **meager** ['miːgəʳ] *adj* escaso, exiguo, pobre.

meal¹ [miːl] *n* (*flour*) harina *f*.

meal² [miːl] **1** *n* comida *f*; **~s on wheels** servicio *m* de comidas a domicilio (para ancianos); **I don't eat between ~s** no como entre horas; **to have a ~** comer; **to have a good ~** comer bien; **to make a ~ of sth** comer algo, contentarse con comer algo; (*fig*) exagerar un asunto, sacar todo el jugo posible de un asunto.

2 *attr*: **~ ticket** vale *m* de comida.

mealtime ['miːltaɪm] *n* hora *f* de comer.

mealy ['miːlɪ] *adj* harinoso.

mealy-mouthed ['miːlɪ'maʊðd] *adj* excesivamente circunspecto; **let us not be ~ about it** hablemos claro sobre esto.

mean¹ [miːn] *adj* **(a)** (*Brit: stingy*) tacaño, agarrado.

(b) (*unpleasant, unkind*) mezquino; **a ~ trick** una mala pasada; **don't be ~!** ¡no seas malo!; **you ~ thing!** ¡qué malo eres!; **you were ~ to me** me has tratado mal; **it made me feel ~** me hizo sentir vergüenza; **that was pretty ~ of them** se han portado bastante mal.

(c) (*inferior*) inferior; *birth* humilde, pobre; (*shabby*) humilde, vil; **the ~est citizen** el menor ciudadano; **obvious**

to the ~est intelligence obvio para quien tiene un poco de sentido común; **he is no ~ player** es un jugador nada despreciable.

(**d**) (*US*) formidable, de primera; **he plays a ~ game** juega estupendamente.

mean[2] [mi:n] **1** *adj* medio; **~ life** (*Phys*) vida *f* media.

2 *n* (**a**) (*middle term*) medio *m*, promedio *m*, término *m* medio; (*Math*) media *f*.

(**b**) **~s** (*method*) medio *m*, manera *f*, método *m*; **~s to an end** medio *m* de conseguir un fin; **there is no ~s of doing it** no hay modo de hacerlo; **he was the ~s of sending it** fue el quien nos proporcionó un medio de enviarlo; **by all ~s** por todos los medios, (*fig*) por cierto; **by all ~s!** ¡naturalmente!, ¡claro que sí!; **by all ~s take one** por favor toma uno; **by any ~s** de cualquier modo, del modo que sea; **by no ~s, not by any ~s** de ningún modo; **by no ~s!** ¡de ningún modo!; **it is by no ~s difficult** no es nada difícil; **by ~s of** por medio de, mediante; **by this ~s** por este medio, de este modo; **by fair ~s** por medios rectos; **by fair ~s or foul** por las buenas o por las malas.

(**c**) (*Fin*) **~s** recursos *mpl*, medios *mpl*, fondos *mpl*, dinero *m*; **a man of ~s** un hombre acaudalado; **we have no ~s to do it** nos faltan recursos para hacerlo; **to have private ~s** tener ingresos privados; **to live beyond one's ~s** vivir por encima de sus posibilidades, gastar más de lo que se gana; **to live within one's ~s** vivir con arreglo a los ingresos, vivir dentro de los medios.

3 *attr*: **~s test** averiguación *f* de los recursos económicos (*del que pide asistencia pública etc*).

mean[3] [mi:n] (*irr*: *pret and ptp* **meant**) *vt* (**a**) (*intend*: *with noun etc*) pretender, intentar; **he ~s well** tiene buenas intenciones; **I ~ it** lo digo en serio; **do you ~ it?** ¿lo dices en serio?; **you can't ~ it!** ¡vaya!; **I ~t it as a joke** lo dije en broma; **I ~ what I say** lo digo muy en serio, lo digo con la mayor seriedad; **he ~s no harm** tiene buenas intenciones; **I ~t no harm by what I said** no lo dije con mala idea; **he ~t no offence** no tenía la intención de ofender a nadie; **8, I ~ 9** 8, quiero decir 9; 8, mejor dicho 9; 8, digo 9.

(**b**) (*intend*: *with verb*) **to ~ to** + *infin* pensar + *infin*, proponerse + *infin*, pretender + *infin*; **what do you ~ to do?** ¿qué piensas hacer?; **I ~t to help** tenía la intención de ayudar; **he didn't ~ to do it** lo hizo sin querer; **this picture is ~t to tell a story** este cuadro se propone contar una historia; **this photo is ~t to be Anne** esta foto quiere ser Ana; **she wasn't ~t to be prime minister** no había intención de que ella llegara a ser primera ministra; **I ~ to be obeyed** insisto en que se me obedezca; **I ~ to have it** quiero tenerlo, me propongo obtenerlo; **if he ~s to be awkward** si quiere ser difícil; **we were ~t to arrive at 8** debíamos llegar a las 8.

(**c**) (*destine*) destinar (*for* a, para); **this present was ~t for you** este regalo era para ti; **do you ~ me?** ¿es a mí?; **was that remark ~t for me?** esa observación ¿iba dirigida contra mí?; **he ~t that for you** lo dijo por ti.

(**d**) (*suppose*) suponer; **it's ~t to be a good car** este coche se supone que es bueno; **parents are ~t to love their children** se supone que los padres quieren a sus hijos; **you're not ~t to drink it!** ¡no te lo dan para que lo bebas!

(**e**) (*signify*: *person, statement etc*) querer decir (*by* con); (*word*) significar (*to* para); **what does 'ohm' ~?** ¿qué quiere decir 'ohmio'?; **what do you ~ by that?** ¿qué quieres decir con eso?; **'vest' ~s sth different in America** en América 'vest' tiene otro significado, en América 'vest' significa otra cosa; **the name ~s nothing to me** el nombre no me suena; **it ~s a lot of expense for us** nos supone unos grandes gastos; **this ~s our ruin** esto es nuestra ruina, esto significa nuestra ruina; **a pound ~s a lot to her** para ella una libra es mucho dinero; **the play didn't ~ a thing to me** poca cosa saqué en claro de la obra; **your friendship ~s much to me** tu amistad es muy importante para mí; **it ~s a lot to have you with us** nos importa mucho tenerte con nosotros; **you know what it ~s to hit a policeman?** ¿Vd sabe qué consecuencias trae el golpear a un policía?; **don't I ~ anything to you?** ¿no significo yo nada para ti?, ¿no tengo yo siquiera un poquito de importancia para ti?; *V* **know 2 (a)**.

meander [mɪ'ændə^{r}] **1** *n* meandro *m*; **~s** (*fig*) meandros *mpl*. **2** *vi* (*river*) serpentear; (*person etc*) andar sin propósito fijo, vagar; (*in speech*) divagar.

meandering [mɪ'ændərɪŋ] *adj river* con meandros; *road* serpenteante; *account, speech etc* largo y confuso, prolijo y poco lógico.

meanderings [mɪ'ændərɪŋz] *npl* (*fig*) divagaciones *fpl*.

meanie* ['mi:nɪ] *n*: **he's an old ~** es un tío agarrado*.

meaning ['mi:nɪŋ] **1** *adj look etc* significativo, lleno de intención.

2 *n* (**a**) (*intention*) intención *f*, propósito *m*; **a look full of ~** una mirada llena de intención; **to mistake sb's ~** interpretar mal la intención de uno.

(**b**) (*sense of words etc*) sentido *m*, significado *m*; (*particular sense of word*) acepción *f*; (*general impact*) significación *f*; **I don't get your ~** no comprendo lo que quieres decir; **if you get my ~** ¿me entiendes?; **what's the ~ of 'hick'?** ¿qué significa 'hick'?, ¿qué quiere decir 'hick'?; **what's the ~ of this?** (*as reprimand*) y esto ¿qué quiere decir?; **life has no ~ for her now** ahora para ella la vida no tiene sentido; **honesty? she doesn't understand the ~ of the word** ¿la honradez? ni sabe lo que eso quiere decir.

meaningful ['mi:nɪŋfʊl] *adj* significativo, que tiene sentido; válido, justificado; útil; *relationship* serio.

meaningless ['mi:nɪŋlɪs] *adj* sin sentido; (*rash, mad*) insensato; **in this situation it is ~** en esta situación no tiene sentido; **to write 'xybj' is ~** escribir 'xybj' carece de sentido.

meanly ['mi:nlɪ] *adv* (**a**) (*stingily*) de manera tacaña, con tacañería. (**b**) (*unkindly*) de manera mezquina, con mezquindad.

meanness ['mi:nnɪs] *n* humildad *f*; vileza *f*, bajeza *f*; tacañería *f*; mezquindad *f*; maldad *f*.

means-test ['mi:nztest] *vt person* averiguar los recursos económicos de; **this benefit is ~ed** este subsidio se otorga después de averiguar los recursos económicos (del que lo pide).

meant [ment] *pret and ptp of* **mean**[3].

meantime ['mi:n'taɪm] *adv*, **meanwhile** ['mi:n'waɪl] *adv* entretanto, mientras tanto; **in the ~** mientras tanto, en el ínterin.

measles ['mi:zlz] *n* sarampión *m*.

measly* ['mi:zlɪ] *adj* miserable, cochino, mezquino.

measurable ['meʒərəbl] *adj* mensurable, que se puede medir; (*perceptible*) apreciable, perceptible.

measure ['meʒə^{r}] **1** *n* (**a**) (*system of ~*) medida *f*; **~ of capacity** medida *f* de capacidad; **I think we have his ~ now** creo que le tenemos calado ya; **to take sb's ~** (*fig*) tomar las medidas a uno.

(**b**) (*rule etc*) regla *f*; (*glass*: *Chem*) probeta *f* graduada.

(**c**) (*limit*) **beyond ~** hasta no más; excesivamente; **better beyond ~** incomparablemente mejor; **in full ~** abundantemente; **for good ~** por añadidura; **in great ~, in large ~** en gran parte; **in some ~** hasta cierto punto; **this is due in no small ~ to X** esto se debe en no pequeña medida a X; **we had some ~ of success** hasta cierto punto tuvimos éxito; **it gives a ~ of protection** da cierta protección.

(**d**) (*step*) medida *f*; (*Parl*) (*bill*) proyecto *m* de ley; (*act*) ley *f*; **to take ~s** tomar medidas (*to* + *infin* para + *infin*); **to take extreme ~s** tomar medidas extremas.

(**e**) (*Geol*) **coal ~s** depósitos *mpl* de carbón.

(**f**) (*Mus*) compás *m*.

(**g**) (*of spirits etc*) ración *f*.

2 *vt* (**a**) medir; *person* (*for height*) tallar, (*for clothes*) tomar las medidas a; *words etc* pesar, pensar bien; *V* **length.** (**b**) (*fig*) medir; **how shall we ~ success?** ¿cómo vamos a medir el éxito?; **in this exercise we ~ performance** en este ejercicio evaluamos la actuación; **can we ~ him against his colleagues?** ¿podemos compararle con sus colegas?

3 *vi* medir; **it ~s 3 metres by 2 metres** mide 3 metros por 2 metros; **what does it ~?** ¿cuánto mide?

◆**measure off** *vt* medir.

◆**measure out** *vt* medir; (*issue*) repartir, distribuir.

◆**measure up** *vt person* valorar, juzgar.

◆**measure up to** *vt*: **to ~ up to sth** estar a la altura de algo.

measured ['meʒəd] *adj tread etc* deliberado, rítmico, acompasado; *tone* mesurado; *statement etc* moderado, circunspecto, prudente.

measureless ['meʒəlɪs] *adj* inmensurable, inmenso.

measurement ['meʒəmənt] *n* (**a**) (*system*) medición *f*. (**b**) (*measure*) medida *f*; dimensión *f*; **to take sb's ~s** tomar las medidas a uno.

measuring ['meʒərɪŋ] **1** *n* medición *f*; **to take ~s of** hacer mediciones de. **2** *attr*: **~ chain** cadena *f* de agrimensor; **~ glass, ~ jug** mesura *f*; **~ rod** vara *f* de medir; **~ spoon** cuchara *f* medidora; **~ tape** cinta *f* métrica.

meat [mi:t] **1** *n* carne *f*; (*fig*) sustancia *f*, meollo *m*, jugo *m*; **cold ~** fiambre *m*, carne *f* fiambre; **a book with some ~ in**

it un libro sólido, un libro jugoso; **one man's ~ is another man's poison** lo que a uno cura a otro mata; **it's ~ and drink to me** no puedo vivir sin él.

2 *attr*: de carne; *industry etc, product* cárnico; **~ extract** extracto *m* de carne; **~ grinder** (*US*) máquina *f* de picar carne; **~ hook** gancho *m* carnicero; **~ loaf** *rollo de carne picada cocida*; **~ pie** pastel *m* de carne, empanada *f*; **~ safe** (*Brit*) fresquera *f*.

meatball ['mi:t'bɔ:l] *n* albóndiga *f*.

meat-eater ['mi:t,i:tər] *n* persona *f* que come carne; (*Zool*) carnívoro *m*, -a *f*; **we're not ~s** no comemos carne.

meat-eating ['mi:t,i:tɪŋ] *adj* carnívoro.

meatfly ['mi:tflaɪ] *n* mosca *f* de la carne.

meathead‡ ['mi:thed] *n* (*US*) idiota *mf*, gilipollas‡ *mf*.

meatless ['mi:tlɪs] *adj*: **~ day** día *m* de vigilia; **~ diet** dieta *f* sin carne.

meaty ['mi:tɪ] *adj* carnoso; (*fig*) sustancioso, jugoso, sólido.

Mecca ['mekə] *n* La Meca; **a ~ for tourists** un lugar (*etc*) de grandes atracciones para el turista.

mechanic [mɪ'kænɪk] *n* mecánico *mf*.

mechanical [mɪ'kænɪkəl] *adj* mecánico; (*fig*) maquinal; **~ drawing** dibujo *m* mecánico; **~ engineer** ingeniero *m* mecánico, ingeniera *f* mecánica; **~ engineering** ingeniería *f* mecánica, mecánica *f* industrial; **~ pencil** (*US*) lapicero *m*.

mechanically [mɪ'kænɪkəlɪ] *adv* mecánicamente; (*fig*) maquinalmente.

mechanics [mɪ'kænɪks] *n* mecánica *f*; mecanismo *m*, técnica *f*.

mechanism ['mekənɪzəm] *n* (*most senses*) mecanismo *m*; (*Philos*) mecanicismo *m*.

mechanistic [,mekə'nɪstɪk] *adj* mecánico, maquinal; (*Philos*) mecanístico.

mechanization [,mekənaɪ'zeɪʃən] *n* mecanización *f*.

mechanize ['mekənaɪz] *vt* mecanizar; motorizar.

mechanized ['mekənaɪzd] *adj process etc* mecanizado; *troops, unit* motorizado.

Med* [med] *n*: **the ~** el Mediterráneo.

M.Ed. *n abbr of* **Master of Education** *título universitario*.

medal ['medl] *n* medalla *f*; **he deserves a ~ for it** merece un galardón; **to have a ~ showing*** tener la farmacia abierta*.

medallion [mɪ'dælɪən] *n* medallón *m*.

medallist, (*US*) **medalist** ['medəlɪst] *n* (*Sport*) medallero *m*, -a *f*; *V* **gold** *etc*.

meddle ['medl] *vi* entrometerse (*in* en); **to ~ with sth** manosear algo, tocar algo, (*and damage*) estropear algo; **who asked you to ~?** ¿quién le mete a Vd en esto?; **he's always meddling** es un entrometido.

meddler ['medlər] *n* entrometido *m*, -a *f*.

meddlesome ['medlsəm] *adj*, **meddling¹** ['medlɪŋ] *adj* entrometido.

meddlesomeness ['medlsəmnɪs] *n* entrometimiento *m*.

meddling² ['medlɪŋ] *n* intromisión *f*.

Mede [mi:d] *n* medo *m*; **the ~s and the Persians** los medos y los persas.

media ['mi:dɪə] **1** *npl* medios *mpl* de comunicación, medios *mpl* de difusión. **2** *attr*: **~ analysis** análisis *m* de los medios; **~ coverage** cobertura *f* periodística; **~ event** acontecimiento *m* periodístico; **~ man** periodista *m*; agente *m* de publicidad; **~ person** personaje *m* de los medios de comunicación; **~ research** investigación *f* de los medios de publicidad; **~ studies** (*Univ*) periodismo *m*.

mediaeval [,medɪ'i:vəl] *adj* (*etc*) *V* **medieval** (*etc*).

medial ['mi:dɪəl] *adj* medial.

median ['mi:dɪən] **1** *adj* mediano. **2** *n* (**a**) (*US*: *also* **~ divider, ~ strip**) mediana *f*, franja *f* central, faja *f* intermedia. (**b**) (*Math*) número *m* medio; punto *m* medio.

mediate ['mi:dɪeɪt] *vi* mediar (*between* entre, *in* en).

mediation [,mi:dɪ'eɪʃən] *n* mediación *f*.

mediator ['mi:dɪeɪtər] *n* mediador *m*, -ora *f*, árbitro *mf*.

medic* ['medɪk] *n* médico *mf*; (*Univ*) estudiante *mf* de medicina.

Medicaid ['medɪ,keɪd] *n* (*US*) ≈ Seguro *m* de Enfermedad.

medical ['medɪkəl] **1** *adj* médico; **~ bulletin** boletín *m* facultativo; **~ care** atención *f* médica; **~ certificate** certificado *m* médico; **~ corps** cuerpo *m* de sanidad; **~ examination** reconocimiento *m* médico; **~ examiner** (*US*) médico *mf* forense; **~ inspection** visita *f* del médico; **~ jurisprudence** medicina *f* legal; **~ kit** botiquín *m*; **~ man** médico *m*; **~ officer** médico *mf*, (*Mil*) oficial *m* médico, (*of town*) jefe *mf* de sanidad municipal; **~ practitioner** médico *mf*; **the ~ profession** la profesión médica; **~ record** historia *f* clínica; **~ school** facultad *f* de medicina; **~ service** servicio *m* médico; **~ student** estudiante *mf* de medicina; **~ treatment** tratamiento *m* médico, asistencia *f* médica.

2 *n* (*) reconocimiento *m* médico.

medically ['medɪkəlɪ] *adv* médicamente; **~ speaking** desde el punto de vista médico; **to be ~ examined** tener un reconocimiento médico.

medicament [me'dɪkəmənt] *n* medicamento *m*.

Medicare ['medɪkɛər] *n* (*US*) seguro *m* médico del Estado.

medicate ['medɪkeɪt] *vt* medicar; impregnar (*with* de); **~d shampoo** champú *m* médico.

medication [,medɪ'keɪʃən] *n* medicación *f*.

medicinal [me'dɪsɪnl] *adj* medicinal.

medicine ['medsɪn,'medɪsɪn] *n* medicina *f*; medicamento *m*; **to take one's ~** (*fig*) sufrir las consecuencias. **2** *attr*: **~ box, ~ cabinet, ~ chest** botiquín *m*.

medicine ball ['medsɪn,bɔ:l] *n* (*Sport*) pelota *f* medicinal.

medicine man ['medsɪnmæn] *n*, *pl* **medicine men** ['medsɪnmen] hechizador *m*.

medico* ['medɪkəʊ] *n* médico *mf*.

medieval [,medɪ'i:vəl] *adj* medieval.

medievalism [,medɪ'i:vəlɪzəm] *n* medievalismo *m*.

medievalist [,medɪ'i:vəlɪst] *n* medievalista *mf*.

mediocre [,mi:dɪ'əʊkər] *adj* mediocre, mediano.

mediocrity [,mi:dɪ'ɒkrɪtɪ] *n* mediocridad *f*, medianía *f* (*also person*).

meditate ['medɪteɪt] **1** *vt* meditar. **2** *vi* meditar (*on sth* algo), reflexionar (*on* en, sobre).

meditation [,medɪ'teɪʃən] *n* meditación *f*.

meditative ['medɪtətɪv] *adj* meditabundo.

Mediterranean [,medɪtə'reɪnɪən] **1** *adj* mediterráneo; **~ Sea** Mar *m* Mediterráneo. **2** *n* Mediterráneo *m*.

medium ['mi:dɪəm] **1** *adj quality etc* mediano, regular; *size* mediano, intermedio; *wave* medio; **of ~ height** de estatura regular; **of ~ difficulty** de mediana dificultad; **~ frequency** media frecuencia *f*; **~ range missile** misil *m* de alcance medio; **~ rare** medio hecho, sonrosado.

2 *n* (**a**) (*pl in some senses* **media** ['mi:dɪə]) medio *m*; **through the ~ of** por medio de.

(**b**) (*spiritualist*) médium *mf*; *V also* **media**.

medium-dry [,mi:dɪəm'draɪ] *adj* semi-seco, semi.

medium-fine ['mi:dɪəm'faɪn] *adj* entrefino.

medium-priced [,mi:dɪəm'praɪst] *adj* de precio medio.

medium-sized ['mi:dɪəm'saɪzd] *adj* mediano, de tamaño mediano; **~ business** empresa *f* mediana.

medlar ['medlər] *n* (*fruit*) níspola *f*; (*tree*) níspero *m*.

medley ['medlɪ] *n* mezcla *f*, mezcolanza *f*; miscelánea *f*; (*Mus*) popurrí *m*.

medulla [me'dʌlə] *n* medula *f*.

meek [mi:k] *adj* manso, dócil, sumiso; **to be very ~ and mild** (*person*) ser como una malva.

meekly ['mi:klɪ] *adv* mansamente, dócilmente, sumisamente.

meekness ['mi:knɪs] *n* mansedumbre *f*, docilidad *f*.

meerschaum ['mɪəʃəm] *n* espuma *f* de mar; (*pipe*) pipa *f* de espuma de mar.

meet¹ [mi:t] *adj* (*liter*) conveniente, apropiado; **it is ~ that ...** conviene que + *subj*; **to be ~ for** ser apto para.

meet² [mi:t] (*irr*: *pret and ptp* **met**) **1** *vt* (**a**) *person etc* (*encounter*) encontrar; (*accidentally*) encontrarse con; (*by arrangement*) reunirse con, (*formally*) entrevistarse con; **to arrange to ~ sb** citarse con uno, dar una cita a uno.

(**b**) *difficulty* encontrar, tropezar con; hacer frente a; *death* hallar, encontrar; *opponent, opposing team* enfrentarse con, (*in duel*) batirse con; **he met his death in 1800** halló la muerte en 1800; **to ~ death calmly** enfrentarse tranquilamente con la muerte; **to ~ death courageously** ir resueltamente a su muerte.

(**c**) (*go to ~*) ir a recibir, ir a buscar, esperar, ir al encuentro de; **I'll ~ you at the garage** te espero en el garaje; **we met her at the station** fuimos a recibirla en la estación; **don't bother to ~ me** no os molestéis viniendo a buscarme; **the car will ~ the train** el coche esperará la llegada del tren; **the bus ~s the aircraft** hay correspondencia entre el autobús y el avión.

(**d**) (*get to know*) conocer; **I never met him** no le conocí nunca, no le llegué a conocer; **I met my wife in 1960** conocí a mi mujer en 1960; **~ Mr Jones** quiero presentarle al Sr Jones; **I am very pleased to ~ you** tengo mucho gusto en conocerle; **pleased to ~ you!** ¡tanto gusto!

(**e**) **what a scene met my eyes!** ¡qué cosas se presentaron a mis ojos!; **I could not ~ his eye** no podía mirarle a los ojos.

(**f**) *charge* refutar; *debt* pagar, honrar, satisfacer;

deficit cubrir; *expense* sostener, correr con, hacer frente a; *liabilities* honrar; *need* satisfacer, cubrir; (*Comm*) *demand* atender, satisfacer; *objection* responder a; *obligation* atender, cumplir; *requirement* satisfacer; *wish* conformarse con, condescender con, satisfacer; *scorn* tener que aguantar.

2 *vi* (**a**) (*encounter each other*) encontrarse, verse; (*by arrangement*) reunirse, verse; (*meeting, society*) reunirse; **the society ~s at 8** la sociedad se reúne a las 8, la sesión de la sociedad comienza a las 8; **let's ~ at 8** citémonos para las 8; **until we ~ again!** ¡hasta la vista!; **keep it until we ~ again** guárdalo hasta que nos veamos.

(**b**) (*get to know*) conocerse; **we met in Seville** nos conocimos en Sevilla; **we have met before** nos conocemos ya; **have we met?** ¿nos conocimos antes?

(**c**) (*fight*) batirse; **Bilbao and Valencia will ~ in the final** el Bilbao se enfrentará con el Valencia en la final, Bilbao y Valencia se disputarán la final.

(**d**) (*join*) encontrarse; **our eyes met** cruzamos una mirada, nos miramos el uno al otro; **where the rivers ~** donde confluyen los ríos; **the roads ~ at Toledo** las carreteras empalman en Toledo; **these qualities ~ in her** estas cualidades se dan cita en ella.

3 *n* (*US Sport*) encuentro *m*, reunión *f*; (*Hunting*) cacería *f*.

◆**meet up** *vi*: **to ~ up with sb** reunirse con uno; **this road ~s up with the motorway** esta carretera empalma con la autopista.

◆**meet with** *vt* (*esp US*) *person* juntarse con, reunirse con; *kindness etc* encontrar; *accident* tener; sufrir; *loss* sufrir; *shock* experimentar; *reaction* suscitar, provocar; *success* tener; *difficulty* tropezar con.

meeting ['mi:tɪŋ] *n* (**a**) (*between 2 persons: accidental*) encuentro *m*, (*arranged*) cita *f*, compromiso *m* (*LAm*), (*formal*) entrevista *f*; **~ of minds** encuentro *m* de inteligencias; **the minister had a ~ with the ambassador** el ministro se entrevistó con el embajador.

(**b**) (*assembly*) reunión *f*; (*esp of legislative body*) sesión *f*; (*popular gathering*) mitin *m*; **~ of creditors** concurso *m* de acreedores; **~ of minds** acuerdo *m*; **to address the ~** tomar la palabra en la reunión, dirigirse a los asistentes; **to call a ~ of shareholders** convocar una junta de accionistas; **to adjourn** (*or* **close**) **the ~** levantar la sesión; **to hold a ~** celebrar una junta, (*Parl*) celebrar sesión; **to open the ~** abrir la sesión.

(**c**) (*Sport: eg athletic*) concurso *m*; (*horse races*) reunión *f*; (*clash between teams*) encuentro *m*.

(**d**) (*of rivers*) confluencia *f*.

meeting-house ['mi:tɪŋ,haʊs] *n*, *pl* **meeting-houses** ['mi:tɪŋ,haʊzɪz] templo *m* (de los cuáqueros).

meeting-place ['mi:tɪŋpleɪs] *n* (*of 2 persons*) lugar *m* de cita, (*of many*) punto *m* de reunión; **this bar was their usual ~** solían citarse en este bar, acostumbraban reunirse en este bar.

Meg [meg] *nf familiar form of* **Margaret**.

mega‡ ['megə] *adj* súper*.

mega... ['megə] *pref* mega...

megabuck* ['megə,bʌk] *n*: **now he's making ~s** (*US*) ahora está ganando una pasta gansa‡, ahora se está forrando de dinero*; **we're talking ~s** hablamos de muchísimos dólares.

megabyte ['megə,baɪt] *n* megabyte *m*, megaocteto *m*.

megacycle ['megə,saɪkl] *n* megaciclo *m*.

megadeath ['megə,deθ] *n* muerte *f* de un millón de personas.

megahertz ['megə,hɜ:ts] *n* megahercio *m*.

megalith ['megəlɪθ] *n* megalito *m*.

megalithic [,megə'lɪθɪk] *adj* megalítico.

megalomania ['megələʊ'meɪnɪə] *n* megalomanía *f*.

megalomaniac ['megələʊ'meɪnɪæk] *n* megalómano *m*, -a *f*.

megalopolis [,megə'lɒpəlɪs] *n* megalópolis *f*.

megaphone ['megəfəʊn] *n* megáfono *m*; **~ diplomacy** diplomacia *f* megafónica.

megaton ['megətʌn] *n* megatón *m*.

megavolt ['megəvəʊlt] *n* megavoltio *m*.

megawatt ['megəwɒt] *n* megavatio *m*.

melamine ['meləmi:n] *n* melamina *f*.

melancholia [,melən'kəʊlɪə] *n* melancolía *f*.

melancholic [,melən'kɒlɪk] *adj* melancólico.

melancholically [,melən'kɒlɪklɪ] *adv* melancólicamente.

melancholy ['melənkəlɪ] **1** *adj* melancólico; *duty, sight etc* triste. **2** *n* melancolía *f*.

melanin ['melənɪn] *n* melanina *f*.

melanism ['melənɪzəm] *n* melanismo *m*.

melanoma [,melə'nəʊmə] *n* melanoma *m*.

Melba toast ['melbə'təʊst] *n* tostada *f* delgada.

melée ['meleɪ] *n* pelea *f* confusa, refriega *f*; tumulto *m*; **there was such a ~ at the booking office** se apiñaba la gente delante de la taquilla; **it got lost in the ~** se perdió en el tumulto.

mellifluous [me'lɪfluəs] *adj* melifluo.

mellow ['meləʊ] **1** *adj fruit etc* maduro, dulce; *wine* añejo; *colour, sound* dulce; *light* suave; *voice* suave, meloso; *instrument* melodioso; *character* maduro y tranquilo; **in ~ old age** en la vejez tranquila; **to be ~*** estar entre dos luces*; **to get ~*** achisparse*.

2 *vt* madurar; suavizar, ablandar.

3 *vi* madurarse; suavizarse, ablandarse.

mellowing ['meləʊɪŋ] *n* maduración *f*.

mellowness ['meləʊnɪs] *n* madurez *f*; dulzura *f*, suavidad *f*; lo melodioso.

melodic [mɪ'lɒdɪk] *adj* melódico.

melodious [mɪ'ləʊdɪəs] *adj* melodioso.

melodiously [mɪ'ləʊdɪəslɪ] *adv* melodiosamente.

melodrama ['meləʊ,drɑ:mə] *n* melodrama *m*.

melodramatic [,meləʊdrə'mætɪk] *adj* melodramático.

melodramatically [,meləʊdrə'mætɪklɪ] *adv* melodramáticamente.

melody ['melədɪ] *n* melodía *f*.

melon ['melən] *n* melón *m*.

melt [melt] **1** *vt metal* fundir; *snow* derretir; *chemical* disolver; (*fig*) *heart etc* ablandar.

2 *vi* fundirse; derretirse; disolverse; ablandarse, enternecerse; **it ~s in the mouth** se derrite en la boca; **to ~ into tears** deshacerse en lágrimas; **the gunman ~ed into the crowd** el pistolero desapareció en la multitud.

◆**melt away** *vi* (*money, confidence etc*) esfumarse, desvanecerse, desaparecer misteriosamente; (*crowd etc*) dispersarse; (*person*) desaparecer silenciosamente, escurrirse.

◆**melt down** *vt* fundir.

meltdown ['meltdaʊn] *n* fusión *f* de un reactor, fundido *m*.

melting ['meltɪŋ] **1** *adj look etc* tierno, dulce. **2** *n* fundición *f*; derretimiento *m*; disolución *f*.

melting-point ['meltɪŋpɔɪnt] *n* punto *m* de fusión.

melting-pot ['meltɪŋpɒt] *n* crisol *m* (*also fig*); **the plan is in the ~** el plan está sujeto a una revisión completa; **it is a nation in the ~** es una nación en formación.

meltwater ['meltwɔ:tə^r] *n* agua *f* de fusión de la nieve.

member ['membə^r] *n* (**a**) (*person*) miembro *m*; (*of company, society*) miembro *mf*, socio *m*; (*of party*) miembro *mf*, militante *mf*, afiliado *m*, -a *f*; (*Parl*) miembro *m*, diputado *m*, -a *f*; **'~s only'** 'reservado a los socios', 'sólo para socios'; **~ of Congress** (*US*) miembro *mf* del Congreso; **~ of the family** miembro *m* de la familia; **~ of parliament** (*Brit*) diputado *m*, -a *f*, miembro *mf* del parlamento, (*Spain*) diputado *m*, -a *f* a Cortes; **~ of the crew** tripulante *mf*; **if any ~ of the audience ...** si cualquiera de los asistentes ...; **the ~ for Woodford** el diputado por Woodford; **full ~** miembro *mf* de número; **the ~ countries** los países miembros (*of* de).

(**b**) (*Anat*) miembro *m*; (*male ~*) miembro *m* viril.

membership ['membəʃɪp] **1** *n* (**a**) (*state*) calidad *f* de miembro (*or* socio); (*Pol: members*) militancia *f*; **Britain's ~ of** (*US:* **in**) **the Common Market** (*act*) el ingreso de Gran Bretaña en el Mercado Común; (*state*) la pertenencia de Gran Bretaña al Mercado Común; **when I applied for ~ of** (*US:* **in**) **the club** cuando solicité el ingreso en el club, cuando quise hacerme socio del club; **~ carries certain rights** el ser miembro da ciertos derechos.

(**b**) (*numerical*) número *m* de miembros (*or* socios); **what is your ~?** ¿cuántos miembros tienes?

2 *attr*: **~ card** tarjeta *f* de afiliación; **~ fee** cuota *f* de socio; **~ list** relación *f* de socios.

membrane ['membreɪn] *n* membrana *f*.

membranous [mem'breɪnəs] *adj* membranoso.

memento [mə'mentəʊ] *n* recuerdo *m*.

memo* ['meməʊ] *n abbr of* **memorandum** memorándum *m*, memo *m*; **~ pad** bloc *m* de notas.

memoir ['memwɑ:^r] *n* memoria *f*; biografía *f*, autobiografía *f*; nota *f* biográfica; **~s** memorias *fpl*.

memorabilia [,memərə'bɪlɪə] *npl* (*objects*) cosas *fpl* memorables, recuerdos *mpl*; (*events*) acontecimientos *mpl* notables.

memorable ['memərəbl] *adj* memorable.

memorably ['memərəblɪ] *adv* memorablemente.

memorandum [,memə'rændəm] *n*, *pl* **memoranda** [,memə'rændə] memorándum *m*, memorando *m*; apunte *m*, nota *f*, memoria *f*.

memorial [mɪ'mɔːrɪəl] **1** *adj* conmemorativo; ~ **park** (*US*) cementerio *m*. **2** *n* (**a**) monumento *m* (conmemorativo). (**b**) (*document*) memorial *m*.

memorize ['meməraɪz] *vt* aprender de memoria.

memory ['memərɪ] **1** *n* (**a**) (*faculty*) memoria *f*; (*capacity for* ~) retentiva *f*; (*Comput*) memoria *f*; **to speak from** ~ hablar fiándose de su memoria; **to the best of my** ~ que yo recuerde; **to commit sth to** ~ aprender algo de memoria; encomendar algo a la memoria; **I have a bad** ~ **for faces** soy mal fisonomista, no recuerdo las caras de las personas; **to have a** ~ **like a sieve** tener malísima memoria; **to lose one's** ~ perder la memoria; **if my** ~ **serves me** si mi memoria no me falla, si mal no recuerdo; **I speak from** ~ hablo de memoria.

(**b**) (*recollection*) recuerdo *m*; **in** ~ **of** en memoria de, en conmemoración de; **of blessed** ~ de feliz recuerdo, de grata memoria; **'Memories of life in Barataria'** 'Recuerdos *mpl* de la vida en Barataria'; **to have happy memories of** tener agradables recuerdos de; **to keep sb's** ~ **alive** guardar el recuerdo de uno, mantener vivo el recuerdo de uno.

2 *attr*: ~ **bank** banco *m* de memoria; ~ **bus** bus *m* de memoria; ~ **chip** chip *m* de memoria; ~ **lane** mundo *m* de los recuerdos (sentimentales); **to go down** ~ **lane** adentrarse en el mundo de los recuerdos; ~ **management** gestión *f* de la memoria.

memsahib ['mem,sɑːhɪb] *n* (*India*) mujer *f* casada.

men [men] *npl of* **man**.

menace ['menɪs] **1** *n* amenaza *f*; **he's a** ~ es peligroso. **2** *vt* amenazar.

menacing ['menɪsɪŋ] *adj* amenazador.

menacingly ['menɪsɪŋlɪ] *adv* de modo amenazador.

ménage [me'nɑːʒ] *n* casa *f*, hogar *m*, menaje *m*; ~ **à trois** menaje *m* de tres.

menagerie [mɪ'nædʒərɪ] *n* casa *f* de fieras, colección *f* de fieras.

mend [mend] **1** *n* (**a**) (*patch*) remiendo *m*; (*darn*) zurcido *m*.

(**b**) **to be on the** ~ ir mejorando.

2 *vt* (*repair*) reparar, componer; (*darn*) zurcir; (*improve*) reformar, mejorar; (*rectify*) remediar.

3 *vi* mejorar, reponerse.

mendacious [men'deɪʃəs] *adj* mendaz.

mendacity [men'dæsɪtɪ] *n* mendacidad *f*.

mendelevium [,mendɪ'liːvɪəm] *n* mendelevio *m*.

Mendelian [men'diːlɪən] *adj* mendeliano.

Mendelianism [men'diːlɪənɪzəm] *n*, **Mendelism** ['mendəlɪzəm] *n* mendelismo *m*.

mendicancy ['mendɪkənsɪ] *n* mendicidad *f*.

mendicant ['mendɪkənt] **1** *adj* mendicante. **2** *n* mendicante *mf*.

mendicity [men'dɪsɪtɪ] *n* mendicidad *f*.

mending ['mendɪŋ] *n* (**a**) (*act*) reparación *f*, compostura *f*; zurcidura *f*. (**b**) (*clothes*) ropa *f* de repaso, ropa *f* por zurcir.

Menelaus [,menɪ'leɪəs] *nm* Menelao.

menfolk ['menfəʊk] *npl* hombres *mpl*.

menhir ['menhɪə^r] *n* menhir *m*.

menial ['miːnɪəl] **1** *adj* doméstico; servil; (*pej*) bajo; ~ **work** trabajo *m* de baja categoría. **2** *n* criado *m*, -a *f*.

meningitis [,menɪn'dʒaɪtɪs] *n* meningitis *f*.

meniscus [mə'nɪskəs] *n* menisco *m*.

menopausal [,menəʊ'pɔːzəl] *adj* menopáusico.

menopause ['menəʊpɔːz] *n* menopausia *f*.

menorrhagia [,menɔː'reɪdʒɪə] *n* menorragia *f*.

menses ['mensiːz] *npl* menstruo *m*.

menstrual ['menstrʊəl] *adj* menstrual; ~ **cycle** ciclo *m* menstrual.

menstruate ['menstrʊeɪt] *vi* menstruar.

menstruation [,menstrʊ'eɪʃən] *n* menstruación *f*.

mensuration [,mensjʊə'reɪʃən] *n* medición *f*, medida *f*, mensuración *f*.

menswear ['menzwɛə^r] *n* ropa *f* de caballero.

mental ['mentl] *adj* (**a**) mental; ~ **age** edad *f* mental; ~ **arithmetic** cálculo *m* mental; ~ **defective** deficiente *mf* mental; ~ **home**, ~ **hospital** manicomio *m*, hospital *m* psiquiátrico; **I made a** ~ **note of it** tomé nota de ello. (**b**) (*Brit**) anormal, tocado; **he must be** ~ debe estar ido*.

mentality [men'tælɪtɪ] *n* mentalidad *f*.

mentally ['mentəlɪ] *adv* mentalmente; ~ **defective**, ~ **deficient** deficiente mental; ~ **disturbed** trastornado; ~ **handicapped** minusválido mental; ~ **retarded** retardado mental.

menthol ['menθɒl] *n* mentol *m*.

mentholated ['menθəleɪtɪd] *adj* mentolado.

mention ['menʃən] **1** *n* (**a**) mención *f*, alusión *f*.

(**b**) (*Mil*) citación *f*.

2 *vt* mencionar, aludir a; hablar de; **to** ~ (**in dispatches**) citar, nombrar (en el parte); **not to** ~ ... sin contar ..., además de ..., amén de ...; **too numerous to** ~ demasiado numerosos para mencionar; **don't** ~ **it!** ¡no hay de qué!, ¡de nada!; **if I may** ~ **it** si se me permite aludir a ello; **I need hardly** ~ **that** ... huelga decir que ..., excusado es decir que ...; **I will** ~ **it to him** se lo diré; **he ~ed no names** no dijo los nombres; **to** ~ **sb in one's will** mencionar a uno en su testamento, legar algo a uno.

mentor ['mentɔː^r] *n* mentor *m*.

menu ['menjuː] *n* (**a**) carta *f*, lista *f* (de platos), menú *m*. (**b**) (*Comput*) menú *m*; **~-driven** guiado por menú.

meow [mɪ'aʊ] **1** *n* maullido *m*, miau *m*. **2** *vi* maullar.

MEP *n* (*Brit*) *abbr of* **Member of the European Parliament** eurodiputado *m*, -a *f*.

Mephistopheles [,mefɪs'tɒfɪliːz] *nm* Mefistófeles.

Mephistophelian [,mefɪstə'fiːlɪən] *adj* mefistofélico.

mercantile ['mɜːkəntaɪl] *adj* mercantil; ~ **agency** agencia *f* mercantil; ~ **marine** marina *f* mercante.

mercantilism ['mɜːkəntɪlɪzəm] *n* mercantilismo *m*.

mercenary ['mɜːsɪnərɪ] **1** *adj* mercenario. **2** *n* mercenario *m*.

merchandise ['mɜːtʃəndaɪz] *n* mercancías *fpl*, géneros *mpl*.

merchandize ['mɜːtʃəndaɪz] *vt* comerciar.

merchandizer ['mɜːtʃəndaɪzə^r] *n* comerciante *m*, tratante *m*.

merchandizing ['mɜːtʃəndaɪzɪŋ] *n* comercialización *f*.

merchant ['mɜːtʃənt] **1** *n* (**a**) comerciante *m*, negociante *m*; **a diamond** ~ un comerciante en diamantes; **'The M~ of Venice'** 'El Mercader de Venecia'.

(**b**) (*) tío* *m*, sujeto *m*.

2 *attr*: ~ **bank** (*Brit*) banco *m* mercantil; ~ **marine** (*US*), ~ **navy** (*Brit*) marina *f* mercante; ~ **seaman** marinero *m* de la marina mercante; ~ **ship** mercante *m*; ~ **shipping** marina *f* mercante; mercantes *mpl*.

merchantable ['mɜːtʃəntəbl] *adj* comercializable; **of** ~ **quality** de calidad comerciable.

merchantman ['mɜːtʃəntmən] *n*, *pl* **merchantmen** ['mɜːtʃəntmən] buque *m* mercante.

merciful ['mɜːsɪfʊl] *adj person* misericordioso, compasivo, clemente; *release etc* afortunado, feliz.

mercifully ['mɜːsɪfəlɪ] *adv act etc* misericordiosamente, con compasión; ~ **it was short** gracias a Dios fue breve.

merciless ['mɜːsɪlɪs] *adj* despiadado.

mercilessly ['mɜːsɪlɪslɪ] *adv* despiadadamente, sin piedad.

mercurial [mɜː'kjʊərɪəl] *adj* (**a**) (*Chem*) mercurial. (**b**) (*lively*) vivo; (*changeable*) veleidoso, voluble.

Mercury ['mɜːkjʊrɪ] *nm* Mercurio.

mercury ['mɜːkjʊrɪ] *n* mercurio *m*.

mercy ['mɜːsɪ] **1** *n* misericordia *f*, compasión *f*, clemencia *f*; **to find sb guilty but with a recommendation to** ~ declarar culpable a uno pero recomendar la clemencia; **to be at the** ~ **of sb** estar a la merced de uno; **it is a** ~ **that** ... gracias a Dios que ..., menos mal que ...; **to beg for** ~ pedir clemencia; **we should be grateful** (*or* **thankful**) **for small mercies** debemos dar las gracias por los pequeños favores; **to have** ~ **on sb** tener compasión de uno, apiadarse de uno; **have** ~**!** ¡por piedad!; **to be left to the tender mercies of sb** verse abandonado en las manos nada piadosas de uno; **to show sb no** ~ tratar a uno con el mayor rigor; **no** ~ **was shown to the rioters** no hubo clemencia para los revoltosos; **to throw o.s. on sb's** ~ abandonarse a la merced de uno.

2 *attr*: ~ **flight** vuelo *m* de emergencia (para rescatar una persona en peligro *etc*); **'~ dash to Palace corgi'** 'fue volando a Palacio para salvar la vida al perro galés'.

mercy-killing ['mɜːsɪ,kɪlɪŋ] *n* eutanasia *f*.

mere[1] [mɪə^r] *n* lago *m*.

mere[2] [mɪə^r] *adj* mero, simple; solo, no más que; **he's a** ~ **clerk** es un simple empleado, no es más que un empleado; **it's** ~ **nonsense, it's the ~st nonsense** es puro disparate; **it's** ~ **talk** son palabras al aire, es pura palabrería; **they quarrelled over a** ~ **nothing** riñeron por una friolera; **it's a** ~ **formality** es pura fórmula.

merely ['mɪəlɪ] *adv* meramente, simplemente; sólo; **I** ~ **said that** ... sólo dije que ..., lo único que dije era que ...; **she's** ~ **a secretary** es una simple secretaria, no es más que una secretaria; **it's not** ~ **broken, it's ruined** no sólo está roto, sino que se ha estropeado del todo.

meretricious [,merɪ'trɪʃəs] *adj* de oropel, charro, postizo; *style, writing* rimbombante.

merge [mɜːdʒ] **1** *vt* unir, combinar (*with* con); mezclar; fundir; (*Comm, Comput*) fusionar.

2 *vi* unirse, combinarse; fundirse; converger; (*Comm*) fusionarse; (*roads*) empalmar; **to ~ into** ir convirtiéndose en; **the bird ~d into its background of leaves** el pájaro se hacía casi invisible contra el fondo de hojas; **this question ~s into that bigger one** esta cuestión se pierde en aquélla mayor.

3 *n* (*Comput*) fusión *f*.

merger [ˈmɜːdʒəʳ] *n* (*Comm*) fusión *f*, concentración *f* (*Mex*).

meridian [məˈrɪdɪən] *n* (*Astron, Geog*) meridiano *m*; (*fig*) cenit *m*, auge *m*.

meridional [məˈrɪdɪənl] *adj* meridional.

meringue [məˈræŋ] *n* merengue *m*.

merino [məˈriːnəʊ] **1** *adj* merino. **2** *n* merino *m*.

merit [ˈmerɪt] **1** *n* mérito *m*; ventaja *f*, bondad *f*; virtud *f*; **it has the ~ of being clear** tiene el mérito de ser claro; **to treat a case on its ~s** considerar un caso según sus méritos; **~ increase** aumento *m* por méritos; **~ pay** (*US*) plus *m* por méritos. **2** *vt* merecer, ser digno de.

meritocracy [ˌmerɪˈtɒkrəsɪ] *n* meritocracia *f*.

meritocrat [ˈmerɪtəʊkræt] *n* meritócrata *mf*.

meritorious [ˌmerɪˈtɔːrɪəs] *adj* meritorio.

meritoriously [ˌmerɪˈtɔːrɪəslɪ] *adv* merecidamente.

merlin [ˈmɜːlɪn] *n* esmerejón *m*.

mermaid [ˈmɜːmeɪd] *n* sirena *f*.

merman [ˈmɜːmæn] *n, pl* **mermen** [ˈmɜːmen] tritón *m*.

Merovingian [ˌmerəʊˈvɪndʒɪən] **1** *adj* merovingio. **2** *n* merovingio *m*, -a *f*.

merrily [ˈmerɪlɪ] *adv* alegremente; regocijadamente, con alborozo.

merriment [ˈmerɪmənt] *n* alegría *f*; regocijo *m*, alborozo *m*; (*laughter*) risas *fpl*; **at this there was much ~** en esto hubo muchas risas.

merry [ˈmerɪ] *adj* alegre; regocijado; alborozado; *joke etc* divertido; **to be as ~ as a lark** (*or* **cricket**) estar como unas pascuas; **to get ~*** achisparse*; **to make ~** divertirse, estar de juerga; **M~ Christmas!** ¡Felices Pascuas!; **M~ England** *la Inglaterra de los buenos tiempos pasados*; **Robin Hood and his ~ men** Robin Hood y sus valientes compañeros.

merry-go-round [ˈmerɪgəʊˌraʊnd] *n* tiovivo *m*, caballitos *mpl*.

merrymaker [ˈmerɪˌmeɪkəʳ] *n* juerguista *mf*, parrandero *m*, -a *f*.

merrymaking [ˈmerɪˌmeɪkɪŋ] *n* festividades *fpl*.

mesa [ˈmeɪsə] *n* (*US*) colina *f* baja, duna *f*.

mescaline [ˈmeskəlɪn] *n* mescalina *f*.

mesentery [ˈmeːzəntrɪ] *n* mesenterio *m*.

meseta [məˈseɪtə] *n* meseta *f*.

mesh [meʃ] **1** *n* malla *f*; (*Mech*) engrane *m*, engranaje *m*; **~es** (*fig*) red *f*, trampa *f*; **to be in ~** (*Mech*) engranar, estar engranado.

2 *vt*: **to get ~ed** enredarse (*in* en).

3 *vi* (*Tech*) engranar (*with* con).

mesmeric [mezˈmerɪk] *adj* mesmeriano.

mesmerism [ˈmezmərɪzəm] *n* mesmerismo *m*.

mesmerize [ˈmezməraɪz] *vt* mesmerizar, hipnotizar; **to ~ sb into doing sth** inducir a uno a hacer algo hipnotizándole.

mesolith [ˈmesəʊlɪθ] *n* mesolito *m*.

mesolithic [mesəʊˈlɪθɪk] **1** *adj* mesolítico. **2** *n*: **the M~** el Mesolítico.

mesomorph [ˈmesəʊˌmɔːf] *n* mesomorfo *m*.

meson [ˈmiːzɒn] *n* mesón *m*.

Mesopotamia [ˌmesəpəˈteɪmɪə] *n* Mesopotamia *f*.

Mesozoic [ˌmesəʊˈzəʊɪk] **1** *adj* mesozoico. **2** *n* mesozoico *m*, -a *f*.

mess [mes] **1** *n* (**a**) (*confusion*) confusión *f*; (*of objects*) revoltijo *m*; (*dirt*) suciedad *f*; (*bungled affair*) lío* *m*; **what a ~!** ¡qué sucio está todo!; ¡qué asco!; ¡qué lío!*; **to be in a ~** (*things*) estar revuelto, (*house etc*) estar desarreglado, (*person*) estar en un aprieto; **his life is in a ~** su vida es un fracaso; **she's a ~*** es un desastre; **to get into a ~** (*person*) meterse en un lío*, (*things*) desarreglarse, (*accounts etc*) enredarse; **to leave things in a ~** dejar las cosas en confusión; **to leave a room in a ~** dejar un cuarto revuelto; **to make a ~ of** *objects* desordenar, *job* fracasar en, hacer muy mal, *sb else's life* llenar de confusión, arruinar, *one's life* fracasar en, (*dirty*) ensuciar.

(**b**) **~ of pottage** plato *m* de lentejas.

(**c**) (*Mil etc*) (*food*) rancho *m*, comida *f*; (*room*) sala *f* de rancho; **officers' ~** comedor *m* de oficiales.

2 *vi* (**a**) (*feed*) hacer rancho, comer (juntos). (**b**) (*****) **no ~ing!** ¡sin bromas!; **no ~ing?** ¿en serio?, ¿sin bromas?

◆**mess about, mess around 1** *vt*: **to ~ sb about** (*Brit*) fastidiar a uno, desorientar a uno (cambiando una cita *etc* con él).

2 *vi* perder el tiempo, ocuparse en fruslerías, trabajar (*etc*) con poca seriedad; **he enjoys ~ing about in boats** le gusta entretenerse con botes; **we ~ed about in Paris for two days** pasamos dos días en París haciendo esto y lo otro; **they kept us ~ing about for an hour** nos hicieron esperar una hora sin decirnos nada; **stop ~ing about!** ¡déjate de tonterías!

◆**mess about with** *vt*: **to ~ about with sth** (*handle*) manosear algo, tocar algo, (*amuse o.s.*) divertirse con algo, (*break*) romper algo, estropear algo; **to ~ about with a girl** andar en líos con una chica.

◆**mess up** *vt* (*disarrange*) desarreglar, desordenar; (*dirty*) ensuciar; (*ruin*) arruinar, estropear, echar a perder; *affair, deal* fracasar en, (*deliberately*) chafar; (*Psych*: *disturb*) perturbar, traumatizar; (*US*: *beat up*) zurrar, dar una paliza a.

◆**mess with*** *vt* perder el tiempo con; andar en líos con*.

message [ˈmesɪdʒ] **1** *n* mensaje *m*, recado *m*; aviso *m*, nota *f*; (*diplomatic etc*) comunicación *f*; (*Comput*) mensaje *m*; (*of telex etc*) texto *m*; (*of speech, book etc*) mensaje *m*, lección *f*, sentido *m*; **to get the ~*** comprender, caer en la cuenta; **do you think he got the ~?*** ¿crees que comprendió?; **to leave a ~** dejar un recado.

2 *attr*: **~ switching** conmutación *f* de mensajes.

messaging [ˈmesɪdʒɪŋ] *n* mensajería *f*.

mess-deck [ˈmesdek] *n* sollado *m*, cubierta *f* de rancho de marineros.

messenger [ˈmesɪndʒəʳ] **1** *n* mensajero *m*, -a *f*, mandadero *m*, -a *f*. **2** *attr*: **~ boy** mensajero *m*.

Messiah [mɪˈsaɪə] *n* Mesías *m*.

messianic [ˌmesɪˈænɪk] *adj* mesiánico.

Messieurs [ˈmesəz] *npl* (*Brit*) señores *mpl*.

messmate [ˈmesmeɪt] *n* compañero *m* de rancho, comensal *m*, (*loosely*) amigo *m*.

Messrs [ˈmesəz] *npl* (*Brit*: *pl of* **Mr**) *abbr of* **Messieurs** señores *mpl*, Sres.

messtin [ˈmestɪn] *n* plato *m* de campaña.

mess-up* [ˈmesʌp] *n* (*Brit*) fracaso *m*; enredo *m*, follón* *m*, lío* *m*; **we had a ~ with the trains** nos hicimos un lío con los trenes*; **what a ~!** ¡qué lío*!

messy [ˈmesɪ] *adj* (*dirty*) sucio; (*untidy*) desaseado, desaliñado, *room etc* en desorden; (*confused*) confuso, nada claro; *divorce* lleno de problemas, lleno de rencores.

met [met] *pret and ptp of* **meet²**.

Met. [met] (**a**) *adj* (*Brit*) *abbr of* **meteorological**; **the ~ Office** la estación meteorológica estatal. (**b**) *n* (*US*) *abbr of* **Metropolitan Opera**. (**c**) *n* (*Brit*) *abbr of* **Metropolitan Police** *policía de Londres*.

meta... [ˈmetə] *pref* meta...

metabolic [ˌmetəˈbɒlɪk] *adj* metabólico.

metabolism [meˈtæbəlɪzəm] *n* metabolismo *m*.

metabolize [meˈtæbəlaɪz] *vt* metabolizar.

metacarpal [ˌmetəˈkɑːpl] *n* metacarpiano *m*.

metal [ˈmetl] **1** *n* (**a**) metal *m*. (**b**) (*Brit*: *on road*) grava *f*. (**c**) (*fig*) temple *m*, ánimo *m*. (**d**) **~s** (*Brit Rail*) rieles *mpl*. **2** *adj* metálico, de metal; **~ detector** detector *m* de metales; **~ fatigue** fatiga *f* del metal; **~ polish** lustre *m* para metales. **3** *vt* (*Brit*) *road* engravar.

metalanguage [ˈmetəˌlæŋgwɪdʒ] *n* metalenguaje *m*.

metallic [mɪˈtælɪk] *adj* metálico.

metallurgic(al) [ˌmetəˈlɜːdʒɪk(əl)] *adj* metalúrgico.

metallurgist [meˈtælədʒɪst] *n* metalúrgico *m*, -a *f*.

metallurgy [meˈtælədʒɪ] *n* metalurgia *f*.

metalwork [ˈmetlwɜːk] *n* metalistería *f*.

metamorphic [ˌmetəˈmɔːfɪk] *adj* metamórfico.

metamorphose [ˌmetəˈmɔːfəʊz] **1** *vt* metamorfosear (*into* en). **2** *vi* metamorfosearse.

metamorphosis [ˌmetəˈmɔːfəsɪs] *n, pl* **metamorphoses** [ˌmetəˈmɔːfəsiːz] metamorfosis *f*.

metaphor [ˈmetəfɔːʳ] *n* metáfora *f*.

metaphorical [ˌmetəˈfɒrɪkəl] *adj* metafórico.

metaphorically [ˌmetəˈfɒrɪklɪ] *adv* metafóricamente.

metaphysical [ˌmetəˈfɪzɪkəl] *adj* metafísico.

metaphysics [ˌmetəˈfɪzɪks] *n* metafísica *f*.

metastasis [mɪˈtæstəsɪs] *n* metástasis *f*.

metatarsal [ˌmetəˈtɑːsl] *n* metatarsiano *m*.

metathesis [meˈtæθəsɪs] *n* metátesis *f*.

mete [miːt] *vt*: **to ~ out** repartir; *punishment etc* dar, imponer.

metempsychosis [ˌmetəmsaɪˈkəʊsɪs] *n* metempsicosis *f*.

meteor [ˈmiːtɪəʳ] **1** *n* meteorito *m*, bólido *m*; (*esp fig*) meteoro *m*. **2** *attr*: ~ **shower** lluvia *f* de meteoritos.

meteoric [ˌmiːtɪˈɒrɪk] *adj* meteórico (*also fig*).

meteorite [ˈmiːtɪəraɪt] *n* meteorito *m*, bólido *m*.

meteoroid [ˈmiːtɪərɔɪd] *n* meteoroide *m*.

meteorological [ˌmiːtɪərəˈlɒdʒɪkəl] *adj* meteorológico.

meteorologist [ˌmiːtɪəˈrɒlədʒɪst] *n* meteorólogo *m*, -a *f*.

meteorology [ˌmiːtɪəˈrɒlədʒɪ] *n* meteorología *f*.

meter [ˈmiːtəʳ] **1** *n* contador *m*, medidor *m* (*LAm*); (*US*) = **metre. 2** *vt* medir (con contador); (*US*) *mail* franquear.

metermaid [ˈmiːtəˌmeɪd] *n* (*US*) controladora *f* de estacionamiento.

methadone [ˈmeθəˌdəʊn] *n* metadona *f*.

methane [ˈmiːθeɪn] *n* metano *m*.

method [ˈmeθəd] **1** *n* método *m*; sistema *m*, procedimiento *m*; ~ **of payment** forma *f* de pago; **there's ~ in his madness** no es tan loco como parece.

2 *attr*: ~ **actor/actress** actor *m* adepto/actriz *f* adepta del método Stanislavski.

methodical [mɪˈθɒdɪkəl] *adj* metódico.

methodically [mɪˈθɒdɪkəlɪ] *adv* metódicamente.

Methodism [ˈmeθədɪzəm] *n* metodismo *m*.

Methodist [ˈmeθədɪst] **1** *adj* metodista. **2** *n* metodista *mf*.

methodology [ˌmeθəˈdɒlədʒɪ] *n* metodología *f*.

meths* [meθs] (*Brit*) **1** *n abbr of* **methylated spirit(s)**. **2** *attr*: ~ **drinker** bebedor *m*, -ora *f* de alcohol metilado.

Methuselah [mɪˈθjuːzələ] *nm* Matusalén.

methylated [ˈmeθɪleɪtɪd] *adj*: ~ **spirit(s)** (*Brit*) alcohol *m* metilado, alcohol *m* desnaturalizado.

meticulous [mɪˈtɪkjʊləs] *adj* meticuloso; minucioso.

meticulously [mɪˈtɪkjʊləslɪ] *adv* meticulosamente.

meticulousness [mɪˈtɪkjʊləsnɪs] *n* meticulosidad *f*.

métier [ˈmeɪtɪeɪ] *n* (*trade*) oficio *m*; (*strong point*) fuerte *m*; (*speciality*) especialidad *f*; **it's not my ~** no es de mi especialidad.

met-man* [ˈmetmæn] *n*, *pl* **met-men** [ˈmetmen] meteorólogo *m*.

metre, (*US*) **meter** [ˈmiːtəʳ] *n* (*all senses*) metro *m*.

metric(al) [ˈmetrɪk(əl)] *adj* métrico; ~ **system** sistema *m* métrico; ~ **ton** tonelada *f* métrica; **to go ~*** adoptar el sistema métrico, cambiar al sistema métrico.

metrication [ˌmetrɪˈkeɪʃən] *n* paso *m* (*or* cambio *m*) al sistema métrico.

metrics [ˈmetrɪks] *n* métrica *f*.

metronome [ˈmetrənəʊm] *n* metrónomo *m*.

metropolis [mɪˈtrɒpəlɪs] *n* metrópoli *f*.

metropolitan [ˌmetrəˈpɒlɪtən] **1** *adj* metropolitano; **M~ Police** *la policía de Londres*. **2** *n* (*Eccl*) metropolitano *m*.

mettle [ˈmetl] *n* temple *m*; ánimo *m*, brío *m*; valor *m*; **to be on one's ~** estar dispuesto a mostrar todo lo que uno vale; **to put sb on his ~** picar a uno en el amor propio; **to show one's ~** mostrar lo que uno vale.

mettlesome [ˈmetlsəm] *adj* animoso, brioso, esforzado.

Meuse [mɜːz] *n* Mosa *m*.

mew [mjuː] **1** *n* maullido *m*. **2** *vi* maullar.

mewl [mjuːl] *vi* (*cat*) maullar; (*baby*) lloriquear.

mews [mjuːz] *n* (*Brit*) caballeriza *f*; calle *f* de casas pequeñas (antes caballerizas).

Mexican [ˈmeksɪkən] **1** *adj* mejicano, (*in Mexico*) mexicano. **2** *n* mejicano *m*, -a *f*, (*in Mexico*) mexicano *m*, -a *f*.

Mexico [ˈmeksɪkəʊ] *n* Méjico *m*, (*in Mexico*) México *m*; ~ **City** (Ciudad *f* de) México.

mezzanine [ˈmezəniːn] *n* entresuelo *m*.

mezzo-soprano [ˈmetsəʊsəˈprɑːnəʊ] *n* mezzosoprano *f*.

mezzotint [ˈmetzəʊtɪnt] *n* grabado *m* mezzotinto.

MF *n abbr of* **medium frequency**.

M.F.A. *n* (*US*) *abbr of* **Master of Fine Arts** *título universitario*.

MFN *n* (*US*) *abbr of* **most favored nation** nación *f* más favorecida; ~ **treatment** trato *m* de nación más favorecida.

mfr(s) *abbr of* **manufacturer(s)** fabricante *m*, fab.

mg *abbr of* **miligramme(s)**.

Mgr (**a**) (*Eccl*) *abbr of* **Monsignor** monseñor *m*, Mons. (**b**) (*Comm etc*) *abbr of* **manager**.

MHR *n* (*US*) *abbr of* **Member of the House of Representatives** *diputado del Congreso de EE.UU.*

MHz (*Rad*) *abbr of* **megahertz** megahercio *m*, MHz.

MI (**a**) *n abbr of* **machine intelligence**. (**b**) (*US Post*) *abbr of* **Michigan**.

mi [miː] (*Mus*) mi *m*.

MI5 *n* (*Brit*) *abbr of* **Military Intelligence 5** *servicio de inteligencia contraespionaje*.

MI6 *n* (*Brit*) *abbr of* **Military Intelligence 6** *servicio de inteligencia*.

MIA *adj* (*Mil*) *abbr of* **missing in action** desaparecido.

miaow [miːˈaʊ] **1** *n* miau *m*. **2** *vi* maullar.

miasma [mɪˈæzmə] *n*, *pl* **miasmas** *or* **miasmata** [mɪˈæzmətə] miasma *m*.

miasmic [mɪˈæzmɪk] *adj* miasmático.

mica [ˈmaɪkə] *n* mica *f*.

mice [maɪs] *npl of* **mouse**.

Mich. (*US*) *abbr of* **Michigan**.

Michael [ˈmaɪkl] *nm* Miguel.

Michaelmas [ˈmɪklməs] **1** *n* fiesta *f* de San Miguel (*29 setiembre*). **2** *attr*: ~ **daisy** margarita *f* de otoño; ~ **term** (*Brit*) trimestre *m* de otoño, primer trimestre *m*.

Michelangelo [ˌmaɪkəlˈændʒɪləʊ] *nm* Miguel Ángel.

Mick [mɪk] *nm familiar form of* **Michael**.

Mickey [ˈmɪkɪ] *nm familiar form of* **Michael**; ~ **Finn** bebida *f* drogada; ~ **Mouse** el ratoncito Mickey; ~ **Mouse money** dinero *m* de jugar; **it's a ~ Mouse set-up** es un montaje poco serio.

mickey‡ [ˈmɪkɪ] *n*: **to take the ~ out of sb** (*Brit*) tomar el pelo a uno*.

micro [ˈmaɪkrəʊ] *n* (**a**) (*Comput*) micro *m*, microordenador *m*. (**b**) (*) microondas *m*.

micro... [ˈmaɪkrəʊ] *pref* micro...

microbe [ˈmaɪkrəʊb] *n* microbio *m*.

microbial [maɪˈkrəʊbɪəl] *adj* microbiano.

microbiological [ˌmaɪkrəʊbaɪəˈlɒdʒɪkəl] *adj* microbiológico.

microbiologist [ˌmaɪkrəʊbaɪˈɒlədʒɪst] *n* microbiólogo *m*, -a *f*.

microbiology [ˌmaɪkrəʊbaɪˈɒlədʒɪ] *n* microbiología *f*.

microchip [ˈmaɪkrəʊˌtʃɪp] *n* microchip *m*, pastilla *f*.

microcircuit [ˈmaɪkrəʊˌsɜːkɪt] *n* microcircuito *m*.

microcircuitry [ˈmaikrəʊˈsɜːkɪtrɪ] *n* microcircuitería *f*.

microclimate [ˈmaɪkrəʊˌklaɪmɪt] *n* microclima *m*.

microcomputer [ˌmaɪkrəʊkəmˈpjuːtəʳ] *n* microordenador *m*, microcomputadora *f*.

microcomputing [ˈmaɪkrəʊkəmˈpjuːtɪŋ] *n* microcomputación *f*.

microcosm [ˈmaɪkrəʊkɒzəm] *n* microcosmo *m*.

microdot [ˈmaɪkrəʊˌdɒt] *n* micropunto *m*.

microeconomic [ˌmaɪkrəʊˌiːkəˈnɒmɪk] *adj* microeconómico.

microeconomics [ˈmaɪkrəʊˌiːkəˈnɒmɪks] *n* microeconomía *f*.

microelectronic [ˈmaɪkrəʊˌiːlekˈtrɒnɪk] *adj* microelectrónico.

microelectronics [ˈmaɪkrəʊˌiːlekˈtrɒnɪks] *n sing* microelectrónica *f*.

microfiche [ˈmaɪkrəʊˌfiːʃ] *n* microfiche *m*, microficha *f*.

microfilm [ˈmaɪkrəʊfɪlm] **1** *n* microfilm *m*, microfilme *m*. **2** *attr*: ~ **reader** lector *m* de microfilm. **3** *vt* microfilmar.

microform [ˈmaɪkrəʊˌfɔːm] *n* microforma *f*.

microgroove [ˈmaɪkrəʊgruːv] *n* microsurco *m*.

microlight, microlite [ˈmaɪkrəʊˌlaɪt] *n* (*also* ~ **aircraft**) (avión *m*) ultraligero *m*, aeroligero *m*.

micromesh [ˈmaɪkrəʊmeʃ] *attr*: ~ **stockings** medias *fpl* de malla fina.

micrometer [maɪˈkrɒmɪtəʳ] *n* micrómetro *m*.

microorganism [ˈmaɪkrəʊˈɔːgənɪzəm] *n* microorganismo *m*.

microphone [ˈmaɪkrəfəʊn] *n* micrófono *m*.

microprocessor [ˌmaɪkrəʊˈprəʊsesəʳ] *n* microprocesador *m*.

microprogramming, (*US, also freq Comput*) **microprograming** [ˌmaɪkrəʊˈprəʊgræmɪŋ] *n* microprogramación *f*.

microscope [ˈmaɪkrəskəʊp] *n* microscopio *m*.

microscopic(al) [ˌmaɪkrəˈskɒpɪk(əl)] *adj* microscópico.

microscopically [ˌmaɪkrəʊˈskɒpɪklɪ] *adv* microscópicamente; ~ **small** microscópico; **to examine sth ~** examinar algo al microscopio.

microscopy [maɪˈkrɒskəpɪ] *n* microscopía *f*.

microsecond [ˈmaɪkrəʊˌsekənd] *n* microsegundo *m*.

microspacing [ˈmaɪkrəʊˈspeɪsɪŋ] *n* microespaciado *m*.

microsurgery [ˌmaɪkrəʊˈsɜːdʒərɪ] *n* microcirugía *f*.

microtechnology [ˌmaɪkrəʊtekˈnɒlədʒɪ] *n* microtecnología *f*.

microtransmitter [ˌmaɪkrəʊtrænzˈmɪtəʳ] *n* microtransmisor *m*.

microwave [ˈmaɪkrəʊˌweɪv] **1** *n* microonda *f*; (~ *oven*) = **2**. **2** *attr*: ~ **oven** horno *m* de microonda, microondas *m*. **3** *vt* poner en el microondas, cocinar al microondas.

micturate [ˈmɪktjʊəreɪt] *vi* orinar.

micturition [ˌmɪktjʊˈrɪʃən] *n* micción *f*.

mid [mɪd] **1** *adj* medio, *eg* **in ~ journey** a medio camino; **in ~ June** a mediados de junio; **in ~ afternoon** a media tarde; **in ~ course** a media carrera; **in ~ channel** en medio del canal. **2** *prep* (*liter, poet*) *V* **amid**.

mid-air [ˈmɪdɛəʳ] **1** *attr*: ~ **collision** colisión *f* en el aire. **2** *n*: **in ~** entre cielo y tierra; **to leave sth in ~** dejar algo en el aire; **to refuel in ~** repostar combustible en pleno vuelo.

Midas [ˈmaɪdəs] *nm* Midas.

mid-Atlantic [mɪdətˈlæntɪk] *attr*: *accent etc* de mitad del Atlántico.

midbrain ['mɪdbreɪn] *n* mesencéfalo *m*, cerebro *m* medio.
midday ['mɪd'deɪ] **1** *n* mediodía *m*; **at ~** a mediodía. **2** *adj* de mediodía.
midden ['mɪdn] *n* muladar *m*.
middle ['mɪdl] **1** *adj* (*of place*) medio, central; de en medio; intermedio; (*in quality, size etc*) mediano; **~ age** mediana edad *f*; **M~ Ages** Edad *f* Media; **M~ America** Centroamérica *f*, (*fig*) el ciudadano norteamericano medio; **~ C** (*Mus*) do *m* mayor; **~ class** clase *f* media; **my ~ daughter** mi segunda hija (de las tres que tengo), la hija de en medio; **in the ~ distance** (*Art*) a medio fondo; **~ ear** oído *m* medio; **M~ East** Oriente *m* Medio; **M~ English** inglés *m* medio; **~ finger** dedo *m* del corazón; **~ ground** terreno *m* neutral; **M~ High German** alto alemán *m* medio; **~ management** gerencia *f* intermedia; **my ~ name is Albert** mi segundo nombre de pila es Alberto; **his ~ name is 'lover'** le han apodado 'Tenorio'; **~ school** primeros años *mpl* de la enseñanza media; **~ voice** voz *f* media.
2 *n* (**a**) medio *m*, centro *m*, mitad *f*; **it divides down the ~** se divide por el medio; **in the ~ of the table** en el centro de la mesa; **in the ~ of the field** en medio del campo; **right in the ~ of the room** en el mismo centro del cuarto; **in the ~ of nowhere** donde Cristo dio las tres voces; **in the ~ of summer** en pleno verano; **in** (*or* **about, towards**) **the ~ of May** a mediados de mayo; **in the ~ of the century** a mediados del siglo; **in the ~ of the morning** a media mañana; **I'm in the ~ of reading it** voy a mitad de su lectura.
(**b**) (*****: *waist*) cintura *f*.
middle-aged ['mɪdl'eɪdʒd] *adj* de mediana edad, de edad madura; cuarentón, cincuentón.
middlebrow ['mɪdlbraʊ] **1** *adj* de (*or* para) gusto medianamente culto, de gusto entre intelectual y plebeyo.
2 *n* persona *f* de gusto medianamente culto, persona *f* de cultura mediana.
middle-class ['mɪdl'klɑːs] *adj* de la clase media.
middle-distance [ˌmɪdl'dɪstəns] *adj*: **~ race** carrera *f* de medio fondo; **~ runner** mediofondista *mf*.
Middle-Eastern [ˌmɪdl'iːstən] *adj* medio-oriental.
middleman ['mɪdlmæn] *n, pl* **middlemen** ['mɪdlmen] intermediario *m*.
middle-of-the-road ['mɪdləvðə'rəʊd] *adj* moderado, de posición intermedia.
middle-sized ['mɪdl,saɪzd] *adj* de tamaño mediano; *person* de estatura mediana.
middleweight ['mɪdlweɪt] *n* peso *m* medio; **light ~** peso *m* medio ligero.
Middle West ['mɪdl'west] *n* (*US*) mediooeste *m* (*llanura central de EE.UU.*).
middling ['mɪdlɪŋ] **1** *adj* mediano, regular. **2** *adv* (**a**) regular; **how are you? ... ~** ¿qué tal estás? ... regular. (**b**) (*****) **~ good** medianamente bueno, regular.
middy* ['mɪdɪ] *n* = **midshipman.**
midfield ['mɪdfiːld] **1** *n* centrocampo *m*, centro *m* del campo. **2** *attr*: **~ player** centrocampista *mf*.
midge [mɪdʒ] *n* mosca *f*, mosquito *m*.
midget ['mɪdʒɪt] **1** *n* enano *m*, -a *f*. **2** *adj* en miniatura, en pequeña escala; *submarine etc* de bolsillo.
midi ['mɪdɪ] *adj*: **~ hi-fi, ~ system** cadena *f* musical compacta.
midiskirt ['mɪdɪskɜːt] *n* midi *m*, midifalda *f*.
midland ['mɪdlənd] **1** *adj* del interior, del centro. **2** *n*: **the M~s** (*Brit*) *la región central de Inglaterra*.
Midlander ['mɪdləndəʳ] *n* nativo *m*, -a *f* (*or* habitante *mf*) de la región central de Inglaterra.
mid-life ['mɪd,laɪf] *attr*: **~ crisis** crisis *f* de los cuarenta.
mid-morning ['mɪd'mɔːnɪŋ] *adj*: **~ coffee** café *m* de media mañana, café *m* de las once.
midnight ['mɪdnaɪt] **1** *n* medianoche *f*. **2** *attr* de medianoche; **~ mass** misa *f* del gallo; **to burn the ~ oil** quemarse las cejas.
midpoint ['mɪd,pɔɪnt] *n* punto *m* medio.
midriff ['mɪdrɪf] *n* diafragma *m*.
midsection ['mɪdsekʃən] *n* sección *f* de en medio.
midshipman ['mɪdʃɪpmən] *n, pl* **midshipmen** ['mɪdʃɪpmən] guardia *m* marina.
midships ['mɪdʃɪps] *adv* en medio del navío.
midst [mɪdst] **1** *n*: **in the ~ of** entre, en medio de; **in our ~** entre nosotros; **in the ~ of plenty** en medio de la abundancia. **2** *prep* (*liter*) = **amid**(**st**).
midstream ['mɪd'striːm] *n*: **in ~** en medio de la corriente, en medio del río.
midsummer ['mɪd'sʌməʳ] **1** *n* pleno verano *m*, (*strictly*) solsticio *m* estival; **M~** (**Day**) fiesta *f* de San Juan (*24 junio*); **'M~ Night's Dream'** 'El sueño de una noche de verano'; **at ~** el día del solsticio de verano; **in ~** en pleno verano.
2 *attr* de pleno verano, estival; **~ madness** locura *f* temporal.
mid-term ['mɪd'tɜːm] *attr*: **~ exam** examen *m* de mitad del trimestre; **~ elections** (*US*) elecciones *fpl* de medio mandato (presidencial).
midtown ['mɪd,taʊn] **1** *n* centro *m* de la ciudad. **2** *attr*: *e.g.* **~ shops** tiendas *fpl* del centro de la ciudad.
midway ['mɪd'weɪ] **1** *adv* a mitad del camino; **~ between X and Y** a mitad del camino (*or* a medio camino) entre X e Y; **we are now ~** ahora estamos a medio camino.
2 *adj* situado a medio camino; **a ~ point** un punto intermedio, un punto equidistante de los dos extremos.
3 *n* (*US*) avenida *f* central, paseo *m* central.
midweek ['mɪd'wiːk] **1** *adv* entre semana. **2** *adj flight etc* de entre semana.
Midwest ['mɪd'west] *n* (*US*) medioeste *m* (*llanura central de EE.UU.*).
Midwestern ['mɪd,westən] *adj* (*US*) del medioeste (*de EE.UU.*).
midwife ['mɪdwaɪf] *n, pl* **midwives** ['mɪdwaɪvz] comadrona *f*, partera *f*.
midwifery ['mɪd,wɪfərɪ] *n* partería *f*.
midwinter ['mɪd'wɪntəʳ] **1** *n* pleno invierno *m*, (*strictly*) solsticio *m* de invierno; **at ~** el día del solsticio de invierno; **in ~** en pleno invierno.
2 *attr* de pleno invierno.
mien [miːn] *n* (*liter*) aire *m*, porte *m*, semblante *m*.
miff* [mɪf] **1** *n* disgusto *m*. **2** *vt* disgustar, ofender; **he was pretty ~ed about it** se ofendió bastante por eso.
might[1] [maɪt] *V* **may.**
might[2] [maɪt] *n* fuerza *f*, poder *m*, poderío *m*; **~ is right** es la ley del más fuerte; **with ~ and main** a más no poder, esforzándose muchísimo; **with all one's ~** con todas sus fuerzas, empleándose a fondo.
might-have-been ['maɪtəv,biːn] *n* esperanza *f* no cumplida.
mightily ['maɪtɪlɪ] *adv* fuertemente; poderosamente; **I was ~ surprised** me sorprendí enormemente.
mightiness ['maɪtɪnɪs] *n* fuerza *f*; poder *m*, poderío *m*.
mightn't ['maɪtnt] = **might not.**
mighty ['maɪtɪ] **1** *adj* (**a**) fuerte; potente, poderoso.
(**b**) (*****) enorme, inmenso.
2 *adv* (*****) muy, terriblemente; **it's ~ awkward** es terriblemente difícil; **I was ~ surprised** me sorprendí enormemente.
mignonette [ˌmɪnjə'net] *n* reseda *f*.
migraine ['miːgreɪn] *n* jaqueca *f*.
migrant ['maɪgrənt] **1** *adj* migratorio. **2** *n* peregrino *m*, -a *f*, nómada *mf*; (*Australia*) inmigrante *mf*; (*bird*) ave *f* migratoria, ave *f* de paso; (*insect*) insecto *m* migratorio.
migrate [maɪ'greɪt] *vi* emigrar, migrar; (*flocks*) trashumar.
migration [maɪ'greɪʃən] *n* migración *f*; trashumancia *f*.
migratory [maɪ'greɪtərɪ] *adj* migratorio; trashumante.
Mike [maɪk] *nm familiar form of* **Michael**; **for the love of ~!*** ¡por Dios!
mike[1] [maɪk] *n*: **to have a good ~⁑** no hacer nada, tirarse a la bartola; gandulear, racanear*.
mike[2]* [maɪk] *n* (*Rad*) micro *m**.
milady [mɪ'leɪdɪ] *n* miladi *f*.
Milan [mɪ'læn] *n* Milán *m*.
milch [mɪltʃ] *attr*: **~ cow** vaca *f* lechera.
mild [maɪld] **1** *adj* (*of character*) apacible, pacífico; manso; *rule etc* blando; *protest* moderado; *climate* templado; *day* blando; *medicine, effect, taste etc* suave, dulce; (*slight*) leve, ligero; (*Med*) benigno. **2** *n tipo de cerveza*.
mildew ['mɪldjuː] *n* moho *m*; (*on wheat*) añublo *m*; (*on vine*) mildiu *m*.
mildewed ['mɪldjuːd] *adj* mohoso; añublado; con mildiu.
mildly ['maɪldlɪ] *adv* (*V adj*) apaciblemente, pacíficamente; blandamente; suavemente, dulcemente; levemente, ligeramente; **to put it ~, and that's putting it ~** para no decir más.
mild-mannered ['maɪld'mænəd] *adj* apacible.
mildness ['maɪldnɪs] *n* (*V adj*) apacibilidad *f*; blandura *f*; suavidad *f*, dulzura *f*; levedad *f*.
mile [maɪl] *n* milla *f* (= 1609,33 *m*); **~s per gallon** *equivalent to* litros por 100 kilómetros; **not a hundred ~s from here** (*fig*) no muy lejos de aquí; **sorry, I was ~s away** lo siento, se me fue el santo al cielo; **we walked ~s!** ¡hemos andado kilómetros y kilómetros!; **they live ~s away** viven lejísimos de aquí; **you were ~s off the target** no te acercaste ni con mucho al objetivo; **you can tell it a ~ off**

eso se ve a la legua; **it smelled for ~s around** olía a muchas leguas a la redonda; **she'll run a ~ from a spider** vuela a la vista de una araña; **it stands out a ~** salta a los ojos, se ve a la legua.

mileage ['maɪlɪdʒ] **1** *n* (**a**) (*distance covered*) número *m* de millas, distancia *f* recorrida en millas; (*Aut*) kilometraje *m*; **~ per gallon** ≃ litros por 100 kilómetros; **what ~ has this car done?** ¿qué kilómetros tiene este coche?

(**b**) (*fig*) **there's no ~ in this story** esta historia sólo tiene un interés pasajero; **he got a lot of ~ out of the affair** explotó el asunto al máximo; **he got a lot of ~ out of it** (*fig*) le sacó mucho partido.

2 *attr*: **~ allowance** gastos *mpl* de viaje por milla recorrida, asignación *f* por kilometraje; **~ indicator** cuentakilómetros *m*; **~ rate** tarifa *f* por distancia; **~ ticket** billete *m* kilométrico.

mileometer ['maɪ'lɒmɪtəʳ] *n* = **milometer**.

milepost ['maɪlpəʊst] *n* (*Hist*) poste *m* miliar, mojón *m*.

miler ['maɪləʳ] *n* corredor *m*, -ora *f* (*etc*) que se especializa en las pruebas de una milla.

milestone ['maɪlstəʊn] *n* (*Hist*) piedra *f* miliaria; (*in Spain etc*) mojón *m* (kilométrico), hito *m* (kilométrico); (*fig*) hito *m*; **these events are ~s in our history** estos acontecimientos hacen época (*or* son hitos) en nuestra historia.

milieu ['miːljɜː] *n, pl* **milieus** *or* **milieux** ['miːljɜː] medio *m*, ambiente *m*, medio *m* ambiente.

militancy ['mɪlɪtənsɪ] *n* militancia *f*; actitud *f* belicosa; activismo *m*.

militant ['mɪlɪtənt] **1** *adj* militante; belicoso, agresivo. **2** *n* militante *mf*; activista *mf*.

militarily ['mɪlɪ'tɜːrɪlɪ] *adv* militarmente.

militarism ['mɪlɪtərɪzəm] *n* militarismo *m*.

militarist ['mɪlɪtərɪst] **1** *adj* militarista. **2** *n* militarista *mf*.

militaristic [ˌmɪlɪtə'rɪstɪk] *adj* militarista.

militarize ['mɪlɪtəraɪz] *vt* militarizar.

military ['mɪlɪtərɪ] **1** *adj* militar; **~ academy** (*US*) escuela *f* militar; **~ attaché** agregado *m* militar; **~ coup** golpe *m* militar; **~-industrial complex** (*esp US*) complejo *m* militar-industrial; **~ operations** operaciones *fpl* militares; **~ police** policía *f* militar; **~ policeman** policía *m* militar; **~ service** servicio *m* militar; **~ training** instrucción *f* militar, (*loosely*) servicio *m*. **2** *n*: **the ~** los militares.

militate ['mɪlɪteɪt] *vi*: **to ~ against** militar contra.

militia [mɪ'lɪʃə] **1** *n* milicia(s) *f*(*pl*). **2** *attr*: **the ~ reserves** (*US*) las reservas (territoriales).

militiaman [mɪ'lɪʃəmən] *n, pl* **militiamen** [mɪ'lɪʃəmən] miliciano *m*.

milk [mɪlk] **1** *n* leche *f*; **~ of magnesia** leche *f* de magnesia; **the ~ of human kindness** la compasión (personificada); **it's no good crying over spilt ~** a lo hecho pecho, agua pasada no mueve molino.

2 *attr* de leche; *diet, product etc* lácteo; **~ chocolate** chocolate *m* con leche; **~ products** productos *mpl* lácteos; **~ pudding** arroz *m* con leche; **~ round** recorrido *m* del lechero; **~ teeth** dentición *f* de leche.

3 *vt* ordeñar; (*fig*) chupar; **they're ~ing the company for all they can get** chupan todo lo que pueden de la compañía.

4 *vi* dar leche.

milk-and-water ['mɪlkən'wɔːtəʳ] *adj* (*fig*) débil, flojo.

milk-bar ['mɪlkbɑːʳ] *n* cafetería *f*.

milk-churn ['mɪlktʃɜːn] *n* lechera *f*.

milk-float ['mɪlkfləʊt] *n* (*Brit*) carro *m* de la leche.

milking ['mɪlkɪŋ] **1** *adj* lechero, de ordeño. **2** *n* ordeño *m*.

milking-machine ['mɪlkɪŋməˌʃiːn] *n* ordeñadora *f* mecánica.

milkmaid ['mɪlkmeɪd] *n* lechera *f*.

milkman ['mɪlkmən] *n, pl* **milkmen** ['mɪlkmən] lechero *m*, repartidor *m* de leche.

milk run ['mɪlkˌrʌn] *n* (*Aer*) vuelo *m* rutinario.

milkshake ['mɪlk'ʃeɪk] *n* batido *m* de leche, malteada *f* (*LAm*).

milksop ['mɪlksɒp] *n* marica *m*.

milk tooth ['mɪlktuːθ] *n, pl* **milk teeth** ['mɪlktiːθ] diente *m* de leche.

milk truck ['mɪlktrʌk] *n* (*US*) carro *m* de la leche.

milkweed ['mɪlkwiːd] *n* algodoncillo *m*.

milk-white ['mɪlk'waɪt] *adj* blanco como la leche.

milky ['mɪlkɪ] *adj* lechoso; **~ coffee** café *m* lechoso; **~ drink** bebida *f* con leche.

Milky Way ['mɪlkɪ'weɪ] *n* Vía *f* Láctea.

mill [mɪl] **1** *n* (**a**) (*wind~*) molino *m*; (*small, for coffee etc*) molinillo *m*; **to go through the ~** pasarlas moradas, sufrir mucho; aprender por experiencia práctica; **to put sb through the ~** someter a uno a un entrenamiento riguroso; hacer que uno aprenda por experiencia práctica; pasar a uno por la piedra.

(**b**) (*factory*) fábrica *f*; (*spinning ~*) hilandería *f*; (*weaving ~*) tejeduría *f*, fábrica *f* de tejidos; (*steel ~*) acería *f*, fábrica *f* de acero; (*workshop*) taller *m*.

2 *vt* (**a**) (*grind*) moler; *cloth* abatanar; *chocolate* batir.

(**b**) (*Mech*) fresar; *coin* acordonar.

◆**mill about, mill around** *vi* circular en masa, moverse por todas partes; **people were ~ing around the booking office** la gente se apiñaba impaciente delante de la taquilla; **stop ~ing around!** ¡quietos!

milled [mɪld] *adj* (**a**) *grain* molido. (**b**) *coin* acordonado; **~ edge** cordoncillo *m*.

millenary [mɪ'lenərɪ] **1** *adj* milenario. **2** *n* milenario *m*.

millennial [mɪ'lenɪəl] *adj* milenario.

millennium [mɪ'lenɪəm] *n, pl* **millenia** [mɪ'lenɪə] milenio *m*, milenario *m*.

miller ['mɪləʳ] *n* molinero *m*.

millet ['mɪlɪt] *n* mijo *m*.

millhand ['mɪlhænd] *n* obrero *m*, -a *f*, operario *m*, -a *f*.

milliard ['mɪlɪɑːd] *n* (*Brit*) mil millones *mpl*; **a ~ marks** mil millones de marcos.

millibar ['mɪlɪbɑːʳ] *n* milibar *m*.

milligram(me) ['mɪlɪgræm] *n* miligramo *m*.

millilitre, (*US*) **milliliter** ['mɪlɪˌliːtəʳ] *n* mililitro *m*.

millimetre, (*US*) **millimeter** ['mɪlɪˌmiːtəʳ] *n* milímetro *m*.

milliner ['mɪlɪnəʳ] *n* sombrerera *f*, modista *f* (de sombreros); **~'s (shop)** sombrerería *f*, tienda *f* de sombreros (de señora).

millinery ['mɪlɪnərɪ] *n* sombrerería *f*, sombreros *mpl* de señora.

milling ['mɪlɪŋ] *n* (**a**) (*grinding*) molienda *f*. (**b**) (*on coin*) cordoncillo *m*.

milling machine ['mɪlɪŋməˌʃiːn] *n* fresadora *f*.

million ['mɪljən] *n* millón *m*; **one ~ fleas** un millón de pulgas; **4 ~ dogs** 4 millones de perros; **she's one in a ~** es una verdadera joya, es un mirlo blanco; **to feel like a ~ dollars** (*US*) sentirse a las mil maravillas; **I've told you ~s of times** te lo he dicho infinidad de veces.

millionaire [ˌmɪljə'nɛəʳ] *n* millonario *m*, -a *f*.

millionth ['mɪljənθ] **1** *adj* millonésimo. **2** *n* millonésimo *m*.

millipede ['mɪlɪpiːd] *n* miriópodo *m*, milpiés *m*.

millisecond ['mɪlɪˌsekənd] *n* milisegundo *m*.

millpond ['mɪlpɒnd] *n* represa *f* de molino.

millrace ['mɪlreɪs] *n* caz *m*.

millstone ['mɪlstəʊn] *n* piedra *f* de molino, muela *f*; (*fig*) carga *f* pesada; lastre *m*; **it's a ~ round his neck** es una losa que lleva encima.

millstream ['mɪlstriːm] *n* corriente *f* de agua que mueve un molino.

millwheel ['mɪlwiːl] *n* rueda *f* de molino.

milometer [maɪ'lɒmɪtəʳ] *n* (*Brit*) cuentakilómetros *m*.

milord [mɪ'lɔːd] *n* milord *m*.

milt [mɪlt] *n* lecha *f*.

mime [maɪm] **1** *n* (**a**) (*action*) pantomima *f*, mímica *f*; (*ancient play*) mímica *f*, teatro *m* de mímica.

(**b**) (*actor*) mimo *m*.

2 *vt* hacer en pantomima, remedar; representar con gestos.

3 *vi* actuar de mimo.

Mimeograph ['mɪmɪəgrɑːf] ® **1** *n* mimeógrafo ® *m*. **2** *vt* mimeografiar.

mimic ['mɪmɪk] **1** *adj* mímico; (*pretended*) fingido, simulado. **2** *n* remedador *m*, -ora *f*, imitador *m*, -ora *f*. **3** *vt* remedar, imitar.

mimicry ['mɪmɪkrɪ] *n* imitación *f*, remedo *m*; (*Bio*) mimetismo *m*.

mimosa [mɪ'məʊzə] *n* mimosa *f*.

Min. (*Brit*) *abbr of* **Ministry** Ministerio *m*, Min.

min. (**a**) *abbr of* **minute**(**s**) minuto(s) *m*(*pl*), m. (**b**) *abbr of* **minimum.**

minaret [mɪnə'ret] *n* alminar *m*.

minatory ['mɪnətərɪ] *adj* (*liter*) amenazador.

mince [mɪns] **1** *n* (*Brit*) carne *f* picada.

2 *vt* (*Brit*) desmenuzar; *meat* picar; **she doesn't ~ her words** no tiene pelos en la lengua; **well, not to ~ matters** bueno, para decirlo francamente.

3 *vi* (*in walking*) andar con pasos menuditos; (*in talking*) hablar remilgadamente.

mincemeat ['mɪnsmiːt] *n* conserva *f* de picadillo de fruta; (*US*) carne *f* picada; **to make ~ of one's opponent** hacer trizas a su contrario, hacer picadillo a su contrario.

mince pie ['mɪns'paɪ] *n* pastel *m* de picadillo de fruta.

mincer ['mɪnsəʳ] *n* máquina *f* de picar carne, picadora *f* de carne.

mincing ['mɪnsɪŋ] *adj* remilgado, afectado; *step* menudito.

mincing-machine ['mɪnsɪŋmə,ʃiːn] *n* máquina *f* de picar carne.

mind [maɪnd] **1** *n* (**a**) mente *f*; (*intellect*) inteligencia *f*, entendimiento *m*; (*memory*) memoria *f*; (*contrasted with matter*) espíritu *m*; (*cast of* ~) mentalidad *f*; (*sanity, judgement*) juicio *m*; (*intention*) intención *f*, voluntad *f*; (*opinion*) opinión *f*, parecer *m*; (*leaning*) inclinación *f*; **~'s eye** imaginación *f*; **state of** ~ estado *m* de ánimo; **of unsound** ~ mentalmente incapacitado; **time out of** ~ tiempo *m* inmemorial; **a triumph of ~ over matter** un triunfo de la inteligencia sobre la materia inerte; **to my** ~ en mi opinión; **with one** ~ unánimemente; **with an open** ~ con espíritu amplio, sin prejuicios, sin ideas preconcebidas; **great ~s think alike** (*hum or iro*) los sabios siempre pensamos igual; **at the back of my ~ I had the feeling that** ... tenía la remota sensación de que ...; **it's all in the** ~ son imaginaciones tuyas; **to be in one's right** ~ estar en su cabal juicio; **nobody in his right ~ would do it** nadie en su cabal juicio lo haría; **she wrote it with publication in** ~ lo escribió con la intención de publicarlo; **to be in two ~s** estar en la duda, no saber a qué carta quedarse (*about* en el asunto de); **I am not clear in my ~ about the incident** no recuerdo el incidente con entera claridad; **I am not clear in my ~ about the plan** no entiendo del todo el proyecto; **to be uneasy in one's** ~ estar algo inquieto; **to be of one** ~ ser unánimes, estar de acuerdo; **I was of the same ~ as my brother** yo compartía el criterio de mi hermano, mi hermano y yo éramos de la misma opinión; **what's on your ~?** ¿qué es lo que te preocupa?; **the child's death was much on his** ~ le angustiaba muchísimo la muerte del niño; **to be out of one's** ~ estar fuera de juicio, estar (como) loco; **you must be out of your ~!** ¿se te ha vuelto el juicio?

(**b**) (*verbal phrases*) **to bear sth in** ~ tener algo presente; **I'll bear you in** ~ me acordaré de ti, no te olvidaré; **we must bear (it) in ~ that** ... tenemos que recordar que ...; **we were bored out of our ~s** nos aburrimos horriblemente; **to bring** (*or* **call**) **sth to** ~ recordar algo; **that calls sth else to** ~ eso me trae otra cosa a la memoria; **to change one's** ~ cambiar de opinión, mudar de parecer; **to change sb else's** ~ hacer que otro cambie de opinión; **it came to my ~ that** ... se me ocurrió que ...; **it crossed my** ~ se me ocurrió (*that* que); **yes, it had crossed my** ~ si, eso se me había ocurrido; **it never crossed** (*or* **entered**) **my** ~ jamás se me pasó por la cabeza; **does it ever cross your ~ that** ...? ¿piensas alguna vez que ...?; **I can't get it out of my** ~ eso no lo puedo quitar de la cabeza; **to give one's ~ to sth** aplicarse a algo; **to go out of one's** ~ volverse loco; **to go over sth in one's** ~ repasar algo mentalmente; **I have a good ~ to do it, I have half a ~ to do it** casi estoy por hacerlo, tengo ganas de hacerlo, por poco lo hago; **to have a closed** ~ tener una mente cerrada; **to have sth in** ~ pensar en algo, tener algo pensado; **to have one's ~ on a matter** tener su atención puesta en un asunto; **to have a ~ to** +*infin*, **to have it in ~ to** + *infin* pensar + *infin*, proponerse + *infin*; **whom have you in ~ for the job?** ¿a quién piensas dar el puesto?; **to have sth on one's** ~ estar preocupado por algo; **to improve one's** ~ edificar su espíritu, educarse, instruirse; **to keep sth in** ~ *V* **to bear sth in** ~; **to keep an open ~ on a subject** evitar tener prejuicios acerca de un asunto; no opinar definitivamente, estar todavía sin decidirse acerca de un asunto; **to know one's own** ~ saber lo que uno quiere; **to let one's ~ run on sth** dejar que la mente se distraiga en algo; **to lose one's** ~ volverse loco; **to make up one's** ~ resolverse, decidirse (*to* + *infin* a + *infin*); tomar partido; **we can't make up our ~s about the house** no nos decidimos a vender (*etc*) la casa; **I can't make up my ~ about him** todavía tengo ciertas dudas con respecto a él; **to pass out of** ~ caer en el olvido; **he puts me in ~ of his father** recuerda a su padre, me hace pensar en su padre; **you can put that right out of your** ~ conviene no pensar más en eso; **if you put your ~ to it** si te concentras en ello; **to read sb's** ~ adivinar el pensamiento de uno; **to set one's ~ on sth** desear algo con vehemencia, estar resuelto a conseguir (*or* hacer *etc*) algo; **it slipped my** ~ se me fue el santo al cielo, se me olvidó; **to speak one's** ~ hablar con franqueza, hablar claro; **the thought that springs to ~ is** ... el pensamiento que se le ocurre a uno es ...; **she stuck in my** ~ quedó grabada en mi recuerdo; **this will take your ~ off it** esto servirá para distraerte.

2 *vt* (**a**) (*pay attention to*) hacer caso de; fijarse en; preocuparse de; *rules etc* obedecer, guiarse por; *person etc* (*US**) obedecer; **never ~ him!** ¡no le hagas caso!; **never ~ that!** ¡no te preocupes por eso!; ¡deja eso en paz!; **buy it and never ~ the expense** cómpralo sin hacer caso del coste; **I don't ~ the cold** el frío me trae sin cuidado, no me molesta el frío; **~ what you're doing!** ¡cuidado lo que haces!; **don't ~ me!** ¡no te ocupes de mí!; (*iro*) ¿y yo que estoy delante?; **~ what I say!** ¡escucha lo que te digo!; **~ you** ... te advierto que ...; **~ you, it was raining at the time** hay que tener en cuenta que en ese momento llovía; **it was a big one, ~ you** era grande, eso sí.

(**b**) (*be put out by*) sentirse molesto por, tener inconveniente en; **do you ~ the noise?** ¿te molesta el ruido?; **I don't ~ 4, but 6 is too many** con 4 estoy bien, pero 6 son muchos; **I shouldn't ~ a cup of tea** no vendría mal una taza de té; **do you ~ coming with me?** ¿me hace el favor de acompañarme?; **would you ~ opening the door?** ¿me haces el favor de abrir la puerta?; **if you don't ~ my** (*or* **me**) **saying so, I think you're wrong** si me lo permites, creo que te equivocas; **I don't ~ having to wait** no tengo inconveniente en esperar, no me importa esperar.

(**c**) (*beware of*) tener cuidado con (*or* de); **~ the stairs!** ¡cuidado con la escalera!; **~ your language!** ¡cuida tu lengua!, ¡cuidado con lo que dices!

(**d**) (*oversee*) cuidar, vigilar, estar al cuidado de; *children etc* cuidar; *shop* ocuparse de, encargarse de; *machine* atender.

(**e**) (††, *: *remember*) acordarse de, recordar; **I ~ the time when** ... me acuerdo de cuando ...

3 *vi* (**a**) (*worry, be concerned*) preocuparse; **never ~!** (*don't worry*) ¡no se preocupe!; (*pay no attention*) ¡no hagas caso!; (*it makes no odds*) ¡es igual!, ¡no importa!, ¡qué más da!; **'who's writing to you?' — 'never you ~'** '¿quién te escribe?' — 'es cosa mía'; **I can't walk, never ~ run** no puedo andar, ni menos correr; **he didn't do it, ~** pero en realidad no lo hizo, la verdad es que no lo hizo.

(**b**) (*be put out*) tener inconveniente; **I don't ~** me es igual, no tengo inconveniente; **do you ~?** ¿se puede?; **do you ~!** (*iro*) ¡por favor!; **a cigarette? - I don't ~** (**if I do**) ¿un cigarrillo? - pues muchas gracias (*or* bueno, no digo que no); **close the door, if you don't ~** haz el favor de cerrar la puerta; **do you ~ if I come?** ¿te importa que yo venga?; **do you ~ if I open the window?** ¿te molesta que abra la ventana?; **if you don't ~, I won't come** si no te importa, yo no vengo.

(**c**) (*be careful*) tener cuidado; **~!** ¡cuidado!; **~ you don't get wet!** ¡cuidado con mojarte!, ¡ten cuidado de no mojarte!; **~ you do it!** ¡hazlo sin falta!, ¡no dejes de hacerlo!; **~ how you go!** (*as farewell*) ¡cuídate!

◆**mind out*** *vi*: **~ out!** ¡cuidado!, ¡atención!; **~ out or you'll break it!** ¡cuidado o lo rompes!

mind-bender* ['maɪnd,bendəʳ] *n* (*US*) (**a**) (*drug*) alucinogénico *m*, droga *f* alucinogénica. (**b**) (*revelation*) noticia *f* (*or* escena *etc*) alucinante*.

mind-bending* ['maɪnd,bendɪŋ] *adj*, **mind-blowing*** ['maɪnd,bləʊɪŋ] *adj*, **mind-boggling*** ['maɪnd,bɒglɪŋ] *adj* increíble; detonante*, alucinante*.

minded ['maɪndɪd] *adj*: **if you are so ~** si estás dispuesto a hacerlo, si quieres hacerlo.

-minded ['maɪndɪd] *adj ending in compounds* de mente ..., de mentalidad ... inclinado a ..., interesado en ..., consciente de ...; **fair~** imparcial; **an industrially~ nation** una nación consciente de sus industrias, una nación que se dedica a la industria; **a romantically~ girl** una joven de pensamientos románticos, una joven con ideas románticas.

minder* ['maɪndəʳ] *n* guardaespaldas *m*; acompañante *m*; escolta *m*.

mindful ['maɪndfʊl] *adj*: **~ of** consciente de, atento a; **we must be ~ of the risks** hay que tener presentes los riesgos, acordémonos de los riesgos.

mindless ['maɪndlɪs] *adj* (**a**) (*stupid*) estúpido, fútil; **the ~ masses** las masas que no piensan; **~ violence** violencia *f* inmotivada. (**b**) **~ of** indiferente a, inconsciente de.

mind-reader ['maɪnd,riːdəʳ] *n* adivinador *m*, -ora *f* de pensamientos.

mind-reading ['maɪnd,riːdɪŋ] *n* adivinación *f* de pensamientos.

mindset ['maɪndset] *n* actitud *f*, disposición *f*.

mine¹ [maɪn] *poss pron* (el) mío, (la) mía *etc*; **~ and thine** lo mío y lo tuyo; **this car is ~** este coche es mío, éste es mi coche; **is this ~?** ¿es mío esto?; **his friends and ~** sus amigos y los míos; **I have what is ~** tengo lo que es mío; **a**

friend of ~ un amigo mío, uno de mis amigos; **it's no business of** ~ no tiene que ver conmigo; **be** ~! († *or hum*) ¡cásate conmigo!; **I want to make her** ~ quiero que sea mi mujer.

mine² [maɪn] **1** *n* (**a**) (*Min*) mina *f*; **to work a** ~ explotar una mina.

(**b**) (*Mil, Naut etc*) mina *f*; **to lay** ~**s** sembrar minas; **to sweep** ~**s** dragar minas, barrer minas.

(**c**) (*fig*) tesoro *m*, pozo *m*; **the book is a** ~ **of information** el libro es un tesoro de datos útiles.

2 *vt* (**a**) *coal, metal* extraer, explotar.

(**b**) (*Mil, Naut*) *channel, road* sembrar minas en; proteger con minas; *ship* hundir con (*or* por medio de) una mina.

3 *vi* extraer minerales; dedicarse a la minería; **to** ~ **for tin** buscar estaño abriendo una mina; explotar los yacimientos de estaño.

mine-detector [ˈmaɪndɪˌtektəʳ] *n* detector *m* de minas.

minefield [ˈmaɪnfiːld] *n* campo de minas, terreno *m* minado (*also fig*).

minelayer [ˈmaɪnˌleɪəʳ] *n* minador *m*.

miner [ˈmaɪnəʳ] *n* minero *m*.

mineral [ˈmɪnərəl] **1** *adj* mineral; ~ **rights** derechos *mpl* al subsuelo; ~ **water** agua *f* mineral, (*Brit*: *loosely*) gaseosa *f*. **2** *n* mineral *m*.

mineralogist [ˌmɪnəˈrælədʒɪst] *n* mineralogista *mf*.

mineralogy [ˌmɪnəˈrælədʒɪ] *n* mineralogía *f*.

Minerva [mɪˈnɜːvə] *nf* Minerva.

mineshaft [ˈmaɪnʃɑːft] *n* pozo *m* de mina.

minestrone [ˌmɪnɪˈstrəʊnɪ] *n* minestrone *f*.

minesweeper [ˈmaɪnˌswiːpəʳ] *n* dragaminas *m*, barreminas *m*.

mingle [ˈmɪŋgl] **1** *vt* mezclar (*with* con).

2 *vi* mezclarse; (*become indistinguishable*) confundirse (*in, with* con); **he** ~**d with people of all classes** se asociaba con personas de todas las clases, vivía con personas de todas las clases.

mingy* [ˈmɪndʒɪ] *adj person* tacaño; *amount, size* escaso, insuficiente, pobre.

Mini [ˈmɪnɪ] *n* (*Aut*) Mini *m*.

mini [ˈmɪnɪ] *n* (*skirt*) minifalda *f*, mini *f*.

mini... [ˈmɪnɪ] *pref* mini..., micro...

miniature [ˈmɪnɪtʃəʳ] **1** *n* miniatura *f*; modelo *m* pequeño; **in** ~ en miniatura, en pequeña escala.

2 *adj* (en) miniatura; ~ **golf** golf *m* miniatura; ~ **poodle** perro *m* de lanas miniatura; ~ **railway** ferrocarril *m* miniatura; ~ **submarine** submarino *m* de bolsillo; ~ **watches** relojes *mpl* miniatura.

miniaturization [ˌmɪnɪtʃəraɪˈzeɪʃən] *n* miniaturización *f*.

miniaturize [ˈmɪnɪtʃəraɪz] *vt* miniaturizar.

minibar [ˈmɪnɪbɑːʳ] *n* minibar *m*.

minibudget [ˈmɪnɪˌbʌdʒɪt] *n* presupuesto *m* interino.

minibus [ˈmɪnɪbʌs] *n* microbús *m*.

minicab [ˈmɪnɪkæb] *n* (*Brit*) (micro)taxi *m*.

minicomputer [ˌmɪnɪkəmˈpjuːtəʳ] *n* miniordenador *m*, minicomputadora *f*.

minicourse [ˈmɪnɪˌkɔːs] *n* (*US*) cursillo *m*.

minidress [ˈmɪnɪdres] *n* minivestido *m*.

minim [ˈmɪnɪm] *n* blanca *f*.

minimal [ˈmɪnɪml] *adj* mínimo.

minimalism [ˈmɪnɪməlɪzəm] *n* minimalismo *m*.

minimalist [ˈmɪnɪməlɪst] **1** *adj* minimalista. **2** *n* minimalista *mf*.

minimarket [ˈmɪnɪˌmɑːkɪt] *n*, **minimart** [ˈmɪnɪˌmɑːt] *n* autoservicio *m*.

minimize [ˈmɪnɪmaɪz] *vt* minimizar; aminorar, minorizar, empequeñecer.

minimum [ˈmɪnɪməm] **1** *adj* mínimo; ~ **lending rate** tipo *m* de interés mínimo; ~ **wage** salario *m* mínimo. **2** *n, pl* **minima** [ˈmɪnɪmə] mínimo *m*, mínimum *m*; **at the** ~ como mínimo; (**down**) **to the** ~ al mínimo; **down to a** ~ **of 5 degrees** hasta 5 grados como mínimum; **to keep costs down to a** (*or* **the**) ~ mantener los costos en el nivel más bajo posible.

mining [ˈmaɪnɪŋ] **1** *n* (**a**) (*Min*) minería *f*; explotación *f*, extracción *f*. (**b**) (*Mil*) minado *m*. **2** *attr area, industry, town* minero; *engineer* de minas.

minion [ˈmɪnjən] *n* (*favourite*) favorito *m*, -a *f*; (*royal favourite*) privado *m*, valido *m*; (*follower*) secuaz *m*; (*servant*) paniaguado *m*.

minipill [ˈmɪnɪˌpɪl] *n* minipíldora *f*.

miniseries [ˈmɪnɪˌsɪərɪz] *n, pl* **miniseries** (*TV*) miniserie *f*.

miniskirt [ˈmɪnɪskɜːt] *n* minifalda *f*.

minister [ˈmɪnɪstəʳ] **1** *n* (**a**) (*Brit Pol etc*) ministro *m*, -a *f* (*for, of* de).

(**b**) (*Eccl*) pastor *m*.

2 *vi*: **to** ~ **to sb** atender a uno; **to** ~ **to sb's needs** ayudar a uno dándole lo que necesita, satisfacer las necesidades de uno; **to** ~ **to a result** contribuir a un resultado.

ministerial [ˌmɪnɪsˈtɪərɪəl] *adj* ministerial, de ministro; ~ **crisis** crisis *f* de gobierno.

ministration [ˌmɪnɪsˈtreɪʃən] *n* ayuda *f*, agencia *f*, servicio *m*; (*Eccl*) ministerio *m*.

ministry [ˈmɪnɪstrɪ] *n* (**a**) (*Pol*) ministerio *m* (*for, of* de), secretaría *f* (*LAm*). (**b**) (*Eccl*) sacerdocio *m*; **to enter the** ~ hacerse sacerdote, (*Protestant*) hacerse pastor.

minium [ˈmɪnɪəm] *n* minio *m*.

mink [mɪŋk] **1** *n* (*Zool*) visón *m*; (*fur*) piel *f* de visón. **2** *attr*: ~ **cape** estola *f* de visón; ~ **coat** abrigo *m* de visón.

Minn. (*US*) *abbr of* **Minnesota**.

minnow [ˈmɪnəʊ] *n* pececillo *m* (*de agua dulce*).

minor [ˈmaɪnəʳ] **1** *adj* menor (*also Eccl, Mus etc*); (*under age*) menor de edad; *writer etc* de segundo orden, secundario; *operation* pequeño, sin trascendencia; *detail* sin importancia; *role, position* secundario, de categoría inferior; **Smith** ~ (*Brit Scol*) Smith el joven; **G** ~ sol *m* menor; ~ **third** tercera *f* menor; ~ **ailment** enfermedad *f* benigna; ~ **offence,** ~ **offense** (*US*) delito *m* de menor cuantía.

2 *n* (**a**) (*Jur*) menor *mf* de edad.

(**b**) (*US Univ*) asignatura *f* secundaria.

3 *vi*: **to** ~ **in Spanish** (*US Univ*) estudiar el español como asignatura secundaria.

Minorca [mɪˈnɔːkə] *n* Menorca *f*.

minority [maɪˈnɒrɪtɪ] **1** *n* minoría *f*; (*age*) minoridad *f*, menor edad *f*; **to be in a** ~ estar en la minoría; **you are in a** ~ **of one** Vd es el único que piensa así.

2 *attr*: ~ **government** gobierno *m* minoritario; ~ **interest** participación *f* minoritaria; ~ **language** lengua *f* minoritaria; ~ **shareholding** accionado *m* minoritario.

Minotaur [ˈmaɪnətɔːʳ] *n* Minotauro *m*.

minster [ˈmɪnstəʳ] *n* catedral *f*; iglesia *f* de un monasterio.

minstrel [ˈmɪnstrəl] juglar *m*; cantor *m*.

minstrelsy [ˈmɪnstrəlsɪ] *n* (*music*) música *f*; (*song*) canto *m*; (*art of epic minstrel*) juglaría *f*; (*art of lyric minstrel*) gaya ciencia *f*.

mint¹ [mɪnt] **1** *n* casa *f* de moneda; ceca *f*; **Royal M~** (*Brit*) Real Casa *f* de la Moneda; **to be worth a** ~ **(of money)** valer un potosí.

2 *adj stamp etc* nuevo, en nuevo, sin usar; **in** ~ **condition** en perfecto estado, sin estrenar.

3 *vt coin* acuñar; *phrase etc* idear, inventar.

mint² [mɪnt] **1** *n* (*Bot*) hierbabuena *f*, menta *f*; (*sweet*) pastilla *f* de menta. **2** *attr*: ~ **julep** (*US*) julepe *m* de menta, (bebida *f* de) whisky *m* con menta; ~ **sauce** salsa *f* de menta; ~ **tea** té *m* a la menta.

minuet [ˌmɪnjʊˈet] *n* minué *m*.

minus [ˈmaɪnəs] **1** *prep* (**a**) menos; **9** ~ **6** 9 menos 6.

(**b**) (*without, deprived of*) sin, desprovisto de, falto de; **he appeared** ~ **his trousers** apareció sin pantalón.

2 *adj* menos; negativo; ~ **sign** signo *m* menos.

3 *n* (*sign*) signo *m* menos; (*amount*) cantidad *f* negativa.

minuscule [ˈmɪnəskjuːl] *adj* minúsculo.

minute¹ [ˈmɪnɪt] **1** *n* (**a**) (*of degree, time*) minuto *m*; (*fig*) momento *m*, instante *m*; **at the last** ~ a última hora; **at 6 o'clock to the** ~ a las 6 en punto; **I'll come in a** ~ vengo al momento, vengo dentro de un momento; **it was all over in a** ~ todo esto ocurrió en un instante; **this very** ~ ahora mismo; **they were on the scene within** ~**s** llegaron a la escena dentro de pocos minutos; **every** ~ **counts** no hay tiempo que perder; **to leave things until the last** ~ dejar las cosas hasta última hora; **up to the** ~ **news** noticias *fpl* de última hora; **tell me the** ~ **he comes** avíseme en cuanto venga; **I shan't be a** ~ vuelvo (*or* termino *etc*) muy pronto; **we expect him any** ~ le esperamos de un momento a otro; **it won't take 5** ~**s** es cosa de pocos minutos; **wait a** ~! ¡un momento!

(**b**) (*draft*) borrador *m*, proyecto *m*, minuta *f*; (*note*) nota *f*, apuntación *f*; ~**s** (*of meeting*) acta *f*, actas *fpl*; **to write up the** ~**s of a meeting** levantar acta de una reunión.

2 *attr*: ~ **hand** minutero *m*; ~ **steak** biftec *m* pequeño (que se cuece rápidamente).

3 *vt meeting* levantar acta de; *remarks* registrar, hacer constar; (*draft*) hacer el borrador de, minutar; **I would like to have that** ~**d** quiero que eso conste en acta.

minute² [maɪˈnjuːt] *adj* (*small*) diminuto, menudo, pequeño; *detail etc* insignificante; (*accurate, searching*) minucioso.

minute book ['mɪnɪtbʊk] *n* libro *m* de actas.

minutely [maɪ'nju:tlɪ] *adv* minuciosamente, con minuciosidad; **a ~ detailed account** un relato completo hasta en los más pequeños detalles; **anything ~ resembling a fish** cualquier cosa que tuviera el más ligero parecido con un pez.

minutiae [mɪ'nju:ʃɪi:] *npl* detalles *mpl* minuciosos.

minx [mɪŋks] *n* picaruela *f*, mujer *f* descarada; **you ~!** ¡lagarta!

Miocene ['maɪəsi:n] **1** *adj* mioceno. **2** *n* mioceno *m*.

MIPS [mɪps] *npl abbr of* **millions of instructions per second** millones *mpl* de instrucciones por segundo, MIPS *mpl*.

miracle ['mɪrəkl] **1** *n* milagro *m*; **by a ~, by some ~** por milagro; **it will be a ~ if ...** será un milagro si ... **2** *attr*: **~ cure** remedio *m* milagro; **~ drug** droga *f* milagro; **~ play** milagro *m*, auto *m*.

miraculous [mɪ'rækjʊləs] *adj* milagroso.

miraculously [mɪ'rækjʊləslɪ] *adv* milagrosamente, por milagro.

mirage ['mɪrɑ:ʒ] *n* espejismo *m* (*also fig*).

mire [maɪəʳ] **1** *n* fango *m*, lodo *m*. **2** *vt* (*US*): **to get ~d in** quedar atascado en, quedar preso en.

mirror ['mɪrəʳ] **1** *n* espejo *m*; (*Aut*) retrovisor *m*; **to look at o.s. in the ~** mirarse en el (*or* al) espejo. **2** *attr*: **~ image** reflejo *m* exacto, contraimagen *f*; **~ writing** escritura *f* invertida. **3** *vt* reflejar.

mirth [mɜ:θ] *n* alegría *f*, regocijo *m*; (*laughter*) risa *f*, risas *fpl*; **at this there was ~** en esto hubo risas; **there was some unseemly ~** se rieron algunos descaradamente.

mirthful ['mɜ:θfʊl] *adj* alegre.

mirthless ['mɜ:θlɪs] *adj* triste, sin alegría.

miry ['maɪrɪ] *adj* fangoso, lodoso; **~ place** lodazal *m*.

MIS *n abbr of* **management information system** sistema *m* informativo de dirección.

misadventure [,mɪsəd'ventʃəʳ] *n* desgracia *f*, percance *m*, accidente *m*; **death by ~** muerte *f* accidental.

misalliance [,mɪsə'laɪəns] *n* casamiento *m* inconveniente, casamiento *m* desigual.

misanthrope ['mɪzənθrəʊp] *n* misántropo *m*.

misanthropic [,mɪzən'θrɒpɪk] *adj* misantrópico.

misanthropist [mɪ'zænθrəpɪst] *n* misántropo *m*.

misanthropy [mɪ'zænθrəpɪ] *n* misantropía *f*.

misapplication ['mɪs,æplɪ'keɪʃn] *n* mala aplicación *f*, aplicación *f* errónea; abuso *m*.

misapply ['mɪsə'plaɪ] *vt* aplicar mal; abusar de.

misapprehend ['mɪs,æprɪ'hend] *vt* comprender mal.

misapprehension ['mɪs,æprɪ'henʃən] *n* equivocación *f*, error *m*, concepto *m* erróneo; **to be under a ~** estar equivocado; **there seems to be some ~** parece haber algún malentendido.

misappropriate ['mɪsə'prəʊprɪeɪt] *vt* malversar.

misappropriation ['mɪsə,prəʊprɪ'eɪʃən] *n* malversación *f*, distracción *f* de fondos.

misbegotten ['mɪsbɪ'gɒtn] *adj* bastardo, ilegítimo; *plan etc* descabellado, llamado a fracasar.

misbehave ['mɪsbɪ'heɪv] *vi* portarse mal; (*child*) ser malo.

misbehaviour, (*US*) misbehavior ['mɪsbɪ'heɪvjəʳ] *n* mala conducta *f*.

misc. *abbr of* **miscellaneous.**

miscalculate ['mɪs'kælkjʊleɪt] *vti* calcular mal.

miscalculation ['mɪs,kælkjʊ'leɪʃən] *n* cálculo *m* erróneo; (*fig*) error *m*, desacierto *m*.

miscall ['mɪs'kɔ:l] *vt* llamar equivocadamente.

miscarriage ['mɪs,kærɪdʒ] *n* (**a**) (*Med*) aborto *m* espontáneo, malparto *m*. (**b**) (*failure*) fracaso *m*, malogro *m*; (*of letter, goods*) extravío *m*; **~ of justice** error *m* judicial, injusticia *f*.

miscarry [mɪs'kærɪ] *vi* (**a**) (*Med*) malparir, abortar. (**b**) (*fail*) fracasar, salir mal, frustrarse; (*letter, goods*) extraviarse.

miscast [,mɪs'kɑ:st] *vt* (*irr*: *V* **cast**) *actor* dar un papel poco apropiado a; *play* distribuir mal los papeles de; **he was ~ as Othello** como Otelo tuvo un papel que no le convenía.

miscegenation [,mɪsɪdʒɪ'neɪʃən] *n* mestizaje *m*, cruce *m* de razas.

miscellaneous [,mɪsɪ'leɪnɪəs] *adj* vario, diverso; **~ expenses** gastos *mpl* diversos.

miscellany [mɪ'selənɪ] *n* miscelánea *f*.

mischance [mɪs'tʃɑ:ns] *n* mala suerte *f*; infortunio *m*, desgracia *f*; **by some ~** por desgracia.

mischief ['mɪstʃɪf] *n* (**a**) (*naughtiness*) travesura *f*, diablura *f*; (*roguishness*) malicia *f*; **he's up to some ~** está haciendo alguna travesura; **there's some ~ going on** están tramando algo mal; **there's no ~ in him** no es capaz de ninguna maldad; **he's always getting into ~** anda siempre metido en alguna travesura; **to keep sb out of ~** impedir a uno hacer travesuras; **to make ~** armar líos; **to make ~ for sb** crear dificultades para uno, amargar la vida a uno.

(**b**) (*person*) diablillo *m*.

(**c**) (*harm*) mal *m*, daño *m*; **to do sb a ~** hacer mal a uno; **to do o.s. a ~** hacerse daño.

mischief-maker ['mɪstʃɪf,meɪkəʳ] *n* revoltoso *m*, -a *f*, persona *f* turbulenta, persona *f* que anda metida en líos; chismoso *m*, -a *f*.

mischievous ['mɪstʃɪvəs] *adj person* malo, dañoso; (*playful*) malicioso, juguetón; *child* travieso; *attack etc* perjudicial; *glance etc* malicioso, lleno de malicia.

mischievously ['mɪstʃɪvəslɪ] *adv* maliciosamente, con malicia; por travesura.

mischievousness ['mɪstʃɪvəsnɪs] *n* travesuras *fpl*.

misconceive ['mɪskən'si:v] *vt* entender mal, juzgar mal; **a ~d plan** un proyecto descabellado.

misconception ['mɪskən'sepʃən] *n* concepto *m* erróneo, idea *f* falsa, equivocación *f*; **but this is a ~** pero esta idea es errónea.

misconduct [mɪs'kɒndʌkt] **1** *n* mala conducta *f*; extravío *m*; (*sexual*) adulterio *m*. **2** [,mɪskən'dʌkt] *vt* manejar mal, dirigir mal. **3** [,mɪskən'dʌkt] *vr*: **to ~ o.s.** portarse mal.

misconstruction ['mɪskəns'trʌkʃən] *n* mala interpretación *f*; mala traducción *f*; (*deliberate*) tergiversación *f*.

misconstrue ['mɪskən'stru:] *vt* interpretar mal; traducir mal; (*deliberately*) tergiversar.

miscount ['mɪs'kaʊnt] **1** *vt* contar mal, equivocarse en la cuenta de. **2** *vi* contar mal.

miscreant ['mɪskrɪənt] *n* sinvergüenza *mf*, bellaco *m*, -a *f*.

misdeal ['mɪs'di:l] **1** *n* reparto *m* erróneo. **2** (*irr*: *V* **deal**) *vt cards* dar mal, repartir mal.

misdeed ['mɪs'di:d] *n* delito *m*, crimen *m*, fechoría *f*.

misdemeanour, (*US*) misdemeanor [,mɪsdɪ'mi:nəʳ] *n* ofensa *f*, delito *m*; (*Brit Jur*) delito *m* de menor cuantía, falta *f*.

misdirect ['mɪsdɪ'rekt] *vt operation etc* manejar mal, dirigir mal; *letter etc* poner unas señas incorrectas en; *person* informar mal (acerca del camino a tomar), hacer perder el camino; *jury* instruir mal.

misdirection ['mɪsdɪ'rekʃən] *n* mal manejo *m*, mala dirección *f*; instrucciones *fpl* erróneas, información *f* errónea.

miser ['maɪzəʳ] *n* avaro *m*, -a *f*, avariento *m*, -a *f*, tacaño *m*, -a *f*.

miserable ['mɪzərəbl] *adj* (**a**) (*filthy, wretched*) indecente, vil; (*contemptible*) vil, despreciable; (*valueless*) sin valor; *show, spectacle* de pena; *weather* muy feo, de perros; *wage* raquítico; **it was a ~ failure** fue un rotundo fracaso.

(**b**) (*unhappy*) triste, desdichado, desgraciado; abatido; **what are you so ~ about?** ¿por qué estás tan triste?; **I feel ~ today** hoy me siento abatido; hoy me siento sin fuerzas para nada; **to make sb ~** entristecer a uno, abatir a uno; **to make sb's life ~** amargar la vida a uno.

miserably ['mɪzərəblɪ] *adv say etc* tristemente; **~ small** lamentablemente pequeño; **~ paid** muy mal pagado; **it failed ~** fracasó rotundamente; **they played ~** jugaron terriblemente mal.

misère [mɪ'zɛəʳ] *n* (*Cards*) nulos *mpl*; **to go ~** jugar a nulos.

miserliness ['maɪzəlɪnɪs] *n* avaricia *f*, tacañería *f*.

miserly ['maɪzəlɪ] *adj person* avariento, tacaño; *amount* muy pequeño, pobre.

misery ['mɪzərɪ] *n* (**a**) (*suffering*) sufrimiento *m*; (*sadness*) pena *f*, tristeza *f*; (*wretchedness*) aflicción *f*, desdicha *f*; (*squalor*) miseria *f*, sordidez *f*; **a life of ~** una vida desgraciada; **to make sb's life a ~** amargar la vida a uno; **to live in ~** vivir en la miseria; **to put an animal out of its ~** acortar la agonía a un animal, rematar un animal; **to put sb out of his ~** (*fig*) satisfacer por fin a uno (contándole una noticia *or* revelándole un secreto *etc*).

(**b**) (*: *person*) aguafiestas *mf*, quejicoso* *m*, -a *f*.

misfile [,mɪs'faɪl] *vt papers* clasificar incorrectamente.

misfire ['mɪs'faɪəʳ] *vi* fallar.

misfit ['mɪsfɪt] *n* (**a**) cosa *f* mal ajustada; (*dress*) traje *m* que no cae bien.

(**b**) (*person*) inadaptado *m*, -a *f*, desplazado *m*, -a *f*, persona *f* reñida con su ambiente; **he's always been a ~ here** no se ha adaptado nunca a las condiciones de aquí, en ningún momento ha estado realmente contento aquí.

misfortune [mɪs'fɔ:tʃən] *n* desgracia *f*, infortunio *m*, desventura *f*; **companion in ~** compañero *m*, -a *f* en la desgracia, compañero *m*, -a *f* de infortunio; **it is his ~ that he is lame** tiene la mala suerte de ser cojo; **I had the ~ to**

meet him tuve la mala suerte de encontrarme con él.

misgiving [mɪsˈgɪvɪŋ] *n* (*mistrust*) recelo *m*, duda *f*, temor *m*; (*apprehension*) presentimiento *m*; **not without some ~** no sin cierto recelo; **I had ~s about the scheme** tuve mis dudas acerca del proyecto.

misgovern [ˈmɪsˈgʌvən] *vti* gobernar mal; administrar mal.

misgovernment [ˈmɪsˈgʌvənmənt] *n* desgobierno *m*, mal gobierno *m*; mala administración *f*.

misguided [ˈmɪsˈgaɪdɪd] *adj* mal aconsejado, equivocado.

misguidedly [ˈmɪsˈgaɪdɪdlɪ] *adv* equivocadamente.

mishandle [ˈmɪsˈhændl] *vt* manejar mal, administrar mal.

mishandling [ˌmɪsˈhændlɪŋ] *n* mal manejo *m*, mala administración *f*.

mishap [ˈmɪshæp] *n* desgracia *f*, contratiempo *m*, accidente *m*; **without ~** sin novedad; **to have a ~** tener un accidente.

mishear [ˈmɪsˈhɪəʳ] (*irr*: *V* **hear**) *vti* oír mal.

mishit 1 [ˈmɪsˌhɪt] *n* golpe *m* defectuoso. **2** [ˌmɪsˈhɪt] *vt* golpear mal.

mishmash [ˈmɪʃmæʃ] *n* masa *f* informe, masa *f* confusa; baturrillo *m*, ensaladilla *f*.

misinform [ˈmɪsɪnˈfɔːm] *vt* informar mal, malinformar, dar informes erróneos a.

misinformation [ˌmɪsɪnfəˈmeɪʃən] *n* desinformación *f*; mala información *f*.

misinterpret [ˈmɪsɪnˈtɜːprɪt] *vt* interpretar mal, malinterpretar; traducir mal; (*deliberately*) tergiversar.

misinterpretation [ˈmɪsɪnˌtɜːprɪˈteɪʃən] *n* mala interpretación *f*; mala traducción *f*; tergiversación *f*.

misjudge [ˈmɪsˈdʒʌdʒ] *vt* juzgar mal, equivocarse sobre.

misjudgement [ˌmɪsˈdʒʌdʒmənt] *n* juicio *m* erróneo.

mislay [mɪsˈleɪ] (*irr*: *V* **lay**[4]) *vt* extraviar, perder.

mislead [mɪsˈliːd] (*irr*: *V* **lead**[2]) *vt* llevar a conclusiones erróneas, despistar; (*deliberately*) engañar; (*morally*) corromper, llevar por mal camino; **I fear you have been misled** me temo que se lo hayan dicho mal.

misleading [mɪsˈliːdɪŋ] *adj* erróneo; (*deliberately*) de apariencia engañosa, engañoso.

mismanage [ˈmɪsˈmænɪdʒ] *vt* manejar mal, administrar mal, gobernar mal.

mismanagement [ˈmɪsˈmænɪdʒmənt] *n* mal manejo *m*, mala administración *f*, desgobierno *m*; incuria *f*.

mismatch [ˈmɪsˈmætʃ] *vt* emparejar mal, hermanar mal.

misname [ˈmɪsˈneɪm] *vt* llamar equivocadamente; **this grotesquely ~d society** esta sociedad con su nombre grotescamente inapropiado.

misnomer [ˈmɪsˈnəʊməʳ] *n* nombre *m* equivocado, nombre *m* inapropiado; denominación *f* errónea; **that is a ~** ese nombre es impropio.

misogamist [mɪˈsɒgəmɪst] *n* misógamo *m*, -a *f*.

misogamy [mɪˈsɒgəmɪ] *n* misogamia *f*.

misogynist [mɪˈsɒdʒɪnɪst] *n* misógino *m*.

misogyny [mɪˈsɒdʒɪnɪ] *n* misoginia *f*.

misplace [ˈmɪsˈpleɪs] *vt* (**a**) colocar mal; poner fuera de su lugar. (**b**) (*lose*) extraviar, perder.

misplaced [ˈmɪsˈpleɪst] *adj* equivocado; inoportuno; inmerecido; descolocado.

misprint [ˈmɪsprɪnt] **1** *n* errata *f*, error *m* de imprenta. **2** [mɪsˈprɪnt] *vt* imprimir mal.

mispronounce [ˈmɪsprəˈnaʊns] *vt* pronunciar mal.

mispronunciation [ˈmɪsprəˌnʌnsɪˈeɪʃən] *n* mala pronunciación *f*.

misquotation [ˈmɪskwəʊˈteɪʃən] *n* cita *f* equivocada.

misquote [ˈmɪsˈkwəʊt] *vt* citar mal; **he was ~d in the press** le citaron mal en la prensa.

misread [ˈmɪsˈriːd] (*irr*: *V* **read**) *vt* leer mal; interpretar mal.

misrepresent [ˈmɪsˌreprɪˈzent] *vt* desfigurar, falsificar; describir engañosamente; tergiversar; **he was ~ed in the papers** los informes de los periódicos falsificaron lo que había dicho.

misrepresentation [ˈmɪsˌreprɪzenˈteɪʃən] *n* desfiguración *f*; falsificación *f*; descripción *f* engañosa; tergiversación *f*; (*Jur*) falsa declaración *f*; **this report is a ~ of what I said** este informe falsifica lo que yo dije.

misrule [ˈmɪsˈruːl] **1** *n* desgobierno *m*, mal gobierno *m*. **2** *vt* desgobernar, gobernar mal.

miss[1] [mɪs] **1** *n* (*shot*) tiro *m* errado, tiro *m* perdido; (*mistake*) error *m*, desacierto *m*; (*failure*) fracaso *m*; **a ~ is as good as a mile** lo mismo da librarse por poco que por mucho; **near ~** (*Aer*) incidente *m* aéreo, air-miss *m*, aproximación *f* peligrosa entre dos aviones; **it was a near ~** (el tiro) anduvo muy cerca; **it was a near ~ with that car** faltó poco para que ese coche chocara con nosotros; **to give sth a ~** (*not go*) dejar de asistir a algo, no asistir a algo, (*not visit*) dejar de visitar algo; **we're giving it a ~ this year** este año no vamos.

2 *vt* (**a**) (*fail to hit*) *aim, target* errar; **the shot just ~ed me** por poco la bala me alcanzó, el tiro me pasó rozando; **the plane just ~ed the tower** faltó poco para que el avión chocara con la torre; **he narrowly ~ed being run over** por poco le atropellan, faltó poco para que se le atropellara.

(**b**) (*fail to find, catch, use etc*) *vocation* errar, equivocarse en la elección de; *solution* no acertar; *thing sought* no encontrar; *bus, train, chance, footing etc* perder; *one's way* equivocarse de; *class, lecture* perder; *appointment* no acudir a; *meeting etc* no asistir a, no poder asistir a; **you haven't ~ed much!** ¡no has perdido nada!; **we ~ed the tide** perdimos la pleamar; **we're afraid of ~ing the market** tememos perder el momento más propicio para la venta; **she ~ed her holiday last year** el año pasado no pudo tomarse las vacaciones; **I ~ed you at the station** no te vi en la estación; **they ~ed each other in the crowd** no lograron encontrarse entre tanta gente; **you mustn't ~ this film** no debes perderte esta película, no dejes de ver esta película; **don't ~ the Prado** no dejes de visitar el Prado; **you can't ~ the house** es imposible equivocarse al venir a la casa.

(**c**) (*fail to hear*) **I ~ed what you said** se me escapó lo que dijiste; **I ~ed that** eso no lo entendí; **you're ~ing the point** no comprendes el punto principal.

(**d**) (*omit*) omitir; (*overlook*) pasar por alto; **let's ~ the next dance** no bailemos la próxima vez.

(**e**) (*notice absence of, regret absence of*) echar de menos; notar la falta de; **I ~ the old trams** echo de menos los viejos tranvías; **I ~ you so** te echo mucho de menos, te extraño mucho (*esp LAm*); **he is much ~ed** se le echa mucho de menos; **then I ~ed my wallet** luego me di cuenta de que no tenía ya cartera; **he won't be ~ed** bien podemos prescindir de él; **we're ~ing 8 dollars** nos faltan 8 dólares; **do take it, I shan't ~ it** tómalo, no me hace falta.

3 *vi* (*shot, person*) errar el blanco, errar el tiro, fallar; (*motor*) fallar; **he ~ed** erró el tiro; **he never ~es*** siempre acierta; **you can't ~!** ¡es imposible fallar!; **I've not ~ed once in 10 years** en 10 años no he faltado ni una sola vez.

◆**miss out** *vt*: **he ~ed out a word** omitió una palabra; **he was ~ed out in the promotions** en los ascensos le pasaron por encima.

◆**miss out on** *vt* perder, dejar pasar, no aprovechar; perder la oportunidad de (*or* para).

miss[2] [mɪs] *n* señorita *f*; (*) niña *f* precoz, niña *f* repipi; **a modern ~** una señorita moderna; **M~ Jennie Smith** (la) Señorita Jennie Smith; **yes, M~ Smith** sí, señorita; **M~ Spain 1999** Miss España 1999.

Miss. (*US*) *abbr of* **Mississippi**.

missal [ˈmɪsəl] *n* misal *m*.

misshapen [ˈmɪsˈʃeɪpən] *adj* deforme.

missile [ˈmɪsaɪl] *n* proyectil *m*; (*javelin etc*) arma *f* arrojadiza; (*modern weapon*) misil *m*.

missile-launcher [ˈmɪsaɪlˌlɔːnʃəʳ] *n* lanzamisiles *m*, lanzadera *f* de misiles.

missing [ˈmɪsɪŋ] *adj* (**a**) *person* ausente, (*Mil etc*) desaparecido; *thing* perdido, extraviado, que falta; **~ in action** desaparecido en combate; **~ link** eslabón *m* perdido, eslabón *m* hipotético; **~ person** desaparecido *m*, -a *f*; **supply the ~ letters** poner las letras que faltan; **the three ~ students are safe** los tres estudiantes desaparecidos están a salvo.

(**b**) **to be ~** faltar; haber desaparecido; **there are 9 books ~, 9 books are ~** faltan 9 libros; **how many are ~?** ¿cuántos faltan?; **two members of the crew are still ~** dos miembros de la tripulación siguen desaparecidos; **one of our aircraft is ~** uno de nuestros aviones no ha vuelto.

mission [ˈmɪʃən] **1** *n* misión *f*; **to send sb on a secret ~** enviar a uno en misión secreta. **2** *attr*: **~ control** centro *m* de control; **~ controller** controlador *m*, -ora *f* de (la) misión.

missionary [ˈmɪʃənrɪ] **1** *adj zeal etc* misional, misionero; **~ position** (*hum*) postura *f* del misionero; **~ society** sociedad *f* misionera. **2** *n* misionero *m*, -a *f*.

missis* [ˈmɪsɪz] *n*: **my ~, the ~** la parienta*; **John and his ~** Juan y su costilla; **yes, ~** sí, señora; **is the ~ in?** ¿está la señora?

Mississippi [ˌmɪsɪˈsɪpɪ] *n* Misisipí *m*.

missive [ˈmɪsɪv] *n* misiva *f*.

Missouri [mɪˈzʊərɪ] *n* Misuri *m*.

misspell [ˈmɪsˈspel] (*irr*: *V* **spell**) *vt* escribir mal.

misspelling [ˈmɪsˈspelɪŋ] *n* error *m* de ortografía.

misspend [ˈmɪsˈspend] (*irr*: *V* **spend**) *vt* malgastar, desperdiciar, perder; **a misspent youth** una juventud mal empleada, una juventud pasada en la disipación.
misstate [ˈmɪsˈsteɪt] *vt* declarar erróneamente; (*deliberately*) declarar falsamente.
misstatement [ˈmɪsˈsteɪtmənt] *n* declaración *f* errónea; declaración *f* falsa.
missus* [ˈmɪsɪz] *n* = **missis.**
missy* [ˈmɪsɪ] *n* (*hum or pej*) = **miss[2].**
mist [mɪst] **1** *n* (*fog*) niebla *f*; (*slight*) neblina *f*; (*summery*; *at sea*) bruma *f*; (*on window*) paño *m*, vaho *m*, velo *m*; (*fig*) nube *f*, velo *m*; **through a ~ of tears** por ojos llenos de lágrimas.
2 *vt* (*fig*) empañar, velar.
3 *vi* (*also* **to ~ over, to ~ up**) empañarse, velarse; (*eyes*) llenarse de lágrimas.
mistakable [mɪsˈteɪkəbl] *adj* confundible.
mistake [mɪsˈteɪk] **1** *n* equivocación *f*, error *m*, falta *f*; **by ~** por equivocación, (*carelessly*) por descuido, (*involuntarily*) sin querer; **it's finished and no ~!** ¡ya lo creo que está terminado!; **he took my hat in ~ for his** confundió mi sombrero con el suyo; **to acknowledge one's ~** confesar su error; **the ~ is mine** la culpa es mía, la culpa la tengo yo; **there must be some ~** ha de haber algún error; **there's no ~ about it** está muy claro, no hay que darle vueltas; **let there be no ~ about it** entiéndase bien que ...; quede perfectamente claro que ...; **to make a ~** equivocarse; **you're making a big ~** te equivocas gravemente, es una decisión totalmente errónea; **make no ~ (about it)** no te hagas ilusiones, y que no queden dudas sobre esto; **to make the ~ of asking too much** cometer el error de pedir demasiado.
2 (*irr*: *V* **take**) *vt* (**a**) *meaning* entender mal, equivocarse sobre; *road etc* equivocar, equivocarse de; **there was no mistaking his intention** su intención era clarísima; **you couldn't ~ her walk** no se podía confundir su manera de andar con la de otras.
(**b**) **to ~ A for B** equivocar A con B, confundir A con B.
(**c**) **to be ~n** equivocarse, estar equivocado, engañarse; **if I am not ~n** si no me equivoco; **he is often ~n for Peter** se le confunde muchas veces con Pedro; **it cannot possibly be ~n for anything else** es imposible confundirlo con otra cosa.
mistaken [mɪsˈteɪkən] **1** *ptp of* **mistake. 2** *adj* equivocado, erróneo; incorrecto; **~ identity** identificación *f* errónea.
mistakenly [mɪsˈteɪkənlɪ] *adv* equivocadamente, erróneamente.
mister [ˈmɪstəʳ] *n* (**a**) (*gen abbr* **Mr**) señor *m* (*gen abbr* Sr). (**b**) (*: *in direct address*) **hey ~!** ¡oiga, usted!; **got a light ~?** ¿tiene fuego, caballero?
mistime [ˈmɪsˈtaɪm] *vt act etc* hacer (*or* decir *etc*) a deshora, hacer en momento poco oportuno; *race etc* cronometrar mal.
mistle thrush [ˈmɪslθrʌʃ] *n* zorzal *m* charlo, tordo *m* mayor.
mistletoe [ˈmɪsltəʊ] *n* muérdago *m*.
mistook [mɪsˈtʊk] *pret of* **mistake.**
mistranslate [ˈmɪstrænsˈleɪt] *vt* traducir mal.
mistranslation [ˈmɪstrænsˈleɪʃən] *n* mala traducción *f*.
mistreat [mɪsˈtriːt] *vt* maltratar, tratar mal.
mistreatment [mɪsˈtriːtmənt] *n* maltrato *m*, maltratamiento *m*, malos tratos *mpl*.
mistress [ˈmɪstrɪs] *n* (**a**) (*of house etc*) señora *f*, ama *f* de casa; **to be ~ of the situation** ser dueña de la situación; **to be one's own ~** ser independiente; trabajar por cuenta propia. (**b**) (*lover*) querida *f*, amante *f*. (**c**) (*Brit*: *teacher, primary*) maestra *f*, (*secondary*) profesora *f*. (**d**) (*abbr* **Mrs** [ˈmɪsɪz]) señora *f* de ...
mistrial [ˌmɪsˈtraɪəl] *n* (*US, Brit*) juicio *m* viciado de nulidad, (*US*) juicio *m* nulo por desacuerdo del jurado.
mistrust [ˈmɪsˈtrʌst] **1** *n* desconfianza *f*, recelo *m*. **2** *vt* desconfiar de, dudar de.
mistrustful [mɪsˈtrʌstfʊl] *adj* desconfiado, receloso; **to be ~ of** recelarse de.
misty [ˈmɪstɪ] *adj* nebuloso, brumoso; *day* de niebla; (*fig*) nebuloso, vaporoso; *glasses, window* empañado; **it's getting ~** se está aneblando, está bajando la niebla; **the window is getting ~** la ventana se está empañando.
misty-eyed [ˈmɪstɪˌaɪd] *adj* sentimental.
misunderstand [ˈmɪsʌndəˈstænd] (*irr*: *V* **stand**) *vti* entender mal, comprender mal; tomar en sentido erróneo; malinterpretar, interpretar mal; **you ~ me** no me entiendes, no entiendes lo que digo; **don't ~ me** entiéndame, no me malinterprete.
misunderstanding [ˈmɪsʌndəˈstændɪŋ] *n* equivocación *f*, error *m*; concepto *m* erróneo; (*disagreement*) desavenencia *f*; malentendido *m*; **there must be some ~** debe de haber alguna equivocación.
misunderstood [ˈmɪsʌndəˈstʊd] *adj* incomprendido; insuficientemente estimado.
misuse [ˈmɪsˈjuːs] **1** *n* abuso *m*, mal uso *m*; (*of word*) empleo *m* erróneo; (*of funds*) malversación *f*; (*of person*) maltrato *m*. **2** [ˈmɪsˈjuːz] *vt* abusar de; *word* emplear mal; *funds* malversar; *person etc* maltratar.
MIT *n* (*US*) *abbr of* **Massachusetts Institute of Technology.**
mite[1] [maɪt] *n* (*Zool*) ácaro *m*.
mite[2] [maɪt] *n* (**a**) (*coin*) ardite *m*, (*as contribution*) óbolo *m*.
(**b**) (*small quantity*) pizca *f*, poquitín *m*; **a ~ of consolation** una pizca de consuelo; **there's not a ~ left** no queda ni una sola gota; **well, just a ~ then** bueno, un poquitín; **we were a ~ surprised** quedamos un tanto atónitos, nos sorprendimos un poquito.
(**c**) (*child*) niño *m* pequeño, niña *f* pequeña, nene *m*, -a *f*; **poor little ~!** ¡pobrecito!
miter [ˈmaɪtəʳ] *n* (*US*) = **mitre.**
Mithraic [mɪθˈreɪɪk] *adj* mitraico.
Mithraism [ˈmɪθreɪɪzəm] *n* mitraísmo *m*.
Mithras [ˈmɪθræs] *nm* Mitra.
mitigate [ˈmɪtɪgeɪt] *vt* mitigar.
mitigating [ˈmɪtɪgeɪtɪŋ] *adj* atenuante; **~ circumstances** circunstancias *fpl* atenuantes.
mitigation [ˌmɪtɪˈgeɪʃən] *n* mitigación *f*; **to say a word in ~** decir algo para mitigar la ofensa (*etc*).
mitre, (*US*) **miter** [ˈmaɪtəʳ] **1** *n* (*Eccl*) mitra *f*; (*Tech*) inglete *m*. **2** *attr*: **~ box** caja *f* de ingletes; **~ joint** ensambladura *f* de inglete. **3** *vt* (*Tech*) ingletear.
mitt [mɪt] *n* (*US*: *Baseball*) guante *m*; = **mitten**; (*) mano *f*, aleta** *f*.
mitten [ˈmɪtn] *n* mitón *m*, guante *m* con solo el pulgar separado; **~s*** guantes *mpl* de boxeo; **to get the ~*** recibir calabazas*; **to give sb the ~*** dar calabazas a uno*.
mix [mɪks] **1** *n* mezcla *f*; ingredientes *mpl*, proporciones *fpl*.
2 *vt* mezclar; combinar, unir; confundir; *concrete, flour, plaster etc* amasar; *drinks* preparar, mezclar; *salad* aderezar; **to ~ sugar into sth** añadir azúcar a algo; **to ~ it*** (*Brit*) venir a las manos, arreglar las cosas a puños.
3 *vi* mezclarse, poder mezclarse; (*ingredients etc*) ir bien juntos; (*persons*: *get on well*) llevarse bien, congeniar; **to ~ with others** asociarse con otros, ir con otros, alternar con otros, frecuentar la compañía de otros; **you should ~ more with people** hay que mezclarse más con la gente; **he's not keen to ~** tiene pocas ganas de alternar; **to ~ in high society** frecuentar la alta sociedad.
◆**mix in 1** *vt*: **to ~ sth in** añadir algo, echar algo.
2 *vi*: **to ~ in with others** asociarse con otros, ir con otros, alternar con otros, frecuentar la compañía de otros; **he's not keen to ~ in** tiene pocas ganas de alternar.
◆**mix up** *vt* (**a**) (*confuse*) mezclar, confundir; **don't ~ me up** no me confundas; **I've ~ed you up with Michael** le he confundido (*or* equivocado) con Miguel. (**b**) (*involve*) **to be ~ed up in an affair** estar metido en un asunto; **to get ~ed up in an affair** meterse en un asunto, mojar en un asunto; **he got ~ed up with some strange people** formó amistades con gente muy rara; **are you ~ed up in this?** ¿tú andas metido en esto? ¿tú tienes que ver con esto?; **to ~ it up*** (*US*) zurrarse*, vapulearse.
mixed [mɪkst] *adj* mixto; mezclado; (*assorted*) variado, surtido; *bathing, choir, school etc* mixto; **a ~ set of people** un grupo de personas variadas; **I wouldn't say it in ~ company** no lo diría estando mujeres delante, no lo diría ante personas del otro sexo; **with ~ results** con resultados diversos, (*pej*) con resultados más bien mediocres; **we had ~ weather** el tiempo ha sido variable; **~ ability class** clase *f* de distinto coeficiente intelectual; **~ doubles** dobles *mpl* mixtos; **~ economy** economía *f* mixta; **~ farming** agricultura *f* mixta; **~ feelings** sentimientos *mpl* encontrados; **~ grill** (*Brit*) parrillada *f* mixta, plato *m* combinado de fritos; **~ marriage** matrimonio *m* mixto (de esposos de diversa religión o raza); **~ metaphor** metáfora *f* disparada; **it got a very ~ reception** suscitó reacciones muy diversas.
mixed-up [ˈmɪkstˈʌp] *adj* (**a**) *things* mezclados; (*disordered*) revueltos, confusos. (**b**) *person* confuso; **I'm all ~** estoy totalmente confuso; **a badly ~ youth** un joven de mentalidad gravemente confusa, un joven lleno de incertidumbre.
mixer [ˈmɪksəʳ] *n* (**a**) (*Culin*: *machine*) batidora *f*, mezcladora *f*; licuadora *f*. (**b**) (*Rad*) mezclador *m*. (**c**) (*drink*) tónica *f*. (**d**) (*person*) persona *f* sociable; **to be a good ~**

tener don de gentes; **he's not much of a ~** tiene pocas ganas de alternar, no tiene don de gentes. (**e**) (*US Univ*) fiesta *f* de bienvenida para nuevos estudiantes.
mixer tap ['mɪksə,tæp] *n* (*Brit*) grifo *m* único de agua fría y caliente.
mixing-bowl ['mɪksɪŋbəʊl] *n* cuenco *m* (de remover).
mixture ['mɪkstʃəʳ] *n* mezcla *f*; (*Med*) medicina *f*; **the ~ as before** la misma receta que antes, (*fig*) lo de siempre; **the family is an odd ~** la familia es una extraña mezcla; **he's an odd ~ of poet and plumber** se reúnen en él de modo bastante raro el poeta y el fontanero.
mix-up ['mɪks'ʌp] *n* confusión *f*, lío *m*; **there was a dreadful ~** hubo un tremendo lío; **we got in a ~ with the trains** nos hicimos un lío con los trenes.
mizzen ['mɪzn] *n* mesana *f*.
mizzenmast ['mɪznmɑːst] *n* palo *m* de mesana.
mizzle ['mɪzl] (* *or dial*) *vi* lloviznar.
Mk *abbr of* **mark** Mk.
mkt *abbr of* **market**.
ml *abbr of* **millilitre(s)**.
M.Litt. *n abbr of* **Master of Literature, Master of Letters** *título universitario*.
MLR *n abbr of* **minimum lending rate** índice *m* base de préstamos.
MM *abbr of* **Messieurs** Señores *mpl*, Sres.
mm *abbr of* **millimetre(s)** milímetro(s) *m(pl)*, mm.
mm ... [mm] *interj* esto ..., pues ..., vamos a ver ...
MMC *n* (*Brit*) *abbr of* **Monopolies and Mergers Commission**.
MN (**a**) *n* (*Brit*) *abbr of* **Merchant Navy**. (**b**) (*US Post*) *abbr of* **Minnesota**.
mnemonic [nɪ'mɒnɪk] **1** *adj* (m)nemotécnico. **2** *n* figura *f* (*or* frase *f etc*) (m)nemotécnica.
mnemonics [nɪ'mɒnɪks] *n* (m)nemotécnica *f*.
MO (**a**) *n abbr of* **medical officer** médico *mf*. (**b**) (*US Post*) *abbr of* **Missouri**. (**c**) (*: *esp US*) *abbr of* **modus operandi** *manera de actuar*.
mo¹* [məʊ] *n* = **moment**.
mo² *abbr of* **month** m.
m.o. *abbr of* **money order** giro *m*, g/.
moan [məʊn] **1** *n* (*groan*) gemido *m*, quejido *m*; (*complaint*) queja *f*, protesta *f*.
2 *vt* decir gimiendo, decir con un gemido.
3 *vi* gemir; quejarse, protestar; **they're ~ing about the food again** han vuelto a quejarse de la comida.
moaner* ['məʊnəʳ] *n* protestón* *m*, -ona *f*.
moaning ['məʊnɪŋ] *n* gemidos *mpl*; quejas *fpl*, protestas *fpl*.
moat [məʊt] *n* foso *m*.
moated ['məʊtɪd] *adj* con foso, rodeado de un foso.
mob [mɒb] **1** *n* (**a**) multitud *f*, muchedumbre *f*, gentío *m*; (*pej*) turba *f*; **the ~** el populacho; **houses were burnt by the ~s** unas casas fueron incendiadas por las turbas; **they went in a ~ to the town hall** fueron en tropel al ayuntamiento; **to join the ~** echarse a las calles; **the army has become a ~** el ejército se ha transformado en una turba.
(**b**) (*) grupo *m*, pandilla *f*, peña *f*; **the M~** (*US*) la Mafia; **Joe and his ~** Pepe y su peña, Pepe y sus amigotes*; **I had nothing to do with that ~** no tuve nada que ver con aquéllos; **which ~ were you in?** (*Mil*) ¿en qué regimiento (*etc*) estuviste?; **they're a hard-drinking ~** son unos borrachos.
2 *attr*: **~ oratory** demagogia *f*, oratoria *f* populachera; **~ rule** ley *f* del pueblo, ley *f* de la calle.
3 *vt* (*molest*) acosar, atropellar; (*attack*) atacar en masa; *actor etc* festejar tumultuosamente, apiñarse entusiastas en torno de; **the minister was ~bed by journalists** los periodistas se apiñaban en torno del ministro; **he was ~bed whenever he went out** al salir siempre se veía acosado por la gente.
mobcap ['mɒbkæp] *n* cofia *f*.
mobile ['məʊbaɪl] **1** *adj* móvil, movible; *canteen etc* ambulante; **now that we're ~*** ahora que tenemos coche; **~ home** caravana *f*, remolque *m*; **~ library** biblioteca *f* móvil, bibliobús *m*; **~ shop** tienda *f* ambulante; **~ unit** (*TV*) unidad *f* móvil. **2** *n* (*Art*) móvil *m*.
mobility [məʊ'bɪlɪtɪ] *n* movilidad *f*; **~ allowance** subsidio *m* de movilidad; **~ of labour** movilidad *f* de la mano de obra.
mobilization [,məʊbɪlaɪ'zeɪʃən] *n* movilización *f*.
mobilize ['məʊbɪlaɪz] **1** *vt* movilizar. **2** *vi* movilizarse.
mobster* ['mɒbstəʳ] *n* (*US*) gángster *m*, pandillero *m*.
moccasin ['mɒkəsɪn] *n* mocasín *m*.
mocha ['mɒkə] *n* moca *m*.
mock [mɒk] **1** *n* (**a**) **to make a ~ of sth** poner algo en ridículo. (**b**) (*Scol*) **~s** exámenes *mpl* de prueba.
2 *adj* (*sham*) fingido, simulado; (*imitated*) imitado; (*parodied*) burlesco; **in ~ anger** con ira simulada; **a ~ battle** un simulacro de combate; **~ exam** examen *m* de prueba.
3 *vt* (*ridicule*) ridiculizar; (*defy*) burlarse de; (*scoff at*) burlarse de, mofarse de; (*mimic*) remedar, imitar; *efforts, plans etc* frustrar, desbaratar.
4 *vi* mofarse (*at* de).
mocker ['mɒkəʳ] *n* (**a**) mofador *m*, -ora *f*. (**b**) **to put the ~s on sb**‡ hacer que uno fracase, joder a uno‡.
mockery ['mɒkərɪ] *n* (*derision*) mofas *fpl*, burlas *fpl*; (*object*) parodia *f*, mal remedo *m*; **this is a ~ of justice** esto es una negación de la justicia; **it was a ~ of a trial** fue una parodia de un proceso; **what a ~ this is!** ¡esto es absurdo!, ¡qué tontería!; **he had to put up with a lot of ~** tuvo que aguantar muchas burlas; **to make a ~ of sth** hacer algo ridículo.
mock-heroic ['mɒkhɪ'rəʊɪk] *adj* heroicoburlesco.
mocking ['mɒkɪŋ] **1** *adj tone etc* burlón. **2** *n* burlas *fpl*.
mockingbird ['mɒkɪŋbɜːd] *n* sinsonte *m*, zenzontle *m* (*LAm*).
mockingly ['mɒkɪŋlɪ] *adv* en tono burlón, con sorna.
mock-orange ['mɒk'ɒrɪndʒ] *n* jeringuilla *f*, celinda *f*.
mock-up ['mɒkʌp] *n* maqueta *f*.
MOD *n* (*Brit*) *abbr of* **Ministry of Defence** Ministerio *m* de Defensa, Min. de D.
modal ['məʊdl] *adj* modal.
modality [məʊ'dælɪtɪ] *n* modalidad *f*.
mod cons [,mɒd'kɒnz] *npl abbr of* **modern conveniences**.
mode [məʊd] *n* (**a**) modo *m* (*also Gram, Mus, Philos*), manera *f*; (*fashion*) moda *f*. (**b**) (*Comput*) modo *m*, modalidad *f*.
model ['mɒdl] **1** *n* (**a**) (*small-scale representation*) modelo *m*; paradigma *m*, patrón *m*, pauta *f*; (*architect's, town planner's etc*) maqueta *f*; **it is made on the ~ of X** está hecho a imitación de X.
(**b**) (*person*) modelo *mf*; **he is a ~ of good behaviour** es un modelo de buenas costumbres; **to hold sb out** (*or* **up**) **as a ~** presentar a uno como modelo.
(**c**) (*dress, car etc*) modelo *m*.
2 *adj* (**a**) (*ideal, experimental*) modelo; modélico; **~ apartment** (*US*) piso *m* modelo; **~ home** casa *f* piloto; **~ prison** cárcel *f* modelo; **~ prisoner** preso *m* modélico; **~ town** ciudad *f* modelo.
(**b**) (*small-scale*) miniatura; **~ aeroplane** aeromodelo *m*; **~ car** coche *m* de juguete; **~ railway** ferrocarril *m* de juguete, ferrocarril *m* miniatura.
3 *vt* (**a**) (*make a ~*) modelar; (*fig*) modelar, formar, planear; **to ~ sth on sth else** modelar algo sobre otra cosa, construir algo a imitación de otra cosa, planear algo según otra cosa.
(**b**) *dress etc* llevar, presentar.
4 *vi* servir de modelo (*for* a, para); ejercer la profesión de modelo, ser modelo.
5 *vr*: **to ~ o.s. on** modelarse sobre.
modeller, (*US*) **modeler** ['mɒdləʳ] *n* modelador *m*, -ora *f*.
modelling, (*US*) **modeling** ['mɒdlɪŋ] **1** *n* (*V* **model 1a, b**) (**a**) modelado *m*; modelismo *m*. (**b**) profesión *f* de modelo. **2** *attr*: **~ clay** plastilina ® *f*.
modem ['məʊdem] *n* módem *m*.
moderate **1** ['mɒdərɪt] *adj* moderado (*also Pol*); (*fair, medium*) regular, mediano, mediocre; *increase, price* módico.
2 ['mɒdərɪt] *n* (*Pol*) moderado *m*, -a *f*.
3 ['mɒdəreɪt] *vt* (**a**) (*lessen*) moderar; mitigar; *wind etc* calmar. (**b**) *exam etc* asesorar.
4 ['mɒdəreɪt] *vi* (**a**) moderarse; mitigarse; (*wind etc*) calmarse, amainar.
(**b**) (*act as moderator*) arbitrar, servir de asesor.
moderately ['mɒdərɪtlɪ] *adv* moderadamente; medianamente, mediocremente; módicamente; **a ~ expensive suit** un traje medianamente caro; **he was ~ successful** tuvo un razonable éxito.
moderation [,mɒdə'reɪʃən] *n* moderación *f*; temperancia *f*; **in ~** con moderación.
moderator ['mɒdəreɪtəʳ] *n* (*Brit Univ*) árbitro *m*, asesor *m*, -ora *f*; **M~** (*Eccl*) *presidente de la asamblea de la Iglesia Escocesa y de otras iglesias protestantes*.
modern ['mɒdən] **1** *adj* moderno. **2** *n* moderno *m*, -a *f*.
modernism ['mɒdənɪzəm] *n* modernismo *m*.
modernist ['mɒdənɪst] **1** *adj* modernista. **2** *n* modernista *mf*.
modernistic [,mɒdə'nɪstɪk] *adj* modernista.
modernity [mɒ'dɜːnɪtɪ] *n* modernidad *f*.
modernization [,mɒdənaɪ'zeɪʃən] *n* modernización *f*; actualización *f*.
modernize ['mɒdənaɪz] **1** *vt* modernizar; actualizar. **2** *vi*

modernizarse; actualizarse.
modest ['mɒdɪst] *adj* (**a**) (*not boastful*) modesto; moderado; (*not grand*) modesto; **to be ~ about one's successes** hablar en términos modestos de sus triunfos; **to be ~ in one's demands** ser moderado en sus reclamaciones. (**b**) (††: *chaste etc*) pudoroso, púdico.
modestly ['mɒdɪstlɪ] *adv* modestamente; con moderación; pudorosamente.
modesty ['mɒdɪstɪ] *n* (**a**) (*gen*) modestia *f*; moderación *f*. (**b**) (††: *chasteness*) pudor *m*.
modicum ['mɒdɪkəm] *n*: **with a ~ of** con una cantidad mínima de, con un poquito de.
modification [ˌmɒdɪfɪ'keɪʃən] *n* modificación *f*.
modifier ['mɒdɪfaɪəʳ] *n* modificante *m*.
modify ['mɒdɪfaɪ] *vt* modificar.
modish ['məʊdɪʃ] *adj* muy de moda, sumamente elegante.
modishly ['məʊdɪʃlɪ] *adv* elegantemente; **to be ~ dressed** ir vestido con suma elegancia.
modiste [məʊ'di:st] *n* modista *f*.
modular ['mɒdjʊləʳ] *adj* modular; **~ program(m)ing** programación *f* modular.
modularity [ˌmɒdjʊ'lærɪtɪ] *n* modularidad *f*.
modulate ['mɒdjʊleɪt] *vti* modular.
modulated ['mɒdjʊleɪtɪd] *adj* modulado.
modulation [ˌmɒdjʊ'leɪʃən] *n* modulación *f*.
module ['mɒdju:l] *n* módulo *m*.
modus operandi ['məʊdəsˌɒpə'rændi:] *n* modus *m* operandi, modo *m* de proceder.
modus vivendi ['məʊdəsvɪ'vendi:] *n* modus *m* vivendi; manera *f* de convivir.
Mogadishu [ˌmɒgə'dɪʃu:] *n* Mogadisio *m*.
moggy* ['mɒgɪ] *n* (*Brit*) gatito *m*, -a *f*, michino* *m*, -a *f*.
mogul ['məʊgəl] *n* magnate *m*; **film ~** magnate *m* de la cinematografía; **the Great M~** el Gran Mogol.
MOH *n abbr of* **Medical Officer of Health**.
mohair ['məʊhɛəʳ] *n* mohair *m*.
Mohammed [məʊ'hæmed] *nm* Mahoma.
Mohammedan [məʊ'hæmɪdən] **1** *adj* mahometano. **2** *n* mahometano *m*, -a *f*.
Mohammedanism [məʊ'hæmɪdənɪzəm] *n* mahometanismo *m*.
moiré ['mwɑ:reɪ] *n* muaré *m*.
moist [mɔɪst] *adj* húmedo; mojado.
moisten ['mɔɪsn] **1** *vt* humedecer, mojar. **2** *vi* humedecerse, mojarse.
moistness ['mɔɪstnɪs] *n*, **moisture** ['mɔɪstʃəʳ] *n* humedad *f*.
moisturize ['mɔɪstʃəraɪz] *vt* humedecer, mojar; *skin etc* hidratar.
moisturizer ['mɔɪstʃəraɪzəʳ] *n* crema *f* hidratante.
moke* [məʊk] *n* (*Brit*) burro *m*.
molar ['məʊləʳ] *n* muela *f*.
molasses [mə'læsɪz] *n sing and pl* melaza *f*, melazas *fpl*.
mold [məʊld] *n etc* (*US*) = **mould** *etc*.
mole¹ [məʊl] *n* (*Anat*) lunar *m*.
mole² [məʊl] *n* (*Zool and fig*) topo *m*.
mole³ [məʊl] *n* (*Naut*) malecón *m*, muelle *m*.
molecular [mə'lekjʊləʳ] *adj* molecular; **~ biology** biología *f* molecular.
molecule ['mɒlɪkju:l] *n* molécula *f*.
molehill ['məʊlhɪl] *n* topera *f*.
moleskin ['məʊlskɪn] *n* piel *f* de topo.
molest [məʊ'lest] *vt* faltar al respeto a, meterse con, importunar, molestar; (*euph*) abordar con propósitos deshonestos.
molestation [ˌməʊles'teɪʃən] *n* importunidad *f*, vejación *f*; (*sexual*) acoso *m*, importunación *f*.
molester [mə'lestəʳ] *n* (*also* **child ~**) maníaco *m* sexual que persigue a niños.
moll* [mɒl] *n* compañera *f* (de gángster).
mollify ['mɒlɪfaɪ] *vt* apaciguar, calmar; **he was somewhat mollified by this** con esto se calmó un poco.
mollusc, (*US*) **mollusk** ['mɒləsk] *n* molusco *m*.
mollycoddle ['mɒlɪkɒdl] **1** *n* marica *m*, niño *m* mimado. **2** *vt* mimar.
mollycoddling ['mɒlɪˌkɒdlɪŋ] *n* mimo *m*.
Molotov ['mɒlətɒf] *attr*: **~ cocktail** *n* cóctel *m* Molotov.
molt [məʊlt] *n etc* (*US*) = **moult** *etc*.
molten ['məʊltən] *adj* fundido, derretido; *lava etc* líquido.
molybdenum [mɒ'lɪbdɪnəm] *n* molibdeno *m*.
mom* [mɒm] **1** *n* (*US*) mamá* *f*. **2** *attr*: **~ and pop store** tienda *f* de la esquina, pequeño negocio *m*.
moment ['məʊmənt] *n* (**a**) (*instant*) momento *m*, instante *m*; (*juncture*) momento *m*, coyuntura *f*; **~ of truth** momento *m* de la verdad; **man of the ~** hombre *m* del momento; **odd ~s** momentos *mpl* de ocio; **at odd ~s** a ratos perdidos; hay veces cuando ...; **at any ~** de un momento a otro; **at the ~** de momento, por ahora; **at the last ~** a última hora; **at this ~** en este momento, ahora mismo; **for the ~** por el momento; **not for a ~** ¡ni pensarlo!, ¡ni soñarlo!; **I'm not saying for a ~ you're wrong** no digo que no tengas razón ni mucho menos; **not for a ~ did I think that ...** en ningún momento pensaba que ...; **from that ~ on** desde entonces, a partir de entonces; **in a ~** en un momento; **yes, in a ~!** ¡sí, en seguida!; **I'll come in a ~** voy en seguida; **it was all over in a ~** todo esto ocurrió en un instante; **to leave things until the last ~** dejar las cosas hasta última hora; **one ~!, half a ~!, wait a ~!** ¡un momento!; **I shan't be a ~** vuelvo muy pronto; termino muy pronto; ahora mismo; **do it this very ~!** ¡hazlo al instante!; **the play has its ~s** la obra tiene sus momentos; **I have just this ~ heard of it** acabo de saberlo; **it won't take a ~** es cosa de unos pocos momentos; **tell me the ~ he comes** avíseme en cuanto venga; **the next ~ he collapsed** al instante sufrió un colapso.
(**b**) (*Mech*) momento *m*; **~ of inertia** momento *m* de inercia.
(**c**) (*importance*) importancia *f*, momento *m*; **of little ~** de poca importancia, de poco momento; **matters of ~** asuntos *mpl* de importancia.
momentarily ['məʊməntərɪlɪ] *adv* (**a**) momentáneamente; *expect etc* de un momento a otro. (**b**) (*US*: *now*) en este momento; (*soon*) dentro de poco, muy pronto.
momentary ['məʊməntərɪ] *adj* momentáneo.
momentous [məʊ'mentəs] *adj* trascendental, muy crítico, de suma importancia, decisivo.
momentousness [məʊ'mentəsnɪs] *n* trascendencia *f*, suma importancia *f*, lo decisivo.
momentum [məʊ'mentəm] *n* momento *m*; (*fig*) impulso *m*, ímpetu *m*; **to gather ~** cobrar velocidad.
momma* ['mɒmə] *n* (*US*), **mommy*** ['mɒmɪ] *n* (*US*) mamá* *f*.
Mon. *abbr of* **Monday** lunes *m*.
Monaco ['mɒnəkəʊ] *n* Mónaco *m*.
monad ['mɒnæd] *n* mónada *f*.
Mona Lisa ['məʊnə'li:zə] *nf* la Gioconda.
monarch ['mɒnək] *n* monarca *m*.
monarchic(al) [mɒ'nɑ:kɪk(əl)] *adj* monárquico.
monarchism ['mɒnəkɪzəm] *n* monarquismo *m*.
monarchist ['mɒnəkɪst] **1** *adj* monárquico. **2** *n* monárquico *m*, -a *f*.
monarchy ['mɒnəkɪ] *n* monarquía *f*.
monastery ['mɒnəstrɪ] *n* monasterio *m*, cenobio *m*.
monastic [mə'næstɪk] *adj* monástico; **~ order** order *f* monástica; **~ vows** votos *mpl* monásticos.
monasticism [mə'næstɪsɪzəm] *n* monacato *m*, vida *f* monástica.
Monday ['mʌndɪ] *n* lunes *m*.
Monegasque [mɒnə'gæsk] **1** *adj* monegasco. **2** *n* monegasco *m*, -a *f*.
monetarism ['mʌnɪtərɪzəm] *n* monetarismo *m*.
monetarist ['mʌnɪtərɪst] **1** *adj* monetarista. **2** *n* monetarista *mf*.
monetary ['mʌnɪtərɪ] *adj* monetario; **~ policy** política *f* monetaria; **~ reserves** reservas *fpl* monetarias; **~ system** sistema *m* monetario; **~ unit** unidad *f* monetaria.
money ['mʌnɪ] **1** *n* dinero *m*; **your ~ or your life!** ¡la bolsa o la vida!; **'~ back if not satisfied'** 'si no queda satisfecho le devolveremos el dinero'; **~ back guarantee** garantía *f* de devolver (*or* reembolsar) el dinero, dinero *m* reembolsable garantizado; **~ talks** poderoso caballero es don Dinero; **~ makes ~** dinero llama dinero; **there's ~ in it** es un buen negocio; **it's a bargain for the ~** a ese precio es una verdadera ganga; **that's the team for my ~!** ¡ése sí es un equipo!, ¡ése es lo que se llama un equipo!; **for my ~ it's not worthwhile** en cuanto a mí no vale la pena; **it's ~ for jam, it's ~ for old rope** (*Brit*) es dinero que se gana sin el menor esfuerzo; **my ~ is on Fred** yo apuesto a Fred; **my ~ is on Fred not coming** yo apuesto a que Fred no vendrá; **he must be coining ~** está forrándose de dinero; **to come into ~** heredar dinero; **bad ~ drives out good** el dinero malo echa fuera al bueno; **to earn good ~** tener un buen sueldo; **he gets his ~ on Fridays** cobra los viernes; **when do I get my ~?** ¿cuándo cobro?, ¿cuándo me vas a pagar?; **~ doesn't grow on trees** el dinero no nace en macetas; **to have ~ to burn** estar cargado de dinero; **after that he was in the ~** con eso se estaba forrando, con eso estaba acuñando dinero; **to keep sb in ~** proveer a uno de dinero; **he's made of ~** es de oro; **do you think I'm made**

of ~? ¿crees que soy millonario?; **to make ~** (*person*) ganar dinero, (*business*) dar dinero, rendir bien; **to make ~ hand over fist** amasar una fortuna; **to put one's ~ where one's mouth is** predicar con el ejemplo; **to be rolling in ~** nadar en dinero; **to throw good ~ after bad** echar la soga tras el caldero.

2 *attr*: **~ economy** economía *f* monetaria; **~ market** mercado *m* de dinero; **~ matters** asuntos *mpl* financieros; **~ order** giro *m* postal; **~ payment** pago *m* en metálico; **~ prize** premio *m* en metálico; **~ spider** araña *f* de la suerte; **~ supply** oferta *f* monetaria, medio *m* circulante, volumen *m* monetario; **~ wage** salario *m* en metálico.

moneybag ['mʌnɪbæg] *n* gato *m*, talega *f*; **~s** (*fig*) talegas *fpl*, riqueza *f*.

moneybox ['mʌnɪbɒks] *n* hucha *f*.

moneychanger ['mʌnɪˌtʃeɪndʒəʳ] *n* cambista *mf*.

moneyed ['mʌnɪd] *adj* adinerado.

moneygrubber ['mʌnɪˌgrʌbəʳ] *n* avaro *m*, -a *f*.

moneygrubbing ['mʌnɪˌgrʌbɪŋ] **1** *adj* avaro, avariento. **2** *n* esfuerzo *m* por enriquecerse, afán *m* de dinero.

moneylender ['mʌnɪˌlendəʳ] *n* prestamista *mf*.

moneylending ['mʌnɪˌlendɪŋ] *n* préstamo *m*.

moneymaker ['mʌnɪˌmeɪkəʳ] *n* artículo *m* (*or* producto *m*, proyecto *m*, inversión *f*) que rinde grandes beneficios, fuente *f* de dinero.

moneymaking ['mʌnɪˌmeɪkɪŋ] **1** *adj* provechoso, rentable, lucrativo. **2** *n* ganancia *f*, lucro *m*.

money-spinner ['mʌnɪˌspɪnəʳ] *n* (*Brit*) = **moneymaker**.

money's-worth ['mʌnɪzwɜːθ] *n*: **to get one's ~** sacar jugo del dinero, estar contento con lo que uno ha adquirido (*etc*); **to get one's ~ out of an investment** salir bien recompensado de una inversión.

-monger ['mʌŋgəʳ] *n ending in compounds* traficante *m* en ..., tratante *m* en ...; *V* **fish~** *etc*.

Mongol ['mɒŋgəl] **1** *adj* mongol; (*Med*) mongólico. **2** *n* (**a**) mongol *m*, -ola *f*; (*Med*) mongólico *m*, -a *f*. (**b**) (*Ling*) mongol *m*.

Mongolia [mɒŋ'gəʊlɪə] *n* Mongolia *f*.

Mongolian [mɒŋ'gəʊlɪən] = **Mongol**.

mongolism ['mɒŋgəlɪzəm] *n* mongolismo *m*.

mongoose ['mɒŋguːs] *n*, *pl* **mongooses** ['mɒŋguːsɪz] mangosta *f*.

mongrel ['mʌŋgrəl] **1** *adj* mestizo; *dog* mestizo, cruzado, (*pej*) callejero. **2** *n* (*person*: *pej*) mestizo *m*, -a *f*; (*dog*) perro *m* mestizo, (*pej*) perro *m* callejero.

monicker‡ ['mɒnɪkəʳ] *n* (*name*) nombre *m*; (*nickname*) apodo *m*; (*signature*) firma *f*; (*initials*) iniciales *fpl*.

monitor ['mɒnɪtəʳ] **1** *n* (**a**) (*Scol*) alumno *m* encargado de la disciplina. (**b**) (*Rad*: *person*) escucha *mf*, monitor *m*; (*TV*, *Comput*) monitor *m*. **2** *vt foreign station* escuchar; *TV programme* controlar; *progress* observar, monitorizar, seguir la marcha de, controlar.

monitoring ['mɒnɪtərɪŋ] **1** *n* supervisión *f*; control *m*; observación *f*; monitorización *f*, monitoreado *m*. **2** *attr body*, *responsibility* de observación, de verificación.

monk [mʌŋk] *n* monje *m*.

monkey ['mʌŋkɪ] **1** *n* mono *m*, -a *f*, mico *m*, -a *f*; (*fig*: *child*) diablillo *m*, golfillo *m*; **I don't care** (*or* **give**) **a ~'s‡** me importa un rábano; **to have a ~ on one's back‡** (*US*) quedar colgado*; **to make a ~ out of sb** poner a uno en ridículo.

2 *attr*: **~ business*** trampas *fpl*; trapisondas *fpl*, tejemanejes *mpl*; **~ tricks*** travesuras *fpl*, diabluras *fpl*.

◆monkey about*, monkey around* *vi* hacer travesuras, juguetear, hacer diabluras; **to ~ about with sth** manosear algo, (*and damage*) estropear algo.

monkeynut ['mʌŋkɪnʌt] *n* (*Brit*) cacahuete *m*, maní *m* (*LAm*).

monkey-puzzle ['mʌŋkɪˌpʌzl] *n* (*Bot*) araucaria *f*.

monkey-wrench ['mʌŋkɪˌrentʃ] *n* llave *f* inglesa; **to throw a ~ into the works*** (*US*) meter un palo en la rueda.

monkfish ['mʌŋkfɪʃ] *n* pejesapo *m*.

monkish ['mʌnkɪʃ] *adj* monacal, de monje; monástico; (*pej*) frailuno.

monkshood ['mʌŋkshʊd] *n* acónito *m*.

mono ['mɒnəʊ] *adj* (= **monophonic**): **~ system** sistema *m* monofónico.

mono... ['mɒnəʊ] *pref* mono...

monochrome ['mɒnəkrəʊm] **1** *adj* monocromo. **2** *n* monocromo *m*.

monocle ['mɒnəkl] *n* monóculo *m*.

monoculture ['mɒnəʊˌkʌltʃəʳ] *n* monocultivo *m*.

monogamous [mɒ'nɒgəməs] *adj* monógamo.

monogamy [mɒ'nɒgəmɪ] *n* monogamia *f*.

monoglot ['mɒnəʊglɒt] **1** *adj* monolingüe. **2** *n* monolingüe *mf*.

monogram ['mɒnəgræm] *n* monograma *m*.

monogrammed ['mɒnəgræmd] *adj* con monograma.

monograph ['mɒnəgræf] *n* monografía *f*.

monohull ['mɒnəʊˌhʌl] *n* monocasco *m*.

monokini [ˌmɒnəʊ'kiːniː] *n* monokini *m*.

monolingual [ˌmɒnəʊ'lɪŋgwəl] *adj* monolingüe.

monolingualism [ˌmɒnəʊ'lɪŋgwəlɪzəm] *n* monolingüismo *m*.

monolith ['mɒnəʊlɪθ] *n* monolito *m*.

monolithic [ˌmɒnəʊ'lɪθɪk] *adj* monolítico.

monolog(ue) ['mɒnəlɒg] *n* monólogo *m*.

monomania [ˌmɒnəʊ'meɪnɪə] *n* monomanía *f*.

monomaniac [ˌmɒnəʊ'meɪnɪæk] **1** *adj* monomaníaco. **2** *n* monomaníaco *m*, -a *f*.

mononucleosis [ˌmɒnəʊˌnjuːklɪ'əʊsɪs] *n* (*US*) (*also* **infectious ~**) mononucleosis *f* infecciosa.

monophonic [ˌmɒnəʊ'fɒnɪk] *adj* monofónico.

monoplane ['mɒnəpleɪn] *n* monoplano *m*.

monopolist [mə'nɒpəlɪst] *n* monopolista *m*.

monopolistic [məˌnɒpə'lɪstɪk] *adj* monopolístico.

monopolization [məˌnɒpəlaɪ'zeɪʃən] *n* monopolización *f*.

monopolize [mə'nɒpəlaɪz] *vt* monopolizar (*also fig*), acaparar.

monopoly [mə'nɒpəlɪ] **1** *n* monopolio *m*. **2** *attr*: **Monopolies and Mergers Commission** (*Brit*) *Comisión de monopolios y fusiones*.

monopsony [mə'nɒpsənɪ] *n* monopsonio *m*.

monorail ['mɒnəʊreɪl] *n* monorail *m*, monocarril *m*.

monoski ['mɒnəʊˌskiː] *n* monoesquí *m*.

monoskier ['mɒnəʊˌskiːəʳ] *n* monoesquiador *m*, -ora *f*.

monoskiing ['mɒnəʊˌskiːɪŋ] *n* monoesquí *m*.

monosodium glutamate ['mɒnəʊˌsəʊdɪəm'gluːtəmeɪt] *n* glutamato *m* monosódico.

monosyllabic ['mɒnəʊsɪ'læbɪk] *adj word* monosílabo; *language*, *utterance* monosilábico.

monosyllable ['mɒnəˌsɪləbl] *n* monosílabo *m*.

monotheism ['mɒnəʊˌθiːɪzəm] *n* monoteísmo *m*.

monotheist ['mɒnəʊˌθiːɪst] *n* monoteísta *mf*.

monotheistic [ˌmɒnəʊθiː'ɪstɪk] *adj* monoteísta.

monotone ['mɒnətəʊn] *n* monotonía *f*; **to speak in a ~** hablar en un solo tono.

monotonous [mə'nɒtənəs] *adj* monótono.

monotony [mə'nɒtənɪ] *n* monotonía *f*.

Monotype ['mɒnəʊtaɪp] ® **1** *n* monotipia ® *f*. **2** *attr*: **~ machine** (máquina *f*) monotipo ® *m*.

monoxide [mɒ'nɒksaɪd] *n* monóxido *m*.

monseigneur [ˌmɒnsen'jɜːʳ] *n* monseñor *m*.

monsignor [mɒn'siːnjəʳ] *n* monseñor *m*.

monsoon [mɒn'suːn] *n* monzón *m or f*; **the ~ rains** las lluvias monzónicas; **~ season** época *f* monzónica.

monster ['mɒnstəʳ] **1** *adj* enorme, monstruoso; (*hum*) grandísimo.

2 *n* monstruo *m*; **a real ~ of a fish** un pez verdaderamente enorme; **a ~ of greed** un monstruo de la avaricia.

monstrance ['mɒnstrəns] *n* custodia *f*, ostensorio *m*.

monstrosity [mɒns'trɒsɪtɪ] *n* monstruosidad *f*.

monstrous ['mɒnstrəs] *adj* (**a**) (*huge*) monstruoso, enorme. (**b**) (*unfair*) injusto, escandaloso.

monstrously ['mɒnstrəslɪ] *adv* enormemente; **~ unfair** terriblemente injusto.

Mont. (*US*) *abbr of* **Montana**.

montage [mɒn'tɑːʒ] *n* montaje *m*.

Mont Blanc [ˌmɔ̃ːm'blɑ̃ːŋ] *n* el Monte Blanco.

month [mʌnθ] *n* mes *m*; **30 dollars a ~** 30 dólares al mes, 30 dólares mensuales; **not in a ~ of Sundays** nunca jamás amén; **it went on for ~s** duró meses y meses.

monthly ['mʌnθlɪ] **1** *adj* mensual; **~ instalment, ~ installment** (*US*), **~ payment** mensualidad *f*; **~ statement** (*Fin*) estado *m* de cuenta mensual.

2 *adv* cada mes, mensualmente; **40 dollars ~** 40 dólares al mes, 40 dólares mensuales.

3 *n* (**a**) (*magazine*) revista *f* mensual. (**b**) **monthlies** (*Med*) regla *f*.

monument ['mɒnjʊmənt] *n* monumento *m* (*to* de, a, que conmemora); **~ to Bolívar** monumento *m* de Bolívar; **~ to the dead** monumento *m* a los muertos.

monumental [ˌmɒnjʊ'mentl] *adj* (**a**) monumental; **~ mason** escultor *m* de monumentos funerarios, marmolista *m*. (**b**) *ignorance etc* enorme, colosal, monumental; *error* garrafal.

moo [muː] **1** *n* mugido *m*. **2** *vi* mugir, hacer mu.

mooch [muːtʃ] **1** *vt* (*) (**a**) (*cadge*) sacar de gorra*. (**b**) (*esp US*: *steal*) birlar*. **2** *vi*: **to ~ along** andar arrastrando los pies.

◆**mooch about*, mooch around*** *vi* no saber qué hacer, no tener nada que hacer, haraganear.

mood[1] [mu:d] *n* (*Gram*) modo *m*.

mood[2] [mu:d] **1** *n* humor *m*; disposición *f* (de ánimo); capricho *m*; **to be in a bad ~** estar de mal humor; **to be in a good ~** estar de buen humor; **he's in a bit of a ~** está de mal humor; **to be in a generous ~** sentirse generoso; **to be in an ugly ~** (*person*) estar de muy mal humor, (*crowd*) amenazar violencia; **to be in a forgiving ~** estar dispuesto a perdonar; **to be in no laughing ~, to be in no ~ for laughing** no tener ganas de reír; **are you in a ~ for chess?** ¿te apetece una partida de ajedrez?, ¿quieres jugar al ajedrez?; **to be in the ~** (**for love**) sentirse amoroso; **I'm not in the ~** no quiero; **I'm not in the ~ for games** no estoy para juegos; **he plays well when he's in the ~** toca bien cuando está de vena; **he's in one of his ~s** está en uno de sus momentos de mal humor; **that depends on his ~** eso es según el humor que tenga; **he has ~s** (*of anger*) tiene arranques de cólera, (*of gloom*) tiene sus rachas de melancolía.

2 *attr*: **~ music** música *f* de fondo (*or* de ambiente).

moodily ['mu:dɪlɪ] *adv answer etc* malhumoradamente; melancólicamente.

moodiness ['mu:dɪnɪs] *n* mal humor *m*; melancolía *f*; humor *m* cambiadizo, propensión *f* a cambiar bruscamente de humor.

moody ['mu:dɪ] *adj*: **to be ~** (*angry*) tener arranques de cólera; (*gloomy*) tener rachas de melancolía; (*variable*) ser caprichoso.

moola(h)⁑ ['mu:lɑ:] *n* (*US*) pasta* *f*, parné⁑ *m*.

moon [mu:n] **1** *n* luna *f*; (*poet*) mes *m*; **full ~** luna *f* llena, plenilunio *m*; **new ~** luna *f* nueva; **once in a blue ~** de higos a brevas, de Pascuas a Ramos; **to ask** (*or* **cry**) **for the ~** pedir la luna; **to be over the ~** estar loco de contento; **to promise the ~** prometer el oro y el moro, prometer la luna.

2 *vi* (*) enseñar el culo.

◆**moon about, moon around** *vi* mirar a las musarañas, pasar el tiempo sin hacer nada; soñar despierto.

◆**moon away** *vt*: **to ~ away a couple of hours** pasar un par de horas sin hacer nada, pasar un par de horas soñando.

◆**moon over** *vt*: **she was ~ing over the photo** miraba amorosamente la foto, contemplaba extasiada la foto.

moonbeam ['mu:nbi:m] *n* rayo *m* de luna.

moonboots ['mu:nbu:ts] *npl* botas *fpl* altas acolchadas.

moon buggy ['mu:n,bʌgɪ] *n* vehículo *m* lunar.

Moonie ['mu:nɪ] *n* miembro *mf* de la Iglesia de la Unificación.

moon-landing ['mu:n,lændɪŋ] *n* alunizaje *m*.

moonless ['mu:nlɪs] *adj* sin luna.

moonlight ['mu:nlaɪt] **1** *n* luz *f* de la luna; **by ~, in the ~** a la luz de la luna; **it was ~** había luna.

2 *attr*: **~ flit** (*Brit*) mudanza *f* a la chita callando.

3 *vi* (*) tener un empleo secundario además del principal, estar pluriempleado, tener un pluriempleo.

moonlighter* ['mu:n,laɪtəʳ] *n* pluriempleado *m*, -a *f*.

moonlighting* ['mu:n,laɪtɪŋ] *n* pluriempleo *m*.

moonlit ['mu:nlɪt] *adj object* iluminado por la luna; *night* de luna.

moonrise ['mu:nraɪz] *n* salida *f* de la luna.

moonscape ['mu:nˌskeɪp] *n* paisaje *m* lunar.

moonshine ['mu:nʃaɪn] *n* (**a**) luz *f* de la luna. (**b**) (*: *nonsense*) pamplinas *fpl*, música *f* celestial. (**c**) (*US**: *illegal spirits*) licor *m* destilado ilegalmente.

moonshiner* ['mu:nʃaɪnəʳ] *n* (*US*) (**a**) (*distiller*) fabricante *m* de licor ilegal. (**b**) (*smuggler*) contrabandista *mf*.

moonshot ['mu:nʃɒt] *n* (lanzamiento *m* de una) nave *f* espacial con destino a la luna.

moonstone ['mu:nstəʊn] *n* feldespato *m*, labradorita *f*.

moonstruck ['mu:nstrʌk] *adj* tocado, trastornado, lunático.

moony* ['mu:nɪ] *adj*: **to be ~** estar distraído, estar soñando despierto.

Moor [mʊəʳ] *n* moro *m*, -a *f*.

moor[1] [mʊəʳ] *n* páramo *m*, brezal *m*; (*for game*) coto *m*.

moor[2] [mʊəʳ] **1** *vt* amarrar, atracar. **2** *vi* echar las amarras.

moorhen ['mʊəhen] *n* polla *f* de agua.

moorings ['mʊərɪŋz] *npl* (*ropes*) amarras *fpl*; (*place*) amarradero *m*, punto *m* de atraque.

Moorish ['mʊərɪʃ] *adj* moro; morisco; (*Archit etc*) árabe; **~ arch** arco *m* de herradura.

moorland ['mʊələnd] *n* páramo *m*, brezal *m*.

moose [mu:s] *n* alce *m* de América.

moot [mu:t] **1** *n* (*Hist*) junta *f*, asamblea *f*.

2 *adj point, question* discutible, dudoso.

3 *vt* proponer para la discusión; **it has been ~ed whether** ... se ha discutido si ...; **when the question was first ~ed** cuando se discutió la cuestión por primera vez.

mop [mɒp] **1** *n* (**a**) (*implement*) fregasuelos *m*, lampazo *m*, trapeador *m* (*LAm*).

(**b**) (*hair*) mata *f*, greña *f*; **~ of hair** pelambrera *f*.

2 *vt* fregar, limpiar; *brow* enjugar.

◆**mop up** *vt* (**a**) *floor, liquid* limpiar, enjugar; (*absorb*) absorber; (*dry up*) secar.

(**b**) (*Mil*) *terrain* limpiar, *remnants* acabar con.

(**c**) (*) *drink* beberse.

mope [məʊp] *vi* estar deprimido, estar abatido; **to ~ for sb** resentirse de la ausencia de uno, estar triste por la pérdida de uno.

◆**mope about, mope around** *vi* andar alicaído.

moped ['məʊped] *n* (*Brit*) ciclomotor *m*.

moquette [mə'ket] *n* moqueta *f*.

moraine [mɒ'reɪn] *n* morena *f*.

moral ['mɒrəl] **1** *adj* moral; *philosophy, support, victory* moral; (*chaste*) virtuoso; (*honourable*) honrado; **the ~ majority** la mayoría moral.

2 *n* (**a**) (*of story*) moraleja *f*; sentido *m* moral; **to draw a ~ from** sacar una moraleja de; **to point the ~** hacer resaltar la moraleja.

(**b**) **~s** moral *f*, ética *f*; moralidad *f*; (*conduct*) costumbres *fpl*; **the ~s of actors** la moralidad de los actores; **she has no ~s** no tiene sentido moral, carece de toda noción de la moralidad.

morale [mɒ'rɑ:l] *n* moral *f*.

moralist ['mɒrəlɪst] *n* moralizador *m*, -ora *f*; (*philosopher, teacher*) moralista *mf*.

moralistic [,mɒrə'lɪstɪk] *adj* moralizador.

morality [mə'rælɪtɪ] **1** *n* moralidad *f*. **2** *attr*: **~ play** moralidad *f*.

moralize ['mɒrəlaɪz] *vti* moralizar.

moralizing ['mɒrəlaɪzɪŋ] **1** *adj* moralizador. **2** *n* instrucción *f* moral, predicación *f* sobre la moralidad.

morally ['mɒrəlɪ] *adv* moralmente.

morass [mə'ræs] *n* cenagal *m*, pantano *m*; **a ~ of problems** un laberinto de problemas; **a ~ of figures** un mar de cifras.

moratorium [,mɒrə'tɔ:rɪəm] *n*, *pl* **moratoriums** *or* **moratoria** [,mɒrə'tɔ:rɪə] moratoria *f*.

moray ['mɒreɪ] *n* (*Fish*) morena *f*.

morbid ['mɔ:bɪd] *adj* insano, malsano; *mind* enfermizo; morboso, patológico; (*Med*) mórbido; (*depressed*) pesimista, melancólico; **don't be so ~!** ¡no digas esas cosas tan feas!

morbidity [mɔ:'bɪdɪtɪ] *n*, **morbidness** ['mɔ:bɪdnɪs] *n* lo insano, lo malsano; lo enfermizo; (*Med*) morbosidad *f*; pesimismo *m*.

morbidly ['mɔ:bɪdlɪ] *adv talk etc* en tono pesimista; *think etc* con pesimismo.

mordacity [mɔ:dæsɪtɪ] *n* mordacidad *f*.

mordant ['mɔ:dənt] *adj* mordaz.

mordent ['mɔ:dənt] *n* mordente *m*.

more [mɔ:ʳ] **1** *adj* (**a**) más; **you have ~ money than I** tienes más dinero que yo; **~ light, please!** ¡más luz, por favor!; **a few ~ weeks** algunas semanas más; **do you want some ~ tea?** ¿quieres más té?; **is there any ~ wine in the bottle?** ¿queda vino en la botella?; **many ~ people** muchas más personas; **much ~ butter** mucha más mantequilla.

(**b**) (*numerals*) **~ than half** más de la mitad; **~ than one** más de uno; **~ than 15** más de 15; **not ~ than one** no más de uno; **not ~ than 15** no más de quince.

2 *n and pron* más; **we can't afford ~** no podemos pagar más; **this house cost ~ than ours** esta casa costó más que la nuestra; **it cost ~ than we had expected** costó más de lo que esperábamos; **I shall have ~ to say about this** volveré a hablar de esto; **and what's ~** ... y además ...; **there's ~ where that came from!** ¡esto no es más que el principio!

3 *adv* más; **~ easily** más fácilmente, con mayor facilidad (*than* que); **~ and ~** más y más, cada vez más; **~ or less** más o menos; **neither ~ nor less** ni más ni menos; **once ~** otra vez, una vez más; **never ~** nunca más; **if he comes here any ~** si vuelve por aquí; **if he says that any ~** si vuelve a decir eso, si dice eso otra vez; **the house is ~ than half built** la casa está más que medio construida; **I had ~ than carried out my obligation** había cumplido con creces mi obligación; **it will ~ than meet the**

demand satisfará ampliamente la demanda; **he was ~ surprised than angry** más que enfadarse se sorprendió; **it's ~ a short story than a novel** más que novela es un cuento.

4 (*the ~*) **the ~ you give him the ~ he wants** cuanto más se le da tanto más quiere; **the ~ he drank the thirstier he got** cuanto más bebía más sed tenía; **it makes me (all) the ~ ashamed** tanto más vergüenza me da; **all the ~ so because** (*or* **as, since**) ... tanto más cuanto que ...; **the ~ the better, the ~ the merrier** cuantos más mejor.

5 (*no ~ etc*) **I have no ~ pennies** no tengo más peniques; **no ~ singing, I can't bear it!** ¡que no se cante más, no lo aguanto!; **let's say no ~ about it** no se hable más de esto; **he doesn't live here any ~** ya no vive aquí; **Queen Anne is no ~** la reina Ana ya no existe; **we shall see her no ~** no la volveremos a ver; **'I don't understand it' ... 'no ~ do I'** 'no lo comprendo' ... 'ni yo tampoco'; **no ~ than is proper** lo justo y nada más; **not much ~ than £5** poco más de 5 libras; **she's no ~ a duchess than I am** tan duquesa es como mi padre; **he no ~ thought of paying me than of flying to the moon** antes iría volando a la luna que pensar pagarme a mí.

moreish* ['mɔːrɪʃ] *adj* apetitoso.

moreover [mɔː'rəʊvəʳ] *adv* además, por otra parte; es más ...

mores ['mɔːreɪz] *npl* costumbres *fpl*, tradiciones *fpl*; moralidad *f*.

morganatic [ˌmɔːgə'nætɪk] *adj* morganático.

morganatically [ˌmɔːgə'nætɪkəlɪ] *adv*: **he married her ~** se casó con ella en casamiento morganático.

morgue [mɔːg] *n* depósito *m* de cadáveres; (*US**) archivo *m*.

MORI ['mɔːrɪ] *n abbr of* **Market & Opinion Research Institute** *compañía especializada en encuestas*.

moribund ['mɒrɪbʌnd] *adj* moribundo (*also fig*).

Mormon ['mɔːmən] **1** *adj* mormónico. **2** *n* mormón *m*, -ona *f*.

Mormonism ['mɔːmənɪzəm] *n* mormonismo *m*.

morn [mɔːn] *n* (*poet*) = **morning**; (*dawn*) alborada *f*.

morning ['mɔːnɪŋ] **1** *n* mañana *f*; (*before dawn*) madrugada *f*; **good ~!** ¡buenos días!; **the ~ after** (*hum*) la mañana después de la juerga; **the next ~** la mañana siguiente, a la mañana; **early in the ~** muy de mañana; **in the ~** por la mañana; (*following day*) a la mañana (siguiente); **at 7 o'clock in the ~** a las 7 de la mañana; **at 3 in the ~** a las 3 de la madrugada; **tomorrow ~** mañana por la mañana; **yesterday ~** ayer por la mañana; **he's generally out ~s** por las mañanas en general no está.

2 *attr* de (la) mañana; mañanero; **~ coat** chaqué *m*; **~ dress** chaqué *m*; **~ mist** bruma *f* del alba; **~ paper** diario *m*; **~ prayers** oraciones *fpl* de la mañana; **~ sickness** náuseas *fpl* matutinas; **~ star** lucero *m* del alba; **~ tea** té *m* mañanero.

morning-after ['mɔːnɪŋ'ɑːftəʳ] *attr*: **~ pill** píldora *f* del día siguiente.

morning-glory ['mɔːnɪŋ'glɔːrɪ] *n* dondiego *m* de día, ipomea *f*.

Moroccan [mə'rɒkən] **1** *adj* marroquí. **2** *n* marroquí *mf*.

Morocco [mə'rɒkəʊ] *n* Marruecos *m*.

morocco [mə'rɒkəʊ] *n* (*also* **~ leather**) marroquí *m*, tafilete *m*.

moron ['mɔːrɒn] *n* imbécil *mf*.

moronic [mə'rɒnɪk] *adj* imbécil.

morose [mə'rəʊs] *adj* malhumorado, hosco, taciturno.

morosely [mə'rəʊslɪ] *adv* malhumoradamente, hoscamente, taciturnamente.

morph [mɔːf] *n* morfo *m*.

morpheme ['mɔːfiːm] *n* morfema *m*.

morphemic [mɔː'fiːmɪk] *adj* morfímico.

morphia ['mɔːfɪə] *n*, **morphine** ['mɔːfiːn] *n* morfina *f*.

morphological [ˌmɔːfə'lɒdʒɪkəl] *adj* morfológico.

morphologist [mɔː'fɒlədʒɪst] *n* morfólogo *m*, -a *f*.

morphology [mɔː'fɒlədʒɪ] *n* morfología *f*.

morris ['mɒrɪs] *n baile tradicional inglés de hombres en el que éstos llevan cascabeles en la ropa*.

morrow ['mɒrəʊ] *n*: **on the ~** (*liter*) al día siguiente.

Morse [mɔːs] **1** *n* morse *m*. **2** *attr*: **~ code** alfabeto *m* morse.

morsel ['mɔːsl] *n* (*small piece*) pedazo *m*, fragmento *m*; (*of food*) bocado *m*.

mort. *abbr of* **mortgage**.

mortadella [ˌmɔːtə'delə] *n* mortadela *f*.

mortal ['mɔːtl] **1** *adj* mortal; **~ combat** combate *m* mortal; **~ remains** restos *mpl* mortales; **~ sin** pecado *m* mortal. **2** *n* mortal *mf*.

mortality [mɔː'tælɪtɪ] **1** *n* mortalidad *f*; (*number killed in war, accident*) número *m* de víctimas; **there was heavy ~** hubo numerosas víctimas, murieron muchos, hubo gran mortandad. **2** *attr*: **~ rate** tasa *f* de mortalidad; **~ table** tabla *f* de mortalidad.

mortally ['mɔːtəlɪ] *adv* mortalmente; **~ wounded** herido de muerte; **~ offended** mortalmente ofendido.

mortar ['mɔːtəʳ] **1** *n* (*Tech, Mil*) mortero *m*. **2** *vt* bombardear con morteros.

mortarboard ['mɔːtəbɔːd] *n* (*Univ*) birrete *m*.

mortgage ['mɔːgɪdʒ] **1** *n* hipoteca *f*; **to pay off a ~** redimir una hipoteca; **to raise a ~, to take out a ~** obtener una hipoteca (*on* sobre).

2 *attr*: **~ broker** especialista *mf* en hipotecas; **~ company** (*US*) = banco *m* hipotecario; **~ loan** préstamo *m* hipotecario; **~ rate** tipo *m* de interés hipotecario.

3 *vt* hipotecar; (*fig*) vender, poner en manos ajenas.

mortgagee [ˌmɔːgə'dʒiː] *n* acreedor *m* hipotecario, acreedora *f* hipotecaria.

mortgager, mortgagor ['mɔːgədʒəʳ] *n* hipotecante *mf*, deudor *m* hipotecario, deudora *f* hipotecaria.

mortice ['mɔːtɪs] *n* = **mortise.**

mortician [mɔː'tɪʃən] *n* (*US*) director *m*, -ora *f* de pompas fúnebres.

mortification [ˌmɔːtɪfɪ'keɪʃən] *n* mortificación *f*; humillación *f*; (*Med*) gangrena *f*.

mortify ['mɔːtɪfaɪ] **1** *vt* mortificar; humillar; **I was mortified to find that** ... me avergoncé al descubrir que ... **2** *vi* (*Med*) gangrenarse.

mortifying ['mɔːtɪfaɪɪŋ] *adj* humillante.

mortise, mortice ['mɔːtɪs] *n* muesca *f*, mortaja *f*; **~ lock** cerradura *f* embutida.

mortuary ['mɔːtjʊərɪ] **1** *adj* mortuorio. **2** *n* (*Brit*) depósito *m* de cadáveres; (*US*) funeraria *f*.

Mosaic [məʊ'zeɪɪk] *adj* mosaico.

mosaic [məʊ'zeɪɪk] *n* mosaico *m*.

Moscow ['mɒskəʊ] *n* Moscú *m*.

Moselle [məʊ'zel] *n* Mosela *m*.

Moses ['məʊzɪs] **1** *nm* Moisés. **2** *attr*: **~ basket** moisés *m*.

mosey* ['məʊzɪ] *vi*: **to ~ along** pasearse, deambular; **to ~ down to the shops** ir (sin prisa) a las tiendas.

Moslem ['mɒzlem] **1** *adj* musulmán. **2** *n* musulmán *m*, -ana *f*.

mosque [mɒsk] *n* mezquita *f*.

mosquito [mɒs'kiːtəʊ] **1** *n*, *pl* **mosquitoes** [mɒs'kiːtəʊz] mosquito *m*. **2** *attr*: **~ bite** picadura *f* de mosquito; **~ net** mosquitero *m*.

moss [mɒs] **1** *n* (**a**) (*Bot*) musgo *m*. (**b**) (*Geog*) pantano *m*, marjal *m*. **2** *attr*: **~ stitch** punto *m* de musgo.

mossy ['mɒsɪ] *adj* musgoso, cubierto de musgo.

most [məʊst] **1** *adj superl* (**a**) (*with sing*) más; **who has ~ money?** ¿quién tiene más dinero?

(**b**) (*with pl*) **~ men** la mayor parte de los hombres, la mayoría de los hombres, los más hombres, casi todos los hombres.

2 *n and pron*: **do the ~ you can** haga todo lo que pueda; **~ of them** casi todos ellos; **~ of those present** la mayor parte de los asistentes; **~ of the time** la mayor parte del tiempo; **at ~, at the ~, at the very ~** a lo más, a lo sumo, todo lo más, cuando más; **20 minutes at the ~** 20 minutos como máximo; **it's the ~!*** ¡es fenomenal!*; **this group is the ~!*** ¡este conjunto es fabuloso!*; **the girl with the ~*** la chica más atractiva; **to get the ~ out of a situation** sacar el máximo partido de una situación; **to make the ~ of an affair** sacar todo el provecho posible de un asunto; **to make the ~ of one's advantages** aprovechar bien sus ventajas; **he made the ~ of the story** explotó todas las posibilidades del cuento, exageró los detalles del cuento.

3 *adv* (**a**) *superl* **he spent ~** él gastó más; **the ~ attractive girl there** la chica más atractiva allí; **the ~ difficult of our problems** el más difícil de nuestros problemas; **which one did it ~ easily?** ¿quién lo hizo con la mayor facilidad?; **~ favoured nation clause** cláusula *f* de la nación más favorecida.

(**b**) (*intensive*) muy, sumamente; **~ likely** muy probable; **a ~ expensive toy** un juguete de los más caros, un juguete carísimo; **a ~ interesting book** un libro de lo más interesante, un libro interesantísimo; **you have been ~ kind** has sido muy amable; **~ holy** santísimo; **~ reverend** reverendísimo; *V* **all** *etc*.

(**c**) (*US**) **~ everybody** casi todos; **~ always** casi siempre.

-most [məʊst] *suf* más; **centre~** más central, **further~** más lejano.

mostly ['məʊstlı] *adv* en su mayor parte; principalmente; en su mayoría; en general; **they are ~ women** en su mayoría son mujeres, casi todas son mujeres; **~ because** ... principalmente porque ...; **we ~ sell retail** en general vendemos al detalle, principalmente vendemos al por menor; **it's ~ finished** está casi terminado.

MOT *n* (*Brit*) (**a**) *abbr of* **Ministry of Transport** ≃ Ministerio *m* de Transportes. (**b**) (*Aut*: *also* **~ test**) *abbr of* **Ministry of Transport test** *examen anual de coches obligatorio*; **~ (test) certificate** ≃ Inspección *f* Técnica de Vehículos, ITV *f*.

mote [məʊt] *n* átomo *m*, mota *f*; **to see the ~ in our neighbour's eye and not the beam in our own** ver la paja en el ojo ajeno y no la viga en el propio.

motel [məʊ'tel] *n* motel *m*, hotel-garaje *m* (*LAm*).

motet [məʊ'tet] *n* motete *m*.

moth [mɒθ] *n* mariposa *f* (nocturna); (*clothes* ~) polilla *f*.

mothball ['mɒθbɔːl] **1** *n* bola *f* de naftalina, bola *f* de la polilla; **in ~s** (*Naut etc*) en la reserva. **2** *vt ship etc* poner en la reserva.

moth-eaten ['mɒθ,iːtn] *adj* apolillado, comido de la polilla.

mother ['mʌðəʳ] **1** *n* madre *f*; (*US***) = **motherfucker****; **M~ of God** Madre *f* de Dios; **M~ Superior** superiora *f*, madre *f* superiora; **to be a ~ to sb** ser como una madre para uno.

2 *attr*: **~ church** iglesia *f* metropolitana; **M~ Church** Santa Madre Iglesia *f*; **~ country** patria *f*; **M~s' Day** fiesta *f* de la Madre; **~ figure** figura *f* maternal; **M~ Goose** la Oca; **~ hen** gallina *f* madre; **~ love** amor *m* maternal; **M~ Nature** Dama *f* Naturaleza; **~ ship** buque *m* nodriza; **~ tongue** lengua *f* materna; **~ wit** sentido *m* común.

3 *vt* (*give birth to*) parir, dar a luz; (*act as ~ to*) servir de madre a; (*spoil*) mimar; *young animal* prohijar.

motherboard ['mʌðə,bɔːd] *n* placa *f* madre.

mothercraft ['mʌðəkrɑːft] *n* arte *m* de cuidar a los niños pequeños, arte *m* de ser madre.

motherfucker** ['mʌðə,fʌkəʳ] *n* (*US*) hijoputa‡ *m*, cabronazo* *m*.

motherfucking** ['mʌðə,fʌkıŋ] *adj* (*US*) pijotero‡, condenado*.

motherhood ['mʌðəhʊd] *n* maternidad *f*; **to prepare for ~** prepararse para ser madre.

mothering ['mʌðərıŋ] **1** *n* cuidados *mpl* maternales. **2** *attr*: **M~ Sunday** (*Brit*) fiesta *f* de la Madre.

mother-in-law ['mʌðərınlɔː] *n*, *pl* **mothers-in-law** suegra *f*.

motherland ['mʌðəlænd] *n* patria *f*, (*more sentimentally*) madre patria *f*.

motherless ['mʌðəlıs] *adj* huérfano de madre, sin madre.

motherly ['mʌðəlı] *adj* maternal.

mother-of-pearl ['mʌðərəv'pɜːl] **1** *n* nácar *m*. **2** *adj* nacarado.

mother-to-be ['mʌðətə'biː] *n*, *pl* **mothers-to-be** futura madre *f*.

moth-hole ['mɒθhəʊl] *n* apolilladura *f*.

mothproof ['mɒθpruːf] *adj* a prueba de polillas.

motif [məʊ'tiːf] *n* (*Art, Mus*) motivo *m*; (*of speech etc*) tema *m*; (*Sew*) adorno *m*.

motion ['məʊʃən] **1** *n* (**a**) (*movement*) movimiento *m*; (*of parts of machine*) marcha *f*, operación *f*, funcionamiento *m*; **to be in ~** estar en movimiento; **to go through the ~s** hacer algo en la debida forma, obrar de acuerdo con las reglas (pero sin creer que se vaya a conseguir nada); obrar por pura fórmula; **to set sth in ~** poner algo en marcha.

(**b**) (*sign*) ademán *m*, señal *f*; **he made a ~ with his hand** hizo una señal con la mano.

(**c**) (*Parl etc*) moción *f*, proposición *f*; **to bring forward** (*or* **propose**, *US* **make**) **a ~** presentar una moción; **to carry a ~** (*person*) hacer adoptar una moción, (*meeting*) adoptar una moción, aprobar una moción; **to vote on a ~** votar una moción; **the ~ is carried** se ha aprobado la moción; **the ~ is lost** se ha rechazado la moción.

(**d**) (*Mech, moving part*) mecanismo *m*.

(**e**) (*Med*) evacuación *f* del vientre.

2 *attr*: **~ sickness** mareo *m*.

3 *vt*: **to ~ sb to do sth** hacer señas a uno para que haga algo, indicar a uno con la mano (*etc*) que haga algo; **he ~ed me to a chair** indicó con la mano que me sentara.

4 *vi*: **to ~ to sb to do sth** hacer señas a uno para que haga algo, indicar a uno con la mano (*etc*) que haga algo.

motionless ['məʊʃənlıs] *adj* inmóvil.

motion picture ['məʊʃən,pıktʃəʳ] (*US*) **1** *n* película *f*. **2** *attr* cinematográfico; **~ camera** cámara *f* cinematográfica; **~ industry** industria *f* del cine; **~ theater** (*US*), **~ theatre** cine *m*.

motivate ['məʊtıveıt] *vt* motivar; **to be ~d to do sth** tener motivo(s) para hacer algo; **he is highly ~d** tiene una fuerte motivación; **the campaign is politically ~d** la campaña tiene una motivación política.

motivation [,məʊtı'veıʃən] *n* motivación *f*.

motivational [,məʊtı'veıʃənl] *adj* motivacional; **~ research** estudios *mpl* motivacionales.

motive ['məʊtıv] **1** *adj* motor (*f*: motora, motriz); **~ power** fuerza *f* motriz.

2 *n* motivo *m* (*for* de); móvil *m*; **what can his ~ have been?** ¿cuál habrá sido su motivo?, ¿qué motivo habrá tenido?; **my ~s were of the purest** lo hice con la mejor intención.

motiveless ['məʊtıvlıs] *adv* sin motivo, inmotivado.

motley ['mɒtlı] **1** *adj* (*many-coloured*) abigarrado, multicolor; (*diversified*) vario, compuesto de elementos muy diversos.

2 *n* botarga *f*, traje *m* de colores; **on with the ~** vistámonos de payaso.

motocross ['məʊtəkrɒs] *n* motocross *m*.

motor ['məʊtəʳ] **1** *adj* (*giving motion*) motor; (*motorized*) automóvil.

2 *n* (**a**) (*engine*) motor *m*. (**b**) (*Brit*: *car*) coche *m*, automóvil *m*, carro *m* (*LAm*).

3 *attr*: **~ accident** accidente *m* de circulación; **~ insurance** seguro *m* de automóvil; **~ launch** lancha *f* motora; **~ mechanic** mecánico *m* de automóviles; **~ road** vía *f* pública, pista *f*, carretera *f*; **~ scooter** motosilla *f*, escúter *m*; **~ ship** motonave *f*; **~ show** exposición *f* de automóviles; **the Paris ~ show** el salón del automóvil de París; **~ spirit** gasolina *f*; **~ torpedo-boat** torpedero *m*; **~ trader** comerciante *mf* en automóviles; **~ transport** transporte *m* motorizado; **~ vehicle** automóvil *m*; **~ vessel** motonave *f*.

4 *vi* ir en coche, viajar en automóvil; **we ~ed down to Ascot** fuimos en coche a Ascot; **we ~ed over to see them** fuimos a visitarles (en coche).

motorail ['məʊtəreıl] *n* motorail *m*.

motorbike* ['məʊtəbaık] *n* moto* *f*.

motorboat ['məʊtəbəʊt] *n* motora *f*, motorbote *m*, lancha *f* rápida, lancha *f* motora.

motorcade ['məʊtəkeıd] *n* (*US*) desfile *m* de automóviles.

motorcar ['məʊtəkɑːʳ] *n* (*Brit*) coche *m*, automóvil *m*, carro *m* (*LAm*).

motor-coach ['məʊtəkəʊtʃ] *n* autocar *m*, autobús *m*, camión *m* (*LAm*).

motorcycle ['məʊtə,saıkl] *n* motocicleta *f*; **~ combination** motocicleta *f* con sidecar.

motorcycling ['məʊtə,saıklıŋ] *n* motociclismo *m*, motorismo *m*.

motorcyclist ['məʊtə,saıklıst] *n* motociclista *mf*; motorista *mf*.

motor-driven ['məʊtə'drıvn] *adj* automóvil, propulsado por motor.

-motored ['məʊtəd] *adj ending in compounds*: **four~** cuatrimotor, tetramotor; **petrol~** propulsado por gasolina.

motoring ['məʊtərıŋ] **1** *adj accident etc* de automóvil, de tránsito (*LAm*), automovilístico, de carretera; **~ holiday** vacaciones *fpl* en coche; **the ~ public** los que viajan en coche; el público aficionado al automovilismo.

2 *n* automovilismo *m*; **school of ~** autoescuela *f*, escuela *f* automovilista.

motorist ['məʊtərıst] *n* (*Brit*) automovilista *mf*; conductor *m*, -ora *f* (de coche), chófer *m*.

motorization [,məʊtəraı'zeıʃən] *n* motorización *f*.

motorize ['məʊtəraız] *vt* motorizar; **to get ~d*** adquirir un coche; **now that we're ~d*** ahora que tenemos coche.

motorized ['məʊtəraızd] *adj* motorizado.

motorman ['məʊtəmən] *n*, *pl* **motormen** ['məʊtəmən] *n* conductor *m* (de locomotora eléctrica *etc*), maquinista *m*.

motor-mower ['məʊtə,məʊəʳ] *n* cortacésped *m* a motor.

motor-oil ['məʊtər,ɔıl] *n* aceite *m* para motores.

motor-racing ['məʊtə,reısıŋ] **1** *n* automovilismo *m* deportivo, carreras *fpl* de coches. **2** *attr*: **~ track** pista *f* de automovilismo.

motorway ['məʊtəweı] *n* (*Brit*) autopista *f*; **~ madness** locura *f* en la autopista; **~ service area** área de servicios de autopista; **~ services** servicios *mpl* en autopista.

mottled ['mɒtld] *adj* abigarrado, multicolor; *marble etc* jaspeado; *complexion* con manchas; *animal, bird* con manchas, moteado; **~ with** manchado de, pintado de.

motto ['mɒtəʊ] *n*, *pl* **mottoes** *or* **mottos** ['mɒtəʊz] lema *m*; (*Heraldry*) divisa *f*; (*watchword*) consigna *f*; (*in cracker*:

verse) versos *mpl,* (*joke*) chiste *m.*

mould¹, (*US*) **mold** [məʊld] *n* (*soil*) mantillo *m.*

mould², (*US*) **mold** [məʊld] **1** *n* (*hollow form*) molde *m*; (*~ed object*) cosa *f* moldeada; (*fig*) carácter *m,* índole *f,* temple *m*; **cast in a heroic ~** de carácter heroico.

2 *vt* (*fashion*) moldear; (*cast*) vaciar; (*Carp*) moldurar; (*fig*) amoldar (*on* a), formar; **~ed plastics** plásticos *mpl* moldeados; **it is ~ed on ...** está hecho según ...

3 *vr*: **to ~ o.s. on sb** amoldarse como uno, modelarse sobre uno, tomar a uno como ejemplo.

mould³, (*US*) **mold** [məʊld] *n* (*fungus*) moho *m*; (*iron ~*) mancha *f* de orín.

moulder¹, (*US*) **molder** ['məʊldəʳ] *n* (*Tech*) moldeador *m,* -ora *f.*

moulder², (*US*) **molder** ['məʊldəʳ] *vi* (*also* **to ~ away**) desmoronarse, convertirse en polvo; (*fig*) desmoronarse, decaer.

mouldering ['məʊldərɪŋ] *adj* podrido; carcomido.

mouldiness, (*US*) **moldiness** ['məʊldɪnɪs] *n* moho *m,* lo mohoso, enmohecimiento *m.*

moulding, (*US*) **molding** ['məʊldɪŋ] *n* (*act*) amoldamiento *m*; (*cast*) vaciado *m*; (*Archit*) moldura *f*; (*fig*) amoldamiento *m,* formación *f.*

mouldy, (*US*) **moldy** ['məʊldɪ] *adj* (**a**) mohoso, enmohecido. (**b**) (*: *fig*) horrible, malísimo; miserable, cochino; **the play was ~** la obra fue horrible; **all he gave me was a ~ old penny** lo único que me dio fue un cochino penique.

moult, (*US*) **molt** [məʊlt] **1** *n* muda *f.* **2** *vt* mudar. **3** *vi* (*snake etc*) mudar la piel, (*bird*) mudar la pluma.

mound [maʊnd] *n* (*pile*) montón *m*; (*earthwork*) terraplén *m*; (*burial ~*) túmulo *m*; (*hillock*) montículo *m.*

mount [maʊnt] **1** *n* (**a**) (*Geog*: ††, *except with names*) monte *m,* montaña *f*; **M~ Everest** (monte *m*) Everest *m.*

(**b**) (*horse etc*) montura *f,* caballería *f.*

(**c**) (*of machine etc*) base *f,* soporte *m*; (*of jewel*) engaste *m*; (*of photo etc*) borde *m,* marco *m*; (*stamp ~*) fijasello *m.*

2 *vt* (**a**) *horse* montar, subir a; (*in mating*) cubrir; *platform etc* subir a, subir en; *ladder* subir; *throne* subir a.

(**b**) *machine etc* montar, armar; *play* poner en escena; *exhibition* organizar; *attack* lanzar, hacer.

(**c**) *picture* poner un borde a, poner un marco a; *stamp* pegar, fijar; *jewel* engastar.

(**d**) *guard* montar.

(**e**) (*provide with horse*) proveer de caballo.

3 *vi* (**a**) (*climb*) subir; (*get on horse*) montar. (**b**) (*also* **to ~ up**; *of quantity, price etc*) subir, aumentar.

mountain ['maʊntɪn] **1** *n* montaña *f*; (*pile*) montón *m*; **to make a ~ out of a molehill** exagerar ridículamente una dificultad, hacer de una pulga un elefante.

2 *attr* montañés, de montaña; montañero, serrano; **~ ash** serbal *m*; **~ bicycle, ~ bike** bicicleta *f* de montaña; **~ chain, ~ range** sierra *f*; **~ hut, ~ refuge** albergue *m* de montaña; **~ lion** (*US*) puma *f*; **~ rescue** servicio *m* de rescate de montañas; **~ sickness** puna *f* (*LAm*), soroche *m* (*LAm*).

mountaineer [ˌmaʊntɪ'nɪəʳ] **1** *n* montañero *m,* -a *f,* alpinista *mf,* andinista *mf* (*LAm*). **2** *vi* dedicarse al montañismo, hacer alpinismo.

mountaineering [ˌmaʊntɪ'nɪərɪŋ] **1** *n* montañismo *m,* alpinismo *m,* andinismo *m* (*LAm*). **2** *attr* montañero, alpinista.

mountainous ['maʊntɪnəs] *adj* montañoso; (*fig*) enorme, colosal.

mountainside ['maʊntɪnˌsaɪd] *n* ladera *f* de montaña, falda *f* de montaña.

mountebank ['maʊntɪbæŋk] *n* saltabanco *m,* saltimbanqui *m.*

mounted ['maʊntɪd] *adj* montado; **~ police** policía *f* montada.

Mountie* ['maʊntɪ] *n* (*Canada*) miembro *m* de la policía montada canadiense; **the ~s** la policía montada canadiense.

mounting ['maʊntɪŋ] *n* (*of machine*: *act*) montaje *m*; (*frame, base*) armadura *f,* base *f,* soporte *m*; (*of jewel*) engaste *m*; (*of photo etc*) marco *m.*

mourn [mɔːn] **1** *vt* llorar, llorar la muerte de, lamentar; (*wear ~ing for*) llevar luto por.

2 *vi* afligirse, lamentarse; (*wear ~ing*) estar de luto; **to ~ for sb** llorar la muerte de uno; **to ~ for sth** llorar la pérdida (*or* desaparición *etc*) de algo; **it's no good ~ing over it** de nada sirve afligirse por eso.

mourner ['mɔːnəʳ] *n* doliente *mf*; (*hired*) plañidero *m,* -a *f*; **the ~s** los que acompañan el féretro, los acompañantes.

mournful ['mɔːnfʊl] *adj person* triste, afligido; *tone, sound* triste, lúgubre, lastimero; *occasion* triste, melancólico.

mournfully ['mɔːnfəlɪ] *adv* tristemente.

mournfulness ['mɔːnfʊlnɪs] *n* tristeza *f*; aflicción *f*; melancolía *f.*

mourning ['mɔːnɪŋ] **1** *n* (*act*) lamentación *f*; (*period etc*) luto *m,* duelo *m*; (*dress*) luto *m*; **to be in ~** estar de luto; **to be in ~ for** llevar luto por; **to come out of ~** dejar el luto; **to go into ~** ponerse de luto; **to plunge a town into ~** enlutar una ciudad.

2 *attr* de luto.

mouse [maʊs] **1** *n, pl* **mice** [maɪs] (**a**) ratón *m.* (**b**) (*Comput*) ratón *m.* **2** *vi* cazar ratones.

mousehole ['maʊshəʊl] *n* ratonera *f.*

mouser ['maʊsəʳ] *n* cazador *m* de ratones.

mousetrap ['maʊstræp] **1** *n* ratonera *f.* **2** *attr*: **~ cheese*** queso *m* corriente.

moussaka [mʊ'sɑːkə] *n* musaca *f.*

mousse [muːs] *n* mousse *f,* crema *f* batida; **chocolate ~** crema *f* batida de chocolate.

moustache [məs'tɑːʃ], (*US*) **mustache** ['mʌstæʃ] *n* bigote *m,* bigotes *mpl,* mostacho *m*; **to wear a ~** tener bigote.

moustachioed [mə'stɑːʃɪəʊd], (*US*) **mustachioed** [mʌstæʃɪəʊd] *adj* bigotudo.

mousy ['maʊsɪ] *adj person* tímido, de personalidad poco fuerte; *colour* pardusco.

mouth [maʊθ] *pl* **mouths** [maʊðz] **1** *n* boca *f*; (*fig, of bottle, cave etc*) boca *f*; (*of river*) desembocadura *f*; (*of channel*) embocadero *m*; (*of wind instrument*) boquilla *f*; **to be down in the ~** estar deprimido, andar alicaído; **to foam** (*or* **froth**) **at the ~** espumajear; **to keep one's ~ shut** (*fig*) tener la boca cerrada, guardar un secreto; **he never opened his ~ at the meeting** en la reunión no abrió la boca; **she didn't dare to open her ~** no se atrevió a decir ni pío; **to put words into sb's ~** poner palabras en boca de uno; **to shoot off one's ~*** hablar inoportunamente, hablar más de la cuenta; **shut your ~!*** ¡cállate ya!; **to stop sb's ~** hacer callar a uno.

2 [maʊð] *vt* (*affectedly*) pronunciar con afectación, articular con rimbombancia; (*soundlessly*) formar con los labios.

3 [maʊð] *vi* hablar exagerando los movimientos de la boca.

mouthed [maʊðd] *adj ending in compounds* de boca ..., que tiene la boca ...; **big-~** de boca grande.

mouthful ['maʊθfʊl] *n* bocado *m*; (*of smoke, air*) bocanada *f*; **the name is a proper ~** es un nombre kilométrico; **you said a ~*** (*US*) ¡y que lo digas!, ¡tú lo has dicho!

mouthorgan ['maʊθˌɔːgən] *n* armónica *f.*

mouthpiece ['maʊθpiːs] *n* (*Mus*) boquilla *f*; (*of bridle*) embocadura *f*; (*Telec*) micrófono *m*; (*fig, person*) portavoz *m.*

mouth-to-mouth ['maʊθtə'maʊθ] *attr*: **~ resuscitation** resucitación *f* boca a boca.

mouthwash ['maʊθwɒʃ] *n* enjuague *m* (bucal).

mouth-watering ['maʊθ'wɔːtərɪŋ] *adj* sumamente apetitoso.

movable ['muːvəbl] **1** *adj* movible; **~ feast** fiesta *f* movible; **not easily ~** nada fácil de mover. **2** *n*: **~s** muebles *mpl,* mobiliario *m*; (*Jur*) bienes *mpl* muebles.

move [muːv] **1** *n* (**a**) (*movement*) movimiento *m*; **Spain is a country on the ~** España es país en marcha; **to be always on the ~** estar siempre en movimiento, (*travelling*) estar siempre de viaje, (*of animal, child*) no saber estar quieto; **you can phone while on the ~** puede telefonear en pleno desplazamiento; **to get a ~ on** (*person*) menearse, darse prisa; **get a ~ on!** ¡menearse!, ¡espabílate!; **they're getting a ~ on with the bridge now** ahora la construcción del puente avanza rápidamente; **to make a ~ (to go)** ponerse en marcha; **it's time we made a ~** es hora de irnos; **it was midnight and no-one had made a ~** era medianoche pero nadie había dado señas de irse.

(**b**) (*in game*) jugada *f*; (*at chess*) jugada *f,* movimiento *m,* movida *f*; **it's my ~** yo juego; **it's your ~** te toca a ti; **whose ~ is it?** ¿a quién le toca jugar?; **he's up to every ~ in the game** se las sabe todas; **to have first ~** empezar, salir, jugar primero; **to make a ~** hacer una jugada, jugar.

(**c**) (*step*) paso *m,* acción *f*; gestión *f*; maniobra *f*; **the government's first ~** la primera gestión del gobierno; **what's the next ~?** ¿qué hacemos ahora?, y ahora ¿qué?; **to make a ~** dar un paso; tomar medidas; **it's up to him to make the first ~** le toca a él dar el primer paso; **without making the least ~ to** + *infin* sin hacer la menor intención de + *infin*; **to watch sb's every ~** observar a uno sin perder detalle, acecharle a uno cada movimiento.

(**d**) (*of house*) mudanza *f*; (*of person to job*) traslado *m*; **it's our third ~ in two years** ésta es la tercera vez en dos años que nos mudamos; **then he made a ~ to Buenos Aires** luego se trasladó a Buenos Aires.

2 *vt* (**a**) (*change place of*) mover; cambiar de sitio, trasladar; (*transport*) transportar; (*propel*) propulsar, impeler; *date, event* cambiar (la fecha *or* el lugar *etc* de); trasladar (a otro sitio); **he was ~d to Quito** le trasladaron a Quito; **if we can ~ the table a few inches** si podemos mover la mesa unos centímetros; **to ~ a piece** (*Chess*) jugar una pieza, mover una pieza; **'we shall not be ~d'** 'no nos moverán'.

(**b**) **to ~ house** (*Brit*) mudarse, cambiarse (*Mex*); **to ~ one's job** cambiar de empleo.

(**c**) (*cause to ~*) remover, agitar, sacudir, menear; **the breeze ~d the leaves gently** la brisa agitaba dulcemente las hojas; **to ~ the bowels** desocupar el vientre.

(**d**) (*person, from opinion*) mover, hacer cambiar de opinión; **he will not be easily ~d** no será fácil moverle.

(**e**) (*emotionally*) conmover, enternecer; impresionar; **to be easily ~d** ser impresionable, ser sensible; **to ~ sb to do sth** mover a uno a hacer algo; **when I feel so ~d** cuando estoy con el ánimo para eso; **to ~ sb to anger** encolerizar a uno; **to ~ sb to tears** hacer llorar a uno.

(**f**) (*Parl*) **to ~ a resolution** proponer una resolución, hacer una moción; **to ~ that ...** proponer que + *subj*.

(**g**) (*Comm*) *merchandise* colocar, vender.

3 *vi* (**a**) (*gen*) moverse; (*to a place*) trasladarse (*to* a); (*shake*) moverse, agitarse, temblar; **~!** ¡menearse!; **she ~d to the next room** pasó a la habitación inmediata; **let's ~ into the garden** vamos al jardín; **she ~s beautifully** anda con garbo; **I'll not ~ from here** no me muevo de aquí; **to ~ freely** (*part, Mech*) moverse libremente, (*person, traffic*) circular libremente; **to keep the traffic moving** mantener fluida la circulación; **keep moving!** ¡circulen!, ¡vayan pasando por delante!; **to ~ in high society** frecuentar la buena sociedad, alternar con personas de la buena sociedad.

(**b**) (*depart*) irse, marcharse; **it's time we were moving** es hora de irnos.

(**c**) (*travel*) ir; estar en movimiento; **the car was not moving** el coche no estaba en movimiento; **the bus was moving at 50 kph** el autobús iba a 50 k/h; **the capsule is moving at 18,000 mph** la cápsula se desplaza a 18.000 m/h; **he was certainly moving!** ¡iba como el demonio!

(**d**) (*progress*) ir adelante, avanzar, hacer progresos; (*of plants*) crecer; **things are moving at last** por fin se están haciendo progresos.

(**e**) (*~ house*) mudarse, mudar de casa; **the family ~d to a new house** la familia se mudó a una casa nueva.

(**f**) (*in games*) jugar, hacer una jugada; **who ~s next?** ¿a quién le toca jugar?; **white ~s** (*Chess*) blanco juega.

(**g**) (*take steps*) dar un paso, hacer una gestión, tomar medidas; **the government must ~ first** el gobierno ha de dar el primer paso; **the council ~d to stop the abuse** el consejo hizo gestiones para corregir el abuso.

◆**move about, move around 1** *vt* cambiar (mucho) de lugar, trasladar (a menudo) a otro sitio; mover de acá para allá. **2** *vi* ir y venir, ir de acá para allá; desplazarse (a menudo); cambiar (mucho) de lugar; **to ~ about freely** circular libremente.

◆**move along 1** *vt crowd* hacer circular; *passengers* hacer pasar hacia adelante. **2** *vi* avanzar; (*on bench etc*) correrse.

◆**move aside 1** *vt* apartar. **2** *vi* apartarse; ponerse a un lado, quitarse de en medio.

◆**move away 1** *vt* alejar, apartar; quitar de en medio. **2** *vi* (**a**) alejarse, apartarse (*from* de); (*depart*) marcharse. (**b**) (*move house*) mudar de casa.

◆**move back 1** *vt* (**a**) *crowd etc* mover hacia atrás, hacer retroceder. (**b**) (*to original place*) devolver a su lugar. (**c**) (*postpone*) aplazar. **2** *vi* (**a**) (*withdraw*) retroceder; retirarse. (**b**) (*to original place*) volver a su lugar. (**c**) **they ~d back to Burgos again** (*move house*) volvieron a Burgos.

◆**move down 1** *vt object etc* bajar. **2** *vi* (**a**) (*person etc*) bajar, descender. (**b**) (*in league*) descender (a la división inferior *etc*).

◆**move forward 1** *vt* (**a**) mover hacia adelante. (**b**) (*help progress*) avanzar, adelantar, promover. (**c**) *meeting etc* adelantar la fecha de. **2** *vi* avanzar.

◆**move in 1** *vt* hacer entrar; llevar dentro, instalar. **2** *vi* (**a**) (*police etc*) avanzar; intervenir, llegar. (**b**) (*to house*) tomar posesión, instalarse.

◆**move in on** *vt* (*police etc*) avanzar hacia; **to ~ in on sb** invadir a uno.

◆**move off** *vi* alejarse; (*depart*) marcharse; ponerse en marcha, ponerse en camino.

◆**move on 1** *vt crowd etc* hacer circular. **2** *vi* (*go on*) seguir, seguir andando; reanudar su viaje; (*go forward*) avanzar; (*time*) pasar; **let us ~ on to the next item** pasemos al próximo asunto; **things have ~d on since your visit** las cosas han cambiado después de tu visita.

◆**move out 1** *vt* desalojar, trasladar a otra parte. **2** *vi* salir; irse; abandonar la casa (*etc*).

◆**move over 1** *vt* apartar, mover a un lado. **2** *vi* apartarse, moverse a un lado; correrse hacia un lado; **we should ~ over to a different system** nos conviene cambiar a otro sistema; **she ~d over to give others a chance** cambió de puesto para dar más oportunidades a otros.

◆**move up 1** *vt* (**a**) *object* subir; *troops* mover hacia el frente. (**b**) (*promote*) ascender; (*in class*) trasladar a una clase superior. **2** *vi* (**a**) (*make room*) hacer sitio, correrse hacia un lado. (**b**) (*rise*) subir. (**c**) (*be promoted*) ser ascendido.

moveable ['mu:vəbl] = **movable**.

movement ['mu:vmənt] *n* (**a**) (*act*) movimiento *m* (*also Mil*); (*of part*) juego *m*, movimiento *m*; (*of traffic etc*) circulación *f*; (*on stock exchange*) actividad *f*, (*change of price*) cambio *m* de precio; **~ of capital** movimiento *m* de capitales; **to be in ~** estar en movimiento; **there was a ~ towards the door** se dirigieron algunos hacia la puerta.

(**b**) (*Pol*) movimiento *m*.

(**c**) (*Mus*) tiempo *m*, movimiento *m*.

(**d**) (*Mech, part*) mecanismo *m*.

(**e**) (*Med*) evacuación *f*.

mover ['mu:vəʳ] *n* (**a**) (*of motion*) autor *m*, -ora *f*, proponente *mf*. (**b**) (*US*) agente *m* de mudanzas. (**c**) **he's a lovely ~** se mueve con mucho garbo, anda con mucha elegancia.

movie ['mu:vɪ] **1** *n* (*US*) película *f*; **the ~s** el cine; **to go to the ~s** ir al cine. **2** *attr*: **~ camera** cámara *f* cinematográfica; **~ house, ~ theater** (*US*) cine *m*; **~ industry** industria *f* cinematográfica; **~ star** estrella *f* cinematográfica (*or* de cine).

moviegoer ['mu:vɪgəʊəʳ] *n* (*US*) aficionado *m*, -a *f* al cine.

movieland ['mu:vɪlænd] *n* (*US*) (*dreamworld*) mundo *m* de ensueño creado por el cine; (*eg Hollywood*) centro *m* de la industria cinematográfica.

moving ['mu:vɪŋ] *adj* (**a**) (*that moves*) movedor; movedizo; (*motive*) motor; **~ average** promedio *m* móvil; **~ part** pieza *f* móvil; **~ staircase** escalera *f* móvil, escalera *f* mecánica; **~ van** (*US*) camión *m* de mudanzas; **they fired from a ~ vehicle** dispararon desde un vehículo en marcha (*or* movimiento); **a ~ target is hard to hit** es difícil dar en el blanco si éste se mueve. (**b**) (*fig*) conmovedor; emocionante.

movingly ['mu:vɪŋlɪ] *adv* de modo conmovedor; **he spoke most ~** conmovió profundamente a los que le escuchaban.

mow [məʊ] (*irr*: *pret* **mowed**, *ptp* **mown** *or* **mowed**) *vt corn etc* segar; *grass* cortar; **to ~ down** segar.

mower ['məʊəʳ] *n* segador *m*, -ora *f*; (*lawn ~*) cortacésped *m*.

mowing ['məʊɪŋ] *n* siega *f*.

mowing-machine ['məʊɪŋmə,ʃi:n] *n* segadora *f* (mecánica).

mown [məʊn] *ptp of* **mow**.

moxie‡, moxy‡ ['mɒksɪ] *n* (*US*) (*courage*) valor *m*; (*nerve*) sangre fría *f*; (*vigor*) vigor *m*, dinamismo *m*.

Mozambican [,məʊzəm'bi:kən] **1** *adj* mozambiqueño. **2** *n* mozambiqueño *m*, -a *f*.

Mozambique [,məʊzəm'bi:k] *n* Mozambique *m*.

Mozarab [mɒz'ærəb] *n* mozárabe *mf*.

Mozarabic [mɒz'ærəbɪk] **1** *adj* mozárabe. **2** *n* mozárabe *m*.

mozzarella [,mɒtsə'relə] *n* mozzarella *f*.

MP *n* (**a**) (*Brit Parl*) *abbr of* **member of parliament** diputado *m*, -a *f*, Dip. (**b**) (*Mil*) *abbr of* **military police** policía *f* militar, P.M. *f*. (**c**) (*Canada*) *abbr of* **mounted police** policía *f* montada.

mpg *n* (*Aut*) *abbr of* **miles per gallon** millas *fpl* por galón.

mph *n abbr of* **miles per hour** millas *fpl* por hora, m/h.

M.Phil. *n abbr of* **Master of Philosophy** *título universitario*.

MPS *n* (*Brit*) *abbr of* **Member of the Pharmaceutical Society.**

Mr ['mɪstəʳ] *n abbr of* **Mister** señor *m*, Sr.

MRC *n* (*Brit*) *abbr of* **Medical Research Council** *departamento estatal que controla la investigación médica*.

MRCP *n* (*Brit*) *abbr of* **Member of the Royal College of Physicians.**

MRCS *n* (*Brit*) *abbr of* **Member of the Royal College of**

Surgeons.

MRCVS *n* (*Brit*) *abbr of* **Member of the Royal College of Veterinary Surgeons.**

MRP *n abbr of* **manufacturer's recommended price** precio *m* recomendado por el fabricante.

Mrs ['mɪsɪz] *n abbr of* **Mistress** señora *f*, Sra.; ~ **Brown** la señora de Brown.

MS (**a**) *n abbr of* **multiple sclerosis** esclerosis *f* múltiple. (**b**) *n* (*US*) *abbr of* **Master of Science** *título universitario.* (**c**) (*US Post*) *abbr of* **Mississippi.**

Ms [mɪz, məz] *prefijo de nombre de mujer que evita expresar su estado civil.*

M.S.A. *n* (*US*) *abbr of* **Master of Science in Agriculture** *título universitario.*

M.Sc. *n* (*Brit*) *abbr of* **Master of Science** *título universitario.*

MS-DOS [,em'esdɒs] *n abbr of* **Microsoft Disk Operating System.**

MSF *n* (*Brit*) *abbr of* **Manufacturing, Science, Finance.**

MSG *n* (*esp US*) *abbr of* **monosodium glutamate.**

Msgr *abbr of* **Monsignor** monseñor *m*, Mons.

MSI *n abbr of* **medium-scale integration** integración *f* a mediana escala.

MS(S) *abbr of* **manuscript**(**s**) manuscrito(s) *m*(*pl*).

MST *n* (*US*) *abbr of* **Mountain Standard Time.**

M.S.W. *n* (*US*) *abbr of* **Master of Social Work** *título universitario.*

MT (**a**) *n abbr of* **machine translation.** (**b**) (*US Post*) *abbr of* **Montana.**

Mt (*Geog*) *abbr of* **Mount, Mountain** monte *m*, m.

MTB *n abbr of* **motor torpedo boat.**

mth *abbr of* **month** mes *m*, m.

much [mʌtʃ] **1** *adj* mucho; ~ **money** mucho dinero; **how ~ money?** ¿cuánto dinero?; **it's too ~!*** (*fantastic*) ¡esto es demasiado!*, ¡qué demasia(d)o!*, ¡esto es estupendo!*; (*excessive*) esto pasa de la raya, esto pasa de castaño oscuro.

2 *adv* (**a**) mucho; (*before ptp*) muy; ~ **better** mucho mejor; ~ **pleased** muy satisfecho; **it doesn't ~ matter** no importa mucho; **he's ~ richer than I** (**am**) es mucho más rico que yo; **ever so ~** muchísimo; **not ~** no mucho, poco; ~ **to my astonishment** con gran sorpresa mía; **that's a bit ~!*** ¡eso es un poco fuerte!

(**b**) (*by far*) con mucho; ~ **the biggest** con mucho el más grande; **I would ~ rather stay** prefiero con mucho quedarme.

(**c**) (*almost*) casi, más o menos; **they are ~ of an age** tienen casi la misma edad; **they're ~ the same size** tienen más o menos el mismo tamaño.

(**d**) **how ~ is it?** ¿cuánto es?, ¿cuánto vale?; **how ~ is it a kilo?** ¿cuánto vale el kilo?

(**e**) **however ~ he tries** por mucho que se esfuerce.

3 *n*: **but ~ remains** pero queda mucho; ~ **of this is true** gran parte de esto es verdad; **we don't see ~ of each other** no nos vemos mucho; **we haven't heard ~ of him lately** desde hace tiempo apenas sabemos nada de él; **there's not ~ to do** no hay mucho que hacer; **it's not up to ~** no vale gran cosa; **I'm not ~ of a musician** sé muy poco de música, entiendo poco de música, como músico no sirvo para nada; **he's not ~ of a player** como jugador no vale mucho; **that wasn't ~ of a dinner** eso apenas se podía llamar cena; **to make ~ of sb** mimar a uno, hacer fiestas a uno; agasajar a uno; **to make ~ of sth** dar mucha importancia a algo; subrayar la importancia de algo.

4 (*with* as, so, too) (**a**) ~ **as I should like to** por más que yo quisiera; ~ **as I would like to go** por mucho que me gustara ir; ~ **as I like him** por mucho que le quiera.

(**b**) (*as ~*) **as ~ again** otro tanto; **three times as ~ tea** tres veces la cantidad de té; **I thought as ~** ya me lo figuraba, lo había previsto ya.

(**c**) (*as ~ as, so ~ as*) **as ~ as possible** todo lo posible; **he has as ~ money as you** tiene tanto dinero como tú; **he spends as ~ as he earns** gasta tanto como gana; **I have three times as ~ as I can eat** tengo tres veces más de lo que puedo comer; **it's as ~ as I can do to stand up** apenas puedo ponerme de pie (*or* pararme: *LAm*); **as ~ as to say** ... como si dijera ...; **the problem is not so ~ one of modernization as of investment** el problema más que de modernización es de inversión; **he went without saying so ~ as a single word** se fue sin decir una palabra siquiera; **I haven't so ~ as a penny** no tengo ni un solo penique.

(**d**) (*so ~*) **so ~ bad weather** tanto mal tiempo; **it has been so ~ exaggerated** se ha exagerado tanto; **we don't go out so ~ now** ahora no salimos tanto; **without so ~ as a phone-call** sin una llamada siquiera; **so ~ the better** tanto mejor; **so ~ for that!** ¡allá eso!; ¡ya se acabó aquello!; **that's so ~ the less to pay** tanto menos habrá que pagar; **at so ~ a pound** a tantas pesetas (*etc*) la libra; **so ~ so that** ... tanto que ...

(**e**) **too ~** demasiado; **he talks too ~** habla demasiado; **too ~ jam** demasiada mermelada *f*, exceso *m* de mermelada; **you gave me a dollar too ~** me dio un dólar de más; **that's too ~ by half** de eso sobra la mitad; **don't make too ~ of it** no exageres la importancia de esto; **it was all too ~ for her** (*emotion*) quedaba postrada con tanta emoción, (*work*) quedaba agobiada por tanto trabajo; **it's too ~ for me to cope with** yo no puedo con tanto trabajo (*etc*); **his rudeness is too ~** su descortesía es intolerable.

muchness ['mʌtʃnɪs] *n*: **they're much of a ~** son poco más o menos lo mismo.

mucilage ['mju:sɪlɪdʒ] *n* mucílago *m*.

mucilaginous [,mju:sɪ'lædʒɪnəs] *adj* mucilaginoso.

muck [mʌk] *n* (**a**) (*dung*) estiércol *m*; (*dirt*) suciedad *f*, inmundicias *fpl*, mierda *f*; **to be in a ~** estar sucio; **she thinks she's Lady M~!*** ¡se cree toda una duquesa!

(**b**) (*fig*) porquería *f*; **the article is just ~** el artículo es una porquería.

◆**muck about, muck around** (*Brit*) **1** *vt*: **to ~ sb about** fastidiar a uno, desorientar a uno (cambiando una cita *etc*) con él.

2 *vi* perder el tiempo, ocuparse en fruslerías, trabajar (*etc*) con poca seriedad; **he enjoys ~ing about in boats** le gusta entretener sus ocios navegando (*etc*) en bote; **stop ~ing about!** ¡déjate de tonterías!; **to ~ about with sth** (*handle*) manosear algo, (*break*) romper algo, estropear algo.

◆**muck in*** *vi* ayudar.

◆**muck out** *vt*: **to ~ out a stable** limpiar una cuadra.

◆**muck up*** (*Brit*) (**a**) (*disarrange*) desarreglar, desordenar; (*ruin*) arruinar, estropear, echar a perder; *affair, deal* fracasar en, (*deliberately*) chafar.

(**b**) (*dirty*) ensuciar.

mucker‡ ['mʌkər] *n* compinche *m*.

muckheap ['mʌk,hi:p] *n* estercolero *m*.

muckiness ['mʌkɪnɪs] *n* suciedad *f*.

muckrake ['mʌkreɪk] *vi* remover el pasado; buscar y revelar cosas vergonzosas en la vida de otros, escarbar vidas ajenas.

muckraker ['mʌk,reɪkər] *n* escarbador *m*, -ora *f* de vidas ajenas.

muckraking ['mʌk,reɪkɪŋ] *n* remoción *f* del pasado; revelación *f* de cosas escandalosas (en la vida de otros).

muck-up* ['mʌkʌp] *n* lío *m* grande; fracaso *m* total; **what a ~!** ¡qué faena!*; **that ~ with the timetable** ese lío que nos armamos con el horario.

mucky ['mʌkɪ] *adj* sucio; puerco; asqueroso; **to get o.s. all ~** ensuciarse; **to get one's dress all ~** ensuciar el vestido.

mucous ['mju:kəs] *adj* mucoso; ~ **membrane** mucosa *f*.

mucus ['mju:kəs] *n* moco *m*, mocosidad *f*.

mud [mʌd] **1** *n* lodo *m*, barro *m*, fango *m*; (*fig*) fango *m*; **to stick in the ~** (*cart*) atascarse, atollarse, (*ship*) embarrancarse; ~ **in your eye!*** ¡salud y pesetas!; **his name is ~** tiene una reputación malísima, no se le estima en nada; **if people hear this my name will be ~** si esto llega a saberse estoy perdido; **to drag sb's name through the ~** llenar a uno de fango; **to sling** (*or* **throw**) **~ at sb** vilipendiar a uno.

2 *attr*: ~ **flap** cortina *f*; ~ **hut** choza *f* de barro; ~ **wall** tapia *f*.

mudbank ['mʌdbæŋk] *n* banco *m* de arena.

mudbath ['mʌdbɑ:θ] *n*, *pl* **mudbaths** ['mʌdbɑ:ðz] baño *m* de lodo, lodos *mpl*.

muddle ['mʌdl] **1** *n* (**a**) (*disorder*) desorden *m*, confusión *f*; **you should have seen what a ~ there was in the room!** ¡había que ver el desorden que había en el cuarto!; **what a ~!** ¡qué confusión!; **how did things get into such a ~?** ¿cómo se produjo tanta confusión?

(**b**) (*perplexity*) perplejidad *f*, confusión *f*; **now I'm all in a ~** ahora estoy totalmente confuso.

(**c**) (*mix-up*) embrollo *m*, lío *m*; **there was a ~ over the seats** hubo un lío con las entradas; **to get into a ~** embrollarse; **to get into a ~ with one's accounts** armarse un lío con las cuentas; **what a ~!** ¡qué lío!, ¡qué faena!

2 *vt* (**a**) *things* embrollar, confundir; introducir el desorden en.

(**b**) *person* aturdir, dejar perplejo, confundir; **I was properly ~d** estaba totalmente confuso; **to get ~d** aturdirse; armarse un lío.

◆**muddle along** *vi* salir del paso sin saber cómo.

◆**muddle on** *vi* hacer las cosas al tuntún.
◆**muddle through** *vi* salir del paso sin saber cómo; **I expect we shall ~ through** espero que lo logremos de algún modo u otro.
◆**muddle up** *vt things* embrollar, confundir; introducir el desorden en; **you've ~d up A and B** has confundido A con B.
muddle-headed ['mʌdl,hedɪd] *adj person* atontado, atolondrado; *ideas* confuso.
muddler ['mʌdlə^r] *n* persona *f* atolondrada, persona *f* atontada.
muddy ['mʌdɪ] **1** *adj place* lodoso, fangoso; *hands, dress etc* cubierto de lodo; *liquid* turbio; *complexion* terroso.
2 *vt* enlodar; cubrir de lodo; *hands, dress etc* manchar de lodo; *liquid* enturbiar.
mudflats ['mʌdflæts] *npl* marisma *f*.
mudguard ['mʌdgɑːd] *n* (*Brit*) guardabarros *m*, guardalodos *m*, tapabarro *m* (*And*).
mudlark ['mʌdlɑːk] *n* galopín *m*.
mudpack ['mʌdpæk] *n* mascarilla *f* facial de barro.
mud pie [,mʌd'paɪ] *n* bola *f* de barro.
mud-slinging ['mʌd,slɪŋɪŋ] *n* injurias *fpl*, vilipendio *m*.
muesli ['mjuːzlɪ] *n* muesli *m*.
muezzin [muː'ezɪn] *n* almuecín *m*, almuédano *m*.
muff¹ [mʌf] *n* manguito *m* (*also Tech*).
muff² [mʌf] *vt ball* dejar escapar; *catch, stop* no lograr por torpeza; *shot* errar; *chance* perder, desperdiciar; (*Theat*) *entrance, lines* estropear; **to ~ it** fracasar, hacerlo malísimamente, no lograrlo por torpeza.
muffin ['mʌfɪn] *n* (*Brit*) ≈ mollete *m*; (*US*) *una especie de pan dulce*, ≈ bollo *m*.
muffle ['mʌfl] *vt* (**a**) envolver; *person etc* embozar, tapar (*with* de). (**b**) *noise* amortiguar, apagar; *noisy thing* amortiguar el ruido de; *bells, oars* envolver con tela; *drum* enfundar.
◆**muffle up** **1** *vt* envolver; *person etc* embozar, tapar (*with* de); **~d up in** embozado de.
2 *vr*: **to ~ o.s. up** embozarse, taparse.
muffled ['mʌfld] *adj sound* sordo, apagado.
muffler ['mʌflə^r] *n* (*scarf*) bufanda *f*; (*Mus*) sordina *f*; (*US Mech*) silenciador *m*, (*on motorbike*) mofle *m*.
mufti ['mʌftɪ] *n* (*Brit*) traje *m* de paisano; **in ~** vestido de paisano.
mug [mʌg] **1** *n* (**a**) (*cup*) taza *f* (alta, sin platillo); (*for beer*) jarro *m*, jarra *f*.
(**b**) (*Brit*‡: *person*) bobo *m*, primo *m*; **what a ~ I've been!** ¡he sido un tonto!; **it's a ~'s game** esto es solamente para tontos.
(**c**) (‡: *face*) jeta* *f*, hocico* *m*; **what a ~ she's got!** ¡qué jeta tiene!*; **he hit him in the ~** le pegó un tortazo en el hocico*.
2 *vt* (*) asaltar, pegar, aporrear.
◆**mug up*** *vt* (**a**) (*Brit*) empollar*, embotellar*, amarrar*.
(**b**) **to ~ it up** (*US*: *grimace*) gesticular, hacer muecas; (*Theat*) actuar exagerando.
mugger* ['mʌgə^r] *n* asaltador *m*.
mugging* ['mʌgɪŋ] *n* asalto *m*, vapuleo *m*.
muggins‡ ['mʌgɪnz] *n* (*Brit*) tonto *m*, primo *m*; **~ will pay for it** este pobre hombre lo pagará; **~ will do it** lo hará este cura*.
muggy ['mʌgɪ] *adj* bochornoso.
mug-shot* ['mʌgʃɒt] *n* fotografía *f* para las fichas.
mugwump ['mʌgwʌmp] *n* (*US*) votante *mf* independiente.
Muhammad [mʊ'hæməd] *nm* Mahoma.
mujaheddin ['muːdʒəhə'diːn] *npl* mujaidín *mpl*.
mulatto [mjuː'lætəʊ] **1** *adj* mulato. **2** *n, pl* **mulattoes** [mjuː'lætəʊz] mulato *m*, -a *f*.
mulberry ['mʌlbərɪ] *n* (*fruit*) mora *f*; (*tree*) morera *f*, moral *m*.
mulch [mʌltʃ] **1** *n* capote *m*, mantillo *m*. **2** *vt* cubrir con capote, cubrir con mantillo.
mulct [mʌlkt] *vt* (**a**) multar. (**b**) **to ~ sb of sth** quitar algo a uno, privar a uno de algo.
mule¹ [mjuːl] *n* (**a**) mulo *m*, -a *f*; (*person*) testarudo *m*, -a *f*. (**b**) (*Tech*) máquina *f* de hilar intermitente, selfactina *f*.
mule² [mjuːl] *n* (*slipper*) babucha *f*.
muleteer [,mjuːlɪ'tɪə^r] *n* mulatero *m*, muletero *m*, arriero *m*.
mule-track ['mjuːltræk] *n* camino *m* de herradura.
mulish ['mjuːlɪʃ] *adj* terco, testarudo.
mulishness ['mjuːlɪʃnɪs] *n* terquedad *f*, testarudez *f*.
mull [mʌl] *vt wine* calentar con especias.
◆**mull over** *vt*: **to ~ sth over** meditar algo, reflexionar sobre algo.
mullah ['mʌlə] *n* mullah *m*.
mullet ['mʌlɪt] *n*: **grey ~** mújol *m*; **red ~** salmonete *m*.
mulligatawny [,mʌlɪgə'tɔːnɪ] *n* sopa *f* de curry angloindia.
mullion ['mʌlɪən] *n* parteluz *m*.
mullioned ['mʌlɪənd] *adj window* dividido con parteluz.
multi... ['mʌltɪ] *pref* multi...
multi-access [,mʌltɪ'ækses] **1** *n* acceso *m* múltiple. **2** *adj* multiacceso, de acceso múltiple.
multicellular [,mʌltɪ'seljʊlə^r] *adj* multicelular.
multichannel ['mʌltɪ'tʃænl] *adj* (*TV*) multicanal.
multicoloured, (*US*) **multicolored** ['mʌltɪ'kʌləd] *adj* multicolor.
multicultural [,mʌltɪ'kʌltʃərəl] *adj* multicultural.
multidimensional [,mʌltɪdɪ'menʃənl] *adj* multidimensional.
multidirectional [,mʌltɪdɪ'rekʃənl] *adj* multidireccional.
multidisciplinary [,mʌltɪ'dɪsɪplɪnərɪ] *adj* multidisciplinario.
multifaceted [,mʌltɪ'fæsɪtɪd] *adj* multifacético.
multifarious [,mʌltɪ'fɛərɪəs] *adj* múltiple(s), diversísimo(s), variadísimo(s).
multiform ['mʌltɪfɔːm] *adj* multiforme.
multifunctional ['mʌltɪ'fʌŋkʃənl] *adj* multifuncional.
multigym ['mʌltɪdʒɪm] *n* gimnasio *m* múltiple.
multilateral ['mʌltɪ'lætərəl] *adj* multilátero, multilateral.
multilayer(ed) [,mʌltɪ'leɪə(d)] *adj* multicapa.
multilevel [,mʌltɪ'levl] *adj* (*US*) de muchos pisos.
multilingual [,mʌltɪ'lɪŋgwəl] *adj* plurilingüe.
multimillionaire ['mʌltɪmɪljə'nɛə^r] *n* multimillonario *m*, -a *f*.
multinational [,mʌltɪ'næʃənl] **1** *adj* multinacional. **2** *n* multinacional *f*.
multiple ['mʌltɪpl] **1** *adj* (*of many parts*) múltiplo; (*in pl, many and various*) múltiple; *firm* con muchas sucursales; **~ accident** (*Aut*) colisión *f* múltiple, colisión *f* en cadena; **~ birth** parto *m* múltiple; **~ choice questions** preguntas *fpl* de tipo elección múltiple; **~ choice test** ejercicio *m* de tipo elección múltiple; **~ ownership** propiedad *f* múltiple; **~ sclerosis** esclerosis *f* múltiple; **~ stores** (*Brit*) cadena *f* de almacenes.
2 *n* múltiplo *m*; (*shop*: *also* **~ store**) (cadena *f* de) grandes almacenes *mpl*; **lowest common ~** mínimo común múltiplo *m*.
multiplex ['mʌltɪ,pleks] *n* (*also* **~ cinema**) multicines *m*.
multiplexor ['mʌltɪ,pleksə^r] *n* multiplexor *m*.
multiplicand [,mʌltɪplɪ'kænd] *n* multiplicando *m*.
multiplication [,mʌltɪplɪ'keɪʃən] **1** *n* multiplicación *f*. **2** *attr*: **~ table** tabla *f* de multiplicar.
multiplicity [,mʌltɪ'plɪsɪtɪ] *n* multiplicidad *f*; **for a ~ of reasons** por múltiples razones; **a ~ of solutions** una gran diversidad de soluciones.
multiply ['mʌltɪplaɪ] **1** *vt* multiplicar; **to ~ 8 by 7** multiplicar 8 por 7. **2** *vi* multiplicarse.
multiprocessing [,mʌltɪ'prəʊsesɪŋ] *n* multiprocesamiento *m*.
multiprocessor [,mʌltɪ'prəʊsesə^r] *n* multiprocesador *m*.
multi-programming, (*US, also freq Comput*) **multiprograming** [,mʌltɪ'prəʊgræmɪŋ] *n* multiprogramación *f*.
multipurpose [,mʌltɪ'pɜːpəs] *adj* de fines múltiples, multiuso.
multiracial ['mʌltɪ'reɪʃəl] *adj* multirracial.
multirisk ['mʌltɪrɪsk] *attr*: **~ insurance** seguro *m* multiriesgo.
multistorey [,mʌltɪ'stɔːrɪ] *adj* de muchos pisos.
multistrike ['mʌltɪ,straɪk] *attr*: **~ ribbon** cinta *f* de múltiples impactos.
multitask(ing) ['mʌltɪ'tɑːsk(ɪŋ)] *n* multitarea *f*.
multitrack ['mʌltɪ,træk] *attr*: **~ recording** grabación *f* en bandas múltiples.
multitude ['mʌltɪtjuːd] *n* multitud *f*; **the ~** (*pej*) las masas, la plebe; **for a ~ of reasons** por múltiples razones; **they came in ~s** acudieron en tropel.
multitudinous [,mʌltɪ'tjuːdɪnəs] *adj* multitudinario; muy numeroso, numerosísimo.
multiuser [,mʌltɪ'juːzə^r] *adj* multiusuario; **~ system** sistema *m* multiusuario.
mum¹ [mʌm] *adj*: **~'s the word!** ¡punto en boca!; **to keep ~** callarse; **see that you keep ~ about it** de esto no digas ni pío; **everybody is keeping very ~ about it** esto lo tienen todos muy secreto.
mum²* [mʌm] *n* (*Brit*) mamá* *f*.
mumble ['mʌmbl] **1** *n*: **he said in a ~** dijo entre dientes. **2** *vt* decir entre dientes. **3** *vi* musitar, hablar entre dientes.
mumbo-jumbo ['mʌmbəʊ'dʒʌmbəʊ] *n* (*cult*) fetiche *m*; (*spell*) conjuro *m*; (*empty ritual*) mistificación *f*, mixtificación *f*, farsa *f*.
mummer ['mʌmə^r] *n* máscara *mf*.
mummery ['mʌmərɪ] *n* (*fig*) mistificación *f*; ceremonia *f*

ridícula, farsa *f.*

mummification [ˌmʌmɪfɪˈkeɪʃən] *n* momificación *f.*

mummify [ˈmʌmɪfaɪ] **1** *vt* momificar. **2** *vi* momificarse.

mummy[1] [ˈmʌmɪ] *n* (*Hist*) momia *f.*

mummy[2]* [ˈmʌmɪ] *n* (*Brit*) mamá* *f.*

mumps [mʌmps] *n* paperas *fpl*, parótidas *fpl.*

munch [mʌntʃ] *vt* mascar, ronzar.

munchie* [mʌntʃɪ] *n* (*US*) piscolabis *m*, algo para picar; **to have the ~s** tener ganas de picar de aquí y de allá.

mundane [ˈmʌnˈdeɪn] *adj* mundano; (*humdrum*) vulgar, trivial.

municipal [mjuːˈnɪsɪpəl] *adj* municipal.

municipality [mjuːˌnɪsɪˈpælɪtɪ] *n* municipio *m.*

munificence [mjuːˈnɪfɪsns] *n* munificencia *f.*

munificent [mjuːˈnɪfɪsnt] *adj* munífico, munificente.

muniments [ˈmjuːnɪmənts] *npl* documentos *mpl* (probatorios); (*also* ~ **room**) archivos *mpl.*

munitions [mjuːˈnɪʃənz] **1** *npl* municiones *fpl*; pertrechos *mpl*. **2** *attr*: ~ **dump** depósito *m* de municiones; ~ **factory** fábrica *f* de municiones.

mural [ˈmjʊərəl] **1** *adj* mural. **2** *n* pintura *f* mural, mural *m.*

murder [ˈmɜːdəʳ] **1** *n* (**a**) asesinato *m*; (*as Jur term*) homicidio *m*; **accused of** ~ acusado de homicidio; ~ **in the first degree** homicidio *m* premeditado; ~ **will out** todo termina por saberse.

(**b**) (*) **it was** ~! ¡un horror!; **this job is** ~ este trabajo es la monda*; **to shout blue** ~ protestar enérgicamente, poner el grito en el cielo; **she gets away with** ~ hace lo que quiere y siempre sale impune.

2 *attr*: ~ **case** caso *m* de homicidio; ~ **inquiry** investigación *f* de un homicidio; **M~ Squad** grupo *m* de homicidios; ~ **trial** juicio *m* por asesinato; **the** ~ **weapon** el arma que se empleó en el homicidio.

3 *vt* asesinar; matar, dar muerte a; *song etc* arruinar, estropear; *play* degollar; (*) *opponent* derrotar.

murderer [ˈmɜːdərəʳ] *n* asesino *m*, (*as Jur term*) homicida *m.*

murderess [ˈmɜːdərɪs] *n* asesina *f*, (*as Jur term*) homicida *f.*

murderous [ˈmɜːdərəs] *adj* homicida; (*fig*) cruel, feroz, sanguinario; *look* homicida, asesino; **this heat is** ~ este calor es cruel; **I felt** ~ me vinieron pensamientos homicidas.

murk [mɜːk] *n* oscuridad *f*, tinieblas *fpl.*

murkiness [ˈmɜːkɪnɪs] *n* oscuridad *f*, lobreguez *f*; (*fig*) lo tenebroso, lo turbio.

murky [ˈmɜːkɪ] *adj* oscuro, lóbrego; (*fig*) tenebroso, turbio.

murmur [ˈmɜːməʳ] **1** *n* (*soft speech*) murmullo *m*; (*of water*) murmullo *m*, murmurio *m*; (*of leaves etc*) susurro *m*; (*of distant traffic etc*) rumor *m*; (*complaint*) queja *f*, murmurio *m*; **there were ~s of disagreement** hubo murmurios de disconformidad.

2 *vt* murmurar, decir en voz baja.

3 *vi* murmullar, murmurar; susurrar; quejarse; **to ~ about, to ~ against** murmurar de, quejarse de.

Murphy [ˈmɜːfɪ] *n*: **~'s law*** ley *f* de la indefectible mala voluntad de los objetos inanimados.

Mus.B., Mus. Bac. *n abbr of* **Bachelor of Music** *título universitario.*

muscatel [ˌmʌskəˈtel] **1** *adj* moscatel. **2** *n* moscatel *m.*

muscle [ˈmʌsl] *n* (**a**) músculo *m*; **he never moved a** ~ se mantuvo inmóvil, no se inmutó en absoluto; **to flex one's ~s** tensar los músculos.

(**b**) (*fig*) fuerza *f* muscular, musculatura *f*; **political** ~ musculatura *f* política.

◆**muscle in*** *vi* (*Brit*) introducirse por fuerza (*on a deal* en un negocio).

musclebound [ˈmʌslbaʊnd] *adj* envarado por exceso de ejercicio.

muscleman* [ˈmʌslmæn] *n, pl* **musclemen** [ˈmʌslmen] forzudo *m.*

Muscovite [ˈmʌskəvaɪt] **1** *adj* moscovita. **2** *n* moscovita *mf.*

muscular [ˈmʌskjʊləʳ] *adj tissue etc* muscular; (*having muscles*) musculoso; (*brawny*) fornido, membrudo; ~ **dystrophy** distrofia *f* muscular.

musculature [ˈmʌskjʊlətjʊəʳ] *n* musculatura *f.*

Mus.D., Mus. Doc. *n abbr of* **Doctor of Music** *título universitario.*

Muse [mjuːz] *n* musa *f*; **the ~s** las Musas.

muse [mjuːz] **1** *vt*: **'should we?' he ~d** '¿debemos hacerlo?', dijo pensativo.

2 *vi* meditar, reflexionar, rumiar; **to ~ about sth, to ~ on sth** meditar algo, reflexionar sobre algo; **to ~ on a scene** contemplar distraído una escena.

museum [mjuːˈzɪəm] *n* museo *m.*

museum piece [mjuːˈzɪəmˌpiːs] *n* (*fig*) cosa *f* anticuada, antigualla *f*; **the car is a real** ~ el coche realmente es digno de estar en un museo.

mush[1] [mʌʃ] *n* (**a**) (*Culin*) gachas *fpl*; masa *f* blanda y espesa. (**b**) (*fig*) sensiblería *f*, sentimentalismo *m.*

mush[2]‡ [muʃ] *n* jeta‡ *f.*

mush[3]‡ [muʃ] *n* (*in direct address*) tronco*.

mushroom [ˈmʌʃrum] **1** *n* seta *f*, hongo *m*; (*as food*) champiñón *m*; **a great ~ of smoke** un enorme hongo de humo; **to grow like ~s** surgir como hongos, crecer de la noche a la mañana.

2 *attr*: ~ **cloud** nube *f* en forma de hongo; ~ **growth** crecimiento *m* rapidísimo; ~ **town** ciudad *f* que crece rapidísimamente.

3 *vi* (*town etc*) surgir como hongos, crecer de la noche a la mañana, crecer rapidísimamente; **the cloud of smoke went ~ing up** subió el humo en forma de hongo; **to ~ into** convertirse rapidísimamente en.

mushy [ˈmʌʃɪ] *adj* (**a**) pulposo, mollar, como gachas. (**b**) (*fig*) sensiblero, muy sentimental.

music [ˈmjuːzɪk] **1** *n* música *f*; ~ **of the spheres** música *f* mundana, armonía *f* celestial; **it was ~ to my ears** daba gusto escucharlo, eran palabras (*etc*) deliciosas para mí; **to face the** ~ afrontar las consecuencias; **to set a work to** ~ poner música a una obra.

2 *attr*: ~ **centre** (*shop*) tienda *f* de aparatos de sonido de alta fidelidad; ~ **critic** crítico *mf* de la música; ~ **festival** festival *m* de música; ~ **lesson** (*instrumental*) clase *f* de música, (*vocal*) clase *f* de solfeo.

musical [ˈmjuːzɪkəl] **1** *adj* (**a**) musical; *composition etc* músico; *sound, voice* armonioso, melodioso; ~ **box** caja *f* de música; ~ **chairs** juego *m* de las sillas; **the politicians are merely playing ~ chairs** estos políticos son los mismos perros con distintos collares; ~ **comedy** comedia *f* musical, (*Sp*) zarzuela *f*; ~ **instrument** instrumento *m* músico.

(**b**) dotado para la música; **he's very** ~ tiene mucho talento para la música; **he comes from a ~ family** es de familia de músicos.

2 *n* comedia *f* musical.

musicale [ˌmjuːzɪˈkɑːl] *n* velada *f* musical.

musically [ˈmjuːzɪkəlɪ] *adv* armoniosamente, melodiosamente.

music-centre [mjuːzɪkˌsentəʳ] *n* equipo *m* estereofónico.

music-hall [ˈmjuːzɪkhɔːl] *n* (*Brit*) teatro *m* de variedades.

musician [mjuːˈzɪʃən] *n* músico *m*, -a *f.*

musicianship [mjuːˈzɪʃənʃɪp] *n* maestría *f* musical.

music-lover [ˈmjuːzɪkˌlʌvəʳ] *n* persona *f* aficionada a la música, melómano *m*, -a *f.*

musicologist [ˌmjuːzɪˈkɒlədʒɪst] *n* musicólogo *m*, -a *f.*

musicology [ˌmjuːzɪˈkɒlədʒɪ] *n* musicología *f.*

music paper [ˈmjuːzɪkˌpeɪpəʳ] *n* papel *m* de música, papel *m* pautado.

music stand [ˈmjuːzɪkstænd] *n* atril *m.*

musingly [ˈmjuːzɪŋlɪ] *adv say etc* con aire distraído, pensativamente.

musings [ˈmjuːzɪŋz] *npl* meditaciones *fpl.*

musk [mʌsk] *n* (*substance*) almizcle *m*; (*scent*) perfume *m* de almizcle; (*smell*) olor *m* a almizcle; (*Bot*) almizcleña *f.*

musket [ˈmʌskɪt] *n* mosquete *m.*

musketeer [ˌmʌskɪˈtɪəʳ] *n* mosquetero *m.*

musketry [ˈmʌskɪtrɪ] *n* (*muskets*) mosquetes *mpl*; (*firing*) fuego *m* de mosquetes, tiros *mpl.*

musk-ox [ˈmʌskɒks] *n, pl* **musk-oxen** [ˈmʌskɒksən] buey *m* almizclado.

muskrat [ˈmʌskræt] *n* rata *f* almizclera.

musk-rose [ˈmʌskrəʊz] *n* rosa *f* almizcleña.

musky [ˈmʌskɪ] *adj* almizcleño, almizclado; *smell* a almizcle.

Muslim [ˈmʊslɪm] = **Moslem.**

muslin [ˈmʌzlɪn] **1** *n* muselina *f*. **2** *attr* de muselina.

musquash [ˈmʌskwɒʃ] *n* ratón *m* almizclero; (*fur*) piel *f* de rata almizclera.

muss [mʌs] *vt* (*also* **to ~ up**) *hair* desarreglar, despeinar; *dress* ajar, chafar.

mussel [ˈmʌsl] *n* mejillón *m.*

mussel-bed [ˈmʌslbed] *n* criadero *m* de mejillones.

must[1] [mʌst] *n* (*of wine*) mosto *m.*

must[2] [mʌst] *n* = **mustiness.**

must[3] [mʌst] *v aux* (*present tense only*) **1** (**a**) (*obligation*) **I ~ do it** debo hacerlo, tengo que hacerlo, he de hacerlo; **one ~ be careful** hay que tener cuidado; **one ~ not be too hopeful** no hay que ser demasiado optimista; **the patient ~ have complete quiet** el enfermo requiere silencio absoluto;

but you ~ come pero es imprescindible que vengas; **I'll do it if I ~** si me obligan, lo haré; lo haré si es necesario; **do it if you ~** hazlo si es necesario, hazlo si no hay más remedio; **if you ~ know, I'm Ruritanian** si es esencial que lo sepa, soy ruritanio; **there ~ be a reason** debe haber una razón, ha de haber una razón.

(**b**) (*probability*) **he ~ be there by now** ya debe de estar allí, ya estará allí; **it ~ be cold up there** hará frío allá arriba; **it ~ be about 3 o'clock** serán las 3; **it ~ have been about 5** serían alrededor de las 5; **but you ~ have seen him!** ¡pero debes haberle visto!; **he ~ be a Mexican** debe de ser mejicano.

2 *n* (*) **this programme is a ~ for everybody** este programa no lo ha de perder nadie, es imprescindible que todos escuchen este programa.

mustache ['mʌstæʃ] *n* (*US*) = **moustache.**

mustang ['mʌstæŋ] *n* potro *m* mesteño, mustang(o) *m*.

mustard ['mʌstəd] **1** *n* mostaza *f*. **2** *adj*: **a ~ (yellow) dress** un vestido mostaza.

mustard-gas ['mʌstədgæs] *n* gas *m* mostaza.

mustard-plaster ['mʌsted'plɑːstə^r] *n* sinapismo *m*, cataplasma *f* de mostaza.

mustard-pot ['mʌstədpɒt] *n* mostacera *f*.

muster ['mʌstə^r] **1** *n* (*gathering*) asamblea *f* (*also Mil*), reunión *f*; (*review*) revista *f*; (*list*) lista *f*, matrícula *f*, (*Naut*) rol *m*; **to pass ~** pasar revista, (*fig*) ser aceptable, ser satisfactorio.

2 *vt* (*call together for inspection*) llamar a asamblea, juntar para pasar revista; (*collect*) juntar, reunir; (*also* **to ~ up**) *courage, strength* cobrar; **the club can ~ 20 members** el club cuenta con 20 miembros, el club consiste en 20 miembros.

3 *vi* juntarse, reunirse.

mustiness ['mʌstɪnɪs] *n* moho *m*; ranciedad *f*; (*of room etc*) olor *m* a humedad, olor *m* a cerrado.

mustn't ['mʌsnt] = **must not.**

musty ['mʌstɪ] *adj* mohoso; rancio; *room etc* que huele a humedad, que huele a cerrado; *joke etc* viejo, gastado.

mutability [,mjuːtə'bɪlɪtɪ] *n* mutabilidad *f*.

mutable ['mjuːtəbl] *adj* mudable.

mutagen ['mjuːtədʒən] *n* mutagene *m*.

mutant ['mjuːtənt] **1** *adj* mutante. **2** *n* mutante *m*.

mutate [mjuː'teɪt] **1** *vt* mudar. **2** *vi* sufrir mutación.

mutation [mjuː'teɪʃən] *n* mutación *f*.

mute [mjuːt] **1** *adj* mudo, silencioso; **with H ~** con hache muda; **to become ~** enmudecer. **2** *n* (**a**) (*person*) mudo *m*, -a *f*. (**b**) (*Mus*) sordina *f*. (**c**) (*Gram*) letra *f* muda. **3** *vt* (*Mus*) poner sordina a; *noise* amortiguar, apagar.

muted ['mjuːtɪd] *adj noise* sordo, apagado; *criticism* callado.

mutilate ['mjuːtɪleɪt] *vt* mutilar.

mutilation [,mjuːtɪ'leɪʃən] *n* mutilación *f*.

mutineer [,mjuːtɪ'nɪə^r] *n* amotinado *m*, amotinador *m*.

mutinous ['mjuːtɪnəs] *adj* amotinado; (*fig*) turbulento, rebelde; **we were feeling pretty ~** estábamos hartos ya, estábamos dispuestos a rebelarnos.

mutiny ['mjuːtɪnɪ] **1** *n* motín *m*, sublevación *f*. **2** *vi* amotinarse, sublevarse.

mutt* [mʌt] *n* (**a**) bobo *m*. (**b**) (*US*) chucho *m*; perro *m* callejero.

mutter ['mʌtə^r] **1** *n* murmullo *m*; **a ~ of voices** un rumor de voces.

2 *vt* murmurar, decir entre dientes; **'yes', he ~ed** 'sí', refunfuñó.

3 *vi* murmurar; (*guns, thunder*) retumbar a lo lejos.

mutton ['mʌtn] *n* (carne *f* de) cordero *m*; **she's ~ dressed up as lamb*** ella es una carantoña*.

mutton chop ['mʌtn'tʃɒp] *n* chuleta *f* de cordero.

mutual ['mjuːtjuəl] *adj* mutuo; (*loosely*) común; **the feeling is ~** yo comparto esa opinión, lo mismo digo yo; **our ~ friend** nuestro común amigo; **their ~ friend** el amigo de los dos, el amigo que tienen en común; **~ benefit society** mutualidad *f*; **~ fund** fondo *m* mutualista; **~ insurance** seguro *m* mutuo; **~ interest** interés *m* mutuo; **~ savings bank** caja *f* mutua de ahorros; **~ understanding** comprensión *f* mutua; acuerdo *m* mutuo.

mutuality [,mjuːtjʊ'ælɪtɪ] *n* mutualidad *f*.

mutually ['mjuːtjʊəlɪ] *adv* mutuamente.

Muzak ['mjuːzæk] ® *n* hilo *m* musical.

muzzle ['mʌzl] **1** *n* (*snout*) hocico *m*; (*for dog*) bozal *m*; (*of gun*) boca *f*. **2** *vt dog* abozalar; *criticism etc* estorbar; *critic* amordazar, imponer silencio a.

muzzle-loader ['mʌzl,ləʊdə^r] *n* arma *f* que se carga por la boca.

muzzle velocity ['mʌzlvɪ,lɒsɪtɪ] *n* velocidad *f* inicial.

muzzy ['mʌzɪ] *adj* (*from drinking*) confuso, atontado; *outline* borroso.

MVP *n* (*US*) *abbr of* **most valuable player.**

MW *n* (*Rad*) *abbr of* **medium wave** onda *f* media, OM *f*.

my [maɪ, mɪ] **1** *poss adj* mi. **2** *interj* ¡caramba!

myalgia [maɪ'ældʒɪə] *n* mialgia *f*.

myalgic [maɪ'ældʒɪk] *adj*: **~ encephalomyelitis** encefalomielitis *f* miálgica.

mycology [maɪ'kɒlədʒɪ] *n* micología *f*.

myopia [maɪ'əʊpɪə] *n* miopía *f*.

myopic [maɪ'ɒpɪk] *adj* miope.

myriad ['mɪrɪəd] (*liter*) **1** *n* miríada *f*. **2** *adj*: **a ~ flies** una miríada de moscas.

myrmidon ['mɜːmɪdən] *n* secuaz *m* fiel, satélite *m*, esbirro *m*.

myrrh [mɜː^r] *n* mirra *f*.

myrtle ['mɜːtl] *n* arrayán *m*, mirto *m*.

myself [maɪ'self] *pron* (*subject*) yo mismo, yo misma; (*acc, dat*) me; (*after prep*) mí (mismo, misma); *V* **oneself.**

mysterious [mɪs'tɪərɪəs] *adj* misterioso.

mysteriously [mɪs'tɪərɪəslɪ] *adv* misteriosamente.

mystery ['mɪstərɪ] **1** *n* (**a**) (*gen*) misterio *m*; **there's no ~ about it** aquí no hay misterio; **it's a ~ to me where it can have gone** no tengo la menor idea de dónde se habrá metido; **to make a great ~ out of a matter** envolver un asunto en un ambiente de misterio.

(**b**) (*Theat*: *also* **~ play**) auto *m*, misterio *m*.

(**c**) (*Liter*: *also* **~ story**) novela *f* de misterio.

2 *attr*: **~ man** hombre *m* misterioso; **~ ship** buque *m* misterioso; **~ tour** viaje *m* sorpresa.

mystic ['mɪstɪk] **1** *adj* místico. **2** *n* místico *m*, -a *f*.

mystical ['mɪstɪkəl] *adj* místico.

mysticism ['mɪstɪsɪzəm] *n* misticismo *m*; (*doctrine, literary genre*) mística *f*.

mystification [,mɪstɪfɪ'keɪʃən] *n* misterio *m*; confusión *f*, perplejidad *f*; **why all the ~?** ¿por qué tanto misterio?; **my ~ increased** creció mi perplejidad.

mystify ['mɪstɪfaɪ] *vt* dejar perplejo, desorientar, desconcertar; **I am mystified** estoy perplejo; **it completely mystified him** le desorientó por completo, le despistó por completo.

mystifying ['mɪstɪ,faɪɪŋ] *adj* inexplicable; desconcertante; hecho para desorientar (*or* despistar).

mystique [mɪs'tiːk] *n* misterio *m* (profesional *etc*), técnica *f* (al parecer) misteriosa, pericia *f* impresionante.

myth [mɪθ] *n* mito *m*.

mythic(al) ['mɪθɪkəl] *adj* mítico.

mythological [,mɪθə'lɒdʒɪkəl] *adj* mitológico.

mythology [mɪ'θɒlədʒɪ] *n* mitología *f*.

myxomatosis ['mɪksəʊmə'təʊsɪs] *n* mixomatosis *f*.

N

N, n [en] *n* (*letter*) N, n *f*; **N for Nellie** *or* (*US*) **Nan** N de Navarra; **nth** enésimo; **to the nth degree***, **to the nth (power)** a la enésima; **for the nth time** por enésima vez; **there are ~ ways of doing it** hay X maneras de hacerlo.
N *abbr of* **north** N. norte *m* (*also adj*).
'n'‡ [ən] *conj* = **and.**
n/a (**a**) *abbr of* **not applicable** no interesa. (**b**) (*Fin*) *abbr of* **no account.** (**c**) (*Comm*) *abbr of* **not available.**
NAACP *n* (*US*) *abbr of* **National Association for the Advancement of Colored People.**
NAAFI ['næfɪ] *n* (*Brit*) *abbr of* **Navy, Army and Air Force Institute** *servicio de cantinas etc para las fuerzas armadas.*
nab* [næb] *vt* coger, echar el guante a; (*arrest*) prender.
nabob ['neɪbɒb] *n* nabab *m.*
nacelle [næ'sel] *n* barquilla *f*, góndola *f.*
nacre ['neɪkəʳ] *n* nácar *m.*
nacreous ['neɪkrɪəs] *adj* nacarino, nacarado, de nácar.
NACU *n* (*US*) *abbr of* **National Association of Colleges and Universities.**
nadir ['neɪdɪəʳ] *n* (*Astron*) nadir *m*; (*fig*) punto *m* más bajo, nadir *m.*
naevus, (*US*) **nevus** ['ni:vəs] *n, pl* **naevi**, (*US*) **nevi** ['ni:vaɪ] nevo *m.*
naff‡ [næf] *adj* inferior, inútil; hortera, ordinario, de mal gusto.
◆**naff off‡** *vi*: **~ off** vete a paseo*, vete al cuerno*.
nag¹ [næg] *n* jaca *f*; (*pej*) rocín *m.*
nag² [næg] **1** *vt* (*scold*) regañar; (*annoy*) importunar, fastidiar, dar la lata a*; criticar; **don't ~ me so!** ¡no machaques!; **his conscience ~ged him** le remordía la conciencia; **he was ~ged by doubts** estaba acosado por las dudas; **she ~s him all day long** ella le importuna con sus quejas todo el día.
2 *vi* ser regañón, ser importuno, dar la lata*; criticar; **to ~ at sb** importunar a uno, criticar a uno; **don't ~, woman!** ¡no machaques, mujer!
nagger ['nægəʳ] *n* regañón *m*, -ona *f*, criticón *m*, -ona *f.*
nagging ['nægɪŋ] **1** *adj person* regañón, criticón, marimandón; *pain* continuo; *conscience* nada tranquilo; *doubt, fear etc* persistente, que no se desvanece.
2 *n* importunar *m*; críticas *fpl*; quejas *fpl.*
naiad ['naɪæd] *n* náyade *f.*
nail [neɪl] **1** *n* (**a**) (*Anat*) uña *f*; (*of animal*) garra *f*; **to bite one's ~s** comerse las uñas.
(**b**) (*metal*) clavo *m*; **~ bomb** bomba *f* de metralla; **this is another ~ in his coffin** éste es otro paso hacia su destrucción; **to hit the ~ on the head** dar en el clavo, acertar; **to pay on the ~** pagar a tocateja.
2 *vt* (**a**) (*fix with ~s*) clavar, enclavar; adornar con clavos, clavetear; **to ~ two things together** fijar (*or* unir) dos cosas con clavos.
(**b**) (*fig*) (*catch, get hold of*) coger (*Sp*), agarrar (*LAm*); *lie* acabar con; *rumour etc* desmentir, demostrar la falsedad de; (*locate*) localizar; (*define*) definir, precisar.
◆**nail down** *vt* (**a**) **to ~ sth down** clavar algo, sujetar algo con clavos. (**b**) *date, price* fijar; *policy etc* concretar, establecer; **to ~ sb down** poner a uno entre la espada y la pared; **we ~ed him down to a date** le forzamos a fijar una fecha; **we ~ed him down to come tomorrow** le comprometimos a que viniera mañana; **you can't ~ him down** es imposible hacerle concretar.
◆**nail up** *vt*: **to ~ sth up** cerrar algo con clavos.
nail-biting ['neɪl,baɪtɪŋ] **1** *adj* tenso, tirante. **2** *n* mala costumbre *f* de comerse las uñas.
nailbrush ['neɪlbrʌʃ] *n* cepillo *m* para las uñas.
nail-clippers ['neɪl,klɪpəz] *npl* cortaúñas *m.*
nailfile ['neɪlfaɪl] *n* lima *f* para las uñas.
nail-polish ['neɪl,pɒlɪʃ] *n* esmalte *m* para las uñas, laca *f* para las uñas; **~ remover** quitaesmalte *m.*
nail-scissors ['neɪlsɪzəz] *npl* tijeras *fpl* para las uñas.
nail-varnish ['neɪl,vɑ:nɪʃ] *n* (*Brit*) = **nail-polish.**
Nairobi [naɪ'rəʊbɪ] *n* Nairobi *m.*
naive, naïve [naɪ'i:v] *adj* ingenuo, cándido, sencillo.
naively, naïvely [naɪ'i:vlɪ] *adv* ingenuamente.
naïveté, naivety, naïvety [naɪ'i:vtɪ] *n* ingenuidad *f*, candor *m*, sencillez *f.*
naked ['neɪkɪd] *adj* desnudo; (*fig*) desabrigado, indefenso; *flame* expuesto al aire; *lamp* sin pantalla; *sword* desenvainado; *attempt* abierto, manifiesto; *emotion* franco, abierto; **the ~ truth** la verdad lisa y llana, la pura verdad; **stark ~** en cueros, en pelota, como le parió su madre; **to go ~** ir desnudo; **to strip sb ~** desnudar a uno completamente, dejar a uno en cueros.
nakedness ['neɪkɪdnɪs] *n* desnudez *f.*
NALGO ['nælgəʊ] *n* (*Brit*) *abbr of* **National and Local Government Officers' Association** *sindicato de funcionarios.*
NAM *n* (*US*) *abbr of* **National Association of Manufacturers.**
namby-pamby ['næmbɪ'pæmbɪ] **1** *adj* soso, ñoño. **2** *n* persona *f* sosa, ñoño *m*, -a *f.*
name [neɪm] **1** *n* (**a**) nombre *m*; designación *f*; (*surname*) apellido *m*; (*nickname*) apodo *m*; (*of book etc*) título *m*; **by ~** de nombre; **Pérez by ~** de nombre Pérez, llamado Pérez; **a lady by the ~ of Dulcinea** una señora llamada Dulcinea; **that's the ~ of the game*** así es la cosa; **no ~s no packdrill** es mejor callar los nombres; **I know him by ~ only** le conozco solamente de nombre; **we know it by** (*or* **under**) **another ~** lo conocemos bajo otro nombre; **to go by** (*or* **under**) **the ~ of** ser conocido por el nombre de, vivir bajo el nombre de; **in ~** de nombre; **he was king in ~ only** era rey tan sólo de nombre, de rey no tenía más que el nombre; **it exists in ~ only** no existe sino de nombre; **he signed on in the ~ of Smith** firmó con el apellido Smith; **at least in ~** al menos nominalmente; **she's the boss in all but ~** para jefa sólo le falta el nombre; **in the ~ of peace** en nombre de la paz; **I thank you in the ~ of all those present** le doy las gracias en nombre de todos los asistentes; **open up, in the ~ of the law!** ¡abran a la justicia!, ¡abran en nombre de la ley!; **what's in a ~?** ¿qué importa un nombre?; **he hasn't a penny to his ~** no tiene donde caerse muerto; **what's your ~?** ¿cómo se llama?; **my ~ is Peter** me llamo Pedro; **I'll do it, or my ~'s not Bloggs!** ¡como me llamo Bloggs, que lo haré!; **to call sb ~s** insultar a uno, poner motes a uno, llenar a uno de injurias; **what ~ are they giving the child?** ¿qué nombre le van a poner al niño?; **they married to give the child a ~** se casaron para darle nombre al niño, se casaron para legitimar al niño; **to lend one's ~ to** prestar su nombre a; **to mention no ~s** no mencionar nombres; **to put one's ~ down for a car** apuntarse para un coche; **what ~ shall I say?** (*Telec*) ¿de parte de quién?; (*announcing arrival*) ¿qué nombre quiere que diga?; **to send in one's ~** presentarse; **to take sb's ~ and address** apuntar las señas de uno; **he had his ~ taken** (*Sport*) el árbitro apuntó su nombre.
(**b**) (*reputation*) nombre *m*; reputación *f*, fama *f*; **the firm has a good ~** la casa tiene buena reputación; **he has a ~ for carelessness** tiene fama de descuidado, ya se sabe que es poco cuidadoso; **his middle ~ is 'lover'** le han apodado 'el amante'; **to get (o.s.) a bad ~** crearse una mala reputación; **he's giving the place a bad ~** le está dando mala fama al lugar; **to make a ~ for o.s.** darse a conocer, empezar a ser conocido (*as* como); **to make one's ~** llegar a ser famoso.
(**c**) (*person*) **big ~** (gran) figura *f*, personaje *m* de relieve; **he's a big ~** es todo un personaje; **he's one of the big ~s in the business** es uno de los personajes importantes en ese campo; **this show has no big ~s** este

show no tiene figuras.

2 *vt* (*call*) *thing* llamar; nombrar; designar, denominar; *person* llamar; (*at birth*) bautizar, poner de nombre a; (*surname*) apellidar; (*mention*) mencionar, mentar; (*nominate*) nombrar; *date, price etc* fijar, señalar; **a man ~d Jack** un hombre llamado Juanito; **they ~d the child Mary** a la niña le pusieron María; **you ~ it, we have it** cualquier cosa que pidas la tenemos; **he is not ~d in this list** no figura en esta lista; **you were not ~d in the speech** no se le mencionó en el discurso; **~ the third president of the USA** diga el nombre del tercer presidente de EE.UU.; **to ~ a boy after** *or* (*US*) **for his grandfather** ponerle a un niño un nombre por su abuelo; **they ~d him Winston after Churchill** le pusieron Winston por Churchill; **he was ~d ambassador to Warsaw** le nombraron embajador en Varsovia.

-named [neɪmd] *adj ending in compounds*: **first~** primero; **last~** último.

name-day ['neɪm'deɪ] *n* (*Rel*) día *m* del santo de uno; fiesta *f* onomástica; (*Fin*) día *m* de ajuste de cuentas.

name-dropper ['neɪm,drɒpəʳ] *n persona dada al 'name-dropping'*.

name-dropping ['neɪm'drɒpɪŋ] *n vicio de procurar impresionar mencionando las personas importantes que uno conoce* (*o finge haber conocido*).

nameless ['neɪmlɪs] *adj* anónimo, sin nombre, innominado; *vice* nefando; *dread etc* vago, indecible; **to remain ~** permanecer en el anonimato; **a person who shall be ~** una persona cuyo nombre callo.

namely ['neɪmlɪ] *adv* a saber; esto es, es decir.

nameplate ['neɪmpleɪt] *n* letrero *m* (*or* placa *f*) con nombre (del dueño *etc*); placa *f* del fabricante.

namesake ['neɪmseɪk] *n* tocayo *m*, -a *f*, homónimo *m*, -a *f*.

nametape ['neɪmteɪp] *n* tirita *f* con el nombre.

Namibia [nɑː'mɪbɪə] *n* Namibia *f*.

Namibian [nɑː'mɪbɪən] **1** *adj* namibio. **2** *n* namibio *m*, -a *f*.

nan* [næn] *n*, **nana*** ['nænə] *n* (*grandmother*) yaya* *f*.

nance‡ [næns] *n*, **nancy(-boy)‡** ['nænsɪbɔɪ] *n* (*Brit*) maricón‡ *m*.

nanny ['nænɪ] *n* (*Brit*) niñera *f* (*also fig*), chacha* *f*; **~ state** estado-niñera *m*.

nanny-goat ['nænɪgəʊt] *n* cabra *f*.

Naomi ['neɪəmɪ] *nf* Naomi.

nap¹ [næp] **1** *n* sueñecito *m*, dormirela *f*; (*in afternoon*) siesta *f*; **to have a ~, to take a ~** descabezar un sueño, echar una siesta, dormir la siesta.

2 *vi* dormitar; dormir la siesta; **to catch sb ~ping** coger a uno desprevenido; **to be caught ~ping** estar desprevenido.

nap² [næp] *n* (*on cloth*) lanilla *f*.

nap³ [næp] (*Cards: game*) napolitana *f*; **to go ~** jugarse el todo (*on* a).

NAPA *n* (*US*) *abbr of* **National Association of Performing Artists** *sindicato de trabajadores del espectáculo*.

napalm ['neɪpɑːm] *n* napalm *m*.

nape [neɪp] *n* (*also* **~ of the neck**) nuca *f*, cogote *m*.

naphtha ['næfθə] *n* nafta *f*.

naphthalene ['næfθəliːn] *n* naftalina *f*.

napkin ['næpkɪn] *n* (*table ~*) servilleta *f*; (*Brit: baby's*) pañal *m*; (*woman's*) compresa *f* higiénica.

napkin-ring ['næpkɪnrɪŋ] *n* servilletero *m*.

Naples ['neɪplz] *n* Nápoles *m*.

Napoleon [nə'pəʊlɪən] *nm* Napoleón.

Napoleonic [nə,pəʊlɪ'ɒnɪk] *adj* napoleónico.

napper* ['næpəʳ] *n* (*head*) coca* *f*.

nappy ['næpɪ] **1** *n* (*Brit*) pañal *m*. **2** *attr*: **~ liner** pañal *m* interior; **~ rash** escaldamiento *m* por pañales húmedos; **to have ~ rash** tener el culito escaldado.

Narbonne [nɑː'bɒn] *n* Narbona *f*.

narc‡ [nɑːk] *n* (*US*) camello* *m*, traficante *mf* de drogas.

narcissi [nɑː'sɪsaɪ] *npl of* **narcissus**.

narcissism [nɑː'sɪsɪzəm] *n* narcisismo *m*.

narcissistic [,nɑːsɪ'sɪstɪk] *adj* narcisista.

Narcissus [nɑː'sɪsəs] *nm* Narciso.

narcissus [nɑː'sɪsəs] *n*, *pl* **narcissi** [nɑː'sɪsaɪ] narciso *m*.

narcosis [nɑː'kəʊsɪs] *n* narcosis *f*, narcotismo *m*.

narcotic [nɑː'kɒtɪk] **1** *adj* narcótico. **2** *n* narcótico *m*. **3** *attr*: **~s agent** agente *mf* de narcóticos; **to be on a ~s charge** estar acusado de traficar con drogas.

narcotism ['nɑːkə,tɪzəm] *n* narcotismo *m*.

narcotize ['nɑːkətaɪz] *vt* narcotizar.

nard [nɑːd] *n* nardo *m*.

nark‡ [nɑːk] (*Brit*) **1** *n* soplón* *m*. **2** *vt* (**a**) **it ~s me** me fastidia terriblemente; **he got properly ~ed** se puso negro*. (**b**) **~ it!** (*stop it*) ¡déjalo!, (*go away*) ¡lárgate!*.

narky‡ ['nɑːkɪ] *adj*: **to get ~** (*Brit*) ponerse negro*.

narrate [nə'reɪt] *vt* narrar, referir, contar.

narration [nə'reɪʃən] *n* narración *f*, relato *m*.

narrative ['nærətɪv] **1** *adj* narrativo. **2** *n* narrativa *f*, narración *f*.

narrator [nə'reɪtəʳ] *n* narrador *m*, -ora *f*.

narrow ['nærəʊ] **1** *adj* estrecho, angosto; *trousers etc* estrecho; *advantage, majority* pequeño; (*restricted*) reducido, corto, restringido; *escape* de milagro, por los pelos; *person* de miras estrechas, intolerante; **~ boat** barcaza *f*; **in the ~ sense of the word** en el sentido estricto de la palabra; **on ~ resources** con escasos recursos.

2 *npl*: **~s** (*Naut*) estrecho *m*.

3 *vt* (*also* **to ~ down**) estrechar, angostar; reducir; **we have ~ed it down to 3 possibilities** lo hemos reducido a 3 posibilidades; **the police have ~ed the search down to Bristol** la policía ha podido limitar sus pesquisas a Bristol.

4 *vi* (*also* **to ~ down**) estrecharse, angostarse, hacerse más angosto; reducirse; **the passage ~s at the end** el pasillo se hace más estrecho hacia el final; **the search has now ~ed to Soho** la búsqueda ha quedado restringida a Soho.

◆narrow down 1 *vt* = **narrow 3.**

2 *vi*: **so the question ~s down to this ...** así que la cuestión se reduce a esto ...

narrow-gauge ['nærəʊgeɪdʒ] *adj* de vía estrecha.

narrowing ['nærəʊɪŋ] *n* (*V adj*) estrechamiento *m*; reducción *f*, restricción *f*.

narrowly ['nærəʊlɪ] *adv* estrechamente; por poco; **the slate ~ missed him** por poco la pizarra le alcanza, faltó poco para que la pizarra le diese; **he ~ missed being elected** no fue elegido por unos pocos votos; **if we define it ~** si lo definimos estrictamente; **they watched me ~** me vigilaban sin quitarme ojo.

narrow-minded ['nærəʊ'maɪndɪd] *adj* de miras estrechas, intolerante.

narrow-mindedness ['nærəʊ'maɪndɪdnɪs] *n* estrechez *f* de miras, intolerancia *f*.

narrowness ['nærəʊnɪs] *n* estrechez *f*.

narwhal ['nɑːwəl] *n* narval *m*.

NAS *n* (*US*) *abbr of* **National Academy of Sciences.**

NASA ['næsə] *n* (*US*) *abbr of* **National Aeronautics and Space Administration** NASA *f*.

nasal ['neɪzəl] **1** *adj* nasal; (*twanging*) gangoso. **2** *n* nasal *f*.

nasality [neɪ'zælɪtɪ] *n* nasalidad *f*.

nasalization [,neɪzəlaɪ'zeɪʃən] *n* nasalización *f*.

nasalize ['neɪzəlaɪz] *vt* nasalizar; (*twangingly*) pronunciar con timbre gangoso.

nasally ['neɪzəlɪ] *adv* nasalmente; con timbre nasal; **to speak ~** hablar por las narices, ganguear.

nascent ['næsnt] *adj* naciente.

Nassau ['næsɔː] *n* Nassau *m*.

nastily ['nɑːstɪlɪ] *adv* (*V adj*) suciamente; horriblemente; groseramente; gravemente; peligrosamente; **he said ~** dijo groseramente; **it was raining quite ~** llovía de muy mala manera.

nastiness ['nɑːstɪnɪs] *n* suciedad *f*; cosas *fpl* horribles; indecencia *f*; lo asqueroso, lo horrible; lo malo; gravedad *f*; lo peligroso; grosería *f*; rencor *m*.

nasturtium [nəs'tɜːʃəm] *n* capuchina *f*.

nasty ['nɑːstɪ] *adj* (**a**) (*dirty*) sucio, puerco; (*obscene*) sucio, indecente, obsceno; (*disagreeable*) asqueroso, horrible, repugnante; *smell, taste* horrible; *remark* feo, horrible; (*rude*) grosero; *weather* feo, malo; *accident* grave; *wound etc* peligroso, de gravedad; *corner, turn etc* peligroso; *temper* vivo; *trick* malo; *habit* feo; **a very ~ film** una película asquerosa, un film de lo más horrible; **a ~ mess** un lío imponente; **what a ~ mind you have!** ¡qué mal pensado eres!; **to smell ~** oler mal, tener un olor desagradable; **to taste ~** saber mal, tener un sabor desagradable; **to turn ~** *situation* ponerse difícil, *weather* volverse malo.

(**b**) *person* antipático; poco afable; (*rude*) grosero; (*malicious*) rencoroso, malévolo; **what a ~ man!** ¡qué hombre más horrible!; **to be ~ to sb** tratar muy mal a uno, portarse mal con uno; **they were ~ to her in the shop** se portaron groseramente con ella en la tienda; **don't be ~!** ¡no digas esas cosas horribles!; ¡no seas mal pensado!; **to turn ~** ponerse negro*, (*weather*) ponerse feo.

NAS/UWT *n* (*Brit*) *abbr of* **National Association of Schoolmasters/Union of Women Teachers** *sindicato de profesores*.

Natal [nə'tæl] *n* Natal *m*.

natal ['neɪtl] *adj* natal.

natality [nə'tælɪtɪ] *n* natalidad *f*.

natatorium [ˌneɪtəˈtɔːrɪəm] *n, pl* **natatoria** [ˌneɪtəˈtɔːrɪə] (*US*) piscina *f.*
natch‡ [nætʃ] *excl* naturalmente, naturaca‡.
nation [ˈneɪʃən] *n* nación *f.*
national [ˈnæʃənl] **1** *adj* nacional; ~ **anthem** himno *m* nacional; ~ **costume,** ~ **dress** vestido *m* nacional; **N~ Curriculum** (*Brit*) *plan de estudios para las escuelas de Inglaterra y Gales*; **N~ Debt** deuda *f* pública; **N~ Enterprise Board** (*Brit*) ≃ Instituto *m* Nacional de Industria (*Sp*); ~ **grid** (*Brit*) red *f* eléctrica nacional; **N~ Guard** (*US*) Guardia *f* Nacional; ~ **holiday** fiesta *f* nacional; ~ **income** renta *f* nacional; **N~ Insurance** (*Brit*) seguro *m* social; ~ **park** parque *m* nacional; ~ **press** prensa *f* nacional; ~ **product** producto *m* nacional; **N~ Savings** (*Brit*) ≃ caja *f* nacional de ahorros; **N~ Savings Bank** (*Brit*) ≃ Caja *f* Postal de Ahorros; **N~ Savings Certificate** ≃ bono *m* del Tesoro; ~ **service** (*Brit*) servicio *m* nacional, conscripción *f*; ~ **serviceman** conscripto *m,* recluta *m*; ~ **socialism** nacionalsocialismo *m*; **N~ Trust** (*Brit*) *instituto encargado del patrimonio histórico-artístico nacional y de parajes de interés ambiental*; **N~ Weather Service** (*US*) *estación meteorológica estatal.*
2 *n* nacional *mf,* súbdito *m,* -a *f.*
nationalism [ˈnæʃnəlɪzəm] *n* nacionalismo *m.*
nationalist [ˈnæʃnəlɪst] **1** *adj* nacionalista. **2** *n* nacionalista *mf.*
nationalistic [ˌnæʃnəˈlɪstɪk] *adj* nacionalista.
nationality [ˌnæʃəˈnælɪtɪ] *n* nacionalidad *f.*
nationalization [ˌnæʃnəlaɪˈzeɪʃən] *n* nacionalización *f.*
nationalize [ˈnæʃnəlaɪz] *vt* nacionalizar.
nationalized [ˈnæʃnəlaɪzd] *adj*: ~ **industry** industria *f* nacionalizada.
nationally [ˈnæʃnəlɪ] *adv* a escala nacional; por toda la nación; nacionalmente, como nación; desde el punto de vista nacional.
nationhood [ˈneɪʃənhʊd] *n* carácter *m* de nación; **to achieve** ~ llegar a constituir una nación, llegar a tener categoría de nación.
nation-state [ˈneɪʃənˈsteɪt] *n* estado-nación *m.*
nationwide [ˈneɪʃənwaɪd] **1** *adj* por toda la nación, a escala nacional; de toda la nación. **2** *adv* por todo el país, a escala nacional.
native [ˈneɪtɪv] **1** *adj* (**a**) (*innate*) natural, innato; ~ **wit** sentido *m* común.
(**b**) (*artless*) sencillo, natural.
(**c**) (*of one's birth*) natal; *town* natal; *language* materno, nativo; ~ **land** patria *f*; **she is not a** ~ **Dutch speaker** el holandés no es su lengua materna.
(**d**) (*Min*) nativo.
(**e**) (*indigenous*) indígena; autóctono; *product, resources etc* natural, nacional, del país; **the animal is** ~ **to Africa** el animal es indígena de Africa, el animal es originario de Africa.
(**f**) (*of natives*) indígena, nativo; **the** ~ **customs** las costumbres de los indígenas; **Minister for N~ Affairs** Ministro *m* de Asuntos Indígenas; **to learn the** ~ **language** aprender el idioma vernáculo; **to go** ~ vivir como los indígenas.
2 *n* (**a**) (*with reference to birth or nationality*) natural *mf*; nacional *mf*; **he was a** ~ **of Seville** nació en Sevilla, era natural de Sevilla, era sevillano; **the plant is a** ~ **of China** la planta es originaria de China; **he speaks German like a** ~ habla alemán como un alemán, habla alemán como si hubiera nacido allí.
(**b**) (*primitive*) nativo *m,* -a *f,* indígena *mf.*
nativity [nəˈtɪvɪtɪ] *n* natividad *f*; **the N~** Navidad *f*; (*Art*) nacimiento *m*; ~ **play** auto *m* del nacimiento.
NATO [ˈneɪtəʊ] *n abbr of* **North Atlantic Treaty Organization** OTAN *f,* Organización *f* del Tratado del Atlántico Norte.
NATSOPA [ˌnætˈsəʊpə] *n* (*Brit*) *abbr of* **National Society of Operative Printers, Graphical and Media Personnel** *sindicato de tipógrafos.*
natter* [ˈnætəʳ] (*Brit*) **1** *n* charla *f*; **to have a** ~ echar un párrafo*, cotillear (*with* con).
2 *vi* (*chat*) charlar; (*chatter*) parlotear, hablar mucho; (*keep on*) machacar; (*complain*) quejarse; **to** ~ **at sb** machacar en un tema con uno.
NATTKE *n* (*Brit*) *abbr of* **National Association of Television, Theatrical and Kinematographic Employees** *sindicato de empleados de televisión, teatro y cine.*
natty* [ˈnætɪ] *adj* (*spruce*) majo, elegante, acicalado; (*deft*) diestro; *gadget etc* ingenioso.
natural [ˈnætʃrəl] **1** *adj* (*in most senses*) natural; normal; instintivo; *person* inafectado, sin afectación; *child* ilegítimo; ~ **break** (*TV etc*) interrupción *f* natural; **to die of** ~ **causes** morir de muerte natural; ~ **childbirth** parto *m* sin dolor; ~ **gas** gas *m* natural; ~ **history** historia *f* natural; ~ **justice** justicia *f* natural; **for the rest of one's** ~ **life** de por vida; ~ **parent** padre *m* biológico, madre *f* biológica; ~ **resources** recursos *mpl* naturales; ~ **sciences** ciencias *fpl* naturales; ~ **selection** selección *f* natural; ~ **wastage** desgaste *m* natural; **it is** ~ **that** ... es natural que ..., es lógico que ...; **it seems** ~ **enough to me** me parece totalmente normal; **he's a** ~ **painter** es un pintor nato, nació para pintor.
2 *n* (**a**) (*person*) imbécil *mf.* (**b**) (*Mus*) nota *f* natural; (*sign*) becuadro *m*; (*key*) tecla *f* blanca. (**c**) (*) cosa *f* de éxito seguro, persona *f* segura de tener éxito; **he's a** ~ tiene dotes innatas, nació para eso.
naturalism [ˈnætʃrəlɪzəm] *n* naturalismo *m.*
naturalist [ˈnætʃrəlɪst] *n* naturalista *mf.*
naturalistic [ˌnætʃrəˈlɪstɪk] *adj* naturalista.
naturalization [ˌnætʃrəlaɪˈzeɪʃən] **1** *n* naturalización *f.* **2** *attr*: ~ **papers** carta *f* de ciudadanía.
naturalize [ˈnætʃrəlaɪz] **1** *vt person* naturalizar; *plant etc* aclimatar, establecer; **to become ~d** naturalizarse. **2** *vi* (*person*) naturalizarse; (*plant etc*) aclimatarse, establecerse.
naturally [ˈnætʃrəlɪ] *adv* (**a**) (*in a natural way*) naturalmente; sin afectación, con naturalidad; instintivamente, por instinto; **a** ~ **optimistic person** una persona optimista por naturaleza; **to write** ~ escribir con naturalidad; **to do what comes** ~ actuar espontáneamente; **it happened** ~ ocurrió de manera natural.
(**b**) (*of course*) naturalmente; desde luego ..., claro que ...; ~! ¡naturalmente!; ~ **it is not true** desde luego no es cierto.
naturalness [ˈnætʃrəlnɪs] *n* naturalidad *f.*
nature [ˈneɪtʃəʳ] **1** *n* (**a**) (*essential quality, character*) naturaleza *f*; índole *f*; modo *m* de ser; esencia *f*; (*of person*) natural *m,* carácter *m,* temperamento *m,* genio *m*; **good** ~ afabilidad *f,* amabilidad *f*; **to abuse sb's good** ~ abusar de la amabilidad de uno; **he has a nice** ~ tiene un temperamento agradable; **it is not in his** ~ **to say that** no es capaz de decir tal cosa, no es típico suyo el decir tal cosa; **that's very much in his** ~ eso es muy de él; **to appeal to sb's better** ~ apelar a los sentimientos nobles de uno; **the** ~ **of birds is to fly** las aves vuelan naturalmente, lo propio de las aves es volar; **outspokenness is second** ~ **with him** la franqueza le es completamente natural; **by its very** ~ de por sí; **to be cautious by** ~ ser cauteloso por naturaleza; **it's against** ~, **it's contrary to** ~ es antinatural, es contrario a la naturaleza; **in the** ~ **of things it's impossible** lógicamente es imposible.
(**b**) (*kind*) género *m,* clase *f*; ~ **of contents** (*Comm*) descripción *f* del contenido; **something of that** ~ algo por el estilo; **of a technical** ~ de carácter técnico; **of quite another** ~ de otra índole; **some conclusions of a** ~ **to amaze one** unas conclusiones de tipo sorprendente; **in the** ~ **of** del género de, algo así como.
(**c**) (*Bio, Phys etc*) naturaleza *f*; **the laws of N~** las leyes de la Naturaleza; **a keen student of** ~ un estudiante entusiasta de la naturaleza (*or* de la historia natural); **in a state of** ~ en su estado natural; **to draw from** ~ dibujar del natural; **to return to** ~ (*area*) volver a su estado natural, (*person*) volver a la naturaleza.
(**d**) **to relieve** ~ hacer de cuerpo, hacer sus necesidades.
2 *attr*: **N~ Conservancy Council** (*Brit*) ≃ Instituto *m* para la Conservación de la Naturaleza, ICONA *m*; ~ **conservation** protección *f* de la naturaleza; ~ **cure** cura *f* natural; ~ **reserve** reserva *f* natural; ~ **study** (estudio *m* de la) historia *f* natural; ~ **trail** paseo *m* por la naturaleza, ruta *f* de interés para el estudio de la naturaleza; ~ **worship** culto *m* de la naturaleza; (*ancient*) panteísmo *m.*
-natured [ˈneɪtʃəd] *adj ending in compounds* de carácter ..., de condición ...; **ill~** malévolo, malicioso; *V* **good-natured** *etc.*
nature-lover [ˈneɪtʃəˌlʌvəʳ] *n* amigo *m,* -a *f* de la naturaleza.
naturism [ˈneɪtʃərɪzəm] *n* naturismo *m,* naturalismo *m.*
naturist [ˈneɪtʃərɪst] *n* naturista *mf,* naturalista *mf.*
naturopath [ˈneɪtʃərəˌpæθ] *n* naturópata *mf.*
naturopathy [ˌneɪtʃəˈrɒpəθɪ] *n* naturopatía *f.*
naught [nɔːt] *n* nada; **there's** ~ **I can do about it** no hay nada que yo pueda hacer; **all for** ~ todo en balde; **to bring to** ~ *attempt, plan* frustrar, *hope* destruir; **to come to** ~ fracasar, malograrse, no dar resultado; **to set at** ~ no hacer caso de, despreciar; *V also* **nought.**

naughtily ['nɔːtɪlɪ] *adv* traviesamente, mal; escabrosamente; con picardía, con malicia.

naughtiness ['nɔːtɪnɪs] *n* (**a**) (*of child etc*) travesuras *fpl,* mala conducta *f,* picardía *f*; desobediencia *f.* (**b**) (*of joke, song etc*) lo verde, lo escabroso; malicia *f.*

naughty ['nɔːtɪ] *adj* (**a**) *child etc* travieso, malo, pícaro; desobediente, revoltoso; **you've been very ~, that was very ~ of you, that was a ~ thing to do** has sido muy malo; **~!** ¡malo!; **don't be ~!** ¡no seas malo!; **you ~ boy!** ¡pillo!, **you ~ girl!** ¡picaruela!

(**b**) *joke, song etc* verde, escabroso, colorado (*LAm*); atrevido, picante; **that ~ jealousy of yours** esos pícaros celos tuyos; **she gave me a ~ look** me miró picaruela; **what ~ times we live in!** ¡qué tiempos más inmorales éstos!; **the N~ Nineties** la Bella Época; **~ bits*** alegrías* *fpl,* paquete* *m.*

nausea ['nɔːsɪə] *n* náusea *f,* bascas *fpl*; (*fig*) asco *m,* repugnancia *f.*

nauseate ['nɔːsɪeɪt] *vt* dar náuseas a; (*fig*) dar asco a, repugnar; **your conduct ~s me** me repugna tu conducta; **that cheese ~s me** ese queso me da asco.

nauseating ['nɔːsɪeɪtɪŋ] *adj* nauseabundo, repugnante, asqueroso.

nauseatingly ['nɔːsɪeɪtɪŋlɪ] *adv* asquerosamente; **~ virtuous** tan virtuoso que da asco.

nauseous ['nɔːsɪəs] *adj* nauseabundo.

nautical ['nɔːtɪkəl] *adj* náutico, marítimo; **~ almanac** almanaque *m* náutico; **~ mile** milla *f* marina.

nautilus ['nɔːtɪləs] *n* nautilo *m.*

naval ['neɪvəl] *adj* naval, de marina; de la marina de guerra; naval militar; *engagement* naval; *forces* de la marina; *power* marítimo; **~ academy** escuela *f* naval; **~ architecture** arquitectura *f* naval; **~ attaché** agregado *m* naval; **~ base** base *f* naval; **~ college** escuela *f* de la Armada; **~ dockyard** astillero *m* naval; **~ officer** oficial *m* de marina; **~ port** puerto *m* naval; **~ power** potencia *f* marítima; **~ station** apostadero *m* naval; **~ warfare** guerra *f* naval.

Navarre [nə'vɑːʳ] *n* Navarra *f.*

Navarrese [ˌnævə'riːz] **1** *adj* navarro. **2** *n* (**a**) navarro *m,* -a *f.* (**b**) (*Ling*) navarro *m.*

nave¹ [neɪv] *n* (*Archit*) nave *f.*

nave² [neɪv] *n* (*wheel*) cubo *m*; **~ plate** (*Aut*) tapacubos *m.*

navel ['neɪvəl] *n* ombligo *m.*

navigable ['nævɪgəbl] *adj* (**a**) *river etc* navegable. (**b**) (*steerable*) gobernable, dirigible.

navigate ['nævɪgeɪt] **1** *vt* (**a**) *ship* marear, gobernar. (**b**) *river etc* navegar por. (**c**) (*fig*) conducir, guiar. **2** *vi* navegar.

navigation [ˌnævɪ'geɪʃən] **1** *n* navegación *f*; (*science of ~*) náutica *f,* navegación *f.* **2** *attr*: **~ lights** (*on ship*) luces *fpl* de navegación; (*in harbour*) baliza *f.*

navigational [ˌnævɪ'geɪʃənl] *adj* relativo a la navegación; **~ aids** ayudas *fpl* a la navegación.

navigator ['nævɪgeɪtəʳ] *n* (*Naut*) navegador *m,* navegante *m*; (*Aer*) navegante *m.*

navvy ['nævɪ] *n* (*Brit*) peón *m* caminero, peón *m* zapador, bracero *m.*

navy ['neɪvɪ] **1** *n* marina *f* de guerra, armada *f,* flota *f.* **2** *attr*: **N~ Department** (*US*) Ministerio *m* de Marina; **~ yard** (*US*) astillero *m* de la Armada.

navy-blue ['neɪvɪ'bluː] **1** *n* azul *m* marino, azul *m* de mar. **2** *adj* azul marino.

nay [neɪ] **1** (†† *or prov*) *adv* no; (*or rather*) más aun, mejor dicho, más bien; **bad, ~ terrible** malo, mejor dicho, horrible; **dozens, ~ hundreds** docenas, digo centenares.

2 *n* (*refusal*) negativa *f*; (*in voting*) voto *m* negativo, voto *m* en contra; **to say sb ~** dar una respuesta negativa a uno.

Nazarene [ˌnæzə'riːn] **1** *adj* nazareno. **2** *n* nazareno *m,* -a *f.*

Nazareth ['næzərəθ] *n* Nazaret *m.*

Nazi ['nɑːtsɪ] **1** *adj* nazi, nazista. **2** *n* nazi *mf.*

Nazism ['nɑːtsɪzəm] *n* nazismo *m.*

NB (**a**) *abbr of* **nota bene; note well** nótese bien, N.B. (**b**) (*Canada*) *abbr of* **New Brunswick.**

NBA *n* (*US*) (**a**) *abbr of* **National Basketball Association.** (**b**) *abbr of* **National Boxing Association.**

NBC *n* (*US*) *abbr of* **National Broadcasting Company.**

NBS *n* (*US*) *abbr of* **National Bureau of Standards** ≃ Oficina *f* Nacional de Normas.

NC (**a**) (*US Post*) *abbr of* **North Carolina.** (**b**) (*Comm etc*) *abbr of* **no charge.**

NCC *n* (**a**) (*Brit*) *abbr of* **Nature Conservancy Council** ≃ Instituto *m* para la Conservación de la Naturaleza, ICONA *m.* (**b**) (*US*) *abbr of* **National Council of Churches.**

NCCL *n* (*Brit*) *abbr of* **National Council for Civil Liberties.**

NCO *n abbr of* **non-commissioned officer** suboficial *m.*

NCV *abbr of* **no commercial value** sin valor comercial.

ND (*US Post*) *abbr of* **North Dakota.**

n.d. *abbr of* **no date** sin fecha, s.f.

N.Dak. *abbr of* **North Dakota.**

NE (**a**) (*US Post*) *abbr of* **Nebraska.** (**b**) (*Geog*) *abbr of* **north east** NE *m.* (**c**) (*US Geog*) *abbr of* **New England.**

Neanderthal [nɪ'ændətɑːl] **1** *n* (*Geog*) Neanderthal *m.* **2** *adj* Neanderthal, de Neanderthal; **~ man** hombre *m* de Neanderthal.

neap [niːp] *n* (*also* **~ tide**) marea *f* muerta.

Neapolitan [nɪə'pɒlɪtən] **1** *adj* napolitano; **~ ice-cream** helado *m* napolitano. **2** *n* napolitano *m,* -a *f.*

near [nɪəʳ] **1** *adv* cerca; **as ~ as I can recall** que yo recuerde; **~ on 30 books*** casi 30 libros; **that's ~ enough** (*fig*) ya basta, con eso vale; no merece la pena precisar más; **it's not anywhere ~ enough** no basta ni con mucho; **to bring sth ~** acercar algo; **to come ~, to draw ~** acercarse; **to come ~ to doing** llegar casi a hacer; **I came ~ to telling her everything** llegué casi a decírselo todo.

2 *prep* (*also* **~ to**) (*of place*) cerca de; junto a, próximo a, al lado de; (*of time*) cerca de, casi; (*of numbers*) casi, cerca de; **~ here** aquí cerca, cerca de aquí; **to be ~ (to) the fire** estar cerca del fuego; **the passage is ~ the end of the book** el trozo está hacia el final del libro; **~ the end of the century** hacia fines del siglo; **she was ~ her end** tocaba a su fin, estaba cerca de la muerte; **she was ~ to crying** estaba a punto de llorar; **we were ~ to being drowned** por poco nos morimos ahogados.

3 *adj place etc* cercano; próximo, inmediato, vecino; *time* próximo; *relationship* estrecho, íntimo; *relative* cercano; *resemblance* grande; *translation etc* aproximativo; **the ~est way** el camino más corto; **the ~est I ever got to winning** lo más cerca que estuve de ganar; **the ~est I ever came to feeling that was when ...** la única vez que llegué a sentir algo parecido fue cuando ...; **work it out to the ~est pound** redondéalo a la libra entera; **one's ~est and dearest** los más allegados y queridos, sus parientes más cercanos; **it was a ~ guess** casi acertamos (*etc*) con la conjetura; **it's the ~est thing to murder** esto es casi un homicidio; *V* **miss 1.**

4 *vt* acercarse a, aproximarse a; **the building is ~ing completion** el edificio está casi terminado, el edificio se terminará dentro de poco; **he is ~ing 50** frisa en los 50, tiene casi 50 años; **the country is ~ing disaster** el país está al borde de la catástrofe.

nearby **1** ['nɪə'baɪ] *adv* cerca. **2** ['nɪəbaɪ] *adj* cercano, próximo, inmediato.

Near East ['nɪər'iːst] *n* Próximo Oriente *m,* Cercano Oriente *m.*

nearly ['nɪəlɪ] *adv* (**a**) (*closely*) **it touches me ~** me toca de cerca.

(**b**) (*numerals*) **~ 100** casi 100; **it's ~ 3 o'clock** son casi las 3; van a ser las 3; **she's ~ 40** tiene casi 40 años, frisa en los 40.

(**c**) (*with adj etc*) **~ finished** casi terminado; **~ black** casi negro, más o menos negro; **very ~!** ¡casi casi!; **it's pretty ~ dead** está casi muerto; **the same number or ~ so** el mismo número o casi.

(**d**) (*with negative*) **it's not ~ ready** no está listo ni con mucho; **it's not ~ good enough** no es bueno ni con mucho (*to + infin* para + *infin*); **she is not ~ so poor as she says** no es ni con mucho tan pobre como ella dice.

(**e**) (*with verb*) **I ~ lost it** por poco lo perdí; **I very ~ caught it** por poco lo cogí; **I ~ did it** estuve a punto de hacerlo.

near-money ['nɪəˌmʌnɪ] *n* (*Comm*) *npl* activos *mpl* realizables.

nearness ['nɪənɪs] *n* proximidad *f,* cercanía *f,* lo cercano; intimidad *f*; inminencia *f;* **because of its ~ to the station** por estar tan cerca de la estación.

near-side ['nɪəsaɪd] (*Aut etc*) **1** *adj* (*Brit*) izquierdo, (*most other countries*) derecho. **2** *n* (*Brit*) lado *m* izquierdo, (*most other countries*) lado *m* derecho.

near-sighted ['nɪə'saɪtɪd] *adj* corto de vista, miope.

near-sightedness ['nɪə'saɪtɪdnɪs] *n* miopía *f.*

neat [niːt] (**a**) (*clean and tidy*) *person etc* pulcro, esmerado, acicalado; *garden, room etc* bien cuidado, bien arreglado, ordenado; *work* primoroso; **her hair is always very ~** lleva el pelo siempre bien peinado; **he made a ~ job of it** lo hizo con esmero.

(**b**) (*pleasing to the eye*) *figure etc* atractivo, esbelto; bien proporcionado.

(**c**) (*skilful*) diestro; *phrase, writing, shot, solution* elegante; *plan* hábil, ingenioso; **that's ~!, very ~!** ¡muy bien!

(**d**) (*Brit*) *drink* puro, solo, sin mezcla; **~ gin** ginebra *f* pura; **I'll take it ~** lo tomo sin mezcla.

(**e**) (*US**) estupendo*, fantástico*.

neaten ['ni:tn] *vt dress* alisarse; *desk* arreglar, ordenar; **to ~ one's hair** retocarse el peinado.

'neath [ni:θ] *prep* (*liter*) = **beneath.**

neatly ['ni:tlɪ] *adv* (*V adj*) (**a**) pulcramente, esmeradamente, con esmero; con primor, primorosamente. (**b**) atractivamente. (**c**) diestramente; elegantemente; hábilmente, ingeniosamente.

neatness ['ni:tnɪs] *n* (*V adj*) (**a**) pulcritud *f*, esmero *m*; lo arreglado, lo cuidado; primor *m*. (**b**) lo atractivo, esbeltez *f*; buena proporción *f*. (**c**) destreza *f*; elegancia *f*; habilidad *f*.

NEB *n abbr of* **New English Bible.**

Nebr. *abbr of* **Nebraska.**

Nebuchadnezzar [,nebjʊkəd'nezər] *nm* Nabucodonosor.

nebula ['nebjʊlə] *n, pl* **nebulae** ['nebjʊli:] nebulosa *f*.

nebulous ['nebjʊləs] *adj* (*also fig*) nebuloso.

NEC *n abbr of* **National Executive Committee** comité *m* ejecutivo nacional.

necessarily ['nesɪsərɪlɪ] *adv* necesariamente; forzosamente; **not ~** cabe otra posibilidad, eso no es cierto del todo, no tiene por qué ser así; **it is not ~ true that ...** no es necesariamente cierto que ...

necessary ['nesɪsərɪ] **1** *adj* necesario; forzoso, preciso, esencial, indispensable, imprescindible; **with the ~ enthusiasm** con el debido entusiasmo; **all the ~ ceremonies** todas las ceremonias obligatorias; **if ~** si es necesario, si es preciso; **it is ~ that ...** es necesario que + *subj*, es preciso que + *subj*; **it is ~ for us to go** es preciso que vayamos; **it made it ~ for us to sell them** hizo inevitable que los vendiésemos; **I shall do everything ~** haré todo lo necesario; **don't do more than is ~** no haga más de lo necesario.

2 *n* (**a**) cosa *f* necesaria, requisito *m* indispensable; (*also* **necessaries** *pl*) lo necesario; **to do the ~*** hacer lo que hace falta, hacer lo que hay que hacer. (**b**) (*: *money*) cumquibus *m*.

necessitate [nɪ'sesɪteɪt] *vt* necesitar, exigir.

necessitous [nɪ'sesɪtəs] *adj* necesitado, indigente.

necessity [nɪ'sesɪtɪ] *n* (**a**) (*need*) necesidad *f*; inevitabilidad *f*; **~ is the mother of invention** la necesidad estimula la invención, el hambre aguza el ingenio; **~ knows no law** la necesidad carece de ley; **the ~ for care** la necesidad del cuidado; **of ~** por necesidad, forzosamente; **out of sheer ~** por fuerza; **in case of ~** si fuese necesario, en caso de urgencia; **it's a case of sheer ~** es un caso de la mayor necesidad; **dire ~ leads me to ask** la más apremiante necesidad me obliga a pedirlo; **there is no ~ for you to do it** no es necesario que lo hagas; **to be under the ~ of** + *ger* verse obligado a + *infin*.

(**b**) (*article*) cosa *f* necesaria, requisito *m* indispensable; **necessities** artículos *mpl* de primera necesidad; **the necessities of life** las cosas necesarias para la vida; **a fridge is a ~ nowadays** hoy día una nevera es una necesidad, es indispensable ahora tener nevera.

(**c**) (*poverty*) indigencia *f*; **to be in ~** estar en la mayor necesidad, estar necesitado.

neck [nek] **1** *n* (**a**) (*Anat*) cuello *m*; garganta *f*; (*of animal*) pescuezo *m*; (*of bottle*) cuello *m*, gollete *m*; (*Geog*) istmo *m*; (*Sew*) cuello *m*, escote *m*; (*Mus: of guitar*) cuello *m*, (*of violin*) mástil *m*; **to race ~ and ~** ir muy iguales, correr parejos; **~ or nothing** (*Brit*) todo o nada; **in this ~ of the woods** en estos pagos; **to beat sb ~ and crop** vencer a uno fácilmente; **they threw him out ~ and crop** le pusieron de patitas en la calle; **to be up to one's ~** (*in work*) tener trabajo hasta la coronilla; **to be in sth up to one's ~** estar muy metido en un asunto; **to break one's ~** desnucarse; **to break sb's ~** romper el pescuezo a uno; **I'll break your ~!** ¡te parto la cara!; **she fell on his ~** ella se le colgó de su cuello; **to get it in the ~*** pagarlas, cargárselas*; (*be told off*) recibir un rapapolvo*; **he's got it all round his ~*** anda hecho un lío con esto*; **to have sb breathing down one's ~** tener a uno encima, tener a uno sobre sus talones; **the rain ran down my ~** la lluvia me corría por el cuello; **to risk one's ~, to stick one's ~ out** arriesgarse, jugarse el tipo; atreverse a expresar una opinión; **to win by a ~** ganar por una cabeza; **to wring a rabbit's ~** torcer el pescuezo a un conejo.

(**b**) (*Brit**) = **nerve 1(d).**

2 *vi* (*) acariciarse, abrazarse amorosamente, besuquear; **to ~ with** acariciar a, besuquear a.

neckband ['nekbænd] *n* tirilla *f*.

neckerchief ['nekətʃi:f] *n* pañuelo *m*.

necking* ['nekɪŋ] *n* caricias *fpl*, abrazos *mpl* amorosos, besuqueo *m*.

necklace ['neklɪs] *n*, **necklet** ['neklɪt] *n* collar *m*.

neckline ['neklaɪn] *n* escote *m*.

necktie ['nektaɪ] *n* (*Brit*) corbata *f*.

necrological [,nekrəʊ'lɒdʒɪkəl] *adj* necrológico.

necrology [ne'krɒlədʒɪ] *n* necrología *f*.

necromancer ['nekrəʊmænsər] *n* nigromante *m*.

necromancy ['nekrəʊmænsɪ] *n* nigromancia *f*, nigromancía *f*.

necrophile ['nekrəʊ,faɪl] *n* necrófilo *m*, -a *f*.

necrophilia [,nekrəʊ'fɪlɪə] *n* necrofilia *f*.

necrophiliac [,nekrəʊ'fɪlɪæk] **1** *adj* necrófilo. **2** *n* necrófilo *m*, -a *f*.

necropolis [ne'krɒpəlɪs] *n* necrópolis *f*.

nectar ['nektər] *n* néctar *m*.

nectarine ['nektəri:n] *n* nectarina *f*.

NEDC, Neddy* ['nedɪ] *n* (*Brit*) *abbr of* **National Economic Development Council** ≈ Consejo *m* Económico y Social.

née [neɪ] *adj* de soltera; **Mrs Minnie Crun, ~ Banister** Señora Minnie Crun, de soltera Banister; Señora Minnie Banister de Crun.

need [ni:d] **1** *n* (**a**) (*necessity*) necesidad *f* (*for, of* de); **if ~(s) be, in case of ~** si fuera necesario, en caso de urgencia; **there is every ~** es totalmente indispensable; **I see no ~** no veo la necesidad; **without the ~ to pay so much** sin necesidad de pagar tanto; **there is no ~ to** + *infin* no hace falta + *infin*; **there's no ~ to worry** no hay para qué inquietarse; **what ~ is there to buy it?** ¿qué necesidad hay de comprarlo?; **no ~ to say that ...** excusado es decir que ...; **no ~ to tell him what to do** no hace falta decirle qué hacer; **to be in ~ of, to have ~ of, to stand in ~ of** necesitar; **I have no ~ of advice** no necesito consejos, no me hacen falta consejos; **you have no ~ to go** no es preciso que vayas; **when I'm in ~ of a drink** cuando siento la necesidad de beber algo, cuando me hace falta tomar algo; **a house in ~ of painting** una casa que hay que pintar, una casa que necesita ser pintada.

(**b**) (*want, lack*) adversidad *f*; apuro *m*; (*absence*) carencia *f*; falta *f*, escasez *f*; **in times of ~** en tiempos de adversidad, en tiempos de carestía; **there is much ~ of food** hay una gran escasez de alimentos.

(**c**) (*poverty*) necesidad *f*, indigencia *f*; **my ~ is great** es grande mi necesidad; **to be in ~** estar necesitado.

(**d**) (*thing needed*) cosa *f* necesaria, requisito *m*; **bodily ~s** necesidades *fpl* corporales; **the ~s of industry** las necesidades de la industria; **my ~s are few** es poco lo que necesito, soy poco exigente; **to supply sb's ~s** proveer lo que necesita uno.

2 *vt* (**a**) (*person*) necesitar; **I ~ it** lo necesito, me hace falta; **it's just what I ~ed** es precisamente lo que necesitaba; **that's all we ~ed!** (*iro*) ¡lo que nos faltaba!; **I ~ this like I ~ a hole in the head** esto me sienta como un tiro; **I ~ two more to make up the series** me faltan dos para completar la serie; **he ~ed no bidding** no se hizo de rogar; **he ~s watching** hay que vigilarle, conviene vigilarle; **who ~s more motorways?** ¿para qué queremos más autopistas?

(**b**) (*thing*) exigir, requerir, reclamar; **it ~s care** requiere cuidado, exige cuidado; **a visa is ~ed** se exige visado; **the report ~s no comment** el informe no deja lugar a comentarios; **a much ~ed holiday** unas vacaciones muy necesarias; **I gave it a much ~ed wash** lo lavé pues le hacía mucha falta; **this will ~ some explaining** no va a ser fácil explicar esto.

(**c**) (**to ~ to** + *infin*) **I ~ to do it** tengo que hacerlo, debo hacerlo; **he ~s to be told everything twice** hay que decírselo todo dos veces; **they don't ~ to be told all the details** no es preciso contarles todos los detalles; **you will hardly ~ to be reminded that ...** apenas es necesario recordarles que ...; **you only ~ed to ask** no había sino pedir; **this room ~s to be painted** hay que pintar este cuarto, conviene pintar este cuarto.

(**d**) (*v aux*) **~ I go?** ¿tengo que ir?; **he ~n't do it, ~ he?** ¿es esencial que lo haga?; **I ~ hardly add that ...** apenas hay que añadir que ...; **~ I say that this is untrue?** ni que decir tiene que esto no es cierto; **but I ~n't have bothered** pero era trabajo perdido; **it ~ not be done now** no es preciso hacerlo ahora.

(**e**) (*impersonal*) **it ~ed a war to alter that** fue necesaria

una guerra para cambiar eso; **it doesn't ~ me to tell him** no hace falta que yo se lo diga.
needful ['ni:dfʊl] **1** *adj* necesario. **2** *n*: **the ~*** el cumquibus*.
neediness ['ni:dɪnɪs] *n* necesidad *f*, pobreza *f*.
needle ['ni:dl] **1** *n* (**a**) aguja *f*; **to look for a ~ in a haystack** buscar una aguja en un pajar; **to be on the ~‡** pincharse*, ser drogadicto; **to get the ~‡** ponerse negro*.
(**b**) (*Bot*) aguja *f*, acícula *f*.
(**c**) (*) mala leche*‡ *f*; rivalidad *f*; hostilidad *f*, rencor *m*.
(**d**) (‡: *drugs*) chuta‡ *f*.
2 *attr*: ~ **match** partido *m* importantísimo, partido *m* muy emocionante, partido *m* muy reñido.
3 *vt* (**a**) (*) *person* pinchar, provocar, fastidiar.
(**b**) (*US*‡) *drink* añadir alcohol a.
needle-case ['ni:dlkeɪs] *n* alfiletero *m*.
needlecraft ['ni:dlkrɑ:ft] *n* arte *m* de la costura.
needle-sharp ['ni:dl'ʃɑ:p] *adj* afiladísimo; (*fig*) agudísimo, de lo más penetrante.
needless ['ni:dlɪs] *adj* innecesario, superfluo, inútil; ~ **to say** ... excusado es decir que ..., está de más decir que ..., huelga decir que ...; **he was, ~ to say, drunk** ni que decir tiene que estaba borracho.
needlessly ['ni:dlɪslɪ] *adv* innecesariamente, inútilmente, en vano; **you worry quite ~** te inquietas sin motivo alguno.
needlessness ['ni:dlɪsnɪs] *n* innecesariedad *f*; (*of remark*) inoportunidad *f*.
needlewoman ['ni:dl,wʊmən] *n*, *pl* **needlewomen** ['ni:dl,wɪmɪn] costurera *f*; **to be a good ~** coser bien.
needlework ['ni:dlwɜ:k] *n* labor *f* de aguja, costura *f*, bordado *m*; **to do ~** hacer costura, coser.
needn't [ni:dnt] = **need not**; *V* **need 2** (**d**).
needs [ni:dz] *adv* necesariamente, forzosamente; **if ~ must** si hace falta; **we must ~ walk** no tenemos más remedio que ir andando.
needy ['ni:dɪ] **1** *adj* necesitado, pobre, indigente. **2** *npl*: **the ~** los necesitados.
ne'er [nɛəʳ] *adv* (*poet*) nunca.
ne'er-do-well ['nɛədʊ,wel] **1** *adj* perdido. **2** *n* perdido *m*, perdulario *m*.
nefarious [nɪ'fɛərɪəs] *adj* nefario, vil, inicuo.
negate [nɪ'geɪt] *vt* anular, invalidar.
negation [nɪ'geɪʃən] *n* negación *f*.
negative ['negətɪv] **1** *adj* negativo; ~ **cashflow** flujo *m* de fondos negativo; ~ **feedback** reacción *f* negativa.
2 *n* (**a**) (*answer*) negativa *f*; **to answer in the ~** dar una respuesta negativa.
(**b**) (*Gram*) negación *f*.
(**c**) (*Phot*) negativo *m*, prueba *f* negativa.
(**d**) (*Elec*) polo *m* negativo.
3 *vt* (*veto*) poner veto a; (*vote down*) rechazar, desaprobar; *statement* negar, desmentir; *effect* anular.
negatively ['negətɪvlɪ] *adv* negativamente.
neglect [nɪ'glekt] **1** *n* (*carelessness*) negligencia *f*, descuido *m*; (*of rule etc*) inobservancia *f*; (*of duty*) incumplimiento *m*; (*neglected state*) abandono *m*; (*of o.s.*) dejadez *f*; (*towards others*) desatención *f*; **to die in ~** morir abandonado.
2 *vt obligations etc* descuidar, desatender; tener descuidado, tener abandonado; *duty etc* no cumplir, faltar a; *friends* dejar de ver; desairar; *advice etc* no hacer caso de; (*omit*) omitir, olvidar; *opportunity* no aprovechar; *garden etc* no cuidar; *wife* dejar sola; **to ~ to** + *infin* olvidarse de + *infin*.
neglected [nɪ'glektɪd] *adj appearance* descuidado, desaliñado; *garden etc* sin cuidar; *wife* abandonada.
neglectful [nɪ'glektfʊl] *adj* negligente, descuidado; **to be ~ of** descuidar, desatender.
negligée ['neglɪʒeɪ] *n* (*nightdress etc*) salto *m* de cama; (*housecoat*) bata *f*.
negligence ['neglɪdʒəns] *n* negligencia *f*, descuido *m*; **through ~** por descuido.
negligent ['neglɪdʒənt] *adj* negligente, descuidado; **to be ~ of** descuidar, desatender.
negligently ['neglɪdʒəntlɪ] *adv* negligentemente, con descuido.
negligible ['neglɪdʒəbl] *adj* insignificante; despreciable; **a ~ quantity** una cantidad insignificante; **a by no means ~ opponent** un adversario nada despreciable.
negotiable [nɪ'gəʊʃɪəbl] *adj* (**a**) (*Fin*) negociable; ~ **instrument** instrumento *m* negociable; **not ~** que no puede negociarse. (**b**) *road etc* transitable.
negotiate [nɪ'gəʊʃɪeɪt] **1** *vt* (**a**) *treaty* negociar; *loan, deal etc* negociar, gestionar, agenciar.
(**b**) *obstacle* salvar, franquear; *river etc* pasar, cruzar; *bend* tomar.
2 *vi* negociar; **to ~ for** negociar para obtener; **to ~ for peace** pedir la paz; **to ~ with sb** negociar con uno.
negotiating [nɪ'gəʊʃɪeɪtɪŋ] *n* negociación *f*, el negociar; ~ **table** mesa *f* de negociaciones; **to sit (down) at the ~ table** sentarse a la mesa de negociaciones.
negotiation [nɪ,gəʊʃɪ'eɪʃən] *n* negociación *f*; gestión *f*; **to be in ~ with sb** estar negociando con uno; **the treaty is under ~** el tratado está siendo negociado; **that will be a matter for ~** eso tendrá que ser discutido, eso tendrá que someterse a discusión; **to break off ~s** romper las negociaciones; **to enter into ~s with sb** entrar en negociaciones con uno.
negotiator [nɪ'gəʊʃɪeɪtəʳ] *n* negociador *m*, -ora *f*.
Negress ['ni:gres] *n* († *pej in US*) negra *f*.
Negro ['ni:grəʊ] († *pej in US*) **1** *adj* negro; ~ **spiritual** espiritual *m*. **2** *n*, *pl* **~es** ['ni:grəʊz] negro *m*.
negroid ['ni:grɔɪd] *adj* negroide.
neigh [neɪ] **1** *n* relincho *m*. **2** *vi* relinchar.
neighbour, (*US*) **neighbor** ['neɪbəʳ] **1** *n* vecino *m*, -a *f*; (*fellow being*) prójimo *m*, -a *f*.
2 *attr*: **Good N~ Policy** (*US*) Política *f* del Buen Vecino.
3 *vi*: **to ~ upon** (*adjoin*) colindar con, estar contiguo a; (*be almost*) rayar en; **to ~ with sb** (*US*) comportarse como buen vecino de uno.
neighbourhood, (*US*) **neighborhood** ['neɪbəhʊd] **1** *n* (**a**) (*area*) vecindad *f*; barrio *m*, sección *f*, sector *m*; **all the girls of the ~** todas las jóvenes del barrio; **not a very nice ~** un barrio poco atractivo; **somewhere in the ~** por allí, cerca de allí; **anyone in the ~ of the crime** cualquier persona que estuviera cerca del lugar del crimen; **the soil in that ~** el suelo de aquel sector; **in the ~ of £80** alrededor de 80 libras.
(**b**) (*surrounding area*) alrededores *mpl*, cercanías *fpl*; **Málaga and its ~** Málaga y sus alrededores.
(**c**) (*persons*) vecinos *mpl*, vecindario *m*.
2 *attr*: ~ **party** fiesta *f* de vecinos, fiesta *f* del barrio; ~ **police** policía *f* de barrio; ~ **watch** grupo *m* de vigilancia de los propios vecinos.
neighbouring, (*US*) **neighboring** ['neɪbərɪŋ] *adj* vecino; cercano, inmediato; (*Jur*) colindante.
neighbourliness, (*US*) **neighborliness** ['neɪbəlɪnɪs] *n*: **good ~** buena vecindad *f*.
neighbourly, (*US*) **neighborly** ['neɪbəlɪ] *adj* de buen vecino, amable, amistoso.
neighing ['neɪɪŋ] *n* relinchos *mpl*.
neither ['naɪðəʳ] **1** *adv, conj*: ~ **he nor I** ni él ni yo; **he ~ smokes nor drinks** no bebe ni fuma.
2 *conj*: **if you aren't going, ~ am I** si tú no vas, yo tampoco; ~ **will he agree to sell it** ni consiente en venderlo tampoco.
3 *pron*: ~ **of them has any money** ninguno de los dos tiene dinero, ni el uno ni el otro tiene dinero; ~ **of them saw it** ni el uno ni el otro lo vio.
4 *adj*: **on ~ side** por ninguno de los dos lados, en ningún lado; ~ **car is for sale** no se vende ninguno de los dos coches.
nelly‡ ['nelɪ] *n*: **not on your ~!** ¡ni hablar!
nelson ['nelsən] *n* (*Wrestling*): **full ~** llave *f*; **half ~** media llave *f*; **to put a half ~ on sb** (*fig*) ponerle trabas a uno.
nem con *abbr of* **nemine contradicente** nemine discrepante.
nemesis ['nemɪsɪs] *n* (*fig*) justo castigo *m*, justicia *f*.
neo... ['ni:əʊ] *pref* neo...
neoclassical ['ni:əʊ'klæsɪkəl] *adj* neoclásico.
neoclassicism ['ni:əʊ'klæsɪsɪzəm] *n* neoclasicismo *m*.
neocolonialism [,ni:əʊkə'ləʊnɪə,lɪzəm] *n* neocolonialismo *m*.
neodymium [,ni:əʊ'dɪmɪəm] *n* neodimio *m*.
neofascism ['ni:əʊ'fæʃɪzəm] *n* neofascismo *m*.
neofascist ['ni:əʊ'fæʃɪst] **1** *adj* neofascista. **2** *n* neofascista *mf*.
neogothic [,ni:əʊ'gɒθɪk] *adj* neogótico.
neolithic [,ni:əʊ'lɪθɪk] *adj* neolítico.
neological [,nɪə'lɒdʒɪkəl] *adj* neológico.
neologism [nɪ'ɒlədʒɪzəm] *n* neologismo *m*.
neon ['ni:ɒn] **1** *n* neón *m*. **2** *attr*: ~ **lamp,** ~ **light** lámpara *f* de neón; ~ **sign** letrero *m* de neón.
neonatal ['ni:əʊ,neɪtl] *adj* neonatal.
neonazi ['ni:əʊ'nɑ:tsɪ] **1** *adj* neonazi, neonazista. **2** *n* neonazi *mf*.
neophyte ['ni:əʊfaɪt] *n* neófito *m*, -a *f*.
neoplatonic ['ni:əʊplə'tɒnɪk] *adj* neoplatónico.
neoplatonism ['ni:əʊ'pleɪtənɪzəm] *n* neoplatonismo *m*.

neoplatonist [ˈniːəʊˈpleɪtənɪst] *n* neoplatonista *mf.*
Nepal [nɪˈpɔːl] *n* Nepal *m.*
Nepalese [ˌnepɔːˈliːz] **1** *adj* nepalés. **2** *n invar* nepalés *m*, -esa *f.*
nephew [ˈnevjuː] *n* sobrino *m.*
nephritic [neˈfrɪtɪk] *adj* nefrítico.
nephritis [neˈfraɪtɪs] *n* nefritis *f.*
nepotism [ˈnepətɪzəm] *n* nepotismo *m.*
Neptune [ˈneptjuːn] *nm* Neptuno.
neptunium [nepˈtjuːnɪəm] *n* neptunio *m.*
nerd‡ [nɜːd] *n* borde* *mf.*
nereid [ˈnɪərɪɪd] *n* nereida *f.*
Nero [ˈnɪərəʊ] *nm* Nerón.
nerve [nɜːv] **1** *n* (**a**) (*Anat, Bot*) nervio *m*; (*Ent*) nervadura *f*; **my ~s are on edge** tengo los nervios de punta; **it gets on my ~s** me pone los nervios de punta, me crispa los nervios, me saca de quicio; **he gets on my ~s** me fastidia terriblemente; **to be living on one's ~s** vivir en estado de nervios constante; **to strain every ~ to** + *infin* hacer un esfuerzo supremo por + *infin.*
(**b**) (*tension*) **~s** nerviosismo *m*, nerviosidad *f*, excitabilidad *f* nerviosa; **a fit of ~s** un ataque de nervios; **to be in a state of ~** estar nervioso, estar hipertenso; **she suffers from ~s** padece de los nervios, sufre trastornos nerviosos.
(**c**) (*courage*) valor *m*, sangre *f* fría; **I hadn't the ~ to do it** no tuve el valor de hacerlo; **to lose one's ~** perder el valor, rajarse; **it takes some ~ to do that** hace falta mucha sangre fría para hacer eso.
(**d**) (*: *cheek*) descaro *m*, valor* *m*, frescura* *f*, caradura* *f*; **of all the ~!, the ~ of it!, what a ~!** ¡qué frescura!*, ¡qué caradura!*; **you've got a ~!** ¡eres un caradura!*, ¡eres un fresco!*; **he had the ~ to ask for money** tuvo el valor de pedir dinero*.
2 *attr*: **~ specialist** neurólogo *m*, -a *f.*
3 *vt*: **to ~ sb to do sth** infundir a uno ánimo(s) para hacer algo.
4 *vr*: **to ~ o.s. to do sth** animarse a hacer algo, esforzarse por hacer algo.
nerve-cell [ˈnɜːvsel] *n* neurona *f.*
nerve-centre, (*US*) **nerve-center** [ˈnɜːvˌsentəʳ] *n* (*Anat*) centro *m* nervioso; (*fig*) punto *m* neurálgico.
nerve-gas [ˈnɜːvgæs] *m* gas *m* nervioso.
nerveless [ˈnɜːvlɪs] *adj* (*fig*) *grasp* flojo; *person* enervado, débil, soso.
nerve-racking [ˈnɜːvˌrækɪŋ] *adj* que crispa los nervios; horripilante, espantoso.
nerviness [ˈnɜːvɪnɪs] *n* nerviosidad *f*, nerviosismo *m.*
nervous [ˈnɜːvəs] *adj* (**a**) *person* nervioso; (*by nature*) tímido; miedoso, aprensivo, asustadizo; *market* nervioso, inquieto; **~ Nellie*** (*US*) miedica* *mf*; **to be ~ of** tener miedo a; **to be ~ of** + *ger* tener miedo a + *infin*; **I was ~ on his account** estaba inquieto por él; **I was ~ about speaking to her** me daba miedo la noción de hablar con ella; **to get ~** ponerse nervioso, sentir miedo; **I get ~ when I'm alone** siento aprensión cuando estoy solo; **it makes me ~** me da miedo.
(**b**) (*Anat*) nervioso; **~ breakdown** colapso *m* nervioso; **~ exhaustion** postración *f* nerviosa; **~ system** sistema *m* nervioso.
nervously [ˈnɜːvəslɪ] *adv* nerviosamente; tímidamente.
nervousness [ˈnɜːvəsnɪs] *n* nerviosidad *f*, nerviosismo *m*, timidez *f*, miedo *m.*
nervy* [ˈnɜːvɪ] *adj* (**a**) (*Brit*: *tense*) nervioso. (**b**) (*US*) = **cheeky.**
nest [nest] **1** *n* (*of bird*) nido *m*; (*of hen*) nidal *m*; (*of animal*) madriguera *f*; (*of wasps*) avispero *m*; (*of ants*) hormiguero *m*; (*clutch of eggs, young birds*) nidada *f*; (*person's house*) nido *m*; (*of thieves etc*) nido *m*, cueva *f*, guarida *f*; (*of boxes, drawers*) juego *m*; **to feather one's ~** ponerse las botas, hacer su agosto; **to foul one's own ~** manchar el propio nido.
2 *vt* (*Comput*) anidar, encajar; **~ed loops** bucles *mpl* anidados.
3 *vi* (**a**) (*bird*) anidar, hacer su nido, nidificar.
(**b**) (*collector*) buscar nidos.
nest-egg [ˈnesteg] *n* nidal *m*; (*fig*) ahorros *mpl*, cantidad *f* ahorrada, buena hucha *f.*
nesting [ˈnestɪŋ] **1** *n* (*Orn*) anidada *f*, anidación *f*; (*Gram, Comput*) anidamiento *m*. **2** *attr*: **~ box** (*for hen*) nidal *m*, ponedero *m*; (*for wild bird*) caja *f* anidadera.
nestle [ˈnesl] *vi* (**a**) **to ~ among leaves** hacerse un nido entre las hojas; **to ~ down among the blankets** hacerse un ovillo entre las mantas; **to ~ up to sb** arrimarse cómodamente a uno, apretarse contra uno.
(**b**) **a house nestling beside a wood** una casa situada al abrigo de un bosque; **a village nestling among hills** un pueblecito protegido por las colinas.
nestling [ˈneslɪŋ] *n* pajarito *m* (en el nido).
NET *n* (*US*) *abbr of* **National Educational Television.**
net¹ [net] **1** *n* red *f* (*also fig*); (*mesh*) malla *f*; (*fabric*) tul *m*; (*for hair etc*) redecilla *f*; **to cast one's ~ wider** ampliar el campo de acción, investigar otras posibilidades; **to slip through the ~** escapar de la red. **2** *attr*: **~ curtains** visillos *mpl.* **3** *vt* coger con red.
net² [net] (*Comm*) **1** *adj* neto, líquido; limpio; *amount, interest* neto; **~ assets** activo *m* neto; **~ income** renta *f* neta; **~ loss** pérdida *f* neta; **~ margin** margen *m* neto; **~ output** producción *f* neta; **~ payment** líquido *m*; **~ price** precio *m* neto; **~ profit** ganancia *f* neta; **~ wage** salario *m* neto; **~ weight** peso *m* neto; **at a ~ profit of 5%** con un beneficio neto de 5 por cien; **'terms strictly ~'** 'sin descuento'. **2** *vt* ganar en limpio, producir en limpio; **he ~s £30,000 a year** tiene una renta neta de 30.000 libras al año.
netball [ˈnetbɔːl] *n* baloncesto *m* (*or* básquet *m*) de mujeres.
nether [ˈneðəʳ] *adj* inferior, más bajo, de abajo; **~ lip** labio *m* inferior; **~ regions** infierno *m*; **down in my ~ regions*** en la parte baja de mi persona.
Netherlander [ˈneðəˌlændəʳ] *n* holandés *m*, -esa *f*, neerlandés *m*, -esa *f.*
Netherlands [ˈneðələndz] *npl* Países *mpl* Bajos.
nethermost [ˈneðəməʊst] *adj superl* (el *etc*) más bajo.
nett [net] = **net².**
netting [ˈnetɪŋ] *n* red *f*, redes *fpl*; (obra *f* de) malla *f*, mallas *fpl.*
nettle [ˈnetl] **1** *n* ortiga *f*; **to grasp the ~** coger el toro por los cuernos. **2** *vt* provocar, irritar, molestar; **somewhat ~d by this** algo molesto por esto.
nettle-rash [ˈnetlræʃ] *n* urticaria *f.*
nettle-sting [ˈnetlˌstɪŋ] *n* picadura *f* de ortiga.
network [ˈnetwɜːk] **1** *n* (*fig*) red *f*; (*Rad, TV*) red *f*, cadena *f*; (*Comput*) red *f*; **the national railway ~** la red nacional de ferrocarriles; **a ~ of spies** una red de espías. **2** *vt* (*Rad, TV*) difundir por la red de emisoras; (*Comput*) conectar a la red. **3** *vi* hacer contactos en el mundo de los negocios.
networking [ˈnetwɜːkɪŋ] *n* (*Comput*) conexión *f* de redes.
neural [ˈnjʊərəl] *adj* neural.
neuralgia [njʊəˈrældʒə] *n* neuralgia *f.*
neurasthenia [ˌnjʊərəsˈθiːnɪə] *n* neurastenia *f.*
neurasthenic [ˌnjʊərəsˈθenɪk] *adj* neurasténico.
neuritis [njʊəˈraɪtɪs] *n* neuritis *f.*
neuro... [ˈnjʊərəʊ] *pref* neuro...
neurobiology [ˌnjʊərəʊbaɪˈɒlədʒɪ] *n* neurobiología *f.*
neurological [ˌnjʊərəˈlɒdʒɪkəl] *adj* neurológico.
neurologist [njʊəˈrɒlədʒɪst] *n* neurólogo *m*, -a *f.*
neurology [njʊəˈrɒlədʒɪ] *n* neurología *f.*
neuron [ˈnjʊərɒn] *n* neurona *f.*
neuropath [ˈnjʊərəpæθ] *n* neurópata *mf.*
neuropsychology [ˈnjʊərəʊsaɪˈkɒlədʒɪ] *n* neuropsicología *f.*
neurosis [njʊəˈrəʊsɪs] *n, pl* **neuroses** [njʊəˈrəʊsiːz] neurosis *f.*
neurosurgeon [ˌnjʊərəʊˈsɜːdʒən] *n* neurocirujano *m*, -a *f.*
neuro-surgery [ˌnjʊərəʊˈsɜːdʒərɪ] *n* neurocirugía *f.*
neurotic [njʊˈrɒtɪk] **1** *adj* neurótico. **2** *n* neurótico *m*, -a *f.*
neurotically [njʊˈrɒtɪkəlɪ] *adv* neuróticamente.
neuter [ˈnjuːtəʳ] **1** *adj* (**a**) (*Gram*) neutro.
(**b**) *cat etc* sin sexo, castrado.
2 *n* (**a**) (*Gram*) género *m* neutro.
(**b**) (*cat etc*) macho *m* castrado, animal *m* sin sexo.
3 *vt cat etc* castrar, capar.
neutral [ˈnjuːtrəl] **1** *adj person, country, opinion* neutral; (*Zool, Bot, Elec, Chem etc*) neutro; *colour* neutro; **~ gear** punto *m* neutro; **to remain ~** permanecer neutral, mantener su neutralidad, no tomar partido.
2 *n* (**a**) neutral *mf*; país *m* neutral.
(**b**) (*Aut*) punto *m* muerto; **in ~** en punto muerto.
neutralism [ˈnjuːtrəlɪzəm] *n* neutralismo *m.*
neutralist [ˈnjuːtrəlɪst] **1** *adj* neutralista. **2** *n* neutralista *mf.*
neutrality [njuːˈtrælɪtɪ] *n* neutralidad *f.*
neutralization [ˌnjuːtrəlaɪˈzeɪʃən] *n* neutralización *f.*
neutralize [ˈnjuːtrəlaɪz] *vt* neutralizar.
neutron [ˈnjuːtrɒn] **1** *n* neutrón *m*. **2** *attr*: **~ bomb** bomba *f* de neutrones; **~ star** estrella *f* de neutrones.
Nev. *abbr of* **Nevada.**
never [ˈnevəʳ] *adv* (**a**) nunca, jamás; **~!** ¡jamás!; **I ~ went** no fui nunca, no fui jamás; **you ~ saw anything like it** nunca se ha visto nada parecido; **I have ~ yet seen anything so horrible** en mi vida he visto cosa más horrible; **~**

in all my life jamás en la vida; **it had ~ been tried before** no se había intentado antes; **you must ~ ever come again** no vuelvas nunca jamás.

(**b**) (*emphatic negative*) **~!, you ~ did!** ¿de veras?; **~ a one** ni uno siquiera; **~ a word did he say** no dijo ni una sola palabra; **I ~ expected it** no contaba con eso de ningún modo; **surely you ~ bought it?** ¿pero lo has comprado de veras?; **well I ~!** ¡caramba!, ¡no me digas!

never-ending ['nevər'endɪŋ] *adj* inacabable, interminable.

never-failing ['nevə'feɪlɪŋ] *adj* infalible; *supply* inagotable.

nevermore ['nevə'mɔːʳ] *adv* nunca más.

never-never ['nevə'nevəʳ] **1** *adj*: **~ land** país *m* de ensueños. **2** *n*: **to buy sth on the ~*** comprar algo a plazos.

nevertheless [,nevəðə'les] *adv* sin embargo, no obstante, con todo; **it is ~ true that ...** con todo es verdad que ...

never-to-be-forgotten ['nevətəbiː,fə'gɒtn] *adj* inolvidable.

nevus ['niːvəs] *n, pl* **nevi** ['niːvaɪ] (*US*) = **naevus**.

new [njuː] *adj* nuevo; reciente; (*fresh*) fresco, nuevo; *bread* tierno; (*different*) nuevo, distinto; **a ~ car** (*different*) un nuevo coche, (*brand new*) un coche nuevo; **the ~ students** los nuevos estudiantes; **the ~ people in No. 5** la nueva familia del núm 5; **N~ Age (music)** música *f* de la Nueva Era; **~ look** nueva moda *f*; **the N~ Man** el nuevo hombre; **~ maths** matemáticas *fpl* modernas; **~ town** pueblo *m* nuevo, ciudad *f* nueva; **~ wool** lana *f* virgen; **'as ~'** (*advert*) 'como nuevo'; **she's very ~, poor girl** no está habituada todavía, la pobre; **are you ~ here?** ¿eres nuevo aquí?; **are you ~ to this?** ¿esto es nuevo para ti?; **he came ~ to us last year** empezó a trabajar con nosotros el año pasado nada más; **what's ~?*** ¿qué hay de nuevo?*; **it's as good as ~** está como nuevo; **there's nothing ~ under the sun** no hay nada nuevo bajo el sol.

new- [njuː] *pref* (*in compounds*) recién ...

newborn ['njuːbɔːn] *adj* recién nacido.

New Caledonia [,njuː,kælɪ'dəʊnjə] *n* Nueva Caledonia *f*.

newcomer ['njuː,kʌməʳ] *n* recién llegado *m*, -a *f*, nuevo *m*, -a *f*.

New Delhi [,njuː'delɪ] *n* Nueva Delhi *f*.

New England [,njuː'ɪŋglənd] *n* la Nueva Inglaterra.

new-fangled ['njuː,fæŋgld] *adj* (*pej*) recién inventado, moderno, novedoso; que está tan de moda.

new-found ['njuː,faʊnd] *adj* recién descubierto; **his ~ zeal** su recién estrenado entusiasmo.

Newfoundland ['njuːfəndlənd] *n* (**a**) (*Geog*) Terranova *f*. (**b**) (*dog*: *also* **~ dog**) perro *m* de Terranova.

Newfoundlander ['njuːfəndləndəʳ] *n* habitante *mf* de Terranova.

New Guinea [,njuː'gɪniː] *n* Nueva Guinea *f*.

newish ['njuːɪʃ] *adj* bastante nuevo.

new-laid ['njuː'leɪd] *adj egg* fresco, recién puesto.

new-look [,njuː'lʊk] *attr* nuevo; renovado; de estilo nuevo.

newly ['njuːlɪ] *adv* nuevamente, recién ...; **~ made** recién hecho, acabado de hacer; **those ~ arrived** los recién llegados; **those ~ arrived from France** los que acaban de llegar de Francia.

newly-weds ['njuːlɪwedz] *npl* recién casados *mpl*.

New Mexico ['njuː'meksɪkəʊ] *n* Nuevo Méjico *m*.

new-mown ['njuː'məʊn] *adj* recién segado.

newness ['njuːnɪs] *n* novedad *f*; (*in a job etc*) inexperiencia *f*, falta *f* de práctica.

New Orleans [njuː'ɔːlɪənz] *n* Nueva Orléans *f*.

news [njuːz] **1** *n* (**a**) noticias *fpl*; nuevas *fpl*; **a piece of ~** una noticia, una nueva; **a sad piece of ~** una triste noticia; **that's good ~** es buena noticia; **no ~ is good ~** la falta de noticias es una buena señal; **it was ~ to me** me cogió de nuevas; **what ~?, what's the ~?** ¿qué hay de nuevo?; **a 700th anniversary is ~** un 700 aniversario es noticia; **they're in the ~** se oye hablar mucho de ellos, figuran mucho en los periódicos (*etc*); **to be bad ~*** (*person*) ser un ave de mal agüero, ser un liante*; (*thing*) ser mal asunto*; **to break the ~ to sb** comunicar una noticia a uno; **when the ~ broke** al saberse la noticia; **I have ~ for you** tengo que darte una noticia (*also iro*).

(**b**) (*Press, Rad, TV*) informaciones *fpl*; **the ~** (*Rad*) noticiario *m*, diario *m* hablado; (*TV*) telediario *m*; **'N~ in Brief'** (*section in newspaper*) 'Brevedades' *fpl*.

2 *attr*: **~ blackout** apagón *m* informativo; **~ conference** rueda *f* de prensa; **~ desk** redacción *f*, sección *f* de informaciones; **~ editor** jefe *mf* de información; **~ headlines** titulares *mpl*; **~ programme,** (*US*) **~ program** transmisión *f* de noticias, (*on TV*) telediario *m*; **~ vendor** vendedor *m*, -ora *f* de periódicos.

news agency ['njuːz,eɪdʒənsɪ] *n* agencia *f* de noticias.

newsagent ['njuːz,eɪdʒənt] *n* (*Brit*) vendedor *m*, -ora *f* de periódicos; **~'s** tienda *f* de periódicos, quiosco *m* de periódicos.

newsboy ['njuːzbɔɪ] *n* chico *m* que reparte (*or* vende) periódicos.

news-bulletin ['njuːz,bʊlɪtɪn] *n* (*Rad*) noticiario *m*, diario *m* hablado; (*TV*) telediario *m*.

newscast ['njuːzkɑːst] *n* telediario *m*.

newscaster ['njuːz'kɑːstəʳ] *n* locutor *m*, -ora *f* de telediario.

newsdealer ['njuːz'diːləʳ] *n* (*US*) vendedor *m*, -ora *f* de periódicos.

news-flash ['njuːzflæʃ] *n* flash *m*, noticia *f* de última hora.

newshound* ['njuːzhaʊnd] *n* reportero *m*.

news-item ['njuːz,aɪtəm] *n* noticia *f*.

newsletter ['njuːz,letəʳ] *n* hoja *f* informativa, informe *m*.

newsman ['njuːzmæn] *n, pl* **newsmen** ['njuːzmen] periodista *m*, reportero *m*.

New South Wales ['njuːsaʊθ'weɪlz] *n* Nueva Gales *f* del Sur.

newspaper ['njuːs,peɪpəʳ] **1** *n* periódico *m*, diario *m*. **2** *attr* de periódico, periodístico; **~ clipping, ~ cutting** recorte *m* de periódico; **~ office** redacción *f* (de periódico); **~ report** reportaje *m*.

newspaperman ['njuːspeɪpəmæn] *n, pl* **newspapermen** ['njuːspeɪpəmen] periodista *m*.

newspeak ['njuːspiːk] *n* neolengua *f*.

newsprint ['njuːzprɪnt] *n* papel *m* prensa, papel *m* continuo.

newsreader ['njuːz,riːdəʳ] *n* (*Brit TV*) locutor *m*, -ora *f* de telediario.

newsreel ['njuːzriːl] *n* noticiario *m*, película *f* de actualidades, (*in Spain*) Nodo *m* (*noticiario m documental*).

newsroom ['njuːzrʊm] *n* (*of newspaper*) (sala *f* de) redacción *f*; (*of library*) sala *f* de periódicos.

news-sheet ['njuːz,ʃiːt] *n* hoja *f* informativa.

news stand ['njuːzstænd] *n* (*US*) quiosco *m* de periódicos y revistas.

newsworthy ['njuːz,wɜːðɪ] *adj* noticioso, de interés periodístico, sensacional; **it's not ~** no es noticia, no tiene interés.

newsy* ['njuːzɪ] *adj* lleno de noticias.

newt [njuːt] *n* tritón *m*.

New Testament ['njuː'testəmənt] *n* Nuevo Testamento *m*.

newton ['njuːtn] *n* newton *m*, neutonio *m*.

Newtonian [njuː'təʊnɪən] *adj* newtoniano.

New Year ['njuː'jɪəʳ] **1** *n* Año *m* Nuevo; **~'s Day** día *m* de Año Nuevo; **~'s Eve** noche *f* vieja; **happy ~!** ¡feliz año nuevo!; **to see the ~ in** festejar el año nuevo. **2** *attr*: **~ resolutions** buenos propósitos *mpl* de fin de año.

New York ['njuː'jɔːk] **1** *n* Nueva York *f*. **2** *attr* neoyorquino.

New Yorker ['njuː'jɔːkəʳ] *n* neoyorquino *m*, -a *f*.

New Zealand [njuː'ziːlənd] **1** *n* Nueva Zelanda *f*, Nueva Zelandia *f*. **2** *attr* neozelandés.

New Zealander [njuː'ziːləndəʳ] *n* neozelandés *m*, -esa *f*.

next [nekst] **1** *adj* (**a**) (*of place*) próximo, inmediato, contiguo, vecino; **the ~ room** la habitación (de) al lado de ésta, la habitación inmediata; **the ~ house** la casa vecina, la casa de al lado; **on the ~ page** a la vuelta, a la página siguiente; **I get out at the ~ stop** yo bajo en la próxima parada.

(**b**) (*of order*) próximo, siguiente; primero; **the ~ in order is ...** el próximo siguiendo el orden es ..., el primero según el orden es ...; **in the ~ volume** en el tomo siguiente, en el tomo después de éste; **the ~ life** la otra vida; **~ time** la próxima vez; **~ time you see him** la próxima vez que le veas; **the ~ but one** el segundo después de éste; **'see ~ page'** 'véase a la página siguiente'; **'continued in the ~ column'** 'sigue en la columna inmediata'; **'to be continued in our ~ ...'** 'continuará'; **as good as the ~ man** tan bueno como cada hijo de vecino; **he's ~ after me** es el primero después de mí; **~ please!** ¡el siguiente por favor!, ¡que pase el siguiente!; **what ~?** y ahora ¿qué?; **what ~, madam?** (*in shop*) ¿algo más, señora?; **who's ~?** ¿quién es el siguiente?; **whatever ~!** ¡qué horror!

(**c**) (*of time*) próximo, siguiente; *week, month, year* próximo, que viene; **~ year** (*looking to future*) el año que viene, (*in past time*) el año siguiente; **~ day** el día siguiente; **the ~ day but one** dos días después, el segundo día después de éste; **the ~ 5 days** los 5 días que vienen; **~ morning** la mañana siguiente, a la mañana; **on 4th May ~** el próximo 4 de mayo; **the year after ~** el segundo año después de éste, en dos años; **by this time ~ year** por estas fechas del año que viene.

2 *adv* (**a**) (*of place, order*) inmediatamente después; **who comes ~?** ¿quién sigue?, ¿a quién le toca?; **what do we**

do ~? ¿qué hacemos ahora?; **the ~ smaller size** el tamaño más pequeño después de éste; **the ~ best thing would be to** + *infin* lo mejor después de esto sería + *infin;* **to take the ~ best** tomar el segundo.

(**b**) (*of time*) luego, después; inmediatamente; la próxima vez; **~ we put the salt in** luego echamos la sal; **what did he do ~?** ¿qué hizo después?, ¿qué hizo entonces?; **when you ~ see him** cuando le veas la próxima vez; **when I ~ saw him** cuando le volví a ver.

3 *prep* (**a**) (*also* **~ to**) junto a, al lado de; **the car ~ to the door** el coche que está junto a la puerta; **his room is ~ to mine** su habitación está al lado de la mía; **to wear silk ~ (to) one's skin** llevar seda sobre la piel.

(**b**) (*fig*) casi; **we got it for ~ to nothing** lo adquirimos por casi nada; **there was ~ to nobody there** no había casi nadie; **there is ~ to no news** apenas hay noticias, no hay noticias casi.

next-door ['neks'dɔːʳ] *adj* de al lado; **~ house** casa *f* de al lado; **~ neighbour** vecino *m*, -a *f* de al lado.

next-of-kin [ˌnekstəv'kɪn] *n* familiar *mf* (*or* pariente *mf*) más cercano, -a.

nexus ['neksəs] *n* nexo *m*.

NF (**a**) *abbr of* **Newfoundland** Terranova *f*. (**b**) *n* (*Brit Pol*) *abbr of* **National Front** *partido político de la extrema derecha.*

n/f (*Fin*) *abbr of* **no funds.**

NFL *n* (*US*) *abbr of* **National Football League.**

Nfld. *abbr of* **Newfoundland.**

NFS *n abbr of* **National Fire Service** *servicio de bomberos.*

NFT *n* (*Brit*) *abbr of* **National Film Theatre.**

NFU *n* (*Brit*) *abbr of* **National Farmers' Union.**

NG (*US*) *abbr of* **National Guard.**

NGA *n* (*Brit*) *abbr of* **National Graphical Association** *sindicato de tipógrafos.*

NGO *n* (*US*) *abbr of* **non-governmental organization.**

NH (*US Post*) *abbr of* **New Hampshire.**

NH(I) *abbr of* **National Health** (**Insurance**).

NHL *n* (*US*) *abbr of* **National Hockey League.**

NHS *n* (*Brit*) *abbr of* **National Health Service** *servicio médico nacional.*

NI (**a**) *abbr of* **Northern Ireland.** (**b**) *abbr of* **National Insurance** *seguro social.*

niacin ['naɪəsɪn] *n* ácido *m* nicotínico.

Niagara [naɪ'ægrə] **1** *n* Niágara *m*. **2** *attr*: **~ Falls** Catarata *f* del Niágara.

nib [nɪb] *n* punta *f*; (*of fountain pen*) plumilla *f*, plumín *m*.

nibble ['nɪbl] **1** *n* (**a**) mordisco *m*; **I never had a ~ all day** (*Fishing*) el corcho no se movió en todo el día; **at £3000 he never got a ~** a las 3000 libras nadie le echó un tiento.

(**b**) (*food*) bocado *m*; **I feel like a ~** podría comer algo, no me vendría mal un bocado.

(**c**) **~s*** (*at party etc*) tapas *fpl*.

2 *vt* mordiscar; *food* mordiscar, mordisquear, picar (*LAm*); (*rat etc*) roer; (*horse*) rozar; (*fish*) picar; **the cheese is all ~d** el queso está lleno de roeduras.

3 *vi*: **to ~ at** mordiscar *etc* (*V vt*); **to ~ at an offer** considerar una oferta, mostrar cierto interés por una oferta.

nibs [nɪbz] *n*: **his ~*** su señoría.

NICAM ['naɪkæm] *n abbr of* **near-instantaneous companding system.**

Nicaragua [ˌnɪkə'rægjʊə] *n* Nicaragua *f*.

Nicaraguan [ˌnɪkə'rægjʊən] **1** *adj* nicaragüense. **2** *n* nicaragüense *mf*.

Nice [niːs] *n* Niza *f*.

nice [naɪs] *adj* (**a**) *person* (*likeable*) simpático; **he's a ~ man** es un hombre simpático.

(**b**) *person* (*kind*) amable; **he was very ~ about it** estuvo muy amable; **it is ~ of you to help** Vd es muy amable ayudándome; **try to be ~ to him** procura ser amable con él; **I find it hard to be ~ to him** encuentro difícil hablar amistosamente con él.

(**c**) *person* (*attractive*) guapo, mono, bonito, lindo (*LAm*); **how ~ you look!** ¡qué guapa estás!

(**d**) *thing* (*pleasant*) agradable, ameno; (*attractive*) mono, bonito, precioso, lindo (*LAm*); *weather etc* bueno; **a ~ photo** una bonita foto; **that's a ~ ring** ¡qué anillo más mono!; **what a ~ idea that was!** ¡ésa sí fue una idea genial!; **what a ~ thing to do!** ¡qué detalle más fino!; **~ one!*** ¡bravo!; **it's ~ here** aquí se está bien; **we had a very ~ holiday in Ibiza** lo pasamos muy bien en Ibiza, hemos pasado unas vacaciones excelentes en Ibiza; **it smells ~** huele bien, tiene un olor agradable; **it doesn't taste at all ~** tiene un sabor nada agradable; **they give you ~ things to do** le dan cosas interesantes que hacer; **they give you ~ things to eat** le dan cosas deliciosas que comer; **it's not very ~ to have to** + *infin* no es muy agradable tener que + *infin.*

(**e**) *things, persons* (*refined*) fino, culto; bien; delicado; **he has ~ manners** tiene modales muy finos; **where are all the ~ girls?** ¿adónde se habrán metido todas las chicas finas?; **only ~ people live here** aquí no vive sino gente culta, (*pej*) aquí no vive sino gente bien; **a ~ district** un barrio elegante; **that's not ~** aquello es feo, eso no es fino.

(**f**) (*intensive*) muy, bastante, bien; **~ and sweet** bien dulce; **~ and early** tempranito; **it's ~ and warm here** aquí hace un calor agradable; **my feet are ~ and warm** tengo los pies a gusto y calientes; **a ~ long holiday** unas vacaciones bien largas; **a ~ cold drink** una bebida bien fría.

(**g**) (*fastidious*) melindroso, delicado; difícil de contentar; (*exacting*) exigente; (*precise*) exacto, meticuloso; (*scrupulous*) escrupuloso; **he's not too ~ about his methods** no es demasiado escrupuloso en cuanto a sus métodos.

(**h**) (*requiring care etc*) fino, delicado, sutil; **a ~ distinction** una distinción sutil; **a ~ point** un punto delicado; **it's a ~ question whether ...** es difícil determinar si ...

(**i**) (*discriminating*) fino, discernidor; **he has a ~ ear** tiene un oído fino.

(**j**) (*iro*) bonito, valiente; **a ~ friend you are!** ¡valiente amigo!; **that's a ~ thing to say!** ¡qué cosas más bonitas me dices!; **a ~ mess** un lío imponente; **a ~ mess!** ¡menudo lío!

nice-looking ['naɪs'lʊkɪŋ] *adj* atractivo; *person* bien parecido, mono, guapo, lindo (*LAm*).

nicely ['naɪslɪ] *adv* (*V adj*) amablemente; agradablemente; con finura, bien; **very ~, thanks** muy bien, gracias; **a ~ situated house** una casa bien situada; **that will do ~** eso está muy bien; **he's doing very ~ (for himself)** levan bien las cosas, (*pej*) se está forrando; **he's getting on ~** hace buenos progresos; **she thanked me very ~** muy amablemente me dio las gracias; **the child behaves quite ~** el niño tiene modales bastante buenos.

niceness ['naɪsnɪs] *n* (**a**) (*of person*) simpatía *f*, lo simpático; amabilidad *f*. (**b**) (*of thing*) lo agradable, amenidad *f*. (**c**) (*refinement*) finura *f*, lo culto. (**d**) (*fastidiousness*) delicadeza *f*; meticulosidad *f*; escrupulosidad *f*; sutileza *f*; discernimiento *m*.

nicety ['naɪsɪtɪ] *n* (**a**) = **niceness.** (**b**) **to judge sth to a ~** juzgar algo con toda precisión; **niceties** detalles *mpl*, puntos *mpl* sutiles.

niche [niːʃ] *n* nicho *m*; hornacina *f*; (*fig*) colocación *f* conveniente, buena posición *f*; **to find a ~ for o.s.** encontrarse una buena posición.

Nicholas ['nɪkələs] *nm* Nicolás.

Nick [nɪk] *nm familiar form of* **Nicholas**; **Old ~** Patillas.

nick [nɪk] **1** (**a**) *n* mella *f*, muesca *f*, corte *m*; **in the ~ of time** a última hora, en el momento crítico.

(**b**) (*Brit‡*) (*prison*) chirona‡ *f*; (*police-station*) comisaría *f*.

(**c**) **in good ~*** (*Brit*) en buen estado.

2 *vt* (**a**) mellar, hacer muescas en, hacer cortes en; cortar; (*with sword etc*) pinchar.

(**b**) (*Brit‡*) (*steal*) robar, birlar*; (*arrest*) trincar‡; **you're ~ed!** ¡queda Vd detenido!

3 *vr*: **to ~ o.s.** cortarse.

nickel ['nɪkl] *n* níquel *m*; (*US*) *moneda de 5 centavos.*

nickel-plated ['nɪkl'pleɪtɪd] *adj* niquelado.

nickel silver [ˌnɪkl'sɪlvəʳ] *n* plata *f* alemana.

nicker‡ ['nɪkəʳ] *n invar* (*Brit*) libra *f* esterlina.

nickname ['nɪkneɪm] **1** *n* apodo *m*, mote *m*. **2** *vt* apodar; **they ~d him Nobby** le dieron el apodo de Nobby; **Clark ~d Nobby** Clark apodado Nobby.

Nicosia [ˌnɪkəʊ'siːə] *n* Nicosia *f*.

nicotine ['nɪkətiːn] **1** *n* nicotina *f*. **2** *attr*: **~ poisoning** nicotinismo *m*.

nicotinic [ˌnɪkə'tɪnɪk] *adj*: **~ acid** ácido *m* nicotínico.

niece [niːs] *n* sobrina *f*.

niff‡ [nɪf] *n* (*Brit*) olorcito *m* (*of* a); tufillo *m*.

niffy‡ ['nɪfɪ] *adj* (*Brit*) maloliente, apestoso.

nifty* ['nɪftɪ] *adj* (*Brit*) (*smart*) elegante, muy pera*; (*skilful*) diestro, hábil, experto, ágil.

Niger ['naɪdʒəʳ] *n* (*country, river*) Níger *m*.

Nigeria [naɪ'dʒɪərɪə] *n* Nigeria *f*.

Nigerian [naɪ'dʒɪərɪən] **1** *adj* nigeriano. **2** *n* nigeriano *m*, -a *f*.

niggardliness ['nɪgədlɪnɪs] *n* tacañería *f*.

niggardly ['nɪgədlɪ] *adj person* tacaño, avariento; *allowance etc* miserable.

nigger ['nɪgər] **1** *n* (*‡ in US*) negro *m*, -a *f*; **to be the ~ in the woodpile** (*Brit*) ser el obstáculo, ser la cosa que estropea el todo. **2** *attr*: **~ brown** (*Brit*) (*colour*) café oscuro; **~ minstrel** cómico *m* disfrazado de negro.

niggle ['nɪgl] **1** *n* queja *f*; duda *f*. **2** *vi* (*worry*) inquietarse por pequeñeces; (*fuss*) perder el tiempo con detalles nimios, preocuparse por minucias; (*complain*) quejarse, murmurar.

niggling ['nɪglɪŋ] **1** *adj detail* nimio, insignificante; *doubt* persistente; (*small-minded*) de miras estrechas. **2** *n* quejas *fpl*; dudas *fpl*; murmurios *mpl*.

nigh [naɪ] († *or prov*) **1** *adv* cerca; casi, **it's ~ on finished** está casi terminado. **2** *prep* cerca de.

night [naɪt] **1** *n* noche *f*; **a Beethoven ~** un concierto dedicado a Beethoven; **first ~** (*Theat etc*) estreno *m*; **good ~!** ¡buenas noches!; **last ~** anoche; **the ~ before last** anteanoche; **tomorrow ~** mañana por la noche; **the ~ before the ceremony** la víspera de la ceremonia; **all ~ (long)** toda la noche; **~ and day** noche y día; **at ~, by ~, in the ~** de noche, por la noche; **11 o'clock at ~** las 11 de la noche; **it is ~** es de noche; **it's the servant's ~ out** es la tarde libre de la criada; **to have a ~ out** salir de juerga (*o* de parranda) por la noche; **to have a bad ~** dormir mal, pasar una mala noche; **to have an early ~** acostarse temprano, retirarse pronto; **to have a late ~** no acostarse hasta (muy) tarde; **she's used to late ~s** ella está acostumbrada a acostarse tarde; **to make a ~ of it** estar de juerga hasta muy entrada la noche; **are you planning to make a ~ of it?** ¿vais a estar fuera toda la noche?

2 *attr* nocturno, de noche; **~ blindness** ceguera *f* nocturna; **~ nurse** enfermera *f* de noche; **~ owl*** ave *f* nocturna; **~ porter** guardián *m* nocturno; **~ safe** caja *f* de seguridad nocturna, depósito *m* nocturno; **~ stand** (*US*) mesilla *f*, mesita *f* de noche; **~ storage heater** acumulador *m* eléctrico nocturno; **~ table** (*US*) = **~ stand**; **~ watch** turno *m* de noche; (*Hist*) ronda *f* nocturna; **~ watchman** vigilante *m* nocturno, sereno *m*; **~ work** trabajo *m* nocturno.

3 *adv*: **to work ~s** trabajar de noche, hacer el turno de noche; **I can't sleep ~s** (*US*) no puedo dormir la noche.

night-bird ['naɪtbɜːd] *n* pájaro *m* nocturno; (*person*) trasnochador *m*, -ora *f*.

nightcap ['naɪtkæp] *n* (**a**) gorro *m* de dormir. (**b**) (*drink*) sosiega *f*, bebida *f* que se toma antes de acostarse.

nightclothes ['naɪtˌkləʊðz] *npl* ropa *f* de dormir.

nightclub ['naɪtklʌb] *n* cabaret *m*, boite *f*, sala *f* de fiestas.

nightdress ['naɪtdres] *n* camisón *m* (de noche).

nightfall ['naɪtfɔːl] *n* anochecer *m*; **at ~** al anochecer; **by ~** antes del anochecer.

night-fighter ['naɪtfaɪtər] *n* caza *m* nocturno.

nightgown ['naɪtgaʊn] *n*, **nightie*** ['naɪtɪ] *n* camisón *m* (de noche).

nighthawk ['naɪthɔːk] *n* chotacabras *m*.

nightingale ['naɪtɪŋgeɪl] *n* ruiseñor *m*.

nightjar ['naɪtdʒɑːr] *n* chotacabras *m*.

night-life ['naɪtlaɪf] *n* vida *f* nocturna.

night-light ['naɪtlaɪt] *n* mariposa *f*, lamparilla *f*.

nightlong ['naɪtˌlɒŋ] *adj* de toda la noche, que dura toda la noche.

nightly ['naɪtlɪ] **1** *adv* todas las noches, cada noche. **2** *adj* de noche, nocturno; (*regular*) de todas las noches.

nightmare ['naɪtmɛər] *n* pesadilla *f* (*also fig*).

nightmarish ['naɪtmɛərɪʃ] *adj* de pesadilla, espeluznante.

night-night* ['naɪtˌnaɪt] *n* (*goodnight*) buenas noches *fpl*.

night-school ['naɪtskuːl] *n* escuela *f* nocturna.

nightshade ['naɪtʃeɪd] *n* dulcamara *f*, hierba *f* mora; **deadly ~** belladona *f*.

nightshift ['naɪtʃɪft] *n* turno *m* de noche; **to be** (*or* **to work**) **on ~** estar (*or* trabajar) en el turno de noche.

nightshirt ['naɪtʃɜːt] *n* camisa *f* de dormir (*de caballero*).

nightsight ['naɪtsaɪt] *n* visor *m* nocturno.

nightspot ['naɪtˌspɒt] *n* lugar *m* de diversión nocturna, (*esp*) club *m* nocturno.

nightstick ['naɪtstɪk] *n* (*US*) porra *f* (de policía).

night-time ['naɪttaɪm] *n* noche *f*; **in the ~** de noche, durante la noche.

nightwear ['naɪtwɛər] *n* ropa *f* de dormir.

nig-nog‡ ['nɪgnɒg] *n* (*pej*) negro *m*, -a *f*.

NIH *n* (*US*) *abbr of* **National Institutes of Health.**

nihilism ['naɪɪlɪzəm] *n* nihilismo *m*.

nihilist ['naɪɪlɪst] *n* nihilista *mf*.

nihilistic [ˌnaɪɪ'lɪstɪk] *adj* nihilista.

nil [nɪl] (*Brit*) **1** *n* cero *m*, nada *f*; **Granada beat Murcia two ~** el Granada venció al Murcia dos-cero; **its merits are ~** sus méritos son nulos, no tiene mérito alguno. **2** *adj* nulo; **~ balance** (*Fin*) balance *m* nulo.

Nile [naɪl] *n* Nilo *m*.

nimble ['nɪmbl] *adj* (*in moving*) ágil, ligero; (*in wit*) listo; *fingers etc* diestro, experto.

nimbleness ['nɪmblnɪs] *n* agilidad *f*; ingenio *m*; destreza *f*.

nimbly ['nɪmblɪ] *adv* ágilmente, ligeramente; diestramente.

nimbostratus [ˌnɪmbəʊ'streɪtəs] *n*, *pl* **nimbostrati** [ˌnɪmbəʊstreɪtaɪ] nimbostrato *m*.

nimbus ['nɪmbəs] *n* nimbo *m*.

NIMBY ['nɪmbɪ] *n abbr of* **not in my backyard** *campaña contra depósito de residuos tóxicos* (*etc*) *'en mi patio'*.

nincompoop ['nɪŋkəmpuːp] *n* bobo *m*, -a *f*, papirote *m*.

nine [naɪn] **1** *adj* nueve; **~-to-five job** trabajo *m* de nueve a cinco; **~ times out of ten** casi siempre; **a ~ days' wonder** una maravilla de un día.

2 *n*: **to be dressed up to the ~s** estar hecho un brazo de mar; **to get dressed up to the ~s** ponerse de punta en blanco.

ninepins ['naɪnpɪnz] *npl* (*objects*) bolos *mpl*; (*game*) juego *m* de bolos; **to go down like ~** caer como bolos en bolera.

nineteen ['naɪn'tiːn] *adj* diecinueve; **to talk ~ to the dozen** (*Brit*) hablar por los codos.

nineteenth ['naɪn'tiːnθ] *adj* decimonoveno, decimonono; **the ~ (hole)** (*hum*) el bar.

ninetieth ['naɪntɪɪθ] *adj* nonagésimo; noventa; **the ~ anniversary** el noventa aniversario.

ninety ['naɪntɪ] *adj* noventa; **the nineties** los años noventa; **to be in one's nineties** tener más de noventa años, ser noventón.

ninny ['nɪnɪ] *n* bobo *m*, -a *f*.

ninth [naɪnθ] *adj* noveno; **Pius IX** Pío Nono.

niobium [naɪ'əʊbɪəm] *n* niobio *m*.

Nip‡ [nɪp] *n* (*pej*) japonés *m*, -esa *f*.

nip¹ [nɪp] **1** *n* pellizco *m*; mordisco *m*; **there's a ~ in the air** hace un poco frío, hay helada.

2 *vt* (*with fingers*) pellizcar, pinchar; (*bite*) mordiscar; (*cut*) cortar; *plant* helar; (*wind*) picar, helar; **to ~ one's fingers in a door** pillarse los dedos en una puerta.

3 *vi* (*Brit*) correr, ir a toda velocidad; **I ~ped round to the shop*** fui a la tienda en una escapadita, me pegué un salto a la tienda.

◆**nip along*** *vi*: **we were ~ping along at 100 kph** (*Brit*) corríamos a 100 kph.

◆**nip in*** *vi* entrar, entrar un momento; entrar sin ser visto; **to ~ in and out of the traffic** colarse por entre el tráfico.

◆**nip off*** **1** *vt* cortar; despuntar.

2 *vi* (*Brit*) pirarse*, largarse‡.

◆**nip out*** *vi*: **I must ~ out for a moment** salgo un momento.

nip² [nɪp] *n* (*of drink*) trago *m*, traguito *m*.

nipper* ['nɪpər] *n* (*Brit*) chiquillo *m*, -a *f*.

nipple ['nɪpl] *n* (*Anat*) pezón *m*; (*of male, bottle*) tetilla *f*; (*Mech*) boquilla *f* roscada, manguito *m* de unión; (*for greasing*) engrasador *m*, pezón *m* de engrase.

nippy* ['nɪpɪ] *adj* (**a**) (*Brit*) *person* ágil, listo; *car etc* rápido, veloz; **be ~ about it!** ¡corre!, ¡menearse!; **we shall have to be ~** tendremos que darnos prisa. (**b**) (*cold*) frío; **it's ~** hace frío.

NIREX ['naɪrɛks] *n* (*Brit*) *abbr of* **Nuclear Industry Radioactive Waste Executive.**

nirvana [nɪə'vaːnə] *n* nirvana *f*.

nit [nɪt] *n* (**a**) (*Zool*) liendre *f*. (**b**) (*Brit‡*) imbécil *mf*, idiota *mf*; **you ~!** ¡imbécil!

niter ['naɪtər] *n* (*US*) = **nitre.**

nit-picker* ['nɪtˌpɪkər] *n* criticón *m*, -ona *f*, chinchorrero *m*, -a *f*.

nit-picking* ['nɪtˌpɪkɪŋ] **1** *adj* criticón. **2** *n* critiquería *f*, chinchorrería *f*.

nitrate ['naɪtreɪt] *n* nitrato *m*.

nitration [naɪ'treɪʃən] *n* nitratación *f*, nitración *f*.

nitre, (*US*) **niter** ['naɪtər] *n* nitro *m*.

nitric ['naɪtrɪk] *adj*: **~ acid** ácido *m* nítrico.

nitrite ['naɪtraɪt] *n* nitrito *m*.

nitrobenzene [ˌnaɪtrəʊben'ziːn] *n* nitrobenceno *m*.

nitrogen ['naɪtrədʒən] **1** *n* nitrógeno *m*. **2** *attr*: **~ cycle** ciclo *m* de nitrógeno; **~ dioxide** dióxido *m* de nitrógeno; **~ oxide** óxido *m* de nitrógeno.

nitrogenous [naɪ'trɒdʒɪnəs] *adj* nitrogenado.

nitroglycerin(e) ['naɪtrəʊ'glɪsəriːn] *n* nitroglicerina *f*.

nitrous ['naɪtrəs] *adj* nitroso; **~ acid** ácido *m* nitroso; **~ oxide** óxido *m* nitroso.

nitty-gritty* [ˌnɪtɪgrɪtɪ] *n* realidad *f* básica, aspectos *mpl*

esenciales; **let's get down to the ~** vamos a lo esencial.
nitwit* ['nɪtwɪt] *n* imbécil *mf*, idiota *mf;* **you ~!** ¡imbécil!
nix‡ [nɪks] **1** *n* nada. **2** *excl* ¡ni hablar!
NJ (*US Post*) *abbr of* **New Jersey.**
NLF *n abbr of* **National Liberation Front.**
NLQ *n* (*Comput*) *abbr of* **near letter quality** calidad *f* casi de correspondencia.
NLRB *n* (*US*) *abbr of* **National Labor Relations Board.**
NM (*US Post*) *abbr of* **New Mexico.**
N. Mex. *abbr of* **New Mexico.**
NMR *n abbr of* **nuclear magnetic resonance.**
NNE *abbr of* **north-north-east** NNE, nornoreste *m* (*also adj*).
NNR *n* (*Brit*) *abbr of* **National Nature Reserve** reserva *f* natural nacional.
NNW *abbr of* **north-north-west** NNO, nornoroeste *m* (*also adj*).
no [nəʊ] **1** *adv* (**a**) no; **whether he comes or ~** si viene o no.
(**b**) (*comp*) **I am ~ taller than you** yo no soy más alto que tú.
2 *adj* (**a**) ninguno, no ... alguno; **no-one** *V* **nobody**; (*often not translated, eg*) **I have ~ money** no tengo dinero; **he made ~ reply** no contestó, no dio respuesta alguna; **~ two of them are alike** no hay dos iguales; **it's ~ distance** no está lejos; **it's ~ trouble** no es molestia; **details of little or ~ interest** detalles *mpl* de poco o ningún interés, detalles *mpl* de poquísimo interés; **problems of ~ easy solution** problemas que no tienen soluciones fáciles, problemas que no se resolverán fácilmente; **it is ~ easy task** es una tarea nada fácil; **he's ~ poet** de poeta no tiene nada; **he was ~ general** no era lo que se llama un general, no merecía el nombre de general; **judge or ~ judge, he's a fool** no importa que sea juez, es un tonto.
(**b**) (*prohibitions*) '**~ admittance**', '**~ entry**' 'se prohíbe la entrada'; **~ kidding?** ¿en serio?; ¿sin bromas?; **~ nonsense!**; ¡déjate de tonterías!; '**~ parking**' 'prohibido estacionar'; '**~ smoking**' 'se prohíbe fumar'; **~ surrender!** ¡no nos rendimos nunca!
(**c**) (*with gerund*) **there's ~ denying it** es imposible negarlo; **there's ~ getting out of it** no hay posibilidad de evitarlo; **there's ~ pleasing him** resulta imposible contentarle, no hay modo de complacerle.
3 *n, pl* **~es** [nəʊz] (**a**) no *m*; **I won't take ~ for an answer** no permito que lo rechaces, no acepto una respuesta negativa.
(**b**) (*Parl*) voto *m* negativo, voto *m* en contra; **there were 7 ~es** votaron 7 en contra; **the ~es have it** se ha rechazado la moción.
no. *abbr of* **number** núm., n°, número *m*.
no-account* ['nəʊə'kaʊnt] (*US*) **1** *adj* inútil, insignificante. **2** *n* cero *m* a la izquierda.
Noah ['nəʊə] *nm* Noé; **~'s ark** arca *f* de Noé.
nob¹‡ [nɒb] *n* (*Anat*) cabeza *f*, cholla‡ *f*.
nob²‡ [nɒb] *n* (*Brit*) (*person of importance*) personaje *m*, pájaro *m* de cuenta; (*toff*) majo *m*, currutaco *m*.
nobble‡ ['nɒbl] *vt* (*Brit*) (**a**) *person* (*bribe*) sobornar; (*win over*) ejercer presión sobre, persuadir por medios nada rectos; (*accost*) procurar hablar con, abordar. (**b**) *horse* narcotizar, drogar, estropear. (**c**) (*arrest*) coger. (**d**) (*steal*) birlar*, pisar*.
Nobel [nəʊ'bel] *attr*: **~ prize** premio *m* Nóbel; **~ prizewinner** ganador *m*, -ora *f* del premio Nóbel.
nobelium [nəʊ'biːlɪəm] *n* nobelio *m*.
nobility [nəʊ'bɪlɪtɪ] *n* (*all senses*) nobleza *f*.
noble ['nəʊbl] **1** *adj* noble; *title* de nobleza; **the ~ art** el boxeo; **~ rot** (*of wine*) podredumbre *f* noble. **2** *n* noble *mf*, aristócrata *mf*, (*Spanish Hist*) hidalgo *m*.
nobleman ['nəʊblmən] *n, pl* **noblemen** ['nəʊblmən] noble *m*, aristócrata *m*, (*Spanish Hist*) hidalgo *m*.
noble-minded [ˌnəʊbl'maɪndɪd] *adj* generoso.
nobleness ['nəʊblnɪs] *n* nobleza *f*.
noblewoman ['nəʊblwʊmən] *n, pl* **noblewomen** ['nəʊblwɪmɪn] dama *f* noble, aristócrata *f*, (*Spanish Hist*) hidalga *f*.
nobly ['nəʊblɪ] *adv* noblemente, con nobleza; (*fig*) generosamente.
nobody ['nəʊbədɪ] **1** *pron* nadie; **~ spoke** nadie habló, no habló nadie; **who spoke? — ~** ¿quién habló? — nadie; **~ has more right to it than she has** no hay nadie que tenga más derecho a ello que ella; **would ~ buy it?** ¿no había quién lo comprara?
2 *n*: **a mere ~** un don nadie, un cero a la izquierda; **I knew him when he was ~** le conocí cuando no era nadie.
no-claim(s) bonus [ˌnəʊ'kleɪm(z)ˌbəʊnəs] *n*, (*US*) **no-claims discount** [ˌnəʊ'kleɪmzˌdɪskaʊnt] *n* bonificación *f* por carencia de reclamaciones, prima *f* de no reclamación.
nocturnal [nɒk'tɜːnl] *adj* nocturno.
nocturne ['nɒktɜːn] *n* nocturno *m*.
nod [nɒd] **1** *n* (*sleepy etc*) cabezada *f*; (*sign*) señal *f* hecha con la cabeza, inclinación *f* de cabeza; **a ~ is as good as a wink** a buen entendedor (pocas palabras bastan); **he gave me a ~** me saludó inclinando la cabeza; **he agreed with a ~** asintió con la cabeza; **to give the ~ to** aprobar, dar luz verde a; **to go through on the ~** ser aprobado sin discusión, ser aprobado sin someterse a votación.
2 *vt head* inclinar, mover, hacer una señal con; **he ~ded his agreement** asintió con la cabeza; **he ~ded a greeting** me saludó inclinando la cabeza; **he ~ded his head** (*saying yes*) asintió con la cabeza, movió la cabeza afirmativamente.
3 *vi* (*sleepily*) dar cabezadas, cabecear; (*say yes*) decir que sí con la cabeza, asentir con la cabeza; (*trees*) mecerse, inclinarse; **Homer ~s** incluso Homero se duerme a veces; **we're on ~ding terms** nos conocemos justo para saludarnos.
◆**nod off** *vi* quedarse dormido.
◆**nod through** *vt*: **the porter ~ded us through** el conserje nos dejó pasar (inclinando la cabeza); **the delegates were ~ded through** los delegados fueron aprobados sin votación.
noddle* ['nɒdl] *n* mollera* *f*.
node [nəʊd] *n* (*Anat, Astron, Phys*) nodo *m*; (*Bot*) nudo *m*.
nodular ['nɒdjʊlə^r] *adj* nodular.
nodule ['nɒdjuːl] *n* nódulo *m*.
Noel [nəʊ'el] *n* Navidad *f*.
no-fault ['nəʊ'fɔːlt] *attr*: **~ agreement** acuerdo *m* de pago respectivo; **~ divorce** divorcio *m* en el que no se culpa a ninguno de los esposos; **~ insurance** seguro *m* en el que no entra el factor de culpabilidad.
no-frills ['nəʊˌfrɪlz] *adj*: **a ~ house** una casa sin adornos, una casa sin lujo.
noggin ['nɒgɪn] *n* (**a**) vaso *m* pequeño, (*loosely*) vaso *m*, caña *f* (de cerveza); **let's have a ~** (*Brit*) tomemos algo.
(**b**) (*measure*) *medida de licor* (= *1,42 decilitros*).
(**c**) (*US‡: head*) cabeza *f*, coco* *m*, calabaza‡ *f*.
no-go [ˌnəʊ'gəʊ] *attr*: **~ area** (*Brit*) zona *f* prohibida.
no-good* ['nəʊgʊd] *adj* (*US*) malísimo, malvado.
no-growth ['nəʊ'grəʊθ] *attr*: **~ economy** economía *f* sin crecimiento, economía *f* de crecimiento cero.
nohow* ['nəʊhaʊ] *adv* de ninguna manera, por ningún medio que sea.
noise [nɔɪz] **1** *n* (**a**) ruido *m*; estrépito *m*; estruendo *m*; clamor *m*; tumulto *m*; alboroto *m*; (*fig*) escándalo *m*; **~ pollution** contaminación *f* auditiva; **~ prevention** medidas *fpl* para evitar el ruido; **to make a ~** hacer ruido; **the book made a lot of ~ when it came out** el libro causó un escándalo cuando apareció, al aparecer se armó un escándalo en torno al libro; **they made a (lot of) ~ about it** protestaron (mucho) por ello, armaron un (tremendo) lío con este motivo; **he made ~s about changing it but did nothing** manifestó la intención de cambiarlo pero no hizo nada; **the minister is making all the right ~s** el ministro se muestra francamente favorable.
(**b**) (*****) **big ~** (*person*) pez *m* gordo*, pájaro *m* de cuenta; **he's a big ~ now** ahora es un personaje.
2 *vt*: **to ~ sth abroad** divulgar la noticia de algo, hacer correr la voz de algo; **we don't want it ~d abroad** no queremos que se publique.
noiseless ['nɔɪzlɪs] *adj* silencioso, sin ruido.
noiselessly ['nɔɪzlɪslɪ] *adv* en silencio, sin (hacer) ruido.
noisily ['nɔɪzɪlɪ] *adv* ruidosamente, estrepitosamente, clamorosamente; escandalosamente.
noisiness ['nɔɪzɪnɪs] *n* ruido *m*, estrépito *m;* lo ruidoso, lo estrepitoso.
noisome ['nɔɪsəm] *adj* (*disgusting*) asqueroso; (*smelly*) fétido, maloliente; (*harmful*) nocivo.
noisy ['nɔɪzɪ] *adj* ruidoso, estrepitoso, clamoroso; *child etc* escandaloso; *protest* ruidoso.
no-jump ['nəʊˌdʒʌmp] *n* salto *m* nulo.
nomad ['nəʊmæd] *n* nómada *mf*.
nomadic [nəʊ'mædɪk] *adj* nómada.
nomadism ['nəʊmədɪzəm] *n* nomadismo *m*.
no-man's ['nəʊmænz] *attr*: **~ land** tierra *f* de nadie.
nom de plume ['nɒmdə'pluːm] *n, pl* **noms de plume** seudónimo *m*, nombre *m* artístico.
nomenclature [nəʊ'menklətʃə^r] *n* nomenclatura *f*.
nominal ['nɒmɪnl] *adj* nominal; **~ partner** socio *mf* nominal; **~ value** valor *m* nominal; **~ wage** salario *m* nominal.
nominalism ['nɒmɪnəlɪzəm] *n* nominalismo *m*.
nominalization [ˌnɒmɪnəlaɪ'zeɪʃən] *n* nominalización *f*.

nominalize ['nɒmɪnəlaɪz] *vt* nominalizar.
nominally ['nɒmɪnəlɪ] *adv* nominalmente.
nominate ['nɒmɪneɪt] *vt* proponer (la candidatura de); nombrar; **to ~ sb as chairman** proponer a uno como candidato a la presidencia, nombrar a uno para presidente; **to ~ sb for a job** nombrar a uno para un cargo.
nomination [,nɒmɪ'neɪʃən] *n* nombramiento *m*; propuesta *f*.
nominative ['nɒmɪnətɪv] **1** *adj* nominativo; **~ case = 2.** **2** *n* nominativo *m*.
nominee [,nɒmɪ'niː] *n* candidato *m*, -a *f*; persona *f* nombrada; **the ~ of sb** el candidato propuesto por uno, el candidato que apoya uno.
non- [nɒn] *pref in compounds*: no..., des..., in...
non-academic ['non,ækə'demɪk] *adj staff* no docente.
non-acceptance ['nɒnək'septəns] *n* rechazo *m*.
non-achiever ['nɒnə'tʃiːvə^r] *n* persona *f* que no alcanza lo que se espera de ella.
non-addictive ['nɒnə'dɪktɪv] *adj drug* que no crea dependencia, no adictivo.
nonagenarian [,nɒnədʒɪ'nɛərɪən] **1** *adj* nonagenario, noventón. **2** *n* nonagenario *m*, -a *f*, noventón *m*, -ona *f*.
non-aggression ['nɒnə'greʃən] **1** *n* no agresión *f*. **2** *attr*: **~ pact** pacto *m* de no agresión.
non-alcoholic ['nɒnælkə'hɒlɪk] *adj* no alcohólico, analcohólico; **~ drink** refresco *m*.
non-aligned ['nɒnə'laɪnd] *adj* neutral, no comprometido; **~ countries** países *mpl* no alineados.
non-alignment ['nɒnə'laɪnmənt] *n* no alineamiento *m*.
non-appearance ['nɒnə'pɪərəns] *n* ausencia *f*; (*Jur*) no comparecencia *f*.
non-arrival ['nɒnə'raɪvəl] *n* ausencia *f*; **the ~ of the mail** el hecho de no haber llegado el correo.
non-attendance ['nɒnə'tendəns] *n* ausencia *f*, falta *f* de asistencia.
non-availability ['nɒnə,veɪlə'bɪlɪtɪ] *n* no disponibilidad *f*.
non-believer ['nɒnbɪ'liːvə^r] *n* no creyente *mf*.
non-belligerent ['nɒnbɪ'lɪdʒərənt] **1** *adj* no beligerante. **2** *n* no beligerante *mf*.
non-biological ['nɒnbaɪəʊ'lɒdʒɪkl] *adj* no biológico.
non-breakable ['nɒn'breɪkəbl] *adj* irrompible.
non-cash ['nɒn'kaeʃ] *adj*: **~ assets** activo *m* no líquido; **~ payment** pago *m* no dinerario.
non-Catholic ['nɒn'kæθlɪk] **1** *adj* no católico, acatólico. **2** *n* no católico *m*, -a *f*.
nonce [nɒns] *adv*: **for the ~** por el momento.
nonce-word ['nɒnswɜːd] *n* palabra *f* efímera creada para un caso especial, hápax *m*.
nonchalance ['nɒnʃələns] *n* indiferencia *f*; negligencia *f*; aplomo *m*; sangre *f* fría, calma *f*.
nonchalant ['nɒnʃələnt] *adj* indiferente, impasible; negligente; despreocupado; **to be ~ about sth** no prestar atención a algo, no tomar algo en serio; **with ~ ease** con aplomo y facilidad, con desenvoltura.
nonchalantly ['nɒnʃələntlɪ] *adv* con indiferencia; negligentemente; con aplomo, con calma; **a ~ knotted tie** una corbata negligentemente anudada.
non-Christian [,nɒn'krɪstɪən] **1** *adj* no cristiano. **2** *n* no cristiano *m*, -a *f*.
non-combatant ['nɒn'kɒmbətənt] **1** *adj* no combatiente. **2** *n* no combatiente *mf*.
non-combustible ['nɒnkəm'bʌstɪbl] *adj* incombustible.
non-commercial ['nɒnkə'mɜːʃl] *adj* no comercial, no lucrativo.
non-commissioned ['nɒnkə'mɪʃənd] *adj*: **~ officer** suboficial *m*, sargento *m or* cabo *m*; **~ officers** ≈ clases *fpl*.
non-committal ['nɒnkə'mɪtl] *adj statement etc* que no compromete a nada; (*pej*) evasivo, equívoco; **he was very ~ about it** se abstuvo de comprometerse a nada, no quiso concretar, evitó tomar una resolución definitiva.
non-committally [,nɒnkə'mɪtlɪ] *adv*: **he said ~** dijo como evitando tomar una resolución definitiva, dijo como si no quisiese comprometerse a nada.
non-completion ['nɒnkəm'pliːʃən] *n* incumplimiento *m*.
non-compliance ['nɒnkəm'plaɪəns] *n* incumplimiento *m*, infracción *f* (*with* de); desobediencia *f* (*with* de).
non-conductor ['nɒnkən'dʌktə^r] *n* (*Elec*) aislante *m*, no conductor *m*, mal conductor *m*.
nonconformism ['nɒnkən'fɔːmɪzəm] *n* inconformismo *m*.
nonconformist ['nɒnkən'fɔːmɪst] **1** *adj* inconformista. **2** *n* inconformista *mf*.
nonconformity ['nɒnkən'fɔːmɪtɪ] *n* inconformismo *m*, disidencia *f*.
non-contagious ['nɒnkən'teɪdʒəs] *adj* no contagioso.
non-contributory [,nɒnkən'trɪbjʊtərɪ] *adj*: **~ pension scheme** sistema *m* de pensión no contributiva, plan *m* de jubilación sin pago de primas.
non-controversial ['nɒnkɒntrə'vɜːʃl] *adj* no conflictivo.
non-conventional ['nɒnkən'venʃənəl] *adj* no convencional.
non-convertible ['nɒnkən'vɜːtɪbl] *adj currency* no convertible.
non-cooperation ['nɒnkəʊ,ɒpə'reɪʃən] *n* (*Pol*) no cooperación *f*.
non-cooperative [,nɒnkəʊ'ɒpərətɪv] *adj* no cooperativo.
non-cumulative ['nɒn'kjuːmjʊlətɪv] *adj* no cumulativo.
non-delivery [,nɒndɪ'lɪvərɪ] *n* falta *f* de entrega.
nondescript ['nɒndɪskrɪpt] *adj* indeterminado, inclasificable; (*pej*) mediocre.
non-distinctive [,nɒndɪs'tɪŋktɪv] *adj* (*Ling*) no distintivo.
non-drinker ['nɒn'drɪŋkə^r] *n* no bebedor *m*, -ora *f*, persona *f* que no bebe; **thanks, I'm a ~** gracias, yo no bebo.
non-drip ['nɒn'drɪp] *adj* que no gotea.
non-durable ['nɒn'djʊərəbl] *adj* perecedero.
non-dutiable ['nɒn'djuːtɪəbl] *adj* libre de aranceles, no sujeto a derechos de aduana.
none [nʌn] **1** *pron* (*person*) nadie; (*person, thing*) ninguno; (*thing*) nada; **~ of them** ninguno de ellos; **~ of you can tell me** ninguno de vosotros sabe decirme; **we have ~ of your books** no tenemos ninguno de sus libros; **~ can tell** nadie lo sabe; **~ but he knows of this** sólo lo sabe él; **~ of this is true** nada de esto es verdad; **any news? — ~** ¿alguna noticia? — ninguna; **I'm sorry, there are ~** lo siento, pero no hay; **there are ~ left** no queda ninguno; **~ of that, now!** ¡déjate de eso!; **I want ~ of your lectures!** ¡basta ya de sermones!; **he is aware, ~ better, that ...** se da cuenta, cómo no, de que ...; **it was ~ other than the bishop** fue el obispo en persona, fue el mismo obispo.

2 *adj* († *or hum*): **riches have I ~** riqueza no la tengo; **reply came there ~** no hubo respuesta.

3 *adv* de ningún modo; **I was ~ too comfortable** no me sentía muy cómodo; **they get on ~ too well** no se llevan del todo bien; **it was ~ too soon** ya era hora; **it's ~ the worse for that** no es peor por eso; **he was still ~ the better off** aun así no había mejorado su posición en lo más mínimo; *V also* **worse.**
nonentity [nɒ'nentɪtɪ] *n* nulidad *f*, cero *m* a la izquierda.
non-essential ['nɒnɪ'senʃəl] **1** *adj* no esencial. **2** *n* cosa *f* no esencial.
nonetheless [,nʌnðə'les] *adv* = **nevertheless.**
non-event [,nɒnɪ'vent] *n* acontecimiento *m* fallido; fracaso *m*; **it was a ~** no pasó estrictamente nada.
non-executive [,nɒnɪg'zekjʊtɪv] *adj*: **~ director** vocal *mf*, consejero *m*, -a *f*.
non-existence ['nɒnɪg'zɪstəns] *n* inexistencia *f*, no existencia *f*.
non-existent ['nɒnɪg'zɪstənt] *adj* inexistente, no existente.
non-fattening [,nɒn'fætnɪŋ] *adj* que no engorda.
non-ferrous ['nɒn'ferəs] *adj* no ferroso, no férreo.
non-fiction ['nɒn'fɪkʃən] *n* literatura *f* no novelesca, no ficción *f*.
non-finite [,nɒn'faɪnaɪt] *adj*: **~ verb** verbo *m* no conjugado.
non-flammable ['nɒn'flæməbl] *adj* ininflamable.
non-fulfilment ['nɒnfʊl'fɪlmənt] *n* incumplimiento *m*.
non-governmental ['nɒn,gʌvn'mentl] *adj* no gubernamental.
non-impact ['nɒn'ɪmpækt] *adj* **~ printer** impresora *f* de no impacto.
non-infectious ['nɒn,ɪn'fekʃəs] *adj* no contagioso.
non-inflammable ['nɒnɪn'flæməbl] *adj* ininflamable.
non-intervention ['nɒn,ɪntə'venʃən] *n* no intervención *f*.
non-iron ['nɒn'aɪən] *adj* de no planchar, que no necesita planchado.
non-laddering ['nɒn'lædərɪŋ] *adj stocking* indesmallable.
non-lethal ['nɒn'liːθl] *adj weapon* no mortífero; *wound* no mortal.
non-malignant ['nɒnmə'lɪgnənt] *adj* no maligno.
non-member ['nɒn,membə^r] *n* no miembro *m*, visitante *mf*.
non-metal [,nɒn'metl] *adj* no metálico.
non-negotiable [,nɒnnɪ'gəʊʃɪəbl] *adj demand* innegociable.
non-nuclear ['nɒn'njuːklɪə^r] *adj defence, policy* no nuclear; *area* desnuclearizado.
no-no* ['nəʊnəʊ] *n* (*US*): **it's a ~** (*undesirable*) eso no se hace; eso es inaceptable; (*not an option*) no existe tal posibilidad.
no-nonsense [,nəʊ'nɒnsəns] *adj* sensato.
non-observance ['nɒnəb'zɜːvns] *n* no observancia *f*, incumplimiento *m*.
non obst. *abbr of* **non obstante, notwithstanding** no obstante.
non-operational ['nɒn,ɒpə'reɪʃənl] *adj* que no funciona,

incapaz de funcionar.

nonpareil ['nɒnpərəl] **1** *adj* sin par. **2** *n* persona *f* sin par, cosa *f* sin par; (*Typ*) nomparell *m*.

non-participating ['nɒnpɑː'tɪsɪpeɪtɪŋ] *adj* no participante.

non-partisan ['nɒn,pɑːtɪ'zæn] *adj* independiente, imparcial.

non-party ['nɒn'pɑːtɪ] *adj* (*Pol*) independiente.

non-paying ['nɒn'peɪɪŋ] *adj member* que no paga, que entra (*etc*) gratis.

non-payment ['nɒn'peɪmənt] *n* impago *m*, falta *f* de pago; **sued for ~ of debts** demandado por no pagar sus deudas.

non-person ['nɒn'pɜːsn] *n* persona *f* que no existe, ser *m* inexistente.

non-playing [,nɒn'pleɪɪŋ] *adj captain* no jugador.

nonplus ['nɒn'plʌs] *vt* dejar perplejo, confundir; **he was completely ~sed** estaba totalmente perplejo; **I confess myself ~sed** confieso que estoy perplejo.

non-poisonous [,nɒn'pɔɪznəs] *adj* no tóxico, atóxico; no venenoso.

non-political [,nɒnpə'lɪtɪkəl] *adj* apolítico.

non-polluting ['nɒnpə'luːtɪŋ] *adj* no contaminante.

non-practising ['nɒn'præktɪsɪŋ] *adj* no practicante.

non-productive [,nɒnprə'dʌktɪv] *adj* improductivo.

non-professional ['nɒnprə'feʃnəl] *adj* no profesional, aficionado.

non-profit [,nɒn'prɒfɪt] *adj* (*US*), **non-profitmaking** ['nɒn'prɒfɪtmeɪkɪŋ] *adj* no lucrativo, no comercial.

non-proliferation ['nɒnprəʊ'lɪfə'reɪʃn] *attr*: **~ treaty** tratado *m* de no proliferación.

non-recurring ['nɒnrɪ'kɜːrɪŋ] *adj* que no se repite, único; **~ expenditure** gasto *m* ocasional.

non-resident ['nɒn'rezɪdənt] **1** *adj* no residente, no fijo, transeúnte. **2** *n* no residente *mf*, huésped *m* no fijo, transeúnte *mf*.

non-residential ['nɒn,rezɪ'denʃl] *adj* no residencial.

non-returnable [,nɒnrɪ'tɜːnəbl] *adj*: **~ bottle** envase *m* sin vuelta, envase *m* no retornable; **~ deposit** depósito *m* sin devolución.

non-scheduled ['nɒn'ʃedjuːld] *adj* no programado; no previsto.

non-sectarian ['nɒnsek'tɛərɪən] *adj* no sectario.

nonsense ['nɒnsəns] **1** *n* disparates *mpl*, tonterías *fpl*, desatinos *mpl*; **a ~, a piece of ~** una tontería; **~!** ¡tonterías!; **what ~!** ¡qué ridículo!; **but that's ~!** ¡eso es absurdo!; **it is ~ to say that ...** es absurdo decir que ...; **this passage makes ~** este pasaje no tiene sentido; **this makes a ~ of our policy** esto es volver de arriba abajo nuestra política; **to talk ~** no decir más que tonterías; **it's just his ~** son cosas de él; **we don't want any of your ~** no queremos escuchar esas tonterías tuyas; **none of your ~!** ¡déjate de tonterías!; **I'll stand no ~ from you!** ¡no tolero tus tonterías!

2 *attr*: **~ verse** disparates *mpl* (en verso), versos *mpl* disparatados.

nonsensical [nɒn'sensɪkəl] *adj* disparatado, absurdo, tonto.

non seq. *abbr of* **non sequitur**.

non sequitur [,nɒn'sekwɪtər] *n* incongruencia *f*, falta *f* de lógica; **it's a ~** aquí hay una falta de lógica.

non-sexist ['nɒn'seksɪst] *adj language etc* no sexista.

non-shrink ['nɒn'ʃrɪŋk] *adj* inencogible.

non-skid ['nɒn'skɪd] *adj*, *surface etc* antideslizante, antirresbaladizo.

non-skilled ['nɒn'skɪld] *adj worker* no cualificado; *work* no especializado.

non-slip ['nɒn'slɪp] *adj* = **non-skid**.

non-smoker ['nɒn'sməʊkər] *n* (*person*) no fumador *m*, -ora *f*, persona *f* que no fuma; (*Rail*) departamento *m* de no fumadores; **I've always been a ~** no he fumado nunca.

non-smoking ['nɒn'sməʊkɪŋ] *adj person* que no fuma; (*Rail*) para no fumadores.

non-specialist ['nɒn'speʃəlɪst] *n* no especialista.

non-standard [,nɒn'stændəd] *adj* (*Ling*) no estándar.

non-starter [,nɒn'stɑːtər] *n*: **that idea is a ~** esa idea es imposible.

non-stick [,nɒn'stɪk] *adj coating, pan* antiadherente.

non-stop ['nɒn'stɒp] **1** *adv* sin parar; (*Rail*) directamente; (*Aer etc*) sin escalas; **he talks ~** no para de hablar. **2** *adj* continuo, incesante; (*Rail*) directo; (*Aer*) sin escalas.

non-taxable ['nɒn'tæksəbl] *adj* no sujeto a impuestos, exento de impuestos, no imponible; **~ income** ingresos *mpl* exentos de impuestos.

non-teaching ['nɒn'tiːtʃɪŋ] *adj staff* no docente.

non-technical ['nɒn'teknɪkl] *adj* no técnico.

non-toxic ['nɒn'tɒksɪk] *adj* no tóxico.

non-trading ['nɒn'treɪdɪŋ] *adj*: **~ partnership** sociedad *f* no mercantil.

non-transferable ['nɒntræns'fɜːrəbl] *adj* intransferible.

non-U* [,nɒn'juː] *adj* (*Brit*) *abbr of* **non-upper class** *que no pertenece a la clase alta*.

non-union ['nɒn'juːnjən] *adj*, **non-unionized** ['nɒn'juːnjənaizd] *adj* no sindicado.

non-verbal ['nɒn'vɜːbl] *adj* sin palabras.

non-viable ['nɒn'vaɪəbl] *adj* inviable.

non-violence ['nɒn'vaɪələns] *n* no violencia *f*.

non-violent ['nɒn'vaɪələnt] *adj* no violento, pacífico.

non-volatile [,nɒn'vɒlətaɪl] *adj*: **~ memory** memoria *f* permanente.

non-voting [,nɒn'vəʊtɪŋ] *adj*: **~ shares** acciones *fpl* sin derecho a votar.

non-white [,nɒn'waɪt] **1** *adj* de color. **2** *n* persona *f* de color.

non-yielding ['nɒn'jiːldɪŋ] *adj* improductivo.

noodle*[1] ['nuːdl] *n* (**a**) (*head*) cabeza *f*. (**b**) (*fool*) bobo *m*, -a *f*.

noodle[2] ['nuːdlz] **1** *npl*: **~s** fideos *mpl*, tallarines *mpl*. **2** *attr*: **~ soup** sopa *f* de fideos.

nook [nʊk] *n* rincón *m*; escondrijo *m*; **we looked in every ~ and cranny** buscamos en todos los sitios.

nookie** ['nʊkɪ] *n*: **to have ~** mojar**; **to want ~** querer mojar**.

noon [nuːn], **noonday** ['nuːndeɪ] **1** *n* mediodía *m*; **at ~** a mediodía; **high noon** (*fig*) apogeo *m*, punto *m* culminante. **2** *attr* de mediodía.

no-one ['nəʊwʌn] *pron* = **nobody**.

noose [nuːs] **1** *n* lazo *m*, nudo *m* corredizo; (*hangman's*) dogal *m*. **2** *vt* coger con lazo.

no-par ['nəʊ'pɑːr] *adj*: **~ securities** títulos *mpl* sin valor nominal.

nope* [nəʊp] *interj* (*esp US*) ¡no!

nor [nɔːr] *conj* ni; **neither A ~ B** ni A ni B; **~ I** ni yo, ni yo tampoco; **I couldn't and ~ could he** yo no pude ni él tampoco; **I don't know, ~ can I guess** no lo sé, ni puedo conjeturarlo; **~ does it seem likely** ni tampoco parece probable; **~ was this all** y esto no fue todo.

Nordic ['nɔːdɪk] *adj* nórdico.

norm [nɔːm] *n* norma *f*; pauta *f*; modelo *m*; (*Bio etc*) tipo *m*; **larger than the ~** más grande que lo normal, (*Bio*) más grande que el tipo; **to exceed one's ~** exceder de la norma.

normal ['nɔːməl] **1** *adj* normal; regular, corriente; **~ distribution** distribución *f* normal; **the child is not ~** el niño es anormal; **it is perfectly ~ to + *infin*** es muy normal + *infin*; **as per ~** como siempre, como es normal.

2 *n* estado *m* normal; nivel *m* normal; normalidad *f*; **the ~ is 20 degrees** lo normal es 20 grados; **things are returning to ~** la situación vuelve a la normalidad, la situación se está normalizando.

normalcy ['nɔːməlsɪ] *n* normalidad *f*.

normality [nɔː'mælɪtɪ] *n* normalidad *f*.

normalization [,nɔːməlaɪ'zeɪʃən] *n* normalización *f*.

normalize ['nɔːməlaɪz] *vt* normalizar.

normally ['nɔːməlɪ] *adv* normalmente.

Norman ['nɔːmən] **1** *adj* normando; **~ architecture** arquitectura *f* románica; **the ~ Conquest** la conquista de los normandos. **2** *n* normando *m*, -a *f*.

Normandy ['nɔːməndɪ] *n* Normandía *f*.

normative ['nɔːmətɪv] *adj* normativo.

Norse [nɔːs] **1** *adj* nórdico, noruego, escandinavo. **2** *n* (*Ling*) nórdico *m*.

Norseman ['nɔːsmən] *n*, *pl* **Norsemen** ['nɔːsmən] vikingo *m*, escandinavo *m*.

north [nɔːθ] **1** *n* norte *m*; **N~ and South** (*Pol*) el Norte y el Sur. **2** *adj* del norte, septentrional; *wind* del norte; **the N~ Country** (*Brit*) los condados del norte (de Inglaterra); **~ star** estrella *f* polar, estrella *f* del norte. **3** *adv* al norte, hacia el norte.

North Africa ['nɔːθ'æfrɪkə] *n* África *f* del Norte.

North African ['nɔːθ'æfrɪkən] **1** *adj* norteafricano. **2** *n* norteafricano *m*, -a *f*.

North America ['nɔːθə'merɪkə] *n* América *f* del Norte, Norteamérica *f*.

North American ['nɔːθə'merɪkən] **1** *adj* norteamericano. **2** *n* norteamericano *m*, -a *f*.

Northants [nɔː'θænts] *n abbr of* **Northamptonshire**.

North Atlantic [,nɔːθət'læntɪk] **1** *n* Atlántico *m* Norte. **2** *attr*: **~ Drift** Corriente *f* del Golfo; **~ Treaty Organization** Organización *f* del Tratado del Atlántico Norte.

northbound ['nɔːθbaʊnd] *adj traffic* que va hacia el norte; *carriageway* dirección norte.

north-country [ˈnɔːθˌkʌntrɪ] *adj* del norte de Inglaterra.
north-east [ˈnɔːθˈiːst] **1** *n* nor(d)este *m.* **2** *adj point, direction* nor(d)este; *wind* del nor(d)este.
north-easterly [ˈnɔːθˈiːstəlɪ] *adj point, direction* nor(d)este; ~ **wind** (viento *m* del) nor(d) este *m.*
north-eastern [ˈnɔːθˈiːstən] *adj* nor(d)este.
north-eastward(s) [ˈnɔːθˈiːstwəd(z)] *adv* hacia el nor(d)este.
northerly [ˈnɔːðəlɪ] *adj point, direction* norte; *wind* del norte; **the most ~ point in Europe** el punto más septentrional de Europa, el punto más nórdico de Europa.
northern [ˈnɔːðən] *adj* del norte, septentrional, norteño; ~ **hemisphere** hemisferio *m* norte; ~ **lights** aurora *f* boreal.
northerner [ˈnɔːðənəʳ] *n* habitante *mf* del norte; (*Nordic*) nórdico *m*, -a *f*; (*US Hist*) nortista *mf*; **he's a ~** es del norte.
Northern Ireland [ˈnɔːðənˈaɪələnd] *n* Irlanda *f* del Norte.
Northern Irish [ˌnɔːðənˈaɪərɪʃ] **1** *adj* norirlandés. **2** *npl* norirlandeses *mpl.*
northernmost [ˈnɔːðənməust] *adj* (el) más norte, situado más al norte; **the ~ town in Europe** la ciudad más septentrional de Europa.
north-facing [ˈnɔːθˌfeɪsɪŋ] *adj* con cara al norte, orientado hacia el norte; ~ **slope** vertiente *f* norte.
North Korea [ˈnɔːθkəˈrɪə] *n* Corea *f* del Norte.
North Korean [ˈnɔːθkəˈrɪən] **1** *adj* norcoreano. **2** *n* norcoreano *m*, -a *f*.
northland [ˈnɔːθlənd] *n* (*US*) región *f* septentrional.
Northman [ˈnɔːθmən] *n*, *pl* **Northmen** [ˈnɔːθmən] vikingo *m*, escandinavo *m.*
north-north-east [ˌnɔːθˌnɔːθˈiːst] **1** *adj* nornordeste. **2** *n* nornordeste *m.*
north-north-west [ˌnɔːθˌnɔːθˈwest] **1** *adj* nornoroeste. **2** *n* nornoroeste *m.*
North Pole [ˌnɔːθˈpəul] *n* Polo *m* Norte.
North Sea [ˈnɔːθˈsiː] **1** *n* Mar *m* del Norte. **2** *attr*: ~ **gas** gas *m* del Mar del Norte; ~ **oil** petróleo *m* del Mar del Norte.
North Vietnam [ˈnɔːθvɪetˈnæm] *n* Vietnam *m* del Norte.
North Vietnamese [ˈnɔːθvɪetnəˈmiːz] **1** *adj* norvietnamita. **2** *n invar* norvietnamita *mf.*
northward [ˈnɔːθwəd] **1** *adj advance etc* hacia el norte, en dirección norte. **2** *adv* (*also* **~s**) hacia el norte, en dirección norte.
north-west [ˈnɔːθˈwest] **1** *n* noroeste *m.* **2** *adj point, direction* noroeste; *wind* del noroeste.
north-westerly [ˈnɔːθˈwestəlɪ] *adj point, direction* noroeste; ~ **wind** (viento *m* del) noroeste *m.*
north-western [ˈnɔːθˈwestən] *adj* noroeste.
north-westward(s) [ˈnɔːθˈwestwəd(z)] *adv* hacia el noroeste.
Norway [ˈnɔːweɪ] *n* Noruega *f*; ~ **lobster** cigala *f.*
Norwegian [nɔːˈwiːdʒən] **1** *adj* noruego. **2** *n* (**a**) noruego *m*, -a *f.* (**b**) (*Ling*) noruego *m.*
nos. *abbr of* **numbers** núms, números *mpl.*
no-score [ˈnəuˌskɔːʳ] *adj*: ~ **draw** empate *m* a cero.
nose [nəuz] **1** *n* (**a**) (*Anat*) nariz *f*; (*pej*) narizota *f*, narices *fpl*; (*of animal*) hocico *m*; **right under one's ~** a ojos vistas, en las barbas de uno, bajo las narices de uno; **with his ~ in the air** con la frente levantada; **to bleed at the ~** echar sangre por las narices; **to blow one's ~** sonarse (las narices); **to count ~s** (*US*) hacer recuento de los presentes; **to cut off one's ~ to spite one's face** ir contra uno mismo; **to follow one's ~** (*go straight*) ir todo seguido, (*by instinct*) dejarse guiar por el instinto; **to get one's ~ in front** conseguir una pequeña ventaja; **he gets up my ~‡** me hace subir por las paredes*; **to have one's ~ in a book** estar enfrascado en un libro; **to hold one's ~** taparse las narices; **to keep one's ~ clean** (*fig*) mantener la reputación, no mancharse; **to keep one's ~ out of sth** no entrometerse en algo; **to lead sb by the ~** tener a uno agarrado por las narices; **to look down one's ~ at** desdeñar, mirar por encima del hombro a; **to make sb pay through the ~** desollar a uno, cobrar a uno un precio elevadísimo; **she paid through the ~ (for it)** pagó gusto y ganas, le costó un ojo de la cara; **to talk through one's ~** hablar por las narices, hablar con voz gangosa; **to poke** (*or* **stick**) **one's ~ into sth** meterse en algo; **who asked you to poke your ~ in?** ¿quién le manda meter las narices en esto?; **to rub sb's ~ in sth** refregar una cosa a uno por las narices; **to see no further than one's ~** no ver más allá de sus narices; **to turn up one's ~** torcer el morro (*at* ante, en presencia de).
(**b**) (*sense of smell*) olfato *m*; **to have a good ~ for** tener buen olfato para.
(**c**) (*of wine*) aroma *m*, buqué *m.*
(**d**) (*Naut*) proa *f*; (*Aer*) morro *m*, proa *f*; (*Aut*) parte *f* delantera; **the traffic stood ~ to tail** los coches estaban pegados unos a otros.
2 *vt*: **to ~ one's way forward** avanzar con precaución.
3 *vi*: **to ~ past sth** pasar algo con mucho cuidado.
◆**nose about, nose around** *vi* curiosear, fisgonear.
◆**nose out** *vt*: **to ~ sth out** husmear algo, olfatear algo; *secret* lograr descubrir.
nosebag [ˈnəuzbæg] *n* morral *m.*
noseband [ˈnəuzbænd] *n* muserola *f.*
nosebleed [ˈnəuzbliːd] *n* hemorragia *f* nasal; **to have a ~** tener una hemorragia nasal, reventarse la nariz*.
nose-cone [ˈnəuzkəun] *n* cabeza *f* separable.
-nosed [nəuzd] *adj ending in compounds* de nariz ...; **red~** de nariz coloradota.
nose-dive [ˈnəuzdaɪv] **1** *n* picado *m* vertical; (*involuntary*) caída *f* de narices; **to take a ~** (*fig*) caer en picado. **2** *vi* descender en picado; (*involuntarily*) caer de morro (*into* en).
nose-drops [ˈnəuzdrɒps] *npl* gotas *fpl* nasales.
nosegay [ˈnəuzgeɪ] *n* ramillete *m.*
nosey* [ˈnəuzɪ] *adj* curioso, fisgón; **don't be so ~!** ¡no seas tan entrometido!
nosey-parker* [ˈnəuzɪˈpɑːkəʳ] *n* (*Brit*) fisgón *m*, -ona *f.*
nosh‡ [nɒʃ] **1** *n* (*Brit*) papeo‡ *m*; **~ up!** ¡la comida está servida! **2** *vi* papear‡.
no-show [ˈnəuˈʃəu] *n* ausente *mf*, *persona que no ocupa una plaza reservada previamente.*
nosh-up‡ [ˈnɒʃʌp] *n* (*Brit*) comilona* *f*, tragadera* *f* (*LAm*).
nosily [ˈnəuzɪlɪ] *adv* entrometidamente.
nostalgia [nɒsˈtældʒɪə] *n* nostalgia *f.*
nostalgic [nɒsˈtældʒɪk] *adj* nostálgico.
nostril [ˈnɒstrɪl] *n* nariz *f*, ventana *f* de la nariz; **~s** narices *fpl.*
nostrum [ˈnɒstrəm] *n* panacea *f* (*also fig*); remedio *m* secreto.
not [nɒt] *adv* (**a**) (*with verb*) no; **he is ~ here** no está aquí; **fear ~!** ¡no temas!; **is it ~ so?** ¿no es verdad?; **you owe me money, do you ~?** ¿me debes algo, no es verdad?; **he is a doctor, is he ~?** es (un) médico, ¿no?; **he asked me ~ to do it** me rogó no hacerlo.
(**b**) **I wish it were ~ so** ¡ojalá no fuera así!; **whether you go or ~** vayas o no; **let me know if ~** avísame en caso contrario; si no, me avisas; **I think ~** creo que no; **~ thinking that ...** sin pensar que ...; **~ that I don't like him** no es que me resulte antipático; **big, ~ to say enormous** grande, por no decir enorme; **why ~?** ¿por qué no?, ¿cómo no?; **~ without some regrets** no sin cierto sentimiento.
(**c**) **absolutely ~!** ¡en absoluto!; **certainly ~!, ~ likely!** ¡de ninguna manera!, ¡ni hablar!; **of course ~!** ¡claro que no!
(**d**) (*with pron etc*) **~ I!** ¡yo no!; **~ one** ni uno; **~ him either** él tampoco, ni él tampoco; **~ everybody can do it** no es cosa que todos sepan hacer; **~ any more** ya no.
(**e**) (*understatement*) **with ~ a little surprise** con no poca sorpresa; **there were ~ a few lions** había no pocos leones; *V* **even, much** *etc.*
notability [ˌnəutəˈbɪlɪtɪ] *n* (**a**) notabilidad *f.* (**b**) (*person*) notabilidad *f*, personaje *m.*
notable [ˈnəutəbl] **1** *adj* notable; señalado, memorable; **it is ~ that ...** es de notar que ... **2** *n* notabilidad *f*, personaje *m*; **~s** notables *mpl.*
notably [ˈnəutəblɪ] *adv* notablemente, señaladamente.
notarial [nəuˈtɛərɪəl] *adj* notarial.
notarize [ˈnəutəraiz] *vt* (*US*) autenticar (legalmente).
notary [ˈnəutərɪ] *n* (*also* **~ public**) notario *m*, -a *f.*
notate [nəuˈteɪt] *vt* (*Mus*) notar.
notation [nəuˈteɪʃən] *n* notación *f.*
notch [nɒtʃ] **1** *n* muesca *f*, mella *f*, corte *m.* **2** *vt* cortar muescas en, mellar; **to ~ up** apuntar.
note [nəut] **1** *n* (**a**) (*Mus etc*) nota *f*; **with a ~ of anxiety in his voice** con una nota de inquietud en la voz; **to hit the right ~** (*fig*) acertar, elegir acertadamente el tono (de un discurso *etc*); **to strike the wrong ~** (*fig*) desentonar.
(**b**) (*sign, stigma*) marca *f*, señal *f*; **~ of infamy** nota *f* de infamia.
(**c**) (*annotation*) nota *f*, apunte *m*; apuntación *f*; (*foot~*) nota *f* (en pie de página); **'N~s on Lucan'** 'Apuntes *mpl* sobre Lucano'; **'editor's ~'** (*in newspaper*) 'nota de la redacción'; **to compare ~s** cambiar impresiones, discutir los resultados; **to make a ~ of sth** apuntar algo, tomar nota de algo; **to speak from ~s** pronunciar un discurso a base de apuntes; **to take a ~ of sth** tomar nota de algo; **to**

take down ~s tomar apuntes.

(**d**) (*letter etc*) nota *f*, carta *f*; recado *m*; esquela *f*; **take a ~, Miss Jones** toma nota, señorita.

(**e**) (*Comm*) vale *m*; (*Brit*: *bank~*) billete *m*; **~ of hand** pagaré *m*.

(**f**) (*eminence*) **of ~** notable, eminente, de importancia; **man of ~** hombre *m* notable.

(**g**) (*notice*) **worthy of ~** digno de atención; **nothing of ~** nada de particular, sin novedad; **to take ~ of** prestar atención a, ocuparse de; **only the critics took ~ of the book** solamente los críticos se ocuparon del libro.

2 *vt* (**a**) (*observe*) notar, observar, advertir.

(**b**) (*write down*; *also* **to ~ down**) apuntar, anotar.

(**c**) **we duly ~ that ...** nos hacemos cuenta de que ...; **your remarks have been ~d** hemos leído con atención sus observaciones.

notebook ['nəʊtbʊk] *n* libro *m* de apuntes, libreta *f*; (*student's etc*) cuaderno *m*.

note-case ['nəʊtkeɪs] *n* (*Brit*) cartera *f*, billetero *m*.

noted ['nəʊtɪd] *adj* célebre, conocido, famoso (*for* por).

note-pad ['nəʊtpæd] *n* (*Brit*) bloc *m*, libreta *f* para notas.

notepaper ['nəʊt,peɪpəʳ] *n* papel *m* para cartas, papel *m* de escribir.

noteworthiness ['nəʊt,wɜːðɪnɪs] *n* notabilidad *f*.

noteworthy ['nəʊt,wɜːðɪ] *adj* notable, digno de notarse; **it is ~ that ...** es notable que ...

nothing ['nʌθɪŋ] **1** *n* (**a**) nada *f*; (*nought*) cero *m*; **I have ~ to give you** no tengo nada que darte, nada tengo que darte; **I see ~ that I like** no veo nada que me guste; **~ else** nada más; **~ much** poca cosa; **there's ~ much to be said** poco es lo que hay que decir; **next to ~** casi nada; **there is ~ mean about him** no tiene nada de tacaño; **there's ~ special about it** no tiene nada de particular; **it's ~ to be proud of** no es motivo para enorgullecerse; **there's ~ to fear** no hay de qué tener miedo.

(**b**) **there is ~ in the rumours** los rumores no tienen ni pizca de verdad; **there's ~ in it** (*in race*) van muy iguales; **there's ~ in it for us** de esto no vamos a sacar ningún provecho; **there's ~ for it but to pay** (*Brit*) no hay más remedio (*or* no nos queda otra *LAm*) que pagar; **there's ~ to it!** ¡es facilísimo!; **she is ~ to him** ella le es indiferente; **it's ~ more than a rumour** es simplemente un rumor; **it is ~ to me whether he comes or not** no me importa que venga o no; **he is ~ if not careful** es prudente por encima de todo; **I'm ~ of a swimmer** yo nado bastante mal.

(**c**) **for ~** (*free*) gratis, (*unpaid*) gratuitamente, sin sueldo, (*in vain*) en vano, en balde; **it is not for ~ that ...** no es sin motivo que ..., por algo será que ...; **to get sth for ~** obtener algo gratis.

(**d**) **to build up a business from ~** crear un negocio de la nada; **to come to ~** fracasar, parar en nada, quedarse en aguas de borraja; **to make ~ of** (*not understand*) no entender, no sacar nada en claro de; (*not use*) no aprovechar; (*not esteem*) no dar importancia a; **to say ~ of ...** sin mencionar ..., amén de ...; **to stop at ~** no pararse en barras; **to stop at ~ to** + *infin* emplear sin escrúpulo todos los medios para + *infin*; **to think ~ of** tener en poco, *task* tener por fácil; **he thinks ~ of walking 30 km** para él no tiene importancia recorrer 30 km a pie; **he thinks ~ of borrowing a fiver** con la mayor frescura pide prestado un billete de 5 libras; **think ~ of it!** ¡no hay de qué!; **he has ~ on her** (*comparison*) no le llega ni a la suela del zapato*.

(**e**) **a mere ~** una friolera, una bagatela; **a mere ~!** ¡una bagatela!; **to whisper sweet ~s to sb** decir mil ternezas a una; *V* **do with, doing, kind** *etc*.

2 *adv* de ninguna manera; **it's ~ like him** el retrato no se le parece en nada; **it was ~ like so big as we thought** era mucho menos grande de lo que nos imaginábamos; **pretty girl ~!*** ¡guapa, ni hablar!; **~ daunted** sin inmutarse.

nothingness ['nʌθɪŋnɪs] *n* nada *f*.

no throw [,nəʊ'θrəʊ] *n* (*Sport*) lanzamiento *m* nulo.

notice ['nəʊtɪs] **1** *n* (**a**) (*intimation, warning*) aviso *m*; **at short ~** a corto plazo, con poca antelación, con poco tiempo de anticipación; **at a moment's ~** en el acto, inmediatamente, casi sin aviso; **you must be ready to leave at a moment's ~** tienes que estar listo para partir en cuanto te avisen; **at 7 days' ~** con 7 días de antelación; **until further ~** hasta nuevo aviso, hasta nueva orden; **without previous ~** sin previo aviso; **he went without ~** se fue sin avisar a nadie; **to give sb at least a week's ~** avisar a uno lo menos con una semana de anticipación; **to give sb ~ that ..., to serve ~ on sb that ...** avisar a uno que ..., hacer saber a uno que ...; **~ is hereby given that ...** se pone en conocimiento del público que ...; **to give sb ~ to do sth** avisar a uno que haga algo; **I must have ~** es imprescindible que me avisen con anticipación; **we require 28 days' ~ for delivery** necesitamos 28 días de aviso para entrega; **we had no ~ of it** no nos habían avisado, no sabíamos nada de ello; **~ to quit** aviso *m* de desalojo.

(**b**) (*order to leave job etc*: *by employer*) despido *m*, (: *by employee*) dimisión *f*, renuncia *f* (*esp LAm*); (*period*) plazo *m*; **to be under ~** estar despedido; estar cesado; **to dismiss sb without ~** despedir a uno sin aviso; **to get one's ~** ser despedido; **to give sb ~** despedir a uno; **to give sb a week's ~** despedir a uno con una semana de plazo; **to hand in one's ~** dimitir; **a week's wages in lieu of ~** el salario de una semana como despido.

(**c**) (*announcement*) aviso *m*; (*in press*) anuncio *m*, nota *f*; comunicado *m*; (*sign*) letrero *m*; (*poster*) cartel *m*; **~ of a meeting** convocatoria *f*, llamada *f*; **to give out a ~** anunciar algo, comunicar algo.

(**d**) (*review*) reseña *f*, crítica *f*.

(**e**) (*attention*) atención *f*; interés *m*; **to be beneath one's ~** no merecer atención; **to attract one's ~** atraer la atención de uno, llamar la atención de uno; **it has attracted a lot of ~** ha suscitado gran interés; **to avoid ~** procurar pasar inadvertido; **to bring a matter to sb's ~** llamar la atención de uno sobre un asunto; **to come to sb's ~** llegar al conocimiento de uno; **it has come to my ~ that ...** ha llegado a mi conocimiento que ..., he llegado a saber que ...; **to escape ~** pasar inadvertido; **to take ~ of sb** hacer caso a uno; **a fat lot of ~ he takes of me!*** ¡maldito el caso que me hace!; **to take ~ of sth** hacer caso de algo, prestar atención a algo; **to take no ~ of sth** no hacer caso de algo; **he took no ~** no hizo caso; **take no ~!** ¡no hagas caso!, ¡no importa!; **I was not taking much ~ at the time** en ese momento iba algo distraído; **to sit up and take ~** aguzar las orejas, empezar a prestar atención.

2 *vt* (**a**) (*perceive*) notar, observar, reparar en, fijarse en; (*heed*) hacer caso de; (*recognize*) ver, reconocer; **I never ~d** no me había fijado; **I don't ~ such things** no me fijo en tales cosas; **eventually he deigned to ~ me** por fin se dignó reconocerme.

(**b**) (*review*) reseñar, escribir una reseña de.

noticeable ['nəʊtɪsəbl] *adj* evidente, obvio; sensible, perceptible; notable; **it was ~ that ...** era evidente que ..., se echaba de ver que ...; **there has been a ~ increase in ...** ha habido un aumento sensible de ...

noticeably ['nəʊtɪsəblɪ] *adv* evidentemente, obviamente; sensiblemente; notablemente; **it has ~ improved** ha mejorado sensiblemente.

notice-board ['nəʊtɪsbɔːd] *n* (*Brit*) tablón *m* (de anuncios).

notifiable ['nəʊtɪfaɪəbl] *adj* de declaración obligatoria.

notification [,nəʊtɪfɪ'keɪʃən] *n* notificación *f*, aviso *m*.

notify ['nəʊtɪfaɪ] *vt* notificar, comunicar, avisar; **to ~ sb of sth** comunicar algo a uno, hacer saber algo a uno.

notion ['nəʊʃən] *n* (**a**) (*idea*) noción *f*, idea *f*; concepto *m*; (*view*) opinión *f*; (*whim*) idea *f*; capricho *m*; inclinación *f*; **what an odd ~!** ¡qué idea más rara!; **I have a ~ that ...** tengo la idea de que ..., se me ocurre pensar que ...; **to have no ~ of sth** no tener concepto alguno de algo; **you have no ~!** ¡no te lo puedes imaginar!; **I haven't the slightest ~** no tengo la más remota idea; **it's a ~ she has** es un capricho suyo, son cosas de ella; **to have a ~ to do sth** estar inclinado a hacer algo, estar dispuesto a hacer algo.

(**b**) **~s** (*US*) (artículos *mpl* de) mercería *f*.

notional ['nəʊʃənl] *adj* nocional; especulativo; hipotético; imaginario; **it is purely ~** existe en el pensamiento nada más, es teórico nada más.

notoriety [,nəʊtə'raɪətɪ] *n* celebridad *f*; (*pej*) mala fama *f*; escándalo *m*; **such was his ~ that ...** tan mala fama tuvo que ...

notorious [nəʊ'tɔːrɪəs] *adj* (*pej*) muy conocido, notorio; célebre (*for* por); de mala fama; escandaloso; **a ~ crime** un crimen muy sonado; **it is ~ that ...** es sabido que ..., es voz pública que ...; **he is ~ for his affairs** es archiconocido por sus amoríos.

notoriously [nəʊ'tɔːrɪəslɪ] *adj* notoriamente; **it is ~ difficult to** + *infin* se sabe perfectamente que es difícil + *infin*; **he is ~ unreliable** tiene fama de informal.

no-trumps ['nəʊ'trʌmps] *n*: **to bid 4 ~** marcar 4 sin triunfos.

Notts [nɒts] *n abbr of* **Nottinghamshire**.

notwithstanding ['nɒtwɪð'stændɪŋ] **1** *adv* no obstante, sin embargo; **this ~** no obstante esto, a pesar de esto; **this rule ~** no obstante esta regla; **I shall go ~** sin embargo iré, de todas formas iré.

2 *prep* a pesar de.

3 *conj* (*also* ~ **that**) a pesar de que, por más que + *subj*.
nougat ['nu:gɑ:] *n* = turrón *m*.
nought [nɔ:t] *n* nada *f*; (*Math etc*) cero *m*; **Murcia beat Granada two** ~ el Murcia venció al Granada dos-cero; **~s and crosses** *juego parecido a tres en raya*; *V also* **naught**.
noun [naʊn] **1** *n* nombre *m*, sustantivo *m*. **2** *attr*: ~ **clause** oración *f* sustantiva, cláusula *f* nominal; ~ **phrase** frase *f* nominal.
nourish ['nʌrɪʃ] *vt* nutrir, alimentar, sustentar; (*fig*) fomentar, nutrir; **to** ~ **sb on sth** alimentar a uno con algo, dar a uno algo de comer.
nourishing ['nʌrɪʃɪŋ] *adj* nutritivo, rico; de gran valor alimenticio.
nourishment ['nʌrɪʃmənt] *n* alimento *m*, sustento *m*; nutrición *f*; **to derive** ~ **from** sustentarse de.
nous* [naʊs] *n* (*Brit*) chirumen* *m*, cacumen* *m*.
nouveau riche ['nu:vəʊ'ri:ʃ] *n*, *pl* **nouveaux riches** ['nu:vəʊri:ʃ] nuevo rico *m*.
nouvelle cuisine ['nu:velkwi:'zi:n] *n* nueva cocina *f*, nouvelle cuisine *f*.
Nov. *abbr of* **November** nov.
Nova Scotia ['nəʊvə'skəʊʃə] *n* Nueva Escocia *f*.
Nova Scotian ['nəʊvə'skəʊʃən] **1** *adj* de Nueva Escocia. **2** *n* habitante *mf* de Nueva Escocia.
novel ['nɒvəl] **1** *adj* nuevo; original; insólito; **this is something** ~ esto es nuevo. **2** *n* novela *f*.
novelette [,nɒvə'let] *n* novela *f* corta; (*pej*) novela *f* sentimental, novela *f* sin valor.
novelettish [,nɒvə'letɪʃ] *adj* sentimental, romántico.
novelist ['nɒvəlɪst] *n* novelista *mf*.
novelty ['nɒvəltɪ] (**a**) *n* (*newness*) novedad *f*; **once the** ~ **has worn off** cuando deja de parecer tan nuevo.
(**b**) (*new thing*) novedad *f*; innovación *f*; (*Comm*) novedad *f*.
November [nəʊ'vembəʳ] *n* noviembre *m*.
novice ['nɒvɪs] *n* principiante *mf*, novato *m*, -a *f*; (*Eccl*) novicio *m*, -a *f*; (*Sport*) aprendiz *m*, -iza *f*; **a** ~ **painter** un pintor principiante, un aspirante a pintor; **he's no** ~ no es ningún principiante; **to be a** ~ **at a job** ser nuevo en un oficio.
noviciate, novitiate [nəʊ'vɪʃɪɪt] *n* período *m* de aprendizaje; (*Eccl*) noviciado *m*.
NOW [naʊ] *n* (*US*) *abbr of* **National Organization for Women**.
now [naʊ] **1** *adv* (**a**) (*at this time*) ahora; actualmente, al presente, hoy día; (*in past time*) luego, entonces; **just** ~ (*right* ~) ahora mismo, en este momento, (*lately*) hace poco; **right** ~ ahora mismo; **even** ~ aun ahora; **even** ~ **we have no rifles** ni siquiera ahora tenemos fusiles; **not** ~, **dear** dejémoslo para después, querido; ahora no quiero, querido; **I must be off** ~ me tengo que marchar ya; **they won't be long** ~ ya no tardarán en venir; **it's** ~ **or never** es ahora o nunca; ~ **I am committed** me he comprometido ya; ~ **I'm ready** ya estoy listo; (**every**) ~ **and again,** (**every**) ~ **and then** de vez en cuando, cada cuando (*LAm*).
(**b**) (*alternation*) ~ **she dances,** ~ **she sings** unas veces baila, otras veces canta; tan pronto baila como canta; ~ **in France,** ~ **in Spain** ora en Francia, ora en España.
(**c**) (*with prep*) **before** ~ (*already*) antes de ahora, antes, ya; (*at other times*) en otras ocasiones; **long before** ~ hace tiempo ya, mucho tiempo ha; **between** ~ **and next Tuesday** entre hoy y el martes que viene; **by** ~ ahora, ya; **they must be there by** ~ habrán llegado ya; **by** ~ **everybody was tired** antes de eso todos se habían cansado; **3 weeks from** ~ de hoy en 3 semanas; **a hundred years from** ~ dentro de cien años; **from** ~ **on** a partir de ahora, de aquí en adelante; **as of** ~ ahora; a partir de ahora; **until** ~, **up to** ~ hasta ahora.
(**d**) (*without temporal force*) ~! ¡a ver!; **come** ~! ¡vamos!, ¡no es para tanto!; **well** ~ ahora bien; ~ **then!** ¡vamos a ver!; ~ **then, what's all this?** ¡eh! ¿qué hacéis aquí?; ¡eh! ¿qué es esto?; ~ ~, **don't get so upset!** ¡oye, que no es para tanto!; ~ **Johnny!** (*warning*) ¡oye, Juanito!
2 *conj* (**a**) ~ (**that**) **you are 16** ahora que tienes 16 años; **take it,** ~ **that I've got 2** tómalo, pues tengo dos.
(**b**) (*without temporal force*) ahora bien, pues; ~ **as you all know** ... pues como sabéis todos ...; ~ **for the matter of your expenses** y por lo que respecta a sus gastos; ~ **Peter was a fisherman** ahora bien, Pedro era pescador.
nowadays ['naʊədeɪz] *adv* hoy (en) día, actualmente, en la actualidad.
noways* ['nəʊweɪz] *adv* (*US*) de ninguna manera.
nowhere ['nəʊwɛəʳ] *adv* (**a**) **I see it** ~ no lo veo en ninguna parte; **you're going** ~ no vas a ninguna parte; ~ **in Europe** en ninguna parte de Europa; ~ **else** en ninguna otra parte; **it's** ~ **you know** no es ningún sitio que conoces; **it's** ~ **you'll ever find it** está en un sitio donde no lo encontrarás nunca; **they seemed to come from** (*or* **out of**) ~ parecían haber salido de la nada.
(**b**) (*fig*) **it's** ~ **near as good** no es tan bueno ni con mucho, dista mucho de ser tan bueno; **A is** ~ **near as big as B** A no es tan grande como B ni con mucho; **the enemy looks** ~ **near giving in** el enemigo no da señales ni por aproximación de ceder; **the rest of the runners came** ~ los demás atletas quedaron muy atrás; **in my opinion the rest come** ~ en mi opinión los demás son muy inferiores; **without me he would be** ~ sin mí no habría llegado a ninguna parte; **this is getting us** ~ así no se llega a ninguna parte, esto no conduce a nada; **I'm getting** ~ **with this analysis** no consigo hacer carrera con este análisis.
no-win ['nəʊ'wɪn] *adj*: **a** ~ **situation** una situación imposible.
nowise ['nəʊwaɪz] *adv* (*US*) de ninguna manera.
nowt [naʊt] *n* (*Brit dialectal*) = **nothing**.
noxious ['nɒkʃəs] *adj* nocivo, dañoso.
nozzle ['nɒzl] *n* (*Mech*) tobera *f*, inyector *m*; (*of hose, vacuum cleaner etc*) boquilla *f*; (*of spray*) pulverizador *m*.
NP *n abbr of* **notary public**.
n.p. *abbr of* **new paragraph** punto *m* y aparte.
n.p. or d. *abbr of* **no place or date** s.l. ni f., sin lugar ni fecha.
nr *abbr of* **near** cerca de.
NRA *n abbr of* **National Rivers Authority**.
NS *abbr of* **Nova Scotia** Nueva Escocia *f*.
NSC *n* (*US*) *abbr of* **National Security Council**.
NSF *n* (*US*) *abbr of* **National Science Foundation**.
NSPCA *n abbr* of **National Society for the Prevention of Cruelty to Animals**.
NSPCC *n abbr of* **National Society for the Prevention of Cruelty to Children**.
NSW *abbr of* **New South Wales**.
NT *n* (**a**) *abbr of* **New Testament**. (**b**) (*Brit*) *abbr of* **National Trust**.
NUAAW *n* (*Brit*) *abbr of* **National Union of Agricultural and Allied Workers** *sindicato de trabajadores del campo*.
nuance ['nju:ɑ:ns] *n* matiz *m*.
nub [nʌb] *n* pedazo *m*, trozo *m*; protuberancia *f*; (*fig*) lo esencial, parte *f* esencial; **that's the** ~ **of the question** ahí está el quid del asunto.
NUBE *n* (*Brit*) *abbr of* **National Union of Bank Employees** *sindicato de empleados bancarios*.
nubile ['nju:baɪl] *adj* núbil.
nuclear ['nju:klɪəʳ] *adj* nuclear; ~ **age** era *f* nuclear; ~ **bomb** bomba *f* nuclear; ~ **confrontation** confrontación *f* nuclear; ~ **device** ingenio *m* nuclear; ~ **energy** energía *f* nuclear; ~ **family** familia *f* nuclear; ~ **fission** fisión *f* nuclear; ~ **fuel** combustible *m* nuclear; ~ **fusion** fusión *f* nuclear; ~ **physics** física *f* nuclear; ~ **power** fuerza *f* nuclear, energía *f* nuclear; ~ **power station** central *f* nuclear; ~ **reaction** reacción *f* nuclear; ~ **reactor** reactor *m* nuclear; ~ **shelter** refugio *m* antinuclear; ~ **submarine** submarino *m* nuclear; ~ **test** prueba *f* nuclear; ~ **waste** vertidos *mpl* nucleares, residuos *mpl* nucleares; ~ **weapon** arma *f* nuclear; ~ **winter** invierno *m* nuclear.
nuclear-free ['nju:klɪə,fri:] *adj* desnuclearizado, no nuclear; ~ **zone** zona *f* desnuclearizada.
nuclei ['nju:klɪaɪ] *npl of* **nucleus**.
nucleic ['nju:klɪɪk] *adj*: ~ **acid** acído *m* nucleico.
nucleus ['nju:klɪəs] *n*, *pl* **nuclei** ['nju:klɪaɪ] núcleo *m*; **the** ~ **of a library** el núcleo de una biblioteca; **we have the** ~ **of a crew** tenemos los elementos indispensables para formar una tripulación.
nude [nju:d] **1** *adj* desnudo. **2** *n* (**a**) (*Art*) desnudo *m*; **a** ~ **of Goya** un desnudo de Goya. (**b**) (*person*) desnudo *m*; mujer *f* desnuda. (**c**) **in the** ~ desnudo.
nudge [nʌdʒ] **1** *n* codazo *m* (ligero); **he said 'she's his secretary,** ~ ~' dijo que 'ella es su secretaria, tú ya me entiendes'. **2** *vt* dar un codazo a; empujar (ligeramente); **to** ~ **sb's memory** refrescar la memoria de uno.
nudie** ['nju:dɪ] *n* (*also* ~ **magazine**) revista *f* porno*.
nudism ['nju:dɪzəm] *n* nudismo *m*.
nudist ['nju:dɪst] **1** *n* nudista *mf*. **2** *attr*: ~ **colony** colonia *f* de nudistas.
nudity ['nju:dɪtɪ] *n* desnudez *f*, desnudo *m*.
nugatory ['nju:gətərɪ] *adj* (*trivial*) insignificante; (*useless*) ineficaz, fútil, baladí.
nugget ['nʌgɪt] *n* (*Min*) pepita *f*; **gold** ~ pepita *f* de oro.
nuisance ['nju:sns] **1** *n* (**a**) (*thing, event*) molestia *f*, incomodidad *f*; fastidio *m*, lata* *f*; **what a** ~! ¡qué lata!*,

¡qué fastidio!; **this hat is a ~** este sombrero me está fastidiando, me estoy armando un lío con este sombrero; **the ~ of having to shave** la incomodidad de tener que afeitarse; **it's a ~ having to shave** es una lata tener que afeitarse; **'commit no ~'** 'mantenga limpio este sitio', (*more specifically*) 'prohibido hacer aguas'.

(**b**) (*person*) moscón *m*, pelmazo *m*; pesado *m*; **what a ~ you are!** ¡eres un pesado!; **you're being a ~** me estás dando la lata; **to make a ~ of o.s.** dar la lata.

(**c**) (*Jur*) perjuicio *m*, daño *m*.

2 *attr*: **~ value** valor *m* como irritante.

NUJ *n* (*Brit*) *abbr of* **National Union of Journalists** *sindicato de periodistas*.

nuke* [nju:k] (*esp US*) **1** *vt* atacar con arma nuclear. **2** *n* bomba *f* atómica.

null [nʌl] *adj* nulo, inválido; **~ and void** nulo, sin efecto, sin fuerza legal; **to render sb's efforts ~** invalidar los esfuerzos de uno.

nullification [ˌnʌlɪfɪ'keɪʃən] *n* anulación *f*, invalidación *f*.

nullify ['nʌlɪfaɪ] *vt* anular, invalidar.

nullity ['nʌlɪtɪ] *n* nulidad *f*.

NUM *n* (*Brit*) *abbr of* **National Union of Mineworkers** *sindicato de mineros*.

numb [nʌm] **1** *adj* entumecido; (*fig*) insensible; **my leg has gone ~** se me ha dormido la pierna; **to be ~ with cold** estar entumecido de frío, (*fig*) estar helado; **to be ~ with fright** estar paralizado de temor. **2** *vt* entumecer, entorpecer.

numbed [nʌmd] *adj* entumecido; (*fig*) insensible.

number ['nʌmbəʳ] **1** *n* (**a**) (*Math*) número *m*; (*figure*) número *m*, cifra *f*; (*Gram, Telec, etc*) número *m*; **a ~ of** algunos, varios, una porción de; **a ~ of people have protested** varias personas han protestado; **a large ~ of people** buen número de personas, muchas personas; **in a small ~ of cases** en unos pocos casos, en contados casos; **on a ~ of occasions** en diversas ocasiones, varias veces; **any ~ of** la mar de; **any ~ of times** muchísimas veces; **to do sth by ~s** (*US*: **by the ~s**) hacer algo siguiendo las instrucciones; (*fig*) hacer algo paso a paso; **to be few in ~** ser pocos; **to be 8 in ~** ser 8; **to come in ~s** venir en tropel, venir en masa; **they exist in ~s in Africa** en África hay muchos, en África son frecuentes; **one of their ~** uno de ellos; **he is not of that ~** no es de ésos, no forma parte de ese grupo; **to the ~ of some 200** en número de unos 200; **times without ~** muchísimas veces; **his ~ is up*** todo se acabó para él; **his ~ came up** su número salió premiado; **I've got his ~ now*** le tengo calado ya.

(**b**) (*of house etc*) número *m*; (*of car etc*) matrícula *f*; **N~ Ten** el Número Diez (*de Downing Street, Londres, residencia del primer ministro*); **we live at No. 15** vivimos en el núm. 15; **the ~ one Spanish player** el jugador número uno de España; **to look after N~ One** mirar por sí, cuidar de sí mismo; **did you get his ~?** ¿has apuntado la matrícula?

(**c**) (*person*) **a nice little ~*** una chica monísima; **my opposite ~ in France** mi equivalente en Francia, mi homólogo francés.

(**d**) **a good ~‡** (*job*) un buen chollo‡.

(**e**) (*of journal*) número *m*.

(**f**) (*Theat etc*) número *m*; **and for my next ~...** ahora voy a cantar (*etc*) ...

(**g**) **~s** (*Poet*) versos *mpl*.

2 *vt* (**a**) (*count*) contar; **the library ~s 30,000 books** la biblioteca cuenta con 30.000 libros, la biblioteca posee 30.000 libros; **to ~ sb among one's friends** contar a uno entre sus amigos; **to be ~ed among** figurar entre, ser de; **his days are ~ed** tiene los días contados; **his days seem to be ~ed** sus días parecen contados.

(**b**) (*amount to*) ascender a, sumar; **they ~ 187** hay 187, ascienden a 187, suman 187; **they ~ several hundreds** hay varios centenares.

(**c**) (*assign ~ to*) numerar, poner número a; *MS pages* foliar; **the houses are not ~ed** las casas no están numeradas, las casas no tienen número; **~ed account** cuenta *f* numerada.

3 *vi*: **to ~ off** numerarse (*from the right* por la derecha).

number-cruncher* ['nʌmbə,krʌntʃəʳ] *n* (*machine*) machacadora *f* de números; **he's the ~** él se encarga de los números.

number-crunching* ['nʌmbə,krʌntʃɪŋ] *n* machaqueo *m* de números, cálculo *m* a gran escala.

numbering ['nʌmbərɪŋ] **1** *n* numeración *f*. **2** *attr*: **~ machine** numerador *m*.

numberless ['nʌmbəlɪs] *adj* innumerable, sin número.

number-plate ['nʌmbəpleɪt] *n* (*Brit Aut etc*) (placa *f* de) matrícula *f*.

numbers game ['nʌmbəz'geɪm] *n*, **numbers racket** ['nʌmbəz'rækɪt] *n* (*US*) *lotería clandestina en Norteamérica*.

numbhead* ['nʌmhed] *n* (*US*) tonto *m*, -a *f*, bobo *m*, -a *f*.

numbness ['nʌmnɪs] *n* entumecimiento *m*; (*fig*) insensibilidad *f*; parálisis *f*.

num(b)skull ['nʌmskʌl] *n* zote *m*, majadero *m*; **you ~!** ¡majadero!

numeracy ['nju:mərəsɪ] *n* competencia *f* en el cálculo, competencia *f* en matemáticas.

numeral ['nju:mərəl] **1** *adj* numeral. **2** *n* número *m*, cifra *f*, guarismo *m*.

numerate ['nju:mərɪt] *adj* competente en el cálculo, competente en las matemáticas.

numeration [ˌnju:mə'reɪʃən] *n* numeración *f*.

numerator ['nju:məreɪtəʳ] *n* numerador *m*.

numeric [nju'merɪk] *adj* numérico; **~ field** campo *m* numérico; **~ keypad** teclado *m* numérico.

numerical [nju:'merɪkəl] *adj* numérico.

numerically [nju:'merɪkəlɪ] *adv* numéricamente; **~ superior to** con superioridad numérica a, superiores en cuanto a su número a.

numerology [ˌnju:mə'rɒlɒdʒɪ] *n* numerología *f*.

numerous ['nju:mərəs] *adj* numeroso; muchos; **a ~ family** una familia numerosa; **in ~ cases** en muchos casos; **~ people believe that ...** mucha gente cree que ...

numismatic [ˌnju:mɪz'mætɪk] *adj* numismático.

numismatics [ˌnju:mɪz'mætɪks] *n* numismática *f*.

numismatist [nju:'mɪzmətɪst] *n* numismático *mf*, numísmata *mf*.

nun [nʌn] *n* monja *f*, religiosa *f*; **to become a ~** tomar el hábito, meterse monja.

nunciature ['nʌnʃɪətjʊəʳ] *n* nunciatura *f*.

nuncio ['nʌnʃɪəʊ] *n* (*also* **papal ~**) nuncio *m* apostólico.

nunnery ['nʌnərɪ] *n* convento *m* de monjas.

NUPE ['nju:pɪ] *n* (*Brit*) *abbr of* **National Union of Public Employees** *sindicato de funcionarios*.

nuptial ['nʌpʃəl] *adj* nupcial.

nuptials ['nʌpʃəlz] *npl* (*hum*) nupcias *fpl*.

NUR *n* (*Brit*) *abbr of* **National Union of Railwaymen** *sindicato de ferroviarios*.

nurd‡ [nɜ:d] *n* borde* *mf*.

nurse [nɜ:s] **1** *n* (*Med*) enfermera *f*; (*male ~*) enfermero *m*; (*wet-~*) nodriza *f*, ama *f* de leche; (*children's*) niñera *f*.

2 *vt* (**a**) *patient* cuidar, atender, asistir; (*US*: *suckle*) criar, amamantar; (*Brit*: *in arms*) mecer; **to ~ sb back to health** cuidar a uno hasta que se reponga; **to ~ a cold** tratar de curarse de un resfriado.

(**b**) (*fig*) **to ~ a constituency** (*Brit Parl*) establecerse (entre elecciones) como candidato en un distrito electoral; **to ~ a business along** fomentar un negocio, promover un negocio.

nursemaid ['nɜ:smeɪd] *n* niñera *f*, chacha* *f*.

nursery ['nɜ:srɪ] **1** *n* (**a**) cuarto *m* de los niños; **from the ~** desde la niñez, desde niño. (**b**) (*Agr etc*) vivero *m*, semillero *m*, plantel *m*; (*fig, Sport*) cantera *f*; **a ~ for new players** una cantera de jóvenes jugadores. **2** *attr*: **~ education** educación *f* preescolar; **~ nurse** puericultor *m*, -ora *f*; **~ schooling = ~ education**; **~ school teacher** maestro *m*, -a *f* de preescolar; **~ slopes** (*Brit Ski*) pistas *fpl* para principiantes.

nurseryman ['nɜ:srɪmən] *n*, *pl* **nurserymen** ['nɜ:srɪmən] horticultor *m*.

nursery-rhyme ['nɜ:srɪraɪm] *n* canción *f* infantil.

nursery-school ['nɜ:srɪ,sku:l] *n* jardín *m* de infancia, parvulario *m*.

nursing ['nɜ:sɪŋ] **1** *adj* (**a**) **~ auxiliary** (*Brit*) auxiliar *mf* de enfermería; **~ college** escuela *f* de enfermería; **~ officer** enfermero *m* jefe, enfermera *f* jefe (*or* jefa); **~ staff** enfermeras *fpl*.

(**b**) **~ mother** madre *f* lactante.

2 *n* (*of patient*) asistencia *f*, cuidado *m*; (*career, course, profession*) enfermería *f*; (*suckling*) lactancia *f*; **to go in for ~** hacerse enfermera, dedicarse a la enfermería.

nursing-home ['nɜ:sɪŋ,həʊm] *n* (*esp Brit*) clínica *f* (particular); (*US*) asilo *m* de ancianos.

nursling ['nɜ:slɪŋ] *n* lactante *mf*, niño *m*, -a *f* de pecho.

nurture ['nɜ:tʃəʳ] **1** *n* (*nourishment*) nutrición *f*; (*bringing-up*) educación *f*, crianza *f*. **2** *vt* alimentar, nutrir (*on* de); educar, criar.

NUS *n* (*Brit*) (**a**) *abbr of* **National Union of Students** *sindicato de estudiantes*. (**b**) *abbr of* **National Union of Seamen** *sindicato de marineros*.

NUT *n* (*Brit*) *abbr of* **National Union of Teachers** *sindicato de profesores*.

nut [nʌt] **1** *n* (**a**) (*Bot*) nuez *f*; **it's a hard ~ to crack** es un hueso duro de roer; **he's a tough ~** es un sujeto duro; **he can't play for ~s*** no juega nada.
(**b**) (‡: *head*) cholla‡ *f*; **he's off his ~** le falta un tornillo*; **you must be off your ~** ¿estás grillado?‡; **to do one's ~** (*Brit*) echar el resto*.
(**c**) (‡: *madman*) chiflado* *m*, -a *f*; (*eccentric*) excéntrico *m*, -a *f*; (*enthusiast*) entusiasta *mf*, maniático *m*, -a *f*.
(**d**) **~s**** (*esp US Anat*) cojones** *mpl*.
(**e**) **~s!*** (*excl*: *US*) ¡narices!*
(**f**) (*Mech*) tuerca *f*; **the ~s and bolts of a scheme** los aspectos prácticos de un proyecto.
2 *attr*: **~ chocolate** chocolate *m* de nueces.

nut-brown ['nʌt'braʊn] *adj* café avellana; *hair* castaño claro.

nutcase‡ ['nʌtkeɪs] *n* pirado‡ *m*, -a *f*.

nutcracker(s) ['nʌt,krækəz] *npl* cascanueces *m*; **a pair of nutcrackers** un cascanueces; **The Nutcracker** (*Mus*) El Cascanueces.

nuthatch ['nʌthætʃ] *n* trepador *m*, trepatroncos *m*.

nuthouse‡ ['nʌthaʊs] *n*, *pl* **nuthouses** ['nʌthaʊziz] manicomio *m*, casa *f* de locos.

nutmeg ['nʌtmeg] *n* nuez *f* moscada.

nutrient ['nju:trɪənt] **1** *adj* nutritivo. **2** *n* nutriente *m*.

nutriment ['nju:trɪmənt] *n* nutrimento *m*, alimento *m*.

nutrition [nju:'trɪʃən] *n* nutrición *f*, alimentación *f*.

nutritional [nju:'trɪʃənl] *adj value etc* nutritivo, nutricional.

nutritionist [nju:'trɪʃənɪst] *n* nutricionista *mf*.

nutritious [nju:'trɪʃəs] *adj*, **nutritive** ['nju:trɪtɪv] *adj* nutritivo, rico.

nuts‡ [nʌts] *adj*: **to be ~** estar chiflado*; **to be ~ about a girl** estar chalado por una*; **to be ~ about sth** pirrarse por algo‡; **to drive sb ~** volver loco a uno; **to go ~** volverse loco.

nutshell ['nʌtʃel] *n* cáscara *f* de nuez; **in a ~** en resumidas cuentas; **to put it in a ~** para decirlo brevemente; **that puts it in a ~** eso lo dice en pocas palabras.

nut-tree ['nʌttri:] *n* (*hazel*) avellano *m*, (*walnut*) nogal *m*.

nutter‡ ['nʌtə^r] *n* (*Brit*) chiflado* *m*, -a *f*.

nutty ['nʌtɪ] *adj* (**a**) *colour* de nuez; *cake* con nueces; *taste* a nueces, que sabe a nueces; *sherry* almendrado, avellanado. (**b**) (‡) loco; **to be ~** estar loco; **to be ~ about sth** estar loco por algo.

nuzzle ['nʌzl] **1** *vt* acariciar con el hocico. **2** *vi* = **snuggle, nestle.**

NV (*US Post*) *abbr of* **Nevada**.

NW *abbr of* **north-west** NO *m*, noroeste *m* (*also adj*).

N.W.T. *abbr of* **Northwest Territories.**

NY (*US Post*) *abbr of* **New York.**

NYC (*US Post*) *abbr of* **New York City.**

nylon ['naɪlɒn] **1** *n* nilón *m*, nailon *m*; **~s** medias *fpl* de nilón. **2** *adj* de nilón, de nailon.

nymph [nɪmf] *n* ninfa *f*.

nymphet(te) [nɪm'fet] *n* nínfula *f*.

nympho* ['nɪmfəʊ], **nymphomaniac** [,nɪmfəʊ'meɪnɪæk] **1** *adj* ninfómano. **2** *n* ninfómana *f*.

nymphomania [,nɪmfəʊ'meɪnɪə] *n* ninfomanía *f*, furor *m* uterino.

NYSE *n* (*US*) *abbr of* **New York Stock Exchange.**

NZ *abbr of* **New Zealand.**

O

O¹, o [əʊ] *n* (*letter*) O, o *f*; **O for Oliver, O for Oboe** (*US*) O de Oviedo; **O-grade** (*Scot Scol*), **O-Level** (*Brit Scol*) *V* **ordinary.**
O² [əʊ] = **oh.**
O & M *n abbr of* **Organization and Methods** organización *f* y métodos.
o/a *abbr of* **on account** a cuenta.
oaf [əʊf] *n* zoquete *m*, patán *m*.
oafish ['əʊfɪʃ] *adj* lerdo, zafio.
oak [əʊk] **1** *n* roble *m*; **to sport one's ~** (*Univ*) cerrar la puerta (para no recibir visitas). **2** *attr* de roble.
oak-apple ['əʊk,æpl] *n* agalla *f* (de roble).
oaken ['əʊkən] *adj* de roble.
oakum ['əʊkəm] *n* estopa *f* (de calafatear).
oakwood ['əʊkwʊd] *n* robledo *m*.
O.A.P. *n* (*Brit*) (**a**) *abbr of* **old age pension** subsidio *m* de vejez. (**b**) *abbr of* **old age pensioner** pensionista *mf*.
OAPEC [əʊ'eɪpek] *n abbr of* **Organization of Arab Petroleum Exporting Countries** Organización *f* de Países Árabes Exportadores de Petróleo, OPAEP *f*.
oar [ɔːʳ] *n* (**a**) remo *m*; **to lie** (*or* **rest**) **on one's ~s** dejar de remar, (*fig*) descansar, dormir sobre sus laureles; **to put** (*or* **shove**) **one's ~ in** meter su cuchara; **to ship the ~s** desarmar los remos.
(**b**) (*person*) remero *m*, -a *f*; **to be a good ~** ser buen remero, remar bien.
oared [ɔːd] *adj* provisto de remos; (*in cpds*) de ... remos, *eg* **eight-~** de ocho remos.
oarlock ['ɔːlɒk] *n* (*US*) tolete *m*, escálamo *m*, chumacera *f*.
oarsman ['ɔːzmən] *n*, *pl* **oarsmen** ['ɔːzmən] remero *m*.
oarsmanship ['ɔːzmənʃɪp] *n* arte *m* de remar.
OAS *n abbr of* **Organization of American States** Organización *f* de Estados Americanos, OEA *f*.
oasis [əʊ'eɪsɪs] *n*, *pl* **oases** [əʊ'eɪsiːz] oasis *m* (*also fig*).
oast-house ['əʊsthaʊs] *n*, *pl* **oast-houses** ['əʊsthaʊzɪz] *n* secadero *m* para lúpulo.
oat bran ['əʊt'bræn] *n* (*US*) salvado *m* de avena.
oatcake ['əʊtkeɪk] *n* torta *f* de avena.
oaten ['əʊtn] *adj* de avena.
oatfield ['əʊtfiːld] *n* avenal *m*.
oath [əʊθ] *n*, *pl* **oaths** [əʊðz] (**a**) (*solemn promise etc*) juramento *m*; **under ~, on ~**, bajo juramento; **to administer an ~ to sb** tomar juramento a uno; **to break one's ~** violar su juramento; **to put sb on ~** hacer prestar juramento a uno; **to take the** (*or* **an**) **~** prestar juramento (*on* sobre); **to take an ~ that ...** jurar que ...; **to take the ~ of allegiance** (*Mil*) jurar la bandera.
(**b**) (*curse*) blasfemia *f*, reniego *m*, palabrota *f*.
oatmeal ['əʊtmiːl] *n* harina *f* de avena.
oats [əʊts] *npl* avena *f*; **to be off one's ~** estar desganado, haber perdido el apetito; **to get one's ~**** mojar (con regularidad)**.
OAU *n abbr of* **Organization of African Unity** Organización *f* para la Unidad Africana, OUA *f*.
OB (*TV*) *n abbr of* **outside broadcast** transmisión *f* exterior.
ob. *abbr of* **obiit, died** murió, m.
Obadiah [,əʊbə'daɪə] *nm* Abdías.
obbligato [,ɒblɪ'gɑːtəʊ] *n* obligado *m*.
obduracy ['ɒbdjʊrəsɪ] *n* obstinación *f*, terquedad *f*; inflexibilidad *f*.
obdurate ['ɒbdjʊrɪt] *adj* obstinado, terco; (*in refusing etc*) inflexible.
O.B.E. *n* (*Brit*) *abbr of* **Officer of the Order of the British Empire** *título ceremonial.*
obedience [ə'biːdɪəns] *n* obediencia *f*; sumisión *f*; docilidad *f*; **in ~ to** conforme a, de acuerdo con; **in ~ to your wishes** accediendo a sus deseos; **to compel ~** exigir obediencia (*from* a).
obedient [ə'biːdɪənt] *adj* obediente; sumiso, dócil; **to be ~ to** ser obediente a, obedecer a.
obediently [ə'biːdɪəntlɪ] *adv* obedientemente; sumisamente, dócilmente; **yours ~** su atento servidor.
obeisance [əʊ'beɪsəns] *n* (*bow etc*) reverencia *f*; (*salutation*) saludo *m*; (*homage*) homenaje *m*; **to do** (*or* **make, pay**) **~ to** tributar homenaje a.
obelisk ['ɒbɪlɪsk] *n* obelisco *m*.
obese [əʊ'biːs] *adj* obeso.
obeseness [əʊ'biːsnɪs] *n*, **obesity** [əʊ'biːsɪtɪ] *n* obesidad *f*.
obey [ə'beɪ] *vt* (*person etc*) obedecer; (*pay heed to*) hacer caso a; *need, controls* responder a; *summons* acudir a; *law* cumplir, observar, obrar de acuerdo con; *instruction* cumplir; **I like to be ~ed** me gusta que se me obedezca.
obfuscate ['ɒbfəskeɪt] *vt* ofuscar.
obit* ['ɒbɪt] *n* = **obituary 2.**
obituary [ə'bɪtjʊərɪ] **1** *adj* necrológico; **~ column** sección *f* necrológica; **~ notice** necrología *f*; esquela *f* (mortuoria). **2** *n* necrología *f*, obituario *m*.
object 1 ['ɒbdʒɪkt] *n* (**a**) (*thing in general*) objeto *m*; cosa *f*, artículo *m*; (*pej: thing*) mamarracho *m*, (*person*) mamarracho *m*, espantajo *m*, estantigua *f*; **she was an ~ of pity to all** daba lástima a cuantos la veían; **he became an ~ of ridicule** se puso en ridículo.
(**b**) (*aim*) objeto *m*, propósito *m*, intento *m*; **~ language** lengua *f* objeto; **~ programme** programa *m* objeto; **with this ~ in view** con este propósito; **with the ~ of** con el propósito de, al objeto de; **what is the ~ of the plan?** ¿qué finalidad tiene el plan?; **expense is no ~** no importan los gastos; **money is no ~** cueste lo que cueste.
(**c**) (*Gram*) complemento *m*.
2 [əb'dʒekt] *vt*: **to ~ that ...** objetar que ...; **to this it was ~ed that ...** a esto se objetó que ...
3 [əb'dʒekt] *vi* hacer objeciones, oponerse; poner reparos; **I ~!** ¡protesto!; **I ~ most strongly!** ¡me opongo rotundamente a ello!; **if you don't ~** si no tienes inconveniente; **I ~ to that remark!** ¡protesto contra esa observación! **to ~ to sb doing sth** oponerse a que uno haga algo; **do you ~ to my going?** ¿te opones a que vaya yo?; **do you ~ to my smoking?** ¿te molesta que fume?; **I don't ~ to an occasional drink** no me opongo a que se tome algo de vez en cuando.
objection [əb'dʒekʃən] *n* objeción *f*, reparo *m*; protesta *f*; (*difficulty*) inconveniente *m*; obstáculo *m*, dificultad *f*; **~!** ¡yo protesto!; **what are the ~s?** ¿qué obstáculo hay?, ¿cuáles son las dificultades?; **there is no ~** no hay inconveniente; **there is no ~ to your going** no hay inconveniente en que vayas; **I can find no ~ to it** no le encuentro ninguna dificultad; **I have no ~** no tengo inconveniente; **if you have no ~** si no tiene inconveniente; **have you any ~ to my smoking?** ¿te molesta que fume?; **have you any ~ to my going?** ¿tienes algún inconveniente en que vaya yo?; **he made no ~** no hizo ninguna objeción, no protestó, no se opuso a ello; **to raise ~s** poner reparos (*to* a), protestar (*to* contra); **I see no ~** no veo inconveniente.
objectionable [əb'dʒekʃnəbl] *adj* desagradable; *person* molesto, pesado; indeseable; *conduct etc* reprensible, censurable; **a most ~ person** una persona inaguantable.
objective [əb'dʒektɪv] **1** *adj* objetivo; **~ test** prueba *f* objetiva. **2** *n* objetivo *m*.
objectively [əb'dʒektɪvlɪ] *adv* objetivamente.
objectivism [əb'dʒektɪvɪzəm] *n* objetivismo *m*.
objectivity [,ɒbdʒɪk'tɪvɪtɪ] *n* objetividad *f*.
object-lesson ['ɒbdʒɪkt,lesn] *n* lección *f* práctica, ejemplo *m*; **it was an ~ in good manners** fue una perfecta demostración de cortesía.
objector [əb'dʒektəʳ] *n* objetante *mf*.

objurgate ['ɒbdʒɜːgeɪt] *vt* increpar, reprender.
objurgation [ˌɒbdʒɜːgeɪʃən] *n* increpación *f*, reprensión *f*.
oblation [əʊ'bleɪʃən] *n* oblación *f*; (*gift*) oblata *f*, ofrenda *f*.
obligate ['ɒblɪgeɪt] *vt*: **to ~ sb to do sth** obligar a uno a hacer algo; **to be ~d to** + *infin* estar obligado a + *infin*.
obligation [ˌɒblɪ'geɪʃən] *n* obligación *f*; deber *m*; compromiso *m*; **of ~** (*Eccl*) de precepto; **without ~** (*in advert*) sin compromiso; **'no ~ to buy'** 'sin compromiso a comprar'; **it is your ~ to see that ...** le cumple a Vd comprobar que + *subj*, es su deber comprobar que + *subj*; **to be under an ~ to sb** deber favores a uno; **to be under an ~ to** + *infin* deber + *infin*, haberse comprometido a + *infin*, tener obligación de + *infin*; **to lay** (*or* **put**) **sb under an ~** poner a uno bajo una obligación; **to meet one's ~s** (*Comm*) cumplir sus compromisos; **to fail to meet one's ~s** no poder cumplir sus compromisos.
obligatory [ɒ'blɪgətərɪ] *adj* obligatorio; **to make it ~ for sb to do sth** imponer a uno la obligación de + *infin*.
oblige [ə'blaɪdʒ] *vt* (**a**) (*force*) obligar, forzar; **to ~ sb to do sth** obligar a uno a hacer algo, forzar a uno a hacer algo; **to be ~d to do sth** verse obligado a hacer algo; **you are not ~d to do it** nada te obliga a hacerlo.
(**b**) (*gratify*) complacer, hacer un favor a; **you would greatly ~ me if ...** agradecería mucho que + *subj*; **anything to ~ a friend!** ¡lo que sea por complacer a un amigo!; **he did it to ~ us** lo hizo como favor, lo hizo para complacernos; **to ~ sb with a match** hacer a uno el favor de (prestarle, darle) una cerilla; **much ~d!** ¡muchísimas gracias!, ¡se agradece!; **I should be much ~d if ...** agradecería que + *subj*; **I am ~d to you for your help** agradezco su ayuda; **to be ~d to sb** estar en deuda con uno.
obligee [ˌɒblɪ'dʒiː] *n* tenedor *m* de una obligación.
obliging [ə'blaɪdʒɪŋ] *adj* servicial, atento, obsequioso.
obligingly [ə'blaɪdʒɪŋlɪ] *adv* atentamente; **he very ~ helped us** muy amablemente nos ayudó.
oblique [ə'bliːk] **1** *adj* oblicuo; *reference etc* indirecto, tangencial; **~ angle** ángulo *m* oblicuo. **2** *n* (*Typ*) barra *f* (oblicua).
obliquely [ə'bliːklɪ] *adv* oblicuamente; indirectamente, tangencialmente.
obliqueness [ə'bliːknɪs] *n*, **obliquity** [ə'blɪkwɪtɪ] *n* oblicuidad *f*; lo indirecto, lo tangencial.
obliterate [ə'blɪtəreɪt] *vt* borrar, eliminar, destruir toda huella de; *town etc* arrasar, destruir; (*Med*) obliterar.
obliteration [əˌblɪtə'reɪʃən] *n* borradura *f*, eliminación *f*; arrasamiento *m*, destrucción *f*; (*Med*) obliteración *f*.
oblivion [ə'blɪvɪən] *n* olvido *m*; **to cast into ~** echar al olvido; **to fall** (*or* **sink**) **into ~** sumirse en el olvido.
oblivious [ə'blɪvɪəs] *adj*: **to be ~ of, to be ~ to** estar inconsciente de; **he, totally ~ of what was happening ...** él, totalmente inconsciente de lo que pasaba ...
oblong ['ɒblɒŋ] **1** *adj* oblongo, apaisado. **2** *n* oblongo *m*.
obloquy ['ɒbləkwɪ] *n* (*abuse*) injurias *fpl*, calumnia *f*; (*shame*) deshonra *f*; **to cover sb with ~** llenar a uno de injurias.
obnoxious [əb'nɒkʃəs] *adj* detestable, repugnante, odioso; *fumes etc* nocivo, desagradable; **it is ~ to me to** + *infin* me repugna + *infin*, me es repugnante + *infin*.
o.b.o. (*US*) *abbr of* **or best offer** abierto ofertas.
oboe ['əʊbəʊ] *n* oboe *m*.
oboist ['əʊbəʊɪst] *n* oboe *mf* (*persona*).
obscene [əb'siːn] *adj* obsceno, indecente, escabroso, procaz.
obscenely [əb'siːnlɪ] *adv* obscenamente, escabrosamente.
obscenity [əb'senɪtɪ] *n* obscenidad *f*, indecencia *f*, escabrosidad *f*, procacidad *f*; **to utter obscenities** proferir obscenidades.
obscurantism [ˌɒbskjʊə'ræntɪzəm] *n* oscurantismo *m*.
obscurantist [ˌɒbskjʊə'ræntɪst] **1** *adj* oscurantista. **2** *n* oscurantista *mf*.
obscure [əb'skjʊəʳ] **1** *adj* oscuro (*also fig*).
2 *vt* oscurecer; (*eclipse*) eclipsar; (*hide*) esconder; *issue* entenebrecer, confundir; *memory, glory etc* oscurecer; **the house is ~d by the trees** la casa está escondida detrás de los árboles; **it served only to ~ the matter further** sirvió para complicar aun más el asunto.
obscurely [əb'skjʊəlɪ] *adv* oscuramente.
obscurity [əb'skjʊərɪtɪ] *n* oscuridad *f* (*also fig*); **to live in ~** vivir en la oscuridad.
obsequies ['ɒbsɪkwɪz] *npl* exequias *fpl*.
obsequious [əb'siːkwɪəs] *adj* servil.
obsequiously [əb'siːkwɪəslɪ] *adj* servilmente.
obsequiousness [əb'siːkwɪəsnɪs] *n* servilismo *m*.
observable [əb'zɜːvəbl] *adj* observable, visible; **as is ~ in rabbits** según se puede apreciar en los conejos; **no ~ difference** ninguna diferencia perceptible.
observably [əb'zɜːvəblɪ] *adv* visiblemente.
observance [əb'zɜːvəns] *n* (**a**) (*of rule etc*) observancia *f* (*of* de), cumplimiento *m* (*of* con); (*rite etc*) práctica *f*; **members of the strict ~** miembros *mpl* de la estricta observancia. (**b**) (*custom*) costumbre *f*.
observant [əb'zɜːvənt] *adj* observador, perspicaz; (*watchful*) vigilante; (*attentive*) atento; **the child is very ~** el niño es muy observador.
observation [ˌɒbzə'veɪʃən] **1** *n* (**a**) (*in most senses*) observación *f*; (*of rule etc*) observancia *f*; **to be under ~** estar vigilado; (*Med*) estar en observación; **we can keep the valley under ~ from here** desde aquí dominamos el valle; **the police are keeping him under ~** la policía le está vigilando; **to escape ~** pasar inadvertido.
(**b**) (*remark*) observación *f*, comentario *m*; **'O~s on Sterne'** 'Apuntes *mpl* sobre Sterne'.
2 *attr*: **~ car** (*Rail*) vagón-mirador *m*, coche *m* panorámico; **~ post** puesto *m* de observación; **~ tower** torre *f* (*or* torreta *f*) de observación.
observatory [əb'zɜːvətrɪ] *n* observatorio *m*.
observe [əb'zɜːv] *vt* (**a**) (*obey*) *rule, custom* observar; cumplir; *Sabbath, silence* guardar; *care* usar de, emplear; *anniversary* celebrar; **failure to ~ the law** incumplimiento *m* de la ley.
(**b**) (*take note of, watch*) observar; examinar; *suspect* vigilar; **I ~d him steal the duck** le vi robar el pato; **now ~ this closely** fijaos bien en esto.
(**c**) (*say*) observar, decir; **I ~d to him that ...** le hice observar que ...; **as Jeeves ~d** según dijo Jeeves.
observer [əb'zɜːvəʳ] *n* observador *m*, -ora *f*.
obsess [əb'ses] *vt* obsesionar, causar obsesión a; **he is ~ed with this idea** está obsesionado por esta idea, le obsesiona esta idea.
obsession [əb'seʃən] *n* obsesión *f*; idea *f* fija, manía *f*; **the ~ about cleanliness** la obsesión de la limpieza, la manía de la limpieza; **to have an ~ about an idea** estar obsesionado por una idea; **it's an ~ with him** es una manía que tiene.
obsessional [əb'seʃənəl] *adj* obsesivo.
obsessive [əb'sesɪv] *adj* obsesionante.
obsessively [əb'sesɪvlɪ] *adv* de modo obsesionante.
obsidian [ɒb'sɪdɪən] *n* obsidiana *f*.
obsolescence [ˌɒbsə'lesns] *n* caída *f* en desuso, obsolescencia *f*.
obsolescent [ˌɒbsə'lesnt] *adj* algo anticuado; **to be ~** irse haciendo anticuado, estar cayendo en desuso.
obsolete ['ɒbsəliːt] *adj* obsoleto.
obstacle ['ɒbstəkl] *n* obstáculo *m*; estorbo *m*, impedimento *m*, inconveniente *m*; **~s to independence** los factores que dificultan la independencia; **one of the ~s is money** uno de los obstáculos es el dinero; **to be an ~ to progress** ser un estorbo al progreso; **that is no ~ to our doing it** eso no impide que lo hagamos; **to put ~s in sb's way** crear dificultades a uno, dificultar el camino a uno.
obstacle course ['ɒbstəklˌkɔːs] *n* pista *f* americana.
obstacle race ['ɒbstəklˌreɪs] *n* carrera *f* de obstáculos.
obstetric(al) [ɒb'stetrɪk(əl)] *adj* obstétrico.
obstetrician [ˌɒbstə'trɪʃən] *n* obstétrico *m*, -a *f*.
obstetrics [ɒb'stetrɪks] *n* obstetricia *f*.
obstinacy ['ɒbstɪnəsɪ] *n* obstinación *f*, terquedad *f*, porfía *f*; tenacidad *f*.
obstinate ['ɒbstɪnɪt] *adj* obstinado, terco, porfiado; *pursuit etc* tenaz; **as ~ as a mule** tan terco como una mula; **to be ~ about sth** insistir con tesón en algo.
obstinately ['ɒbstɪnɪtlɪ] *adv* obstinadamente, tercamente, porfiadamente; tenazmente.
obstreperous [əb'strepərəs] *adj* (*noisy*) ruidoso, estrepitoso; (*unruly*) turbulento, desmandado; protestón; **he became ~** empezó a desmandarse.
obstreperously [əb'strepərəslɪ] *adv* ruidosamente, estrepitosamente; de modo turbulento.
obstruct [əb'strʌkt] **1** *vt* obstruir; (*Parl, Sport*) obstruir; *plan, progress etc* dificultar, estorbar; *person* estorbar, impedir; *road* cerrar, bloquear, obstruir; *pipe etc* obstruir, atascar, atorar.
2 *vi* estorbar.
obstruction [əb'strʌkʃən] *n* obstrucción *f* (*also Parl*); estorbo *m*, obstáculo *m*; (*Med*) oclusión *f*; **to cause an ~** causar un estorbo, (*Aut etc*) obstruir el tráfico.
obstructionism [əb'strʌkʃənɪzəm] *n* obstruccionismo *m*.
obstructionist [əb'strʌkʃənɪst] **1** *adj* obstruccionista. **2** *n* obstruccionista *mf*.
obstructive [əb'strʌktɪv] *adj* obstructivo, estorbador; **you're**

being ~ Vd nos está estorbando.

obstructiveness [əb'strʌktɪvnɪs] *n* carácter *m* obstructivo; obstructivismo *m*.

obtain [əb'teɪn] **1** *vt* obtener; adquirir; lograr, conseguir; **oil can be ~ed from coal** el aceite se puede extraer del carbón; **his uncle ~ed the job for him** su tío le consiguió el puesto; **a work for which he ~ed a prize** un trabajo que le valió un premio, un trabajo por el que le dieron un premio.

2 *vi* prevalecer, predominar; privar; regir; **the price which ~s now** el precio que rige ahora; **in the conditions then ~ing** en las condiciones que existían entonces; **that did not ~ in my day** en mis tiempos no existía eso, en mis tiempos no era así.

obtainable [əb'teɪnəbl] *adj*: **to be ~** ser asequible, poderse adquirir; (*in shop*) estar a la venta; **'~ at all chemists'** 'de venta en todas las farmacias'; **it is no longer ~** ya no se puede conseguir.

obtrude [əb'tru:d] **1** *vt tongue etc* sacar, extender; **to ~ sth on sb** imponer algo a uno.

2 *vi* (*person*) entrometerse; **he does not let his opinions ~** no hace gala de sus opiniones, no impone sus opiniones a los demás.

obtrusion [əb'tru:ʒən] *n* imposición *f*; importunidad *f*; entrometimiento *m*.

obtrusive [əb'tru:sɪv] *adj* importuno, molesto; intruso; indiscreto; *building etc* demasiado visible, llamativo; *smell* penetrante; *person* entrometido, intruso.

obtrusively [əb'tru:sɪvlɪ] *adv* importunamente; indiscretamente; de modo demasiado visible; de modo penetrante.

obtuse [əb'tju:s] *adj* (**a**) (*Math etc*) obtuso. (**b**) *person* obtuso, estúpido, duro de mollera; *remark* poco inteligente; **now you're just being ~** te has empeñado en no comprender; **he can be very ~ at times** a veces puede ser muy obtuso.

obtuseness [əb'tju:snɪs] *n* (*fig*) estupidez *f*, torpeza *f*, obtusidad *f*.

obverse ['ɒbvɜ:s] **1** *adj* del anverso. **2** *n* anverso *m*; (*fig*) complemento *m*.

obviate ['ɒbvɪeɪt] *vt* obviar, evitar, eliminar.

obvious ['ɒbvɪəs] **1** *adj* (*clear, perceptible*) evidente, obvio, manifiesto, patente; (*expected*) obvio, natural; (*unsubtle*) poco sutil, transparente; (*suitable*) indicado; **the ~ thing to do is ...** lo lógico es ...; **he's the ~ man for the job** es el hombre más indicado para el puesto; **it's ~, isn't it?** ¿es obvio, no?; **it's not ~ to me** para mí no está tan claro; **we must not be too ~ about it** en esto conviene ser algo astuto.

2 *n*: **to state the ~** afirmar lo obvio.

obviously ['ɒbvɪəslɪ] *adv* evidentemente, obviamente; **~!** ¡naturalmente!; **it's ~ the best** evidentemente es el mejor; **he was not ~ drunk** no estaba visiblemente borracho.

OC *n abbr of* **Officer Commanding** jefe *m*.

o/c *abbr of* **overcharge.**

ocarina [,ɒkə'ri:nə] *n* ocarina *f*.

OCAS *n abbr of* **Organization of Central American States** Organización *f* de Estados Centroamericanos, ODECA *f*.

occasion [ə'keɪʒən] **1** *n* (**a**) (*suitable juncture*) coyuntura *f*; oportunidad *f*, ocasión *f*; **he was awaiting a suitable ~** aguardaba una coyuntura favorable, esperaba un momento propicio; **to take ~ to + infin** aprovechar la oportunidad de + *infin*.

(**b**) (*reason*) razón *f*, motivo *m*; **there is no ~ for alarm** no hay motivo para inquietarse, no hay por qué inquietarse; **there was no ~ for it** no había necesidad de eso; **to give ~ for scandal** provocar el escándalo; **he has given me no ~ for saying so** no me ha dado ocasión para decirlo; **I had ~ to reprimand him** tuve que reprenderle; **if you have ~ to use it** si te ves en el caso de usarlo.

(**c**) **to go about one's lawful ~s** ocuparse en sus negocios legítimos.

(**d**) (*time, occurrence*) ocasión *f*, vez *f*; **on the ~ of the cup final** cuando la final de copa; **on the ~ of his retirement** con motivo de su jubilación, para festejar su jubilación, para conmemorar su jubilación; **on ~** de vez en cuando; **on one ~** una vez; **on other ~s** otras veces; **on just such an ~** otra vez exactamente igual que ésta; **on that ~** esa vez, en aquella ocasión; **as the ~ requires** según el caso; **if the ~ arises** si se da el caso; **should the ~ so demand** si lo exigen las circunstancias; **to leave sth for another ~** dejar algo para otra vez; **to rise to the ~** ponerse a la altura de las circunstancias.

(**e**) (*event, function*) función *f*, acontecimiento *m*; **this is an important ~** esto es un acontecimiento importante; **it will be a big ~** será una función impresionante; **the three big ~s of the university year** las tres grandes funciones del año universitario; **it was quite an ~** realmente fue un acontecimiento; **music written for the ~** música *f* compuesta para la función.

2 *vt* ocasionar, causar.

occasional [ə'keɪʒənl] *adj* (**a**) **an ~ event** algo que pasa de vez en cuando, un acontecimiento poco frecuente; **~ paper** monografía *f*; **~ table** mesita *f*; **~ worker** (*US*) jornalero *m* temporero; **we have an ~ visitor** recibimos de vez en cuando una visita; **we're just ~ visitors** estamos de visita nada más.

(**b**) *music etc* de circunstancia, compuesto para una función determinada.

occasionally [ə'keɪʒnəlɪ] *adv* de vez en cuando, a veces, cada cuando (*LAm*); **very ~** muy de tarde en tarde.

occident ['ɒksɪdənt] *n* occidente *m*.

occidental [,ɒksɪ'dentl] *adj* occidental.

occipital [ɒk'sɪpɪtəl] *adj* occipital.

occiput ['ɒksɪpʌt] *n* occipucio *m*.

occlude [ɒ'klu:d] *vt* obstruir.

occluded [ɒ'klu:dɪd] *adj*: **~ front** oclusión *f*.

occlusion [ɒ'klu:ʒən] *n* oclusión *f*.

occlusive [ɒ'klu:sɪv] **1** *adj* oclusivo. **2** *n* oclusiva *f*.

occult [ɒ'kʌlt] **1** *adj reason etc* oculto, misterioso; (*mystic*) oculto, sobrenatural, mágico.

2 *n*: **the ~** lo oculto, lo sobrenatural; **to study the ~** dedicarse al ocultismo, estudiar las ciencias ocultas.

occultism ['ɒkəltɪzəm] *n* ocultismo *m*.

occultist ['ɒkəltɪst] *n* ocultista *mf*.

occupancy ['ɒkjʊpənsɪ] *n* ocupación *f*, tenencia *f*.

occupant ['ɒkjʊpənt] *n* (*of boat, car etc*) ocupante *mf*; pasajero *m*, -a *f*; (*of house*) habitante *mf*, inquilino *m*, -a *f*; **all the ~s were killed** perecieron todos los viajeros; **the ~s could not be reached** resultó imposible socorrer a los que iban dentro.

occupation [,ɒkjʊ'peɪʃən] *n* (**a**) (*of house etc*) tenencia *f*, inquilinato *m*; (*of country*) ocupación *f*; (*of office*) tenencia *f*; **a house unfit for ~** una casa inhabitable; **to be in ~ of** ocupar; **we found them already in ~** encontramos que ya se habían instalado allí.

(**b**) (*act of taking*) ocupación *f*; **the ~ of Paris in 1940** la ocupación de París en 1940; **the house is ready for ~** la casa está lista para su ocupación.

(**c**) (*work*) trabajo *m*; (*employment*) empleo *m*; oficio *m*; (*calling*) oficio *m*; profesión *f*; (*pastime*) pasatiempo *m*; **a harmless enough ~** un pasatiempo inocente; **a tailor by ~** de oficio sastre; **what is he by ~?, what is his ~?** ¿cuál es su profesión?; **it gives ~ to 50 men** emplea a 50 hombres, da trabajo a 50 hombres; **this will give some ~ to your mind** esto le servirá para entretener la inteligencia.

occupational [,ɒkjʊ'peɪʃənl] *adj* de oficio, relativo al oficio, profesional, laboral; ocupacional; **~ accident** accidente *m* laboral; **~ disease** enfermedad *f* profesional; **~ guidance** orientación *f* profesional; **~ hazard, ~ risk** (*hum*) gajes *mpl* del oficio; **~ pension plan, ~ pension scheme** plan *m* profesional de jubilación; **~ therapy** terapia *f* laboral, terapia *f* ocupacional; **~ training** formación *f* ocupacional.

occupier ['ɒkjʊpaɪəʳ] *n* inquilino *m*, -a *f*.

occupy ['ɒkjʊpaɪ] *vt* ocupar (*also Mil*); *house* habitar, vivir en; *time* emplear, pasar; *attention, mind* entretener; **in occupied France** en la Francia ocupada (por los alemanes); **to be occupied in** (*or* **with**) ocuparse de (*or* en, con); **to be occupied** (*US Telec*) estar comunicando; **he is occupied in research** se dedica a la investigación; **he is very occupied at the moment** de momento está muy ocupado.

occur [ə'kɜ:ʳ] *vi* (**a**) (*happen*) ocurrir, suceder, acontecer, pasar; **to ~ again** volver a suceder, producirse de nuevo; **if a vacancy ~s** si se produce una vacante; **if the opportunity ~s** si se presenta la oportunidad; **don't let it ever ~ again** y que esto no vuelva a ocurrir nunca.

(**b**) (*be found*) encontrarse, existir; **the plant ~s all over Spain** la planta existe en todas partes en España.

(**c**) (*come to mind*) **it ~s to me that ...** se me ocurre que ...; **it ~red to me to ask him** se me ocurrió preguntárselo; **such an idea would never have ~red to her** tal idea no se le hubiera ocurrido nunca.

occurrence [ə'kʌrəns] *n* (**a**) (*happening*) acontecimiento *m*; incidente *m*; caso *m*; **a common ~** un caso frecuente; **an everyday ~** un suceso de todos los días; **that is a common**

~ eso sucede a menudo, ese caso se da con frecuencia.

(**b**) (*existence*) existencia *f*; aparición *f*; **its ~ in the south is well known** se sabe que existe en el sur, es conocida su existencia en el sur; **its ~ here is unexpected** su aparición aquí es inesperada.

ocean [ˈəʊʃən] **1** *n* océano *m*; **~s of** (*fig*) la mar de. **2** *attr*: **~ bed** lecho *m* marino; **~ cruise** crucero *m*; **~ liner** transatlántico *m*.

oceanarium [ˌəʊʃəˈnɛərɪəm] *n* oceanario *m*.

ocean-going [ˈəʊʃənˌgəʊɪŋ] *adj* de alta mar, de altura.

Oceania [ˌəʊʃɪˈeɪnɪə] *n* Oceanía *f*.

oceanic [ˌəʊʃɪˈænɪk] *adj* oceánico.

oceanographer [ˌəʊʃəˈnɒgrəfəʳ] *n* oceanógrafo *m*, -a *f*.

oceanographic [ˌəʊʃənɒˈgræfɪk] *adj* oceanográfico.

oceanography [ˌəʊʃəˈnɒgrəfɪ] *n* oceanografía *f*.

ocelot [ˈəʊsɪlɒt] *n* ocelote *m*.

ochre, (*US*) **ocher** [ˈəʊkəʳ] **1** *n* ocre *m*. **2** *attr*: **red ~** ocre *m* rojo, almagre *m*; **yellow ~** ocre *m* amarillo.

ochreous [ˈəʊkrɪəs] *adj* de color ocre.

o'clock [əˈklɒk] **1** *adv*: **it is 1 ~** es la una; **it is 3 ~** son las 3; **at 9 ~** a las 9; **at exactly 9 ~** a las 9 en punto; **it is just after 2 ~** son un poco más de las 2; **it is nearly 8 ~** son casi las 8. **2** *as n*: *eg* **the six ~** (*train etc*) el tren (*etc*) de las seis.

OCR *n* (**a**) *abbr of* **optical character reader** lector *m* óptico de caracteres, LOC *m*. (**b**) *abbr of* **optical character recognition** reconocimiento *m* óptico de caracteres, ROC *m*.

Oct. *abbr of* **October** octubre *m*, oct.

octagon [ˈɒktəgən] *n* octágono *m*.

octagonal [ɒkˈtægənl] *adj* octagonal.

octahedron [ˈɒktəˈhiːdrən] *n* octaedro *m*.

octal [ˈɒktəl] **1** *adj* octal. **2** *n* octal *m*.

octane [ˈɒkteɪn] *n* octano *m*; **~ number** grado *m* octánico.

octave [ˈɒktɪv] *n* (*Mus, Poet*) octava *f*.

Octavian [ɒkˈteɪvɪən] *nm* Octavio.

octavo [ɒkˈteɪvəʊ] **1** *adj* en octavo. **2** *n* libro *m* en octavo.

octet(te) [ɒkˈtet] *n* octeto *m*.

October [ɒkˈtəʊbəʳ] *n* octubre *m*.

octogenarian [ˌɒktəʊdʒɪˈnɛərɪən] **1** *adj* octagenario. **2** *n* octagenario *m*, -a *f*.

octopus [ˈɒktəpəs] *n* pulpo *m*.

octosyllabic [ˈɒktəʊsɪˈlæbɪk] *adj* octosílabo.

octosyllable [ˈɒktəʊˈsɪləbl] *n* octosílabo *m*.

ocular [ˈɒkjʊləʳ] *adj* ocular.

oculist [ˈɒkjʊlɪst] *n* oculista *mf*.

OD, O/D (**a**) *adv abbr of* **on demand** a solicitud. (**b**) *n abbr of* **overdraft.** (**c**) *adj abbr of* **overdrawn** en descubierto.

OD* [əʊˈdiː] (*US*) *abbr of* **overdose 1** *n* sobredosis *f*. **2** *vi* administrarse una sobredosis de droga.

odalisk, odalisque [ˈəʊdəlɪsk] *n* odalisca *f*.

odd [ɒd] *adj* (**a**) (*extra, left over*) sobrante, de más; (*isolated*) suelto; (*unpaired*) sin pareja, desparejado, desparejo, de non; **the ~ dollar** el dólar que sobra, el dólar que hace falta; **the team and the ~ supporter** el equipo y algún hincha; **to be ~ man out** (*surplus*) estar de más, sobrar; (*left out*) quedar excluido; (*different*) ser distinto, diferenciarse de los demás.

(**b**) (*Math*) impar; **~ or even** par o impar.

(**c**) (*and a few more*) **30 ~** treinta y pico, treinta y tantos; **£20 ~** unas 20 libras.

(**d**) (*casual*) **~ job** tarea *f* suelta, chapuza; **~ job man** hombre que hace de todo; **he has done the ~ job for us** ha trabajado para nosotros de vez en cuando; **~ lot** (*St Ex*) cantidad *f* irregular (y normalmente pequeña) de acciones (*o* valores); **at ~ times** de vez en cuando; **he has written the ~ article** ha escrito algún que otro artículo.

(**e**) (*strange*) raro, extraño, singular; misterioso; estrambótico; **how ~!, very ~!, most ~!** ¡qué raro!; **the ~ thing about it is ...** lo raro es que ...; **he's very ~ in his ways** tiene manías; **he's got rather ~ lately** recientemente se ha vuelto algo raro.

oddball* [ˈɒdbɔːl] (*esp US*) **1** *adj* raro, excéntrico. **2** *n* bicho *m* raro, excéntrico *m*.

oddbod* [ˈɒdˌbɒd] *n* bicho *m* raro, excéntrico *m*.

oddity [ˈɒdɪtɪ] *n* (**a**) (*strangeness*) rareza *f*, singularidad *f*, excentricidad *f*. (**b**) (*peculiar trait*) rareza *f*, manía *f*; (*odd person*) genio *m* raro, original *m*; (*odd thing*) cosa *f* rara; **he has his oddities** tiene sus manías; **one of the oddities of the situation** uno de los aspectos raros que tiene la situación.

odd-looking [ˈɒdˌlʊkɪŋ] *adj* de aspecto singular.

oddly [ˈɒdlɪ] singularmente, extrañamente; **they are ~ similar** tienen un extraño parecido; **~ attractive** extrañamente atractivo; **~ enough, ...** aunque parezca mentira, ...; **he is behaving most ~** se está comportando de una manera muy rara.

oddment [ˈɒdmənt] *n* artículo *m* suelto, artículo *m* que sobra; (*pej*) bagatela *f*, baratija *f*; (*Brit Comm*) retal *m*.

oddness [ˈɒdnɪs] *n* rareza *f*, singularidad *f*.

odds [ɒdz] *npl* (**a**) (*difference*) **what's the ~?** ¿qué importa?, ¿qué más da?; **it makes no ~** no importa, lo mismo da; **it makes no ~ to me** me es igual.

(**b**) (*variance, strife*) **to be at ~** estar reñidos (*over* por causa de), estar de punta; **to be at ~ with sb** estar reñido con uno (*about, over* con motivo de); estar incomodado con uno; **to set 2 people at ~** enemistar a 2 personas, hacer que riñan 2 personas.

(**c**) (*balance of advantage*) ventaja *f*, superioridad *f*; **the ~ are in his favour** tiene muchas probabilidades (de ganar); **the ~ are too great** nuestra desventaja es insuperable; los peligros son demasiado grandes; **to fight against overwhelming ~** luchar contra fuerzas abrumadoras; **to succeed against all the ~** triunfar a pesar de todos los factores en contra.

(**d**) (*equalizing allowance*) ventaja *f*; (*in betting*) puntos *mpl* de ventaja; **the ~ on the horse are 5 to 1** los puntos de ventaja del caballo son de 5 a 1; **to give ~ of 3 to 1** ofrecer 3 puntos de ventaja a 1; **what ~ will you give me?** ¿cuánta ventaja me da?; **to shout the ~*** (*fig*) vocear, gritar mucho; **to pay over the ~** (*Brit*) pagar en demasía.

(**e**) (*chances*) probabilidades *fpl*; **the ~ are that ...** lo más probable es que + *subj*; **the ~ are against it** es poco probable.

(**f**) **~ and ends** (*of cloth etc*) retazos *mpl*, materiales *mpl* sobrantes; (*trinkets*) baratijas *fpl*, chucherías *fpl*; (*things in disorder*) cosas *fpl* sin arreglar; (*possessions*) chismes *mpl*; **there were ~ and ends of machinery** había piezas sueltas de máquinas.

(**g**) (‡) **all the ~ and sods** todo quisque*, todo hijo de vecina*.

odds-on [ˈɒdzˈɒn] *adj*: **~ favourite** caballo *m* favorito, caballo *m* con puntos de ventaja; **he's ~ favourite for the job** él tiene las mejores posibilidades de ganar el puesto; **it's ~ he won't come** lo más probable es que no venga.

odd-sounding [ˈɒdˌsaʊndɪŋ] *adj name etc* raro, de sonido extraño.

ode [əʊd] *n* oda *f*.

odious [ˈəʊdɪəs] *adj* odioso, detestable.

odiously [ˈəʊdɪəslɪ] *adv* odiosamente, detestablemente.

odium [ˈəʊdɪəm] *n* odio *m*; oprobio *m*; **to bring ~ on sb** hacer que uno sea odiado; **to incur the ~ of having** + *ptp* suscitar el odio de la gente por haber + *ptp*.

odometer [ɒˈdɒmɪtəʳ] *n* (*US*) cuentakilómetros *m*.

odontologist [ˌɒdɒnˈtɒlədʒɪst] *n* odontólogo *m*, -a *f*.

odontology [ˌɒdɒnˈtɒlədʒɪ] *n* odontología *f*.

odor [ˈəʊdəʳ] *n* (*US*) = **odour.**

odoriferous [ˌəʊdəˈrɪfərəs] *adj* odorífero.

odorless [ˈəʊdəlɪs] *adj* (*US*) = **odourless.**

odorous [ˈəʊdərəs] *adj* oloroso.

odour, (*US*) **odor** [ˈəʊdəʳ] *n* olor *m* (*of* a); fragancia *f*, perfume *m*; (*fig*) sospecha *f*; **~ of sanctity** olor *m* de santidad; **bad ~** mal olor *m*; **to be in bad ~** tener mala fama, estar bajo sospecha; **to be in bad ~ with sb** llevarse mal con uno.

odourless, (*US*) **odorless** [ˈəʊdəlɪs] *adj* inodoro.

Odysseus [əˈdɪsjuːs] *nm* Odiseo.

Odyssey [ˈɒdɪsɪ] *n* Odisea *f*; **o~** (*fig*) odisea *f*.

OE *n* (*Ling*) *abbr of* **Old English** inglés *m* antiguo.

OECD *n abbr of* **Organization for Economic Cooperation and Development** Organización *f* de Cooperación y Desarrollo Económico, OCDE *f*.

oecumenical, ecumenical [ˌiːkjuːˈmenɪkəl] *adj* ecuménico.

OED *n abbr of* **Oxford English Dictionary.**

oedema, edema [ɪˈdiːmə] *n* edema *m*.

Oedipus [ˈiːdɪpəs] **1** *nm* Edipo. **2** *attr*: **~ complex** complejo *m* de Edipo.

oenologist [iːˈnɒlədʒɪst] *n* enólogo *m*, -a *f*.

oenology [iːˈnɒlədʒɪ] *n* enología *f*.

oenophile [ˈiːnəʊfaɪl] *n* enófilo *m*, -a *f*.

o'er [ˈəʊəʳ] (*poet*) = **over.**

oesophagus, (*US*) **esophagus** [iːˈsɒfəgəs] *n* esófago *m*.

oestrogen, (*US*) **estrogen** [ˈiːstrəʊdʒən] *n* estrógeno *m*.

oestrous, (*US*) **estrous** [ˈiːstrəs] *adj* en celo; **~ cycle** ciclo *m* de celo.

oestrus, (*US*) **estrus** [ˈiːstrəs] *n* estro *m*.

œuvre [œvrə] *n* obra *f*.

of [ɒv,əv] *prep* (**a**) (*possession*) de; **the pen ~ my aunt** la pluma de mi tía; **a friend ~ mine** un amigo mío; **love ~**

country el amor a la patria; **it's no business ~ yours** aquí no te metas, no tienes que ver con esto.

(**b**) (*partitive etc*) de; **how much ~ this do you want?** ¿cuánto quieres de esto?; **there were 4 ~ us** éramos 4; **all ~ them** todos ellos; **~ the 12 two were bad** de los 12, dos estaban pasados; **most ~ all** más que nada; **you ~ all people ought to know** debieras saberlo más que nadie; **the best ~ friends** el mejor amigo; **they became the best ~ friends** se hicieron muy amigos; **the book ~ books** el libro de los libros; **king ~ kings** rey de reyes.

(**c**) (*descriptive genitive*) **the city ~ Burgos** la ciudad de Burgos; **a boy ~ 8** un muchacho de 8 años; **cakes ~ her making** pasteles que ella había hecho; **by the name ~ Green** llamado Green; **bright ~ eye** de ojos claros; **hard ~ heart** duro de corazón; **that idiot ~ a minister** ese idiota de ministro; **a real palace ~ a house** una casa que es un verdadero palacio.

(**d**) (*origin, cause etc*) **to buy sth ~ sb** comprar algo a uno; **'~ all chemists'** 'de venta en todas las farmacias'; **~ necessity** por necesidad, forzosamente; **~ itself** de por sí; **to die ~ a disease** morir de una enfermedad.

(**e**) (*material*) de; **made ~ metal** hecho de metal.

(**f**) (*agent*) **beloved ~ all** querido de todos; **it was very harsh ~ him to** + *infin* ha sido durísimo en + *infin*; **it is kind ~ you** eres muy amable.

(**g**) (*with certain verbs*) **to dream ~ sth** soñar con algo; **to judge ~ sth** juzgar algo, opinar sobre algo; **to smell ~ sth** oler a algo; **he was robbed ~ his watch** le robaron el reloj, se le robó el reloj.

(**h**) (*****) **he died ~ a Friday** murió un viernes; **it was fine ~ a morning** por la mañana hacía buen tiempo.

(**i**) (*with hours: US*) **it is 10 (minutes) ~ 4** son las 4 menos 10.

off [ɒf] **1** *adv* (**a**) (*away*) **a place 2 miles ~** un lugar a 2 millas (de distancia); **it landed not 50 metres ~** cayó a menos de 50 metros de nosotros; **noises ~** ruidos *mpl* de fondo, (*Theat*) efectos *mpl* sonoros; **a voice ~** voz de fondo, (*Cine*) voz en off.

(**b**) (*of removal*) **with his hat ~** sin el sombrero puesto, sombrero en mano; **with his shoes ~** sin zapatos, descalzo; **hats ~!** ¡descúbranse!; **~ with those wet socks!** ¡quítate esos calcetines mojados!; **~ with his head!** ¡que le corten la cabeza!; **hands ~!** ¡fuera las manos!; ¡no tocar!; **the lid is ~** la tapa está quitada; **~ with you!** ¡fuera de aquí!, (*tenderly*) ¡vete ya!; **~ we go!** ¡vamos!; **'10% ~'** 'descuento de 10 por cien'; **I'll give you 5% ~** te hago un descuento de 5 por cien; **to have a day ~** tomarse un día de asueto.

(**c**) **~ and on** de vez en cuando, a ratos, a intervalos; ya bien ya mal; **right ~, straight ~** sin parar, sin interrupción; **3 days straight ~** 3 días seguidos.

2 *adv* (*with* to be) (**a**) (*of distance, time*) **it's some way ~** está algo lejos; **the game is 3 days ~** faltan 3 días para el partido.

(**b**) (*depart*) **to be ~** irse; **I'm ~** me voy; **I must be ~** tengo que marcharme; **I'm ~ to Paris** voy a París, salgo para París; **she's ~ at 4** sale del trabajo a las 4; **be ~!** ¡fuera de aquí!, ¡lárgate!; **they're ~!** (*race etc*) ¡ya!; **he's ~ fishing every Sunday** todos los domingos sale a pescar, todos los domingos va de pesca.

(**c**) (*be absent*) **to be ~** estar fuera, no estar; estar libre, no trabajar; tener día franco; **to be ~ sick** estar de baja; **he's ~ fishing** ha ido a pescar; **she's ~ on Tuesdays** los martes no viene (a trabajar); **are you ~ this weekend?** ¿vas a estar fuera este fin de semana?; **salmon is ~** (*on menu*) no hay salmón ya, se acabó el salmón; **there are 2 buttons ~** faltan 2 botones; **the game is ~** se ha cancelado el partido; **sorry, but the party's ~** lo siento, pero no hay guateque; **their engagement is ~** han roto el noviazgo; **the talks are ~** se han cancelado las conversaciones.

(**d**) (*of switches etc*) **to be ~** estar en posición de desconectado; (*apparatus, radio, TV*) estar desenchufado, estar desconectado; (*light*) estar apagado; (*tap*) estar cerrado; (*Mech*) estar parado; (*water etc*) estar cortado; (*brake*) no estar puesto, estar quitado.

3 *adj* (**a**) (*be bad*) **to be ~** estar pasado; (*milk*) estar cortado; (*fig*) **it's a bit ~, isn't it?** esto no lo apruebo, ¿sabes?; **I thought his behaviour was rather ~** me pareció que su conducta era bastante censurable; **she's feeling rather ~** se siente algo mal.

(**b**) (*financial etc*) **to be well ~** estar acomodado, tener dinero; **he's better ~ where he is** está mejor allí donde está ahora; **we should be no better ~** no ganaríamos nada; **to be badly ~** andar mal de dinero; **to be badly ~ for potatoes** andar escaso de patatas, sufrir escasez de patatas; **how are you ~ for money?** ¿qué tal andas de dinero?; *V* **well-off, worse 2** *etc*.

(**c**) (*non*) **to have an ~ day** tener un día malo; **~ season** temporada *f* baja, estación *f* muerta; **in the ~ season** fuera de temporada; **in the ~ position** en posición de cerrado (*etc*); *V* **off-side.**

4 *prep* (**a**) de; **height ~ the ground** altura *f* del suelo, altura *f* sobre el suelo; **to fall ~ a table** caer de una mesa; **to fall ~ a cliff** caer por un precipicio; **to eat ~ a dish** comer en un plato; **to dine ~ fish** cenar pescado; **to allow 5% ~ the price** rebajar el precio en un 5 por cien.

(**b**) **a street ~ the square** una calle que sale de la plaza; **a house ~ the main road** una casa algo apartada de la carretera.

(**c**) **~ Portland Bill** a la altura de Portland Bill, frente a Portland Bill.

(**d**) **there are 2 buttons ~ my coat** le faltan 2 botones a mi chaqueta; **to be ~ one's food** no tener apetito; **he was ~ work for 3 weeks** durante 3 semanas no pudo trabajar; **to take 3 days ~ work** tomarse 3 días libres.

5 *n* (*****) comienzo *m*: (*Sport*) salida *f*; **at the ~** en la salida; **ready for (the) ~** listos para comenzar, (*Sport*) listos para salir.

offal ['ɒfəl] *n* asaduras *fpl*, menudencias *fpl*.

offbeat ['ɒf,biːt] *adj* excéntrico, insólito; inconformista, nada convencional.

off-centre, (*US*) **off-center** ['ɒf'sentəʳ] *adj*: **to be ~** estar descentrado.

off-chance ['ɒftʃɑːns] *n* posibilidad *f* remota; **we'll go on the ~** iremos por si acaso, iremos aunque hay poca posibilidad; **he bought it on the ~ that it would come in useful** lo compró pensando que tal vez resultaría útil algún día.

off-colour, (*US*) **off-color** ['ɒf'kʌləʳ] *adj fabric etc* descolorido, desteñido; (*Brit: ill*) indispuesto, (*of child*) pachucho; *joke etc* verde, subido de tono.

offcut ['ɒf,kʌt] *n* trozo *m*; **~s** restos *mpl*, sobras *fpl*.

offence, (*US*) **offense** [ə'fens] *n* (**a**) (*insult*) ofensa *f*; **no ~!, no ~ meant** sin ofender a Vd; **no ~ was intended, he intended no ~** no quería ofender a nadie; **to give ~** ofender; **to take ~** ofenderse (*at* por), resentirse (*at* de).

(**b**) (*crime*) delito *m*, crimen *m*, infracción *f* de la ley; (*moral*) transgresión *f*, pecado *m*; **first ~** primer delito *m*; **second ~** reincidencia *f*; **it is an ~ to** + *infin* la ley castiga a los que ...; **to commit an ~** cometer un delito.

offend [ə'fend] **1** *vt* ofender; **it ~s my sense of justice** ofende mi sentido de justicia; **to be ~ed** ofenderse (*at, by* por), tomarlo a mal; **he wasn't a bit ~ed** no se ofendió en lo más mínimo; **don't be ~ed** no te vayas a ofender, no lo tomes a mal; **he is easily ~ed** es algo picajoso; **to become ~ed** ofenderse.

2 *vi* ofender; (*criminally*) cometer una infracción (de la ley *etc*); **to ~ again** reincidir.

◆**offend against** *vt* pecar contra.

offender [ə'fendəʳ] *n* (**a**) (*insulter*) ofensor *m*, -ora *f*.

(**b**) (*criminal*) delincuente *mf*, culpable *mf*; (*against traffic code etc*) infractor *m*, -ora *f* (*against* de); **first ~** *V* **first.**

(**c**) (*moral*) transgresor *m*, -ora *f*, pecador *m*, -ora *f*.

offending [ə'fendɪŋ] *adj* delincuente, culpable; **the ~ words are ...** las palabras ofensivas son ...

offense [ə'fens] *n* (*US*) = **offence.**

offensive [ə'fensɪv] **1** *adj* (**a**) *warfare etc* ofensivo.

(**b**) (*insulting*) ofensivo, injurioso; (*disgusting*) repugnante; **don't be ~!** ¡hable con más educación!; **to be ~ to sb** ser grosero con uno, decir injurias a uno.

2 *n* ofensiva *f*; **to go over to the ~, to take the ~** tomar la ofensiva.

offensively [ə'fensɪvlɪ] *adv* injuriosamente; repugnantemente; groseramente.

offer ['ɒfəʳ] **1** *n* oferta *f*, ofrecimiento *m*; (*Comm*) oferta *f*; **~ of marriage** oferta *f* de matrimonio, petición *f* de mano; **~ of peace** ofrecimiento *m* de paz; **to be on ~** estar en oferta, ofrecerse; **it was on ~ at £400** se ofrecía a 400 libras; **to be under ~** estar en oferta; **to make an ~ for sth** hacer una oferta por algo, ofrecerse a comprar algo; **make me an ~!** ¡hágame una oferta!; **it's the best ~ I can make** no puedo ofrecer más.

2 *attr*: **~ price** precio *m* de oferta.

3 *vt* (**a**) *help, love, money, services etc* ofrecer; *opportunity, prospect etc* brindar, facilitar, deparar; **to ~ sth to sb** ofrecer algo a uno; **to ~ one's flank to the enemy** exponer su flanco al enemigo; **to ~ resistance** ofrecer (*or* oponer) resistencia (*to* a); **he ~ed no resistance** no se resistió; **the plan ~s us nothing new** el plan no nos ofrece nada nuevo; **the garden ~s a fine spectacle** el jardín se muestra espléndido.

(**b**) **to ~ to do sth** ofrecerse a hacer algo; **he ~ed to strike me** hizo ademán de pegarme, hizo como si fuera a pegarme.

(**c**) *comment, remark* hacer; **he ~ed no comment** no hizo comentario alguno; **I wish to ~ two comments** quiero hacer dos observaciones.

(**d**) *prayers*; *V* **offer up**.

4 *vi*: **if the opportunity ~s** si se me da la oportunidad, si se da el caso.

5 *vr*: **to ~ o.s. for a mission** ofrecerse a ir a una misión; **to ~ o.s. for a post** presentarse para un puesto.

◆**offer up** *vt prayers* rezar, ofrecer.

offering ['ɒfərɪŋ] *n* ofrecimiento *m*; (*Rel*) ofrenda *f*; (*gift*) regalo *m*, don *m*; (*sacrifice*) sacrificio *m*.

offertory ['ɒfətərɪ] *n* ofertorio *m*.

offertory box ['ɒfətərɪ,bɒks] *n* cepillo *m*.

offhand ['ɒf'hænd] **1** *adj* informal, brusco, descortés; poco ceremonioso; **to treat sb in an ~ manner** tratar a uno con bastante informalidad; **he was very ~ about it** lo discutió sin darle importancia.

2 *adv* de improviso, sin pensarlo; **~ I couldn't tell you** así de improviso no te lo puedo decir.

offhandedly ['ɒf'hændɪdlɪ] *adv* con informalidad, bruscamente, descortésmente; sin ceremonias, sin miramientos; **to treat sb ~** tratar a uno con bastante informalidad; **he said ~** dijo en tono brusco.

offhandedness ['ɒf'hændɪdnɪs] *n* informalidad *f*; brusquedad *f*; descortesía *f*.

office ['ɒfɪs] **1** *n* (**a**) (*place*) oficina *f*; (*room*) despacho *m*; (*lawyer's*) bufete *m*; (*as part of organization*) sección *f*, departamento *m*; (*ministry*) ministerio *m*; (*branch*) sucursal *f*; (*US*: *Med etc*) consultorio *m*; **O~ of Fair Trading** (*Brit*) *oficina de normas comerciales justas*.

(**b**) (*function*) oficio *m*; (*post*) cargo *m*; **it is my ~ to** + *infin* yo tengo el deber de + *infin*, me incumbe + *infin*; **to be in ~, to hold ~** (*person*) estar en funciones, desempeñar un cargo, (*govt*) estar en el poder; **he is in ~ for one year** ocupa el cargo durante un año; **to be out of ~** no estar en el poder; **to come into ~, to take ~** (*person*) asumir un cargo, (*govt*) entrar en el poder; **to leave ~** (*person*) dimitir un cargo, (*govt*) salir del poder; **to perform the ~ of sb** hacer las veces de uno.

(**c**) **good ~s** buenos oficios *mpl*; **to offer one's good ~s** ofrecer sus buenos oficios; **through the ~s of** gracias a la mediación de.

(**d**) **O~ for the Dead** (*Eccl*) oficio *m* de difuntos.

2 *attr work etc* de oficina; **~ automation** ofimática *f*, buromática *f*; **~ bearer** alto cargo *m*; **~ block** (*Brit*) bloque *m* de oficinas; **~ boy** chico *m* de los recados, ordenanza *m*, mandadero *m*; **~ building** edificio *m* de oficinas; **~ equipment, ~ furniture** muebles *m* de oficina, equipo *m* de oficina; **~ holder** funcionario *m*, -a *f*; **~ hours** (*Brit*) horas *fpl* de oficina, (*US*) horas *fpl* de consulta; **~ job** trabajo *m* de oficina; **~ manager** gerente *m*, jefe *m* de oficina; **~ party** fiesta *f* de oficina; **~ staff** personal *m* de oficina; **~ supplies** material *m* de oficina; **~ worker** oficinista *mf*.

officer ['ɒfɪsəʳ] **1** *n* (*Mil, Naut, Aer*) oficial *mf*; (*of society*) dignatario *m*, -a *f*; (*of local govt*) magistrado *m*, -a *f*; funcionario *m*, -a *f*; (*of company*) director *m*, -ora *f*; (*of police*) policía *m*, agente *mf* de policía; **~ of the day** oficial *mf* del día; **~ of the watch** oficial *m* de guardia; **the ~s of a company** los directores de una sociedad, la junta directiva de una sociedad; **an ~ and a gentleman** oficial y caballero; **'Yes, ~'** (*to policeman*) 'Sí, señor guardia'.

2 *vt* (*command*) mandar; (*staff*) proveer de oficiales; **to be well ~ed** tener buena oficialidad.

official [ə'fɪʃəl] **1** *adj* oficial; autorizado; *voice, style etc* ceremonioso, solemne; **in ~ circles** en círculos oficiales; **is that ~?** ¿se ha confirmado eso (oficialmente)?; **O~ Receiver** (*Brit Fin*) síndico *m*, depositario *m* judicial; **O~ Secrets Act** (*Brit*) *ley relativa a los secretos de Estado*; **~ strike** huelga *f* oficial.

2 *n* oficial *mf*, oficial *m* público, oficial *f* pública, funcionario *m*, -a *f*; **an ~ of the ministry** un funcionario del Ministerio.

officialdom [ə'fɪʃəldəm] *n* (*pej*) burocracia *f*.

officialese [ə,fɪʃə'li:z] *n* lenguaje *m* burocrático, estilo *m* oficial burocrático.

officially [ə'fɪʃəlɪ] *adv* oficialmente; de modo autorizado.

officiate [ə'fɪʃɪeɪt] *vi* oficiar (*as* de).

officious [ə'fɪʃəs] *adj* oficioso.

officiously [ə'fɪʃəslɪ] *adv* oficiosamente.

officiousness [ə'fɪʃəsnɪs] *n* oficiosidad *f*.

offing ['ɒfɪŋ] *n*: **to be in the ~** (*Naut*) estar a la vista, estar cerca, (*fig*) estar en perspectiva.

off-key [,ɒf'ki:] **1** *adj* desafinado. **2** *adv* desafinadamente.

off-licence ['ɒf,laɪsəns] *n* (*Brit*) *tienda donde se venden bebidas alcohólicas para llevar*.

off-limits ['ɒf'lɪmɪts] *adj, adv* fuera de los límites.

off-line ['ɒf'laɪn] **1** *adj* (*Comput*) off-line, fuera de línea; (*switched off*) desconectado. **2** *adv* fuera de línea, off-line.

offload ['ɒfləʊd] *vt* = **unload**.

off-peak [,ɒf'pi:k] *adj holiday* de temporada baja; *electricity* de banda económica.

off-piste ['ɒf'pi:st] **1** *adj* fuera de pista. **2** *adv* fuera de pista.

offprint ['ɒfprɪnt] *n* separata *f*, tirada *f* aparte.

off-putting ['ɒf,pʊtɪŋ] *adj* (*Brit*) poco atractivo, que quita las ganas; *person* difícil, poco amable; *reception* nada amistoso; **it's very ~ when ...** es desalentador cuando ..., es para desanimarse cuando ...

off ramp ['ɒfræmp] *n* (*US*) vía *f* de salida.

off sales ['ɒfseɪlz] *n* (*Brit*) tienda *f* de bebidas alcohólicas.

offset ['ɒfset] **1** *n* compensación *f*; (*Typ*) offset *m*; (*Hort*: *layer*) acodo *m*, (*bulb*) bulbo *m* reproductor; (*Archit*) retallo *m*.

2 *attr*: **~ lithography** = **~ printing**; **~ press** prensa *f* offset; **~ printing** impresión *f* en offset.

3 *vt* (*irr*: *V* **set**) compensar; contrarrestar, contrapesar; **to ~ A against B** contrapesar A y B; **higher prices will be ~ by wage increases** los aumentos de precios serán compensados por incrementos salariales.

offshoot ['ɒfʃu:t] *n* (*Bot*) renuevo *m*, vástago *m*; (*fig*) ramal *m* (*from* de), retoño *m*.

offshore ['ɒf'ʃɔ:ʳ] **1** *adv* a cierta distancia, a lo largo; (*oil parlance*) off-shore, costa afuera. **2** *adj breeze* terral, que sopla de tierra; *island* a poca distancia de la costa; **~ exploration** exploración *f* costa afuera; **~ fishing** pesca *f* de bajura; **~ investments** inversiones *fpl* off-shore; **~ oil** petróleo *m* de costa afuera; **~ oilfield** campo *m* petrolífero submarino.

offside ['ɒf'saɪd] **1** *adv*: **to be ~** estar fuera de juego; **the goal was disallowed for ~** el gol fue anulado por fuera de banda (de un jugador).

2 *adj* (**a**) **~ rule** regla *f* de fuera de juego; **~ trap** trampa *f* de fuera de juego.

(**b**) (*Aut etc*) (*Brit*) derecho, (*most other countries*) izquierdo.

3 *interj* ¡orsay!, ¡offside!

4 *n* (*Aut etc*) (*Brit*) lado *m* derecho, (*most other countries*) lado *m* izquierdo.

offspring ['ɒfsprɪŋ] *n* (*sing*) vástago *m*, descendiente *mf*; (*pl*) descendencia *f*, hijos *mpl*, prole *f*; **to die without ~** morir sin dejar descendencia.

offstage ['ɒf'steɪdʒ] **1** *adv* entre bastidores. **2** *adj* de entre bastidores.

off-the-cuff [,ɒfðə'kʌf] **1** *adj remark* dicho sin pensar, espontáneo; *speech* improvisado. **2** *adv* de improviso; *V also* **cuff**[2].

off-the-job ['ɒfðə'dʒɒb] *adj*: **~ training** formación *f* fuera del trabajo.

off-the-peg ['ɒfðə'peg] (*Brit*) *adj*, **off-the-rack** ['ɒfðə'ræk] (*US*) *adj* confeccionado, de percha.

off-the-record [,ɒfðə'rekəd] *adj* no oficial, extraoficial; confidencial.

off-the-wall* [,ɒfðə'wɔ:l] *adj idea etc* nuevo, inesperado; hecho de improviso; espontáneo.

off-white ['ɒf'waɪt] *adj* blancuzco, color hueso.

OFT *n* (*Brit*) *abbr of* **Office of Fair Trading**.

oft [ɒft] *adv* (*poet*) = **often**; **many a time and ~** repetidas veces.

often ['ɒfən] *adv* muchas veces, mucho, a menudo, con frecuencia; **very ~** muchísimas veces, repetidas veces, muy a menudo; **not ~** pocas veces; **how ~?** ¿cuántas veces?; **so ~** tantas veces; **as ~ as** tantas veces como, siempre que; **as ~ as not, more ~ than not** las más veces; **every so ~** (*time*) cada cierto tiempo, (*distance, spacing*) cada cierta distancia; **it is not ~ that ...** no es frecuente que ...; no es corriente que ...; **it cannot be said too ~ that ...** nunca huelga repetir que ...

oft-times ['ɒftaɪmz] *adv* (*liter*) a menudo.

ogival [əʊ'dʒaɪvəl] *adj* ojival.

ogive ['əʊdʒaɪv] *n* ojiva *f*.

ogle ['əʊgl] *vt* echar miradas amorosas (*or* incitantes) a, comerse con los ojos.

O-grade ['əʊgreɪd] *n* (*Scot Scol*) *abbr of* **Ordinary grade**; *V* **ordinary 1**(**b**).

ogre ['əʊgəʳ] *n* ogro *m*.

OH (*US Post*) *abbr of* **Ohio.**

oh [əʊ] *interj* (**a**) (*vocative*) ~ **king!** ¡oh rey!

(**b**) (*pain*) ¡ay!

(**c**) (*preceding questions and excls*) ~ **really?** ¿de veras?; ~ **is he?** ¿en serio?; ~ **what a surprise!** ¡qué sorpresa!; ~ **yes?** ¿ah sí?; ~ **no you don't!** ¡eso no!; ~ **for a horse!** ¡quién tuviera un caballo!; ~ **to be in Splotz!** ¡ojalá estuviera en Splotz!

ohm [əʊm] *n* ohmio *m*, ohm *m*.

OHMS (*Brit*) *abbr of* **On Her** (**His**) **Majesty's Service.**

oik‡ [ɔɪk] *n* palurdo *m*, patán *m*.

oil [ɔɪl] **1** *n* (*in most senses*) aceite *m*, (*Geol, as mineral*) petróleo *m*; (*Art*) óleo *m*; (*holy* ~) crisma *f*, santo óleo *m*; **an ~ by Rembrandt** un óleo de Rembrandt; **to burn the midnight** ~ quemarse las cejas; **to check the** ~ (*Aut etc*) revisar el nivel del aceite; **to paint in ~s** pintar al óleo; **to pour ~ on troubled waters** tratar de calmar la tempestad (*or* las pasiones *etc*); **to strike** ~ encontrar un pozo de petróleo, (*fig*) encontrar un filón, enriquecerse de súbito.

2 *attr*: ~ **deposits** yacimientos *mpl* de petróleo; ~ **industry** industria *f* del petróleo, industria *f* petrolera; ~ **pipeline** oleoducto *m*; ~ **pollution** contaminación *f* de petróleo; ~ **pressure** presión *f* del aceite; ~ **spill** (*act*) fuga *f* de petróleo, (*slick*) marea *f* negra; ~ **terminal** terminal *f* petrolífera.

3 *vt* lubricar, lubrificar, engrasar; **to be well ~ed*** ir a la vela*.

oil-based ['ɔɪlbeɪst] *adj*: ~ **product** producto *m* derivado del petróleo.

oil-burning ['ɔɪl,bɜːnɪŋ] *adj* (alimentado) al petróleo, de petróleo.

oilcake ['ɔɪlkeɪk] *n* torta *f* de borujo, torta *f* de linaza.

oilcan ['ɔɪlkæn] *n* aceitera *f*.

oil-change ['ɔɪl,tʃeɪndʒ] *n* cambio *m* de aceite.

oilcloth ['ɔɪlklɒθ] *n* hule *m*, encerado *m*.

oildrum ['ɔɪldrʌm] *n* bidón *m* de aceite.

oilfield ['ɔɪlfiːld] *n* yacimiento *m* petrolífero.

oil-filter ['ɔɪl,fɪltəʳ] *n* filtro *m* de aceite.

oil-fired ['ɔɪlfaɪəd] *adj* (alimentado) al petróleo; ~ **central heating** calefacción *f* central al petróleo; ~ **power-station** central *f* térmica de fuel.

oil-gauge ['ɔɪlgeɪdʒ] *n* manómetro *m* de aceite; indicador *m* de nivel del aceite.

oiliness ['ɔɪlɪnɪs] *n* (**a**) lo aceitoso, oleaginosidad *f*; lo grasiento. (**b**) (*fig*) zalamería *f*.

oil-lamp ['ɔɪllæmp] *n* velón *m*, quinqué *m*, candil *m*.

oil-level ['ɔɪllevl] *n* nivel *m* del aceite.

oilman ['ɔɪlmæn] *n*, *pl* **oilmen** ['ɔɪlmen] petrolero *m*; magnate *m* del petróleo.

oil-painting ['ɔɪl,peɪntɪŋ] *n* pintura *f* al óleo; **she's no ~*** no es tan hermosa que digamos.

oilpan ['ɔɪlpæn] *n* (*US Aut*) cárter *m*.

oil-refinery ['ɔɪlrɪ,faɪnərɪ] *n* refinería *f* de petróleo.

oil-rig ['ɔɪlrɪg] *n* torre *f* de perforación; (*Naut*) plataforma *f* de perforación submarina.

oilskin ['ɔɪlskɪn] *n* hule *m*, encerado *m*; **~s** (*Brit*) traje *m* de encerado, chubasquero *m*, ahulado *m* (*Mex*).

oil-slick ['ɔɪlslɪk] *n* (*large*) marea *f* negra; (*small*) mancha *f* de petróleo, capa *f* de petróleo (en el agua).

oil-stove ['ɔɪlstəʊv] *n* (*cooking*) cocina *f* de petróleo; (*heating*) estufa *f* de petróleo.

oil-tanker ['ɔɪltæŋkəʳ] *n* petrolero *m*.

oilwell ['ɔɪlwel] *n* pozo *m* de petróleo.

oily ['ɔɪlɪ] *adj* (**a**) *liquid etc* aceitoso, oleaginoso; *meal* grasiento, grasoso (*LAm*). (**b**) *person* zalamero, empalagoso.

oink [ɔɪŋk] *vi* gruñir.

ointment ['ɔɪntmənt] *n* pomada *f*, ungüento *m*.

OJT *n* (*US*) *abbr of* **on-the-job training** aprendizaje *m* en el trabajo.

OK (*US Post*) *abbr of* **Oklahoma.**

O.K.* ['əʊ'keɪ] **1** *interj* (*all right*) ¡está bien!; (*yes*) ¡sí!; (*understood*) ¡comprendo!; (*I agree*) ¡vale!; **I'm coming too, ~?** yo vengo también, ¿vale?

2 *adj* (*agreed*) aprobado; (*satisfactory*) satisfactorio; **it's ~ with me** lo apruebo, estoy de acuerdo; **is it ~ with you if ...?** ¿te importa que ... + *subj*?, ¿me permites + *infin* ...?; **I'm ~, thanks** estoy bien, gracias; **that may have been ~ last year** eso puede haber estado bien el año pasado; ~ **it's difficult but ~ ...** estoy de acuerdo que es difícil pero ...; **the ~ hair-do of 1999** el peinado elegante de 1999, el peinado que está de moda en 1999.

3 *adv*: **he's doing ~** las cosas le van bien.

4 *n* visto *m* bueno; **to give sth one's ~** dar el visto bueno a algo, aprobar algo.

5 *vt* dar el visto bueno a, aprobar.

okapi [əʊ'kɑːpɪ] *n* okapi *m*.

okay* [əʊ'keɪ] = **O.K.***

okey-doke(y)‡ [,əʊkɪ'dəʊk(ɪ)] *excl* de acuerdo, vale.

Okla. (*US*) *abbr of* **Oklahoma.**

okra ['əʊkrə] *n* kimbombó *m*.

old [əʊld] **1** *adj* (**a**) (*person: aged*) viejo; anciano; **an ~ man** un viejo, un anciano; **an ~ woman** una vieja, una anciana; ~ **and young** grandes y pequeños; ~ **Peter** Pedro el viejo; ~ **Mrs Brown** la vieja señora de Brown; **he's a good ~ horse** es un valiente caballo (aunque bastante viejo ya); **to grow ~** envejecerse; **to live to be ~** llegar a una edad avanzada; **if I live to be that ~** si llego a esa edad.

(**b**) (*ancient*) *thing* viejo; *clothes etc* viejo; usado, gastado; *bread* duro; *wine* añejo; **it's too ~ to be any use** es demasiado viejo para servir.

(**c**) (*with expression of years: person*) **how ~ are you?** ¿cuántos años tienes?, ¿qué edad tienes?; **I am 7 years ~** tengo 7 años; **she's 3 years ~ today** hoy cumple 3 años; **she is ~er than I** tiene más años que yo, es más vieja que yo; **she is the ~est** es la mayor; **to be 4 years ~er than sb** tener 4 años más que uno; **she's ~ enough to go alone** tiene bastante edad para ir sola; **he's ~ enough to know his own mind** tiene bastante edad para saber lo que quiere; **he's ~ enough to know better** a su edad debe portarse mejor; **he's ~ enough to be her father** tiene tanta edad como para ser su padre.

(**d**) (*with expression of years: thing*) **the building is 300 years ~** el edificio tiene 300 años (de construido); **the company is a century ~** la sociedad existe desde hace un siglo, la sociedad se fundó hace un siglo.

(**e**) (*old-established, long-standing*) viejo, antiguo; **an ~ friend of mine** un viejo amigo mío; **that's as ~ as the hills** eso es de tiempos de Maricastaña, eso es tan viejo como el mundo.

(**f**) (*former*) antiguo; **an ~ boy of the school** (*Brit*) un antiguo alumno (*or* ex alumno) del colegio; **my ~ school** mi antiguo colegio; ~ **school tie** (*Brit*) corbata *f* del colegio; (*fig*) amiguismo* *m*, nepotismo *m* escolar; **in the ~ days** antaño, en el pasado; **O~ French** antiguo francés *m*.

(**g**) (*affectionate*) **the ~ country** la patria, (mi *etc*) país *m* natal; **O~ Glory** (*US*) bandera *f* de EE.UU.; ~ **Lucas** el tío Lucas; **the ~ man*** el jefe, el patrón; **my ~ man*** el pariente*, **my ~ woman*** la parienta*; **I say, ~ man*** oye, chico; **any ~ thing does for me** me contento con cualquier cosa; **any ~ thing you like** lo que quieras; **it's not just any ~ painting, it's a Zurburán** no es un cuadro cualquiera, es un Zurburán; **he leaves his things any ~ how*** deja sus cosas de cualquier modo.

2 *n* (**a**) **the ~** (*people*) los viejos, los mayores, los ancianos (*LAm*).

(**b**) **of ~** antiguamente, antaño; **knights of ~** los caballeros de antaño; **I know him of ~** le conozco de antiguo.

old-age ['əʊldeɪdʒ] *attr*: ~ **pension** jubilación *f*; ~ **pensioner** (*Brit*) pensionista *mf*.

old-clothes ['əʊld'kləʊðz] *attr*: ~ **dealer** ropavejero *m*, -a *f*, prendero *m*, -a *f*; ~ **shop** ropavejería *f*, prendería *f*.

olden ['əʊldən] *adj* (†† *or liter*) antiguo; **in the ~ days** antaño, en el pasado.

Old English ['əʊld'ɪŋglɪʃ] **1** *n* (*Ling*) inglés *m* antiguo. **2** *adj*: ~ **sheepdog** pastor *m* ovejero inglés.

old-established ['əʊldɪ'stæblɪʃt] *adj* viejo, antiguo.

olde-worlde ['əʊldɪ'wɜːldɪ] *adj* (*hum*) viejísimo, antiquísimo; de antaño; arcaizante; **with ~ lettering** con letras al estilo antiguo; **a very ~ interior** un interior pintoresco de antaño; **Stratford is terribly ~** Stratford tiene sabor arcaico en exceso.

old-fashioned ['əʊld'fæʃnd] *adj thing* anticuado, pasado de moda; de estilo antiguo; *person* de ideas anticuadas, chapado a la antigua; **to give sb an ~ look*** mirar a uno con extrañeza.

oldie* ['əʊldɪ] *n* (*song*) melodía *f* del ayer; (*joke*) chiste *m* anticuado.

oldish ['əʊldɪʃ] *adj* algo viejo, más bien viejo, que va para viejo.

old-looking ['əʊld,lʊkɪŋ] *adj* de aspecto viejo.

old-maidish ['əʊld'meɪdɪʃ] *adj* de solterona; remilgado.

old-stager ['əʊld'steɪdʒə^r] *n* veterano *m*, -a *f*.

oldster ['əʊldstə^r] *n* (*US*) viejo *m*, vieja *f*.

old-style ['əʊld'staɪl] *adj* antiguo, al estilo antiguo, a la antigua; ~ **calendar** calendario *m* juliano.

Old Testament [ˌəʊld'testəmənt] *n* Antiguo Testamento *m*.

old-time ['əʊldtaɪm] *adj* de antaño, del tiempo viejo; ~ **dancing** bailes *mpl* de antaño.

old-timer [ˌəʊld'taɪmə^r] *n* veterano *m*, viejo *m*.

old-wives' tale ['əʊld'waɪvz,teɪl] *n* patraña *f*, cuento *m* de viejas.

old-world ['əʊld'wɜːld] *adj* (*Bio, Geog*) del Viejo Mundo; *character etc* antiguo, arcaico, rancio; **the ~ charm of Toledo** la atractiva ranciedad de Toledo, el sabor arcaico de Toledo.

oleaginous [əʊlɪ'ædʒɪnəs] *adj* oleaginoso.

oleander [ˌəʊlɪ'ændə^r] *n* adelfa *f*.

oleo... ['əʊlɪəʊ] *pref* oleo...

O-Level ['əʊ,levl] *n* (*Brit Scol*) *abbr of* **Ordinary Level**; **to take 8 ~s** presentarse como candidato en 8 asignaturas de *Ordinary Level*; *V* **ordinary 1(b)**.

olfactory [ɒl'fæktərɪ] *adj* olfativo, olfatorio.

oligarchic(al) [ˌɒlɪ'gɑːkɪk(əl)] *adj* oligárquico.

oligarchy ['ɒlɪgɑːkɪ] *n* oligarquía *f*.

oligo... ['ɒlɪgəʊ] *pref* oligo...

Oligocene ['ɒlɪgəʊsiːn] **1** *adj* oligocénico. **2** *n*: **the ~** el Oligoceno.

oligopoly [ˌɒlɪ'gɒpəlɪ] *n* oligopolio *m*.

oligopsony [ˌɒlɪ'gɒpsənɪ] *n* oligopsonio *m*.

olive ['ɒlɪv] **1** *n* (*fruit*) aceituna *f*, oliva *f*; (*tree*) olivo *m*. **2** *adj* aceitunado, oliváceo; (*colour*: *also* **~green**) verde oliva.

olive-branch ['ɒlɪvbrɑːntʃ] *n* ramo *m* de olivo (*also fig*); **to hold out the ~ to sb** ofrecer el ramo de olivo a uno.

olive-green ['ɒlɪv'griːn] *adj* verde oliva; **~ uniforms** uniformes *mpl* verde oliva.

olive-grove ['ɒlɪvgrəʊv] *n* olivar *m*.

olive-grower ['ɒlɪv,grəʊə^r] *n* oleicultor *m*, -ora *f*, oleícola *mf*.

olive-growing ['ɒlɪv,grəʊɪŋ] **1** *n* oleicultura *f*. **2** *attr*: **~ region** región *f* olivera.

olive-oil ['ɒlɪv'ɔɪl] *n* aceite *m* (de oliva).

Oliver ['ɒlɪvə^r] *nm* Oliverio.

Olympia [ə'lɪmpɪə] *n* Olimpia *f*.

Olympiad [əʊ'lɪmpɪæd] *n* olimpíada *f*.

Olympian [əʊ'lɪmpɪən] *adj* olímpico.

Olympic [əʊ'lɪmpɪk] **1** *adj* olímpico; **O~ Games** Juegos *mpl* Olímpicos; **O~ medallist** medallero *m* olímpico, medallera *f* olímpica; **O~ torch** antorcha *f* olímpica. **2** *npl*: **O~s** Juegos *mpl* Olímpicos.

Olympus [əʊ'lɪmpəs] *n* Olimpo *m*.

OM *n* (*Brit*) *abbr of* **Order of Merit** *título ceremonial*.

Oman [əʊ'mɑːn] *n* Omán *m*.

Omani [əʊ'mɑːnɪ] **1** *adj* omaní. **2** *n* omaní *mf*.

OMB *n* (*US*) *abbr of* **Office of Management and Budget** servicio *m* que asesora al presidente en materia presupuestaria.

ombudsman ['ɒmbʊdzmən] *n, pl* **ombudsmen** ['ɒmbʊdzmən] ombudsman *m*, defensor *m* del pueblo (*Sp*).

omega ['əʊmɪgə] *n* omega *f*.

omelet(te) ['ɒmlɪt] *n* tortilla *f*, tortilla *f* de huevo (*Méx*); **you can't make an ~ without breaking eggs** no se puede hacer tortillas sin romper huevos.

omen ['əʊmen] *n* agüero *m*, presagio *m*; **bird of ill ~** ave *f* de mal agüero; **it is a good ~ that ...** es un buen presagio que ...

ominous ['ɒmɪnəs] *adj* siniestro, de mal agüero, ominoso, amenazador; **the silence was ~** el silencio no auguraba nada bueno; **in an ~ tone** en tono amenazador; **that's ~** eso es mala señal.

ominously ['ɒmɪnəslɪ] *adv*: **the thunder rumbled ~** retumbaba amenazador el trueno; **it was ~ familiar to us** nos era siniestramente familiar; **he spoke ~** habló en tono amenazador.

omission [əʊ'mɪʃən] *n* omisión *f*; supresión *f*; olvido *m*, descuido *m*; **it was an ~ on my part** fue un descuido mío.

omit [əʊ'mɪt] *vt* omitir; suprimir; olvidar, descuidar; *person, person's name* pasar por alto; **to ~ to** + *infin* olvidar de + *infin*, dejar de + *infin*; **don't ~ to visit her** no dejes de visitarla.

omni... ['ɒmnɪ] *pref* omni...

omnibus ['ɒmnɪbəs] **1** *adj* general, para todo; *edition* completo. **2** *n* **(a)** (*Aut*) autobús *m*. **(b)** (*Liter*) antología *f*, tomo *m* colectivo. **3** *attr*: **~ edition** edición *f* colectiva.

omnidirectional [ˌɒmnɪdɪ'rekʃənəl] *adj* omnidireccional.

omnipotence [ɒm'nɪpətəns] *n* omnipotencia *f*.

omnipotent [ɒm'nɪpətənt] *adj* omnipotente.

omnipresence ['ɒmnɪ'prezəns] *n* omnipresencia *f*.

omnipresent ['ɒmnɪ'prezənt] *adj* omnipresente.

omniscience [ɒm'nɪsɪəns] *n* omnisciencia *f*.

omniscient [ɒm'nɪsɪənt] *adj* omnisciente, omniscio.

omnivore ['ɒmnɪvɔː^r] *n* omnívoro *m*, -a *f*.

omnivorous [ɒm'nɪvərəs] *adj* omnívoro; **she is an ~ reader** en sus lecturas lo devora todo, es lectora insaciable.

ON (*Canada*) *abbr of* **Ontario**.

on [ɒn] **1** *adv* **(a)** **to have one's boots ~** llevar las botas puestas; **what had he got ~?** ¿cómo estaba vestido?; **she had not got much ~** iba muy ligera de ropa; **the lid is ~** la tapa está puesta; **it's not ~ properly** no está bien puesto.

(b) (*continuation*) **to drive ~, to go ~, to ride ~, to walk ~** *etc* seguir adelante (*V also* **go on** *etc*); **to read ~** seguir leyendo; **and so ~** y así sucesivamente, y así los demás; etcétera; **to talk ~ and ~** hablar sin parar, hablar incansablemente.

(c) (*time*) **from that time ~** desde entonces, a partir de entonces; **well ~ in June** bien entrado junio; **well ~ in years** entrado en años, que va para viejo.

(d) (*with* to be: *of switches etc*) **to be ~** estar conectado; (*apparatus, Rad, TV*) estar conectado, estar puesto, estar enchufado, estar prendido (*LAm*); (*light*) estar encendido, estar puesto, estar prendido (*LAm*); (*tap*) estar abierto; (*Mech*) estar en marcha, estar funcionando; (*brake*) estar puesto.

(e) (*with* to be: *of shows etc*) **the show is now ~** ha comenzado el espectáculo; **the show is now ~ in London** se ha estrenado el espectáculo en Londres; **the show was ~ for only 2 weeks** el show estuvo solamente 15 días en cartelera; **~ with the show!** ¡que empiece (*or* continúe) el espectáculo!; **~ with the dancing girls!** ¡que salgan las bailarinas!; **what's ~ at the cinema?** ¿qué ponen en el cine?; **what's ~ at the theatre?** ¿qué dan en el teatro?; **'what's ~ in London'** 'cartelera de los espectáculos londinenses'; **have you anything ~ this evening?** ¿tienes compromiso para esta noche?; **is the meeting ~ or not?** ¿se celebra la reunión o no?; **the deal is ~** se ha cerrado el trato, ya está concertado el trato; **that's not ~!*** ¡eso no se hace!, ¡no hay derecho!; eso es imposible.

(f) (*idioms with* to be) **to be ~** (*actor*) estar en escena; **you're ~ in 5 minutes** sales en 5 minutos; **are you ~ next?** ¿te toca a ti la próxima vez?; ¿viene ahora tu número?; **are you ~ tomorrow?** ¿estás de turno mañana?; **to be ~ to sth** creer haber encontrado algo, seguir una pista interesante; **he's ~ to sth good** se ha encontrado algo bueno; **he knows he's ~ to a good thing** sabe que ha encontrado algo que vale la pena; **the police are ~ to the villain** la policía tiene una pista que le conducirá al criminal; **we're ~ to them** les conocemos el juego; **they were ~ to him at once** le calaron en seguida, le identificaron en el acto; **he's always ~ to me about it*** me está majando continuamente con eso*.

(g) **~ and off** de vez en cuando, a intervalos; **to have one day ~ and the next off** trabajar un día y el otro no.

2 *interj* ¡adelante!

3 *prep* **(a)** (*of place etc*) en, sobre; encima de; **~ the Continent** en el continente; **~ the table** en la mesa, sobre la mesa; **a meal ~ the train** una comida en el tren; **~ all sides** por todas partes, por todos lados; **~ the ceiling** sobre el techo; **~ the high seas** en alta mar; **hanging ~ the wall** colgado de (*or* en) la pared; **with her hat ~ her head** con el sombrero puesto; **a house ~ the square** una casa en la plaza; **~ page 2** en la página 2; **~ the right** a la derecha; **~ foot** a pie; **~ horseback** a caballo; **I've no money ~ me** no llevo dinero encima, no llevo dinero; **to drift ~ to the shore** llegar a la deriva sobre la playa; **so they came ~ to me** así que los hicieron pasar a mí, así que vinieron a mis manos.

(b) (*fig*) **a story based ~ fact** una historia basada en hechos; **the march ~ Rome** la marcha sobre Roma; **an attack ~ the government** un ataque contra el gobierno; **to swear ~ the Bible** prestar juramento sobre la Biblia; **all the children play ~ the piano** todos los chicos saben tocar el piano; **so he played it ~ the violin** así que lo tocó al violín; **he's ~ the committee** es miembro del comité; **he's ~ the permanent staff** es de plantilla; **~ average** por término medio; **~ good authority** de buena tinta; **~ his authority** con su autorización; **~ my responsibility** bajo mi responsabilidad; **~ a charge of murder** acusado de homicidio; **~ pain of** so pena de; **~ account of** a causa de; **~ sale** de venta, en venta; **a student ~ a grant** un estudiante con beca; **I'm ~ £30,000** yo gano 30.000 libras (al año); **we're ~ irregular verbs** estamos estudiando los verbos irregulares; **I'm ~ a milk diet** sigo un régimen lácteo; **I'm ~ 3 pills a day** tomo 3 píldoras al día; **he's back ~ drugs** ha vuelto a drogarse; **many live ~ less than that** muchos viven con menos; (*for many expressions, eg* **~ duty, ~ hand,** *V the noun*).

(**c**) (*of time*) **~ Friday** el viernes; **~ Fridays** los viernes; **~ the next day** al día siguiente; **~ 14th May** el catorce de mayo; **~ the evening of the 2nd July** el 2 de julio por la tarde; **~ a day like this** un día como éste; **~ some days it is** hay días cuando lo es; **~ and after the 15th** el día 15 y a partir de la misma fecha; **~ or about the 8th** el día 8 o por ahí; **~ my arrival** al llegar yo, a mi llegada.

(**d**) (+ *ger*) **~ seeing him** al verle; **~ my calling to him** al llamarle yo.

(**e**) (*concerning*) sobre, acerca de; **a book ~ physics** un libro de física, un libro sobre física; **an examination ~ maths** un examen de matemáticas; **Eden ~ the events of 1956** lo que dice Eden acerca de los acontecimientos de 1956; **Bentley ~ Horace** los comentarios de Bentley sobre Horacio; **have you heard the boss ~ the new tax?** ¿has oído lo que dice el jefe acerca de la nueva contribución?; **while we're ~ the subject** como hablamos de esto.

(**f**) (*after, according to*) según; **~ this model** según este modelo.

(**g**) (*engaged in*) **he's away ~ business** está fuera por negocios; **the company is ~ tour** la compañía está en gira; **to be ~ holiday** estar de vacaciones; **I'm ~ a new project** trabajo sobre un nuevo proyecto.

(**h**) (*at the expense of*) **this round's ~ me** esto corre de mi cuenta, invito yo; **it's ~ the house** la casa invita, está pagado (por el dueño); **the tour was ~ the Council** la gira la pagó el Consejo, corrió el Consejo con los gastos de la gira.

(**i**) **woe ~ woe** dolor sobre dolor; **snow ~ snow** nieve y más nieve.

(**j**) (*as against*) **prices are down ~ last year's** los precios son inferiores a los del año pasado, han bajado los precios con relación al año pasado.

4 *adj* (**a**) **in the ~ position** *tap* abierto, en posición de abierto; (*Elec*) encendido, puesto, prendido (*LAm*); **~-off switch** botón *m* de conexión.

(**b**) *V* **on-side.**

onanism [ˈəʊnənɪzəm] *n* onanismo *m*.

on-board [ˌɒnˈbɔːd] *adj*: **~ computer** computadora *f* (*or* ordenador *m*) de a bordo.

ONC *n* (*Brit Scol*) *abbr of* **Ordinary National Certificate**; *V* **ordinary 1** (**b**).

once [wʌns] **1** *adv* (**a**) (*on one occasion*) una vez; **~ before** una vez antes; **we were here ~ before** estuvimos aquí una vez; **~ or twice** alguna que otra vez; **~ a week** una vez por semana; **~ only** sólo una vez, una vez nada más; **~ again, ~ more** otra vez, una vez más; **~ in a while** de vez en cuando, cada cuando (*LAm*); **~ and for all** de una vez por todas; **just this ~** esta vez nada más; **for ~** por una vez; **more than ~** más de una vez; **not ~** ni una vez siquiera; **~ a thief always a thief** el ladrón siempre sigue ladrón.

(**b**) (*formerly*) antes, antiguamente, en otro tiempo; **~ when we were young** hace tiempo, cuando éramos jóvenes; **~ upon a time** en tiempos de Maricastaña, (*as start of story*) érase una vez ..., hubo una vez ...; **it had ~ been white** antes había sido blanco; **I knew him ~** le conocía hace tiempo.

(**c**) **at ~** en seguida, inmediatamente; sin pérdida de tiempo; (*in one go*) de una vez; **at ~ a food and a tonic** alimento y tónico a la vez, juntamente alimento y tónico; **all at ~** (*suddenly*) de repente, de golpe; (*in one go*) de una vez; (*all together*) todo junto, todos juntos, a un mismo tiempo.

2 *conj* una vez que ..., si ...; **~ allow this all is lost** en cuanto esto se permita se acaba todo; **~ you give him the chance** una vez que le des la oportunidad, si le das la oportunidad.

once-over* [ˈwʌnsˌəʊvəʳ] *n* (**a**) (*search etc*) **to give sth the ~** dar un vistazo a algo, examinar algo (rápidamente); **they gave the house the ~** registraron superficialmente la casa. (**b**) (*beating*) paliza *f*.

oncologist [ɒŋˈkɒlədʒɪst] *n* oncólogo *m*, -a *f*.

oncology [ɒŋˈkɒlədʒɪ] *n* oncología *f*.

oncoming [ˈɒnˌkʌmɪŋ] *adj* (**a**) *event* que se acerca, venidero. (**b**) *traffic* que viene en dirección contraria.

oncosts [ˈɒnˌkɒsts] *npl* gastos *mpl* generales.

OND *n* (*Brit Scol*) *abbr of* **Ordinary National Diploma**; *V* **ordinary 1** (**b**).

one [wʌn] **1** *adj* (**a**) (*numeral*) uno, una; (*before sing n*) un, *eg* **one man** un hombre; **~ or two people** algunas personas; **~ man out of two** uno de cada dos hombres; **there is only ~ left** queda uno solamente; **the last but ~** el penúltimo; **that's ~ way of doing it** es uno de los métodos de hacerlo; **you've got it in ~!** ¡has acertado la primera vez!; **they came in ~s and twos** entraron solos o en parejas; **they waited in ~s and twos** esperaban en pequeños grupos; *V* **number.**

(**b**) (*sole*) solo, único; **the ~ and only difficulty** la única dificultad; **the ~ and only Charlie Chaplin** el irrepetible Charlot, el inimitable Charlot; **his ~ care** su único cuidado; **the ~ way to do it** el único método de hacerlo; **no ~ man could do it** nadie podría hacerlo por sí sólo.

(**c**) (*same*) mismo; **all in ~ direction** todos en la misma dirección; **they are ~ and the same** son el mismo; **it's all ~** es lo mismo; **it's all ~ to me** me da igual, me da lo mismo; **God is ~** Dios es uno; **to be ~ with sth** formar un conjunto con algo; **to become ~** casarse; **they all shouted as ~** todos gritaron como un solo hombre.

2 *n*: **price of ~** precio *m* de la unidad; **it's made all in ~** está hecho en una sola pieza; **he's president and secretary all in ~** es presidente y secretario todo junto; **to be at ~ with sb** estar completamente de acuerdo con uno; **to be ~ up** tener la ventaja; tener un punto (*or* gol *etc*) de ventaja; haber ganado un partido más que los adversarios; **to be ~ up on sb** llevar ventaja a uno; **that puts us ~ up** eso nos da un punto (*or* gol *etc*) de ventaja; **to go ~ better than sb** quedar por encima de uno, aventajar a uno; **but John went ~ better** pero Juan hizo más; **he dotted her ~*** la pegó; **to have a quick ~*** echarse un traguito*; **to have ~ for the road*** beberse un trago antes de partir*, tomar la espuela*.

3 *dem pron*: **this ~** éste, ésta; **that ~** ése, ésa, aquél, aquélla; **this ~ is better than that ~** éste es mejor que ése; **~ or two** algunos; **which ~ do you want?** ¿cuál quieres?

4 *rel pron* (**a**) **the ~ on the floor** el que está en el suelo; **the ~ who, the ~ that** el que, la que; **the ~s who, the ~s that** los que, las que; **they were the ~s who told us** ellos eran quienes nos lo dijeron.

(**b**) **the white dress and the grey ~** el traje blanco y el gris; **who wants these red ~s?** ¿quién quiere estos colorados?; **what about this little ~?** ¿y el pequeño éste?

(**c**) **that's a good ~!** ¡ésa sí que es buena!; **to pull a fast ~ on sb** jugar una mala pasada a uno, embaucar a uno; **that's a difficult ~** eso es un problema difícil; **our dear ~s** nuestros seres queridos; **the Evil O~** el demonio, el malo; **the little ~s** los pequeños, los chiquillos, la gente menuda; **he's a clever ~** es un taimado; **you're a fine ~!** ¡estás tú bueno!, ¡qué tío!; **you are a ~!** ¡qué cosas dices! (*or* haces *etc*); **he's the troublesome ~** él es el elemento revoltoso; **he's a great ~ for chess** es estupendo para el ajedrez, es un entusiasta del ajedrez; **he's ~ for the ladies** es Perico entre ellas; **he's not much of a ~ for sweets** no le gustan mucho los dulces; **he is not the ~ to protest** no es de los que protestan.

5 *indef adj*: **~ day** un día, cierto día; **~ hot July evening** una tarde de julio de mucho calor.

6 *indef pron* (**a**) **have you got ~?** ¿tienes uno?; **the book is ~ which I have never read** el libro es de los que no he leído nunca; **his message is ~ of pessimism** su mensaje es pesimista, su mensaje termina con tono de pesimismo; **~ of them** uno de ellos; **any ~ of us** cualquiera de nosotros; **he's ~ of the group** es del grupo, forma parte del grupo; **he's ~ of the family now** ya es de la familia; **I for ~ am not going** de todas formas yo no voy.

(**b**) **never a ~** ni uno siquiera; **~ and all** todos sin excepción; **the ~..., the other ...** el uno ..., el otro ...; **you can't buy ~ without the other** no se puede comprar el uno sin el otro; **~ after the other** uno tras otro; **for ~ reason or another** por una razón u otra, por alguna razón; **~ by ~** uno a uno, uno tras otro.

(**c**) (*one another*) **they kissed ~ another** se besaron, se besaron el uno al otro; **they all kissed ~ another** se besaron unos a otros; **do you see ~ another much?** ¿os visitáis mucho?; **it's a year since we saw ~ another** hace un año que no nos vemos.

(**d**) **he looked like ~ who had seen a ghost** tenía el aspecto del que acababa de ver un fantasma; **~ more sensitive would have fainted** una persona de mayor sensibilidad se hubiera desmayado; **to ~ who can read between the lines** para el que sabe leer entre líneas; ~

Pérez un tal Pérez.

(**e**) (*subject etc*) ~ **never knows** nunca se sabe; ~ **must wash** hay que lavarse; ~ **has one's pride** uno tiene cierto amor propio.

(**f**) (*possessive*) ~**'s life is not really safe** la vida de uno no es realmente segura; ~**'s opinion does not count** la opinión de uno no cuenta; **to cut** ~**'s finger** cortarse el dedo.

one- [wʌn] *pref in compounds*: de un ..., de un solo ..., uni-; un-, *eg* **a** ~**line message** un mensaje de una sola línea; **a** ~**celled animal** un animal unicelular; **he's a** ~**woman man** es un hombre para el que no existe más que una mujer; **a** ~**day excursion** (*US*) un billete de ida y vuelta en un día.

one-act ['wʌn'ækt] *adj* de un solo acto.

one-armed ['wʌn'ɑːmd] *adj* manco; ~ **bandit** máquina *f* tragaperras.

one-eyed ['wʌnaɪd] *adj* tuerto.

one-handed ['wʌn'hændɪd] **1** *adv*: **to catch the ball** ~ recoger la pelota con una sola mano. **2** *adj* manco.

one-horse ['wʌn'hɔːs] *adj* (**a**) *carriage* de un solo caballo. (**b**) (*) insignificante, de poca monta; ~ **town** pueblucho* *m*.

one-legged ['wʌn'legɪd] *adj* con una sola pierna.

one-liner [,wʌn'laɪnəʳ] *n* chiste *m* breve, observación *f* sucinta.

one-man ['wʌn'mæn] *adj* individual; de un solo hombre; ~ **band** hombre *m* orquesta; ~ **exhibition,** ~ **show** exposición *f* de un solo artista; ~ **woman** mujer *f* que dedica su vida a un solo hombre.

oneness ['wʌnnɪs] *n* unidad *f*; identidad *f*.

one-night ['wʌnnaɪt] *adj*: ~ **stand** función *f* de una sola noche, representación *f* única; (*) ligue* *m*, cama *f* de una noche*.

one-off* ['wʌnɒf] **1** *adj* único; aislado; fuera de serie, excepcional, irrepetible; ~ **job** acontecimiento *m* único. **2** *n*: **it's a** ~ es un caso único; es una oportunidad (*etc*) fuera de serie; es una oferta (*etc*) irrepetible.

one-parent ['wʌn,pɛərənt] *adj*: ~ **family** familia *f* monoparental, hogar *m* sin pareja.

one-party ['wʌn'pɑːtɪ] *adj state etc* de partido único.

one-piece ['wʌn'piːs] *adj* enterizo, de una pieza.

onerous ['ɒnərəs] *adj* oneroso.

oneself [wʌn'self] *pron* (*subject*) uno mismo, una misma; (*acc, dative*) se; (*after prep*) sí (mismo, misma); **to wash** ~ lavarse (a sí mismo); **to be** ~ conducirse con naturalidad; ser fiel a su propia manera de ser; **to be by** ~ estar solo, estar a solas; **to do sth by** ~ hacer algo solo, hacer algo por sí mismo; **to look out for** ~ mirar por sí; **to come to** ~ volver en sí; **to say to** ~ decir para sí, decir entre sí; **to talk to** ~ hablar consigo mismo; **it's nice to have the museum to** ~ es agradable estar solo en el museo.

one-shot* ['wʌnʃɒt] (*US*) **1** *adj* = **one-off. 2** *n* artículo *m* fuera de serie.

one-sided ['wʌn'saɪdɪd] *adj* unilateral; asimétrico; (*unbalanced*) desequilibrado; *contest, game* desigual; *view etc* parcial, injusto.

one-sidedness [,wʌn'saɪdɪdnɪs] *n* carácter *m* unilateral; asimetría *f*; desequilibrio *m*; desigualdad *f*; parcialidad *f*, injusticia *f*.

one-stop ['wʌnstɒp] *adj*: ~ **shopping** tiendas *fpl* y servicios *mpl* bajo el mismo techo.

one-time ['wʌntaɪm] *adj* antiguo; otrora; ~ **butler to Lord Yaxley** antiguo mayordomo de Lord Yaxley; ~ **prime minister** ex primer ministro *m*; **the** ~ **revolutionary** el otrora revolucionario.

one-to-one ['wʌntə'wʌn] (*Brit*) **1** *adj* exacto, en correspondencia exacta; ~ **relationship** relación *f* de uno a uno, relación *f* de persona a persona. **2** *adv* exactamente, en correspondencia exacta.

one-track ['wʌntræk] *adj* (*Rail*) de vía única; *mind* que tiene un solo pensamiento.

one-upmanship [wʌn'ʌpmənʃɪp] *n* (*hum*) *arte de llevar siempre la ventaja, arte de establecerse en una posición superior con respecto a otra persona (logrando una ventaja táctica en una conversación etc)*.

one-way ['wʌnweɪ] *adj admiration etc* que el otro (*etc*) no comparte, no correspondido; ~ **journey** viaje *m* sin retorno; ~ **street** calle *f* de dirección única, sentido *m* único (*LAm*), calle *f* de un (solo) sentido (*Mex*); '~ **traffic**' 'dirección única', 'dirección obligatoria'; ~ **ticket** billete *m* sencillo.

one-woman ['wʌn'wʊmən] *adj* individual; de una sola mujer; ~ **business** empresa *f* dirigida por una sola mujer; ~ **man** hombre *m* que dedica su vida a una sola mujer.

one-year ['wʌnjɪəʳ] *adj* de un año; para un año; ~ **unconditional warranty** garantía *f* incondicional de un año.

ongoing ['ɒn,gəʊɪŋ] *adj* que continúa, que sigue funcionando, que cursa, en marcha.

onion ['ʌnjən] **1** *n* cebolla *f*; (‡) cabeza *f*; **to know one's** ~**s** (*Brit*) conocer a fondo su oficio, conocer el paño.

2 *attr*: ~ **johnny** vendedor *m* ambulante de cebollas; ~**-shaped** acebollado, con forma de cebolla; ~ **skin** papel *m* de cebolla.

on-line ['ɒnlaɪn] **1** *adj* (*Comput*) on-line, en línea; (*switched on*) conectado. **2** *adv* on-line, en línea.

onlooker ['ɒn,lʊkəʳ] *n* espectador *m*, -ora *f*; observador *m*, -ora *f*; (*esp pej*) mirón *m*, -ona *f*; **I was a mere** ~ yo era un simple espectador.

only ['əʊnlɪ] **1** *adv* sólo, solamente, únicamente; no ... más que; nada más; **we have** ~ **5** tenemos solamente 5, tenemos 5 solamente, tenemos 5 nada más; **what,** ~ **5?** ¿cómo, 5 nada más?; **'Ladies** ~' 'Señoras'; ~ **God can tell** sólo Dios lo sabe; ~ **time will show** sólo el tiempo lo dirá; **I'm** ~ **the porter** yo soy simplemente el conserje, yo no soy más que el conserje; **I** ~ **touched it** no hice más que tocarlo; **you** ~ **have to ask** no hay sino preguntar; **I will** ~ **say that ...** diré solamente que ...; ~ **to think of it!** ¡sólo pensar en ello!; ~ **too glad!** ¡con mucho gusto!; **if** ~ **I could!** ¡ojalá!, ¡ojalá pudiese ...!; ~ **just** apenas; **not** ~ **A but also B** no sólo A sino tambien B; *V* **if** *etc*.

2 *adj* único, solo; **their** ~ **son** su hijo único; **your** ~ **hope is to** + *infin* tu única posibilidad es + *infin*; **his** ~ **response was to laugh** por toda respuesta se rió; **to be the** ~ **one to** + *infin* ser el único en + *infin;* **you are not the** ~ **one** no eres el único en hacer (*etc*) eso.

3 *conj*: **it's very good** ~ **rather dear** es muy bueno pero algo caro; **I would gladly do it** ~ **I shall be away** lo haría de buena gana sólo que voy a estar fuera.

o.n.o. *abbr of* **or near offer** abierto ofertas.

onomastic [,ɒnəʊ'mæstɪk] *adj* onomástico.

onomastics [,ɒnəʊ'mæstɪks] *nsing* onomástica *f*.

onomatopoeia [,ɒnəʊmætəʊ'piːə] *n* onomatopeya *f*.

onomatopoeic [,ɒnəʊmætəʊ'piːɪk] *adj* onomatopéyico.

onrush ['ɒnrʌʃ] *n* arremetida *f*, embestida *f*; avalancha *f*, riada *f*; fuerza *f*, ímpetu *m*.

onset ['ɒnset] *n* (**a**) (*attack*) ataque *m*, arremetida *f*. (**b**) (*beginning*) comienzo *m*; **the** ~ **of winter** el comienzo del invierno.

onshore ['ɒnʃɔːʳ] **1** *adv* hacia la tierra. **2** *adj breeze* que sopla del mar hacia la tierra.

onside ['ɒnsaɪd] (*Aut etc*) **1** *adj* (*Brit*) izquierdo, (*most other countries*) derecho; (*Football etc*: [,ɒn'saɪd]) **to be** ~ estar en posición correcta. **2** *n* (*Brit*) lado *m* izquierdo, (*most other countries*) lado *m* derecho.

on-site ['ɒn,saɪt] *adj* in situ.

onslaught ['ɒnslɔːt] *n* ataque *m* violento, embestida *f* furiosa; **to make a furious** ~ **on a critic** atacar violentamente a un crítico.

Ont. (*Canada*) *abbr of* **Ontario.**

on-the-job ['ɒnðə'dʒɒb] *adj*: ~ **training** formación *f* en el trabajo (*or* sobre la práctica).

on-the-spot ['ɒnðə'spɒt] *adj decision* instantáneo; *investigation* en el terreno, en el propio lugar (del crimen *etc*); *report* inmediato, de lo más actual; **our** ~ **reporter** nuestro reportero que está allí mismo.

onto* ['ɒntʊ] *prep* = **on to.**

ontological [,ɒntə'lɒdʒɪkəl] *adj* ontológico.

ontology [ɒn'tɒlədʒɪ] *n* ontología *f*.

onus ['əʊnəs] *n* (*no pl*) carga *f*, responsabilidad *f*; **the** ~ **is upon the makers** la responsabilidad es de los fabricantes; **the** ~ **is upon him to** + *infin* le incumbe a él + *infin*; **the** ~ **of proof is on the prosecution** le incumbe al fiscal probar la acusación.

onward ['ɒnwəd] *adj march etc* progresivo, hacia adelante.

onward(s) ['ɒnwəd(z)] **1** *adv* adelante, hacia adelante; **from that time** ~ desde entonces; **from the 12th century** ~ desde el siglo XII en adelante, a partir del siglo XII.

2 *interj* ¡adelante!

onyx ['ɒnɪks] *n* ónice *m*, ónix *m*.

oodles* ['uːdlz] *npl*: **we have** ~ tenemos montones*, tenemos muchísimo; **we have** ~ **of** tenemos la mar de*, tenemos montones de*.

ooh [uː] **1** *excl* ¡oh! **2** *vi* exclamar con placer.

oolite ['əʊəlaɪt] *n* oolito *m*.

oolitic [,əʊə'lɪtɪk] *adj* oolítico.

oompah ['uːmpɑː] *n* chumpa *f*.

oomph‡ [ʊmf] *n* aquél* *m*, atracción *f* sexual, sexy *m*.

oophorectomy [ˌəʊəfəˈrektəmɪ] *n* ooforectomía *f*, ovariotomía *f*.

oops* [ʊps] *excl* ¡ay!

ooze [uːz] **1** *n* cieno *m*, lama *f*.

2 *vt* rezumar; (*fig*) rezumar, rebosar de; **the wound was oozing blood** la herida sangraba lentamente; **he simply ~s confidence** rebosa confianza.

3 *vi* (*liquid*) rezumar, rezumarse; (*blood*) manar suavemente; (*barrel etc*) rezumar.

◆**ooze away** *vi* rezumarse; agotarse poco a poco.

◆**ooze out** *vi* rezumarse.

op* [ɒp] *n* = **operation.**

op (*Mus*) *abbr of* **opus.**

opacity [əʊˈpæsɪtɪ] *n* opacidad *f*.

opal [ˈəʊpəl] *n* ópalo *m*.

opalescence [ˌəʊpəˈlesns] *n* opalescencia *f*.

opalescent [ˌəʊpəˈlesnt] *adj* opalescente.

opaque [əʊˈpeɪk] *adj* opaco.

op.cit. *abbr of* **opere citato, in the work cited** en la obra *f* citada, obr. cit.

OPEC [ˈəʊpek] *n abbr of* **Organization of Petroleum Exporting Countries** Organización *f* de Países Exportadores de Petróleo, OPEP *f*.

open [ˈəʊpən] **1** *adj* (**a**) (*not closed*) abierto; *book, grave, parcel, pores, wound etc* abierto; *bottle etc* destapado; ~ **prison** cárcel *f* abierta, prisión *m* de régimen abierto; ~ **and shut case** asunto *m* clarísimo; **the door is ~** la puerta está abierta; **a dress ~ at the neck** un vestido abierto por el cuello; **with his shirt ~** con la camisa desabotonada; ~ **to the public on Mondays** se abre al público los lunes; **to break a safe ~** forzar una caja fuerte; **to cut a sack ~** abrir un saco cortándolo, abrir un saco de un tajo; **to fling** (*or* **throw**) **a door ~** abrir una puerta de golpe, abrir una puerta de par en par.

(**b**) (*unobstructed*) abierto, sin límites, no limitado; *road* franco, abierto, no obstruido; ~ **country** campo *m* raso; ~ **end trust** (*US*) sociedad *f* inversionista; ~ **market** (*open-air*) mercado *m* al aire libre; (*Fin*) mercado *m* libre, mercado *m* abierto; ~ **sea** mar *m* abierto; **in the ~ air** al aire libre; **with ~ views** con amplias vistas, con extensas vistas; **the way to Paris lay ~** el camino de París quedaba abierto.

(**c**) (*permissible*) **it is ~ to you to** + *infin* puedes perfectamente + *infin*, tienes derecho a + *infin*; **what choices are ~ to me?** ¿qué posibilidades hay?

(**d**) (*exposed*) abierto, descubierto; *town* abierto; *boat, car, carriage* descubierto; **the map was ~ on the table** el mapa estaba desplegado sobre la mesa; **the book was ~ at page 7** el libro estaba abierto por la página 7; **books on ~ access** libros *mpl* en libre acceso; ~ **to every wind** expuesto a todos los vientos; ~ **to influence from advertisers** accesible a la influencia de los anunciantes; **it is ~ to doubt whether ...** es discutible si ..., es dudoso que + *subj*; **it is ~ to criticism on several counts** se le puede criticar por diversas razones, es criticable desde diversos puntos de vista; **I am ~ to persuasion** estoy dispuesto a dejarme convencer; **I am ~ to advice** escucho de buena gana los consejos; **I am ~ to offers** estoy dispuesto a recibir ofertas; **to lay ~** abrir; *secret etc* poner al descubierto; **to lay o.s. ~ to criticism** exponerse a ser criticado.

(**e**) (*public, unrestricted*) público; para todos; *championship, competition, race, scholarship, ticket etc* abierto; *trial* público; ~ **day,** ~ **house** día *m* para el público, jornada *f* de puertas abiertas; ~ **letter** carta *f* abierta; ~ **policy** (*Insurance*) póliza *f* abierta; ~ **secret** secreto *m* a voces; ~ **shop** (*factory etc*) empresa *f* con personal agremiado y no agremiado; **O~ University** (*Brit*) ≃ (*Sp*) Universidad *f* Nacional de Educación a Distancia; **he bought it on the ~ market** lo compró en el mercado público; **the competition is ~ to all** todos pueden participar en el certamen, el certamen se abre a todos; **membership is not ~ to women** la sociedad no admite a las mujeres; *V* **house** *etc*.

(**f**) (*declared, frank*) abierto, franco; *admiration etc* franco; **an ~ enemy of the Church** un enemigo declarado de la Iglesia; **to be in ~ revolt** estar en franca rebeldía, estar en plena rebeldía; **he was not very ~ with us** no se portó del todo honradamente con nosotros, no fue muy sincero con nosotros.

(**g**) (*undecided*) *mind* receptivo; imparcial, sin prejuicios; *race* abierto, muy igual; *cheque* sin cruzar, abierto; ~ **question** cuestión *f* pendiente, cuestión *f* sin resolver; **it is an ~ question whether ...** queda por resolver si ..., el tiempo dirá si ...; ~ **verdict** juicio *m* en el que se determina el crimen sin designar el culpable; **let's leave it ~** dejémoslo sin decidir, dejémoslo pendiente.

2 *n* (**a**) **to be out in the ~** (*in the country*) estar en el campo; (*in bare country*) estar al raso; (*out of doors*) estar al aire libre; **to sleep in the ~** dormir al raso, dormir a cielo abierto; **to bring a dispute into the ~** hacer que una disputa llegue a ser del dominio público; **their true feelings came into the ~** sus verdaderos sentimientos salieron a flor de piel; **why don't you come into the ~ about it?** ¿por qué no lo declara abiertamente?

(**b**) **the O~** (*Golf*) el campeonato 'open'.

3 *vt* (**a**) (*gen*) abrir; *arms, eyes, heart, mouth, case, letter etc* abrir; (*unfold*) desplegar, extender; *legs etc* abrir, separar; *abscess* cortar; *bottle etc* destapar; *parcel* abrir, desenvolver; *shop* abrir, poner; (*tear*) romper; (*leave exposed*) dejar al descubierto; **to ~ a road to traffic** abrir una carretera al tráfico.

(**b**) (*drive*) **to ~ a hole in a wall** hacer un agujero en una pared; **to ~ a road through a forest** construir una carretera a través de un bosque.

(**c**) (*begin*) *conversation, debate, negotiations etc* iniciar, empezar; **to ~ an account in sb's name** abrir una cuenta a nombre de uno; **to ~ the case** (*Jur*) exponer los detalles de la acusación, presentar los hechos en que se basa la acusación; **to ~ 3 hearts** (*Bridge*) abrir de 3 corazones.

(**d**) (*declare ~, inaugurate*) inaugurar; **the exhibition was ~ed by the Queen** la exposición fue inaugurada por la Reina.

4 *vi* (**a**) (*gen*) abrirse (*also* abrir); *flower etc* abrirse; **the door ~ed** se abrió la puerta; **a door that ~s on to the garden** una puerta que da al jardín; **this room ~s into a larger one** este cuarto se comunica con (*or* se junta con) otro más grande; **the shops ~ at 9** el comercio abre a las 9; **the heavens ~ed** se abrieron los cielos.

(**b**) (*begin*) empezar, comenzar, iniciarse; (*Bridge*) abrir (la declaración); **the season ~s in June** la temporada comienza en junio; **when we ~ed in Bradford** cuando dimos la primera representación en Bradford; **the play ~ed to great applause** el estreno de la obra fue muy aplaudido; **to ~ for the Crown** (*Jur*) exponer los detalles de la acusación, presentar los hechos en que se basa la acusación; **the book ~s with a long description** el libro comienza con una larga descripción; **to ~ with 2 hearts** (*Bridge*) abrir de 2 corazones.

◆**open out 1** *vt* abrir; (*unfold*) extender, desplegar.

2 *vi* (**a**) (*unfold*) extenderse, desplegarse; (*flower*) abrirse.

(**b**) (*widen*) hacerse más ancho.

(**c**) (*person*) hacerse menos reservado, perder la reserva; **the company is ~ing out a bit now** ahora la compañía está extendiendo el campo de sus actividades; **the team ~ed out in the second half** en el segundo tiempo el equipo se mostró más enérgico.

◆**open up 1** *vt* (**a**) *box etc* abrir; *map etc* extender, desplegar; *jacket* abrir.

(**b**) *business, branch* abrir; inaugurar; **to ~ up a market** abrirse un mercado, conquistar un mercado.

(**c**) *route* abrir; *blocked road* franquear, despejar; *country* explorar; *secret, new vista* revelar; *new possibility* crear; **to ~ up a country for trade** abrir un país al comercio; **when the oilfield was ~ed up** cuando se empezó a explotar el campo petrolífero.

2 *vi* (**a**) ~ **up!** ¡abran!, (*police order*) ¡abran a la autoridad!

(**b**) (*Comm etc*) empezar, comenzar.

(**c**) (*Mil*) romper el fuego.

(**d**) (*emotionally*) franquearse, abrir su pecho.

(**e**) (*car*) acelerar (a fondo).

open-air [ˈəʊpnˈɛəʳ] *adj* al aire libre.

opencast [ˈəʊpənˈkɑːst] *adj* (*Brit*) a cielo abierto, de cielo abierto.

open-door [ˈəʊpənˈdɔːʳ] *adj*: ~ **policy** política *f* de puerta abierta.

open-ended [ˈəʊpənˈendɪd] *adj discussion etc* abierto, sin límites fijos, no limitado de antemano.

opener [ˈəʊpnəʳ] *n* (**a**) (*tin~*) abrelatas *m*. (**b**) (*Theat etc*) primer número *m*. (**c**) **for ~s*** (*US*) de entrada.

open-eyed [ˈəʊpnˈaɪd] *adj* con los ojos abiertos; (*amazed*) con ojos desorbitados.

open-handed [ˈəʊpnˈhændɪd] *adj* liberal, generoso.

open-handedness [ˈəʊpnˈhændɪdnɪs] *n* liberalidad *f*; generosidad *f*.

open-heart [ˈəʊpnˌhɑːt] *attr*: ~ **surgery** cirugía *f* de corazón abierto.

open-hearted [ˌəʊpn'hɑːtɪd] *adj* franco, generoso.

opening ['əʊpnɪŋ] **1** *adj remark etc* primero; *ceremony, speech,* de apertura; ~ **hours** horas *fpl* de abrir; ~ **night** primera noche *f*; (*Theat*) estreno *m*; (*of club etc*) inauguración *f*; ~ **price** cotización *f* de apertura; ~ **stock** existencias *fpl* iniciales; ~ **time** (*Brit*) hora *f* de abrir. **2** *n* (**a**) (*gap*) abertura *f*; (*in walls etc*) brecha *f*; (*in wood*) claro *m*; (*in clouds*) abertura *f*, claro *m*. (**b**) (*beginning*) comienzo *m*, principio *m*; (*of play*) estreno *m*. (**c**) (*of exhibition etc*) inauguración *f*; (*Chess*) apertura *f*. (**d**) (*chance*) oportunidad *f*, entrada *f*; (*Comm*) salida *f*; (*post*) puesto *m*, vacante *f*; **an unusual ~ occurs for ...** se ofrece un puesto interesante de ...; **it's a fine ~ for a young man** es una magnífica oportunidad para un joven; **to give sb an ~ for sth** dar a uno la oportunidad de hacer algo.

openly ['əʊpənlɪ] *adv* abiertamente, francamente; públicamente.

open-minded ['əʊpn'maɪndɪd] *adj* libre de prejuicios, imparcial; **I am still ~ about it** no me he decidido todavía, sigo sin resolverme.

open-mindedness ['əʊpn'maɪndɪdnɪs] *n* ausencia *f* de prejuicios, imparcialidad *f*.

open-mouthed ['əʊpn'maʊðd] *adj* boquiabierto.

open-necked ['əʊpn'nekt] *adj* sin cuello, sin corbata.

openness ['əʊpnnɪs] *n* franqueza *f*.

open-plan ['əʊpn,plæn] *adj*: ~ **office** oficina *f* de plan abierto.

openwork ['əʊpnwɜːk] *n* (*Sew*) calado *m*, enrejado *m*.

opera ['ɒpərə] *n* ópera *f*; (*building*) (teatro *m* de la) ópera *f*.

operable ['ɒpərəbl] *adj* operable.

opera-glasses ['ɒpərəglɑːsɪz] *npl* gemelos *mpl* de teatro.

opera-goer ['ɒpərə,gəʊəʳ] *n* aficionado *m*, -a *f* a la ópera.

opera-hat ['ɒpərəhæt] *n* clac *m*.

opera-house ['ɒpərəhaus] *n*, *pl* **opera-houses** ['ɒpərəhaʊzɪz] teatro *m* de la ópera.

operand ['ɒpərænd] *n* operando *m*.

opera-singer ['ɒpərə,sɪŋəʳ] *n* cantante *mf* de (la) ópera, operista *mf*.

operate ['ɒpəreɪt] **1** *vt motor etc* impulsar; *machine* hacer funcionar, (*as driver etc*) manejar; *switchboard* atender a; *company etc* dirigir; *eg canal* explotar, administrar; **a machine ~d by electricity** una máquina que funciona con electricidad; **can you ~ this tool?** ¿sabes manejar esta herramienta?; **he has been operating a clever swindle** ha estado manejando una hábil estafa, ha andado en una estafa muy hábil.

2 *vi* (**a**) (*person etc*) obrar, actuar; (*Mech*) funcionar; *drug etc* surtir efecto (*on* en); (*Mil, St Ex etc*) operar; **to ~ on** producir efecto en, afectar, influir; **his words ~d on all our minds** sus palabras influyeron en nuestro ánimo; **it ~s on two levels** funciona a dos niveles.

(**b**) (*Med*) **to ~ on sb for sth** operar a uno de algo; **to ~ for appendicitis** operar a uno de apendicitis; **he has still not been ~d on** todavía no se le ha operado; **to ~ on sb's liver** operar de hígado a uno.

operatic [ˌɒpə'rætɪk] *adj* de ópera, operístico.

operating ['ɒpəreɪtɪŋ] *adj* operante; ~ **assets** activo *m* operante; ~ **budget** presupuesto *m* operante; ~ **costs,** ~ **expenses** gastos *mpl* de funcionamiento, gastos *mpl* operacionales; ~ **cycle** ciclo *m* de operaciones; ~ **loss** pérdida *f* en operaciones; ~ **margin** margen *m* operacional; ~ **profit** beneficio *m* neto; ~ **room** (*US*) = ~ **theatre;** ~ **statement** (*Comm*) estado *m*, balance *m*, cuenta *f* (de pérdidas y ganancias); ~ **system** (*Comput*) sistema *m* de explotación, sistema *m* operativo; ~ **table** mesa *f* de operaciones; ~ **theatre** (*Brit*) quirofáno *m*, sala *f* de operaciones.

operation [ˌɒpə'reɪʃən] **1** *n* (**a**) funcionamiento *m*; manejo *m*; dirección *f*; explotación *f*, administración *f*; (*Mil, St Ex etc*) operación *f*; (*of person*) actuación *f*; (*manoeuvre*) maniobra *f*; **the company's ~s during the year** las actividades de la compañía durante el año; **~s of doubtful legality** maniobras *fpl* de dudosa legalidad; **to be in ~** (*Mech*) funcionar, estar en funcionamiento, estar funcionando; (*Jur*) estar en vigor, ser vigente; **to be in full ~** estar en pleno funcionamiento; **to bring a machine into ~** poner una máquina en funcionamiento; **to come into ~** (*Jur*) entrar en vigor; **to put into ~** (*Jur*) hacer entrar en vigor, poner en obra.

(**b**) (*Med*) operación *f*, intervención *f* quirúrgica; **a liver ~** una operación de hígado; **to perform an ~ on sb for sth** operar a uno de algo; **to undergo an ~** ser operado (*for sth* de algo).

2 *attr*: ~ **code** código *m* de operación; **~s research** investigaciones *fpl* operacionales; **~s room** (*Police etc*) centro *m* de coordinación, sala *f* de dirección de operaciones.

operational [ˌɒpə'reɪʃənl] *adj* (**a**) (*relating to operations*) de operaciones; ~ **research** investigaciones *fpl* operacionales.

(**b**) (*fit*: *Mil*) en condiciones de servicio, operacional; (*Mech*) en buen estado, capaz de funcionar; **it will not be ~ until next year** no será operacional hasta el año que viene; **when the service is fully ~** cuando el servicio esté en pleno funcionamiento.

operative ['ɒpərətɪv] **1** *adj* (**a**) **the ~ word is ...** la palabra clave es ...; **to be ~** (*Jur*) estar en vigor; **to become ~ from the 9th** (*Jur*) entrar en vigor a partir del 9.

(**b**) (*Med*) operatorio.

2 *n* (*worker*) operario *m*, -a *f*; (*spy*) agente *mf*.

operator ['ɒpəreɪtəʳ] *n* (**a**) (*of machine*) operario *m*, -a *f*; maquinista *mf*; (*Cine, Med*) operador *m*; (*Telec*) telefonista *mf*; (*Comm*) agente *mf*, corredor *m*, -ora *f* de bolsa. (**b**) (*pej*) vivales *m*, vividor *m*; **he's a very clever ~** es un vividor de los más hábiles.

operetta [ˌɒpə'retə] *n* opereta *f*; (*Sp*) zarzuela *f*.

Ophelia [ɒ'fiːlɪə] *nf* Ofelia.

ophthalmia [ɒf'θælmɪə] *n* oftalmía *f*.

ophthalmic [ɒf'θælmɪk] *adj* oftálmico.

ophthalmologist [ˌɒfθæl'mɒlədʒɪst] *n* oftalmólogo *m*, -a *f*.

ophthalmology [ˌɒfθæl'mɒlədʒɪ] *n* oftalmología *f*.

ophthalmoscope [ɒf'θælməskəʊp] *n* oftalmoscopio *m*.

opiate ['əʊpɪɪt] *n* opiata *f*, opiáceo *m*, narcótico *m* (*also fig*).

opine [əʊ'paɪn] *vi* opinar.

opinion [ə'pɪnjən] **1** *n* opinión *f*, parecer *m*; juicio *m*; concepto *m*; **in my ~** en mi opinión, a mi juicio; **in the ~ of those who know** en la opinión de los que saben, según los que saben; **well, that's my ~** por lo menos eso pienso yo; **I am of the ~ that ...** soy del parecer de que; **I am entirely of your ~** estoy completamente de acuerdo contigo; **it's a matter of ~** es cuestión de opinión; **what is your ~ of him?** ¿qué concepto tienes de él?, ¿qué piensas de él?; **to ask sb's ~** pedir el parecer de uno; **his ~ doesn't count** no vale su opinión; **to echo sb's ~** compartir el sentir de uno; **to form an ~** formarse una opinión; **to give one's ~** dar su parecer; **to have a high ~ of sb** tener muy buen concepto de uno, tener a uno en mucho; **to have a high ~ of o.s.** estar pagado de sí mismo; **to have a low** (*or* **poor**) **~ of sb** tener un mal concepto de uno; **I do not share your ~** no comparto esa opinión.

2 *attr*: ~ **poll,** ~ **survey** sondeo *m* (de la opinión pública).

opinionated [ə'pɪnjəneɪtɪd] *adj* porfiado, terco, dogmático.

opium ['əʊpɪəm] **1** *n* opio *m*. **2** *attr*: ~ **addict** opiómano *m*, -a *f*; ~ **addiction** opiomanía *f*; ~ **den** fumadero *m* de opio.

opossum [ə'pɒsəm] *n* zarigüeya *f*, opos(s)um *m*.

opp. *abbr of* **opposite** en frente, enfrente de.

opponent [ə'pəʊnənt] *n* adversario *m*, -a *f*, contrario *m*, -a *f*, contrincante *m*.

opportune ['ɒpətjuːn] *adj* oportuno, a propósito; **to be ~** venir al caso, (*of time etc*) ser propicio; **at an ~ moment** en el momento oportuno; **his arrival was most ~** su llegada fue muy oportuna.

opportunely ['ɒpətjuːnlɪ] *adv* oportunamente, a propósito; **this comes most ~** esto viene al pelo.

opportunism [ˌɒpə'tjuːnɪzəm] *n* oportunismo *m*.

opportunist [ˌɒpə'tjuːnɪst] **1** *adj* oportunista. **2** *n* oportunista *mf*.

opportunistic [ˌɒpətjʊ'nɪstɪk] *adj* oportunista.

opportunity [ˌɒpə'tjuːnɪtɪ] *n* oportunidad *f*, ocasión *f*, chance *m* (*LAm*); **equality of ~** igualdad *f* de oportunidades; **at the earliest** (*or* **first**) **~** en la primera ocasión; cuanto antes; **they helped at every ~** ayudaban siempre cuando podían; **to have the ~ to** + *infin* tener la oportunidad (*or* el chance *LAm*) de + *infin*; **to make the most of one's ~** aprovechar la ocasión; **to miss one's ~** perder la ocasión, desperdiciar la ocasión; **I take this ~ to** + *infin* aprovecho esta ocasión para + *infin*.

oppose [ə'pəʊz] *vt* oponerse a; resistir, combatir; **but he ~d it** pero él se opuso (a ello); **they ~d the motion** se opusieron a la moción; **we shall ~ this by all the means in our power** lucharemos contra esto por todos los medios.

opposed [ə'pəʊzd] *adj* opuesto; **to be ~ to sth** oponerse a algo, hablar en contra de algo, resistirse a aceptar algo; **it is ~ to all our experience** va en contra de toda nuestra experiencia; **savings as ~ to investments** los ahorros y no las inversiones, los ahorros en comparación con las inversiones.

opposing [ə'pəʊzɪŋ] *adj* opuesto, contrario; ~ **team** equipo *m* adversario.

opposite ['ɒpəzɪt] **1** *adv* en frente; **they sat ~** se sentaran frente a frente, se sentaron uno enfrente del otro; **it is immediately ~** está exactemente en frente; **they are directly ~** están frente por frente.

2 *prep* (*also* **~ to**) enfrente de, frente a; **a house ~ the school** una casa enfrente de la escuela; **~ the bus stop** frente a la parada del autobús; **it was ~ the setting sun** estaba de cara al sol que se ponía; **to sit ~ sb** sentarse enfrente de uno; **we were ~ Calais at the time** (*Naut*) entonces estábamos a la altura de Calais.

3 *adj* (**a**) (*of position*) de enfrente; opuesto; **the house ~** la casa de enfrente; **on the ~ bank** en la ribera opuesta; **on the ~ page** en la página de enfrente; **in the ~ direction** en sentido contrario.

(**b**) (*point of view etc*) opuesto, contrario; (*hostile*) antagónico; **we take an ~ view** nosotros pensamos al contrario, nosotros creemos lo contrario; **of the ~ sex** del otro sexo; *V* **number.**

4 *n*: **the ~ is true** la verdad es al contrario; **quite the ~!** ¡todo lo contrario!; **he maintains the ~** él sostiene lo contrario; **it's the ~ of what we wanted** es totalmente distinto de lo que queríamos.

opposition [,ɒpə'zɪʃən] **1** *n* oposición *f* (*also Pol*); resistencia *f*; (*Comm*) competencia *f*; (*Sport*: *team*) equipo *m* contrario, equipo *m* opuesto; (*persons*) (demás) competidores *mpl*; **he made his ~ known** indicó su disconformidad; **to advance a kilometre without ~** avanzar un kilómetro sin encontrar resistencia; **to act in ~ to the chairman** obrar de modo contrario al presidente; **the party in ~** el partido de la oposición; **the O~** (*Pol*) la Oposición; **to be in ~** (*Pol*) estar en la oposición; **to start up a business in ~ to another** montar un negocio en competencia con otro.

2 *attr member, party* de la oposición; **the O~ benches** los escaños de la Oposición, la Oposición.

oppress [ə'pres] *vt* oprimir; (*of moral cause etc*) agobiar; (*heat etc*) agobiar, ahogar; **the ~ed** los oprimidos.

oppression [ə'preʃən] *n* opresión *f*; agobio *m*.

oppressive [ə'presɪv] *adj* (*Pol etc*) opresivo; tiránico, oprimente, cruel; *burden* agobiante, oneroso; *tax* gravoso; *heat etc* agobiante, agobiador, sofocante.

oppressively [ə'presɪvlɪ] *adv* opresivamente; cruelmente; de modo agobiante, de modo sofocante; **an ~ hot day** un día de calor agobiante.

oppressor [ə'presəʳ] *n* opresor *m*, -ora *f*.

opprobrious [ə'prəʊbrɪəs] *adj* oprobioso.

opprobrium [ə'prəʊbrɪəm] *n* oprobio *m*.

opt [ɒpt] *vi* optar; **to ~ for sth** optar por algo, elegir algo, escoger algo; **to ~ to** + *infin* optar por + *infin*.

◆**opt out** *vi* optar por no tomar parte (*of* en), decidir no participar (*of* en).

optative ['ɒptətɪv] **1** *adj* optativo. **2** *n* optativo *m*.

optic ['ɒptɪk] *adj* óptico; **~ nerve** nervio *m* óptico.

optical ['ɒptɪkəl] *adj* óptico; **~ character reader** lector *m* óptico de caracteres; **~ character recognition** reconocimiento *m* óptico de caracteres; **~ disk** disco *m* óptico; **~ fiber** (*US*), **~ fibre** fibra *f* óptica; **~ illusion** ilusión *f* óptica; **~ reader** lector *m* óptico.

optician [ɒp'tɪʃən] *n* óptico *mf*; **~'s (shop)** óptica *f*.

optics ['ɒptɪks] *n* óptica *f*.

optimal ['ɒptɪml] *adj* óptimo.

optimism ['ɒptɪmɪzəm] *n* optimismo *m*.

optimist ['ɒptɪmɪst] *n* optimista *mf*.

optimistic [,ɒptɪ'mɪstɪk] *adj* optimista; **I am not ~ about it** no lo veo tan fácil, no soy optimista (respecto de ello).

optimistically [,ɒptɪ'mɪstɪklɪ] *adv* con optimismo; *speak etc* en tono optimista.

optimization [,ɒptɪmaɪ'zeɪʃən] *n* optimización *f*.

optimize ['ɒptɪmaɪz] *vt* optimizar.

optimum ['ɒptɪməm] **1** *adj* óptimo, mejor; más favorable; **the ~ number is 8** el mejor número es 8; **in ~ conditions** en las condiciones más favorables.

2 *n, pl* **optima** ['ɒptɪmə] lo óptimo, lo mejor; cantidad *f* óptima, grado *m* óptimo (*etc*).

option ['ɒpʃən] *n* opción *f* (*also Comm, Scol*); **~s** (*US Aut*) accesorios *mpl*, extras *mpl*; **with an ~ on 10 more aircraft** con opción para la compra de 10 aviones más; **6 months without the ~ (of a fine)** una condena de 6 meses sin la posibilidad de pagar una multa; **at the ~ of the purchaser** a opción del comprador; **to have the ~ of doing sth** tener la posibilidad de hacer algo; **I have no ~** no tengo otro recurso, no tengo más remedio; **to keep one's ~s open** no comprometerse; **to take out an ~ on another 100** suscribir una opción para la compra de otros 100.

optional ['ɒpʃənl] *adj* discrecional, facultativo; potestativo; *part, fitting etc* opcional, de opción, optativo; (*Comm*) opcional; **dress ~** traje de etiqueta o de calle, traje a voluntad; **~ extras** (*Aut*) accesorios *mpl*, extras *mpl*; **the heater is ~** el calentador es de opción, el calentador es optativo; **that is completely ~** eso es según lo desee Vd.

optionally ['ɒpʃənlɪ] *adv* opcionalmente; **~ you can have a blue one** Vd puede optar por uno azul.

optometrist [ɒp'tɒmətrɪst] *n* optometrista *mf*.

opulence ['ɒpjʊləns] *n* opulencia *f*.

opulent ['ɒpjʊlənt] *adj* opulento.

opus ['əʊpəs] *n, pl* **opera** ['ɒpərə] (*Mus*) opus *m*, obra *f*; (*hum*) obra *f*.

OR (**a**) *n abbr of* **operations research, operational research** investigaciones *fpl* operacionales. (**b**) (*US Post*) *abbr of* **Oregon.**

or [ɔːʳ] *conj* (**a**) o; (*before* o-, ho-) u; **7 ~ 8** siete u ocho, **this one ~ another** éste u otro; **either A ~ B** o A o B; **~ else** o bien, si no; de otro modo; **an hour ~ so** una hora más o menos; **20 ~ so** unos veinte, veinte más o menos; **let me go ~ I'll scream!** ¡suélteme, que voy a gritar!; **rain ~ no rain, you've got to go** con lluvia o sin lluvia, tienes que ir.

(**b**) (*after negative*) ni; **without relatives ~ friends** sin parientes ni amigos; **without fear ~ favour** imparcialmente; **he didn't write ~ telephone** no escribió ni telefoneó.

o.r. *abbr of* **at owner's risk** a riesgo del propietario.

oracle ['ɒrəkl] *n* oráculo *m*; **to work the ~** dirigirlo todo entre bastidores, ingeniárselas.

oracular [ɒ'rækjʊləʳ] *adj* profético, fatídico; sentencioso; misterioso.

oral ['ɔːrəl] **1** *adj* oral; (*Anat*) bucal; *message* verbal, hablado; *examination, history* oral. **2** *n* examen *m* oral.

orally ['ɔːrəlɪ] *adv* oralmente; *tell etc* por boca, en palabras; (*Anat, Med*) por vía bucal.

orange ['ɒrɪndʒ] **1** *n* (*fruit*) naranja *f*; (*tree*) naranjo *m*; (*colour*) color *m* naranja; (*orangeade*) naranjada *f*. **2** *adj* naranjado, anaranjado, color naranja.

orangeade ['ɒrɪndʒ'eɪd] *n* naranjada *f*.

orange-blossom ['ɒrɪndʒ,blɒsəm] *n* azahar *m*.

orange-coloured, (*US*) **orange-colored** ['ɒrɪndʒ,kʌləd] *adj* = **orange 2.**

orange-grove ['ɒrɪndʒgrəʊv] *n* naranjal *m*.

orange-juice ['ɒrɪndʒdʒuːs] *n* zumo *m* de naranja, jugo *m* de naranja (*LAm*).

Orangeman ['ɒrɪndʒmən] *n, pl* **Orangemen** ['ɒrɪndʒmən] (*Ir*) orangista *m* (*protestante de Irlanda del Norte*).

orangery ['ɒrɪndʒərɪ] *n* invernadero *m* de naranjos.

orang-outang, orang-utan [ɔː'ræŋ'uːtæn] *n* orangután *m*.

orate [ɔː'reɪt] *vi* (*hum*) perorar.

oration [ɔː'reɪʃən] *n* oración *f*, discurso *m*.

orator ['ɒrətəʳ] *n* orador *m*, -ora *f*.

oratorical [,ɒrə'tɒrɪkəl] *adj* oratorio; retórico.

oratorio [,ɒrə'tɔːrɪəʊ] *n* (*Mus*) oratorio *m*.

oratory[1] ['ɒrətərɪ] *n* oratoria *f*.

oratory[2] ['ɒrətərɪ] *n* (*Eccl*) oratorio *m*.

orb [ɔːb] *n* orbe *m*; esfera *f*, globo *m*.

orbit ['ɔːbɪt] **1** *n* órbita *f* (*also fig*); **to be in ~** estar en órbita; **to go into ~ round the moon** entrar en órbita alrededor de la luna.

2 *vt* orbitar, girar alrededor de.

3 *vi* orbitar, girar.

orbital ['ɔːbɪtl] *adj* orbital.

orchard ['ɔːtʃəd] *n* huerto *m*; (*apple* **~**) pomar *m*.

orchestra ['ɔːkɪstrə] **1** *n* orquesta *f*; (*US*: *seating part of theatre*) platea *f*, patio *m* de butacas.

2 *attr*: **~ pit** foso *m* de orquesta; **~ stall** butaca *f* de platea.

orchestral [ɔː'kestrəl] *adj* orquestal.

orchestrate ['ɔːkɪstreɪt] *vt* orquestar, instrumentar; *campaign* orquestar.

orchestration [,ɔːkɪs'treɪʃən] *n* orquestación *f*, instrumentación *f*.

orchid ['ɔːkɪd] *n*, **orchis** ['ɔːkɪs] *n* orquídea *f*.

ordain [ɔː'deɪn] **1** *vt* (**a**) (*order*) ordenar, decretar; **to ~ that ...** ordenar que + *subj*; **to ~ sb's exile** decretar el destierro de uno.

(**b**) (*Eccl*) ordenar; **to ~ sb priest** ordenar a uno de sacerdote; **to be ~ed** ordenarse de sacerdote.

2 *vi* mandar, disponer; **as God ~s** según Dios manda, como Dios manda.

ordeal [ɔː'diːl] *n* (**a**) (*Hist*) ordalías *fpl*; **~ by fire** ordalías *fpl* del fuego.

(**b**) (*fig*) prueba *f* rigurosa, experiencia *f* penosa; sufrimiento *m*; **it was a terrible ~** fue una experiencia terrible; **after such an ~** después de tanto sufrir; **exams are an ~ for me** para mí los exámenes son una cosa horrible, sufro lo indecible con los exámenes.

order ['ɔːdəʳ] **1** *n* (**a**) (*of society etc, Bio*) orden *m*; clase *f*, categoría *f*; **the lower ~s** la clase baja, la plebe; **talents of the first ~** talentos *mpl* de primer orden; **of the ~ of 500** del orden de 500.

(**b**) (**holy**) **~s** órdenes *fpl* sagradas.

(**c**) (*society, decoration*) (*Eccl*) orden *f*; (*secular*) orden *f*, sociedad *f*; (*worn on dress*) condecoración *f*, insignia *f*; **~ of knighthood** orden *f* de caballería; **O~ of the Garter** Orden *f* de la Jarretera.

(**d**) (*Archit*) orden *m*; **Doric ~** orden *m* dórico.

(**e**) (*succession, disposition*) orden *m*; clasificación *f*; método *m*; **in ~** en orden, por orden, por su orden; **in alphabetical ~** por orden alfabético; **in chronological ~** por orden cronológico; **in ~ of seniority** por orden de antigüedad; **to be out of ~** (*sequence*) estar mal arreglados; estar fuera de serie; **to get out of ~** desarreglarse; **to put in ~** poner en orden, arreglar, ordenar; clasificar.

(**f**) (*Mil*) **in close ~** en filas apretadas; **in battle ~** en orden de batalla; **in marching ~** en orden de marchar.

(**g**) (*good ~*) estado *m*; **in ~** en regla; **in good ~** en buen estado, en buenas condiciones; **his papers are in ~** tiene los papeles en regla; **everything is in ~** todo está en regla; **is this passport in ~?** ¿este pasaporte está en regla?; **beer would be in ~** sería indicado tomarse una cerveza; **what sort of an ~ is it in?** ¿en qué estado está?; **to put a matter in ~** arreglar un asunto; **a machine in working ~** una máquina en funcionamiento; **is it in ~ for me to go to Rome?** ¿tengo permiso para ir a Roma?; **'out of ~'** 'no funciona'; **to be out of ~** estar desarreglado; (*Mech*) no funcionar, estar descompuesto; **my liver is out of ~** no estoy bien del hígado; **to get out of ~** (*Mech*) descomponerse, estropearse, averiarse.

(**h**) (*Parl*) **~!** ¡orden! **to be out of ~** estar fuera de orden, estar fuera de la cuestión; ser improcedente; **it is not in ~ to discuss Ruritania** Ruritania está fuera de la cuestión; **to call sb to ~** llamar a uno al orden; **to call the meeting to ~** abrir la sesión; **to rise to a point of ~** levantarse para discutir una cuestión de procedimiento; **to rule a matter out of ~** decidir que un asunto no se puede discutir.

(**i**) (*peace*) orden *m*; **the forces of ~** las fuerzas del orden; **to keep ~** mantener el orden; **she can't keep ~** es incapaz de imponer la disciplina, no puede hacerse obedecer; **to keep children in ~** mantener a los niños en orden.

(**j**) **in ~ to** + *infin* para + *infin*; **in ~ that** ... para que + *subj*.

(**k**) (*command*) orden *f*; decreto *m*, mandato *m*; (*of court etc*) sentencia *f*, fallo *m*; **~ of the day** orden *f* del día; (*fig*) moda *f*, lo que es de rigor; **strikes are the ~ of the day** las huelgas están a la orden del día; **O~ in Council** Orden *f* Real; **~ of the court** sentencia *f* del tribunal; **by ~ of** por orden de; **by ~ of the king** por Real Orden; **on the ~s of** por orden de; **till further ~s** hasta nueva orden; **that's an ~!** ¡es una orden!; **~s are ~s** las órdenes no se discuten; **to be under the ~s of** estar bajo el mando de; **to be under starter's ~s** estar listo para la salida; **we are under ~s not to allow it** tenemos orden de no permitirlo; **to get one's marching ~s*** ser despedido; **to give an ~** dar una orden; **to give sb ~s to do sth** ordenar a uno hacer algo; **to give ~s that sth should be done** mandar que se haga algo; **to obey ~s** cumplir las órdenes; **I don't take ~s from anyone** a mí no me da órdenes nadie.

(**l**) (*Comm*) pedido *m*, encargo *m*; **~ department** sección *f* de pedidos; **~ number** número *m* de pedido; **made to ~** hecho por encargo especial, hecho a la orden; **to the ~ of** a la orden de; **we can't do things to ~** no podemos proveer en seguida todo cuanto se nos pide; **to give an ~ for sth** pedir algo, hacer un pedido de algo; **to place an ~ for sth with sb** pedir algo a uno; **we have it on ~ for you** está pedido para Vd; **we will put it on ~ for you** se lo pediremos para Vd al fabricante; **that's rather a tall ~** eso es mucho pedir; **an ~ of French fries** (*US*) una ración de patatas fritas.

(**m**) (*Fin*) libranza *f*; giro *m*.

2 *vt* (**a**) (*put in ~*) disponer, arreglar, poner en orden; clasificar; **to ~ one's life properly** organizar bien su vida, vivir de acuerdo a cierto método.

(**b**) (*command*) **to ~ sb to do sth** mandar a uno hacer algo, ordenar a uno hacer algo; **to ~ sb a new drug** recetar un nuevo medicamento para uno; **to ~ sb a complete rest** mandar a uno reposo absoluto; **to be ~ed to pay costs** ser condenado en costas.

(**c**) (*Comm*) pedir, encargar; *meal, taxi* encargar; **to ~ a suit of clothes** mandar hacer un traje; **have you ~ed yet?** ¿has escogido ya?, ¿has pedido ya?

◆**order about, order around** *vt* mandar de acá para allá, marimandonear.

◆**order back** *vt* mandar volver.

◆**order in** *vt* mandar entrar.

◆**order off** *vt* despedir, echar; decir que se vaya; (*Sport*) expulsar.

◆**order out** *vt* echar; mandar que se vaya; *troops* llamar, enviar.

order-book ['ɔːdəbʊk] *n* libro *m* de pedidos, cartera *f* de pedidos.

ordered ['ɔːdəd] *adj* ordenado, metódico, disciplinado.

order-form ['ɔːdəfɔːm] *n* hoja *f* de pedido, boletín *m* de pedido.

ordering ['ɔːdərɪŋ] *n* (*Comm*) pedido *m*; el pedir.

orderliness ['ɔːdəlɪnɪs] *n* orden *m*, método *m*, disciplina *f*.

orderly ['ɔːdəlɪ] **1** *adj* (*methodical*) ordenado, metódico; (*tidy*) aseado, en orden, en buen estado; (*well-behaved*) formal; *crowd etc* pacífico, obediente; disciplinado; **~ officer** oficial *m* del día.

2 *n* (*Mil*) ordenanza *m*, asistente *m*; (*Med*) asistente *mf*.

orderly room ['ɔːdəlɪˌrʊm] *n* oficina *f*.

order-paper ['ɔːdəˌpeɪpəʳ] *n* (*Brit Parl etc*) orden *m* del día.

ordinal ['ɔːdɪnl] **1** *adj* ordinal; **~ number** número *m* ordinal. **2** *n* ordinal *m*.

ordinance ['ɔːdɪnəns] *n* ordenanza *f*, decreto *m*.

ordinand ['ɔːdɪnænd] *n* ordenando *m*.

ordinarily [ɔːdɪ'nɛərɪlɪ] *adv* ordinariamente, de ordinario; **~ we buy 6 at a time** generalmente compramos 6 a la vez; **more than ~ polite** más cortés de lo común.

ordinary ['ɔːdnrɪ] **1** *adj* (**a**) corriente, común, normal; **the ~ Frenchman** el francés corriente; **an ~ citizen** un simple ciudadano; **for the ~ reader** para el lector medio; **in the ~ way I wouldn't allow it** normalmente no lo permitiría; **it's not what you'd call an ~ present** no es lo que se diría un regalo de todos los días.

(**b**) **~ degree** (*Brit*) diploma *m*; **O~ grade** (*Scot Scol*), **O~ Level** (*Brit*) ≈ bachillerato *m* elemental (*examen oficial que se suele realizar en el cuarto curso de secundario*); **O~ National Certificate** (*Brit*) ≈ diploma *m* de técnico especialista; **O~ National Diploma** (*Brit*) *diploma profesional*, ≈ diploma *m* de técnico especialista.

(**c**) *share* ordinario; **~ seaman** marinero *m*.

(**d**) (*pej*) vulgar, ordinario; mediocre; **just an ~ man** un hombre vulgar; **they're very ~ people** son gente muy modesta; **neither good nor bad, just ~** ni bueno ni malo, solamente regular.

2 *n*: **a man above the ~** un hombre fuera de serie, un hombre que no es del montón; **sth out of the ~** algo fuera de lo común, algo extraordinario.

ordination [ˌɔːdɪ'neɪʃən] *n* (*Eccl*) ordenación *f*.

ordnance ['ɔːdnəns] **1** *n* (*guns*) artillería *f*, cañones *mpl*; (*supplies*) pertrechos *mpl* de guerra. **2** *attr*: **O~ Corps** Cuerpo *m* de Armamento y Material; **~ factory** fábrica *f* de artillería; **O~ Survey** (*Brit*) *servicio oficial de topografía;* **O~ (Survey) map** (*Brit*) ≈ mapa *m* del Estado Mayor.

Ordovician [ˌɔːdəʊ'vɪʃɪən] *adj* ordoviciense.

ordure ['ɔːdjʊəʳ] *n* inmundicia *f* (*also fig*).

ore [ɔːʳ] *n* mineral *m*, mena *f*; **copper** (*etc*) **~** mineral *m* de cobre (*etc*).

Ore. (*US*) *abbr of* **Oregon**.

ore-carrier ['ɔːkærɪəʳ] *n* mineralero *m*.

oregano [ˌɒrɪ'gɑːnəʊ] *n* orégano *m*.

organ ['ɔːgən] *n* (*all senses*) órgano *m*.

organdie, (*US*) **organdy** ['ɔːgəndɪ] *n* organdí *m*.

organ-grinder ['ɔːgənˌgraɪndəʳ] *n* organillero *m*.

organic [ɔː'gænɪk] *adj* (**a**) (*gen*) orgánico; **~ analysis** análisis *m* orgánico; **~ chemistry** química *f* orgánica. (**b**) (*free of chemicals*) orgánico, exento de productos químicos; **~ farming** agricultura *f* orgánica, agricultura *f* que no emplea productos químicos; **~ food products** alimentos *mpl* orgánicos (*or* naturales); **~ restaurant** restaurante *m* de cocina natural.

organically [ɔː'gænɪkəlɪ] *adv* orgánicamente; **he's farming ~** se dedica a la agricultura orgánica; **~ grown foods** alimentos *mpl* orgánicos; **there's nothing ~ wrong with you** Vd está en buen estado en cuanto a lo físico.

organism ['ɔːgənɪzəm] *n* organismo *m*.

organist [ˈɔːgənɪst] *n* organista *mf.*
organization [ˌɔːgənaɪˈzeɪʃən] **1** *n* (**a**) (*act*) organización *f.*
(**b**) (*body*) organización *f*, organismo *m.*
2 *attr*: ~ **chart** organigrama *m*; ~ **man** especialista *m* en ciencias administrativas.
organizational [ˌɔːgənaɪˈzeɪʃənl] *adj* organizativo.
organize [ˈɔːgənaɪz] **1** *vt* (**a**) (*gen*) organizar; **to get ~d** organizarse, arreglárselas.
(**b**) (*US Ind*) organizar en sindicatos, sindicar.
2 *vi* (**a**) (*gen*) organizarse (*for* para).
(**b**) (*US Ind*) sindicarse, afiliarse a un sindicato.
organized [ˈɔːgənaɪzd] *adj* (**a**) *crime etc* organizado. (**b**) *person* metódico, ordenado.
organizer [ˈɔːgənaɪzəʳ] *n* organizador *m*, -ora *f.*
organizing [ˈɔːgənaɪzɪŋ] *adj*: ~ **committee** comisión *f* organizadora.
organ loft [ˈɔːgənlɒft] *n* tribuna *f* del órgano, galería *f* del órgano.
organ pipe [ˈɔːgənpaɪp] *n* cañón *m* de órgano.
organ stop [ˈɔːgənstɒp] *n* registro *m* de órgano.
organza [ɔːˈgænzə] *n* organza *f*, organdí *m* de seda.
orgasm [ˈɔːgæzəm] *n* orgasmo *m.*
orgasmic [ɔːˈgæzmɪk] *adj* orgásmico.
orgiastic [ˌɔːdʒɪˈæstɪk] *adj* orgiástico.
orgy [ˈɔːdʒɪ] *n* orgía *f*; **an ~ of destruction** una orgía de destrucción; **the flowers were an ~ of colour** las flores eran una explosión de colores.
oriel [ˈɔːrɪəl] *n* mirador *m.*
Orient [ˈɔːrɪənt] *n* Oriente *m.*
orient [ˈɔːrɪənt] *vt etc* = **orientate.**
oriental [ˌɔːrɪˈentəl] **1** *adj* oriental. **2** *n* oriental *mf* (*also* **O~**).
orientalism [ˌɔːrɪˈentəlɪzəm] *n* orientalismo *m.*
orientalist [ˌɔːrɪˈentəlɪst] **1** *adj* orientalista. **2** *n* orientalista *mf.*
orientate [ˈɔːrɪenteɪt] **1** *vt* orientar (*to, towards* hacia). **2** *vr*: **to ~ o.s.** orientarse.
orientated [ˈɔːrɪenteɪtɪd] *adj in compounds eg* **career-~** orientado hacia una carrera; **commercially-~** orientado hacia el comercio.
orientation [ˌɔːrɪenˈteɪʃən] *n* orientación *f*; ~ **course** curso *m* de orientación.
oriented [ˈɔːrɪentɪd] = **orientated.**
orienteering [ˌɔːrɪənˈtɪərɪŋ] *n* orientación *f.*
orifice [ˈɒrɪfɪs] *n* orificio *m.*
origami [ˌɒrɪˈgɑːmɪ] *n* papiroflexia *f.*
origin [ˈɒrɪdʒɪn] *n* origen *m*; (*point of departure*) procedencia *f*; **country of ~** país *m* de origen, país *m* de procedencia; **to be of humble ~, to have humble ~s** ser de nacimiento humilde.
original [əˈrɪdʒɪnl] **1** *adj* (**a**) (*first etc*) original, primero; *meaning, sin etc* original; (*earlier*) primitivo; **the ~ sense was ...** el sentido primitivo era ...; **one of the ~ members** uno de los primeros miembros, uno de los socios fundadores; **its ~ inventor** su inventor primitivo.
(**b**) (*inventive, new*) original.
2 *n* (**a**) (*manuscript, painting etc*) original *m*; (*archetype*) original *m*, prototipo *m*; **the ~ is lost** el original está perdido; **he reads Cervantes in the ~** lee a Cervantes en su idioma original, lee a Cervantes en su propia lengua.
(**b**) (*person*) original *m*, excéntrico *m.*
originality [əˌrɪdʒɪˈnælɪtɪ] *n* originalidad *f.*
originally [əˈrɪdʒənəlɪ] *adv* (**a**) (*at first*) al principio, en sus orígenes; originariamente, originalmente; **as they were ~ written** tal como fueron escritas originariamente; **~ they were in Athens** al principio estuvieron en Atenas, antiguamente estuvieron en Atenas.
(**b**) (*in an original manner*) **it is quite ~ written** está escrito con bastante originalidad; **he deals with the subject ~** trata el asunto con inventiva.
originate [əˈrɪdʒɪneɪt] **1** *vt* producir, originar, dar lugar a; (*of person*) idear, inventar, crear.
2 *vi* originarse, nacer, surgir; **to ~ from, to ~ in** traer su origen de; **to ~ with sb** ser obra de uno, ser invento de uno; **where did the fire ~?** ¿dónde empezó el incendio?; **with whom did the idea ~?** ¿quién tuvo la idea primero?
originator [əˈrɪdʒɪneɪtəʳ] *n* inventor *m*, -ora *f*, autor *m*, -ora *f.*
oriole [ˈɔːrɪəʊl] *n*: **golden ~** oropéndola *f.*
Orkney Islands [ˈɔːknɪˌaɪləndz] *npl*, **Orkneys** [ˈɔːknɪz] *npl* Órcadas *fpl.*
Orlon [ˈɔːlɒn] ® *n* orlón ® *m.*
ormolu [ˈɔːməʊluː] *n* similor *m*, bronce *m* dorado.
ornament 1 [ˈɔːnəmənt] *n* adorno *m*, ornato *m*, ornamento *m*; (*trinket*) chuchería *f*; (*vase etc*) objeto *m* de adorno; **he is the chief ~ of his country** es el máximo valor de su patria; **~s** (*Eccl*) ornamentos *mpl.*
2 [ˈɔːnəment] *vt* adornar, ornamentar (*with* de).
ornamental [ˌɔːnəˈmentl] *adj* ornamental (*also Bot*); decorativo, de adorno.
ornamentation [ˌɔːnəmenˈteɪʃən] *n* ornamentación *f.*
ornate [ɔːˈneɪt] *adj* muy ornado, vistoso; *style* florido.
ornately [ɔːˈneɪtlɪ] *adv* vistosamente; en estilo florido.
ornateness [ɔːˈneɪtnɪs] *n* vistosidad *f*; estilo *m* florido; lo florido.
ornithological [ˌɔːnɪθəˈlɒdʒɪkəl] *adj* ornitológico.
ornithologist [ˌɔːnɪˈθɒlədʒɪst] *n* ornitólogo *m*, -a *f.*
ornithology [ˌɔːnɪˈθɒlədʒɪ] *n* ornitología *f.*
orphan [ˈɔːfən] **1** *adj* huérfano.
2 *n* huérfano *m*, -a *f.*
3 *vt* dejar huérfano a; **the children were ~ed by the accident** el accidente dejó huérfanos a los niños; **she was ~ed at the age of 9** quedó huérfana a los 9 años.
orphanage [ˈɔːfənɪdʒ] *n* orfanato *m*, orfelinato *m*, asilo *m* de húerfanos.
Orpheus [ˈɔːfɪuːs] *nm* Orfeo.
ortho... [ˈɔːθəʊ] *pref* orto...
orthodontics [ˌɔːθəʊˈdɒntɪks] *n* ortodoncia *f.*
orthodontist [ˌɔːθəʊˈdɒntɪst] *n* ortodoncista *mf.*
orthodox [ˈɔːθədɒks] *adj* ortodoxo.
orthodoxy [ˈɔːθədɒksɪ] *n* ortodoxia *f.*
orthographic(al) [ˌɔːθəˈgræfɪk(əl)] *adj* ortográfico.
orthography [ɔːˈθɒgrəfɪ] *n* ortografía *f.*
orthopaedic, (*US*) **orthopedic** [ˌɔːθəʊˈpiːdɪk] *adj* ortopédico; ~ **surgeon** cirujano *m* ortopédico, cirujana *f* ortopédica; ~ **surgery** cirujía *f* ortopédica.
orthopaedics, (*US*) **orthopedics** [ˌɔːθəʊˈpiːdɪks] *n* ortopedia *f.*
orthopaedist, (*US*) **orthopedist** [ˌɔːθəʊˈpiːdɪst] *n* ortopedista *mf.*
oryx [ˈɒrɪks] *n* orix *m.*
OS (**a**) *n* (*Brit Geog*) *abbr of* **Ordnance Survey** *servicio oficial de topografía.* (**b**) (*Hist*) *abbr of* **old style** según el calendario juliano.
O.S. *n* (*Brit*) *abbr of* **ordinary seaman.**
O/S *abbr of* **out of stock.**
o/s (*Comm*) *abbr of* **outsize** de tamaño extraordinario.
Oscar [ˈɒskəʳ] *n* (*Cine*) Oscar *m.*
oscillate [ˈɒsɪleɪt] **1** *vt* hacer oscilar.
2 *vi* (**a**) oscilar (*between* entre; *from A to Z* de A a Z); fluctuar, variar.
(**b**) (*person*) oscilar, vacilar; **he ~s between boredom and keenness** pasa del aburrimiento al entusiasmo, oscila entre el aburrimiento y el entusiasmo.
oscillating [ˈɒsɪleɪtɪŋ] *adj* oscilante.
oscillation [ˌɒsɪˈleɪʃən] *n* oscilación *f*; fluctuación *f*, variación *f*; vacilación *f.*
oscillator [ˈɒsɪleɪtəʳ] *n* oscilador *m.*
oscillatory [ˌɒsɪˈleɪtərɪ] *adj* oscilatorio.
oscilloscope [ɒˈsɪləˌskəʊp] *n* osciloscopio *m.*
osculate [ˈɒskjʊleɪt] (*hum*) **1** *vt* besar. **2** *vi* besar(se).
osculation [ˌɒskjʊˈleɪʃən] *n* (*hum*) ósculo *m.*
OSHA *n* (*US*) *abbr of* **Occupational Safety and Health Administration.**
osier [ˈəʊʒəʳ] **1** *n* mimbre *f.* **2** *attr*: ~ **bed** mimbrera *f.*
Oslo [ˈɒzləʊ] *n* Oslo *m.*
osmium [ˈɒzmɪəm] *n* osmio *m.*
osmosis [ɒzˈməʊsɪs] *n* ósmosis *f* (*also fig*).
osmotic [ɒzˈmɒtɪk] *adj* osmótico.
osprey [ˈɒspreɪ] *n* águila *f* pescadora, quebrantahuesos *m.*
osseous [ˈɒsɪəs] *adj* óseo.
ossification [ˌɒsɪfɪˈkeɪʃən] *n* osificación *f.*
ossify [ˈɒsɪfaɪ] **1** *vt* osificar. **2** *vi* osificarse.
ossuary [ˈɒsjʊərɪ] *n* osario *m.*
OST *n* (*US*) *abbr of* **Office of Science and Technology.**
Ostend [ɒsˈtend] *n* Ostende *m.*
ostensible [ɒsˈtensəbl] *adj* pretendido, aparente.
ostensibly [ɒsˈtensəblɪ] *adv* aparentemente, en apariencia.
ostensive [ɒˈstensɪv] *adj* ostensivo.
ostentation [ˌɒstenˈteɪʃən] *n* ostentación *f*; aparato *m*, boato *m*; fausto *m.*
ostentatious [ˌɒstenˈteɪʃəs] *adj* ostentoso; aparatoso; *person* ostentativo.
ostentatiously [ˌɒstenˈteɪʃəslɪ] *adv* ostentosamente, con ostentación; aparatosamente; con boato; **he remained ~ silent** permaneció ostentosamente silencioso.
osteo... [ˈɒstɪəʊ] *pref* osteo...
osteoarthritis [ˈɒstɪəʊɑːˈθraɪtɪs] *n* osteoartritis *f.*
osteomalacia [ˌɒstɪəʊməˈleɪʃɪə] *n* osteomalacia *f.*

osteomyelitis [ˌɒstɪəʊmaɪɪˈlaɪtɪs] *n* osteomielitis *f.*
osteopath [ˈɒstɪəpæθ] *n* osteópata *mf.*
osteopathy [ˌɒstɪˈɒpəθɪ] *n* osteopatía *f.*
osteoporosis [ˌɒstɪəʊpɔːˈrəʊsɪs] *n* osteoporosis *f.*
ostler [ˈɒsləʳ] *n* (*esp Brit* ††) mozo *m* de cuadra.
ostracism [ˈɒstrəsɪzəm] *n* ostracismo *m.*
ostracize [ˈɒstrəsaɪz] *vt* condenar al ostracismo, excluir de la sociedad (*or* del trato, del grupo *etc*); **he was ~d** vivió en el ostracismo.
ostrich [ˈɒstrɪtʃ] *n* avestruz *m.*
OT *n abbr of* **Old Testament** Antiguo Testamento *m*, A.T.
OTB *n* (*US*) *abbr of* **off-track betting** apuestas *fpl* ilegales hechas fuera del hipódromo.
OTC (**a**) *adv* (*Comm*) *abbr of* **over the counter** al contado. (**b**) *n* (*Brit*) *abbr of* **Officer Training Corps** cuerpo *m* de cadetes militares.
OTE (*Brit*) *abbr of* **on-target earnings** beneficios *mpl* según objetivos.
Othello [əˈθeləʊ] *nm* Otelo.
other [ˈʌðəʳ] **1** *adj* otro; **the ~ one** el otro; **the ~ five** los otros cinco; **the ~ day** el otro día; **come some ~ day** venga otro día; **all the ~ books have been sold** todos los otros libros se han vendido, todos los demás libros se han vendido; **~ people have done it** otros lo han hecho; **~ people's property** la propiedad ajena; **~ people's ideas** las ideas ajenas; **among ~ things she is a writer** entre otras cosas es escritora; **together with every ~ woman** así como todas las mujeres (*V also* **every**); **I do not wish him ~ than he is** no quiero que sea distinto de lo que es; **no book ~ than this** ningún libro que no sea éste; **he had no clothes ~ than those he stood up in** no tenía más ropa que la que llevaba puesta; **it was no ~ than the bishop** fue el obispo en persona, fue el mismo obispo.
2 *pron*: **the ~** el otro; **the ~s** los otros, los demás; **one after the ~** uno tras otro; **among ~s** entre otros; **some do, ~s don't** algunos sí, otros no; los hay que sí, otros no; **are there any ~s?** ¿hay otros?; **and these 5 ~s** y estos otros 5; **she and no ~** ella y no otra; **some fool or ~** algún tonto; **somebody or ~** alguien, alguno, -a (*LAm*); **one or ~ of us** uno de nosotros; **no ~** ningún otro; **our happiness depends on that of ~s** nuestra felicidad depende de la de otros; **we must respect ~s' rights** hay que respetar los derechos ajenos; *V* **each.**
3 *adv*: **~ than** de otra manera que; otra cosa que; **he could not act ~ than as he did** no podía hacer otra cosa que la que hizo; **I did not read it ~ than cursorily** no le di sino una lectura superficial.
otherness [ˈʌðənɪs] *n* alteridad *f.*
otherwise [ˈʌðəwaɪz] **1** *adv* (**a**) (*in another way*) de otra manera; **it cannot be ~** no puede ser de otra manera; **we had no reason to think ~** no teníamos motivo para creer otra cosa; **Miller, ~ known as Dusty** Miller, por otro nombre Dusty; **goods whether sold or ~** géneros vendidos o sin vender.
(**b**) (*in other respects*) por lo demás, por otra parte; **~ it's a very good car** por lo demás es un coche muy bueno, aparte de esto es un coche muy bueno; **a car better than I would ~ have bought** un coche mejor que hubiera comprado normalmente.
2 *conj* (*if not*) si no; **~ we shall have to walk** pues si no (*or* pues de lo contrario) tendremos que ir a pie.
other-worldly [ˈʌðəˈwɜːldlɪ] *adj* (**a**) *person* espiritual, poco realista. (**b**) *experience* (como) de otro mundo; *being* extraterrestre.
otiose [ˈəʊtɪəʊs] *adj* ocioso, inútil.
otitis [əʊˈtaɪtɪs] *n* otitis *f.*
OTT* *adj abbr of* **over the top.**
otter [ˈɒtəʳ] *n* nutria *f.*
Otto [ˈɒtəʊ] *nm* Otón.
Ottoman [ˈɒtəmən] **1** *adj* otomano. **2** *n* otomano *m*, -a *f.*
ottoman [ˈɒtəmən] *n* otomana *f.*
OU *n* (*Brit*) *abbr of* **Open University** ≃ Universidad *f* Nacional de Educación a Distancia, UNED *f.*
ouch [aʊtʃ] *excl* ¡ay!
ought¹ [ɔːt] *n* = **aught.**
ought² [ɔːt] *v aux* (**a**) (*obligation*) deber; **I ~ to do it** debo hacerlo, debiera hacerlo; **I ~ to have done it** debiera haberlo hecho; **one ~ not to do it** no se debe hacer; **to behave as one ~** comportarse como se debe; **one ~ to be able to find it** ha de ser posible encontrarlo; **I thought I ~ to tell you** me creí en el deber de decírselo, pensé que debía decírselo.
(**b**) (*vague desirability*) **you ~ to go and see it** vale la pena ir a verlo; **you ~ to have seen it!** ¡era de ver!; **you ~ to have seen him!** ¡había que verle!
(**c**) (*probability*) **that car ~ to win** ese coche tiene más probabilidades de ganar; **that ~ to be enough** eso ha de bastar; **he ~ to have arrived by now** debe de haber llegado ya.
Ouija [ˈwiːdʒə] ® *n* (*also* **~ board**) tabla *f* de espiritismo.
ounce [aʊns] *n* (**a**) onza *f* (= *28,35 gr*).
(**b**) (*fig*) pizca *f*; **there's not an ~ of truth in it** no tiene ni pizca de verdad; **if you had an ~ of common sense** si tuvieras una gota de sentido común.
OUP *n abbr of* **Oxford University Press.**
our [aʊəʳ] *poss adj* nuestro(s), nuestra(s).
ours [aʊəz] *poss pron* (el) nuestro, (la) nuestra *etc.*
ourselves [ˌaʊəˈselvz] *pron* (*subject*) nosotros mismos, nosotras mismas; (*acc, dat*) nos; (*after prep*) nosotros (mismos), nosotras (mismas); *V* **oneself.**
oust [aʊst] *vt* desalojar; expulsar, echar; (*from house etc*) desahuciar; **to ~ sb from a post** lograr que uno renuncie a un puesto; **we ~ed them from the position** les hicimos abandonar la posición; **'fab' ~ed 'smashing'** 'fantástico' sustituyó a 'fabuloso'.
out [aʊt] **1** *adv* (**a**) (*gen*) fuera, afuera; hacia fuera; **'~'** (*notice*) 'salida'; **~ you go!** ¡fuera!; **~ with him!** ¡fuera con él!, ¡que le echen fuera!; **~ with it!** ¡desembucha!*, ¡suelta la lengua! (*LAm*); **seconds ~!** (*Boxing*) ¡segundos fuera!; **you're ~** (*in games*) quedas fuera, te has eliminado; **I'm ~** (*in games*) termino; **the voyage ~** el viaje de ida; **murder will ~** el asesinato se descubrirá; **~ here** aquí fuera; aquí, aquí en este sitio tan remoto; **~ there** allí fuera; allí, allí en ese sitio tan remoto; **it carried us ~ to sea** nos llevó mar adentro; **to have a day ~** pasar un día fuera de casa, pasar un día en el campo, pasar un día al aire libre; **it's her evening ~** es su tarde libre; **to have a night ~** salir de juerga por la noche; *V other verbs, eg* **to come ~, to go ~** salir; **to run ~** salir corriendo.
(**b**) **to be ~** (*person*) no estar (en casa), estar fuera; haber salido; **Mr Green is ~** el Sr Green no está; **he's ~ a good deal** pasa bastante tiempo fuera; **to be ~ and about again** estar repuesto y activo, estar de nuevo en pie; **now that the Liberals are ~** ahora que los liberales están fuera del poder; **the railwaymen are ~** los ferroviarios están en huelga; **I was ~ for some minutes** (*unconscious*) estuve varios minutos sin conocimiento; **he was ~ cold** estuvo completamente sin conocimiento.
(**c**) (*incorrect*) **I'm 2 dollars ~** he perdido 2 dólares en el cálculo; **he was ~ in his reckoning** había hecho mal el cálculo, había calculado mal; **I was not far ~** lo acerté casi; **and he was not far ~ either** y su conjetura resultó ser casi exacta.
(**d**) (*fig*) **when the sun is ~** cuando brilla el sol; **the dahlias are ~** las dalias están en flor; **the book is ~** se ha publicado el libro, ha salido el libro; **the secret is ~** el secreto ha salido a luz; **the ball is ~** el balón está fuera del terreno; **the tide is ~** la marea está baja; **long dresses are ~** los vestidos largos ya no están de moda; **your watch is 5 minutes ~** su reloj lleva 5 minutos de atraso (*or* de adelanto); **before the week is ~** antes del fin de la semana; **to be ~** *fire, light, gas* estar apagado; **'lights ~ at 10 pm'** 'se apagan las luces a las 10'; **my pipe is ~** se me ha apagado la pipa.
(**e**) (*purpose*) **to be ~ for** buscar; ambicionar, aspirar a; **he's ~ for all he can get** está resuelto a hacerse con todo lo que pueda; **we're ~ for a quick decision** buscamos una pronta decisión; **they're ~ for trouble** quieren armar un escándalo; buscan camorra; **we are ~ after duck** estamos cazando ánades; **she's ~ to find a husband** se propone pescar un marido, está dedicada a conseguir marido.
(**f**) (*of clothes etc*) **the coat is ~ at the elbows** la chaqueta está rota por los codos.
(**g**) (*intensive*) **it's the biggest swindle ~** es la mayor estafa que hay; **he's the best footballer ~** es el mejor futbolista que se ha visto, es el mejor futbolista que se ha conocido jamás.
(**h**) **~ loud** en alta voz; **right ~, straight ~** francamente, sin rodeos.
2 ~ of *prep* (**a**) (*outside, beyond*) fuera de; **to be ~ of range** estar fuera de alcance; **to be ~ of danger** estar fuera de peligro; **to be ~ of sight** estar invisible, no estar a la vista, no poderse ver; **to be ~ of season** estar fuera de temporada; **we're well ~ of it** de buena nos hemos librado; **to feel ~ of it** sentirse aislado, no tomar parte en las actividades sociales (*etc*).
(**b**) (*incompatible with*) **to be ~ of proportion with** no

guardar proporción con; ~ **of measure** fuera de medida; **times** ~ **of number** innumerables veces; *V* **mind, sort** *etc.*

(**c**) (*verbs of motion etc*) **to go** ~ **of the house** salir de la casa; **to go** ~ **of the door** salir por la puerta; **to throw sth** ~ **of a window** tirar algo por una ventana; **we looked** ~ **of the window** nos asomamos a la ventana, miramos por la ventana; **to turn sb** ~ **of the house** echar a uno de la casa.

(**d**) (*origin*) de; **a chapter** ~ **of a novel** un capítulo de una novela; **like a princess** ~ **of a fairy tale** como una princesa de un cuento de hadas; **to drink** ~ **of a glass** beber de un vaso; **to eat** ~ **of the same dish** comer del mismo plato; **to take sth** ~ **of a drawer** sacar algo de un cajón; **to read** ~ **of a novel** leer en una novela; **to copy sth** ~ **of a book** copiar algo de un libro.

(**e**) (*from among*) **1** ~ **of 10** de cada 10, 1; **1** ~ **of every 3 smokers** 1 de cada 3 fumadores.

(**f**) (*material*) de; **a box made** ~ **of wood** una caja hecha de madera.

(**g**) (*because of*) por; ~ **of respect for you** por el respeto que te tengo; ~ **of spite** por despecho; ~ **of necessity** por necesidad; **to do sth** ~ **of sympathy** hacer algo por compasión.

(**h**) (*lacking*) **we're** ~ **of petrol** no hay gasolina, se acabó la gasolina, nos hemos quedado sin gasolina; **it's** ~ **of stock** no hay, no tenemos; **to be** ~ **of a suit** (*Bridge*) estar fallo; **to be** ~ **of hearts** tener fallo a corazones.

3 *n*: *V* **in 3.**

outage ['aʊtɪdʒ] *n* (*esp US Elec*) apagón *m*, corte *m*.

out-and-out ['aʊtən'aʊt] *adj believer etc* firme, acérrimo, cien por cien; de tomo y lomo; *scoundrel* consumado, redomado.

outback ['aʊtbæk] *n* (*Australia*) despoblado *m*, interior *m*, campo *m*.

outbid [aʊt'bɪd] (*irr*: *V* **bid**) *vt* licitar más que, hacer mejor oferta que; sobrepujar.

outboard ['aʊtbɔːd] *adj* fuera de borda; ~ **motor** motor *m* fuera de borda, motor *m* fuera-bordo, fuera bordo *m*, propela *f* (*Carib*).

outbound ['aʊtˌbaʊnd] (*US*) **1** *adv* hacia fuera, hacia el exterior. **2** *adj* que va hacia fuera, que va hacia el exterior; *flight* de ida.

outbreak ['aʊtbreɪk] *n* (*of spots*) erupción *f*; (*of disease*) epidemia *f*, brote *m*; (*of revolt*) estallido *m*; (*of war*) comienzo *m*, declaración *f*, (*of hostilities*) rompimiento *m*; (*of feeling, violence etc*) arranque *m*; (*of crimes etc*) ola *f*; **at the** ~ **of war** al declararse la guerra.

outbuilding ['aʊtˌbɪldɪŋ] *n* dependencia *f*, edificio *m* accesorio; (*shed*) cobertizo *m*.

outburst ['aʊtbɜːst] *n* explosión *f*; arranque *m*, acceso *m*; **an** ~ **of anger** una explosión de cólera; **there was an** ~ **of applause** hubo una salva de aplausos, estallaron ruidosos los aplausos; **forgive my** ~ **last week** te ruego perdonar el que perdiera los estribos la semana pasada.

outcast ['aʊtkɑːst] *n* paria *mf*, proscrito *m*, -a *f*; marginado *m*, -a *f*; **he is a social** ~ vive rechazado por la sociedad, ha sido marginado por la sociedad.

outclass [aʊt'klɑːs] *vt* ser netamente superior a, aventajar con mucho a.

outcome ['aʊtkʌm] *n* resultado *m*, consecuencia *f*.

outcrop ['aʊtkrɒp] **1** *n* afloramiento *m*, afloración *f*. **2** *vi* aflorar.

outcry ['aʊtkraɪ] *n* grito *m*, protesta *f* clamorosa; **to raise an** ~ **about sth** poner el grito en el cielo por motivo de algo; **there was a great** ~ hubo fuertes protestas, se armó la gorda*.

outdated ['aʊt'deɪtɪd] *adj* anticuado, fuera de moda.

outdistance [aʊt'dɪstəns] *vt* dejar atrás.

outdo [aʊt'duː] (*irr*: *V* **do**) *vt* exceder, sobrepujar; **to** ~ **sb in sth** exceder a uno en algo; **he was not be outdone** no se quedó en menos; **I, not to be outdone ...** pues yo, para no quedar en menos ...; **not to be outdone, he added ...** ni corto ni perezoso, añadió que ...

outdoor ['aʊtdɔːʳ] *adj* al aire libre; ~ **activities** actividades *fpl* al aire libre; ~ **clothes** ropa *f* de calle; **the** ~ **life** la vida al aire libre; ~ **market** mercado *m* al aire libre.

outdoors ['aʊt'dɔːz] **1** *adv* al aire libre; fuera de casa; **go and play** ~ id a jugar fuera. **2** *n*: **the great** ~ el gran mundo al aire libre.

outer ['aʊtəʳ] *adj* exterior; externo; ~ **leaves** hojas *fpl* de afuera; **O~ Mongolia** Mongolia *f* Exterior; ~ **space** espacio *m* exterior.

outermost ['aʊtəməʊst] *adj place* extremo, (el) más remoto; *cover etc* (el) más exterior, primero.

outface [aʊt'feɪs] *vt* desafiar.

outfall ['aʊtfɔːl] *n* (*of drain*) desagüe *m*, desaguadero *m*; (*of river*) desembocadura *f*.

outfield ['aʊtfiːld] *n* (*Sport*) parte *f* más lejana del campo, (*Baseball*) jardín *m*.

outfit ['aʊtfɪt] *n* (**a**) (*gear*) equipo *m*; (*tools*) herramientas *fpl*, juego *m* de herramientas; (*of clothes*) traje *m*; **a complete camper's** ~ un equipo completo de campista; **why are you wearing that** ~**?** ¿por qué te has trajeado así?

(**b**) (*) (*Mil*) unidad *f*, cuerpo *m*, equipo *m*; grupo *m*; organización *f*; (*Sport*) equipo *m*; **when I joined this** ~ cuando vine a formar parte de esta unidad; **it's a rotten** ~ es una sección horrible.

outfitter ['aʊtfɪtəʳ] *n* camisero *m*; **sports** ~**'s** tienda *f* especializada en ropa deportiva.

outflank [aʊt'flæŋk] *vt* (*Mil*) flanquear, rebasar; (*fig*) superar en táctica, burlar.

outflow ['aʊtfləʊ] *n* efusión *f*; desagüe *m*; pérdida *f*; (*of capital etc*) fuga *f*, salida *f*; (*Mech*) tubo *m* de salida.

outfox [aʊt'fɒks] *vt* ser más listo que.

outgeneral [aʊt'dʒenərəl] *vt* superar en estrategia (*or* táctica).

outgo ['aʊtgəʊ] *n* (*US*) gastos *mpl*.

outgoing ['aʊtˌgəʊɪŋ] **1** *adj* (**a**) *president etc* saliente; *government* cesante; *ministry* que acaba de dimitir; *mail* que sale; *tide* que baja; *flight* de ida. (**b**) *character* extrovertido, abierto. **2** *npl*: ~**s** (*Brit*) gastos *mpl*.

outgrow [aʊt'grəʊ] (*irr*: *V* **grow**) *vt* (*person*) crecer más que; *habit etc* pasar de la edad de, ser ya viejo para; *defect, illness* curarse de ... con la edad; *clothes* hacerse demasiado grande para; **she has** ~**n her gloves** se le han quedado chicos los guantes; **we've** ~**n all that** todo eso ha quedado ya a la espalda.

outgrowth ['aʊtˌgrəʊθ] *n* excrecencia *f*; (*fig*) extensión *f*.

outhouse ['aʊthaʊs] *n*, *pl* **outhouses** ['aʊthaʊzɪz] (**a**) (*Brit*) = **outbuilding.** (**b**) (*US*) retrete *m* fuera de la casa.

outing ['aʊtɪŋ] *n* (*walk*) paseo *m*; (*trip*) excursión *f*, jira *f* campestre; **I took a brief** ~ di un pequeño paseo, di una vuelta; **everyone went on an** ~ **to Toledo** todos fueron de excursión a Toledo.

outlandish [aʊt'lændɪʃ] *adj* estrafalario, extravagante.

outlast [aʊt'lɑːst] *vt* durar más tiempo que; (*person*) sobrevivir a.

outlaw ['aʊtlɔː] **1** *n* proscrito *m*, forajido *m*. **2** *vt* proscribir; *drug etc* ilegalizar; *practice etc* declarar ilegal, declarar fuera de la ley.

outlawry ['aʊtlɔːrɪ] *n* bandolerismo *m*.

outlay ['aʊtleɪ] *n* desembolso *m*, inversión *f*.

outlet ['aʊtlet] *n* salida *f* (*also fig, Comm*); (*retail* ~) concesionario *m*; (*of drain etc*) desagüe *m*, desaguadero *m*; (*of stream etc*) desembocadura *f*; (*Mech*) salida *f*, tubo *m* de salida; (*US Elec*) toma *f* de corriente; **to find an** ~ **for a product** encontrar una salida (*or* un mercado) para un producto; **it provides an** ~ **for his energies** ofrece un empleo para sus energías.

outline ['aʊtlaɪn] **1** *n* (*profile*) contorno *m*, perfil *m*; (*of plan*) trazado *m*; (*sketch*) esbozo *m*, bosquejo *m*; (*general idea, also* ~**s**) idea *f* general, nociones *fpl* generales; **'O~s of History'** (*as title*) 'Introducción a la Historia'; **in broad** ~ a grandes líneas, a grandes rasgos; **in broad** ~ **the plan is as follows ...** el trazado general del plan es el siguiente ...; **I'll give you a rapid** ~ **of the scheme** te esbozaré el proyecto, te daré un resumen del proyecto.

2 *adj*: ~ **drawing** esbozo *m*; ~ **history** resumen *m* de historia; ~ **programme** borrador *m* de programa.

3 *vt* (*draw profile of*) perfilar; (*sketch*) trazar, bosquejar; *policy etc* explicar en términos generales, dar una idea general de; **to be** ~**d against** destacarse contra, dibujarse contra; **the building was** ~**d in the distance** el edificio se perfilaba a lo lejos; **let me** ~ **the scheme for you** te doy un resumen del proyecto.

outlive [aʊt'lɪv] *vt* (**a**) sobrevivir a; (*thing*) durar más tiempo que.

(**b**) (*live down*) hacer olvidar.

outlook ['aʊtlʊk] *n* (**a**) (*view, future promise*) perspectiva *f*, perspectivas *fpl*; panorama *m*; (*Met*) pronóstico *m*; **the** ~ **for the wheat crop is good** son favorables las perspectivas de la cosecha de trigo; **it's a grim** ~ es una perspectiva nada halagüeña, el futuro no promete nada bueno.

(**b**) (*opinion*) punto *m* de vista; actitud *f*; **one's** ~ **on life** su concepto de la vida, la actitud de uno ante la vida; **what is his** ~ **on the matter?** ¿cuál es su punto de vista en este asunto?; **his** ~ **is always pessimistic** su actitud siempre es pesimista; **a person with a broad** ~ una persona de amplias miras.

outlying ['aʊt,laɪɪŋ] *adj* (*distant*) remoto, lejano, aislado; *suburb etc* exterior, periférico.

outmanoeuvre, (*US*) **outmaneuver** [,aʊtmə'nu:vəʳ] *vt* superar en la táctica.

outmatch [aʊt'mætʃ] *vt* superar, aventajar.

outmoded [aʊt'məʊdɪd] *adj* anticuado, pasado de moda.

outnumber [aʊt'nʌmbəʳ] *vt* exceder en número, ser más numeroso que; **we were ~ed 10 to 1** ellos eran diez veces más que nosotros.

out-of-bounds [,aʊtəv'baʊndz] *adj V* **bound[2]**.

out-of-date ['aʊtəv'deɪt] *adj* anticuado; *V also* **date[1] 1**.

out-of-doors ['aʊtəv'dɔ:z] *adv* = **outdoors**.

out-of-pocket ['aʊtəv'pɒkɪt] *adj*: **~ expenses** gastos *mpl* realizados.

out-of-school [,aʊtəv'sku:l] *adj*: **~ activities** actividades *fpl* extraescolares.

out-of-the-way ['aʊtəvðə'weɪ] *adj* (*remote*) remoto, apartado, aislado; inaccesible; (*unusual*) insólito; poco conocido, poco común; (*recherché*) rebuscado.

out-of-towner [,aʊtəv'taʊnəʳ] *n* (*US*) forastero *m*, -a *f*.

outpace [aʊt'peɪs] *vt* dejar atrás.

outpatient ['aʊt,peɪʃənt] *n* paciente *m* externo, paciente *f* externa (del hospital); **~s' department** departamento *m* de consulta externa.

outperform ['aʊtpə'ʃɔ:m] *vt* hacer mejor que, superar a.

outplay [aʊt'pleɪ] *vt* superar en la táctica, jugar mejor que; **we were ~ed in every department** ellos resultaron ser mejores que nosotros en todos los aspectos del juego, nos dominaron por completo.

outpost ['aʊtpəʊst] *n* avanzada *f* (*also fig*), puesto *m* avanzado.

outpouring ['aʊt,pɔ:rɪŋ] *n* efusión *f*; **the ~s of a sick mind** la efusión de una mente enferma; **an ~ of emotion** una efusión de emoción.

output ['aʊtpʊt] **1** *n* producción *f*, volumen *m* de producción; (*of machine*) rendimiento *m*; (*Elec*) potencia *f* de salida; (*Comput*) salida *f*, output *m*; **to raise ~** aumentar la producción.

2 *attr*: **~ bonus** prima *f* por rendimiento; **~ device** dispositivo *m* de salida.

3 *vt* (*Comput*) imprimir.

outrage 1 ['aʊtreɪdʒ] *n* atrocidad *f*; atropello *m*; (*by terrorists*) atentado *m*; (*committed during riot etc*) desmán *m*, desafuero *m*; (*public scandal*) escándalo *m*; (*suffered by sb*) indignidad *f*; **bomb ~** atentado *m* con bomba; **it's an ~!** ¡es un escándalo!, ¡qué barbaridad!, ¡no hay derecho!; **to commit an ~ against** (*or* **on**) **sb** cometer un desafuero contra uno.

2 [aʊt'reɪdʒ] *vt* ultrajar, violentar, atropellar; (*rape*) violar; **it ~s justice** atropella la justicia.

outrageous [aʊt'reɪdʒəs] *adj* atroz, terrible; monstruoso; escandaloso; indignante; **your ~ conduct** tu conducta escandalosa; **it is absolutely ~ that ...** es indignante que + *subj*; **it's ~!** ¡es un escándalo!, ¡qué barbaridad!, ¡no hay derecho!

outrageously [aʊt'reɪdʒəslɪ] *adv behave etc* de modo escandaloso.

outrank [aʊt'ræŋk] *vt* ser de categoría superior a.

outré ['u:treɪ] *adj* extravagante, estrafalario.

outrider ['aʊt,raɪdəʳ] *n* motociclista *m* de escolta.

outrigger ['aʊt,rɪgəʳ] *n* (*beam, spar*) batanga *f*, balancín *m*; (*rowlock*) portarremos *m* exterior; (*boat*) bote *m* con batanga, bote *m* con portarremos exterior.

outright 1 ['aʊtraɪt] *adj* (*complete*) completo, entero, total; *sale etc* en su totalidad, definitivo; (*forthright*) franco; *supporter etc* incondicional, declarado; *refusal* rotundo.

2 [aʊt'raɪt] *adv* (*once and for all*) de una vez, de un golpe; (*forthrightly*) abiertamente, francamente; **to buy sth ~** comprar algo en su totalidad, comprar algo definitivamente; **to reject an offer ~** rechazar una oferta de pleno; **to laugh ~ at sth** reírse abiertamente de algo; **they won the cup ~** ganaron la copa definitivamente; **he was killed ~** murió en el acto, murió al instante.

outrun [aʊt'rʌn] (*irr*: *V* **run**) *vt* correr más que; (*fig*) exceder, rebasar, pasar los límites de.

outsell [,aʊtsel] (*irr*: *V* **sell**) *vt* vender más que, superar en las ventas a; **this product ~s all the competition** este producto se vende más que todos los competidores.

outset ['aʊtset] *n* principio *m*, comienzo *m*; **at the ~** al principio; **from the ~** desde el principio.

outshine [aʊt'ʃaɪn] (*irr*: *V* **shine**) *vt* brillar más que; (*fig*) eclipsar, superar en brillantez.

outside ['aʊt'saɪd] **1** *adv* fuera; **to be ~** estar fuera; **to leave a car ~** dejar un coche fuera, (*at night etc*) dejar un coche en la calle, dejar un coche al descubierto; **to put the cat ~** hacer salir al gato; **seen from ~** visto desde fuera; **to ride ~** (*on bus*) viajar en el piso superior; **~ of** = **2**.

2 *prep* fuera de; al exterior de; (*beyond*) más allá de, al otro lado de; **he's waiting ~ the door** espera a la puerta; **one could hear everything that was said ~ the door** se oía todo cuanto se estaba diciendo al otro lado de la puerta; **it's ~ the normal range** cae fuera del alcance normal; **it's ~ our scheme** no forma parte de nuestro proyecto; **that's ~ our terms of reference** eso no está comprendido en nuestro mandato.

3 *adj* (*outer*) exterior, externo; (*outermost*) extremo; *chance etc* remoto, poco prometedor; (*relating to other people*) ajeno; (*brought from ~*) traído desde fuera; *TV broadcast* exterior; *forward* (*Sport*) extremo; **thanks to ~ influence** gracias a la influencia de personas ajenas al asunto, gracias a influencias extrañas; **to get an ~ opinion** buscar una opinión independiente; **~ call** llamada *f* de fuera; **~ contractor** contratista *mf* independiente; **~ lane** carril *m* de adelantamiento; **~ line** línea *f* exterior.

4 *n* (*outer part*) exterior *m*; (*surface*) superficie *f*; (*outward aspect*) aspecto *m* exterior, apariencia *f*; (*of bus*) piso *m* superior; **at the ~** a lo sumo, cuando más; **from the ~** desde fuera, desde el exterior; **to open a window from the ~** abrir una ventana desde fuera; **on the ~** por fuera; **to pass sb on the ~** adelantar (*LAm*: rebasar) a uno por el exterior; **the window opens to the ~** la ventana se abre hacia fuera.

outside-forward ['aʊtsaɪd'fɔ:wəd] *n* delantero *m* extremo, delantera *f* extrema.

outside-left ['aʊtsaɪd'left] *n* extremo *m* izquierdo, extrema *f* izquierda.

outsider ['aʊt'saɪdəʳ] *n* (*stranger*) forastero *m*, -a *f*, desconocido *m*, -a *f*, (*pej*) intruso *m*, -a *f*; (*in racing*) caballo *m* que no figura entre los favoritos, (*in election*) candidato *m* poco conocido; (*cad*) canalla *m*, persona *f* indeseable; (*independent*) persona *f* independiente, persona *f* ajena al asunto, persona *f* no comprometida; **I'm an ~ in these matters** yo soy un profano en estos asuntos.

outside-right ['aʊtsaɪd'raɪt] *n* extremo *m* derecho, extrema *f* derecha.

outsize ['aʊtsaɪz] *adj* muy grande, de tamaño extraordinario; (*hum*) enorme.

outskirts ['aʊtskɜ:ts] *npl* afueras *fpl*; alrededores *mpl*; barrios *mpl* (exteriores).

outsmart [aʊt'smɑ:t] *vt* ser más listo que, burlar; (*deceive*) engañar, burlar.

outspoken [aʊt'spəʊkən] *adj* franco, abierto; **to be ~** no tener pelos en la lengua.

outspokenly [aʊt'spəʊkənlɪ] *adv* francamente.

outspokenness [aʊt'spəʊkənnɪs] *n* franqueza *f*.

outspread ['aʊt'spred] *adj* extendido; desplegado.

outstanding [aʊt'stændɪŋ] *adj* (**a**) (*exceptional*) destacado; excepcional, relevante, sobresaliente. (**b**) *problem* pendiente, no resuelto; *account* por pagar; *debt, interest, shares* pendiente.

outstandingly [aʊt'stændɪŋlɪ] *adv* excepcionalmente, extraordinariamente.

outstare [,aʊt'stɛəʳ] *vt*: **to ~ sb** desconcertar a uno mirándole fijamente.

outstation ['aʊt,steɪʃən] *n* dependencia *f*.

outstay [aʊt'steɪ] *vt person* quedarse más tiempo que; **to ~ one's welcome** permanecer tanto tiempo que uno resulta pesado, quedarse más tiempo de lo conveniente; **I don't want to ~ my welcome** no quiero ser un pesado, no quiero abusar.

outstretched ['aʊtstretʃt] *adj* extendido; alargado; **with ~ arms** con los brazos tendidos.

outstrip [aʊt'strɪp] *vt* dejar atrás, aventajar, superar, adelantarse a.

out-take ['aʊt,teɪk] *n* trozo *m* de película desechado.

out-tray ['aʊt,treɪ] *n* bandeja *f* de salida.

outturn ['aʊttɜ:n] *n* (*US*) rendimiento *m*, producción *f*.

outvote [aʊt'vəʊt] *vt person* vencer en las elecciones; *proposal* rechazar por votación; **but I was ~d** pero en la votación perdí.

outward ['aʊtwəd] *adj* exterior, externo, *journey* de ida.

outwardly ['aʊtwədlɪ] *adv* por fuera, aparentemente.

outward(s) ['aʊtwəd(z)] *adv* hacia fuera; exteriormente; **to be ~ bound from Vigo** haber salido de Vigo; **to be ~ bound for Gijón** ir con rumbo a Gijón.

outwear [aʊt'wɛəʳ] (*irr*: *V* **wear**) *vt* (*last longer than*) durar más tiempo que; (*wear out*) gastar.

outweigh [aʊt'weɪ] *vt* pesar más que, tener mayor peso que; (*fig*) pesar más que; **this ~s all other considerations** éste vale más que todos los demás factores.
outwit [aʊt'wɪt] *vt* ser más listo que, burlar.
outworn [aʊt'wɔːn] *adj* gastado, cansado.
ouzo ['uːzəʊ] *n* ouzo *m*.
ova ['əʊvə] *npl of* **ovum**.
oval ['əʊvəl] **1** *adj* oval, ovalado. **2** *n* óvalo *m*.
ovarian [əʊ'vɛərɪən] *adj* ovárico.
ovary ['əʊvərɪ] *n* ovario *m*.
ovate ['əʊveɪt] *adj* aovado.
ovation [əʊ'veɪʃən] *n* ovación *f*; **to give sb an ~** ovacionar a uno; **to receive an ~** ser ovacionado; **he got a standing ~ from the delegates** fue ovacionado por los delegados puestos de pie.
oven ['ʌvn] *n* (*Tech*) horno *m*, (*Culin*) horno *m*, cocina *f* (*LAm*); **Huelva was like an ~** Huelva era un horno; **it's like an ~ in there** allí dentro es el mismo infierno.
oven-glove ['ʌvn,glʌv] *n* (*Brit*) guante *m* para el horno.
ovenproof ['ʌvnpruːf] *adj* refractario, (a prueba) de horno.
oven-ready [,ʌvn'redɪ] *adj* listo para hornear.
oven-tray ['ʌvntreɪ] *n* bandeja *f* para horno.
ovenware ['ʌvnwɛəʳ] *n* utensilios *mpl* para horno, utensilios *mpl* termorresistentes.
over ['əʊvəʳ] **1** *adv* **(a)** (*of place*) encima; por encima; arriba (*LAm*); por arriba (*LAm*); **this goes under and that goes ~** éste pasa por debajo y ése por encima.
(b) (*in another place*) **~ here** acá; **~ there** allá; **~!** (*Radio*) ¡cambio!; **~ and out!** ¡cambio y corto!; **~ to you!** (*Telec etc*) ¡a ti!; **so now it's ~ to you** así que te toca a ti decidir, así que ahora dirás tú; **~ now to our reporter** (*Rad, TV*) ahora pasamos la palabra a nuestro reportero; **~ in France** allá en Francia; **they're ~ for the day** han venido a pasar el día; **when we were ~ in the States** cuando estábamos de visita en Estados Unidos; **~ against the wall** contra la pared; **~ against the church** al lado de la iglesia, junto a la iglesia.
(c) (*everywhere*: **all ~** *etc*) **the world ~** en todo el mundo; **to search the whole country ~** registrar el país de arriba abajo; **embroidered all ~** todo bordado; **to tremble all ~** estar todo tembloroso; **I ache all ~** me duele en todas partes; **I looked for you all ~** te busqué por todas partes; **it happens all ~** ocurre en todas partes, ocurre por doquier; **he was all ~ flour** estaba todo harina; **that's him all ~** eso es muy de él; **suddenly, he was all ~ me** de repente, se puso a manosearme.
(d) (*with verbs*) **to bend ~** inclinarse, encorvarse, doblarse (*LAm*); **to bend sth ~** doblar algo; **to boil ~** irse, rebosar; **to flow ~** desbordarse; *V* **fall over, lean over, look over** *etc.*
(e) (*of number, quantity*) **persons of 21 and ~** las personas de 21 años para arriba; **4 into 29 goes 7 and 1 ~** 29 dividido entre 4 son 7 y queda 1; **we have 4 pounds and a bit ~** tenemos 4 libras y algo más; **there are 3 ~** sobran 3, quedan 3; **I have a card ~** me sobra una carta, tengo una carta de más; **we did it two or three times ~** lo hicimos dos o tres veces (a fondo).
(f) (*finished*) **to be ~ (and done with)** estar terminado; **when this is all ~** cuando esto haya terminado, cuando se acabe esto; **as soon as the war is ~** en cuanto termine la guerra; **the storm is ~** ya pasó la tormenta; **it's all ~!** ¡se acabó!; **it's all ~ with him** se acabó con él, está perdido, (*relationship*) he roto con él.
(g) it happened (all) ~ again volvió a ocurrir, ocurrió otra vez; **it's happening ~ and ~ (again)** esto pasa repetidas veces; **we shall have to start all ~ again** tendremos que volver a comenzar desde el principio.
2 *prep* **(a)** (*place: above*) encima de, por encima de, arriba de (*LAm*); (*on, in contact with*) sobre; **~ our heads** por encima de nuestras cabezas; **to spread a sheet ~ sth** extender una sábana sobre algo; **to jump ~ sth** saltar por encima de algo; **we looked ~ the wall** miramos por encima de la tapia; **with a sign ~ the door** con un rótulo sobre la puerta; **it sticks out ~ the street** sobresale por encima de la calle; **to bend ~ a table** inclinarse sobre una mesa; **to fall ~ a cliff** caer por un precipicio; **to trip ~ sth** tropezar con algo; **to sit ~ the fire** estar sentado junto a la lumbre; **the water came ~ her knees** el agua le cubrió las rodillas; **a change came ~ him** se operó en él un cambio; **she's ~ it now** se ha repuesto de eso ya, eso queda ya a la espalda.
(b) (*place: across*) **the pub ~ the road** la taberna de enfrente; **it's just ~ the road from us** está justamente enfrente de nuestra casa; **it's ~ the river** está tras el río, está en la otra orilla del río; **the bridge ~ the river** el puente que cruza el río.
(c) (*place: with* **all**) **all ~ Spain** por toda España; **known all ~ the world** conocido en el mundo entero; **he had mud all ~ himself** estaba totalmente cubierto de lodo; **they were all ~ him** le recibieron con el mayor entusiasmo, le dieron grandes testimonios de su afecto; **Zaragoza were all ~ Bilbao** el Zaragoza dominó al Bilbao por completo.
(d) (*place: fig*) **to rule ~ a people** reinar sobre un pueblo; **he's ~ me** es mi superior; **they gave me the preference ~ him** me prefirieron a él; **to have an advantage ~ sb** llevar ventaja a uno.
(e) (*numbers*) **the numbers ~ 20** los números superiores a 20, los números más allá de 20; **~ 200** más de 200; **well ~ 200** 200 y muchos más; **she's ~ 21 now** tiene más de 21 años ya; **he must be ~ 60** tendrá más de 60 años; **~ and above last year's figure** en exceso de la cifra del año pasado; **an increase of 5% ~ last year's total** un aumento de 5 por cien sobre el año anterior; **~ and above what has been said** además de lo que se ha dicho; **~ and above our needs** más allá de nuestras necesidades.
(f) (*time*) **~ the last few years** durante los últimos años; **payments spread ~ some years** pagos espaciados por varios años; **we stayed on ~ the weekend** nos quedamos a pasar el fin de semana.
(g) (*motive*) **they fell out ~ money** riñeron por cuestión de dinero; **to pause ~ a difficulty** detenerse a considerar un punto difícil.
(h) (*means*) **I heard it ~ the radio** lo supe por la radio.
over- ['əʊvəʳ] *pref*: sobre..., super...; demasiado ...
overabundance ['əʊvərə'bʌndəns] *n* sobreabundancia *f*.
overabundant ['əʊvərə'bʌndənt] *adj* sobreabundante.
overact ['əʊvər'ækt] *vi* sobreactuar, exagerar (el papel).
overacting [,əʊvər'æktɪŋ] *n* sobreactuación *f*, exageración *f* (del papel).
overactive ['əʊvər'æktɪv] *adj* demasiado activo.
overall 1 [,əʊvər'ɔːl] *adv* en conjunto, en su totalidad; **~, we are well pleased** en resumen, estamos muy contentos.
2 ['əʊvərɔːl] *adj study, view etc* de conjunto; *length etc* total; (*total*) global.
overalls ['əʊvərɔːlz] *npl* guardapolvo *m*, mono *m*, traje *m* de faena, bata *f*, overol *m* (*LAm*).
overambitious ['əʊvəræm'bɪʃəs] *adj* demasiado ambicioso.
overanxious ['əʊvər'æŋkʃəs] *adj* **(a)** (*worried*) demasiado preocupado, preocupado sin motivo.
(b) (*eager*) demasiado deseoso (*for* de; *to do* de hacer); **I'm not ~ to go** tengo pocas ganas de ir.
overarm ['əʊvərɑːm] *adv throw, bowl* por encima de la cabeza.
overawe [,əʊvər'ɔː] *vt* intimidar; imponer respeto a.
overbalance [,əʊvə'bæləns] **1** *vt* hacer perder el equilibrio. **2** *vi* perder el equilibrio.
overbearing [,əʊvə'bɛərɪŋ] *adj* imperioso, altivo; despótico.
overbid 1 ['əʊvəbɪd] *n* (*at auction*) mejor oferta *f*, mejor postura *f*; (*Bridge*) sobremarca *f*.
2 [,əʊvə'bɪd] (*irr: V* **bid**) *vt* (*at auction*) licitar más que, hacer mejor oferta que; (*Bridge*) marcar más que.
3 [,əʊvə'bɪd] *vi* (*Bridge*) hacer una sobremarca, (*foolishly*) declarar demasiado.
overbill ['əʊvəbɪl] *vt* (*US*) cobrar demasiado a, presentar una factura excesiva a; **I was ~ed** trataron de cobrarme demasiado.
overblown ['əʊvə'bləʊn] *adj* **(a)** *flower* marchito, pasado. **(b)** *style* pomposo, pretencioso.
overboard ['əʊvəbɔːd] *adv*: **man ~!** ¡hombre al agua!; **to fall ~** caer al agua; **to throw sth ~** echar algo por la borda (*also fig*); **to go ~ for sth*** entusiasmarse locamente por algo.
overbold ['əʊvə'bəʊld] *adj* demasiado atrevido; temerario; descarado.
overbook [,əʊvə'bʊk] *vt* sobrereservar, reservar con exceso.
overbooking [,əʊvə'bʊkɪŋ] *n* sobrecontrata *f*, sobrecontratación *f*, exceso *m* de contratación.
overburden [,əʊvə'bɜːdn] *vt* sobrecargar; oprimir, agobiar (*with* de); **not exactly ~ed with worries** no precisamente agobiado de preocupaciones.
overcall [,əʊvə'kɔːl] *vti* = **overbid.**
over-capacity ['əʊvəkə'pæsɪtɪ] *n* sobrecapacidad *f*.
overcapitalization [,əʊvə,kæpɪtəlaɪ'zeɪʃən] *n* sobrecapitalización *f*, capitalización *f* inflada.
overcapitalize [,əʊvə'kæpɪtəlaɪz] *vt* sobrecapitalizar.
overcast ['əʊvəkɑːst] *adj sky* encapotado, cubierto, nublado; **to grow ~** anublarse.
overcautious ['əʊvə'kɔːʃəs] *adj* demasiado cauteloso,

prudente con exceso.
overcautiousness [ˌəʊvəˈkɔːʃəsnɪs] *n* excesiva cautela *f*.
overcharge **1** [ˈəʊvəˌtʃɑːdʒ] *n* precio *m* excesivo, cargo *m* excesivo. **2** [ˈəʊvəˈtʃɑːdʒ] *vt* sobrecargar (*also Elec*); *person* cobrar demasiado a. **3** [ˈəʊvəˈtʃɑːdʒ] *vi* cobrar un precio excesivo, hacer pagar demasiado.
overcoat [ˈəʊvəkəʊt] *n* abrigo *m*, sobretodo *m*, gabán *m*.
overcome [ˌəʊvəˈkʌm] (*irr*: *V* **come**) **1** *vt enemy, temptation etc* vencer; *difficulty* salvar, superar; **sleep overcame him** le rindió el sueño; **he was ~ by remorse** le rindieron los remordimientos; **he was ~ by grief** estaba postrado de dolor.
2 *vi* vencer, triunfar; **we shall ~** venceremos.
overcompensate [ˌəʊvəˈkɒmpenˌseɪt] *vi*: **to ~ for sth** compensar algo excesivamente.
overcompensation [ˈəʊvəˌkɒmpenˈseɪʃən] *n* compensación *f* excesiva.
overconfidence [ˈəʊvəˈkɒnfɪdəns] *n* confianza *f* excesiva, exceso *m* de confianza.
overconfident [ˈəʊvəˈkɒnfɪdənt] *adj* demasiado confiado (*of* en).
overconsumption [ˈəʊvəkənˈsʌmpʃən] *n* superconsumo *m*, exceso *m* de consumo.
overcook [ˈəʊvəˈkʊk] *vt* cocer demasiado, recocer.
overcritical [ˌəʊvəˈkrɪtɪkəl] *adj* hipercrítico; **let's not be ~** seamos justos en nuestra crítica.
overcrowd [ˌəʊvəˈkraʊd] *vt* atestar, superpoblar, congestionar.
overcrowded [ˈəʊvəˈkraʊdɪd] *adj room etc* atestado de gente, muy lleno; *suburb etc* congestionado; *country* superpoblado.
overcrowding [ˌəʊvəˈkraʊdɪŋ] *n* superpoblación *f*, congestionamiento *m*; masificación *f*; amontonamiento *m*; (*in tenement etc*) hacinamiento *m*, número *m* excesivo de inquilinos.
overdependence [ˌəʊvədɪˈpendəns] *n* dependencia *f* excesiva.
overdependent [ˌəʊvədɪˈpendənt] *adj* excesivamente dependiente (*on* de).
overdeveloped [ˈəʊvədɪˈveləpt] *adj* (*gen*) superdesarrollado; (*Phot*) sobreprocesado.
overdo [ˌəʊvəˈduː] (*irr*: *V* **do**) *vt food* cocer demasiado, recocer; (*exaggerate*) exagerar; (*use to excess*) usar demasiado; llevar a extremos, excederse en; **to ~ it, to ~ things** (*work too hard*) trabajar demasiado, fatigarse; (*exaggerate*) exagerar; pasarse, irse de la mano; (*in description, sentiment etc*) cargar la mano; **she rather overdoes the scent** tiende a cargar la mano con el perfume; **see that you don't ~ it** cuidado con no fatigarte; **Espronceda overdoes the passion** Espronceda exagera la pasión.
overdone [ˌəʊvəˈdʌn] *adj* exagerado; *food* muy hecho, demasiado asado (*or* cocido *etc*).
overdose [ˈəʊvədəʊs] **1** *n* sobredosis *f*. **2** *vi* tomar una sobredosis (*on* de).
overdraft [ˈəʊvədrɑːft] **1** *n* (*Comm*) sobregiro *m*, (giro *m* en) descubierto *m*; (*on account*) saldo *m* deudor; (*loan*) préstamo *m*; **to have an ~ at the bank** tener un saldo deudor con el banco, deber dinero al banco.
2 *attr*: **~ charges** cargos *mpl* por descubierto; **~ facility** crédito *m* al descubierto; **~ limit** límite *m* del descubierto.
overdraw [ˈəʊvəˈdrɔː] (*irr*: *V* **draw**) *vt* girar en descubierto; **your account is ~n (by £50)** su cuenta tiene un saldo deudor (de 50 libras); **I'm ~n at the bank** tengo deudas en el banco, tengo un saldo deudor en el banco.
overdress [ˈəʊvəˈdres] *vi* vestirse con demasiada elegancia.
overdrive [ˈəʊvədraɪv] *n* sobremarcha *f*, superdirecta *f*; **to go into ~** (*fig*) ponerse en superdirecta.
overdue [ˈəʊvəˈdjuː] *adj* (*Comm*) vencido y no pagado; *train etc* atrasado, con retraso; **the bus is 30 minutes ~** el autobús tiene 30 minutos de retraso; **this baby is two weeks ~** este niño debió nacer hace quince días, se ha retrasado el parto quince días; **the book is 5 days ~** se acabó hace 5 días el plazo de préstamo de este libro; **that change was long ~** ese cambio debió hacerse mucho tiempo antes.
overeager [ˈəʊvərˈiːgəʳ] *adj* demasiado deseoso (*for* de; *to do* de hacer); demasiado entusiasta, entusiasta con exceso; muy afanado; **she was not ~ to help** tenía pocas ganas de ayudar.
overeat [ˈəʊvərˈiːt] (*irr*: *V* **eat**) *vi* comer con exceso; (*at 1 meal*) atracarse, darse un atracón.
overeating [ˌəʊvərˈiːtɪŋ] *n* comida *f* excesiva.
overelaborate [ˈəʊvərɪˈlæbərɪt] *adj* demasiado complicado; demasiado detallado; rebuscado; *courtesy etc* estudiado.
overemphasize [ˌəʊvərˈemfəsaɪz] *vt* sobreenfatizar.
overemployment [ˈəʊvərɪmˈplɔɪmənt] *n* superempleo *m*.
overenthusiastic [ˈəʊvərɪnˌθjuːzɪˈæstɪk] *adj* demasiado entusiasta.
overestimate **1** [ˈəʊvərˈestɪmɪt] *n* sobre(e)stimación *f*, estimación *f* excesiva; (*Fin*) presupuesto *m*-excesivo.
2 [ˈəʊvərˈestɪmeɪt] *vt* sobre(e)stimar, apreciar en una cantidad (*etc*) excesiva; estimar en valor excesivo; *person* tener un concepto exagerado de; **to ~ one's strength** creerse uno más fuerte de lo que es.
overexcite [ˈəʊvərɪkˈsaɪt] *vt* sobre(e)xcitar.
overexcited [ˈəʊvərɪkˈsaɪtɪd] *adj* sobre(e)xcitado; **to get ~** sobre(e)xcitarse.
overexcitement [ˈəʊvərɪkˈsaɪtmənt] *n* sobre(e)xcitación *f*.
overexert [ˈəʊvərɪgˈzɜːt] *vr*: **to ~ o.s.** hacer un esfuerzo excesivo.
overexertion [ˈəʊvərɪgˈzɜːʃən] *n* (*effort*) esfuerzo *m* excesivo; (*weariness*) fatiga *f*.
overexpenditure [ˌəʊvəɪksˈpendɪtʃəʳ] *n* gasto *m* excesivo.
overexpose [ˈəʊvərɪksˈpəʊz] *vt* sobre(e)xponer.
overexposure [ˈəʊvərɪksˈpəʊʒəʳ] *n* sobre(e)xposición *f*.
overfamiliar [ˈəʊvəfəˈmɪlɪəʳ] *adj* demasiado familiar, que emplea demasiada confianza.
overfeed [ˈəʊvəˈfiːd] (*irr*: *V* **feed**) **1** *vt* sobrealimentar; dar demasiado de comer a. **2** *vi* sobrealimentarse; comer demasiado, atracarse.
overfeeding [ˌəʊvəˈfiːdɪŋ] *n* sobrealimentación *f*.
overflow **1** [ˈəʊvəfləʊ] *n* (*liquid*) exceso *m* de líquido, líquido *m* derramado; (*pipe etc*) rebosadero *m*, cañería *f* de desagüe; (*of people*) exceso *m*, número *m* excesivo.
2 [ˈəʊvəfləʊ] *attr*: **~ meeting** reunión *f* para el público sobrante.
3 [ˌəʊvəˈfləʊ] *vt banks* desbordarse de, salir de; *fields, surrounds* inundar.
4 [ˌəʊvəˈfləʊ] *vi* (*vessel*) rebosar, desbordarse; (*river*) desbordarse, salir de madre; **to ~ with** (*fig*) rebosar de; **to fill a cup to ~ing** llenar una taza hasta que se derrame el líquido; **the crowd filled the stadium to ~ing** el estadio estaba a rebosar de público.
overfly [ˈəʊvəˈflaɪ] (*irr*: *V* **fly**) *vt* sobrevolar.
overfull [ˈəʊvəˈfʊl] *adj* demasiado lleno (*of* de), más que lleno, rebosante.
overgenerous [ˈəʊvəˈdʒenərəs] *adj* demasiado generoso; **an ~ helping** una porción excesivamente grande; **they were ~ in their praise of him** le elogiaron con exceso.
overgrown [ˈəʊvəˈgrəʊn] *adj* (**a**) *boy etc* demasiado grande para su edad. (**b**) *garden etc* abandonado, descuidado; cubierto de malas hierbas; **~ with** cubierto de, revestido de; **the path is quite ~ now** la senda está ya totalmente cubierta de vegetación.
overhand [ˈəʊvəhænd] (*US*) **1** *adj stroke* hecho (*or* dado *etc*) por lo alto. **2** *adv* por lo alto.
overhang **1** [ˈəʊvəhæŋ] *n* proyección *f*; (*of roof*) alero *m*; (*in rock climbing*) extraplomo *m*, panza *f* de burro, saliente *m*.
2 [əʊvəˈhæŋ] (*irr*: *V* **hang**) *vt* sobresalir por encima de; estar pendiente sobre, estar colgado sobre; (*fig*) amenazar.
3 [ˌəʊvəˈhæŋ] *vi* sobresalir; estar pendiente, estar colgado.
overhanging [ˈəʊvəˈhæŋɪŋ] *adj* sobresaliente, voladizo.
overhastily [ˌəʊvəˈheɪstɪlɪ] *adv* apresuradamente, precipitadamente.
overhasty [ˌəʊvəˈheɪstɪ] *adj* apresurado, precipitado.
overhaul **1** [ˈəʊvəhɔːl] *n* repaso *m* general, revisión *f*. **2** [ˌəʊvəˈhɔːl] *vt* (**a**) (*check*) *machine* revisar, repasar, dar un repaso general a; *plans etc* volver a pensar, rehacer, examinar. (**b**) (*overtake*) alcanzar, adelantarse a.
overhead **1** [ˌəʊvəˈhed] *adv* por lo alto, en alto, por encima de la cabeza; **a bird flew ~** pasó un pájaro.
2 [ˈəʊvəhed] *adj* de arriba, encima de la cabeza; *crane* de techo; *railway* elevado, aéreo, suspendido; *camshaft etc* superior, superpuesto; **~ cable** línea *f* eléctrica aérea; **~ expenses** gastos *mpl* generales; **~ kick** chilena *f*, tijereta *f*; **~ light** luz *f* de techo; **~ projector** retroproyector *m*.
3 [ˈəʊvəhed] *n*: **~** (*US*), **~s** (*Brit*) gastos *mpl* generales.
overhear [ˌəʊvəˈhɪəʳ] (*irr*: *V* **hear**) *vt* oír, oír por casualidad; acertar a oír; **she was ~d complaining** le alcanzaron a oír quejándose.
overheat [ˈəʊvəˈhiːt] **1** *vt* recalentar, sobrecalentar (*also fig, Econ*); **to get ~ed** recalentarse. **2** *vi* recalentarse, sobrecalentarse.
overheating [ˌəʊvəˈhiːtɪŋ] *n* sobrecalentamiento *m* (*also fig,*

Econ).

overindulge ['əʊvərɪn'dʌldʒ] **1** *vt child* mimar con exceso; *passion etc* dar rienda suelta a; *taste etc* consentir.

2 *vi* darse demasiada buena vida; **to ~ in alcohol** (*etc*) abusar del alcohol (*etc*).

overindulgence ['əʊvərɪn'dʌldʒəns] *n* (**a**) (*excess*) abuso *m* (*in* de), exceso *m* vicioso; **by his ~ in ...** por su abandono vicioso a ...(**b**) (*kindness*) exceso *m* de tolerancia (*towards* con).

overindulgent ['əʊvərɪn'dʌldʒənt] *adj* demasiado indulgente (*towards* con).

overinvestment [,əʊvərɪn'vestmənt] *n* sobreinversión *f*.

overissue ['əʊvər,ɪʃuː] (*St Ex*) **1** *n* emisión *f* excesiva. **2** *vt* emitir con exceso.

overjoyed [,əʊvə'dʒɔɪd] *adj*: **they were ~** estuvieron llenos de alegría, se alegraron muchísimo; **he was ~ at the news** no cabía en sí de contento con la noticia; **she will be ~ to see you** estará encantada de veros.

overkill ['əʊvəkɪl] *n* capacidad *f* excesiva de destrucción; (*fig*) exceso *m* de medios; **there is a danger of ~ here** aquí hay peligro de excedernos en los medios.

overladen [,əʊvə'leɪdn] *adj* sobrecargado (*with* de).

overland 1 [,əʊvə'lænd] *adv* por tierra, por vía terrestre. **2** ['əʊvəlænd] *adj* terrestre; **~ vehicle** vehículo *m* todo terreno; **by ~ mail** por vía terrestre.

overlap 1 ['əʊvəlæp] *n* traslapo *m*, solapo *m*; (*fig*) coincidencia *f* parcial; superposición *f*. **2** [,əʊvə'læp] *vt* traslapar. **3** [,əʊvə'læp] *vi* traslaparse; (*fig*) coincidir en parte.

overlay 1 ['əʊvəleɪ] *n* capa *f* sobrepuesta; incrustación *f*. **2** [,əʊvə'leɪ] (*irr*: *V* **lay**[4]) *vt* cubrir (*with* con); **to get overlaid with** formarse una capa de, cubrirse con, incrustarse de.

overleaf ['əʊvə'liːf] *adv* a la vuelta; **'see ~'** 'véase al dorso'.

overload 1 ['əʊvələʊd] *n* sobrecarga *f*. **2** ['əʊvə'ləʊd] *vt* sobrecargar (*with* de); **to be ~ed with** estar sobrecargado de, estar agobiado de.

overlong [,əʊvə'lɒŋ] *adj* demasiado largo, muy largo.

overlook [,əʊvə'lʊk] *vt* (**a**) (*of view*: *person*) dominar; (*of building*) dar a, mirar hacia, tener vista a; **the house ~s the park** la casa tiene vistas al parque; **the garden is not ~ed** el jardín no tiene ningún edificio al lado que lo domine.

(**b**) (*watch over*) vigilar; (*inspect*) inspeccionar, examinar.

(**c**) (*leave out*) pasar por alto; olvidar; no hacer caso de; (*tolerate*) dejar pasar, disimular; (*forgive*) perdonar; (*wink at*) hacer la vista gorda a; **we'll ~ it this time** se perdona esta vez; **the plant is easily ~ed** es fácil dejar de ver la planta.

overlord ['əʊvəlɔːd] *n* (*feudal etc*) señor *m*; (*leader*) jefe *m* supremo.

overlordship ['əʊvəlɔːdʃɪp] *n* señoría *f*; jefatura *f* suprema.

overly ['əʊvəlɪ] *adv* (*US*) demasiado; **~ fond of** demasiado aficionado a.

overman [,əʊvə'mæn] *vt* proveer exceso de mano de obra a; **an ~ned industry** una industria con exceso de mano de obra.

overmanning [,əʊvə'mænɪŋ] *n* exceso *m* de mano de obra.

overmuch ['əʊvə'mʌtʃ] **1** *adj* demasiado. **2** *adv* demasiado; en demasía.

overnice ['əʊvə'naɪs] *adj* melindroso, remilgado.

overnight ['əʊvə'naɪt] **1** *adv*: **it happened ~** ocurrió durante la noche, ocurrió de la noche a la mañana; **to stay ~** pasar la noche, pernoctar (*at* en); **we drove ~** viajamos por la noche; **will it keep ~?** ¿se conservará fresco hasta mañana?; **we can't solve this one ~** no podemos resolver este problema de la noche a la mañana.

2 *adj*: **~ bag** fin *m* de semana, neceser *m* de viaje; **~ journey** viaje *m* de noche; **~ stay** estancia *f* de una noche.

overparticular ['əʊvəpə'tɪkjʊlə^r] *adj* melindroso, remilgado; escrupuloso en exceso; **he's not ~ about money** le importa poco el dinero; (*pej*) es poco escrupuloso en asuntos de dinero; **I'm not ~** me da igual.

overpass ['əʊvəpɑːs] *n* (*US*) paso *m* superior, paso *m* a desnivel (*LAm*).

overpay ['əʊvə'peɪ] (*irr*: *V* **pay**) *vt* pagar demasiado a.

overpayment ['əʊvə'peɪmənt] *n* pago *m* excesivo.

overplay [,əʊvə'pleɪ] *vt*: **to ~ (one's hand)** exagerar.

overpopulated ['əʊvə'pɒpjʊleɪtɪd] *adj* superpoblado.

overpopulation [,əʊvəpɒpjʊ'leɪʃən] *n* superpoblación *f*.

overpower [,əʊvə'paʊə^r] *vt* (*defeat*) sobreponerse a, vencer, subyugar; (*subdue physically*) dominar, asir y tener quieto; (*fig*) dominar; dejar estupefacto; *senses* embargar; **we were ~ed by a sense of tragedy** se apoderó de nosotros un sentimiento de tragedia.

overpowering [,əʊvə'paʊərɪŋ] *adj* abrumador, arrollador.

overpraise ['əʊvə'preɪz] *vt* elogiar demasiado.

overprice [,əʊvə'praɪs] *vt* cargar demasiado sobre el precio de; **these goods are ~d** el precio de estas mercancías es excesivo.

overprint ['əʊvə'prɪnt] **1** *n* sobrecarga *f*. **2** *vt* sobrecargar (*with* de).

overproduce [,əʊvəprə'djuːs] **1** *vt* producir demasiado. **2** *vi* producir demasiado.

overproduction ['əʊvəprə'dʌkʃən] *n* superproducción *f*, exceso *m* de producción.

overprotect [,əʊvəprə'tekt] *vt* proteger demasiado.

overprotection [,əʊvəprə'tekʃən] *n* sobreprotección *f*.

overprotective [,əʊvəprə'tektɪv] *adj* excesivamente solícito.

overqualified [,əʊvə'kwɒlɪfaɪd] *adj* sobrecualificado.

overrate ['əʊvə'reɪt] *vt* supervalorar, sobre(e)stimar.

overrated [,əʊvə'reɪtɪd] *adj* sobre(e)stimado.

overreach [,əʊvə'riːtʃ] *vr*: **to ~ o.s.** ir demasiado lejos, extralimitarse.

overreact [,əʊvərɪ'ækt] *vi* reaccionar demasiado, sobrereaccionar.

overreaction [,əʊvərɪ'ækʃən] *n* sobrerreacción *f*.

overreliance [,əʊvərɪ'laɪəns] *n* confianza *f* excesiva (*on* en); dependencia *f* excesiva (*on* de).

overreliant [,əʊvərɪ'laɪənt] *adj* excesivamente confiado (*on* en); excesivamente dependiente (*on* de).

override [,əʊvə'raɪd] (*irr*: *V* **ride**) *vt* (*ignore*) no hacer caso de; (*invalidate*) anular, invalidar, restar valor a; desautorizar; (*set aside*) poner a un lado; **this fact ~s all others** este hecho domina todos los demás; **our protests were overridden** no hicieron caso de nuestras protestas; **the court can ~ all earlier decisions** el tribunal puede anular toda decisión anterior.

overriding [,əʊvə'raɪdɪŋ] *adj* predominante, decisivo; *importance* primero, primordial; *need etc* imperioso.

overripe ['əʊvə'raɪp] *adj* demasiado maduro, pasado; *fruit* pocho.

overrule [,əʊvə'ruːl] *vt* (*override*) desautorizar, anular; *request etc* denegar, rechazar; **but we were ~d** pero fuimos desautorizados.

overrun 1 ['əʊvə,rʌn] *n* (*on costs*) exceso *m* de costos, costos *mpl* excesivos, sobrecoste *m*.

2 [,əʊvə'rʌn] (*irr*: *V* **run**) *vt* (**a**) cubrir enteramente, invadir; **the field is ~ with weeds** las malas hierbas han invadido el campo, el campo está cubierto de malas hierbas; **the town is ~ with tourists** la ciudad ha sido invadida por los turistas.

(**b**) *costs, time limit etc* rebasar, exceder.

3 [,əʊvə'rʌn] *vi* rebasar el límite; **his speech overran by 15 minutes** su discurso se excedió en 15 minutos.

overscrupulous ['əʊvə'skruːpjʊləs] *adj* = **overparticular**.

overseas ['əʊvə'siːz] **1** *adv* en ultramar, allende el mar; **to be ~** estar en el extranjero; **to go ~** ir al extranjero; **to travel ~** viajar por el extranjero; **visitors from ~** visitantes *mpl* de ultramar; **to send a regiment to fight ~** enviar un regimiento a servir en el extranjero.

2 *adj* de ultramar; **~ agent** agente *m* extranjero; **~ debt** deuda *f* exterior; **~ market** mercado *m* exterior; **~ service** (*Mil etc*) servicio *m* en el extranjero; **~ trade** comercio *m* exterior.

oversee ['əʊvə'siː] (*irr*: *V* **see**) *vt* superentender, vigilar.

overseer ['əʊvəsɪə^r] *n* superintendente *mf*; inspector *m*, -ora *f*; (*foreman*) capataz *m*.

oversell ['əʊvə'sel] (*irr*: *V* **sell**) *vt product* hacer una propaganda excesiva a favor de; (*fig*) insistir demasiado en.

oversensitive [,əʊvə'sensɪtɪv] *adj* hipersensible, demasiado sensible.

oversexed [,əʊvə'sekst] *adj* de deseo sexual excesivo; sexualmente obsesionado.

overshadow [,əʊvə'ʃædəʊ] *vt* sombrear, ensombrecer; (*fig*) eclipsar; hacer minúsculo; **it was ~ed by greater events** fue eclipsado por sucesos de mayor trascendencia.

overshoe ['əʊvəʃuː] *n* chanclo *m*.

overshoot ['əʊvə'ʃuːt] (*irr*: *V* **shoot**) *vti*: **to ~ (the mark)** pasar de la raya, excederse; **to ~ (the target) by 40 tons** producir 40 toneladas más de lo provisto; **to ~ (the runway)** aterrizar largo; **to ~ a turning** ir más allá de una bocacalle.

oversight ['əʊvəsaɪt] *n* (**a**) (*omission*) descuido *m*, inadvertencia *f*, equivocación *f*; **by an ~** por descuido; **it was an ~** ha sido una distracción.

(**b**) (*supervision*) superintendencia *f*, vigilancia *f*.
oversimplification ['əʊvə,sɪmplɪfɪ'keɪʃən] *n* simplificación *f* excesiva.
oversimplify ['əʊvə'sɪmplɪfaɪ] *vt* simplificar demasiado.
oversize(d) [,əʊvə'saɪz(d)] *adj* demasiado grande, descomunal; (*US*) *clothes* de talla grande.
oversleep ['əʊvə'sli:p] (*irr*: *V* **sleep**) *vi* dormir demasiado, no despertar a tiempo; **I overslept** durmiendo se me pasó la hora, se me pegaron las sábanas.
overspend ['əʊvə'spend] (*irr*: *V* **spend**) **1** *vt*: **to ~ one's allowance** gastar más de lo que permite su pensión.
2 *vi* gastar demasiado, gastar más de la cuenta; **we have overspent by 50 dollars** hemos gastado 50 dólares más de lo que debíamos.
overspending [,əʊvə'spendɪŋ] *n* gasto *m* excesivo.
overspill ['əʊvəspɪl] *n* (*Brit*) (*act*) desparramamiento *m* de población; (*quantity*) exceso *m* de población; **an ~ town for Manchester** una ciudad vecinal de absorción de Manchester.
overstaffed [,əʊvə'stɑ:ft] *adj* con exceso de empleados.
overstaffing [,əʊvə'stɑ:fɪŋ] *n* exceso *m* de plantilla.
overstate ['əʊvə'steɪt] *vt* exagerar.
overstatement ['əʊvə'steɪtmənt] *n* exageración *f*.
overstay ['əʊvə'steɪ] *vt*: **to ~ one's leave** quedarse más tiempo de lo que la licencia permite; **to ~ one's welcome** quedarse más tiempo de lo conveniente.
overstep ['əʊvə'step] *vt* exceder, pasar de, traspasar; **to ~ the limit** pasarse de la raya; *V* **mark**[2] *etc*.
overstock ['əʊvə'stɒk] *vt* abarrotar; **to be ~ed with** tener existencias excesivas de.
overstrain ['əʊvə'streɪn] **1** *n* fatiga *f* excesiva; (*nervous*) hipertensión *f*.
2 *vt person* fatigar excesivamente; provocar una hipertensión en; *metal* deformar, torcer; *resources* exigir demasiado de, someter a exigencias excesivas.
3 *vr*: **to ~ o.s.** fatigarse excesivamente.
overstrict [,əʊvə'strɪkt] *adj* demasiado estricto; excesivamente riguroso.
overstrike [,əʊvə'straɪk] (*Comput*) **1** *n* superposición *f*. **2** *vt* superponer.
overstrung ['əʊvə'strʌŋ] *adj* sobre(e)xcitado, hipertenso.
oversubscribed [,əʊvəsəb'skraɪbd] *adj* suscrito en exceso; **the issue was ~** se pidieron más acciones de las que había; **the issue was ~ 4 times** la solicitud de acciones rebasó 4 veces la cantidad de títulos ofrecidos.
oversupply ['əʊvəsə'plaɪ] *vt* proveer en exceso (*with* de); **we are oversupplied with cars** tenemos exceso de coches.
overt [əʊ'vɜ:t] *adj* abierto, público; evidente.
overtake [,əʊvə'teɪk] (*irr*: *V* **take**) **1** *vt* (**a**) alcanzar; (*Brit Aut*) adelantar, rebasar; pasar, sobrepasar; **he doesn't want to be ~n** no quiere dejarse adelantar; **we overtook a lorry near Burgos** cerca de Burgos pasamos un camión; **you can't ~ that car on the bend** no puedes adelantar ese coche en la curva; **X has ~n Y in steel production** X se ha adelantado a Y en la producción de acero.
(**b**) (*fig*) coger de improviso, sorprender; **to be ~n by events** ser sorprendido por los sucesos.
2 *vi* adelantar, pasar; **'no overtaking'** (*Brit*) 'prohibido adelantar', 'prohibido rebasar' (*LAm*).
overtaking [,əʊvə'teɪkɪŋ] *n* adelantamiento *m*, paso *m*.
overtax 1 ['əʊvə'tæks] *vt* (*Fin*) oprimir con tributos, exigir contribuciones excesivas a; (*with effort*) agobiar, exigir esfuerzos excesivos a.
2 *vr*: **to ~ o.s.** fatigarse demasiado, exigirse demasiados esfuerzos a sí mismo.
over-the-counter ['əʊvəθə'kaʊntə^r] *adj method etc* limpio, honrado.
overthrow 1 ['əʊvəθrəʊ] *n* derrumbamiento *m*, derrocamiento *m*.
2 [,əʊvə'θrəʊ] *vt* (*irr*: *V* **throw**) echar abajo, tumbar, derribar; (*overturn*) volcar; *dictator, system, empire etc* derrumbar, derrocar.
overtime ['əʊvətaɪm] **1** *n* (**a**) horas *fpl* extra(ordinarias); tiempo *m* suplementario; **to do ~, to work ~** trabajar horas extra(ordinarias), hacer horas; **we shall have to work ~ to catch up** (*fig*) tendremos que esforzarnos al máximo para recuperar lo que hemos perdido. (**b**) (*US*: *Sport*) prórroga *f*.
2 *attr*: **~ ban** prohibición *f* de horas extra(ordinarias); **~ pay, ~ rate** pago *m* de horas extra(ordinarias).
overtly [əʊ'vɜ:tlɪ] *adv* abiertamente, públicamente.
overtone ['əʊvətəʊn] *n* (*Mus*) armónico *m*; (*fig*) trasfondo *m*; matiz *m*; sugestión *f*; **a speech with a hostile ~** un discurso con alguna nota de hostilidad.
overtop ['əʊvə'tɒp] *vt* descollar sobre.
overtrick ['əʊvətrɪk] *n* baza *f* de más.
overtrump ['əʊvə'trʌmp] *vt* contrafallar.
overture ['əʊvətjʊə^r] *n* (*Mus*) obertura *f*; (*fig*) proposición *f*, propuesta *f*; sondeo *m*; **to make ~s to sb** hacer una propuesta a uno; **to make ~s for an armistice** hacer sondeos de armisticio, hacer propuestas de armisticio (*to* a).
overturn [,əʊvə'tɜ:n] **1** *vt car, saucepan etc* volcar; (*disarrange*) trastornar; *government etc* derrumbar, derrocar; *decision* revocar, anular; **they managed to have the ruling ~ed** lograron hacer anular la decisión.
2 *vi car, aircraft etc* volcar, capotar, dar una vuelta de campana; *boat* zozobrar.
overuse ['əʊvə'ju:z] *vt* usar demasiado.
overvalue ['əʊvə'vælju:] *vt* sobrevalorar, sobre(e)estimar.
overview ['əʊvəvju:] *n* visión *f* de conjunto.
overweening [,əʊvə'wi:nɪŋ] *adj* arrogante, presuntuoso, altivo; **~ pride** desmesurado orgullo *m*.
overweight ['əʊvə'weɪt] **1** *adj* demasiado pesado; **to be ~** pesar demasiado, *person* ser gordo, tener exceso de carnes; **he is 8 kilos ~** tiene 8 kilos de más; **the parcel is a kilo ~** el paquete tiene un exceso de un kilo. **2** *n* exceso *m* de peso, sobrepeso *m*.
overwhelm [,əʊvə'welm] *vt opponent, team etc* arrollar, aplastar; (*in argument*) aplastar; (*of waves etc*) fundir, inundar; (*of grief etc*) vencer, postrar; (*of work etc*) abrumar, agobiar; **he speedily ~ed his opponent** arrolló a su contrincante en muy poco tiempo; **to ~ sb with favours** colmar a uno de favores; **to ~ sb with kindness** colmar a uno de atenciones; **he was ~ed with joy** rebosaba alegría, no cabía en sí de contento; **we have been ~ed with offers of help** estamos inundados de ofertas de ayuda; **Venice just ~s me** Venecia me deja boquiabierto, Venecia es pasmosa; **you ~ me!** ¡basta ya, te lo ruego!
overwhelming [,əʊvə'welmɪŋ] *adj defeat etc* arrollador, aplastante, contundente; *success* arrollador; *majority* abrumador; *pressure etc* irresistible; **one's ~ impression is of heat** la más fuerte impresión de todas es la del calor.
overwhelmingly [,əʊvə'welmɪŋlɪ] *adv* de modo arrollador; abrumadoramente; irresistiblemente; **they voted ~ for X** la abrumadora mayoría de ellos votó por X; **he was ~ defeated** sufrió una derrota arrolladora.
overwind ['əʊvə'waɪnd] (*irr*: *V* **wind**[2]) *vt watch* dar demasiada cuerda a.
overwork ['əʊvə'wɜ:k] **1** *n* trabajo *m* excesivo; **to suffer from ~** haberse cansado trabajando demasiado.
2 *vt person* hacer trabajar demasiado; exigir un esfuerzo excesivo a; *word, concept* usar en exceso, hacer uso excesivo de.
3 *vi* trabajar demasiado, cansarse trabajando demasiado.
overwrite [,əʊvə'raɪt] (*irr*: *V* **write**) *vt* (**a**) exagerar; cargar los efectos literarios de; **this passage is overwritten** este pasaje tiene un estilo recargado. (**b**) (*Comput*) sobreescribir.
overwrought ['əʊvə'rɔ:t] *adj*: **to be ~** estar nerviosísimo, haberse agotado por la emoción (*etc*), estar sobre(e)xcitado.
overzealous ['əʊvə'zeləs] *adj* demasiado entusiasta, demasiado apasionado.
Ovid ['ɒvɪd] *nm* Ovidio.
oviduct ['əʊvɪdʌkt] *n* oviducto *m*.
oviform ['əʊvɪfɔ:m] *adj* oviforme.
ovine ['əʊvaɪn] *adj* ovino.
oviparous [əʊ'vɪpərəs] *adj* ovíparo.
ovoid ['əʊvɔɪd] **1** *adj* ovoide. **2** *n* ovoide *m*.
ovulate ['ɒvjʊleɪt] *vi* ovular.
ovulation [,əʊvjʊ'leɪʃən] *n* ovulación *f*.
ovule ['əʊvju:l] *n* óvulo *m*.
ovum ['əʊvəm] *n*, *pl* **ova** ['əʊvə] óvulo *m*.
ow [aʊ] *excl* ¡ay!
owe [əʊ] **1** *vt* deber; **to ~ sb £2** deber 2 libras a uno; **I'll ~ it to you** te lo quedo a deber; **to ~ allegiance to sb** deber lealtad a uno; **to ~ sb a grudge** guardar rencor a uno; **to ~ sb thanks for his help** estar agradecido a uno por su ayuda, deber las gracias a uno por su ayuda; **to ~ one's life to a lucky chance** deber su vida a una casualidad; **he ~s his talent to his mother** le debe su talento a su madre; **to whom do I ~ this honour?** ¿a quién le debo este honor?; **I ~ it to her to confess** mi deber con ella me obliga a confesarlo; **you ~ it to yourself to come** venir es un deber que tienes contigo mismo.
2 *vi* tener deudas; **to ~ sb for a meal** estar en deuda con

uno por una comida.

owing ['əʊɪŋ] **1** *adj*: **the £5 ~** las 5 libras que debemos, las 5 libras que se nos deben; **how much is ~ to you now?** ¿cuanto se te debe ahora?

2: **~ to** *prep* debido a, por causa de; **~ to the bad weather** debido al mal tiempo, por el mal tiempo; **it is ~ to lack of time** se debe a la falta de tiempo.

owl [aʊl] *n* (*barn* ~) lechuza *f*; (*little* ~) mochuelo *m*; (*long-eared* ~) búho *m*; (*tawny* ~) cárabo *m*.

owlet ['aʊlɪt] *n* mochuelo *m*.

owlish ['aʊlɪʃ] *adj look etc* de búho; solemne.

own [əʊn] **1** *adj* propio; **it's all my ~ money** todo el dinero es el mío propio; **but his ~ brother said so** pero su propio hermano lo dijo; **in her ~ house** en su propia casa; **the house has its ~ garage** la casa tiene garaje propio; **~ goal** autogol *m*.

2 *pron* lo suyo *etc*; **all my ~** todo lo mío; **he has a style all his ~** tiene un estilo muy suyo; **the house is her** (**very**) **~** la casa es la suya propia, la casa le pertenece únicamente a ella; **my time is my ~** dispongo de mi tiempo como quiero; **the decision was his ~** la decisión fue suya (y no de otro); **may I keep it for my** (**very**) **~?** ¿me lo puedo guardar como mío propio?; **she has money of her ~** tiene dinero particular; **I'll give you a copy of your ~** te daré un ejemplar propio, te daré un ejemplar para guardar; **for reasons of his ~** por motivos particulares, por motivos propios; **a place of one's ~** una casa propia, una casa para sí; **to come into one's ~** entrar en posesión de lo suyo, (*fig*) justificarse, encontrar su plena justificación; obtener el éxito merecido; **to be on one's ~** estar a solas, estar solo; ser independiente; **now we're on our ~** ya estamos solos; **she was all on her ~ for a week** pasó una semana enteramente sola; **if I can get him on his ~** si puedo hablar con él a solas; **to do sth on one's ~** hacer algo por su cuenta, hacer algo sólo; **each to his ~** cada uno a lo suyo, cada cual a lo suyo; **to call sth one's ~** ser dueño de algo, disponer de algo como de cosa propia; **without a chair to call my ~** sin una silla que pueda decir que es mía; **I am so busy I can scarcely call my time my ~** estoy tan ocupado que apenas dispongo de mi tiempo; **he made the theory his ~** hizo suya la teoría, adoptó la teoría; **to get one's ~ back** desquitarse, tomar su revancha; **to hold one's ~** no cejar, mantenerse firme; no ceder terreno; mantenerse al nivel de los demás; poder competir; **he can hold his ~ with anybody** no le va a la zaga a nadie; **I can hold my ~ in German** me defiendo en alemán; **we all look after our ~** todos cuidamos lo nuestro.

3 *vt* (**a**) (*possess*) poseer, tener; ser dueño de; **he ~s 2 tractors** posee 2 tractores; **he ~s 3 newspapers** es dueño de 3 periódicos; **who ~s the newspaper?** ¿quién es el dueño del periódico?; **who ~s this pen?** ¿a quién pertenece esta pluma?; **to come in as if one ~ed the place** entrar como Pedro en su casa; **a cat nobody wants to ~** un gato que nadie quiere reclamar.

(**b**) (*acknowledge, recognize*) reconocer; **he ~ed the child as his** reconoció al niño como suyo; **I ~ my mistake** reconozco mi error.

(**c**) (*confess*) confesar; **I ~ it** lo confieso; **I ~ I was wrong** confieso que me equivoqué.

4 *vi*: **to ~ to a mistake** confesar un error, reconocer un error; **I ~ed to debts of £47** confesé tener deudas de 47 libras.

◆**own up** *vi* confesar, confesar de plano; **~ up!** ¡confiésalo!; **she ~ed up to being 40** confesó tener 40 años; **they ~ed up to having stolen the apples** confesaron haber robado las manzanas.

own brand ['əʊn,brænd] **1** *n* marca *f* propia. **2** *attr*: **~ products** productos *mpl* de establecimiento.

owner ['əʊnəʳ] **1** *n* dueño *m*, -a *f*, propietario *m*, -a *f*, amo *m*, -a *f*; poseedor *m*, -ora *f*; (*Naut**) capitán *m*; **the ~ of car no. NBG 999** el dueño del coche matrícula NBG 999; **~'s equity** participación *f* del dueño; **is the ~ about?** ¿está el dueño?

2 *attr*: **~ driver** conductor *m* propietario, conductora *f* propietaria; **there's a growing level of ~ occupancy** hay cada vez más propietarios de la vivienda; **~ occupier** ocupante *m* propietario, ocupante *f* propietaria.

ownerless ['əʊnəlɪs] *adj* sin dueño.

ownership ['əʊnəʃɪp] *n* posesión *f*; propiedad *f*; **'under new ~'** 'nuevo propietario', 'nuevo dueño'; **books in** (*or* **under**) **the ~ of ...** libros que son de la propiedad de ...; **under his ~ the business flourished** el negocio prosperó bajo su dirección.

ownsome* ['əʊnsəm] *n*: **on one's ~** a solas.

owt [aʊt] *n* (*Brit dialect*) algo, alguna cosa.

ox [ɒks] *n*, *pl* **oxen** ['ɒksən] buey *m*.

oxalic [ɒk'sælɪk] *adj*: **~ acid** ácido *m* oxálico.

oxblood ['ɒksblʌd] *adj* de color rojo oscuro.

oxbow lake ['ɒks,bəʊ'leɪk] *n* lago *m* en forma de herradura.

Oxbridge ['ɒksbrɪdʒ] *n* (*Brit*) Universidades *fpl* de Oxford y Cambridge.

oxcart ['ɒkskɑːt] *n* carro *m* de bueyes.

oxen ['ɒksən] *npl of* **ox**.

ox-eye daisy [,ɒksaɪ'deɪzɪ] *n* margarita *f*.

Oxfam ['ɒksfæm] *n abbr of* **Oxford Committee for Famine Relief.**

oxford ['ɒksfəd] *n* (*US*) zapato *m* (de tacón bajo).

oxhide ['ɒkshaɪd] *n* cuero *m* de buey.

oxidation [,ɒksɪ'deɪʃən] *n* oxidación *f*.

oxide ['ɒksaɪd] *n* óxido *m*.

oxidize ['ɒksɪdaɪz] **1** *vt* oxidar. **2** *vi* oxidarse.

oxlip ['ɒkslɪp] *n* prímula *f*.

Oxon ['ɒksən] *adj* (*Brit*) *abbr of* **Oxoniensis, of Oxford.**

Oxonian [ɒk'səʊnɪən] **1** *adj* oxoniense. **2** *n* oxoniense *mf*.

oxtail ['ɒksteɪl] *n*: **~ soup** sopa *f* de cola de buey.

oxyacetylene ['ɒksɪə'setɪliːn] *adj* oxiacetilénico; **~ burner, ~ lamp, ~ torch** soplete *m* oxiacetilénico; **~ welding** soldadura *f* oxiacetilénica.

oxygen ['ɒksɪdʒən] *n* oxígeno *m*.

oxygenate [ɒk'sɪdʒəneɪt] *vt* oxigenar.

oxygenation [,ɒksɪdʒə'neɪʃən] *n* oxigenación *f*.

oxygen-mask ['ɒksɪdʒən,mɑːsk] *n* máscara *f* de oxígeno, mascarilla *f* con oxígeno.

oxygen-tent ['ɒksɪdʒən,tent] *n* tienda *f* de oxígeno.

oyez [əʊ'jez] *interj* ¡oíd!

oyster ['ɔɪstəʳ] *n* ostra *f*; **the world is his ~** tiene el mundo a sus pies.

oysterbed ['ɔɪstəbed] *n* criadero *m* (*o* vivero) de ostras.

oystercatcher ['ɔɪstə,kætʃəʳ] *n* ostrero *m*.

oyster-farm ['ɔɪstəfɑːm] *n* criadero *m* de ostras.

oyster-shell ['ɔɪstəʃel] *n* concha *f* de ostra.

oz. *abbr of* **ounce**(**s**) onza(s) *f*(*pl*).

ozone ['əʊzəʊn] *n* ozono *m*; **~ hole** agujero *m* de ozono; **~ layer** capa *f* de ozono.

ozone-friendly ['əʊzəʊn'frendlɪ] *adj* que no daña la capa de ozono.

ozonosphere [əʊ'zəʊnə,sfɪəʳ] *n* ozonosfera *f*.

P

P, p [piː] *n* (*letter*) P, p *f*; **P for Paris** P de París; **to mind one's Ps and Qs** cuidarse de no meter la pata.
P (**a**) *abbr of* **president** presidente *m*, P. (**b**) *abbr of* **prince** príncipe *m*, P.
p (**a**) *n abbr of* **penny, pence** penique(s) *m*(*pl*). (**b**) *abbr of* **page** página *f*, pág.
p.&h. (*US*) *abbr of* **postage and handling** gastos *mpl* de envío.
P.&L. *n abbr of* **profit and loss** pérdidas *fpl* y ganancias, Pérd. y Gan.
p.&p. *n abbr of* **postage and packing** correo *m* y embalaje.
PA *n* (**a**) *abbr of* **personal assistant** ayudante *mf* personal. (**b**) *abbr of* **public address system** (sistema *m* de) megafonía *f*. (**c**) *abbr of* **Press Association.** (**d**) (*US Post*) *abbr of* **Pennsylvania.** (**d**) (*Theat etc*) *abbr of* **personal appearance**.
p.a. *abbr of* **per annum, yearly** por año, al año.
pa* [pɑː] *n* papá* *m*.
PAC *n* (*US*) *abbr of* **political action committee.**
pace¹ [peɪs] **1** *n* (**a**) (*step*) paso *m*; **12 ~s off** a 12 pasos; **to put a horse through its ~s** ejercitar un caballo, entrenar un caballo; **to put sb through his ~s** poner a uno a prueba, demostrar las cualidades de uno; **to show one's ~s** demostrar su capacidad, demostrar lo que puede uno.
(**b**) (*speed*) paso *m*, marcha *f*, velocidad *f*; ritmo *m*; **at a good ~, at a smart ~** a paso rápido; **at a slow ~** a paso lento; **at a walking ~** a la velocidad del que camina a pie; **at a snail's ~** a paso de tortuga; **we kept up a good ~ with the work** mantuvimos un buen ritmo de trabajo; **the present ~ of development** el actual ritmo del desarrollo; **to keep ~** ir al mismo paso; **he does it at his own ~** lo hace a su propio ritmo; **to keep ~ with sb** llevar el mismo paso que uno; **industry has not kept ~ with technology** la industria no ha avanzado al mismo paso que la tecnología; **I can't keep ~ with events** no puedo mantenerme al corriente de los sucesos; **to make the ~, to set the ~** establecer el paso, marcar el ritmo; **to quicken one's ~** apretar el paso; **he can't stand the ~** no puede mantener el ritmo (de la marcha *etc*), (*fig*) las cosas se desarrollan demasiado rápidamente para él.
2 *vt distance* medir a pasos; *floor, room* pasearse preocupado (*etc*) por; *competitor* marcar el paso para; **to ~ off 10 metres** medir 10 metros a pasos.
3 *vi*: **~ up and down** pasearse de un lado a otro.
◆**pace out** *vt distance* mediar a pasos.
pace² [ˈpeɪsɪ] *prep* según, de acuerdo con.
pacemaker [ˈpeɪsˌmeɪkəʳ] *n* (**a**) (*Sport*) liebre *f*. (**b**) (*Med*) marcapasos *m*.
pacesetter [ˈpeɪsˌsetəʳ] *n* (*Sport*) liebre *f*; (*fig*) persona *f* que da la pauta.
pachyderm [ˈpækɪdɜːm] *n* paquidermo *m*.
pacific [pəˈsɪfɪk] *adj* pacífico.
pacifically [pəˈsɪfɪkəlɪ] *adv* pacíficamente.
pacification [ˌpæsɪfɪˈkeɪʃən] *n* pacificación *f*.
Pacific Ocean [pəˈsɪfɪkˈəʊʃən] *n* Océano *m* Pacífico.
pacifier [ˈpæsɪfaɪəʳ] *n* (*US*: *baby's*) chupete *m*.
pacifism [ˈpæsɪfɪzəm] *n* pacifismo *m*.
pacifist [ˈpæsɪfɪst] **1** *adj* pacifista. **2** *n* pacifista *mf*.
pacify [ˈpæsɪfaɪ] *vt* pacificar; apaciguar, calmar; **we managed to ~ him eventually** por fin logramos apaciguarle.
pack [pæk] **1** *n* (**a**) (*bundle*) lío *m*, fardo *m*; (*on animal*) carga *f*; (*rucksack, also Mil*) mochila *f*; (*packet*) paquete *m*; (*of cigarettes*: *US*) paquete *m*, cajetilla *f*; (*wrapping*) envase *m*; (*Med*) compresa *f*; **a ~ of lies** un montón de mentiras; **it's a ~ of lies!** ¡mentira!, ¡es una sarta (*LAm*: bola *f*) de mentiras!
(**b**) (*of hounds*) jauría *f*; (*of wolves*) manada *f*; (*Rugby*) los delanteros; **they're a ~ of fools** son todos tontos; **they're like a ~ of kids** son como una pandilla de chavales.
(**c**) (*Cards*) baraja *f*.
2 *vt* (**a**) *container* llenar, ir llenando; *case, trunk etc* hacer; *things in case etc* poner; *fish, meat in tin* enlatar; (*wrap*) envasar; (*put into parcel*) empaquetar; **~ed lunch** bolsa *f* de comida, merienda *f*, bocadillos *mpl*; **articles ~ed in dozens** artículos en caja de a docena; **it comes ~ed in polythene** viene envasado en politeno; **I'm ~ed and ready** tengo las maletas hechas y estoy listo para salir.
(**b**) (*excessively*) *container* llenar, atestar (*with* de); *articles* meter apretadamente; **to ~ earth round a plant** acollar una planta; **the place was ~ed (out)** el local estaba de bote en bote; **the Costa Brava is ~ed (out) with tourists** la Costa Brava está llena de turistas.
(**c**) *meeting* llenar de partidarios; *jury* nombrar de modo fraudulento.
(**d**) **he ~s a gun*** (*US*) lleva revólver.
(**e**) (*Comput*) comprimir.
3 *vi* (**a**) (*pack cases*) hacer las maletas, hacer el equipaje.
(**b**) (*form a mass*) endurecerse, consolidarse, formar una masa compacta; (*people*) apiñarse; **they ~ed round the speaker** se apiñaron en torno al orador.
(**c**) **to send sb ~ing** echar a uno con cajas destempladas; despedir a uno sin más.
◆**pack away** *vt* guardar.
◆**pack down** *vt* apretar, comprimir; (*with feet etc*) apisonar.
◆**pack in** *vt* (**a**) **to ~ more people in** ir introduciendo más personas; **can you ~ 2 more in?** ¿caben 2 más?; **they were ~ed in like sardines** estaban como sardinas en banasta; **the show's ~ing them in*** el show tiene un lleno todas las noches.
(**b**) (*) dejarlo; **~ it in!** ¡déjalo!; **it's time we ~ed it in** es hora de dejarlo ya.
◆**pack off** *vt* despachar, despedir, deshacerse de; **they ~ed him off to London** le enviaron sin más a Londres; **to ~ a child off to bed** mandar a un niño a la cama.
◆**pack up 1** *vt* (**a**) = **pack 3** (**a**).
2 *vi* (**a**) (*) terminar; (*and depart*) liar el petate*.
(**b**) (*: *engine etc*) averiarse, pararse.
package [ˈpækɪdʒ] **1** *n* paquete *m*; bulto *m*; (*fig*: *of measures etc*) paquete *m*.
2 *attr*: **~ bomb** (*US*) paquete-bomba *m*; **~ deal** paquete *m*, acuerdo *m* global; **~ holiday, ~ tour, ~ vacation** (*US*) vacaciones *fpl* todo pagado; **~ store** (*US*) = **off-licence.**
3 *vt* (*US*: *also* **to ~ up**) empaquetar, envasar.
packaging [ˈpækɪdʒɪŋ] *n* envasado *m*, embalaje *m*; **~ material** material *m* de envasado.
pack-animal [ˈpækˌænɪməl] *n* animal *m* de carga, acémila *f*.
packer [ˈpækəʳ] *n* embalador *m*, -ora *f*, empaquetador *m*, -ora *f*.
packet [ˈpækɪt] **1** *n* (**a**) paquete *m*; (*of cigarettes*) paquete *m*, cajetilla *f*; (*of stamps*) sobre *m*; (*of crisps etc*) bolsa *f*; **a new ~ of proposals** un paquete de nuevas propuestas; **a whole ~ of trouble** la mar de disgustos; **to make a ~*** ganarse un dineral; **to make one's ~*** hacer su pacotilla; **that must have cost a ~*** eso habrá costado un dineral.
(**b**) (*Naut*: *also* **~ boat**) paquebote *m*.
2 *attr*: **~ switching** conmutación *f* de paquetes.
packhorse [ˈpækhɔːs] *n* caballo *m* de carga.
pack-ice [ˈpækaɪs] *n* témpanos *mpl* flotantes.
packing [ˈpækɪŋ] **1** *n* (**a**) (*act*) embalaje *m*, envase *m*, envasado *m*; **to do one's ~** hacer sus maletas, arreglar el equipaje.
(**b**) (*material*) (*outer*) envase *m*; (*inner*) relleno *m*, empaquetadura *f*.
2 *attr*: **~ density** densidad *f* de compacidad; **~ house, ~**

plant fábrica *f* de conservas cárnicas.
packing-case ['pækɪŋkeɪs] *n* cajón *m* de embalaje.
packing-slip ['pækɪŋ,slɪp] *n* hoja *f* de embalaje.
packsaddle ['pæk,sædl] *n* albarda *f*.
pact [pækt] *n* pacto *m*; (*on wages etc*) convenio *m*; **to make a ~ with sb** pactar con uno.
pad¹ [pæd] *vi*: **to ~ about, to ~ along** andar, pisar (sin hacer ruido).
pad² [pæd] **1** *n* (**a**) (*gen*) almohadilla *f*, cojinete *m*; (*of fox etc*) pata *f*; (*for inking*) tampón *m*, almohadilla *f* para entintar; (*of paper*) bloc *m*, taco *m*; (*blotting ~*) secafirmas *m*; (*on shoulder*) hombrera *f*.
(**b**) (*for helicopter*) plataforma *f*; (*launching*) plataforma *f* de lanzamiento.
2 *vt* (**a**) (*gen*) almohadillar; acolchar; rellenar, forrar; *shoulders etc* acolchar, bombear; *armour* enguatar.
(**b**) *book etc* meter paja en, hinchar con mucha paja.
◆**pad out** *vt book etc* meter paja en, hinchar con mucha paja; **the speech was ~ded out with references to** ... el discurso estaba hinchado con referencias a ...
pad³‡ [pæd] *n* (*home*) casa *f*; (*flat*) piso *m*; (*room*) agujero‡ *m*, habitación *f*; (*bed*) pulguero‡ *m*, cama *f*.
padded ['pædɪd] *adj shoulders* acolchado, con hombrera(s), bombeado; *dashboard etc* almohadillado; *armour* enguatado; *envelope* acolchado; *cell* acolchado, de aislamiento.
padding ['pædɪŋ] *n* (**a**) relleno *m*, almohadilla *f*; acolchamiento *m*; (*material*) borra *f*. (**b**) (*fig*) paja *f*.
paddle ['pædl] **1** *n* (**a**) (*oar*) canalete *m*, zagual *m*; (*blade of wheel*) paleta *f*; (*wheel*) rueda *f* de paletas; (*US*) raqueta *f*.
(**b**) **to go for a ~, to have a ~** ir a mojarse los pies, chapotear en el mar (*etc*).
2 *vt* (**a**) *boat* impulsar con canalete, remar con canalete.
(**b**) **to ~ one's feet in the sea** mojarse los pies en el mar, chapotear en el mar.
(**c**) (*US**) *child* azotar, zurrar*.
3 *vi* (**a**) (*in boat*) palear, remar con canalete; **they ~d to the bank** dirigieron el bote a la orilla.
(**b**) (*with feet*) mojarse los pies, chapotear.
paddle-boat ['pædlbəʊt] *n*, **paddle-steamer** ['pædl,stiːməʳ] *n* (*Brit*) vapor *m* de ruedas, vapor *m* de paletas.
paddle-wheel ['pædlwiːl] *n* rueda *f* de paletas.
paddling-pool ['pædlɪŋpuːl] *n* (*Brit*) estanque *m* para chapotear, estanque *m* (*or* piscina *f*) para niños.
paddock ['pædək] *n* (*field*) prado *m*; (*of racecourse*) corral *m*, explanada *f* de ensillado, paddock *m*; (*of cars*) parque *m*.
Paddy ['pædɪ] *nm familiar form of* **Patrick**; (*pej*) irlandés *m*.
paddy¹ ['pædɪ] *n* (*rice*) arroz *m*; (*field*) arrozal *m*.
paddy²* ['pædɪ] *n* rabieta* *f*; **to get into a ~** coger una rabieta.
paddy waggon* ['pædɪ,wægən] *n* (*US*) coche *m* celular.
paddywhack* ['pædɪwæk] *n* rabieta* *f*.
padlock ['pædlɒk] **1** *n* candado *m*. **2** *vt* cerrar con candado.
padre* ['pɑːdrɪ] *n* (*Mil*) capellán *m* militar; (*Univ*) capellán *m* de colegio; (*in direct address*) padre.
paean ['piːən] *n* himno *m* de alegría; **~s of praise** alabanzas *fpl*.
paediatric, (*US*) **pediatric** [,piːdɪ'ætrɪk] *adj* pediátrico; **~ ward** sala *f* de pediatría.
paediatrician, (*US*) **pediatrician** [,piːdɪə'trɪʃən] *n* pediatra *mf*, pedíatra *mf*, médico *m* puericultor.
paediatrics, (*US*) **pediatrics** [,piːdɪ'ætrɪks] *n* pediatría *f*.
paedological, (*US*) **pedological** [,piːdə'lɒdʒɪkl] *adj* pedológico.
paedology, (*US*) **pedology** [pɪ'dɒlədʒɪ] *n* pedología *f*.
paedophile, (*US*) **pedophile** ['piːdəʊfaɪl] *n* pedófilo *m*.
paedophilia, (*US*) **pedophilia** [,piːdəʊ'fɪlɪə] *n* pedofilia *f*.
pagan ['peɪgən] **1** *adj* pagano. **2** *n* pagano *m*, -a *f*.
paganism ['peɪgənɪzəm] *n* paganismo *m*.
page¹ [peɪdʒ] **1** *n* (*boy-servant*) paje *m*; (*squire*) escudero *m*.
2 *vt*: **to ~ sb** buscar a uno llamando (su nombre), hacer llamar a uno por el altavoz.
page² [peɪdʒ] **1** *n* página *f*; (*Typ, of newspaper*) plana *f*; **a glorious ~ in our history** una página gloriosa de nuestra historia; **the news was on the front ~** la noticia figuraba en la primera plana; **on ~ 14** a la página 14, en la página 14; **'see ~ 20'** 'véase la página 20'.
2 *attr*: **~ break** (*Comput*) límite *m* de la página.
3 *vt* paginar.
-page [peɪdʒ] *n ending in compounds*: **a 4-~ pamphlet** un folleto de 4 páginas.
pageant ['pædʒənt] *n* (*show*) espectáculo *m* brillante; representación *f* escénica; (*procession*) desfile *m*; **a ~ of Elizabethan times** una representación de la época isabelina en una serie de cuadros; **the town held a ~ to mark the anniversary** la ciudad organizó una serie de fiestas públicas para celebrar el aniversario.
pageantry ['pædʒəntrɪ] *n* pompa *f*, boato *m*; **the ~ of the occasion** lo espectacular del acontecimiento, lo vistoso del acontecimiento; **all the ~ of History** toda la magnificencia de la Historia; **it was celebrated with much ~** se celebró con gran boato.
pageboy ['peɪdʒbɔɪ] *n* paje *m*; **~ hairstyle** peinado *m* de paje.
page-proofs ['peɪdʒpruːfs] *npl* pruebas *fpl* de planas.
pager ['peɪdʒəʳ] *n* localizador *m*, busca* *m*.
paginate ['pædʒɪneɪt] *vt* paginar.
pagination [,pædʒɪ'neɪʃən] *n* paginación *f*; **without ~** sin paginar.
paging ['peɪdʒɪŋ] **1** *n* (*Comput, Typ*) paginación *f*. **2** *attr*: **~ device** localizador *m*, busca* *m*.
pagoda [pə'gəʊdə] *n* pagoda *f*.
paid [peɪd] **1** *pret and ptp of* **pay**.
2 *adj* (**a**) *official* asalariado, que recibe un sueldo; *work* remunerado, rentado (*SC*); **a ~ hack** un escritorzuelo a sueldo.
(**b**) *bill, holiday etc* pagado; **to put ~ to sth** acabar con algo.
paid-up ['peɪd'ʌp], (*US*) **paid-in** ['peɪd'ɪn] *adj share* liberado; **fully ~ share** acción *f* totalmente liberada; **~ capital** capital *m* pagado; **a fully ~ member** miembro *m* que ha pagado su cuota.
pail [peɪl] *n* cubo *m*, balde *m*; (*child's*) cubito *m*.
pailful ['peɪlfʊl] *n* cubo *m*, contenido *m* de un cubo.
paillasse ['pælɪæs] *n* jergón *m*.
pain [peɪn] **1** *n* (**a**) (*Med*) dolor *m*; sufrimiento *m*; **~ barrier** barrera *f* del dolor; **to be in ~** estar con dolor; **to be in great ~** tener mucho dolor, sufrir mucho; **cucumber gives me a ~** el pepino me sienta mal; **I have a ~ in my leg** me duele la pierna; **to put a wounded animal out of its ~** acortar la agonía de un animal herido, despachar un animal herido.
(**b**) **~s** (*efforts*) trabajos *mpl*, cuidados *mpl*, esfuerzos *mpl*; **to be at great ~s over sth, to take ~s over sth** esmerarse en algo, tomarse trabajo en algo; **he was at ~s to be reasonable** se esforzó por parecer razonable; **all he got for his ~s was ...** lo único que logró después de tantos trabajos fue ...; **to spare no ~s** no perdonar esfuerzos (*to + infin* por + *infin*); **to take ~s to + infin** poner especial cuidado en + *infin*.
(**c**) (*penalty*) pena *f*; **on ~ of death** so pena de muerte; **with all the ~s and penalties of fame** con todas las dificultades y disgustos que acarrea la fama.
(**d**) (*: *nuisance*) (*person*) persona *f* latosa*; **she's a real ~** es una persona realmente latosa*; **what a ~!** ¡qué lata!*; **it's a ~ having to + infin** es una lata tener que* + *infin*; **he's a ~ in the arse**** (*Brit*), **he's a ~ in the ass**** (*US*) es más pesado que el plomo*, da mucho la tabarra*; **he's a ~ in the neck, it gives me a ~ in the neck** me da cien patadas*.
2 *vt* (*physically*) doler; (*mentally*) dar lástima a; **my leg ~s me** me duele la pierna; **you ~ me!** (*iro*) ¡me das lástima!; **where does it ~ you?** ¿dónde te duele?
pained [peɪnd] *adj expression* de disgusto, afligido; ofendido; *voice* dolorido; **he looked ~** hizo una mueca, torció el gesto.
painful ['peɪnfʊl] *adj* (**a**) (*physically*) doloroso, dolorido; (*difficult*) difícil, penoso, angustioso; *duty* desagradable, nada grato; **it is my ~ duty to tell you that ...** tengo el deber desagradable de decirle que ...; **my arm was becoming ~** empezaba a dolerme el brazo; **it was ~ to behold** daba lástima verlo.
(**b**) (*) horrible, malísimo; **~, isn't it?** ¿es horrible, no?; **she gave a ~ performance** dio una actuación lamentable, actuó pésimamente.
painfully ['peɪnfəlɪ] *adv* (**a**) dolorosamente, con dolor; penosamente. (**b**) (*fig*) terriblemente.
painkiller ['peɪnkɪləʳ] *n* analgésico *m*.
painkilling ['peɪn,kɪlɪŋ] *adj drug* analgésico.
painless ['peɪnlɪs] *adj* (*without pain*) indoloro, sin dolor; (*easy*) fácil; **~ childbirth** parto *m* sin dolor.
painlessly ['peɪnlɪslɪ] *adv* (*without pain*) sin causar dolor; (*easily*) fácilmente.
painstaking ['peɪnz,teɪkɪŋ] *adj person* laborioso, concienzudo,

esmerado; *work* hecho con cuidado, esmerado.
painstakingly ['peɪnz,teɪkɪŋlɪ] *adv* laboriosamente, concienzudamente, esmeradamente.
paint [peɪnt] **1** *n* pintura *f*; (*for face*) colorete *m*; **box of ~s** caja *f* de pinturas; **'wet~'** ¡(ojo,) recién pintado!
2 *vt* pintar; **to ~ sth black** pintar algo de negro; **to ~ one's face** pintarse, ponerse colorete.
3 *vi* pintar; ser pintor.
◆**paint in** *vt* pintar; añadir (con pintura).
◆**paint out** *vt* tachar (*or* tapar) con una mano de pintura.
◆**paint over** *vt* (**a**) = **paint out.** (**b**) (*repaint*) repintar, volver a pintar.
paintbox ['peɪntbɒks] *n* caja *f* de pinturas.
paintbrush ['peɪntbrʌʃ] *n* (*Art*) pincel *m*; (*for decorating*) brocha *f*.
painter¹ ['peɪntəʳ] *n* (*Art*) pintor *m*, -ora *f*; (*decorator*) pintor *m* (de brocha gorda).
painter² ['peɪntəʳ] *n* (*Naut*) amarra *f*; **to cut the ~** (*fig*) cortar las amarras, independizarse.
painting ['peɪntɪŋ] *n* (*art*) pintura *f*; (*picture*) cuadro *m*, pintura *f*.
paintpot ['peɪntpɒt] *n* bote *m* de pintura.
paint-remover ['peɪntrɪ,muːvəʳ] *n* quitapintura *f*.
paint-roller ['peɪnt,rəʊləʳ] *n* rodillo *m* (pintor).
paint-spray ['peɪntspreɪ] *n* pistola *f* (rociadora) de pintura.
paint-stripper ['peɪnt,strɪpəʳ] *n* quitapintura *f*.
paintwork ['peɪntwɜːk] *n* pintura *f*.
pair [pɛəʳ] **1** *n* (*of gloves, shoes, etc*) par *m*; (*of people, animals, cards, stamps*) pareja *f*; (*of oxen*) yunta *f*; **a ~ of trousers** un pantalón, unos pantalones; **a carriage and ~** un landó con dos caballos; **a ~ of scissors** unas tijeras; **the happy ~** la feliz pareja, los novios; **arranged in ~s** arreglados (*or* colocados) de dos en dos.
2 *vt* aparear (*also Bio*).
3 *vi* aparearse (*also Bio*); **to ~ with** aparearse con, juntarse con.
◆**pair off, pair up** *vi* aparearse, formar pareja (*with* con).
pair-bond(ing) ['pɛə,bɒnd(ɪŋ)] *n* unión *f* de pareja, emparejamiento *m*.
pairing ['pɛərɪŋ] *n* (*Bio*) apareamiento *m*.
paisley ['peɪzlɪ] **1** *n* (*fabric*) cachemira *f*; (*design*: *also* **~ pattern**) cachemira *f*. **2** *attr*: **~ shawl** chal *m* de cachemira.
pajamas [pə'dʒɑːməz] *npl* (*US*) pijama *m*.
Paki‡ ['pækɪ] *n* (*Brit pej*) *abbr of* **Pakistani.**
Pakistan [,pɑːkɪs'tɑːn] *n* Pakistán *m*, Paquistán *m*.
Pakistani [,pɑːkɪs'tɑːnɪ] **1** *adj* pakistaní, paquistaní. **2** *n* pakistaní *mf*, paquistaní *mf*.
PAL [pæl] *n abbr of* **phase alternation line** línea *f* de fase alternante.
pal* [pæl] *n* camarada *mf*, compinche *m*, compañero *m*, -a *f*, cuate *mf* (*Mex*); **old ~'s act** acto *m* de amiguismo*; **be a ~!** ¡vamos, pórtate como un amigo!; **you've always been a ~ to me** siempre has sido muy amable conmigo; **they're great ~s** son íntimos amigos.
◆**pal up** *vi* hacerse amigos; **to ~ up with sb** hacerse amigo de uno.
palace ['pælɪs] *n* palacio *m*.
palaeo- ['pælɪəʊ] *etc* = **paleo-** *etc.*
palatable ['pælətəbl] *adj* sabroso, apetitoso; (*just passable*) comible; (*fig*) aceptable (*to* a); **it may not be ~ to the government** puede no ser del gusto (*or* agrado) del gobierno.
palatal ['pælətl] **1** *adj* palatal. **2** *n* palatal *f*.
palatalize ['pælətəlaɪz] **1** *vt* palatalizar. **2** *vi* palatalizarse.
palate ['pælɪt] *n* paladar *m* (*also fig*); **hard ~** paladar *m*; **soft ~** velo *m* del paladar; **to have a delicate ~** tener un paladar delicado; **to have no ~ for wine** no tener paladar para el vino; **I have no ~ for that kind of activity** no aguanto (*or* no puedo tragar) ese tipo de actividad.
palatial [pə'leɪʃəl] *adj* suntuoso, espléndido.
palatinate [pə'lætɪnɪt] *n* palatinado *m*.
palaver [pə'lɑːvəʳ] **1** *n* (**a**) (*conference*) conferencia *f*, parlamento *m*. (**b**) (*) (*fuss*) lío* *m*; (*trouble*) molestias *fpl*, trámites *mpl* engorrosos; (*US*: *chatter*) palabrería *f*; **that ~ about the car** aquel lío que se armó acerca del coche*; **can't we do it without a lot of ~?** ¿no podemos hacerlo sin tantas molestias?, ¿no podemos hacerlo sin meternos en tantos líos*? **2** *vi* parlamentar.
pale¹ [peɪl] **1** *adj complexion, face* pálido; *colour* claro; *light* tenue; **a ~ blue dress** un vestido azul claro; **she was deathly ~** estaba pálida como la muerte; **to go ~, to grow ~, to turn ~** palidecer, ponerse pálido.
2 *vi* palidecer, ponerse pálido; **but X ~s beside Y** pero X pierde al lado de Y.
pale² [peɪl] *n* (*stake*) estaca *f*; **to be beyond the ~** estar excluido de la buena sociedad; ser inaceptable, ser un indeseable; **to be outside the ~ of** quedar fuera de los límites de.
paleface ['peɪlfeɪs] *n* rostropálido *m*, -a *f*; (*US term*) blanco *m*, -a *f*.
pale-faced [,peɪl'feɪst] *adj* pálido.
paleness ['peɪlnɪs] *n* palidez *f*; tenuidad *f*.
paleo... ['pælɪəʊ] *pref* paleo...
paleographer [,pælɪ'ɒgrəfəʳ] *n* paleógrafo *m*, -a *f*.
paleography [,pælɪ'ɒgrəfɪ] *n* paleografía *f*.
paleolithic [,pælɪəʊ'lɪθɪk] **1** *adj* paleolítico. **2** *n*: **the P~** el Paleolítico.
paleontology [,pælɪɒn'tɒlədʒɪ] *n* paleontología *f*.
Palestine ['pælɪstaɪn] *n* Palestina *f*.
Palestinian [,pæləs'tɪnɪən] **1** *adj* palestino. **2** *n* palestino *m*, -a *f*.
palette ['pælɪt] *n* paleta *f*.
palette knife ['pælɪtnaɪf] *n*, *pl* **palette knives** ['pælɪtnaɪvz] espátula *f*.
palfrey ['pɔːlfrɪ] *n* palafrén *m*.
palimony* ['pælɪmənɪ] *n* alimentos *mpl* pagados a una ex compañera.
palimpsest ['pælɪmpsest] *n* palimpsesto *m*.
palindrome ['pælɪndrəʊm] *n* palindromo *m*.
paling ['peɪlɪŋ] *n* (*stake*) estaca *f*; (*fence*) valla *f*, estacada *f*, (em)palizada *f*.
palisade [,pælɪ'seɪd] *n* palizada *f*, estacada *f*, vallada *f*.
pall¹ [pɔːl] *n* (*on coffin*) paño *m* mortuorio; (*robe, Eccl*) palio *m*; (*fig*) manto *m*, capa *f*; **a ~ of smoke** una capa de humo.
pall² [pɔːl] *vi* perder su sabor (*on* para), dejar de gustar (*on* a); empalagar (*on* a); **it ~s after a time** después de cierto tiempo deja de gustar; **it never ~s** nunca pierde su sabor; **I found the book ~ed** encontré que el libro empezaba a aburrirme.
palladium [pə'leɪdɪəm] *n* paladio *m*.
pallbearer ['pɔːl,bɛərəʳ] *n* portador *m* del féretro.
pallet ['pælɪt] *n* (*bed*) jergón *m*; (*platform*) paleta *f*, plataforma *f*.
palletization [pælɪtaɪ'zeɪʃən] *n* paletización *f*.
pallet truck ['pælɪttrʌk] *n* carretilla *f* elevadora de paletas.
palliasse ['pælɪæs] *n* = **paillasse.**
palliate ['pælɪeɪt] *vt* paliar, mitigar.
palliative ['pælɪətɪv] **1** *adj* paliativo, lenitivo. **2** *n* paliativo *m*, lenitivo *m*.
pallid ['pælɪd] *adj* pálido.
pallidness ['pælɪdnɪs] *n*, **pallor** ['pæləʳ] *n* palidez *f*.
pally* ['pælɪ] *adj*: **he's a ~ sort** es una persona afable; **they're very ~** son muy amigos; **to be pretty ~ with sb** ser muy amigo de uno.
palm¹ [pɑːm] **1** *n* (*Bot*) palma *f*, palmera *f*; (*English sallow*) sauce *m*; (*as carried at Easter*) ramo *m*; **to bear the ~** llevarse la palma; **to yield the ~ to sb** reconocer la superioridad de uno, conceder la victoria a uno.
2 *attr*: **P~ Sunday** Domingo *m* de Ramos.
palm² [pɑːm] (*Anat*) **1** *n* palma *f*; **you must cross the gipsy's ~ with silver** hay que pagar a la gitana con una moneda de plata; **to grease sb's ~** untar la mano a uno; **to have an itching ~** ser muy codicioso; (*be bribable*) estar dispuesto a dejarse sobornar; **to read sb's ~** leer la mano a uno.
2 *vt card* escamotear.
◆**palm off** *vt* (**a**) **to ~ sth off on sb** encajar algo a uno; **I managed to ~ the visitor off on John** logré que Juan se encargara de la visita.
(**b**) **I ~ed him off with the excuse that ...** logré satisfacerle con la excusa de que ...; **I will not be ~ed off with such nonsense** a mí no se me aparta del propósito con tonterías así.
palm-grove [,pɑːm'grəʊv] *n* palmar *m*, palmeral *m*.
palmist ['pɑːmɪst] *n* quiromántico *m*, -a *f*, palmista *mf* (*Carib, Mex*).
palmistry ['pɑːmɪstrɪ] *n* quiromancia *f*.
palm-oil ['pɑːmɔɪl] *n* aceite *m* de palma.
palm-tree ['pɑːmtriː] *n* palma *f*, palmera *f*, palmero *m* (*And, SC, Mex*).
palmy ['pɑːmɪ] *adj* floreciente; próspero, feliz; **those ~ days** aquellos días tan prósperos.
palpable ['pælpəbl] *adj* palpable; (*fig*) palpable, sensible.
palpably ['pælpəblɪ] *adv* palpablemente; sensiblemente; **a ~ unjust sentence** una condena manifiestamente injusta; **that is ~ untrue** eso es a todas luces falso.
palpitate ['pælpɪteɪt] *vi* palpitar.

palpitating [ˈpælpɪteɪtɪŋ] *adj* palpitante.

palpitation [ˌpælpɪˈteɪʃən] *n* palpitación *f*; **to have ~s** tener vahidos.

palsied [ˈpɔːlzɪd] *adj* paralítico.

palsy [ˈpɔːlzɪ] *n* perlesía *f*, parálisis *f*.

paltry [ˈpɔːltrɪ] *adj* insignificante, baladí; vil; miserable; **for a few ~ pesetas** por unas pesetillas, por unas miserables pesetas; **for some ~ reason** por alguna razón insignificante.

pampas [ˈpæmpəs] *npl* pampa *f*, pampas *fpl*; **the P~** la Pampa.

pamper [ˈpæmpəʳ] *vt* mimar.

pampered [ˈpæmpəd] *adj child etc* mimado, consentido; *life* regalado; **he had a ~ childhood** se crió entre algodones.

pamphlet [ˈpæmflɪt] *n* (*informative, brochure*) folleto *m*, impreso *m*; (*literary*) panfleto *m*; (*political, handed out in street*) octavilla *f*, hoja *f* de propaganda.

pamphleteer [ˌpæmflɪˈtɪəʳ] *n* folletista *mf*, panfletista *mf*.

pan[1] [pæn] **1** *n* (*utensil*) cazuela *f*, cacerola *f*; perol *m*; (*frying ~*) sartén *f*; (*of lavatory*) taza *f*; (*of firearm*) cazoleta *f*.

2 *vt* (**a**) *gold* separar en la gamella.

(**b**) (*) *play* dar un palo a.

3 *vi*: **to ~ for gold** lavar con batea para obtener el oro.

◆**pan out 1** *vt* repartir.

2 *vi* resultar, salir (bien *etc*); **if it ~s out as we hope** si sale como nosotros lo esperamos; **it didn't ~ out at all well** no dio ningún resultado satisfactorio; **we must wait and see how it ~s out** tenemos que esperar hasta ver cómo sale esto.

pan[2] [pæn] (*Cine*) *vti* panoramizar.

pan... [pæn] *pref* pan...; **pan-African** panafricano.

panacea [ˌpænəˈsɪə] *n* panacea *f*.

panache [pəˈnæʃ] *n* aire *m*, garbo *m*, brío *m*, brillantez *f*; **to do sth with ~** hacer algo con brío, hacer algo con aire triunfal.

Pan-Africanism [ˈpænˈæfrɪkənɪzəm] *n* panafricanismo *m*.

Panama [ˌpænəˈmɑː] **1** *n* Panamá *m*. **2** *attr*: **~ Canal** Canal *m* de Panamá; **~ hat** (sombrero *m* de) jipijapa *f*, panamá *m*.

Panamanian [ˌpænəˈmeɪnɪən] **1** *adj* panameño. **2** *n* panameño *m*, -a *f*.

Pan-American [ˈpænəˈmerɪkən] *adj* panamericano; **~ Union** Unión *f* Panamericana.

Pan-Americanism [ˈpænəˈmerɪkənɪzəm] *n* panamericanismo *m*.

pancake [ˈpænkeɪk] **1** *n* crep *m*, hojuela *f*, tortita *f*, panqueque *m* (*LAm*).

2 *attr*: **~ day** martes *m* de carnaval (*en que en Inglaterra se sirven hojuelas*); **~ landing** aterrizaje *m* de panza.

panchromatic [ˈpænkrəʊˈmætɪk] *adj* pancromático.

pancreas [ˈpæŋkrɪəs] *n* páncreas *m*.

pancreatic [ˌpæŋkrɪˈætɪk] *adj* pancreático.

panda [ˈpændə] *n* panda *mf*; **~ car** coche *m* patrulla.

pandemic [pænˈdemɪk] **1** *adj* pandémico. **2** *n* pandemia *f*.

pandemonium [ˌpændɪˈməʊnɪəm] *n* pandemonio *m*, ruido *m* de todos los diablos, estruendo *m* infernal; **it's sheer ~!** ¡es la monda!; **at this there was ~** en esto se armó las de Caín, en esto se armó un tremendo jaleo.

pander [ˈpændəʳ] **1** *n* alcahuete *m*. **2** *vi* alcahuetear; **to ~ to sb** consentir a uno, mimar a uno, desvivirse por complacer a uno; **to ~ to sb's desires** tratar por todos los medios de satisfacer los deseos de uno; **this is ~ing to the public's worst tastes** esto es condescender con los peores gustos del público.

Pandora [pænˈdɔːrə] *nf*: **~'s box** caja *f* de Pandora.

pane [peɪn] *n* cristal *m*, (hoja *f* de) vidrio *m*.

panegyric [ˌpænɪˈdʒɪrɪk] *n* panegírico *m*.

panel [ˈpænl] **1** *n* (**a**) panel *m*; (*of wall*) panel *m*; (*of ceiling*) artesón *m*; (*of door*) entrepaño *m*, panel *m*; (*Sew*) paño *m*; (*Art*) tabla *f*; (*of instruments, switches*) tablero *m*, panel *m*.

(**b**) (*Brit Med etc*) lista *f* de pacientes; (*in competition*) jurado *m*; (*TV etc*) panel *m*; (*of assessors*) grupo *m* de asesores.

2 *attr*: **~ discussion** mesa *f* redonda; **~ game** concurso *m* por equipos.

3 *vt* poner paneles (*etc*) a, adornar con paneles (*etc*).

panel-beater [ˈpænl,biːtəʳ] *n* chapista *m*.

panel-beating [ˈpænl,biːtɪŋ] *n* chapistería *f*.

panelled, (*US*) **paneled** [ˈpænld] *adj* con paneles, adornado de paneles; artesonado.

panelling, (*US*) **paneling** [ˈpænəlɪŋ] *n* paneles *mpl*; artesonado *m*; entrepaños *mpl*.

panellist, (*US*) **panelist** [ˈpænəlɪst] *n* miembro *mf* del jurado (de un concurso *etc*), miembro *mf* del panel.

pang [pæŋ] *n* punzada *f*, dolor *m* súbito, dolor *m* agudo; **~ of conscience** remordimiento *m*; **I felt a ~ of conscience** me remordió la conciencia; **~s of childbirth** dolores *mpl* del parto; **the ~s of hunger** el acometimiento del hambre.

panhandle [ˈpænhændl] (*US*) **1** *n faja angosta de territorio de un estado que entra en el de otro.* **2** *vi* (*US**) mendigar, pedir limosna.

panic [ˈpænɪk] **1** *n* pánico *m*, terror *m* pánico; **to flee in ~** huir aterrado; **the country was thrown into a ~** el pánico cundió en el país, el país fue preso del pánico; **there's no ~, tomorrow will do** no hay ninguna prisa loca, lo haremos mañana; **they were in their usual mad ~** todos corrían de acá para allá como locos.

2 *attr*: **~ button** botón *m* de alarma; **~ buying** compras *fpl* debidas al pánico; **~ measures** medidas *fpl* inducidas por el pánico; **it was ~ stations*** reinaba el pánico.

3 *vt* aterrar, infundir pánico a.

4 *vi* llenarse de terror, aterrarse, ser preso de un terror pánico; **the crew ~ked** la tripulación se abandonó al terror; **don't ~!** ¡con calma!, ¡no te asustes!

panicky [ˈpænɪkɪ] *adj* (**a**) *person* asustadizo; lleno de pánico; **to get ~** llenarse de pánico; **don't get ~!** ¡con calma!, ¡no te asustes!

(**b**) *act, measure etc* influido por el terror.

panic-stricken [ˈpænɪk,strɪkən] *adj* preso de pánico, muerto de miedo.

panjandrum [pænˈdʒændrəm] *n* jefazo *m*, mandamás *m*; **he's the great ~** es el archipámpano.

pannier [ˈpænɪəʳ] **1** *n* cuévano *m*, serón *m*, banasta *f*. **2** *attr*: **~ bag** (*on cycle etc*) cartera *f*, bolsa *f* (para equipaje); (*for mule etc*) alforja *f*.

panoply [ˈpænəplɪ] *n* (*armour*) panoplia *f*; (*fig*) pompa *f*, esplendor *m*.

panorama [ˌpænəˈrɑːmə] *n* panorama *m*.

panoramic [ˌpænəˈræmɪk] *adj* panorámico; **~ screen** pantalla *f* panorámica; **~ view** visión *f* panorámica.

pansy [ˈpænzɪ] *n* (**a**) (*Bot*) pensamiento *m*. (**b**) (‡) maricón‡ *m*.

pant [pænt] **1** *n* jadeo *m*; resuello *m*.

2 *vt*: **to ~ out** decir jadeando, decir con palabras entrecortadas.

3 *vi* jadear; resollar; (*heart*) palpitar; **to ~ for water** jadear sediento; **to ~ for breath** jadear; **to ~ with desire for sth** desear algo ardientemente.

◆**pant for** *vt* (*fig*) suspirar por, anhelar.

pantechnicon [pænˈteknɪkən] *n* (*Brit*) camión *m* de mudanzas.

pantheism [ˈpænθiːɪzəm] *n* panteísmo *m*.

pantheist [ˈpænθiːɪst] *n* panteísta *mf*.

pantheistic [ˌpænθiːˈɪstɪk] *adj* panteísta.

pantheon [ˈpænθɪən] *n* panteón *m*.

panther [ˈpænθəʳ] *n* pantera *f*.

panties [ˈpæntɪz] *npl* bragas *fpl*, braga *f*, braguitas *fpl*; **a pair of ~** unas bragas.

panting [ˈpæntɪŋ] *n* jadeo *m*; respiración *f* difícil.

panto* [ˈpæntəʊ] *n abbr of* **pantomime.**

pantomime [ˈpæntəmaɪm] *n* (*classical*) pantomima *f*; (*Brit*) *revista musical en época de Navidades, a base de cuentos de hadas etc*; **what a ~!** ¡qué farsa!; **it was a real ~** fue una verdadera comedia.

pantry [ˈpæntrɪ] *n* despensa *f*.

pants [pænts] *npl* (*Brit*) (*man's*) calzoncillos *mpl*; (*US*) pantalones *mpl*; (*woman's*) bragas *fpl*; **a pair of ~** (*Brit*) unos calzoncillos, (*US*) unos pantalones, un pantalón; **to bore the ~ off sb*** aburrir terriblemente a uno; **to catch sb with his ~ down*** coger a uno desprevenido; **she wears the ~*** ella manda.

pants press [ˈpænts,pres] *n* (*US*) prensa *f* para pantalones.

pantsuit [ˈpæntsuːt] *n* (*US*) traje *m* de chaqueta y pantalón.

panty [ˈpæntɪ] *attr*: **~ girdle** faja *f* pantalón; **~ hose** pantys *mpl*, pantimedias *fpl*.

Panzer [ˈpæntsəʳ] (*German army*) **1** *adj* motorizado; **~ division** división *f* motorizada. **2** *n*: **the ~s** las tropas motorizadas.

pap [pæp] *n* papilla *f*, gachas *fpl*.

papa [pəˈpɑː] *n* papá *m*.

papacy [ˈpeɪpəsɪ] *n* papado *m*, pontificado *m*.

papadum [ˈpæpədəm] *n* torta *f* india.

papal [ˈpeɪpəl] *adj* papal, pontificio; **~ nuncio** nuncio *m* apostólico.

papaya [pəˈpaɪə] *n* (*fruit*) papaya *f*, mamón *m* (*And, SC*); (*tree*) árbol *m* de la papaya.

paper [ˈpeɪpəʳ] **1** *n* (**a**) (*material, gen*) papel *m*; (*wall~*)

papel *m* pintado; **a piece of ~** un papel, una hoja de papel, un trozo de papel; **on ~** sobre el papel, teóricamente; **to commit sth to ~, to get** (*or* **put**) **sth down on ~** poner algo por escrito; **it's not worth the ~ it's written on** no vale para nada.

(**b**) (*document*) papel *m*, documento *m*; **~s** (*identity etc*) papeles *mpl*, documentación *f*; **your ~s, please** la documentación, por favor; **ship's ~s** documentación *f* del barco; **Churchill's private ~s** los papeles personales de Churchill.

(**c**) (*Univ etc exercise*) ejercicio *m*, ensayo *m*; (*exam*) cuestionario *m* de examen; **to do a good ~ in maths** hacer un buen examen de matemáticas; **to set a ~ in physics** poner un examen de física.

(**d**) (*learned: written*) artículo *m*, (*read aloud*) comunicación *f*, ponencia *f*; **we heard a good ~ on place-names** escuchamos una buena ponencia sobre toponimia.

(**e**) (*newspaper*) periódico *m*; **to write for the ~s** colaborar en los periódicos, escribir artículos para los periódicos; **to write to the ~ about sth** escribir una carta al director de un periódico.

2 *attr* de papel; **~ advance** avance *m* de papel; **~ bag** saco *m* de papel, bolsa *f* de papel; **~ credit** papel *m* crédito; **~ cup** vaso *m* de cartón; **~ currency** papel *m* moneda; **~ handkerchief, ~ hankie** pañuelo *m* de papel; **~ industry** industria *f* papelera; **~ lantern** farolillo *m* de papel; **~ loss** pérdida *f* que tiene lugar cuando baja el valor de una acción (*etc*) sin venderse ésta; **~ money** papel *m* moneda, billetes *mpl* de banco; **~ profit** beneficio *m* no realizado; **~ round** reparto *m* de periódicos (por las casas); **~ tape** cinta *f* de papel; **~ tiger** tigre *m* de papel; **~ tissue** pañuelo *m* de papel, tisú *m*; **~ towel** toallita *f* de papel.

3 *vt wall, room* empapelar, tapizar (*LAm*).

◆paper over *vt* (*fig*) disimular.

paperback ['peɪpəbæk] *n* libro *m* en rústica, (*loosely*) libro *m* de bolsillo.

paperbacked ['peɪpəbækt] *adj*, **paperbound** ['peɪpəbaʊnd] *adj* en rústica.

paperboy ['peɪpəbɔɪ] *n* repartidor *m* de periódicos.

paper-chain ['peɪpətʃeɪn] *n* cadeneta *f* de papel.

paperchase ['peɪpətʃeɪs] *n* rallye-paper *m*.

paperclip ['peɪpəklɪp] *n* clip *m*, sujetapapeles *m*, broche *m* (*SC*), ataché *m* (*Carib*).

paper-fastener ['peɪpə,fɑːsnəʳ] *n* grapa *f*.

paper-feed(er) ['peɪpə'fiːd(əʳ)] *n* alimentador *m* de papel.

paperhanger ['peɪpə,hæŋəʳ] *n* (*Brit*) empapelador *m*.

paper-knife ['peɪpənaɪf] *n*, *pl* **paper-knives** ['peɪpənaɪvz] abrecartas *m*, plegadera *f*, cortapapeles *m*.

paperless ['peɪpəlɪs] *adj* sin papel; **the ~ society** la sociedad sin papel.

paper-mill ['peɪpəmɪl] *n* fábrica *f* de papel, papelera *f*.

paper-shop* ['peɪpəʃɒp] *n* = kiosco *m* (de periódicos).

paperweight ['peɪpəweɪt] *n* pisapapeles *m*.

paperwork ['peɪpəwɜːk] *n* trabajo *m* administrativo; trabajo *m* de oficina; aspecto *m* teórico; (*pej*) papeleo *m*, trámites *mpl* burocráticos.

papery ['peɪpərɪ] *adj* parecido al papel; delgado como el papel.

papier-mâché ['pæpɪeɪ'mæʃeɪ] **1** *adj* de cartón piedra.

2 *n* cartón *m* piedra.

papist ['peɪpɪst] *n* papista *mf*.

papistry ['peɪpɪstrɪ] *n* papismo *m*.

paprika ['pæprɪkə] *n* pimienta *f* húngara, paprika *f*.

Pap test ['pæptest] *n* frotis *m* (cervical).

Papua New Guinea ['pæpjʊənjuː'gɪnɪ] **1** *n* Nueva Guinea *f* Papúa. **2** *adj* de Nueva Guinea Papúa.

Papua New Guinean ['pæpjʊənjuː'gɪnɪən] *n* papú *mf*.

papyrus [pə'paɪərəs] *n*, *pl* **papyruses** *or* **papyri** [pə'paɪəraɪ] papiro *m*.

par [pɑːʳ] **1** *adj value etc* nominal, a la par; **~ value** valor *m* a la par.

2 *n* (*Comm*) par *f*; (*Golf*) par *m*; **~ for the course** par *m* del campo; **it's about ~ for the course** (*fig*) es más o menos normal, es más o menos lo que era de esperar; **5 under ~** 5 bajo par; **2 over ~** 2 sobre par; **to be above** (*or* **over**) **~** (*Comm*) estar por encima de (*or* sobre) la par; **to be under** (*or* **below**) **~** (*Comm*) estar por debajo de (*or* bajo) la par, (*Med*) estar indispuesto, sentirse mal, (*thing: also* **to be not up to ~**) ser inferior a la calidad normal; **to be at ~** (*Comm*) estar a la par; **to be on a ~ with** ser equivalente a, correr parejas con; **to place sth on a ~ with** parangonar algo con, equiparar algo con.

para. *n abbr of* **paragraph** párrafo *m*.

parable ['pærəbl] *n* parábola *f*.

parabola [pə'ræbələ] *n* parábola *f*.

parabolic [,pærə'bɒlɪk] *adj* parabólico; **~ aerial** antena *f* parabólica.

paracetamol [pærə'siːtəmɒl] *n* paracetamol *m*.

parachute ['pærəʃuːt] **1** *n* paracaídas *m*.

2 *attr*: **~ drop** lanzamiento *m* en paracaídas; **~ jump** salto *m* en paracaídas; **~ regiment** regimiento *m* de paracaidistas.

3 *vt* lanzar en paracaídas; **to ~ food to sb** suministrar víveres a uno en paracaídas.

4 *vi* lanzarse en paracaídas; (*also* **to ~ down**) bajar en paracaídas; **to ~ to safety** salvarse utilizando el paracaídas.

parachutist ['pærəʃuːtɪst] *n* paracaidista *mf*.

parade [pə'reɪd] **1** *n* (*procession*) desfile *m*; (*Mil*) desfile *m*, parada *f*; (*of models*) desfile *m*, presentación *f*; (*road*) paseo *m*; (*fig*) alarde *m*; **to be on ~** (*fig*) estar visible, estar a la vista del público; **to make a ~ of** hacer alarde de, ostentar.

2 *vt troops* formar, formar en parada; *streets* recorrer, desfilar por; *placard, image etc* pasear (*through the streets* por las calles); (*show off*) hacer alarde de, hacer ostentación de, lucir; **to ~ one's learning** hacer alarde de su erudición.

3 *vi* (*Mil*) formar en parada, pasar revista; (*group of people*) desfilar; (*one person*) pasearse; **the strikers ~d through the town** los huelguistas desfilaron por la ciudad; **she ~d up and down with the hat on** se paseó de un lado a otro con el sombrero puesto, andaba de acá para allá para lucir el sombrero.

◆parade about, parade around *vi* pavonearse.

parade-ground [pə'reɪdgraʊnd] *n* plaza *f* de armas.

paradigm ['pærədaɪm] *n* paradigma *m*.

paradigmatic [,pærədɪg'mætɪk] *adj* paradigmático.

paradise ['pærədaɪs] *n* paraíso *m*; **this is ~!** ¡esto es jauja!; *V* **fool¹, earthly**.

paradox ['pærədɒks] *n* paradoja *f*.

paradoxical ['pærə'dɒksɪkəl] *adj* paradójico.

paradoxically [,pærə'dɒksɪkəlɪ] *adv* paradójicamente.

paraffin ['pærəfɪn] **1** *n* (*Brit*: *also* **~ oil**) petróleo *m* (de alumbrado), queroseno *m*; (*wax*) parafina *f*.

2 *attr*: **~ lamp** quinqué *m* de petróleo; **~ wax** parafina *f*.

paragon ['pærəgən] *n* dechado *m*; **a ~ of virtue** un dechado de virtudes.

paragraph ['pærəgrɑːf] **1** *n* párrafo *m*, acápite *m* (*LAm*); (*Typ*: *short article in newspaper*) suelto *m*; **'new ~'** '(punto y) aparte'. **2** *vt* dividir en párrafos.

Paraguay ['pærəgwaɪ] *n* el Paraguay.

Paraguayan [,pærə'gwaɪən] **1** *adj* paraguayo. **2** *n* paraguayo *m*, -a *f*.

parakeet ['pærəkiːt] *n* perico *m*, periquito *m*.

paralanguage ['pærə,læŋgwɪdʒ] *n* paralenguaje *m*.

paralinguistic [,pærəlɪŋ'gwɪstɪk] *adj* paralingüístico.

parallel ['pærəlel] **1** *adj* paralelo; (*Comput, Elec*) en paralelo; (*fig*) semejante, análogo (*to* a); **~ bars** paralelas *fpl*; **~ printer** impresora *f* en paralelo; **in a ~ direction to** en dirección paralela a; **to run ~ to** ir en línea paralela a, correr paralelo con;; **this is a ~ case to the last one** este caso es análogo al anterior.

2 *n* (*Geom*) paralela *f*, línea *f* paralela; (*Geog, fig*) paralelo *m*; **the 49th ~** el paralelo 49; **in ~** (*Elec*) en paralelo; **a case without ~** un caso sin paralelo, un caso nunca visto; **it has no ~ as far as I know** que yo sepa no tiene paralelo, que yo sepa no hay nada parecido; **to draw a ~ between X and Y** establecer un paralelo entre X e Y; **these things occur in ~** estas cosas corren parejas (*with* con), estas cosas ocurren paralelamente.

3 *vt* (*fig*) ser paralelo a, ser análogo a, correr parejas con; **it is ~led by ...** corre parejas con ..., tiene su paralelo en ...

parallelism ['pærəlelɪzəm] *n* paralelismo *m*.

parallelogram [,pærə'leləʊgræm] *n* paralelogramo *m*.

paralysis [pə'ræləsɪs] *n* parálisis *f*; (*fig*) paralización *f*, parálisis *f*.

paralytic [,pærə'lɪtɪk] **1** *adj* (**a**) paralítico. (**b**) **he was ~** (*Brit**) estaba como una cuba*. **2** *n* paralítico *m*, -a *f*.

paralyzation [,pærəlaɪ'zeɪʃən] *n* paralización *f*.

paralyze ['pærəlaɪz] *vt* paralizar (*also fig*); **to be ~d in both legs** estar paralizado de las dos piernas; **to be ~d with fright** estar paralizado de miedo.

paramedic [,pærə'medɪk] *n* paramédico *m*, -a *f*.

paramedical [,pærə'medɪkəl] *adj* paramédico.

parameter [pə'ræmɪtəʳ] *n* parámetro *m*.

paramilitary [ˌpærəˈmɪlɪtərɪ] *adj* paramilitar.
paramount [ˈpærəmaʊnt] *adj* supremo; **of ~ importance** de la mayor importancia, primordial; **solvency must be ~** la solvencia es lo más importante, ante todo la solvencia.
paramour [ˈpærəmʊəʳ] *n* (*esp hum*) amante *mf*, querido *m*, -a *f*.
paranoia [ˌpærəˈnɔɪə] *n* paranoia *f*.
paranoiac [ˌpærəˈnɔɪɪk] **1** *adj* paranoico. **2** *n* paranoico *m*, -a *f*.
paranoid [ˈpærənɔɪd] *adj* paranoide.
paranormal [ˌpærəˈnɔːməl] **1** *adj* paranormal. **2** *n*: **the ~** lo paranormal.
parapet [ˈpærəpɪt] *n* parapeto *m*; (*of well etc*) brocal *m*.
paraphernalia [ˈpærəfəˈneɪlɪə] *n* parafernalia *f*.
paraphrase [ˈpærəfreɪz] **1** *n* paráfrasis *f*. **2** *vt* parafrasear.
paraplegia [ˌpærəˈpliːdʒə] *n* paraplejía *f*.
paraplegic [ˌpærəˈpliːdʒɪk] **1** *adj* parapléjico. **2** *n* parapléjico *m*, -a *f*.
parapsychology [ˌpærəsaɪˈkɒlədʒɪ] *n* parapsicología *f*.
Paras* [ˈpærəz] *npl abbr of* **Parachute Regiment** paras* *mpl*, paracas* *mpl*.
parasite [ˈpærəsaɪt] *n* parásito *m* (*also fig*: *on* de).
parasitic(al) [ˌpærəˈsɪtɪk(əl)] *adj* parasítico, parasitario; **to be ~ on** ser parásito de.
parasitism [ˈpærəsɪtɪzəm] *n* parasitismo *m*.
parasitize [ˈpærəsɪˌtaɪz] *vt* parasitar (en).
parasitology [ˌpærəsɪˈtɒlədʒɪ] *n* parasitología *f*.
parasol [ˌpærəˈsɒl] *n* sombrilla *f*, quitasol *m*, parasol *m*.
parataxis [ˌpærəˈtæksɪs] *n* parataxis *f*.
paratrooper [ˈpærətruːpəʳ] *n* paracaidista *m*.
paratroops [ˈpærətruːps] *npl* paracaidistas *mpl*.
paratyphoid [ˈpærəˈtaɪfɔɪd] *n* paratifoidea *f*.
parboil [ˈpɑːbɔɪl] *vt* sancochar.
Parcae [ˈpɑːkiː] *npl*: **the ~** las Parcas.
parcel [ˈpɑːsl] *n* paquete *m*; (*of land*) parcela *f*.
◆**parcel out** *vt* repartir; dividir; *land* parcelar.
◆**parcel up** *vt* empaquetar, embalar.
parcel-bomb [ˈpɑːslbɒm] *n* paquete-bomba *m*.
parcel-office [ˈpɑːslˌɒfɪs] *n* departamento *m* de paquetes.
parcel-post [ˈpɑːslpəʊst] *n* servicio *m* de paquetes postales.
parch [pɑːtʃ] **1** *vt* secar, resecar; agostar; quemar. **2** *vi* secarse.
parched [pɑːtʃt] *adj land etc* seco; **to be ~ (with thirst)** estar muerto de sed.
parchment [ˈpɑːtʃmənt] *n* pergamino *m*.
parchment-like [ˈpɑːtʃməntˌlaɪk] *adj* apergaminado.
pardon [ˈpɑːdn] **1** *n* perdón *m*; (*Jur*) indulto *m*; **free ~** indulto *m* absoluto; **general ~** amnistía *f*; **to beg sb's ~** pedir perdón a uno; **I beg your ~, but could you ...?** perdone la molestia, pero ¿podría Vd ...?; **I beg your ~!** ¡perdone Vd!, ¡ay perdone!, ¡disculpe! (*LAm*); **~?, (I beg your) ~?,** (*US*) **~ me?** ¿cómo?, ¿mande? (*Mex*).
2 *vt* perdonar, dispensar; (*Jur*) indultar; **to ~ sb sth** perdonar algo a uno; dispensar a uno de hacer (*etc*) algo; **~ me, but could you ...?** perdone la molestia, pero ¿podría Vd ...?; **~ me!** ¡perdone Vd!, ¡ay perdone!; **~ my mentioning it** siento tener que decirlo, perdona que te lo diga.
pardonable [ˈpɑːdnəbl] *adj* perdonable.
pardonably [ˈpɑːdnəblɪ] *adv*: **he was ~ angry** es fácil disculpar su enojo, se comprende fácilmente que se encolerizara.
pare [pɛəʳ] *vt nails* cortar; *fruit etc* mondar; *stick etc* adelgazar; **to ~ away, to ~ down** (*fig*) reducir, ir reduciendo; **to ~ sth down to the minimum** reducir algo al mínimum.
parent [ˈpɛərənt] **1** *n* padre *m*, madre *f*; **~s** padres *mpl*. **2** *adj, attr*: **the ~ plant** la planta madre; **the ~ company** la casa matriz; **~-teacher association** ≃ asociación *f* de padres de alumnos.
parentage [ˈpɛərəntɪdʒ] *n* familia *f*, linaje *m*; **of humble ~** de nacimiento humilde; **of unknown ~** de padres desconocidos.
parental [pəˈrentl] *adj care etc* de padre y madre, de los padres; paternal, maternal; **~ authority** patria potestad *f*.
parenteral [pæˈrentərəl] *adj* parenteral.
parenthesis [pəˈrenθɪsɪs] *n*, *pl* **parentheses** [pəˈrenθɪsiːz] paréntesis *m*; **in ~** entre paréntesis.
parenthetic(al) [ˌpærənˈθetɪk(əl)] *adj* entre paréntesis; explicativo.
parenthetically [ˌpærənˈθetɪkəlɪ] *adv* entre paréntesis; a modo de explicación.
parenthood [ˈpɛərənthʊd] *n* el ser padre (*or* madre), el tener hijos; paternidad *f*, maternidad *f*.
parenting [ˈpɛərəntɪŋ] *n* el ser padres; **shared ~** participación *f* conjunta en la vida familiar; **~ is a full-time occupation** el cuidar de los hijos es una labor de plena dedicación.
parer [ˈpɛərəʳ] *n* pelalegumbres *m*.
par excellence [pɑːrˈeksəlɑːns] *adv* por excelencia.
pariah [ˈpærɪə] *n* paria *mf*.
parietal [pəˈraɪɪtl] *adj* parietal.
paring [ˈpɛərɪŋ] *attr*: **~ knife** cuchillo *m* de mondar.
parings [ˈpɛərɪŋz] *npl* peladuras *fpl*, mondaduras *fpl*; desperdicios *mpl*.
pari passu [ˈpærɪˈpæsuː] *adv* a ritmo parecido, al igual; **~ with** a ritmo parecido al de, al igual que.
Paris [ˈpærɪs] **1** *n* París *m*. **2** *attr* parisiense.
parish [ˈpærɪʃ] **1** *n* parroquia *f*. **2** *attr* parroquial, de la parroquia; **~ church** iglesia *f* parroquial; **~ council** concejo *m* parroquial; **~ priest** párroco *m*; **~ register** libro *m* parroquial, registro *m* parroquial.
parishioner [pəˈrɪʃənəʳ] *n* feligrés *m*, -esa *f*.
parish-pump [ˈpærɪʃˈpʌmp] *attr* (*Brit pej*) de campanario, de aldea, pueblerino; **~ attitude** espíritu *m* de campanario.
Parisian [pəˈrɪzɪən] **1** *adj* parisiense, parisino, parisién. **2** *n* parisiense *mf*.
parity [ˈpærɪtɪ] *n* paridad *f*, igualdad *f*; (*Fin*) paridad *f*; **exchange at ~** cambio *m* a la par.
park [pɑːk] **1** *n* parque *m*; jardines *mpl*; (*Sport**) campo *m*; (*Aut*) aparcamiento *m*, parque *m* (de automóviles).
2 *vt* (*Aut*) estacionar, aparcar (*Sp*); (*) poner, dejar, depositar; **can I ~ my car here?** ¿puedo aparcar mi coche aquí?
3 *vi* (*Aut*) estacionarse, aparcar (*Sp*); (*) quedarse.
parka [ˈpɑːkə] *n* anorak *m*.
park-and-ride [ˌpɑːkənd'raɪd], **park-ride** [ˌpɑːkˈraɪd] *n aparcamiento en estaciones periféricas conectadas con el transporte urbano colectivo*.
parking [ˈpɑːkɪŋ] **1** *n* estacionamiento *m*; aparcamiento *m*; **'no ~'** 'prohibido estacionar'; **'good ~ for cars'** 'amplio aparcamiento para coches'; **'~ for 50 cars'** 'aparcamiento para 50 coches'.
2 *attr*: **~ attendant** guardacoches *mf*; **~ bay** área *f* de aparcamiento (*or* estacionamiento *m LAm*) de coches; **~ lights** luces *fpl* de estacionamiento; **~ lot** (*esp US*) aparcamiento *m*, estacionamiento *m* (*LAm*); **~ meter** parquímetro *m*, contador *m* de aparcamiento, estacionómetro *m* (*Mex*); **~ offence, ~ violation** (*US*) ofensa *f* por aparcamiento indebido; **~ place, ~ space** sitio *m* para aparcar, aparcamiento *m*; **~ ticket** multa *f* de aparcamiento (*or* estacionamiento *LAm*).
Parkinson [ˈpɑːkɪnsən] *n*: **~'s disease** enfermedad *f* de Parkinson; **~'s law** ley *f* de Parkinson.
park-keeper [ˈpɑːkˌkiːpəʳ] *n* guardián *m* (de parque), guardabosque *m*.
parkland [ˈpɑːklænd] *n* zonas *fpl* verdes.
parkway [ˈpɑːkweɪ] *n* (*US*) carretera *f* principal, alameda *f*.
parky* [ˈpɑːkɪ] *adj* (*Brit*) frío; **it's pretty ~** hace un frío glacial.
parlance [ˈpɑːləns] *n* lenguaje *m*; **in common ~** en lenguaje corriente; **in technical ~** en lenguaje técnico.
parley [ˈpɑːlɪ] **1** *n* parlamento *m*. **2** *vi* parlamentar (*with* con).
parliament [ˈpɑːləmənt] *n* parlamento *m*; (*Spanish*) Cortes *fpl*; **to get into ~** llegar a ser diputado, ser elegido (a las Cortes *etc*).
parliamentarian [ˌpɑːləmenˈtɛərɪən] **1** *adj* parlamentario. **2** *n* parlamentario *m*, -a *f*.
parliamentary [ˌpɑːləˈmentərɪ] *adj* parlamentario; **~ agent** agente *m* parlamentario, agente *f* parlamentaria; **~ democracy** democracia *f* parlamentaria; **~ election** elecciones *fpl* parlamentarias; **~ government** gobierno *m* parlamentario; **~ immunity** inmunidad *f* parlamentaria; **~ privilege** privilegio *m* parlamentario.
parlour, (*US*) **parlor** [ˈpɑːləʳ] **1** *n* sala *f* de recibo, salón *m*, living *m* (*LAm*); (*Eccl*) locutorio *m*. **2** *attr*: **~ car** (*US*) coche-salón *m*.
parlour game, (*US*) **parlor game** [ˈpɑːləgeɪm] *n* juego *m* de salón.
parlourmaid, (*US*) **parlormaid** [ˈpɑːləmeɪd] *n* camarera *f*.
parlous [ˈpɑːləs] *adj state* lamentable, crítico, pésimo, peligroso, alarmante.
Parma [ˈpɑːmə] *attr*: **~ ham** jamón *m* de Parma; **~ violet** violeta *f* de Parma.
Parmesan [ˌpɑːmɪˈzæn] *n* (*cheese*) parmesano *m*.
Parnassus [pɑːˈnæsəs] *n* Parnaso *m*.
parochial [pəˈrəʊkɪəl] *adj* (*Eccl*) parroquial; (*fig*) estrecho, limitado, restringido; de miras estrechas.

parochialism [pəˈrəʊkɪəlɪzəm] *n* (*fig*) estrechez *f*, lo limitado, lo restringido; estrechez *f* de miras; mentalidad *f* pueblerina.
parodic [pəˈrɒdɪk] *adj* paródico.
parodist [ˈpærədɪst] *n* parodista *mf*.
parody [ˈpærədɪ] **1** *n* parodia *f*. **2** *vt* parodiar.
parole [pəˈrəʊl] **1** *n* (*promise*) palabra *f*, palabra *f* de honor; (*freedom*) libertad *f* bajo palabra, libertad *f* condicional; **to be on ~** estar libre bajo palabra; **to break one's ~** faltar a su palabra; **to put sb on ~** dejar a uno libre bajo palabra.
2 *vt* dejar libre bajo palabra.
paroxysm [ˈpærəksɪzəm] *n* paroxismo *m*.
parquet [ˈpɑːkeɪ] *n* parquet *m*, parqué *m*; entarimado *m* (de hojas quebradas *or* de maderas finas).
parquetry [ˈpɑːkɪtrɪ] *n* entarimado *m*, obra *f* de entarimado.
parricide [ˈpærɪsaɪd] *n* (**a**) (*act*) parricidio *m*. (**b**) (*person*) parricida *mf*.
parrot [ˈpærət] **1** *n* loro *m*, papagayo *m*; **they repeated it like ~s** lo repitieron como loros. **2** *vt words* repetir como un loro, (*person*) imitar como un loro.
parrot-cry [ˈpærətkraɪ] *n* eslogan *m* (*etc*) que se repite mecánicamente; cantilena *f*.
parrot-fashion [ˈpærət,fæʃən] *adv learn etc* mecánicamente.
parry [ˈpærɪ] *vt* (*Fencing*) parar, quitar; *blow* parar, desviar; *attack* rechazar, defenderse de; (*fig*) esquivar, eludir, desviar hábilmente.
parse [pɑːz] *vt* analizar.
Parsee [pɑːˈsiː] *n* parsi *mf*.
parser [ˈpɑːzəʳ] *n* analizador *m* sintáctico.
parsimonious [,pɑːsɪˈməʊnɪəs] *adj* parco; escaso, corto; frugal.
parsimoniously [,pɑːsɪˈməʊnɪəslɪ] *adv* parcamente; escasamente; frugalmente.
parsimony [ˈpɑːsɪmənɪ] *n* parquedad *f*; escasez *f*; frugalidad *f*.
parsing [ˈpɑːzɪŋ] *n* análisis *m* gramatical, análisis *m* sintáctico.
parsley [ˈpɑːslɪ] *n* perejil *m*.
parsnip [ˈpɑːsnɪp] *n* chirivía *f*, pastinaca *f*.
parson [ˈpɑːsn] *n* clérigo *m*, cura *m*; (*esp*) párroco *m*, (*Protestant*) pastor *m*; **~'s nose** (*of chicken*) rabadilla *f*.
parsonage [ˈpɑːsnɪdʒ] *n* casa *f* del párroco; casa *f* del pastor.
parsonical [pɑːˈsɒnɪkəl] *adj* (*hum*) frailuno.
part [pɑːt] **1** *n* (**a**) (*portion, fragment*) parte *f*; porción *f*; trozo *m*; **this ~ is blue** esta parte es azul; **the funny ~ of it is that ...** lo gracioso es que ...; **you haven't heard the best ~ yet** todavía no te he dicho lo mejor; **that's the awkward ~** eso es lo difícil; **it is ~ and parcel of the scheme** es parte esencial del proyecto, es parte integrante del proyecto; **the book is good in ~s** hay partes del libro que son buenas; **a good ~ of, a large ~ of** buena parte de; **the greater ~ of it is done** la mayor parte está hecha; **this is in great ~ due to ...** esto se debe ante todo a ..., más que nada esto se debe a ...; **for the most ~** por la mayor parte; **it went on for the best ~ of an hour** continuó casi una hora; **we lost the best ~ of a month** perdimos casi un mes; **for the better ~ of the day** durante la mayor parte del día; **in the latter ~ of the year** en los últimos meses del año; **in ~** en parte; **it is ready in ~** en parte está listo; **to pay a debt in ~** pagar parte de una deuda; **5 ~s of sand to 1 of cement** 5 partes de arena y 1 de cemento; **three ~s** tres cuartos; **it's 3 ~s gone** las tres cuartas partes se han usado ya.
(**b**) (*Mech*) pieza *f*.
(**c**) (*Gram*) parte *f*; **~ of speech** parte *f* de la oración; **principal ~s of a verb** partes *fpl* principales de un verbo.
(**d**) (*of journal*) número *m*; (*of series*) tomo *m*; (*of serial*) entrega *f*; (*of reference work*) fascículo *m*.
(**e**) (*share*) parte *f*; **to do one's ~** cumplir con sus obligaciones; **each one did his ~** cada uno hizo lo que le tocaba; **to have no ~ in sth** (*not be active*) no participar en algo, (*have nothing to do with*) no tener nada que ver con algo, ser ajeno a algo, desentenderse de algo; **he had no ~ in stealing it** no tuvo que ver con el robo; **to take** (**a**) **~ in** tomar parte en, intervenir en, participar en; **are you taking ~?** ¿vas a tomar parte?
(**f**) (*Theat, fig*) papel *m*; **it is not my ~ to** + *infin* no me toca a mí + *infin*; **to look the ~** vestir el cargo; **to play a ~** hacer un papel, (*fig*) desempeñar un papel; **what ~ do you play?** ¿qué papel haces?; **he's just playing a ~** está haciendo un papel, nada más; **the climate has played a ~ in** + *ger* el clima ha contribuido a + *infin*.
(**g**) (*Mus*) parte *f*; **the soprano ~** la parte de soprano; **to sing in ~s** cantar por partes.
(**h**) (*region*) **~s** lugar *m*; comarca *f*, región *f*; **from all ~s** de todas partes; **in these ~s** por aquí; en estos pagos, en estos contornos; **the biggest thief in these ~s** el mayor ladrón en estos contornos; **in foreign ~s** en el extranjero; **what ~ are you from?** ¿de dónde es Vd?; **he's not from these ~s** no es de aquí; **it's a lovely ~** es una región hermosa.
(**i**) (*side*) parte *f*; **for my ~, on my ~** por mi parte; **a mistake on the ~ of ...** un error por parte de ..., un error debido a ...; **on the one ~..., on the other ...** por una parte ..., por otra ...; **there is opposition on the ~ of some** hay oposición por parte de algunos; **to take sb's ~** ponerse del lado de uno, tomar el partido de uno.
(**j**) **to take sth in good ~** tomar algo en buena parte.
(**k**) **a man of ~s** un hombre de talento.
(**l**) (*US: in hair*) raya *f*, vereda *f* (*Mex*).
2 *adv*: **~ one and ~ the other** parte esto y parte lo otro; **it is ~ brass and ~ copper** parte es latón y parte es cobre; **it was ~ eaten** había sido comido en parte; **she is ~ French** ella es en parte francesa.
3 *attr*: **a 4 ~ song** una canción a 4 voces; **~ load** carga *f* parcial; **~ work** revista *f* con entregas coleccionables.
4 *adj* parcial; co..., con...; **~-author** coautor *m*, -ora *f*; **~-owner** condueño *m*, -a *f*, copropietario *m*, -a *f*.
5 *vt* separar, dividir (*from* de); (*break*) romper, partir; **to ~ sth in two** partir algo en dos; **he ~ed the grass with his hand** con la mano apartó la hierba; **to ~ one's hair** hacerse la raya.
6 *vi* (**a**) (*crowd etc*) apartarse; **the branches ~ed** se apartaron las ramas; **the people ~ed to let her through** la gente se hizo a un lado para dejarla pasar.
(**b**) (*2 persons*) separarse; **they ~ed 5 years ago** se separaron hace 5 años; **the best of friends must ~** los mejores amigos han de separarse alguna vez; **to ~ from sb** separarse de uno, despedirse de uno; **when we ~ed from Seville** cuando nos despedimos de Sevilla.
(**c**) (*roads etc*) bifurcarse.
(**d**) (*snap, break*) romperse, partirse (*LAm*); (*fall away*) separarse, desprenderse.
(**e**) **to ~ with** ceder, entregar; *money* pagar, dar, soltar; (*get rid of*) deshacerse de; **I hate ~ing with it** siento mucho tener que cederlo, me da pena perderlo.
partake [pɑːˈteɪk] (*irr*: *V* **take**) *vti* (**a**) **to ~ of** *food* comer, comer de, aceptar; *drink* tomar, beber; **do you ~?** ¿bebes vino? (*etc*); **will you ~?** ¿quieres de esto?
(**b**) **to ~ of a quality** tener algo de una cualidad, tener rasgos de una cualidad.
(**c**) **to ~ in** tomar parte en, participar en; **are you partaking?** ¿vas a tomar parte?
part-exchange [ˈpɑːtɪksˈtʃeɪndʒ] *n* (*Brit*): **to offer sth in ~** ofrecer algo como parte del pago; **'we take your old car in ~'** 'admitimos su coche usado a cambio'.
parthenogenesis [ˈpɑːθɪnəʊˈdʒenɪsɪs] *n* partenogénesis *f*.
Parthenon [ˈpɑːθənɒn] *n* Partenón *m*.
partial [ˈpɑːʃəl] *adj* (**a**) (*in part*) parcial. (**b**) (*biased*) parcial. (**c**) **to be ~ to sth*** ser aficionado a algo, tener gusto por algo.
partiality [,pɑːʃɪˈælɪtɪ] *n* (**a**) (*bias*) parcialidad *f*; predisposición *f*, prejuicio *m*. (**b**) (*liking*) **~ for, ~ to** afición *f* a, gusto *m* por.
partially [ˈpɑːʃəlɪ] *adv* (**a**) (*partly*) parcialmente, en parte. (**b**) (*with bias*) con parcialidad.
participant [pɑːˈtɪsɪpənt] *n* partícipe *mf*, participante *mf*; (*in competition*) concursante *mf*; (*in fight*) combatiente *mf*.
participate [pɑːˈtɪsɪpeɪt] *vi* participar, tomar parte (*in* en); **participating countries** países *mpl* participantes.
participation [pɑː,tɪsɪˈpeɪʃən] *n* participación *f*.
participial [,pɑːtɪˈsɪpɪəl] *adj* participial.
participle [ˈpɑːtɪsɪpl] *n* participio *m*; **past ~** participio *m* pasivo, participio *m* pasado, participio *m* (de) pretérito; **present ~** participio *m* activo, participio *m* (de) presente.
particle [ˈpɑːtɪkl] *n* (**a**) partícula *f*; (*of dust etc*) átomo *m*, grano *m*; (*fig*) pizca *f*; **~ accelerator** acelerador *m* de partículas; **~ physics** física *f* de partículas; **there's not a ~ of truth in it** eso no tiene ni pizca de verdad. (**b**) (*Gram*) partícula *f*.
particleboard [ˈpɑːtɪklbɔːd] *n* (*US*) madera *f* aglomerada.
parti-coloured, (*US*) **parti-colored** [ˈpɑːtɪ,kʌləd] *adj* de diversos colores, multicolor, abigarrado.
particular [pəˈtɪkjʊləʳ] **1** *adj* (**a**) (*special*) particular; especial; concreto; determinado; individual; **that ~ person** esa persona en particular, esa persona (y no otra);

a ~ thing una cosa determinada; **in ~ cases** en casos especiales; **it varies according to the ~ case** varía según el caso individual; **in this ~ case** en este caso concreto; **for no ~ reason** por ninguna razón especial; **to take ~ care** tomar especial cuidado, ser especialmente cuidadoso.

(**b**) *account etc* detallado, minucioso.

(**c**) (*fastidious*) exigente, quisquilloso (*about, as to, as to what* en cuanto a, en asuntos de, para); (*scrupulous*) escrupuloso; (*about food etc*) delicado; **he's ~ about his food** es delicado con lo que come; **he is very ~ about cleanliness** es muy exigente para la limpieza; **he's ~ about his car** cuida mucho del coche; **I'm ~ about my friends** escojo mis amigos con cierto cuidado; **I'm not too ~ (about it)** lo mismo da, me es igual; **he was most ~ about it** insistió mucho sobre esto; **he was very ~ to say that ...** subrayó que ..., dijo con toda claridad que ...

2 *n* (**a**) (*detail*) detalle *m*, pormenor *m*, dato *m*; **~s** detalles *mpl*; **in this ~** en este caso particular; **correct in every ~** correcto en todos los detalles; **for further ~s apply to ...** para más informes escriban a ...; **to give ~s** citar los detalles; **please give full ~s** se ruega hacer constar todos los detalles, se ruega dar un informe detallado.

(**b**) **in ~** en particular; en concreto, concretamente; **nothing in ~** nada concreto, nada en particular; **are you looking for anything in ~?** ¿busca Vd algo en concreto?

particularity [pə,tɪkjʊ'lærɪtɪ] *n* particularidad *f*.

particularize [pə'tɪkjʊləraɪz] **1** *vt* particularizar, especificar, señalar; **he did not ~ which one he wanted** no especificó cuál quería.

2 *vi* dar todos los detalles, concretar; **he did not ~** no concretó.

particularly [pə'tɪkjʊləlɪ] *adv*: **this is ~ true of his later novels** sobre todo es esto verdad de sus novelas de última epoca; **notice ~ that ...** observen Vds sobre todo que ...; **he said most ~ not to do it** dijo de modo particular que no se hiciera; **do you want it ~ for tomorrow?** ¿lo necesitas especialmente para mañana?; **he was not ~ pleased** no se puso loco de contento que digamos; **not ~!** ¡no mucho!

parting ['pɑːtɪŋ] **1** *adj* de despedida; **a ~ present** un regalo de despedida; **~ shot** última observación, palabra *f* dicha al despedirse, golpe *m* final; **his ~ words** sus palabras al despedirse; **he made a ~ threat** al separarse de nosotros pronunció una amenaza, nos dejó con una amenaza.

2 *n* (**a**) separación *f*; despedida *f*; **the ~ of the ways** el momento de la separación, (*fig*) el punto decisivo.

(**b**) (*Brit*: *in hair*) raya *f*, vereda *f* (*Mex*).

partisan [,pɑːtɪ'zæn] **1** *adj* partidista; (*Mil*) de partisanos, de guerrilleros; **~ spirit** partidismo *m*; **~ warfare** guerra *f* de guerrilleros.

2 *n* partidario *m*, -a *f*, (*of* de); (*Mil*) partisano *m*, -a *f*, guerrillero *m*, -a *f*.

partisanship [,pɑːtɪ'zænʃɪp] *n* partidismo *m*.

partition [pɑː'tɪʃən] **1** *n* (**a**) (*Pol etc*) partición *f*, división *f*.

(**b**) (*wall*) tabique *m*, medianía *f* (*LAm*).

2 *vt* (**a**) *country etc* partir, dividir; (*share*) repartir (*among* entre).

(**b**) *room etc* tabicar, dividir con tabique; **to ~ a part off** separar una parte con tabique.

partitive ['pɑːtɪtɪv] *adj* partitivo.

partly ['pɑːtlɪ] *adv* en parte; en cierto modo; **only ~ true** verdad sólo en parte; **it was ~ destroyed** quedaba destruido en parte, quedaba parcialmente destruido.

partner ['pɑːtnəʳ] **1** *n* compañero *m*, -a *f* (*also Cards*); (*Comm*) socio *mf*; (*in dance, at tennis etc*) pareja *f*; (*in crime*) codelincuente *mf*; (*spouse*) cónyuge *mf*; (*sexual*) pareja *f*; (*lover*) compañero *m*, -a *f*; **Britain's EC ~s** los socios comunitarios de Gran Bretaña.

2 *vt* acompañar; **to be ~ed by** ir acompañado de; tener a uno por pareja (*etc*).

partnership ['pɑːtnəʃɪp] *n* asociación *f*, (*Comm*) sociedad *f* (comanditaria); (*of spouses*) vida *f* conyugal, vida *f* en común; **A is in ~ with Z** A es socio de Z; **to enter into ~, to form a ~** asociarse (*with* con); **to take sb into ~** tomar a uno como socio.

part-owner ['pɑːt'əʊnəʳ] *n* condueño *m*, -a *f*, copropietario *m*, -a *f*.

part-payment ['pɑːt'peɪmənt] *n* pago *m* parcial; **to offer sth in ~** ofrecer algo como parte del pago.

partridge ['pɑːtrɪdʒ] *n* perdiz *f*.

part-song ['pɑːtsɒŋ] *n* canción *f* a varias voces.

part-time ['pɑːt'taɪm] **1** *adv*: **to work ~** trabajar en horario de jornada reducida, trabajar parte de la jornada. **2** *adj person* en dedicación parcial, que trabaja por horas; *work* por horas, de horario partido. **3** *n* jornada *f* reducida; **to be on ~** trabajar en horario de jornada reducida.

part-timer [,pɑːt'taɪməʳ] *n* trabajador *m*, -ora *f* a tiempo partido.

parturition [,pɑːtjʊə'rɪʃən] *n* parturición *f*, parto *m*.

part-way ['pɑːt,weɪ] *adv*: **~ through the week** a mitad de la semana; **we're only ~ into** (*or* **through**) **the work** hemos hecho sólo una parte del trabajo; **the window was ~ open** la ventana estaba medio abierta.

party ['pɑːtɪ] **1** *n* (**a**) (*Pol*) partido *m*; **to be a member of the ~** ser miembro del partido; **to join the ~** hacerse miembro del partido.

(**b**) (*group*) grupo *m*; (*Mil*) pelotón *m*, destacamento *m*; **a ~ of travellers** un grupo de viajeros; **hunting ~** partida *f* de caza; **we were a ~ of 5** éramos un grupo de 5; **we were only a small ~** éramos pocos; **I was one of the ~** yo formaba parte del grupo; **to join sb's ~** unirse al grupo de uno.

(**c**) (*gathering*) reunión *f*; (*tea ~ etc*) tertulia *f*; (*merry*) fiesta *f*, guateque *m*; **that little ~ at El Alamein*** la fiestecita de El Alamain*; **that was quite a ~*!** ¡eso fue de miedo*!; **the ~'s over** se acabó la fiesta; **to crash a ~*** colarse, entrar de rondón; **to give a ~** ofrecer una fiesta, organizar una fiesta; **to go to a ~** ir a una fiesta; **keep the ~ clean!** ¡nada de chistes verdes!

(**d**) (*Jur etc*) parte *f*; interesado *m*, -a *f*; **third ~** tercera persona *f*, tercero *m*; **the parties to a dispute** las partes de una disputa, los interesados; **the high contracting parties** las altas partes contratantes; **to be a ~ to an agreement** firmar un acuerdo; **to be a ~ to a crime** ser cómplice en un crimen; **were you a ~ to this?** ¿tuvo Vd algo que ver con esto?; **I will not be a ~ to any violence** no quiero tener nada que ver con la violencia; **I will not be a ~ to any such attempt** no me presto a ninguna tentativa de ese tipo.

(**e**) (*: *person*) individuo *m*, -a* *f*; **a ~ of the name of Pérez** un individuo llamado Pérez*.

2 *attr* (**a**) (*Pol*) **~ line** línea *f* de partido; **~ machine** aparato *m* del partido; **~ political broadcast** ≈ espacio *m* electoral; **~ politics** política *f* de partidos, (*pej*) partidismo *m*, politiqueo *m*.

(**b**) **~ dress** traje *m* de fiesta; **~ piece, ~ trick** numerito *m* (de fiesta); **~ pooper*** (*US*) aguafiestas *mf*.

(**c**) **~ line** (*Telec*) línea *f* compartida.

(**d**) **~ wall** pared *f* medianera.

(**e**) **~ plan** venta *f* directa a través de círculos sociales.

3 (*) *vi* ir a fiestas, ir (mucho) a guateques; **we partied at John's** fuimos a la fiesta de Juan; **where shall we ~ tonight?** ¿a qué fiesta vamos esta noche?

party-goer ['pɑːtɪ,gəʊəʳ] *n* (*gen*) asiduo *m*, -a *f* a fiestas; (*on specific occasion*) invitado *m*, -a *f*; **I'm not much of a ~** yo voy poco a las fiestas.

party-going ['pɑːti,gəʊɪŋ] *n*: **he spends his time ~ instead of working** se pasa el tiempo en ir a fiestas y no en trabajar.

parvenu ['pɑːvənjuː] *n* advenedizo *m*, -a *f*.

paschal ['pɑːskəl] *adj* pascual; **the P~ Lamb** el cordero pascual.

pas de deux ['pɑːdə'dɜː] *n* paso *m* a dos.

pasha ['pæʃə] *n* bajá *m*, pachá *m*.

pass [pɑːs] **1** *n* (**a**) (*permit*) permiso *m*, pase *m*; (*Mil etc*) salvoconducto *m*; (*of journalist, worker etc*) permiso *m*; (*Theat*) entrada *f* de favor; (*Rail etc*) billete *m* de favor; (*membership card*) carnet *m*.

(**b**) (*Sport, Fencing, by conjuror, mesmerist*) pase *m*; **forward ~** pase *m* adelantado.

(**c**) (*in exams*) aprobado *m*, nota *f* de aprobado; **to get a ~ in German** aprobar en alemán; **I need a ~ in physics still** todavía tengo que aprobar la física.

(**d**) **things have come to a pretty ~** las cosas han llegado a una situación crítica, estamos en una situación crítica.

(**e**) **to make a ~ at*** echar un tiento a*.

(**f**) (*Geog*) puerto *m*, paso *m* (*LAm*); (*small*) desfiladero *m*; **to sell the ~** tracionar la causa; ceder lo que bien podría ser defendido.

2 *vt* (**a**) (*move past*) pasar; pasar por delante de; *person* (*on street etc*) cruzarse con; *competitor* pasar; (*Aut*: *overtake*) pasar, adelantar a, rebasar (*LAm*); **they ~ed each other on the way** se cruzaron en el camino; **we are now ~ing the Tower of London** pasamos ahora delante de la Torre de Londres.

(**b**) (*cross*) *frontier etc* cruzar.

(**c**) **it ~es belief** es increíble (*that* que); **it ~es my comprehension that ...** para mí resulta incomprensible que ...

(**d**) (*Univ etc*) *exam* aprobar, ser aprobado en.

(**e**) *censor* ser aprobado por; *critic* merecer la

aprobación de.

(**f**) (*approve*) *motion, plan, candidate etc* aprobar; **to ~ sb fit** dar a uno de alta; **to ~ sb for the army** declarar a uno apto para el servicio militar.

(**g**) *ball etc* pasar; **to ~ sth from hand to hand** pasar algo de mano a mano; **~ me the salt, please** ¿me haces el favor de pasar (*or* alcanzar *SC*) la sal?

(**h**) *false coin* pasar.

(**i**) **to ~ a cloth over sth** limpiar algo con un paño, frotar algo con un trapo; **to ~ one's hand between two bars** introducir la mano entre dos rejas.

(**j**) (*spend*) *time* pasar; **we ~ed the weekend pleasantly** pasamos el fin de semana agradablemente; **just to ~ the time** para pasar el rato; **I ~ed the time of day with him** me detuve un rato a charlar con él, cambié algunas palabras con él.

(**k**) *remark* hacer; *opinion* expresar; *sentence* pronunciar, dictar (*on* sobre, en el asunto de).

(**l**) *blood, water* evacuar.

3 *vi* (**a**) (*come, go*) pasar; **to ~ into a tunnel** entrar en un túnel; **to ~ into oblivion** ser olvidado; **to ~ out of sight** perderse de vista; **~ along the car please!** ¡vayan pasando por delante!; **words ~ed between them** se cambiaron algunas palabras (fuertes); **no money has ~ed** ningún dinero ha cambiado de dueño; **to let sth ~** no hacer caso de algo, no protestar contra algo; **we can't let that ~!** ¡eso no lo podemos consentir!; **let it ~** conviene dejarlo, conviene no protestar.

(**b**) (*of time*) (*also* **to ~ by**) pasar; **how time ~es!** ¡cómo pasa el tiempo!

(**c**) (*disappear*) pasar; desaparecer; (*clouds etc*) disiparse; **it'll ~** eso pasará, eso se olvidará.

(**d**) (*be acceptable*) ser aceptable, aprobarse; **what ~es in New York may not be good enough here** lo que se aprueba en Nueva York puede resultar inaceptable aquí.

(**e**) (*be considered as*) **it ~es for a restaurant** pasa por ser restaurante; **in her day she ~ed for a great beauty** en sus tiempos se le consideraba una gran belleza; **or what ~es nowadays for a hat** o lo que se llama sombrero hoy día.

(**f**) (*Univ etc*) aprobar, ser aprobado; **I ~ed!** ¡aprobé!; **did you ~ in chemistry?** ¿aprobaste en química?

(**g**) **it came to ~ that ...** (*liter*) aconteció que ...

(**h**) (*Cards etc*) **I ~** paso.

◆**pass about, pass around** *vt* = **pass round.**

◆**pass along 1** *vt* pasar de uno a otro, hacer circular.

2 *vi* pasar, circular.

◆**pass away** *vi* (**a**) (*die*) fallecer. (**b**) = **pass 3** (**c**).

◆**pass back** *vt* devolver (*to* a).

◆**pass by 1** *vt* no hacer caso de, no fijarse en, pasar por alto.

2 *vi* pasar de largo; pasar cerca.

◆**pass down 1** *vt* transmitir, pasar.

2 *vi* transmitirse, pasar.

◆**pass off 1** *vt* (**a**) *coin* pasar; *offence* disimular; **to ~ sth off as a joke** pasar algo por chiste; **he ~ed the girl off as his sister** hizo creer que la chica era su hermana, hizo pasar a la chica por su hermana.

(**b**) **to ~ sth off on sb** encajar algo a uno.

2 *vi* (**a**) (*subside*) pasar, desaparecer.

(**b**) (*occur*) pasar, tener lugar; **it all ~ed off without incident** todo transcurrió normalmente.

3 *vr*: **to ~ o.s. off as a doctor** hacerse pasar por médico.

◆**pass on 1** *vt* (*hand down*) pasar, transmitir; *message* dar, decir, comunicar; **we shall have to ~ the increase on to the consumer** tendremos que hacer que el consumidor cargue con el incremento.

2 *vi* (**a**) (*die*) fallecer. (**b**) (*continue*) pasar adelante; seguir su camino; **to ~ on to a new subject** pasar a un nuevo asunto.

◆**pass out 1** *vt leaflets etc* distribuir, repartir.

2 *vi* (**a**) (*emerge*) salir (*of* de).

(**b**) (*Mil*) graduarse; (*US Scol*) salir, terminar los estudios.

(**c**) (*: *faint*) caer redondo*, perder el conocimiento.

◆**pass over 1** *vt* (*neglect*) pasar por alto, omitir; **I think we can ~ that bit over** creo que podemos dejar ese trozo a un lado; **he was ~ed over again for promotion** en los ascensos volvieron a postergarle.

2 *vi* (*die*) fallecer.

◆**pass round** *vt bottle etc* pasar de uno a otro; pasar de mano en mano; *note* hacer circular.

◆**pass through 1** *vt hardships* pasar por, aguantar. **2** *vi* pasar; **I'm just ~ing through** estoy de paso nada más.

◆**pass up** *vt chance* no aprovechar; *claim* renunciar a.

passable ['pɑːsəbl] *adj* (**a**) (*tolerable*) pasable; tolerable, admisible. (**b**) (*usable, crossable*) transitable.

passably ['pɑːsəblɪ] *adv* medianamente, pasablemente.

passage ['pæsɪdʒ] *n* (**a**) (*act of passing*) paso *m*, tránsito *m*; (*voyage*) viaje *m*, travesía *f*; (*fare*) pasaje *m*; (*Parl: process*) trámites *mpl*, (*final*) aprobación *f*; **the ~ of time** el paso del tiempo; **in the ~ of time** andando el tiempo, con el tiempo.

(**b**) (*corridor*) pasillo *m*, galería *f*, pasadizo *m*; (*alley*) callejón *m*; (*Mech*) tubo *m*, conducto *m*; (*Anat*) tubo *m*.

(**c**) **~ of arms** combate *m*.

(**d**) (*Liter, Mus etc*) pasaje *m*; trozo *m*; episodio *m*, sección *f*; **'selected ~s from Caesar'** 'selecciones de César'.

passage money ['pæsɪdʒ,mʌnɪ] *n* pasaje *m*.

passageway ['pæsɪdʒweɪ] *n* pasillo *m*, galería *f*, pasadizo *m*.

passbook ['pɑːsbʊk] *n* libreta *f* de depósitos.

passé ['pæseɪ] *adj* pasado de moda.

passel ['pæsəl] *n* (*US*) muchedumbre *f*.

passenger ['pæsndʒəʳ] **1** *n* (**a**) pasajero *m*, -a *f*; viajero *m*, -a *f*; **the ~s** (*collectively*) el pasaje, los pasajeros; **will ~s please rejoin the train?** ¡señores viajeros, al tren! (**b**) (*pej*) **for many years he was a ~** durante muchos años fue una nulidad; **there's no room for ~s in this company** en esta empresa no toleramos a los gandules.

2 *attr* de pasajeros; **~ list** lista *f* de pasajeros; **~ seat** (*Aut*) asiento *m* de pasajero; **~ ship** buque *m* de pasajeros; **~ train** tren *m* de pasajeros.

passenger-miles ['pæsndʒə'maɪlz] *npl* millas-pasajero *fpl*.

passe-partout ['pæspɑːtuː] *n* paspartú *m*, passe partout *m*.

passer-by ['pɑːsə'baɪ] *n*, *pl* **passers-by** ['pɑːsəz'baɪ] transeúnte *mf*.

passim ['pæsɪm] *adv* passim.

passing ['pɑːsɪŋ] **1** *adj* (*fleeting*) pasajero; *glance etc* rápido, superficial; **a ~ car** un coche que pasaba; **~ fancy** capricho *m*; **~ grade** (*US*) aprobado *m*; **~ lane** (*US Aut*) carril *m* de adelantamiento; **~ place** (*Brit Aut*) apartadero *m*; **~ remark** comentario *m* hecho de paso; **~ shot** (*Sport*) tiro *m* pasado; **with each ~ day it gets more difficult** día tras día se hace más difícil.

2 *n* (**a**) paso *m*; (*Parl*) aprobación *f*; (*disappearance*) desaparición *f*; (*euph*: *death*) fallecimiento *m*; **in ~** de paso, de pasada. (**b**) (*US Aut*) adelantamiento *m*, paso *m*.

passing bell ['pɑːsɪŋbel] *n* toque *m* de difuntos.

passing-out [,pɑːsɪŋ'aʊt] *attr*: **~ parade** desfile *m* de promoción.

passion ['pæʃən] **1** *n* (**a**) pasión *f*; (*anger*) cólera *f*, arranque *m* de cólera; **crime of ~** crimen *m* pasional; **he said with ~** dijo con pasión; **political ~s are strong here** aquí son muy fuertes las pasiones políticas; **to be in a ~** estar encolerizado; **to burst** (*or* **fly**) **into a ~** montar en cólera, encolerizarse; **to conceive a ~ for sb** enamorarse con verdadera pasión de uno, apasionarse por uno; **I have a ~ for shellfish** adoro los mariscos, me apasionan los mariscos.

(**b**) **the P~** la Pasión.

2 *attr*: **P~ play** drama *m* de la Pasión; **P~ Sunday** domingo *m* de la Pasión.

passionate ['pæʃənɪt] *adj embrace, speech, temperament etc* apasionado; *believer, desire* vehemente, ardiente; (*angry*) colérico.

passionately ['pæʃənɪtlɪ] *adv* apasionadamente, con pasión; con vehemencia, ardientemente; coléricamente; **to love sb ~** amar a uno con pasión.

passionflower ['pæʃən,flaʊəʳ] *n* pasionaria *f*.

passionfruit ['pæʃənfruːt] *n* granadilla *f*, fruta *f* de la pasión.

passionless ['pæʃənlɪs] *adj affair etc* sin pasión, frío; desapasionado; (*dispassionate*) imparcial.

passive ['pæsɪv] **1** *adj* pasivo (*also Gram*); inactivo, inerte; **~ resistance** resistencia *f* pasiva; **~ smoking** fumar *m* pasivo. **2** *n* voz *f* pasiva.

passively ['pæsɪvlɪ] *adv* pasivamente.

passiveness ['pæsɪvnɪs] *n*, **passivity** [pæ'sɪvɪtɪ] *n* pasividad *f*; inercia *f*.

passkey ['pɑːskiː] *n* llave *f* maestra.

passmark ['pɑːsmɑːk] *n* aprobado *m*.

Passover ['pɑːsəʊvəʳ] *n* Pascua *f* (de los judíos).

passport ['pɑːspɔːt] *n* pasaporte *m*; **the ~ to fame** el pasaporte de la fama.

password ['pɑːswɜːd] *n* santo *m* y seña, contraseña *f*; (*Comput*) contraseña *f* de acceso.

past [pɑːst] **1** *adv* por delante; **to fly ~** pasar volando; **to march ~** desfilar; **to rush ~** pasar precipitadamente; **he**

went ~ without stopping pasó sin detenerse; **she walked slowly ~** pasó despacio.

2 *prep* (**a**) (*place*: *in front of*) por delante de; (*beyond*) más allá de; **just ~ the town hall** un poco más allá del Ayuntamiento; **to run ~ sb** pasar a uno corriendo; alcanzar y pasar a uno corriendo.

(**b**) (*with numbers*) más de; **we're ~ 100 already** ya vamos a más de 100; hemos contado más de 100 ya; **she's ~ 40** tiene más de 40 años.

(**c**) (*with time*) después de; **10 ~ 3** (*Brit*) las 3 y 10; **half ~ 4** (*Brit*) las 4 y media; **at a quarter ~ 9** (*Brit*) a las 9 y cuarto; **it's ~ 12** dieron las 12 ya, son las 12 dadas.

(**d**) (*other expressions*) **it is ~ belief** es increíble; **it is ~ endurance** es intolerable; **we're ~ caring** ya nos trae sin cuidado, ya no tenemos por qué preocuparnos de eso; **he's ~ it** ya no puede, ya no tiene fuerzas para eso; **I wouldn't put it ~ him** le creo capaz hasta de eso, no me extrañaría en él.

3 *adj* pasado (*also Gram*); (*former*) antiguo, ex ..., que fue; *master etc* consumado; **~ perfect** pluscuamperfecto *m*; **~ tense** tiempo *m* pasado; **for some time ~** de algún tiempo a esta parte; **in times ~** en otro tiempo, antiguamente; **all that is now ~** todo eso ha quedado ya a la espalda; **in ~ years** en otros años, en años pasados; **~ president of ...** antiguo presidente de ..., ex presidente de ..., presidente que fue de ...

4 *n* el pasado (*also Gram*), lo pasado; (*early history*) historia *f*, antecedentes *mpl*; **in the ~** en el pasado, antes, antiguamente; **as we did in the ~** como hacíamos antes; **it's a thing of the ~** pertenece a la historia; **silent pictures are things of the ~** las películas mudas han quedado anticuadas; **that belongs to my murky ~** eso pertenece a mi turbio pasado; **what's his ~?** ¿cuáles son sus antecedentes?; **a town with a ~** una ciudad de abolengo histórico, una ciudad llena de historia; **she's a woman with a ~** es una mujer que tiene historia.

pasta ['pæstə] *n* pastas *fpl* alimenticias.

paste [peɪst] **1** *n* (**a**) (*material in general*) pasta *f*; (*for sticking*) engrudo *m*; (*fish-~*) pasta *f*. (**b**) (*gems*) diamante *m* de imitación, bisutería *f*.

2 *vt* (**a**) (*apply ~ to*) engrudar; engomar; (*affix, stick together*) pegar; **to ~ sth to a wall** pegar algo a una pared. (**b**) (*) (*beat*) pegar; (*Sport*) cascar*, dar una paliza a.

◆**paste up** *vt*: **to ~ up a notice** pegar un anuncio.

pasteboard ['peɪstbɔːd] **1** *n* cartón *m*. **2** *attr* de cartón.

pastel ['pæstəl] **1** *n* (**a**) (*material*) pastel *m*; (*crayon*) lápiz *m* de color; (*drawing etc*) pintura *f* al pastel. (**b**) **~s** (*colours*) colores *mpl* pastel. **2** *attr*: **~ blue** azul *m* pastel; **~ drawing** pintura *f* al pastel; **~ shade** tono *m* pastel.

pastern ['pæstɜːn] *n* cuartilla *f* (del caballo).

pasteurization [ˌpæstəraɪ'zeɪʃən] *n* paste(u)rización *f*.

pasteurize ['pæstəraɪz] *vt* paste(u)rizar.

pasteurized ['pæstəraɪzd] *adj* paste(u)rizado.

pastiche [pæs'tiːʃ] *n* pastiche *m*, imitación *f*.

pastille ['pæstɪl] *n* pastilla *f*.

pastime ['pɑːstaɪm] *n* pasatiempo *m*.

pasting* ['peɪstɪŋ] *n* paliza *f*; **to give sb a ~** dar una paliza a uno; **he got a ~ from the critics** los críticos le dieron una paliza.

pastor ['pɑːstəʳ] *n* pastor *m*.

pastoral ['pɑːstərəl] **1** *adj care, economy* pastoral; (*Eccl*) pastoral; (*Liter*) pastoril; **~ letter = 2. 2** *n* (*Eccl*) pastoral *f*.

pastrami [pə'strɑːmɪ] *n especie de embutido ahumado a base de carne de vaca con especias.*

pastry ['peɪstrɪ] *n* (*dough*) pasta *f*; (*collectively*) pastas *fpl*, pasteles *mpl*; (*art*) pastelería *f*; **pastries** pastas *fpl*, pasteles *mpl*.

pastryboard ['peɪstrɪˌbɔːd] *n* tabla *f* de amasar.

pastrybrush ['peɪstrɪˌbrʌʃ] *n* cepillo *m* de repostería.

pastrycase ['peɪstrɪˌkeɪs] *n* cobertura *f* de pasta.

pastrycook ['peɪstrɪkʊk] *n* pastelero *m*, -a *f*, repostero *m*, -a *f*.

pastry shop ['peɪstrɪʃɒp] *n* pastelería *f*, repostería *f*.

pasturage ['pɑːstjʊrɪdʒ] *n* = **pasture 1**.

pasture ['pɑːstʃəʳ] **1** *n* (*grass*) pasto *m*; (*land*) pasto *m*, prado *m*, dehesa *f*; **to put** (*or* **send**) **animals out to ~** echar los animales al pasto; **they're putting me out to ~** me echan al pasto (como a caballo viejo); **he's gone to ~s new** (*euph, hum*) ha pasado a mejor vida. **2** *vt animals* apacentar, pastorear; *grass* comer, pacer. **3** *vi* pastar, pacer.

pastureland ['pɑːstʃəlænd] *n* pasto *m*, prado *m*, dehesa *f*.

pasty 1 ['peɪstɪ] *adj material* pastoso; *colour* pálido; **to look ~** estar pálido. **2** ['pæstɪ] *n* (*Brit*) pastel *m* (de carne), empanada *f*.

pasty-faced ['peɪstɪˌfeɪst] *adj* pálido, de cara pálida.

Pat [pæt] *nm and nf familiar form of* **Patrick, Patricia.**

pat¹ [pæt] **1** *n* (**a**) (*with hand*) palmadita *f*, golpecito *m*; (*on shoulder*) palmada *f*; (*caress*) caricia *f*; **to give sb a ~ on the back** dar a uno una palmada en la espalda, (*fig*) pronunciar unas palabras elogiosas para uno, felicitar a uno; **to give o.s. a ~ on the back** felicitarse a sí mismo.

(**b**) (*of butter*) pastelillo *m*.

2 *vt* (*touch*) tocar, pasar la mano por, posar la mano sobre; (*tap, with hand*) dar una palmadita en, *shoulder* dar una palmada en; *child's head, dog etc* acariciar; **he ~ted the chair with the book** tocó la silla con el libro; **to ~ sb on the back** dar a uno una palmada en la espalda, (*fig*) pronunciar unas palabras elogiosas para uno, felicitar a uno.

3 *vr*: **to ~ o.s. on the back** (*fig*) felicitarse a sí mismo.

pat² [pæt] **1** *adv*: **he knows it** (**off**) **~** lo sabe al dedillo; **he always has an excuse just ~** siempre tiene su excusa lista; **the answer came too ~** dio su respuesta con demasiada prontitud; **to stand ~** (*US*) mantenerse firme, mantenerse en sus trece.

2 *adj answer etc* oportuno, a propósito; pronto; convincente.

Patagonia [ˌpætə'gəʊnɪə] *n* Patagonia *f*.

Patagonian [ˌpætə'gəʊnɪən] **1** *adj* patagón, patagónico. **2** *n* patagón *m*, -ona *f*.

patch [pætʃ] **1** *n* (**a**) (*piece of cloth etc*) pedazo *m*; (*mend*) remiendo *m*; (*on tyre, wound*) parche *m*, guarache *m* (*Mex*); (*beauty-spot*) lunar *m* postizo; (*Comput*) ajuste *m*. (**b**) (*stain etc*) mancha *f*; (*small area*) pedazo *m*, pequeña extensión *f*; (*Agr*) terreno *m*, parcela *f*; **they must get off our ~*** tienen que largarse de lo nuestro*; **but this is their ~*** pero éste es territorio de ellos; **a ~ of oil** una mancha de aceite; **a ~ of blue flowers** una masa de flores azules, una extensión de flores azules; **a ~ of blue sky** un pedazo de cielo azul, un claro. (**c**) **the team is having a bad ~** el equipo pasa por un momento difícil, el equipo tiene una mala racha; **we have had our bad ~es** hemos tenido nuestros momentos malos; **then we hit a bad ~ of road** dimos luego con un tramo de carretera bastante malo; **it's not a ~ on the other one** no se puede comparar con el otro.

2 *vt* remendar, poner remiendo a.

◆**patch together** *vt materials* ir componiendo (de modo provisional); *coalition etc* formar (de modo poco satisfactorio).

◆**patch up** *vt*: **to ~ sth up** componer algo de modo provisional; **we'll see if we can ~ sth up for you** trataremos de arreglarlo para Vd; **after a time they ~ed things up** después de un rato se la arreglaron; **to ~ up a quarrel** hacer las paces (*with* con).

patchwork ['pætʃwɜːk] **1** *n* labor *f* de retazos; (*fig*) masa *f* confusa; mosaico *m*; **a ~ of fields** un mosaico de campos.

2 *attr*: **~ quilt** centón *m*, edredón *m* de trozos multicolores.

patchy ['pætʃɪ] *adj* desigual, poco uniforme; *pattern etc* manchado.

pate [peɪt] *n* mollera *f*; testa *f*; **bald ~** calva *f*.

pâté ['pæteɪ] *n* paté *m*; pastel *m* (de carne *etc*).

patella [pə'telə] *n* rótula *f*.

paten ['pætən] *n* patena *f*.

patent ['peɪtənt] **1** *adj* (**a**) (*obvious*) patente, evidente, palmario. (**b**) (*Comm*) de patente, patentado.

2 *n* (**a**) (*also* **~ leather**) charol *m*. (**b**) (*Comm*) patente *f*; **~ applied for, ~ pending** patente en trámite; **to take out a ~** obtener una patente.

3 *attr* de patentes; **~ agent** agente *m* de patentes; **~ law** derecho *m* de patentes; **~ leather = 2** (**a**); **~ medicine** específico *m*; **~ office** oficina *f* de patentes; **P~ Office** (*Brit*), **P~ and Trademark Office** (*US*) *registro de la propiedad industrial*; **~ rights** derechos *mpl* de patente.

4 *vt* patentar.

patentable ['peɪtəntəbl] *adj* patentable.

patentee [ˌpeɪtən'tiː] *n* poseedor *m*, -ora *f* de patente, concesionario *m*, -a *f* de la patente.

patently ['peɪtəntlɪ] *adv* evidentemente, a las claras; **a ~ untrue statement** una declaración de evidente falsedad.

patentor ['peɪtəntəʳ] *n* dueño *m*, -a *f* de patente.

pater* ['peɪtəʳ] *n*: **the ~** (*esp Brit*) el viejo*.

paterfamilias ['peɪtəfə'mɪlɪæs] *n* padre *m* de familia.

paternal [pə'tɜːnl] *adj quality* paternal; *relation* paterno.

paternalism [pə'tɜːnəlɪzəm] *n* gobierno *m* paternal.

paternalist [pə'tɜːnəlɪst] *n* paternalista *m*.

paternalistic [pə,tɜːnə'lɪstɪk] *adj* paternalista.

paternally [pə'tɜːnəlɪ] *adv* paternalmente; **he said ~** dijo paternal.

paternity [pə'tɜːnɪtɪ] **1** *n* paternidad *f.* **2** *attr*: **~ leave** licencia *f* de paternidad; **~ suit** litigio *m* de paternidad.

paternoster ['pætə'nɒstəʳ] *n* padrenuestro *m.*

path [pɑːθ] *n, pl* **paths** [pɑːðz] camino *m,* senda *f,* sendero *m,* vereda *f;* (*fig*) camino *m;* trayectoria *f,* curso *m;* (*person's track*) pista *f;* (*of bullet*) trayectoria *f;* (*of hurricane etc*) rastro *m,* marcha *f;* (*Comput*) camino *m;* **the ~ to power** el camino del poder; **to beat a ~ to sb's door** asediar a uno; **to cross sb's ~** tropezar con uno; crear dificultades a uno; **to keep to the straight and narrow ~** ir por la vereda, no apartarse del buen camino; **to smooth sb's ~ for him** allanarle el camino a uno; **to tread the ~ of moderation** ir por el camino de la moderación.

pathetic [pə'θetɪk] *adj* (**a**) patético, lastimoso, conmovedor; **a ~ sight** una escena lastimosa; **a ~ creature** un infeliz, un pobre hombre; **it was ~ to see it** daba pena verlo.

(**b**) (*very bad*) horrible, malísimo; **~, isn't it?** ¿es horrible, no?; **it was a ~ performance** fue una exhibición que daba pena.

(**c**) **~ fallacy** (*Liter*) engaño *m* sentimental.

pathetically [pə'θetɪklɪ] *adv* patéticamente, lastimosamente; **a ~ inadequate answer** una respuesta tan poco satisfactoria que da pena.

pathfinder ['pɑːθ,faɪndəʳ] *n* explorador *m,* piloto *m;* pionero *m.*

pathogen ['pæθəʊdʒen] *n* patógeno *m.*

pathological [,pæθə'lɒdʒɪkəl] *adj* patológico.

pathologist [pə'θɒlədʒɪst] *n* patólogo *m,* -a *f.*

pathology [pə'θɒlədʒɪ] *n* patología *f.*

pathos ['peɪθɒs] *n* patetismo *m,* lo patético.

pathway ['pɑːθweɪ] *n* = **path.**

patience ['peɪʃəns] *n* (**a**) paciencia *f;* **my ~ is exhausted** se me ha acabado la paciencia, no tengo más paciencia; **you must have ~** hay que tener paciencia; **I have no ~ with you** ya no aguanto más, estoy para desesperarme; **to lose one's ~** perder la paciencia; **to possess one's soul in ~** armarse de paciencia; **she taxes** (*or* **tries**) **my ~ very much** me cuesta no impacientarme con ella.

(**b**) (*Brit Cards*) solitario *m.*

patient ['peɪʃənt] **1** *adj* paciente; sufrido; **to be ~ with sb** ser paciente con uno; **you must be very ~ about it** hay que tener mucha paciencia; **we have been ~ long enough!** ¡ya no aguantamos más!, ¡se nos agota la paciencia!

2 *n* paciente *mf,* enfermo *m,* -a *f.*

patiently ['peɪʃəntlɪ] *adv* pacientemente, con paciencia.

patina ['pætɪnə] *n* pátina *f.*

patio ['pætɪəʊ] **1** *n* patio *m.* **2** *attr*: **~ doors** puertas *fpl* que dan al patio.

patois ['pætwɑː] *n* dialecto *m,* jerga *f.*

pat. pend. *abbr of* **patent pending.**

patriarch ['peɪtrɪɑːk] *n* patriarca *m.*

patriarchal [,peɪtrɪ'ɑːkəl] *adj* patriarcal.

patriarchy ['peɪtrɪ,ɑːkɪ] *n* patriarcado *m.*

Patricia [pə'trɪʃə] *nf* Patricia.

patrician [pə'trɪʃən] **1** *adj* patricio. **2** *n* patricio *m,* -a *f.*

patricide ['pætrɪsaɪd] *n* (*crime*) patricidio *m;* (*person*) patricida *mf.*

Patrick ['pætrɪk] *nm* Patricio.

patrimony ['pætrɪmənɪ] *n* patrimonio *m.*

patriot ['peɪtrɪət] *n* patriota *mf.*

patriotic [,pætrɪ'ɒtɪk] *adj* patriótico.

patriotically [,pætrɪ'ɒtɪkəlɪ] *adv* patrióticamente.

patriotism ['pætrɪətɪzəm] *n* patriotismo *m.*

patrol [pə'trəʊl] **1** *n* patrulla *f;* **to be on ~** estar de patrulla, patrullar.

2 *vt* (**a**) patrullar por; *frontier etc* guardar, defender; **they ~led the streets at night** patrullaban por las calles de noche; **the frontier is not ~led** la frontera no tiene patrullas.

(**b**) (*fig*) rondar, pasearse por.

3 *vi* (**a**) patrullar.

(**b**) (*fig*) rondar, pasearse; **he ~s up and down** se pasea de un lado a otro.

patrol-boat [pə'trəʊlbəʊt] *n* patrullero *m,* (lancha *f*) patrullera *f.*

patrol-car [pə'trəʊlkɑːʳ] *n* coche *m* patrulla.

patrol leader [pə'trəʊl'liːdəʳ] *n* jefe *m* de patrulla.

patrolman [pə'trəʊlmən] *n, pl* **patrolmen** [pə'trəʊlmən] (*Brit Aut*) mecánico *m* del servicio de ayuda en carretera; (*US*) guardia *m,* policía *m.*

patrol wagon [pə'trəʊl,wægən] *n* (*US*) coche *m* celular.

patron ['peɪtrən] *n* (*Comm*) cliente *mf;* (*of enterprise*) patrocinador *m;* (*Liter, Art*) mecenas *m;* (*Eccl, also* **~ saint**) patrón *m,* patrono *m,* patrona *f.*

patronage ['pætrənɪdʒ] *n* (*of enterprise*) patrocinio *m;* (*Liter, Art*) mecenazgo *m,* protección *f;* (*Eccl*) patronato *m;* **under the ~ of** bajo el patronato de, patrocinado por, bajo los auspicios de.

patronize ['pætrənaɪz] *vt* (**a**) *shop* ser cliente de, comprar en; *services etc* usar, utilizar; *enterprise* patrocinar, favorecer, fomentar, apoyar; **the shop is well ~d** la tienda tiene mucha clientela, la tienda está muy acreditada.

(**b**) (*treat condescendingly*) tratar con condescendencia.

patronizing ['pætrənaɪzɪŋ] *adj* paternalista, desdeñoso, altivo; superior, lleno de superioridad; **a few ~ remarks** algunas observaciones dichas con aire protector; **he's a ~ person** es una persona llena de superioridad.

patronizingly ['pætrənaɪzɪŋlɪ] *adv* protectoramente, con aire paternalista, con aire de superioridad; desdeñosamente, altivamente.

patronymic [,pætrə'nɪmɪk] **1** *adj* patronímico. **2** *n* patronímico *m.*

patsy* ['pætsɪ] *n* (*US*) bobo *m,* -a *f,* primo* *m.*

patten ['pætn] *n* zueco *m,* chanclo *m.*

patter[1] ['pætəʳ] **1** *n* (*jargon*) jerga *f;* labia *f;* (*of salesman*) jerga *f* publicitaria; (*rapid speech*) parloteo *m;* **~ song** aria *f* (*or* canción *f*) de letra rapidísima; **the fellow has some very clever ~** el tío tiene unos argumentos muy hábiles, hablando el tío es muy listo.

2 *vi* (*also* **to ~ on**) charlar, parlotear (*about* de).

patter[2] ['pætəʳ] **1** *n* (*of feet*) pasos *mpl* ligeros, pataditas *fpl,* ruido *m* sordo; (*taps*) golpecitos *mpl;* golpeteo *m;* (*of rain*) tamborileo *m;* **we shall soon hear the ~ of tiny feet** pronto habrá un niño en la casa, pronto sentiremos pataditas.

2 *vi* (*also* **to ~ about**) andar con pasos ligeros, pisar con ruido sordo; (*rain*) tamborilear; **he ~ed over to the door** fue con pasos ligeros a la puerta.

pattern ['pætən] **1** *n* modelo *m;* (*sample*) muestra *f;* (*design*) diseño *m,* dibujo *m;* (*Sew*) patrón *m,* modelo *m,* molde *m* (*SC*); (*fig*) pauta *f,* norma *f;* **~ of distribution** patrón *m* de distribución; **~ of expenditure** composición *f* de los gastos; **~ of trade** estructura *f* del comercio; **~ recognition** reconocimiento *m* de modelos; **on the ~ of** sobre el modelo de, según el diseño de; **it set a ~ for other conferences** estableció una pauta para otros congresos; **it is following the usual ~** se está desarrollando como siempre, sigue la norma.

2 *vt* modelar (*on* sobre), diseñar (*on* según).

pattern-book ['pætənbʊk] *n* libro *m* de muestras.

patterned ['pætənd] *adj material, fabric, china* estampado.

patterning ['pætənɪŋ] *n* diseño *m,* dibujo *m.*

pattern-maker ['pætən'meɪkəʳ] *n* carpintero *m* modelista.

patty ['pætɪ] *n* empanada *f.*

paucity ['pɔːsɪtɪ] *n* escasez *f,* insuficiencia *f,* corto número *m.*

Paul [pɔːl] *nm* Pablo; (*Saint*) Pablo; (*Pope*) Paulo (*V also* **John**).

Pauline[1] ['pɔːlaɪn] *adj*: **the ~ Epistles** las Epístolas de San Pablo.

Pauline[2] ['pɔːliːn] *nf* Paulina.

paunch [pɔːntʃ] **1** *n* panza *f,* barriga *f.* **2** *vt rabbit etc* destripar.

paunchy ['pɔːntʃɪ] *adj* panzudo, barrigudo.

pauper ['pɔːpəʳ] *n* pobre *mf,* indigente *mf.*

pauperism ['pɔːpərɪzəm] *n* pauperismo *m.*

pauperization [,pɔːpəraɪ'zeɪʃən] *n* empobrecimiento *m.*

pauperize ['pɔːpəraɪz] *vt* empobrecer, reducir a la miseria.

pause [pɔːz] **1** *n* pausa *f* (*also Mus*); intervalo *m;* interrupción *f;* silencio *m;* **there was a ~ while ...** hubo un silencio mientras ...; **we carried on without ~** continuamos sin interrupción, seguíamos trabajando (*etc*) sin descansar; **to give sb ~** dar que pensar a uno, hacer vacilar a uno.

2 *vi* hacer una pausa; (*speaker etc*) detenerse (brevemente), callarse (momentáneamente), interrumpirse; **~ before you act** reflexione antes de obrar; **he ~d for breath** se calló para cobrar aliento; **he spoke for 30 minutes without once pausing** habló durante 30 minutos sin interrumpirse una sola vez; **let's ~ here** detengámonos aquí un rato; **it made him ~** le hizo vacilar.

pave [peɪv] *vt* pavimentar; (*with flags*) enlosar, solar; (*with stones*) empedrar; adoquinar; (*with bricks*) enladrillar; **to ~ the way** preparar el terreno (*for* a); **the streets are ~d with gold** las calles tienen pavimento de oro.

paved [peɪvd] *adj* pavimentado; enlosado; empedrado; enladrillado; *road* asfaltado, afirmado.

pavement ['peɪvmənt] **1** *n* (*Brit*) pavimento *m*; (*sidewalk*) acera *f*, vereda *f* (*LAm*), andén *m* (*CAm*), banqueta *f* (*CAm, Mex*); (*US*) calzada *f*, camino *m* asfaltado; **brick ~** enladrillado *m*; **stone ~** empedrado *m*; **to leave the ~** (*US Aut*) salir de la calzada.

2 *attr*: **~ artist** pintor *m* callejero; **~ café** café *m* con terraza, café *m* al aire libre.

pavilion [pə'vɪlɪən] *n* pabellón *m*; (*for band etc*) quiosco *m*; (*Sport*) caseta *f*, vestuario *m*; (*at trade-fair etc*) pabellón *m*.

paving ['peɪvɪŋ] *n* pavimento *m*, pavimentación *f*, enlosado *m*, adoquinado *m*, enladrillado *m*.

paving-stone ['peɪvɪŋstəʊn] *n* adoquín *m*; (*flagstone*) losa *f*.

Pavlovian [pæv'ləʊvɪən] *adj* pavloviano.

paw [pɔː] **1** *n* (**a**) (*of animal*) pata *f*; (*of cat*) garra *f*; (*of lion*) zarpa *f*.

(**b**) (*: *hand*) manaza *f*, manota *f*.

2 *vt* (**a**) (*animal*) tocar con la pata; (*lion*) dar zarpazos a; **to ~ the ground** (*horse*) piafar.

(**b**) (*) (*person*: *pej*) tocar, manosear, (*amorously*) sobar, palpar; **stop ~ing me!** ¡fuera las manos!, ¡manos quietas!

3 *vi*: **to ~ at sth** tocar algo con la pata, (*to wound*) dar zarpazos a algo.

pawl [pɔːl] *n* trinquete *m*.

pawn¹ [pɔːn] *n* (*Chess*) peón *m*; (*fig*) instrumento *m*; **they simply used me as a ~** se aprovecharon de mí como mero instrumento.

pawn² [pɔːn] **1** *n*: **in ~** en prenda; **to leave** (*or* **put**) **sth in ~** dejar algo en prenda; **the country is in ~ to foreigners** el país está empeñado a extranjeros.

2 *vt* empeñar, pignorar, dejar en prenda.

pawnbroker ['pɔːn,brəʊkəʳ] *n* prestamista *m*, prendero *m*, agenciero *m* (*SC*); **~'s (shop)** casa *f* de empeños, prendería *f*, monte *m* de piedad.

pawnshop ['pɔːnʃɒp] *n* casa *f* de empeños, prendería *f*, monte *m* de piedad, agencia *f* (*SC*).

pawn-ticket ['pɔːn,tɪkɪt] *n* papeleta *f* de empeño.

pawpaw ['pɔːpɔː] *n* papaya *f*.

pax [pæks] *n* (**a**) **~!** (*Brit*) ¡me rindo! (**b**) (*Eccl*) beso *m* de la paz.

pay [peɪ] **1** *n* paga *f*; remuneración *f*, retribución *f*; (*of professional person*) sueldo *m*; (*of worker*) salario *m*, sueldo *m*; (*of day labourer*) jornal *m*; **equal ~** igualdad *f* de retribución (para hombres y mujeres); **to be in sb's ~** ser asalariado de uno, estar al servicio de uno; **agents in the enemy's ~** agentes *mpl* al servicio del enemigo; **to draw** (*or* **get**) **one's ~** cobrar.

2 *attr*: **~ as you earn** (*Brit*), **~-as-you-go** (*US*) retención *f* fiscal en la fuente; **~ award** adjudicación *f* de aumento de salarios; **~ increase, ~ rise** incremento *m* salarial, subida *f* de salario; **~ negotiations** negociaciones *fpl* salariales; **~ policy** política *f* salarial; **~ round** serie *f* de negociaciones salariales; **~ structure** estructura *f* salarial; **~ talks = ~ negotiations**; **~ TV** TV *f* de pago.

3 (*irr*: *pret and ptp* **paid**) *vt* (**a**) pagar (*for* por); **to ~ sb £10** pagar 10 libras a uno; **what did you ~ for it?** ¿cuánto pagaste por él?; **it's a service that has to be paid for** es un servicio que hay que pagar; **to ~ money into an account** ingresar dinero en una cuenta; **how much is there to ~?** ¿cuánto hay que pagar?; **to be** (*or* **get**) **paid on Fridays** cobrar los viernes; **when do you get paid?** ¿cuándo cobras?; **to ~ cash (down)** pagar al contado; **shares that ~ 5%** acciones *fpl* que producen un 5 por 100; **the company paid 12% last year** el año pasado la sociedad pagó 12 por 100; **to ~ sb to do a job** pagar a uno para que haga un trabajo; **a badly paid worker** un obrero mal retribuido; **a badly paid job** un empleo mal remunerado; *V also* **paid**.

(**b**) *account, debt* liquidar; satisfacer; *bill, duty, fee* pagar; **'paid'** (*on receipted bill*) 'pagado'.

(**c**) (*be profitable to*) ser provechoso a; **it wouldn't ~ him to do it** no le saldría a cuenta hacerlo, (*fig*) no le sería aconsejable hacerlo, no le valdría la pena hacerlo; **it doesn't ~ you to be kind nowadays** hoy día no vale la pena mostrarse amable; **but it paid him in the long run** pero a la larga le fue provechoso.

(**d**) *attention* prestar (*to* a); *homage* rendir (*to* a); *respects* ofrecer, presentar; *visit* hacer; *V also* **address** *etc*.

4 *vi* (**a**) pagar; **who ~s?** ¿quién paga?; **to ~ on account** pagar a cuenta; **to ~ in advance** pagar por adelantado; **to ~ in full** pagarlo todo, pagar la cantidad íntegra; **to ~ in instalments** pagar a plazos; **'please ~ at the door'** 'por favor: paguen a la entrada'; **to ~ for sth** pagar algo; costear algo, correr con los gastos de algo; **they made him ~ dearly for it** le hicieron pagarlo muy caro; **she paid for it with her life** lo pagó con la vida; **he paid for his rashness with his life** su temeridad le costó la vida; **they paid for her to go** pagaron para que fuera; **I'll make you ~ for this!** ¡me las pagarás!

(**b**) (*be profitable*) rendir, rendir bien, ser provechoso; **it's a business that ~s** es un negocio que rinde, es un negocio rentable; **it's ~ing at last** por fin produce ganancias; **his job ~s well** tiene un buen sueldo, el trabajo le paga bien; **it ~s to be courteous** vale la pena mostrarse cortés; **it doesn't ~ to paint it** vale más no pintarlo, es mejor no pintarlo; **it ~s to advertise** compensa hacer publicidad.

◆**pay away** *vt* pagar, desembolsar.

◆**pay back** *vt* (**a**) *money* devolver; restituir, reintegrar.

(**b**) *person* pagar. (**c**) **to ~ sb back (in his own coin)** (*fig*) pagar a uno en la misma moneda.

◆**pay down** *vt* (*cash*) pagar al contado; (*deposit*) pagar como desembolso inicial.

◆**pay in 1** *vt cheque, money* ingresar.

2 *vi* (**a**) (*at bank*) ingresar dinero.

(**b**) (*to scheme etc*) pagar contribuciones; **he was ~ing in for 20 years** llevaba 20 años pagando contribuciones.

◆**pay off 1** *vt* (**a**) *debt* pagar, liquidar, saldar; *mortgage etc* amortizar, redimir; *old score* ajustar.

(**b**) *workers, crew* pagar y despedir.

2 *vi* (*fig*) valer la pena, merecer la pena; tener éxito; reportar beneficios, dar buenos resultados; **the rule paid off** la estratagema salió bien; **it has paid off many times over** ha demostrado su valor muchísimas veces; **when do you think it will begin to ~ off?** ¿cuándo piensas que empezará a dar resultado?

◆**pay out 1** *vt* (**a**) *money* pagar, desembolsar.

(**b**) (*fig*) *person* pagar en la misma moneda; desquitarse con; **I'll ~ you out for this!** ¡me las pagarás!

(**c**) *rope* ir dando.

2 *vi*: **to ~ out on a policy** pagar una póliza.

◆**pay over** *vt* pagar, entregar.

◆**pay up 1** *vt* pagar (de mala gana).

2 *vi* pagar; pagar lo que se debe; **~ up!** ¡a pagar!

payable ['peɪəbl] *adj* pagadero; **~ to bearer** pagadero al portador; **~ on demand** pagadero a presentación; **~ at sight** pagadero a vista; **to make a cheque ~ to sb** extender un cheque a favor de uno.

payback ['peɪbæk] *n* restitución *f*; **~ period** período *m* de restitución.

paybed ['peɪbed] *n* cama *f* de pago.

paycheck ['peɪtʃek] *n* (*US*) sueldo *m*, pago *m*.

payday ['peɪdeɪ] *n* día *m* de paga.

paydesk ['peɪdesk] *n* caja *f*.

paydirt ['peɪdɜːt] *n* (*US*) grava *f* provechosa (*also fig*).

PAYE *n* (*Brit*) *abbr of* **pay as you earn**; *V* **pay 2**.

payee [peɪ'iː] *n* portador *m*, -ora *f*, tenedor *m*, -ora *f*; (*on cheque*) orden *f*, beneficiario *m*, -a *f*; **account ~ only** (*on cheque*) cuenta *f* nominal.

pay envelope ['peɪ,envələʊp] *n* (*US*) sobre *m* de paga.

payer ['peɪəʳ] *n* pagador *m*, -ora *f*; **slow ~, bad ~** moroso *m*, -a *f*.

paying ['peɪɪŋ] *adj* provechoso, que rinde bien; rentable; **~ bank** banco *m* pagador; **~ guest** huésped *m*, -a *f* de pago, pensionista *mf*; **it's a ~ proposition** es un negocio provechoso.

paying-in slip [,peɪɪŋ'ɪn,slɪp] *n*, **pay-in slip** [,peɪ'ɪn,slɪp] *n* hoja *f* de ingreso.

payload ['peɪləʊd] *n* carga *f* útil.

paymaster ['peɪmɑːstəʳ] *n* (*Mil etc*) (oficial *m*) pagador *m*; **the spy's Ruritanian ~s** los oficiales ruritanios que pagaban al espía.

payment ['peɪmənt] *n* pago *m*; remuneración *f*, retribución *f*; **~ on account** pago *m* a cuenta; **~ in cash** pago *m* al contado; **~ after delivery** pago *m* a la entrega; **~ by instalments** pago *m* a plazos; **~ on invoice** pago *m* a la presentación de factura; **~ by results** pago *m* por resultados; **~ terms** condiciones *fpl* de pago; **as ~ for, in ~ for** en pago de; **as ~ for your services** en concepto de sus servicios; **on ~ of £5** pagando 5 libras, mediante el pago de 5 libras; **without ~** sin remuneración; **to make a ~** efectuar un pago; **to present sth for ~** presentar algo al cobro; **to stop ~s** (*bank*) suspender los pagos; **to stop ~ of a cheque** detener el cobro de un cheque.

payoff ['peɪɒf] *n* (**a**) (*payment*) pago *m*; (*of debt*) liquidación *f* (total). (**b**) (*reward*) recompensa *f*; retribución *f*; (*venge-*

ance) ajuste *m* de cuentas, castigo *m*; (*bribe*) soborno *m*; (*spin-off*) beneficios *mpl.* (**c**) (*outcome*) resultado *m*, consecuencia *f*; (*climax*) momento *m* de la verdad.
pay office ['peɪ,ɒfɪs] *n* caja *f*, pagaduría *f*.
payola* [peɪ'əʊlə] *n* (*US*) soborno *m*.
pay-out ['peɪaʊt] *n* pago *m*; (*share-out*) reparto *m*.
pay packet ['peɪ,pækɪt] *n* (*Brit*) sobre *m* de paga.
pay pause ['peɪpɔːz] *n* congelación *f* de sueldos y salarios.
payphone ['peɪfəʊn] *n* teléfono *m* público.
payroll ['peɪrəʊl] **1** *n* nómina *f* (de sueldos); **to be on a firm's ~** estar en la nómina *f* de una empresa; **he has 1000 people on his ~** tiene una nómina de 1000 personas. **2** *attr*: **~ tax** impuesto *m* sobre la nómina.
paysheet ['peɪʃiːt] *n* nómina *f*.
payslip ['peɪslɪp] *n* hoja *f* de sueldo.
pay station ['peɪ,steɪʃən] *n* (*US*) teléfono *m* público.
pay-television ['peɪ'telɪ,vɪʒən] *n* televisión *f* de pago.
PB *n abbr of* **personal best**.
PBAB *abbr of* **please bring a bottle**.
PBS *n* (*US*) *abbr of* **Public Broadcasting Service**.
PBX *n* (*Telec*) *abbr of* **private branch exchange** *centralita para extensiones*.
PC *n* (**a**) (*Brit*) *abbr of* **police constable** policía *m*. (**b**) *abbr of* **personal computer** ordenador *m* (*or* computadora *f*) personal, CP, PC. (**c**) (*Brit*) *abbr of* **Privy Councillor**.
p.c. (**a**) *abbr of* **postcard** tarjeta *f* postal. (**b**) *abbr of* **per cent** por cien, por ciento, p.c.
P/C (**a**) (*St Ex*) *abbr of* **prices current** cotizaciones *fpl.* (**b**) (*Comm*) *abbr of* **petty cash**.
PCB *n* (**a**) *abbr of* **printed circuit board** tarjeta *f* de circuito(s) impreso(s), TCI *f*. (**b**) *abbr of* **polychlorinated biphenyl** bifenilo *m* policlorinado.
PCFC *n abbr of* **Polytechnics and Colleges Funding Council**.
pcm *adv abbr of* **per calendar month** por mes, p/mes.
PD *n* (*US*) *abbr of* **police department**.
pd *abbr of* **paid** pagado, pgdo.
PDSA *n abbr of* **People's Dispensary for Sick Animals**.
PDT *n* (*US*) *abbr of* **Pacific Daylight Time**.
PE *n abbr of* **physical education** cultura *f* física, educación *f* física, ed. física.
pea [piː] **1** *n* guisante *m*, arveja *f* (*LAm*), chícharo *m* (*LAm*). **2** *attr*: **~ soup** sopa *f* de guisantes.
peace [piːs] *n* paz *f*; (*peacefulness*) paz *f*, tranquilidad *f*, sosiego *m*; **~ of mind** tranquilidad *f* de ánimo; **the (King's) ~** el orden público; **to be at ~** estar en paz; **to break** (*or* **disturb**) **the ~** perturbar la paz, alterar el orden público; **to hold one's ~** guardar silencio, callarse; **to keep the ~** mantener el orden; mantener la paz; **he was bound over to keep the ~** se le ordenó respetar el orden público; **to make ~** hacer las paces (*with* con).
2 *attr*: **~ campaign** campaña *f* pacifista; **~ campaigner** *persona que participa en una campaña pacifista*; **P~ Corps** (*US*) Cuerpo *m* de la Paz; **~ initiative** iniciativa *f* de paz; **P~ Movement** Movimiento *m* Pacifista; **~ sign** señal *f* de paz; **~ talks** negociaciones *fpl* de paz; **~ treaty** tratado *m* de paz.
peaceable ['piːsəbl] *adj* pacífico.
peaceful ['piːsfʊl] *adj* (*not warlike*) pacífico; (*quiet*) tranquilo, sosegado; *coexistence* pacífico; **it's very ~ here** aquí todo está perfectamente tranquilo; **on a ~ June evening** una tranquila tarde de junio.
peacefully ['piːsfəlɪ] *adv* pacíficamente, en paz; tranquilamente; **to die ~** morirse tranquilamente.
peacefulness ['piːsfʊlnɪs] *n* tranquilidad *f*, sosiego *m*, calma *f*; (*of nation*) carácter *m* pacífico.
peacekeeper ['piːs,kiːpəʳ] *n* (*Mil*) pacificador *m*.
peace-keeping ['piːs,kiːpɪŋ] **1** *adj*: **~ force** fuerzas *fpl* de pacificación; **~ operation** operación *f* pacificadora. **2** *n* pacificación *f*; mantenimiento *m* de la paz.
peace-loving ['piːs,lʌvɪŋ] *adj nation* amante de la paz.
peacemaker ['piːs,meɪkəʳ] *n* pacificador *m*, -ora *f*; (*between 2 sides*) árbitro *m*, conciliador *m*, -ora *f*.
peace-offering ['piːs,ɒfərɪŋ] *n* prenda *f* de paz, ramo *m* de olivo; (*to gods*) sacrificio *m* propiciatorio.
peacetime ['piːstaɪm] *n*: **in ~** en tiempo de paz.
peach¹ [piːtʃ] **1** *n* (**a**) (*fruit*) melocotón *m*, durazno *m* (*LAm*); (*tree*) melocotonero *m*, durazno *m* (*LAm*).
(**b**) (*****) **she's a ~** es un bombón*, es una monada*; **it's a ~** es una monada*; **a ~ of a girl** una real moza; **a ~ of a dress** un vestido monísimo.
(**c**) (*colour*) color *m* de melocotón.
2 *adj* color melocotón.
peach²** [piːtʃ] *vi* soplar (*on* contra)*.
peach-tree ['piːtʃtriː] *n* melocotonero *m*, durazno (*LAm*).
peacock ['piːkɒk] *n* pavo *m* real, pavón *m*; **~ blue** azul *m* pavo.
pea-green ['piː'griːn] *adj* verde claro.
peahen ['piːhen] *n* pava *f* real.
peak [piːk] **1** *n* (*point*) punta *f*; (*of mountain*) cumbre *f*, cima *f*; (*mountain*) pico *m*; (*of cap*) visera *f*; (*fig*) cumbre *f*; apogeo *m*, punto *m* más alto; **when the empire was at its ~** cuando el imperio estaba en su apogeo; **when demand is at its ~** cuando la demanda alcanza su punto más alto; **he was at the ~ of his fame** estaba en la cumbre de su fama.
2 *adj*: **~ hours** horas *fpl* punta; **~ load** carga *f* máxima; **~ period** período *m* de máxima actividad; **~ production** producción *f* máxima; **~ season** temporada *f* más popular del año, temporada *f* alta; **~(-hour) traffic** movimiento *m* máximo (de tráfico), tráfico *m* de horas punta; **~ viewing time** banda *f* horaria caliente.
3 *vi* alcanzar su punto más alto, llegar al máximo.
peaked¹ [piːkt] *adj*: **~ cap** gorra *f* de visera.
peaked² [piːkt] *adj*, **peaky** ['piːkɪ] *adj* pálido, enfermizo; **to look ~** tener la cara pálida.
peal [piːl] **1** *n* (*sound of bells*) repique *m*, campanillazo *m*, toque *m* de campanas; **~ of bells** (*set*) juego *m* de campanas; **~ of laughter** carcajada *f*; **~ of the organ** sonido *m* del órgano; **~ of thunder** trueno *m*.
2 *vt* repicar, tocar a vuelo.
3 *vi* (*bell*) repicar, tocar a vuelo; (*organ*) sonar.
peanut ['piːnʌt] **1** *n* cacahuete *m*, maní *m* (*LAm*); **it's mere ~s to him*** para él es una bagatela; **we're not playing for ~s*** esto no es ninguna bagatela, esto va en serio. **2** *attr*: **~ butter** manteca *f* de cacahuete; **~ oil** aceite *m* de cacahuete.
peapod ['piːpɒd] *n* vaina *f* de guisante.
pear [pɛəʳ] *n* (*fruit*) pera *f*; (*tree*) peral *m*.
pearl [pɜːl] **1** *n* perla *f* (*also fig*); (*mother-of-pearl*) nácar *m*; **to cast ~s before swine** echar margaritas a los puercos.
2 *attr necklace etc* de perla, de perlas; (*in colour*) color de perla; **~ barley** cebada *f* perlada; **~ diver** pescador *m* de perlas; **~ fishery** pescadería *f* de perlas; **~ necklace** collar *m* de perlas; **~ oyster** madre perla *f*.
pearl-grey ['pɜːl'greɪ] *adj* gris perla.
pearly ['pɜːlɪ] *adj* (*made of pearl*) de perla, de perlas; (*in colour*) color de perla, perlino; *mother of pearl* nacarado; **the P~ Gates** (*hum*) las puertas del Paraíso.
pear-shaped ['pɛəʃeɪpt] *adj* de forma de pera.
pear-tree ['pɛətriː] *n* peral *m*.
peasant ['pezənt] **1** *n* campesino *m*, -a *f*; labrador *m*, -ora *f*; (*pej*) palurdo *m*, -a *f*. **2** *attr* campesino; rústico; **~ farmer** campesino *m*.
peasantry ['pezəntrɪ] *n* campesinos *mpl*, campesinado *m*.
peashooter ['piː,ʃuːtəʳ] *n* cerbatana *f*.
pea-souper* ['piː'suːpəʳ] *n* puré *m* de guisantes*, niebla *f* muy densa.
peat [piːt] *n* turba *f*.
peatbog ['piːtbɒg] *n* turbera *f*, turbal *m*.
peaty ['piːtɪ] *adj* turboso.
pebble ['pebl] *n* guija *f*, guijarro *m*, china *f*; **he's not the only ~ on the beach** no es el único en el mundo.
pebbledash [,pebl'dæʃ] **1** *n* enguijarrado *m*. **2** *vt* enguijarrar.
pebbly ['peblɪ] *adj* guijarroso.
pecan ['piːkæn] *n* pacana *f*.
peccadillo [,pekə'dɪləʊ] *n* falta *f* leve, pecadillo *m*.
peck¹ [pek] *n medida de áridos*: = 9,087 *litros*; (*fig*) montón *m*; **a ~ of troubles** la mar de disgustos.
peck² [pek] **1** *n* picotazo *m*; (*kiss*) besito *m*, beso *m* rápido.
2 *vt* picotear; (*kiss*) dar un besito a, dar un beso rápido a.
3 *vi* picotear; **to ~ at** (*bird*) intentar picotear, (*in eating*) comer melindrosamente.
pecker ['pekəʳ] *n* (**a**) (*Brit**) **to keep one's ~ up** no dejarse desanimar; **keep your ~ up!** ¡ánimo! (**b**) (*US***) polla** *f*.
pecking-order ['pekɪŋ'ɔːdəʳ] *n* (*Bio*) orden *m* en que picotean las gallinas; (*fig*) jerarquía *f* social.
peckish* ['pekɪʃ] *adj* (**a**) hambriento, con hambre; **I'm ~, I feel ~** me anda el gusanillo. (**b**) (*US*) irritable.
pectin ['pektɪn] *n* pectina *f*.
pectoral ['pektərəl] **1** *adj* pectoral. **2 ~s** *npl* (músculos *mpl*) pectorales *mpl*.
peculate ['pekjʊleɪt] *vi* desfalcar.
peculation [,pekjʊ'leɪʃən] *n* desfalco *m*, peculado *m*.
peculiar [pɪ'kjuːlɪəʳ] *adj* (**a**) (*belonging exclusively*) peculiar; propio, característico; (*marked*) particular, especial; **an**

animal ~ to Africa un animal autóctono de África, un animal que existe únicamente en África; **it is a phrase ~ to him** es una frase propia de él; **the region has its ~ dialect** la región tiene su dialecto especial.

(**b**) (*strange*) singular, extraño, raro; sui generis; **a most ~ flavour** un sabor muy extraño; **he's a ~ chap** es un tío raro; **how very ~!** ¡qué raro!; **it's really most ~** es realmente extraño; **I'm feeling a bit ~** no me siento del todo bien.

peculiarity [pɪ,kjʊlɪ'ærɪtɪ] *n* (*V adj*) (**a**) peculiaridad *f*; particularidad *f*; rasgo *m* característico; **it has the ~ that ...** tiene la particularidad de que ...; **'special peculiarities'** (*on passport etc*) 'señas *fpl* particulares'.

(**b**) singularidad *f*, rareza *f*; extravagancia *f*, manía *f*; **there is some ~ which I cannot quite define** hay alguna rareza que no puedo precisar; **it's a ~ he has** es una manía que tiene; **he has his peculiarities** tiene sus manías.

peculiarly [pɪ'kju:lɪəlɪ] *adv* (*V adj*) (**a**) particularmente, especialmente; **a ~ difficult work** una obra particularmente difícil.

(**b**) extrañamente, de modo raro; **he has been acting very ~** se ha comportado de modo rarísimo.

pecuniary [pɪ'kju:nɪərɪ] *adj* pecuniario.

pedagogic(al) [,pedə'gɒdʒɪk(əl)] *adj* pedagógico.

pedagogically [,pedə'gɒdʒɪkəlɪ] *adv* pedagógicamente.

pedagogue, (*US sometimes*) **pedagog** ['pedəgɒg] *n* pedagogo *m*, -a *f*.

pedagogy ['pedəgɒgɪ] *n* pedagogía *f*.

pedal ['pedl] **1** *n* pedal *m* (*also Mus*); **loud ~** pedal *m* fuerte; **soft ~** sordina *f*. **2** *vt* impulsar pedaleando; **he came up ~ling his bicycle furiously** llegó en su bicicleta dándoles duro a los pedales. **3** *vi* pedalear. **4** *attr*: **~ (bi)cycle** bicicleta *f* a pedales; **~ bin** cubo *m* con pedal; **~ cyclist** ciclista *mf*.

pedal-boat ['pedl,bəʊt] *n*, **pedalo** ['pedələʊ] *n* patín *m* a pedal, pedaló *m*.

pedant ['pedənt] *n* pedante *mf*.

pedantic [pɪ'dæntɪk] *adj person* pedante; *manner etc* pedantesco.

pedantically [pɪ'dæntɪkəlɪ] *adv* con pedantería, pedantescamente.

pedantry ['pedəntrɪ] *n* pedantería *f*.

peddle ['pedl] *vt* vender como buhonero, vender por las casas, andar vendiendo (de puerta en puerta); (*fig*) *scandal etc* contar, repetir, difundir.

peddler ['pedlə^r] *n* (*US*) = **pedlar**.

pederast ['pedəræst] *n* pederasta *m*.

pederasty ['pedəræstɪ] *n* pederastia *f*.

pedestal ['pedɪstl] **1** *n* pedestal *m*, basa *f*; **to knock sb off his ~** tumbar a uno, derrocar a uno; **to put sb on a ~** poner a uno sobre un pedestal. **2** *attr*: **~ lamp** lámpara *f* de pie.

pedestrian [pɪ'destrɪən] **1** *adj* (**a**) (*lit*) pedestre. (**b**) (*fig*) prosaico, pedestre. **2** *n* peatón *m*. **3** *attr* de peatones, para peatones; **~ area** zona *f* peatonal, zona *f* peatonizada; **~ crossing** paso *m* para peatones; **~ precinct** (*Brit*) = **~ area**; **~ traffic** circulación *f* de peatones.

pedestrianize [pɪ'destrɪənaɪz] *vt* peatonizar.

pediatrician *etc* = **paediatrician** *etc*.

pedicure ['pedɪkjʊə^r] *n* pedicura *f*, quiropedia *f*.

pedigree ['pedɪgri:] **1** *n* (*lineage*) genealogía *f*, linaje *m*; (*of animal*) pedigree *m*, pedigrí *m*; (*tree*) árbol *m* genealógico; (*document*) certificado *m* de genealogía. **2** *attr* de raza, de casta, de pura sangre; (*fig*) certificado, garantizado.

pediment ['pedɪmənt] *n* frontón *m*.

pedlar ['pedlə^r] *n* vendedor *m* ambulante, buhonero *m*, pacotillero *m* (*And, Carib*).

pedological [,pi:də'lɒdʒɪkl] *adj* (*US*) = **paedological**.

pedology [pɪ'dɒlədʒɪ] *n* (*US*) = **paedology**.

pedometer [pɪ'dɒmɪtə^r] *n* podómetro *m*.

pedophile ['pi:dəʊfaɪl] *n* (*US*) = **paedophile**.

pedophilia [,pi:dəʊ'fɪlɪə] *n* (*US*) = **paedophilia**.

pee [pi:] = **piss**.

peek [pi:k] **1** *n* mirada *f* rápida, mirada *f* furtiva; **to take a ~ at** echar una mirada rápida (*or* furtiva) a.

2 *vi* mirar a hurtadillas; **to ~ at** echar una mirada rápida (*or* furtiva) a.

peel [pi:l] **1** *n* piel *f*; (*after removal*) pieles *fpl*, monda *f*, cáscara *f*, peladuras *fpl*; (*fragment in cocktail etc*) corteza *f*.

2 *vt fruit etc* pelar, mondar, quitar la piel a; *bark* descortezar; *layer of paper etc* quitar, quitar una capa de.

3 *vi* (*layer of paper etc*) quitarse, despegarse, desprenderse; (*paint etc*) desconcharse; (*bark*) descortezarse; **I'm ~ing** se me despega la piel.

◆**peel away 1** *vt rind, skin* mondar; *film, covering* pelar.

2 *vi* (*Med, skin*) pelarse; (*paint*) caerse a tiras; (*wallpaper*) despegarse.

◆**peel back** *vt film, covering* despegar.

◆**peel off 1** *vt dress etc* quitarse rápidamente, quitarse lisamente.

2 *vi* (**a**) (*separate*) separarse (*from* de); desviarse (*from* de); **this is where we ~ off from the main road** aquí es donde salimos de la carretera principal. (**b**) (*) desnudarse rápidamente.

peeler ['pi:lə^r] *n* (**a**) (*gadget*) mondador *m*; (*electric*) pelacables *m*. (**b**) (*US*‡) estriptista *f*.

peeling ['pi:lɪŋ] *n* (*Med: of face etc*) descamación *f*; (*cosmetic trade*) peeling *m*; **~s** monda *f*, peladuras *fpl*.

peep[1] [pi:p] **1** *n* (*of bird etc*) pío *m*; **there hasn't been a ~ out of them** no han dicho ni pío; **we can't get a ~ out of them** no les podemos hacer contestar; **I don't want a single ~ out of you** tú ni chistar, tú ni pío.

2 *vi* piar.

peep[2] [pi:p] **1** *n* mirada *f* rápida, mirada *f* furtiva, ojeada *f*; **at ~ of day** al primer amanecer; **to get a ~ at sth** lograr ver algo brevemente; **let's take a ~** vamos a verlo; **take a ~ at this** echa una ojeada a esto.

2 *vi* mirar rápidamente, mirar furtivamente; **to ~ at sth** echar una mirada rápida (*or* furtiva) a algo; **to ~ from behind a tree** mirar a hurtadillas desde detrás de un árbol; **to ~ over a wall** atisbar por encima de una tapia, asomar cuidadosamente la cabeza por encima de una tapia para mirar; **to ~ through a window** atisbar a través de una ventana.

◆**peep out 1** *vt* asomar; **she ~ed her head out** asomó la cabeza.

2 *vi* asomar; **the book is ~ing out of his pocket** el libro se deja ver en su bolsillo, asoma el libro por su bolsillo; **a head ~ed out** se asomó una cabeza; **the sun ~ed out from behind the clouds** el sol atisbó por las nubes.

peepers* ['pi:pəz] *npl* ojos *mpl*.

peephole ['pi:phəʊl] *n* mirilla *f*, atisbadero *m*.

Peeping Tom [,pi:pɪŋ'tɒm] *nm* curioso *m*, mirón *m*.

peepshow ['pi:pʃəʊ] *n* mundonuevo *m*; (*) vistas *fpl* sicalípticas, espectáculo *m* deshonesto.

peeptoe ['pi:ptəʊ] *adj*: **~ sandal** sandalia *f* abierta; **~ shoe** zapato *m* abierto.

peer[1] [pɪə^r] **1** *n* (**a**) (*noble*) par *m*; **~ of the realm** par *m* del reino. (**b**) (*equal*) igual *mf*, par *mf*; **as a musician he has no ~** como músico no tiene par. **2** *attr*: **~ group** grupo *m* paritario; **~ review** evaluación *f* por los iguales.

peer[2] [pɪə^r] *vi* (**a**) (*person*) mirar con ojos de miope; **to ~ at sth** mirar algo de cerca, mirar algo con ojos de miope; **to ~ into a room** mirar dentro de un cuarto; **to ~ out of a window** asomarse (curioso) a una ventana; **to ~ over a wall** atisbar por encima de una tapia.

(**b**) (*fig*) **two eyes ~ed out** aparecieron dos ojos, se asomaron dos ojos.

peerage ['pɪərɪdʒ] *n* (*persons*) nobleza *f*, aristocracia *f*; (*rank*) título *m* de nobleza, dignidad *f* de par; (*book*) (libro *m*) nobiliario *m*, guía *f* nobiliaria; **to get a ~** recibir un título de nobleza; **so they gave him a ~** así que le dieron un título de nobleza; **to marry into the ~** casarse con un título.

peeress ['pɪərɪs] *n* paresa *f*.

peerless ['pɪəlɪs] *adj* sin par, incomparable.

peeve* [pi:v] *vt* enojar, irritar.

peeved* [pi:vd] *adj*: **to be ~** estar enojado, estar furioso; **to get ~** sulfurarse*; ofenderse; **he got a bit ~** se ofendió.

peevish ['pi:vɪʃ] *adj* malhumorado, displicente, picajoso; impaciente.

peevishly ['pi:vɪʃlɪ] *adv* malhumoradamente, con mal humor; impacientemente; **he said ~** dijo malhumorado.

peevishness ['pi:vɪʃnɪs] *n* mal humor *m*, displicencia *f*; impaciencia *f*.

peewee* [pi:wi:] *adj* (*US*) diminuto, pequeñito.

peewit ['pi:wɪt] *n* avefría *f*.

peg [peg] **1** *n* clavija *f*, claveta *f*; (*Mus*) clavija *f*; (*in ground*) estaca *f*, estaquilla *f*; (*tent-~*) estaca *f*; (*clothes-~*) pinza *f*, broche *m* (*LAm*); (*for coat*) gancho *m*, colgadero *m*, percha *f* (*LAm*); (*in barrel*) estaquilla *f*; (*fig*) pretexto *m*; (*for argument etc*) punto *m* de apoyo, punto *m* de partida; **a ~ of whisky** (*Brit*) un trago de whiskey; **clothes off the ~** (*Brit*) ropa *f* de percha; **to buy a suit off the ~** (*Brit*) comprar un traje de percha; **it was just a ~ on which to hang personal rivalries** era simplemente un clavo en que colgar las rivalidades personales; **to be a square ~**

in a round hole no cuadrar (donde se está); ser un inadaptado; **to take sb down a ~** bajar los humos a uno.
2 *vt* (**a**) (*fix ~s to*) enclavijar.
(**b**) *currency* vincular (*to* a); *prices* fijar, estabilizar (a cierto nivel).
◆**peg away*** *vi* machacar, batir el yunque; **to ~ away at sth** persistir en algo, afanarse por lograr algo.
◆**peg down** *vt* estaquillar, fijar con estacas, sujetar con estacas.
◆**peg out 1** *vt area* señalar con estacas; *clothes* tender (con pinzas).
2 *vi* (‡) estirar la pata*.
Pegasus ['pegəsəs] *n* Pegaso *m*.
pegboard ['pegbɔːd] *n* tablero *m* de clavijas.
pegleg ['pegleg] *n* pata *f* de palo.
PEI (*Canada*) *abbr of* **Prince Edward Island**.
peignoir ['peɪnwɑːʳ] *n* bata *f* (de señora), peinador *m*.
pejorative [pɪ'dʒɒrɪtɪv] *adj* peyorativo (*also Gram*), despectivo.
peke* [piːk] *n*, **pekinese** [ˌpiːkɪ'niːz] *n* pequinés *m*, -esa *f*.
Pekin [piː'kɪn] *n*, **Peking** [piː'kɪŋ] *n* Pekín *m*.
pelagic [pɪ'lædʒɪk] *adj* pelágico.
pelican ['pelɪkən] *n* pelícano *m*; **~ crossing** semáforo *m* sonoro.
pellet ['pelɪt] *n* bolita *f*; (*pill etc*) píldora *f*; (*shot*) perdigón *m*; (*of fertilizer etc*) gránulo *m*.
pell-mell ['pel'mel] *adv* en tropel, atropelladamente.
pellucid [pe'luːsɪd] *adj* diáfano, translúcido.
pelmet ['pelmɪt] *n* galería *f* (para cubrir la barra de las cortinas).
Peloponnese [ˌpeləpə'niːs] *n*: **the ~** el Peloponeso.
Peloponnesian [ˌpeləpə'niːʃən] *adj* peloponense.
pelota [pɪ'ləʊtə] **1** *n* pelota *f* (vasca). **2** *attr*: **~ player** pelotari *m*.
pelt¹ [pelt] *n* (*skin*) pellejo *m*; (*fur*) piel *f*.
pelt² [pelt] **1** *vt* (**a**) (*throw*) tirar, arrojar (*at* a).
(**b**) **to ~ sb with eggs** tirar huevos a uno; **to ~ sb with stones** apedrear a uno; **they ~ed him with questions** le acribillaron a preguntas.
2 *vi* (**a**) (*of rain*: *also* **to ~ with rain**) llover a cántaros.
(**b**) (*) ir a máxima velocidad; **to go ~ing past** pasar como un rayo; **to go ~ing off** partir como un rayo.
3 *n*: **to go full ~** ir a todo correr, ir a máxima velocidad.
◆**pelt down** *vi*: **it was ~ing down** (*rain*) llovía de verdad, diluviaba.
pelvic ['pelvɪk] *adj* pélvico.
pelvis ['pelvɪs] *n* pelvis *f*.
pen¹ [pen] **1** *n* (*enclosure*) corral *m*; (*sheep-~*) redil *m*, aprisco *m*; (*bull-~*) toril *m*; (*play-~*) parque *m* (de niño); (*US**) chirona *f*. **2** *vt* encerrar, acorralar.
pen² [pen] **1** *n* pluma *f*; (*fountain ~*) estilográfica *f*, plumafuente *f* (*LAm*); **to put ~ to paper** empuñar la pluma, escribir algo; **to wield a ~** menear cálamo. **2** *attr*: **~-and-ink drawing** dibujo *m* a pluma. **3** *vt* escribir; redactar, formular.
pen³ [pen] *n* (*Orn*) cisne *m* hembra.
penal ['piːnl] *adj* (**a**) (*gen*) penal; **~ code** código *m* penal; **~ colony** colonia *f* penal; **~ servitude** trabajos *mpl* forzados; **~ settlement** = **~ colony.** (**b**) *taxation etc* muy gravoso, perjudicial.
penalization [ˌpiːnəlaɪ'zeɪʃən] *n* castigo *m*.
penalize ['piːnəlaɪz] *vt* penar; (*accidentally, unfairly*) perjudicar; (*Sport*) castigar, sancionar, penalizar; **to be ~d for a foul** ser castigado por una falta; **we are ~d by not having a car** somos perjudicados por no tener coche; **the decision ~s those who ...** la decisión perjudica a los que ....
penalty ['penəltɪ] **1** *n* pena *f*, castigo *m*; (*fine*) multa *f*; (*Sport*) castigo *m*, sanción *f*, (*football etc*) penálty *m*, penalti *m*; (*golf*) penalización *f*, (*Bridge*) multa *f*, castigo *m*; **'~ £5'** 'la infracción se castigará con una multa de 5 libras'; **on ~ of** so pena de; **the ~ for this is death** esto se castiga con la muerte; **to pay the ~** sufrir el castigo (*for* de).
2 *attr*: **~ area, ~ box** área *f* de castigo; **~ clause** cláusula *f* penal; **~ goal** gol *m* de penálty (*or* de tiro de castigo); **~ kick** penálty *m*, penalti *m*; **~ point** punto *m* de castigo; **~ shoot-out** desempate *m* a penaltis, tanda *f* de penaltis; **~ spot** punto *m* del penálty.
penance ['penəns] *n* penitencia *f*; **to do ~** hacer penitencia (*for* por).
pence [pens] *npl of* **penny**.
penchant [ˌpɑ̃ːŋʃɑ̃ːŋ] *n* predilección *f* (*for* por), inclinación *f* (*for* hacia); **to have a ~ for** tener predilección por.
pencil ['pensl] **1** *n* lápiz *m*, lapicero *m* (*LAm*); (*propelling ~*) lapicero *m*; (*for eyebrows*) lápiz *m* de cejas; (*of light*) rayo *m* delgado; **to draw in ~** dibujar con lápiz.
2 *attr*: **~ drawing** dibujo *m* a lápiz; **~ mark** señal *f* hecha a lápiz.
3 *vt* (*also* **to ~ in**) escribir con lápiz; **a ~led note** un apunte escrito a lápiz.
◆**pencil in** *vt* apuntar (con lápiz); (*fig*) apuntar con carácter provisional.
pencil-box ['penslbɒks] *n* cajita *f* de lápices.
pencil-case ['penslkeɪs] *n* plumier *m*.
pencil-sharpener ['pensl,ʃɑːpnəʳ] *n* sacapuntas *m*.
pendant ['pendənt] *n* pendiente *m*, medallón *m*.
pending ['pendɪŋ] **1** *adj* pendiente; **~ tray** cajón *m* para documentos pendientes; **to be ~** estar pendiente, estar en trámite; **and other matters ~** y otros asuntos todavía por resolver.
2 *prep*: **~ the arrival of ...** hasta que llegue ...; **~ your decision** mientras se decida Vd.
pendulous ['pendjʊləs] *adj* colgante.
pendulum ['pendjʊləm] *n* péndulo *m*.
Penelope [pə'neləpɪ] *nf* Penélope.
penetrable ['penɪtrəbl] *adj* penetrable.
penetrate ['penɪtreɪt] *vt* penetrar (por).
penetrating ['penɪtreɪtɪŋ] *adj* penetrante (*also fig*).
penetratingly ['penɪtreɪtɪŋlɪ] *adv* con penetración, de manera penetrante.
penetration [ˌpenɪ,treɪʃən] *n* penetración *f* (*also fig*).
penetrative ['penɪtrətɪv] *adj* penetrante.
penfriend ['penfrend] *n* (*Brit*) amigo *m*, -a *f* por correspondencia.
penguin ['peŋgwɪn] *n* pingüino *m*.
penholder ['pen,həʊldəʳ] *n* portaplumas *m*.
penicillin [ˌpenɪ'sɪlɪn] *n* penicilina *f*.
peninsula [pɪ'nɪnsjʊlə] *n* península *f*.
peninsular [pɪ'nɪnsjʊləʳ] *adj* peninsular; **the P~ War** la Guerra de Independencia.
penis ['piːnɪs] *n* pene *m*.
penitence ['penɪtəns] *n* penitencia *f*, arrepentimiento *m*.
penitent ['penɪtənt] **1** *adj* penitente (*also Eccl*); arrepentido, compungido. **2** *n* penitente *mf*.
penitential [ˌpenɪ'tenʃəl] *adj* penitencial.
penitentiary [ˌpenɪ'tenʃərɪ] *n* (*US*) cárcel *f*, presidio *m*, penitenciaria *f*.
penitently ['penɪtəntlɪ] *n* penitentemente; arrepentidamente, compungidamente.
penknife ['pennaɪf] *n*, *pl* **penknives** ['pennaɪvz] navaja *f* (pequeña), cortaplumas *m*.
penman ['penmən] *n*, *pl* **penmen** ['penmən] pendolista *m*, calígrafo *m*.
penmanship ['penmənʃɪp] *n* caligrafía *f*.
Penn., Penna. (*US*) *abbr of* **Pennsylvania**.
pen-name ['pen'neɪm] *n* seudónimo *m*, nombre *m* de guerra.
pennant ['penənt] *n* banderola *f*; banderín *m*; (*Naut*) gallardete *m*.
pen-nib ['pennɪb] *n* punta *f* (de pluma); plumilla *f*, plumín *m* (de estilográfica).
penniless ['penɪlɪs] *adj* pobre; sin dinero; **to be ~** no tener un céntimo; **to be left ~** quedar completamente sin dinero.
Pennine ['penaɪn] *n*: **the ~s** los (Montes) Peninos.
pennon ['penən] *n* pendón *m*.
Pennsylvania [ˌpensl'veɪnɪə] *n* Pensilvania *f*.
penny ['penɪ] *n*, *pl* **pennies** ['penɪz] *or* **pence** [pens] penique *m*; (*US*) centavo *m*; (*Spanish equivalent*) perra *f*; **~ arcade** (*US*) galería *f* de máquinas tragaperras; **for two pence I'd ...** por menos de nada yo ...; **in for a ~, in for a pound** preso por mil, preso por mil quinientos; **a ~ for your thoughts!** ¿en qué piensas?; **I'm not a ~ the wiser** lo entiendo menos que antes; **that must have cost a pretty ~** eso habrá costado un dineral; **to earn an honest ~** emplearse en un oficio honrado; ganarse unos duros honradamente; **he hasn't a ~ to his name, he hasn't two pennies to rub together** no tiene donde caerse muerto; **take care of the pennies and the pounds will take care of themselves** muchos pocos hacen un montón; **then the ~ dropped** luego se dio cuenta, por fin cayó en la cuenta; **to spend a ~*** cambiar el agua al canario*; **he turns up like a bad ~** aparece una y otra vez como la falsa moneda.
Penny ['penɪ] *nf familiar form of* **Penelope**.
penny-a-liner ['penɪə'laɪnəʳ] *n* escritorzuelo *m*, -a *f*, gacetillero *m*, -a *f*.
penny dreadful ['penɪ'dredfʊl] *n* (*Brit*) tebeo *m* (*or* revista *f* juvenil) de bajísima calidad.

penny-in-the-slot ['penɪɪnðə'slɒt] *attr*: ~ **machine** (máquina *f*) tragaperras *m*.

penny-pinching ['penɪ,pɪntʃɪŋ] **1** *n* tacañería *f*. **2** *adj person* tacaño, avaro.

pennyweight ['penɪweɪt] *n* *peso de 24 granos* (= 1,555 gramos).

penny whistle [,penɪ'wɪsl] *n* flauta *f* metálica.

pennyworth ['penəθ] *n* valor *m* de un penique, cantidad *f* que se compra con un penique; (*fig*) pizca *f*.

penologist [piː'nɒlədʒɪst] *n* penalista *mf*, criminólogo *m*, -a *f*.

penology [piː'nɒlədʒɪ] *n* ciencia *f* penal, criminología *f*.

pen-pal* ['penpæl] *n* = **penfriend**.

penpusher ['pen,pʊʃəʳ] *n* (*Liter*) plumífero *m*; (*clerk*) empleadillo *m*, -a *f*.

pension ['penʃən] **1** *n* pensión *f*; (*Mil*) retiro *m*; (*superannuation etc*) jubilación *f*; **to retire on a** ~ jubilarse.

2 *attr*: ~ **book** libreta *f* de pensión; ~ **fund** caja *f* de pensiones; ~ **rights** derechos *mpl* de pensión; ~ **scheme** plan *m* de pensiones.

3 *vt* pensionar, dar una pensión a.

◆**pension off** *vt*: **to** ~ **sb off** jubilar a uno.

pensionable ['penʃənəbl] *adj*: ~ **age** edad *f* de jubilación; ~ **post** empleo *m* con derecho a pensión.

pensioner ['penʃənəʳ] *n* pensionado *m*, -a *f*, pensionista *mf*; (*Mil*) inválido *m*; ~**s** clases *fpl* pasivas.

pensive ['pensɪv] *adj* pensativo, meditabundo; preocupado; triste.

pensively ['pensɪvlɪ] *adv* pensativamente; tristemente; **he said** ~ dijo pensativo.

pent [pent] *adj* *V* **pent-up**.

pentagon ['pentəgən] *n* pentágono *m*; **the P**~ (*Washington*) el Pentágono.

pentagonal [pen'tægənl] *adj* pentagonal.

pentameter [pen'tæmɪtəʳ] *n* pentámetro *m*.

Pentateuch ['pentətjuːk] *n* Pentateuco *m*.

pentathlon [pen'tæθlən] *n* pentatlón *m*.

pentatonic [,pentə'tɒnɪk] *adj* pentatónico; ~ **scale** escala *f* pentatónica.

Pentecost ['pentɪkɒst] *n* Pentecostés *m*.

Pentecostal [,pentɪ'kɒstl] *adj* de Pentecostés.

penthouse ['penthaʊs] *n*, *pl* **penthouses** ['penthaʊzɪz] cobertizo *m*; (*flat*) ático *m*, casa *f* de azotea.

pent-up ['pentʌp] *adj* (**a**) **to be** ~, **to feel** ~ (*person etc*) estar encerrado, sentirse como enjaulado. (**b**) *emotion etc* reprimido; ~ **demand** demanda *f* reprimida.

penult [pɪ'nʌlt] *n* penúltima *f*.

penultimate [pɪ'nʌltɪmɪt] *adj* penúltimo.

penumbra [pɪ'nʌmbrə] *n* penumbra *f*.

penurious [pɪ'njʊərɪəs] *adj* miserable, pobrísimo.

penury ['penjʊrɪ] *n* (**a**) (*poverty*) miseria *f*, pobreza *f*; **to live in** ~ vivir en la miseria. (**b**) (*lack*) falta *f*, escasez *f* (*of* de).

penwiper ['pen,waɪpəʳ] *n* limpiaplumas *m*.

peon ['piːən] *n* peón *m*.

peonage ['piːənɪdʒ] *n* condición *f* de peón; estado *m* en que viven los peones; (*fig*) servidumbre *f*, esclavitud *f*.

peony ['pɪənɪ] *n* peonía *f*, saltaojos *m*.

people ['piːpl] **1** *n* (**a**) (*Pol etc*) pueblo *m*; ciudadanos *mpl*; **the** ~ (*pej*), **the common** ~ el pueblo, la plebe; **the** ~ **at large** el pueblo en general; **a man of the** ~ un hombre del pueblo; **the king and his** ~ el rey y su pueblo, el rey y sus súbditos; **government by the** ~ gobierno *m* por el pueblo; ~**'s democracy** democracia *f* popular; **Chinese P**~**s' Republic** República *f* Popular China.

(**b**) (*race*) pueblo *m*, nación *f*; **English** ~ los ingleses; **the English** ~ el pueblo inglés; **the British** ~ la nación británica; **the Beaker P**~ la gente de las copas, el pueblo de las copas.

(**c**) (*parents*) padres *mpl*; (*relatives*) parientes *mpl*, familia *f*; **my** ~ mis padres, mi familia; **how are your** ~? ¿cómo están los tuyos?, ¿cómo está tu familia?; **have you met his** ~? ¿conoces a sus padres?

(**d**) (*persons*) gente *f*; **the good** ~, **the little** ~ las hadas; **old** ~ los viejos; **young** ~ los jóvenes, la juventud; **what do you** ~ **think?** y ustedes, ¿qué opinan?; **the place was full of** ~ el local estaba lleno de gente; **they're strange** ~ son gente rara; **I like the** ~ **here** aquí la gente es simpática, la gente de aquí me gusta; **the gas** ~ **are coming tomorrow** los del gas vienen mañana; **try the idea with our design** ~ prueba la idea con la gente de diseño.

(**e**) (*inhabitants*) habitantes *mpl*; **the** ~ **of London** los habitantes de Londres, los londinenses; **Madrid has over 4 million** ~ Madrid tiene más de 4 millones de habitantes.

(**f**) (*with numerals*) **20** ~ 20 personas; **many** ~ **think that** ... muchas personas creen que ..., son muchos los que creen que ...; **some** ~ algunos, algunas personas.

(**g**) (*vague subject use*) ~ **say that** ... dicen que ..., se dice que ..., la gente dice que ...; **here** ~ **quarrel a lot** aquí se riñe mucho; ~ **get worried** la gente se inquieta; **it's enough to worry** ~ basta para inquietar a la gente.

2 *vt* poblar; **the country is** ~**d by** ... el país está poblado por ..., el país está habitado por ...

people mover ['piːpl,muːvəʳ] *n* (*US*) cinta *f* transbordadora, pasillo *m* móvil.

pep* [pep] *n* empuje *m*, dinamismo *m*, ímpetu *m*, energía *f*.

◆**pep up*** *vt* estimular, animar, hacer más dinámico; *drink etc* fortalecer.

pepper ['pepəʳ] **1** *n* (*spice*) pimienta *f*; (*vegetable*) pimiento *m*; (~-*plant*) pimentero *m*; ~ **steak** filete *m* a la pimienta.

2 *vt* (**a**) (*spice*) sazonar con pimienta, añadir pimienta a. (**b**) **to** ~ **a work with quotations** salpicar una obra de citas; **to** ~ **sb with shot** acribillar a uno a tiros.

pepperbox ['pepəbɒks] *n* pimentero *m*.

peppercorn ['pepəkɔːn] **1** *n* grano *m* de pimienta. **2** *attr*: ~ **rent** alquiler *m* nominal.

peppermill ['pepəmɪl] *n* molinillo *m* de pimienta.

peppermint ['pepəmɪnt] *n* (*plant, flavour*) menta *f*, hierbabuena *f*; (*sweet*) pastilla *f* de menta.

pepperpot ['pepəpɒt] *n*, **pepper shaker** ['pepə,ʃeɪkəʳ] *n* (*US*) pimentero *m*.

peppery ['pepərɪ] *adj taste* picante; mordiscante; (*fig*) enojadizo, de malas pulgas.

pep-pill ['peppɪl] *n* píldora *f* antifatiga, estimulante *m*.

pepsin ['pepsɪn] *n* pepsina *f*.

pep-talk* ['peptɔːk] *n*: **to give a** ~ **to** dar ánimos a, arengar a.

peptic ['peptɪk] *adj* péptico; ~ **ulcer** úlcera *f* péptica.

peptone ['peptəʊn] *n* peptona *f*.

per [pɜːʳ] *prep* por; (*with year etc*) a; **£20** ~ **annum** 20 libras al año; **£7** ~ **week** 7 libras a la semana; **45p** ~ **dozen** 45 peniques la docena; **60 miles** ~ **hour** 60 millas por hora; **4 litres** ~ **100 km** 4 litros por 100 km; ~ **cent**, ~**cent** por ciento, por cien; **20** ~ **cent** 20 por cien(to); **it has increased by 8** ~ **cent** ha aumentado en un 8 por cien(to); **there is a 10** ~ **cent discount** hay un descuento de un 10 por cien(to); **at so much** ~ **cent** a un tanto por ciento; ~ **person** por persona; ~ **se** de por sí; **as** ~ **invoice** según factura; *V* **usual**.

perambulate [pə'ræmbjʊleɪt] **1** *vt* recorrer (para inspeccionar). **2** *vi* pasearse, deambular.

perambulation [pə,ræmbjʊ'leɪʃən] *n* (*visit*) visita *f* de inspección; (*stroll*) paseo *m*; (*journey*) viaje *m*.

perambulator ['præmbjʊleɪtəʳ] *n* (*Brit*) cochecito *m* de niño.

perborate [pə'bɔːreɪt] *n* perborato *m*.

per capita [pə'kæpɪtə] *adv* per cápita; ~ **income** ingresos *mpl* per cápita.

perceive [pə'siːv] *vt* percibir; (*see*) notar, observar; divisar; (*hear*) percibir; (*understand*) comprender; (*realize*) darse cuenta de; **now I** ~ **that** ... ahora veo que ...; **do you** ~ **anything strange?** ¿notas algo raro?; **I do not** ~ **how it can be done** no comprendo cómo se puede hacer.

percentage [pə'sentɪdʒ] **1** *n* porcentaje *m*, tanto *m* por ciento; proporción *f*; (*: *rake-off*) tajada* *f*; (*commission*) comisión *f* porcentual; **the figure is expressed as a** ~ la cifra está expresada como un tanto por ciento; **a high** ~ **are girls** un elevado porcentaje son chicas; **to get a** ~ **on all sales** recibir un tanto por ciento sobre todas las ventas.

2 *attr* porcentual; **on a** ~ **basis** según un sistema porcentual; ~ **increase** aumento *m* porcentual; ~ **point** punto *m* porcentual; ~ **sign** signo *m* del tanto por ciento.

percentile [pə'sentaɪl] *n* percentil *m*.

perceptible [pə'septəbl] *adj* perceptible; sensible.

perceptibly [pə'septəblɪ] *adv* perceptiblemente; sensiblemente; **it has improved** ~ ha mejorado sensiblemente.

perception [pə'sepʃən] *adj* percepción *f*; perspicacia *f*; penetración *f*; agudeza *f*.

perceptive [pə'septɪv] *adj* perspicaz; penetrante, agudo; *function* perceptivo.

perceptiveness [pə'septɪvnɪs] *n* penetración *f*; sensibilidad *f*; facultad *f* perceptiva.

perch¹ [pɜːtʃ] *n*, *pl invar or* **perches** ['pɜːtʃɪz] (*Fish*) perca *f*.

perch² [pɜːtʃ] **1** *n* (**a**) *medida de longitud* = 5,029 *m*.

(**b**) (*of bird*) percha *f*; (*fig*) posición *f* elevada; posición *f* peligrosa, posición *f* poco segura; **to knock sb off his** ~ (*fig*) destronar a uno, tumbar a uno.

2 *vt* encaramar, colocar (en una posición elevada, poco segura *etc*); **he** ~**ed his hat on his head** posó el sombrero en la cabeza; **we ~ed the child on the wall** encaramamos al niño en la tapia.

3 *vi* (*bird*) posarse (*on* en); (*person etc*) sentarse (en un sitio elevado, poco seguro *etc*); colocarse en una posición elevada; **we ~ed in a tree to see the procession** nos subimos a un árbol para ver el desfile; **the village ~es on a hilltop** el pueblo ocupa la cumbre de una colina; **she ~ed on the arm of my chair** se acomodó en el brazo de mi butaca.

perchance [pə'tʃɑːns] *adv* (*liter*) por ventura, acaso.

percipient [pə'sɪpɪənt] *adj* perspicaz; penetrante, agudo.

percolate ['pɜːkəleɪt] **1** *vt* filtrar, colar; (*fig*) filtrarse en, filtrarse por; *coffee* preparar, filtrar.

2 *vi* (**a**) filtrarse, colarse; **to ~ down to** penetrar hasta; **to ~ through** penetrar por.

(**b**) (*coffee*) prepararse.

percolator ['pɜːkəleɪtəʳ] *n* percolador *m.*

percussion [pɜ'kʌʃən] **1** *n* percusión *f.* **2** *attr instrument etc* de percusión; **~ cap** cápsula *f* fulminante.

percussionist [pɜ'kʌʃənɪst] *n* percusionista *mf.*

per diem ['pɜː'diːem] *adv* por día.

perdition [pɜː'dɪʃən] perdición *f.*

peregrination [,perɪgrɪ'neɪʃən] *n* peregrinación *f*; **~s** (*hum*) vagabundeo *m*, periplo *m.*

peregrine ['perɪgrɪn] **1** *n* halcón *m* común, neblí *m.* **2** *attr*: **~ falcon** halcón *m* peregrino.

peremptory [pə'remptərɪ] *adj* perentorio; *person* imperioso, autoritario.

perennial [pə'renɪəl] **1** *adj* perenne (*also Bot*); eterno, perpetuo; **it's a ~ complaint** es una queja constante. **2** *n* (*Bot*) perenne *m*, planta *f* vivaz.

perennially [pə'renɪəlɪ] *adv* perennemente; perpetuamente, constantemente.

perfect 1 ['pɜːfɪkt] *adj* (**a**) perfecto; *host etc* perfecto, modélico, ejemplar; **it's just ~!** ¡qué maravilla!; **with ~ assurance** con la más completa confianza; **she's a ~ terror** es una arpía; **he's a ~ stranger to me** me es completamente desconocido; **he's a ~ idiot** es un idiota completo; **he's a ~ gentleman** es un cumplido caballero; **his Spanish is far from ~** su español dista mucho de ser perfecto.

(**b**) (*Gram*) perfecto.

2 ['pɜːfɪkt] *n* (*Gram*) perfecto *m.*

3 [pə'fekt] *vt* perfeccionar.

perfectibility [pə,fektɪ'bɪlɪtɪ] *n* perfectibilidad *f.*

perfectible [pə'fektəbl] *adj* perfectible.

perfection [pə'fekʃən] *n* perfección *f*; **she does it to ~** lo hace a la perfección, lo hace a las mil maravillas.

perfectionism [pə'fekʃənɪzm] *n* perfeccionismo *m.*

perfectionist [pə'fekʃənɪst] *n* perfeccionista *mf.*

perfective [pə'fektɪv] **1** *adj aspect, verb* perfectivo. **2** *n* perfectivo *m.*

perfectly ['pɜːfɪktlɪ] *adv* (**a**) perfectamente; **she does it ~** lo hace perfectamente, lo hace a la perfección.

(**b**) **it's ~ marvellous** es de lo más maravilloso; **how ~ marvellous!** ¡qué maravilla!; **it's ~ ridiculous** es completamente absurdo; **we're ~ happy about it** estamos completamente contentos con esto.

perfidious [pɜː'fɪdɪəs] *adj* pérfido.

perfidiously [pɜː'fɪdɪəslɪ] *adv* pérfidamente.

perfidy ['pɜːfɪdɪ] *n* perfidia *f.*

perforate ['pɜːfəreɪt] *vt* perforar, horadar, agujerear; **to ~ holes in sth** practicar agujeros en algo.

perforated ['pɜːfəreɪtɪd] *adj stamp* dentado.

perforation [,pɜːfə'reɪʃən] *n* perforación *f*; agujero *m*; (*of stamp*) trepado *m*, dentado *m.*

perforce [pə'fɔːs] *adv* (*liter*) forzosamente.

perform [pə'fɔːm] **1** *vt* (**a**) *task etc* hacer, cumplir, realizar; *duty* cumplir; *function* desempeñar; ejercer; *operation* llevar a cabo, realizar; (*Ling*) realizar. (**b**) (*Theat*) *play* representar, dar, poner, *part* interpretar, hacer; (*Mus*) ejecutar, interpretar.

2 *vi* (**a**) (*Mus*: *play*) tocar, (*sing*) cantar; (*Theat*) representar, actuar; trabajar; hacer un papel, tener un papel; (*trained animal*) hacer trucos; **to ~ on the violin** tocar el violín, interpretar una obra al violín; **how did he ~?** ¿qué tal lo hizo?; **he ~ed brilliantly as Hamlet** interpretó brillantemente el papel de Hamlet, en el papel de Hamlet se lució; **when we ~ed in Seville** cuando nos presentamos en Sevilla; **I'm not ~ing this time** esta vez no hago ningún papel, esta vez no tomo parte.

(**b**) (*Mech etc*) funcionar, comportarse; **the car is not ~ing properly** el coche no funciona bien; **how does the metal ~ under pressure?** ¿cómo se comporta el metal bajo presión?

performance [pə'fɔːməns] *n* (**a**) (*of task etc*) cumplimiento *m*, ejecución *f*, realización *f*; resultado *m*; (*of function*) desempeño *m*; ejercicio *m*; acción *f*, actuación *f*; (*Ling*) realización *f*; **in the ~ of his duties** en el ejercicio de su cargo.

(**b**) (*Theat*: *of play*) representación *f*, (*by actor, of a part*) actuación *f*, desempeño *m*; interpretación *f*; (*Mus*) ejecución *f*; interpretación *f*; (*sitting*: *Theat*) función *f*, (*cinema*) sesión *f*; **the late ~** la función de la noche, la sesión de la noche; **'no ~ tonight'** 'no hay representación esta noche'; **first ~** estreno *m*; **we didn't like his ~ as Don Juan** no nos gustó su interpretación del papel de don Juan, su modo de entender el papel de don Juan no nos gustó; **he gave a splendid ~** su actuación fue estupenda; **the play had 300 ~s** la obra tuvo 300 representaciones, la obra siguió en la cartelera durante 300 representaciones; **it has not had a ~ since 1950** no se ha representado desde 1950.

(**c**) (*Mech etc*) comportamiento *m*; funcionamiento *m*; (*economic, of person, by motor*) rendimiento *m*; (*Aut etc*) prestaciones *fpl*; (*of team in match*) actuación *f*, desempeño *m*; (*of athlete, car, horse in race*) performance *f*; **the team gave a poor ~** el equipo tuvo una actuación nada satisfactoria; **they eventually put up a good ~** por fin estuvieron a su altura.

(**d**) (***: *fuss*) lío* *m*, jaleo *m*; **what a ~!** ¡qué lata!*; **it's such a ~ getting here** llegar aquí supone un tremendo jaleo.

performative [pə'fɔːmətɪv] *n*: **~ (verb)** (verbo *m*) performativo *m.*

performer [pə'fɔːməʳ] *n* (*Theat*) actor *m*, actriz *f*; artista *mf*; (*Mus*) intérprete *mf*, ejecutante *mf*, músico *m*; **a skilled ~ on the piano** un pianista experto.

performing [pə'fɔːmɪŋ] *adj* (**a**) *animal* amaestrado, sabio. (**b**) **~ arts** artes *fpl* teatrales.

perfume 1 ['pɜːfjuːm] *n* perfume *m.* **2** [pə'fjuːm] *vt* perfumar.

perfumery [pə'fjuːmərɪ] *n* (*perfumes*) perfumes *mpl*; (*factory*) perfumería *f.*

perfunctorily [pə'fʌŋktərɪlɪ] *adv* superficialmente, someramente, a la ligera.

perfunctory [pə'fʌŋktərɪ] *adj* superficial, somero; hecho (*etc*) a la ligera; *service etc* rutinario; **he gave a ~ performance** tocó (*etc*) por cumplir.

pergola ['pɜːgələ] *n* pérgola *f.*

perhaps [pə'hæps, præps] *adv* tal vez, quizá(s), puede que; **~!** ¡quizá!; **~ not** puede que no; **~ so** quizá, quizá sea así; **~ he did it** quizá lo hizo; **~ he's in Segovia** puede que esté en Segovia; **~ he'll come** quizá venga, puede que venga.

peri... ['perɪ] *pref* peri...

perigee ['perɪdʒiː] *n* perigeo *m.*

peril ['perɪl] *n* peligro *m*, riesgo *m*; **to be in ~** estar en peligro; **to be in ~ of one's life** correr riesgo de perder la vida; **do it at your ~** hágalo a su riesgo.

perilous ['perɪləs] *adj* peligroso, arriesgado; **it would be ~ to +** *infin* sería arriesgado + *infin.*

perilously ['perɪləslɪ] *adv* peligrosamente; **to come ~ close to ...** acercarse de modo peligroso a ..., (*fig*) rayar en ....

perimeter [pə'rɪmɪtəʳ] *n* perímetro *m.*

perinatal [,perɪ'neɪtl] *adj* perinatal.

perineum [,perɪ'niːəm] *n* perineo *m.*

period ['pɪərɪəd] **1** *n* (**a**) período *m*; época *f*, edad *f*; (*time limit*) plazo *m*; (*Sport*) tiempo *m*; **at that ~** en aquel entonces; **within a 3 month ~** en 3 meses; dentro de un plazo de 3 meses; **this is a bad ~ for ...** ésta es una mala época para ...; **a painting of his early ~** un cuadro de su primera época, un cuadro de su juventud; **the postwar ~** la posguerra.

(**b**) (*Scol*) hora *f*, clase *f*; **we have two French ~s** tenemos dos clases de francés.

(**c**) (*Gram*) período *m*; (*full stop*: *esp US*) punto *m*; **I said no, ~** he dicho que no, y punto.

(**d**) (*menstruation*) período *m*, regla *f.*

2 *attr*: **~ cost** costo *m* fijo; **in ~ dress** en traje de la época; **~ furniture** muebles *mpl* de época, muebles *mpl* clásicos; **~ piece** mueble *m* (*etc*) clásico.

periodic [,pɪərɪ'ɒdɪk] *adj* periódico; **~ table** tabla *f* periódica.

periodical [,pɪərɪ'ɒdɪkəl] **1** *adj* periódico. **2** *n* revista *f*, publicación *f* periódica. **3** *attr*: **~s library** hemeroteca *f.*

periodically [,pɪərɪ'ɒdɪkəlɪ] *adv* periódicamente; (*from time to time*) de vez en cuando, cada cierto tiempo.

periodicity [,pɪərɪə'dɪsɪtɪ] *n* periodicidad *f.*

peripatetic [,perɪpə'tetɪk] *adj* ambulante, que no tiene

residencia fija; (*Philos*) peripatético; **to lead a ~ existence** cambiar mucho de domicilio, no tener residencia fija.
peripheral [pəˈrɪfərəl] **1** *adj* periférico; **~ device** dispositivo *m* periférico; **~ unit** unidad *f* periférica. **2** *n* periférico *m*, unidad *f* periférica.
peripheralize [pəˈrɪfərəlaɪz] *vt* marginar.
periphery [pəˈrɪfərɪ] *n* periferia *f*.
periphrasis [pəˈrɪfrəsɪs] *n*, *pl* **periphrases** [pəˈrɪfrəsiːz] perífrasis *f*.
periphrastic [ˌperɪˈfræstɪk] *adj* perifrástico.
periscope [ˈperɪskəʊp] *n* periscopio *m*.
perish [ˈperɪʃ] **1** *vt* deteriorar, estropear, echar a perder; **to be ~ed (with cold)*** estar helado.
2 *vi* (**a**) (*person*) *etc* perecer, fallecer; **we shall do it or ~ in the attempt** lo conseguiremos o moriremos intentándolo; **he ~ed at sea** murió en el mar; **~ the thought!** ¡ni por pensamiento!, ¡Dios me libre!
(**b**) (*food, material*) deteriorarse, estropearse.
perishable [ˈperɪʃəbl] **1** *adj* perecedero. **2** *n*: **~s** artículos *mpl* perecederos, productos *mpl* perecederos.
perisher‡ [ˈperɪʃəʳ] *n* (*Brit*) tío* *m*; **little ~** tunante *m*; **you little ~!** ¡tunante!
perishing* [ˈperɪʃɪŋ] *adj* (**a**) (*) **it's ~ (cold)** hace un frío glacial; **I'm ~** estoy helado. (**b**) (*Brit* ‡) condenado*.
peristalsis [ˌperɪˈstælsɪs] *n*, *pl* **peristalses** [ˌperɪˈstælsiːz] peristalsis *f*.
peristyle [ˈperɪstaɪl] *n* peristilo *m*.
peritoneum [ˌperɪtəˈniːəm] *n* peritoneo *m*.
peritonitis [ˌperɪtəˈnaɪtɪs] *n* peritonitis *f*.
periwig [ˈperɪwɪg] *n* peluca *f*.
periwinkle [ˈperɪˌwɪŋkl] *n* (*Bot*) vincapervinca *f*; (*Zool*) litorina *f*, caracol *m* de mar.
perjure [ˈpɜːdʒəʳ] *vt*: **to ~ o.s.** perjurar, perjurarse.
perjured [ˈpɜːdʒəd] *adj evidence* falso.
perjurer [ˈpɜːdʒərəʳ] *n* perjuro *m*, -a *f*.
perjury [ˈpɜːdʒərɪ] *n* perjurio *m*; **to commit ~** jurar en falso, perjurar.
perk[1] [pɜːk] **1** *vt*: **to ~ sb up** reanimar a uno, infundir nuevo vigor a uno; **this will ~ you up!** ¡anímate con esto!, ¡esto te animará!; **to ~ one's ears up** aguzar las orejas; **to ~ one's head up** levantar la cabeza.
2 *vi*: **to ~ up** (*person*) reanimarse, cobrar ánimo; (*in health*) sentirse mejor, reponerse; **business is ~ing up** los negocios van mejor.
perk[2]* [pɜːk] gaje *m*, prebenda* *f*; **~s** gajes *mpl* (y emolumentos *mpl*), beneficios *mpl* adicionales; (*tips*) propinas *fpl*; **a salary and ~s** un sueldo y otros beneficios; **company ~s** beneficios *mpl* corporativos; **there are no ~s in this job** en este empleo no hay nada aparte del sueldo.
perk[3] [pɜrk] *vi* (*abbr of* **percolate**) (*coffee*) filtrarse.
perkiness [ˈpɜːkɪnɪs] *n* alegría *f*, buen humor *m*; despejo *m*; frescura *f*.
perky [ˈpɜːkɪ] *adj* (*gay*) alegre, de excelente humor; (*wide-awake*) despabilado; (*pert*) fresco; **to feel ~** estar alegre, estar de buen humor.
perm[1]* [pɜːm] **1** *n* permanente *f*; **to have a ~** hacerse una permanente. **2** *vt*: **to ~ sb's hair** hacer una permanente a una; **to have one's hair ~ed** hacerse una permanente.
perm[2] [pɜːm] *n abbr of* **permute, permutation.**
permafrost [ˈpɜːməfrɒst] *n* permagel *m*.
permanence [ˈpɜːmənəns] *n* permanencia *f*.
permanency [ˈpɜːmənənsɪ] *n* (*permanence*) permanencia *f*; (*permanent arrangement*) arreglo *m* permanente, cosa *f* fija; **the post is not a ~** no es un puesto permanente; **I hope this is now a ~** espero que esto sea un arreglo definitivo.
permanent [ˈpɜːmənənt] *adj* permanente (*also Comput*); estable, fijo; *finish on steel etc* inalterable; *wave* permanente; **~ staff** personal *m* de plantilla; **I'm not ~ here** yo no estoy fijo aquí; **we cannot make any ~ arrangements** no podemos arreglar las cosas de modo definitivo.
permanently [ˈpɜːmənəntlɪ] *adv* permanentemente; de modo estable, de modo definitivo; **we seem to be ~ stuck here** parece que nos vamos a quedar aquí para siempre; **he is ~ drunk** está borracho todo el tiempo.
permanent-press [ˌpɜːmənəntˈpres] *adj trousers* de raya permanente; *skirt* inarrugable.
permanganate [pɜːˈmæŋgənɪt] *n* permanganato *m*; **~ of potash** permanganato *m* de potasio.
permeability [ˌpɜːmɪəˈbɪlɪtɪ] *n* permeabilidad *f*.
permeable [ˈpɜːmɪəbl] *adj* permeable.
permeate [ˈpɜːmɪeɪt] **1** *vt* penetrar; calar; saturar, impregnar (*with* de); **to be ~d with** estar impregnado de. **2** *vi* penetrar, filtrarse; (*fig*) extenderse, propagarse.
permissible [pəˈmɪsəbl] *adj* permisible, lícito; **it is not ~ to** + *infin* no se permite + *infin*; **would it be ~ to say that ...?** ¿podemos decir que ...? ¿sería lícito decir que ...?
permission [pəˈmɪʃən] *n* permiso *m*; licencia *f*; autorización *f*; **with your ~** con permiso de Vds; **without ~** sin licencia; **'by kind ~ of Pérez Ltd'** 'con permiso de la Cía. Pérez'; **to give sb ~ to** + *infin* autorizar a uno para que + *subj*; **no ~ is needed** no hay que pedir permiso; **to withhold one's ~** negar su permiso.
permissive [pəˈmɪsɪv] *adj* (**a**) (*tolerant*) permisivo; **~ society** sociedad *f* permisiva. (**b**) (*optional*) facultativo, opcional.
permissively [pəˈmɪsɪvlɪ] *adv* permisivamente; facultativamente.
permissiveness [pəˈmɪsɪvnɪs] *n* permisividad *f*.
permit 1 [ˈpɜːmɪt] *n* permiso *m*, licencia *f*; (*allowing free entry etc*) pase *m*; **~ holder** titular *mf* de un permiso.
2 [pəˈmɪt] *vt* permitir; autorizar; tolerar, sufrir; **to ~ sb to do sth** permitir a uno hacer algo; **is it ~ted to smoke?** ¿se puede fumar?; **whoever ~ted this was a fool** el que dio permiso para eso fue un tonto; **we could never ~ it to happen** no podríamos nunca tolerar eso; **~ me!** ¡permítame!
3 [pəˈmɪt] *vi* (**a**) permitir; **weather ~ing** si el tiempo lo permite.
(**b**) **to ~ of** permitir; dar lugar a; posibilitar; **it ~s of certain changes** nos permite hacer varios cambios; **it does not ~ of doubt** no deja lugar a dudas.
permutation [ˌpɜːmjʊˈteɪʃən] *n* permutación *f*.
permute [pəˈmjuːt] *vt* permutar.
pernicious [pɜːˈnɪʃəs] *adj* pernicioso (*also Med*); nocivo, dañoso; peligroso; funesto; **~ anaemia** anemia *f* perniciosa; **the ~ custom of ...** la funesta costumbre de ...
perniciously [pɜːˈnɪʃəslɪ] *adv* perniciosamente.
pernickety* [pəˈnɪkɪtɪ] *adj* (*person*) quisquilloso, remirado; *talk* delicado; **he's very ~ about clocks** tiene ideas raras sobre los relojes; **he's terribly ~ about punctuality** tiene la manía de la puntualidad; **she's ~ about food** es exigente para la comida.
peroration [ˌperəˈreɪʃən] *n* peroración *f*.
peroxide [pəˈrɒksaɪd] **1** *n* peróxido *m*. **2** *attr*: **~ blonde** rubia *f* de bote, rubia *f* oxigenada.
perpendicular [ˌpɜːpənˈdɪkjʊləʳ] **1** *adj* perpendicular. **2** *n* perpendicular *f*; **to be out of (the) ~** salir de la perpendicular, no estar a plomo.
perpetrate [ˈpɜːpɪtreɪt] *vt* cometer; (*Jur*) perpetrar.
perpetration [ˌpɜːpɪˈtreɪʃən] *n* comisión *f*; (*Jur*) perpetración *f*.
perpetrator [ˈpɜːpɪtreɪtəʳ] *n* autor *m*, -ora *f*; responsable *mf*; (*Jur*) perpetrador *m*, -ora *f*.
perpetual [pəˈpetjʊəl] *adj* perpetuo; incesante, constante, continuo; *motion etc* perpetuo, continuo; **~ motion** movimiento *m* perpetua; **these ~ complaints** este continuo quejarse.
perpetually [pəˈpetjʊəlɪ] *adv* perpetuamente; constantemente, continuamente; **we were ~ hungry** teníamos hambre siempre; **they complain ~** se quejan constantemente.
perpetuate [pəˈpetjʊeɪt] *vt* perpetuar.
perpetuation [pəˌpetjʊˈeɪʃən] *n* perpetuación *f*.
perpetuity [ˌpɜːpɪˈtjuːɪtɪ] *n* perpetuidad *f*; **in ~** para siempre.
Perpignan [ˈpɜːpiːnjɒn] *n* Perpiñán *m*.
perplex [pəˈpleks] *vt* dejar perplejo, confundir.
perplexed [pəˈplekst] *adj* perplejo; confuso, desconcertado; **to look ~** parecer confuso.
perplexedly [pəˈpleksɪdlɪ] *adv* perplejamente.
perplexing [pəˈpleksɪŋ] *adj* confuso, que causa perplejidad; complicado; misterioso; **it's all very ~** no entiendo nada; **it's a ~ situation** es una situación complicada, es una situación que deja a todos perplejos.
perplexity [pəˈpleksɪtɪ] *n* perplejidad *f*, confusión *f*; **to be in some ~** estar algo perplejo.
per pro. *abbr of* **per procurationem, by proxy** por poder, p.p.
perquisite [ˈpɜːkwɪzɪt] *n* gaje *m*, prebenda *f*.
perry [ˈperɪ] *n* sidra *f* de peras.
persecute [ˈpɜːsɪkjuːt] *vt* perseguir; (*harass*) atormentar, importunar, molestar, acosar; **under the Nazis they were ~d** bajo los nazis se les persiguió, bajo los nazis sufrieron la persecución.
persecution [ˌpɜːsɪˈkjuːʃən] **1** *n* persecución *f*. **2** *attr*: **~ complex** complejo *m* persecutorio; **~ mania** manía *f* persecutoria.
persecutor [ˈpɜːsɪkjuːtəʳ] *n* perseguidor *m*, -ora *f*.
Persephone [pəˈsefənɪ] *n* Perséfone *f*.

Perseus ['pɜːsjuːs] *n* Perseo *m.*
perseverance [,pɜːsɪ'vɪərəns] *n* perseverancia *f,* tenacidad *f.*
persevere [,pɜːsɪ'vɪəʳ] *vi* perseverar, persistir (*in* en); **to ~ with** continuar con, no abandonar.
persevering [,pɜːsɪ'vɪərɪŋ] *adj* perseverante, tenaz.
perseveringly [,pɜːsɪ'vɪərɪŋlɪ] *adv* con perseverancia, perseverantemente.
Persia ['pɜːʃə] *n* (*Hist*) Persia *f.*
Persian ['pɜːʃən] **1** *adj* persa; **~ carpet** alfombra *f* persa; **~ cat** gato *m* de Angora, gata *f* de Angora; **~ lamb** (*animal*) oveja *f* caracul, (*skin*) caracul *m.* **2** *n* (**a**) (*person*) persa *mf.* (**b**) (*Ling*) persa *m.*
Persian Gulf ['pɜːʃən'gʌlf] *n* Golfo *m* Pérsico.
persiflage [,pɜːsɪ'flɑːʒ] *n* burlas *fpl,* zumba *f,* guasa *f.*
persimmon [pɜː'sɪmən] *n* placaminero *m,* caqui *m.*
persist [pə'sɪst] *vi* (**a**) persistir; continuar; **we must ~** hay que persistir, tenemos que mantenernos firmes; **we shall ~ in our efforts to** + *infin* seguiremos esforzándonos por + *infin*; **it will ~ some time yet** durará todavía algún tiempo.
(**b**) (*insist*) porfiar, empeñarse, obstinarse; **if he ~s** si se empeña en ello, si se obstina; **to ~ in doing sth** empeñarse en hacer algo, obstinarse en hacer algo.
persistence [pə'sɪstəns] *n,* **persistency** [pə'sɪstənsɪ] *n* persistencia *f*; porfía *f,* empeño *m*; (*of disease etc*) pertinacia *f*; **as a reward for her ~** en premio a su perseverancia.
persistent [pə'sɪstənt] *adj* persistente; continuo; porfiado; *disease etc* pertinaz; **~ offender** multirreincidente *mf,* delincuente *mf* habitual; **he is most ~** es muy porfiado, se porfía mucho; **despite our ~ warnings** a pesar de nuestras continuas advertencias.
persistently [pə'sɪstəntlɪ] *adv* con persistencia, persistentemente; constantemente; **he ~ refuses to help** se niega constantemente a prestar su ayuda.
persnickety [pəː'nɪkɪtɪ] *adj* (*US*) = **pernickety**.
person ['pɜːsn] *n* (**a**) persona *f*; **private ~** particular *m*; **in ~** en persona; **in the ~ of** en la persona de; **he is neat in his ~** es muy pulcro; **per ~** por persona; **murder by ~ or ~s unknown** homicidio *m* por mano desconocida.
2 *attr*: **~ to ~ call** (*US*) llamada *f* de persona a persona.
(**b**) (*Gram*) persona *f*; **in the first ~** en primera persona.
persona [pɜː'səʊnə] *n, pl* **personae** [pɜː'səʊnaɪ] persona *f*; **~ grata** persona *f* grata; **~ non grata** persona *f* no grata.
personable ['pɜːsnəbl] *adj* bien parecido, atractivo.
personage ['pɜːsnɪdʒ] *n* personaje *m.*
personal ['pɜːsnl] **1** *adj* personal; (*private*) privado, íntimo, particular; (*for one's sole use*) de uso personal; *liberty etc* individual; *interview* en persona; **~ account** (*story*) narración *f* personal; (*Fin*) cuenta *f* personal; **~ allowance** desgravación *f* personal; **~ appearance** aspecto *m* personal, aspecto *m* físico; (*Theat etc*) presentación *f* en directo, presentación *f* en vivo; **to make a ~ appearance** aparecer en persona; **~ assets** bienes *mpl* muebles; **~ assistant** ayudante *mf* personal; **~ call** (*Brit Telec*) llamada *f* a una persona especificada; **~ check** (*US*), **~ cheque** cheque *m* personal; **~ cleanliness** aseo *m* personal; **~ column** (sección *f* de) anuncios *mpl* personales; **~ computer** ordenador *m* personal; **~ effects** efectos *mpl* personales; **~ foul** falta *f* personal; **~ identification number** número *m* personal de identificación; **~ income** ingresos *mpl* personales; **~ income tax** impuesto *m* sobre la renta de las personas físicas; **~ investment** inversión *f* personal; **~ letter** carta *f* particular; **~ loan** préstamo *m* personal; **~ organizer** organizador *m* personal; **~ pronoun** pronombre *m* personal; **~ property** cosas *fpl* personales; bienes *mpl* muebles; **to ask ~ questions** hacer preguntas sobre asuntos íntimos; **~ relief** (*on tax*) desgravación *f* (de impuestos) personal; **~ secretary** secretario *m,* -a *f* particular; **~ security** (*on loan*) garantía *f* personal; **~ stereo** estéreo *m* personal; **don't be ~!** ¡Vd es un maleducado!; **to become ~** pasar a hacer crítica personal, empezar a hacer referencias de tipo personal; **I have no ~ knowledge of it** no lo conozco directamente; **my ~ view is that ...** creo para mí que ...; **to make a ~ application for sth** solicitar algo en persona.
2 *n* (*US* : *in magazine etc*) nota *f* de sociedad; (*message*) mensaje *m* personal.
personality [,pɜːsə'nælɪtɪ] **1** *n* (*character*) personalidad *f*; (*person, figure*) personaje *m*; figura *f*; **a well-known radio ~** una conocida figura de la radio; **to indulge in personalities** hacer crítica personal, cambiar personalismos, hacer referencias de tipo personal.
2 *attr*: **~ cult** culto *m* a la personalidad.
personalize ['pɜːsənəlaɪz] *vt* (**a**) *garment etc* marcar con iniciales (*etc*). (**b**) *argument etc* llevar al terreno de lo personal.
personalized ['pɜːsənəlaɪzd] *adj garment etc* con las iniciales (*etc*) de uno; *service etc* personal, creado para el individuo.
personally ['pɜːsnəlɪ] *adv* (**a**) (*for my etc part*) personalmente; **~ I think that ...** creo personalmente que ..., creo para mí que ...; **~ I am willing, but others ...** en cuanto a mí digo que sí, pero otros ...; **don't take it too ~** no vayas a creer que lo digo contra ti, no te des por aludido.
(**b**) (*in person*) **to hand sth over ~** entregar algo en persona; **the manager saw her ~** el gerente habló con ella en persona.
personalty ['pɜːsnltɪ] *n* bienes *mpl* muebles.
personate ['pɜːsəneɪt] *vt* (*impersonate*) hacerse pasar por; (*Theat*) hacer el papel de.
personification [pɜː,sɒnɪfɪ'keɪʃən] *n* personificación *f*; **he is the ~ of good taste** es la personificación del buen gusto, es el buen gusto en persona.
personify [pɜː'sɒnɪfaɪ] *vt* personificar; representar; **he personified the spirit of resistance** encarnó el espíritu de la resistencia; **he is greed personified** es la codicia en persona, es la personificación de la codicia.
person mover ['pɜːsən,muːvəʳ] *n* (*US*) cinta *f* transbordadora, pasillo *m* móvil.
personnel [,pɜːsə'nel] **1** *n* personal *m.* **2** *attr*: **~ agency** agencia *f* de personal; **~ carrier** transporte *m* de tropas; camión *m* blindado; **~ department** sección *f* de personal; **~ management** administración *f* del personal, gestión *f* de personal; **~ manager, ~ officer** jefe *mf* del personal.
perspective [pə'spektɪv] *n* perspectiva *f*; **from our ~** desde nuestro punto de vista; **in ~** en perspectiva; **let's get things in ~** pongamos las cosas en su sitio; **to see things in their proper ~** apreciar debidamente las cosas, apreciar las cosas en su justo valor; **he gets things out of ~** ve las cosas distorsionadas.
Perspex ['pɜːspeks] ® *n* (*esp Brit*) plexiglás ® *m.*
perspicacious [,pɜːspɪ'keɪʃəs] *adj* perspicaz.
perspicacity [,pɜːspɪ'kæsɪtɪ] *n* perspicacia *f.*
perspicuous [,pə'spɪkjʊəs] *adj* perspicuo.
perspicuity [,pɜːspɪ'kjuːɪtɪ] *n* perspicuidad *f.*
perspiration [,pɜːspə'reɪʃən] *n* transpiración *f*; sudor *m*; **beads of ~** gotitas *fpl* de sudor; **to be bathed in ~** estar bañado en sudor, estar todo sudoroso.
perspire [pəs'paɪəʳ] *vi* transpirar, sudar; **to ~ freely** sudar mucho.
perspiring [pəs'paɪərɪŋ] *adj* sudoroso.
persuadable [pə'sweɪdəbl] *adj* influenciable, persuasible; **he may be ~** quizá le podamos persuadir.
persuade [pə'sweɪd] *vt* persuadir, convencer; **to ~ sb to do sth** persuadir a uno a hacer algo, convencer a uno para que haga algo, inducir a uno a hacer algo; **but they ~d me not to** pero ellos me disuadieron, pero ellos me persuadieron a dejarlo; **to ~ sb that sth is true** convencer a uno de que algo es verdad; **I am ~d that ...** estoy convencido de que ...; **to ~ sb of the truth of a theory** convencer a uno de que una teoría es verdadera; **she is easily ~d** se deja convencer fácilmente; **it does not take much to ~ him** no se necesita mucho esfuerzo para persuadirle.
persuasion [pə'sweɪʒən] *n* (**a**) (*act*) persuasión *f.*
(**b**) (*persuasiveness*; *also* **power of ~**) persuasiva *f*; **he needed a lot of ~** había que ejercer mucha persuasiva; **I don't need much ~ to stop working** me cuesta poco dejar el trabajo.
(**c**) (*creed*) creencia *f,* secta *f*; opinión *f*; **I am not of that ~** no es ésa mi opinión, yo lo veo de otro modo; **the Methodist ~** la secta metodista; **and others of that ~** y otros que creen así.
persuasive [pə'sweɪsɪv] *adj* persuasivo; **I had to be very ~** tuve que ejercer mucha persuasión.
persuasively [pə'sweɪsɪvlɪ] *adv* de modo persuasivo.
persuasiveness [pə'sweɪsɪvnɪs] *n* persuasiva *f.*
PERT [pɜːt] *n abbr of* **programme evaluation and review technique** técnica *f* de evaluación y revisión de proyectos.
pert [pɜːt] *adj* (**a**) (*saucy*) impertinente, respondón, fresco*.
(**b**) (*jaunty*) elegante; coqueto.
pertain [pɜː'teɪn] *vi*: **to ~ to** (*concern*) tener que ver con, estar relacionado con; (*belong to*) pertenecer a; (*be the province of*) incumbir a; **and other matters ~ing to it** y otros asuntos relacionados, y otros asuntos pertenecientes.
pertinacious [,pɜːtɪ'neɪʃəs] *adj* pertinaz.
pertinaciously [,pɜːtɪ'neɪʃəslɪ] *adv* con pertinacia.
pertinacity [,pɜːtɪ'næsɪtɪ] *n* pertinacia *f.*
pertinence ['pɜːtɪnəns] *n* pertinencia *f,* oportunidad *f.*

pertinent ['pɜːtɪnənt] *adj* pertinente, oportuno, a propósito; **not very ~** poco oportuno, no muy a propósito.
pertinently ['pɜːtɪnəntlɪ] *adv* oportunamente, a propósito, atinadamente.
pertly ['pɜːtlɪ] *adv* de modo impertinente, descaradamente, con frescura.
pertness ['pɜːtnɪs] *n* (**a**) impertinencia *f*, frescura *f**. (**b**) elegancia *f*.
perturb [pə'tɜːb] *vt* perturbar, inquietar; **we are all very ~ed** todos estamos muy inquietos.
perturbation [,pɜːtɜː'beɪʃən] *n* perturbación *f*, inquietud *f*; **she asked in some ~** preguntó algo perturbada.
perturbing [pə'tɜːbɪŋ] *adj* perturbador, inquietante.
Peru [pə'ruː] *n* el Perú.
perusal [pə'ruːzəl] *n* lectura *f* (cuidadosa), examen *m* (detenido).
peruse [pə'ruːz] *vt* leer (con atención), examinar (con detenimiento).
Peruvian [pə'ruːvɪən] **1** *adj* peruano; **~ bark** quina *f*. **2** *n* peruano *m*, -a *f*.
perv* [pɜːv] *n* pervertido *m*, -a *f*.
pervade [pɜː'veɪd] *vt* extenderse por, difundirse por, empapar (de), impregnar, saturar; **to be ~d with** estar impregnado de, estar saturado de.
pervasive [pɜː'veɪsɪv] *adj* penetrante; omnipresente, generalizado.
perverse [pə'vɜːs] *adj* (*wicked*) perverso; (*obstinate*) terco, contumaz; (*wayward*) travieso, díscolo.
perversely [pə'vɜːslɪ] *adv* perversamente; tercamente; traviesamente.
perverseness [pə'vɜːsnɪs] *n* perversidad *f*; terquedad *f*, contumacia *f*; lo travieso.
perversion [pə'vɜːʃən] *n* perversión *f* (*also Med*); (*of facts, truth*) desnaturalización *f*, tergiversación *f*.
perversity [pə'vɜːsɪtɪ] *n* = **perverseness.**
pervert 1 ['pɜːvɜːt] *n* pervertido *m*, -a *f*. **2** [pə'vɜːt] *vt* pervertir (*also Med*); *taste etc* estragar, estropear; *words* torcer, forzar; *facts, truth* desnaturalizar, tergiversar; *talent* emplear mal.
perverted [pə'vɜːtɪd] *adj* (*all senses*) pervertido.
pervious ['pɜːvɪəs] *adj* permeable (*to* a).
peseta [pə'setə] *n* peseta *f*.
pesky* ['peskɪ] *adj* (*US*) molesto, fastidioso.
pessary ['pesərɪ] *n* pesario *m*, óvalo *m* (*Mex*).
pessimism ['pesɪmɪzəm] *n* pesimismo *m*.
pessimist ['pesɪmɪst] *n* pesimista *mf*.
pessimistic [,pesɪ'mɪstɪk] *adj* pesimista.
pessimistically [,pesɪ'mɪstɪkəlɪ] *adv* con pesimismo.
pest [pest] *n* (**a**) (*Zool*) plaga *f*; insecto *m* nocivo, animal *m* dañino; **the moth is a ~ of pinewoods** la mariposa es una plaga de los pinares; **rabbits are a ~ in Australia** el conejo es muy dañino en Australia; **this will kill the ~s on your roses** esto matará los insectos nocivos de sus rosas.
(**b**) (*fig*) (*person*) machaca *f*, mosca *f*, pelma *m*; (*thing*) molestia *f*, lata *f*; **what a ~ that child is!** ¡cómo me fastidia ese niño!; **it's a ~ having to go** es una lata tener que ir.
pest-control ['pestkən,trəʊl] **1** *n* lucha *f* contra los insectos nocivos, lucha *f* contra las plagas. **2** *attr*: **~ officer** oficial *m* del departamento de lucha contra plagas.
pester ['pestəʳ] *vt* molestar, acosar, importunar; **he's constantly ~ing me** no me deja a sol ni a sombra; **is this man ~ing you?** ¿le molesta este hombre?; **she ~ed me for the book** me pidió el libro repetidas veces; **he ~s me with his questions** me molesta con sus preguntas, me fastidia haciendo tantas preguntas; **stop ~ing!** ¡no machaques!; **to ~ sb to do sth** insistir constantemente en que uno haga algo, rogar repetidas veces que uno haga algo.
pesticide ['pestɪsaɪd] *n* pesticida *m*.
pestilence ['pestɪləns] *n* pestilencia *f*, peste *f*.
pestilent ['pestɪlənt] *adj* pestilente.
pestilential [,pestɪ'lenʃəl] *adj* pestilente; (*****) engorroso, latoso*****.
pestle ['pesl] *n* mano *f* (de mortero).
pet¹ [pet] **1** *adj animal* doméstico, domesticado, de casa, familiar; (*favourite*) favorito; *name etc* cariñoso; **a ~ lion** un león domesticado; **a ~ rabbit** un conejo casero; **her two ~ dogs** sus dos perros de casa; **it's my ~ subject** es mi tema predilecto; **~ aversion** bestia *f* negra, pesadilla *f*; **~ name** nombre *m* cariñoso, nombre *m* hipocorístico, (*short form*) diminutivo *m* cariñoso.
2 *n* (**a**) (*animal*) animal *m* doméstico, animal *m* de casa; animal *m* de compañía; perro *m*, gato *m* (*etc*); **no ~s are allowed in school** no se permite llevar animales a la escuela.
(**b**) (*person*) favorito *m*, -a *f*; persona *f* querida; persona *f* muy mimada; **yes, my ~** sí, mi cielo; **she's teacher's ~** es la favorita de la maestra; **he's rather a ~** es simpatiquísimo, es un ángel.
3 *vt* acariciar; (*****: *amorously*) acariciar, sobar, magrear******; (*spoil*) mimar.
4 *vi* (*****) acariciarse, besuquearse, sobarse, hacerse arrumacos.
pet² [pet] *n* rabieta***** *f*; **to be in a ~** estar de mal humor, estar enojado.
petal ['petl] *n* pétalo *m*.
petard [pe'tɑːd] *n* petardo *m*; **he was hoist with his own ~** le salió el tiro por la culata.
pet door [pet'dɔːʳ] *n* (*US*) gatera *f*.
Pete [piːt] *nm familiar form of* **Peter** (Perico); **for ~'s sake!*** ¡por Dios!
Peter ['piːtəʳ] *nm* Pedro; **~'s pence** dinero *m* de San Pedro; **to rob ~ to pay Paul** desnudar a un santo para vestir a otro; **~ the Great** Pedro el Grande; **~ Rabbit** el Conejo Peter.
peter¹ ['piːtəʳ] *vi*: **to ~ out** (*supply*) agotarse, acabarse; (*vein of metal etc*) desaparecer; (*plan etc*) quedar en agua de borrajas, parar en nada.
peter²** ['piːtəʳ] *n* (*US*) verga****** *f*, picha****** *f*.
peter³* ['piːtəʳ] *n* (*safe*) caja *f* de caudales; (*cell*) celda *f*.
petfood ['petfuːd] *n* comida *f* para animales.
petite [pə'tiːt] *adj* chiquita.
petition [pə'tɪʃən] **1** *n* petición *f*, instancia *f*, demanda *f*; súplica *f*; **~ for divorce** petición *f* de divorcio; **to file a ~** presentar una petición.
2 *vt person* dirigir una instancia a; **to ~ for sth** pedir algo, solicitar algo; **to ~ sb to do sth** rogar a uno hacer algo, pedir que uno haga algo.
3 *vi*: **to ~ for** pedir, solicitar.
petitioner [pə'tɪʃnəʳ] *n* suplicante *mf*, demandante *mf*.
Petrarch ['petrɑːk] *nm* Petrarca.
Petrarchan [pe'trɑːkən] *adj* petrarquista.
Petrarchism ['petrɑːkɪzəm] *n* petrarquismo *m*.
petrel ['petrəl] *n* petrel *m*, paíño *m*.
petrifaction [,petrɪ'fækʃən] *n*, **petrification** [,petrɪfɪ'keɪʃən] *n* petrificación *f*.
petrified ['petrɪfaɪd] *adj* petrificado; *V* **petrify.**
petrify ['petrɪfaɪ] **1** *vt* (**a**) (*lit*) petrificar; **to become petrified** petrificarse.
(**b**) (*fig*) pasmar, horrorizar; **I was simply petrified** me quedé de piedra; **to be petrified with fear** estar muerto de miedo.
2 *vi* petrificarse.
petrochemical [,petrəʊ'kemɪkəl] **1** *adj* petroquímico. **2** *n*: **~s** productos *mpl* petroquímicos.
petrodollar ['petrəʊ,dɒləʳ] *n* petrodólar *m*.
petrol ['petrəl] *n* (*Brit*) gasolina *f*, gas *m* (*Carib*), nafta *f* (*Argentina*), bencina *f* (*Chile*); (*for lighter*) bencina *f*; **to run out of ~** quedarse sin gasolina.
petrol-bomb ['petrəlbɒm] *n* (*Brit*) bomba *f* de gasolina.
petrol-can ['petrəlkæn] *n* (*Brit*) bidón *m* de gasolina.
petrol-engine ['petrəl,endʒɪn] *n* (*Brit*) motor *m* de gasolina.
petroleum [pɪ'trəʊlɪəm] **1** *n* petróleo *m*. **2** *attr*: **~ jelly** jalea *f* de petróleo; **~ products** derivados *mpl* del petróleo.
petrol (filler)-cap ['petrəl(,fɪlə),kæp] *n* tapón *m* de depósito.
petrol-gauge ['petrəlgeɪdʒ] *n* (*Brit*) indicador *m* de nivel de gasolina.
petrology [pe'trɒlɪdʒɪ] *n* petrología *f*.
petrol-pump ['petrəlpʌmp] *n* (*Brit*) (*in engine*) bomba *f* de gasolina; (*at garage*) surtidor *m* de gasolina.
petrol-station ['petrəl,steɪʃən] *n* (*Brit*) estación *f* de gasolina, gasolinera *f*, grifo *m* (*And*), estación *f* de servicio (*SC*).
petrol-tank ['petrəltæŋk] *n* (*Brit*) depósito *m* de gasolina.
petrol-tanker ['petrəl,tæŋkəʳ] *n* (*Brit*) gasolinero *m*.
petshop ['petʃɒp] *n* pajarería *f*.
petticoat ['petɪkəʊt] **1** *n* enaguas *fpl*; (*slip*) combinación *f*; (*stiff*) falda *f* can-can.
pettifogging ['petɪfɒgɪŋ] *adj detail etc* insignificante, pequeño, nimio; *lawyer etc* pedante, charlatán; *suggestion etc* hecho para entenebrecer el asunto.
pettily ['petɪlɪ] *adv* mezquinamente.
pettiness ['petɪnɪs] *n* (*V adj*) (**a**) insignificancia *f*, pequeñez *f*; nimiedad *f*; frivolidad *f*.
(**b**) mezquindad *f*; estrechez *f* de miras; rencor *m*; manía *f* de criticar; intolerancia *f*.
petting* ['petɪŋ] *n* caricias *fpl*, magreo***** *m*.
pettish ['petɪʃ] *adj* malhumorado.

petty ['petɪ] *adj* (**a**) *detail etc* insignificante, pequeño, nimio; de poca monta; *excuse* frívolo, baladí; **the ~ wars of the time** las pequeñas guerras de la época; **the ~ kings of Moslem Spain** los reyezuelos de la España musulmana.

(**b**) (*Brit: minor*) **~ cash** (dinero *m* para) gastos *mpl* menores; caja *f* chica*; **~ cash book** libro *m* de caja auxiliar; **~ claims** reclamaciones *mpl* menores; **~ expenses** gastos *mpl* menores; **~ larceny** robo *m* de menor cuantía; **~ officer** suboficial *m* de marina; **~ sessions** tribunal *m* de primera instancia.

(**c**) (*small-minded*) mezquino; de miras estrechas; (*preoccupied with detail*) quisquilloso; (*spiteful*) rencoroso; (*faultfinding*) reparón, criticón; (*intolerant*) intolerante; **you're being very ~ about it** en esto te estás mostrando poco comprensivo, en esto muestras que guardas rencor.

petulance ['petjʊləns] *n* mal humor *m*, irritabilidad *f*.

petulant ['petjʊlənt] *adj* malhumorado, irritable.

petulantly ['petjʊləntlɪ] *adv* malhumoradamente, con mal humor.

petunia [pɪ'tju:nɪə] *n* petunia *f*.

pew [pju:] *n* (*Eccl*) banco *m* (de iglesia, de los fieles); (*) asiento *m*; **take a ~!** ¡siéntate!; **can you find a ~?** ¿puedes buscarte un asiento?

pewter ['pju:tə^r] **1** *n* peltre *m*. **2** *attr* de peltre.

Pfc (*US Mil*) *abbr of* **private first class**.

PFLP *n abbr of* **Popular Front for the Liberation of Palestine** Frente *m* Popular de Liberación Palestina, FPLP *m*.

PG *n* (*Cine*) *abbr of* **Parental Guidance** = menores de 15 años acompañados.

PH *n* (*US Mil*) *abbr of* **Purple Heart**.

pH *n abbr of* **potential of hydrogen** potencial *m* de hidrógeno.

PHA *n* (*US*) *abbr of* **Public Housing Administration**.

phagocyte ['fægəʊsaɪt] *n* fagocito *m*.

phalange ['fælændʒ] *n* falange *f*; **P~** (*Spain*) Falange *f*.

phalangist [fæ'lændʒɪst] **1** *adj* falangista. **2** *n* falangista *mf*.

phalanx ['fælæŋks] *n* falange *f*.

phalarope ['fælərəʊp] *n* falaropo *m*.

phallic ['fælɪk] *adj* fálico.

phallus ['fæləs] *n*, *pl* **phalli** ['fælaɪ] *or* **phalluses** ['fæləsɪz] falo *m*.

phantasm ['fæntæzəm] *n* fantasma *m*.

phantasmagoria [,fæntæzmə'gɔ:rɪə] *n* fantasmagoría *f*.

phantasmagoric [,fæntæzmə'gɒrɪk] *adj* fantasmagórico.

phantasy ['fæntəzɪ] *n* fantasía *f*.

phantom ['fæntəm] **1** *n* fantasma *m*. **2** *adj* fantasmal; **~ pregnancy** embarazo *m* nervioso, pseudoembarazo *m*; **~ ship** buque *m* fantasma.

Pharaoh ['fɛərəʊ] *nm* Faraón.

Pharisaic(al) [,færɪ'seɪɪk(əl)] *adj* farisaico.

Pharisee ['færɪsi:] *n* fariseo *m*.

pharmaceutical [,fɑ:mə'sju:tɪkəl] **1** *adj* farmacéutico. **2 ~s** *npl* productos *mpl* farmacéuticos.

pharmacist ['fɑ:məsɪst] *n* farmacéutico *m*, -a *f*; **to go to the ~'s** ir a la farmacia.

pharmacological [,fɑ:məkə'lɒdʒɪkəl] *adj* farmacológico.

pharmacologist [,fɑ:mə'kɒlədʒɪst] *n* farmacólogo *m*, -a *f*.

pharmacology [,fɑ:mə'kɒlədʒɪ] *n* farmacología *f*.

pharmacopoeia, (*US sometimes*) **pharmacopeia** [,fɑ:məkə'pi:ə] *n* farmacopea *f*.

pharmacy ['fɑ:məsɪ] *n* farmacia *f*.

pharyngitis [,færɪn'dʒaɪtɪs] *n* faringitis *f*.

pharynx ['færɪŋks] *n* faringe *f*.

phase [feɪz] **1** *n* fase *f* (*also Astron*); etapa *f*; **to be in ~** estar en fase; **to be out of ~** estar desfasado, estar fuera de fase.

2 *vt plan etc* proyectar en una serie de etapas, escalonar; arreglar, organizar; **we must ~ this carefully** hay que organizar esto con cuidado; **~d development** desarrollo *m* por etapas; **a ~d withdrawal** una retirada progresiva, una retirada programada.

◆**phase in** *vt* escalonar; introducir poco a poco.

◆**phase out** *vt* reducir progresivamente, eliminar (*or* retirar) por etapas.

phase-out ['feɪz,aʊt] *n* (*esp US*) reducción *f* progresiva.

phatic ['fætɪk] *adj* fático.

Ph.D. *n abbr of* **Doctor of Philosophy** doctor *m*, -ora *f* en filosofía.

pheasant ['feznt] *n* faisán *m*.

phenobarbitone ['fi:nəʊ'bɑ:bɪtəʊn] *n* fenobarbitona *f*.

phenol ['fi:nɒl] *n* fenol *m*.

phenomena [fɪ'nɒmɪnə] *npl of* **phenomenon**.

phenomenal [fɪ'nɒmɪnl] *adj* fenomenal.

phenomenally [fɪ'nɒmɪnəlɪ] *adv* de modo fenomenal; **~ rich** rico en un grado fenomenal.

phenomenon [fɪ'nɒmɪnən] *n*, *pl* **phenomena** [fɪ'nɒmɪnə] fenómeno *m*.

pheromone ['ferəməʊn] *n* feromona *f*.

phew [fju:] *interj* ¡puf!; ¡caramba!, ¡uy!

phial ['faɪəl] *n* ampolla *f*, redoma *f*, frasco *m*.

Phi Beta Kappa ['faɪ'beɪtə'kæpə] *n* (*US Univ*) *asociación de antiguos alumnos sobresalientes*.

Phil [fɪl] *nm familiar form of* **Philip**.

Philadelphia [,fɪlə'delfɪə] *n* Filadelfia *f*.

philander [fɪ'lændə^r] *vi* flirtear, mariposear (*with* con).

philanderer [fɪ'lændərə^r] *n* tenorio *m*, mariposón *m*.

philandering [fɪ'lændərɪŋ] **1** *adj* mariposón. **2** *n* flirteo *m*.

philanthropic [,fɪlən'θrɒpɪk] *adj* filantrópico.

philanthropist [fɪ'lænθrəpɪst] *n* filántropo *m*, -a *f*.

philanthropy [fɪ'lænθrəpɪ] *n* filantropía *f*.

philatelic [,fɪlə'telɪk] *adj* filatélico.

philatelist [fɪ'lætəlɪst] *n* filatelista *mf*.

philately [fɪ'lætəlɪ] *n* filatelia *f*.

-phile [faɪl] *suf* -filo, *eg* **francophile** francófilo *m*, -a *f*.

philharmonic [fɪlɑ:'mɒnɪk] *adj* filarmónico.

-philia ['fɪlɪə] *suf* -filia, *eg* **francophilia** francofilia *f*.

Philip ['fɪlɪp] *nm* Felipe.

philippic [fɪ'lɪpɪk] *n* filípica *f*.

Philippine ['fɪlɪpi:n] **1** *adj* filipino. **2** *n* filipino *m*, -a *f*.

Philippines ['fɪlɪpi:nz] *npl*, **Philippine Islands** ['fɪlɪpi:n,aɪləndz] *npl* Filipinas *fpl*.

Philistine ['fɪlɪstaɪn] **1** *adj* filisteo (*also fig*). **2** *n* filisteo *m*, -a *f* (*also fig*).

philistinism ['fɪlɪstɪnɪzəm] *n* filisteísmo *m*.

Phillips ['fɪlɪps] ® *attr*: **~ screw** tornillo *m* de cabeza cruciforme; **~ screwdriver** destornillador *m* cruciforme.

philological [,fɪlə'lɒdʒɪkəl] *adj* filológico.

philologist [fɪ'lɒlədʒɪst] *n* filólogo *m*, -a *f*.

philology [fɪ'lɒlədʒɪ] *n* filología *f*.

philosopher [fɪ'lɒsəfə^r] *n* filósofo *m*, -a *f*; **~'s stone** piedra *f* filosofal.

philosophic(al) [,fɪlə'sɒfɪk(əl)] *adj* filosófico.

philosophically [,fɪlə'sɒfɪkəlɪ] *adv* filosóficamente.

philosophize [fɪ'lɒsəfaɪz] *vi* filosofar.

philosophy [fɪ'lɒsəfɪ] *n* filosofía *f*; **~ of life** filosofía *f* de la vida.

philtre, (*US*) **philter** ['fɪltə^r] *n* filtro *m*, poción *f*.

phiz* [fɪz] *n* jeta* *f*.

phlebitis [flɪ'baɪtɪs] *n* flebitis *f*.

phlegm [flem] *n* flema *f* (*also fig*).

phlegmatic [fleg'mætɪk] *adj* flemático.

phlegmatically [fleg'mætɪkəlɪ] *adv* con flema; **he said ~** dijo flemático.

phlox [flɒks] *n* flox *m*.

Phnom Penh, Pnom Penh ['nɒm'pen] *n* Phnom Penh *m*.

-phobe [fəʊb] *suf* -fobo, *eg* **francophobe** francófobo *m*, -a *f*.

phobia ['fəʊbɪə] *n* fobia *f*.

-phobia ['fəʊbɪə] *suf* -fobia, *eg* **anglophobia** anglofobia *f*.

phobic ['fəʊbɪk] *adj* fóbico.

Phoebus ['fi:bəs] *nm* Febo.

Phoenicia [fɪ'nɪʃɪə] *n* Fenicia *f*.

Phoenician [fɪ'nɪʃɪən] **1** *adj* fenicio. **2** *n* fenicio *m*, -a *f*.

phoenix ['fi:nɪks] *n* fénix *m*.

phone^1* [fəʊn] **1** *n* = **telephone**. **2** *attr*: **~ book** *etc* = **telephone book** *etc*.

◆**phone up** *vti* llamar (al teléfono).

phone^2 [fəʊn] *n* (*Ling*) fono *m*.

phonecard ['fəʊnkɑ:d] *n* tarjeta *f* telefónica.

phone-in ['fəʊnɪn] *n* (*also* **~ programme**) (programa *m*) coloquio *m* (por teléfono).

phoneme ['fəʊni:m] *n* fonema *m*.

phonemic [fəʊ'ni:mɪk] *adj* fonémico.

phonetic [fəʊ'netɪk] *adj* fonético.

phonetician [,fəʊnɪ'tɪʃən] *n* fonetista *mf*.

phonetics [fəʊ'netɪks] *n* fonética *f*.

phon(e)y* ['fəʊnɪ] **1** *adj* falso, postizo; fingido, simulado; mixtificado; sospechoso; insincero; **the ~ war** (*1939*) la extraña guerra; **it's completely ~** no es lo que parece ser en absoluto; **there's sth ~ about it** esto huele a camelo.

2 *n* (*person*) farsante* *mf*; (*thing*) cosa *f* falsa, cosa *f* postiza; **it's a ~** es falso, es un engaño.

phonic ['fɒnɪk] *adj* fónico.

phono... ['fəʊnəʊ] *pref* fono...

phonograph ['fəʊnəgrɑ:f] *n* (*US*) gramófono *m*, fonógrafo *m*, tocadiscos *m*.

phonological [,fəʊnə'lɒdʒɪkəl] *adj* fonológico.

phonology [fəʊ'nɒlədʒɪ] *n* fonología *f*.

phony* ['fəʊnɪ] *adj* = **phoney**.

phooey* ['fu:ɪ] *excl* (*rubbish*) ¡bobadas!; (*annoyance*) ¡qué

tonto soy!; (*disappointment*) ¡ay!
phosgene ['fɒzdʒiːn] *n* fosgeno *m.*
phosphate ['fɒsfeɪt] *n* fosfato *m.*
phosphide ['fɒsfaɪd] *n* fosfito *m.*
phosphine ['fɒsfiːn] *n* fosfino *m.*
phosphoresce [ˌfɒsfə'res] *vi* fosforecer.
phosphorescence [ˌfɒsfə'resns] *n* fosforescencia *f.*
phosphorescent [ˌfɒsfə'resnt] *adj* fosforescente.
phosphoric [fɒs'fɒrɪk] *adj* fosfórico.
phosphorous ['fɒsfərəs] *adj* fosforoso.
phosphorus ['fɒsfərəs] *n* fósforo *m.*
photo ['fəʊtəʊ] *n* foto *f*; ~ **booth** fotomatón *m*, cabina *f* de fotos; ~ **opportunity** = **photocall**; = **photograph.**
photo... ['fəʊtəʊ] *pref* foto...
photocall ['fəʊtəʊkɔːl] *n* rueda *f* fotográfica, oportunidad *f* fotográfica.
photochemical [ˌfəʊtəʊ'kemɪkəl] *adj* fotoquímico.
photocomposer [ˌfəʊtəʊkəm'pəʊzər] *n* fotocomponedora *f.*
photocopier ['fəʊtəʊ'kɒpɪər] *n* fotocopiadora *f.*
photocopy ['fəʊtəʊˌkɒpɪ] **1** *n* fotocopia *f.* **2** *vt* fotocopiar.
photocopying ['fəʊtəʊˌkɒpɪɪŋ] *n* fotocopia *f.*
photocoverage ['fəʊtəʊˌkʌvərɪdʒ] *n* reportaje *m* gráfico.
photodisk ['fəʊtəʊˌdɪsk] *n* fotodisco *m.*
photoelectric ['fəʊtəʊɪ'lektrɪk] *adj* fotoeléctrico; ~ **cell** célula *f* fotoeléctrica.
photoelectron [ˌfəʊtəʊɪ'lektrɒn] *n* fotoelectrón *m.*
photoengraving ['fəʊtəʊen'greɪvɪŋ] *n* fotograbado *m.*
photo-finish ['fəʊtəʊ'fɪnɪʃ] *n* resultado *m* comprobado por fotocontrol; (*fig*) final *m* muy reñido.
Photofit ['fəʊtəʊfɪt] ® *attr*: ~ **picture** retrato *m* robot.
photoflash ['fəʊtəʊflæʃ] *n* flash *m*, relámpago *m.*
photogenic [ˌfəʊtəʊ'dʒenɪk] *adj* fotogénico.
photograph ['fəʊtəgræf] **1** *n* fotografía *f* (*foto*); **to take a ~** sacar una foto.
2 *attr*: ~ **album** álbum *m* de fotos.
3 *vt* fotografiar, hacer una fotografía de, sacar una foto de; **'~ed by X'** 'fotografía de X'.
4 *vi*: **to ~ well** ser fotogénico, sacar buena foto.
photographer [fə'tɒgrəfər] *n* fotógrafo *m*, -a *f.*
photographic [ˌfəʊtə'græfɪk] *adj* fotográfico.
photographically [ˌfəʊtə'græfɪkəlɪ] *adv* fotográficamente; **to record sth ~** registrar algo por medio de fotografías, hacer una historia fotográfica de algo.
photography [fə'tɒgrəfɪ] *n* fotografía *f.*
photogravure [ˌfəʊtəgrə'vjʊər] *n* fotograbado *m.*
photojournalism ['fəʊtəʊ'dʒɜːnəˌlɪzəm] *n* fotoperiodismo *m.*
photokit ['fəʊtəʊkɪt] *n* retrato *m* robot.
photometer [fə'tɒmɪtər] *n* fotómetro *m.*
photomontage [ˌfəʊtəʊmɒn'tɑːʒ] *n* fotomontaje *m.*
photon ['fəʊtɒn] *n* fotón *m.*
photosensitive [ˌfəʊtəʊ'sensɪtɪv] *adj* fotosensible.
photosetting ['fəʊtəʊˌsetɪŋ] **1** *n* fotocomposición *f.* **2** *attr*: ~ **machine** fotocompositora *f.*
photostat ['fəʊtəʊstæt] (® *in US*) **1** *n* fotóstato *m.* **2** *vt* fotostatar.
photosynthesis [ˌfəʊtəʊ'sɪnθəsɪs] *n* fotosíntesis *f.*
phototropism ['fəʊtəʊ'trəʊpɪzəm] *n* fototropismo *m.*
phototype ['fəʊtəʊˌtaɪp] *n* fototipo *m.*
photovoltaic [ˌfəʊtəʊvɒl'teɪɪk] *adj* fotovoltaico; ~ **cell** célula *f* fotovoltaica.
phrasal ['freɪzəl] *adj* frasal; ~ **verb** verbo *m* frasal, verbo *m* con preposición (*or* adverbio).
phrase [freɪz] **1** *n* frase *f* (*also Mus*), expresión *f*, locución *f*; **to coin a ~** para decirlo así; si se me permite la frase; **he knows how to turn a ~** a veces es muy elocuente, sabe crear frases muy expresivas.
2 *vt* expresar; **a carefully ~d letter** una carta redactada con cuidado; **can we ~ that differently?** ¿podemos poner eso de otro modo?
3 *attr*: ~ **marker** marcador *m* de frase; ~ **structure** estructura *f* de frase.
phrasebook ['freɪzbʊk] *n* libro *m* de frases.
phraseology [ˌfreɪzɪ'ɒlədʒɪ] *n* fraseología *f.*
phrasing ['freɪzɪŋ] *n* (*act*) redacción *f*; (*style*) estilo *m*, fraseología *f*, términos *mpl*; (*Mus*) fraseo *m*; **the ~ is rather unfortunate** la forma de expresarse no es apropiada.
phrenetic [frɪ'netɪk] *adj* frenético.
phrenologist [frɪ'nɒlədʒɪst] *n* frenólogo *m*, -a *f.*
phrenology [frɪ'nɒlədʒɪ] *n* frenología *f.*
phthisis ['θaɪsɪs] *n* tisis *f.*
phut* [fʌt] *adj*: **to go ~** estropearse, romperse, hacer kaput*; (*fig*) fracasar, acabarse.
phylactery [fɪ'læktərɪ] *n* filacteria *f.*
phylloxera [ˌfɪlɒk'sɪərə] *n* filoxera *f.*
physic ['fɪzɪk] *n* (††) medicina *f.*
physical ['fɪzɪkəl] *adj* (**a**) (*of the body*) físico; ~ **condition** estado *m* físico; ~ **culture** cultura *f* física; ~ **education** educación *f* física; ~ **examination** reconocimiento *m* físico; ~ **geography** geografía *f* física; ~ **jerks*** (*Brit*) ejercicios *mpl* físicos, gimnasia *f*; ~ **record** registro *m* físico; ~ **science** ciencias *fpl* físicas; ~ **training** gimnasia *f.*
(**b**) (*fig*) material; **a ~ impossibility** una imposibilidad material; ~ **inspection** inspección *f* material.
(**c**) (*Sport*: *euph*) *play* duro.
physically ['fɪzɪkəlɪ] *adv* físicamente.
physician [fɪ'zɪʃən] *n* médico *m*, -a *f.*
physicist ['fɪzɪsɪst] *n* físico *m*, -a *f.*
physics ['fɪzɪks] *n* física *f.*
physio* ['fɪzɪəʊ] *n* (*Sport*) = **physiotherapist.**
physio... ['fɪzɪəʊ] *pref* fisio...
physiognomy [ˌfɪzɪ'ɒnəmɪ] *n* fisonomía *f.*
physiological ['fɪzɪə'lɒdʒɪkəl] *adj* fisiológico.
physiologist [ˌfɪzɪ'ɒlədʒɪst] *n* fisiólogo *m*, -a *f.*
physiology [ˌfɪzɪ'ɒlədʒɪ] *n* fisiología *f.*
physiotherapist [ˌfɪzɪə'θerəpɪst] *n* fisioterapeuta *mf*, fisioterapista *mf.*
physiotherapy [ˌfɪzɪə'θerəpɪ] *n* fisioterapia *f.*
physique [fɪ'ziːk] *n* físico *m*, complexión *f.*
phytobiology [ˌfaɪtəʊbaɪ'ɒlədʒɪ] *n* fitobiología *f.*
phytofagous [faɪ'tɒfəgəs] *adj* fitófago.
phytopathology [ˌfaɪtəʊpə'θɒlədʒɪ] *n* fitopatología *f.*
pi[1]* [paɪ] *adj* piadoso, devoto.
pi[2] [paɪ] *n* (*Math*) pi *m.*
pianist ['pɪənɪst] *n* pianista *mf.*
piano ['pjɑːnəʊ] **1** *n* piano *m.*
2 *attr*: ~ **concerto** concierto *m* para piano; ~ **duet** dúo *m* de piano; ~ **lesson** lección *f* de piano; ~ **piece** música *f* para piano; ~ **teacher** profesor *m*, -ora *f* de piano.
piano-accordion ['pjɑːnəʊə'kɔːdɪən] *n* acordeón-piano *m.*
pianoforte [ˌpjɑːnəʊ'fɔːtɪ] *n* = **piano.**
pianola [pɪə'nəʊlə] *n* pianola *f.*
piano-stool ['pjɑːnəʊˌstuːl] *n* taburete *m* de piano.
piano-tuner ['pjɑːnəʊˌtjuːnər] *n* afinador *m*, -ora *f* de pianos.
piastre, (*US*) **piaster** [pɪ'æstər] *n* piastra *f.*
piazza [pɪ'ætsə] *n* (*US*) pórtico *m*, galería *f.*
pic* [pɪk], *pl* **pics** *or* **pix** [pɪks] *n abbr of* **picture** foto *f.*
pica ['paɪkə] *n* (*Med, Vet*) pica *f*; (*Typ*) cícero *m.*
Picardy ['pɪkədɪ] *n* Picardía *f.*
picaresque [ˌpɪkə'resk] *adj* picaresco; ~ **novel** novela *f* picaresca.
picayune [ˌpɪkə'juːn] (*US*) **1** *adj* de poca monta. **2** *n* (*person*) persona *f* insignificante; (*thing*) bagatela *f.*
piccalilli ['pɪkəˌlɪlɪ] *n* legumbres *fpl* en escabeche, encurtidos *mpl* picantes.
piccaninny ['pɪkəˌnɪnɪ] *n* negrito *m*, -a *f.*
piccolo ['pɪkələʊ] *n* flautín *m*, píccolo *m.*
pick [pɪk] **1** *n* (**a**) (*tool*) pico *m*, zapapico *m*, piqueta *f.*
(**b**) (*choice, right to choose*) derecho *m* de elección; **it's your ~** a ti te toca elegir; **whose ~ is it?** ¿a quién le toca elegir?; **he had his ~ of the books** él escogió los libros que quería; él pudo llevarse los mejores libros; **take your ~!** ¡a elegir!
(**c**) (*best*) lo mejor, lo más escogido; flor *f* y nata; **it's the ~ of the bunch** es el mejor del grupo.
2 *vt* (**a**) *hole etc* picar, hacer; *teeth* mondarse, limpiarse; *nose* hurgarse; *bone* roer; *bird* desplumar; *sore etc* rascar; manosear; *lock* forzar, abrir con ganzúa.
(**b**) (*choose*) escoger, elegir; escoger con cuidado; *team* seleccionar; **to ~ one's way** andar con mucho tiento (*across* por), abrirse camino (*among* entre, *through* por).
(**c**) **to ~ pockets** ratear, robar carteras, ser carterista; **to ~ sb's pocket** robar algo del bolsillo de uno; **he had his pocket ~ed** le robaron la cartera (*etc*).
(**d**) (*pluck*) coger (*Sp*), recoger (*LAm*).
3 *vi*: **to ~ and choose** tardar en decidirse; hacer melindres al escoger, mostrarse difícil; **I like to ~ and choose** me gusta elegir con cuidado.
◆**pick at** *vt* (**a**) *sore etc* rascar; manosear; **to ~ at one's food** comer con poco apetito, picar.
(**b**) (*US**) = **pick on** (**b**).
◆**pick off** *vt* (**a**) *paint* arrancar, separar; **to ~ sth off the ground** recoger algo del suelo.
(**b**) (*shoot*) matar de un tiro; matar con tiros sucesivos; *opponents* acabar uno a uno con.
◆**pick on** *vt* (**a**) (*single out*) esoger; designar, nombrar; **why ~ on me?** ¿por qué lo dices a mí y no a otro?
(**b**) (*harass*) perseguir; criticar mucho; fastidiar; **he's always ~ing on me** me tiene manía.

(c) (*US*: *choose*) = **pick out** (a).

◆**pick out** *vt* (a) (*choose*) elegir, escoger; entresacar.

(b) (*distinguish*) distinguir (*among* entre, *from* de); (*recognize*) conocer, identificar (*by* por); (*discern*) alcanzar a ver.

(c) *tune* tocar de oído (*on the piano* al piano).

(d) (*highlight*) destacar, hacer resaltar.

◆**pick over, pick through** *vt* ir revolviendo y examinando.

◆**pick up 1** *vt* (a) (*lift*) recoger; levantar, alzar; *telephone* descolgar; *child* levantar en los brazos.

(b) (*collect*) recoger, buscar (*esp LAm*); **I'll call and ~ it up** pasaré por casa a recogerlo.

(c) (*Aut*) *hitch-hiker* recoger.

(d) (*: *sexually*) ligar*, ligar con*.

(e) (*acquire*) adquirir; (*buy*) comprar, adquirir; (*find*) encontrar; (*learn*) aprender, adquirir; *information* saber, indagar; saber por casualidad; *disease* contagiarse con; *habit* adquirir; **he ~s up £400 a week** gana 400 libras a la semana; **he ~s up a living selling antiques** se gana la vida vendiendo antigüedades.

(f) (*Rad*) captar, sintonizar; **the dog ~ed up the scent** el perro cogió el rastro; **our ears cannot ~ up that sound** nuestro oído no percibe ese sonido.

(g) (*Naut etc*: *rescue*) recoger, rescatar.

(h) (*arrest*) detener.

(i) (*focus on*) destacar; subrayar; **I want to ~ up three points** quiero subrayar tres temas.

(j) (*reprimand*) reprender; **he ~ed me up on my grammar** me señaló diversas faltas de gramática; **may I ~ you up on one point?** ¿me permites criticarte en un punto?

(k) **to ~ up speed** acelerar, cobrar velocidad.

(l) (*: *steal*) birlar*.

2 *vi* (a) (*improve*) mejorar; (*Med*) reponerse; (*business etc*) ir mejor; **the game ~ed up in the second half** se jugó mejor en el segundo tiempo.

(b) (*put on speed*) acelerarse, ir cobrando velocidad.

(c) **we ~ed up where we had left off** reanudamos la conversación (*etc*) donde la habíamos dejado.

3 *vr*: **to ~ o.s. up** ponerse de pie, levantarse; (*fig*) restablecerse.

pickaback ['pɪkəbæk] *adv*: **to carry sb ~** llevar a uno sobre los hombros, llevar a uno a cuestas.

pickaxe, (*US*) **pickax** ['pɪkæks] *n* pico *m*, zapapico *m*, piqueta *f*.

picked [pɪkt] *adj* escogido, selecto.

picker ['pɪkəʳ] *n* (*of fruit etc*) recolector *m*, -ora *f*.

picket ['pɪkɪt] **1** *n* (a) (*stake*) estaca *f*.

(b) (*all other senses*) piquete *m*.

2 *attr*: **~ duty** servicio *m* de piquetes.

3 *vt factory* piquetear, estacionar piquetes a la puerta de.

4 *vi* estar de guardia (los piquetes).

picketing ['pɪkɪtɪŋ] *n* piquete *m*, el piquetear.

picket-line ['pɪkɪtlaɪn] *n* piquete *m*; **to cross a ~** no hacer caso de un piquete.

picking ['pɪkɪŋ] *n* (a) (*of fruit etc*) recolección *f*, cosecha *f*; (*act of choosing*) elección *f*, selección *f*.

(b) **~s** (*leftovers*) sobras *fpl*, desperdicios *mpl*; (*profits*) ganancias *fpl*; (*stolen goods*) artículos *mpl* robados.

pickle ['pɪkl] **1** *n* (a) (*as condiment*: *also* **~s**) encurtido *m*; (*of fish, olives*) escabeche *m*; (*of meat*) adobo *m*; (*in salt solution*) salmuera *f*.

(b) (*) (*plight*) apuro *m*; **to be in a ~** (*person*) estar en un apuro, (*room*) estar en desorden, estar revuelto; **to get into a ~** meterse en líos*; **what a ~!** ¡qué lío!*

(c) (*: *child*) diablillo *m*, pillo *m*.

2 *vt* encurtir; escabechar; adobar; conservar, conservar en vinagre; (*Bio*) conservar en alcohol, conservar en formalina.

pickled ['pɪkld] *adj* (a) *food* escabechado, encurtido, en conserva; **~ onions** cebollas *fpl* en vinagre; **~ herrings** arenques *mpl* en escabeche; **~ walnuts** nueces *fpl* adobadas.

(b) **to be ~‡** (*drunk*) estar jumado*.

picklock ['pɪklɒk] *n* ganzúa *f*.

pick-me-up ['pɪkmiːʌp] *n* (*Brit*) (*Med*) tónico *m*; (*alcohol*) bebida *f*, trago *m*.

pickpocket ['pɪk,pɒkɪt] *n* carterista *m*, ratero *m*, bolsista *m* (*Mex*).

pick-up ['pɪkʌp] **1** *n* (a) (*Mus*) pick-up *m*.

(b) (*Aut*: *also* **~ truck,** (*Brit*) **~ van**) furgoneta *f*, camioneta *f* (de reparto).

(c) (*) ligue* *m*.

2 *attr*: **~ arm** pick-up *m*, fonocaptor *m*; **~ point** punto *m* de recogida.

picky* ['pɪkɪ] *adj* (*US*) (a) (*critical*) criticón. (b) (*choosy*) melindroso, delicado.

picnic ['pɪknɪk] **1** *n* jira *f*, excursión *f* campestre, merienda *f* en el campo, picnic *m*; **to go for a ~, to go on a ~** ir de jira, merendar en el campo; **we found a nice place for a ~** encontramos un buen sitio para merendar; **it was no ~*** no era nada fácil; no tenía nada de agradable.

2 *attr*: **~ basket** canasta *f* para bocadillos; **~ site** lugar *m* destinado para picnics.

3 *vi* ir de jira, merendar en el campo; llevar la merienda al campo; **we ~ked by the river** merendamos junto al río; **we go ~king every Sunday** todos los domingos vamos de jira.

picnicker ['pɪknɪkəʳ] *n* excursionista *mf*.

pics* [pɪks] *npl abbr of* **pictures** (a) (*Cine*) cine *m*, películas *fpl*. (b) (*Phot*) fotos *fpl*.

Pict [pɪkt] *n* picto *m*, -a *f*.

Pictish ['pɪktɪʃ] **1** *adj* picto. **2** *n* picto *m*.

pictogram ['pɪktəʊgræm] *n* pictograma *m*.

pictograph ['pɪktəgrɑːf] *n* (a) (*record, chart etc*) pictografía *f*. (b) (*Ling*) (*symbol*) pictograma *m*; (*writing*) pictografía *f*.

pictorial [pɪk'tɔːrɪəl] **1** *adj* pictórico; *magazine* gráfico, ilustrado. **2** *n* revista *f* ilustrada.

pictorially [pɪk'tɔːrɪəlɪ] *adv* pictóricamente; *represent etc* gráficamente, por imágenes.

picture ['pɪktʃəʳ] **1** *n* (a) (*Art*) cuadro *m*, pintura *f*; (*portrait*) retrato *m*; (*photo*) fotografía *f*; (*in book*) lámina *f*, estampa *f*, grabado *m*.

(b) (*TV*) cuadro *m*, imagen *f*.

(c) (*Cine*) película *f*, film *m*; **the ~s** (*esp Brit*) el cine; **to go to a ~** ir a ver una película; **to go to the ~s** (*esp Brit*) ir al cine.

(d) (*spoken etc*) descripción *f*; (*mental*) imagen *f*; idea *f*; recuerdo *m*; (*outlook*) perspectiva *f*; (*overall view*) visión *f* de conjunto; **the other side of the ~** el reverso de la medalla; **she looked a ~!** ¡estaba guapísima!; **the garden is a ~ in June** en junio el jardín es de lo más hermoso; **his face was a ~!** ¡había que ver la cara que puso!; **it was a ~ of devastation** todo fue devastación; **she looked a ~ of health** era la salud personificada; **he gave us a grim ~** nos hizo una descripción horrorosa; **he painted a black ~ of the future** nos hizo un cuadro muy negro del porvenir; **I have no very clear ~ of it** no lo recuerdo con claridad; **these figures give the general ~** estas cifras ofrecen una visión de conjunto; **are you in the ~?*** ¿estás enterado?; **I get the ~*** ya comprendo; **to put sb in the ~*** poner a uno al corriente, poner a uno en antecedentes.

2 *attr* de pinturas, de cuadros; *paper* gráfico, ilustrado; **~ card** (*Cards*) carta *f* de figura; **~ hat** pamela *f*; **~ window** ventanal *m*, ventana *f* grande.

3 *vt* (*paint*) pintar; (*describe*) pintar, describir; **to ~ sth to o.s.** imaginarse algo, representarse algo en la imaginación; **~ the scene** figúraos la escena; **~ if you can a winkle** imaginaos, si podéis, un bígaro.

picture-book ['pɪktʃəbʊk] *n* libro *m* de imágenes.

picture-frame ['pɪktʃəfreɪm] *n* marco *m* (para cuadro).

picture gallery ['pɪktʃə'gælərɪ] *n* museo *m* de pintura, museo *m* de bellas artes, pinacoteca *f*; **the Prado ~** el Museo del Prado.

picturegoer ['pɪktʃə,gəʊəʳ] *n* aficionado *m*, -a *f* al cine.

picture-palace ['pɪktʃə,pælɪs] *n* (†) cine *m*.

picture postcard ['pɪktʃə'pəʊstkɑːd] *n* tarjeta *f* postal.

picture-rail ['pɪktʃəreɪl] *n* moldura *f* (*pegada a la pared para colgar cuadros*).

picturesque [,pɪktʃə'resk] *adj* pintoresco; (*quaint, of tourist interest*) típico.

picturesquely [,pɪktʃə'resklɪ] *adv* de modo pintoresco.

picturesqueness [,pɪktʃə'resknɪs] *n* lo pintoresco; pintoresquismo *m*.

piddle ['pɪdl] = **piss**.

piddling* ['pɪdlɪŋ] *adj* de poca monta, insignificante.

pidgin ['pɪdʒɪn] *n* (*also* **~ English**) *lengua franca* (*inglés-chino*) *comercial del Lejano Oriente*.

pie [paɪ] *n* (*of fruit etc*) pastel *m*, tarta *f*, pay *m* (*LAm*); (*of meat*) empanada *f*, pastel *m*; **it's ~ in the sky** es como prometer la luna; **to eat humble ~** humillarse y pedir perdón, morder el polvo.

piebald ['paɪbɔːld] **1** *adj* pío, de varios colores. **2** *n* caballo *m* pío.

piece [piːs] **1** *n* (a) (*fragment*) pedazo *m*, trozo *m*, fragmento *m*; (*Mech, Mil*) pieza *f*; (*coin*) moneda *f*, pieza *f*; (*Liter, Theat, Mus*) obra *f*, pieza *f*; (*Chess*) pieza *f*; **a 50-pence ~** una moneda de 50 peniques; **that nice ~ in the third movement** aquel pasaje tan bonito del tercer tiempo; **to buy sth by the ~** comprar algo por piezas; **it is made all in one ~** está hecho de una pieza, forma pieza única, las partes no son separables; **the back is all of a ~ with the seat** el respaldo forma pieza única con el asiento; **to get back all in one ~** volver sano y salvo; **we got it back all in one ~** nos lo devolvieron en buen estado; **this is of a ~ with the other** éste es de la misma clase que el otro, éste se parece al otro; **this is of a ~ with what he told us** esto es conforme con lo que nos dijo, esto concuerda con lo que nos dijo; **to pick up the ~s** recoger los platos rotos; **to leave sb to pick up the ~s** dejar que otro pague los platos rotos; **I said my ~ and left** dije lo que tenía que decir y salí; **when do I say my ~?** ¿cuándo digo lo mío?

(**b**) **a nice little ~**‡ (*girl*) una pizpireta*, una chica muy mona.

(**c**) (*examples of* **a ~ of**) **a ~ of paper** un trozo de papel, una hoja de papel, un papel; **a ~ of soap** un cacho de jabón; **a ~ of string** un cabo; **a ~ of bread** un pedazo de pan; **a ~ of cake** una porción de tarta; **it's a ~ of cake*** es pan comido, está tirado; **another ~ of cake?** ¿quieres más tarta?; **a ~ of my work** una de mis obras, una muestra de mi trabajo; **a ~ out of a book** un trozo de un libro; **a ~ of advice** un consejo; **a ~ of carelessness** un descuido, un acto de imprudencia; **a ~ of clothing** una prenda (de vestir); **a ~ of folly** una locura, un acto de locura; **a ~ of furniture** un mueble; **a ~ of ground** un lote de terreno, un terreno, (*for building*) un solar; **by a ~ of good luck** por suerte; **a ~ of luggage** un bulto; **3 ~s of luggage** 3 bultos; **a ~ of news** una noticia, una nueva; **a ~ of poetry** una poesía; **to give sb a ~ of one's mind** decir cuatro verdades a uno, cantar las cuarenta a uno.

(**d**) **to be in ~s** (*taken apart*) estar desmontado, (*broken*) estar hecho pedazos, estar roto; **to break sth to** (*or* **in**) **~s** hacer algo pedazos; **to break** (*vi*) **in ~s** hacerse pedazos; **to come to ~s, to fall to ~s** hacerse pedazos, romperse; **it comes to ~s** se desmonta, es desmontable; **to go to ~s** (*person*) sufrir un ataque de nervios, perder el control, (*government etc*) venirse abajo, (*Med*) perder la salud, (*team etc*) desanimarse por completo; **to hack sth to ~s** cortar algo en pedazos (violentamente, despiadadamente *etc*); **to pull to ~s** deshacer, despedazar, hacer pedazos, *argument* deshacer, *person* criticar duramente; **to say one's ~** decir lo que uno quiere decir; **to smash sth to ~s** destrozar algo violentamente, romper algo a golpes; **the boat was smashed to ~s on the rocks** el barco se estrelló contra las rocas y se hizo astillas; **to take sth to ~s** desmontar algo; **it takes to ~s** se desmonta, es desmontable; **to tear sth to ~s** romper algo violentamente, (*prey etc*) desgarrar algo; **the crowd will tear him to ~s** la gente le hará pedazos; **he tore the theory to ~s** destrozó la teoría por completo.

2 *attr*: **~ rate** (*Comm*) tarifa *f* a destajo.

◆**piece together** *vt* juntar, juntar las partes de; (*Mech*) montar, ir montando; (*fig*) atar cabos e ir comprendiendo; **we eventually ~d the story together** por fin logramos saber toda la historia, por fin logramos atar todos los cabos.

pièce de résistance [ˌpjɛsdərezɪs'tɑ̃:s] *n* lo principal, lo más importante; (*on menu*) plato *m* principal; (*in programme*) atracción *f* principal, número *m* más importante.

piecemeal ['pi:smi:l] **1** *adv* (*bit by bit*) poco a poco, a pedacitos, a trozos, por etapas; (*haphazard*) sin sistema fijo. **2** *adj* poco sistemático.

piecework ['pi:swɜ:k] *n* trabajo *m* a destajo; **to be on ~, to do ~** trabajar a destajo.

pieceworker ['pi:swɜ:kəʳ] *n* destajista *mf*.

pie-chart ['paɪtʃɑ:t] *n* (*Math*) gráfico *m* circular, gráfico *m* de sectores (*or* de tarta); (*Comput*) tarta *f*.

piecrust ['paɪkrʌst] **1** *n* pasta *f* de pastel. **2** *attr*: **~ pastry** (*US*) pasta *f* quebradiza.

pied [paɪd] *adj animal* pío, de varios colores; *bird* manchado; **the P~ Piper of Hamelin** el flautista de Hamelín.

pied-à-terre [ˌpɪeɪdæ'tɛəʳ] *n* apeadero *m*.

Piedmont ['pi:dmɒnt] *n* Piamonte *m*.

Piedmontese [ˌpi:dmɒn'ti:z] **1** *adj* piamontés. **2** *n* piamontés *m*, -esa *f*.

pie-eyed* ['paɪ'aɪd] *adj* jumado*.

pier [pɪəʳ] *n* (**a**) (*Archit*) pilar *m*, columna *f*; (*of bridge*) estribo *m*, pila *f*. (**b**) (*Naut*) dique *m*, malecón *m*, embarcadero *m*; paseo *m* marítimo (sobre malecón).

pierce [pɪəs] *vt* penetrar; atravesar, traspasar; (*hole*) agujerear; (*bore*) horadar, perforar; (*punch*) taladrar; (*puncture*) pinchar; **the bullet ~d the armour** la bala penetró en la coraza; **the bullet ~d his lung** la bala le atravesó el pulmón, la bala entró en el pulmón; **to have one's ears ~d** hacerse abrir las orejas; **the rock is ~d by numerous holes** la roca está agujereada (*or* horadada) en muchos sitios; **a nail ~d the tyre** un clavo pinchó el neumático; **the dam had been ~d in various places** se habían abierto brechas en distintas partes de la presa; **a wall ~d with loopholes** un muro en el que se abrían aspilleras; **to ~ sth through and through** perforar algo una y otra vez; **a cry ~d the silence** un grito desgarró el silencio; **a light ~d the darkness** una luz hendió la oscuridad; **the news ~d him to the heart** la noticia le hirió en el alma.

piercing ['pɪəsɪŋ] *adj wind* cortante; *cry* agudo, desgarrador, penetrante; *look* penetrante; *pain* lancinante.

piercingly ['pɪəsɪŋlɪ] *adv blow* de modo cortante; *cry* agudamente, en tono penetrante.

pierhead ['pɪəhed] *n* punta *f* del muelle.

pierrot ['pɪərəʊ] *n* pierrot *m*.

pietism ['paɪətɪzəm] *n* piedad *f*, devoción *f*; (*pej*) beatería *f*, mojigatería *f*.

pietistic [paɪə'tɪstɪk] *adj* (*pej*) pietista, beato, mojigato.

piety ['paɪətɪ] *n* piedad *f*, devoción *f*; **affected ~** beatería *f*.

piffle* ['pɪfl] *n* disparates *mpl*, tonterías *fpl*; **~!** ¡tonterías!

piffling* ['pɪflɪŋ] *adj* de poca monta, insignificante.

pig [pɪg] **1** *n* (**a**) cerdo *m*, puerco *m*, cochino *m*, chancho *m* (*LAm*); **roast ~** cochinillo *m* asado, lechón *m* asado; **to buy a ~ in a poke** cerrar un trato a ciegas; **to sell sb a ~ in a poke** dar gato por liebre; **when ~s (learn to) fly** cuando las ranas críen pelos; **it was a ~ of a job** fue un trabajo horrible; **he made a right ~'s ear of it** se armó un tremendo lío con eso; lo hizo malísimamente; **in a ~'s eye!*** (*US*) ¡ni hablar!, ¡que te lo has creído!

(**b**) (*fig: person*) cochino *m*, marrano *m*, chancho *m* (*LAm*); (‡: *policeman*) poli* *m*; **you ~!** (*hum*) ¡bandido!; **the boss is a ~** el jefe es un bruto; **you're a ~, sir!** ¡Vd es un maleducado!; **to make a ~ of o.s.** comer demasiado; darse un atracón* (*over* de).

(**c**) (*Metal*) lingote *m*.

2 *vt*: **to ~ it** vivir como cerdos.

pig-breeding ['pɪgˌbri:dɪŋ] *n* cría *f* de cerdos.

pigeon ['pɪdʒən] *n* (**a**) paloma *f*, palomo *m*; (*young*) palomino *m*, pichón *m*; (*as food*) pichón *m*. (**b**) (*) **that's his ~** allá él; **it's not my ~** eso no tiene que ver conmigo.

pigeon-fancier ['pɪdʒənˌfænsɪəʳ] *n* colombófilo *m*, -a *f*.

pigeon-fancying ['pɪdʒənˌfænsɪɪŋ] *n* colombofilia *f*.

pigeonhole ['pɪdʒənhəʊl] **1** *n* casilla *f*; **set of ~s** casillas *fpl*, casillero *m*.

2 *vt* (*classify*) encasillar, clasificar; (*store away*) archivar; archivar en la memoria; (*shelve*) dar carpetazo a.

pigeon-house ['pɪdʒənhaʊs] *n*, *pl* **pigeon-houses** ['pɪdʒənˌhaʊzɪz], **pigeon-loft** ['pɪdʒənlɒft] *n* palomar *m*.

pigeon-post ['pɪdʒənˌpəʊst] *n* correo *m* de palomas; **by ~** por paloma mensajera.

pigeon-shooting ['pɪdʒənˌʃu:tɪŋ] *n* tiro *m* de pichón.

pigeon-toed ['pɪdʒən'təʊd] *adj* con los pies torcidos hacia dentro.

piggery ['pɪgərɪ] *n* pocilga *f*, porqueriza *f*, cochiquera *f*.

piggish ['pɪgɪʃ] *adj* (*in manners*) puerco; (*greedy*) glotón; (*stubborn*) tozudo, testarudo.

piggy ['pɪgɪ] **1** *n* cerdito *m*, cochinillo *m*, lechón *m*; **to be ~ in the middle** sufrir por estar entre otros dos que se riñen (*etc*). **2** *adj*: **with little ~ eyes** con ojos pequeños como de cerdo.

piggy-back ['pɪgɪbæk] *n*: **to give a child a ~** llevar a un niño sobre los hombros, llevar a un niño a cuestas.

piggy-bank ['pɪgɪbæŋk] *n* hucha *f* (en forma de cerdito).

pigheaded ['pɪg'hedɪd] *adj person* terco, testarudo; *attitude etc* obstinado; **it was a ~ thing to do** fue un acto que reveló su terquedad.

pigheadedly ['pɪg'hedɪdlɪ] *adv* tercamente; obstinadamente.

pigheadedness ['pɪg'hedɪdnɪs] *n* terquedad *f*, testarudez *f*; obstinación *f*.

pig-ignorant* [ˌpɪg'ɪgnərənt] *adj* bruto.

pig-iron ['pɪgˌaɪən] *n* hierro *m* en lingotes.

piglet ['pɪglɪt] *n* cerdito *m*, cochinillo *m*, lechón *m*.

pigman ['pɪgmæn] *n*, *pl* **pigmen** ['pɪgmen] porquerizo *m*, porquero *m*.

pigmeat ['pɪgmi:t] *n* carne *f* de cerdo.

pigment ['pɪgmənt] *n* pigmento *m*.

pigmentation [ˌpɪgmən'teɪʃən] *n* pigmentación *f*.

pigmented [pɪg'mentɪd] *adj* pigmentado.

pigmy ['pɪgmɪ] **1** *adj* pigmeo; (*fig*) enano; miniatura, pequeñito. **2** *n* pigmeo *m*, -a *f*, enano *m*, -a *f*.
pigpen ['pɪgpen] *n* (*US*) = **pigsty.**
pigskin ['pɪgskɪn] *n* piel *f* de cerdo.
pigsty ['pɪgstaɪ] *n* (*Brit*) pocilga *f*, porqueriza *f*, cochiquera *f* (*also fig*).
pigswill ['pɪgswɪl] *n* bazofia *f* (*also fig*).
pigtail ['pɪgteɪl] *n* (*of Chinese, bullfighter etc*) coleta *f*; (*girl's*) trenza *f*.
pike¹ [paɪk] *n* (*Mil*) pica *f*, chuzo *m*.
pike² [paɪk] *n*, *pl invar* (*Fish*) lucio *m*.
pikeman ['paɪkmən] *n*, *pl* **pikemen** ['paɪkmən] piquero *m*.
piker‡ ['paɪkəʳ] *n* (*US*) (*mean person*) cicatero *m*; (*unimportant person*) persona *f* de poco fuste; (*coward*) cobarde *m*.
pikestaff ['paɪkstɑːf] *n V* **plain 1.**
pilaf(f) ['pɪlæf] *n plato oriental a base de arroz.*
pilaster [pɪ'læstəʳ] *n* pilastra *f*.
Pilate ['paɪlət] *nm* Pilatos.
pilau [pɪ'laʊ] *n* = **pilaff.**
pilchard ['pɪltʃəd] *n* sardina *f*.
pile¹ [paɪl] *n* (*Archit*) pilote *m*.
pile² [paɪl] **1** *n* (**a**) (*heap*) montón *m*, pila *f*, rimero *m*; **to make a ~ of things, to put things in a ~** amontonar cosas, juntar cosas en un montón.
(**b**) (*****) fortuna *f*; **to make one's ~** hacer su agosto; **he made his ~ in oil** se hizo una fortuna en el petróleo; **~s of*** montones de*.
(**c**) (*of buildings*) mole *f*, masa *f* imponente, conjunto *m* grandioso; **the Escorial, that noble ~** El Escorial, aquel edificio tan imponente.
(**d**) (*Phys etc*) pila *f*; **atomic ~** pila *f* atómica.
2 *vt* amontonar, apilar, juntar en un montón; acumular; **a table ~d high with books** una mesa cargada de libros; **to ~ coal on the fire** echar carbón al fuego.
3 *vi* (**a**) amontonarse, apilarse; acumularse.
(**b**) **we all ~d into the car*** entramos todos en el coche.
◆pile in* *vi*: **~ in!** ¡dentro todos, que nos vamos!
◆pile off* *vi* (*of people*) salir en avalancha.
◆pile on *vt*: **to ~ it on** exagerar; **he does rather ~ it on** es un exagerado; **to ~ on the agony** aumentar el dolor, añadir dolor sobre dolor; **to ~ on the pressure** ir aumentando la presión, (*fig*) presionar cada vez más fuerte.
◆pile out* *vi*: **everybody ~d out** todos salieron en desorden.
◆pile up 1 *vt* amontonar, apilar, juntar en un montón; acumular; **we ~d it all up high** lo amontonamos todo muy alto; **he went on piling up the evidence** fue acumulando los datos, fue amontonando las pruebas; **to ~ the fire up with coal** echar carbón al fuego.
2 *vi* (**a**) amontonarse, apilarse; acumularse; **the evidence is piling up** las pruebas van acumulándose.
(**b**) (*****) **the car ~d up against the wall** el coche se estrelló contra el muro; **the ship ~d up on the rocks** el buque se estrelló contra las rocas.
pile³ [paɪl] *n* (*of carpet*) pelo *m*.
pile-driver ['paɪl,draɪvəʳ] *n* martinete *m*.
pile-dwelling ['paɪl,dwelɪŋ] *n* (*Hist*) vivienda *f* construida sobre pilotes.
piles [paɪlz] *npl* (*Med*) almorranas *fpl*, hemorroides *fpl*.
pile-up* ['paɪlʌp] *n* (*Aut etc*) accidente *m* múltiple, colisión *f* (*or* choque *m*) en cadena; **there was a ~ at the corner** chocaron varios coches en la esquina, hubo un accidente múltiple en la esquina.
pilfer ['pɪlfəʳ] **1** *vt article* ratear, hurtar; (*by servant etc*) sisar; **the crate had been ~ed** algunos artículos habían sido robados del cajón; **they often ~ the trucks** con frecuencia roban cosas de los vagones.
2 *vi* ratear, robar cosas.
pilferage ['pɪlfərɪdʒ] *n* hurto *m*, robo *m*.
pilferer ['pɪlfərəʳ] *n* ratero *m*, -a *f*, ladronzuelo *m*, -a *f*.
pilfering ['pɪlfərɪŋ] *n* ratería *f*, hurto *m*.
pilgrim ['pɪlgrɪm] **1** *n* peregrino *m*, -a *f*, romero *m*, -a *f*. **2** *attr*: **the P~ Fathers** los padres peregrinos.
pilgrimage ['pɪlgrɪmɪdʒ] *n* peregrinación *f*, romería *f*; **to go on a ~, to make a ~** ir en peregrinación, ir en romería (*to* a).
pill [pɪl] *n* gragea *f*; píldora *f*; **the ~** (*contraceptive*) la píldora; **she's on the ~** toma la píldora; **it was a bitter ~ (to swallow)** fue una píldora amarga, fue un trago amargo; **to sugar** (*or* **sweeten**) **the ~** dorar la píldora.
pillage ['pɪlɪdʒ] **1** *n* pillaje *m*, saqueo *m*. **2** *vt* pillar, saquear.
pillar ['pɪləʳ] *n* pilar *m*, columna *f*; (*fig*) sostén *m*, pilar *m*; **~ of salt** estatua *f* de sal; **the P~s of Hercules** las Columnas de Hércules; **to be a ~ of strength** ser firme como una roca, ser una columna de sostén; **to chase sb from ~ to post** acosar a uno, no dejar a uno a sol ni a sombra.
pillarbox ['pɪləbɒks] *n* (*Brit*) buzón *m*.
pillbox ['pɪlbɒks] *n* (*Med*) pastillero *m*, cajita *f* de píldoras; (*Mil*) fortín *m*.
pillion ['pɪljən] **1** *n* (*also* **~ seat**) asiento *m* de atrás, asiento *m* de pasajero; (*on horse*) grupera *f*.
2 *attr*: **~ passenger** pasajero *m*, -a *f* que va detrás.
3 *adv*: **to ride ~** ir en el asiento de atrás.
pillock‡ ['pɪlək] *n* (*Brit*) gili* *mf*.
pillory ['pɪlərɪ] **1** *n* picota *f*. **2** *vt* (*fig*) poner en ridículo, satirizar; censurar duramente.
pillow ['pɪləʊ] **1** *n* almohada *f*.
2 *vt* apoyar sobre una almohada; apoyar, servir de almohada a; **she ~ed her head on my shoulder** apoyó la cabeza en mi hombro.
pillowcase ['pɪləʊkeɪs] *n*, **pillowslip** ['pɪləʊslɪp] *n* funda *f* de almohada.
pillow-talk ['pɪləʊ,tɔːk] *n* charla *f* de enamorados (en la cama).
pilot ['paɪlət] **1** *n* (**a**) (*Aer*) piloto *mf*, aviadora *f*; (*Naut*) práctico *m*, piloto *m*. (**b**) = **~ light.** (**c**) = **~ programme.**
2 *adj* piloto, experimental; **~ jet, ~ light** (*on stove*) mechero *m*, encendedor *m*; **~ light** (*Aut*) luz *f* de situación; **~ plant** planta *f* piloto; **~ program** (*US*), **~ programme** programa *m* piloto; **~ scheme** proyecto *m* experimental; **~ series** serie *f* piloto; **~ study** estudio *m* piloto.
3 *vt* pilotar; (*fig*) guiar, conducir; dirigir; **a plane ~ed by ...** un avión pilotado por ...; **he ~ed the negotiations through** dirigió las negociaciones, condujo las negociaciones a buen fin; **to ~ a bill through the House** encargarse de un proyecto de ley durante los debates parlamentarios, asegurar la aprobación de un proyecto de ley.
pilot boat ['paɪlətbəʊt] *n* bote *m* del práctico.
pilot house ['paɪləthaʊs] *n*, *pl* **pilot houses** ['paɪləthaʊzɪz] (*Naut*) timonera *f*.
pilot officer ['paɪlət,ɒfɪsəʳ] *n* oficial *m* piloto.
pimento [pɪ'mentəʊ] *n* pimiento *m*.
pimp [pɪmp] **1** *n* alcahuete *m*; coime *m*, chulo *m* de putas, cafiche *m* (*LAm*). **2** *vi* alcahuetear; ser coime, ser chulo de putas; **to ~ for sb** servir de alcahuete a uno.
pimpernel ['pɪmpənel] *n* murajes *mpl*, pimpinela *f*.
pimple ['pɪmpl] *n* grano *m*; **she came out in ~s** le salieron granos.
pimply ['pɪmplɪ] *adj* lleno de granos, cubierto de granos; granujiento; **~ youth** (*fig*) mocoso *m*, mozalbete *m*.
PIMS *n abbr of* **personal information management system.**
PIN [pɪn] *n* (*Comput, Fin*) *abbr of* **personal identification number**; **~ number** número *m* personal de identificación, NPI *m*.
pin [pɪn] **1** *n* (**a**) (*Sew etc*) alfiler *m*; (*Mech*: *bolt*) perno *m*, (*cotter*) chaveta *f*; (*of grenade*) arandela *f*; (*wooden*) clavija *f*; **~s and needles** hormiguillo *m*, hormigueo *m*; **like a new ~** como una patena; **for two ~s I'd knock his head off** por menos de nada le rompo la crisma; **you could have heard a ~ drop** se oía el vuelo de una mosca.
(**b**) (*Elec*) polo *m*.
(**c**) **~s*** (*legs*) piernas *fpl*.
2 *attr*: **two ~ plug** clavija *f* bipolar; **three ~ plug** clavija *f* de 3 polos.
3 *vt* (**a**) (*put pin in*) prender con alfiler, prender con alfileres; (*with bolt*) sujetar (con perno *etc*); **to ~ a medal to sb's uniform** prender una medalla al uniforme de uno; **to ~ sb's arms to his side** sujetar los brazos de uno; **to ~ sb against a wall** apretar a uno contra una pared; **the battalion was ~ned against the river** el batallón estaba copado junto al río, el batallón quedó inmovilizado junto al río.
(**b**) **to ~ one's hopes** (*or* **faith**) **on sb** cifrar sus esperanzas en uno.
(**c**) (*****) **to ~ sth on sb** acusar (falsamente) a uno de algo; **you can't ~ it on me** no podéis lograr que yo cargue con la culpa, es imposible probar que yo lo hiciera; **they ~ned a number of robberies on him** le acusaron (falsamente) de haber participado en una serie de robos.
◆pin back *vt* (*lit*) doblar hacia atrás y sujetar con alfileres; **now ~ your ears back** escuchadme muy atentos; **to ~ sb's ears back** (*fig*: *startle*) meter a uno el susto en el cuerpo*; (*US**: *scold*) reñir a uno, regañar a uno; (*US**: *beat up*) darle una zurra a uno*.

◆**pin down** *vt* (*fig*) **to ~ sb down** obligar a uno a que concrete; **we were ~ned down by the bombardment** el bombardeo nos inmovilizó; **it's impossible to ~ him down** es imposible hacerle concretar; **you can't ~ him down to a date** es imposible lograr que nos diga una fecha concreta; **there's something odd I can't quite ~ down** hay algo raro que no puedo precisar; **the idea is rather hard to ~ down** es un concepto de difícil concreción.
◆**pin on** *vt* prender.
◆**pin together** *vt*: **to ~ papers together** prender unos papeles con una grapa, grapar papeles.
◆**pin up** *vt clothing* recoger con alfileres (*or* imperdible); *hair* recoger con horquilla; **to ~ a notice up** fijar un anuncio con chinches; poner un anuncio, pegar un anuncio.
pinafore ['pɪnəfɔːʳ] *n* delantal *m* (de niña); **~ dress** mandil *m*.
pinball ['pɪnbɔːl] *n* (*also* **~ machine**) millón *m*, flíper *m*.
pince-nez ['pɛːnsneɪ] *npl* quevedos *mpl*.
pincer ['pɪnsəʳ] **1** *n* (**a**) (*Zool*) pinza *f*. (**b**) (*Tech*) **~s** tenazas *fpl*, pinzas *fpl*; **a pair of ~s** unas tenazas. **2** *attr*: **~ movement** (*Mil*) movimiento *m* de pinza.
pinch [pɪntʃ] **1** *n* (**a**) (*with fingers*) pellizco *m*; **to give sb a ~ on the arm** pellizcar el brazo a uno.
(**b**) (*small quantity*) pizca *f*; pulgarada *f*; **a ~ of salt** una pizca de sal; **to take sth with a ~ of salt** tomar algo con un grano de sal; **a ~ of snuff** un polvo de rapé.
(**c**) (*fig*) apuro *m*; **to feel the ~** (empezar a) pasar apuros; **to feel the ~ of hunger** empezar a tener hambre; **to feel the ~ of poverty** saber lo que significa ser pobre; **at a ~** si es realmente necesario, en caso de necesidad.
2 *vt* (**a**) (*with fingers*) pellizcar, dar un pellizcón a; (*squeeze, crush*) apretar, estrujar, aplastar; (*of shoe*) apretar; **to ~ one's finger in the door** pillarse el dedo en la puerta.
(**b**) (*: *steal*) birlar*, guindar‡, pisar*; **I had my pen ~ed** me guindaron la pluma; **he ~ed that idea from Shaw** esa idea la robó de Shaw; **A ~ed B's girl** A le pisó la novia a B.
(**c**) (‡: *arrest etc*) coger (*Sp*), pescar*; **he got ~ed for a parking offence** le pescaron en una infracción de aparcamiento.
3 *vi* (**a**) (*shoe*) apretar; **to know where the shoe ~es** (*fig*) saber dónde aprieta el zapato.
(**b**) (*economize*) economizar; privarse de lo necesario; **we had to ~ and scrape** tuvimos que hacer muchas economías; **they ~ed and scraped to send her to college** se privaron de muchas cosas a fin de poder enviarla a la universidad.
◆**pinch back, pinch off** *vt*: **to ~ off a bud** quitar un brote con los dedos, separar un brote con la uña.
pinchbeck ['pɪntʃbek] **1** *n* similor *m*. **2** *attr* de similor; (*fig*) falso.
pinched ['pɪntʃt] *adj* (**a**) (*drawn*) **to look ~** tener la cara pálida; **to look ~ with cold** estar aterido, estar chupado. (**b**) **to be ~ for money** andar escaso de dinero; **we're very ~ for space** tenemos muy poco espacio.
pinch-hit ['pɪntʃhɪt] *vi* (*US*) batear de suplente; (*fig*) sustituir a otro en un apuro.
pinchpenny ['pɪntʃpenɪ] *adj* tacaño.
pincushion ['pɪn,kʊʃən] *n* acerico *m*, almohadilla *f*.
Pindar ['pɪndəʳ] *nm* Píndaro.
Pindaric [pɪn'dærɪk] *adj* pindárico.
pine¹ [paɪn] *n* pino *m*.
pine² [paɪn] *vi* (*also* **to ~ away**) languidecer, consumirse; **to ~ for** suspirar por, perecer por, consumirse pensando en.
pineal ['pɪnɪəl] *adj*: **~ body, ~ gland** glándula *f* pineal.
pineapple ['paɪn,æpl] *n* piña *f* (de América), ananás *m*.
pinecone ['paɪnkəʊn] *n* piña *f*.
pine-grove ['paɪngrəʊv] *n* pinar *m*.
pine-kernel ['paɪn,kɜːnl] *n* piñón *m*.
pine-marten ['paɪn,mɑːtɪn] *n* marta *f*.
pine-needle ['paɪn,niːdl] *n* aguja *f* de pino.
pine-nut ['paɪn,nʌt] *n* piña *f*, piñón *m*.
pine-tree ['paɪntriː] *n* pino *m*.
pinewood ['paɪnwʊd] *n* pinar *m*.
ping [pɪŋ] **1** *n* (*of bullet, through air*) silbido *m*, (*on striking*) sonido *m* metálico; (*of bell*) tintín *m*.
2 *vi* silbar (como una bala); hacer un sonido metálico (como una bala); tintinear, hacer tintín.
ping-pong ['pɪŋpɒŋ] ® **1** *n* ping-pong *m*, pimpón *m*. **2** *attr*: **~ ball** pelota *f* de ping-pong.
pinhead ['pɪnhed] *n* (*lit*) cabeza *f* de alfiler; (*) mentecato *m*, cabeza de chorlito*.
pinhole ['pɪnhəʊl] *n* agujero *m* de alfiler; **~ camera** cámara *f* de agujero de alfiler.
pinion¹ ['pɪnjən] **1** *n* (*poet*) ala *f*. **2** *vt bird* cortar las alas a; *person* atar los brazos a; **he was ~ed against the wall** estaba contra la pared sin poderse mover, le tuvieron apretado contra la pared.
pinion² ['pɪnjən] *n* (*Mech*) piñón *m*.
pink¹ [pɪŋk] **1** *n* (**a**) (*Bot*) clavel *m*, clavellina *f*.
(**b**) (*colour*) color *m* de rosa.
(**c**) **hunting ~** levitín *m* rojo de caza.
(**d**) (*Pol*) rojillo *m*, -a *f*.
(**e**) (*fig*) **to be in the ~** vender salud, rebosar salud; estar como un reloj; **to be in the ~ of condition** estar en perfecto estado.
2 *adj* (*colour*) rosado, color de rosa; (*Pol*) rojillo; **~ gin** ginebra *f* con angostura; **~ slip** (*US*) notificación *f* de despido; **strike me ~!‡** ¡caray!*; **to be tickled ~ about sth*** (*pleased*) estar encantado con algo, (*joke*) reírse mucho con algo.
pink² [pɪŋk] *vt* (*Sew*) ondear, picar; **to ~ sb with a sword** herir a uno levemente con un florete.
pink³ [pɪŋk] *vi* (*Brit Aut*) picar.
pinking shears ['pɪŋkɪŋ,ʃiːəz] *npl* tijeras *fpl* dentadas.
pinkish ['pɪŋkɪʃ] *adj* rosáceo; (*Pol*) rojillo.
pinko* ['pɪŋkəʊ] (*Pol pej*) **1** *adj* rojillo. **2** *n* rojillo *m*, -a *f*.
pin-money ['pɪn,mʌnɪ] *n* alfileres *mpl*, dinero *m* para gastos menores.
pinnace ['pɪnɪs] *n* pinaza *f*.
pinnacle ['pɪnəkl] *n* (*Archit*) pináculo *m*, remate *m*; chapitel *m*; (*of rock etc*) punta *f*; (*of mountain*) pico *m*, cumbre *f*; (*fig*) cumbre *f*, cúspide *m*; **the ~ of fame** la cumbre de la fama.
pinny* ['pɪnɪ] *n* = **pinafore**.
Pinocchio [pɪ'nɒkɪəʊ] *nm* Pinocho.
pinpoint ['pɪnpɔɪnt] **1** *n* punta *f* de alfiler; (*fig*) punto *m* muy pequeño. **2** *vt* indicar con toda precisión; concretar; poner el dedo en.
pinprick ['pɪnprɪk] *n* alfilerazo *m*; pinchazo *m*; (*fig*) alfilerazo *m*, molestia *f* pequeña.
pinstripe ['pɪnstraɪp] **1** *adj* a rayas, rayado; **~ suit** traje *m* a rayas. **2** *n* traje *m* (*etc*) a rayas.
pint [paɪnt] **1** *n* (**a**) pinta *f* (= 0,57 *litros*, *US* = 0,47 *litros*).
(**b**) (*Brit*: *loosely*) vaso *m* grande de cerveza, caña *f* de cerveza; **we had a ~ together** tomamos una caña; **he likes his ~** le gusta la cerveza, es algo aficionado a la cerveza; **we had a few ~s** bebimos unas cuantas.
2 *attr*: **~-size(d)*** diminuto, pequeñito.
pinta* ['paɪntə] *n* pinta *f* (de leche).
pin-table ['pɪnteɪbl] *n* billar *m* romano, billar *m* automático.
pintail ['pɪnteɪl] *n* ánade *m* rabudo.
pin-up ['pɪnʌp] *n* pin-up *mf*.
pinwheel ['pɪn,wiːl] *n* (*esp US*) rueda *f* catalina.
pioneer [,paɪə'nɪəʳ] **1** *n* pionero *m*, -a *f*; (*explorer*) explorador *m*, -ora *f*; (*early settler*) colonizador *m*, -ora *f*; (*Mil*) zapador *m*; (*of scheme, in study*) iniciador *m*, -ora *f*; promotor *m*, -ora *f*; **he was one of the ~s** él era de los pioneros; **he was a ~ in the study of bats** fue uno de los primeros en estudiar los murciélagos.
2 *attr*: **~ corps** cuerpo *m* de zapadores; **~ work** trabajo *m* de pioneros.
3 *vt settlement etc* preparar el terreno para, hacer los preparativos para; *scheme, study* iniciar, promover; echar los cimientos de, sentar las bases de.
4 *vi* explorar, abrir nuevos caminos.
pioneering [,paɪə'nɪərɪŋ] *adj work, research, study* pionero.
pious ['paɪəs] *adj* piadoso, devoto; **~ hopes** esperanzas *fpl* piadosas.
piously ['paɪəslɪ] *adv* piadosamente, devotamente.
pip¹ [pɪp] *n* (*Med*) pepita *f*; **it gives me the ~*** me fastidia terriblemente; **it's enough to give you the ~*** es para volverse loco; **he's got the ~*** está de muy mal humor.
pip² [pɪp] *n* (**a**) (*Bot*) pepita *f*, pepa *f* (*LAm*); (*on card, dice*) punto *m*; (*Brit*: *on uniform*) estrella *f*.
(**b**) (*sound*) bip *m*, pitido *m*; **the 6 ~s** (*Rad*) los 6 pitidos; **wait till you hear the ~** esperar a que se oiga el pitido.
pip³* [pɪp] **1** *vt* (*wound*) herir (levemente); (*defeat*) vencer; **A ~ped B at the post** A le ganó a B en el último momento; **he was ~ped at the post by another candidate** por muy escaso margen dieron el puesto a otro; **I ~ped French again** volvieron a escabecharme en francés*.
2 *vi* (*) (*lose*) perder; (*fail*) fracasar; (*in exam*) catearse*, cargarse*.
pipe [paɪp] **1** *n* (**a**) (*tube*) tubo *m*, caño *m*, conducto *m*;

(*also* ~**s**) tubería *f*, cañería *f*; (*of a hose etc*) manga *f*; (*of wine*) pipa *f*.

(**b**) (*Mus*: *of organ*) cañón *m*, tubo *m*; (*instrument*) caramillo *m*, (*boatswain's*) pito *m*; ~**s** (*Scot*) gaita *f*, (*Pan's*) flauta *f*.

(**c**) (*smoker's*) pipa *f*; ~ **of peace** pipa *f* de la paz; **to fill one's ~** cargar la pipa; **put that in your ~ and smoke it!*** ¡chúpate eso!*

2 *vt* (**a**) *water etc* conducir en cañerías; ~**d music** hilo *m* musical, música *f* ambiental; **water is ~d to the farm** se conduce el agua a la granja por unas cañerías; **the oil is ~d across the desert** el petróleo es conducido a través del desierto en un oleoducto.

(**b**) (*Mus*) *tune* tocar; **to ~ the admiral aboard** tocar el pito al subir el almirante a bordo.

(**c**) (*Sew*) adornar con rib etc.

3 *vi* (*Mus*) tocar el caramillo, tocar la flauta; tocar la gaita; (*bird*) trinar.

◆**pipe down*** *vi* callarse.

◆**pipe up*** *vi* decir (inesperadamente), echar a hablar (inesperadamente).

pipeclay ['paɪpkleɪ] **1** *n* albero *m*. **2** *vt* blanquear con albero.

pipe-cleaner ['paɪpˌkliːnəʳ] *n* limpiapipas *m*, limpiador *m* de pipa.

pipe-dream ['paɪpdriːm] *n* esperanza *f* imposible, sueño *m* imposible, castillos *mpl* en el aire.

pipefitter ['paɪpˌfɪtəʳ] *n* fontanero *m*.

pipeful ['paɪpfʊl] *n* pipa *f*; **a ~ of tobacco** una pipa de tabaco.

pipeline ['paɪplaɪn] *n* tubería *f*, cañería *f*; tubería *f* de distribución; (*for oil*) oleoducto *m*; (*for gas*) gasoducto *m*; **it is in the ~** (*fig*) está en trámite, se está tramitando.

piper ['paɪpəʳ] *n* flautista *mf*; (*Scot*) gaitero *m*; **to pay the ~** cargar con los gastos; **he who pays the ~ calls the tune** el que paga tiene derecho a escoger.

pipe-rack ['paɪpræk] *n* soporte *m* para pipas.

pipe-smoker ['paɪpˌsməʊkəʳ] *n* fumador *m* de pipa, pipero *m*.

pipe-tobacco ['paɪptəˌbækəʊ] *n* tabaco *m* de pipa.

pipette [pɪ'pet] *n* pipeta *f*.

piping ['paɪpɪŋ] **1** *n* (**a**) (*in house etc*) tubería *f*, cañería *f*.

(**b**) (*Mus*) sonido *m* del caramillo, música *f* de flauta; (*of bird*) trinar *m*, trinos *mpl*.

(**c**) (*Sew*) ribete *m*, cordoncillo *m*.

2 *adj voice* agudo.

3 *adv*: ~ **hot** bien caliente, que casi quema.

pipistrelle [ˌpɪpɪ'strel] *n* pipistrelo *m*.

pipit ['pɪpɪt] *n* bisbita *f*, pitpit *m*.

pipkin ['pɪpkɪn] *n* ollita *f* de barro.

pippin ['pɪpɪn] *n* camuesa *f*, manzana *f* reineta.

pipsqueak ['pɪpskwiːk] *n* persona *f* insignificante, fantoche *m*.

piquancy ['piːkənsɪ] *n* picante *m*, lo picante.

piquant ['piːkənt] *adj* (**a**) (*Culin*) picante. (**b**) (*fig*) picante; *attitude, remark* agudo, provocativo; *situation* picante.

piquantly ['piːkəntlɪ] *adv* de modo picante.

pique [piːk] **1** *n* pique *m*, resentimiento *m*; **to be in a ~** estar resentido; **to do sth in a fit of ~, to do sth out of ~** hacer algo motivado por el rencor.

2 *vt* picar, herir; **to be ~d at** ofenderse por, estar resentido por.

3 *vr*: **to ~ o.s. on sth** preciarse de algo, enorgullecerse de algo.

piquet [pɪ'ket] *n* piquet *m*.

piracy ['paɪərəsɪ] *n* piratería *f*; (*of book*) publicación *f* pirata.

piranha [pɪ'rɑːnjə] *n* piraña *f*.

pirate ['paɪərɪt] **1** *n* pirata *m*. **2** *adj*: ~ **broadcasting** radiodifusión *f* no autorizada; ~ **radio** emisora *f* pirata. **3** *vt book, tape* piratear.

pirated ['paɪərɪtɪd] *adj*: ~ **edition** edición *f* pirata.

piratical [paɪ'rætɪkəl] *adj* pirático.

pirouette [ˌpɪrʊ'et] **1** *n* pirueta *f*. **2** *vi* piruetear.

Pisces ['paɪsiːz] *n* (*Zodiac*) Piscis *m*.

piss** [pɪs] **1** *n* orina *f*, meados** *mpl*; ~ **artist** privota** *mf*; **to have a ~** mear**; **to take the ~ out of sb** cachondearse de uno*.

2 *vt* mear**.

3 *vi* mear**; **it's ~ing with rain** está lloviendo a chuzos.

◆**piss about**** *vi* hacer el oso.

◆**piss down**** *vi*: **it's fair ~ing down** llueve a torrentes.

◆**piss off**** **1** *vt* (*annoy*) irritar; sacar de quicio; (*depress*) desalentar; (*disappoint*) decepcionar; **I feel thoroughly ~ed off about it** estoy hasta la coronilla con esto*; **he's feeling ~ed off** está de mala leche**. **2** *vi* largarse*; ~ **off!** ¡vete al cuerno!*

pissed** [pɪst] *adj*: **to be ~** (*Brit*) estar ajumado*, (*US*) estar de mala leche**.

piss-up** ['pɪsʌp] *n* juerga *f* de borrachera*.

pistachio [pɪs'tɑːʃɪəʊ] *n* pistacho *m*.

piste [piːst] *n* (*Ski*) pista *f*.

pistil ['pɪstɪl] *n* pistilo *m*.

pistol ['pɪstl] **1** *n* pistola *f*, revólver *m*. **2** *attr*: **at ~ point** a punta de pistola.

pistol-shot ['pɪstlˌʃɒt] *n* pistoletazo *m*; **to be within ~** estar a tiro de pistola.

piston ['pɪstən] **1** *n* pistón *m*, émbolo *m*; (*Mus*) pistón *m*, llave *f*. **2** *attr*: ~ **engine** motor *m* de pistón.

piston-engined ['pɪstənˌendʒɪnd] *adj* con motor de pistón.

piston-ring ['pɪstənˌrɪŋ] *n* aro *m* de pistón, segmento *m* de pistón.

piston-rod ['pɪstənˌrɒd] *n* vástago *m* de émbolo.

piston-stroke ['pɪstənˌstrəʊk] *n* carrera *f* del émbolo.

pit[1] [pɪt] **1** *n* (**a**) (*hole in ground*) hoyo *m*, hoya *f*, foso *m*; (*small depression in surface*) hoyo *m*; (*as trap*) trampa *f*; (*at garage*) foso *m* de inspección, foso *m* de reparación; (*in motor-racing*) box *m*; (*of stomach*) boca *f*; (*Min*) mina *f*, (*quarry*) cantera *f*; (*fig*) abismo *m*; **the ~** (*fig*: *hell*) el infierno; **the ~ of hell** lo más profundo del infierno.

(**b**) (*Brit Theat*) platea *f*; (*for cockfighting*) cancha *f*, reñidero *m*; (*US St Ex*) parquet *m* de la Bolsa; **the cotton ~** la bolsa del algodón.

(**c**) (*US**) **the ~s** (*gloom*) estado *m* de depresión; (*low point*) punto *m* más bajo; **this game is the ~s** este partido es una basura; **he's the ~s** es la reoca*; **it really sent her to the ~s** la mandó a lo último.

2 *vt* (**a**) *surface* hacer hoyos en, marcar con hoyos; (*with smallpox*) marcar con viruelas; **the surface was ~ted with ...** en la superficie había hoyos formados por ...

(**b**) **to ~ A against B** oponer A a B; **we ~ted all our strength against him** nos opusimos a él con todas nuestras fuerzas; **we are ~ting our wits against the experts** nos enfrentamos a los expertos en un certamen de inteligencia; **he found himself ~ted against the champion** encontró que tenía que habérselas con el campeón.

3 *vr*: **to ~ o.s. against an opponent** medirse con un contrario.

pit[2] [pɪt] (*US*) **1** *n* (*Bot*) hueso *m*. **2** *vt* deshuesar, quitar el hueso a.

pitapat ['pɪtə'pæt] *adv*: **my heart went ~** mi corazón latía rápidamente, mi corazón palpitaba.

pitch[1] [pɪtʃ] **1** *n* pez *f*, brea *f*. **2** *vt* embrear.

pitch[2] [pɪtʃ] **1** *n* (**a**) (*throw*) tiro *m*, lanzamiento *m*; echada *f*; **it came full ~ into my hands** llegó a mis manos sin tocar el suelo; **it fell full ~ into the garden** cayó de plano en el jardín.

(**b**) (*Naut*) cabezada *f*.

(**c**) (*Brit Sport*) campo *m*, terreno *m*, cancha *f* (*LAm*).

(**d**) (*place in market etc*) puesto *m*; (*fig*) terreno *m*; **this is my usual ~** éste es mi puesto habitual; **keep off our ~!** ¡cuidado con no meteros en lo nuestro!

(**e**) (*slope*) grado *m* de inclinación; (*of roof*) pendiente *f*.

(**f**) (*height, degree*) punto *m*, extremo *m*; (*height*) elevación *f*; (*of propeller etc*) paso *m*; **to such a ~ that ...** a tal punto que ...; **excitement is at a high ~** la emoción está al rojo vivo; **matters reached such a ~ that ...** las cosas llegaron a tal extremo que ...

(**g**) (*Mus*) tono *m*; diapasón *m*; **to adjust the ~ of an instrument** ajustar el tono de un instrumento; **to have perfect ~** tener oído perfecto, poder dar el tono exacto; **to queer sb's ~** chafar la guitarra a uno; frustrar el intento de uno.

(**h**) (*: *spiel*) rollo* *m*, explicaciones *fpl*.

(**i**) (*) **to make a ~ for sth** tratar de asegurarse algo; **he made a ~ for the women's vote** procuró acaparar los votos de las mujeres; **he made a ~ for her** (*US*) le dio un tiento.

2 *vt* (**a**) (*throw*) arrojar, lanzar, tirar; (*Baseball etc*) lanzar.

(**b**) (*Mus*) *note* dar, producir, entonar; (*play*) tocar, (*sing*) cantar; *instrument* graduar el tono de; **she can't ~ a note properly** es incapaz de producir una nota buena; **I'll ~ you a note** os doy la nota para empezar; **you're ~ing it too high for me** lo tocas demasiado alto para mí; **to ~ one's aspirations too high** picar muy alto; **it is ~ed in rather high-flown terms** está redactado en términos algo retóricos; **it must be ~ed at the right level for the audience** el tono ha de ajustarse al público.

(**c**) *tent* armar.

(**d**) (*) **to ~ it strong** exagerar, no perdonar detalle; **to ~ sb a story** contar a uno un cuento (inverosímil); **he ~ed me this hard-luck story** me contó esta historia tan trágica.

3 *vi* (**a**) (*fall*) caer, caerse; **the ball ~ed in front of him** la pelota cayó delante de él, la pelota vino a parar a sus pies; **after ~ing it bounced high** después de tocar el suelo rebotó muy alto; **the aircraft ~ed into the sea** el avión se precipitó en el mar.

(**b**) (*Naut*) cabecear.

◆**pitch forward** *vi* caer de bruces, caer de cabeza.

◆**pitch in*** *vi* (**a**) (*start*) empezar, (*esp*) empezar a comer; **~ in!** ¡vamos!; ¡a ello!; ¡manos a la obra! (**b**) (*cooperate*) cooperar; (*contribute*) contribuir; **so we all ~ed in together** así que todos nos pusimos a trabajar (*etc*) juntos.

◆**pitch into*** *vt* (**a**) **to ~ into the work** emprender enérgicamente el trabajo, ponerse enérgicamente a trabajar; **they ~ed into the food** atacaron las viandas.

(**b**) (*attack*) atacar; (*verbally*) arremeter contra; (*scold*) poner como un trapo*.

◆**pitch off 1** *vt* quitar de encima, sacudir; **he was ~ed off his horse** fue desarzonado, cayó del caballo.

2 *vi* caer; **he ~ed off the roof** cayó del techo.

◆**pitch out** *vt object* tirar; *person* echar, expulsar, poner de patitas en la calle.

◆**pitch over 1** *vt* tirar; **~ it over!** ¡tíramelo!

2 *vi* (*vehicle etc*) volcarse.

◆**pitch (up)on** *vt* (**a**) (*choose*) elegir, escoger.

(**b**) (*find*) encontrar, dar con.

pitch-and-putt [ˌpɪtʃən'pʌt] *n* minigolf *m*.

pitch-and-toss ['pɪtʃən'tɒs] *n* (juego *m* de) cara *f* o cruz, chapas *fpl*.

pitch-black ['pɪtʃ'blæk] *adj* negro como boca de lobo.

pitchblende ['pɪtʃblend] *n* pec(h)blenda *f*.

pitch-dark ['pɪtʃ'dɑːk] *adj* negro como boca de lobo.

pitched [pɪtʃt] *adj*: **~ battle** batalla *f* campal.

pitcher[1] ['pɪtʃəʳ] *n* (*jug*) cántaro *m*, jarro *m*.

pitcher[2] ['pɪtʃəʳ] *n* (*Baseball*) lanzador *m*.

pitchfork ['pɪtʃfɔːk] **1** *n* horca *f*, bielda *f*.

2 *vt* (*fig*) **to ~ sb into a job** imponer inesperadamente a uno una tarea, hacer que uno se encargue de algo de buena o mala gana; **I was ~ed into it** tuve que aceptarlo a la fuerza, me metieron en esto a la fuerza.

pitchpine ['pɪtʃpaɪn] *n* pino *m* de tea.

pitch pipe ['pɪtʃpaɪp] *n* (*Mus*) diapasón *m*.

piteous ['pɪtɪəs] *adj* lastimero, lastimoso, patético.

piteously ['pɪtɪəslɪ] *adv* lastimosamente.

pitfall ['pɪtfɔːl] *n* escollo *m*, peligro *m*; trampa *f*; **it's a ~ for the unwary** es una trampa para los imprudentes; **'P~s of English'** 'Escollos *mpl* del inglés'; **there are many ~s ahead** hay muchos peligros por delante.

pith [pɪθ] *n* (*Bot*) médula *f*; (*fig*) meollo *m*, médula *f*, jugo *m*, esencia *f*.

pithead ['pɪthed] *n* bocamina *f*.

pithiness ['pɪθɪnɪs] *n* jugosidad *f*; lo sentencioso, lo expresivo; lo sucinto, lo lacónico, concisión *f*.

pithy ['pɪθɪ] *adj* (*full of sense*) jugoso; sentencioso, expresivo; (*terse*) sucinto, lacónico, conciso; **~ saying** dicho *m* sentencioso.

pitiable ['pɪtɪəbl] *adj* lastimoso, digno de compasión; **in a ~ state** en un estado que da lástima; **it was most ~ to see** daba lástima verlo.

pitiful ['pɪtɪfʊl] *adj* (**a**) (*moving to pity*) lastimero, lastimoso; conmovedor. (**b**) (*contemptible*) lamentable, miserable, despreciable; **a ~ display** una exhibición lamentable; **it was just ~** daba lástima.

pitifully ['pɪtɪfəlɪ] *adv* (**a**) (*pathetically*) lastimosamente; de modo conmovedor; **she was crying most ~** lloraba que daba lástima. (**b**) (*contemptibly*) lamentablemente; **a ~ bad play** una comedia tan mala que da lástima.

pitiless ['pɪtɪlɪs] *adj* despiadado, implacable, inmisericorde.

pitilessly ['pɪtɪlɪslɪ] *adv* despiadadamente, implacablemente.

pitman ['pɪtmən] *n*, *pl* **pitmen** ['pɪtmən] minero *m*.

piton ['piːtɒn] *n* pitón *m*, clavija *f* de escala.

pit pony ['pɪtˌpəʊnɪ] *n poney usado antiguamente en las minas.*

pit-prop ['pɪtprɒp] *n* puntal *m*, peón *m*.

pit-stop ['pɪtstɒp] *n* (*motor racing*) entrada *f* a boxes; (*: *on journey*) parada *f* en ruta.

pittance ['pɪtəns] *n* miseria *f*, renta *f* miserable; **a mere ~!** ¡una miseria!; **to live on a ~** vivir de una renta miserable.

pitted ['pɪtɪd] *adj* (**a**) *skin* picado (de viruelas), cacarañado; *surface* picado. (**b**) (*US*) *fruit* deshuesado, sin hueso.

pitter-patter ['pɪtə'pætəʳ] *n etc* = **patter**[2].

pituitary [pɪ'tjuːɪtərɪ] **1** *adj* pituitario; **~ gland** = **2**. **2** *n* glándula *f* pituitaria.

pit worker ['pɪtˌwɜːkəʳ] *n* minero *m*.

pity ['pɪtɪ] **1** *n* (**a**) (*compassion*) compasión *f*, piedad *f*; **for ~'s sake!** ¡por piedad!; (*less seriously*) ¡por Dios!, ¡por el amor de Dios!; **I did it out of ~ for him** se lo hice por compasión; **to feel no ~ for sb** no sentir compasión por uno; **to move sb to ~** mover a uno a compasión, dar lástima a uno; **to take ~ on sb** tener piedad de uno, apiadarse de uno, compadecerse de uno.

(**b**) (*misfortune*) lástima *f*; **what a ~!** ¡qué lástima!, ¡qué pena!; **more's the ~!** ¡desgraciadamente!; **it is a ~ that ...** es una lástima que + *subj*, es una pena que + *subj*; **the ~ of it was that ...** lo lamentable fue que ..., lo peor del caso fue que ...; **it is a thousand pities that ...** es muy de lamentar que + *subj*.

2 *vt* compadecer(se de), tener lástima a; apiadarse de.

pitying ['pɪtɪɪŋ] *adj glance etc* de lástima, lleno de compasión, compasivo.

pityingly ['pɪtɪɪŋlɪ] *adv* con lástima, compasivamente.

Pius ['paɪəs] *nm* Pío.

pivot ['pɪvət] **1** *n* pivote *m*, gorrón *m*; (*fig*) eje *m*, punto *m* central.

2 *vt* montar sobre un pivote; **he ~ed it on his hand** lo hizo girar sobre la mano, lo mantuvo en equilibrio sobre la mano.

3 *vi* girar (*on* sobre); **to ~ on** (*fig*) depender de.

pivotal ['pɪvətl] *adj* (*fig*) central, fundamental.

pix* [pɪks] = **pics**.

pixel ['pɪksel] *n* pixel *m*, punto *m*.

pixie, pixy ['pɪksɪ] *n* duendecito *m*.

pixie hood ['pɪksɪhʊd] *n* caperucita *f*.

pizza ['piːtsə] *n* pizza *f*.

piz(z)azz* [pə'zæz] *n* energía *f*, dinamismo *m*.

pizzeria [ˌpiːtsə'rɪə] *n* pizzería *f*.

PL a/c *abbr of* **profit and loss account** cuenta *f* de pérdidas y ganancias.

placard ['plækɑːd] **1** *n* (*on wall etc*) cartel *m*; (*sign, announcement*) letrero *m*; (*carried in procession etc*) pancarta *f*.

2 *vt*: **the wall is ~ed all over** la pared está llena de carteles; **the town is ~ed with slogans** en todas partes de la ciudad se ven carteles con slogans.

placate [plə'keɪt] *vt* aplacar, apaciguar.

placatory [plə'keɪtərɪ] *adj act, gesture, smile* apaciguador.

place [pleɪs] **1** *n* (**a**) (*gen*) sitio *m*, lugar *m*; **a ~ in the sun** (*fig*) una posición envidiable; **this is the ~** éste es el lugar, aquí es; **we came to a ~ where ...** llegamos a un sitio donde ...; **any ~ will do** cualquier lugar será conveniente, donde quiera sirve; **I don't see it any ~** (*US*) no lo veo en ninguna parte; **it must be some ~ else** (*US*) estará en otra parte; **it's a pretty low sort of ~** no es un lugar muy decente; **people in high ~s** los que ocupan puestos relevantes; **this is no ~ for you** éste no es sitio conveniente para ti; **from ~ to ~** de lugar en lugar; de un lugar para otro; **in another ~** en otra parte, (*Brit Parl*) en la otra cámara; **in high ~s** allá arriba, en las altas esferas, en el gobierno (*etc*); **when the new law is in ~** cuando la nueva ley entre en vigor; **the furniture was all over the ~** los muebles estaban por todas partes; **we're all over the ~** vivimos en la mayor confusión; **your work is all over the ~** haces tu trabajo de cualquier modo; **it all began to fall into ~** todo empezó a tener sentido; todo empezó a parecer lógico; **to find one's ~ in a book** encontrar la página; **to lose one's ~** no encontrar el lugar, (*in reading*) no encontrar la página; perder el hilo; **to mark one's ~ in a book** registrar un libro; **to laugh at the right ~** reírse en el momento oportuno; **to go ~s** (*travel*) viajar, visitar muchos países (*etc*); **we like to go ~s at weekends** durante los fines de semana nos gusta salir de excursión; **he's going ~s** es un ambicioso; llegará lejos; es un hombre de empuje; **we're going ~s at last** por fin empezamos a hacer progresos; **to run in ~** (*US*) correr en parada.

(**b**) (*specific*) sitio *m*, local *m*; **~ of amusement** lugar *m* de diversión; **~ of business** oficina *f*, (*shop*) comercio *m*; **~ of employment, ~ of work** lugar *m* de trabajo; **~ of refuge** refugio *m*, asilo *m*; **~ of residence** residencia *f*, domicilio *m*; **~ of worship** templo *m*, edificio *m* de culto.

(**c**) (*town etc*) lugar *m*; ciudad *f* (*etc*); **fortified ~** plaza *f*, fortaleza *f*; **find a native of the ~** busca un natural de aquí, busca a uno que sea realmente de aquí; **it's a small ~** es un pueblo pequeño; **it's just a small country ~** no es más que un pequeño pueblo rural.

(**d**) (*house*) casa *f*; **his ~ in the country** su casa de campo; **they have a new ~ now** tienen una nueva casa ya; **it's a vast great ~** es una casa inmensa; **we were at Peter's ~** estuvimos en casa de Pedro, estuvimos donde Pedro*; **come to our ~** ven (a visitarnos) a casa; **my ~ or yours?** ¿en mi cama o en la tuya?

(**e**) (*in street names*) plaza *f*.

(**f**) (*~ in relation to owner etc*) sitio *m*, lugar *m*, puesto *m*; **does this have a ~?** ¿tiene esto un sitio determinado?; **to be in ~** estar en su lugar; **to put sth back in its ~** volver algo a su sitio; **to hold sth in ~** sujetar algo en su lugar; **in ~ of** en lugar de, en vez de; **if I were in your ~** yo en tu lugar, yo que tú; **to be out of ~** estar fuera de lugar; desentonar; estar fuera de serie; haberse equivocado de sitio; **that remark was quite out of ~** esa observación estaba fuera de propósito, no cabía tal observación; **it looks out of ~ here** aquí no está bien, aquí parece que está fuera de (su) lugar; **I feel rather out of ~ here** aquí me siento algo desplazado, me siento como que estoy de más aquí; **to change ~s** cambiar de sitio; **to change ~s with sb** trocarse con uno; **to give ~ to** ceder el paso a; **to take ~** tener lugar, verificarse; (*meeting etc*) celebrarse; **the marriage will not now take ~** ahora la boda no se celebrará, ahora no habrá boda; **Z has taken the ~ of A** Z ha sustituido a A; **nobody could ever take his ~** nadie sería capaz de sustituirle; **he managed to keep his ~ in the team** logró conservar su puesto en el equipo.

(**g**) (*seat*) plaza *f*, asiento *m*; (*at table*) cubierto *m*; **a theatre with 2000 ~s** un teatro de 2000 asientos, un teatro que tiene un aforo de 2000; **are there any ~s left?** ¿quedan plazas?; **is this ~ taken?** ¿está ocupado este asiento?; **to lay an extra ~ for sb** poner otro cubierto para uno.

(**h**) (*post*) puesto *m*, empleo *m*; colocación *f*; **~s for 500 workers** 500 puestos *mpl* de trabajo; **school ~** puesto *m* escolar; **it is not my ~ to** + *infin* no me cumple a mí + *infin*; **he found a ~ for his nephew in the firm** le dio un puesto en la compañía a su sobrino; **to seek a ~ in publishing** buscarse una colocación en una casa editorial.

(**i**) (*in series, as rank etc*) lugar *m*, puesto *m*; (*in exam*) calificación *f*; (*rank*) posición *f*, rango *m*; **in the first ~** en primer lugar; **in the second ~** en segundo lugar; **in the next ~** luego, después; **to three ~s of decimals** en milésimas; **to work sth out to three ~s of decimals** calcular algo hasta las milésimas; **P won, with Q in second ~** ganó P, con Q en segunda posición; **to attain a high ~** llegar muy alto, alcanzar un rango alto; **to back a horse for a ~** apostar algo a un caballo para colocado; **to give up one's ~** (*in a queue*) ceder la vez, ceder su turno; **to keep one's ~** mantenerse en la misma posición, lograr seguir como antes; **to know one's ~** ser respetuoso, guardar las distancias; **to put sb in his ~** bajar los humos a uno; **if he gets fresh put him in his ~** si se pone fresco vuélvele a su sitio; **that properly put him in his ~** eso sí le hizo sentirse humilde; **A took (over) B's ~** A ocupó el lugar de B.

2 *vt* (**a**) (*gen*) poner, colocar; fijar; situar, emplazar; **~ it on the table** ponlo en la mesa; **it is ~d rather high up** está en una posición más bien alta, se ha fijado un poco alto; **the house is well ~d** la casa está bien situada; **the shop is awkwardly ~d** la tienda está en una posición de difícil acceso; **the town is ~d on a hill** la ciudad está emplazada en una colina; **to ~ confidence in sb** poner confianza en uno, confiar a uno; **we should ~ no trust in that** no hay que fiarse de eso.

(**b**) (*of orders etc*) **to ~ an advert in a paper** poner un anuncio en un periódico; **to ~ a book with a publisher** colocar un libro con una editorial; **I shall ~ the book elsewhere** ofreceré el libro a otra editorial; **to ~ a contract for machinery with a French firm** firmar un contrato con una compañía francesa para adquirir unas máquinas; **to ~ money** invertir dinero; **to ~ money at interest** colocar dinero a interés; **to ~ an order** colocar un pedido (*for* de), pedir; **goods that are difficult to ~** unos géneros que no encuentran salida; **Cuba was trying to ~ her sugar** Cuba trataba de colocar su azúcar; **the child was ~d with a loving family** el niño fue a vivir con una familia muy cariñosa.

(**c**) (*of jobs*) dar un puesto a, emplear, colocar; **we could ~ 200 men if we had them** de tenerlos podríamos colocar a 200 hombres.

(**d**) (*of series, rank etc*) colocar, clasificar; **to be ~d** (*in race*) colocarse; **to be ~d second** colocarse en segundo lugar; **Vigo is well ~d in the League** Vigo tiene un buen puesto en la Liga; **she was ~d in the first class in maths** le dieron un sobresaliente en matemáticos; **where shall we ~ this candidate?** ¿cómo clasificamos a este candidato?; **he is well ~d to see it all** está en una buena posición para observarlo todo; **we are better ~d than a month ago** estamos mejor colocados que hacia un mes; **we are well ~d to attack** estamos en una buena posición para pasar a la ofensiva.

(**e**) (*recall etc*) recordar, traer a la memoria; (*recognize*) reconocer; (*identify*) identificar, ubicar (*LAm*); **I can't ~ him** no le recuerdo; **I can't quite ~ it** no puedo identificarlo con precisión; **she ~d him at once** le reconoció en seguida.

placebo [plə'si:bəʊ] *n* (*Med, fig*) placebo *m*.

placecard ['pleɪskɑ:d] *n* tarjeta *f que indica el puesto que uno ha de ocupar en la mesa*.

placekick ['pleɪskɪk] *n* puntapié *m* colocado, tiro *m* libre.

placemat ['pleɪsmæt] *n* tapete *m* individual, reposaplatos *m*.

placement ['pleɪsmənt] *n* colocación *f*.

place-name ['pleɪsneɪm] *n* nombre *m* de lugar, topónimo *m*; **~s** (*as study, in general*) toponimia *f*; **the ~s of Aragon** la toponimia aragonesa.

placenta [plə'sentə] *n* placenta *f*.

place-setting ['pleɪs,setɪŋ] *n* cubierto *m*.

placid ['plæsɪd] *adj* plácido; apacible; tranquilo, sosegado.

placidity [plə'sɪdɪtɪ] *n* placidez *f*; apacibilidad *f*; tranquilidad *f*; sosiego *m*.

placidly ['plæsɪdlɪ] *adv* plácidamente; apaciblemente; tranquilamente; sosegadamente.

placing ['pleɪsɪŋ] *n* (*act*) colocación *f*; clasificación *f*; (*~ in table, rank*) puesto *m*, calificación *f*.

plagal ['pleɪgəl] *adj* plagal.

plagiarism ['pleɪdʒɪərɪzəm] *n* plagio *m*.

plagiarist ['pleɪdʒɪərɪst] *n* plagiario *m*, -a *f*.

plagiarize ['pleɪdʒɪəraɪz] *vt* plagiar.

plague [pleɪg] **1** *n* (*Med*) peste *f*; (*fig*) plaga *f*; **what a ~ he is!** ¡es un pesado!; **to avoid sth like the ~** huir de algo como de la peste, evitar algo a toda costa; **to hate sth like the ~** tener un odio visceral a algo.

2 *vt* plagar, infestar; (*fig*) acosar, atormentar; fastidiar; **a thought is plaguing me** me atormenta una idea; **to ~ the life out of sb** fastidiar a uno terriblemente, amargar la vida a uno; **to ~ sb with questions** importunar a uno con preguntas.

plague-ridden ['pleɪg,rɪdn] *adj*, **plague-stricken** ['pleɪg,strɪkən] *adj* apestado.

plaguey* ['pleɪgɪ] *adj* latoso*, engorroso.

plaice [pleɪs] *n, pl invar* platija *f*, solla *f*.

plaid [plæd] *n* (*cloth*) tela *f* a cuadros, tartán *m*; (*cloak*) manta *f* escocesa, plaid *m*.

plain [pleɪn] **1** *adj* (**a**) (*clear*) claro, evidente; **a ~ case of jealousy** un caso evidente de celos; **it is ~ that ...** es evidente que ..., está claro que ...; **it must be ~ to all that ...** ha de ser obvio para todos que ...; **it's as ~ as a pikestaff** está claro como la luz del día; **to make sth ~ to sb** explicar algo a uno con toda claridad; decir algo a uno de modo que no quede lugar a dudas; **I must make it ~ that ...** conste que ..., quede bien claro que ..., tengo que subrayar que ...; **to make one's meaning ~** explicar lo que uno quiere decir; **do I make myself ~?** ¿me entiendes?

(**b**) (*outspoken*) franco, abierto; **to be ~ with sb** hablar claro a uno; **let me be ~ with you** dejémonos de rodeos, pongamos las cosas en su sitio.

(**c**) (*unadorned*) sencillo, llano; sin adornos; *answer* franco; *dealing* honrado; *language, style* corriente, llano; *living* sencillo, sin lujo; *cooking* corriente, casero; *truth* liso y llano; **in ~ clothes** en traje de calle, de paisano; **under ~ cover** en un paquete discreto; **~ knitting** punto *m* de media, punto *m* del derecho; **in ~ language** hablando sin rodeos; para decirlo como es, para llamar las cosas por su nombre; **~ speaking** franqueza *f*; **they're very ~ people** son gente muy sencilla; **I'm a ~ man** soy un hombre llano; **it's a ~ guess** evidentemente es una conjetura; **they used to be called ~ Smith** antes se llamaban Smith sin más.

(**d**) (*unmixed*) natural, puro, sin mezcla; **~ chocolate** chocolate *m* negro, chocolate *m* sin leche; **~ flour** harina *f* normal; **I like ~ whisky** me gusta el whisky sin añadidura, me gusta el whisky sin mezcla.

(**e**) (*of appearance*) sin atractivo, algo feo, ordinario; **she's terribly ~, poor girl** no tiene atractivo alguno, la pobre; **pretty girls and ~ ones** las guapas y las feas.

2 *adv* claro, claramente; **so I told him pretty ~** así que se lo dije con toda claridad; **I can't say it any ~er** no lo puedo decir de modo más claro; **he's ~ wrong** no tiene razón, y punto.

3 *n* llano *m*, llanura *f*; **the Great P~s** (*US*) la Pradera (norteamericana).

plain-clothes ['pleɪn'kləʊðz] *adj*: ~ **policeman** policía *m* en paisano, policía *m* no uniformado.

plainly ['pleɪnlɪ] *adv* (**a**) (*clearly*) claramente, evidentemente; ~ **I was not welcome** evidentemente no iban a recibirme con placer; **to put sth** ~ explicar algo con claridad; **to speak** ~ **to sb** hablar claro a uno.

(**b**) (*frankly*) francamente, con franqueza; categóricamente.

(**c**) (*simply*) sencillamente, claramente.

plainness ['pleɪnnɪs] *n* (**a**) (*clarity*) claridad *f*; evidencia *f*.

(**b**) (*frankness*) franqueza *f*.

(**c**) (*simplicity*) sencillez *f*, llaneza *f*.

(**d**) (*of face*) falta *f* de atractivo, fealdad *f*.

plainsman ['pleɪnzmən] *n*, *pl* **plainsmen** ['pleɪnzmən] llanero *m*, hombre *m* de la llanura.

plainsong ['pleɪnsɒŋ] *n* canto *m* llano.

plain-spoken ['pleɪn'spəʊkən] *adj* franco, llano.

plaintiff ['pleɪntɪf] *n* demandante *mf*, querellante *mf*.

plaintive ['pleɪntɪv] *adj* lastimero, dolorido, quejumbroso.

plaintively ['pleɪntɪvlɪ] *adv* lastimeramente, con dolor.

plait [plæt] **1** *n* trenza *f*; **in ~s** trenzado, en trenzas. **2** *vt* trenzar.

plan [plæn] **1** *n* (**a**) (*Archit*) plano *m*; **to make a** ~ **of** trazar el plano de.

(**b**) (*schedule etc*) programa *m*; (*system*) sistema *m*; **if everything goes according to** ~ si todo se realiza tal como se prevé; **everything went according to** ~ todo salió bien, todo resultó como se había previsto.

(**c**) (*Pol, Econ etc*) plan *m*; ~ **of action** plan *m* de acción, (*loosely*) propósito *m*, programa *m*; **what's our** ~ **of action?** ¡qué nos proponemos hacer?; ~ **of campaign** plan *m* de campaña; **the Badajoz P~** el Plan Badajoz; **the Marshall P~** el Plan Marshall; **the Divine P~** el Diseño Divino; **to draw up a** ~ hacer un plan, redactar un plan.

(**d**) (*personal project etc*) proyecto *m*; **the** ~ **is to come back later** pensamos volver más tarde, tenemos la idea de volver más tarde; **the best** ~ **is to** + *infin* lo mejor es + *infin*; **to change one's** ~ cambiar de proyecto, cambiar de idea; **what ~s have you for the holiday?** ¿qué proyectos tienes para las vacaciones?; **have you any ~s for tonight?** ¿tienes programa para esta noche?; **I have no fixed ~s** no he arreglado nada en definitivo; **what ~s have you for Jim?** ¿qué proyectos hay para Jaimito?, ¿qué ideas tienes sobre el porvenir de Jaimito?; **to make ~s** hacer proyectos; **to upset sb's ~s** dar al traste con los proyectos de uno.

2 *vt* (**a**) (*devise, work out*) planear, planificar; proyectar; preparar; idear; **to** ~ **a robbery** planear un robo; **to** ~ **the future of an industry** planificar el porvenir de una industria; **the mania of ~ning everything** la manía de planificarlo todo; **this trip was ~ned by him** este viaje lo preparó él, fue él quien hizo los preparativos para este viaje.

(**b**) (*intend*) **to** ~ **to do sth, to** ~ **on doing sth** proponerse hacer algo, pensar hacer algo, proyectar hacer algo; **we weren't ~ning to** no teníamos tal intención; no se nos había ocurrido; **how long do you** ~ **to stay?** ¿cuánto tiempo piensas quedarte?

3 *vi* hacer proyectos; hacer los preparativos; **to** ~ **for months** hacer proyectos durante meses enteros; **we are ~ning for next April** hacemos proyectos para el abril que viene; **one has to** ~ **months ahead** hay que hacer los preparativos con varios meses de antelación.

◆**plan out** *vt* planear detalladamente.

planchette [plɑːn'ʃet] *n* tabla *f* de escritura espiritista.

plane¹ [pleɪn] *n* (*Bot*: *also* ~ **tree**) plátano *m*.

plane² [pleɪn] **1** *adj* plano; ~ **geometry** geometría *f* plana.

2 *n* (**a**) (*Math*) plano *m*.

(**b**) (*fig*) nivel *m*, esfera *f*; **he seems to exist on another** ~ parece existir en una esfera distinta; **on this** ~ en este nivel, a esta altura.

(**c**) (*tool*) (*small*) cepillo *m* (de carpintero); (*large*) garlopa *f*.

(**d**) (*Aer*) avión *m*; **to go by** ~ ir en avión; **to send goods by** ~ enviar artículos por avión.

3 *vt* acepillar; **to** ~ **down** acepillar, desbastar, alisar.

plane³ [pleɪn] *vi* (*bird, glider, boat*) planear; (*car*) aquaplanear.

planet ['plænɪt] *n* planeta *m*.

planetarium [,plænɪ'tɛərɪəm] *n* planetario *m*.

planetary ['plænɪtərɪ] *adj* planetario.

plangent ['plændʒənt] *adj* plañidero.

plank [plæŋk] **1** *n* tabla *f* (gruesa), tablón *m*; (*fig*: *Pol*) principio *m*, artículo *m* (de un programa político); **~s** (*planking*) tablaje *m*; **deck ~s** tablazón *f* de la cubierta.

2 *vt* (**a**) entablar, entarimar.

(**b**) **to** ~ **sth down** tirar algo violentamente, arrojar algo violentamente.

3 *vr*: **to** ~ **o.s. down** sentarse (*etc*) de modo agresivo.

planking ['plæŋkɪŋ] *n* tablas *fpl*, tablaje *m*; (*Naut*) tablazón *f* de la cubierta.

plankton ['plæŋktən] *n* plancton *m*.

planned [plænd] *adj economy* dirigido; *development, redundancy etc* programado; *crime, murder* premeditado.

planner ['plænəʳ] **1** *n* planificador *m*, -ora *f*. **2** *attr*: ~ **board** diagrama *m* de planificación.

planning ['plænɪŋ] **1** *n* (*Pol, Econ etc*) planificación *f*; (*personal projects*) proyectos *mpl*.

2 *attr*: ~ **board** comisión *f* planificadora; ~ **permission** permiso *m* de construcción; **we're still in the** ~ **stage** estamos todavía en la etapa de la planificación.

plant [plɑːnt] **1** *n* (**a**) (*Bot*) planta *f*.

(**b**) (*Tech*: *machinery*) equipo *m*, maquinaria *f*, instalación *f*; (*factory*) planta *f*, fábrica *f*.

(**c**) (*: *trick*) truco *m* para incriminar a uno; **it's a** ~ aquí hay trampa.

(**d**) (*: *person*) agente *mf*, espía *f*.

2 *attr* vegetal; ~ **life** vida *f* vegetal, las plantas; ~ **kingdom** reino *m* vegetal; ~ **louse** pulgón *m*.

3 *vt* (**a**) *plant* plantar; *seed* sembrar; **to** ~ **a field with turnips** sembrar un campo de nabos; **the field is ~ed with wheat** el campo está sembrado de trigo.

(**b**) (*place*) poner, colocar; fijar; *people* establecer; *informer, spy* colar, colocar, introducir (*on* en); *blow* plantar, asestar; *idea etc* inculcar (*in* en), imbuir (*in* con); **to** ~ **sth on sb** ocultar algo en la ropa (*or* en la habitación *etc*) de uno para incriminarle.

4 *vr*: **to** ~ **o.s. in the middle of the road** ponerse en medio de la calle.

◆**plant out** *vt seedlings* trasplantar.

◆**plant up** *vt land* plantar, sembrar.

plantain ['plæntɪn] *n* llantén *m*, plátano *m* (*LAm*).

plantation [plæn'teɪʃən] *n* (*of tea, sugar etc*) plantación *f*; (*large estate*) hacienda *f*; (*of trees*) arboleda *f*; (*of young trees*) plantel *m*; (*Hist*) colonia *f*.

planter ['plɑːntəʳ] *n* plantador *m*, -ora *f*; cultivador *m*, -ora *f*; (*loosely*) colono *m*.

planting ['plɑːntɪŋ] *n* plantación *f*, el plantar; ~ **season** estación *f* de plantar.

plantpot ['plɑːntpɒt] *n* tiesto *m*, maceta *f*.

plaque [plæk] *n* placa *f*; (*on teeth*) sarro *m*.

plash [plæʃ] = **splash**.

plasm ['plæzəm] *n*, **plasma** ['plæzmə] *n* plasma *m*.

plaster ['plɑːstəʳ] **1** *n* (**a**) (*lime material*) yeso *m*; (*in building*) argamasa *f*, (*layer on wall*) enlucido *m*.

(**b**) (*Brit Med*: *applied to wound*) emplasto *m*, parche *m*; (*for injured arm etc*) escayola *f*, tablilla *f* de yeso; (*Brit*: *adhesive* ~) esparadrapo *m*, tirita *f*; ~ **of Paris** yeso *m* mate; **with his leg in** ~ con la pierna escayolada; **to have one's neck in** ~ tener el cuello escayolado.

2 *attr*: ~ **cast** vaciado *m*; (*death mask*) mascarilla *f* mortuoria; (*Med*) escayola *f*.

3 *vt* (**a**) *wall* enyesar, enlucir; (*Med*) emplastar, aplicar un emplasto a; **to** ~ **a wall with posters** llenar (*or* cubrir) una pared de carteles; **to** ~ **posters on a wall** pegar carteles a una pared; **to** ~ **over a hole** llenar un hoyo de argamasa; **the story was ~ed all over the front page** el reportaje llenaba la primera plana; **the children came back ~ed with mud** los niños volvieron cubiertos de lodo.

(**b**) (*) dar una paliza a, pegar.

plasterboard ['plɑːstəbɔːd] *n* cartón *m* de yeso y fieltro.

plastered‡ ['plɑːstəd] *adj*: **to be** ~ estar ajumado*, estar tomado* (*LAm*).

plasterer ['plɑːstərəʳ] *n* yesero *m*, enlucidor *m*.

plastering ['plɑːstərɪŋ] *n* enlucido *m*.

plastic ['plæstɪk] **1** *adj* (**a**) (*gen*) plástico; ~ **bag** bolsa *f* de plástico; ~ **bomb** bomba *f* de goma 2; ~ **bullet** bala *f* de goma; ~ **explosive** goma *f* 2; ~ **money** dinero *m* plástico; ~ **surgeon** cirujano *m* especializado en cirugía plástica; ~ **surgery** cirugía *f* plástica, cirugía *f* estética. (**b**) (*: *sham*) falso, de imitación. **2** *n* plástico *m*; (*credit cards*) dinero *m* plástico.

Plasticine ['plæstɪsiːn] ® *n* plasticina ® *f*, plastilina *f*, arcilla *f* de modelar.

plasticity [plæs'tɪsɪtɪ] *n* plasticidad *f*.

plate [pleɪt] **1** *n* (*dish*) plato *m*; (*of metal etc*) lámina *f*, chapa *f*, plancha *f*; (*on cooker*) quemador *m*, fuego *m*, placa *f*; (*plaque*) placa *f*; (*silver*) vajilla *f* de plata; (*for taking collection*) platillo *m*; (*Geol*) placa *f*; (*Typ*) lámina *f*; (*Phot*: *of microscope*) placa *f*; (*prize, in racing*) premio *m*; (*also* **dental** ~) placa *f* de la dentadura postiza; (*US Baseball*) plato *m*; **~s**‡ (*feet*) tachines‡ *mpl*; **gold** ~ vajilla *f* de oro; **to hand sb sth on a** ~ (*fig*) servir algo a uno en bandeja de plata; **to go to the** ~ (*US*) entrar a batear; (*fig*) afrontar el problema; reconocer sus responsabilidades; **to have a lot on one's** ~ estar muy ocupado, tener muchos asuntos entre manos, tener grandes responsabilidades.

2 *attr*: ~ **armor** (*US*), ~ **armour** blindaje *m*; ~ **glass** vidrio *m* cilindrado, luna *f*.

3 *vt* (*with metal*) planchear, chapear; (*with armour*) blindar; (*with silver*) platear; (*with nickel*) niquelar.

Plate [pleɪt] *n*: **the River** ~ el Río de la Plata.

plateau ['plætəʊ] *n*, *pl* **plateaux** ['plætəʊz] meseta *f*, altiplanicie *f*, altiplano *m* (*LAm*).

plated ['pleɪtɪd] *adj* chapeado (*with* de); niquelado; (*armoured*) blindado.

plateful ['pleɪtfʊl] *n* plato *m*.

plateholder ['pleɪtˌhəʊldəʳ] *n* (*Phot*) portaplacas *m*.

platelayer ['pleɪtˌleɪəʳ] *n* obrero *m* (de ferrocarriles).

platen ['plætən] *n* rodillo *m*.

plate-rack ['pleɪtræk] *n* portaplatos *m*.

plate-warmer ['pleɪtˌwɔːməʳ] *n* calentador *m* de platos.

platform ['plætfɔːm] **1** *n* (**a**) plataforma *f*; (*at meeting*) tribuna *f*; (*for band etc*) estrado *m*; (*roughly-built*) tarima *f*, tablado *m*; (*Pol*) programa *m* electoral, plataforma *f*; **the society offered him a** ~ la sociedad le ofreció una tribuna (para exponer sus ideas); **last year they shared a** ~ el año pasado ocuparon la misma tribuna.

(**b**) (*Brit Rail*) andén *m*; (*with number mentioned*) vía *f*; **the 5.15 is at** (*or* **on**) ~ **8** el tren de las 5.15 está en la vía número 8.

2 *attr*: **the** ~ **speakers** los oradores de la tribuna; ~ **ticket** (*Brit*) billete *m* (*LAm*: boleto *m*) de andén.

plating ['pleɪtɪŋ] *n* enchapado *m*; capa *f* metálica; (*armour*-~) blindaje *m*; (*of nickel*) niquelado *m*.

platinum ['plætɪnəm] **1** *n* platino *m*. **2** *attr*: ~ **blonde** rubia *f* platino.

platitude ['plætɪtjuːd] *n* lugar *m* común, tópico *m*, perogrullada *f*; **it is a** ~ **to say that** ... es un tópico decir que ...

platitudinize [ˌplætɪ'tjuːdɪnaɪz] *vi* decir tópicos.

platitudinous [ˌplætɪ'tjuːdɪnəs] *adj speech* lleno de lugares comunes (*etc*); *speaker* aficionado a los lugares comunes (*etc*), que peca por exceso de tópicos.

Plato ['pleɪtəʊ] *nm* Platón.

platonic [plə'tɒnɪk] *adj* platónico; ~ **love** amor *m* platónico.

platonism ['pleɪtənɪzəm] *n* platonismo *m*.

platonist ['pleɪtənɪst] *n* platonista *mf*.

platoon [plə'tuːn] *n* pelotón *m*, sección *f*.

platter ['plætəʳ] *n* (**a**) (*dish*) fuente *f*. (**b**) (*US**) disco *m*.

platypus ['plætɪpəs] *n* ornitorrinco *m*.

plaudits ['plɔːdɪts] *npl* aplausos *mpl*.

plausibility [ˌplɔːzə'bɪlɪtɪ] *n* verosimilitud *f*, admisibilidad *f*, credibilidad *f*; **his** ~ **is such that** ... habla tan bien que ..., tiene tanto cuento que ...

plausible ['plɔːzəbl] *adj argument etc* verosímil, admisible, creíble; *person* bien hablado pero no del todo confiable, que casi convence; **he's a** ~ **sort** tiene mucho cuento.

plausibly ['plɔːzəblɪ] *adv* de modo verosímil, creíblemente; **he tells it most** ~ lo cuenta de modo que casi convence.

play [pleɪ] **1** *n* (**a**) (*amusement etc*) juego *m*, recreo *m*, diversión *f*; ~ **on words** juego *m* de palabras; **to be at** ~ estar jugando; **to make** ~ **of** burlarse de; **to say sth in** ~ decir algo en broma.

(**b**) (*Sport etc*: *act of* ~*ing*) jugada *f*; **neat** ~ una bonita jugada; **a clever piece of** ~ una hábil jugada; **fair** ~ juego *m* limpio; **foul** ~ juego *m* sucio; **to be in** ~ estar en juego; **to be out of** ~ estar fuera de juego; ~ **began at 3 o'clock** el partido comenzó a las 3, se empezó a jugar a las 3.

(**c**) (*activity etc*) juego *m*, actividad *f*; **to bring into** ~ poner en juego; **to come into** ~ entrar en juego; **to give full** ~ **to one's imagination** dar rienda suelta a la imaginación; **to make great** ~ **with sth** recalcar algo, insistir en algo.

(**d**) (*Mech*) juego *m*, holgura *f*, movimiento *m* libre.

(**e**) **the** ~ **of light on the water** el rielar de la luz sobre el agua; **the** ~ **of light and dark in this picture** el efecto de luz y sombra en este cuadro.

(**f**) (*Theat*) obra *f*, obra *f* dramática, comedia *f*; **the** ~**s of Lope** las obras dramáticas de Lope, el teatro de Lope; **to go to the** ~ ir al teatro.

(**g**) **to make a** ~ **for sth** tratar de conseguir algo, hacer una tentativa de obtener algo; **he made a** ~ **for her** le echó un tiento.

2 *vt* (**a**) (*Theat etc*) *play* representar, poner, dar; *part* hacer, hacer el papel de, (*fig*) desempeñar; **when we** ~**ed 'Hamlet'** cuando representamos 'Hamlet'; **when I** ~**ed Hamlet** cuando hice el papel de Hamlet; **what did you** ~**?** ¿qué papel tuviste?; **we shall be** ~**ing the West End** pondremos la obra en el West End; **when we last** ~**ed Blackpool** cuando representamos la última vez en Blackpool; **we** ~**ed 'Lear' as a comedy** representamos 'Lear' como comedia; **we** ~**ed 'Charley's Aunt' straight** representamos 'Charley's Aunt' como obra seria; **let's** ~ **it for laughs** hagámoslo de manera burlesca; **he likes to** ~ **the soldier** se las echa de soldado, se da aires de militar; *V* **fool**[1] *etc*.

(**b**) **to** ~ **a joke on sb** gastar una broma a uno; **to** ~ **a dirty trick on sb** hacer una mala pasada a uno.

(**c**) *card* jugar; *ball* golpear; *chess piece etc* mover; *fish* dejar que se canse, agotar; **to** ~ **the market** jugar a la bolsa; **to** ~ **both ends against the middle** beneficiarse de la diversidad de factores en juego.

(**d**) *cards, game etc* jugar a; **to** ~ **a game of tennis** jugar un partido de tenis; **to** ~ **a game of cards with sb** echar una partida de cartas con uno; **do you** ~ **football?** ¿juegas al fútbol?

(**e**) *opponent* jugar con, jugar contra; **I** ~**ed him at chess** jugué contra él al ajedrez; **I** ~**ed him twice** jugué contra él dos veces; **I'll** ~ **you for the drinks** quien pierde paga.

(**f**) (*make member of team*) incluir, incluir en el equipo; **are they** ~**ing Wooster?** ¿juega Wooster?, ¿van a incluir a Wooster?

(**g**) (*Sport*: *in position*) jugar de; **I** ~**ed back** jugué de defensa; **can you** ~ **goalkeeper?** ¿puedes jugar de portero?

(**h**) **to** ~ **sb false** traicionar a uno.

(**i**) (*direct*) dirigir (*on* hacia, sobre); **to** ~ **hoses on a fire** dirigir mangueras sobre un incendio; ~ **the hose this way a bit** dirige la manguera más hacia este lado; **to** ~ **a searchlight on an aircraft** dirigir un reflector hacia un avión, hacer de un avión el blanco de un reflector.

(**j**) (*Mus*) *instrument* tocar; *record, tape* poner; **to learn to** ~ **the piano** aprender a tocar el piano; **they** ~**ed the 5th Symphony** tocaron la Quinta Sinfonía, interpretaron la Quinta Sinfonía.

3 *vi* (**a**) (*amuse o.s.*) jugar; divertirse; (*frolic*) jugar, juguetear; (*gambol*) retozar; **run away and** ~**!** ¡idos a jugar!; **to** ~ **with a stick** jugar con un palo; **to** ~ **with fire** jugar con fuego; **to** ~ **with one's food** comiscar, jugar con la comida; **he's just** ~**ing with you** se está burlando de ti; **to** ~ **with an idea** acariciar una idea; **he's got money to** ~ **with** tiene dinero de sobra; **this is not a question to be** ~**ed with** éste no es asunto para reírse, éste no es asunto para tomar en broma; *V* **fast**[1] *etc*.

(**b**) (*at a game etc*) **to** ~ **at chess** jugar al ajedrez; **he just** ~**s at it** lo hace con poca seriedad; **the little girl** ~**s at being a woman** la niña juega a ser mujer; **to** ~ **at soldiers** jugar a los soldados; **to** ~ **at trains** jugar con los trenes; **what are you** ~**ing at?** ¿a qué esto?; ~**!** ¡listo!; **who** ~**s first?** ¿quién juega primero?; **are you** ~**ing today?** ¿tu juegas hoy?; **I've not** ~**ed for a long time** hace mucho tiempo que no juego; **to** ~ **fair** jugar limpio; **to** ~ **for time** tratar de ganar tiempo; **to** ~ **into sb's hands** hacer el caldo gordo a uno, hacer el juego a uno.

(**c**) (*Mus*) tocar; **to** ~ **on the piano** tocar el piano; **do you** ~**?** ¿sabes tocar?; **to** ~ **to sb** tocar para uno; **when the organ** ~**s** cuando suena el órgano.

(**d**) (*light*) rielar; **the sun was** ~**ing on the water** rielaba el sol sobre el agua.

(**e**) (*fountain*) correr; funcionar.

(**f**) (*act*) **to** ~ **in a film** tener (*or* hacer) un papel en una película; **we have** ~**ed all over the South** hemos representado en todas partes del Sur; **to** ~ **ill** fingirse enfermo; **to** ~ **hard to get** hacerse de rogar; (*woman*) hacerse la difícil; **to** ~ **safe** obrar con cautela, ser prudente.

◆**play about, play around** *vi* (**a**) (*children*) jugar, divertirse; (*sleep around*) dormir con cualquiera.

(**b**) **to** ~ **about with** (*fiddle*) jugar con, manosear; (*damage*) estropear; (*test*) explorar, ensayar (de varias maneras); **I** ~**ed around with the programme till it worked** ensayé el programa de varias maneras hasta hacerle funcionar bien.

◆**play along** *vi*: **to** ~ **along with sb** seguir el humor a uno; ajustarse a las ideas de uno.

◆**play back** *vt* repetir, reproducir.
◆**play down** *vt* quitar (*or* restar) importancia a, tratar de minimizar, relativizar.
◆**play in 1** *vt*: **the band ~ed the procession in** tocaba la orquesta mientras entraba el desfile.
2 *vr*: **to ~ o.s. in** acostumbrarse a las condiciones de juego.
◆**play off 1** *vt* (**a**) **to ~ off A against B** contraponer A a B.
(**b**) **to ~ off a tie** jugar el desempate.
2 *vi* (*Sport*) jugar el desempate.
◆**play on 1** *vt*: **to ~ on words** jugar con las palabras; **to ~ on sb's emotions** jugar con las emociones de uno; **to ~ on sb's nerves** poner los nervios de uno de punta; **to ~ on sb's credulity** explotar la credulidad de uno.
2 *vi* (*Mus*) seguir tocando; (*Sport*) seguir jugando; **~ on!** ¡adelante!
◆**play out** *vt* (**a**) **to ~ out time** entretener el tiempo que queda, seguir jugando por pura fórmula hasta el fin.
(**b**) **the organ ~ed the congregation out** tocaba el órgano mientras salían los fieles.
(**c**) **to be ~ed out*** (*person, seam etc*) estar agotado.
(**d**) *fantasy etc* realizar, dar forma práctica a, expresar en la realidad; **they are ~ing out a drama of revenge** están representando un drama de venganza.
◆**play over, play through** *vt music* tocar, ensayar.
◆**play up 1** *vt* (**a**) (*give trouble*) dar guerra a; causar molestias a; **the kids ~ her up dreadfully** los chavales le dan guerra de mala manera.
(**b**) (*magnify*) exagerar, encarecer.
2 *vi* (**a**) (*Sport*) jugar mejor, jugar con más ánimo; **~ up!** ¡ánimo!, ¡aúpa!
(**b**) (*Brit**) dar guerra; causar problemas, causar molestias; **my stomach is ~ing up again** mi estómago vuelve a darme problemas; **the car is ~ing up** el coche no marcha bien.
(**c**) **to ~ up to sb*** hacer la pelotilla a uno*, bailar el agua a uno.
◆**play upon** *vt* = **play on 2.**
playact ['pleɪækt] *vi* hacer la comedia; (*exaggerate*) hacer teatro.
playacting ['pleɪˌæktɪŋ] *n* comedia *f*, farsa *f*; **this is mere ~** esto es puro teatro, no es más que una comedia.
playactor ['pleɪˌæktəʳ] *n* actor *m* (*also fig*).
playback ['pleɪbæk] *n* repetición *f*, reproducción *f*; (*TV etc*) playback *m*, previo *m*.
playbill ['pleɪbɪl] *n* cartel *m* (de teatro).
playboy ['pleɪbɔɪ] *n* señorito *m*, córrelas *m*, botarate *m*.
played-out* ['pleɪd'aʊt] *adj person, seam etc* agotado, rendido; quemado.
player ['pleɪəʳ] *n* (**a**) (*Theat*) actor *m*, actriz *f*, representante *mf*. (**b**) (*Mus*) músico *m*, -a *f*. (**c**) (*Sport*) jugador *m*, -ora *f*; **football ~** jugador *m* de fútbol.
playfellow ['pleɪˌfeləʊ] *n* compañero *m*, -a *f* de juego.
playful ['pleɪfʊl] *adj person* juguetón; *mood* alegre; *remark* dicho en broma, festivo.
playfully ['pleɪfəlɪ] *adv* jugando, en juego; alegremente; en broma; **he said ~** dijo guasón.
playfulness ['pleɪfʊlnɪs] *n* carácter *m* juguetón; alegría *f*; tono *m* guasón.
playgoer ['pleɪˌgəʊəʳ] *n* aficionado *m*, -a *f* al teatro; **we are regular ~s** vamos con regularidad al teatro.
playground ['pleɪgraʊnd] *n* (*in school*) patio *m*; campo *m* de recreo; (*of millionaires*) paraíso *m*, lugar *m* favorito.
playgroup ['pleɪˌgruːp] *n* guardería *f* infantil, jardín *m* de infancia.
playhouse ['pleɪhaʊs] *n*, *pl* **playhouses** ['pleɪˌhaʊzɪz] teatro *m*; (*US*) casita *f* de muñecas.
playing ['pleɪɪŋ] *n* (**a**) (*Sport*) juego *m*; **~ in the wet is tricky** es difícil jugar cuando llueve. (**b**) (*Mus*) **the orchestra's ~ of the symphony was uninspired** la interpretación de la orquesta de la sinfonía fue poco inspirada; **there was some fine ~ in the violin concerto** el concierto de violín estuvo muy bien interpretado.
playing-card ['pleɪɪŋkɑːd] *n* carta *f*, naipe *m*.
playing-field ['pleɪɪŋfiːld] *n* campo *m* (*LAm*: cancha *f*) de deportes.
playmate ['pleɪmeɪt] *n* camarada *mf*, compañero *m*, -a *f* de juego.
play-off ['pleɪɒf] *n* (partido *m* de) desempate *m*; (*of top teams in league*) liguilla *f*.
playpen ['pleɪpen] *n* parque *m* de jugar, corralito *m* (de niño).
play-reading ['pleɪˌriːdɪŋ] *n* lectura *f* (de una obra dramática).
playroom ['pleɪrʊm] *n* cuarto *m* de los niños.
playschool ['pleɪˌskuːl] *n* parvulario *m*.
plaything ['pleɪθɪŋ] *n* juguete *m* (*also fig*).
playtime ['pleɪtaɪm] *n* recreo *m*.
playwright ['pleɪraɪt] *n* dramaturgo *mf* (*also* -a *f*), autor *m* dramático, autora *f* dramática.
plaza ['plɑːzə] *n* (*US*) (**a**) (*motorway services*) zona *f* de servicios. (**b**) (*toll*) peaje *m*.
PLC, plc *n* (*Brit*) *abbr of* **public limited company** Sociedad *f* Anónima por acciones, S.A.
plea [pliː] *n* (**a**) (*excuse*) pretexto *m*, disculpa *f*. (**b**) (*entreaty*) ruego *m*, súplica *f*, petición *f*; **he made a ~ for mercy** pidió clemencia. (**c**) (*Jur*) alegato *m*, defensa *f*; contestación *f* a la demanda, declaración *f*; **a ~ of insanity** un alegato de desequilibrio mental.
plea bargaining ['pliːˌbɑːgɪnɪŋ] *n acuerdo táctico entre fiscal y defensor para agilizar los trámites judiciales*.
plead [pliːd] (*irr in US*: *pret, ptp* **pled**) **1** *vt* (**a**) **to ~ sb's cause** hablar por uno, interceder por uno; (*Jur*) defender a uno en juicio.
(**b**) (*give as excuse*) alegar; pretextar; **to ~ ignorance** pretextar ignorancia; **he ~ed certain difficulties** alegó ciertas dificultades; **to ~ that ...** alegar que ..., pretextar que ...
2 *vi* (**a**) suplicar, rogar; **to ~ with sb** suplicar a uno; **to ~ with sb for sth** rogar a uno que conceda (*or* permita *etc*) algo; **I ~ed and ~ed but it was no use** le supliqué mil veces pero de nada sirvió; **the village has ~ed for a new bridge for 10 years** durante 10 años el pueblo viene reclamando un nuevo puente.
(**b**) (*Jur*: *as barrister*) abogar.
(**c**) (*Jur*: *as defendant*) declarar; **how do you ~?** ¿qué contestación hace Vd a la demanda?; **to ~ guilty** confesarse culpable; **to ~ not guilty** negar la acusación.
pleading ['pliːdɪŋ] **1** *n* súplicas *fpl*; (*Jur*) alegatos *mpl*; **special ~** argumentos *mpl* especiosos. **2** *adj tone etc* suplicante, de súplica.
pleasant ['pleznt] *adj* agradable; *surprise etc* grato; *manner, style* ameno; *person* simpático, afable, amable; **we had a ~ time** lo pasamos muy bien; **it's very ~ here** aquí se está muy bien; **it made a ~ change from our usual holiday** fueron unas vacaciones distintas de las acostumbradas y muy agradables; **it's a ~ surprise to find that ...** es una grata sorpresa descubrir que ...; **it did not make ~ reading** su lectura no fue nada agradable; **to make o.s. ~ to sb** procurar ser amable con uno.
pleasantly ['plezntlɪ] *adv* agradablemente; gratamente; en estilo ameno; afablemente, amablemente; **I am ~ surprised that ...** para mí es una grata sorpresa que + *subj*; **it is ~ warm** hace un calor agradable.
pleasantness ['plezntnɪs] *n* agrado *m*, lo agradable; amenidad *f*; simpatía *f*, amabilidad *f*.
pleasantry ['plezntrɪ] *n* chiste *m*, dicho *m* gracioso.
please [pliːz] **1** *vti* (**a**) (*give pleasure to*) dar gusto a, dar satisfacción a, agradar, contentar; caer en gracia a; **I did it just to ~ you** lo hice únicamente para darte gusto; **there's no pleasing him** es imposible contentarle; **he is easily ~d** se contenta con cualquier cosa; **she's hard to ~** es muy exigente; **the joke ~d him** el chiste le cayó en gracia; **he is anxious to ~** procura dar satisfacción; **a gift that is sure to ~** un regalo que siempre agrada; **music that ~s the ear** una música grata para el oído; **to lay o.s. out to ~ sb** desvivirse por contentar a uno; **it ~d him to order that ...** tuvo a bien ordenar que + *subj*.
(**b**) (*impers*) **~ God!** ¡plegue a Dios!; **~ God that ...!** ¡plegue a Dios que + *subj*!
(**c**) (*expressing wish*) **~!** ¡por favor!, (*as protest*) ¡por Dios!; **my bill ~** la cuenta, por favor; **two pints ~!** ¡dos cañas (por favor)!; **two to Victoria ~** a Victoria, dos (por favor); **~ pass the salt, pass the salt ~** ¿me haces el favor de pasar la sal?; **~ tell me** haz el favor de decírmelo, dímelo por favor; **~ be seated** siéntense; **~ sit down!** ¡hagan el favor de sentarse!; **~ accept this book** le ruego acepte este libro; **'~ do not open this door'** 'se ruega no abrir esta puerta'; **~ don't cry!** ¡no llores, te lo suplico!; **now ~ DO let me know if ...** no dejes de decirme si ...; **may I? ... ~ do!** ¿se puede? ... ¡por supuesto!
(**d**) (*think fit*) **if you ~** si te parece; con tu permiso; **he wanted 10, if you ~!** quería llevarse 10, ¡fíjate!; **to do as one ~s** hacer lo que le da la gana; **I shall do what I ~** haré lo que me parezca bien; **as you ~** como quieras; **do as you ~** haz lo que quieras.
2 *vr*: **to ~ o.s.** hacer lo que le da la gana; **~ yourself!** ¡como quieras!; **he has always ~d himself about holidays**

en asunto de vacaciones siempre ha hecho lo que le venía en gana.

pleased [pliːzd] *adj* (**a**) (*happy*) alegre, contento; **to be ~** estar contento; **to be as ~ as Punch** estar como unas pascuas; **to look ~** estar alegre, parece estar contento; tener aire satisfecho.

(**b**) **to be ~ with sth** estar satisfecho de algo; **to be ~ with sb** mostrarse satisfecho con uno; **to be ~ with o.s.** estar satisfecho de sí mismo; **they were anything but ~ with the news** no estaban nada contentos con la noticia, distaban mucho de estar contentos con la noticia; **I am ~ at the decision** me alegro de la decisión; **I am ~ to hear it** me alegro de saberlo; (**I am**) **~ to meet you** (tengo) mucho gusto en conocerle, (estoy) encantado de conocerle; **I am ~ to be able to announce that ...** me es grato poderles anunciar que ...; **we are ~ to inform you that ...** (*Comm*) nos complacemos en comunicarles que ..., nos es grato informarles que ...

(**c**) (*royal usage*) **Her Majesty has been graciously ~ to accept ...** su Majestad aceptó sumamente complacida ...

pleasing ['pliːzɪŋ] *adj* agradable; grato; halagüeño; **with ~ results** con resultados halagüeños; **a most ~ piece of news** una noticia muy grata.

pleasingly ['pliːzɪŋlɪ] *adv* agradablemente; gratamente.

pleasurable ['pleʒərəbl] *adj* agradable, deleitoso.

pleasurably ['pleʒərəblɪ] *adv* agradablemente, deleitosamente; **we were ~ surprised** para nosotros fue una grata sorpresa.

pleasure ['pleʒəʳ] **1** *n* (**a**) (*in general*) placer *m*, gusto *m*, satisfacción *f*; **with ~** con mucho gusto; **it's a ~ to see him** da gusto verle; **it's a ~ to know that ...** es un motivo de satisfacción saber que ...; **it's a real ~** es un verdadero placer; **~!, the ~ is mine!** (*returning thanks*) ¡no hay de qué!; **to find ~ in chess** disfrutar jugando al ajedrez; **what ~ can you find in shooting partridges?** ¿qué placer encuentras en matar perdices?; **to give sb ~** dar gusto a uno; **if it gives you any ~** si te gusta; **I have much ~ in informing you that ...** me es grato informarle que ...; **may I have the ~?** (*at dance*) ¿quieres bailar?; **to take ~ in books** disfrutar leyendo; **I take great ~ in watching them grow** disfruto muchísimo viéndolos crecer; **to take ~ in doing damage** complacerse en hacer daño; **Mr and Mrs X request the ~ of Y's company** los señores de X solicitan el placer de la compañía del Sr Y.

(**b**) (*amusements*) placeres *mpl*; diversión *f*, recreo *m*; **all the ~s of London** todos los placeres de Londres, todas las diversiones de Londres; **sexual ~** placer *m* sexual; **to be fond of ~** ser amante de los placeres.

(**c**) (*will*) voluntad *f*; **at ~** a voluntad; **do it at your ~** hazlo cuando quieras, hazlo cuando tengas tiempo; **during the royal ~** mientras quiera el monarca; **what is your ~, sir?** ¿en qué puedo servirle, señor?, ¿qué manda Vd, señor?

2 *attr* de recreo; **~ trip** viaje *m* de recreo.

pleasure-boat ['pleʒəbəʊt] *n*, **pleasure-craft** ['pleʒəkrɑːft] *n* barco *m* de recreo; embarcación *f* deportiva.

pleasure-cruise ['pleʒəkruːz] *n* crucero *m* de recreo.

pleasure-ground ['pleʒəgraʊnd] *n* parque *m* de atracciones.

pleasure-loving ['pleʒə,lʌvɪŋ] *adj* amante de los placeres.

pleasure-seeker ['pleʒə,siːkəʳ] *n* hedonista *mf*.

pleasure-seeking ['pleʒə,siːkɪŋ] *adj* hedonista, que busca el placer.

pleasure-steamer ['pleʒə,stiːməʳ] *n* vapor *m* de recreo.

pleat [pliːt] **1** *n* pliegue *m*, doblez *m*; (*of skirt*) tabla *f*. **2** *vt* plegar, plisar.

pleb* [pleb] **1** *n* plebeyo *m*, -a *f*, persona *f* ordinaria; **the ~s** la plebe. **2** *adj* plebeyo, aplebeyado.

plebeian [plɪ'biːən] **1** *adj* plebeyo. **2** *n* plebeyo *m*, -a *f*.

plebiscite ['plebɪsɪt] *n* plebiscito *m*.

plectrum ['plektrəm] *n* plectro *m*.

pled [pled] (*US*) *irr*: *pret, ptp of* **plead.**

pledge [pledʒ] **1** *n* (*given as security*) prenda *f*; (*promise*) promesa *f*, voto *m*; garantía *f*; (*to flag etc*) acto *m* de acatamiento; (*between governments etc*) compromiso *m*; (*toast*) brindis *m*; **as a ~ of** en señal de, como garantía de; **I give you this ~** os hago esta promesa; **the government will honour its ~s** el gobierno hará honor a sus compromisos; **to sign the ~** jurar abstenerse del alcohol.

2 *vt* (**a**) (*pawn*) empeñar, pignorar, dejar en prenda.

(**b**) (*promise*) prometer; *one's word* dar; **to ~ support for sb** prometer su apoyo a uno, prometer apoyar a uno; **to ~ one's allegiance to sb** jurar ser fiel a uno; **I am ~d to secrecy** he jurado guardarlo secreto; **we are ~d to go to their aid** hemos prometido ir a ayudarles, nos hemos comprometido a ayudarles.

(**c**) (*toast*) brindar por.

3 *vr*: **to ~ o.s. to** + *infin* comprometerse a + *infin*.

Pleiades ['plaɪədiːz] *npl* Pléyades *fpl*.

plenary ['pliːnərɪ] **1** *adj* plenario; **~ paper** ponencia *f* en sesión plenaria, ponencia *f* general; **~ session** sesión *f* plenaria, pleno *m*. **2** *n* = **~ paper.**

plenipotentiary [,plenɪpə'tenʃərɪ] *n* plenipotenciario *m* -a *f*.

plenitude ['plenɪtjuːd] *n* plenitud *f*.

plenteous ['plentɪəs] *adj*, **plentiful** ['plentɪfʊl] *adj* copioso, abundante; **a ~ supply of ...** una buena provisión de ..., un buen surtido de ...; **eggs are now ~** hay abundancia de huevos, abundan los huevos.

plentifully ['plentɪfəlɪ] *adv* copiosamente, abundantemente.

plenty ['plentɪ] **1** *n* (**a**) abundancia *f*; cantidad *f* suficiente; **land of ~** tierra *f* de la abundancia; **in ~** en abundancia; **it rained in ~** llovió copiosamente; **it grows here in ~** por aquí existe en abundancia; **to live in ~** vivir en el lujo; **that's ~, thanks!** ¡basta, gracias!; **we have ~** tenemos bastante; **there's ~ to go on** hay suficientes datos, son muchas las pruebas; **we know ~ about you** sabemos mucho acerca de Vd.

(**b**) **~ of** bastante; muchos, muchísimos; una cantidad suficiente de; **we have ~ of money** tenemos bastante dinero; **they have ~ of money** tienen mucho dinero; **we have ~ of tea** tenemos mucho té; **there are ~ of them** los hay en cantidad; **we see ~ of them** (*numbers*) vemos muchos de ellos, (*as friends*) les vemos mucho, nos vemos con frecuencia; **we have ~ of time** tenemos tiempo de sobra; **it takes ~ of courage** exige bastante valor; **~ of people do** hay muchos que lo hacen, son muchos los que lo hacen.

2 *adv* (*) **it's ~ big enough** claro que es bastante grande; **they're ~ rich enough to pay for two** son lo bastante ricos para pagar por dos de ellos; **it rained ~** (*US*) y ¡como llovió!; **we like it ~** (*US*) nos gusta mucho.

plenum ['pliːnəm] *n* pleno *m*.

pleonasm ['pliːənæzəm] *n* pleonasmo *m*.

pleonastic [plɪə'næstɪk] *adj* pleonástico.

plethora ['pleθərə] *n* plétora *f*.

plethoric [ple'θɒrɪk] *adj* pletórico.

pleurisy ['plʊərɪsɪ] *n* pleuresía *f*, pleuritis *f*.

Plexiglas ['pleksɪglɑːs] ® *n* (*US*) plexiglás ® *m*.

pliability [,plaɪə'bɪlɪtɪ] *n* flexibilidad *f* (*also fig*).

pliable ['plaɪəbl] *adj*, **pliant** ['plaɪənt] *adj* flexible (*also fig*); plegable.

pliers ['plaɪəz] *npl* alicates *mpl*, tenazas *fpl*; **a pair of ~, some ~** unos alicates, unas tenazas.

plight[1] [plaɪt] *vt word* dar, empeñar; **to ~ one's troth** (†† *or hum*) prometerse, dar su palabra de casamiento (*to* a).

plight[2] [plaɪt] *n* condición *f* (inquietante), situación *f* (difícil), situación *f* apremiante; crisis *f*; **the ~ of the shellfish industry** la crisis de la industria marisquera; **the country's economic ~** la situación económica del país; los apuros económicos del país; **to be in a sad** (*or* **sorry**) **~** estar en un estado lamentable.

Plimsoll ['plɪmsəl] *attr*: **~ line** línea *f* de máxima carga.

plimsolls ['plɪmsəlz] *npl* (*Brit*) zapatos *mpl* de tenis.

plinth [plɪnθ] *n* plinto *m*.

Pliny ['plɪnɪ] *nm* Plinio; **~ the Elder** Plinio el Viejo; **~ the Younger** Plinio el Joven.

PLO *n abbr of* **Palestine Liberation Organization** Organización *f* para la Liberación de Palestina, OLP *f*.

plod [plɒd] **1** *n* (**a**) **to go at a steady ~** caminar despacio pero sin desanimarse.

(**b**) **it's a long ~ to the village** queda mucho camino para llegar al pueblo.

2 *vt* recorrer despacio; **we ~ded the road for another hour** seguimos andando con dificultad durante una hora más; **we ~ded our way homeward** volvimos penosamente hacia casa.

3 *vi* (**a**) (*also* **to ~ along, to ~ on**) caminar despacio, andar penosamente, avanzar con dificultad; **keep ~ding!** ¡ánimo!, ¡no os dejéis desanimar!

(**b**) (*at work etc*) trabajar laboriosamente, trabajar lentamente pero sin desanimarse; **to ~ away at a task** dedicarse laboriosamente a un trabajo, seguir trabajando a pesar de las dificultades.

plodder ['plɒdəʳ] *n* estudiante *mf* más aplicado que brillante, persona *f* que trabaja con más aplicación que talento.

plodding ['plɒdɪŋ] *adj* perseverante, laborioso; *student* empollón; *worker* más aplicado que brillante.

plonk[1] [plɒŋk] **1** *n* golpe *m* seco, ruido *m* seco; **it fell with a**

~ **to the floor** cayó al suelo con un ruido seco.

2 *adv*: **he went ~ into the stream** cayó ¡zas! en el arroyo; **it landed ~ on his cheek** le dio de lleno en la mejilla.

3 *vt* (**a**) (*Mus*) puntear.

(**b**) **to ~ sth down** arrojar algo con fuerza, dejar caer algo pesadamente.

4 *vr*: **to ~ o.s. down in a chair** dejarse caer pesadamente en una silla, desplomarse en una silla.

plonk²* [plɒŋk] *n* (*Brit*) vino *m* corriente, vino *m* peleón, purrela* *f*.

plonker‡ ['plɒŋkəʳ] *n* (*Brit*) gili* *mf*.

plop [plɒp] **1** *n* paf *m*; **~!** ¡paf! **2** *vt* (*also* **to ~ down**) arrojar dejando oír un paf. **3** *vi* caer dejando oír un paf.

plosive ['pləʊsɪv] **1** *adj* explosivo. **2** *n* explosiva *f*.

plot¹ [plɒt] *n* (*Agr*) terreno *m*; parcela *f*; (*of vegetables, flowers etc*) cuadro *m*; (*for building*) solar *m*; **~ of grass** cuadro *m* de cesped; **vegetable ~** cuadro *m* de hortalizas.

plot² [plɒt] **1** *n* (**a**) (*conspiracy*) complot *m*, compló *m*, conspiración *f*, conjura *f*.

(**b**) (*Liter, Theat*) argumento *m*; estructura *f*; trama *f*, intriga *f*; **the ~ thickens** (*fig*) la cosa se complica.

2 *vt* (**a**) *progress, course* (*on graph etc*) trazar; **to ~ A against Z** trazar A como función de Z.

(**b**) *downfall etc* urdir, tramar, maquinar.

3 *vi* conspirar, conjurarse; intrigar; **to ~ to do sth** conspirar para hacer algo, conjurarse para hacer algo.

plotter¹ ['plɒtəʳ] *n* conspirador *m*, -ora *f*, conjurado *m*, -a *f*.

plotter² ['plɒtəʳ] *n* (*Comput*) trazador *m* (de gráficos), tabla *f* trazadora, plotter *m*.

plotting ['plɒtɪŋ] **1** *n* conspiración *f*, intrigas *fpl*, maquinaciones *fpl*. **2** *attr*: **~ board** tablero *m* trazador; **~ paper** (*US*) papel *m* cuadriculado; **~ table** mesa *f* trazadora.

plough, (*US*) **plow** [plaʊ] **1** *n* arado *m*; **the P~** (*Astron*) el Carro, la Osa Mayor.

2 *attr*: **~ horse** caballo *m* de labranza.

3 *vt* (**a**) arar; (*fig*) surcar; **to ~ one's way through snow** abrirse con dificultad paso por la nieve; **to ~ one's way through a book** leer un libro con dificultad; **I ~ed my way through it eventually** por fin acabé de leerlo pero resultó pesadísimo.

(**b**) **to ~ money into a project** invertir (grandes cantidades de) dinero en un proyecto.

(**c**) (*Brit Univ**) cargar*, dar calabazas a*; **I was ~ed in German, they ~ed me in German** me cargaron en alemán.

4 *vi* (**a**) arar; **to ~ through = to ~ one's way; the lorry ~ed into the crowd** el camión se lanzó (violentamente) en medio de la multitud, el camión se metió en la multitud; *V* **3** (**a**).

(**b**) (*Brit Univ**) **I ~ed again** volvieron a cargarme*.

◆**plough back** *vt profits* reinvertir.

◆**plough in, plough under** *vt* cubrir arando, enterar arando.

◆**plough up** *vt new ground* roturar; *bushes etc* arrancar con el arado, *pathway* hacer desaparecer arando; **the train ~ed up the track for 100 metres** el tren destrozó unos 100 metros de la vía.

ploughing, (*US*) **plowing** ['plaʊɪŋ] *n* arada *f*; **~ back** inversión *f* de ganancias.

ploughland, (*US*) **plowland** ['plaʊlænd] *n* tierra *f* de labrantío, tierra *f* labrantía.

ploughman, (*US*) **plowman** ['plaʊmən] *n*, *pl* **ploughmen,** (*US*) **plowmen** ['plaʊmən] arador *m*, labrador *m*; **~'s lunch** *almuerzo de pub consistente en pan con queso y encurtidos.*

ploughshare, (*US*) **plowshare** ['plaʊʃɛəʳ] *n* reja *f* del arado.

plover ['plʌvəʳ] *n* chorlito *m*.

plow [plaʊ] (*US*) *etc* = **plough** *etc*.

ploy [plɔɪ] *n* truco *m*, estratagema *f*, táctica *f*.

PLP *n abbr of* **Parliamentary Labour Party.**

PLR *n abbr of* **Public Lending Right.**

pluck¹ [plʌk] *n* (*courage*) valor *m*, ánimo *m*; (*guts*) agallas *fpl*; **it takes ~ to do that** hace falta mucho valor para conseguir eso; **he's got plenty of ~** sí tiene agallas; **I didn't have the ~ to own up** no tuve el valor para confesar.

pluck² [plʌk] **1** *n* (*tug*) tirón *m*.

2 *vt fruit, flower* coger, recoger (*LAm*); *bird* desplumar; *guitar* pulsear, puntear; **to ~ one's eyebrows** depilarse las cejas; **the helicopter ~ed him from the sea** el helicóptero le recogió del mar; **he seemed to ~ the answer out of the air** parecía sacar la solución de la nada; **it's an idea I've just ~ed out of the air** es una idea que he cogido al vuelo.

3 *vi*: **to ~ at** tirar de, dar un tirón a; **to ~ at sb's sleeve** tirar ligeramente de la manga de uno.

◆**pluck off, pluck out** *vt* arrancar con los dedos, arrancar de un tirón.

◆**pluck up** *vt* (**a**) = **pluck off; he ~ed it up off the table** lo recogió bruscamente de la mesa. (**b**) **to ~ up courage** cobrar ánimo.

pluckily ['plʌkɪlɪ] *adv* valientemente; con resolución.

pluckiness ['plʌkɪnɪs] *n* valor *m*, ánimo *m*; resolución *f*.

plucky ['plʌkɪ] *adj* valiente, valeroso; resuelto.

plug [plʌg] **1** *n* (**a**) (*bung*) tapón *m*, taco *m*; (*in bath etc*) tapón *m*; (*Med*: *of cotton wool etc*) tampón *m*; (*US*: *of tobacco*) rollo *m*, tableta *f* (de tabaco de mascar); **the bank pulled the ~ on my overdraft*** el banco dejó de tolerar mi saldo deudor.

(**b**) (*Elec*: *free, on wire, on apparatus*) clavija *f*, enchufe *m*; (*in wall*) toma *f*; (*Telec*) clavija *f*; (*Aut*) bujía *f*.

(**c**) (*) enchufe* *m*; anuncio *m* (incidental), publicidad *f* (incidental); **to give sb a ~** dar publicidad a uno; **to put in a ~ for a product** lograr anunciar un producto (de modo solapado).

2 *vt* (**a**) *hole etc* tapar, llenar, obturar; (*Archit*) rellenar; *tooth* empastar; **to ~ a lead into a socket** enchufar un hilo en una toma; **~ this cloth into the hole** tapa el agujero con este trapo; **to ~ the drain on the reserves** acabar con las pérdidas de divisas.

(**b**) (‡) (*hit*) pegar; (*shoot*) pegar un tiro a.

(**c**) (*) (*Comm*) anunciar (de modo solapado), dar publicidad (incidental) a; (*repeat*) repetir, machacar en; **he's been ~ging that line for years** hace años que viene diciendo lo mismo.

◆**plug away*** *vi* seguir trabajando (*etc*) a pesar de todo, batir el yunque; no dejarse desanimar.

◆**plug in 1** *vt* (*Elec*) enchufar, conectar; **to ~ in a radio** conectar una radio. **2** *vi* (*esp US*) ponerse en la onda; **~ in to** ponerse en la onda de, sintonizar, compenetrarse de.

◆**plug up** *vt* tapar, obturar.

plughole ['plʌghəʊl] *n* tubo *m* de salida, salida *f*; **all that work has gone down the ~** todo ese trabajo se perdió, todo ese trabajo vale para nada.

plug-in ['plʌg'ɪn] *adj* (*Elec*) enchufable, con enchufe.

plum [plʌm] *n* (**a**) (*fruit*) ciruela *f*; (*tree*) ciruelo *m*. (**b**) (*fig*: *the best*) lo mejor; (*also* **~ job**) pingüe destino *m*, turrón *m**, breva* *f*.

plumage ['pluːmɪdʒ] *n* plumaje *m*.

plumb [plʌm] **1** *n* plomada *f*.

2 *adj* vertical, a plomo.

3 *adv* (**a**) (*vertically*) verticalmente, a plomo.

(**b**) (*wholly*) totalmente, completamente; **~ crazy** completamente loco; **~ in the middle** exactamente en el centro; **it hit him ~ on the nose** le dio de lleno en las narices.

4 *vt* (*also fig*) sondar, sondear; **to ~ the depths of despair** conocer la mayor desesperación.

◆**plumb in** *vt* conectar (con el suministro de agua).

plumbago [plʌm'beɪgəʊ] *n* plombagina *f*.

plumber ['plʌməʳ] *n* fontanero *m*, plomero *m* (*LAm*), gasfitero *m* (*SC*); **~'s helper** (*US*), **~'s mate** desatascador *m* de fregaderos.

plumbic ['plʌmbɪk] *adj* plúmbico, plúmbeo.

plumbing ['plʌmɪŋ] *n* (**a**) (*craft*) fontanería *f*, plomería *f* (*LAm*), gasfitería *f* (*SC*). (**b**) (*piping*) instalación *f* de cañerías; (*bathroom fittings*) aparatos *mpl* sanitarios.

plumbline ['plʌmlaɪn] *n* (cuerda *f* de) plomada *f*.

plume [pluːm] **1** *n* pluma *f*; (*on helmet*) penacho *m*; (*of smoke etc*) penacho *m*, hilo *m*.

2 *vr*: **the bird ~s itself** el ave se limpia las plumas, el ave se arregla las plumas.

plumed [pluːmd] *adj* plumado; con plumas; *helmet* empenachado.

plummet ['plʌmɪt] **1** *n* plomada *f*. **2** *vi*: **to ~ down, to come ~ing down** caer a plomo (*also fig*).

plummy* ['plʌmɪ] *adj voice* pastoso.

plump¹ [plʌmp] **1** *adj body* rechoncho, rollizo; *face* mofletudo; *chicken etc* gordo. **2** *vt* (*fatten*) engordar; (*swell*) hinchar. **3** *vi* engordar; hincharse.

plump² [plʌmp] **1** *adv* de lleno; **it fell ~ on the roof** cayó de lleno en el techo.

2 *vi* (*fall*) caer pesadamente, dejarse caer pesadamente.

◆**plump down 1** *vt*: **to ~ sth down** arrojar algo pesadamente, dejar caer algo pesadamente (en el suelo *etc*).

2 *vi*: **to ~ down on to a chair** dejarse caer pesadamente en un sillón, desplomarse en un sillón.

3 *vr*: **to ~ o.s. down** dejarse caer pesadamente, desplomarse.

◆**plump for** *vt* decidir por, optar por; (*vote*) votar por.

◆**plump up** *vt* hinchar.

plumpness ['plʌmpnɪs] *n* gordura *f*; lo rollizo.

plum-pudding ['plʌm'pʊdɪŋ] *n* budín *m*.

plum-tree ['plʌmtri:] *n* ciruelo *m*.

plunder ['plʌndəʳ] **1** *n* (*act*) pillaje *m*, saqueo *m*; (*loot*) botín *m*.

2 *vt* saquear, pillar; *tomb* robar; *safe* robar el contenido de, robar (las alhajas de); **they ~ed my cellar** saquearon mi bodega.

plunderer ['plʌndərəʳ] *n* saqueador *m*, -ora *f*.

plundering ['plʌndərɪŋ] *n* saqueo *m*.

plunge [plʌndʒ] **1** *n* (**a**) (*dive from bank etc*) salto *m*; (*submersion by swimmer, bird etc*) zambullida *f*; (*by professional diver*) inmersión *f*; (*bathe*) baño *m*; **the diver rested after each ~** el buzo descansó después de cada inmersión; **he had a ~ before breakfast** se fue a bañar antes de desayunar.

(**b**) (*bath*) baño *m*; (*pool*) piscina *f*; **cold ~** baño *m* frío.

(**c**) (*fig*: *fall*) baja *f*, caída *f*, descenso *m*.

(**d**) (*fig*) **to take the ~** dar el paso decisivo, aventurarse; resolverse; jugarse el todo; (*esp hum*: *get married*) decidir casarse; **we are about to take the ~** estamos al punto de dar el paso decisivo; **I took the ~ and bought it** por fin me resolví a comprarlo.

2 *vt* (**a**) (*immerse*) sumergir; hundir (*into* en); **he ~d his hands into the water** hundió las manos en el agua; **he ~d his hand into his pocket** metió la mano bien dentro del bolsillo; **to ~ a dagger into sb's chest** hundir (*or* clavar) un puñal en el pecho de uno.

(**b**) **to ~ a room into darkness** sumir un cuarto en la oscuridad; **New York was suddenly ~d into darkness** Nueva York se encontró de repente sumida en la oscuridad; **to ~ sb into sadness** hundir (*or* sumir, abismar) a uno en la tristeza; **we were ~d into gloom by the news** la noticia nos sumió en la tristeza.

3 *vi* (**a**) (*dive*) saltar; zambullirse; sumergirse; (*sink*) hundirse; **then the submarine ~d** luego se sumergió el submarino; **she ~d into 10 metres of water** se zambulló en 10 metros de agua.

(**b**) (*fall*) caer; (*road, cliff*) precipitarse; **he ~d to his death** tuvo una caída mortal; **he ~d from a 5th storey window** se arrojó desde una ventana del 5° piso; **the aircraft ~d into the sea off Dover** el avión cayó al (*or* se precipitó en el) mar a la altura de Dover.

(**c**) (*dress*) tener mucho escote, ser muy escotado.

(**d**) (*ship*) cabecear; (*horse*) corcovear.

(**e**) (*person*: *rush*) arrojarse, lanzarse, precipitarse; **to ~ forward** precipitarse hacia adelante; **to ~ into one's work** emprender resuelto su trabajo, engolfarse en el trabajo; **to ~ heedlessly into danger** meterse en los peligros sin hacer caso de ellos; **he ~d into a discussion of Plato** se lanzó a una discusión de Platón.

(**f**) (*: *gamble*) apostar el todo; jugar fuerte; (*Comm*) arriesgar mucho dinero.

(**g**) (*: *decide*) resolverse, dar el paso decisivo.

plunger ['plʌndʒəʳ] *n* (*Mech*) émbolo *m*; (*for sink*) desatascador *m* (de fregaderos).

plunging ['plʌndʒɪŋ] *adj*: **~ neckline** escote *m* muy bajo.

plunk [plʌŋk] *n etc* (*US*) = **plonk**¹.

pluperfect ['plu:'pɜ:fɪkt] *n* pluscuamperfecto *m*.

plural ['plʊərəl] **1** *adj* plural; **the ~ form of the noun** la forma del sustantivo en plural. **2** *n* plural *m*; **in the ~** en el plural.

pluralism ['plʊərəlɪzəm] *n* pluralismo *m*.

pluralist ['plʊərəlɪst] **1** *adj* pluralista. **2** *n* pluralista *mf*.

pluralistic [,plʊərə'lɪstɪk] *adj* pluralista.

plurality [,plʊə'rælɪtɪ] *n* pluralidad *f*.

plus [plʌs] **1** *prep* más, y; además de; juntamente con; **3 ~ 4** 3 más 4; **~ what I have to do already** además de (*or* más) lo que tengo que hacer ya; **we're ~ 500** (*Bridge*) tenemos una ventaja de 500 puntos.

2 *adj* (**a**) (*Math, Elec*: *quantity*) positivo, de signo positivo; **~ sign** signo *m* de más, signo *m* de sumar.

(**b**) **two pounds ~** dos libras y algo más, más de dos libras; **twenty ~** veinte y pico, veintitantos.

3 *n* (**a**) (*Math*: *sign*) signo *m* de más, signo *m* de sumar; (*amount*) cantidad *f* positiva.

(**b**) (*fig*) punto *m* a favor; aspecto *m* positivo; **that is a ~ for him** es un punto a su favor.

4 *conj* (*esp US*) además; **~ we haven't got the money** además no tenemos el dinero.

plus fours ['plʌs'fɔ:z] *npl* pantalones *mpl* de golf, pantalones *mpl* holgados de media pierna.

plush [plʌʃ] **1** *n* felpa *f*. **2** *adj* de felpa; felpado; (*) *V* **plushy**.

plushy* ['plʌʃɪ] *adj* lujoso, elegante, de buen tono.

Plutarch ['plu:tɑ:k] *nm* Plutarco.

Pluto ['plu:təʊ] *nm* Plutón.

plutocracy [,plu:'tɒkrəsɪ] *n* plutocracia *f*.

plutocrat ['plu:təʊkræt] *n* plutócrata *mf*.

plutocratic [,plu:təʊ'krætɪk] *adj* plutocrático.

plutonium [plu:'təʊnɪəm] *n* plutonio *m*.

pluviometer [,plu:vɪ'ɒmɪtəʳ] *n* pluviómetro *m*.

ply¹ [plaɪ] *n*: **three ~** (*wood*) de tres capas; (*wool*) triple, de tres hebras.

ply² [plaɪ] **1** *vt* (**a**) *needle, tool etc* manejar, menear (vigorosamente); *oars etc* emplear; *trade* ejercer; *seas, river* navegar por.

(**b**) **to ~ sb with questions** acosar a uno con preguntas, importunar a uno haciéndole muchas preguntas; **to ~ sb for information** importunar a uno pidiéndole informes; **to ~ sb with drink** dar a uno repetidas veces de beber, emborrachar a uno; **to ~ sb with cakes** ofrecer repetidas veces los pastelitos a uno.

2 *vi*: **to ~ between** hacer el servicio entre, ir y venir entre; **to ~ for hire** ofrecerse para alquilar.

plywood ['plaɪwʊd] *n* madera *f* contrachapada, madera *f* multilaminar, panel *m*.

PM *n* (**a**) (*Brit*) *abbr of* **Prime Minister**. (**b**) (*Jur, Med*) *abbr of* **post-mortem**.

p.m. *adv abbr of* **post meridiem** después del mediodía, de la tarde.

PMG *n* (*Brit*) *abbr of* **Postmaster General** Director *m* General de Correos.

PMT *n abbr of* **premenstrual tension** síndrome *m* premenstrual, SPM.

PN, P/N *n abbr of* **promissory note** pagaré *m*.

PND *n abbr of* **postnatal depression** depresión *f* posparto.

pneumatic [nju:'mætɪk] *adj* neumático; **~ drill** taladradora *f* neumática.

pneumoconiosis [,nju:məʊ,kəʊnɪ'əʊsɪs] *n* neumoconiosis *f*.

pneumonia [nju:'məʊnɪə] *n* pulmonía *f*.

Pnom Penh ['nɒm'pen] *n* = **Phnom Penh**.

PO *n* (**a**) *abbr of* **Post Office** oficina *f* de correos. (**b**) *abbr of* **PO Box** apartado *m*, apdo, casilla *f*. (**c**) (*Aer*) *abbr of* **Pilot Officer** oficial *m* piloto. (**d**) (*Naut*) *abbr of* **Petty Officer** suboficial *m* de marina.

po‡ [pəʊ] *n* (*Brit*) orinal *m*.

p.o. *abbr of* **postal order** giro *m* postal.

POA *n* (**a**) (*Brit*) *abbr of* **Prison Officers' Association** *sindicato de empleados de cárcel*. (**b**) (*Comm*) *abbr of* **prices on application** los precios, a solicitud.

poach¹ [pəʊtʃ] *vt* (*Culin*) *egg* escalfar; *fish etc* hervir.

poach² [pəʊtʃ] **1** *vt* cazar (*or* pescar *etc*) en vedado; cazar (*or* pescar *etc*) ilegalmente; (*fig*: *steal*) robar, *advantage etc* pisar, tomar.

2 *vi* cazar (*or* pescar *etc*) en finca ajena; cazar furtivamente; **to ~ on sb's preserves** (*fig*) cazar en finca ajena, meterse en los asuntos ajenos.

poached [pəʊtʃt] *adj egg* escalfado; *fish etc* hervido.

poacher¹ ['pəʊtʃəʳ] *n* cazador *m* furtivo.

poacher² ['pəʊtʃəʳ] *n* (*for eggs*) escalfador *m* (de huevos).

poaching ['pəʊtʃɪŋ] *n* furtivismo *m*, caza *f* furtiva, pesca *f* furtiva.

POB *abbr of* **post office box** apartado *m* de correos.

pochard ['pəʊtʃəd] *n* porrón *m* común.

pock [pɒk] *n* (*also* **~mark**) pústula *f*; picadura *f*, hoyuelo *m*.

pocked [pɒkt] *adj* = **pockmarked**.

pocket ['pɒkɪt] **1** *n* bolsillo *m*, bolsa *f* (*Méx*); (*Billiards*) tronera *f*; (*fig*: *Geol, Mil etc*) bolsa *f*; hoyo *m*, cavidad *f*, hueco *m*; (*Aer*) bolsa *f* de aire; **~ of resistance** bolsa *f* de resistencia; **to be in ~** salir ganando; **to be £5 in ~** haber ganado 5 libras; **to be out of ~** salir perdiendo; **to be £5 out of ~** haber perdido 5 libras; **he has the game in his ~** tiene el partido en el bote; **to have sb in one's ~** tener a uno en el bolsillo; **that hurts his ~** eso le duele en el bolsillo; **to line one's ~s** ponerse las botas; *V* **pick**.

2 *attr* de bolsillo; **~ battleship** acorazado *m* de bolsillo; **~ calculator** calculadora *f* de bolsillo; **~ diary** agenda *f* de bolsillo; **~ edition** edición *f* de bolsillo.

3 *vt* meter en el bolsillo, guardar en el bolsillo; (*Billiards*) entronerar; (*earn, make*) ganar; (*pej*) apropiarse, alzarse con, embolsar; **he ~ed half the takings** se embolsó la mitad de la recaudación; *V* **pride** *etc*.

pocketbook ['pɒkɪtbʊk] *n* (*US*) (**a**) (*wallet*) cartera *f*, portamonedas *m*; (*handbag*) bolso *m* (de mano), cartera *f* (*LAm*). (**b**) (*book*) libro *m* de bolsillo.

pocketful ['pɒkɪtfʊl] *n* bolsillo *m*; cantidad *f* que cabe en el bolsillo; **a ~ of nuts** un bolsillo de nueces.

pocket-handkerchief [,pɒkɪt'hæŋkətʃɪf] *n* pañuelo *m*.

pocketknife ['pɒkɪtnaɪf] *n*, *pl* **pocketknives** ['pɒkɪtnaɪvz] navaja *f*.

pocket-money ['pɒkɪt,mʌnɪ] *n* (*Brit*) asignación *f*, dinero *m* para pequeños gastos personales.

pocket-size ['pɒkɪtsaɪz] *adj* de bolsillo.

pockmark ['pɒkmɑːk] *n* picadura *f*, hoyuelo *m*.

pockmarked ['pɒkmɑːkt] *adj face* picado de viruelas; *surface* marcado de hoyuelos; **to be ~ with** estar marcado de, estar acribillado de.

POD *n abbr of* **payment on delivery** pago *m* a la entrega.

pod [pɒd] *n* vaina *f*.

podgy ['pɒdʒɪ] *adj* gordinflón; *face* mofletudo.

podiatrist [pɒ'diːətrɪst] *n* (*US*) pedicuro *mf*.

podiatry [pɒ'diːətrɪ] *n* (*US*) pedicura *f*.

podium ['pəʊdɪəm] *n*, *pl* **podia** ['pəʊdɪə] podio *m*.

POE *n* (**a**) *abbr of* **port of embarkation** puerto *m* de embarque. (**b**) *abbr of* **port of entry** puerto *m* de entrada.

poem ['pəʊɪm] *n* (*short*) poesía *f*; (*long, narrative*) poema *m*; **P~ of the Cid** Poema *m* de mío Cid, Cantar *m* de mío Cid; **Lorca's ~s** las poesías de Lorca, la obra poética de Lorca, las obras en verso de Lorca.

poet ['pəʊɪt] *n* poeta *mf*; **P~ Laureate** (*Brit*) Poeta *m* laureado.

poetaster [,pəʊɪ'tæstə^r] *n* poetastro *m*.

poetess ['pəʊɪtes] *n* poetisa *f*.

poetic(al) [pəʊ'etɪk(əl)] *adj* poético; **~ justice** justicia *f* poética; **~ licence, ~ license** (*US*) licencia *f* poética.

poetically [pəʊ'etɪkəlɪ] *adv* poéticamente.

poeticize [pəʊ'etɪsaɪz] *vt* (*enhance*) poetizar, adornar con detalles poéticos; (*translate into verse*) hacer un poema de, hacer una versión poética de.

poetics [pəʊ'etɪks] *n* poética *f*.

poetry ['pəʊɪtrɪ] **1** *n* poesía *f*. **2** *attr*: **~ magazine** revista *f* de poesía; **~ reading** lectura *f* de poemas.

po-faced‡ [,pəʊ'feɪst] *adj* que mira con desaprobación, severo.

pogrom ['pɒgrəm] *n* pogrom *m*, pogromo *m*, persecución *f* antisemítica.

poignancy ['pɔɪnjənsɪ] *n* patetismo *m*; intensidad *f*, profundidad *f*.

poignant ['pɔɪnjənt] *adj* (*moving*) conmovedor, patético; (*profound*) intenso, agudo, profundo.

poignantly ['pɔɪnjəntlɪ] *adv* de modo conmovedor, patéticamente; intensamente, agudamente.

poinsettia [pɔɪn'setɪə] *n* flor *f* de pascua.

point [pɔɪnt] **1** *n* (**a**) (*Typ etc: dot*) punto *m*; **7.6 (seven ~ six)** 7,6 (siete coma seis, seite con seis, siete enteros con seis décimos).

(**b**) (*on scale: place, time*) punto *m*; **~ of the compass** cuarta *f*; **~ of departure** punto *m* de partida; **Slough and all ~s west** Slough y las estaciones más hacia el oeste; **~ of reference** punto *m* de referencia; **~ of no return** punto *m* de no retorno; **at the ~ where the road forks** donde se bifurca el camino; **at this ~** en esto, llegado a este punto; **at that ~ in time** en aquel momento; **at all ~s** por todas partes, en todos los sitios; **matters are at such a ~ that ...** las cosas han llegado a tal extremo que ...; **to be on the ~ of** + *ger* estar a punto de + *infin*; **delivered free to all ~s in Spain** entrega gratuita en cualquier punto de España; **he is severe to the ~ of cruelty** es tan severo que resulta cruel, su severidad raya en la crueldad; **up to a ~** hasta cierto punto; en cierto modo.

(**c**) (*aspect*) punto *m*, aspecto *m*; **~ of interest** punto *m* interesante, aspecto *m* interesante; **~ of honour** cuestión *f* de honor, punto *m* de honor; **~ of order** cuestión *f* de procedimiento, cuestión *f* de orden; **in ~ of** en cuanto a, por lo que se refiere a; **in ~ of fact** en realidad; **in ~ of numbers** en cuanto al número; **in ~ of sheer strength** en cuanto a la fuerza sola.

(**d**) **~ of view** punto *m* de vista; **from the ~ of view of** desde el punto de vista de; **to come round to sb's ~ of view** adoptar el criterio de uno, llegar a compartir la opinión de uno; **to look at a matter from all ~s of view** considerar una cuestión bajo todos sus aspectos; **to see** (*or* **understand**) **sb's ~ of view** comprender el punto de vista de uno.

(**e**) (*of argument etc*) punto *m*; **to argue ~ by ~** razonar punto por punto; **the ~ at issue** el punto en cuestión, el asunto en litigio; **the ~s to remember are ...** los puntos a retener son los siguientes ...; **to be beside the ~** no venir al caso; **it is beside the ~ that ...** no importa que + *subj*; **it's off the ~** está fuera de propósito; **to get off the ~, to wander off the ~** salirse del tema, apartarse del tema; **on this ~** sobre este punto; **on that ~** en cuanto a eso; **on that ~ we agree** sobre eso estamos de acuerdo; **to differ on a ~** no estar de acuerdo en un particular; **an argument very much to the ~** un argumento muy a propósito; **that is hardly to the ~** eso apenas hace al caso; **to come to the ~** ir al grano; **let's come to the ~!** ¡vamos al grano!, ¡dejémonos de historias!; **to get back to the ~** volver al tema; **now, to get back to the ~** bueno, para volver al tema; **to keep to the ~** no salirse del tema; **to carry one's ~** salirse con la suya; **it gave ~ to the argument** hizo ver la importancia del argumento; **to speak to the ~** (*relevantly*) hablar acertadamente, hablar con tino; **I think she has a ~** creo que tiene un poco de razón; **to make a ~** establecer un punto, hacer aceptar una opinión; **you've made your ~** nos (*etc*) has convencido; **he made the following ~s** dijo lo siguiente; **to make the ~ that ...** hacer ver que ..., hacer comprender que ...; **to make a ~ of** + *ger* no dejar de + *infin*, insistir en + *infin*; **to press the ~** insistir (*that* en que); **to pursue one's ~** seguir su tema; **to stretch a ~** hacer una excepción, hacer una concesión; **I take your ~** acepto lo que dices; **~ taken!** ¡de acuerdo!, ¡tienes razón!

(**f**) (*significant part, important thing*) lo significativo, lo importante; **this is the ~** esto es lo importante; **the ~ is, ...** lo importante es ...; **the whole ~ is ...** lo único que importa es ...; **the ~ is that ...** el hecho es que ...; **that's just the ~!** ¡si eso es lo más importante!, ¡eso es!; **that's not the ~** no es eso; **the ~ of the joke is that ...** la gracia del chiste consiste en que ...; **to get the ~** comprender; **to miss the ~** no comprender; no ver lo esencial.

(**g**) (*purpose*) fin *m*, finalidad *f*, objeto *m*; (*usefulness*) utilidad *f*; **what's the ~ of railways?** ¿qué utilidad tienen los ferrocarriles?, ¿de qué sirven los ferrocarriles?; **what's the ~ of trying?** ¿de qué sirve esforzarse?; **there is no ~ in** + *ger* no vale la pena + *infin*, no hay para qué + *infin*; **I don't see the ~ of doing it** no entiendo por qué sea necesario hacerlo, no veo el motivo por hacerlo.

(**h**) (*of character*) rasgo *m*, característica *f*; cualidad *f*; **weak ~** flaco *m*, punto *m* flaco, punto *m* débil; **~s of a horse** características *fpl* de un caballo; **he has his ~s** tiene algunas cualidades buenas; **it was always his strong ~** siempre ha sido su punto fuerte; **maths is not a strong ~ of mine** nunca he sido muy fuerte en matemáticas; **what ~s should I look for?** ¿qué puntos debo buscar?

(**i**) (*Games*) punto *m*, tanto *m*; **~s against** puntos *mpl* en contra; **~s for** puntos *mpl* a favor; **to give sb ~s** dar una ventaja a uno; **to score 10 ~s** marcar 10 puntos; **to win on ~s** ganar a los puntos.

(**j**) (*unit*) **the thermometer went up 3 ~s** el termómetro subió 3 grados; **the shares went down 2 ~s** las acciones bajaron 2 enteros.

(**k**) (*sharp end*) (*of needle etc*) punta *f*; (*of pen*) puntilla *f*; (*Geog*) punta *f*, promontorio *m*, cabo *m*; (*Elec*) enchufe *m*, toma *m*; **~s** (*Brit Rail*) agujas *fpl*; **to dance on ~s** bailar sobre las puntas; **to put a ~ on a pencil** sacar punta a un lápiz; **not to put too fine a ~ on it** para decirlo como es, hablando sin rodeos.

(**l**) (*Typ*) cuerpo *m*; **9 ~ black** negritas *fpl* del cuerpo 9.

(**m**) (*Brit Elec: also* **power ~**) toma *f* de corriente.

2 *attr*: **~s decision** (*Boxing*) decisión *f* a los puntos; **a five-~ star** una estrella de cinco puntas; **~s system** sistema *m* de puntos; **~s win** victoria *f* a los puntos.

3 *vt* (**a**) (*sharpen*) afilar, aguzar; *pencil* sacar punta a.

(**b**) **to ~ a moral** inculcar una lección, subrayar una moraleja.

(**c**) *gun, telescope etc* apuntar (*at* a); **to ~ a gun at sb** apuntar a uno con un fusil; **to ~ a finger at sb** señalar a uno con el dedo; **would you ~ me in the direction of the town hall?** ¿me quiere decir dónde está el ayuntamiento?; **we ~ed him in the right direction** le indicamos el camino.

(**d**) *path, way* indicar, señalar.

(**e**) *wall* rejuntar.

(**f**) *text* puntuar; *Hebrew etc* puntar.

4 *vi* (**a**) **to ~ at sb** señalar (*or* indicar) a uno con el dedo.

(**b**) (*of dog*) mostrar la caza, parar.

(**c**) **it ~s north** está orientado hacia el norte; **the hand ~ed to midnight** la aguja marcaba las 12; **this ~s to the**

fact that ... esto indica que ...; **everything ~s that way** todo parece indicarlo; **everything ~s to his success** todo anuncia su éxito; **everything ~s to the festival being a lively one** el festival se anuncia animado; **the evidence ~s to her** las pruebas indican que ella es la culpable.

◆**point out** *vt* indicar, señalar; **to ~ out sth to sb** señalar algo a uno, enseñar algo a uno; (*in speaking*) hacer ver algo a uno, indicar algo a uno; **to ~ out sb's mistakes** señalar los errores de uno; **to ~ out to sb the advantages of a car** explicar a uno las ventajas de tener coche; **to ~ out that** ... indicar que ..., señalar que ...; **may I ~ out that** ... permítaseme observar que ...

◆**point up** *vt* destacar, poner de relieve.

point-blank ['pɔɪnt'blæŋk] **1** *adv* a quemarropa (*also fig*); **to ask sb sth ~** preguntar algo a uno a quemarropa; **to refuse ~** dar una negativa rotunda.

2 *adj question, shot* hecho a quemarropa.

point-by-point ['pɔɪntbaɪ'pɔɪnt] *adj* punto por punto.

point duty ['pɔɪnt,djuːtɪ] *n* (*Brit*) control *m* de la circulación.

pointed ['pɔɪntɪd] *adj* (**a**) *shape* puntiagudo; (*sharp*) afilado, agudo; (*Archit*) *arch, window* ojival. (**b**) *remark etc* intencionado, lleno de intención; inequívoco, directo; enfático.

pointedly ['pɔɪntɪdlɪ] *adv say etc* con intención; inequívocamente, directamente; enfáticamente.

pointer ['pɔɪntəʳ] *n* (**a**) (*needle*) indicador *m*, aguja *f*; (*of balance*) fiel *m*; (*long stick*) puntero *m*. (**b**) (*dog*) perro *m* de muestra, braco *m*. (**c**) (*fig*) índice *m* (*to* de); indicación *f*; pista *f*; **it is a ~ to a possible solution** es una indicación de una solución posible; **there is at present no ~ to the outcome** por ahora nada indica qué resultado tendrá; **this is a ~ to the guilty man** es una pista que conducirá al criminal.

pointillism ['pwæntɪlɪzəm] *n* puntillismo *m*.

pointing ['pɔɪntɪŋ] *n* (*Constr*) rejuntado *m*.

pointless ['pɔɪntlɪs] *adj* (*useless*) inútil; (*motiveless*) sin motivo, inmotivado; (*meaningless*) sin sentido; insensato; **it is ~ to complain** es inútil quejarse, de nada sirve quejarse; **an apparently ~ crime** un crimen que parece carecer de motivo; **a ~ existence** una vida sin sentido, una vida que carece de propósito.

pointlessly ['pɔɪntlɪslɪ] *adv* inútilmente; sin motivo.

pointlessness ['pɔɪntlɪsnɪs] *n* inutilidad *f*; falta *f* de motivo; falta *f* de sentido; **the ~ of war** la insensatez de la guerra.

point of sale [,pɔɪntəv'seɪl] **1** *n* punto *m* de venta. **2 point-of-sale** *attr advertising etc* en el punto de venta.

pointsman ['pɔɪntsmən] *n, pl* **pointsmen** ['pɔɪntsmən] (*Rail*) encargado *m* del cambio de agujas.

point-to-point ['pɔɪnttə'pɔɪnt] *n* (*also* **~ race**) *carrera de caballos a campo traviesa*.

poise [pɔɪz] **1** *n* (**a**) (*balance*) equilibrio *m*.

(**b**) (*fig*: *of body*) aire *m*, porte *m*; elegancia *f*; **she dances with such ~** baila con tanta elegancia, baila con tal garbo.

(**c**) (*of mind*) serenidad *f*; aplomo *m*; confianza *f* en sí mismo; **she does it with great ~** lo hace con el mayor aplomo; **he lacks ~** le falta confianza en sí mismo.

2 *vt* equilibrar; balancear; **he ~d it on his hand** lo puso en equilibrio sobre la mano; **to be ~d** estar suspendido; (*hover*) cernerse, estar inmóvil (en el aire *etc*); **they are ~d to attack, they are ~d for the attack** están listos para atacar, están aprestados para el ataque.

poised [pɔɪzd] *adj* (*in temperament*) sereno, ecuánime, confiado en sí mismo.

poison ['pɔɪzn] **1** *n* veneno *m*; tóxico *m*; (*fig*) ponzoña *f*, veneno *m*; **to die of ~** morir envenenado; **to take ~** envenenarse; **they hate each other like ~** se odian a muerte.

2 *attr*: **~ gas** gas *m* tóxico, gas *m* asfixiante.

3 *vt* envenenar; (*chemically*) intoxicar; (*fig*) envenenar, emponzoñar; corromper; **to ~ sb's mind** envenenar el pensamiento de uno (*against* contra); **the wells were ~ed** echaron sustancias tóxicas a los pozos.

poisoner ['pɔɪznəʳ] *n* envenenador *m*, -ora *f*.

poisoning ['pɔɪznɪŋ] *n* envenenamiento *m*; intoxicación *f*.

poisonous ['pɔɪznəs] *adj snake etc* venenoso; *substance, plant, fumes etc* tóxico; (*fig*: *damaging*) pernicioso, (*very bad*) horrible, malísimo; **this ~ propaganda** esta propaganda perniciosa; **the play was ~** la obra fue horrible; **he's a ~ individual** es una persona odiosa.

poison-pen ['pɔɪzn'pen] *adj*: **~ letter** anónimo *m* ofensivo.

poke¹ [pəʊk] *n* (*esp Scot*: *sack*) saco *m*, bolsa *f*.

poke² [pəʊk] **1** *n* (**a**) (*push*) empuje *m*, empujón *m*; (*with elbow*) codazo *m*; (*jab*) pinchazo *m*; hurgonazo *m*; (*with poker*) hurgonada *f*, hurgonazo *m*; **to give the fire a ~** atizar la lumbre, remover la lumbre; **to give sb a ~ in the ribs** dar a uno un codazo en las costillas.

(**b**) **to have a ~**⁑ (*Brit*) echar un polvo⁑.

2 *vt* (*push*) empujar; *fire* hurgar, atizar, remover; (*Comput*) almacenar; **to ~ sb in the ribs** dar a uno un codazo en las costillas; **to ~ sb in the ribs with a stick** dar a uno un empujón con un palo en las costillas; **to ~ a stick into a crack** meter un palo en una grieta; **to ~ a rag into a tube** introducir un trapo en un tubo; **to ~ a stick into the ground** clavar un palo en el suelo; **to ~ a hole in a picture** hacer un agujero en un cuadro; **to ~ fun at sb** ridiculizar a uno.

3 *vi*: **to ~ at sth with a stick** tratar de remover (*etc*) algo con un bastón; **to ~ into sb's business** meterse en los asuntos de uno.

◆**poke about, poke around** *vi* andar buscando; (*pej*) fisgar, hacer indagaciones a hurtadillas; **we spent a day poking about in the shops** pasamos un día curioseando en las tiendas; **and now you come poking about!** ¡y ahora te metes a husmear!

◆**poke out** *vt*: **to ~ sb's eye out** saltar el ojo a uno, quebrar el ojo a uno; **to ~ one's head out** sacar la cabeza, asomar la cabeza.

poker¹ ['pəʊkəʳ] *n* atizador *m*, hurgón *m*.

poker² ['pəʊkəʳ] *n* (*Cards*) póquer *m*, póker *m*; **to have a ~ face** tener una cara impasible.

poker-faced ['pəʊkə'feɪst] *adj* de cara impasible; **they looked on ~** miraron impasibles, miraron sin expresión.

poky ['pəʊkɪ] *adj room* estrecho, muy pequeño; **a ~ little room** un cuartucho.

Polack⁑ ['pəʊlæk] *n* (*US pej*) polaco *m*, -a *f*.

Poland ['pəʊlənd] *n* Polonia *f*.

polar ['pəʊləʳ] *adj* polar; **~ bear** oso *m* blanco, oso *m* polar; **~ cap** casquete *m* polar; **P~ Circle** Círculo *m* Polar.

polarity [pəʊ'lærɪtɪ] *n* polaridad *f*.

polarization [,pəʊləraɪ'zeɪʃən] *n* polarización *f*.

polarize ['pəʊləraɪz] **1** *vt* polarizar. **2** *vi* polarizarse.

Polaroid ['pəʊlərɔɪd] ® **1** *adj* Polaroid ®. **2** *n* (*also* **~ camera**) Polaroid ® *f*.

Pole [pəʊl] *n* polaco *m*, -a *f*.

pole¹ [pəʊl] **1** *n* (**a**) *medida de longitud* = 5,029 *m*.

(**b**) palo *m*, palo *m* largo, vara *f* larga; (*flag~*) asta *f*; (*tent~*) mástil *m*; (*for fencing*) estaca *f*; (*Telec*) poste *m*; (*for gymnastics*) percha *f*; (*for vaulting*) pértiga *f*; (*for punting*) pértiga *f*; (*of cart*) vara *f*, lanza *f*; **to be up the ~**⁑ estar chiflado*.

2 *vt punt* etc impeler con pértiga.

pole² [pəʊl] *n* (*Elec, Geog etc*) polo *m*; **~ star** estrella *f* polar; **North P~** Polo *m* Norte; **South P~** Polo *m* Sur; **from ~ to ~** de polo a polo; **they're ~s apart** son polos opuestos.

poleaxe, (*US*) **poleax** ['pəʊlæks] *vt* desnucar; (*fig*) pasmar, aturdir.

pole bean ['pəʊl,biːn] *n* (*US*) judía *f* trepadora.

polecat ['pəʊlkæt] *n* turón *m*; (*US*) mofeta *f*.

polemic [pɒ'lemɪk] **1** *adj* polémico. **2** *n* polémica *f*; **~s** polémica *f*.

polemical [pɒ'lemɪkəl] *adj* polémico.

polemicist [pɒ'lemɪsɪst] *n* polemista *mf*.

pole position ['pəʊlpə'zɪʃn] *n* posición *f* de cabeza, pole *f*; (*fig*) posición *f* de ventaja.

polevault ['pəʊlvɔːlt] **1** *n* salto *m* de pértiga. **2** *vi* saltar con pértiga.

polevaulter ['pəʊl,vɔːltəʳ] *n* saltador *m* de pértiga, pertiguista *m*.

polevaulting ['pəʊl,vɔːltɪŋ] *n* salto *m* de pértiga.

police [pə'liːs] **1** *n* policía *f*.

2 *attr*: **~ captain** (*US*) subjefe *mf*; **~ car** coche *m* de policía, coche-patrulla *m*; **~ constable** policía *m*, guardia *m*; **~ court** tribunal *m* de policía, tribunal *m* correccional; **in ~ custody** bajo custodia policial; **~ department** (*US*) policía *f*; **~ dog** perro *m* policía; **~ escort** escolta *f* policial; **~ force** policía *f*; **~ inspector** inspector *m*, -ora *f* de policía; **~ officer** policía *m*; **~ protection** protección *f* policial; **~ record** antecedentes *mpl* penales; **~ state** estado *m* policíaco; **~ station** comisaría *f*; delegación *f* (*Mex*); **~ work** trabajo *m* policial, trabajo *m* de la policía.

3 *vt frontier* vigilar, patrullar por; *area* mantener servicio de policía en, mantener el orden público en; *process* vigilar, controlar; **the frontier is ~d by UN patrols** la frontera la vigilan las patrullas de la ONU; **the area used to be ~d by Britain** antes Gran Bretaña proveía la policía para la región.

policeman [pə'liːsmən] *n, pl* **policemen** [pə'liːsmən] policía *m*, guardia *m*.

policewoman [pəˈliːsˌwʊmən] *n, pl* **policewomen** [pəˈliːsˌwɪmɪn] mujer *f* policía, agente *f*.

policing [pəˈliːsɪŋ] *n* servicio *m* policial.

policy[1] [ˈpɒlɪsɪ] *n* (**a**) política *f*; (*loosely*) principios *mpl*; criterio *m*, actitud *f*; sistema *m*; (*of party, at election*) programa *m*; (*of newspaper*) normas *fpl* de conducta; ~ **decision** decisión *f* de principio; ~ **statement** declaración *f* de política; **that's not my** ~ ése no es mi sistema; **to change one's** ~ cambiar de táctica; **it would be contrary to public** ~ **to** + *infin* no sería conforme con el interés nacional + *infin*.

(**b**) (*wisdom*) prudencia *f*; **it is** ~ **to** + *infin* es prudente + *infin*.

policy[2] [ˈpɒlɪsɪ] *n* (*insurance*) póliza *f*; **to take out a** ~ hacerse un seguro, sacar un seguro.

policyholder [ˈpɒlɪsɪˌhəʊldəʳ] *n* tenedor *m*, -ora *f* de una póliza, asegurado *m*, -a *f*.

polio [ˈpəʊlɪəʊ] *n* polio *f*.

poliomyelitis [ˈpəʊlɪəʊmaɪəˈlaɪtɪs] *n* poliomielitis *f*.

Polish [ˈpəʊlɪʃ] **1** *adj* polaco. **2** *n* (*Ling*) polaco *m*.

polish [ˈpɒlɪʃ] **1** *n* (**a**) (*material*) (*shoe* ~) betún *m*; (*floor* ~, *furniture* ~) cera *f* (de lustrar); (*metal* ~) líquido *m* para limpiar metales; (*nail* ~) esmalte *m* para las uñas, laca *f* para las uñas.

(**b**) (*act*) pulimento *m*; **to give sth a** ~ sacar brillo a algo, pulir algo; **my shoes need a** ~ hace falta limpiar mis zapatos.

(**c**) (*shine*) brillo *m*, bruñido *m*, lustre *m*; **high** ~ lustre *m* brillante; **the buttons have lost their** ~ los botones han perdido su brillo, los botones se han deslustrado; **to put a** ~ **on sth** sacar brillo a algo; **the water takes the** ~ **off** el agua quita el brillo.

(**d**) (*fig: refinement*) finura *f*, cultura *f*, urbanidad *f*; (*of artistry etc*) elegancia *f*; perfección *f*; **his style needs** ~ le hace falta limar el estilo; **he lacks** ~ le falta finura.

2 *vt* (**a**) *shoes* limpiar, bolear (*Mex*); *floor, furniture* encerar, sacar brillo a; *pans, metal, silver* pulir; (*mechanically, industrially*) pulimentar.

(**b**) (*also* **to** ~ **up**) *person* civilizar; *manners* refinar; *style etc* pulir, limar; *one's French etc* repasar, refrescar.

◆**polish off** *vt work* despachar; *person etc* acabar con; *food, drink* despachar, dar cuenta de.

◆**polish up** *vt* = **polish 2** (**b**).

polished [ˈpɒlɪʃt] *adj* pulido; *style etc* limado, elegante; *person* culto, distinguido, fino; *manners* fino.

polisher [ˈpɒlɪʃəʳ] *n* (*person*) pulidor *m*, -ora *f*; (*machine*) enceradora *f*.

polishing machine [ˈpɒlɪʃɪŋməˌʃiːn] *n* pulidor *m*; (*for floors*) enceradora *f*.

polite [pəˈlaɪt] *adj* cortés, atento, fino; educado, correcto; **that's not very** ~ eso no es fino; **I can't deny he was very** ~ **to me** no niego que estuvo muy correcto conmigo; **in** ~ **society** en la buena sociedad.

politely [pəˈlaɪtlɪ] *adv* cortésmente, atentamente; correctamente.

politeness [pəˈlaɪtnɪs] *n* cortesía *f*, finura *f*; educación *f*, corrección *f*; **with exquisite** ~ con la mayor finura; **to do sth out of** ~ hacer algo por cortesía.

politic [ˈpɒlɪtɪk] *adj* prudente.

political [pəˈlɪtɪkəl] *adj* político; ~ **correspondent** corresponsal *m* político, corresponsal *f* política; ~ **economy** economía *f* política; ~ **editor** editor *m* político, editora *f* política; ~ **levy** impuesto *m* político; ~ **prisoner** preso *m* político, presa *f* política; ~ **science** ciencias *fpl* políticas; ~ **scientist** experto *m*, -a *f* en ciencias políticas.

politically [pəˈlɪtɪkəlɪ] *adv* políticamente.

politician [ˌpɒlɪˈtɪʃən] *n* político *mf*; (*pej*) politicastro *m*; (*manipulator*) politiquero *m*, -a *f*.

politicization [pəˌlɪtɪsaɪˈzeɪʃən] *n* politización *f*.

politicize [pəˈlɪtɪsaɪz] *vt* politizar.

politicking [ˈpɒlɪtɪkɪŋ] *n* politiqueo *m*.

politico [pəˈlɪtɪkəʊ] *n* (*hum*) político *m*.

politics [ˈpɒlɪtɪks] *n* política *f*; (*Univ etc*) estudios *mpl* políticos; **to go into** ~ dedicarse a la política; **to talk** ~ hablar de política.

polity [ˈpɒlɪtɪ] *n* gobierno *m*, forma *f* de gobierno; estado *m*.

polka [ˈpɒlkə] *n* polca *f*.

polka dot [ˈpɒlkədɒt] *n* punto *m*; diseño *m* de puntos.

poll [pəʊl] **1** *n* (**a**) (*election*) votación *f*; elección *f*; **in the** ~ **of 1945, at the** ~**s in 1945** en las elecciones de 1945; **a** ~ **was demanded** reclamaron una votación, insistieron en una votación; **to go to the** ~**s** acudir a las urnas; **to head the** ~ obtener la mayoría de los votos, ser elegido, ocupar el primer puesto en la elección; **to take a** ~ someter un asunto a votación; **a** ~ **was taken among those present** votaron los asistentes.

(**b**) (*total votes*) votos *mpl*; **the candidate achieved a** ~ **of 5000 votes** el candidato obtuvo 5000 votos; **there was a** ~ **of 84%** votaron el 84 por cien; **the** ~ **has been a heavy one** ha votado un elevado porcentaje del electorado.

(**c**) (*public opinion organization*) organismo *m* de sondaje; (*inquiry*) encuesta *f*, sondeo *m*; **the Gallup** ~ la encuesta Gallup, el sondeo Gallup; **to take a** ~ hacer una encuesta.

(**d**) (*Telec*) interrogación *f*.

2 *vt* (**a**) *cattle* descornar.

(**b**) *votes* obtener, recibir; **he** ~**ed only 50 votes** obtuvo solamente 50 votos.

(**c**) *persons* encuestar, hacer una encuesta de; **1068 people were** ~**ed** figuraron 1068 personas en la encuesta.

3 *vi*: **he** ~**ed badly** recibió pocos votos, tuvo escaso apoyo; **we shall** ~ **heavily** obtendremos muchos votos.

pollack [ˈpɒlək] *n* abadejo *m*.

pollard [ˈpɒləd] **1** *n* árbol *m* desmochado. **2** *vt* desmochar.

pollen [ˈpɒlən] *n* polen *m*; ~ **allergy** alergia *f* polínica; ~ **count** recuento *m* polínico; ~ **grain** grano *m* de polen.

pollinate [ˈpɒlɪneɪt] *vt* fecundar (con polen), polinizar.

pollination [ˌpɒlɪˈneɪʃən] *n* polinización *f*, fecundación *f*.

polling [ˈpəʊlɪŋ] *n* votación *f*; ~ **will be on Thursday** las elecciones se celebrarán el jueves, se votará el jueves; ~ **has been heavy** ha votado un elevado porcentaje de los electores.

polling-booth [ˈpəʊlɪŋˌbuːð] *n* cabina *f* de votar.

polling-day [ˈpəʊlɪŋˌdeɪ] *n* día *m* de elecciones.

polling-station [ˈpəʊlɪŋˌsteɪʃən] *n* (*Brit*) colegio *m* electoral, centro *m* electoral.

polliwog [ˈpɒlɪwɒg] *n* (*US*) renacuajo *m*.

pollster [ˈpəʊlstəʳ] *n* encuestador *m*, -ora *f*.

poll-tax [ˈpəʊltæks] *n* (contribución *f* de) capitación *f*, impuesto *m* (municipal *etc*) por cabeza.

pollutant [pəˈluːtənt] *n* contaminante *m*, agente *m* contaminador.

pollute [pəˈluːt] *vt* contaminar; ensuciar; (*fig*) corromper; **to become** ~**d** contaminarse (*with* de).

polluter [pəˈluːtəʳ] *n* contaminador *m*, -ora *f*.

pollution [pəˈluːʃən] *n* contaminación *f*, polución *f*; (*fig*) corrupción *f*.

Pollyanna [pɒlɪˈænə] *n* (*US*) persona *f* que todo lo ve color de rosa, optimista *m* redomado, optimista *f* redomada.

pollywog [ˈpɒlɪwɒg] *n* (*US*) renacuajo *m*.

polo [ˈpəʊləʊ] *n* polo *m*.

polonaise [ˌpɒləˈneɪz] *n* polonesa *f*.

poloneck [ˈpəʊləʊnek] *n* cuello *m* cisne; ~ **sweater** suéter *m* con cuello cisne.

polonecked [ˈpəʊləʊnekt] *adj* con cuello cisne.

polonium [pəˈləʊnɪəm] *n* polonio *m*.

poltergeist [ˈpɔːltəgaɪst] *n* poltergeist *m*, duende *m* travieso.

poltroon [pɒlˈtruːn] *n* cobarde *m*.

poly... [pɒlɪ] *pref* poli...

poly* [ˈpɒlɪ] *n* = **polytechnic**.

polyandrous [ˌpɒlɪˈændrəs] *adj* poliándrico.

polyandry [ˈpɒlɪændrɪ] *n* poliandria *f*.

polyanthus [ˌpɒlɪˈænθəs] *n* prímula *f*, primavera *f*, hierba *f* de San Pablo mayor.

poly bag* [ˈpɒlɪbæg] *n* bolsa *f* de politeno.

polychromatic [ˌpɒlɪkrəʊˈmætɪk] *adj* policromo.

polyester [ˌpɒlɪˈestəʳ] *n* poliéster *m*.

polyethylene [ˌpɒlɪˈeθəliːn] *n* (*US*) polietileno *m*.

polygamist [pɒˈlɪgəmɪst] *n* polígamo *m*.

polygamous [pɒˈlɪgəməs] *adj* polígamo.

polygamy [pɒˈlɪgəmɪ] *n* poligamia *f*.

polygenesis [ˌpɒlɪˈdʒenɪsɪs] *n* poligénesis *f*.

polyglot [ˈpɒlɪglɒt] **1** *adj* poligloto. **2** *n* poligloto *m*, -a *f*.

polygon [ˈpɒlɪgən] *n* polígono *m*.

polygonal [pɒˈlɪgənl] *adj* poligonal.

polygraph [ˈpɒlɪgrɑːf] *n* polígrafo *m*, detector *m* de mentiras.

polyhedron [ˌpɒlɪˈhiːdrən] *n* poliedro *m*.

polymath [ˈpɒlɪmæθ] *n* polímata *mf*, erudito *m*, -a *f*.

polymer [ˈpɒlɪməʳ] *n* polímero *m*.

polymerization [ˈpɒlɪməraɪˈzeɪʃən] *n* polimerización *f*.

polymorphic [ˌpɒlɪˈmɔːfɪk] *adj* polimorfo.

polymorphism [ˌpɒlɪˈmɔːfɪzəm] *n* polimorfismo *m*.

Polynesia [ˌpɒlɪˈniːzɪə] *n* la Polinesia.

Polynesian [ˌpɒlɪˈniːzɪən] **1** *adj* polinesio. **2** *n* polinesio *m*, -a *f*.

polyp [ˈpɒlɪp] *n* (*Med, Zool*) pólipo *m*.

Polyphemus [ˌpɒlɪˈfiːməs] *nm* Polifemo.

polyphonic [ˌpɒlɪ'fɒnɪk] *adj* polifónico.
polyphony [pə'lɪfənɪ] *n* polifonía *f.*
polypropylene [ˌpɒlɪ'prɒpɪliːn] *n* polipropileno *m.*
polypus ['pɒlɪpəs] *n* (*Zool*) pólipo *m.*
polysemic [ˌpɒlɪ'siːmɪk] *adj* polisémico.
polysemy [pɒ'lɪsəmɪ] *n* polisemia *f.*
polystyrene [ˌpɒlɪ'staɪriːn] *n* poliestireno *m.*
polysyllabic ['pɒlɪsɪ'læbɪk] *adj* polisílabo.
polysyllable ['pɒlɪˌsɪləbl] *n* polisílabo *m.*
polytechnic [ˌpɒlɪ'teknɪk] *n* (*Brit*) politécnico *m,* escuela *f* politécnica.
polytheism ['pɒlɪθiːɪzəm] *n* politeísmo *m.*
polytheistic [ˌpɒlɪθiː'ɪstɪk] *adj* politeísta.
polythene ['pɒlɪθiːn] *n* (*Brit*) politene *m,* politeno *m.*
polyunsaturated [ˌpɒlɪʌn'sætʃəreɪtɪd] *adj* poliinsaturado.
polyurethane [ˌpɒlɪ'jʊərɪθeɪn] *n* poliuretano *m.*
pom[1]* [pɒm] *n* = **pommy.**
pom[2]* [pɒm] *n* (*dog*) perro *m* de Pomerania, lulú *mf* (de Pomerania).
pomade [pə'mɑːd] *n* pomada *f.*
pomander [pəʊ'mændəʳ] *n recipiente de porcelana que contiene hierbas perfumadas.*
pomegranate ['pɒməgrænɪt] *n* (*fruit*) granada *f;* (*tree*) granado *m.*
pomelo ['pɒmɪˌləʊ] *n* pomelo *m.*
pommel ['pʌml] **1** *n* pomo *m.* **2** *vt* apuñear, dar de puñetazos; aporrear.
pommy* ['pɒmɪ] (*pej*) **1** *n* inglés *m,* -esa *f* (*inmigrante en Australia*). **2** *adj* inglés.
pomp [pɒmp] *n* pompa *f;* fausto *m,* boato *m,* ostentación *f;* ~ **and circumstance** pompa *f* y solemnidad.
Pompeii [pɒm'peɪɪ] *n* Pompeya *f.*
Pompey ['pɒmpɪ] *nm* Pompeyo.
pompom ['pɒmpɒm] *n,* **pompon** ['pɒmpɒn] *n* pompón *m,* borla *f.*
pomposity [pɒm'pɒsɪtɪ] *n* pomposidad *f;* fausto *m,* ostentación *f;* ampulosidad *f,* hinchazón *f.*
pompous ['pɒmpəs] *adj* pomposo; fastuoso, ostentoso; *language* ampuloso, hinchado.
pompously ['pɒmpəslɪ] *adv* pomposamente; ampulosamente, hinchadamente.
ponce [pɒns] *n* (*Brit*) coime *m,* chulo *m* de putas, rufián *m.*
◆ponce about*, ponce around* *vi* chulear*.
poncho ['pɒntʃəʊ] *n* poncho *m.*
pond [pɒnd] *n* (*natural*) charca *f;* (*artificial*) estanque *m;* (*fish*~) vivero *m.*
ponder ['pɒndəʳ] **1** *vt* ponderar, meditar, considerar con especial cuidado. **2** *vi* reflexionar, pensar; **to ~ on sth, to ~ over sth** meditar algo.
ponderous ['pɒndərəs] *adj* (*all senses*) pesado.
ponderously ['pɒndərəslɪ] *adv* pesadamente; *say etc* en tono pesado, lentamente y con énfasis.
pondlife ['pɒndlaɪf] *n* fauna *f* de las charcas.
pondweed ['pɒndwiːd] *n* planta *f* acuática.
pone [pəʊn] *n* (*US*) pan *m* de maíz.
pong‡ [pɒŋ] (*Brit*) **1** *n* hedor *m,* tufo *m.* **2** *vi* apestar, heder.
pongy‡ ['pɒŋɪ] *adj* foche*, maloliente.
poniard ['pɒnjəd] *n* (*liter*) puñal *m.*
pontiff ['pɒntɪf] *n* pontífice *m.*
pontifical [pɒn'tɪfɪkəl] *adj* pontificio, pontifical; (*fig*) dogmático, autoritario.
pontificate 1 [pɒn'tɪfɪkɪt] *n* pontificado *m.* **2** [pɒn'tɪfɪkeɪt] *vi* pontificar (*also fig*).
Pontius Pilate ['pɒnʃəs'paɪlət] *nm* Poncio Pilato.
pontoon[1] [pɒn'tuːn] **1** *n* pontón *m.* **2** *attr:* ~ **bridge** puente *m* de pontones.
pontoon[2] [pɒn'tuːn] *n* (*Brit Cards*) veintiuna *f.*
pony ['pəʊnɪ] *n* (**a**) caballito *m,* jaca *f,* poni *m,* poney *m,* potro *m* (*LAm*). (**b**) (*Brit*‡) *25 libras.* (**c**) (*US**) chuleta* *f.*
ponytail ['pəʊnɪteɪl] *n* trenza *f,* (peinado *m* de) cola *f* de caballo.
pony trekking ['pəʊnɪˌtrekɪŋ] *n* excursión *f* en poney.
pooch* [puːtʃ] *n* (*US*) perro *m.*
poodle ['puːdl] *n* perro *m* de lanas, caniche *m.*
poof‡ [pʊf] *n* (*Brit*), **poofter‡** ['pʊftəʳ] *n* (*Brit*) maricón‡ *m.*
poofy‡ ['pʊfɪ] *adj* (*Brit*) de maricón‡, afeminado.
pooh [puː] *interj* ¡bah!, ¡qué va!
pooh-pooh [puː'puː] *vt proposal etc* rechazar con desdén; *danger etc* negar la importancia de.
pool[1] [puːl] *n* (*natural*) charca *f;* (*artifical*) estanque *m;* (*swimming* ~) piscina *f,* alberca *f* (*LAm*), pileta *f* (*SC*); (*in river*) pozo *m,* remanso *m;* (*of spilt liquid*) charco *m.*
pool[2] [puːl] **1** *n* (**a**) (*game*) chapolín *m;* (*Cards*) polla *f;* (*football* ~) quinielas *fpl;* (*Comm*) consorcio *m,* asociación *f;* mancomunidad *f;* fusión *f* de intereses; (*of typists*) sala *f* de mecanógrafas; servicio *m* de mecanógrafas; **coal and steel** ~ comunidad *f* de carbón y acero; **that's dirty ~*** (*US*) eso no es jugar limpio; **to shoot** ~ (*US*) jugar al chapolín.
(**b**) (*reserve*) reserva *f;* (*source*) fuente *f;* (*of genes etc*) fondo *m,* reserva *f;* **an untapped ~ of ability** una reserva de inteligencia no utilizada aún.
2 *vt* juntar, mancomunar; *resources* consociar, utilizar (*etc*) en forma consociada.
pooling ['puːlɪŋ] *n* consocio *m,* utilización *f* en forma consociada.
poolroom ['puːlruːm] *n* (*US*) sala *f* de billar.
pool table ['puːlˌteɪbl] *n* mesa *f* de billar.
poop[1] [puːp] *n* (*Naut*) popa *f.*
poop[2]*‡ [puːp] *n* (*excrement*) caca‡ *f.*
poop[3]* [puːp] *n* (*US: information*) onda* *f,* información *f.*
pooped‡ [puːpt] *adj:* **to be** ~ (*esp US*) (*tired*) estar hecho polvo; (*drunk*) estar ajumado*.
pooper-scooper* ['puːpə'skuːpəʳ] *n* caca-can* *m.*
poo-poo‡ ['puː'puː] *n* caca‡ *f.*
poor [pʊəʳ] **1** *adj* (**a**) (*not rich*) pobre; *soil etc* pobre, estéril; **a ~ man** un pobre; **a ~ woman** una mujer pobre; ~ **law** ley *f* de asistencia pública; ~ **white** (*US etc*) blanco *m,* -a *f* pobre; **an ore ~ in metal** un mineral de escaso contenido metálico; **a food ~ in vitamins** un alimento pobre en vitaminas; **to be as ~ as a church-mouse** ser más pobre que las ratas, ser pobre de solemnidad.
(**b**) (*bad*) malo; de baja calidad; (*in spirit*) apocado, mezquino; **my ~ memory** mi mala memoria; **it's ~ stuff** no es bueno; **the game was pretty** ~ el partido fue bastante malo; **to be in ~ health** estar mal (de salud); **to be ~ at maths** ser malo en matemáticas; **to have a ~ opinion of sb** tener un concepto poco favorable de uno.
(**c**) (*pitying*) pobre; ~ **me!** ¡pobre de mí!; ~ **you!, ~ old you!, you ~ old thing!** ¡pobrecito!; ~ **Mary!** ¡pobre María!; ~ **Mary's lost all her money** la pobre de María ha perdido todo su dinero; **he's very ill, ~ old chap** está grave el pobre.
2 *npl:* **the** ~ los pobres.
poorbox ['pʊəbɒks] *n* cepillo *m* de los pobres.
poorhouse ['pʊəhaʊs] *n, pl* **poorhouses** ['pʊəhaʊzɪz] asilo *m* de los pobres.
poorly ['pʊəlɪ] **1** *adv* (**a**) pobremente; **they live very** ~ viven en la mayor pobreza.
(**b**) (*badly*) mal; **the team is doing** ~ el equipo juega mal; **exports are doing** ~ las exportaciones no van bien; **I used to do ~ at chemistry** tenía malas notas en química.
2 *adj* (*ill*) mal, enfermo, malucho; en mal estado; **to be ~, to look** ~ estar malo; **I found him very** ~ le encontré en muy mal estado.
poorness ['pʊənɪs] *n* (**a**) (*lack of wealth*) pobreza *f.* (**b**) (*badness*) mala calidad *f;* ~ **of spirit** apocamiento *m,* mezquindad *f.*
poor-spirited ['pʊə'spɪrɪtɪd] *adj* apocado, mezquino.
poove‡ [puːv] *n* = **poof.**
POP (**a**) *abbr of* **publish or perish** publica o perece. (**b**) *abbr of* **Post Office Preferred.**
pop[1] [pɒp] **1** *n* (**a**) (*sound*) ligera detonación *f;* (*of cork*) taponazo *m;* (*of fastener etc*) ruido *m* seco; (*imitative sound*) ¡pum!; **to go** ~ (*bottle etc*) hacer ¡pum!
(**b**) (*: *drink*) gaseosa *f.*
2 *vt* (**a**) *balloon* hacer reventar; pinchar.
(**b**) (*place*) poner, poner rápidamente; **to ~ sth into a drawer** poner algo (rápidamente, sin ser visto *etc*) en un cajón; **to ~ pills** drogarse (con pastillas).
(**c**) (‡: *pawn*) empeñar.
(**d**) (*) **to ~ the question** declararse.
3 *vi* (**a**) (*burst etc*) estallar, reventar (con ligera detonación); pincharse; **there were corks ~ping all over** por todas partes saltaban los tapones; **my ears ~ped on landing** al aterrizar se me han taponado los oídos; **to make sb's eyes** ~ dejar a uno con los ojos fuera de órbita.
(**b**) **we ~ped over to see them** fuimos a hacerles una breve visita; **let's ~ round to Joe's** vamos a casa de Pepe.
◆pop back 1 *vt lid etc* poner de nuevo, volver a poner.
2 *vi* volver un momento.
◆pop in *vi* entrar de sopetón, dar un vistazo; **to ~ in to see sb** ir a saludar a uno, pasar por la casa de uno; **I just ~ped in** me acerqué a veros, me asomé a veros, no tuve la intención de quedarme.
◆pop off‡ *vi* estirar la pata*.
◆pop on *vt light, oven* poner, encender; *kettle* poner (a

calentar); *clothing* ponerse (de prisa); **I'll just ~ my hat on** voy a ponerme el sombrero.

◆**pop out 1** *vt*: **she ~ped her head out** asomó de repente la cabeza. **2** *vi* salir un momento; **he ~ped out for some cigarettes** fue en una escapadita a buscar tabaco; **he ~ped out from his hiding place** salió de repente de su escondite.

◆**pop up** *vi* aparecer inesperadamente.

pop²* [pɒp] *adj abbr of* **popular** pop; **~ art** arte *m* pop; **~ artist** artista *mf* pop; **~ music** música *f* pop; **~ star** estrella *f* de la música pop.

pop³* [pɒp] *n* (*esp US*) papá* *m*.

pop. *abbr of* **population** habitantes *mpl*, h.

popcorn ['pɒpkɔːn] *n* rosetas *fpl*, palomitas *fpl* (de maíz).

pope [pəʊp] *n* papa *m*; **P~ John XXIII** el Papa Juan XXIII.

popemobile ['pəʊpməʊˌbiːl] *n* papamóvil *m*.

popery ['pəʊpərɪ] *n* (*pej*) papismo *m*; **no ~!** ¡abajo el papa!, ¡papa no!

pop-eyed ['pɒp'aɪd] *adj* (*permanently*) de ojos saltones; **they were ~ with amazement** se les desorbitaron los ojos con el asombro; **they looked at me ~** me miraron con los ojos desorbitados.

popgun ['pɒpgʌn] *n* fusil *m* de juguete, taco *m*.

popinjay ['pɒpɪndʒeɪ] *n* pisaverde *m*.

popish ['pəʊpɪʃ] *adj* (*pej*) papista, católico.

poplar ['pɒpləʳ] *n* (*black*) chopo *m*, álamo *m*; (*white*) álamo *m* blanco.

poplin ['pɒplɪn] *n* popelina *f*.

poppa* ['pɒpə] *n* (*US*) papá* *m*.

poppadum ['pɒpədəm] *n* = **papadum**.

popper⁑ ['pɒpəʳ] *n* cápsula *f* de nitrito amílico.

poppet* ['pɒpɪt] *n* (*Brit*): **yes, my ~** sí, hija; sí, querida; **hullo, ~!** ¡oye, ricura!*; **isn't she a ~?** ¡qué preciosidad!; **the boss is a ~** el jefe es muy amable.

poppy ['pɒpɪ] *n* amapola *f*, adormidera *f*; **P~ Day** aniversario *m* del Armisticio (*de noviembre 1918*); **~ seed** semilla *f* de amapola.

poppycock* ['pɒpɪkɒk] *n* tonterías *fpl*; **~!** ¡tonterías!

Popsicle ['pɒpsɪkl] ® *n* (*US*) polo *m*.

popsy⁑ ['pɒpsɪ] *n* chica *f*.

populace ['pɒpjʊlɪs] *n* pueblo *m*; (*pej*) plebe *f*, populacho *m*.

popular ['pɒpjʊləʳ] *adj* (**a**) (*well-liked*) popular; **to be ~** (*enjoy wide esteem*) ser popular, (*be in fashion*) estar de moda; **it's a ~ work** es una obra popular; **the show is proving very ~** el espectáculo está muy concurrido; **there is a ~ belief that** ... muchos creen que ..., se cree generalmente que ...; **he's ~ with the girls** tiene mucho éxito con las chicas; **I'm not very ~ in the office just now** por ahora no me quieren mucho en la oficina.

(**b**) (*of the people*) popular; **~ front** frente *m* popular; **by ~ request, we offer** ... respondiendo a la demanda general, ofrecemos ...; **it's a ~ work** es una obra de vulgarización.

popularity [ˌpɒpjʊ'lærɪtɪ] *n* popularidad *f*.

popularization ['pɒpjʊləraɪ'zeɪʃən] *n* popularización *f*; vulgarización *f*.

popularize ['pɒpjʊləraɪz] *vt* (*make popular*) popularizar; (*make available to laymen*) vulgarizar.

popularly ['pɒpjʊləlɪ] *adv*: **X ~ known as Y** X conocido por regla general como Y, X al que se llama vulgarmente Y; **it is ~ thought that** ... muchos creen que ...

populate ['pɒpjʊleɪt] *vt* poblar.

population [ˌpɒpjʊ'leɪʃən] *n* población *f*; (*in numbering inhabitants*) habitantes *mpl*; **~ explosion** explosión *f* demográfica; **~ growth** crecimiento *m* demográfico; **~ pressures** presiones *fpl* demográficas.

populism ['pɒpjʊlɪzəm] *n* populismo *m*.

populist ['pɒpjʊlɪst] **1** *adj* populista. **2** *n* populista *mf*.

populous ['pɒpjʊləs] *adj* populoso; **the most ~ city in the world** la ciudad más poblada del mundo.

pop-up ['pɒpʌp] *attr*: **~ book** libro *m* con dibujos en relieve; **~ toaster** tostador *m* automático.

porcelain ['pɔːslɪn] *n* porcelana *f*.

porch [pɔːtʃ] *n* pórtico *m*; entrada *f*; (*of house, church*) porche *m*.

porcine ['pɔːsaɪn] *adj* porcino, porcuno.

porcupine ['pɔːkjʊpaɪn] *n* puerco *m* espín.

porcupine fish ['pɔːkjʊpaɪnˌfɪʃ] *n* pez *m* globo.

pore¹ [pɔːʳ] *n* poro *m*.

pore² [pɔːʳ] *vi*: **to ~ over sth** estar absorto en el estudio de algo, estudiar algo larga y detenidamente; **we ~d over it for hours** lo estudiamos durante horas y horas.

pork [pɔːk] *n* (carne *f* de) cerdo *m*, (carne *f* de) chancho *m* (*LAm*); **~ butcher** tocinero *m*; **~ sausage** salchicha *f* de cerdo.

porker ['pɔːkəʳ] *n* cerdo *m*, cochino *m*.

porkies⁑ ['pɔːkɪz] *npl* mentiras *fpl*.

porkpie ['pɔːk'paɪ] *n* pastel *m* de carne de cerdo.

porky* ['pɔːkɪ] *adj* gordo, gordinflón*.

porn* [pɔːn] *n abbr of* **pornography**; **~ merchant** traficante *m* en pornografía; **~ shop** tienda *f* de pornografía, tienda *f* porno*.

pornographer [pɔː'nɒgrəfəʳ] *n* editor *m* (*or* artista *m etc*) porno, pornografista *mf*.

pornographic [ˌpɔːnə'græfɪk] *adj* pornográfico.

pornography [pɔː'nɒgrəfɪ] *n* pornografía *f*.

porosity [pɔː'rɒsɪtɪ] *n* porosidad *f*.

porous ['pɔːrəs] *adj* poroso.

porousness ['pɔːrəsnɪs] *n* porosidad *f*.

porphyria [pɔː'fɪrɪə] *n* porfirismo *m*.

porphyry ['pɔːfɪrɪ] *n* pórfido *m*.

porpoise ['pɔːpəs] *n* marsopa *f*, puerco *m* de mar.

porridge ['pɒrɪdʒ] *n* (**a**) (*approx*) gachas *fpl* de avena; (*baby's*) papilla *f*; **~ oats** copos *mpl* de avena. (**b**) **to do 2 years' ~⁑** (*Brit*) pasar 2 años a la sombra⁑.

port¹ [pɔːt] **1** *n* (**a**) (*Naut: harbour*) puerto *m*; **~ of call** puerto *m* de escala; **his next ~ of call was the chemist's** luego fue a la farmacia; **which is your next ~ of call?** ¿adónde se dirige ahora?; **~ of entry** puerto *m* de entrada; **any ~ in a storm** en el peligro cualquier refugio es bueno; la necesidad carece de ley; **to come into ~, to put into ~** entrar a puerto; **to leave ~** hacerse a la mar, zarpar.

(**b**) (*Comput*) puerta *f*, puerto *m*, port *m*.

2 *attr* de puerto, portuario; **~ authority** autoridad *f* portuaria; **~ dues** derechos *mpl* de puerto; **~ facilities** facilidades *fpl* portuarias.

port² [pɔːt] *n* (*Naut: ~hole*) portilla *f*; (*Mech*) lumbrera *f*; (*Mil* ††) tronera *f*.

port³ [pɔːt] (*Naut: also* **~ side**) **1** *n* babor *m*; **the sea to ~** la mar a babor; **land to ~!** ¡tierra a babor!

2 *attr lighter etc* de babor; **on the ~ side** a babor.

3 *vt*: **to ~ the helm** poner el timón a babor, virar a babor.

port⁴ [pɔːt] *n* (*wine*) vino *m* de Oporto, oporto *m*.

portability [ˌpɔːtə'bɪlɪtɪ] *n* (*esp Comput*) portabilidad *f*, portatilidad *f*; (*of software*) transferibilidad *f*.

portable ['pɔːtəbl] **1** *adj* portátil. **2** *n* máquina *f* (*etc*) portátil.

portage ['pɔːtɪdʒ] *n* porteo *m*.

Portakabin ['pɔːtəˌkæbɪn] ® *n* (*gen*) caseta *f* prefabricada; (*extension to office etc*) anexo *m* prefabricado; (*works office etc*) barracón *m* de obras.

portal ['pɔːtl] *n* puerta *f* (grande, imponente).

portcullis [pɔːt'kʌlɪs] *n* rastrillo *m*.

portend [pɔː'tend] *vt* presagiar, anunciar; **what does this ~?** ¿qué quiere decir esto?

portent ['pɔːtent] *n* presagio *m*, augurio *m*, señal *f*; (*prodigy*) portento *m*; **a ~ of doom** un presagio de la catástrofe.

portentous [pɔː'tentəs] *adj* (**a**) (*ominous, prodigious*) portentoso. (**b**) (*pompous*) pomposo.

portentously [pɔː'tentəslɪ] *adv* (**a**) portentosamente. (**b**) pomposamente.

porter ['pɔːtəʳ] *n* (**a**) (*Brit: of hotel, office etc*) portero *m*, conserje *m*; (*Brit Rail: uniformed*) mozo *m* de estación, (*US Rail*) mozo *m* de los coches-cama, (*touting for custom*) mozo *m* de cuerda; (*Sherpa*) porteador *m*; **~'s lodge** portería *f*, conserjería *f*.

(**b**) (*beer*) cerveza *f* negra.

porterage ['pɔːtərɪdʒ] *n* porte *m*.

porterhouse ['pɔːtəhaʊs] **1** *n*, **1** *pl* **porterhouses** ['pɔːtəhaʊzɪz] (††) mesón *m*. **2** *attr*: **~ steak** (*Brit*) biftec *m* de filete.

portfolio [pɔːt'fəʊlɪəʊ] *n* cartera *f*, carpeta *f*; (*Pol*) cartera *f*; **~ management** administración *f* de la cartera de acciones; **~ of shares** cartera *f* de acciones; **minister without ~** ministro *m* sin cartera.

porthole ['pɔːthəʊl] *n* portilla *f*.

Portia ['pɔːʃə] *nf* Porcia.

portico ['pɔːtɪkəʊ] *n* pórtico *m*.

portion ['pɔːʃən] **1** *n* porción *f*, parte *f*; (*helping*) ración *f*; (*also* **marriage ~**) dote *f*; (*quantity, in relation to a whole*) porción *f*; sección *f*; porcentaje *m*. **2** *vt* (*also* **to ~ out**) repartir, dividir.

portliness ['pɔːtlɪnɪs] *n* gordura *f*, corpulencia *f*.

portly ['pɔːtlɪ] *adj* gordo, corpulento.

portmanteau [pɔːt'mæntəʊ] *n* baúl *m* de viaje; **~ word** palabra *f* híbrida, palabra *f* entrecruzada (*p.ej. motel, smog*).

Porto Rico [ˌpɔːtəʊ'riːkəʊ] *etc* = **Puerto Rico** *etc*.

portrait ['pɔːtrɪt] *n* retrato *m*; ~ **gallery** museo *m* de retratos, galería *f* iconográfica; **National P~ Gallery** Museo *m* Iconográfico Nacional; ~ **orientation** formato *m* vertical; **to have one's ~ painted, to sit for one's ~** retratarse, hacerse retratar.

portraitist ['pɔːtrɪtɪst] *n*, **portrait painter** ['pɔːtrɪt,peɪntəʳ] *n* retratista *mf*.

portraiture ['pɔːtrɪtʃəʳ] *n* (*portrait*) retrato *m*; (*portraits collectively*) retratos *mpl*; (*art of* ~) arte *m* de retratar; **Spanish ~ in the 16th century** retratos *mpl* españoles del siglo XVI.

portray [pɔː'treɪ] *vt* (*Art*) retratar; (*fig*) pintar, describir; representar.

portrayal [pɔː'treɪəl] *n* (*Art*) retrato *m*; (*fig*) descripción *f*; descripción *f* gráfica, representación *f*; **a most unflattering ~** una representación nada halagüeña.

portress ['pɔːtrɪs] *n* portera *f*.

Portugal ['pɔːtjʊgəl] *n* Portugal *m*.

Portuguese [,pɔːtjʊ'giːz] **1** *adj* portugués. **2** *n* (**a**) portugués *m*, -esa *f*. (**b**) (*Ling*) portugués *m*.

POS *n abbr of* **point of sale** punto *m* de venta.

pose [pəʊz] **1** *n* (**a**) (*of body*) postura *f*, actitud *f*.

(**b**) (*fig*) afectación *f*, pose *f*; **it's just a big ~** todo esto no es más que afectación.

2 *vt* (**a**) (*place*) colocar; **he ~d the model in the position he wanted** hizo que la modelo adoptara la postura que él quería.

(**b**) *problem* plantear; *question* hacer, formular; *threat* representar, encerrar.

3 *vi* (**a**) (*place o.s.*) colocarse; (*as model*) posar; **she once ~d for Picasso** una vez posó para Picasso.

(**b**) (*affectedly*) darse tono; tomar una postura afectada; **to ~ as** hacerse pasar por, echárselas de.

Poseidon [pə'saɪdən] *nm* Poseidón.

poser ['pəʊzəʳ] *n* (**a**) (*problem*) pregunta *f* difícil, problema *m* difícil. (**b**) (*person*) = **poseur**.

poseur [pəʊ'zɜːʳ] *n* persona *f* afectada, farsante *mf*, vacilón*, -ona *f*, maniquí *mf*.

posh* [pɒʃ] **1** *adj* elegante, de lujo, lujoso; (~ *but in bad taste*) cursi; *wedding etc* de mucho rumbo; *accent* afectado; *school* de buen tono; ~ **people** gente *f* bien; **a ~ car** un coche de lujo; **it's a very ~ neighbourhood** es un barrio de lo más elegante.

2 *adv*: **to talk ~** hablar con acento afectado.

3 *vt*: **to ~ a place up** procurar que un local parezca más elegante, renovar la pintura (*etc*) de un local; **it's all ~ed up** está totalmente renovado, se ha reformado por completo.

4 *vr*: **to ~ o.s. up** arreglarse, ataviarse, emperejilarse.

posit ['pɒzɪt] *vt* proponer como principio (*that* que), postular.

position [pə'zɪʃən] **1** *n* (**a**) (*place, in physical sense*) posición *f*, situación *f*; (*of body, posture*) posición *f*, postura *f*, actitud *f*; (*sexual*) postura *f*; (*Sport*) posición *f*; **to be in ~** estar en posición, estar en su lugar; **to be in a dangerous ~** estar en una posición peligrosa; **what ~ was the body in?** ¿cuál era la postura del cadáver?; **you are in the best ~ to see it** estás en la mejor posición para verlo, estás en el mejor sitio para verlo; **to place sth in ~** colocar algo, poner algo en su lugar; **put yourself in my ~** ponte en mi lugar; **to be out of ~** estar fuera de su lugar, estar desplazado; **what ~ do you play (in)?** ¿qué posición tienes?; **my usual ~ is goalkeeper** en general yo juego de portero.

(**b**) (*Naut*) posición *f*; **to fix one's ~** determinar su posición, averiguar su posición; **to take up ~ astern** ponerse a popa.

(**c**) (*Mil*) posición *f*; (*post*) puesto *m*; (*for gun*) emplazamiento *m*; **our ~s before the attack** nuestras posiciones antes del ataque; **to manoeuvre for ~** hacer maniobras para mejorar de posición; **to storm an enemy ~** tomar una posición enemiga al asalto.

(**d**) (*rank*) posición *f*; (*social*) posición *f*, rango *m*, categoría *f*; (*in class, league etc*) puesto *m*; **of good social ~** de buena posición social, de categoría; **to have a high social ~** ocupar una posición social elevada; **to lose one's ~ at the top of the league** perder su puesto a la cabeza de la liga.

(**e**) (*post*) puesto *m*, empleo *m*; colocación *f*; situación *f*; cargo *m*; **the ~ of ambassador in Bogotá** el puesto de embajador en Bogotá; **to have a good ~ in a bank** tener un buen puesto en un banco; **to look for a ~** buscar una colocación.

(**f**) (*state*) situación *f*; **the country's economic ~** la situación económica del país; **the ~ is that ...** es que ..., el hecho es que ...; **our ~ is improving** estamos mejorando de situación; **to be in a ~ to** + *infin* estar en condiciones de + *infin*; **to be in no ~ to** + *infin* no estar en condiciones de + *infin*; **to consider one's ~** (*euph*) pensar en dimitir, estudiar la conveniencia de dimitir.

(**g**) (*opinion*) postura *f*; opinión *f*; actitud *f*; **what is our ~ on Greece?** ¿cuál es nuestra actitud hacia (*or* para con) Grecia?, ¿cuál es nuestra política con Grecia?; **to take up a ~ on a matter** adoptar una postura en un asunto; **to change one's ~** cambiar de opinión, cambiar de idea.

2 *vt* colocar, disponer.

positive ['pɒzɪtɪv] **1** *adj* (**a**) (*definite*) positivo; definitivo; real, verdadero; ~ **proof** prueba *f* concluyente; **there are some ~ results at last** por fin hay unos resultados positivos; **it's a ~ miracle!** ¡es un auténtico milagro!; **he's a ~ nuisance** realmente es un pesado.

(**b**) (*of person: sure*) seguro; **he is ~ about it** está seguro de ello; **I'm quite ~ on that point** estoy completamente convencido de ello; **you don't sound very ~** no pareces estar muy seguro.

(**c**) (*of things: sure*) enfático, categórico; **in a ~ tone of voice** con énfasis.

(**d**) (*of character*) de fuerte personalidad, enérgico, activo; **she's a ~ sort of person** es una persona enérgica, es una persona que sabe lo que quiere.

(**e**) (*Gram*) *degree* positivo; (*affirmative*) afirmativo; ~ **cash flow** flujo *m* positivo de efectivo; ~ **discrimination** discriminación *f* positiva; ~ **vetting** investigación *f* positiva.

(**f**) (*Elec, Math, Phot*) positivo.

2 *n* (*Phot*) positiva *f*.

positively ['pɒzɪtɪvlɪ] *adv* (**a**) (*definitely*) positivamente; definitivamente; verdaderamente; **it's ~ marvellous!** ¡es realmente maravilloso!

(**b**) (*emphatically*) con énfasis, categóricamente.

(**c**) (*energetically*) con energía, enérgicamente.

positivism ['pɒzɪtɪvɪzəm] *n* positivismo *m*.

positivist ['pɒzɪtɪvɪst] **1** *adj* positivista. **2** *n* positivista *mf*.

positron ['pɒzɪ,trɒn] *n* positrón *m*.

poss.* [pɒs] *adj, adv abbr of* **possible, possibly**.

posse ['pɒsɪ] *n* (*US*) pelotón *m*, grupo *m* (*esp fuerza civil armada bajo el mando del Sheriff*).

possess [pə'zes] **1** *vt* (**a**) (*have, own, also* **to be ~ed of**) poseer; **it ~es many advantages** posee muchas ventajas; **they ~ a fortune** poseen una fortuna, tienen una fortuna.

(**b**) **to be ~ed by demons** estar poseso (*or* poseído) por los demonios; **to be ~ed by an idea** estar dominado por una idea; **we are ~ed by many doubts** son muchas las dudas que tenemos; **whatever can have ~ed you?** ¿cómo lo has podido hacer?; **what can have ~ed you to think like that?** ¿cómo has podido pensar así?

2 *vr* (**a**) **to ~ o.s. of** tomar posesión de; (*violently*) apoderarse de.

(**b**) **to ~ o.s. in patience** armarse de paciencia.

possessed [pə'zest] *adj* poseso, poseído; **like one ~** como un poseso, como un energúmeno.

possession [pə'zeʃən] *n* (**a**) (*act, state*) posesión *f*; ~ **of arms** tenencia *f* de armas; **to get ~ of** adquirir, hacerse con; (*improperly*) apoderarse de; **to take ~ of** tomar posesión de; *house etc* ocupar, entrar en; (*improperly*) apoderarse de, hacerse dueño de; (*confiscate*) incautarse de; **to be in ~ of** poseer, tener; **to be in full ~ of one's faculties** poseer todas sus facultades; **to be in the ~ of** estar en manos de, ser de la propiedad de, pertenecer a; **to come into ~ of** adquirir; **to come** (*or* **pass**) **into the ~ of** pasar a manos de; **to have ~** (**of the ball**) estar en posesión (del balón); **to have sth in one's ~** poseer algo; **a house with vacant ~** una casa (que se vende) desocupada; **'with vacant ~'** 'llave en mano'.

(**b**) (*object*) posesión *f*; **~s** posesiones *fpl*; (*as legal term*) bienes *mpl*; **Spain's overseas ~s** las posesiones de España en ultramar.

(**c**) (*by devil*) posesión *f*.

possessive [pə'zesɪv] **1** *adj* (**a**) *love etc* dominante, tiránico, absorbente; **to be ~ towards sb** ser absorbente con uno.

(**b**) (*Gram*) posesivo; ~ **pronoun** pronombre *m* posesivo.

2 *n* posesivo *m*.

possessively [pə'zesɪvlɪ] *adv* tiránicamente; de modo absorbente.

possessiveness [pə'zesɪvnɪs] *n* posesividad *f*.

possessor [pə'zesəʳ] *n* poseedor *m*, -ora *f*; dueño *m*, -a *f*; **he was the proud ~ of ...** se preciaba de poseer ...

possibility [,pɒsə'bɪlɪtɪ] *n* (**a**) (*chance*) posibilidad *f*; (*outlook*) perspectiva *f*; **the ~ of severe losses** la posibilidad de sufrir pérdidas cuantiosas; **there is no ~ of his agreeing to**

it no existe posibilidad alguna de que consienta en ello; **if by any ~...** si por casualidad ...; **it is within the bounds of ~** cabe dentro de lo posible; **it's a grim ~** es una perspectiva aterradora.

(**b**) (*event etc*) acontecimiento *m* posible; posibilidad *f*; **to allow for the ~ that it may happen** tener en cuenta la posibilidad de que una cosa ocurra; **to foresee all the possibilities** prever todas las posibilidades.

(**c**) (*promise*) **he has possibilities** promete, es prometedor; **the subject has possibilities** es un tema prometedor, es un tema de gran potencial.

possible ['pɒsəbl] **1** *adj* (**a**) posible; **a ~ defeat** una posible derrota; **a ~ candidate** un candidato aceptable; **all ~ concessions** todas las concesiones posibles; **one has to foresee all ~ outcomes** hay que prever todos los resultados posibles; **to make sth ~** hacer algo posible, posibilitar algo; **we will help whenever ~** ayudaremos siempre cuando sea posible; **where ~, wherever ~** donde sea posible.

(**b**) (*with verb* to be *etc*) **if ~** si es posible, de ser posible, a ser posible; si cabe; **it is just ~** existe una pequeña posibilidad (*that* de que + *subj*); **it is ~ that ...** es posible que + *subj*, puede ser que + *subj*; **it is ~ to** + *infin* es posible + *infin*; **it is not ~ to do more** es imposible hacer más; **it will be ~ for you to return the same day** te será posible volver el mismo día, podrás volver el mismo día.

(**c**) (*with* as) **we will help as far as ~** ayudaremos en lo posible, ayudaremos en cuanto podamos; **as much as ~** todo lo posible; **as often as ~** lo más frecuentemente posible; **as well as ~** lo mejor posible; **as soon as ~** cuanto antes, lo antes posible, lo más pronto posible; **as heavy as ~** lo más pesado que pueda ser, todo lo pesado que pueda ser; el más pesado que haya.

2 *n*: **a list of ~s for the job** una lista de candidatos aceptables para el puesto; **he's a ~ for the team** tiene posibilidades de formar parte del equipo; **P~s versus Probables** la selección B contra la selección A.

possibly ['pɒsəblɪ] *adv* posiblemente; tal vez; **yes, ~** sí, es posible; **if I ~ can** si me es posible; **~ they've gone already** es posible que hayan ido ya, puede que hayan ido ya, han ido ya quizá; **he did all he ~ could** hizo todo lo que pudo; **I come as often as I ~ can** vengo todas las veces que puedo, vengo lo más a menudo posible; **I cannot ~ allow it** no lo puedo permitir de ninguna manera, me es totalmente imposible autorizarlo; **it can't ~ be true!** ¡no puede ser!, ¡no es posible!

possum ['pɒsəm] *n* zarigüeya *f*; **to play ~** (*sleeping*) fingir estar dormido; (*dead*) hacerse el muerto.

post[1] [pəʊst] **1** *n* (*of timber etc*) poste *m*; (*goal ~*) poste *m* (de la portería); (*for fencing, marking*) estaca *f*; **the ~** (*Sport*) (*starting*) poste *m* de salida, (*finishing*) poste *m* de llegada, meta *f*; **to be left at the ~** quedar atrás desde la salida; **to win on the ~** ganar junto al mismo poste de llegada.

2 *vt* (*announce*) anunciar; *bills etc* (*also* **to ~ up**) fijar, pegar; '**~ no bills**' 'prohibido fijar carteles'; **to ~ sb missing** declarar a uno desaparecido.

post[2] [pəʊst] **1** *n* (*Brit*) (**a**) (*mail*) correo *m*; (*office*) casa *f* de correos, correos *mpl*; (*numbered*: *collection*) recogida *f*, (*delivery*) entrega *f*; **first ~** primera recogida *f*; **last ~** última recogida *f*, última entrega *f*; **by ~** por correo; **~ free** libre de franqueo; **~ paid** porte *m* pagado; **your cheque is in the ~** su cheque está en el correo; **the ~ has come** ha llegado el correo; **it came with the ~** vino con el correo; **to drop a card in the ~** echar una postal al buzón; **to go to the ~** ir a correos, ir al buzón; **to open one's ~** abrir sus cartas; **to sort the ~** clasificar las cartas; **to take a parcel to the ~** llevar un paquete a correos.

(**b**) **there has been a general ~ among the staff** muchos miembros del personal han intercambiado sus puestos.

2 *vt* (**a**) (*Brit*) *mail* echar al buzón, llevar a correos; **this was ~ed on Monday** esto se echó al buzón el lunes; **to ~ sth to sb** mandar algo a uno por correo.

(**b**) (*inform*) **to keep sb ~ed** tener a uno al corriente; **please keep me ~ed** no dejes de mantenerme al corriente.

3 *vi* (††) viajar en posta; **he went ~ing off to India** se fue (inesperadamente, a toda prisa *etc*) a la India.

post[3] [pəʊst] **1** *n* (**a**) (*job*) puesto *m*, empleo *m*; destino *m*; cargo *m*; **to look for a ~** buscar un puesto; **the duties of the ~** las funciones del cargo; **to take up one's ~** ocupar el puesto, entrar en funciones.

(**b**) (*Mil*) puesto *m*; **Last P~** toque *m* de retreta; **to die at one's ~** morir en su puesto.

2 *vt* (**a**) (*station*) situar, apostar; **to ~ sentries** apostar centinelas; **to ~ a man at the gate** apostar un hombre a la puerta.

(**b**) (*Brit*: *send*) **to ~ sb to Buenos Aires** enviar a uno a Buenos Aires, nombrar a uno en Buenos Aires, destinar a uno para Buenos Aires; **to be ~ed to a regiment** ser ordenado a incorporarse a un regimiento; **he was ~ed first to a destroyer** se le mandó primero a un destructor; **to be ~ed captain** ser ascendido a capitán.

post... [pəʊst] *pref* post..., pos...

postage ['pəʊstɪdʒ] *n* porte *m*, franqueo *m*; **~s** (*in account*) gastos *mpl* de correo; **~ due** a pagar; **~ machine** (*US*), **~ meter** (*US*) franqueadora *f*; **~ paid** porte pagado, franco de porte; **~ rates** tarifa *f* de correo.

postage-stamp ['pəʊstɪdʒ,stæmp] *n* sello *m* (de correo), estampilla *f* (*LAm*), timbre *m* (*Mex*).

postal ['pəʊstəl] *adj* postal, de correos; **~ area, ~ district** distrito *m* postal; **~ charges, ~ rates** tarifa *f* de correo; **~ order** giro *m* postal; **~ packet** paquete *m* postal; **~ service** servicio *m* postal; **~ system** sistema *m* postal, correo *m*; **~ vote** voto *m* postal; **~ worker** empleado *m*, -a *f* de correos.

postbag ['pəʊstbæg] *n* (*Brit*) saco *m* postal; **it arrived in my ~** llegó en mi correo; **he received a heavy ~** recibió muchas cartas.

postbox ['pəʊstbɒks] *n* (*Brit*) buzón *m*.

postcard ['pəʊstkɑːd] *n* tarjeta *f* postal, postal *f*.

postcode ['pəʊstkəʊd] *n* (*Brit*) código *m* postal.

post-coital [pəʊst'kəʊɪtəl] *adj* de después del coito.

postdate ['pəʊst'deɪt] *vt* poner fecha adelantada a, posfechar.

postdated ['pəʊst'deɪtɪd] *adj cheque* con fecha adelantada.

post-doctoral ['pəʊst'dɒktərəl] *adj* posdoctoral; **~ fellow** becario *m*, -a *f* posdoctoral; **~ fellowship** beca *f* posdoctoral.

poster ['pəʊstəʳ] *n* cartel *m*; póster *m*, afiche *m* (*And, Mex, SC*); **~ artist, ~ designer** cartelista *mf*; **~ paint** pintura *f* al agua.

poste restante ['pəʊst'restɑːnt] *n* (*Brit*) lista *f* de correos, poste *f* restante (*LAm*).

posterior [pɒs'tɪərɪəʳ] **1** *adj* posterior. **2** *n* trasero *m*.

posterity [pɒs'terɪtɪ] *n* posteridad *f*.

postern ['pəʊstɜːn] *n* postigo *m*.

post-free ['pəʊst'friː] *adv* porte pagado, franco de porte, libre de franqueo.

postglacial ['pəʊst'gleɪsɪəl] *adj* posglacial.

postgraduate ['pəʊst'grædjʊɪt] **1** *adj* (pos)graduado; **~ course** curso *m* para (pos)graduados. **2** *n* (pos)graduado *m*, -a *f*.

post-haste ['pəʊst'heɪst] *adv* a toda prisa, con toda urgencia.

post-hole ['pəʊsthəʊl] *n* agujero *m* de poste.

post-horn ['pəʊst,hɔːn] *n* corneta *f* del correo.

posthumous ['pɒstjʊməs] *adj* póstumo.

posthumously ['pɒstjʊməslɪ] *adv* póstumamente, con carácter póstumo, después de la muerte.

postilion [pəs'tɪlɪən] *n* postillón *m*.

post-imperial ['pəʊstɪm'pɪərɪəl] *adj* posimperial.

post-impressionism ['pəʊstɪm'preʃənɪzəm] *n* posimpresionismo *m*.

post-impressionist ['pəʊstɪm'preʃənɪst] **1** *adj* posimpresionista. **2** *n* posimpresionista *mf*.

post-industrial [,pəʊstɪn'dʌstrɪəl] *adj* posindustrial.

posting ['pəʊstɪŋ] *n* (**a**) (*Brit Mil etc*) destino *m*. (**b**) (*Fin*) asiento *m*, traspaso *m* al libro mayor.

postman ['pəʊstmən] *n, pl* **postmen** ['pəʊstmən] cartero *m*.

postmark ['pəʊstmɑːk] **1** *n* matasellos *m*; **date as ~** según fecha del matasellos. **2** *vt* matar (el sello de), timbrar; **it is ~ed 'León'** lleva el matasellos de León.

postmaster ['pəʊst,mɑːstəʳ] *n* administrador *m* de correos; **P~ General** (*Brit*) Director *m*, -ora *f* General de Correos.

postmistress ['pəʊst,mɪstrɪs] *n* administradora *f* de correos.

postmodern ['pəʊst'mɒdən] *adj* posmoderno.

postmodernism ['pəʊst'mɒdənɪzəm] *n* posmodernismo *m*.

postmodernist ['pəʊst'mɒdənɪst] **1** *adj* posmodernista. **2** *n* posmodernista *mf*.

post-mortem ['pəʊst'mɔːtəm] *n* autopsia *f*; **to carry out a ~** practicar una autopsia; **to hold a ~ on sth** (*fig*) analizar los resultados de algo, examinar algo críticamente, pasar algo en revista.

postnatal ['pəʊst'neɪtl] *adj* posnatal; **~ depression** depresión *f* posparto.

post office ['pəʊst,ɒfɪs] **1** *n* (oficina *f*, casa *f* de) correos; **General P~** Administración *f* General de Correos; **I was in the ~** estaba en correos; **I'm going to the ~** voy a correos.

2 *attr*: **~ box** apartado *m* de correos, casilla *f* de correos (*LAm*); ~ **savings-bank** caja *f* postal de ahorros; ~ **worker** empleado *m*, -a *f* de correos.

post-operative [ˌpəustˈɒpərətɪv] *adj* posoperativo, posoperatorio.

post-paid [ˈpəustˈpeɪd] *adv* porte pagado, franco de porte.

postpone [pəustˈpəun] *vt* aplazar; diferir; **to ~ sth for a month** aplazar algo por un mes; **it has been ~d till Tuesday** ha sido aplazado hasta el martes.

postponement [pəustˈpəunmənt] *n* aplazamiento *m*.

postpositive [pəustˈpɒzɪtɪv] *adj* pospositivo.

postprandial [ˈpəustˈprændɪəl] *adj speech, talk etc* de sobremesa; *walk etc* que se da después de comer.

postscript [ˈpəusskrɪpt] *n* posdata *f*; (*fig*) añadidura *f*; epílogo *m*; **there is a ~ to this story** esta historia tiene epílogo.

poststructuralism [ˈpəustˈstrʌktʃərəlɪzm] *n* posestructuralismo *m*.

postulant [ˈpɒstjʊlənt] *n* postulante *m*, -a *f*.

postulate 1 [ˈpɒstjʊlɪt] *n* postulado *m*. **2** [ˈpɒstjʊleɪt] *vt* postular.

postulation [ˌpɒstjʊˈleɪʃən] *n* postulación *f*.

posture [ˈpɒstʃəʳ] **1** *n* postura *f*, actitud *f*. **2** *vi* tomar una postura, adoptar una actitud; (*pej*) adoptar una actitud afectada.

postviral [ˌpəustˈvaɪrəl] *adj*: ~ **syndrome** síndrome *m* posvírico.

postvocalic [ˌpəustvəʊˈkælɪk] *adj* posvocálico.

postwar [ˈpəustˈwɔːʳ] *adj* de pos(t)guerra, de la pos(t)guerra, posbélico; **the ~ period** la pos(t)guerra.

posy [ˈpəuzɪ] *n* ramillete *m*.

pot[1] [pɒt] **1** *n* **(a)** (*for cooking*) olla *f*, puchero *m*, marmita *f*; (*for preserving*) tarro *m*, pote *m*; (*coffee~*) cafetera *f*; (*tea~*) tetera *f*; (*US*: *kitty*) bote *m*; (*flower~*) tiesto *m*, maceta *f*; (*chamber~*) orinal *m*; **big ~*** pez *m* gordo*, personaje *m*; **the ~ calling the kettle black** el puchero dijo a la sartén 'apártate de mí que me tiznas'; **a ~ of coffee for two** café *m* para dos; **~s and pans** cacharros *mpl*; (*modern*) batería *f* de cocina; **we have ~s of it*** tenemos montones*; **to have ~s of money*** ser muy rico; **to go to ~*** echarse a perder, arruinarse; **to keep the ~ boiling** (*earn living*) ganarse la vida; (*make things progress*) mantener las cosas en marcha; **to make a ~ of tea** hacer el té.

(b) (*Sport**) copa *f*.

(c) (*Anat**) barriga *f*, panza *f*.

(d) (*Snooker*) golpe *m*; (*~shot*) tiro *m*; **he took a ~ at the wolf** tiró al lobo.

2 *attr*: ~ **cheese** (*US*) ≃ requesón *m*.

3 *vt* **(a)** *food* conservar (en botes *etc*); (*also* **to ~ up**) *seedling* enmacetar, *plant* poner en tiesto.

(b) *game* derribar; abatir (a tiros); *person* herir; (*Snooker*) *ball* embolsar, entronerar.

4 *vi*: **to ~ at sb** disparar sobre uno; **to ~ away** seguir disparando.

pot[2]‡ [pɒt] *n* marijuana *f*.

potable [ˈpəutəbl] *adj* potable.

potash [ˈpɒtæʃ] *n* potasa *f*.

potassium [pəˈtæsɪəm] *n* potasio *m*; ~ **cyanide** cianuro *m* de potasio; ~ **nitrate** nitrato *m* de potasio; ~ **sulphate** sulfato *m* potásico.

potations [pəʊˈteɪʃənz] *npl* libaciones *fpl*.

potato [pəˈteɪtəʊ] **1** *n*, *pl* **potatoes** [pəˈteɪtəʊz] patata *f*, papa *f* (*LAm*); **potatoes in their jackets** patatas *fpl* enteras, patatas *fpl* con su piel.

2 *attr*: ~ **beetle** dorífora *f*, escarabajo *m* de la patata; ~ **blight** roña *f* de la patata; ~ **cake** croqueta *f* de patata; ~ **chips** (*US*), ~ **crisps** (*Brit*) patatas *fpl* fritas (a la inglesa), papas *fpl* fritas (*LAm*); ~ **field** patatal *m*; ~ **masher** *utensilio para aplastar las patatas al hacer puré*; ~ **peeler** pelapatatas *m*.

potbellied [ˈpɒtˌbelɪd] *adj* barrigón, tripudo, panzudo; (*from malnutrition*) con la barriga hinchada.

potbelly [ˌpɒtˈbelɪ] *n* (*from overeating*) panza *f*; (*from malnutrition*) barriga *f* hinchada.

potboiler [ˈpɒtˌbɔɪləʳ] *n* obra *f* (mediocre) compuesta para ganar dinero.

pot-bound [ˈpɒtbaʊnd] *adj*: **this plant is ~** esta planta ya no cabe en la maceta, esta planta ha crecido demasiado para esta maceta.

poteen [pɒˈtiːn, pɒˈtʃiːn] *n* aguardiente *m*, whiskey *m* (*irlandés, destilado ilegalmente*).

potency [ˈpəutənsɪ] *n* potencia *f*; fuerza *f*; eficacia *f*; (*Physiol*) potencia *f*.

potent [ˈpəutənt] *adj* potente, poderoso; *drink* fuerte; *remedy* eficaz.

potentate [ˈpəutənteɪt] *n* potentado *m*.

potential [pəˈtenʃəl] **1** *adj* potencial; posible, eventual, en potencia; futuro; ~ **earnings** ganancias *fpl* potenciales; **a ~ prime minister** un primer ministro en ciernes, un primer ministro en potencia; **a ~ threat** una posible amenaza.

2 *n* potencial *m* (*also Elec, Math, Phys*); potencialidad *f*, capacidad *f*; **the war ~ of Ruritania** el potencial bélico de Ruritania.

potentiality [pəˌtenʃɪˈælɪtɪ] *n* potencialidad *f*; aptitud *f*, capacidad *f*.

potentially [pəˈtenʃəlɪ] *adv* potencialmente, en potencia.

potentiate [pəˈtenʃɪˌeɪt] *vt* potenciar.

pother [ˈpɒðəʳ] *n* alharaca *f*, aspaviento *m*; lío *m*; **all this ~!** ¡qué lío!; **to make a ~ about sth** armar un lío a causa de algo.

pot-herb [ˈpɒthɜːb] *n* hierba *f* de (*or* para) cocina.

pothole [ˈpɒthəʊl] **1** *n* (*in road*) bache *m*; (*Geol*) sima *f*, marmita *f* de gigante, (*loosely*) cueva *f*, caverna *f* profunda, gruta *f*.

2 *vi*: **to ~, to go potholing** dedicarse a la espeleología; ir a explorar una gruta.

potholer [ˈpɒthəʊləʳ] *n* espeleólogo *m*, -a *f*.

potholing [ˈpɒthəʊlɪŋ] *n* espeleología *f*.

pothunter [ˈpɒthʌntəʳ] *n* cazador *m*, -ora *f* de premios.

potion [ˈpəuʃən] *n* poción *f*, pócima *f*.

potluck [ˈpɒtˈlʌk] *n*: **to take ~** comer lo que haya; (*fig*) tomar lo que haya, contentarse con lo que haya.

pot-plant [ˈpɒtplɑːnt] *n* planta *f* de maceta, planta *f* de interior.

potpourri [pəʊˈpʊrɪ] *n* (*leaves, Mus*) popurrí *m*; (*Liter etc*) mezcla *f*, centón *m*, popurrí *m*.

pot-roast [ˈpɒtrəʊst] **1** *n* carne *f* asada. **2** *vt* asar.

potsherd [ˈpɒtˌʃɜːd] *n* tiesto *m*, casco *m*.

potshot [ˈpɒtˌʃɒt] *n* tiro *m* sin apuntar, tiro *m* al azar; **to take a ~ at sth** tirar a algo sin apuntar.

potted [ˈpɒtɪd] *adj* **(a)** *food* en conserva, cocido y conservado en bote; *plant* en tiesto, en maceta. **(b)** (*fig*) *account, version* resumido, breve.

potter[1] [ˈpɒtəʳ] *n* alfarero *m*; (*artistic*) ceramista *mf*; **~'s clay** arcilla *f* de alfarería; **~'s field** (*US*) cementerio *m* de pobres; **~'s wheel** torno *m* de alfarero.

potter[2] [ˈpɒtəʳ] *vi* ocuparse en fruslerías; no hacer nada de particular; **I ~ed round the house all day** hice bagatelas en casa todo el día; **I ~ed round to see him** fui a verle; **we ~ed round the shops** nos paseamos por las tiendas.

◆**potter about** *vi* ocuparse en fruslerías; no hacer nada de particular; **he likes ~ing about in the garden** le gusta pasar el tiempo haciendo pequeños trabajos en el jardín.

◆**potter along** *vi* hacerse el remolón; **we ~ along** vamos tirando.

◆**potter around, potter away** *vi* = **potter along**.

pottery [ˈpɒtərɪ] *n* **(a)** (*workshop*) alfar *m*, alfarería *f*. **(b)** (*craft*) alfarería *f*, (*art*) cerámica *f*. **(c)** (*pots*) cacharros *mpl*, (*of fine quality*) loza *f*; (*archaeological remains*) cerámicas *fpl*.

potting-shed [ˈpɒtɪŋʃed] *n* cobertizo *m* de enmacetar.

potty[1] [ˈpɒtɪ] *n* orinal *m* de niño, orinal *m* pequeño, bacinica *f*.

potty[2]* [ˈpɒtɪ] *adj* (*Brit*) **(a)** (*small*) insignificante, fútil, miserable.

(b) (*mad*) chiflado*; **you must be ~!** ¿has perdido el juicio?; **to drive sb ~** volver loco a uno; **it's enough to drive you ~** es para volverse loco; **she's ~ about him** se chifla por él*, anda loca por él.

potty-trained [ˈpɒtɪˌtreɪnd] *adj* acostumbrado a la bacinica, que ya no necesita pañales.

pouch [paʊtʃ] *n* bolsa *f* (*also Anat, Zool*); (*hunter's*) morral *m*, zurrón *m*; (*tobacco ~*) petaca *f*; (*Mil*) cartuchera *f*.

pouf(fe) [puːf] *n* pouf *m*, puff *m*.

poulterer [ˈpəʊltərəʳ] *n* pollero *m*, -a *f*; **~'s (shop)** pollería *f*.

poultice [ˈpəʊltɪs] **1** *n* cataplasma *f*, emplasto *m*. **2** *vt* poner una cataplasma a, emplastar (*with* con).

poultry [ˈpəʊltrɪ] *n* (*alive*) aves *fpl* de corral; (*dead*) pollos *mpl*, volatería *f*; ~ **breeding** avicultura *f*; ~ **dealer** recovero *m*, -a *f*, pollero *m*, -a *f*; ~ **shop** (*US*) pollería *f*.

poultry-farm [ˈpəʊltrɪfɑːm] *n* granja *f* avícola.

poultry-farmer [ˈpəʊltrɪˌfɑːməʳ] *n* avicultor *m*, -ora *f*.

poultry-farming [ˈpəʊltrɪˌfɑːmɪŋ] *n* avicultura *f*.

poultry-house [ˈpəʊltrɪhaʊs] *n*, *pl* **poultry-houses** [ˈpəʊltrɪhaʊzɪz] gallinero *m*.

poultry-keeper [ˈpəʊltrɪˌkiːpəʳ] *n* avicultor *m*, -ora *f*.

poultry-keeping [ˈpəʊltrɪˌkiːpɪŋ] *n* avicultura *f*.

pounce [paʊns] **1** *n* salto *m*; ataque *m* súbito; (*swoop by* *bird*) calada *f*.

2 *vi* atacar súbitamente; saltar, precipitarse; (*by bird*) calarse; **to ~ on sth** saltar sobre algo, precipitarse sobre algo, arrojarse sobre algo; **to ~ on sb's mistake** saltar sobre el error de uno.

pound[1] [paʊnd] **1** *n* (**a**) (*weight*) libra *f* (= *453,6 gr*); **half a ~** media libra *f*; **two dollars a ~** dos dólares la libra; **they sell it by the ~** lo venden por libras; **to have one's ~ of flesh** (*fig*) exigir el cumplimiento completo (de un contrato *etc*); exprimir a uno hasta la última gota.

(**b**) (*money*) libra *f*; **~ sterling** libra *f* esterlina; **it must have cost ~s** habrá costado un dineral.

2 *attr*: **~ note** billete *m* de a libra.

pound[2] [paʊnd] *n* corral *m* de concejo; (*police ~, for cars*) depósito *m*.

pound[3] [paʊnd] **1** *vt* (*crush etc*) machacar, majar; (*with hammer*) martillar; (*grind*) moler; (*beat*) golpear, aporrear; (*of sea*) azotar, batir; (*Mil*) bombardear; **he used to ~ the table with his fists** aporreaba la mesa con los puños, golpeaba la mesa con los puños; **to ~ sb with one's fists** dar de puñetazos a uno; **he was ~ing the piano** aporreaba el piano; **to ~ sth to pieces** romper algo a martillazos; **to ~ a fort into surrender** bombardear una fortaleza hasta que se rinda.

2 *vi* (*heart*) palpitar; **to ~ at, to ~ on** aporrear, dar golpes en, descargar golpes sobre; **the sea was ~ing against the rocks** el mar azotaba las rocas; **he was ~ing along the road** corría pesadamente por la carretera; **the train ~ed past us** el tren pasó estrepitosamente delante de nosotros.

◆**pound away** *vi*: **to ~ away at** (*also fig*) machacar en, seguir machacando en.

◆**pound down** *vt drugs, spices* moler; *rocks* machacar; *earth* apisonar; **to ~ sth down to a pulp** hacer algo papilla.

◆**pound out** *vt*: **he was ~ing out a tune on the piano** a golpes violentos tocaba una melodía al piano.

◆**pound up** *vt* = **pound down**.

poundage [ˈpaʊndɪdʒ] *n* impuesto *m* (*or* comisión *f etc*) que se exige por cada libra (esterlina) (*or* de peso).

-pounder [ˈpaʊndəʳ] *n ending in compounds*: **four~** (pez *m etc*) de cuatro libras; **twenty-five~** (*Mil*) cañón *m* de veinticinco.

pounding [ˈpaʊndɪŋ] *n* (*of heart*) palpitación *f*; (*noise*) martilleo *m*, golpeo *m*, el aporrear *etc*; (*of sea*) azote *m*, embate *m*; (*Mil*) bombardeo *m*; **the ship took a ~ from the waves** el barco tuvo que aguantar la violencia de las olas; **the city took a ~ last night** la ciudad sufrió terriblemente en el bombardeo de anoche; **Barcelona gave us a real ~** el Barça nos dio una paliza de las buenas.

pour [pɔːʳ] **1** *vt* (**a**) verter, echar; derramar; *a drink, tea etc* servir, echar; preparar; **he ~ed me a sherry** me sirvió un jerez; **shall I ~ the tea?** ¿sirvo el té?, ¿echo el té?; **he ~ed himself some coffee** se sirvió café; **to ~ money into a project** invertir muchísimo dinero en un proyecto, proveer abundantes fondos para un proyecto; **he has ~ed good ideas into the book** ha llenado el libro de excelentes ideas; **to ~ it on*** (*US*) volcarse, echar el resto*.

(**b**) (*of rain*) **to ~ cats and dogs, to ~ torrents** llover a cántaros.

2 *vi* (**a**) (*rain*) llover mucho, diluviar, llover a cántaros; (*of water etc*) correr, fluir (abundantemente); **it's ~ing, it's ~ing with rain** está lloviendo a cántaros; **it ~ed for 4 days** llovió seguido durante 4 días; **water came ~ing into the room** el agua entraba a raudales en el cuarto; **water ~ed from the broken pipe** el agua salía a raudales del tubo roto; **blood ~ed from the wound** la sangre salía a borbotones de la herida, la herida sangraba a chorros; **confessions ~ed from his lips** las confesiones salían atropelladamente de su boca.

(**b**) **they came ~ing into the shop** entraban a raudales en la tienda.

◆**pour away** *vt* vaciar, verter.

◆**pour down** *vi*: **the rain** (*or* **it**) **was ~ing down** llovía a cántaros.

◆**pour in 1** *vt*: **to ~ in a broadside** hacer fuego con todos los cañones.

2 *vi* (*persons etc*) entrar a raudales, entrar en tropel; **tourists are ~ing in from all sides** acuden los turistas en tropel de todas partes; **requests are ~ing in** nos llegan las solicitudes a montones.

◆**pour off** *vt* vaciar, verter.

◆**pour out 1** *vt coffee etc* servir, echar; *unwanted remainder* vaciar; *smoke* arrojar; **to ~ out one's feelings** expresar tumultuosamente sus sentimientos; **to ~ out one's heart to sb** abrir su pecho a uno; **to ~ out one's thanks** expresar efusivamente sus gracias; **to ~ out threats against sb** desatarse en amenazas contra uno.

2 *vi* (*persons etc*) salir a raudales, salir en tropel; **they ~ed out into the streets** invadieron las calles; **secrets came ~ing out of the inquiry** los secretos se revelaron a docenas en la investigación.

pouring [ˈpɔːrɪŋ] **1** *adj*: **~ rain** lluvia *f* torrencial. **2** *adv*: **a ~ wet day** un día de lluvia torrencial.

pout [paʊt] **1** *n* puchero *m*, mala cara *f*; **to say with a ~** decir con mala cara. **2** *vt*: **'Never!', she ~ed** '¡Nunca!', dijo con mala cara; **to ~ one's lips** = **3**. **3** *vi* hacer pucheros, poner mala cara, hacer morros.

poverty [ˈpɒvətɪ] **1** *n* pobreza *f*, miseria *f*; (*of ideas etc*) falta *f*, escasez *f*; **~ is no crime** pobreza no es vileza; **to live in ~** vivir en la miseria; **~ of ideas** carencia *f* de ideas; **~ of resources** escasez *f* de recursos.

2 *attr*: **~ line** mínimo *m* vital; **to live below the ~ line** vivir en la indigencia; **to live on the ~ line** vivir del salario mínimo; **~ trap** (*Brit*) trampa *f* de la pobreza.

poverty-stricken [ˈpɒvətɪˌstrɪkn] *adj* menesteroso, indigente, necesitado.

P.O.W. *n abbr of* **prisoner of war** prisionero *m*.

powder [ˈpaʊdəʳ] **1** *n* polvo *m*; (*face ~*) polvos *mpl*; (*gun ~*) pólvora *f*; **to keep one's ~ dry** no gastar la pólvora en salvas, reservarse para mejor ocasión; **to reduce sth to ~** reducir algo a polvo, pulverizar algo.

2 *vt* (**a**) (*reduce to ~*) reducir a polvo, pulverizar.

(**b**) (*apply ~ to*) polvorear, (*Culin etc*) espolvorear (*with* de); **to ~ one's face, to ~ one's nose** ponerse polvos, empolvarse; **I must go and ~ my nose** (*euph*) voy donde la propia reina tiene que ir en persona.

3 *vi* (**a**) pulverizarse, hacerse polvo.

(**b**) (*person*) = **4**.

4 *vr*: **to ~ o.s.** ponerse polvos, empolvarse.

powder-blue [ˈpaʊdəˈbluː] **1** *adj* azul pálido. **2** *n* azul *m* pálido.

powder-compact [ˈpaʊdəˌkɒmpækt] *n* polvera *f*.

powdered [ˈpaʊdəd] *adj* en polvo; **~ milk** leche *f* en polvo; **~ sugar** (*US*) azúcar *m* extrafino.

powdering [ˈpaʊdərɪŋ] *n*: **a ~ of snow** una leve capa de nieve.

powder-keg [ˈpaʊdəkeg] *n* (*fig*) polvorín *m*, barril *m* de pólvora; **the country is a ~** el país es un polvorín.

powder magazine [ˈpaʊdəmægəˌziːn] *n* santabárbara *f*.

powder-puff [ˈpaʊdəpʌf] *n* borla *f* (para empolvarse).

powder-room [ˈpaʊdərʊm] *n* aseos *mpl* (de señora), tocador *m*; **'P~'** 'Señoras'.

powdery [ˈpaʊdərɪ] *adj substance* en polvo, polvoriento; *snow* polvoriento; *surface* polvoriento, empolvado.

power [paʊəʳ] **1** *n* (**a**) (*gen*) poder *m*; (*physical strength*) fuerza *f*, energía *f*, vigor *m*; (*Mil*) potencia *f*, poder *m*; **a painting of great ~** un cuadro de gran impacto, un cuadro que causa honda impresión; **our ~ in the air** nuestra potencia en el aire; **more ~ to your elbow!** ¡que tengas éxito!; **it is beyond his ~ to save her** no está dentro de sus posibilidades salvarla, no puede hacer nada para salvarla; **to be in the ~ of** estar en manos de; **to do all in one's ~ to** + *infin* hacer lo posible por + *infin*; **to have sb in one's ~** tener a uno en su poder; **to fall into sb's ~** caer en manos de uno; **it does not lie within my ~** no está dentro de mis posibilidades, eso no es de mi competencia; **as far as lies within my ~** en cuanto me sea posible; **to the utmost of one's ~** hasta más no poder.

(**b**) (*mental*) facultad *f* (*of* de); (*drive*) empuje *m*, energía *f*; **mental ~s** facultades *fpl* mentales; **to be at the height of one's ~s** estar en la cumbre de sus facultades mentales; **his ~s are failing** decaen sus facultades; **to lose the ~ of speech** perder el habla.

(**c**) (*Mech etc*) potencia *f*; energía *f*, fuerza *f*; (*output*) rendimiento *m*; **engines at half ~** motores *mpl* a medio vapor, motores *mpl* a potencia mitad; **the ship returned to port under her own ~** el buque volvió al puerto impulsado por sus propios motores.

(**d**) (*Elec*) fuerza *f*, energía *f*, fluido *m*; (*electric ~*) electricidad *f*, fuerza *f* eléctrica, energía *f* eléctrica; **they cut off the ~** cortaron la corriente.

(**e**) (*Pol etc*) poder *m*; poderío *m*; autoridad *f*; influencia *f*; **~ to the people!** ¡el pueblo al poder!; **~ of life and death** poder *m* de vida y de muerte; **the ~s of darkness** las fuerzas del mal; **the ~s that be** los poderes fácticos, los que mandan, las autoridades (actuales); **he's a ~ in the land** es de los que mandan en el país; **in that year the Prime Minister was at the height of her ~** aquel año fue la cumbre del poderío de la primera ministra; **to be in ~** estar en el poder; **to come to ~** subir al poder, empezar a gobernar, tomar el mando; **to raise sb to ~** alzar a uno al poder; **to share ~** compartir el poder.

(**f**) (*specific ~*) ~ **of attorney** poder *m*, procuración *f*; **full ~s** plenos poderes *mpl*; **to exceed one's ~s** excederse, ir demasiado lejos.

(**g**) (*nation*) potencia *f*; **the Great P~s** las Grandes Potencias.

(**h**) (*) **a ~ of people** muchísima gente; **to make a ~ of money** hacerse una pingüe ganancia; **that did me a ~ of good!** ¡con eso me siento mucho mejor!, ¡ahora sí que estoy mucho mejor!; **beer does you a ~ of good** la cerveza le hace pero que mucho bien*.

(**i**) (*Math*) potencia *f*; **7 to the ~ of 3** 7 elevado al cubo, 7 elevado a la 3ª potencia; **to the nth ~** a la enésima potencia.

2 *attr* (**a**) (*Pol etc*) ~ **base** base *f* de poder; ~ **game** juego *m* del poder; ~ **structure** estructura *f* del poder; ~ **struggle** lucha *f* por el poder.

(**b**) (*Mech*) ~ **cable** cable *m* de energía eléctrica; ~ **consumption** consumo *m* de energía; ~ **cut** (*Brit*), ~ **outage** (*US*) corte *m* de corriente, apagón *m*; ~ **drill** taladro *m* mecánico, taladradora *f* de fuerza; ~ **failure** fallo *m* del suministro de electricidad; ~ **hammer** martillo *m* mecánico; ~ **line** línea *f* de conducción eléctrica; ~ **loader** rompedora-cargadora *f*; ~ **plant** grupo *m* electrógeno, (*US*) central *f* eléctrica; ~ **point** (*Brit*) toma *f* de corriente; ~ **saw** motosierra *f*, sierra *f* mecánica; ~ **shovel** excavadora *f*; ~ **station** central *f* eléctrica; ~ **steering** dirección *f* asistida; ~ **tool** herramienta *f* mecánica; ~ **unit** grupo *m* electrógeno; ~ **workers** trabajadores *mpl* del sector energético.

3 *vt* accionar, impulsar; **a car ~ed by electricity** un coche impulsado por electricidad; **a plane ~ed by 4 jets** un avión impulsado por 4 motores a reacción.

power-assisted ['paʊərə,sɪstɪd] *adj*: ~ **brakes** servofrenos *mpl*; ~ **steering** dirección *f* asistida.

powerboat ['paʊə,bəʊt] *n* motora *f*, motorbote *m*.

powerboating ['paʊə,bəʊtɪŋ] *n* motonáutica *f*.

power-driven ['paʊədrɪvn] *adj* con motor; *tool, saw etc* mecánico.

powered ['paʊəd] *adj* con motor; mecánico.

-powered ['paʊəd] *adj ending in compounds*: **wind~** impulsado por el viento, que funciona con energía eólica.

powerful ['paʊəfʊl] *adj person, government etc* poderoso; *engine etc* potente; *build* fuerte, fornido; *blow, kick* fuerte; *light, smell, swimmer, voice* fuerte; *emotion* intenso, profundo; *argument* convincente; *painting etc* de gran impacto, que produce honda emoción; **a ~ lot of people*** muchísima gente; **it is a ~ film** es una película muy emocionante; **he gave a ~ performance** su actuación fue magistral.

powerfully ['paʊəfəlɪ] *adv* poderosamente; fuertemente; intensamente; profundamente; de modo convincente; **to be ~ built** ser fornido; **I was ~ affected by the book** el libro me conmovió profundamente.

powerhouse ['paʊəhaʊs] *n, pl* **powerhouses** ['paʊəhaʊzɪz] central *f* eléctrica; (*fig*) fuente *f* de energía; **he's a ~ of ideas** es una fuente inagotable de ideas.

powerless ['paʊəlɪs] *adj* impotente; ineficaz; **to be ~ to resist** no tener fuerzas para resistir, no poder resistir; **we are ~ to help you** estamos sin fuerzas para ayudarle, somos incapaces de prestarle ayuda; **they are ~ in the matter** no tienen autoridad para intervenir en el asunto, el asunto no es de su competencia.

powerlessness ['paʊəlɪsnɪs] *n* impotencia *f*; ineficacia *f*.

power-sharing ['paʊə,ʃɛərɪŋ] **1** *adj*: **a ~ government** un gobierno de poder compartido. **2** *n* compartimiento *m* del poder.

powwow ['paʊwaʊ] **1** *n* conferencia *f*. **2** *vi* conferenciar.

pox* [pɒks] *n* (*VD*) sífilis *f*; (*small~*) viruelas *fpl*; **a ~ on them!** (††) ¡malditos sean!

poxy‡ ['pɒksɪ] *adj* puñetero‡.

pp (**a**) *abbr of* **parcel post**.
(**b**) *abbr of* **post-paid**.
(**c**) *abbr of* **prepaid**.

pp. *abbr of* **pages** páginas *fpl*, págs.

p.p. *adv abbr of* **per procurationem, by proxy** por poder, p.p.

PPE *n abbr of* **philosophy, politics, economics** *grupo de asignaturas de la Universidad de Oxford*.

ppm *npl abbr of* **parts per million** partes *fpl* por millón.

PPP *n abbr of* **personal pension plan**.

PPS *n* (**a**) (*Brit*) *abbr of* **Parliamentary Private Secretary**. (**b**) *abbr of* **post-postscriptum** posdata *f* adicional.

PR (**a**) *n* (*Pol*) *abbr of* **proportional representation**. (**b**) *n* (*Comm*) *abbr of* **public relations** relaciones *fpl* públicas, R.P. (**c**) (*US Post*) *abbr of* **Puerto Rico**.

Pr. *abbr of* **prince** príncipe, P.

practicability [,præktɪkə'bɪlɪtɪ] *n* practicabilidad *f*, factibilidad *f*; **I doubt its ~** dudo que sea factible.

practicable ['præktɪkəbl] *adj* factible, practicable, hacedero.

practical ['præktɪkəl] **1** *adj* (**a**) práctico; **for all ~ purposes** en la práctica, desde el punto de vista práctico; ~ **joke** broma *f* pesada, trastada *f*, mistificación *f*; ~ **nurse** (*US*) enfermera *f* práctica, enfermera *f* sin título. (**b**) **it's a ~ certainty** es prácticamente cierto; **it's a ~ sell-out** es casi una traición. **2** *nm* (*Univ etc*) examen *m* práctico.

practicality [,præktɪ'kælɪtɪ] *n* (**a**) (*of temperament*) espíritu *m* práctico; (*of scheme etc*) factibilidad *f*; **I doubt its ~** dudo que sea factible. (**b**) (*thing*) cosa *f* práctica; **practicalities** aspectos *mpl* prácticos.

practically ['præktɪklɪ] *adv* (**a**) (*in a practical way*) prácticamente. (**b**) (*almost*) prácticamente, casi; ~ **everybody** casi todos; ~ **nothing** casi nada; **there has been ~ no rain** casi no ha llovido.

practice ['præktɪs] **1** *n* (**a**) (*habit*) costumbre *f*, uso *m*; **according to his usual ~** según su costumbre; **it is not our ~ to** + *infin* no acostumbramos + *infin*; **to make a ~ of** + *ger*, **to make it a ~ to** + *infin* acostumbrar + *infin*.

(**b**) (*exercise*) ejercicio *m*; (*training*) adiestramiento *m*, (*period*) período *m* de entrenamiento; clase *f* práctica; (*Sport*) entrenamiento *m*; **to be in ~** estar entrenado, estar en forma; **to be out of ~** estar desentrenado, no estar en forma; **to learn by ~** aprender por la práctica, aprender por la experiencia; ~ **makes perfect** la práctica (*or* el uso) hace maestro; **it needs a lot of ~** hace falta bastante experiencia.

(**c**) (*reality*) práctica *f*; **in ~** en la práctica; **to put sth into ~** poner algo en obra.

(**d**) (*of profession etc*) práctica *f*, ejercicio *m*; **the ~ of medicine** el ejercicio de la medicina; **he was in ~ in Bilbao** ejercía en Bilbao; **he is no longer in ~** ya no ejerce; **to set up in ~** (*Jur*) poner su bufete; (*Med*) empezar a ejercer de médico; **to set up in ~ as** empezar a trabajar como.

(**e**) (*Med, Jur: patients, clients*) clientela *f*.

2 *attr*: ~ **flight** vuelo *m* de entrenamiento; ~ **run** carrera *f* de entrenamiento.

practise, (*US*) **practice** ['præktɪs] **1** *vt* (**a**) (*carry out in action*) practicar; tener por costumbre; **we ~ this method** nosotros empleamos (*or* seguimos) este método; **to ~ charity** ejercitar la caridad; **to ~ patience** tener paciencia; **to ~ what one preaches** predicar con el ejemplo.

(**b**) *profession* ejercer; **to ~ medicine** practicar la medicina, ejercer de médico.

(**c**) (*train o.s. at*) hacer ejercicios de, hacer prácticas de; **to ~ the piano** hacer ejercicios en el piano, estudiar el piano; **to ~ football** entrenarse en el fútbol; **to ~ a shot at golf** ensayar un golpe de golf; **to ~** + *ger* ensayarse + *infin*.

2 *vi* (**a**) (*Mus*) tocar, estudiar, hacer ejercicios; (*Sport*) ejercitarse, entrenarse, adiestrarse; ensayarse; **to ~ every day** hacer ejercicios todos los días; **one has to ~ a lot** hace falta estudiar mucho.

(**b**) **to ~ as a doctor** ejercer de médico, practicar la medicina.

practised, (*US*) **practiced** ['præktɪst] *adj eye etc* experto; *teacher etc* experto, de gran experiencia; *performance* pulido.

practising, (*US*) **practicing** ['præktɪsɪŋ] *adj* activo, que ejerce, practicante; **a ~ Christian** un cristiano practicante.

practitioner [præk'tɪʃənəʳ] *n* (*of an art*) practicante *mf*; (*Med: also* **medical ~**) médico *m*, -a *f*; *V* **general**.

pr(a)esidium [prɪ'sɪdɪəm] *n* (*Pol*) presidio *m*.

praetorian, (*US*) **pretorian** [prɪ'tɔːrɪən] *adj*: ~ **guard** guardia *f* pretoriana.

pragmatic [præg'mætɪk] **1** *adj* pragmático. **2** **~s** *n sing* pragmática *f*.

pragmatically [præg'mætɪklɪ] *adv* pragmáticamente.

pragmatism ['prægmətɪzəm] *n* pragmatismo *m*.

pragmatist ['prægmətɪst] *n* pragmatista *mf*.

Prague [prɑːg] *n* Praga *f*.

prairie ['prɛərɪ] **1** *n* pradera *f*, llanura *f*, pampa *f* (*LAm*). **2** *attr* (*US*): ~ **oyster** *huevo crudo y sazonado que se toma en una bebida alcohólica*; ~ **wolf** coyote *m*.

praise [preɪz] **1** *n* alabanza *f*, elogio *m*; alabanzas *fpl*, elogios *mpl*; **in ~ of** en alabanza de; **all ~ to him!** ¡enhorabuena!; ~ **be!**, ~ **be to God!** ¡gracias a Dios!; **it's**

beyond ~ queda por encima de todo elogio; **to be loud** (*or* **warm**) **in one's ~s of sth** alabar algo sinceramente, elogiar algo con entusiasmo; **he is not much given to** ~ no acostumbra pronunciar palabras de elogio; **I have nothing but ~ for him** merece todos mis elogios; **to heap ~s on sb** amontonar alabanzas sobre uno; **to sing the ~s of sb** cantar las alabanzas de uno, elogiar con efusión a uno; **to sound** (*or* **sing**) **one's own ~s** cantar sus propias alabanzas

2 *vt* alabar, elogiar; **to ~ God** glorificar a Dios.

◆praise up *vt*: **to ~ sth up** poner algo por las nubes.

praiseworthily ['preɪz,wɜːðɪlɪ] *adv* loablemente, plausiblemente, de modo digno de elogio.

praiseworthiness ['preɪz,wɜːðɪnɪs] *n* lo loable, lo plausible, mérito *m*.

praiseworthy ['preɪz,wɜːðɪ] *adj* loable, plausible, digno de elogio.

pram [præm] *n* (*Brit*) cochecito *m* de niño.

prance [prɑːns] *vi* (*horse*) hacer cabriolas, hacer corvetas, encabritarse; (*person*) saltar, bailar; andar con cierta afectación; **he came prancing into the room** entró en la habitación como cabriolando; **to ~ with rage** saltar de rabia.

prang‡ [præŋ] *vt* (*Brit*) (**a**) *town etc* bombardear, destruir. (**b**) *plane* estrellar; *car etc* estropear.

prank [præŋk] *n* travesura *f*; broma *f*; **a childish ~** una travesura, una diablura; **a student ~** una broma estudiantil; **to play a ~ on sb** gastar una broma a uno.

prankish ['præŋkɪʃ] *adj* travieso, pícaro.

prankster ['præŋkstəʳ] *n* bromista *mf*.

praseodymium [,preɪzɪəʊ'dɪmɪəm] *n* praseodimio *m*.

prat‡ [præt] *n* inútil* *mf*; imbécil *mf*; **you ~!** ¡imbécil!

prate [preɪt] *vi* parlotear, charlar; **to ~ of** hablar interminablemente de.

pratfall‡ ['prætfɔːl] *n* (*US*) culada‡ *f*, caída *f* de culo‡.

prating ['preɪtɪŋ] *adj* parlanchín.

prattle ['prætl] **1** *n* parloteo *m*; (*child's*) balbuceo *m*. **2** *vi* parlotear; balbucear.

prawn [prɔːn] **1** *n* gamba *f*; (*small*) quisquilla *f*, camarón *m*; (*Dublin Bay ~, large ~*) langostino *m*. **2** *attr*: **~ cocktail** cóctel *m* de gambas.

pray [preɪ] **1** *vt* (*liter*) rogar, suplicar; **I ~ you** se lo suplico; **~ tell me, I ~ you tell me ...** le ruego decirme ...; **to ~ sb to do sth** rogar a uno hacer algo, rogar a uno que haga algo; **~ be seated, ~ take a seat** siéntese, por favor.

2 *vi* (**a**) (*say prayers*) rezar, orar; **to ~ to God** rogar a Dios; **to ~ for sth** rogar algo, orar por algo; **to ~ for sb's soul** orar por el alma de uno; **to ~ for sb** orar por uno, rezar por uno; **to ~ that sth may not happen** hacer votos para que algo no ocurra, hacer rogativas para que algo no ocurra; **he's past ~ing for** es un caso desahuciado, ya no le valen oraciones.

(**b**) **what good is that, ~?** ¿de qué sirve eso, pues?

prayer [prɛəʳ] *n* (**a**) (*to God*) oración *f*, rezo *m*; **~s** (*as service*) rezo *m*, oficio *m*; **~s for peace** oraciones *fpl* por la paz; **Book of Common P~** *liturgia de la Iglesia Anglicana*; **to be at one's ~s** estar rezando, estar en oración; **to offer up ~s for** orar por, rezar por; **to say one's ~s** orar, rezar; **he didn't have a ~*** (*US*) no tenía nada que hacer, no tenía ni la menor posibilidad.

(**b**) (*entreaty*) ruego *m*, súplica *f*; (*Jur*) petición *f*.

prayer-beads ['prɛə,biːdz] *npl* rosario *m*.

prayerbook ['prɛəbʊk] *n* devocionario *m*, misal *m*.

prayer-mat ['prɛə,mæt] *n* alfombra *f* de oración.

prayer meeting ['prɛə,miːtɪŋ] *n* reunión *f* para rezar.

praying ['preɪɪŋ] *adj*: **~ mantis** mantis *f* religiosa.

pre... [priː] *pref* pre...; ante...

preach [priːtʃ] **1** *vt* (**a**) predicar; **to ~ a sermon** predicar un sermón; **to ~ the gospel** predicar el Evangelio.

(**b**) *advantages etc* celebrar; *patience etc* aconsejar.

2 *vi* predicar; **to ~ at sb** predicar a uno, dar un sermón a uno; **to ~ to a congregation** predicar a los fieles.

preacher ['priːtʃəʳ] *n* predicador *m*, -ora *f*; (*US*) pastor *m*, -ora *f*.

preachify* ['priːtʃɪfaɪ] *vi* sermonear largamente; (*fig*) disertar largamente.

preaching ['priːtʃɪŋ] *n* predicación *f*; (*pej*) sermoneo *m*.

preachy* ['priːtʃɪ] *adj* dado a sermonear.

preamble [priː'æmbl] *n* preámbulo *m*.

prearrange ['priːə'reɪndʒ] *vt* arreglar de antemano, predeterminar.

prearranged [,priːə'reɪndʒd] *adj* predeterminado.

prebend ['prebənd] *n* (*stipend*) prebenda *f*; (*person*) prebendado *m*.

prebendary ['prebəndərɪ] *n* prebendado *m*.

precarious [prɪ'kɛərɪəs] *adj* precario.

precariously [prɪ'kɛərɪəslɪ] *adv* precariamente.

precariousness [prɪ'kɛərɪəsnɪs] *n* precariedad *f*.

precast ['priː'kɑːst] *adj*: **~ concrete** hormigón *m* precolado.

precaution [prɪ'kɔːʃən] *n* precaución *f*; **by way of ~** como precaución, para mayor seguridad; **to take ~s** tomar precauciones; **to take the ~ of** + *ger* tomar la precaución de + *infin*.

precautionary [prɪ'kɔːʃənərɪ] *adj* de precaución, precautorio; **~ measure** medida *f* de precaución, medida *f* cautelar.

precede [prɪ'siːd] *vti* preceder; **for a month preceding this** durante un mes antes de esto; **to ~ a lecture with a joke** empezar una conferencia contando un chiste.

precedence ['presɪdəns] *n* precedencia *f*; prioridad *f*; primacía *f*; **to take ~ over sb** preceder a uno, tener precedencia sobre uno, primar sobre uno.

precedent ['presɪdənt] *n* precedente *m*; **according to ~** de acuerdo con los precedentes; **against all the ~s** contra todos los precedentes; **without ~** sin precedentes; **to establish** (*or* **lay down, set up**) **a ~** establecer un precedente, sentar un precedente (*for* a).

preceding [prɪ'siːdɪŋ] *adj* precedente; **the ~ day** el día anterior.

precentor [prɪ'sentəʳ] *n* chantre *m*.

precept ['priːsept] *n* precepto *m*.

preceptor [prɪ'septəʳ] *n* preceptor *m*.

precinct ['priːsɪŋkt] *n* recinto *m*; (*US*: *area*) barrio *m*; (*US Pol*) distrito *m* electoral, circunscripción *f*; (*US*: *of policeman*) ronda *f*; **~s** contornos *mpl*; **within the ~s of** dentro de los límites de.

preciosity [,presɪ'ɒsɪtɪ] *n* preciosidad *f*.

precious ['preʃəs] **1** *adj* (**a**) precioso; *metal, stone* precioso; *person etc* amado, querido; **the book is very ~ to me** para mí el libro tiene gran valor.

(**b**) *style etc* preciosista, afectado, rebuscado.

(**c**) (*: *iro*) **that ~ marrow of yours** aquel estimable calabacín tuyo; **your ~ son** tu magnífico hijo.

2 *adv* (*) muy; **there are ~ few left** quedan bien pocos; **to take ~ good care to see that ...** velar de modo muy particular para que + *subj*; **~ little has been gained** se ha logrado muy poco.

3 *n*: (**my**) **~!** ¡querida!

precipice ['presɪpɪs] *n* precipicio *m*, despeñadero *m*.

precipitancy [prɪ'sɪpɪtənsɪ] *n* precipitación *f*.

precipitate 1 [prɪ'sɪpɪtɪt] *n* (*Chem*) precipitado *m*.

2 [prɪ'sɪpɪteɪt] *vt* precipitar (*also Chem*); (*hasten*) acelerar; *trouble etc* causar, motivar, producir.

3 [prɪ'sɪpɪtɪt] *adj* precipitado, apresurado.

precipitately [prɪ'sɪpɪtɪtlɪ] *adv* precipitadamente.

precipitation [prɪ,sɪpɪ'teɪʃən] *n* (*all senses*) precipitación *f*; **to act with ~** obrar con precipitación.

precipitous [prɪ'sɪpɪtəs] *adj* (**a**) (*steep*) escarpado, cortado a pico. (**b**) (*hasty*) precipitado, apresurado.

precipitously [prɪ'sɪpɪtəslɪ] *adv* en escarpa, en precipicio.

précis ['preɪsiː] **1** *n* resumen *m*; **to make a ~ of** = **3**. **2** *attr*: **~ writer** redactor *m*, -ora *f* de actas resumidas. **3** *vt* hacer un resumen de, resumir.

precise [prɪ'saɪs] *adj* (**a**) *thing* preciso, exacto; (*clearly stated*) claro; **at that ~ moment** en ese mismo momento; **they gave me the ~ book I wanted** me dieron justo el libro que buscaba; **let's be ~ about this** pongamos las cosas en su punto, concretemos; **well, to be ~...** bueno, en rigor ...; **there were 6, to be ~** había 6, para ser exacto.

(**b**) (*meticulous*) meticuloso, puntual, escrupuloso; (*over~*) afectado, pedante; **he's very ~ in everything** es meticuloso en todo; **in that ~ voice of hers** con su tono un poco pedante, con ese tono suyo un tanto afectado.

precisely [prɪ'saɪslɪ] *adv* (*V adj*) (**a**) precisamente, con precisión, exactamente; claramente; **~!** ¡perfectamente!, ¡eso es!, ¡justo!; **at ~ 7 o'clock** a las 7 en punto; **~ what was it you wanted?** ¿qué era lo que quería Vd exactamente?

(**b**) meticulosamente, puntualmente; (*over ~*) afectadamente, con pedantería; **he said very ~** dijo con énfasis.

preciseness [prɪ'saɪsnɪs] *n* (*V adj*) (**a**) precisión *f*, exactitud *f*. (**b**) puntualidad *f*, escrupulosidad *f*; afectación *f*, pedantería *f*.

precision [prɪ'sɪʒən] **1** *n* = **preciseness**. **2** *attr* de precisión; **~ bombing** bombardeo *m* de precisión; **~ instrument** instrumento *m* de precisión; **~-made** de precisión.

preclude [prɪ'kluːd] *vt* excluir; imposibilitar; **this does not ~ the possibility of ...** esto no excluye (*or* quita) la posibilidad de ...; **so as to ~ all doubt** para disipar

cualquier duda; **we are ~d from** + *ger* nos vemos imposibilitados para + *infin*; nos está vedado + *infin*.
precocious [prɪ'kəʊʃəs] *adj* precoz.
precociously [prɪ'kəʊʃəslɪ] *adv* de modo precoz, con precocidad.
precociousness [prɪ'kəʊʃəsnɪs] *n* precocidad *f*.
precocity [prə'kɒsɪtɪ] *n* precocidad *f*.
precognition [,pri:kɒg'nɪʃən] *n* precognición *f*.
pre-Columbian ['pri:kə'lʌmbɪən] *adj* precolombino.
preconceived ['pri:kən'si:vd] *adj* preconcebido.
preconception ['pri:kən'sepʃən] *n* preconcepción *f*, idea *f* preconcebida.
preconcerted ['pri:kən'sɜ:tɪd] *adj* preconcertado.
precondition ['pri:kən'dɪʃən] *n* condición *f* previa, estipulación *f* hecha de antemano; **without ~s** sin condiciones previas.
precook [,pri:'kʊk] *vt* precocinar.
precooked [,pri:'kʊkt] *adj* precocinado.
precool ['pri:'ku:l] *vt* preenfriar.
precursor [pri:'kɜ:səʳ] *n* precursor *m*, -ora *f*.
precursory [prɪ'kɜ:sərɪ] *adj* preliminar.
predate ['pri:'deɪt] *vt* preceder, ser anterior a, antedatar.
predator ['predətəʳ] *n* depredador *m*, animal *m* (*etc*) de rapiña.
predatory ['predətərɪ] *adj animal* rapaz, de rapiña; *person* agresivo, depredador.
predecease ['pri:dɪ'si:s] *vt* morir antes que.
predecessor ['pri:dɪsesəʳ] *n* predecesor *m*, -ora *f*, antecesor *m*, -ora *f*.
predestination [pri:,destɪ'neɪʃən] *n* predestinación *f*.
predestine [pri:'destɪn] *vt* predestinar; **to be ~d to** + *infin* ser predestinado a + *infin*.
predetermination ['pri:dɪ,tɜ:mɪ'neɪʃən] *n* predeterminación *f*.
predetermine ['pri:dɪ'tɜ:mɪn] *vt* predeterminar.
predicament [prɪ'dɪkəmənt] *n* apuro *m*, situación *f* difícil; **to be in a ~** estar en un apuro; **what a ~ to be in!** ¡qué lío!
predicate 1 ['predɪkɪt] *n* predicado *m*. **2** ['predɪkeɪt] *vt* (**a**) (*base*) basar, fundar (*on* en); **to be ~d on** estar basado en. (**b**) (*imply*) implicar.
predicative [prɪ'dɪkətɪv] *adj* predicativo.
predicatively [prɪ'dɪkətɪvlɪ] *adv* predicativamente.
predict [prɪ'dɪkt] *vt* pronosticar, profetizar, predecir.
predictable [prɪ'dɪktəbl] *adj* previsible, que se puede prever; *person* de reacciones previsibles; **it is ~ that** ... se prevé que ...
predictably [prɪ'dɪktəblɪ] *adv* previsiblemente; **he was ~ angry** como era de esperar, se enfadó.
prediction [prɪ'dɪkʃən] *n* pronóstico *m*, profecía *f*, predicción *f*.
predictive [prɪ'dɪktɪv] *adj* profético, que vale como pronóstico.
predigested [,pri:daɪ'dʒestɪd] *adj* predigerido.
predilection [,pri:dɪ'lekʃən] *n* predilección *f*; **to have a ~ for** tener predilección por.
predispose ['pri:dɪs'pəʊz] *vt* predisponer.
predisposition ['pri:,dɪspə'zɪʃən] *n* predisposición *f*.
predominance [prɪ'dɒmɪnəns] *n* predominio *m*.
predominant [prɪ'dɒmɪnənt] *adj* predominante.
predominantly [prɪ'dɒmɪnəntlɪ] *adv* de modo predominante, en un grado predominante; en su mayor parte.
predominate [prɪ'dɒmɪneɪt] *vi* predominar.
preemie* ['pri:mɪ] *n* (*US Med*) bebé *m* prematuro.
pre-eminence [pri:'emɪnəns] *n* preeminencia *f*.
pre-eminent [pri:'emɪnənt] *adj* preeminente.
pre-eminently [pri:'emɪnəntlɪ] *adv* especialmente; **a ~ political stance** una actitud marcadamente política; **it was ~ created for** ... fue creado especialmente para ...
pre-empt [pri:'empt] *vt* (*Brit*) (**a**) *person* adelantarse a; **we found they had ~ed us in buying it** encontramos que se nos habían adelantado a comprarlo. (**b**) **to ~ sth** asegurarse de algo adelantándose a otros; hacer valer sus derechos sobre algo.
pre-emption [pri:'empʃən] *n* preempción *f*; prioridad *f*; derecho *m* de preferencia (de compra); anticipación *f*.
pre-emptive [prɪ(:)'emptɪv] *adj claim etc* por derecho de prioridad, preferente; **~ bid** oferta *f* con derecho preferente; propuesta *f* hecha con intención de excluir cualquier otra; **~ right** derecho *m* preferencial; **~ strike** ataque *m* anticipado; ataque *m* preventivo.
preen [pri:n] **1** *vt feather* limpiar, arreglar con el pico.
2 *vr*: **to ~ o.s.** (*bird*) limpiarse, arreglarse las plumas con el pico; (*person*) pavonearse, atildarse; **to ~ o.s. on** enorgullecerse de, jactarse de.
pre-established ['pri:ɪs'tæblɪʃt] *adj* establecido de antemano.
pre-exist ['pri:ɪg'zɪst] *vi* preexistir.
pre-existence ['pri:ɪg'zɪstəns] *n* preexistencia *f*.
pre-existent ['pri:ɪg'zɪstənt] *adj* preexistente.
prefab* ['pri:fæb] *n* casa *f* prefabricada.
prefabricate ['pri:'fæbrɪkeɪt] *vt* prefabricar.
prefabricated ['pri:'fæbrɪkeɪtɪd] *adj* prefabricado.
preface ['prefɪs] **1** *n* prólogo *m*, prefacio *m*.
2 *vt*: **he ~d this by saying that** ... a modo de prólogo a esto dijo que ..., introdujo este tema diciendo que ...; **the book is ~d by an essay** el libro tiene un ensayo a modo de prólogo.
prefaded [,pri:'feɪdɪd] *adj jeans etc* desteñido de origen.
prefatory ['prefətərɪ] *adj* preliminar, a modo de prólogo.
prefect ['pri:fekt] *n* prefecto *m*; (*Brit Scol*) tutor *m*, monitor *m*.
prefecture ['pri:fektjʊəʳ] *n* prefectura *f*.
prefer [prɪ'fɜ:ʳ] **1** *vt* (**a**) preferir; **to ~ coffee to tea** preferir el café al té; **to ~ walking to going by car** preferir ir a pie a ir en coche; **to ~ to** + *infin* preferir + *infin*; **I ~ not to say** prefiero no decirlo; **which do you ~?** ¿cuál prefieres?, ¿cuál te gusta más?; **A is much to be ~red over B** A es mucho mejor que B.
(**b**) (*esp Eccl*: *promote*) ascender, promover; (*appoint*) nombrar; **he was ~red to the see of Toledo** le nombraron al arzobispado de Toledo.
(**c**) (*charge*) hacer, presentar; **to ~ a charge against sb** poner a uno un juicio, acusar a uno.
(**d**) **~red stock** (*US*) acciones *fpl* preferentes.
2 *vi*: **as you ~** como Vd quiera.
preferable ['prefərəbl] *adj* preferible (*to* a).
preferably ['prefərəblɪ] *adv* preferentemente, más bien.
preference ['prefərəns] **1** *n* preferencia *f*, prioridad *f*; **for ~** de preferencia; **A in ~ to B** A más que B, A antes que B; **to give sth ~** preferir algo, tener preferencia por algo; **to give sth ~ over sth else** anteponer algo a otra cosa; **what is your ~?** ¿cuál te gusta más?; **I have no ~** no tengo preferencia.
2 *attr* (*Brit*) *share* preferente.
preferential [,prefə'renʃəl] *adj* preferente, de preferencia, preferencial; **on ~ terms** con condiciones preferenciales.
preferentially [,prefə'renʃəlɪ] *adv* de manera preferente.
preferment [prɪ'fɜ:mənt] *n* (*esp Eccl*) ascenso *m*, promoción *f*; nombramiento *m* (*to* a); **to get ~** ser ascendido.
prefiguration [,pri:fɪgə'reɪʃən] *n* prefiguración *f*.
prefigure [pri:'fɪgəʳ] *vt* prefigurar.
prefix 1 ['pri:fɪks] *n* prefijo *m*. **2** [pri:'fɪks] *vt* prefijar.
preggers* ['pregəz] *adj*: **to be ~ = to be pregnant**.
pregnancy ['pregnənsɪ] **1** *n* embarazo *m*, preñez *f*. **2** *attr*: **~ test** test *m* de embarazo.
pregnant ['pregnənt] *adj* (**a**) embarazada; **to be ~** estar embarazada, estar en estado, estar encinta; **to be 6 months ~** estar embarazada de 6 meses; **to become ~, to get ~** quedarse embarazada.
(**b**) (*fig*) **~ with** cargado de, preñado de; **a ~ pause** una pausa llena de expectación; **a ~ silence** un silencio elocuente (*or* significativo).
preheat ['pri:'hi:t] *vt* precalentar.
prehensile [prɪ'hensaɪl] *adj* prensil.
prehistoric ['pri:hɪs'tɒrɪk] *adj* prehistórico.
prehistory ['pri:'hɪstərɪ] *n* prehistoria *f*.
preignition ['pri:ɪg'nɪʃən] *n* preignición *f*.
prejudge ['pri:'dʒʌdʒ] *vt* prejuzgar.
prejudice ['predʒʊdɪs] **1** *n* (**a**) (*bias*) parcialidad *f*; (*biased view*) prejuicio *m*; (*hostility*) mala voluntad *f*, prevención *f*; **there are many ~s about this** sobre esto existen muchos prejuicios; **to have a ~ against sb** tener mala voluntad contra uno, tener prevención contra uno, estar predispuesto contra uno.
(**b**) (*injury, detriment*) perjuicio *m*; daño *m*; **to the ~ of** con perjuicio de, con menoscabo de; **without ~** (*Jur*) sin detrimento de sus propios derechos; **without ~ to** sin perjuicio de.
2 *vt* (**a**) (*predispose, bias*) prevenir, predisponer (*against* contra).
(**b**) (*damage*) perjudicar; **to ~ one's chances** perjudicar las posibilidades de uno.
prejudiced ['predʒʊdɪst] *adj* (**a**) *view etc* parcial, interesado; **he's very ~** tiene muchos prejuicios.
(**b**) **to be ~d against sb** tener mala voluntad contra uno, tener prevención contra uno, estar predispuesto contra uno.
prejudicial [,predʒʊ'dɪʃəl] *adj* perjudicial (*to* para).
prelate ['prelɪt] *n* prelado *m*.

prelim [ˈpriːlɪm] *n abbr of* **preliminary.**
preliminary [prɪˈlɪmɪnərɪ] **1** *adj* preliminar. **2** *n* preliminar *m*; **preliminaries** preliminares *mpl*, preparativos *mpl*.
prelude [ˈpreljuːd] **1** *n* preludio *m* (*also Mus*; *to* de). **2** *vt* preludiar.
premarital [ˈpriːˈmærɪtl] *adj* premarital, prematrimonial, prenupcial.
premature [ˈpremətʃʊəʳ] *adj* prematuro; ~ **baby** niño *m* prematuro, niña *f* prematura; ~ **baldness** calvicie *f* precoz; **it seems** ~ **to think of it** parece prematuro pensar en ello; **he was (born) 5 weeks** ~ nació con 5 semanas de antelación; **I think you're being a little** ~ creo que te has adelantado.
prematurely [ˈpremətʃʊəlɪ] *adv* prematuramente; antes de su debido tiempo; ~ **bald** con calvicie precoz.
pre-med [ˈpriːmed] **1** *n* (*Brit*) *abbr of* **premedication**. **2** *adj* (*US*) *abbr of* **premedical**; ~ **course** curso *m* preparatorio a los estudios en la Facultad de Medicina.
premedication [ˌpriːmedɪˈkeɪʃən] *n* premedicación *f*, medicación *f* previa.
premeditate [priːˈmedɪteɪt] *vt* premeditar.
premeditated [priːˈmedɪteɪtɪd] *adj* premeditado.
premeditation [priːˌmedɪˈteɪʃən] *n* premeditación *f*.
premenstrual [ˌpriːˈmenstrʊəl] *adj* premenstrual; ~ **tension** síndrome *m* premenstrual.
premier [ˈpremɪəʳ] **1** *adj* primero, principal. **2** *n* primer ministro *m*, primera ministra *f*.
première [ˌpremɪˈɛəʳ] **1** *n* estreno *m*; **world** ~ estreno *m* mundial; **the film had its** ~ se estrenó la película. **2** *vt* estrenar.
premiership [ˈpremɪəʃɪp] *n* cargo *m* del primer ministro, puesto *m* de primer ministro; período *m* de gobierno.
premise [ˈpremɪs] **1** *n* (**a**) (*gen, Philos*: *also* **premiss**) premisa *f*. (**b**) ~**s** local *m*; (*house*) casa *f*; (*building*) edificio *m*; (*shop etc*) tienda *f*, establecimiento *m*; (*as property*) local *m*, propiedad *f*; **on the** ~**s** en el local (*etc*); **for consumption on the** ~**s** para tomarse en el local. **2** *vt*: **to be** ~**d on** estar basado en, tener como premisa.
premium [ˈpriːmɪəm] **1** *n* (*prize*) premio *m*; (*Comm, insurance*) prima *f*; ~ **price** precio *m* con prima; **to be at a** ~ (*Comm*) estar sobre la par, (*fig*) tener mucha demanda, ser muy solicitado; **to put a** ~ **on sth** estimular algo, fomentar algo; hacer que suba el valor de algo (debido a su escasez); **to sell sth at a** ~ vender algo en más de su valor nominal.
2 *attr*: ~ **bond** (*Brit*) bono *m* de la caja de ahorros; ~ **deal** oferta *f* extraordinaria; ~ **gasoline** (*US*) (gasolina *f*) súper *f*.
premolar [priːˈməʊləʳ] *n* premolar *m*.
premonition [ˌpriːməˈnɪʃən] *n* presentimiento *m*, premonición *f*; **to have a** ~ **that** ... presentir que ...
premonitory [prɪˈmɒnɪtərɪ] *adj* premonitorio.
prenatal [ˈpriːˈneɪtl] *adj* prenatal, antenatal; ~ **clinic** clínica *f* prenatal.
preoccupation [priːˌɒkjʊˈpeɪʃən] *n* preocupación *f*.
preoccupied [priːˈɒkjʊpaɪd] *adj* preocupado; absorto; abstraído; **to be** ~ **about** estar preocupado por, inquietarse por; **to be** ~ **with sth** estar absorto en algo; **he was too** ~ **to notice** estaba demasiado absorto para darse cuenta.
preoccupy [priːˈɒkjʊpaɪ] *vt* preocupar.
preordain [ˈpriːɔːˈdeɪn] *vt* predestinar.
pre-owned [ˈpriːˈəʊnd] *adj* (*US*) seminuevo.
prep* [prep] **1** *n* (*Brit Scol*) *abbr of* **preparation** tareas *fpl*, deberes *mpl*.
2 *adj*: ~ **school** (*Brit*) = **preparatory school**; *V* **preparatory**.
3 *vi* (*US**) (**a**) **to** ~ **for sth** prepararse para algo.
(**b**) (*Scol*) hacer el curso de preparación a los estudios universitarios.
4 *vr*: **to** ~ **o.s.** (*US*) prepararse.
prepack [ˌpriːˈpæk] *vt*, **prepackage** [ˌpriːˈpækɪdʒ] *vt* preempaquetar.
prepackaged [ˈpriːˈpækɪdʒd] *adj*, **prepacked** [ˌpriːˈpækt] *adj* empaquetado.
prepaid [ˈpriːˈpeɪd] *adj* pagado con antelación; (*Post*) porte pagado, franco de porte.
preparation [ˌprepəˈreɪʃən] *n* preparación *f*; ~**s** preparativos *mpl* (*for* para); **to be in** ~ (*book*) estar en preparación; **to do sth without** ~ hacer algo sin preparación; **to make one's** ~**s** hacer sus preparativos (*to* + *infin* para + *infin*); **Latin is a good** ~ **for Greek** el latín es buena preparación para el griego.
preparatory [prɪˈpærətərɪ] **1** *adj* preparatorio, preliminar; ~ **school** (*Brit*) *escuela privada para muchachos de 8 a 12 años* (*que pasan después a una public school*), (*US*) colegio *m* privado. **2** ~ **to** *as prep* como preparación para; con miras a, antes de.
prepare [prɪˈpɛəʳ] **1** *vt* preparar; disponer; aparejar; **how is it** ~**d?** ¿cómo se prepara?; ¿cómo se hace?; **to** ~ **a surprise for sb** preparar una sorpresa para uno; **to** ~ **the way for a treaty** preparar el terreno para un tratado; **to** ~ **sb for bad news** prevenir a uno para recibir una mala noticia.
2 *vi* prepararse; disponerse; hacer preparativos; prevenirse; **to** ~ **for sb's arrival** hacer preparativos para recibir a uno; **to** ~ **for a storm** prepararse para una tempestad; **to** ~ **for an examination** estudiar para un examen; **to** ~ **to** + *infin* disponerse a + *infin*, hacer preparativos para + *infin*.
prepared [prɪˈpɛəd] *adj* (**a**) listo; ~ **food** producto *m* previamente elaborado; **'be** ~**'** (*motto*) '¡está preparado!'
(**b**) **to be** ~ **for anything** estar preparado para todo; no dejarse sorprender por nada; **we were not** ~ **for this** esto no lo esperábamos, no contábamos con esto; **we were** ~ **for it** lo habíamos previsto; **to be** ~ **to** + *infin* estar dispuesto a + *infin*; **he was not** ~ **to listen to us** no estaba dispuesto a escucharnos.
preparedness [prɪˈpɛərɪdnɪs] *n* preparación *f*, estado *m* de preparación; **military** ~ preparación *f* militar.
prepay [ˈpriːˈpeɪ] (*irr*: *V* **pay**) *vt* pagar por adelantado.
prepayment [ˈpriːˈpeɪmənt] *n* pago *m* adelantado, pago *m* anticipado.
preponderance [prɪˈpɒndərəns] *n* preponderancia *f*, predominio *m*.
preponderant [prɪˈpɒndərənt] *adj* preponderante, predominante.
preponderantly [prɪˈpɒndərəntlɪ] *adv* de modo predominante, en un grado predominante; en su mayor parte.
preponderate [prɪˈpɒndəreɪt] *vi* preponderar, predominar.
preposition [ˌprepəˈzɪʃən] *n* preposición *f*.
prepositional [ˌprepəˈzɪʃənl] *adj* preposicional.
prepossess [ˌpriːpəˈzes] *vt* (*preoccupy*) preocupar; (*bias, impress favourably*) predisponer.
prepossessing [ˌpriːpəˈzesɪŋ] *adj* atractivo, agradable; **not very** ~ no muy atractivo.
preposterous [prɪˈpɒstərəs] *adj* absurdo, ridículo.
preposterously [prɪˈpɒstərəslɪ] *adv* absurdamente.
preposterousness [prɪˈpɒstərəsnɪs] *n* lo absurdo.
preppy* [ˈprepɪ] *adj* (*US*) de muy buen tono; guapón*, elegantón*.
preprogramme, (*US, freq Comput*) **preprogram** [ˌpriːˈprəʊgræm] *vt* preprogramar.
preprogrammed, (*US*) **preprogramed** [ˌpriːˈprəʊgræmd] *adj* preprogramado.
prepuce [ˈpriːpjuːs] *n* prepucio *m*.
pre-Raphaelite [ˈpriːˈræfəlaɪt] **1** *adj* prerrafaelista. **2** *n* prerrafaelista *mf*.
prerecord [ˈpriːrɪ(ː)ˈkɔːd] *vt* grabar (*or* registrar) de antemano.
prerecorded [ˌpriːrɪˈkɔːdɪd] *adj* pregrabado, ya grabado.
prerequisite [ˈpriːˈrekwɪzɪt] **1** *adj* previamente necesario. **2** *n* requisito *m* previo; condición *f* previa; cosa *f* necesaria, esencial *m*; ~**s for success** las cosas necesarias para asegurar el éxito.
prerogative [prɪˈrɒgətɪv] *n* prerrogativa *f*.
presage [ˈpresɪdʒ] **1** *n* presagio *m*. **2** *vt* presagiar.
Presbyterian [ˌprezbɪˈtɪərɪən] **1** *adj* presbiteriano. **2** *n* presbiteriano *m*, -a *f*.
presbytery [ˈprezbɪtərɪ] *n* casa *f* paroquial; (*Archit*) presbiterio *m*.
preschool [ˈpriːˈskuːl] *adj* preescolar; ~ **education** educación *f* preescolar.
prescience [ˈpresɪəns] *n* presciencia *f*.
prescient [ˈpresɪənt] *adj* presciente.
prescribe [prɪsˈkraɪb] **1** *vt* (**a**) (*also Jur*) prescribir; ordenar; **in the** ~**d way** de conformidad con la ley, en el modo que ordena la ley; **in the** ~**d time** dentro del plazo que fija la ley.
(**b**) (*Med*) recetar; **to** ~ **a medicine for sb** recetar una medicina para uno; **he** ~**d complete rest** recomendó el reposo completo; **what do you** ~**?** ¿qué me recomiendas?
2 *vi* (**a**) prescribir (*also Jur*); ordenar.
(**b**) (*Med*) recetar; **to** ~ **for boils** recetar una medicina para curar los diviesos.
prescription [prɪsˈkrɪpʃən] **1** *n* (**a**) prescripción *f* (*also Jur*); precepto *m*.
(**b**) (*Med*) receta *f*, prescripción *f*; **made according to** ~ hecho según receta; **available only on** ~ obtenible sólo con receta.

2 *attr*: ~ **lenses** (*US*) lentes *fpl* graduadas.
prescriptive [prɪs'krɪptɪv] *adj* legal; sancionado por la costumbre; (*Ling*) prescriptivo.
prescriptivism [prɪ'skrɪptɪ,vɪzəm] *n* prescriptivismo *m*.
presealed ['pri:'si:ld] *adj* precintado (de antemano).
presence ['prezns] *n* (**a**) presencia *f*; (*attendance*) asistencia *f* (*at* a); ~ **of mind** aplomo *m*, serenidad *f*, sangre *f* fría; **saving your** ~ con perdón de los presentes, con la venia de los presentes; **in the** ~ **of** en presencia de, (*fig*) ante; **to be admitted to the P~** ser conducido ante el rey (*etc*); **to make one's** ~ **felt** (saber) imponerse, hacerse notar; **your** ~ **is requested** se ruega su asistencia.
(**b**) (*bearing etc*) presencia *f*.
present 1 ['preznt] *adj* (**a**) (*in attendance*) presente; ~! ¡presente!; **those** ~ los presentes, los asistentes; **to be** ~ asistir (*at* a); **all were** ~ **to hear it** todos asistieron para oírlo, acudieron todos a oírlo; **he was** ~ **at the accident** fue testigo del accidente; **he was** ~ **at the foundation** presenció la fundación; **nobody else was** ~ no había nadie más; **how many others were** ~? ¿cuántos más había?
(**b**) (*of time, current*) actual; presente; *month etc* corriente; ~ **methods include** ... los métodos actuales incluyen ..., los métodos en uso incluyen ...; **the** ~ **Queen of England** la actual Reina de Inglaterra; **the** ~ **letter** la presente; **the** ~ **writer** el que esto escribe; **its** ~ **value** su valor actual; **in the** ~ **year** en el año que corre.
(**c**) (*Gram*) *tense* presente; *participle* activo, (de) presente.
2 ['preznt] *n* (**a**) (*of time*) presente *m*, actualidad *f*; **the** ~ el presente; **at** ~ al presente, actualmente; **for the** ~ por ahora, por el momento; **up to the** ~ hasta ahora.
(**b**) (*gift*) regalo *m*, presente *m*; obsequio *m*; **to make sb a** ~ **of sth** regalar algo a uno, (*fig*) dar algo a uno medio regalado, servir algo a uno en bandeja.
(**c**) (*Gram*) (tiempo *m*) presente *m*; ~ **perfect** pretérito *m* perfecto.
3 [prɪ'zent] *vt* (**a**) (*introduce*) presentar; **to** ~ **X to Y** presentar a X a Y; **may I** ~ **Miss Blandish?** permítame presentarle a la señorita Blandish; **to be ~ed at court** ser presentado en la corte.
(**b**) (*Theat*) **to** ~ **a play** representar una obra; **'~ing Garbo as Mimi'** 'con Garbo en el papel de Mimi'.
(**c**) (*expound*) *case etc* exponer; **to** ~ **a plan to a meeting** exponer (*or* explicar) un proyecto a una reunión.
(**d**) (*give*) presentar, ofrecer, dar; (*show*) *documents, tickets etc* presentar, mostrar; (*TV*) *programme* presentar; (*represent, portray*) presentar; **to** ~ **sth to sb, to** ~ **sb with sth** regalar algo a uno, (*more formally*) obsequiar a uno con algo; **to** ~ **an account** (*Comm*) pasar factura; **to** ~ **a report** presentar un informe; **to** ~ **one's compliments to sb** cumplimentar a uno, saludar a uno, ofrecer sus saludos a uno; **the report ~s him in a favourable light** el informe le presenta bajo una luz favorable.
(**e**) (*provide*) ofrecer; **it ~s a magnificent sight** ofrece un espectáculo maravilloso; **the case ~s some odd features** el caso tiene ciertas características algo raras; **it ~s some difficulties** nos plantea algunas dificultades; **the boy ~s a problem** el chico nos plantea un problema.
(**f**) (*Mil*) **to** ~ **arms** presentar las armas; ~ **arms!** ¡presenten armas!
4 [prɪ'zent] *vr*: **to** ~ **o.s.** presentarse (*at a time* a una hora, *at a place* en un sitio); **to** ~ **o.s. for examination** examinarse (*in* de); **when the chance ~s itself** cuando se ofrece la ocasión; **a problem has ~ed itself** ha surgido un problema.
presentable [prɪ'zentəbl] *adj* presentable; **are you** ~? (*dressed etc*) ¿estás visible?; **I must go and make myself** ~ voy a arreglarme un poco.
presentably [prɪ'zentəblɪ] *adv*: ~ **dressed** vestido de manera presentable.
presentation [,prezən'teɪʃən] **1** *n* (**a**) (*act*) presentación *f*; (*of case etc*) exposición *f*; (*Theat*) representación *f*; **on** ~ **of the voucher** al presentarse el vale.
(**b**) (*present*) obsequio *m*; (*ceremony*) entrega *f* ceremoniosa de un regalo; **to make sb a** ~ **on his retirement** hacer un obsequio a uno en su jubilación.
(**c**) (*Scol, Univ*) exposición *f* oral de un ejercicio escrito.
2 *attr*: ~ **case** estuche *m* de regalo; ~ **copy** ejemplar *m* con dedicatoria del autor.
presentational [,prezən'teɪʃənəl] *adj* relativo a la presentación.
present-day ['preznt'deɪ] *adj* actual, de hoy en día.
presenter [prɪ'zentə^r] *n* (*Brit TV etc*) presentador *m*, -ora *f*.
presentiment [prɪ'zentɪmənt] *n* presentimiento *m*, corazonada *f*; **to have a** ~ **about sth** tener un presentimiento acerca de algo; **to have a** ~ **that** ... presentir que ...
presently ['prezntlɪ] *adv* (*Brit*) luego, dentro de poco; (*esp US*) ahora, actualmente; en el momento presente.
preservation [,prezə'veɪʃən] **1** *n* conservación *f*; preservación *f*; **in a good state of** ~, **in good** ~ bien conservado, en buen estado.
2 *attr*: ~ **order** (*Brit*) orden *f* de preservación; ~ **society** (*Brit*) sociedad *f* para la preservación.
preservative [prɪ'zɜ:vətɪv] **1** *adj* preservativo. **2** *n* preservativo *m*.
preserve [prɪ'zɜ:v] **1** *n* (**a**) (*Brit Culin*) conserva *f*; confitura *f*; compota *f*.
(**b**) (*Hunting*) coto *m*, vedado *m*; (*game* ~) coto *m* de caza; (*fig*) dominio *m*, territorio *m*; **it's a female** ~ es un coto cerrado femenino.
2 *vt* (**a**) (*keep*) conservar; mantener en buen estado; (*keep from harm*) preservar (*against, from* contra), guardar, proteger (*against, from* de); **may God** ~ **you** que Dios os guarde.
(**b**) (*Culin*) hacer una conserva de; (*in syrup*) almibarar, (*in salt*) salar, salpresar.
preserved [prɪ'zɜ:vd] *adj food* en conserva.
preset ['pri:'set] *vt* (*irr*: *V* **set**) programar.
pre-shrunk ['pri:'ʃrʌŋk] *adj* inencogible.
preside [prɪ'zaɪd] *vi* presidir; **to** ~ **at** (*or* **over**) **a meeting** presidir una reunión.
presidency ['prezɪdənsɪ] *n* presidencia *f*.
president ['prezɪdənt] *n* (*Pol etc*) presidente *m*, -a *f*; (*US Comm*) director *m*, -ora *f*; (*US Univ*) rector *m*, -ora *f*; **~-elect** presidente *m* electo, presidenta *f* electa.
presidential [,prezɪ'denʃəl] *adj* presidencial.
presidium [prɪ'sɪdɪəm] *n* (*Pol*) presidio *m*.
press [pres] **1** *n* (**a**) (*pressure*) presión *f*; (*of hand etc*) apretón *m*, presión *f*; (*Weightlifting*) presa *f*; **give it a** ~ **here** presione aquí.
(**b**) (*crush etc of people*) apiñamiento *m*, agolpamiento *m*; (*of affairs*) urgencia *f*; **there was such a** ~ **of people** había tal multitud de gente, era tal el apiñamiento; **in the** ~ **of the battle** en lo más reñido de la batalla.
(**c**) (*Mech*) prensa *f*.
(**d**) (*Typ*) (*printing press, publishing firm*) imprenta *f*; (*newspapers in general*) prensa *f*; **the P~** la Prensa; **to be in** ~ estar en prensa; **to get** (*or* **have**) **a bad** ~ tener mala prensa; **to get** (*or* **have**) **a good** ~ tener buena prensa; **to go to** ~ entrar en prensa, entrar en máquina; **to pass sth for the** ~ aprobar algo para la prensa.
2 *attr*: ~ **baron** magnate *m* de la prensa; ~ **card** tarjeta *f* de periodista, pase *m* de periodista; ~ **corps** cuerpo *m* de periodistas; ~ **office** oficina *f* de prensa; ~ **officer**, ~ **secretary** secretario *m*, -a *f* de prensa.
3 *vt* (**a**) *button, switch, doorbell etc* apretar, pulsar, presionar, empujar; *hand, trigger* apretar; *hand* (*painfully*) apretujar; *grapes* pisar, prensar; *metal, olives etc* (*Tech*) prensar; *suit* planchar; (*crush, squeeze*) estrujar; **to** ~ **sb's hand** apretar la mano a uno; **to** ~ **the juice out of an orange** exprimir el zumo de una naranja; **it ~es me here** me aprieta aquí; **he ~ed his face to the window** pegó la cara al cristal; **to** ~ **sb to one's heart** abrazar a uno estrechamente; **to** ~ **books into a case** meter libros apretadamente en una maleta.
(**b**) (*put pressure on enemy etc*) acosar, hostigar, (*in game*) apretar, (*in pursuit*) seguir muy de cerca, pisar los talones de; **to** ~ **sb hard** apretar mucho a uno; **to** ~ **sb for payment** insistir en que uno pague algo, exigir el pago a uno, apremiar a uno a que pague; **to** ~ **sb for an answer** pedir insistentemente que uno conteste a algo; **to** ~ **charges against sb** hacer acusaciones contra uno; **to** ~ **a claim** insistir en una demanda; **to** ~ **a point** insistir en su punto de vista; **to** ~ **home an advantage** aprovecharse todo lo posible de una ventaja; **to** ~ **a gift on sb** insistir en que uno acepte un regalo; **to** ~ **sb to do sth** instar a uno a que haga algo, apremiar a uno para que haga algo, hacer presión sobre uno para que haga algo; **he didn't need much ~ing** no hacía falta convencerle; **he was being ~ed by creditors** le acosaban los acreedores; **to be ~ed for money** andar muy escaso de dinero; **to be ~ed for time** tener poco tiempo, tener mucha prisa.
4 *vi* (**a**) (*in physical sense*) apretar; ejercer presión, hacer presión; **to** ~ **hard** apretar mucho; **to** ~ **close up to sb** arrimarse a uno; **to** ~ **on one's pen** escribir haciendo más presión con la pluma; **the people ~ed round him** la gente se apiñó en torno a él.

(**b**) (*fig*) ejercer presión, hacer presión; presionar; **time ~es** el tiempo apremia; **responsibilities ~ hard on him** las responsabilidades pesan sobre él.

(**c**) **to ~ for sth** presionar por algo, presionar para conseguir algo; reclamar algo, exigir algo, pedir algo con urgencia; **to ~ for sb to resign** presionar para que uno dimita.

◆**press ahead** *vi* = **press forward.**

◆**press back** *vt crowd, enemy* rechazar.

◆**press down 1** *vt*: **to ~ sth down** comprimir algo.

2 *vi*: **to ~ down on sth** apretar algo comprimiéndolo; pesar sobre algo.

◆**press forward, press on** *vi* avanzar; seguir su camino; (*hasten*) apretar el paso; **~ on!** ¡adelante!

◆**press out** *vt*: **to ~ the juice out of an orange** exprimir el zumo de una naranja.

press-agency ['pres,eɪdʒənsɪ] *n* agencia *f* de prensa.

press-agent ['pres,eɪdʒənt] *n* agente *mf* de publicidad.

press attaché ['presə'tæʃeɪ] *n* agregado *m* de prensa.

press-box ['presbɒks] *n* tribuna *f* de la prensa.

press-button ['pres'bʌtn] **1** *n* botón *m* (de control).
2 *attr* mandado por botón.

press-clipping ['pres,klɪpɪŋ] = **press-cutting.**

press-conference ['pres,kɒnfərəns] *n* rueda *f* de prensa, conferencia *f* de prensa.

press-cutting ['pres,kʌtɪŋ] *n* recorte *m* (de periódico).

press gallery ['pres,gælərɪ] *n* tribuna *f* de la prensa.

press-gang ['presgæŋ] **1** *n* leva *f*, ronda *f* de enganche. **2** *vt*: **to ~ sb into sth** obligar a uno muy contra su voluntad a hacer algo.

pressing ['presɪŋ] *adj* urgente, apremiante, acuciante.

pressman ['presmæn] *n, pl* **pressmen** ['presmen] (*Brit*) periodista *m*; (*US*) tipógrafo *m*.

pressmark ['presmɑːk] *n* (*Brit*) signatura *f*.

press photographer ['presfə'tɒgrəfə^r] *n* fotógrafo *m*, -a *f* de prensa.

press-release ['presrɪ,liːs] *n* boletín *m* de prensa, comunicado *m* de prensa, nota *f* de prensa.

press-report ['presrɪ,pɔːt] *n* reportaje *m* de prensa.

press run ['presrʌn] *n* (*US*) tirada *f*.

press-stud ['presstʌd] *n* (*Brit*) botón *m* de presión.

press-up ['presʌp] *n* flexión *f*, abdominal *m*, plancha *f*.

pressure ['preʃə^r] **1** *n* (**a**) (*Met, Phys, Tech*) presión *f*; (*weight*) peso *m*; (*strength*) fuerza *f*; **a ~ of x kilogrammes to the square metre** una presión de x kg al m^2.

(**b**) (*urgency*) urgencia *f*, apremio *m*; (*influence*) influencia *f*, persuasión *f*; (*Med*) tensión *f* nerviosa; **because of the ~ of business** (*Comm*) debido a la cantidad de negocios, (*at meeting etc*) por el número de los asuntos a tratar; **to act under ~** obrar bajo persuasión; **he is under ~ to sign the agreement** le están presionando para que firme el acuerdo; **to do sth under ~ from the bankers** hacer algo presionado por los banqueros; **to bring ~ to bear on sb** hacer presión sobre uno (*to do sth* para que haga algo); **to live at high ~** tener una vida muy activa; **to work under ~** trabajar con urgencia.

2 *vt* = **pressurize.**

pressure-cook ['preʃə,kʊk] *vt* cocer en olla a presión.

pressure-cooker ['preʃə,kʊkə^r] *n* olla *f* a presión.

pressure-feed ['preʃəfiːd] *n* tubo *m* de alimentación a presión.

pressure-gauge ['preʃəgeɪdʒ] *n* manómetro *m*.

pressure-group ['preʃəgruːp] *n* grupo *m* de presión.

pressure pan ['preʃəpæn] *n* (*US*) olla *f* a presión.

pressure-point ['preʃə,pɔɪnt] *n* (*Anat*) punto *m* de presión.

pressure-suit ['preʃə,suːt] *n* traje *m* de presión compensada.

pressurize ['preʃəraɪz] *vt* presionar, hacer presión sobre, ejercer presión sobre; **to ~ sb into doing sth** forzar a uno a hacer algo, presionar a uno para que haga algo.

pressurized ['preʃəraɪzd] *adj cabin* a presión, presurizado; **~ water reactor** reactor *m* de agua a presión.

press view ['presvjuː] *n* preestreno *m* (para prensa).

Prestel ['prestel] ® *n* videotex *m*.

prestidigitation ['prestɪ,dɪdʒɪ'teɪʃən] *n* prestidigitación *f*.

prestige [pres'tiːʒ] *n* prestigio *m*.

prestigious [pres'tɪdʒəs] *adj* prestigioso.

presto ['prestəʊ] *adv*: **hey ~!** ¡abracadabra!

prestressed ['priː'strest] *adj*: **~ concrete** hormigón *m* pretensado.

presumably [prɪ'zjuːməblɪ] *adv* probablemente, presumiblemente, según cabe presumir; **~ he will come** imagino que vendrá; **~ he did** cabe presumir que lo hizo.

presume [prɪ'zjuːm] **1** *vt* (**a**) (*suppose*) presumir; suponer; **his death must be ~d** hay que presumir que ha muerto, es de suponer que murió; **to ~ that ...** suponer que ...; **it may be ~d that ...** es de suponer que ...; **to ~ sb to be innocent** suponer que uno es inocente; **Dr Livingstone, I ~** Dr Livingstone según creo, cabe conjeturar que Vd es el Dr Livingstone.

(**b**) (*venture*) **to ~ to** + *infin* atreverse a + *infin*; pretender + *infin*, tomarse la libertad de + *infin*; **if I may ~ to advise you** si me permites ofrecerte un consejo.

2 *vi*: **to ~ on sb's friendship** abusar de la amistad de uno; **you ~ too much** no sabes lo que pides, eso es mucho pedir.

presumption [prɪ'zʌmpʃən] *n* (**a**) (*arrogance*) presunción *f*; atrevimiento *m*; **pardon my ~** le ruego perdonar mi atrevimiento.

(**b**) (*thing presumed*) suposición *f*; pretensión *f*; **the ~ is that ...** es de suponer que ..., puede presumirse que ...

presumptive [prɪ'zʌmptɪv] *adj heir* presunto; **~ evidence** pruebas *fpl* presuntivas.

presumptuous [prɪ'zʌmptjʊəs] *adj* presumido, presuntuoso; atrevido; **in that I was rather ~** en eso fui algo atrevido; **it would be ~ of me to express an opinion** sería osado que yo opinara.

presumptuously [prɪ'zʌmptjʊəslɪ] *adv* con presunción, presuntuosamente.

presumptuousness [prɪ'zʌmptjʊəsnɪs] *n* presunción *f*, atrevimiento *m*.

presuppose [,priːsə'pəʊz] *vt* presuponer.

presupposition [,priːsʌpə'zɪʃən] *n* presuposición *f*.

pre-tax [,priː'tæks] *adj* anterior al impuesto; **~ profits** beneficios *mpl* preimpositivos.

pre-teen [,priː'tiːn] (*US*) **1** *adj* preadolescente. **2** *npl*: **the ~s** los preadolescentes.

pretence, (*US*) **pretense** [prɪ'tens] *n* (**a**) (*claim*) pretensión *f*; **to make no ~ to learning** no pretender ser erudito.

(**b**) (*display*) ostentación *f*; afectación *f*; **without ~, devoid of all ~** sin ostentación, sin afectación.

(**c**) (*pretext*) pretexto *m*; **on the ~ of, under the ~ of** so pretexto de.

(**d**) (*make-believe*) fingimiento *m*; ficción *f*; fraude *m*, engaño *m*; **it's all a ~** todo es fingido; **to make a ~ of sth** fingir algo.

pretend [prɪ'tend] **1** *vt* (**a**) (*feign*) fingir, aparentar, simular; **to ~ ignorance** fingir ignorancia, fingir ignorar, aparentar no saber; **to ~ that ...** (querer) hacer creer que ...; **let's ~ I'm the doctor and you're the nurse** yo era el médico y tú eras la enfermera; **to ~ to** + *infin* fingir + *infin*, aparentar + *infin*; **to ~ to go away** fingir marcharse; **to ~ to be mad** fingirse loco; **to ~ to be asleep, to ~ to sleep** fingir dormir, fingirse dormido, hacerse el dormido; **he ~s to be a poet** se dice poeta, se hace el poeta, las echa de poeta; **to ~ not to be listening** hacerse el distraído; **to ~ not to understand** hacerse el desentendido.

(**b**) (*claim*) pretender; **I do not ~ to know the answer** no pretendo saber la respuesta; **I don't ~ to understand art** no pretendo entender de arte.

2 *vi* (**a**) (*feign*) fingir; **it's just ~, we're only ~ing** (*to child etc*) es de mentirijillas; **let's ~** imaginémoslo; **let's not ~ to each other** no nos engañemos uno a otro.

(**b**) (*claim*) **to ~ to the throne** pretender el trono; **to ~ to intelligence** afirmar tener inteligencia, pretender ser inteligente.

3 *adj*: **~ money*** dinero *m* de juego.

pretended [prɪ'tendɪd] *adj* pretendido.

pretender [prɪ'tendə^r] *n* pretendiente *mf*; **~ to the throne** pretendiente *mf* al trono; **the Young P~** el joven Pretendiente.

pretense [prɪ'tens] *n* (*US*) = **pretence.**

pretension [prɪ'tenʃən] *n* (**a**) (*claim*) pretensión *f*; **to have ~s to culture** tener pretensiones de cultura, pretender ser culto.

(**b**) (*pretentiousness*) presunción *f*; afectación *f*.

pretentious [prɪ'tenʃəs] *adj* pretencioso; *person* presumido; (*ostentatious*) ostentoso, aparatoso, ambicioso; (*and vulgar*) cursi.

pretentiously [prɪ'tenʃəslɪ] *adv* con presunción; ostentosamente, aparatosamente.

pretentiousness [prɪ'tenʃəsnɪs] *n* pretenciosidad *f*; presunción *f*; lo ostentoso, lo aparatoso; cursilería *f*.

preterite ['pretərɪt] *n* pretérito *m*.

preterm [,priː'tɜːm] **1** *adj* prematuro. **2** *adv* prematuramente.

preternatural [,priːtə'nætʃrəl] *adj* preternatural.

pretext ['priːtekst] *n* pretexto *m*; **under ~ of** so pretexto de; **it's just a ~** es sólo un pretexto.

pretorian [prɪˈtɔːrɪən] *adj* (*US*) = **praetorian.**

prettify [ˈprɪtɪfaɪ] *vt* (*pej*) embellecer, adornar (de modo ridículo); ataviar.

prettily [ˈprɪtɪlɪ] *adv* con gracia, elegantemente; preciosamente; ~ **adorned with** con adornos elegantes de.

pretty [ˈprɪtɪ] **1** *adj* (**a**) *person* guapo, bonito, lindo (*LAm*); *dress, object etc* precioso, mono, bonito; *scene* hermoso; **a ~ girl** una muchacha guapa; **a ~ little house** una casita preciosa; **what a ~ hat!** ¡qué sombrero más mono!, ¡qué monada de sombrero!; **yes, my ~** (*to child*) sí, ricura; **she's as ~ as a picture** es guapísima; **he has a ~ wit** (*liter*) tiene un ingenio muy vivo, es muy ingenioso.

(**b**) *sum etc* importante, considerable.

(**c**) (*iro*) bueno; **a ~ mess we're in!** ¡vaya lío!

2 *adv* bastante; casi; **~ good** bastante bueno, muy bueno; **~ hard** bastante difícil; **it's ~ much the same** llega a ser como lo mismo, es lo mismo más o menos; **he got ~ cross** se enfadó bastante; **I have a ~ fair idea who did it** yo sé casi seguramente quién lo hizo; **it's ~ near ruined** está casi arruinado; **that's ~ well everything** eso es todo más o menos; **~ well, thanks!** ¡regular, gracias!; **to be sitting ~** estar bien sentado.

◆**pretty up** *vt* = **prettify.**

pretty-pretty* [ˌprɪtɪˈprɪtɪ] *adj* (*pej*): **he's very ~** es un guapito de cara*; **she's very ~** es una niña mona.

pretzel [ˈpretsl] *n* (*US*) *galleta tostada en forma de rosquilla, polvoreada con sal.*

prevail [prɪˈveɪl] *vi* (**a**) (*gain mastery*) prevalecer, imponerse; **to ~ against** (*or* **over**) **one's enemies** triunfar sobre los enemigos; **finally good sense ~ed** por fin se impuso el buen sentido; **eventually peace ~ed** por fin se restableció la paz.

(**b**) (*be current*) reinar, imperar; predominar; (*be in fashion*) estar de moda, estar en boga; **the conditions that now ~** las condiciones que ahora imperan.

(**c**) (*persuade*) **to ~ upon sb to do sth** convencer a uno para que haga algo, inducir a uno a hacer algo; **he was eventually ~ed upon to** + *infin* por fin se dejó persuadir a + *infin*; **he could not be ~ed upon** era imposible persuadirle, no se convenció.

prevailing [prɪˈveɪlɪŋ] *adj* reinante, imperante; vigente; predominante; usual, corriente; *price* imperante; **the ~ fashion** la moda actual, la moda reinante; **under ~ conditions** bajo las condiciones actuales; **the ~ wind** el viento predominante.

prevalence [ˈprevələns] *n* predominio *m*; frecuencia *f*; uso *m* corriente, costumbre *f*.

prevalent [ˈprevələnt] *adj* predominante; frecuente, común, corriente; (*fashionable*) en boga, de moda; *custom etc* extendido; (*present-day*) actual.

prevaricate [prɪˈværɪkeɪt] *vi* buscar evasivas, usar sofismas, tergiversar.

prevarication [prɪˌværɪˈkeɪʃən] *n* evasivas *fpl*, sofismas *mpl*, tergiversación *f*.

prevent [prɪˈvent] *vt person* impedir, estorbar; *event etc* impedir, evitar; estorbar; prevenir; *illness etc* evitar; **it was impossible to ~ it** fue imposible impedirlo; **to ~ sb** + *ger*, **to ~ sb from** + *ger* impedir a uno + *infin*.

preventable [prɪˈventəbl] *adj* evitable.

preventative [prɪˈventətɪv] *adj* = **preventive.**

prevention [prɪˈvenʃən] *n* prevención *f*; el impedir, el evitar; **~ is better than cure** es más fácil prevenir que curar; **the ~ of errors is not easy** no es fácil evitar los errores; **for the ~ of accidents** para evitar los accidentes; **a society for the ~ of cruelty to animals** una sociedad protectora de animales.

preventive [prɪˈventɪv] *adj* preventivo, impeditivo; **~ dentistry** odontología *f* preventiva; **~ detention** arresto *m* preventivo; **~ measure** medida *f* preventiva; **~ medicine** medicina *f* preventiva.

preview [ˈpriːvjuː] **1** *n* preestreno *m*; (*fig*) anticipo *m*, vista *f* anticipada; (*Cine*) tráiler *m*, avance *m*; **to have a ~ of sth** ver algo con anticipación, lograr ver algo antes que otros.

2 *vt* preestrenar.

previous [ˈpriːvɪəs] **1** *adj* (**a**) previo, anterior; **in ~ years** en años anteriores; **no ~ experience necessary** no hace falta experiencia previa; **because of a ~ engagement** por tener compromiso anterior.

(**b**) (*hasty*) prematuro; **this seems somewhat ~** esto parece algo prematuro; **you have been rather ~** has obrado con cierta prisa.

2 *prep*: **~ to** antes de; **~ to doing this** antes de hacer esto.

previously [ˈpriːvɪəslɪ] *adv* (*already*) previamente, con anticipación, anteriormente; (*in early times*) antes.

prewar [ˈpriːˈwɔːʳ] *adj* de antes de la guerra, de (la) preguerra, prebélico; **the ~ period** la preguerra.

prewash [ˈpriːwɒʃ] *n* prelavado *m*.

prey [preɪ] **1** *n* presa *f*, víctima *f*; **bird of ~** ave *f* de rapiña; **to be a ~ to** ser víctima de; **he fell (a) ~ to the disease** llegó a ser víctima de la enfermedad.

2 *vi* (**a**) **to ~ on** (*feed on*) atacar, alimentarse de, comer, devorar; (*plunder*) robar, pillar; (*sponge on*) vivir a costa de; **rabbits are ~ed on by foxes** los conejos son presa de los zorros.

(**b**) **to ~ on** (*mind*) atormentar, remorder, preocupar; **doubts ~ed on him** le obsesionaban las dudas; **the tragedy so ~ed on his mind that ...** la tragedia le afectó de tal modo que ...

prezzie* [ˈprezɪ] *n abbr of* **present** regalo *m*.

price [praɪs] **1** *n* precio *m*; (*quotation, Fin*) cotización *f*; (*in betting*) puntos *mpl* de ventaja; **at a ~ of £500** a un precio de 500 libras; **at a reduced ~** a un precio reducido, con descuento; **at any ~** (*fig*) a toda costa; **peace at any ~** la paz a toda costa; **they need to win at any ~** tienen que ganar a cualquier precio; **you can buy it at a ~** se puede comprar pero cuesta bastante; **not at any ~!** de ningún modo; **I don't want that at any ~** eso no lo quiero ni regalado; **what ~ these pigs?** ¿cuánto se me ofrece por estos cerdos?; **what ~ liberty?** y la libertad, ¿qué?; **what ~ Joe Soap now?** ¿qué me dicen ahora sobre Joe Soap?; **what ~ she'll change her mind?** ¿qué posibilidades hay de que cambie de opinión?; **what's the ~ of this?** ¿cuánto vale esto?; **to pay top ~ for sth** pagar algo al precio máximo; **she paid a high ~ for her success** compró muy caro su triunfo; **that was the ~ that had to be paid for progress** así había que pagar el progreso; **that is a small ~ to pay for independence** ése es un precio módico para comprar la independencia; **to rise in ~** subir de precio; **houses have risen in ~** ha aumentado el valor de las casas.

2 *attr*: **~ bracket** categoría *f* de precio; **~ control** control *m* de precios; **~ cut** rebaja *f*; **~ cutting** reducción *f* de precios; **~ fixing** fijación *f* de precios; **~ freeze** congelación *f* de los precios; **~ index** (*Brit*) índice *m* de precios; **~ level** nivel *m* de precios; **to put a ~ limit on sth** poner un precio límite a algo; **~ range** escala *f* de precios; **~ ring** confabulación *f* de comerciantes (formada para fijar los precios de los productos); **~ support** subsidio *m* de precios; **~ sticker, ~ tag, ~ ticket** etiqueta *f* del precio; **~ war** guerra *f* de precios; **~s and incomes policy** política *f* de ingresos y precios.

3 *vt* estimar, valuar, valorar (*at* en); tasar (*at* en), fijar el precio de; **it is ~d rather high at £80** está valorado en 80 libras, lo cual es mucho; **it's not ~d in the window** en el escaparate no lleva precio.

◆**price down** *vt* rebajar.

◆**price out 1** *vt*: **to be ~d out of the market** dejar de ser competitivo (en el mercado), perder competetividad de precios. **2** *vr*: **to ~ o.s. out of the market = 1.**

◆**price up** *vt* aumentar el precio de.

-priced [praɪst] *adj ending in compounds*: **high~** muy caro; *V* **low.**

priceless [ˈpraɪslɪs] *adj* (**a**) inapreciable, que no tiene precio. (**b**) (*) divertidísimo, impagable; **it was ~!** ¡fue para morirse de risa!*

price-list [ˈpraɪslɪst] *n* lista *f* de precios.

price-rigging [ˈpraɪsˌrɪgɪŋ] *n* (*pej*) manipulación *f* de precios.

price-tag [ˈpraɪstæg] *n* etiqueta *f* de precio, escandallo *m*.

pricey* [ˈpraɪsɪ] *adj* caro.

pricing [ˈpraɪsɪŋ] **1** *n* fijación *f* de precios. **2** *attr*: **~ policy** política *f* tarifaria.

prick [prɪk] **1** *n* (**a**) pinchazo *m*, punzada *f*; (*sting etc*) picadura *f*; (*with pin*) alfilerazo *m*; (*of spur*) espolada *f*; (*with goad*) aguijonazo *m*; **~ of conscience** escrúpulo *m* de conciencia, remordimiento *m*; **to kick against the ~s** dar coces contra el aguijón.

(**b**) (**: *penis*) polla** *f*.

(**c**) (**: *person*) gilipollas** *m*.

2 *vt* (**a**) pinchar, punzar, picar; (*sting*) picar; (*with spur*) dar con las espuelas; (*goad*) aguijar; (*make hole in*) agujerear; (*mark with holes*) marcar con agujerillos.

(**b**) **it ~ed his conscience** le remordió la conciencia, le dio un escrúpulo de conciencia.

3 *vi*: = **prickle 3.**

◆**prick out** *vt* (*Hort*) plantar.

◆**prick up 1** *vt*: **to ~ up one's ears** aguzar el oído.

2 *vi* aguzar el oído, empezar a prestar atención.

pricked [prɪkt] *adj wine* picado.

prickings ['prɪkɪŋz] *npl*: ~ **of conscience** remordimientos *mpl*.

prickle ['prɪkl] **1** *n* (**a**) (*Bot*) espina *f*; (*Zool*) púa *f*. (**b**) (*on skin etc*) escozor *m*. **2** *vt* picar. **3** *vi* hormiguear; picar; **my eyes are prickling** me duelen los ojos; **I could feel my skin prickling** me escocía la piel.

prickly ['prɪklɪ] *adj* espinoso, lleno de espinas; lleno de púas; *person* poco afable, malhumorado, difícil; ~ **heat** salpullido *m* causado por exceso de calor; ~ **pear** higo *m* chumbo, chumbera *f*; **he's rather ~ about that** sobre ese tema es algo quisquilloso.

pride [praɪd] **1** *n* (**a**) orgullo *m*; (*pej*) orgullo *m*, soberbia *f*, arrogancia *f*; **it's the ~ of Navarre** es el blasón de Navarra; **he's the ~ of the family** es el orgullo de la familia; **his roses are his ~ and joy** sus rosas son su tesoro, sus rosas son un gran motivo de orgullo; ~ **comes before a fall**, ~ **must have a fall** el orgullo excesivo conduce a la caída; **it is a source of ~ to us that ...** es para nosotros un motivo de orgullo el que ...; **to nurse one's ~** conservar el amor propio; tratar de restaurar el amor propio; **to swallow one's ~** tragarse el amor propio; tragar una afrenta; **to take (a) ~ in sth** enorgullecerse de algo, ufanarse de algo; **to take ~ of place** venir primero, ocupar el primer puesto.

(**b**) (*of lions*) grupo *m*, manada *f*.

2 *vr*: **to ~ o.s. on sth** enorgullecerse de algo, ufanarse de algo; **he ~s himself on his punctuality** se precia de puntual; **to ~ o.s. on** + *ger* enorgullecerse de + *infin*.

priest [priːst] *n* (*gen, pagan*) sacerdote *m*; (*Christian*) sacerdote *m*, cura *m*.

priestess ['priːstɪs] *n* sacerdotisa *f*.

priesthood ['priːsthʊd] *n* (*function*) sacerdocio *m*; (*priests collectively*) clero *m*; **to enter the ~** ordenarse de sacerdote.

priestly ['priːstlɪ] *adj* sacerdotal.

prig [prɪg] *n* presumido *m*, -a *f*; pedante *mf*; mojigato *m*, -a *f*, gazmoño *m*, -a *f*; **don't be such a ~!** ¡no seas tan pedante!; ¡no presumas!

priggish ['prɪgɪʃ] *adj* presumido; pedante; mojigato, gazmoño.

priggishness ['prɪgɪʃnɪs] *n* presunción *f*; pedantería *f*; mojigatería *f*, gazmoñería *f*.

prim [prɪm] *adj* (*formal*) etiquetero, estirado; (*affected*) remilgado; (*prudish*) gazmoño.

primacy ['praɪməsɪ] *n* primacía *f*.

prima donna ['priːmə'dɒnə] *n* primadonna *f*, diva *f*; (*fig*) persona *f* difícil, persona *f* de reacciones imprevisibles.

prima facie ['praɪmə'feɪʃɪ] **1** *adv* a primera vista.

2 *adj* (*Jur*): ~ **case** presunciones *fpl* razonables; ~ **evidence** prueba *f* semiplena; **there are ~ reasons why ...** hay suficientes razones que justifican el que + *subj*; **he has a ~ case** (*fig*) a primera vista parece que tiene razón.

primal ['praɪməl] *adj* (*first in time*) original; (*first in importance*) principal; ~ **scream** grito *m* primal.

primarily ['praɪmərɪlɪ] *adv* ante todo; en primer lugar; principalmente.

primary ['praɪmərɪ] **1** *adj* primario; principal; central; *colour, education* primario; ~ **education** educación *f* primaria, educación *f* primera; ~ **products** productos *mpl* primarios; ~ **school** (*Brit*) escuela *f* primaria; ~ **storage** almacenamiento *m* primario; **that is not the ~ reason** ésa no es la razón principal.

2 *n* (*US Pol*: *also* ~ **election**) (elección *f*) primaria *f*.

primate¹ ['praɪmɪt] *n* (*Eccl*) primado *m*.

primate² ['praɪmeɪt] *n* (*Zool*) primate *m*.

prime [praɪm] **1** *adj* (**a**) (*Math*) primo.

(**b**) (*chief*) primero, principal; fundamental; **the ~ reason** la razón principal; **of ~ importance** de primera importancia; **of ~ necessity** de primera necesidad; ~ **cost** costo *m* neto, costo *m* de producción; ~ **factor** factor *m* primordial; ~ **minister** primer ministro *m*, primera ministra *f*; ~ **ministerial** (*Sp*) presidencial; (*elsewhere*) del primer ministro; ~ **ministership** (*tenure*) (*Sp*) presidencia *f*, (*elsewhere*) período *m* de funciones de primer ministro; (*office*) cargo *m* de(l) primer ministro; ~ **mover** (*Mech*) máquina *f* motriz; (*Philos*) primer motor *m*; (*person*) promotor *m*, -ora *f*; ~ **rate** tipo *m* de interés preferente; ~ **time** (*TV*) banda *f* horaria caliente, horas *fpl* de mayor sintonía; (*Comm*) tiempo *m* preferencial.

(**c**) (*excellent*) selecto, de primera clase; ~ **quality beef** carne *f* de vaca de primera calidad; **in ~ condition** en excelente estado.

2 *n* (**a**) flor *f*, lo mejor; **the ~ of life** la flor de la vida, la edad viril; **to be in one's ~** estar en la flor de la vida; **to be past one's ~** haber dado lo mejor de sí, estar en decadencia; **to be cut off in one's ~** morir en la flor de la vida.

(**b**) (*Eccl*) prima *f*.

3 *vt gun, pump* cebar; *surface etc* preparar, aprestar; **to ~ sb** informar a uno de antemano; **they ~d him about what he should say** le dieron instrucciones acerca de lo que había de decir; **to ~ sb with drink** emborrachar a uno, hacer que uno beba; **he arrived well ~d** llegó ya medio borracho.

primer ['praɪmər] *n* (**a**) (*book*) cartilla *f*, libro *m* de texto elemental; **a French ~** un libro elemental de francés. (**b**) (*paint*) apresto *m*. (**c**) (*of bomb*) iniciador *m*.

primeval [praɪ'miːvəl] *adj* primitivo.

priming ['praɪmɪŋ] **1** *n* preparación *f*; (*of pump etc*) cebo *m*; (*Art*) primera capa *f*. **2** *attr*: ~ **device** iniciador *m*.

primitive ['prɪmɪtɪv] **1** *adj* (*early, original, primary*) primitivo; (*old-fashioned*) anticuado; (*simple, rude*) rudimentario, sencillo; (*uncivilized*) inculto; (*sordid*) sucio, miserable, asqueroso; (*Art*) primitivo.

2 *n* (*Art*) primitivo *m*.

primly ['prɪmlɪ] *adv* remilgadamente; con gazmoñería.

primness ['prɪmnɪs] *n* lo etiquetero, lo estirado; remilgo *m*; gazmoñería *f*.

primogeniture [,praɪməʊ'dʒenɪtʃər] *n* primogenitura *f*.

primordial [praɪ'mɔːdɪəl] *adj* primordial.

primp [prɪmp] = **prink**.

primrose ['prɪmrəʊz] **1** *n* (*Bot*) primavera *f*; (*colour*) color *m* amarillo pálido. **2** *adj* amarillo pálido. **3** *attr*: ~ **path** caminito *m* de rosas.

primula ['prɪmjʊlə] *n* oreja *f* de oso.

Primus (stove) ['praɪməs(stəʊv)] ® *n* cocinilla *f* de camping, hornillo *m*, infernillo *m* campestre.

prince [prɪns] *n* príncipe *m*; **P~ Charming** el Príncipe Azul, el Príncipe Encantador; **the ~ of darkness** el príncipe de las tinieblas, Satanás *m*; ~ **consort** príncipe *m* consorte; ~ **regent** príncipe *m* regente; **P~ of Wales** Príncipe *m* de Gales (*heredero del trono del Reino Unido, equivalente al Príncipe de Asturias en España*).

princely ['prɪnslɪ] *adj* principesco; magnífico, noble; **a ~ gesture** un gesto magnífico, un gesto digno de un príncipe; **the ~ sum of 5 dollars** (*iro*) la bonita cantidad de 5 dólares.

princess [prɪn'ses] *n* princesa *f*; ~ **royal** hija *f* mayor del soberano.

principal ['prɪnsɪpəl] **1** *adj* principal; mayor; ~ **boy** joven héroe *m* (*papel de actriz en la 'pantomime' navideña*). **2** *n* (**a**) principal *mf*, jefe *m*, -a *f*; (*of school, college*) director *m*, -ora *f*; (*Univ*) rector *m*, -ora *f*. (**b**) (*Fin*) principal *m*, capital *m*.

principality ['prɪnsɪ'pælɪtɪ] *n* principado *m*.

principally ['prɪnsɪpəlɪ] *adv* principalmente.

principle ['prɪnsəpl] *n* principio *m*; **in ~** en principio; **agreement in ~** acuerdo *m* de principio; **on ~** por principio; **to argue from first ~s** construir su argumento sobre los principios (fundamentales); **to go back to first ~s** volver a los principios (fundamentales); **to have high ~s** tener principios nobles; **to lay it down as a ~ that ...** sentar el principio de que ...; **I make it a ~ never to** + *infin* me hago una regla de nunca + *infin*.

principled ['prɪnsɪpld] *adj person* de fuertes principios; *behaviour, stand* basado en fuertes principios.

prink [prɪŋk] **1** *vt* acicalar, ataviar; arreglar elegantemente. **2** *vi* acicalarse, ataviarse; arreglarse elegantemente.

print [prɪnt] **1** *n* (**a**) (*mark, imprint*) marca *f*, señal *f*, impresión *f*; (*foot~*) huella *f*, pisada *f*; (*finger~*) huella *f* dactilar.

(**b**) (*Typ*) tipo *m*, letra *f* de molde; caracteres *mpl*; (*printed matter*) impreso *m*; **large ~** tipo *m* grande; **fine ~, small ~** tipo *m* menudo; **one must read the small ~** hay que leer la letra menuda; **in (cold) ~** en letras de molde; **books in ~** libros *mpl* en venta; **to be in ~** (*be published as book etc*) estar impreso; (*be available*) estar disponible, estar en existencia; **to be out of ~** estar fuera de catálogo, estar agotado; **he likes to see himself in ~** se enorgullece de que se impriman sus artículos (*etc*); le agrada que le mencionen en los periódicos; **to get into ~** imprimirse, publicarse; **we don't want that to get into ~** no queremos que eso se publique; **I've got into ~ at last!** ¡por fin me van a publicar el artículo! (*etc*); **to rush into ~** publicar una obra sin reflexionar, lanzarse a publicar.

(**c**) (*Art*) estampa *f*, grabado *m*; (*Phot*) positiva *f*, copia *f*; (*dress, fabric*) estampado *m*.

2 *attr dress* estampado; ~ **queue** cola *f* de espera para impresión; ~ **speed** velocidad *f* de impresión; ~ **wheel** rueda *f* impresora.

3 *vt* imprimir; (*on the mind etc*) grabar; *book etc* imprimir; sacar a luz, dar a la estampa, publicar; (*Phot*) imprimir; *cloth, pattern* estampar; (*write plainly*) escribir en caracteres de imprenta, escribir en letras de molde; **the ~ed word** la palabra impresa; **~ed by** impreso por; **they ~ed 300 copies** tiraron 300 ejemplares, hicieron una tirada de 300 ejemplares.

◆**print off** *vt* imprimir.

◆**print out** *vt* imprimir.

printable ['prɪntəbl] *adj* imprimible.

printed ['prɪntɪd] *adj* impreso; *dress* estampado; ~ **circuit** circuito *m* impreso; ~ **matter** impresos *mpl*; ~ **paper rate** (*Brit*) tarifa *f* de impreso.

printer ['prɪntəʳ] *n* (**a**) (*person*) impresor *m*; **~'s ink** tinta *f* de imprenta; **~'s mark** pie *m* de imprenta. (**b**) (*Comput*) impresora *f*.

printhead ['prɪnthed] *n* cabeza *f* impresora.

printing ['prɪntɪŋ] **1** *n* (**a**) (*art*) tipografía *f*, imprenta *f*; **'16th century ~ in Toledo'** 'la imprenta en Toledo en el siglo XVI'.

(**b**) (*act*) impresión *f*; (*quantity*) **4th** ~ 4ª impresión; **a ~ of 500 copies** una tirada de 500 ejemplares.

2 *attr*: ~ **frame** prensa *f* de copiar; ~ **ink** tinta *f* de imprenta; ~ **office** imprenta *f*; ~ **press** imprenta *f*, prensa *f*; ~ **queue** cola *f* de impresión; ~ **works** imprenta *f*.

printout ['prɪntaʊt] *n* print-out *m*, output *m*, listado *m*, impresión *f*.

print-run ['prɪntrʌn] *n* tirada *f*.

print-shop ['prɪntʃɒp] *n* (*Typ*) taller *m* de impresión; (*art shop*) tienda *f* de cuadros.

prior ['praɪəʳ] **1** *adj* anterior, previo; *claim etc* preferente.

2 *adv* (**a**) ~ **to** antes de; hasta; ~ **to this discovery** antes de este descubrimiento. (**b**) (*US*) antes; **it happened 2 days** ~ ocurrió 2 días antes.

3 *n* (*Eccl*) prior *m*.

prioress ['praɪərɪs] *n* priora *f*.

prioritize [praɪ'ɒrɪtaɪz] *vt* (*esp US*) priorizar.

priority [praɪ'ɒrɪtɪ] **1** *n* prioridad *f*; (*in time*) anterioridad *f*, antelación *f*, precedencia *f*; **to give sth first** (*or* **top**) ~ dar la máxima prioridad a algo, priorizar algo de modo absoluto; **to have** (*or* **take**) ~ tener prioridad (*over sb* sobre uno); **they will be given out in strict order of** ~ se distribuirán estrictamente de acuerdo con prioridades; **we must get our priorities right** hemos de establecer un justo orden de prioridades. **2** *attr* prioritario; preferente; ~ **case** caso *m* prioritario; ~ **share** acción *f* prioritaria; ~ **treatment** trato *m* preferente.

priory ['praɪərɪ] *n* priorato *m*.

prise [praɪz] *vt* (*Brit*): **to ~ open** abrir por fuerza, abrir con una palanca; **to ~ a lid up** levantar una tapa con una palanca; **we had to ~ the secret out of him** tuvimos que sacarle el secreto a la fuerza; **to ~ sb out of his post** lograr que uno renuncie a su puesto, desahuciar a uno.

◆**prise off** *vt* arrancar.

prism ['prɪzəm] *n* prisma *m*.

prismatic [prɪz'mætɪk] *adj* prismático.

prison ['prɪzn] **1** *n* cárcel *f*, prisión *f*; **to be in** ~ estar en la cárcel; **to go to ~ for 5 years** ser condenado a 5 años de prisión; pasar 5 años en la cárcel; **to put sb in ~, to send sb to** ~ encarcelar a uno; **to send sb to ~ for 2 years** condenar a uno a 2 años de prisión.

2 *attr* carcelario; ~ **break** fuga *f* (de la cárcel); ~ **camp** campamento *m* para prisioneros; ~ **governor** (*Brit*), ~ **warden** (*US*) director *m*, -ora *f* de (la) prisión; ~ **life** vida *f* en la cárcel; ~ **officer** carcelero *m*, -a *f*; ~ **population** población *f* reclusa; ~ **riot** motín *m* carcelario; ~ **system** sistema *m* penitenciario; ~ **term** condena *f*; ~ **van** coche *m* celular; ~ **visitor** visitante *mf* de un prisionero; ~ **yard** patio *m* de (la) cárcel.

prisoner ['prɪznəʳ] *n* (*under arrest*) detenido *m*, -a *f*; (*facing charge*, ~ **at the bar**) acusado *m*, -a *f*; (*convicted*) preso *m*, -a *f*; (*Mil*) prisionero *m*, -a *f*; ~ **of conscience** preso *m*, -a *f* de conciencia; ~ **of war** prisionero *m*, -a *f* de guerra; **to hold sb** ~ detener a uno; **to take sb** ~ hacer prisionero a uno.

prissy* ['prɪsɪ] *adj* remilgado, repipi*.

pristine ['prɪstaɪn] *adj* prístino.

privacy ['prɪvəsɪ] *n* soledad *f*, retiro *m*, aislamiento *m*; vida *f* privada; intimidad *f*; (*secrecy*) secreto *m*, reserva *f*; sigilo *m*; (*Comput*) privacidad *f*, confidencialidad *f*; **desire for** ~ deseo *m* de estar a solas; **in search of some** ~ en busca de soledad; **there is no ~ in these flats** en estos pisos no hay vida privada; **in the ~ of one's home** en la intimidad de su casa; **in the strictest** ~ en el mayor secreto, con el mayor sigilo; **to invade sb's** ~ invadir la soledad de uno; **P~ Act** ≃ Ley *f* del Derecho a la Intimidad.

private ['praɪvɪt] **1** *adj* privado; particular; (*for ~ use*) propio, personal; (*confidential*) secreto, reservado, confidencial; *life* privado, íntimo; *conversation, letter* íntimo, entre los dos; *opinion* personal; *arrangement, car, company, entrance, house, interview, lesson, room, school, etc* particular; *hearing, sitting* secreto, a puertas cerradas; *report* secreto, confidencial; **'~'** 'propiedad particular'; **'~ and confidential'** 'privado y confidencial'; ~ **detective** detective *m* privado; ~ **enterprise** iniciativa *f* privada; ~ **eye*** detective *m*; ~ **finance** finanzas *fpl* privadas; ~ **income,** ~ **means** renta *f* de fuente particular; ~ **limited company** sociedad *f* de responsabilidad limitada; ~ **health care** servicio *m* médico privado; ~ **line** (*Telec*) línea *f* particular; ~ **member** miembro *mf* (que no es ministro); ~ **member's bill** proyecto *m* de ley presentado por un miembro (no por el gobierno); ~ **patient** paciente *m* privado, paciente *f* privada; ~ **parts** partes *fpl* pudendas; ~ **practice** (*Med*) consulta *f* privada; ~ **property** propiedad *f* privada; ~ **prosecution** demanda *f* civil; ~ **secretary** secretario *m*, -a *f* particular; ~ **sector** sector *m* privado; ~ **soldier** soldado *m* raso; ~ **view** inauguración *f*; **my ~ opinion is that** ... yo creo para mí que ..., mi opinión personal es que ...; **the wedding was** ~ la ceremonia se celebró en la intimidad; **to keep a matter** ~ guardar el secreto de un asunto, no divulgar un asunto; **he's a very ~ person** es una persona muy reservada; **they want to be** ~ quieren estar a solas; **to go** ~ (*Med*) ir a lo privado, ir a particular.

2 *n* (**a**) (*Mil*) soldado *m* raso; **P~ Jones** el soldado Jones; **P~ Jones!** ¡Jones!

(**b**) **in** ~ en privado; en secreto; de persona a persona, entre los dos; confidencialmente; **I have been told in ~ that** ... me han dicho confidencialmente que ...; **the committee sat in** ~ la comisión se reunió puerta cerrada; **the wedding was held in** ~ la ceremonia se celebró en la intimidad.

(**c**) **~s** (*Anat*) partes *fpl* pudendas.

privateer [,praɪvə'tɪəʳ] *n* corsario *m*.

privately ['praɪvɪtlɪ] *adv* privadamente, en privado; en secreto; particularmente; **the meeting was held** ~ la reunión fue a puerta cerrada; **the wedding took place** ~ la ceremonia se celebró en la intimidad; ~ **I think that** ... personalmente creo que ...; **I have been told ~ that** ... me han dicho confidencialmente que ...; **but ~ he was very upset** pero en su corazón se sintió muy molesto; **so he spoke ~ to me** así que me habló privadamente; **he is being ~ educated** está en un colegio particular; tiene un profesor particular.

privation [praɪ'veɪʃən] *n* (**a**) (*state*) privación *f*, miseria *f*, estrechez *f*; **to live in** ~ vivir en la miseria. (**b**) (*hardship*) privaciones *fpl*, apuro *m*; **to suffer many ~s** pasar muchos apuros.

privative ['prɪvətɪv] **1** *adj* privativo. **2** *n* privativo *m*.

privatization [,praɪvətaɪ'zeɪʃən] *n* privatización *f*.

privatize ['praɪvətaɪz] *vt* privatizar.

privatizing ['praɪvətaɪzɪŋ] *n* privatización *f*.

privet ['prɪvɪt] *n* ligustro *m*, alheña *f*.

privilege ['prɪvɪlɪdʒ] **1** *n* privilegio *m*; prerrogativa *f*; (*Jur, Parl*) inmunidad *f*; **to have parliamentary** ~ gozar de la inmunidad parlamentaria.

2 *vt*: **to be ~d to** + *infin* tener el privilegio de + *infin*.

privileged ['prɪvɪlɪdʒd] *adj* privilegiado; *information* confidencial; *speech* que goza de la inmunidad parlamentaria (*etc*); **for a ~ few** para unos pocos afortunados.

privily ['prɪvɪlɪ] *adv* privadamente, en privado; *tell etc* confidencialmente.

privy ['prɪvɪ] **1** *adj* (**a**) **to be ~ to sth** estar enterado secretamente de algo. (**b**) (*Brit*) **P~ Council** Consejo *m* Privado (del monarca); **P~ Councillor** consejero *m*, -a *f* del Consejo Privado; **P~ Purse** gastos *mpl* personales del monarca. **2** *n* retrete *m*.

prize¹ [praɪz] **1** *n* (**a**) premio *m*; galardón *m*; **first** ~ primer premio *m*; (*in lottery*) el gordo; ~ **day** día *m* de distribución de premios; **to carry off the ~, to win the** ~ ganar el premio.

(**b**) (*Naut*) presa *f*; ~ **court** tribunal *m* de presas marítimas.

2 *adj entry, rose etc* galardonado, premiado; (*fig*) digno de premio; excelente, de primera clase; **he's a ~ idiot** es un tonto de capirote; **what a ~ idiot you are!** ¡imbécil!

3 *vt* apreciar, estimar; **to ~ sth highly** estimar algo en mucho.

prize² [praɪz] *vt* = **prise.**

prize draw ['praɪz,drɔː] *n* tómbola *f.*

prize fight ['praɪzfaɪt] *n* partido *m* de boxeo profesional.

prize fighter ['praɪzfaɪtəʳ] *n* boxeador *m* profesional.

prize fighting ['praɪz,faɪtɪŋ] *n* boxeo *m* profesional.

prize-giving ['praɪz,gɪvɪŋ] *n* distribución *f* de premios.

prize money ['praɪz,mʌnɪ] *n* (*Naut*) parte *f* de presa; (*cash*) premio *m* en metálico; (*Boxing*) bolsa *f.*

prize ring ['praɪz,rɪŋ] *n* (*Boxing*) ring *m.*

prizewinner ['praɪz,wɪnəʳ] *n* premiado *m*, -a *f.*

prizewinning ['praɪz,wɪnɪŋ] *adj* premiado.

PRO *n* (**a**) *abbr of* **Public Record Office** Archivo *m* Nacional.

(**b**) (*Comm etc*) *abbr of* **public relations officer.**

pro¹ [prəʊ] **1** *prep* (**a**) (*in favour of*) pro; en pro de.

(**b**) (*in compounds*) pro-; *eg* **~-Soviet** pro-soviético; **~-Spanish** hispanófilo; **~-European** europeísta; **they were terribly ~-Franco** eran unos franquistas furibundos, eran partidarios acérrimos de Franco.

(**c**) **~ forma** pro forma; **~ forma invoice** factura *f* pro forma, factura *f* simulada; **~ forma letter** carta *f* pro forma; **~ rata** a prorrateo, proporcionalmente; **the money will be shared out ~ rata** el dinero será repartido a prorrateo, se prorrateará el dinero; **a ~ rate agreement** (*US*) un acuerdo a prorrateo; **~ tempore, ~ tem*** por ahora, por el momento, interinamente.

2 *n*: **the ~s and the cons** el pro y el contra; **we are weighing up the ~s and the cons** estudiamos los argumentos a favor y en contra.

pro²* [prəʊ] *n* profesional *mf.*

pro³* [prəʊ] *n* (*prostitute*) puta *f.*

probability [,prɒbə'bɪlɪtɪ] *n* probabilidad *f*; **in all ~** sin duda, según toda probabilidad; **the ~ is that** ... es probable que + *subj.*

probable ['prɒbəbl] *adj* (**a**) (*likely*) probable; **it is ~ that** ... es probable que + *subj.* (**b**) (*credible*) verosímil.

probably ['prɒbəblɪ] *adv* probablemente; **he will ~ come, ~ he will come** es probable que venga; **he ~ forgot** lo habrá olvidado, a lo mejor lo olvidó; **~ not** quizá no; **very ~, but** ... bien puede ser, pero ...

probate ['prəʊbɪt] *n* verificación *f* oficial de los testamentos; **~ court** tribunal *m* de testamentarías; **to value sth for ~** evaluar algo para la verificación oficial de testamentos.

probation [prə'beɪʃən] **1** *n* (*Jur*) libertad *f* condicional, libertad *f* vigilada; **release on ~** libertad *f* a prueba; **to be on ~** estar en libertad condicional; **to put sb on ~** (*fig*) asignar a uno un período a prueba; **to take sth on ~** tomar algo a prueba.

2 *attr*: **~ officer** *oficial que vigila las personas que están en libertad condicional.*

probationary [prə'beɪʃnərɪ] *adj* de prueba; **~ period** (*Jur*) período *m* de libertad condicional, (*fig*) período *m* a (*or* de) prueba.

probationer [prə'beɪʃnəʳ] *n* (*Jur*) persona *f* en libertad condicional; (*Med*) aprendiz *mf* de ATS (*Sp*), aprendiz *mf* de enfermero; (*Eccl*) novicio *m*, -a *f.*

probe [prəʊb] **1** *n* (**a**) (*Med*) sonda *f*, tienta *f*; (*rocket*) cohete *m*, proyectil *m*; (*space ~*) vehículo *m* espacial, sonda *f.*

(**b**) (*inquiry*) investigación *f*, indagación *f*, encuesta *f*; **a ~ into the drug traffic** una investigación del tráfico de drogas.

2 *vt* (*Med*) sondar, tentar; *ground etc* sondar; (*explore*) explorar; (*search*) registrar; (*investigate*) investigar, indagar; **to ~ a mystery** investigar un misterio.

3 *vi* investigar; **to ~ into sb's past** investigar el pasado de uno; **you should have ~d more deeply** convenía hacer una investigación más a fondo.

probing ['prəʊbɪŋ] **1** *adj question etc* agudo, penetrante. **2** *n* sondeo *m*; investigación *f*; exploración *f.*

probity ['prəʊbɪtɪ] *n* probidad *f.*

problem ['prɒbləm] **1** *n* problema *m*; **the housing ~** el problema de la vivienda; (*more serious*) la crisis de la vivienda; **it's not my ~** no tiene que ver conmigo; **no ~!** ¡no hay problema!

2 *attr*: **~ child** niño *m*, -a *f* difícil, niño *m*, -a *f* problema; **~ page** consultorio *m*; **~ play** drama *m* de tesis.

problematic(al) [,prɒblɪ'mætɪk(əl)] *adj* problemático, dudoso; **it is ~ whether** ... es dudoso si ...

proboscis [prəʊ'bɒsɪs] *n* probóscide *f*, trompa *f*; (**: hum*) trompa* *f.*

procedural [prə'siːdjʊrəl] *adj* relativo al procedimiento; (*Jur*) procesal; **a ~ question** una cuestión de procedimiento.

procedure [prə'siːdʒəʳ] *n* procedimiento *m*; proceder *m*; trámites *mpl*, tramitación *f*; **the usual ~ is to** + *infin* lo que se hace por lo general es + *infin*; **the correct ~ would be to** + *infin* lo correcto sería + *infin.*

proceed [prə'siːd] *vi* (**a**) (*go*) proceder; **before we ~ any further** antes de ir más lejos, antes de seguir; **to ~ on one's way** seguir adelante, seguir su camino; **we ~ed to London** seguimos (viaje) a Londres; **we ~ed to the bar** nos trasladamos al bar; **the ship ~ed at 10 knots** el barco continuó a una velocidad de 10 nudos, el barco reanudó el viaje a una velocidad de 10 nudos; **cars should ~ slowly** los automóviles deberán seguir despacio; **let us ~ with caution** avancemos con precaución.

(**b**) (*go on to*) **how should we ~?** ¿cómo hemos de proceder?; **to ~ to blows** llegar a las manos; **to ~ to business** pasar a discutir los asuntos a tratar; **let us ~ to the next item** pasemos al punto siguiente; **to ~ to do sth** pasar a hacer algo, ponerse a hacer algo, empezar a hacer algo; **he ~ed to drink the lot** en seguida se lo bebió todo; **he ~ed to say that** ... dijo a continuación que ...

(**c**) (*continue*) continuar, seguir; **the text ~s thus** el texto sigue así; **things are ~ing according to plan** las cosas se están desarrollando según previsto; **how does the story ~ after that?** ¿cómo se desarrolla el argumento después de eso?; **they ~ed with their plan** prosiguieron su proyecto; **~!** ¡siga!

(**d**) **to ~ against sb** (*Jur etc*) proceder contra uno, procesar a uno.

(**e**) (*emerge*) **to ~ from** salir de; (*fig*) proceder de, provenir de; **sounds ~ed from the box** unos ruidos salían de la caja; **this ~s from ignorance** esto proviene de la ignorancia.

proceeding [prə'siːdɪŋ] *n* (**a**) (*way*) procedimiento *m*, modo *m* de proceder; proceder *m*; **the best ~** el mejor modo de proceder; **a somewhat dubious ~** un proceder sospechoso.

(**b**) **~s** (*ceremony etc*) acto *m*, actos *mpl*, función *f*; **the ~s began at 7 o'clock** el acto comenzó a las 7; **the ~s were orderly** en estos actos no sufrió alteración el orden público.

(**c**) **~s** (*of learned society*) actas *fpl*, transacciones *fpl*; **P~s of the Royal Society** Actas *fpl* de la Real Sociedad.

(**d**) **~s** (*measures*) medidas *fpl*; **to take ~s** tomar medidas; **to take ~s against sb** (*Jur*) proceder contra uno, procesar a uno; **to take legal ~s** entablar demanda, instruir causa.

proceeds ['prəʊsiːdz] *npl* importe *m* (de la recaudación *etc*); producto *m*, ingresos *mpl.*

process¹ ['prəʊses] **1** *n* (**a**) (*proceeding*) procedimiento *m*; proceso *m*; **the ~es of government** los trámites gubernamentales; **the ~es of the mind** los procedimientos de la mente; **by due ~ of law** por los justos procedimientos de la ley; **by a ~ of elimination** por un proceso de eliminación; **it's a very slow ~** es un proceso muy lento.

(**b**) (*course*) **in ~ of construction** bajo construcción, en construcción; **it is in ~ of reform** está siendo reformado; **it is in ~ of demolition** está siendo derribado; **in the ~ of time** con el tiempo, andando el tiempo; **in the ~ of cleaning the picture, they discovered** ... mientras limpiaban el cuadro, descubrieron ...; **we are in ~ of removal to** ... estamos en vía de trasladarnos a ...

(**c**) (*method*) método *m*, sistema *m*; (*Tech*) proceso *m*; **the Bessemer ~** el proceso de Bessemer.

(**d**) (*Jur*) proceso *m.*

(**e**) (*Anat, Bot etc*) proceso *m.*

2 *vt* (*Tech*) preparar; tratar; someter a un tratamiento especial; elaborar; *food* procesar, tratar; (*Phot*) revelar; *application* tramitar; *data* tratar, manejar.

process² [prə'ses] *vi* (*Brit*) desfilar.

process³ ['prəʊses] *adj* (*US*), **processed** ['prəʊsest] *adj food* procesado, tratado.

processing ['prəʊsesɪŋ] *n* preparación *f*; tratamiento *m*; elaboración *f*; **~ language** lenguaje *m* de procesamiento; **~ speed** velocidad *f* de procesamiento; **~ plant** planta *f* depuradora; **~ unit** unidad *f* central de proceso.

procession [prə'seʃən] *n* desfile *m*; (*Eccl*) procesión *f*; (*of funeral*) cortejo *m*, comitiva *f*; **to go** (*or* **walk**) **in ~** desfilar; (*Eccl*) ir en procesión.

processional [prə'seʃənl] *adj* procesional.

processor ['prəʊsesəʳ] *n* unidad *f* central, procesador *m.*

process-server ['prəʊses,sɜːvəʳ] *n* notificador *m*, -ora *f*, ujier *m.*

proclaim [prəˈkleɪm] **1** *vt* (**a**) (*announce*) proclamar; **to ~ sb king** proclamar a uno rey.
(**b**) (*reveal*) revelar, anunciar; **his tone ~ed his confidence** su tono declaraba su optimismo; **their faces ~ed their guilt** su culpabilidad se revelaba en las caras.
2 *vr*: **to ~ o.s. king** proclamarse rey.
proclamation [ˌprɒkləˈmeɪʃən] *n* (*act*) proclamación *f*; (*document*) proclama *f*.
proclivity [prəˈklɪvɪtɪ] *n* propensión *f*, inclinación *f*.
proconsul [ˌprəʊˈkɒnsəl] *n* procónsul *m*.
procrastinate [prəʊˈkræstɪneɪt] *vi* aplazar una decisión, no resolverse; andarse con dilaciones; procurar ganar tiempo.
procrastination [prəʊˌkræstɪˈneɪʃən] *n* dilación *f*, falta *f* de resolución.
procreate [ˈprəʊkrɪeɪt] *vt* procrear.
procreation [ˌprəʊkrɪˈeɪʃən] *n* procreación *f*.
Procrustean [prəʊˈkrʌstɪən] *adj* de Procusto.
Procrustes [prəʊˈkrʌstiːz] *nm* Procusto.
proctor [ˈprɒktəʳ] **1** *n* (*Jur*) procurador *m*; (*Brit Univ*) censor *m*, *oficial que cuida de la disciplina*, (*US Univ*) celador *m*, -ora *f*. **2** *vti* (*US*) vigilar.
procurable [prəˈkjʊərəbl] *adj* asequible; **easily ~** muy asequible.
procurator [ˈprɒkjʊreɪtəʳ] *n* procurador *m*, -ora *f*; **P~ Fiscal** (*Scot*) fiscal *mf*.
procure [prəˈkjʊəʳ] **1** *vt* (**a**) (*obtain*) obtener, conseguir; lograr; gestionar; **to ~ sb sth, to ~ sth for sb** obtener algo para uno; **to ~ some relief** conseguir cierto alivio.
(**b**) **to ~ a girl** (*Jur*) obtener una joven para una casa de prostitución.
2 *vi* alcahuetear, dedicarse al proxenetismo.
procurement [prəˈkjʊəmənt] **1** *n* obtención *f*, consecución *f*. **2** *attr*: **~ agency** agencia *f* de aprovisionamiento; **~ price** precio *m* al productor.
procurer [prəˈkjʊərəʳ] *n* alcahuete *m*, proxeneta *m*.
procuress [prəˈkjʊərɪs] *n* alcahueta *f*, proxeneta *f*.
procuring [prəˈkjʊərɪŋ] *n* alcahuetería *f*, proxenetismo *m*.
prod [prɒd] **1** *n* (*push*) empuje *m*; (*with elbow*) codazo *m*; (*jab*) pinchazo *m*; **to give sb a ~** dar un pinchazo a uno (*also fig*); **he needs an occasional ~** hay que pincharle de vez en cuando.
2 *vt* (*push*) empujar; (*with elbow*) codear, dar un codazo a; (*jab*) pinchar, punzar; (*with goad*) agujar; **he has to be ~ded along** hay que empujarle constantemente hacia adelante; **he needs to be ~ded** hay que pincharle; **to ~ sb to do sth** instar a uno a hacer algo.
3 *vi*: **he ~ded at the picture with a finger** indicó el cuadro con un movimiento brusco del dedo, dio con el dedo en el cuadro.
prodigal [ˈprɒdɪgəl] **1** *adj* pródigo; **~ of** pródigo de, pródigo en; **the ~ son** el hijo pródigo. **2** *n* pródigo *m*, -a *f*.
prodigality [ˌprɒdɪˈgælɪtɪ] *n* prodigalidad *f*.
prodigious [prəˈdɪdʒəs] *adj* prodigioso; enorme, vasto, ingente.
prodigiously [prəˈdɪdʒəslɪ] *adv* prodigiosamente, maravillosamente.
prodigy [ˈprɒdɪdʒɪ] *n* prodigio *m*; portento *m*; **child ~, infant ~** niño *m* prodigio.
produce 1 [ˈprɒdjuːs] *n* producto *m*; (*Agr*) productos *mpl* agrícolas; **'~ of Spain'** 'producto *m* de España'.
2 [ˈprɒdjuːs] *attr*: **~ dealer** (*US*) verdulero *m*, -a *f*.
3 [prəˈdjuːs] *vt* (**a**) (*bring forward, show*) presentar, mostrar; *proof* aducir, presentar; **he ~d it from his pocket** lo sacó del bolsillo; **he seemed to ~ it out of thin air** parece que lo sacó de la nada; **how can I ~ £500?** ¿dónde voy yo a buscar 500 libras?; **'please ~ your tickets'** 'se ruega mostrar los billetes'; **he could ~ no witnesses** no pudo nombrar ningún testigo.
(**b**) (*Theat*) *play* presentar, poner en escena; representar, dar; (*Cine, TV*) realizar; *actors* dirigir; **when we last ~d 'Hamlet'** cuando representamos 'Hamlet' la última vez; **a well ~d play** una obra bien montada, una obra bien realizada.
(**c**) *line* prolongar.
(**d**) (*manufacture*) producir, fabricar; (*yield*) producir; *crop, fruit* dar; *interest, profit* rendir; *offspring* dar a luz, tener; **he ~s 3 novels a year** escribe (*or* publica) 3 novelas al año; **it ~s 200 watts** da 200 vatios, produce 200 vatios; **the mine ~s 20 tons of lead** la mina produce 20 toneladas de plomo; **Ireland does not ~ atomic bombs** Irlanda no fabrica bombas atómicas.
(**e**) (*cause*) causar, motivar, ocasionar, producir; acarrear; **it ~d great alarm** causó mucha alarma; **this ~d a sensation** esto causó una sensación; **what impression does it ~ on you?** ¿qué impresión te produce?
4 [prəˈdjuːs] *vi* (**a**) (*mine etc*) producir.
(**b**) (*Theat etc*) dirigir; **who is going to ~?** ¿quién va a dirigir?
producer [prəˈdjuːsəʳ] *n* productor *m*, -ora *f*; (*Theat*) director *m*, -ora *f* de escena; (*Cine*) productor *m*, -ora *f*; (*TV*) productor *m*, -ora *f*, realizador *m*, -ora *f*.
-producing [prəˈdjʊsɪŋ] *adj ending in compounds* productor de ...; **oil~** productor de petróleo; **one of the most important coal~ countries** uno de los principales países productores de carbón.
product [ˈprɒdʌkt] **1** *n* (**a**) (*thing produced*) producto *m*; (*result*) fruto *m*, resultado *m*, consecuencia *f*; **meat ~** derivado *m* cárnico. (**b**) (*Math*) producto *m*. **2** *attr*: **~ liability** responsabilidad *f* del fabricante; **~ research** investigación *f* del producto.
production [prəˈdʌkʃən] **1** *n* (**a**) (*act of showing*) presentación *f*; **on ~ of this card** presentando esta tarjeta, mediante presentación de esta tarjeta.
(**b**) (*Tech etc*) producción *f*, rendimiento *m*; **the country's steel ~** la producción nacional de acero; **the factory is in full ~** la fábrica trabaja a plena capacidad.
(**c**) (*product*) producto *m*; (*Art, Liter etc*) obra *f*.
(**d**) (*Theat*: *performance*) presentación *f*; representación *f*; (*by producer, of actor*) dirección *f*; (*Cine, TV*) realización *f*; **'Peribáñez: a new ~ by ...'** 'Peribáñez: nueva presentación a cargo de ...'.
2 *attr* (**a**) **~ agreement** (*US*) acuerdo *m* de productividad; (*Comm*) **~ bonus** prima *f* por rendimiento; **~ control** control *m* de producción; **~ line** línea *f* de montaje; **~ manager** encargado *m*, -a *f* (*or* jefe *mf*) de producción.
(**b**) (*Cine, TV*) **~ assistant** ayudante *mf* de realización; **~ manager** jefe *mf* de realización.
productive [prəˈdʌktɪv] *adj* (**a**) productivo; provechoso; eficaz; **the factory is not yet fully ~** la fábrica todavía no trabaja a plena capacidad.
(**b**) **~ of** fértil en, prolífico en; **to be ~ of error** tener tendencia a causar errores; **it is ~ of nothing but trouble** no produce sino disgustos.
productively [prəˈdʌktɪvlɪ] *adv* de manera productiva; provechosamente, de manera provechosa; eficazmente.
productivity [ˌprɒdʌkˈtɪvɪtɪ] **1** *n* productividad *f*; rendimiento *m*; **when it is in full ~** cuando esté trabajando a plena capacidad.
2 *attr*: **~ agreement** (*Brit*) acuerdo *m* de productividad; **~ bonus** prima *f* por rendimiento, bono *m* de productividad.
Prof. [prɒf] *n abbr of* **professor** profesor *m*, -ora *f*, Prof.
prof* [prɒf] *n* profe *m*.
profanation [ˌprɒfəˈneɪʃən] *n* profanación *f*.
profane [prəˈfeɪn] **1** *adj* (**a**) (*secular, uninitiated, lay*) profano; (*irreverent*) profano, sacrílego, blasfemo.
(**b**) *language etc* fuerte, indecente; **he's very ~** es un malhablado; **don't be ~!** ¡no digas palabrotas!; **he became ~** empezó a jurar.
2 *vt* profanar.
profanity [prəˈfænɪtɪ] *n* (*V adj*) (**a**) profanidad *f*; blasfemia *f*, impiedad *f*.
(**b**) lenguaje *m* indecente, palabrotas *fpl*; **to utter a string of profanities** soltar una serie de palabrotas.
profess [prəˈfes] **1** *vt faith, belief etc* profesar; (*assent*) afirmar, declarar; *regret etc* manifestar; *ignorance etc* confesar; **I do not ~ to be an expert** no pretendo ser un experto; **he ~es to know all about it** afirma estar enterado de ello; **she ~es to be 25** dice tener 25 años, afirma tener 25 años.
2 *vr*: **to ~ o.s. satisfied** declararse satisfecho; **to ~ o.s. unable to** + *infin* declararse incapaz de + *infin*.
professed [prəˈfest] *adj* declarado; (*pej*) supuesto, ostensible; (*Eccl*) profeso.
professedly [prəˈfesɪdlɪ] *adv* declaradamente; (*pej*) supuestamente.
profession [prəˈfeʃən] *n* (**a**) (*declaration*) profesión *f*, declaración *f*; **~ of faith** profesión *f* de fe. (**b**) (*calling*) profesión *f*; oficio *m*; carrera *f*; **by ~ he is an engineer** es ingeniero de oficio.
professional [prəˈfeʃənl] **1** *adj* (**a**) profesional; de profesión, de oficio; **~ charges, ~ fees** honorarios *mpl*, derechos *mpl*; **~ diplomat** diplomático *m*, -a *f* de carrera; **~ foul** falta *f* profesional; **~ liability** responsabilidad *f* profesional; **~ man** hombre *m* profesional; **~ qualifications** títulos *mpl* profesionales; **~ services** servicios *mpl*

profesionales; ~ **standing** reputación *f* profesional; **he's a ~ thug** es un matón de oficio.

(**b**) (*competent*) experto, perito.

2 *n* profesional *mf*; (*of golf-club*) maestro *m*, -a *f*.

professionalism [prəˈfeʃnəlɪzəm] *n* (**a**) (*of person, employment*) profesionalismo *m*. (**b**) (*of book etc*) excelencia *f*, alta calidad *f*, pericia *f*.

professionally [prəˈfeʃnəlɪ] *adv* (**a**) profesionalmente; **I never met him ~** no le conocí nunca en su cargo profesional; **X, known ~ as Y** X conocido por Y en la profesión.

(**b**) (*fig*) expertamente, con pericia; **they did it most ~** lo hicieron expertamente.

professor [prəˈfesəʳ] *n* profesor *m* (universitario), profesora *f* (universitaria), catedrático *m*, -a *f*.

professorial [ˌprɒfəˈsɔːrɪəl] *adj* de profesor, de catedrático; profesoral.

professorship [prəˈfesəʃɪp] *n* cátedra *f*; **to be appointed to a ~** obtener una cátedra, ser nombrado a una cátedra.

proffer [ˈprɒfəʳ] *vt* ofrecer.

proficiency [prəˈfɪʃənsɪ] **1** *n* pericia *f*, habilidad *f*, competencia *f*. **2** *attr*: ~ **test** examen *m* de suficiencia.

proficient [prəˈfɪʃənt] *adj* perito, hábil, competente (*at, in* en).

profile [ˈprəʊfaɪl] **1** *n* perfil *m* (*also fig*); **in ~** de perfil; **to keep** (*or* **maintain**) **a high ~** tratar de llamar la atención; **to keep** (*or* **maintain**) **a low ~** tratar de pasar inadvertido, adoptar una actitud discreta. **2** *vt* (*fig*) *person* retratar, hacer el retrato de; *situation* describir, analizar.

profit [ˈprɒfɪt] **1** *n* (*Comm*) ganancia *f*; (*fig*) provecho *m*, beneficio *m*; utilidad *f*, ventaja *f*; **~s** ganancias *fpl*, utilidades *fpl*, beneficios *mpl*; ~ **and loss** ganancias *fpl* y pérdidas; **to make a ~ of two millions** ganar dos millones, sacar una ganancia de dos millones; **to make a ~ on a deal** salir ganando en un negocio; **to show** (*or* **yield**) **a ~** dar dinero, rendir una ganancia; **to sell sth at a ~** vender algo con ganancia; **to turn sth to ~** aprovecharse de algo.

2 *attr*: ~ **and loss account** cuenta *f* de ganancias y pérdidas; ~ **center** (*US*), ~ **centre** centro *m* de beneficios; ~ **margin** margen *m* de beneficios, margen *m* de utilidad; ~ **motive** afán *m* de lucro; ~ **squeeze** reducción *f* de los márgenes de beneficio; **~s tax** impuesto *m* sobre los beneficios, impuesto *m* sobre las utilidades.

3 *vt* servir a, aprovechar a, ser de utilidad a; **what will it ~ him to go?** ¿qué le aprovechará ir?

4 *vi* ganar; (*Comm*) sacar ganancia; **he does not seem to have ~ed** no parece haber sacado provecho de ello; **to ~ by, to ~ from** aprovechar, beneficiarse de, sacar partido de; **to ~ by the mistakes of others** escarmentar en cabeza ajena.

profitability [ˌprɒfɪtəˈbɪlɪtɪ] *n* rentabilidad *f*.

profitable [ˈprɒfɪtəbl] *adj* provechoso, útil; ventajoso; (*Comm*) lucrativo; (*economic to run etc*) rentable; **a most ~ trip** un viaje sumamente provechoso; **a ~ investment** una inversión lucrativa; **the line is no longer ~** la línea ya no es rentable; **it would be ~ to you to read this** te beneficiarás de leer esto, te sería útil leer esto.

profitably [ˈprɒfɪtəblɪ] *adv* con provecho, provechosamente; (*Comm*) lucrativamente, con lucro.

profiteer [ˌprɒfɪˈtɪəʳ] **1** *n* acaparador *m*, -ora *f*, él (*or* la) que hace ganancias excesivas; (*black marketeer*) estraperlista *mf*. **2** *vi* hacer ganancias excesivas, cobrar más de lo justo.

profiteering [ˌprɒfɪˈtɪərɪŋ] *n* ganancias *fpl* excesivas.

profitless [ˈprɒfɪtlɪs] *adj* inútil.

profitlessly [ˈprɒfɪtlɪslɪ] *adv* inútilmente.

profit-making [ˈprɒfɪtˌmeɪkɪŋ] *adj*: **a ~ organization** una organización lucrativa.

profit-related [ˈprɒfɪtrəˈleɪtɪd] *adj*: ~ **bonus** prima *f* relacionada con los beneficios.

profit-seeking [ˈprɒfɪtˌsiːkɪŋ] *adj* de fines lucrativos, lucrativo.

profit-sharing [ˈprɒfɪtˌʃɛərɪŋ] *n* (*by workers*) participación *f* directa en los beneficios; (*by company*) reparto *m* de los beneficios.

profit-taking [ˈprɒfɪtˌteɪkɪŋ] *n* realización *f* de beneficios.

profligacy [ˈprɒflɪgəsɪ] *n* libertinaje *m*; prodigalidad *f*.

profligate [ˈprɒflɪgɪt] **1** *adj* (*dissolute*) libertino, disoluto; (*extravagant*) manirroto, pródigo. **2** *n* libertino *m*; manirroto *m*, despilfarrador *m*.

pro-form [ˈprəʊˌfɔːm] *n* (*Ling*) pro forma *f*.

profound [prəˈfaʊnd] *adj* profundo.

profoundly [prəˈfaʊndlɪ] *adv* profundamente.

profundity [prəˈfʌndɪtɪ] *n* profundidad *f*.

profuse [prəˈfjuːs] *adj* profuso; pródigo (*in* en); **to be ~ in one's apologies** disculparse con efusión.

profusely [prəˈfjuːslɪ] *adv* profusamente; pródigamente; **he apologized ~** se disculpó con efusión; **to sweat ~** sudar muchísimo.

profusion [prəˈfjuːʒən] *n* profusión *f*, abundancia *f*; prodigalidad *f*; derroche *m*; **a ~ of colour** un derroche de color; **a ~ of flowers** una abundancia de flores; **trees in ~** árboles *mpl* abundantes, muchísimos árboles *mpl*.

progenitor [prəʊˈdʒenɪtəʳ] *n* progenitor *m*.

progeny [ˈprɒdʒɪnɪ] *n* progenie *f*, prole *f*.

progesterone [prəʊˈdʒestərəʊn] *n* progesterona *f*.

prognosis [prɒgˈnəʊsɪs] *n*, *pl* **prognoses** [prɒgˈnəʊsiːz] pronóstico *m*.

prognostic [prɒgˈnɒstɪk] *n* pronóstico *m*.

prognosticate [prɒgˈnɒstɪkeɪt] *vt* pronosticar.

prognostication [prɒgˌnɒstɪˈkeɪʃən] *n* (*act, art*) pronosticación *f*; (*forecast*) pronóstico *m*.

programmable, (*US, also freq Comput*) **programable** [ˈprəʊgræməbl] *adj* programable.

programme, (*US, also freq Comput*) **program** [ˈprəʊgræm] **1** *n* programa *m*. **2** *attr*: ~ **music** música *f* de programa; ~ **notes** notas *fpl* de programa. **3** *vt* (*Comput*) programar; **it is ~d to** + *infin* está programado para + *infin*.

programmed, (*US*) **programed** [ˈprəʊgræmd] *adj* programado; ~ **learning,** ~ **teaching** enseñanza *f* programada.

programmer, (*US*) **programer** [ˈprəʊgræməʳ] *n* programador *m*, -ora *f*.

programming, (*US*) **programing** [ˈprəʊgræmɪŋ] **1** *n* programación *f*. **2** *attr*: ~ **environment** entorno *m* de programación; ~ **language** lenguaje *m* de programación.

progress 1 [ˈprəʊgres] *n* progreso *m*; progresos *mpl*; (*of events etc*) marcha *f*, desarrollo *m*; (*of disease*) desarrollo *m*, evolución *f*; **the ~ of events** la marcha de los acontecimientos; **the ~ of a student** los progresos de un estudiante; **it is in ~** está en vía de realizarse (*etc*); **harvesting is in full ~** la cosecha está en plena marcha; **the game was already in ~** había comenzado ya el partido; **to make** (**some**) **~** hacer progresos, progresar; **to make slow ~** avanzar despacio; **I can't make any ~ with this child** no hago carrera con esta niño.

2 [ˈprəʊgres] *attr*: ~ **report** informe *m* sobre la labor realizada; informe *m* interino.

3 [prəˈgres] *vi* hacer progresos, progresar; avanzar; desarrollarse; **as the game ~ed** a medida que iba desarrollándose el partido; **matters are ~ing slowly** las cosas avanzan lentamente; **how is the student ~ing?** ¿qué progresos hace el estudiante?; **the patient is ~ing favourably** el enfermo está mejorando de modo satisfactorio.

4 [prəˈgres] *vt* seguir adelante con.

progression [prəˈgreʃən] *n* progresión *f*.

progressive [prəˈgresɪv] **1** *adj* progresivo; (*Pol*) progresista; ~ **tax** impuesto *m* progresivo. **2** *n* progresista *mf*.

progressively [prəˈgresɪvlɪ] *adv* progresivamente; (*Pol*) de modo progresista; **it diminishes ~** disminuye progresivamente; **it's getting ~ better** se va haciendo cada vez mejor.

progressiveness [prəˈgresɪvnɪs] *n* carácter *m* progresista.

prohibit [prəˈhɪbɪt] *vt* (**a**) (*forbid*) prohibir; **to ~ sb from doing sth** prohibir a uno hacer algo; **'it is ~ed to feed the animals'** 'se prohibe dar de comer a los animales'; **'smoking ~ed'** 'se prohibe fumar', 'prohibido fumar'; **~ed area** zona *f* prohibida.

(**b**) (*prevent*) impedir; **to ~ sb from doing sth** impedir a uno hacer algo; **his health ~s him from swimming** su salud le impide nadar.

prohibition [ˈprəʊɪˈbɪʃən] *n* prohibición *f*; (*US*) prohibicionismo *m*; ley *f* seca.

prohibitionism [ˌprəʊɪˈbɪʃənɪzəm] *n* prohibicionismo *m*.

prohibitionist [ˌprəʊɪˈbɪʃənɪst] **1** *adj* prohibicionista. **2** *n* prohibicionista *mf*.

prohibitive [prəˈhɪbɪtɪv] *adj* prohibitivo; *price* imposible.

prohibitively [prəˈhɪbɪtɪvlɪ] *adv*: ~ **expensive** imposiblemente caro.

prohibitory [prəˈhɪbɪtərɪ] *adj* prohibitorio.

project 1 [ˈprɒdʒekt] *n* proyecto *m*. **2** [prəˈdʒekt] *vt* proyectar; **~ed costs** gastos *mpl* previstos, gastos *mpl* presupuestados. **3** [prəˈdʒekt] *vi* salir, sobresalir, resaltar; **to ~ beyond** sobresalir más allá de; **to ~ over** sobresalir por encima de.

projectile [prəˈdʒektaɪl] *n* proyectil *m*.

projecting [prəˈdʒektɪŋ] *adj* saliente, saledizo.

projection [prəˈdʒekʃən] *n* (**a**) proyección *f*; (*overhang etc*) saliente *m*, resalto *m*; (*knob etc*) protuberancia *f*. (**b**)

(*Fin*) proyección *f*.
projectionist [prəˈdʒekʃnɪst] *n* operador *m*, -ora *f* (de proyector), proyectista *mf*.
projection room [prəˈdʒekʃən,rʊm] *n* cabina *f* (de proyección).
project manager [ˈprɒdʒekt,mænɪdʒəʳ] *n* director *m*, -ora *f* de proyecto.
projector [prəˈdʒektəʳ] *n* proyector *m* (de películas).
prolapse [ˈprəʊlæps] *n* prolapso *m*.
proles [prəʊlz] *npl* proletarios *mpl*.
proletarian [,prəʊləˈtɛərɪən] **1** *adj* proletario. **2** *n* proletario *m*, -a *f*.
proletarianize [,prəʊləˈtɛərɪənaɪz] *vt* proletariar.
proletariat [,prəʊləˈtɛərɪət] *n* proletariado *m*.
proliferate [prəˈlɪfəreɪt] **1** *vt* multiplicar; extender. **2** *vi* proliferar, multiplicarse; extenderse.
proliferation [prə,lɪfəˈreɪʃən] *n* proliferación *f*, multiplicación *f*; extensión *f*.
prolific [prəˈlɪfɪk] *adj* prolífico (*of* en).
prolix [ˈprəʊlɪks] *adj* prolijo.
prolixity [prəʊˈlɪksɪtɪ] *n* prolijidad *f*.
prologue, (*US*) **prolog** [ˈprəʊlɒg] *n* prólogo *m* (*to* de).
prolong [prəˈlɒŋ] *vt* (*in space*) prolongar, extender; (*in time*) alargar, extender.
prolongation [,prəʊlɒŋˈgeɪʃən] *n* prolongación *f*, alargamiento *m*, extensión *f*.
prolonged [prəˈlɒŋd] *adj absence, leave etc* prolongado; *event, period, struggle* (muy) largo; **at this there was ~ applause** esto fue aplaudido durante varios minutos.
prom* [prɒm] *n* (**a**) (*Brit*) = **promenade concert.** (**b**) (*seaside* ~) paseo *m* marítimo. (**c**) (*US*) *baile de gala bajo los auspicios de los alumnos de un colegio.*
promenade [,prɒmɪˈnɑːd] **1** *n* (**a**) (*act*) paseo *m*.
(**b**) (*avenue*) paseo *m*, avenida *f*; (*at seaside*) paseo *m* marítimo.
2 *attr*: ~ **concert** (*Brit*) *concierto en el que una parte del público permanece de pie*; ~ **deck** cubierta *f* de paseo.
3 *vt* pasear.
4 *vi* pasearse.
Prometheus [prəˈmiːθjuːs] *nm* Prometeo.
prominence [ˈprɒmɪnəns] *n* prominencia *f*; (*fig*) eminencia *f*, importancia *f*; **to bring sth into ~** hacer que algo destaque; **he came into ~ in the Cuba affair** empezó a sobresalir cuando lo de Cuba; **that aspect is coming into ~** ese aspecto está adquiriendo importancia.
prominent [ˈprɒmɪnənt] *adj* (*jutting out*) prominente; *cheekbone, tooth etc* saliente; *eye* saltón; (*fig*) eminente, importante, notable, destacado; **the most ~ article in the window** el objeto que más salta a la vista en el escaparate; **the most ~ feature of this theory** el aspecto más notable de esta teoría; **put it in a ~ position** ponlo muy a la vista; **to be ~ in a deal** desempeñar un papel importante en un negocio; **she is ~ in London society** es una figura destacada de la buena sociedad londinense.
prominently [ˈprɒmɪnəntlɪ] *adv*: **to display sth ~** exponer algo muy a la vista, poner algo en un sitio donde resulta perfectamente visible; **he figured ~ in the case** desempeñó un papel importante en el proceso.
promiscuity [,prɒmɪsˈkjuːɪtɪ] *n* (*V adj*) (**a**) libertad *f* en las relaciones sexuales, inmoralidad *f*, libertinaje *m*. (**b**) promiscuidad *f*.
promiscuous [prəˈmɪskjʊəs] *adj* (**a**) *person* libre en las relaciones sexuales, inmoral, libertino; *relationship* ilícito; *conduct* inmoral, libre. (**b**) (*mixed*) promiscuo.
promiscuously [prəˈmɪskjʊəslɪ] *adv* (*V adj*) (**a**) libremente, de modo inmoral; ilícitamente. (**b**) promiscuamente.
promise [ˈprɒmɪs] **1** *n* (**a**) (*pledge*) promesa *f*; **~ of marriage** palabra *f* de matrimonio; **under ~ of** bajo palabra de; **a ~ is a ~** lo promitido es deuda; **to break one's ~** faltar a su palabra; **to hold** (*or* **keep**) **sb to his ~** obligar a uno a cumplir su promesa, hacer que uno cumpla su promesa; **to keep one's ~** cumplir su promesa; **to release sb from his ~** absolver a uno de su promesa.
(**b**) (*hope*) promesa *f*; esperanza *f*; porvenir *m*; **full of ~** muy prometedor; **a young man of ~** un joven que promete, un joven de porvenir; **to hold out a ~ of** dar esperanzas de; **to show ~** prometer, demostrar tener aptitudes.
2 *vt* prometer; (*forecast*) prometer, augurar, pronosticar; **no, I ~ you** no, se lo aseguro; **to ~ to do sth** prometer hacer algo; **to ~ sb sth, to ~ sth to sb** prometer dar algo a uno; **it ~s trouble** nos augura algo malo; **they ~ us rain tomorrow** nos pronostican lluvia para mañana; **this does not ~ to be easy** esto me parece que no va a ser fácil.
3 *vi* (**a**) prometer; **~?** ¿me lo prometes?; **I can't ~** no lo puedo prometer.
(**b**) (*fig*) **to ~ well** prometer, ser prometedor; **the crop ~s well** la cosecha se muestra buena, la cosecha se anuncia espléndida; **this does not ~ well** esto no nos anuncia nada bueno.
4 *vr*: **to ~ o.s. sth** prometerse algo.
promised [ˈprɒmɪst] *adj* prometido; **the P~ Land** la tierra de promisión.
promising [ˈprɒmɪsɪŋ] *adj* prometedor, que promete; *future prospect* esperanzador, halagüeño; **a ~ young man** un joven que promete, un joven de porvenir; **two ~ candidates** dos candidatos buenos; **it doesn't look very ~** no parece muy halagüeño, es una perspectiva poco atractiva.
promisingly [ˈprɒmɪsɪŋlɪ] *adv* de manera prometedora; esperanzadoramente; **it's going quite ~** va bastante bien; **she plays ~** tocando se ve que promete, toca lo bastante bien para demostrar que tiene aptitudes.
promissory [ˈprɒmɪsərɪ] *adj*: **~ note** pagaré *m*.
promo* [ˈprəʊməʊ] *n* (*Comm*) *abbr of* **promotion** promoción *f*.
promontory [ˈprɒməntrɪ] *n* promontorio *m*.
promote [prəˈməʊt] *vt* (**a**) *trade etc* promover, fomentar; *good feeling* fomentar; *campaign* apoyar; *product* (*advertise*) dar publicidad a, hacer propaganda por, (*sell*) promover, impulsar, aumentar las ventas de; *discussion etc* estimular, favorecer, facilitar; (*Parl*) *bill* presentar; *company* fundar, crear, financiar.
(**b**) (*in rank*) ascender; **to be ~d** ser ascendido (*to colonel* a coronel); **Tarifa was ~d to the first division** Tarifa fue promovida a primera división, Tarifa ascendió a primera división.
(**c**) (*Chem*) *reaction* provocar.
promoter [prəˈməʊtəʳ] *n* promotor *m*, -ora *f*; agente *mf* de negocios; (*of company*) fundador *m*, -ora *f*; (*Boxing*) empresario *m*, promotor *m*; **sales ~** promotor *m*, -ora *f* de ventas.
promotion [prəˈməʊʃən] *n* (**a**) promoción *f*, fomento *m*; apoyo *m*; gestión *f*; facilitación *f*; presentación *f*; fundación *f*, creación *f*; **sales ~** promoción *f* de ventas; **'a ~ by Bloggs Enterprises'** 'presentación de la Empresa Bloggs'.
(**b**) (*in rank*) ascenso *m*; promoción *f*; **to get ~** ser ascendido (*to* a); **to move up the ~ ladder** subir en el escalafón; **to win ~** (*Sport*) ser promovido, ganar la promoción, ascender.
(**c**) (*Chem*) provocación *f*.
promotional [prəˈməʊʃənl] *adj* promocional.
prompt [prɒmpt] **1** *adj* pronto; *action, delivery, reply etc* pronto, inmediato; *service* rápido; *payment* puntual; *person's character* puntual; **they're very ~** son muy puntuales; **'please be ~'** 'se ruega mucha puntualidad'.
2 *adv* puntualmente; **at 6 o'clock ~** a las 6 en punto.
3 *vt* (**a**) (*urge*) **to ~ sb to do sth** mover a uno a hacer algo, incitar a uno a hacer algo; **I felt ~ed to protest** me encontré en la necesidad de protestar; **what ~ed you to do it?** ¿qué te movió a hacerlo?
(**b**) (*suggest*) inspirar; provocar; sugerir; **what ~ed that question?** ¿cuál fue el motivo de esa pregunta?; **a decision ~ed by fear** una decisión influida por el temor; **a poem ~ed by a memory** una poesía inspirada por un recuerdo; **it ~s the thought that ...** sugiere la noción de que ..., hace pensar que ...
(**c**) (*Theat*) apuntar; **don't ~ her!** ¡no la ayudes a recordar!, ¡no le soples cosas al oído!; **the witness had to be ~ed** fue necesario recordar unos hechos al testigo, hubo que traer ciertas cosas a la memoria del testigo.
4 *vi* (*Theat*) apuntar.
5 *n* (**a**) (*Theat*) apuntador *m*, -ora *f*.
(**b**) (*Comput*) aviso *m*, guía *f*, carácter *m* de petición.
6 *attr*: **~ side** (*Theat*) lado *m* izquierdo (del actor).
prompt-box [ˈprɒmptbɒks] *n* concha *f* (del apuntador).
prompter [ˈprɒmptəʳ] *n* apuntador *m*, -ora *f*.
prompting [ˈprɒmptɪŋ] *n*: **without ~** sin ayuda de nadie, sin tener que consultar el texto (*etc*); **the ~s of conscience** los escrúpulos de la conciencia; **the ~s of love** los dictados del amor.
promptitude [ˈprɒmptɪtjuːd] *n* = **promptness.**
promptly [ˈprɒmptlɪ] *adv* puntualmente, con prontitud; inmediatamente; rápidamente; **they do it very ~** lo hacen con toda prontitud; **they left ~ at 6** partieron a las 6 en punto.

promptness ['prɒmptnɪs] *n* prontitud *f*, puntualidad *f*; rapidez *f*.
promulgate ['prɒməlgeɪt] *vt* promulgar.
promulgation [,prɒməl'geɪʃən] *n* promulgación *f*.
prone [prəʊn] *adj* (**a**) (*face down*) **to be ~** estar postrado (boca abajo).
(**b**) (*liable*) **to be ~ to** + *n* ser propenso a + *n*, estar inclinado a + *n*; **to be ~ to** + *infin* ser propenso a + *infin*.
proneness ['prəʊnnɪs] *n* propensión *f* (*to* a), predisposición *f* (*to* a).
prong [prɒŋ] *n* punta *f*, púa *f*, diente *m*.
-pronged [prɒŋd] *adj ending in compounds*: **three~** de tres puntas.
pronominal [prəʊ'nɒmɪnl] *adj* pronominal.
pronoun ['prəʊnaʊn] *n* pronombre *m*.
pronounce [prə'naʊns] **1** *vt* (**a**) (*Ling*) pronunciar. (**b**) (*Jur*) pronunciar; (*with adj*) declarar; **they ~d him unfit to** + *infin* le declararon incapaz de + *infin*.
2 *vi*: **to ~ in favour of sth** pronunciarse en favor de algo; **to ~ on sth** expresar una opinión sobre algo, juzgar algo.
pronounceable [prə'naʊnsəbl] *adj* pronunciable.
pronounced [prə'naʊnst] *adj* marcado, acusado, fuerte; pronunciado; decidido.
pronouncement [prə'naʊnsmənt] *n* declaración *f*; opinión *f*; **to make a ~** pronunciarse, hacer una declaración (*about* sobre).
pronto* ['prɒntəʊ] *adv* pronto.
pronunciation [prə,nʌnsɪ'eɪʃən] *n* pronunciación *f*.
proof [pru:f] **1** *n* (**a**) (*gen*) prueba *f* (*also Math etc*); comprobación *f*; **~ positive** prueba *f* concluyente; **..., ~ positive that ......**, lo cual es prueba concluyente de que ...; **in ~ of** en prueba de, en comprobación de; como señal de; **in ~ whereof** en fe de lo cual; **it is ~ that he is poor** es prueba de su pobreza; **to adduce ~ to the contrary** aducir hechos que prueban lo contrario; **to give** (*or* **show**) **~ of** dar prueba de; **the onus of ~ lies with the accuser** le cumple al acusador probar lo que dice; **the ~ of the pudding is in the eating** al probar se ve el mosto; los melones, a cata.
(**b**) (*Typ*) prueba *f*; **~s, ~ sheets** pruebas *fpl*; **to read the ~s** corregir las pruebas.
(**c**) (*of alcohol*) graduación *f* normal; **this drink is 40% ~** esta bebida tiene una graduación de 40 por 100.
2 *adj* (**a**) *alcohol* de graduación normal; **~ spirit** licor *m* de graduación normal.
(**b**) **to be ~ against sth** ser (*or* estar) a prueba de algo; **it is ~ against moisture** está a prueba de la humedad; **I'm not ~ against temptation** yo no soy insensible a la tentación.
(**c**) *eg* **bullet-~** a prueba de balas.
3 *vt* impermeabilizar.
proofread ['pru:fri:d] (*irr*: *V* **read**) *vt* corregir las pruebas de.
proofreader ['pru:f,ri:də^r] *n* corrector *m*, -ora *f* de pruebas.
proofreading ['pru:f,ri:dɪŋ] *n* corrección *f* de pruebas.
prop [prɒp] **1** *n* apoyo *m*; (*Archit*) puntal *m*; (*Hort*) horca *f*, rodrigón *m*; (*Min*) peón *m*, entibo *m*, puntal *m*; (*Naut*) escora *f*; (*fig*) sostén *m*; **~ forward** pilier *m*.
2 *vt* (*also* **to ~ up**) apoyar; apuntalar; apoyar con rodrigón (*etc*); (*fig*) apoyar, sostener; **to ~ a ladder against a wall** apoyar una escalera contra una pared; **the company was ~ped up by a big loan** la compañía recibió el apoyo de un préstamo cuantioso.
3 *vr*: **to ~ o.s. against a tree** apoyarse contra un árbol.
prop. (**a**) (*Comm*) *abbr of* **proprietor** propietario *m*, -a *f*. (**b**) [prɒp] *n* (*Theat**) *abbr of* **property** accesorio *m*. (**c**) [prɒp] *n* (*Aer**) *abbr of* **propeller** hélice *f*.
propaganda [,prɒpə'gændə] *n* propaganda *f*.
propagandist [,prɒpə'gændɪst] *n* propagandista *mf*.
propagandize [prɒpə'gændaɪz] **1** *vt doctrine* propagar; *person* hacer propaganda a. **2** *vi* hacer propaganda.
propagate ['prɒpəgeɪt] **1** *vt* propagar. **2** *vi* propagarse.
propagation [,prɒpə'geɪʃən] *n* propagación *f*.
propane ['prəʊpeɪn] *n* propano *m*.
propel [prə'pel] *vt* impulsar, propulsar; (*push*) empujar; **it is ~led by turbines** está propulsado por turbinas.
propellant, propellent [prə'pelənt] *n* propulsor *m*; (*aerosol etc*) propelente *m*.
propeller [prə'pelə^r] *n* hélice *f*.
propeller shaft [prə'peləʃɑ:ft] *n* (*Aer*) eje *m* de la hélice; (*Aut*) árbol *m* de mando, eje *m* cardón; (*Naut*) eje *m* portahélice.
propelling pencil [prə'pelɪŋ'pensl] *n* (*Brit*) lapicero *m*, portaminas *m*.
propensity [prə'pensɪtɪ] *n* propensión *f* (*to* a).
proper ['prɒpə^r] **1** *adj* (**a**) (*peculiar, characteristic*) propio, peculiar; característico; **~ name, ~ noun** nombre *m* propio; **the qualities which are ~ to it** las cualidades que le son propias, las cualidades que son propias de él.
(**b**) (*correct*) verdadero, exacto, apropiado; **physics ~** la física propiamente dicha; **in the ~ sense of the word** en el sentido estricto de la palabra; **I'm not a ~ Londoner** no soy un auténtico londinense, no soy un londinense de verdad.
(**c**) (*) **he's a ~ rogue** es un verdadero pillo; **it's a ~ nuisance** es una verdadera molestia; **he's a ~ gentleman now** ya es un caballero hecho y derecho; **we got a ~ beating** nos dieron una paliza de las buenas; **there was a ~ row** hubo un lío de todos los diablos*.
(**d**) (*right, suitable*) apropiado, conveniente; oportuno; debido; justo, exacto; **in ~ condition** en buen estado; **at the ~ time** en el momento oportuno; **in the ~ way** convenientemente, del modo conveniente; **as you think ~** según te parezca, según tu criterio; **do as you think ~** haz lo que te parezca bien; **to do the ~ thing by sb** tratar a uno con justicia, cumplir con uno; **to say the ~ thing** decir lo que piden las circunstancias; **it was the ~ thing to say** fue lo que había que decir; **in a style ~ to his station** en un estilo que conviene a su rango; **I think it ~ to** + *infin* creo hacer bien en + *infin*.
(**e**) (*seemly*) decente; correcto; **~ behaviour** conducta *f* correcta; **what is ~** lo que está bien, lo que conviene; **it is not ~ for you to** + *infin* no está bien que + *subj*; **it's not ~ with children about** no es decente si hay niños delante.
(**f**) (*prim and ~*) etiquetero, relamido; formal.
(**g**) (*Her*) natural.
2 *adv* (*) (**a**) (*really*) **it's ~ difficult** es realmente difícil, es dificilísimo; **we were ~ puzzled** quedamos francamente perplejos.
(**b**) = **properly** (**b**).
properly ['prɒpəlɪ] *adv* (**a**) (*correctly etc*) correctamente, apropiadamente, debidamente; **a word ~ used** una palabra correctamente empleada; **~ speaking** propiamente dicho; en el sentido estricto de la palabra; **it is not ~ so called** no es correcto llamarlo así, no se llama así en propiedad, en propiedad no se dice así; **she very ~ refused** se negó a ello e hizo bien; **to do sth ~** hacer algo bien, hacer algo como se debe, hacer algo como Dios manda.
(**b**) (*in seemly fashion*) decentemente; correctamente; **not ~ dressed** incorrectamente vestido; **to behave ~** portarse correctamente; **behave ~!** ¡pórtate bien!, ¡estáte formal!
(**c**) (*intensive*) **we were ~ ashamed** nos avergonzamos de verdad; **we got ~ beaten** nos dieron una paliza de las buenas; **we were ~ puzzled** quedamos requeteperplejos.
propertied ['prɒpətɪd] *adj* adinerado, acaudalado; **the ~ classes** la clase acaudalada.
property ['prɒpətɪ] **1** *n* (**a**) (*quality*) propiedad *f*; **the properties of this substance** las propiedades de esta sustancia.
(**b**) (*thing owned*) propiedad *f*; bienes *mpl*; (*estate*) hacienda *f*, finca *f*, propiedad *f*; **that's my ~** eso es mío; **whose ~ is this?** ¿de quién es esto?; **it doesn't seem to be anyone's ~** no parece que tenga dueño, no parece que pertenezca a nadie; **that news is common ~** eso lo saben todos ya, esa noticia es ya del dominio público; **it is common ~ that ...** todos saben que ...; **it became the ~ of Mr Jones** pasó a ser propiedad del Sr Jones; **she left her ~ to X** dejó sus bienes a X.
(**c**) (*Theat*) accesorio *m*; **properties** accesorios *mpl*, at(t)rezzo *m*.
2 *attr* inmobiliario; **~ company** compañía *f* inmobiliaria; **~ developer** promotor *m* inmobiliario, promotora *f* inmobiliaria, promotor *m*, -ora *f* (de construcciones); **~ market** mercado *m* inmobiliario, mercado *m* de bienes raíces; **~ mart** sección *f* de ventas de inmuebles y viviendas (de un periódico); **~ mistress** accesorista *f*, attrezzista *f*; **~ owner** hacendado *m*, -a *f*, terrateniente *mf*; **~ speculation** especulación *f* inmobiliaria; **~ tax** contribución *f* territorial, impuesto *m* sobre la propiedad; **~ transfer tax** impuesto *m* sobre transmisiones patrimoniales.
prophecy ['prɒfɪsɪ] *n* profecía *f*.
prophesy ['prɒfɪsaɪ] *vt* profetizar; (*fig*) predecir, prever, augurar (*that* que).
prophet ['prɒfɪt] *n* profeta *m*.
prophetess ['prɒfɪtɪs] *n* profetisa *f*.
prophetic [prə'fetɪk] *adj* profético.

prophetically [prəˈfetɪkəlɪ] *adv* proféticamente.
prophylactic [ˌprɒfɪˈlæktɪk] **1** *adj* profiláctico. **2** *n* profiláctico *m*.
prophylaxis [ˈprɒfɪˈlæksɪs] *n* profilaxis *f*.
propinquity [prəˈpɪŋkwɪtɪ] *n* (*nearness*) propincuidad *f*; (*kinship*) consanguinidad *f*, parentesco *m*.
propitiate [prəˈpɪʃɪeɪt] *vt* propiciar.
propitiation [prəˌpɪʃɪˈeɪʃən] *n* propiciación *f*.
propitiatory [prəˈpɪʃɪətərɪ] *adj* propiciatorio, conciliatorio.
propitious [prəˈpɪʃəs] *adj* propicio, favorable.
propitiously [prəˈpɪʃəslɪ] *adv* de modo propicio, bajo signo propicio, favorablemente.
proponent [prəˈpəʊnənt] *n* defensor *m*, -ora *f*.
proportion [prəˈpɔːʃən] *n* (**a**) (*ratio, relationship*: *also Math*) proporción *f*; parte *f*, porción *f*, porcentaje *m*; **the ~ of blacks to whites** la proporción entre negros y blancos; **what ~ is in private hands?** ¿qué porción queda en manos de particulares?; **in equal ~s** por partes iguales; **in due ~** en su justa medida; **in ~ as** a medida que; **in ~ to** en proporción con, a medida de; **and the rest in ~** y lo demás en proporción, (*Comm*) y lo demás a prorrata; **to be out of ~** ser desproporcionado; **to be out of ~ with** (*or* **to**) no guardar proporción con; **it has been magnified out of all ~** se ha exagerado mucho.
(**b**) **sense of ~** (*lit, fig*) sentido *m* de la medida.
(**c**) **~s** (*size*) dimensiones *fpl*.
proportional [prəˈpɔːʃənl] *adj* proporcional; **~ representation** representación *f* proporcional; **~ to** en proporción con, a medida de; **X is not ~ to Y** X no guarda proporción con Y; **~ spacing** (*Comput*: *on printer*) espaciado *m* proporcional.
proportionally [prəˈpɔːʃnəlɪ] *adv* proporcionalmente, en proporción.
proportionate [prəˈpɔːʃnɪt] *adj* proporcionado.
proportionately [prəˈpɔːʃnɪtlɪ] *adv* proporcionadamente, en proporción.
proportioned [prəˈpɔːʃnd] *adj*: **well ~** bien proporcionado.
proposal [prəˈpəʊzl] *n* (**a**) (*offer*) propuesta *f*, proposición *f*; oferta *f*; (*to girl*) declaración *f* (de amor); **~ of marriage** oferta *f* de matrimonio, (*formally*) petición *f* de mano; **to make a ~** hacer una propuesta; **to make the ~ that ...** proponer que ...
(**b**) (*plan*) proyecto *m*; (*notion*) idea *f*; (*suggestion*) sugerencia *f*; **my ~ was to** + *infin* mi idea era de + *infin*; **it is a new ~ to reform the currency** es un nuevo proyecto para reformar la moneda.
propose [prəˈpəʊz] **1** *vt* (**a**) (*suggest*) proponer; ofrecer; *motion* proponer; *candidate* proponer (la candidatura de); **the ~d motorway** la autopista que se propone; **to ~ marriage to sb** hacer una oferta de matrimonio a una, (*formally*) pedir la mano de una a su padre; **to ~ sb for membership of a club** proponer la candidatura de uno para socio de un club; **what course do you ~?** ¿qué línea de acción nos recomiendas?
(**b**) **to ~ sb's health** brindar por uno, beber a la salud de uno.
(**c**) **to ~ to** + *infin* proponerse + *infin*; pensar + *infin*, tener la intención de + *infin*; **what do you ~ doing?** ¿qué piensas hacer?
2 *vi* (**a**) **Man ~s, God disposes** el hombre propone y Dios dispone.
(**b**) (*to girl*) declararse (*to* a); **to ~ to sb** (*formally*) hacer una oferta de matrimonio a una, pedir la mano de una a su padre.
proposer [prəˈpəʊzəʳ] *n* (*Parl etc*) proponente *mf* autor *m*, -ora *f* (de una moción).
proposition [ˌprɒpəˈzɪʃən] **1** *n* (**a**) (*statement, Math, Logic etc*) proposición *f*; (*proposal*) propuesta *f*, proposición *f*; oferta *f*; (*plan*) proyecto *m*.
(**b**) (*job*) tarea *f*; (*enterprise*) empresa *f*; (*problem*) problema *m*; (*objective*) propósito *m*; (*opponent*) adversario *m*, -a *f*; (*prospect*) perspectiva *f*; **it's a tough ~** es mucho pedir; **he's a tough ~** es un adversario formidable; **the journey alone is quite a ~** sólo el viaje pide grandes esfuerzos; **it will be a paying ~** dará dinero; **it's not an economic ~** no es rentable.
2 *vt girl* echar un tiento a*.
propound [prəˈpaʊnd] *vt* proponer, exponer, presentar.
proprietary [prəˈpraɪətərɪ] *adj* propietario; *article* patentado; **~ brand** marca *f* comercial; **~ goods** artículos *mpl* de marca; **~ interest** interés *m* patrimonial; **~ name** nombre *m* propietario.
proprietor [prəˈpraɪətəʳ] *n* propietario *m*, -a *f*, dueño *m*, -a *f*.
proprietorial [prəˌpraɪəˈtɔːrɪəl] *adj attitude etc* protector.
proprietorship [prəˈpraɪətəʃɪp] *n* propiedad *f*, posesión *f*.
proprietress [prəˈpraɪətrɪs] *n* propietaria *f*, dueña *f*.
propriety [prəˈpraɪətɪ] *n* (*seemliness*) decoro *m*, decencia *f*, corrección *f*; (*fitness*) conveniencia *f*; **the proprieties** las convenciones, los cánones sociales, el decoro; **breach of ~** ofensa *f* contra el decoro, incorrección *f*; **to observe the proprieties** atenerse a los cánones sociales; **to throw ~ to the winds** abandonar totalmente el decoro.
props* [prɒps] *npl* (*Theat*) *V* **property 1 (c)**.
propulsion [prəˈpʌlʃən] *n* propulsión *f*.
pro rata [ˌprəʊˈrɑːtə] *adj, adv V* **pro 1 (c)**.
prorate [ˈprəʊreɪt] (*US*) **1** *n* prorrata *f*. **2** *vt* prorratear.
prorogation [ˌprəʊrəˈgeɪʃən] *n* prorrogación *f*.
prorogue [prəˈrəʊg] *vt* prorrogar.
prosaic [prəʊˈzeɪɪk] *adj* prosaico.
prosaically [prəʊˈzeɪɪkəlɪ] *adv* prosaicamente.
Pros. Atty. (*US*) *abbr of* **prosecuting attorney**.
proscenium [prəʊˈsiːnɪəm] *n* proscenio *m*; **~ arch** embocadura *f*; **~ box** palco *m* de proscenio.
proscribe [prəʊsˈkraɪb] *vt* proscribir.
proscription [prəʊsˈkrɪpʃən] *n* proscripción *f*.
prose [prəʊz] **1** *n* (**a**) (*Liter*) prosa *f*. (**b**) (*Scol etc*: *also* **~ composition**) traducción *f* inversa. **2** *attr* de prosa; en prosa, prosístico.
prosecute [ˈprɒsɪkjuːt] *vt* (**a**) (*Jur*) procesar; enjuiciar; *claim* demandar en juicio; **to ~ sb for theft** procesar a uno por ladrón; **to be ~d for a traffic offence** ser procesado por una infracción del código; **'trespassers will be ~d'** 'se procederá contra los intrusos'.
(**b**) (*follow up*) proseguir, continuar, llevar adelante.
prosecuting [ˈprɒsɪkjuːtɪŋ] *adj*: **~ counsel** fiscal *mf*.
prosecution [ˌprɒsɪˈkjuːʃən] *n* (**a**) (*Jur*: case) proceso *m*, causa *f*, juicio *m*; (*act*) acusación *f*, procesamiento *m*; (*side*) parte *f* actora; **counsel for the ~** fiscal *mf*; **~ witness** testigo *mf* de cargo; **to start a ~ against sb** entablar juicio contra uno, entablar una acción judicial contra uno.
(**b**) (*furtherance*) prosecución *f*; **in the ~ of his duty** en el cumplimiento de su deber.
prosecutor [ˈprɒsɪkjuːtəʳ] *n* acusador *m*, -ora *f*; (*also* **public ~**) fiscal *mf*.
proselyte [ˈprɒsɪlaɪt] *n* prosélito *m*, -a *f*.
proselytism [ˈprɒsɪlɪtɪzəm] *n* proselitismo *m*.
proselytize [ˈprɒsɪlɪtaɪz] *vi* ganar prosélitos.
prose writer [ˈprəʊzˌraɪtəʳ] *n* prosista *mf*.
prosody [ˈprɒsədɪ] *n* métrica *f*.
prospect 1 [ˈprɒspekt] *n* (**a**) (*view*) vista *f*, panorama *m*; **the ~ from the window** la vista desde la ventana; **a ~ of Toledo** una vista de Toledo; **where every ~ pleases** donde todo deleita la vista.
(**b**) (*outlook*) perspectiva *f*; (*hope*) esperanza *f*; expectativa *f*; (*future*) porvenir *m*; **what a ~!** (*iro*) ¡qué perspectiva!; **future ~s** perspectivas *fpl* del futuro; **~s are really good** las perspectivas son francamente buenas; **'good ~s'** (*advert for job*) 'buen provenir', 'porvenir risueño', 'posibilidades de superación'; **it's a grim ~** es una perspectiva nada atractiva; **there are ~s of a fine day** el día se presenta muy bueno; **~s for the harvest are poor** la cosecha se anuncia más bien mediocre; **his ~s are outstandingly good** le espera un gran porvenir; **he has no ~s** no tiene porvenir; **this ~ cheered him up** se alegró con esta perspectiva; **we are faced with the ~ of** + *ger* nos encontramos ante la perspectiva de + *infin*; **to have sth in ~** esperar algo; **to hold out a ~ of** dar esperanzas de.
(**c**) (*chance*) probabilidad *f*, **the ~ of an early peace** la posibilidad de una pronta paz; **there is little ~ of his coming** hay pocas posibilidades de que venga; **to dangle a ~ before sb** ofrecer a uno la posibilidad de + *infin*, tentar a uno con la posibilidad de + *infin*; **I see no ~ of that** eso no lo creo probable.
(**d**) (*person*) persona *f* en perspectiva; (*Comm*) cliente *m* posible, comprador *m* (*etc*) probable; **is he a ~ for the team?** ¿vale considerarle como posible miembro del equipo?; **he's not much of a ~ for her** no vale gran cosa como partido para ella.
2 [prəsˈpekt] *vt* explorar.
3 [prəsˈpekt] *vi*: **to ~ for** buscar.
prospecting [prəsˈpektɪŋ] *n* (*Min*) prospección *f*.
prospective [prəsˈpektɪv] *adj* anticipado, prospectivo, esperado; probable; *son-in-law etc* futuro; *heir* presunto; *legislation etc* en perspectiva.
prospector [prəsˈpektəʳ] *n* explorador *m*; **gold ~** buscador *m* de oro.
prospectus [prəsˈpektəs] *n* prospecto *m*; programa *m*; folleto *m* informativo.

prosper ['prɒspəʳ] **1** *vt* favorecer, fomentar. **2** *vi* prosperar; medrar; florecer.
prosperity [prɒs'perɪtɪ] *n* prosperidad *f.*
prosperous ['prɒspərəs] *adj* próspero.
prosperously ['prɒspərəslɪ] *adv* prósperamente.
prostaglandin [,prɒstə'glændɪn] *n* prostaglandina *f.*
prostate ['prɒsteɪt] *n* próstata *f.*
prosthesis [prɒs'θiːsɪs] *n, pl* **prostheses** [prɒs'θiːsiːs] prótesis *f.*
prosthetic [prɒs'θetɪk] *adj* prostético.
prostitute ['prɒstɪtjuːt] **1** *n* prostituta *f.* **2** *vt* prostituír (*also fig*).
prostitution [,prɒstɪ'tjuːʃən] *n* prostitución *f.*
prostrate 1 ['prɒstreɪt] *adj* postrado; (*Bot*) procumbente; (*fig*) postrado, abatido (*with* por).
2 [prɒs'treɪt] *vt* postrar; (*fig*) postrar, abatir; **to be ~d by grief** estar postrado por el dolor.
3 [prɒs'treɪt] *vr*: **to ~ o.s.** postrarse.
prostration [prɒs'treɪʃən] *n* postración *f*; (*fig*) postración *f*, abatimiento *m.*
prosy ['prəʊzɪ] *adj* prosaico, aburrido, monótono.
Prot. *abbr of* **Protestant.**
protagonist [prəʊ'tægənɪst] *n* protagonista *mf.*
protean ['prəʊtɪən] *adj* proteico.
protect [prə'tekt] *vt* proteger (*against, from* contra, de); amparar, resguardar.
protection [prə'tekʃən] **1** *n* protección *f*; (*Comm*) protección *f*, proteccionismo *m*; **the policy gives ~ against ...** la póliza protege contra ...; **to be under sb's ~** estar bajo la protección de uno.
2 *attr*: **he pays 200 dollars a week ~ money** paga 200 dólares de protección a la semana; **~ factor** factor *m* de protección; **~ racket** chantaje *m* ejercido contra un comerciante so pretexto de protegerle.
protectionism [prə'tekʃənɪzəm] *n* proteccionismo *m.*
protectionist [prə'tekʃənɪst] **1** *adj* proteccionista. **2** *n* proteccionista *mf.*
protective [prə'tektɪv] *adj* protector; (*Comm*) proteccionista; **~ coloration** colores *mpl* protectores; **~ cream** crema *f* protectora; **~ custody** detención *f* preventiva; **~ duty** impuesto *m* proteccionista; **~ mimicry** mimetismo *m* protector.
protectively [prə'tektɪvlɪ] *adv* protectoramente, de modo protector.
protectiveness [prə'tektɪvnɪs] *n* actitud *f* (*or* cualidad *f etc*) protectora.
protector [prə'tektəʳ] *n* protector *m*, -ora *f.*
protectorate [prə'tektərɪt] *n* protectorado *m.*
protectress [prə'tektrɪs] *n* protectora *f.*
protégé ['prɒteʒeɪ] *n* protegido *m*, ahijado *m.*
protégée ['prɒteʒeɪ] *n* protegida *f*, ahijada *f.*
protein ['prəʊtiːn] **1** *n* proteína *f.* **2** *attr*: **~ content** contenido *m* proteínico.
pro tem ['prəʊ'tem] *adv abbr of* **pro tempore = for the time being** provisionalmente.
protest 1 ['prəʊtest] *n* protesta *f*; **under ~** bajo protesta, haciendo objeciones; **I'll do it but under ~** lo haré pero que conste mi protesta; **to make a ~** hacer una protesta.
2 ['prəʊtest] *attr*: **~ demonstration** manifestación *f* de protesta; **~ march** marcha *f* de protesta; **~ movement** movimiento *m* de protesta, movimiento *m* contestatario; **~ song** canción *f* (de) protesta; **~ vote** voto *m* de protesta.
3 [prə'test] *vt* (**a**) (*complain*) protestar; **to ~ that ...** protestar de que ...
(**b**) (*affirm*) afirmar, declarar (enérgicamente, solemnemente *etc*).
4 [prə'test] *vi* protestar; **to ~ at** (*or* **against**) protestar de, protestar contra.
Protestant ['prɒtɪstənt] **1** *adj* protestante. **2** *n* protestante *mf.*
Protestantism ['prɒtɪstəntɪzəm] *n* protestantismo *m.*
protestation [,prɒtes'teɪʃən] *n* (**a**) (*complaint*) protesta *f.* (**b**) (*affirmation*) afirmación *f*, declaración *f* (enérgica, solemne *etc*).
protester, protestor [prə'testəʳ] *n* protestador *m*, -ora *f*; (*on march, in demonstration etc*) manifestante *mf.*
proto... ['prəʊtəʊ] *pref* proto...
protocol ['prəʊtəkɒl] *n* protocolo *m.*
proton ['prəʊtɒn] *n* protón *m.*
protoplasm ['prəʊtəʊplæzəm] *n* protoplasma *m.*
prototype ['prəʊtəʊtaɪp] *n* prototipo *m.*
protract [prə'trækt] *vt* prolongar; extender, alargar.
protracted [prə'træktɪd] *adj* largo, prolongado.
protraction [prə'trækʃən] *n* prolongación *f*; extensión *f*, alargamiento *m.*
protractor [prə'træktəʳ] *n* transportador *m.*
protrude [prə'truːd] **1** *vt* sacar fuera. **2** *vi* salir (fuera), sobresalir.
protruding [prə'truːdɪŋ] *adj* saliente; *eye, tooth* saltón.
protrusion [prə'truːʒən] *n* saliente *m*, protuberancia *f.*
protuberance [prə'tjuːbərəns] *n* protuberancia *f*, saliente *m.*
protuberant [prə'tjuːbərənt] *adj* protuberante, saliente; prominente; *eye, tooth* saltón.
proud [praʊd] *adj* (**a**) (*of person etc*) orgulloso; (*pej*) soberbio, arrogante, altanero; **as ~ as a peacock** más orgulloso que un pavo real; **to be ~ of** estar orgulloso de, enorgullecerse de, preciarse de, ufanarse de; **to be ~ that ...** estar orgulloso de que ...; **to be ~ to +** *infin* tener el honor de + *infin*, estar orgulloso de + *infin*; **to do o.s. ~** permitirse toda clase de lujos; darse buena vida, vivir a cuerpo de rey; **to do sb ~*** hacer muchas fiestas a uno, regalar a uno, (*with food*) dar de comer opíparamente a uno.
(**b**) (*imposing*) espléndido, imponente; (*glorious*) glorioso; **it is a ~ day for us** es un día glorioso para nosotros; **a ~ ship** un magnífico buque, un soberbio buque; **it is the town's ~est possession** es la posesión más importante de la ciudad.
(**c**) **~ flesh** bezo *m.*
proudly ['praʊdlɪ] *adv* (*V adj*) (**a**) orgullosamente; *say etc* con orgullo; arrogantemente. (**b**) de modo imponente.
prove [pruːv] **1** *vt* demostrar; probar; (*verify*) comprobar; (*show*) demostrar; (*confirm*) confirmar; *will* verificar; **this ~s that ...** esto demuestra que ...; **the exception ~s the rule** la excepción confirma la regla; **can you ~ it?** ¿tiene Vd prueba (de ello)?; **you can't ~ anything against me** Vd no puede demostrar nada contra mí; **it remains to be ~d whether ...** queda por demostrar si ...; **it all goes to ~ that ...** todo sirve para demostrar que ...; **he was ~d right in the end** al fin se demostró que tenía razón; **to ~ sb innocent** demostrar la inocencia de uno.
2 *vi* resultar; **if it ~s useful** si resulta útil; **the news ~d false** resultó que la noticia era falsa; **she ~d unequal to the job** ella resultó no estar al nivel del puesto; **if it ~s otherwise** si sale al contrario, si resulta que no es así.
3 *vr*: **to ~ o.s.** dar prueba de su valor, probar su valor.
proven ['pruːvən] *adj* probado; **of ~ quality** de calidad probada; **it's a ~ fact that ...** es un hecho comprobado que ...; **he's a ~ liar** es un mentiroso probado como tal; **the case was found not ~** el acusado fue absuelto por falta de pruebas; **there are ~ oil reserves** hay reservas de petróleo conocidas.
provenance ['prɒvɪnəns] *n* procedencia *f*, origen *m*, punto *m* de origen.
Provençal [,prɒvɑːn'sɑːl] **1** *adj* provenzal. **2** *n* (**a**) provenzal *mf.* (**b**) (*Ling*) provenzal *m.*
Provence [prɒ'vɑːns] *n* Provenza *f.*
provender ['prɒvɪndəʳ] *n* forraje *m*; (*hum*) provisiones *fpl*, comida *f.*
proverb ['prɒvɜːb] *n* refrán *m*, proverbio *m.*
proverbial [prə'vɜːbɪəl] *adj* proverbial.
proverbially [prə'vɜːbɪəlɪ] *adv* proverbialmente.
provide [prə'vaɪd] **1** *vt* (**a**) (*supply, furnish*) suministrar, surtir; dar, proporcionar; **to ~ sb with sth** (*supply*) proveer a uno de algo, suministrar algo a uno; (*give*) proporcionar algo a uno; **the car is ~d with a heater** el coche está provisto de un calentador; **can you ~ a substitute?** ¿podéis encontrar un suplente?; **the government ~d half the money** el gobierno proporcionó la mitad del dinero; **the plant will ~ an output of ...** la fábrica permitirá una producción de ...; **it ~s shade for the cows** da sombra para las vacas.
(**b**) **to ~ that ...** (*stipulate*) estipular que ..., disponer que ...
2 *vi* (**a**) **God will ~** Dios proveerá; **a husband who ~s well** un marido que mantiene debidamente a su familia.
(**b**) **to ~ against** precaverse de, tomar precauciones contra; **to ~ for sb** mantener a uno, proporcionar medios de vida a uno, (*with an allowance*) señalar una pensión a uno; **they are well ~d for** tienen medios adecuados; **to ~ for one's dependants** asegurar el porvenir de su familia; **to ~ for every contingency** prevenir cualquier posibilidad; **we have ~d for that** eso lo hemos previsto.
(**c**) **the treaty ~s for ...** el tratado estipula ...; **as ~d for in the 1990 contract** de acuerdo con lo estipulado en el contrato de 1990.
3 *vr*: **to ~ o.s. with sth** proveerse de algo.
provided [prə'vaɪdɪd] *conj*: **~, ~ that** con tal que + *subj*,

siempre que + *subj*; a condición de que + *subj*.

providence ['prɒvɪdəns] *n* (*all senses*) providencia *f*; **P~** Divina Providencia *f*.

provident ['prɒvɪdənt] *adj* providente, previsor, próvido; **~ fund** fondo *m* de previsión; **~ society** (*Brit*) sociedad *f* de socorro mutuo, mutualidad *f*.

providential [,prɒvɪ'denʃəl] *adj* providencial; (*lucky*) afortunado, milagroso.

providentially [,prɒvɪ'denʃəlɪ] *adv* providencialmente; afortunadamente, milagrosamente.

providently ['prɒvɪdəntlɪ] *adv* próvidamente.

provider [prə'vaɪdəʳ] *n* proveedor *m*, -ora *f*.

providing [prə'vaɪdɪŋ] *conj* = **provided.**

province ['prɒvɪns] *n* (**a**) provincia *f*; **they live in the ~s** viven en provincia.
(**b**) (*fig*: *field*) esfera *f*; especialidad *f*; (*jurisdiction etc*) competencia *f*; **it's not within my ~** no es de mi competencia.

provincial [prə'vɪnʃəl] **1** *adj* provincial, de provincia; (*pej*) provinciano. **2** *n* provinciano *m*, -a *f*.

provincialism [prə'vɪnʃəlɪzəm] *n* provincialismo *m*.

provision [prə'vɪʒən] **1** *n* (**a**) (*gen*) provisión *f*; (*supply*) provisión *f*, suministro *m*; abastecimiento *m*; **the ~ of new capital** la provisión de nuevos capitales; **the ~ of new housing** la provisión de nuevas viviendas; **to make ~ for** prevenir, prever; **to make ~ for one's family** asegurar el porvenir de su familia.
(**b**) **~s** (*food*) provisiones *fpl*, comestibles *mpl*, víveres *mpl*.
(**c**) (*stipulation*) estipulación *f*, disposición *f*; **according to the ~s of the treaty** de acuerdo con lo estipulado en el tratado; **there is no ~ to the contrary** no hay estipulación que lo prohíba; **it comes within the ~s of this law** está comprendido dentro de lo estipulado por esta ley.
2 *vt* aprovisionar, abastecer.

provisional [prə'vɪʒənl] **1** *adj* provisional; interino. **2** *npl*: **the P~s** los Provisionales (*tendencia activista del IRA*).

provisionally [prə'vɪʒnəlɪ] *adv* provisionalmente; con carácter provisional; interinamente.

proviso [prə'vaɪzəʊ] *n* condición *f*, estipulación *f*; salvedad *f*; **with the ~ that ...** con la condición de que + *subj*.

Provo* ['prəʊvəʊ] *n* = **provisional 2.**

provocation [,prɒvə'keɪʃən] *n* provocación *f*; **to act under ~** obrar bajo provocación; **to suffer great ~** sufrir una gran provocación.

provocative [prə'vɒkətɪv] *adj* *remark etc* provocador, provocativo; *title* provocador; *book etc* sugestivo, que invita a pensar; *person* seductor; **now you're trying to be ~** ahora sí que intentas provocarme.

provocatively [prə'vɒkətɪvlɪ] *adv* de modo provocador, de modo provocativo.

provoke [prə'vəʊk] *vt* (**a**) (*cause*) provocar, causar, producir, motivar; facilitar; (*rouse, move*) provocar, incitar, mover (*to* a); **it ~d us to action** nos incitó a obrar; **it ~d the town to revolt** incitó la ciudad a sublevarse.
(**b**) (*anger*) provocar; irritar; **he is easily ~d** se irrita por cualquier cosa.

provoking [prə'vəʊkɪŋ] *adj* provocativo; irritante, fastidioso; **how very ~!** ¡qué lata!*

provost ['prɒvəst] **1** *n* (*Univ*) rector *m*, -ora *f*; director *m*, -ora *f*; (*Scot*) alcalde *m*, -esa *f*. **2** *attr*: **~ marshal** capitán *m* preboste.

prow [praʊ] *n* proa *f*.

prowess ['praʊɪs] *n* (*skill*) destreza *f*, habilidad *f*; (*courage*) valor *m*.

prowl [praʊl] **1** *n* ronda *f* (en busca de presa, botín *etc*); **to be on the ~** merodear, rondar.
2 *attr*: **~ car** (*US*) coche-patrulla *m*.
3 *vt*: **to ~ the streets** rondar las calles, vagar por las calles.
4 *vi* rondar (en busca de presa, botín *etc*), merodear; **he ~s round the house at night** (*outside*) ronda la casa de noche, (*inside*) se pasea por la casa de noche.

prowler ['praʊləʳ] *n* rondador *m*, hombre *m* que ronda en busca de presa (*or* mujeres *etc*); merodeador *m*; ladrón *m*.

prox. *abbr of* **proximo** próximo futuro, pr. fr.

proximity [prɒk'sɪmɪtɪ] *n* proximidad *f*; **in ~ to** cerca de, junto a.

proximo ['prɒksɪməʊ] *adv* (*Comm*) del mes próximo; **before the 7th ~** antes del 7 del mes que viene.

proxy ['prɒksɪ] **1** *n* (*power*) poder *m*, procuración *f*; (*person*) apoderado *m*, -a *f*; sustituto *m*, -a *f*; **by ~** por poder, por poderes; **to be married by ~** casarse por poderes.
2 *attr*: **~ vote** voto *m* por poderes.

prude [pru:d] *n* remilgado *m*, -a *f*, mojigato *m*, -a *f*, gazmaño *m*, -a *f*.

prudence ['pru:dəns] *n* prudencia *f*.

prudent ['pru:dənt] *adj* prudente.

prudential [prʊ(:)'denʃəl] prudencial.

prudently ['pru:dəntlɪ] *adv* prudentemente, con prudencia.

prudery ['pru:dərɪ] *n* remilgo *m*, mojigatería *f*, gazmoñería *f*.

prudish ['pru:dɪʃ] *adj* remilgado, mojigato, gazmoño.

prudishness ['pru:dɪʃnɪs] *n* = **prudery.**

prune¹ [pru:n] *n* (**a**) (*fruit*) ciruela *f* pasa. (**b**) (*) bobo *m*, -a *f*, majadero *m*, -a *f*.

prune² [pru:n] *vt* podar; (*fig*) reducir, recortar.

◆prune away *vt branches* podar; (*fig*) *words* cortar.

pruning ['pru:nɪŋ] *n* poda *f*.

pruning-hook ['pru:nɪŋhʊk] *n*, **pruning-knife** ['pru:nɪŋnaɪf] *n*, *pl* **pruning-knives** ['pru:nɪŋnaɪvz], **pruning-shears** ['pru:nɪŋʃɪəz] *npl* podadera *f*.

prurience ['prʊərɪəns] *n* salacidad *f*, lascivia *f*.

prurient ['prʊərɪənt] *adj* salaz, lascivo.

Prussia ['prʌʃə] *n* Prusia *f*.

Prussian ['prʌʃən] **1** *adj* prusiano; **~ blue** azul *m* de Prusia.
2 *n* prusiano *m*, -a *f*.

prussic ['prʌsɪk] *adj*: **~ acid** ácido *m* prúsico.

pry¹ [praɪ] *vi* (*watch*) fisgonear, curiosear; (*meddle*) entrometerse; **to ~ into sb's affairs** entrometerse en lo ajeno; **to ~ into sb's secrets** ir curioseando los secretos de uno.

pry² [praɪ] *vt* (*US*) = **prise.**

prying ['praɪɪŋ] *adj* fisgón, curioso; entrometido.

PS *n* (**a**) *abbr of* **postscript** posdata *f*, P.D. (**b**) (*Parl*) *abbr of* **Parliamentary Secretary.**

psalm [sɑ:m] *n* salmo *m*.

psalmist ['sɑ:mɪst] *n* salmista *m*.

psalmody ['sælmədɪ] *n* salmodia *f*.

psalter ['sɔ:ltəʳ] *n* salterio *m*.

PSAT *n* (*US*) *abbr of* **Preliminary Scholastic Aptitude Test.**

PSBR *n* (*Econ*) *abbr of* **public sector borrowing requirement** necesidades *fpl* de endeudamiento del sector público.

psephologist [se'fɒlədʒɪst] *n* psefólogo *m*, -a *f*.

psephology [se'fɒlədʒɪ] *n* psefología *f*.

pseud* [sju:d] *n* (*Brit*) farsante* *mf*.

pseudo* ['sju:dəʊ] *adj* falso, fraudulento; *person* fingido; (*of person's character*) artificial, afectado.

pseudo... ['sju:dəʊ] *pref* seudo...; falso, fingido; **a ~-artist** un seudo artista.

pseudohistory [,sju:dəʊ'hɪstərɪ] *n* seudohistoria *f*.

pseudonym ['sju:dənɪm] *n* seudónimo *m*.

pseudonymous [sju:'dɒnɪməs] *adj* seudónimo.

pshaw [pʃɔ:] *interj* ¡bah!

psittacosis [,psɪtə'kəʊsɪs] *n* psitacosis *f*.

psoriasis [sə'raɪəsɪs] *n* soriasis *f*.

PST (*US*) *abbr of* **Pacific Standard Time.**

PSV *n abbr of* **public service vehicle** vehículo *m* de servicio público.

psych* [saɪk] (*abbr of* **psychoanalyse**) *vt* (**a**) (*guess, anticipate*) *reactions etc* adivinar, anticipar. (**b**) (*make uneasy*: *also* **to ~ out**) poner nervioso; **that doesn't ~ me** no me da ni frío ni calor, me tiene sin cuidado. (**c**) (*prepare psychologically*: *also* **to ~ up**) mentalizar; **to get o.s. ~ed up for sth** mentalizarse para algo; **he was all ~ed up to start, when ...** ya estaba mentalizado para empezar, cuando ...

◆psych out* **1** *vt* (*unhinge*) desquiciar. **2** *vi* (**a**) desquiciarse. (**b**) (*make uneasy*) = **psych** (**b**).

◆psych up* *vt V* **psych** (**c**).

psych... [saɪk] *pref* psic..., psiqu..., sic..., siqu...

Psyche ['saɪkɪ] *nf* Psique.

psyche ['saɪkɪ] *n* psique *f*.

psychedelic [,saɪkə'delɪk] *adj* psiquedélico, psicodélico.

psychiatric [,saɪkɪ'ætrɪk] *adj* psiquiátrico.

psychiatrist [saɪ'kaɪətrɪst] *n* psiquiatra *mf*.

psychiatry [saɪ'kaɪətrɪ] *n* psiquiatría *f*.

psychic(al) ['saɪkɪk(əl)] *adj* psíquico; **I'm not psychic*** no soy psicológico, no tengo psicología; **you must be ~*** tienes que ser psicológico.

psycho* ['saɪkəʊ] *n* caso *m* psicológico, persona *f* anormal.

psycho... ['saɪkəʊ] *pref* psico...

psychoactive [,saɪkəʊ'æktɪv] *adj*: **~ drug** droga *f* psicoactiva.

psychoanalyse, (*US*) **psychoanalyze** [,saɪkəʊ'ænəlaɪz] *vt* psicoanalizar.

psychoanalysis [,saɪkəʊə'nælɪsɪs] *n* psicoanálisis *m*.

psychoanalyst [ˌsaɪkəʊˈænəlɪst] *n* psicoanalista *mf*.

psychoanalytic(al) [ˌsaɪkəʊˌænəˈlɪtɪk(əl)] *adj* psicoanalítico.

psychodrama [ˈsaɪkəʊˌdrɑːmə] *n* psicodrama *m*.

psychodynamics [ˌsaɪkəʊdaɪˈnæmiks] *n sing* psicodinámica *f*.

psychokinesis [ˌsaɪkəʊkɪˈniːsɪs] *n* psicoquinesis *f*.

psychokinetic [ˌsaɪkəʊkɪˈnetɪk] *adj* psicoquinético.

psycholinguistic [ˌsaɪkəʊlɪŋˈgwɪstɪk] *adj* psicolingüístico.

psycholinguistics [ˌsaɪkəʊlɪŋˈgwɪstɪks] *n* psicolingüística *f*.

psychological [ˌsaɪkəˈlɒdʒɪkəl] *adj* psicológico; ~ **block** bloqueo *m* psicológico; ~ **make-up** perfil *m* psicológico; ~ **moment** momento *m* psicológico; ~ **warfare** guerra *f* psicológica.

psychologically [ˌsaɪkəˈlɒdʒɪkəlɪ] *adv* psicológicamente.

psychologist [saɪˈkɒlədʒɪst] *n* psicólogo *m*, -a *f*.

psychology [saɪˈkɒlədʒɪ] *n* psicología *f*.

psychoneurosis [ˈsaɪkəʊnjʊəˈrəʊsɪs] *n*, *pl* **psychoneuroses** [ˈsaɪkəʊnjʊəˈrəʊsiːz] psiconeurosis *f*.

psychopath [ˈsaɪkəʊpæθ] *n* psicópata *mf*.

psychopathic [ˌsaɪkəʊˈpæθɪk] *adj* psicopático.

psychopathology [ˈsaɪkəʊpəˈθɒlədʒɪ] *n* psicopatología *f*.

psychosexual [ˌsaɪkəʊˈseksjʊəl] *adj* psicosexual.

psychosis [saɪˈkəʊsɪs] *n* psicosis *f*.

psychosomatic [ˈsaɪkəʊsəʊˈmætɪk] *adj* psicosomático.

psychosurgery [ˌsaɪkəʊˈsɜːdʒərɪ] *n* psicocirugía *f*.

psychotherapist [ˌsaɪkəʊˈθerəpɪst] *n* psicoterapeuta *mf*.

psychotherapy [ˈsaɪkəʊˈθerəpɪ] *n* psicoterapia *f*.

psychotic [saɪˈkɒtɪk] **1** *adj* psicótico. **2** *n* psicótico *m*, -a *f*.

psychotropic [ˌsaɪkəʊˈtrɒpɪk] *adj* psicotrópico.

PT *n abbr of* **physical training** gimnasia *f*, cultura *f* física.

Pt (*Geog*) *abbr of* **Point** Punta *f*, Pta.

pt (**a**) *abbr of* **part** parte *f*. (**b**) *abbr of* **pint(s)**. (**c**) *abbr of* **point** punto *m*. (**d**) (*Comm*) *abbr of* **payment** pago *m*.

P/T *abbr of* **part-time**.

PTA *n abbr of* **Parent-Teacher Association** ≃ Asociación *f* de Padres de Alumnos, APA *f*.

ptarmigan [ˈtɑːmɪgən] *n* perdiz *f* blanca, perdiz *f* nival.

Pte *abbr of* **Private** soldado *m* raso.

pterodactyl [ˌterəʊˈdæktɪl] *n* pterodáctilo *m*.

PTO *abbr of* **please turn over** véase al dorso, sigue.

Ptolemaic [ˌtɒləˈmeɪɪk] *adj*: ~ **system** sistema *m* de Tolomeo, sistema *m* tolemaico.

Ptolemy [ˈtɒləmɪ] *nm* Tolomeo.

ptomaine [ˈtəʊmeɪn] *n* (p)tomaína *f*; ~ **poisoning** envenenamiento *m* (p)tomaínico.

PTV *n* (*US*) *abbr of* **pay television, public television**.

pub [pʌb] *n* (*Brit*) taberna *f*, tasca *f*, bar *m*.

pub-crawl* [ˈpʌbkrɔːl] (*Brit*) **1** *n* chateo* *m* (de tasca* en tasca); **to go on a** ~ = **2**. **2** *vi* ir de chateo* (*or* parranda* *LAm*), copear*, alternar*.

puberty [ˈpjuːbətɪ] *n* pubertad *f*.

pubescence [pjuːˈbesəns] *n* pubescencia *f*.

pubescent [pjuːˈbesənt] *adj* pubescente.

pubic [ˈpjuːbɪk] *adj* púbico; ~ **hair** vello *m* púbico.

pubis [ˈpjuːbɪs] *n* pubis *m*.

public [ˈpʌblɪk] **1** *adj* público; ~ **address system** sistema *m* de altavoces, sistema *m* amplificador; ~ **bar** bar *m*; ~ **body** corporación *f* estatal; ~ **company** compañía *f* pública; ~ **convenience** (*Brit*) aseos *mpl* públicos, sanitarios *mpl* (*LAm*); ~ **debt** deuda *f* pública; ~ **enemy** enemigo *m* público; ~ **enemy number one** enemigo *m* público número uno; ~ **enterprise** (*firm*) empresa *f* pública, (*endeavour*) iniciativa *f* pública; ~ **expenditure** gastos *mpl* públicos; ~ **holiday** fiesta *f* oficial; ~ **house** (*Brit*) taberna *f*; ~ **housing** (*US*) viviendas *fpl* protegidas; ~ **issue** (*St Ex*) emisión *f* pública; ~ **lavatory** urinarios *mpl*; ~ **library** biblioteca *f* pública; ~ **life** vida *f* pública; ~ **limited company** sociedad *f* anónima; ~ **nuisance** (*Jur*) perjuicio *m* público, daño *m* público; **he's a** ~ **nuisance** perjudica al bienestar público; ~ **opinion** opinión *f* pública; ~ **ownership** nacionalización *f*, propiedad *f* pública; **P~ Records Office** (*Brit*) Archivo *m* Nacional; ~ **relations** relaciones *fpl* públicas; ~ **relations adviser** asesor *m*, -ora *f* de imagen; ~ **relations officer** encargado *m*, -a *f* de relaciones públicas, public relations* *mf*; ~ **school** (*Brit*: *approx*) internado *m* privado, (*Scot*, *US*) escuela *f* pública; ~ **sector** sector *m* público; ~ **servant** funcionario *mf*; ~ **service vehicle** vehículo *m* de servicio público; ~ **speaking** oratoria *f*; ~ **spending** gastos *mpl* públicos; ~ **spirit** civismo *m*; ~ **transport**, ~ **transportation** (*US*) transportes *mpl* públicos; ~ **utilities** empresas *fpl* del servicio público; ~ **utility** servicio *m* público; ~ **works** obras *fpl* públicas; **it's too** ~ **here** aquí la gente nos mira, aquí estamos a la vista de todos; **to be in the** ~ **eye** estar muy a la vista; **to go** ~ (*Comm*) hacerse cotizar en la Bolsa, ofrecer acciones a la venta pública; (*: *reveal*) hablar en público, revelar secretos al público; **to make a matter** ~ publicar un asunto, hacer público un asunto.

2 *n* público *m*; **in** ~ en público; **the general** ~ el gran público; **the sporting** ~ los aficionados al deporte; **the great British** ~ (*hum*) los ingleses, los súbditos de su Majestad.

publican [ˈpʌblɪkən] *n* (**a**) (*Brit*) tabernero *m*. (**b**) (*Bible*) publicano *m*.

publication [ˌpʌblɪˈkeɪʃən] **1** *n* publicación *f*. **2** *attr*: ~ **date** fecha *f* de publicación; ~ **details** detalles *mpl* de publicación.

publicist [ˈpʌblɪsɪst] *n* publicista *mf*.

publicity [pʌbˈlɪsɪtɪ] **1** *n* publicidad *f*. **2** *attr*: ~ **agent** agente *mf* de publicidad; ~ **campaign** campaña *f* publicitaria; ~ **manager** director *m*, -ora *f* de publicidad; **~-shy** reacio a la publicidad; ~ **stunt** truco *m* publicitario.

publicize [ˈpʌblɪsaɪz] *vt* publicar, dar publicidad a, anunciar.

publicly [ˈpʌblɪklɪ] *adv* públicamente, en público.

public-spirited [ˈpʌblɪkˈspɪrɪtɪd] *adj act* de buen ciudadano; *person* lleno de civismo, consciente del bien público.

publish [ˈpʌblɪʃ] *vt* publicar; *banns* correr.

publisher [ˈpʌblɪʃəʳ] *n* editor *m*, -ora *f*.

publishing [ˈpʌblɪʃɪŋ] **1** *n* publicación *f* (de libros); **he's in** ~ publica libros, está con una casa editorial. **2** *attr*: ~ **company**, ~ **house** casa *f* editorial.

puce [pjuːs] **1** *n* color *m* castaño rojizo. **2** *adj* de color castaño rojizo; (*with shame etc*) colorado.

puck¹ [pʌk] *n* (*imp*) duende *m* (malicioso).

puck² [pʌk] *n* (*Sport*) puck *m*, disco *m*.

pucker [ˈpʌkəʳ] **1** *n* arruga *f*; (*Sew*) frunce *m*, fruncido *m*; (*accidentally formed*) buche *m*.

2 *vt* (*also* **to** ~ **up**) arrugar; (*brow*, *Sew*) fruncir.

3 *vi* (*also* **to** ~ **up**) arrugarse, formar buches.

puckish [ˈpʌkɪʃ] *adj* malicioso, juguetón.

pud* [pʊd] *n* = **pudding**.

pudding [ˈpʊdɪŋ] *n* púding *m*; (*as course*) postre *m* (dulce).

pudding-basin [ˈpʊdɪŋˌbeɪsn] *n* cuenco *m*.

pudding-rice [ˈpʊdɪŋˌraɪs] *n* arroz *m* redondo.

puddingstone [ˈpʊdɪŋstəʊn] *n* pudinga *f*.

puddle [ˈpʌdl] **1** *n* charco *m*. **2** *vt* (*Tech*) pudelar.

pudenda [puːˈdendə] *npl* partes *fpl* pudendas.

pudgy [ˈpʌdʒɪ] *adj* = **podgy**.

puerile [ˈpjʊəraɪl] *adj* pueril.

puerility [pjʊəˈrɪlɪtɪ] *n* puerilidad *f*.

puerperal [pjʊ(ː)ˈɜːpərəl] *adj* puerperal; ~ **fever** fiebre *f* puerperal; ~ **psychosis** psicosis *f* puerperal.

Puerto Rican [ˈpwɜːtəʊˈriːkən] **1** *adj* puertorriqueño. **2** *n* puertorriqueño *m*, -a *f*.

Puerto Rico [ˈpwɜːtəʊˈriːkəʊ] *n* Puerto *m* Rico.

puff [pʌf] **1** *n* (**a**) (*of air*) soplo *m*, (*of wind*) soplo *m*, racha *f*; (*of smoke*) humareda *f*, (*at cigarette*, *pipe*) chupada *f*, fumada *f*; (*from mouth*) bocanada *f*; (*sound*: *of breathing*, *of engine*) resoplido *m*, resuello *m*, bufido *m*.

(**b**) (*powder* ~) borla *f*; (*Culin*: *cream* ~) petisú *m*, pastelillo *m* de crema.

(**c**) (*advert*) bombo *m*.

(**d**) (‡: *drug*) canabis *m*.

2 *vt* (*blow*) soplar; *pipe etc* chupar; **to** ~ **smoke in sb's face** echar humo a la cara de uno.

3 *vi* (*blow*) soplar; (~ *and blow*) jadear, resollar, acezar; **to** ~ **(away) at one's pipe** chupar su pipa.

◆puff along *vi* (*train*) avanzar bufando; (*person*) correr (*etc*) jadeando.

◆puff away *vi V* **puff 3**.

◆puff out 1 *vt* (**a**) *smoke etc* echar, arrojar, despedir. (**b**) *cheeks, chest, sails* hinchar, inflar (*LAm*); *feathers* erizar.

2 *vi*: **the train ~ed out of the station** el tren salió bufando, el tren salió echando humo.

◆puff up 1 *vt* (**a**) = **puff out** (**b**). (**b**) *tyre etc* inflar, hinchar. (**c**) (*fig**) dar bombo a.

2 *vr*: **to** ~ **o.s. up** darse bombo, engreírse.

puff-adder [ˈpʌfˌædəʳ] *n* víbora *f* puff.

puffball [ˈpʌfbɔːl] *n* bejín *m*, pedo *m* de lobo.

puffed [pʌft] *adj eye* hinchado (*also* ~ **up**); **to be ~*** (*out of breath*) estar sin aliento, estar acezando; **to be** ~ **up** (*with pride*) estar engreído.

puffer* [ˈpʌfəʳ] *n* locomotora *f*.

puffin [ˈpʌfɪn] *n* frailecillo *m*.

puffiness [ˈpʌfɪnɪs] *n* hinchazón *f*.

puff-pastry [ˈpʌfˈpeɪstrɪ] *n*, (*US*) **puff paste** [ˈpʌfˈpeɪst] *n* hojaldre *m*.

puff sleeves [ˌpʌfˈsliːvz] *npl* mangas *fpl* filipinas.

puffy [ˈpʌfɪ] *adj eye etc* hinchado.

pug [pʌg] *n* doguillo *m*; ~ **nose** nariz *f* chata.
pugilism ['pju:dʒɪlɪzəm] *n* pugilato *m*, pugilismo *m*.
pugilist ['pju:dʒɪlɪst] *n* púgil *m*, pugilista *m*.
pugnacious [pʌg'neɪʃəs] *adj* belicoso, agresivo, pugnaz.
pugnaciously [pʌg'neɪʃəslɪ] *adv* con pugnacidad, agresivamente.
pugnacity [pʌg'næsɪtɪ] *n* pugnacidad *f*, belicosidad *f*, agresividad *f*, pugnacidad *f*.
pug-nosed ['pʌg'nəʊzd] *adj* chato, braco.
puke‡ [pju:k] **1** *n* **(a)** *(matter)* vómito *m*. **(b) to have a** ~ = **2**. **2** *vi* cambiar la peseta*, vomitar; **it makes me** ~ me da asco.
pukka* ['pʌkə] *adj* *(real)* auténtico, genuino; *(posh)* esnob, elegante, lujoso.
pulchritude ['pʌlkrɪtju:d] *n* *(hum)* belleza *f*.
pulchritudinous [,pʌlkrɪ'tju:dɪnəs] *adj* *(hum)* bello.
pull [pʊl] **1** *n* **(a)** *(tug)* tirón *m*, jalón *m* *(LAm)*, jalada *f* *(Mex)*; estirón *m*; *(with oar etc)* golpe *m*; *(of a magnet, also fig)* atracción *f*, fuerza *f* atractiva; *(of current)* fuerza *f*, ímpetu *m*; **the** ~ **of the south** la atracción del Sur, lo atractivo del Sur; **it was a long** ~ fue mucho camino; **we had a long** ~ **up the hill** nos costó mucho trabajo subir la cuesta; **give the rope a** ~ tira de la cuerda; **suddenly it gave a** ~ de repente dio un tirón.
(b) *(advantage)* ventaja *f*; *(influence)* enchufe* *m*; palanca* *f* *(LAm)*, influencia *f*, poder *m*; **they have a** ~ **over us now** ahora nos llevan ventaja; **he has a slight** ~ tiene una pequeña ventaja; **he has** ~ **in the right places** tiene influencia donde hace falta.
(c) *(at one's pipe)* chupada *f*; *(drink)* trago *m*; **he took a** ~ **at his pipe** chupó la pipa; **he took a** ~ **from the bottle** dio un tiento a la botella.
(d) *(handle of drawer etc)* tirador *m*; *(of bell)* cuerda *f*.
(e) *(Typ)* primeras pruebas *fpl*.
2 *vt* **(a)** *(tug at)* *bell rope, hair etc* tirar de, jalar *(LAm)*; *trigger* apretar; *oar* tirar de; *boat* remar; *(Naut)* *rope* halar, jalar; *weeds* arrancar; *muscle* torcerse, dislocarse; **to** ~ **a gun on sb** sacar una pistola para amenazar a uno; **his ideas** ~**ed me the same way** sus ideas me llevaron por el mismo camino; ~ **the other one!‡** ¡cuéntaselo a tu abuela*!
(b) *(extract, take out)* sacar; *beer* servir.
(c) *(draw along)* tirar, arrastrar, remolcar; **the engine** ~**s 6 coaches** la locomotora arrastra 6 vagones; ~ **your chair over** acerca la silla.
(d) *(Typ)* *proof* imprimir.
(e) *ball (at golf, etc)* golpear oblicuamente (a la izquierda).
(f) (*): **he knows how to** ~ **the birds** sabe ligar con las chicas; **this will really** ~ **the punters** esto seguramente atraerá clientela.
(g) to ~ **a fast one** (*or* **a trick**) **on sb** jugar una mala pasada a uno, embaucar a uno.
3 *vi* **(a)** tirar (*at* de); dar un tirón; **to** ~ **at a rope** tirar de una cuerda; **the steering** ~**s to the right** la dirección tira a la derecha.
(b) *(vehicle)* ir; *(oarsmen etc)* remar; **we** ~**ed for the shore** remamos hacia la orilla; **he** ~**ed sharply to one side to avoid the lorry** torció bruscamente a un lado para no chocar con el camión; **the car** ~**ed slowly up the hill** el coche subía despacio la cuesta; **it** ~**ed to a stop** se paró, se detuvo.
(c) to ~ **at one's pipe** dar chupadas a la pipa; **to** ~ **at a bottle** dar un tiento a una botella.
◆**pull about** *vt* manosear, estroprear.
◆**pull along 1** *vt* arrastrar.
2 *vr*: **to** ~ **o.s. along** arrastrarse.
◆**pull apart 1** *vt* **(a)** *(pull to pieces)* romper; partir en dos; *(take to pieces)* desmontar; *(criticize)* criticar duramente.
(b) *(separate)* separar; despegar, desunir.
2 *vi*: **they** ~ **apart easily** se separan fácilmente.
◆**pull away 1** *vt* arrancar (*from* a), quitar arrancando (*from* a).
2 *vi* **(a)** *(vehicle)* adelantarse (*from* a); **boat A** ~**ed away from B** el bote A dejaba atrás a B.
(b) to ~ **away at the oars** seguir remando; tirar (enérgicamente) de los remos.
(c) to ~ **away from sb** apartarse bruscamente de uno.
◆**pull back 1** *vt* **(a)** *(withdraw)* retirar; *(hold back)* retener, tirar hacia atrás.
(b) *lever etc* tirar hacia sí; *curtains* descorrer.
(b) *(Sport)* **to** ~ **one back** remontar un gol.
2 *vi* *(withdraw)* retirarse; *(refrain)* contenerse, *(pej)* rajarse.
◆**pull down** *vt* **(a)** *(lower)* bajar; tirar hacia abajo; *price etc* rebajar; *person* hacer caer, tumbar; **he** ~**ed his hat down** se caló el sombrero, se encasquetó el sombrero.
(b) *(demolish)* derribar, demoler; *government* derribar.
(c) *(weaken)* debilitar; **the mark in chemistry** ~**s her down** la nota de química es la razán de que salga mal.
(d) *(US*: earn)* ganar.
◆**pull in 1** *vt* **(a)** tirar hacia sí; *net* recoger; *rope* cobrar.
(b) *suspect* detener.
(c) *horse* enfrenar.
(d) (*: *earn*) ganar.
(e) (*: *attract*) **the film is** ~**ing them in** la película atrae un público numeroso, la película es muy popular; **this will** ~ **them in** esto les hará venir en masa.
2 *vi* *(Aut)* parar (junto a la acera); *(Rail)* llegar (a la estación).
3 *vr*: **to** ~ **o.s. in** apretarse el cinturón.
◆**pull off 1** *vt* **(a)** *(remove)* arrancar, separar; quitar de un tirón; *clothes* quitarse (de prisa); **the buses were** ~**ed off the road at once** en seguida los autobuses dejaron de circular.
(b) *plan etc* llevar a cabo; *deal* cerrar, concluir con éxito (algo inesperadamente); *game* ganar (algo inesperadamente); **to** ~ **it off** lograrlo, llevarlo a cabo, vencer.
2 *vi* *(Aut)* **we** ~**ed off (the road) into a layby** salimos de la carretera y paramos en un apartadero.
◆**pull on 1** *vt* *gloves etc* ponerse (de prisa). **2** *vi* tirar de.
◆**pull out 1** *vt* **(a)** *(take out)* sacar; *tooth* sacar, extraer; *lever etc* tirar hacia fuera; **to** ~ **sb out of a hole** tirar a uno de un hoyo a estirones; **to** ~ **sb out of a river** sacar a uno de un río.
(b) *(stretch)* estirar, extender.
(c) *(withdraw)* retirar; **everybody was** ~**ed out on strike** todos fueron llamados a la huelga.
2 *vi* **(a)** *(leave)* irse, marcharse (*from* de); *(Mil)* retirarse (*from* de); **we're** ~**ing out** nos marchamos ya.
(b) *(Aut)* salirse; *(Rail)* salir (de la estación); **he** ~**ed out and disappeared into the traffic** arrancó y se perdió en el tráfico; **the red car** ~**ed out from behind that black one** el coche rojo se salió de detrás de aquel negro.
(c) it ~**s out easily** *(drawer etc)* sale fácilmente.
◆**pull over 1** *vt* **(a)** *(move)* acercar tirando.
(b) *(topple)* derribar; volcar.
2 *vi* *(Aut)* hacerse a un lado, desviarse hacia un lado.
◆**pull round 1** *vt*: **to** ~ **sb round** ayudar a uno a reponerse.
2 *vi* reponerse.
◆**pull through 1** *vt*: **to** ~ **sb through** sacar a uno de un apuro (*or* de una enfermedad *etc*).
2 *vi* salir de un apuro; *(Med)* reponerse, recobrar la salud.
◆**pull together 1** *vt*: **this essay needs** ~**ing together** hay que reorganizar este ensayo, este ensayo conviene remodelarlo; **he has** ~**ed the team together** gracias a él los jugadores han recuperado su espíritu de equipo.
2 *vi* *(fig)* trabajar con un propósito común, trabajar (*etc*) con espíritu de equipo.
3 *vr*: **to** ~ **o.s. together** sobreponerse, serenarse, recobrar la calma; ~ **yourself together!** ¡cálmate!, ¡anímate!
◆**pull up 1** *vt* **(a)** *(raise)* alzar, levantar; tirar hacia arriba; *socks etc* alzar; *chair* acercar.
(b) *plant* arrancar, desarraigar.
(c) *(strengthen)* fortalecer; **his mark in French has** ~**ed him up** la nota de francés es la razón de que salga bien; **it has** ~**ed the pound up** ha fortalecido la libra.
(d) *(halt)* parar; *horse* refrenar.
(e) *(scold)* reprender.
2 *vi* **(a)** *(stop)* pararse, detenerse; *(Aut)* parar(se); *(restrain o.s.)* contenerse; *(stop talking etc)* interrumpirse.
(b) *(improve position)* mejorar, mejorar su posición.
pull-down ['pʊl,daʊn] *adj*: ~ **menu** menú *m* desplegable.
pullet ['pʊlɪt] *n* polla *f*, pollita *f*.
pulley ['pʊlɪ] *n* polea *f*.
pull-in ['pʊl,ɪn] *n* *(Brit Aut: lay-by)* apartadero *m*; *(for food)* café *m* de carretera, restaurante *m* de carretera.
Pullman car ['pʊlmən,kɑ:ʳ] *n* coche *m* Pullman, *(US)* coche-cama *m*.
pull-off ['pʊlɒf] *n* *(US Aut)* apartadero *m*.
pull-out ['pʊlaʊt] **1** *n* *(of magazine)* separable *m*, suplemento *m*. **2** *attr* separable.
pullover ['pʊləʊvəʳ] *n* pullover *m*, pull *m*.
pull-ring ['pʊlrɪŋ] *n*, **pull-tab** ['pʊltæb] *n* anilla *f*.

pullulate ['pʌljʊleɪt] *vi* pulular.
pull-up ['pʊlʌp] *n* (**a**) (*Brit*) = **pull-in.** (**b**) (*US*) = **press-up.**
pulmonary ['pʌlmənərɪ] *adj* pulmonar.
pulp [pʌlp] **1** *n* pulpa *f*; (*Bot*) pulpa *f*, carne *f*; (*paper* ~, *wood*~) pasta *f*; (*also* ~ **magazines** *etc*) prensa *f* amarilla; ~ **literature** literatura *f* para tirar, literatura *f* de bajísima calidad; **a leg crushed to** ~ una pierna hecha trizas; **to beat sb to a** ~ dar a uno una tremenda paliza; **to reduce sth to** ~ hacer algo pulpa, reducir algo a pulpa.
2 *vt* hacer pulpa, reducir a pulpa.
pulping ['pʌlpɪŋ] *n* reducción *f* a pulpa.
pulpit ['pʊlpɪt] *n* púlpito *m*.
pulpy ['pʌlpɪ] *adj* (**a**) pulposo. (**b**) *literature* para tirar, de bajísima calidad.
pulsar ['pʌlsɑːʳ] *n* pulsar *m*.
pulsate [pʌl'seɪt] *vi* pulsar, latir.
pulsation [pʌl'seɪʃən] *n* pulsación *f*, latido *m*.
pulse¹ [pʌls] **1** *n* (*Anat*) pulso *m*; (*throb*) pulsación *f*, latido *m*; **to feel** (*or* **take**) **sb's** ~ tomar el pulso a uno; **he keeps his finger on the company's** ~ está tomando constantemente el pulso a la compañía. **2** *vi* pulsar, latir.
pulse² [pʌls] *n* (*Bot*) legumbre *f*, legumbres *fpl*.
pulsebeat ['pʌlsbiːt] *n* latido *m* del pulso.
pulse rate ['pʌlsreɪt] *n* frecuencia *f* del pulso.
pulverization [ˌpʌlvəraɪ'zeɪʃən] *n* pulverización *f*.
pulverize ['pʌlvəraɪz] **1** *vt* pulverizar; (*fig*) hacer polvo; anonadar; (*) cascar*. **2** *vi* pulverizarse.
puma ['pjuːmə] *n* puma *f*.
pumice ['pʌmɪs] *n*, **pumice-stone** ['pʌmɪsstəʊn] *n* piedra *f* pómez.
pummel ['pʌml] = **pommel.**
pump¹ [pʌmp] **1** *n* bomba *f*; (*Naut*) pompa *f*; (*Aut*: *at garage*) surtidor *m* de gasolina.
2 *vt* (**a**) sacar (*or* elevar, llevar *etc*) con una bomba; bombear; **to** ~ **shots into sb** pegar muchos tiros a uno, acribillar a uno a tiros; **to** ~ **air along a tube** hacer que pase el aire por un tubo por medio de una bomba; **to** ~ **a tank dry** secar (*or* vaciar) un tanque con una bomba; **to** ~ **money into a company** invertir (grandes cantidades de) dinero en una compañía.
(**b**) *arm, handle* mover rápidamente de arriba para abajo; **to** ~ **hands** (*US**) estrechar la mano con fuerza; estrechar muchas manos.
(**c**) (*) *person* sonsacar (*for information* para obtener información); **it's no good trying to** ~ **me** es inútil tratar de sonsacarme.
3 *vi* (*person*) dar a la bomba; (*heart*: *also* **to** ~ **away**) pulsar, latir (fuertemente).
◆**pump in** *vt water etc* introducir bombeando; ~ **some more air in** pon más aire.
◆**pump out 1** *vt* (**a**) *liquid* sacar con una bomba. (**b**) *flooded cellar etc* sacar el agua de (con bomba); *stomach* vaciar (bombeando). **2** *vi*: **the blood was ~ing out of the wound** la sangre salía a borbotones de la herida.
◆**pump up** *vt tyre* inflar (con una bomba), bombear (*LAm*).
pump² [pʌmp] *n* (*shoe*) zapatilla *f*; (*US*) escarpín *m*.
pumper ['pʌmpəʳ] *n* (*US*) coche *m* bomba.
pumpernickel ['pʌmpənɪkl] *n* (*US*) pan *m* de centeno entero.
pumphouse ['pʌmphaʊs] *n*, *pl* **pumphouses** ['pʌmphaʊzɪz] casa *f* de bombas.
pumping-station ['pʌmpɪŋˌsteɪʃən] *n* estación *f* de bombeo.
pumpkin ['pʌmpkɪn] *n* (*vegetable*) calabaza *f*; (*plant*) calabacera *f*.
pump-priming ['pʌmp'praɪmɪŋ] *n* (*fig*) inversión *f* inicial con carácter de estímulo; (*US*) inversión *f* estatal en nuevos proyectos que se espera beneficien la economía.
pumproom ['pʌmprʊm] *n* pabellón *m* de hidroterapia.
pun [pʌn] **1** *n* juego *m* de palabras (*on* sobre), equívoco *m*, retruécano *m*, albur *m* (*Mex*). **2** *vi* hacer un juego de palabras (*on* sobre), jugar del vocablo, alburear (*Mex*).
Punch [pʌntʃ] *nm* Polichinela; **~-and-Judy show** guiñol *m*, teatro *m* de polichinelas.
punch¹ [pʌntʃ] **1** *n* (**a**) (*tool*) punzón *m*; (*for tickets*) sacabocados *m*, taladro *m*.
(**b**) (*blow*) puñetazo *m*, golpe *m*; **he packs a ~*** pega duro*; **to pull one's ~es** no emplear toda su fuerza; **he didn't pull any ~es** (*fig*) no se mordió la lengua, no anduvo con chiquitas.
(**c**) (*fig*) empuje *m*, vigor *m*, fuerza *f*; **he has** ~ es hombre de empuje; **he's a speaker with some** ~ es un orador dinámico; **think of a phrase that's got some** ~ **to it** dame una frase que tenga garra.
2 *vt* (**a**) (*with tool*) punzar, taladrar; agujerear; perforar; *card* perforar; *ticket* picar, ponchar (*Carib*); **~ed tape** cinta *f* perforada; **to** ~ **holes in a sheet** practicar agujeros en una lámina.
(**b**) (*with fist*) dar un puñetazo a, pegar, golpear.
(**c**) *button, key* presionar, tocar; **you have to** ~ **the code in first** primero hay que introducir el código.
3 *vi* pegar.
◆**punch in** *vi* fichar, picar.
◆**punch out 1** *vt hole* taladrar, perforar; (*machine parts*) troquelar; (*design*) estampar.
2 *vi* (**a**) (*on time clock*) fichar al salir, picar la salida. (**b**) (*US**) estirar la pata*.
punch² [pʌntʃ] *n* (*drink*) ponche *m*.
punchball ['pʌntʃbɔːl] *n* (*Brit*) saco *m* de arena, punching *m*.
punchbowl ['pʌntʃbəʊl] *n* ponchera *f*.
punch-drunk ['pʌntʃ'drʌŋk] *adj*: **to be** ~ estar groggy, estar grogui, estar sonado*.
punch(ed) card ['pʌntʃ(t)kɑːd] *n* tarjeta *f* perforada.
puncher ['pʌntʃəʳ] *n* (**a**) (*tool*) perforador *m*. (**b**) **he's a hard** ~ pega fuerte.
punch(ing)-bag ['pʌntʃ(ɪŋ)bæg] *n* saco *m* de arena, punching *m*.
punch-line ['pʌntʃlaɪn] *n* frase *f* clave; **the** ~ **of his speech was ...** remató su discurso con la frase ...
punch-operator ['pʌntʃɒpəreɪtəʳ] *n* operador *m*, -ora *f* de máquina perforadora.
punch-up‡ ['pʌntʃʌp] *n* (*Brit*) riña *f*, pendencia *f*.
punchy* ['pʌntʃɪ] *adj* (*US*) *person etc* de empuje, dinámico; *phrase, remark* tajante, contundente; *style* vigoroso.
punctilio [pʌŋk'tɪlɪəʊ] *n* puntillo *m*, etiqueta *f*; puntualidad *f*.
punctilious [pʌŋk'tɪlɪəs] *adj* puntilloso, etiquetero, puntual.
punctiliously [pʌŋk'tɪlɪəslɪ] *adv* de modo puntilloso; puntualmente.
punctual ['pʌŋktjʊəl] *adj* puntual; **'please be ~'** 'se ruega la mayor puntualidad'; **will the train be ~?** ¿llegará el tren a la hora?
punctuality [ˌpʌŋktjʊ'ælɪtɪ] *n* puntualidad *f*.
punctually ['pʌŋktjʊəlɪ] *adv* puntualmente; **~ at 6 o'clock** a las 6 en punto; **the bus arrived** ~ el autobús llegó a la hora.
punctuate ['pʌŋktjʊeɪt] *vt* puntuar; (*fig*) interrumpir; **his speech was ~d by bursts of applause** su discurso fue interrumpido por salvas de aplausos.
punctuation [ˌpʌŋktjʊ'eɪʃən] **1** *n* puntuación *f*. **2** *attr*: ~ **mark** signo *m* de puntuación.
puncture ['pʌŋktʃəʳ] **1** *n* perforación *f*; (*of skin etc*) puntura *f*, punzada *f*; (*Aut*) pinchazo *m*; (*Med*) punción *f*; **I have a** ~ tengo un neumático pinchado, se me ha reventado un neumático (una llanta *LAm*).
2 *vt* (*gen*) perforar; *leather, paper etc* punzar, pinchar; *balloon, tyre* pinchar, ponchar (*Carib*); (*Med*) perforar; **this ~d his confidence** esto destruyó su confianza; **we'll see if it ~s his pride** veremos si esto le baja los humos.
3 *vi* (*tyre*) pincharse.
pundit ['pʌndɪt] *n* (*iro*) lumbrera *f*, erudito *m* a la violeta.
pungency ['pʌndʒənsɪ] *n* lo acre; picante *m*; mordacidad *f*, acerbidad *f*.
pungent ['pʌndʒənt] *adj smell* acre; (*piquant*) picante; *satire etc* mordaz, acerbo.
pungently ['pʌndʒəntlɪ] *adv* acremente; de modo picante; mordazmente, acerbamente.
Punic ['pjuːnɪk] **1** *adj* púnico. **2** *n* púnico *m*.
punish ['pʌnɪʃ] *vt* (**a**) castigar; **to** ~ **sb for sth** castigar a uno por algo; **to** ~ **sb for doing sth** castigar a uno por haber hecho algo.
(**b**) (*fig*) (*maltreat*) maltratar; (*in race etc*) exigir esfuerzos sobrehumanos a; (*Boxing*) castigar; (*take advantage of*) aprovecharse al máximo de; *food* devorar, no perdonar.
punishable ['pʌnɪʃəbl] *adj* punible, castigable; **a** ~ **offence** una infracción que castiga la ley; **a crime** ~ **by death** un delito que merece la pena de muerte.
punishing ['pʌnɪʃɪŋ] **1** *adj race etc* duro, agotador. **2** *n* castigo *m*; (*fig*) castigo *m*, malos tratos *mpl*; **to take a** ~ sufrir un duro castigo.
punishment ['pʌnɪʃmənt] *n* castigo *m*; **to make the** ~ **fit the crime** señalar un castigo de acuerdo con el crimen; **the boxer took a lot of** ~ el boxeador sufrió un duro castigo; **to take one's** ~ **like a man** sufrir el castigo sin quejarse.
punitive ['pjuːnɪtɪv] *adj* punitivo; (*Jur*) *damages* punitorio.
Punjabi [pʌn'dʒɑːbɪ] **1** *adj* punjabí. **2** *n* (**a**) punjabí *mf*. (**b**) (*Ling*) punjabí *m*.

punk [pʌŋk] **1** *adj* (**a**) (*) malo, baladí, de baja calidad. (**b**) (*1980s*) punki. **2** *n* (**a**) (*US*‡) pobre hombre *m*; novato *m*; bobo *m*; (*hoodlum*) matón *m*. (**b**) (‡: *nonsense*) bobadas *fpl*. (**c**) (*1980s*) punki *mf*.

punnet ['pʌnɪt] *n* (*Brit*) canastilla *f*.

punster ['pʌnstəʳ] *n* persona *f* aficionada a los juegos de palabras, equivoquista *mf*.

punt¹ [pʌnt] **1** *n* batea *f*. **2** *vt* impulsar con percha. **3** *vi* ir en batea, pasearse en batea.

punt² [pʌnt] **1** *n* puntapié *m* de volea. **2** *vt* dar un puntapié de volea a.

punt³ [pʌnt] *vi* (*Brit*: *bet*) jugar, hacer apuestas.

punter ['pʌntəʳ] *n* (*Brit*) (**a**) (*who bets*) apostante *mf*. (**b**) (*person**) tío* *m*, sujeto *m*; (*Comm, also of prostitute*) cliente *m*.

puntpole ['pʌntpəʊl] *n* percha *f*, pértiga *f* (de batea).

puny ['pju:nɪ] *adj person etc* débil, encanijado; *effort* débil, flojo; (*petty*) insignificante.

pup [pʌp] **1** *n* cachorro *m*, -a *f*; **to sell sb a ~** dar a uno gato por liebre. **2** *vi* parir (*la perra*).

pupa ['pju:pə] *n, pl* **pupae** ['pju:pi:] crisálida *f*.

pupate ['pju:peɪt] *vi* crisalidar.

pupil¹ ['pju:pl] *n* alumno *m*, -a *f*, escolar *mf*, educando *m*, -a *f*.

pupil² ['pju:pl] *n* (*Anat*) pupila *f*.

puppet ['pʌpɪt] **1** *n* títere *m*; (*fig*) títere *m*, marioneta *mf*. **2** *attr*: **~ régime** gobierno *m* títere; **~ show, ~ theater** (*US*), **~ theatre** (*Brit*) títeres *mpl*, teatro *m* de títeres.

puppeteer [,pʌpɪ'tɪəʳ] *n* titiritero *m*, -a *f*.

puppetry ['pʌpɪtrɪ] *n* títeres *mpl*, arte *m* del titiritero.

puppy ['pʌpɪ] **1** *n* cachorro *m*, -a *f*, perrito *m*, -a *f*. **2** *attr*: **~ fat** carnes *fpl* de adolescente; **~ love** amor *m* de jóvenes.

purblind ['pɜ:blaɪnd] *adj* cegato; (*fig*) ciego, falto de comprensión.

purchase ['pɜ:tʃɪs] **1** *n* (**a**) (*Comm etc*) compra *f*; adquisición *f*; **to make a ~** hacer una compra.

(**b**) (*on rock etc*) agarre *m* firme, pie *m* firme; (*Mech*) apalancamiento *m*; **to get a ~ on the surface** tener donde agarrarse a la superficie, lograr pegarse a la superficie.

2 *attr*: **~ order** orden *f* de compra; **~ price** precio *m* de compra; **~ tax** (*Brit*) impuesto *m* de venta.

3 *vt* comprar, adquirir.

purchaser ['pɜ:tʃɪsəʳ] *n* comprador *m*, -ora *f*.

purchasing ['pɜ:tʃɪsɪŋ] *n* compra *f*, el comprar; **~ power** poder *m* de compra, poder *m* adquisitivo.

purdah ['pɜ:də] *n* (*India etc*) costumbre *f* de mantener recluida a la mujer, reclusión *f* femenina; **to be in ~** (*fig*) estar en cuarentena.

pure [pjʊəʳ] *adj* puro; **~ mathematics** matemáticas *fpl* puras; **~ science** ciencias *fpl* puras; **~ and simple** puro y sencillo; **it's a ~ waste of time** es sencillamente perder el tiempo; **as ~ as the driven snow** puro como la nieve.

purebred ['pjʊə'bred] **1** *adj* de pura sangre, de raza. **2** *n* pura sangre *mf*.

purée ['pjʊəreɪ] *n* puré *m*.

purely ['pjʊəlɪ] *adv* puramente; **~ and simply** sencillamente, simplemente.

pure-minded ['pjʊə'maɪndɪd] *adj* de mente pura.

pureness ['pjʊənɪs] *n* pureza *f*.

purgation [pɜ:'geɪʃən] *n* purgación *f*.

purgative ['pɜ:gətɪv] **1** *adj* purgativo, purgante. **2** *n* purgante *m*.

purgatory ['pɜ:gətərɪ] *n* purgatorio *m*; **it was ~!** ¡fue un purgatorio!

purge [pɜ:dʒ] **1** *n* (*act*) purga *f*; (*medicine*) purga *f*, purgante *m*; (*Pol*) purga *f*, depuración *f*. **2** *vt* purgar; purificar, depurar; *offence, sin* purgar; (*Pol*) *party* purgar, depurar, *member* liquidar.

purification [,pjʊərɪfɪ'keɪʃən] *n* purificación *f*, depuración *f*.

purifier ['pjʊərɪfaɪəʳ] *n* depurador *m*.

purify ['pjʊərɪfaɪ] *vt* purificar, depurar; *metal* acrisolar, refinar; *town etc* depurar.

purism ['pjʊərɪzəm] *n* purismo *m*.

purist ['pjʊərɪst] *n* purista *mf*, casticista *mf*.

puritan ['pjʊərɪtən] **1** *adj* puritano. **2** *n* puritano *m*, -a *f*.

puritanical [,pjʊərɪ'tænɪkəl] *adj* puritano.

puritanism ['pjʊərɪtənɪzəm] *n* puritanismo *m*.

purity ['pjʊərɪtɪ] *n* pureza *f*.

purl [pɜ:l] **1** *n* puntada *f* invertida, punto *m* del revés. **2** *vt* hacer a puntadas invertidas; **'~ two'** 'dos puntadas invertidas'.

purler* ['pɜ:ləʳ] *n*: **to come a ~** caer pesadamente, caer aparatosamente; (*fig*) fracasar estrepitosamente, darse un batacazo.

purlieus ['pɜ:lju:z] *npl* alrededores *mpl*, inmediaciones *fpl*.

purloin [pɜ:'lɔɪn] *vt* robar, hurtar.

purple ['pɜ:pl] **1** *adj* purpúreo; *bruise etc* morado; **~ heart** (píldora *f* de) anfetamina *f*; **P~ Heart** (*US Mil*) *condecoración otorgada a los heridos de guerra*; **~ passage, ~ patch** trozo *m* de estilo hinchado; **to go ~ (in the face)** enrojecerse. **2** *n* púrpura *f*. **3** *vt* purpurar.

purplish ['pɜ:plɪʃ] *adj* purpurino, algo purpúreo.

purport 1 ['pɜ:pət] *n* (*meaning*) significado *m*, sentido *m*; (*purpose*) intención *f*.

2 [pɜ:'pɔ:t] *vt* (*mean*) significar; (*convey meaning*) dar a entender (*that* que); (*profess*) pretender (*to be* ser); **this ~s to be a statement of ...** esto pretende ser una declaración de ...

purportedly [pɜ:'pɔ:tɪdlɪ] *adv* supuestamente; **~ written by ...** supuestamente escrito por ...

purpose ['pɜ:pəs] **1** *n* (**a**) (*intention*) propósito *m*, intención *f*, objeto *m*; **'~ of visit'** (*official form*) 'motivo *m* del viaje'; **novel with a ~** novela *f* de tesis, novela *f* de intención seria; **my ~ in doing this** mi propósito al hacer esto; **for the ~** al efecto; **for this ~** para este fin; **in a box placed for that ~** en una caja colocada a ese efecto; **for our ~s we may disregard this** para nuestros fines podemos hacer caso omiso de esto; **for the ~ of** + *ger* con el fin de + *infin*, al efecto de + *infin*; **for the ~s of this meeting** por lo que toca a esta reunión; **on ~** a propósito, aposta, adrede; **to speak to the ~** hablar oportunamente, hablar muy a propósito; **to good ~, to some ~** con buenos resultados, provechosamente; **to little ~** para poco; **to no ~** inútilmente, en vano; **to answer** (*or* **serve**) **sb's ~** servir para el caso, servir para lo que quiere uno; **it serves no useful ~** no tiene utilidad práctica; **it serves a variety of ~s** sirve para diversos efectos.

(**b**) (*sense of* ~) resolución *f*; **infirmity of ~** falta *f* de resolución; **strength of ~** resolución *f*, firmeza *f*.

2 *vt* proponerse, proyectar, intentar; **to ~ to do sth** proponerse hacer algo.

purpose-built [,pɜ:pəs'bɪlt] *adj* construido con propósitos específicos.

purposeful ['pɜ:pəsfʊl] *adj* resuelto, determinado; *activity* intencionado.

purposefully ['pɜ:pəsfəlɪ] *adv* resueltamente.

purposefulness ['pɜ:pəsfʊlnɪs] *n* resolución *f*.

purposeless ['pɜ:pəslɪs] *adj person's character* irresoluto; *person's state* indeciso; *act* sin propósito, sin objeto, sin finalidad.

purposely ['pɜ:pəslɪ] *adv* a propósito, adrede, expresamente; **a ~ vague statement** una declaración hecha adrede en términos vagos.

purposive ['pɜ:pəsɪv] *adj* = **purposeful.**

purr [pɜ:ʳ] **1** *n* ronroneo *m*. **2** *vt* (*say*) decir suavemente, susurrar. **3** *vi* (*cat, engine*) ronronear; (*person*) estar satisfecho.

purse [pɜ:s] **1** *n* bolsa *f*; monedero *m*, portamonedas *m*; (*handbag: US*) bolso *m*, cartera *f* (*LAm*); (*prize*) premio *m*; (*collection*) colecta *f*; **a well-lined ~** una bolsa llena; **it is beyond my ~** mis recursos no llegan a tanto, está fuera de mi alcance.

2 *vt*: **to ~ (up) one's lips** fruncir los labios.

purser ['pɜ:səʳ] *n* contador *m* (de navío), comisario *m*, -a *f*.

purse-snatcher ['pɜ:ssnætʃəʳ] *n* (*US*) tironista *mf*.

purse-strings ['pɜ:sstrɪŋz] *npl*: **to hold the ~** manejar los cuartos.

pursuance [pə'sju:əns] *n* prosecución *f*, cumplimiento *m*; **in ~ of** con arreglo a, en cumplimiento de.

pursuant [pə'sju:ənt] *adv*: **~ to** de acuerdo con, conforme a.

pursue [pə'sju:] *vt* (*hunt*) seguir, seguir la pista de, perseguir, cazar, dar caza a; (*chase, molest*) acosar, dar caza a, asediar; *line of conduct, inquiry* seguir; *aim, objective* buscar, aspirar a; *study* proseguir; *profession* dedicarse a, ejercer; *plan* proceder de acuerdo con, obrar con arreglo a; *pleasures etc* dedicarse a; **they ~d the fox into the wood** siguieron la zorra dentro del bosque; **he ~d the girl home** siguió a la chica hasta casa; **he won't stop pursuing me!** ¡no me deja a sol ni a sombra!

pursuer [pə'sju:əʳ] *n* perseguidor *m*, -ora *f*.

pursuit [pə'sju:t] *n* (**a**) (*chase*) caza *f*; perseguimiento *m*, persecución *f*; (*search*) busca *f*; **in ~ of** en busca de, en pos de; **with two policemen in hot ~** con dos policías que le seguían muy de cerca; **to go in ~ of sb** ir en pos de uno; **to set out in ~ of sb** salir a buscar a uno.

(**b**) **the ~ of happiness** la busca de la felicidad; **the ~ of wealth** el afán de riqueza.

(**c**) (*occupation*) ocupación *f*, carrera *f*, empleo *m*; (*pastime*) pasatiempo *m*; **her favourite** ~ su pasatiempo predilecto; **literary ~s** intereses *mpl* literarios, actividades *fpl* literarias.

pursuit plane [pə'sju:tpleɪn] *n* avión *m* de caza.

purulence ['pjʊərʊləns] *n* purulencia *f*.

purulent ['pjʊərʊlənt] *adj* purulento.

purvey [pɜ:'veɪ] *vt* proveer, suministrar, abastecer.

purveyance [pɜ:'veɪəns] *n* provisión *f*, suministro *m*, abastecimiento *m*.

purveyor [pɜ:'veɪə^r] *n* proveedor *m*, -ora *f*, abastecedor *m*, -ora *f*.

purview ['pɜ:vju:] *n* alcance *m*, esfera *f*; **it comes within the ~ of the law** está comprendido dentro de los límites de la ley.

pus [pʌs] *n* pus *m*, postema *f* (*Mex*).

push [pʊʃ] **1** *n* (**a**) (*shove*) empuje *m*, empujón *m*; **with one** ~ de un empuje; **to give sb a** ~ dar un empujón a uno; **to give sb a helping** ~ ayudar a uno empujando su coche (*etc*).

(**b**) (*Mil*) ataque *m*, ofensiva *f*; avance *m*; **the final** ~ el último esfuerzo.

(**c**) (*Brit**) **to get the** ~ (*worker*) ser despedido; (*lover*) recibir calabazas; **to give sb the** ~ (*member, worker*) poner a uno de patitas en la calle, (*lover*) dar calabazas a uno*.

(**d**) (*pushfulness*) dinamismo *m*, empuje *m*, energía *f*; **he's got no** ~ no tiene empuje, le falta energía; **he's a man with plenty of** ~ es hombre de empuje.

(**e**) (*) **at a** ~ si es necesario, en caso de necesidad; **when it comes to the** ~ en el momento de la verdad, llegado el punto crítico.

2 *vt* (**a**) (*press*) empujar; (*down, with foot*) pisar, apretar; *button etc* apretar, pulsar, presionar; **to ~ a car into the garage** empujar un coche dentro del garaje; **to ~ one's finger into a hole** introducir el dedo en un agujero; **he ~ed his finger into my eye** me metió el dedo en el ojo.

(**b**) *person* empujar; **don't ~ me!** ¡no me empujes!; **to ~ sb off the pavement** echar a uno de la acera a empujones; **they ~ed me off the ball** me quitaron el balón a empujones.

(**c**) (*press*) *advantage* aprovecharse de; *claim* proseguir, insistir en; *enterprise* promover, fomentar; *person* proteger, ayudar, ayudar en su carrera; *product etc* promocionar; **to ~ an attack home** esforzarse por asegurar el éxito de un ataque; **don't ~ your luck** no te fíes demasiado de tu buena suerte, no te arriesgues demasiado.

(**d**) (*force*) empujar; **to ~ sb to do sth** empujar a uno a hacer algo; incitar a uno a hacer algo; **I was ~ed into it** me obligaron a ello; **when we ~ed her, she explained it all** cuando insistimos con ella, lo explicó todo; **to ~ sb for payment** ejercer presión sobre uno para que pague; **we are ~ed for time** tenemos poco tiempo, tenemos mucha prisa; **to be ~ed for money** andar muy escaso de dinero; **I'm rather ~ed for boxes just now** ahora ando algo escaso de cajas; **we shall be (hard) ~ed to finish it** tendremos grandes dificultades para terminarlo.

(**e**) *drugs* vender, traficar en.

(**f**) (*) **he's ~ing 60** tiene casi 60 años.

3 *vi* (**a**) empujar; dar un empujón, dar empujones; '~' (*on doors*) 'empujad'; **don't ~!** ¡no empujen!

(**b**) (*fig*) hacer esfuerzos, obrar con energía; **they're ~ing for better conditions** hacen campaña para mejorar sus condiciones (de trabajo).

(**c**) **to ~ into enemy territory** avanzar en territorio enemigo.

◆**push along 1** *vt* (**a**) *object* empujar.

(**b**) *work* acelerar, agilizar.

2 *vi* (**a**) (*Aut etc*) rodar, circular, ir.

(**b**) (*: *leave*) largarse*.

◆**push around** *vt* (**a**) empujar (de acá para allá).

(**b**) (*bully*) mandar, dar órdenes a; tratar brutalmente; **he's not one to be ~ed around** no da su brazo a torcer.

◆**push aside, push away** *vt object* apartar (con la mano); **to ~ sb aside** apartar a uno empujándole, (*fig*) arrinconar a uno.

◆**push at** *vt door etc* empujar.

◆**push back** *vt enemy* echar atrás, rechazar; *crowd* hacer retroceder; *hair etc* echar hacia atrás; **he's ~ing back the frontiers of knowledge** está ampliando nuestros conocimientos.

◆**push down** *vt* (**a**) (*press down*) comprimir; (*lower*) bajar, hacer bajar; *price, value* hacer bajar.

(**b**) (*topple*) derribar, hacer caer.

◆**push forward 1** *vt* (**a**) *person etc* empujar hacia adelante.

(**b**) *plan, work* llevar adelante.

2 *vi* avanzar.

3 *vr*: **to ~ o.s. forward** ofrecer (con poca modestia) sus servicios; ofrecerse, proponerse; darse mucha importancia.

◆**push in 1** *vt* (**a**) *screw etc* introducir a la fuerza; empujar; clavar, hincar.

(**b**) **to ~ one's way in** = **2** (**a**).

2 *vi* (**a**) entrar a empujones; introducirse a la fuerza.

(**b**) (*interfere*) injerirse, entrometerse.

◆**push off 1** *vt* (**a**) *lid etc* quitar a la fuerza.

(**b**) (*Naut*) desatracar.

2 *vi* (**a**) (*Naut*) desatracar; apartarse de la orilla.

(**b**) (*) largarse*; **~ off!** ¡lárgate*!

(**c**) **the top ~es off** la tapa se quita empujando.

◆**push on 1** *vt* (**a**) *lid etc* poner (presionando).

(**b**) (*incite*) empujar, incitar (*to + infin* a + *infin*).

(**c**) *work* acelerar, agilizar.

2 *vi* seguir adelante, continuar (a pesar de todo); **they ~ed on another 5 km** avanzaron 5 km más; **we ~ed on to the camp** seguimos hasta el campamento; **it's time to ~ on** es hora de ponernos otra vez en camino.

◆**push out 1** *vt* (**a**) *person* empujar hacia fuera; expulsar, hacer salir; *boat* desatracar.

(**b**) *tentacle etc* sacar, extender.

(**c**) (*produce*) producir.

2 *vi* (*root etc*) extenderse.

◆**push over** *vt* (**a**) **to ~ one's way over** acercarse a empujones.

(**b**) *object* empujar (*to* hacia).

(**c**) (*topple*) derribar, hacer caer; *car* volcar.

◆**push through 1** *vt* (**a**) *hand etc* pasar (a la fuerza); hacer pasar (empujando).

(**b**) *deal* concluir rápidamente, concluir a pesar de la oposición; (*Parl*) *bill* hacer aceptar a la fuerza.

(**c**) **to ~ one's way through a crowd** abrirse camino a empujones por la muchedumbre, abrirse paso empujando a través de una multitud.

2 *vi* (*plant*) aparecer; **to ~ through** (*also* **to ~ one's way through**) abrirse camino a empujones.

◆**push to** *vt door* cerrar.

◆**push up** *vt* (**a**) *lever etc* alzar, levantar; empujar hacia arriba.

(**b**) (*increase*) hacer subir, aumentar.

pushbike* ['pʊʃbaɪk] *n* (*Brit*) bici* *f*.

push-button ['pʊʃ,bʌtn] **1** *n* pulsador *m*, botón *m* (de control *etc*). **2** *attr* dotado de pulsador, con botón (de mando *etc*), de botones; **with ~ control** con mando de botón.

pushcart ['pʊʃkɑ:t] *n* carretilla *f* de mano.

pushchair ['pʊʃtʃɛə^r] *n* (*Brit*) sillita *f* de ruedas.

pusher ['pʊʃə^r] *n* (**a**) persona *f* emprendedora; (*pej*) persona *f* de ambición desmesurada. (**b**) (*: *of drugs*) camello* *m*, traficante *m* de drogas.

pushful ['pʊʃfʊl] *adj* emprendedor, dinámico, enérgico; ambicioso; (*pej*) agresivo.

pushfulness ['pʊʃfʊlnɪs] *n* empuje *m*, dinamismo *m*, espíritu *m* emprendedor; ambición *f*; (*pej*) agresividad *f*.

pushing ['pʊʃɪŋ] *adj* = **pushful.**

pushover* ['pʊʃ,əʊvə^r] *n*: **it's a ~** es pan comido*, está tirado*; **he was a ~** era fácil convencerle (*or* sonsacarle *etc*); **I'm a ~ when a woman asks me** no resisto cuando me lo pide una mujer.

push-pull ['pʊʃpʊl] *attr*: **~ circuit** circuito *m* de contrafase, circuito *m* equilibrado.

push-rod ['pʊʃrɒd] *n* (*Aut*) barra *f* de presión.

push-up ['pʊʃʌp] *n* (*US*) = **press-up.**

pushy* ['pʊʃɪ] *adj* = **pushful.**

pusillanimity [,pju:sɪlə'nɪmɪtɪ] *n* pusilanimidad *f*.

pusillanimous [,pju:sɪ'lænɪməs] *adj* pusilánime.

puss [pʊs] *n* (**a**) minino *m*, micho *m*; **~, ~!** ¡miz, miz!; **P~ in Boots** el gato con botas. (**b**) (‡) jeta* *f*.

pussy ['pʊsɪ] *n* (**a**) = **puss (a).** (**b**) (***) coño*** *m*.

pussycat ['pʊsɪkæt] *n* minino *m*.

pussyfoot* ['pʊsɪfʊt] *vi* (*esp US*) (*also* **to ~ around**) andar sigilosamente, moverse a paso de gato; andar a tientas; (*fig*) no decidirse, no declararse.

pussy-willow [,pʊsɪ'wɪləʊ] *n* sauce *m*.

pustule ['pʌstju:l] *n* pústula *f*.

put [pʊt] (*irr: pret and ptp* **put**) **1** *vt* (**a**) (*place*) poner; colocar; (*esp into, inside*) meter; **~ it here** ponlo aquí; **~ it there*!** (*handshake*) ¡chócala*!, ¡vengan esos cinco!; **to ~**

milk in one's coffee echar (*or* añadir) leche a su café; **to ~ sth to one's ear** acercar algo al oído; **to ~ one's signature to sth** poner su firma en algo, firmar algo; **I've ~ a lot of time into this** he dedicado mucho tiempo a esto; **to ~ a field under oats** sembrar un campo de avena; **to ~ sb under an obligation** poner a uno bajo una obligación; **to ~ virtue before success** anteponer la virtud al éxito, preferir la virtud al éxito; **he ~s the Italians before the Spaniards** estima a los italianos más que a los españoles.

(**b**) (*versions*) **to ~ a text into verse** poner un texto en verso, versificar un texto; **to ~ a passage into Greek** traducir un pasaje al griego.

(**c**) (*invest etc*) **to ~ money into a company** invertir dinero en una sociedad; **to ~ one's money into shares** comprar acciones con su dinero; **to ~ one's savings into marks** cambiar sus ahorros en marcos; **to ~ money on a horse** apostar dinero a un caballo.

(**d**) (*state etc*) declarar; (*express*) expresar; (*in writing*) redactar; *plan etc* exponer, explicar (*to* a); *problem* plantear; **as Lope ~s it** como lo expresa Lope; **if I may ~ it so** si se me permite decirlo así; **all that can be ~ in 2 sentences** todo eso se puede expresar en 2 frases; **as the Portuguese ~ it** como dicen los portugueses; **to ~ it bluntly** para decirlo como es, hablando sin rodeos; **to ~ it briefly** para decirlo en pocas palabras; **to ~ it simply** para decirlo sencillamente; **~ it to him nicely** díselo de buen modo, díselo con finura; **how will you ~ it to him?** ¿cómo se lo vas a explicar?; **he ~s a convincing case** se explica con argumentos convincentes; **I ~ it to you that ...** les sugiero que ..., me veo en el caso de decirles que ...; **to ~ a question to sb** hacer una pregunta a uno; **I should like to ~ a resolution** quiero proponer una moción; **the chairman ~ it to the committee** el presidente lo sometió a votación en el comité.

(**e**) (*estimate*) calcular; computar, estimar (*at* en); **the population is ~ at 2500** se calcula la población en 2500; **what would you ~ it at?** ¿en cuánto lo estimas?; **I would ~ her at about 40** diría que tiene unos 40 años.

(**f**) (*with personal object*) **to ~ sb to bed** acostar a uno; **to ~ the enemy to flight** poner en fuga al enemigo; **they ~ the lad to a trade** le pusieron al muchacho de aprendiz en un oficio; **to ~ sb to a new kind of work** poner a uno a trabajar en un nuevo oficio; **to ~ sb through his paces** poner a uno a prueba, demostrar las cualidades de uno; **to ~ sb through a test** hacer pasar a uno por una prueba, someter a uno a una prueba; **they really ~ him through it** le sometieron a las pruebas más rigurosas; de veras le dieron un mal rato; **to ~ a horse at a fence** hacer que un caballo salte una valla.

(**g**) (*direct*) **to ~ a bullet through sb** atravesar a uno de una bala; **to ~ one's pen through a word** tachar una palabra; **to ~ the weight** lanzar el peso.

(**h**) (*ptp*) **~ option** opción *f* de venta a precio fijado; **to stay ~** no moverse, seguir en el mismo sitio.

2 *vr*: **where would you like me to ~ myself?** ¿dónde quieres que me coloque?, (*at meal*) ¿dónde quieres que me siente?; **I didn't know where to ~ myself** creí morir de vergüenza.

◆put about, put around 1 *vt* (**a**) *rumour* diseminar, hacer correr; **to ~ it about that ...** dar a entender que ..., hacer creer que ...; hacer correr el rumor de que ...; **she's ~ting it about a bit‡** se está ofreciendo a todo quisque*.

(**b**) (*Naut*) hacer virar.

2 *vi* (*Naut*) virar, cambiar de bordada.

◆put across 1 *vt* (**a**) *information* comunicar; *meaning* hacer entender; *idea, product* hacer aceptar; *personality* presentar.

(**b**) *deal etc* cerrar.

(**c**) **to ~ it across sb*** (*deceive*) engañar a uno, embaucar a uno; (*defeat*) dar una paliza a uno.

2 *vr*: **to ~ o.s. across** impresionar con su personalidad, presentarse de manera eficaz; comunicar eficazmente lo que uno quiere decir.

◆put apart *vt*: **that ~s him apart from the others** (*fig*) eso le separa de los demás.

◆put aside *vt* (**a**) (*reject*) rechazar; *fears etc* desechar; *work* dejar, poner a un lado.

(**b**) (*save*) dejar de lado, poner aparte.

◆put away *vt* (**a**) (*store*) guardar, poner aparte; *money* ahorrar.

(**b**) (*replace*) devolver a su lugar; *car* poner en el garaje; *sword* envainar; (*in pocket etc*) guardar.

(**c**) (*reject*) *thought* desechar, descartar; *wife* repudiar.

(**d**) (*imprison*) encarcelar; *lunatic* recluir en un manicomio; (*banish*) alojar.

(**e**) (*) *food* zamparse; **he can certainly ~ it away** ése sí sabe comer.

◆put back 1 *vt* (**a**) (*replace*) devolver a su lugar; restituir, volver a poner; (*in pocket, drawer etc*) guardar, volver; (*to post*) restituir; **~ that back!** ¡déjalo!

(**b**) (*retard*) retrasar; **this will ~ us back 10 years** esto nos retrasará 10 años; **to ~ a clock back one hour** retrasar un reloj una hora.

(**c**) (*postpone*) aplazar.

(**d**) (*) *drink* beber(se); **I've already ~ back seven gins** me he bebido siete copitas de ginebra ya.

2 *vi*: **to ~ back to port** volver a puerto.

◆put by *vt*: **to have money ~ by** tener ahorros, tener dinero ahorrado; **I had it ~ by for you** te lo tenía guardado, *V also* **put away** (**a**).

◆put down *vt* (**a**) *burden* poner en tierra, poner en el suelo, depositar; *blinds etc* bajar; (*let go*) soltar, dejar; *passengers* dejar apearse; **~ it down!** ¡déjalo!, ¡suéltalo!; **I couldn't ~ the book down** me era imposible dejar de leer el libro.

(**b**) (*Aer*) poner en tierra.

(**c**) *umbrella etc* cerrar.

(**d**) (*pay*) pagar como desembolso inicial.

(**e**) *wine* poner en cava.

(**f**) (*suppress*) *abuse etc* suprimir; *revolt* sofocar, dominar.

(**g**) (*silence*) hacer callar, dejar sin réplica posible; (*humiliate*) humillar.

(**h**) (*record*) apuntar; poner por escrito; *name on list* poner, inscribir; **~ me down for two, please** por favor, apúntame para dos.

(**i**) (*reduce in rank*) degradar; (*Sport etc*) pasar a una división inferior.

(**j**) (*attribute*) **we ~ it down to his account** lo sentamos en su cuenta; **we ~ it down to nerves** lo atribuimos a los nervios; **what do you ~ it down to?** ¿a qué lo atribuyes?, ¿cuál crees que es la causa?

(**k**) (*consider*) **I ~ him down as a disaster** le creí una calamidad; **I used to ~ her down as a troublemaker** la creía revoltosa, la tenía por revoltosa; **I should ~ her down as about 30** le daría unos 30 años, creo que tendría unos 30 años.

(**l**) (*Brit: kill*) sacrificar.

◆put forth *vt hand* alargar, tender; *arm* extender; *leaves etc* echar; *effort* emplear, desplegar.

◆put forward 1 *vt* (**a**) (*propose*) *candidate* nombrar, presentar; *idea* proponer; *suggestion* hacer; *case, theory* presentar, proponer, exponer.

(**b**) (*advance*) adelantar; **to ~ a clock forward one hour** adelantar un reloj una hora.

2 *vr*: **to ~ o.s. forward** ofrecerse (con poca modestia); ponerse en evidencia; llamar la atención sobre sí.

◆put in 1 *vt* (**a**) (*into box etc*) meter, introducir.

(**b**) (*insert*) insertar; *remark* interponer.

(**c**) (*present*) *claim etc* presentar; *evidence* aducir.

(**d**) (*Pol*) *party* votar a, elegir.

(**e**) (*devote*) dedicar; **I ~ in 2 hours reading** pasé 2 horas leyendo; **to ~ in time on a project** invertir tiempo en un proyecto, dedicar tiempo a un proyecto; **you've ~ in a good day's work** has trabajado bien hoy; **more effort has to be ~ in** hay que esforzarse más.

(**f**) (*instal*) instalar; conectar; (*plant*) plantar; (*sow*) sembrar.

2 *vi* (**a**) **to ~ in to a port** entrar a puerto, (*on route*) hacer escala en un puerto.

(**b**) (*apply*) **to ~ in for a post** presentarse a un puesto, solicitar un puesto; **are you ~ting in?** ¿te vas a presentar?

◆put off 1 *vt* (**a**) (*postpone*) aplazar, posponer, dejar para después.

(**b**) (*dissuade*) disuadir; (*confuse*) desconcertar; (*discourage*) desanimar; **to ~ sb off with a promise** dar largas a uno con una promesa; **he's not easily ~ off** no es fácil apartarle de su propósito; **we shall have to ~ the guests off** tendremos que decir a los invitados que no vengan; **he tried to ~ me off my stroke** trató de distraerme en el golpe, trató de hacerme errar el golpe; **her face is enough to ~ anyone off** su cara basta para desanimar al más fuerte; **you quite ~ me off my meal** me has quitado todo el apetito; **what you say ~s me off prawns** lo que dices me quita las ganas de las gambas; **it almost ~ me off opera for good** casi mató mi gusto por la ópera para siempre; **we managed to ~ them off the scent** logramos despistarlos.

(**c**) *passenger* dejar; *dress* quitarse.

(**d**) (*extinguish*) apagar.

2 *vi* (*Naut*) hacerse a la mar; salir (*from* de).

◆**put on** *vt* (**a**) *clothes, make-up* ponerse; *ointment etc* aplicar.

(**b**) (*add*) **to ~ on speed** acelerar; cobrar velocidad; **they ~ £2 on** (**to**) **the price** añadieron 2 libras al precio; *V* **weight** *etc.*

(**c**) (*assume*) asumir; *accent* poner; **to ~ on an innocent air** adoptar una postura de inocencia; **to ~ it on** (*exaggerate*) exagerar, (*overact*) exagerar el papel; **she does ~ it on** (**so**) se emociona demasiado, es una persona muy exagerada; se da tanto tono.

(**d**) (*present*) *play* representar, poner en escena; *extra train* poner; *dish on menu* poner.

(**e**) *light, radio etc* poner, encender; *disc, tape* poner; *brake* aplicar, echar; *kettle, stew etc* poner (a calentar).

(**f**) *clock* adelantar; **to ~ a clock on one hour** adelantar un reloj una hora.

(**g**) **Sue ~ us on to you** Sue nos dio su nombre, Sue nos sugirió su nombre; **what ~ you on to it?** ¿qué te hizo pensar en esto?; ¿qué te dio la pista?; **one of the thieves ~ the police on to the others** uno de los ladrones denunció a los otros a la policía.

(**h**) (*****: *kid, esp US*) tomar el pelo a.

◆**put out 1** *vt* (**a**) (*put outside*) *chairs etc* sacar, poner fuera; *cat* mandar a pasearse; (*eject*) echar, expulsar; poner en la calle; *tenant, squatter* desahuciar; **to ~ clothes out to dry** tender la ropa, poner la ropa a secar.

(**b**) (*Naut*) *boat* echar al mar.

(**c**) (*extend*) *hand* alargar, tender, (*Aut*) sacar; *arm* extender; *tongue* sacar; *head* asomar, sacar; *horns* sacar; *leaves etc* echar.

(**d**) (*set out*) ordenar, disponer; desplegar.

(**e**) (*extinguish*) *light* apagar; *fire* apagar, sofocar.

(**f**) (*disconcert*) desconcertar; (*anger*) enojar, irritar; (*inconvenience*) incomodar; **I don't want to ~ you out at all** no quiero molestarte en lo más mínimo; **she was very ~ out** estaba muy enfadada; **she never seems to be ~ out** no parece alterarse por nada.

(**g**) (*dislocate*) dislocarse.

(**h**) (*publish*) *book etc* publicar, sacar a luz; *announcement* hacer; *rumour* diseminar, hacer correr.

(**i**) **to ~ money out at interest** poner el dinero a interés.

2 *vi* (*Naut*) hacerse a la mar; salir (*from* de).

3 *vr*: **to ~ o.s. out** tomarse la molestia, molestarse; **don't ~ yourself out!** ¡no te molestes!, ¡no te incomodes!

◆**put over** *vt* (**a**) = **put across.**

(**b**) **to ~ one over on sb*** (*forestall*) ganar por la mano a uno, (*deceive*) engañar a uno, dar a uno gato por liebre.

◆**put through** *vt* (**a**) *deal* cerrar; *business* despachar; *proposal* hacer aprobar.

(**b**) (*Telec*) **to ~ a call through** poner una llamada; **~ me through to Sr Blanco** póngame (comuníqueme *LAm*) con el Sr Blanco.

(**c**) **to ~ sb through a test** someter a uno a una prueba; **we'll ~ him through the course** le haremos estudiar el curso; **they really ~ him through it at the interview** en la entrevista le han hecho sudar la gota gorda.

◆**put together** *vt* (**a**) (*place together*) poner juntos; juntar, reunir; (*add*) añadir, (*Math*) sumar; **more than all the rest ~ together** más que todos los demás reunidos; **if all the cigars in the world are ~ together end to end** si se ponen uno tras otro todos los puros del mundo.

(**b**) (*assemble*) *machine* montar, armar; *collection* juntar, reunir, formar; *scheme* crear, formar, organizar; *meal* confeccionar; **I like to know how it's ~ together** me gusta saber cómo está hecho.

(**c**) **then the team really ~ it together*** luego el equipo jugó realmente bien.

◆**put up 1** *vt* (**a**) (*raise*) *hand* alzar, levantar, poner en alto; *window etc* levantar; *umbrella* abrir; *collar* alzar; *ladder* montar, poner; *flag, sail* izar; *picture* colgar; *notice* pegar, fijar, poner; *sword* envainar; *building* construir; **~ your hands up!** ¡arriba las manos!; **to ~ one's hair up** recoger el pelo, (*stylishly*) hacerse un peinado alto.

(**b**) (*increase*) aumentar, subir.

(**c**) (*offer*) *prayer, prize* ofrecer; *plan* presentar; *suggestion* hacer; *resistance* oponer; *candidate* nombrar, proponer (*for* a); **to ~ a house up for sale** poner una casa en venta.

(**d**) (*provide*) dar, poner; **to ~ up the money for sth** poner el dinero para algo.

(**e**) (*prepare*) *meal etc* preparar, hacer.

(**f**) (*lodge*) hospedar, alojar.

(**g**) (*incite*) incitar; **to ~ sb up to sth** incitar a uno a hacer algo; **sb must have ~ him up to it** alguien ha debido sugerírselo.

(**h**) *game* levantar.

(**i**) *petition* presentar.

2 *vi* (**a**) **to ~ up at a hotel** hospedarse en un hotel.

(**b**) (*offer o.s.*) **to ~ up for president** ser candidato a la presidencia; **to ~ up for the Greens** ser candidato de los Verdes; **to ~ up for Bognor** ser candidato por Bognor.

(**c**) **to ~ up with** aguantar; resignarse a, conformarse con; **I can't ~ up with her** no la puedo ver, no la aguanto; **I can't ~ up with it any longer** no aguanto más; **she ~s up with a lot** es muy tolerante, tiene mucho aguante.

◆**put upon** *vt*: **to ~ upon sb** molestar a uno, incomodar a uno; pedir mucho a uno; abusar de la amabilidad de uno.

putative ['pju:tətɪv] *adj* supuesto; *relation* putativo.

put-down* ['pʊt,daʊn] *n* (*act*) humillación *f*; (*words*) frase *f* despectiva.

put-in ['pʊt,ɪn] *n* (*Rugby*) introducción *f*.

put-on* ['pʊt,ɒn] **1** *n* (*pretence*) burla *f*, cachondeo* *m*; (*hoax*) broma *f* (de mal gusto). **2** *adj* (*feigned*) fingido.

putrefaction [,pju:trɪ'fækʃən] *n* putrefacción *f*.

putrefy ['pju:trɪfaɪ] **1** *vt* pudrir. **2** *vi* pudrirse.

putrescence [pju:'tresns] *n* pudrición *f*.

putrescent [pju:'tresnt] *adj* putrescente, podrido.

putrid ['pju:trɪd] *adj* (**a**) podrido, putrefacto. (**b**) (*****) horrible, malísimo.

putsch [pʊtʃ] *n* golpe *m* de estado.

putt [pʌt] **1** *n* putt *m*, pat *m*, golpe *m* corto. **2** *vti* patear.

putter ['pʌtə^r] **1** *n* putter *m*. **2** *vi* (*US*) = **potter**².

putting ['pʊtɪŋ] *n*: **~ the weight** lanzamiento *m* del peso.

putting green ['pʌtɪŋgri:n] *n* green *m*, minigolf *m*.

putty ['pʌtɪ] *n* masilla *f*.

putty-knife ['pʌtɪnaɪf] *n*, *pl* **putty-knives** ['pʌtɪnaɪvz] espátula *f* para masilla.

put-up* ['pʊtʌp] *adj*: **~ job** cosa *f* proyectada y preparada de antemano; asunto *m* fraudulento; **it was a ~ job to give him the post** fue un truco para darle el puesto.

put-upon ['pʊtə'pɒn] *adj*: **she's feeling very ~** cree que los demás la están explotando; se siente agobiada por las muchas exigencias (*etc*).

put-you-up ['pʊtjʊ,ʌp] *n* (*Brit*) cama *f* plegable, sofá-cama *m*.

puzzle ['pʌzl] **1** *n* (**a**) (*game*) rompecabezas *m*, puzzle *m*; (*riddle*) acertijo *m*; (*crossword*) crucigrama *m*; (*jigsaw*) rompecabezas *m*.

(**b**) (*mystery*) problema *m*, enigma *m*, misterio *m*; **it's a real ~** es un verdadero problema; **the ~ of their origin** el enigma de su origen; **your friends are ~s to me** no llego a entender a tus amigos.

2 *vt* dejar perplejo, confundir; **that properly ~d him** eso le dejó totalmente perplejo; **I am ~d to know why** no llego a comprender por qué, no acabo de entender por qué; **I was ~d to know what to answer** no sabía en absoluto lo que debía contestar.

3 *vi*: **to ~ over sth** esforzarse por resolver algo, devanarse los sesos para descifrar algo; tratar de comprender algo.

◆**puzzle out** *vt*: **to ~ sth out** resolver algo, descifrar algo; **we're still trying to ~ out why he did it** seguimos tratando de comprender por qué lo hizo.

puzzle book ['pʌzl,bʊk] *n* libro *m* de puzzles.

puzzled ['pʌzld] *adj look etc* perplejo.

puzzlement ['pʌzlmənt] *n* perplejidad *f*, confusión *f*.

puzzler ['pʌzlə^r] *n* problema *m*, enigma *m*, misterio *m*.

puzzling ['pʌzlɪŋ] *adj* enigmático, misterioso; incomprensible; **it is ~ that** ... es curioso que ...

PVC *n abbr of* **polyvinyl chloride** cloruro *m* de polivinilo.

PVS *n abbr of* **postviral syndrome.**

Pvt. (*US*) *abbr of* **Private** soldado *m* raso.

PW *n* (*US*) *abbr of* **prisoner of war** prisionero *m*.

p.w. *abbr of* **per week** por semana, a la semana.

PWR *abbr of* **pressurized water reactor** reactor *m* de agua a presión.

PX *n* (*US Mil*) *abbr of* **Post Exchange** *economato militar*.

pygmy ['pɪgmɪ] **1** *adj* pigmeo; (*fig*) miniatura, minúsculo. **2** *n* pigmeo *m*, -a *f*.

pyjamas [pɪ'dʒɑ:məz] *npl* (*Brit*) pijama *m*.

pylon ['paɪlən] *n* pilón *m*, poste *m*; (*Elec*) torre *f* (de conducción eléctrica, de alta tensión).

pyorrhoea, (*US*) **pyorrhea** [,paɪə'rɪə] *n* piorrea *f*.

pyramid ['pɪrəmɪd] **1** *n* pirámide *f*. **2** *attr*: **~ selling** venta *f*

piramidal.
pyramidal [pɪ'ræmɪdl] *adj* piramidal.
pyre ['paɪəʳ] *n* pira *f*; (*fig*) hoguera *f*.
Pyrenean [,pɪrə'ni:ən] *adj* pirenaico, pirineo.
Pyrenees [,pɪrə'ni:z] *npl* Pirineo *m*, Pirineos *mpl*.
pyrethrum [paɪ'ri:θrəm] *n* piretro *m*.
pyretic [paɪ'retɪk] *adj* pirético.
Pyrex ['paɪreks] ® **1** *n* pírex ® *m*. **2** *attr dish* de pírex ®.
pyrites [paɪ'raɪti:z] *n* pirita *f*.
pyro- ['paɪərəʊ] *pref* piro...
pyromania [,paɪrəʊ'meɪnɪə] *n* piromanía *f*, incendiarismo *m*.
pyromaniac ['paɪərəʊ'meɪnɪæk] *n* pirómano *m*, -a *f*, incendiario *m*, -a *f*.
pyrotechnic [,paɪərəʊ'teknɪk] **1** *adj* pirotécnico. **2** *npl*: **~s** pirotecnia *f*.
Pyrrhic ['pɪrɪk] *adj*: ~ **victory** victoria *f* pírrica.
Pyrrhus ['pɪrəs] *nm* Pirro.
Pythagoras [paɪ'θægərəs] *nm* Pitágoras.
Pythagorean [paɪ,θægə'rɪən] *adj* pitagóreo.
python ['paɪθən] *n* pitón *m*.
pythonesque [,paɪθə'nesk] *adj* pitonesco (*del estilo de Monty Python*).
pyx [pɪks] *n* píxide *f*.
pzazz* [pə'zæz] *n* = **piz(z)azz**.

Q

Q, q [kju:] *n* (*letter*) Q, q *f*; **Q for Queen** Q de Quebec.

Q. (**a**) *abbr of* **Queen** reina *f*. (**b**) *abbr of* **question** pregunta *f*, p.

Qatar [kæ'tɑːʳ] *n* Katar *m*, Qatar *m*.

QC *n* (*Brit*) *abbr of* **Queen's Counsel.**

QED (*Math etc*) *abbr of* **quod erat demonstrandum** que es lo que había que probar, Q.E.D.

QM *abbr of* **Quartermaster.**

qr *abbr of* **quarter**(**s**).

q.t. [kju:ti:] *n abbr of* **quiet**; **on the ~*** a hurtadillas.

qty *abbr of* **quantity** cantidad *f*, ctdad.

Qu. *abbr of* **Queen** reina *f*.

qua [kweɪ] *prep* como, en cuanto; **let us consider man ~ animal** consideremos al hombre en cuanto animal.

quack[1] [kwæk] **1** *n* graznido *m* (del pato). **2** *vi* graznar.

quack[2] [kwæk] **1** *n* charlatán *m*; (*Med*) curandero *m*, matasanos *m*. **2** *adj* falso, fingido; *remedy* de curandero; **~ doctor** medicucho *m*, curandero *m*.

quackery ['kwækərɪ] *n* charlatanismo *m*; curanderismo *m*.

quack-quack ['kwæk'kwæk] *n* cuac cuac *m*.

quad [kwɒd] *n* (**a**) (*Archit**) = **quadrangle.** (**b**) (*Typ*) cuadratín *m*. (**c**) *abbr of* **quadruple.** (**d**) (*) *abbr of* **quadruplet.**

Quadragesima [ˌkwɒdrə'dʒesɪmə] *n* Cuadragésima *f*.

quadrangle ['kwɒdræŋgl] *n* cuadrilátero *m*, cuadrángulo *m*; (*court*) patio *m*.

quadrangular [kwɒ'dræŋgjʊləʳ] *adj* cuadrangular.

quadrant ['kwɒdrənt] *n* cuadrante *m*.

quadraphonic [ˌkwɒdrə'fɒnɪk] *adj* cuatrifónico.

quadratic [kwɒ'drætɪk] *adj*: **~ equation** ecuación *f* de segundo grado, cuadrática *f*.

quadrature ['kwɒdrətʃəʳ] *n* cuadratura *f*.

quadrennial [kwɒ'drenɪəl] *adj* cuatrienal.

quadrilateral [ˌkwɒdrɪ'lætərəl] **1** *adj* cuadrilátero. **2** *n* cuadrilátero *m*.

quadrille [kwə'drɪl] *n* cuadrilla *f*.

quadripartite ['kwɒdrɪ'pɑːtaɪt] *adj* cuadripartido.

quadriplegia [ˌkwɒdrɪ'pliːdʒə] *n* cuadriplegia *f*, tetraplegia *f*.

quadriplegic [ˌkwɒdrɪ'pliːdʒɪk] **1** *adj* cuadripléjico. **2** *n* cuadripléjico *m*, -a *f*.

quadrivium [kwɒ'drɪvɪəm] *n* cuadrivio *m*.

quadroon [kwɒ'druːn] *n* cuarterón *m*.

quadrophonic [ˌkwɒdrə'fɒnɪk] *adj* cuadrafónico.

quadruped ['kwɒdrʊped] *n* cuadrúpedo *m*.

quadruple **1** ['kwɒdrʊpl] *adj* cuádruple, cuádruplo. **2** ['kwɒdrʊpl] *n* cuádruple *m*, cuádruplo *m*. **3** ['kwɒ'druːpl] *vt* cuadruplicar. **4** ['kwɒ'druːpl] *vi* cuadruplicarse.

quadruplet [kwɒ'druːplɪt] *n* cuatrillizo *m*, -a *f*.

quadruplicate **1** [kwɒ'druːplɪkɪt] *adj* cuadruplicado. **2** [kwɒ'druːplɪkɪt] *n*: **in ~** por cuadruplicado. **3** [kwɒ'druːplɪkeɪt] *vt* cuadruplicar.

quaestor, (*US sometimes*) **questor** ['kwiːstəʳ] *n* cuestor *m*.

quaff [kwɒf] *vt* (†† *or hum*) beber(se).

quagmire ['kwægmaɪəʳ] *n* tremedal *m*, cenegal *m*, lodazal *m*; (*fig*) atolladero *m*, cenegal *m*.

quail[1] [kweɪl] *n* codorniz *f*.

quail[2] [kweɪl] *vi* acobardarse, amedrentarse (*before* ante); **her heart ~ed** se le desfalleció el corazón.

quaint [kweɪnt] *adj* (*odd*) curioso, original, singular; *workmanship etc* rebuscado; *person* singular, original; (*picturesque, of tourist interest etc*) típico, pintoresco.

quaintly ['kweɪntlɪ] *adv* curiosamente; singularmente; típicamente; **he described it ~ as ...** le dio la calificación curiosa de ...

quaintness ['kweɪntnɪs] *n* curiosidad *f*, originalidad *f*, singularidad *f*; lo rebuscado; tipismo *m*, lo pintoresco.

quake [kweɪk] **1** *n* = **earthquake.**

2 *vi* temblar, estremecerse; **to ~ at the knees** flaquearle a uno las piernas, temblarle a uno las rodillas; **to ~ at the sight** estremecerse viendo tal cosa; **to ~ with fright** temblar de miedo; **the earth ~d 3 times** la tierra tembló 3 veces.

Quaker ['kweɪkəʳ] **1** *adj* cuáquero. **2** *n* cuáquero *m*, -a *f*.

Quakerism ['kweɪkərɪzəm] *n* cuaquerismo *m*.

qualification [ˌkwɒlɪfɪ'keɪʃən] *n* (**a**) (*reservation*) reserva *f*; salvedad *f*; modificación *f*, restricción *f*; **to accept sth without ~** aceptar algo sin reserva.

(**b**) (*for a post etc*) requisito *m*, calificación *f* (*LAm*); **the ~s for the post are ...** los requisitos del puesto son ...; **the ~s for membership** lo que se requiere para ser socio.

(**c**) (*of person*) **~s** aptitud *f*, capacidad *f*; (*paper ~s*) títulos *mpl*; **to have the ~s for a post** llenar los requisitos de un puesto, tener los títulos exigidos para un puesto, estar capacitado para ocupar un puesto; **what are his ~s?** ¿qué títulos tiene?

(**d**) (*act, description*) calificación *f*; **without ~** sin reserva; (*pej*) sin paliativos.

qualified ['kwɒlɪfaɪd] *adj* (**a**) *person* (*fit*) apto, competente (*to + infin* para + *infin*); (*trained*) capacitado, cualificado, calificado, habilitado; (*professionally*) titulado, que tiene título, con título; **a ~ engineer** un ingeniero titulado; **to be ~ to do sth** estar capacitado para hacer algo; ser competente para hacer algo; **to be ~ to vote** tener los requisitos para votar; **I don't feel ~ to judge that** no me creo calificado para juzgar eso.

(**b**) (*limited*) modificado, limitado; **~ acceptance** aceptación *f* condicional; **he gave it his ~ approval** lo aprobó pero con reservas; **it was a ~ success** obtuvo un éxito moderado.

qualifier ['kwɒlɪfaɪəʳ] *n* calificador *m*.

qualify ['kwɒlɪfaɪ] **1** *vt* (**a**) (*describe*) calificar (*as* de); (*Gram*) calificar a.

(**b**) (*make competent*) habilitar, capacitar; **this should ~ you for the post** esto deberá darte los requisitos para el puesto; **her skills ~ her for the job** reúne las condiciones necesarias para el puesto; **to ~ sb to do sth** habilitar a uno para hacer algo; **that doesn't ~ him to speak on this** eso no le da derecho para hablar sobre este asunto.

(**c**) (*modify*) modificar; restringir; **I think you should ~ that** creo que te conviene modificar eso.

(**d**) (*diminish*) atenuar, moderar, disminuir.

2 *vi* habilitarse, capacitarse; ser apto; reunir las condiciones necesarias; (*professionally*) cursar los estudios profesionales, estudiar; (*graduate*) obtener el título, graduarse; **to ~ as an engineer** (*as student*) estudiar para ingeniero, (*finally*) obtener el título de ingeniero, calificarse de ingeniero (*LAm*); **to ~ for a post** llenar los requisitos para un puesto; reunir las condiciones necesarias para un puesto; **does he ~?** ¿tiene los requisitos?; **I qualified in 1968** yo saqué el título en 1968; **we shall marry when he qualifies** nos casaremos en cuanto termine la carrera; **he hardly qualifies as a poet** apenas se le puede calificar de poeta.

qualifying ['kwɒlɪfaɪɪŋ] *adj* (**a**) (*Gram*) calificativo. (**b**) *round etc* eliminatorio; **~ examination** examen *m* eliminatorio, examen *m* de ingreso.

qualitative ['kwɒlɪtətɪv] *adj* cualitativo.

qualitatively ['kwɒlɪtətɪvlɪ] *adv* bajo el aspecto cualitativo.

quality ['kwɒlɪtɪ] **1** *n* (**a**) (*nature, kind*) calidad *f*; categoría *f*, clase *f*; **~ of life** calidad *f* de la vida; **of the best ~** de la mejor calidad; **of good ~, of high ~** de buena calidad; **of low ~** de baja calidad; **fibres of ~** fibras *fpl* de calidad; **he's a man of some ~** es hombre de cierta categoría; **he has real ~** tiene verdadera excelencia.

(**b**) (*characteristic, moral ~ etc*) cualidad *f*; **among her qualities** entre sus cualidades; **he has many good qualities** tiene muchas buenas cualidades.

(**c**) (††) **the** ~ la aristocracia; **people of** ~ la gente bien nacida, las personas cultas.

(**d**) (*of sound*) timbre *m*, tono *m*.

2 *attr*: **a** ~ **carpet** una alfombra de calidad; ~ **control** control *m* de (la) calidad; **the** ~ **papers** los periódicos serios; ~ **product** producto *m* de calidad.

qualm [kwɑːm] *n* (**a**) (*Med*) bascas *fpl*, náusea *f*; mareo *m*.

(**b**) (*scruple*) escrúpulo *m*, duda *f*; **to have** ~**s about doing sth** sentir escrúpulo al hacer algo; **now she's having** ~**s about it** ahora le está remordiendo la conciencia por ello, ahora le están asaltando las dudas; **to have no** ~**s about doing sth** no dudar en hacer algo, hacer algo sin escrúpulos, hacer algo sin remordimientos.

quandary [ˈkwɒndərɪ] *n* dilema *m*, apuro *m*; **to be in a** ~ estar perplejo, estar en un dilema; encontrarse ante una encrucijada; **to get sb out of a** ~ sacar a uno de un apuro.

quango [ˈkwæŋgəʊ] *n* (*Brit*) *abbr of* **quasi-autonomous non-governmental organization.**

quanta [ˈkwɒntə] *npl of* **quantum.**

quantifiable [ˈkwɒntɪfaɪəbl] *adj* cuantificable.

quantifier [ˈkwɒntɪfaɪəʳ] *n* cuantificador *m*.

quantify [ˈkwɒntɪfaɪ] *vt* cuantificar.

quantitative [ˈkwɒntɪtətɪv] *adj* cuantitativo.

quantitatively [ˈkwɒntɪtətɪvlɪ] *adv* bajo el aspecto cuantitativo.

quantity [ˈkwɒntɪtɪ] **1** *n* cantidad *f*; **unknown** ~ incógnita *f*; **in large quantities, in** ~ en grandes cantidades; **what** ~ **do you want?** ¿cuánto quiere?

2 *attr*: ~ **discount** descuento *m* por cantidad; ~ **mark** signo *m* prosódico; ~ **surveyor** (*Brit*) aparejador *m*, medidor *m* de cantidad de obra.

quantum [ˈkwɒntəm] **1** *n*, *pl* **quanta** [ˈkwɒntə] cuanto *m*, quántum *m*. **2** *attr*: ~ **leap** salto *m* espectacular; ~ **mechanics** mecánica *f* cuántica; ~ **number** número *m* cuántico; ~ **physics** física *f* cuántica; ~ **theory** teoría *f* cuántica.

quarantine [ˈkwɒrəntiːn] **1** *n* cuarentena *f*; **to be in** ~ estar en cuarentena; **to place a dog in** ~ poner un perro en cuarentena. **2** *vt* poner en cuarentena.

quark [kwɑːk] *n* cuark *m*.

quarrel [ˈkwɒrəl] **1** *n* (*argument*) riña *f*, disputa *f*; (*with blows*) reyerta *f*, pendencia *f*, pelea *f*; **to have a** ~ **with sb** reñir con uno, pelearse con uno (*esp LAm*); **we had a** ~ reñimos; **I have no** ~ **with you** no tengo nada en contra de Vd, no tengo queja de Vd; **to pick a** ~ buscar camorra; **to pick a** ~ **with sb** meterse con uno, armar pleito con uno; **to take up sb's** ~ ponerse de la parte de uno.

2 *vi* reñir, pelearse (*esp LAm*); disputar; **they** ~**led about** (*or* **over**) **money** riñeron por cuestión de dinero; **to** ~ **with sb** reñir con uno, pelearse con uno; **we** ~**led and I never saw him again** reñimos y no volví a verle; **to** ~ **with sb for doing sth** reñir a uno por haber hecho algo; **you can't** ~ **with that** es imposible quejarse de eso; **what we** ~ **with is ...** nuestro motivo de queja es ...

quarrelling, (*US*) **quarreling** [ˈkwɒrəlɪŋ] *n* disputas *fpl*, altercados *mpl*; **there was constant** ~ se reñía constantemente.

quarrelsome [ˈkwɒrəlsəm] *adj* pendenciero, discutón, peleón.

quarrelsomeness [ˈkwɒrəlsəmnɪs] *n* espíritu *m* pendenciero.

quarrier [ˈkwɒrɪəʳ] *n* cantero *m*.

quarry¹ [ˈkwɒrɪ] *n* (*Hunting*) presa *f*; (*fig*) presa *f*, víctima *f*.

quarry² [ˈkwɒrɪ] **1** *n* cantera *f*; (*fig*) mina *f*, cantera *f*; ~ **tile** baldosa *f* (no vidriada). **2** *vt* sacar, extraer. **3** *vi* explotar una cantera, extraer piedra (*etc*) de una cantera; **to** ~ **for marble** sacar mármol de una cantera.

◆**quarry out** *vt* extraer.

quarryman [ˈkwɒrɪmən] *n*, *pl* **quarrymen** [ˈkwɒrɪmən] cantero *m*, picapedrero *m*.

quart [kwɔːt] *n cuarto de galón* (*Brit = 1,136 litros*); **we drank** ~**s** bebimos cantidades.

quarter [ˈkwɔːtəʳ] **1** *n* (**a**) (*fourth part*) cuarto *m*, cuarta parte *f*; (*Brit weight*) = *28 libras* (= *12.7 kg, approx* = arroba *f*); (*US, Can Fin*) *moneda de 25 centavos*, cuarto *m* de dólar; (*Her*) cuartel *m*; ~**s** (*of horse*) anca *f*; **a** ~ **of a century** un cuarto de siglo; **for a** ~ **of the price** por la cuarta parte del precio; **it's a** ~ **gone already** ya se ha gastado la cuarta parte; **it's only a** ~ **as long** tiene solamente la cuarta parte de largo; **to divide sth into** ~**s** dividir algo en cuartos.

(**b**) (*of moon*) cuarto *m*; (*3 months*) trimestre *m*; **to pay by the** ~ pagar cada 3 meses, pagar trimestralmente.

(**c**) (*time*) **a** ~ **of an hour** un cuarto de hora; **it's a** ~ **to 3, it's a** ~ **of 3** (*US*) son las 3 menos cuarto, es un cuarto para las 3 (*LAm*); **it's a** ~ **past 3, it's a** ~ **after 3** (*US*) son las 3 y cuarto.

(**d**) (*of compass*) cuarta *f*; (*region*) región *f*; (*fig*) fuente *f*, origen *m*; procedencia *f*; dirección *f*; **the 4** ~**s of the globe** las 4 partes del mundo; **from all** ~**s** de todas partes; **at close** ~**s** de cerca, (*fight*) casi cuerpo a cuerpo; **from an unknown** ~ de procedencia desconocida, de origen desconocido; **we may expect trouble in that** ~ podemos tener dificultades en esa región; **the wind is in the right** ~ el viento sopla en dirección favorable; **what** ~ **is the wind in?** ¿qué dirección lleva el viento?

(**e**) (*of town*) barrio *m*; **the business** ~ el barrio comercial.

(**f**) (*lodging*) ~**s** vivienda *f*; alojamiento *m*; (*Mil*) alojamiento *m*; (*barracks*) cuartel *m*; **to have free** ~**s** tener alojamiento gratis; **to live in cramped** ~**s** tener un cuarto (*etc*) muy estrecho; **to shift one's** ~**s** cambiar de alojamiento; **to take up one's** ~**s** ocupar su cuarto (*etc*); establecerse, alojarse.

(**g**) **to give no** ~ no dar cuartel.

2 *adj*: **for a** ~ **century** durante un cuarto de siglo; **a** ~ **mile** un cuarto de milla; ~ **note** (*US*) negra *f*; **the** ~ **part of** la cuarta parte de; **he has a** ~ **share** tiene una cuarta parte.

3 *vt* (**a**) (*divide into 4*) cuartear, dividir en cuartos; *meat* descuartizar; (*Her*) cuartelar.

(**b**) (*Mil*) acuartelar, alojar; **to be** ~**ed on sb** estar alojado en casa de uno.

(**c**) **to** ~ **the ground** (*dog*) buscar olfateando.

quarter-day [ˈkwɔːtədeɪ] *n* primer día *m* del trimestre; (*Fin*) día *m* en que se paga un trimestre.

quarter-deck [ˈkwɔːtədek] *n* alcázar *m*.

quarter-final [ˈkwɔːtəˌfaɪnl] *n* cuarto *m* de final.

quarter-finalist [ˈkwɔːtəˈfaɪnəlɪst] *n* cuartofinalista *mf*.

quarter-hour [ˈkwɔːtəˈaʊəʳ] *n* cuarto *m* de hora.

quarter-hourly [ˈkwɔːtəˈaʊəlɪ] **1** *adv* cada cuarto de hora. **2** *adj*: **at** ~ **intervals** cada cuarto de hora.

quartering [ˈkwɔːtərɪŋ] *n* (*Her*) cuartel *m*.

quarter light [ˈkwɔːtəˌlaɪt] *n* (*Brit*) ventanilla *f* direccional.

quarterly [ˈkwɔːtəlɪ] **1** *adv* cada tres meses, trimestralmente, por trimestres. **2** *adj* trimestral; ~ **account** cuenta *f* trimestral; ~ **return** informe *m* trimestral; ~ **statement** relato *m* trimestral. **3** *n* publicación *f* trimestral.

quartermaster [ˈkwɔːtəˌmɑːstəʳ] **1** *n* (*approx*) furriel *m*, comisario *m*. **2** *attr*: ~ **general** intendente *m* general; ~ **sergeant** ≃ brigada *m*.

quartern [ˈkwɔːtən] *n* cuarta *f*; ~ **loaf** pan *m* de 4 libras.

quarterstaff [ˈkwɔːtəstɑːf] *n* (*Hist*) barra *f*.

quarter-tone [ˈkwɔːtətəʊn] *n* cuarto *m* de tono.

quartet(te) [kwɔːˈtet] *n* (*Mus*) cuarteto *m*; (*set of 4*) grupo *m* de cuatro.

quartile [ˈkwɔːtaɪl] *n* cuartil *m*.

quarto [ˈkwɔːtəʊ] **1** *adj* en cuarto; (*paper size*) tamaño *m* holandesa. **2** *n* libro *m* en cuarto.

quartz [ˈkwɔːts] **1** *n* cuarzo *m*. **2** *attr*: ~ **clock,** ~ **watch** reloj *m* de cuarzo; ~ **crystal** cristal *m* de cuarzo; ~ **lamp** lámpara *f* de cuarzo.

quartzite [ˈkwɔːtsaɪt] *n* cuarcita *f*.

quasar [ˈkweɪzɑːʳ] *n* cuasar *m*.

quash [ˈkwɒʃ] *vt verdict* anular, invalidar; *rebellion* sofocar, reprimir; *proposal* rechazar.

quasi [ˈkweɪzaɪ, ˈkwɑːzɪ] *adv* cuasi; **a** ~ **monarch** un cuasi monarca.

quatercentenary [ˌkwɒtəsenˈtiːnərɪ] *n* cuarto centenario *m*.

quaternary [kwəˈtɜːnərɪ] **1** *adj* cuaternario. **2** *n* cuaternario *m*.

quatrain [ˈkwɒtreɪn] *n* cuarteto *m*, estrofa *f* de cuatro versos.

quaver [ˈkweɪvəʳ] **1** *n* temblor *m*; vibración *f*; (*esp Brit Mus*: *trill*) trémolo *m*, (*note*) corchea *f*; **with a** ~ **in her voice** con voz trémula.

2 *vt* decir con voz temblorosa; **'yes', she** ~**ed** 'sí', dijo temblorosa.

3 *vi* temblar; vibrar.

quavering [ˈkweɪvərɪŋ] *adj* tembloroso, trémulo; **in** ~ **tones** en tono tembloroso.

quaver rest [ˈkweɪvəˈrest] *n* (*Brit*) pausa *f* de corchea.

quavery [ˈkweɪvərɪ] *adj* = **quavering.**

quay [kiː] *n*, **quayside** [ˈkiːsaɪd] *n* muelle *m*; **on the** ~ en el muelle.

Que. (*Canada*) *abbr of* **Quebec.**

queasiness [ˈkwiːzɪnɪs] *n* (*Med*) bascas *fpl*; propensión *f* a la náusea; (*of conscience*) delicadeza *f*, escrupulosidad *f*.

queasy ['kwi:zɪ] *adj* (*Med*) bascoso; *stomach* delicado; *conscience* delicado, escrupuloso; **I feel** ~ me siento mal.

queen [kwi:n] **1** *n* (**a**) reina *f*; (*Chess*) reina *f*; (*Cards*) dama *f*, (*in Spanish pack*) caballo *m*; ~ **consort** reina *f* consorte; **she was** ~ **to Charles II** era la reina de Carlos II; **Q~'s Bench** (*Brit*) *departamento del Tribunal Supremo de Justicia*; **Q~'s Counsel** (*Brit*) abogado *mf* (*de categoría superior*).

(**b**) (*Zool*) (*also* ~ **bee**) abeja *f* reina, (*ant*) hormiga *f* reina.

(**c**) (‡) marica‡ *m*, homosexual *m*.

2 *attr*: ~ **mother** reina *f* madre.

3 *vt pawn* coronar; **to** ~ **it** conducirse como una reina, (*fig*) pavonearse.

4 *vi* (*Chess*) ser coronado.

queenly ['kwi:nlɪ] *adj* regio, de reina.

queer [kwɪəʳ] **1** *adj* (**a**) (*odd*) raro, extraño, singular; misterioso; excéntrico; sospechoso; ~ **fish*** tío *m* raro*; **it's very** ~ es muy raro; **there's something** ~ **going on** pasa algo raro; **what's** ~ **about it?** ¿qué tiene esto de raro?; **to be in Q~ Street** (*Brit*) estar en la miseria.

(**b**) (‡) maricón‡.

(**c**) (*Brit Med*) malucho; **to come over** ~, **to feel** ~ tener vahidos, sentirse mal, sentirse indispuesto.

2 *n* (‡) maricón *m*.

3 *vt* estropear; *V* **pitch 1** (**g**).

queer-bashing‡ ['kwɪə,bæʃɪŋ] *n*: **to go in for** ~ atacar a homosexuales.

queerly ['kwɪəlɪ] *adv* de modo raro, extrañamente; misteriosamente; **to behave** ~ comportarse de modo raro.

queerness ['kwɪənɪs] *n* rareza *f*, singularidad *f*; lo misterioso; lo excéntrico.

quell [kwel] *vt passion etc* reprimir; calmar; *revolt* sofocar, dominar; *opposition* sobreponerse a, dominar; *fears* desechar.

quench [kwentʃ] *vt flames, thirst etc* apagar; *desire, hope* matar, sofocar; *enthusiasm* enfriar.

quenchless ['kwentʃlɪs] *adj* inapagable.

quern [kwɜ:n] *n* molinillo *m* de mano.

querulous ['kwerʊləs] *adj* quejumbroso.

querulously ['kwerʊləslɪ] *adv* quejumbrosamente; en tono quejumbroso.

query ['kwɪərɪ] **1** *n* (**a**) (*question*) pregunta *f*; interrogante *m*; (*doubt*) duda *f*; ~ **language** lenguaje *m* de interrogación; **there are many queries about it** hay muchos interrogantes acerca de esto; **did you have a** ~**?** ¿querías preguntar algo?; ~: **who killed Cock Robin?** pregunta: ¿quién mató a Cock Robin?

(**b**) (*Gram*) signo *m* de interrogación.

2 *vt* (*ask*) preguntar; (*doubt*) dudar de, expresar dudas acerca de; (*Comput*) interrogar; (*disagree with*) no estar conforme con; **to** ~ **whether** ... dudar si ...; **I** ~ **that** dudo si eso es cierto, tengo mis dudas acerca de eso; **do you** ~ **the evidence?** ¿tienes dudas acerca del testimonio?

quest [kwest] **1** *n* busca *f*, búsqueda *f* (*for* de); (*Hist*) demanda *f* (*for* de); **to go in** ~ **of** ir en busca de. **2** *vti* buscar (*for sth* algo).

question ['kwestʃən] **1** *n* (**a**) (*interrogative*) pregunta *f*; interrogante *m*; ~**s and answers** preguntas *fpl* y respuestas; **are there any** ~**s?** ¿hay alguna pregunta?; **to ask sb a** ~, **to put a** ~ **to sb** hacer una pregunta a uno; **many** ~**s were left unanswered** muchas preguntas quedaron sin contestar; **to pop the** ~* declararse.

(**b**) (*matter*) asunto *m*, cuestión *f*; problema *m*; **the German** ~ el problema alemán; **the** ~ **is,** ... el caso es, ...; **it is a** ~ **of** se trata de ...; **it is a** ~ **of whether** ... se trata de saber si ...; **that is the** ~ ahí está la dificultad; **that is not the** ~ no se trata de eso; **it is not simply a** ~ **of money** no se trata simplemente de dinero, no es cuestión de dinero y nada más; **there is no** ~ **of outside help** no hay posibilidad de ayuda exterior; **there can be no** ~ **of your resigning** no se puede consentir en que dimitas; **there was some** ~ **of John coming** se hablaba de que pudiera venir Juan; **at the time in** ~ a la hora que nos (*etc*) interesa; **the person in** ~ la persona de quien hablamos (*etc*); **it's out of the** ~ es imposible; **that begs the** ~ eso es una petición de principio.

(**c**) (*at meeting*) asunto *m*; interpelación *f*; ~**!** ¡que se vuelva al tema de la discusión!; ~ **time** (*Brit Parl*) sesión *f* de interpelaciones (dirigidas a ministros); **to move the previous** ~ plantear la cuestión previa; **to put the** ~ someter la moción a votación.

(**d**) (*doubt etc*) **beyond** ~, **past** ~ incuestionable, fuera de toda duda; **in** ~ en cuestión; **without** ~ sin duda, indudablemente; **there is no** ~ **about it** no existen dudas sobre ello; **it is open to** ~ **whether** ... es discutible si ...; **to bring** (*or* **call**) **sth in(to)** ~ poner algo en duda; **to come into** ~ empezar a discutirse; **I make no** ~ **but that it is so** no dudo que es así.

2 *vt* (**a**) (*interrogate*) hacer preguntas a; (*by police etc*) interrogar; (*by examiner etc*) examinar; (*at meeting*) interpelar; **we** ~**ed him closely to find out whether** ... le interrogamos del modo más apremiante para saber si ...; **I will not be** ~**ed about it** no permito que se me interrogue sobre eso.

(**b**) (*doubt*) cuestionar, poner en duda; dudar de, desconfiar de; **I** ~ **whether it is worthwhile** me pregunto si vale la pena; **I don't** ~ **your honesty** no dudo de tu honradez.

questionable ['kwestʃənəbl] *adj* cuestionable, dudoso, discutible; **it is** ~ **whether** ... es dudoso si ...; **in** ~ **taste** de gusto dudoso.

questionary ['kwestʃənərɪ] *n* cuestionario *m*, encuesta *f*.

questioner ['kwestʃənəʳ] *n* interrogador *m*, -ora *f*; (*at meeting*) interpelante *mf*.

questioning ['kwestʃənɪŋ] **1** *adj* interrogativo. **2** *n* preguntas *fpl*; (*by police etc*) interrogatorio *m*.

question-mark ['kwestʃənmɑ:k] *n* signo *m* de interrogación; (*fig*) interrogante *m*; **a big** ~ **hangs over him** sobre él pende un interrogante mayúsculo.

question-master ['kwestʃən,mɑ:stəʳ] *n* interrogador *m*.

questionnaire [,kwestʃə'neəʳ] *n* cuestionario *m*, encuesta *f*.

question tag ['kwestʃəntæg] *n* pregunta *f* coletilla.

questor ['kwi:stəʳ] *n* (*US*) = **quaestor**.

queue [kju:] **1** *n* (*Brit*) cola *f*; **to form a** ~, **to stand in a** ~ hacer cola; **to jump the** ~ salirse de su turno, colarse.

2 *vi* (*Brit*: *also* **to** ~ **up**) hacer cola; **to** ~ **for sth** hacer cola para comprar (*etc*) algo; **to** ~ **for 3 hours** pasar 3 horas haciendo cola.

queue-jump ['kju:,dʒʌmp] *vi* salirse de su turno, colarse.

queue-jumper ['kju:,dʒʌmpəʳ] *n* colón *m*, -ona *f*.

queue-jumping ['kju:,dʒʌmpɪŋ] *n* colarse *m*.

quibble ['kwɪbl] **1** *n* sofistería *f*, sutileza *f*; objeción *f* de poca monta; **that's just a** ~ eso es pura sofistería, eso es mucho sutilizar.

2 *vi* usar sofisterías, sutilizar, buscar evasivas; hacer objeciones de poca monta; **he always** ~**s** es un quisquilloso, es un sofista; **you can't** ~ **about that** no puedes hacer objeciones acerca de eso.

quibbler ['kwɪbləʳ] *n* sofista *mf*.

quibbling ['kwɪblɪŋ] **1** *adj* quisquilloso, sofista. **2** *n* sofistería *f*, sofismas *mpl*; sutilezas *fpl*; objeciones *fpl* de poca monta.

quiche [ki:ʃ] *n* quiche *m*.

quick [kwɪk] **1** *adj* (*speedy*) rápido; veloz; (*early*) pronto; (*of foot*) ligero, veloz; (*agile*) ágil; (*in mind*) listo, inteligente; *ear* fino; *eye, wit etc* agudo; *temper* vivo; **a** ~ **train** un tren rápido; **the** ~**est method** el método más rápido; **a** ~ **reply** una pronta contestación; **for a** ~ **sale** para poder venderlo pronto; **as** ~ **as a flash, as** ~ **as lightning** como un relámpago, como un rayo (*LAm*); ~ **on the draw** rápido en sacar la pistola; **be** ~**!** ¡pronto! ¡date prisa!; **and just be** ~ **about it!** ¡no te entretengas!; **you have been very** ~ **about it** lo has hecho con la mayor prontitud; **he's too** ~ **for me** (*in speech*) habla demasiado de prisa para mí; (*in escaping*) corre más que yo; (*in intelligence*) es demasiado listo para mí; **to be** ~ **to act** obrar con prontitud; **to be** ~ **to take offence** ofenderse por poca cosa; **to be** ~ **to anger** tener repentinos enojos; **to be** ~ **to pity** tener repentina compasión; **to have a** ~ **one** echarse un traguito; **let's have a** ~ **one** entremos a tomar algo.

2 *n* (**a**) (*Anat*) carne *f* viva; **to cut sb to the** ~ herir a uno en lo vivo.

(**b**) (*liter*) **the** ~ (*living*) los vivos; **the** ~ **and the dead** los vivos y los muertos.

3 *adv* = **quickly**.

quick-acting ['kwɪk'æktɪŋ] *adj* extrarrápido, de acción rápida.

quick-change ['kwɪk'tʃeɪndʒ] *adj*: ~ **actor,** ~ **artist** transformista *m*.

quick-eared ['kwɪk'ɪəd] *adj* de oído fino.

quicken ['kwɪkən] **1** *vt* acelerar, apresurar; avivar; **to** ~ **one's pace** apretar (*LAm*: acelerar) el paso. **2** *vi* acelerarse, apresurarse; avivarse; (*embryo*) empezar a moverse.

quick-eyed ['kwɪk'aɪd] *adj* de vista aguda.

quick-fire ['kwɪkfaɪəʳ] *adj gun* de tiro rápido; *question etc* rápido, hecho a quemarropa.

quick-firing ['kwɪk,faɪərɪŋ] *adj* de tiro rápido.

quick-freeze ['kwɪk'fri:z] *vt* congelar rápidamente.

quickie* ['kwɪkɪ] *n* (*question*) pregunta *f* relámpago; (*drink*) trago* *m* (*etc*) rápido.

quicklime ['kwɪklaɪm] *n* cal *f* viva.

quickly ['kwɪklɪ] *adv* rápidamente; de prisa; pronto; **~!** ¡pronto!; **they answered ~** contestaron pronto; **the next phase followed ~** la etapa siguiente empezó inmediatamente; **he talks too ~ for me to understand** habla demasiado rápidamente para que pueda entenderle; **come as ~ as you can** ven cuanto antes, ven lo más pronto que puedas; **the firemen were ~ on the spot** los bomberos se presentaron sin pérdida de tiempo.

quickness ['kwɪknɪs] *n* rapidez *f*, velocidad *f*; prontitud *f*, presteza *f*; agilidad *f*; inteligencia *f*; penetración *f*, finura *f*; agudeza *f*; viveza *f*.

quicksand ['kwɪksænd] *n* arena *f* movediza.

quickset ['kwɪkset] **1** *adj* compuesto de plantas vivas (*esp* de espinos). **2** *n* (*slip*) plantón *m*; (*hawthorn*) espino *m*; (*hedge*) seto *m* vivo (*esp* de espinos).

quick-setting ['kwɪk,setɪŋ] *adj*: **~ glue** pegamento *m* rápido.

quick-sighted ['kwɪk'saɪtɪd] *adj* de vista aguda; (*fig*) perspicaz.

quicksilver ['kwɪk,sɪlvəʳ] **1** *n* azogue *m*, mercurio *m*. **2** *adj* azogado; (*fig*) inconstante, caprichoso. **3** *vt* azogar.

quickstep ['kwɪkstep] *n baile formal a ritmo rápido.*

quick-tempered ['kwɪk'tempəd] *adj* de genio vivo, irascible, de prontos enojos.

quick-witted ['kwɪk'wɪtɪd] *adj* agudo, perspicaz; **that was very ~ of you** en eso has estado muy listo.

quid[1]** [kwɪd] *n* (*Brit*) libra *f* esterlina; **3 ~** 3 libras; **to be ~s in** haber ganado bastante.

quid[2] [kwɪd] *n* mascada *f* (de tabaco).

quiddity ['kwɪdɪtɪ] *n* (*Philos*) esencia *f*; (*quibble*) sutileza *f*, sofistería *f*.

quid pro quo ['kwɪdprəʊ'kwəʊ] *n* quid pro quo *m*, compensación *f*, recompensa *f* (*for* de).

quiescence [kwaɪ'esns] *n* quietud *f*, inactividad *f*; reposo *m*.

quiescent [kwaɪ'esnt] *adj* quieto, inactivo; reposado.

quiet ['kwaɪət] **1** *adj* **(a)** (*silent*) silencioso, callado; *person* (*by nature*) callado, reservado; *place, town etc* tranquilo; (*pej*) *town, life etc* aburrido; *engine etc* sin ruido, que no hace ruido, silencioso; (*not excited*) tranquilo, reposado; **~!, be ~!** (*to people*) ¡silencio!, (*more forcefully*) ¡a callar!, (*to 1 person*) ¡cállate!; **to be ~** (*person: after speaking*) callarse, (*in moving about*) no hacer ruido; **isn't it ~?** ¡qué silencio!; **it was as ~ as the grave** había un silencio sepulcral; **to keep ~** no hacer ruido; no decir nada, quedar callado, callarse; **keep those bottles ~!** ¡no hagas tanto ruido con esas botellas!; **to keep as ~ as a mouse** estar a la chita callando; **they paid £100 to keep him ~** pagaron 100 libras para callarle.

(b) *temperament* tranquilo, sosegado; *animal* manso; **'The Q~ American'** 'El americano impasible'.

(c) *dress etc* no llamativo, discreto; *colour* suave, apagado.

(d) (*not overt*) discreto; (*private*) más bien privado; íntimo, que se celebra en la intimidad; (*informal*) íntimo, sin ceremonias; **with ~ humour he said ...** con su humor discreto dijo ...; **all ~ here** aquí sin novedad; **all ~ on the Western Front** sin novedad en el frente del oeste; **it was a ~ wedding** la boda se celebró en la intimidad; **we had a ~ supper** cenamos en la intimidad; **business is very ~** el negocio está muy flojo; **to have a ~ dig at sb** burlarse discretamente de uno; **they lead a ~ life** llevan una vida tranquila.

2 *n* silencio *m*; paz *f*; tranquilidad *f*; reposo *m*; **an hour of blessed ~** una hora de paz bendita; **on the ~** a la sordina, a hurtadillas; **let's have complete ~** quiero que se callen completamente todos.

3 *vt* calmar; *V* **quieten.**

quieten ['kwaɪətn] **1** *vt* (*esp Brit*) (*also* **to ~ down**) (*calm*) calmar, tranquilizar; (*silence*) hacer callar; **he managed to ~ the crowd** logró tranquilizar a la multitud.

2 *vi* (*also* **to ~ down**) calmarse, tranquilizarse; callarse; (*after unruly youth etc*) sentar los cascos, hacerse más juicioso.

quietism ['kwaɪɪtɪzəm] *n* quietismo *m*.

quietist ['kwaɪɪtɪst] *n* quietista *mf*.

quietly ['kwaɪətlɪ] *adv* (*V adj*) **(a)** silenciosamente, en silencio, calladamente; tranquilamente; sin hacer ruido; **he said ~** dijo dulcemente, dijo en tono bajo; **please play more ~** procure tocar con menos ruido, por favor; **she came in ~** entró sin hacer ruido.

(b) sosegadamente; mansamente; **are you coming ~ or are you going to make trouble?** ¿nos acompaña Vd pacíficamente o va a armar un lío*?

(c) discretamente; **to be ~ dressed** ir vestido con discreción.

(d) discretamente; en la intimidad, en privado; sin ceremonias; **let's get married ~** casémonos sin ceremonias; **we dined ~ at home** cenamos en la intimidad del hogar.

quietness ['kwaɪətnɪs] *n* (*V adj*) **(a)** silencio *m*; paz *f*; tranquilidad *f*; reposo *m*; **the ~ of her voice** lo dulce de su voz, su voz dulce.

(b) sosiego *m*, lo sosegado; mansedumbre *f*.

(c) discreción *f*.

(d) discreción *f*; intimidad *f*.

quietude ['kwaɪətju:d] *n* quietud *f*.

quietus [kwaɪ'i:təs] *n* golpe *m* de gracia; (*death*) muerte *f*; (*Comm*) quitanza *f*, finiquito *m*.

quiff [kwɪf] *n* copete *m*.

quill [kwɪl] *n* (*Zool*) pluma *f* de ave; (*part of feather*) cañón *m* de pluma; (*pen*) pluma *f* (de ganso); (*in fishing*) cañón *m* de pluma; (*of hedgehog etc*) púa *f*; (*bobbin*) canilla *f*; **~ pen** pluma *f* (de ganso).

quilt [kwɪlt] **1** *n* (*Brit*) colcha *f*, edredón *m*. **2** *vt* acolchar.

quilted ['kwɪltɪd] *adj* acolchado.

quilting ['kwɪltɪŋ] *n* colchadura *f*; (*Sew*) piqué *m*, acolchado *m*.

quim** [kwɪm] *n* coño** *m*.

quin* [kwɪn] *n* (*Brit*) = **quintuplet.**

quince [kwɪns] **1** *n* (*fruit, tree*) membrillo *m*. **2** *attr*: **~ cheese, ~ jelly** carne *f* de membrillo.

quincentenary [,kwɪnsen'ti:nərɪ] *n* quinto centenario *m*.

quinine [kwɪ'ni:n] *n* quinina *f*.

Quinquagesima [,kwɪŋkwə'dʒesɪmə] *n* Quincuagésima *f*.

quinquennial [kwɪŋ'kwenɪəl] *adj* quinquenal.

quinquennium [kwɪŋ'kwenɪəm] *n* quinquenio *m*.

quinsy ['kwɪnzɪ] *n* angina *f*.

quint* [kwɪnt] *n* (*US*) quintillizo *m*, -a *f*.

quintessence [kwɪn'tesns] *n* quintaesencia *f*.

quintessential [,kwɪntɪ'senʃəl] *adj* quintaesencial.

quintet(te) [kwɪn'tet] *n* quinteto *m*.

quintuple 1 ['kwɪntjʊpl] *adj* quíntuplo. **2** ['kwɪntjʊpl] *n* quíntuplo *m*. **3** ['kwɪn'tju:pl] *vt* quintuplicar. **4** ['kwɪn'tju:pl] *vi* quintuplicarse.

quintuplet [kwɪn'tju:plɪt] *n* quintillizo *m*, -a *f*.

quip [kwɪp] **1** *n* chiste *m*, agudeza *f*, ocurrencia *f*, pulla *f*. **2** *vt*: **'~', he ~ped '~',** dijo humorísticamente. **3** *vi* hacer un chiste.

quire ['kwaɪəʳ] *n* mano *f* (de papel).

quirk [kw3:k] *n* **(a)** (*oddity*) peculiaridad *f*, rasgo *m* peculiar; capricho *m*; **by some ~ of fate** por algún capricho de la suerte; **it's just a ~ he has** son cosas suyas, es un rasgo peculiar suyo.

(b) (*flourish*) rasgo *m*; (*Archit*) avivador *m*.

quirkiness ['kw3:kɪnɪs] *n* carácter *m* caprichoso; rareza *f*, lo estrafalario.

quirky ['kw3:kɪ] *adj* caprichoso; raro, estrafalario.

quisling ['kwɪzlɪŋ] *n* quisling *mf*; colaboracionista *mf*.

quit [kwɪt] (*irr: pret and ptp* **quit** *or* **quitted**) **1** *vt* dejar, abandonar (*also Comput*); *place* abandonar, salir de; *premises etc* desocupar; **to ~ one's job** abandonar su puesto, dimitir; **to ~ work** suspender el trabajo, dejar de trabajar; **to ~ +** *ger* (*esp US*) dejar de + *infin*, desistir de + *infin*; **~ fooling!** ¡déjate de tonterías!; **it's time to ~ dreaming** es hora de renunciar a los sueños.

2 *vi* (*esp US*) (*go away*) irse, marcharse; (*withdraw*) retirarse; (*Comput*) terminar, abandonar; (*resign*) dimitir; (*give up, in game etc*) rajarse, abandonar; (*stop work*) suspender el trabajo, dejar de trabajar; (*be a quitter*) renunciar a una empresa, abandonar, rajarse; **I ~!** ¡me rajo!

3 *adj*: **to be ~ of sb** estar libre de uno, haberse librado de uno.

quite [kwaɪt] *adv* **(a)** (*completely*) totalmente, completamente; **~ new** completamente nuevo; **~ a hero** todo un héroe (*also iro*); **~!, ~ so!** ¡se comprende!, ¡así es!, perfectamente; **oh, ~ that!** ¡lo menos eso!; **that's ~ enough** eso basta y sobra; **that's ~ enough for me** eso me basta a mí; **not ~ as many as last time** algo menos que la última vez; **I ~ understand** lo comprendo perfectamente; **I don't ~ understand it** no acabo de entenderlo; **that's not ~ right** eso no está del todo bien; **he has not ~ recovered yet** no se ha repuesto todavía del todo; **it was ~ 3 months** era lo menos 3 meses; **it's not ~ what we wanted** no es exactamente lo que buscábamos; **we don't ~ know** no sabemos exactamente; **he's ~ grown up now** ahora está hecho un hombre; es todo un hombre.

(**b**) (*rather*) bastante; **it's ~ good** es bastante bueno; **it was ~ a** (*or* **some**) **surprise** me sorprendió bastante; **I ~ believe that** ... casi tengo la certeza de que ...

Quito ['ki:təʊ] *n* Quito *m*.

quits [kwɪts] *adv*: **to be ~ with sb** estar en paz con uno, estar desquitado con uno; **now we're ~!** ¡ahora no nos debemos nada!; **let's call it ~** hagamos las paces; **to cry ~** (querer) hacer las paces.

quitter ['kwɪtə^r] *n* remolón *m*, -ona *f*; persona *f* que deja fácilmente lo empezado; inconstante *mf*, rajado *m*, -a *f*.

quiver¹ ['kwɪvə^r] *n* carcaj *m*, aljaba *f*.

quiver² ['kwɪvə^r] **1** *n* temblor *m*, estremecimiento *m*, palpitación *f*. **2** *vi* temblar, estremecerse, palpitar (*with* de).

qui vive [ki:'vi:v] *n*: **to be on the ~** estar alerta.

Quixote ['kwɪksət] *nm* Quijote.

quixotic [kwɪk'sɒtɪk] *adj* quijotesco.

quixotism ['kwɪksətɪzəm] *n* quijotismo *m*.

quiz [kwɪz] **1** *n* (*interrogation*) interrogatorio *m*; examen *m*; (*US*) test *m*; (*inquiry*) encuesta *f*; (*Rad etc*; *also* **~ programme, ~ show**) concurso *m* de preguntas y respuestas; **~ master** moderador *m*.

2 *vt* (*stare at*) mirar con curiosidad; (*question*) interrogar (*about* sobre).

quizzical ['kwɪzɪkəl] *adj* burlón.

quizzically ['kwɪzɪkəlɪ] *adv*: **he looked at me ~** me miró burlón.

quod‡ [kwɒd] *n* (*Brit*) chirona‡ *f*.

quoin [kɔɪn] *n* (*angle*) esquina *f*, ángulo *m*; (*stone*) piedra *f* angular; (*Typ*) cuña *f*.

quoit [kwɔɪt] *n* aro *m*, tejo *m*; **~s** juego *m* de aros, juego *m* de tejos.

quondam ['kwɒndæm] *adj* (††) antiguo.

quorate ['kwɔ:reɪt] *adj*: **the meeting was not ~** no había suficiente quórum en la reunión.

quorum ['kwɔ:rəm] *n* quórum *m*; **to constitute a ~** constituir un quórum; **what number constitutes a ~?** ¿cuántos constituyen un quórum?

quot. *n abbr of* **quotation** (**b**).

quota ['kwəʊtə] *n* cuota *f*; (*Comm etc*) contingente *m*, cupo *m*; (*of production*) cuota *f*, cupo *m*; **import ~** cupo *m* de importación; **~ system** sistema *m* de cuota.

quotable ['kwəʊtəbl] *adj* citable; digno de citarse; (*Fin*) cotizable.

quotation [kwəʊ'teɪʃən] *n* (**a**) (*words*) cita *f*; (*act*) citación *f*; **~ marks** comillas *fpl*; **in ~ marks** entre comillas; **dictionary of ~s** diccionario *m* de frases. (**b**) (*Fin*) cotización *f*; (*Comm*) presupuesto *m*.

quote [kwəʊt] **1** *vt* (**a**) citar; *reference number etc* dar, expresar; *example* dar, aducir; **he ~d Góngora** citó a Góngora; **he can ~ Góngora all day long** es capaz de seguir recitando versos de Góngora hasta cuando sea; **he said, and I ~,** ... dijo textualmente ...; **but don't ~ me** pero no me menciones, pero sin mencionar mi nombre; **please ~ the number of the postal order** por favor exprese el número del giro postal; **can you ~ me an example?** ¿puedes darme un ejemplo?

(**b**) (*Fin*) cotizar (*at* en); (*Comm*) estimar; **~d company** empresa *f* cotizada en la Bolsa; **it is not ~d on the Stock Exchange** no se cotiza en la Bolsa.

2 *vi* (**a**) citar; **to ~ from an author** citar versos (*etc*) de un autor, repetir las palabras de un autor; **and I ~** y aquí cito sus propias palabras.

(**b**) **to ~ for** (*Comm*) preparar el presupuesto para, presupuestar; estimar el precio de.

3 *n* cita *f*; **~s** (*inverted commas*) comillas *fpl*; **in ~s** entre comillas; **'~'** 'comienza la cita'; **'close the ~', 'end of ~'** 'fin de la cita'; **she said the minister was (~) "as tired as a newt" (un~)** dijo que el ministro estaba — entre comillas — "más cansado que una cuba".

quoth [kwəʊθ] *vi* (††): **~ I** dije yo; **~ he** dijo él.

quotient ['kwəʊʃənt] *n* cociente *m*.

q.v. *abbr of* **quod vide** = 'which see' véase, q.v.

R

R, r [ɑːʳ] *n* (*letter*) R *f,* r *f;* **R for Robert, R for Roger** (*US*) R de Ramón; **the 3 Rs** (= *reading, writing, [a]rithmetic*) las enseñanzas básicas.

R (**a**) (*Brit*) *abbr of* **Rex** Rey *m,* R.
(**b**) (*Brit*) *abbr of* **Regina** Reina *f,* R.
(**c**) (*Geog*) *abbr of* **river** río *m,* R.
(**d**) *abbr of* **right** derecha *f,* dcha.
(**e**) *adj* (*US Cine*) *abbr of* **restricted** sólo mayores.
(**f**) *abbr of* **Réaumur (scale)**.
(**g**) (*US Pol*) *abbr of* **Republican**.

® *n abbr of* **registered trade mark** marca *f* registrada.

R&B *n abbr of* **Rhythm and Blues**.

R&D *n abbr of* **research and development** investigación *f* y desarrollo, I. y D.

R&R *n* (*US Mil*) *abbr of* **rest and recreation** descanso *m.*

RA *n* (**a**) (*Brit Art*) *abbr of* **Royal Academy** ≈ Real Academia *f* de Bellas Artes. (**b**) (*Brit Art*) *abbr of* **Royal Academician** ≈ miembro *mf* de la Real Academia de Bellas Artes. (**c**) (*Mil*) *abbr of* **Royal Artillery**. (**d**) *abbr of* **Rear Admiral**.

Rabat [rəˈbɑːt] *n* Rabat *m.*

rabbi [ˈræbaɪ] *n* rabino *m;* (*before name*) rabí *m;* **chief ~** gran rabino *m.*

rabbinical [rəˈbɪnɪkəl] *adj* rabínico.

rabbit [ˈræbɪt] **1** *n* conejo *m;* (*Sport**) jugador *m,* -ora *f* inhábil; **~ ears*** (*US TV*) antena *f* de conejo.
2 *vi* (**a**) **to go ~ing** (ir a) cazar conejos.
(**b**) **to ~ on*** (*Brit*) dar el rollo*, no parar de hablar, hablar sin ton ni son.

rabbit burrow [ˈræbɪt,bʌrəʊ] *n* madriguera *f* (de conejos).

rabbit-hole [ˈræbɪthəʊl] *n* hura *f* de conejos.

rabbit-hutch [ˈræbɪthʌtʃ] *n* conejera *f.*

rabbit punch [ˈræbɪtpʌntʃ] *n* golpe *m* de nuca.

rabbit warren [ˈræbɪt,wɒrən] *n* conejera *f,* madriguera *f* (de conejos).

rabble [ˈræbl] *n* (*the ~*) canalla *f,* chusma *f;* **a ~ of** una multitud turbulenta de.

rabble-rouser [ˈræbl,raʊzəʳ] *n* agitador *m,* -ora *f,* demagogo *m,* -a *f.*

rabble-rousing [ˈræblˈraʊzɪŋ] **1** *adj* demagógico. **2** *n* agitación *f,* demagogia *f.*

Rabelaisian [,ræbəˈleɪzɪən] *adj* rabelasiano.

rabid [ˈræbɪd] *adj* (*Med*) rabioso; (*fig*) rabioso, fanático.

rabies [ˈreɪbiːz] *n* rabia *f.*

RAC *n* (*Brit*) (**a**) (*Aut*) *abbr of* **Royal Automobile Club** ≈ Real Automóvil Club *m* de España, RACE *m.* (**b**) (*Mil*) *abbr of* **Royal Armoured Corps.**

raccoon [rəˈkuːn] *n* mapache *m.*

race¹ [reɪs] **1** *n* (**a**) (*contest*) carrera *f,* prueba *f,* (*on water*) regata *f;* **~s** carreras *fpl;* **the ~ for the moon** la carrera hacia la luna; **~ against the clock,** (*fig*) **~ against time** carrera *f* contra (el) reloj; **to go to the ~s** ir a las carreras; **to run a ~** tomar parte en una carrera; **you ran a good ~** corriste muy bien.
(**b**) (*rush*) carrera *f,* corrida *f;* **the ~ to the bus** la carrera precipitada para coger el autobús; **it was a ~ to finish it in time** nos costó para terminarlo a tiempo.
(**c**) (*current*) corriente *f* fuerte; (*of mill*) caz *m,* saetín *m.*
2 *attr:* **~ car** (*US*) coche *m* de carreras; **~ (car) driver** (*US*) corredor *m,* -ora *f* de coches.
3 *vt* (**a**) *horse etc* hacer correr, (*at race meeting*) presentar.
(**b**) **to ~ sb** competir con uno en una carrera (*or* regata); **I'll ~ you!** ¡te echo una carrera!, ¡a ver quién corre más!; **I'll ~ you home!** ¡a ver quién llega primero a casa!
(**c**) **to ~ an engine** acelerar un motor al máximo, hacer funcionar un motor a velocidad excesiva.
(**d**) **to ~ a plan through** hacer que se apruebe un proyecto de prisa; no permitir que se discuta debidamente un proyecto.
4 *vi* (**a**) (*go fast*) correr de prisa, (*Aut etc*) ir a máxima velocidad; **to ~ along** ir corriendo; **to ~ down a hill** ir cuesta abajo a toda carrera; **he ~d past us** pasó delante de nosotros corriendo como un demonio, nos pasó a toda carrera.
(**b**) (*pulse*) latir a ritmo acelerado; (*engine*) girar a velocidad excesiva.
(**c**) (*in contest*) competir; presentarse; **they will ~ at 3 o'clock** empezarán la carrera a las 3; **we're not racing today** no tomamos parte hoy; **when did you last ~?** ¿cuándo corriste (*etc*) la última vez?

race² [reɪs] **1** *n* (*Bio*) raza *f;* casta *f,* estirpe *f,* familia *f;* **the white ~** la raza blanca; **he comes from a ~ of smugglers** es de linaje de contrabandistas.
2 *attr:* **~ relations** relaciones *fpl* raciales; **~ riot** disturbio *m* racial.

racecard [ˈreɪskɑːd] *n* programa *m* de carreras.

racecourse [ˈreɪskɔːs] *n* (*esp Brit*) hipódromo *m.*

racegoer [ˈreɪsgəʊəʳ] *n* el *m* (*or* la *f*) que asiste a las carreras, aficionado *m,* -a *f* a las carreras (de caballos).

race-hatred [ˈreɪsˈheɪtrɪd] *n* odio *m* racial, racismo *m.*

racehorse [ˈreɪshɔːs] *n* caballo *m* de carreras.

raceme [ˈræsiːm] *n* racimo *m.*

race-meeting [ˈreɪs,miːtɪŋ] *n* carreras *fpl* (de caballos).

racer [ˈreɪsəʳ] *n* corredor *m,* -ora *f;* (*horse*) caballo *m* de carreras; (*Aut*) coche *m* de carreras.

racetrack [ˈreɪstræk] *n* (*Brit: horses*) pista *f,* (*US*) hipódromo *m;* (*Aut etc*) autódromo *m.*

Rachel [ˈreɪtʃəl] *nf* Raquel.

rachitic [ræˈkɪtɪk] *adj* raquítico.

racial [ˈreɪʃəl] *adj* racial; racista; **~ discrimination** discriminación *f* racial; **~ integration** integración *f* racial.

racialism [ˈreɪʃəlɪzəm] *n* racismo *m.*

racialist [ˈreɪʃəlɪst] **1** *adj* racista. **2** *n* racista *mf.*

racially [ˈreɪʃəlɪ] *adv* racialmente; de manera racista; **children of ~ mixed parents** hijos *mpl* de padres racialmente mixtos.

raciness [ˈreɪsɪnɪs] *n* picante *m,* sal *f,* vivacidad *f.*

racing [ˈreɪsɪŋ] **1** *n* carreras *fpl.*
2 *attr* de carreras; **~ bicycle** bicicleta *f* de carreras; **~ calendar** calendario *m* de carreras (de caballos); **~ car** coche *m* de carreras; **~ cyclist** corredor *m,* -ora *f* ciclista; **~ driver, ~ motorist** piloto *m,* corredor *m,* -ora *f* automovilista; **~ man** aficionado *m* a las carreras (de caballos); experto *m* en caballos; **~ pigeon** paloma *f* de carreras; **the ~ world** el mundo de las carreras (de caballos); **~ yacht** yate *m* de regatas.

racism [ˈreɪsɪzəm] *n* racismo *m.*

racist [ˈreɪsɪst] **1** *adj* racista. **2** *n* racista *mf.*

rack¹ [ræk] **1** *n* (*shelf*) estante *m,* estantería *f,* anaquel *m;* (*for clothes etc*) percha *f,* perchero *m,* cuelgacapas *m,* colgadero *m* (*LAm*); (*Aut*) baca *f;* (*Rail*) rejilla *f;* (*Mech*) cremallera *f;* (*for torture*) potro *m;* (*for arms*) armero *m;* (*for billiard cues*) taquera *f;* **~ and pinion** cremallera *f* y piñón; **to be on the ~** (*fig*) estar en ascuas; **to buy clothes off the ~** (*US*) comprar ropa de percha.
2 *vt* (**a**) atormentar; **to be ~ed by pains** tener dolores atroces por todas partes; **to be ~ed by remorse** estar atormentado por el remordimiento; *V* **brain.**
(**b**) *wine* (*also* **to ~ off**) trasegar.

◆**rack up** *vt* (*accumulate*) conseguir, ganar.

rack² [ræk] *n:* **to go to ~ and ruin** arruinarse, echarse a perder.

racket¹ [ˈrækɪt] *n,* **racquet** [ˈrækɪt] *n* raqueta *f;* **~s** (*game*) *especie de tenis jugado contra frontón.*

racket² ['rækɪt] **1** *n* (**a**) (*din*) ruido *m*, estrépito *m*; (*confused noise*) barahúnda *f*, jaleo *m*; **you never heard such a ~!** ¡no se había oído nunca tal ruido!; **to kick up** (*or* **make**) **a ~** armar un jaleo, meter ruido.

(**b**) (*: *trick*) trampa *f*, trapacería *f*; (*criminal*) fraude *m* sistematizado, estafa *f*, timo *m*; (*blackmail, protection*) chantaje *m*; **the drug ~** el tráfico de drogas; **the car ~** (*hum*) el negocio del automóvil; **it's a ~!** ¡aquí hay trampa!; **what ~ are you in?** ¿a qué se dedica Vd?; **he was in on the ~** era de los que operaban la trampa; **to stand the ~** pagar los platos rotos.

2 *vi* (*make noise*) (*also* **to ~ about**) hacer ruido, armar un jaleo.

racketeer [ˌrækɪ'tɪəʳ] *n* estafador *m*, timador *m*; chantajista *m*.

racketeering [ˌrækɪ'tɪərɪŋ] *n* chantaje *m* sistematizado, crimen *m* organizado.

racking ['rækɪŋ] *adj pain* atroz.

rack railway ['ræk'reɪlweɪ] *n* ferrocarril *m* de cremallera.

rack-rent ['rækrent] *n* alquiler *m* exorbitante.

raconteur [ˌrækɒn'tɜːʳ] *n* anecdotista *m*, narrador *m*, (*esp*) el que cuenta con gracia los chistes.

racoon [rə'kuːn] *n* mapache *m*.

racquet ['rækɪt] *n* = **racket¹**.

racy ['reɪsɪ] *adj* picante, salado, vivo.

rad‡ [ræd] *adj* (*esp US*) = **radical (b)**.

RADA ['rɑːdə] *n* (*Brit*) *abbr of* **Royal Academy of Dramatic Art**.

radar ['reɪdɑːʳ] **1** *n* radar *m*.

2 *attr*: **~ beacon** faro *m* de radar; **~ scanner** antena *f* giratoria de radar; **~ screen** pantalla *f* de radar; **~ station** estación *f* de radar; **~ trap** trampa *f* de radar.

raddled ['rædld] *adj* depravado, decaído.

radial ['reɪdɪəl] *adj* radial; **~ engine** motor *m* radial; **~ tyre** (*Brit*), **~-ply (tire)** (*US*) neumático *m* radial.

radiance ['reɪdɪəns] *n* brillantez *f*, brillo *m*, resplandor *m*.

radiant ['reɪdɪənt] *adj* radiante, brillante, resplandeciente; **a ~ smile** una sonrisa radiante; **the bride was ~** la novia estaba hermosísima; **to be ~ with happiness** estar radiante de felicidad, rebosar felicidad.

radiantly ['reɪdɪəntlɪ] *adv* brillantemente; **to be ~ happy** irradiar felicidad; **to smile ~ at sb** echar una sonrisa radiante a uno.

radiate **1** ['reɪdɪeɪt] *vt* radiar, irradiar; *happiness etc* difundir; **lines that ~ from the centre** líneas *fpl* que se extienden desde el centro. **2** ['reɪdɪeɪt] *vi* irradiar, radiar (*from* de); (*roads etc*) salir (*from* de). **3** ['reɪdɪɪt] *adj* radiado.

radiation [ˌreɪdɪ'eɪʃən] *n* radiación *f*; **~ sickness** enfermedad *f* de radiación; **~ therapy** terapéutica *f* por radiaciones; **~ treatment** tratamiento *m* por radiaciones.

radiator ['reɪdɪeɪtəʳ] *n* radiador *m*; **~ cap** tapón *m* de radiador; **~ grille** reja *f* de radiador.

radical ['rædɪkəl] **1** *adj* (**a**) radical. (**b**) (*US‡*) guay*, súper*. **2** *n* (*all senses*) radical *m*.

radicalism ['rædɪkəlɪzəm] *n* radicalismo *m*.

radicalize ['rædɪkəˌlaɪz] *vt* radicalizar.

radically ['rædɪkəlɪ] *adv* radicalmente.

radicle ['rædɪkl] *n* (*Bot*) radícula *f*; (*Chem*) radical *m*.

radii ['reɪdɪaɪ] *npl of* **radius**.

radio ['reɪdɪəʊ] **1** *n* (*as science etc*) radio *f*, radiofonía *f*; (*set*) radio *f* (*m in parts of LAm*), receptor *m* de radio, radiorreceptor *m*; **by ~, on the ~, over the ~** por radio; **to talk on the ~** hablar por radio.

2 *attr*: **~-alarm clock** radio-reloj *m* despertador; **~ announcer** locutor *m*, -ora *f* de radio; **~ astronomy** radioastronomía *f*; **~ beacon, ~ beam** radiofaro *m*; **~ broadcast** emisión *f* de radio; **~ contact** radiocomunicación *f*; **~ engineer** radiotécnico *m*; **~ engineering** radiotécnica *f*; **~ frequency** frecuencia *f* de radio; **~ ham** radioaficionado *m*, -a *f*; **~ link** enlace *m* radiofónico; **~ mast, ~ tower** (*US*) torre *f* de radio; **~ network** cadena *f* (*or* red *f*) de emisoras; **~ operator** radiotelegrafista *mf*; **~ play** comedia *f* radiofónica; **~ program** (*US*), **~ programme** programa *m* de radio; **~ set** radio *f*; **~ silence** silencio *m* radiofónico; **~ station** emisora *f*; **~ taxi** radiotaxi *m*; **~ telescope** radiotelescopio *m*; **~ transmitter** emisora *f*; **~ wave** onda *f* de radio.

3 *vt* radiar, transmitir por radio.

4 *vi*: **to ~ for help** pedir socorro por radio; **to ~ to sb** enviar un mensaje a uno por radio.

radio... ['reɪdɪəʊ] *pref* radio...

radioactive ['reɪdɪəʊ'æktɪv] *adj* radiactivo; **~ waste** residuos *mpl* radiactivos.

radioactivity ['reɪdɪəʊæk'tɪvɪtɪ] *n* radiactividad *f*.

radiobiology [ˌreɪdɪəʊbaɪ'ɒlədʒɪ] *n* radiobiología *f*.

radiocarbon [ˌreɪdɪəʊ'kɑːbən] *n* radiocarbono *m*; **~ analysis** análisis *m* por radiocarbono; **~ test** test *m* por radiocarbono.

radiocassette [ˌreɪdɪəʊkə'set] *n* (*also* **~ recorder**) radiocaset(t)e *m*.

radio-controlled ['reɪdɪəʊkən'trəʊld] *adj* teledirigido.

radiogram ['reɪdɪəʊgræm] *n* (*Brit*: *set*) radiogramola *f*; (*message*) radiograma *m*.

radiograph ['reɪdɪəʊgrɑːf] **1** *n* radiografía *f*. **2** *vt* radiografiar.

radiographer [ˌreɪdɪ'ɒgrəfəʳ] *n* radiógrafo *m*, -a *f*.

radiography [ˌreɪdɪ'ɒgrəfɪ] *n* radiografía *f*.

radioisotope ['reɪdɪəʊ'aɪsətəʊp] *n* radioisótopo *m*.

radiolocation [ˌreɪdɪəʊlə'keɪʃən] *n* radiolocalización *f*.

radiological [ˌreɪdɪə'lɒdʒɪkəl] *adj* radiológico.

radiologist [ˌreɪdɪ'ɒlədʒɪst] *n* radiólogo *m*, -a *f*.

radiology [ˌreɪdɪ'ɒlədʒɪ] *n* radiología *f*.

radiopager ['reɪdɪəʊˌpeɪdʒəʳ] *n* localizador *m*, busca* *m*.

radioscopy [ˌreɪdɪ'ɒskəpɪ] *n* radioscopia *f*.

radiotelephone ['reɪdɪəʊ'telɪfəʊn] *n* radioteléfono *m*.

radiotelephony [ˌreɪdɪəʊtə'lefənɪ] *n* radiotelefonía *f*.

radiotherapist [ˌreɪdɪəʊ'θerəpɪst] *n* radioterapeuta *mf*.

radiotherapy ['reɪdɪəʊ'θerəpɪ] *n* radioterapia *f*.

radish ['rædɪʃ] *n* rábano *m*.

radium ['reɪdɪəm] *n* radio *m*.

radius ['reɪdɪəs] *n*, *pl* **radii** ['reɪdɪaɪ] (*most senses*) radio *m*; (*Aer*: *also* **operational ~**) autonomía *f*; **within a ~ of 50 km** en un radio de 50 km.

radix ['reɪdɪks] *n*, *pl* **radices** ['reɪdɪsiːz] (*Bot, Gram*) raíz *f*; (*Math*) base *f*.

radon ['reɪdɒn] *n* radón *m*.

RAF *n* (*Brit*) *abbr of* **Royal Air Force** fuerzas *fpl* aéreas británicas.

raffia ['ræfɪə] *n* rafia *f*.

raffish ['ræfɪʃ] *adj* disipado, disoluto.

raffle ['ræfl] **1** *n* rifa *f*, sorteo *m*. **2** *vt* rifar, sortear; **10 bottles will be ~d for charity** se sortearán 10 botellas con fines benéficos.

raft [rɑːft] *n* (**a**) balsa *f*, almadía *f*. (**b**) (*) (*quantity*) cantidad *f*; montón *m*; (*set*) serie *f*; grupo *m*.

rafter ['rɑːftəʳ] *n* par *m*; **the ~s** (*loosely*) el techo.

rag¹ [ræg] **1** *n* (**a**) (*piece of cloth*) trapo *m*; (*for cleaning*) trapo *m*, paño *m*; (*shred of clothing*) andrajo *m*, harapo *m*; **~s** (*: *clothes*) trapos* *mpl*; **from ~s to riches** de los andrajos a la riqueza; **to be in ~s** estar harapiento, estar en andrajos; **to chew the ~** (*US*: *chat*) charlar, pasar el rato, (*argue*) discutir; **to feel like a ~** estar hecho cisco; **she hasn't a ~ to her back** no tiene con qué vestirse; **to put on one's glad ~s** endomingarse; **it's like a red ~ to a bull** es lo que más le provoca a cólera, no hay nada que más le enfurezca.

(**b**) (*: *newspaper*) periodicucho* *m*.

2 *attr*: **~ doll** muñeca *f* de trapo; **~ fair** rastro *m*, feria *f* de ropa y objetos usados; **~ trade*** industria *f* del vestido.

rag²* [ræg] (*Brit*) **1** *n* (*practical joke*) broma *f* pesada; (*Univ*) broma *f* estudiantil; novatada *f*, (*for charity*) función *f* estudiantil benéfica; **~ week** semana *f* de funciones benéficas (estudiantiles); **we did it just for a ~** lo hicimos en broma nada más.

2 (*) *vt* dar guerra a, tomar el pelo a*; **they were ~ging him about his new tie** le estaban tomando el pelo por la nueva corbata*.

3 *vi* guasearse, bromearse; **I was only ~ging** lo dije en broma.

ragamuffin ['rægəˌmʌfɪn] *n* granuja *m*, galopín *m*.

rag-and-bone man [ˌrægən'bəʊnmæn] *n*, *pl* **rag-and-bone men** [ˌrægən'bəʊnmen] (*Brit*) trapero *m*.

ragbag ['rægbæg] *n* talego *m* de recortes; (*Brit fig*) mezcolanza *f*, cajón *m* de sastre; **it's a ~ of a book** es un libro todo revuelto, el libro es todo un fárrago.

rage [reɪdʒ] **1** *n* (**a**) (*anger*) rabia *f*, furor *m*, ira *f*; (*of wind etc*) furia *f*; **to be in a ~** estar furioso (*about* por, *with sb* contra uno); **to fly into a ~** montar en cólera, encolerizarse; **to vent one's ~ on sb** descargar su indignación sobre uno.

(**b**) (*fashion*) boga *f*, moda *f* (*for* de); (*craze*) manía *f* (*for* de); **it's all the ~** es la moda, es la última; **his dresses are all the ~ in New York** sus vestidos hacen furor en Nueva York.

2 *vi* (**a**) (*be angry*) estar furioso, rabiar; **to ~ against sb** estar furioso con uno; culpar amargamente a uno; **to ~ against sth** protestar furiosamente contra algo.

(**b**) (*of pain*) doler atrozmente; (*sea etc*) embravecerse, enfurecerse; (*wind*) bramar; (*fire, plague etc*) desencadenarse; continuar con pleno vigor; **fire ~d in the building for 3 hours** durante 3 horas el fuego hizo estragos en el edificio.

ragged ['rægɪd] *adj* (**a**) *dress* roto; *person* andrajoso, harapiento; *edge* desigual, mellado; *coastline etc* accidentado; *line, procession* confuso, desordenado, sin orden; *style* desigual, descuidado; (*Mus*) *note* poco suave, imperfecto.

(**b**) (*text*) ~ **left** margen *m* izquierdo irregular; ~ **right** margen *m* derecho irregular.

(**c**) (*US**) **to run sb** ~ cansar a uno, agobiar a uno.

raggedly ['rægɪdlɪ] *adv*: **he was ~ dressed** estaba muy mal vestido, estaba en andrajos; **the engine is running** ~ el motor marcha mal.

ragged robin ['rægɪd'rɒbɪn] *n* (*Bot*) cuclillo *m*.

raging ['reɪdʒɪŋ] *adj* rabioso, furioso; *storm etc* violento; *pain* atroz, agudo; **to be in a ~ temper** estar furiosísimo.

raglan ['ræglən] *n* raglán *m*.

ragman ['rægmæn] *n, pl* **ragmen** ['rægmen] trapero *m*.

ragout [ræ'gu:] *n* guisado *m*.

ragpicker ['rægpɪkəʳ] *n* trapero *m*.

rag-tag* ['rægtæg] *n* chusma *f* (*also* ~ **and bobtail**).

ragtime ['rægtaɪm] *n* tiempo *m* sincopado, rag-time *m*; **in** ~ sincopado.

ragweed ['rægwi:d] *n* ambrosía *f*.

ragwort ['rægwɜ:t] *n* hierba *f* cana, zuzón *m*, hierba *f* de Santiago.

raid [reɪd] **1** *n* (*into territory, across border etc*) incursión *f*, correría *f*, razzia *f*; (*Aer*) ataque *m* (*on* contra), bombardeo *m* (*on* de); (*sweep by police*) redada *f*, batida *f*; (*by criminals*) asalto *m* (*on* a); **the men are away on a** ~ los hombres están fuera en una correría; **only 5 aircraft returned from the** ~ solamente 5 aviones regresaron después del ataque; **there was a ~ on the jeweller's last night** anoche fue asaltada la joyería.

2 *vt* (*by land*) invadir, atacar, hacer una incursión en; (*Aer*) atacar, bombardear; (*by criminals*) asaltar; **the boys ~ed the orchard** los muchachos pillaron el huerto; **the police ~ed the club** la policía registró el club; **shall we ~ the larder?** ¿asaltamos la despensa?, ¿vamos a coger algo en la despensa?; **the king's tomb had already been ~ed** la tumba del rey había sido ya saqueada.

3 *vi* hacer una incursión, ir en razzia, razziar; **they ~ed deep into enemy territory** penetraron profundamente en tierras enemigas.

raider ['reɪdəʳ] *n* (*across frontier*) invasor *m*, incursor *m*; (*Aer*) bombardero *m*; (*Naut*) buque *m* corsario; (*criminal*) criminal *m*, asaltante *m*, ladrón *m*.

raiding party ['reɪdɪŋ,pɑ:tɪ] *n* grupo *m* de ataque.

rail[1] [reɪl] **1** *n* (**a**) (*hand~*) baranda *f*, barandilla *f*, pasamanos *m*; (*Naut*) barandilla *f*; borda *f*; (*of bar*) apoyo *m* para los pies; **~s** (*fence*) cerca *f*, palizada *f*.

(**b**) (*Rail*) carril *m*, raíl *m*, riel *m*; **~s** (*freq*) vía *f*; **~s** (*Fin*) acciones *fpl* de sociedades ferroviarias; **to come off** (*or* **run off, jump, leave**) **the ~s** descarrilar; **to go** (*or* **run**) **off the ~s** (*fig*) extraviarse; (*morally*) echarse a perder; **by** ~ por ferrocarril.

2 *attr*: ~ **accident** accidente *m* de ferrocarril; ~ **journey** viaje *m* por ferrocarril; ~ **strike** huelga *f* de ferroviarios; ~ **system** red *f* ferroviaria, sistema *m* ferroviario; ~ **traffic** tráfico *m* por ferrocarril.

3 *vt* (**a**) (*also* **to ~ in, to ~ off**) cercar con una barandilla, poner barandilla a.

(**b**) (*Rail*) transportar por ferrocarril, mandar por ferrocarril.

rail[2] [reɪl] *n* (*Orn*) rascón *m*.

rail[3] [reɪl] *vi*: **to ~ at, to ~ against** denostar, despotricar contra, maldecir de.

railcar ['reɪlkɑ:ʳ] *n* automotor *m*.

railcard ['reɪlkɑ:d] *n* carnet *m* para obtener descuento en los ferrocarriles; **family** ~ carnet *m* de familia (de la RENFE); **student's** ~ carnet *m* de estudiante.

railhead ['reɪlhed] *n* estación *f* terminal, cabeza *f* de línea.

railing ['reɪlɪŋ] *n* baranda *f*, barandilla *f*, pasamanos *m*; **~s** verja *f*, enrejado *m*.

raillery ['reɪlərɪ] *n* burlas *fpl*, chanzas *fpl*.

railroad ['reɪlrəʊd] **1** *n, attr* (*US*) = **railway**.

2 *vt*: **to ~ sth through** llevar algo a cabo muy precipitadamente; **to ~ a bill through** hacer que se apruebe un decreto de ley sin discutirse; **to ~ sb into doing sth** obligar a uno a hacer algo (sin darle tiempo para reflexionar).

railroader ['reɪlrəʊdəʳ] *n* (*US*) = **railwayman**.

railway ['reɪlweɪ] **1** *n* (*Brit*) ferrocarril *m*; (*as track*) vía *f*, vía *f* férrea; (*as route*) línea *f* (de ferrocarril).

2 *attr* ferroviario; de ferrocarril; ~ **bridge** puente *m* de ferrocarril; ~ **carriage** vagón *m*, coche *m* (de ferrocarril); ~ **engine** máquina *f*, locomotora *f*; ~ **line** (*track*) vía *f*, vía *f* férrea, (*route*) línea *f* (de ferrocarril); ~ **network** red *f* ferroviaria; ~ **porter** mozo *m*; ~ **station** estación *f* (de ferrocarril); ~ **ticket** billete *m* de ferrocarril; ~ **timetable** horario *m* de trenes; ~ **track** vía *f* (de ferrocarril); ~ **yard** cochera *f*.

railwayman ['reɪlweɪmən] *n, pl* **railwaymen** ['reɪlweɪmən], **railworker** ['reɪl,wɜ:kəʳ] *n* ferroviario *m*, ferrocarrilero *m* (*LAm*).

raiment ['reɪmənt] *n* (*liter*) vestido *m*, vestimenta *f*.

rain [reɪn] **1** *n* lluvia *f* (*also fig*); **the ~s** la época de las lluvias; **a ~ of gifts** una lluvia de regalos; **a walk in the** ~ un paseo bajo la lluvia; **to be out in the** ~ estar fuera aguantando la lluvia; **come in out of the ~!** ¡entra, que te vas a mojar!; **come ~ or shine** pase lo que pase, contra viento y marea; **if the ~ keeps off** si no llueve; **it looks like** ~ parece que va a llover.

2 *vt* llover; **to ~ blows on sb** llover golpes sobre uno; **to ~ gifts on sb** colmar a uno de regalos; **hereabouts it ~s soot** por aquí llueve hollín; **to ~ cats and dogs** llover a cántaros.

3 *vi* llover; **blows ~ed upon him** llovieron sobre él los golpes; **gifts ~ed upon him** le llovieron regalos encima; **it ~s on the just as well as on the unjust** la lluvia cae sobre los buenos como sobre los malos; **it never ~s but it pours** (*fig*) llueve sobre mojado, las desgracias nunca vienen solas.

◆**rain down** *vi* llover.

◆**rain off,** (*US*) **rain out** *vt*: **the match was ~ed off** se canceló (*or* se abandonó) el partido debido a la lluvia; **we were ~ed off** tuvimos que abandonarlo por la lluvia.

rainbelt ['reɪnbelt] *n* zona *f* de lluvias.

rainbow ['reɪnbəʊ] **1** *n* arco *m* iris. **2** *attr*: **the ~ coalition** la coalición multicolor; ~ **trout** trucha *f* arco iris.

raincheck ['reɪntʃek] *n* (*US*) contraseña *f* para usar otro día (en caso de cancelación por lluvia); **to take a** ~ (*fig*) esperar que la invitación se renueve para otro día, apuntarse para la próxima vez.

raincloud ['reɪnklaʊd] *n* nubarrón *m*.

raincoat ['reɪnkəʊt] *n* impermeable *m*, gabardina *f*.

raindrop ['reɪndrɒp] *n* gota *f* de agua.

rainfall ['reɪnfɔ:l] *n* (*act*) precipitación *f*; (*quantity*) lluvia *f*, cantidad *f* de lluvia; **the region has 3″ of ~ a year** la región tiene 3 pulgadas de lluvia al año.

rain-forest ['reɪn,fɒrɪst] *n* (*also* **tropical** ~) pluviselva *f*, selva *f* tropical.

rain-gauge ['reɪngeɪdʒ] *n* pluviómetro *m*.

rain-hood ['reɪnhʊd] *n* capucha *f* impermeable.

raininess ['reɪnɪnɪs] *n* lo lluvioso, pluviosidad *f*.

rainless ['reɪnlɪs] *adj* sin lluvia, seco.

rainproof ['reɪnpru:f] *adj* impermeable.

rainstorm ['reɪnstɔ:m] *n* tempestad *f* de lluvia, temporal *m*.

rainwater ['reɪnwɔ:təʳ] *n* agua *f* llovediza, agua *f* de lluvia.

rainwear ['reɪnwɛəʳ] *n* ropa *f* impermeable.

rainy ['reɪnɪ] *adj climate, region* lluvioso; ~ **day** día *m* de lluvia, (*fig*) tiempo (futuro) *m* de escasez; ~ **season** estación *f* de las lluvias; **it was so ~ yesterday** llovió tanto ayer.

raise [reɪz] **1** *n* (*esp US*) aumento *m*, subida *f*; (*of salary*) aumento *m*; (*Cards*) sobremarca *f*.

2 *vt* (**a**) (*lift*) *fallen object, weight, arm, eyes etc* levantar, alzar, elevar; *hat* quitarse; *flag* izar, enarbolar; *dust* levantar; *dough* fermentar; *sunken ship* sacar a flote; *camp, siege* levantar; *spirits* (*conjure*) evocar; *embargo etc* levantar; (*from the dead*) resucitar; (*Math*) elevar (a una potencia); **to ~ one's glass** alzar el vaso; **to ~ sb to power** alzar a uno al poder; **to ~ the standard of revolt** pronunciarse, sublevarse; **to ~ tribesmen in revolt** sublevar a las tribus; **to ~ the people against a tyrant** hacer que el pueblo se subleve contra un tirano; **to ~ sb's hopes excessively** hacer a uno concebir esperanzas desmesuradas; **to ~ sb's spirits** dar aliento a uno, reanimar a uno.

(**b**) (*erect*) *building* erigir, edificar; *statue* erigir.

(**c**) (*increase*) *price, salary* aumentar, subir; *production* aumentar; *person* (*in rank*) ascender (*to* a); *voice* levantar; **don't ~ your voice!** ¡no levantes la voz!; **you are not to ~ your voice to me** Vd no me levanta a mí la voz; **I'll ~ you 10 dollars** (*bet*) apuesto 10 dólares más, (*bid*) ofrezco 10 dólares más.

(**d**) (*bring up etc*) *family, livestock* criar; mantener; *crop* cultivar.

(**e**) (*produce*) causar, producir; dar lugar a; *bump etc* causar; *laughter* suscitar, provocar; *doubts* suscitar; *problem, question* plantear; *objection* poner, hacer; *cry etc* dar; *outcry* armar; **I'll ~ the point with them** se lo mencionaré; **it ~s many problems for us** nos plantea muchos problemas; **this ~s the question of whether** ... esto plantea el problema de si ...; **can't you ~ a smile?** ¿no sonríes siquiera?

(**f**) (*get together*) *army* reclutar; *funds* reunir; obtener, movilizar; *loan* lograr, obtener; *new taxes* imponer; **to ~ money on an estate** obtener un préstamo sobre una propiedad.

(**g**) (*) (*contact*) contactar con; (*find*) localizar; **I'll see if I can ~ him by phone** trataré de localizarle por teléfono.

(**h**) (*improve*) mejorar; **to ~ one's game** mejorar su juego, jugar mejor.

3 *vr*: **to ~ o.s.** alzarse, levantarse.

◆**raise up 1** *vt* (*lift*) levantar, alzar, elevar; **to ~ sb up from poverty** sacar a uno de la pobreza, ayudar a uno a salir de la miseria.

2 *vr*: **he ~d himself up on one elbow** se apoyó en un codo; **he has ~d himself up from nothing** ha salido de la nada.

raised [reɪzd] *adj* (*in relief*) en relieve.

raisin ['reɪzən] *n* pasa *f*, uva *f* pasa.

raison d'être ['reɪzɔːn'deːtr] *n* razón *f* de ser.

raj [rɑːdʒ] *n*: **the British ~** el imperio británico (en la India); la soberanía británica (en la India).

rajah ['rɑːdʒə] *n* rajá *m*.

rake[1] [reɪk] **1** *n* (*garden ~*) rastrillo *m*; (*Agr*) rastro *m*; (*fire ~*) hurgón *m*.

2 *vt* (*Agr etc*) rastrillar; *fire* hurgar; (*with shots etc*) barrer; (*with eyes*) examinar, escudriñar; (*search, ransack*) registrar, buscar en.

◆**rake in** *vt* (**a**) *gambling chips* recoger. (**b**) (*) **they ~d in a profit of £1000** se sacaron 1000 libras de ganancia limpia; **he ~s in £50 on every deal** se toma una tajada de 50 libras de cada negocio*; **he must be raking it in** está acuñando dinero.

◆**rake off** *vt* quitar con el rastrillo.

◆**rake over** *vt flowerbed* rastrillar; *memories, past* remover.

◆**rake together** reunir (*or* recoger) con el rastrillo; (*fig*) reunir (con dificultad); **we managed to ~ a team together** por fin logramos formar un equipo.

◆**rake up** *vt subject* sacar a relucir; *the past etc* remover; **why did you have to ~ that up?** ¿para qué has vuelto a mencionar eso?

rake[2] [reɪk] *n* (*person*) libertino *m*, calavera *m*; **old ~** viejo *m* verde.

rake[3] [reɪk] **1** *n* (*Archit, Naut*) inclinación *f*. **2** *vt* inclinar.

rake-off* ['reɪkɒf] *n* comisión *f*, tajada* *f*, porcentaje *m*.

rakish[1] ['reɪkɪʃ] *adj* (*dissolute*) libertino, disoluto.

rakish[2] ['reɪkɪʃ] *adj ship* de palos inclinados; (*fast-looking*) veloz, ligero; (*smart*) elegante, gallardo; desenvuelto; de mucho garbo; **with his hat at a ~ angle** con el sombrero echado de lado, con el sombrero a lo chulo.

rakishly ['reɪkɪʃlɪ] *adv* (*of hat etc*) echado al lado, a lo chulo; elegantemente.

rally[1] ['rælɪ] **1** *n* (**a**) (*Pol etc*) reunión *f*, mitin *m*, manifestación *f*; (*of scouts etc*) reunión *f*, congreso *m*; (*Aut*) rallye *m*.

(**b**) (*Tennis*) peloteo *m*.

(**c**) (*Mil*) repliegue *m*; (*Med, Fin etc*) recuperación *f*.

2 *vt* (*gather*) reunir; (*Mil*) rehacer; *faculties* concentrar; (*encourage*) reanimar, infundir ánimo a, fortalecer.

3 *vi* (**a**) (*gather*) reunirse (*around sb, to sb* en torno a uno); (*demonstrate*) manifestarse; **they rallied to him** se reunieron en torno a él, afirmaron su adhesión, se solidarizaron con él; **to ~ to the call** responder a la llamada.

(**b**) (*Mil*) replegarse, rehacerse; (*Med, Fin etc*) recuperarse, mejorar.

◆**rally round** *vi*: **everyone must ~ round** todos hemos de afirmar nuestra unidad; todos tenemos que cooperar; **they have all rallied round nobly** todos han hecho maravillas en un esfuerzo común.

rally[2] ['rælɪ] *vt* (*tease*) tomar el pelo a.

rallying-cry ['rælɪɪŋ,kraɪ] *n* llamamiento *m* (para reanimar la resistencia *etc*).

rallying-point ['rælɪɪŋ,pɔɪnt] *n* punto *m* de reunión.

RAM [ræm] *n abbr of* **random access memory.**

ram [ræm] **1** *n* (**a**) (*Zool*) carnero *m*, morueco *m*; (*Astron*) Aries *m*.

(**b**) (*Mil*) ariete *m*; (*Naut*) espolón *m*; (*Tech*: *rammer*) pisón *m*, (*pile driver*) martillo *m* pilón.

2 *vt* (**a**) (*tread down*) (*also* **to ~ down**) apisonar; (*squeeze*) apretar; (*fill*) rellenar (*with* de); **to ~ a charge home** atacar una carga; **they ~med it down his throat** se lo hicieron tragar a la fuerza; **to ~ clothes into a case** poner la ropa apretadamente en una maleta; **to ~ sth into a hole** meter algo apretadamente en un agujero, introducir algo a la fuerza en un agujero; **we had Campoamor ~med into us at school** nos dimos un atracón de Campoamor en el colegio.

(**b**) (*collide with*) chocar con, dar contra; (*Naut*: *deliberately*) atacar con el espolón; **the car ~med the lamppost** el coche chocó con el farol.

Ramadan [,ræmə'dæn] *n* ramadán *m*.

ramble ['ræmbl] **1** *n* paseo *m* por el campo, excursión *f* a pie, caminata *f*; **to go for a ~** salir de excursión a pie, dar una caminata.

2 *vi* (**a**) (*walk*) salir de excursión a pie, dar una caminata; pasearse, ir de paseo (en el campo); **we spent a week rambling in the hills** pasamos una semana explorando la montaña a pie (*or* paseándonos por la montaña).

(**b**) (*in speech*) divagar; (*lose thread*) perder el hilo, salirse del tema; (*of river etc*) serpentear; (*of plant*) trepar, enredarse; extenderse como una enredadera; **he just ~d on and on** siguió divagando.

rambler ['ræmblə^r] *n* (**a**) (*person*) excursionista *mf* (a pie). (**b**) (*Bot*) trepadora *f*; **~ rose** rosal *m* trepador.

rambling ['ræmblɪŋ] **1** *adj plant* trepador; *speech* divagador, prolijo y confuso, enmarañado; *house* laberíntico, sin plan.

2 *n* (**a**) excursionismo *m* a pie; excursiones *fpl* a pie.

(**b**) (*also* **~s**) desvaríos *mpl*, divagaciones *fpl*.

rambunctious* [ræm'bʌŋkʃəs] *adj* bullicioso, pendenciero.

RAMC *n* (*Brit*) *abbr of* **Royal Army Medical Corps.**

ramification [,ræmɪfɪ'keɪʃən] *n* ramificación *f*; **in all its ~s** en toda su complejidad; **with numerous ~s** con innumerables ramificaciones.

ramify ['ræmɪfaɪ] *vi* ramificarse.

ramjet ['ræmdʒet] *n* estatorreactor *m*.

rammer ['ræmə^r] *n* (*roadmaking*) pisón *m*; (*for rifle*) baqueta *f*.

ramp[1] [ræmp] *n* (*incline*) rampa *f*; (*on road*) desnivel *m*.

ramp[2]* [ræmp] *n* (*Brit*) estafa *f*, timo *m*; **the housing ~** el escándalo (del precio) de la vivienda; **it's a ~!** ¡no hay derecho!, ¡esto no se puede consentir!

rampage [ræm'peɪdʒ] **1** *n*: **to be on the ~** = **2**. **2** *vi* desbocarse, desmandarse; alborotar; comportarse como un loco; **the crowd ~d through the market** la multitud corrió alocada por el mercado.

rampancy ['ræmpənsɪ] *n* exuberancia *f*, lozanía *f*; furia *f*, desenfreno *m*; agresividad *f*; predominio *m*.

rampant ['ræmpənt] *adj* (*Her*) rampante; (*Bot*) exuberante, lozano; *person* furioso, desenfrenado; agresivo; *inflation* galopante; **to be ~** (*be common*) cundir, predominar; **he's a ~ anarchist** es un anarquista furibundo; **anarchism is ~ here** aquí el anarquismo está muy extendido, aquí ha cundido mucho el anarquismo.

rampart ['ræmpɑːt] *n* terraplén *m*, defensa *f*; (*city wall*) muralla *f*; **the ~s of York** la muralla de York.

ramrod ['ræmrɒd] *n* baqueta *f*, atacador *m*.

ramshackle ['ræm,ʃækl] *adj* desvencijado, destartalado.

ram's-horn ['ræmzhɔːn] *n* cuerno *m* de carnero.

ran [ræn] *pret of* **run**; *V* **also-~**.

ranch [rɑːntʃ] **1** *n* (*US*) hacienda *f*; estancia *f*, rancho *m* (*LAm*). **2** *attr*: **~ hand** peón *m*; **~ house** casa *f* de rancho.

rancher ['rɑːntʃə^r] *n* (*US*) ganadero *m*, estanciero *m* (*LAm*), ranchero *m* (*LAm*).

ranching ['rɑːntʃɪŋ] *n* (*US*) ganadería *f*.

rancid ['rænsɪd] *adj* rancio.

rancidity [ræn'sɪdɪtɪ] *n*, **rancidness** ['rænsɪdnɪs] *n* rancidez *f*, ranciedad *f*.

rancorous ['ræŋkərəs] *adj* rencoroso.

rancour, (*US*) **rancor** ['ræŋkə^r] *n* rencor *m*.

rand [rænd] *n* rand *m*.

randiness* ['rændɪnɪs] *n* cachondez *f*, rijosidad *f*.

random ['rændəm] **1** *adj* fortuito, casual; hecho al azar, hecho sin pensar; sin orden ni concierto; (*Math*) *distribution, variant* aleatorio; *sample* seleccionado al azar; **~ access** acceso *m* aleatorio; **~ access memory** memoria *f* de acceso aleatorio; **~ shot** disparo *m* hecho sin apuntar, bala *f* perdida.

2 *n*: **at ~** al azar; sin pensar; **to choose sth at ~** escoger algo sin pensar; **to hit out at ~** repartir golpes por todos lados; **to talk at ~** hablar sin pesar las palabras.

randomize ['rændəmaɪz] *vt* aleatorizar.

randomly ['rændəmlɪ] *adv*: **~ chosen** elegidos al azar.

randomness ['rændəmnɪs] *n* aleatoriedad *f*.

randy* ['rændɪ] *adj* cachondo, rijoso, con ganas (*LAm*); **to feel ~** estar cachondo.

rang [ræŋ] *pret of* **ring²**.

range [reɪndʒ] **1** *n* (**a**) (*row*) línea *f*, hilera *f*; (*of buildings*) grupo *m*; (*of mountains*) sierra *f*, cadena *f*, cordillera *f*.

(**b**) (*US Agr*) dehesa *f*, terreno *m* de pasto.

(**c**) (*for shooting*: *in open*) campo *m* de tiro, (*at fair*) galería *f* de tiro, barraca *f* de tiro.

(**d**) (*extent*) extensión *f*; intervalo *m*, banda *f*; recorrido *m*; (*of voice*) extensión *f*, alcance *m*, compás *m*; (*series*) serie *f*; escala *f*, abanico *m*, gama *f*; (*Comm*) surtido *m*; **~ of action** esfera *f* de acción; **~ of vision** campo *m* visual; **the present ~ of knowledge** la extensión de los conocimientos actuales; **~ of variation** gama *f* de variación (permisible); **~ of colours** gama *f* de colores; **~ of prices** escala *f* de precios; **~ of speeds** escala *f* de velocidades; **~ of possibilities** abanico *m* de posibilidades; **~ of frequencies** gama *f* de frecuencias; **the ~ of sb's mind** el alcance de la inteligencia de uno; **over the whole ~ of politics** sobre todo el campo de la política; **that's outside my ~** eso no pertenece a mi esfera de actividades; **to go outside one's normal ~** salir de su acostumbrada esfera de actividades; **she has a wide ~ of interests** tiene una extensa gama de intereses; **they have a new ~ of models** tienen una nueva gama (*or* un nuevo surtido) de modelos.

(**e**) (*Bio*) distribución *f*, zona *f* de distribución; **the plant has a limited ~** la planta tiene una distribución restringida; **this is outside its normal ~** este sitio queda fuera de su zona acostumbrada; **its ~ extends to León** alcanza la provincia de León.

(**f**) (*distance attainable*: *Mil*) alcance *m*, alcance *m* de tiro; distancia *f*; **a gun with a ~ of 3 miles** un cañón con un alcance de 3 millas; **at a ~ of 5 miles** a una distancia de 5 millas; **at close ~** de cerca, (*point-blank*) a quemarropa; **within ~** al alcance, a tiro, a tiro de fusil (*etc*); **the plane is out of ~** el avión está fuera de alcance; **to correct the ~** corregir la puntería; **to take the ~** averiguar la distancia.

(**g**) (*of plane, ship*) autonomía *f*, radio *m* de acción; **the ~ is 3,000 miles** la autonomía es de 3.000 millas.

(**h**) (*kitchen ~*) cocina *f* económica, fogón *m*.

2 *attr*: **intermediate ~ missile** misil *m* de medio alcance; **shorter ~ missile** misil *m* de corto alcance.

3 *vt* (**a**) (*arrange*) arreglar, ordenar; clasificar; (*line up*) alinear; (*place*) colocar; **he ~d them along the wall** los colocó a lo largo de la pared.

(**b**) (*go about*) recorrer; **they ~d the countryside** recorrieron el campo; **his eye ~d the horizon** escudriñó el horizonte.

(**c**) **to ~ a gun** apuntar un cañón.

(**d**) (*text*) **~d left** alineado a la izquierda; **~d right** alineado a la derecha.

4 *vi* (**a**) (*extend*) extenderse; (*wander over*) recorrer; vagar por; **the insect ~s from Andalusia to Burgos** el insecto se extiende desde Andalucía hasta Burgos; **research ranging over a wide field** investigaciones *fpl* que se extienden sobre un ancho campo; investigaciones *fpl* de gran alcance; **his mind ~s widely** tiene una mentalidad de gran alcance; **the troops ~d over the whole province** las tropas recorrieron toda la provincia.

(**b**) (*of numbers etc*) oscilar, variar, fluctuar; **temperatures ~ from 5 to 30 degrees** las temperaturas oscilan entre los 5 y 30 grados; **they ~ as high as 40 degrees at times** a veces suben hasta los 40 grados.

5 *vr*: **to ~ o.s. with sb** ponerse al lado de uno; **to ~ o.s. with a group** sumarse a un grupo.

rangefinder ['reɪndʒˌfaɪndəʳ] *n* telémetro *m*.

ranger ['reɪndʒəʳ] *n* guardabosque *m*.

Rangoon [ræŋ'guːn] *n* Rangún *m*.

rangy ['reɪndʒɪ] *adj* (*US*) alto y delgado.

rank¹ [ræŋk] **1** *n* (**a**) (*row*) fila *f*, hilera *f*, línea *f*; (*Mil*) fila *f*; **the ~s of poplars** las hileras de álamos; **in serried ~s** en filas apretadas; **the ~s, the ~ and file** las masas, la gente común, (*of club*) los socios ordinarios, (*Mil*) los soldados rasos; **in the ~s of the party** en las filas del partido; **to break ~s** romper filas; **to close (the) ~s** (*Mil, fig*) apretar las filas, cerrar filas; **to join the ~s of** (*fig*) unirse con, llegar a ser uno de; **to reduce sb to the ~s** degradar a uno a soldado raso; **to rise from the ~s** ascender desde soldado raso, llegar a oficial.

(**b**) (*status*) posición *f*, categoría *f*, dignidad *f*, calidad *f*; (*Mil*) graduación *f*, grado *m*, rango *m*; **persons of ~** gente *f* de calidad; **other ~s** (*esp Brit*) soldados *mpl* que no son oficiales; **a writer of the first ~** un escritor de primera categoría; **4 officers of high ~** 4 oficiales de alta graduación; **their ~s range from lieutenant to colonel** sus graduaciones van de teniente a coronel; **to attain the ~ of major** ser ascendido a comandante, llegar a comandante; **to pull ~*** tratar de conseguir una ventaja (*or* colocarse en situación superior *etc*) empleando su categoría más alta.

(**c**) (*taxi ~*) (*Brit*) parada *f*.

2 *attr*: **as a ~ and file policeman I must say ...** como policía de filas, debo decir ...

3 *vt* clasificar, ordenar; jerarquizar; **I ~ him 6th** le pongo en 6ª posición; **to ~ A with B** considerar iguales A y B, poner A y B en el mismo nivel; **where would you ~ him?** ¿qué posición le darías?

4 *vi* clasificarse; figurar; **to ~ 4th** ocupar el 4° puesto; **to ~ 2nd to sb else** tener el segundo lugar después de otra persona; **to ~ high** ocupar una alta posición; **where does she ~?** ¿qué posición ocupa?; **the shares will ~ for dividend** se pagará el dividendo que corresponda a estas acciones; **to ~ above** ser superior a; **to ~ among** figurar entre; estar al nivel de; **to ~ as** equivaler a, figurar como; **to ~ with** ser igual a, equipararse con, estar al nivel de.

rank² [ræŋk] *adj* (**a**) (*Bot*) lozano, exuberante; *soil* fértil; (*thick*) espeso, tupido.

(**b**) (*smelly*) maloliente, fétido, rancio; **to smell ~** oler mal.

(**c**) (*fig*) *beginner, outsider etc* completo, puro; **that's ~ nonsense!** ¡puras tonterías!; **it's a ~ bad play** es una obra francamente mala; **it's ~ injustice** es una injusticia manifiesta; **he's a ~ liar** es un mentiroso redomado.

ranker ['ræŋkəʳ] *n* (*Mil*) oficial *m* patatero*.

ranking ['ræŋkɪŋ] **1** *adj* (*chiefly US*) superior, de (mucha) categoría; **a ~ scientist** un científico de categoría. **2** *n* ránking *m*; categoría *f*, clase *f*, posición *f*; jerarquización *f*; (*Mil*) graduación *f*.

rankle ['ræŋkl] *vi* doler; **to ~ with sb** afligir continuamente a uno, roer a uno, amargar la vida a uno; **it still ~s** duele todavía.

rankly ['ræŋklɪ] *adv* lozanamente, con exuberancia; espesamente.

rankness ['ræŋknɪs] *n* (*V* **rank²**) (**a**) lozanía *f*, exuberancia *f*; fertilidad *f*; espesura *f*. (**b**) mal olor *m*, fetidez *f*, ranciedad *f*. (**c**) (*of injustice etc*) enormidad *f*.

ransack ['rænsæk] *vt* (*search*) registrar (de arriba abajo); escudriñar (minuciosamente); (*pillage*) desvalijar; saquear; **they ~ed the house for arms** registraron toda la casa buscando armas; **the place had been ~ed** el local había sido saqueado.

ransom ['rænsəm] **1** *n* rescate *m*; (*Rel*) redención *f*; **~ money** rescate *m*, dinero *m* exigido a cambio del rehén; **to hold sb to ~** pedir un rescate por uno, (*fig*) hacer chantaje a uno. **2** *vt* rescatar; (*Rel*) redimir.

ransoming ['rænsəmɪŋ] *n* rescate *m*; redención *f*.

rant [rænt] **1** *n* lenguaje *m* campanudo, lenguaje *m* declamatorio.

2 *vi* vociferar, despotricar; hablar en tono violento, hablar en un estilo hinchado; **he ~ed and raved for hours** despotricó durante varias horas; **he ~ed on about the Pope** siguió vociferando injurias (*or* echando pestes) contra el papa.

ranter ['ræntəʳ] *n* fanfarrón *m*; orador *m* campanudo, orador *m* populachero.

ranting ['ræntɪŋ] **1** *adj* fanfarrón; campanudo, vociferador, chillón.

2 *n* lenguaje *m* campanudo, lenguaje *m* declamatorio; vociferación *f*; **for all his ~** por más que despotrique.

ranunculus [rə'nʌŋkjʊləs] *n* ranúnculo *m*.

rap [ræp] **1** *n* (**a**) golpecito *m*, golpe *m* seco; (*at door*) llamada *f*, aldabada *f*; **there was a ~ at the door** llamaron a la puerta.

(**b**) (*) **to take the ~** pagar el pato*; **to take the ~ for sth** sufrir las consecuencias de algo; cargar con la culpa de algo.

(**c**) (*esp US**) acusación *f*; **murder ~** acusación *f* de homicidio; **to beat the ~** (lograr) ser absuelto.

(**d**) (*Mus*) rap *m*.

2 *vt* (**a**) golpear, dar un golpecito en, tocar. (**b**) (*)

criticar severamente.

3 *vi* (**a**) (*US**) charlar. (**b**) **to ~ at the door** llamar a la puerta. (**c**) (*Mus*) hacer rap.

◆**rap out** *vt* decir en tono brusco; **to ~ out an order** espetar una orden.

rapacious [rəˈpeɪʃəs] *adj* rapaz.

rapaciously [rəˈpeɪʃəslɪ] *adv* con rapacidad.

rapacity [rəˈpæsɪtɪ] *n* rapacidad *f*.

rape[1] [reɪp] **1** *n* violación *f*, estupro *m*; (*fig*) destrucción *f*, ruina *f*; **attempted ~** intento *m* de violación; **the ~ of Poland** la destrucción de Polonia. **2** *vt* violar, estuprar, forzar.

rape[2] [reɪp] *n* (*Bio*) colza *f*; **~ oil** (*also* **~seed oil**) aceite *m* de colza.

rapeseed [ˈreɪpsiːd] *n* semilla *f* de colza.

Raphael [ˈræfeɪel] *nm* Rafael.

rapid [ˈræpɪd] *adj* rápido.

rapidity [rəˈpɪdɪtɪ] *n* rapidez *f*.

rapidly [ˈræpɪdlɪ] *adv* rápidamente.

rapids [ˈræpɪdz] *npl* rápido(s) *m(pl)*, rabión *m*, rabiones *mpl*.

rapier [ˈreɪpɪəʳ] *n* estoque *m*.

rapine [ˈræpaɪn] *n* rapiña *f*.

rapist [ˈreɪpɪst] *n* violador *m*.

rapping [ˈræpɪŋ] *n* golpecitos *mpl*, golpes *mpl* secos; llamadas *fpl*, aldabadas *fpl*.

rapport [ræˈpɔːʳ] *n* buena relación *f*; entendimiento *m*; conformidad *f*; compenetración *f*; **we often find ourselves in ~** nos entendemos casi siempre bien; **to be in ~ with** estar conforme con, estar de acuerdo con.

rapprochement [ræˈprɒʃmɑ̃ːŋ] *n* acercamiento *m*, aproximación *f*.

rapscallion [ræpˈskælɪən] *n* bribón *m*, golfo *m*.

rapt [ræpt] *adj* arrebatado; (*absorbed*) absorto, ensimismado; (*enraptured*) extático, extasiado; **with ~ attention** con atención fija; **to be ~ in contemplation** estar absorto en la contemplación.

rapture [ˈræptʃəʳ] *n* éxtasis *m*, rapto *m*, arrobamiento *m*; **what ~!** ¡qué encanto!; **to be in ~s** estar extasiado, extasiarse; **to go into ~s** extasiarse (*over, about* ante, con).

rapturous [ˈræptʃərəs] *adj* extático; *applause etc* delirante, extático.

rapturously [ˈræptʃərəslɪ] *adv* extáticamente; con entusiasmo.

rare[1] [rɛəʳ] *adj* (**a**) raro, poco común, nada frecuente; excepcional; (*Phys*) ralo; **at ~ intervals** muy de tarde en tarde; **in a moment of ~ generosity** en un momento de generosidad poco frecuente en él; **it is ~ to find that ...** es poco frecuente encontrar que ...; **the plant is ~ in Wales** la planta es poco común en Gales.

(**b**) (*) maravilloso, estupendo*; **we had a ~ old time last night** lo pasamos pipa anoche*; **we had a ~ old time getting here** nos ha costado un ojo de la cara llegar aquí*; **you gave me a ~ old fright!** ¡vaya susto que me diste!

rare[2] [rɛəʳ] *adj meat* poco hecho, algo crudo.

rarebit [ˈrɛəbɪt] *n*: **Welsh ~** pan *m* con queso tostado.

rarefaction [ˌrɛərɪˈfækʃən] *n* rarefacción *f*.

rarefied [ˈrɛərɪfaɪd] *adj atmosphere* enrarecido (*also fig*).

rarefy [ˈrɛərɪfaɪ] **1** *vt* enrarecer. **2** *vi* enrarecerse.

rarely [ˈrɛəlɪ] *adv* raramente, con poca frecuencia; rara vez, pocas veces, casi nunca; **it is ~ found here** aquí se encuentra con poca frecuencia; **that method is ~ satisfactory** ese método no es satisfactorio casi nunca.

rareness [ˈrɛənɪs] *n*, **rarity** [ˈrɛərɪtɪ] *n* rareza *f*; **it's a rarity here** aquí es una rareza.

raring [ˈrɛərɪŋ] *adj*: **to be ~ to do sth** tener muchas ganas de hacer algo; **to be ~ to go** tener muchas ganas de empezar.

rascal [ˈrɑːskəl] *n* pillo *m*, pícaro *m*.

rascality [rɑːsˈkælɪtɪ] *n* picardía *f*.

rascally [ˈrɑːskəlɪ] *adj* pícaro, truhanesco.

rash[1] [ræʃ] *n* (**a**) (*Med*) erupción *f* (cutánea); sarpullido *m*; **she came out in a ~** le salieron erupciones en la piel. (**b**) (*fig*) brote *m*; serie *f*, racha *f*; **a ~ of complaints** una serie de quejas.

rash[2] [ræʃ] *adj* temerario; imprudente; precipitado; **that was very ~ of you** en eso has sido muy imprudente.

rasher [ˈræʃəʳ] *n* (*Brit*) lonja *f*, loncha *f*.

rashly [ˈræʃlɪ] *adv* temerariamente; imprudentemente; precipitadamente, a la ligera.

rashness [ˈræʃnɪs] *n* temeridad *f*; imprudencia *f*; precipitación *f*.

rasp [rɑːsp] **1** *n* (**a**) (*tool*) escofina *f*, raspador *m*. (**b**) (*sound*) sonido *m* desapacible; (*of voice*) tono *m* áspero. **2** *vt* (**a**) (*Tech*) escofinar, raspar. (**b**) (*say*) decir con tono áspero; *order* (*also* **to ~ out**) espetar. **3** *vi* hacer un sonido desapacible.

raspberry [ˈrɑːzbərɪ] *n* (**a**) (*fruit*) frambuesa *f*; (*bush*) frambueso *m* (*also* **~ bush, ~ cane**).

(**b**) (*) sonido *m* grosero, sonido *m* despectivo, sonido *m* ofensivo; **to blow sb a ~** hacer un gesto grosero a uno; **to get the ~** recibir una bronca, sufrir una repulsa.

rasping [ˈrɑːspɪŋ] *adj voice etc* áspero, desapacible.

Rasta* [ˈræstə], **Rastafarian** [ˌræstəˈfɛərɪən] **1** *adj* rastafario. **2** *n* rastafario *m*, -a *f*.

rat [ræt] **1** *n* rata *f*; (*) (*rotter*) canalla *m*; (*deserter*) desertor *m*; **~s!*** (*Brit*) ¡narices!*; **you ~!*** ¡bestia!*; **to smell a ~** oler el poste; **I smell a ~** aquí hay gato encerrado.

2 *vi* (**a**) cazar ratas, matar ratas.

(**b**) (*) chaquetear, desertar; **to ~ on sb** (*abandon*) abandonar a uno, (*inform*) chivarse de uno‡, soplar contra uno*.

ratable [ˈreɪtəbl] *adj* = **rateable**.

rat-a-tat [ˌrætəˈtæt] *n* (*at door*) golpecitos *mpl*; (*imitating sound*) ¡toc, toc!; (*of machine-gun*) tableteo *m*.

ratcatcher [ˈrætˌkætʃəʳ] *n* cazarratas *m*, cazador *m* de ratas.

ratchet [ˈrætʃɪt] *n* trinquete *m*; **~ wheel** rueda *f* de trinquete.

rate[1] [reɪt] **1** *n* (**a**) (*proportion, ratio*) proporción *f*, relación *f*, razón *f*; tanto *m* por ciento; **~ of births** (índice *m* de) natalidad *f*; **at a ~ of 5%** a un 5 por ciento; **at a ~ of 5 in every 30** a razón de 5 por cada 30; **at the ~ of 3 per person** a razón de 3 por persona; **at any ~** de todas formas, de todos modos; por lo menos; **at that ~** de ese modo; **if things go on at this ~** de seguir las cosas así.

(**b**) (*price etc*) precio *m*, tasa *f*; tarifa *f*; (*of interest etc*) tipo *m*; (*of hotel etc*) tarifa *f*; **at a cheap ~** a un precio reducido; **the ~ for the job** el pago por el trabajo; **advertising ~s** tarifa *f* de anuncios; **~ of exchange** (tipo *m* de) cambio *m*; **~ of interest** tipo *m* de interés; **~s of pay** escala *f* de sueldos, escalafón *m*; **~ of return** (*Fin*) tasa *f* de rentabilidad (*or* rendimiento); **~ of taxation** nivel *m* de impuestos.

(**c**) **~s** (*Brit*: *local tax*) contribución *f* municipal, impuestos *mpl* municipales; **~s and taxes** contribuciones *fpl* e impuestos; **we pay £900 in ~s** pagamos 900 libras de contribuciones.

(**d**) **first-~** de primera clase; **some third-~ author** algún autor de baja categoría, algún escritorcillo.

(**e**) (*speed*) velocidad *f*; (*of work etc*) ritmo *m*; **~ of climb** (*Aer*) velocidad *f* de subida; **~ of flow** velocidad *f* de flujo; **~ of growth** ritmo *m* de expansión; **a high ~ of growth** un elevado ritmo de crecimiento; **at a great ~** rapidísimamente, (*of vehicle*) a gran velocidad; **at a ~ of 20 knots** a una velocidad de 20 nudos.

2 *attr*: **~ rebate** devolución *f* de contribución municipal.

3 *vt* (**a**) (*estimate*) estimar; (*estimate value*) tasar, valorar (*at* en); (*classify*) clasificar; **I ~ it at £20** lo valoro en 20 libras; **I don't ~ your chances** creo que tienes pocas posibilidades; **I ~ the book highly** estimo el libro en mucho; **I ~ him highly** tengo un muy buen concepto de él; **how do you ~ her?** ¿qué opinas de ella?; **I ~ him among my best 3 pupils** le pongo entre mis 3 mejores alumnos.

(**b**) (*Fin*) imponer contribución municipal a; **we are highly ~d here** aquí nos exigen una contribución elevada; **the house is ~d at £840 per annum** se impone una contribución de 840 libras al año a esta casa, pagamos por esta casa una contribución de 840 libras al año.

(**c**) (*deserve*) merecer; **it didn't ~ a mention** no mereció ser mencionado, no logró una mención; **this hotel doesn't ~ 4 stars** este hotel no merece 4 estrellas.

4 *vi*: **to ~ as** ser considerado como, ser tenido por; **he just doesn't ~** no cuenta para nada, no vale para nada; **this case does not ~ for a grant** en este caso no se justifica un subsidio.

rate[2] [reɪt] *vt* regañar, reñir.

-rate [reɪt] *suf V* **rate**[1] **1** (**d**).

rateable [ˈreɪtəbl] *adj property* imponible; **~ value** valor *m* catastral.

rate-capping [ˈreɪtˌkæpɪŋ] *n* (*Brit Pol*) *limitación de la contribución municipal impuesta por el Estado.*

ratepayer [ˈreɪtpeɪəʳ] *n* contribuyente *mf*.

rather 1 [ˈrɑːðəʳ] *adv* (**a**) (*more accurately*) antes, más bien; mejor dicho; **or ~** mejor dicho; **~ it is a matter of money** antes es cuestión de dinero, es al contrario cuestión de dinero, es más bien cuestión de dinero.

(**b**) (*somewhat*) algo, un poco, bastante; **~ good**

bastante bueno; ~ **difficult** algo difícil; **it's** ~ **wet** está un poco mojado; **I'm** ~ **tired** estoy un poco cansado; **there's** ~ **a lot** hay bastante; **I** ~ **think he won't come** me inclino a creer que no vendrá; **I** ~ **expected as much** ya lo preveía; **are you keen to go?... yes, I am** ~ ¿quieres ir en efecto?... sí quiero; **isn't she pretty?... yes, she is** ~ ¿es guapa, eh?... sí, bastante.

(**c**) (*for preference*) **A** ~ **than B** A antes que B, más bien A que B; **this** ~ **than that** esto antes que eso; **anything** ~ **than that!** ¡todo menos eso!; **play anything** ~ **than that** toca cualquier cosa que no sea eso; **'I'm going to have it out with the boss' — '~ you than I!'** 'voy a plantéarselo al jefe' — '¡allá tú!'; **I would** ~ **not say** prefiero no decirlo; **I would** ~ **have sherry** me gustaría más un jerez; **I would** ~ **not** más bien no quiero hacerlo (*etc*).

2 ['rɑːðɜːʳ] *interj* **would you like some? ...** ~! ¿quieres algo de esto? ... ¡ya lo creo! (*or* ¡por supuesto!).

ratification [ˌrætɪfɪ'keɪʃən] *n* ratificación *f*.

ratify ['rætɪfaɪ] *vt* ratificar.

rating[1] ['reɪtɪŋ] **1** *n* (**a**) (*act of valuing*) tasación *f*, valuación *f*; derrama *f*; (*value*) valor *m*; (*Brit*: *local tax*) contribución *f*.

(**b**) (*standing*) clasificación *f*; puesto *m*, posición *f*; (*of audience, TV etc*: *also* ~**s**) índice *m*; (*of ship*) clase *f*; ~**s** (*Comm, Fin*) clasificación *f*, ránking *m*; **what's his ~?** ¿qué puesto ocupa?; ¿qué opinión hay de él?

(**c**) (*Brit Naut*) marinero *m*.

2 *attr*: ~ **service** servicio *m* de clasificación de valores.

rating[2] ['reɪtɪŋ] *n* reprensión *f*.

ratio ['reɪʃɪəʊ] *n* razón *f*, relación *f*, proporción *f*; **in direct ~ to** en razón directa con; **in the ~ of 5 to 2** a razón de 5 a 2; **the ~ of wages to raw materials** la relación entre los sueldos y las materias primas.

ratiocinate [rætɪ'ɒsɪneɪt] *vi* raciocinar.

ratiocination [ˌrætɪɒsɪ'neɪʃən] *n* raciocinación *f*.

ration ['ræʃən] **1** *n* ración *f*; ~**s** (*Mil etc*) víveres *mpl*, suministro *m*; **it's off the ~ now** ya no está racionado; **to be on short ~s** andar escaso de víveres, tener poco que comer; **to draw one's ~s** recibir los víveres; **when they put bread on the ~** cuando racionaron el pan.

2 *vt* (*also* **to ~ out**) racionar; **they are ~ed to 1 kilo a day** están racionados a 1 kilo por día.

rational ['ræʃənl] *adj* racional; lógico, razonable; (*sane, of person*) sensato, cuerdo; ~ **number** número *m* racional; **the ~ thing to do would be ...** lo lógico sería ...; **he seemed quite ~** parecía estar perfectamente cuerdo; **a long skirt is hardly ~ dress for the beach** una falda larga es poco práctica en la playa; **let's be ~ about this** seamos razonables.

rationale [ræʃə'nɑːl] *n* razón *f* fundamental, base *f* lógica.

rationalism ['ræʃnəlɪzəm] *n* racionalismo *m*.

rationalist ['ræʃnəlɪst] **1** *adj* racionalista. **2** *n* racionalista *mf*.

rationalistic [ˌræʃnə'lɪstɪk] *adj* racionalista.

rationality [ˌræʃə'nælɪtɪ] *n* racionalidad *f*; lógica *f*.

rationalization [ˌræʃnəlaɪ'zeɪʃən] *n* racionalización *f*; **industrial ~** (*euph*) reconversión *f* industrial.

rationalize ['ræʃnəlaɪz] *vt* racionalizar; (*Math*) quitar los radicales a, racionalizar.

rationally ['ræʃnəlɪ] *adv* racionalmente; lógicamente, razonablemente; **he spoke quite ~** habló cuerdamente, habló de modo juicioso.

ration-book ['ræʃənbʊk] *n*, **ration-card** ['ræʃənkɑːd] *n* cartilla *f* de racionamiento.

rationing ['ræʃnɪŋ] *n* racionamiento *m*.

Ratisbon ['rætɪzbɒn] *n* Ratisbona *f*.

rat-poison ['ræt'pɔɪzn] *n* matarratas *m*, raticida *m*.

rat-race ['rætreɪs] *n* lucha *f* incesante por adelantar, competencia *f* sin tregua para adelantar; **it's a ~** es una arrebatiña.

rats'-tails [ˌræts'teɪlz] *npl* greñas *fpl*.

rattan [rə'tæn] *n* rota *f*, junco *m* (*or* caña *f*) de Indias.

rat-tat-tat ['rættæt'tæt] *n* = **rat-a-tat**.

rattle ['rætl] **1** *n* (**a**) (*noise*: *banging*) golpeteo *m*; (*of cart, train etc*) traqueteo *m*; (*of machine gun etc*) traqueteo *m*, tableteo *m*; (*eg of stone in tin*) ruido *m*, castañeteo *m*; (*of hail, rain*) tamborileo *m*; (*of window etc*) crujido *m*; (*of teeth*) castañeteo *m*; (*in throat*) estertor *m*.

(**b**) (*instrument*) carraca *f*, matraca *f*; (*child's*) sonajero *m*; (*snake's*) cascabel *m*.

2 *vt* (**a**) (*shake*) agitar, sacudir; (*play*) hacer sonar; (*vibrate*) hacer vibrar; (*jolt*) traquetear; **the wind ~d the window** el viento hacía crujir la ventana; **he ~d the tin** agitó la lata, sacudió la lata.

(**b**) (*: *disconcert*) desconcertar, confundir; poner nervioso; **he was badly ~d** quedó muy desconcertado; **that ~d him badly** eso le desconcertó de mala manera; **to get ~d** ponerse nervioso; **he never gets ~d** nunca pierde la calma.

3 *vi* (**a**) golpear; traquetear, tabletear; sonar, hacer ruido; tamborilear; crujir; castañetear.

(**b**) **we were rattling along at 50** corríamos a 50 (kilómetros por hora).

◆**rattle away** *vi* = **rattle on**.

◆**rattle off** *vt* enumerar rápidamente, decir de carretilla.

◆**rattle on** *vi*: **he ~d on** seguía parloteando; **he was rattling on about the war** seguía hablando incansablemente de la guerra.

◆**rattle through** *vt* darse prisa con.

rattler* ['rætləʳ] *n* (*US*), **rattlesnake** ['rætlsneɪk] *n* serpiente *f* de cascabel, yarará *f* (*And*).

rattletrap ['rætltræp] **1** *adj* desvencijado. **2** *n* armatoste *m*.

rattling ['rætlɪŋ] **1** *adj*: **at a ~ pace** muy rápidamente, a gran velocidad. **2** *adv*: ~ **good*** realmente estupendo*.

rattrap ['rættræp] *n* trampa *f* para ratas, ratonera *f*.

ratty* ['rætɪ] *adj*: (**a**) (*Brit*) **he was pretty ~ about it** se picó mucho por ello; **to get ~** ponerse negro*. (**b**) (*US*) andrajoso.

raucous ['rɔːkəs] *adj* estridente, ronco, chillón.

raucously ['rɔːkəslɪ] *adv* de modo estridente, roncamente, en tono chillón.

raucousness ['rɔːkəsnɪs] *n* estridencia *f*, ronquedad *f*.

raunchy* ['rɔːntʃɪ] *adj* (*US*: *smutty*) lascivo, verde; (*randy*) cachondo.

ravage ['rævɪdʒ] **1** *n* estrago *m*, destrozo *m*; ~**s** destrucción *f*, estragos *mpl*; **the ~s of time** los estragos del tiempo.

2 *vt* estragar, destruir, destrozar; (*plunder*) saquear, pillar; **the region was ~d by floods** la región fue asolada por las inundaciones; **a picture ~d by time** un cuadro muy deteriorado por el tiempo; **a body ~d by disease** un cuerpo desfigurado por la enfermedad.

rave [reɪv] **1** *n* (*) **it's a ~** es lo último*, es la monda*.

2 *adj*: **the play got ~ notices*** la obra fue reseñada con el mayor entusiasmo, se escribieron reseñas entusiastas de la obra; **the film got ~ reviews** la película obtuvo críticas excelentes.

3 *vi* delirar, desvariar; **to ~ about sb** pirrarse por uno, hablar en términos entusiastas de uno; **to ~ about sth** entusiasmarse por algo; **to ~ at sb** despotricar contra uno.

rave-in* ['reɪvɪn] *n* orgía *f*.

ravel ['rævəl] *vt* enredar, enmarañar (*also fig*).

raven ['reɪvn] **1** *n* cuervo *m*. **2** *adj hair* negro.

raven-haired [ˌreɪvn'hɛəd] *adj* de pelo negro.

ravening ['rævnɪŋ] *adj* rapaz, salvaje.

ravenous ['rævənəs] *adj* (*starving*) famélico, hambriento; (*voracious*) voraz; **I'm ~!** ¡me comería un toro!; **he was ~** tenía un hambre canina.

ravenously ['rævənəslɪ] *adv* vorazmente; **to be ~ hungry** tener una hambre canina.

raver* ['reɪvəʳ] *n* juerguista* *mf*; persona *f* totalmente desinhibida.

rave-up* ['reɪvʌp] *n* (*Brit*) juerga* *f*.

ravine [rə'viːn] *n* barranco *m*, garganta *f*, quebrada *f* (*LAm*).

raving ['reɪvɪŋ] **1** *adj*: ~ **lunatic** loco *m* de atar. **2** *adv*: ~ **mad** loco de atar.

ravings ['reɪvɪŋz] *npl* delirio *m*, desvarío *m*.

ravioli [ˌrævɪ'əʊlɪ] *npl* ravioles *mpl*.

ravish ['rævɪʃ] *vt* (**a**) (*charm*) encantar, embelesar. (**b**) (*liter*: *carry off*) raptar, robar; (*rape*) violar.

ravisher ['rævɪʃəʳ] *n* raptor *m*; violador *m*.

ravishing ['rævɪʃɪŋ] *adj* encantador, embelesador.

ravishingly ['rævɪʃɪŋlɪ] *adv* encantadoramente, embelesadoramente; ~ **beautiful** bellísimo.

ravishment ['rævɪʃmənt] *n* (*V vt*) (**a**) embeleso *m*, éxtasis *m*. (**b**) rapto *m*, robo *m*; violación *f*.

raw [rɔː] **1** *adj* (**a**) (*uncooked*) *food* crudo; *spirit* puro, sin mezcla; de baja calidad; *leather, silk etc* bruto, sin refinar, crudo; *cotton* en rama; *account, piece of writing* sin pulir, sin refinar; tosco; ~ **data** datos *mpl* brutos, datos *mpl* en bruto; ~ **material** materia *f* prima.

(**b**) (*inexperienced*) novato, inexperto; (*socially coarse*) tosco, grosero; ~ **recruit** (*Mil*) soldado *m* bisoño, quinto *m*, (*fig*) novicio *m*.

(**c**) (*sore*) *flesh* sensible; *wound* abierto; **in the ~ flesh** en carne viva; **I touched a ~ nerve** le di en lo más sensible, le herí en lo vivo; **his nerves are very ~** tiene los nervios a flor de piel.

(**d**) *day, weather* crudo, áspero; *wind* fuerte.

(**e**) (*unfair*) inequitativo; ~ **deal** injusticia *f*, trato *m* inequitativo; **he got a ~ deal** le trataron mal; **that's pretty ~** eso es injusto, no hay derecho a eso.

2 *n* carne *f* viva; **in the ~** (*US**) desnudo; **life in the ~** la vida tal como es, la vida bajo su aspecto más inculto; **it got him on the ~** le hirió en lo más vivo.

rawboned ['rɔː'bəʊnd] *adj* huesudo.

rawhide ['rɔːhaɪd] **1** *adj* de cuero crudo. **2** *n* (*US*) cuero *m* de vaca.

Rawlplug ['rɔːlplʌg] ® *n* taco *m*.

rawness ['rɔːnɪs] *n* (**a**) crudeza *f*. (**b**) (*inexperience*) inexperiencia *f*; tosquedad *f*.

Ray [reɪ] *nm familiar form of* **Raymond.**

ray[1] [reɪ] *n* rayo *m*; ~ **of light** rayo *m* de luz; **without a ~ of hope** sin la más tenue esperanza; **I see a ~ of hope** (*or* **light**) hay un rayo de esperanza.

ray[2] [reɪ] *n* (*Fish*) raya *f*.

ray[3] [reɪ] *n* (*Mus*) re *m*.

Raymond ['reɪmənd] *nm* Raimundo, Ramón.

rayon ['reɪɒn] *n* rayón *m*.

raze [reɪz] *vt* (*also* **to ~ to the ground**) arrasar, asolar.

razor ['reɪzə^r] *n* (*open*) navaja *f*, chaveta *f* (*Mex*); (*safety* ~) maquinilla *f* de afeitar, gillette *f*; (*electric* ~) maquinilla *f* eléctrica, rasuradora *f*; ~ **burn** erosión *f* cutánea; **it's on a ~'s edge** está al filo de la navaja.

razorbill ['reɪzəbɪl] *n* alca *f* (común).

razorblade ['reɪzəbleɪd] *n* hoja *f* de afeitar, cuchilla *f* de afeitar.

razor-cut ['reɪzə,kʌt] *n* (*Hairdressing*) corte *m* a la navaja.

razor-sharp ['reɪzə'ʃɑːp] *adj* afiladísimo; *mind* agudísimo, de lo más penetrante.

razor-strop ['reɪzəstrɒp] *n* suavizador *m*.

razz* [ræz] *vt* (*US*) tomar el pelo a*.

razzle* ['ræzl] *n* borrachera *f*; **to go on the ~** ir de juerga*, ir de borrachera; **to be on the ~** estar de juerga*.

razzle-dazzle* ['ræzl,dæzl] *n* (**a**) = **razzle.** (**b**) = **razzmatazz.**

razzmatazz* [,ræzmə'tæz] *n* (*US*) bombo *m* publicitario, actividad *f* frenética, juerga* *f* (con que se lanza a un candidato, un producto *etc*); animación *f*, bullicio *m*.

RC *n abbr of* **Roman Catholic** católico *m*, -a *f*; *also adj*.

RCAF *n abbr of* **Royal Canadian Air Force.**

RCMP *n abbr of* **Royal Canadian Mounted Police** *fuerza de policía canadiense montada*.

RCN *n abbr of* **Royal Canadian Navy.**

RD (*US Post*) *abbr of* **rural delivery.**

Rd *abbr of* **road** calle *f*, c/.

R/D *vt abbr of* **refer to drawer** protestar este cheque por falta de fondos.

RDC *n* (**a**) *abbr of* **Rural District Council.** (**b**) *abbr of* **regional distribution centre.**

RE *n* (**a**) (*Scol*) *abbr of* **religious education** educación *f* religiosa, ed. religiosa. (**b**) (*Brit Mil*) *abbr of* **Royal Engineers.**

re[1] [riː] *prep* respecto a, con referencia a; ~ **yours of the 8th** me refiero a su carta del día 8.

re[2] [reɪ] *n* (*Mus*) re *m*.

re... [riː] *pref* re...

reabsorb ['riːəb'zɔːb] *vt* reabsorber.

reabsorption ['riːəb'zɔːpʃən] *n* reabsorción *f*.

reach [riːtʃ] **1** *n* (**a**) (*accessibility*) alcance *m*; extensión *f*; distancia *f*; (*Boxing etc*) envergadura *f*; **to have a long ~** tener brazos largos; **to be beyond sb's ~, to be out of sb's ~** estar fuera del alcance de uno; **to be within ~ of the hand** estar al alcance de la mano; **to be within (easy) ~** estar al alcance, estar a la mano; **cars within the ~ of all families** coches *mpl* al alcance de todas las familias; **a house within easy ~ of the station** una casa a corta distancia de la estación; **it's within easy ~ by bus** es fácilmente accesible en autobús.

(**b**) (*of river*) recto *m*, extensión *f* entre dos recodos; (*of canal*) recto *m*, extensión *f* entre dos compuertas; **the upper ~es of the Seine** la parte alta del Sena.

2 *vt* (**a**) (*stretch out*) alargar, extender; **he ~ed out a hand** alargó la mano.

(**b**) (*pass*) alcanzar, pasar, dar; **please ~ me down that case** por favor bájeme la maleta esa; **can you ~ me (over) the oil?** ¿me das (*LAm*: alcanzas) el aceite, por favor?

(**c**) (*arrive at, attain*) alcanzar; llegar a, llegar hasta; lograr; extenderse a, abarcar; **to ~ home** llegar a casa; **it doesn't ~ the bottom** no llega al fondo; **the child hardly ~ed my waist** el niño apenas me llegaba a la cintura; **the door is ~ed by a long staircase** se sube a la puerta por una larga escalera; **your letter ~ed me this morning** su carta me llegó esta mañana; **when this news ~ed my ears** cuando supe esta noticia; **to ~ 21** cumplir los 21 años; **to ~ perfection** lograr la perfección; **to ~ a compromise** llegar a un arreglo; **production now ~es 3,400 megawatts** la producción actual alcanza 3.400 megavatios; **the law does not ~ such cases** la ley no se extiende a tales casos.

(**d**) *person* ponerse en contacto con, contactar (*esp LAm*); **to ~ sb by telephone** hablar con uno por teléfono; **you can always ~ me at the office** me puedes llamar en todo momento en la oficina.

(**e**) (*US Jur*) *witness* sobornar.

3 *vi* (**a**) **to ~ out (with one's hand) for sth** alargar (*or* tender) la mano para tomar algo; **don't ~ over people** no alargues la mano delante de otros; **see if you can ~ up for it** a ver si puedes alcanzarlo; **to ~ for the sky** aspirar al cielo; **~ for the sky!** (*US‡*) ¡arriba las manos!

(**b**) (*stretch*) alcanzar; extenderse; llegar; **it won't ~** no llega; **it ~es to the sea** se extiende hasta el mar; **as far as the eye could ~** hasta donde alcanzaba la vista; **the beer won't ~ till Friday** la cerveza no llega al viernes; **it ~es back to 1700** se remonta a 1700; **it's a tradition that ~es back for centuries** es una tradición de varios siglos; **the water ~ed up to the windows** el agua llegó a las ventanas.

reachable ['riːtʃəbl] *adj* alcanzable; accesible.

reach-me-down ['riːtʃmɪ,daʊn] **1** *adj clothes, ideas* común y corriente; de segunda mano. **2 ~s** *npl* ropa *f* burda, traje *m* de segunda mano; ropa *f* de percha.

react [riː'ækt] *vi* reaccionar (*against* contra; *on* sobre; *to* a, ante; *with* (*Chem*) con); **how did she ~?** ¿cómo reaccionó?

reaction [riː'ækʃən] *n* reacción *f*; **what was your ~?** ¿cómo reaccionaste?, ¿qué impresión te produjo?; **it produced no ~** no surtió efecto.

reactionary [riː'ækʃənrɪ] **1** *adj* reaccionario; retrógrado. **2** *n* reaccionario *m*, -a *f*.

reactivate [riː'æktɪveɪt] *vt* reactivar.

reactivation [riː,æktɪ'veɪʃən] *n* reactivación *f*.

reactive [riː'æktɪv] *adj* reactivo.

reactor [riː'æktə^r] *n* reactor *m*.

read [riːd] (*irr*: *pret and ptp* **read** [red]) **1** *vt* (**a**) leer; (*with difficulty*) lograr leer, interpretar, descifrar; **do you ~ Russian?** ¿sabes leer el ruso?; **I ~ it differently** lo entiendo de otro modo; **I ~ you loud and clear** (*Aer etc*) te oigo perfectamente; **do you ~ me?** (*Aer etc*) ¿me oyes?; **to take the minutes as ~** dar las actas por leídas; **we can take that as ~** (*fig*) eso lo podemos dar por sentado.

(**b**) **to ~ sth aloud** leer algo en voz alta; **to ~ the news** leer las noticias; **to ~ a report to a meeting** leer un informe a una reunión.

(**c**) **to ~ sb to sleep** adormecer a uno leyéndole.

(**d**) (*Univ*) estudiar, cursar; **to ~ Romance languages** estudiar lenguas románicas; **what are you ~ing?** ¿qué asignatura estudias?

(**e**) **to ~ music** leer música; **to ~ sb's hand** leer la mano a uno; **she can ~ me like a book** me conoce a fondo; **to ~ the future** adivinar el porvenir; **to ~ sb's thoughts** adivinar el pensamiento de uno.

(**f**) (*take a reading from*) leer, consultar; **when I ~ the thermometer** cuando consulté el termómetro; **they come to ~ the meter once a month** vienen una vez al mes a leer el contador; **he wants to ~ the gas meter** quiere ver el contador de gas.

(**g**) **you're ~ing too much into it** le atribuyes demasiada importancia; **to ~ into a sentence what is not there** ver en una frase un significado que no tiene.

2 *vi* (**a**) leer; **to ~ aloud** leer en voz alta; **I ~ about it in the papers** lo leí en los periódicos; **I'm ~ing about Napoleon** me estoy documentando sobre Napoleón; estoy leyendo acerca de Napoleón; **to ~ between the lines** leer entre líneas; **to ~ to sb** leer un libro (*etc*) a uno.

(**b**) (*notice etc*) decir, rezar; (*of thermometer etc*) indicar, marcar; **it should ~ 'Urraca'** debiera decir 'Urraca'.

(**c**) (*of text*) **how does the letter ~ now?** ¿qué tal te parece la carta ahora?, ¿a ver cómo te suena la carta ahora?; **the book ~s well** el libro está bien escrito; **it would ~ better if you said ...** causaría mejor impresión si pusieras ..., sería más elegante si escribieras ...; **the play acts better than it ~s** la obra es mejor representada que leída.

(**d**) (*study*) estudiar; **to ~ for a degree** estudiar la licenciatura; **to ~ for the Bar** estudiar derecho (para hacerse abogado).

3 *n*: **I was having a quiet ~ in the garden** leía tranquilamente en el jardín; **I like a good ~** me gusta leer; **it's a good solid ~** el libro dará muchas horas de lectura amena; **I managed to have a good ~ whilst waiting** pude leer bastante mientras esperaba.

◆**read back** *vt* releer, volver a leer.

◆**read off** *vt* leer; leer de un tirón.

◆**read on** *vi* seguir leyendo; **'now ~ on'** 'prosigue el cuento'.

◆**read out** *vt* leer, leer en voz alta; leer para que lo oigan todos (*etc*); **please ~ it out** por favor léenoslo.

◆**read over** *vt* repasar, volver a leer.

◆**read through** *vt* leer (de cabo a rabo); repasar.

◆**read up** *vt* estudiar; preparar; repasar.

◆**read up on** *vt* leer bibliografía sobre.

readability [ˌriːdəˈbɪlɪtɪ] *n* legibilidad *f* (*also Comput*); amenidad *f*, interés *m*.

readable [ˈriːdəbl] *adj writing* legible; que se deja leer; *book etc* digno de leerse, ameno, interesante.

readdress [ˈriːəˈdres] *vt letter* poner señas nuevas (*or* correctas) en, reexpedir; **to ~ a letter to sb** volver a dirigir una carta a uno.

reader [ˈriːdəʳ] *n* (**a**) lector *m*, -ora *f*; (*in library*) usuario *m*, -a *f*; (*Typ*) corrector *m*, -a *f*; **he's a great ~** lee mucho, es muy aficionado a la lectura; **I'm not much of a ~** leo poco, no me interesan mucho los libros.

(**b**) (*Brit Univ*) profesor *m* adjunto, profesora *f* adjunta.

(**c**) (*book*) libro *m* de lectura.

(**d**) (*machine*) máquina *f* lectora, aparato *m* lector.

readership [ˈriːdəʃɪp] *n* (**a**) lectorado *m*, número *m* total de lectores (de un periódico). (**b**) (*Brit Univ*) *puesto del* **reader**.

read head [ˈriːdhed] *n* cabeza *f* de lectura.

readily [ˈredɪlɪ] *adv* (*quickly*) en seguida, pronto; (*willingly*) de buena gana; (*easily*) fácilmente.

readiness [ˈredɪnɪs] *n* prontitud *f*; disponibilidad *f*; buena disposición *f*, buena voluntad *f*; (*preparedness*) preparación *f*; **~ of wit** viveza *f* de ingenio; **everything is in ~** todo está listo, todo está preparado; **to hold o.s. in ~ for sth** estar listo para algo; **hold yourself in ~ for ...** prepárese para ...

reading [ˈriːdɪŋ] **1** *n* (**a**) (*gen*) lectura *f*; (*aloud*) lectura *f*, recitación *f*.

(**b**) (*understanding*) interpretación *f*.

(**c**) (*of thermometer etc*) indicación *f*, lectura *f*; medición *f*.

(**d**) (*in text*) lección *f*.

(**e**) (*Parl*) lectura *f*; **second ~** segunda lectura *f*; **to give a bill a second ~** leer un proyecto de ley por segunda vez.

2 *adj*: **the ~ public** el público que lee, el público lector; **he's a great ~ man** es un hombre que lee mucho, es hombre muy aficionado a la lectura.

3 *attr* de lectura; **he has a ~ age of 8** tiene el nivel de lecturas de un niño de ocho años; **~ book** libro *m* de lectura; **~ comprehension test** ejercicio *m* de comprensión lectora; **~ glass** lente *m* para leer; **~ glasses** gafas *fpl* de leer (*or* de lectura); **she has a ~ knowledge of Spanish** sabe leer el español; **~ lamp** lámpara *f* para leer (en la cama *etc*), lámpara *f* portátil; **~ list** lista *f* de lecturas; **~ matter** lectura *f*; **~ room** sala *f* de lectura; **~ speed** velocidad *f* de lectura.

readjust [ˈriːəˈdʒʌst] **1** *vt* reajustar; reorientar. **2** *vi* reajustarse; reorientarse.

readjustment [ˈriːəˈdʒʌstmənt] *n* reajuste *m*; reorientación *f*.

readmit [ˈriːədˈmɪt] *vt* readmitir, volver a admitir.

read-only [ˌriːdˈəʊnlɪ] *adj*: **~ memory** memoria *f* muerta, memoria *f* de sola lectura.

read-out [ˈriːdaʊt] *n* lectura *f* de salida.

read-write [ˌriːdˈraɪt] *adj*: **~ head** cabeza *f* de lectura-escritura; **~ window** ventana *f* de lectura-escritura.

ready [ˈredɪ] **1** *adj* (**a**) (*prepared*) listo, preparado; pronto; (*available*) disponible; **~?, are you ~?** ¿estás listo?, ¿vamos?; **~, steady, go!** ¡preparados, listos, ya!; **~ when you are!** ¡todo listo!; **we're all ~ and waiting** todos estamos listos y dispuestos; **~ for action** dispuesto para el combate, (*fig*) lanza en ristre; **~ for use** listo para usar; **I'm ~ for bed** tengo sueño; **I'm ~ for a drink** muero por echarme un trago; **~ cash, ~ money** dinero *m* contante, dinero *m* efectivo, fondos *mpl* disponibles; **to be ~ to hand** estar a la mano, estar disponible; **to be ~ to do sth** estar listo para hacer algo; **the aircraft will be ~ to fly in 6 months** el avión estará listo para volar en 6 meses; **I am ~ to face him now** ahora estoy con ánimo para enfrentarme con él; **~ to serve** preparado; **~ to use** listo para usar; **to get ~, to make ~** prepararse; disponerse (*to* + *infin* a + *infin*); **to get sth ~, to make sth ~** preparar algo, disponer algo; **to hold o.s. ~** estar listo (*for* para); **hold yourselves ~ to leave at any moment** prepárense para partir en cualquier momento.

(**b**) (*willing*) dispuesto (*to* + *infin* a + *infin*); **he's a ~ helper** presta su ayuda de buena gana.

(**c**) (*about*) **I was ~ to die of hunger** estaba para morirme de hambre; **we were ~ to give up there and then** estábamos a punto de abandonarlo sin más.

(**d**) (*prompt*) fácil, pronto; *wit* agudo, vivo; **to have a ~ wit** ser ingenioso, tener chispa; **to have a ~ pen** escribir con soltura; **to have a ~ tongue** no morderse la lengua; **to find a ~ sale** venderse fácilmente, tener una salida fácil.

2 *n* (**a**) **with rifles at the ~** con los fusiles listos para tirar, con los fusiles apercibidos; **pen at the ~** pluma en ristre.

(**b**) **some of the ~‡** algo de parné‡, algún dinero *m* contante.

3 *vt* (*esp US*) preparar, disponer; poner a punto.

ready-cooked [ˈredɪˈkʊkt] *adj* listo para comer.

ready-made [ˈredɪˈmeɪd] *adj* hecho, confeccionado; *clothing* hecho, de percha.

ready-reckoner [ˈredɪˈreknəʳ] *n* baremo *m*, libro *m* de cálculos hechos.

ready-to-serve [ˌredɪtəˈsɜːv] *adj* preparado.

ready-to-wear [ˈredɪtəˈwɛəʳ] *adj* hecho, confeccionado, de percha.

reaffirm [ˈriːəˈfɜːm] *vt* reafirmar, reiterar, afirmar de nuevo.

reaffirmation [ˈriːæfəˈmeɪʃən] *n* reafirmación *f*, reiteración *f*.

reafforest [ˈriːəˈfɒrɪst] *vt*, (*US*) **reforest** [ˈriːˈfɒrɪst] repoblar de árboles.

reafforestation [ˈriːəˌfɒrɪsˈteɪʃən], (*US*) **reforestation** [ˌriːfɒrɪsˈteɪʃən] *n* repoblación *f* forestal.

reagent [riːˈeɪdʒənt] *n* reactivo *m*.

real [rɪəl] **1** *adj* (**a**) real; verdadero; auténtico; legítimo; *income, value, wages* real; **the ~ world** el mundo real; **a ~ man** todo un hombre; **~ ale** cerveza *f* legítima; **in ~ terms** en términos reales; **the ~ McCoy** lo auténtico, lo realmente genuino; **you're a ~ friend** eres un verdadero amigo; **the ~ power is in the hands of X** el poder efectivo está en manos de X; **this is ~ coffee** esto es auténtico café, esto es lo que se llama café; **we have had days of ~ heat** hemos tenido días de auténtico calor; **is he the ~ king?** ¿él es el rey legítimo?; **this is the ~ thing at last** por fin lo tenemos sin trampa ni cartón.

(**b**) **~ assets** propiedad *f* inmueble, bienes *mpl* raíces; **~ estate, ~ property** bienes *mpl* raíces; **~ estate agent** (*US*) agente *m* inmobiliario, agente *f* inmobiliaria; **~ estate market** (*US*) mercado *m* inmobiliario.

(**c**) **~ time** tiempo *m* real.

2 *adv* (*) **~ good** muy bueno, realmente bueno; **a ~ nice guy** un chico de los más amables; **it's ~ heavy** pesa una barbaridad.

3 *n* (**a**) **the ~** (*Philos*) lo real.

(**b**) (*) **it's for ~** esto va de veras; **don't worry, it's not for ~** no te preocupes, no es de veras.

realign [riːəˈlaɪn] *vt* reordenar.

realignment [riːəˈlaɪnmənt] *n* reordenación *f*.

realism [ˈrɪəlɪzəm] *n* realismo *m*; autenticidad *f*.

realist [ˈrɪəlɪst] *n* realista *mf*.

realistic [rɪəˈlɪstɪk] *adj* realista; auténtico; objetivo.

realistically [rɪəˈlɪstɪkəlɪ] *adv* de modo realista; auténticamente.

reality [riːˈælɪtɪ] *n* realidad *f*; **in ~** en realidad; **the realities of power** la realidad del poder; **let's get back to ~** volvamos a la realidad; **let's stick to realities** atengámonos a la realidad.

realizable [ˈrɪəlaɪzəbl] *adj* realizable, factible.

realization [ˌrɪəlaɪˈzeɪʃən] *n* (**a**) comprensión *f*; **this ~ came too late** esto lo comprendió tarde; **it was a sudden ~** cayó de repente en la cuenta. (**b**) (*Comm*) realización *f*.

realize [ˈrɪəlaɪz] *vt* (**a**) (*comprehend*) darse cuenta de, hacerse cargo de, comprender; caer en la cuenta de; **without realizing it** sin darse cuenta; **I ~ that ...** me doy cuenta de que ..., comprendo que ..., reconozco que ...; **once I ~d how it was done** tan pronto como caí en la cuenta de cómo se hacía; **do you ~ what you've done?** ¿te das cuenta de lo que has hecho?

(**b**) (*carry out*) realizar, llevar a cabo, poner por obra; *one's potential* realizar; **my worst fears were ~d** resultaron ser ciertos mis temores.

(**c**) (*Comm*) *assets etc* realizar.

real-life [ˌrɪəlˈlaɪf] *adj* de la vida real, auténtico.

reallocate [riːˈæləˌkeɪt] *vt resources* redistribuir.

really [ˈrɪəlɪ] *adv* (**a**) (*used alone*) **~?** ¿de veras?, ¿ah sí?;

not ~? ¿lo dices en serio?; **~!** ¡ca!; ¡eh!; ¡mire Vd!; **~, whatever next!** ¡qué cosas pasan!

(**b**) (*with adj*) verdaderamente, realmente, francamente; **a ~ good film** una película realmente buena, una película francamente buena; **~ ugly** lo que se dice feo, lo que se llama feo; **I'm ~ very cross with you** estoy francamente disgustado contigo; **now it's ~ true** ahora sí es verdad; **this time we're ~ done for*** esta vez hemos pringado de verdad*.

(**c**) (*with verb*) en realidad; realmente; en el fondo; en rigor; **I don't ~ know** en realidad no lo sé; **you ~ must see it** realmente tienes que verlo; **can it ~ be expected that ...?** ¿cabe realmente esperar que ...?; **has he ~ gone?** ¿es cierto que se ha ido?; **how a gentleman who is ~ a gentleman lives** cómo vive un señor señor; **as for ~ talking Chinese, I can't** hablar chino, lo que se dice hablar chino, no sé.

realm [relm] *n* reino *m*; (*fig*) esfera *f*, campo *m*; dominio *m*; **in the ~ of speculation** en la esfera de la especulación; **in the ~s of fantasy** en el país de la fantasía.

realtor [ˈrɪəltɔː^{r}] *n* (*US*) corredor *m* de bienes raíces, corredor *m* de fincas.

realty [ˈrɪəltɪ] *n* bienes *mpl* raíces.

ream^{1} [riːm] *n* resma *f*; (*fig*) montón *m*, gran cantidad *f*.

ream^{2} [riːm] *vt* (*Tech*: *also* **to ~ out**) escariar.

reamer [ˈriːmə^{r}] *n* escariador *m*.

reanimate [ˈriːˈænɪmeɪt] *vt* reanimar.

reap [riːp] *vt* segar; (*fig*) cosechar, recoger; **to ~ what one has sown** cosechar lo que uno ha sembrado; **to ~ no profit from sth** no obtener ganancia de algo, (*fig*) no sacarse ventaja de algo; **who ~s the reward?** ¿quién se lleva el beneficio?

reaper [ˈriːpə^{r}] *n* (**a**) (*person*) segador *m*, -ora *f*. (**b**) (*machine*) segadora *f*, agavilladora *f*.

reaping [ˈriːpɪŋ] *n* siega *f*.

reaping hook [ˈriːpɪŋhʊk] *n* hoz *f*.

reappear [ˈriːəˈpɪə^{r}] *vi* reaparecer, volver a aparecer.

reappearance [ˈriːəˈpɪərəns] *n* reaparición *f*.

reapply [ˈriːəˈplaɪ] **1** *vt* aplicar de nuevo; *paint etc* dar otra capa de. **2** *vi* volver a presentarse, mandar una nueva solicitud (*for* pidiendo).

reappoint [ˈriːəˈpɔɪnt] *vt* volver a nombrar.

reappointment [ˈriːəˈpɔɪntmənt] *n* nuevo nombramiento *m*.

reapportion [ˈriːəˈpɔːʃən] *vt* volver a repartir (*among* entre).

reappraisal [ˈriːəˈpreɪzəl] *n* reevaluación *f*.

reappraise [ˈriːəˈpreɪz] *vt* reevaluar.

rear^{1} [rɪə^{r}] **1** *adj* trasero, posterior; de cola; (*Mil*) de retaguardia; **~ door** puerta *f* de atrás; **~ gunner** artillero *m* de cola; **~ lamp, ~ light** luz *f* trasera, calavera *f* (*Mex*); **~ wheel** rueda *f* trasera; **~-wheel drive** tracción *f* trasera; **~ window** ventanilla *f* de atrás, (*Aut*) luneta *f* trasera.

2 *n* parte *f* trasera, parte *f* posterior; cola *f*; (*Anat**) trasero *m*; (*Mil*: *row*) última fila *f*, (*rearguard*) retaguardia *f*; **at the ~ of, in (the) ~ of** detrás de; **in the ~** (*Mil*) a retaguardia; **3 miles to the ~** 3 millas a retaguardia; **to be well to the ~** quedar muy atrasado; **to bring up the ~** cerrar la marcha; **to take the enemy in the ~** atacar al enemigo por detrás.

rear^{2} [rɪə^{r}] **1** *vt* (**a**) (*build*) erigir. (**b**) (*raise*) levantar, alzar; **violence ~s its ugly head again** la violencia vuelve a levantar la cabeza. (**c**) (*bring up*) criar. **2** *vi* (*also* **to ~ up**) encabritarse, ponerse de manos.

rear-admiral [ˈrɪərˈædmərəl] *n* contraalmirante *m*.

rear-engined [ˈrɪərˌendʒɪnd] *adj* con motor trasero.

rearguard [ˈrɪəgɑːd] **1** *n* retaguardia *f*. **2** *attr*: **~ action** combate *m* para cubrir una retirada; **to fight a ~ action** (*fig*) resistir en lo posible.

rearm [ˈriːˈɑːm] **1** *vt* rearmar. **2** *vi* rearmarse.

rearmament [ˈriːˈɑːməmənt] *n* rearme *m*.

rearmost [ˈrɪəməʊst] *adj* trasero, último de todos.

rear-mounted [ˈrɪəˈmaʊntɪd] *adj*: **~ engine** motor *m* trasero, motor *m* posterior.

rearrange [ˈriːəˈreɪndʒ] *vt* volver a arreglar; ordenar de nuevo, arreglar de otro modo; (*Liter*) refundir.

rearrangement [ˈriːəˈreɪndʒmənt] *n* nuevo arreglo *m*, nueva disposición *f*; (*Liter*) refundición *f*.

rear-view [ˈrɪəˌvjuː] *attr* retrovisor; **~ mirror** espejo *m* retrovisor.

rearward [ˈrɪəwəd] *adj* trasero, de atrás, posterior.

rearward(s) [ˈrɪəwəd(z)] *adv* hacia atrás.

reason [ˈriːzn] **1** *n* (**a**) (*motive*) razón *f*; motivo *m*; causa *f*; **the ~ for my departure** el motivo de mi ida; **the ~ for my going** la razón por la que me marcho; **the ~ why** la razón por qué, el por qué; **~s of state** razón *f* de estado; **by ~ of** a causa de; en virtud de; **for this ~** por eso, por esta razón; **for that very ~** por esa misma razón; **for some ~ or other** por alguna razón que otra; **for no good ~, for no ~ at all** sin razón, sin motivo; **for ~s best known to himself** por motivos que se sabe él; **with good ~** con razón; **all the more ~ why you should not sell it** razón de más para no venderlo, motivo más que sobrado para no venderlo; **what ~ can there be for it?** ¿qué razón puede haber?; **you had ~ to complain** Vd tuvo motivo de queja; **we have ~ to believe that ...** tenemos motivo para creer que ...; **as I have good ~ to know** según ciertos indicios que tengo.

(**b**) (*faculty*) razón *f*; **to lose one's ~** perder la razón.

(**c**) (*good sense*) sensatez *f*; moderación *f*; **everything in ~** todo con moderación; **we cannot in ~ agree** no podemos razonablemente consentir; **it's out of all ~** está fuera de razón; **to listen to ~, to see ~** ponerse en razón; **we'll make him see ~** le haremos entrar en razón; **it stands to ~** es evidente, es lógico (*that* que); **within ~** dentro de lo razonable.

2 *vt* (**a**) **to ~ that ...** razonar que ..., calcular que ..., estimar que ...; **ours not to ~ why** no nos cumple a nosotros averiguar por qué.

(**b**) **to ~ out a problem** resolver un problema meditándolo.

(**c**) **to ~ sb out of sth** disuadir a uno de algo (alegando razones en contra).

3 *vi* razonar, discurrir; **to ~ about the universe** especular acerca del universo; **to ~ from data** razonar partiendo de ciertos datos; **to ~ with sb** alegar razones para convencer a uno, tratar de convencer a uno.

reasonable [ˈriːznəbl] *adj* (*in most senses*) razonable; *person* sensato, juicioso; tolerante; **be ~!** ¡sé razonable!

reasonableness [ˈriːznəblnɪs] *n* lo razonable; sensatez *f*; juicio *m*; tolerancia *f*; **in an atmosphere of sweet ~** en un ambiente de moderación, en un ambiente de tolerancia.

reasonably [ˈriːznəblɪ] *adv* razonablemente; **a ~ good price** un precio razonable; **a ~ accurate report** un informe bastante exacto; **he acted very ~** obró con mucho tino.

reasoned [ˈriːznd] *adj* razonado.

reasoning [ˈriːznɪŋ] **1** *adj* racional. **2** *n* razonamiento *m*; argumentos *mpl*; **I don't follow your ~** no comprendo tus argumentos.

reassemble [ˈriːəˈsembl] **1** *vt* volver a reunir; (*Tech*) montar de nuevo. **2** *vi* volver a reunirse; (*Parl etc*) volver a celebrar sesión.

reassembly [ˌriːəˈsemblɪ] *n* (**a**) (*Parl etc*) (inauguración *f* de la) nueva sesión *f*. (**b**) (*Tech*) nuevo montaje *m*.

reassert [ˈriːəˈsɜːt] *vt* reafirmar, reiterar.

reassertion [ˌriːəˈsɜːʃən] *n* reafirmación *f*, reiteración *f*.

reassess [ˈriːəˈses] *vt* (*Fin*) tasar de nuevo, revalorar, valorar de nuevo (*at* en); *amount of tax* fijar de nuevo (*at* en); (*Liter etc*) hacer una nueva apreciación de; **we shall have to ~ the situation** tendremos que estudiar la situación de nuevo.

reassessment [ˌriːəˈsesmənt] *n* (*Fin*) revaloración *f*; (*Liter etc*) nueva apreciación *f*.

reassurance [ˈriːəʃʊərəns] *n* (**a**) noticia *f* tranquilizadora, promesa *f* tranquilizadora; alivio *m*, seguridades *fpl*. (**b**) (*Fin*) reaseguro *m*.

reassure [ˈriːəˈʃʊə^{r}] *vt* (**a**) tranquilizar; alentar; **to feel ~d** estar más tranquilo. (**b**) (*Fin*) reasegurar.

reassuring [ˈriːəˈʃʊərɪŋ] *adj* tranquilizador; alentador; **to make ~ noises** decir cosas tranquilizadoras.

reassuringly [ˈriːəˈʃʊərɪŋlɪ] *adv* de modo tranquilizador; **he spoke ~** nos alentó con sus palabras; **a ~ strong performance** una actuación cuya fuerza nos alentó.

reawaken [ˈriːəˈweɪkən] **1** *vt* volver a despertar. **2** *vi* (volver a) despertarse.

reawakening [ˈriːəˈweɪknɪŋ] *n* despertar *m*.

REB *n abbr of* **Revised English Bible** *versión revisada de la Biblia*.

rebarbative [rɪˈbɑːbətɪv] *adj* repugnante, repelente.

rebate [ˈriːbeɪt] **1** *n* rebaja *f*, descuento *m*. **2** *vt* rebajar, descontar.

Rebecca [rɪˈbekə] *nf* Rebeca.

rebel 1 [ˈrebl] *adj* rebelde; **the ~ government** el gobierno rebelde; **~ leader** cabecilla *m*. **2** [ˈrebl] *n* rebelde *mf*. **3** [rɪˈbel] *vi* rebelarse, sublevarse; (*legs, stomach etc*) rebelarse, negarse a funcionar.

rebellion [rɪˈbeljən] *n* rebelión *f*, sublevación *f*.

rebellious [rɪˈbeljəs] *adj* rebelde; *child etc* revoltoso, díscolo.

rebelliousness [rɪˈbeljəsnɪs] *n* rebeldía *f*; carácter *m* revoltoso, naturaleza *f* díscola.

rebind [ˈriːˈbaɪnd] (*irr*: *V* **bind**) *vt* volver a atar; *book* reencuadernar.

rebirth [ˈriːˈbɜːθ] *n* renacimiento *m.*

reboot [ˌriːˈbuːt] *vti* reinicializar, reiniciar.

rebore [ˈriːˈbɔːʳ] (*Tech*) **1** *n* rectificado *m.* **2** *vt* rectificar.

reborn [ˈriːˈbɔːn] *ptp*: **to be ~** renacer.

rebound 1 *n* [ˈriːbaʊnd] rebote *m*; **on the ~** de rebote, de rechazo; **she married him on the ~** se casó con él de rechazo.

2 [rɪˈbaʊnd] *vi* rebotar (*off* después de chocar con), dar un rebote; (*fig*) repercutir (*on* en).

rebroadcast [ˈriːˈbrɔːdkɑːst] **1** *n* retransmisión *f.* **2** *vt* retransmitir.

rebuff [rɪˈbʌf] **1** *n* repulsa *f*, desaire *m*; **to meet with a ~** ser repulsado, aguantar un desaire. **2** *vt* rechazar; desairar.

rebuild [ˈriːˈbɪld] (*irr*: *V* **build**) *vt* reconstruir, reedificar; reconstituir.

rebuilding [ˈriːˈbɪldɪŋ] *n* reconstrucción *f*, reedificación *f*; reconstitución *f.*

rebuke [rɪˈbjuːk] **1** *n* reprensión *f*; reprimenda *f.* **2** *vt* reprender, censurar; **to ~ sb for having done sth** reprender a uno por haber hecho algo.

rebus [ˈriːbəs] *n* jeroglífico *m.*

rebut [rɪˈbʌt] *vt* rebatir, refutar, rechazar.

rebuttal [rɪˈbʌtl] *n* refutación *f.*

recalcitrance [rɪˈkælsɪtrəns] *n* obstinación *f*, terquedad *f.*

recalcitrant [rɪˈkælsɪtrənt] *adj* reacio, refractorio, recalcitrante.

recall [rɪˈkɔːl] **1** *n* aviso *m*, llamada *f* (para hacer volver a uno); retirada *f*; destitución *f*; **to be beyond** (*or* **past**) **~** ser irrevocable; (*person*) haberse ido definitivamente; **those days are gone beyond ~** aquellos días son irrevocables; **to have total ~** poder recordarlo todo, tener una memoria infalible.

2 *vt* (**a**) (*call back*) *person* llamar, hacer volver; *ambassador, capital* retirar; (*dismiss*) destituir; *library book* reclamar; *defective product* retirar del mercado; (*Comput*) volver a llamar.

(**b**) (*remember*) recordar, traer a la memoria; **I can't quite ~ whether ...** no recuerdo del todo si ...; **it ~s the time when ...** hace pensar en aquella ocasión cuando ...

recant [rɪˈkænt] **1** *vt* retractar, desdecirse de; renunciar a. **2** *vi* retractarse, desdecirse; confesar su error.

recantation [ˈriːkænˈteɪʃən] retractación *f*; confesión *f* de error.

recap* [ˈriːkæp] **1** *n* recapitulación *f*, resumen *m.* **2** *vti* recapitular, resumir.

recapitulate [ˌriːkəˈpɪtjʊleɪt] *vti* recapitular, resumir.

recapitulation [ˈriːkəˌpɪtjʊˈleɪʃən] *n* recapitulación *f*, resumen *m.*

recapture [ˈriːˈkæptʃəʳ] **1** *n* recobro *m;* reconquista *f.*

2 *vt prisoner etc* recobrar, volver a prender; *town* reconquistar, volver a tomar; *memory, scene* hacer revivir.

recast [ˈriːˈkɑːst] (*irr*: *V* **cast**) *vt* (*Tech, Liter etc*) refundir; *play* repartir de otra manera los papeles de.

recce* [ˈrekɪ] (*Mil*) *abbr of* (**a**) *n* **reconnaissance** reconocimiento *m.* (**b**) *vt* **reconnoitre** reconocer.

recd, rec'd (*Comm*) *abbr of* **received** recibido, rbdo.

recede [rɪˈsiːd] *vi* retroceder, retirarse; (*floods, price*) bajar; (*danger etc*) alejarse, disminuir; (*memory*) desvanecerse; **his hair is receding** se le están formando entradas.

receding [rɪˈsiːdɪŋ] *adj prospect* que va disminuyendo; *tide* que está bajando; *forehead* huidizo, achatado; **with a ~ hairline** con acusadas entradas capilares.

receipt [rɪˈsiːt] **1** *n* (**a**) (*act of receiving*) recepción *f*, recibo *m*; **to acknowledge ~ of** acusar recibo de; **I am in ~ of your letter** he recibido su carta, (*more formally*) obra su carta en mi poder; **on ~ of** al recibo de; **on ~ of these goods** a la recepción de estas mercancías; **on ~ of this news** al saber esta noticia, al recibir esta noticia; **pay on ~** pago *m* contra entrega, pago *m* al recibo.

(**b**) (*document*) recibo *m*, abono *m* (*Mex*); **please give me a ~** haga el favor de darme un recibo.

(**c**) **~s** (*Comm, Fin*: *money taken*) ingresos *mpl*; (*of function, game etc*) entrada *f.*

2 *vt goods* dar recibo por; *bill* poner el 'recibí' en.

receipt book [rɪˈsiːtbʊk] *n* libro *m* talonario.

receivable [rɪˈsiːvəbl] **1** *adj* recibidero; (*Comm*) por (*or* a) cobrar. **2 ~s** *npl* cuentas *fpl* por cobrar.

receive [rɪˈsiːv] **1** *vt* recibir; *money* recibir, *payment, salary* cobrar, recibir; (*accept*) aceptar, admitir; *guests* acoger, (*to stay*) hospedar, alojar; *broadcast* captar; *stolen goods* encubrir, ocultar, receptar; *wound* sufrir; *blow, thrashing* cobrar; (*stand weight of*) sufrir, apoyar; *ball* restar; (*approve*) aprobar; **'~d with thanks'** 'recibí'; **are you receiving me?** (*Rad*) ¿me oye?; **to ~ sb into the Academy** recibir a uno en la Academia; **to ~ sb as a partner** admitir a uno como socio; **to ~ sb into the Church** bautizar a uno, recibir a uno en el seno de la Iglesia; **to ~ sb into one's home** hospedar a uno en su casa; **the idea was well ~d** la idea tuvo buena acogida; **the book was not well ~d** el libro tuvo una acogida poco entusiasta; **he ~d a wound in the leg** sufrió una herida en la pierna; **to ~ a blank refusal** encontrar una negativa rotunda; **what treatment did you ~?** ¿qué tratamiento te dieron?

2 *vi* (**a**) (*Jur*) receptar, ser receptador.

(**b**) (*Sport*) ser restador.

(**c**) (*socially*) recibir; **the Duchess ~s on Thursdays** la duquesa recibe los jueves.

received [rɪˈsiːvd] *adj* (*Brit*) *pronunciation etc* admitido, normativo; *opinion* admitido, aceptado, recibido.

receiver [rɪˈsiːvəʳ] *n* (**a**) (*person*) recibidor *m*, -ora *f*; (*addressee*) destinatario *m*, -a *f*; (*of stolen goods*) receptador *m*, -ora *f*, perista* *mf*; (*in bankruptcy, also* **official ~**) síndico *m*, administrador *m* jurídico; (*Sport*) restador *m*, -ora *f*; **to call in the ~** entrar en liquidación.

(**b**) (*Rad*) receptor *m*, radiorreceptor *m*; (*Telec*) auricular *m*, fono *m* (*SC*).

(**c**) (*Chem etc*) recipiente *m.*

receivership [rɪˈsiːvəʃɪp] *n*: **to go into ~** entrar en liquidación.

receiving [rɪˈsiːvɪŋ] **1** *n* recepción *f*; (*of stolen goods*) receptación *f*, encubrimiento *m.* **2** *adj* (**a**) **~ set** receptor *m*, radiorreceptor *m.* (**b**) **to be at the ~ end** ser la víctima, ser el blanco.

recension [rɪˈsenʃən] *n* recensión *f.*

recent [ˈriːsnt] *adj* reciente; nuevo; **in ~ years** en estos últimos años; **in the ~ past** en el próximo pasado.

recently [ˈriːsntlɪ] *adv* (**a**) recientemente; hace poco, últimamente; **as ~ as 1990** todavía en 1990; **until ~** hasta hace poco, hasta fecha reciente. (**b**) (*before ptps*) recién; **~ arrived** recién llegado.

receptacle [rɪˈseptəkl] *n* recipiente *m.*

reception [rɪˈsepʃən] **1** *n* (**a**) (*act*) recepción *f*, recibimiento *m*; (*welcome*) acogida *f*; **to get a warm ~** tener buena acogida, ser recibido con entusiasmo; **they'll get a warm ~ if they come here** (*iro*) estamos listos para recibirles si se presentan aquí.

(**b**) (*social function*) recepción *f.*

(**c**) (*Rad etc*) recepción *f.*

(**d**) (*in hotel etc*) recepción *f.*

2 *attr*: **~ center** (*US*), **~ centre** centro *m* de recepción; **~ class** clase *f* de primer año; **~ desk** (mesa *f* de) recepción *f*; **~ room** sala *f* de recibo.

receptionist [rɪˈsepʃənɪst] *n* (*hotel*) recepcionista *f;* (*dentist's etc*) chica *f*, chica *f* enfermera; (*other*) secretaria *f.*

receptive [rɪˈseptɪv] *adj* receptivo.

receptiveness [rɪˈseptɪvnɪs] *n*, **receptivity** [rɪsepˈtɪvɪtɪ] *n* receptividad *f.*

recess [rɪˈses] **1** *n* (**a**) (*vacation*) vacaciones *fpl*; (*US*: *short rest*) descanso *m*; (*esp US*: *in school*) recreo *m*; (*Parl*) suspensión *f*, (*between sittings*) intermedio *m*; **parliament is in ~** la sesión del parlamento está suspendida.

(**b**) (*Tech*) rebajo *m*; (*Archit*) hueco *m*; nicho *m*; (*hiding place*) escondrijo *m.*

(**c**) **~es** (*fig*) seno *m*; lo más hondo, lo más recóndito.

2 *vi* (*US Jur, Parl*) prorrogarse, suspenderse la sesión.

recession [rɪˈseʃən] *n* retroceso *m*, retirada *f*; (*fall*) baja *f*; (*lessening*) disminución *f*; (*Fin, Comm*) recesión *f.*

recessional [rɪˈseʃənl] *n* himno *m* de fin de oficio.

recessive [rɪˈsesɪv] *adj* recesivo.

recharge [ˈriːˈtʃɑːdʒ] *vt* volver a cargar, recargar; **to ~ one's batteries** (*fig*) reponerse.

rechargeable [rɪˈtʃɑːdʒəbl] *adj* recargable.

recherché [rəˈʃeəʃeɪ] *adj* rebuscado.

rechristen [ˈriːˈkrɪsn] *vt* (*Eccl*) rebautizar; (*rename*) poner nuevo nombre a; **they have ~ed the boat 'Gloria'** han puesto al barco el nuevo nombre de 'Gloria'.

recidivism [rɪˈsɪdɪvɪzəm] *n* reincidencia *f.*

recidivist [rɪˈsɪdɪvɪst] *n* reincidente *mf.*

recipe [ˈresɪpɪ] *n* receta *f* (*for* de); **it's a ~ for disaster** es una receta para el desastre.

recipient [rɪˈsɪpɪənt] *n* recibidor *m*, -ora *f*, recipiente *mf*; el que recibe, la que recibe; (*of gift etc*) beneficiario *m*, -a *f.*

reciprocal [rɪˈsɪprəkəl] **1** *adj* recíproco, mutuo. **2** *n* (*Math*) recíproca *f.*

reciprocally [rɪˈsɪprəkəlɪ] *adv* recíprocamente, mutuamente.

reciprocate [rɪ'sɪprəkeɪt] **1** *vt good wishes etc* intercambiar, devolver; corresponder a; **and this feeling is ~d** y correspondemos plenamente, y queremos expresar idénticos sentimientos; **her kindness was not ~d** no correspondieron a su amabilidad.

2 *vi* (**a**) (*Mech*) oscilar, alternar.

(**b**) (*fig*) usar de reciprocidad, corresponder; **but they did not ~** pero ellos no correspondieron a esto; **he ~d with a short speech** pronunció un breve discurso a modo de contestación.

reciprocation [rɪˌsɪprə'keɪʃən] *n* reciprocación *f*; reciprocidad *f*, correspondencia *f*.

reciprocity [ˌresɪ'prɒsɪtɪ] *n* reciprocidad *f*.

recital [rɪ'saɪtl] *n* relación *f*, narración *f*; (*Mus*) recital *m*.

recitation [ˌresɪ'teɪʃən] *n* (*act*) recitación *f*; (*text, piece for* ~) recitado *m*; **with humorous ~s** con recitados humorísticos.

recitative [ˌresɪtə'tiːv] **1** *adj* recitativo. **2** *nm* recitado *m*.

recite [rɪ'saɪt] **1** *vt* narrar, referir; enumerar; *recitation* recitar; **she ~d her troubles all over again** volvió a enumerar todas sus dificultades. **2** *vi* dar un recitado.

reckless ['reklɪs] *adj person* temerario, imprudente; *act* imprudente; *speed etc* excesivo, peligroso; *statement* inconsiderado; (*daring*) osado; (*scatterbrained*) atolondrado; **~ driver** conductor *m* temerario, conductora *f* temeraria; **~ driving** conducción *f* temeraria.

recklessly ['reklɪslɪ] *adv* temerariamente, imprudentemente; **to drive ~** conducir temerariamente; **to spend ~** derrochar dinero.

recklessness ['reklɪsnɪs] *n* temeridad *f*, imprudencia *f*; inconsideración *f*; **the ~ of youth** la temeridad de la juventud; **the ~ of her driving** su modo imprudente de conducir.

reckon ['rekən] **1** *vt* (**a**) (*count number*) contar, calcular; computar; (*ascertain quantity*) calcular, estimar.

(**b**) (*believe*) considerar, estimar; **to ~ sb among one's friends** contar a uno entre los amigos; **to ~ sb as** considerar a uno como.

(**c**) (*think*) pensar, creer; considerar; **I ~ we can start** creo que podemos empezar; **to ~ that ...** estimar que ..., considerar que ..., creer que ...; **I ~ he's worth more** considero que vale más; **she'll come, I ~** según creo vendrá; **I ~ so** así lo creo, creo que sí; cierto.

2 *vi* (**a**) (*do sum*) calcular; hacer cálculos; **to learn to ~** aprender a calcular; **~ing from today** contando desde hoy.

(**b**) **you ~?*** ¿tú crees?; **to ~ on** contar con; **to ~ on** + *ger* contar con + *infin;* **to ~ to** + *infin* contar con poder + *infin*, esperar poder ~ *infin*; **to ~ with** tener en cuenta, contar con; **he's a person to be ~ed with** es una persona de cuenta; **if you offend him you'll have to ~ with the whole family** si le ofendes tendrás que ver con toda la familia; **we didn't ~ with that** no contábamos con eso; **we hadn't ~ed with having to walk** no habíamos contado con ir a pie; **to ~ without sb** dejar fuera a uno, omitir a uno en sus cálculos; **we ~ed without that** no contábamos con eso.

◆reckon in *vt* incluir.

◆reckon up *vt* calcular, computar; **to ~ up one's losses** calcular sus pérdidas.

reckoning ['reknɪŋ] *n* (**a**) (*calculation*) cálculo *m*, cuenta *f*; **by any ~** a todas luces; **according to my ~** según mis cálculos; **to be out in one's ~** hacer mal el cálculo, calcular mal.

(**b**) (*bill*) cuenta *f*.

(**c**) (*fig*) ajuste *m* de cuentas.

reclaim [rɪ'kleɪm] **1** *n*: **to be beyond** (*or* **past**) **~** ser irremediable, no tener remedio; estar definitivamente perdido.

2 *vt* (*claim back*) reclamar; *baggage* recoger, reclamar; *sinner etc* reformar; (*tame*) amansar, domesticar; *land* recuperar, hacer utilizable; (*from sea*) ganar, rescatar; *swamp* sanear, entarquinar; *rubber etc* regenerar, volver a hacer utilizable.

reclaimable [rɪ'kleɪməbl] *adj* reclamable; utilizable.

reclamation [ˌreklə'meɪʃən] *n* reclamación *f*; reformación *f*; domesticación *f*; recuperación *f*; utilización *f*; **land ~** rescate *m* de terrenos, entarquinamiento *m*.

recline [rɪ'klaɪn] **1** *vt* (*lean, lay*) apoyar, recostar, reclinar; (*rest*) descansar. **2** *vi* reclinarse, recostarse; apoyarse; descansar; **to ~ upon** (*fig*) contar con, fiarse de.

reclining [rɪ'klaɪnɪŋ] *adj* acostado; tumbado; *figure, statue* yacente; **~ chair** sillón *m* reclinable; (*Med*) silla *f* de extensión; **~ seat** asiento *m* abatible.

recluse [rɪ'kluːs] *n* solitario *m*, -a *f*, recluso *m*, -a *f*.

reclusion [rɪ'kluːʒən] *n* reclusión *f*.

reclusive [rɪ'kluːzɪv] *adj* dado a la reclusión, solitario.

recognition [ˌrekəg'nɪʃən] *n* reconocimiento *m*; **a smile of ~** una sonrisa de reconocimiento; **in ~ of** en reconocimiento de, en premio de; en señal de; **in ~ of this fact** reconociendo este hecho; **to change sth beyond ~** cambiar algo de modo que resulta irreconocible.

recognizable ['rekəgnaɪzəbl] *adj* reconocible; identificable; **it is ~ as** se puede reconocer como, se puede identificar como.

recognizance [rɪ'kɒgnɪzəns] *n* reconocimiento *m*; obligación *f* contraída; (*sum*) fianza *f*; **to enter into ~s to** + *infin* comprometerse legalmente a + *infin*.

recognize ['rekəgnaɪz] *vt* (**a**) (*know again*) reconocer, identificar; conocer; **you don't ~ me** no me reconoce; **I ~d him by his walk** le conocí por su modo de andar; **his own mother would not have ~d him** su propia madre no le hubiera conocido; **he was ~d by 2 policemen** le reconocieron 2 policías; **do you ~ this handbag?** ¿conoce Vd este bolso?

(**b**) (*acknowledge*) admitir, confesar; reconocer; **we ~ that ...** reconocemos que ..., confesamos que ...; **we do not ~ the government of Ruritania** no reconocemos el gobierno de Ruritania; **does the Academy ~ the word?** ¿admite la Academia la palabra?; **we do not ~ your claim** no admitimos (*or* aceptamos) su pretensión; **to ~ sb as king** reconocer a uno por rey.

(**c**) **the Chair ~s Mr X** (*US Parl*) el Sr X tiene la palabra.

recognized ['rekəgnaɪzd] *adj expert etc* reconocido como tal; *feature* conocido; *agent etc* acreditado, oficial; **it's the ~ method** es el sistema normal.

recoil [rɪ'kɔɪl] **1** *n* retroceso *m*; (*of gun*) retroceso *m*, rebufo *m*, culatazo *m*.

2 *vi* recular, retroceder; (*Mil*) retroceder, rebufar; **to ~ in fear** retroceder espantado; **to ~ from sth** retroceder ante algo, cejar ante la perspectiva de algo; **to ~ from doing sth** sentir repugnancia por hacer algo, no animarse a hacer algo; **it ~ed on him** recayó sobre él, resultó contraproducente para él.

recoilless [rɪ'kɔɪllɪs] *adj gun* sin retroceso.

recollect [ˌrekə'lekt] **1** *vt* recordar, acordarse de. **2** *vi* recordar, acordarse.

recollection [ˌrekə'lekʃən] *n* recuerdo *m*; **to the best of my ~** que yo recuerde.

recommence ['riːkə'mens] **1** *vt* reanudar, recomenzar, volver a comenzar. **2** *vi* reanudarse, recomenzar, volver a comenzar.

recommend [ˌrekə'mend] *vt* recomendar; **to ~ a candidate for a post** recomendar a un candidato para un puesto; **I ~ him to you most warmly** se lo recomiendo con la mayor confianza; **to ~ sb to do sth** recomendar a uno que haga algo, aconsejar a uno hacer algo; **~ed retail price** precio *m* de venta recomendado, precio *m* de venta al público.

recommendable [ˌrekə'mendəbl] *adj* recomendable.

recommendation [ˌrekəmen'deɪʃən] *n* recomendación *f*; **the ~s of a report** las recomendaciones de un informe.

recommendatory [ˌrekə'mendətərɪ] *adj* recomendatorio.

recompense ['rekəmpens] **1** *n* recompensa *f*. **2** *vt* recompensar (*for* por).

reconcilable ['rekənsaɪləbl] *adj* conciliable, reconciliable.

reconcile ['rekənsaɪl] **1** *vt persons* reconciliar; *theories etc* conciliar; *quarrel* componer; **to become ~d to sth** resignarse a algo, acomodarse con algo; **what ~d him to the place was the weather** lo que le hizo conformarse con el lugar fue el tiempo.

2 *vr*: **to ~ o.s. to sth** resignarse a algo, acomodarse con algo, conformarse con algo.

reconciliation [ˌrekənsɪlɪ'eɪʃən] *n* reconciliación *f*; conciliación *f*; composición *f*; **~ statement** (*Fin*) estado *m* de reconciliación.

recondite [rɪ'kɒndaɪt] *adj* recóndito.

recondition ['riːkən'dɪʃən] *vt* reacondicionar.

reconnaissance [rɪ'kɒnɪsəns] *n* reconocimiento *m*; **~ flight** vuelo *m* de reconocimiento; **to make a ~** reconocer el terreno, explorar el terreno.

reconnoitre, (*US*) **reconnoiter** [ˌrekə'nɔɪtəʳ] **1** *vt* reconocer, explorar. **2** *vi* reconocer el terreno, explorar el terreno.

reconquer ['riː'kɒŋkəʳ] *vt* reconquistar.

reconquest ['riː'kɒŋkwest] *n* reconquista *f*; **the R~** (*of Spain*) la Reconquista.

reconsider ['riːkən'sɪdəʳ] **1** *vt* volver a considerar, volver a examinar; reconsiderar, repensar. **2** *vi* volver a considerarlo.

reconsideration ['ri:kən,sɪdə'reɪʃən] *n* reconsideración *f*; **on ~** después de volver sobre ello.
reconstitute ['ri:'kɒnstɪtju:t] *vt* reconstituir.
reconstitution ['ri:,kɒnstɪ'tju:ʃən] *n* reconstitución *f*.
reconstruct ['ri:kən'strʌkt] *vt* reconstruir; reedificar; *crime etc* reconstituir.
reconstruction ['ri:kən'strʌkʃən] *n* reconstrucción *f*; reedificación *f*; reconstitución *f*.
reconvert ['ri:kən'vɜ:t] *vt* volver a convertir (*to* en); reorganizar.
record 1 ['rekɔ:d] *n* (**a**) (*document, report etc*) documento *m*; registro *m*, partida *f*; relación *f*; (*Jur*) acta *f*; (*note*) nota *f*, apunte *m*; (*Comput*) registro *m*; **~ of attendances** registro *m* de asistencias; **~ of a case** acta *f* de un proceso; **for the ~, I disagree** que conste, no estoy de acuerdo; **to write sth into the ~** añadir algo a la relación escrita; **off the ~** (*adj*) no oficial, extraoficial, confidencial, (*adv*) de modo no oficial, extraoficialmente, confidencialmente; **it is on ~ that ..., it is a matter of ~ that ...** consta que ...; **the fact is on ~** consta el hecho; **the highest temperatures on ~** las temperaturas más altas de que hay constancia; **the minister is on ~ as saying that ...** consta que el ministro ha dicho que ...; **to place** (*or* **put**) **sth on ~** hacer constar algo, dejar constancia de algo; **there is no ~ of it** no hay constancia de ello, no consta en los documentos; **to keep** (*or* **make**) **a ~ of** apuntar, tomar nota de; **he left no ~ of it** no dejó relación de ello; **let me put** (*or* **set**) **the ~ straight** que consten los hechos; les diré la verdad de los hechos.
(**b**) **~s** archivos *mpl*; (*of police*) archivo *m* del servicio de identificación; **the ~s of a society** los archivos de una sociedad; **I will have the ~s searched** mandaré buscar en los archivos.
(**c**) (*person's past in general*) historia *f*; reputación *f*; antecedentes *mpl*; (*as dossier*) expediente *m*; (*written with application for post*) carrera *f*, curriculum *m* vitae; (*of person, organization etc*) historial *m*; (*Mil*) hoja *f* de servicios; **criminal ~** antecedentes *mpl* delictivos; **her past ~** su historia, su historial; **this company's splendid ~** el brillante historial de esta compañía; **his ~ is against him** su historial obra en perjuicio suyo; **has he a ~?** ¿tiene antecedentes penales?, ¿tiene ficha? (*esp LAm*); **he has a clean ~** no hay nada en su historial que le perjudique; **he left behind a splendid ~ of achievements** dejó un magnífico historial de éxitos.
(**d**) (*Sport etc*) récord *m*, marca *f*; **is this a ~?** ¿es esto un récord?; ¿es excepcional esto?; **to beat** (*or* **break**) **the ~** batir el récord, superar la marca; **to establish** (*or* **set up**) **a ~** establecer un récord; **to hold the ~ for the 100 metres** ostentar el récord de los 100 metros.
(**e**) (*Mus etc*) disco *m*; **to make a ~** grabar un disco.
2 ['rekɔ:d] *attr*: **~ album** álbum *m* de discos; **~ cabinet** armario *m* para discos; **~ company** casa *f* discográfica; **~ dealer** (*person*) vendedor *m*, -ora *f* de discos; (*shop*) tienda *f* de discos; **~ library** discoteca *f*; **~ player** tocadiscos *m*; **~ token** cupón *m* para discos.
3 ['rekɔ:d] *adj* récord (*invar*), sin precedentes, máximo, nuevo; **a ~ output** una producción sin precedentes; **in a ~ time** en un tiempo récord; **in the ~ time of 12 seconds** en el tiempo récord de 12 segundos.
4 [rɪ'kɔ:d] *vt* (**a**) (*set down*) registrar; inscribir; apuntar; hacer constar, dejar constancia de, consignar; **it is not ~ed anywhere** no consta en ninguna parte; **I will ~ your order** apuntaré su pedido.
(**b**) (*on dial etc*) indicar, marcar.
(**c**) (*Mus etc*) grabar, registrar; **she ~ed the song in 1989** grabó la canción en 1989; **to have one's voice ~ed** hacer grabar su voz.
(**d**) (*Comput*) registrar.
5 [rɪ'kɔ:d] *vi* (*Mus etc*) grabar, hacer una grabación.
record-breaker ['rekɔ:d,breɪkəʳ] *n* recordman *m*, plusmarquista *mf*.
record-breaking ['rekɔ:d,breɪkɪŋ] *adj person, team* brillante, excepcional; que tantos récords ostenta; *effort, run* récord (*invar*).
record-card ['rekɔ:d,kɑ:d] *n* ficha *f*.
record-changer ['rekɔ:d,tʃeɪndʒəʳ] *n* cambiadiscos *m*.
recorded [rɪ'kɔ:dɪd] *adj* (**a**) **~ music** música *f* grabada. (**b**) **never in ~ history** nunca en la historia escrita; **it is a ~ fact that ...** consta el hecho de que ...; **~ delivery** (*Brit Post*) entrega *f* con acuse de recibo.
recorder [rɪ'kɔ:dəʳ] *n* (**a**) (*person*) registrador *m*, -ora *f*, archivero *m*, -a *f*; **he was a faithful ~ of the facts** registró puntualmente los hechos.
(**b**) (*Brit Jur*) juez *m* municipal.
(**c**) (*Mus*) flauta *f* dulce, flauta *f* de pico.
(**d**) (*Mech*) contador *m*, indicador *m*; (*tape~*) magnetofón *m*.
record-holder ['rekɔ:d,həʊldəʳ] *n* recordman *m*, titular *mf*, plusmarquista *mf*; **the 100 metres ~** el (*or* la) que ostenta el récord de los 100 metros.
recording [rɪ'kɔ:dɪŋ] **1** *n* grabación *f*; registro *m*.
2 *attr*: **~ angel** ángel *m* que registra las acciones buenas o malas de los hombres; **~ artist** músico *m* (*etc*) que hace grabaciones; **~ density** densidad *f* de grabación; **~ studio** estudio *m* de grabación, sala *f* de grabaciones; **~ tape** cinta *f* de grabación, cinta *f* magnetofónica; **~ van** camión *m* de grabación.
recordist [rɪ'kɔ:dɪst] *n* (*Cine, TV*) sonista *mf*.
recount [rɪ'kaʊnt] *vt* contar, referir.
re-count ['ri:'kaʊnt] **1** *n* (*Parl*) segundo escrutinio *m*; **to have a ~** someter los votos a un segundo escrutinio. **2** *vt* volver a contar.
recoup [rɪ'ku:p] *vt* recobrar, recuperar; indemnizarse por.
recourse [rɪ'kɔ:s] *n* recurso *m*; **to have ~ to** recurrir a.
recover [rɪ'kʌvəʳ] **1** *vt* recobrar, recuperar (*also Comput*); *money* reembolsarse; *stolen property* recuperar; (*rescue*) rescatar; **to ~ lost time** recuperar el tiempo perdido; **to ~ consciousness** recobrar el conocimiento, volver en sí; **to ~ one's health** recobrar la salud, reponerse; **to ~ sth from sb** hacer que uno devuelva algo; **to ~ one's property** (*Jur*) reivindicar su propiedad; **to ~ damages from sb** ser indemnizado por daños y perjuicios por uno.
2 *vi* (*Med, Fin etc*) restablecerse, reponerse; (*Econ etc*) reactivarse; **to ~ from an illness** reponerse de una enfermedad; **has she quite ~ed?** ¿se ha curado del todo?; **shares have ~ed** las acciones han vuelto a subir; **when I had ~ed from my astonishment** cuando me había sobrepuesto a mi asombro.
3 *vr*: **to ~ o.s.** reponerse, sobreponerse.
re-cover ['ri:'kʌvəʳ] *vt* volver a cubrir.
recoverable [rɪ'kʌvərəbl] adj recuperable; (*at law*) reivindicable.
recovery [rɪ'kʌvərɪ] **1** *n* recobro *m*, recuperación *f*; (*Comput, Fin*) recuperación *f*; (*Econ*) reactivación *f*; (*rescue*) rescate *m*; (*Med etc*) restablecimiento *m*, mejoría *f*; (*Jur*) reivindicación *f*; **an action for ~ of damages** una demanda del pago de daños y perjuicios; **to be past ~** haberse perdido definitivamente, ser irrecuperable, (*Med*) estar desahuciado; **to make a rapid ~** restablecerse rápidamente; **to make a slow ~** restablecerse lentamente; **prices made a slow ~** las cotizaciones tardaron en restablecerse.
2 *attr*: **~ room** (*Med*) sala *f* de posoperatorio; **~ service** (*Aut*) servicio *m* de rescate; **~ ship, ~ vessel** nave *f* de salvamento.
recreant†† ['rekrɪənt] **1** *n* cobarde *mf*. **2** *adj* cobarde.
recreate ['rekrɪeɪt] *vt* recrear.
re-create ['ri:krɪ'eɪt] *vt* (*create again*) recrear, volver a crear.
recreation [,rekrɪ'eɪʃən] **1** *n* (**a**) (*act*) recreación *f*. (**b**) (*play, amusement*) recreo *m*; (*Scol*) recreo *m*, hora *f* de recreo. **2** *attr*: **~ center** (*US*), **~ centre** centro *m* de recreo; **~ ground** campo *m* de deportes; **~ room** salón *m* de recreo.
recreational [,rekrɪ'eɪʃənəl] *adj* recreativo; **~ facilities** facilidades *fpl* de recreo, instalaciones *fpl* recreativas; **~ vehicle** (*US*) caravana *f* pequeña, rulota *f* pequeña; **this is only ~** esto es sólo un pasatiempo.
recreative ['rekrɪ,eɪtɪv] *adj* recreativo.
recriminate [rɪ'krɪmɪneɪt] *vi* recriminar.
recrimination [rɪ,krɪmɪ'neɪʃən] *n* recriminación *f*.
recross ['ri:'krɒs] *vti* volver a cruzar.
recrudesce [,ri:kru:'des] *vi* recrudecer.
recrudescence [,ri:kru:'desns] *n* recrudescencia *f*, recrudecimiento *m*.
recrudescent [,ri:kru:'desnt] *adj* recrudescente.
recruit [rɪ'kru:t] **1** *n* recluta *m*. **2** *vt* (*Mil*) reclutar; *strength etc* restablecer. **3** *vi* alistar reclutas.
recruiting [rɪ'kru:tɪŋ] **1** *n* reclutamiento *m*. **2** *attr*: **~ office** caja *f* de reclutas; **~ officer** oficial *m* de reclutamiento.
recruitment [rɪ'kru:tmənt] *n* reclutamiento *m*; **~ agency** agencia *f* de colocaciones, agencia *f* de selección de personal.
rec't *n abbr of* **receipt**.
rectal ['rektəl] *adj* rectal.
rectangle ['rek,tæŋgl] *n* rectángulo *m*.
rectangular [rek'tæŋgjʊləʳ] *adj* rectangular.
rectifiable ['rektɪfaɪəbl] *adj* rectificable.

rectification [ˌrektɪfɪ'keɪʃən] *n* rectificación *f*.
rectifier ['rektɪfaɪəʳ] *n* (*Elec, Chem etc*) rectificador *m*; (*Mech*) rectificadora *f*.
rectify ['rektɪfaɪ] *vt* (*all senses*) rectificar.
rectilinear [ˌrektɪ'lɪnɪəʳ] *adj* rectilíneo.
rectitude ['rektɪtjuːd] *n* rectitud *f*.
rector ['rektəʳ] *n* (*Eccl*) párroco *m*, -ora *f*; (*Univ etc*) rector *m*, -ora *f*; (*Scot Scol*) director *m*, -ora *f*.
rectory ['rektərɪ] *n* casa *f* del párroco.
rectum ['rektəm] *n* recto *m*.
recumbent [rɪ'kʌmbənt] *adj* recostado, acostado; *statue* yacente.
recuperate [rɪ'kuːpəreɪt] **1** *vt* recuperar. **2** *vi* restablecerse, reponerse; **to ~ after an illness** reponerse de una enfermedad.
recuperation [rɪˌkuːpə'reɪʃən] *n* recuperación *f*; (*Med*) restablecimiento *m*.
recuperative [rɪ'kuːpərətɪv] *adj* recuperativo.
recur [rɪ'kɜːʳ] *vi* repetirse, producirse de nuevo, volver a producirse; (*revert to*) volver a; (*come to mind again*) volver a la mente; **the idea ~s constantly in his work** la idea se repite constantemente en su obra.
recurrence [rɪ'kʌrəns] *n* repetición *f*, reaparición *f*.
recurrent [rɪ'kʌrənt] *adj* repetido; constante; (*Anat, Med*) recurrente; **it is a ~ theme** es un tema constante, es un tema que se repite a menudo.
recurring [rɪ'kɜːrɪŋ] *adj*: **~ decimal** decimal *f* periódica.
recusant ['rekjʊzənt] **1** *adj* recusante. **2** *n* recusante *mf*.
recyclable [ˌriː'saɪkləbl] *adj* reciclable.
recycle [ˌriː'saɪkl] *vt* reciclar.
recycling [ˌriː'saɪklɪŋ] *n* reciclado *m*, reciclaje *m*; **~ plant** planta *f* de reciclaje.
red [red] **1** *adj* rojo, colorado; *face* (*high-coloured*) encarnado; (*with anger*) encendido (de ira); (*with shame*) encendido, ruboroso; *hair* rojo; *wine* tinto; *ink* colorado; (*Pol*) rojo; **~ admiral (butterfly)** vanesa *f* roja; **~ alert** alarma *f* roja; **R~ Army** Ejército *m* Rojo; **~ cabbage** col *f* lombarda; **~ card** tarjeta *f* roja, cartulina *f* roja; **R~ Cross** Cruz *f* Roja; **~ deer** ciervo *m* (común); **~ diesel (oil)** gasóleo *m* B; **~ flag** bandera *f* roja; **~ heat** calor *m* rojo; **~ herring** pista *f* falsa, ardid *m* para apartar la atención del asunto principal; **R~ Indian** piel roja *mf*; **~ lead** minio *m*; **~ light** luz *f* roja; **~ pepper** pimiento *m* rojo, chile *m* rojo (*LAm*); **~ squirrel** ardilla *f* roja; **~ tape** (*rules*) reglas *fpl*; (*formalities*) formalidades *fpl* burocráticas, trámites *mpl*; (*paperwork*) papeleo *m*; **to be ~ in the face** tener la cara encendida, tener el rostro sofocado; **was my face ~!** ¡cómo me avergoncé!; **to go** (*or* **turn**) **as ~ as a beetroot** (*or* **lobster** *or* **tomato**) ponerse como un tomate; **to go** (*or* **turn**) **~ with shame** ponerse colorado, ruborizarse.
2 *n* (**a**) rojo *m*, color *m* rojo; (*Pol*) rojo *m*, -a *f*; **to be in the ~** estar en números rojos; **to be £1000 in the ~** deber 1000 libras; **to get into the ~** contraer deudas; **to get out of the ~** salirse de deudas, liquidar sus deudas; **to see ~** sulfurarse, salirse de sus casillas; **this makes me see ~** esto me saca de quicio.
(**b**) (*Pol*) rojo *m*, -a *f*.
(**c**) (*wine*) (vino *m*) tinto *m*.
redact [rɪ'dækt] *vt* redactar.
redaction [rɪ'dækʃən] *n* redacción *f*.
red-berried ['red'berɪd] *adj* con bayas rojas.
red-blooded ['red'blʌdɪd] *adj* viril, vigoroso, enérgico, de pelo en pecho.
redbreast ['redbrest] *n* (*also* **robin ~**) petirrojo *m*.
red-brick ['redbrɪk] *adj*: **~ building** edificio *m* de ladrillo; **~ university** (*Brit*) universidad *f* de reciente fundación.
redcap ['redkæp] *n* (*Brit Mil*) policía *m* militar; (*US*) mozo *m* de estación.
redcoat ['redkəʊt] *n* (*Brit*) soldado *m* inglés (del siglo XVIII *etc*).
redcurrant ['red'kʌrənt] *n* (*fruit*) grosella *f* roja, (*bush*) grosellero *m* rojo.
redden ['redn] **1** *vt* enrojecer, teñir de rojo. **2** *vi* enrojecerse, ponerse rojo; (*person: with anger*) enrojecerse, (*with shame*) ponerse colorado, ruborizarse.
reddish ['redɪʃ] *adj* rojizo.
redecorate ['riː'dekəreɪt] *vt room* renovar, pintar de nuevo, volver a decorar.
redecoration [riːˌdekə'reɪʃən] *n* renovación *f*.
redeem [rɪ'diːm] **1** *vt* redimir (*also Rel*), rescatar; *mortgage, bonds* amortizar; (*from pawn*) desempeñar; *promise* cumplir; *fault* expiar. **2** *vr*: **to ~ o.s.** salvarse, expiar su falta.
redeemable [rɪ'diːməbl] *adj* redimible; (*Fin*) amortizable; (*Comm*) reembolsable.
Redeemer [rɪ'diːməʳ] *n* Redentor *m*.
redeeming [rɪ'diːmɪŋ] *adj*: **~ feature** rasgo *m* bueno, (*fig*) punto *m* favorable; **~ virtue** virtud *f* compensadora; **I see no ~ feature in it** no le encuentro ningún aspecto bueno.
redefine [ˌriːdɪ'faɪn] *vt* redefinir.
redemption [rɪ'dempʃən] *n* redención *f* (*also Rel*), rescate *m*; (*Fin*) amortización *f*; desempeño *m*; cumplimiento *m*; expiación *f*; **~ price** precio *m* de retroventa; **to be beyond** (*or* **past**) **~** no tener remedio, ser irremediable.
redemptive [rɪ'demptɪv] *adj* redentor.
redeploy ['riːdɪ'plɔɪ] *vt resources, men* disponer de otro modo, reorganizar; utilizar de modo distinto.
redeployment ['riːdɪ'plɔɪmənt] *n* nueva disposición *f*, reorganización *f*; utilización *f* más económica (*or* lógica).
redevelop [ˌriːdɪ'veləp] *vt* reorganizar.
redevelopment [ˌriːdɪ'veləpmənt] *n* reorganización *f*.
red-eyed ['red'aɪd] *adj* con los ojos enrojecidos.
red-faced ['red'feɪst] *adj* (*with anger*) con la cara encendida, con la cara colorada; (*with shame*) colorado, ruboroso, avergonzado.
red-haired ['red'hɛəd] *adj* pelirrojo.
red-handed ['red'hændɪd] *adj*: **to catch sb ~** coger (*LAm*: pillar) a uno con las manos en la masa, coger (*LAm*: pillar) a uno in fraganti.
redhead ['redhed] *n* pelirroja *f*.
red-headed ['red'hedɪd] *adj* pelirrojo.
red-hot ['red'hɒt] *adj* candente; (*fig*) *news* de última hora; *issue* peligrosísimo; de máxima importancia, de la mayor actualidad; *supporter etc* vehemente, acérrimo; **~ player** as *m*.
redial [riː'daɪəl] **1** *vti* volver a marcar. **2** *n*: **automatic ~** marcación *f* automática.
redirect ['riːdaɪ'rekt] *vt letter* reexpedir; *energies* emplear de otro modo; *traffic* desviar, dirigir por otra ruta.
rediscover ['riːdɪs'kʌvəʳ] *vt* volver a descubrir, redescubrir.
rediscovery ['riːdɪs'kʌvərɪ] *n* redescubrimiento *m*.
redistribute ['riːdɪs'trɪbjuːt] *vt* distribuir de nuevo, volver a distribuir.
redistribution ['riːˌdɪstrɪ'bjuːʃən] *n* redistribución *f*, nueva distribución *f*.
red-letter ['red'letəʳ] *adj*: **~ day** día *m* señalado, día *m* especial.
red-light ['red'laɪt] *adj*: **~ district** barrio *m* chino, barrio *m* de los lupanares, zona *f* de tolerancia.
redneck ['rednek] *n* (*US*) campesino *m* blanco (de los estados del Sur); patán *m*.
redness ['rednɪs] *n* rojez *f*, color *m* rojo, lo rojo, lo encarnado.
redo ['riː'duː] (*irr: V* **do**) *vt* rehacer, volver a hacer.
redolence ['redəʊləns] *n* fragancia *f*, perfume *m*.
redolent ['redəʊlənt] *adj*: **~ of** perfumado como, con perfume como el de; **to be ~ of** (*fig*) recordar, hacer pensar en.
redouble [riː'dʌbl] **1** *vt* redoblar, intensificar; (*Bridge*) redoblar. **2** *vi* redoblarse, intensificarse; (*Bridge*) redoblar.
redoubt [rɪ'daʊt] *n* reducto *m*; **the last ~ of ...** el último reducto de ...
redoubtable [rɪ'daʊtəbl] *adj* temible, formidable.
redound [rɪ'daʊnd] *vi*: **to ~ to** redundar en, redundar en beneficio de; **this will hardly ~ to his credit** esto no va a beneficiar su buen nombre.
redraft ['riː'drɑːft] *vt* volver a redactar, hacer un nuevo borrador de, rehacer.
redraw ['riː'drɔː] (*irr: V* **draw**) *vt* volver a dibujar; *map, plan* volver a trazar.
redress [rɪ'dres] **1** *n* reparación *f*, compensación *f*; remedio *m* (legal), derecho *m* a satisfacción; **in such a case you have no ~** en tal caso Vd no tiene ningún derecho a satisfacción; **to seek ~ for** solicitar compensación por, reclamar satisfacción por.
2 *vt* (*readjust*) reajustar; *balance etc* rectificar, corregir; (*make up for*) reparar, compensar; *fault* remediar; *offence* desagraviar, enmendar.
Red Riding Hood ['red'raɪdɪŋhʊd] *nf* Caperucita *f* Roja.
Red Sea ['red'siː] *n* Mar *m* Rojo.
redshank ['redʃæŋk] *n* archibebe *m*.
redskin ['redskɪn] *n* piel roja *mf*.
redstart ['redstɑːt] *n* colirrojo *m* real.
reduce [rɪ'djuːs] **1** *vt* (**a**) reducir (*to* a; *also Math etc*), disminuir; *price* rebajar; (*in rank*) degradar; (*Culin*) hervir y espesar; **to ~ an article by a quarter** abreviar un artículo en la cuarta parte; **to ~ everything to simple terms** ex-

presarlo todo en términos sencillos; **to ~ sth to ashes** reducir algo a cenizas; **to ~ speed** reducir la velocidad; **this ~d him to silence** esto le hizo callar; **we were ~d to begging in the streets** nos vimos sin otro recurso que el de pedir por las calles.
(**b**) (*Mil*: *capture*) tomar, conquistar.
2 *vi* (**a**) reducirse, disminuir; (*Culin*) espesarse.
(**b**) (*slim*) adelgazar.

reduced [rɪ'dju:st] *adj*: **a ~ income** una renta mermada, unos ingresos disminuidos; **at a ~ price** con rebaja, con descuento; **~ goods** mercancías *fpl* rebajadas; **'greatly ~ prices'** 'grandes rebajas'; **'~ to clear'** 'rebajas por liquidación'.

reducible [rɪ'dju:səbl] *adj* reducible.

reduction [rɪ'dʌkʃən] *n* (**a**) reducción *f* (*in, of* de), disminución *f*; (*in price*) rebaja *f*; (*in rank*) degradación *f*; (*shortening*) abreviación *f*; **'great ~s'** (*Comm*) 'grandes rebajas'; **there has been no ~ in demand** no ha disminuido la demanda.
(**b**) (*Mil*) toma *f*, conquista *f*.

redundance [rɪ'dʌndəns] *n* redundancia *f*.

redundancy [rɪ'dʌndənsɪ] **1** *n* exceso *m*, superfluidad *f*; (*of worker*: *euph*) despido *m*; (*among workers*) desempleo *m*; *V* **compulsory** *etc*.
2 *attr*: **~ compensation, ~ payment** (*Brit*) (compensación *f* por) despido *m*, indemnización *f* por desempleo.

redundant [rɪ'dʌndənt] *adj* excesivo, superfluo; (*Gram*) redundante; **to be ~** (*Brit*) estar de más; **the workers now made ~** (*Brit*) los obreros que quedan ahora sin trabajo; **automation may make some workers ~** (*Brit*) la automatización puede hacer que varios obreros pierdan sus puestos.

reduplicate [rɪ'dju:plɪkeɪt] *vt* reduplicar.

reduplication [rɪ,dju:plɪ'keɪʃən] *n* reduplicación *f*.

reduplicative [rɪ'dju:plɪkətɪv] *adj* reduplicativo.

redwing ['redwɪŋ] *n* malvís *m*.

redwood ['redwʊd] *n* secoya *f*.

redye ['ri:'daɪ] *vt* reteñir, volver a teñir.

re-echo ['ri:'ekəʊ] **1** *vt* repetir, resonar con. **2** *vi* resonar, repercutirse.

reed [ri:d] **1** *n* (*Bot*) carrizo *m*, junco *m*, caña *f*; (*Mus*: *in mouthpiece*) lengüeta *f*, (*pipe*) caramillo *m*; **broken ~** (*fig*) persona *f* quemada.
2 *attr* **~ instrument** instrumento *m* de lengüeta; **~ stop** registro *m* de lengüetas.

reedbed ['ri:dbed] *n* carrizal *m*, juncal *m*, cañaveral *m*.

reed bunting ['ri:d'bʌntɪŋ] *n* verderón *m* común.

re-edit ['ri:'edɪt] *vt* reeditar.

reedmace ['ri:dmeɪs] *n* anea *f*, espadaña *f*.

re-educate ['ri:'edjʊkeɪt] *vt* reeducar.

re-education ['ri:,edjʊ'keɪʃən] *n* reeducación *f*.

reed-warbler ['ri:d'wɔ:bləʳ] *n* carricero *m* común.

reedy ['ri:dɪ] *adj* (**a**) *place* lleno de cañas, cubierto de carrizos (*etc*). (**b**) (*Mus*) aflautado, atiplado.

reef¹ [ri:f] (*Naut*) **1** *n* rizo *m*; **to let out a ~** largar rizos, (*fig*) aflojar el cinturón (*etc*); **to take in a ~** tomar rizos, (*fig*) apretar el cinturón (*etc*).
2 *vt* arrizar.

reef² [ri:f] *n* (*Geog*) escollo *m*, arrecife *m*.

reefer¹ ['ri:fəʳ] *n* chaquetón *m*.

reefer²‡ ['ri:fəʳ] *n* porro‡ *m*.

reefknot ['ri:fnɒt] *n* nudo *m* de marino.

reek [ri:k] **1** *n* mal olor *m*, hedor *m* (*of* a).
2 *vi* (*smoke*) humear, vahear; (*smell*) oler, heder, apestar (*of* a); trascender (*of* a); **this ~s of treachery** esto huele a traición; **she ~s with affectation** su afectación es inaguantable; **he comes home simply ~ing** (*of drink*) vuelve a casa que apesta a vino.

reel [ri:l] **1** *n* (*in fishing etc*) carrete *m*; (*for tape recorder etc*) carrete *m*, bobina *f*; (*Sew*) broca *f*, devanadera *f*; (*Phot*: *for small camera*) carrete *f*, película *f*, rollo *m*, (*of cine film*) bobina *f*, cinta *f*; (*Mus*) *baile escocés muy vivo*; **about 20 right off the ~** (*US*) unos 20 seguidos, unos 20 sin parar.
2 *vt* (*Sew*) devanar.
3 *vi* tambalear, tambalearse; (*retreat*) cejar, retroceder; **he was ~ing about drunkenly** andaba haciendo eses; **the boxer ~ed to his corner** el boxeador se fue tambaleando a su rincón; **the mind ~s** la mente queda atolondrada; **we ~ed at the news** la noticia nos atolondró; **to make sb's mind ~** atolondrar a uno; **my head is ~ing** mi cabeza está dando vueltas.
◆reel in *vt*: **to ~ in one's line** ir cobrando el sedal; **to ~ in a fish** tirar de un pez haciendo girar el carrete.
◆reel off *vt* enumerar rápidamente, recitar de una tirada, ensartar.

re-elect ['ri:ɪ'lekt] *vt* reelegir.

re-election ['ri:ɪ'lekʃən] *n* reelección *f*.

re-eligible ['ri:'elɪdʒəbl] *adj* reelegible.

reel-to-reel ['ri:ltə'ri:l] *adj*: **~ tape-recorder** grabadora *f* de bobina.

re-emerge ['ri:ɪ'mɜ:dʒ] *vi* volver a salir, reaparecer.

re-employ [,ri:ɪm'plɔɪ] *vt* volver a emplear.

re-enact ['ri:ɪ'nækt] *vt* (**a**) (*Parl*) volver a promulgar; decretar de nuevo. (**b**) (*Theat etc*) volver a representar; *crime* reconstruir.

re-enactment [,ri:ɪ'næktmənt] *n* reconstrucción *f*.

re-engage ['ri:ɪn'geɪdʒ] *vt* contratar de nuevo.

re-enlist ['ri:ɪn'lɪst] *vi* reengancharse, alistarse de nuevo.

re-enter ['ri:'entəʳ] *vt* reingresar en, volver a entrar en.

re-entry ['ri:'entrɪ] *n* reingreso *m*, segunda entrada *f*; (*of spacecraft*) reentrada *f*, reingreso *m*.

re-equip ['ri:ɪ'kwɪp] *vt* equipar de nuevo (*with* con).

re-erect [,ri:ɪ'rekt] *vt* reerigir.

re-establish ['ri:ɪs'tæblɪʃ] *vt* restablecer.

re-establishment ['ri:ɪs'tæblɪʃmənt] *n* restablecimiento *m*.

reeve¹ [ri:v] *vt* (*Naut*) asegurar (con cabo); pasar por un ojal.

reeve² [ri:v] *n* (*Hist*) baile *m*, juez *m* local.

re-examination ['ri:ɪg,zæmɪ'neɪʃən] *n* reexaminación *f*.

re-examine ['ri:ɪg'zæmɪn] *vt* reexaminar.

re-export ['ri:'ekspɔ:t] **1** *vt* reexportar. **2** *n* reexportación *f*.

ref¹* [ref] *n* (*Sport*) árbitro *m*.

ref² (**a**) *prep abbr of* **with reference to** respecto de. (**b**) (*in letter-head*) *n abbr of* **reference** referencia *f*.

reface ['ri:'feɪs] *vt* revestir de nuevo, forrar de nuevo (*with* de), poner un nuevo revestimiento a.

refashion ['ri:'fæʃən] *vt* formar de nuevo, rehacer.

refectory [rɪ'fektərɪ] *n* refectorio *m*.

refer [rɪ'fɜ:ʳ] **1** *vt* (**a**) (*send, direct*) remitir; **to ~ sth (back) to sb** remitir algo a uno; **to ~ sb to sth** remitir a uno a algo; **the reader is ~red to page 15** remito al lector a la página 15; **it is ~red to us for decision** se remite a nosotros para que decidamos; **to ~ a matter to a lawyer** entregar un asunto a un abogado; **a cheque ~red to drawer (R/D)** un cheque protestado por falta de fondos.
(**b**) (*ascribe*) atribuir, referir (*to* a); relacionar (*to* con); **he ~s his mistake to tiredness** el error lo achaca a su cansancio; **he ~s the painting to the 14th century** atribuye el cuadro al siglo XIV; **this insect is to be ~red to the genus Pieris** este insecto ha de clasificarse en el género Pieris.
2 *vi*: **to ~ to** referirse a, aludir a, mencionar, hacer referencia a; **I ~ to our worthy president** me refiero a nuestro digno presidente; **we will not ~ to it again** no lo volveremos a mencionar; **~ring to yours of the 5th** me refiero a su carta del 5; **please ~ to section 3** véase la sección 3; **you must ~ to the original** hay que recurrir al original; **to ~ to one's notes** consultar sus notas.
◆refer back *vt* remitir.

referable [rɪ'fɜ:rəbl] *adj*: **~ to** referible a; atribuible a; que ha de clasificarse en.

referee [,refə'ri:] **1** *n* (**a**) (*in dispute, Sport etc*) árbitro *mf*; (*of learned paper*) evaluador *m*, -ora *f*.
(**b**) (*Brit*: *of person, for post*) referencia *f*; **Pérez has named you as a ~** Pérez dice que Vd está dispuesto a dar informes sobre él.
2 *vt* (**a**) *game* dirigir, arbitrar en. (**b**) *learned paper* evaluar.
3 *vi* arbitrar.

reference ['refrəns] **1** *n* (**a**) (*act of referring*) remisión *f*; **it was agreed without ~ to me** se acordó sin consultarme, se decidió sin que se pidiera mi parecer.
(**b**) (*bearing*) relación *f* (*to* con); **for future ~, please note that ...** por si importa en el futuro, obsérvese que ...; **I'll keep it for future ~** lo guardo por si importa en el futuro; **with ~ to** en cuanto a, respecto de; **with ~ to yours of the 8th** me refiero a su carta del 8; **without ~ to any particular case** sin referirme (*etc*) a ningún caso concreto; **what ~ has A to B?** ¿qué tiene que ver A con B?; **it has no ~ to what I asked** no tiene que ver con lo que yo pregunté.
(**c**) (*allusion*) referencia *f*, alusión *f*, mención *f*; **he spoke without any ~ to you** habló sin mencionarte para nada; **to make ~ to** referirse a, hacer referencia de.
(**d**) (*directive*) referencia *f*; número *m* de referencia *f*; sigla *f*; (*Typ*: *also* **~ mark**) llamada *f*; **'~ XYZ2'** 'número

de referencia: XYZ2'; **a ~ in the margin** una referencia al margen.

(**e**) (*testimonial*) referencia *f*; informe *m*; (*person*) persona *f* a quien se puede acudir para pedir una referencia; **to have good ~s** tener buenas referencias; **to take up sb's ~s** pedir referencias (*or* informes) acerca de uno.

2 *attr* de referencia; **~ book** libro *m* de consulta; **~ library** biblioteca *f* de consulta; **~ number** número *m* de referencia; **~ point** punto *m* de referencia; **~ price** (*Agr*) precio *m* de referencia.

referendum [ˌrefə'rendəm] *n, pl* **~s** *or* **referenda** [ˌrefə'rendə] referéndum *m.*

refill 1 ['riːfɪl] *n* repuesto *m*, recambio *m*; (*for pencil*) mina *f*; **would you like a ~?** ¿te pongo más vino? (*etc*), ¿otro vaso? **2** ['riː'fɪl] *vt* rellenar, volver a llenar.

refinance [rɪː'faɪ'næns] *vt* refinanciar.

refine [rɪ'faɪn] **1** *vt* refinar; purificar; *society etc* refinar, educar, hacer más culto; *methods* refinar; *style* limar, purificar; *oil etc* refinar; *metal* acrisolar, acendrar; *fats* clarificar.

2 *vi*: **to ~ upon sth** refinar algo, mejorar algo; (*discuss*) discutir algo con mucha sutileza.

refined [rɪ'faɪnd] *adj* (**a**) refinado. (**b**) *society, person* fino, culto; (*pej*) redicho, afectado; *style* elegante, pulido.

refinement [rɪ'faɪnmənt] *n* (**a**) refinamiento *m*; (*act, Tech*) refinación *f*; purificación *f*.

(**b**) (*of society, person*) finura *f*, cultura *f*, educación *f*; (*pej*) afectación *f*; (*of style*) elegancia *f*, urbanidad *f*; **a person of some ~** una persona fina; **that is a ~ of cruelty** eso es ser más cruel todavía; **with every possible ~ of cruelty** con las formas más refinadas de la crueldad.

refiner [rɪ'faɪnə^r] *n* refinador *m.*

refinery [rɪ'faɪnərɪ] *n* refinería *f.*

refit ['riː'fɪt] **1** *n* reparación *f*, compostura *f*; (*Naut*) reparación *f*, carenadura *f*.

2 *vt* reparar, componer; (*Naut*) reparar, carenar; **to ~ sth with a device** volver a equipar algo con un dispositivo.

3 *vi* (*Naut*) repararse.

refitting ['riː'fɪtɪŋ] *n*, **refitment** ['riː'fɪtmənt] *n* reparación *f*, compostura *f*; (*Naut*) reparación *f*, carenadura *f*.

reflate [ˌriː'fleɪt] *vt* reflacionar.

reflation [riː'fleɪʃən] *n* reflación *f.*

reflationary [riː'fleɪʃnərɪ] *adj* reactivador, reflacionario.

reflect [rɪ'flekt] **1** *vt* (**a**) reflejar; **plants ~ed in the water** plantas *fpl* reflejadas en el agua; **the difficulties are ~ed in his report** el informe se hace eco de las dificultades, las dificultades se reflejan en su informe; **the speech ~s credit on him** el discurso le hace honor.

(**b**) **to ~ that ...** pensar que ...

2 *vi* (*think*) reflexionar, pensar; meditar; **~ before you act** reflexione antes de obrar; **if we but ~ a moment** sí sólo reflexionamos un instante.

◆**reflect (up)on** *vt*: **~ (up)on it!** ¡medítelo!; **that ~s well (up)on him** eso le hace honor; **that ~s ill (up)on him** eso le muestra bajo una luz poco favorable; **it ~s (up)on all of us** eso tiende a perjudicarnos (*or* desprestigiarnos) a todos; **it ~s (up)on her reputation** eso pone en tela de duda su fama.

reflection [rɪ'flekʃən] *n* (**a**) (*of light*: *act*) reflexión *f*, (*image*) reflejo *m*; **the ~ of the light in the mirror** el reflejo de la luz en el espejo; **a pale ~ of former glories** un pálido reflejo de glorias pasadas; **to see one's ~ in a shop window** verse reflejado en un escaparate.

(**b**) (*aspersion*) reproche *m* (*on* a), crítica *f*; **this is no ~ on your honesty** esto no dice nada en contra de su honradez, esto no es ningún reproche a su honradez; **to cast ~s on sb** reprochar a uno.

(**c**) (*reconsideration*) **on ~** después de volver a pensarlo, pensándolo bien; **without due ~** sin pensarlo bastante; **mature ~ suggests that ...** una meditación más profunda indica que ...

(**d**) (*idea*) pensamiento *m*, idea *f*; **'R~s on Ortega'** 'Meditación *f* sobre Ortega'.

reflective [rɪ'flektɪv] *adj* (**a**) *surface* brillante, lustroso. (**b**) (*thoughtful*) pensativo, meditabundo. (**c**) **to be ~ of** reflejar.

reflectively [rɪ'flektɪvlɪ] *adv* pensativamente; **he said ~** dijo pensativo; **she looked at me ~** me miró pensativa.

reflector [rɪ'flektə^r] *n* reflector *m*; (*Aut*: *also* **rear ~**) reflectante *m*, captafaros *m.*

reflex ['riːfleks] **1** *adj* reflejo. **2** *n* reflejo *m.*

reflexive [rɪ'fleksɪv] **1** *adj* reflexivo; **~ pronoun** pronombre *m* reflexivo; **~ verb** verbo *m* reflexivo. **2** *n* pronombre *m* reflexivo; verbo *m* reflexivo.

reflexively [rɪ'fleksɪvlɪ] *adv* reflexivamente.

refloat ['riː'fləʊt] *vt* desencallar, desvarar, poner a flote, reflotar.

reflux ['riːflʌks] *n* reflujo *m.*

reforest ['riː'fɒrɪst] *vt* repoblar de árboles.

reforestation ['riːˌfɒrɪs'teɪʃən] *n* repoblación *f* forestal.

reform [rɪ'fɔːm] **1** *n* reforma *f*; **~ school** (*US*) reformatorio *m.* **2** *vt* reformar. **3** *vi* reformarse.

re-form ['riː'fɔːm] **1** *vt* formar de nuevo, volver a formar; reorganizar, reconstituir. **2** *vi* formarse de nuevo, volver a formarse; reconstituirse; (*Mil*) rehacerse.

reformat ['riː'fɔːmæt] *vt* reformatear.

reformation [ˌrefə'meɪʃən] *n* reformación *f*; **R~** (*Eccl*) Reforma *f*.

reformatory [rɪ'fɔːmətərɪ] *n* (*Brit*) reformatorio *m.*

reformed [rɪ'fɔːmd] *adj* reformado.

reformer [rɪ'fɔːmə^r] *n* reformador *m*, -ora *f*.

reformist [rɪ'fɔːmɪst] **1** *adj* reformista. **2** *n* reformista *mf.*

refract [rɪ'frækt] *vt* refractar.

refracting [rɪ'fræktɪŋ] *adj*: **~ telescope** telescopio *m* de refracción, telescopio *m* refractor.

refraction [rɪ'frækʃən] *n* refracción *f.*

refractive [rɪ'fræktɪv] *adj* refractivo.

refractor [rɪ'fræktə^r] *n* refractor *m.*

refractoriness [rɪ'fræktərɪnɪs] *n* obstinacia *f.*

refractory [rɪ'fræktərɪ] *adj* (**a**) refractario, obstinado. (**b**) (*Tech*) refractario.

refrain[1] [rɪ'freɪn] *n* estribillo *m*; **his constant ~ is ...** siempre está con la misma canción ...

refrain[2] [rɪ'freɪn] *vi*: **to ~ from sth** abstenerse de algo; **to ~ from** + *ger* abstenerse de + *infin*; **I couldn't ~ from laughing** no pude menos de reír, no pude contener la risa, no pude dejar de reír.

refresh [rɪ'freʃ] **1** *vt* refrescar; **to ~ sb's memory** recordar algo a uno. **2** *vr*: **to ~ o.s.** refrescarse, tomar un refresco.

refresher [rɪ'freʃə^r] **1** *n* (**a**) refresco *m.* (**b**) (*Jur*) honorarios *mpl* suplementarios. **2** *attr*: **~ course** curso *m* de actualización, curso *m* de repaso.

refreshing [rɪ'freʃɪŋ] *adj* (**a**) refrescante. (**b**) (*fig*) interesante, estimulante; **it's a ~ change to find this** es interesante encontrar esta novedad, es alentador encontrar esto; **it's ~ to hear some new ideas** da gusto escuchar nuevas ideas.

refreshingly [rɪ'freʃɪŋlɪ] *adv*: **~ different** tan nuevo que resulta alentador.

refreshment [rɪ'freʃmənt] **1** *n* refresco *m*; refrigerio *m*; **'R~s'** 'Refrescos'; **'R~s will be served'** 'se servirá un refrigerio'; **to take some ~** tomar algo, comer (*or* beber *etc*).

2 *attr*: **~ bar** chiringuito *m* de refrescos; **~ room** (*Rail*) cantina *f*, comedor *m* (*LAm*); **~ stall, ~ stand** puesto *m* de refrescos.

refrigerant [rɪ'frɪdʒərənt] *n* refrigerante *m.*

refrigerate [rɪ'frɪdʒəreɪt] *vt* refrigerar.

refrigeration [rɪˌfrɪdʒə'reɪʃən] *n* refrigeración *f.*

refrigerator [rɪ'frɪdʒəreɪtə^r] **1** *n* frigorífico *m*, refrigerador *m*, nevera *f*, refrigeradora *f* (*LAm*), heladera *f* (*SC*). **2** *attr*: **~ lorry** camión *m* frigorífico; **~ ship** buque *m* frigorífico.

refuel ['riː'fjʊəl] **1** *vt* reabastecer (*or* rellenar) de combustible; *speculation etc* renovar, volver a despertar. **2** *vi* repostar, repostar combustible.

refuelling, (*US*) **refueling** ['riː'fjʊəlɪŋ] *n* reabastecimiento *m* (*or* rellenado *m*) de combustible, repostaje *m*; **~ stop** escala *f* para repostar.

refuge ['refjuːdʒ] *n* refugio *m*, asilo *m*; (*resort*) recurso *m*; (*hut*) albergue *m*; **God is my ~** Dios es mi amparo; **to seek ~** buscar dónde guarecerse; **to take ~** ponerse al abrigo, guarecerse; **to take ~ in** refugiarse en, (*fig*) acogerse a, recurrir a.

refugee [ˌrefjʊ'dʒiː] *n* refugiado *m*, -a *f*; **~ camp** campamento *m* de refugiados; **~ from justice** prófugo *m* de la justicia; **~ status** status *m* de refugiado.

refulgence [rɪ'fʌldʒəns] *n* refulgencia *f.*

refulgent [rɪ'fʌldʒənt] *adj* refulgente.

refund 1 ['riːfʌnd] *n* (*act*) devolución *f*; (*amount*) reembolso *m.* **2** [rɪ'fʌnd] *vt* devolver, reintegrar, reembolsar.

refundable [rɪ'fʌndəbl] *adj* reintegrable, reembolsable.

refurbish ['riː'fɜːbɪʃ] *vt* restaurar; (*decorate*) renovar; *literary work* refundir.

refurnish ['riː'fɜːnɪʃ] *vt* amueblar de nuevo.

refusal [rɪ'fjuːzəl] *n* (**a**) negativa *f*, denegación *f*; **a blank** (*or* **flat**) **~** una rotunda negativa; **the offer met a flat ~** rechazaron la oferta de plano.

(**b**) (*Comm etc*) opción *f*, opción *f* exclusiva; **you have first** ~ Vd tiene opción al artículo, lo ofreceré primero a Vd.

refuse[1] ['refju:s] **1** *n* basura *f*, desperdicios *mpl*, desecho *m*. **2** *attr*: ~ **bin** cubo *m* (*LAm*: bote *m*) de la basura; ~ **chute** rampa *f* de desperdicios, rampa *f* de la basura; ~ **collection** recolección *f* de basuras; ~ **collector** basurero *m*; ~ **disposal** eliminación *f* de basuras; ~ **disposal unit** triturador *m* de basura; ~ **dump** vertedero *m*; ~ **lorry** camión *m* de la basura.

refuse[2] [rɪ'fju:z] **1** *vt* rehusar, rechazar, denegar; no querer aceptar; negar; **to** ~ **to** + *infin* negarse a + *infin*, rehusar + *infin*; **to** ~ **sb sth** negar algo a uno; **they can** ~ **her nothing** son incapaces de privarla de nada; **I have never been ~d here** aquí no se han negado nunca a servirme; **she ~d my offer** rechazó mi oferta; **I regret to have to** ~ **your invitation** siento no poder aceptar su invitación.

2 *vi* (**a**) **he ~d** se negó a hacerlo.

(**b**) (*of horse*) rehusar, plantarse, resistirse a saltar.

3 *vr*: **to** ~ **o.s. sth** privarse de algo.

refutable [rɪ'fju:təbl] *adj* refutable.

refutation [,refjʊ'teɪʃən] *n* refutación *f*.

refute [rɪ'fju:t] *vt* refutar, rebatir.

regain [rɪ'geɪn] *vt* cobrar, recobrar, recuperar; *breath* cobrar; **to** ~ **consciousness** recobrar el conocimiento, volver en sí.

regal ['ri:gəl] *adj* regio, real.

regale [rɪ'geɪl] **1** *vt* agasajar, festejar; **to** ~ **sb on oysters** agasajar a uno con ostras; **he ~d the company with a funny story** para divertirles les contó a los comensales un chiste.

2 *vr*: **to** ~ **o.s. on** (*or* **with**) **sth** regalarse con algo, darse el lujo de algo.

regalia [rɪ'geɪlɪə] *n* insignias *fpl* (*esp* reales).

regally ['ri:gəlɪ] *adv* regiamente; con pompa (*etc*) regia.

regard [rɪ'gɑ:d] **1** *n* (**a**) (*gaze*) mirada *f*.

(**b**) (*aspect, point*) respecto *m*; aspecto *m*; **in** ~ **to, with** ~ **to** con respecto a, en cuanto a, por lo que se refiere a; **in this** ~ con respecto a esto.

(**c**) (*attention, care*) atención *f*; **without** ~ **to** sin hacer caso de, sin considerar; **having** ~ **to** en atención a, teniendo en cuenta; **to have no** ~ **to** (*of person*) no prestar atención a, no tener en cuenta; (*of relationship*) no guardar relación con, no tener que ver con; ~ **must be had to this matter** hay que tener en cuenta este asunto.

(**d**) (*esteem*) respeto *m*, consideración *f*, estimación *f*; **my** ~ **for him** el respeto que le tengo; **out of** ~ **for** por respeto a; **to have a high** ~ **for sb, to hold sb in high** ~ tener un gran concepto de uno, estimar mucho a uno; **to show** ~ **for sb** mostrar respeto por uno; **he shows little** ~ **for their feelings** le importan poco sus susceptibilidades.

(**e**) (*in messages*) **~s** recuerdos *mpl*; **~s to X, please give my ~s to X** recuerdos a X, saluda de mi parte a X; **with kind ~s** con muchos recuerdos.

2 *vt* (**a**) (*look at*) mirar; observar; **she ~ed me with astonishment** me miró atónita.

(**b**) (*consider*) considerar; **we** ~ **it as worth doing** consideramos que vale la pena hacerlo; **we don't** ~ **it as necessary** no creemos que sea necesario; **they** ~ **it with horror** lo ven con horror; **to** ~ **sb with suspicion** recelarse de uno.

(**c**) **as ~s** (*regarding*) en cuanto a, por lo que se refiere a.

(**d**) **highly ~ed** muy estimado, muy bien reputado.

regardful [rɪ'gɑ:dfʊl] *adj*: ~ **of** atento a.

regarding [rɪ'gɑ:dɪŋ] *prep* en cuanto a, por lo que se refiere a; **and other things** ~ **money** y otras cosas relativas al dinero.

regardless [rɪ'gɑ:dlɪs] **1** *adj*: ~ **of** indiferente a; insensible a; sin hacer caso de, sin pensar para nada en, sin miramientos de; **buy it** ~ **of the cost** cómpralo cueste lo que cueste; **they shot them all** ~ **of rank** los fusilaron a todos sin miramientos a su graduación; **we did it** ~ **of the consequences** lo hicimos sin tener en cuenta las consecuencias.

2 *adv* a pesar de todo; pese a quien pese; **he went on** ~ continuó sin prestar atención a esto, a pesar de esto siguió adelante; **press on ~!** ¡echa por la calle de en medio!

regatta [rɪ'gætə] *n* regata *f*.

regd *adj* (**a**) (*Comm*) *abbr of* **registered** registrado. (**b**) (*Post*) *abbr of* **registered.**

regency ['ri:dʒənsɪ] *n* regencia *f*; **R~ furniture** mobiliario *m* Regencia, mobiliario *m* estilo Regencia.

regenerate 1 [rɪ'dʒenərɪt] *adj* regenerado. **2** [rɪ'dʒenəreɪt] *vt* regenerar.

regeneration [rɪ,dʒenə'reɪʃən] *n* regeneración *f*.

regenerative [rɪ'dʒenərətɪv] *adj* regenerador.

regent ['ri:dʒənt] **1** *adj*: **prince** ~ príncipe *m* regente. **2** *n* regente *mf*.

reggae ['regeɪ] *n* reggae *m*.

regicide ['redʒɪsaɪd] *n* (**a**) (*act*) regicidio *m*. (**b**) (*person*) regicida *mf*.

régime [reɪ'ʒi:m] *n* régimen *m*; **ancien** ~ antiguo régimen *m*; **under the Nazi** ~ bajo el régimen de los nazis.

regimen ['redʒɪmən] *n* régimen *m*.

regiment 1 ['redʒɪmənt] *n* (*Mil*) regimiento *m*; **a whole** ~ **of mice** todo un ejército de ratones.

2 ['redʒɪment] *vt* organizar muy estrictamente; reglamentar; **we are very ~ed at the college** en el colegio nuestra vida está muy reglamentada.

regimental [,redʒɪ'mentl] **1** *adj* de regimiento, del regimiento; (*fig*) militar; **with** ~ **precision** con precisión militar. **2** *npl*: **~s** (*Mil*) uniforme *m*.

regimentation [,redʒɪmen'teɪʃən] reglamentación *f*, organización *f* estricta.

Reginald ['redʒɪnld] *nm* Reinaldo, Reginaldo.

region ['ri:dʒən] *n* región *f*; comarca *f*; zona *f*; **a fertile** ~ una región fértil; **the lower ~s** (*fig*) el infierno; **in the** ~ **of 40** alrededor de 40, unos 40; **I felt a pain in the kidney** ~ sentí un dolor de riñones, sentí un dolor a la altura de los riñones.

regional ['ri:dʒənl] *adj* regional; ~ **council** (*Scot*) consejo *m* regional; ~ **development** desarrollo *m* regional; ~ **development grant** subsidio *m* para el desarrollo regional.

regionalism ['ri:dʒənəlɪzəm] *n* regionalismo *m*.

regionalist ['ri:dʒənəlɪst] **1** *adj* regionalista. **2** *n* regionalista *mf*.

register ['redʒɪstə[r]] **1** *n* registro *m*; (*Mus, Typ, of hotel*) registro *m*; (*in school*) lista *f*; (*of members*) lista *f*, padrón *m*; (*Univ, Naut*) matrícula *f*; (*Tech*) indicador *m*; (*Ling*) registro *m*, estilo *m*; (*US*: **cash** ~) caja *f* registradora; ~ **of births** registro *m* de nacimientos; **R~ of Companies** Registro *m* de Empresas; ~ **of deaths** registro *m* de defunciones; ~ **of marriages** registro *m* de casamientos; ~ **of voters** registro *m* electoral; **to be in** ~ (*Typ*) estar en registro; **to call the** ~ (*Scol*) pasar lista; **to sign the** ~ (*in hotel*) firmar el registro.

2 *attr*: ~ **office** *V* **registry**; **a ship of 50,000 gross** ~ **tons** un buque de 50.000 toneladas de registro bruto.

3 *vt* (**a**) (*record*) registrar; *birth etc* declarar; *trademark etc* registrar; (*record*) apuntar, registrar, hacer constar; (*Univ, Naut*) matricular; (*by post*) certificar, (*by rail*) facturar.

(**b**) (*show, indicate*) marcar, indicar; *emotion* acusar, mostrar, manifestar; **the thermometer ~s 40 degrees** el termómetro marca 40 grados; **he ~ed no surprise** no acusó sorpresa alguna; **the patient has ~ed a marked improvement** el enfermo ha acusado una notable mejoría; **production has ~ed a big fall** la producción ha experimentado un descenso considerable.

(**c**) (*take note of*) darse cuenta de; **I ~ed the fact that she had gone** me di cuenta de que se había ido.

4 *vi* (**a**) (*sign on etc*) inscribirse, matricularse; (*for conference*) inscribirse; **to** ~ **at an hotel** registrarse en un hotel; **to** ~ **for a course** matricularse en un curso; **to** ~ **with a doctor** inscribirse en la lista de un médico.

(**b**) (*Typ*) estar en registro.

(**c**) (*be understood*) producir impresión (*with* en); **it doesn't seem to have ~ed with her** parece no haber producido impresión en ella; **when it finally ~ed** cuando por fin cayó en la cuenta, cuando por fin comprendió; **things like that just don't** ~ las cosas así pasan inadvertidas.

registered ['redʒɪstəd] *adj letter, mail, post* certificado, *baggage* facturado; *design, trademark etc* registrado; *student etc* matriculado; *charity* legalizado, legalmente constituido; ~ **company** sociedad *f* legalmente constituida; ~ **nurse** (*US*) enfermero *m* calificado, enfermera *f* calificada; ~ **office** domicilio *m* social.

registrar [,redʒɪs'trɑ:[r]] *n* registrador *m*, -ora *f*; archivero *m*, -a *f*; (*of society*) secretario *m*, -a *f*; (*Brit Univ*) secretario *m*, -a *f* general; (*Brit*: *of births etc*) secretario *m*, -a *f* del registro civil; (*Brit Med*) médico *m*, -a *f* asistente.

registration [,redʒɪs'treɪʃən] **1** *n* (*act*) registro *m*; inscripción *f*; matrícula *f*; declaración *f*; certificación *f*, facturación *f*; (*Aut, Naut, Univ etc*: *number*) matrícula *f*.

2 *attr*: ~ **document** (*Brit Aut*) documento *m* de matriculación; ~ **fee** derechos *mpl* de matriculación; ~ **form** formulario *m* de inscripción; ~ **number** (*Brit Aut*) matrícula *f*; ~ **tag** (*US Aut*) (placa *f* de) matrícula *f*.

registry [ˈredʒɪstrɪ] **1** *n* registro *m*, archivo *m*; (*Univ etc*) secretaría *f* general; **servants'** ~ agencia *f* de colocaciones.

2 *attr*: ~ **office** (*Brit*) juzgado *m* municipal, registro *m* civil; **to get married at a** ~ **office** casarse por lo civil, casarse por el juzgado.

Regius [ˈriːdʒjəs] *adj* (*Brit Univ*) regio.

regress 1 [ˈriːgres] *n* regreso *m*. **2** [rɪˈgres] *vi* regresar.

regression [rɪˈgreʃən] *n* regresión *f*.

regressive [rɪˈgresɪv] *adj* regresivo.

regret [rɪˈgret] **1** *n* (**a**) sentimiento *m*, pesar *m*; remordimiento *m*; **much to my** ~, **to my great** ~ con gran pesar mío; **to express one's** ~ **to sb** (*for act*) expresar su sentimiento a uno, disculparse con uno, (*for death etc*) enviar el pésame a uno; **to feel** ~ sentirlo, sentir pesar; **I have no** ~**s** no me arrepiento de ello; **I say it with** ~ lo digo con pesar.

(**b**) (*in messages*) ~**s** (*excuses*) excusas *fpl*; **to send one's** ~**s for not being able to come** mandar sus excusas por no poder venir.

2 *vt* sentir, lamentar; arrepentirse de; **I** ~ **the error** lamento el error; **it is to be** ~**ted** es de sentir, es de lamentar; **to** ~ **that** ... sentir que + *subj*, lamentar que + *subj*; **we** ~ **to inform you that** ... lamentamos tener que informarle que ...; **he** ~**s saying it** lamenta haberlo dicho, se arrepiente de haberlo dicho.

regretful [rɪˈgretfʊl] *adj* pesaroso; arrepentido; **to be** ~ **that** ... lamentar que + *subj*; **he was most** ~ **about it** lo lamentó profundamente; **we are not** ~ **about leaving** no nos pesa tener que partir.

regretfully [rɪˈgretfəlɪ] *adv* con pesar, sentidamente; **she spoke** ~ habló con sentimiento; ~ **I have to tell you that** ... siento tener que decirles que ...

regrettable [rɪˈgretəbl] *adj* lamentable, deplorable; *loss etc* sensible.

regrettably [rɪˈgretəblɪ] *adv* lamentablemente; **there were** ~ **few replies** hubo tan pocas respuestas que daba lástima.

regroup [ˈriːˈgruːp] **1** *vt* reagrupar; (*Mil etc*) reorganizar.

2 *vi* reagruparse; (*Mil etc*) reorganizarse.

regrouping [ˈriːˈgruːpɪŋ] *n* reagrupación *f*; reorganización *f*.

Regt. *abbr of* **Regiment** regimiento *m*, regto.

regular [ˈregjʊləʳ] **1** *adj* (**a**) (*gen*) regular; (*Eccl, Mil, Gram etc*) regular; uniforme; normal, corriente, constante; *meeting* ordinario; *attender, reader etc* habitual, asiduo; **our** ~ **waiter** el camarero que suele servirnos; **the** ~ **travellers on a train** los que siempre viajan en un tren; ~ **customer** cliente *mf* habitual; ~ **feature** (*of newspaper*) crónica *f* regular; ~ **size** (*US*) tamaño *m* normal; **the** ~ **staff** los empleados permanentes; ~ **troops** tropas *fpl* regulares; **as a** ~ **reader of your journal, may I** ... como lector habitual de su revista, me permito ...; **as** ~ **as clockwork** como un reloj; **X has been Y's** ~ **escort** X ha sido el acompañante fijo de Y; **to have a** ~ **time for doing sth** tener hora fija para hacer algo, hacer algo siempre a la misma hora; **to make** ~ **use of sth** usar algo con regularidad.

(**b**) (*systematic*) sistemático, regular; (*consistent*) constante; ~ **features** facciones *fpl* correctas; **a man of** ~ **habits** un hombre ordenado (en sus costumbres).

(**c**) (*normal*) normal, corriente; **the** ~ **word is 'looking glass'** la palabra corriente es 'espejo'; **it's perfectly** ~ es completamente normal; **it's quite** ~ **to see deer here** es corriente ver ciervos por aquí.

(**d**) (*****) cabal, verdadero; **a** ~ **feast** un verdadero banquete; **there was a** ~ **quarrel** se riñó de verdad; **he's a** ~ **guy** (*US*) es buen chico, es un tipo estupendo*.

2 *n* (*Eccl*) regular *m*; (*Mil*) soldado *m* de línea; (*client etc*) parroquiano *m*, -a *f*, cliente *mf* habitual; (*US*: *gas*) gasolina *f* normal; **one of the café** ~**s** un asiduo del café; **we keep the best goods for our** ~**s** guardamos lo mejor para nuestros clientes habituales.

regularity [ˌregjʊˈlærɪtɪ] *n* regularidad *f*; **with great** ~ con la mayor regularidad.

regularize [ˈregjʊləraɪz] *vt* regularizar; formalizar; normalizar; arreglar, poner en orden; **in order to** ~ **your position** para arreglar su situación.

regularly [ˈregjʊləlɪ] *adv* regularmente, con regularidad; **'use brand X** ~**'** 'use la marca X con regularidad'; **he's** ~ **late** siempre llega con retraso; **a** ~ **declined noun** un sustantivo de declinación regular; **this ground has been** ~ **fought over** sobre este terreno se ha luchado constantemente.

regulate [ˈregjʊleɪt] *vt* regular (*also Mech etc*); arreglar, ajustar; (*make regulations for*) reglamentar; **to** ~ **one's life by** ... vivir según las normas establecidas por ..., vivir con arreglo a ...; **a well** ~**d life** una vida ordenada; **to** ~ **prices** regular los precios.

regulation [ˌregjʊˈleɪʃən] **1** *n* (**a**) (*act*) regulación *f*; arreglo *m*.

(**b**) (*rule*) regla *f*; reglamento *m*.

2 *attr* reglamentario, de reglamento; normal; **it's** ~ **wear in school** es el uniforme del reglamento en la escuela.

regulative [ˈregjʊlətɪv] *adj* reglamentario.

regulator [ˈregjʊleɪtəʳ] *n* regulador *m*.

regulatory [ˈregjʊˌleɪtərɪ] *adj* regulador.

regulo [ˈregjʊləʊ] *n número del mando de temperatura de un horno a gas.*

regurgitate [rɪˈgɜːdʒɪteɪt] **1** *vt* volver a arrojar, vomitar (sin esfuerzo); (*fig*) reproducir maquinalmente. **2** *vi* regurgitar.

regurgitation [rɪˈgɜːdʒɪˈteɪʃən] *n* regurgitación *f*; (*fig*) reproducción *f* maquinal.

rehabilitate [ˌriːəˈbɪlɪteɪt] *vt* rehabilitar.

rehabilitation [ˈriːəˌbɪlɪˈteɪʃən] *n* rehabilitación *f*.

rehash [ˈriːˈhæʃ] **1** *n* refrito *m*. **2** *vt* hacer un refrito de.

rehearsal [rɪˈhɜːsəl] *n* enumeración *f*, repetición *f*; (*Mus, Theat etc*) ensayo *m*; **it was just a** ~ **for bigger things to come** fue a modo de ensayo para las empresas mayores que habían de venir después.

rehearse [rɪˈhɜːs] *vt* enumerar, repetir; (*Mus, Theat etc*) ensayar.

rehouse [ˈriːˈhaʊz] *vt family* dar nueva vivienda a, proveer de vivienda nueva; trasladar a otra casa; **200 families have been** ~**d** 200 familias tienen vivienda nueva ya.

reification [ˌriːɪfɪˈkeɪʃən] *n* cosificación *f*.

reify [ˈriːɪˌfaɪ] *vt* cosificar.

reign [reɪn] **1** *n* reinado *m*; (*fig*) dominio *m*, predominio *m*; **the** ~ **of the miniskirt** la moda de la minifalda; ~ **of terror** régimen *m* del terror; **in** (*or* **under**) **the** ~ **of** bajo el reinado de.

2 *vi* reinar; (*fig*) predominar, imperar, prevalecer; **total silence** ~**ed** reinaba el silencio más absoluto; **it is better to** ~ **in hell than serve in heaven** más vale ser cabeza de ratón que cola de león.

reigning [ˈreɪnɪŋ] *adj monarch* reinante, actual; (*fig*) predominante, que impera.

reimburse [ˌriːɪmˈbɜːs] *vt* reembolsar; **to** ~ **sb for sth** pagar (*or* reembolsar) a uno por algo.

reimbursement [ˌriːɪmˈbɜːsmənt] *n* reembolso *m*.

reimpose [ˈriːɪmˈpəʊz] *vt* volver a imponer, reimponer.

rein [reɪn] *n* rienda *f*; **to draw** ~ detenerse, tirar de la rienda (*also fig*); **to give** (**free**) ~ **to** dar rienda suelta a; **to keep a tight** ~ **on sb** atar corto a uno; **we must keep a tight** ~ **on expenditure** tenemos que restringir los gastos.

◆rein back *vt* refrenar.

◆rein in 1 *vt* refrenar. **2** *vi* detenerse.

reincarnate [ˌriːɪnˈkɑːneɪt] *vt* reencarnar; **to be** ~**d** reencarnar, volver a encarnar.

reincarnation [ˈriːɪnkɑːˈneɪʃən] *n* reencarnación *f*.

reindeer [ˈreɪndɪəʳ] *n* reno *m*.

reinforce [ˌriːɪnˈfɔːs] *vt* reforzar (*also fig*); *concrete etc* armar.

reinforced [ˌriːɪnˈfɔːst] *adj* reforzado; *concrete* armado.

reinforcement [ˌriːɪnˈfɔːsmənt] *n* (*act*) reforzamiento *m*; ~**s** refuerzos *mpl*.

reinsert [ˈriːɪnˈsɜːt] *vt* volver a insertar, reinsertar; volver a introducir.

reinstate [ˈriːɪnˈsteɪt] *vt suppressed passage etc* reintegrar (*in* a), volver a incluir; (*rehabilitate*) rehabilitar; *dismissed worker* volver a emplear; *dismissed official* restituir a su puesto, reintegrar, reinstalar.

reinstatement [ˈriːɪnˈsteɪtmənt] *n* reintegración *f* (*in* a); rehabilitación *f*; vuelta *f* a su empleo; restitución *f* a su puesto, reinstalación *f*.

reinsurance [ˈriːɪnˈʃʊərəns] *n* reaseguro *m*.

reinsure [ˈriːɪnˈʃʊəʳ] *vt* reasegurar.

reintegrate [ˈriːˈɪntɪgreɪt] *vt* reintegrar; (*socially*) reinsertar (*into* en).

reintegration [ˈriːɪntɪˈgreɪʃən] *n* reintegración *f*; reinserción *f*.

reinter [ˈriːɪnˈtɜːʳ] *vt* enterrar de nuevo.

reinvest [ˈriːɪnˈvest] *vt* reinvertir, volver a invertir.

reinvestment [ˈriːɪnˈvestmənt] *n* reinversión *f*.

reinvigorate [ˈriːɪnˈvɪgəreɪt] *vt* vigorizar, infundir nuevo vigor a; **to feel** ~**d** sentirse con nuevas fuerzas, sentirse vigorizado.

reissue ['riː'ɪʃjuː] **1** *n* nueva emisión *f*; reedición *f*; reimpresión *f*; reexpedición *f*; reestreno *m*.

2 *vt stamp* volver a emitir; *book* reeditar; reimprimir; *patent etc* reexpedir; *film* reestrenar.

reiterate [riː'ɪtəreɪt] *vt* reiterar, repetir; subrayar; **I must ~ that** ... tengo que subrayar que ...

reiteration [riːɪtə'reɪʃən] *n* reiteración *f*, repetición *f*.

reiterative [riː'ɪtərətɪv] *adj* reiterativo.

reject 1 ['riːdʒekt] *n* cosa *f* rechazada, cosa *f* defectuosa; producto *m* defectuoso; persona *f* rechazada.

2 ['riːdʒekt] *attr*: **~ shop** tienda *f* de taras.

3 [rɪ'dʒekt] *vt offer etc* rechazar; *application* denegar; *motion* rechazar, desestimar; *plan etc* desechar; *solution* descartar; *advance* repulsar; *bad coin, damaged goods* rechazar, no aceptar; (*of stomach etc*) arrojar; (*Med*) *tissue* rechazar; *person* rechazar; marginar.

rejection [rɪ'dʒekʃən] **1** *n* rechazamiento *m*, rechazo *m*; denegación *f*; desestimación *f*; **to meet with a ~** sufrir una repulsa; **the novel has already had 3 ~s** ya han rechazado la novela 3 veces.

2 *attr*: **~ slip** nota *f* de rechazo.

rejoice [rɪ'dʒɔɪs] **1** *vt* alegrar, regocijar, causar alegría a; **to ~ that** ... alegrarse de que + *subj*.

2 *vi* (**a**) alegrarse, regocijarse (*at, about, over* de); **let us not ~ too soon** es aconsejable no alegrarse demasiado pronto.

(**b**) **to ~ in the name of Anastasius** (*hum, iro*) ser el afortunado poseedor del nombre de Anastasio.

rejoicing [rɪ'dʒɔɪsɪŋ] *n* (*also* **~s** *pl*) regocijo *m*, júbilo *m*, alegría *f*; (*general, public*) fiestas *fpl*; **the ~ lasted far into the night** continuaron las fiestas hasta una hora avanzada.

rejoin[1] [rɪ'dʒɔɪn] *vt* replicar, contestar.

rejoin[2] ['riː'dʒɔɪn] *vt* reunirse con, volver a juntarse con; *regiment etc* reincorporarse a.

rejoinder [rɪ'dʒɔɪndə^r] *n* réplica *f*; **as a ~ to ...** como contestación a ...

rejuvenate [rɪ'dʒuːvɪneɪt] *vt* rejuvenecer.

rejuvenating [rɪ'dʒuːvɪneɪtɪŋ] *adj effect etc* rejuvenecedor.

rejuvenation [rɪˌdʒuːvɪ'neɪʃən] *n* rejuvenecimiento *m*.

rekindle ['riː'kɪndl] *vt* volver a encender, reencender; (*fig*) despertar, reavivar.

relapse [rɪ'læps] **1** *n* (*Med*) recaída *f*; (*into crime, error*) reincidencia *f*, recaída *f*; **to have a ~** (*Med*) recaer, tener una recaída.

2 *vi* (*Med*) recaer; (*into crime, error*) reincidir (*into* en).

relate [rɪ'leɪt] **1** *vt* (**a**) (*tell*) contar, narrar, relatar; **strange to ~** aunque parece mentira, por raro que parezca.

(**b**) (*establish relation between*) relacionar (*to, with* con), establecer una conexión entre.

2 *vi*: **to ~ to** relacionarse con, tener que ver con, referirse a; **this ~s to what I said yesterday** esto se refiere a lo que dije ayer.

related [rɪ'leɪtɪd] *adj* (**a**) *subject* afín, conexo; **~ to** relativo a, referente a; **they are ~ subjects** son temas afines; **this murder is not ~ to the other** este asesinato no tiene que ver con el otro, no hay relación entre este asesinato y el otro.

(**b**) *person* emparentado; **they are ~** son parientes, están emparentados; **they are closely ~** son parientes cercanos; **we are ~ but only distantly** somos parientes pero lejanos; **are you ~ to the prisoner?** ¿es Vd pariente del acusado?; **they became ~ by marriage to the Borgias** emparentaron con los Borja.

-related [rɪ'leɪtɪd] *adj in compounds*: *eg* **football~ hooliganism** gamberrismo *m* relacionado con el fútbol.

relating [rɪ'leɪtɪŋ] *as prep*: **details ~ to X** detalles *mpl* acerca de X, detalles *mpl* relativos a X; **and other matters ~ to Y** y otros asuntos concernientes a Y.

relation [rɪ'leɪʃən] *n* (**a**) (*narration*) narración *f*; relato *m*, relación *f*.

(**b**) (*relationship*) conexión *f*, relación *f*, nexo *m* (*to, with* con); (*between persons*) parentesco *m*; **the ~ between A and B** la relación entre A y B; **in ~ to** respecto de, con relación a; **Proust in ~ to the French novel** Proust en relación con la novela francesa; **to bear a certain ~ to ...** guardar cierta relación con ...; **it bears no ~ to the facts** no tiene que ver con los hechos, se desentiende por completo de los hechos.

(**c**) (*contact*) **~s** relaciones *fpl*; **good ~s** buenas relaciones *fpl*; **~s are rather strained** las relaciones están algo tirantes; **to break off ~s with sb** romper con uno; **we have broken off ~s with Ruritania** hemos roto las relaciones con Ruritania; **to enter into ~s with sb** establecer relaciones con uno; **we have business ~s with them** tenemos relaciones comerciales con ellos; **to have sexual ~s with sb** tener relaciones sexuales con uno.

(**d**) (*relative*) pariente *m*, -a *f*, familiar *mf*; **friends and ~s** amigos *mpl* y familiares; **close ~** pariente *m* cercano, parienta *f* cercana; **two distant ~s** dos parientes lejanos; **all my ~s** todos mis parientes, toda mi familia; **what ~ is she to you?** ¿qué parentesco hay entre ella y Vd?; **she's no ~** no es parienta mía.

relational [rɪ'leɪʃənl] *adj* relacional.

relationship [rɪ'leɪʃənʃɪp] *n* relación *f*, conexión *f* (*to, with* con); afinidad *f*; (*kinship*) parentesco *m*; (*between persons*) relaciones *fpl*; amistad *f*; trato *m*; **~ by marriage** parentesco *m* por enlace matrimonial, parentesco *m* político; **~ by blood** consanguinidad *f*, parentesco *m* natural; **our ~ lasted 5 years** nuestras relaciones continuaron durante 5 años; **they have a beautiful ~** (*US*) les unen los lazos de la más fina amistad; se llevan maravillosamente bien; **what is your ~ to the prisoner?** ¿qué parentesco hay entre Vd y el acusado?; **the ~ of A to B, the ~ between A and B** la relación entre A y B.

relative ['relətɪv] **1** *adj* (**a**) relativo (*to* a); (*respective*) respectivo; **with ~ ease** con relativa facilidad. (**b**) (*Gram*) relativo; **~ clause** oración *f* relativa; **~ pronoun** pronombre *m* relativo. **2** *n* (**a**) (*Gram*) relativo *m*. (**b**) (*person*) pariente *m*, -a *f*, familiar *mf*; = **relation (d)**.

relatively ['relətɪvlɪ] *adv* relativamente; **there are ~ few** hay relativamente pocos.

relativism ['relətɪvɪzəm] *n* relativismo *m*.

relativist ['relətɪvɪst] *n* relativista *mf*.

relativistic [ˌrelətɪv'ɪstɪk] *adj* relativista.

relativity [ˌrelə'tɪvɪtɪ] *n* relatividad *f*.

relaunch ['riː'lɔːntʃ] *vt plan etc* relanzar.

relaunching ['riː'lɔːntʃɪŋ] *n* relanzamiento *m*.

relax [rɪ'læks] **1** *vt grip etc* relajar, aflojar; *restrictions, severity* relajar, mitigar, suavizar; **to ~ one's muscles** aflojar los músculos; **to ~ one's hold on sth** dejar de agarrarse de (*or* a) algo tan apretadamente, soltar algo.

2 *vi* (**a**) (*grip etc*) relajarse, aflojarse; (*restrictions, severity*) mitigarse, suavizarse; **his face ~ed into a smile** se le aflojaron los músculos de la cara y empezó a sonreír; **we must not ~ in our efforts** es preciso no cejar en nuestros esfuerzos (*to + infin* por + *infin*).

(**b**) (*rest*) relajarse; descansar; (*amuse o.s.*) esparcirse, expansionarse; **~!** ¡cálmate!; ¡no te apures!; ¡tranquilo!; **now there is time to ~ a little** ahora hay tiempo para esparcirse un poco; **we ~ed in the sun of Majorca** nos expansionamos bajo el sol de Mallorca; **I like to ~ with a book** me gusta relajarme leyendo.

relaxation [ˌriːlæk'seɪʃən] *n* (**a**) (*act*) relajación *f*, aflojamiento *m;* mitigación *f*.

(**b**) (*rest*) relajamiento *m*; descanso *m*; (*amusement*) esparcimiento *m*, recreo *m*; **to seek ~ in painting** esparcirse dedicándose a la pintura; **to take some ~** esparcirse, expansionarse.

(**c**) (*pastime*) pasatiempo *m*, recreo *m*, diversión *f*; **a favourite ~ of the wealthy** un pasatiempo favorito de los ricos.

relaxed [rɪ'lækst] *adj* relajado, tranquilo, sosegado, ecuánime; **in a ~ atmosphere** en un clima de distensión; **he always seems so ~** siempre parece tan sosegado; **try to be more ~** procura ser más tranquilo.

relaxing [rɪ'læksɪŋ] *adj* relajante.

relay ['riːleɪ] **1** *n* (**a**) (*of workmen*) tanda *f*; (*of horses*) parada *f*, posta *f*; **to work in ~s** trabajar por tandas.

(**b**) (*Sport*: *also* **~ race**) carrera *f* de relevos; **the 400 metres ~** los 400 metros relevos.

(**c**) (*Elec*) relaï(s) *m*, relé *m*.

2 *attr*: **~ station** (*Elec*) estación *f* retransmisora, estación *f* repetidora.

3 *vt* (*Rad etc*) retransmitir; **to ~ a message to sb** pasar un mensaje a uno, hacer llegar un mensaje a uno.

re-lay ['riː'leɪ] *vt* volver a colocar; *cable, rail etc* volver a tender.

release [rɪ'liːs] **1** *n* (**a**) (*freeing etc*) liberación *f*; excarcelación *f*; libertad *f*; emisión *f*; lanzamiento *m*; disparo *m*; aflojamiento *m*; descargo *m*, absolución *f*; **a sudden ~ of gas** un súbito escape de gas; **a sudden ~ of creative energy** un repentino estallar de energía creadora; **death came as a merciful ~** la muerte fue una liberación feliz; **his ~ came through on Monday** se aprobó su excarcelación el lunes, la orden de su puesta en libertad llegó el lunes.

(**b**) (*Mech, Phot etc*) disparador *m*.

(**c**) (*for press etc*) boletín *m*, comunicado *m*; (*book, film* *etc*) novedad *f*.

(**d**) (*act of publishing*) publicación *f*; (*of news*) divulgación *f*; (*of film*) estreno *m*; (*of record, video*) puesta *f* en venta, puesta *f* en circulación; **to be on general ~** exhibirse en todos los cines.

2 *vt* (**a**) (*set free*) soltar, libertar; *prisoner* poner en libertad, *convict* excarcelar; *person from obligation* descargar, absolver; **~ me, sir!** ¡suélteme, señor!; **to ~ sb on bail** poner a uno en libertad bajo fianza; **to ~ sb from a debt** absolver a uno de una deuda; **they ~d him to go to a new post** permitieron que se fuera a ocupar un nuevo puesto; **can you ~ him for a few hours each week?** ¿nos lo ceden algunas horas cada semana?

(**b**) (*let go*) soltar; *bomb* lanzar; *gas, smoke* despedir, arrojar, emitir; (*Phot*) disparar; (*Mech*) desenganchar, disparar; *brake* soltar; *grip, hold* soltar, aflojar.

(**c**) *book* publicar; *record, video* poner a la venta; *film* estrenar; *news, report* publicar, autorizar la publicación de; divulgar, dar a conocer.

relegate ['relɪgeɪt] *vt* relegar (*to* a); **Mérida is ~d to the second division** Mérida pasa a la segunda división, Mérida desciende a la segunda división.

relegation [,relɪ'geɪʃən] *n* relegación *f*; (*Sport*) descenso *m*.

relent [rɪ'lent] *vi* ablandarse, apiadarse, ceder.

relentless [rɪ'lentlɪs] *adj* implacable, inexorable; despiadado; **with ~ severity** con implacable severidad; **he is quite ~ about it** en esto se muestra totalmente implacable.

relentlessly [rɪ'lentlɪslɪ] *adv* implacablemente, inexorablemente; **he presses on ~** avanza implacable.

relet ['riː'let] *vt* realquilar.

relevance ['reləvəns], (*US*) **relevancy** ['reləvənsɪ] *n* pertinencia *f*; conexión *f*, relación *f*; aplicabilidad *f*; **matters of doubtful ~** asuntos *mpl* de dudosa pertinencia; **what is the ~ of that?** y eso ¿tiene que ver (con lo que estamos discutiendo)?

relevant ['reləvənt] *adj* (**a**) (*related*) pertinente; conexo, relacionado (*to* con); aplicable; **details ~ to this affair** detalles *mpl* relacionados con este asunto, detalles *mpl* concernientes a este asunto; **that is hardly ~** eso apenas tiene que ver (con lo que estamos discutiendo).

(**b**) (*fitting*) apropiado, oportuno, adecuado; **bring the ~ papers** traiga los documentos pertinentes; **we have all the ~ data** tenemos todos los datos que hacen al caso.

reliability [rɪ,laɪə'bɪlɪtɪ] *n* exactitud *f*, veracidad *f*; seguridad *f*; confianza *f*; confiabilidad *f*, fiabilidad *f*; formalidad *f*, seriedad *f*.

reliable [rɪ'laɪəbl] *adj news etc* fidedigno, fehaciente, digno de crédito; *account* exacto, veraz; *machine etc* seguro; *person* (*trustworthy*) de confianza, de fiar, fiable; (*businesslike*) formal, serio; **it's a most ~ firm** es una casa de toda confianza; **I have it from a ~ source** lo sé de fuente fidedigna (*or* competente, solvente); **he's not very ~** no es de fiar, no hay que fiarse de él; **I've always found him very ~** siempre me ha parecido de mucha formalidad.

reliably [rɪ'laɪəblɪ] *adv*: **I am ~ informed that ...** sé de fuente fidedigna que ...

reliance [rɪ'laɪəns] *n* confianza *f* (*on* en); dependencia *f* (*on* de); **our excessive ~ on him** nuestra excesiva dependencia con respecto de él, el que dependamos tanto de él; **you can place no ~ on that** eso no es de fiar, no hay que tener confianza en eso.

reliant [rɪ'laɪənt] *adj* confiado; **to be ~ on sth** confiar en algo, tener confianza en algo.

relic ['relɪk] *n* reliquia *f*, vestigio *m*; (*Eccl*) reliquia *f*.

relict ['relɪkt] *n* (††) viuda *f*.

relief [rɪ'liːf] **1** *n* (**a**) (*alleviation*) alivio *m*; desahogo *m*; consuelo *m*; aligeramiento *m*; (*of taxation*) desgravación *f*; (*of congestion*) descongestión *f*; **by way of light ~** a modo de diversión; **there is a comic scene by way of ~** para aliviar la tensión sigue una escena cómica; **that's a ~!** ¡menos mal!, ¡qué alivio!; **it is a ~ to find that ...** me consuela encontrar que ..., me alegro de encontrar que ...; **the medicine brings ~** la medicina alivia; **it came as a general ~ when they left** se aliviaron todos cuando ellos se marcharon; **to heave a sigh of ~** dar un suspiro de alivio.

(**b**) (*aid*) socorro *m*, ayuda *f*; **poor ~** socorro *m*, beneficencia *f*; **to be on ~** vivir de la beneficencia, cobrar del seguro; **to go to sb's ~** acudir a socorrer a uno.

(**c**) (*Mil*: *of town*) descerco *m*, socorro *m*.

(**d**) (*Mil*: *also* **~ party, ~ troops**) relevo *m*; (*substitute*) relevo *m*, sustituto *m*.

(**e**) (*Jur*) satisfacción *f*, remedio *m*.

(**f**) (*Art, Geog*) relieve *m*, realce *m*; **high ~** alto relieve *m*; **low ~** bajo relieve *m*; **to stand out in ~** destacar; **to throw sth into ~** hacer resaltar algo, (*fig*) servir para destacar (*or* subrayar) algo.

2 *attr*: **~ fund** fondo *m* de auxilio (a los damnificados); **~ map** mapa *m* en relieve; **~ organization** organización *f* de beneficencia, beneficencia *f*; **~ road** (*Brit*) carretera *f* de decongestión; **~ supplies** provisiones *fpl* de auxilio; **~ work** trabajos *mpl* de socorro; **~ works** obras *fpl* públicas (de alivio al paro).

relieve [rɪ'liːv] **1** *vt* (**a**) (*mitigate*) *sufferings etc* aliviar, mitigar; *person's mind* tranquilizar; *feelings* desahogar; *burden* aligerar; *pain, headache etc* quitar, suprimir, aliviar; **to feel ~d** sentirse aliviado, sentir un alivio; **I am ~d to hear that ...** me alegro de saber que ...; **to ~ one's feelings** desahogarse; **I ~ed my feelings in a letter** me desahogué escribiendo una carta; **to ~ the boredom of the journey** para aliviar el aburrimiento del viaje; **the plain is ~d by an occasional hill** de vez en cuando una colina alivia la monotonía de la llanura.

(**b**) **to ~ the poor** (*help*) socorrer a los pobres.

(**c**) (*release*) **to ~ sb from doing sth** librar a uno de la necesidad de hacer algo; **to ~ sb of anxiety** tranquilizar a uno; **this ~s us of financial worries** esto acaba con nuestras preocupaciones económicas; **to ~ sb of a duty** exonerar a uno de un deber; **to ~ sb of a post** destituir a uno; **he was ~d of his command** fue relevado de su mando; **to ~ sb of his wallet** quitar la cartera a uno, robar la cartera a uno; **let me ~ you of your coat** permítame tomarle el abrigo.

(**d**) (*Mil*) *city* descercar, socorrer; *troops* relevar; **I'll come and ~ you at 6** vengo a las 6 a relevarte.

2 *vr* (**a**) **to ~ o.s.** (*euph*) hacer del cuerpo, hacer sus necesidades.

(**b**) **to ~ o.s. of a burden** deshacerse de un peso, quitarse un peso de encima.

religion [rɪ'lɪdʒən] *n* religión *f*; **to get ~*** darse a la religión.

religiosity [rɪ,lɪdʒɪ'ɒsɪtɪ] *n* religiosidad *f*.

religious [rɪ'lɪdʒəs] **1** *adj* (**a**) religioso; **~ instruction** enseñanza *f* religiosa; **~ toleration** libertad *f* de cultos.

(**b**) (*fig*) puntual; exacto, fiel.

2 *n* religioso *m*, -a *f*.

religiously [rɪ'lɪdʒəslɪ] *adv* (**a**) religiosamente. (**b**) (*fig*) puntualmente, exactamente, fielmente.

religiousness [rɪ'lɪdʒəsnɪs] *n* religiosidad *f*.

reline ['riː'laɪn] *vt* reforrar, poner nuevo forro a.

relinquish [rɪ'lɪŋkwɪʃ] *vt* abandonar, renunciar a; *grip* soltar; *post* renunciar a, dimitir de.

relinquishment [rɪ'lɪŋkwɪʃmənt] *n* abandono *m*, renuncia *f*; dimisión *f*.

reliquary ['relɪkwərɪ] *n* relicario *m*.

relish ['relɪʃ] **1** *n* (**a**) (*flavour*) sabor *m*, gusto *m*; (*smack*) dejo *m* (*of* de), sabor *m* (*of* a).

(**b**) (*Culin*: *sauce*) salsa *f*, condimento *m*.

(**c**) (*enjoyment*) gusto *m*; (*attractive quality*) apetencia *f*; (*appetite*) apetito *m*; (*zest*) entusiasmo *m*; (*liking*) afición *f*; **to eat sth with ~** comer algo con apetito; **to do sth with ~** hacer algo de buena gana, hacer algo con entusiasmo; **to have a ~ for sth** apetecer algo, gustar de algo, ser aficionado a algo; **hunting has no ~ for me now** ya no me apetece la caza; **the ~ for hunting does not seem to be so strong** no parece que la caza atraiga tanto, parece que hay menos afición a la caza.

2 *vt taste, savour* paladear, saborear; (*like*) gustar de, tener buen apetito para; **I don't ~ the idea** no me gusta la idea; **I ~ a day's fishing** apetece salir de pesca un día, me gusta pasar el día pescando; **do you ~ some fishing?** ¿quieres ir a pescar?; **I don't ~ the idea of staying up all night** no me hace gracia la idea de estar levantado toda la noche.

relive ['riː'lɪv] *vt* vivir de nuevo, volver a vivir.

reload ['riː'ləʊd] *vt* recargar, volver a cargar.

relocate ['riːləʊ'keɪt] **1** *vt* volver a colocar, volver a situar.

2 *vi* moverse (a otro solar), trasladarse.

relocation [riːləʊ'keɪʃən] *n* nueva ubicación *f*, nueva colocación *f*; **~ package** prima *f* de traslado.

reluctance [rɪ'lʌktəns] *n* desgana *f*, renuencia *f*, reticencia *f*; repugnancia *f*; **with ~** a desgana, de mala gana; **to affect ~** aparentar no querer.

reluctant [rɪ'lʌktənt] *adj* (**a**) (*unwilling, disinclined*) **he was ~** no quiso, se mostró poco dispuesto a hacerlo; **to be ~ to do sth** estar poco dispuesto a hacer algo, tener pocas ganas de hacer algo; **he was ~ to decide** vaciló en decidirse; **I should be most ~ to let you go** me resistiría a permitirte ir, no consentiría de buena gana en que fueras.

(**b**) (*done etc unwillingly*) **it had his ~ agreement** consintió pero de mala gana; **the ~ dragon** el dragón que no quería; **I should make a ~ secretary** yo, de ser secretario, sería a desgana.

reluctantly [rɪˈlʌktəntlɪ] *adv* de mala gana, a regañadientes; **she went ~** se fue de mala gana; **I ~ agree** consiento pero contra mi voluntad.

rely [rɪˈlaɪ] *vi*: **to ~ on** confiar en, fiarse de, contar con; **you can't ~ on the trains** es imposible fiarse de los trenes; **one can't ~ on the weather** no puede uno fiarse del tiempo; **we are ~ing on you to do it** contamos con Vd para hacerlo, confiamos en que Vd lo haga.

REM [rem] *n* (**a**) (*Physiol*) *abbr of* **rapid eye movement** movimiento *m* rápido del ojo. (**b**) (*Phys*) *abbr of* **roentgen equivalent man.**

remain [rɪˈmeɪn] *vi* (**a**) (*be left over*) sobrar; (*survive*) quedar; **if any ~** si sobra alguno; **few ~** quedan pocos; **the few pleasures that ~ to me** los pocos placeres que me quedan; **nothing ~s but to sell up** no queda otro remedio sino venderlo todo; **it ~s to be done** queda por hacer; **it ~s to be seen whether** ... queda por ver si ...; **more than half ~s to be built** queda por construir más de la mitad.

(**b**) (*continue*) quedar, quedarse, permanecer; seguir, continuar; **we ~ed there 3 weeks** nos quedamos allí 3 semanas; **how long do you expect to ~?** ¿cuánto tiempo piensas quedarte aquí?; **that objection ~s** queda (en pie) esa objeción; **it will ~ in my memory** quedará grabado en mi memoria; **the fact ~s that** ... sigue siendo un hecho que ..., no es menos cierto que ...; **to ~ behind** quedarse; **to ~ seated, to ~ sitting** permanecer sentado; **to ~ standing** permanecer de pie.

(**c**) (*with adj complement*) **to ~ faithful to** seguir fiel a; **the problem ~s unsolved** el problema sigue sin solucionarse; **it ~s true that** ... no es menos cierto que ...; **it ~s the same** sigue siendo lo mismo; **if the weather ~s fine** si el tiempo sigue bueno.

(**d**) (*in letters*) **I ~ yours faithfully** le saluda atentamente.

◆**remain behind** *vi* (*fall back*) quedarse atrás, rezagarse; (*after school*) quedarse después de la clase.

remainder [rɪˈmeɪndəʳ] **1** *n* (**a**) (*sth left over*) resto *m*; (*Math*) residuo *m*, resto *m*, resta *f*; **the ~** lo que sobra, lo que queda; los (*etc*) demás; **the ~ of the debt** el resto de la deuda; **during the ~ of the day** durante el resto del día; **the ~ would not come** los otros (*or* los demás) no quisieron venir.

(**b**) **~s** (*Comm*) artículos *mpl* no vendidos; (*books*) restos *mpl* de edición.

2 *vt books etc* saldar.

remaining [rɪˈmeɪnɪŋ] *adj* que queda; **the 3 ~ possibilities** las 3 posibilidades que quedan; **the ~ passengers** los otros pasajeros, los demás pasajeros.

remains [rɪˈmeɪnz] *npl* (*human, archaeological etc*) restos *mpl*; (*left-overs*) sobras *fpl*, desperdicios *mpl*; restos *mpl*, despojos *mpl*.

remake (*irr*: *V* **make**) **1** [ˈriːˈmeɪk] *vt* rehacer, volver a hacer. **2** [ˈriːmeɪk] *n* (*Cine*) nueva versión *f*, refundición *f*.

remand [rɪˈmɑːnd] **1** *n*: **prisoner on ~** preso *m* preventivo, presa *f* preventiva; **to be on ~ (in custody)** estar en prisión preventiva, estar detenido (mientras se investiga una acusación *or* se prepara el proceso).

2 *attr* (*Brit*): **~ centre** cárcel *f* transitoria; **~ home** cárcel *f* transitoria para menores; **~ wing** galería *f* de prisión preventiva.

3 *vt*: **to ~ sb (in custody)** poner a uno en prisión preventiva, reencarcelar a uno (para que se investigue una acusación *or* se prepare el proceso); **to ~ sb on bail** libertar a uno bajo fianza (mientras se prepara el proceso); **to ~ sb for a week** reencarcelar a uno durante una semana; **he was ~ed to Brixton** volvieron a encarcelarle en Brixton.

remark [rɪˈmɑːk] **1** *n* (**a**) (*notice*) **worthy of ~** notable, digno de notar; **to let sth pass without ~** dejar pasar algo sin comentario.

(**b**) (*comment*) observación *f*; comentario *m*; **'R~s on the Press'** 'Observaciones *fpl* sobre la Prensa'; **after some introductory ~s** después de hacer algunas observaciones a modo de prefacio; **to make a ~** hacer una observación; **to make the ~ that** ... observar que ...; **to pass ~s on sb** hacer observaciones acerca de uno, (*freq*) hacer un comentario desfavorable sobre uno.

2 *vt* (**a**) (*notice*) observar, notar.

(**b**) (*say*) **to ~ that** ... decir que ..., observar que ...; **'it's a pity' she ~ed** 'es una lástima' dijo.

3 *vi*: **to ~ on sth** hacer una observación sobre algo, comentar algo.

remarkable [rɪˈmɑːkəbl] *adj* notable, singular; extraordinario; **~!, most ~!** ¡qué raro!; **with ~ skill** con singular habilidad; **it is in no way ~** no tiene nada que sea digno de notar; **what's ~ about that?** ¿es que eso te parece singular?, y eso ¿qué tiene de raro?; **he's a most ~ man** es un hombre extraordinario.

remarkably [rɪˈmɑːkəblɪ] *adv* extraordinariamente.

remarriage [ˈriːˈmærɪdʒ] *n* segundas nupcias *fpl*, segundo casamiento *m*.

remarry [ˈriːˈmærɪ] *vi* volver a casarse, casarse en segundas nupcias.

rematch [ˈriːˌmætʃ] *n* partido *m* de vuelta, revancha *f*.

remediable [rɪˈmiːdɪəbl] *adj* remediable.

remedial [rɪˈmiːdɪəl] *adj* remediador; (*Med*) curativo, terapéutico; **~ course** curso *m* correctivo; **~ exercises** gimnasia *f* terapéutica; **~ teaching** enseñanza *f* de los niños (*etc*) atrasados.

remedy [ˈremədɪ] **1** *n* remedio *m* (*for* para curar); (*Jur etc*) recurso *m*; **there's no ~ for that** eso no tiene remedio; **the best ~ for that is to protest** eso se remedia protestando; **to have no ~ at law** no tener recurso legal.

2 *vt* remediar; curar; **that's soon remedied** eso es fácil remediarlo, eso fácilmente queda arreglado.

remember [rɪˈmembəʳ] **1** *vt* (**a**) (*recall*) acordarse de, recordar; (*commemorate*) conmemorar; **I ~ seeing it, I ~ having seen it** recuerdo haberlo visto; **she ~ed to do it** se acordó de hacerlo; **don't you ~ me?** ¿no se acuerda Vd de mí?; **it is worth ~ing that** ... vale la pena recordar que ...; **give me sth to ~ you by** dame algún recuerdo tuyo; **so I gave him sth to ~ me by** (*fig*) así que le di algo para que no me olvidara; **to ~ sb in one's will** mencionar a uno en su testamento.

(**b**) (*bear in mind*) tener presente, no olvidar; **~ that he carries a gun** ten presente que lleva revólver; **~ what happened before** no te olvides de lo que pasó antes, acuérdate de lo que pasó antes; **~ to turn out the light** no te olvides de apagar la luz; **'please ~ the guide'** 'se ruega no olvidar los servicios del guía'; **~ who you're with!** ¡piensa con quién estás!

(**c**) (*with wishes*) **~ me to him!** ¡dale recuerdos míos!, salúdale de mi parte; **she asks to be ~ed to you all** ella manda recuerdos para todos.

2 *vi*: **yes, I ~** sí, me acuerdo; **if I ~ aright** si bien me acuerdo; **as far as I can ~** que yo recuerde.

remembrance [rɪˈmembrəns] **1** *n* (*remembering*) recordación *f*; memoria *f*; (*souvenir*) recuerdo *m*; **~s** recuerdos *mpl*; **in ~ of** en conmemoración de, para conmemorar; **I have no ~ of it** no lo recuerdo en absoluto.

2 *attr*: **R~ Day** (*Brit*) *conmemoración del fin de la guerra en 1918 (y de las dos guerras mundiales), 11 de noviembre.*

remind [rɪˈmaɪnd] **1** *vt* recordar; **to ~ sb of sth** recordar algo a uno; **that ~s me of last time** eso me recuerda la vez pasada; **she ~s me of Anne** me recuerda a Ana, me hace pensar en Ana, tiene mucho parecido con Ana; **that ~s me!** y a propósito ...; **to ~ sb to do sth** recordar a uno que haga algo; **you have to keep ~ing him to do it** hay que traérselo constantemente a la memoria.

2 *vr*: **to ~ o.s. that** ... recordarse que ...; **I ~ myself about it all the time** me lo recuerdo constantemente.

reminder [rɪˈmaɪndəʳ] **1** *n* (**a**) (*note etc*) recordatorio *m*; advertencia *f*; (*Comm*) notificación *f*; **it's a gentle ~** es una advertencia amistosa; **we will send a ~** le enviaremos un recordatorio.

(**b**) (*memento*) recuerdo *m*; **it's a ~ of the good old days** recuerda los buenos tiempos pasados.

2 *attr*: **subscription ~ card** tarjeta *f* recordatoria de renovación de suscripción.

reminisce [ˌremɪˈnɪs] *vi* contar los recuerdos, recordar viejas historias (*about* de).

reminiscence [ˌremɪˈnɪsəns] *n* reminiscencia *f*, recuerdo *m*; **'R~s of life in the Congo'** 'Recuerdos *mpl* de la vida en el Congo'; **the symphony has ~s of Mozart** la sinfonía tiene reminiscencias de Mozart.

reminiscent [ˌremɪˈnɪsənt] *adj* (**a**) **it's a ~ work** es una obra evocadora; es una obra llena de reminiscencias; **to be in a ~ mood** estar de humor para contar los recuerdos, estar de humor para evocar el pasado.

(**b**) **to be ~ of sth** recordar algo; (*pej*) oler a algo, sonar a algo; **that bit is ~ of Rossini** ese trozo recuerda a Rossini, ese trozo tiene reminiscencia de Rossini; **that's ~ of another old joke** eso suena a otro chiste viejo.

reminiscently [ˌremɪˈnɪsəntlɪ] *adv*: **he spoke ~** habló pensando en el pasado.

remiss [rɪˈmɪs] *adj* negligente, descuidado; **I have been very ~ about it** he sido muy descuidado en eso; **you have been**

~ in not attending to it Vd merece que se le censure por no atenderlo, el no atenderlo ha sido un descuido suyo.

remission [rɪ'mɪʃən] *n* (*all senses*) remisión *f*; **~ of sins** remisión *f* de los pecados.

remissness [rɪ'mɪsnɪs] *n* negligencia *f*, descuido *m*.

remit 1 ['ri:mɪt] *n* cometido *m*, deber *m*; (*of committee etc*) puntos *mpl* de consulta. **2** [rɪ'mɪt] *vt* (**a**) (*send*) remitir, enviar. (**b**) (*excuse*) perdonar; **3 months of the sentence were ~ted** se le redujo la pena en 3 meses. **3** [rɪ'mɪt] *vi* disminuir, reducirse.

remittal [rɪ'mɪtl] *n* (*Jur*) remisión *f*.

remittance [rɪ'mɪtəns] **1** *n* remesa *f*, envío *m*. **2** *attr*: **~ advice** aviso *m* de pago.

remittee [rɪmɪ'ti:] *n* consignatario *m*, -a *f*.

remittent [rɪ'mɪtənt] *adj fever etc* remitente.

remitter [rɪ'mɪtə^r] *n* remitente *mf*.

remnant ['remnənt] **1** *n* (*remainder*) resto *m*, residuo *m*; (*of cloth*) retazo *m*. **2** *attr*: **~ day** (*Comm*) día *m* de venta de restos de serie; **~ sale** venta *f* de restos de serie, remate *m* total.

remodel ['ri:'mɒdl] *vt* modelar de nuevo, remodelar; reestructurar; reorganizar; (*Liter etc*) refundir.

remold ['ri:məʊld] (*US*) = **remould**.

remonstrance [rɪ'mɒnstrəns] *n* protesta *f*, reconvención *f*.

remonstrate ['remənstreɪt] *vi* protestar, objetar; **to ~ about sth** protestar contra algo, poner reparos a algo; **to ~ with sb** reconvenir a uno.

remorse [rɪ'mɔ:s] *n* remordimiento *m*; **to feel ~** arrepentirse, compungirse.

remorseful [rɪ'mɔ:sfʊl] *adj* arrepentido, compungido; **now he's ~** ahora está lleno de remordimientos, ahora le remuerde la conciencia.

remorsefully [rɪ'mɔ:sfəlɪ] *adv* con remordimiento; **he said ~** dijo compungido.

remorsefulness [rɪ'mɔ:sfʊlnɪs] *n* remordimiento *m*, compunción *f*.

remorseless [rɪ'mɔ:slɪs] *adj* implacable, despiadado, inexorable.

remorselessly [rɪ'mɔ:slɪslɪ] *adv* implacablemente, despiadadamente, inexorablemente.

remorselessness [rɪ'mɔ:slɪsnɪs] *n* inexorabilidad *f*.

remote [rɪ'məʊt] *adj* (**a**) (*distant*) remoto (*also Comput*); distante, lejano; aislado; **~ control** mando *m* a distancia, telecontrol *m*; telemando *m*; **~ job entry** entrada *f* de trabajos a distancia; **~ learning** aprendizaje *m* a distancia; **~ viewing** (*US*) clarividencia *f*; **in a ~ spot** en un lugar remoto; **in a ~ farmstead** en una alquería aislada, en una alquería apartada; **it's ~ from the town** está lejos de la ciudad; **she is ~ from such things** queda alejada de tales cosas, tales cosas le son ajenas; **in some ~ future** en un futuro lejano.

(**b**) (*slight*) ligero; leve, tenue; **it's a ~ prospect** es poco probable, de eso existe poca probabilidad; **there is a ~ resemblance** hay un ligero parecido; **he hasn't the ~st chance** no tiene la más remota posibilidad; **I haven't the ~st idea** no tengo la más remota idea; **all the while there remains a ~ chance** mientras haya una tenue posibilidad.

remote-controlled [rɪ'məʊtkən'trəʊld] *adj* con mando a distancia, teledirigido.

remotely [rɪ'məʊtlɪ] *adv* (**a**) remotamente; **it is ~ situated** está situado en un lugar remoto; **they are ~ related** hay un parentesco lejano entre ellos. (**b**) **it's not even ~ likely** de eso no hay la más remota posibilidad.

remoteness [rɪ'məʊtnɪs] *n* distancia *f*; aislamiento *m*, alejamiento *m*; **her ~ from everyday life** su alejamiento de la vida diaria.

remould, (*US*) **remold 1** ['ri:məʊld] *n* recauchutado *m*. **2** ['ri:'məʊld] *vt tyre* recauchutar.

remount ['ri:'maʊnt] **1** *n* (*Mil etc*) remonta *f*. **2** *vt* volver a subir (a), subir de nuevo (a); *horse* montar de nuevo. **3** *vi* subir de nuevo.

removable [rɪ'mu:vəbl] *adj* separable, amovible; desmontable; *collar etc* de quita y pon.

removal [rɪ'mu:vəl] **1** *n* remoción *f*, el quitar (*etc*); supresión *f*; separación *f*; eliminación *f*; extirpación *f*; destitución *f*; el tachar; solución *f*; disipación *f*; apartamiento *m*, alejamiento *m*; (*of house*) mudanza *f*; **his ~ to a new post** su traslado a un nuevo puesto; **the ~ of this threat** la eliminación de esta amenaza.

2 *attr*: **~ allowance** subvención *f* de mudanza; **~ expenses** gastos *mpl* de traslado de efectos personales; **~ man** mozo *m* de mudanzas; **~ van** (*Brit*) camión *m* de mudanzas.

remove [rɪ'mu:v] **1** *n*: **this is but one ~ from disaster** esto raya en la catástrofe; **this is several ~s from our official policy** en esto nos apartamos bastante de nuestra política oficial.

2 *vt* (*take away*) quitar; llevarse; (*take off*) quitar, *clothes etc* quitarse; (*steal*) llevarse, robar; (*get out of the way*) quitar de en medio; *letter, passage, tax etc* suprimir; *name from list* tachar, borrar (*from* de); (*Mech*) *part etc* separar, retirar, quitar; *obstacle, threat, waste* eliminar; (*Med*) *appendix etc* extirpar; *person from post* destituir; *problem* solucionar; *doubt* disipar; *fear* acabar con; (*do away with*) *person* quitar de en medio, eliminar; *competitor* apartar, alejar, deshacerse de; **~ hats on entering** se ruega descubrirse al entrar; **he ~d his hat** se descubrió, se quitó el sombrero; **first ~ the lid** primero quitar la tapa; **~ that bauble** que se quite esa chuchería de en medio; **this effectively ~d him from the scene** esto terminó de alejarle de allí; **illness ~d him from politics** la enfermedad le hizo abandonar la política; **to ~ sth to another place** trasladar algo a otro sitio, cambiar algo de sitio; **that is far ~d from what we wanted** eso se aparta mucho de lo que queríamos; **cousin once ~d** hijo *m*, -a *f* de primo carnal, sobrino *m* segundo, sobrina *f* segunda.

3 *vi* mudarse, trasladarse (*to* a), cambiarse (*Mex*).

4 *vr*: **to ~ o.s.** irse, marcharse; quitarse de en medio; **kindly ~ yourself at once** haga el favor de irse inmediatamente; **to ~ o.s. to another place** irse a otro sitio; **I must ~ myself** tengo que marcharme.

remover [rɪ'mu:və^r] *n* (*owner*) agente *m* de mudanzas; (*workman*) mozo *m* de mudanzas.

remunerate [rɪ'mju:nəreɪt] *vt* remunerar.

remuneration [rɪ,mju:nə'reɪʃən] *n* remuneración *f*.

remunerative [rɪ'mju:nərətɪv] *adj* remunerador, remunerativo, lucrativo.

renaissance [rə'neɪsɑ:ns] **1** *n* renacimiento *m*; **R~** (*Hist*) Renacimiento *m*; **the 12th century R~** el Renacimiento del siglo XII.

2 *attr*: **R~** renacentista, del Renacimiento.

renal ['ri:nl] *adj* renal; **~ failure** insuficiencia *f* renal.

rename ['ri:'neɪm] *vt* poner nuevo nombre a, rebautizar; **they have ~d it 'Mon Repos'** le han puesto el nuevo nombre de 'Mon Repos'.

renascence [rɪ'næsns] *n* renacimiento *m*; **a spiritual ~** un renacimiento espiritual, un despertar espiritual.

renascent [rɪ'næsnt] *adj* renaciente, que renace.

renationalization ['ri:,næʃnəlaɪ'zeɪʃən] *n* renacionalización *f*.

renationalize ['ri:'næʃnəlaɪz] *vt* renacionalizar.

rend [rend] (*irr*: *pret and ptp* **rent**) *vt* (*liter*) (*tear*) rasgar, desgarrar; (*split*) hender, rajar; **to ~ sth in twain** partir algo por medio, hender algo; **to ~ one's dress** rasgar su ropa; **to turn and ~ sb** perder por fin la paciencia y arremeter contra uno; **a cry rent the air** un grito desgarró los aires; **the air was rent with cries** los gritos hendieron el aire.

render ['rendə^r] *vt* (**a**) (*return*) **to ~ good for evil** devolver bien por mal; **to ~ thanks to sb** dar las gracias a uno.

(**b**) (*hand over*) entregar; **~ unto Caesar** ... al César lo que es del César (y a Dios lo que es de Dios).

(**c**) (*give*) *service* hacer, prestar; *assistance* dar, prestar; *honour* dar.

(**d**) (*send in*) **to ~ an account** (*Comm*) pasar factura; **to account ~ed** según factura anterior; **to ~ an account of one's stewardship** dar cuenta de su gobierno, justificar su conducta durante su mando; **to ~ an account to God** dar cuenta de sí ante Dios.

(**e**) (*reproduce*) reproducir, representar; (*Mus*) interpretar, ejecutar; (*translate*) traducir, verter (*into* a); **no photograph could adequately ~ the scene** ninguna fotografía podría representar adecuadamente la escena; **how does one ~ 'cursi'?** ¿cómo se traduce 'cursi'?

(**f**) (*make*) hacer, volver; **this ~s it impossible** esto lo hace imposible, esto lo imposibilita; **you have ~ed our efforts useless** Vd ha inutilizado nuestros esfuerzos, Vd ha hecho inútiles nuestros esfuerzos.

(**g**) *fat* derretir.

(**h**) *building etc* enlucir.

◆render down *vt fat* derretir.

◆render up *vt* ceder, entregar; **the earth ~s up its treasures** la tierra rinde sus tesoros.

rendering ['rendərɪŋ] *n* reproducción *f*, representación *f*; (*Mus*) interpretación *f*; traducción *f*, versión *f*; **her ~ of the sonata** su interpretación de la sonata; **an elegant ~ of Machado** una elegante versión de Machado.

rendezvous ['rɒndɪvu:] **1** *n, pl* **rendezvous** ['rɒndɪvu:z] cita *f*; lugar *m* de una cita; **~ in space** cita *f* espacial; **to have**

a ~ with sb tener cita con uno; **to make a ~ with another ship at sea** efectuar un enlace con otro buque en el mar.
2 *vi* reunirse, verse; (*spaceship*) efectuar una reunión espacial (*with* con); **we will ~ at 8** nos reuniremos a las 8; **the ships will ~ off Vigo** los buques efectuarán el enlace a la altura de Vigo.
rendition [ren'dɪʃən] *n* (*Mus*) interpretación *f*, ejecución *f*.
renegade ['renɪgeɪd] **1** *adj* renegado. **2** *n* renegado *m*, -a *f*.
renege [rɪ'ni:g] *vi* faltar a su palabra; **to ~ on a promise** no cumplir una promesa.
renew [rɪ'nju:] *vt* renovar; (*resume*) reanudar; *lease, loan etc* extender, prorrogar; *subscription* renovar; *promise* reafirmar; *attack etc* volver a; *effort etc* volver a hacer, redoblar; **to ~ acquaintance with sb** reanudar la amistad con uno; **to ~ the attack on sb** volver a arremeter contra uno; **to ~ the attack on a town** volver a atacar una ciudad; **to ~ one's strength** restablecer sus fuerzas, cobrar nuevo vigor.
renewable [rɪ'nju:əbl] *adj* renovable; **~ energy** energías *fpl* alternativas.
renewal [rɪ'nju:əl] *n* renovación *f*; reanudación *f*; extensión *f*; prorrogación *f*; reafirmación *f*; **~ of subscriptions** renovación *f* de suscripciones; **the ~ of the attack** el nuevo ataque; **a spiritual ~** una renovación espiritual; **urban ~** renovación *f* urbana.
renewed [rɪ'nju:d] *adj* renovado; nuevo; **with ~ vigour** con nuevo vigor, con redoblado vigor; con nuevos bríos; **to feel spiritually ~** sentirse con nuevas fuerzas espirituales.
rennet ['renɪt] *n* cuajo *m*.
renounce [rɪ'naʊns] **1** *vt right, inheritance, offer etc* renunciar; *plan, post, the world etc* renunciar a. **2** *vi* (*Cards*) renunciar.
renouncement [rɪ'naʊnsmənt] *n* renuncia *f*.
renovate ['renəʊveɪt] *vt* renovar, restaurar.
renovation [ˌrenəʊ'veɪʃən] *n* renovación *f*, restauración *f*.
renown [rɪ'naʊn] *n* renombre *m*, nombradía *f*, fama *f*.
renowned [rɪ'naʊnd] *adj* renombrado; **it is ~ for ...** es famoso por ..., es célebre por ...
rent¹ [rent] **1** *pret and ptp of* **rend. 2** *n* (*tear*) rasgón *m*, rasgadura *f*; (*split*) abertura *f*, raja *f*, hendedura *f*; (*fig*) escisión *f*, cisma *m*.
rent² [rent] **1** *n* alquiler *m*, arriendo *m*; **we pay £350 in ~** pagamos 350 libras de alquiler; **to build flats for ~** construir pisos para alquilarlos; **'for ~'** (*US*) 'se alquila'.
2 *attr*: **~ book** librito *m* del alquiler; **~ rebate** devolución *f* de alquiler.
3 *vt* (*also* **to ~ out**) alquilar, rentar (*Mex*); **to ~ a flat from sb** alquilar un piso de uno; **to ~ a house (out) to sb** alquilar una casa a uno; **it is ~ed out at £400 a week** está alquilado a 400 libras por semana.
rental ['rentl] **1** *n* alquiler *m*, arriendo *m*. **2** *attr*: **~ car** (*US*) coche *m* de alquiler; **~ value** valor *m* de alquiler.
rent-a-mob ['rentəmɒb] *n* turba *f* alquilada.
rentboy* ['rentbɔɪ] *n* chapero* *m*.
rent-collector ['rentkəˌlektəʳ] *n* recaudador *m*, -ora *f* de alquileres.
rent-control ['rentkənˌtrəʊl] *n* control *m* de alquileres.
rent-controlled ['rentkənˌtrəʊld] *adj*: **a ~ flat** un piso de alquiler controlado.
rent-free ['rent'fri:] **1** *adj house etc* exento de alquiler, gratuito. **2** *adv*: **to live ~** ocupar una casa (*etc*) sin pagar alquiler.
rentier ['rɒntɪeɪ] *n* rentista *m*.
renting ['rentɪŋ] *n* arrendamiento *m*.
rent-roll ['rentrəʊl] *n* lista *f* de alquileres; (total *m* de) ingresos *mpl* de alquileres.
renumber ['ri:'nʌmbəʳ] *vt* volver a numerar; corregir la numeración de.
renunciation [rɪˌnʌnsɪ'eɪʃən] *n* renuncia *f*.
reoccupy ['ri:'ɒkjʊpaɪ] *vt* volver a ocupar.
reopen ['ri:'əʊpən] **1** *vt* volver a abrir, reabrir; **to ~ a case** (*Jur*) rever un pleito, rever un proceso, (*fig*) reconsiderar un asunto.
2 *vi* volver a abrirse, reabrirse; **school ~s on the 8th** el nuevo curso comienza el día 8.
reopening ['ri:'əʊpnɪŋ] *n* reapertura *f*; (*Jur*) revisión *f*; reconsideración *f*.
reorder ['ri:'ɔ:dəʳ] *vt* (**a**) *objects* ordenar (*or* arreglar *etc*) de nuevo, volver a poner en orden. (**b**) (*Comm*) volver a pedir, repetir el pedido de.
reorganization ['ri:ˌɔ:gənaɪ'zeɪʃən] *n* reorganización *f*.
reorganize ['ri:'ɔ:gənaɪz] **1** *vt* reorganizar. **2** *vt* reorganizarse.
rep¹ [rep] *n* (*fabric*) reps *m*.
rep²* [rep] **1** *n* (*Comm*) viajante *mf*, agente *mf*; (*of union etc*) representante *mf*. **2** *vi*: **to ~ for** ser agente de.
rep³* [rep] *n* (*Theat*) = **repertory**.
Rep. (**a**) *abbr of* **Republic** República *f*. (**b**) (*US Pol*) *abbr of* **Republican** republicano *m*, -a *f* (*also adj*). (**c**) (*US Pol*) *abbr of* **Representative** diputado *m*, -a *f*.
repack ['ri:'pæk] *vt object* reembalar, reenvasar, devolver a su caja (*etc*); *suitcase* volver a hacer.
repaint ['ri:'peɪnt] *vt* repintar; **to ~ sth blue** repintar algo de azul.
repair¹ [rɪ'pɛəʳ] *vi*: **to ~ to** (*move to*) trasladarse a, dirigirse a; (*go regularly to*) acudir a, reunirse en.
repair² [rɪ'pɛəʳ] **1** *n* (**a**) (*act*) reparación *f*, compostura *f*; (*patch etc*) remiendo *m*; **~s** reparaciones *fpl*, (*Archit*) obras *fpl*, reformas *fpl*; **'closed for ~s'** 'cerrado por obras', 'cerrado por reformas'; **cost of ~s** coste *m* de las reparaciones; **to be under ~** estar siendo reparado; (*Archit*) estar en obras; **it is beyond ~** no tiene arreglo, no se puede reparar; (*fig*) no tiene remedio; **it is damaged beyond ~** ha sufrido tantos desperfectos que no se puede reparar.
(**b**) (*state*) **to be in good ~** estar en buen estado; **it's in very bad ~** está en muy mal estado.
2 *attr*: **~ kit** caja *f* de herramientas (para reparaciones); **~ shop** taller *m* de reparaciones.
3 *vt* reparar, componer; *shoes etc* remendar.
repairable [rɪ'pɛərəbl] *adj* que se puede reparar.
repairer [rɪ'pɛərəʳ] *n* reparador *m*, -ora *f*.
repairman [rɪ'pɛəmæn] *n*, *pl* **repairmen** [rɪ'pɛəmen] reparador *m*, mecánico *m*, técnico *m*.
repaper ['ri:'peɪpəʳ] *vt* empapelar de nuevo.
reparable ['repərəbl] *adj* reparable.
reparation [ˌrepə'reɪʃən] *n* reparación *f*; satisfacción *f*; **~s** (*Fin*) indemnización *f*; **to make ~s** dar satisfacción (*for* por).
repartee [ˌrepɑ:'ti:] *n* (intercambio *m* de) réplicas *fpl* agudas, réplicas *fpl* chistosas.
repass ['ri:'pɑ:s] *vt* repasar.
repast [rɪ'pɑ:st] *n* comida *f*.
repatriate 1 [ri:'pætrɪət] *n* repatriado *m*, -a *f*. **2** [ri:'pætrɪeɪt] *vt* repatriar.
repatriation [ri:ˌpætrɪ'eɪʃən] *n* repatriación *f*.
repay [ri:'peɪ] (*irr*: *V* **pay**) *vt money* devolver, reembolsar, reintegrar; *person* pagar; *debt* pagar, liquidar; *person* (*in compensation*) resarcir, compensar; *person* (*pej*) pagar en la misma moneda; *kindness etc* devolver, corresponder a; *visit* devolver, pagar; **to ~ sb in full** pagar a uno todo lo que se le debe, devolver a uno la suma entera; **how can I ever ~ you?** ¿cómo podré nunca corresponder?; **it ~s a visit** vale la pena visitarlo; **it ~s study** merece que se le estudie; **it ~s reading** vale la pena leerlo.
repayable [ri:'peɪəbl] *adj* reembolsable, reintegrable; **£5 deposit not ~** desembolso *m* inicial de 5 libras no reembolsable; **~ in 10 instalments** a pagar en 10 cuotas; **~ on demand** reembolsable a petición; **the money is ~ on the 5th of June** el dinero ha de ser devuelto el 5 de junio.
repayment [ri:'peɪmənt] **1** *n* devolución *f*, reembolso *m*; pago *m*; **now he asks for ~** ahora pide que se le devuelva el dinero; **in 6 ~s of £8** en 6 cuotas de 8 libras cada uno.
2 *attr*: **~ schedule** plan *m* de amortización.
repeal [rɪ'pi:l] **1** *n* revocación *f*, abrogación *f*. **2** *vt* revocar, abrogar.
repeat [rɪ'pi:t] **1** *n* repetición *f*; (*Rad etc*) retransmisión *f*.
2 *attr*: **~ broadcast** retransmisión *f*; **~ mark(s)** (*Mus*) símbolo(s) *m(pl)* de repetición; **~ mortgage** hipoteca *f* amortizable; **~ order** (*Brit*) pedido *m* de repetición; **~ performance** repetición *f*; **~ sign** (*Mus*) = **~ mark.**
3 *vt* repetir; *thanks etc* reiterar, volver a dar; (*aloud*) recitar; **she went and ~ed it to the boss** fue a contárselo al jefe; **don't ~ it to anybody** no lo digas a nadie; **this offer cannot be ~ed** esta oferta no se repetirá; **can you ~ the design of this house?** ¿puede Vd construir otra casa igual que ésta?
4 *vi* repetirse; (*clock, rifle, taste*) repetir; **radishes ~ on me** me repite el rábano.
repeated [rɪ'pi:tɪd] *adj* repetido; reiterado; **in spite of ~ reminders** a pesar de habérselo recordado infinitas veces.
repeatedly [rɪ'pi:tɪdlɪ] *adv* repetidamente, repetidas veces; reiteradamente; **I have told you so ~** te lo he dicho repetidas veces.
repeater [rɪ'pi:təʳ] *n* (**a**) (*watch*) reloj *m* de repetición; (*rifle*) rifle *m* de repetición. (**b**) (*US Jur*) reincidente *mf*.
repeating [rɪ'pi:tɪŋ] *adj* (*Math*) periódico.
repechage [ˌrepɪ'ʃɑ:ʒ] *n* repesca *f*.

repel [rɪ'pel] **1** *vt* rechazar, repeler; (*fig*) repugnar; **he ~s me** me da asco; **it ~s me to have to** + *infin* me repugna tener que + *infin.* **2** *vi* repelerse mutuamente.
repellent [rɪ'pelənt] **1** *adj* repugnante; **it is ~ to insects** ahuyenta los insectos. **2** *n*: **insect ~** repelente *m* de insectos, crema *f* anti-insectos.
repent [rɪ'pent] **1** *vt* arrepentirse de. **2** *vi* arrepentirse.
repentance [rɪ'pentəns] *n* arrepentimiento *m*.
repentant [rɪ'pentənt] *adj* arrepentido; contrito, compungido.
repeople ['riː'piːpl] *vt* repoblar.
repercussion [ˌriːpə'kʌʃən] *n* repercusión *f*; **~s** (*fig*) repercusiones *fpl*; resonancia *f*; **as for the political ~s** en cuanto a las repercusiones políticas; **it had great ~s in Ruritania** tuvo gran resonancia en Ruritania.
repertoire ['repətwɑːʳ] *n* repertorio *m*.
repertory ['repətərɪ] **1** *n* repertorio *m*; **to be** (*or* **act**) **in ~** formar parte de una compañía de repertorio. **2** *attr*: **~ company** compañía *f* de repertorio; **~ theater** (*US*), **~ theatre** (*Brit*) teatro *m* de repertorio.
repetition [ˌrepɪ'tɪʃən] *n* repetición *f*; recitación *f*.
repetitious [ˌrepɪ'tɪʃəs] *adj* repetidor, que se repite; monótono.
repetitive [rɪ'petɪtɪv] *adj* reiterativo; **the book is a bit ~** el libro tiene sus repeticiones.
rephrase [riː'freɪz] *vt* expresar de otro modo, decir con otras palabras.
repine [rɪ'paɪn] *vi* quejarse (*at* de), afligirse (*at* por).
replace [rɪ'pleɪs] *vt* (**a**) (*put back*) reponer, poner en su lugar, devolver a su sitio, colocar nuevamente; **please ~ the receiver** cuelgue, por favor.
(**b**) (*take the place of*) reemplazar, sustituir; **to ~ sth by** (*or* **with**) **sth else** sustituir a algo por otra cosa; **the Matisse was ~d by a Klee** el Matisse fue sustituido por un Klee, un cuadro de Klee sustituyó al de Matisse; **nobody could ever ~ him in my heart** nadie podría reemplazarle en mi corazón; **he asked to be ~d** rogó que se le sustituyera (*or* relevara); **he had to be ~d** tuvo que ser destituido; **we will ~ the broken glasses** nosotros pagaremos los vasos rotos.
replaceable [rɪ'pleɪsəbl] *adj* reemplazable, sustituible; **it will not easily be ~** no será fácil encontrar un repuesto; **he will not easily be ~** no será fácil encontrar un sustituto.
replacement [rɪ'pleɪsmənt] **1** *n* (**a**) (*act*) reposición *f*; devolución *f*; reemplazo *m*, sustitución *f*.
(**b**) (*substitute*: *thing*) reemplazo *m*, repuesto *m*, (*person*) sustituto *m*, suplente *mf*; **it took 3 days to find a ~** tardaron 3 días en encontrar un repuesto.
2 *attr*: **~ cost** costo *m* de sustitución; **~ engine** motor *m* de repuesto; **~ part** repuesto *m*; **~ value** valor *m* de sustitución.
replant ['riː'plɑːnt] *vt* replantar.
replay 1 ['riːpleɪ] *n* (*TV*) repetición *f*; (*Sport*) (partido *m* de) desempate *m*. **2** [ˌriː'pleɪ] *vt* (*TV*) repetir; (*Sport*) volver a jugar; (*Mus*) volver a tocar. **3** [ˌriː'pleɪ] *vi* (*Sport*) jugar el desempate.
replenish [rɪ'plenɪʃ] *vt* (*refill*) rellenar; (*with supplies*) reaprovisionar, repostar (*with* de); *stocks* reponer; (*with fuel*) repostar.
replenishment [rɪ'plenɪʃmənt] *n* rellenado *m*; reaprovisionamiento *m*; reposición *f*.
replete [rɪ'pliːt] *adj* repleto, totalmente lleno (*with* de).
repletion [rɪ'pliːʃən] *n* saciedad *f*, repleción *f*; **to eat to ~** darse un atracón, comer realmente bien.
replica ['replɪkə] *n* (*Art etc*) copia *f*, reproducción *f* (exacta); réplica *f*; (*fig*: *person etc*) segunda edición *f*.
replicate ['replɪˌkeɪt] *vt* reproducir exactamente.
reply [rɪ'plaɪ] **1** *n* respuesta *f*, contestación *f*; **~ card** tarjeta *f* respuesta; **'~ paid'** 'porte pagado'; **~ paid postcard** tarjeta *f* de respuesta pagada; **in ~ he said ...** contestando a esto dijo que ...; **he had nothing to say in ~** no podía darme (*etc*) respuesta; **what is your ~ to this?** ¿qué contestas a esto?; **we await your ~** (*ending letter*) en espera de sus noticias.
2 *attr*: **~ coupon** cupón-respuesta *m*; **international ~ coupon** cupón-respuesta *m* internacional.
3 *vi* responder, contestar; **to ~ to sb** contestar a uno; **to ~ to a letter** contestar una carta.
repoint [riː'pɔɪnt] *vt* rejuntar.
repointing [riː'pɔɪntɪŋ] *n* rejuntamiento *m*.
repopulate ['riː'pɒpjʊleɪt] *vt* repoblar.
repopulation ['riːˌpɒpjʊ'leɪʃən] *n* repoblación *f*.
report [rɪ'pɔːt] **1** *n* (**a**) (*account*) relato *m*, relación *f*; (*Mil etc*) parte *m*; (*official*) informe *m*; (*piece of news*) noticia *f*; (*in newspaper*) reportaje *m*, crónica *f*, información *f*; (*school*) papeleta *f*, nota *f*, certificado *m* escolar; (*annual* ~) memoria *f* anual; **the Robbins R~** el Informe Robbins; **'R~ on the Motor Industry'** 'Informe *m* sobre la Industria del Automóvil'; **the ~ of his death upset us** la noticia de su muerte nos causó pesar; **to present a ~** presentar un informe.
(**b**) (*rumour*) rumor *m*, voz *f*; **there is a ~ that ...** corre la voz de que ..., se rumorea que ...; **I only know of it by ~** lo sé de oídas nada más.
(**c**) (*reputation*: *liter*) reputación *f*, fama *f*; **a person of good ~** una persona de buena fama.
(**d**) (*bang*) estampido *m*, estallido *m*; explosión *f*; **there was a ~** se oyó una explosión.
2 *vt* (*recount*) relatar, narrar, dar cuenta de; (*Mil*) dar parte de; *event etc* informar acerca de; *crime etc* denunciar (*to* a); *meeting* (*as secretary*) levantar las actas de, (*as reporter*) escribir la crónica de; **to ~ that ...** informar que ..., comunicar que ...; **it is ~ed from Berlin that ...** se informa desde Berlín que ..., comunican desde Berlín que ...; **he is ~ed to have said that ...** parece que dijo que ..., habría dicho que ...; **she is ~ed to be in Italy** se cree que está en Italia; **~ed speech** discurso *m* indirecto, discurso *m* referido; **what have you to ~?** ¿qué tienes que decirnos?; **nothing to ~** sin novedad; **nothing to ~ from the front** sin novedad en el frente; **to ~ progress** dar cuenta de los progresos; **I shall have to ~ this** tendré que denunciar esto; **you have been ~ed for idleness** Vd ha sido denunciado por vago, le han acusado de ser holgazán; **he was ~ed for swearing at the referee** se le denunció por dirigir palabrotas al árbitro.
3 *vi* (**a**) (*make report*) hacer un informe, presentar un informe (*on* acerca de); **a committee was set up to ~ on the pill** se creó una comisión para investigar la píldora; **Professor X ~s on his discovery in the next issue** el Profesor X informará de su descubrimiento en el próximo número; **the committee will ~ to the cabinet** la comisión elevará su informe al consejo de ministros; **he ~s to the marketing director** es responsable al director de márketing; **Jim Bloggs ~s from Chicago** (*Rad, TV*) Jim Bloggs informa desde Chicago.
(**b**) (*as reporter*) ser reportero; **he ~ed for the 'Daily Echo' for 40 years** durante 40 años fue reportero del 'Daily Echo'.
(**c**) (*present o.s.*) presentarse; personarse; **to ~ at a place at 18.00 hours** presentarse en un sitio a las 18.00 horas; **~ to me when you are better** venga a verme cuando te hayas repuesto; **he is to ~ to the court tomorrow** tiene que personarse mañana ante el tribunal; **to ~ sick** darse de baja por enfermo; **to ~ fit** darse de alta; **to ~ to one's unit** reincorporarse a su unidad.
◆**report back** *vi*: **to ~ back to sb** rendir cuentas a uno; presentarse para informar a uno; **~ back at 6 o'clock** preséntese a las 6.
reportage [ˌrepɔː'tɑːʒ] *n* reportaje *m*.
report card [rɪ'pɔːtˌkɑːd] *n* (*Scol*) cartilla *f* escolar.
reportedly [rɪ'pɔːtɪdlɪ] *adv* según se dice, según se informa; **he is ~ living in Australia** se dice que está viviendo en Australia.
reporter [rɪ'pɔːtəʳ] *n* reportero *m*, -a *f*, periodista *mf*; (*TV, Radio*) locutor *m*, -ora *f*.
reporting [rɪ'pɔːtɪŋ] **1** *n* reportaje *m*. **2** *adj*: **~ structure** estructura *f* laboral jerárquica.
repose [rɪ'pəʊz] **1** *n* reposo *m*.
2 *vt* (*lay etc*) reposar, descansar; recostar; **to ~ confidence in sb** poner confianza en uno.
3 *vi* reposar, descansar; **to ~ on** descansar sobre, (*fig*) descansar en, estribar en, estar basado en.
repository [rɪ'pɒzɪtərɪ] *n* depósito *m*, almacén *m*; (*furniture* ~) guardamuebles *m*; (*person*) depositario *m*, -a *f*.
repossess ['riːpə'zes] **1** *vt* recobrar. **2** *vr*: **to ~ o.s. of sth** recobrar algo, volver a tomar algo.
repossession [ˌriːpə'zeʃən] *n* recuperación *f* de un artículo no pagado.
repot [riː'pɒt] *vt* poner en nueva maceta, cambiar de maceta.
reprehend [ˌreprɪ'hend] *vt* reprender.
reprehensible [ˌreprɪ'hensɪbl] *adj* reprensible, censurable.
reprehensibly [ˌreprɪ'hensɪblɪ] *adv* censurablemente.
reprehension [ˌreprɪ'henʃən] *n* reprensión *f*.
represent [ˌreprɪ'zent] *vt* representar; (*Jur*) ser apoderado de, (*fig*) hablar en nombre de; (*Comm*) ser agente de; **the goods are not as ~ed** las mercancías no son como nos las describieron; **his early work is well ~ed in the exhibition** su

obra juvenil tiene una fuerte representación en la exposición; **you ~ed it falsely to us** Vd nos lo describió falsamente; **it has been ~ed to us that** ... se ha pretendido que ..., se nos ha dicho que ...; **he ~s nobody but himself** no representa a nadie sino a sí mismo.

re-present ['riːprɪ'zent] *vt* volver a presentar.

representation [ˌreprɪzen'teɪʃən] *n* (**a**) representación *f* (*also Pol*).

(**b**) (*protest etc*) petición *f*; declaración *f*; **to make ~s to sb** presentar una petición a uno, dirigir un memorial a uno, (*complain*) quejarse ante uno; **to make ~s about sth** quejarse de algo.

(**c**) **to make false ~s** describir algo falsamente.

representational [ˌreprɪzen'teɪʃənəl] *adj* (*Art*) figurativo.

representative [ˌreprɪ'zentətɪv] **1** *adj* representativo; **~ government** gobierno *m* representativo; **these figures are more ~** estas cifras son más representativas; **a person not fully ~ of the group** una persona que no representa adecuadamente el grupo.

2 *n* representante *mf* (*also Comm*); (*Jur*) apoderado *m*; (*US Pol*) diputado *m*, -a *f*.

repress [rɪ'pres] *vt* reprimir.

repressed [rɪ'prest] *adj* reprimido.

repression [rɪ'preʃən] *n* represión *f*.

repressive [rɪ'presɪv] *adj* represivo.

reprieve [rɪ'priːv] **1** *n* (*breathing space*) respiro *m*, alivio *m* temporal; (*Jur*) indulto *m*, suspensión *f* (*esp* de la pena de muerte); **to win a last-minute ~** ser indultado a última hora; **the wood got a ~** se retiró la orden de talar el bosque.

2 *vt* indultar, suspender la pena de; **to ~ sb from death** indultar a uno de muerte, suspender la pena de muerte de uno.

reprimand ['reprɪmɑːnd] **1** *n* reprimenda *f*, reprensión *f*. **2** *vt* reprender, reconvenir.

reprint **1** ['riːprɪnt] *n* reimpresión *f*; (*offprint*) tirada *f* aparte, separata *f*. **2** ['riː'prɪnt] *vt* reimprimir; **'~ed from the Transactions of ...'** 'tirada aparte de las Actas de ...'

reprisal [rɪ'praɪzəl] *n* represalia *f*; **as a ~ for** como represalia por; **by way of ~** a modo de represalia; **to take ~s** tomar represalias.

reproach [rɪ'prəʊtʃ] **1** *n* (*spoken etc*) reproche *m*, censura *f*; (*stain, disgrace*) tacha *f*, baldón *m*, oprobio *m*; **beyond ~** por encima de toda crítica, intachable; **term of ~** término *m* oprobioso; **this is a ~ to us all** esto es deshonroso para todos nosotros; **poverty is a ~ to civilization** la pobreza es una vergüenza para la civilización.

2 *vt*: **to ~ sb for sth, to ~ sb with sth** reprochar algo a uno, censurar algo a uno, echar algo en cara a uno.

3 *vr*: **to ~ o.s. for sth** reprocharse algo; **you have no reason to ~ yourself** Vd no tiene motivo para reprocharse (nada).

reproachful [rɪ'prəʊtʃfʊl] *adj look etc* acusador, lleno de reproches; **next day she was ~** el día siguiente me reprochó.

reproachfully [rɪ'prəʊtʃfəlɪ] *adv look etc* con reproche; *speak etc* en tono acusador.

reprobate ['reprəʊbeɪt] *n* réprobo *m*, -a *f*.

reprobation [ˌreprəʊ'beɪʃən] *n* reprobación *f*.

reprocess [ˌriː'prəʊses] *vt* reprocesar.

reprocessing [ˌriː'prəʊsesɪŋ] *n* reprocesamiento *m*; **~ plant** planta *f* de reprocesamiento.

reproduce [ˌriːprə'djuːs] **1** *vt* reproducir. **2** *vi* reproducirse.

reproduction [ˌriːprə'dʌkʃən] **1** *n* reproducción *f*. **2** *attr*: **~ furniture** mobiliario *m* estilo.

reproductive [ˌriːprə'dʌktɪv] *adj* reproductor.

reprography [rɪ'prɒgrəfɪ] *n* reprografía *f*.

reproof [rɪ'pruːf] *n* reprensión *f*, reconvención *f*; **to administer a ~ to sb** reprender a uno.

re-proof [ˌriː'pruːf] *vt* reimpermeabilizar.

reproval [rɪ'pruːvəl] *n* reprobación *f*.

reprove [rɪ'pruːv] *vt* reprender, reconvenir; **to ~ sb for sth** reprender algo a uno.

reproving [rɪ'pruːvɪŋ] *adj* reprobador, lleno de reproches.

reprovingly [rɪ'pruːvɪŋlɪ] *adv* en tono reprobador, reprobadoramente, con reprobación; **she looked at me ~** me miró severa, me reprendió con la mirada.

reptile ['reptaɪl] *n* reptil *m*.

reptilian [rep'tɪlɪən] **1** *adj* reptil. **2** *n* reptil *m*.

republic [rɪ'pʌblɪk] *n* república *f*.

republican [rɪ'pʌblɪkən] **1** *adj* republicano. **2** *n* republicano *m*, -a *f*.

republicanism [rɪ'pʌblɪkənɪzəm] *n* republicanismo *m*.

republication ['riːˌpʌblɪ'keɪʃən] *n* reedición *f*.

republish ['riː'pʌblɪʃ] *vt* reeditar.

repudiate [rɪ'pjuːdɪeɪt] *vt charge etc* rechazar, negar, desechar; *attitude etc* repudiar; *possibility* descartar; *obligation etc* rechazar, desconocer; *wife* repudiar; *debt, treaty* anular, cancelar.

repudiation [rɪˌpjuːdɪ'eɪʃən] *n* rechazamiento *m*; desconocimiento *m*; repudio *m*; incumplimiento *m*; anulación *f*, cancelación *f*.

repugnance [rɪ'pʌgnəns] *n* repugnancia *f*.

repugnant [rɪ'pʌgnənt] *adj* repugnante; **it is ~ to me** me repugna.

repulse [rɪ'pʌls] **1** *n* repulsa *f*, repulsión *f*; rechazo *m*; **to suffer a ~** ser repulsado, ser rechazado. **2** *vt* rechazar, repulsar.

repulsion [rɪ'pʌlʃən] *n* repulsión *f*, repugnancia *f*; (*Phys*) repulsión *f*.

repulsive [rɪ'pʌlsɪv] *adj* repulsivo, repelente.

repulsively [rɪ'pʌlsɪvlɪ] *adv* de modo repulsivo; **~ ugly** terriblemente feo.

repulsiveness [rɪ'pʌlsɪvnɪs] *n* lo repulsivo; lo repelente; **of such ~** tan repelente.

repurchase ['riː'pɜːtʃɪs] **1** *n* readquisición *f*. **2** *vt* readquirir, volver a comprar.

reputable ['repjʊtəbl] *adj firm, brand etc* acreditado, de toda confianza; *person* honroso, formal, estimable.

reputation [ˌrepjʊ'teɪʃən] *n* reputación *f*, fama *f*; **of good ~** de buena fama; **to have a bad ~** tener mala fama; **to have a ~ for meanness** tener fama de tacaño; **the hotel has a ~ for good food** el hotel es célebre por su buena comida; **he has the ~ of being awkward** se dice que es difícil, tiene fama de difícil; **to ruin a girl's ~** acabar con la buena fama de una joven.

repute [rɪ'pjuːt] **1** *n* reputación *f*, fama *f*; **by ~** según la opinión común, según se dice; **a firm of (good) ~** una casa acreditada; **a café of ill ~** un café de mala fama; **a house of ill ~** (*euph*) una casa de mala fama; **to hold sb in (high) ~** tener un alto concepto de uno; **his skill was held in high ~** su destreza era muy estimada; **to know sb by ~ only** conocer a uno sólo por su reputación, conocer a uno de oídas nada más.

2 *vt* reputar; **to be ~d as** tener fama de, pasar por; **to be ~d to be clever** tener fama de inteligente, pasar por ser inteligente; **he is ~d to be a millionaire** se dice que es millonario.

reputed [rɪ'pjuːtɪd] *adj* supuesto, presunto.

reputedly [rɪ'pjuːtɪdlɪ] *adv* según se dice, según la opinión común.

request [rɪ'kwest] **1** *n* ruego *m*, petición *f*; instancia *f*; (*formal*) solicitud *f*; **a ~ for help** una petición de socorro; **at the ~ of** a petición de, a instancia de; **at the urgent ~ of X I have decided to** + *infin* accediendo al ruego insistente de X he decidido + *infin*; **by ~** a petición; **to play a record by ~** tocar un disco a petición de un oyente; **it is much in ~** tiene mucha demanda, está muy solicitado; **on ~** a solicitud; **to grant sb's ~** acceder al ruego de uno; **to make a ~ for sth** pedir algo, hacer una petición de algo.

2 *attr programme* a petición de los radioyentes; *stop* discrecional, a petición.

3 *vt* pedir, rogar; solicitar; **to ~ sth of sb** pedir algo a uno; **to ~ sb to do sth** rogar a uno hacer algo, pedir que uno haga algo; **'visitors are ~ed not to talk'** 'se ruega a los visitantes respetar el silencio'.

requiem ['rekwɪem] *n* réquiem *m*.

require [rɪ'kwaɪəʳ] *vt* (**a**) (*need*) necesitar; exigir; pedir, requerir; **we ~ another chair** necesitamos otra silla más; **it ~s great care** exige mucho cuidado; **the lock ~s attention** hace falta reparar la cerradura; **the battery ~s regular attention** hay que comprobar la pila con regularidad; **no maintenance ~d** no necesita manutención alguna; **it ~d all his strength to lift it** hacía falta que emplease todas sus fuerzas para levantarlo; **this plant ~s watering frequently** esta planta hay que regarla con frecuencia; **is my presence ~d?** ¿es necesario que asista yo?; **your presence is ~d** se exige que asista Vd; **if ~d** en caso de necesidad, si es necesario; **when ~d** cuando hace falta; **as the situation may ~** según lo exija la situación; **we will do all that is ~d** haremos todo lo que haga falta; **what qualifications are ~d?** ¿qué títulos se requieren?

(**b**) **to ~ sth of sb** pedir algo a uno; **what do you ~ of me?** ¿qué piden Vds que haga?

(**c**) (*demand*) **to ~ that ...** exigir que + *subj*, requerir que + *subj*, insistir en que + *subj*; **the law ~s that it should be done** la ley exige que se haga.

required [rɪ'kwaɪəd] *adj* necesario, obligatorio, que hace falta; **a pipe of the ~ length** un tubo del largo que hace falta; **by the ~ date** antes de la fecha prescrita; **within the ~ time** dentro del plazo establecido; **has he got the ~ qualities?** ¿tiene las cualidades necesarias?; **the qualities ~ for the job** las cualidades que se requieren para el puesto; **it is a ~ course for the degree** (*US*) es una asignatura obligatoria para el título.

requirement [rɪ'kwaɪəmənt] *n* requisito *m*; estipulación *f*; necesidad *f*; condición *f*; exigencia *f*; **~s** requisitos *mpl*; **our ~s are few** nuestras necesidades son pocas, necesitamos poco; **Latin is a ~ for the course** el latín es un requisito para este curso, para este curso se exige el latín; **it is one of the ~s of the contract** es una de las estipulaciones del contrato; **to meet all the ~s for sth** llenar todos los requisitos para algo.

requisite ['rekwɪzɪt] **1** *adj* preciso, indispensable, imprescindible. **2** *n* requisito *m*; **office ~s** material *m* de oficina; **toilet ~s** artículos *mpl* de tocador.

requisition [,rekwɪ'zɪʃən] **1** *n* pedido *m*, solicitud *f* (*for* de); (*Mil*) requisa *f*, requisición *f*. **2** *vt* (*Mil*) requisar.

requital [rɪ'kwaɪtl] *n* compensación *f*, satisfacción *f*; desquite *m*.

requite [rɪ'kwaɪt] *vt* (*make return for*) compensar, recompensar, pagar; **to ~ sb's love** corresponder al amor de uno; **that love was not ~d** ese amor no fue correspondido.

reread ['riː'riːd] (*irr*: *V* **read**) *vt* releer, volver a leer.

reredos ['rɪədɒs] *n* retablo *m*.

reroute ['riː'ruːt] *vt* desviar; **the train was ~ed through Burgos** el tren se desvió de la ruta normal y pasó por Burgos.

rerun 1 ['riːrʌn] *n* repetición *f*; (*Theat etc*) reestreno *m*, reposición *f*. **2** ['riː'rʌn] (*irr*: *V* **run**) *vt race* correr de nuevo; (*Theat etc*) reestrenar, reponer.

resale ['riː'seɪl] **1** *n* reventa *f*. **2** *attr*: **~ price maintenance** mantenimiento *m* del precio de venta; **~ value** valor *m* de reventa.

reschedule [riː'ʃedjuːl] *vt* reprogramar.

rescind [rɪ'sɪnd] *vt* rescindir, anular, revocar.

rescission [rɪ'sɪʒən] *n* rescisión *f*, anulación *f*, revocación *f*.

rescue ['reskjuː] **1** *n* salvamento *m*, rescate *m*; liberación *f* (*from* de); **the hero of the ~ was ...** el héroe del salvamento fue ...; **to come** (*or* **go**) **to the ~ of** ir al socorro de, acudir al rescate de; **to the ~!** ¡al socorro!; **Batman to the ~!** ¡Batman acude a la llamada!

2 *attr*: **~ attempt** tentativa *f* de salvamento; **~ dig** excavación *f* de urgencia; **~ operations** operaciones *fpl* de salvamento; **~ party, ~ team** equipo *m* de salvamento; **~ services** servicios *mpl* de rescate; **~ vessel** buque *m* de salvamento; **~ work** operación *f* de salvamento.

3 *vt* salvar, rescatar; librar, libertar (*from* de); **three men were ~d** tres hombres fueron salvados; **they waited 3 days to be ~d** esperaron 3 días hasta ser rescatados; **to ~ sb from death** librar a uno de la muerte; **the ~d man is in hospital** el hombre rescatado está en el hospital.

rescuer ['reskjʊəʳ] *n* salvador *m*, -ora *f*.

research [rɪ'sɜːtʃ] **1** *n* investigación *f*, investigaciones *fpl* (*in, into* de); **~ and development** investigación *f* y desarrollo; **atomic ~** investigaciones *fpl* atómicas; **our ~ shows that ...** nuestras investigaciones demuestran que ...; **a piece of ~** una investigación.

2 *attr*: **~ establishment** instituto *m* de investigaciones; **~ fellow** investigador *m*, -ora *f*; **~ laboratory** laboratorio *m* de investigación; **~ staff** personal *m* investigador; **~ student** estudiante *m* investigador, estudiante *f* investigadora; **~ team** equipo *m* de investigación; **~ work** investigaciones *fpl*, trabajos *mpl* de investigación; **~ worker** investigador *m*, -ora *f*.

3 *vi* investigar; **to ~ into sth** investigar algo, hacer investigaciones de algo.

4 *vt* (*US*) investigar; **to ~ an article** preparar el material para un estudio, reunir datos para escribir un artículo; **a well ~ed study** un estudio bien preparado.

researcher [rɪ'sɜːtʃəʳ] *n* investigador *m*, -ora *f*.

reseat [,riː'siːt] *vt chair* poner nuevo asiento a.

resection [riː'sekʃən] *n* (**a**) (*Survey*) triangulación *f*. (**b**) (*Med*) resección *f*.

resell ['riː'sel] (*irr*: *V* **sell**) *vt* revender, volver a vender.

resemblance [rɪ'zembləns] *n* semejanza *f*, parecido *m*; **to bear a strong ~ to sb** parecerse mucho a uno; **to bear no ~ to sb** no parecerse en absoluto a uno; **there is no ~ between them** los dos no se parecen en absoluto; **there is hardly any ~ between this version and the one I gave you** apenas existe parecido entre esta versión y la que te di.

resemble [rɪ'zembl] *vt* parecerse a; **he doesn't ~ his father** no se parece a su padre; **they do ~ one another** sí se parecen uno a otro.

resent [rɪ'zent] *vt* ofenderse por, tomar a mal, resentirse de (*or* por); **I ~ that!** ¡protesto contra esa observación!, ¡no permito que se diga eso!, ¡eso no!; **he ~s my being here** se ofende por mi presencia aquí, no está conforme con mi presencia aquí; **I don't ~ your saying it** no me ofende que lo digas.

resentful [rɪ'zentfʊl] *adj person* resentido, ofendido, agraviado; *tone* resentido, ofendido; **to be** (*or* **feel**) **~ of** ofenderse por, sentirse agraviado por; **no wonder she feels ~** no me extraña que se sienta ofendida; **he is still ~ about it** todavía guarda rencor por ello.

resentfully [rɪ'zentfəlɪ] *adv* con resentimiento; **he said ~** dijo resentido.

resentment [rɪ'zentmənt] *n* resentimiento *m* (*about, at* por).

reservation [,rezə'veɪʃən] *n* (**a**) (*act*) reservación *f*, reserva *f*; (*mental*) reserva *f*, (*in contract etc*) salvedad *f*, (*in argument*) distingo *m*; **with certain ~s** con ciertas reservas; **to accept sth without ~** aceptar algo sin reserva; **I had ~s about it** tenía ciertas dudas sobre ese punto.

(**b**) (*booking*) reservación *f*; (*seat*) plaza *f* reservada; (*in restaurant*) mesa *f* reservada; **to make a ~ in a hotel** reservar una habitación en un hotel.

(**c**) (*on road*) mediana *f*, franja *f* central.

(**d**) (*US*) reserva *f* (de pieles rojas).

reservation desk [,rezə'veɪʃən,desk] *n* (*Brit*) mostrador *m* de reservas, (*US*: *in hotels*) recepción *f*.

reserve [rɪ'zɜːv] **1** *n* (**a**) (*of money etc*) reserva *f*; **to have sth in ~** tener algo de reserva; **to have a ~ of strength** tener una reserva de fuerzas; **there are untapped ~s of energy** hay reservas de energía que quedan sin explotar; **Spain possesses half the world's ~s of pyrites** España tiene la mitad de las reservas mundiales de piritas.

(**b**) (*Mil*) **the ~** la reserva.

(**c**) (*Sport etc*) suplente *mf*; **to play in** (*or* **with**) **the ~s** jugar en el segundo equipo.

(**d**) (*land*) reserva *f*; (*game*) coto *m* (de caza); (*nature*) reserva *f* natural.

(**e**) (*restriction*) **without ~** sin reserva.

(**f**) (*shyness*) reserva *f*.

2 *attr*: **~ currency** divisa *f* de reserva; **~ fund** fondo *m* de reserva; **~ gas tank** (*US*), **~ petrol tank** (*Brit*) depósito *m* de gasolina de reserva; **~ player** suplente *mf*; **~ price** (*Brit*) precio *m* mínimo (fijado en una subasta); **~ team** segundo equipo *m*.

3 *vt* (**a**) (*keep, book*) reservar; **that's being ~d for me** eso está reservado para mí; **I ~ the right to +** *infin* me reservo el derecho de + *infin*; **did you ~ the seats?** ¿has reservado las plazas?

(**b**) (*Jur*) aplazar, diferir; **the judge ~d sentence** el juez difirió la sentencia.

4 *vr*: **I'm reserving myself for later** me reservo para más tarde.

reserved [rɪ'zɜːvd] *adj* (*all senses*) reservado.

reservedly [rɪ'zɜːvɪdlɪ] *adv* con reserva.

reservist [rɪ'zɜːvɪst] *n* reservista *mf*.

reservoir ['rezəvwɑːʳ] *n* (**a**) (*small*) depósito *m*, represa *f*; (*tank*) depósito *m*, cisterna *f*; (*large, for irrigation, hydroelectric power*) pantano *m*, embalse *m*, represa *f* (*LAm*); **natural underground ~** embalse *m* subterráneo natural.

(**b**) (*fig*: *of strength etc*) reserva *f*.

reset ['riː'set] (*irr*: *V* **set**) **1** *vt machine etc* reajustar; (*Typ*) recomponer; (*Comput*) reinicializar; *bone* volver a encajar; *jewel* reengastar.

2 *attr*: **~ switch** conmutador *m* de reajuste.

resettle ['riː'setl] **1** *vt persons* restablecer, volver a establecer; *land* volver a colonizar, volver a poblar; **the lands were ~d by the Poles** las tierras fueron nuevamente colonizadas por los polacos.

2 *vi* restablecerse, volver a establecerse.

resettlement ['riː'setlmənt] *n* restablecimiento *m*; nueva colonización *f*, repoblación *f*.

reshape ['riː'ʃeɪp] *vt* reformar, formar de nuevo, rehacer; reorganizar.

reshuffle ['riː'ʃʌfl] **1** *n* (*Pol*) reconstrucción *f*, remodelación *f*, reajuste *m*. **2** *vt cards* volver a barajar; (*Pol*) reconstruir, remodelar, reajustar.

reside [rɪ'zaɪd] *vi* residir, vivir; **to ~ in** (*fig*) residir en.

residence ['rezɪdəns] **1** *n* (**a**) (*stay*) residencia *f*; (*stay, in official parlance*) permanencia *f*, estancia *f*; **after 6 months' ~** después de 6 meses de permanencia; **when the students are in ~** cuando están los estudiantes; **there is a doctor in ~** hay un médico interno; **to take up one's ~** establecerse.

(**b**) (*house*) residencia *f*, domicilio *m*; (*Univ*: *also* **hall of ~**) residencia *f*; **'town and country ~s for sale'** 'se ofrecen fincas urbanas y rurales'; **the minister's official ~** la residencia oficial del ministro.

2 *attr*: ~ **permit** (*Brit*) permiso *m* de permanencia.

residency ['rezɪdənsɪ] *n* residencia *f*.

resident ['rezɪdənt] **1** *adj* (*gen, Comput*) residente; *population etc* fijo, permanente; *doctor etc* interno; *servant* permanente, que duerme en casa; *bird* no migratorio; **to be ~ in a town** residir en una ciudad, tener domicilio fijo en una ciudad; **we were ~ there for some years** residimos allí durante varios años.

2 *n* residente *mf*; vecino *m*, -a *f*; (*in hotel etc*) huésped *m*, -eda *f*; **~s' association** asociación *f* de vecinos; **the ~s got together to protest** los vecinos se reunieron para protestar.

residential [ˌrezɪ'denʃəl] *adj* residencial; **~ area** barrio *m* residencial.

residual [rɪ'zɪdjʊəl] **1** *adj* residual. **2** *n*: **~s** derechos *mpl* residuales de autor.

residuary [rɪ'zɪdjʊərɪ] *adj* restante, remanente, residual; **~ legatee** legatario *m*, -a *f* universal.

residue ['rezɪdjuː] *n* resto *m*, residuo *m*; (*Fin etc*) saldo *m*, superávit *m*; **a ~ of bad feeling** un residuo de rencor, un rencor que queda.

residuum [rɪ'zɪdjʊəm] *n* residuo *m*.

resign [rɪ'zaɪn] **1** *vt office etc* dimitir, renunciar a; *claim, task etc* renunciar a; **to ~ a task to others** ceder un cometido a otros; **when he ~ed the leadership** cuando dimitió la jefatura.

2 *vi* (**a**) dimitir; renunciar; **to ~ in favour of sb else** renunciar en favor de otro.

(**b**) (*Chess*) abandonar.

3 *vr*: **to ~ o.s.** resignarse; **to ~ o.s. to** resignarse a, conformarse con; **I ~ed myself to never seeing her again** me resigné a no volverla a ver jamás.

resignation [ˌrezɪg'neɪʃən] *n* (**a**) (*act*) dimisión *f* (*from* de), renuncia *f*; **to offer** (*or* **send in, submit, tender**) **one's ~** dimitir, presentar su dimisión.

(**b**) (*state*) resignación *f* (*to* a), conformidad *f* (*to* con); **to await sth with ~** esperar algo resignado, esperar algo con resignación.

resigned [rɪ'zaɪnd] *adj* resignado.

resignedly [rɪ'zaɪnɪdlɪ] *adv* con resignación.

resilience [rɪ'zɪlɪəns] *n* elasticidad *f*; (*fig*) resistencia *f*; poder *m* de recuperación; flexibilidad *f*, capacidad *f* para adaptarse.

resilient [rɪ'zɪlɪənt] *adj* elástico; (*fig*) resistente; que tiene poder de recuperación; flexible, que tiene capacidad para adaptarse.

resin ['rezɪn] *n* resina *f*.

resinous ['rezɪnəs] *adj* resinoso.

resist [rɪ'zɪst] **1** *vt* resistir (a); oponerse a; oponer resistencia a; **to ~ arrest** resistirse a ser detenido, oponer resistencia a la policía; **to ~ temptation** resistir la tentación; **they ~ed the attack vigorously** resistieron vigorosamente el ataque; **we ~ this change** nos oponemos a este cambio; **I can't ~ squid** me apasionan los calamares; **I couldn't ~ buying it** no me resistí a comprarlo, no pude menos de comprarlo, me fue imposible dejar de comprarlo; **I can't ~ saying that ...** no resisto al impulso de decir que ...

2 *vi* resistirse, oponer resistencia.

resistance [rɪ'zɪstəns] **1** *n* (*all senses*) resistencia *f*; **the R~** (*Pol*) la Resistencia; **to offer ~** oponer resistencia (*to* a); **to have good ~ to disease** tener mucha resistencia a la enfermedad; **to take the line of least ~** seguir la línea de menor resistencia, optar por lo más fácil.

2 *attr*: **~ fighter, ~ worker** militante *mf* de la Resistencia; **~ movement** (movimiento *m* de) resistencia *f*.

resistant [rɪ'zɪstənt] *adj* resistente (*to* a).

resistible [rɪ'zɪstɪbl] *adj* resistible.

resistor [rɪ'zɪstəʳ] *n* resistor *m*.

resit (*Brit*) **1** ['riːsɪt] *n* reválida *f*.

2 [ˈriːˈsɪt] (*irr*: *V* **sit**) *vt exam* presentarse otra vez a; *subject* examinarse otra vez de.

3 ['riː'sɪt] *vi* presentarse otra vez, volver a examinarse.

resole ['riː'səʊl] *vt* sobresolar, remontar.

resolute ['rezəluːt] *adj* resuelto.

resolutely ['rezəluːtlɪ] *adv* resueltamente.

resoluteness ['rezəluːtnɪs] *n* resolución *f*.

resolution [ˌrezə'luːʃən] *n* (**a**) (*resoluteness*) resolución *f*; **to show ~** mostrarse resuelto.

(**b**) (*separation, solving*) resolución *f*.

(**c**) (*motion*) resolución *f*, proposición *f*; (*Parl*) acuerdo *m*; **to pass a ~** tomar un acuerdo; **to put a ~ to a meeting** someter una moción a votación.

(**d**) (*resolve*) propósito *m*; **good ~s** buenos propósitos *mpl*; **to make a ~ to** + *infin* resolverse a + *infin*.

(**e**) (*Comput*) resolución *f*, definición *f* (de la pantalla).

resolvable [rɪ'zɒlvəbl] *adj* soluble.

resolve [rɪ'zɒlv] **1** *n* (**a**) (*resoluteness*) resolución *f*; **unshakeable ~** resolución *f* inquebrantable.

(**b**) (*decision*) propósito *m*; **to make a ~ to** + *infin* resolverse a + *infin*.

2 *vt* (*all senses*) resolver (*into* en); **this will ~ your doubts** esto ha de resolver sus dudas; **the problem is still not ~d** el problema queda por resolver; **it was ~d that ...** se acordó que ...

3 *vi* (**a**) (*separate*) resolverse (*into* en); **the question ~s into 4 parts** la cuestión se resuelve en 4 partes.

(**b**) (*decide*) **to ~ on sth** optar por algo, resolverse por algo; **to ~ on** + *ger* acordar + *infin*; **to ~ to** + *infin* resolverse a + *infin*; **to ~ that ...** acordar que ...

resolved [rɪ'zɒlvd] *adj* resuelto; **to be ~ to** + *infin* estar resuelto a + *infin*.

resonance ['rezənəns] *n* resonancia *f*.

resonant ['rezənənt] *adj* resonante.

resonate ['rezəˌneɪt] *vi* resonar (*with* de).

resonator ['rezəneɪtəʳ] *n* resonador *m*.

resorption [rɪ'zɔːpʃən] *n* resorción *f*.

resort [rɪ'zɔːt] **1** *n* (**a**) (*recourse*) recurso *m*; **as a last ~, in the last ~** en último caso; **without ~ to force** sin recurrir a la fuerza.

(**b**) (*place*) punto *m* de reunión, lugar *m* de reunión; (*holiday ~*) punto *m* de veraneo; (*coastal, seaside*) playa *f*, punto *m* marítimo (de veraneo); **it is a ~ of thieves** es lugar frecuentado por los ladrones, es donde se reúnen los ladrones.

2 *vi*: **to ~ to** (**a**) *place* frecuentar, concurrir a, acudir a.

(**b**) (*have recourse to*) recurrir a; acudir a; hacer uso de; **to ~ to violence** recurrir a la violencia; **then they ~ed to throwing stones** pasaron luego a tirar piedras; **then you ~ to me for help** así que acudes a mí a pedir ayuda.

resound [rɪ'zaʊnd] *vi* resonar, retumbar; **the valley ~ed with shouts** resonaron los gritos por el valle; **the whole house ~s with laughter** resuenan las risas por toda la casa.

resounding [rɪ'zaʊndɪŋ] *adj* sonoro; (*fig*) *success etc* clamoroso, resonante; *failure* estrepitoso.

resoundingly [rɪ'zaʊndɪŋlɪ] *adv*: **to defeat sb ~** obtener una victoria resonante sobre uno.

resource [rɪ'sɔːs] **1** *n* (**a**) (*expedient*) recurso *m*, expediente *m*.

(**b**) **~s** (*wealth, supplies etc*) recursos *mpl*; **financial ~s** recursos *mpl* financieros; **natural ~s** recursos *mpl* naturales; **to be at the end of one's ~s** haber agotado sus recursos; **he has great ~s of energy** tiene una gran reserva de energía; **those ~s are as yet untapped** esos recursos quedan todavía sin explotar.

(**c**) (*resourcefulness*) inventiva *f*.

2 *vt* proveer fondos para, financiar; **we are ~d by X** nuestra fuente de fondos es X; **they are generously ~d** su fuente de fondos los trata generosamente; **an inadequately ~d project** un proyecto insuficientemente financiado.

resourceful [rɪ'sɔːsfʊl] *adj* inventivo, ingenioso.

resourcefully [rɪ'sɔːsfəlɪ] *adv* ingeniosamente, mostrando tener inventiva.

resourcefulness [rɪ'sɔːsfʊlnɪs] *n* inventiva *f*, iniciativa *f*, ingeniosidad *f*.

re-sow [ˌriː'səʊ] *vt* resembrar, volver a sembrar.

re-sowing [ˌriː'səʊɪŋ] *n* resembrado *m*.

respect [rɪs'pekt] **1** *n* (**a**) (*relation*) respecto *m*; **in every ~** desde todos los puntos de vista; **in many ~s** desde muchos puntos de vista; en cierto modo; **in one ~** desde un punto de vista; bajo uno de los aspectos; **in other ~s** por lo demás; **in some ~s** desde varios puntos de vista; **in this ~** por lo que se refiere a esto; en cuanto a esto; **in ~ of** respecto a, respecto de; **with ~ to** con respecto a.

(**b**) (*frm*) **without ~ of persons** sin acepción de personas.

(**c**) (*consideration*) respeto *m*, consideración *f*; **~ for one's parents** respeto *m* a sus padres; **~ for the truth** respeto *m* por la verdad; **out of ~ for sb** por consideración a uno; **with all ~ to you** sin menoscabo del respeto que se le debe a Vd; **with all due ~** con el respeto debido; **if I may say so with ~** si puedo decirlo con el mayor respeto;

worthy of ~ digno de respeto, respetable; **to command** ~ imponer respeto, hacerse respetar; **to have ~ for sb, to hold sb in** ~ tener respeto a uno, respetar a uno; **we have the greatest ~ for him** le respetamos muchísimo; **to pay ~ to sb** respetar a uno; **to pay one's last ~s to sb** hacer honor al muerto, acompañar por última vez a uno; (*in official ceremony*) rendir el último homenaje a uno; **to show no ~ to sb** faltar al respeto debido a uno; **he shows scant ~ for our opinions** poco respeta nuestras opiniones; **to treat sb with** ~ tratar a uno respetuosamente; **to win sb's** ~ ganarse el respeto de uno.

(**d**) (*in messages*) **~s** recuerdos *mpl*, saludos *mpl*; **to pay one's ~s to sb** cumplimentar a uno, presentar sus respetos a uno; **to send one's ~s to sb** mandar recuerdos a uno.

2 *vt* respetar; acatar; **to ~ sb's opinions** respetar las opiniones de uno; **to ~ sb's wishes** atenerse a los deseos de uno; **to make o.s. ~ed** hacerse respetar.

respectability [rɪs,pektə'bɪlɪtɪ] *n* respetabilidad *f*.

respectable [rɪs'pektəbl] *adj* (**a**) (*deserving respect*) respetable; **for perfectly ~ reasons** por motivos perfectamente respetables.

(**b**) (*of fair social standing, decent*) respetable, decente, honrado; **~ people** gente *f* bien; **in ~ society** en la buena sociedad, entre personas educadas; **that's not** ~ eso no se hace, eso no es decente, eso es de mala educación; **that skirt isn't** ~ esa falda no es decente.

(**c**) *amount etc* respetable; apreciable, importante; **at a ~ distance** a respetable distancia; a distancia prudencial; **she lost a ~ sum** perdió una cantidad importante.

(**d**) (*passable*) pasable, tolerable; **we made a ~ showing** lo hicimos pasablemente; **his work is ~ but not brilliant** su obra es pasable pero no brillante.

respectably [rɪs'pektəblɪ] *adv* (**a**) (*decently*) respetablemente; decentemente. (**b**) (*passably*) pasablemente.

respected [rɪs'pektɪd] *adj* respetado, estimado; **a much ~ person** una persona muy respetada.

respecter [rɪs'pektə^{r}] *n*: **to be no ~ of persons** no ser aceptador de personas.

respectful [rɪs'pektfʊl] *adj* respetuoso.

respectfully [rɪs'pektfəlɪ] *adv* respetuosamente; **Yours** ~ le saluda respetuosamente.

respectfulness [rɪs'pektfʊlnɪs] *n* respetuosidad *f*, acatamiento *m*.

respecting [rɪs'pektɪŋ] *prep* (con) respecto a; en cuanto a; por lo que se refiere a.

respective [rɪs'pektɪv] *adj* respectivo.

respectively [rɪs'pektɪvlɪ] *adv* respectivamente.

respiration [,respɪ'reɪʃən] *n* respiración *f*.

respirator ['respɪreɪtə^{r}] *n* (*Mil etc*) careta *f* antigás; (*Med*) resucitador *m*.

respiratory [rɪs'paɪərətərɪ] *adj* respiratorio; **~ tract** vías *fpl* respiratorias.

respire [rɪs'paɪə^{r}] *vti* respirar.

respite ['respaɪt] *n* respiro *m*, respiradero *m*; (*Jur*) plazo *m*, prórroga *f*; **without** ~ sin tregua, sin respirar; **to get no** ~ no tener alivio, no poder descansar; **we got no ~ from the heat** el calor apenas nos dejó respirar; **they gave us no** ~ nos hicieron trabajar (*etc*) sin tregua, no nos dejaron respirar.

resplendence [rɪs'plendəns] *n* resplandor *m*, refulgencia *f*.

resplendent [rɪs'plendənt] *adj* resplandeciente, refulgente; **to be** ~ resplandecer, refulgir; **to be ~ in a new dress** lucir un nuevo vestido; **the car is ~ in green** luce el coche su pintura verde.

respond [rɪs'pɒnd] *vi* (**a**) (*answer*) responder. (**b**) (*be responsive*) reaccionar, ser sensible (*to* a); atender (*to* a); **it ~s to sunlight** reacciona a la luz solar, es sensible a la luz solar; **it is ~ing to treatment** responde al tratamiento; **the cat ~s to kindness** el gato es sensible a los buenos tratos.

respondent [rɪs'pɒndənt] *n* (*Jur*) demandado *m*, -a *f*, acusado *m*, -a *f*; (*to questionnaire*) persona *f* que responde.

response [rɪs'pɒns] *n* (**a**) (*answer*) respuesta *f*; (*Eccl*) responsorio *m*; **~ time** tiempo *m* de respuesta; **his only ~ was to yawn** por toda respuesta dio un bostezo. (**b**) (*reaction*) reacción *f*, correspondencia *f* (*to* a); (*to charity appeal*) acogida *f*; **in ~ to many requests ...** accediendo a muchos ruegos ...; **the ~ was not favourable** la reacción no fue favorable; **we got a 73%** ~ respondió el 73 por cien; **we had hoped for a bigger** ~ habíamos esperado más correspondencia; **it found no** ~ no tuvo correspondencia alguna, no encontró eco alguno; **it met with a generous** ~ tuvo una generosa acogida.

responsibility [rɪs,pɒnsə'bɪlɪtɪ] **1** *n* (**a**) (*liability*) responsabilidad *f* (*for* de); **joint** ~ responsabilidad *f* solidaria; **on one's own** ~ bajo su propia responsabilidad; **to accept ~ for sth** hacerse responsable de algo; **that's his** ~ eso le incumbe a él, eso le toca a él; **it is my ~ to decide** me toca a mí decidir; **to claim ~ for an outrage** reivindicar un atentado, responsabilizarse de un atentado.

(**b**) (*sense of* ~) seriedad *f*; formalidad *f*; **try to show some** ~ procure tener un poco de seriedad.

2 *attr*: **~ payment** (*Brit Scol*) *prima de responsabilidad basada en el número de alumnos a su cargo.*

responsible [rɪs'pɒnsəbl] *adj* (**a**) (*liable*) responsable (*for* de); **to be ~ to sb for sth** ser responsable ante uno de algo; **those ~ will be punished** se castigará a las personas responsables; **who was ~ for the delay?** ¿a quién se debe el retraso?; **the fog was not ~ this time** no se puede culpar a la niebla esta vez; **she is ~ for 40 children** tiene a su cargo 40 niños; **the committee is ~ to the council** la comisión depende del consejo; **he is not ~ for his actions** no es responsable de sus actos; **to hold sb ~ for an accident** echar a uno la culpa de un accidente, hacer a uno responsable de un accidente; **to make o.s.** ~ responsabilizarse, tomar sobre sí la responsabilidad.

(**b**) (*of character*) serio, formal; **he is a fully ~ person** es una persona de toda formalidad; **to act in a ~ fashion** obrar con seriedad.

(**c**) *post etc* de confianza, de gran responsabilidad, de autoridad.

responsibly [rɪs'pɒnsəblɪ] *adv*: **to act** ~ obrar con seriedad, obrar con formalidad.

responsive [rɪs'pɒnsɪv] *adj audience etc* que reacciona con entusiasmo (*or* interés *etc*); **he was not very** ~ apenas dio indicio de interés, apenas parecía interesarle la cosa; **to be ~ to sth** ser sensible a algo.

responsiveness [rɪs'pɒnsɪvnɪs] *n* interés *m*; sensibilidad *f* (*to* a); grado *m* de reacción.

rest[1] [rest] **1** *n* (**a**) (*repose*) descanso *m*, reposo *m*; (*fig*) paz *f*; **day of** ~ día *m* de descanso, asueto *m*, (*as calendar item*) día *m* festivo; **to be at** ~ estar en reposo, descansar; (*of insect etc*) estar posado; (*of the dead*) estar en paz; **to come to** ~ (*vehicle*) pararse, detenerse, (*machine*) pararse, (*insect etc*) posarse; **give it a ~!*** ¡déjalo!, ¡no machaques!; **give the piano a ~!*** ¡deja el piano!; **to go to (one's)** ~ ir a acostarse; **to have a 10-minute** ~ descansar durante 10 minutos; **to have a good night's** ~ dormir bien, pasar una buena noche; **to lay sb to** ~ enterrar a uno; **this puts that theory to** ~ esto permite enterrar esa teoría; **to set sb's mind at** ~ tranquilizar a uno; **to take a** ~ descansar, descansar un rato.

(**b**) (*Mus*) silencio *m*, pausa *f*.

(**c**) (*support*) apoyo *m*, soporte *m*; (*base*) base *f*; (*Telec*) horquilla *f*; (*for lance etc*) ristre *m*.

2 *attr*: **~ area, ~ stop** (*US Aut*) apartadero *m*; **~ camp** campamento *m* de reposo; **~ cure** cura *f* de reposo; **~ day** día *m* de descanso; **~ home** casa *f* de reposo; asilo *m* (de ancianos), residencia *f* para jubilados.

3 *vt* (**a**) (*give ~ to*) descansar; dejar descansar; **to ~ one's men** dejar descansar a sus hombres; **horses have to be ~ed** hay que dejar descansar a los caballos; **I feel very ~ed** he descansado mucho; me encuentro mejor con el descanso; **these colours ~ your eyes** estos colores descansan la vista; **God ~ his soul!** ¡Dios le acoja en su seno!; **to ~ one's case** (*Jur*) terminar la presentación de su alegato.

(**b**) (*support*) descansar, apoyar (*against* contra, *on* sobre); **~ your head on the pillow** apoya la cabeza en la almohada; **~ the ladder against the tree** apoya la escalera contra el árbol; **she ~ed her eyes on the picture** clavó la vista en el cuadro.

4 *vi* (**a**) (*repose*) descansar (*from* de), reposar; (*stop*) detenerse, pararse; (*Theat*: *euph*) no tener trabajo, estar sin trabajo; **where my caravan has ~ed** donde se ha detenido mi caravana; **he never ~s** no descansa nunca; **the waves never** ~ las olas no descansan nunca; **may he ~ in peace** descanse en paz; **we shall never ~ until it is settled** no nos tranquilizaremos hasta que se arregle el asunto; **let us not ~ until he is avenged** no descansemos hasta vengarle.

(**b**) (*lean, be supported*) **to ~ on** (*perch*) posar en, posarse en; (*be supported*) descansar sobre, apoyarse en; (*fig*) estribar en, estar basado en; **her arm ~ed on my chair** su brazo estaba apoyado en mi silla; **her head ~ed on her hand** su cabeza se apoyaba en la mano; **the case ~s on the following facts** la teoría está basada en los siguientes datos; **his eye ~ed on me** su mirada se clavó en mí, clavó su mirada en mí; **a heavy responsibility ~s on**

him pesa sobre él una grave responsabilidad.

(**c**) (*remain*) quedar; **and there the matter ~s** así que ahí queda el asunto; **we cannot let the matter ~ there** no podemos permitir que las cosas sigan en ese punto, no podemos dejar ahí el asunto; **please ~ assured that ...** tenga la seguridad de que ...; **to ~ with** depender de; residir en; **it does not ~ with me** no depende de mí; **the authority ~s with him** la autoridad reside en él.

◆**rest up*** *vi* tomar un descanso.

rest² [rest] *n* resto *m*; **the ~** el resto, lo demás, los demás (*etc*); **she was a deb and all the ~ of it*** era debutante y todo lo demás; **for the ~** por lo demás; **the ~ stayed outside** los demás quedaron fuera; **what shall we give the ~ of them?** ¿qué daremos a los otros?; **the ~ of them couldn't care less** a los otros les trae sin cuidado; **the ~ of the soldiers** los otros soldados, los demás soldados.

restart ['riː'stɑːt] **1** *vt* empezar de nuevo, volver a empezar; reanudar; (*engine*) volver a arrancar. **2** *vi* empezar de nuevo, reempezar; reanudarse.

restate ['riː'steɪt] *vt* repetir, reafirmar; *case* volver a exponer; *problem* volver a plantear.

restatement ['riː'steɪtmənt] *n* repetición *f*, reafirmación *f*; nueva exposición *f*; nuevo planteamiento *m*.

restaurant ['restərɒŋ] *n* restaurante *m*, restorán *m*.

restaurant car ['restərɒŋ,kɑːʳ] *n* (*Brit*) coche-comedor *m*.

restaurateur [,restərə'tɜːʳ] *n* propietario *m* de un restaurante, restaurador *m*, restorador *m*.

restful ['restfʊl] *adj* descansado, reposado, sosegado.

restfully ['restfəlɪ] *adv* reposadamente, sosegadamente.

resting-place ['restɪŋpleɪs] *n* (*also* **last ~**) última morada *f*.

restitution [,restɪ'tjuːʃən] *n* restitución *f*; **to make ~ for sth** indemnizar a uno por algo.

restive ['restɪv] *adj* inquieto, intranquilo; *horse* repropio; **to get ~** agitarse, impacientarse, (*horse*) ponerse repropio.

restiveness ['restɪvnɪs] *n* inquietud *f*, intranquilidad *f*; agitación *f*, impaciencia *f*.

restless ['restlɪs] *adj* inquieto, intranquilo, desasosegado; descontentadizo; (*sleepless*) insomne, desvelado; (*Pol etc*) turbulento; (*roving*) andariego; **the poet's ~ genius** el genio inquieto del poeta; **he's the ~ sort** es un tipo inquieto*, (*pej*) es un culo de mal asiento*; **he is ~ to be gone** se impacienta por partir; **he's been ~ in the job** no ha estado contento en el puesto; **the spectators were getting ~** los espectadores se estaban impacientando; **the unions are getting ~** se están agitando los sindicatos; **I had a ~ night** pasé una mala noche, pasé una noche agitada.

restlessly ['restlɪslɪ] *adv* inquietamente, desasosegadamente; turbulentamente; **she moved ~ in her sleep** se movió inquieta mientras dormía.

restlessness ['restlɪsnɪs] *n* inquietud *f*, intranquilidad *f*, desasosiego *m*; agitación *f*, impaciencia *f*; descontento *m*; insomnio *m*, desvelo *m*; turbulencia *f*; lo andariego; **there is much ~ in the provinces** existe gran descontento en las provincias.

restock ['riː'stɒk] *vt larder etc* reaprovisionar, repostar; *pond etc* repoblar (*with* de); **we ~ed with Brand X** renovamos las existencias de Marca X.

restoration [,restə'reɪʃən] *n* restauración *f*; devolución *f*; restablecimiento *m*; **the R~** (*Brit Hist*) la Restauración (*de la monarquía inglesa en 1660*).

restorative [rɪs'tɔːrətɪv] **1** *adj* reconstituyente, regenerador, fortalecedor. **2** *n* reconstituyente *m*.

restore [rɪs'tɔːʳ] *vt* (**a**) (*return*) *object to owner etc* devolver (*to* a); *strength etc* restablecer; *law, tax* reimponer, volver a imponer; **to ~ sth to sb** devolver algo a uno; **to ~ sth to its place** devolver algo a su lugar; **to ~ sb to health** devolver la salud a uno; **to ~ sb to liberty** devolver la libertad a uno; **to ~ sb's sight** devolver la vista a uno; **to ~ sb's strength** restaurar las fuerzas a uno, reconstituir las fuerzas de uno; **to ~ the value of the pound** restablecer el valor de la libra; **they ~d the king to his throne** volvieron a poner al rey sobre su trono; **order was soon ~d** pronto se restableció el orden, se volvió pronto a la normalidad.

(**b**) *building, painting etc* restaurar.

restorer [rɪs'tɔːrəʳ] *n* (**a**) (*Art etc*) restaurador *m*, -ora *f*. (**b**) (*hair ~*) loción *f* capilar, regenerador *m* del cabello.

restrain [rɪs'treɪn] **1** *vt* contener, refrenar, reprimir; moderar; tener a raya; **to ~ sb from** + *ger* disuadir a uno de + *infin*, (*physically etc*) impedir a uno + *infin*; **kindly ~ your friend** haga el favor de refrenar a su amigo; **I managed to ~ my anger** logré contener mi enojo.

2 *vr*: **to ~ o.s.** contenerse, dominarse; **but I ~ed myself** pero me contuve, pero me dominé; **please ~ yourself!** ¡por favor, cálmese!; **to ~ o.s. from** + *ger* dominarse para que no + *subj*.

restrained [rɪs'treɪnd] *adj* moderado, comedido; *style etc* refrenado, moderado; **he was very ~ about it** estuvo muy comedido.

restraint [rɪs'treɪnt] *n* (**a**) (*check, control*) freno *m*, control *m*; restricción *f*, limitación *f*; (*on wages etc*) moderación *f*; **a ~ on trade** una restricción del comercio, (*on free enterprise*) una limitación de la libre competencia; **without ~** sin restricción, libremente; **to be under a ~** estar cohibido; **to fret under a ~** impacientarse por una restricción; **to put sb under a ~** refrenar a uno; (*Jur*) imponer una restricción legal a uno.

(**b**) (*constraint*) (*of manner*) reserva *f*, (*of character*) moderación *f*, comedimiento *m*; (*self-control*) dominio *m* de sí mismo, autodominio *m*; **to cast aside all ~** abandonar toda moderación, abandonar toda reserva; **he showed great ~** mostró poseer gran autodominio, se mostró muy comedido.

restrict [rɪs'trɪkt] **1** *vt* restringir, limitar (*to* a).

2 *vr*: **I ~ myself to the facts** me limito a exponer los hechos; **nowadays I ~ myself to a litre a day** hoy día me limito a beber un litro diario.

restricted [rɪs'trɪktɪd] *adj* (*small*) *area, circulation etc* reducido; *distribution etc* restringido; *horizon* limitado; (*prohibited*) prohibido; (*Mil*) **~ area** zona *f* prohibida; **~ document** documento *m* de circulación restringida; **~ market** mercado *m* restringido; **he has rather a ~ outlook** tiene miras más bien estrechas; **the plant is ~ to Andalusia** la planta está restringida a Andalucía; **his output is ~ to novels** su producción consiste únicamente en novelas.

restriction [rɪs'trɪkʃən] *n* restricción *f*, limitación *f*; **without ~ as to ...** sin restricción de ...; **to place ~ on the sale of a drug** restringir la venta de una droga; **to place ~s on sb's liberty** restringir la libertad de uno.

restrictive [rɪs'trɪktɪv] *adj* restrictivo; **~ practices** normas *fpl* restrictivas, prácticas *fpl* restrictivas.

re-string [,riː'strɪŋ] (*irr*: *pret, ptp* **re-strung**) *vt pearls, necklace* ensartar de nuevo; *violin, racket* poner nuevas cuerdas a; *bow* poner una nueva cuerda a.

restroom ['restrʊm] *n* cuarto *m* de descanso; (*US euph*) aseos *mpl*, sanitarios *mpl* (*LAm*).

restructure [,riː'strʌktʃəʳ] *vt* reestructurar; (*Econ etc*) sanear.

restructuring [,riː'strʌktʃərɪŋ] *n* reestructuración *f*; saneamiento *m*.

restyle [,riː'staɪl] *vt car etc* remodelar.

restyling [,riː'staɪlɪŋ] *n* remodelación *f*.

result [rɪ'zʌlt] **1** *n* resultado *m*; **~s** (*of election, exam etc*) resultados *mpl*; **as a ~** por consiguiente; **as a ~ of** de resultas de, a consecuencia de; **as a ~ of a misunderstanding** debido a un malentendido; **in the ~** finalmente; **with the ~ that ...** resultando que ..., con la consecuencia de que ...; **without ~** sin resultado; **the ~ is that ...** el resultado es que ...; **what will be the ~ of it all?** ¿en qué va a parar todo esto?

2 *attr*: **~s bonus** bonificación *f* según resultados.

3 *vi*: **to ~ from** resultar de; **to ~ in** producir, motivar, terminar en, dar por resultado, dar como resultado; traducirse en; acarrear; **it ~ed in his death** causó su muerte, condujo a su muerte; **it ~ed in a large increase** produjo un aumento apreciable; **it didn't ~ in anything useful** no produjo nada útil, no dio ningún resultado útil.

resultant [rɪ'zʌltənt] *adj* consiguiente, resultante.

resume [rɪ'zjuːm] **1** *vt* (**a**) (*continue*) reanudar, continuar; *office etc* reasumir; **to ~ one's seat** volver a sentarse; **to ~ one's work** reanudar su trabajo; **'Now then', he ~d** 'Ahora bien', dijo reanudando la conversación (*or* su discurso *etc*).

(**b**) (*summarize*) resumir.

2 *vi* continuar; comenzar de nuevo.

résumé ['reɪzjuːmeɪ] *n* resumen *m*; (*US*) currículum *m* (vitae).

resumption [rɪ'zʌmpʃən] *n* reanudación *f*, continuación *f*; reasunción *f*; **on the ~ of the sitting** al reanudarse la sesión.

resurface ['riː'sɜːfɪs] **1** *vt* poner nueva superficie a; volver a allanar; *road* rehacer el firme de.

2 *vi* (*submarine*) volver a emerger, volver a salir a la superficie; (*person*) reaparecer, presentarse de nuevo.

resurgence [rɪ'sɜːdʒəns] *n* resurgimiento *m*.

resurgent [rɪ'sɜːdʒənt] *adj* resurgente, renaciente, que está en trance de renacer.

resurrect [ˌrezəˈrekt] *vt* resucitar.
resurrection [ˌrezəˈrekʃən] *n* resurrección *f.*
resuscitate [rɪˈsʌsɪteɪt] *vti* resucitar.
resuscitation [rɪˌsʌsɪˈteɪʃən] *n* resucitación *f.*
resuscitator [rɪˈsʌsɪteɪtəʳ] *n* resucitador *m.*
ret. *abbr of* **retired** jubilado, (*Mil*) retirado.
retail [ˈriːteɪl] **1** *n* venta *f* al por menor, venta *f* al detalle.
2 *attr*: ~ **business** comercio *m* (*or* negocio *m*) al por menor (*or* al detalle); ~ **dealer,** ~ **trader** comerciante *mf* al por menor, detallista *mf*; ~ **outlet** punto *m* de venta al por menor (*or* al detalle); ~ **price** precio *m* al por menor, precio *m* al detalle; ~ **price index** índice *m* de precios al consumo (*or* al por menor); ~ **sales** ventas *fpl* al detalle; ~ **trade** comercio *m* al por menor, comercio *m* detallista, comercio *m* menorista (*LAm*).
3 *adv*: **to sell sth** ~ vender algo al por menor, vender algo al detalle.
4 *vt* (**a**) (*Comm*) vender al por menor, vender al detalle.
(**b**) [rɪˈteɪl] *gossip* repetir, *story* contar.
5 *vi* venderse al por menor (*at* a).
retailer [ˈriːteɪləʳ] *n* comerciante *mf* al por menor, detallista *mf*, menorista *mf* (*LAm*).
retain [rɪˈteɪn] *vt* (**a**) (*keep*) retener; conservar; (*keep in one's possession*) guardar, quedarse con; (*in memory*) retener; **~ed earnings, ~ed profit** beneficios *mpl* retenidos; **the sponge ~s the water** la esponja retiene el agua; **it ~s sth of its past glories** conserva una parte de sus viejas glorias; **the customer ~s that part** el cliente se queda con esa porción.
(**b**) (*sign up*) *lawyer* ajustar; *player* contratar, fichar.
retainer [rɪˈteɪnəʳ] *n* (**a**) (*follower*) secuaz *m*; adherente *m*, partidario *m*, -a *f*; (*servant*) criado *m*; **family ~, old ~** viejo criado *m* (que lleva muchos años sirviendo en la misma familia).
(**b**) (*Jur*) anticipo *m* (sobre los honorarios); (*on flat etc*) depósito *m*, señal *f* (para que se guarde el piso *etc*).
retake 1 [ˈriːteɪk] *n* (*Cine*) repetición *f*, nueva toma *f*. **2** [ˌriːˈteɪk] (*irr*: *V* **take**) *vt* (**a**) (*Mil*) volver a tomar, reconquistar. (**b**) (*Cine*) repetir, volver a tomar. (**c**) *exam* presentarse segunda vez a; *subject* examinarse otra vez de.
retaliate [rɪˈtælɪeɪt] *vi* desquitarse, tomar represalias, tomar su revancha; **to ~ by** + *ger* vengarse + *ger*; **to ~ on sb** tomar represalias contra uno; vengarse de uno.
retaliation [rɪˌtælɪˈeɪʃən] *n* desquite *m*, represalias *fpl*, revancha *f*; venganza *f*; **by way of ~, in ~** en revancha, para desquitarse, para vengarse.
retaliatory [rɪˈtælɪətərɪ] *adj*: ~ **raid** ataque *m* vengativo, ataque *m* de desquite; **to take ~ measures** tomar medidas para desquitarse, tomar represalias.
retard [rɪˈtɑːd] *vt* retardar, retrasar.
retarded [rɪˈtɑːdɪd] **1** *adj* retardado, retrasado. **2** *npl*: **the ~** los retrasados (mentales).
retch [retʃ] *vi* vomitar; esforzarse por vomitar; darle a uno arcadas.
retching [ˈretʃɪŋ] *n* esfuerzo *m* por vomitar; náusea *f*, bascas *fpl.*
retd *adj abbr of* **retired** jubilado, (*Mil*) retirado.
retell [ˈriːˈtel] (*irr*: *V* **tell**) *vt* volver a contar.
retention [rɪˈtenʃən] *n* retención *f* (*also Med*); conservación *f.*
retentive [rɪˈtentɪv] *adj* retentivo.
retentiveness [rɪˈtentɪvnɪs] *n* retentiva *f*, poder *m* de retención.
rethink [ˈriːˈθɪŋk] **1** *n*: **to have a ~** volver a pensarlo. **2** (*irr*: *V* **think**) *vt* repensar, volver a pensar; reformular.
reticence [ˈretɪsəns] *n* reticencia *f*, reserva *f.*
reticent [ˈretɪsənt] *adj* reticente, reservado; **he has been very ~ about it** no ha querido decirnos nada acerca de ello, ha tratado el asunto con la mayor reserva.
reticently [ˈretɪsəntlɪ] *adv* con reserva.
reticle [ˈretɪkl] *n* retículo *m.*
reticulate [rɪˈtɪkjʊlɪt] *adj*, **reticulated** [rɪˈtɪkjʊleɪtɪd] *adj* reticular.
reticule [ˈretɪkjuːl] *n* (**a**) (*Opt etc*) retículo *m*. (**b**) (*Hist*: *bag*) ridículo *m.*
retina [ˈretɪnə] *n* retina *f.*
retinue [ˈretɪnjuː] *n* séquito *m*, comitiva *f.*
retire [rɪˈtaɪəʳ] **1** *vt* jubilar; **he was compulsorily ~d** le obligaron a jubilarse.
2 *vi* (**a**) (*withdraw*) retirarse (*also Mil*); **to ~ to bed, to ~ for the night** ir a dormir, ir a acostarse, recogerse; **to ~ from the world** retirarse del mundo; **to ~ into o.s.** encerrarse en sus pensamientos, huir del mundo exterior.
(**b**) (*of age limit*) jubilarse; (*Mil*) retirarse; **to ~ from business** dejar los negocios; **to ~ from a post** dimitir un cargo, renunciar a un puesto; **to ~ on a pension** jubilarse; **they ~d to the countryside** se jubiló él (*or* ella) y fueron a vivir en el campo.
(**c**) (*Sport*) abandonar; **he had to ~ in the 5th lap** tuvo que abandonar en la 5ª vuelta.
retired [rɪˈtaɪəd] *adj* jubilado, (*esp Mil*) retirado; **a ~ person** un jubilado, una jubilada; **to place sb on the ~ list** dar el retiro a uno.
retiree [rɪˈtaɪəˌriː] *n* (*US*) jubilado *m*, -a *f.*
retirement [rɪˈtaɪəment] **1** *n* (**a**) (*state of being retired*) retiro *m*; **to live in ~** vivir en el retiro; **to spend one's ~ growing roses** ocuparse después de la jubilación cultivando rosas; **how will you spend your ~?** ¿qué piensa hacer después de jubilarse?
(**b**) (*act of retiring*) jubilación *f*; (*esp Mil*) retiro *m.*
(**c**) (*Mil*: *withdrawal*) retirada *f.*
2 *attr*: ~ **age** edad *f* de jubilación, (*Mil*) edad *f* de retiro; ~ **benefit** prestaciones *fpl* por jubilación; ~ **pay,** ~ **pension** jubilación *f*, (*Mil*) retiro *m.*
retiring [rɪˈtaɪərɪŋ] *adj* (**a**) *member etc* saliente, dimitente; *age, pay etc* de jubilación, (*Mil*) de retiro; **the ~ members of staff** los miembros que se jubilan.
(**b**) *character* reservado, retraído, modesto.
retort [rɪˈtɔːt] **1** *n* (**a**) (*answer*) réplica *f*. (**b**) (*Chem*) retorta *f*. **2** *vt insult etc* devolver; **he ~ed that ...** replicó que ...
retouch [ˈriːˈtʌtʃ] *vt* retocar.
retrace [riːˈtreɪs] *vt* volver a trazar; (*in memory*) recordar, ir recordando, rememorar; *sb's journey etc* seguir las huellas de; **to ~ one's steps** desandar lo andado, volver sobre los pasos.
retract [rɪˈtrækt] **1** *vt* retractar, retirar; (*draw in*) retraer, encoger; *undercarriage etc* replegar.
2 *vi* retractarse; (*be drawn in*) retraerse; (*undercarriage etc*) replegarse; **he refuses to ~** se niega a retractarse.
retractable [rɪˈtræktəbl] *adj* retractable; (*Aer etc*) replegable, retráctil.
retraction [rɪˈtrækʃən] *n* retractación *f*, retracción *f.*
retrain [ˈriːˈtreɪn] *vt workers* recapacitar, reciclar, reeducar.
retraining [ˈriːˈtreɪnɪŋ] *n* recapacitación *f*, reciclaje *m*, reeducación *f* profesional.
retransmit [ˈriːtrænzˈmɪt] *vt* retransmitir.
retread (*Brit*) **1** [ˈriːtred] *n* recauchutado *m*, reencauchado *m* (*CAm*). **2** [ˈriːˈtred] *vt tyre* recauchutar, reencauchar (*CAm*).
re-tread [ˌriːˈtred] *vt path etc* volver a pisar.
retreat [rɪˈtriːt] **1** *n* (**a**) (*place*) retiro *m*; refugio *m*, asilo *m*; (*state*) retraimiento *m*, apartamiento *m.*
(**b**) (*Mil*) retirada *f*; (*fig*) vuelta *f* atrás, marcha *f* hacia atrás; **the ~ from Mons** la retirada de Mons; **to beat the ~** dar el toque de retreta; **to beat a ~** retirarse, batirse en retirada; (*fig*) emprender la retirada; **to beat a hasty ~** retirarse precipitadamente; **the government is in ~ on this issue** en este asunto el gobierno se está echando atrás; **this represents a ~ from his promise** con esto se está volviendo atrás de su promesa; **to be in full ~** retirarse en masa, retirarse en todo el frente.
(**c**) (*Eccl*: *house*) retiro *m*; casa *f* de ejercicios; (*act*) ejercicios *mpl.*
2 *vi* retirarse, batirse en retirada; **they ~ed to Dunkirk** se retiraron a Dunquerque; **the waters are ~ing** las aguas están bajando.
retrench [rɪˈtrentʃ] **1** *vt* reducir, cercenar. **2** *vi* economizar, hacer economías.
retrenchment [rɪˈtrentʃmənt] *n* reducción *f*, cercenadura *f*; economías *fpl.*
retrial [ˈriːˈtraɪəl] *n* (*of person*) nuevo proceso *m*; (*of case*) revisión *f.*
retribution [ˌretrɪˈbjuːʃən] *n* justo castigo *m*, pena *f* merecida; desquite *m.*
retributive [rɪˈtrɪbjʊtɪv] *adj* castigador, de castigo.
retrievable [rɪˈtriːvəbl] *adj* recuperable; *error etc* reparable.
retrieval [rɪˈtriːvəl] *n* recuperación *f*; (*Hunting*) cobra *f*; reparación *f*; subsanación *f*; rescate *m*; (*Comput*) recuperación *f.*
retrieve [rɪˈtriːv] *vt* (*recover*) cobrar, recobrar, recuperar; (*Hunting*) cobrar; *information, loss* recuperar; *fortunes* reparar; *error* reparar, subsanar; **to ~ sth from the water** rescatar algo del agua; **she ~d her handkerchief** recogió su pañuelo, volvió a tomar su pañuelo; **we shall ~ nothing from this disaster** no salvaremos nada de esta catástrofe.
retriever [rɪˈtriːvəʳ] *n* perro *m* cobrador, perdiguero *m.*
retro... [ˈretrəʊ] *pref* retro...

retroactive [ˌretrəʊ'æktɪv] *adj* retroactivo.
retroflex ['retrəʊfleks] *adj* vuelto hacia atrás.
retrograde ['retrəʊgreɪd] *adj* retrógrado; **a ~ step** un paso hacia atrás, una medida reaccionaria.
retrogress [ˌretrəʊ'gres] *vi* retroceder; (*fig*) empeorar, degenerar, decaer.
retrogression [ˌretrəʊ'greʃən] *n* retroceso *m*, retrogradación *f*.
retrogressive [ˌretrəʊ'gresɪv] *adj* retrógrado.
retrorocket ['retrəʊ'rɒkɪt] *n* retrocohete *m*.
retrospect ['retrəʊspekt] *n* retrospección *f*, mirada *f* retrospectiva; **in ~** retrospectivamente; mirando hacia atrás, volviendo a considerar el pasado; **in ~ it seems a happy time** visto desde esta altura parece haber sido un período feliz.
retrospection [ˌretrəʊ'spekʃən] *n* retrospección *f*, consideración *f* del pasado.
retrospective [ˌretrəʊ'spektɪv] **1** *adj* retrospectivo; *law etc* retroactivo, de efecto retroactivo. **2** *n* (*Art*) (exposición *f*) retrospectiva *f*.
retrospectively [ˌretrəʊ'spektɪvlɪ] *adv* retrospectivamente; de modo retroactivo.
retroussé [rə'tru:seɪ] *adj*: **~ nose** nariz *f* respingona.
retrovirus ['retrəʊˌvaɪrəs] *n* retrovirus *m*.
retry ['ri:'traɪ] *vt person* procesar de nuevo, volver a procesar; *case* rever.
retune [ˌri:'tju:n] *vt* afinar de nuevo.
return [rɪ'tɜ:n] **1** *n* (**a**) (*going back*) vuelta *f*, regreso *m*; (*Med etc*) reaparición *f*; **the ~ home** la vuelta a casa; **the ~ to school** la vuelta al colegio; **the ~ of King Kong** la vuelta de King Kong; **his ~ to his old habits** su vuelta a sus costumbres de antes; **by ~ (of post)**, **by ~ mail** (*US*) a vuelta de correo; **on my ~** a mi regreso, a la vuelta; **many happy ~s (of the day)!** ¡feliz cumpleaños!, ¡felicidades!
(**b**) (*Comm*) ganancia *f*, retorno *m*; ingresos *mpl*; (*interest*) rédito *m*; **~ on capital** rendimiento *m* del capital; **the ~ on investments is only 2%** las inversiones rinden sólo el 2 por ciento; **~ on sales** rendimiento *m* de las ventas; **law of diminishing ~s** ley *f* de rendimiento decreciente; **to bring in a good ~** rendir bien, dar un buen rédito.
(**c**) (*of thing borrowed, of merchandise*) devolución *f*; restitución *f*; **3 dozen on a sale or ~ basis** 3 docenas a devolver si no se venden.
(**d**) (*Tennis etc*) resto *m*.
(**e**) (*reward*) recompensa *f*; **in ~** en cambio; **in ~ for** en cambio de, en recompensa de; **in ~ you ...** en cambio Vd ...; **in ~ for this service** en recompensa de este servicio.
(**f**) (*report*) informe *m*, relación *f*; (*answer*) respuesta *f*; (*figures*) estadística *f*; (*tax ~*) declaración *f*; **~s** estadísticas *fpl*, tablas *fpl* de estadísticas (*for* de); **~ of income** declaración *f* de renta.
(**g**) (*Parl etc*: *of member*) elección *f*; (*voting*) resultado *m* (del escrutinio).
(**h**) (*Brit*: *~ ticket*) billete *m* de ida y vuelta.
(**i**) = **~ key**.
2 *attr* (**a**) **~ fare** (*Brit*), **~ half** parte *f* de vuelta; **~ flight** vuelo *m* de regreso; **~ journey** viaje *m* de vuelta, viaje *m* de regreso; **~ key** tecla *f* de retorno; **~ ticket** (*Brit*) billete *m* de ida y vuelta.
(**b**) **~ match** (partido *m* de) desquite *m*, partido *m* de vuelta, revancha *f*.
(**c**) **~ address** señas *fpl* del remitente.
3 *vt* (**a**) (*give back*) devolver, regresar (*LAm*); restituir; (*send back*) *light* reflejar; *ball* restar; (*Mil*) *fire* devolver, responder a; *suit of cards* devolver; *answer, thanks* dar; *favour, kindness, love* corresponder a; *visit* pagar; **to ~ sth to its place** devolver algo a su lugar; **to ~ partner's lead** devolver el palo que sirvió el compañero; **'~ to sender'** 'devuélvase al remitente'; **to ~ blow for blow** devolver golpe por golpe; **to ~ like for like** pagar a uno en la misma moneda; **I hope to ~ your kindness** espero poder corresponder a su amabilidad; **her love was not ~ed** su amor no fue correspondido.
(**b**) (*declare*) declarar; **to ~ an income of £X** declarar tener una renta de X libras; **to ~ a verdict** pronunciar una sentencia, dar un fallo; **to ~ a verdict of guilty on sb** declarar culpable a uno.
(**c**) (*Parl etc*) elegir, votar a; **he was ~ed by an overwhelming majority** resultó elegido por una abrumadora mayoría; **Old Sarum used to ~ two members to Parliament** Old Sarum tenía antes el derecho a dos escaños en el Parlamento.
(**d**) (*reply*) responder, contestar.
(**e**) (*Fin*) *profit etc* producir, dar.
4 *vi* (**a**) (*go back*) volver, regresar (*to* a); (*Jur*) revertir (*to* a); **to ~ home** volver a casa; **to ~ from town** volver de la ciudad; **to ~ from a journey** volver de un viaje, regresar después de un viaje; **his good spirits ~ed** renació su alegría, se restableció su buen humor.
(**b**) **to ~ to a task** volver a una tarea, emprender de nuevo una tarea; **to ~ to a theme** volver a un asunto.
(**c**) (*Med*: *symptoms etc*) reaparecer.
returnable [rɪ'tɜ:nəbl] *adj* restituible; *deposit* reintegrable, reembolsable; *bottle etc* retornable; (*Jur*) devolutivo; (*on approval*) a prueba; **~ empties** envases *mpl* a devolver; **the book is ~ on the 14th** el libro deberá devolverse el 14; **the deposit is not ~** no se reembolsa el depósito.
returnee [rɪtɜ:'ni:] *n* (*US*) persona *f* que vuelve.
returning officer [rɪ'tɜ:nɪŋˌɒfɪsəʳ] *n* escrutador *m*, -ora *f*.
reunification ['ri:ˌju:nɪfɪ'keɪʃən] *n* reunificación *f*.
reunify ['ri:'ju:nɪfaɪ] *vt* reunificar.
reunion [ri:'ju:njən] *n* reunión *f*.
reunite ['ri:ju:'naɪt] **1** *vt* reunir; (*in friendship etc*) reconciliar; **eventually the family was ~d** por fin la familia volvió a verse unida; **she was ~d with her husband** volvió a verse al lado de su marido.
2 *vi* reunirse; reconciliarse; volver a verse unido.
re-usable [ˌri:'ju:zəbl] *adj* reutilizable, que se puede volver a emplear.
re-use [ˌri:'ju:z] *vt* volver a usar, reutilizar.
rev* [rev] (*Aut etc*) **1** *n* revolución *f*.
2 *vt* (*also* **to ~ up**) girar (el motor de); acelerar (la marcha de).
3 *vi* (*also* **to ~ up**) girar (rápidamente); acelerarse; **the plane was ~ving up** se aceleraban los motores del avión.
Rev(d). *abbr of* **Reverend** Reverendo, R., Rdo., Rvdo.; **the ~*** (*Catholic*) el cura, (*Protestant*) el pastor.
revaluation [ri:ˌvælju'eɪʃən] *n* revaluación *f*, revalorización *f*.
revalue ['ri:'vælju:] *vt* revaluar, revalorizar.
revamp ['ri:'væmp] *vt* remendar; (*fig*) rehacer, refundir, renovar; modernizar.
revanchism [rɪ'væntʃɪzəm] *n* revanchismo *m*.
revanchist [rɪ'væntʃɪst] **1** *adj* revanchista. **2** *n* revanchista *mf*.
reveal [rɪ'vi:l] *vt* revelar; desplegar, demostrar; *feelings* exteriorizar; **on that occasion he ~ed great astuteness** en aquella ocasión desplegó gran astucia.
revealing [rɪ'vi:lɪŋ] *adj* revelador.
revealingly [rɪ'vi:lɪŋlɪ] *adv* de modo revelador.
reveille [rɪ'vælɪ] *n* diana *f*, toque *m* de diana.
revel ['revl] **1** *vi* jaranear, estar de parranda, divertirse tumultuosamente; **to ~ in** deleitarse en, deleitarse con; **to ~ in** + *ger* deleitarse en + *infin*.
2 ~s *npl* jolgorio *m*, jarana *f*, diversión *f* tumultuosa; (*organized*) fiestas *fpl*, festividades *fpl*; **let the ~s begin!** ¡que comience la fiesta!; **the ~s lasted for 3 days** continuaron las fiestas durante 3 días.
revelation [ˌrevə'leɪʃən] *n* revelación *f*; (**Book of**) **R~s** el Apocalipsis; **it was a ~ to me** fue una revelación para mí.
reveller, (*US*) **reveler** ['revləʳ] *n* jaranero *m*, juerguista *mf*; (*drunk*) borracho *m*.
revelry ['revlrɪ] *n* jolgorio *m*, juerga *f*, jarana *f*, diversión *f* tumultuosa; (*organized*) fiestas *fpl*, festividades *fpl*; **the spirit of ~** el espíritu de carnaval.
revenge [rɪ'vendʒ] **1** *n* venganza *f*; **in ~** para vengarse (*for* de); **to take ~ on sb for sth** vengarse de algo en uno.
2 *vt* vengar; **to be ~d on sb** vengarse en uno.
3 *vi*: **to ~ o.s.** vengarse (*on sb* en uno, *for sth* de algo).
revengeful [rɪ'vendʒfʊl] *adj* vengativo.
revengefully [rɪ'vendʒfəlɪ] *adv* vengativamente.
revenger [rɪ'vendʒəʳ] *n* vengador *m*, -ora *f*.
revenue ['revənju:] **1** *n* (**a**) (*income*: *also* **~s**) ingresos *mpl*; renta *f*; (*on investments*) rédito *m*; (*profit*) ganancia *f*, beneficio *m* (*from* de).
(**b**) (*of state*) rentas *fpl* públicas; (*Inland ~*, *US Internal ~*) Fisco *m*, Hacienda *f*.
2 *attr*: **~ account** cuenta *f* de ingresos presupuestarios; **~ expenditure** gasto *m* corriente; **~ stamp** timbre *m* fiscal.
reverberate [rɪ'vɜ:bəreɪt] *vi* (**a**) (*sound*) resonar, retumbar; **the sound ~d in the distance** el sonido retumbaba a lo lejos; **the valley ~d with the sound** el ruido resonaba por el valle.
(**b**) (*Tech*: *light*) reverberar.
reverberation [rɪˌvɜ:bə'reɪʃən] *n* (**a**) (*of sound*) retumbo *m*, el retumbar, eco *m*. (**b**) (*of light*) reverberación *f*.
reverberator [rɪ'vɜ:bəreɪtəʳ] *n* reverberador *m*.
revere [rɪ'vɪəʳ] *vt* reverenciar, venerar; **a ~d figure** una

figura venerada.

reverence ['revərəns] **1** *n* reverencia *f*; **Your R~** Reverencia. **2** *vt* reverenciar.

reverend ['revərənd] **1** *adj* reverendo; **right ~** reverendísimo. **2** *n* (*: *Catholic*) padre *m*, cura *m*; (*Protestant*) pastor *m*.

reverent ['revərənt] *adj* reverente.

reverential [,revə'renʃəl] *adj* reverencial.

reverently ['revərəntlı] *adv* reverentemente, con reverencia.

reverie ['revərı] *n* ensueño *m*; **to be lost in ~** estar absorto, estar ensimismado.

revers [rı'vıəʳ] *n* solapa *f*.

reversal [rı'vɜ:səl] *n* (*of order*) inversión *f*; (*of direction, policy*) cambio *m* completo; (*of decision*) revocación *f*.

reverse [rı'vɜ:s] **1** *adj* (**a**) *order* inverso, invertido; *direction* contrario, opuesto; **in the ~ order** en orden inverso, al revés; **in the ~ direction** en sentido contrario; **~ turn** vuelta *f* al revés; **~ video** vídeo *m* inverso.

(**b**) (*Mech*) *gear* de marcha atrás.

2 *n* (**a**) (*opposite*) **the ~** lo contrario; **quite the ~** todo lo contrario; **but the ~ is true** pero es al contrario; **it was the ~ of what we had expected** fue todo lo contrario de lo que habíamos esperado; **his remarks were the ~ of flattering** sus observaciones eran poco halagueñas, todo lo contrario; **it's the same process in ~** es el mismo proceso al revés, es una forma invertida del mismo proceso.

(**b**) (*face*: *of coin*) reverso *m*; (*of cloth*) revés *m*; (*of paper etc*) dorso *m*.

(**c**) (*Mech*) marcha *f* atrás, contramarcha *f*, reversa *f* (*LAm*); **to go into ~** dar marcha atrás; **my luck went into ~** mi suerte dio marcha atrás; **to put a car into ~** dar marcha atrás a un coche.

(**d**) (*setback*) revés *m*, contratiempo *m*; (*defeat*) derrota *f*.

3 *vt* (**a**) (*invert order of*) invertir, invertir el orden de; trastrocar; (*turn other way*) volver al revés; *arms* llevar a la funerala; **to ~ A and B** invertir el orden de A y B, anteponer B a A; **~(d) charge call** (*Brit*) llamada *f* a cobro revertido; *V* **charge**.

(**b**) (*change*) *opinion* cambiar completamente de; *decision* revocar, anular, cancelar.

(**c**) (*Mech*) poner en marcha atrás; invertir la marcha de; **he ~d the car into the garage** dio marcha atrás y entró en el garaje; **he ~d the car into a pillarbox** al dar marcha atrás chocó con un buzón.

4 *vi* (*Brit*) dar marcha atrás; **I ~d into a van** al dar marcha atrás choqué con una furgoneta.

reversible [rı'vɜ:səbl] *adj* reversible.

reversing [rı'vɜ:sıŋ] *n* marcha *f* atrás; **~ light** luz *f* de marcha atrás.

reversion [rı'vɜ:ʃən] *n* reversión *f* (*also Bio, Jur*); **~ to type** reversión *f* al tipo, salto *m* atrás.

reversionary [rı'vɜ:ʃnərı] *adj* reversionario, reversible.

revert [rı'vɜ:t] *vi* (*Jur*) revertir (*to* a); (*Bio*) saltar atrás; **to ~ to a subject** volver a un tema; **~ing to the matter under discussion ...** volviendo al tema de la discusión ...; **to ~ to type** saltar atrás en la cadena natural.

revetment [rı'vetmənt] *n* revestimiento *m*.

revictual ['ri:'vıtl] **1** *vt* reabastecer. **2** *vi* reabastecerse.

review [rı'vju:] **1** *n* (**a**) (*Jur*: *revision*) revisión *f*; (*examination*) repaso *m*; examen *m*; análisis *m*; (*of research etc*) evaluación *f*; **the annual ~ of expenditure** el examen anual de los gastos; **the sentence is subject to ~ in the high court** la sentencia puede volver a ser vista en el tribunal supremo; **salaries are under ~** los sueldos están sujetos a revisión; **we shall keep your case under ~** volveremos a considerar su caso; **when the case comes up for ~** cuando el asunto se someta a revisión.

(**b**) (*Mil etc*) revista *f*; **the Spithead R~** la revista naval de Spithead; **the general passed the troops in ~** el general pasó revista a las tropas; **the troops passed in ~ before the general** las tropas desfilaron en revista ante el general.

(**c**) (*critique*) reseña *f*; **~ copy** ejemplar *m* para reseñar.

(**d**) (*journal*) revista *f*.

(**e**) (*show*) revista *f*.

2 *vt* (**a**) (*Jur*) rever; (*US Scol*: *take stock of*) repasar; examinar, analizar, estudiar; *research etc* evaluar; **we will ~ the position in a month** volveremos a estudiar la situación dentro de un mes; **we shall have to ~ our policy** tendremos que reconsiderar nuestra política.

(**b**) (*Mil etc*) pasar revista a, revistar.

(**c**) (*write ~ of*) reseñar.

reviewer [rı'vju:əʳ] *n* crítico *m*, -a *f*; (*of book*) reseñante *mf*.

revile [rı'vaıl] *vt* injuriar, llenar de injurias, vilipendiar.

revise [rı'vaız] **1** *vt* (*look over*) revisar, volver a examinar, volver a estudiar; (*Brit*) *lesson etc* repasar; (*amend*) modificar, corregir; *proofs* corregir; *text* refundir; *decision* modificar.

2 *vi*: **to ~ for exams** repasar para los exámenes.

revised [rı'vaızd] *adj text* refundido; **R~ Version** (*Brit*) Versión *f* Revisada (*traducción inglesa de la Biblia, 1884*).

reviser [rı'vaızəʳ] *n* revisor *m*, -ora *f*; refundidor *m*, -ora *f*; (*Typ*) corrector *m*, -ora *f*.

revision [rı'vıʒən] *n* revisión *f*; repaso *m*; modificación *f*, corrección *f*; refundición *f*; **I need 2 weeks for ~** necesito 2 semanas para repasar mis libros (*etc*).

revisionism [rı'vıʒənızəm] *n* revisionismo *m*.

revisionist [rı'vıʒənıst] **1** *adj* revisionista. **2** *n* revisionista *mf*.

revisit ['ri:'vızıt] *vt* volver a visitar; **'Brideshead R~ed'** 'Retorno *m* a Brideshead'.

revitalize ['ri:'vaıtəlaız] *vt* revivificar; vigorizar; infundir fuerzas a.

revival [rı'vaıvəl] *n* resucitación *f*; reanimación *f*; restablecimiento *m*; despertamiento *m*; (*Theat*) reposición *f*, reestreno *m*; (*of learning, art*) renacimiento *m*; (*Pol etc*) resurgimiento *m*; **the R~ of Learning** el Renacimiento.

revivalism [rı'vaıvə,lızəm] *n* evangelismo *m*.

revivalist [rı'vaıvəlıst] **1** *n* evangelista *mf*; (*preacher*) predicador *m* evangelista. **2** *attr*: **~ meeting** reunión *f* evangelista.

revive [rı'vaıv] **1** *vt* (*restore to life*) resucitar; (*fig*) reanimar; restablecer; *fire* avivar; *accusation* volver a, volver a hacer; *hopes* despertar; *suspicion* hacer revivir; *play* reponer, reestrenar; **this will ~ you** esto te reanimará; **to ~ sb's courage** infundir nuevo ánimo a uno.

2 *vi* (*come back to life*) resucitar; (*recover*) reponerse, restablecerse; cobrar fuerzas; (*after unconsciousness*) volver en sí; (*after apparent death*) revivir; **the pound has ~d** la libra se ha repuesto; **interest in Gongora has ~d** ha renacido el interés por Góngora; **his courage ~d** se sintió con nuevo ánimo.

revivify [ri:'vıvıfaı] *vt* revivificar.

revocation [,revə'keıʃən] *n* revocación *f*.

revoke [rı'vəʊk] **1** *n* (*Cards*) renuncio *m*. **2** *vt* revocar. **3** *vi* (*Cards*) renunciar.

revolt [rı'vəʊlt] **1** *n* rebelión *f*, sublevación *f*; **to be in open ~** estar en franca (*or* plena) rebeldía; **to rise in ~** rebelarse, sublevarse.

2 *vt* repugnar, dar asco a; **the book ~ed me** el libro me dio asco.

3 *vi* rebelarse, sublevarse (*against* contra).

revolting [rı'vəʊltıŋ] *adj* asqueroso, repugnante.

revoltingly [rı'vəʊltıŋlı] *adv* asquerosamente, de modo repugnante; **they're ~ rich** son tan ricos que da asco.

revolution [,revə'lu:ʃən] *n* (**a**) (*Pol*) revolución *f*.

(**b**) (*turn*) revolución *f*; vuelta *f*, rotación *f*; **600 ~s per minute** 600 revoluciones por minuto.

revolutionary [,revə'lu:ʃənərı] **1** *adj* revolucionario. **2** *n* revolucionario *m*, -a *f*.

revolutionize [,revə'lu:ʃənaız] *vt* revolucionar.

revolve [rı'vɒlv] **1** *vt* girar, hacer girar; (*in the mind*) dar vueltas a, revolver, meditar.

2 *vi* (**a**) (*Mech etc*) girar (*on* sobre, *round* alrededor de); dar vueltas; (*Astron*) revolverse.

(**b**) (*fig*) **everything ~s round him** todo depende de él, todo se centra en él; **the discussion ~d round 3 topics** el debate se centró en 3 temas.

revolver [rı'vɒlvəʳ] *n* revólver *m*.

revolving [rı'vɒlvıŋ] *adj* giratorio; **~ credit** crédito *m* rotativo (*or* renovable); **~ door** puerta *f* giratoria; **~ stage** escena *f* giratoria.

revue [rı'vju:] *n* revista *f*.

revulsion [rı'vʌlʃən] *n* (**a**) (*disgust*) asco *m*, repugnancia *f*; (*Med*) revulsión *f*. (**b**) (*change*) reacción *f*, cambio *m* repentino.

reward [rı'wɔ:d] **1** *n* recompensa *f*, premio *m*; (*for finding sth*) gratificación *f*, hallazgo *m*; **as a ~ for** en recompensa de, como premio a; **'£50 ~'** '50 libras de hallazgo', '50 libras de recompensa'; **'a ~ will be paid for information about ...'** 'se recompensará al que dé informes acerca de ...'

2 *vt* recompensar, premiar; **to ~ sb for his services** recompensar a uno por sus servicios; **she ~ed me with a smile** me premió con una sonrisa; **it might ~ your attention** podría valer la pena ir a verlo (*etc*); **the case would ~ your investigation** le valdría la pena investigar el

asunto.
rewarding [rɪ'wɔːdɪŋ] *adj* remunerador; (*fig*) provechoso, útil, valioso.
rewind ['riː'waɪnd] (*irr*: *V* **wind**) *vt watch* dar cuerda a; *wool etc* devanar; (*Elec, Cine*) rebobinar.
rewinding ['riː'waɪndɪŋ] *n* (*Elec*) rebobinado *m*.
rewire ['riː'waɪəʳ] *vt house* renovar (completamente) el alambrado de.
reword ['riː'wɜːd] *vt* expresar en otras palabras, redactar en otra forma.
rework [riː'wɜːk] *vt* rehacer; refundir.
rewrite **1** ['riː'raɪt] (*irr*: *V* **write**) *vt* volver a escribir, escribir de nuevo; *text* rehacer, refundir; redactar en otras palabras. **2** ['riːraɪt] *n* nueva versión *f*, refundición *f*.
Reykjavik ['reɪkjəviːk] *n* Reikiavik *m*.
RFD *n* (*US Post*) *abbr of* **rural free delivery**.
Rgt *abbr of* **Regiment** Regimiento *m*.
Rh *n abbr of* **Rhesus** Rhesus *m*, Rh.
r.h. *abbr of* **right hand** derecha *f*, der., derª.
rhapsodic [ræp'sɒdɪk] *adj* rapsódico; (*fig*) extático, locamente entusiasmado, delirante.
rhapsodize ['ræpsədaɪz] *vi*: **to ~ over sth** extasiarse ante algo, entusiasmarse por algo; hablar de algo en términos elogiosos.
rhapsody ['ræpsədɪ] *n* rapsodia *f*; (*fig*) transporte *m* de admiración (*etc*); **to be in rhapsodies** estar extasiado; **to go into rhapsodies over sth** extasiarse ante algo, entusiasmarse por algo; hablar de algo en términos elogiosos.
rhea ['riːə] *n* ñandú *m*.
Rhenish ['renɪʃ] **1** *adj* renano. **2** *n* vino *m* del Rin.
rhenium ['riːnɪəm] *n* renio *m*.
rheostat ['riːəʊstæt] *n* reóstato *m*.
rhesus ['riːsəs] **1** *n* macaco *m* de la India; **~ negative** Rhesus negativo; **~ positive** Rhesus positivo.
2 *attr*: **~ baby** bebé *m* con factor Rhesus; **~ factor** factor *m* Rhesus; **~ monkey** macaco *m* de la India.
rhetic ['riːtɪk] *adj* rético.
rhetoric ['retərɪk] *n* retórica *f*.
rhetorical [rɪ'tɒrɪkəl] *adj* retórico; **~ question** pregunta *f* a la que no se espera contestación.
rhetorically [rɪ'tɒrɪkəlɪ] *adv* retóricamente; **I speak ~** hablo en metáfora.
rhetorician [ˌretə'rɪʃən] *n* retórico *m*.
rheumatic [ruː'mætɪk] **1** *adj* reumático; **~ fever** fiebre *f* reumática. **2** *npl*: **~s*** reumatismo *m*.
rheumaticky* [ruː'mætɪkɪ] *adj* reumático.
rheumatism ['ruːmətɪzəm] *n* reumatismo *m*.
rheumatoid ['ruːmətɔɪd] *adj* reumatoideo; **~ arthritis** reumatismo *m* articular crónico, reúma *m* articular.
rheumatologist [ˌruːmə'tɒlədʒɪst] *n* reumatólogo *m*, -a *f*.
rheumatology [ˌruːmə'tɒlədʒɪ] *n* reumatología *f*.
rheumy ['ruːmɪ] *adj eyes* legañoso, pitañoso.
Rhine [raɪn] **1** *n* Rin *m*. **2** *attr*: **~ wine** vino *m* blanco del Rin.
Rhineland ['raɪnlənd] *n* Renania *f*.
rhinestone ['raɪnˌstəʊn] *n* diamante *m* de imitación.
rhino* ['raɪnəʊ] *n*, **rhinoceros** [raɪ'nɒsərəs] *n* rinoceronte *m*.
rhizome ['raɪzəʊm] *n* rizoma *m*.
Rhodes [rəʊdz] *n* Rodas *f*.
Rhodesia [rəʊ'diːʒə] *n* (*Hist*) Rodesia *f*.
Rhodesian [rəʊ'diːʒən] (*Hist*) **1** *adj* rodesiano. **2** *n* rodesiano *m*, -a *f*.
rhodium ['rəʊdɪəm] *n* rodio *m*.
rhododendron [ˌrəʊdə'dendrən] *n* rododendro *m*.
rhomb [rɒm] *n* rombo *m*.
rhomboid ['rɒmbɔɪd] **1** *adj* romboidal. **2** *n* romboide *m*.
rhombus ['rɒmbəs] *n* rombo *m*.
Rhône [rəʊn] *n* Ródano *m*.
rhubarb ['ruːbɑːb] *n* (**a**) (*Bot, Culin*) ruibarbo *m*. (**b**) (*Theat*) *palabra que se repite para representar la conversación callada en escenas de comparsas.*
rhyme [raɪm] **1** *n* (**a**) (*identical sound*) rima *f*; **without ~ or reason** sin ton ni son. (**b**) (*poem*) poesía *f*, versos *mpl*; **in ~** en verso. **2** *vti* rimar; **rhyming slang** argot *m* basado en rimas (*p.ej.*, **'apples and pears'** = **'stairs'**). **3** *attr*: **~ scheme** esquema *m* de la rima, combinación *f* de rimas.
rhymed [raɪmd] *adj* rimado.
rhymer ['raɪməʳ] *n*, **rhymester** ['raɪmstəʳ] *n* rimador *m*, -ora *f*.
rhythm ['rɪðəm] *n* ritmo *m*; **~ method** método *m* de Ogino-Knaus.
rhythmic(al) ['rɪðmɪk(əl)] *adj* rítmico.
rhythmically ['rɪðmɪkəlɪ] *adv* rítmicamente, de modo rítmico.
RI *n* (**a**) (*US*) *abbr of* **Rhode Island**. (**b**) (*Scol*) *abbr of* **religious instruction** religión *f*.
rib [rɪb] **1** *n* (*Anat, Culin*) costilla *f*; (*Bot*) nervio *m*, nervadura *f*; (*in fabric*) cordoncillo *m*; (*Archit*) nervadura *f*; (*of umbrella*) varilla *f*; (*Naut*) costilla *f*, cuaderna *f*; **~ cage** tórax *m*.
2 *vt*: **to ~ sb*** tomar el pelo a uno*.
RIBA *n abbr of* **Royal Institute of British Architects**.
ribald ['rɪbəld] *adj* verde, obsceno, escabroso; irreverente y regocijado.
ribaldry ['rɪbəldrɪ] *n* (*character*) lo verde, obscenidad *f*, escabrosidad *f*; (*jokes etc*) cosas *fpl* verdes, cosas *fpl* obscenas.
ribbed [rɪbd] *adj*: **~ sweater** jersey *m* de cordoncillo.
ribbing ['rɪbɪŋ] *n* (*in fabric*) cordoncillos *mpl*; (*Archit*) nervaduras *fpl*.
ribbon ['rɪbən] **1** *n* cinta *f*; (*Mil*) galón *m*; **to tear sth to ~s** hacer algo trizas; **with his jacket torn to ~s** con su chaqueta hecha trizas.
2 *attr*: **~ development** desarrollo *m* línea, desarrollo *m* a lo largo de la carretera.
riboflavin [ˌraɪbəʊ'fleɪvɪn] *n* riboflavina *f*.
ribonucleic [ˌraɪbəʊnjuː'kleɪɪk] *adj*: **~ acid** ácido *m* ribonucleico.
rib-tickler* ['rɪb'tɪkləʳ] *n* (*Brit*) chiste *m* desternillante*, historia *f* desternillante*.
rice [raɪs] **1** *n* arroz *m*. **2** *attr*: **~ paddy** (*US*) arrozal *m*; **~ paper** papel *m* de paja de arroz; **~ pudding** arroz *m* con leche, arequipa *f* (*Méx*); **~ wine** vino *m* de arroz.
ricefield ['raɪsfiːld] *n* arrozal *m*.
rice-growing ['raɪsˌgrəʊɪŋ] *adj* arrocero.
rich [rɪtʃ] **1** *adj* rico; (*in price, workmanship*) costoso, precioso, exquisito; *colour* vivo, brillante; *profit* pingüe; *smell* rico; *soil* fértil; *voice* sonoro; *clothing, fabric* rico; *banquet* suntuoso, opíparo; *food* sabroso, suculento, (*pej*) pesado, fuerte, muy dulce, empalagoso; *wine* generoso; *style* copioso; *experience, history* rico; (*: *funny*) muy divertido; **that's ~!** ¡qué gracioso!; **to be ~ in** abundar de, abundar en; **a gallery ~ in Impressionists** un museo que posee gran caudal de impresionistas; **a style ~ in metaphors** un estilo en el que abundan las metáforas; **the soil is ~ in nitrates** el suelo tiene abundantes nitratos; **to become** (*or* **get, grow**) **~** enriquecerse (*on* con); **to get ~ quick** enriquecerse pronto; **to strike it ~*** ponerse las botas.
2 *npl* (**a**) **the ~** (*people*) los ricos *mpl*.
(**b**) **~es** (*wealth*) riqueza *f*, riquezas *fpl*; **the earth's ~es** las riquezas de la tierra.
Richard ['rɪtʃəd] *nm* Ricardo; **~ (the) Lionheart** Ricardo Corazón de León.
richly ['rɪtʃlɪ] *adv* (*V adj*) ricamente; preciosamente, exquisitamente; suntuosamente; sabrosamente; copiosamente; **a ~ adorned chair** una silla de exquisitos adornos; **a ~ humorous situation** una situación divertidísima; **a ~ endowed library** una biblioteca de fondos copiosos; **she ~ deserves it** muy bien merecido lo tiene.
richness ['rɪtʃnɪs] *n* (*V adj*) riqueza *f*; preciosidad *f*, exquisitez *f*; viveza *f*, brillantez *f*; fertilidad *f*; sonoridad *f*; suntuosidad *f*; suculencia *f*; lo pesado, lo fuerte; copia *f*; abundancia *f*.
Richter ['rɪçtəʳ] *n*: **~ scale** escala *f* (de) Richter.
rick¹ [rɪk] (*Agr*) **1** *n* almiar *m*, niara *f*. **2** *vt* almiarar, recoger en niaras (*etc*), amontonar.
rick² [rɪk] *vt* = **wrick**.
rickets ['rɪkɪts] *n* raquitismo *m*, raquitis *f*.
rickety ['rɪkɪtɪ] *adj* (**a**) (*Med*) raquítico. (**b**) (*unsafe*) desvencijado; (*unsteady*) tambaleante, inseguro.
rickshaw ['rɪkʃɔː] *n* jinrikisha *f*, carro *m* de culí.
ricochet ['rɪkəʃeɪ] **1** *n* rebote *m*. **2** *vi* rebotar (*off* de).
rictus ['rɪktəs] *n* rictus *m*.
rid [rɪd] (*irr*: *pret* **rid, ridded**, *ptp* **rid**) **1** *vt* (**a**) **to ~ a place of rats** librar un lugar de ratas, eliminar las ratas de un lugar; **to ~ sb of a difficulty** librar a uno de una dificultad; **the medicine ~ me of the cough** la medicina me curó (*or* quitó) la tos.
(**b**) **to be ~ of** estar libre de; **we're ~ of him at last!** ¡por fin nos vemos libres de él!
(**c**) **to get ~ of** deshacerse de, desembarazarse de; hacer desaparecer; **the body gets ~ of waste** el cuerpo elimina los desechos; **get ~ of it at any price** véndelo a cualquier precio; **to get ~ of sb** deshacerse de uno, (*euph*) eliminar a uno matándole.
2 *vr*: **to ~ o.s. of** librarse de, desembarazarse de; **to ~ o.s. of evil thoughts** librarse de los malos pensamientos.
riddance ['rɪdəns] *n*: **good ~ (to bad rubbish)!** (*iro*) ¡enhoramala!; ¡vete con viento fresco!; **it was a good ~**

de buena nos libramos; **and good ~ to him** que se pudra.

ridden ['rɪdn] *ptp of* **ride**; **a horse ~ by ...** un caballo montado por ...

riddle¹ ['rɪdl] *n* (*conundrum*) acertijo *m*, adivinanza *f*; (*mystery*) enigma *m*, misterio *m*; (*person etc*) enigma *m*; **to ask sb a ~** proponer un acertijo a uno; **to speak in ~s** hablar en enigmas.

riddle² ['rɪdl] **1** *n* (*sieve*) criba *f*, criba *f* gruesa; (*potato sorter etc*) escogedor *m*.

2 *vt* (**a**) (*sieve*) cribar; *potatoes etc* pasar por el escogedor.

(**b**) **to ~ a door with bullets** acribillar una puerta a balazos; **the organization is ~d with communists** el organismo está plagado de comunistas; **the army is ~d with subversion** el ejército está lleno de subversionismo.

ride [raɪd] **1** *n* (**a**) (*on horse*) cabalgata *f*, paseo *m* a caballo; (*in car etc*) paseo *m* en coche, viaje *m* en coche (*or* bicicleta *etc*); (*US*) viaje *m* gratuito, aventón *m* (*LAm*); (*distance ridden*) viaje *m*, recorrido *m*; **the ~ of the Valkyries** la cabalgata de las valquirias; **'50p a ~'** '50 peniques por persona', '50 peniques la vuelta'; **it was a rough ~** fue un viaje nada cómodo; **to give sb a rough ~** (*fig*) hacer pasar un mal rato a uno; **it's only a short ~** es poco camino, es poca distancia; **it's a 10-minute ~ by bus** el viaje dura 10 minutos en autobús; **it's a 70p ~ from the station** el viaje desde la estación cuesta 70 peniques; **they gave me a ~ into town** me llevaron (en coche) a la ciudad; **I got a ~ all the way to Bordeaux** un automovilista me llevó hasta todo Burdeos; **to go for a ~ over the fields** pasearse a caballo por los campos; **to go for a ~ in a car** dar un paseo en coche; **it's my first ~ in a Rolls** es la primera vez que viajo en un Rolls; **to take a ~ in a helicopter** dar un paseo en helicóptero; **to take sb for a ~*** dar gato por liebre a uno, embaucar a uno, (*US‡*) dar el paseo a uno‡; **to be taken for a ~*** hacer el primo*.

(**b**) (*in a wood*) vereda *f*.

2 (*irr*: *pret* **rode**, *ptp* **ridden**) *vt* (**a**) **to ~ a horse** montar a caballo; **to ~ a bicycle** ir en bicicleta; **to ~ an elephant** ir montado en un elefante; **he rode his horse up the stairs** hizo que el caballo subiese la escalera; **he rode his horse into the shop** entró a caballo en la tienda; **it has never been ridden** hasta ahora nadie ha montado en él; **he rode it in two races** lo corrió en dos carreras; **to ~ a horse hard** castigar mucho a un caballo; **can you ~ a bicycle?** ¿sabes montar en bicicleta?

(**b**) (*esp US fig*) **to ~ sb** tiranizar a uno, dominar a uno; **don't ~ him too hard** no seas demasiado severo con él; **to ~ an idea to death** explotar una idea con demasiado entusiasmo, acabar con una idea a fuerza de repetirla demasiado.

(**c**) (*Naut*) *waves* hender, surcar.

(**d**) **to ~ a good race** hacer bien una carrera, dar buena cuenta de sí (en una carrera).

3 *vi* (**a**) (*on animal*) montar, cabalgar; (*on a bicycle, in a car*) ir; pasearse, viajar; **to ~ on an elephant** ir montado en un elefante; **to ~ in a car** ir en coche; **some rode but I had to walk** algunos fueron en coche pero yo tuve que ir a pie; **to ~ astride** montar a horcajadas; **to ~ like mad** correr como el demonio; **to ~ home on sb's shoulders** ser llevado a casa en los hombros de uno; **she ~s every day** monta a diario; **he ~s for a different stable** monta para otra cuadra.

(**b**) (*with expressions of distance and time, often not translated*) **to ~ to Jaén** ir (a caballo) a Jaén; **we'll ~ over to see you** vendremos a verte; **he rode straight at me** arremetió contra mí; **he rode 12 miles** recorrió 12 millas, hizo 12 millas.

(**c**) (*fig*) **to ~ at anchor** estar al ancla, estar anclado; **the moon was riding high in the sky** la luna estaba en lo alto del cielo; **to be riding high** (*person*) estar alegre, estar en la cumbre de la felicidad; **when I'm riding high** cuando mis cosas van bien, cuando todo me va bien.

◆**ride about, ride around** *vi* pasearse a caballo (*or* en coche, en bicicleta *etc*).

◆**ride away** *vi* alejarse, irse, partir.

◆**ride back** *vi* volver (a caballo, en bicicleta *etc*).

◆**ride behind** *vi* ir después, caminar a la zaga; (*in rear seat*) ir en el asiento de atrás; (*on same horse*) cabalgar a la grupa.

◆**ride by** *vi* pasar (a caballo).

◆**ride down** *vt* (**a**) (*trample*) atropellar. (**b**) (*catch*) coger, alcanzar.

◆**ride off** *vi* = **ride away**.

◆**ride on** *vi* seguir adelante.

◆**ride out** *vt storm* aguantar (*also fig*).

◆**ride up** *vi* (**a**) (*horseman, motorcyclist etc*) llegar, acercarse. (**b**) (*dress*) subirse.

rider ['raɪdəʳ] *n* (**a**) (*horse ~*) jinete *m*, -a *f*; caballero *m*; (*cyclist*) ciclista *mf*; (*motorcyclist*) motociclista *mf*; (*US Aut*) pasajero *m*, -a *f*, viajero *m*, -a *f*; **I'm not much of a ~** apenas sé montar; **he's a fine ~** es un jinete destacado.

(**b**) (*clause*) aditamento *m*; corolario *m*; **I must add the ~ that ...** tengo que añadir que ...

ridge [rɪdʒ] *n* (*of hills*) cadena *f*, sierra *f*; estribación *f*; (*of hill*) cresta *f*; (*of nose, roof*) caballete *m*; (*on cloth etc*) cordoncillo *m*; (*wrinkle*) arruga *f*; (*Agr*) caballón *m*, camellón *m*; **~ of high pressure** zona *f* de alta presión.

ridgepole ['rɪdʒpəʊl] *n* parhilera *f*, cumbrera *f*.

ridge tent ['rɪdʒ,tent] *n* tienda *f* canadiense.

ridgetile ['rɪdʒtaɪl] *n* teja *f* de caballete.

ridgeway ['rɪdʒweɪ] *n* ruta *f* de las crestas.

ridicule ['rɪdɪkju:l] **1** *n* irrisión *f*; burlas *fpl*, mofa *f*; **to expose sb to public ~** exponer a uno a la mofa pública; **to hold sb up to ~** ridiculizar a uno, mofarse de uno; **to lay o.s. open to ~** exponerse al ridículo.

2 *vt* ridiculizar, poner en ridículo, mofarse de.

ridiculous [rɪ'dɪkjʊləs] *adj* ridículo, absurdo; **~!, how ~!** ¡qué ridículo!; **to make o.s. ~** ponerse en ridículo.

ridiculously [rɪ'dɪkjʊləslɪ] *adv* ridículamente, absurdamente; de modo ridículo; **it is ~ easy** es ridículamente fácil.

riding ['raɪdɪŋ] **1** *n* equitación *f*, montar *m* a caballo. **2** *attr* de montar; de equitación.

riding-boots ['raɪdɪŋbu:ts] *npl* botas *fpl* de montar.

riding-breeches ['raɪdɪŋ,brɪtʃɪz] *npl* pantalones *mpl* de montar.

riding-crop ['raɪdɪŋkrɒp] *n* fusta *f*.

riding-habit ['raɪdɪŋ,hæbɪt] *n* amazona *f*, traje *m* de montar.

riding-jacket ['raɪdɪŋ,dʒækɪt] *n* chaqueta *f* de montar.

riding-master ['raɪdɪŋ,mɑ:stəʳ] *n* profesor *m* de equitación.

riding-school ['raɪdɪŋsku:l] *n* picadero *m*, escuela *f* de equitación, escuela *f* hípica.

riding-stables ['raɪdɪŋ,steɪblz] *npl* cuadras *fpl*.

riding-whip ['raɪdɪŋwɪp] *n* fusta *f*.

rife [raɪf] *adj* (**a**) (*widespread*) **to be ~** abundar, ser muy común; ser endémico; **corruption is ~** la corrupción existe en todas partes; **measles is ~** hay mucho sarampión; **the abuse has become ~ of late** recientemente ha cundido el abuso, recientemente se ha extendido mucho el abuso.

(**b**) **to be ~ with** estar lleno de, abundar de (*or* en).

riffle ['rɪfəl] *vi*: **to ~ through a book** hojear (rápidamente) un libro, volver rápidamente las hojas de un libro.

riffraff ['rɪfræf] *n* gentuza *f*, chusma *f*; **and all the ~ of the neighbourhood** y todos los sinvergüenzas del barrio.

rifle¹ ['raɪfl] *vt* robar, saquear; desvalijar; **to ~ a case** desvalijar una maleta; **the house had been ~d** habían saqueado la casa; **they ~d the house in search of money** saquearon la casa buscando dinero.

rifle² ['raɪfl] **1** *n* (**a**) rifle *m*, fusil *m*. (**b**) **~s** (*as regiment etc*) fusileros *mpl*. **2** *vt* estriar, rayar.

rifle-butt ['raɪflbʌt] *n* culata *f* de rifle.

rifled ['raɪfld] *adj* (*Tech*) estriado, rayado.

rifle-fire ['raɪflfaɪəʳ] *n* fuego *m* de fusilería.

rifleman ['raɪflmən] *n*, *pl* **riflemen** ['raɪflmən] fusilero *m*.

rifle-range ['raɪflreɪndʒ] *n* campo *m* de tiro, polígono *m* de tiro; (*at fair*) barraca *f* de tiro al blanco.

rifle-shot ['raɪflʃɒt] *n* tiro *m* de fusil; **within ~** a tiro de fusil.

rifling ['raɪflɪŋ] *n* (*Tech*) estría *f*, estriado *m*, rayado *m*.

rift [rɪft] *n* hendedura *f*, grieta *f*, rendija *f*; (*in clouds etc*) claro *m*, abertura *f*; (*in relations etc*) grieta *f*; (*between friends*) desavenencia *f*; (*in party*) escisión *f*, cisma *m*.

rig [rɪg] **1** *n* (**a**) (*Naut*) aparejo *m*.

(**b**) (*: *dress*) atuendo *m*.

(**c**) (*oil~*) torre *f* de perforación; (*Naut*) plataforma *f* de perforación submarina.

2 *vt* (**a**) (*Naut*) aparejar, enjarciar.

(**b**) (*falsify*) amañar; falsificar; **to ~ an election** amañar unas elecciones, dar pucherazo; **the government had got it all ~ged** el gobierno lo había arreglado de modo fraudulento; **to ~ the market** manipular la lonja; **it's been ~ged!** ¡aquí hay tongo!

◆**rig out** *vt* (*Naut*) proveer (*with* de), equipar (*with* con); **to ~ sb out in sth** ataviar a uno de algo; **to be ~ged out in a new dress** lucir un vestido nuevo.

◆**rig up** *vt* (*build*) armar, construir; (*arrange*) arreglar; (*improvise*) improvisar; **we'll see what we can ~ up** veremos si podemos arreglar algo.

rigger ['rɪgəʳ] *n* (*Naut*) aparejador *m*; (*Aer*) mecánico *m*.

rigging ['rɪgɪŋ] *n* jarcia *f*, cordaje *m*, aparejo *m*.

right [raɪt] **1** *adj* (**a**) (*just*) justo; equitativo; (*suitable*) debido, indicado; (*proper*) apropiado, propio, conveniente; (*reasonable*) razonable; **it is ~ that ...** es justo que ...; **it is only ~ to add that ...** es de justicia añadir que ...; **it is only ~ and proper to** + *infin* la justicia exige que + *subj*; **it cannot be ~ for you to** + *infin* no puede ser justo que Vd + *subj*; **would it be ~ for me to ask him?** ¿conviene que yo se lo pregunte?; **it's not ~!** ¡no hay derecho!; **I thought it ~ to** + *infin* me pareció conveniente + *infin*; **to do the ~ thing** hacer lo que hay que hacer; **to do the ~ thing by sb** tratar a uno con justicia, obrar honradamente con respecto a uno; **she's on the ~ side of 40** tiene menos de 40 años; **if the price is ~** si el precio es razonable; **we'll do it when the time is ~** lo haremos en el momento oportuno.

(**b**) (*correct*) correcto, exacto; (*true*) verdadero; *conditions etc* favorable, propicio; *thing sought etc* que hace falta, que se busca; **Mr R~** el novio soñado, el marido ideal; **~!** ¡conforme!, ¡bueno!, ¡muy bien!; sí, eso es; ¡justo!; (*answering call*) ¡voy!; **~ you are!** ¡bueno!; **quite ~!** ¡exacto!, ¡perfectamente!; **that's ~** eso es; **the ~ answer** la respuesta correcta, (*Math: to problem etc*) la solución correcta; **the ~ word** la palabra exacta, la palabra apropiada; **the ~ time** la hora exacta; **have you the ~ time?** ¿tienes la hora exacta?; **~ side of cloth** lado *m* derecho de un paño, haz *f* de un paño; **to choose the ~ moment** elegir el momento oportuno (*or* favorable); **is this the ~ house?** ¿es ésta la casa?; **is this the ~ road for Segovia?** ¿es éste el camino de Segovia?, ¿por aquí se va a Segovia?; **are we on the ~ road?** ¿vamos por buen camino?; **am I ~ for the station?** ¿por aquí se va a la estación?; **he's the ~ man for the job** es el hombre más indicado para el cargo, es el hombre que hace falta para el puesto; **he knows all the ~ people** conoce a todas las personas que pueden serle útiles; **they holiday in all the ~ places** toman sus vacaciones en todos los sitios que están de moda; **it's not the ~ length** de largo no sirve, de largo no vale; **he's one of the ~ sort** es buen chico, es un tío simpático; **he's clever but not the ~ sort for us** es inteligente pero no nos conviene; **to say the ~ thing** decir lo que conviene, decir lo que se debe decir; **we must get it ~ this time** esta vez tenemos que acertarlo, tenemos que hacerlo bien esta vez; **to put a clock ~** poner un reloj en hora; **to put** (*or* **set**) **sth ~** arreglar algo, poner algo en orden; **that's soon put ~** eso se corrige fácilmente; **to put a mistake ~** corregir un error, rectificar un error; **to put sb ~** corregir a uno, señalar a uno su error, (*unpleasantly*) enmendar la plana a uno.

(**c**) **to be ~** (*person*) tener razón, estar en lo cierto (*esp LAm*); **you're dead ~, you're quite ~** estás en lo cierto; **to be ~ to** + *infin* hacer bien en + *infin*; **am I ~ in thinking that ...?** ¿me equivoco al afirmar que ...?

(**d**) (*in mind*) cuerdo; **to be in one's ~ mind** estar en su cabal juicio; **she's not ~ in the head** no está en sus cabales.

(**e**) (*in order, settled*) **all's ~ with the world** todo le va bien al mundo; **to be as ~ as rain** (*Brit*) estar perfectamente; **I'm as ~ as rain, thanks** gracias, estoy perfectamente; **she'll be as ~ as rain in a few days** en unos pocos días se repondrá completamente de esto; **it all came ~ in the end** al fin todo se arregló, al fin todo salió bien; **it will all come ~ in the end** todo se arreglará.

(**f**) *V* **all right**.

(**g**) (*not left*) derecho; (*Pol*) derechista; **~ back** defensa *m* derecho, defensa *f* derecha; **~ half** medio *m* derecho, medio *m* volante derecho; **~ wing** (*Mil, Sport*) ala *f* derecha.

(**h**) (*Math*) *angle* recto.

(**i**) (*) **he's a ~ idiot** es un puro idiota; **a ~ twit I should feel if ...** bien tonto me creería si ...; **he made a ~ mess of it** lo hizo malísimamente, lo embrolló todo de mala manera.

2 *adv* (**a**) (*straight etc*) derecho; directamente; **~ away** en seguida, ahorita mismo (*Mex*); **~ away!** (*Rail etc*) ¡en marcha!; **~ here** aquí mismo; **~ now** ahora mismo; **I'll be ~ over** voy en seguida; **to go ~ on** seguir, seguir derecho, seguir adelante; **~ on!**‡ ¡eso es!, ¡de acuerdo!; **he just went ~ on talking** siguió hablando tan fresco; **to speak ~ out** hablar claramente, hablar sin rodeos.

(**b**) (*quite, exactly*) completamente; exactamente; **~ in the middle** exactamente en el centro, por toda la mitad; **~ at the top** en todo lo alto; **it hit him ~ on the chest** le dio de lleno en el pecho; **he filled it ~ up** lo llenó del todo; **the wind is ~ behind us** sopla el viento precisamente detrás de nosotros; **~ at the end of his speech** precisamente al fin de su discurso; **there is a fence ~ round the house** hay una valla que rodea la casa por completo; **it goes ~ to the end** llega hasta el final (sin dejar espacio *etc*); **he put his hand in ~ to the bottom** introdujo la mano hasta el mismo fondo.

(**c**) (*rightly*) bien; correctamente; **to do ~** obrar bien, obrar correctamente; **you did ~** hiciste bien; **if I remember ~** si mal no recuerdo; **nothing goes ~ with them** nada les sale bien; **it was him all ~** fue él sin sombra de duda; **it's a big one all ~** ya lo creo que es grande; **~ enough!** ¡muy bien!; ¡razón tienes!; **it was there ~ enough** sí estaba allí; *V* **serve**.

(**d**) (*not left*) a la derecha, hacia la derecha; **~ (about) turn!** ¡media vuelta a la derecha!; **to turn ~** torcer a la derecha; **he looked neither ~ nor left** no miró a ningún lado; **they owe money ~ and left** deben dinero a todos, tienen deudas por doquier; **we are a ~ of centre party** somos un partido del centro derecho.

(**e**) **R~ Reverend** Reverendísimo *m*.

3 *n* (**a**) (*what is lawful*) derecho *m*; (*what is just*) justicia *f*; (*what is morally ~*) bien *m*; **~ and wrong** el bien y el mal; **might and ~** la fuerza y el derecho; **to be in the ~** tener razón; **to fight for the ~** luchar por la justicia; **to have ~ on one's side** tener la razón de su parte; **to know ~ from wrong** saber distinguir el bien del mal.

(**b**) (*title, claim*) derecho *m*; título *m*; privilegio *m*; **~ of abode** derecho *m* a domicilio; **~ of assembly** derecho *m* de reunión; **~s of the citizen** derechos *mpl* del ciudadano; **~s of man** derechos *mpl* del hombre; **~ to reply** derecho *m* de réplica; **~ of way** derecho *m* de paso, (*Jur*) servidumbre *f* de paso, (*Aut etc*) prioridad *f*; **sole ~** (*Comm*) exclusiva *f*; **as of ~** por derecho propio; de oficio; **by ~s** según derecho, en justicia; **by ~ of** por razón de; **by what ~?** ¿con qué derecho ...?; **to be within one's ~s** estar en su derecho; **to exercise one's ~** usar de su derecho (*to* + *infin* de + *infin*); **to have a ~ to sth** tener derecho a algo; **to have the ~ to** + *infin* tener el derecho de + *infin*; **you had no ~ to** + *infin* no le correspondía a Vd + *infin*; **to own sth in one's own ~** poseer algo por derecho propio; **to reserve the ~ to** + *infin* reservarse el derecho de + *infin*.

(**c**) (*of authorship etc*) derechos *mpl*; propiedad *f*; **film ~s** derechos *mpl* cinematográficos; **'all ~s reserved'** 'es propiedad', 'reservados todos los derechos'.

(**d**) **~s: I don't know the ~s of the matter** no sé quién tiene razón en el asunto; **to set sth to ~s** arreglar algo; componer algo.

(**e**) (*not left*) derecha *f*; (*Pol: also* **~ wing**) derecha *f*; (*Boxing*) derechazo *m*; **on the ~, to the ~** a la derecha; **to keep to the ~** (*Aut*) circular por la derecha; **reading from ~ to left** leyendo de derecha a izquierda; **he is of the ~** es de derechas; **he's further to the ~ than I am** es más derechista que yo.

4 *attr*: **~s issue** emisión *f* gratuita de acciones.

5 *vt* (**a**) (*set upright etc*) enderezar.

(**b**) (*correct*) corregir, rectificar; **to ~ a wrong** deshacer un agravio, acabar con un abuso.

right angle ['raɪt,æŋgl] *n* ángulo *m* recto; **to be at ~s to** estar en (*or* formar) ángulo recto con.

right-angled ['raɪt,æŋgld] *adj* rectangular; *triangle* rectángulo; *bend etc* en ángulo recto.

righteous ['raɪtʃəs] *adj* justo, honrado, recto; *indignation etc* virtuoso, justificado.

righteously ['raɪtʃəslɪ] *adv* honradamente, rectamente; virtuosamente; con justicia.

righteousness ['raɪtʃəsnɪs] *n* honradez *f*, rectitud *f*; virtud *f*; justicia *f*.

rightful ['raɪtfʊl] *adj* legítimo; verdadero; **~ claimant** derechohabiente *mf*.

rightfully ['raɪtfəlɪ] *adv* legítimamente; verdaderamente.

right-hand ['raɪthænd] *adj*: **~ drive** conducción *f* por la derecha; **~ man** brazo *m* derecho, hombre *m* de confianza; **~ side** derecha *f*; **~ turn** vuelta *f* a la derecha.

right-handed ['raɪt'hændɪd] *adj* diestro, que usa la mano derecha; *tool* para persona que usa la mano derecha.

right-hander [,raɪt'hændə^r] *n* (*Sport*) diestro *m*, -a *f*.

right-ho* [,raɪt'həʊ] *excl* ¡vale!, ¡bien!

rightism ['raɪtɪzəm] *n* derechismo *m*.

rightist ['raɪtɪst] **1** *adj* derechista. **2** *n* derechista *mf*.

rightly ['raɪtlɪ] *adv* correctamente; debidamente; bien; **~ or wrongly** mal que bien; con razón o sin ella; **and ~ so** y con razón, a justo título; **to act ~** obrar correctamente, obrar bien; **as he ~ believed** según creía correctamente; **he was ~ dismissed** con toda justicia le despidieron; **I**

don't ~ know, I couldn't ~ say no lo sé muy bien, no estoy muy seguro.

right-minded ['raɪt'maɪndɪd] *adj* (*sensible*) prudente; (*decent*) honrado.

rightness ['raɪtnɪs] *n* (*correctness*) exactitud *f*; (*justice*) justicia *f*.

right-thinking ['raɪt'θɪŋkɪŋ] *adj* juicioso, sensato; honrado.

rightward ['raɪtwəd] *adj movement etc* a (*or* hacia) la derecha.

rightward(s) ['raɪtwəd(z)] *adv move etc* a (*or* hacia) la derecha.

right-wing ['raɪt'wɪŋ] *adj* derechista.

right-winger ['raɪt'wɪŋər] *n* derechista *mf*.

rigid ['rɪdʒɪd] *adj* rígido; yerto; (*in attitude*) inflexible, severo; **he is quite ~ about it** es inflexible sobre ese punto; **we were ~ with fear** quedamos helados de miedo; **to shake sb ~*** pasmar a uno, dejar frío a uno*.

rigidity [rɪ'dʒɪdɪtɪ] *n* rigidez *f*; inflexibilidad *f*, severidad *f*.

rigidly ['rɪdʒɪdlɪ] *adv* rígidamente; inflexiblemente, severamente; **he is ~ opposed to it** está totalmente en contra de esto.

rigmarole ['rɪgmərəʊl] *n* galimatías *m*, relación *f* disparatada.

rigor ['rɪgər] *n* (*US*) = **rigour**.

rigor mortis ['rɪgə'mɔːtɪs] *n* rigidez *f* cadavérica.

rigorous ['rɪgərəs] *adj* riguroso.

rigorously ['rɪgərəslɪ] *adv* rigurosamente.

rigour, (*US*) **rigor** ['rɪgər] *n* rigor *m*, severidad *f*; **the full ~ of the law** el máximo rigor de la ley; **the ~s of the climate** los rigores del clima.

rig-out* ['rɪgaʊt] *n* atuendo *m*, atavío *m*.

rile* [raɪl] *vt* sulfurar*, reventar*, sacar de quicio a; **it ~s me terribly** me irrita muchísimo; **there's nothing that ~s me more** no hay nada que me reviente más*.

rill [rɪl] *n* (*liter*) arroyo *m*, riachuelo *m*.

rim [rɪm] *n* (*of cup etc*) borde *m*, canto *m*; (*of wheel*) llanta *f*; (*of spectacles*) montura *f*, aro *m*; (*of dirt etc*) cerco *m*; **the ~ of the sun** el borde del sol.

rime¹ [raɪm] *n* (*poet*) rima *f*.

rime² [raɪm] *n* (*frost*) escarcha *f*.

rimless ['rɪmlɪs] *adj glasses* sin aros.

rimmed [rɪmd] *adj*: **~ with ...** con un borde de ..., bordeado de ...; **glasses ~ with gold** gafas *fpl* con montura de oro.

rind [raɪnd] *n* (*of fruit etc*) corteza *f*, cáscara *f*, piel *f*; (*of cheese*) costra *f*; (*of bacon*) piel *f*.

ring¹ [rɪŋ] **1** *n* (**a**) (*circle*: *of metal etc*) aro *m*; argolla *f*; (*on finger*) anillo *m*, sortija *f*; alianza *f*; (*on bird's leg, for curtain*) anilla *f*; (*ear~*) arete *m*; (*on stove*) hornillo *m*, quemador *m*; (*Bot*: *annual ~*) anillo *m* anual, cerco *m* anual; **~s** (*Gymnastics*) anillas *fpl*; **~ of smoke** anillo *m* de humo, (*from mouth*) bocanada *f* de humo; **~s of Saturn** anillos *mpl* de Saturno; **to have ~s round one's eyes** tener ojeras.

(**b**) (*of people*) círculo *m*, grupo *m*; (*of children, gossips etc*) corro *m*; (*coterie*) camarilla *f*; (*gang*) pandilla *f*; (*Comm*) confabulación *f*, (*on large scale*) cartel *m*; **there was a ~ of children round her** los niños estaban reunidos en torno suyo, ella estaba rodeada de niños; **they were sitting in a ~** estaban sentados en círculo; **to make** (*or* **run**) **~s round sb** dar quince y raya a uno.

(**c**) (*Boxing*: *arena etc*) cuadrilátero *m*; (*at circus*) pista *f*; (*bull~*) ruedo *m*, redondel *m*, plaza *f*; (*at horse race*) cercado *m*; **the ~** (*fig*) el boxeo.

2 *attr*: **~ exercise** anillas *fpl*; **~ finger** dedo *m* anular.

3 *vt* cercar, rodear (*by, with* de); *bird* anillar, poner anilla a; **the town is ~ed by hills** la ciudad está rodeada de colinas; **we are ~ed by enemies** estamos rodeados de enemigos, nos cercan los enemigos.

◆**ring round** *vt* rodear (*with* de).

ring² [rɪŋ] **1** *n* (**a**) (*metallic sound*) sonido *m* metálico; (*resonance*) resonancia *f*; (*tinkle*) retintín *m*; (*of voice*) timbre *m*; (*tone*) tono *m*, entonación *f*; (*of large bell*) repique *m*, tañido *m*; (*of handbell*) campanilleo *m*; (*of electric bell*) toque *m* de timbre; (*at door*) llamada *f*; **there was a ~ at the door** llamaron a la puerta; **give 3 ~s for the maid** tocar el timbre 3 veces para llamar a la camarera; **with a ~ of defiance** en son de reto; **with a sarcastic ~ in his voice** con retintín, con énfasis sarcástico; **that has the ~ of truth about it** eso tiene traza de ser verdad.

(**b**) **a ~ of bells** (*set*) un juego de campanas.

(**c**) (*Telec*) llamada *f* telefónica, telefonazo *m*; **I'll give you a ~** te llamaré.

2 (*irr*: *pret* **rang**, *ptp* **rung**) *vt* (**a**) (*strike, make sound*) hacer sonar; *large bell* repicar, tañer; *electric bell* tocar; **~ the bell, please** por favor toque el timbre.

(**b**) **to ~ sb** (*Brit Telec*) llamar a uno al (*or* por) teléfono, telefonear a uno.

3 *vi* (*sound*) sonar; resonar (*with* con); (*large bell*) repicar; (*small bell*) sonar; (*tinkle*) campanillear, tintinear; (*at door*) llamar; (*ears*) zumbar; **the telephone rang** (*Brit*) sonó el teléfono; **the valley rang with cries** resonaron los gritos por el valle; **his words were ~ing in my head** sus palabras resonaban en mi cabeza; **you rang, madam?** ¿me llama Vd, señora?; **we'll ~ for some sugar** llamaremos para pedir azúcar; **his words rang false** sus palabras sonaban falsas; **his story ~s true** su narración parece verídica.

◆**ring back 1** *vt* volver a llamar a, llamar otra vez a.

2 *vi* volver a llamar.

◆**ring down** *vt curtain* bajar.

◆**ring in 1** *vt* anunciar; **to ~ in the New Year** celebrar el Año Nuevo (con campanas).

2 *vi* (**a**) telefonear (una noticia *etc*).

(**b**) (*US Ind*) fichar.

◆**ring off** *vi* colgar.

◆**ring out 1** *vt*: **to ~ out the old year** tañer las campanas para señalar el fin del año.

2 *vi* (**a**) oírse, sonar; **a shot rang out** se oyó un tiro, sonó un tiro.

(**b**) (*US Ind*) fichar la salida.

◆**ring round** *vt* llamar (al teléfono).

◆**ring up** *vt* (**a**) (*Telec*) llamar (por teléfono).

(**b**) *curtain* levantar; **to ~ up the curtain on** (*fig*) dar comienzo a, iniciar.

(**c**) *amount* (*on cash-register*) registrar.

ring-a-ring-a-roses ['rɪŋə'rɪŋə'rəʊzɪz] *n* corro *m*; **to play ~** jugar al corro.

ring binder ['rɪŋbaɪndər] *n* carpeta *f* de anillos.

ringbolt ['rɪŋbəʊlt] *n* perno *m* con anillo, (*Naut*) cáncamo *m*.

ringdove ['rɪŋdʌv] *n* paloma *f* torcaz.

ringer ['rɪŋər] *n* (**a**) campanero *m*, -a *f*. (**b**) (‡) **dead ~** doble *m*, viva imagen *f*; **A is a dead ~ for B** A se le parece en todo a B. (**c**) (*US Racing*) caballo *m* sustituido.

ringing¹ ['rɪŋɪŋ] *n* (*Orn*) anillado *m*, anillamiento *m*.

ringing² ['rɪŋɪŋ] **1** *adj* resonante, sonoro; **in ~ tones** en tono vibrante, en tono enérgico; **~ tone** (*Brit Telec*) tono *m* de llamada.

2 *n* (*of large bell*) repique *m*, tañido *m*; (*of handbell*) campanilleo *m*; (*of electric bell*) toque *m* de timbre; (*in ears*) zumbido *m*.

ringleader ['rɪŋˌliːdər] *n* cabecilla *m*.

ringlet ['rɪŋlɪt] *n* rizo *m*, bucle *m*, tirabuzón *m*.

ringmaster ['rɪŋˌmɑːstər] *n* jefe *m* de pista, director *m* de circo; (*trainer*) domador *m*.

ring-pull ['rɪŋpʊl] *n* anilla *f*; **~ can** lata *f* de anilla.

ringroad ['rɪŋ'rəʊd] *n* (*Brit*) carretera *f* de circunvalación, carretera *f* radial, periférico *m* (*LAm*).

ringside ['rɪŋsaɪd] *n*: **to be at the ~** estar junto al cuadrilátero; **a ~ seat** una butaca de primera fila; **to have a ~ seat** (*fig*) verlo todo desde muy cerca.

ring-spanner ['rɪŋˌspænər] *n* llave *f* dentada.

ringway ['rɪŋweɪ] *n* (*US*) = **ringroad**.

ringworm ['rɪŋwɜːm] *n* tiña *f*.

rink [rɪŋk] *n* pista *f*.

rinse [rɪns] **1** *n* (**a**) (*of dishes etc*) enjuague *m*; (*of clothes*) aclarado *m*; **to give one's stockings a ~** aclarar las medias.

(**b**) (*colouring*) reflejo *m*; **to give one's hair a blue ~** dar reflejos azules a su pelo.

2 *vt* (**a**) (*also* **to ~ out**) enjuagar; aclarar; *mouth* lavar, limpiar.

(**b**) (*colour*) dar reflejos a.

Rio de Janeiro [ˌriːəʊdədʒə'nɪərəʊ] *n* Río *m* de Janeiro.

riot ['raɪət] **1** *n* motín *m*, disturbio *m*; tumulto *m*; (*fig*) orgía *f*; alboroto *m*; (*in prison*) amotinamiento *m*, sublevación *f*; **it was a ~ of colour** había una exhibición brillante de colores; **there was nearly a ~** hubo casi un motín; **it was a ~!** (*fig*) ¡fue divertidísimo!, ¡fue la monda!*; **to run ~** desmandarse, cometer excesos, librarse de toda traba; (*spread*) extenderse por todas partes, cubrirlo todo; **to let one's imagination run ~** dejar volar la imaginación, dar rienda suelta a la imaginación.

2 *attr*: **to read the ~ act** mandar que cese el disturbio, imponer la paz; **to read the ~ act to sb** leerle la cartilla a uno; **~ gear** uniforme *m* antidisturbios; **~ police** brigada *f* antidisturbios; **~ shield** escudo *m* antidisturbios; **~ squad** = **~ police**.

3 *vi* amotinarse.

rioter ['raɪətəʳ] *n* amotinado *m*, -a *f*, manifestante *mf*, revoltoso *m*.

riotous ['raɪətəs] *adj person, populace* amotinado; *assembly* desordenado, alborotado; *party* bullicioso, ruidoso; *life* desenfrenado; **it was a ~ success** obtuvo un éxito ruidoso; **we had a ~ time** nos divertimos una barbaridad.

riotously ['raɪətəslɪ] *adv* con desorden, alborotadamente; bulliciosamente, ruidosamente; desenfrenadamente; **a ~ funny play** una comedia tremendamente divertida.

R.I.P. *abbr of* **requiescat in pace, (may he** (*etc*) **rest in peace)** que en paz descanse, E.P.D., D.E.P.

rip [rɪp] **1** *n* rasgón *m*, rasgadura *f*.

2 *vt* rasgar, desgarrar; **to ~ a box open** abrir una caja rompiéndola, quitar violentamente la tapa de una caja; **to ~ an envelope open** abrir un sobre rompiéndolo.

3 *vi* (**a**) (*cloth*) rasgarse, romperse.

(**b**) (*****) **to ~ along** correr a toda mecha, ir a buen tren; **let her ~!** ¡más rápido!, ¡más gas!*

◆**rip off** *vt* (**a**) arrancar, quitar (de un tirón). (**b**) (‡) *person* timar, robar; *object* pulir‡, birlar*.

◆**rip out** *vt* arrancar.

◆**rip through** *vt* desgarrar, romper (violentamente); destrozar.

◆**rip up** *vt* (*tear*) desgarrar, romper; **the train ~ped up 100 metres of track** el tren destrozó 100 metros de la vía.

riparian [raɪ'pɛərɪən] *adj* ribereño.

ripcord ['rɪpkɔːd] *n* cabo *m* de desgarre.

ripe [raɪp] *adj* (**a**) *fruit etc* maduro; **to be ~ for picking** estar bastante maduro para poderse coger; **to grow ~** madurar.

(**b**) (*fig*) listo; perfecto, en su punto; **a plan ~ for execution** un plan listo para ponerse en obra; **to be ~ for mischief** estar dispuesto a emprender cualquier diablura; **the company is ~ for a takeover** la empresa está en su punto para que la adquiera otro; **the country is ~ for revolution** la revolución está a punto de estallar en el país; **to live to a ~ old age** llegar a muy viejo; **when the time is ~** cuando se nos depare la oportunidad, cuando llegue el momento oportuno.

(**c**) (*****) *language* grosero, verde; *smell* fuerte, desagradable; **that's pretty ~!** ¡eso no se puede consentir!

ripen ['raɪpən] *vti* madurar.

ripeness ['raɪpnɪs] *n* madurez *f*.

rip-off‡ ['rɪpɒf] *n* timo *m*, robo *m*, estafa *f*.

riposte [rɪ'pɒst] **1** *n* (*Fencing*) estocada *f*; (*reply*) respuesta *f* aguda, réplica *f*. **2** *vi* replicar, responder con viveza.

ripper ['rɪpəʳ] *n*: **Jack the R~** Juanito el Destripador.

ripping*† ['rɪpɪŋ] *adj* (*Brit*) estupendo*, bárbaro*.

ripple ['rɪpl] **1** *n* (*wave*) rizo *m*, onda *f*; (*sound*) murmullo *m*; **~ effect = knock-on effect**; **a ~ of excitement** un susurro de emoción; **a ~ of applause** unos cuantos aplausos.

2 *vt* rizar.

3 *vi* rizarse; correr con rizos; murmurar; **the crowd ~d with excitement** el público se estremeció emocionado.

rip-roaring* ['rɪp,rɔːrɪŋ] *adj party etc* bullicioso, animadísimo, de lo más ruidoso; *speech* apasionado, violento; *success* apoteósico.

riptide ['rɪptaɪd] *n* aguas *fpl* revueltas.

rise [raɪz] **1** *n* (**a**) (*act of rising*) subida *f*, ascensión *f*, elevación *f*; (*of sun, moon*) salida *f*; (*of river*) crecida *f*; **a ~ in the voice** una elevación de tono; **~ and fall** (*of water etc*) subida *f* y bajada; (*of music, voice*) cadencia *f*.

(**b**) (*act of rising, fig*) **the ~ of the middle class** el desarrollo de la clase media; **the ~ of Bristol** el crecimiento de Bristol; **Napoleon's ~ to power** la subida de Napoleón al poder; **the ~ and fall of the empire** la grandeza y caída del imperio; **inflation is on the ~ again** la inflación vuelve a subir; **to take a ~ out of sb*** burlarse de uno; poner a uno en ridículo; **nobody takes a ~ out of me*** a mí nadie me tose.

(**c**) (*in price, temperature*) subida *f*, alza *f*; (*in value*) aumento *m*; (*in salary*) aumento *m*, subida *f*; (*promotion*) ascenso *m*; **to ask for a ~** (*Brit*) pedir un aumento de sueldo; **they got a ~ of 50 dollars** les aumentaron el sueldo en 50 dólares; **prices are on the ~** los precios están subiendo; **a ~ of 5 degrees in temperature** una subida de temperatura de 5 grados.

(**d**) (*of spring, river*) nacimiento *m*; (*fig*) origen *m*; **the river takes its ~ in the mountains** el río nace en las montañas; **to give ~ to** dar origen a, motivar, ocasionar, (*doubts etc*) suscitar, dar lugar a.

(**e**) (*high ground*) altura *f*, eminencia *f*; (*slope*) cuesta *f*, pendiente *f*.

2 (*irr*: *pret* **rose,** *ptp* **risen**) *vi* (**a**) (*of person*: *to one's feet etc*) levantarse, ponerse en pie; **he rose to greet us** se levantó para recibirnos; **to ~ from table** levantarse de la mesa; **to ~ at 6** levantarse a las 6; **to ~ early** levantarse temprano, madrugar; **to ~** (**again**) **from the dead** resucitar; **Slobodia shall ~ again** Eslobodia renacerá.

(**b**) **to ~** (**in revolt**) sublevarse, rebelarse (*against* contra); **to ~** (**up**) **in arms** alzarse en armas.

(**c**) (*sun, moon*) salir; (*smoke etc*) subir, elevarse, alzarse; (*building, mountain*) elevarse; **it rose 3 metres off the ground** se elevó 3 metros sobre el suelo; **the mountain ~s to 3,500 metres** la montaña alcanza 3.500 metros, la montaña se eleva a 3.500 metros; **to ~ to the surface** salir a la superficie; **she could feel a blush rising to her cheeks** sentía que sus mejillas se ponían coloradas; **the partridge rose** se levantó la perdiz, la perdiz alzó el vuelo; **to ~ to the bait** picar, morder el anzuelo (*also fig*); **he wouldn't ~** (**to the bait**) no quería picar; **to ~ to the challenge** ponerse a la altura del reto, responder al desafío como se debe.

(**d**) (*ground*) subir (en pendiente); (*dough*) leudarse; (*barometer, temperature, sea etc*) subir; (*river*) crecer; (*sound, voice*) hacerse más fuerte, sonar más fuerte; (*wind*) hacerse más fuerte, soplar más fuerte; (*swell*) hincharse, crecer; (*price*) subir, avanzar; (*St Ex*) estar en alza, cotizarse en alza; (*number*) subir, aumentar; **prices are rising** suben los precios; **tension is rising** aumenta la tensión; **it has risen 20% in price** su precio ha subido en un 20 por cien; **a thought rose in my mind** se me ocurrió algo; **laughter rose from the audience** en el público estallaron las risas; **our spirits rose** volvimos a animarnos, nos reanimamos.

(**e**) **to ~ above petty rancour** mostrarse superior a los pequeños rencores; **to ~ to the occasion** ponerse a la altura de las circunstancias.

(**f**) (*in rank*) ascender, avanzar; **he rose to colonel** ascendió a coronel; **he rose from nothing** salió de la nada; **to ~ in the world** hacer carrera, avanzar en su carrera; **to ~ in sb's opinion** ganar en la opinión de uno.

(**g**) (*river*) nacer.

(**h**) **then the House rose** luego se suspendió la sesión.

◆**rise up** *vi V* **rise 2.**

risen ['rɪzn] *ptp of* **rise.**

riser ['raɪzəʳ] *n*: **to be an early ~** madrugar, ser madrugador; **to be a late ~** levantarse tarde.

risibility [,rɪzɪ'bɪlɪtɪ] *n* risibilidad *f*.

risible ['rɪzɪbl] *adj* risible.

rising ['raɪzɪŋ] **1** *adj number, quantity* creciente; *tide* creciente; *sun etc* naciente; *trend* (*Fin*) alcista; (*promising*) prometedor, que promete, de porvenir; **the ~ number of murders** el creciente número de homicidios; **with ~ alarm** con creciente alarma; **~ damp** humedad *f*; **the ~ generation** las nuevas generaciones; **~ ground** terreno *m* ascendente; **~ politician** político *m* en alza.

2 *n* (**a**) (*rebellion*) sublevación *f*, rebelión *f*.

(**b**) (*of river*) nacimiento *m*; (*of sun etc*) salida *f*.

(**c**) **on the ~ of the House** al suspenderse la sesión.

3 *adv*: **he's ~ 12*** pronto tendrá 12 años.

risk [rɪsk] **1** *n* riesgo *m*, peligro *m*; **against all ~s** contra todo riesgo; **persons at ~** personas *fpl* en peligro, personas *fpl* vulnerables; **at the ~ of** a riesgo de; **at the ~ of one's life** con peligro de la vida, arriesgando la vida; **at one's own ~** bajo su propia responsabilidad; **at owner's ~** bajo la responsabilidad del dueño; **there is a fire ~** hay peligro de provocar un incendio; **it's not worth the ~** no vale la pena correr tanto peligro; **to put sth at ~** poner algo en peligro; **to run the ~ of defeat** correr riesgo de ser derrotado; **to run the ~ of +** *ger* correr el riesgo de + *infin*; **to take ~s** arriesgarse; **he takes a lot of ~s** se arriesga mucho; **will you take the ~?** ¿te atreves?; **I can't take the ~** no me puedo exponer a eso.

2 *attr*: **~ capital** capital *m* (de) riesgo.

3 *vt* arriesgar; atreverse a, exponerse a; **I'll ~ it** acepto; **I can't ~ it** no me puedo exponer a eso; **shall we ~ it?** ¿nos atrevemos?; **to ~ defeat** correr riesgo de ser derrotado, exponerse a una posible derrota; **to ~ +** *ger* arriesgarse a + *infin*; **I can't ~ going alone** no puedo arriesgarme a ir solo, no me atrevo a ir solo.

riskiness ['rɪskɪnɪs] *n* peligro *m*, lo peligroso, lo arriesgado; **in view of the ~ of the plan** visto lo peligroso del plan.

risky ['rɪskɪ] *adj* (**a**) *plan, deed etc* peligroso, arriesgado, aventurado; **a ~ enterprise** una empresa arriesgada; **it is ~ to suppose that ...** es arriesgado (*or* temerario) suponer que ... (**b**) = **risqué.**

risotto [rɪ'zɒtəʊ] *n* arroz *m* (*con pollo, verduras, etc*).

risqué [ˈriːskeɪ] *adj* verde, indecente, de color subido.

rissole [ˈrɪsəʊl] *n* (*Brit*) ≃ croqueta *f*.

rite [raɪt] *n* rito *m*; (*funeral* **~s**) exequias *fpl*; **last ~s** extremaunción *f*; **'The R~ of Spring'** 'La Consagración de la Primavera'.

ritual [ˈrɪtjʊəl] **1** *adj* ritual; (*fig*) consagrado, formulario; **in the ~ phrase** en la expresión consagrada. **2** *n* ritual *m*, ceremonia *f*.

ritualism [ˈrɪtjʊəlɪzəm] *n* ritualismo *m*.

ritualist [ˈrɪtjʊəlɪst] *n* ritualista *mf*.

ritualistic [ˌrɪtjʊəˈlɪstɪk] *adj* ritualista; (*fig*) consagrado, sacramental.

ritually [ˈrɪtjʊəlɪ] *adv* ritualmente.

ritzy* [ˈrɪtsɪ] *adj* (*US*) muy pera*, lujoso.

rival [ˈraɪvəl] **1** *adj* rival, opuesto; **a ~ firm** una firma competidora. **2** *n* rival *mf*, competidor *m*, -ora *f*. **3** *vt* rivalizar con, competir con.

rivalry [ˈraɪvəlrɪ] *n* rivalidad *f*; competencia *f*; **to enter into ~ with sb** empezar a competir con uno.

riven [ˈrɪvən] *adj, ptp* (*liter*) rajado, hendido; **~ by** desgarrado por, dividido por, escindido por.

river [ˈrɪvəʳ] **1** *n* río *m*; **down ~** río abajo; **up ~** río arriba; **up ~ from Toledo** aguas arriba de Toledo; **to sell sb down the ~*** traicionar a uno.

2 *attr* de río, del río; fluvial; **~ fish** pez *m* de río; **~ fishing** pesca *f* de río; **~ police** brigada *f* fluvial; **~ traffic** tráfico *m* fluvial.

riverbank [ˈrɪvəbæŋk] **1** *n* orilla *f* del río, margen *f* del río. **2** *attr* ribereño.

riverbasin [ˈrɪvəˌbeɪsn] *n* cuenca *f* de río.

riverbed [ˈrɪvəbed] *n* lecho *m*, cauce *m* (del río).

riverine [ˈrɪvəraɪn] *adj* fluvial, ribereño.

rivermouth [ˈrɪvəmaʊθ] *n, pl* **rivermouths** [ˈrɪvəmaʊðz] estuario *m*, ría *f*.

riverside [ˈrɪvəsaɪd] **1** *n* ribera *f*, orilla *f* (del río). **2** *attr* ribereño.

rivet [ˈrɪvɪt] **1** *n* roblón *m*, remache *m*.

2 *vt* remachar; (*fig*) clavar (*on, to* en); **to ~ one's eyes on sth** clavar la vista en algo; **it ~ed our attention** nos llamó fuertemente la atención, lo miramos fascinados.

riveter [ˈrɪvɪtəʳ] *n* remachador *m*.

rivet(t)ing [ˈrɪvɪtɪŋ] **1** *n* remachado *m*. **2** *adj* fascinante, cautivador.

Riviera [ˌrɪvɪˈɛərə] *n* (*French*) Riviera *f* (francesa), Costa *f* Azul; (*Italian*) Riviera *f* italiana.

rivulet [ˈrɪvjʊlɪt] *n* riachuelo *m*, arroyuelo *m*.

Riyadh [rɪˈjɑːd] *n* Riyadh *m*.

RK *n* (*Scol*) *abbr of* **Religious Knowledge** instrucción *f* religiosa.

Rly *abbr of* **Railway** ferrocarril, f.c.

RM *n abbr of* **Royal Marines.**

RN *n* (**a**) (*Brit*) *abbr of* **Royal Navy.** (**b**) (*US*) *abbr of* **registered nurse.**

RNA *n abbr of* **ribonucleic acid** ácido *m* ribonucleico, ARN *m*.

RNLI *n abbr of* **Royal National Lifeboat Institution** *servicio de lanchas de socorro.*

RNVR *n abbr of* **Royal Naval Volunteer Reserve.**

roach [rəʊtʃ] *n* (**a**) (*Fish*) escarcho *m*; (*US*) cucaracha *f*. (**b**) (*US*‡: *drug*) cucaracha‡ *f*.

road [rəʊd] **1** *n* camino *m* (*to* de; *also fig*); (*main* **~**) carretera *f*; (*in town*) calle *f*; (*surface*) firme *m*; (*roadway, not pavement*) calzada *f*; **~s** (*Naut*) rada *f*; **'~ narrows'** 'estrechamiento de la calzada'; **'~ up'** 'cerrado por obras'; **the ~ to Teruel** el camino de Teruel; **at the 23rd kilometre on the Valencia ~** en el kilómetro 23 de la carretera de Valencia; **the ~ to success** el camino del éxito; **one for the ~*** el trago del estribo*, la del estribo; **across the ~** al otro lado de la calle, enfrente; **she lives across the ~ from us** vive en frente de nosotros; **by ~** por carretera; **my car is off the ~** mi coche está en el garaje; **to be on the ~** estar en camino; (*Comm*) ser viajante; (*Theat*) estar de gira; **my car is on the ~ again** he vuelto a tener coche en carretera; **he's on the ~ to recovery** se está reponiendo; **we're on the ~ to disaster** vamos camino del desastre; **the dog was wandering on the ~** el perro andaba por la calzada; **to get** (*or* **take**) **a show on the ~, to take to the ~** echarse a la carretera; **to be on the right ~** ir por buen camino (*also fig*); **to get out of the ~** (*fig*) quitarse de en medio; **our relationship has reached the end of the ~** nuestras relaciones han llegado al punto final; **to hold the ~** (*Aut*) agarrarse al camino; **to take the ~** ponerse en camino (*to X* para ir a X).

2 *attr* de carretera; vial; **~ accident** accidente *m* de tráfico, accidente *m* de tránsito; **~ construction** construcción *f* de carreteras; **~ haulage** transportes *mpl* por carretera; **~ haulier** compañía *f* de transportes por carretera; transportista *mf*; **~ hump** banda *f* de desaceleración; **~ junction** empalme *m*; **~ racer** (*Cycling*) ciclista *mf* de fondo en carretera; **~ safety** seguridad *f* en la carretera, seguridad *f* vial; **~ sense** instinto *m* del automovilista; **~ tax** impuesto *m* de rodaje; **~ test, ~ trial** prueba *f* en carretera; **~ traffic** circulación *f* por carretera; tránsito *m* rodado; **~ transport** transportes *mpl* por carretera; **~ vehicle** vehículo *m* carretero.

roadbed [ˈrəʊdbed] *n* (*US*) firme *m*; (*Rail*) capa *f* de balasto.

roadblock [ˈrəʊdblɒk] *n* control *m*; barricada *f*.

roadbook [ˈrəʊdbʊk] *n* (*Aut*) libro *m* de mapas e itinerarios (*etc*).

roadbridge [ˈrəʊdbrɪdʒ] *n* puente *m* de carretera.

roadhog [ˈrəʊdhɒg] *n* loco *m* del volante, loca *f* del volante.

roadhouse [ˈrəʊdhaʊs] *n, pl* **roadhouses** [ˈrəʊdhaʊzɪz] albergue *m* de carretera, motel *m*.

roadie* [ˈrəʊdɪ] *n* (*Mus*) encargado *m* del transporte del equipo.

roadmaking [ˈrəʊdˌmeɪkɪŋ] *n* construcción *f* de carreteras.

roadmap [ˈrəʊdmæp] *n* mapa *m* de carreteras, mapa *m* vial.

roadmender [ˈrəʊdmendəʳ] *n* peón *m* caminero.

road metal [ˈrəʊdmetl] *n* grava *f*, lastre *m*.

roadrace [ˈrəʊdreɪs] *n* carrera *f* en carretera.

roadroller [ˈrəʊdˌrəʊləʳ] *n* apisonadora *f*.

roadshow [ˈrəʊdʃəʊ] *n* (*Theat*) bolo* *m*.

roadside [ˈrəʊdsaɪd] **1** *n* borde *m* (*LAm*: orilla *f*) del camino, borde *m* (*LAm*: orilla *f*) de la carretera. **2** *attr* de camino, de carretera; **~ inn** fonda *f* de carretera; **~ repairs** reparaciones *fpl* al borde de la carretera; **~ restaurant** (*US*) café-restaurante *m* (de carretera).

roadsign [ˈrəʊdsaɪn] *n* señal *f* de tráfico, señal *f* de carretera, señal *f* vertical.

roadstead [ˈrəʊdsted] *n* rada *f*.

roadster [ˈrəʊdstəʳ] *n* (*car*) coche *m* de turismo; (*cycle*) bicicleta *f* de turismo.

roadsweeper [ˈrəʊdˌswiːpəʳ] *n* barrendero *m*.

roaduser [ˈrəʊdˌjuːzəʳ] *n* usuario *m* de la vía pública.

roadway [ˈrəʊdweɪ] *n* calzada *f*.

roadworks [ˈrəʊdwɜːks] *npl* obras *fpl* de carretera.

roadworthy [ˈrəʊdˌwɜːðɪ] *adj car* en condiciones para circular, apto para circular.

roam [rəʊm] **1** *vt* vagar por, errar por, recorrer. **2** *vi* vagar.

◆roam about, roam around *vi* andar sin propósito fijo.

roamer [ˈrəʊməʳ] *n* hombre *m* errante, andariego *m*; (*tramp*) vagabundo *m*.

roaming [ˈrəʊmɪŋ] *n* vagabundeo *m*; (*as tourist etc*) excursiones *fpl*, paseos *mpl*.

roan [rəʊn] **1** *adj* ruano. **2** *n* caballo *m* ruano.

roar [rɔːʳ] **1** *n* (*of animal*) rugido *m*, bramido *m*; (*of person*) rugido *m*; (*loud noise*) estruendo *m*, fragor *m*; (*of fire*) crepitación *f*; (*of river, storm etc*) estruendo *m*; (*of laughter*) carcajada *f*; **with great ~s of laughter** con grandes carcajadas; **he said with a ~** dijo rugiendo; **to set the room in a ~** hacer reír a todo el mundo a carcajadas.

2 *vt* rugir, decir a gritos; **to ~ one's disapproval** manifestar su disconformidad a gritos; **he ~ed out an order** lanzó una orden a voz en grito.

3 *vi* rugir, bramar; hacer estruendo; (*of guns, thunder*) retumbar; (*with laughter*) reírse a carcajadas; **to ~ with pain** rugir de dolor; **the lorry ~ed past** el camión pasó ruidosamente; **this will make you ~** esto os hará moriros de risa.

4 *vr*: **to ~ o.s. hoarse** ponerse ronco gritando, gritar hasta enronquecerse.

roaring [ˈrɔːrɪŋ] *adj*: **the R~ Forties** los cuarenta rugientes; **he was ~ drunk** estaba borracho y despotricaba; **in front of a ~ fire** junto a la lumbre que arde furiosamente; **it was a ~ success** fue un éxito clamoroso; **to do a ~ trade** hacer un tremendo negocio.

roast [rəʊst] **1** *n* carne *f* asada, asado *m*.

2 *adj* asado; *coffee* torrefacto, tostado; **~ beef** rosbif *m*.

3 *vt meat* (**a**) asar; *coffee* tostar; **the sun which was ~ing the city** el sol que achicharraba la ciudad; **to ~ one's feet by the fire** asarse los pies junto al fuego.

(**b**) (*) **to ~ sb** (*mock*) mofarse de uno; (*criticize*) criticar a uno, censurar a uno; (*scold*) desollar vivo a uno, poner a uno como un trapo*.

4 *vi* (*meat*) asarse; (*person*) tostarse; **we ~ed there for a whole month** nos asamos allí durante un mes entero.

roaster ['rəʊstəʳ] *n* (**a**) (*implement*) asador *m*, tostador *m*. (**b**) (*bird*) pollo *m* para asar.
roasting ['rəʊstɪŋ] **1** *adj* (**a**) *chicken etc* para asar. (**b**) *day, heat* abrasador. **2** *n* (**a**) (*Culin*) asado *m*; (*of coffee*) tostadura *f*, tueste *m*. (**b**) **to give sb a ~*** = **roast 3** (**b**).
roasting-jack ['rəʊstɪŋdʒæk] *n*, **roasting-spit** ['rəʊstɪŋspɪt] *n* asador *m*.
rob [rɒb] *vt* robar; *bank etc* atracar; **to ~ sb of sth** robar algo a uno; **I've been ~bed!** ¡me han robado!; **we were ~bed!*** (*Sport*) ¡hubo tongo!
robber ['rɒbəʳ] *n* ladrón *m*; (*bank~*) atracador *m*; (*footpad*) salteador *m* (de caminos); (*brigand*) bandido *m*.
robbery ['rɒbərɪ] *n* robo *m*; latrocinio *m*; **~ with violence** robo *m* a mano armada, atraco *m*, asalto *m*.
robe [rəʊb] **1** *n* (††) manto *m*, túnica *f*; (*monk's*) hábito *m*; (*priest's*) sotana *f*; (*lawyer's, Univ*) toga *f*, traje *m* talar; (*bath~*) albornoz *m*; (*christening ~*) traje *m* de bautismo; **~s** traje *m* de ceremonia, traje *m* talar.
2 *vt*: **to ~ sb in black** vestir a uno de negro; **to appear ~d in a long dress** aparecer vestido de un traje largo.
3 *vr*: **to ~ o.s.** vestirse.
Robert ['rɒbət] *nm* Roberto.
robin ['rɒbɪn] *n* (*Orn*) petirrojo *m*.
robot ['rəʊbɒt] *n* robot *m*, autómata *m*.
robotics [rəʊ'bɒtɪks] *n* robótica *f*.
robust [rəʊ'bʌst] *adj* robusto; fuerte, vigoroso; **a ~ defence** una defensa vigorosa, una defensa enérgica; **a ~ sense of humour** un fuerte sentido del humor.
robustly [rəʊ'bʌstlɪ] *adv* robustamente; fuertemente, vigorosamente.
robustness [rəʊ'bʌstnɪs] *n* robustez *f*; fuerza *f*, vigor *m*, energía *f*.
rock¹ [rɒk] *n* roca *f*; (*standing stone, ~face*) peña *f*, peñasco *m*; (*US*) piedra *f*, piedrecilla *f*; (*Naut*) escollo *m*; (‡: *diamond*) diamante *m*; (‡: *drug*) crack *m*; **the R~ (of Gibraltar)** el Peñón (de Gibraltar); **whisky on the ~s*** whisky *m* con (cubitos de) hielo; **to be on the ~s*** (*broke*) no tener un céntimo; **their marriage is on the ~s*** su matrimonio anda mal; **to run on to the ~s** (*Naut*) dar en un escollo, (*fig*) peligrar, estar en peligro.
rock² [rɒk] **1** *vt* (*gently*) mecer, balancear; (*violently*) sacudir; **to ~ a child to sleep** arrullar a un niño, adormecer a un niño meciéndole en la cuna (*etc*); **the country was ~ed by strikes** el país fue sacudido por las huelgas; **the news ~ed us all** la noticia pasmó a todos.
2 *vi* mecerse, balancearse; sacudirse; **the ship ~ed gently on the waves** el buque se balanceaba en las olas; **the train ~ed violently** el tren se sacudió violentamente; **we just ~ed (with laughter)** nos morimos de risa; **the theatre ~ed with laughter** las risas estremecieron el teatro.
3 *n* (*Mus*) rock *m*; **~ concert** concierto *m* de rock; **~ festival** festival *m* de rock; **~ music** música *f* rock; **~ and roll** rocanrol *m*.
rock-bottom ['rɒk'bɒtəm] **1** *n* fondo *m*, parte *f* más profunda; (*fig*) punto *m* más bajo; **prices are at ~** los precios están por los suelos; **to reach ~, to touch ~** (*fig*) llegar a su punto más bajo.
2 *attr price* más bajo, mínimo.
rock-carving ['rɒk,kɑːvɪŋ] *n* escultura *f* rupestre.
rock-climber ['rɒk,klaɪməʳ] *n* escalador *m*, -ora *f* (de rocas).
rock-climbing ['rɒk,klaɪmɪŋ] *n* escalada *f* en rocas.
rock crystal ['rɒk,krɪstl] *n* cristal *m* de roca, cuarzo *m*.
rocker ['rɒkəʳ] *n* (**a**) (*Mech*) balancín *m*, eje *m* de balancín; (*chair*) mecedora *f*. (**b**) (‡) cabeza *f*; **he's off his ~** le falta un tornillo*; **you must be off your ~!** ¡estás majareta!* (**c**) (*Mus*) rockero *m*, -a *f*.
rockery ['rɒkərɪ] *n* jardincito *m* rocoso, cuadro *m* alpino.
rocket¹ ['rɒkɪt] *n* (*Bot*) oruga *f*.
rocket² ['rɒkɪt] **1** *n* (**a**) cohete *m*.
(**b**) (*) peluca* *f*; **to get a ~ from sb** (*Brit*) recibir una peluca de uno; **to give sb a ~** echar un rapapolvo a uno* (*for the mistake* por el error).
2 *vt* (*Mil*) atacar con cohetes.
3 *vi*: **to ~ upwards** subir como un cohete; **to ~ to the moon** ir en cohete a la luna; **to ~ to fame** hacerse famoso de la noche a la mañana, llegar repentinamente a la fama; **prices have ~ed** los precios se han puesto por las nubes.
rocket attack ['rɒkɪtə,tæk] *n* ataque *m* con cohetes.
rocket-launcher ['rɒkɪt,lɔːntʃəʳ] *n* lanzacohetes *m*.
rocket-propelled ['rɒkɪtprə,peld] *adj* propulsado por cohete(s).
rocket propulsion ['rɒkɪtprə,pʌlʃən] *n* propulsión *f* a cohete.
rocket-range ['rɒkɪtreɪndʒ] *n* base *f* de lanzamiento de cohetes.
rocketry ['rɒkɪtrɪ] *n* cohetería *f*.
rockface ['rɒkfeɪs] *n* pared *f* de roca.
rockfall ['rɒkfɔːl] *n* deslizamiento *m* de montaña.
rock-garden ['rɒk,gɑːdn] *n* jardincito *m* rocoso, cuadro *m* alpino.
rock-hard ['rɒk'hɑːd] *adj* duro como la roca.
Rockies ['rɒkɪz] *npl* Montañas *fpl* Rocosas.
rocking ['rɒkɪŋ] *n* balanceo *m*.
rocking-chair ['rɒkɪŋtʃɛəʳ] *n* mecedora *f*.
rocking-horse ['rɒkɪŋhɔːs] *n* caballo *m* de balancín.
rock-painting ['rɒk,peɪntɪŋ] *n* pintura *f* rupestre.
rock-plant ['rɒkplɑːnt] *n* planta *f* rupestre, planta *f* rupícola.
rock-pool ['rɒkpuːl] *n* charca *f* (de agua de mar) entre rocas.
rockrose ['rɒkrəʊz] *n* jara *f*, heliantemo *m*.
rock-salmon ['rɒk'sæmən] *n* (*Brit*) perro *m* marino, cazón *m*.
rock-salt ['rɒksɔːlt] *n* sal *f* gema, sal *f* sin refinar.
rocky¹ ['rɒkɪ] *adj substance* de roca, parecido a roca; *slope etc* rocoso; fragoso, escabroso.
rocky² ['rɒkɪ] *adj* (**a**) (*unstable*) que se bambolea, inestable. (**b**) (*) débil, flojo, nada firme.
Rocky Mountains ['rɒkɪ'maʊntɪnz] *npl* Montañas *fpl* Rocosas.
rococo [rəʊ'kəʊkəʊ] **1** *adj* rococó. **2** *n* rococó *m*.
rod [rɒd] *n* (*Mech etc*) vara *f*, varilla *f*, barra *f*; (*stick, of authority*) vara *f*; (*fishing ~*) caña *f*; (*Survey*) jalón *m*; (*curtain ~*) barra *f*; (*connecting ~*) biela *f*; (*measure*) *medida de longitud = 5,029 metros*; (*US* ‡) pipa‡ *f*, pistola *f*; **to have a ~ in pickle for sb** guardársela a uno; **to make a ~ for one's own back** hacer algo que después resultará contraproducente; **to rule with a ~ of iron** gobernar con mano de hierro; **to spare the ~** excusar la vara; **this is to spare the ~ and spoil the child** quien bien te quiere te hará llorar.
Rod [rɒd] *nm*, **Roddy** ['rɒdɪ] *nm familiar forms of* **Roderick**.
rode [rəʊd] *pret of* **ride**.
rodent ['rəʊdənt] *n* roedor *m*.
rodeo ['rəʊdɪəʊ] *n* rodeo *m*.
Roderick ['rɒdərɪk] *nm* Rodrigo; **~, the last of the Goths** Rodrigo el último godo.
rodomontade [,rɒdəmɒn'teɪd] *n* fanfarronada *f*.
roe¹ [rəʊ] *n* (*Zool*: *also* **~ deer**) corzo *m*, -a *f*.
roe² [rəʊ] *n* (*Fish*): **hard ~** hueva *f*; **soft ~** lecha *f*.
roebuck ['rəʊbʌk] *n* corzo *m*.
Rogation [rəʊ'geɪʃən]: **~ Days** Rogativas *fpl* de la Ascensión; **~ Sunday** Domingo *m* de la Ascensión.
rogations [rəʊ'geɪʃənz] *npl* (*Eccl*) rogativas *fpl*.
Roger ['rɒdʒəʳ] *nm* Rogelio; **~!** (*Telec etc*) ¡bien!, ¡de acuerdo!
roger** ['rɒdʒəʳ] *vt* joder**.
rogue [rəʊg] **1** *n* pícaro *m*, pillo *m*; (*hum*) picaruelo *m*; **you ~!** ¡canalla!; **~s' gallery** fichero *m* de delincuentes. **2** *adj* solitario; que actúa solo (y de modo sospechoso); **~ elephant** elefante *m* solitario (y peligroso).
roguery ['rəʊgərɪ] *n* picardía *f*, truhanería *f*; (*mischief*) travesuras *fpl*, diabluras *fpl*; **they're up to some ~** están haciendo alguna diablura.
roguish ['rəʊgɪʃ] *adj* picaresco; (*mischievous*) pillo, travieso; *look, smile etc* picaruelo, malicioso.
roguishly ['rəʊgɪʃlɪ] *adv look, smile etc* con malicia; **she looked at me ~** me miró picaruela.
ROI *n abbr of* **return on investments** rendimiento *m* de las inversiones.
roil [rɔɪl] *vt* (*US*) = **rile**.
roister ['rɔɪstəʳ] *vi* jaranear.
roisterer ['rɔɪstərəʳ] *n* jaranero *m*.
Roland ['rəʊlənd] *nm* Roldán, Rolando.
role, rôle [rəʊl] *n* (*Theat, fig*) papel *m*; **to cast sb in the ~ of** dar a uno el papel de (*also fig*); **to play** (*or* **take**) **a ~** (*Theat*) hacer un papel, (*fig*) desempeñar un papel.
role-model ['rəʊl,mɒdl] *n* modelo *m* a imitar.
role-playing ['rəʊl,pleɪɪŋ] *n* juego *m* de imitación, juego *m* de roles.
roll [rəʊl] **1** *n* (**a**) (*of paper, tobacco, film etc*) rollo *m*; (*of cloth*) pieza *f*; (*of fat on body*) rodete *m*, rosca *f*, michelín *m* (*hum*); (*US*: *of banknotes*) fajo *m*; (*of bread*) panecillo *m*, bolillo *m* (*Méx*).
(**b**) (*list*) lista *f*; rol *m*, nómina *f*; **~s** (*Hist*) archivos *mpl*; **~ of honour** lista *f* de honor; **to call the ~** pasar lista; **to have 500 pupils on ~** tener inscritos 500 alumnos; **to strike sb off the ~** tachar a uno de la lista.

(**c**) (*sound*) (*of thunder*) retumbo *m*; (*of drum*) redoble *m*.

(**d**) (*movement*) (*of gait*) bamboleo *m*; (*of ship*) balanceo *m*; **to walk with a ~** andar bamboleándose; **the ship gave a sudden ~** el buque se balanceó de repente.

2 *vt vehicle, furniture etc* hacer rodar; (*move*) mover; (*push*) empujar; *eyes* poner en blanco; *soil* allanar; *lawn, pitch* apisonar; *pastry* aplanar; *metal* laminar; *cigarette* liar, hacer; *tongue* vibrar; *one's Rs* pronunciar con énfasis, exagerar, (*in Spanish*) pronunciar bien; **to ~ a car to the side of the road** empujar un coche al borde de la carretera; **to ~ a ball along the pavement** hacer rodar una pelota sobre la acera; **to ~ a stone downhill** hacer rodar una piedra cuesta abajo; **he's judge and jury ~ed into one** es a la vez juez y jurado.

3 *vi* (**a**) (*go ~ing*) rodar, ir rodando, dar vueltas; (*on ground, in pain etc*) revolcarse; (*land*) ondular; (*camera, machine*) funcionar; **it ~ed under the chair** rodó debajo de la silla; **it went ~ing downhill** fue rodando cuesta abajo; **when the tanks ~ed into the city** cuando los tanques entraron en la ciudad; **the bus ~ed to a stop** el autobús se paró; **to be ~ing in plenty** nadar en la abundancia; **they're ~ing in money*, they're ~ing in it*** nadan en oro.

(**b**) (*sound*) (*thunder*) retumbar; (*drum*) redoblar; (*organ*) sonar.

(**c**) (*in walking*) bambolearse; (*Naut*) balancearse; **he ~ed from side to side as he walked** iba bamboleándose de un lado para otro.

◆**roll about, roll around** *vi* (*coins etc*) rodar, ir rodando; (*dog etc*) rodar por el suelo; (*ship*) balancearse.

◆**roll along** *vi* (**a**) (*ball etc*) rodar, ir.

(**b**) (*: *arrive*) llegar, venir, presentarse.

◆**roll away 1** *vt table etc* apartar, quitar.

2 *vi* (*mist etc*) disiparse; (*ball*) alejarse (rodando).

◆**roll back** *vt carpet* quitar, enrollar; **to ~ back the years** remontarse en el tiempo, volver a los tiempos pasados.

◆**roll by** *vi* (*cart, procession, years*) pasar.

◆**roll down 1** *vt sleeve etc* bajar; desenrollar. **2** *vi* rodar por, bajar rodando por; **tears ~ed down her cheeks** las lágrimas le corrieron por las mejillas.

◆**roll in** *vi* (**a**) llegar; **the waves came ~ing in** llegaban grandes olas a la playa; **the money is ~ing in*** nos entra el dinero a raudales.

(**b**) (*: *person*) llegar, volver, presentarse; **he ~ed in at 2 am** entró en la casa (*etc*) a las 2.

◆**roll off** *vi* caer rodando.

◆**roll on** *vi* (*vehicle*) seguir su marcha; (*river*) correr, seguir su curso; (*offensive, time*) avanzar; **~ on the summer!*** ¡que venga el verano!

◆**roll out** *vt* (**a**) *barrel, table* sacar (rodando).

(**b**) *excuse etc* ensartar; presentar (otra vez); *speech* pronunciar (pesadamente).

(**c**) *pastry* extender (con el rodillo); *metal* laminar.

◆**roll over 1** *vt* (**a**) remover; volver.

(**b**) *debt* extender el plazo de.

2 *vi* dar una vuelta, volverse al otro lado.

◆**roll past** *vi* = **roll by**.

◆**roll up 1** *vt map, umbrella* arrollar, enrollar; *sleeve* arremangar, remangar; **to ~ sth up in paper** envolver algo en papel; **he was ~ed up in the blankets** estaba envuelto en las mantas.

2 *vi* (**a**) (*hedgehog etc*) enroscarse, arrollarse, hacerse un ovillo.

(**b**) (*car etc*) llegar; (*: *person*) aparecer, presentarse, llegar; acudir, venir; **~ up, ~ up!** ¡vengan todos!

3 *vr*: **to ~ o.s. up into a ball** arrollarse, hacerse un ovillo; **to ~ o.s. up in a blanket** envolverse en una manta.

rollaway ['rəʊləweɪ] *n* (*US*: *also* **~ bed**) cama *f* desmontable (sobre ruedas), cama *f* abatible (sobre ruedas).

rollbar ['rəʊlbɑːʳ] *n* (*Aut*) barra *f* estabilizadora.

rollcall ['rəʊlkɔːl] *n* lista *f*, acto *m* de pasar lista.

rolled [rəʊld] *adj umbrella etc* arrollado; *metal* laminado; **~ gold** oro *m* laminado; **~ oats** copos *mpl* de avena.

roller ['rəʊləʳ] *n* (**a**) (*Agr, Tech*) rodillo *m*; (*castor*) rueda *f*; (*steam~*) apisonadora *f*; (*for hair, sports field*) rulo *m*. (**b**) (*wave*) ola *f* larga, ola *f* grande.

roller bandage ['rəʊlə'bændɪdʒ] *n* venda *f* enrollada.

roller blind ['rəʊlə,blaɪnd] *n* persiana *f* enrollable.

roller-coaster ['rəʊlə'kəʊstəʳ] *n* montaña *f* rusa.

roller-skate ['rəʊlə,skeɪt] **1** *n* patín *m* de ruedas. **2** *vi* ir en patines de ruedas.

roller-skating ['rəʊlə,skeɪtɪŋ] *n* patinaje *m* sobre ruedas.

roller towel ['rəʊlə'taʊəl] *n* toalla *f* de rodillo, toalla *f* sin fin.

rollick ['rɒlɪk] *vi* jugar, divertirse; jaranear.

rollicking ['rɒlɪkɪŋ] **1** *adj* alegre, divertido; **we had a ~ time** nos divertimos una barbaridad; **it was a ~ party** fue una fiesta animadísima; **it's ~ nonsense** son disparates de los más divertidos; **it's a ~ farce** es una farsa de lo más divertido. **2** *n* (*Brit*‡): **to give sb a ~** poner a uno como un trapo*.

rolling ['rəʊlɪŋ] **1** *adj* rodante; *countryside* ondulado; *programme* continuo; **~ stone** (*fig*) canto *m* rodante; **a ~ stone gathers no moss** piedra movediza nunca moho la cobija; **to walk with a ~ gait** andar bamboleándose. **2** *n* (*Naut*) balanceo *m*.

rolling-mill ['rəʊlɪŋmɪl] *n* taller *m* de laminación; tren *m* de laminaje.

rolling-pin ['rəʊlɪŋpɪn] *n* rodillo *m* (de cocina).

rolling-stock ['rəʊlɪŋstɒk] *n* material *m* rodante, material *m* móvil.

rollmop ['rəʊlmɒp] *n* arenque *m* adobado.

roll-neck ['rəʊlnek] *n* (*Brit*) jersey *m* cuello cisne.

roll-on ['rəʊlɒn] **1** *n* faja *f* elástica, tubular *m*. **2** *adj* elástico. **3** *attr*: **~ deodorant** bola *f* desodorante; **roll-on-roll-off facility** facilidad *f* para la carga y descarga autopropulsada; **roll-on-roll-off ship** ro-ro *m*, rolón *m*.

roll-top ['rəʊltɒp] *adj*: **~ desk** buró *m*, escritorio *m* de tapa rodadera.

roly-poly ['rəʊlɪ'pəʊlɪ] **1** *n* (*Brit*: *also* **~ pudding**) brazo *m* de gitano. **2** *adj* regordete.

ROM [rɒm] *n abbr of* **read-only-memory** ROM *f*, memoria *f* muerta, memoria *f* de sola lectura.

romaine [rəʊ'meɪn] *n* (*US, Canada*: *also* **~ lettuce**) lechuga *f* romana, lechuga *f* cos.

Roman ['rəʊmən] **1** *adj* romano; **~ alphabet** alfabeto *m* romano; **~ candle** candela *f* romana; **~ Catholic** (*adj*) católico (romano), (*n*) católico *m* (romano), católica *f* (romana); **~ Catholicism** catolicismo *m*; **~ law** derecho *m* romano; **~ nose** nariz *f* aguileña; **~ numeral** número *m* romano. **2** *n* (**a**) romano *m*, -a *f*. (**b**) (*Typ*) tipo *m* romano.

romance [rəʊ'mæns] **1** *n* (**a**) (*tale*) novela *f* (sentimental), cuento *m* (de amor); (*medieval*) libro *m* de caballerías, poema *m* caballeresco; libro *m* de aventuras; (*Mus*) romanza *f*.

(**b**) (*love-affair*) amores *mpl*, amorío *m*, aventura *f* sentimental; **their ~ lasted exactly 6 months** sus amores duraron exactamente 6 meses; **a young girl waiting for ~** una joven que espera su primer amor; **I've finished with ~** para mí no más amores.

(**c**) (*romantic character*) lo romántico, lo pintoresco, lo poético; **the ~ of the sea** el encanto del mar; **the ~ of travel** lo romántico del viajar; **the ~ of history** lo atractivo de la historia, lo poético de la historia.

(**d**) (*Ling*) romance *m*.

2 *adj language* romance, románico, neolatino.

3 *vi* soñar, inventar fábulas; exagerar; fantasear.

Romanesque [,rəʊmə'nesk] *adj*, **Romanic** [rəʊ'mænɪk] *adj* románico.

Romania [rəʊ'meɪnɪə] *n* Rumania *f*, Rumanía *f*.

Romanian [rəʊ'meɪnɪən] **1** *adj* rumano. **2** *n* (**a**) rumano *m*, -a *f*. (**b**) (*Ling*) rumano *m*.

romanize ['rəʊmənaɪz] *vt* romanizar.

Romansch [rəʊ'mænʃ] **1** *adj* rético. **2** *n* (**a**) rético *m*, -a *f*. (**b**) (*Ling*) rético *m*.

romantic [rəʊ'mæntɪk] **1** *adj* romántico. **2** *n* romántico *m*, -a *f*.

romantically [rəʊ'mæntɪkəlɪ] *adv* románticamente, de modo romántico.

romanticism [rəʊ'mæntɪsɪzəm] *n* romanticismo *m*.

romanticist [rəʊ'mæntɪsɪst] *n*: **he's a bit of a ~** es un romántico.

romanticize [rəʊ'mæntɪsaɪz] **1** *vt* hacer romántico; añadir detalles románticos (*or* ambiente romántico) a. **2** *vi* hablar (*or* escribir *etc*) de modo romántico; soñar, fantasear.

Romany ['rɒmənɪ] **1** *adj* gitano. **2** *n* (**a**) gitano *m*, -a *f*. (**b**) (*Ling*) romanó *m*, lengua *f* gitana; (*in Spain*) caló *m*.

Rome [rəʊm] *n* (**a**) Roma *f*; **~ was not built in a day** no se ganó Zamora en una hora; **all roads lead to ~** por todas partes se va a Roma; **when in ~ do as the Romans do** allí donde fueres haz lo que vieres.

(**b**) (*Eccl*) la Iglesia, el catolicismo; **Manning turned to ~** Manning se convirtió al catolicismo.

Romeo ['rəʊmɪəʊ] *nm* Romeo.

Romish ['rəʊmɪʃ] *adj* (*pej*) católico.

romp [rɒmp] **1** *n* retozo *m*, juego *m*; **to have a ~ in the hay** retozar en el heno, revolcarse en el pajar; **the play was**

just a ~ la obra era una farsa alegre nada más.

2 *vi* retozar, jugar, divertirse; (*lambs etc*) brincar, correr alegremente; **the horse ~ed home to win by 19 lengths** el caballo ganó fácilmente por 19 cuerpos; **she ~ed through the examination** encontró que el examen era muy fácil.

rompers ['rɒmpəz] *npl* pelele *m*, mono *m*.

Romulus ['rɒmjʊləs] *nm* Rómulo.

rondeau ['rɒndəʊ] *n* (*Liter*) rondó *m*.

rondo ['rɒndəʊ] *n* (*Mus*) rondó *m*.

Roneo ['rəʊnɪəʊ] ® *vt* reproducir con multicopista.

rood [ru:d] *n* cruz *f*, crucifijo *m*.

roodscreen ['ru:dskri:n] *n* reja *f* entre la nave y el coro.

roof [ru:f] **1** *n, pl* **roofs** [ru:fs *or* ru:vz] techo *m*, tejado *m*; (*outside of bus, car*) baca *f*, (*of coach*) imperial *f*; (*tiled*) tejado *m*; (*of heaven*) bóveda *f* celeste; **~ of the mouth** paladar *m*, cielo *m* de la boca; **prices are going through the ~** los precios están por las nubes; **they haven't a ~ over their heads** no tienen donde cobijarse; **he hit the ~*** se subió por las paredes*; **they live under the same ~** viven bajo el mismo techo; **to raise the ~** (*protest*) poner el grito en el cielo; (*sing etc*) cantar (*etc*) como para levantar el techo.

2 *vt* (*also* **to ~ in, to ~ over**) techar, poner techo a; **it is ~ed in wood** tiene techo de madera; **to ~ a hut in wood** (*or* **with wood**) poner techo de madera a una caseta.

roof-garden ['ru:f,gɑ:dn] *n* azotea *f* con flores y plantas.

roofing ['ru:fɪŋ] **1** *n* techumbre *f*; material *m* para techado.

2 *attr felt etc* para techos.

roofless ['ru:flɪs] *adj* sin techo.

roof-rack ['ru:fræk] *n* (*Brit*) baca *f*, portaequipajes *m*.

rooftop ['ru:ftɒp] **1** *n* techo *m*; azotea *f*; **we will proclaim it from the ~s** lo proclamaremos a los cuatro vientos. **2** *attr*: **~ restaurant** restaurante *m* de azotea.

rook¹ [rʊk] **1** *n* (*Orn*) grajo *m*, -a *f*.

2 *vt* estafar, timar; **you've been ~ed** te han cobrado demasiado, te han desollado; **they always ~ the customer in that shop** en esa tienda siempre le timan al cliente.

rook² [rʊk] *n* (*Chess*) torre *f*.

rookery ['rʊkərɪ] *n* colonia *f* de grajos.

rookie* ['rʊkɪ] *n* (*Mil*) bisoño *m*, novato *m*.

room [rʊm] **1** *n* (**a**) (*in house*) cuarto *m*, habitación *f*; pieza *f*; (*large, public*) sala *f*; **~s** (*lodging*) alojamiento *m*, (*flat*) piso *m*; **this is my ~** ésta es mi habitación; **in ~ 504** (*hotel*) en la habitación número 504; **in the professor's ~** en el cuarto del profesor; **he has ~s in college** tiene un cuarto en el colegio; **they've always lived in ~s** han vivido siempre en pisos alquilados.

(**b**) (*space*) sitio *m*, espacio *m*; cabida *f*, cupo *m* (*Méx*); **is there ~?** ¿hay sitio?; **is there ~ for this?** ¿cabe esto?; **there is no ~ for that** eso no cabe; **there's no ~ for anything else** no cabe más; **is there ~ for me?** ¿quepo yo?, ¿hay sitio para mí?; **there is plenty of ~** queda mucho espacio libre; **there is still ~ on Tuesday** quedan todavía localidades para el martes; **to be cramped for ~** tener poco espacio; **to make ~ for sb** hacer sitio para uno, hacer lugar para uno; **make ~!** ¡abran paso!

(**c**) (*fig*) **there is no ~ for doubt** no queda lugar a dudas; **there is ~ for improvement** esto se puede mejorar todavía; **to leave ~ for imponderables** dar cabida a un margen de imponderables.

2 *attr*: **~ clerk** (*US*) recepcionista *mf* (de hotel); **~ temperature** temperatura *f* ambiente.

3 *vi*: **to ~ with a landlady** alojarse en casa de una patrona; **to ~ with 3 other students** estar en una pensión con otros 3 estudiantes, compartir un piso con otros 3 estudiantes.

room divider ['rʊmdɪ'vaɪdəʳ] *n* biombo *m*; tabique *m*.

-roomed [rʊmd] *adj* de ... piezas, *eg* **seven~** de siete piezas.

roomer ['rʊməʳ] *n* (*US*) inquilino *m*, -a *f*; huésped *m*, -eda *f*.

roomette [ru:'met] *n* (*US*) departamento *m* de coche-cama.

roomful ['rʊmfʊl] *n*: **a ~ of priests** un cuarto lleno de curas; **they have Picassos by the ~** tienen salas enteras llenas de cuadros de Picasso.

roominess ['rʊmɪnɪs] *n* espaciosidad *f*, amplitud *f*; holgura *f*.

rooming house ['rʊmɪŋhaʊs] *n, pl* **rooming houses** ['rʊmɪŋ,haʊzɪz] (*US*) casa *f* de huéspedes, pensión *f*.

roommate ['rʊmmeɪt] *n* compañero *m*, -a *f* de cuarto.

room-service ['rʊm,sɜ:vɪs] *n* servicio *m* en la habitación, servicio *m* de habitación.

roomy ['rʊmɪ] *adj room* espacioso, amplio; *garment* capaz, holgado.

roost [ru:st] **1** *n* percha *f*; (*hen~*) gallinero *m*; **to rule the ~** mandar, dirigir el cotarro.

2 *vi* dormir (*or* descansar) en una percha; (*fig*) pasar la noche; **the birds ~ in that tree** los pájaros pasan la noche en ese árbol; **now his policies have come home to ~** ahora su política produce su fruto amargo, ahora se están viendo los malos resultados de su política.

rooster ['ru:stəʳ] *n* gallo *m*.

root [ru:t] **1** *n* raíz *f* (*also fig*); (*Gram*) radical *m*; **~ and branch** de raíz, completamente, del todo; **money is the ~ of all evil** el dinero es la raíz de todos los males; **the ~ of the problem is that** ... lo fundamental del problema es que ..., la esencia del problema es que ...; **what lies at the ~ of his attitude?** ¿qué razón fundamental tiene su actitud?; **to put down one's ~s in a country** radicarse en un país, echar raíces en un país; **to strike** (*or* **take**) **~** echar raíces, arraigar; **to strike at the ~ of sth** afectar la parte fundamental de algo, atacar la misma esencia de algo.

2 *adj*: **~ beer** (*US*) cerveza *f* no alcohólica; **~ cause** causa *f* primordial; **~ crops** (cultivos *mpl* de) raíces *fpl*; **~ idea** idea *f* fundamental, idea *f* esencial; **~ sign** (*Math*) raíz *f*; **~ vegetable** raíz *f*; **~ word** palabra *f* radical.

3 *vt* (**a**) (*plant*) hacer arraigar.

(**b**) (*fig*) **to be** (*or* **stand**) **~ed to the spot** quedar helado (de miedo *etc*), quedar inmovilizado, estar sin poderse mover; **it is firmly ~ed in all minds that** ... está grabado en la mente de todos que ..., todos creen firmemente que ...; **a ~ed prejudice** un prejuicio muy arraigado.

4 *vi* (**a**) (*Bot*) echar raíces, arraigar(se). (**b**) (*animal*) hozar, hocicar.

◆**root about, root around** *vi* (*pig*) hozar, hocicar, (*fig*) andar buscando por todas partes (*for sth* algo); investigar.

◆**root for*** *vt* (*esp US*) *team etc* gritar por; *cause etc* hacer propaganda por, apoyar a.

◆**root out** *vt* arrancar (de raíz), desarraigar; (*fig*) desarraigar, extirpar; suprimir del todo.

◆**root through** *vt* hocicar; (*fig*) examinar, explorar.

◆**root up** *vt* arrancar.

rootless ['ru:tlɪs] *adj person etc* desarraigado.

rootstock ['ru:tstɒk] *n* rizoma *m*.

rope [rəʊp] **1** *n* cuerda *f*, mecate *m* (*Mex*); soga *f*; (*Naut*: *hawser*) maroma *f*, cable *m*, (*in rigging*) cabo *m*; (*hangman's*) dogal *m*; (*of pearls*) collar *m*; (*of onions etc*) ristra *f*; **the ~s** (*Boxing*) las cuerdas; **to be on the ~s** (*fig*) estar en las cuerdas; **to give sb more ~** dar a uno mayor libertad de acción; **if you give him enough ~ he'll hang himself** déjale actuar y él se condenará a sí mismo; **to jump ~, to skip ~** (*US*) saltar a la comba; **to know the ~s** conocer un negocio a fondo, saber cuántas son dos y dos; **to learn the ~s** aprender el oficio; **I'll show you the ~s** te voy a mostrar lo que hay que hacer, te enseñaré el oficio; **there were 3 of us on the ~** (*Mountaineering*) éramos 3 los encordados.

2 *attr*: **~ burn** quemadura *f* por fricción; **~ ladder** escala *f* de cuerda; **~ trick** truco *m* de la cuerda.

3 *vt* atar con una cuerda, amarrar con una cuerda; (*US*) *animal* coger con lazo; **to ~ two things together** atar dos cosas con una cuerda; **there were 4 ~d together** había 4 que iban encordados.

4 *vr*: **they are roping themselves together** se están encordando.

◆**rope in*** *vt*: **to ~ sb in** enganchar a uno (*to do sth* para hacer algo); **they managed to ~ in their friends** consiguieron arrastrar a sus amigos.

◆**rope off** *vt*: **to ~ off a space** acordonar un espacio, cercar un espacio con cuerdas.

◆**rope up** *vt* cordar.

ropemaker ['rəʊp,meɪkəʳ] *n* cordelero *m*.

ropewalker ['rəʊp,wɔ:kəʳ] *n* funámbulo *m*, -a *f*, volatinero *m*, -a *f*.

rop(e)y ['rəʊpɪ] *adj* (**a**) *liquid* viscoso. (**b**) (*) deteriorado, desvencijado; inestable; *plan, argument etc* nada convincente, flojo; **I feel a bit ~** no me siento del todo bien.

RO/RO *abbr of* **roll-on/roll-off**.

rosary ['rəʊzərɪ] *n* rosario *m*; **to say one's ~** rezar el rosario.

Rose [rəʊz] *nf* Rosa.

rose¹ [rəʊz] **1** *n* (**a**) (*Bot*) rosa *f*; (*colour*) color *m* de rosa; **wild ~** rosal *m* silvestre; **life isn't all ~s** la vida no es un lecho de rosas; **there's no ~ without a thorn** no hay rosa sin espina.

(**b**) (*of watering-can*) roseta *f*.

(**c**) (*Archit*) rosetón *m*.

2 *adj* color de rosa, rosado, rosáceo; **~ pink** rosa.

rose² [rəʊz] *pret of* **rise**.

rosé ['rəʊzeɪ] **1** *adj* rosado. **2** *n* rosado *m.*
roseate ['rəʊzɪɪt] *adj* róseo, rosado.
rosebay ['rəʊzbeɪ] *n* adelfa *f.*
rosebed ['rəʊzbed] *n* rosaleda *f.*
rosebowl ['rəʊzbəʊl] *n* jarrón *m* (*or* florero *m*) para rosas.
rosebud ['rəʊzbʌd] *n* capullo *m* de rosa, botón *m* de rosa.
rosebush ['rəʊzbʊʃ] *n* rosal *m.*
rose-coloured, (*US*) **rose-colored** ['rəʊz,kʌləd] *adj* color de rosa, rosado, rosáceo; **to see everything through ~ spectacles** verlo todo color de rosa.
rose garden ['rəʊz,gɑːdn] *n* rosaleda *f.*
rose hip ['rəʊzhɪp] **1** *n* escaramujo *m.* **2** *attr*: **~ syrup** jarabe *m* de escaramujo.
rosemary ['rəʊzmərɪ] *n* romero *m.*
rose-red ['rəʊz'red] *adj* color de rosa.
rosetree ['rəʊztriː] *n* rosal *m.*
rosette [rəʊ'zet] *n* (*Archit*) rosetón *m*; (*emblem*) escarapela *f.*
rosewater ['rəʊz,wɔːtə^r] *n* agua *f* de rosas.
rose window ['rəʊz'wɪndəʊ] *n* rosetón *m.*
rosewood ['rəʊzwʊd] *n* palo *m* de rosa, palisandro *m.*
Rosicrucian [,rəʊzɪ'kruːʃən] **1** *n* rosacruz *mf.* **2** *adj* rosacruz.
rosin ['rɒzɪn] *n* colofonia *f.*
ROSPA ['rɒspə] *n abbr of* **Royal Society for the Prevention of Accidents.**
roster ['rɒstə^r] **1** *n* lista *f.* **2** *attr*: **~ duty** lista *f* de deberes.
rostrum ['rɒstrəm], *pl* **~s** *or* **rostra** ['rɒstrə] **1** *n* tribuna *f.* **2** *attr*: **~ cameraman** (*TV*) cámara-truca *m.*
rosy ['rəʊzɪ] *adj* (**a**) rosado, sonrosado; **with ~ cheeks** con mejillas sonrosadas. (**b**) (*fig*) *prospects etc* prometedor, halagueño.
rot [rɒt] **1** *n* (**a**) putrefacción *f,* podredumbre *f*; **it has ~** está podrido.
(**b**) (*fig*) decadencia *f*; **a ~ set in** comenzó un período de decadencia, todo empezó a decaer; **to stop the ~** acabar con la degeneración, impedir que la situación vaya de mal en peor, reformarlo todo.
(**c**) (*: *nonsense*) tonterías *fpl,* bobadas *fpl,* babosadas *fpl* (*LAm*); **oh ~!, what ~!** ¡tonterías!; **don't talk ~!** ¡no digas bobadas!; **it is utter ~ to say that** ... es una sandez decir que ...
2 *vt* pudrir, corromper, descomponer (*also fig*).
3 *vi* pudrirse, corromperse, descomponerse; **to ~ in jail** pudrirse en la cárcel; **you can ~ for all I care!** ¡que te pudras!
◆**rot away** *vi* pudrirse, corromperse, descomponerse; **it had ~ted away with the passage of time** con el tiempo se había descompuesto; **it had quite ~ted away** se había descompuesto del todo.
rota ['rəʊtə] *n* lista *f* (de tandas *etc*).
Rotarian [rəʊ'tɛərɪən] **1** *adj* rotario. **2** *n* rotario *m.*
rotary ['rəʊtərɪ] *adj* rotativo; giratorio; **R~ Club** Sociedad *f* Rotaria; **~ press** prensa *f* rotativa.
rotate [rəʊ'teɪt] **1** *vt wheel etc* hacer girar; dar vueltas a; (*Comput*) *graphics* rotar, girar; *crops* alternar, cultivar en rotación; (*vary*) alternar; **to ~ A and B** alternar A con B.
2 *vi* girar; dar vueltas; alternarse.
rotating [rəʊ'teɪtɪŋ] *adj* rotativo; giratorio.
rotation [rəʊ'teɪʃən] *n* rotación *f* (*also Agr, Astron*); alternación *f*; **~ of crops** rotación *f* de cultivos; **in ~** por turno; **A and B in ~** A y B alternadamente; **orders are dealt with in strict ~** los pedidos se sirven por riguroso orden.
rotational [rəʊ'teɪʃənəl] *adj* rotacional.
rotatory [rəʊ'teɪtərɪ] *adj* rotativo; giratorio.
rotavate ['rəʊtəveɪt] *vt* trabajar con motocultor.
rotavator ['rəʊtəveɪtə^r] *n* (*Brit*) motocultor *m.*
rote [rəʊt] *n*: **by ~** de memoria; **to learn sth by ~** aprender algo maquinalmente, aprender algo a fuerza de repetirlo (en coro); **~ learning was the fashion** era costumbre aprender cosas a fuerza de repetirlas.
rotgut* ['rɒtgʌt] *n* matarratas *m.*
rotisserie [rəʊ'tɪsərɪ] *n* rotisserie *f.*
rotor ['rəʊtə^r] **1** *n* rotor *m.* **2** *attr*: **~ arm** (*Aut*) rotor *m*; **~ blade** paleta *f* de rotor.
rotproof ['rɒtpruːf] *adj* a prueba de putrefacción, imputrescible.
rotten ['rɒtn] **1** *adj* (**a**) podrido, putrefacto, corrompido; *tooth* cariado; *wood* carcomido; (*fig*) corrompido; **to smell ~** oler a podredumbre.
(**b**) (*) (*morally*) vil, despreciable; (*of bad quality*) malísimo, lamentable, fatal*; (*Med*) malo; **what a ~ thing to do!** ¡qué cosa más vil!; **what a ~ thing to happen!** ¡qué mala suerte!; **how ~ for you!** ¡cuánto te compadezco!, ¡lo que habrás sufrido!; **what ~ weather!** ¡qué tiempo de perros!; **his English is ~** tiene un inglés fatal*; **he's ~ at chess** para el ajedrez es un desastre; **it's a ~ novel** es una novela que huele*, es una novela lamentable; **I feel ~** me siento fatal*; **beer always makes me feel ~** la cerveza siempre me pone malo; **he's ~ with money** está que huele de dinero*, está podrido de dinero*; **to be ~ to sb*** portarse como un canalla con uno.
2 *adv* (‡) malísimamente, fatal*; **they played real ~** jugaron fatal*; **they made me suffer something ~** me hicieron pasarlas negras.
rottenly* ['rɒtnlɪ] *adv*: **to behave ~ to sb** portarse como un canalla con uno.
rottenness ['rɒtnnɪs] *n* podredumbre *f,* putrefacción *f*; (*fig*) corrupción *f.*
rotter* ['rɒtə^r] *n* (*Brit*) caradura* *m,* sinvergüenza *m*; **you ~!** ¡canalla!
rotting ['rɒtɪŋ] *adj* podrido, que se está pudriendo.
rotund [rəʊ'tʌnd] *adj* rotundo; (*fat*) gordo.
rotunda [rəʊ'tʌndə] *n* rotonda *f.*
rotundity [rəʊ'tʌndɪtɪ] *n* rotundidad *f*; gordura *f.*
rouble, (*US*) **ruble** ['ruːbl] *n* rublo *m.*
roué ['ruːeɪ] *n* libertino *m.*
Rouen ['ruːɑ̃ːŋ] *n* Ruán *m.*
rouge [ruːʒ] **1** *n* colorete *m,* carmín *m.* **2** *vt*: **to ~ one's cheeks** ponerse colorete.
rough [rʌf] **1** *adj* (**a**) *surface, skin etc* áspero; *ground* quebrado, fragoso, escabroso; *road* desigual, lleno de baches; *cloth* basto; *hand* calloso; *hair* despeinado; *edge* desigual; **~ to the touch** áspero al tacto; **~ diamond** diamante *m* (en) bruto (*also fig*).
(**b**) *treatment, behaviour etc* brutal; inconsiderado; *person* inculto, sin educación; *sea* bravo; encrespado, picado; *weather* borrascoso, tormentoso; *wind* violento; *play, sport* duro; *neighbourhood* malo, de mala vida, peligroso; **to be ~ with sb** tratar a uno de modo brutal; **to get ~** (*sea*) embravecerse; **to get ~ with sb** empezar a pegar a uno; **he got a ~ handling in the press** le dieron una paliza en la prensa; **he got ~ justice** recibió un castigo duro pero apropiado.
(**c**) *manners* tosco, grosero; *voice* bronco, áspero; *speech* rudo; *style* tosco; *work* chapucero; *workman* torpe, desmañado; *material* crudo, bruto.
(**d**) *calculation, estimate* aproximado; *guess* aproximativo; *plan, sketch* a grandes rasgos; *draft* primero; *work* de preparación, preliminar; *translation* no muy exacto; preliminar; aproximativo; **~ copy** borrador *m*; **I would say 50 at a ~ guess** diría que 50 aproximadamente.
2 *adv*: **to cut up ~** (*Brit**) cabrearse*; **to live ~** vivir sin comodidades, vivir como un vagabundo; **to play ~** jugar duro; **to sleep ~** pasar la noche al raso, dormir al descubierto, dormir a la intemperie.
3 *n* (**a**) (*ground etc*) terreno *m* quebrado, superficie *f* áspera; (*Golf*) rough *m,* zona *f* de matojos; **in (the) ~** en bruto, (*plan etc*) a grandes rasgos; **we'll do it first in ~** lo haremos primero sólo en forma preliminar (*or* en forma de bosquejo); **to take the ~ with the smooth** tomar las duras con las maduras, aceptar la vida como es.
(**b**) (*person*) matón *m.*
4 *vt*: **to ~ it** pasar apuros, luchar contra dificultades, vivir sin comodidades.
◆**rough out** *vt*: **to ~ out a plan** esbozar un plan, bosquejar un plan, trazar un plan a grandes rasgos.
◆**rough up*** *vt hair* despeinar; *person* dar una paliza a.
roughage ['rʌfɪdʒ] *n* sustancia *f* celulósica, forraje *m.*
rough-and-ready ['rʌfən'redɪ] *adj* tosco pero eficaz; improvisado; provisional; (*person*) inculto pero estimable.
rough-and-tumble ['rʌfən'tʌmbl] *n* (*quarrel, fight*) riña *f,* pendencia *f*; (*activity etc*) actividad *f* frenética; **the ~ of life** la confusión y violencia de la vida; **the ~ of politics** los avatares de la política, los altibajos de la política.
roughcast ['rʌfkɑːst] *n* mezcla *f* gruesa.
roughen ['rʌfn] **1** *vt* poner áspero; hacer más tosco. **2** *vi* ponerse áspero; hacerse más tosco; (*sea*) embravecerse.
rough-hew ['rʌf'hjuː] (*irr*: *V* **hew**) *vt* desbastar.
rough-hewn ['rʌf'hjuːn] *adj* toscamente labrado; desbastado; (*fig*) tosco, inculto.
roughhouse* ['rʌfhaʊs] *n, pl* **roughhouses** ['rʌfhaʊzɪz] trifulca* *f,* riña *f* general, reyerta *f.*
roughly ['rʌflɪ] *adv* (*V adj*) (**a**) ásperamente. (**b**) brutalmente; incultamente; violentamente; duramente. (**c**) toscamente; groseramente; broncamente; torpemente. (**d**) aproximadamente, más o menos; de modo preliminar.

roughneck* [ˈrʌfnek] *n* matón *m*.
roughness [ˈrʌfnɪs] *n* (*V adj*) (**a**) aspereza *f*; lo quebrado, fragosidad *f*; desigualdad *f*; callosidad *f*.
(**b**) brutalidad *f*; incultura *f*; falta *f* de educación; braveza *f*; violencia *f*; dureza *f*.
(**c**) tosquedad *f*; rudeza *f*; lo chapucero; torpeza *f*, desmaña *f*.
rough puff pastry [ˌrʌfˌpʌfˈpeɪstrɪ] *n* hojaldre *m*.
roughrider [ˈrʌfˌraɪdəʳ] *n* domador *m* de caballos.
roughshod [ˈrʌfʃɒd] *adv*: **to ride ~ over sb** tratar a uno sin miramientos, no hacer caso alguno de uno.
rough-spoken [ˈrʌfˈspəʊkən] *adj* inculto, de habla inculta, malhablado.
roulette [ruːˈlet] *n* ruleta *f*.
Roumania [ruːˈmeɪnɪə] *etc* = **Romania** *etc*.
round [raʊnd] **1** *adj* redondo; *sum* redondo; *denial etc* rotundo, terminante; *trip* de ida y vuelta, completo; *dance* en ruedo; **a ~ dozen** una docena redonda; **~ arch** arco *m* redondo; **in ~ figures** en números redondos; **~ number** número *m* redondo; **in ~ numbers** en números redondos; **~ robin** (*request*) petición *f* firmada en rueda, (*protest*) protesta *f* firmada en rueda; **R~ Table** (*Hist*) Mesa *f* Redonda; **~ table conference** conferencia *f* de mesa redonda; **~ trip** ida *f* y vuelta, viaje *m* redondo (*LAm*); **~ trip ticket** (*US*) billete *m* de ida y vuelta.
2 *adv* alrededor; **all ~** por todos lados; **all the year ~** durante todo el año; **it has a fence all ~** tiene una cerca que lo rodea completamente; **taking it all ~** (considerándolo) en conjunto; **drinks all ~!** ¡pago la ronda para todos!; **it is 200 metres ~** tiene 200 metros en redondo; **for 5 miles ~ about** en 5 millas a la redonda, en 5 millas en torno; **it's a long way ~** es mucho rodeo; **when you're ~ this way** cuando pases por aquí; **we were ~ at John's** estábamos en casa de Juan; **we shall be ~ at the pub** estaremos en el bar; **it flew ~ and ~** voló dando vueltas.
3 *prep* (**a**) (*place etc*) alrededor de; **a trip ~ the world** un viaje alrededor del mundo; **the wall ~ the town** la muralla que rodea la ciudad; **a walk ~ the town** un paseo por la ciudad; **all the people ~ about** toda la gente alrededor; **it's just ~ the corner** está precisamente a la vuelta de la esquina; **we were sitting ~ the table** estábamos sentados alrededor de la mesa; **we were sitting ~ the fire** estábamos sentados al amor de la lumbre; **it's written ~ the Suez episode** tiene por tema principal el episodio de Suez; **she's 36 inches ~ the bust** mide de pecho 36 pulgadas; **to sing hymns ~ the pubs** cantar himnos de bar en bar; **to deliver papers ~ the houses** repartir periódicos por las casas.
(**b**) (*approximately*) alrededor de; cerca de, cosa de; **~ 2 o'clock** a eso de las 2; **~ about £50** cerca de 50 libras, cosa de 50 libras, 50 libras más o menos; **somewhere ~ that sum** esa cantidad más o menos.
4 *n* (**a**) (*circle*) círculo *m*; esfera *f*; (*slice*) tajada *f*, rodaja *f*; **a ~ of toast** una tostada.
(**b**) (*routine*) rutina *f*; **one long ~ of pleasures** una sucesión de placeres, una serie sin fin de placeres.
(**c**) (*esp Brit*: *beat*: *of watchman etc*) ronda *f*; (*of postman, milkman etc*) recorrido *m*; (*of golf etc*) recorrido *m*, ronda *f*, vuelta *f*; (*of doctor*) visitas *fpl*; **a ~ of talks** una serie de conferencias; **the first ~ of negotiations** la primera ronda de negociaciones; **he's out on his ~s** está fuera visitando sus enfermos; **she did** (*or* **went, made**) **the ~s of the agencies** visitó todas las agencias, recorrió todas las agencias; **to go the ~s** (*watchman etc*) estar de ronda, hacer su ronda de inspección; **the story is going the ~s that ...** se dice que ..., se rumorea que ...; **the story went the ~s of the club** el chiste se contó en todos los corrillos del club.
(**d**) (*Boxing*) asalto *m*; (*Golf*) round *m*; (*in tournament*) vuelta *f*, rueda *f*; (*of election*) vuelta *f*; (*lap*) circuito *m*; (*in show jumping*) recorrido *m*; **to have a clear ~** hacer un recorrido sin penalizaciones.
(**e**) **~ (of drinks)** ronda *f* (de bebidas); **~ of applause** salva *f* de aplausos; **~ of ammunition** tiro *m*, cartucho *m*, bala *f*; **whose ~ is it?** ¿a quién le toca (pagar)?
(**f**) **in the ~** (*Theat*) en redondo; (*fig*) *develop etc* en conjunto, en su totalidad, globalmente.
5 *vt*: **to ~ a corner** doblar una esquina; **the ship ~ed the headland** el buque dobló el promontorio.
◆**round down** *vt price etc* redondear (rebajando).
◆**round off** *vt* redondear; acabar, terminar; perfeccionar; **to ~ the series off** para completar la serie.
◆**round on** *vt* volverse contra.
◆**round out** *vt* redondear, completar.
◆**round up** *vt* (**a**) (*bring together*) acorralar, rodear (*LAm*); **we ~ed up a few friends to help** reunimos a unos amigos para ayudar.
(**b**) *figure etc* redondear.
◆**round upon** *vt* volverse contra.
roundabout [ˈraʊndəbaʊt] **1** *adj* indirecto; **by a ~ way** dando un rodeo, por una ruta indirecta; **to speak in a ~ way** ir con rodeos, hablar con circunloquios.
2 *n* (*Brit*) (*at fair*) tiovivo *m*; (*Aut*) glorieta *f*, (cruce *m* de) circulación *f* giratoria, redoma *f* (*Carib*), rotonda *f* (*SC*).
rounded [ˈraʊndɪd] *adj end* redondeado; esférico; *end of boat* redondo; *style* maduro, expresivo.
roundelay [ˈraʊndɪleɪ] *n* (*song*) canción *f* que se canta en rueda; (*dance*) baile *m* en círculo.
rounders [ˈraʊndəz] *n* (*Brit*) *juego similar al béisbol*.
round-eyed [ˈraʊndˈaɪd] *adj, adv*: **to look at sb ~** mirar a uno con los ojos desorbitados.
round-faced [ˈraʊndˈfeɪst] *adj* de cara redonda.
Roundhead [ˈraʊndhed] *n* (*Brit Hist*) cabeza *f* pelada.
roundhouse [ˈraʊndhaʊs] *n, pl* **roundhouses** [ˈraʊndhaʊzɪz] (*US Rail*) cocherón *m* circular, rotonda *f* para locomotoras; (*Naut*) chupeta *f*.
roundly [ˈraʊndlɪ] *adv* (*fig*) rotundamente, terminantemente.
round-necked [ˈraʊndˌnekt] *adj*: **~ pullover** jersey *m* de cuello cerrado (*or* redondo).
roundness [ˈraʊndnɪs] *n* redondez *f*.
round-shouldered [ˈraʊndˈʃəʊldəd] *adj* cargado de espaldas.
roundsman [ˈraʊndzmən] *n, pl* **roundsmen** [ˈraʊndzmən] (*Brit*) repartidor *m*, proveedor *m* casero.
round-the-clock [ˈraʊndðəˈklɒk] *adj surveillance etc* de veinticuatro horas, permanente.
round-up [ˈraʊndʌp] *n* (*Agr*) rodeo *m*; (*of suspects etc*) detención *f*; (*by police*) redada *f*; **~ of the latest news** resumen *m* de las últimas noticias.
roundworm [ˈraʊndwɜːm] *n* lombriz *f* intestinal.
rouse [raʊz] **1** *vt* (*wake*) despertar; *emotion* excitar, suscitar, despertar; (*from torpor*) animar, reanimar; *game* levantar; **to ~ sb from sleep** despertar a uno; **to ~ sb to action** mover a uno a la acción; **to ~ sb to fury** provocar a uno a la furia; **it ~d the whole house** despertó a todo el mundo.
2 *vi* despertar(se).
3 *vr*: **to ~ o.s.** despertarse; (*to act etc*) animarse a hacer algo.
rousing [ˈraʊzɪŋ] *adj welcome etc* emocionado, entusiasta; *song etc* vivo, lleno de vigor; *speech* conmovedor.
Roussillon [ˈruːsɪjɔ̃ŋ] *n* Rosellón *m*.
roustabout* [ˈraʊstəbaʊt] *n* (*US*) peón *m*.
rout [raʊt] **1** *n* (*defeat*) derrota *f* (completa); (*flight*) fuga *f* desordenada. **2** *vt* derrotar (completamente).
◆**rout out** *vt*: **to ~ sb out** hacer salir a uno; **to ~ sb out of bed** hacer que uno se levante apresuradamente, hacer que uno abandone la cama.
route [ruːt] **1** *n* (**a**) (*gen*) ruta *f*, camino *m*; itinerario *m*; (*of bus*) recorrido *m*, línea *f*; (*Naut*) rumbo *m*, derrota *f*; **R~ 31** (*US*) Ruta *f* 31; **to go by a new ~** seguir una nueva ruta; **the ~ to the coast** el camino de la costa. (**b**) (*US*: *often* [raʊt]: *delivery round*) recorrido *m*. **2** *vt* fijar el itinerario de; (*Comput*) encaminar; **the train is now ~ed through X** ahora el tren pasa por X.
route-map [ˈruːtmæp] *n* mapa *m* de carreteras.
route-march [ˈruːtmɑːtʃ] *n* marcha *f* de entrenamiento, marcha *f* de maniobras.
routine [ruːˈtiːn] **1** *n* rutina *f*; **the daily ~** la rutina cotidiana; **as a matter of ~** por rutina.
2 *adj* rutinario, de rutina; **a ~ inspection** una inspección rutinaria; **it's just ~** es cosa de rutina.
routinely [ruːˈtiːnlɪ] *adv* rutinariamente, por rutina.
routing [ˈraʊtɪŋ] *n* (*Comput*) encaminamiento *m*.
rove [rəʊv] **1** *vt* vagar por, errar por, recorrer.
2 *vi* vagar; **to ~ about** andar sin propósito fijo; **his eye ~d over the room** su mirada pasó por todo el cuarto.
rover [ˈrəʊvəʳ] *n* vagabundo *m*, andariego *m*; (*Naut*) pirata *m*; (*Scout*) escultista *m*.
roving [ˈrəʊvɪŋ] *adj* (*wandering*) errante; *salesman etc* ambulante; *ambassador* itinerante; *reporter* volante; *disposition* andariego; **to have a ~ commission** no tener puesto fijo, tener el cometido de hacer investigaciones (*etc*) donde le parezca a uno; **he has a ~ eye** se le van los ojos tras las mujeres.
row[1] [rəʊ] **1** *n* (*line*) fila *f*, hilera *f*; renglón *m*; (*Theat etc*)

fila *f*; (*of books, houses etc*) hilera *f*; (*in knitting*) pasada *f*; vuelta *f*; **in the front ~** en primera fila; **in the fourth ~** en la cuarta fila, en la fila cuatro; **he killed four in a ~** mató cuatro seguidos, mató cuatro uno tras otro; **for 5 days in a ~** durante 5 días seguidos.

2 *attr*: **~ houses** (*US*) casas *fpl* adosadas.

row² [rəʊ] **1** *n* (**a**) (*trip*) paseo *m* en bote de remos; **to go for a ~** pasearse en bote, hacer una excursión en bote.

(**b**) **it was a hard ~ to the shore** nos costó llegar a la playa remando; **you'll have a hard ~ upstream** os costará trabajo remar contra la corriente.

2 *vt boat* conducir remando; **to ~ a race** tomar parte en una regata (de botes de remos); **you ~ed a good race** habéis remado muy bien; **he ~ed the Atlantic** cruzó el Atlántico a remo; **to ~ sb across a river** llevar a uno en bote a través de un río; **can you ~ me out to the yacht?** ¿me lleva en bote al yate?

3 *vi* remar, bogar; **to ~ hard** esforzarse remando, hacer fuerza de remos; **to ~ against sb** competir con uno en una regata a remo; **we ~ed for the shore** remamos (para llegar) a la playa, remamos hacia la playa; **he ~ed for Oxford** remó en el bote de Oxford; **to ~ round an island** dar la vuelta a una isla a remo.

row³ [raʊ] **1** *n* (**a**) (*noise*) ruido *m*, estrépito *m*, estruendo *m*; **hold your ~!, stop your ~!** ¡cállate!; **the ~ from the engine** el ruido del motor; **it makes a devil of a ~** hace un ruido de todos los demonios.

(**b**) (*dispute*) bronca *f*, pelea *f*; **the ~ about wages** la disputa acerca de los salarios; **now don't let's start a ~** no riñamos.

(**c**) (*fuss, disturbance, incident*) jaleo *m*, lío *m*, follón *m* (*Sp*), bronca *f* (*LAm*); escándalo *m*; **what's the ~ about?** ¿a qué se debe el lío?; **there was a devil of a ~ about it** sobre esto se armó un tremendo follón (*LAm*: lío); **to kick up a ~, to make a ~** armar un jaleo, armar un follón, armar bronca (*LAm*); (*protest*) poner el grito en el cielo; **he makes a ~ about nothing** se queja por nada; **make a ~ with your member of parliament** quéjese a su diputado.

(**d**) (*scolding*) regaño *m*; **you'll get into a ~** te van a regañar (*for* por).

2 *vt*: **to ~ sb** echar un rapapolvo a uno.

3 *vi* reñir, reñirse, pelear (*esp LAm*); **they're always ~ing** siempre están riñendo; **to ~ with sb** pelearse con uno.

rowan ['raʊən] *n* (*also* **~ tree**) serbal *m*; (*berry*) serba *f*.

rowboat ['rəʊbəʊt] *n* (*US*) bote *m* de remos.

rowdiness ['raʊdɪnɪs] *n* lo ruidoso, ruido *m*; carácter *m* pendenciero; alboroto *m*, desorden *m*.

rowdy ['raʊdɪ] **1** *adj person* (*noisy*) ruidoso; (*quarrelsome*) pendenciero, quimerista; *meeting etc* alborotado, desordenado. **2** *n* quimerista *mf*.

rowdyism ['raʊdɪɪzəm] *n* disturbios *mpl*, pendencias *fpl*; gamberrismo *m*.

rower ['rəʊəʳ] *n* remero *m*, -a *f*.

rowing ['rəʊɪŋ] *n* remo *m*; **~ machine** máquina *f* de remo.

rowing-boat ['rəʊɪŋbəʊt] *n* (*Brit*) bote *m* de remos.

rowing-club ['rəʊɪŋklʌb] *n* club *m* de remo.

rowlock ['rɒlək] *n* tolete *m*, escálamo *m*, chumacera *f*.

royal ['rɔɪəl] **1** *adj* (**a**) (*gen*) real; (*esp fig*) regio; **R~ Academy** (*Brit*) Real Academia *f*; **~ blue** azul *m* marino; **R~ Commission** (*Brit*) Comisión *f* Real; **R~ Engineers** (*Brit*) Cuerpo *m* de Ingenieros; **~ family** familia *f* real; **~ household** casa *f* real; **~ line** familia *f* real, casa *f* real; **the ~ 'we'** el plural mayestático.

(**b**) (*splendid*) magnífico, espléndido, suntuoso; **a ~ feast** un banquete suntuoso; **to have a right ~ time** pasarlo en grande.

2 *n* (*) personaje *m* real, miembro *m* de la familia real; **the ~s** la realeza.

royalism ['rɔɪəlɪzəm] *n* sentimiento *m* monárquico, monarquismo *m*.

royalist ['rɔɪəlɪst] **1** *adj* monárquico. **2** *n* monárquico *m*, -a *f*.

royally ['rɔɪəlɪ] *adv* (*fig*) magníficamente, espléndidamente.

royalty ['rɔɪəltɪ] *n* (**a**) realeza *f*; personajes *mpl* reales, familia *f* real; **in the presence of ~** estando presente un miembro de la familia real; **a shop patronized by ~** una tienda que visita la familia real, una tienda donde la familia real hace compras.

(**b**) (*payment*; *also* **royalties**) derechos *mpl* de autor, regalías *fpl* (*LAm*); derechos *mpl* de patente; **the royalties on oil** los derechos del petróleo.

rozzer‡ ['rɒzəʳ] *n* (*Brit*) guindilla‡ *m*, guiri‡ *m*.

RP *n* (**a**) (*Brit Ling*) *abbr of* **Received Pronunciation** *pronunciación estándar del inglés*. (**b**) (*Post*) *abbr of* **reply paid** contestación *f* pagada, CP.

RPI *n abbr of* **Retail Price Index** Indice *m* de precios al consumidor, IPC *m*.

RPM *n abbr of* **resale price maintenance** mantenimiento *m* del precio de venta.

rpm *n abbr of* **revolutions per minute** revoluciones *fpl* por minuto, r.p.m.

RR (*US*) *abbr of* **Railroad** ferrocarril *m*, FC *m*.

RRP *n abbr of* **recommended retail price** precio *m* al por menor recomendado, precio *m* orientativo de venta al público, PVP *m*.

RSA *n* (**a**) *abbr of* **Republic of South Africa.** (**b**) (*Brit*) *abbr of* **Royal Society of Arts.** (**c**) *abbr of* **Royal Scottish Academy.**

RSI *n abbr of* **repetitive strain injury** lesión *f* de la tensión repetida.

RSM *n abbr of* **Regimental Sergeant-Major** ≈ brigada *m* de regimiento.

RSPB *n* (*Brit*) *abbr of* **Royal Society for the Protection of Birds.**

RSPCA *n* (*Brit*) *abbr of* **Royal Society for the Prevention of Cruelty to Animals.**

RSVP *abbr of* **répondez s'il vous plaît** = *please reply* se ruega contestación, S.R.C.

rt *abbr of* **right.**

Rt.Hon. (*Brit*) *abbr of* **Right Honourable** *título honorífico de diputado*.

Rt Rev. *abbr of* **Right Reverend** reverendo, Rvdo.

RU *abbr of* **Rugby Union.**

rub [rʌb] **1** *n* (**a**) frotamiento *m*; (*accidental friction*) roce *m*, rozadura *f*; **to give sb's back a ~** frotar las espaldas de uno; **to give one's shoes a ~ (up)** limpiar los zapatos; **to give the silver a ~** sacar brillo a la plata.

(**b**) (*fig*) **there's the ~** ahí está el problema, ésa es la dificultad; **but here we come to the ~** pero aquí tropezamos con la dificultad principal; **the ~ is that ...** la dificultad es que ...

2 *vt* (*apply friction*) frotar, (*Med etc*) friccionar; (*hard*) estregar, restregar; (*to clean*) limpiar frotando; (*polish*) sacar brillo a; **to ~ sth dry** secar algo frotándolo; **to ~ a surface bare** alisar una superficie a fuerza de frotarla; **to ~ one's hands together** frotarse las manos.

◆**rub against** *vt* rozar.

◆**rub along*** *vi* ir tirando; **I can ~ along in Arabic** me defiendo en árabe.

◆**rub away** *vt* quitar frotando; desgastar.

◆**rub down 1** *vt body* secar frotando, *horse* almohazar, *wall etc* alisar frotando.

2 *vi* (*person*) secarse frotándose con una toalla.

◆**rub in** *vt*: **to ~ an ointment in** frotar con un ungüento, dar fricciones con un ungüento; **to ~ an idea in** reiterar una idea; (*pej*) insistir en una idea; **the lesson has to be ~bed in** hay que insistir en la lección; **don't ~ it in!** ¡no machaques!, ¡no insistas!

◆**rub off 1** *vt* quitar, frotar; hacer desaparecer.

2 *vi* borrarse debido al roce; **some of their ideas have ~bed off on him** una parte de sus opiniones ha influido en él, él ha hecho suyas algunas de las opiniones de ellos.

◆**rub on** *vt* (**a**) *ointment etc* aplicar frotando.

(**b**) (**~ *against***) rozar.

◆**rub out 1** *vt* (*erase*) borrar; **to ~ sb out‡** cargarse a uno*, despenar a uno‡.

2 *vi* borrarse; **it ~s out easily** es fácil quitarlo.

◆**rub up** *vt* limpiar; pulir, sacar brillo a; (*fig*) refrescar; *V* **way 1 (h)**.

rub-a-dub ['rʌbə'dʌb] *n* rataplán *m*.

rubber¹ ['rʌbəʳ] **1** *n* (*material*) caucho *m*, goma *f*, hule *m* (*LAm*); (*Brit*: *eraser*) goma *f* de borrar; (*Mech etc*) paño *m* de pulir; (*) condón *m*, goma *f*; **~s** (*shoes*) chanclos *mpl*, zapatos *mpl* de goma.

2 *attr* de caucho, de goma; **~ band** goma *f*, gomita *f*; **~ bullet** bala *f* de goma; **~ cement** adhesivo *m* de goma; **~ cheque*** (*Brit*) cheque *m* sin fondos; **~ dinghy** lancha *f* neumática; **~ goods** artículos *mpl* de goma; (*euph*) gomas *fpl* higiénicas; **~ industry** industria *f* gomera; **~ plant** ficus *m*; **~ plantation** cauchal *m*; **~ raft** balsa *f* neumática; **~ solution** disolución *f* de goma; **~ stamp** estampilla *f* (de goma) (*V also* **~-stamp**); **~ tree** árbol *m* gomero, árbol *m* de caucho.

rubber² ['rʌbəʳ] *n* (*Bridge etc*) juego *m*, coto *m*.

rubberize ['rʌbəraɪz] *vt* engomar, cauchutar.

rubberized ['rʌbəraɪzd] *adj* engomado, cauchutado, cubierto de goma.

rubberneck* ['rʌbənek] (*US*) **1** *n* mirón *m*, -ona *f*. **2** *vi*

curiosear.
rubber-stamp [ˌrʌbəˈstæmp] *vt* (*fig*) aprobar maquinalmente; aprobar con carácter oficial; poner su firma a.
rubbery [ˈrʌbərɪ] *adj* gomoso, parecido a la goma.
rubbing [ˈrʌbɪŋ] **1** *n* (**a**) (*act*) frotamiento *m*. (**b**) (*brass* ~) calco *m*. **2** *attr*: ~ **alcohol** (*US*) alcohol *m*.
rubbish [ˈrʌbɪʃ] **1** *n* (**a**) (*waste*) basura *f*; desperdicios *mpl*, desecho *m*, desechos *mpl*.
(**b**) (*fig*: *goods*) pacotilla *f*; (*production, work of art etc*) basura *f*, porquería *f*; (*spoken, written*) tonterías *fpl*, bobadas *fpl*; ~!, **what** ~! ¡tonterías!; **he talks a lot of** ~ no dice más que tonterías; **it's all** ~ todo son bobadas; **the novel is** ~ la novela es una basura.
2 *vt* (*) condenar como inútil, criticar duramente, poner por los suelos.
rubbish-bin [ˈrʌbɪʃbɪn] *n* (*Brit*) cubo *m* de la basura, basurero *m*.
rubbish-chute [ˈrʌbɪʃˌʃuːt] *n* rampa *f* de la basura.
rubbish collection [ˈrʌbɪʃkəˌlekʃən] *n* recogida *f* de basuras, recolección *f* de la basura.
rubbish-dump [ˈrʌbɪʃdʌmp] *n*, **rubbish-heap** [ˈrʌbɪʃhiːp] *n* vertedero *m*, basurero *m*.
rubbishy [ˈrʌbɪʃɪ] *adj goods* de pacotilla; *production, work of art etc* que no vale para nada, de bajísima calidad.
rubble [ˈrʌbl] *n* escombros *mpl*, cascote *m*; (*filling*) cascajo *m*; **the town was reduced to** ~ el pueblo quedó reducido a escombros.
rub-down [ˈrʌbdaʊn] *n* masaje *m*; secada *f* con toalla; frotación *f*, frotada *f*; **to give o.s. a** ~ secarse (con toalla).
rube* [ruːb] *n* (*US*) patán *m*, palurdo *m*.
rubella [rʊˈbelə] *n* rubéola *f*.
Rubicon [ˈruːbɪkən] *n* Rubicón *m*; **to cross the** ~ pasar el Rubicón.
rubicund [ˈruːbɪkənd] *adj* rubicundo.
rubidium [ruːˈbɪdɪəm] *n* rubidio *m*.
ruble [ˈruːbl] *n* (*US*) = **rouble**.
rubric [ˈruːbrɪk] *n* rúbrica *f*.
rub-up [ˈrʌbʌp] *n* frotada *f*; **to give a table a** ~ encerar una mesa, sacar brillo a una mesa.
ruby [ˈruːbɪ] **1** *n* rubí *m*. **2** *adj necklace etc* de rubíes; *ring* de rubí, con un rubí; *colour* color de rubí.
RUC *n abbr of* **Royal Ulster Constabulary** *Policía de Irlanda del Norte*.
ruck[1] [rʌk] *n* (*Racing*) grueso *m* del pelotón; (*Rugby*) melé *f*; (*fig*) gente *f* común, personas *fpl* corrientes; **to get out of the** ~ empezar a destacar, adelantarse a los demás.
ruck[2] [rʌk], **ruckle** [ˈrʌkl] **1** *n* (*in clothing etc*) arruga *f*. **2** (*also* **to** ~ **up**) *vt* arrugar. **3** *vi* arrugarse.
rucksack [ˈrʌksæk] *n* mochila *f*.
ruckus* [ˈrʌkəs] *n* (*US*) = **ruction**.
ruction* [ˈrʌkʃən] *n* lío* *m*, jaleo *m*, bronca *f*; **there will be** ~**s** se va a armar la gorda*.
rudder [ˈrʌdəʳ] *n* (*Naut*) timón *m*, gobernalle *m*; (*Aer*) timón *m*.
rudderless [ˈrʌdəlɪs] *adj* sin timón.
ruddiness [ˈrʌdɪnɪs] *n* rubicundez *f*; lo rojizo; lo frescote, frescura *f*.
ruddy[1] [ˈrʌdɪ] *adj* rubicundo; rojizo; *complexion* coloradote, frescote.
ruddy[2‡] [ˈrʌdɪ] *adj* (*Brit euph*) condenado*, puñetero‡.
rude [ruːd] *adj* (**a**) (*offensive*) grosero, descortés, ofensivo; **don't be** ~! ¡Vd es un maleducado!, ¡Vd es un fresco!; **you were very** ~ **to me once** Vd estuvo muy descortés conmigo una vez; **it's** ~ **to eat noisily** es de mala educación hacer ruido al comer; **would it be** ~ **of me to ask if** ...? ¿puedo sin ser descortés preguntar si ...?; **how** ~! ¡qué ordinario!
(**b**) (*indecent*) indecente; *joke etc* verde, colorado (*LAm*); **they sing** ~ **songs** cantan canciones verdes; **there's nothing** ~ **about that picture** ese cuadro no tiene nada de indecente.
(**c**) (*uncivilized etc*) rudo, grosero, tosco; inculto.
(**d**) (*sudden*) repentino; (*violent*) violento; **a** ~ **shock** un golpe inesperado; **a** ~ **awakening** una sorpresa desagradable.
(**e**) (*vigorous*) **to be in** ~ **health** gastar salud, vender salud.
rudely [ˈruːdlɪ] *adv* (**a**) (*offensively*) groseramente, con descortesía, de modo ofensivo. (**b**) (*indecently*) toscamente. (**c**) (*suddenly*) de repente; violentamente.
rudeness [ˈruːdnɪs] *n* (**a**) grosería *f*, descortesía *f*. (**b**) indecencia *f*. (**c**) rudeza *f*, tosquedad *f*. (**d**) violencia *f*.
rudiment [ˈruːdɪmənt] *n* (*Bio*) rudimento *m*; ~**s** rudimentos *mpl*, primeras nociones *fpl*.
rudimentary [ˌruːdɪˈmentərɪ] *adj* (*Bio*) rudimental; (*fig*) rudimentario; **he has** ~ **Latin** tiene las primeras nociones de latín, sabe un poquito de latín.
rue[1] [ruː] *vt* arrepentirse de, lamentar; **you shall** ~ **it** te arrepentirás de haberlo hecho; **I** ~ **the day when I did it** ojalá no lo hubiera hecho nunca; **he lived to** ~ **it** vivió para arrepentirse.
rue[2] [ruː] *n* (*Bot*) ruda *f*.
rueful [ˈruːfʊl] *adj* triste; arrepentido; lamentable.
ruefully [ˈruːfəlɪ] *adv* tristemente.
ruefulness [ˈruːfʊlnɪs] *n* tristeza *f*.
ruff[1] [rʌf] *n* gorguera *f*, gola *f*; (*Orn, Zool*) collarín *m*.
ruff[2] [rʌf] (*Cards*) **1** *n* fallada *f*. **2** *vt* fallar.
ruffian [ˈrʌfɪən] *n* matón *m*, criminal *m*; **you** ~! ¡canalla!
ruffianly [ˈrʌfɪənlɪ] *adj* brutal, criminal.
ruffle [ˈrʌfl] **1** *n* arruga *f*; (*Sew*) volante *m* fruncido; (*ripple*) rizo *m*.
2 *vt* (*wrinkle*) arrugar; *surface* agitar, rizar; (*Sew*) fruncir; *hair* despeinar; *feathers* encrespar, erizar; *sb's composure* descomponer, perturbar; **to** ~ **sb's feelings** ofender a uno, herir los sentimientos de uno; **nothing** ~**s him** no se altera por nada; **she wasn't at all** ~**d** no se perturbó en lo más mínimo; **to smooth sb's** ~**d feathers** (*fig*) alisar las plumas erizadas de uno.
3 *vi* arrugarse; agitarse, rizarse.
rug [rʌg] *n* (*on floor*) tapete *m*, alfombrilla *f*; (*travelling* ~) manta *f* (de viaje); **to pull the** ~ **from under sb** (*fig*) mover la silla para que uno se caiga.
rugby [ˈrʌgbɪ] *n* (*also* ~ **football**) rugby *m*; ~ **player** jugador *m* de rugby.
rugged [ˈrʌgɪd] *adj terrain* escabroso, áspero, accidentado, bravo; (*harsh*) duro, severo; *character* robusto; *construction* fuerte, robusto; *features* fuerte, acentuado; *workmanship* tosco; *independence etc* vigoroso; *style* desigual.
ruggedness [ˈrʌgɪdnɪs] *n* escabrosidad *f*, aspereza *f*, lo accidentado; severidad *f*; robustez *f*; lo fuerte; tosquedad *f*; vigor *m*; desigualdad *f*.
rugger* [ˈrʌgəʳ] *n* (*Brit*) rugby *m*.
ruin [ˈruːɪn] **1** *n* (**a**) ruina *f*; ~**s** ruinas *fpl*; restos *mpl*; **to be in** ~**s** estar en ruinas, estar arruinado; **her hopes were in** ~**s** sus esperanzas estaban arruinadas; **to lay a town in** ~**s** asolar una ciudad; **the city rose from the** ~**s** la ciudad volvió a nacer sobre las ruinas.
(**b**) (*act*) ruina *f*, arruinamiento *m*.
(**c**) (*fig*) ruina *f*; perdición *f*; **the** ~ **of sb's hopes** la destrucción de las esperanzas de uno; **it will be the** ~ **of him** será su ruina; **drink will be his** ~ el alcohol le perderá, el alcohol será su perdición; **to bring sb to** ~ arruinar a uno; ~ **stared us in the face** nos encontramos frente a la ruina.
2 *vt* arruinar; asolar; (*spoil*) estropear; *taste etc* estragar; (*morally*) perder; **her extravagance** ~**ed him** sus despilfarros le arruinaron; **what** ~**ed him was gambling** lo que le perdió fue el juego; **he** ~**ed my new car** estropeó mi nuevo coche.
ruination [ˌruːɪˈneɪʃən] *n* ruina *f*, arruinamiento *m*, perdición *f*.
ruined [ˈruːɪnd] *adj* arruinado (*also fig*), en ruinas, ruinoso.
ruinous [ˈruːɪnəs] *adj* (*all senses*) ruinoso.
ruinously [ˈruːɪnəslɪ] *adv* de modo ruinoso; ~ **expensive** carísimo, de lo más caro.
rule [ruːl] **1** *n* (**a**) (*ruling*) regla *f*; norma *f*; costumbre *f*; principio *m*; ~**s** (*of competition*) bases *fpl*; **as a** ~ en general, por regla general; normalmente; ~ **of the road** reglamento *m* del tráfico; ~ **of three** (*Math*) regla *f* de tres; ~ **of thumb** regla *f* empírica; **by** ~ **of thumb** por experiencia, por rutina; mediante una prueba práctica; **the** ~**s of the game** las reglas del juego; ~**s and regulations** reglamento *m*; **it's the** ~ es de regla; **it's against the** ~**s** es contra la regla, eso no se permite; **our** ~ **is** ... nuestro principio es ...; **bad weather is the** ~ **here** el mal tiempo es normal aquí; **the golden** ~ **is** ... la regla principal es ...; **there is no hard-and-fast** ~ **about it** sobre eso no existe ninguna regla terminante; **to bend** (*or* **stretch**) **the** ~ ajustar la regla; **to do everything by** ~ obrar siempre por sistema; **to make it a** ~ **to** + *infin* hacerse una regla de + *infin*; **I make it a** ~ **never to drink** yo por sistema nunca bebo; **to work to** ~ trabajar al mínimo legal, hacer huelga de celo, estar en paro técnico.
(**b**) (*Jur*) fallo *m*; decisión *f*.
(**c**) (*dominion etc*) dominio *m*, imperio *m*; autoridad *f*; mando *m*; **under British** ~ bajo la autoridad británica; **under the** ~ **of Louis XV** bajo el reinado de Luis XV; ~ **of law** imperio *m* de la ley; **under the** ~ **of fear** bajo el imperio del miedo.

(**d**) (*ruler*) metro *m.*
(**e**) (*Eccl*) regla *f*; **the Benedictine ~** la regla benedictina.
2 *vt* (**a**) (*govern*: *also* **to ~ over**) gobernar, mandar, regir; **to ~ an empire** gobernar un imperio; **he ~d the company for 40 years** durante 40 años rigió la compañía; **he's ~d by his wife** le domina su mujer; **be ~d by my advice** déjate guiar por mis consejos, guíate por mí.
(**b**) (*Jur*) decidir; (*of chairman etc*) disponer, determinar; **to ~ that ...** decidir que ..., decretar que ...; **to ~ sth out of order** decidir que un asunto no se puede discutir.
(**c**) (*draw*) *line* trazar, tirar; *paper* rayar, reglar.
3 *vi* (**a**) (*govern*) gobernar; (*of monarch*) reinar.
(**b**) (*decide*) fallar, decidir (*against* contra, en contra de, *for* en favor de).
(**c**) (*of price*) regir.
◆**rule off** *vt* cerrar con una línea, tirar una línea debajo de.
◆**rule out** *vt*: **to ~ sth out** excluir algo, descartar algo; **we can't ~ out the possibility that ...** no podemos excluir la posibilidad de que + *subj*; **you are not ~d out because of that** no se te excluye por eso.
rulebook ['ru:lbʊk] *n* libro *m* de normas, libro *m* de reglamento; **we'll do it by the ~** lo haremos de acuerdo con el reglamento.
ruled [ru:ld] *adj paper* rayado.
ruler ['ru:ləʳ] *n* (**a**) (*person*) gobernante *mf*, gobernador *m*, -ora *f*; soberano *m*, -a *f*. (**b**) (*for measuring*) regla *f*.
ruling ['ru:lɪŋ] **1** *adj passion* dominante, predominante; *price* que rige; **the ~ classes** la clase que gobierna, la clase que manda.
2 *n* fallo *m*, decisión *f*; **to give a ~** fallar, decidir; **to give a ~ on a dispute** pronunciar un fallo sobre una disputa.
rum¹ [rʌm] **1** *n* ron *m*. **2** *attr*: **~ toddy** *ron con agua caliente y azúcar.*
rum²* [rʌm] *adj* (*Brit*) extraño, raro.
Rumania *etc* (*Brit*) = **Romania** *etc.*
rumba ['rʌmbə] *n* rumba *f*.
rumble¹ ['rʌmbl] **1** *n* retumbo *m*, ruido *m* sordo, rumor *m*; (*of thunder etc*) redoble *m*; (*in stomach*) ruido *m* (de tripas); (*of tank etc*) rodar *m*; **~s of discontent** ruidos *mpl* sordos de descontento.
2 *vi* retumbar; hacer un ruido sordo; redoblar; rodar; (*stomach*) sonar, hacer ruidos; **the train ~d past** el tren pasó con estruendo; **the talk ~d on** se siguió charlando pesadamente; **he ~d on another half-hour** continuó media hora más con el rollo*.
rumble²* ['rʌmbl] *vt* (*Brit*) calar; **he's ~d us** nos ha calado, nos ha pillado (*LAm*); **I soon ~d what was going on** pronto me olí lo que estaban haciendo.
rumble seat ['rʌmbl'si:t] *n* (*US Aut*) asiento *m* trasero exterior.
rumble strip ['rʌmbl,strɪp] *n superficie rugosa en la calzada para frenado.*
rumbling ['rʌmblɪŋ] *n* = **rumble¹**.
rumbustious [rʌm'bʌstʃəs] *adj* bullicioso, ruidoso.
ruminant ['ru:mɪnənt] **1** *adj* rumiante. **2** *n* rumiante *m*.
ruminate ['ru:mɪneɪt] *vti* rumiar (*also fig*).
rumination [,ru:mɪ'neɪʃən] *n* (*act*) rumia *f*; (*thought*) meditación *f*, reflexión *f*.
ruminative ['ru:mɪnətɪv] *adj* (*Bio*) rumiante; (*fig*) pensativo, meditabundo.
ruminatively ['ru:mɪnətɪvlɪ] *adv* pensativamente; **'I hope so', he said ~** 'espero que sí', dijo pensativo.
rummage ['rʌmɪdʒ] *vi* hurgar; **to ~ about** revolverlo todo, buscar revolviéndolo todo; **he was rummaging about in the drawer** estaba hurgando en el cajón; **he ~d in his pocket and produced a key** hurgando en el bolsillo sacó una llave.
rummage sale ['rʌmɪdʒseɪl] *n* (*US*) venta *f* de objetos usados (con fines benéficos).
rummy¹* ['rʌmɪ] **1** *adj* extraño, raro. **2** *n* (*US**: *drunk*) borracho *m*, -a *f*.
rummy² ['rʌmɪ] *n* (*Cards*) rummy *m*.
rumour, (*US*) **rumor** ['ru:məʳ] **1** *n* rumor *m*; **as ~ has it** según se dice; **~ has it that ...** se rumorea que ... **2** *vt*: **it is ~ed that ...** se rumorea que ..., se dice que ...; **he is ~ed to be rich** se dice que es rico.
rump [rʌmp] *n* (**a**) (*Anat*) (*of horse etc*) ancas *fpl*, grupa *f*; (*of bird*) rabadilla *f*; (*: *of person*) trasero *m*; (*Culin*) cuarto *m* trasero, cadera *f*. (**b**) (*of party etc*) parte *f* que queda; núcleo *m* irreductible; **there's just a ~ left** quedan solamente unos pocos miembros.
rumple ['rʌmpl] *vt* ajar, arrugar, chafar.
rumpsteak ['rʌmp'steɪk] *n* filete *m*.
rumpus* ['rʌmpəs] *n* lío* *m*, jaleo *m*; batahóla* *f*, revuelo *m*; **to have a ~ with sb** pelearse con uno; **to kick up a ~** armar un lío*, armar una bronca (*LAm*).
rumpus room ['rʌmpəs,rum] *n* (*US*) cuarto *m* de los niños, cuarto *m* de juegos.
run [rʌn] **1** *n* (**a**) (*act of running*) corrida *f*, carrera *f*; (*Athletics, Baseball, Cricket*) carrera *f*; (*in stocking*) carrera *f*, acarraladura *f* (*And, SC*); (*of fish*) migración *f*; **at a ~** corriendo; **to go at a steady ~** correr a un paso regular; **to break into a ~** echar a correr, empezar a correr; **to be on the ~** estar huido; **a prisoner on the ~** un preso fugado, un preso evadido; **he's on the ~ from prison** escapó de la cárcel; **he was on the ~ for 6 weeks** estuvo libre durante 6 semanas; **he's on the ~ from his creditors** se está escapando de sus acreedores; **to keep sb on the ~** hacer que uno corra de acá para allá; mantener a uno en constante actividad; acosar a uno, (*Mil*) hostigar a uno; **we soon had the enemy on the ~** pronto pusimos al enemigo en fuga; **we've got them on the ~ now** ya están casi vencidos; **it came down with a ~** bajó repentinamente, cayó todo junto; **prices came down with a ~** los precios bajaron de golpe; **I had a ~ to catch it** tuve que correr bastante para cogerlo; **I have a ~ before breakfast** corro antes del desayuno; **to make a ~ for it** tratar de fugar, tratar de escaparse; **we shall have to make a ~ for it** tendremos que correr; **they gave us** (*or* **we had**) **a** (**good**) **~ for our money** nos dieron bastante satisfacción por nuestro dinero; **never mind, we gave him a** (**good**) **~ for his money** no importa, le hicimos sudar.
(**b**) (*Aut etc*: *outing*) paseo *m* (en coche), excursión *f* (en coche); (*Aer etc*: *raid*) ataque *m*; **it was a very pleasant ~** fue un viaje muy agradable; **to go for a ~, to have a ~** dar un paseo (en coche), dar una vuelta (en coche); **we'll have a ~ down to the coast** iremos de excursión a la costa.
(**c**) (*Rail etc*: *distance travelled*) trayecto *m*, recorrido *m*; **day's ~** (*Naut*) singladura *f*; **the Plymouth-Santander ~** el servicio de Plymouth a Santander, la línea de Plymouth a Santander; **it's a short car ~** es un breve viaje en coche.
(**d**) (*Typ*) tirada *f*; **a ~ of 5,000 copies** una tirada de 5.000 ejemplares.
(**e**) (*tendency*) tendencia *f*; **the ~ of the market** la tendencia del mercado; **the ~ of the play was favourable to us** el partido se desarrolló de modo favorable para nosotros; **they scored against the ~ of play** marcaron un gol cuando menos se podía esperar.
(**f**) (*series*) serie *f*; (*of product*) cantidad *f*, total *m*; **a ~ of four** (*Cards*) una escalera de cuatro; **a ~ of luck** una racha de suerte; **a ~ of bad luck** una temporada de mala suerte; **a ~ of 5 wins** una racha de 5 victorias; **to have a long ~** (*fashion*) estar en boga mucho tiempo, conservar su popularidad durante mucho tiempo; **the play had a long ~** la obra se mantuvo mucho tiempo en la cartelera; **when the London ~ was over** al terminarse la serie de representaciones en Londres; **in the long ~** a la larga; **in the short ~** a plazo corto.
(**g**) (*Comm*) **~ on a bank** asedio *m* de un banco; **there is a ~ on soap** hay una gran demanda de jabón, el jabón tiene mucha demanda.
(**h**) (*generality*) **the common ~ of people** el común de las gentes; **the common ~ of books** la generalidad de los libros; **it's above the common ~** es superior al nivel general.
(**i**) (*access*) **to have the ~ of sb's house** poder entrar libremente en la casa de uno; **to have the ~ of sb's library** tener libre uso de la biblioteca de uno, poder usar a discreción la biblioteca de uno.
(**j**) (*Agr etc*) terreno *m* de pasto; (*hen~*) corral *m*, gallinero *m*; (*ski~*) pista *f* de esquí.
(**k**) (*Mus*) fermata *f*; carrerilla *f*.
(**l**) **to have the ~s‡** tener el vientre descompuesto, tener cagueruelas‡.
2 (*irr*: *pret* **ran**, *ptp* **run**) *vt* (**a**) (*gen*) correr; **she ran 20 km** corrió 20 km; **to ~ a race** tomar parte en una carrera; **you ran a good race** corriste muy bien; **they're not ~ning the race this year** este año no hay carrera; **the race is ~ over 4 km** la distancia de la carrera es de 4 km.
(**b**) **to ~ a risk** correr un riesgo.
(**c**) (*cause to run*) hacer correr; (*hunt, chase*) cazar, dar caza a; **to ~ sb off his legs** correr hasta cansar al compañero; agotar a uno corriendo; **to ~ sb close, to ~ sb hard** casi alcanzar a uno, ir pisándole los talones a uno

(*also fig*); **to ~ it close, to ~ it fine** llegar con muy poco tiempo, dejarse muy poco margen.

(**d**) **to ~ sheep in a field** pacer las ovejas en un campo.

(**e**) (*move, transport etc*) llevar; transportar; **he ran the car into the garage** puso el coche en el garaje; **he ran the car into a tree** chocó con un árbol; **this will ~ you into debt** esto te endeudará; **it ran him into a lot of trouble** le causó muchas molestias; **I'll ~ you up to town** te llevo a la ciudad; **to ~ a boat ashore** varar una embarcación; **to ~ guns across a frontier** pasar fusiles de contrabando a través de una frontera; **the stream ran blood** el arroyo iba tinto de sangre; **to ~ messages** llevar recados; **to ~ a new bus service** establecer un nuevo servicio de autobuses; **they're ~ning an extra train** ponen un tren suplementario; **they don't ~ that bus on Sundays** no ponen ese autobús los domingos.

(**f**) **to ~ the blockade** forzar el bloqueo, burlar el bloqueo; **to ~ a stoplight** (*US*) saltarse un semáforo en rojo.

(**g**) (*have, possess*) tener, poseer; **he ~s two cars** tiene dos coches; **we don't ~ a car** no tenemos coche; **to ~ a (high) temperature** tener fiebre; **to ~ a temperature of 104°** tener 4 grados de fiebre.

(**h**) (*direct, operate etc*) *business* dirigir; controlar, gobernar, regir; administrar; organizar; *machine* hacer funcionar; manejar; (*Comput*) *program* ejecutar, rodar; *campaign* dirigir, organizar; *course* ofrecer, organizar; **to ~ the house for sb** llevar la casa a uno; **a house which is easy to ~** (*or* **easily ~**) una casa de fácil manejo; **she's the one who really ~s everything** la que en realidad lo dirige todo es ella; **I want to ~ my own life** quiero organizar mi propia vida; **you can ~ this machine on gas** puedes hacer funcionar esta máquina a gas; **you can ~ it on** (*or* **off**) **the mains** funciona con corriente de la red.

(**i**) (*present in contest*) **to ~ a horse** correr un caballo; **he ran 3 horses last season** en la última temporada corrió 3 caballos; **to ~ a candidate** presentar un candidato; **the liberals are not ~ning anybody this time** esta vez los liberales no tienen candidato.

(**j**) (*pass*) pasar; (*pierce*) traspasar; (*introduce*) introducir; **to ~ one's hand over a chair** pasar la mano por un sillón, recorrer un sillón con la mano; **to ~ one's eye over a text** dar una ojeada a un texto; **~ your eye over this** mira esto un poco; **let me ~ this idea past you** (*US*) a ver qué piensas de esta idea; **to ~ a line round sth** trazar una línea alrededor de algo; **to ~ water into a bath** hacer correr agua en un baño, llenar un baño de agua; **would you ~ my bath?** ¿me preparas el baño?; **we'll ~ a fence round it** pondremos un cerco alrededor de él; **to ~ a pipe through a wall** pasar un tubo a través de una pared; **he ran his pencil through the phrase** tachó la frase con el lápiz; **I ran a thorn into my finger** me clavé una espina en el dedo.

(**k**) *report, story* publicar, imprimir, presentar; *product* vender, poner a la venta.

3 *vi* (**a**) (*gen*) correr; (*hasten*) correr, darse prisa, apresurarse; (*in race*) competir, tomar parte; **to ~ for all one is worth, to ~ like the devil** correr a todo correr; **to ~ downstairs** bajar la escalera corriendo; **to ~ down the garden** correr por el jardín; **to ~ for a bus** correr para coger un autobús; **to ~ to meet sb** correr al encuentro de uno, acudir corriendo para recibir a uno; **to ~ to help sb** acudir corriendo en ayuda de uno.

(**b**) (*flee*) huir; **we shall have to ~ for it** tendremos que correr; **~ for your lives!** ¡sálvese el que pueda!

(**c**) (*present o.s.*) **to ~ for office** ser candidato para un puesto, presentarse como candidato para un puesto; **are you ~ning?** ¿vas a presentar tu candidatura?

(**d**) (*Naut*) **to ~ before the wind** navegar con viento a popa; **to ~ aground** encallar, embarrancar.

(**e**) (*function: engine etc*) funcionar, marchar, andar; estar en marcha; **the lift isn't ~ning** el ascensor no funciona; **the car ~s smoothly** el coche marcha bien; **things did not ~ smoothly for them** las cosas no les fueron bien; **it ~s on petrol** funciona con gasolina, tiene motor de gasolina; **it ~s off the mains** funciona con corriente de la red.

(**f**) (*function: service etc*) circular, ir; **the trains ~ning between Madrid and Ávila** los trenes que circulan entre Madrid y Ávila, los trenes que hacen el servicio entre Madrid y Ávila; **there are no trains ~ning to Toboso** no hay servicio de trenes a Toboso; **that train does not ~ on Sundays** ese tren no circula los domingos; **the buses ~ every 10 minutes** los autobuses salen cada 10 minutos; **the train is ~ning late** el tren lleva retraso; **the service usually ~s on time** el servicio generalmente es puntual; **steamers ~ daily between X and Y** hay servicio diario de vapores entre X e Y.

(**g**) (*pass*) **a rumour ran round the school** un rumor corrió por la escuela; **a ripple ran through the crowd** la multitud se estremeció (de emoción *etc*); **it ~s through the whole history of art** afecta toda la historia del arte, se observa en toda la historia del arte; **it ~s in the family** viene de familia; **the thought ran through my head that ...** se me ocurrió pensar que ...; **that tune keeps ~ning in my head** esa melodía la tengo metida en la cabeza; **the conversation ran on wine** el tema de la conversación era el vino; **my thoughts ran on Mary** mi pensamiento se concentró en María.

(**h**) (*go, continue*) seguir; **the contract ran for 7 years** el contrato fue válido durante 7 años; **the play ran for 40 performances** la obra tuvo 40 representaciones seguidas; **the play ~ for 3 months** la obra se mantuvo en la cartelera durante 3 meses; **things must ~ their course** las cosas tienen que seguir su curso; **the affair has ~ its course** el asunto ha terminado; **where his writ does not ~** donde su autoridad no vale, donde él no tiene jurisdicción.

(**i**) (*extend*) **to ~ to** extenderse a; (*of amounts*) subir a, ascender a, sumar; **the book has ~ into 20 editions** el libro ha alcanzado 20 ediciones; **the cost will ~ into millions** el coste se elevará a varios millones; **the talk ran to 2 hours** la charla se extendió a 2 horas; **the book will ~ to 700 pages** el libro tendrá 700 páginas en total; **my salary won't ~ to a second car** mi sueldo no me permite adquirir un segundo coche; **we can't possibly ~ to a grand piano** nos es imposible comprar un piano de cola.

(**j**) (*colour*) desteñirse, correrse; (*melt*) derretirse; (*Med: sore*) supurar; **colours that will not ~** colores *mpl* sólidos, colores *mpl* inalterables, colores *mpl* que no se corren; **my ice is ~ning** mi helado se está derritiendo.

(**k**) (*flow*) correr, fluir; (*tears*) correr; (*drip*) gotear; **the milk ran all over the floor** la leche se derramó por todo el suelo; **tears ran down her cheeks** las lágrimas le corrían por las mejillas; **my pen ~s** mi pluma gotea; **the streets were ~ning with water** el agua corría por las calles; **we were ~ning with sweat** chorreábamos de sudor; **a land ~ning with milk and honey** una tierra que abunda en leche y miel; **to leave a tap ~ning** dejar abierto un grifo, dejar abierta una llave (*LAm*); **the Tagus ~s past Toledo** el Tajo pasa por Toledo; **the river ~s for 300 miles** el río corre 300 millas; **it ~s into the sea at Lisbon** desemboca en el mar en Lisboa; **the street ~s into the square** la calle desemboca en la plaza; **blood ran from the wound** la sangre manaba de la herida, la herida manaba sangre; **a heavy sea was ~ning** el mar estaba muy picado; había una fuerte corriente; **when the tide is ~ning strongly** cuando sube la marea rápidamente; **to ~ dry** (*river*) secarse, (*resources*) agotarse.

(**l**) (*go, pass*) ir; **the road ~s along the river** la carretera sigue el río, la carretera va a lo largo del río; **a fence ~s along that side** hay un cerco por ese lado; **a balcony ~s round the hall** una galería se extiende todo lo largo de la sala; **a fence ~s round the field** el campo está rodeado por una cerca; **York has walls that ~ right round it** York tiene una muralla que la rodea completamente; **the road ~s by our house** la carretera pasa junto a nuestra casa; **it ~s north and south** va de norte a sur.

(**m**) (*say*) **so the story ~s** así dice el cuento; **the text ~s like this** el texto dice así, el texto reza así.

(**n**) (*develop*) **to ~ to seed** granar; **to ~ to fat** engordar; tener tendencia a engordar; *V* **high, low**[1] *etc*.

(**o**) (*stocking*) hacerse una carrera.

(**p**) (*Comput*) ejecutarse.

◆**run about, run around** *vi* correr (por todas partes); (*have fun*) divertirse corriendo; **to ~ around with** (*fig*) salir con, alternar con; ser compañero de, acompañar (mucho) a.

◆**run across 1** *vt* (*encounter*) *person* toparse con; *object etc* encontrar.

2 *vi* cruzar corriendo; **the water ran across the road** el agua cruzó la calle.

◆**run after** *vt* correr tras; *girl* correr detrás de, dar caza a, perseguir.

◆**run along** *vi* correr; (*depart*) marcharse; **~ along (now)!** ¡anda ya!

◆**run at** *vt* lanzarse sobre, precipitarse sobre.

◆**run away** *vi* (**a**) (*escape*) evadirse, huir, escaparse; (*horse*) dispararse; **to ~ away from home** huir de casa; **to**

~ **away from prison** fugarse de la cárcel; **to ~ away from the facts** no prestar atención a los hechos, no hacer caso de los hechos; **to ~ away from one's responsibilities** evadir sus responsabilidades; **to ~ away with sb** fugarse con uno; **to ~ away with the cash** alzarse con el dinero; **to ~ away with a race** ganar fácilmente una carrera; **it simply ~s away with the money** es que devora el dinero; **don't let your feelings ~ away with you** no te dejes dominar por las emociones; **don't ~ away with the idea that** ... no te imagines que ..., no te dejes arrastrar por la idea de que ...; *V also* ~ **along.**

(**b**) (*water etc*) irse, salir.

◆**run back 1** *vt* (**a**) *person* llevar (a su casa *etc*) en coche.

(**b**) *film* rebobinar.

2 *vi* volver corriendo.

◆**run down 1** *vt* (**a**) (*Aut*) atropellar.

(**b**) (*Naut*) hundir.

(**c**) (*reduce*) reducir, restringir; *battery etc* agotar, descargar; *company* restringir la producción de; *supply* reducir; (*Med*) agotar; **to be ~ down** (*Med*) no estar bien de salud, estar agotado, estar debilitado; (*battery*) estar descargado; (*clock*) estar parado.

(**d**) (*: *denigrate*) hablar mal de, vilipendiar; desacreditar.

(**e**) (*find*) localizar, encontrar; (*catch up with*) alcanzar; (*capture*) coger, cazar.

(**f**) **he ran down the list** pasó (rápidamente) el ojo por la lista.

2 *vi* (**a**) bajar corriendo.

(**b**) (*clock*) parar; (*battery*) acabarse; ir perdiendo fuerza; **the spring has ~ down** se ha acabado la cuerda.

◆**run in 1** *vt* (**a**) (*Brit Aut*) rodar; **'~ning in'** 'en rodaje'.

(**b**) (*: *arrest*) detener, meter en la cárcel.

2 *vi* entrar corriendo.

◆**run into** *vt* (**a**) (*crash*) chocar con, dar contra; **the two cars ran into each other** chocaran los dos coches.

(**b**) (*meet*) topar a, tropezar con.

(**c**) (*fig*) **to ~ into debt** contraer deudas, endeudarse, endrogarse (*LAm*); **to ~ into trouble** tropezar con dificultades, encontrar problemas; **to ~ into danger** exponerse a un peligro.

◆**run off 1** *vt* (**a**) *water etc* vaciar; dejar correr, dejar salir.

(**b**) (*recite*) enumerar rápidamente; (*compose*) componer en el acto; (*print*) tirar, imprimir.

(**c**) (*Sport*) *heats* decidir, correr.

2 *vi* = ~ **away** (**a**).

◆**run on 1** *vt* (*Typ*) continuar sin dejar espacio; unir al párrafo anterior.

2 *vi* (**a**) seguir corriendo.

(**b**) (*in talking etc*) continuar, continuar sin interrupción; **the Wagner ran on for 9 hours** el Wagner continuó durante 9 horas; **he's good but he does ~ on** es bueno pero continúa más de lo necesario; **she does ~ on so** es tan habladora, no termina de hablar.

◆**run out 1** *vt rope* ir dando; pasar, extender.

2 *vi* (**a**) (*person etc*) salir corriendo; (*liquid*) irse; (*tide*) bajar.

(**b**) (*come to an end*) acabarse, agotarse; (*time*) acabarse, vencerse (*LAm*); (*lease, term*) expirar; (*contract, permit*) vencer, caducar; (*stock, supply*) acabarse; **when the money ~s out** cuando se acabe el dinero; **the tide is ~ning out, the sands are ~ning out** (*fig*) queda poco tiempo.

(**c**) **we ran out of petrol** nos quedamos sin gasolina; **I ran out of patience** se me acabó la paciencia; **I ran out of road on the bend** se me acabó la carretera en la curva.

(**d**) **she ran out on her husband** abandonó a su marido; **you're not going to ~ out on us now?** ¿ahora nos abandonas?

◆**run over 1** *vt* (**a**) (*Aut*) atropellar.

(**b**) (*rehearse*) volver a hacer, repasar, volver a ensayar; (*read rapidly*) repasar, leer por encima.

2 *vi* (**a**) (*go*) ir; **to ~ over to** ir (corriendo) a; (*Aut*) ir (en coche) a visitar a, ir en una escapada a.

(**b**) (*overflow*) irse, desbordarse, rebosar.

(**c**) (*in time*) rebasar el límite; **the show ran over by 5 minutes** la función duró 5 minutos más de lo debido; **this text ~s over by 200 words** este texto tiene 200 palabras más de lo estipulado.

◆**run through** *vt* (**a**) (*with sword etc*) traspasar.

(**b**) (*use up*) gastar, consumir.

(**c**) (*read*) *book* hojear, leer a la ligera; *instructions etc* repasar; (*rehearse*) repasar.

◆**run up 1** *vt* (**a**) *flag* izar.

(**b**) *account, bill* crear, hacerse; *debt* incurrir en, contraer.

(**c**) *dress* hacer de prisa; *building* construir.

2 *vi* (**a**) subir corriendo; (*approach*) acudir corriendo; **to ~ up to sb** acercarse corriendo a uno; **to ~ up a hill** subir un cerro corriendo.

(**b**) (*plant*) trepar por.

(**c**) (*fig: encounter*) **to ~ up against sb** tener que habérselas con uno; **to ~ up against difficulties** tropezar con dificultades.

runabout ['rʌnəbaʊt] *n* (**a**) (*Aut*) coche *m* pequeño. (**b**) (*Rail etc*) billete *m* kilométrico.

runaround* ['rʌnəraʊnd] *n*: **to give sb the ~** traer a uno al retortero.

runaway ['rʌnəweɪ] **1** *adj prisoner, slave* fugitivo; *soldier* desertor; *horse* desbocado; *lorry* sin frenos, fuera de control; *inflation* galopante, desenfrenado; *success* arrollador; *victory* abrumador, fácil; *marriage* clandestino, fugitivo.

2 *n* (*person*) fugitivo *m*, -a *f*; (*horse*) caballo *m* desbocado.

run-down ['rʌn'daʊn] *adj battery* descargado; *health* debilitado; *building* descuidado, mal cuidado; *organization etc* en decadencia.

rundown ['rʌndaʊn] *n* (**a**) (*of industry etc*) cierre *m* gradual; (*of activity*) disminución *f*, reducción *f*; declive *m*; deterioro *m*. (**b**) (*briefing*) resumen *m* (oral) (*on* de), informe *m* (oral); **to give sb a ~** poner a uno al día.

rune [ru:n] *n* runa *f*.

rung[1] [rʌŋ] *n* escalón *m*, peldaño *m*.

rung[2] [rʌŋ] *ptp of* **ring**[2].

runic ['ru:nɪk] *adj* rúnico.

run-in ['rʌnɪn] *n* (**a**) (*Typ*) palabras *fpl* insertadas en un párrafo. (**b**) (*in contest, election*) desempate *m*. (**c**) (*rehearsal*) ensayo *m*. (**d**) (*approach*) aproximación *f*; etapa *f* previa. (**e**) (*: *argument*) altercado *m*.

runlet ['rʌnlɪt] *n*, **runnel** ['rʌnl] *n* arroyuelo *m*.

runner ['rʌnəʳ] **1** *n* (**a**) (*athlete*) corredor *m*, -ora *f*, atleta *mf*; (*horse, in race*) caballo *m*; (*messenger*) mensajero *m*, (*Mil*) ordenanza *m*, (*Fin*) corredor *m*.

(**b**) (*ring: of curtain etc*) anillo *m* movible; (*wheel*) ruedecilla *f*; (*of sledge, aircraft*) patín *m*.

(**c**) (*carpet*) alfombra *f* de pasillo; (*table ~*) tapete *m*.

(**d**) (*Bot*) tallo *m* rastrero, estolón *m*.

(**e**) (‡) **to do a ~** largarse*.

2 *attr*: ~ **bean** (*Brit*) judía *f* (escarlata), habichuela *f*.

runner-up ['rʌnər'ʌp] *n* subcampeón *m*, -ona *f*, segundo *m*, -a *f*.

running ['rʌnɪŋ] **1** *adj water* corriente; *knot* corredizo; *writing* cursivo; *commentary* en directo; *start* lanzado; ~ **costs** gastos *mpl* de explotación, gastos *mpl* corrientes; ~ **fight** acción *f* de retirada; combate *m* continuo; ~ **head** encabezamiento *m* normal; ~ **kick** puntapié *m* dado mientras corre el jugador (*etc*); ~ **mate** (*Pol etc*) compañero *m*, -a *f* de candidatura; ~ **repairs** reparaciones *fpl* provisionales; ~ **sore** úlcera *f*, (*fig*) llaga *f*; ~ **total** suma *f* parcial; suma y sigue; **in ~ order** en buen estado; **5 days ~** 5 días seguidos; **for the sixth time ~** por sexta vez consecutiva.

2 *n* (**a**) (*act of ~*) el correr; footing *m*, jogging *m*; **to be in the ~** tener posibilidades de ganar; **to be in the ~ for a chair** tener posibilidades de ganar una cátedra; **to be out of the ~** no tener posibilidad de ganar; **to make (all) the ~** ir a la cabeza, ir delante; ser el promotor (principal).

(**b**) (*of business etc*) dirección *f*; control *m*; gobierno *m*; administración *f*; organización *f*; manejo *m*.

(**c**) (*of machine*) marcha *f*, funcionamiento *m*.

running-board ['rʌnɪŋbɔ:d] *n* estribo *m*.

running-in ['rʌnɪŋ'ɪn] *n* rodaje *m*.

running mate ['rʌnɪŋ'meɪt] *n* (*US Pol*) candidato *m*, -a *f* a la vicepresidencia.

running-shoe ['rʌnɪŋ,ʃu:] *n* zapatilla *f* para correr.

running-track ['rʌnɪŋ,træk] *n* pista *f* (de atletismo).

runny ['rʌnɪ] *adj* líquido; derretido; ~ **nose** narices *fpl* que moquean.

run-off ['rʌnɒf] *n* (**a**) (*Sport*) carrera *f* de desempate; (*Pol*) desempate *m*, segunda vuelta *f*. (**b**) (*Agr*) escorrentía *f*; ~ **water** aguas *fpl* de escorrentía.

run-of-the-mill ['rʌnəvðə'mɪl] *adj* corriente y moliente, ordinario.

runproof ['rʌnpru:f] *adj mascara* que no se corre; *tights* indesmallable.

runt [rʌnt] *n* (*also fig*) redrojo *m*, enano *m*; **you little ~!** ¡canalla!

run-through ['rʌnθruː] *n* prueba *f* preliminar, ensayo *m*.
run-up ['rʌnʌp] *n* (**a**) (*Brit*) período *m* previo (*to* a); preparativos *mpl* (*to* para). (**b**) (*Sport*) corrida *f*.
runway ['rʌnweɪ] *n* (*Aer*) pista *f*; (*US*: *Theat etc*) pasarela *f*; ~ **lights** baliza *f*.
rupee [ruː'piː] *n* rupia *f*.
rupture ['rʌptʃəʳ] **1** *n* (*Med*) hernia *f*, quebradura *f*; (*fig*) ruptura *f*, rompimiento *m*.
2 *vt* (**a**) causar una hernia en, quebrarse. (**b**) (*fig*) romper, destruir.
3 *vr*: **to ~ o.s.** causarse una hernia, quebrarse.
rural ['rʊərəl] *adj* rural; ~ **free delivery** (*US*) entrega *f* gratuita en zona rural.
ruse [ruːz] *n* ardid *m*, treta *f*, estratagema *f*.
rush¹ [rʌʃ] **1** *n* (*Bot*) junco *m*. **2** *attr*: ~ **mat** estera *f*; ~ **matting** esteras *fpl*.
rush² [rʌʃ] **1** *n* (**a**) (*act of ~ing*) ímpetu *m*; (*Mil*) ataque *m*; acometida *f*; asalto *m*; **general ~** desbandada *f* general; **the gold ~** la rebatiña del oro; **there was a ~ to the door** se precipitaron todos hacia la puerta; **there was a ~ for safety** todos hicieron lo posible por ponerse a salvo; **to make a ~ at sb** arremeter contra uno, precipitarse sobre uno; **it got lost in the ~** se perdió en la confusión; **2 were injured in the ~** al precipitarse todos 2 resultaron heridos.
(**b**) (*haste*) prisa *f*, precipitación *f*, apuro *m* (*LAm*); (*tumult*) bullicio *m*, ajetreo *m*; **the ~ of modern life** el ajetreo de la vida moderna; **the ~ of London** el bullicio de Londres; **what's all the ~ about?** ¿por qué tanta prisa?; **is there any ~ for this?** ¿te corre prisa esto?; **we're in a ~** tenemos prisa, tenemos apuro (*LAm*), llevamos prisa; **we're in a ~ to finish it** tenemos prisa por terminarlo; **I did it in a ~** lo hice de prisa; **we had a ~ to get it ready** tuvimos que darnos prisa para tenerlo listo; **everything happened with a ~** todo ocurrió de repente; **it came down with a ~** cayó de repente.
(**c**) (*Comm*) demanda *f* (*for, on* de); **there has been a ~ on matches** ha habido una demanda extraordinaria de cerillas.
(**d**) (*current*) **a ~ of air** una fuerte corriente de aire, una ráfaga de aire; **a ~ of water** un torrente de agua; **a ~ of words** un torrente de palabras; **a ~ of people** un tropel; **in a ~ of sympathy** en un arrebato de compasión; **we've had a ~ of orders** estamos inundados de pedidos; **he had a ~ of blood to the head** (*fig*) le pasó algo totalmente inesperado; tuvo un momento de locura.
(**e**) **~es** (*Cine*) primeras pruebas *fpl*.
2 *adj*: ~ **hours** horas *fpl* punta, horas *fpl* de máximo tránsito; ~ **hour traffic** tráfico *m* de hora punta; **Barcelona in the ~ hour** Barcelona a la hora punta; ~ **job** trabajo *m* urgente; trabajo *m* hecho de prisa; ~ **order** pedido *m* urgente; ~ **work** trabajo *m* hecho precipitadamente.
3 *vt* (**a**) *person* dar prisa a, apresurar; **I hate being ~ed** me ofende que me metan prisa, no aguanto a los que piden que vaya más de prisa; **we're ~ed off our feet** tenemos trabajo (*etc*) hasta encima de la coronilla; **I don't want to ~ you** quiero que lo hagas con tranquilidad.
(**b**) *work* hacer precipitadamente, ejecutar de mucha prisa.
(**c**) (*carry etc*) llevar rápidamente; **to ~ medicine to sb** llevar con toda prisa medicina a uno; **he was ~ed to hospital** le llevaron al hospital con la mayor urgencia.
(**d**) (*Mil*) *position etc* asaltar, tomar al asalto; *troops* atacar repentinamente; **the crowd ~ed the barriers** el público asaltó las barreras.
(**e**) (*) **how much did they ~ you?** ¿cuánto te cobraron?; **they ~ed me £20** me hicieron pagar 20 libras.
4 *vi* precipitarse, lanzarse; correr (*etc*) rápidamente, ir de prisa, ir a máxima velocidad; **I must ~** me voy corriendo; tengo mucha prisa; **to ~ across a road** cruzar una calle a toda prisa; **you mustn't ~ across roads like that** es peligroso cruzar las calles con tanta precipitación; **everyone ~ed to the windows** se precipitaron todos hacia las ventanas; **the rocket was ~ing through space** el cohete iba a gran velocidad por el espacio; **don't ~!** ¡con calma!; **to ~ past** pasar como un rayo; **to ~ into the fray** lanzarse a la batalla; **I ~ed to her side** corrí a su lado; **I was ~ing to finish it** me daba prisa por terminarlo.
◆**rush about, rush around** *vi* correr de acá para allá.
◆**rush at** *vt* precipitarse hacia, lanzarse sobre; **to ~ at sb** arremeter contra uno, abalanzarse sobre uno.
◆**rush away** *vi* partir como un rayo.
◆**rush by** *vi* pasar como un rayo.
◆**rush down** *vi* bajar corriendo.
◆**rush in** *vi* entrar precipitadamente.
◆**rush off** *vi* = **rush away**.
◆**rush out 1** *vt book etc* publicar con toda prisa. **2** *vi* salir precipitadamente.
◆**rush through** *vt work etc* hacer apresuradamente, hacer urgentemente; **to ~ a bill through** (*Parl*) hacer aprobar de prisa un proyecto de ley.
◆**rush up** *vi* subir corriendo; **he ~ed up to a policeman** se acercó corriendo a un policía.
rushed [rʌʃt] *adj*: **it was a ~ job** el trabajo se hizo con mucha prisa.
rushlight ['rʌʃlaɪt] *n* vela *f* de junco.
rushy ['rʌʃɪ] *adj* juncoso.
rusk [rʌsk] *n* bizcocho *m* tostado, tostada *f*, biscote *m*.
russet ['rʌsɪt] **1** *n* color *m* bermejo, color *m* rojizo. **2** *adj* bermejo, rojizo.
Russia ['rʌʃə] *n* Rusia *f*.
Russian ['rʌʃən] **1** *adj* ruso; ~ **roulette** ruleta *f* rusa; ~ **salad** ensalada *f* rusa. **2** *n* (**a**) ruso *m*, -a *f*. (**b**) (*Ling*) ruso *m*.
Russki* ['rʌskɪ] *adj*, *n* = **Russian**.
rust [rʌst] **1** *n* (*action*) oxidación *f*, corrosión *f*; (*visible*) óxido *m*, herrumbre *f*, moho *m*; (*colour*) color *m* de orín; (*Agr*) roya *f*.
2 *vt* oxidar, corroer; aherrumbrar.
3 *vi* oxidarse, corroerse; aherrumbrarse, tomarse de orín.
rusted ['rʌstɪd] *adj* oxidado, aherrumbrado.
rustic ['rʌstɪk] **1** *adj* rústico; aldeano; (*pej*) rústico; (*person*) palurdo. **2** *n* rústico *m*, palurdo *m*.
rusticate ['rʌstɪkeɪt] **1** *vt* (*Brit Univ*) suspender temporalmente. **2** *vi* rusticar.
rustication [ˌrʌstɪ'keɪʃən] *n* (*Univ*) suspensión *f* temporal.
rusticity [rʌs'tɪsɪtɪ] *n* rusticidad *f*.
rustiness ['rʌstɪnɪs] *n* (**a**) herrumbre *f*, lo aherrumbrado. (**b**) (*fig*) falta *f* de práctica, torpeza *f*.
rustle¹ ['rʌsl] **1** *n* (*of leaves, wind*) susurro *m*; (*of paper*) crujido *m*; (*of silk, dress*) frufrú *m*. **2** *vt* (*V n*) hacer susurrar, mover ligeramente; hacer crujir. **3** *vi* susurrar; crujir; hacer frufrú.
◆**rustle up*** *vt* (*find*) buscar; (*obtain*) conseguir, (lograr) reunir; *meal etc* improvisar; **I'll see what I can ~ up** veré lo que hay; **can you ~ up some coffee?** ¿podrías hacerme un café?
rustle²* ['rʌsl] *vt* (*US*) robar, hurtar.
rustler ['rʌsləʳ] *n* (*US*) ladrón *m* de ganado; (*) persona *f* dinámica.
rustless ['rʌstlɪs] *adj* inoxidable.
rustling¹ ['rʌslɪŋ] *n* = **rustle¹ 1**.
rustling² ['rʌslɪŋ] *n*: **cattle ~** (*US*) robo *m* de ganado.
rustproof ['rʌstpruːf] **1** *adj* inoxidable. **2** *vt* tratar contra la corrosión.
rustproofing ['rʌstˌpruːfɪŋ] *n* tratamiento *m* anticorrosión.
rust-resistant ['rʌstrɪzɪstənt] *adj* inoxidable.
rusty ['rʌstɪ] *adj* (**a**) (*lit*) oxidado, herrumbroso, aherrumbrado, mohoso; *colour* color de orín. (**b**) (*fig*) falto de práctica, torpe; **my Catalan is pretty ~** mi catalán está bastante oxidado.
rut¹ [rʌt] *n* rodera *f*, rodada *f*, carril *m*; bache *m*; (*fig*) rutina *f*, sendero *m* trillado; **to be in a ~** estar sin poder salir de la rutina, ir encarrilado; **you've got into a ~** te has hecho esclavo de la rutina; **to get out of the ~** salir del bache.
rut² [rʌt] (*Bio*) **1** *n* celo *m*; **to be in ~** estar en celo. **2** *vi* (*be*) estar en celo; (*begin to ~*) caer en celo.
rutabaga [ˌruːtə'beɪgə] *n* (*US*) nabo *m* sueco, naba *f*.
ruthenium [ruː'θiːnɪəm] *n* rutenio *m*.
ruthless ['ruːθlɪs] *adj* despiadado; sin piedad; implacable, inexorable.
ruthlessly ['ruːθlɪslɪ] *adv* despiadadamente; implacablemente, inexorablemente.
ruthlessness ['ruːθlɪsnɪs] *n* crueldad *f*; implacabilidad *f*.
rutinize [ruː'tiːnaɪz] *vt* (*US*) organizar de manera rutinaria.
rutted ['rʌtɪd] *adj* lleno de baches.
rutting ['rʌtɪŋ] *adj* (*Bio*) en celo; ~ **season** época *f* de celo.
rutty ['rʌtɪ] *adj* lleno de baches.
RV *n* (**a**) *abbr of* **Revised Version** *versión revisada de la Biblia*. (**b**) *n* (*US*) *abbr of* **recreational vehicle**.
rye [raɪ] **1** *n* centeno *m*. **2** *attr*: ~ **(bread)** pan *m* de centeno; ~ **(whisky)** (*US*) whisky *m* de centeno.
ryegrass ['raɪgrɑːs] *n* ballico *m*, joyo *m*.

S

S, s [es] *n* (*letter*) S, s *f*; **S for sugar** S de Soria; **S-bend** curva *f* en S.
S (**a**) *abbr of* **south** sur *m*; *also adj*. (**b**) *abbr of* **Saint** santo *m*, santa *f*, Sto., Sta. (**c**) (*US Scol*) *abbr of* **satisfactory** suficiente.
s. (**a**) *abbr of* **second** segundo *m*. (**b**) *abbr of* **son** hijo *m*. (**c**) (*Brit Fin* †) *abbr of* **shilling(s)** chelín *m*, chelines *mpl*.
SA (**a**) *abbr of* **South Africa** África *f* del Sur. (**b**) *abbr of* **South America** América *f* del Sur. (**c**) *abbr of* **South Australia.**
Saar [zɑːʳ] *n* Sarre *m*.
sabbatarian [ˌsæbəˈtɛərɪən] **1** *adj* sabatario. **2** *n* sabatario *m*, -a *f*, partidario *m* de guardar estrictamente el domingo.
Sabbath [ˈsæbəθ] *n* (*Christian*) domingo *m*; (*Jewish*) sábado *m*.
sabbatical [səˈbætɪkəl] **1** *adj* (*Rel*) sabático; dominical; ~ **year** = **2**. **2** *n* año *m* sabático.
saber [ˈseɪbəʳ] (*US*) = **sabre.**
sable [ˈseɪbl] **1** *n* (*animal, fur*) marta *f* (cebellina); (*colour*) negro *m*; (*Her*) sable *m*. **2** *adj* negro.
sabot [ˈsæbəʊ] *n* zueco *m*.
sabotage [ˈsæbətɑːʒ] **1** *n* sabotaje *m*. **2** *vt* sabotear (*also fig*).
saboteur [ˌsæbəˈtɜːʳ] *n* saboteador *m*.
sabre, (*US*) **saber** [ˈseɪbəʳ] **1** *n* sable *m*. **2** *vt* herir (*or* matar *etc*) a sablazos.
sabre-rattler, (*US*) **saber-rattler** [ˈseɪbəˌrætləʳ] *n* patriotero *m*, jingoísta *m*.
sabre-rattling, (*US*) **saber-rattling** [ˈseɪbəˌrætlɪŋ] *n* patriotería *f*, jingoísmo *m*.
sac [sæk] *n* (*Anat etc*) saco *m*.
saccharin [ˈsækərɪn] *n* (*US*) = **saccharine 2.**
saccharine [ˈsækəriːn] **1** *adj* sacarino; (*fig*) azucarado, empalagoso. **2** *n* sacarina *f*.
sacerdotal [ˌsæsəˈdəʊtl] *adj* sacerdotal.
sachet [ˈsæʃeɪ] *n* saquito *m*, bolsita *f*; (*of perfume*) almohadilla *f* perfumada.
sack¹ [sæk] **1** *n* (**a**) (*bag*) saco *m*, costal *m*.
(**b**) (*****) (*dismissal*) despido *m*; **to get the** ~ ser despedido; **to give sb the** ~ despedir a uno.
(**c**) (**‡**: *esp US*: *bed*) pulguero‡ *m*; **to hit the** ~ acostarse.
2 *vt* (**a**) ensacar, meter en sacos.
(**b**) (*****) despedir.
sack² [sæk] (*Mil*) **1** *n* saqueo *m*. **2** *vt* saquear.
sackbut [ˈsækbʌt] *n* sacabuche *m*.
sackcloth [ˈsækklɒθ] *n* (h)arpillera *f*; **to wear ~ and ashes** ponerse el hábito de penitencia, ponerse cenizas en la cabeza.
sackful [ˈsækfʊl] *n* saco *m*, contenido *m* de un saco.
sacking¹ [ˈsækɪŋ] *n* (**a**) (*material*) (h)arpillera *f*. (**b**) (*****) despido *m*.
sacking² [ˈsækɪŋ] *n* (*Mil*) saqueo *m*.
sack race [ˈsækreɪs] *n* carrera *f* de sacos.
sacral [ˈseɪkrəl] *adj* sacral.
sacrament [ˈsækrəmənt] *n* sacramento *m*; Eucaristía *f*; **to receive the last ~s** recibir los últimos sacramentos.
sacramental [ˌsækrəˈmentl] *adj* sacramental.
sacred [ˈseɪkrɪd] *adj* sagrado; santo; consagrado; ~ **cow** vaca *f* sagrada (*also fig*); **S~ History** Historia *f* Sagrada; ~ **music** música *f* sacra; ~ **to the memory of ...** consagrado a la memoria de ...; **is nothing ~ to you?** ¿no hay nada sagrado para ti?, ¿no respetas nada?
sacrifice [ˈsækrɪfaɪs] **1** *n* sacrificio *m*; (*person etc*) víctima *f*; **the ~ of the mass** el sacrificio de la misa; **to make ~s** privarse de algo, renunciar a algo; **to sell sth at a ~** vender algo con pérdida.
2 *vt* sacrificar; (*Comm*) vender con pérdida, vender a precio de sacrificio.
3 *vr*: **to ~ o.s.** sacrificarse.
sacrificial [ˌsækrɪˈfɪʃəl] *adj* de sacrificio.
sacrilege [ˈsækrɪlɪdʒ] *n* sacrilegio *m*.
sacrilegious [ˌsækrɪˈlɪdʒəs] *adj* sacrílego.
sacrist [ˈsækrɪst] *n*, **sacristan** [ˈsækrɪstən] *n* sacristán *m*.
sacristy [ˈsækrɪstɪ] *n* sacristía *f*.
sacrosanct [ˈsækrəʊsæŋkt] *adj* sacrosanto.
sacrum [ˈsækrəm] *n* (*Anat*) sacro *m*.
sad [sæd] *adj* (**a**) (*sorrowful*) triste; melancólico; **how ~!** ¡qué triste!; **to be ~ at heart** estar profundamente triste, tener el corazón oprimido; **to grow ~** entristecerse, ponerse triste; **to make sb ~** entristecer a uno, poner triste a uno; **he left a ~der and a wiser man** partió habiendo aprendido una dura lección.
(**b**) (*deplorable*) lamentable; **a ~ mistake** un error lamentable; **it's a ~ business** es un asunto lamentable.
sadden [ˈsædn] *vt* entristecer; afligir.
saddle [ˈsædl] **1** *n* (**a**) silla *f* (de montar); (*cycle* ~) asiento *m*, sillín *m*; **Red Rum won with X in the ~** ganó Red Rum montado por X; **to be in the ~** (*fig*) estar en el poder, mandar; **to leap into the ~** saltar a la silla.
(**b**) (*hill*) collado *m*.
(**c**) (*of meat*) cuarto *m* trasero.
2 *vt* (**a**) *horse* (*also* **to ~ up**) ensillar. (**b**) (*****) **to ~ sb with sth** echar algo a cuestas a uno, echar a uno la responsabilidad de algo; **now we're ~d with it** ahora tenemos que cargar con ello; **to get ~d with sth** tener que cargar con algo.
3 *vr*: **to ~ o.s. with sth** cargar con algo.
saddle-backed [ˈsædlbækt] *adj* (*Zool*) ensillado.
saddlebag [ˈsædlbæg] *n* alforja *f*.
saddlebow [ˈsædlbəʊ] *n* arzón *m* delantero.
saddlecloth [ˈsædlklɒθ] *n* sudadero *m*.
saddler [ˈsædləʳ] *n* talabartero *m*, guarnicionero *m*.
saddlery [ˈsædlərɪ] *n* talabartería *f*, guarnicionería *f*.
saddle-sore [ˈsædlˌsɔːʳ] *adj*: **he was ~** le dolían las posaderas de tanto montar.
sadism [ˈseɪdɪzəm] *n* sadismo *m*.
sadist [ˈseɪdɪst] *n* sadista *mf*, sádico *m*, -a *f*.
sadistic [səˈdɪstɪk] *adj* sádico.
sadly [ˈsædlɪ] *adv* (**a**) (*unhappily*) tristemente. (**b**) (*regrettably*) muy; **~ lacking in** muy deficiente en; **a ~ incompetent headmaster** un director (de colegio) de lo más ineficaz; **you are ~ mistaken** estás muy equivocado, te equivocas gravemente.
sadness [ˈsædnɪs] *n* tristeza *f*, melancolía *f*.
sadomasochism [ˌseɪdəʊˈmæsəˌkɪzəm] *n* sadomasoquismo *m*.
sadomasochist [ˌseɪdəʊˈmæsəkɪst] *n* sadomasoquista *mf*.
sadomasochistic [ˌseɪdəʊˌmæsəˈkɪstɪk] *adj* sadomasoquista.
s.a.e. *n abbr of* **stamped addressed envelope** *sobre m con las propias señas de uno y con sello*.
safari [səˈfɑːrɪ] **1** *n* safari *m*; **to be on ~** estar de safari. **2** *attr*: **~ jacket** chaqueta *f* safari; **~ park** parque *m* de fieras.
safe [seɪf] **1** *adj* seguro; salvo, fuera de peligro; (*from injury*) ileso, incólume; *journey, trip* feliz; sin novedad; *birth* feliz; (*Parl*) *seat, investment* seguro; *bet etc* seguro, cierto; *person* (*trustworthy*) digno de confianza, formal; (*sound*) prudente, sensato; **~ and sound** sano y salvo; **~ from** a salvo de, al abrigo de; **~ house** piso *m* franco, vivienda *f* segura; **~ period** período *m* sin peligro; **~ sex** sexo *m* seguro; **better ~ than sorry!** ¡la prudencia ante todo!; **as ~ as houses** completamente seguro; **the ~st thing is to** + *infin* lo más seguro es + *infin*; **just to be ~** por precaución, para mayor seguridad; **all the passengers are ~** todos los pasajeros están ilesos, no ha habido víctimas entre los pasajeros; **these stairs are not very ~** esta escalera no es

muy segura; **it's a ~ beach** es una playa sin peligro; **no girl is ~ with him** ninguna joven está sin peligro estando con él; **is that dog ~?** ¿es peligroso ese perro?; **he's ~ with children** es de fiar con los niños, no es un peligro para los niños; **your reputation is ~** su reputación está a salvo; **the secret is ~ with me** el secreto seguirá siéndolo conmigo; **the book is ~ now** ahora el libro está en buenas manos; **you'll be perfectly ~ here** aquí estás fuera de todo peligro; **his life was not ~** no estaba seguro de su vida; **is it ~ to go out?** ¿se puede salir sin peligro?; **the ice isn't ~** el hielo no es sólido, el hielo no es de fiar; **there is ~ bathing here** aquí se baña sin peligro; **it is in ~ hands** está en buenas manos; **it is ~ to say that ...** se puede decir con confianza que ...; **to come ~ home** volver a casa sin novedad; **I don't feel very ~ up here** no me siento muy seguro aquí arriba; **to keep sth ~** tener algo seguro; **he plays a ~ game** es un jugador prudente.

2 *adv*: *V* **play 3(f)**.

3 *n* caja *f* de caudales; (*for meat*) fresquera *f*.

safe-blower ['seɪf,bləʊəʳ] *n*, **safe-breaker** ['seɪf,breɪkəʳ] *n* ladrón *m*, -ona *f* de cajas fuertes.

safe-conduct ['seɪf'kɒndəkt] *n* salvoconducto *m*.

safe-cracker ['seɪf,krækəʳ] *n* (*US*) ladrón *m*, -ona *f* de cajas fuertes.

safe deposit ['seɪfdɪ,pɒzɪt] *n* (*vault*) cámara *f* acorazada; (*box*: *also* ~ **box**) caja *f* fuerte, caja *f* de seguridad.

safeguard ['seɪfgɑːd] **1** *n* salvaguardia *f*; protección *f*, garantía *f*; **as a ~** por precaución; **as a ~ against ...** como defensa contra ..., para evitar ... **2** *vt* salvaguardar, proteger, defender.

safe-keeping [,seɪf'kiːpɪŋ] *n* custodia *f*; **in his ~** bajo su custodia.

safely ['seɪflɪ] *adv* seguramente, con seguridad; sin peligro; *arrive, travel etc* sin novedad, sin accidente; **you may ~ do it now** ahora puedes hacerlo sin peligro; **to put sth away ~** guardar algo en un lugar seguro; **we can ~ say that ...** podemos decir con confianza que ...

safeness ['seɪfnɪs] *n* seguridad *f*.

safety ['seɪftɪ] **1** *n* seguridad *f*; **~ on the roads** seguridad *f* en la carretera; '**~ first!**' (*as slogan*) '¡prudencia ante todo!'; **~ first campaign** campaña *f* pro seguridad; **~ first policy** política *f* de seguridad; **in a place of ~** en un lugar seguro; **for ~'s sake** por precaución, para mayor seguridad, en interés de la seguridad; **with complete ~** con la mayor seguridad; **there's ~ in numbers** cuantos más, menos peligro; **to play for ~** obrar prudentemente; **to reach ~** ponerse a salvo; **to seek ~ in flight** salvarse huyendo.

2 *attr* de seguridad; **~ belt** cinturón *m* de seguridad; **~ catch** fiador *m*; (*on door*) cadena *f* de seguridad; (*on gun*) seguro *m*; **~ chain** seguro *m* de pulsera; **~ curtain** (*Theat*) telón *m* de seguridad; **~ deposit box** caja *f* fuerte, caja *f* de seguridad; **~ device** dispositivo *m* de seguridad; **~ factor** factor *m* de seguridad; **~ glass** vidrio *m* inastillable; **~ harness** arnés *m* de seguridad; **~ lamp** lámpara *f* de seguridad; **~ lock** seguro *m*, cerradura *f* de seguridad; **~ margin** margen *m* de seguridad; **~ match** cerilla *f* de seguridad; **~ measure** medida *f* de seguridad, precaución *f*, prevención *f*; **~ mechanism** mecanismo *m* de seguridad; **~ net** red *f* de seguridad; **~ officer** encargado *m*, -a *f* de seguridad; **~ pin** imperdible *m*, seguro *m* (*LAm*); (*of grenade*) arandela *f*; **~ precaution** medida *f* de seguridad; **~ razor** maquinilla *f* de afeitar, gillette *f*; **~ regulations** normas *fpl* de seguridad; **~ valve** válvula *f* de seguridad.

saffron ['sæfrən] **1** *n* azafrán *m*. **2** *adj* azafranado, color azafrán.

sag [sæg] **1** *n* comba *f*. **2** *vi* (*bulge, warp*) combarse, hundirse, pandear; (*slacken*) aflojarse, ceder; (*price etc*) bajar; (*spirit*) flaquear.

saga ['sɑːgə] *n* saga *f*; (*fig*) saga *f*, epopeya *f*; (*novel*) saga *f*, novela *f* río.

sagacious [sə'geɪʃəs] *adj* sagaz.

sagaciously [sə'geɪʃəslɪ] *adv* sagazmente.

sagacity [sə'gæsɪtɪ] *n* sagacidad *f*.

sage[1] [seɪdʒ] *n* (*Bot*) salvia *f*; **~ green** verde salvia.

sage[2] [seɪdʒ] **1** *adj* sabio. **2** *n* sabio *m*.

sagebrush ['seɪdʒbrʌʃ] *n* (*US*) artemisa *f*.

sagely ['seɪdʒlɪ] *adv* sabiamente.

sagging ['sægɪŋ] *adj ground* hundido; *beam* pandeado; *cheek* fofo; *rope* flojo; *gate, hemline* caído.

Sagittarius [,sædʒɪ'tɛrɪəs] *n* (*Zodiac*) Sagitario *m*.

sago ['seɪgəʊ] **1** *n* sagú *m*. **2** *attr*: **~ palm** palmera *f* sagú.

Sahara [sə'hɑːrə] *n* Sáhara *m*, Sájara *m*.

Sahel [sɑː'hel] *n* Sahel *m*.

sahib ['sɑːhɪb] *n* (*India*) (**a**) señor *m*; **Smith S~** (el) señor Smith. (**b**) (*hum*) caballero *m*; **pukka ~** caballero *m* de verdad.

said [sed] **1** *pret and ptp of* **say**. **2** *adj* dicho, antedicho; **the ~ animals** dichos animales, los cuales animales; **the ~ general** dicho general.

Saigon [saɪ'gɒn] *n* Saigón *m*.

sail [seɪl] **1** *n* (**a**) (*cloth*) vela *f*; **in full ~, under full ~, with all ~s set** a toda vela, a vela llena; **to set ~** hacerse a la vela, zarpar (*for* con rumbo a); **to lower the ~s** arriar las velas; **to take in the ~s** amainar.

(**b**) (*of mill*) aspa *f*.

(**c**) (*trip*) paseo *m* (en barco), paseo *m* en balandro (*etc*); **it is 3 days' ~ from here** desde aquí es un viaje de 3 días en barco; **to go for a ~** dar un paseo en barco, salir en balandro (*etc*).

(**d**) (*boat*) barco *m* de vela, velero *m*; **20 ~** 20 barcos.

2 *vt* (**a**) *ship* (*steer*) gobernar; *boat* manejar; **they ~ed the ship to Cadiz** fueron con el barco a Cádiz, fueron en el barco a Cádiz; **he ~s his own boat** tiene barco propio.

(**b**) **to ~ the seas** navegar los mares; **to ~ the Atlantic** cruzar el Atlántico.

3 *vi* (**a**) (*Naut*) navegar; **to ~ at 12 knots** navegar a 12 nudos, ir a 12 nudos; **we ~ed into Lisbon** llegamos a Lisboa; **we ~ed into harbour** entramos a puerto; **to go ~ing** (*as sport*) hacer vela; **to ~ round the world** dar la vuelta al mundo; **to ~ round a headland** doblar un cabo; **to ~ up the Tagus** entrar en el Tajo, subir el Tajo.

(**b**) (*Naut*: *leave*) hacerse a la vela, zarpar (*for* con rumbo a); (*gen*) salir, partir; **she ~s on Monday** sale el lunes; **we ~ for Australia** partimos para Australia.

(**c**) (*fig*: *swan etc*) deslizarse; (*cloud*) flotar; (*object*) volar; **it ~ed over my head** voló por encima de mi cabeza; **it ~ed over into the next garden** voló por los aires y cayó en el jardín de al lado.

◆**sail into** *vt* (**a**) **to ~ into sb** (*: *scold*) poner a uno como un trapo*, (*attack*) arremeter contra uno, atacar a uno. (**b**) **she ~ed into the room*** entró en la sala a vela tendida.

◆**sail through*** *vt*: **she ~ed through the exam** aprobó el examen volando; **don't worry, you'll ~ through it** no te preocupes, todo sera facilísimo.

sailboard ['seɪlbɔːd] **1** *n* plancha *f* de windsurf. **2** *vi* hacer windsurf.

sailboarder ['seɪlbɔːdəʳ] *n* windsurfista *mf*.

sailboarding ['seɪlbɔːdɪŋ] *n* windsurf *m*, surf *m* a vela.

sailboat ['seɪlbəʊt] *n* (*US*) barco *m* de vela.

sailcloth ['seɪlklɒθ] *n* lona *f*.

sailfish ['seɪlfɪʃ] *n* aguja *f* de mar, pez *m* vela.

sailing ['seɪlɪŋ] **1** *n* (**a**) (*gen*) navegación *f*; (*as sport*) (deporte *m* de la) vela *f*, balandrismo *m*; **to go ~** salir en balandro; **now it's all plain ~** ahora es muy sencillo, ahora es cosa de coser y cantar; **it's not exactly plain ~** no es tan sencillo que digamos.

(**b**) (*departure*) salida *f*, partida *f*.

2 *attr*: **~ boat** (*Brit*) barco *m* de vela; **~ date** fecha *f* de salida; **~ orders** últimas instrucciones *fpl* (dadas al capitán de un buque); **~ time** hora *f* de salida (de un barco).

sailing ship ['seɪlɪŋʃɪp] *n* velero *m*, buque *m* de vela.

sailmaker ['seɪl,meɪkəʳ] *n* velero *m*.

sailor ['seɪləʳ] **1** *n* marinero *m*, marino *m*; **to be a bad ~** marearse fácilmente; **to be a good ~** no marearse. **2** *attr*: **~ hat** sombrero *m* de marinero; **~ suit** traje *m* de marinero (*de niño*).

sainfoin ['sænfɔɪn] *n* pipirigallo *m*.

saint [seɪnt] *n* (**a**) santo *m*, -a *f*; **~'s day** fiesta *f* (de santo).

(**b**) *before m names abbreviated to* San, *eg* **St John** San Juan; *except* **St Dominic** Santo Domingo, **St Thomas** Santo Tomás.

(**c**) (*as name of church*) **at St Mark's** en San Marcos, en la iglesia de San Marcos.

(**d**) **St Andrew** (*patrón de Escocia*) San Andrés; **St Bernard** (*dog*) perro *m* de San Bernardo; **St Elmo's fire** fuego *m* de Santelmo; **St George** (*patrón de Inglaterra*) San Jorge; **St James** (*patrón de España*) Santiago; **St John the Baptist** San Juan Bautista; **St Kitts** (*WI*) San Cristóbal; **St Patrick** (*patrón de Irlanda*) San Patricio; **St Theresa** Santa Teresa; **St Valentine's Day** día *m* de San Valentín (14 *febrero, día de los enamorados*); **St Vitus' dance** baile *m* de San Vito.

sainted ['seɪntɪd] *adj* santo; bendito; (*of dead*) que en santa gloria esté; **my ~ aunt!*** (*hum*) ¡caray!*

sainthood ['seɪnthʊd] *n* santidad *f*.

saint-like ['seɪntlaɪk] *adj* = **saintly**.
saintliness ['seɪntlɪnɪs] *n* santidad *f*.
saintly ['seɪntlɪ] *adj* santo, piadoso.
sake¹ [seɪk] *n*: **for the ~ of** por; por motivo de; en consideración a, en atención a; **for God's ~** por el amor de Dios; **for God's ~!, for heaven's ~!** ¡por Dios!; **for my ~** por mí; **for your own ~** por tu propio bien, en interés propio; **for old times' ~** por respeto al pasado, por los tiempos pasados; **for the ~ of peace** por amor a la paz, en interés de la paz; para obtener la paz; **art for art's ~** el arte por el arte; **to talk for talking's ~** hablar por hablar; **she likes this kind of music for its own ~** le gusta este tipo de música por sí misma.
sake² ['sɑːkɪ] *n* sake *m*.
sal [sæl] *n* sal *f*.
salaam [sə'lɑːm] **1** *n* zalema *f*. **2** *vi* hacer zalemas.
salable ['seɪləbl] *adj* (*US*) = **saleable**.
salacious [sə'leɪʃəs] *adj* salaz.
salaciousness [sə'leɪʃəsnɪs] *n*, **salacity** [sə'læsɪtɪ] *n* salacidad *f*.
salad ['sæləd] *n* ensalada *f*.
salad-bowl ['sælədbəʊl] *n* ensaladera *f*.
salad-cream ['sæləd,kriːm] *n* (*Brit*) mayonesa *f*.
salad-days ['sæləddeɪz] *npl* juventud *f*; ingenuidad *f* juvenil.
salad-dish ['sæləddɪʃ] *n* ensaladera *f*.
salad-dressing ['sæləd,dresɪŋ] *n* mayonesa *f*, aliño *m*.
salad-oil ['sælədɔɪl] *n* aceite *m* para ensaladas.
salamander ['sælə,mændə^r] *n* salamandra *f*.
salami [sə'lɑːmɪ] *n* salami *m*.
sal ammoniac [,sælə'məʊnɪæk] *n* sal *f* amoníaca.
salaried ['sælərɪd] *adj* asalariado; **~ person** persona *f* asalariada; **~ post** puesto *m* retribuido; **~ staff** personal *m* asalariado.
salary ['sælərɪ] **1** *n* sueldo *m*. **2** *attr*: **~ bracket** categoría *f* salarial; **~ package** paquete *m* salarial; **~ range** margen *m* salarial; **~ review** revisión *f* de sueldos; **~ scale** banda *f* salarial; **~ structure** estructuración *f* salarial.
salary-earner ['sælərɪ,ɜːnə^r] *n* persona *f* que gana un sueldo, persona *f* que cobra cada mes.
sale [seɪl] **1** *n* (**a**) (*act*) venta *f*; **~ and lease back** venta *f* y arrendamiento al vendedor; **'for ~'** 'se vende'; **'horse for ~'** 'se vende caballo'; **is it for ~?** ¿se vende?; **'not for ~'** 'no se vende'; **it's going cheap for a quick ~** se ofrece a un precio módico para venderlo pronto; **it found a ready ~** se vendió pronto; **to put a house up for ~** ofrecer una casa en venta; **on a ~ or return basis** a base de vender o devolver; **to be on ~** estar en venta; **'on ~ at all fishmongers'** 'de venta en todas las pescaderías'.
(**b**) (*event*: *clearance ~*) liquidación *f*; (*annual etc*) saldo *m*, rebaja *f* (*LAm*); (*auction, public ~*) subasta *f*; **'~'** (*in shop window*) 'grandes rebajas'; **the ~s are on** es la temporada de los saldos.
2 *attr*: **~s agent** agente *mf* de ventas; **~s assistant** (*Brit*), **~s clerk** (*US*) vendedor *m*, -ora *f*, dependiente *m*, -a *f*; **~ brochure** folleto *m* publicitario; **~ budget** presupuesto *m* de ventas; **~s campaign** campaña *f* de ventas; **~s check** (*US*) hoja *f* de venta; **~s conference** conferencia *f* de ventas; **~s department** sección *f* de ventas; **~s drive** promoción *f* de ventas; **~s executive** ejecutivo *m*, -a *f* de ventas; **~s figures** cifras *fpl* de ventas; **~s force** personal *m* de ventas; **~s forecast** previsión *f* de ventas; **~(s) invoice** factura *f* de venta(s); **~s leaflet** folleto *m* publicitario; **~s ledger** libro *m* de ventas; **~s literature** folletos *mpl* de venta; propaganda *f* de venta; **~s manager** jefe *mf* de ventas; **~s meeting** reunión *f* de ventas; **~s office** oficina *f* de ventas; **~s pitch*** rollo* *m* publicitario; **~s potential** potencial *m* de ventas; **~ price** precio *m* de venta; **~ promotion** promoción *f* de ventas; **~s rep(resentative)** agente *mf* de ventas; **~s resistance** resistencia *f* a comprar; **~s slip** hoja *f* de venta; **~s talk** jerga *f* de vendedor; **~ value** valor *m* comercial, valor *m* en el mercado.
saleability [,seɪlə'bɪlɪtɪ] *n* vendibilidad *f*.
saleable ['seɪləbl] *adj* vendible.
saleroom ['seɪlrʊm] *n*, (*US*) **salesroom** ['seɪlzrʊm] *n* sala *f* de subastas.
salesgirl ['seɪlzgɜːl] *n* dependienta *f*, vendedora *f*.
salesman ['seɪlzmən] *n*, *pl* **salesmen** ['seɪlzmən] (*in shop*) dependiente *m*, vendedor *m*; (*traveller*) viajante *m*; **'Death of a S~'** 'La muerte de un viajante'.
salesmanship ['seɪlzmənʃɪp] *n* arte *m* de vender.
salesperson ['seɪlz,pɜːsn] *n* (*esp US*) vendedor *m*, -ora *f*, dependiente *m*, -a *f*.
sales tax ['seɪlztæks] *n* (*US*) impuesto *m* sobre las ventas.
saleswoman ['seɪlzwʊmən] *n*, *pl* **saleswomen** ['seɪlzwɪmɪn] dependienta *f*, vendedora *f*.
salient ['seɪlɪənt] **1** *adj* saliente; (*fig*) sobresaliente, destacado, notable; **~ points** puntos *mpl* principales. **2** *n* saliente *m*.
salina [sə'liːnə] *n* (*marsh etc, saltworks*) salina *f*; (*mine*) mina *f* de sal, salina *f*.
saline ['seɪlaɪn] *adj* salino; **~ drip** gota-a-gota *m* salino.
salinity [sə'lɪnɪtɪ] *n* salinidad *f*.
saliva [sə'laɪvə] *n* saliva *f*.
salivary ['sælɪvərɪ] *adj* salival; **~ gland** glándula *f* salival.
salivate ['sælɪveɪt] *vi* salivar.
salivation [,sælɪ'veɪʃən] *n* salivación *f*.
sallow¹ ['sæləʊ] *n* (*Bot*) sauce *m* cabruno.
sallow² ['sæləʊ] *adj* cetrino, amarillento.
sallowness ['sæləʊnɪs] *n* lo cetrino, amarillez *f*.
Sallust ['sæləst] *nm* Salustio.
Sally ['sælɪ] *nf familiar form of* **Sarah**.
sally ['sælɪ] **1** *n* (*all senses*) salida *f*; **to make a ~** hacer una salida. **2** *vi* hacer una salida.
◆**sally forth, sally out** *vi* salir resueltamente.
salmon ['sæmən] **1** *n*, *pl invar* salmón *m*; (*colour*) color *m* salmón. **2** *adj* color salmón. **3** *attr*: **~ fishing** pesca *f* de salmón; **~ ladder** paso *m* salmonero; **~ trout** trucha *f* asalmonada, trucha *f* de mar.
salmonella [,sælmə'nelə] *n* salmonela *f*; **~ food-poisoning** salmonelosis *f*.
salmonellosis [,sælməne'ləʊsɪs] *n* salmonelosis *f*.
Salome [sə'ləʊmɪ] *nf* Salomé.
salon ['sælɒn] *n* salón *m*.
saloon [sə'luːn] *n* salón *m*; (*Naut*) cámara *f*, salón *m*; (*Brit Aut*) turismo *m*; (*US*: *bar*) bar *m*; taberna *f*, cantina *f* (*Mex*).
saloon-car [sə'luːnkɑː^r] *n* (*Rail*) coche-salón *m*; (*Aut*) turismo *m*.
salopettes [,sælə'pets] *npl* peto *m* de esquiar.
salsify ['sælsɪfɪ] *n* salsifí *m*.
SALT [sɔːlt] *n abbr of* **Strategic Arms Limitation Talks.**
salt [sɔːlt] **1** *n* sal *f*; **~s** sales *fpl* medicinales; **~ of the earth** (*fig*) sal *f* de la tierra; **to rub ~ in the wound** (*fig*) poner sal en la llaga; **to be worth one's ~** (*fig*) merecer el pan que se come.
2 *adj meat, water etc* salado; *taste* salobre; **~ beef** carne *f* de vaca salada; **~ lake** lago *m* de agua salada; **it's very ~** está muy salado.
3 *vt* (*cure*) salar; (*flavour*) poner sal en, añadir sal a; *road* poner sal en, tratar con sal; **to ~ a dig** poner objetos en una excavación para que se encuentren después.
◆**salt away** *vt* ahorrar, ocultar para uso futuro.
◆**salt down** *vt* conservar en sal, salar.
salt-cellar ['sɔːlt,selə^r] *n* salero *m*.
salted ['sɔːltɪd] *adj* salado, con sal.
salt-flats ['sɔːltflæts] *npl* salinas *fpl*.
salt-free ['sɔːltfriː] *adj* sin sal.
saltiness ['sɔːltɪnɪs] *n* salinidad *f*; sabor *m* de sal; salobridad *f*.
saltings ['sɔːltɪŋz] *npl* saladar *m*.
saltmarsh ['sɔːltmɑːʃ] *n* saladar *m*, salina *f*.
saltmine ['sɔːltmaɪn] *n* mina *f* de sal.
saltpan ['sɔːltpæn] *n* salina *f*.
saltpetre, (*US*) **saltpeter** ['sɔːlt,piːtə^r] *n* salitre *m*.
salt-shaker ['sɔːlt,ʃeɪkə^r] *n* salero *m*.
salt-spoon ['sɔːltspuːn] *n* cucharita *f* de sal.
saltwater ['sɔːlt,wɔːtə^r] *attr fish etc* de mar, de agua salada.
saltworks ['sɔːltwɜːks] *n* salinas *fpl*.
salty ['sɔːltɪ] *adj* salado (*also fig*); salobre.
salubrious [sə'luːbrɪəs] *adj* salubre, sano.
salubrity [sə'luːbrɪtɪ] *n* salubridad *f*.
salutary ['sæljʊtərɪ] *adj* saludable.
salutation [,sæljʊ'teɪʃən] *n* salutación *f*, saludo *m*.
salute [sə'luːt] **1** *n* (*with hand etc*) saludo *m*; (*of guns*) salva *f*; **to fire a ~ of 21 guns for sb** saludar a uno con una salva de 21 cañonazos; **to take the ~** tomar el saludo. **2** *vti* saludar.
Salvadorian [,sælvə'dɔːrɪən] **1** *adj* salvadoreño. **2** *n* salvadoreño *m*, -a *f*.
salvage ['sælvɪdʒ] **1** *n* (**a**) (*act*) salvamento *m*; recuperación *f*.
(**b**) (*objects*) objetos *mpl* salvados; (*material*) material *m* aprovechable.
(**c**) (*fee*) derechos *mpl* de salvamento.
2 *attr*: **~ operation** salvamento *m*; **~ value** valor *m* de desecho; **~ vessel** buque *m* de salvamento.
3 *vt* salvar; recuperar; **to ~ sth from the wreckage**

salvar algo de las ruinas.
salvation [sæl'veɪʃən] *n* salvación *f*; **S~ Army** Ejército *m* de Salvación.
salvationist [sæl'veɪʃnɪst] *n* miembro *mf* del Ejército de Salvación.
salve[1] [sælv] *vt* (*Naut etc*) salvar; recuperar.
salve[2] [sælv] **1** *n* (*fig*) ungüento *m*, bálsamo. **2** *vt* curar (con ungüento); **to ~ one's conscience** tranquilizar la conciencia.
salver ['sælvəʳ] *n* bandeja *f*.
salvia ['sælvɪə] *n* salvia *f*.
salvo[1] ['sælvəʊ] *n* salvedad *f*, reserva *f*.
salvo[2] ['sælvəʊ] *n* (*Mil*) salva *f*; **a ~ of applause** una salva de aplausos.
sal volatile [,sælvə'lætəlɪ] *n* sal *f* volátil.
Salzburg ['sæltsbɜːg] *n* Salsburgo *m*.
SAM [sæm] *n abbr of* **surface-(to)-air missile.**
Sam [sæm], **Sammy** ['sæmɪ] *nm familiar form of* **Samuel**; **Sam Browne (belt)** correaje *m* de oficial.
Samaritan [sə'mærɪtn] **1** *adj* samaritano. **2** *n* samaritano *m*, -a *f*; **good ~** buen samaritano *m*.
samarium [sə'mɛərɪəm] *n* samario *m*.
samba ['sæmbə] *n* samba *f*.
sambo ['sæmbəʊ] *n* (*pej*) mestizo *m*; negro *m*.
same [seɪm] **1** *adj* mismo; igual; idéntico; **the ~ day** el mismo día; **~ day delivery** entrega *f* en el mismo día, entrega *f* inmediata; **it's the very ~ dog** es el mismísimo perro; **we sat at the ~ table as usual** nos sentamos a la mesa de siempre; **it's the ~ thing again** es lo mismo, es lo de siempre; **it comes to the ~ thing** viene a ser lo mismo.
2 *pron* el mismo, la misma; **the ~ as ...** el mismo que ...; **we all have the ~** todos tenemos lo mismo; **do the ~ as he does** haz lo que él, haz lo mismo que él; **(the) ~ again, please** lo mismo, por favor; **it's the ~ with us** es igual para nosotros, nosotros tenemos lo mismo; **and I did the ~** y yo hice lo mismo; **I'd do the ~ again** yo volvería a hacer lo mismo; **and the ~ to you!** ¡igualmente!; ¡a Vd!; **all the ~** con todo, de todas formas; a pesar de todo; **it's all the ~** es lo mismo, es todo uno; **it's all the ~ to me** me es igual, lo mismo me da; **if it's all the ~ to you** si a ti te da lo mismo; **no, but thanks all the ~** no, pero en todo caso, gracias; **it's just the ~** es exactamente igual; **things go on just the ~** eso continúa como siempre; **they are much the ~** son más o menos idénticos; **she's much about the ~** sigue más o menos igual; **I still feel the ~ about you** yo para contigo sigo igual; **to repair of door and repainting ~** ... reparación de la puerta y pintar lo mismo ...; **~ here!** ¡yo también!
sameness ['seɪmnɪs] *n* igualdad *f*; identidad *f*; (*pej*) monotonía *f*.
Samoa [sə'məʊə] *n* Samoa *f*.
Samoan [sə'məʊən] **1** *adj* samoano. **2** *n* samoano *m*, -a *f*.
samovar [,sæməʊ'vɑːʳ] *n* samovar *m*.
sampan ['sæmpæn] *n* sampán *m*.
sample ['sɑːmpl] **1** *n* (*all senses*) muestra *f*; **free ~** muestra *f* gratuita; **~ pack** paquete *m* de muestra; **~ survey** estudio *m* de muestra. **2** *vt* probar; (*in blending*) catar; (*Statistics*) muestrear.
sample book ['sɑːmplbʊk] *n* muestrario *m*.
sampler ['sɑːmpləʳ] *n* (**a**) (*person*) catador *m*. (**b**) (*Sew*) dechado *m*.
sampling ['sɑːmplɪŋ] *n* muestreo *m*; **~ technique** método *m* de muestreo.
Samson ['sæmsn] *nm* Sansón.
Samuel ['sæmjʊəl] *nm* Samuel.
San Andreas [,sænæn'dreɪəs] *n*: **~ Fault** falla *f* de San Andrés.
sanatorium [,sænə'tɔːrɪəm] *n, pl* **sanatoriums** *or* **sanatoria** [,sænə'tɔːrɪə] (*Brit*) sanatorio *m*.
sanctification [,sæŋ*k*tɪfɪ'keɪʃən] *n* santificación *f*.
sanctify ['sæŋ*k*tɪfaɪ] *vt* santificar.
sanctimonious [,sæŋ*k*tɪ'məʊnɪəs] *adj* mojigato, santurrón, beato.
sanctimoniously [,sæŋ*k*tɪ'məʊnɪəslɪ] *adv* con mojigatería; **she said ~** dijo mojigata.
sanctimoniousness [,sæŋ*k*tɪ'məʊnɪəsnɪs] *n* mojigatería *f*, santurronería *f*, beatería *f*.
sanction ['sæŋ*k*ʃən] **1** *n* (**a**) (*permission*) sanción *f*, autorización *f*, aprobación *f*. (**b**) (*penalty*) sanción *f*; **~ busting** ruptura *f* de sanciones; **to impose trade ~s against a country** imponer sanciones comerciales contra un país. **2** *vt* (**a**) (*permit*) sancionar, autorizar, aprobar. (**b**) (*penalize*) sancionar.
sanctity ['sæŋ*k*tɪtɪ] *n* santidad *f*; inviolabilidad *f*.
sanctuary ['sæŋ*k*tjʊərɪ] *n* santuario *m*; (*high altar*) sagrario *m*; (*Hist*: *place of refuge*) sagrado *m*, (*modern*) refugio *m*, asilo *m*; (*for wildlife*) reserva *f*; **to seek ~** acogerse a sagrado; **to seek ~ in** refugiarse en; **to seek ~ with** acogerse a.
sanctum ['sæŋ*k*təm] *n* lugar *m* sagrado; (*fig*) despacho *m* particular.
sand [sænd] **1** *n* arena *f*; **~s** (*of desert*) arenas *fpl*, (*beach*) playa *f* (arenosa); **the plan ran into the ~** el proyecto quedó estancado; **the ~s are running out** queda poco tiempo. **2** *vt* enarenar.
◆**sand down** *vt* alisar con arena.
sandal ['sændl] *n* sandalia *f*; (*rope-soled*) alpargata *f*.
sandal(wood) ['sændl(wʊd)] *n* sándalo *m*.
sandbag ['sæn*d*bæg] **1** *n* saco *m* de arena, saco *m* terrero. **2** *vt* proteger con sacos de arena.
sandbank ['sæn*d*bæŋk] *n* banco *m* de arena.
sand-bar ['sæn*d*bɑːʳ] *n* barra *f* de arena, banco *m* de arena.
sandblast ['sæn*d*blɑːst] *n* chorro *m* de arena.
sandbox ['sæn*d*bɒks] *n* (*US*) cajón *m* de arena.
sand-boy ['sæn*d*bɔɪ] *n*: **to be as happy as a ~** estar como unas pascuas.
sandcastle ['sæn*d*,kɑːsl] *n* castillo *m* de arena.
sand-dune ['sæn*d*djuːn] *n* duna *f*.
sander ['sændəʳ] *n* (*tool*) pulidora *f*.
sandglass ['sæn*d*glɑːs] *n* reloj *m* de arena.
sanding ['sændɪŋ] *n* (*of road*) enarenamiento *m*; (*of floor*) pulimiento *m*; (*sandpapering*) lijamiento *m*.
sandlot ['sændlɒt] (*US*) **1** *n terreno en una ciudad que se usa para el béisbol* (*etc*). **2** *adj* (*Sport*) de barrio, de vecindad; **~ baseball** béisbol *m* de barrio.
sandman ['sæn*d*mæn] *n ser imaginario que les trae el sueño a los niños.*
sand-martin ['sæn*d*,mɑːtɪn] *n* avión *m* zapador.
sandpaper ['sæn*d*,peɪpəʳ] **1** *n* papel *m* de lija. **2** *vt* lijar.
sandpiper ['sæn*d*'paɪpəʳ] *n* andarríos *m*, lavandera *f*.
sandpit ['sæn*d*pɪt] *n* (*esp Brit*) arenal *m*; (*in garden*) cuadro *m* de arena.
sandshoes ['sæn*d*ʃuːz] *npl* playeras *fpl*.
sandstone ['sæn*d*stəʊn] *n* piedra *f* arenisca.
sandstorm ['sæn*d*stɔːm] *n* tempestad *f* (*or* tormenta *f*) de arena.
sandwich ['sænwɪdʒ] **1** *n* sándwich *m*, emparedado *m*, bocadillo *m*; **~ course** (*Univ etc*) *programa que intercala períodos de estudio con prácticas profesionales.*
2 *vt* insertar; intercalar; (*Sport*) apretujar; **to ~ sth between two things** poner algo (apretadamente) entre dos cosas; **the house is ~ed between two big hotels** la casa se encuentra entre dos grandes hoteles, la casa ocupa un espacio estrecho entre dos grandes hoteles; **I was ~ed between two fat ladies** me tocó estar apretujado entre dos señoras gordas.
sandwich-bar ['sænwɪdʒ,bɑːʳ] *n* bocadillería *f*.
sandwich-board ['sænwɪdʒ,bɔːd] *n* cartelón *m* (*que lleva el hombre-anuncio*).
sandwich-man ['sænwɪdʒmæn] *n*, *pl* **sandwich-men** ['sænwɪdʒmen] hombre-anuncio *m*, anuncio *m* ambulante.
sandworm ['sæn*d*wɜːm] *n* gusano *m* de arena.
sandy ['sændɪ] *adj* (**a**) arenoso. (**b**) (*in colour*) rojizo, dorado; *hair* rojo.
sane [seɪn] *adj person* cuerdo, sensato, de juicio sano; *policy etc* prudente.
sanely ['seɪnlɪ] *adv* sensatamente; prudentemente.
Sanforized ['sænfəraɪzd] ® *adj* sanforizado ®.
sang [sæŋ] *pret of* **sing.**
sangfroid ['sɑ̃ːŋ'frwɑː] *n* sangre *f* fría.
sanguinary ['sæŋgwɪnərɪ] *adj* sanguinario; sangriento.
sanguine ['sæŋgwɪn] *adj* (*fig*) optimista.
sanguineous [sæŋ'gwɪnɪəs] *adj* sanguíneo.
sanitarium [,sænɪ'tɛərɪəm] *n* (*esp US*) sanatorio *m*.
sanitary ['sænɪtərɪ] *adj* (**a**) (*clean*) higiénico. (**b**) *system etc* sanitario; **~ engineer** ingeniero *m* sanitario; **~ inspector** inspector *m* de sanidad; **~ napkin** (*US*), **~ towel** (*Brit*) paño *m* higiénico, compresa *f* (higiénica).
sanitation [,sænɪ'teɪʃən] **1** *n* sanidad *f*; higiene *f*; (*domestic ~*) instalación *f* sanitaria, saneamiento *m*, (*euph*) servicios *mpl* higiénicos; (*in town*) servicio *m* de desinfección.
2 *attr*: **~ department** (*US*) departamento *m* de limpieza y recogida de basuras.
sanitize ['sænɪtaɪz] *vt* sanear; **to ~ the image of war** sanear la imagen de la guerra.
sanitized ['sænɪtaɪzd] *adj* saneado.
sanity ['sænɪtɪ] *n* cordura *f*, sensatez *f*, juicio *m* sano; prudencia *f*; **~ demands that ...** la razón exige que ...; **for-**

tunately ~ prevailed afortunadamente se impuso el buen juicio; **to be restored to ~** recobrar su juicio; **to return to ~** ponerse en razón, volver a la razón.
sank [sæŋk] *pret of* **sink[1]**.
San Marino [ˌsænmə'riːnəʊ] *n* San Marino *m.*
Sanskrit ['sænskrɪt] **1** *adj* sánscrito. **2** *n* sánscrito *m.*
sans serif [ˌsæn'serɪf] *n* grotesca *f.*
Santa Claus [ˌsæntə'klɔːz] *nm* San Nicolás, Papá Noel.
Santiago [ˌsæntɪ'ɑːgəʊ] *n* (*Chile*) Santiago *m* (de Chile); (*Spain*) **~ de Compostela** Santiago *m* (de Compostela).
sap[1] [sæp] *n* (*Bot*) savia *f*; (*fig*) jugo *m* (vital), vitalidad *f.*
sap[2] [sæp] (*Mil*) **1** *n* zapa *f.* **2** *vt* zapar; socavar; *strength etc* minar, agotar.
sap[3]* [sæp] *n* bobo *m*; **you ~!** ¡bobo!
sapling ['sæplɪŋ] *n* pimpollo *m*, árbol *m* nuevo, arbolito *m.*
sapper ['sæpəʳ] *n* (*Brit*) zapador *m.*
sapphire ['sæfaɪəʳ] **1** *n* zafiro *m.* **2** *attr*: **~ blue** azul zafiro; **~ (blue) sky** cielo *m* azul zafiro.
sappiness ['sæpɪnɪs] *n* jugosidad *f.*
sappy[1] ['sæpɪ] *adj* (*Bot*) lleno de savia, jugoso.
sappy[2]* ['sæpɪ] *adj* bobo.
SAR *n abbr of* **Search and Rescue** Servicio *m* de Búsqueda y Salvamento.
saraband ['særəbænd] *n* zarabanda *f.*
Saracen ['særəsn] **1** *adj* sarraceno. **2** *n* sarraceno *m*, -a *f.*
Saragossa [ˌsærə'gɒsə] *n* Zaragoza *f.*
Sarah ['sɛərə] *nf* Sara.
sarcasm ['sɑːkæzəm] *n* sarcasmo *m.*
sarcastic [sɑː'kæstɪk] *adj* sarcástico.
sarcastically [sɑː'kæstɪkəlɪ] *adv* con sarcasmo, sarcásticamente.
sarcoma [sɑː'kəʊmə] *n* sarcoma *m.*
sarcophagus [sɑː'kɒfəgəs] *n, pl* **sarcophagi** [sɑː'kɒfəgaɪ] sarcófago *m.*
sardine [sɑː'diːn] *n* sardina *f.*
Sardinia [sɑː'dɪnɪə] *n* Cerdeña *f.*
Sardinian [sɑː'dɪnɪən] **1** *adj* sardo. **2** *n* sardo *m*, -a *f.*
sardonic [sɑː'dɒnɪk] *adj* burlón, irónico, sarcástico, sardónico.
sardonically [sɑː'dɒnɪkəlɪ] *adv* con aire burlón, irónicamente, con sarcasmo.
sarge* [sɑːdʒ] *n* = **sergeant**; **yes ~** sí, mi sargento.
sari ['sɑːrɪ] *n* sari *m.*
sarky* ['sɑːkɪ] *adj* = **sarcastic.**
sarnie* ['sɑːnɪ] *n* (*Brit*) bocata* *f.*
sarsaparilla [ˌsɑːsəpə'rɪlə] *n* zarzaparrilla *f.*
sartorial [sɑː'tɔːrɪəl] *adj* relativo al vestido; **~ elegance** elegancia *f* en el vestido; **~ taste** gusto *m* en vestidos.
SAS *n* (*Brit Mil*) *abbr of* **Special Air Service.**
s.a.s.e. *n* (*US*) *abbr of* **self-addressed stamped envelope** *sobre m con las propias señas de uno y con sello.*
sash[1] [sæʃ] *n* faja *f*; (*Mil*: *of order*) fajín *m.*
sash[2] [sæʃ] *n* (*window ~*) marco *m* corredizo de ventana.
sashay* [sæ'ʃeɪ] *vi* pasearse; **to ~ off** largarse*.
sashcord ['sæʃkɔːd] *n* cuerda *f* de ventana (de guillotina).
sash-window ['sæʃˌwɪndəʊ] *n* ventana *f* de guillotina.
Sask. (*Canada*) *abbr of* **Saskatchewan.**
sass* [sæs] (*US*) **1** *n* réplicas *fpl*, descoco *m.* **2** *vt*: **to ~ sb** replicar a uno.
sassafras ['sæsəfræs] *n* sasafrás *m.*
Sassenach ['sæsənæx] *n* (*Scot*: *sometimes pej*) inglés *m*, -esa *f.*
sassy* ['sæsɪ] *adj* (*US*) fresco*, descarado.
SAT *n* (*US*) *abbr of* **Scholastic Aptitude Test.**
sat [sæt] *pret and ptp of* **sit.**
Sat. *n abbr of* **Saturday** sábado *m*, sáb.
Satan ['seɪtn] *nm* Satanás, Satán.
satanic [sə'tænɪk] *adj* satánico.
satchel ['sætʃəl] *n* bolsa *f*, cartera *f*; (*schoolboy's*) cartera *f*, cabás *m*, mochila *f* (*LAm*).
sate [seɪt] *vt* saciar, hartar.
sateen [sæ'tiːn] *n* satén *m.*
satellite ['sætəlaɪt] **1** *n* satélite *m.* **2** *attr*: **~ broadcasting** transmisión *f* por satélite; **~ country** país *m* satélite; **~ dish** antena *f* parabólica para TV por satélite; **~ town** ciudad *f* satélite; **~ TV** TV *f* por satélite.
satiate ['seɪʃɪeɪt] *vt* saciar, hartar.
satiated ['seɪʃɪeɪtɪd] *adj* (*with food*) harto; (*with pleasures*) saciado.
satiation [ˌseɪʃɪ'eɪʃən] *n*, **satiety** [sə'taɪətɪ] *n* saciedad *f*, hartura *f*; **to ~** hasta la saciedad.
satin ['sætɪn] **1** *n* raso *m.* **2** *adj* (*also* **satiny** ['sætɪnɪ]) terso, liso; lustroso; **with a ~ finish** satinado.
satinwood ['sætɪnwʊd] *n* madera *f* satinada de las Indias, doradillo *m*, satín *m.*
satire ['sætaɪəʳ] *n* sátira *f.*
satiric(al) [sə'tɪrɪk(əl)] *adj* satírico.
satirically [sə'tɪrɪkəlɪ] *adv* satíricamente.
satirist ['sætərɪst] *n* escritor *m* satírico, escritora *f* satírica.
satirize ['sætəraɪz] *vt* satirizar.
satisfaction [ˌsætɪs'fækʃən] *n* satisfacción *f*; (*of debt*) pago *m*, liquidación *f*; **to the general ~** con la satisfacción de todos; **has it been done to your ~?** ¿se ha hecho a tu satisfacción?; **to demand ~** pedir satisfacción; **to express one's ~ at a result** expresar su satisfacción con un resultado, declararse satisfecho con un resultado; **it gives every** (*or* **full**) **~** es completamente satisfactorio; **it gives me much ~ to introduce ...** es para mí un verdadero placer presentar a ...
satisfactorily [ˌsætɪs'fæktərɪlɪ] *adv* satisfactoriamente, de modo satisfactorio.
satisfactory [ˌsætɪs'fæktərɪ] *adj* satisfactorio.
satisfy ['sætɪsfaɪ] **1** *vt* satisfacer; *debt* pagar, liquidar; *condition* satisfacer, llenar; (*convince*) convencer; **he is never satisfied** no está contento nunca, no se da nunca por satisfecho; **it completely satisfies me** me satisface completamente; **to ~ sb that ...** convencer a uno de que ...; **I am not satisfied that ...** no estoy convencido de que ...; **to ~ the requirements** llenar los requisitos; **to ~ the examiners** aprobar; **you'll have to be satisfied with that** tendrás que contentarte con eso; **we are very satisfied with it** estamos perfectamente satisfechos con él, nos satisface completamente.

2 *vr*: **to ~ o.s. about sth** satisfacerse con algo; **to ~ o.s. that ...** convencerse de que ...
satisfying ['sætɪsfaɪɪŋ] *adj* satisfactorio, que satisface; agradable; *food, meal* bueno, que llena.
satsuma [ˌsæt'suːmə] *n* satsuma *f.*
saturate ['sætʃəreɪt] **1** *vt* saturar, empapar (*with* de); **to be ~d with** (*fig*) estar empapado de. **2** *vr*: **to ~ o.s. in** (*fig*) empaparse en.
saturated ['sætʃəreɪtɪd] *adj*: **~ fat** grasa *f* saturada.
saturation [ˌsætʃə'reɪʃən] **1** *n* saturación *f.* **2** *attr*: **~ bombing** bombardeo *m* por saturación; **~ diving** buceo *m* de saturación; **~ point** punto *m* de saturación.
Saturday ['sætədɪ] *n* sábado *m.*
Saturn ['sætən] *nm* Saturno.
Saturnalia [ˌsætə'neɪlɪə] *npl* saturnales *fpl.*
saturnine ['sætənaɪn] *adj* saturnino.
satyr ['sætəʳ] *n* sátiro *m.*
sauce [sɔːs] *n* **(a)** (*Culin*) salsa *f*; (*sweet*) crema *f*; (*apple ~*) compota *f*; **what's ~ for the goose is ~ for the gander** lo que es bueno para uno es bueno para el otro.

(b) (*) frescura* *f*; **what ~!** ¡qué fresco*!; **none of your ~!** ¡eres un fresco*!
sauceboat ['sɔːsbəʊt] *n* salsera *f.*
saucepan ['sɔːspən] *n* cacerola *f*, cazo *m.*
saucer ['sɔːsəʳ] *n* platillo *m.*
saucily ['sɔːsɪlɪ] *adv reply etc* con frescura; con coquetería.
sauciness ['sɔːsɪnɪs] *n* frescura *f*, descaro *m*, desfachatez *f*; coquetería *f.*
saucy ['sɔːsɪ] *adj* fresco, descarado, desfachatado; *girl* coqueta; *hat etc* coquetón; **don't be ~!** ¡qué fresco!
Saudi ['saʊdɪ] **1** *adj* saudí, saudita. **2** *n* saudí *mf*, saudita *mf.*
Saudi Arabia ['saʊdɪə'reɪbɪə] *n* Arabia *f* Saudí, Arabia *f* Saudita.
Saudi Arabian ['saʊdɪə'reɪbɪən] *adj* = **Saudi.**
sauerkraut ['saʊəkraʊt] *n* chucrut *m*, chucrú *m.*
Saul [sɔːl] *nm* Saúl.
sauna ['sɔːnə] *n* sauna *f.*
saunter ['sɔːntəʳ] **1** *n* paseo *m* (lento y tranquilo); **to have a ~ in the park** dar un paseo tranquilo en el parque.

2 *vi* pasearse (despacio y tranquilamente); **to ~ up and down** deambular, pasearse despacio de acá para allá; **he ~ed up to me** se acercó a mí con mucha calma.
saurian ['sɔːrɪən] *n* saurio *m.*
sausage ['sɒsɪdʒ] *n* (*gen*) embutido *m*; (*small*) salchicha *f*; **not a ~*!** ¡ni un botón!, ¡nada de nada!
sausage dog* ['sɒsɪdʒˌdɒg] *n* perro *m* salchicha*.
sausage-machine ['sɒsɪdʒməˌʃiːn] *n* embutidora *f.*
sausage-meat ['sɒsɪdʒmiːt] *n* masa *f* del embutido; carne *f* de salchicha.
sausage-roll ['sɒsɪdʒ'rəʊl] *n* (*esp Brit*) empanadilla *f* de salchicha.
sauté ['səʊteɪ] **1** *adj* salteado. **2** *vt* saltear.
savage ['sævɪdʒ] **1** *adj* salvaje; *attack* feroz, furioso, violento; **to be ~*** estar rabioso; **to get ~*** ponerse ne-

gro*.

2 *n* salvaje *mf.*

3 *vt* (*of animal*) embestir, atacar, morder; (*fig*) atacar ferozmente.

savagely ['sævɪdʒlɪ] *adv* de modo salvaje; ferozmente, furiosamente, violentamente; **he said ~** dijo furioso.

savageness ['sævɪdʒnɪs] *n*, **savagery** ['sævɪdʒrɪ] *n* salvajismo *m*, salvajería *f*; ferocidad *f*, furia *f*, violencia *f*.

savannah [sə'vænə] *n* sabana *f*.

savant ['sævənt] *n* sabio *m*, erudito *m*, intelectual *m*.

save[1] [seɪv] **1** *vt* (**a**) (*rescue*) salvar; rescatar; **to ~ sb's life** salvar la vida a uno; **to ~ sb from death** salvar a uno de la muerte, rescatar a uno de la muerte; **to ~ sb from falling** impedir que caiga uno, agarrarse a uno para que no se caiga; **to ~ appearances** salvar las apariencias; **to ~ the situation** salvar la situación; **to ~ one's soul** salvarse; **I couldn't do it to ~ my soul** (*or* **life**) no lo podría hacer por nada del mundo; **God ~ the Queen** Dios guarde a la Reina, Dios salve a la Reina; **God ~ us all!** ¡que Dios nos ayude!; **to ~ a building for posterity** lograr conservar un edificio para la posteridad; **to ~ one's eyes** cuidarse la vista; **to ~ sth from the wreck** salvar algo de las ruinas.

(**b**) (*put by*; *also* **to ~ up**) guardar, reservar; (*preserve*) conservar; *money etc* ahorrar; *stamps etc* coleccionar; (*Comput*) salvar, grabar, guardar; **~ as you earn** (*savings scheme*) ahorre mientras gana; **I ~d this for you** guardé esto para ti; **~ me a seat** resérvame un asiento; **she has £2000 ~d** sus ahorros suman 2000 libras.

(**c**) (*avoid using up*) *time etc* ahorrar; economizar; **to ~ time ...** para ahorrar tiempo ..., para ganar tiempo ...; **this way you ~ £8** por este sistema te ahorras 8 libras; **this way you ~ 4 miles** por esta ruta te ahorras 4 millas; **it ~s fuel** economiza combustible; **he's saving his strength for tomorrow** se reserva para mañana.

(**d**) (*prevent*) evitar, impedir; **to ~ a goal** parar un tiro, impedir que se marque un gol; **it ~d a lot of trouble** evitó muchas molestias, evitó muchos disgustos; **to ~ sb trouble** evitar molestias a uno.

2 *vi* ahorrar, economizar, hacer economías; **to ~ on petrol** ahorrar gasolina.

3 *vr*: **to ~ o.s. for** reservarse para.

4 *n* (*Sport*) parada *f*.

◆**save up 1** *vt dinero* ahorrar.

2 *vi*: **to ~ up for a new bicycle** ahorrar dinero para comprar una bicicleta.

save[2] [seɪv] *prep and conj* (*esp liter*) salvo, excepto, con excepción de; **all ~ one** todos excepto uno, todos menos uno; **~ for** excepto; si no fuera por; **~ that ...** excepto que ...

saveloy ['sævəlɔɪ] *n salchicha seca muy sazonada.*

saver ['seɪvə^r] *n* (**a**) (*having account*) ahorrador *m*, -ora *f*; **small ~** ahorrador *m* pequeño, ahorradora *f* pequeña. (**b**) (*by nature*) persona *f* ahorrativa. (**c**) (*ticket*) billete-abono *m*.

saving ['seɪvɪŋ] **1** *adj* (**a**) económico; (*pej*) tacaño; **she's not the ~ sort** no es de las que economizan.

(**b**) **~ clause** cláusula *f* que contiene una salvedad; **~ grace** virtud *f*, mérito *m*; **it has the ~ grace that ...** tiene el mérito excepcional de que ...

2 *n* (**a**) (*act*: *rescue*) salvamento *m*, rescate *m*; (*Eccl*) salvación *f*.

(**b**) (*of money etc*) ahorro *m*; (*of cost etc*) economía *f*; **~s** ahorros *mpl*; **she has ~s of £3000** sus ahorros suman 3000 libras; **to live on one's ~s** vivir de sus ahorros; **we must make ~s** tenemos que economizar.

3 *attr*: **~s account** cuenta *f* de ahorros; **~s bond** bono *m* de ahorros; **~s certificate** bono *m* de caja de ahorros; **~s and loan association** (*US*) sociedad *f* inmobiliaria, cooperativa *f* de construcciones.

savings-bank ['seɪvɪŋzbæŋk] *n* caja *f* de ahorros.

savings-stamp ['seɪvɪŋz,stæmp] *n* sello *m* de ahorros.

saviour, (*US*) **savior** ['seɪvjə^r] *n* salvador *m*, -ora *f*; **S~** Salvador *m*.

savoir-faire ['sævwɑː'fɛə^r] *n* desparpajo *m*; habilidad *f* práctica; sentido *m* común; don *m* de gentes.

savor ['seɪvə^r] *etc* (*US*) = **savour** *etc*.

savory[1] ['seɪvərɪ] *n* (*Bot*) tomillo *m* salsero.

savory[2] ['seɪvərɪ] (*US*) = **savoury**.

savour, (*US*) **savor** ['seɪvə^r] **1** *n* sabor *m*, gusto *m*; (*aftertaste*) dejo *m*; (*fig*) sabor *m* (*of* a); **it has lost its ~** ha perdido su sabor.

2 *vt* saborear, paladear; (*fig*) saborear.

3 *vi*: **to ~ of** saber a, oler a (*also fig*).

savouriness, (*US*) **savoriness** ['seɪvərɪnɪs] *n* sabor *m*, buen sabor *m*, lo sabroso.

savourless, (*US*) **savorless** ['seɪvəlɪs] *adj* soso, insípido.

savoury, (*US*) **savory**[2] ['seɪvərɪ] **1** *adj* (*appetizing*) sabroso, apetitoso; (*not sweet*) no dulce; (*salted*) salado; **not very ~** (*fig*) no muy respetable, poco decente; **it's not a very ~ district** es un barrio de mala fama.

2 *n* plato *m* salado (*que empieza o termina una comida*).

Savoy [sə'vɔɪ] *n* Saboya *f*.

savoy [sə'vɔɪ] *n* berza *f* de Saboya.

savvy* ['sævɪ] **1** *n* inteligencia *f*; desparpajo *m*. **2** *vt* comprender; **~?** ¿comprende?

saw[1] [sɔː] **1** *n* sierra. **2** *attr*: **~ edge** filo *m* dentado (*or* de sierra). **3** (*irr*: *pret* **sawed**, *ptp* **sawed** *or* **sawn**) *vt* serrar.

◆**saw away 1** *vt* quitar con la sierra.

2 *vi*: **she was ~ing away at the violin** iba rascando el violín.

◆**saw off** *vt* quitar con la sierra.

◆**saw up** *vt* cortar con la sierra.

saw[2] [sɔː] *n* refrán *m*, dicho *m*.

saw[3] [sɔː] *pret of* **see**[1].

sawbench ['sɔːbentʃ] *n*, **sawbuck** ['sɔːbʌk] *n* (*US*) caballete *m* para serrar.

sawbones* ['sɔːbəʊnz] *n* matasanos *m*.

sawdust ['sɔːdʌst] *n* serrín *m*.

sawed-off ['sɔːdɒf] *adj* (*US*), **sawn-off** ['sɔːnɒf] *adj*: **~ shotgun** escopeta *f* de cañones recortados, recortada *f*, recortado *m* (*SC*).

sawfish ['sɔːfɪʃ] *n* pez *m* sierra.

sawhorse ['sɔːhɔːs] *n* caballete *m* para serrar.

sawmill ['sɔːmɪl] *n* aserradero *m*.

sawn [sɔːn] *ptp of* **saw**[1] **3**.

sawyer ['sɔːjə^r] *n* aserrador *m*.

sax* [sæks] *n* saxo* *m*.

saxhorn ['sækshɔːn] *n* bombardino *m*.

saxifrage ['sæksɪfrɪdʒ] *n* saxífraga *f*.

Saxon ['sæksn] **1** *adj* sajón. **2** *n* sajón *m*, -ona *f*.

Saxony ['sæksənɪ] *n* Sajonia *f*.

saxophone ['sæksəfəʊn] *n* saxofón *m*, saxófono *m*.

saxophonist [,sæk'sɒfənɪst] *n* saxofón *m*, saxófono *m*, saxofonista *mf*.

say [seɪ] **1** *n*: **to have a** (*or* **some**) **~ in sth** tener voz y voto; **to have no ~ in sth** no tener voz en capítulo; **I had no ~ in it** no tuve nada que ver con ello, no pidieron mi parecer acerca de ello; **if I had had a ~ in it** si hubieran pedido mi parecer; **I have had my ~** he dicho lo que quería; **to let sb have his ~** dejar hablar a uno; **let him have his ~!** ¡que hable él!

2 (*irr*: *pret and ptp* **said**) *vt* (**a**) (*gen*) decir; *mass* decir; *prayer* rezar; *lesson* recitar; **to ~ yes** decir que sí; **to ~ no** decir que no; **to ~ yes to an invitation** aceptar una invitación; **to ~ no to a proposal** rechazar una propuesta; **to ~ good-bye to sb** despedirse de uno; **to ~ good morning to sb** dar los buenos días a uno; **they ~** se dice, dicen; **to ~ to o.s.** decir para sí; **who shall I ~?** ¿qué nombre digo?

(**b**) (*idioms*) **that is to ~** es decir, esto es; **to ~ nothing of the rest** y no digamos de los demás; **to ~ nothing of swearing** sin mencionar lo de decir palabrotas (*and V* **nothing 1 (d)**); **his suit ~s a lot about him** su traje dice mucho de él; **I will ~ this about him: he's bright** reconozco (a pesar de todo) que es listo; **it's an original, not to ~ revolutionary, idea** la idea es original y hasta revolucionaria; **~ what you like about her hat, she's charming** dígase lo que se quiera acerca de su sombrero, es encantadora; **to ~ the least** para no decir más; **as one might ~** como si dijéramos; **that's ~ing a lot** ya es decir; **would you really ~ so?** ¿lo crees de veras?; **what would you ~ to that?** ¿qué contestas a eso?; **what would you ~ to a cup of tea?** ¿te apetece una taza de té?, ¿se te antoja una taza de té? (*LAm*); **I wouldn't ~ no to a gin** no me vendría mal una ginebra; **what have you got to ~ for yourself?** ¿qué puedes decir en tu defensa?; ¿cómo te vas a justificar?; **she hasn't much to ~ for herself** es muy reservada, no es nada habladora; **that doesn't ~ much for her** eso no dice mucho en su favor; **it doesn't ~ much for his intelligence** eso no dice mucho a favor de su inteligencia; **it ~s much for his courage that he stayed** el que permaneciera allí demuestra su valor; **it goes without ~ing that ...** ni que decir tiene que ...; **that goes without ~ing** eso cae de su peso; **there's no ~ing** nadie lo sabe; **there's no ~ing what he'll do** podría hacer cualquier cosa; **though I ~** (*or* **~s***) **it myself, though I ~** (*or* **~s***) **it as shouldn't** aunque soy yo el que lo dice.

(**c**) (*exclamatory idioms*) **~!** (*US*), **I ~!** (*calling attention*) ¡oiga!, (*in surprise*) ¡caramba!; **you don't ~** (**so**)! ¡parece mentira!, ¿de veras?; **I should ~ so!, you can ~ that again!** ¡ya lo creo!; ¡bien dicho!; **you've said it!** ¡eso es!; **so you ~!** ¡es Vd quien lo dice!; **~ no more!** ¡basta!, ¡ni una palabra más!

(**d**) (*phrases with ptp* **said**) **it is said that ...** se dice que ...; **he is said to be worth a million** se dice que es millonario; **there is sth to be said for it** hay algunas razones a favor de esa opinión (*etc*); **there is a lot to be said for doing it now** hay buenas razones por las que conviene hacerlo ahora; **there is sth to be said on both sides** hay algo que decir en pro y en contra; **when all is said and done there's no money for it** total que no hay dinero para ello, a fin de cuentas no hay dinero para ello; **it's easier said than done** eso se dice muy pronto; del dicho al hecho hay gran trecho; **no sooner said than done** dicho y hecho; **well said!** ¡muy bien dicho!; **enough said!** ¡basta!; al buen entendedor pocas palabras le bastan.

(**e**) (*suppose*) **~ it is worth £20** pongamos por caso que vale 20 libras; **we sell it at ~ £25** pongamos que lo vendemos por 25 libras; **we were going at ~ 80 kph** íbamos a 80 kph más o menos; **shall we ~ £5?** ¿convenimos en 5 libras?; **shall we ~ Tuesday?** ¿para el martes, pues?

(**f**) (*admit*) decir; confesar, admitir; **I must ~ she's very pretty** tengo que reconocer que es muy guapa; **it's difficult, I must ~** es difícil, lo confieso.

(**g**) (*register*: *dial etc*) marear, señalar; (*text*) decir, rezar; **my watch ~s 3 o'clock** mi reloj marca las 3; **it ~s 30 degrees** marca 30 grados.

SAYE *abbr of* **save as you earn.**

saying ['seɪɪŋ] *n* dicho *m*, refrán *m*; **as the ~ goes** como dice el refrán, como dijo el otro; **it's just a ~** es un refrán, es un decir.

say-so* ['seɪsəʊ] *n* (**a**) (*rumour*) rumor *m* (infundado); (*statement*) aserto *m*; **we have only his ~ for this accusation** esta acusación depende solamente de su aserto.

(**b**) (*authority*) autoridad *f*; aprobación *f*; decisión *f*; **it depends on his ~** necesita su visto bueno.

SBA *n* (*US*) *abbr of* **Small Business Administration.**

SC (**a**) *n* (*US*) *abbr of* **Supreme Court.** (**b**) (*US Post*) *abbr of* **South Carolina.**

s.c. *abbr of* **self-contained.**

scab [skæb] *n* (**a**) (*Med*) costra *f*. (**b**) (*Vet*) roña *f*. (**c**) (*) esquirol *m*.

scabbard ['skæbəd] *n* vaina *f* (de espada).

scabby ['skæbɪ] *adj* (**a**) costroso; lleno de costras. (**b**) (*Vet*) roñoso.

scabies ['skeɪbiːz] *n* sarna *f*.

scabious¹ ['skeɪbɪəs] *adj* (*Med*) sarnoso.

scabious² ['skeɪbɪəs] *n* (*Bot*) escabiosa *f*.

scabrous ['skeɪbrəs] *adj* escabroso.

scads* [skædz] *npl* montones* *mpl*; **we have ~ of it** lo tenemos a montones*, tenemos montones de eso*.

scaffold ['skæfəld] *n* (*Archit*) andamio *m*; (*for execution*) cadalso *m*, patíbulo *m*.

scaffolding ['skæfəldɪŋ] *n* andamio *m*, andamiaje *m*.

scalawag ['skæləwæg] *n* (*US*) = **scallywag.**

scald [skɔːld] **1** *n* escaldadura *f*.

2 *vt o.s., skin etc* escaldar, quemar con agua caliente; *milk* calentar; *instruments* esterilizar con agua caliente; **to ~ out a saucepan** escaldar una cacerola.

scalding ['skɔːldɪŋ] *adj*: **~ hot** hirviendo, hirviente; **the soup is ~** la sopa está muy caliente.

scale¹ [skeɪl] **1** *n* (*of fish etc*) escama *f*; (*flake*) hojuela *f*; laminita *f*; (*of skin*) costra *f*; (*on teeth*) sarro *m*.

2 *vt fish* escamar; (*Tech*) raspar; *teeth* quitar el sarro a.

3 *vi* (*also* **to ~ off**) descamarse; desconcharse.

scale² [skeɪl] **1** *n* (*of balance*) platillo *m*; **~s** balanza *f*, (*for heavy weights*) báscula *f*; **the S~** (*Zodiac*) Libra *f*; **to turn** (*or* **tip**) **the ~s** (*fig*) inclinar la balanza, decidirlo; **he turns the ~s at 80 kilos** pesa 80 kilos.

2 *vi* pesar; **it ~s 4 kilos** pesa 4 kilos.

scale³ [skeɪl] **1** *n* escala *f* (*also Math, Mus*); (*of salaries*) escalafón *m*, banda *f*; **~ of charges** tarifa *f*, lista *f* de precios; **on a ~ of 5 km to the centimetre** a escala de 5 km al centímetro; **on a big** (*or* **large**) **~** a gran escala, a grande escala; **on a small ~** a pequeña escala; **on a national ~** a escala nacional; **to draw sth to ~** dibujar algo a escala; **the drawing is not to ~** el dibujo no está a escala.

2 *attr*: **~ drawing** dibujo *m* a escala; **~ model** modelo *m* a escala, maqueta *f*.

3 *vt mountain etc* escalar; *tree etc* trepar a.

◆**scale back** (*US*), **scale down** *vt* (*gen*) reducir a escala, reducir proporcionalmente; (*Econ*) reducir, rebajar; (*Comput*) escalar.

◆**scale up** *vt* aumentar a escala, aumentar proporcionalmente; (*Comput*) escalar.

scallion ['skæljən] *n* cebolleta *f* (para ensalada), cebollita *f* (*LAm*), chalote *m*.

scallop ['skɒləp] **1** *n* (**a**) (*Zool*) venera *f*, vieira *f*; **~ shell** venera *f*. (**b**) (*Sew*) festón *m*. **2** *vt* (**a**) (*Culin*) guisar en conchas. (**b**) (*Sew*) festonear.

scallywag ['skælɪwæg] *n* = **scamp¹.**

scalp [skælp] **1** *n* cuero *m* cabelludo, cabellera *f*; (*Anat*) pericráneo *m*; (*fig*) trofeo *m*. **2** *vt* (**a**) escalpar, quitar el cuero cabelludo a. (**b**) (*US**) revender. **3** *vi* (*US**) revender.

scalpel ['skælpəl] *n* escalpelo *m*.

scalper* ['skælpəʳ] *n* (*US*) revendedor *m*, -ora *f*.

scalping ['skælpɪŋ] *n* (*US**) reventa *f*.

scaly ['skeɪlɪ] *adj* escamoso.

scam‡ [skæm] *n* estafa *f*, timo *m*.

scamp¹ [skæmp] *n* tunante *mf*, bribón *m*, -ona *f*; (*child*) diablillo *m*, travieso *m* (*LAm*); **you little ~!** ¡pícaro!

scamp² [skæmp] *vt* chapucear, frangollar.

scamper ['skæmpəʳ] **1** *n* carrera *f* rápida; huida *f* precipitada.

2 *vi* correr, darse prisa; **to ~ along** ir corriendo; **to ~ for the bus** correr para coger el autobús; **to ~ past** pasar corriendo.

◆**scamper about** *vi* corretear.

◆**scamper away, scamper off** *vi* escabullirse, escaparse corriendo.

scampi ['skæmpɪ] *npl* gambas *fpl*.

scan [skæn] **1** *vt* (**a**) (*examine*) escudriñar, examinar; (*Comput*) examinar, explorar; (*glance at*) dar un vistazo a; *horizon etc* explorar con la vista; (*by radar etc*) explorar, registrar.

(**b**) *verse* medir, escandir.

2 *vi* estar bien medido; **it does not ~** no está bien medido.

3 *n* escáner *m*; **to go for a ~, to have a ~** hacerse un escáner.

scandal ['skændl] *n* (**a**) (*disgrace*) escándalo *m*; (*Jur*) difamación *f*; **the groundnuts ~** el escándalo de los cacahuetes; **to cause a ~, to create a ~** hacer un escándalo, armar un lío; **what a ~!, it's a ~!** ¡qué vergüenza!; **it is a ~ that ...** es una vergüenza que ...

(**b**) (*gossip*) chismorreo *m*, murmuración *f*; (*pieces of gossip*) habladurías *fpl*, chismes *mpl*; **the local ~** los chismes del pueblo (*or* del barrio *etc*); **have you heard the latest ~?** ¿te han contado el último chisme?, ¿has oído lo que están diciendo ahora?; **there's a lot of ~ going round about the vicar** se cuentan muchos chismes acerca del pastor; **to talk ~** murmurar, contar chismes.

scandalize ['skændəlaɪz] *vt* escandalizar; **she was ~d** se escandalizó.

scandalmonger ['skændl,mʌŋgəʳ] *n* chismoso *m*, -a *f*.

scandalous ['skændələs] *adj* escandaloso; (*libellous*) difamatorio, calumnioso; **~ talk** habladurías *fpl*, chismes *mpl*; **it's simply ~!** ¡es una vergüenza!, ¡no hay derecho!

scandalously ['skændələslɪ] *adv* escandalosamente.

Scandinavia [,skændɪ'neɪvɪə] *n* Escandinavia *f*.

Scandinavian [,skændɪ'neɪvɪən] **1** *adj* escandinavo. **2** *n* escandinavo *m*, -a *f*.

scandium ['skændɪəm] *n* escandio *m*.

scanner ['skænəʳ] *n* (*Radar*) antena *f* direccional giratoria; (*TV*) dispositivo *m* explorador; (*Comput, Med*) escáner *m*.

scanning ['skænɪŋ] *n* (*Med*) visualización *f* radiográfica; **~ device** detector *m*.

scansion ['skænʃən] *n* escansión *f*; medida *f*.

scant [skænt] *adj* escaso.

scantily ['skæntɪlɪ] *adv* insuficientemente; **~ provided with ...** con escasa provisión de...; **~ dressed** ligeramente vestido, ligero de ropa.

scantiness ['skæntɪnɪs] *n* escasez *f*, cortedad *f*, insuficiencia *f*.

scanty ['skæntɪ] *adj* escaso, corto, insuficiente; *clothing* ligero.

scapegoat ['skeɪpgəʊt] *n* cabeza *f* de turco, chivo *m* expiatorio, víctima *f* propiciatoria; **to be a ~ for** pagar el pato por, pagar los cristales rotos por.

scapegrace ['skeɪpgreɪs] *n* pícaro *m*, bribón *m*.

scapula ['skæpjʊlə] *n* escápula *f*.

scar¹ [skɑːʳ] **1** *n* (*Med*) cicatriz *f*, señal *f*; (*fig*) señal *f*; **it left a deep ~ on his mind** dejó una profunda señal en su espíritu.

2 *vt* dejar una cicatriz en; marcar con una cicatriz,

marcar con cicatrices; (*fig*) señalar, dejar señales en; **he was ~red with many wounds** llevaba las cicatrices de muchas heridas; **he was ~red for life** quedó marcado para toda la vida; **the walls are ~red with bullets** las balas han dejado señales en las paredes.

3 *vi* (*also* **to ~ over**) cicatrizarse.

scar² [skɑːʳ] *n* (*Geog*) paraje *m* rocoso, pendiente *f* rocosa.

scarab [ˈskærəb] *n* escarabajo *m*.

scarce [ˈskɛəs] **1** *adj* escaso; poco común, poco frecuente; **money is ~** escasca el dinero, hay poco dinero; **such people are ~** tales personas son poco frecuentes; **the plant is ~ in the north** en el norte la planta es poco común; **to grow ~** ir escaseando; **to make o.s.* ~** largarse*, esfumarse, rajarse (*LAm*); no dejarse ver.

2 *adv* = **scarcely**.

scarcely [ˈskɛəslɪ] *adv* apenas; **~ 200** apenas 200; **~ anybody** casi nadie; **~ ever** casi nunca; **it will ~ be enough** escasamente alcanzará, apenas bastará; **I could ~ stand up** apenas (si) pude levantarme; **I ~ know what to say** en realidad no sé qué decir.

scarceness [ˈskɛəsnɪs] *n* escasez *f*; poca frecuencia *f*.

scarcity [ˈskɛəsɪtɪ] **1** *n* escasez *f*; poca frecuencia *f*; (*shortage*) carestía *f*; **in years of ~** en años de carestía; **due to the ~ of money** debido a la escasez de dinero.

2 *attr*: **~ value** valor *m* de escasez, valor *m* excesivo debido a la poca frecuencia (de un artículo *etc*).

scare [ˈskɛəʳ] **1** *n* susto *m*, sobresalto *m*; the invasion ~ el pánico de la invasión; los rumores alarmistas de una invasión; **to create** (*or* **raise**) **a ~** infundir miedo a la gente, alarmar a las personas; **to give sb a ~** dar un susto a uno; **what a ~ you gave me!** ¡qué susto me diste!

2 *attr*: **~ campaign** campaña *f* alarmista, campaña *f* de intimidación; **it's only a ~ story** se trata de un reportaje alarmista.

3 *vt* asustar, espantar, infundir miedo a; **to be ~d to death, to be ~d stiff** estar muerto de miedo; **to ~ the hell** (*or* **life**) **out of sb*** meter a uno el ombligo para dentro*; **she was too ~d to talk** estaba demasiado asustada para poder hablar, no podía hablar por el susto; **he's ~d of women** tiene miedo a las mujeres; **don't be ~d** no te asustes, no tengas miedo.

4 *vi*: **he doesn't ~ easily** no se asusta por poca cosa.

◆scare away, scare off *vt* ahuyentar.

scarecrow [ˈskɛəkrəʊ] *n* espantapájaros *m*; (*fig*) espantajo *m*.

scarehead [ˈskɛəhed] *n* (*US*) titulares *mpl* sensacionales.

scaremonger [ˈskɛəmʌŋgəʳ] *n* alarmista *mf*.

scaremongering [ˈskɛəˌmʌŋgərɪŋ] *n* alarmismo *m*.

scarf [skɑːf] *n*, *pl* **scarfs** *or* **scarves** [skɑːvz] bufanda *f*; (*head~*) pañuelo *m*.

scarface [ˈskɑːfeɪs] *n* (*as nickname*) caracortada *mf*.

scarify [ˈskɛərɪfaɪ] *vt* (*Med, Agr*) escarificar; (*fig*) despellejar, desollar, criticar severamente.

scarifying [ˈskɛərɪfaɪɪŋ] *adj attack etc* mordaz, severo.

scarlatina [ˌskɑːləˈtiːnə] *n* escarlatina *f*.

scarlet [ˈskɑːlɪt] **1** *n* escarlata *f*. **2** *adj* color escarlata; **~ fever** escarlatina *f*; **~ pimpernel** mujares *mpl*; **~ runner** judía *f* escarlata; **to blush ~, to turn ~** enrojecer, ponerse colorado; **he was ~ with rage** se puso rojo de furia.

scarp [skɑːp] *n* escarpa *f*, declive *m*.

scarper‡ [ˈskɑːpəʳ] *vi* (*Brit*) largarse*.

scarves [skɑːvz] *npl of* **scarf**.

scary* [ˈskɛərɪ] *adj person etc* asustadizo; *experience* espeluznante; *place* que infunde miedo.

scat* [skæt] *interj* ¡zape!

scathing [ˈskeɪðɪŋ] *adj attack, criticism* mordaz, duro; **he was ~ about our trains** criticó duramente nuestros trenes; **he was pretty ~** tuvo cosas bastante duras que decir.

scathingly [ˈskeɪðɪŋlɪ] *adv* mordazmente, duramente; **he spoke ~ of ...** criticó duramente ...

scatological [ˌskætəˈlɒdʒɪkəl] *adj* escatológico.

scatology [skæˈtɒlədʒɪ] *n* escatología *f*.

scatter [ˈskætəʳ] **1** *n* (*Math, Tech*) dispersión *f*; **a ~ of houses** unas casas dispersas; **a ~ of raindrops** unas cuantas gotas de lluvia.

2 *vt* (*dot about*) esparcir, desparramar; salpicar; *benefits etc* (*also* **to ~ about**) derramar aquí y allá; (*put to flight*) dispersar; *clouds etc* disipar; **the flowers were ~ed about on the floor** las flores estaban desparramadas por el suelo; **the floor was ~ed with flowers** el suelo estaba sembrado de flores dispersas.

3 *vi* desparramarse; dispersarse; **the family ~ed to distant parts** los miembros de la familia se desparramaron por sitios lejanos; **the crowd ~ed** la multitud se dispersó.

4 *attr*: **~ cushions** almohadones *mpl*.

scatterbrain [ˈskætəbreɪn] *n* cabeza *mf* de chorlito.

scatterbrained [ˈskætəbreɪnd] *adj* ligero de cascos, atolondrado.

scattered [ˈskætəd] *adj* disperso; **~ showers** lluvias *fpl* aisladas; **the village is very ~** las casas del pueblo son muy dispersas.

scattering [ˈskætərɪŋ] *n*: **a ~ of books** unos cuantos libros aquí y allá.

scattiness* [ˈskætɪnɪs] *n* (*Brit*) ligereza *f* de cascos, atolondramiento *m*.

scatty* [ˈskætɪ] *adj* (*Brit*) ligero de cascos, atolondrado; **to drive sb ~** volver majareta a uno*, poner chalupa a uno*.

scavenge [ˈskævɪndʒ] **1** *vt* limpiar las calles (*etc*), recoger la basura. **2** *vi*: **to ~ for food** andar buscando comida (entre la basura).

scavenger [ˈskævɪndʒəʳ] *n* (**a**) basurero *m*, barrendero *m*. (**b**) (*Zool*) animal *m* (*or* ave *f etc*) que se alimenta de carroña.

Sc.D. *n abbr of* **Doctor of Science**.

scenario [sɪˈnɑːrɪəʊ] *n* (**a**) (*Cine*) guión *m*. (**b**) (*forecast*) pronóstico *m*; marco *m* hipotético.

scenarist [ˈsiːnərɪst] *n* guionista *mf*.

scene [siːn] **1** *n* (**a**) (*Theat*) escena *f*; **the bedroom ~** la escena del dormitorio; **the big ~ in the film** la principal escena de la película; **behind the ~s** entre bastidores; **the ~ is set in a castle** la acción se desarrolla en un castillo, la escena es en un castillo; **to set the ~ for a love affair** (*fig*) crear el ambiente para una aventura sentimental; **now let our reporter set the ~ for you** ahora permitan que nuestro reportero les describa la escena; **there were unhappy ~s at the meeting** en la reunión pasaron cosas nada agradables.

(**b**) (*place in general*) escenario *m*, teatro *m*, lugar *m*; **the ~ of operations** el teatro de las operaciones; **the ~ of the disaster** el lugar de la catástrofe; **the ~ of the crime** el lugar del crimen, el escenario del crimen; **the ~s of one's early life** los lugares frecuentados por uno en su juventud; **the political ~ in Italy** el escenario político italiano; **to appear** (*or* **come** *etc*) **on the ~** presentarse, llegar; **when I came on the ~** cuando llegué; **he appeared unexpectedly on the ~** se presentó inesperadamente; **to disappear from the political ~** desaparecer del escenario político.

(**c**) (*sight, vision*) vista *f*, perspectiva *f*, panorama *m*; (*landscape*) paisaje *m*; **the ~ from the top is marvellous** desde la cumbre se abarca un panorama maravilloso; **the ~ spread out before you** el panorama que se extiende delante de uno; **it was a ~ of utter destruction** fue una perspectiva de destrucción total; **it is a lonely ~** es un paisaje solitario; **a change of ~ would do you good** le vendría bien un cambio de aire.

(**d**) (*: *environment etc*) ambiente *m*; panorama *m*; movida* *f*; **the pop ~** el mundo pop; **it's not my ~** esto no es lo mío, en este ambiente no estoy bien; **to be part of the Madrid ~** estar en la movida madrileña*.

(**e**) (*: *fuss*) escándalo *m*, lío* *m*, jaleo *m*; **try to avoid a ~** procura no armar un lío*; **I hate ~s** detesto los jaleos; **to make a ~** armar un lío*, armar un escándalo; **she had a ~ with her husband** riñó con su marido.

2 *attr*: **~ change** (*Theat*) cambio *m* de escena.

scene-painter [ˈsiːnˌpeɪntəʳ] *n* (*designer*) escenógrafo *m*, -a *f*, (*workman*) pintor *m*, -ora *f* de decoraciones.

scenery [ˈsiːnərɪ] *n* (**a**) (*landscape*) paisaje *m*. (**b**) (*Theat*) decoraciones *fpl*, decorado *m*.

scene-shifter [ˈsiːnˌʃɪftəʳ] *n* tramoyista *mf*.

scenic [ˈsiːnɪk] *adj* (**a**) (*Theat*) escénico, dramático. (**b**) (*picturesque*) pintoresco; **~ railway** montaña *f* rusa; **~ road** (*US*) ruta *f* turística; **an area of ~ beauty** una región de bellos paisajes.

scenography [siːˈnɒgrəfɪ] *n* escenografía *f*.

scent [sent] **1** *n* (**a**) (*smell*) olor *m*; (*pleasant smell*) perfume *m*, aroma *m*, fragancia *f*; (*Hunting*) rastro *m*, pista *f*; **to be on the ~** seguir la pista (*also fig*; *of* de); **to lose the ~** perder la pista; **to throw sb off the ~** despistar a uno.

(**b**) (*liquid*) perfume *m*.

(**c**) (*sense of smell*) olfato *m*.

2 *vt* (**a**) (*add ~ to*) perfumar (*with* de).

(**b**) (*smell*) oler; *danger etc* percibir, sospechar; **to ~ sth out** olfatear algo, husmear algo.

scent-bottle [ˈsentˌbɒtl] *n* frasco *m* de perfume.

scented [ˈsentɪd] *adj* perfumado.

scentless [ˈsentlɪs] *adj* inodoro.

scent-spray [ˈsentspreɪ] *n* atomizador *m* (de perfume), pulverizador *m* (de perfume).

scepter ['septəʳ] *n* (*US*) = **sceptre.**

sceptic, (*US*) **skeptic** ['skeptɪk] *n* escéptico *m*, -a *f*.

sceptical, (*US*) **skeptical** ['skeptɪkəl] *adj* escéptico; **he was ~ about it** se mostró escéptico acerca de ello, tenía dudas sobre ello.

sceptically, (*US*) **skeptically** ['skeptɪkəlɪ] *adv* escépticamente.

scepticism, (*US*) **skepticism** ['skeptɪsɪzəm] *n* escepticismo *m*.

sceptre, (*US*) **scepter** ['septəʳ] *n* cetro *m*.

schedule ['ʃedju:l, *US* 'skedju:l] **1** *n* (*list*) lista *f*; (*timetable*) horario *m*; (*of events etc*) programa *m*; (*of charges, prices*) lista *f*; (*of questions*) cuestionario *m*; (*legal document*) inventario *m*, apéndice *m*; (*of work to be done etc*) programa *m*, plan *m*; **the train is behind ~** el tren lleva un retraso; **the bus was on ~** el autobús llegó a la hora debida, el autobús llegó sin retraso; **the work is up to ~** los trabajos llevan el ritmo adecuado, los trabajos avanzan de acuerdo con lo previsto; **we are working to a very tight ~** trabajamos de acuerdo con un plan riguroso; **our ~ did not include the Prado** nuestro programa de visitas no incluía el Museo del Prado.

2 *vt* (*list*) poner en una lista, hacer una lista de; catalogar, inventariar; (*plan*) proyectar, redactar el plan de; *trains etc* establecer el horario de; (*Rad, TV etc*) programar; *visit, lecture etc* fijar la hora de, programar; **as ~d** según (lo) previsto; **~d building** monumento *m* histórico, edificio *m* declarado de interés histórico-artístico; **~d flight** vuelo *m* regular; **~d stop** parada *f* prevista, escala *f* prevista; **this stop is not ~d** esta parada no es oficial; **the plane is ~d for 2 o'clock, the plane is ~d to land at 2 o'clock** según el horario el avión debe llegar a las 2; **you are ~d to speak for 20 minutes** según el programa hablarás durante 20 minutos; **this building is ~d for demolition** se prevé la demolición de este edificio.

scheduling ['ʃedju:lɪŋ] *n* (*Comput*) planificación *f*.

Scheldt [ʃelt] *n* Escalda *m*.

schema ['ski:mə] *n, pl* **schemata** ['ski:mətə] esquema *m*.

schematic [skɪ'mætɪk] *adj* esquemático.

scheme [ski:m] **1** *n* (**a**) (*arrangement*) disposición *f*; combinación *f*; (*of colours etc*) combinación *f*; (*of rhymes*) esquema *m*, combinación *f*; **man's place in the ~ of things** el puesto del hombre en el diseño divino; **in the government's ~ of things there is no place for protest** la política del gobierno no deja espacio para la protesta.

(**b**) (*systematic table*) plan *m*, esquema *m*; (*diagram*) diagrama *m*; (*summary*) resumen *m*.

(**c**) (*plan*) plan *m*, proyecto *m*; (*idea*) idea *f*; (*US: shady deal*) asunto *m* poco limpio, negocio *m* turbio; **the ~ for the new bridge** el proyecto del nuevo puente; **it's some crazy ~ of his** es una idea estrafalaria de las de él; **it's not a bad ~** no es mala idea.

(**d**) (*plot*) intriga *f*; (*ruse*) treta *f*, ardid *m*; **it's a ~ to get him out of the way** es una jugada para quitarle de en medio.

2 *vt* (*plan*) proyectar; (*pej*) tramar, urdir.

3 *vi* (*plan*) hacer proyectos, formar planes; (*pej*) intrigar; **they're scheming to get me out** están intrigando para expulsarme.

schemer ['ski:məʳ] *n* intrigante *mf*.

scheming ['ski:mɪŋ] **1** *adj* intrigante; astuto, mañoso. **2** *n* intrigas *fpl*.

scherzo ['skɜ:tsəʊ] *n* scherzo *m*.

schism ['sɪzəm, 'skɪzəm] *n* cisma *m*.

schismatic [sɪz'mætɪk, skɪz'mætɪk] **1** *adj* cismático. **2** *n* cismático *m*.

schismatical [sɪz'mætɪkəl, skɪz'mætɪkəl] *adj* cismático.

schist [ʃɪst] *n* esquisto *m*.

schizo* ['skɪtsəʊ] *n* (*Brit*) esquizo* *m*, -a *f*.

schizoid ['skɪtsɔɪd] **1** *adj* esquizoide. **2** *n* esquizoide *mf*.

schizophrenia [ˌskɪtsəʊ'fri:nɪə] *n* esquizofrenia *f*.

schizophrenic [ˌskɪtsəʊ'frenɪk] **1** *adj* esquizofrénico. **2** *n* esquizofrénico *m*, -a *f*.

schlemiel* [ʃlə'mi:l] *n* (*US*) (*clumsy*) persona *f* desmañada; (*unlucky*) persona *f* desgraciada.

schmaltz* [ʃmɔ:lts] *n* (*US*) sentimentalismo *m*, sensiblería *f*.

schmaltzy* ['ʃmɔ:ltsɪ] *adj* (*US*) sentimental, sensiblero, empalagoso.

schmuck‡ [ʃmʌk] *n* (*US*) imbécil *mf*.

schnapps [ʃnæps] *n* schnapps *m*.

schnozzle‡ ['ʃnɒzəl] *n* (*esp US*) napia‡ *f*, nariz *f*.

scholar ['skɒləʳ] *n* (**a**) (*pupil*) colegial *m*, -ala *f*, alumno *m*, -a *f*, escolar *mf*.

(**b**) (*learned person*) erudito *m*, -a *f*; sabio *m*, -a *f*; **he's a Tirso ~** es especialista en Tirso; **the famous Cervantes ~** el docto cervantista; **I'm no ~** yo apenas sé nada, yo no soy nada intelectual.

(**c**) (*scholarship holder*) becario *m*, -a *f*.

scholarly ['skɒləlɪ] *adj* erudito.

scholarship ['skɒləʃɪp] **1** *n* (**a**) (*learning*) erudición *f*. (**b**) (*money award*) beca *f*. **2** *attr*: **~ holder** becario *m*, -a *f*.

scholastic [skə'læstɪk] **1** *adj* (**a**) (*relative to school*) escolar; **~ books** libros *mpl* escolares; **the ~ year** el año escolar; **the ~ profession** el magisterio. (**b**) (*relative to scholasticism*) escolástico. **2** *n* escolástico *m*.

scholasticism [skə'læstɪsɪzəm] *n* escolasticismo *m*.

school¹ [sku:l] **1** *n* (**a**) (*gen*) escuela *f*; (*primary, specialist, military etc*) escuela *f*; colegio *m*; academia *f*; **the ~s** (*Hist*) las escuelas; **~ of art** escuela *f* de bellas artes; **~ of dancing** escuela *f* de baile, escuela *f* de ballet; **~ of music** academia *f* de música, conservatorio *m*; **to be at ~** estar en la escuela; **we have to be at ~ by 9** tenemos que estar en la clase para las 9; **you weren't at ~ yesterday** ayer faltaste a la clase; **which ~ were you at?** ¿dónde cursó Vd los estudios (del bachillerato)?; **we were at ~ together** fuimos al mismo instituto (*etc*); **to go to ~** ir a la escuela; **to learn in a tough ~** formarse en una escuela dura.

(**b**) (*lessons*) clases *fpl*, clase *f*; curso *m*; **~ starts again in September** el curso empieza de nuevo en septiembre; **there's no ~ today** hoy no hay clase.

(**c**) (*Univ*) departamento *m*, facultad *f*; **in the History ~** en el departamento de Historia; **S~ of Arabic Studies** Escuela *f* de Estudios Árabes.

(**d**) (*US freq*) universidad *f*; **I went back to ~ at 35** a la edad de 35 volví a la universidad.

(**e**) (*of thought etc*) escuela *f*; **Plato and his ~** Platón y su escuela, Platón y sus discípulos; **the Dutch ~** la escuela holandesa; **I am not of that ~** yo no sigo esa opinión; **I am not of the ~ that ...** yo no soy de los que ...; **people of the old ~** gente *f* de la vieja escuela, gente *f* chapada a la antigua.

2 *attr*: **~-age child** niño *m* en edad escolar; **~ attendance** asistencia *f* a la escuela; **~ attendance officer** *funcionario encargado del cumplimiento del reglamento de asistencia*; **~ bus** bus *m* escolar; **~ dinner** comida *f* escolar; **~ doctor** médico *mf* de escuela; **~ fees** cuota *f* de enseñanza; pensión *f* (escolar); **~ holidays** vacaciones *fpl* escolares; **~ hours** horas *fpl* de escuela; **~ inspector** inspector *m*, -ora *f* de enseñanza; **~ life** vida *f* escolar; **~ lunch** almuerzo *m* proveído por la escuela; **to take ~ lunches** comer (*or* almorzar) en la escuela; **~ meal** comida *f* proveída por la escuela; **~ population** población *f* escolar, (cifra *f* de) escolaridad *f*; **~ report** informe *m* escolar, nota *f* escolar; **in ~ time** durante las horas de escuela; **~ uniform** uniforme *m* escolar; **to go on a ~ visit** (*or* **outing** *or* **trip**) **to the zoo** ir de visita al zoo con el colegio; **~ year** año *m* escolar.

3 *vt* instruir, enseñar; disciplinar; **to ~ sb in a technique** instruir a uno en una técnica; **to ~ sb to do sth** enseñar a uno a hacer algo; entrenar a uno para que haga algo; **he has been well ~ed** ha sido bien instruido.

4 *vr*: **to ~ o.s.** instruirse, enseñarse; disciplinarse; **to ~ o.s. in patience** aprender paciencia, disciplinarse para ser paciente.

school² [sku:l] *n* (*Fish*) banco *m*, cardumen *m*.

schoolbag ['sku:lbæg] *n* bolso *m*, cabás *m*.

schoolbook ['sku:lbʊk] *n* libro *m* escolar.

schoolboy ['sku:lbɔɪ] *n* colegial *m*, escolar *m*.

schoolchild ['sku:ltʃaɪld] *n* alumno *m*, -a *f*, escolar *mf*.

schooldays ['sku:ldeɪz] *npl* años *mpl* de colegio.

schoolfellow ['sku:lˌfeləʊ] *n* compañero *m*, -a *f* de clase.

schoolfriend ['sku:lfrend] *n* amigo *m*, -a *f* de clase.

schoolgirl ['sku:lgɜ:l] **1** *n* colegiala *f*, escolar *f*. **2** *attr*: **~ complexion** cutis *m* de colegiala; **~ crush*** amartelamiento *m* de colegiala.

schoolhouse ['sku:lhaʊs] *n, pl* **schoolhouses** ['sku:lhaʊzɪz] escuela *f*.

schooling ['sku:lɪŋ] *n* (*teaching etc*) instrucción *f*, enseñanza *f*; disciplina *f*; **compulsory ~ up to 16** escolaridad *f* obligatoria hasta los 16 años; **~ is free** la enseñanza es gratuita; **he had little formal ~** apenas asistió a la escuela.

school-leaver ['sku:lˌli:vəʳ] *n* joven *mf* que ha terminado los estudios.

school-leaving age [ˌsku:l'li:vɪŋˌeɪdʒ] *n* fin *m* de la escolaridad obligatoria; **to raise the ~** elevar el fin de la escolaridad obligatoria.

schoolman ['sku:lmən] *n, pl* **schoolmen** ['sku:lmən] escolástico *m.*
schoolmarm* ['sku:lmɑ:m] *n (pej)* institutriz *f.*
schoolmaster ['sku:l,mɑ:stəʳ] *n (secondary school)* profesor *m* (de instituto); *(other)* maestro *m.*
schoolmate ['sku:lmeɪt] *n* compañero *m,* -a *f* de clase.
schoolmistress ['sku:l,mɪstrɪs] *n (secondary school)* profesora *f* (de instituto); *(other)* maestra *f.*
schoolroom ['sku:lrʊm] *n* clase *f.*
schoolteacher ['sku:l,ti:tʃəʳ] *n* maestro *m,* -a *f,* profesor *m,* -ora *f.*
schoolteaching ['sku:l,ti:tʃɪŋ] *n* enseñanza *f;* pedagogía *f;* magisterio *m;* **to go in for ~** dedicarse al magisterio.
schoolwork ['sku:lwɜ:k] *n* trabajo *m* de clase.
schoolyard ['sku:ljɑ:d] *n* patio *m* (de recreo).
schooner ['sku:nəʳ] *n* goleta *f.*
schwah [ʃwɑ:] *n* vocal *f* neutra.
sciatic [saɪ'ætɪk] *adj* ciático.
sciatica [saɪ'ætɪkə] *n* ciática *f.*
science ['saɪəns] **1** *n* ciencia *f;* **to blind sb with ~** impresionar *(or* deslumbrar) a uno citándole muchos datos científicos; lucir sus conocimientos para impresionar a uno.
2 *attr:* **~ park** zona *f* de ciencias; **~ teacher** profesor *m,* -ora *f* de ciencias.
science-fiction ['saɪəns,fɪkʃən] *n* ciencia-ficción *f.*
scientific [,saɪən'tɪfɪk] *adj* científico.
scientifically [,saɪən'tɪfɪkəlɪ] *adv* científicamente.
scientist ['saɪəntɪst] *n* científico *m,* -a *f.*
scientologist [,saɪən'tɒlədʒɪst] *n* cientólogo *m,* -a *f.*
scientology [,saɪən'tɒlədʒɪ] *n* cienciología *f,* cientología *f.*
sci-fi* ['saɪ'faɪ] *n abbr of* **science-fiction.**
Scillies ['sɪlɪz] *npl,* **Scilly Isles** ['sɪlɪaɪlz] *npl* Islas *fpl* Sorlinga.
scimitar ['sɪmɪtəʳ] *n* cimitarra *f.*
scintillate ['sɪntɪleɪt] *vi* centellear, chispear; *(fig)* brillar.
scintillating ['sɪntɪleɪtɪŋ] *adj (fig)* brillante; ingenioso; de lo más vivo, animadísimo.
scion ['saɪən] *n (Bot, fig)* vástago *m;* **~ of a noble family** vástago *m* de una familia noble.
Scipio ['skɪpɪəʊ] *nm* Escipión.
scissors ['sɪzəz] *npl* tijeras *fpl;* **a pair of ~** unas tijeras; **~ jump** tijera *f;* **~ kick** chilena *f,* tijereta *f.*
sclerosis [sklɪ'rəʊsɪs] *n* esclerosis *f.*
scoff¹ [skɒf] *vi* mofarse, burlarse *(at* de).
scoff²* [skɒf] **1** *n* comida *f;* **~ up!** ¡la comida está servida!
2 *vt (esp Brit)* zamparse, engullir; **she ~ed the lot** se lo comió todo.
scoffer ['skɒfəʳ] *n* mofador *m,* -ora *f.*
scoffing ['skɒfɪŋ] *n* mofas *fpl,* burlas *fpl.*
scold [skəʊld] **1** *n* virago *f.* **2** *vt* reprender, regañar *(for* por).
scolding ['skəʊldɪŋ] *n* reprensión *f,* regaño *m;* **to give sb a ~** reprender a uno.
scoliosis [,skəʊlɪ'əʊsɪs] *n* escoliosis *f.*
scollop ['skɒləp] = **scallop.**
sconce [skɒns] *n* candelabro *m* de pared.
scone [skɒn] *n* bollo *m.*
scoop [sku:p] **1** *n* **(a)** *(instrument)* pala *f,* paleta *f,* cuchara *f;* *(for bailing)* achicador *m;* *(kitchen implement)* paleta *f;* *(carpenter's)* gubia *f;* *(of dredger)* cuchara *f* (de draga), cangilón *m;* *(Med)* espátula *f.*
(b) *(profit)* ganancia *f* grande; golpe *m* financiero; *(by newspaper)* primicia *f* informativa, exclusiva *f,* pisotón* *m,* escupe* *m;* **it was a ~ for the paper** fue un gran éxito para el periódico; **we brought off the ~** logramos un triunfo con la exclusiva.
2 *vt* **(a)** *grain, liquid etc (also* **to ~ out, to ~ up)** sacar con pala, sacar con cuchara; sacar con achicador.
(b) to ~ the pool llevar las diez de últimas; ganar todas las bazas; **we ~ed the other papers** nos adelantamos a los demás periódicos con nuestra exclusiva.
◆**scoop out** *vt (hollow)* excavar, ahuecar; hacer; *V* **scoop 2.**
◆**scoop up** *vt cards etc* recoger rápidamente; *V* **scoop 2.**
scoot* [sku:t] *vi (also* **to ~ away, to ~ off)** escabullirse, largarse*; correr precipitadamente; ir en una escapadita; **I must ~** tengo que marcharme.
scooter ['sku:təʳ] *n (child's)* patinete *m;* *(adult's)* scooter *m,* escúter *m,* moto *f,* motoneta *f (CAm).*
scope [skəʊp] *n* alcance *m;* envergadura *f;* esfera *f* de acción; ámbito *m;* campo *m,* campo *m* de aplicación; **there is ~ for** hay campo para; **a programme of considerable ~** un programa de gran alcance, un programa de mucha envergadura; **the ~ of the new measures must be defined** conviene delimitar el campo de aplicación de las nuevas medidas; **I'm looking for a job with more ~** busco un puesto que ofrezca más posibilidades; **to give sb full ~** dar carta blanca a uno; **this should give you plenty of ~ for your talents** esto ha de darte grandes posibilidades para explotar tus talentos; **it is outside my ~** eso está fuera de mi alcance; **it is well within his ~** está dentro de su alcance, está bien dentro de su competencia.
scorbutic [skɔ:'bju:tɪk] *adj* escorbútico.
scorch [skɔ:tʃ] **1** *vt* chamuscar; *(of sun, wind)* abrasar; *plants etc* quemar, secar; **~ mark** señal *f* que deja una quemadura; **~ed earth policy** política *f* de tierra quemada; **to ~ the earth** quemar la tierra, destruir todo lo útil; arrasarlo todo.
2 *vi* **(a)** chamuscarse; quemarse, secarse.
(b) to ~ along* *(Brit)* ir volando, correr a gran velocidad.
scorcher* ['skɔ:tʃəʳ] *n* día *m* de mucho calor.
scorching ['skɔ:tʃɪŋ] *adj sun etc* abrasador; *day* de mucho calor; *speed* grande, excesivo; **it's ~ hot** hace un tremendo calor; **a few ~ remarks** algunas observaciones mordaces.
score [skɔ:ʳ] **1** *n* **(a)** *(notch)* muesca *f,* entalladura *f;* señal *f;* *(line)* raya *f,* línea *f.*
(b) *(reckoning)* cuenta *f;* **to pay one's ~** pagar la cuenta; **to pay off old ~s** ajustar cuentas viejas; **to settle an old ~ with sb** desquitarse con uno; **I have a ~ to settle with him** tengo cuentas pendientes con él.
(c) *(in exam, test)* puntuación *f;* *(Sport)* tanteo *m;* tantos *mpl,* puntos *mpl (etc);* **what's the ~?** ¿cómo estamos?, ¿cómo va esto?; **the ~ was Toboso 9, Barataria 1** el resultado fue Toboso 9, Barataria 1; **there was no ~ at half-time** en el primer tiempo no hubo goles; **to keep (the) ~** tantear, llevar la cuenta *(LAm);* **do you know the ~?** ¿sabes cuántos goles han marcado?; **he doesn't know the ~*** no está al tanto, *(pej)* es un despistado, es un pobre hombre; **we all know what the ~ is*** todos estamos al cabo de la calle (en cuanto a eso); **to make a ~** marcar un tanto, marcar un gol *(etc).*
(d) *(Mus)* partitura *f;* *(of film etc)* música *f;* **piano ~** partitura *f* para piano.
(e) *(twenty)* veinte, veintena *f;* **a ~ of people** veinte personas, una veintena de personas; **3 ~ years and 10** 70 años; **there were ~s of mistakes** había muchísimas erratas, había erratas a granel; **actresses by the ~** actrices en cantidades.
(f) *(ground, reason)* **on the ~ of illness** por enfermedad, con motivo de su enfermedad; **on that ~** a ese respecto, por lo que se refiere a eso; **on what ~?** ¿con qué motivo?
2 *vt* **(a)** *(notch)* hacer muescas en, hacer cortes en; señalar; *(line)* rayar; **the wall is heavily ~d with lines** las paredes están profundamente rayadas; **the plane ~d the runway as it landed** al aterrizar el avión hizo rayas en la pista; **to ~ sth through** tachar algo.
(b) *(in exam, test)* obtener una puntuación ...; obtener una nota...; ser calificado de...; *(Sport) goal, points* ganar, apuntar, marcar; *runs* hacer; **to ~ 70%** obtener una puntuación de 70 por ciento; **to ~ well in a test** obtener buena nota en un test; **to ~ a goal** marcar un gol; **they went 5 games without scoring a point** en 5 partidos no apuntaron un solo punto; **they had 14 goals ~d against them** sus adversarios metieron 14 goles contra ellos; **to ~ a great success** marcar un gran triunfo.
(c) *(Mus)* instrumentar, orquestar; **it is ~d for 5 bassoons** está instrumentado para 5 fagots; **the film was ~d by X** la banda musical de la película es de X.
(d) (‡) *drugs* comprar, obtener.
3 *vi* **(a)** *(Sport etc)* marcar un tanto, marcar un gol, ganar puntos *(etc);* **to fail to ~** no marcar ningún gol; **that's where he ~s** en eso es donde tiene más ventajas *(over the others* sobre los otros), es en ese aspecto donde sobresale; **to ~ with a girl*** ligar con una chica*; **to ~ off sb** triunfar a costa de uno, *(with witty remark)* hacer un chiste a costa de uno; **she's easy to ~ off** es fácil hacer chistes a costa suya.
(b) *(keep ~)* tantear, llevar el tanteo.
(c) *(count)* puntuar; **that doesn't ~** eso no puntúa, eso no vale.
(d) (‡) comprar droga.
◆**score off, score out, score through** *vt* tachar.
◆**score up** *vt:* **~ it up to me** apúntelo en mi cuenta.
scoreboard ['skɔ:bɔ:d] *n* tanteador *m,* marcador *m.*
scorebook ['skɔ:bʊk] *n* cuaderno *m* de tanteo.
scorecard ['skɔ:kɑ:d] *n* marcador *m,* tarjeta *f* en que se

lleva el tanteo.
scorekeeper ['skɔːˌkiːpəʳ] *n* tanteador *m*, -ora *f*.
scoreless ['skɔːlɪs] *adj*: ~ **draw** empate *m* a cero.
scorer ['skɔːrəʳ] *n* (*player*) marcador *m*, -ora *f*; (*recorder*) tanteador *m*, -ora *f*; **he is top ~ in the league** es el principal goleador en la liga, ha marcado más goles que ningún otro en la liga; **the ~s were A and B** marcaron los goles A y B.
scoresheet ['skɔːʃiːt] *n* acta *f* (*or* hoja *f*) de tanteo.
scoring ['skɔːrɪŋ] *n* (**a**) (*Sport*) tanteo *m*; **rules for ~** reglas *fpl* para el tanteo; **a low ~ match** un partido de pocos goles (*etc*); **all the ~ was in the second half** todos los goles se marcaron en el segundo tiempo.
(**b**) (*cuts*) muescas *fpl*, cortes *mpl*.
(**c**) (*Mus*) orquestación *f*.
scorn [skɔːn] **1** *n* desprecio *m*, desdén *m* (*for* de); **to laugh sth to ~, to pour ~ on sth** ridiculizar algo, poner algo en ridículo.
2 *vt* despreciar, desdeñar; **to ~ to do sth** desdeñarse de hacer algo, no dignarse hacer algo.
scornful ['skɔːnfʊl] *adj* desdeñoso; **to be ~ about sth** desdeñar algo.
scornfully ['skɔːnfəlɪ] *adv* desdeñosamente, con desprecio.
Scorpio ['skɔːpɪəʊ] *n* (*Zodiac*) Escorpión *m*.
scorpion ['skɔːpɪən] *n* escorpión *m*, alacrán *m*.
Scot [skɒt] *n*, escocés *m*, -esa *f*.
Scotch [skɒtʃ] **1** *adj* escocés; ~ **broth** sopa *f* escocesa; ~ **egg** huevo *m* escocés; ~ **mist** llovizna *f*; ~ **tape** (*US*) ® escotch *m* ®, cinta *f* adhesiva, durex *m* (*Mex*); ~ **terrier** terrier *m* escocés; ~ **whisky** = **2** (**a**). **2** *n* (**a**) whisky *m* (escocés). (**b**) **the** ~ los escoceses.
scotch [skɒtʃ] **1** *n* calza *f*, cuña *f*. **2** *vt wheel* calzar, engalgar; *rumour* desmentir; *idea* hacer abandonar; *plan etc* frustrar.
scot-free ['skɒt'friː] *adj* impune; **to get off ~** (*unpunished*) salir impune, quedar sin castigo, (*unhurt*) salir ileso.
Scotland ['skɒtlənd] **1** *n* Escocia *f*. **2** *attr*: ~ **Yard** *oficina central de la policía de Londres*.
Scots [skɒts] **1** *adj* escocés; ~ **pine** pino *m* escocés. **2** *n* (*Ling*) escocés *m*.
Scotsman ['skɒtsmən] *n*, *pl* **Scotsmen** ['skɒtsmən] escocés *m*.
Scotswoman ['skɒtsˌwʊmən] *n*, *pl* **Scotswomen** ['skɒtsˌwɪmɪn] escocesa *f*.
Scotticism ['skɒtɪsɪzəm] *n* giro *m* escocés, escocesismo *m*.
scottie ['skɒtɪ] *n* terrier *m* escocés.
Scottish ['skɒtɪʃ] *adj* escocés; ~ **Office** Ministerio *m* de Asuntos Escoceses.
scoundrel ['skaʊndrəl] *n* canalla *m*, sinvergüenza *m*.
scoundrelly ['skaʊndrəlɪ] *adj* canallesco, vil.
scour¹ ['skaʊəʳ] *vt pan etc* fregar, estregar, limpiar fregando, restregar (*esp LAm*); *channel* limpiar; (*Med*) purgar.
◆**scour out** *vt pan etc* fregar, estregar, limpiar fregando; *channel* limpiar; (*Med*) purgar; **the river had ~ed out part of the bank** el río se había llevado una parte de la orilla.
scour² ['skaʊəʳ] **1** *vt area* recorrer, registrar; **we are ~ing the countryside for him** recorremos el campo buscándole.
2 *vi*: **to ~ about for sth** buscar algo por todas partes.
scourer ['skaʊrəʳ] *n* (*pad*) estropajo *m*; (*powder*) limpiador *m*, desgrasador *m*.
scourge [skɜːdʒ] **1** *n* azote *m*; (*fig*) azote *m*, flagelo *m*; plaga *f*; **the ~ of malaria** el azote del paludismo; **Attila, the ~ of God** Atila, el azote de Dios; **it is the ~ of our times** es la plaga de nuestros tiempos; **God sent it as a ~** Dios lo envió como castigo.
2 *vt* azotar, flagelar; (*fig*) hostigar.
scouring pad ['skaʊrɪŋpæd] *n* estropajo *m*.
scouring powder ['skaʊrɪŋpaʊdəʳ] *n* limpiador *m*, desgrasador *m*.
Scouse* [skaʊs] **1** *adj* de Liverpool. **2** *n* (**a**) habitante *mf* de Liverpool. (**b**) (*Ling*) dialecto *m* de Liverpool.
scout¹ [skaʊt] **1** *n* (**a**) (*person*: *Mil*) explorador *m*, escucha *m*; (*Univ*) criado *m*; **boy ~** explorador *m*.
(**b**) (*) (*reconnaissance*) reconocimiento *m*; (*search*) búsqueda *f*; **to have a ~ round** reconocer el terreno; **we'll have a ~ for it** lo buscaremos.
2 *vi* explorar; reconocer el terreno; hacer una batida; **to ~ for sth** buscar algo.
◆**scout about, scout around** *vi* (*Mil*) ir de reconocimiento, reconocer el terreno.
◆**scout round** *vi*: **to ~ round for sth** buscar algo.
scout² [skaʊt] *vt proposal* rechazar con desdén; *rumour etc* desmentir.
scout-car ['skaʊtkɑːʳ] *n* (*Mil*) vehículo *m* de reconocimiento.
scouting ['skaʊtɪŋ] *n* escutismo *m*.
scoutmaster ['skaʊtˌmɑːstəʳ] *n* jefe *m* de sección de exploradores.
scow [skaʊ] *n* gabarra *f*.
scowl [skaʊl] **1** *n* ceño *m*; **he said with a ~** dijo ceñudo. **2** *vi* fruncir el ceño, poner mal gesto; **to ~ at sb** mirar con ceño a uno.
scowling ['skaʊlɪŋ] *adj* ceñudo.
scrabble ['skræbl] *vi* (*in writing*) garrapatear; **to ~ about** escarbar; revolverlo todo al buscar algo; **she was scrabbling about in the coal** iba revolviendo el carbón mientras buscaba.
scrag [skræg] **1** *n* pescuezo *m*. **2** *vt animal* torcer el pescuezo a; (*) *person* dar una paliza a.
scragginess ['skrægɪnɪs] *n* flaqueza *f*.
scraggy ['skrægɪ] *adj* flaco, descarnado, escuálido, esquelético.
scram* [skræm] *vi* largarse*, rajarse (*LAm*); ~! ¡lárgate*!
scramble ['skræmbl] **1** *n* (**a**) (*climb*) subida *f*; (*outing*) excursión *f* (de montaña, sobre terreno escabroso *etc*).
(**b**) (*fight etc*) arrebatiña *f*, pelea *f* (*for* por); (*race*) carrera *f* (confusa).
(**c**) (*Sport*) carrera *f* de motocross.
2 *vt* (**a**) *eggs* revolver, hacer un revoltillo de; **~d eggs** huevos *mpl* revueltos *or* pericos (*And*).
(**b**) *message* cifrar, poner en cifra; (*Rad, Telec*) desmodular; (*TV*) codificar.
(**c**) *aircraft* hacer despegar con urgencia (por alarma).
3 *vi* (**a**) **to ~ out** salir de prisa, salir con dificultad, salir a gatas; **to ~ through a hedge** abrirse paso con dificultad a través de un seto; **to ~ up** trepar a, subir gateando a.
(**b**) **to ~ for coins** andar a la rebatiña por unas monedas, disputarse unas monedas a gritos, pelearse entre sí para recoger unas monedas.
scrambler ['skræmbləʳ] *n* (**a**) (*Telec*: *device*) scrambler *m*, aparato *m* de interferencia radiofónica. (**b**) (*motorcyclist*) motociclista *mf* de motocross.
scrambling ['skræmblɪŋ] *n* (*Sport*) motocross *m* campo a través; (*TV*) codificación *f*.
scran‡ [skræn] *n* comida *f*.
scrap¹ [skræp] **1** *n* (**a**) (*small piece*) pedacito *m*, fragmento *m*; ~ **of paper** (*iro*) papel *m* mojado.
(**b**) (*fig*) pizca *f*; **a few ~s of news** algunas noticias de escasa importancia; **it's a ~ of comfort** es una migaja de consolación; **I overheard a ~ of conversation** logré escuchar algunas palabras de la conversación; **there is not a ~ of truth in it** eso no tiene ni pizca de verdad; **not a ~!** ¡ni pizca!, ¡en absoluto!
(**c**) **~s** (*left-overs*) sobras *fpl*, desperdicios *mpl*; **the dog feeds on ~s** el perro come las sobras de la mesa.
(**d**) (~ *iron*) chatarra *f*, hierro *m* viejo; **to sell a ship for ~** vender un barco para chatarra; **what is it worth as ~?** ¿cuánto vale como chatarra?
2 *attr iron etc* viejo; ~ **metal** chatarra *f*, desecho *m* de metal; ~ **paper** (*waste*) papeles *mpl* viejos; (*for notes*) papel *m* para apuntes; **its ~ value is £30** como chatarra vale 30 libras.
3 *vt car, ship etc* desguazar, reducir a chatarra; vender para chatarra; *old equipment etc* tirar; *plan etc* desechar, descartar; **we had to ~ that idea** tuvimos que descartar esa idea.
scrap²* [skræp] **1** *n* riña *f*, camorra *f*, bronca *f*; **to get into** (*or* **have**) **a ~ with sb** armar una bronca con uno, pelearse con uno; **there was a tremendous ~ over the steel bill** se armó una bronca fenomenal sobre el proyecto de ley del acero.
2 *vi* reñir, armar una bronca, pelearse; **they were ~ping in the street** se estaban peleando en la calle.
scrapbook ['skræpbʊk] *n* álbum *m* de recortes.
scrap dealer ['skræpˌdiːləʳ] *n* chatarrero *m*.
scrape [skreɪp] **1** *n* (**a**) (*act*) raspadura *f*; **to give sth a ~** raspar algo, limpiar algo raspándolo; **to give one's knee a ~** rasguñarse la rodilla.
(**b**) (*) lío* *m*; apuro *m*; **to get into a ~** armarse un lío*, meterse en un lío*; **to get sb out of a ~** ayudar a uno a salir de un apuro.
2 *vt* raspar, raer; (*flesh etc*) rasguñar, raer; *surface* (*in decorating*) rascar; (~ *against*) rozar; (*Mus, hum*) rascar; *shoes* restregar; **the lorry ~d the wall** el camión rozó la pared; **the ship ~d the bottom** el barco rozó el fondo; **to ~ one's boots** limpiarse las botas; **to ~ one's feet across the floor** arrastrar los pies por el suelo.
3 *vi* (**a**) (*make noise*) rechinar. (**b**) (*economize*) hacer

economías; vivir muy justo. (**c**) **to ~ past** pasar rozando; **we just managed to ~ through the gap** pudimos con dificultad pasar por la abertura sin tocar las paredes.

◆**scrape along** *vi* rozar; (*fig*) ir tirando; **I can ~ along in Arabic** me defiendo en árabe.

◆**scrape away** **1** *vt* raspar, quitar raspando. **2** *vi*: **to ~ away at the violin** ir rascando el violín.

◆**scrape off** *vt* = **scrape away 1**.

◆**scrape out** *vt contents* remover raspando.

◆**scrape through** **1** *vt*: **to ~ through an exam** aprobar un examen por los pelos.

2 *vi*: **I just ~d through** aprobé por los pelos.

◆**scrape together, scrape up** *vt* arañar, (*fig*) reunir poco a poco, rebañar.

scraper ['skreɪpəʳ] *n* (*tool*) rascador *m*, raspador *m*; (*in road-making*) niveladora *f*; (*at door*) limpiabarros *m*.

scraperboard ['skreɪpəbɔːd] *n cartulina entintada sobre la cual se realiza un dibujo rascando la capa de tinta.*

scrap-heap ['skræphiːp] *n* montón *m* de desechos; **this is for the ~** esto es para tirar; **to throw sth on the ~** desechar algo, descartar algo; **workers are being thrown on the ~** los obreros van al basurero.

scrapings ['skreɪpɪŋz] *npl* raspaduras *fpl*; **~ of the gutter** (*fig*) hez *f* de la sociedad.

scrap-iron ['skræp'aɪən] *n* chatarra *f*, hierro *m* viejo.

scrap merchant ['skræpˌmɜːtʃənt] *n* chatarrero *m*.

scrappy ['skræpɪ] *adj meal etc* pobre, escaso; *text etc* muy imperfecto, fragmentario; *speech* inconexo, descosido; *knowledge* superficial.

scrapyard ['skræpjɑːd] *n* depósito *m* de chatarra; (*for cars*) cementerio *m* de coches.

scratch ['skrætʃ] **1** *n* (**a**) (*from claw, on flesh etc*) rasguño *m*, arañazo *m*; (*on surface*) raya *f*, marca *f*; **it's just a ~** es un rasguño nada más; **the cat gave her a ~** el gato la arañó; **he hadn't a ~ on him** no tuvo la más leve herida; **to have a good ~** rascarse vigorosamente.

(**b**) (*Sport*) línea *f* de salida; **to be** (*or* **come**) **up to ~** (*thing*) estar en buen estado, llenar los requisitos, ser de buena calidad, (*person*) ser tan bueno como siempre, estar a la altura de las circunstancias; **to start from ~** (*with no resources*) empezar sin nada, empezar sin ventaja alguna, (*from beginning*) empezar desde el principio; **we shall have to start from ~ again** tendremos que partir nuevamente de cero, tendremos que comenzar desde el principio otra vez.

2 *adj competitor* sin ventaja; *team* improvisado, sin experiencia, reunido de prisa; **~ meal** comida *f* improvisada, comistrajo *m*.

3 *vt* (**a**) (*with claw etc*) rasguñar, arañar; (*to relieve itch*) rascar; *hard surface* rayar, marcar; (*of chicken etc*) escarbar; **to ~ a hole in sth** hacer un agujero en algo rascándolo; **she ~ed the dog's ear** le rascó la oreja al perro; **he ~ed his head** se rascó la cabeza; **the glass of this watch cannot be ~ed** el cristal de este reloj no puede rayarse; **we ~ed our names on the wood** grabamos nuestros nombres en la madera; **to ~ sb's eyes out** sacar los ojos a uno con las uñas; **to ~ sb off a list** tachar el nombre de uno de una lista.

(**b**) (*Sport*) retirar (tachando el nombre de); **that horse has been ~ed** ese caballo ha sido retirado.

(**c**) (*Comput*: *erase*) borrar.

4 *vi* (**a**) rasguñar; (*to relieve itch*) rascarse; (*of chicken etc*) escarbar; (*pen*) raspear; **the dog ~ed at the door** el perro arañó la puerta.

(**b**) (*Sport*) retirarse.

◆**scratch together** *vt* (*fig*) *money* arañar.

scratch file ['skrætʃfaɪl] *n* fichero *m* de trabajo.

scratchpad ['skrætʃpæd] *n* (*US*) cuadernillo *m* de apuntes, bloc *m*.

scratch score [ˌskrætʃ'skɔːʳ] *n* (*Golf*) puntuación *f* par.

scratch tape ['skrætʃteɪp] *n* cinta *f* reutilizable.

scratchy ['skrætʃɪ] *adj pen* que raspea; *tone* áspero; *writing* flojo, irregular.

scrawl [skrɔːl] **1** *n* garabatos *mpl*, garrapatos *mpl*; **the word finished in a ~** la palabra terminó en un garabato; **I can't read her ~** no soy capaz de leer sus garabatos.

2 *vt*: **to ~ a note to sb** garabatear una nota para uno; **a wall ~ed all over with rude words** una pared llena de palabras feas.

3 *vi* garrapatear, hacer garabatos.

scrawny ['skrɔːnɪ] *adj* descarnado, escuálido.

scream [skriːm] **1** *n* (**a**) chillido *m*, grito *m* (agudo); **there were ~s of laughter** hubo grandes carcajadas; **to give a ~** chillar, dar un grito.

(**b**) (*) **it was a ~** fue para morirse de risa*; **he's a ~** es célebre, es impagable.

2 *vt abuse etc* vociferar (*at* contra).

3 *vi* chillar, gritar; **to ~ with pain** lanzar gritos de dolor; **to ~ with laughter** reírse a carcajadas.

4 *vr*: **to ~ o.s. hoarse** enronquecer a fuerza de gritar.

◆**scream out** **1** *vt* = **scream 2**. **2** *vi* = **scream 3**.

screamingly* ['skriːmɪŋlɪ] *adv*: **a ~ funny joke** un chiste de lo más divertido; **it was ~ funny** fue para morirse de risa*.

scree ['skriː] *n* cono *m* de desmoronamiento.

screech [skriːtʃ] = **scream** (*in most senses*); *vi* (*brakes, wheels etc*) chirriar.

screech-owl ['skriːtʃaʊl] *n* lechuza *f*.

screed [skriːd] *n* escrito *m* largo y pesado, documento *m* aburrido; **to write ~s** escribir esta vida y la otra.

screen [skriːn] **1** *n* (**a**) (*protective*) pantalla *f*; (*folding*) biombo *m*; (*Mil etc*) cortina *f*; (*Phot*) retícula *f*; (*on window*) red *f* metálica; (*sieve*) tamiz *m*, criba *f*.

(**b**) (*Cine, TV*) pantalla *f*; **the small ~** la pequeña pantalla; **stars of the ~** estrellas *fpl* de la pantalla, estrellas *fpl* del cine; **to write for the ~** escribir para el cine.

2 *attr*: **~ actor** actor *m* de cine, **~ actress** actriz *f* de cine; **~ editing** corrección *f* en pantalla; **~ memory** memoria *f* de la pantalla; **~play** guión *m* (cinematográfico); **~ rights** derechos *mpl* cinematográficos; **~ test** prueba *f* cinematográfica; **~ writer** guionista *mf*.

3 *vt* (**a**) (*hide*) ocultar, esconder; tapar; (*protect*) proteger (con una pantalla), abrigar; **the house is ~ed by trees** la casa se oculta detrás de unos árboles; **in order to ~ our movements from the enemy** para impedir que el enemigo observara nuestros movimientos.

(**b**) (*sift*) tamizar, pasar por una criba; *suspects etc* investigar; (*select*) seleccionar, pasar por el tamiz; **he was ~ed by Security** la Seguridad le investigó, tuvo que someterse a las investigaciones de la Seguridad.

(**c**) (*Cine, TV*) *film* proyectar; *novel etc* adaptar para el cine, hacer una película de, hacer una versión cinematográfica de.

(**d**) (*Med*) hacer una exploración a.

◆**screen off** *vt* tapar.

screening ['skriːnɪŋ] *n* (**a**) ocultación *f*; protección *f*. (**b**) (*by security etc*) investigación *f*; (*selection*) selección *f*. (**c**) (*Cine, TV*) proyección *f*. (**d**) (*Med*) exploración *f*.

screw [skruː] **1** *n* (**a**) (*Mech*) tornillo *m*; rosca *f* (*also* **~ thread**); (*Sport*: *of ball*) efecto *m*; **he's got a ~ loose*** le falta un tornillo*; **to put the ~s on sb*** apretar los tornillos a uno.

(**b**) (*Aer, Naut*) hélice *f*.

(**c**) (‡: *income*) sueldo *m*; **he gets a good ~** tiene un buen sueldo.

(**d**) (‡: *warder*) boca‡ *m*.

(**e**) (**‡) polvo**‡ *m*; **to have a ~** echar un polvo**‡.

2 *vt* (**a**) *screw* atornillar; *nut* apretar; *ball* torcer, dar efecto a.

(**b**) **to ~ money out of sb** arrancar dinero a uno; **to ~ the truth out of sb** arrancar la verdad a uno.

(**c**) (**‡) joder**‡, tirarse a**‡; **~ the government!** ¡que se joda el gobierno**‡!; **~ the cost, it's got to be done!** ¡no importa el gasto, hay que hacerlo!

(**d**) (*: *defraud*) timar, estafar.

3 *vi* (*ball*) torcerse.

◆**screw around** *vi* (**a**) (‡: *waste time*) hacer el vago.

(**b**) (**‡: *sexually*) ligar*.

◆**screw down** *vt*: **to ~ sth down** fijar algo con tornillos.

◆**screw off** **1** *vt* desenroscar.

2 *vi* desenroscarse; **the lid ~s off** la tapadera se desenrosca.

◆**screw on** **1** *vt*: **to ~ sth on to a board** fijar algo en un tablón con tornillos; **he's got his head ~ed on** sabe cuántas son cinco.

2 *vi*: **it ~s on here** se fija aquí con tornillos.

◆**screw together** *vt* unir con tornillos.

◆**screw up** **1** *vt* (**a**) *screw* atornillar; *nut* apretar; *V* **courage**.

(**b**) *paper* arrugar; **to ~ up one's eyes** entornar los ojos; **to ~ up one's face** arrugar la cara, hacer visajes.

(**c**) (‡: *spoil*) estropear, arruinar, joder‡; armarse un lío con*; **the experience really ~ed him up** la experiencia le afectó de mala manera.

2 *vi*: **it will ~ up tighter than that** se puede apretar todavía más.

3 *vr*: **to ~ o.s. up to do sth** obligarse a hacer algo; cobrar bastante ánimo para hacer algo.

screwball* ['skruːbɔːl] (*US*) **1** *adj* excéntrico, estrafalario.

2 *n* chalado* *m*, -a *f*, tarado* *m*, -a *f* (*LAm*).
screwdriver ['skru:,draɪvəʳ] *n* destornillador *m*, desarmador *m* (*CAm*); (*: *drink*) destornillador *m*.
screw-top ['skru:tɒp] *n* tapa *f* de tornillo; ~ **jar** pote *m* con tapa de tornillo.
screw-up‡ ['skru:ʌp] *n* lío* *m*, embrollo *m*, cacao* *m*.
screwy* ['skru:ɪ] *adj* chiflado*.
scribble ['skrɪbl] **1** *n* garabatos *mpl*; **I can't read her** ~ no soy capaz de leer sus garabatos; **a wall covered in ~s** una pared llena de garabatos.
2 *vt*: **to ~ one's signature** escribir con mucha prisa su firma; **a word ~d on a wall** una palabra mal escrita en una pared; **a sheet of paper ~d (over) with notes** una hoja de papel emborronada de notas.
3 *vi* garrapatear, hacer garabatos; escribir con mucha prisa; (*pej, hum*) ser escritor, ser periodista.
◆**scribble down** *vt notes* escribir de prisa.
scribbler ['skrɪbləʳ] *n* escritorzuelo *m*, -a *f*, plumífero *m*.
scribbling ['skrɪblɪŋ] *n* garabato *m*.
scribbling pad ['skrɪblɪŋ,pæd] *n* borrador *m*, bloc *m*.
scribe [skraɪb] *n* (*professional letter-writer etc*) escribiente *m*; amanuense *m*; (*of manuscript*) copista *m*; (*Bible*) escriba *m*; (*pej, hum*) escritorzuelo *m*, -a *f*, plumífero *m*.
scrimmage ['skrɪmɪdʒ] *n* (**a**) (*fight*) arrebatiña *f*, pelea *f*. (**b**) (*US Sport*) = **scrum**.
scrimp [skrɪmp] **1** *vt* escatimar. **2** *vi* economizar, escatimar, hacer economías; **to ~ and save** hacer grandes economías, vivir muy justo.
scrimpy ['skrɪmpɪ] *adj person* tacaño; *supply etc* escaso.
scrimshank* ['skrɪmʃæŋk] *vi* (*Brit Mil*) racanear*, hacer el rácano*.
scrimshanker* ['skrɪm,ʃæŋkəʳ] *n* (*Brit Mil*) rácano* *m*.
scrip [skrɪp] *n* (*Fin*) vale *m*, abonaré *m*.
script [skrɪpt] **1** *n* (**a**) (*writing*) escritura *f*, letra *f* (cursiva).
(**b**) (*manuscript*) manuscrito *m*; (*Scol, Univ*) trabajo *m* escrito, examen *m*; (*Cine*) guión *m*.
2 *attr*: ~ **editor** (*Cine, TV*) revisor *m*, -ora *f* de guión; ~ **girl** (*Cine*) script *f*, anotadora *f*, secretaria *f* de dirección.
3 *vt film* escribir el guión de; **the film was not well ~ed** la película no tenía un buen guión.
scriptural ['skrɪptʃərəl] *adj* escriturario, bíblico.
Scripture ['skrɪptʃəʳ] *n* (*also* **Holy ~**) Sagrada Escritura *f*; (*as school subject, lesson*) Historia *f* Sagrada.
scriptwriter ['skrɪpt,raɪtəʳ] *n* guionista *mf*.
scrofula ['skrɒfjʊlə] *n* escrófula *f*.
scrofulous ['skrɒfjʊləs] *adj* escrofuloso.
scroll [skrəʊl] **1** *n* rollo *m*; (*ancient*) rollo *m* de escritura; rollo *m* de pergamino; (*Art, Archit*) voluta *f*; ~ **of fame** lista *f* de la fama; ~ **key** tecla *f* de desplazamiento; **the Dead Sea ~s** los manuscritos del Mar Muerto. **2** *vti* desplazar.
◆**scroll down 1** *vt* desplazar hacia abajo. **2** *vi* desplazarse hacia abajo.
◆**scroll up 1** *vt* desplazar hacia arriba. **2** *vi* desplazarse hacia arriba.
scrolling ['skrəʊlɪŋ] *n* (*Comput*) corrimiento *m*.
Scrooge [skru:dʒ] *n el avariento típico* (*personaje del* 'Christmas Carol', *de Dickens*).
scrotum ['skrəʊtəm] *n* escroto *m*.
scrounge* [skraʊndʒ] **1** *n*: **to be on the ~** ir de gorra*, ir sableando*; tratar de adquirir cosas sin pagar; tratar de pedir algo prestado; **to have a ~ round for sth** buscar algo.
2 *vt* obtener por medio de gorronería*, obtener sin pagar, agenciarse*; **can I ~ a drink from you?** ¿me invitas a un trago?*; **I ~d a ticket** me agencié una entrada; **to ~ sth from sb** gorronear algo a uno*.
3 *vi* ir de gorra*, gorronear*, sablear*; **to ~ around for sth** buscar algo; **to ~ on sb** vivir a costa de uno.
scrounger* ['skraʊndʒəʳ] *n* gorrón* *m*, sablista* *mf*.
scrub[1] [skrʌb] *n* (*Bot*) maleza *f*, monte *m* bajo, matas *fpl*; ~ **fire** incendio *m* de monte bajo.
scrub[2] [skrʌb] **1** *n* fregado *m*, fregadura *f*; **to give sth a ~** limpiar algo fregándolo; **it needs a hard ~** hay que fregarlo con fuerza.
2 *vt* (**a**) fregar, restregar; limpiar fregando.
(**b**) (*: *cancel*) cancelar, borrar; **let's ~ it** bueno, lo borramos.
3 *vi* (*fig*) **let's ~ round it*** pasemos la esponja, borrón y cuenta nueva.
◆**scrub away** *vt dirt* quitar restregando; *stain* quitar frotando.
◆**scrub down 1** *vt room, walls* fregar a fondo. **2** *vr*: **to ~ o.s. down** lavarse a fondo.
◆**scrub off** *vt* = **scrub away**.
◆**scrub out** *vt stain* limpiar restregando; *pan* fregar; *name* tachar.
◆**scrub up** *vi* (*of surgeon etc*) lavarse las manos.
scrubber ['skrʌbəʳ] *n* (**a**) (*also* **pan-~**) estropajo *m*. (**b**) (‡) tía *f* fea*; (*whore*) putilla‡ *f*.
scrubbing-brush ['skrʌbɪŋ,brʌʃ] *n*, (*US*) **scrub brush** ['skrʌb,brʌʃ] *n* cepillo *m* de fregar.
scrubby ['skrʌbɪ] *adj* (**a**) *person* achaparrado, enano. (**b**) *land* cubierto de maleza.
scrubland ['skrʌblænd] *n* monte *m* bajo.
scrubwoman ['skrʌb,wʊmən] *n*, *pl* **scrubwomen** ['skrʌb-,wɪmɪn] (*US*) fregona *f*.
scruff[1] [skrʌf] *n*: ~ **of the neck** pescuezo *m*; **to take sb by the ~ of the neck** agarrar a uno por el pescuezo.
scruff[2]* [skrʌf] *n* persona *f* desaliñada.
scruffily ['skrʌfɪlɪ] *adv*: ~ **dressed** mal vestido, vestido con desaliño.
scruffiness ['skrʌfɪnɪs] *n* desaliño *m*; suciedad *f*.
scruffy ['skrʌfɪ] *adj* desaliñado, dejado (*LAm*); sucio, piojoso.
scrum [skrʌm] *n*, **scrummage** ['skrʌmɪdʒ] *n* melé *f*; **loose ~** melé *f* abierta; **set ~** melé *f* cerrada.
◆**scrum down** *vi* formar la melé cerrada.
scrum-half [,skrʌm'hɑ:f] *n* medio *m* (de) melé.
scrumptious* ['skrʌmpʃəs] *adj* de rechupete*, riquísimo.
scrunch [skrʌntʃ] *vt* (*also* **to ~ up**) ronzar.
scruple ['skru:pl] **1** *n* (**a**) (*weight*) escrúpulo *m* (*Pharm* = *20 granos* = *1.296 gramos*).
(**b**) (*fig*) escrúpulo *m*; **a person of no ~s** una persona sin escrúpulos; **he is entirely without ~** no tiene conciencia en absoluto; **to have no ~s about** ... no tener escrúpulos acerca de ...; **to make no ~ to** + *infin* no vacilar en + *infin*.
2 *vi*: **not to ~ to** + *infin* no vacilar en + *infin*.
scrupulous ['skru:pjʊləs] *adj* escrupuloso (*about* en cuanto a).
scrupulously ['skru:pjʊləslɪ] *adv* escrupulosamente; **a ~ fair decision** una decisión completamente justa; **a ~ clean room** un cuarto completamente limpio.
scrupulousness ['skru:pjʊləsnɪs] *n* escrupulosidad *f*.
scrutineer [,skru:tɪ'nɪəʳ] *n* (*Brit*) escudriñador *m*, -ora *f*.
scrutinize ['skru:tɪnaɪz] *vt* escudriñar, examinar; *votes* escrutar.
scrutiny ['skru:tɪnɪ] *n* escrutinio *m*, examen *m*; **it does not stand up to ~** no resiste al examen; **to submit sth to a close ~** someter algo a un cuidadoso examen; **under his ~ she felt nervous** bajo su mirada se sintió nerviosa; **to keep sb under close ~** vigilar a uno de cerca.
scuba ['sku:bə] *attr*: ~ **diving** buceo *m* con escafandra autónoma; ~ **suit** escafandra *f* autónoma.
scud [skʌd] *vi*: **to ~ along** correr (llevado por el viento), deslizarse rápidamente; **the clouds were ~ding across the sky** las nubes pasaban rápidamente a través del cielo; **the ship ~ded before the wind** el barco iba viento en popa.
scuff [skʌf] **1** *vt shoes* desgastar, rayar; *feet* arrastrar. **2** *attr*: ~ **marks** rozaduras *fpl*. **3** *vi* andar arrastrando los pies.
scuffle ['skʌfl] **1** *n* refriega *f*, pelea *f*. **2** *vi* pelearse; **to ~ with the police** pelearse con la policía.
scull [skʌl] **1** *n* espadilla *f*. **2** *vti* remar (con espadilla).
scullery ['skʌlərɪ] *n* (*esp Brit*) trascocina *f*, fregadero *m*, office *m*.
scullery-maid ['skʌlərɪmeɪd] *n* fregona *f*.
sculpt [skʌlpt] *vt* esculpir.
sculptor ['skʌlptəʳ] *n* escultor *m*, -ora *f*.
sculptress ['skʌlptrɪs] *n* escultora *f*.
sculptural ['skʌlptʃərəl] *adj* escultural.
sculpture ['skʌlptʃəʳ] **1** *n* (*art, object*) escultura *f*. **2** *vt* esculpir.
scum [skʌm] *n* (**a**) (*on liquid*) espuma *f*, nata *f*; (*on pond*) verdín *m*; (*on metal*) escoria *f*. (**b**) (*fig*) heces *fpl*; **the ~ of the earth** las heces de la sociedad; **you ~!** ¡canalla!
scumbag‡* ['skʌm,bæg] *n* cabronazo‡ *m*, puta mierda‡* *mf*.
scummy ['skʌmɪ] *adj* (*V n*) (**a**) lleno de espuma; cubierto de verdín. (**b**) (*fig*) canallesco, vil.
scupper ['skʌpəʳ] **1** *n* imbornal *m*. **2** *vt* (*Naut*) abrir los imbornales de; (*loosely*) hundir; (*fig*: *ruin*) arruinar, destruir, acabar con; (*fig*: *frustrate*) frustrar.
scurf [skɜ:f] *n* caspa *f*.
scurfy ['skɜ:fɪ] *adj* casposo.
scurrility [skʌ'rɪlɪtɪ] *n* grosería *f*, procacidad *f*, chocarrería *f*; lo difamatorio.
scurrilous ['skʌrɪləs] *adj* grosero, procaz, chocarrero;

difamatorio; **a ~ journal** una revista chocarrera; **to make a ~ attack on sb** atacar a uno de modo grosero.
scurrilously ['skʌrɪləslɪ] *adv* groseramente, con procacidad; de modo difamatorio.
scurry ['skʌrɪ] *vi* correr, ir a toda prisa; **to ~ along** ir corriendo; **to ~ for shelter** correr para ponerse al abrigo.
◆scurry away, scurry off *vi* escabullirse.
scurvy ['skɜːvɪ] **1** *adj* vil, canallesco; ruin. **2** *n* escorbuto *m*.
scut [skʌt] *n* rabito *m* (*esp* de conejo).
scutcheon ['skʌtʃən] *n* = **escutcheon**.
scuttle¹ ['skʌtl] *n* cubo *m*, carbonera *f*.
scuttle² ['skʌtl] **1** *vt* (*Naut*) barrenar, dar barreno a, echar a pique.
2 *vi* (*fig*) abandonar, renunciar; **a policy of ~** una política de abandonarlo todo.
scuttle³ ['skʌtl] **1** *n* huida *f* precipitada, retirada *f* precipitada.
2 *vi*: **to ~ along** correr, ir a toda prisa; **we must ~** tenemos que marcharnos.
◆scuttle away, scuttle off *vi* escabullirse.
scuzzy‡ ['skʌzɪ] *adj* (*esp US*) cutre*.
Scylla ['sɪlə] *nf*: **~ and Charybdis** Escila y Caribdis.
scythe [saɪð] **1** *n* guadaña *f*. **2** *vt* guadañar, segar con guadaña.
SD (*US Post*) *abbr of* **South Dakota**.
S.Dak. (*US*) *abbr of* **South Dakota**.
SDI *n abbr of* **Strategic Defence Initiative** Iniciativa *f* de Defensa Estratégica, IDE *f*.
SDLP *n abbr of* **Social Democratic and Labour Party** *partido político de Irlanda del Norte*.
SDP *n* (*Brit Pol, formerly*) *abbr of* **Social Democratic Party**.
SDR *n abbr of* **special drawing rights** derechos *mpl* especiales de giro, DEG *mpl*.
SE *abbr of* **south east** sudeste *m*, *also adj*, SE.
sea [siː] **1** *n* (**a**) (*not land*) mar *m* (*or f in some phrases*; *V below*); **the seven ~s** todos los mares del mundo; **in Spanish ~s** en aguas españolas; **at ~** en el mar; **beyond the ~s** allende el mar; **from beyond the ~s** desde allende el mar; **by ~** por mar, por vía marítima; **by the ~** a la orilla del mar, junto al mar; **out at ~** en alta mar; **to be all at ~** estar despistado, estar en un mar de confusiones; **to be all at ~ about sth** (*or* **with sth**) no saber nada en absoluto de algo; **on the high ~s** en alta mar; **to follow the ~, to go to ~** hacerse marinero; **to put to ~** hacerse a la mar; **to remain 2 months at ~** estar navegando durante 2 meses, pasar 2 meses en el mar; **to stand out to ~** apartarse de la costa.
(**b**) (*state of the ~*) **heavy ~, strong ~** oleada *f*, marejada *f*; **to ship a heavy** (*or* **green**) **~** ser inundado por una ola grande.
(**c**) (*fig*) **a ~ of faces** una multitud de caras; **a ~ of corn** un mar de espigas; **a ~ of flame** una vasta extensión de llamas; **a ~ of troubles** un piélago de penas; **~s of blood** ríos *mpl* de sangre.
2 *attr* de mar; marino, marítimo; **~ air** aire *m* de mar; **~ battle** batalla *f* naval; **~ change** (*fig*) viraje *m*, cambiazo *m*; **~ power** potencia *f* naval; **~ transport** transporte *m* por mar, transporte *m* marítimo; **~ trip** viaje *m* por mar.
sea-anemone ['siːə'nemənɪ] *n* anémona *f* de mar.
sea-bass ['siːbæs] *n* corvina *f*.
sea-bathing ['siːˌbeɪðɪŋ] *n* baños *mpl* de mar.
seabed ['siːbed] *n* lecho *m* del mar, lecho *m* marino.
seabird ['siːbɜːd] *n* ave *f* marina.
seaboard ['siːbɔːd] *n* litoral *m*.
seaboots ['siːbuːts] *npl* botas *fpl* de marinero.
seaborne ['siːbɔːn] *adj* transportado por mar.
seabream ['siː'briːm] *n* besugo *m*.
sea-breeze ['siː'briːz] *n* brisa *f* de mar.
seacoast ['siːkəʊst] *n* litoral *m*, costa *f* marítima, orilla *f* del mar.
sea-cow ['siː'kaʊ] *n* manatí *m*.
sea-crossing ['siːkrɒsɪŋ] *n* travesía *f*.
sea-dog ['siːdɒg] *n* lobo *m* de mar.
seafarer ['siːˌfɛərəʳ] *n* marinero *m*.
seafaring ['siːˌfɛərɪŋ] **1** *adj community* marinero, *life* de marinero. **2** *n* marinería *f*; vida *f* de marinero.
sea-fight ['siːfaɪt] *n* combate *m* naval.
sea-fish ['siːfɪʃ] *n* pez *m* de mar.
seafood ['siːfuːd] *n* mariscos *mpl*; **~ restaurant** marisquería *f*.
seafront ['siːfrʌnt] *n* (*beach*) playa *f*; (*promenade*) paseo *m* marítimo.
seagirt [siːgɜːt] *adj* (*liter*) rodeado por el mar.
seagoing ['siːˌgəʊɪŋ] *adj* de alta mar, de altura.
sea-green ['siːgriːn] *adj* verdemar.
seagull ['siːgʌl] *n* gaviota *f*.
seahorse ['siːhɔːs] *n* caballito *m* de mar, hipocampo *m*.
seakale ['siːkeɪl] *n* col *f* marina.
seal¹ [siːl] **1** *n* (*Zool*) foca *f*. **2** *attr*: **~ cull, ~ culling** matanza *f* (selectiva) de focas. **3** *vi*: **to go ~ing** ir a cazar focas.
seal² [siːl] **1** *n* sello *m*; precinto *m*; (*Mec*) sello *m*; **under the ~ of secrecy** bajo promesa de guardar el secreto; **under my hand and ~** firmado y sellado por mí; **he gave it his ~ of approval** lo aprobó, le dio su aprobación; **to set** (*or* **put**) **one's ~ to sth** sellar algo, poner su sello en algo.
2 *vt* (**a**) sellar; precintar; cerrar, cerrar herméticamente; (*with wax*) lacrar; (*with lead*) emplomar; **~ed bid** oferta *f* cerrada; **~ed orders** órdenes *fpl* secretas; **to ~ a letter** cerrar una carta; **my lips are ~ed** he prometido no decir nada, soy una tumba.
(**b**) (*fig*) *fate etc* decidir; **this ~ed his fate** esto acabó de perderle; **the ship's fate is ~ed** la suerte del barco está decidida.
◆seal in *vt* encerrar herméticamente.
◆seal off *vt* obturar; separar, aislar.
◆seal up *vt* cerrar; (*Comm*) *packet* precintar.
sea lamprey ['siː'læmprɪ] *n* lamprea *f* marina.
sea-lane ['siːleɪn] *n* ruta *f* marítima.
sealant ['siːlənt] *n* (*device*) sellador *m*, tapador *m*; (*substance*) silicona *f* selladora.
sea-legs ['siːlegz] *npl*: **to get one's ~** acostumbrarse a la vida de a bordo.
sealer ['siːləʳ] *n* (*person*) cazador *m* de focas; (*boat*) barco *m* para la caza de focas.
sea-level ['siː'levl] *n* nivel *m* del mar; **800 metres above ~** 800 metros sobre el nivel del mar.
sealing ['siːlɪŋ] *n* caza *f* de focas.
sealing-wax ['siːlɪŋwæks] *n* lacre *m*.
sealion ['siːlaɪən] *n* león *m* marino.
sealskin ['siːlskɪn] *n* piel *f* de foca.
seam [siːm] **1** *n* (**a**) (*Sew*) costura *f*; (*Tech*) juntura *f*; (*line on skin*) arruga *f*; (*Anat*) sutura *f*; (*Naut*) costura *f* de los tablones; **to burst** (*or* **come apart**) **at the ~s** descoserse; **we're bursting at the ~s in the office** en la oficina ya no cabemos.
(**b**) (*Geol*) filón *m*, veta *f*.
2 *vt* (*Sew*) coser; (*Tech*) juntar; *face* arrugar.
seaman ['siːmən] *n*, *pl* **seamen** ['siːmən] marinero *m*.
seamanlike ['siːmənlaɪk] *adj* de buen marinero.
seamanship ['siːmənʃɪp] *n* náutica *f*, marinería *f*.
sea-mist ['siː'mɪst] *n* bruma *f*.
seamless ['siːmlɪs] *adj* sin costura.
seamstress ['semstrɪs] *n* costurera *f*.
seamy ['siːmɪ] *adj* miserable, vil; asqueroso; **the ~ side** (*fig*) el revés de la medalla.
séance ['seɪɑːns] *n* sesión *f* de espiritismo.
sea-perch ['siːˌpɜːtʃ] *n* perca *f* de mar.
seapiece ['siːpiːs] *n* (*Art*) marina *f*.
seaplane ['siːpleɪn] *n* hidroavión *m*.
seaport ['siːpɔːt] *n* puerto *m* de mar.
SEAQ ['siːˌæk] *n abbr of* **Stock Exchange Automated Quotations**.
sear [sɪəʳ] *vt* (*wither*) secar, marchitar; (*Med*) cauterizar; (*of pain etc*) punzar; (*of sun, wind*) abrasar; (*scorch*) chamuscar, quemar; **it was ~ed into my memory** quedó grabado en la memoria.
◆sear through *vt walls, metal* penetrar a través de.
search [sɜːtʃ] **1** *n* (*quest*) busca *f*, búsqueda *f* (*for* de); (*of person, of house etc*) registro *m*, cateo *m* (*Mex*); (*inspection*) reconocimiento *m*; (*Comput*) búsqueda *f*; (*Video*) búsqueda *f* de imagen; **right of ~** derecho *m* de visita; **in ~ of** en busca de; en demanda de; **to do a ~ and replace** hacer una operación de buscar y reemplazar; **to make a ~ in a house** practicar un registro en una casa; **a ~ is being made for the missing child** se está buscando al niño desaparecido; **I am having a ~ made in the archives** estoy organizando un registro de los archivos.
2 *attr*: **~ and destroy operation** operación *f* de acoso y derribo.
3 *vt* (*scan*) examinar, escudriñar; *place* explorar, registrar; buscar en; *conscience* examinar; *house, luggage etc* registrar, catear (*Mex*); *person* registrar, (*for weapon*) cachear; **we have ~ed the whole library for it** lo hemos buscado en todas partes de la biblioteca, hemos registrado la biblioteca de arriba abajo; **the police are ~ing the woods** la policía está registrando el bosque; **~ me!*** ¡yo

qué sé!, ¡ni idea!

4 *vi* buscar (*also Comput*); (*Med*) tentar, sondar; '**~ and replace**' (*Comput*) 'buscar y reemplazar'; **to ~ after, to ~ for** buscar; **to ~ into** investigar.

◆**search about, search around** *vi* buscar por todas partes.

◆**search out** *vt*: **to ~ sb out** buscar a uno, (*and find*) descubrir a uno tras una búsqueda; **it ~es out the weak spots** identifica los puntos débiles.

searcher ['sɜːtʃəʳ] *n* buscador *m*, -ora *f*; investigador *m*, -ora *f*.

searching ['sɜːtʃɪŋ] *adj look* penetrante; *question* agudo, perspicaz.

searchingly ['sɜːtʃɪŋlɪ] *adv* con penetración; agudamente, con perspicacia.

searchlight ['sɜːtʃlaɪt] *n* reflector *m*, proyector *m*.

search-party ['sɜːtʃ,pɑːtɪ] *n* pelotón *m* de salvamento.

search-warrant ['sɜːtʃ,wɒrənt] *n* mandamiento *m* judicial de registro, auto *m* de registro domiciliario.

searing ['sɪərɪŋ] *adj heat etc* abrasador; *pain* punzante; *criticism* mordaz, acerbo.

sea-room ['siːrʊm] *n* espacio *m* para maniobrar.

seascape ['siːskeɪp] *n* marina *f*.

sea-serpent ['siː,sɜːpənt] *n* serpiente *f* de mar.

sea-shanty ['siː,ʃæntɪ] *n* saloma *f*.

seashell ['siːʃel] *n* concha *f* (marina), caracol *m* (marino).

seashore ['siːʃɔːʳ] *n* playa *f*; orilla *f* del mar.

seasick ['siːsɪk] *adj* mareado; **to be ~** estar mareado; **to get ~** marearse.

seasickness ['siːsɪknɪs] *n* mareo *m*.

seaside ['siːsaɪd] **1** *n* playa *f*; costa *f*; orilla *f* del mar; **to go to the ~** ir a una playa (a veranear); **to take the family to the ~ for a day** llevar a la familia a pasar un día junto al mar.

2 *attr*: **~ resort** playa *f*, punto *m* marítimo de veraneo; **we like ~ holidays** nos gusta pasar las vacaciones en la costa, nos gusta veranear junto al mar.

season ['siːzn] **1** *n* (*of the year*) estación *f*; (*indefinite*) época *f*, período *m*; (*eg social ~, sporting ~*) temporada *f*; (*opportune time*) sazón *f*; **at this ~** en esta época del año; **at that ~** a la sazón; **at the height of the ~** en plena temporada; **for a ~** durante una temporada; **in due ~** a su tiempo; **a word in ~** una palabra a propósito; **in ~ and out of ~** a tiempo y a destiempo; **to be in ~** (*fruit*) estar en sazón; (*animal*) estar en celo; **prices are higher in (the) ~** suben los precios en la temporada alta; **the open ~** (*Hunting*) la temporada de caza, (*Fishing*) la temporada de pesca; **to be out of ~** estar fuera de temporada; **the London ~** la temporada social de Londres; **it was not the ~ for jokes** no era el momento oportuno para chistes; **we did a ~ at La Scala** representamos en la Scala durante una temporada; **did you have a good ~?** ¿qué tal la temporada?

2 *attr*: **~ ticket** billete *m* de abono; (*Theat*) abono *m* (de temporada); **~ ticket holder** abonado *m*, -a *f*.

3 *vt* (**a**) *food* sazonar, condimentar; **a speech ~ed with wit** un discurso salpicado de agudezas.

(**b**) *wood* curar; (*moderate*) moderar, templar; *person etc* acostumbrar (*to* a); ejercitar (*to* en).

seasonable ['siːznəbl] *adj* (*suitable*) oportuno; *weather etc* propio de la estación.

seasonal ['siːzənl] *adj unemployment etc* estacional; *worker* temporal; *dress etc* apropiado a la estación; **it's very ~** varía mucho según la estación.

seasonally ['siːzənlɪ] *adv* estacionalmente, según la estación; **~ adjusted** ajustado a la estación.

seasoned ['siːznd] *adj* (**a**) *food* sazonado. (**b**) *timber* curado, maduro; *person* experto, perito; (*Mil*) veterano, aguerrido; **a ~ campaigner** un veterano, una veterana.

seasong ['siːsɒŋ] *n* canción *f* de marineros; (*shanty*) saloma *f*.

seasoning ['siːznɪŋ] *n* (**a**) (*Culin*) condimento *m*; (*fig*) salsa *f*, sal *f*; **with a ~ of jokes** con una salpicadura de chistes. (**b**) (*of timber*) cura *f*.

seat [siːt] **1** *n* (**a**) (*chair*) asiento *m*, silla *f*; (*bench*) banco *m*; (*in counting numbers of ~s in bus, plane etc*) plaza *f*, asiento *m*; (*Theat etc*) localidad *f*, (*as ticket*) localidad *f*, entrada *f*; (*of cycle*) asiento *m*, sillín *m*; **an aircraft with 250 ~s** un avión de 250 plazas; **are there any ~s left?** ¿quedan entradas?; **to have a ~ on the board** ser miembro de la junta directiva; **to keep one's ~** permanecer sentado; **we need 2 ~s on an early flight** necesitamos 2 plazas en el primer vuelo disponible; **to take a ~** sentarse, tomar asiento; **please take your ~s for supper** la cena está servida; **do take a ~** siéntese por favor.

(**b**) (*Parl*) escaño *m*; **a majority of 50 ~s** una mayoría de 50 (miembros, votos *etc*); **to gain a ~ for the liberals** ganar un escaño para los liberales; **to keep one's ~** retener su escaño; **to win 4 ~s from the nationalists** ganar 4 escaños a los nacionalistas; **to take one's ~** prestar juramento como diputado.

(**c**) (*of chair*) fondo *m*; (*of trousers*) fondillos *mpl*; (*Anat**) trasero *m*; **he does it by the ~ of his pants** lo hace por instinto; **to get a bump on one's ~** darse un golpe en el trasero.

(**d**) (*centre*: *of government etc*) sede *f*; (*of governor etc*) residencia *f*; (*of nobleman*) casa *f* solariega; (*of infection, fire, trouble*) foco *m*; **~ of learning** centro *m* de estudios.

(**e**) (*of rider*) **to have a good ~** montar bien, **to keep one's ~** seguir en la silla; **to lose one's ~** caer del caballo.

2 *vt* (**a**) *person etc* sentar; **to be ~ed** estar sentado; **please be ~ed** siéntese por favor; **where shall we ~ the bishop?** ¿dónde ponemos al obispo?; **to remain ~ed** permanecer sentado, no levantarse; **when you are comfortably ~ed** cuando estén sentados cómodamente.

(**b**) (*of capacity*) tener asientos para; **the car ~s 5** el coche tiene 5 asientos, caben 5 personas en el coche; **the table ~s 12** hay sitio para 12 en esta mesa; **the theatre ~s 900** el teatro tiene un aforo de 900.

(**c**) (*Mech*) *valve etc* asentar, ajustar.

3 *vr*: **to ~ o.s.** sentarse.

seatback ['siːtbæk] *n* respaldo *m*.

seatbelt ['siːtbelt] *n* cinturón *m* de seguridad.

-seater ['siːtəʳ] *adj, n ending in compounds*: **a 10~ plane** un avión de 10 plazas, un avión con capacidad para 10 plazas.

seating ['siːtɪŋ] **1** *n* asientos *mpl*. **2** *attr*: **~ accommodation** plazas *fpl*, asientos *mpl*; **~ arrangements, ~ plan** distribución *f* de asientos; **~ capacity** cabida *f*, número *m* de asientos.

SEATO ['siːtəʊ] *n abbr of* **Southeast Asia Treaty Organization** Organización *f* del Tratado de Asia Sudeste, OTASE *f*.

sea-trout ['siːtraʊt] *n* trucha *f* marina, reo *m*.

sea-urchin ['siː,ɜːtʃɪn] *n* erizo *m* de mar.

sea-wall ['siː'wɔːl] *n* dique *m* marítimo.

seaward ['siːwəd] *adj* de hacia el mar, de la parte del mar; **on the ~ side** en el lado del mar.

seaward(s) ['siːwəd(z)] *adv* hacia el mar; **to ~** en la dirección del mar.

sea-water ['siː,wɔːtəʳ] *n* agua *f* de mar.

seaway ['siːweɪ] *n* vía *f* marítima.

seaweed ['siːwiːd] *n* alga *f* (marina).

seaworthiness ['siː,wɜːðɪnɪs] *n* navegabilidad *f*.

seaworthy ['siː,wɜːðɪ] *adj* marinero, navegable, en condiciones de navegar.

sea-wrack ['siːræk] *n* algas *fpl* (en la playa).

sebaceous [sɪ'beɪʃəs] *adj* sebáceo.

SEC *n* (*US*) *abbr of* **Securities and Exchange Commission.**

Sec. *abbr of* **Secretary** Secretario *m*, -a *f*, Srio, Sria.

sec. *n abbr of* **second(s)** segundo *m*, segundos *mpl*; *V* **second 3 (a).**

secant ['siːkənt] *n* secante *f*.

secateurs [,sekə'tɜːz] *npl* tijeras *fpl* de podar, podadera *f*.

secede [sɪ'siːd] *vi* secesionarse, separarse (*from* de).

secession [sɪ'seʃən] *n* secesión *f*, separación *f*.

secessionist [sɪ'seʃnɪst] **1** *adj* secesionista, separatista. **2** *n* secesionista *m*, separatista *m*.

secluded [sɪ'kluːdɪd] *adj* retirado, apartado.

seclusion [sɪ'kluːʒən] *n* retiro *m*, apartamiento *m*; **to live in ~** vivir en el retiro, vivir lejos del tumulto.

second 1 ['sekənd] *adj* segundo; otro; **a ~ Manolete** otro Manolete; **every ~ post** cada dos postes, un poste sí y otro no; **the ~ largest fish** el mayor pez después del primero; **this is the ~ largest fish** este pez es el segundo en tamaño; **this is the ~ largest city of Slobodia** ésta es la segunda ciudad de Eslobodia; **to be ~ to none** no ser inferior a nadie; no ir a la zaga a nadie (*in* en); **A is ~ only to B as a tourist attraction** como atracción turística A vale casi lo que B; **to be ~ in command** ser el segundo después del jefe, (*fig*) ser el segundo de a bordo; **will you have a ~ cup?** ¿quieres otra taza?; **you won't get a ~ chance** no tendrás otra oportunidad; **~ coming** segundo advenimiento *m*; **~ cousin** primo *m* segundo, prima *f* segunda; **~ floor** (*Brit*) segundo piso *m*, tercer piso *m* (*LAm*); (*US*) primer piso *m*, segundo piso *m* (*LAm*); **~ gear** segunda velocidad *f*; **~ generation** segunda generación *f*; **a ~ generation model** un modelo de segunda generación; **~ half** (*Sport*) segundo tiempo *m*; (*Fin*) segundo semestre *m* (del año económico); **~ home** segunda vivienda *f*, casa *f* de veraneo; ~ **language** segunda lengua *f*; ~ **lieutenant** (*Mil*) alférez *m*, subteniente *m*; ~ **mate,** ~ **officer** (*Naut*) segundo *m* de a bordo; ~ **mortgage** segunda hipoteca *f*; ~ **person** segunda persona *f*; ~ **sight** doble vista *f*; clarividencia *f*.

2 *adv* en segundo lugar; **to come** ~ (*in race*) ocupar el segundo puesto; **to go** ~, **to travel** ~ (*Rail*) viajar en segunda.

3 *n* (**a**) (*time*) segundo *m*; ~ **hand** (*of watch*) segundero *m*; **just a** ~! ¡un momento!, ¡momentito! (*LAm*); **it won't take a** ~ es cosa de unos momentos; **at that very** ~ en ese mismo instante; **I'll be with you in (just) a** ~ un momento y estoy contigo; **in a split** ~ en un instante, en un abrir y cerrar de ojos; **the operation is timed to a split** ~ la operación está concebida con la mayor precisión en cuanto al tiempo.

(**b**) (*Mus*) segunda *f*.

(**c**) (*Brit Univ*) segunda clase *f*.

(**d**) (*Boxing*) segundo *m*, cuidador *m*; (*in duel*) padrino *m*.

(**e**) (*Aut*) segunda velocidad *f*; **in** ~ en segunda.

(**f**) (*in race, exam etc*) **to come in** ~ llegar el segundo, ocupar el segundo puesto; **to come a poor** ~ resultar ser muy inferior al que gana.

(**g**) (*Comm*) ~**s** artículos *mpl* de segunda calidad, artículos *mpl* con algún desperfecto.

(**h**) (*Culin**) **will you have some** ~**s?** ¿quieres más?, ¿quieres servirte otra porción?

4 *vt* (**a**) secundar, apoyar; ayudar; *motion* apoyar; **I** ~ **that!** ¡yo digo lo mismo!

(**b**) [sɪ'kɒnd] (*Brit*) trasladar temporalmente (*to* a).

secondary ['sekəndərɪ] *adj* secundario; ~ **education** segunda enseñanza *f*; ~ **explosion** explosión *f* por simpatía; ~ **picket(ing)** piquete *m* secundario; ~ **production** producción *f* secundaria; ~ **school** instituto *m* (de segunda enseñanza); ~ **storage** almacenamiento *m* secundario.

second-best ['sekənd'best] **1** *adj* segundo; (el) mejor después del primero; **our** ~ **car** nuestro coche número dos.

2 *adv*: **to come off** ~ quedarse en segundo lugar.

3 *n* expediente *m*; sustituto *m*; **it's a** ~ es un sustituto, no es todo lo que hubiéramos deseado, sabemos que es inferior.

second-class ['sekənd'klɑːs] **1** *adj* de segunda clase; inferior, más bien mediocre; ~ **citizen** ciudadano *m* de segunda clase; ~ **mail,** ~ **post** correo *m* de segunda clase; ~ **ticket** billete *m* de segunda clase. **2** *adv*: **to send a letter** ~ enviar una carta por correo de segunda clase.

seconder ['sekəndəʳ] *n* el (la) que apoya una moción; **there was no** ~ nadie apoyó la moción.

secondhand ['sekənd'hænd] **1** *adj* de segunda mano, de lance; usado, no nuevo; ~ **bookseller** librero *m* de viejo; ~ **bookshop** librería *f* de viejo; ~ **car** coche *m* de segunda mano; ~ **clothes** ropa *f* usada; ~ **information** información *f* de segunda mano; ~ **shop** compraventa *f*. **2** *adv*: **to buy sth** ~ comprar algo de segunda mano (*or* usado *etc*); **I heard it only** ~ yo lo supe solamente por otro.

second-in-command ['sekəndɪnkə'mɑːnd] *n* (*Mil*) subjefe *m*, segundo *m* en el mando.

secondly ['sekəndlɪ] *adv* en segundo lugar.

secondment [sɪ'kɒndmənt] *n* (*Brit*) traslado *m* temporal (*to* a); **she is on** ~ **to section B** se ha trasladado temporalmente a la Sección B.

second-rate ['sekənd'reɪt] *adj* de segunda categoría; inferior, más bien mediocre; **some** ~ **writer** algún escritor de segunda categoría.

secrecy ['siːkrəsɪ] *n* secreto *m*; reserva *f*, discreción *f*; **in** ~ en secreto; **in strict** ~ en el mayor secreto; **to swear sb to** ~ hacer que uno jure no revelar algo.

secret ['siːkrɪt] **1** *adj* secreto; *information etc* secreto, confidencial; (*secretive*) reservado; (*hidden*) oculto, encubierto; ~ **agent** agente *m* secreto, agente *f* secreta; ~ **drawer** secreto *m*; ~ **police** policía *f* secreta; ~ **service** servicio *m* secreto, servicio *m* de contraespionaje; **to keep sth** ~ tener algo secreto, no revelar algo; **it's all highly** ~ todo es de lo más secreto.

2 *n* secreto *m*; **the** ~**s of nature** los misterios de la naturaleza; **in** ~ en secreto; clandestinamente; **to be in on the** ~ estar en el secreto; **there's no** ~ **about it** esto no tiene nada de secreto; **to keep a** ~ guardar un secreto, no revelar un secreto; **to let sb into a** ~ revelar a uno un secreto; **shall I let you into a** ~? ¿quieres que te revele un secreto?; **to make no** ~ **of sth** no tratar de tener algo secreto; **he made no** ~ **that** ... no trató de negar que ...; **to tell sb sth as a** ~ contar algo a uno como un secreto, decir algo a uno en confianza.

secretarial [,sekrə'tɛərɪəl] *adj* de secretario; ~ **college** colegio *m* de secretaría; ~ **course** curso *m* de secretaría; ~ **services** servicios *mpl* de secretaria; ~ **skills** técnicas *fpl* de secretaria; ~ **work** trabajo *m* de secretaria, trabajo *m* de oficina.

secretariat [,sekrə'tɛərɪət] *n* secretaría *f*, secretariado *m*.

secretary ['sekrətrɪ] **1** *n* secretario *m*, -a *f*; **S**~ **of State** (*Brit*) Ministro *m*, -a *f* (*for* de); (*US*) Ministro *m*, -a *f* de Asuntos Exteriores. **2** *attr*: ~ **pool** (*US*) servicio *m* de mecanógrafas.

secretary-general ['sekrətrɪ'dʒenərəl] *n* secretario *m*, -a *f* general.

secretaryship ['sekrətrɪʃɪp] *n* secretaría *f*, secretariado *m*.

secrete [sɪ'kriːt] *vt* (**a**) (*hide*) esconder, ocultar. (**b**) (*Med*) secretar, segregar.

secretion [sɪ'kriːʃən] *n* (**a**) escondimiento *m*, ocultación *f*. (**b**) (*Med*) secreción *f*, segregación *f*.

secretive ['siːkrətɪv] *adj* reservado, callado; sigiloso; **to be** ~ **about sth** hacer un secreto de algo, hacer algo con secreto.

secretively ['siːkrətɪvlɪ] *adv* calladamente; sigilosamente.

secretiveness ['siːkrətɪvnɪs] *n* reserva *f*; sigilo *m*.

secretly ['siːkrɪtlɪ] *adv* secretamente, en secreto; a escondidas; **to be** ~ **pleased about sth** alegrarse en el fondo de su corazón de algo.

sect [sekt] *n* secta *f*.

sectarian [sek'tɛərɪən] **1** *adj* sectario. **2** *n* sectario *m*, -a *f*.

sectarianism [sek'tɛərɪənɪzəm] *n* sectarismo *m*.

section ['sekʃən] *n* sección *f*; parte *f*, porción *f*; (*of city*) barrio *m*; (*of country*) región *f*; (*of code, document, law etc*) artículo *m*; (*of pipeline, road etc*) tramo *m*; (*of opinion*) sector *m*; (*in diagram, dissection*) sección *f*, corte *m*; (*of orange etc*) gajo *m*; (~ *mark*) párrafo *m*; **passports** ~ sección *f* de pasaportes; **in all** ~**s of the public** en todos los sectores del público.

◆**section off** *vt* cortar, seccionar, vallar.

sectional ['sekʃənl] *adj* seccional; relativo a una sección; regional, local; *furniture* combinado, desmontable, fabricado en secciones.

sectionalism ['sekʃənəlɪzəm] *n* faccionalismo *m*.

section mark ['sekʃənmɑːk] *n* párrafo *m*.

sector ['sektəʳ] *n* sector *m* (*also Comput*).

secular ['sekjʊləʳ] *adj* secular, seglar; ~ **school** escuela *f* laica.

secularism ['sekjʊlərɪzəm] *n* laicismo *m*.

secularization ['sekjʊləraɪ'zeɪʃən] *n* secularización *f*.

secularize ['sekjʊləraɪz] *vt* secularizar.

secure [sɪ'kjʊəʳ] **1** *adj* (*safe, certain*) seguro; (*firm*) firme, fijo, estable; ~ **in the knowledge that** ... sabiendo perfectamente que ...; **to be** ~ **against, to be** ~ **from** estar asegurado contra, estar protegido contra; **to feel** ~ sentirse seguro; **to make a door** ~ asegurar una puerta.

2 *vt* (**a**) (*make firm*) asegurar, fijar, afianzar; cerrar; *loan* asegurar, garantizar; ~**d creditor** acreedor *m* con garantía; ~**d loan** préstamo *m* con garantía.

(**b**) (*obtain*) obtener, conseguir; **to** ~ **the services of sb** obtener los servicios de uno; **I** ~**d two fine specimens** obtuve dos bellos ejemplares; **he** ~**d it for £900** lo adquirió por 900 libras.

securely [sɪ'kjʊəlɪ] *adv* seguramente; firmemente, fijamente; **it is** ~ **fastened** está bien sujetado; **we are now** ~ **established** ahora estamos firmemente establecidos.

security [sɪ'kjʊərɪtɪ] **1** *n* (**a**) seguridad *f*; protección *f*; (*against spying etc*) seguridad *f*; (*Fin*: *on loan*) fianza *f*; (*on small loan*) prenda *f*; (*person*) fiador *m*, -ora *f*; **to live on (social)** ~ vivir del Seguro; ~ **of tenure** tenencia *f* asegurada; **up to £100 without** ~ hasta 100 libras sin fianza; **to lend money on** ~ prestar dinero sobre fianza; **to stand** ~ **for sb** (*Fin*) salir fiador de uno, (*fig*) salir por uno.

(**b**) **securities** (*Fin*) títulos *mpl*, valores *mpl*, obligaciones *fpl*.

2 *attr*: ~ **agreement** (*Fin*) acuerdo *m* de garantía; ~ **blanket** (*Psych*: *of a child*) manta *f* de seguridad; (*secrecy*) colchón *m* de seguridad; **S**~ **Council** Consejo *m* de Seguridad; ~ **firm** empresa *f* de seguridad; ~ **forces** fuerzas *fpl* de seguridad; ~ **guard** guarda *m* jurado; ~ **leak** filtración *f* de información secreta; ~ **man** hombre *m* de seguridad; **securities market** mercado *m* bursátil; ~ **officer** oficial *mf* de seguridad; ~ **police** policía *f* de seguridad; **securities portfolio** cartera *f* de valores; **a** ~ **risk** persona *f* de dudosa lealtad, persona *f* no enteramente confiable (desde el punto de vista de la seguridad nacional); ~ **services** servicios *mpl* de seguridad; ~ **system** sistema *m*

de seguridad; ~ **vetting** acreditación *f* por la Seguridad.
Secy. *abbr of* **Secretary** Secretario *m*, -a *f*, Srio, Sria.
sedan [sɪ'dæn] *n* (*also* ~ **chair**) silla *f* de manos; (*US Aut*) sedán *m*.
sedate [sɪ'deɪt] **1** *adj* tranquilo, sosegado; serio. **2** *vt* (*Med*) administrar sedantes a, sedar.
sedately [sɪ'deɪtlɪ] *adv* tranquilamente, sosegadamente; seriamente.
sedateness [sɪ'deɪtnɪs] *n* tranquilidad *f*, sosiego *m*; seriedad *f*.
sedation [sɪ'deɪʃən] *n* sedación *f*, tratamiento *m* con calmantes; **under** ~ bajo calmantes, bajo sedación.
sedative ['sedətɪv] **1** *adj* sedante, calmante. **2** *n* sedante *m*, calmante *m*.
sedentary ['sedntrɪ] *adj* sedentario.
sedge [sedʒ] *n* junco *m*, juncia *f*.
sediment ['sedɪmənt] *n* sedimento *m* (*also Geol*); poso *m*.
sedimentary [,sedɪ'mentərɪ] *adj* sedimentario.
sedimentation [,sedɪmen'teɪʃən] *n* sedimentación *f*.
sedition [sə'dɪʃən] *n* sedición *f*.
seditious [sə'dɪʃəs] *adj* sedicioso.
seduce [sɪ'dju:s] *vt* seducir; **to ~ sb from his duty** apartar a uno de su deber.
seducer [sɪ'dju:sə^r] *n* seductor *m*.
seduction [sɪ'dʌkʃən] *n* seducción *f*.
seductive [sɪ'dʌktɪv] *adj* seductor.
seductively [sɪ'dʌktɪvlɪ] *adv* de modo seductor; en tono seductor.
seductiveness [sɪ'dʌktɪvnɪs] *n* atractivo *m*.
seductress [sɪ'dʌktrɪs] *n* seductora *f*.
sedulous ['sedjʊləs] *adj* asiduo, diligente.
sedulously ['sedjʊləslɪ] *adv* asiduamente, diligentemente.
see[1] [si:] (*irr*: *pret* **saw**, *ptp* **seen**) **1** *vt* (**a**) (*gen*) ver; **'~ page 8'** 'véase la página 8'; **he's ~n a lot of the world** ha visto mucho mundo; **she'll not ~ 40 again** los 40 ya no los cumple; **I'll ~ what I can do** veré si puedo hacer algo; **I can ~ to read** veo bastante bien para poder leer; **to ~ sb do sth** ver a uno hacer algo; **I saw him coming** lo vi venir; **he was ~n to fall** se le vio caer; **I saw it done in 1968** lo vi hacer en 1968; **I'll ~ him damned first** antes le veré colgado; **there was not a house to be ~n** no se veía ni una sola casa; **this dress is not fit to be ~n** este vestido no se puede ver; **he's not fit to be ~n in public** no se le puede presentar a los ojos del público.

(**b**) (*accompany*) acompañar; **to ~ sb to the door** acompañar a uno a la puerta; **to ~ a girl home** acompañar a una chica a su casa; **may I ~ you home?** ¿puedo acompañarte a casa?; **he was so drunk we had to ~ him to bed** estaba tan borracho que tuvimos que llevarle a la cama.

(**c**) (*understand*) comprender, entender, ver; **I don't ~ why** no veo por qué, no comprendo por qué; **I fail to ~ how** no comprendo cómo; **as far as I can ~** según mi modo de entender las cosas; a mi ver; **this is how I ~ it** éste es mi modo de entenderlo, yo lo entiendo así; **the Russians ~ it differently** los rusos lo miran desde otro punto de vista, el criterio de los rusos es distinto; **I don't ~ it** (*fig*) no creo que sea posible; no veo cómo se podría hacer.

(**d**) (*look, learn, perceive*) mirar; observar; percibir; **I saw only too clearly that ...** percibí demasiado bien que ...; **I ~ in the paper that ...** veo en el periódico que ...; **did you ~ that Queen Anne is dead?** ¿has oído que ha muerto la reina Ana?; **I ~ nothing wrong in it** no le encuentro nada indebido; **I don't know what she ~s in him** no sé lo que ella le encuentra.

(**e**) (*ensure*) **to ~ (to it) that...** procurar que + *subj*, asegurar que + *subj*; **~ that he has all he needs** cuida que tenga todo lo que necesita; **~ that it does not happen again** y que no vuelva a ocurrir; **~ that you have it ready for Monday** procura tenerlo listo para el lunes; **to ~ that sth is done** procurar que algo se haga.

(**f**) (*visit, frequent*) ver, visitar; **to ~ the doctor** consultar al médico; **I want to ~ you about my daughter** quiero hablar con Vd acerca de mi hija; **what did he want to ~ you about?** ¿qué asunto quería discutir contigo?, ¿qué motivo tuvo su visita?; **we don't ~ much of them nowadays** ahora les vemos bastante poco; **we shall be ~ing them for dinner** vamos a cenar con ellos; **to call** (*or* **go**) **and ~ sb** ir a visitar a uno; **the minister saw the Queen yesterday** el ministro se entrevistó con la Reina ayer; **I'm afraid I can't ~ you tomorrow** lamento no poder verle mañana; **~ you*!**, **~ you soon!**, **~ you later!**, **be ~ing you*!** ¡hasta pronto!; **~ you on Sunday!** ¡hasta el domingo!

(**g**) (*imagine*) **I don't ~ her as a minister** no me imagino verla como ministra; **I can't ~ myself doing that** no me imagino con capacidad para hacer eso; **I can't really ~ myself being elected** en realidad no creo que me vayan a elegir.

(**h**) (*experience*) **he's ~n it all** está de vuelta de todo; **this hat has ~n better days** este sombrero ha conocido mejores días; **I never thought I'd ~ the day when ...** parece imposible que llegara el día en que ...; **she's certainly ~ing life** es seguro que está viendo muchas cosas; **we'll not ~ his like again** no veremos otro como él.

2 *vi* (**a**) (*gen*) ver; **let me ~** déjame ver; (*fig*: *also* **let's ~**) vamos a ver, veamos; a ver; **I'll go and ~** voy a ver; **~ for yourself!** ¡véalo Vd!; **now just ~ here!** ¡mire!; **so I ~** lo veo, lo estoy viendo; **as far as the eye can ~** hasta donde alcanza la vista; **from here you can ~ for miles** desde aquí se ve muy lejos; desde aquí se domina un gran panorama; **he was trying to ~ in** se esforzaba por ver el interior; **we shan't be able to ~ out** no podremos ver el exterior.

(**b**) (*understand*) comprender; **I ~** lo veo; **I ~!** ¡ya!, ¡ya caigo!, ¡ya comprendo!; **it's all over, ~?*** se acabó, ¿comprendes?; **he's dead, don't you ~?** está muerto, me entiendes?; **as far as I can ~** a mi ver, según mi modo de entender las cosas.

◆**see about** *vt* (**a**) (*attend to*) atender a, encargarse de; **I'll ~ about it** lo haré, me encargo de eso; **he came to ~ about our TV** vino a ver nuestra televisión; (*and repair*) vino a reparar nuestra televisión.

(**b**) (*consider*) **I'll ~ about it** lo veré, lo pensaré; **we'll ~ about that!** ¡es lo que hay que ver!; ¡y cómo!; **we must ~ about getting a new car** tenemos que pensar en comprar un nuevo coche.

◆**see in** *vt person* hacer entrar, hacer pasar; **to ~ the New Year in** celebrar (*LAm*: festejar) el Año Nuevo.

◆**see into** *vt* investigar, examinar.

◆**see off** *vt* (**a**) (*say goodbye*) despedirse de; **we went to ~ him off at the station** fuimos a despedirnos de él en la estación.

(**b**) (*****: *send away*) **the policeman saw them off** el policía los acompañó a la puerta; el policía les dijo que se fueran.

(**c**) (*****: *defeat*) vencer, cascar*; deshacerse de; acabar con; **the minister saw the miners off** el ministro acabó con los mineros.

◆**see out** *vt* (**a**) *person* acompañar a la puerta.

(**b**) **to ~ a film out** quedarse hasta el fin de una película, permanecer sentado hasta que termine una película; **we wondered if he would ~ the month out** nos preguntábamos si viviría hasta el fin del mes.

◆**see over** *vt* visitar, hacer la visita de; recorrer.

◆**see through** *vt* (**a**) *deal* llevar a cabo; **don't worry, we'll ~ it through** no te preocupes, nosotros lo haremos todo.

(**b**) **to ~ sb through** ayudar a uno a salir de un apuro, ayudar a uno en un trance difícil; **£100 should ~ you through** tendrás bastante con 100 libras, con 100 libras estarás bien.

(**c**) **to ~ through sb** calar a uno, conocer el juego de uno; **to ~ through a mystery** penetrar un misterio.

◆**see to** *vt* atender a; encargarse de; (*repair*) reparar, componer; **he ~s to everything** se encarga de todo, lo hace todo; **the rats saw to that** las ratas se encargaron de eso; **to ~ to it that ...** procurar que + *subj*, asegurar que + *subj*.

see[2] [si:] *n* sede *f*; (*of archbishop*) arzobispado *m*; (*of bishop*) obispado *m*; *V* **holy**.
seed [si:d] **1** *n* (**a**) (*Bot*; *for sowing*) semilla *f*, simiente *f*; (*within fruit*) pepita *f*; (*grain*) grano *m*; **to go to ~**, **to run to ~** granar, dar en grana; (*fig*) echarse a perder; ir a menos; **to sow ~s of doubt in sb's mind** sembrar la duda en la mente de uno.

(**b**) (*sperm*) simiente *f*; (*offspring*) descendencia *f*.
(**c**) (*of idea etc*) germen *m*.
(**d**) (*Sport*) preseleccionado *m*, -a *f*.
2 *vt* (**a**) *land* sembrar (*with* de); (*extract ~s from*) despepitar.
(**b**) (*Sport*) preseleccionar.
3 *vi* granar, dar en grana; dejar caer semillas.
seedbed ['si:dbed] *n* semillero *m*.
seedbox ['si:dbɒks] *n* caja *f* de simientes, semillero *m*.
seedcake ['si:dkeɪk] *n* torta *f* de alcaravea.
seedcorn ['si:dkɔ:n] *n* trigo *m* de siembra.
seed-drill ['si:ddrɪl] *n* sembradora *f*.
seedily ['si:dɪlɪ] *adv dress* andrajosamente.

seediness ['si:dɪnɪs] *n* (*shabbiness*) desaseo *m*; (*illness*) indisposición *f*.
seedless ['si:dlɪs] *adj* sin semillas.
seedling ['si:dlɪŋ] *n* plántula *f*.
seed merchant ['si:d,mɜ:tʃənt] *n* comerciante *mf* de semillas.
seed pearl ['si:dpɜ:l] *n* aljófar *m*.
seed pod ['si:dpɒd] *n* vaina *f*.
seed potato ['si:dpə,teɪtəʊ] *n, pl* **seed potatoes** ['si:dpə,teɪtəʊz] patata *f* (*or* papa *f LAm*) de siembra.
seedsman ['si:dzmən] *n, pl* **seedsmen** ['si:dzmən] vendedor *m* de semillas.
seed-time ['si:dtaɪm] *n* siembra *f*.
seedy ['si:dɪ] *adj* (**a**) (*Med*) enfermo, indispuesto; pachucho, ojeroso. (**b**) *appearance* desaseado; *clothing* raído; *place* pobre, sórdido.
seeing ['si:ɪŋ] **1** *n* vista *f*, visión *f*; ~ **is believing** ver y creer; **a film worth** ~ una película que vale la pena de verse.
2 *conj*: ~ **that** ..., ~ **as*** ... visto que ..., puesto que ...
seek [si:k] (*irr*: *pret and ptp* **sought**) **1** *vt* (**a**) buscar; *post* pretender, solicitar; *honour* ambicionar; (*search*) registrar, recorrer buscando; **to** ~ **death** buscar la muerte; **to** ~ **shelter** buscar dónde refugiarse; **to** ~ **advice from sb** pedir consejos a uno; **it is much sought after** está muy cotizado; **the reason is not far to** ~ no es difícil indicar la causa; **he has been sought in many countries** se le ha buscado en muchos países.
(**b**) (*attempt*) **to** ~ **to** + *infin* intentar + *infin*, procurar + *infin*; esforzarse por + *infin*.
2 *vi* buscar; **to** ~ **after, to** ~ **for** buscar; **to** ~ **to** + *infin* intentar + *infin*, procurar + *infin*; esforzarse por + *infin*.
◆**seek out** *vt* buscar.
seeker ['si:kəʳ] *n* buscador *m*, -ora *f*.
seem [si:m] *vi* parecer; **so it** ~**s** así parece; **how does it** ~ **to you?** ¿qué te parece?; **it** ~**s that** ... parece que ...; **it does not** ~ **that** ... no parece que + *subj*; **he** ~**s honest** parece honrado; **he** ~**ed absorbed in** ... parecía estar absorto en ...; **she** ~**s not to want to go** parece que no quiere ir; **I** ~ **to have heard that before** me parece que ya me contaron eso antes; **what** ~**s to be the trouble?** ¿pasa algo?
seeming ['si:mɪŋ] **1** *adj* aparente. **2** *n* apariencia *f*; **to all** ~ según todas las apariencias.
seemingly ['si:mɪŋlɪ] *adv* aparentemente, según parece (*or* parecía *etc*); **it is** ~ **finished** parece que está terminado.
seemliness ['si:mlɪnɪs] *n* decoro *m*, decencia *f*, corrección *f*.
seemly ['si:mlɪ] *adj* decoroso, decente, correcto.
seen [si:n] *ptp of* **see**[1].
seep [si:p] *vi* filtrarse, rezumarse.
◆**seep away** *vi* escurrirse.
◆**seep in** *vi* filtrarse.
◆**seep out** *vi* escurrirse.
seepage ['si:pɪdʒ] *n* filtración *f*.
seer [sɪəʳ] *n* vidente *mf*, profeta *mf*.
seersucker ['sɪə,sʌkəʳ] *n* sirsaca *f*.
seesaw ['si:sɔ:] **1** *n* balancín *m*, columpio *m* de tabla, subibaja *m*; (*fig*) vaivén *m*. **2** *adj movement* de vaivén, oscilante; ~ **motion** movimiento *m* oscilante (*or* de balanceo). **3** *vi* columpiarse; (*fig*) oscilar.
seethe [si:ð] *vi* hervir; **to** ~ **with** hervir de, hervir en; **he's seething** está furioso; **to** ~ **with anger** indignarse muchísimo, estar furioso.
see-through ['si:θru:] *adj dress* diáfano, transparente.
segment ['segmənt] *n* segmento *m*.
segmentation [,segmən'teɪʃən] *n* segmentación *f*.
segregate ['segrɪgeɪt] *vt* segregar, separar (*from* de); **to be** ~**d from** estar separado de.
segregated ['segrɪgeɪtɪd] *adj* segregado, separado.
segregation ['segrɪ'geɪʃən] *n* segregación *f*, separación *f*; (*esp*) segregación *f* racial.
segregationist [,segrɪ'geɪʃnɪst] *n* segregacionista *mf*.
Seine [seɪn] *n* Sena *m*.
seine [seɪn] *n* jábega *f*.
seismic ['saɪzmɪk] *adj* sísmico.
seismograph ['saɪzməgrɑ:f] *n* sismógrafo *m*.
seismography [saɪz'mɒgrəfɪ] *n* sismografía *f*.
seismologist [saɪz'mɒlədʒɪst] *n* sismólogo *m*, -a *f*.
seismology [saɪz'mɒlədʒɪ] *n* sismología *f*.
seize [si:z] *vt* (*clutch*) agarrar, asir, coger; (*Jur*) *person* detener, prender, *property* embargar, secuestrar; *contraband etc* incautarse de; *territory etc* apoderarse de; *opportunity* aprovechar sin vacilar; **to** ~ **sb by the arm** asir a uno por el brazo; **to be** ~**d with fear** sobrecogerse, ser preso del miedo; **he was** ~**d with a desire to** + *infin* le entró un súbito deseo de + *infin*.
◆**seize up** *vi* (*Mech*) agarrotarse (*also fig*).
◆**seize (up)on** *vt* fijarse en; *pretext etc* valerse de.
seizure ['si:ʒəʳ] *n* (**a**) (*V vt*) asimiento *m*; detención *f*; prendimiento *m*; embargo *m*, secuestro *m*; incautación *f*; **the** ~ **of Slobodia** el acto de apoderarse de Eslobodia. (**b**) (*Med*) ataque *m*; convulsión *f*, crisis *f*; acceso *m*; **to have a** ~ sufrir un ataque (*esp* epiléptico).
seldom ['seldəm] *adv* rara vez, raramente; ~ **if ever** rara vez por no decir jamás.
select [sɪ'lekt] **1** *vt* escoger, elegir; (*Sport*) seleccionar.
2 *adj* selecto, escogido; exclusivista; *tobacco etc* fino; ~ **committee** comité *m* de investigación; **a very** ~ **neighbourhood** un barrio de muy buen tono; **a** ~ **group of people** un grupo selecto de personas.
selection [sɪ'lekʃən] **1** *n* selección *f*; elección *f*; (*Comm*) surtido *m*; **'~s from Rossini'** 'selecciones *fpl* de Rossini'; **'~s from Cervantes'** 'páginas *fpl* escogidas de Cervantes'; **~s for the big race** pronósticos *mpl* para la carrera principal; **one has to make a** ~ hay que escoger, hay que tomar unos y dejar otros.
2 *attr*: ~ **committee** tribunal *m* de selección, jurado *m*.
selective [sɪ'lektɪv] *adj* selectivo; **one has to be** ~ hay que escoger, hay que tomar unos y dejar otros.
selectively [sɪ'lektɪvlɪ] *adv* selectivamente.
selectivity [sɪlek'tɪvɪtɪ] *n* selectividad *f*.
selector [sɪ'lektəʳ] *n* (*Tech*) selector *m*; (*Sport*) seleccionador *m*, -ora *f*.
selenium [sɪ'li:nɪəm] *n* selenio *m*.
self [self] **1** *reflexive pron* se (*etc*); (*after prep*) sí mismo (*etc*); (*Comm, hum**) = **myself** *etc*; **a room reserved for wife and** ~ una habitación reservada para mi esposa y yo.
2 *adj* (*esp Bot*) unicolor.
3 *n, pl* **selves** [selvz] uno mismo, una misma; **the** ~ el yo; **my better** ~ mi mejor parte; **my former** ~ mi ser anterior; **one's other** ~ su otro yo; **if your good** ~ **could possibly** ... si Vd tuviera tanta amabilidad como para ...; **my humble** ~ este servidor; **is it for** ~ **or someone else?** ¿es para Vd o para otra persona?; **he's quite his old** ~ **again** vuelve a ser el mismo de antes, se ha repuesto completamente; **he thinks of nothing but** ~ no piensa sino en sí mismo.
self- [self] *pref* auto...; ... de sí mismo.
self-abasement ['selfə'beɪsmənt] *n* rebajamiento *m* de sí mismo, autodegradación *f*.
self-absorbed ['selfəb'zɔ:bd] *adj* absorto en sí mismo; ensimismado.
self-abuse ['selfə'bju:s] *n* (*euph*) masturbación *f*.
self-acting ['self'æktɪŋ] *adj* automático.
self-addressed ['selfə'drest] *adj*: ~ **envelope** sobre *m* con el nombre y dirección de uno mismo.
self-adhesive ['selfəd'hi:zɪv] *adj* autoadhesivo.
self-advertisement ['selfəd'vɜ:tɪsmənt] *n* autobombo *m*.
self-aggrandizement [,selfə'grændɪzmənt] *n* autobombo *m*.
self-analysis [,selfə'næləsɪs] *n* autoanálisis *m*.
self-apparent ['selfə'pærənt] *adj* evidente, patente.
self-appointed ['selfə'pɔɪntɪd] *adj* que se ha nombrado a sí mismo.
self-appraisal [,selfə'preɪzl] *n* autovaloración *f*.
self-assertion ['selfə'sɜ:ʃən] *n* asertividad *f*.
self-assertive ['selfə'sɜ:tɪv] *adj* asertivo; que insiste en reafirmarse, que trata de imponerse.
self-assertiveness ['selfə'sɜ:tɪvnɪs] *n* asertividad *f*; insistencia *f* en reafirmarse.
self-assessment ['selfə'sesmənt] *n* autoevaluación *f*.
self-assurance ['selfə'ʃʊərəns] *n* confianza *f* en sí mismo.
self-assured ['selfə'ʃʊəd] *adj* seguro de sí mismo.
self-awareness [,selfə'weənɪs] *n* conocimiento *m* (*or* conciencia *f*) de sí mismo.
self-catering ['self'keɪtərɪŋ] *attr*: ~ **apartment** piso *m* sin pensión; ~ **holiday** vacaciones *fpl* en piso (*or* chalet *or* casita *etc*) con cocina propia.
self-centred, (*US*) **self-centered** ['self'sentəd] *adj* egocéntrico.
self-cleaning [,self'kli:nɪŋ] *adj oven etc* autolimpiable.
self-closing [,self'kləʊzɪŋ] *adj* de cierre automático.
self-coloured, (*US*) **self-colored** ['self'kʌləd] *adj* de color uniforme, unicolor.
self-command ['selfkə'mɑ:nd] *n* dominio *m* sobre sí mismo, autodominio *m*.
self-complacent ['selfkəm'pleɪsənt] *adj* satisfecho de sí mismo.
self-composed ['selfkəm'pəʊzd] *adj* ecuánime, dueño de sí

mismo, sereno.

self-composure ['selfkəm'pəʊʒəʳ] *n* ecuanimidad *f*, serenidad *f*.

self-conceit ['selfkən'siːt] *n* presunción *f*, vanidad *f*, engreimiento *m*.

self-conceited ['selfkən'siːtɪd] *adj* presumido, vanidoso, engreído.

self-confessed [ˌselfkən'fest] *adj* confeso, autoconfesado.

self-confidence ['self'kɒnfɪdəns] *n* confianza *f* en sí mismo.

self-confident ['self'kɒnfɪdənt] *adj* seguro de sí mismo, lleno de confianza en sí mismo.

self-congratulation ['selfkənˌgrætjʊ'leɪʃən] *n* autofelicitación *f*.

self-conscious ['self'kɒnʃəs] *adj* cohibido, tímido, encogido, inseguro.

self-consciously [ˌself'kɒnʃəslɪ] *adv* cohibidamente, tímidamente.

self-consciousness ['self'kɒnʃəsnɪs] *n* timidez *f*, encogimiento *m*, inseguridad *f*.

self-contained ['selfkən'teɪnd] *adj* independiente; que tiene sus propios recursos, que no necesita ayuda de afuera; (*Brit*) *flat* independiente, con entrada particular; *person* independiente; reservado, poco comunicativo.

self-contradiction ['selfˌkɒntrə'dɪkʃən] *n* contradicción *f* en sí.

self-contradictory ['selfˌkɒntrə'dɪktərɪ] *adj* que se contradice a sí mismo, que lleva implícita una contradicción.

self-control ['selfkən'trəʊl] *n* autodominio *m*, dominio *m* sobre sí mismo, control *m* de sí mismo; **to exercise one's ~** contenerse, dominarse; **to lose one's ~** perder la calma, ponerse nervioso.

self-controlled ['selfkən'trəʊld] *adj* ecuánime, sereno.

self-correcting [ˌselfkə'rektɪŋ] *adj* autocorrector.

self-critical [ˌself'krɪtɪkl] *adj* autocrítico.

self-criticism ['self'krɪtɪsɪzəm] *n* autocrítica *f*.

self-deception ['selfdɪ'sepʃən] *n* engaño *m* de sí mismo; **this is mere ~** son ilusiones, esto es engañarse a sí mismo.

self-defeating ['selfdɪ'fiːtɪŋ] *adj* contraproducente.

self-defence, (*US*) **self-defense** ['selfdɪ'fens] *n* autodefensa *f*, defensa *f* propia; **to act in ~** obrar en defensa propia.

self-delusion [ˌselfdɪ'luːʒən] *n* autoengaño *m*.

self-denial ['selfdɪ'naɪəl] *n* abnegación *f*.

self-denying ['selfdɪ'naɪɪŋ] *adj* abnegado; **~ ordinance** resolución *f* abnegada.

self-destruct [ˌselfdɪs'trʌkt] *vi* autodestruirse.

self-destruction ['selfdɪs'trʌkʃən] *n* suicidio *m*; (*of weapon*) autodestrucción *f*.

self-destructive [ˌselfdɪs'trʌktɪv] *adj* autodestructivo.

self-determination ['selfdɪˌtɜːmɪ'neɪʃən] *n* autodeterminación *f*.

self-determined [ˌselfdɪ'tɜːmɪnd] *adj* autodeterminado, independiente.

self-discipline ['self'dɪsɪplɪn] *n* autodisciplina *f*, autodominio *m*.

self-disciplined ['self'dɪsɪplɪnd] *adj* autodisciplinado.

self-doubt [ˌself'daʊt] *n* desconfianza *f* de sí mismo.

self-drive [ˌself'draɪv] *attr*: **~ hire** (*Brit Aut*) alquiler *m* sin chófer.

self-educated ['self'edjʊkeɪtɪd] *adj* autodidacta.

self-effacement ['selfɪ'feɪsmənt] *n* modestia *f*, humildad *f*.

self-effacing ['selfɪ'feɪsɪŋ] *adj* modesto, humilde.

self-employed ['selfɪm'plɔɪd] *adj* autónomo, que trabaja por cuenta propia.

self-employment ['selfɪm'plɔɪmənt] *n* trabajo *m* autónomo, trabajo *m* por cuenta propia.

self-esteem ['selfɪs'tiːm] *n* amor *m* propio, autoestima *f*.

self-evident ['self'evɪdənt] *adj* evidente, patente.

self-examination [ˌselfɪgˌzæmɪ'neɪʃən] *n* autoexamen *m*, introspección *f*, examen *m* de conciencia.

self-explanatory ['selfɪks'plænɪtərɪ] *adj* que se explica por sí mismo.

self-expression ['selfɪks'preʃən] *n* autoexpresión *f*; arte *m* de expresarse, expresión *f* de la personalidad de uno.

self-filling ['self'fɪlɪŋ] *adj* de relleno automático.

self-financing [ˌselffaɪ'nænsɪŋ] **1** *n* autofinanciación *f*, autofinanzamiento *m*. **2** *adj* autofinanciado.

self-fulfilling ['selffʊl'fɪlɪŋ] *adj*: **~ prophecy** profecía *f* que por su propia naturaleza contribuye a cumplirse.

self-fulfilment, (*US*) **self-fulfillment** ['selffʊl'fɪlmənt] *n* realización *f* de los más íntimos deseos de uno, realización *f* completa de la potencialidad de uno.

self-governing ['self'gʌvənɪŋ] *adj* autónomo.

self-government ['self'gʌvnmənt] *n* autonomía *f*, autogobierno *m*.

self-help ['self'help] *n* ayuda *f* propia, autoayuda *f*, esfuerzo *m* personal; **~ group** grupo *m* de apoyo mutuo.

self-image ['self'ɪmɪdʒ] *n* autoimagen *f*, imagen *f* del propio ego.

self-importance ['selfɪm'pɔːtəns] *n* presunción *f*, vanidad *f*, engreimiento *m*.

self-important ['selfɪm'pɔːtənt] *adj* presumido, vanidoso, engreído.

self-imposed ['selfɪm'pəʊzd] *adj punishment etc* autoimpuesto, que uno se impone a sí mismo, voluntario.

self-improvement [ˌselfɪm'pruːvmənt] *n* autosuperación *f*.

self-induced ['selfɪn'djuːst] *adj* autoinducido.

self-indulgence ['selfɪn'dʌldʒəns] *n* falta *f* de moderación, excesos *mpl* (en el comer *etc*); egoísmo *m*; comodonería *f*.

self-indulgent ['selfɪn'dʌldʒənt] *adj* inmoderado, que se permite excesos (en el comer *etc*); egoísta; comodón, regalón.

self-inflicted ['selfɪn'flɪktɪd] *adj wound* autoinfligido, infligido a sí mismo.

self-interest ['self'ɪntrɪst] *n* egoísmo *m*; interés *m* propio.

self-interested ['self'ɪntrɪstɪd] *adj* egoísta.

selfish ['selfɪʃ] *adj* egoísta; interesado.

selfishly ['selfɪʃlɪ] *adv* con egoísmo, de modo egoísta.

selfishness ['selfɪʃnɪs] *n* egoísmo *m*.

self-justification [ˌselfˌdʒʌstɪfɪ'keɪʃən] *n* autojustificación *f*.

self-knowledge ['self'nɒlɪdʒ] *n* conocimiento *m* de sí mismo.

selfless ['selflɪs] *adj* desinteresado.

selflessly ['selflɪslɪ] *adv* desinteresadamente.

selflessness ['selflɪsnɪs] *n* desinterés *m*.

self-loading ['self'ləʊdɪŋ] *adj* autocargador, de autocarga.

self-locking ['self'lɒkɪŋ] *adj* de cierre automático.

self-love ['self'lʌv] *n* egoísmo *m*; narcisismo *m*; egolatría *f*.

self-made ['self'meɪd] *adj*: **~ man** hombre *m* que ha llegado a su posición actual por sus propios esfuerzos, hijo *m* de sus propias obras.

self-management ['self'mænɪdʒmənt] *n* autogestión *f*.

self-mockery [ˌself'mɒkərɪ] *n* burla *f* de sí mismo.

self-neglect ['selfnɪ'glekt] *n* abandono *m* de sí mismo.

self-opinionated ['selfə'pɪnjəneɪtɪd] *adj* terco.

self-perpetuating [ˌselfpə'petjʊeɪtɪŋ] *adj* autoperpetuable.

self-pity ['self'pɪtɪ] *n* compasión *f* de sí mismo, lástima *f* de sí mismo, autocompasión *f*.

self-pitying [ˌself'pɪtɪɪŋ] *n* autocompasión *f*.

self-pollination ['selfˌpɒlɪ'neɪʃən] *n* autopolinización *f*.

self-portrait ['self'pɔːtrɪt] *n* autorretrato *m*.

self-possessed ['selfpə'zest] *adj* sereno, dueño de sí mismo.

self-possession ['selfpə'zeʃən] *n* serenidad *f*, dominio *m* de sí mismo, autodominio *m*.

self-praise ['self'preɪz] *n* autobombo *m*.

self-preservation ['selfˌprezə'veɪʃən] *n* autopreservación *f*, propia conservación *f*.

self-proclaimed [ˌselfprə'kleɪmd] *adj* autoproclamado.

self-propelled ['selfprə'peld] *adj* autopropulsado, automotor (*f* automotriz).

self-raising ['selfˌreɪzɪŋ] *adj* (*Brit*): **~ flour** harina *f* con levadura, harina *f* de fuerza.

self-regard ['selfrɪ'gɑːd] *n* amor *m* propio; (*pej*) egoísmo *m*.

self-regulating ['self'regjʊleɪtɪŋ] *adj* de regulación automática.

self-regulation ['selfˌregjʊleɪʃən] *n* autorregulación *f*.

self-regulatory [ˌself'regjʊlətərɪ] *adj* autorregulado.

self-reliance ['selfrɪ'laɪəns] *n* confianza *f* en sí mismo; independencia *f*.

self-reliant ['selfrɪ'laɪənt] *adj* seguro de sí mismo; independiente.

self-reproach ['selfrɪ'prəʊtʃ] *n* remordimiento *m*.

self-respect ['selfrɪs'pekt] *n* amor *m* propio, dignidad *f*.

self-respecting ['selfrɪs'pektɪŋ] *adj* que tiene amor propio, consciente de su dignidad personal.

self-restraint ['selfrɪs'treɪnt] *n* = **self-control**.

self-righteous ['self'raɪtʃəs] *adj* santurrón, farisaico.

self-righteousness [ˌself'raɪtʃəsnɪs] *n* santurronería *f*, farisaísmo *m*.

self-rising ['self'raɪzɪŋ] *adj* (*US*): **~ flour** harina *f* con levadura.

self-rule [ˌself'ruːl] *n* autonomía *f*.

self-sacrifice ['self'sækrɪfaɪs] *n* (*act*) sacrificio *m* de sí mismo; (*spirit*) abnegación *f*.

self-sacrificing ['self'sækrɪfaɪsɪŋ] *adj* abnegado.

selfsame ['selfseɪm] *adj* mismo, mismísimo.

self-satisfaction ['selfˌsætɪs'fækʃən] *n* satisfacción *f* de sí mismo; suficiencia *f*.

self-satisfied ['self'sætɪsfaɪd] *adj* satisfecho de sí mismo,

pagado de sí mismo; suficiente.
self-sealing ['self'si:lɪŋ] *adj tank* de cierre automático; *envelope* autoadhesivo, autopegado.
self-seeking ['self'si:kɪŋ] **1** *adj* egoísta. **2** *n* egoísmo *m*.
self-service ['self'sɜ:vɪs] *adj*: ~ **laundry** lavandería *f* de autoservicio; ~ **restaurant** autoservicio *m*, self-service *m*, automático *m* (*SC*).
self-serving ['self'sɜ:vɪŋ] *adj* egoísta, interesado.
self-starter ['self'stɑ:təʳ] *n* (**a**) (*Aut*) arranque *m* automático. (**b**) (*Comm etc*) persona *f* dinámica.
self-styled ['self'staɪld] *adj* supuesto, sediciente.
self-sufficiency ['selfsə'fɪʃənsɪ] *n* independencia *f*; (*economic*) autosuficiencia *f*, autarquía *f*; (*of person*) confianza *f* en sí mismo.
self-sufficient ['selfsə'fɪʃənt] *adj* independiente; (*economically*) autosuficiente; *person* seguro de sí mismo.
self-supporting ['selfsə'pɔ:tɪŋ] *adj* independiente; que tiene sus propios recursos (económicos); que vive de su propio trabajo; **you can marry her when you are** ~ te puedes casar con ella cuando ganes un sueldo adecuado.
self-taught ['self'tɔ:t] *adj* autodidacta.
self-test ['self,test] **1** *n* autocomprobación *f*. **2** *vi* autocomprobarse.
self-willed ['self'wɪld] *adj* terco, voluntarioso.
self-winding ['self'waɪndɪŋ] *adj*: ~ **watch** reloj *m* de cuerda automática.
sell [sel] (*irr*: *pret and ptp* **sold**) **1** *vt* (**a**) vender (*at* a, *for* por); **'car to ~'** 'se vende coche'; **'to be sold'** 'se vende'; **to ~ one's life dearly** vender cara la vida; **I was sold this in Valencia** esto me lo vendieron en Valencia; **to ~ sb for a slave, to ~ sb into slavery** vender a uno como esclavo; *V* **auction, loss** *etc*.
(**b**) (*: *put over*) comunicar, hacer aceptar; **if we can ~ coexistence to Ruritania** si podemos hacer aceptar en Ruritania la idea de la coexistencia; **he doesn't manage to ~ his personality** no consigue comunicar su personalidad.
(**c**) (*: *cheat, betray*) vender, traicionar; **sold again!** ¡la estafa de siempre!; **you've been sold** te han dado gato por liebre.
(**d**) (*) **to be sold on** estar cautivado por; **I'm not exactly sold on the idea** no me estusiasma la idea, estoy lejos de dejarme cautivar por la idea.
2 *vi* (**a**) venderse (*at* a, *for* por); estar de venta; **it ~s well** tiene buena venta, se vende bien, tiene mucha demanda; **that line doesn't ~** ese género no tiene demanda.
(**b**) (*fig*) ser aceptable; **the idea didn't ~** la idea no resultó aceptable.
3 *vr*: **to ~ o.s.** venderse; (*fig*) comunicar con el público, comunicar su personalidad.
4 *n* (**a**) (*) decepción *f*; engaño *m*, estafa *f*; **what a ~!** ¡cómo nos han decepcionado!; ¡todo ha sido engaño!
(**b**) (*Comm*) *V* **hard, soft.**
◆**sell back** *vt*: **to ~ sth back to sb** revender algo a uno.
◆**sell off** *vt* vender (todas las existencias de); liquidar, saldar.
◆**sell out 1** *vt* (*Comm*) vender (todas las existencias de); liquidar, saldar; **we are sold out of bananas** hemos agotado las existencias de plátanos; **stocks of umbrellas are sold out** las existencias de paraguas están agotadas.
2 *vi* (**a**) (*Comm*) venderlo todo, vender todas las existencias; realizar.
(**b**) (*fig*) abandonar, renunciar; (*compromise*) transigir, transar (*LAm*); **to ~ out to the Slobodians** abandonar y dejar el paso a los eslobodios.
◆**sell up** *vi* (*esp Brit*) venderlo todo; vender todas las existencias; realizar.
sell-by date ['selbaɪ,deɪt] *n* fecha *f* de caducidad; fecha *f* límite de venta.
seller ['seləʳ] *n* (**a**) (*person who sells*) vendedor *m*, -ora *f*; (*dealer*) comerciante *m* (*of* en); **~'s market** mercado *m* de demanda, mercado *m* de signo favorable al vendedor, mercado *m* de vendedores. (**b**) **good ~** artículo *m* que tiene mucha demanda.
selling ['selɪŋ] **1** *n* venta *f*, el vender; **a career in ~** una carrera en el márketing. **2** *attr*: **~ point** punto *m* fuerte, aspecto *m* interesante; **~ price** precio *m* de venta; **~ rate** (*Fin*) precio *m* de venta medio.
Sellotape ['seləʊteɪp] ® (*Brit*) **1** *n* Sellotape ® *m*, cinta *f* adhesiva, scotch *m* (*LAm*), durex *m* (*Mex*). **2** *vt* cerrar (*or* pegar *etc*) con cinta adhesiva.
sellout ['selaut] *n* (**a**) (*betrayal*) traición *f*; abandono *m*, renuncia *f*. (**b**) (*Theat, Sport etc*) lleno *m*, venta *f* total.
seltzer (water) ['seltsəʳ(,wɔ:təʳ)] *n* agua *f* de seltz.
selvage, selvedge ['selvɪdʒ] *n* orillo *m*, borde *m*.
selves [selvz] *pl of* **self.**
semantic [sɪ'mæntɪk] *adj* semántico.
semantically [sɪ'mæntɪkəlɪ] *adv* semánticamente.
semanticist [sɪ'mæntɪsɪst] *n* semasiólogo *m*, -a *f*, semantista *mf*.
semantics [sɪ'mæntɪks] *n* semántica *f*.
semaphore ['seməfɔ:ʳ] **1** *n* semáforo *m*. **2** *vt* comunicar por semáforo.
semblance ['sembləns] *n* apariencia *f*; **without a ~ of regret** sin mostrar siquiera el remordimiento; **without a ~ of fear** sin dar señal alguna de miedo; **to put on a ~ of gaiety** procurar parecer alegre, fingir alegría.
seme [si:m] *n* sema *m*.
semen ['si:mən] *n* semen *m*.
semester [sɪ'mestəʳ] *n* (*esp US*) semestre *m*.
semi... ['semɪ] *pref* semi...; medio...
semi* ['semɪ] *n* (**a**) (*Brit*) casa *f* semiseparada, chalet *m* adosado, dúplex *m*. (**b**) (*US, also* **~ trailer**) trailer *m*.
semiautomatic [,semɪ,ɔ:tə'mætɪk] **1** *adj* semiautomático. **2** *n* arma *f* semiautomática.
semibasement ['semɪ'beɪsmənt] *n* semisótano *m*.
semibreve ['semɪbri:v] *n* (*esp Brit*) semibreve *f*.
semicircle ['semɪ,sɜ:kl] *n* semicírculo *m*.
semicircular ['semɪ'sɜ:kjʊləʳ] *adj* semicircular; *archway* de medio punto.
semicolon ['semɪ'kəʊlən] *n* punto *m* y coma.
semiconductor [,semɪkən'dʌktəʳ] *n* semiconductor *m*.
semiconscious ['semɪ'kɒnʃəs] *adj* semiconsciente.
semiconsonant ['semɪ'kɒnsənənt] *n* semiconsonante *f*.
semidarkness ['semɪ'dɑ:knɪs] *n*: **in the ~** en la casi oscuridad.
semidetached ['semɪdɪ'tætʃt] *adj*: **~ house** casa *f* semiseparada, chalet *m* adosado, dúplex *m*.
semifinal ['semɪ'faɪnl] *n* semifinal *f*.
semifinalist ['semɪ'faɪnəlɪst] *n* semifinalista *mf*.
semifinished [,semɪ'fɪnɪʃt] *adj product* semiacabado, semielaborado.
semiliterate [,semɪ'lɪtərɪt] *adj* semialfabetizado.
seminal ['semɪnl] *adj* seminal.
seminar ['semɪnɑ:ʳ] *n* (*Univ*: *class*) seminario *m*, clase *f* de discusión; (*group*) grupo *m* de investigadores; (*conference*) congreso *m*; reunión *f*; (*institute*) instituto *m*.
seminarist ['semɪnərɪst] *n* seminarista *m*.
seminary ['semɪnərɪ] *n* seminario *m*.
semiofficial ['semɪə'fɪʃəl] *adj* semioficial.
semiology [,semɪ'ɒlədʒɪ] *n* semiología *f*.
semiotic [,semɪ'ɒtɪk] *adj* semiótico.
semiotics [,semɪ'ɒtɪks] *n* semiótica *f*.
semiprecious ['semɪ,preʃəs] *adj* fino, semiprecioso; **~ stone** piedra *f* semipreciosa.
semiquaver ['semɪ,kweɪvəʳ] *n* (*esp Brit*) semicorchea *f*.
semiskilled ['semɪ'skɪld] *adj person* semiexperto, semicualificado; *work* para persona semiexperta.
semi-skimmed ['semɪ'skɪmd] *adj*: **~ milk** leche *f* semidesnatada.
Semite ['si:maɪt] *n* semita *mf*.
Semitic [sɪ'mɪtɪk] *adj* semítico.
semitone ['semɪtəʊn] *n* semitono *m*.
semitrailer ['semɪ'treɪləʳ] *n* (*US*) trailer *m*.
semivowel ['semɪ'vaʊəl] *n* semivocal *f*.
semolina [,semə'li:nə] *n* sémola *f*.
sempiternal [,sempɪ'tɜ:nl] *adj* sempiterno.
sempstress ['sempstrɪs] *n* costurera *f*.
SEN *n* (*Brit*) *abbr of* **State Enrolled Nurse.**
Sen. (**a**) *abbr of* **Senior.** (**b**) (*US Pol*) *abbr of* **Senator.** (**c**) (*US Pol*) *abbr of* **Senate.**
senate ['senɪt] *n* senado *m*; (*Univ*) ≃ claustro *m*; **the S~** (*US*) el Senado.
senator ['senɪtəʳ] *n* senador *m*, -ora *f*.
senatorial [,senə'tɔ:rɪəl] *adj* senatorial.
send [send] (*irr*: *pret and ptp* **sent**) **1** *vt* (**a**) (*gen*) enviar, mandar; despachar; remitir; *message, signal* enviar; *telegram* poner; **the gods ~ it as a punishment** los dioses nos lo envían como castigo; **to ~ a child to school** poner a un niño en la escuela; **in Britain children are sent to school at 5** en Gran Bretaña los niños van a la escuela a los 5 años; **some children are sent to school without breakfast** hay niños que van a la escuela sin desayunar; **I wrote the letter but didn't ~ it** escribí la carta pero no la eché al correo; **to ~ sb for sth** enviar a uno a buscar algo; enviar a uno a comprar algo; **they sent him here to help** le enviaron para que nos ayudara; **the rain sent us indoors** la lluvia nos obligó a buscar abrigo; **please ~ me further**

details le ruego enviarme más detalles; **they sent a party to look for him** enviaron un pelotón a buscarle; **the sight sent her running to her mother** viendo esto se echó a correr a su madre.

(**b**) (*propel*) *ball etc* lanzar; *arrow* enviar, lanzar, arrojar; **he sent everything flying** lo echó todo a rodar; **the blow sent him sprawling** el golpe le hizo caer redondo.

(**c**) (*with adj*) hacer, volver, poner; **it ~s the wool green** vuelve la lana verde; **it's enough to ~ you barmy‡** es para volverse loco; **the speech sent everybody wild** el discurso llenó a todos de entusiasmo.

(**d**) (‡) entusiasmar, llenar de emoción, chiflar*, embelesar; **that tune ~s me** esa melodía me chifla*; **he ~s me** me vuelve loca; **it doesn't ~ me** me trae sin cuidado.

2 *vi* mandar; **she sent to say that ...** envió un recado diciendo que ..., mandó a decir que ...

◆**send away 1** *vt* (**a**) enviar (fuera).

(**b**) (*dismiss*) despedir.

(**c**) *goods* despachar, expedir; enviar.

2 *vi*: **to ~ away for** pedir (por correo), encargar (por correo).

◆**send back** *vt goods etc* devolver; *person* hacer volver.

◆**send down** *vt* (**a**) (hacer) bajar; *diver* enviar.

(**b**) *price etc* hacer bajar.

(**c**) (*Brit Univ*) expulsar; *criminal* encarcelar; **they sent him down for 2 years** le condenaron a 2 años de prisión.

◆**send for** *vt* (**a**) *doctor etc* llamar; enviar por.

(**b**) (*order*) pedir, encargar; requerir; mandar buscar, mandar traer.

◆**send forth** *vt smoke etc* emitir, arrojar; *sparks* lanzar; **to ~ sb forth into the world** enviar a uno a vivir en el mundo.

◆**send in** *vt* (**a**) *person* hacer entrar; *visitor* hacer pasar; **~ him in!** ¡que pase!; **to ~ in the troops** enviar los soldados.

(**b**) *bill, name, resignation* presentar.

◆**send off 1** *vt* (**a**) *person* enviar; (*say goodbye to*) despedir.

(**b**) *goods* despachar, expedir; (*by post*) enviar por correo; echar al correo.

(**c**) (*Sport*) expulsar.

2 *vi*: **to ~ off for** pedir, encargar.

◆**send on** *vt* (*Brit*) *letter* hacer seguir; *application etc* dar curso a; *instructions* dar, transmitir.

◆**send out 1** *vt* (**a**) *person* enviar; (*of room*) mandar fuera.

(**b**) *invitations etc* mandar.

(**c**) (*emit*) *smoke etc* arrojar, despedir; *signal* emitir; (*Bot*) *shoot* echar.

2 *vi*: **to ~ out for** mandar traer, mandar buscar.

◆**send round** *vt* (**a**) (*circulate*) hacer circular; pasar; distribuir.

(**b**) **I'll ~ it round to you** te lo enviaré; **to ~ sb round to the shop** enviar a uno a la tienda.

◆**send up** *vt* (**a**) (hacer) subir; *balloon* lanzar; **~ him up!** ¡que suba!

(**b**) *price etc* hacer subir, aumentar.

(**c**) (*Brit**: *parody*) parodiar, satirizar.

(**d**) (*blow up*) volar, destruir.

sender [ˈsendə^{r}] *n* remitente *mf*; (*Elec*) transmisor *m*.

sending-off [ˈsendɪŋˌɒf] *n* (*Sport*) expulsión *f*.

send-off [ˈsendɒf] *n* (*farewell*) despedida *f*; (*start*) inauguración *f*, apertura *f*; principio *m*; **to give a project a good ~** inaugurar felizmente un proyecto, hacer que un proyecto comience felizmente.

send-up* [ˈsendʌp] *n* (*Brit*) parodia *f*, sátira *f*.

Seneca [ˈsenɪkə] *nm* Séneca.

Senegal [ˌsenɪˈgɔːl] *n* el Senegal.

Senegalese [ˈsenɪgəˈliːz] **1** *adj* senegalés. **2** *n* senegalés *m*, -esa *f*.

senile [ˈsiːnaɪl] *adj* senil; **~ dementia** demencia *f* senil; **to go ~** padecer debilidad senil.

senility [sɪˈnɪlɪtɪ] *n* senilidad *f*.

senior [ˈsiːnɪə^{r}] **1** *adj* (*in age*) mayor (de edad), más viejo; (*on a staff*) más antiguo (*to* que); *position, rank* superior, de categoría superior; *section* (*in competition etc*) para mayores; **Joseph Bloggs, ~** Joseph Bloggs, padre; **~ citizen** (*euph*) ciudadano *m*, -a *f* de la tercera edad; **~ high school** (*US*) ≈ instituto *m* de enseñanza media, instituto *m* de BUP (*Sp*); **~ management** altos cargos *mpl* directivos; **~ partner** socio *mf* principal, socio *mf* más antiguo; **S~ Service** marina *f*; **he is ~ to me** (*in age*) tiene más años que yo, es más viejo que yo; (*in rank*) tiene categoría superior a la mía.

2 *n* mayor *mf*; (*in group*) miembro *mf* más antiguo, -a; decano *m*; (*in company etc*) socio *mf* más antiguo, -a; (*US*) alumno *m*, -a *f* del último año; **he is my ~** (*in age*) tiene más años que yo, es más viejo que yo; (*in rank*) tiene categoría superior a la mía; **he is 2 years my ~, he is my ~ by 2 years** tiene 2 años más que yo, él me lleva 2 años.

seniority [ˌsiːnɪˈɒrɪtɪ] *n* antigüedad *f*.

senna [ˈsenə] *n* sena *f*.

sensation [senˈseɪʃən] *n* sensación *f*; **to be a ~, to cause a ~, to create a ~** causar sensación; **it was a ~ in New York** en Nueva York causó sensación; **it's a ~!** ¡es formidable*!, ¡es una bomba!

sensational [senˈseɪʃənl] *adj* sensacional.

sensationalism [senˈseɪʃnəlɪzəm] *n* sensacionalismo *m*.

sensationalist [senˈseɪʃnəlɪst] *adj, n* sensacionalista *mf*.

sensationalize [senˈseɪʃnəlaɪz] *vt* sensacionalizar, presentar en términos sensacionales.

sensationally [senˈseɪʃnəlɪ] *adv report, describe* sensacionalmente; **it was ~ successful** tuvo un éxito sensacional; **it was ~ popular** era increíblemente popular.

sense [sens] **1** *n* (**a**) (*bodily*) sentido *m*; **the 5 ~s** los 5 sentidos; **~ of hearing** oído *m*; **~ of sight** vista *f*; **~ of smell** olfato *m*; **~ of taste** gusto *m*; **~ of touch** tacto *m*; **to have a keen ~ of smell** tener buen olfato; **sixth ~** sexto sentido *m*.

(**b**) **~s** (*right mind*) juicio *m*; **any man in his ~s** cualquier hombre sensato; **to be out of one's ~s** haber perdido el juicio, no estar en sus cabales; **to bring sb to his ~s** obligar a uno a sentar la cabeza, hacer entrar en razón a uno; (*Med*) hacer a uno volver en sí; **to come to one's ~s** sentar la cabeza; (*Med*) volver en sí; **to take leave of one's ~s** perder el juicio; **have you taken leave of your ~s?** ¿se te ha vuelto el juicio?

(**c**) (*good ~*) buen sentido *m*, juicio *m*; inteligencia *f*; **good ~, sound ~** sentido *m* común; **a man of ~** un hombre sensato, un hombre juicioso; **there is no ~ in that** eso no sirve para nada, eso es inútil; **there is no ~ in +** *ger* es inútil + *infin*; **what is the ~ of +** *ger*? ¿de qué sirve + *infin*?; **I couldn't get any ~ out of him** no pude sacar nada en claro de él; **he had the ~ to call the doctor** tuvo bastante inteligencia como para llamar al médico; **didn't you have the ~ to shout?** ¿no se te ocurrió gritar?; **it doesn't make ~** no tiene sentido; **it doesn't make ~ to me** para mí no tiene sentido; **can you make any ~ of it?** ¿has logrado descifrar el misterio?; **to make sb see ~** hacer que uno entre en razón; **I can't see any ~ in it** no encuentro ningún sentido en eso, no veo para qué vale eso; **to talk ~** hablar con juicio, hablar razonablemente; **now you're talking ~** esto es más razonable.

(**d**) (*feeling*) sensación *f*; **a ~ of pleasure** una sensación de placer; **the picture conveys a ~ of occasion** el cuadro comunica una sensación de acontecimiento importante; **to labour under a ~ of injustice** creer que uno ha sido tratado injustamente.

(**e**) (*instinct, insight*) sentido *m*; talento *m*, instinto *m*; aptitud *f*; **~ of colour** sentido *m* del color; **~ of direction** sentido *m* de la dirección; **~ of humour** sentido *m* del humor; **she lacks all ~ of humour** no tiene sentido del humor en absoluto; **~ of proportion** sentido *m* de la medida; **business ~** aptitud *f* para los negocios.

(**f**) (*sentiment*) opinión *f*; **to take the ~ of the meeting** interpretar la opinión colectiva de la reunión.

(**g**) (*meaning*) sentido *m*, significado *m*; acepción *f*; significación *f*; **in a ~** hasta cierto punto; **in the broad ~** en el sentido amplio; **in the full ~ of that word** en toda la extensión de la palabra; **in the strict ~** en el sentido estricto; **in what ~ do you use the word?** ¿qué significado le das a la palabra?; **in no ~ can it be said that ...** de ninguna manera se puede decir que ...; **it has various ~s** tiene diversas acepciones; **there are ~s in which that may be true** desde algunos puntos de vista eso puede ser cierto; **he's an amateur in the best ~** es un aficionado en el buen sentido de la palabra.

2 *vt* sentir, percibir, barruntar; **to ~ that ...** percibir que ..., barruntar(se) que ..., darse cuenta de que ..., formarse la impresión de que ...

senseless [ˈsenslɪs] *adj* (**a**) (*stupid*) estúpido, insensato. (**b**) (*Med*) sin sentido, sin conocimiento; **to fall ~** caer sin sentido; **to knock sb ~** derribar a uno y dejarle sin sentido.

senselessly [ˈsenslɪslɪ] *adv* estúpidamente, insensatamente.

senselessness [ˈsenslɪsnɪs] *n* insensatez *f*.

sense organ [ˈsensˌɔːgən] *n* órgano *m* sensorio.

sensibility [ˌsensɪˈbɪlɪtɪ] *n* sensibilidad *f* (*to* a); **sensibilities**

delicadeza *f*, sentimientos *mpl* delicados.

sensible ['sensəbl] *adj* (**a**) (*having good sense*) juicioso, sensato; prudente, discreto; inteligente; **he's a ~ sort** es una persona sensata, es una persona de buen criterio; **try to be ~ about it** procura ser razonable.

(**b**) (*reasonable*) *act, decision etc* prudente; razonable, lógico; *reply, taste* acertado; *clothing etc* práctico; **that's a ~ thing to do** eso me parece razonable; **the ~ course would be to** + *infin* lo más prudente sería + *infin*; **that is very ~ of you** en eso haces muy bien, me parece muy lógico.

(**c**) (*appreciable*) apreciable, perceptible.

(**d**) (†: *aware*) **to be ~ of** ser consciente de, darse cuenta de; **I am ~ of the honour you do me** agradezco el honor que se me hace.

sensibleness ['sensəblnɪs] *n* (*V adj*) (**a**) juicio *m*, sensatez *f*; prudencia *f*, discreción *f*; inteligencia *f*. (**b**) lo razonable, lógica *f*; lo práctico.

sensibly ['sensəblɪ] *adv* sensatamente; prudentemente; discretamente; inteligentemente; razonablemente, lógicamente; acertadamente; **she acted very ~** obró muy prudentemente; **he ~ answered that ...** contestó con tino que ...; **try to behave ~** procura ser más formal.

sensitive ['sensɪtɪv] *adj* (**a**) (*impressionable*) impresionable, susceptible, sensible, delicado; (*touchy*) susceptible; (*quick to react*) sensible; **to be ~ to** ser sensible a; **to be ~ about one's hair** preocuparse mucho por su pelo, tener vergüenza de (*LAm*: pena por) su pelo; **you're too ~ about your suit** te preocupas demasiado por el traje.

(**b**) *skin etc* delicado, sensible; (*Phot*) *paper etc* sensibilizado; *market* volátil.

(**c**) (*relating to the senses*) sensitivo, sensorio.

(**d**) (*secret*) secreto, confidencial.

sensitively ['sensɪtɪvlɪ] *adv* susceptiblemente, sensiblemente, impresionablemente.

sensitiveness ['sensɪtɪvnɪs] *n*, **sensitivity** [ˌsensɪ'tɪvɪtɪ] *n* (**a**) lo impresionable, susceptibilidad *f*. (**b**) delicadeza *f*; sensibilidad *f* (*to* a).

sensitize ['sensɪtaɪz] *vt* sensibilizar; (*US*) mentalizar, concienciar.

sensitized ['sensɪtaɪzd] *adj* sensibilizado.

sensor ['sensəʳ] *n* sensor *m*.

sensory ['sensərɪ] *adj* sensorio, sensorial; **~ deprivation** aislamiento *m* sensorial.

sensual ['sensjʊəl] *adj* sensual.

sensualism ['sensjʊəlɪzəm] *n* sensualismo *m*.

sensualist ['sensjʊəlɪst] *n* sensualista *mf*.

sensuality [ˌsensjʊ'ælɪtɪ] *n* sensualidad *f*.

sensually ['sensjʊəlɪ] *adv* sensualmente.

sensuous ['sensjʊəs] *adj* sensual, sensorio.

sensuousness ['sensjʊəsnɪs] *n* sensualidad *f*.

sent [sent] *pret and ptp of* **send**.

sentence ['sentəns] **1** *n* (**a**) (*Gram*) frase *f*; oración *f*; **he writes very long ~s** escribe frases larguísimas.

(**b**) (*Jur*) sentencia *f*, fallo *m*; (*with expression of time etc*) condena *f*; **~ of death** (condena *f* a la) pena *f* de muerte; **to be under ~ of death** estar condenado a muerte; **the judge gave him a 6-month ~** el juez le condenó a 6 meses de prisión; **he got a 5-year ~** se le condenó a 5 años de prisión; **to pass ~** pronunciar sentencia, fallar (*on sb* en el proceso de uno); **to serve one's ~** cumplir su condena.

2 *attr*: **~ structure** estructura *f* de la frase.

3 *vt* condenar (*to* a).

sententious [sen'tenʃəs] *adj* sentencioso.

sententiously [sen'tenʃəslɪ] *adv* sentenciosamente.

sententiousness [sen'tenʃəsnɪs] *n* sentenciosidad *f*, estilo *m* sentencioso.

sentient ['senʃənt] *adj* sensitivo, sensible.

sentiment ['sentɪmənt] *n* (**a**) (*feeling*) sentimiento *m*; (*opinion*) opinión *f*, sentir *m*; **those are my ~s too** ése es mi criterio también, así lo pienso yo también. (**b**) (*sentimentality*) sentimentalismo *m*, sensiblería *f*; **to wallow in ~** nadar en el sentimentalismo.

sentimental [ˌsentɪ'mentl] *adj* sentimental; (*pej*) sentimental, sensiblero; romántico; **~ value** valor *m* sentimental.

sentimentalism [ˌsentɪ'mentəlɪzəm] *n* sentimentalismo *m*.

sentimentalist [ˌsentɪ'mentəlɪst] *n* persona *f* sentimental, romántico *m*, -a *f*.

sentimentality [ˌsentɪmen'tælɪtɪ] *n* sentimentalismo *m*, sensiblería *f*.

sentimentalize [ˌsentɪ'mentəlaɪz] **1** *vt* sentimentalizar, imbuir de sentimiento. **2** *vi* dejarse llevar por el sentimentalismo.

sentimentally [ˌsentɪ'mentəlɪ] *adv* de modo sentimental; *say* en tono sentimental.

sentinel ['sentɪnl] *n* centinela *m*.

sentry ['sentrɪ] *n* centinela *m*, guardia *m*; **to be on ~ duty** estar de guardia, hacer guardia.

sentry-box ['sentrɪbɒks] *n* garita *f* de centinela.

sentry-go ['sentrɪgəʊ] *n* turno *m* de centinela; **to be on ~** estar de guardia.

Seoul [səʊl] *n* Seúl *m*.

sepal ['sepəl] *n* sépalo *m*.

separable ['sepərəbl] *adj* separable.

separate 1 ['seprɪt] *adj* separado (*from* de); distinto; suelto; independiente (*from* de); **under ~ cover** por separado; **they sleep in ~ rooms** duermen en habitaciones distintas; **could we have ~ bills?** queremos cuentas individuales; **I wrote it on a ~ sheet** lo escribí en otra hoja; **take a ~ sheet for the next part** toma una nueva hoja para lo que viene después; **everybody has a ~ cup** cada uno tiene su taza particular (*or* individual); **they live very ~ lives** viven muy independientes uno de otro; **they went their ~ ways** fueron cada uno por su lado; **to sign a ~ peace** firmar un tratado de paz por separado; **'with ~ toilet'** 'con inodoro separado'; **this is quite ~ from his profession** esto no tiene nada que ver con su profesión.

2 ['seprɪt] *n* (**a**) (*US*) separata *f*. (**b**) **~s** *pl* (*clothes*) coordinados *mpl*.

3 ['sepəreɪt] *vt* separar (*from* de); dividir, desunir; **to ~ truth from error** separar lo falso de lo verdadero, distinguir entre lo falso y lo verdadero; **he is ~d from his wife** está separado de su mujer.

4 ['sepəreɪt] *vi* separarse; **they ~d in 1990** se separaron en 1990.

◆**separate out** *vt* apartar.

separately ['seprɪtlɪ] *adv* separadamente; por separado; aparte.

separation [ˌsepə'reɪʃən] *n* separación *f*.

separatism ['sepərətɪzəm] *n* separatismo *m*.

separatist ['sepərətɪst] **1** *adj* separatista. **2** *n* separatista *mf*.

separator ['sepəreɪtəʳ] *n* separador *m*.

Sephardi [se'fɑːdɪ] *n*, *pl* **Sephardim** [se'fɑːdɪm] sefardí *mf*.

Sephardic [se'fɑːdɪk] *adj* sefardí.

sepia ['siːpɪə] **1** *n* (*fish*) sepia *f*, jibia *f*; (*colour*) sepia *f*. **2** *attr* color sepia.

sepoy ['siːpɔɪ] *n* cipayo *m*.

sepsis ['sepsɪs] *n* sepsis *f*.

Sept. *abbr of* **September** se(p)tiembre *m*, sep.

September [sep'tembəʳ] *n* se(p)tiembre *m*.

septet [sep'tet] *n* septeto *m*.

septic ['septɪk] *adj* séptico; **~ tank** pozo *m* séptico; **to go ~, to turn ~** infectarse.

septicaemia, (*US*) **septicemia** [ˌseptɪ'siːmɪə] *n* septicemia *f*.

septuagenarian [ˌseptjʊədʒɪ'neərɪən] **1** *adj* septuagenario. **2** *n* septuagenario *m*, -a *f*.

Septuagesima [ˌseptjʊə'dʒesɪmə] *n* Septuagésima *f*.

Septuagint ['septjʊədʒɪnt] *n* versión *f* de los setenta.

septuplet [sep'tjʊplɪt] *n* septillizo *m*, -a *f*.

sepulchral [sɪ'pʌlkrəl] *adj* sepulcral (*also fig*).

sepulchre, (*US*) **sepulcher** ['sepəlkəʳ] *n* (*liter*) sepulcro *m*; **whited ~** sepulcro *m* blanqueado.

sequel ['siːkwəl] *n* consecuencia *f*, resultado *m*; desenlace; (*of story*) continuación *f*; **in the ~** como consecuencia; **it had a tragic ~** tuvo un desenlace trágico, la cosa terminó trágicamente.

sequence ['siːkwəns] *n* sucesión *f*, orden *m* de sucesión; serie *f*; (*Cards*) serie *f*, escalera *f*; (*Cine*) secuencia *f*; **~ of tenses** concordancia *f* de tiempos; **to arrange things in ~** ordenar cosas secuencialmente.

sequential [sɪ'kwenʃəl] *adj* secuencial; **~ access** acceso *m* secuencial.

sequester [sɪ'kwestəʳ] *vt* (**a**) (*isolate, shut up*) aislar. (**b**) (*Jur*) *property* secuestrar, confiscar.

sequestered [sɪ'kwestəd] *adj* (**a**) (*isolated*) aislado, remoto. (**b**) *property* secuestrado, confiscado.

sequestrate [sɪ'kwestreɪt] *vt* secuestrar.

sequestration [ˌsiːkwes'treɪʃən] *n* secuestración *f*.

sequin ['siːkwɪn] *n* lentejuela *f*.

sequinned ['siːkwɪnd] *adj* con lentejuelas, cubierto de lentejuelas.

sequoia [sɪ'kwɔɪə] *n* secoya *f*.

seraglio [se'rɑːlɪəʊ] *n* serallo *m*.

seraph ['serəf] *n*, *pl* **seraphim** ['serəfɪm] serafín *m*.

seraphic [sə'ræfɪk] *adj* seráfico.
Serb [sɜːb] *n* serbio *m*, -a *f*.
Serbia ['sɜːbɪə] *n* Serbia *f*.
Serbian ['sɜːbɪən] **1** *adj* serbio. **2** *n* serbio *m*, -a *f*.
Serbo-Croat ['sɜːbəʊ'krəʊæt] *n* (*Ling*) serbocroata *m*.
Serbo-Croatian ['sɜːbəʊkrəʊ'eɪʃən] **1** *adj* serbocroata. **2** *n* serbocroata *mf*.
SERC *n* (*Brit*) *abbr of* **Science and Engineering Research Council.**
sere [sɪəʳ] *adj* seco, marchito.
serenade [,serə'neɪd] **1** *n* serenata *f*. **2** *vt* dar serenata a.
serendipity [,serən'dɪpɪtɪ] *n* serependismo *m*.
serene [sə'riːn] *adj* sereno, tranquilo; **all ~!** ¡sin novedad!
serenely [sə'riːnlɪ] *adv* serenamente, tranquilamente; **~ indifferent to the noise** sin molestarse en lo más mínimo por el ruido; **'No' he said ~** 'No' dijo con mucha tranquilidad.
serenity [sɪ'renɪtɪ] *n* serenidad *f*, tranquilidad *f*.
serf [sɜːf] *n* siervo *m*, -a *f* (de la gleba).
serfdom ['sɜːfdəm] *n* servidumbre *f* (de la gleba); (*fig*) servidumbre *f*.
serge [sɜːdʒ] *n* estameña *f*, sarga *f*.
sergeant ['sɑːdʒənt] *n* sargento *m*; **~ at arms** (*Parl*) oficial *m* de orden, ujier *m*; **~ first class, top ~** (*US*) primer sargento *m*; **yes, ~** sí, mi sargento.
sergeant-major ['sɑːdʒənt'meɪdʒəʳ] *n* (*Brit*) = brigada *m*.
serial ['sɪərɪəl] **1** *adj* consecutivo, en serie; **~ access** acceso *m* en serie; **~ interface** interface *m* en serie; **~ number** número *m* de serie; **~ printer** impresora *f* en serie; **~ rights** derechos *mpl* de publicación por entregas; **~ story** = **2**.
2 *n* (*Liter*) serial *m*, novela por entregas; (*TV*) serial *m*, telenovela *f*, serie *f* televisiva.
serialization [,sɪərɪəlaɪ'zeɪʃən] *n* serialización *f*, publicación *f* por entregas.
serialize ['sɪərɪəlaɪz] *vt* serializar, publicar como serial, publicar por entregas; **it has been ~d in the papers** ha aparecido en una serie de entregas en los periódicos.
serially ['sɪərɪəlɪ] *adv* en serie.
seriatim [,sɪərɪ'eɪtɪm] *adv* en serie.
sericulture [,serɪ'kʌltʃəʳ] *n* sericultura *f*.
series ['sɪərɪz] **1** *n, pl* **series** serie *f*; sucesión *f*; (*Math*) serie *f*, progresión *f*; (*of lectures etc*) ciclo *m*; **to connect in ~** (*Elec*) conectar en serie.
2 *attr*: **~ producer** (*TV*) productor *m*, -ora *f* de la serie.
series-wound ['sɪərɪz'waʊnd] *adj* arrollado en serie.
serious ['sɪərɪəs] *adj* (**a**) (*in earnest*) serio; *character* serio, formal; **are you ~ (about it)?**, **you can't be ~!** ¿lo dices en serio?; **gentlemen, let's be ~** señores, un poco de formalidad; **he's ~ about her** está enamorado de verdad de ella; **when we're alone he gets ~** cuando estamos a solas se pone muy serio; **to give ~ thought to** pensar seriamente en; **the ~ student of jazz would say that ...** el que se interese seriamente en el jazz diría que ...
(**b**) (*causing concern*) grave; de consideración, importante; **the injury is not ~** la lesión no es de gravedad; **things are getting ~** las cosas van poniéndose graves.
(**c**) (*) **that's a ~ wine** ése es un vino de verdad; **now, that's ~ money!** ¡eso sí que es dinero!
seriously ['sɪərɪəslɪ] *adv* (**a**) seriamente; en serio; **~, though ...** pero en serio ...; **do you say so ~?** ¿me lo dices en serio?; **I can't take Campoamor ~** no puedo tomar a Campoamor en serio; **he takes himself ~** se toma muy en serio.
(**b**) (*dangerously*) gravemente; **~ wounded** herido de gravedad; **he is ~ ill** está grave; **we are ~ worried** estamos gravemente preocupados.
seriousness ['sɪərɪəsnɪs] *n* (*V adj*) (**a**) seriedad *f*; **in all ~** en serio, seriamente. (**b**) gravedad *f*; **the ~ of the situation** la gravedad de la situación.
sermon ['sɜːmən] *n* sermón *m* (*also fig*); **the S~ on the Mount** el Sermón de la Montaña.
sermonize ['sɜːmənaɪz] *vti* sermonear.
serology [sɪ'rɒlədʒɪ] *n* serología *f*.
seropositive [,sɪərəʊ'pɒzɪtɪv] *adj* seropositivo.
serous ['sɪərəs] *adj* seroso.
serpent ['sɜːpənt] *n* serpiente *f*, sierpe *f*; (*fig*) serpiente *f*.
serpentine ['sɜːpəntaɪn] **1** *adj* serpentino. **2** *n* (*Min*) serpentina *f*.
SERPS [sɜːps] *n abbr of* **state earnings-related pension scheme.**
serrated [se'reɪtɪd] *adj* serrado, dentellado.
serration [se'reɪʃən] *n* borde *m* dentado.
serried ['serɪd] *adj* apretado; **in ~ ranks** en filas apretadas.
serum ['sɪərəm] *n* suero *m*.
servant ['sɜːvənt] **1** *n* (*domestic*) criado *m*, -a *f*, muchacho *m*, -a *f* (*LAm*); (*of company etc*) empleado *m*, -a *f*; (*gen fig*) servidor *m*, -ora *f*; **your devoted ~, your humble ~** un servidor, servidor de Vd; **your obedient ~** (*in letters*) suyo afmo, att. y s.s. (= atento y seguro servidor); **the ~s** (*collectively*) la servidumbre.
2 *attr*: **~ girl** criada *f*; **the ~ problem** el problema del servicio.
serve [sɜːv] **1** *vt* (**a**) (*of person*) servir; estar al servicio de; **to ~ the Queen** servir a la Reina; **he ~d his country well** sirvió dignamente a la patria, prestó valiosos servicios a la patria.
(**b**) (*of thing*) servir; ser útil a; **if my memory ~s me** si mi memoria no me falla, si tengo buena memoria.
(**c**) (*Rail etc*) **in towns ~d by this line** en las ciudades por donde pasa esta línea; **the villages used to be ~d by buses** antes en estos pueblos había servicio de autobuses.
(**d**) (*in shop*) *goods* vender; despachar; *customer* servir, atender; *food, meal* servir; **to ~ sb with 5 kilos of potatoes** vender 5 kilos de patatas a uno; **to ~ sb with hors d'oeuvres** servir los entremeses a uno; **dinner is ~d** la cena está servida; **this recipe ~s 6** esta receta es suficiente para 6 personas; **are you being ~d, madam?** ¿le están despachando, señora?; **they ~d cod as halibut** hicieron pasar bacalao por halibut.
(**e**) (*Tennis etc*) sacar.
(**f**) *writ* entregar.
(**g**) (*treat*) tratar; **he ~d me very ill** me trató muy mal; **it ~s her right** le está bien empleado, se lo ha buscado; **it ~s you right!** ¡bien merecido lo tienes!; **it ~d him right for being so greedy** lo mereció por ser tan glotón; **it would have ~d them right if he had** bien merecido lo hubieran tenido ellos si lo hubiese hecho él.
(**h**) (*of stallion etc*) cubrir.
(**i**) (*work out*) *apprenticeship, time* hacer; *sentence* cumplir; **to ~ one's time** (*Mil*) hacer su servicio.
2 *vi* (**a**) servir; **to ~ 10 years in the army** servir 10 años en el ejército; **to ~ at table** servir a la mesa; **to ~ on the jury** formar parte del jurado, ser miembro del jurado; **to ~ on the council** ser concejal; **to ~ in parliament** ser diputado; **he is not willing to ~** no quiere servir, no está dispuesto a ofrecer sus servicios.
(**b**) **to ~ as, to ~ for** servir de; servir para; **it will ~** servirá para el caso; **when the occasion ~s** cuando se presente una ocasión propicia; **it ~s to show that ...** sirve para demostrar que ...
(**c**) (*Tennis etc*) sacar.
3 *n* (*Tennis etc*) saque *m*; **whose ~ is it?** ¿quién saca?; **he has a strong ~** saca muy fuerte.
◆**serve out** *vt* (**a**) *meal* servir; *rations etc* repartir, distribuir.
(**b**) **to ~ sb out** ajustar cuentas con uno; **I'll ~ you out for this!** ¡me las pagarás!
(**c**) *period, time* hacer, cumplir.
◆**serve up** *vt food* servir; presentar; **he ~d that up as an excuse*** eso lo ofreció como excusa.
server ['sɜːvəʳ] *n* (**a**) (*Tennis*) saque *mf*; (*Eccl*) acólito *m*. (**b**) (*US*) camarero *m*, -a *f*. (**c**) (*for fish etc*) pala *f*.
service ['sɜːvɪs] **1** *n* (**a**) (*gen*) servicio *m*; **he has 10 years' ~** lleva 10 años en el servicio, sirve desde hace 10 años; **he saw long ~** sirvió durante muchos años; **to see ~ as** prestar servicio de; **is ~ included in the bill?** ¿se incluye el servicio en la cuenta?; **15% ~ is included** se incluye un 15 por ciento de servicio.
(**b**) (*branch, department etc*) servicio *m*; **the S~** (*Mil*) el ejército; (*Aer*) la aviación; (*Naut*) la marina; **the (three) S~s** las fuerzas armadas, los tres ejércitos; **'all main ~s'** 'todos servicios'; **the train ~ to Pamplona** el servicio de trenes a Pamplona; **the number 13 bus ~** el servicio de autobuses número 13; **to be on government ~** estar al servicio del gobierno.
(**c**) (*domestic*) **to be in ~** ser criado, ser criada; servir; **she was in ~ at Lord Copper's** era criada en la casa de Lord Copper; **to go into ~** entrar a servir (*with* a).
(**d**) (*act of serving etc*) servicio *m*; **for ~s to education** en premio a sus servicios a la educación; **his ~s to industry were most valuable** prestó valiosísimos servicios a la industria; **I don't need any lawyer's ~s** no necesito los servicios de ningún abogado; **the ~ is really poor in this hotel** en este hotel el servicio es francamente malo; **to dispense with sb's ~s** despedir a uno; **to do sb a ~** prestar un servicio a uno; **to do good ~** servir bien, ser muy útil; **Tristram Shandy, at your ~** Tristram Shandy, para servirle

(*or* a su disposición): **I am at your ~** estoy a su disposición; **Brand X is always at your ~** la marca X está siempre lista para servirle; **to bring into ~** empezar a usar, introducir; **to come into ~** entrar en servicio; **to press into ~** *thing* utilizar; echar mano de; *person* hacer trabajar, hacer prestar servicio; **to be of ~** servir, ayudar; **can I be of ~?** ¿puedo ayudarle?, ¿puedo servirle? (*LAm*); **it's of no ~ in an emergency** en caso de urgencia no sirve para nada; **to be out of ~** (*Mech*) no funcionar.

(**e**) (*Eccl*) (*Catholic*) misa *f*; (*other*) culto *m*, oficio *m* divino.

(**f**) (*Tennis*) saque *m*, servicio *m*.

(**g**) (*Jur*) entrega *f*.

(**h**) (*set*) vajilla *f*, juego *m*, servicio *m* de mesa.

(**i**) (*Aut, Mech*) revisión *f*, mantenimiento *m*; **the car is in for a ~** están revisando el coche; **to send one's car in for a ~** mandar el coche a revisar.

2 *attr*: **~ agreement** contrato *m* de mantenimiento; **~ area** área *f* de servicios; **~ bus** coche *m* de línea; **~ charge** (*Brit*) servicio *m*; (*of flat etc*) gastos *mpl* de servicio, gastos *mpl* de escalera; **~ corps** cuerpo *m* de intendencia; **~ department** (*office etc*) departamento *m* (*or* sección *f*) de mantenimiento; (*repair shop*) taller *m* de reparaciones; **~ families** familias *fpl* de miembros de las fuerzas armadas; **~ flat** (*Brit*) piso *m* con servicio de criada, conserje *etc*; **~ industry** industria *f* de servicios; **~ lift** (*Brit*), **~ elevator** (*US*) ascensor *m* de carga; **~ line** (*Tennis*) línea *f* de saque; **~ road** vía *f* de acceso; **~ sector** (*Econ*) sector *m* de servicios, sector *m* terciario; **~ station** estación *f* de servicio.

3 *vt* (**a**) (*Aut, Mech*) revisar, mantener. (**b**) *debt* pagar el interés de. (**c**) *committee etc* proveer a las necesidades de, atender.

serviceable ['sɜːvɪsəbl] *adj* servible, utilizable, útil; práctico; (*lasting*) duradero.

serviceman ['sɜːvɪsmən] *n*, *pl* **servicemen** ['sɜːvɪsmən] militar *m*.

service tree ['sɜːvɪstriː] *n* serbal *m*.

servicing ['sɜːvɪsɪŋ] *n* (*of car*) revisión *f*; (*of washing machine etc*) servicio *m* de reparaciones.

serviette [ˌsɜːvɪ'et] *n* servilleta *f*.

serviette-ring [ˌsɜːvɪ'etrɪŋ] *n* servilletero *m*.

servile ['sɜːvaɪl] *adj* servil.

servility [sɜː'vɪlɪtɪ] *n* servilismo *m*.

serving ['sɜːvɪŋ] **1** *adj officer* en activo; **~ cart** (*US*), **~ trolley** carrito *m*; **~ dish** plato *m* de servir. **2** *n* (*of meal etc*) servicio *m*.

servitude ['sɜːvɪtjuːd] *n* servidumbre *f*.

servo ['sɜːvəʊ] *n* servo *m*.

servoassisted ['sɜːvəʊə'sɪstɪd] *adj* servoasistido.

sesame ['sesəmɪ] **1** *n* (*Bot*) sésamo *m*; **open ~!** ¡ábrete sésamo! **2** *attr*: **~ oil** aceite *m* de sésamo; **~ seeds** semillas *fpl* de sésamo.

sesquipedalian [ˌseskwɪpɪ'deɪlɪən] *adj* sesquipedal; polisilábico; **~ word** palabra *f* kilométrica.

sessile ['sesaɪl] *adj* sésil.

session ['seʃən] *n* sesión *f* (*also Comput*); (*Scol, Univ*) curso *m*; **to be in ~** estar celebrando sesión, sesionar; **to go into secret ~** celebrar una sesión secreta.

sessional ['seʃənl] *adj* de una sesión; *exam* de fin de curso.

sestet [ses'tet] *n* sesteto *m*.

set [set] **1** *n* (**a**) (*group: of tools, cups, chairs, golf clubs etc*) juego *m*; (*of kitchen utensils*) batería *f*; (*of cutlery*) cubierto *m*; (*of turbines etc*) equipo *m*; (*of gears*) tren *m*; (*of stamps*) serie *f*; (*of rooms*) grupo *m*; apartamento *m*; (*of books, works*) colección *f*; (*of songs etc*) grupo *m*, serie *f*; (*Math*) conjunto *m*; **~ of teeth** dentadura *f*; **a complete ~ of Galdós novels** una colección completa de las novelas de Galdós; **that one makes up the ~** ése completa la serie; **it makes a ~ with those over there** hace juego con los que ves allá; **I need two to make up the ~** me faltan dos para completar la serie (*or* colección).

(**b**) (*Tennis*) set *m*, manga *f*.

(**c**) (*Elec etc*) aparato *m*; (*Rad*) aparato *m* de radio, radiorreceptor *m*; (*TV*) televisión *f*, televisor *m*.

(**d**) (*of persons*) grupo *m*; clase *f*; (*pej*) pandilla *f*, camarilla *f*; **the fast ~** la gente de vida airada; **the literary ~** los literatos, la gente literaria; **the smart ~** el mundo elegante, los elegantes; **we're not in their ~** no formamos parte de su mundo; **they're a ~ of thieves** son unos ladrones; **they form a ~ by themselves** forman un grupo aparte.

(**e**) (*Brit Scol*) clase *f*; **the mathematics ~** la clase de matemáticas.

(**f**) **to make a dead ~ at sb** (*pick on*) emprenderla resueltamente con uno, escoger a uno como víctima; (*amorously*) proponerse conquistar a uno.

(**g**) **to have a shampoo and ~** hacerse lavar y marcar el pelo.

(**h**) (*of fabric*) caída *f*; (*of dress*) corte *m*, ajuste *m*; (*of head*) porte *m*, manera *f* de llevar; (*of saw*) triscamiento *m*; (*of tide, wind*) dirección *f*; (*of person's mind etc*) inclinación *f*, sesgo *m*, tendencia *f*.

(**i**) (*Hort*) planta *f* de transplantar; esqueje *m*; **onion ~s** cebollitas *fpl* de transplantar.

(**j**) (*Theat*) decorado *m*, decorados *mpl*; (*Cine*) plató *m*; **to be on the ~** estar en plató.

2 *attr*: **~ designer** director *m*, -ora *f* de arte, decorador *m*, -ora *f*; **~ point** punto *m* de set.

3 *adj and ptp* (**a**) (*rigid*) rígido, inflexible; *face* rígido, sin expresión; *smile* forzado; permanente; (*in belief*) inflexible; **the fruit is ~** el fruto está formado.

(**b**) (*ready*) listo; **all ~?, are we all ~?** ¿estamos?, ¿estamos listos?; **to be all ~ for** estar listo para; **with their cameras all ~ to shoot** con las máquinas a punto para disparar.

(**c**) (*fixed, decided in advance*) fijo; decidido de antemano; *menu, price, purpose* fijo; *task* asignado; *subject* prescrito, establecido; *time* señalado; (*usual*) reglamentario; (*customary*) acostumbrado; **~ phrase** frase *f* hecha, frase *f* estereotipada; **~ piece** (*Art*) grupo *m*; (*fireworks*) cuadro *m*; (*Liter etc*) escena *f* importante, episodio *m* central; **at a ~ time** a la hora señalada; **there is no ~ time for it** para eso no hay hora fija; **~ books** autores *mpl* del programa; **with no ~ limits** sin límites determinados; **he gave us a ~ speech** pronunció un discurso preparado de antemano (*or* formal); **he has a ~ speech for these occasions** para estas ocasiones tiene un discurso estereotipado.

(**d**) (*resolved*) resuelto, decidido; **to be ~ in one's purpose** tener un propósito firme, mantenerse firme en su propósito; **to be ~ in one's ways** tener costumbres profundamente arraigadas; **to be ~ on sth** estar empeñado en algo; **to be ~ on** + *ger* estar resuelto a + *infin*; **since you are so ~ on it** puesto que te empeñas en ello; **to be dead ~ against sth** estar completamente opuesto a algo.

(**e**) **the tide is ~ in our favour** la marea fluye para llevarnos adelante; (*fig*) la tendencia actual nos favorece, llevamos el viento en popa; **the wind is ~ strong from the north** el viento sopla recio del norte.

4 (*irr*: *pret and ptp* **set**) *vt* (**a**) (*place*) poner, colocar; situar; *jewel* engastar, montar; **bricks ~ in mortar** ladrillos puestos en argamasa; **to ~ places for 14** poner cubiertos para 14 personas; **to ~ the table** poner la mesa; **~ the chairs by the window** pon las sillas junto a la ventana; **to ~ a poem to music** poner música a un poema; **she ~ the dish before me** puso el plato delante de mí; **to ~ a plan before a committee** exponer un plan ante una comisión; **I ~ him above Greene** le creo superior a Greene, le antepongo a Greene; **what value do you ~ on it?** ¿en cuánto lo valoras?; (*fig*) ¿qué valor tiene para ti?; **the ruins are ~ in a valley** las ruinas están enclavadas en un valle; **the scene is ~ in Rome** la escena es Roma, la acción pasa en Roma; **his stories, ~ in the society of 1890 ...** sus cuentos, ambientados en la sociedad de 1890 ...

(**b**) (*adjust*) ajustar, arreglar; *clock* poner en hora; *alarm clock* poner; *bone* reducir, encasar, componer; *specimen* montar; *hair* marcar, fijar; *sail* desplegar; *saw* triscar; *trap* armar; *snare* tender (*also fig*); *type* componer; *cement etc* solidificar, endurecer; *jelly* cuajar; *teeth* apretar; **the alarm clock is ~ for 7** el despertador está puesto para las 7; **he ~s his watch by Big Ben** pone su reloj por el Big Ben; **I'll ~ your room** (*US*) voy a limpiar y arreglar su habitación.

(**c**) (*fix*) fijar, señalar; **to ~ a time for a meeting** fijar una hora para una reunión; **to ~ limits to sth** señalar límites a algo; **to ~ a period of 3 months** señalar un plazo de 3 meses; **to ~ the fashion** imponer la moda (*for* de); **to ~ a record of 10 seconds** establecer un récord de 10 segundos; **to ~ course for** hacer rumbo a; **the meeting is ~ for Tuesday** (*US*) la reunión se celebrará el martes.

(**d**) (*give*) *example* dar; *task* imponer, asignar; *problem* plantear, (*as test etc*) poner; **to ~ Lorca for 1999** poner una obra de Lorca en el programa de estudios para 1999; **Cela is not ~ this year** este año Cela no figura en el programa; **to ~ an exam paper in German** poner un examen en alemán.

(**e**) **to ~ a dog on sb** azuzar un perro contra uno; **I was**

~ **on by 3 dogs** me atacaron 3 perros; **we ~ the police on to him** le denunciamos a la policía; **what ~ the police on the trail?** ¿qué puso a la policía sobre la pista?

(**f**) (*start*) **the noise ~ the dogs barking** el ruido hizo ladrar a los perros; **to ~ sth going** poner algo en marcha; **to ~ sb laughing** hacer reír a uno; **to ~ everyone talking** dar que hablar a todos; **this ~ me thinking** esto me hizo pensar; **to ~ sb to work** poner a uno a trabajar; **to ~ a fire** (*US*) provocar un incendio.

5 *vi* (**a**) (*sun etc*) ponerse.

(**b**) (*bone*) componerse.

(**c**) (*jelly etc*) cuajarse; (*blood*) coagularse; (*cement*) fraguar; (*gum, mud*) endurecerse, solidificarse; (*fruit, seed*) formarse.

(**d**) (*dog*) estar de muestra.

(**e**) **to ~ to work** (*start*) ponerse a trabajar; poner manos a la obra.

◆**set about** *vt* (**a**) *task* emprender, comenzar; **to ~ about** + *ger* ponerse a + *infin*.

(**b**) (*attack*) atacar, agredir; empezar a pegar.

◆**set against** *vt* (**a**) (*provoke enmity*) **to ~ A against B** indisponer a A con B, enemistar a A con B.

(**b**) (*contrast*) compensar; **these costs can be ~ against tax** estos gastos son desgravables; **one has to ~ X against Z** hay que contrapesar X y Z, hay que pesar X contra Z.

(**c**) **to ~ sb against an idea** hacer que uno se oponga a una idea; **he is very ~ against it** se opone rotundamente a ello.

◆**set apart** *vt* (**a**) = **set aside** (**a**), (**b**).

(**b**) (*make difference*) diferenciar, hacer distinto (*from* de).

◆**set aside** *vt* (**a**) (*save*) poner aparte; reservar, guardar; *land* abandonar definitivamente, retirar de la producción.

(**b**) (*put away*) poner a un lado.

(**c**) (*reject*) *proposal* desechar, rechazar; *petition* desestimar; *law, sentence, will* anular.

◆**set back** *vt* (**a**) (*replace*) devolver a su lugar.

(**b**) **a house ~ back from the road** una casa algo apartada de la carretera.

(**c**) (*retard*) *clock* retrasar; *progress* detener, entorpecer; poner obstáculos a; **this has ~ us back some years** esto representa una pérdida de varios años, esto nos ha costado varios años de progreso.

(**d**) (*: *cost*) costar; **the dinner ~ me back £40** la cena me costó 40 libras.

◆**set by** *vt* = **set aside** (**a**).

◆**set down** *vt* (**a**) (*put down*) dejar; poner en tierra, poner en el suelo; depositar; **the taxi ~ us down here** el taxi nos dejó aquí; **the train ~s down passengers at ...** los viajeros se apean en ...

(**b**) (*Aer*) poner en tierra.

(**c**) (*in writing*) poner por escrito; consignar, registrar.

(**d**) (*attribute*) **we ~ it down to ...** lo atribuimos a ..., lo achacamos a ...; **I ~ him down as a liar** le juzgué mentiroso.

◆**set forth 1** *vt theory* exponer, explicar; (*display*) mostrar.

2 *vi* = **set out 2** (**a**).

◆**set in** *vi* (*begin*) comenzar; (*night, winter*) cerrar; **the reaction ~ in after the war** la reacción se afianzó después de la guerra; **the rain has ~ in for the night** la lluvia continuará toda la noche; **the rain has really ~ in now** ahora está lloviendo de verdad.

◆**set off 1** *vt* (**a**) *bomb* explotar, hacer estallar; accionar.

(**b**) (*enhance*) hacer resaltar, dar énfasis a; **the black ~s off the red** el negro hace resaltar el rojo, el negro pone de relieve el rojo; **her dress ~s off her figure** su vestido le acentúa el tipo.

(**c**) (*balance*) contraponer; **to ~ off profits against losses** contraponer las ganancias a las pérdidas; **these expenses are ~ off against tax** estos gastos son desgravables.

(**d**) (*start*) causar, provocar, motivar; **that was what ~ off the riot** eso fue lo que provocó el motín; **to ~ sb off** (*laughing*) hacer reír a uno; (*talking*) dar a uno la oportunidad de hablar; **that really ~ him off** con eso se puso furioso.

2 *vi* (*leave*) partir, ponerse en camino.

◆**set on** *vt* (*attack*) agredir, atacar; **he was ~ on by 4 of them** fue agredido por 4 de ellos.

◆**set out 1** *vt* (*arrange*) arreglar, ordenar; sacar y disponer; clasificar; (*on paper etc*) disponer; (*state*) exponer, explicar.

2 *vi* (**a**) (*leave*) partir, salir (*for* para); ponerse en camino.

(**b**) (*intend*) **to ~ out to** + *infin* ponerse a + *infin*; proponerse + *infin*; **what are you ~ting out to do?** ¿qué os proponéis?, ¿cuál es vuestro objetivo?; **we did not ~ out to do that, we did not ~ out with that idea** no teníamos esa intención al principio.

◆**set to** *vi* (**a**) (*start*) empezar; (*work*) ponerse (resueltamente) a trabajar; aplicarse con vigor; (*start eating*) empezar a comer (con buen apetito); **~ to!** ¡a ello!

(**b**) **they ~ to with their fists** empezaron a pegarse, se liaron a golpes.

◆**set up 1** *vt* (**a**) (*place*) *monument* erigir, levantar; *fence etc* construir, poner.

(**b**) (*start*) *company etc* crear, fundar, establecer; *committee* constituir; *fund* crear; (*Tech*) armar, montar; *house* poner; *government* establecer, instaurar; *record* establecer; *precedent* sentar; **he ~ her up in a flat** la instaló en un piso; **to ~ sb up in business** establecer a uno en un negocio, ayudar a uno a establecerse en un negocio; **to ~ sb up as a model** poner a uno como modelo; **to ~ sb up as a judge** erigir a uno como juez.

(**c**) (*after illness etc*) fortalecer; **now he's ~ up for life** ahora tiene una carrera (*or* recursos *etc*) para toda la vida, ahora tiene el porvenir asegurado.

(**d**) (*equip*) equipar, proveer (*with* de); **to be well ~ up for** estar bien provisto de, tener buena provisión de.

(**e**) (*Typ*) componer.

(**f**) *cry* levantar, lanzar, dar; *protest* levantar, formular.

(**g**) (*) (*select*) escoger como víctima; (*frame*) incriminar dolosamente.

2 *vi*: **to ~ up in business** establecerse en un negocio; **to ~ up as a plumber** establecerse como fontanero, empezar a trabajar como fontanero.

3 *vr*: **to ~ o.s. up as a model** ofrecerse como modelo; **to ~ o.s. up as judge** erigirse en juez, constituirse en juez.

◆**set upon** *vt* = **set on**.

set-aside ['setə'saɪd] *adj*: **~ land** tierras *fpl* en abandono definitivo, tierras *fpl* retiradas de la producción.

setback ['setbæk] *n* revés *m*, contratiempo *m*; **to suffer a ~** sufrir un revés.

setscrew ['setskruː] *n* tornillo *m* de presión.

setsquare ['setskwɛəʳ] *n* cartabón *m*, escuadra *f*.

settee [se'tiː] *n* sofá *m*.

settee-bed [se'tiː'bed] *n* sofá-cama *m*.

setter ['setəʳ] *n* (**a**) (*of puzzle etc*) autor *m*, -ora *f*. (**b**) (*dog*) perro *m* de muestra inglés, setter *m*.

setting ['setɪŋ] *n* (**a**) (*of sun*) puesta *f*; (*act of placing*) colocación *f*; (*of bone*) reducción *f*, composición *f*; (*of machine etc*) ajuste *m*; (*Typ*) composición *f*.

(**b**) (*of jewel*) engaste *m*, montadura *f*, montura *f*.

(**c**) (*Theat etc*) escena *f*, escenario *m*; (*of action etc*) marco *m*; encuadre *m*; (*natural ~, landscape etc*) marco *m*.

(**d**) (*Mus*) arreglo *m*, versión *f*; **a ~ for 2 violins** un arreglo para 2 violines.

setting-up ['setɪŋ'ʌp] *n* (*of monument*) erección *f*; (*of institution, company*) creación *f*, fundación *f*, establecimiento *m*; (*Typ*) composición *f*.

settle[1] ['setl] *n* banco *m*.

settle[2] ['setl] **1** *vt* (**a**) (*place*) colocar; (*place firmly*) asentar; (*fix*) asegurar, fijar, afirmar; *gaze* fijar; **to ~ one's feet in the stirrups** afirmarse en los estribos.

(**b**) *persons* establecer; *land* colonizar, poblar (*with* de); **it was first ~d by the French** los primeros colonos fueron los franceses; **he ~d her in a little flat** la instaló en un modesto piso.

(**c**) **to ~ an income on sb** (*assign*) asignar (*or* señalar) una renta a uno.

(**d**) (*arrange*) **to ~ one's affairs** arreglar sus asuntos; **to ~ an invalid for the night** poner a un enfermo cómodamente para la noche.

(**e**) (*calm*) *nerves* calmar, sosegar; *doubts* disipar, desvanecer; *stomach* asentar.

(**f**) (*resolve*) *account* ajustar, liquidar, saldar; *claim* satisfacer; *differences, quarrel* componer; *date etc* fijar, acordar; *deal* firmar; *problem* resolver, solucionar; **several points remain to be ~d** quedan varios puntos por resolver; **the terms were ~d by negotiation** se acordaron las condiciones mediante una negociación; **to ~ an affair out of court** arreglar una disputa; **the result was ~d in the first half** se decidió el resultado en el primer tiempo; **it's all ~d** todo está resuelto; ya no hay problema; **so that's ~d then** así que todo está arreglado; **that ~s it!** ¡ya no hay más que decir!; **~ it among yourselves!** ¡allá vosotros!, ¡arregladlo vosotros!

(**g**) (*) **I'll soon** ~ **him** me lo cargaré*; **that** ~**d him** ya no hay problema con él, ya no volverá a molestarnos.

2 *vi* (**a**) (*establish o.s.*: *in a house etc*) establecerse, instalarse; (*in a country*) arraigarse; (*first settlers*) asentarse; (*bird, insect*) posarse; **to** ~ **comfortably in an armchair** sentarse cómodamente en una butaca; **the snow is settling** la nieve cuaja; **the wind** ~**d in the east** el viento siguió soplando del este; **a deep gloom has** ~**d on the party** un profundo pesimismo se ha apoderado del partido; **a smile** ~**d on his face** siguió con su sonrisa fija; **my eyes** ~**d on her immediately** en seguida se fijó mi mirada en ella.

(**b**) (*building*) asentarse; (*liquid*) clarificarse; (*sediment*) depositarse, sedimentarse; (*food*) digerirse, asimilarse; asentarse en el estómago; (*ship*) hundirse lentamente; **things are settling into shape** las cosas empiezan a adquirir una forma.

(**c**) (*calm down*: *passion etc*) calmarse; (*weather*) serenarse; (*conditions*) normalizarse, volver a la normalidad.

(**d**) (*resolve*) **to** ~ **on sth** decidirse por algo; (*choose*) escoger algo, optar por algo; **to** ~ **on a date** fijar una fecha.

(**e**) (*agree*) llegar a un arreglo, llegar a un acuerdo; transigir; **now they want to** ~ ahora quieren llegar a un arreglo; **I'll** ~ **for all of us** pago la cuenta para todos, pago por todos; **to** ~ **for** *solution etc* decidir por, aceptar; **to** ~ **for £250** convenir en aceptar 250 libras; **will you** ~ **for a draw?** ¿quedamos en empate?; **I'll** ~ **for the smaller one** me conformo con el pequeño.

◆**settle down 1** *vi* (**a**) (*establish o.s.*: *in a house etc*) establecerse, instalarse; (*in a country*) arraigarse; (*first settlers*) asentarse; (*of bird, insect*) posarse; **to** ~ **down comfortably in an armchair** sentarse cómodamente en una butaca.

(**b**) (*after wild period etc*) sentar la cabeza; **to marry and** ~ **down** casarse y empezar a tomar las cosas en serio; **to** ~ **down to a new life** adaptarse a una vida nueva; **he's settling down at school** se está acostumbrando a la escuela; **things are beginning to** ~ **down** las cosas empiezan a volver a la normalidad; **he** ~**d down with two mistresses** se las arregló para vivir con dos queridas; **he can't** ~ **down anywhere** es un culo de mal asiento*; **to** ~ **down to work** aplicarse al trabajo, dedicarse a trabajar (en serio).

2 *vr*: **to** ~ **o.s. down in an armchair** sentarse cómodamente en una butaca; **to** ~ **o.s. down for the night** arreglarse para pasar la noche.

◆**settle in** *vi* (*get things straight*) acostumbrarse, habituarse; (*get used to things*) adaptarse bien.

◆**settle up** *vi* (*also fig*) ajustar cuentas (*with sb* con uno).

settled [ˈsetld] *adj* fijo; permanente; **a** ~ **social order** un orden social fijo; **the first** ~ **civilization** la primera civilización de carácter fijo; **I feel very** ~ **in this job** me siento perfectamente establecido en este puesto.

settlement [ˈsetlmənt] *n* (**a**) (*of account*) ajuste *m*, liquidación *f*; (*of claim*) satisfacción *f*; (*of difference, quarrel*) arreglo *m*; (*of problem*) solución *f*; **please find enclosed my cheque in full** ~ **of ...** adjunto le remito el talón a cuenta de la total liquidación de ...

(**b**) (*agreement*) acuerdo *m*, convenio *m*; composición *f*; (*of marriage*) contrato *m*; **to reach a** ~ llegar a un acuerdo.

(**c**) (*act of settling persons*) establecimiento *m*; (*of land*) colonización *f*; asentamiento *m*.

(**d**) (*colony*) colonia *f*; (*village*) pueblo *m*; núcleo *m* rural; (*homestead*) caserío *m*; (*for social work*) centro *m* social; (*archaeological site*) asentamiento *m*.

settler [ˈsetləʳ] *n* colono *m*, -a *f*; (*pioneer*) colonizador *m*, -ora *f*.

set-to* [ˈsetˈtuː] *n* bronca *f*, pelea *f*, agarrada *f*; **to have a** ~ **with sb** pelearse con uno.

set-up* [ˈsetʌp] *n* tinglado *m*, sistema *m*, organización *f*; estructura *f*; plan *m*; (*persons*) equipo *m*; **it's an odd** ~ **here** aquí tienen un extraño sistema; **you have to know the** ~ hay que conocer el tinglado; **what's the** ~? ¿cuál es el sistema?, ¿cómo está organizado?; **he's joining our** ~ formará parte de nuestro equipo.

seven [ˈsevn] **1** *adj* siete. **2** *n* siete *m*.

sevenfold [ˈsevnfəʊld] **1** *adj* séptuplo. **2** *adv* siete veces.

seventeen [ˈsevnˈtiːn] *adj* diecisiete.

seventeenth [ˈsevnˈtiːnθ] *adj* decimoséptimo.

seventh [ˈsevnθ] **1** *adj* séptimo; **S~ Cavalry** (*US*) Séptimo *m* de Caballería. **2** *n* séptimo *m*, séptima parte *f*; (*Mus*) séptima *f*.

seventieth [ˈsevntɪɪθ] *adj* septuagésimo; setenta; **the** ~ **anniversary** el setenta aniversario.

seventy [ˈsevntɪ] *adj* setenta; **the seventies** (*eg* 1970s) los años setenta; **to be in one's seventies** tener más de setenta años, ser setentón.

sever [ˈsevəʳ] *vt* cortar; separar, dividir; *relations* romper.

several [ˈsevrəl] **1** *adj* (**a**) (*of number*) varios, algunos; diversos; ~ **times already** varias veces ya; **I bought** ~ **books** compré algunos libros.

(**b**) (*respective*) respectivos, distintos; **they have their** ~ **colours** tienen sus respectivos colores; **they went their** ~ **ways** se fueron cada uno por su lado; **joint and** ~ (*Jur*) solidario.

2 *pron* algunos; varios; ~ **of them wore hats** algunos de ellos llevaban sombrero; ~ **were dead** algunos estaban muertos.

severally [ˈsevrəlɪ] *adv* respectivamente; (*one by one*) por separado, individualmente.

severance [ˈsevərəns] **1** *n* corte *m*; separación *f*, división *f*; (*of relations*) ruptura *f*; (*from work*) despido *m*. **2** *attr*: ~ **pay** (indemnización *f* por) despido *m*.

severe [sɪˈvɪəʳ] *adj* severo; riguroso, fuerte; duro; *weather, winter, critic, restriction etc* riguroso; *illness, loss, wound* grave; *pain* intenso, agudo; *storm* violento; *reprimand* áspero; *blow* duro; *style* adusto, austero; **to be** ~ **on sb** tratar a uno con rigor; **to be too** ~ (**on sb**) cargar la mano.

severely [sɪˈvɪəlɪ] *adv* severamente; rigurosamente, fuertemente; duramente; gravemente; intensamente; agudamente; ásperamente; austeramente; ~ **wounded** herido de gravedad; **a** ~ **plain style** un estilo de lo más austero; **to leave sth** ~ **alone** no tener nada en absoluto que ver con algo.

severity [sɪˈverɪtɪ] *n* severidad *f*; rigor *m*; gravedad *f*; intensidad *f*, agudeza *f*; aspereza *f*; austeridad *f*.

Seville [səˈvɪl] **1** *n* Sevilla *f*. **2** *attr*: ~ **orange** naranja *f* amarga.

Sevillian [səˈvɪlɪən] **1** *adj* sevillano. **2** *n* sevillano *m*, -a *f*.

sew [səʊ] (*irr*: *pret* **sewed,** *ptp* **sewn**) **1** *vt* coser. **2** *vi* coser.

◆**sew on** *vt* coser, pegar.

◆**sew up** *vt* (**a**) coser, zurcir. (**b**) (*) **to get a matter all** ~**n up*** arreglar un asunto de modo definitivo; **the deal is all** ~**n up** el negocio está hecho definitivamente; **we've got the game all** ~**n up now*** tenemos el partido en el bote*.

sewage [ˈsjuːɪdʒ] **1** *n* aguas *fpl* residuales, aguas *fpl* fecales. **2** *attr*: ~ **disposal** depuración *f* de aguas residuales; ~ **farm,** ~ **works** estación *f* depuradora (de aguas residuales).

sewer [ˈsjʊəʳ] *n* albañal *m*, alcantarilla *f*, cloaca *f*; (*fig*) letrina *f*, sentina *f*.

sewerage [ˈsjʊərɪdʒ] *n* alcantarillado *m*; (*as service on estate etc*) saneamiento *m*.

sewing [ˈsəʊɪŋ] **1** *n* costura *f*; labor *f* de costura. **2** *attr* de coser.

sewing-basket [ˈsəʊɪŋˌbɑːskɪt] *n* cesta *f* de costura.

sewing-machine [ˈsəʊɪŋməˌʃiːn] *n* máquina *f* de coser.

sewing-silk [ˈsəʊɪŋsɪlk] *n* torzal *m*, seda *f* de coser.

sewn [səʊn] *ptp of* **sew**.

sex [seks] **1** *n* sexo *m*; **to have** ~ tener relaciones sexuales (*con* with).

2 *attr* sexual; ~ **act** acto *m* carnal, coito *m*; ~ **aids** ayudas *fpl* sexuales; ~ **crime** crimen *m* sexual; ~ **discrimination** discriminación *f* sexual; ~ **education** educación *f* sexual; ~ **hormone** hormona *f* sexual; ~ **maniac** maníaco *m* sexual; ~ **object** objeto *m* sexual; ~ **offender** delincuente *m* sexual; ~ **organ** órgano *m* sexual (*or* genital); ~ **symbol** sex-símbol *mf*.

3 *vt chicks* sexar, determinar el sexo de.

sexagenarian [ˌseksədʒɪˈnɛərɪən] **1** *adj* sexagenario. **2** *n* sexagenario *m*, -a *f*.

Sexagesima [ˌseksəˈdʒesɪmə] *n* Sexagésima *f*.

sex-appeal [ˈseksəˌpiːl] *n* sexy *m*, sex-appeal *m*, sexapel *m*.

sex-change [ˈsekstʃeɪndʒ] **1** *n* cambio *m* de sexo. **2** *attr*: ~ **operation** operación *f* de cambio de sexo.

sex-crazed [ˈsekskreɪzd] *adj* obsesionado por el sexo.

sexed [sekst] *adj* (*Bio, Zool*) sexuado; **to be highly** ~ estar obsesionado con el sexo.

sexiness [ˈseksɪnɪs] *n* sexy *m*; carácter *m* sexual; cachondez *f*.

sexism [ˈseksɪzəm] *n* sexismo *m*.

sexist [ˈseksɪst] **1** *adj* sexista. **2** *n* sexista *mf*.

sexless [ˈsekslɪs] *adj* asexuado, desprovisto de instinto sexual; desprovisto de atractivo sexual; (*Bio*) sin sexo, asexual.

sex-life ['sekslaif] *n* vida *f* sexual.

sex-linked ['seks'lıŋkt] *adj* (*Bio*) ligado al sexo.

sex-mad [,seks'mæd] *adj* obsesionado por el sexo.

sexologist [sek'sɒlədʒıst] *n* sexólogo *m*, -a *f*.

sexology [sek'sɒlədʒı] *n* sexología *f*.

sexpot* ['sekspɒt] *n* (*hum*) cachonda *f*.

sex-shop ['seksʃɒp] *n* sexería *f*, sex-shop *m*.

sex-starved ['seksstɑːvd] *adj* sexualmente frustrado.

sextant ['sekstənt] *n* sextante *m*.

sextet(te) [seks'tet] *n* sexteto *m*.

sexton ['sekstən] *n* sacristán *m*; (*gravedigger*) sepulturero *m*.

sextuplet ['sekstjuplıt] *n* sextillizo *m*, -a *f*.

sexual ['seksjuəl] *adj* sexual; ~ **abuse** abuso *m* sexual; ~ **act** acto *m* carnal, coito *m*; ~ **assault** atentado *m* contra el pudor; ~ **desire** deseo *m* sexual; ~ **harassment** importunación *f* sexual, acoso *m* sexual; ~ **intercourse** comercio *m* sexual, trato *m* sexual, coito *m*; ~ **organs** órganos *mpl* sexuales; ~ **orientation** orientación *f* sexual.

sexuality [,seksju'ælıtı] *n* sexualidad *f*.

sexually ['seksjuəlı] *adv* sexualmente; ~ **transmitted disease** enfermedad *f* de transmisión sexual.

sexy ['seksı] *adj* *person* sexy; cachondo; *dress etc* sexy, provocativo; *joke, film etc* verde, escabroso.

Seychelles [seı'ʃelz] *npl* Seychelles *fpl*.

sez‡ [sez] = **says**; ~ **you!** ¡lo dices tú!

SF *n abbr of* **science-fiction** ciencia-ficción *f*.

SFA‡ *n abbr of* **sweet Fanny Adams.**

SFO *n* (*Brit*) *abbr of* **Serious Fraud Office.**

SG *n* (*US*) *abbr of* **Surgeon General** jefe *m* del servicio federal de sanidad.

sgd *abbr of* **signed** firmado.

Sgt *abbr of* **Sergeant** sargento *m*.

sh [ʃ] *interj* ¡chitón!, ¡chist!

shabbily ['ʃæbılı] *adv* (**a**) (*lit*) pobremente. (**b**) (*fig*) injustamente; vilmente; de manera poco honrada.

shabbiness ['ʃæbınıs] *n* (**a**) (*lit*) pobreza *f*, lo desharrapado; lo raído, lo viejo; mal estado *m*. (**b**) (*fig*) injusticia *f*; vileza *f*.

shabby ['ʃæbı] *adj* (**a**) *person* pobremente vestido, desharrapado; *garment* raído, gastado, viejo; *area* pobre; *building etc* de aspecto pobre, en mal estado; **to feel** ~ sentirse mal vestido; **to look** ~ tener aspecto pobre, tener aspecto poco elegante.

(**b**) *treatment etc* injusto; *trick* vil, malo; *behaviour* poco honrado; *excuse* poco convincente.

shabby-looking ['ʃæbı,lukıŋ] *adj* de aspecto pobre.

shack [ʃæk] *n* chabola *f*, choza *f*, jacal *m* (*Carib*), bohío *m* (*CAm*).

◆**shack up‡** *vi*: **to ~ up with sb** amontonarse con uno*; **to ~ up together** vivir amontonados*.

shackle ['ʃækl] **1** *vt* encadenar; poner grilletes a; (*fig*) poner trabas a, estorbar; **we are ~d by tradition** las trabas de la tradición nos tienen presos.

2 *npl*: **~s** grillos *mpl*, grilletes *mpl*; (*fig*) trabas *fpl*; **the ~ of convention** las trabas de la convención.

shad [ʃæd] *n* sábalo *m*.

shade [ʃeıd] **1** *n* (**a**) (*shadow*) sombra *f*; **~s of night** tinieblas *fpl*, oscuridad *f*; **the ~s of night were falling fast** se hacía rápidamente de noche; **in the** ~ a la sombra (*of* de); **temperature in the** ~ temperatura *f* a la sombra; **35° in the** ~ 35 grados a la sombra; **to put sth in the** ~ (*fig*) eclipsar algo, dejar algo chico; **to put sb in the** ~ (*fig*) hacer sombra a uno.

(**b**) (*lamp~*) pantalla *f*; (*eye~*) visera *f*; (*US*: *blind*) persiana; **~s** (*esp US*: *glasses*) gafas *fpl* de sol.

(**c**) (*of colour*) matiz *m*; tonalidad *f*, tono *m*; (*of meaning, opinion*) matiz *m*, modalidad *f*; **a new ~ of lipstick** una nueva tonalidad de lápiz labial; **have you a lighter ~?** ¿tiene una tonalidad más clara?; **all ~s of opinion are represented** todas las modalidades de la opinión están representadas.

(**d**) (*small quantity*) poquito *m*; pizca *f*; **just a ~ more** un poquito más; **he's a ~ better** está un poquito mejor; **it's a ~ awkward** es un tanto difícil.

(**e**) (*ghost*) fantasma *m*; **the S~s** el Averno, el infierno; **~s of Professor X!** ¡eso recuerda al profesor X!

2 *vt* (**a**) dar sombra a, sombrear; *face etc* proteger contra el sol (*etc*); resguardar de la luz; **to ~ one's eyes with one's hand** llevar la mano a los ojos para protegerlos contra el sol; **to ~ a light** poner pantalla a una lámpara; **her face was ~d by a big hat** un sombrero ancho le daba sombra a la cara; **the garden is ~d by a large tree** el jardín está sombreado por un árbol grande.

(**b**) (*Art*) sombrear, esfumar; (*cross-hatch*) sombrear; *eyes* poner sombreador en, sombrear; **the dark ~d area** (*Typ etc*) la zona en trama oscura.

◆**shade away** = **shade off.**

◆**shade off 1** *vt* (*Art*) *colours* degradar.

2 *vi* cambiar poco a poco (*into* hasta hacerse), transformarse gradualmente (*into* en); **blue that ~s off into black** azul que se transforma (*or* se funde) gradualmente en negro.

shadeless ['ʃeıdlıs] *adj* sin sombra, privado de sombra.

shadiness ['ʃeıdınıs] *n* (**a**) (*shade*) sombra *f*, lo umbroso. (**b**) (*fig*) dudosa honradez *f*; tenebrosidad *f*.

shading ['ʃeıdıŋ] *n* (*for eyes*) sombreado *m*; (*of colours*) degradación *f*; transformación *f* gradual (*into* en); (*cross-hatching*) sombreado *m*; trama *f* oscura.

shadow ['ʃædəu] **1** *n* (**a**) sombra *f*; **the ~s** la oscuridad, las tinieblas; **the ~ of death** la sombra de la muerte; **in the ~ of** dentro de la sombra de, (*fig*) amenazado por; **under the ~ of serious charges** amenazado por unas acusaciones graves; **without a ~ of doubt** sin sombra de duda, sin la menor duda; **without a ~ of truth** sin tener la más pequeña parte de verdad; **he is but a ~ of his former self** es apenas una sombra de lo que fue; **to cast a ~** proyectar una sombra; **to cast a ~ over the festivities** ser una nota triste en la fiesta; **to wear o.s. to a ~** extenuarse, agotarse.

(**b**) (*person*: *tail*) sombra *f*, policía *m* (*or* detective *m etc*) que sigue a un sospechoso; (*companion*) sombra *f*.

2 *adj*: ~ **cabinet** (*Brit*) gobierno *m* en la sombra; ~ **leader** (*Brit*) dirigente *mf* en la sombra; ~ **Foreign Secretary** (*Brit*) portavoz *mf* de Asuntos Exteriores del gobierno en la sombra.

3 *vt* (**a**) (*darken*) oscurecer; (*Art*) sombrear; **to ~ forth** anunciar, indicar vagamente, simbolizar.

(**b**) (*follow*) seguir y vigilar; **have that man ~ed** que se vigile a ese hombre; **I was ~ed all the way home** me siguieron todo el camino hasta mi casa.

shadow-box ['ʃædəubɒks] *vi* boxear con un adversario imaginario; (*fig*) disputar con un adversario imaginario.

shadow-boxing ['ʃædəu,bɒksıŋ] *n* boxeo *m* con un adversario imaginario; (*fig*) disputa *f* con un adversario imaginario.

shadowy ['ʃædəuı] *adj* oscuro; (*fig*) oscuro; indistinto, vago, indefinido; **a ~ form** un bulto, una forma indistinta; **the company leads a ~ existence** la compañía tiene una existencia misteriosa.

shady ['ʃeıdı] *adj* (**a**) *place* sombreado, umbroso, de sombra; a la sombra; **a ~ tree** un árbol que da sombra; **it's ~ here** aquí hay sombra.

(**b**) (*fig*) *person* sospechoso; *deal* turbio; *past etc* tenebroso; **the ~ side of politics** el aspecto turbio de la política; **to be on the ~ side of 40** tener más de 40 años.

shaft [ʃɑːft] **1** *n* (**a**) (*arrow etc*) flecha *f*, dardo *m*, saeta *f*; (*part of arrow*) astil *m*; (*of column*) caña *f*, fuste *m*; (*of tool, golf-club etc*) mango *m*; (*of cart, carriage*) vara *f*; (*Mech*) eje *m*, árbol *m*; (*of light*) rayo *m*; **the ~s of Cupid** las flechas de Cupido; ~ **of wit** agudeza *f*.

(**b**) (*Min*) pozo *m*.

2 *vt* (*US‡*) timar, joder‡.

shag¹ [ʃæg] *n* tabaco *m* picado, picadura *f*.

shag² [ʃæg] *n* (*Orn*) cormorán *m* moñudo.

shag³** [ʃæg] **1** *n* polvo** *m*; **to have a ~** echar un polvo**. **2** *vt* joder**. **3** *vi* joder**.

shag⁴ [ʃæg] *n* (*carpet*) tripe *m*.

shagged‡ [ʃægd] *adj* (*also* ~ **out‡**) hecho polvo*.

shaggy ['ʃægı] *adj* velludo, peludo, lanudo; ~ **dog story** chiste *m* goma.

shagreen [ʃæ'griːn] *n* chagrín *m*, zapa *f*.

Shah [ʃɑː] *n* cha *m*, chah *m*, sha *m*.

shake [ʃeık] **1** *n* (**a**) sacudida *f*, sacudimiento *m*; (*quiver*) temblor *m*; (*of vehicle etc*) vibración *f*; (*Mus*) trino *m*; (*of head*) movimiento *m*; **with a ~ in his voice** con voz temblorosa; **with a ~ of her head** moviendo la cabeza, con un movimiento de la cabeza; **to be all of a ~** estar todo tembloroso; **to give sb a good ~** sacudir violentamente a uno; **to give a rug a good ~** sacudir bien una alfombrilla; **to have the ~s** temblar como un azogado.

(**b**) (*milk ~*) batido *m*.

(**c**) **he's no great ~s* at swimming, he's no great ~s* as a swimmer** como nadador no vale mucho; **in a brace of ~s*, in two ~s*** en un decir Jesús, en un abrir y cerrar de ojos.

2 (*irr*: *pret* **shook**, *ptp* **shaken**) *vt* (**a**) sacudir; *building* *etc* hacer temblar, hacer retemblar; *head* mover, menear; *hand* estrechar; *bottle* agitar; *cocktail etc* agitar, remover; '**~ the bottle**' 'agitar la botella'; '**~ well before using**' 'agítese bien antes de usar'; **we had to ~ him to rouse him** tuvimos que sacudirle para despertarle; **to ~ one's finger at sb** negar con el dedo lo que dice (*etc*) uno; **to ~ one's fist at sb** amenazar a uno con el puño; **to ~ hands** estrecharse la mano, darse las manos; **to ~ hands on a deal** darse las manos para cerrar un trato; **to ~ hands with sb** estrechar la mano a uno; **to ~ one's head** negar con la cabeza, mover la cabeza negativamente.

(**b**) (*fig*) (*weaken*) debilitar; hacer flaquear; (*impair*) perjudicar, afectar; **it has ~n his health** ha afectado su salud; **nothing will ~ our resolve** nada hará flaquear nuestra resolución; **the firm's credit has been badly ~n** ha sido perjudicada la buena fama de la casa; **the prosecutor could not ~ his evidence** el fiscal no logró hacerle modificar su testimonio; el fiscal no pudo desacreditar su testimonio.

(**c**) (*fig*: *alarm*) inquietar, perturbar; (*amaze*) sorprender, pasmar, dejar estupefacto; (*upset composure of*) desconcertar; (*shock*) dar una sacudida a; **the news shook me** la noticia me pasmó; **that shook him** eso le desconcertó; **7 days which shook the world** 7 días que estremecieron el mundo; **it shook me rigid** (*or* **solid**)* me pasmó, me dejó frío; **he needs to be ~n out of his smugness** hay que darle una sacudida para que deje su presunción.

3 *vi* estremecerse; temblar, retemblar (*at, with* de); (*of voice*) temblar; (*Mus*) trinar; **to ~ like a leaf** temblar como un azogado; **to ~ with fear** temblar de miedo; **to ~ with laughter** desternillarse de risa; **the house shook with merry singing** la casa retemblaba con alegres canciones; **the walls shook at the sound** se estremecían las paredes con el ruido; **to ~ in one's shoes** temblar de aprensión; **it shook in the wind** bamboleaba al viento; **his voice shook** le tembló la voz; **~*!, ~ on it*!** ¡chócala*!; **to ~ on a deal** darse las manos para cerrar un trato.

4 *vr*: **to ~ o.s. free** librarse de una sacudida.

◆**shake down 1** *vt* (**a**) *fruit etc* hacer caer, sacudir; bajar sacudiendo.

(**b**) (*US**) **to ~ sb down** sacar dinero a uno por chantaje; **they shook him down for 5000 dollars** le sacaron 5000 dólares.

(**c**) **to ~ sb down for weapons*** cachear a uno.

2 *vi* (*: *settle for sleep*) acostarse, echarse a dormir; **I can ~ down anywhere** yo me duermo en cualquier sitio.

◆**shake off** *vt* (**a**) *dust etc* sacudirse.

(**b**) *cold etc* quitarse (de encima); deshacerse de, librarse de; *habit* dejar; *yoke* sacudirse; *pursuer* zafarse de, dar esquinazo a.

◆**shake out** *vt* (**a**) *flag etc* desplegar; *blanket etc* abrir y sacudir; **to ~ dust out** sacudir el polvo.

(**b**) *company* reorganizar, reestructurar; *work-force* reducir.

◆**shake up** *vt* (**a**) *bottle etc, contents* agitar, remover; *travellers* sacudir.

(**b**) (*emotionally*) chocar; perturbar, desconcertar; **she was badly ~n up** sufrió una profunda conmoción.

(**c**) (*rouse, stir up*) *person etc* dar una sacudida a, dar un pinchazo a; estimular, reanimar; infundir nueva energía a; *organization* reorganizar, reestructurar.

shakedown* ['ʃeɪkdaʊn] *n* (**a**) (*bed*) cama *f* improvisada. (**b**) (*US*) exacción *f* de dinero; chantaje *m*. (**c**) (*search*) registro *m* a fondo.

shaken ['ʃeɪkən] *ptp of* **shake**.

shake-out ['ʃeɪkaʊt] *n* reorganización *f*, reestructuración *f*; reducción *f*.

shaker ['ʃeɪkə^r] *n* (*cocktail ~*) coctelera *f*.

Shakespeare ['ʃeɪkspɪə^r] *nm* Shakespeare, Chéspir.

Shakespearian [ʃeɪks'pɪərɪən] *adj* shakespeariano, chespiriano.

shake-up ['ʃeɪkʌp] *n* conmoción *f*; reorganización *f*; sacudida *f*, pinchazo *m*; infusión *f* de nueva energía; **the company needs a big ~** la compañía necesita una reorganización completa.

shakily ['ʃeɪkɪlɪ] *adv* de modo inestable; con poca firmeza; **he said ~** dijo en voz trémula; **to walk ~** andar con paso vacilante.

shakiness ['ʃeɪkɪnɪs] *n* inestabilidad *f*, falta *f* de firmeza; temblor *m*; debilidad *f*; (*of knowledge*) deficiencia *f*, mala calidad *f*.

shaking ['ʃeɪkɪŋ] **1** *adj*: **a ~ experience** una experiencia desconcertante.

2 *n*: **to give sb a good ~** sacudir violentamente a uno; **he needs a good ~** (*fig*) hay que darle un pinchazo.

shako ['ʃækəʊ] *n* chacó *m*.

shaky ['ʃeɪkɪ] *adj* (*unstable*) inestable, poco firme, poco sólido; movedizo; *hands etc* tembloroso; *health* delicado; *voice* trémula, débil; *writing* poco firme; *start* incierto; *situation* precario; **his Spanish is rather ~** su español es algo defectuoso; **to be ~ on one's legs** tener las piernas débiles, andar con paso vacilante.

shale [ʃeɪl] *n* esquisto *m*.

shale oil ['ʃeɪlɔɪl] *n* petróleo *m* de esquisto.

shall [ʃæl] (*irr*: *V also* **should**) *v aux* (**a**) (*used to form future tense*) **I ~ go** iré; **no I ~ not, no I shan't** no, yo no; **it ~ be done** así se hará; **~ I hear from you soon?** ¿me escribirás pronto?

(**b**) (*emphatic*) **you ~ pay for this!** ¡me las pagarás!; **they ~ not pass!** ¡no pasarán!

(**c**) (*in commands, of duty etc*) **passengers ~ not cross the line** se prohibe a los señores viajeros cruzar la vía; **it ~ be done this way** ha de hacerse de este modo; **you ~ do it!** ¡sí lo harás!; **thou shalt not kill** no matarás.

(**d**) (*in questions*) **~ I go now?** ¿me voy ahora?, ¿quieres que me vaya ahora?; **I'll buy 3, ~ I?** compro 3, ¿no te parece?; **let's go in, ~ we?** ¿entramos?; **~ we let him?** ¿se lo permitimos?

shallot [ʃə'lɒt] *n* chalote *m*, cebollita *f*, cebolleta *f* (*LAm*).

shallow ['ʃæləʊ] **1** *adj* (**a**) *water etc* poco profundo, no muy profundo, bajo; *dish etc* llano; *breathing* poco profundo.

(**b**) *person* superficial, frívolo, sin carácter; *knowledge etc* superficial, somero.

2 *n*: **~s** bajos *mpl*, bajío *m*.

3 *vi* hacerse menos profundo.

shallowness ['ʃæləʊnɪs] *n* (**a**) (*lit*) poca profundidad *f*. (**b**) (*fig*) superficialidad *f*, frivolidad *f*, falta *f* de carácter.

shalt†† [ʃælt] = **shall**.

sham [ʃæm] **1** *adj* falso, fingido, simulado; **~ fight** simulacro *m* de combate; **she's terribly ~** es la mar de afectada; **with ~ politeness** con fingida cortesía.

2 *n* (**a**) (*imposture*) impostura *f*, fraude *m*, engaño *m*; imitación *f*; **it's all a ~** todo es engaño; **the ~ of these elections** el fraude de estas elecciones; **the declaration was a mere ~** la declaración no fue sino una impostura.

(**b**) (*person*) impostor *m*, -ora *f*; **he's just a big ~** es un grandísimo farsante.

3 *vt* fingir, simular; **to ~ illness** fingirse enfermo.

4 *vi* fingir, fingirse; **he's just ~ming** lo está fingiendo; **to ~ dead** fingir estar muerto; **to ~ ill** fingirse enfermo.

shamateur* ['ʃæmətə^r] *n* amateur *m* fingido, amateur *f* fingida.

shamble ['ʃæmbl] *vi* (*also* **to ~ along**) andar arrastrando los pies; **he ~d across to the window** fue arrastrando los pies a la ventana.

shambles ['ʃæmblz] *n sing* (*scene of carnage*) lugar *m* de gran matanza; (*carnage*) matanza *f*, carnicería *f*; (*ruined place*) ruina *f*, escombrera *f*; (*muddle*) caos *m*, confusión *f*; **the place was a ~** el sitio era todo escombros; **this room is a ~!** ¡has visto qué desorden en este cuarto!; **the game was a ~** el partido degeneró en follón.

shambolic* [ʃæm'bɒlɪk] *adj* caótico.

shame [ʃeɪm] **1** *n* (**a**) (*feeling, humiliation*) vergüenza *f*; deshonra *f*; **the ~ of that defeat** la vergüenza de esa derrota; **the street is the ~ of the town** la calle es la vergüenza (*or* el baldón) de la ciudad; **~!, for ~!, ~ on you!, the ~ of it!** ¡qué vergüenza!; **to my eternal** (*or* **lasting**) **~ I did nothing** con gran vergüenza mía no hice nada; **to be without ~, to be lost to all sense of ~** no tener vergüenza; **to bring ~ upon sb** deshonrar a uno; **have you no ~?** ¿no te da vergüenza esto?; ¡qué cinismo!; **to put sb to ~** avergonzar a uno, (*fig*) superar con mucho a uno, dejar chico a uno.

(**b**) (*pity*) lástima *f*, pena *f*; **it's a ~ that ...** es una lástima que + *subj*, es una pena que + *subj*; **it's a ~ to have to + *infin*** es una pena tener que + *infin*; **what a ~!** ¡qué lástima!, ¡qué pena!

2 *vt* avergonzar; deshonrar; **they ~d me into contributing** me obligaron a contribuir por vengüenza.

shamefaced ['ʃeɪmfeɪst] *adj* avergonzado; vergonzoso, tímido.

shamefacedly ['ʃeɪmfeɪsɪdlɪ] *adv* con vergüenza, avergonzado; tímidamente.

shamefacedness ['ʃeɪmfeɪstnɪs] *n* vergüenza *f*; timidez *f*.

shameful ['ʃeɪmfʊl] *adj* vergonzoso; **how ~!** ¡qué vergüenza!

shamefully ['ʃeɪmfəlɪ] *adv* vergonzosamente; **~ ignorant** tan ignorante que da vergüenza; **they are ~ underpaid** se les paga terriblemente mal.

shamefulness ['ʃeɪmfʊlnɪs] *n* vergüenza *f*; ignominia *f*.

shameless ['ʃeɪmlɪs] *adj* desvergonzado, descarado, descocado; impúdico; cínico; **~ person** sinvergüenza *mf*; **are you completely ~?** ¿no tienes vergüenza?; ¡qué cinismo!

shamelessly ['ʃeɪmlɪslɪ] *adv* desvergonzadamente, descaradamente; impúdicamente; cínicamente.

shamelessness ['ʃeɪmlɪsnɪs] *n* desvergüenza *f*, descaro *m*, descoco *m*; impudor *m*; cinismo *m*.

shaming ['ʃeɪmɪŋ] *adj* vergonzoso; **this is too ~!** ¡qué vergüenza!

shammy ['ʃæmɪ] *n* gamuza *f*.

shampoo [ʃæm'puː] **1** *n* champú *m*; **to give o.s. a ~** lavarse la cabeza, darse un champú; **a ~ and set** un lavado y marcado.

2 *vt person* lavar la cabeza a, dar un champú a; *hair* lavar; *carpet* limpiar, lavar; **to have one's hair ~ed and set** hacerse lavar y marcar el pelo.

shamrock ['ʃæmrɒk] *n* trébol *m* (*emblema nacional irlandés*).

shandy ['ʃændɪ] *n* (*Brit*), **shandygaff** ['ʃændɪ,gæf] *n* (*US*) cerveza *f* con gaseosa.

Shanghai [,ʃæŋ'haɪ] *n* Shanghai *m*.

shanghai* [ʃæŋ'haɪ] *vt*: **to ~ sb** (*Naut*) narcotizar (*or* emborrachar) a uno y llevarle como marinero; (*fig*) secuestrar a uno.

Shangri-la ['ʃæŋrɪ'lɑː] *n* jauja *f*, paraíso *m* terrestre.

shank [ʃæŋk] *n* (*part of leg*) caña *f*; (*bird's leg*) zanca *f*; (*Bot*) tallo *m*; (*handle*) mango *m*; **~s*** piernas *fpl*; **to go on S~s' pony** ir en el coche de San Francisco, ir a golpe de calcetín.

shan't [ʃɑːnt] = **shall not.**

shanty¹ ['ʃæntɪ] *n* (*hut*) choza *f*, chabola *f*.

shanty² ['ʃæntɪ] *n* (*Brit Mus*) saloma *f*.

shanty-town ['ʃæntɪ,taʊn] *n* barrio *m* de chabolas, suburbio *m*; callampas *fpl* (*Chile*), colonia *f* proletaria (*Mex*), barriadas *fpl* (*Perú*), cantegriles *mpl* (*Uruguay*), ranchos *mpl* (*Venezuela*), villa *f* miseria (*Argentina*).

shape [ʃeɪp] **1** *n* forma *f*; figura *f*; configuración *f*; (*of garment*) corte *m*; (*of person*) talle *m*, tipo *m*; (*for jelly etc*) molde *m*; (*thing dimly seen*) bulto *m*, forma *f*; **the ~ of things to come** la configuración del futuro; **not in any ~ or form** de ningún modo, en absoluto; **they come in all ~s and sizes** se sirven en todas las formas y todos los tamaños; **royalty was present in the ~ of Princess Ida** asistió la Realeza, en persona de la Princesa Ida; **stamps of all ~s** sellos *mpl* de todas las formas; **it is rectangular in ~** es de forma rectangular, tiene forma rectangular; **what ~ is it?** ¿de qué forma es?; **to be in good ~** estar en buenas condiciones, (*person*) estar bien de salud, estar en forma; **to be in bad ~** estar en mal estado, (*person*) estar enfermo, estar en malas condiciones físicas; **to beat sth into ~** dar forma a algo a martillazos; **to keep in ~** mantener(se) en forma; **to knock** (*or* **lick**) **sb into ~** desbastar a uno; disciplinar a uno; adiestrar a uno; **to lick a team into ~** ir entrenando un equipo; **to put an essay into ~** corregir un ensayo, preparar un ensayo para publicarlo (*etc*); **to get out of ~, to lose ~** perder la forma; **to take ~** tomar forma, irse formando, (*fig*) irse perfilando.

2 *vt* formar, dar forma a; moldear; *stone* labrar; *wood* tallar; *jug etc* modelar, hacer; *course etc* condicionar, determinar; plasmar, amoldar; **~d like a tank** de forma de un carro de combate; **Plato helped to ~ his ideas** Platón ayudó a formar sus ideas; **the factors which ~ one's life** los factores que determinan el desarrollo de la vida de uno; **he did not ~ the course of events** él no influyó en la marcha de los acontecimientos; **there is a destiny which ~s our ends** hay un destino que gobierna nuestra vida.

3 *vi* formarse, tomar forma; **to ~ well** desarrollarse de modo esperanzador, prometer; **he is shaping (up) nicely as a goalkeeper** como guardameta promete, es un guardameta que promete; **how are things shaping?** ¿cómo van las cosas?; **as things are shaping** tal y como van las cosas.

◆**shape up** *vi* (*US*) comportarse mejor; trabajar mejor, rendir más.

-shaped [ʃeɪpt] *adj ending in compounds* en forma de, *eg* **heart~** acorazonado, en forma de corazón; **U~** en forma de U.

shapeless ['ʃeɪplɪs] *adj* informe, sin forma definida.

shapelessness ['ʃeɪplɪsnɪs] *n* falta *f* de forma.

shapeliness ['ʃeɪplɪnɪs] *n* proporción *f*; elegancia *f* (de forma).

shapely ['ʃeɪplɪ] *adj* bien formado, bien proporcionado; *leg etc* torneado; *person* de buen talle; **~ columns** columnas *fpl* elegantes; **the ~ Miss Galicia** la bien modelada Miss Galicia.

shard [ʃɑːd] *n* tiesto *m*, casco *m*, fragmento *m* (de loza *etc*).

share¹ [ʃɛəʳ] **1** *n* (**a**) (*thing received*) parte *f*, porción *f*; (*proportion*) cuota *f*; participación *f*; proporción *f*; **~ in the market** participación *f* del mercado; **~ in the profits** participación *f* en los beneficios; **the lion's ~** la parte del león; **fair ~s for all** la equidad para todos, un trato equitativo para todos; **in equal ~s** por partes iguales; **your ~ is £5** le tocan a Vd 5 libras; **how much will my ~ be?** ¿cuánto me corresponderá a mí?; **to come in for one's full ~ of work** tener que hacer una buena parte del trabajo; **the minister came in for a full ~ of criticism** el ministro recibió una amplia dosis de críticas; **it fell to my ~** me tocó a mí, me correspondió a mí; **to go ~s** dividir lo recibido; contribuir por partes iguales; **to go half ~s with sb** dividir lo recibido con otro por partes iguales; **we've had our ~ of misfortunes** hemos sufrido bastante infortunio.

(**b**) (*contribution*) contribución *f*; cuota *f*; parte *f*; **to bear one's ~ of the cost** pagar la parte del coste que le corresponde a uno; **to do one's ~** cumplir con su obligación; **he doesn't do his ~** no hace todo lo que debiera, no hace todo lo que le cumple; **to have a ~ in sth** participar en algo; **I had no ~ in that** no tuve nada que ver con eso; **to go ~s** ir a escote, escotar cada uno lo suyo; **to pay one's ~** pagar su cuota.

(**c**) (*Brit Fin*) acción *f*; **to hold 1000 ~s in a company** tener 1000 acciones en una compañía, poseer 1000 acciones de una compañía.

2 *attr*: **~ capital** capital *m* social en acciones; **~ certificate** (*Brit*) (certificado *m* *or* título *m* de una) acción *f*; **~ index** índice *m* de cotización en bolsa; **~ issue** emisión *f* de acciones; **~ option** plan *m* de compra de acciones de una empresa por sus empleados (*a precios ventajosos*); **~ premium** prima *f* de emisión; **~ prices** cotizaciones *fpl* (de acciones); **~ prospectus** prospecto *m* de acciones; **~ warrant** certificado *m* de acción.

3 *vt* (**a**) (*have in common*) compartir, poseer en común; usar juntos de; **they ~ a room** comparten un cuarto; **to ~ certain characteristics** poseer en común ciertas características; **I do not ~ that view** no comparto ese criterio.

(**b**) (*divide*) partir (*with sb* con uno), dividir.

4 *vi*: **to ~ and ~ alike** participar por partes iguales; **children have to learn to ~** los niños tienen que aprender a compartir con otros; **there were no rooms free so I had to ~** no había habitación libre y por tanto tuve que compartir una con otra persona; **to ~ in** tener parte en, participar en, (*fig*) participar de; **to ~ in sb's success** contribuir al éxito de uno.

◆**share out** *vt* repartir, distribuir.

share² [ʃɛəʳ] *n* (*Agr*) reja *f*.

sharecropper ['ʃɛə,krɒpəʳ] *n* (*US*) aparcero *m*, mediero *m* (*Mex*).

sharecropping ['ʃɛə,krɒpɪŋ] *n* (*US*) aparcería *f*.

shared [ʃɛəd] *adj* compartido; *facilities etc* comunitario; **~ line** línea *f* compartida.

shareholder ['ʃɛə,həʊldəʳ] *n* (*Brit*) accionista *mf*.

shareholding ['ʃɛə,həʊldɪŋ] *n* accionariado *m*, acciones *fpl*; participación *f* accionaria.

share-out ['ʃɛəraʊt] *n* reparto *m*, distribución *f*.

shark [ʃɑːk] *n* (**a**) (*Fish*) tiburón *m*. (**b**) (*****: *swindler*) estafador *m*; **the ~s of the building trade** los piratas de la construcción. (**c**) (*US**) experto *m*, -a *f*, as* *m*.

sharkskin ['ʃɑːkskɪn] *n* zapa *f*.

sharon ['ʃærən] *n* (*also* **~ fruit**) sharon *m*.

sharp [ʃɑːp] **1** *adj* (**a**) (*cutting*) afilado, cortante; *point* puntiagudo; *angle* agudo; *curve, bend* cerrado, fuerte; *turn by car* repentino, brusco; *feature* bien marcado, anguloso; *outline* definido; *photo* nítido; *contrast* neto, marcado; **to be at the ~ end*** estar en situación peligrosa; ser el que va a sufrir las consecuencias; ser la víctima, ser el blanco.

(**b**) (*of person*) *mind* listo, vivo, despalilado, inteligente; *hearing* fino; *sight* agudo, penetrante; *glance* penetrante; **the child is quite ~** el niño es bastante listo; **he's as ~ as they come** es de lo más avispado; **that was pretty ~ of you** en eso has estado muy perspicaz; **you'll have to be ~er than that** tendrás que espabilarte.

(**c**) (*of person*: *pej*) astuto, mañoso; poco escrupuloso; *trick* poco honrado; **he's too ~ for me** es demasiado astuto para mi gusto; **~ practice** trampa *f*, maña *f*.

(**d**) (*fig*) *shower, storm* fuerte, repentino; *frost* fuerte; *wind* penetrante; *pain* agudo, intenso; *fight* encarnizado; *pace* rápido, vivo; *walk* rápido; *fall in price etc* brusco; *temper* áspero, vivo; *retort* áspero; *tongue* mordaz; *rebuke* severo; *tone* acerbo, áspero, severo; **that was ~ work!** ¡qué rápido!

(**e**) *taste* acerbo, acre; *wine* ácido.

(**f**) *sound* agudo, penetrante; (*Mus*) sostenido; **C ~** (*Mus*) do *m* sostenido.

2 *adv* (**a**) (*Mus*) desafinadamente.

(**b**) **at 5 o'clock ~** a las 5 en punto; **and be ~ about it** y date prisa; **look ~!** ¡pronto!, ¡rápido!; **look ~ about it!** ¡menearse!; **if you don't look ~** si no te meneas; **to pull up ~** frenar en seco; **you turn ~ left at the lights** a las luces se tuerce muy cerrado a la izquierda.

3 *n* (**a**) (*Mus*) sostenido *m*.

(**b**) (*: *person*) estafador *m*, (*card*~) fullero *m*.

sharp-edged [ˈʃɑːpˈedʒd] *adj* afilado, de filo cortante.

sharpen [ˈʃɑːpən] **1** *vt* (**a**) *tool* afilar, aguzar; amolar; *pencil* sacar punta a.

(**b**) *appetite* (*also* **to ~ up**) abrir; *wits* despabilar; *conflict, emotion, sensation* agudizar.

2 *vi* (*fig*) agudizarse.

sharpener [ˈʃɑːpnəʳ] *n* afilador *m*, máquina *f* de afilar; (*pencil* ~) sacapuntas *m*.

sharper [ˈʃɑːpəʳ] *n* estafador *m*; (*card*~) fullero *m*.

sharp-eyed [ˈʃɑːpˈaɪd] *adj* de vista aguda, de ojos de lince.

sharp-faced [ˈʃɑːpˈfeɪst] *adj* de facciones angulosas.

sharpish* [ˈʃɑːpɪʃ] *adv* prontito, bien pronto; **we'll be leaving ~ tomorrow** mañana partimos tempranito; **it needs to be ready ~** hay que tenerlo listo bien pronto.

sharply [ˈʃɑːplɪ] *adv* (*abruptly*) bruscamente; (*clearly*) claramente; (*harshly*) severamente; **~ pointed** puntiagudo; **shares rose ~** las acciones subieron bruscamente.

sharpness [ˈʃɑːpnɪs] *n* (*V adj*) (**a**) lo afilado, lo cortante; lo puntiagudo; lo cerrado; lo repentino, brusquedad *f*; definición *f*; nitidez *f*; lo marcado.

(**b**) viveza *f*, inteligencia *f*; finura *f*; agudeza *f*.

(**c**) fuerza *f*; lo fuerte, lo repentino; agudeza *f*, intensidad *f*; brusquedad *f*, aspereza *f*; mordacidad *f*; severidad *f*; **there was a note of ~ in his voice** se notaba cierta aspereza en su tono; **there is a ~ in the air** empieza a notarse el frío.

sharpshooter [ˈʃɑːpˌʃuːtəʳ] *n* tirador *m* certero.

sharp-sighted [ˈʃɑːpˈsaɪtɪd] *adj* de vista aguda, de ojos de lince.

sharp-tempered [ˌʃɑːpˈtempəd] *adj* de genio áspero.

sharp-tongued [ˈʃɑːpˈtʌŋd] *adj* de lengua mordaz.

sharp-witted [ˈʃɑːpˈwɪtɪd] *adj* listo, perspicaz.

shat** [ʃæt] *pret and ptp of* **shit.**

shatter [ˈʃætəʳ] **1** *vt* romper, hacer añicos, hacer pedazos; *health* quebrantar; *nerves* destrozar; *hopes etc* destruir, acabar con; **to ~ sth against a wall** estrellar algo contra una pared; **I was ~ed to hear it** al saberlo quedé estupefacto; **this will ~ you** tengo que decirte algo pasmoso; **she was ~ed by his death** su muerte la anonadó.

2 *vi* romperse, hacerse añicos; hacerse pedazos; estrellarse (*against* contra); **the windscreen ~ed** el parabrisas se hizo añicos.

shattered [ˈʃætəd] *adj* (*grief-stricken*) destrozado; (*aghast, overwhelmed*) abrumado, confundido; (*: *exhausted*) hecho polvo*.

shattering [ˈʃætərɪŋ] *adj attack* demoledor; *news etc* pasmoso, fulgurante; *defeat* contundente; *experience* fulgurante; *day, journey* agotador.

shatterproof [ˈʃætəpruːf] *adj glass* inastillable.

shave [ʃeɪv] **1** *n* (**a**) afeitado *m*, rasurado *m*; **to have a ~** afeitarse.

(**b**) **close ~** (*lit*) afeitado *m* apurado; (*fig*) **to have a close** (*or* **narrow**) **~** escaparse por un pelo; **that was a close ~** eso fue cosa de milagro.

2 (*irr*: *pret* **shaved,** *ptp* **shaved** *or* **shaven**) *vt face* afeitar, rasurar; *wood* acepillar; (*skim*) casi tocar, pasar rozando; *price etc* reducir; **to ~ one's legs** afeitarse las piernas, depilarse las piernas.

3 *vi* (*person*) afeitarse, rasurarse; **that razor ~s well** esa navaja afeita bien.

◆shave off *vt*: **to ~ off one's beard** afeitarse la barba, quitarse la barba.

shaven [ˈʃeɪvn] **1** *ptp of* **shave. 2** *adj head etc* rapado.

shaver [ˈʃeɪvəʳ] *n* (**a**) (*electric* ~) máquina *f* de afeitar eléctrica, afeitadora *f* eléctrica, rasuradora *f*. (**b**) **young ~***† muchachuelo *m*, rapaz *m*, chaval* *m*.

Shavian [ˈʃeɪvɪən] *adj* shaviano, típico de G.B. Shaw.

shaving [ˈʃeɪvɪŋ] **1** *n* (**a**) (*with razor etc*) afeitado *m*, el afeitarse, rasurado *m*; **~ is a nuisance** es una pesadez tener que afeitarse.

(**b**) (*piece of wood, metal etc*) **~s** virutas *pl*, acepilladuras *fpl*; **wood ~s** virutas *fpl* de madera.

2 *attr* de afeitar.

shaving-brush [ˈʃeɪvɪŋbrʌʃ] *n* brocha *f* (de afeitar).

shaving-cream [ˈʃeɪvɪŋkriːm] *n* crema *f* de afeitar.

shaving-foam [ˈʃeɪvɪŋfəʊm] *n* espuma *f* de afeitar.

shaving-lotion [ˈʃeɪvɪŋˌləʊʃən] *n* loción *f* para el afeitado.

shaving-mirror [ˈʃeɪvɪŋmɪrəʳ] *n* espejo *m* de bolsillo.

shaving-soap [ˈʃeɪvɪŋsəʊp] *n* jabón *m* de afeitar.

shaving-stick [ˈʃeɪvɪŋstɪk] *n* barra *f* de jabón de afeitar.

shawl [ʃɔːl] *n* chal *m*.

shawm [ʃɔːm] *n* chirimía *f*.

she [ʃiː] **1** *pron* ella; **~ who** la que, quien.

2 *n* hembra *f*.

3 *attr* hembra, *eg* **the ~-hedgehog** el erizo hembra, la hembra del erizo; **~-bear** osa *f*; **~-cat** gata *f*.

sheaf [ʃiːf] *n, pl* **sheaves** [ʃiːvz] (*Agr*) gavilla *f*; (*of arrows etc*) haz *m*; (*of papers*) fajo *m*, lío *m*.

shear [ʃɪəʳ] (*irr*: *pret* **sheared,** *ptp* **shorn**) **1** *vt sheep* esquilar, trasquilar; *cloth* tundir.

2 *n*: **~s** tijeras *fpl* (grandes); (*Hort*) tijeras *fpl* de jardín; (*for metals*) cizalla *f*.

◆shear off *vt* cortar, quitar cortando; **the machine ~ed off two fingers** la máquina cercenó dos dedos; **the ship had its bows shorn off in the collision** la colisión cortó la proa al buque.

◆shear through *vt* cortar, hender.

shearer [ˈʃɪərəʳ] *n* esquilador *m*, -ora *f*.

shearing [ˈʃɪərɪŋ] *n* esquileo *m*; **~s** lana *f* esquilada.

shearing machine [ˈʃɪərɪŋməˌʃiːn] *n* esquiladora *f*.

shearwater [ʃɪəwɔːtəʳ] *n* pardela *f*.

sheath [ʃiːθ] *n* vaina *f*; funda *f*, cubierta *f*; (*Bot etc*) vaina *f*; (*Brit*) (*contraceptive*) condón *m*, preservativo *m*.

sheathe [ʃiːð] *vt sword* envainar; enfundar; **to ~ sth in metal** revestir algo de metal, poner cubierta metálica a algo.

sheathing [ˈʃiːðɪŋ] *n* revestimiento *m*, cubierta *f*.

sheath-knife [ˈʃiːθnaɪf] *n, pl* **sheath-knives** [ʃiːθnaɪvz] cuchillo *m* de funda.

sheaves [ʃiːvz] *pl of* **sheaf.**

Sheba [ˈʃiːbə] *n* Sabá; **Queen of ~** reina *f* de Sabá.

shebang‡ [ʃəˈbæŋ] *n*: **the whole ~** (*esp US*) todo ello, todo el negocio.

shebeen [ʃɪˈbiːn] *n* (*Ir*) taberna *f* ilícita.

shed¹ [ʃed] (*irr*: *pret and ptp* **shed**) *vt* (**a**) (*get rid of*) *clothes, leaves etc* despojarse de; *skin* mudar; *unwanted thing* deshacerse de; desprenderse de, quitarse; **the party tried to ~ its leader** el partido intentó deshacerse de su jefe; **the lorry ~ its load** la carga cayó del camión; **the roof is built to ~ water** el techo está construido para que el agua no quede en él; **I'm trying to ~ 5 kilos** estoy tratando de perder 5 kilos.

(**b**) (*send out*) *tears* verter; *blood* verter, derramar; *light* dar, (*fig*) echar, arrojar; *happiness etc* difundir, irradiar; **much blood has been ~** se ha vertido mucha sangre; **no blood was ~** no hubo efusión de sangre.

shed² [ʃed] *n* (*garden ~ etc*) cobertizo *m*, alpende *m*; (*workmen's*) barraca *f*; (*industrial*) nave *f*.

she'd [ʃiːd] = **she would; she had.**

sheen [ʃiːn] *n* lustre *m*; brillo *m*; **to take the ~ off sth** deslustrar algo.

sheeny [ˈʃiːnɪ] *adj* lustroso, brillante.

sheep [ʃiːp] *n, pl invar* oveja *f*; (*ram*) carnero *m*; (*pl, collectively*) ganado *m* lanar; **to count ~** fingir contar ovejas (para dormirse); **to separate the ~ from the goats** (*fig*) apartar las ovejas de los cabritos; **to make ~'s eyes at sb** mirar tiernamente a uno; **they followed like a lot of ~** le (*etc*) siguieron como manada de borregos; *V* **black 1.**

sheep-dip [ˈʃiːpdɪp] *n* (baño *m*) desinfectante *m* para ovejas.

sheepdog [ˈʃiːpdɒg] *n* perro *m* pastor; **~ trials** pruebas *fpl* de trabajo para perros pastores, concurso *m* de pastoreo.

sheep-farm [ˈʃiːpfɑːm] *n* granja *f* de ovejas.

sheep-farmer [ˈʃiːpˌfɑːməʳ] *n* dueño *m* de ganado lanar, ganadero *m*.

sheep-farming [ˈʃiːpˌfɑːmɪŋ] *n* pastoreo *m*, industria *f* del ganado lanar, ganadería *f*.

sheepfold [ˈʃiːpfəʊld] *n* redil *m*, aprisco *m*.

sheepish [ˈʃiːpɪʃ] *adj* tímido, vergonzoso.

sheepishly [ˈʃiːpɪʃlɪ] *adv* tímidamente.

sheepishness [ˈʃiːpɪʃnɪs] *n* timidez *f*, vergüenza *f*.

sheepmeat [ˈʃiːpmiːt] *n* carne *f* de oveja.
sheep-run [ˈʃiːprʌn] *n* pasto *m* de ovejas, dehesa *f* de ovejas.
sheepshearer [ˈʃiːp,ʃɪərə^{r}] *n* (*person*) esquilador *m*, -ora *f*; (*machine*) esquiladora *f*.
sheepskin [ˈʃiːpskɪn] *n* piel *f* de carnero; zamarra *f*, badana *f*; ~ **jacket** zamarra *f*, gamulán *m* (*SC*).
sheep-track [ˈʃiːptræk] *n* cañada *f*.
sheepwalk [ˈʃiːpwɔːk] *n* = **sheep-run.**
sheep-worrying [ˈʃiːp,wʌrɪɪŋ] *n* acoso *m* de ovejas.
sheer[1] [ʃɪə^{r}] **1** *adj* (**a**) (*absolute*) puro, completo, absoluto; **the ~ impossibility of ...** la total imposibilidad de ...; **~ nonsense!** ¡puro disparate!; **this is ~ robbery** esto es puro robo; **by ~ force** a viva fuerza; **by ~ hard work** gracias simplemente al trabajo, por puro esfuerzo de trabajo; **in ~ desperation** en último extremo.
(**b**) (*steep*) escarpado, cortado a pico; perpendicular; **there is a ~ fall of 200 metres** hay una caída de 200 metros sin obstáculo alguno.
(**c**) (*of cloth etc*) diáfano; **~ curtain** visillos *mpl*.
2 *adv*: **it falls ~ to the sea** baja sin obstáculo alguno hasta el mar; **it rises ~ above the town** está cortado a pico por encima de la ciudad; **it rises ~ for 100 metres** se levanta verticalmente unos 100 metros.
3 *npl*: **~s** (*US*) visillos *mpl*.
sheer[2] [ʃɪə^{r}] *vi*: **to ~ away from a topic** desviarse de un tema, evitar hablar de un tema.
◆**sheer off** *vi* (*Naut*) desviarse; (*fig*) largarse.
sheet [ʃiːt] **1** *n* (*bed~*) sábana *f*; (*shroud*) mortaja *f*; (*of paper, newspaper*) hoja *f*; (*of tin*) hoja *f*, (*of other metal*) chapa *f*, lámina *f*; (*of glass*) lámina *f*; (*of water etc*) extensión *f*; (*Naut*) escota *f*; (*cover*) cubierta *f*; (*tarpaulin*) alquitranado *m*; **a ~ of flame** unas lenguas de fuego; **a ~ of ice** una capa de hielo; **to start again with a clean ~** volver a comenzar sin nota adversa.
2 *attr*: **~ feed** alimentador *m* de papel; **~ glass** vidrio *m* plano; **~ lightning** relámpago *m* difuso, fucilazo *m*; **~ music** (hojas *fpl* de) partitura *f*; **~ steel** chapa *f* de acero; láminas *fpl* de acero, acero *m* en láminas.
3 *vt*: **to ~ sth in, to ~ sth over** cubrir algo con un alquitranado.
sheet anchor [ˈʃiːt,æŋkə^{r}] *n* ancla *f* de la esperanza.
sheeting [ˈʃiːtɪŋ] *n* (*cloth*) lencería *f* para sábanas; (*metal*) placas *fpl* de metal, laminado *m*, cobertura *f* metálica.
sheik(h) [ʃeɪk] *n* jeque.
sheik(h)dom [ˈʃeɪkdəm] *n* reino *m* (*or* territorio *m*) de un jeque.
shekel [ˈʃekl] *n* siclo *m*; **~s*** pasta* *f*, parné‡ *m*.
sheldrake [ˈʃeldreɪk] *n*, **shelduck** [ˈʃeldʌk] *n* tadorna *f*.
shelf [ʃelf] **1** *n*, *pl* **shelves** [ʃelvz] (**a**) tabla *f*, anaquel *m*; (*of cupboard, kitchen*) repisa *f*; **shelves** (*collectively*) estante *m*, estantería *f*; **to be (left) on the ~** (*girl*) quedarse para vestir santos; (*proposal etc*) quedar arrinconado; **to leave sth on the ~** (*fig*) arrinconar algo, dar carpetazo a algo; **to buy a product off the ~** comprar un producto ya hecho.
(**b**) (*Geog*: *on rock face*) repisa *f*; (*Naut*) banco *m* de arena, bajo *m*; plataforma *f*.
2 *attr* (*Comm*) **~ life** tiempo *m* de durabilidad antes de la venta; **~ mark** código *m*; **~ space** cantidad *f* de estanterías (para exponer la mercancía).
she'll [ʃiːl] = **she will, she shall.**
shell [ʃel] **1** *n* (**a**) (*Zool*: *of egg*) cáscara *f*, cascarón *m*; (*of nut*) cáscara *f*; (*of mollusc*) concha *f*; (*of tortoise, turtle*) caparazón *m*; (*of insect, lobster etc*) caparazón *m*, carapacho *m*; (*of pea*) vaina *f*; **to come out of one's ~** salir de su concha; **to retire into one's ~** meterse en su concha.
(**b**) (*Tech*: *framework*) armazón *f*, esqueleto *m*; (*of house, after bombardment etc*) casco *m*; (*Naut*) casco *m*; (*outer covering*) cubierta *f*, exterior *m*.
(**c**) (*boat*) bote *m* de construcción lisa.
(**d**) (*Mil*) proyectil *m*, obús *m*, granada *f*; (*US*) cartucho *m*.
2 *vt* (**a**) *peas* desenvainar; *eggs, nuts* descascarar, quitar la cáscara a.
(**b**) (*Mil*) bombardear.
◆**shell out*** **1** *vt money* aflojar*, desembolsar.
2 *vi* retratarse* (*for sth* para pagar algo).
shellac [ʃəˈlæk] *n* laca *f*, goma *f* laca.
shelled [ʃeld] *adj*: **~ nuts** nueces *fpl* sin cáscara.
shellfire [ˈʃelfaɪə^{r}] *n* cañoneo *m*, fuego *m* de artillería, bombardeo *m*; **to be under ~** sufrir un bombardeo; **the ~ lasted all night** el cañoneo duró toda la noche.
shellfish [ˈʃelfɪʃ] *n* (*Zool*) crustáceo *m*; (*as food*) marisco *m*, (*collectively*) mariscos *mpl*.
shell-hole [ˈʃelhəʊl] *n* hoyo *m* que forma un obús al explotar.
shelling [ˈʃelɪŋ] *n* bombardeo *m*.
shellproof [ˈʃelpruːf] *adj* a prueba de bombas.
shellshock [ˈʃelʃɒk] *n* neurosis *f* de guerra, shock *m* (causado por bombardeos).
shell-shocked [ˈʃelʃɒkt] *adj* que padece neurosis de guerra; (*fig*) que sufre estrés.
shell suit [ˈʃelsuːt] *n* chandal *m* holgado.
shelter [ˈʃeltə^{r}] **1** *n* abrigo *m*, asilo *m*, refugio *m*; (*air-raid ~ etc*) refugio *m*; (*bus ~*) refugio *m* (de espera); (*mountain ~*) albergue *m*; (*fig*) protección *f*, resguardo *m*; **under ~** al abrigo; **under the ~ of the mountain** al abrigo de la montaña; **to seek ~** buscar dónde cobijarse; **to seek ~ for the night** buscar dónde pasar la noche; **to take ~** ponerse al abrigo (*from* de), cobijarse (*from* de).
2 *vt* abrigar (*from* de); (*aid*) amparar, proteger (*from* de); (*hide*) esconder, ocultar; **to ~ a criminal** proteger a un criminal, dar albergue a un criminal.
3 *vi* abrigarse, ponerse al abrigo, cobijarse (*from* de); refugiarse; **to ~ from the rain** ponerse al abrigo de la lluvia.
sheltered [ˈʃeltəd] *adj place* abrigado; *industry* protegido (contra la competencia extranjera); **~ accommodation** residencia *f* vigilada; **~ life** vida *f* protegida; **she has led a very ~ life** se ha criado bajo las faldas de mamá, se ha criado en la inocencia; **a spot ~ from the wind** un sitio al abrigo del viento.
shelve [ʃelv] **1** *vt* (*fig*) dar carpetazo a, arrinconar, aplazar indefinidamente; (*Parl etc*) aparcar*.
2 *vi* formar declive, estar en declive; **the beach ~s rapidly** el fondo está en fuerte declive; **it ~s down to the sea** baja hacia el mar.
shelves [ʃelvz] *pl of* **shelf.**
shelving [ˈʃelvɪŋ] *n* estante *m*, estantería *f*.
shemozzle* [ʃəˈmɒzl] *n* (*Brit*) lío* *m*; bronca *f*, follón* *m*.
shenanigans* [ʃəˈnænɪgənz] *npl* trampas *fpl*, artimañas *fpl*; travesuras *fpl*; bromas *fpl*.
shepherd [ˈʃepəd] **1** *n* pastor *m*; **the Good S ~** el Buen Pastor; **~'s crook** cayado *m*; **~'s pie** (*Brit*) *plato a base de carne picada y puré de patatas*; **~'s purse** (*Bot*) zurrón *m* de pastor.
2 *vt* guiar, conducir; **to ~ children across a road** conducir niños a través de una calle.
shepherd-boy [ˈʃepədbɔɪ] *n* zagal *m*.
shepherdess [ˈʃepədɪs] *n* pastora *f*, zagala *f*.
sherbert [ˈʃɜːbɔːt] *n* = **sherbet.**
sherbet [ˈʃɜːbət] *n* polvos *mpl* de limón; gaseosa *f* en polvo; (*US*) sorbete *m*.
sherd [ʃɜːd] = **shard.**
sheriff [ˈʃerɪf] *n* sheriff *m*, alguacil *m* (*oficial de justicia inglés, escocés, o norteamericano*).
Sherpa [ˈʃɜːpə] *n* sherpa *mf*.
sherry [ˈʃerɪ] *n* jerez *m*.
she's [ʃiːz] = **she is; she has.**
Shetland Islands [ˈʃetlənd,aɪləndz] *npl*, **Shetlands** [ˈʃetləndz] *npl* Islas *fpl* Shetland, Islas *fpl* de Zetlandia.
shew [ʃəʊ] *vti* (††) = **show.**
shewn [ʃəʊn] *ptp* (††) *of* **show.**
shibboleth [ˈʃɪbəleθ] *n* (*Bible*) lema *m*, santo *m* y seña; (*fig*) dogma *m* hoy desacreditado, doctrina *f* que ha quedado anticuada.
shield [ʃiːld] **1** *n* (*also Her*) escudo *m*; (*round*) rodela *f*; (*Tech*) blindaje *m*, capa *f* protectora; (*fig*) escudo *m*, defensa *f*.
2 *vt* proteger, resguardar, amparar; *criminal* proteger; (*Tech*) blindar, revestir de una capa protectora; **to ~ one's eyes from the sun** proteger los ojos contra el sol.
shieling [ˈʃiːlɪŋ] *n* (*Scot*) (*pasture*) pasto *m*, prado *m*; (*hut*) choza *f*, cabaña *f*; albergue *m*; (*sheepfold*) aprisco *m*.
shift [ʃɪft] **1** *n* (**a**) (*change*) cambio *m* (*in, of* de); cambio *m* de sitio, traslado *m*, movimiento *m*; desplazamiento *m*; **~ of emphasis** cambio *m* de énfasis; **~ of wind** cambio *m* (de dirección) del viento; **consonant ~** cambio *m* consonántico; **~ in demand** desplazamiento *m* de la demanda; **there has been a ~ in policy** ha habido un cambio de política; **the ~ from north to south is increasing** el movimiento de norte a sur se acelera; **to make a ~** cambiar de sitio, (*person*) irse, largarse; **it's time we made a ~** ya es hora de cambiar de sitio.
(**b**) (*at work*) turno *m*; (*of workers*) tanda *f*; **an 8-hour ~** un turno de 8 horas; **to work in ~s** trabajar por turnos.
(**c**) (*expedient*) recurso *m*, expediente *m*; (*pej*) maña *f*, astucia *f*; **to make ~ with** arreglárselas con, contentarse

con; **to make ~ without** arreglárselas sin, prescindir de, pasarse sin; **to make ~ to** + *infin* arreglárselas para + *infin*, ingeniarse por + *infin*.

(**d**) (††) camisa *f* (de mujer).

(**e**) (*US Aut*: *gear* ~) palanca *f* de velocidades, cambio *m* de marcha (*LAm*).

2 *attr*: **three-~ system** (*work*) sistema *m* de tres turnos.

3 *vt* cambiar; (*move*) cambiar de sitio, trasladar a otro sitio, mover; (*budge*) mover; *stain etc* quitar, hacer salir; (*get rid of*) quitarse de encima, librarse de; *gears* (*US*) cambiar de; **to ~ scenery** cambiar el decorado; **~ it over to the wall** ponlo contra la pared; **we could not ~ him (from his opinion)** no logramos hacerle cambiar de opinión; **I can't ~ this cold** no me quito este catarro; **they ~ed him to Valencia** le trasladaron a Valencia; **we shall have to ~ 20 tons** hará falta mover 20 toneladas; **to ~ the blame on to sb else** echar (*or* pasar) la culpa a otro.

4 *vi* (**a**) (*move*) moverse; cambiar; cambiar de sitio; (*person*) cambiar de puesto, trasladarse a otro sitio; (*move house*) mudar; (*of ballast, cargo*) correrse; (*of wind*) cambiar; (*in attitude etc*) cambiar de actitud, modificar su postura; **can you please ~ along a little?** ¿te corres un poco a ese lado?; **to ~ into second (gear)** (*US*) cambiar a segunda (velocidad); **the scene ~s to Burgos** la escena cambia a Burgos; **he ~ed to Lima** se trasladó a Lima; **we couldn't get him to ~** no logramos hacerle cambiar de actitud.

(**b**) (*: *car etc*) ir a gran velocidad, correr; (*person*) darse prisa, menearse; **~ !** ¡menearse!

(**c**) **to ~ for o.s.** valerse por sí mismo, arreglárselas solo.

◆**shift about, shift around** *vi* cambiar (mucho) de sitio, (*in job*) cambiar de empleo.

◆**shift over** *vi* correrse.

shiftily [ˈʃɪftɪlɪ] *adv* astutamente; furtivamente; **to behave ~** comportarse de modo sospechoso.

shiftiness [ˈʃɪftɪnɪs] *n* lo tramposo, lo taimado, astucia *f*; lo sospechoso; lo furtivo.

shifting [ˈʃɪftɪŋ] *adj sand etc* movedizo.

shift-key [ˈʃɪftkiː] *n* tecla *f* de mayúsculas.

shiftless [ˈʃɪftlɪs] *adj* (*lazy*) vago, holgazán; (*useless*) inútil, incompetente.

shiftlessness [ˈʃɪftlɪsnɪs] *n* holgazanería *f*; inutilidad *f*.

shift register [ˈʃɪftˌredʒɪstəʳ] *n* registro *m* de desplazamiento.

shift-worker [ˈʃɪftˌwɜːkəʳ] *n* (*Brit*) trabajador *m*, -ora *f* por turnos.

shift-work(ing) [ˈʃɪftwɜːk(ɪŋ)] *n* (*Brit*) trabajo *m* por turno.

shifty [ˈʃɪftɪ] *adj* tramposo, taimado, astuto; *conduct* sospechoso; *glance etc* furtivo.

shifty-eyed [ˈʃɪftɪˈaɪd] *adj* de mirada furtiva.

Shi'ite [ˈʃiːaɪt] **1** *adj* chiíta. **2** *n* chiíta *mf*.

shillelagh [ʃəˈleɪlə, ʃəˈleɪlɪ] *n* (*Ir*) cachiporra *f*.

shilling [ˈʃɪlɪŋ] *n* chelín *m*; **6 ~s in the pound** 6 chelines por libra; **to cut sb off with a ~** desheredar a uno; **to take the Queen's** (*or* **King's**) **~** (*Hist*) alistarse en el ejército.

shilly-shally [ˈʃɪlɪˌʃælɪ] *vi* vacilar, no resolverse, no saber qué hacer; **you've shilly-shallied long enough** has estado bastante tiempo ya sin resolverte.

shilly-shallying [ˈʃɪlɪˌʃælɪɪŋ] *n* vacilación *f*, titubeos *mpl*.

shimmer [ˈʃɪməʳ] **1** *n* reflejo *m* trémulo, resplandor *m* trémulo. **2** *vi* rielar, relucir.

shimmering [ˈʃɪmərɪŋ] *adj*, **shimmery** [ˈʃɪmərɪ] *adj* reluciente; *light* trémulo.

shimmy* [ˈʃɪmɪ] *n* camisa *f* (de mujer).

shin [ʃɪn] *n* espinilla *f*; (*of meat*) jarrete *m*, corvejón *m*.

◆**shin up** *vi* trepar; **to ~ up a tree** trepar a un árbol.

shinbone [ˈʃɪnbəʊn] *n* espinilla *f*, tibia *f*.

shindig* [ˈʃɪndɪg] *n* juerga* *f*, guateque *m*.

shindy* [ˈʃɪndɪ] *n* (*noise*) ruido *m* grande, conmoción *f*; (*dispute*) lío* *m*, bronca *f*; **to kick up a ~** meter ruido; armar un lío*.

shine [ʃaɪn] **1** *n* (**a**) (*brilliance*) brillo *m*, lustre *m*; **to give one's shoes a ~** sacar brillo a los zapatos, limpiar los zapatos; **to take the ~ off sth** deslustrar algo; (*fig*) quitarle el encanto a algo; **to take the ~ out of sb** eclipsar a uno, dejar a uno muy atrás; **to take a ~ to*** tomar simpatía por, encontrar simpático a.

(**b**) (*Met*) buen tiempo *m*, tiempo *m* de sol; **we'll go rain or ~** iremos no importa el tiempo que haga.

2 (*irr*: *pret and ptp* **shone**) *vt* (**a**) *shoes* sacar brillo a, limpiar, bolear (*Mex*); *silver etc* pulir.

(**b**) **to ~ a light on sth** proyectar una luz sobre algo; **~ the torch this way** dirige la linterna hacia este lado.

3 *vi* (**a**) brillar; relucir, resplandecer; **a lamp was shining** brillaba una lámpara; **the sun is shining** hay sol; **the metal shone in the sun** el metal relucía al sol; **her face shone with happiness** su cara irradiaba felicidad; **a certain quiet confidence ~s through** trasciende cierta confianza.

(**b**) (*fig*) brillar, lucirse, distinguirse; **he doesn't exactly ~ at his work** no brilla en sus estudios que digamos; **he shone as a footballer** se distinguió como futbolista.

◆**shine down** *vi* (*of sun, moon, stars*) brillar.

shiner* [ˈʃaɪnəʳ] *n* (*black eye*) ojo *m* a la funerala.

shingle[1] [ˈʃɪŋgl] **1** *n* (**a**) (*Archit*) ripia *f*. (**b**) (†: *hair style*) corte *m* a lo garçon. (**c**) (*US*) rótulo *m* de oficina (*or* de consultorio *etc*); **to hang out one's ~** colgar un cartel; abrir una oficina (*etc*). **2** *vt* (†) *hair* cortar a lo garçon.

shingle[2] [ˈʃɪŋgl] *n* (*pebbles*) guijos *mpl*, guijarral *m*; (*beach*) playa *f* guijarrosa.

shingles [ˈʃɪŋglz] *n* (*Med*) herpes *m or fpl*.

shingly [ˈʃɪŋglɪ] *adj* guijarroso.

shinguard [ˈʃɪngɑːd] *n* espinillera *f*.

shininess [ˈʃaɪnɪnɪs] *n* brillo *m*.

shining [ˈʃaɪnɪŋ] *adj* brillante, lustroso; *face etc* radiante; *example* notable; **their ~ hour** su momento cumbre.

shinpad [ˈʃɪnpæd] *n* espinillera *f*.

Shintoism [ˈʃɪntəʊɪzəm] *n* sintoísmo *m*.

shinty [ˈʃɪntɪ] *n* (*Scot*) *especie de hockey*.

shiny [ˈʃaɪnɪ] *adj* brillante, lustroso; *cloth* (*with wear*) gastado, con brillo.

ship [ʃɪp] **1** *n* buque *m*, barco *m*, navío *m*; **the good ~ Venus** el buque Venus, el Venus; **Her** (*or* **His**) **Majesty's S~** (*abbr* **HMS**) buque *m* de guerra inglés; **to serve on HMS Warspite** servir en el Warspite; **~'s boat** lancha *f*, bote *m* salvavidas; **~'s company** tripulación *f*; **~'s doctor** médico *m* de a bordo; **~'s manifest** manifiesto *m* del buque; **~'s papers** documentación *f* del buque; **the ~ of the desert** el camello; **~ of the line** buque *m* de línea; **on board ~** a bordo; **to abandon ~** abandonar el barco; **to clear a ~ for action** alistar un buque para el combate; **when my ~ comes in** cuando lleguen las vacas gordas, cuando la suerte me favorezca; **to jump ~** desertar del buque; **to pump ~**** mear**; **to take ~ for** embarcarse para.

2 *vt* (**a**) (*put on board*) *goods, passengers* embarcar; *mast* izar; *oars* desarmar; **to ~ a sea** embarcar agua.

(**b**) (*transport*) transportar (por vía marítima), enviar, expedir.

3 *vi* embarcarse (*on* en).

◆**ship off** *vt* expedir.

◆**ship out** *vt* enviar, mandar; **a new engine had to be ~ped out to them** hubo que enviarles un nuevo motor.

shipboard [ˈʃɪpbɔːd] *n*: **on ~** a bordo.

shipbreaker [ˈʃɪpˌbreɪkəʳ] *n* desguazador *m*.

ship-broker [ˈʃɪpˌbrəʊkəʳ] *n* agente *m* marítimo.

shipbuilder [ˈʃɪpˌbɪldəʳ] *n* constructor *m* de buques, arquitecto *m* naval.

shipbuilding [ˈʃɪpˌbɪldɪŋ] *n* construcción *f* de buques, construcción *f* naval.

ship canal [ˈʃɪpkəˌnæl] *n* canal *m* de navegación.

shipload [ˈʃɪpləʊd] *n* cargamento *m* (entero) de un buque; (*loosely*) envío *m*, cantidad *f* enviada; (*) montón* *m*; **we have jam by the ~*** tenemos mermelada a montones*; **the tourists are arriving by the ~*** los turistas vienen en masa.

shipmate [ˈʃɪpmeɪt] *n* camarada *m* de a bordo.

shipment [ˈʃɪpmənt] *n* (*act*) embarque *m*; transporte *m*; (*quantity*) envío *m*, remesa *f*.

shipowner [ˈʃɪpəʊnəʳ] *n* naviero *m*, armador *m*.

shipper [ˈʃɪpəʳ] *n* exportador *m*; importador *m*; (*sender*) remitente *m*, transportista *m*.

shipping [ˈʃɪpɪŋ] **1** *n* (**a**) (*act*) embarque *m*; transporte *m* (por vía marítima).

(**b**) (*ships*) buques *mpl*, barcos *mpl*; (*ships of a country*) flota *f*, marina *f*; **dangerous to ~** peligroso para la navegación; **~ losses in 1942** cantidad *f* (*or* tonelaje *m*) de buques perdidos en 1942; **the canal is closed to British ~** el canal está cerrado para la marina británica.

2 *attr*: **~ agent** agente *m* marítimo; **~ company** compañía *f* naviera; **~ department** departamento *m* de envíos; **~ instructions** instrucciones *fpl* de embarque; **~ lane** ruta *f* de navegación; **~ line** compañía *f* naviera; **~ office** oficina *f* de compañía naviera; **~ specification** especificaciones *fpl* de embarque.

ship's chandler [ˈʃɪpsˌtʃɑːndləʳ] *n* (*also* **ship chandler**) abastecedor *m* de buques, proveedor *m* de efectos navales.

shipshape [ˈʃɪpʃeɪp] *adv, adj* en buen orden, en regla; **to get everything ~** ponerlo todo en orden.

ship-to-shore [ˈʃɪptəˌʃɔːʳ] *attr*: **~ radio** radio *f* de barco a costa.

shipwreck ['ʃɪprek] 1 n naufragio m (also fig).
2 vt: to be ~ed naufragar; ~ person náufrago m, -a f.

shipwright ['ʃɪpraɪt] n carpintero m de navío.

shipyard ['ʃɪpjɑ:d] n astillero m.

shire ['ʃaɪəʳ] 1 n (Brit) condado m; the S~s los condados centrales de Inglaterra. 2 attr: ~ horse percherón m.

-shire [ʃɪəʳ] n ending in compounds: condado m.

shirk [ʃɜ:k] 1 vt eludir, esquivar; obligation faltar a; work no hacer, rehuir; difficulty, issue escamotear; to ~ doing sth esquivar el deber de hacer algo.
2 vi faltar al deber; ponerse al socaire; escamotear; (not work) gandulear; you're ~ing! ¡eres un gandul!

shirker ['ʃɜ:kəʳ] n gandul m, flojo m (LAm).

shirr [ʃɜ:ʳ] vt (a) (Sew) fruncir. (b) ~ed eggs (US) huevos mpl al plato.

shirring ['ʃɜ:rɪŋ] n frunce m.

shirt [ʃɜ:t] n camisa f; (Sport) camiseta f; to keep one's ~ on* quedarse sereno; keep your ~ on!* ¡con calma!; to put one's ~ on a horse apostar todo lo que tiene uno a un caballo.

shirt-collar ['ʃɜ:t,kɒləʳ] n cuello m de camisa.

shirtdress ['ʃɜ:tdres] n camisa f vestido.

shirt-front ['ʃɜ:tfrʌnt] n pechera f.

shirtless ['ʃɜ:tlɪs] adj sin camisa, descamisado.

shirt-sleeves ['ʃɜ:tsli:vz] npl: to be in ~ estar en mangas de camisa.

shirttail ['ʃɜ:tteɪl] n faldón m (de camisa).

shirtwaist ['ʃɜ:tweɪst] n (US) blusa f (de mujer).

shirty* ['ʃɜ:tɪ] adj (esp Brit): he was pretty ~ about it la cosa no le gustó en absoluto, la cosa no le cayó en gracia; to get ~ ponerse negro*, amostazarse*.

shish kebab ['ʃɪ:ʃkə'bæb] n V kebab.

shit** [ʃɪt] 1 n (a) (excrement) mierda** f, caca** f; ~!, oh ~! ¡mierda!**; tough ~! ¡mala suerte!; to beat (or knock etc) the ~ out of sb dar una tremenda paliza a uno*; I don't give a ~ me importa un rábano; to have the ~s tener el vientre descompuesto; he landed (or dropped) us in the ~ nos dejó en la mierda**.
(b) (person) mierda** f, cabrón‡ m.
(c) (nonsense) cagadas** fpl.
2 (pret and ptp shit, shitted or shat) vt cagar**; to ~ bricks (etc) cagarse de miedo**.
3 vi cagar.
4 vr: to ~ o.s. cagarse de miedo**.

shitlist** ['ʃɪtlɪst] n lista n negra.

shitty** ['ʃɪtɪ] adj (fig) de mierda**.

shiver1 ['ʃɪvəʳ] 1 n (a) temblor m, estremecimiento m; (with cold) tiritón m; (of horror etc) escalofrío m; to give a ~ estremecerse; it sent ~s down my back me dio escalofríos.
(b) the ~s (fig) dentera f, grima f; it gives me the ~s (of fear) me da miedo, (of taste etc) me da dentera.
2 vi temblar, estremecerse; vibrar; (with fear) temblar, dar diente con diente; (with cold) tiritar.

shiver2 ['ʃɪvəʳ] 1 vt (break) romper, hacer añicos. 2 vi romperse, hacerse añicos.

shivery ['ʃɪvərɪ] adj estremecido; (sensitive to cold) friolero, friolento (LAm); to feel ~ tener frío, tener escalofríos.

shoal1 [ʃəʊl] 1 n (sandbank etc) banco m de arena, bajío m, bajo m. 2 vi disminuir en profundidad, hacerse menos profundo.

shoal2 [ʃəʊl] n (of fish) banco m, cardumen m; (of people etc) multitud f; muchedumbre f; to come in ~s venir en tropel; we have ~s of applications tenemos montones de solicitudes.

shock1 [ʃɒk] 1 n (a) (Elec) descarga f (eléctrica); sacudida f, calambre m; (collision) choque m, colisión f; (jolt) sacudida f; (of earthquake) seísmo m, temblor m de tierra; she got a ~ from the refrigerator la nevera le dio una descarga; the ~ of the explosion was felt 5 miles away se sintió el choque de la explosión a una distancia de 5 millas; the house collapsed at the first ~ al primer seísmo se hundió la casa.
(b) (emotional) conmoción f (desagradable); impresión f (fuerte); (start) sobresalto m, susto m; our feeling is one of ~ lo que sentimos es un enorme disgusto; the ~ was too much for him la conmoción que le produjo la noticia le anonadó; the ~ killed him el disgusto le mató; it comes as a ~ to hear that ... nos asombramos al saber que ...; to give sb a ~ sobresaltar a uno; asombrar a uno; it gave me a nasty ~ me produjo una conmoción desagradable; the news gave me quite a ~ la noticia me afectó muchísimo, la noticia me disgustó bastante; what a ~ you gave me! ¡qué susto me diste!
(c) (Med) shock m, postración f nerviosa, conmoción f; to be in (a state of) ~ estar conmocionado; to be suffering from ~ padecer una postración nerviosa.
2 attr: ~ result resultado m sorprendente; ~ tactics táctica f de ataque repentino; ~ therapy, ~ treatment terapia f de choque (also fig); ~ troops tropas fpl de asalto; ~ wave onda f de choque, onda f expansiva.
3 vt (startle) sobresaltar, dar un susto a; (affect emotionally) dar un disgusto a, producir una conmoción desagradable a; impresionar (fuertemente); (make indignant) indignar; (because of impropriety) escandalizar; ofender; she is easily ~ed se ofende por cualquier cosa, se escandaliza por poca cosa; I was ~ed to hear the news la noticia me dio un enorme disgusto, la noticia me asombró; now don't be ~ed at what I'm going to say no te escandalices de lo que te voy a decir; you can't ~ me yo no me asombro de nada; to ~ sb into doing sth dar una sacudida a uno para animarle a hacer algo; we managed to ~ him out of his complacency con el susto pudimos sacarle de su suficiencia.

shock2 [ʃɒk] (Agr) 1 n tresnal m, garbera f. 2 vt poner en tresnales.

shock3 [ʃɒk] n: ~ of hair greña f; melena f.

shockable ['ʃɒkəbl] adj impresionable; sensible; she's very ~ se escandaliza por poca cosa; I am not easily ~ yo no me asombro de nada.

shock-absorber ['ʃɒkəb,zɔ:bəʳ] n amortiguador m.

shocked [ʃɒkt] adj (taken aback) sorprendido; (disgusted) ofendido; (scandalized) escandalizado; (Med) en estado de shock, conmocionado; a ~ silence un silencio conmocionado.

shocker* ['ʃɒkəʳ] n (a) (Liter) novelucha f. (b) it's a ~ es horrible; es de lo más vil; he's a ~ es un sinvergüenza, es un canalla; you ~! (hum) ¡canalla!

shock-headed ['ʃɒk'hedɪd] adj greñudo; melenudo.

shocking ['ʃɒkɪŋ] 1 adj (appalling) espantoso, horrible; (morally improper) escandaloso, vergonzoso, ofensivo, chocante (esp LAm); ~ pink rosa m estridente; how ~! ¡qué horror!; isn't it ~? ¿es espantoso, eh?; it was a ~ sight fue un espectáculo horrible; she has ~ taste tiene un pésimo gusto; the book is not all that ~ el libro es menos escandaloso de lo que se dice.
2 adv (*) a ~ bad film una película de bajísima calidad; it was ~ awful fue de lo más horrible.

shockingly ['ʃɒkɪŋlɪ] adv horriblemente; escandalosamente; ~ dear terriblemente caro; a ~ bad film una película de bajísima calidad; to behave ~ comportarse de modo escandaloso.

shockproof ['ʃɒkpru:f] adj a prueba de choques; person imperturbable.

shod [ʃɒd] pret and ptp of shoe; ~ with calzado de.

shoddily ['ʃɒdɪlɪ] adv (behave) ruinmente; ~ made mal hecho.

shoddiness ['ʃɒdɪnɪs] n baja calidad f; mala hechura f.

shoddy ['ʃɒdɪ] 1 adj de pacotilla, de bajísima calidad; muy mal hecho.
2 n (cloth) paño m burdo de lana; (wool) lana f regenerada; (as waste, fertilizer) desechos mpl de lana.

shoe [ʃu:] 1 n zapato m; (horse~) herradura f; (brake~) zapata f; I wouldn't like to be in his ~s no quisiera estar en su pellejo; to cast a ~ (horse) perder una herradura; to know where the ~ pinches saber dónde aprieta el zapato; to put on one's ~s calzarse; to take off one's ~s quitarse los zapatos, descalzarse; to step into sb's ~s pasar a ocupar el puesto de uno; to be waiting for dead men's ~s esperar a que muera uno (para pasar luego a ocupar su puesto).
2 (irr: pret and ptp shod) vt calzar (with de); horse herrar.

shoeblack ['ʃu:blæk] n limpiabotas m, lustrabotas m (LAm).

shoeblacking ['ʃu:,blækɪŋ] n betún m, lustre m (LAm).

shoebrush ['ʃu:brʌʃ] n cepillo m para zapatos.

shoecap ['ʃu:kæp] n puntera f.

shoehorn ['ʃu:hɔ:n] n calzador m.

shoelace ['ʃu:leɪs] n cordón m, agujeta f (Mex), trenza f (Carib).

shoe-leather ['ʃu:,leðəʳ] n cuero m para zapatos; to wear out one's ~ gastarse el calzado (andando de acá para allá).

shoemaker ['ʃu:,meɪkəʳ] n zapatero m; ~'s (shop) zapatería f.

shoe-polish ['ʃu:,pɒlɪʃ] n betún m, crema f (para el calzado), lustre m (LAm).

shoe-repairer [ˈʃuːrɪˌpɛərəʳ] *n* zapatero *m* remendón.
shoe-repairs [ˈʃuːrɪˌpɛəz] *npl* reparación *f* de calzado.
shoeshine [ˈʃuːʃaɪn] (*US*) **1** *n*: **to have a ~** hacerse limpiar los zapatos. **2** *attr*: **~ boy** limpiabotas *m*, lustrabotas *m* (*LAm*).
shoeshop [ˈʃuːʃɒp] *n* zapatería *f*, tienda *f* de calzado, peletería *f* (*Carib*).
shoestring [ˈʃuːstrɪŋ] **1** *n* (*US*) cordón *m*; **on a ~** a lo barato; con cuatro cuartos; **to do sth on a ~** hacer algo con muy poco dinero; **to live on a ~** vivir muy justo (*or* con escasos recursos).
2 *attr*: **~ budget** presupuesto *m* muy limitado.
shoetree [ˈʃuːtriː] *n* horma *f*.
shone [ʃɒn] *pret and ptp of* **shine**.
shoo [ʃuː] **1** *interj* ¡zape!, ¡ox!, ¡os!; (*to child*) ¡vete!, ¡fuera de aquí!
2 *vt* (*also* **to ~ away, to ~ off**) ahuyentar; **I had to ~ the children away** tuve que mandar a los niños ir a otra parte; **sb ~ed us away** alguien nos mandó ir a otra parte.
3 *attr*: **it's a ~-in** (*US**) es cosa de coser y cantar.
shook [ʃʊk] *pret of* **shake**.
shoot [ʃuːt] **1** *n* (**a**) (*Bot*) renuevo *m*, retoño *m*, vástago *m*.
(**b**) (*inclined plane*) conducto *m* inclinado; (*on ice*) resbaladero *m*; *V* **chute**.
(**c**) (*shooting party, hunt*) partida *f* de caza, cacería *f*; (*competition*) certamen *m* de tiro al blanco.
(**d**) (*preserve*) coto *m*, vedado *m*.
2 *interj*: **oh, ~!** (*****: *euph*) ¡caracoles!
3 (*irr*: *pret and ptp* **shot**) *vt* (**a**) (*Mil etc*) *bullet* disparar, tirar; *arrow etc* disparar; *gun* disparar, descargar; *lava etc* arrojar.
(**b**) *person, animal* matar con arma de fuego, herir con arma de fuego; (*execute*) fusilar; **to ~ sb dead, to ~ sb to death** matar a uno a tiros; **he was shot dead by a policeman** fue muerto a tiros por un policía; **he was shot in the leg** una bala le hirió en la pierna; **he had been shot through the heart** la bala le había atravesado el corazón; **I'll ~ you a rabbit** te cazaré un conejo; **he shot his wife** pegó un tiro a su mujer; **he was shot as a spy** le fusilaron por espía; **you'll get me shot** si hago esto me harás fusilar; **people have been shot for less** han fusilado a muchos por menos motivos.
(**c**) (*fig*) *film* rodar; *film scene* fotografiar, filmar; *subject of snapshot* tomar, sacar una instantánea de; *goal* marcar, meter; *bolt* correr; *coal, rubbish etc* verter, vaciar; *dice* echar; *net* echar; *ray of light* echar; *glance* echar, lanzar; **'~ no rubbish'** (*US*) 'prohibido verter basuras'; **to ~ the sun** tomar la altura del sol; **to ~ a question at sb** disparar una pregunta inesperada a uno.
(**d**) (*pass*) *rapids* salvar, atravesar; *bridge* pasar por debajo de; **to ~ the lights** (*Aut**) saltarse un semáforo en rojo.
4 *vi* (**a**) (*with gun: as sport*) practicar el deporte del tiro al blanco, (*as hunter*) cazar; **do you ~?** ¿Vd caza?; **I haven't shot for years** hace tiempo que no manejo la escopeta; **he ~s for Oxford** forma parte del equipo de tiro de Oxford; **we can ~ over Lord Emsworth's ground** podemos cazar en la finca de Lord Emsworth; **if they attack you, ~** si os atacan, disparad; **~ to kill** tirad a matar; **~ to kill policy** programa *m* de tirar a matar; **don't ~!** ¡no dispare!; **to ~ at sb** tirar a uno, disparar a uno; pegar un tiro a uno; **he shot at me but missed** disparó contra mí pero erró el tiro; **to ~ wide of the mark** errar el tiro.
(**b**) **~!*** (*in conversation*) ¡adelante!, ¡suelta!, ¡bien, dime!
(**c**) (*Ftbl etc*) chutar, tirar; **~!** ¡chuta!; **to ~ at goal** tirar a gol.
(**d**) (*pain*) punzar, dar punzadas.
(**e**) (*Bot*) brotar.
(**f**) (*move rapidly*: *person*) lanzarse, precipitarse; **he shot to the door** se lanzó hacia la puerta; **to ~ ahead** adelantarse rápidamente, adelantarse mucho (*of* a); **we were ~ing along** íbamos a gran velocidad; **to ~ by, to ~ past** pasar como un meteoro; **to ~ in** entrar como una bala; **he shot into space** se lanzó al espacio; **the car shot past us** el coche pasó como un rayo.
(**g**) (*Phot*) disparar.
◆**shoot away 1** *vt* = **shoot off 1** (**b**).
2 *vi* (**a**) (*Mil*) seguir tirando.
(**b**) (*move*) partir como una bala, salir disparado.
◆**shoot back 1** *vt* devolver rápidamente, devolver en el acto.
2 *vi* (**a**) (*Mil*) devolver el tiro, responder con disparos.
(**b**) (*move*) volver como una bala (*to* a).
◆**shoot down** *vt* (**a**) (*Aer*) derribar, abatir; *argument* rebatir, destruir; *arguer* anonadar.
(**b**) (*kill*) matar de un tiro, balear (*Mex*).
◆**shoot off 1** *vt* (**a**) *gun* disparar; *V* **mouth**.
(**b**) **he had a leg shot off** un disparo le cercenó una pierna.
2 *vi* = **shoot away 2** (**b**).
◆**shoot out 1** *vt* (**a**) *arm* extender rápidamente; extender inesperadamente; *tongue* sacar; *sparks etc* arrojar.
(**b**) *lights* apagar a tiros.
(**c**) **to ~ it out** resolverlo a tiros.
(**d**) **we were literally shot out of bed by the noise** nos vimos materialmente arrancados de la cama por el estruendo.
2 *vi* (*flame, water*) salir (con gran fuerza); (*arm*) extenderse rápidamente (*or* inesperadamente); (*person*) salir como una bala, salir disparado.
◆**shoot up 1** *vt aerodrome* destrozar a tiros; *town, district* aterrorizar a tiros; *person* acribillar a tiros, balacear (*Mex*).
2 *vi* (**a**) (*flame etc*) salir (con gran fuerza); (*hand*) alzarse rápidamente; (*price etc*) subir vertiginosamente.
(**b**) (*grow quickly*) crecer, espigar.
(**c**) (**‡**: *drugs*) chutarse‡, inyectarse.
shooter* [ˈʃuːtəʳ] *n* (*pistol*) pistola *f*; (*shotgun*) escopeta *f*.
shooting [ˈʃuːtɪŋ] **1** *n* (**a**) (*shots*) tiros *mpl*, disparos *mpl*; (*continuous* ~) tiroteo *m*; (*by artillery*) cañoneo *m*, bombardeo *m*.
(**b**) (*act: murder*) asesinato *m*; (*execution*) fusilamiento *m*.
(**c**) (*Hunting*) caza *f* (con escopeta); **he comes each year for the ~** viene cada año para la caza; **there is good ~ in Asturias** Asturias es buen terreno para la caza; **to go ~** ir de caza, ir a cazar; **good ~!** ¡buen tiro!; ¡bravo!
(**d**) (*Cine*) rodaje *m*.
2 *attr* de tiro; de caza; *pain* punzante; **~ affray** refriega *f* con tiros; **~ incident** incidente *m* de tiroteo; **within ~ range** a tiro; **~ war** guerra *f* a tiros.
shooting-box [ˈʃuːtɪŋbɒks] *n*, **shooting-lodge** [ˈʃuːtɪŋlɒdʒ] *n* pabellón *m* de caza.
shooting-brake [ˈʃuːtɪŋbreɪk] *n* (*Brit*: †) rubia *f*, furgoneta *f*, camioneta *f* (*LAm*).
shooting-gallery [ˈʃuːtɪŋˌgælərɪ] *n* galería *f* de tiro al blanco.
shooting-jacket [ˈʃuːtɪŋˌdʒækɪt] *n* chaquetón *m*.
shooting-match [ˈʃuːtɪŋmætʃ] *n* certamen *m* de tiro al blanco; **the whole ~*** (*Brit*) el todo, todo el negocio.
shooting-party [ˈʃuːtɪŋˌpɑːtɪ] *n* partida *f* de caza.
shooting-range [ˈʃuːtɪŋreɪdʒ] *n* campo *m* de tiro.
shooting-star [ʃuːtɪŋˈstɑːʳ] *n* estrella *f* fugaz.
shooting-stick [ˈʃuːtɪŋstɪk] *n* bastón *m* taburete.
shoot-out [ˈʃuːtaʊt] *n* (**a**) tiroteo *m*, balacera *f* (*Mex*). (**b**) (*Sport*) desempate *m* a penaltis.
shop [ʃɒp] **1** *n* (**a**) (*esp Brit*: *Comm*) tienda *f*, negocio *m* (*And, SC*); (*large store*) almacén *m*; **~!** ¿quién despacha?; **to keep a ~** poseer un negocio; **to set up ~** poner una tienda; **to shut up ~** cerrar; (*fig*) dar por terminado un asunto; desistir de una empresa; **to talk ~** hablar del propio trabajo, hablar de asuntos profesionales; **it's all over the ~*** está en el mayor desorden; **she leaves things all over the ~*** deja sus cosas de cualquier modo; **they're all over the ~*** no tienen ni idea, carecen de todo sentido del buen orden; **the papers were all over the ~*** los papeles estaban en la mayor confusión.
(**b**) (*Tech*) taller *m*.
2 *attr* (**a**) (*Comm*) **~ assistant** (*Brit*) vendedor *m*, -ora *f*, dependiente *m*, -a *f*, empleado *m*, -a *f* (de una tienda) (*LAm*); **~ hours** horas *fpl* de apertura; **~ talk** temas *mpl* del oficio, conversación *f* sobre el trabajo, asuntos *mpl* de interés profesional.
(**b**) (*Brit Tech*) **~ floor** (*fig*) taller *m*, fábrica *f*; **~ floor (workers)** obreros *mpl*; **~ floor opinion** opinión *f* de las bases sindicales, opinión *f* de los obreros; **~ steward** enlace *mf* sindical.
3 *vt* **to ~ sb‡** (*esp Brit*) traicionar a uno, delatar a uno; denunciar a uno a la policía.
4 *vi* comprar, hacer compras; **to go ~ping** ir de compras, ir de tiendas; **to send sb ~ping** enviar a uno a hacer compras; **to ~ at Joe's** hacer sus compras en la tienda de Joe; **to ~ for fish** ir a buscar pescado en las tiendas.
◆**shop around** *vi* comparar los precios en diversas tiendas (*for sth* antes de comprar algo).
shopfront [ˈʃɒpfrʌnt] *n* escaparate *m*.

shopgirl [ˈʃɒpgɜːl] *n* (*Brit*) dependienta *f*, empleada *f* (de una tienda) (*LAm*).
shopkeeper [ˈʃɒpˌkiːpəʳ] *n* tendero *m*, -a *f*.
shoplift [ˈʃɒplɪft] *vi* hurtar en tiendas.
shoplifter [ˈʃɒpˌlɪftəʳ] *n* mechera *f*, ratero *m* de tiendas.
shoplifting [ˈʃɒpˌlɪftɪŋ] *n* ratería *f*, hurto *m* (en las tiendas).
shopper [ˈʃɒpəʳ] *n* comprador *m*, -ora *f*.
shopping [ˈʃɒpɪŋ] **1** *n* (**a**) (*act*) **I like ~** me gusta ir de tiendas; **we have to go a long way for our ~** para comprar cosas tenemos que ir muy lejos. (**b**) (*goods bought*) compras *fpl*.
2 *attr*: **~ bag** bolsa *f* de compras; **~ basket** cesta *f* de compras; **~ cart** (*US*), **~ trolley** carrito *m* de la compra; **~ centre,** (*US*) **~ center, ~ mall** centro *m* comercial, zona *f* de tiendas; **~ list** lista *f* de compras; **~ precinct** centro *m* comercial; **~ trip** viaje *m* de compras.
shop-soiled [ˈʃɒpsɔɪld] *adj* (*Brit*) usado, deteriorado; (*fig*) trasnochado.
shopwalker [ˈʃɒpˌwɔːkəʳ] *n* (*Brit*) vigilante *m*, -a *f*.
shopwindow [ˈʃɒpˌwɪndəʊ] *n* escaparate *m*, vitrina *f* (*LAm*), vidriera *f* (*SC*).
shopworn [ˈʃɒpwɔːn] *adj* (*US*) = **shop-soiled.**
shore[1] [ʃɔːʳ] **1** *n* playa *f*; orilla *f*, ribera *f*; **these ~s** (*fig*) estas tierras, esta parte; **on ~** en tierra. **2** *attr*: **~ leave** licencia *f* para ir a tierra.
shore[2] [ʃɔːʳ] **1** *n* puntal *m*; (*Min*) entibo *m*. **2** *vt* (*also* **to ~ up**) apuntalar; entibar.
◆**shore up** *vt* (*fig*) apoyar, reforzar, sostener.
shoreline [ˈʃɔːlaɪn] *n* línea *f* de la costa.
shoreward(s) [ˈʃɔːwəd(z)] *adv* hacia la costa, hacia la playa.
shorn [ʃɔːn] *ptp of* **shear** mocho; **~ of** sin, desprovisto de; despojado de; **~ of its verbiage, this means ...** quitando la palabrería, esto quiere decir ...; **~ of outside aid we cannot go on** sin la ayuda exterior no podemos continuar.
short [ʃɔːt] **1** *adj* (**a**) (*in length, distance*) corto; *message etc* corto, breve, sucinto; *person* bajo, chaparro (*Mex*); *radio wave* corto; **~ sight** miopía *f*; **to have ~ sight** ser miope, ser corto de vista; **~ story** cuento *m*; **~ story writer** escritor *m*, -ora *f* de cuentos; **the ~est route** la ruta más corta; **a few ~ words** algunas palabritas; **a ~ way off** a poca distancia, no muy lejos; **by a ~ head** por una cabeza escasa; **to be ~ in the leg** tener las piernas cortas; **these trousers are a bit ~ in the leg** estos pantalones tienen la pierna algo pequeña; **the ~ answer is that ...** en pocas palabras la razón es que ...; **to have a ~ back-and-sides** llevar el pelo corto por detrás y por los lados; **to have sb by the ~ and curlies‡** tener a alguien por los huevos**‡; **to take ~ steps** dar pequeños pasos; **to take a ~ walk** dar un paseíto.
(**b**) (*of words*) **'Joss' is ~ for 'Jocelyn'** 'Joss' es diminutivo de 'Jocelyn'; **'living' is ~ for 'living room'** 'living' es apócope de 'living room'; **he's called Fred for ~** su diminutivo es Fred; **'TV' is ~ for 'television'** 'TV' es abreviatura de 'televisión'.
(**c**) (*in time*) corto, breve; de poca duración; *vowel* breve; *memory* flaco, malo; **for a ~ time** por poco tiempo; **in ~ order** con toda rapidez; sin demora; **it was ~ and sweet** fue corto y bueno; **February is a ~ month** febrero es un mes corto; **the days are getting ~er** los días se hacen más breves; **time is getting ~er** nos queda poco tiempo.
(**d**) (*curt*) *reply* brusco, seco; *manner* brusco, corto (*LAm*); *temper* vivo; **to be ~ with sb** tratar a uno con sequedad.
(**e**) (*insufficient*) insuficiente; **~ delivery** (*Comm*) entrega *f* incompleta; **~ ton** (*US*: = *2,000 lb*) tonelada *f* corta; **5 ~** faltan 5, 5 de menos; **I'm £3 ~** me faltan 3 libras; **it's 2 kilos ~** faltan 2 kilos; **we were ~ last week** la semana pasada nos faltó; **oranges are in ~ supply** escasean las naranjas, hay escasez de naranjas, hay poca naranja; **to give ~ weight** vender algo con peso insuficiente; **to give sb ~ change** faltarle a uno en la vuelta; **to be on ~ time** trabajar jornadas reducidas; **not far ~ of £100** poco menos de 100 libras; **nothing ~ of total surrender** nada menos que la rendición incondicional; **it's little ~ of madness** dista poco de la locura; **nothing ~ of a bomb would stop him** fuera de una bomba nada le impediría.
(**f**) (*lacking*) **to be ~ of** estar falto de, andar escaso de; **we are ~ of petrol** andamos escasos de gasolina; **we're not ~ of volunteers** se han ofrecido muchos voluntarios, no andamos escasos de voluntarios; **I was ~ of clubs** tenía poco trébol; **the plan is ~ on details** el proyecto tiene pocos detalles; **he's ~ on brains*** le falta chirumen*; **bananas are very ~** escasean los plátanos, casi no hay plátanos; **to go ~ of** pasarse sin; **no one goes ~ in this house** en esta casa nadie padece hambre; **to run ~** escasear; **we ran ~ of petrol** se nos acabó la gasolina, quedamos sin gasolina.
(**g**) *pastry* quebradizo.
2 *adv* (**a**) **in ~** en resumen; en fin; **to cut ~** acortar, abreviar; interrumpir; terminar inesperadamente; **they had to cut ~ their holiday** tuvieron que interrumpir sus vacaciones; **to fall ~** resultar ser insuficiente, no alcanzar; **production has fallen ~ by 100 tons** la producción arroja un déficit de 100 toneladas; **to fall ~ of the target** no alcanzar el blanco, no llegar al blanco; **to fall ~ of expectations** no cumplir las esperanzas; **it falls far ~ of what we require** dista mucho de satisfacer nuestras exigencias; **to sell ~** vender al descubierto; **to sell sb ~** (*deceive*) engañar a uno en un negocio; (*belittle*) despreciar a uno, quitar méritos a uno; **to stop ~** parar en seco; parar de repente; **to stop ~ of** detenerse antes de llegar a; **to be taken ~** necesitar urgentemente ir al wáter.
(**b**) **~ of blowing it up** a menos que lo volemos, a no ser que lo volemos; **~ of murder I'll do anything** lo haré todo menos matar; **it's nothing ~ of robbery** es nada menos que un robo.
3 *n* (**a**) (*Cine*) cortometraje *m*; complemento *m*.
(**b**) (*Elec*) cortocircuito *m*.
(**c**) (*drink*) licor *m*, bebida *f* corta, copa *f* (de licor).
(**d**) (*garment*) **~s** pantalón *m* corto; (*US*) calzoncillos *mpl*.
4 *vt* (*Elec*) poner en cortocircuito.
5 *vi* ponerse en cortocircuito.
shortage [ˈʃɔːtɪdʒ] *n* escasez *f*, falta *f*; insuficiencia *f*; penuria *f*; **the housing ~** la crisis de la vivienda; **~ of staff** insuficiencia *f* de personal; **in times of ~** en las épocas de escasez; **there is no ~ of advice** no es que falten los consejos.
shortbread [ˈʃɔːtbred] *n torta dulce seca y quebradiza.*
shortcake [ˈʃɔːtkeɪk] *n* torta *f* de frutas; = **shortbread.**
short-change [ˈʃɔːtˈtʃeɪndʒ] *vt*: **to ~ sb** faltarle a uno en la vuelta; (*fig*) defraudar a uno, decepcionar a uno; **to do this is to ~ the project** (*esp US*) hacer esto es tratar inadecuadamente el proyecto.
short-circuit [ˈʃɔːtˈsɜːkɪt] **1** *n* cortocircuito *m*. **2** *vt* (**a**) (*Elec*) poner en cortocircuito. (**b**) (*fig*: *bypass*) evitar (la necesidad de pasar por); (*cause to fail*) dar al traste con, arruinar, estropear. **3** *vi* ponerse en cortocircuito.
shortcoming [ˈʃɔːtkʌmɪŋ] *n* defecto *m*, deficiencia *f*, fallo *m*.
shortcrust pastry [ˈʃɔːtkrʌstˌpeɪstrɪ] *n* (*Brit*) pasta *f* quebradiza; *V also* **short 1 (g).**
short-dated [ˈʃɔːtˈdeɪtɪd] *adj* a corto plazo.
shorten [ˈʃɔːtn] **1** *vt* acortar; abreviar; reducir; *holiday, journey etc* acortar.
2 *vi* acortarse; abreviarse; reducirse; **the odds have ~ed** los puntos de ventaja se han reducido.
shortening [ˈʃɔːtnɪŋ] *n* (*V vt*) (**a**) acortamiento *m*; abreviación *f*; reducción *f*. (**b**) (*Culin*) manteca *f* (de hojaldre).
shortfall [ˈʃɔːtfɔːl] *n* déficit *m*, deficiencia *f*.
short-haired [ˈʃɔːtˈhɛəd] *adj* pelicorto.
shorthand [ˈʃɔːthænd] (*Brit*) **1** *n* taquigrafía *f*; **to take ~** escribir en taquigrafía; **to take sth down in ~** apuntar algo taquigráficamente.
2 *attr*: **~ note** nota *f* taquigráfica; **~ notebook** cuaderno *m* de taquigrafía; **~ speed** palabras *fpl* por minuto (en taquigrafía); **~ typing** taquimecanografía; **~ typist** taquimeca(nógrafa) *f*; **~ writer** taquígrafo *m*, -a *f*.
short-handed [ˈʃɔːtˈhændɪd] *adj* falto de personal, falto de mano de obra.
short-haul [ˈʃɔːthɔːl] *adj* de corto recorrido.
shortish [ˈʃɔːtɪʃ] *adj* algo pequeño, más bien bajo, bajito.
shortlist [ˈʃɔːtˈlɪst] **1** *n* (*Brit*) preselección *f*, terna *f*, lista *f* de candidatos escogidos.
2 *vt*: **to ~ sb** poner a uno en la lista de candidatos escogidos, preseleccionar a uno.
short-lived [ˈʃɔːtˈlɪvd] *adj* efímero.
shortly [ˈʃɔːtlɪ] *adv* (**a**) (*soon*) en breve, dentro de poco; luego; próximamente; **~ after** poco después; **~ before this** poco tiempo antes de esto; **you shall see it very ~** lo va a ver muy pronto.
(**b**) (*curtly*) bruscamente, secamente.
shortness [ˈʃɔːtnɪs] *n* (**a**) (*in length, distance*) cortedad *f*; (*of message etc*) brevedad *f*; (*of person*) pequeñez *f*; (*in time*) brevedad *f*, poca duración *f*; **because of the ~ of my memory** debido a mi mala memoria; **~ of sight** miopía *f*; **~ of breath** falta *f* de aliento, respiración *f* difícil.

(**b**) (*curtness*) brusquedad *f*, sequedad *f*.

short-range [ˈʃɔːtˈreɪndʒ] *adj gun* de corto alcance; *aircraft* de autonomía limitada, de corto radio en acción.

short-run [ˈʃɔːtrʌn] *adj* breve, de alcance limitado.

short-sighted [ˈʃɔːtˈsaɪtɪd] *adj* (*esp Brit*) miope, corto de vista; (*fig*) miope, *person* falto de previsión, imprevisor; *measure etc* imprudente.

short-sightedly [ˈʃɔːtˈsaɪtɪdlɪ] *adv* con ojos de miope; (*fig*) imprudentemente.

short-sightedness [ˈʃɔːtˈsaɪtɪdnɪs] *n* miopía *f*; cortedad *f* de vista; (*fig*) falta *f* de previsión, imprevisión *f*; imprudencia *f*.

short-sleeved [ˈʃɔːtsliːvd] *adj* de manga corta.

short-staffed [ˌʃɔːtˈstɑːft] *adj* falto de personal.

short-tempered [ˈʃɔːtˈtempəd] *adj* de genio vivo, enojadizo.

short-term [ˈʃɔːttɜːm] *adj* a corto plazo; **~ car park** zona *f* de estacionamiento limitado.

short-time [ˈʃɔːtˈtaɪm] **1** *adj*: **~ working** sistema *m* de jornadas reducidas, sistema *m* de jornada limitada, trabajo *m* de horario reducido; **to be on ~ working** trabajar jornadas reducidas.

2 *adv*: **to work ~** trabajar jornadas reducidas.

shortwave [ˈʃɔːtˌweɪv] *adj* de onda corta.

short-winded [ˈʃɔːtˈwɪndɪd] *adj* corto de resuello.

shortly* [ˈʃɔːtɪ] *n* persona *f* bajita.

shot [ʃɒt] **1** *n* (**a**) (*missile*) bala *f*; proyectil *m*; (*sound of ~*) tiro *m*, disparo *m*; (*causing wound*) balazo *m*; (*pellets*) perdigones *mpl*; (*weight, Sport*) peso *m*; **~ across the bows** cañonazo *m* de advertencia; **~ in the dark** (*fig*) tiro *m* al azar; **good ~!** ¡muy bien!; **I'll do it like a ~** lo haré de buena gana; **he did it like a ~** lo hizo como un relámpago, lo hizo como un resorte; **he was off like a ~** partió como una bala; **it's a long ~, but we could try** no es fácil, pero podemos probar; **that guess was a very long ~** fue una conjetura muy arriesgada; **to fire a ~ at sb** disparar sobre uno, tirar a uno; **who fired that ~?** ¿quién disparó?; **it surrendered without firing a ~** (*or* **without a ~ being fired**) se rindió sin resistencia alguna; **we captured it without firing a ~** lo tomamos sin disparar una sola vez; **to exchange ~s** tirotearse; **to put the ~** lanzar el peso; **to take a ~ at sb** tirar a uno.

(**b**) (*person*) tirador *m*, -ora *f*; **to be a crack ~** ser un tirador experto; **I'm rather a poor ~** no tiro muy bien; *V* **big 1**.

(**c**) (*in space exploration*) lanzamiento *m*; cohete *m*, vehículo *m* espacial.

(**d**) (*Sport: with club etc*) golpe *m*; (*Snooker etc*) golpe *m*, jugada *f*; (*throw*) tirada *f*, echada *f*; (*at goal*) tiro *m*, disparo *m*; **to call the ~s** (*fig*) mandar, dirigirlo todo.

(**e**) (*attempt*) tentativa *f*; (*guess*) conjetura *f*; **it's your ~** te toca a ti; **to have a ~** probar suerte; **to have a ~ at** + *ger* hacer una tentativa de + *infin*; **will you have a ~ at it?** ¿quieres probar?

(**f**) (*injection*) inyección *f*; (*dose*) dosis *f*; (*: *of drug*) pico** *m*, chute** *m*; **a ~ of rum** un trago de ron*; **it's a ~ in the arm for ...** es un estimulazo para ...; **the industry needs a ~ in the arm** la industria necesita una fuerte ayuda económica.

(**g**) (*Phot*) foto *f*, instantánea *f*; (*in film*) fotograma *m*, toma *f*, plano *m*.

2 *pret and ptp of* **shoot**; **~ silk** seda *f* tornasolada; **to get ~ of*** deshacerse de, quitarse de encima; **black ~ (through) with blue** negro con visos azules; **his story is ~ through with inconsistencies** su narración está plagada de incongruencias.

shotgun [ˈʃɒtgʌn] **1** *n* escopeta *f*. **2** *attr*: **~ marriage, ~ wedding** casamiento *m* a la fuerza; **to have a ~ wedding** casarse a la fuerza, casarse de penalty*.

shot-put [ˈʃɒtpʊt] *n* (*Sport*) lanzamiento *m* de pesos.

shot-putter [ˈʃɒtˌpʊtər] *n* lanzador *m*, -ora *f* de pesos.

should [ʃʊd] (*irr: pret and conditional of* **shall**) *v aux* (**a**) (*used to form conditional tense*) **I ~ go if they sent for me** iría si me llamasen; **~ I be out at the time** si estoy fuera en aquel momento; **I ~n't be surprised if ...** no me sorprendería si ...; **I ~n't if I were you** yo en tu lugar no lo haría; **he ordered that it ~ be done** mandó que se hiciera así; **thanks, I ~ like to** gracias, me gustaría; **I ~n't like to say** prefiero no decirlo.

(**b**) (*statements of duty and command*) **all cars ~ carry lights** todos los coches deben llevar luces; **you ~n't do that** no debes hacer eso; **all is as it ~ be** todo está en regla; **..., which is as it ~ be ...** como es razonable; **why ~ I?** ¿por qué lo voy a hacer?; **why ~ he (have done it)?** ¿por qué lo iba a hacer?; **why ~ you want to know?** ¿por qué has de saberlo tú?; **he ~ know that ...** debiera saber que ...; **he ~ have paid it** debiera haberlo pagado.

(**c**) (*statements of probability*) **he ~ be there by now** debe haber llegado ya; **they ~ arrive tomorrow** deberán llegar mañana; **this ~ be good** esto promete ser bueno.

shoulder [ˈʃəʊldər] **1** *n* (**a**) (*Anat*) hombro *m*; espaldas *fpl*; (*of meat*) espalda *f*; (*of coat etc*) hombrera *f*; **to carry sth on one's ~s** llevar algo a hombros; **he was carried out on their ~s** le sacaron a hombros; **all the responsibilities fell on his ~s** tuvo que cargar con todas las responsabilidades; **they carried him ~ high** le llevaron a hombros; **to give sb the cold ~, turn a cold ~ on** (*or* **to**) **sb** (*US*) volver la espalda a uno; **to give sb sth straight from the ~** decir algo a uno sin rodeos; **to look over one's ~** mirar por encima del hombro; **to put one's ~ to the wheel** arrimar el hombro; **to rub ~s with sb** codearse con uno; **to stand ~ to ~** estar hombro con hombro.

(**b**) (*of hill*) lomo *m*; (*Brit: of motorway*) arcén *m*.

2 *vt* (**a**) (*carry*) llevar al hombro; (*pick up*) poner al hombro; (*fig*) *responsibilities etc* cargar con; **~ arms!** ¡armas al hombro!

(**b**) **to ~ sb aside** apartar a uno con el hombro; abrirse paso empujando a uno con el hombro; (*fig*) dejar a uno al lado; **to ~ one's way through** abrirse paso a empujones.

shoulder-bag [ˈʃəʊldəˌbæg] *n* bolso *m* de bandolera.

shoulderblade [ˈʃəʊldəbleɪd] *n* omóplato *m*.

shoulder-flash [ˈʃəʊldəˌflæʃ] *n* charretera *f*.

shoulder-holster [ˈʃəʊldəˌhəʊlstər] *n* pistolera *f*.

shoulder-joint [ˈʃəʊldəˌdʒɔɪnt] *n* articulación *f* del hombro.

shoulderknot [ˈʃəʊldənɒt] *n* dragona *f*, charretera *f*.

shoulder-length [ˈʃəʊldəˌleŋθ] *adj hair* hasta el hombro.

shoulderpad [ˈʃəʊldəpæd] *n* hombrera *f*.

shoulder-strap [ˈʃəʊldəstræp] *n* (*Mil*) dragona *f*; (*of dress*) tirante *m*; (*of satchel etc*) correa *f*, bandolera *f*.

shouldn't [ˈʃʊdnt] = **should not**.

shout [ʃaʊt] **1** *n* grito *m*, voz *f*; **a ~ of protest** un grito de protesta; **there were ~s of applause** hubo grandes aplausos; **there were ~s of laughter** hubo grandes carcajadas; **to give sb a ~** llamar a uno; **it's my ~*** me toca a mí; **he's still in with a ~*** todavía tiene una posibilidad de ganar.

2 *vt* gritar; **to ~ abuse at sb** lanzar improperios contra uno; **to ~ a protest** protestar en alta voz.

3 *vi* gritar; dar voces; (*talk loudly*) hablar a voz en grito; **he ~ed for his servant** llamó a su criado a voz en grito; **to ~ for help** pedir socorro a voces; **to ~ with laughter** reírse a grandes carcajadas.

4 *vr*: **to ~ o.s. hoarse** enronquecer gritando.

◆**shout down** *vt*: **to ~ sb down** abuchear a uno, hundir a uno en gritos; **to ~ a play down** hundir una obra a gritos.

◆**shout out 1** *vt* gritar, decir a voz en grito. **2** *vi* gritar, dar gritos.

shouting [ˈʃaʊtɪŋ] **1** *n* gritos *mpl*, vocerío *m*, clamoreo *m*; *V* **bar 3**. **2** *attr*: **within ~ distance** al alcance de la voz.

shove [ʃʌv] **1** *n* empujón *m*; **to give sb a ~** empujar a uno; **can you give me a ~, please?** (*Aut etc*) ¿por favor, me ayuda a arrancar empujándolo?; **one more ~ and we're there** empujad una vez más y ya está; **give it a good ~** dale un buen empujón.

2 *vt* (**a**) (*push*) empujar; **to ~ sb aside** apartar a uno empujándole, apartar a uno a codazos; **his friends ~d him forward** sus amigos le empujaron hacia adelante.

(**b**) (*) poner, meter; dejar; **~ it here** ponlo aquí.

3 *vi* empujar, dar empujones; **stop shoving!** ¡dejen de empujar!

◆**shove about, shove around** *vt* (*lit*) *object* empujar de un lado a otro; *person* mandar de un lado a otro; (*) tiranizar.

◆**shove away** *vt person, object* empujar.

◆**shove back** *vt*: **to ~ sb back** hacer retroceder a uno empujándole.

◆**shove off 1** *vt*: **to ~ a boat off** echar afuera un bote.

2 *vi* (*Naut*) alejarse del muelle (*etc*); (*) largarse*; **~ off!** ¡lárgate*!

◆**shove on*** *vt hat, coat etc* ponerse; **~ another record on** pon otro disco.

◆**shove out** *vt*: **to ~ a boat out** echar afuera un bote; **they ~d him out** le empujaron fuera, (*fig*) le obligaron a salir de su puesto (*etc*).

◆**shove over 1** *vt* (**a**) (*knock over*) *chair etc* derribar; *person* derribar de un golpe.

(**b**) **they ~d the car over the cliff** fueron empujando el coche hasta que cayó por el acantilado.

(**c**) **~ it over to me*** trae pa'acá*.

2 (*) *vi* correrse; ~ **over!** ¡córrete!, ¡échate pa'allá*!
◆**shove up*** *vi* = **shove over 2.**
shovel ['ʃʌvl] **1** *n* pala *f*; (*mechanical*) pala *f* mecánica.
2 *vt* traspalar, mover con pala; **to ~ earth into a pile** amontonar tierra con una pala; **he was ~ling food into his mouth** iba zampando la comida; **to ~ coal on to a fire** añadir carbón a la lumbre con pala; **they were ~ling out the mud** estaban sacando el lodo con palas.
◆**shovel up** *vt coal etc* levantar con una pala; *snow* quitar con pala.
shovelboard ['ʃʌvlbɔːd] *n* juego *m* de tejo.
shoveler ['ʃʌvləʳ] *n* (**a**) (*Orn*) espátula *f* común, pato *m* cuchareta. (**b**) (*tool*) paleador *m*.
shovelful ['ʃʌvlfʊl] *n* paletada *f*.
show [ʃəʊ] **1** *n* (**a**) (*showing*) demostración *f*; **~ of hands** votación *f* a mano alzada; **an impressive ~ of power** una impresionante exhibición de poder; **the garden is a splendid ~** el jardín está muy vistoso; **the dahlias make a fine ~** las dalias se muestran espléndidas.
(**b**) (*exhibition*) exposición *f*; (*of agriculture, trade*) feria *f*; **to be on ~** estar expuesto; **he's holding his first London ~** está organizando su primera exposición en Londres; *V* **horse ~, motor ~** *etc*.
(**c**) (*Theat etc*) función *f*, espectáculo *m*; show *m*; **on with the ~!** ¡que comience (*or* continúe) la función!; **the ~ goes on** (*Theat*) la función continúa, (*fig*) seguimos adelante a pesar de todo; **the last ~ starts at 11** la última función empieza a las 11; **there is no ~ on Sundays** el domingo no hay función; **let's get this ~ on the road** (*fig*) echémosnos a la carretera; **to go to a ~** ir a un teatro, ir a un espectáculo; **to steal the ~** acaparar toda la atención; **Lord Mayor's S~** desfile *m* del alcalde de Londres (el día de su inauguración).
(**d**) (*: *undertaking, organization*) negocio *m*, empresa *f*, cosa *f*, organización *f*; **who's in charge of this ~?** ¿quién manda aquí?; **this is my ~** esto es mío, aquí mando yo; **he runs the ~** manda él, él es el amo.
(**e**) (*Brit**: *performance*) **bad ~!** ¡malo!; **good ~!** ¡muy bien!, ¡bravo!; **to put up a good ~** hacer un buen papel, dar buena cuenta de sí; **it's a pretty poor ~, isn't it?** esto es un desastre, ¿no?; **to give the ~ away** (*deliberately*) tirar de la manta, (*involuntarily*) clarearse.
(**f**) (*outward ~*) apariencia *f*; ostentación *f*; (*pomp*) boato *m*, aparato *m*, pompa *f*; **it's just for ~** es sólo para impresionar; **it's all ~ with him** todo lo hace para impresionar; **to do sth for ~** hacer algo para impresionar; **to make a ~ of resistance** aparentar resistir, fingir resistir; **to make a ~ of unwillingness** fingir no querer; **to make a great ~ of sympathy** hacer alarde de su mucha compasión.
2 *attr*: **~ bill** cartel *m*; **~ house** (*Brit*) casa *f* piloto, casa *f* modelo; **~ trial** proceso *m* organizado con fines propagandísticos, proceso *m* espectacular.
3 (*irr*: *pret* **showed**, *ptp* **shown**) *vt* (**a**) (*manifest*) mostrar, enseñar; *film* proyectar, poner; *slides* proyectar; *picture* exhibir; *goods* exponer; **to ~ sb sth, to ~ sth to sb** mostrar (*or* enseñar) algo a uno; **to ~ one's passport** mostrar su pasaporte, presentar su pasaporte; **to ~ a picture at the Academy** exhibir un cuadro en la Academia; **to ~ a film at Cannes** presentar una película en Cannes; **the film was first ~n in 1968** la película se estrenó en 1968; **to ~ sb a light** alumbrar a uno, dar luz a uno; **he had nothing to ~ for his trouble** se quedó sin nada después de tantos trabajos, no sacó provecho alguno de tantos trabajos; **they ~ed us round the garden** nos mostraron el jardín, con ellos visitamos el jardín; **who is going to ~ us round?** ¿quién actuará de guía?
(**b**) (*indicate*) indicar; (*Comm*) arrojar; **it ~s 200°** indica 200°, marca 200°; **it ~s a speed of ...** indica una velocidad de ...; **as ~n in the illustration** según se indica en la lámina, como lo indica el grabado; **the roads are ~n in red** las carreteras están marcadas en rojo; **to ~ a loss** dejar una pérdida; **to ~ a profit** arrojar un saldo positivo; **the figures ~ a rise** las cifras arrojan un aumento.
(**c**) (*demonstrate*) mostrar, manifestar; acusar; (*prove*) probar, demostrar; **I'll ~ you!** (*indignant*) ¡ya lo verás!; **to ~ intelligence** mostrar tener inteligencia, mostrar ser inteligente; **to ~ his disagreement, he ...** para mostrar su disconformidad, él ...; **she ~ed no reaction** no acusó reacción alguna; **her face ~ed her happiness** su felicidad se acusaba en la cara; **to ~ one's affection** demostrar su cariño; **a big crowd turned up to ~ its feeling for him** una gran multitud acudió para testimoniarle su simpatía; **the choice of dishes ~s excellent taste** la selección de platos demuestra un gusto muy fino; **she's beginning to ~ her age** ya empieza a aparentar su edad; **to ~ that ...** demostrar que ..., hacer ver que ...; **I ~ed him that this could not be true** le hice ver que esto no podía ser cierto.
(**d**) (*reveal*) revelar; **the gap ~s her legs** el espacio deja ver sus piernas; **she likes to ~ her legs** le gusta hacer exhibición de sus piernas; **a dress which ~s the slip** un vestido que deja ver la combinación; **this ~s him to be a swindler** esto le revela como estafador, esto demuestra que es estafador.
(**e**) (*direct*) **to ~ sb the way** enseñar a uno el camino; **let me ~ you** se lo voy a enseñar; **to ~ sb into a room** hacer que pase uno, hacer entrar a uno en un cuarto; **I was ~n into a large hall** me hicieron pasar a un vestíbulo grande; **to ~ sb to his seat** enseñar a uno su asiento, acompañar a uno a su asiento.
4 *vi* mostrarse, verse, revelarse; aparecer; (*film*) proyectarse; **your slip's ~ing, madam** señora, se le ve la combinación; **it doesn't ~** no se nota; **don't worry, it won't ~** no te preocupes, no se notará; **the tulips are beginning to ~** empiezan a brotar los tulipanes; **a little colour is beginning to ~ now** ahora se empieza a verles un poco de color; **it just goes to ~!** ¡hay que ver!: **it all goes to ~ that ...** todo sirve para demostrar que ...
5 *vr*: **to ~ o.s.** presentarse; hacer acto de presencia; **to ~ o.s. incompetent** descubrir su incompetencia, mostrarse incompetente; **it ~s itself in his speech** se revela en su forma de hablar, se le nota en el habla.
◆**show in** *vt* hacer pasar; **~ him in!** ¡que pasé!
◆**show off 1** *vt* (**a**) (*display*) hacer gala de, lucir; *beauty etc* hacer resaltar, destacar.
(**b**) (*pej*) hacer ostentación de.
2 *vi* darse importancia, presumir; fachendear; **to ~ off in front of one's friends** presumir ante las amistades; **stop ~ing off!** ¡no presumas!
◆**show out** *vt* acompañar a la puerta.
◆**show through** *vi* verse; transparentarse, trascender; clarearse.
◆**show up 1** *vt* (**a**) *visitor* hacer subir; **~ her up!** ¡que suba!
(**b**) *fraud etc* descubrir; *person* desenmascarar; *defect etc* revelar, patentizar.
(**c**) (*present*) presentar; *beauty etc* hacer resaltar, destacar.
(**d**) (*embarrass*) avergonzar.
2 *vi* (**a**) (*stand out*) destacar.
(**b**) (*: *appear*) acudir, presentarse, aparecer.
show biz* ['ʃəʊbɪz] *n* = **show business.**
showboat ['ʃəʊbəʊt] *n* (*US*) barco-teatro *m*.
show business ['ʃəʊbɪznɪs] *n* los espectáculos, el mundo del espectáculo, el negocio del espectáculo; la vida de actor.
showcase ['ʃəʊkeɪs] **1** *n* vitrina *f* (de exposición), (*fig*) escaparate *m*. **2** *attr*: **~ project** proyecto *m* modelo.
showdown ['ʃəʊdaʊn] *n* confrontación *f*, enfrentamiento *m* decisivo; ajuste *m* de cuentas definitivo; momento *m* decisivo; hora *f* de la verdad; **the Suez ~** la crisis de Suez; **if it comes to a ~** si llega a un conflicto, si llega el momento decisivo; **to have a ~ with sb** enfrentarse con uno, confrontarse con uno; **I'm going to have a ~ with the boss** le voy a decir cuatro verdades al jefe.
shower ['ʃaʊəʳ] **1** *n* (**a**) (*of rain*) chaparrón *m*, chubasco *m*, aguacero *m*.
(**b**) (*fig*: *of arrows, stones etc*) lluvia *f*.
(**c**) (*Brit*‡) gentuza *f*; **they were an utter ~** eran horribles, eran unos pesados; **what a ~!** ¡qué pesados!
(**d**) (*~bath*) ducha *f*, regadera *f* (*Mex*); **to take** (*or* **have**) **a ~** ducharse, tomar una ducha.
(**e**) (*US*) fiesta *f* con motivo de un nacimiento (*or* matrimonio *etc*).
2 *attr*: **~ gel** gel *m* de baño; **~ unit** ducha *f*.
3 *vt* (*fig*: *also* **to ~ down**) llover, derramar; **to ~ sb with honours, to ~ honours on sb** colmar a uno de honores; **he was ~ed with invitations** le llovieron encima las invitaciones, le abrumaron de invitaciones.
4 *vi* (**a**) (*rain*) llover, caer un chaparrón. (**b**) (*in ~bath*) ducharse, tomar una ducha.
showerbath ['ʃaʊəbɑːθ] *n*, *pl* **showerbaths** ['ʃaʊəbɑːðz] ducha *f*; **to take a ~** ducharse, tomar una ducha.
showercap ['ʃaʊəkæp] *n* gorro *m* de ducha.
shower-curtain ['ʃaʊə,kɜːtən] *n* cortina *f* de ducha.
shower-head ['ʃaʊəhed] *n* alcachofa *f* de ducha.
showerproof ['ʃaʊəpruːf] *adj* impermeable.
showery ['ʃaʊərɪ] *adj day etc* de chaparrones; *weather* lluvioso; **it will be ~ tomorrow** mañana habrá chapa-

rrones.
showgirl ['ʃəʊgɜːl] *n* corista *f.*
showground ['ʃəʊgraʊnd] *n* real *m* (de la feria), ferial *m.*
showily ['ʃəʊɪlɪ] *adv* vistosamente, llamativamente; aparatosamente; de modo espectacular; ostentosamente.
showiness ['ʃəʊɪnɪs] *n* vistosidad *f,* lo llamativo; espectacularidad *f,* ostentación *f;* boato *m.*
showing ['ʃəʊɪŋ] *n* **(a)** (*of pictures etc*) exposición *f;* (*of film*) proyección *f,* presentación *f;* **a second ~ of 'The Blue Angel'** un reestreno de 'El Ángel Azul'.
(b) (*performance*) actuación *f;* **the team's ~ this season** la actuación del equipo durante la temporada actual; **the poor ~ of the team** la pobre actuación del equipo; **to make a good ~** hacer un buen papel, dar buena cuenta de sí.
(c) on his own ~ según él mismo confiesa.
showing-off [,ʃəʊɪŋ'ɒf] *n* lucimiento *m;* (*pej*) fachenda *f.*
show-jumper ['ʃəʊ,dʒʌmpəʳ] *n* participante *mf* en concursos de saltos.
show-jumping ['ʃəʊ,dʒʌmpɪŋ] *n* concurso *m* de saltos.
showman ['ʃəʊmən] *n, pl* **showmen** ['ʃəʊmən] empresario *m,* director *m* de espectáculos; (*fig*) persona *f* ostentosa, exhibicionista *m;* (*pej*) comediante *m,* fantoche *m,* charlatán *m;* **the prime minister is a consummate ~** el primer ministro es un brillante actor.
showmanship ['ʃəʊmənʃɪp] *n* instinto *m* del buen actor; teatralidad *f;* talento *m* para organizar grandes espectáculos.
shown [ʃəʊn] *ptp of* **show.**
show-off* ['ʃəʊɒf] *n* fantasmón* *m,* comediante *m,* fantoche *m.*
showpiece ['ʃəʊpiːs] *n* objeto *m* de valor (*or* interés *etc*) excepcional; **the ~ of the exhibition is ...** la joya de la exposición es ...; **this vase is a real ~** este florero es realmente excepcional.
showplace ['ʃəʊpleɪs] *n* lugar *m* de gran atractivo, centro *m* turístico, monumento *m;* **Granada is a ~** Granada es una ciudad de gran atractivo, Granada es un monumento artístico e histórico; **the new school is not typical but is a ~** el nuevo colegio no es un colegio corriente, es más bien una cosa excepcional para mostrar a los visitantes.
showroom ['ʃəʊrʊm] *n* salón *m* de demostraciones; (*in shop*) sala *f* de muestras; (*Art*) sala *f* de exposición.
show-stopper* ['ʃəʊ,stɒpəʳ] *n*: **he** (*or* **it**) **was a ~** fue un éxito clamoroso.
show window ['ʃəʊ,wɪndəʊ] *n* escaparate *m.*
showy ['ʃəʊɪ] *adj* vistoso, llamativo; aparatoso, espectacular; *person* ostentoso.
shrank [ʃræŋk] *pret of* **shrink.**
shrapnel ['ʃræpnl] *n* metralla *f.*
shred [ʃred] **1** *n* (*bit*) fragmento *m,* pedazo *m;* (*of cloth*) triza *f,* jirón *m;* (*narrow strip*) tira *f;* **there isn't a ~ of truth in it** eso no tiene ni pizca de verdad; **if you had a ~ of decency** si Vd tuviese una gota de honradez; **without a ~ of clothing on** sin ni asomo de vestido; **to be in ~s** estar roto, estar destrozado; **her dress hung in ~s** su vestido estaba hecho jirones; **to tear sth to ~s** hacer algo trizas; **to tear an argument to ~s** hacer un argumento pedazos; **the crowd will tear him to ~s** la gente le hará pedazos.
2 *vt* hacer trizas, hacer tiras; *food etc* desmenuzar; *meat* deshilar; *paper* desfibrar, triturar.
shredder ['ʃredəʳ] *n,* **shredding-machine** ['ʃredɪŋmə,ʃiːn] *n* (*document ~*) desfibradora *f,* trituradora *f;* (*vegetable ~*) picadora *f.*
shrew [ʃruː] *n* **(a)** (*Zool*) musaraña *f.* **(b)** (*fig*) arpía *f,* fiera *f;* **'The Taming of the S~'** 'La fierecilla domada'.
shrewd [ʃruːd] *adj person* sagaz, perspicaz; listo; *plan etc* prudente, astuto; **~ reasoning** razonamiento *m* inteligente; **that is a ~ thing to do** eso es lo más prudente; **that was very ~ of you** en eso has sido muy perspicaz; **I have a ~ idea that ...** se me ocurre pensar que ..., me parece razonable suponer que ...
shrewdly ['ʃruːdlɪ] *adv* sagazmente, con perspicacia; prudentemente, astutamente.
shrewdness ['ʃruːdnɪs] *n* sagacidad *f,* perspicacia *f;* inteligencia *f;* prudencia *f,* astucia *f.*
shrewish ['ʃruːɪʃ] *adj* regañona, de mal genio.
shriek [ʃriːk] **1** *n* chillido *m,* grito *m* agudo; **a ~ of pain** un grito de dolor; **with ~s of laughter** con grandes carcajadas.
2 *vt* gritar; **to ~ abuse at sb** lanzar improperios contra uno.
3 *vi* chillar, gritar; **to ~ with pain** chillar de dolor; **to ~ with laughter** reírse a grandes carcajadas; **the colour simply ~s at one** es un color de lo más chillón.
shrieking ['ʃriːkɪŋ] **1** *adj child, colour* chillón. **2** *n* chillidos *mpl,* gritos *mpl.*
shrift [ʃrɪft] *n*: **to give sb short ~** echar a uno con cajas destempladas; **he gave that idea short ~** mostró su completa disconformidad con tal idea, desechó muy pronto tal posibilidad; **he got short ~ from the boss** el jefe se mostró poco compasivo con él; **he'll get short ~ from me!** ¡que no venga a mí a pedir compasión!
shrike [ʃraɪk] *n* alcaudón *m.*
shrill [ʃrɪl] **1** *adj* chillón, agudo, estridente. **2** *vt* gritar (con voz estridente). **3** *vi* chillar.
shrillness ['ʃrɪlnɪs] *n* lo chillón, estridencia *f.*
shrilly ['ʃrɪlɪ] *adv* agudamente, de modo estridente.
shrimp [ʃrɪmp] **1** *n* **(a)** (*Zool*) camarón *m.* **(b)** (*fig*) enano *m,* renacuajo *m.* **2** *attr*: **~ cocktail** cóctel *m* de camarones; **~ sauce** salsa *f* de camarones. **3** *vi* (*also* **to go ~ing**) pescar camarones.
shrine [ʃraɪn] *n* (*tomb*) sepulcro *m* (de santo), santuario *m;* relicario *m;* (*chapel*) capilla *f;* (*altar*) altar *m;* (*fig*) lugar *m* sagrado.
shrink [ʃrɪŋk] (*irr: pret* **shrank,** *ptp* **shrunk**) **1** *vt* encoger; contraer; *quality* reducir, disminuir; **to ~ a part on** (*Tech*) montar una pieza en caliente.
2 *vi* **(a)** (*get smaller*) encoger(se); contraerse; (*quantity*) reducirse, disminuir, mermar; **to ~ in the wash** encogerse al lavar; **'will not ~'** 'no (se) encoge', 'inencogible'; **to ~ away to nothing** reducirse a nada, desaparecer.
(b) (*recoil: also* **to ~ away, to ~ back**) retroceder (*from* ante); acobardarse, retirarse (*from, at* ante); **I ~ from doing it** no me atrevo a hacerlo, me repugna hacerlo; **he did not ~ from touching it** no vaciló en tocarlo.
3 *n* (*esp US*‡) psiquiatra *mf.*
shrinkage ['ʃrɪŋkɪdʒ] *n* encogimiento *m;* contracción *f;* reducción *f,* disminución *f.*
shrinking ['ʃrɪŋkɪŋ] *adj clothes* que se encoge; *resources etc* que escasea; **~ violet** (*fig*) tímido *m,* -a *f,* vergonzoso *m,* -a *f.*
shrink-wrap ['ʃrɪŋkræp] *vt* empaquetar (*or* envasar) al vacío.
shrink-wrapped ['ʃrɪŋkræpt] *adj* empaquetado (*or* envasado) al vacío.
shrink-wrapping ['ʃrɪŋkræpɪŋ] *n* envasado *m* al vacío.
shrivel ['ʃrɪvl] **1** *vt* (*also* **to ~ up**) secar, marchitar; *skin* arrugar.
2 *vi* (*also* **to ~ up**) secarse, marchitarse; (*skin etc*) arrugarse, avellanarse, apergaminarse; (*fruit*) consumirse.
shrivelled, (*US*) **shriveled** ['ʃrɪvld] *adj plant etc* seco, marchito; *skin* arrugado, apergaminado.
shroud [ʃraʊd] **1** *n* **(a)** sudario *m,* mortaja *f;* (*fig*) velo *m;* **the S~ of Turin** el Santo Sudario de Turín; **a ~ of mystery** un velo de misterio.
(b) ~s (*Naut*) obenques *mpl.*
2 *vt* amortajar; (*fig*) velar, cubrir; **the castle was ~ed in mist** el castillo estaba envuelto en niebla; **the whole thing is ~ed in mystery** el asunto entero está envuelto en un velo de misterio.
Shrovetide ['ʃrəʊvtaɪd] *n* carnestolendas *fpl.*
Shrove Tuesday ['ʃrəʊv'tjuːzdɪ] *n* martes *m* de carnaval.
shrub [ʃrʌb] *n* arbusto *m.*
shrubbery ['ʃrʌbərɪ] *n* arbustos *mpl,* plantío *m* de arbustos.
shrug [ʃrʌg] **1** *n* encogimiento *m* de hombros; **he said with a ~** dijo encogiéndose de hombros.
2 *vt*: **to ~ one's shoulders = 3.**
3 *vi* encogerse de hombros.
◆**shrug off** *vt*: **to ~ sth off** negar importancia a algo, minimizar algo; **you can't just ~ that off** no puedes negar la importancia de eso.
shrunk [ʃrʌŋk] *ptp of* **shrink.**
shrunken ['ʃrʌŋkən] *adj* encogido; (*shrivelled*) seco; marchito; apergaminado; *head* reducido; *quantity* reducido, mermado.
shtoom‡ [ʃtʊm] *adj*: **to keep ~** achantar*, estar achantado*.
shuck [ʃʌk] **1** *n* **(a)** (*husk*) vaina *f,* hollejo *m.* **(b)** (*US: of shellfish*) concha *f* (de marisco); **~s!** (*US*) ¡cáscaras! **2** *vt* **(a)** *peas etc* desenvainar. **(b)** (*US*) *shellfish* desbullar.
shudder ['ʃʌdəʳ] **1** *n* estremecimiento *m,* escalofrío *m;* (*of vehicle etc*) vibración *f,* sacudida *f;* **a ~ ran through her** se estremeció; **she realized with a ~ that ...** se estremeció al darse cuenta de que ...; **it gives me the ~s** me da escalofríos.
2 *vi* estremecerse (*with* de); vibrar, sacudirse; **I ~ to think of it** sólo pensar en eso me da escalofríos; **I ~ to**

think what he will do next me da escalofríos pensar en lo que hará luego.

shuffle [ˈʃʌfl] **1** *n* (**a**) **to walk with a ~** caminar arrastrando los pies.

(**b**) (*Cards*) barajadura *f*; **to give the cards a ~** barajar las cartas; **whose ~ is it?** ¿a quién le toca barajar?

2 *vt* (**a**) *feet* arrastrar.

(**b**) (*mix up*) mezclar, revolver; *cards* barajar, mezclar.

(**c**) **to ~ sb aside** apartar a uno, relegar a uno a un puesto menos importante.

3 *vi* (**a**) (*walk*) arrastrar los pies; caminar (*or* bailar *etc*) arrastrando los pies; **he ~d across to the door** fue hacia la puerta arrastrando los pies; **he managed to ~ out of the job** logró zafarse del compromiso.

(**b**) (*Cards*) barajar.

◆**shuffle off 1** *vi* marcharse arrastrando los pies.

2 *vt garment* despojarse de; (*fig*) *responsibility* rechazar; **to ~ sth off** deshacerse de algo.

shuffleboard [ˈʃʌflbɔːd] *n* juego *m* de tejo.

shufti‡ [ˈʃʊftɪ] *n* ojeada *f*; **let's have a ~** a ver, déjame ver; **we went to take a ~** fuimos a echar un vistazo.

shun [ʃʌn] *vt* evitar, esquivar, rehuir; volver la espalda a; **to ~ doing sth** evitar hacer algo; **to feel ~ned by the world** sentirse rechazado por la gente.

shunt [ʃʌnt] **1** *vt* (*Rail*) maniobrar; **to ~ sb aside** apartar a uno, relegar a uno a un puesto menos importante; **to ~ sb off** apartar a uno de su propósito; **he was ~ed into retirement** lograron con maña que se jubilase; **to ~ sb to and fro** mandar a uno de acá para allá.

2 *vi*: **to ~ to and fro** trajinar de acá para allá.

shunter [ˈʃʌntəʳ] *n* (*Brit*) guardagujas *m*.

shunting [ˈʃʌntɪŋ] **1** *n* maniobras *fpl*. **2** *attr*: **~ engine** locomotora *f* de maniobra; **~ yard** estación *f* de maniobras, playa *f* de clasificación.

shush [ʃʊʃ] **1** *interj* ¡chitón! **2** *vt* hacer callar, imponer silencio a.

shut [ʃʌt] (*irr*: *pret and ptp* **shut**) **1** *vt* cerrar; **to find the door ~** encontrar que la puerta está cerrada; **he had the door ~ in his face** le dieron con la puerta en las narices; **to ~ one's fingers in the door** pillarse los dedos en la puerta.

2 *vi* cerrarse; **we ~ at 5** cerramos a las 5; **the lid doesn't ~** la tapa no cierra (bien).

◆**shut away 1** *vt* encerrar; recluir.

2 *vr*: **to ~ o.s. away** encerrarse; recluirse; **he ~s himself away all day in his room** permanece encerrado todo el día en su habitación.

◆**shut down 1** *vt* (**a**) *lid etc* cerrar.

(**b**) *business, factory* cerrar.

(**c**) *machine* parar.

2 *vi* (*business etc*) cerrar, cerrarse.

◆**shut in** *vt person etc* encerrar; (*surround*) cercar, rodear; **to feel ~ in** sentirse encerrado; **the runner was ~ in** el atleta se encontró tapado.

◆**shut off** *vt* (**a**) (*stop, cut*) *water etc* cortar; interrumpir; *engine* parar; *pipe etc* obturar, cegar.

(**b**) (*isolate*) aislar, separar (*from* de); **to be ~ off from** estar aislado de.

◆**shut out** *vt* (**a**) (*by door etc*) excluir; negar la entrada a; *workers* dejar sin trabajo por lock-out.

(**b**) (*block*) tapar, ocultar; impedir ver.

◆**shut to 1** *vt* cerrar.

2 *vi* cerrarse.

◆**shut up 1** *vt* (**a**) (*close*) cerrar.

(**b**) (*block*) cegar, obturar.

(**c**) *person etc* encerrar; recluir.

(**d**) *factory etc* cerrar.

(**e**) (*: *silence*) hacer callar, reducir al silencio.

2 *vi* (*: *be quiet*) callarse; **~ up!** ¡calla!, ¡cállate!; **to ~ up like a clam** callarse como un muerto.

shutdown [ˈʃʌtdaʊn] *n* cierre *m*.

shut-eye* [ˈʃʌtaɪ] *n* sueño *m*; **to get some ~** echar un sueñecito*.

shut-in [ˈʃʌtɪn] *adj* encerrado.

shutoff [ˈʃʌtɒf] *n* interruptor *m*.

shut-out [ˈʃʌtaʊt] *n* cierre *m* (para impedir la entrada); (*US Sport*) victoria *f* fácil, victoria *f* abrumadora; (*Brit Sport*) **the goalkeeper had 10 successive ~s** el portero salió imbatido en 10 partidos sucesivos; **~ record** récord *m* de imbatibilidad; **~ bid** declaración *f* aplastante.

shutter [ˈʃʌtəʳ] **1** *n* (*of window*) contraventana *f*; (*Phot*) obturador *m*; **to put up the ~s** (*shop*) cerrar del todo, (*fig*) abandonar, (*Sport etc*) resolverse a no correr riesgo alguno.

2 *attr*: **~ speed** velocidad *f* de obturación.

shuttered [ˈʃʌtəd] *adj* (*having shutters*) con contraventanas; (*with shutters closed*) con las contraventanas cerradas.

shuttle [ˈʃʌtl] **1** *n* (**a**) (*of loom, sewing machine*) lanzadera *f*.

(**b**) (*Aer*) puente *m* aéreo.

(**c**) (*Space*) transbordador *m* espacial.

2 *attr*: **~ diplomacy** viajes *mpl* diplomáticos; **~ service** (*Aer*) puente *m* aéreo; (*Rail etc*) servicio *m* de lanzadera.

3 *vt*: **to ~ sb about** mandar a uno de acá para alla; **we were ~d about all day** pasamos todo el día trajinando de acá para allá; **the form was ~d about between different departments** la solicitud fue enviada de departamento a departamento (sin que nadie la atendiese).

4 *vi* (*Aer, Rail etc*) hacer el servicio rápido y continuo (*between 2 points* entre 2 puntos).

shuttlecock [ˈʃʌtlkɒk] *n* volante *m*, rehilete *m*.

shy[1] [ʃaɪ] **1** *adj* (**a**) tímido; (*bashful*) vergonzoso; (*reserved*) reservado; (*unsociable*) huraño; *animal* huraño, asustadizo; **I can't do it, I'm ~** no puedo hacerlo, me da vergüenza; **to be ~ of, to fight ~ of** procurar evitar; **to be ~ of** + *ger* procurar evitar + *infin*, no atreverse a + *infin*; **don't be ~** no tengas miedo; **he makes me ~** él me hace sentirme miedoso.

(**b**) **I'm 10 dollars ~** (*US*) me faltan 10 dólares, he perdido 10 dólares.

2 *vi* (*of horse*) espantarse, respingar (*at sth* al ver algo); **to ~ at a fence** negarse a saltar una valla.

◆**shy away** *vi*: **to ~ away from sth** alejarse asustado de algo; **they shied away from the idea** se asustaron de la idea; **to ~ away from** + *ger* asustarse y negarse a + *infin*.

shy[2] [ʃaɪ] (*Brit*) **1** *n* (*throw*) tirada *f*; (*fig*) tentativa *f*; **to have a ~ at sth** probar algo, intentar algo; **to have a ~ at** + *ger* hacer una tentativa de + *infin*; **'50 pesetas a ~'** '50 pesetas la tirada'. **2** *vt* lanzar, echar.

shyly [ˈʃaɪlɪ] *adv* tímidamente; con vergüenza, vergonzosamente.

shyness [ˈʃaɪnɪs] *n* timidez *f*; vergüenza *f*; reserva *f*; lo huraño, lo asustadizo.

shyster* [ˈʃaɪstəʳ] *n* (*US*) abogado *m* trampista; persona *f* poco honrada.

SI *n abbr of* **Système Internationale** *system of metric units*.

Siam [saɪˈæm] *n* Siam *m*.

Siamese [ˌsaɪəˈmiːz] **1** *adj* siamés; **~ cat** gato *m* siamés, gata *f* siamesa; **~ twins** gemelos *mpl* siameses, gemelas *fpl* siamesas. **2** *n* (**a**) siamés *m*, -esa *f*. (**b**) (*Ling*) siamés *m*.

Siberia [saɪˈbɪərɪə] *n* Siberia *f*.

Siberian [saɪˈbɪərɪən] **1** *adj* siberiano. **2** *n* siberiano *m*, -a *f*.

sibilant [ˈsɪbɪlənt] **1** *adj* sibilante. **2** *n* sibilante *f*.

sibling [ˈsɪblɪŋ] **1** *n* hermano *m* (*or* hermana *f*); **it turned out they were ~s** resultó que eran hermanos. **2** *attr*: **~ rivalry** rivalidad *f* de hermanos.

Sibyl [ˈsɪbɪl] *nf* Sibila.

sibyl [ˈsɪbɪl] *n* sibila *f*.

sibylline [ˈsɪbɪlaɪn] *adj* sibilino.

sic [sɪk] *adv*: **he said '...'** dijo '...' (palabras textuales *or* la cita es textual).

Sicilian [sɪˈsɪlɪən] **1** *adj* siciliano. **2** *n* (**a**) siciliano *m*, -a *f*. (**b**) (*Ling*) siciliano *m*.

Sicily [ˈsɪsɪlɪ] *n* Sicilia *f*.

sick [sɪk] **1** *adj* (**a**) (*ill*) enfermo; **~ building syndrome** *síndrome causado por el aire acondicionado*; **to be (off) ~** estar enfermo; **to fall ~, to go ~, to take ~** caer enfermo, enfermar; (*be absent*) ausentarse debido a enfermedad; **the cow took ~ and died** la vaca cayó enferma y murió; **to report ~** darse de baja por enfermo.

(**b**) (*Brit*: *dizzy, about to vomit*) mareado; **to be ~** vomitar; arrojar*; **to feel ~** estar mareado; **I get ~ in aeroplanes** me mareo en los aviones; **too much beer makes me ~** un exceso de cerveza me da ganas de vomitar.

(**c**) (*fig*) **to be ~ at heart** estar muy deprimido, sentirlo en el alma; **they were all as ~ as parrots*** todos arrojaron hasta los huesos*; **to be ~ (and tired) of, to be ~ to death of** estar harto de; **I get ~ of that** eso se me hace pesado, cojo asco a eso; **he just did look ~** estaba la mar de abatido; estaba furioso consigo mismo; **it's enough to make you ~** es para volverse loco; **you make me ~!** ¡me das asco!; **it makes me ~ to think that ...** me da asco pensar que ...; **she worried herself ~ about it** se inquietó terriblemente por esto.

(**d**) *humour* negro, malsano; **~ joke** chiste *m* negro.

2 *npl* (**a**) **the ~** los enfermos. (**b**) (*) vómito *m*.

◆**sick up*** *vt* arrojar*, devolver*.

sickbay [ˈsɪkbeɪ] *n* enfermería *f*.

sickbed ['sɪkbed] *n* lecho *m* de enfermo.

sicken ['sɪkn] **1** *vt* dar asco a (*also fig*); **it ~s me** me da asco, me repugna.

2 *vi* caer enfermo, enfermar; **to ~ at sth** sentir náuseas ante algo; **I ~ at the sight of blood** el ver sangre me da náuseas; **to ~ for, to be ~ing for** (*Med*) mostrar síntomas de; **to ~ for want of** enfermar por.

sickening ['sɪknɪŋ] *adj* nauseabundo; (*fig*) asqueroso, repugnante; **it's ~ that** ... me ofende en el alma que + *subj*.

sickeningly ['sɪknɪŋlɪ] *adv* (*fig*) asquerosamente; **~ sentimental** tan sensiblero que da asco.

sickle ['sɪkl] *n* hoz *f*.

sick-leave ['sɪkli:v] *n* permiso *m* por enfermedad; **to be on ~** estar ausente con permiso por enfermedad.

sickle-cell ['sɪkl,sel] *attr*: **~ anaemia, ~ anemia** (*US*) anemia *f* de células falciformes, drepanocitosis *f*.

sickliness ['sɪklɪnɪs] *n* lo enfermizo, lo achacoso; palidez *f*; lo nauseabundo; debilidad *f*; lo empalagoso.

sick-list ['sɪklɪst] *n* lista *f* de enfermos; **to be on the ~** estar enfermo.

sickly ['sɪklɪ] *adj person* enfermizo, achacoso; *plant* débil, de mal aspecto; *appearance* pálido; (*Brit*) *smell* nauseabundo; *smile* débil, forzado; *cake, sweet* empalagoso; **~ sweet** dulzón, empalagoso.

sick-making* ['sɪkmeɪkɪŋ] *adj* asqueroso.

sickness ['sɪknɪs] *n* (*Med*) enfermedad *f*, mal *m*; (*fig*) mal *m*, malestar *m*; **~ benefit** subsidio *m* por invalidez; **there is ~ on board** hay epidemia a bordo, hay enfermedad contagiosa a bordo.

sick-pay ['sɪkpeɪ] *n* subsidio *m* de enfermedad; **to be on ~** recibir el subsidio de enfermedad.

sickroom ['sɪkrʊm] *n* cuarto *m* del enfermo.

side [saɪd] **1** *n* (**a**) (*Anat etc*) costado *m*, lado *m*; (*of animal*) flanco *m*, ijada *f*; **~ of bacon** hoja *f* de tocino; **the assistant was at** (*or* **by**) **his ~** el ayudante estaba a su lado; **by the ~ of** al lado de; **he had the telephone by his ~** tenía el teléfono a su lado; **to sit by sb's ~** estar sentado al lado de uno; **to sit ~ by ~ with sb** estar sentado al lado de uno; **to sleep on one's ~** dormir de costado; **to split one's ~s** desternillarse de risa.

(**b**) (*flank etc, fig*) lado *m*, flanco *m*; (*of triangle*) lado *m*; (*of ship*) costado *m*; (*of hill*) falda *f*, ladera *f*; (*of lake*) orilla *f*; (*of small pond etc*) borde *m*; (*of wood*) límite *m*, borde *m*.

(**c**) (*face, surface*) lado *m*, superficie *f*; (*of record, slice of bread, solid etc*) cara *f*; **wrong ~** revés *m*, envés *m*; **to be wrong ~ out** estar al revés; **what's on the other ~?** (*of record*) ¿qué hay a la vuelta?; **these are two ~s of the same coin** son dos caras de la misma moneda; **let us look at the other ~ of the coin** véamos el revés de la medalla; **please write on both ~s of the paper** escribir en ambas caras del papel.

(**d**) (*part, region*) lado *m*; **left-hand ~** izquierda *f*; **right-hand ~** derecha *f*; **to be on the left-hand ~** estar a la izquierda; **on one ~..., on the other** ... por una parte ..., por otra ...; **on this ~** por este lado; **on all ~s** por todas partes, por todos lados; **on both ~s** por ambos lados; **on my mother's ~** por parte de mi madre; **on the ~** (*as adv*) incidentalmente; de paso; (*unofficially*) de modo extraoficial; **to make a bit on the ~** ganarse algo bajo cuerda; **to get out of bed on the wrong ~** levantarse con el pie izquierdo; **to be on the right ~ of 40** no haber cumplido todavía los 40 años; **to put sth on one ~** poner algo aparte, guardarse algo; ahorrar; **I'll put it on one ~ for you** te lo guardaré; **from ~ to ~** de un lado al otro; **leaving that to one ~ for the moment, ...** dejando eso a un lado por ahora, ...; **to move to one ~** apartarse, hacerse a un lado; **it's this ~ of Segovia** está más acá de Segovia; **it's the other ~ of Illescas** está más allá de Illescas; **it won't happen this ~ of Christmas** no será antes de Navidades; **he's the wrong ~ of 40** tiene más de 40 años, ha pasado ya de los 40.

(**e**) (*aspect*) aspecto *m*, lado *m*; **the other ~ (of the picture), the seamy ~** el reverso de la medalla; **to be on the safe ~ ...** para mayor seguridad ..., por precaución ...; **let's be on the safe ~** atengámonos a lo más seguro; **to hear both ~s of the question** escuchar los argumentos en pro y en contra; **to see only one ~ of the question** sólo ver un aspecto de la cuestión; **to get on the good ~ of sb** procurar congraciarse con uno; **to get on the wrong ~ of sb** ponerse a malas con uno; **to look on the bright ~** ser optimista, ver el lado risueño de las cosas.

(**f**) (*fig*) **it's on the large ~** es algo grande; **the results are on the poor ~** los resultados son más bien mediocres; **the weather's on the cold ~** el tiempo es algo frío.

(**g**) (*Brit**: *conceit, superiority*) tono *m*, postín* *m*; **there's no ~ about** (*or* **to**) **him** no presume, no se da aires de superioridad; **to put on ~** darse tono.

(**h**) (*party*) partido *m*; (*team*) equipo *m*; (*Bridge etc*) bando *m*, campo *m*; **our ~** nuestro campo (*etc*), los nuestros; **the science ~ of the school** los estudios científicos en el instituto; **he went on the science ~** optó por estudiar ciencias; **to change ~s** pasar al otro bando, cambiar de partido; cambiar de opinión; **to let the ~ down** hacer algo indigno de su colegio (*etc*), hacer algo que desmerece de su partido (*etc*); **to pick a ~** seleccionar un equipo; **to take ~s** tomar partido; **he's on our ~** es de los nuestros, es partidario nuestro; **whose ~ are you on?** ¿a quiénes apoyas?; **you have tradition on your ~** la tradición está de parte de Vd, la tradición le apoya a Vd; **with a few concessions on the government ~** con algunas concesiones por parte del gobierno.

2 *attr* lateral, de lado; *entrance* accesorio; *elevation* lateral; **~ door** puerta *f* accesoria; **~ effect** efecto *m* secundario; **~ entrance** entrada *f* lateral; **~ issue** cuestión *f* secundaria; **~ plate** plato *m* pequeño.

◆**side against** *vt*: **to ~ against sb** tomar el partido contrario a uno, alinearse con los que se oponen a uno.

◆**side with** *vt*: **to ~ with sb** declararse por uno, tomar el partido de uno; **I'm siding with nobody** yo no tomo partido.

side-arms ['saɪdɑ:mz] *npl* armas *fpl* de cinto.

sideboard ['saɪdbɔ:d] *n* aparador *m*.

sideboards ['saɪdbɔ:dz] *npl* (*Brit*), **sideburns** ['saɪdbɜ:nz] *npl* patillas *fpl*.

sidecar ['saɪdkɑ:ʳ] *n* sidecar *m*.

-sided ['saɪdɪd] *adj ending in compounds* de ... lados, *eg* **six~** de seis lados.

side dish ['saɪddɪʃ] *n* plato *m* adicional (servido con el principal).

side drum ['saɪddrʌm] *n* tamboril *m*.

side face ['saɪdfeɪs] **1** *n* perfil *m*. **2** *attr* de perfil. **3** *adv* de perfil.

side glance ['saɪdglɑ:ns] *n* mirada *f* de soslayo.

sidekick* ['saɪdkɪk] *n* compañero *m* (de trabajo *etc*), compinche *m*.

sidelight ['saɪdlaɪt] *n* (**a**) (*Brit Aut etc*) luz *f* lateral, luz *f* de posición. (**b**) (*fig*) detalle *m* incidental, información *f* incidental (*on* relativo a).

sideline ['saɪdlaɪn] **1** *n* (**a**) (*Rail*) apartadero *m*, vía *f* secundaria. (**b**) (*Sport, Ftbl etc*) línea *f* lateral, (*Tennis etc*) línea *f* de banda; **to stand** (*or* **stay**) **on the ~s** (*fig*) no tomar parte, mantenerse aparte; mantener su neutralidad. (**c**) (*fig*) empleo *m* suplementario, negocio *m* suplementario; **it's just a ~** es solamente una cosa secundaria; **he breeds parrots as a ~** como negocio suplementario se dedica a criar loros.

2 *vt* (*esp US*) apartar, marginar, dejar a un lado; **we won't be ~d** no permitimos que se nos margine; **he was ~d by injury the whole season** quedó fuera del equipo durante toda la temporada debido a una lesión.

sidelong ['saɪdlɒŋ] **1** *adv* de lado, lateralmente; oblicuamente; *glance* de soslayo. **2** *adj* lateral; oblicuo; *glance* de soslayo.

sidereal [saɪ'dɪ:rɪəl] *adj* sidéreo.

side road ['saɪdrəʊd] *n* (*Brit*) calle *f* lateral; calle *f* secundaria.

sidesaddle ['saɪd,sædl] **1** *n* silla *f* de mujer. **2** *adv*: **to ride ~** montar a mujeriegas, montar a asentadillas.

sideshow ['saɪdʃəʊ] *n* (*at fair*) barraca *f*, caseta *f* (de feria); (*fig*) función *f* secundaria.

sideslip ['saɪdslɪp] *n* (*Aer*) deslizamiento *m* lateral.

side-slipping ['saɪd,slɪpɪŋ] *n* (*Ski*) derrapaje *m*.

sidesman ['saɪdzmən] *n*, *pl* **sidesmen** ['saɪdzmən] acólito *m*.

side-splitting ['saɪd,splɪtɪŋ] *adj joke* divertidísimo.

side-step ['saɪdstep] **1** *n* paso *m* hacia un lado; (*dodge*) esquivada *f*. **2** *vt* (*fig*) evitar, esquivar; **he neatly ~ped the question** esquivó hábilmente la pregunta. **3** *vi* dar un paso hacia un lado, moverse a un lado.

side street ['saɪdstri:t] *n* calle *f* lateral; calle *f* secundaria.

sidestroke ['saɪdstrəʊk] *n* natación *f* de costado.

side-swipe ['saɪdswaɪp] *n* golpe *m* de refilón (*also fig*).

sidetable ['saɪd,teɪbl] *n* trinchero *m*.

sidetrack ['saɪdtræk] **1** *n* (*Rail*) apartadero *m*, vía *f* muerta; (*fig*) cuestión *f* secundaria.

2 *vt person* apartar de su propósito, desviar del asunto principal; *discussion* conducir por cuestiones de poca importancia; **I got ~ed** me aparté del asunto principal, me despisté.

side view ['saɪdvjuː] *n* perfil *m*.

sidewalk ['saɪdwɔːk] *n* (*US*) acera *f*, vereda *f* (*LAm*), andén *m* (*CAm*), banqueta *f* (*CAm, Mex*).

sidewards ['saɪdwədz] *adv* de lado; hacia un lado; oblicuamente; **it goes in** ~ entra de lado.

sideways ['saɪd,weɪz] **1** *adv* (**a**) = **sidewards**. (**b**) (*fig*) **to move** ~ (*in career etc*) trasladarse a otro puesto equivalente al actual, ir a tomar un puesto de la misma categoría.

side whiskers ['saɪd,wɪskəz] *npl* patillas *fpl*.

sidewind ['saɪdwɪnd] *n* viento *m* lateral.

siding ['saɪdɪŋ] *n* apartadero *m*, vía *f* muerta.

sidle ['saɪdl] *vi*: **to** ~ **up** acercarse cautelosamente (*or* sigilosamente, servilmente; *to* a).

Sidon ['saɪdən] *n* Sidón *m*.

SIDS *n abbr of* **sudden infant death syndrome** muerte *f* en la cuna.

siege [siːdʒ] **1** *n* cerco *m*, sitio *m*; **to lay** ~ **to** poner sitio a, sitiar, cercar; *person* asediar; **to raise the** ~ levantar el cerco. **2** *attr*: ~ **economy** economía *f* de sitio (*or* de asedio).

sienna [sɪ'enə] *n* siena *f*.

Sierra Leone [sɪ'erəlɪ'əʊn] *n* Sierra *f* Leona.

Sierra Leonean [sɪ,erəlɪ'əʊnɪən] **1** *adj* sierraleonés. **2** *n* sierraleonés *m*, -esa *f*.

siesta [sɪ'estə] *n* siesta *f*; **to have a** ~ dormir la siesta.

sieve [sɪv] **1** *n* tamiz *m*, cedazo *m*, criba *f*; (*Culin*) coladera *f*. **2** *vt* = **sift**.

sift [sɪft] *vt* tamizar, cerner, cribar; (*fig*) escudriñar, examinar.

sigh [saɪ] **1** *n* suspiro *m*; (*of wind*) susurro *m*; **to breathe a** ~ **of relief** suspirar, suspirar aliviado; **to heave a** ~ dar un suspiro. **2** *vi* suspirar; (*wind*) susurrar; **to** ~ **for** suspirar por.

sighing ['saɪɪŋ] *n* suspiros *mpl*; (*of wind*) susurro *m*.

sight [saɪt] **1** *n* (**a**) (*faculty, act of seeing*) vista *f*; visión *f*; **30 days' (after)** ~ (a) 30 días vista; **at** ~, **at first** ~ a primera vista, a la vista; **to hate sb at first** ~ **on (or at)** detestar a uno desde el principio, odiar a uno desde el primer momento; **payable at** ~ pagadero a la vista; **to shoot at** ~ disparar nada más ver; **to translate at** ~ traducir oralmente, traducir a libro abierto; **it was love at first** ~ fue un flechazo; **to know sb by** ~ conocer a uno de vista; **land in** ~! ¡tierra a la vista!; **to be in** (*or* **within**) ~ estar a la vista (*of* de); **our goal is in** ~ ya vemos la meta; **we are in** ~ **of victory** estamos a las puertas de la victoria; **to keep sb in** ~ no perder a uno de vista; **to find favour in sb's** ~ (*plan etc*) ser aceptable a uno, (*person*) merecerse la aprobación de uno; **to come into** ~ aparecer, asomarse; **to heave in(to)** ~ aparecer; **on** ~ = **at** ~; **to be out of** ~ estar invisible, no estar a la vista, no poderse ver; **to drop out of** ~ desaparecer; **not to let sb out of one's** ~ no perder a uno de vista, vigilar constantemente a uno; **out of** ~* (*US*) fabuloso*, fantástico*; **out of** ~, **out of mind** ojos que no ven, corazón que no siente; **to be lost to** ~ desaparecer, perderse de vista; **I can't bear the** ~ **of blood** no aguanto la vista de la sangre; **I can't bear the** ~ **of him** no le puedo ver; **to buy sth** ~ **unseen** comprar algo sin verlo; **to catch** ~ **of** (*glimpse*) vislumbrar; (*happen to see*) ver por casualidad; (*on appearance of object*) alcanzar a ver; **to get a** ~ **of sth** lograr ver algo; **I hate the** ~ **of him** no le puedo ver; **to lose** ~ **of sb** perder a uno de vista; **to lose** ~ **of the fact that ...** no tener presente el hecho de que ...; **to lose one's** ~ perder la vista, quedar ciego; **to regain one's** ~ recobrar la vista.

(**b**) (*on gun*) mira *f*, alza *f*, guión *m* de mira; visor *m*; **to set one's** ~**s too high** (*fig*) apuntar muy alto, ser demasiado ambicioso; **to set one's** ~**s on sth** resolverse a adquirir (*or* obtener *etc*) algo.

(**c**) (*scene, spectacle*) vista *f*, escena *f*, espectáculo *m*; **it is a** ~ **to see** es cosa digna de verse; **it's a sad** ~ es una cosa triste; **it's not a pretty** ~ no es muy agradable para la vista; **it was a** ~ **for sore eyes** daba gusto verlo; **his face was a** ~! ¡había que ver su cara!, (*after injury etc*) ¡había que ver el estado en que quedaba su cara!

(**d**) (*spectacle: of person*) **I must look a** ~ debo parecer horroroso, ¿no?; **doesn't she look a** ~ **in that hat!** ¡con ese sombrero parece un espantajo!; **what a** ~ **you are!** ¡qué adefesio!

(**e**) (*for tourists etc*) ~**s** monumentos *npl*, cosas *fpl* de interés (turístico), curiosidades *fpl*; **the** ~**s of Córdoba** los monumentos de Córdoba; **to see the** ~**s** visitar los monumentos, visitar los puntos de interés.

2 *attr*: ~ **draft** letra *f* a la vista; ~ **translation** traducción *f* oral, traducción *f* a libro abierto.

3 *adv* (*) **it's a (long)** ~ **better than the other one** es muchísimo mejor que el otro; **he's a** ~ **too clever** es demasiado listo; **it's a** ~ **dearer** es mucho más caro.

4 *vt* (**a**) (*see*) ver, divisar, avistar; **to** ~ **land** ver tierra; **we** ~**ed him coming down the street** le vimos bajar la calle.

(**b**) (*aim*) **to** ~ **a gun** apuntar un cañón (*at, on* a).

sighted ['saɪtɪd] *adj* vidente, que ve, de vista normal; **a blind man and a** ~ **companion** un ciego y su compañero de vista normal.

-sighted ['saɪtɪd] *adj ending in compounds*: **weak**~ corto de vista, miope.

sighting ['saɪtɪŋ] *n* observación *f*.

sightless ['saɪtlɪs] *adj* ciego, invidente.

sightly ['saɪtlɪ] *adj*: **not very** ~ no muy agradable para la vista.

sight-read ['saɪtriːd] (*irr*: *V* **read**) *vti* leer sin preparación; (*Mus*) ejecutar a la primera lectura, repentizar.

sight-reading ['saɪt,riːdɪŋ] *n* lectura *f* sin preparación; (*Mus*) ejecución *f* a la primera vista.

sightseeing ['saɪt,siːɪŋ] *n* excursionismo *m*, turismo *m*, visita *f* de puntos de interés; **'S~ in Ruritania'** 'Monumentos *mpl* de Ruritania'; **to go** ~ visitar los monumentos.

sightseer ['saɪt,sɪə^r^] *n* excursionista *mf*, turista *mf*; visitante *mf*.

sight-singing ['saɪt,sɪŋɪŋ] *n* ejecución *f* a la primera lectura.

sign [saɪn] **1** *n* (**a**) (*with hand etc*) señal *f*, seña *f*; ~ **of recognition** señal *f* de reconocimiento *m*; **to communicate by** ~**s** hablar por señas; **to make a** ~ **to sb** hacer una señal a uno; **to make a rude** ~ hacer una señal grosera; **to make the** ~ **of the Cross** hacer la señal de la cruz; **to make the** ~ **of the Cross over sth** santiguar algo.

(**b**) (*indication*) señal *f*, indicio *m*; asomo *m*; (*Med*) síntoma *m*; **the** ~**s of measles are ...** los síntomas del sarampión son ...; **at the slightest** ~ **of disagreement** ante cualquier asomo de discrepancia; **it's a** ~ **of rain** es indicio de lluvia; **it's a sure** ~ es un indicio inconfundible; **it's a** ~ **of the true expert** esto indica el verdadero experto; **it's a** ~ **of the times** así son los tiempos actuales; **there's no** ~ **of their agreeing** no hay indicio de que se vayan a poner de acuerdo; **it's a good** ~ es buena señal; **to show** ~**s of** dar muestras de, dar indicios de; **as a** ~ **of, in** ~ **of** en señal de.

(**c**) (*trace*) huella *f*, vestigio *m*, rastro *m*; **there was no** ~ **of it** no quedaba rastro de él; **there was no** ~ **of him anywhere** no se le veía en ninguna parte; **there was no** ~ **of the former inhabitants** no quedaba huella de los antiguos habitantes; **there was no** ~ **of life in the village** no había vestigio de ser viviente en el pueblo.

(**d**) (*road* ~) señal *f* de carretera; indicador *m*; (*inn* ~) letrero *m*; (*shop* ~) rótulo *m*; (*US: carried in demonstration*) pancarta *f*; **there was a big** ~ **which said 'Danger'** había un grande letrero que decía 'Peligro (de muerte)'.

(**e**) (*written symbol*) signo *m*; símbolo *m*; (*Astron, Math, Mus, Zodiac*) signo *m*.

2 *vt* firmar; ~**ed and sealed** firmado y lacrado, firmado y sellado.

3 *vi* (**a**) **to** ~ **to sb to do sth** hacer señas a uno para que haga algo, decir a uno por medio de señas que haga algo.

(**b**) (*with signature*) firmar, firmar su nombre.

4 *vr*: **he** ~**s himself Joe Soap** usa la firma Joe Soap, firma con el nombre Joe Soap.

◆**sign away** *vt* firmar la cesión de, (*fig*) ceder, abandonar.

◆**sign for** *vt key, parcel etc* firmar el recibo de; **he** ~**ed for Real Madrid** fichó por el Madrid.

◆**sign in 1** *vt*: **to** ~ **sb in** (*at club etc*) firmar el registro para avalar la admisión de uno. **2** *vi* (*in factory*) firmar la entrada; (*in hotel*) firmar en el registro, registrarse.

◆**sign off** *vi* terminar; (*Rad, TV*) terminar el programa, terminar la emisión; (*Bridge*) terminar la declaración; (*ending letter*) terminar.

◆**sign on 1** *vt*: **to** ~ **sb on** contratar a uno.

2 *vi* (*Comm*) contratarse; apuntarse, inscribirse; firmar un contrato; (*Sport etc*) fichar (*for* por); (*as unemployed*) registrarse (para cobrar el subsidio de paro); **to** ~ **on at a hotel** firmar el registro (de un hotel).

◆**sign out 1** *vt*: **the book is** ~**ed out to Professor Q** el libro está prestado al profesor Q; **you must** ~ **all books out** tienes que firmar al tomar prestado cualquier libro.

2 *vi*: **to** ~ **out of a hotel** firmar el registro al salir de un hotel.

◆**sign over** *vt*: **to** ~ **sth over to sb** firmar el traspaso de algo a uno.

◆**sign up** = **sign on.**

signal ['sɪgnl] **1** *n* (**a**) (*sign*) señal *f*, seña *f*; (*Rad, TV*) señal *f*; **it was the ~ for revolt** fue la señal para la sublevación; **to give the ~ for** dar la señal de (*or* para); **to make a ~ to sb** hacer una señal a uno.

(**b**) (*apparatus*) señal *f*; **the ~ is at red** la señal está en rojo.

(**c**) **S~s** (*Mil*) transmisiones *fpl*, cuerpo *m* de transmisiones.

2 *adj* notable, señalado, insigne.

3 *vt*: **to ~ one's approval** hacer una seña de aprobación; **to ~ sb to do sth** hacer señas a uno para que haga algo; **to ~ sb on** hacer señas a uno para que avance; **to ~ that ...** comunicar por señales que ...; **to ~ a turn to the right** indicar que uno va a torcer a la derecha; **to ~ a train** anunciar por señales la llegada de un tren; **the train is ~led** la señal indica la llegada del tren.

4 *vi* hacer una señal, hacer señales; **to ~ before stopping** hacer una señal antes de parar.

signal book ['sɪgnlbʊk] *n* (*Naut*) código *m* de señales.

signalbox ['sɪgnlbɒks] *n* garita *f* de señales; casilla *f* de maniobras.

signal flag ['sɪgnlflæg] *n* bandera *f* de señales.

signalize ['sɪgnəlaɪz] *vt* distinguir, señalar.

signal lamp ['sɪgnllæmp] *n* reflector *m* de señales, lámpara *f* de señales.

signally ['sɪgnəlɪ] *adv* notablemente, señaladamente; **he has ~ failed to do it** ha sufrido un notable fracaso al tratar de hacerlo.

signalman ['sɪgnlmən] *n, pl* **signalmen** ['sɪgnlmən] guardavía *m*.

signatory ['sɪgnətərɪ] **1** *adj* firmante, signatario; **the ~ powers to an agreement** las potencias firmantes de un acuerdo. **2** *n* firmante *mf*, signatario *m*, -a *f*.

signature ['sɪgnətʃəʳ] *n* firma *f*; (*Mus, Typ*) signatura *f*; **to put one's ~ to a document** firmar un documento, poner su firma en un documento.

signature-tune ['sɪgnətʃə,tju:n] *n* (*esp Brit*) sintonía *f*.

signboard ['saɪnbɔ:d] *n* letrero *m*, muestra *f*.

signer ['saɪnəʳ] *n* firmante *mf*.

signet ['sɪgnɪt] **1** *n* sello *m*. **2** *attr*: **~ ring** anillo *m* de sello.

significance [sɪg'nɪfɪkəns] *n* significación *f*, significado *m*; trascendencia *f*.

significant [sɪg'nɪfɪkənt] *adj* significativo; trascendente, importante; *improvement etc* sensible; *look* expresivo; **calculate it to 4 ~ figures** calcúlelo a 4 cifras significativas; **it is ~ that ...** es significativo que ...

significantly [sɪg'nɪfɪkəntlɪ] *adv* significativamente; expresivamente; **it has improved ~** ha mejorado sensiblemente; **it is not ~ different** no hay diferencia importante; **she looked at me ~** me lanzó una mirada expresiva.

signify ['sɪgnɪfaɪ] **1** *vt* (**a**) (*mean*) significar, querer decir; **it signifies that ...** significa que ...; **what does it ~?** ¿qué quiere decir?

(**b**) (*make known*) indicar; *opinion* comunicar, hacer saber; **to ~ that ...** dar a entender que ...; **to ~ one's approval** indicar su aprobación.

2 *vi*: **it does not ~** no importa; **in the wider context it does not ~** en el contexto más amplio no tiene importancia.

sign-language ['saɪn,læŋgwɪdʒ] *n* lenguaje *m* de señas, lenguaje *m* mímico, mímica *f*; **to talk in ~** hablar por señas.

sign-painter ['saɪn,peɪntəʳ] *n* rotulista *mf*.

signpost ['saɪnpəʊst] **1** *n* poste *m* indicador, indicador *m* de dirección. **2** *vt* señalizar; **the road is well ~ed** la carretera tiene buena señalización.

signposting ['saɪnpəʊstɪŋ] *n* señalización *f*.

sign-writer ['saɪn,raɪtəʳ] *n* rotulista *mf*.

Sikh [si:k] **1** *adj* sij. **2** *n* sij *mf*.

silage ['saɪlɪdʒ] *n* ensilaje *m*.

silence ['saɪləns] **1** *n* silencio *m*; **~!** ¡silencio!; **~ is golden** el silencio es de oro; **in dead ~** en el silencio más absoluto; **there was ~** hubo un silencio; **~ gives consent** quien calla otorga; **to pass over sth in ~** silenciar algo; pasar algo por alto; **to reduce sb to ~** hacer callar a uno; **to reduce guns to ~** reducir los cañones al silencio.

2 *vt* hacer callar, acallar; *guns etc* reducir al silencio; (*Tech*) silenciar; *critic* imponer silencio a, amordazar.

silencer ['saɪlənsəʳ] *n* (*Brit*) silenciador *m*.

silent ['saɪlənt] *adj* silencioso; callado; *letter* mudo; **~ film, ~ picture** película *f* muda; **~ majority** mayoría *f* silenciosa; **~ partner** (*esp US*) socio *m* comanditario; **to be ~, to keep ~, to remain ~** callarse, guardar silencio, permanecer silencioso; **to become ~** callarse, enmudecer; **it was as ~ as the grave** había un silencio sepulcral.

silently ['saɪləntlɪ] *adv* silenciosamente, en silencio.

silhouette [,sɪlu:'et] **1** *n* silueta *f*; **in ~** en silueta. **2** *vt* destacar, hacer aparecer en silueta; **to be ~d against** destacarse contra, destacarse sobre.

silica ['sɪlɪkə] *n* sílice *f*.

silicate ['sɪlɪkɪt] *n* silicato *m*.

siliceous [sɪ'lɪʃəs] *adj* silíceo.

silicon ['sɪlɪkən] **1** *n* silicio *m*. **2** *attr*: **~ carbide** carburo *m* de silicio; **~ chip** chip *m* de silicio, pastilla *f* de silicio.

silicone ['sɪlɪkəʊn] *n* silicona *f*.

silicosis [,sɪlɪ'kəʊsɪs] *n* silicosis *f*.

silk [sɪlk] **1** *n* seda *f*; **to take ~** (*Brit*) ser ascendido a la abogacía superior. **2** *attr* de seda; **with a ~ finish** *cloth, paintwork* satinado; **~ hat** sombrero *m* de copa; **~ industry** industria *f* sedera; **~ screen printing** serigrafía *f*; **~ thread** hilo *m* de seda.

silken ['sɪlkən] *adj* (*of silk*) de seda; (*like silk*) sedoso, sedeño; *manner, voice* suave, mimoso.

silkiness ['sɪlkɪnɪs] *n* sedosidad *f*, lo sedoso; suavidad *f*, lo mimoso.

silkmoth ['sɪlkmɒθ] *n* mariposa *f* de seda.

silk-raising ['sɪlk,reɪzɪŋ] *n* sericultura *f*.

silkworm ['sɪlkwɜ:m] *n* gusano *m* de seda.

silky ['sɪlkɪ] *adj* sedoso.

sill [sɪl] *n* antepecho *m*; (*window~*) alféizar *m*, repisa *f* (*LAm*); (*door ~*) umbral *m*.

silliness ['sɪlɪnɪs] *n* tontería *f*, necedad *f*; insensatez *f*; lo absurdo.

silly ['sɪlɪ] *adj person* tonto, bobo, necio; *act* tonto, insensato; *idea etc* absurdo; **~ season** temporada *f* boba, canícula *f*; **~ (of) me!** ¡qué tonto soy!; **you ~ child!, you big ~!** ¡bobo!; **don't be ~** no seas bobo; **that was ~ of you, that was a ~ thing to do** eso fue muy bobo, eso fue una estupidez; **I've done a ~ thing** he hecho una tontería, he sido un tonto; **I feel ~ in this hat** temo hacer el ridículo con este sombrero; **you look ~ carrying that fish** pareces un tonto llevando ese pez; **to knock sb ~*** dar una paliza a uno; **the blow knocked him ~** el golpe le dejó sin sentido; **to laugh o.s. ~*** desternillarse de risa*; **to make sb look ~** poner a uno en ridículo.

silo ['saɪləʊ] *n* (*Agr*) silo *m*, ensiladora *f*; (*Mil*) silo *m*.

silt [sɪlt] **1** *n* sedimento *m*, aluvión *m*. **2** *vt* (*also* **to ~ up**) obstruir con sedimentos. **3** *vi* (*also* **to ~ up**) obstruirse con sedimentos.

silting ['sɪltɪŋ] *n* (*also* **~ up**) obstrucción *f* con sedimentos.

silver ['sɪlvəʳ] **1** *n* (**a**) (*metal*) plata *f*.

(**b**) (*Fin*) monedas *fpl* de plata.

(**c**) (*US: cutlery*) cubertería *f*.

2 *attr* de plata, plateado; **~ beet** (*US*) acelga *f*, acelgas *fpl*; **~ birch** abedul *m* (plateado); **'~ collection'** 'contribuya generosamente'; **~ fir** abeto *m* blanco, pinabete *m*; **~ foil** hoja *f* de plata, (*paper*) papel *m* de plata; **~ fox** zorro *m* plateado; **~ gilt** plata *f* dorada; **~ jubilee** vigésimo quinto aniversario *m*; **~ lining** (*fig*) resquicio *m* de esperanza; **~ medal** medalla *f* de plata; **~ medallist** medallero *m*, -a *f* de plata; **~ paper** (*Brit*) papel *m* de plata, papel *m* de estaño; **~ plate** vajilla *f* de plata; **the ~ screen** la pantalla cinematográfica; **~ wedding** bodas *fpl* de plata.

3 *vt metal* platear; *mirror* azogar; *hair* blanquear.

4 *vi* (*hair*) blanquear.

silverfish ['sɪlvəfɪʃ] *n* lepisma *f*.

silver-grey ['sɪlvə'greɪ] *adj* gris perla.

silver-haired ['sɪlvə'hɛəd] *adj* de pelo entrecano.

silver-plate ['sɪlvə'pleɪt] *vt* platear.

silver-plated [,sɪlvə'pleɪtɪd] *adj* chapado en plata, plateado.

silversmith ['sɪlvəsmɪθ] *n* platero *m*; **~'s (shop)** platería *f*.

silver-tongued ['sɪlvə'tʌŋd] *adj* elocuente, con pico de oro.

silverware ['sɪlvəwɛəʳ] *n* plata *f*, vajilla *f* de plata.

silvery ['sɪlvərɪ] *adj* plateado; *voice etc* argentino.

silviculture ['sɪlvɪ,kʌltʃəʳ] *n* silvicultura *f*.

simian ['sɪmɪən] *adj* símico.

similar ['sɪmɪləʳ] *adj* parecido, semejante; **A and B are ~, A is ~ to B** A y B se parecen; **they are not at all ~** no se parecen en absoluto; **they are ~ in size** son de tamaño parecido; **this is ~ to what happened before** esto es parecido a lo que pasó antes.

similarity [,sɪmɪ'lærɪtɪ] *n* parecido *m*, semejanza *f*; **there is a certain ~** hay cierto parecido.

similarly ['sɪmɪləlɪ] *adv* de un modo parecido; **and ~, ...** y asimismo, ...

simile ['sɪmɪlɪ] *n* símil *m*.

similitude [sɪ'mɪlɪtjuːd] *n* similitud *f*, semejanza *f*.

simmer ['sɪməʳ] **1** *n*: **to be on the ~, to keep on the ~** hervir a fuego lento.

2 *vt* cocer a fuego lento.

3 *vi* (**a**) (*Culin*) hervir a fuego lento.

(**b**) (*fig*) estar hirviendo, estar a punto de estallar (*with rage* de ira).

◆**simmer down** *vi* (*fig*) calmarse poco a poco, tranquilizarse lentamente; **~ down!** ¡cálmate!

Simon ['saɪmən] *nm* Simón.

simony ['saɪmənɪ] *n* simonía *f*.

simp* [sɪmp] *n* (*US*) bobo *m*, -a *f*.

simper ['sɪmpəʳ] **1** *n* sonrisa *f* afectada, sonrisa *f* boba. **2** *vi* sonreírse afectadamente, sonreírse bobamente. **3** *vt*: **'Yes', she ~ed** 'Sí', dijo sonriendo afectada.

simpering ['sɪmpərɪŋ] *adj* afectado; bobo y remilgado.

simperingly ['sɪmpərɪŋlɪ] *adv* afectadamente; bobamente.

simple ['sɪmpl] *adj* (**a**) (*uncomplicated, easy, plain*) sencillo; **it's as ~ as ABC** es de lo más sencillo; **the ~ life** la vida sencilla; **I'm a ~ soul** soy un hombre sencillo; **it's very ~** es muy sencillo; **it's ~ madness** es una locura ni más ni menos; **he's a ~ craftsman** es un simple artesano.

(**b**) (*not compound*) *fracture, interest, sentence etc* simple.

(**c**) (*foolish*) simple; imbécil; (*innocent*) ingenuo, inocente; crédulo; **S~ Simon** Simón el Bobito; **he's a bit ~** es algo bobo, está algo tocado; **I am not so ~ as to believe that ...** no soy lo bastante ingenuo como para creer que ...

simple-hearted ['sɪmpl'hɑːtɪd] *adj* candoroso, ingenuo.

simple-minded ['sɪmpl'maɪndɪd] *adj* candoroso, ingenuo; (*pej*) simple, mentecato; **I am not so ~** no soy tan ingenuo; **in their ~ way** en su modo ingenuo.

simple-mindedness ['sɪmpl'maɪndɪdnɪs] *n* candor *m*, ingenuidad *f*; (*pej*) simpleza *f*, mentecatez *f*.

simpleton ['sɪmpltən] *n* inocentón *m*, -ona *f*, simplón *m*, -ona *f*, bobalicón *m*, -ona *f*.

simplicity [sɪm'plɪsɪtɪ] *n* sencillez *f*; simpleza *f*, ingenuidad *f*, credulidad *f*; **it's ~ itself** es de lo más sencillo.

simplifiable ['sɪmplɪfaɪəbl] *adj* simplificable.

simplification [,sɪmplɪfɪ'keɪʃən] *n* simplificación *f*.

simplify ['sɪmplɪfaɪ] *vt* simplificar.

simplistic [sɪm'plɪstɪk] *adj* simplista.

simply ['sɪmplɪ] *adv* sencillamente; simplemente; **a ~ furnished room** un cuarto amueblado sencillamente; **I ~ said that ...** dije sencillamente que ...; **it's ~ impossible!** ¡es sencillamente imposible!; **but you ~ must!** ¡pero no tienes más remedio que hacerlo!; **I was ~ amazed** me quedé completamente asombrado.

simulacrum [,sɪmjʊ'leɪkrəm] *n*, *pl* **simulacra** [,sɪmjʊ'leɪkrə] simulacro *m*.

simulate ['sɪmjʊleɪt] *vt* simular, fingir.

simulated ['sɪmjʊ,leɪtɪd] *adj* simulado; **~ attack** simulacro *m* de ataque; **~ leather** cuero *m* de imitación.

simulation [,sɪmjʊ'leɪʃən] *n* simulación *f*, fingimiento *m*; (*Comput*) simulación *f*.

simulator ['sɪmjʊleɪtəʳ] *n* simulador *m*.

simulcast ['sɪməl,kɑːst] **1** *n* emisión *f* simultánea por radio y televisión. **2** *vt* emitir simultáneamente por radio y televisión.

simultaneity [,sɪməltə'nɪətɪ] *n* simultaneidad *f*.

simultaneous [,sɪməl'teɪnɪəs] *adj* simultáneo; **~ equations** sistema *m* de ecuaciones; **~ interpreting** interpretación *f* simultánea; **~ processing** procesamiento *m* simultáneo; **~ translation** traducción *f* simultánea.

simultaneously [,sɪməl'teɪnɪəslɪ] *adv* simultáneamente.

sin [sɪn] **1** *n* pecado *m*; **like ~** con vehemencia; **for my ~s** por mis pecados; **his besetting ~ is ...** su mayor defecto es ..., tiene la manía de ...; **it would be a ~ to** + *infin* sería un crimen + *infin*, sería un pecado + *infin*; **to fall into ~** caer en el pecado; **to live in ~** estar amancebados.

2 *vi* pecar; **he was more ~ned against than ~ning** era más bien el ofendido y no el ofensor.

Sinai ['saɪnɪaɪ] **1** *n* Sinaí *m*; **Mount ~** el monte Sinaí. **2** *attr*: **the ~ Desert** el desierto del Sinaí.

Sinbad ['sɪnbæd] *nm* Simbad; **~ the Sailor** Simbad el marino.

sin bin* ['sɪnbɪn] *n* banquillo *m* de los expulsados.

since [sɪns] **1** *adv* desde entonces, después; **ever ~** desde entonces; **a long time ~** hace mucho (tiempo); **not long ~, a short time ~** hace poco.

2 *prep* desde; a partir de, después de; **~ Monday** desde el lunes; **~ arriving** desde que llegué, desde mi llegada; **I've been waiting ~ 10** espero desde las 10; **ever ~ 1900** a partir de 1900, de 1900 acá; **how long is it ~ the accident?** ¿cuánto tiempo ha pasado desde el accidente?; *V* **then.**

3 *conj* (**a**) (*time*) desde que; **~ I arrived** desde que llegué; **it is a week ~ he left** hace una semana que salió, salió hace una semana; **~ I've been here** desde que estoy aquí.

(**b**) (*because*) ya que, puesto que; **~ you can't come** puesto que no puedes venir; **~ he is Spanish** como es español, siendo él español.

sincere [sɪn'sɪəʳ] *adj* sincero.

sincerely [sɪn'sɪəlɪ] *adv* sinceramente; **Yours ~** le saluda atentamente, le saluda cordialmente.

sincerity [sɪn'serɪtɪ] *n* sinceridad *f*; **in all ~** con toda sinceridad, con toda franqueza.

sine [saɪn] *n* (*Math*) seno *m*.

sinecure ['saɪnɪkjʊəʳ] *n* sinecura *f*; canonjía *f*, prebenda *f*.

sine qua non ['saɪnɪkweɪ'nɒn] *n* sine qua non *m*.

sinew ['sɪnjuː] *n* tendón *m*; **~s** (*fig*) nervio *m*, fibra *f*; recursos *mpl*; **the ~s of war** el dinero.

sinewy ['sɪnjuːɪ] *adj* nervudo, nervioso, vigoroso.

sinfonietta [,sɪnfən'jetə] *n* sinfonieta *f*.

sinful ['sɪnfʊl] *adj person* pecador; *act, thought* pecaminoso; *town etc* inmoral, depravado.

sinfully ['sɪnfəlɪ] *adv* de modo pecaminoso.

sinfulness ['sɪnfʊlnɪs] *n* maldad *f*; pecaminosidad *f*; vicio *m*, depravación *f*.

sing [sɪŋ] (*irr*: *pret* **sang**, *ptp* **sung**) **1** *vt* cantar; **~ us a song!** ¡cántanos algo!; **to ~ a child to sleep** arrullar a un niño, adormercer a un niño cantando.

2 *vi* (**a**) cantar; (*bird*) trinar, gorjear; (*ears*) zumbar; (*wind*) susurrar; (*kettle*) silbar (al hervir); **to ~ flat, to ~ out of tune** desafinar, cantar mal; **to ~ small** achantarse, ser más humilde.

(**b**) (*US*‡) cantar*.

◆**sing out** *vi* cantar más fuerte; (*fig*) vocear, gritar; **if you want anything ~ out*** si necesitas algo me llamas; **to ~ out for sth** reclamar algo a gritos.

◆**sing up** *vi* cantar más fuerte; **~ up!** ¡más fuerte!

Singapore [,sɪŋgə'pɔːʳ] *n* Singapur *m*.

Singaporean [,sɪŋgə'pɔːrɪən] **1** *adj* de Singapur. **2** *n* nativo *m*, -a *f* (*or* habitante *mf*) de Singapur.

singe [sɪndʒ] *vt* chamuscar; *hair* quemar las puntas de.

singer ['sɪŋəʳ] *n* cantor *m*, -ora *f*; (*professional*) cantante *mf*; (*in cabaret etc*) vocalista *mf*.

Singhalese [,sɪŋgə'liːz] **1** *adj* cingalés. **2** *n* (**a**) cingalés *m*, -esa *f*. (**b**) (*Ling*) cingalés *m*.

singing ['sɪŋɪŋ] **1** *n* canto *m*; cantos *mpl*, canciones *fpl*; (*in the ears*) zumbido *m*.

2 *attr*: **~ lesson** lección *f* de canto; **~ teacher** profesor *m*, -ora *f* de canto; **~ telegram** telegrama *m* cantado; **to have a good ~ voice** tener una buena voz para cantar.

single ['sɪŋgl] **1** *adj* (**a**) (*only*) único, solo; (*not double*) simple, sencillo; *bed, room* individual, sencillo (*LAm*); *ticket, spacing* sencillo; **~ combat** combate *m* singular; **~ density disk** disco *m* de densidad sencilla; **S~ European Act** Acta *f* Única Europea; **in ~ file** en fila de a uno; **~ market** mercado *m* único; **~ track** vía *f* única; **~ user** (*adj*) monousuario; **the greatest ~ problem** el mayor problema; **every ~ day** todos los días sin excepción; **every ~ book I looked at** todos los libros que miré sin excepción; **not a ~ one spoke up** no habló ni uno solo; **there was a ~ rose in the garden** en el jardín había una rosa única.

(**b**) (*unmarried*) soltero, no casado; **~ parent** madre *f* sin pareja, madre *f* sola, padre *m* sin pareja, padre *m* solo; **~ parent family** familia *f* monoparental, hogar *m* sin pareja; **~ parenthood** monoparentalidad *f*; **~ people** personas *fpl* no casadas; **the ~ state** el estado célibe; **she's a ~ woman** es soltera; **she remained ~** siguió sin casarse.

2 *n* (**a**) (*Brit Rail etc*) billete *m* sencillo.

(**b**) (*Mus*) single *m*, sencillo *m*.

(**c**) **~s** solteros *mpl*; **~s bar** bar *m* para solteros.

(**d**) **~s** (*Tennis*) juego *m* de individuales; **ladies' ~s** individual *m* femenino; **men's ~s** individual *m* masculino.

(**e**) (*record*) single *m*.

(**f**) (*Fin*) moneda *f* de una libra, billete *m* de un dólar, *etc*; **he paid me 200 dollars in ~s** me pagó 200 dólares en billetes de a uno.

(**g**) (*measure of drink*) ración *f* normal.

◆**single out** *vt* (*choose*) escoger; (*distinguish*) distinguir, singularizar; **he was ~d out to lead the team** se le escogió para ser capitán del equipo; **to ~ (out) plants** entresacar plantas.

single-barrelled ['sɪŋgl'bærəld] *adj gun* de cañón único.

single-breasted ['sɪŋgl'brestɪd] *adj jacket* sin cruzar, recto.

single-cell(ed) ['sɪŋgl'sel(d)] *adj* unicelular.

single-chamber ['sɪŋgl'tʃeɪmbəʳ] *adj* unicameral.

single-engined ['sɪŋgl'endʒɪnd] *adj* monomotor.
single-entry ['sɪŋgl'entrɪ] **1** *n* partida *f* simple. **2** *attr*: ~ **book-keeping** contabilidad *f* por partida simple.
single-family ['sɪŋgl,fæmlɪ] *attr* unifamiliar.
single-figure ['sɪŋgl,fɪgəʳ] *attr*: ~ **inflation** inflación *f* de un solo dígito.
single-handed ['sɪŋgl'hændɪd] *adj, adv* sin ayuda (de nadie).
single-hearted ['sɪŋgl'hɑːtɪd] *adj* sincero, leal; resuelto.
single-masted ['sɪŋgl'mɑːstɪd] *adj* de palo único.
single-minded ['sɪŋgl'maɪndɪd] *adj* resuelto, firme.
single-mindedness [,sɪŋgl'maɪndɪdnɪs] *n* resolución *f*, firmeza.
singleness ['sɪŋglnɪs] *n*: ~ **of purpose** resolución *f*. firmeza *f*.
single-party ['sɪŋgl'pɑːtɪ] *adj state etc* de partido único.
single-seater ['sɪŋgl'siːtəʳ] *n* monoplaza *m*.
single-sex ['sɪŋglseks] *adj*: ~ **school** escuela *f* para sólo niños (*or* sólo niñas).
single-sided ['sɪŋgl,saɪdɪd] *adj*: ~ **disk** disco *m* de una cara.
single-space ['sɪŋgl'speɪs] *vt text* mecanografiar a espacio sencillo.
single spacing ['sɪŋgl'speɪsɪŋ] *n* interlineado *m* simple; **in** ~ a espacio sencillo.
singlet ['sɪŋglɪt] *n* (*Brit*) camiseta *f*.
singleton ['sɪŋgltən] *n* semifallo *m* (*in* a).
single-track ['sɪŋgl'træk] *adj* de vía única.
singly ['sɪŋglɪ] *adv* uno a uno, individualmente, separadamente.
singsong ['sɪŋ,sɒŋ] **1** *adj tone* monótono, cantarín.
2 *n* (*tone*) salmodia *f*, sonsonete *m*; (*songs*) concierto *m* espontáneo; **to get together for a** ~ reunirse para cantar (canciones populares, folklóricas *etc*).
singular ['sɪŋgjʊləʳ] **1** *adj* (**a**) (*Gram*) singular; **a** ~ **noun** un sustantivo en singular.
(**b**) (*odd*) raro, extraño, singular; **a most** ~ **occurrence** un acontecimiento muy extraño; **how very** ~! ¡qué raro!
2 *n* singular *f*; **in the** ~ en singular.
singularity [,sɪŋgjʊ'lærɪtɪ] *n* singularidad *f*, particularidad *f*.
singularly ['sɪŋgjʊləlɪ] *adv* singularmente; **a** ~ **inappropriate remark** una observación de lo más inoportuno.
Sinhalese [,sɪŋə'liːz] = **Singhalese**.
sinister ['sɪnɪstəʳ] *adj* siniestro.
sink¹ [sɪŋk] (*irr*: *pret* **sank**, *ptp* **sunk**) **1** *vt* (**a**) *ship* hundir, echar a pique; sumergir; (*fig*) *theory* destruir, acabar con; *person* acabar con.
(**b**) *mine* abrir, excavar; *hole* hacer, excavar; *well* perforar; (*) *drink* tragarse, embaular*; *ball, putt* embocar; **to** ~ **a post 2 metres in the ground** fijar un poste 2 metros bajo tierra; **to** ~ **one's teeth into sth** hincar los dientes en algo; **he can** ~ **a glass of beer in 12 seconds** se traga una caña de cerveza en 12 segundos.
(**c**) *differences* suprimir, olvidar; **to** ~ **one's identity in that of a group** olvidar su individualidad en la solidaridad de un grupo.
(**d**) **to** ~ **money in an enterprise** invertir dinero en una empresa.
(**e**) (*phrases with* **sunk**) **to be sunk in thought** estar absorto en la meditación, estar ensimismado; **to be sunk in depression** estar sumido en el abatimiento; **to be sunk in debt** estar agobiado por las deudas; **now we're sunk!*** ¡estamos perdidos!
2 *vi* (**a**) (*ship etc*) hundirse; irse a pique, naufragar; sumergirse; **to** ~ **by the bow** hundirse de proa; **to** ~ **to the bottom** ir al fondo; **it** ~**s instead of floating** se hunde en lugar de flotar; **he was left to** ~ **or swim** (*fig*) le abandonaron a su suerte.
(**b**) (*subside*) hundirse; (*building, land etc*) hundirse; (*fire*) estarse apagando, morir; (*person*) debilitarse, morirse; (*sun*) ponerse; **he sank in the mud up to his knees** se hundió en el lodo hasta las rodillas; **to** ~ **into a chair** dejarse caer en una silla, arrellanarse en una silla; **to** ~ **into insignificance** perder su importancia; **to** ~ **deeper into degradation** hundirse cada vez más en la degradación, envilecerse más y más; **to** ~ **into poverty** caer en la miseria; **to** ~ **to one's knees** caer de rodillas; **his voice sank to a whisper** pasó a hablar en tono muy bajo; **my spirits sank, my heart sank** se me cayeron las alas del corazón; **to** ~ **out of sight** desaparecer.
(**c**) (*in quantity*) disminuir; (*in value*) perder su valor; (*decline*) declinar, menguar; **he has sunk in my estimation** ha bajado en mi estima; **the shares have sunk to 3 dollars** las acciones han bajado a 3 dólares.
◆**sink away** *vi* (*liquid*) irse, desaparecer.
◆**sink back** *vi* arrellanarse, arrepanchigarse; **he sank back into his chair** se arrellanó en la silla.
◆**sink down** *vi*: **to** ~ **down into a chair** dejarse caer en una silla, arrellenarse en una silla.
◆**sink in** *vi* penetrar, calar; **to let the paint** ~ **in** dejar que penetre la pintura; **the water** ~**s in in time** con el tiempo va penetrando el agua; **his words seem to have sunk in** sus palabras parecen haber surtido efecto, parece que sus palabras han hecho mella.
sink² [sɪŋk] *n* fregadero *m*, pila *f*; (*Tech*) sumidero *m*; (*fig*) sentina *f*; ~ **of iniquity** sentina *f*, lugar *m* de todos los vicios; ~ **tidy** cubeta *f* para basura.
sinker ['sɪŋkəʳ] *n* (*Fishing*) plomo *m*.
sinking ['sɪŋkɪŋ] **1** *adj*: ~ **fund** fondo *m* de amortización; **that** ~ **feeling** esa sensación de que todo se va a pique; **with** ~ **heart** con alma aprensiva.
2 *n* hundimiento *m*.
sink-unit ['sɪŋk'juːnɪt] *n* lavadero *m*, fregadero *m* (de cocina).
sinless ['sɪnlɪs] *adj* libre de pecado, puro, inmaculado.
sinner ['sɪnəʳ] *n* pecador *m*, -ora *f*.
Sino... ['saɪnəʊ] *pref* sino..., chino...
Sinologist [,saɪ'nɒlədʒɪst] *n* sinólogo *m*, -a *f*.
Sinology [,saɪ'nɒlədʒɪ] *n* sinología *f*.
sinuosity [,sɪnjʊ'ɒsɪtɪ] *n* sinuosidad *f*.
sinuous ['sɪnjʊəs] *adj* sinuoso.
sinus ['saɪnəs] *n* (*Anat*) seno *m*.
sinusitis [,saɪnə'saɪtɪs] *n* sinusitis *f*.
sip [sɪp] **1** *n* sorbo *m*. **2** *vt* sorber, beber a sorbitos; probar. **3** *vi* (*also* **to** ~ **at**) sorber, beber a sorbitos.
siphon ['saɪfən] **1** *n* sifón *m*. **2** *vt* sacar con sifón; *funds etc* (*also* **to** ~ **off**) desviar, malversar.
◆**siphon off** *vt* (*lit*) sacar con sifón; (*fig*) quitar poco a poco, reducir gradualmente; separar; desviar; *funds etc* (*illegally*) malversar.
◆**siphon out** *vt* sacar con sifón.
sir [sɜːʳ] *n* (*in direct address*) señor *m*; (*as title*) sir *m*; **yes,** ~ (*Mil*) sí, mi capitán (*etc*); **S**~ (*to editor of paper*) señor director; **S**~**s** (*US*) muy señores nuestros; **Dear S**~ muy señor mío; **my dear** ~**!, my good** ~! ¡pero amigo ...!
sire ['saɪəʳ] **1** *n* (*Zool*) padre *m*; (*stallion*) semental *m*, caballo *m* padre; **S**~ (*to monarch*: ††) Señor *m*.
2 *vt* ser el padre de; engendrar; **he** ~**d 49 children** tuvo 49 hijos; **the horse A,** ~**d by B** el caballo A, cuyo padre fue B.
siren ['saɪərən] *n* (*all senses*) sirena *f*; ~ **song** canto *m* de sirena.
Sirius ['sɪrɪəs] *nm* Sirio.
sirloin ['sɜːlɔɪn] *n* solomillo *m*, diezmillo *m* (*Mex*).
sirocco [sɪ'rɒkəʊ] *n* siroco *m*.
sis* [sɪs] *n* = **sister**.
sisal ['saɪsəl] *n* henequén *m*, fique *m*, pita *f*.
sissy⁑ ['sɪsɪ] *n* (**a**) (*effeminate*) marica⁑ *m*, mariquita⁑ *m*; **the last one's a** ~! ¡maricón el último⁑! (**b**) (*coward*) gallina* *f*.
sister ['sɪstəʳ] **1** *n* (**a**) hermana *f*. (**b**) (*Eccl*) hermana *f*; **S**~ **Manuela** Sor Manuela. (**c**) (*Brit Med*) enfermera *f*, hermana *f* enfermera, (*of higher rank*) enfermera *f* jefa. **2** *adj*: ~ **city** (*US*) ciudad *f* gemela; ~ **college** colegio *m* hermano; ~ **company** empresa *f* hermana; ~ **organizations** organizaciones *fpl* hermanas.
sisterhood ['sɪstəhʊd] *n* hermandad *f*.
sister-in-law ['sɪstərɪnlɔː] *n*, *pl* **sisters-in-law** cuñada *f*, hermana *f* política.
sisterly ['sɪstəlɪ] *adj* de hermana, como hermana.
sister-ship ['sɪstəʃɪp] *n* buque *m* gemelo; **X is the** ~ **of Z** X es buque gemelo de Z.
Sistine ['sɪstiːn] *adj*: **the** ~ **Chapel** la Capilla Sixtina.
Sisyphus ['sɪsɪfəs] *nm* Sísifo.
sit [sɪt] (*irr*: *pret and ptp* **sat**) **1** *vt* (**a**) (*also* **to** ~ **down**) sentar; **to** ~ **sb (down) in a chair** sentar a uno en una silla; **to** ~ **a child (down) on one's knees** sentar a un niño sobre las rodillas.
(**b**) **to** ~ **a horse well** montar bien (a caballo).
(**c**) (*esp Brit*) **to** ~ **an examination** presentarse a un examen, pasar un examen (*LAm*); **to** ~ **an examination in French** examinarse de francés.
2 *vi* (**a**) (*gen*: *act*) sentarse; (*state*) estar sentado; ~! (*to dog*) ¡quieto!; ~ **here** siéntate aquí; **I was** ~**ting there** estaba sentado allí; ~ **by me** siéntate a mi lado, siéntate conmigo; **to** ~ **at home all day** pasar todo el día en casa (sin hacer nada); **to** ~ **at table** sentarse a la mesa; **he** ~**s on the board** (*Comm etc*) es miembro de la junta directiva, forma parte de la junta directiva; **he sat over his books all night** pasó toda la noche con sus libros; **don't just** ~ **there, do something!** ¡no te quedes ahí sin hacer

nada!

(**b**) (*assembly*) reunirse; celebrar junta, celebrar sesión; **the House sat all night** la sesión de la Cámara duró toda la noche; **the House sat for 22 hours** la Cámara tuvo una sesión de 22 horas.

(**c**) (*bird, insect*) posarse; (*hen*) empollar, incubar; **the hen is ~ting on 12 eggs** la gallina empolla 12 huevos.

(**d**) (*fig: dress*) caer, sentar (*on sb* a uno); **that pie ~s heavy on the stomach** la empanada esa no me sienta; **how ~s the wind?** ¿de dónde sopla el viento?; **it sat heavy on his conscience** le remordió la conciencia.

(**e**) (*model*) **to ~ for a painter** posar para un pintor, servir de modelo a un pintor; **she sat for Goya** se hizo retratar por Goya; **to ~ for one's portrait** hacerse retratar, hacerse un retrato.

(**f**) (*esp Brit: candidate*) presentarse (*for an exam* a un examen).

(**g**) (*Brit Pol*) **to ~ for Bury** representar a Bury, ser diputado por Bury; **to ~ in Parliament** ser diputado (*Sp*: a Cortes), ser miembro del Parlamento.

◆**sit about, sit around** *vi* estar sin hacer nada.

◆**sit back** *vi* sentarse cómodamente; **to ~ back (and do nothing)** cruzarse de brazos.

◆**sit down 1** *vt* = **sit 1** (**a**).

2 *vi* sentarse; **do ~ down!** ¡siéntese, por favor!; **to ~ down to table** sentarse a la mesa; **to ~ down to a big supper** sentarse a comer una cena fuerte; **to ~ down under an insult** tragar un insulto, aguantar un insulto; **we sat down 13 to supper** éramos 13 a la mesa para cenar.

3 *vr*: **to ~ o.s. down** sentarse.

◆**sit in** *vi* (*students, workers*) hacer una sentada, ocupar las aulas (*or* la fábrica *etc*); **to ~ in for a friend** sustituir a un amigo; **to ~ in on talks** asistir a una conferencia (sin ser delegado oficial), participar como observador en unas discusiones.

◆**sit on 1** *vt* (**a**) (*****) *secret* guardar secreto, no revelar; no publicar; guardar para sí; *plan etc* dar carpetazo a.

(**b**) (*****) *person* (*silence*) hacer callar; (*suppress*) reprimir a; (*be hard on*) ser severo con; **he won't be sat on** no quiere callar, no da su brazo a torcer.

2 *vi* permanecer sentado, seguir en su asiento.

◆**sit out 1** *vt* (**a**) **to ~ a lecture out** aguantar hasta el fin de una conferencia; **to ~ sb out** resistir más tiempo que uno, demostrar tener más aguante que uno; **to ~ out a strike** aguantar una huelga (sin ofrecer concesiones).

(**b**) **to ~ out a dance** no bailar; **let's ~ this one out** no bailemos esta vez.

2 *vi* sentarse fuera; estar sentado al aire libre.

◆**sit through** *vt concert, lecture* permanecer hasta el fin de, aguantar toda la extensión de.

◆**sit up 1** *vt doll, patient* sentar, poner derecho; **to ~ an invalid up** incorporar a un enfermo (en la cama).

2 *vi* (**a**) (*after lying*) incorporarse; **to ~ up in bed** incorporarse en la cama; **to ~ up with a start** incorporarse sobresaltado; **to ~ up at the table** sentarse a la mesa.

(**b**) (*straighten o.s.*) ponerse derecho, erguirse en la silla.

(**c**) (*stay awake*) velar, trasnochar, no acostarse; **to ~ up for sb** esperar a que vuelva uno, estar sin acostarse hasta que vuelva uno; **to ~ up with a child** velar a un niño.

(**d**) **to ~ up (and take notice)** empezar a prestar atención; darse cuenta; **to make sb ~ up** dar en qué pensar a uno; impresionar fuertemente a uno; sorprender a uno.

sitar [sɪ'tɑːʳ] *n* sitar *m*.

sitcom* ['sɪtkɒm] *n* (*TV*) *abbr of* **situation comedy.**

sit-down ['sɪtdaʊn] **1** *n*: **I must have a ~*** tengo que descansar (sentado). **2** *attr*: **we had a ~ lunch** hemos comido a la mesa; **~ strike** sentada *f*, huelga *f* de brazos caídos.

site [saɪt] **1** *n* sitio *m*, local *m*; (*for building*) solar *m*; (*archaeological, Geol*) yacimiento *m*; **the ~ of the battle** el lugar de la batalla; **a late Roman ~** un emplazamiento romano tardío; **the only ~ for the plant in Spain** la única localidad para la planta en España.

2 *vt* situar; localizar; **a badly ~d building** un edificio mal situado.

sit-in ['sɪtɪn] *n* sentada *f*, ocupación *f*, encierro *m*.

siting ['saɪtɪŋ] *n* situación *f*; emplazamiento *m*; **the ~ of new industries** la localización de las nuevas industrias.

Sits Vac. [ˌsɪts'væk] *n abbr of* **Situations Vacant** Ofrecen trabajo.

sitter ['sɪtəʳ] *n* (**a**) (*Art*) modelo *mf* de pintor. (**b**) (*baby~*) canguro* *mf*. (**c**) (*****) cosa *f* fácil; **it was a ~*** (*Sport*) fue un gol (*etc*) que se canta*; **you missed a ~*** erraste un tiro de lo más fácil.

sitting ['sɪtɪŋ] **1** *adj* sentado; **a ~ bird** una ave que está posada, una ave que está inmóvil; **a ~ hen** una gallina clueca; **~ duck** (*fig*) blanco *m* fácil, presa *f* fácil; **~ member** miembro *mf* actual, miembro *mf* en funciones; **~ tenant** inquilino *m*, -a *f* en posesión.

2 *n* (*Pol etc*) sesión *f*; (*of eggs*) nidada *f*; **~ and standing room** sitio *m* para sentarse y para estar de pie; **at one ~** en una sesión; de una vez, de un tirón; **second ~ for lunch** segundo turno *m* de comedor.

sitting-room ['sɪtɪŋrʊm] *n* cuarto *m* de estar, living *m*.

situate ['sɪtjʊeɪt] *vt* situar; **it is ~d in the High Street** está situado en la Calle Mayor; **how are you ~d?** ¿cuál es su situación actual?; **a pleasantly ~d house** una casa bien situada.

situation [ˌsɪtjʊ'eɪʃən] **1** *n* (**a**) (*location*) situación *f*; emplazamiento *m*.

(**b**) (*circumstances*) situación *f*; (*Econ, Pol etc*) coyuntura *f*: **to save the ~** salvar la situación.

(**c**) (*job*) puesto *m*, empleo *m*, colocación *f*; **'S~s Vacant'** 'Ofrecen trabajo'; **'S~s Wanted'** 'Buscan trabajo'.

2 *attr*: **~ comedy** comedia *f* de situación.

sit-up ['sɪtʌp] *n* ejercicio *m* de abdominales boca arriba.

six [sɪks] **1** *adj* seis; **~ of the best** (*Brit*) seis azotes *mpl* (*castigo escolar*); **it's ~ of one and half-a-dozen of the other** lo mismo da; olivo y aceituno es todo uno.

2 *n* seis *m*; **to be at ~es and sevens** (*things*) estar en confusión, estar en desorden, (*persons*) estar reñidos; **to knock sb for ~*** dejar pasmado a uno.

six-eight ['sɪk'seɪt] *attr*: **in ~ time** en un compás de seis por ocho.

sixfold ['sɪksfəʊld] **1** *adj* séxtuplo. **2** *adv* seis veces.

six-footer ['sɪks'fʊtəʳ] *n* hombre *m* (*or* mujer *f*) que mide 6 pies.

six-pack ['sɪkspæk] *n* paquete *m* de seis.

sixpence ['sɪkspəns] *n* (*Brit* †) 6 peniques *mpl*.

sixpenny ['sɪkspənɪ] *adj* (*Brit* †) de 6 peniques; (*pej*) insignificante, inútil.

six-shooter ['sɪks'ʃuːtəʳ] *n* revólver *m* de 6 tiros.

sixteen ['sɪks'tiːn] *adj* dieciséis.

sixteenth ['sɪks'tiːnθ] *adj* decimosexto; **~ note** (*US*) semicorchea *f*.

sixth [sɪksθ] **1** *adj* sexto; **~ form** clase *f* de alumnos del sexto año (*de 16 a 18 años de edad*); **~ former** alumno *m*, -a *f* de 16 a 18 años. **2** *n* sexto *m*, sexta parte *f*.

sixth-form [sɪksθfɔːm] *attr*: **~ college** instituto *m* para alumnos de 16 a 18 años.

sixtieth ['sɪkstɪɪθ] *adj* sexagésimo; sesenta; **the ~ anniversary** el sesenta aniversario.

sixty ['sɪkstɪ] *adj* sesenta; **the sixties** (*eg* 1960s) los años sesenta; **to be in one's sixties** tener más de sesenta años, ser sesentón.

sixtyish ['sɪkstɪɪʃ] *adj* de unos sesenta años.

size[1] [saɪz] **1** *n* tamaño *m*; dimensiones *fpl*; extensión *f*; magnitud *f*; (*of person*) talla *f*, estatura *f*; (*measurement: of gloves, shoes etc*) número *m*; (*of dress, shirt etc*) talla *f*; **a hall of immense ~** una sala de vastas dimensiones; **the ~ of the problem daunted him** la magnitud del problema le asombró; **the great ~ of the operation** la gran envergadura de la operación; **it's the ~ of a brick** es del tamaño de un ladrillo; **what ~ is it?** ¿de qué tamaño es?, ¿cómo es de grande?; **it's quite a ~** es bastante grande; **it's 2 ~s too big** lo quisiera 2 números más pequeño; **he's about your ~** tiene más o menos la talla de Vd; **that's about the ~ of it** eso es lo que puedo decirle acerca del asunto, es más o menos eso, (*as answer*) así es; **to be of a ~** ser del mismo tamaño, tener el mismo tamaño; **they're all of a ~** tienen todos el mismo tamaño; **to cut sth to ~** cortar algo del tamaño preciso que se necesita; **to cut sb down to ~** bajarle los humos a uno, ponerle a uno en su sitio; **it is drawn to natural ~** está dibujado a tamaño natural; **what ~ shoe do you take?** ¿qué número calza Vd?; **I take ~ 9** uso el número 9; **what ~ shirt do you take?** ¿qué talla de camisa es la de Vd?; **try this (on) for ~** prueba esto a ver si te conviene, a ver si esta medida es la tuya.

2 *vt* clasificar según el tamaño.

◆**size up** *vt*: **to ~ sb up** medir a uno con la vista; **to ~ up a problem** formarse una idea de un problema, tomar la medida de un problema; **I've got him all ~d up** le tengo calado; **I can't quite ~ him up** no llego a entenderle bien.

size[2] [saɪz] **1** *n* cola *f*, apresto *m*. **2** *vt* encolar, aprestar.

sizeable ['saɪzəbl] *adj* bastante grande, considerable, importante; **a ~ sum** una cantidad importante; **it's quite a ~ house** es una casa bastante grande.

sizeably ['saɪzəblɪ] *adv* considerablemente.
-sized [saɪzd] *adj ending in compounds* de tamaño ...; **medium~** de tamaño mediano.
sizzle ['sɪzl] *vi* chisporrotear, churruscar, crepitar; (*in frying*) crepitar (al freírse).
sizzling ['sɪzlɪŋ] **1** *adj heat* sofocante; *shot etc* fulminante. **2** *n* chisporroteo *m*, crepitación *f*.
SK (*Canada*) *abbr of* **Saskatchewan**.
skate¹ [skeɪt] *n* (*Brit*: *fish*) raya *f*.
skate² [skeɪt] **1** patín *m*; **get your ~s on!*** ¡date prisa!, ¡apúrate!
2 *vi* patinar; **it went skating across the floor** se deslizó velozmente sobre el suelo; **I ~d into a tree** (en un patinazo) di contra un árbol.
◆skate around, skate over, skate round *vt problem* evitar, esquivar.
skateboard ['skeɪtbɔːd] *n* monopatín *m*.
skateboarder ['skeɪtbɔːdəʳ] *n* monopatinador *m*, -ora *f*.
skateboarding ['skeitbɔːdɪŋ] *n* monopatinaje *m*.
skater ['skeɪtəʳ] *n* patinador *m*, -ora *f*.
skating ['skeɪtɪŋ] *n* patinaje *m*.
skating-rink ['skeɪtɪŋrɪŋk] *n* pista *f* de patinaje.
skedaddle* [skɪ'dædl] *vi* escabullirse, salir pitando*, poner pies en polvorosa*; **they ~d in all directions** huyeron por todos lados.
skein [skeɪn] *n* madeja *f*; **a tangled ~** (*fig*) un asunto enmarañado.
skeletal ['skelɪtl] *adj* esquelético.
skeleton ['skelɪtn] **1** *n* (*Anat*) esqueleto *m*; (*fig*) esquema *m*, plan *m*; (*Tech*) armazón *f*, armadura *f*; **the ~ at the feast** el aguafiestas; **~ in the cupboard, ~ in the closet** (*US*) secreto *m* vergonzoso de la familia, cadáver *m* en el armario.
2 *adj staff etc* reducido; *outline* esquemático; **~ key** llave *f* maestra, ganzúa *f*.
skeptic ['skeptɪk] *etc* (*US*) = **sceptic** *etc*.
sketch [sketʃ] **1** *n* **(a)** (*rough draft*) esbozo *m*, boceto *m*, bosquejo *m*, croquis *m* (*for* de); (*drawing*) dibujo *m*, diseño *m*; **~ for a costume** diseño *m* de un traje.
(b) (*Theat*) sketch *m*.
2 *attr*: **~ map** mapa *m* esbozado.
3 *vt* (*also* **to ~ out**) (*outline*) esbozar, trazar a grandes líneas; (*draw*) bosquejar, dibujar; hacer un dibujo de.
4 *vi* dibujar, hacer dibujos.
◆sketch in *vt*: **he ~ed in the details for me** me explicó los detalles.
sketchbook ['sketʃbʊk] *n* libro *m* de dibujos.
sketchily ['sketʃɪlɪ] *adv* incompletamente, superficialmente.
sketching ['sketʃɪŋ] *n* dibujo *m*, arte *m* de dibujar.
sketch(ing)-pad ['sketʃ(ɪŋ),pæd] *n* bloc *m* de dibujo.
sketchy ['sketʃɪ] *adj* incompleto, superficial, somero; difuminado; impreciso.
skew [skjuː] **1** *n*: **to be on the ~** estar desviado, estar sesgado; estar puesto mal.
2 *adj* sesgado, oblicuo, torcido.
3 *vt* sesgar, desviar; poner mal.
4 *vi* (*also* **to ~ round**) desviarse, ponerse al sesgo, torcerse.
skewbald ['skjuːbɔːld] **1** *adj* pintado, con pintas. **2** *n* pinto *m*.
skewed ['skjuːd] *adj* sesgado, torcido (*also fig*).
skewer ['skjʊəʳ] **1** *n* broqueta *f*, espetón *m*. **2** *vt* espetar; pasar una broqueta por.
skew-whiff* [,skjuː'wɪf] *adj* (*Brit*) sesgado, oblicuo, torcido; **to be on ~** estar puesto mal.
ski [skiː] **1** *n* esquí *m*. **2** *attr*: **~ instructor** instructor *m*, -ora *f* de esquí; **~ rack** baca *f* portaesquís; **~ resort** estación *f* de esquí; **~ stick** bastón *m* de esquiar. **3** *vi* esquiar.
ski-boot ['skiːbuːt] *n* bota *f* de esquí.
skid [skɪd] **1** *n* **(a)** (*Aut etc*) patinazo *m*, derrape *m*, deslizamiento *m*.
(b) (*Aer*) patín *m*; **to grease the ~s*** (*US*) engrasar el mecanismo; **to put the ~s under sb*** deshacerse de uno con maña, lograr con maña que uno abandone un puesto (*etc*).
2 *attr*: **~ row*** (*US*) barrio *m* de mala vida; calles *fpl* donde se refugian los borrachos, drogadictos *etc*.
3 *vi* (*Aut etc*) patinar, derrapar; (*of person*) resbalar; **it went ~ding across the floor** se deslizó velozmente sobre el suelo; **I ~ded into a tree** en un patinazo di contra un árbol; **the car ~ded to a halt** el coche se resbaló y paró.
skiddoo* [skɪ'duː] *vi* (*US*) largarse*.
skidlid* ['skɪdlɪd] *n* casco *m* protector (de motorista).
skidmark ['skɪdmɑːk] *n* huella *f* del patinazo.
skidproof ['skɪdpruːf] *adv* a prueba de patinazos.
skier ['skɪːəʳ] *n* esquiador *m*, -ora *f*.
skiff [skɪf] *n* esquife *m*.
skiing ['skiːɪŋ] **1** *n* esquí *m*; **to go ~** ir a esquiar. **2** *attr*: **~ holiday** vacaciones *fpl* de esquí; **~ resort** estación *f* de esquí.
ski-jump ['skiːdʒʌmp] *n* pista *f* para saltos de esquí.
ski-jumper ['skiː,dʒʌmpəʳ] *n* saltador *m*, -ora *f* de esquí.
ski-jumping ['skiː,dʒʌmpɪŋ] *n* salto *m* de esquí.
skilful, (*US*) **skillful** ['skɪlfʊl] *adj* hábil, diestro, experto (*at, in* en).
skilfully, (*US*) **skillfully** ['skɪlfəlɪ] *adv* hábilmente, diestramente.
skilfulness, (*US*) **skillfulness** ['skɪlfʊlnɪs] *n* habilidad *f*, destreza *f*.
ski-lift ['skiːlɪft] *n* remonte *m*, telesquí *m*, telesilla *m*.
skill [skɪl] *n* **(a)** (*ability*) habilidad *f*, destreza *f*; pericia *f*; **linguistic ~s** destrezas *fpl* lingüísticas; **his ~ at billiards** su habilidad en el billar; **he shows no small ~** muestra tener no poca habilidad; **we could make good use of his ~** podríamos utilizar su pericia.
(b) (*in craft etc*) arte *m*, técnica *f*; oficio *m*; **it's a ~ that has to be acquired** es una técnica que se aprende.
skilled [skɪld] *adj* (*skilful*) hábil, diestro; (*qualified*) cualificado, especializado; *work* especializado, que requiere técnicas especiales; **~ labor** (*US*), **~ labour** mano *f* de obra cualificada (*or* especializada); **to be ~ in a craft** ser perito en una artesanía; **a man ~ in diplomacy** un hombre de gran habilidad diplomática.
skillet ['skɪlɪt] *n* sartén *f*; cacerola *f* de mango largo.
skillful ['skilfʊl] *adj etc* (*US*) = **skilful** *etc*.
skim [skɪm] **1** *vt* **(a)** *liquid* espumar; *milk* desnatar, descremar.
(b) (*graze*) rozar, rasar, casi tocar al pasar.
2 *vi*: **to ~ over** pasar rasando, pasar casi tocando; **to ~ through** examinar superficialmente, hojear.
3 *adj*: **~(med) milk** leche *f* desnatada, leche *f* descremada.
◆skim off *vt cream, grease* desnatar, despumar, espumar; **they ~med off the brightest pupils** separaron a la flor y nata de los alumnos.
ski-mask ['skiːmɑːsk] *n* (*US*) pasamontaña(s) *m*.
skimmer ['skɪməʳ] *n* (*Orn*) picotijera *m*, rayador *m*.
skimp [skɪmp] **1** *vt* escatimar; *work* chapucear, frangollar.
2 *vi* economizar, ser parsimonioso (*on* con).
skimpily ['skɪmpɪlɪ] *adv serve, provide* escasamente; *live* mezquinamente.
skimpy ['skɪmpɪ] *adj allowance etc* escaso, pequeño; mezquino; *skirt etc* muy abreviado, muy corto; *person* tacaño.
skin [skɪn] **1** *n* **(a)** piel *f*; (*with reference to texture etc*) cutis *m*; **by the ~ of one's teeth** por los pelos; **it's no ~ off my nose‡** no me va ni me viene; **he's nothing but ~ and bone** está en los huesos; **to have a thick ~** ser bastante insensible, tener mucha cara dura; **to have a thin ~** ser muy susceptible; **he gets under my ~*** me hace subir por las paredes*; **I've got you under my ~*** el recuerdo de ti no se me quita de la cabeza; **to jump out of one's ~** llevarse un tremendo susto; **to save one's ~** salvar el pellejo; **to wear wool next to one's ~** llevar prenda de lana sobre la piel.
(b) (*Zool*) piel *f*, pellejo *m*; (*as hide*) piel *f*, cuero *m*; (*for wine*) odre *m*.
(c) (*Bot*) piel *f*, pellejo *m*; corteza *f*.
(d) (*fig*) (*on milk*) nata *f*; (*for duplicating*) clisé *m*; (*Aer, Naut*) revestimiento *m*.
(e) (*) = **skinhead**.
2 *attr* de la piel; **~ disease** enfermedad *f* cutánea, enfermedad *f* dérmica; **~ trade** publicación *f* de revistas porno; **~ wound** herida *f* superficial.
3 *vt* **(a)** *animal* despellejar, desollar; *fruit* pelar, quitar la piel a; *tree* descortezar; **to ~ sb alive** desollar vivo a uno; **to ~ one's knee** despellejarse la rodilla.
(b) (‡: *steal from*) despellejar, esquilmar.
◆skin over *vi* (*Med*) cicatrizarse.
skin-deep ['skɪn'diːp] *adj* epidérmico, superficial; **beauty is only ~** la hermosura es cosa pasajera, la hermosura atañe a lo superficial.
skindiver ['skɪndaɪvəʳ] *n* buceador *m*, -ora *f*.
skindiving ['skɪn,daɪvɪŋ] *n* natación *f* submarina, exploración *f* submarina, pesca *f* submarina.
skinflick‡ ['skɪnflɪk] *n* película *f* porno*.
skinflint ['skɪnflɪnt] *n* tacaño *m*, cicatero *m*.
skinful* ['skɪnfʊl] *n*: **to have had a ~** llevar una copa de más, haber bebido más de la cuenta.
skin game ['skɪngeɪm] *n* (*US*) estafa *f*.

skin graft(ing) ['skɪn,grɑːft(ɪŋ)] *n* injerto *m* de piel.
skinhead ['skɪnhed] *n* (*Brit*) pelado *m*, cabeza rapada *m*.
-skinned [skɪnd] *adj ending in compounds* de piel ...; **dark~** de piel morena; **rough~** de piel áspera.
skinny ['skɪnɪ] *adj* flaco, magro, escuálido, descarnado.
skint‡ [skɪnt] *adj* (*Brit*): **to be ~** no tener ni un céntimo, estar pelado* (*LAm*).
skin-tight ['skɪntaɪt] *adj* muy ajustado, muy ceñido.
skip¹ [skɪp] **1** *n* brinco *m*, salto *m* (pequeño).
2 *vt passage* (*in reading etc*) omitir, pasar por alto; (*) *class, work* fumarse*; **to ~ lunch** saltarse el almuerzo, no almorzar; **~ it!*** ¡déjalo!, ¡no te preocupes más de eso!; **oh, ~ it!*** bueno, ¡no importa!
3 *vi* (**a**) brincar, saltar; (*with rope*) saltar a la comba; **to ~ with joy** brincar de alegría; **he ~ped out of the way** se apartó de un salto; **to ~ from one subject to another** saltar de un tema a otro; **the book ~s about a lot** el libro da muchos saltos; **to ~ over sth** saltar por encima de algo; (*omit*) omitir algo, pasar algo por alto.
(**b**) (*) largarse*, escabullirse; **we ~ped up to London yesterday** ayer fuimos en una escapadita a Londres.
skip² [skɪp] *n* (*cage*) jaula *f*; (*bucket*) cuba *f*; (*basket*) cesta *f*, canasta *f*; (*builder's*) contenedor *m* de escombros.
ski-pants ['skiː'pænts] *npl* pantalones *mpl* de esquí.
skipper ['skɪpəʳ] **1** *n* capitán *m* (*also Sport*); (*Naut*) patrón *m*; **well, you're the ~** bueno, tú eres el jefe. **2** *vt boat* patronear.
skipping ['skɪpɪŋ] *n* saltar *m* a la comba.
skipping-rope ['skɪpɪŋrəʊp] *n*, (*US*) **skip rope** ['skɪprəʊp] *n* comba *f*, cuerda *f* de saltar.
skirl [skɜːl] *n* (*Scot*): **the ~ of the pipes** el son de la gaita, la música de la gaita.
skirmish ['skɜːmɪʃ] **1** *n* escaramuza *f*; (*fig*) roce *m*; **to have a ~ with** (*fig*) tener un roce con. **2** *vi* escaramuzar.
skirmisher ['skɜːmɪʃəʳ] *n* escaramuzador *m*.
skirt [skɜːt] **1** *n* falda *f*, pollera *f* (*LAm*); (*of coat etc*) faldón *m*; (‡: *girl*) falda* *f*.
2 *attr*: **a ~ length** tela *f* suficiente para una falda.
3 *vt* (*surround*) ceñir, rodear; (*go round*) orillar, ladear, seguir el borde (*or* la orilla) de; (*avoid*) evitar entrar en, mantenerse a distancia de; **we ~ed Seville to the north** pasamos al norte de Sevilla.
4 *vi*: **to ~ round = 3.**
skirting(-board) ['skɜːtɪŋ(bɔːd)] *n* rodapié *m*, cenefa *f*.
ski-run ['skiːrʌn] *n*, **ski-slope** ['skiːsləʊp] pista *f* de esquí.
ski-suit ['skiːsuːt] *n* traje *m* de esquiar.
skit [skɪt] *n* sátira *f*, parodia *f* (*on* de); (*Theat*) número *m* corto satírico.
skitter ['skɪtəʳ] *vi*: **to ~ across the water/along the ground** (*bird*) volar rozando el agua/el suelo; (*stone*) saltar por encima del agua/por el suelo.
skittish ['skɪtɪʃ] *adj horse etc* nervioso, asustadizo; *playful* juguetón; *girl* coqueta; caprichoso.
skittishly ['skɪtɪʃlɪ] *adv* nerviosamente; de modo juguetón; con coquetería; caprichosamente.
skittle ['skɪtl] *n* bolo *m*; **~s** juego *m* de bolos, boliche *m*.
skittle alley ['skɪtl,ælɪ] *n* bolera *f*.
skive‡ [skaɪv] (*Brit*) **1** *n*: **to be on the ~, to have a good ~** gandulear, no hacer nada. **2** *vi* gandulear, no hacer nada.
◆skive off‡ *vi* (*Brit*) escabullirse, rajarse (*LAm*).
skiver‡ ['skaɪvəʳ] *n* (*Brit*) gandul *m*.
skivvy* ['skɪvɪ] *n* (*Brit*) fregona *f*.
skua ['skjuːə] *n* págalo *m*.
skulduggery* [skʌl'dʌgərɪ] *n* trampas *fpl*, embustes *mpl*; **piece of ~** trampa *f*, embuste *m*.
skulk [skʌlk] *vi* estar escondido, permanecer oculto; acechar sin ser visto, procurar no ser visto.
skull [skʌl] *n* calavera *f*; (*Anat*) cráneo *m*; **~ and crossbones** calavera *f*, bandera *f* negra (*de los piratas*).
skullcap ['skʌlkæp] *n* casquete *m*, solideo *m*.
skunk [skʌŋk] *n* (*Zool*) mofeta *f*; (*) canalla *m*; **you ~!** ¡canalla!
sky [skaɪ] *n* cielo *m*; **under blue skies** bajo un cielo azul; **the skies over England** el cielo sobre Inglaterra; **out of a clear blue ~** (*fig*) de repente, inesperadamente; **the ~'s the limit** no hay límite; **to praise sb to the skies** poner a uno por las nubes.
sky-blue ['skaɪ'bluː] **1** *n* azul *m* celeste. **2** *adj* azul celeste.
sky-dive ['skaɪdaɪv] **1** *n* caída *f* libre. **2** *vi* saltar en caída libre.
sky-diver ['skaɪdaɪvəʳ] *n* paracaidista *mf* de caída libre, paracaidista *m* acrobático, paracaidista *f* acrobática.
sky-diving ['skaɪdaɪvɪŋ] *n* caída *f* libre, paracaidismo *m* acrobático.
sky-high ['skaɪ'haɪ] *adv* hasta las nubes; por las nubes; **the smoke rose ~** el humo se elevaba hasta las nubes; **to blow sth ~** volar algo en mil pedazos; **to blow a theory ~** refutar completamente una teoría; **prices have gone ~** los precios se han puesto por las nubes.
skyjack* ['skaɪdʒæk] *vt plane* atracar, piratear.
skyjacking* ['skaɪdʒækɪŋ] *n* atraco *m* (aéreo), piratería *f* (aérea).
skylark ['skaɪlɑːk] **1** *n* alondra *f*. **2** (*) *vi* jaranear, juguetear.
skylarking* ['skaɪlɑːkɪŋ] *n* jarana *f*; bromas *fpl*; pelea *f* amistosa.
skylight ['skaɪlaɪt] *n* tragaluz *m*, claraboya *f*.
skyline ['skaɪlaɪn] *n* horizonte *m*, línea *f* del horizonte; (*of building*) silueta *f*, perfil *m*; (*of city*) perfil *m*.
skyrocket ['skaɪ,rɒkɪt] **1** *n* cohete *m*. **2** *vi* subir (como un cohete); (*fig, of price etc*) ponerse por las nubes, dispararse.
skyscraper ['skaɪ,skreɪpəʳ] *n* rascacielos *m*.
skytrain ['skaɪtreɪn] *n* puente *m* aéreo.
skyward(s) ['skaɪwəd(z)] *adv* hacia el cielo.
skyway ['skaɪweɪ] *n* ruta *f* aérea.
skywriting ['skaɪ,raɪtɪŋ] *n* escritura *f* aérea, publicidad *f* aérea.
SL *n abbr of* **source language** lenguaje *m* fuente.
slab [slæb] *n* bloque *m*; (*of wood etc*) plancha *f*, tabla *f*; (*of stone*) bloque *m*, (*flat*) losa *f*; (*of meat etc*) tajada *f* (gruesa); (*of cake*) porción *f* gruesa; (*of chocolate*) tableta *f*.
slack [slæk] **1** *adj* (**a**) (*not tight*) flojo; **~ tide, ~ water** repunte *m* de la marea.
(**b**) (*lax*) descuidado, negligente; (*lazy*) vago, perezoso; *student* desaplicado, inerte, poco serio; **to be ~** (*student etc*) gandulear, racanear*; **to be ~ about one's work** desatender su trabajo, ser negligente en su trabajo; **to be ~ about** (*or* **in**) **doing sth** dejar de hacer algo por desidia.
(**c**) (*inactive*) *demand* flojo; *market* flojo, encalmado; *period* de inactividad; *season* muerto; **business is ~** el mercado está flojo, hay poca actividad en el mercado.
2 *n* (**a**) (*part of rope etc*) lo flojo, parte *f* floja; **to take up the ~** quitar la parte floja, tensar la cuerda (*etc*); **to take up the ~ in the economy** utilizar toda la capacidad productiva de la economía.
(**b**) (*period*) período *m* de inactividad; (*season*) estación *f* muerta.
(**c**) (*Min*) cisco *m*.
(**d**) (*trousers*) **~s** pantalones *mpl* (flojos).
3 *vt* (**a**) = **slacken.**
(**b**) = **slake.**
4 *vi* gandulear, racanear*, flojear (*LAm*); **he's been ~ing** ha sido muy gandul.
slacken ['slækn] **1** *vt* (*also* **to ~ off**) aflojar; (*reduce*) disminuir; **to ~ speed** (*person*) aflojar el paso, ir más despacio, (*car etc*) disminuir la velocidad, moderar la marcha.
2 *vi* aflojarse; disminuir, reducirse; (*wind*) amainar; (*activity etc*) hacerse menos intenso; (*Comm*) aflojarse.
◆slacken off 1 *vi* dejar de trabajar (*etc*) tanto. **2** *vt* = **slacken 1.**
◆slacken up *vi* (*person*) aflojar el paso, ir más despacio.
slackening ['slæknɪŋ] *n* aflojamiento *m*; disminución *f*.
slacker ['slækəʳ] *n* vago *m*, -a *f*, gandul *m*, rácano* *m*.
slackly ['slæklɪ] *adv hang* flojamente, laxamente; (*fig*) *work* negligentemente.
slackness ['slæknɪs] *n* (*V adj*) (**a**) flojedad *f*, lo flojo; (**b**) descuido *m*, negligencia *f*; vaguedad *f*, pereza *f*; desaplicación *f*, inercia *f*, falta *f* de seriedad. (**c**) inactividad *f*; (*Comm*) flojedad *f*, inactividad *f*.
slag¹ [slæg] *n* (*of metal*) escoria *f*.
slag²‡ [slæg] *n* (*whore*) putilla‡ *f*.
slag³‡ [slæg] *vt* (*also* **to ~ off**: *criticize*) poner como un trapo*, dar una paliza a; (*get rid of*) deshacerse de.
slagheap ['slæghiːp] *n* escorial *m*, escombrera *f*.
slain [sleɪn] **1** *ptp of* **slay. 2** *npl*: **the ~** los muertos, los caídos.
slake [sleɪk] *vt lime, thirst* apagar; **~d lime** cal *f* muerta.
slalom ['slaləm] *n* eslálom *m*, eslalon *m*.
slam [slæm] **1** *n* (**a**) golpe *m*; (*of door*) portazo *m*; **to close the door with a ~** dar un portazo, cerrar la puerta ruidosamente.
(**b**) (*Cards*) bola *f*, capote *m*; slam *m*; **grand ~** gran slam *m*; **small ~** pequeño slam *m*.
2 (**a**) *vt* (*strike*) golpear; **to ~ the door** dar un portazo, cerrar la puerta ruidosamente (*V also* **door**); **he ~med the**

ball into the net disparó la pelota a la red; **Ruritania ~med in 5 goals*** Ruritania marcó 5 goles.

(**b**) (*: *defeat*) cascar*, dar una paliza a.

(**c**) (*: *criticize*) vapulear, dar una paliza a; condenar, criticar duramente.

(**d**) (‡) **to get ~med** (*drunk*) ajumarse*.

3 *vi* (*of door*) cerrarse de golpe; **the door ~med shut** la puerta se cerró de golpe.

◆**slam down** *vt* : **to ~ sth down on the table** arrojar algo violentamente sobre la mesa.

◆**slam on** *vt*: **she ~med the brakes on** frenó violentamente.

◆**slam to** *vi*: **the door ~med to** la puerta se cerró de golpe.

slammer‡ ['slæməʳ] *n* trena‡ *f*, talego‡ *m*.

slander ['slɑːndəʳ] **1** *n* calumnia *f*, difamación *f*; **to sue sb for ~** demandar a uno por calumnia.

2 *vt* calumniar, difamar; decir mal de, hablar mal de.

slanderer ['slɑːndərəʳ] *n* calumniador *m*, -ora *f*, defamador *m*, -ora *f*.

slanderous ['slɑːndərəs] *adj* calumnioso, difamatorio.

slanderously ['slɑːndərəslɪ] *adv* calumniosamente.

slang [slæŋ] **1** *n* argot *m*; (*of a group, trade etc*) jerga *f*; (*thieves' ~*) germanía *f*; (*gipsy ~*) caló *m*; **that word is ~** esa palabra es del argot; **to talk ~** hablar en argot.

2 *adj*: **~ word** palabra *f* del argot, palabra *f* argótica.

3 *vt* (*) (*insult*) llenar de insultos; (*criticize*) criticar duramente, poner como un trapo*, poner verde*.

slangily ['slæŋɪlɪ] *adv*: **to talk ~** hablar con mucho argot.

slanging-match* ['slæŋiŋ'mætʃ] *n* discusión *f* violenta.

slangy ['slæŋɪ] *adj person* que emplea mucho argot, que habla en argot; *style etc* lleno de argot.

slant [slɑːnt] **1** *n* (**a**) inclinación *f*, sesgo *m*; **to be on the ~** estar inclinado, estar sesgado; **the situation is taking on a new ~** la situación está tomando un nuevo giro.

(**b**) (*fig*) punto *m* de vista; modo *m* de ver una cosa, modo *m* de enfocar un problema; **what is your ~ on this?** ¿cuál es su punto de vista en esto?; **to get a ~ on a topic** pedir pareceres sobre un asunto.

2 *vt* inclinar, sesgar; **to ~ a report** escribir un informe parcial, escribir un informe desde un punto de vista particular.

3 *vi* inclinarse, sesgarse; **the light ~ed in at the window** la luz entraba oblicuamente por la ventana.

slant-eyed ['slɑːnt'aɪd] *adj* de ojos almendrados.

slanting ['slɑːntɪŋ] *adj* inclinado, oblicuo, sesgado.

slantwise ['slɑːntwaɪz] *adj* oblicuamente, al sesgo.

slap [slæp] **1** *n* palmada *f*, manotada *f*; **~ in the face** cachete *m*, bofetada *f*, (*fig*) palmetazo *m*, golpe *m* rudo, desaire *m*; **~ on the back** espaldarazo *m*; **they were having a bit of the old ~ and tickle*** los dos se estaban sobando; **to give sb a ~ on the wrist** (*fig*) dar un aviso a uno.

2 *interj* ¡zas!

3 *adv* de lleno, de plano; directamente; **it fell ~ in the middle** cayó en todo el medio, cayó en el mismo centro; **he ran ~ into a tree** dio de lleno contra un árbol.

4 *vt* (**a**) (*strike*) dar una palmada (*or* bofetada) a; pegar, golpear; **to ~ sb's face, to ~ sb on the face** dar una bofetada a uno, pegar un tortazo a uno; **to ~ sb on the back** dar un espaldarazo a uno; **to ~ one's knees** palmotearse las rodillas.

(**b**) (*place*) **he ~ped the book on the table** arrojó el libro en la mesa.

◆**slap down** *vt* : **to ~ sb down** derribar a uno de una bofetada; (*fig*) aplastar a uno, apabullar a uno.

◆**slap on** *vt* : **they've ~ped another storey on the house** han añadido un piso a la casa (como si tal cosa); **the judge ~ped £100 on the fine** el juez aumentó la multa en 100 libras; **~ a coat of paint on it** échale una mano de pintura.

slap-bang ['slæp'bæŋ] *adv* ruidosamente, violentamente; directamente, exactamente.

slapdash ['slæpdæʃ] *adj person* descuidado; despreocupado; *work* de brocha gorda, descuidado, chapucero.

slap-happy* ['slæp'hæpɪ] *adj* alegre y despreocupado; totalmente inconsciente.

slapstick ['slæpstɪk] *n* payasadas *fpl*; **~ comedy** comedia *f* de payasadas, comedia *f* de golpe y porrazo.

slap-up* ['slæpʌp] *adj* (*Brit*) muy pera*, de lujo, de primera; **~ meal** banquetazo* *m*, comilona* *f*; **it was ~** fue un banquetazo.

slash [slæʃ] **1** *n* (**a**) (*with knife*) cuchillada *f*; (*with whip*) latigazo *m*.

(**b**) (*US Typ*) barra *f* oblicua.

(**c**) (‡) **to go for a ~, to have a ~** cambiar el agua al canario‡.

2 *vt* (**a**) (*with knife etc*) acuchillar; rasgar; *tyre* rajar; (*Sew*) acuchillar; (*with whip*) azotar; **~ and burn agriculture** agricultura *f* de rozas y quema.

(**b**) (*reduce*) *price* machacar, quemar; *estimate etc* reducir radicalmente; *speech, text* abreviar sensiblemente.

(**c**) (*: *attack*) atacar, criticar severamente.

3 *vi*: **to ~ at sb** tirar tajos a uno, tratar de acuchillar a uno.

slashing ['slæʃɪŋ] *adj attack etc* fulminante.

slat [slæt] *n* tablilla *f*, hoja *f*, listón *m*; (*of blind*) lama *f*.

slate [sleɪt] **1** *n* (**a**) pizarra *f*; **put it on the ~*** (*Brit*) apúntalo en mi cuenta; **to start with a clean ~, to wipe the ~ clean** hacer borrón y cuenta nueva.

(**b**) (*US Pol*) lista *f* de candidatos.

2 *attr* de pizarra; color pizarra; **~ pencil** pizarrín *m*; **~ roof** empizarrado *m*.

3 *vt* (**a**) cubrir de pizarras.

(**b**) (*US*) anunciar; **it is ~d to start at 9** según el programa comienza a las 9, deberá comenzar a las 9.

(**c**) (*US Pol*) *candidate* nombrar.

(**d**) (*Brit**) vapulear, dar una paliza a.

slate-blue ['sleɪt'bluː] *adj* color azul pizarra.

slate-coloured, (*US*) **slate-colored** ['sleɪt,kʌləd] *adj* color pizarra.

slate-grey [,sleɪt'greɪ] **1** *adj* gris pizarra. **2** *n* gris *m* pizarra.

slate quarry ['sleɪt,kwɒrɪ] *n* pizarral *m*.

slater ['sleɪtəʳ] *n* pizarrero *m*.

slatted ['slætɪd] *adj* de tablillas, hecho de listones.

slattern ['slætən] *n* mujer *f* dejada, mujer *f* sucia, pazpuerca *f*.

slatternly ['slætənlɪ] *adj* sucio, puerco, desaseado.

slaty ['sleɪtɪ] *adj* (*of material*) parecido a pizarra, pizarroso; (*in colour*) color pizarra.

slaughter ['slɔːtəʳ] **1** *n* (*of animals*) matanza *f*, sacrificio *m*; (*of persons*) carnicería *f*, mortandad *f*; **the ~ on the roads** la carnicería en las carreteras; **the S~ of the Innocents** la Degollación de los Inocentes; **like a lamb to the ~** como borrego al matadero; **there was great ~** hubo gran mortandad.

2 *vt animals* matar, sacrificar, carnear (*LAm*); *persons* matar (brutalmente), hacer una carnicería de; (*: *Sport etc*) cascar*.

slaughterer ['slɔːtərəʳ] *n* jifero *m*, matarife *m*.

slaughterhouse ['slɔːtəhaʊs] *n*, *pl* **slaughterhouses** ['slɔːtəhaʊzɪz] matadero *m*.

slaughterman ['slɔːtəmən] *n*, *pl* **slaughtermen** ['slɔːtəmən] jifero *m*, matarife *m*.

Slav [slɑːv] **1** *adj* eslavo. **2** *n* eslavo *m*, -a *f*.

slave [sleɪv] **1** *n* esclavo *m*, -a *f*; **to be a ~ to tobacco** ser esclavo del tabaco; **to be a ~ to duty** ser esclavo del deber.

2 *attr*: **~ labour** (*work*) trabajo *m* de esclavos; (*persons*) esclavos *mpl*.

3 *vi* (*also* **to ~ away**) trabajar como un negro (*at* en), sudar tinta.

slavedriver ['sleɪv,draɪvəʳ] *n* negrero *m* (*also fig*).

slaver¹ ['sleɪvəʳ] *n* (*ship*) barco *m* negrero; (*person*) negrero *m*.

slaver² ['slævəʳ] **1** *n* baba *f*. **2** *vi* babear.

slavery ['sleɪvərɪ] *n* esclavitud *f*; **his ~ to tobacco** la esclavitud en que el tabaco le tiene; **to sell sb into ~** vender a uno como esclavo.

slave-trade ['sleɪvtreɪd] *n* comercio *m* de esclavos, tráfico *m* de esclavos.

slave-trader ['sleɪv,treɪdəʳ] *n* traficante *m* en esclavos; negrero *m*.

slavey* ['sleɪvɪ] *n* fregona *f*.

Slavic ['slævɪk] **1** *adj* eslavo. **2** *n* eslavo *m*.

slavish ['sleɪvɪʃ] *adj* servil.

slavishly ['sleɪvɪʃlɪ] *adv* servilmente.

slavishness ['sleɪvɪʃnɪs] *n* servilismo *m*.

Slavonic [slə'vɒnɪk] **1** *adj* eslavo. **2** *n* eslavo *m*.

slaw [slɔː] *n* (*US*) ensalada *f* de col.

slay [sleɪ] (*irr*: *pret* **slew**, *ptp* **slain**) *vt* (**a**) (*lit, hum*) matar, asesinar. (**b**) (*) hacer morir de risa*; **this will ~ you** esto os hará morir de risa*; **you ~ me!** (*iro*) ¡qué divertido!

slayer ['sleɪəʳ] *n* asesino *m*.

SLD *n* (*Brit*) *abbr of* **Social and Liberal Democratic (Party)**.

sleaze* [sliːz] *n*, **sleaziness*** ['sliːzɪnɪs] *n* desaseo *m*, desaliño *m*; sordidez *f*, asco *m*; mala fama *f*; **the ~ factor in**

these dealings la poca limpieza de estas operaciones (de la Bolsa *etc*).

sleazy* ['sli:zɪ] *adj person* desaseado, desaliñado; *place* sórdido, asqueroso; de mala fama; *deal etc* poco limpio, moralmente sospechoso.

sled [sled] (*esp US*), **sledge¹** [sledʒ] **1** *n* trineo *m*. **2** *vt* transportar por trineo, llevar en trineo. **3** *vi* ir en trineo.

sledge² [sledʒ] *n*, **sledgehammer** ['sledʒ,hæməʳ] *n* macho *m*, acotillo *m*, almádena *f*.

sleek [sli:k] **1** *adj* liso y brillante, lustroso; (*of general appearance*) pulcro, muy aseado; *boat, car* de líneas puras; *animal* gordo y de buen aspecto.

2 *vt* alisar, pulir.

◆**sleek down** *vt* : **to ~ one's hair down** alisar y arreglarse el pelo.

sleekly ['sli:klɪ] *adv smile, reply* zalameramente.

sleekness ['sli:knɪs] *n* lisura *f* y brillantez, lustre *m*; pulcritud *f*, aseo *m*; pureza *f* de líneas; gordura *f*.

sleep [sli:p] **1** *n* sueño *m*; **to drop off to ~, to go to ~** dormirse, quedarse dormido; **to go to ~** (*limb*) dormirse; **to have a ~** dormir, (*briefly*) descabezar un sueño; **to have a good night's ~** dormir bien durante la noche; **I shan't lose any ~ over it** eso no me hará desvelarme; **to put sb to ~** acostar a uno; dormir a uno, adormecer a uno; **to put an animal to ~** sacrificar un animal; **to send sb to ~** dormir a uno; **to sleep the ~ of the just** dormir con la conciencia tranquila; dormir a pierna suelta; **to walk in one's ~** ser sonámbulo, pasearse dormido; **she walked downstairs in her ~** estando dormida bajó la escalera.

2 (*irr: pret and ptp* **slept**) *vt* **we can ~ 4** tenemos camas para 4; **can you ~ all of us?** ¿hay camas para todos nosotros?

3 *vi* dormir; **to ~ like a log** (*or* **top**) dormir como un lirón; **to ~ heavily, to ~ soundly** dormir profundamente; **he was ~ing soundly** estaba profundamente dormido; **to ~ with sb** dormir con uno; **to get to ~** conciliar el sueño.

◆**sleep around*** *vi* dormir con todo el mundo, acostarse con cualquiera.

◆**sleep away** *vt* : **to ~ the hours away** pasar las horas durmiendo.

◆**sleep in** *vi* (**a**) (*late*) dormir tarde, seguir dormido. (**b**) (*in house*) dormir en casa.

◆**sleep off** *vt* : **to ~ it off, to ~ off a hangover** dormir la mona*, dormir la cruda* (*LAm*); **she's ~ing off the effects of the drug** duerme hasta que desaparezcan los efectos de la droga.

◆**sleep on 1** *vt*: **to ~ on a problem** consultar algo con la almohada. **2** *vi* = **sleep in** (**a**).

◆**sleep out** *vi* (*not at home*) dormir fuera de casa; (*in open air*) dormir al aire libre, pasar la noche al raso.

◆**sleep through 1** *vt*: **he slept through the alarm clock** no oyó el despertador.

2 *vi*: **I slept through till the afternoon** dormí hasta la tarde.

◆**sleep together** *vi* dormir juntos, acostarse juntos.

sleeper ['sli:pəʳ] *n* (**a**) (*person*) durmiente *mf*, persona *f* dormida; **to be a heavy ~** tener el sueño profundo; **to be a light ~** tener el sueño ligero.

(**b**) (*Brit Rail: tie*) traviesa *f*, durmiente *m;* (*coach*) coche-cama *m*.

(**b**) (*US: for baby*) pijama *m* de niño.

sleepily ['sli:pɪlɪ] *adv* soñolientamente; **she said ~** dijo soñolienta.

sleepiness ['sli:pɪnɪs] *n* somnolencia *f*; (*fig*) letargo *m*, carácter *m* soporífero.

sleeping ['sli:pɪŋ] **1** *adj* durmiente, dormido; *pill etc* para dormir; **S~ Beauty** la Bella Durmiente (del Bosque); **~ partner** (*Brit*) socio *m* comanditario, socia *f* comanditaria; **~ policeman** policía *m* muerto.

2 *n* sueño *m*, el dormir; **between ~ and waking** entre duerme y vela.

sleeping-bag ['sli:pɪŋbæg] *n* saco-manta *m*, saco *m* de dormir; (*baby's*) camiseta *f* de dormir.

sleeping-car ['sli:pɪŋkɑ:ʳ] *n* coche-cama *m*.

sleeping-draught ['sli:pɪŋdrɑ:ft] *n* soporífero *m*.

sleeping-pill ['sli:pɪŋpɪl] *n* comprimido *m* para dormir, somnífero *m*.

sleeping-quarters ['sli:pɪŋ,kwɔ:təz] *npl* dormitorio *m*; espacio *m* para dormir.

sleeping sickness ['sli:pɪŋ,sɪknɪs] *n* enfermedad *f* del sueño, encefalitis *f* letárgica.

sleeping-tablet ['sli:pɪŋ,tæblɪt] *n* comprimido *m* para dormir, somnífero *m*.

sleepless ['sli:plɪs] *adj person* insomne, desvelado; **to have a ~ night** pasar la noche en blanco.

sleeplessness ['sli:plɪsnɪs] *n* insomnio *m*.

sleep-talk ['sli:ptɔ:k] *vi* (*US*) hablar estando dormido.

sleepwalk ['sli:p,wɔ:k] *vi* ser sonámbulo, pasearse dormido.

sleepwalker ['sli:p,wɔ:kəʳ] *n* sonámbulo *m*, -a *f*.

sleepwalking ['sli:p,wɔ:kɪŋ] *n* sonambulismo *m*.

sleepwear ['sli:pwɛəʳ] *n* (*US*) ropa *f* de dormir.

sleepy ['sli:pɪ] *adj person, voice etc* soñoliento; *place* soporífero; *pear* pasado, fofo; **to be ~** (*person*) tener sueño; **to feel ~** sentirse con sueño; **I feel very ~ at midnight** a medianoche empiezo a tener mucho sueño.

sleepyhead ['sli:pɪhed] *n* dormilón *m*, -ona *f*.

sleet [sli:t] **1** *n* aguanieve *f*. **2** *vi*: **it was ~ing** caía aguanieve.

sleeve [sli:v] *n* (*of dress*) manga *f*; (*of record*) portada *f*, funda *f*; (*Mech*) manguito *m*, enchufe *m*; **to have sth up one's ~** guardar una carta en la manga, tener algo en reserva; **to laugh up one's ~** reírse para su capote; **to roll up one's ~s** arremangarse.

sleeved [sli:vd] *adj* con mangas.

-sleeved [sli:vd] *adj ending in compounds* con mangas ..., *eg* **long~** con mangas largas.

sleeveless ['sli:vlɪs] *adj* sin mangas.

sleigh [sleɪ] **1** *n, vti* = **sled. 2** *attr*: **~ bell** cascabel *m*; **to go for a ~ ride** ir a pasear en trineo.

sleight [slaɪt] *n*: **~ of hand** escamoteo *m*, prestidigitación *f*; destreza *f*; **by ~ of hand** con maña, mañosamente.

slender ['slendəʳ] *adj* (*not thick*) delgado, tenue; fino; *hand, waist etc* delgado; *figure* esbelto; *resources etc* escaso, limitado, reducido; *chance* pequeño, escaso; *hope* remoto; *excuse* poco convincente.

slenderize ['slendəraɪz] *vt* (*US*) adelgazar.

slenderly ['slendəlɪ] *adv*: **~ built** (*person*) delgado; de talle esbelto; **~ made** de construcción delicada.

slenderness ['slendənɪs] *n* delgadez *f*, tenuidad *f*; esbeltez *f*; escasez *f*, lo limitado; lo remoto.

slept [slept] *pret and ptp of* **sleep**.

sleuth [slu:θ] *n* detective *m*, sabueso *m*.

slew¹ [slu:] **1** *vt* (*also* **to ~ round**) torcer; girar; **to ~ sth to the left** torcer algo a la izquierda; girar algo a la izquierda; **to be ~ed‡** estar ajumado*. **2** *vi* (*also* **to ~ round**) torcerse.

slew² [slu:] *pret of* **slay**.

slew³* [slu:] *n* (*US*) montón* *m*.

slice [slaɪs] **1** *n* (**a**) (*of meat etc*) tajada *f*, lonja *f*; (*of sausage*) raja *f*; (*of bread*) rebanada *f*, trozo *m*; (*of lemon, cucumber etc*) rodaja *f*.

(**b**) (*fig: portion*) parte *f*, porción *f*; **a ~ of life** un trozo de la vida tal como es; **it took quite a ~ of our profits** nos quitó una buena parte de nuestras ganancias; **it affects a large ~ of the population** afecta a buena parte de la población.

(**c**) (*tool*) estrelladera *f*, pala *f*.

(**d**) (*Golf*) golpe *m* con efecto a la derecha.

2 *vt* (**a**) cortar, tajar; cortar en rodajas; *bread* rebanar; **to ~ sth in two** cortar algo en dos.

(**b**) *ball* cortar, torcer, dar efecto a; (*Golf*) golpear oblicuamente (a derecha).

◆**slice off** *vt* cercenar.

◆**slice through** *vt rope* cortar; (*fig*) *restrictions etc* pasarse por encima; **to ~ through the air/the waves** cortar el aire/las olas.

◆**slice up** *vt* cortar en rebanadas.

sliced [slaɪst] *adj bread* rebanado, en rebanadas; **it's the best thing since ~ bread** (*hum*) es un magnífico parto del ingenio humano; **~ lemon** limón *m* en rodajas.

slicer ['slaɪsəʳ] *n* rebanadora *f*, máquina *f* de cortar.

slick [slɪk] **1** *adj* (*skilful*) hábil, diestro; (*quick*) rápido; (*pej*) *person* astuto, mañoso; **he's the ~ sort** es un astuto; **he's too ~ for me** es demasiado hábil para mi gusto; **be ~ about it!** ¡date prisa!

2 *n* (*of oil etc*) masa *f* flotante, mancha *f*, capa *f* (en el agua).

3 *vt* = **sleek 2.**

slicker ['slɪkəʳ] *n* embaucador *m*, tramposo *m*; **city ~*** capitalino* *m*.

slickly ['slɪklɪ] *adv* hábilmente, diestramente; rápidamente; astutamente, mañosamente.

slickness ['slɪknɪs] *n* habilidad *f*, destreza *f*; rapidez *f*; maña *f*.

slid [slɪd] *pret and ptp of* **slide**.

slide [slaɪd] **1** *n* (**a**) (*place: on ice, mud etc*) resbaladero *m*; (*for logs etc*) deslizadero *m*; (*in playground, swimming pool*) tobogán *m*.

(**b**) (*Tech: part*) corredera *f*, cursor *m*; (*for hair*) pasador *m*; (*Mus*) vara *f*, corredera *f*.
(**c**) (*microscope* ~) platina *f*, portaobjeto *m*; (*Phot*) diapositiva *f*, filmina *f*; **a lecture with ~s** una conferencia con diapositivas, una conferencia con proyecciones.
(**d**) (*act*) resbalón *m*; (*of land*) desprendimiento *m*; **the ~ in share prices** la baja de las cotizaciones; **the ~ in temperature** el descenso de la temperatura.
2 (*irr: pret and ptp* **slid**) *vt* correr, pasar, deslizar; **to ~ furniture across the floor** deslizar un mueble sobre el suelo; **~ the top on when you've finished** pon la tapa cuando termines.
3 *vi* (*slip*) resbalar; (*glide*) deslizarse; **they were sliding across the floor** se deslizaban sobre el suelo; **it ought to ~ gently into place** debiera correr suavemente a su lugar; **to ~ into a habit** caer en un hábito (sin darse cuenta); **to let things ~** no ocuparse de las cosas, no prestar atención a lo que pasa, dejar rodar la bola; **these last months he's let everything ~** estos últimos meses se ha desatendido de todo.
◆**slide down** *vt*: **to ~ down the banisters** bajar deslizándose por la barandilla; **the ring ~s down this rope** el anillo corre por esta cuerda.
◆**slide off** *vi top, lid etc* resbalar.
slideholder ['slaɪd,həʊldəʳ] *n* portadiapositiva *m*.
slide-magazine ['slaɪd,mægə,ziːn] *n* cartucho *m* (*or* guía *f*) para diapositivas.
slide-projector ['slaɪdprə,dʒektəʳ] *n* proyector *m* de diapositivas.
sliderule ['slaɪdruːl] *n* regla *f* de cálculo.
sliding ['slaɪdɪŋ] *adj part* corredizo; **~ door** puerta *f* deslizante, puerta *f* de corredera; **~ roof** techo *m* corredizo, techo *m* de corredera; **~ scale** escala *f* móvil; **~ seat** bancada *f* corrediza.
slight [slaɪt] **1** *adj* (**a**) *figure* delgado, fino; *stature* pequeño, bajo; (*of weak appearance*) débil, frágil, delicado.
(**b**) (*trivial*) leve; insignificante, de poca importancia; (*small*) leve; pequeño, escaso; **a ~ pain in the arm** un leve dolor de brazo; **the wound is only ~** la herida es más bien leve, la herida no es de consideración; **of ~ importance** de escasa importancia; **a ~ improvement** una pequeña mejora; **of ~ intelligence** de escasa inteligencia; **to a ~ extent** en un grado pequeño; **he showed some ~ optimism** mostró cierto optimismo; **the future does not justify the ~est optimism** el futuro no autoriza el más leve optimismo; **there's not the ~est possibility of that** de eso no existe la más remota posibilidad; **not in the ~est** en absoluto, ni en lo más mínimo.
2 *n* desaire *m*, insulto *m* (*on* a, para).
3 *vt* desairar, ofender, insultar.
slighting ['slaɪtɪŋ] *adj* despreciativo, menospreciativo, despectivo.
slightingly ['slaɪtɪŋlɪ] *adv* con desprecio, despectivamente.
slightly ['slaɪtlɪ] *adv* un poco; **yes, ~** sí, un poco; **~ better** un poco mejor; **~ built** de talle delgado, menudo; **to know sb ~** conocer a uno ligeramente, conocer a uno un poco.
slightness ['slaɪtnɪs] *n* (**a**) (*of size etc*) delgadez *f*, finura *f*; pequeñez *f*; fragilidad *f*. (**b**) (*of importance etc*) insignificancia *f*, poca importancia *f*.
slim [slɪm] **1** *adj* (**a**) (*of figure*) delgado, esbelto; **to get ~** adelgazar.
(**b**) *resources etc* escaso, insuficiente; **his chances are pretty ~** sus posibilidades son escasas.
2 *vt* adelgazar.
3 *vi* adelgazar.
◆**slim down 1** *vt* (**a**) = **slim 2.**
(**b**) (*fig*) **~med down** *business, industry* reconvertido, saneado.
2 *vi* bajar de peso, adelgazar.
slime [slaɪm] *n* limo *m*, légamo *m*, cieno *m*; (*of snail*) baba *f*; (*fig*) lodo *m*.
sliminess ['slaɪmɪnɪs] *n* (**a**) (*lit*) lo limoso; lo baboso; viscosidad *f*. (**b**) (*of person*) lo rastrero; zalamería *f*.
slimline ['slɪm,laɪn] *adj*: **~ food** alimento *m* reductivo, alimento *m* que no engorda.
slimmer ['slɪməʳ] *n* persona *f* que está a dieta.
slimming ['slɪmɪŋ] **1** *n* adelgazamiento *m*. **2** *attr* reductivo; **to be on a ~ diet** seguir un régimen para adelgazar, estar a dieta; **to eat only ~ foods** comer solamente cosas que no engordan.
slimness ['slɪmnɪs] *n* delgadez *f*.
slimy ['slaɪmɪ] *adj* (**a**) limoso, legamoso; *snail* baboso; viscoso. (**b**) *person* rastrero; zalamero; odioso.
sling [slɪŋ] **1** *n* (*weapon*) honda *f*; (*Med*) cabestrillo *m*; (*for rifle etc*) portafusil *m*; (*Naut*) eslinga *f*; (*toy*) tirador *m*; **to have one's arm in a ~** llevar el brazo en cabestrillo.
2 *vt* (*irr: pret and ptp* **slung**) (**a**) (*throw*) lanzar, tirar, arrojar.
(**b**) (*hang*) colgar, suspender; alzar; (*Naut*) eslingar; **with a rifle slung across his shoulder** con un fusil en bandolera.
◆**sling away*** *vt*: **to ~ sth away** tirar algo.
◆**sling out*** *vt object* tirar, botar*; *person* echar, botar, expulsar.
◆**sling over*** *vt* : **to ~ sth over to sb** tirar algo a uno, pasar algo a uno.
slingshot ['slɪŋʃɒt] *n* (*weapon*) honda *f*, tirador *m*; (*US*) tirador *m*, tirachinas *m*, (*shot*) hondazo *m*.
slink [slɪŋk] (*irr: pret and ptp* **slunk**) *vi*: **to ~ along** andar furtivamente; **to ~ away, to ~ off** largarse*, escabullirse, irse cabizbajo.
slinky* ['slɪŋkɪ] *adj* seductor, provocativo; *walk etc* sinuoso, ondulante.
slip[1] [slɪp] **1** *n* (**a**) (*slide*) resbalón *m*; (*trip*) traspié *m*, tropezón *m*; (*of earth*) desprendimiento *m* (de tierras).
(**b**) (*mistake*) falta *f*, error *m*, equivocación *f*; (*moral*) desliz *m*; (*by neglect*) descuido *m*; **~ of the pen** lapsus *m* calami; **~ of the tongue** lapsus *m* linguae; **it was a bad ~** fue una grave equivocación; **there's many a ~ 'twixt cup and lip** de la mano a la boca desaparece la sopa.
(**c**) (*pillow~*) funda *f*; (*undergarment*) combinación *f*; (*gym~ etc*) túnica *f*.
(**d**) (*Naut*) **~s** grada *f*, gradas *fpl*.
(**e**) **to give sb the ~** dar esquinazo a uno, zafarse de uno.
2 *vt* (**a**) (*slide*) deslizar; **to ~ a coin into a slot** introducir una moneda en una ranura; **~ that nut on here** pon esa tuerca aquí; **to ~ sth across to sb** pasar algo (furtivamente) a uno; **would you ~ the salt across, please?** ¿me das la sal, por favor?; **to ~ an arm round sb's waist** pasar el brazo por la cintura de una; **to ~ sb a fiver** pasar a uno un billete de 5 libras (como propina o para comprar su ayuda).
(**b**) (*escape from*) eludir, escaparse de; **to ~ a disc** dislocarse una vértebra; **to ~ a cable** soltar una amarra; **the dog ~ped its chain** el perro soltó la cadena; **it ~ped my memory** se me olvidó, se me fue de la cabeza; **to ~ sb's notice** no ser advertido por uno, pasar inadvertido ante uno.
3 *vi* (**a**) (*glide*) deslizarse (*along* por, sobre); (*stumble*) tropezar, resbalar; (*of bone etc*) dislocarse; (*of earth*) caer, correrse; **I ~ped on the ice** resbalé en el hielo; **my foot ~ed** se me fue el pie; **it ~s easily along the wire** se desliza suavemente por el hilo; **the knot has ~ped** el nudo se ha desatado; **it ~ped from her hand** se le escapó de entre las manos; **the clutch ~s** el embrague patina.
(**b**) (*move quickly*) ir (rápidamente); **I'll ~ round to the shop** voy a la tienda en una escapadita; **to ~ into bed** meterse en la cama; **she ~ped into the room** se caló dentro del cuarto, se introdujo (sin llamar la atención) en el cuarto; **to ~ into a dress** ponerse un vestido; **the motorcycle ~s through the traffic** la moto se cuela por entre la circulación.
(**c**) (*with* let) **to let it ~ that ...** revelar inadvertidamente que ...; **he let a secret ~** se le escapó un secreto; **to let a chance ~** perder una oportunidad, no aprovechar una oportunidad.
(**d**) (*decline*) declinar, decaer; **you're ~ping** no eres lo que eras antes; se te nota un ir a menos.
◆**slip away** *vi* marcharse desapercibido, irse sin ser notado; (*pej*) largarse*, escabullirse; **time is ~ping away** se nos escapa el tiempo, el tiempo corre; **her life was ~ping away** se le estaba acabando la vida.
◆**slip back** *vi* regresar con sigilo.
◆**slip by** *vi* pasar inadvertido.
◆**slip down** *vi object, car* resbalar pendiente abajo; *person* resbalar; **I'll just ~ down and get it** bajo un momento y lo traigo.
◆**slip in 1** *vt* deslizar, introducir suavemente (*or* sin ruido *etc*); *comment, word* insinuar.
2 *vi* entrar desapercibido; colarse dentro.
◆**slip off 1** *vt dress* quitarse; *cover, lid* quitar.
2 *vi* (**a**) = **slip away.**
(**b**) (*cover, lid*) quitarse, deslizarse.
◆**slip on** *vt dress, ring etc* ponerse; *cover, lid* poner.
◆**slip out** *vi* (*person*) salir un instante; salir en una escapada; **the name ~ped out** se me escapó el nombre, dije el nombre sin querer; **to ~ out of a dress** quitarse un

vestido.

◆**slip over** 1 *vt*: to ~ one over on sb* jugar una mala pasada a uno; ganar por la mano a uno; encajar algo a uno.
 2 *vi* = slip up (a).

◆**slip past** *vi* pasar desapercibido.

◆**slip up** *vi* (a) resbalar, tropezar.
 (b) (*fig*: *make mistake*) equivocarse; cometer un desliz; meter la pata*.

slip² [slɪp] *n* estaca *f*, plantón *m*; ~ of paper papeleta *f*, papelito *m*; (*in filing system etc*) ficha *f*; (*packer's*) hoja *f* de embalaje, hoja *f* de control; a ~ of a girl una jovenzuela, una chicuela.

slipcase ['slɪpkeɪs] *n* estuche *m*.

slipcovers ['slɪpˌkʌvəz] *npl* (*US*) fundas *fpl* que se pueden quitar.

slipknot ['slɪpnɒt] *n* nudo *m* corredizo.

slip-on ['slɪpɒn] *adj* que se pone por la cabeza; de quitaipón; ~ shoes zapatos *mpl* sin cordón.

slipover ['slɪpəʊvəʳ] *n* pullover *m* sin mangas.

slippage ['slɪpɪdʒ] *n* (*slip*) deslizamiento *m*; (*loss*) pérdida *f*; (*shortage*) déficit *m*; (*delay*) retraso *m*.

slipped [slɪpt] *adj*: ~ disc hernia *f* discal, vértebra *f* dislocada.

slipper ['slɪpəʳ] *n* zapatilla *f*; babucha *f*, pantufla (*LAm*), chancla *f* (*Mex*).

slippery ['slɪpərɪ] *adj* (a) *surface* resbaladizo; *skin etc* viscoso; to be on a ~ slope (*fig*) estar en terreno resbaladizo.
 (b) *person* astuto, escurridizo, evasivo, (*pej*) escurridizo, nada confiable; he's as ~ as they come (*or* as an eel) tiene más conchas que un galápago.

slippy* ['slɪpɪ] *adv* (*Brit*): to be ~, to look ~ about it darse prisa, menearse; look ~! ¡menearse!; we shall have to look ~ tendremos que darnos prisa.

slip-road ['slɪprəʊd] *n* (*Brit*) carretera *f* de acceso.

slipshod ['slɪpʃɒd] *adj* descuidado, poco correcto.

slipstream ['slɪpstriːm] *n* viento *m* de la hélice, estela *f*.

slip-up ['slɪpʌp] *n* (*mistake*) falta *f*, error *m*, equivocación *f*; metedura *f* de pata*; (*moral*) desliz *m*; (*by neglect*) descuido *m*.

slipway ['slɪpweɪ] *n* grada *f*, gradas *fpl*.

slit [slɪt] 1 *n* hendedura *f*, raja *f*; resquicio *m*; corte *m* largo; to make a ~ in sth hacer un corte en algo.
 2 (*irr*: *pret and ptp* slit) *vt* hender, rajar; cortar; to ~ a sack open abrir un saco con un cuchillo (*etc*); to ~ sb's throat degollar a uno.

slit-eyed [ˌslɪt'aɪd] *adj* de ojos rasgados.

slither ['slɪðəʳ] *vi* deslizarse (*down a rope* por una cuerda); ir rodando (*down a slope* por una pendiente); to ~ about on ice ir resbalando sobre el hielo.

sliver ['slɪvəʳ] *n* raja *f*; (*of wood etc*) astilla *f*.

Sloane Ranger* ['sləʊn'reɪndʒəʳ] *n* señorito *m* (londinense), niño *m* bien* (londinense), niña *f* bien.

slob* [slɒb] *n* haragán *m*, -ana *f*, gandul *m*, gandula *f*; you ~! ¡patán!

slobber ['slɒbəʳ] 1 *n* baba *f*.
 2 *vi* babear; to ~ over besuquear; (*fig*) caerse la baba por; tratar con mucha sensiblería, entusiasmarse tontamente por.

slobbery ['slɒbərɪ] *adj kiss* mojado, baboso; *person* sensiblero, tontamente sentimental.

sloe [sləʊ] 1 *n* (*fruit*) endrina *f*; (*tree*) endrino *m*. 2 *attr*: ~ gin licor *m* de endrinas.

slog [slɒg] 1 *n*: it was a ~ me costó trabajo; it's a hard ~ to the top cuesta mucho trabajo llegar a la cumbre.
 2 *vt ball* golpear (sin arte).
 3 *vi* (a) (*work etc*) afanarse, sudar tinta.
 (b) (*walk etc*) caminar penosamente.

◆**slog along** *vi* = slog on.

◆**slog away** *vi* : to ~ away at sth afanarse por hacer algo, trabajar como un negro para terminar algo.

◆**slog on** *vi*: we ~ged on for 8 kilometres caminamos con dificultad 8 kilómetros más.

◆**slog out** *vt*: to ~ it out (*fighting*) luchar hasta el fin, seguir luchando; (*arguing*) discutir sin ceder terreno; (*working etc*) aguantarlo todo, no cejar.

slogan ['sləʊgən] *n* slogan *m*, eslogan *m*; (*graffiti*) pintada *f*.

slogger ['slɒgəʳ] *n* trabajador *m*, -ora *f*.

sloop [sluːp] *n* balandra *f*; corbeta *f*.

slop [slɒp] 1 *npl*: ~s (*food*) gachas *fpl*; (*of wine*) heces *fpl*; (*waste*) agua *f* sucia, lavazas *fpl*.
 2 *vt* derramar, verter.
 3 *vi* (*also* to ~ over) derramarse; desbordarse.

◆**slop about** *vi*: to ~ about in the mud chapotear en el lodo; the water was ~ping about in the bucket el agua chapoteaba en el cubo.

◆**slop over** *vi* = slop 3.

slop-basin ['slɒpˌbeɪsn] *n* recipiente *m* para agua sucia; (*at table*) taza *f* para los posos del té.

slope [sləʊp] 1 *n* inclinación *f*; (*up*) cuesta *f*, pendiente *f*; (*down*) declive *m*; (*of hill*) falda *f*; vertiente *f*, ladera *f*; the ~s of Mulacén las laderas de Mulacén; the southern ~ of the Guadarrama la vertiente sur del Guadarrama; the car got stuck on a ~ el coche se quedó parado en una cuesta; there is a ~ down to the town la tierra está en declive hacia la ciudad.
 2 *vt* inclinar; sesgar; ~ arms! ¡armas al hombro!
 3 *vi* inclinarse, estar inclinado; declinar, estar en declive; to ~ forwards estar inclinado hacia delante.

◆**slope away, slope down** *vi* estar en declive; the garden ~s down to the sea el jardín baja hacia el mar.

◆**slope off*** *vi* largarse*.

◆**slope up** *vi* estar en pendiente, subir, ascender.

sloping ['sləʊpɪŋ] *adj* inclinado; (*up*) en pendiente, (*down*) en declive.

slop-pail ['slɒppeɪl] *n* cubeta *f* para agua sucia.

sloppily ['slɒpɪlɪ] *adv* (a) (*carelessly*) descuidadamente, de modo poco sistemático; to dress ~ vestir con poca elegancia. (b) (*sentimentally*) de modo sentimental, con sensiblería.

sloppiness ['slɒpɪnɪs] *n* (a) (*carelessness*) descuido *m*, lo descuidado, falta *f* de sistema; desaseo *m*. (b) (*sentimentality*) sentimentalismo *m*, sensiblería *f*.

sloppy ['slɒpɪ] *adj* (a) (*in consistency*) poco sólido, casi líquido; *road etc* lleno de charcos, lleno de barro; (*wet*) mojado. (b) *work etc* descuidado, poco sistemático; *thought* poco riguroso; mal presentado; *dress* desgalichado; *appearance* desaseado. (c) (*sentimental*) sentimental, sensiblero.

slop shop ['slɒpʃɒp] *n* (*US**) bazar *m* de ropa barata, tienda *f* de pacotilla.

slosh* [slɒʃ] *vt* (*esp Brit*) *person* pegar; to ~ some water over sth echar agua sobre algo.

◆**slosh about, slosh around** *vi*: to ~ about in the puddles chapotear en los charcos; the water was ~ing about in the pail el agua chapoteaba en el cubo.

sloshed* [slɒʃt] *adj* (*esp Brit*): to be ~ estar ajumado*; to get ~ ajumarse*, agarrar una trompa*.

slot [slɒt] 1 *n* (a) muesca *f*, ranura *f*; to put a coin in the ~ meter una moneda en la ranura.
 (b) (*job* ~) vacante *f*; (*in programme etc*) espacio *m*; lugar *m*; (*advertising* ~) cuña *f* (publicitaria).
 (c) (*for aircraft*) espacio *m*.
 2 *vt*: to ~ a part into another part encajar una pieza en (la ranura de) otra pieza; to ~ sth into place colocar algo en su lugar; we can ~ you into the programme te podemos dar un espacio en el programa, te podemos incluir en el programa.

◆**slot in** *vi* : it ~s in here entra en esta ranura, encaja aquí.

sloth [sləʊθ] *n* (a) (*idleness*) pereza *f*, indolencia *f*, desidia *f*. (b) (*Zool*) perezoso *m*.

slothful ['sləʊθfʊl] *adj* perezoso.

slot-machine ['slɒtməˌʃiːn] *n* (*Comm*) aparato *m* vendedor automático; (*in fun fair etc*) tragaperras *m*.

slouch [slaʊtʃ] 1 *n* (a) to walk with a ~ andar con un aire gacho, caminar arrastrando los pies.
 (b) he's no ~* (*in skill*) no es ningún principiante, (*at work*) no es ningún vago; he's no ~ in the kitchen tiene buena mano para cocina.
 2 *adj*: ~ hat sombrero *m* flexible.
 3 *vi* andar con un aire gacho, caminar con los hombros caídos; to sit ~ed in a chair repanchigarse en un sillón; he was ~ed over his desk estaba inclinado sobre su mesa de trabajo en postura desgarbada.

◆**slouch about, slouch around** *vi* (a) andar con un aire gacho, caminar arrastrando los pies; andar de un lado para otro (sin saber qué hacer). (b) (*fig*) gandulear, golfear.

◆**slouch along** *vi* = slouch about, slouch around (a).

◆**slouch off** *vi* irse cabizbajo, alejarse con un aire gacho.

slough¹ [slaʊ] *n* fangal *m*, cenegal *m*; (*fig*) abismo *m*; the ~ of despond el abatimiento más profundo, el abismo de la desesperación.

slough² [slʌf] 1 *n* (*Zool*) camisa *f*, piel *f* vieja (que muda la serpiente); (*Med*) escara *f*.
 2 *vt* mudar, echar de sí; (*fig*) deshacerse de, desechar.
 3 *vi* desprenderse, caerse.

◆**slough off** **1** *vt* mudar, echar de sí; (*fig*) deshacerse de, desechar. **2** *vi* = **slough² 3.**
Slovak ['sləʊvæk] **1** *adj* eslovaco. **2** *n* eslovaco *m*, -a *f*.
Slovakia [sləʊ'vækɪə] *n* Eslovaquia *f*.
Slovakian [sləʊ'vækɪən] *adj* eslovaco.
sloven ['slʌvn] *n* (*in appearance*) persona *f* desgarbada, persona *f* desaseada; (*at work*) vago *m*, -a *f*.
Slovene ['sləʊviːn] **1** *adj* esloveno. **2** *n* esloveno *m*, -a *f*.
Slovenia [sləʊ'viːnɪə] *n* Eslovenia *f*.
slovenliness ['slʌvnlɪnɪs] *n* desaseo *m*; despreocupación *f*, dejadez *f*; descuido *m*, chapucería *f*.
slovenly ['slʌvnlɪ] *adj appearance* desgarbado, desaseado; *person* despreocupado, dejado, descuidado; *work* descuidado, chapucero.
slow [sləʊ] **1** *adj* (**a**) *person, progress, vehicle etc* lento; pausado; ~ **fuse** espoleta *f* retardada; ~ **lane** (*Brit Aut*) carril *m* de la izquierda, (*most countries*) carril *m* de la derecha; carril *m* de los lentos; ~ **match** mecha *f* tardía; ~ **train** (*Brit*) tren *m* correo, tren *m* ómnibus; ~ **but sure**! ¡despacio pero seguro!; **it's ~ work** es (un) trabajo lento; **he's a ~ worker** trabaja despacio; **this car is ~er than my old one** este coche anda menos que el que tenía antes; **business is very ~** el negocio está muy flojo; **life here is ~** aquí se vive a un ritmo lento.
(**b**) (*not prompt*) **to be ~ to do sth** tardar en hacer algo; **they were ~ to act** tardaron en obrar; **he was not ~ to notice that ...** no tardó en observar que ...; **to be ~ to anger** ser ecuánime, tener mucho aguante; **to be ~ to pay** ser moroso.
(**c**) *clock* atrasado; **my watch is ~** mi reloj (se) atrasa; **my watch is 20 minutes ~** mi reloj (se) atrasa 20 minutos, mi reloj lleva 20 minutos de atraso.
(**d**) *character* (*phlegmatic*) flemático, cachazudo; (*stupid*) torpe, lerdo.
(**e**) (*boring*) aburrido; **the game is very ~** el partido es la mar de aburrido.
(**f**) *surface, pitch* pesado.
2 *adv* despacio, lentamente; **to go ~** ir despacio, (*in industrial dispute*) trabajar a ritmo lento, trabajar al mínimo legal.
3 *vt* (*also* **to ~ down, to ~ up**) retardar; *engine, machine* reducir la velocidad de, moderar la marcha de; *economy etc* ralentizar; *development* retardar; **that car ~s up the traffic** ese coche entorpece la circulación.
4 *vi* (*also* **to ~ down, to ~ up**) ir más despacio; (*in walking etc*) aflojar el paso; (*Aut*) moderar la marcha, desacelerar, reducir la velocidad; (*economy etc*) ralentizarse; **'S~ down'** (*road sign*) 'Disminuir velocidad'; **the car ~ed to a stop** el coche moderó su marcha y paró; **production has ~ed to almost nothing** la producción se ha reducido casi a cero.
◆**slow down** *vt, vi* = **slow 3, 4.**
◆**slow up** *vt, vi* = **slow 3, 4.**
slow-burning ['sləʊ'bɜːnɪŋ] *adj* que se quema lentamente; ~ **fuse** espoleta *f* retardada.
slowcoach* ['sləʊkəʊtʃ] *n* (*Brit*) (*idler*) perezoso *m*, -a *f*, vago *m*, -a *f*; (*stupid person*) torpe *mf*.
slow cooker ['sləʊ,kʊkəʳ] *n* bote *m* eléctrico de cocción lenta.
slowdown ['sləʊdaʊn] *n* (*US: strike*) huelga *f* de manos caídas; = **slowing-down.**
slowing-down ['sləʊɪŋ'daʊn] *n* disminución *f* de velocidad; retardación *f*; (*of economy etc*) ralentización *f*.
slowly ['sləʊlɪ] *adv* despacio, lentamente; poco a poco; ~ **but surely** lenta pero seguramente.
slow-mo*, slomo* ['sləʊ,məʊ] *adj, n* = **slow-motion.**
slow-motion ['sləʊ'məʊʃən] **1** *adj*: ~ **film** película *f* a cámara lenta. **2** *n*: **to show a film in ~** pasar una película a cámara lenta, pasar una película ralentizada.
slow-moving [,sləʊ'muːvɪŋ] *adj* lento; de acción lenta; de movimiento pesado.
slowness ['sləʊnɪs] *n* (V *adj*) (**a**) lentitud *f*. (**b**) flema *f*; torpeza *f*; aburrimiento *m*. (**c**) pesadez *f*.
slowpoke* ['sləʊ,pəʊk] *n* (*US*) = **slowcoach.**
slow-witted ['sləʊ'wɪtɪd] *adj* torpe, lerdo.
slowworm ['sləʊwɜːm] *n* lución *m*.
sludge [slʌdʒ] *n* (*mud*) lodo *m*, fango *m*; (*sediment*) sedimento *m* fangoso; (*sewage*) aguas *fpl* de albañal.
slue [sluː] *vti* (*US*) = **slew¹, slew³.**
slug¹ [slʌg] *n* (*Zool*) babosa *f*; (*bullet*) posta *f*; (*Typ*) lingote *m*; (*US: for slot-machine*) ficha *f*; (*US**: *of drink*) trago *m*.
slug²* [slʌg] *vt* pegar, aporrear.
◆**slug out** *vt* : **to ~ it out** (**with sb**) pegarse, aporrearse; resolver un asunto con los puños.
sluggard ['slʌgəd] *n* haragán *m*, -ana *f*.
sluggish ['slʌgɪʃ] *adj* (*indolent*) perezoso; (*slow-moving*) lento; *animal etc* inactivo, inerte, perezoso; *business, market* flojo; *person's temperament* flemático, cachazudo.
sluggishly ['slʌgɪʃlɪ] *adv* perezosamente; lentamente; inactivamente; flojamente; con flema.
sluggishness ['slʌgɪʃnɪs] *n* pereza *f*; lentitud *f*; inactividad *f*, inercia *f*; flojedad *f*; flema *f*.
sluice [sluːs] *n* (**a**) (*gate*) compuerta *f*, esclusa *f*; (*barrier*) dique *m* de contención; (*waterway*) canal *m*. (**b**) **to give sth a ~ down** echar agua sobre algo (para lavarlo), regar algo; **to give sb a ~ down** dar una ducha a uno.
◆**sluice down** *vt*: **to ~ sth down** (**with water**) echar agua sobre algo (para lavarlo), regar algo con agua.
sluicegate ['sluːsgeɪt] *n* compuerta *f*.
sluiceway ['sluːsweɪ] *n* canal *m*.
slum [slʌm] **1** *n* (*area*) barrio *m* bajo, barrio *m* pobre, barriada *f* (*LAm*); (*house*) casucha *f*, tugurio *m*; **the ~s** los barrios bajos, los suburbios; **they live in a ~** viven en una casucha; **this house will be a ~ in 10 years** dentro de 10 años esta casa será una ruina; **they've made their house a ~** su casa es un desastre.
2 *attr* : ~ **area** barrio *m* bajo; ~ **clearance programme** programa *m* de demolición y reconstrucción de los barrios pobres; ~ **dwelling** tugurio *m*.
3 *vt*: **to ~ it*** (*esp Brit*) vivir como pobres; vivir muy barato.
4 *vi*: **to ~, to go ~ming** visitar los barrios bajos; investigar los bajos fondos sociales, conocer los lugares de la baja vida.
slumber ['slʌmbəʳ] **1** *n* (*lit*) sueño *m*; (*fig*) inactividad *f*, inercia *f*; **~s** sueño *m*; **my ~s were rudely interrupted** mis sueños fueron bruscamente interrumpidos.
2 *vi* dormir; estar dormido; (*fig*) permanecer inactivo, estar inerte.
slumb(e)rous ['slʌmbərəs] *adj* soñoliento; (*fig*) inactivo, inerte.
slum-dweller ['slʌm,dweləʳ] *n* barriobajero *m*, -a *f*.
slummy* ['slʌmɪ] *adj* muy pobre, sórdido.
slump [slʌmp] **1** *n* (*economic*) depresión *f*, declive *m* económico, retroceso *m*; **the 1929 ~** la depresión de 1929, la crisis económica de 1929; ~ **in prices** hundimiento *m* de los precios; **the ~ in the price of copper** la baja repentina del precio del cobre; ~ **in morale** bajón *m* en la moral.
2 *vi* (**a**) (*price etc*) hundirse, bajar repentinamente; (*production*) bajar catastróficamente; (*morale etc*) sufrir un bajón, decaer gravemente.
(**b**) **to ~ into a chair** dejarse caer pesadamente en un sillón; **he was ~ed over the wheel** se había desplomado sobre el volante; **he was ~ed on the floor** estaba tumbado en el suelo.
slung [slʌŋ] *pret and ptp of* **sling.**
slunk [slʌŋk] *pret and ptp of* **slink.**
slur [slɜːʳ] **1** *n* (**a**) (*stigma*) borrón *m*, mancha *f*, nota *f* infamante; calumnia *f*; **to cast a ~ on sb** calumniar a uno, hacer un reparo (injustificado) a uno; **it is no ~ on him to say that ...** no es hacer un reparo a él decir que ... no es baldonarle a él decir que ...
(**b**) (*Mus*) ligado *m*.
2 *vt* (*also* **to ~ over**) pasar por alto de, omitir, suprimir; (*hide*) ocultar; *word* articular mal, *syllable* comerse; (*Mus*) ligar.
◆**slur over** *vt* = **slur 2.**
slurp [slɜːp] **1** *vt* sorber. **2** *vi* sorber.
slurred [slɜːd] *adj speech* indistinto, poco correcto.
slurry [slʌrɪ] *n* compuesto *m* acuoso; lodo *m* (*etc*) líquido; (*Agr*) estiércol *m* líquido.
slush [slʌʃ] **1** *n* (**a**) (*watery snow*) nieve *f* a medio derretir; (*mud*) fango *m*, lodo *m* (líquido).
(**b**) (*) sentimentalismo *m*, tonterías *fpl* sentimentales, cursilería *f*.
2 *attr*: ~ **fund** caja *f* B, fondos *mpl* para sobornar.
slushy [slʌʃɪ] *adj* (**a**) *snow* a medio derretir, casi líquido; *mud* casi líquido; *path etc* lleno de lodo, fangoso. (**b**) (*) sentimentaloide*, sensiblero, cursi.
slut [slʌt] *n* tía *f* guarra *f*, marrana *f*.
sluttish ['slʌtɪʃ] *adj* puerco, desaliñado.
sly [slaɪ] **1** *adj* (*wily*) astuto; (*hypocritical*) taimado; (*secretive*) furtivo, disimulado, sigiloso; (*arch*) malicioso; (*bantering*) guasón; (*insinuating*) intencionado.
2 *n*: **on the ~** a hurtadillas; disimuladamente, sigilosamente.
slyboots ['slaɪ,buːts] *n sing* taimado *m*, -a *f*.
slyly ['slaɪlɪ] *adv* astutamente; furtivamente, disi-

muladamente, sigilosamente; maliciosamente; con intención.

slyness ['slaɪnɪs] *n* astucia *f*; lo taimado, carácter *m* taimado; disimulo *m*, sigilo *m*; malicia *f*; guasa *f*; intención *f*.

smack¹ [smæk] **1** *n* (*taste*) sabor *m*, saborcillo *m*, dejo *m* (*of* a).

2 *vi* tener un saborcillo un poco raro; saber mal; **to ~ of** saber a, tener un saborcillo a; (*fig, pej*) tener resabios de; oler a; **the whole thing ~s of bribery** el asunto entero huele a corrupción.

smack² [smæk] **1** *n* (**a**) (*slap*) manotada *f*, palmada *f*; (*blow, stroke*) golpe *m*; (*sound*) ruido *m* de un golpe, chasquido *m*; **it hit the wall with a great ~** dio ¡zas! contra la pared; **the ~ of firm government** la mano dura del gobierno resuelto; **it was a ~ in the eye for them*** (*esp Brit*) fue un golpe duro para ellos; **to give a child a ~** dar una manotada a un niño; **stop it or you'll get a ~** déjalo o te pego.

(**b**) (*esp Brit**) tentativa *f*; **I'll have a ~ at it** lo voy a tentar, probaré.

2 *vt* (*slap*) dar una manotada a, pegar (con la mano); **he ~ed it on to the table** dio con él ¡zas! en la mesa; **to ~ one's lips** relamerse, chuparse los labios.

3 *adv*: **it fell ~ in the middle** cayó en el mismo centro; **he went ~ into a tree** dio de golpe contra un árbol, dio de lleno contra un árbol.

4 *interj* ¡zas!

smack³ [smæk] *n* (*Naut*) queche *m*, barco *m* de pesca.

smack⁴‡ [smæk] *n* (*US*) heroína *f*.

smacker‡ ['smækəʳ] *n* (**a**) (*kiss*) beso *m* sonado; (*blow*) golpe *m* ruidoso. (**b**) (*Brit Fin*) libra *f*; (*US*) dólar *m*.

smacking ['smækɪŋ] **1** *adj*: **at a ~ pace** a gran velocidad, muy rápidamente. **2** *n* zurra *f*, paliza *f*; **to give sb a ~** dar una paliza a uno.

small [smɔːl] **1** *adj* pequeño; chico; menudo; (*person*) pequeño, bajo (de estatura), chaparro (*Mex*); *stock, supply etc* escaso, corto, exiguo; (*lesser*) menor; (*unimportant*) insignificante; *voice* humilde; (*the idea of ~ is often expressed by a diminutive, eg*) **a ~ house** una casita, **a ~ book** un librillo; **I'm sorry it's so ~** siento que sea tan chiquito; **the fish here are very ~** aquí los peces son chiquitines; **~ ad*** (*Brit*) anuncio *m* breve; **~ business** negocio *m* pequeño; **~ capitals** (*Typ*: *also* **~ caps**) versalitas *fpl*; **~ change** cambio *m*, calderilla *f*, sencillo *m* (*LAm*), feria *f* (*Mex*); **~ claims court** tribunal *m* de instancia (que se ocupa de asuntos menores); **he's just ~ fry** es un don nadie; **~ hours** altas horas *fpl*; **~ intestine** intestino *m* delgado; **~ investor** pequeño inversionista *m*, pequeña inversionista *f*; **~ letter** minúscula *f*; **~ print** letra *f* menuda; **the ~ screen** la pequeña pantalla; **with no ~ surprise** con no poca sorpresa; **~ trader** comerciante *mf* minorista; **to be in business in a ~ way** tener un negocio modesto; **we started in just a ~ way** empezamos a escala pequeña; **I do my best in my own ~ way** hago lo que puedo con mis modestos objetivos; **when we were ~** cuando éramos pequeños; **to be a ~ eater** comer poco; **to feel ~** sentirse humillado, tener vergüenza; **it made me feel pretty ~** me hizo sentirme poca cosa; **to make sb look ~** humillar a uno, dar vergüenza a uno; **this house makes the other one look ~** esta casa hace que la otra quede pequeña; **to make o.s. ~** achicarse, agacharse; **the ~er of the two** el menor (de los dos); **the Earth is 75 times ~er than Uranus** la Tierra es 75 veces menor que Urano.

2 *n* (**a**) **~ of the back** parte *f* más estrecha de la espalda.

(**b**) **~s** (*Brit**) paños *mpl* menores, ropa *f* interior, ropa *f* íntima (*LAm*).

small-arms ['smɔːl'ɑːmz] *npl* armas *fpl* cortas, armas *fpl* portátiles.

small-boned [ˌsmɔːl'bəʊnd] *adj* de huesos pequeños.

smallholder ['smɔːlˌhəʊldəʳ] *n* (*Brit*) cultivador *m*, -ora *f* de una granja pequeña, minifundista *mf*.

smallholding ['smɔːlˌhəʊldɪŋ] *n* (*Brit*) parcela *f*, granja *f* pequeña; minifundio *m*.

smallish ['smɔːlɪʃ] *adj* más bien pequeño.

small-minded ['smɔːl'maɪndɪd] *adj* de miras estrechas; mezquino.

small-mindedness ['smɔːl'maɪndɪdnɪs] *n* estrechez *f* de miras; mezquindad *f*.

smallness ['smɔːlnɪs] *n* (*V* **small**) pequeñez *f*, pequeño tamaño *m*, tamaño *m* reducido; escasez *f*; insignificancia *f*.

smallpox ['smɔːlpɒks] *n* viruela *f*, viruelas *fpl*.

small-scale ['smɔːl'skeɪl] *adj* en pequeña escala.

small-talk ['smɔːltɔːk] *n* conversación *f* sin trascendencia, cháchara *f*, palique *m*; banalidades *fpl*; **she has no ~** no sabe hablar de trivialidades; **to swap ~ with sb** intercambiar banalidades con uno.

small-time ['smɔːl'taɪm] *adj* de poca monta; de escasa importancia; en pequeña escala.

small-town ['smɔːl'taʊn] *adj* pueblerino, lugareño.

smarm* [smɑːm] *vt*: **to ~ one's hair down** alisarse y fijarse el pelo.

smarmy* ['smɑːmɪ] *adj* (*Brit*) cobista*; **he's a ~ sort** es un cobista*.

smart [smɑːt] **1** *adj* (**a**) (*elegant*) elegante; pulcro, elegante; (*not shabby*) aseado; *society* elegante, de buen tono; **that's a ~ car** qué coche más elegante; **in a ~ shop on Serrano** en una tienda elegante de Serrano; **you're looking very ~!** ¡qué elegante estás!, ¡qué guapo estás!

(**b**) (*bright*) listo, vivo, inteligente; *computer, missile etc* inteligente; (*pej*) ladino, astuto, cuco; **~ Alec(k)***, **~ ass‡** (*US*) sabelotodo* *m*, listillo *m*; **~ card** tarjeta *f* electrónica, tarjeta *f* de cajero automático, tarjeta *f* inteligente; **~ money** dinero *m* en busca de utilidades excepcionales; dinero *m* del inversionista con información confidencial; **he's a ~ one** es un cuco; **he was too ~ for me** era muy listo para mí; **that's a ~ trick** es un truco hábil; **he thinks it's ~ to** + *infin* él se cree la mar de listo al + *infin*; **that was pretty ~ of you** listo fuiste.

(**c**) (*quick*) pronto, rápido, vivo; *pace* vivo; *attack etc* repentino; **that's ~ work** lo has hecho con toda rapidez; **~ work by the police led to ...** una pronta acción de parte de la policía condujo a ...; **and look ~ about it!** ¡y dáte prisa!, y ¡menearse!, ¡apúrate! (*LAm*).

2 *n* (**a**) escozor *m*; (*fig*) dolor *m*, resentimiento *m*.

(**b**) **~s** (*US‡*) picardía *f*.

3 *vi* (**a**) (*Med*) escocer, picar; **it makes my mouth ~** escuece en la boca; **my eyes are ~ing** me duelen los ojos; **it ~s for a few minutes** escuece durante algunos minutos.

(**b**) (*fig*) **to ~ under, to ~ with** sufrir bajo, resentirse de; **to ~ under criticism** resentirse de la crítica; **you shall ~ for this!** ¡me las pagarás!

smarten ['smɑːtn] = **smarten up**.

◆**smarten up** **1** *vt* arreglar, mejorar el aspecto de; hermosear; **we'll ~ the house up for the summer** arreglaremos la casa para el verano.

2 *vr*: **to ~ o.s. up** arreglarse; mejorarse de aspecto; **I must go and ~ myself up** tengo que ir a arreglarme un poco; **she has ~ed herself up a lot in the last year** durante el año pasado ha mejorado mucho de aspecto.

smartly ['smɑːtlɪ] *adv* (*V adj*) (**a**) elegantemente; pulcramente, de modo distinguido; **she dresses very ~** viste con mucha elegancia.

(**b**) inteligentemente; (*pej*) astutamente.

(**c**) pronto, rápidamente; a paso vivo; de repente, repentinamente; **they marched him ~ off to the police station** le llevaron sin más a la comisaría.

smartness ['smɑːtnɪs] *n* (*V adj*) (**a**) elegancia *f*; pulcritud *f*, distinción *f*; aseo *m*; buen tono *m*.

(**b**) viveza *f*, inteligencia *f*; (*pej*) astucia *f*, cuquería *f*.

(**c**) viveza *f*, rapidez *f*.

smarty* ['smɑːtɪ] *n* sabelotodo* *m*.

smash [smæʃ] **1** *n* (**a**) (*collision, also* **~-up**) choque *m* (violento), colisión *f*, encontronazo *m*; accidente *m*; (*breakage*) rotura *f*, quiebra *f* (*LAm*); (*noise of ~*) estruendo *m*; **he died in a car ~** murió en accidente de automóvil; **the 1969 rail ~** el accidente de ferrocarril de 1969.

(**b**) (*Tennis etc*) smash *m*, mate *m*.

(**c**) (*Fin*) quiebra *f*; crisis *f* económica; **the 1929 ~** la crisis de 1929.

2 *adj* (*) **~ hit** éxito *m* fulminante, exitazo *m*; **the ~ hit of 1920** el mayor éxito de 1920.

3 *adv*: **to go ~ into sth** dar de lleno contra algo, dar violentamente contra algo.

4 *vt* (*break*) romper, quebrar (*esp LAm*); (*shatter*) hacer pedazos; (*annihilate*) destruir; *ball* golpear violentamente; *attack* desbaratar; *opponent* aplastar; *crime ring, conspiracy* deshacer, acabar con, descoyuntar; **when they ~ed the atom** cuando desintegraron el átomo; **he ~ed it against the wall** lo estrelló contra la pared; **the waves threatened to ~ the boat on the rocks** las olas amenazaban con estrellar el barco contra las rocas; **I've ~ed my watch** he estropeado mi reloj; **A ~ed his fist into B's face** A dio a B un puñetazo violento en la cara.

5 *vi* (*break*) romperse; hacerse pedazos, quebrarse (*esp LAm*); estropearse; (*collide*) chocar (*against, into* con, con-

tra), estrellarse (*against, into* contra); (*Fin*) quebrar.
◆**smash down** *vt door etc* romper.
◆**smash in** *vt door etc* romper; **I'll ~ your face in** te rompo la cara.
◆**smash up** *vt car* hacer pedazos; *room* destrozar; **he was all ~ed up in the accident** sufrió grandes lesiones en el accidente.
smash-and-grab raid ['smæʃən'græb,reɪd] *n* robo *m* relámpago (con rotura de escaparate; en joyería *etc*).
smashed⁑ [smæʃt] *adj* (*drunk*) colocado⁑; (*drugged*) flipado⁑.
smasher⁑ ['smæʃəʳ] *n* (*esp Brit*) cosa *f* estupenda, (*esp girl*) bombón* *m*, guayabo* *m*; **it's a ~!** ¡es estupendo!
smashing* ['smæʃɪŋ] *adj* (*esp Brit*) imponente*, bárbaro*, pistonudo*; **a ~ dress** un vestido monísimo; **we had a ~ time** lo pasamos en grande*; **isn't it ~?** ¿es estupendo, no?
smash-up ['smæʃʌp] *n* choque *m* violento, colisión *f* violenta, accidente *m*.
smattering ['smætərɪŋ] *n* conocimientos *mpl* elementales, conocimiento *m* superficial, nociones *fpl*; **I have a ~ of Catalan** tengo algunas nociones de catalán.
smear [smɪəʳ] **1** *n* mancha *f*; (*fig*) calumnia *f*, mancha *f*; (*Med*) frotis *m*.
2 *attr*: **~ campaign** campaña *f* denigratoria, campaña *f* de desprestigio; **~ tactics** tácticas *fpl* de difamación; **~ test** análisis *m* citológico.
3 *vt* (**a**) manchar (*with* de), untar (*with* de); **to ~ one's face with blood** untarse la cara de sangre; **to ~ wet paint** manchar la pintura fresca.
(**b**) (*fig*) calumniar, difamar; desprestigiar; **to ~ sb as a traitor** tachar a uno de traidor; **to ~ sb because of his past** tachar a uno por su pasado.
(**c**) (*US*⁑) derrotar sin esfuerzo.
4 *vi* mancharse.
smell [smel] **1** *n* (**a**) (*sense of ~*) olfato *m*; **to have a keen sense of ~** tener buen olfato.
(**b**) (*odour*) olor *m* (*of* a); **bad ~** mal olor *m*, hedor *m*; **it has a nice ~** tiene un olor agradable.
(**c**) **let's have a ~** déjame olerlo.
2 (*irr*: *pret and ptp* **smelled** *or* **smelt**) *vt* oler; *danger, difficulty etc* percebir, presentir; (*esp of animals*) olfatear.
3 *vi* (**a**) oler (*of* a); **it ~s good** huele bien; **it ~s bad** huele mal, tiene mal olor; **that flower doesn't ~** esa flor no tiene olor; **it's a gas which doesn't ~** es un gas inodoro; **it ~s damp in here** aquí dentro huele a húmedo.
(**b**) **since the accident he cannot ~** después del accidente no tiene olfato; **the dog ~ed at my shoes** el perro olfateó mis zapatos.
◆**smell out** *vt* (**a**) (*find by scent*) olfatear, husmear; (*identify*) identificar, descubrir. (**b**) (*cause to smell*) apestar; **it's ~ing the room out** hace oler mal todo el cuarto, apesta el cuarto.
smelliness ['smelɪnɪs] *n* hediondez *f*.
smelling-bottle ['smelɪŋ,bɒtl] *n* frasco *m* de sales.
smelling-salts ['smelɪŋsɔːlts] *npl* sales *fpl* (aromáticas).
smelly ['smelɪ] *adj* que huele mal, de mal olor, apestoso, hediondo; **it's ~ in here** aquí dentro huele (mal).
smelt[1] [smelt] *pret and ptp of* **smell**.
smelt[2] [smelt] *vt* fundir.
smelt[3] [smelt] *n* (*Fish*) eperlano *m*.
smelter ['smeltəʳ] *n* horno *m* de fundición.
smelting ['smeltɪŋ] **1** *n* fundición *f*. **2** *attr*: **~ furnace** horno *m* de fundición.
smidgen*, smidgin* ['smɪdʒən] *n*: **a ~ of** un poquito de, un poquitín de, una pizca de; (*of truth*) una pizca de.
smile [smaɪl] **1** *n* sonrisa *f*; **with a ~ on one's lips** con una sonrisa en los labios; **a face wreathed in ~s** una cara con una sonrisa radiante; **to give sb a ~** sonreír a uno; **come on, give me a ~!** ¡vamos, una sonrisa!; **to knock the ~ off sb's face** quitarle a uno las ganas de sonreír; **to raise a ~** forzar una sonrisa; **can't you even raise a ~?** ¿no sonríes siquiera?
2 *vt emotion* expresar con una sonrisa; **she ~d her thanks** dio las gracias con una sonrisa; **to ~ a bitter ~** sonreír amargamente.
3 *vi* sonreír, sonreírse (*at* de); **to keep smiling** seguir con la sonrisa en los labios; **to ~ at danger** reírse del peligro; **fortune ~d on him** le favoreció la fortuna; **if she ~s on me** si me mira con buenos ojos.
smiling ['smaɪlɪŋ] *adj* sonriente, risueño.
smilingly ['smaɪlɪŋlɪ] *adv* sonriendo, con cara risueña, con una sonrisa.
smirch [smɜːtʃ] *vt* (*liter*) mancillar, desdorar.
smirk [smɜːk] **1** *n* sonrisa *f* satisfecha; sonrisa *f* afectada. **2** *vi* sonreírse satisfecho; sonreírse afectadamente.
smirkingly ['smɜːkɪŋlɪ] *adv* con una sonrisa satisfecha (*or* afectada).
smite [smaɪt] (*irr*: *pret* **smote**, *ptp* **smitten**) *vt* (*liter*) (*strike*) golpear; (*punish*) castigar; (*pain*) doler, afligir; (*of light, sound etc*) herir; **an idea smote me** se me ocurrió una idea; **my conscience smote me** me remordió la conciencia; **he smote the ball hard** golpeó la pelota duro; *V also* **smitten**.
smith [smɪθ] *n* herrero *m*.
smithereens ['smɪðə'riːnz] *npl*: **to smash sth to ~** hacer algo añicos; **it was in ~** estaba hecho añicos.
smithy ['smɪðɪ] *n* herrería *f*.
smitten ['smɪtn] *ptp of* **smite**; **to be ~ with the plague** sufrir el azote de la peste, ser afligido por la peste; **to be ~ with an idea** entusiasmarse por una idea; **to be ~ with sb** estar chalado por uno; **I was ~ by the urge to** + *infin* me entraron deseos vehementes de + *infin*.
smock [smɒk] **1** *n* (*artist's, labourer's*) blusa *f*; (*child's*) delantal *m*; (*expectant mother's*) bata *f* corta, tontón *m*; (*US*: *overall*) guardapolvo *m*. **2** *vt* fruncir, adornar con frunces.
smocking ['smɒkɪŋ] *n* adorno *m* de frunces.
smog [smɒg] *n* niebla *f* con humo, calina *f*; niebla *f* tóxica.
smoke [sməʊk] **1** *n* (**a**) humo *m*; **the S~**⁑ (*Brit*) Londres; **there's no ~ without fire** cuando el río suena agua lleva, lo que hace humo es porque está ardiendo; **to go up in ~** (*building etc*) quedar destruido en un incendio, quemarse totalmente; (*: *person*) subirse por las paredes*; (*plans*) fracasar, quedar en agua de borrajas; **his fortune went up in ~** su fortuna se hizo humo.
(**b**) (*cigarette etc*) pitillo *m*, tabaco *m*, cigarro *m* (*LAm*); **to have a ~** echar un pitillo, fumar un cigarrillo; **I like to have a ~ after meals** me gusta fumar después de comer; **will you have a ~?** ¿quieres fumar?; **I've no ~s**⁑ no tengo tabaco.
2 *vt tobacco* fumar; *bacon, glass etc* ahumar; **he ~s a pipe** fuma en pipa; **he's smoking his pipe** está fumando su pipa.
3 *vi* (**a**) (*chimney etc*) humear, echar humo.
(**b**) (*smoker*) fumar; (*esp US**) fumar marijuana; **do you ~?** ¿fuma Vd?; **will you ~?** ¿quieres fumar?; **do you mind if I ~?** ¿te molesta que fume?; **he ~s like a chimney** fuma como un carretero.
◆**smoke out** *vt*: **to ~ insects out** ahuyentar insectos con humo; **to ~ a gang out** hacer que salga una pandilla de su escondite pegándole fuego; **to ~ out a beehive** ahumar una colmena; **that lamp is smoking the room out** esa lámpara está llenando el cuarto de humo.
smoke-bomb ['sməʊkbɒm] *n* bomba *f* de humo, granada *f* de humo.
smoked [sməʊkt] *adj bacon, glass etc* ahumado.
smoke-detector ['sməʊkdɪ,tektəʳ] *n* detector *m* de humo.
smoke-dried ['sməʊkdraɪd] *adj* ahumado, curado al humo.
smoke-filled ['sməʊkfɪld] *adj* lleno de humo.
smokehood ['sməʊkhʊd] *n* capucha *f* antihumo.
smokeless ['sməʊklɪs] *adj* sin humo; **~ fuel** combustible *m* sin humo; **~ zone** zona *f* libre de humo.
smoker ['sməʊkəʳ] *n* (**a**) (*person*) fumador *m*, -ora *f*; **~'s cough** tos *f* de fumador; **I'm not a ~** no fumo; **to be a heavy ~** fumar mucho. (**b**) (*Rail*) coche *m* fumador.
smokescreen ['sməʊkskriːn] *n* (*also fig*) cortina *f* de humo; **to put up a ~** (*fig*) entenebrecer un asunto, enmarañar un asunto (para despistar a la gente).
smoke shop ['sməʊkʃɒp] *n* (*US*) estanco *m*, tabaquería *f*.
smokesignal ['sməʊk,sɪgnl] *n* ahumada *f*.
smokestack ['sməʊkstæk] *n* chimenea *f*; **~ industries** industrias *fpl* con chimeneas.
smoking ['sməʊkɪŋ] **1** *adj* humeante, que humea.
2 *n* el fumar; **~ is bad for you** el fumar te hace daño; **'no ~'** 'se prohíbe fumar'; **no ~ area** zona *f* de no fumar; **to give up ~** dejar de fumar.
3 *attr* de fumar; de (*or* para) fumador; **~ compartment**, (*US*) **~ car** departamento *m* de fumadores, coche *m* fumador; **~ jacket** chaqueta *f* casera, medio batín *m*; **~ room** salón *m* de fumar.
smoky ['sməʊkɪ] *adj chimney, fire* humeante, que humea; *room* lleno de humo; *flavour, surface etc* ahumado; **it's ~ in here** aquí hay mucho humo.
smolder ['sməʊldəʳ] *vi* (*US*) = **smoulder**.
smooch* [smuːtʃ] *vi* besuquearse, manosearse, acariciarse, abrazarse amorosamente.
smoochy* ['smuːtʃɪ] *adj record etc* sentimental; erótico.
smooth [smuːð] **1** *adj* (**a**) *surface* liso, terso; suave; llano,

igual, uniforme, parejo (*LAm*); *skin etc* liso, suave; *brow* sin arrugas; *sea* tranquilo, en calma.

(**b**) (*in consistency*) *paste etc* liso, sin grumos; *running of engine, take-off etc* suave; *voice* suave; *style* fluido, suave; *passage, trip* tranquilo, sin novedad; *person's manner* afable.

(**c**) *person* afable, culto; (*pej*) zalamero, meloso; **he's a ~ operator** es muy persuasivo; **he's a ~ talker** tiene pico de oro.

2 *vt hair etc* alisar; *surface* allanar, igualar; *dress etc* arreglar; *wood* desbastar; *style etc* suavizar; **to ~ the way** (*or* **path**) **for sb** allanar el camino a uno, preparar el terreno para uno.

◆smooth away *vt* = **smooth over.**

◆smooth back *vt hair* peinarse hacia atrás, alisarse; *sheet* estirar, alisar.

◆smooth down *vt hair etc* alisar; *surface* allanar, igualar; *wood* desbastar; **to ~ sb down** calmar a uno, apaciguar a uno.

◆smooth out *vt dress* arreglar.

◆smooth over *vt*: **to ~ over difficulties** allanar dificultades, zanjar dificultades.

smooth-chinned ['smuːð'tʃɪnd] *adj*, **smooth-faced** ['smuːð'feɪst] *adj* barbilampiño; bien afeitado; **some ~ youth** algún joven imberbe.

smoothie* ['smuːðɪ] *n* zalamero *m*; lameculos* *m*.

smoothing-iron ['smuːðɪŋˌaɪən] *n* plancha *f*.

smoothly ['smuːðlɪ] *adv* (*V adj*) (**a**) lisamente; suavemente; de modo uniforme; tranquilamente; **everything went ~** todo fue sobre ruedas, todo fue viento en popa. (**b**) afablemente; **he said ~** dijo sin alterarse.

smoothness ['smuːðnɪs] *n* (*V adj*) lisura *f*, tersura *f*; suavidad *f*; igualdad *f*, uniformidad *f*; tranquilidad *f*, calma *f*; fluidez *f*; afabilidad *f*; (*pej*) zalamería *f*.

smooth-running ['smuːð'rʌnɪŋ] *adj engine etc* que funciona bien.

smooth-shaven ['smuːð'ʃeɪvn] *adj* apurado.

smooth-spoken ['smuːð'spəʊkən] *adj*, **smooth-talking** ['smuːðˌtɔːkɪŋ] *adj* afable; (*pej*) zalamero, meloso.

smooth-tongued ['smuːð'tʌŋd] *adj* zalamero, meloso.

smorgasbord ['smɔːgəsˌbɔːd] *n* smorgasbord *m*; ambigú *m* escandinavo.

smote [sməʊt] *pret of* **smite.**

smother ['smʌðəʳ] **1** *vt* (*stifle*) ahogar, sofocar, asfixiar; *fire* apagar; *yawn* contener; *criticism, doubt etc* ahogar, suprimir; **fruit ~ed in cream** fruta *f* cubierta de crema; **a book ~ed in dust** un libro cubierto de polvo; **the child was ~ed in dirt** el niño estaba todo sucio; **she ~ed the child with kisses** cubrió al nino de besos. **2** *vi* ahogarse, sofocarse.

smoulder, (*US*) **smolder** ['sməʊldəʳ] *vi* arder sin llama, arder lentamente; (*fig*: *hatred etc*) estar latente, estar sin apagarse.

smouldering, (*US*) **smoldering** ['sməʊldərɪŋ] *adj* que arde lentamente; (*fig*) latente; **she gave me a ~ look** me miró provocativa.

smudge [smʌdʒ] **1** *n* mancha *f*, tiznón *m*. **2** *vt* manchar; tiznar (*with* de). **3** *vi* mancharse.

smudgy ['smʌdʒɪ] *adj* manchado; lleno de manchas; *writing etc* borroso.

smug [smʌg] *adj* pagado de sí (mismo), suficiente; presumido; **he said with ~ satisfaction** dijo muy pagado de sí; **don't be so ~!** ¡no presumas!

smuggle ['smʌgl] **1** *vt* pasar (de contrabando); **~d goods** géneros *mpl* de contrabando; **to ~ goods in** introducir artículos de contrabando; **to ~ sth past** (*or* **through**) **the customs** pasar algo por la aduana sin declararlo; **to ~ sb out in disguise** pasar a uno disfrazado.

2 *vi* hacer contrabando, dedicarse a pasar cosas de contrabando.

smuggler ['smʌgləʳ] *n* contrabandista *mf*.

smuggling ['smʌglɪŋ] **1** *n* contrabando *m*. **2** *attr*: **~ ring** red *f* de contrabando, red *f* de contrabandistas.

smugness ['smʌgnɪs] *n* satisfacción *f* de sí (mismo), suficiencia *f*; presunción *f*.

smut [smʌt] *n* (**a**) (*piece of dirt*) tizne *m*; (*in eye*) mota *f* de carbonilla; (*on paper*) tiznón *m*, mancha *f*. (**b**) (*Bot*) tizón *m*. (**c**) (*fig*) obscenidades *fpl*, cosas *fpl* verdes; **to talk ~** contar cosas verdes.

smuttiness ['smʌtɪnɪs] *n* (*fig*) obscenidad *f*.

smutty ['smʌtɪ] *adj* (**a**) tiznado. (**b**) (*Bot*) atizonado. (**c**) (*fig*) obsceno, verde; **a lot of ~ talk** muchos cuentos verdes.

Smyrna ['smɜːnə] *n* Esmirna *f*.

snack [snæk] *n* bocadillo *m*, tentempié *m*, piscolabis *m*; **to have a ~** tomar un bocadillo, comer algo.

snackbar ['snækbɑːʳ] *n* cafetería *f*, bar *m*, lonchería *f* (*LAm*).

snaffle[1] ['snæfl] *n* bridón *m*.

snaffle[2]* ['snæfl] *vt* (*Brit*) afanar*, birlar*.

snag [snæg] **1** *n* (**a**) (*in wood*) nudo *m*; (*of tree*) tocón *m*; (*of tooth*) raigón *m*.

(**b**) (*fig*) dificultad *f*, obstáculo *m*, estorbo *m*, pega *f*; **there's a ~** hay una dificultad; **the ~ is that ...** la dificultad es que ...; **that's the ~** ahí está el problema; **what's the ~?** ¿qué obstáculo hay?; **to hit** (*or* **run into**) **a ~** encontrar una pega, tropezar con una dificultad.

2 *vt* enganchar, coger (*on* en).

3 *vi* engancharse, quedar cogido (*on* en).

snail [sneɪl] **1** *n* caracol *m*; **at a ~'s pace** a paso de tortuga.

2 *attr*: **~ shell** concha *f* de caracol.

snake [sneɪk] **1** *n* culebra *f*, serpiente *f*; **the (European Monetary) S~** la Serpiente; **he's the ~ in the grass** él es el traidor, él es el enemigo oculto, él es el peligro oculto; **~s and ladders** juego *m* de escaleras y serpientes.

2 *vi*: **a hand ~d out of the curtain** una mano se deslizó de la cortina.

◆snake about, snake along *vi* serpentear.

snakebite ['sneɪkbaɪt] *n* mordedura *f* de serpiente.

snake-charmer ['sneɪkˌtʃɑːməʳ] *n* encantador *m* de serpientes.

snakepit ['sneɪkpɪt] *n* nido *m* de serpientes.

snakeskin ['sneɪkskɪn] *n* piel *f* de serpiente.

snaky ['sneɪkɪ] *adj* serpentino, tortuoso.

snap [snæp] **1** *n* (**a**) (*sound*: *of fingers*) castañetazo *m*; (*of whip etc*) chasquido *m*; (*report*) estallido *m*; (*click*) golpe *m* seco, ruido *m* seco; **it shut with a ~** se cerró de golpe, se cerró con un ruido seco.

(**b**) **cold ~** ola *f* de frío, período *m* breve de frío.

(**c**) (*) vigor *m*, energía *f*; **put some ~ into it!** ¡menearse!

(**d**) (*US*: *fastener*) automático *m*, clec *m*.

(**e**) (*Phot*) foto *f*, instantánea *f*; **to take a ~ of sb** tomar una foto de uno; **these are our holiday ~s** éstas son las fotos de nuestras vacaciones.

(**f**) **it's a ~** (*US**) eso está tirado*, es muy fácil.

2 *adj* repentino; **~ answer** respuesta *f* sin pensar, respuesta *f* instantánea; **~ decision** decisión *f* tomada de repente; **~ judgement** juicio *m* instantáneo; **~ vote** votación *f* improvista.

3 *adv*: **~!** ¡crac!; **to go ~** hacer crac.

4 *excl* ¡lo mismo!; ¡yo también!

5 *vt* (**a**) *fingers* castañetear (*V also* **finger**); *whip* chasquear; **to ~ a box shut** cerrar una caja de golpe; **to ~ sth into place** colocar algo con un golpe seco.

(**b**) (*break*) romper, quebrar, hacer saltar.

(**c**) (*Phot*) **to ~ sb** tomar una foto de uno.

6 *vi* (**a**) **to ~ at sb** (*dog*) querer morder a uno, tratar de morder a uno; (*person*) contestar (*or* hablar *etc*) bruscamente (*or* con brusquedad) a uno; **don't ~ at me!** ¡habla con más educación!

(**b**) (*whip etc*) chasquear; (*fastener etc*) hacer un ruido seco; **it ~ped shut** se cerró de golpe.

(**c**) (*break*) romperse, quebrarse; separarse, desprenderse; saltar.

(**d**) **she ~ped into action** echó a trabajar (*etc*) en seguida.

◆snap back *vi*: **to ~ back at sb** contestar (*or* hablar *etc*) bruscamente a uno.

◆snap off 1 *vt* romper, separar; (*dog etc*) morder y separar, separar con los dientes; **to ~ sb's head off** echar un rapapolvo a uno; interrumpir bruscamente a uno.

2 *vi*: **it ~ped off** se desprendió, se partió.

◆snap out 1 *vt*: **to ~ out an order** espetar una orden.

2 *vi* (*) **to ~ out of sth** dejarse de algo, quitarse algo de encima; **~ out of it!** ¡déjate de eso!, ¡ánimo!

◆snap up *vt*: **to ~ up a bargain** lanzarse sobre un saldo, agarrarse de una ganga; **our stock was ~ped up at once** nuestras existencias quedaron agotadas al instante.

snapdragon ['snæpˌdrægən] *n* dragón *m*, boca *f* de dragón.

snap fastener ['snæp'fɑːsnəʳ] *n* (*US*) automático *m*, clec *m*.

snappish ['snæpɪʃ] *adj* brusco, abrupto; irritable.

snappishness ['snæpɪʃnɪs] *n* brusquedad *f*; irritabilidad *f*.

snappy* ['snæpɪ] *adj* (**a**) (*quick*) rápido; (*energetic*) enérgico, vigoroso; *answer* instantáneo; *slogan* conciso; **to be ~ about sth** hacer algo con toda rapidez; **and be ~ about it!** ¡y date prisa!; **make it ~!** ¡rápido! (**b**) (*smart*) elegante; **he's a ~ dresser** se viste con elegancia.

snapshot ['snæpʃɒt] *n* foto *f*, instantánea *f*.

snare [snɛəʳ] **1** *n* lazo *m*, trampa *f*; (*fig*) trampa *f*, engaño *m*; **it's a ~ and delusion** es una pura trampa.
2 *vt* coger (*LAm*: agarrar) con trampas; (*fig*) hacer caer en el lazo, engañar.
snare drum ['snɛədrʌm] *n* tambor *m* militar pequeño.
snarl[1] [snɑːl] **1** *n* gruñido *m*; **he said with a ~** dijo gruñendo. **2** *vt* gruñir, decir gruñendo. **3** *vi* gruñir; **to ~ at sb** decir algo a uno gruñendo.
snarl[2] [snɑːl] **1** *vt* (*also* **to ~ up**) enmarañar, enredar; **it's got all ~ed up** ha quedado en la mayor confusión; **the traffic was all ~ed up** la circulación quedó bloqueada.
2 *vi* (*also* **to ~ up**) enmarañarse, enredarse.
◆snarl up *vt, vi* = **snarl 1, 2.**
snarl-up ['snɑːlʌp] *n* (**a**) (*Aut etc*) congestión *f*, embotellamiento *m*; bloque *m*. (**b**) lío *m*; caos *m*, confusión *f*.
snatch [snætʃ] **1** *n* (**a**) (*act*) arrebatamiento *m*; (*Weightlifting*) arrancada *f*; **~ squad** unidad *f* de arresto; **to make a ~ at sth** tratar de arrebatar algo.
(**b**) (*: *robbery*) robo *m*; (*of handbag*) tirón *m* (de bolso); (*kidnapping*) secuestro *m*; **jewellery ~** robo *m* de joyas.
(**c**) (*Mus etc*) trocito *m*; **to whistle ~es of Mozart** silbar trocitos de Mozart.
(**d**) (*US***) coño*** *m*.
2 *vt* (**a**) (*pick up*) asir, coger, agarrar; (*from sb's hold*) arrebatar (*from* a); (*out of the air*) coger al vuelo; **to ~ a meal** comer algo a toda prisa; **to ~ an opportunity** asir una ocasión; **to ~ an hour of happiness** procurarse (a pesar de todo) una hora de felicidad.
(**b**) (*: *steal*) robar, (*kidnap*) secuestrar.
3 *vi*: **don't ~!** ¡no arrebates las cosas!; **to ~ at sth** tratar de arrebatar algo; tratar de coger algo al vuelo; **to ~ at an opportunity** agarrar una ocasión al vuelo.
◆snatch away *vt*: **to ~ sth away** arrebatar algo (*from a*).
◆snatch up *vt* agarrar; **to ~ up a knife** asir un cuchillo; **to ~ up a child** coger a un niño en brazos.
snatchy* ['snætʃɪ] *adj work* irregular, intermitente; *conversation* intermitente, inconexo.
snazzy* ['snæzɪ] *adj*: **a ~ dress** un vestido de lo más elegante.
sneak [sniːk] **1** *n* soplón* *m*, -ona *f*; (*Brit*) acusón* *m*, -ona *f*.
2 *adj* furtivo; imprevisto; **~ preview** anticipo *m* no autorizado; **~ visit** visita *f* furtiva.
3 *vt* (**a**) (*steal*) robar a hurtadillas, afanar, birlar.
(**b**) **to ~ a look at sth** ver algo de tapadillo; **I managed to ~ one in** logré meter uno sin ser visto.
4 *vi* (**a**) **to ~ about** ir a hurtadillas, moverse furtivamente; **to ~ away, to ~ off** largarse a hurtadillas*; **to ~ in** entrar a hurtadillas, entrar sin ser visto.
(**b**) **to ~ on sb*** (*Brit*) soplarse de uno*; **to ~ to the teacher** soplarse al profesor*.
◆sneak away, sneak off *vi* escabullirse; **to ~ off with sth** alzarse con algo.
sneakers* ['sniːkəz] *npl* zapatos *mpl* de lona, deportivos *mpl*, zapatillas *fpl*.
sneaking ['sniːkɪŋ] *adj manner* furtivo, sigiloso; **to have a ~ regard for sb** respetar a uno a pesar de todo, respetar a uno sin querer confesarlo abiertamente.
sneak-thief ['sniːkθiːf] *n*, *pl* **sneak-thieves** ['sniːkθiːvz] ratero *m*, garduño *m*.
sneaky ['sniːkɪ] *adj manner* furtivo, sigiloso; (*of character*) soplón.
sneer [snɪəʳ] **1** *n* (*expression*) visaje *m* de burla y desprecio, sonrisa *f* de sarcasmo; (*remark*) burla *f*, mofa *f*; comentario *m* despreciativo; **he said with a ~** dijo con desprecio; **the book is full of ~s about ...** el libro se mofa constantemente de ...
2 *vi* hacer un visaje de burla y desprecio; **to ~ at sb** mofarse de uno, hablar con desprecio de uno.
sneerer ['snɪərəʳ] *n* mofador *m*, -ora *f*.
sneering ['snɪərɪŋ] *adj tone etc* burlador y despreciativo, lleno de desprecio.
sneeringly ['snɪərɪŋlɪ] *adv* en tono burlador y despreciativo; con una sonrisa de desprecio.
sneeze [sniːz] **1** *n* estornudo *m*. **2** *vi* estornudar; **an offer not to be ~d at** una oferta que no es de despreciar.
snick [snɪk] **1** *n* (**a**) (*cut*) corte *m*, tijeretada *f*.
(**b**) (*Sport*) toque *m* ligero.
2 *vt* (**a**) (*cut*) cortar (un poco), tijeretear; **to ~ sth off** cortar algo con un movimiento rápido.
(**b**) *ball* desviar ligeramente.
snicker ['snɪkəʳ] = **snigger.**
snide [snaɪd] *adj* despreciativo, sarcástico.

sniff [snɪf] **1** *n* sorbo *m* por las narices; inhalación *f*; (*of dog etc*) husmeo *m*; **to go out for a ~ of air** salir a tomar el fresco; **we never got a ~ of the vodka*** no llegamos siquiera a oler el vodka*; **one ~ of that would kill you** una inhalación de eso te mataría.
2 *vt* sorber por las narices; inhalar; *glue etc* esnifar, inhalar; (*of dog etc, also* **to ~ out**) husmear, olfatear; **just ~ these flowers** huele un poco estas flores; **you can ~ the sea air here** aquí se huele ese aire de mar; **~ the gas deeply** aspire profundamente el gas.
3 *vi* (**a**) (*person*) sorber por las narices; inhalar; **to ~ at** oler; **don't ~!** ¡no hagas ese ruido con las narices!
(**b**) (*dog etc*) oler, husmear, olfatear; **the dog ~ed at my shoes** el perro olió mis zapatos.
(**c**) **to ~ at sth** (*fig*) despreciar algo, tratar algo con desdén; **an offer not to be ~ed at** una oferta que no es de despreciar.
sniffer ['snɪfəʳ] *adj*: **~ dog** (*drugs*) perro *m* antidroga; (*explosives*) perro *m* antiexplosivos.
sniffle ['snɪfl] **1** *n*: **to have the ~s** hacer ruido con las narices; estar un poco acatarrado. **2** *vi* = **1.**
sniffy* ['snɪfɪ] *adj* estirado, desdeñoso; **he was pretty ~ about it** trató el asunto con bastante desdén.
snifter ['snɪftəʳ] *n* (**a**) (*) trago *m*. (**b**) (*US*) copita *f* para coñac.
snigger ['snɪgəʳ] **1** *n* risa *f* disimulada. **2** *vi* reírse con disimulo (*at* de).
sniggering ['snɪgərɪŋ] **1** *n* risitas *fpl*, cachondeo* *m*. **2** *adj* que se ríe tontamente.
snip [snɪp] **1** *n* (**a**) (*cut*) tijeretada *f*, tijeretazo *m*; (*incision*) tijeretada *f*; (*piece of material etc*) recorte *m*; **to have the ~*** esterilizarse.
(**b**) (*Brit**) ganga *f*.
2 *vt* tijeretear.
◆snip off *vt* recortar.
snipe [snaɪp] **1** *n* (*Orn*) agachadiza *f*, becacina *f*.
2 *vi*: **to ~ at sb** tirar a uno desde un escondite; **to ~ from the shelter of ...** tirar desde la protección de ...; **to ~ at one's critics** contestar (con precaución) a los críticos de uno; **he was really sniping at the Minister** en realidad sus ataques iban dirigidos contra el Ministro.
sniper ['snaɪpəʳ] *n* tirador *m* escondido, francotirador *m*.
snippet ['snɪpɪt] *n* (*of cloth*) retazo *m*, retal *m*; (*of information etc*) retazo *m*; **~s** retazos *mpl*; **'S~s'** (*heading in press etc*) 'Breverías'.
snitch* [snɪtʃ] **1** *n* (*nose*) napias* *fpl*; (*informer*) soplón* *m*, -ona *f*. **2** *vt* birlar*. **3** *vi* soplarse* (*on sb* de uno).
snivel ['snɪvl] *vi* lloriquear.
sniveller ['snɪvləʳ], (*US*) **sniveler** *n* quejica* *mf*.
snivelling ['snɪvlɪŋ], (*US*) **sniveling 1** *adj* llorón. **2** *n* lloriqueo *m*.
snob [snɒb] *n* (e)snob *mf*.
snobbery ['snɒbərɪ] *n* (e)snobismo *m*.
snobbish ['snɒbɪʃ] *adj* (e)snob.
snobbishness ['snɒbɪʃnɪs] *n* (e)snobismo *m*.
snobby* ['snɒbɪ] *adj* (e)snob.
snog* [snɒg] **1** *n*: **to have a ~** = **2.** **2** *vi* sobarse, besuquearse*.
snood [snuːd] *n* (*band*) cintillo *m*; (*net*) redecilla *f*.
snook* [snuːk] *n*: **to cock a ~ at sb** hacer burla de uno con la mano; (*fig*) dejar a uno con un palmo de narices; mofarse abiertamente de uno.
snooker ['snuːkəʳ] **1** *n* (*Brit*) snooker *m*.
2 *vt* (*) **to ~ sb** (*US*) poner a uno en un aprieto; **now we're properly ~ed** (*Brit*) ahora no hay nada que hacer, en buen lío nos hemos metido*.
snoop* [snuːp] **1** *n* (**a**) (*person*) fisgón *m*, -ona *f*; **he's a regular ~** (*US*) es un cuzo*.
(**b**) (*act*) **I'll have a ~ round** voy a reconocer el terreno; **I had a ~ round the kitchen** fui fisgando por la cocina, estuve husmeando por la cocina.
2 *vi* (*also* **to ~ about, to ~ around**) curiosear, fisgonear; practicar un registro furtivo, hacer una investigación furtiva; **he comes ~ing around here** viene aquí a fisgonear.
snooper* ['snuːpəʳ] *n* (*official*) investigador *m* (*or* inspector *m*) encubierto, investigadora *f* (*or* inspectora *f*) encubierta; (*nosey person*) fisgón *m*, -ona *f*; (*spy*) espía *mf*.
snooty* ['snuːtɪ] *adj* fachendoso*, presumido; **people hereabouts are very ~** por aquí la gente se da mucho tono; **there's no call to be ~ about it** Vd no tiene motivo para presumir.
snooze* [snuːz] **1** *n* siestecita *f*, sueñecillo *m*; **to have a ~** = **2.** **2** *vi* dormitar, echar una siestecita.
snore [snɔːʳ] **1** *n* ronquido *m*. **2** *vi* roncar.

snorer ['snɔːrəʳ] *n* persona *f* que ronca mucho.
snoring ['snɔːrɪŋ] *n* ronquidos *mpl*.
snorkel ['snɔːkl] **1** *n* tubo *m* snorkel, esnórquel *m*, tubo *m* de respiración. **2** *vi* nadar respirando por un tubo.
snort [snɔːt] **1** *n* (**a**) bufido *m*; **with a ~ of rage** con un bufido de enojo. (**b**) (‡) (*drink*) trago *m*; (*drug*) esnife* *m*. **2** *vt* (**a**) bufar; **'No!' he ~ed** '¡No!' dijo bufando. (**b**) (*Drugs*‡) inhalar, esnifar*. **3** *vi* esnifar*.
snorter‡ ['snɔːtəʳ] *n* (**a**) **a real ~ of a song** una canción estupenda*; **a ~ of a question** una pregunta dificilísima; **it was a ~ of a game** fue un partido maravilloso. (**b**) (‡) = **snort 1 (b)**.
snot* [snɒt] (**a**) *n* (*mucus*) mocarro *m*. (**b**) (*person*) mocoso *m*, -a *f* insolente*.
snotty* ['snɒtɪ] *adj* (**a**) mocoso. (**b**) (*fig*) (*snooty*) fachendoso*, presumido; (*angry*) enojado.
snotty-faced* ['snɒtɪ,feɪst] *adj* mocoso.
snotty-nosed* ['snɒtɪ,nəʊzd] *adj* (**a**) (*lit*) = **snotty-faced***. (**b**) (*fig*) engreído.
snout [snaʊt] *n* (**a**) hocico *m*, morro *m*; (‡: *of person*) napias‡ *fpl*. (**b**) (‡) tabaco *m*, cigarrillos *mpl*.
snow [snəʊ] **1** *n* (**a**) nieve *f*. (**b**) (‡) nieve‡ *f*, cocaína *f*. (**c**) (*TV*) nieve *f*. **2** *vt*: **to ~ sb*** (*US*) camelar a uno*. **3** *vi* nevar.
◆**snow in** *vt*: **to be ~ed in** estar encerrado (*or* aprisionado) por la nieve.
◆**snow under** *vt*: **to be ~ed under** (*fig*) estar inundado (*by, with* por).
◆**snow up** *vt* (*Brit*) = **snow in**.
snowball ['snəʊbɔːl] **1** *n* bola *f* de nieve.
2 *vt* lanzar bolas de nieve a.
3 *vi* (*fig*) aumentar progresivamente, aumentar rápidamente.
snow-blind ['snəʊ,blaɪnd] *adj* cegado por la nieve.
snow-blindness ['snəʊ,blaɪndnɪs] *n* ceguera *f* causada por la nieve.
snowbound ['snəʊbaʊnd] *adj* aprisionado por la nieve.
snow-cap ['snəʊ,kæp] *n* casquete *m* de nieve, corona *f* de nieve.
snow-capped ['snəʊkæpt] *adj* coronado de nieve, nevado.
snow-covered ['snəʊ'kʌvəd] *adj* cubierto de nieve, nevado.
snowdrift ['snəʊdrɪft] *n* montón *m* de nieve, nieve *f* amontonada, (*on mountain*) ventisquero *m*.
snowdrop ['snəʊdrɒp] *n* campanilla *f* de febrero, flor *f* de nieve, campanilla *f* blanca.
snowfall ['snəʊfɔːl] *n* nevada *f*.
snowfence ['snəʊfens] *n* valla *f* paranieves.
snowfield ['snəʊfiːld] *n* campo *m* de nieve.
snowflake ['snəʊfleɪk] *n* copo *m* de nieve.
snowgoose ['snəʊ,guːs] *n*, *pl* **snowgeese** ['snəʊ,giːs] ánsar *m* nival.
snow-leopard ['snəʊ,lepəd] *n* onza *f*.
snowline ['snəʊlaɪn] *n* límite *m* de las nieves perpetuas.
snow machine ['snəʊmə,ʃiːn] *n* cañón *m* de nieve artificial.
snowman ['snəʊmæn] *n*, *pl* **snowmen** ['snəʊmen] figura *f* de nieve, monigote *m* de nieve; **the abominable ~** el abominable hombre de las nieves.
snowmobile ['snəʊmə,biːl] *n* motonieve *f*.
snowplough, (*US*) **snowplow** ['snəʊplaʊ] *n* quitanieves *m*.
Snow Queen ['snəʊ,kwiːn] *n* Reina *f* de las nieves.
snowshoe ['snəʊʃuː] *n* raqueta *f* (de nieve).
snowslide ['snəʊslaɪd] *n* (*US*) alud *m* (de nieve), avalancha *f*.
snowstorm ['snəʊstɔːm] *n* nevada *f*, nevasca *f*.
snowsuit ['snəʊsuːt] *n* mono *m* acolchado de nieve.
snow-tyre, (*US*) **snow tire** ['snəʊ,taɪəʳ] *n* neumático *m* antideslizante.
Snow White ['snəʊwaɪt] *nf* Blancanieves; **'~ and the Seven Dwarfs'** 'Blancanieves y los siete enanitos'.
snow-white ['snəʊ'waɪt] *adj* blanco como la nieve; (*poet*) níveo, cándido.
snowy ['snəʊɪ] *adj* (**a**) (*Met*) *climate, region* de mucha nieve, que tiene mucha nieve; *countryside etc* cubierto de nieve; **~ day** día *m* de nieve; **~ season** estación *f* de las nieves; **it was very ~ yesterday** ayer nevó mucho, ayer cayó mucha nieve.
(**b**) (*fig*) blanco como la nieve, (*poet*) níveo, cándido.
SNP *n abbr of* **Scottish National Party**.
Snr *abbr of* **Senior**.
snub¹ [snʌb] **1** *n* desaire *m*; repulsa *f*. **2** *vt person* desairar, ofender; repulsar; *offer etc* despreciar.
snub² [snʌb] *adj*: **~ nose** nariz *f* respingona.
snub-nosed ['snʌb'nəʊzd] *adj* chato, de nariz respingona, ñato (*LAm*).
snuff [snʌf] **1** *n* rapé *m*, tabaco *m* en polvo; **to take ~** tomar rapé.
2 *vt* (**a**) (*breathe in*) aspirar, sorber por la nariz.
(**b**) *candle* despabilar; **to ~ it‡** estirar la pata*.
◆**snuff out** *vt* apagar; (*fig*) extinguir.
snuffbox ['snʌfbɒks] *n* tabaquera *f*.
snuffer ['snʌfəʳ] *n* matacandelas *m*; **~s** (*scissors*; *also* **pair of ~s**) apagaderas *fpl*.
snuffle ['snʌfl] **1** *n* ruido *m* de la nariz; (*twang*) gangueo *m*.
2 *vi* respirar con ruido, hacer ruido con la nariz; (*in speaking*) ganguear.
snuff movie* ['snʌf,muːvɪ] *n* película *f* porno en que muere realmente uno de los participantes.
snug [snʌg] **1** *adj* (*cosy*) cómodo y bien caliente; (*sheltered*) abrigado, al abrigo; (*of dress*) ajustado; *income etc* respetable, nada despreciable; **to be ~ in bed** estar cómodamente acostado; **it's nice and ~ here** aquí se está bien. **2** *n* (*Brit*) salón *m* pequeño.
◆**snuggle down** *vi*: **to ~ down in bed** acomodarse en la cama, hacerse un ovillo en la cama; **they'll ~ down together** se acurrucarán juntos.
◆**snuggle up** *vi*: **to ~ up to sb** arrimarse (*or* abrazarse) (amorosamente *etc*) a uno, apretarse contra uno; **~ up to me** arrímate a mí; **I like to ~ up with a book** me gusta ponerme cómodamente y leer.
snugly ['snʌglɪ] *adv* cómodamente; al abrigo; **it fits ~** se ajusta perfectamente.
SO, S/O *abbr of* **standing order** giro *m* regular.
so¹ [səʊ] **1** *adv* (**a**) (*in comparisons*: *before adj and adv*) tan; **~ quick** tan rápido, **~ quickly** tan rápidamente; **it's about ~ high** es más o menos así de alto; **it is ~ big that ...** es tan grande que ...; **it's not ~ very difficult** no es tan difícil, la dificultad no es tan grande; **he's not ~ silly as to do that** no es bastante tonto para hacer eso, no es tan tonto como para hacer eso; **~ many flies** tantas moscas; **~ much tea** tanto té (*and V* **many, much**); **we spent ~ much** gastamos tanto; **I love you ~** te quiero tanto; **he who ~ loved Spain** él que amó tanto a España; *V* **kind, sure** *etc*.
(**b**) (*thus*) así; (*in this way*) de este modo, de esta manera; **he does it ~** lo hace de este modo; **if ~** si es así; en ese caso; **only more ~** pero en mayor grado; **how ~?** ¿por qué?, ¿cómo?; **why ~?** ¿cómo es eso?; **just ~!** ¡eso!, ¡eso es!, ¡perfectamente!, ¡precisamente!; **he likes things just ~** quiere tener cada cosa en su lugar, le gusta una vida bien ordenada; **you do it like ~*** se hace así, se hace de esta manera; **not ~!** ¡nada de eso!; **~ would I** yo también; **~ do I** yo también, yo hago lo mismo; **he's wrong and ~ are you** él se equivoca y tú también; **and ~ forth, and ~ on** y así sucesivamente, y así los demás; etcétera; **it is ~** es así; **~ it is!, ~ it does!** ¡es verdad!, ¡es cierto!; **that's ~** eso es; **is that ~?** ¿de veras?, ¿es cierto eso?; **isn't that ~?** ¿no es así?; ¿no es verdad?; **~ be it** así sea; **~ it was that ...** así fue que ...; **we ~ arranged things that ...** lo arreglamos de modo que ...; **and he did ~** y lo hizo; **by ~ doing** haciéndolo así; **it ~ happens that ...** da la casualidad que ...; **I hope ~** espero que sí; **~ saying, he walked out** diciendo esto, se marchó; **~ to speak** por decirlo así; **I think ~** creo que sí, lo creo; **I told you ~** te lo dije ya; **I tell you it is ~** te digo que es así; **30 or ~** unos 30, 30 o así.
(**c**) **~ that** (*purpose*) para que + *subj*, a fin de que + *subj*; **I brought it ~ that you should see it** lo traje para que lo vieras.
(**d**) **~ that** (*result*) de modo que + *indic*; **he stood ~ that nobody could get past** estaba en tal posición que nadie podía pasar.
(**e**) **~ as to** + *infin* para + *infin*, a fin de + *infin*; **we hurried ~ as not to be late** nos dimos prisa para no llegar tarde.
2 *conj* (**a**) **it rained and ~ we could not go out** llovió y por tanto (*or* por consiguiente) no pudimos salir.
(**b**) (*exclamatory etc*) **~?, ~ what?** ¿y qué?; **~ you're Spanish?** ¿conque Vd es español?, así que ¿Vd es español?; **~ you're not going?** ¿de suerte que no vas?; **~ there you are!** ¡ahí estás!; **~ you're not selling?** ¿de modo que no lo vende?, así que ¿no lo vende?; *V* **there** *etc*.
so² [səʊ] *n* (*Mus*) = **soh**.
soak [səʊk] **1** *vt* (**a**) **to ~ sth in a liquid** remojar algo en un líquido, empapar algo en un líquido; **to be ~ed (to the skin)** estar calado hasta los huesos; **to get ~ed (to the skin)** calarse hasta los huesos.
(**b**) (*) **to ~ sb** desplumar a uno*, clavar un precio excesivo a uno*; **to ~ sb for a loan** pedir prestado dinero

a uno; **to ~ the rich** cargar la mano con los ricos; **~ the rich!** ¡que paguen los ricos!

2 *vi* (**a**) remojarse, estar a remojo; **to leave sth to ~** dejar algo a remojo.

(**b**) (‡) beber mucho; emborracharse.

3 *vr*: **to ~ o.s.** calarse hasta los huesos; **to ~ o.s. in** (*fig*) empaparse en.

4 *n* (**a**) (*rain*) diluvio *m*; **to have a good ~ in the bath** descansar bañándose largamente; **give your shirt a ~ overnight** deja la camisa en remojo por la noche.

(**b**) (‡) borrachín *m*.

◆**soak in** *vi* (*liquid*) calar, penetrar; (*fig*) penetrar; hacer mella, tener efecto.

◆**soak through** *vi* calar, penetrar.

◆**soak up** *vt* (*absorb*) absorber, embeber.

soaking ['səʊkɪŋ] **1** *adj*: **to be ~** (**wet**) (*person*) estar hecho una sopa, (*object*) estar totalmente mojado, estar empapado; **a ~ wet day** un día de muchísima lluvia.

2 *n* (*in liquid*) remojo *m*; (*of rain*) diluvio *m*; **to get a ~** calarse hasta los huesos.

so-and-so ['səʊənsəʊ] *n* (**a**) **Mr ~** don Fulano (de Tal); **old ~ up at the shop** fulano el de la tienda; **any ~ could pinch it*** cualquiera pudiera apañarlo*.

(**b**) **he's a ~*** (*pej*) es un tío*; **you old ~!** (*hum*) ¡sinvergüenza!

soap [səʊp] **1** *n* (**a**) jabón *m*. (**b**) (*) = **soap-opera**. **2** *vt* jabonar, enjabonar.

◆**soap up** *vt*: **to ~ sb up*** dar coba a uno*.

soapbox ['səʊpbɒks] **1** *n* caja *f* vacía empleada como tribuna (en la calle). **2** *attr*: **~ orator** orador *m* callejero.

soapdish ['səʊpdɪʃ] *n* jabonera *f*.

soapflakes ['səʊpfleɪks] *npl* jabón *m* en escamas.

soap-opera* ['səʊp,ɒpərə] *n* (*Rad*) radionovela *f*; (*TV*) telenovela *f*, serial *m* (doméstico, sentimental *etc*), culebrón* *m*.

soap-powder ['səʊp,paʊdər] *n* jabón *m* en polvo.

soapstone ['səʊpstəʊn] *n* esteatita *f*.

soapsuds ['səʊpsʌdz] *npl* jabonaduras *fpl*, espuma *f* de jabón.

soapy ['səʊpɪ] *adj* (**a**) jabonoso; cubierto de jabón; (*like soap*) parecido a jabón, jabonoso; **it tastes ~** sabe a jabón. (**b**) (*) zalamero, cobista*.

soar [sɔːr] *vi* (**a**) (*rise*) remontarse, encumbrarse, subir muy alto; (*hover*) cernerse.

(**b**) (*fig*: *tower etc*) elevarse mucho sobre el suelo, elevarse hacia el cielo; (*price etc*) subir vertiginosamente, ponerse por las nubes; **the new tower ~s over the city** la nueva torre se eleva sobre la ciudad; **after this his ambition ~ed** después de esto se extendió mucho más su ambición; **our spirits ~ed** nos reanimamos de golpe; renació nuestra esperanza.

soaring ['sɔːrɪŋ] *adj flight* encumbrado, por lo alto; *building* altísimo; *ambition* inmenso; *price* que va subiendo vertiginosamente.

sob [sɒb] **1** *n* sollozo *m*; **she said with a ~** dijo sollozando.

2 *attr*: **~ story*** historia *f* sentimental; dramón* *m*; narración *f* patética; **~ stuff*** sentimentalismo *m*, sensiblería *f*.

3 *vt*: **'No', she ~bed** 'no', dijo sollozando; **to ~ o.s. to sleep** dormirse sollozando.

4 *vi* sollozar.

◆**sob out** *vt*: **to ~ one's heart out** llorar a lágrima viva; **she ~bed out her woes** contó sus penas llorando.

S.O.B.‡ *n* (*US*) *abbr of* **son of a bitch** hijo *m* de puta‡.

sobbing ['sɒbɪŋ] *n* sollozos *mpl*.

sober ['səʊbər] *adj* (**a**) (*moderate, sedate*) sobrio, serio, moderado; (*sensible*) sensato, juicioso; *colour* discreto; **a ~ assessment of the facts** una seria valoración de los hechos; **a ~ statement** una declaración razonada.

(**b**) (*not drunk*) no embriagado, que no ha bebido, sereno; **to be as ~ as a judge, to be stone-cold ~** estar totalmente sereno; **I'm perfectly ~** no he bebido en absoluto, tengo la cabeza perfectamente despejada; **one has to be ~ to drive** para conducir es necesario no haber bebido nada; **tomorrow, when you're ~** mañana, cuando te hayas despejado de la borrachera.

◆**sober down 1** *vt*: **to ~ sb down** calmar a uno.

2 *vi* calmarse; **he's ~ed down recently** recientemente ha sentado la cabeza.

◆**sober up 1** *vt*: **to ~ sb up** quitar la sopa a uno*; **this will ~ you up** esto te quitará la merluza*.

2 *vi* (*after drinking*) espabilar la borrachera; (*calm o.s.*) recuperar la sobriedad.

sober-headed ['səʊbə'hedɪd] *adj person* sensato, sobrio; *decision* sensato.

sobering ['səʊbərɪŋ] *adj*: **it had a ~ effect** moderó el entusiasmo (*etc*); hizo que la gente (*etc*) pensara en las consecuencias; **it's a ~ thought** eso hace reflexionar, eso da en qué pensar.

soberly ['səʊbəlɪ] *adv* sobriamente, seriamente, moderadamente; sensatamente; discretamente; **~ dressed** discretamente vestido.

sober-minded ['səʊbə'maɪndɪd] *adj* serio, formal.

soberness ['səʊbənɪs] *n*, **sobriety** [səʊ'braɪətɪ] *n* (**a**) sobriedad *f*, seriedad *f*; moderación *f*; sensatez *f*; discreción *f*. (**b**) estado *m* del que no ha bebido, serenidad *f*; moderación *f* en beber.

sobersides* ['səʊbəsaɪdz] *n* persona *f* muy reservada.

sobriquet ['səʊbrɪkeɪ] *n* apodo *m*, mote *m*.

Soc. (**a**) *abbr of* **society** sociedad *f*. (**b**) *abbr of* **Socialist** socialista *mf*, *also adj*.

so-called ['səʊ'kɔːld] *adj* llamado, denominado; supuesto, presunto; **in the ~ rush hours** en las llamadas horas punta; **all these ~ journalists** todos estos presuntos periodistas.

soccer ['sɒkər] **1** *n* fútbol *m*. **2** *attr* futbolístico; **~ player** futbolista *mf*.

sociability [,səʊʃə'bɪlɪtɪ] *n* sociabilidad *f*; afabilidad *f*.

sociable ['səʊʃəbl] *adj* sociable; afable; amistoso.

sociably ['səʊʃəblɪ] *adv* sociablemente; afablemente; amistosamente; **to live ~ together** vivir juntos amistosamente.

social ['səʊʃəl] **1** *adj* social; sociable; **a ~ outcast** una persona desterrada de la sociedad; **man is a ~ animal** el hombre es un animal sociable; **~ administration** administración *f* social; **~ anthropology** antropología *f* social; **~ class** clase *f* social; **~ climber** trepador *m*, -ora *f*; **~ climbing** arribismo *m* (social); **~ club** club *m* social; **~ column** notas *fpl* de sociedad; **~ contract** contrato *m* social; **~ cost** costo *m* en términos sociales; **S~ Democrat** socialdemócrata *mf*; **S~ Democratic** socialdemocrático; **I'm a ~ drinker only** yo no bebo a solas, yo bebo solamente en compañía de los amigos; **~ engineering** ingeniería *f* social; **~ insurance** (*US*), **~ welfare** seguro *m* social; **~ life** vida *f* social; **~ mobility** movilidad *f* social; **~ science** ciencia *f* social; **~ scientist** sociólogo *m*, -a *f*; **~ secretary** secretario *m*, -a *f* social; **~ security** seguridad *f* social; **~ security benefit** subsidio *m* del seguro social; **to be on ~ security** cobrar el seguro de desempleo; **~ services** servicios *mpl* sociales; **~ studies** estudios *mpl* sociales; **one's ~ superiors** los socialmente superiores a uno; **~ work** asistencia *f* social; **~ worker** trabajador *m*, -ora *f* social, asistente *mf* social.

2 *n* velada *f*, tertulia *f*, peña *f* (*LAm*).

socialism ['səʊʃəlɪzəm] *n* socialismo *m*.

socialist ['səʊʃəlɪst] **1** *adj* socialista. **2** *n* socialista *mf*.

socialistic [,səʊʃə'lɪstɪk] *adj* socialista.

socialite ['səʊʃəlaɪt] *n* persona *f* mundana, persona *f* conocidísima en la buena sociedad.

socialization [,səʊʃəlaɪ'zeɪʃən] *n* socialización *f*.

socialize ['səʊʃəlaɪz] **1** *vt* socializar. **2** *vi* alternar con la gente, mezclarse con la gente; conversar, charlar; **you should ~ more** debes ver más gente; **we don't ~ much these days** no salimos mucho estos días.

socially ['səʊʃəlɪ] *adv* socialmente; sociablemente; **we meet ~** nos vemos en las reuniones de tipo social.

societal [sə'saɪətəl] *adj* societal.

society [sə'saɪətɪ] **1** *n* (**a**) (*community*) sociedad *f*; **to live in ~** vivir en la sociedad; **he's a danger to ~** es un peligro para la sociedad.

(**b**) (*high ~*) alta sociedad *f*; buena sociedad *f*, mundo *m* elegante; **to go into ~** (*girl*) ponerse de largo; **to move in ~** frecuentar la buena sociedad.

(**c**) (*companionship*) sociedad *f*, compañía *f*; **in the ~ of** en compañía de, acompañado por; **I enjoy his ~** me gusta su compañía.

(**d**) (*group*) sociedad *f*; asociación *f*; **S~ of Friends** los cuáqueros; **S~ of Jesus** Compañía *f* de Jesús.

2 *attr*: **~ news** notas *fpl* de sociedad; **~ wedding** boda *f* de la buena sociedad; **~ woman** mujer *f* conocida en la buena sociedad.

sociobiology [,səʊsɪəʊbaɪ'ɒlədʒɪ] *n* sociobiología *f*.

socioeconomic ['səʊsɪəʊ,iːkə'nɒmɪk] *adj* socioeconómico.

sociolect ['səʊsɪəʊ,lekt] *n* sociolecto *m*.

sociolinguistic [,səʊsɪəʊlɪŋ'gwɪstɪk] *adj* sociolingüístico.

sociolinguistics [,səʊsɪəʊlɪŋ'gwɪstɪks] *n* sociolingüística *f*.

sociological [,səʊsɪə'lɒdʒɪkəl] *adj* sociológico.

sociologist [,səʊsɪ'ɒlədʒɪst] *n* sociólogo *m*, -a *f*.

sociology [ˌsəʊsɪ'ɒlədʒɪ] *n* sociología *f*.
sociopolitical [ˌsəʊsɪəʊpə'lɪtɪkəl] *adj* sociopolítico.
sock[1] [sɒk] *n* calcetín *m*, media *f* (*LAm*); (*insole*) plantilla *f*; **to pull one's ~s up** (*fig*) hacer un esfuerzo, procurar hacer mejor; **put** (*or* **shove**) **a ~ in it!*** ¡a callar!, ¡cállate!
sock[2]* [sɒk] **1** *n* tortazo* *m*. **2** *vt* pegar; **~ him one!** ¡pégale!; **~ it to me!** ¡dímelo!
socket ['sɒkɪt] *n* (*of eye*) cuenca *f*, órbita *f*; (*of tooth*) alvéolo *m*; (*of joint*) fosa *f*; (*Brit Elec*) enchufe *m*, toma *f*; (*Mech*) encaje *m*, cubo *m*.
socket joint ['sɒkɪtˌdʒɔɪnt] *n* (*Carp*) machihembrado *m*; (*Anat*) articulación *f* esférica.
socko* ['sɒkəʊ] (*US*) **1** *adj* estupendo*, extraordinario. **2** *n* gran éxito *m*.
Socrates ['sɒkrətiːz] *nm* Sócrates.
Socratic [sɒ'krætɪk] *adj* socrático.
sod[1] [sɒd] *n* césped *m*.
sod[2]** [sɒd] (*Brit*) **1** *n* bestia* *f*, bruto *m*; **you ~!** ¡cabrón!**; **~'s law** ley *f* de la indefectible mala voluntad de los objetos inanimados; **he's a real ~** es una mala bestia; **this job is a real ~** este trabajo es la monda*; **the lid is a ~ to get off** quitar la tapa hace sudar la gota gorda; **some poor ~** algún pobre diablo.
2 *vt*: **~ it!** ¡mierda!**; **~ him!** ¡que se joda!**
◆**sod off**** *vi* irse a la porra*, ir a hacer puñetas**; **~ off!** ¡vete a la porra!*
soda ['səʊdə] *n* (**a**) (*Chem*) sosa *f*, soda *f*; (*Culin*) bicarbonato *m* (sódico).
(**b**) (*drink*) soda *f*, agua *f* de seltz, gaseosa *f*; **gin and ~** ginebra *f* con sifón; **do you like ~ with it?** ¿te echo un poco de sifón?, ¿con soda?
sod-all** ['sɒdɔːl] = **damn-all**.
soda ash ['səʊdəˌæʃ] *n* sosa *f* comercial, ceniza *f* de soda.
soda fountain ['səʊdəˌfaʊntɪn] *n* (*US*) sifón *m*; bar *m* de bebidas no alcohólicas.
sodality [səʊ'dælɪtɪ] *n* hermandad *f*, cofradía *f*.
soda-siphon ['səʊdəˌsaɪfən] *n* sifón *m*.
soda-water ['səʊdəˌwɔːtə'] *n* soda *f*, agua *f* de seltz, gaseosa *f*; **...with ~** ... con sifón, ... con soda.
sodden ['sɒdn] *adj* empapado, mojado, saturado; **to be ~ with drink** estar embrutecido por el alcohol.
sodding** ['sɒdɪŋ] *adj* jodido**, puñetero**.
sodium ['səʊdɪəm] **1** *n* sodio *m*. **2** *attr*: **~ bicarbonate** bicarbonato *m* sódico; **~ carbonate** carbonato *m* sódico; **~ chloride** cloruro *m* sódico; **~ nitrate** nitrato *m* sódico; **~ sulphate** sulfato *m* sódico.
Sodom ['sɒdəm] *n* Sodoma *f*.
sodomite ['sɒdəmaɪt] *n* sodomita *m*.
sodomize ['sɒdəmaɪz] *vt* sodomizar.
sodomy ['sɒdəmɪ] *n* sodomía *f*.
sofa ['səʊfə] *n* sofá *m*.
sofa-bed ['səʊfəbed] *n* sofá-cama *m*.
Sofia ['səʊfɪə] *n* Sofía *f*.
soft [sɒft] *adj* (**a**) *material etc* blando; muelle; (*flabby*) flojo; *skin* suave, terso, fino; *metal* dúctil; *hat* flexible; *fruit* blando; **~ centre** relleno *m* blando; **~ coal** huella *f* grasa; **~ collar** cuello *m* blando; **~ furnishings** tejidos *mpl* para casa (*cortinas, fundas, etc*); **~ goods** géneros *mpl* textiles; **~ ice cream** helado *m* de máquina; **~ money** (*US*) papel *m* moneda; **~ palate** velo *m* del paladar; **~ shoulder** = **~ verge**; **~ top** (*esp US*) descapotable *m*; **~ toy** muñeco *m* de peluche; **~ verge** (*Brit*) borde *m* blando; **~ to the touch** blando al tacto; **as ~ as silk, as ~ as velvet** tan suave como la seda; **to go ~** ablandarse, ponerse blando; **his muscles have gone ~** sus músculos han perdido su fuerza, sus músculos ya están flojos.
(**b**) (*fig*) *air, sound* suave; *voice* dulce; *step* suave; *water* blando; *rain* suave; *colour* delicado; *loan* favorable, privilegiado; *heart, words* tierno, compasivo; *job* fácil; *character* débil; muelle, afeminado; (*lenient*) indulgente, tolerante; **~ copy** copia *f* transitoria; **~ currency** moneda *f* blanda; **~ drink** bebida *f* no alcohólica, bebida *f* refrescante, gaseosa *f*; **~ drug** droga *f* suave, droga *f* blanda; **~ focus** flou *m*, desenfoque *m*; **in ~ focus** desenfocado; **~ job*** prebenda* *f*, chollo* *m*; **~ landing** aterrizaje *m* suave; **~ lighting** luz *f* baja; **~ lights and sweet music** poca luz y música sentimental; **~ option** alternativa *f* más fácil; **~ porn*** pornografía *f* blanda; **~ sell*** venta *f* persuasiva, venta *f* con publicidad discreta; venta *f* fácil; **~ soap*** coba* *f*; **~ touch*** persona *f* que se deja convencer fácilmente; **~ water** agua *f* blanda; **to be ~ on sb** tratar a uno con demasiada indulgencia; **to be ~ on crime** ser blando con el delito; **he's ~ on communism** es demasiado tolerante para con el comunismo.
(**c**) (*foolish*) estúpido, tonto; **you must be ~!** ¿has perdido el juicio?; **he's ~** (**in the head**) es un poco tocado; **he's going ~** (**in the head**) está perdiendo el juicio.
softback ['sɒftbæk] *attr* = **soft-bound**.
softball ['sɒftbɔːl] *n* (*US*) *especie de béisbol sobre un terreno más pequeño que el normal, con pelota grande y blanda*.
soft-boiled ['sɒftˌbɔɪld] *adj*: **~ egg** huevo *m* pasado por agua, huevo *m* tibio (*And*), huevo *m* amelcochado (*Carib*).
soft-bound ['sɒftbaʊnd] *adj*, **soft-cover** ['sɒftkʌvə'] *attr*: **~ book** libro *m* en rústica.
soften ['sɒfn] **1** *vt* ablandar, reblandecer; (*weaken*) debilitar; (*mitigate*) mitigar, suavizar, templar; *blow* amortiguar.
2 *vi* ablandarse, reblandecerse; debilitarse, aflojarse; suavizarse, templarse.
◆**soften up** **1** *vt*: **to ~ up resistance** debilitar la resistencia.
2 *vi*: **to ~ up on sb** hacerse menos severo con uno, mitigar su severidad con uno; **we must not ~ up on communism** tenemos que seguir tan opuestos como siempre al comunismo.
softener ['sɒfnə'] *n* (*water ~*) descalcificador *m*; (*fabric ~*) suavizante *m*.
softening ['sɒfnɪŋ] *n* reblandecimiento *m*; debilitación *f*; mitigación *f*, suavización *f*; **~ of the brain** reblandecimiento *m* cerebral; **there has been a ~ of his attitude** se ha suavizado su actitud.
soft-headed ['sɒftˌhedɪd] *adj* bobo, tonto.
soft-hearted ['sɒft'hɑːtɪd] *adj* compasivo, bondadoso.
soft-heartedness ['sɒft'hɑːtɪdnɪs] *n* bondad *f*.
softie* ['sɒftɪ] *n* = **softy**.
soft-liner [ˌsɒft'laɪnə'] *n* blando *m*, -a *f*.
softly ['sɒftlɪ] *adv* blandamente; suavemente; dulcemente; delicadamente; **she said ~** dijo dulcemente; **to move ~** moverse silenciosamente, moverse sin ruido; **to adopt a ~ ~ approach** avanzar con cautela, ir con pies de plomo.
softness ['sɒftnɪs] *n* (*V adj*) (**a**) blandura *f*; flojedad *f*; suavidad *f*, tersura *f*; ductilidad *f*. (**b**) dulzura *f*; delicadeza *f*; ternura *f*; debilidad *f*; indulgencia *f*, tolerancia *f*. (**c**) estupidez *f*.
soft-pedal ['sɒft'pedl] *vt* (*fig*) no dar tanto énfasis a, dejar de insistir en, conceder menos importancia a.
soft-soap* [ˌsɒft'səʊp] *vt* dar coba a*.
soft-spoken ['sɒft'spəʊkən] *adj* de voz suave, de tono dulce.
software ['sɒftwɛə'] **1** *n* software *m*, elementos *mpl* de programación, logicial *m*, soporte *m* lógico, componentes *mpl* lógicos. **2** *attr*: **~ engineering** ingeniería *f* de software; **~ house** compañía *f* especializada en programación; **~ package** paquete *m* de programas.
softwood ['sɒftwʊd] *n* madera *f* blanda.
SOGAT ['səʊgæt] *n* (*Brit*) *abbr of* **Society of Graphical and Allied Trades** *sindicato de tipógrafos*.
softy* ['sɒftɪ] *n* mollejón* *m*, -ona *f*; memo *m*, -a *f*.
soggy ['sɒgɪ] *adj* empapado, saturado; esponjoso.
soh [səʊ] *n* sol *m*.
soi-disant ['swɑː'diːsɔːŋ] *adj* supuesto, presunto, sediciente.
soigné ['swɑːnjeɪ] *adj* pulcro, acicalado.
soil[1] [sɔɪl] *n* tierra *f*, suelo *m*; **one's native ~** su tierra, su patria.
soil[2] [sɔɪl] **1** *vt* ensuciar; manchar (*also fig*).
2 *vi* ensuciarse.
3 *vr*: **to ~ o.s.** ensuciarse; **I would not ~ myself by contact with ...** no me rebajaría a tener contacto con ...
soiled [sɔɪld] *adj* sucio.
soilpipe ['sɔɪlpaɪp] *n* tubo *m* de desagüe sanitario.
soirée ['swɑːreɪ] *n* velada *f*.
sojourn ['sɒdʒɜːn] **1** *n* permanencia *f*, estancia *f*. **2** *vi* permanecer, residir, morar; pasar una temporada.
solace ['sɒlɪs] **1** *n* consuelo *m*; **to seek ~ with ...** procurar consolarse con ...
2 *vt* consolar.
3 *vr*: **to ~ o.s.** consolarse (*with* con).
solar ['səʊlə'] *adj* solar, del sol; **~ battery** pila *f* solar; **~ calculator** calculadora *f* solar; **~ cell** célula *f* solar; **~ eclipse** eclipse *m* solar; **~ energy** energía *f* solar; **~ flare** erupción *f* solar; **~ heat** calor *m* solar; **~ heating** calefacción *f* solar; **~ panel** panel *m* solar; **~ plexus** plexo *m* solar; **~ system** sistema *m* solar; **~ wind** viento *m* solar.
solarium [səʊ'lɛərɪəm] *n, pl* **solaria** [səʊ'lɛərɪə] solario *m*, solárium *m*, solana *f*.
solar-powered ['səʊlə'paʊəd] *adj* que funciona con energía solar.
sold [səʊld] *pret and ptp of* **sell**.

solder ['səʊldəʳ] **1** *n* soldadura *f*. **2** *vt* soldar.
soldering-iron ['səʊldərɪŋ,aɪən] *n* soldador *m*.
soldier ['səʊldʒəʳ] **1** *n* soldado *mf*; militar *m*; ~ **of fortune** aventurero *m* militar; **common** ~ soldado *m* raso; **old** ~ veterano *m*, excombatiente *m*; **a young woman** ~ una joven soldado; **to come the old** ~ **with sb*** tratar de imponerse a uno (por más experimentado).
2 *vi* militar, ser soldado; servir; **he** ~**ed for 10 years in the East** sirvió durante 10 años en el Oriente.
◆**soldier on** *vi* (*Brit*) continuar a pesar de todo.
soldierly ['səʊldʒəlɪ] *adj* militar.
soldiery ['səʊldʒərɪ] *n* soldadesca *f*; **a brutal and licentious** ~ la soldadesca indisciplinada.
sole[1] [səʊl] **1** *n* (*Anat*) planta *f*; (*of shoe*) suela *f*, piso *m*. **2** *vt* poner suela a, poner piso a.
sole[2] [səʊl] *n* (*Fish*) lenguado *m*.
sole[3] [səʊl] *adj* único, solo; exclusivo; ~ **agency** agencia *f* única; ~ **agent** agente *m* único, agente *f* única; **to be** ~ **agent for** tener la representación exclusiva de; ~ **owner** propietario *m* único, propietaria *f* única; ~ **trader** comerciante *m* exclusivo; **the** ~ **reason is that ...** la única razón es que ...
solecism ['sɒləsɪzəm] *n* solecismo *m*.
solely ['səʊllɪ] *adv* únicamente, solamente, sólo.
solemn ['sɒləm] *adj* solemne.
solemnity [sə'lemnɪtɪ] *n* solemnidad *f*.
solemnization [,sɒləmnaɪ'zeɪʃən] *n* solemnización *f*.
solemnize ['sɒləmnaɪz] *vt* solemnizar.
solemnly ['sɒləmlɪ] *adv* solemnemente.
solenoid ['səʊlənɔɪd] *n* solenoide *m*.
solfa ['sɒl'fɑː] *n* solfa *f*.
solicit [sə'lɪsɪt] **1** *vt* (*request*) solicitar; implorar, pedir insistentemente; (*importune*) importunar; (*prostitute*) abordar, importunar; **to** ~ **sb for sth, to** ~ **sth of sb** solicitar algo a uno. **2** *vi* (*prostitute*) importunar.
solicitation [sə,lɪsɪ'teɪʃən] *n* solicitación *f*.
soliciting [sə'lɪsɪtɪŋ] *n* abordamiento *m*.
solicitor [sə'lɪsɪtəʳ] *n* (**a**) (*US*) representante *mf*, agente *mf*; (*US Jur*) abogado *m* asesor adscrito a un municipio (*etc*).
(**b**) (*Brit Jur*) procurador *m*, abogado *mf*; (*for oaths, wills etc*) notario *m*; **S~ General** (*Brit*) subfiscal *m* de la Corona, (*US*) fiscal *m* general del Estado.
solicitous [sə'lɪsɪtəs] *adj* solícito (*about, for* por); preocupado, ansioso; atento.
solicitude [sə'lɪsɪtjuːd] *n* solicitud *f*; preocupación *f*, ansiedad *f*; atención *f*.
solid ['sɒlɪd] **1** *adj* (**a**) (*gen*) sólido; *gold, silver, oak etc* macizo; *tyre* macizo, sin cámara; (*of consistency of soup etc*) sustancioso; *meal* fuerte; *crowd* denso, apretado; *vote* unánime; *person's character* enteramente serio, muy formal; *conviction* firme; *argument* sólido, fundado; *supporter* incondicional; **the** ~ **South** (*US*) el bloque sólido constituido por los estados del Sur (que apoyaban siempre al Partido Democrático); ~ **compound** (*Ling*) compuesto *m* cuyos términos están gráficamente soldados; ~ **fuel** combustible *m* sólido; ~ **fuel heater** calentador *m* de combustible sólido; ~ **geometry** geometría *f* del espacio; ~ **word** palabra *f* simple; **Slobodia is** ~ **for Smith** Eslobodia apoya unánimemente a Smith; **the house is** ~ **enough** la casa es perfectamente sólida; **the square was** ~ **with cars** la plaza estaba totalmente llena de coches, la plaza estaba atestada de coches; **to be frozen** ~ estar completamente helado; **it was cut into** ~ **rock** se excavó en peña viva; **to have** ~ **grounds for thinking that ...** tener buenos motivos para creer que ...; **it makes good** ~ **sense** hace muy buen sentido; **we walked 14** ~ **miles** anduvimos 14 millas largas; **we waited 2** ~ **hours** esperamos dos horas enteras.
(**b**) (*US: excellent*) excelente, extraordinario.
2 *n* sólido *m*; ~**s** (*food*) alimentos *mpl* sólidos.
solidarity [,sɒlɪ'dærɪtɪ] *n* solidaridad *f*; ~ **strike** huelga *f* por solidaridad; **out of** ~ **with the workers** por solidaridad con los obreros.
solidification [sə,lɪdɪfɪ'keɪʃən] *n* solidificación *f*.
solidify [sə'lɪdɪfaɪ] **1** *vt* solidificar. **2** *vi* solidificarse.
solidity [sə'lɪdɪtɪ] *n* solidez *f*.
solidly ['sɒlɪdlɪ] *adv* sólidamente; densamente, apretadamente; unánimemente; **a** ~ **reasoned argument** un argumento sólidamente razonado; **to vote** ~ **for sb** votar unánimemente por uno; **we were** ~ **for Smith** apoyamos unánimemente a Smith; **a** ~**-built house** una casa de sólida construcción.
solid-state ['sɒlɪd'steɪt] *attr* del estado sólido; ~ **physics** física *f* del estado sólido.
solidus ['sɒlɪdəs] *n* (*Typ*) barra *f*.
soliloquize [sə'lɪləkwaɪz] *vi* soliloquiar; '~', **he** ~**d** '~' dijo para sí.
soliloquy [sə'lɪləkwɪ] *n* soliloquio *m*.
solipsism ['səʊlɪpsɪzəm] *n* solipsismo *m*.
solitaire [,sɒlɪ'teəʳ] *n* (*game, gem*) solitario *m*.
solitary ['sɒlɪtərɪ] **1** *adj* (**a**) (*living alone*) solitario, solo; (*secluded*) retirado, apartado; **to be in** ~ **confinement** estar incomunicado, estar en pelota‡; **to take a** ~ **walk** dar un paseo solo, pasearse sin compañía; **to feel rather** ~ sentirse solo, sentirse aislado.
(**b**) (*sole*) único, solo; **not a** ~ **one** ni uno (solo); **there has been one** ~ **case** ha habido un caso único; **there has not been one** ~ **case** no ha habido ni un solo caso.
2 *n* (**a**) (*person*) solitario *m*, -a *f*.
(**b**) (*) = ~ **confinement**; *V* **1a.**
solitude ['sɒlɪtjuːd] *n* soledad *f*.
solo ['səʊləʊ] **1** *n*, *pl* **solos** ['səʊləʊz] (*Cards, Mus*) solo *m*; **to sing a** ~ cantar un solo; **a tenor** ~ un solo para tenor.
2 *adj*: ~ **flight** vuelo *m* a solas; **passage for** ~ **violin** pasaje *m* para violín solo; ~ **trip round the world** vuelta *f* al mundo en solitario.
3 *adv*: **to fly** ~ volar a solas; **to sing** ~ cantar solo.
soloist ['səʊləʊɪst] *n* solista *mf*.
Solomon ['sɒləmən] **1** *nm* Salomón. **2** *attr*: ~ **Islands** Islas *fpl* Salomón.
solstice ['sɒlstɪs] *n* solsticio *m*; **summer** ~ solsticio *m* de verano; **winter** ~ solsticio *m* de invierno.
solubility [,sɒljʊ'bɪlɪtɪ] *n* solubilidad *f*.
soluble ['sɒljʊbl] *adj* soluble; ~ **in water** soluble en agua.
solution [sə'luːʃən] *n* (*all senses*) solución *f* (*to a problem* de un problema); **in** ~ en solución.
solvable ['sɒlvəbl] *adj* soluble, que se puede resolver.
solve [sɒlv] *vt* resolver, solucionar; *riddle* adivinar.
solvency ['sɒlvənsɪ] *n* solvencia *f*.
solvent ['sɒlvənt] **1** *adj* solvente. **2** *n* solvente *m*. **3** *attr*: ~ **abuse** esnifamiento *m* de disolvente.
solver ['sɒlvəʳ] *n* solucionista *mf*.
Somali [səʊ'mɑːlɪ] **1** *adj* somalí. **2** *n* somalí *mf*.
Somalia [səʊ'mɑːlɪə] *n* Somalia *f*.
Somalian [səʊ'mɑːlɪən] **1** *adj* somalí. **2** *n* somalí *mf*.
Somaliland [səʊ'mɑːlɪlænd] *n* Somalia *f*.
sombre, (*US*) **somber** ['sɒmbəʳ] *adj* sombrío; pesimista; **in** ~ **hues** en colores sombríos; **a** ~ **prospect** una perspectiva sombría; **he was** ~ **about our chances** se mostró pesimista acerca de nuestras posibilidades.
sombrely, (*US*) **somberly** ['sɒmbəlɪ] *adv* sombríamente; con pesimismo, en tono pesimista.
sombreness, (*US*) **somberness** ['sɒmbənɪs] *n* lo sombrío; pesimismo *m*.
some [sʌm] **1** *adj* (**a**) alguno, (*before m sing n*) algún; unos, unos cuantos; ~ **day** algún día; ~ **man** algún hombre; ~ **people** algunos, algunas personas; ~ **very big cars** algunos coches muy grandes, unos coches muy grandes; ~ **distance away** a cierta distancia; **after** ~ **time** después de cierto tiempo; **it took** ~ **courage to do that** hacer eso exigió bastante valor, quien hizo eso tenía bastante valor; ~ **books I could name** ciertos libros que pudiera mencionar; ~ **days ago** hace unos días; **in** ~ **form or other** en alguna forma; **for** ~ **reason or other** por alguna razón; ~ **politician or other** algún político; ~ **other time** otro día; ~ **idiot of a driver** algún imbécil de conductor; ~ **people just don't care** hay gente que no se preocupa en lo más mínimo.
(**b**) (*partitive*) un poco de, algo de; (*freq not translated, eg*) **have you** ~ **money?** ¿tienes dinero?, **will you have** ~ **tea?** ¿quieres té?; **all I have left is** ~ **chocolate** solamente me queda un poco de chocolate; **here is** ~ **water for you** te he traído un poco de agua; ~ **water, please** agua, por favor.
(**c**) (*intensive*) **that's** ~ **fish!** ¡eso es lo que se llama un pez!; ¡eso es un pez de verdad!; ~ **expert!** (*iro*) ¡valiente experto!; **that's** ~ **woman** es mucha mujer; **it was** ~ **party** menuda fiesta fue; **you're** ~ **friend!** ¡menudo amigo tú!
2 *pron* (**a**) (*a certain number*) algunos; ~ **went this way and** ~ **that** algunos fueron por aquí y otros por allá; ~ **say yes and** ~ **say no** algunos dicen que sí y otros que no; ~ **of them are crazy** algunos de ellos están locos; ~ **believe that ...** algunos creen que ..., hay quien cree que ...
(**b**) (*a certain amount*) algunos; algo, un poco; **do take** ~ (*pl*) toma algunos, (*sing*) toma algo, toma un poco; **thanks, I have** ~ gracias, ya tengo; **could I have** ~ **of that cheese?** ¿me puedes servir un poco de ese queso?; **I like** ~ **of what you said in the speech** me gusta una parte de lo que Vd dijo en el discurso; ~ **of what you say is true** parte

de lo que dices es cierto; **and then ~*** y luego más, y más todavía.

3 *adv* (**a**) (*about*) ~ **20 people** unas 20 personas, aproximadamente 20 personas, una veintena de personas; ~ **£30** unas 30 libras, más o menos 30 libras; ~ **few difficulties** unas pocas dificultades.

(**b**) (*esp US**) mucho; **we laughed** ~ nos reímos mucho; **it sure bothered us** ~ ya lo creo que nos preocupó bastante; **he's travelling** ~ lleva gran velocidad.

-some [səm] *n ending in compounds* grupo *m* de ...; **three~** grupo *m* de tres personas; **we'll go in a three~** iremos los tres, iremos como grupo de tres; **have we a four~ for bridge?** ¿tenemos cuatro para jugar al bridge?; **to make up a four~** formar un grupo de cuatro.

somebody ['sʌmbədɪ] **1** *pron* alguien; ~ **else** algún otro, otra persona; ~ **told me so** alguien me lo dijo, me lo dijo alguno; ~ **or other must have taken it** alguien se lo habrá llevado; ~ **up there loves me** tengo una buena racha; ~ **up there hates me** tengo una mala racha.

2 *n*: **to be** ~ ser un personaje, ser alguien; **he thinks he's ~ now** ahora se cree un personaje.

someday ['sʌmdeɪ] *adv* algún día.

somehow ['sʌmhaʊ] *adv* (**a**) (*in some way*) de algún modo, de un modo u otro; **it must be done ~ or other** de un modo u otro tiene que hacerse; ~ **or other I never liked him** por alguna razón no me era simpático.

(**b**) **it seems ~ odd, it seems odd** ~ no sé por qué pero me parece extraño.

someone ['sʌmwʌn] *pron* = **somebody**.

someplace ['sʌmpleɪs] *adv* (*US*) = **somewhere**.

somersault ['sʌməsɔːlt] **1** *n* (*by person*) salto *m* mortal; (*by car etc*) vuelco *m*, vuelta *f* de campana; **to turn a** ~ dar un salto mortal; volcar; **to turn ~s** dar saltos mortales; dar vueltas de campana.

2 *vi* dar un salto mortal; dar una vuelta de campana.

something ['sʌmθɪŋ] **1** *pron* (**a**) algo; alguna cosa; ~ **else** otra cosa; ~ **or other is bothering him** algo le trae preocupado; **there's ~ the matter** pasa algo; **did you say ~?** ¿dijiste algo?; **there's ~ odd here** aquí hay algo raro; ~ **of the kind** algo por el estilo; **it's come to ~ when ...** llegamos a un punto grave cuando ...; **there's ~ in what you say** hay gran parte de verdad en lo que dices; **well, that's** ~ eso ya es algo; **she has a certain** ~ tiene un no sé qué (de atractivo); **that certain ~ that makes all the difference** ese no sé qué que importa tanto; **her hat was quite** ~ su sombrero era de ver; **her win was quite** ~ su victoria era extraordinaria; **that's quite** (*or* **really**) **~!** ¡eso sí que es algo!; **you've got ~ there*** no es mala idea (*etc*); es un punto clave; **he's called John** ~ se llama Juan y no sé qué más; **there were 30** ~ había treinta y algunos más; **will you have ~ to drink?** ¿quieres tomar algo?; **I need ~ to eat** necesito comer; **I gave him ~ for himself** le di algo para sí; **it gives her ~ to live for** le da un motivo para vivir; **do you want to make ~ of it?** ¿quién le mete a Vd en esto?; y a Vd ¿qué le importa?

(**b**) (*or* ~) **are you mad or ~?** ¿estás loco o qué?; **her name is Camilla or** ~ se llama algo así como Camila; **he's got flu or** ~ tiene gripe o algo parecido.

(**c**) **it's ~ of a problem** en cierto sentido representa un problema, viene a ser un problema; **he's ~ of a musician** es en cierto modo un músico, tiene cierto talento para la música; **let's see ~ of you soon** ven a vernos pronto.

2 *adv* (**a**) ~ **over 200** algo más de 200; **he left ~ over £10,000** dejó más de 10.000 libras; **he left ~ like £10,000** dejó algo así como 10.000 libras; **now that's ~ like a rose!** ¡eso es lo que se llama una rosa!

(**b**) (*****) **it's ~ chronic** es horrible, es fatal*; **the weather was ~ shocking** el tiempo fue asqueroso.

sometime ['sʌmtaɪm] **1** *adv* (**a**) (*in future*) algún día; alguna vez; ~ **or other it will have to be done** tarde o temprano tendrá que hacerse; **write to me ~ soon** escríbeme pronto, escríbeme algún día de éstos; ~ **before tomorrow** antes de mañana; ~ **next year** el año que viene.

(**b**) (*in past*) ~ **last month** el mes pasado; ~ **last century** en el siglo pasado, durante el siglo pasado; **it was ~ before 1950** fue antes de 1950 (no lo sé más exactamente).

2 *adj* (**a**) ex ..., antiguo; ~ **mayor of Wapping** ex alcalde de Wapping.

(**b**) (*US*: *occasional*) intermitente.

sometimes ['sʌmtaɪmz] *adv* algunas veces; a veces.

somewhat ['sʌmwɒt] *adv* algo, algún tanto; **we are ~ worried** estamos algo inquietos; **it was done ~ hastily** se hizo con demasiada prisa.

somewhere ['sʌmwɛəʳ] *adv* (**a**) (*be*) en alguna parte; (*go*) a alguna parte; ~ **else** (*be*) en otra parte; (*go*) a otra parte; **I left it ~ or other** lo dejé en alguna parte, lo dejé por ahí; **he's ~ around** anda por ahí; **now we're getting** ~ estamos haciendo progresos; ~ **near Huesca** cerca de Huesca; ~ **in Aragón** en alguna parte de Aragón; **to broadcast from ~ in Europe** emitir de algún lugar de Europa.

(**b**) (*approximately*) alrededor de; ~ **about 3 o'clock** alrededor de las 3, a eso de las 3; **he paid ~ about £12** pagó alrededor de 12 libras; **she's ~ about 50** tiene 50 años más o menos.

Somme [sɒm] *n* Somme *m*; **the Battle of the** ~ la batalla del Somme.

somnambulism [sɒm'næmbjʊlɪzəm] *n* so(m)nambulismo *m*.

somnambulist [sɒm'næmbjʊlɪst] *n* so(m)námbulo *m*, -a *f*.

somniferous [sɒm'nɪfərəs] *adj* somnífero.

somnolence ['sɒmnələns] *n* somnolencia *f*.

somnolent ['sɒmnələnt] *adj* soñoliento.

son [sʌn] *n* hijo *m*; ~ **of a bitch‡** hijo *m* de puta‡; **S~ of God** Hijo *m* de Dios; **S~ of Man** Hijo *m* del Hombre.

sonar ['səʊnɑːʳ] *n* sonar *m*.

sonata [sə'nɑːtə] *n* sonata *f*.

son et lumière [ˌsɔ̃elym'jɛːr] *n* (espectáculo *m* de) luz *f* y sonido.

song [sɒŋ] **1** *n* (*a* ~) canción *f*; (*art of singing*) canto *m*; (*epic*) cantar *m*; **festival of Spanish** ~ festival *m* de la canción española; **'A S~ for Europe'** 'Canción *f* para Europa'; **S~ of Roland** Cantar *m* de Roldán; **S~ of Solomon, S~ of S~s** Cantar *m* de los Cantares; **to burst into** ~ romper a cantar; **give us a ~!** ¡cántanos algo!; **to make a great ~ and dance about sth** hacer algo a bombo y platillos; **he made a ~ and dance about the carpet** armó la gorda por lo de la alfombra; **there's no need to make a ~ and dance** no es para tanto; **to give sb the same old ~ and dance*** (*US*) andar siempre con las mismas disculpas; **to sell sth for a** (**mere**) ~ vender algo medio regalado; **I got it for a** ~ lo adquirí muy barato; **to sing another** ~ (*fig*) bajar el tono, desdecirse.

2 *attr*: ~ **and dance routine** número *m* de canción y baile.

songbird ['sɒŋbɜːd] *n* pájaro *m* cantor, ave *f* canora.

songbook ['sɒŋbʊk] *n* cancionero *m*.

song-cycle ['sɒŋ'saɪkl] *n* ciclo *m* de canciones.

songfest ['sɒŋfest] *n* festival *m* de canciones.

song-hit ['sɒŋhɪt] *n* canción *f* de moda, canción *f* popular del momento, impacto *m*.

songster ['sɒŋstəʳ] *n* pájaro *m* cantor.

songthrush ['sɒŋθrʌʃ] *n* tordo *m* cantor, tordo *m* melodioso.

songwriter ['sɒŋˌraɪtəʳ] *n* compositor *m*, -ora *f* de canciones.

sonic ['sɒnɪk] *adj* sónico; ~ **boom** estampido *m* sónico.

sonics ['sɒnɪks] *n* sónica *f*.

son-in-law ['sʌnɪnlɔː] *n*, *pl* **sons-in-law** ['sʌnzɪnlɔː] yerno *m*, hijo *m* político.

sonnet ['sɒnɪt] *n* soneto *m*.

sonny* ['sʌnɪ] *n* hijito *m*; (*in direct address*) hijo.

son-of-a-gun‡ [ˌsʌnəvə'gʌn] *n* hijo *m* de tu madre*, hijo *m* de la gran pu‡.

sonority [sə'nɒrɪtɪ] *n* sonoridad *f*.

sonorous ['sɒnərəs] *adj* sonoro.

sonorousness ['sɒnərəsnɪs] *n* sonoridad *f*.

soon [suːn] *adv* (**a**) (*before long*) pronto, dentro de poco; (*early*) temprano; **come back** ~ vuelve pronto; ~ **afterwards** poco después; **how ~ can you come?** ¿cuando puedes venir?; **how ~ can you be ready?** ¿para cuando estarás listo?; **we got there too** ~ llegamos demasiado pronto; **Friday is too** ~ el viernes es muy pronto; **all too ~ it was over** la función terminó desmasiado pronto; **we were none too** ~ llegamos en el momento oportuno; no llegamos antes de tiempo.

(**b**) (*with* **as**) **as ~ as** en cuanto, tan pronto como, así que; **as ~ as you've seen him** en cuanto le veas, en cuanto le hayas visto; **as ~ as it was finished** en cuanto se terminó; **as ~ as possible** cuanto antes, lo antes posible, lo más pronto posible; **I would as ~ not go** más prefiero no ir, más me gustaría no ir; **she'd marry him as ~ as not** se casaría con él y tan contenta; *V also* **sooner**.

sooner ['suːnəʳ] *adv* (**a**) (*time*) más temprano, antes; **we got there** ~ nosotros llegamos antes; ~ **or later** tarde o temprano; **the ~ the better** cuanto antes, mejor; **no ~ had we arrived, than ...** apenas habíamos llegado, cuando ..., no bien llegamos, cuando ...; **no ~ said than done** dicho y hecho; **in 5 years or at his death, whichever is the** ~ al cabo de 5 años o a su muerte, lo que suceda antes; **the ~ we start the ~ we finish** cuanto más pronto empecemos, más pronto podremos concluir.

(**b**) (*preference*) **I had ~ not do it, I would ~ not do it** preferiría no hacerlo; **which would you ~?** ¿cuál prefieres?; **~ you than me!** ¡me alegro de no estar en tu lugar!

soot [sʊt] *n* hollín *m*.

sooth†† [suːθ] *n*: **in ~** en realidad.

soothe [suːð] *vt* tranquilizar, calmar; *pain* aliviar.

soothing [ˈsuːðɪŋ] *adj* tranquilizador, calmante; (*pain-killing*) analgésico; *tone, words etc* dulce, consolador.

soothingly [ˈsuːðɪŋlɪ] *adv speak etc* dulcemente, con dulzura, en tono consolador.

soothsayer [ˈsuːθˌseɪəʳ] *n* adivino *m*, -a *f*.

soothsaying [ˈsuːθˌseɪɪŋ] *n* adivinación *f*.

sooty [ˈsʊtɪ] *adj* hollinoso, cubierto de hollín; (*fig*) negro como el hollín.

SOP *n abbr of* **standard operating procedure.**

sop [sɒp] *n* (**a**) (*food*) sopa *f*. (**b**) (*fig*) regalo *m*, dádiva *f*; compensación *f*; **as a ~ to his pride** para ayudarle a salvar las apariencias, como compensación a su amor propio; **this is a ~ to Cerberus** esto es para comprar la benevolencia de ... (**c**) (*) bobo *m*, -a *f*.

◆**sop up** *vt* absorber.

Sophia [səʊˈfaɪə] *nf* Sofía.

sophism [ˈsɒfɪzəm] *n* sofisma *m*.

sophist [ˈsɒfɪst] *n* sofista *mf*.

sophistical [səˈfɪstɪkəl] *adj* sofístico.

sophisticated [səˈfɪstɪkeɪtɪd] *adj* (*all senses*) sofisticado.

sophistication [səˌfɪstɪˈkeɪʃən] *n* sofisticación *f*.

sophistry [ˈsɒfɪstrɪ] *n* sofistería *f*; **a ~** un sofisma.

Sophocles [ˈsɒfəkliːz] *nm* Sófocles.

sophomore [ˈsɒfəmɔːʳ] *n* (*US*) estudiante *mf* de segundo año.

soporific [ˌsɒpəˈrɪfɪk] *adj* soporífero.

sopping [ˈsɒpɪŋ] *adj*: **it's ~ (wet)** está empapado, está totalmente mojado; **he was ~ wet** estaba hecho una sopa.

soppy* [ˈsɒpɪ] *adj* (*Brit*) (**a**) (*foolish*) bobo, tonto. (**b**) (*mushy*) sentimental, sensiblero.

soprano [səˈprɑːnəʊ] **1** *n*, *pl* **sopranos** [səˈprɑːnəʊz] *n* (*person*) soprano *f*, tiple *f*; (*voice and part*) soprano *m*. **2** *adj part etc* de soprano, para soprano; *voice* de soprano.

sorb [sɔːb] *n* (*tree*) serbal *m*; (*fruit*) serba *f*.

sorbet [ˈsɔːbeɪ, ˈsɔːbɪt] *n* (*water ice*) sorbete *m*; **lemon ~** sorbete *m* de limón.

sorbitol [ˈsɔːbɪtɒl] *n* sorbitol *m*.

sorcerer [ˈsɔːsərəʳ] *n* hechicero *m*, brujo *m*; **~'s apprentice** aprendiz *m* de brujo.

sorceress [ˈsɔːsəres] *n* hechicera *f*, bruja *f*.

sorcery [ˈsɔːsərɪ] *n* hechicería *f*, brujería *f*.

sordid [ˈsɔːdɪd] *adj* (*squalid, dirty*) sórdido, asqueroso, sucio; *place, room* miserable; *deal, motive etc* vil; **it's a pretty ~ business** es un asunto de lo más desagradable.

sordidness [ˈsɔːdɪdnɪs] *n* sordidez *f*, lo asqueroso, suciedad *f*; lo miserable; vileza *f*.

sore [sɔːʳ] **1** *adj* (**a**) (*Med*) inflamado, dolorido, que duele; **~ throat** dolor *m* de garganta; **my eyes are ~, I have ~ eyes** me duelen los ojos; **I'm ~ all over** me duele todo el cuerpo; **where are you ~?** ¿dónde te duele?

(**b**) (*fig*) **to be ~ at heart** dolerle a uno el corazón; **to be ~ about sth** estar resentido por algo; **to be ~ with sb** estar enojado con uno; **what are you so ~ about?** ¿por qué estás tan ofendido?; **now don't get ~** no te vayas a ofender; **it's a ~ point** es un asunto delicado.

(**c**) (*liter*) **there is a ~ need of ...** hay gran necesidad de ...; **it was a ~ temptation** era una gran tentación.

2 *n* (*Med*) llaga *f*, úlcera *f*; (*caused by harness etc*) matadura *f*; (*fig*) llaga *f*, herida *f*; recuerdo *m* doloroso; **to open an old ~** (*fig*) renovar la herida.

sorehead* [ˈsɔːhed] *n* (*US*) persona *f* resentida, resentido *m*, -a *f*.

sorely [ˈsɔːlɪ] *adv*: **~ wounded** herido de gravedad, gravemente herido; **I am ~ tempted** tengo grandes tentaciones; **I am ~ tempted to** + *infin* casi estoy por + *infin*; **he has been ~ tried** ha sufrido lo indecible.

soreness [ˈsɔːnɪs] *n* (*Med*) inflamación *f*, dolor *m*.

sorghum [ˈsɔːgəm] *n* sorgo *m*.

sorority [səˈrɒrɪtɪ] *n* (*US Univ*) hermandad *f* de mujeres.

sorrel[1] [ˈsɒrəl] *n* (*Bot*) acedera *f*.

sorrel[2] [ˈsɒrəl] **1** *adj* alazán. **2** *n* alazán *m*, caballo *m* alazán.

sorrow [ˈsɒrəʊ] **1** *n* pesar *m*, pena *f*, dolor *m*; tristeza *f*; **more in ~ than in anger** con más pesar que enojo; **to my (great) ~** con gran pesar mío, con gran sentimiento mío; **this was a great ~ to me** esto me causó mucha pena; **the ~s of their race** las aflicciones de su raza; **to drown one's ~s** olvidar su tristeza emborrachándose, ahogar sus penas en alcohol.

2 *vi* apenarse, afligirse (*at, for, over* de, por), dolerse (*at, for, over* de).

sorrowful [ˈsɒrəfʊl] *adj* afligido, triste, pesaroso.

sorrowfully [ˈsɒrəfəlɪ] *adv* con pena, tristemente.

sorrowing [ˈsɒrəʊɪŋ] *adj* afligido.

sorry [ˈsɒrɪ] *adj* (**a**) (*regretful*) arrepentido; (*sad*) triste, afligido, apenado; **~!** ¡perdón!, ¡perdone!; **awfully ~!, so ~!, very ~!** lo siento mucho, lo siento en el alma, ¡cuánto lo siento!; **to be ~** sentirlo; **I am very ~** lo siento mucho; **I can't say I'm ~** no puedo decir que lo sienta; **he wasn't in the least bit ~** no se arrepintió en lo más mínimo; **I'm ~ to say it was no use** desgraciadamente no sirvió para nada; **to be ~ about sth** afligirse por algo; **I'm ~ about that vase** te pido perdón por lo del florero; me da pena el florero ese; **to be (*or* feel) ~ for sb** compadecer a uno, tener lástima a uno; **I feel ~ for the child** el niño me da lástima; **to feel ~ for o.s.** sentirse desgraciado; **there's no need to be ~ for him** no hace falta compadecerle; **you'll be ~ for this!** ¡lo arrepentirás!, ¡me las pagarás!; **to be (*or* feel, look) ~ for o.s.** estar muy abatido; **to be ~ that ...** sentir que + *subj*; **to be ~ to** + *infin* sentir + *infin*, lamentar + *infin*; **I am ~ to have to tell you that ...** lamento tener que decirle que ...; **we are ~ to inform you that ...** lamentamos informarle que ...; **I am ~ for the inconvenience caused by ...** lamento las molestias que se han debido a ...

(**b**) (*bad*) *condition, plight* lastimoso; *sight* triste; *figure* ridículo; *excuse* nada convincente; *joke* pobre; **it was a ~ tale of defeat** fue una triste narración de derrotas.

sort [sɔːt] **1** *n* (**a**) (*class, kind*) clase *f*, género *m*, especie *f*; tipo *m*; **what ~ do you want?** ¿qué clase quiere Vd?; **the ~ you gave me last time** la misma que Vd me dio la última vez; **but not that ~** pero no de ese tipo, pero no como eso; **I know his ~** ésos me los conozco, conozco el paño; **he's the ~ who will cheat you** es de los que te engañarán; **books of all ~s** toda clase de libros, libros de toda clase; **he's a painter of a ~, he's a painter of ~s** es en cierto modo pintor; **it's coffee of a ~** es café pero bastante inferior, es lo que apenas se puede llamar café; **perfect of its ~** perfecto en su línea; **something of the ~** algo por el estilo; **nothing of the ~!** ¡nada de eso!, ¡ni hablar!; **I shall do nothing of the ~** no haré eso bajo ningún concepto; **in some ~** en cierta medida; **it takes all ~s (to make a world)** de todo hay en la viña del Señor.

(**b**) (*with* **of**) **what ~ of car?** ¿qué clase de coche?; **what ~ of man is he?** ¿qué tipo de hombre es?; **this ~ of house** una casa de este tipo; **an odd ~ of novel** una novela rara, una novela de tipo extraño; **all ~s of dogs** toda clase de perros, perros de toda clase; **he's a ~ of agent** es algo así como un agente; **he's some ~ of painter** es pintor pero no sé de qué género; **I felt a ~ of shame** sentí algo parecido a la vergüenza, en cierto modo sentí vergüenza; **it's a ~ of dance** es una especie de baile; **I have a ~ of idea that ...** tengo cierta idea de que ...; **that's the ~ of thing I need** eso es lo que me hace falta; **that's the ~ of thing I mean** eso es precisamente lo que quiero decir; **and all that ~ of thing** y otras cosas por el estilo; **that's the ~ of person I am** yo soy así; **he's not that ~ of person** no es capaz de hacer eso, no es de los que hacen tales cosas; **I'm not that ~ of girl** yo no soy de ésas.

(**c**) (*: **~ of**) **it's ~ of awkward** es bastante (*LAm*: medio) difícil; **it's ~ of blue** es más bien azul; **I'm ~ of lost** estoy como perdido; **it's ~ of finished** está más o menos terminado; **I ~ of feel that ...** en cierto modo creo que ...; **it ~ of made me laugh** no sé por qué pero me hizo reír; **aren't you pleased? ... ~ of** ¿no te alegras? ... en cierto modo.

(**d**) (*person*) **he's a good ~** es buena persona, es buena gente (*LAm*), es un buen chico; **she sounds a good ~** da la impresión de ser buena persona; **he's an odd ~** es un tipo extraño; **your ~ never did any good** las personas como Vd nunca hicieron nada bueno.

(**e**) **to be out of ~s** (*Med*) estar indispuesto, no estar del todo bien; (*in mood*) estar molesto, sentirse incómodo.

(**f**) (*Comput*) ordenación *f*.

2 *vt problems* arreglar; *papers* clasificar; (*Comput*) ordenar.

◆**sort out** *vt* (**a**) (*classify*) clasificar; **to ~ out the bad ones** (*select*) separar los malos, quitar los malos.

(**b**) (*fig*) *problem etc* arreglar; solucionar; **we've got it ~ed out now** lo hemos arreglado ya; **can you ~ this out for me?** ¿puede ayudarme con esto?; **to ~ sb out*** (*Brit*) ajustar cuentas con uno; **I'll come down there and ~ you out!*** ¡si bajo allá te pego una paliza!

(**c**) (*explain*) **to ~ sth out for sb** explicar algo a uno, aclarar algo a uno.

sort code [ˈsɔːtkəʊd] *n* número *m* de agencia.

sorter [ˈsɔːtəʳ] *n* clasificador *m*, -ora *f*; (*Post*) oficial *mf* de correos.

sortie [ˈsɔːtɪ] *n* salida *f*; **to make a ~** hacer una salida.

sorting [ˈsɔːtɪŋ] *n* clasificación *f*; (*Comput*) ordenación *f*.

sorting-office [ˈsɔːtɪŋˌɒfɪs] *n* sala *f* de batalla.

sort-out* [ˈsɔːtaʊt] *n*: **to have a ~** hacer limpieza; arreglar las cosas.

SOS *n* (*signal*) s.o.s. *m*; (*fig*) llamada *f* de socorro.

so-so [ˈsəʊˈsəʊ] *adv* regular, así así.

sot [sɒt] *n* borrachín *m*.

sottish [ˈsɒtɪʃ] *adj* embrutecido (por el alcohol).

sotto voce [ˈsɒtəʊˈvəʊtʃɪ] *adv* en voz baja.

Soudan [suˈdɑːn] *etc* = **Sudan** *etc*.

soufflé [ˈsuːfleɪ] **1** *n* suflé *m*, soufflé *m*. **2** *attr*: **~ dish** fuente *f* de soufflé.

sough [saʊ] **1** *n* susurro *m*. **2** *vi* susurrar.

sought [sɔːt] *pret and ptp of* **seek**.

sought-after [ˈsɔːtˌɑːftəʳ] *adj* codiciado; solicitado, deseado, que tiene mucha demanda; **this much ~ title** este codiciado título.

soul [səʊl] *n* (**a**) alma *f*; **like a lost ~** como alma en pena; **upon my ~!, (God) bless my ~!** ¡caramba!; ¡Dios mío!; **with all one's ~** con toda el alma; **God rest his ~!** ¡Dios le tenga en su gloria!; **to bare one's ~** abrir su pecho (*to sb* a uno); **to possess one's ~ in patience** armarse de paciencia.

(**b**) (*fig*: *person*) alma *f*; **3,000 ~s** 3.000 almas; **poor ~!** ¡pobrecito!; **the poor ~ had nowhere to sleep** el pobre no tenía dónde dormir; **he's a good ~** es un bendito; **she's a simple ~** es un alma de Dios; **without seeing a ~** sin ver bicho viviente; **every living ~** todo ser viviente; **the ship was lost with all ~s** el buque se hundió con toda la tripulación (y pasajeros); **he's the ~ of discretion** es la misma discreción, es la discreción en persona.

(**c**) (*US*) *se aplica a la cultura de los negros de EE.UU*; **~ food** cocina *f* negra del sur de EE.UU; **~ music** soul *m*.

soul-destroying [ˈsəʊldɪsˈtrɔɪɪŋ] *adj* (*fig*) de lo más aburrido (*or* monótono *etc*); totalmente desprovisto de interés, de nulo interés intelectual (*or* estético *etc*).

soulful [ˈsəʊlfʊl] *adj* sentimental; conmovedor; (*pej*) patético, lacrimoso.

soulfully [ˈsəʊlfəlɪ] *adv* de modo sentimental; de modo conmovedor.

soulless [ˈsəʊllɪs] *adj person* sin alma, desalmado; *work etc* mecánico, monótono, sin interés humano.

soulmate [ˈsəʊlmeɪt] *n* perfecto compañero *m* espiritual, perfecta compañera *f* espiritual.

soul-searching [ˈsəʊlˌsɜːtʃɪŋ] *n* examen *m* de conciencia, examen *m* introspectivo.

soul-stirring [ˈsəʊlˌstɜːrɪŋ] *adj* conmovedor, emocionante, inspirador.

sound¹ [saʊnd] **1** *adj* sano; firme, sólido; *constitution* robusto; (*Comm*) solvente; *person* formal, digno de confianza; *argument, idea, opinion* razonable, lógico, bien fundado; ortodoxo; *policy* prudente; *investment* bueno, seguro; *move* acertado, lógico; *rule* bueno; *training etc* sólido; *sleep* profundo; **in ~ condition** en buenas condiciones; **to be as ~ as a bell** estar en perfecta salud; **to be ~ in wind and limb** estar en buen estado físico; **to be ~ in mind and body** ser sano de cuerpo y de espíritu; **he's a very ~ man** es persona de la mayor confianza; **he's a ~ worker** es buen trabajador, trabaja con toda seriedad; **he is ~ enough on the theory** tiene una preparación sólida en cuanto a la teoría; tiene opiniones ortodoxas acerca de la teoría.

2 *adv*: **to be ~ asleep** estar profundamente dormido; **I shall sleep the ~er for it** por eso dormiré más tranquilamente.

sound² [saʊnd] **1** *n* sonido *m*, son *m*; ruido *m*; **to the ~(s) of the national anthem** a los sones del himno nacional; **by the ~ of it** según parece, al parecer; **within ~ of** al alcance de; **they were within ~ of the camp** el campamento estaba al alcance del oído; **the Glenn Miller ~** la música de Glenn Miller; **not a ~ was heard** no hubo ruido alguno; **there came the ~ of breaking glass** se oyó el ruido de cristales que se rompían; **I don't like the ~ of it** esto no nos promete nada bueno, me inquieta la noticia, no me gusta la idea.

2 *attr*: **~ archive** archivo *m* del sonido; **~ bite** frase *f* pegadiza; **~ engineer** sonista *mf*; **~ law** ley *f* fonética; **~ library** fonoteca *f*; **~-producing** productor de sonido; **~ shift** cambio *m* de pronunciación; **~ system** (*of language*) sistema *m* fonológico, (*hi-fi*) cadena *f* de sonido; **~ truck** (*US*) furgón *m* publicitario.

3 *vt* sonar; *alarm, bell, horn, trumpet* tocar; *warning* dar; *praises* cantar, entonar; **to ~ the 'd' in 'hablado'** pronunciar la 'd' en 'hablado'; **to ~ the charge** tocar la carga; **to ~ the retreat** tocar a retirada.

4 *vi* (**a**) sonar, resonar; **the bell ~ed** sonó el timbre; **it ~s hollow** suena a hueco; **it ~s like Dutch to me** me suena a holandés; **a gun ~ed a long way off** se oyó un cañón a lo lejos.

(**b**) (*fig*: *seem*) sonar, parecer; **that ~s very odd** eso parece muy raro; **he ~s like a good sort** parece buena persona, da la impresión de ser buena persona; **how does it ~ to you?** ¿a ti qué te parece?; **it ~s as if she's not coming** parece que no viene.

◆**sound off*** *vi* (*speak firmly*) hablar en tono autoritario; (*complain*) quejarse; (*protest*) protestar, poner el grito en el cielo.

sound³ [saʊnd] **1** *n* (*Med*) sonda *f*.

2 *vt* (*Med, Naut*) sondar; *chest* auscultar.

◆**sound out** *vt person, intentions* sondear, tantear; **to ~ sb out about sth** tratar de averiguar lo que piensa uno acerca de un asunto; **to ~ out one's conscience** consultar su conciencia.

sound⁴ [saʊnd] *n* (*Geog*) estrecho *m*, brazo *m* de mar.

sound-barrier [ˈsaʊndˌbærɪəʳ] *n* barrera *f* del sonido.

soundbox [ˈsaʊndˌbɒks] *n* (*Mus*) caja *f* de resonancia.

sound-effects [ˈsaʊndɪˌfekts] *npl* efectos *mpl* sonoros.

sounding¹ [ˈsaʊndɪŋ] *n* (**a**) (*of trumpet, bell etc*) sonido *m*, son *m*; **the ~ of the retreat/the alarm** el toque de retirada/de generala. (**b**) (*Med*) sondeo *m*.

sounding² [ˈsaʊndɪŋ] *n* (*Naut*) sondeo *m*; **~s** (*for oil etc*) sondeos *mpl*; **to take ~s** (*fig*) sondear la opinión, pulsar las opiniones.

sounding-board [ˈsaʊndɪŋbɔːd] *n* (*Mus*) secreto *m*, tabla *f* armónica, tablero *m* sonoro, caja *f* de resonancia; (*fig*) piedra *f* de toque, caja *f* de resonancia.

soundless [ˈsaʊndlɪs] *adj* silencioso, sin ruido; insonoro.

soundlessly [ˈsaʊndlɪslɪ] *adv* silenciosamente, sin ruido.

soundly [ˈsaʊndlɪ] *adv* sólidamente; razonablemente, lógicamente, prudentemente; **to beat sb ~** derrotar a uno completamente; **to thrash sb ~** dar a uno una paliza de verdad; **to sleep ~** dormir bien, dormir profundamente.

soundness [ˈsaʊndnɪs] *n* firmeza *f*, solidez *f*; robustez *f*; solvencia *f*; formalidad *f*; lo razonable, lógica *f*, sólida fundación *f*; ortodoxia *f*; prudencia *f*; seguridad *f*; **the ~ of sb's health** la buena salud de uno; **the ~ of a proposal** la solidez de una proposición.

soundproof [ˈsaʊndpruːf] **1** *adj* insonorizado, a prueba de ruidos. **2** *vt* insonorizar.

soundproofing [ˈsaʊndpruːfɪŋ] *n* insonorización *f*.

sound recording [ˈsaʊndrɪˌkɔːdɪŋ] *n* grabación *f* sonora.

sound recordist [ˈsaʊndrɪˌkɔːdɪst] *n* (*TV*) registrador *m*, -ora *f* de sonido.

soundtrack [ˈsaʊndtræk] *n* banda *f* sonora.

soundwave [ˈsaʊndweɪv] *n* onda *f* sonora, onda *f* acústica.

soup [suːp] *n* (*clear, thin*) caldo *m*, consomé *m*; (*thick*) puré *m*, sopa *f*; **to be in the ~*** estar en apuros; **now we're properly in the ~*** ahora la hemos pringado de verdad*.

◆**soup up*** *vt* (*Aut*) sobrealimentar, trucar*; (*fig*) mejorar, aumentar la eficacia de.

soupçon [ˈsuːpsɔ̃] *n* pizca *f*; olorcillo *m* (*of* a); **with a ~ of ginger** con una pizca de jengibre.

souped-up* [ˈsuːptˌʌp] *adj* (*Aut*) sobrealimentado, trucado*.

soup-kitchen [ˈsuːpˌkɪtʃɪn] *n* comedor *m* de beneficencia, olla *f* común.

soup-plate [ˈsuːppleɪt] *n* plato *m* sopero.

soupspoon [ˈsuːpspuːn] *n* cuchara *f* sopera.

soup tureen [ˈsuːptəˌriːn] *n* sopera *f*.

soupy [ˈsuːpɪ] *adj liquid* espeso, turbio; *atmosphere* pesado, espeso; viciado.

sour [ˈsaʊəʳ] **1** *adj* agrio, acre; *milk* cortado; *land* maleado; *person* agrio, desabrido, poco afable; *tone, reply* áspero, desabrido; **~ cream** (*Culin*) nata *f* cortada, crema *f* agria; **to go ~** (*milk*) cortarse; **to turn ~** agriarse, volverse agrio.

2 *vt* agriar; *land* malear; *person* agriar, amargar.

3 *vi* agriarse, volverse agrio; (*land*) malearse.

source [sɔːs] **1** *n* (*of river*) fuente *f*, nacimiento *m*; (*fig*) fuente *f*, origen *m*; procedencia *f*; (*Liter etc*) fuente *f*; (*of infection*) foco *m*; **what is the ~ of this information?** ¿de

dónde proceden estos informes?; **I have it from a good ~ that** ... sé de fuente fidedigna que ...; **we have other ~s of supply** tenemos otras fuentes de suministro.
2 *attr*: **~ file** archivo *m* fuente; **~ language** lengua *f* de partida, lengua *f* original, lengua *f* (de) base; (*Comput*) lenguaje *m* fuente; **~ materials** materiales *mpl* de referencia; **~ program(me)** programa *m* fuente.
sourdine [sʊə'diːn] *n* sordina *f*.
sourdough ['saʊə,dəʊ] *attr*: **~ bread** (*US*) pan *m* de masa fermentada.
sour-faced ['saʊəfeɪst] *adj* con cara de pocos amigos.
sourish ['saʊərɪʃ] *adj* agrete.
sourly ['saʊəlɪ] *adv* (*fig*) agriamente; **to answer ~** contestar en tono áspero.
sourness ['saʊənɪs] *n* agrura *f*, acidez *f*; (*fig*) agrura *f*, aspereza *f*.
sourpuss* ['saʊəpʊs] *n* persona *f* desabrida, persona *f* poco afable.
souse [saʊs] **1** *vt* (**a**) (*pickle*) escabechar. (**b**) (*plunge*) zambullir (*into* en); (*soak*) empapar (*with* de, en), mojar (*with* de); **to ~ sb with soup** empapar a uno de sopa; **to get ~d** mojarse, calarse. (**c**) **to be ~d‡** estar ajumado*.
2 *n* (*US‡*) borracho *m*, -a *f*.
south [saʊθ] **1** *n* sur *m*; mediodía *m*. **2** *adj* del sur, meridional; *wind* del sur. **3** *adv* al sur, hacia el sur.
South Africa [saʊθ'æfrɪkə] *n* África *f* del Sur.
South African [saʊθ'æfrɪkən] **1** *adj* sudafricano. **2** *n* sudafricano *m*, -a *f*.
South America [,saʊθə'merɪkə] *n* América *f* del Sur, Sudamérica *f*.
South American [,saʊθə'merɪkən] **1** *adj* sudamericano. **2** *n* sudamericano *m*, -a *f*.
South Australia [,saʊθɒs'treɪlɪə] *n* Australia *f* del Sur.
southbound ['saʊθbaʊnd] *adj traffic* que va hacia el sur; *carriageway* dirección sur.
South Carolina [,saʊθkærə'laɪnə] *n* Carolina *f* del Sur.
South Dakota [,saʊθdə'kəʊtə] *n* Dakota *f* del Sur.
south-east ['saʊθ'iːst] **1** *n* sudeste *m*. **2** *adj point, direction* sudeste; *wind* del sudeste.
South-East Asia [,saʊθiːst'eɪʃə] *n* Asia *f* Sudoriental.
south-easterly [saʊθ'iːstəlɪ] *adj point, direction* sudeste; *wind* del sudeste.
south-eastern [saʊθ'iːstən] *adj* sudeste.
south-eastward(s) [saʊθ'iːstwəd(z)] *adv* hacia el sudeste.
southerly ['sʌðəlɪ] *adj point, direction* sur; *wind* del sur; **the most ~ point in Europe** el punto más meridional de Europa.
southern ['sʌðən] *adj* del sur, meridional; **S~ Cross** Cruz *f* del Sur; **~ hemisphere** hemisferio *m* sur.
southerner ['sʌðənəʳ] *n* habitante *mf* del sur; meridional *mf*, sureño *m*, -a *f* (*LAm*); (*US Hist*) sudista *mf*; **she's a ~** es del Sur; **~s are shorter than northerners** los meridionales son menos altos que los septentrionales.
southernmost ['sʌðənməʊst] *adj* (el) más meridional, situado más al sur; **the ~ town in Europe** la ciudad más meridional de Europa.
south-facing ['saʊθ,feɪsɪŋ] *adj* con cara al sur, orientado hacia el sur; **~ slope** vertiente *f* sur.
South Georgia [,saʊθ'dʒɔːdʒɪə] *n* Georgia *f* del Sur.
South Korea ['saʊθkə'rɪə] *n* Corea *f* del Sur.
South Korean ['saʊθkə'rɪən] **1** *adj* surcoreano. **2** *n* surcoreano *m*, -a *f*.
South Pacific [,saʊθpə'sɪfɪk] *n* Pacífico *m* Sur.
southpaw ['saʊθpɔː] *n* (*esp US*) zurdo *m*.
South Pole [,saʊθ'pəʊl] *n* Polo *m* Sur.
South Sea Islands [,saʊθsiː'aɪləndz] *npl* Islas *fpl* de los mares del Sur.
South Seas ['saʊθ'siːz] *npl* mares *mpl* del Sur.
south-south-east [,saʊθsaʊθ'iːst] **1** *n* sudsudeste *m*. **2** *adj* sudsudoriental, sudsudeste. **3** *adv* hacia el sudsudeste.
south-south-west [,saʊθsaʊθ'west] **1** *n* sudsudoeste *m*. **2** *adj* sudsudoccidental, sudsudoeste. **3** *adv* hacia el sudsudoeste.
South Vietnam ['saʊθ,vjet'næm] *n* Vietnam *m* del Sur.
South Vietnamese ['saʊθ,vjetnə'miːz] **1** *adj* survietnamita. **2** *n* survietnamita *mf*.
southward ['saʊθwəd] **1** *adj advance etc* hacia el sur, en dirección sur. **2** *adv* (*also* **~s**) hacia el sur, en dirección sur.
south-west ['saʊθ'west] **1** *n* suroeste *m*. **2** *adj point, direction* suroeste; *wind* del suroeste.
South West Africa [,saʊθwest'æfrɪkə] *n* África *f* del Suroeste.
south-wester [saʊθ'westəʳ] *n* (*wind*) suroeste *m*; (*hat*) sueste *m*.
south-westerly [saʊθ'westəlɪ] *adj point, direction* suroeste; *wind* del suroeste.
south-western [saʊθ'westən] *adj* suroeste.
south-westward(s) [saʊθ'westwəd(z)] *adv* hacia el suroeste.
souvenir [,suːvə'nɪəʳ] *n* recuerdo *m*.
sou'wester [saʊ'westəʳ] *n* sueste *m*.
sovereign ['sɒvrɪn] **1** *adj* soberano; **~ state** estado *m* soberano. **2** *n* soberano *m*, -a *f*; (*Brit*: *coin*) soberano *m*.
sovereignty ['sɒvrəntɪ] *n* soberanía *f*.
soviet ['səʊvɪət] **1** *n* (**a**) soviet *m*. (**b**) **S~** (*person*) soviético *m*, -a *f*, ruso *m*, -a *f*. **2** *adj* soviético; **S~ Russia** Rusia *f* Soviética; **S~ Union** Unión *f* Soviética.
sow[1] [səʊ] (*irr*: *pret* **sowed**, *ptp* **sown**) *vt* sembrar (*with* de; *also fig*); esparcir; *doubts* sembrar; **to ~ mines in a strait, to ~ a strait with mines** sembrar un estrecho de minas, colocar minas en un estrecho.
sow[2] [saʊ] *n* cerda *f*, puerca *f*, marrana *f*; (*of wild boar*) jabalina *f*; (*of badger*) tejón *m* hembra; (*Tech*) galápago *m*.
sower ['səʊəʳ] *n* sembrador *m*, -ora *f*.
sowing ['səʊɪŋ] *n* siembra *f*.
sowing-machine ['səʊɪŋmə,ʃiːn] *n* sembradora *f*.
sowing time ['səʊɪŋ,taɪm] *n* época *f* de la siembra, sementera *f*.
sown [səʊn] *ptp of* **sow**.
sow-thistle ['saʊθɪsl] *n* cerraja *f*.
soy [sɔɪ] (*esp US*), **soya** ['sɔɪə] (*esp Brit*) **1** *n* soja *f*. **2** *attr*: **~ bean** haba *f* de soja, fríjol *m* de soja; **~ flour** harina *f* de soja; **~ oil** aceite *m* de soja; **~ sauce** salsa *f* de soja.
sozzled‡ ['sɒzld] *adj*: **to be ~** estar ajumado*; **to get ~** ajumarse*.
spa [spɑː] *n* balneario *m*, estación *f* termal.
space [speɪs] **1** *n* (**a**) (*gen*) espacio *m*; (*room*) espacio *m*, sitio *m*; **for a ~** durante cierta distancia, durante cierto tiempo; **in a confined ~** en un espacio restringido; **in the ~ of one hour** en el espacio de una hora; **in the ~ of 3 generations** en el espacio de 3 generaciones; **to buy ~ in a newspaper** comprar un espacio en un periódico; **to clear a** (*or* **make**) **~ for** hacer un sitio para, hacer lugar para; **to leave ~ for** dejar un sitio para; **leave a ~ for the name** deje un espacio para el nombre; **to stare into ~** mirar al vacío; mirar distraído; **it takes up a lot of ~** ocupa bastante espacio.
(**b**) (*Astron, Phys*) espacio *m*.
2 *attr* espacial; **~ age** era *f* espacial; **~ exploration** exploración *f* espacial; **S~ Invaders** (*game*) Marcianitos *mpl*; **~ lab** laboratorio *m* espacial; **~ platform** plataforma *f* espacial; **~ probe** sonda *f* espacial; **~ race** carrera *f* espacial; **~ research** investigaciones *fpl* espaciales; **~ sickness** enfermedad *f* espacial; **~ travel** viajes *mpl* espaciales.
3 *vt* (**a**) (*also* **to ~ out**) espaciar (*also Typ*); **well ~d out** bastante distanciados.
(**b**) **to be ~d out‡** (*on drugs*) estar colocado‡; (*drunk*) estar ajumado*.
space-bar ['speɪsbɑːʳ] *n* barra *f* espaciadora, espaciador *m*.
space-capsule ['speɪs,kæpsjuːl] *n* cápsula *f* espacial.
space-centre, (*US*) **space-center** ['speɪs,sentəʳ] *n* centro *m* espacial.
spacecraft ['speɪskrɑːft] *n*, *pl invar* nave *f* espacial, astronave *f*.
space-flight ['speɪsflaɪt] *n* vuelo *m* espacial.
space-helmet ['speɪs,helmɪt] *n* casco *m* espacial.
spaceman ['speɪsmæn] *n*, *pl* **spacemen** ['speɪsmen] astronauta *m*, cosmonauta *m*.
space-saving ['speɪs,seɪvɪŋ] *adj* que economiza espacio; de tamaño reducido.
spaceship ['speɪsʃɪp] *n* nave *f* espacial, astronave *f*.
space-shot ['speɪsʃɒt] *n* (lanzamiento *m* de un) vehículo *m* espacial.
space-shuttle ['speɪs,ʃʌtl] *n* transbordador *m* espacial, lanzadera *f* espacial.
space-station ['speɪs,steɪʃən] *n* estación *f* espacial, cosmódromo *m*.
spacesuit ['speɪssuːt] *n* traje *m* espacial.
space-time ['speɪs'taɪm] *n* (*also* **~ continuum**) continuo *m* espacio-tiempo.
space-vehicle ['speɪs,viːɪkl] *n* vehículo *m* espacial.
spacewalk ['speɪswɔːk] **1** *n* paseo *m* espacial. **2** *vi* pasear por el espacio.
spacewoman ['speɪs,wʊmən] *n*, *pl* **spacewomen** ['speɪs,wɪmɪn] astronauta *f*, cosmonauta *f*.
spacing ['speɪsɪŋ] *n* espaciamiento *m*; (*Typ*) espaciado *m*;

with double ~ a doble espacio; **in single ~** a espacio sencillo.

spacing-bar [ˈspeɪsɪŋbɑːʳ] *n* barra *f* espaciadora, espaciador *m*.

spacious [ˈspeɪʃəs] *adj* espacioso, amplio; extenso; *living* holgado, lujoso.

spaciousness [ˈspeɪʃəsnɪs] *n* espaciosidad *f*, amplitud *f*; extensión *f*.

spade [speɪd] *n* (**a**) (*tool*) pala *f*, laya *f*; **to call a ~ a ~** llamar al pan pan y al vino vino. (**b**) **~s** (*Cards*) picas *fpl*, picos *mpl*, (*in Spanish pack*) espadas *fpl*. (**c**) (*pej*‡) negro *m*, -a *f*.

spadeful [ˈspeɪdfʊl] *n* pala *f*; **by the ~** (*fig*) en grandes cantidades.

spadework [ˈspeɪdwɜːk] *n* (*fig*) trabajo *m* preliminar.

spaghetti [spəˈgetɪ] *n* espaguetis *mpl*; fideos *mpl*; **~ junction*** scalextric *m*; **~ western** película *f* de vaqueros hecha por un director italiano, spaghetti western *m*.

Spain [speɪn] *n* España *f*.

spake†† [speɪk] *pret of* **speak**.

Spam [spæm] ® *n* carne *f* de cerdo en conserva.

span[1] [spæn] **1** *n* (**a**) (*extent*) (*of time*) lapso *m*, espacio *m*; duración *f*; (*of wing*) envergadura *f*; (*of bridge*: *referring to space*) ojo *m*, luz *f*, (*referring to structure*) arcada *f*, tramo *m*; (*of roof*) vano *m*; **a ~ of 50 metres** (*bridge*) una luz de 50 metros; **a bridge with 7 ~s** un puente de 7 arcadas, un puente de 7 ojos; **the longest single-~ bridge in the world** el puente más largo del mundo de una sola arcada; **the average ~ of life** la duración media de la vida; **for a brief ~** durante una breve temporada; **the whole ~ of world affairs** toda la extensión de los asuntos mundiales, los asuntos mundiales en toda su amplitud.

(**b**) (††: *measure*) palmo *m*.

(**c**) (*yoke*: *of oxen*) yunta *f*, (*horses*) pareja *f*.

2 *vt* (**a**) (*bridge*) extenderse sobre, cruzar; (*builder*) tender un puente sobre; (*in time etc*) abarcar; **his life ~ned 4 reigns** su vida abarcó 4 reinados.

(**b**) (*measure*) medir (a palmos).

span[2] [spæn] *pret of* **spin**.

spangle [ˈspæŋgl] **1** *n* lentejuela *f*. **2** *vt* adornar con lentejuelas; **~d with** (*fig*) sembrado de.

Spanglish [ˈspæŋglɪʃ] *n* (*hum*) angliparla *f*, hispinglés *m*, espinglés *m*.

Spaniard [ˈspænjəd] *n* español *m*, -ola *f*.

spaniel [ˈspænjəl] *n* perro *m* de aguas.

Spanish [ˈspænɪʃ] **1** *adj* español; **~ America** Hispanoamérica *f*; **~ Armada** la Invencible (*1588*); **~ chestnut** castaña *f* dulce; **~ fly** cantárida *f*; **~ guitar** guitarra *f* española. **2** *n* (**a**) **the ~** los españoles. (**b**) (*Ling*) español *m*, castellano *m*.

Spanish-American [ˈspænɪʃəˈmerɪkən] **1** *adj* hispanoamericano. **2** *n* hispanoamericano *m*, -a *f*.

Spanishness [ˈspænɪʃnɪs] *n* carácter *m* español, cualidad *f* española *f*; españolismo *m*.

Spanish-speaking [ˈspænɪʃˈspiːkɪŋ] *adj* hispanohablante, hispanoparlante, de habla española.

spank [spæŋk] **1** *n* azote *m*, manotada *f* (en las nalgas); **to give sb a ~** dar un azote a uno (en las nalgas).

2 *vt* zurrar, manotear; **I'll ~ you!** ¡te voy a pegar!

3 *vi*: **to ~ along** correr, ir volando.

spanking [ˈspæŋkɪŋ] **1** *adj* (*) *pace* grande, rápido; *breeze* fuerte; **we had a ~ (good) time** lo pasamos en grande*.

2 *n* zurra* *f*; **to give sb a ~** zurrar a uno*.

spanner [ˈspænəʳ] *n* (*Brit*) llave *f*, llave *f* de tuercas; **to throw** (*or* **put**) **a ~ in the works** meter un palo en la rueda.

spar[1] [spɑːʳ] *n* (*Naut*) palo *m*, verga *f*.

spar[2] [spɑːʳ] *vi* (*Boxing*) hacer fintas, fintar; entrenarse en el boxeo, hacer ejercicios de boxeo; **to ~ at sb** amagar a uno; **to ~ with sb about sth** (*fig*) disputar algo amistosamente con uno; **he's only ~ring with the problem** no intenta seriamente resolver el problema.

spar[3] [spɑːʳ] *n* (*Min*) espato *m*.

spare [speəʳ] **1** *adj* (**a**) (*left over*) sobrante, que sobra, de más; (*available*) disponible; *room* para convidados; *time* libre, desocupado; *part* (*Mech*) de repuesto, de recambio; **~ collar** cuello *m* de repuesto; **~ part = 2**; **~ part surgery*** cirugía *f* de trasplantes; **~ time** ratos *mpl* libres, ratos *mpl* de ocio; horas *fpl* libres; **if you have any ~ time** si dispones de tiempo, si tienes tiempo; **~ tire** (*US*), **~ tyre** neumático *m* de repuesto, (*hum*) michelín *m*, rosca *f*, rodete *m*; **there are 2 going ~** sobran 2, quedan 2; **if you have any ~ bottles** si dispones de algunas botellas; **it's all the ~ cash I have** es todo el dinero que me sobra.

(**b**) (*of build etc*) enjuto; **~ rib** costilla *f* de cerdo (con poca carne).

(**c**) **to go ~** (*Brit*‡) enloquecerse, subirse por las paredes*.

2 *n* pieza *f* de repuesto, repuesto *m*, recambio *m*, refacción *f* (*Mex*); **we stock ~s** tenemos existencia de repuestos.

3 *vt* (**a**) (*be grudging with*) excusar; escatimar; **to ~ no expense** no escatimar dinero; **to ~ no pains to do sth** no escatimar esfuerzos por hacer algo.

(**b**) (*do without*) pasarse sin, prescindir de; ahorrar; economizar; **we can't ~ him now** ahora no podemos estar sin él, ahora no podemos prescindir de él; **can you ~ this for a moment?** ¿me puedo llevar esto un momento?, ¿me permite llevarme esto un momento?; **if you can ~ it** si puedes pasarte sin él, si puedes cedérmelo; **can you ~ the time?** ¿dispones del tiempo?; **I can ~ you 5 minutes** estoy libre para verle durante 5 minutos, le puedo dedicar 5 minutos.

(**c**) (*left over*) **to ~** de sobra; **there is none to ~** apenas queda nada; no tenemos nada de sobra, no nos sobra nada; **we have 9 bottles to ~** nos sobran 9 botellas; **there's enough and to ~** basta y sobra, hay más que suficiente para todos.

(**d**) (*show mercy to*) *life* perdonar; **the fire ~d nothing** el incendio no perdonó nada; **he was ~d another 3 years** Dios le dio 3 años más de vida; **he ~s nobody** hace trabajar a todos; es severo con todos sin excepción; **to ~ sb's feelings** procurar no herir los sentimientos de uno; **I will ~ you the details** te evitaré los detalles; **to ~ sb the trouble of doing sth** evitar a uno la molestia de hacer algo; **~ my blushes!** ¡considera mi modestia!, ¡qué cosas me dices!

spare-time [ˈspeətaɪm] *attr*: **~ job** actividad *f* que ocupa las horas libres.

sparing [ˈspeərɪŋ] *adj* escaso; (*thrifty*) económico; controlado, limitado; **his ~ use of colour** su parquedad con los colores; **to be ~ of, to be ~ with** ser parco en, ser avaro de; **to be ~ of praise** escatimar los elogios; **to be ~ of words** ser persona de pocas palabras; ser parco en hablar.

sparingly [ˈspeərɪŋlɪ] *adv* escasamente; económicamente; **we used water ~** empleamos poca agua; **he uses colour ~** es parco en el uso de los colores; **use it very ~** úselo en pequeñas cantidades, úselo con moderación; **to eat ~** comer poco, comer frugalmente.

sparingness [ˈspeərɪŋnɪs] *n* parquedad *f*; economía *f*, moderación *f*.

spark [spɑːk] **1** *n* (**a**) chispa *f*; (*of wit*) chispazo *m*; **bright ~*** tipo *m* muy listo*; **there's not a ~ of life about it** no tiene ni un átomo de vida; **the book hasn't a ~ of interest** el libro no tiene ni pizca de interés; **to make the ~s fly** provocar una bronca; **they struck ~s off each other** por efecto mutuo hacían chispear el ingenio.

(**b**) **~s*** (*Naut*) telegrafista *m*; (*Film, TV*) iluminista *mf*.

2 *vt* (*also* **to ~ off**) hacer estallar; (*fig*) hacer estallar, precipitar, provocar.

3 *vi* chispear, echar chispas.

spark-gap [ˈspɑːkgæp] *n* entrehierro *m*.

sparking-plug [ˈspɑːkɪŋplʌg] *n*, **spark-plug** [ˈspɑːkplʌg] *n* bujía *f*, chispero *m* (*CAm*).

sparkle [ˈspɑːkl] **1** *n* centelleo *m*, destello *m*; (*fig*) brillo *m*, viveza *f*, vida *f*; **a person without ~** una persona sin viveza.

2 *vi* centellear, destellar, chispear; (*shine*) brillar, relucir; **she doesn't exactly ~** no tiene mucha viveza que digamos; **the conversation ~d** la conversación fue animadísima, en la conversación hubo muchas salidas ingeniosas.

sparkler [ˈspɑːkləʳ] *n* (*firework*) bengala *f*; (‡) diamante *m*.

sparkling [ˈspɑːklɪŋ] *adj* centelleante; brillante, reluciente; *wine* espumoso; *eyes, wit, conversation* chispeante.

sparky [ˈspɑːkɪ] *adj* vivaracho, marchoso*.

sparring match [ˈspɑːrɪŋˌmætʃ] *n* combate *m* con spárring.

sparring-partner [ˈspɑːrɪŋˌpɑːtnəʳ] *n* spárring *m*; (*hum*) contertulio *m*, -a *f*.

sparrow [ˈspærəʊ] *n* gorrión *m*.

sparrowhawk [ˈspærəʊhɔːk] *n* gavilán *m*.

sparse [spɑːs] *adj* disperso, esparcido; poco denso; escaso; *hair* ralo; **~ furnishings** muebles *mpl* escasos; **~ population** población *f* poco densa.

sparsely [ˈspɑːslɪ] *adv* de modo poco denso; escasamente; **a ~ furnished room** un cuarto con pocos muebles; **a ~ inhabited area** una región de población poco densa.

Sparta [ˈspɑːtə] *n* Esparta *f*.

Spartacus [ˈspɑːtəkəs] *nm* Espartaco.

Spartan ['spɑːtən] **1** *adj* espartano (*also fig*). **2** *n* espartano *m*, -a *f*.

spasm ['spæzəm] *n* (*Med*) espasmo *m*; (*fig*) acceso *m*, arranque *m*; **in a ~ of fear** en un acceso de miedo; **a sudden ~ of activity** un arranque repentino de actividad; **to work in ~s** trabajar a rachas.

spasmodic [spæz'mɒdɪk] *adj* espasmódico; irregular, intermitente.

spasmodically [spæz'mɒdɪkəlɪ] *adv* de modo espasmódico; de modo irregular, de modo intermitente; a rachas.

spastic ['spæstɪk] **1** *adj* espástico. **2** *n* espástico *m*, -a *f*.

spasticity [spæs'tɪsɪtɪ] *n* espasticidad *f*.

spat[1] [spæt] *n* (*Fish*) freza *f*; (*of oysters*) hueva *f* de ostras.

spat[2] [spæt] *n* (*gaiter*) polaina *f* corta, botín *m*.

spat[3]* [spæt] (*US*) **1** *n* riña *f*, disputa *f* (sin trascendencia).
2 *vi* reñir.

spat[4] [spæt] *pret and ptp of* **spit**.

spate [speɪt] *n* avenida *f*, crecida *f*; (*fig*) torrente *m*; avalancha *f*; **to be in ~** estar crecido; **to be in full ~** estar muy crecido.

spatial ['speɪʃəl] *adj* espacial.

spatio-temporal [,speɪʃɪəʊ'tempərəl] *adj* espaciotemporal.

spatter ['spætə^r] *vt* salpicar, rociar (*with* de); **a dress ~ed with mud** un vestido manchado de lodo; **a wall ~ed with blood** una pared salpicada de sangre.

spatula ['spætjʊlə] *n* espátula *f*.

spavin ['spævɪn] *n* esparaván *m*.

spawn [spɔːn] **1** *n* (*Fish*) freza *f*, hueva *f*; (*of frog etc*) huevas *fpl*; (*of mushroom*) semillas *fpl*; (*fig: pej*) prole *f*.
2 *vt* (*pej*) engendrar, producir.
3 *vi* desovar, frezar.

spawning ['spɔːnɪŋ] *n* desove *m*, freza *f*.

spay [speɪ] *vt animal* sacar los ovarios a.

S.P.C.A. *n* (*US*) *abbr of* **Society for the Prevention of Cruelty to Animals.**

S.P.C.C. *n* (*US*) *abbr of* **Society for the Prevention of Cruelty to Children.**

speak [spiːk] (*irr: pret* **spoke**, *ptp* **spoken**) **1** *vt* (**a**) (*gen*) decir, hablar; **to ~ the truth** decir la verdad; **to ~ one's mind** hablar con franqueza, hablar claro; **nobody spoke a word** nadie habló, nadie dijo palabra.
(**b**) *language* hablar; **do you ~ Arabic?** ¿hablas árabe?; **'English spoken here'** 'se habla inglés'.
2 *vi* (**a**) (*gen*) hablar; **did you ~?** ¿dijiste algo?; **since they quarrelled they don't ~** desde que riñeron no se hablan; **to ~ to sb** hablar con uno; **she never spoke to me again** no volvió a dirigirme la palabra; **I'll ~ to him about it** hablaré con él sobre eso; discutiré el asunto con él; **to ~ harshly to sb** hablar a uno en tono severo; **I don't know him to ~ to** no le conozco bastante como para hablar con él; **I know him to ~ to** le conozco bastante bien para cambiar algunas palabras con él; **so to ~** por decirlo así, como quien dice; **roughly ~ing** más o menos, aproximadamente; **technically** (*etc*) **~ing** en términos técnicos (*etc*), desde el punto de vista técnico (*etc*); **~ing personally, ...** en cuanto a mí ..., yo por mi parte; **~ing as a member, I ...** como miembro, digo que ...; **to ~ of** hablar de; **~ing of lions ...** a propósito de los leones ...; **... lions, not to ~ of tigers ...** leones, para no hablar de tigres; **it's nothing to ~ of** no tiene importancia, no es nada; **there are no trees to ~ of** no hay árboles que digamos; **everything ~s of hatred** por todas partes late el odio; **everything ~s of luxury** todo indica el lujo; **to ~ well of sb** hablar bien de uno; **~ now or forever hold your peace** hable ahora o guarde para siempre silencio.
(**b**) **to ~ for sb** hablar por uno; hablar en nombre de uno; interceder por uno; **he ~s for the miners** habla por los mineros, representa a los mineros; **~ing for myself** en cuanto a mí, yo por mi parte; **~ for yourself!** ¡eso lo dices tú!; **it ~s for itself** es evidente, habla por sí mismo; **the facts ~ for themselves** los datos hablan por sí solos; **that is already spoken for** eso está reservado ya.
(**c**) (*gun*) oírse, sonar; (*dog*) ladrar; **the gun spoke** se oyó un tiro.
(**d**) (*formally, in assembly*) hablar, pronunciar un discurso; intervenir (en un debate); (*begin to ~*) tomar la palabra, hacer uso de la palabra; **are you ~ing in the debate?** ¿interviene Vd en el debate?; **it's years since he spoke** hace años que no pronuncia ningún discurso; **the member rose to ~** el diputado se levantó para tomar la palabra; **the speaker asked Mr X to ~** el presidente le concedió la palabra al Sr X.
(**e**) (*Telec*) **~ing!** ¡al aparato!, ¡al habla!; **John ~ing!** ¡soy Juan!; **who is that ~ing?** ¿quién habla?, ¿de parte (de quién)?

◆**speak out** *vi* hablar claro; hablar francamente; osar hablar; **~ out!** ¡más fuerte!

◆**speak up** *vi* (**a**) hablar alto; **to ~ up for sb** (*fig*) hablar en favor de uno.
(**b**) = **speak out.**

-speak [spiːk] *n* (*pej*) *ending in compounds*: **computer~** lenguaje *m* de los ordenadores, jerga *f* informática.

speakeasy* ['spiːk,iːzɪ] *n* (*US*) taberna *f* (clandestina).

speaker ['spiːkə^r] *n* (**a**) (*gen*) el (*or* la) que habla; (*public ~*) orador *m*, -ora *f*; (*lecturer*) conferenciante *mf*; (*at conference*) ponente *mf*; (*Parl*) presidente *mf*; **as the last ~ said** como dijo el señor (*or* la señora) que acaba de hablar; **he's a good ~** es buen orador, habla bien.
(**b**) (*of language*) hablante *mf*; **are you a Welsh ~?** ¿habla Vd galés?; **all ~s of Spanish** todos los que hablan español, todos los hispanohablantes; **Catalan has several million ~s** el catalán es hablado por varios millones.
(**c**) (*loud~*) altavoz *m*; **~s** (*of hi-fi system*) pantallas *fpl* acústicas.

speaking ['spiːkɪŋ] *adj* hablante; **~ likeness** retrato *m* vivo; **~ part** papel *m* hablado; **to be within ~ distance** estar al habla, estar al alcance de la voz; **to be on ~ terms with sb** estar en buenas relaciones con uno; **we're not on ~ terms** no nos hablamos; **a pleasant ~ voice** una voz agradable.

-speaking ['spiːkɪŋ] *adj ending in compounds*: **English~** anglófono, anglohablante, de habla inglesa.

speaking trumpet ['spiːkɪŋ,trʌmpɪt] *n* bocina *f*.

speaking-tube ['spiːkɪŋtjuːb] *n* tubo *m* acústico.

spear [spɪə^r] **1** *n* (*Mil*) lanza *f*; (*fishing ~*) arpón *m*.
2 *vt* alancear, herir (*or* matar) con lanza; *fish* arponear; (*fig*) pasar, atravesar, pinchar; **he ~ed the paper on his fork** atravesó el papel en su tenedor.

speargun ['spɪəgʌn] *n* harpón *m* submarino.

spearhead ['spɪəhed] **1** *n* punta *f* de lanza (*also fig*). **2** *attr*: **~ industry** sector *m* puntero, industria *f* de vanguardia. **3** *vt attack etc* encabezar, dirigir.

spearmint ['spɪəmɪnt] *n* menta *f* verde, menta *f* romana.

spec* [spek] *n* (*Comm*): **to buy sth on ~** comprar algo como especulación; **to go along on ~** ir a ver lo que sale, ir a probar fortuna.

special ['speʃəl] **1** *adj* especial, particular; *edition etc* extraordinario; **~ agent** agente *mf* especial; **S~ Branch** (*Brit*) *sección de la policía que vigila la seguridad política*; **~ correspondent** enviado *m*, -a *f* especial; **~ delivery** (*Post*) entrega *f* urgente; **~ effects** efectos *mpl* especiales; **~ feature** (*Press*) artículo *m*, crónica *f*; (*of product*) característica *f*, prestación *f*; **~ general meeting** junta *f* general extraordinaria; **~ interest group** grupo *m* de presión que persigue un tema específico; **~ jury** jurado *m* especial; **~ licence** licencia *f* especial de matrimonio; una tasa especial; **~ measures** medidas *fpl* especiales; **~ offer** oferta *f* especial; **~ price** precio *m* de ocasión; **my ~ friend** mi mejor amigo, uno de mis amigos más íntimos; **we can offer you a ~ rate** podemos ofrecerle una tasa especial; **what happened? ... nothing ~** ¿qué tal? ... sin novedad (*or* nada de particular); **what's so ~ about this house?** ¿qué tiene de particular esta casa?; **what's so ~ about that?** y eso ¿qué tiene de particular?
2 *n* (*constable*) guardia *m* auxiliar; (*edition*) número *m* extraordinario; (*train*) tren *m* extraordinario, tren *m* especial; (*US Comm*) oferta *f* extraordinaria, ganga *f*; (*US Culin*) plato *m* del día.

specialism ['speʃə,lɪzəm] *n* especialidad *f*, campo *m* de conocimientos (*or* estudios *etc*) especializados.

specialist ['speʃəlɪst] **1** *n* especialista *mf*. **2** *attr*: **~ knowledge** conocimientos *mpl* especializados; **~ teacher** (*primary*) maestro *m* especializado, maestra *f* especializada; (*secondary*) profesor *m* especializado, profesora *f* especializada; **that's ~ work** es trabajo para un profesional, es trabajo que pide conocimientos especializados.

speciality [,speʃɪ'ælɪtɪ] *n*, (*US*) **specialty** ['speʃəltɪ] *n* especialidad *f*; **it's a ~ of the house** es una especialidad de la casa, es un plato especial de la casa; **to make a ~ of sth** especializarse en algo, dedicarse a algo de modo especial.

specialization [,speʃəlaɪ'zeɪʃən] *n* especialización *f*.

specialize ['speʃəlaɪz] *vi* especializarse (*in*, (*US*) *on* en).

specialized ['speʃəlaɪzd] *adj*: **~ knowledge** conocimientos *mpl* especializados.

specially ['speʃəlɪ] *adv* especialmente, particularmente; sobre todo, ante todo; **a ~ difficult task** un cometido especialmente difícil; **we asked for it** ~ lo pedimos especialmente; ~ **the yellow ones** sobre todo los amarillos.

specialty ['speʃəltɪ] *n* (*US*) = **speciality**.

specie ['spiːʃiː] *n* metálico *m*, efectivo *m*; **in** ~ en metálico.

species ['spiːʃiːz] *n, pl* **species** especie *f*.

specific [spə'sɪfɪk] **1** *adj* específico; expreso, explícito; ~ **gravity** peso *m* específico. **2** *n* (**a**) específico *m*. (**b**) ~**s** (*esp US*) detalles *mpl*; aspectos *mpl* concretos.

specifically [spə'sɪfɪkəlɪ] *adv* específicamente; expresamente, explícitamente.

specification [ˌspesɪfɪ'keɪʃən] *n* especificación *f*; ~**s** (*plan*) presupuesto *m*, plan *m* detallado.

specify ['spesɪfaɪ] *vti* especificar; designar (en un plan); concretar, precisar, indicar, puntualizar; **he did not** ~ no concretó, no mencionó nada concreto; **at a specified time** a una hora indicada; **unless otherwise specified** a no ser que se especifique lo contrario, salvo indicación al contrario.

specimen ['spesɪmɪn] **1** *n* ejemplar *m*, espécimen *m*; muestra *f*; **a fine** ~ **of trout** un bello ejemplar de trucha; **he's an odd** ~ es un tipo extraño; **you're a pretty poor** ~ no vales para mucho.

2 *attr*: ~ **copy** ejemplar *m* de muestra; ~ **page** página *f* que sirve de muestra; ~ **signature** espécimen *m* de firma.

specious ['spiːʃəs] *adj* especioso.

speciousness ['spiːʃəsnɪs] *n* lo especioso.

speck [spek] **1** *n* (*of dirt*) pequeña mancha *f*, manchita *f*; (*of dust*) grano *m*; (*smut*) mota *f* (de carbonilla *etc*); (*small portion*) partícula *f*, pizca *f*; (*dot, point*) punto *m*; **just a** ~ **on the horizon** solamente un punto en el horizonte; **just a** ~, **thanks** (*of drink etc*) un poquitín, gracias; **there's not a** ~ **of truth in it** no tiene ni pizca de verdad.

2 *vt* = **speckle**.

speckle ['spekl] **1** *n* punto *m*, mota *f*. **2** *vt* salpicar, motear (*with* de); salpicar de manchitas.

speckled ['spekld] *adj* con puntos, con manchas, moteado.

specs* [speks] *npl* (**a**) gafas *fpl*, lentes *mpl* (*LAm*). (**b**) *abbr of* **specifications**.

spectacle ['spektəkl] *n* (**a**) (*sight*) espectáculo *m*; **a sad** ~ un triste espectáculo; **to make a** ~ **of o.s.** ponerse en ridículo.

(**b**) ~**s** (*Brit*) gafas *fpl*, anteojos *mpl*, lentes *mpl* (*LAm*); **a pair of** ~**s** unas gafas; **to see everything through rose-coloured** ~**s** verlo todo color de rosa.

spectacle-case ['spektəkl,keɪs] *n* estuche *m* de gafas.

spectacled ['spektəkld] *adj* con gafas.

spectacular [spek'tækjʊləʳ] *adj* espectacular; *fall etc* aparatoso; *show, success etc* impresionante.

spectacularly [spek'tækjʊləlɪ] *adv* de manera espectacular, espectacularmente; aparatosamente; de manera impresionante.

spectator [spek'teɪtəʳ] *n* espectador *m*, -ora *f*; ~**s** (*collectively, at game etc*) público *m*; ~ **sport** deporte *m* para espectadores.

spectral ['spektrəl] *adj* espectral.

spectre, (*US*) **specter** ['spektəʳ] *n* espectro *m*, fantasma *m*.

spectrogram ['spektrəʊgræm] *n* espectrograma *m*.

spectrograph ['spektrəʊgrɑːf] *n* espectrógrafo *m*.

spectrometer [spek'trɒmɪtəʳ] *n* espectrómetro *m*.

spectrometry [spek'trɒmɪtrɪ] *n* espectrometría *f*.

spectroscope ['spektrəskəʊp] *n* espectroscopio *m*.

spectroscopy [spek'trɒskəpɪ] *n* espectroscopia *f*.

spectrum ['spektrəm], *pl* **spectra** ['spektrə] *n* espectro *m*; (*fig*) gama *f*, abanico *m*; ~ **analysis** análisis *m* espectral; **a wide** ~ **of opinions** un amplio abanico de opiniones.

speculate ['spekjʊleɪt] *vi* (**a**) especular (*on* en); **to** ~ **about** especular sobre, hacer conjeturas acerca de, formular teorías acerca de. (**b**) (*Fin*) especular (*in* en).

speculation [ˌspekjʊ'leɪʃən] *n* (**a**) especulación *f*; **it is the subject of much** ~ es tema de muchas conjeturas, sobre esto existen muchas teorías. (**b**) (*Fin*) especulación *f*; **to buy sth on** ~ comprar algo como especulación; **it's a good** ~ vale como especulación.

speculative ['spekjʊlətɪv] *adj* especulativo.

speculator ['spekjʊleɪtəʳ] *n* especulador *m*, -ora *f*.

speculum ['spekjʊləm] *n* espéculo *m*.

sped [sped] *pret and ptp of* **speed**.

speech [spiːtʃ] **1** *n* (**a**) (*faculty of* ~) habla *f*; palabra *f*; **to be slow of** ~ hablar lentamente, ser torpe de palabra; **to lose the power of** ~ perder el habla, perder la palabra; **to recover one's** ~ recobrar el habla, recobrar la palabra.

(**b**) (*words*) palabras *fpl*; **without further** ~ sin decir más.

(**c**) (*language*) (*national*) idioma *m*; (*of class etc*) lenguaje *m*; (*of region*) dialecto *m*, habla *f* regional; **in dockers'** ~ en el lenguaje de los portuarios; **in the** ~ **of Leon** en el dialecto de León, en leonés.

(**d**) (*oration*) discurso *m*, oración *f*; parlamento *m*; **to deliver a** ~, **to make a** ~ pronunciar un discurso.

(**e**) (*Gram*) oración *f*.

2 *attr*: ~ **act** acto *m* de habla; ~ **analysis** análisis *m* de la voz; ~ **command** comando *m* vocal; ~ **community** comunidad *f* lingüística; ~ **day** (*Brit*) (día *m* de) distribución *f* de premios; ~ **defect** defecto *m* del habla; ~ **impediment** impedimento *m* del habla; ~ **organ** órgano *m* del habla; ~ **synthesizer** sintetizador *m* de la voz humana; ~ **therapist** logopeda *mf*, logoterapeuta *mf*; ~ **therapy** terapia *f* lingüística, logopedia *f*, logoterapia *f*; ~ **training** lecciones *fpl* de elocución.

speechify ['spiːtʃɪfaɪ] *vi* (*pej*) disertar prolijamente, perorar.

speechifying ['spiːtʃɪfaɪɪŋ] *n* (*pej*) disertaciones *fpl* prolijas, peroratas *fpl*.

speechless ['spiːtʃlɪs] *adj* mudo, estupefacto; **I'm** ~! ¡estoy mudo!; **everybody was** ~ **at this** con esto todos quedaron estupefactos; **to be** ~ **with rage** enmudecer de rabia.

speechmaking ['spiːtʃ,meɪkɪŋ] *n* (**a**) pronunciación *f* de discursos; (*speeches collectively*) discursos *mpl*. (**b**) (*pej*) = **speechifying**.

speechwriter ['spiːtʃ,raɪtəʳ] *n* escritor *m*, -ora *f* de discursos, redactor *m*, -ora *f* de discursos.

speed [spiːd] **1** *n* (**a**) velocidad *f*; rapidez *f*; (*haste*) prisa *f*; (*promptness*) prontitud *f*; **at** ~ a gran velocidad; **at full** ~, **at top** ~ a máxima velocidad, a toda máquina, a todo correr; **full** ~ **ahead!** ¡avante toda!*, ¡avante a toda máquina!; **with all possible** ~ con toda prontitud; **the maximum** ~ **is 90 mph** la velocidad máxima es de 90 mph; **what** ~ **were you doing?** ¿a qué velocidad ibas?; **to pick up** ~ acelerar, cobrar velocidad.

(**b**) (*gear*) velocidad *f*; **four forward** ~**s** cuatro velocidades hacia adelante; **five-**~ **gearbox** caja *f* de cambios de cinco velocidades.

(**c**) **good** ~!†† ¡buen viaje!

(**d**) (‡) anfetamina *f*.

2 *vt* (*regular*) **to** ~ **sb on his way** despedir a uno, desear un feliz viaje a uno.

3 *vi* (*irr*: *pret and ptp* **sped**) (**a**) (*person etc*) darse prisa, apresurarse; **he sped down the street** corrió a toda prisa por la calle; **to** ~ **off** irse a toda prisa.

(**b**) (*Aut*) exceder la velocidad permitida.

◆**speed along** *vi* (*pret, ptp* **sped along**) ir a gran velocidad, ir a toda rapidez.

◆**speed up 1** *vt* (*pret, ptp* **speeded up**) *engine* acelerar; *process* acelerar, agilizar, activar; fomentar; *person* dar prisa a, apurar (*LAm*).

2 *vi* (*process*) acelerarse; (*person*) darse prisa, apurarse (*LAm*).

speedball ['spiːdbɔːl] *n* (**a**) (*game*) speedball *m*. (**b**) (‡: *drugs*) chute *m* de cocaína con heroína‡.

speedboat ['spiːd,bəʊt] *n* motora *f*, lancha *f* rápida.

speed bump ['spiːd,bʌmp] *n* banda *f* de frenado.

speed cop* ['spiːdkɒp] *n* (*Brit*) policía *m* de tráfico, policía *m* de tránsito (*LAm*).

speeder ['spiːdəʳ] *n* (*fast driver*) automovilista *mf* que conduce a gran velocidad; (*convicted*) infractor *m*, -ora *f* de los límites de velocidad.

speedily ['spiːdɪlɪ] *adv* rápidamente; prontamente, con toda prontitud; **it** ~ **became obvious that ...** pronto se hizo manifiesto que ...; **as** ~ **as possible** lo más pronto posible.

speediness ['spiːdɪnɪs] *n* velocidad *f*, rapidez *f*; prontitud *f*.

speeding ['spiːdɪŋ] *n* (*Aut*) exceso *m* de velocidad; **he was fined for** ~ se le impuso una multa por exceso de velocidad.

speed-limit ['spiːd,lɪmɪt] *n* velocidad *f* máxima, límite *m* de velocidad; **to exceed the** ~ exceder la velocidad permitida.

speedometer [spɪ'dɒmɪtəʳ] *n* velocímetro *m*, cuentakilómetros *m*.

speed restriction ['spiːdrɪs,trɪkʃən] *n* limitación *f* de velocidad.

speed-skating ['spiːd,skeɪtɪŋ] *n* patinaje *m* de velocidad.

speed trap ['spiːdtræp] *n* control *m* por radar.

speed-up ['spiːdʌp] *n* aceleración *f*, agilización *f*.

speedway ['spiːdweɪ] *n* (**a**) (*track*) pista *f* de ceniza, carretera *f* para carreras. (**b**) (*motor-cycle racing*) carreras *fpl* de motocicleta. (**c**) (*US*) autopista *f*.

speedwell ['spiːdwel] *n* verónica *f*.

speedy ['spiːdɪ] *adj* veloz, rápido; *answer etc* pronto; *service etc* rápido.

speleologist [ˌspiːlɪˈɒlədʒɪst] *n* espeleólogo *m*, -a *f*.
speleology [ˌspiːlɪˈɒlədʒɪ] *n* espeleología *f*.
spell¹ [spel] *n* encanto *m*, hechizo *m*; ensalmo *m*; **to be under a ~** estar hechizado; **to be under sb's ~** estar hechizado por uno; **to break the ~** romper el encanto; **to cast a ~ over sb, to put sb under a ~** hechizar a uno (*also fig*); **Seville casts its ~ over the tourists** Sevilla hechiza a los turistas.
spell² [spel] (*irr: pret and ptp* **spelled** *or* **spelt**) *vti* (**a**) escribir; **she can't ~** no sabe escribir correctamente, sabe poco de ortografía; **how do you ~ 'onyx'?** ¿cómo se escribe 'ónice'?; **what do these letters ~?** ¿qué palabra se forma con estas letras?; **c-a-t ~s 'cat'** c-a-t hacen 'cat'.
(**b**) (*denote*) anunciar, presagiar; significar; **it ~s disaster for us** representa un desastre para nosotros; **it ~s ruin** significa la ruina.
◆spell out *vt* (**a**) (*read letter by letter*) deletrear.
(**b**) **to ~ sth out for sb** (*fig*) explicar algo a uno de un modo muy sencillo, explicar algo a uno detalladamente.
spell³ [spel] *n* (**a**) (*at work*) tanda *f*, turno *m*; **to take a ~ with the saw** trabajar su turno con la sierra.
(**b**) (*period in general*) rato *m*; temporada *f*, período *m*; **by ~s** a rachas, a ratos; **cold ~** período *m* de frío; **a prolonged ~ of bad weather** una larga temporada de mal tiempo; **we had a ~ in Chile** pasamos una temporada en Chile; **I had a ~ as a traveller** durante cierto tiempo trabajé como viajante; **they're going through a bad ~** atraviesan un mal rato.
spellbinder [ˈspelˌbaɪndəʳ] *n* orador *m*, -ora *f* fascinante.
spellbinding [ˈspelˌbaɪndɪŋ] *adj* cautivador, fascinante.
spellbound [ˈspelbaʊnd] *adj* embelesado, hechizado; **to hold one's audience ~** tener a sus oyentes embelesados.
speller [ˈspeləʳ] *n*: **to be a bad ~** no saber escribir correctamente, tener mala ortografía.
spelling [ˈspelɪŋ] *n* ortografía *f*; **~ checker** corrector *m* ortográfico, consultor *m* de ortografía; **~ error** error *m* de ortografía; **~ pronunciation** pronunciación *f* ortográfica; **the correct ~ is ...** la buena ortografía es ...
spelling bee [ˈspelɪŋˌbiː] *n* certamen *m* de ortografía.
spelt¹ [spelt] *n* (*Bot*) espelta *f*.
spelt² [spelt] *pret and ptp of* **spell²**.
spelunker [spɪˈlʌŋkəʳ] *n* (*esp US*) espeleólogo *m*, -a *f*.
spelunking [spɪˈlʌŋkɪŋ] *n* (*esp US*) espeleología *f*.
spend [spend] (*irr: pret and ptp* **spent**) **1** *vt* (**a**) *money* gastar (*on* en).
(**b**) *time* pasar; (*on journey, project etc*) invertir (*on* en), dedicar (*on* a); **I spent an hour reading** pasé una hora leyendo; **where are you ~ing your holiday?** ¿dónde vas a pasar tus vacaciones?
(**c**) (*consume*) *anger, emotion* agotar, consumir; *effort* gastar; **the storm has spent its fury** la tempestad ha agotado su violencia.
2 *vi* gastar dinero; **he ~s freely** gasta mucho, gasta bastante.
spender [ˈspendəʳ] *n* gastador *m*, -ora *f*; **big ~** persona *f* generosa, (*pej*) derrochador *m*, -ora *f*; **to be a free ~** gastar libremente su dinero, ser derrochador.
spending [ˈspendɪŋ] **1** *n* gasto *m*; gastos *mpl*. **2** *attr*: **~ limit** límite *m* de gastos; **~ money** dinero *m* para gastos personales; **~ power** poder *m* de compra, poder *m* adquisitivo; **~ spree** derroche *m* de dinero; **we went on a ~ spree** gastamos como locos.
spendthrift [ˈspendθrɪft] **1** *adj* derrochador, pródigo. **2** *n* derrochador *m*, -ora *f*, pródigo *m*, -a *f*.
spent [spent] **1** *pret and ptp of* **spend. 2** *adj* agotado; *bullet* frío; **he's a ~ force** es una vieja gloria, ya no vale lo que antes.
sperm [spɜːm] *n* esperma *f*; **~ bank** banco *m* de espermas; **~ count** recuento *m* de espermas; **~ whale** cachalote *m*.
spermaceti [ˌspɜːməˈsetɪ] *n* esperma *f* de ballena.
spermatozoon [ˌspɜːmətəʊˈzəʊɒn] *n*, *pl* **spermatozoa** [ˌspɜːmətəʊˈzəʊə] espermatozoo *m*.
spermicidal [ˌspɜːmɪˈsaɪdl] *adj* espermicida.
spermicide [ˈspɜːmɪsaɪd] *n* espermicida *m*.
spew [spjuː] *vt* (*also* **to ~ forth, to ~ out, to ~ up**) vomitar; (*fig*) vomitar, arrojar, echar fuera; **it makes me ~*** (*fig*) me da asco.
sphagnum [ˈsfægnəm] *n* esfagno *m*.
sphere [sfɪəʳ] *n* (**a**) (*lit*) esfera *f*. (**b**) (*fig*) esfera *f*, campo *m*; competencia *f*; **~ of influence** esfera *f* de influencia; **~ of activity** campo *m* de actividad; **in the ~ of music** en la esfera de la música, en el mundo de la música; **that's outside my ~** eso no es de mi competencia.
spherical [ˈsferɪkəl] *adj* esférico.
spheroid [ˈsfɪərɔɪd] *n* esferoide *m*.
sphincter [ˈsfɪŋktəʳ] *n* esfínter *m*.
sphinx [sfɪŋks] *n* esfinge *f*.
spice [spaɪs] **1** *n* (*Culin*) especia *f*, olor *m* (*Mex, SC*); (*fig*) sabor *m*, picante *m*; **it's the ~ of life** es la sal de la vida; **the detail added ~ to the story** el detalle dio más sabor a la narración; **the papers like stories with some ~** a los periódicos les gusta reportajes con cierto picante.
2 *vt* condimentar; (*fig*) dar picante a; **gossip ~d with scandal** unos chismes con el sabor adicional de detalles escandalosos; **a highly ~d account** un relato de mucho picante.
spice-rack [ˈspaɪsˌræk] *n* especiero *m*.
spiciness [ˈspaɪsɪnɪs] *n* lo picante, picante *m*, sabor *m* (*also fig*).
Spick‡ [spɪk] *n* (*US*) hispano *m*, -a *f*.
spick-and-span [ˈspɪkənˈspæn] *adj* impecablemente limpio; *house etc* como una tacita de plata; *person* pulcro, aseado, acicalado.
spicy [ˈspaɪsɪ] *adj* condimentado, picante; (*fig*) picante, sabroso.
spider [ˈspaɪdəʳ] *n* araña *f*; **~ crab** centollo *m*, centolla *f*; **~'s web** telaraña *f*.
spiderman [ˈspaɪdəmæn] *n*, *pl* **spidermen** [ˈspaɪdəmen] obrero *m* que trabaja en la construcción de edificios altos.
spider-plant [ˈspaɪdəplɑːnt] *n* arañonero *m*.
spidery [ˈspaɪdərɪ] *adj* delgado; *writing* de patas de araña.
spiel [spiːl] *n* (*speech*) arenga *f*, discurso *m*; (*of salesman etc*) rollo* *m*, material *m* publicitario; (*tale*) relato *m* con que uno procura convencer a otro.
spiffing*† [ˈspɪfɪŋ] *adj* fetén†*, estupendo*, fenomenal*.
spigot [ˈspɪgət] *n* (*of cask*) espita *f*, grifo *m*; (*Tech*) espiga *f*, macho *m*.
spike [spaɪk] **1** *n* (**a**) (*point*) punta *f*; (*tool*) escarpia *f*; (*on shoes, for letters etc*) clavo *m*; (*Zool: of hedgehog etc*) pincho *m*, púa *f*; (*Elec*) pico *m* parásito; (*Bot*) espiga *f*; (*US*) **~ heel** talón *m* de aguja.
(**b**) *npl* (*Sport*) **~s** zapatillas *fpl* con clavos.
2 *vt* (**a**) atravesar con un pincho; sujetar con un clavo (*etc*); *gun* clavar, (*fig*) inutilizar, hacer inútil; (*) *news item etc* rechazar, desestimar; **to ~ a quote** cancelar una cita.
(**b**) (*US*) *drink* echar licor a, fortalecer.
spiked [spaɪkt] *adj shoe* claveteado.
spikenard [ˈspaɪknɑːd] *n* nardo *m*.
spiky [ˈspaɪkɪ] *adj* (**a**) puntiagudo; armado de púas, cubierto de púas, erizado. (**b**) *person* quisquilloso, susceptible.
spill¹ [spɪl] **1** *n* (**a**) caída *f*; vuelco *m*; **to have a ~** sufrir una caída, tener un accidente.
(**b**) (*US*) vertido *m*, vertidos *mpl*.
2 (*irr: pret and ptp* **spilled** *or* **spilt**) *vt* derramar, verter; *rider* hacer caer, desarzonar.
3 *vi* derramarse, verterse.
◆spill out **1** *vt* derramar. **2** *vi* derramarse, desparramarse; (*people etc*) salir en avalancha; **the crowd ~ed out into the streets** la gente salió a la calle en avalancha.
◆spill over *vi* irse, desbordarse; (*fig*) desbordarse.
spill² [spɪl] *n* pajuela *f*.
spillage [ˈspɪlɪdʒ] *n* vertido *m*.
spillover [ˈspɪləʊvəʳ] *n* (*act of spilling*) derrame *m*; (*quantity spilt*) cantidad *f* derramada; (*fig: excess part*) excedente *m*; (*Econ: effect*) incidencia *f* indirecta en el gasto público.
spillway [ˈspɪlweɪ] *n* (*US*) derramadero *m*, aliviadero *m*.
spilt [spɪlt] *pret and ptp of* **spill**.
spin [spɪn] **1** *n* (**a**) (*revolution*) vuelta *f*, revolución *f*; **to give a wheel a ~** poner una rueda en movimiento, hacer que una rueda gire.
(**b**) (*: *trip*) paseo *m* (en coche *etc*); **to go for a ~** dar un paseo (en coche), salir de excursión en coche.
(**c**) (*Aer*) barrena *f*; **to go into a ~** entrar en barrena; **to be in a flat ~*** estar completamente confuso, estar totalmente despistado.
(**d**) (*on ball*) efecto *m*, torcimiento; **to put a ~ on a ball** dar efecto a una pelota, torcer una pelota.
2 (*irr: pret* **spun** *or* **span**, *ptp* **spun**) *vt* (**a**) *thread* hilar; *cocoon* devanar, hacer.
(**b**) (*turn*) girar, hacer girar; dar una vuelta a; *top* hacer bailar; *ball* dar efecto a, torcer; *coin* echar a cara o cruz; *clothes* (*Brit*) centrifugar.
(**c**) *story* contar.
3 *vi* (*revolve*: *also* **to ~ round**) girar, dar vueltas; (*top*) girar, bailar; (*Aer*) entrar en barrena; descender en barrena; **to ~ along** correr rápidamente, ir a buen tren; **my**

head is ~ning estoy mareado; **it makes my head ~** me marea; **to send sth ~ning** echar algo a rodar; **the blow sent him ~ning** el golpe le echó a rodar por los suelos.
◆spin out *vt* alargar, prolongar.
spina bifida [ˌspaɪnəˈbɪfɪdə] *n* espina *f* bífida.
spinach [ˈspɪnɪdʒ] *n* (*plant*) espinaca *f*; (*dish*) espinacas *fpl*.
spinal [ˈspaɪnl] *adj* espinal; **~ column** columna *f* vertebral; **~ cord** médula *f* espinal.
spindle [ˈspɪndl] *n* (*for spinning*) huso *m*; (*Mech*) eje *m*.
spindleshanks* [ˈspɪndlʃæŋks] *n* zanquivano *m*, -a *f*.
spindly [ˈspɪndlɪ] *adj* largo y delgado, larguirucho; *leg* zanquivano.
spindrift [ˈspɪndrɪft] *n* rocío *m* del mar, espuma *f*.
spin-dry [ˌspɪnˈdraɪ] *vt washing* centrifugar.
spin-dryer [ˈspɪnˈdraɪəʳ] *n* (*Brit*) secador *m* centrífugo.
spine [spaɪn] *n* (**a**) (*Anat*) espinazo *m*, columna *f* vertebral; (*Zool*) púa *f*; (*Bot*) espina *f*; (*of book*) lomo *m*. (**b**) (*US fig*) decisión *f*, valor *m*.
spine-chiller [ˈspaɪnˌtʃɪləʳ] *n* libro *m* (*or* película *f etc*) escalofriante.
spine-chilling [ˈspaɪnˌtʃɪlɪŋ] *adj* escalofriante.
spineless [ˈspaɪnlɪs] *adj* débil, flojo, falto de voluntad, sin carácter.
spinelessly [ˈspaɪnlɪslɪ] *adv* débilmente, flojamente.
spinet [spɪˈnet] *n* espineta *f*.
spinnaker [ˈspɪnəkəʳ] *n* balón *m*, espinaquer *m*.
spinner [ˈspɪnəʳ] *n* hilandero *m*, -a *f*.
spinneret [ˌspɪnəˈret] *n* pezón *m* hilador.
spinney [ˈspɪnɪ] *n* bosquecillo *m*.
spinning [ˈspɪnɪŋ] *n* (**a**) (*motion*) rotación *f*, girar *m*. (**b**) (*of thread*) (*act*) hilado *m*, hilatura *f*; (*art*) hilandería *f*; arte *m* de hilar.
spinning-jenny [ˈspɪnɪŋˈdʒenɪ] *n* máquina *f* de hilar de husos múltiples.
spinning-mill [ˈspɪnɪŋmɪl] *n* hilandería *f*.
spinning-top [ˈspɪnɪŋtɒp] *n* peonza *f*.
spinning-wheel [ˈspɪnɪŋwiːl] *n* torno *m* de hilar, rueca *f*.
spin-off [ˈspɪnɒf] *n* subproducto *m*; efecto *m* indirecto, producto *m* suplementario (*or* adicional); beneficios *mpl* incidentales, beneficios *mpl* indirectos.
spinster [ˈspɪnstəʳ] *n* soltera *f*; (*pej*) solterona *f*.
spiny [ˈspaɪnɪ] *adj* con púas, erizado de púas; espinoso.
spiracle [ˈspɪrəkl] *n* espiráculo *m*.
spiraea, (*US*) **spirea** [spaɪˈrɪə] *n* espirea *f*.
spiral [ˈspaɪərəl] **1** *adj* espiral, helicoidal; en espiral; **~ staircase** escalera *f* de caracol.
2 *n* espiral *f*; hélice *f*; **the inflationary ~** la espiral inflacionista.
3 *vi* dar vueltas en espiral.
◆spiral down *vi*: **the plane ~led down** el avión bajó en espiral.
◆spiral up *vi*: **the smoke ~led up, the smoke went ~ling up** el humo subió en espiral; **prices have ~led up** los precios han subido vertiginosamente.
spirally [ˈspaɪərəlɪ] *adv* en espiral.
spire [ˈspaɪəʳ] *n* aguja *f*, chapitel *m*.
spirit [ˈspɪrɪt] **1** *n* (**a**) (*soul*) espíritu *m*, alma *f*; ánima *f*; **an unquiet ~** un alma inquieta; **to be vexed in ~** sentirlo en el alma.
(**b**) (*ghost*) aparecido *m*, fantasma *m*; (*evil etc*) espíritu *m* (maligno); **to cast out ~s** exorcizar espíritus.
(**c**) (*person*) alma *f*; **the leading** (*or* **moving**) **~ in the party** el alma del partido, la figura más destacada del partido; **a few restless ~s** algunas personas descontentadizas.
(**d**) (*humour, mood*) espíritu *m*; temple *m*, humor *m*; **the ~ of the age** el espíritu de la época; **in a ~ of friendship** con espíritu de amistad; **in a ~ of mischief** estando de humor para hacer alguna travesura; **we are with you in ~** os acompañamos en el sentimiento; nos alineamos con vosotros; **everyone is in a party ~** todo el mundo quiere divertirse; **it's in the ~ of the book** representa bien el espíritu del libro; **that's the ~!** ¡muy bien!; **to enter into the ~ of sth** dejarse emocionar por algo; empaparse en el ambiente de algo; **to take sth in the wrong ~** interpretar mal el espíritu con que se ha hecho algo; **it depends on the ~ in which it is done** depende del humor con que se hace.
(**e**) (*courage*) valor *m*; (*energy*) energía *f*; (*panache*) brío *m*, ánimo *m*; **a man of some ~** un hombre de cierta energía; **to catch sb's ~** ser influido por el valor de uno; **they lack ~** carecen de energía, no tienen carácter; **to show some ~** mostrar algún brío; **to sing with ~** cantar con brío.
(**f**) **~s** (*frame of mind*) ánimo *m*; humor *m*; **high ~s** optimismo *m*; alegría *f*; **to be in high ~s** estar animadísimo, estar muy alegre; **low ~s** pesimismo *m*, abatimiento *m*; **to be in low ~s** estar abatido; **to keep up one's ~s** no dejarse desanimar, no perder su optimismo; **we kept our ~s up by singing** nos animamos cantando; **to raise sb's ~s** dar aliento a uno, reanimar a uno; **to recover one's ~s** volver a estar alegre, reanimarse; **my ~s rose somewhat** me sentí algo más alegre, me sentí un poco más optimista.
(**g**) (*Chem*) alcohol *m*; (*Aut*: *also* **motor ~**) gasolina *f*; (*drink*) licor *m*; **~s of wine** espíritu *m* de vino; **I keep off ~s** no bebo licores.
2 *attr*: **~ duplicator** copiadora *f* al alcohol.
◆spirit away, spirit off *vt* llevarse misteriosamente, hacer desaparecer.
spirited [ˈspɪrɪtɪd] *adj person* animoso, brioso; *attack etc* enérgico, vigoroso; *horse* fogoso; *other animal* bravo.
spirit-lamp [ˈspɪrɪtlæmp] *n* lamparilla *f* de alcohol.
spiritless [ˈspɪrɪtlɪs] *adj* apocado, sin ánimo.
spirit-level [ˈspɪrɪtˌlevl] *n* nivel *m* de aire.
spirit-stove [ˈspɪrɪtstəʊv] *n* infernillo *m* de alcohol.
spiritual [ˈspɪrɪtjʊəl] **1** *adj* espiritual. **2** *n* (*Mus*: *negro ~*) espiritual *m* negro.
spiritualism [ˈspɪrɪtjʊəlɪzəm] *n* espiritismo *m*.
spiritualist [ˈspɪrɪtjʊəlɪst] *n* espiritista *mf*.
spirituality [ˌspɪrɪtjʊˈælɪtɪ] *n* espiritualidad *f*.
spiritually [ˈspɪrɪtjʊəlɪ] *adv* espiritualmente.
spirituous [ˈspɪrɪtjʊəs] *adj* espirit(u)oso.
spirt [spɜːt] **1** *n* chorro *m*, chorretada *f*.
2 *vt* hacer salir en chorro, arrojar un chorro de.
3 *vi* (*also* **to ~ out, to ~ up**) salir en chorro, salir a chorros; brotar a borbotones; *V also* **spurt**.
spit¹ [spɪt] **1** *n* (*Culin*) asador *m*, espetón *m*; (*of land*) lengua *f*; (*sandbank*) banco *m* de arena; **~ roast** asado *m*.
2 *vt* espetar.
spit² [spɪt] **1** *n* saliva *f*; esputo *m*; **a ~ of rain** unas gotas de lluvia; **that table needs a bit of ~ and polish*** esa mesa hay que limpiarla (y sacarle brillo); **they're very keen on ~ and polish here*** aquí lo tienen todo relimpio; **to be the dead** (*or* **very**) **~ of sb** ser la segunda edición de uno, ser la viva imagen de uno.
2 (*irr*: *pret and ptp* **spat**) *vt* escupir.
3 *vi* escupir (*at* a, *on* en); (*cat*) bufar; (*fat, fire*) chisporrotear; **to ~ in sb's face** escupir a la cara a uno; **the fish is ~ting in the pan** chisporrotea el pescado en la sartén; **it is ~ting (with rain)** caen algunas gotas de lluvia, empieza a llover.
◆spit forth *vt* = **spit out**.
◆spit out *vt* escupir (*also fig*); **~ it out!*** ¡dilo!, ¡desembucha!
◆spit up *vt blood* soltar un esputo de.
spit³ [spɪt] *n* (*Agr*) azadada *f*; **to dig 3 ~s deep** excavar a una profundidad de 3 azadadas.
spite [spaɪt] **1** *n* rencor *m*, ojeriza *f*, despecho *m*; **in ~ of** a pesar de, a despecho de; **in ~ of all he says** a pesar de todo lo que dice; **to do sth out of** (*or* **from**) **~** hacer algo por despecho.
2 *vt* mortificar, herir, causar pena a; **she just does it to ~ me** lo hace solamente para causarme pena.
spiteful [ˈspaɪtfʊl] *adj* rencoroso, malévolo; **to be ~ to sb** tratar a uno con malevolencia.
spitefully [ˈspaɪtfəlɪ] *adv* con rencor, malévolamente; por despecho; **she said ~** dijo malévola.
spitefulness [ˈspaɪtfʊlnɪs] *n* rencor *m*, malevolencia *f*.
spitfire [ˈspɪtˌfaɪəʳ] *n* fierabrás *m*.
spitroast [ˈspɪtrəʊst] *vt* rostizar.
spitting [ˈspɪtɪŋ] **1** *n*: **'~ prohibited'** 'prohibido escupir'. **2** *adj*: **it's within ~ distance*** está muy cerca, está justo al lado; *V* **image**.
spittle [ˈspɪtl] *n* saliva *f*, baba *f*.
spittoon [spɪˈtuːn] *n* escupidera *f*.
spiv* [spɪv] *n* (*Brit*) chanchullero* *m*, caballero *m* de industria; (*slacker*) gandul *m*; (*black marketeer*) estraperlista *m*.
splash [splæʃ] **1** *n* (*spray*) salpicadura *f*, rociada *f*; (*~ing noise*) chapoteo *m*; (*of colour*) mancha *f*; **whisky with a ~ of water** whisky *m* con un poquitín de agua; **it fell with a great ~ into the water** cayó ruidosamente al agua, cayó al agua levantando mucha espuma; **with a great ~ of publicity*** con mucho bombo publicitario*; **to make a ~*** causar una sensación, impresionar; hacer algo en grande*.
2 *vt* (**a**) salpicar (*with* de). (**b**) (*fig*) **they ~ed the news**

across the front page publicaron la noticia con mucho bombo en la primera plana.

3 *vi* (*liquid*) esparcirse, rociarse; (*person in water*) chapotear.

◆**splash about 1** *vt*: **to ~ water about** desparramar (el) agua; **to ~ one's money about** derrochar su dinero por todas partes.

2 *vi* (*person in water*) chapotear; **to ~ about in the water** chapotear en el agua.

◆**splash down** *vi* (*Aer*) amerizar.

◆**splash out*** *vi* derrochar dinero; **so we ~ed out and bought it** así que en un derroche lo compramos.

◆**splash up 1** *vt* salpicar. **2** *vi* salpicar.

splashback ['splæʃbæk] *n* salpicadero *m*.

splashboard ['splæʃbɔːd] *n* guardabarros *m*, alero *m*.

splashdown ['splæʃdaʊn] *n* amaraje *m*, amerizaje *m*, chapuzón *m*.

splashy ['splæʃɪ] *adj* líquido; fangoso.

splatter ['splætəʳ] = **spatter**.

splay [spleɪ] *vt* extender (sin gracia); (*Tech*) biselar, achaflanar.

spleen [spliːn] *n* (*Anat*) bazo *m*; (*fig*) spleen *m*, esplín *m*, rencor *m*; **to vent one's ~** descargar la bilis (*on* contra).

splendid ['splendɪd] *adj* espléndido; **~!** ¡magnífico!; **that's simply ~!** ¡pero qué bien!; **but how ~ for you!** ¡cuánto me alegro por ti!; **a ~ joke** un chiste excelente; **he has done ~ work** ha hecho una magnífica labor.

splendidly ['splendɪdlɪ] *adv* espléndidamente; magníficamente; **a ~ dressed man** un hombre brillantemente vestido; **you did ~** hiciste muy bien, lo has hecho rebién; **everything went ~** todo fue a las mil maravillas; **we get along ~** nos llevamos muy bien.

splendiferous* [splen'dɪfərəs] *adj* = **splendid.**

splendour, (*US*) **splendor** ['splendəʳ] *n* esplendor *m*; magnificencia *f*; (*of achievement etc*) brillo *m*, gloria *f*.

splenetic [splɪ'netɪk] *adj* (*Anat*) esplénico; (*fig*) enojadizo, de genio vivo; malhumorado.

splice [splaɪs] **1** *n* empalme *m*, junta *f*. **2** *vt* empalmar, juntar; (*Naut*) ayustar; **to get ~d‡** casarse.

splicer ['splaɪsəʳ] *n* (*for film*) máquina *f* de montaje.

splint [splɪnt] **1** *n* tablilla *f*; (*Vet*) sobrecaña *f*; **to put sb's arm in ~s** entablillar el brazo a uno. **2** *vt* entablillar.

splinter ['splɪntəʳ] **1** *n* astilla *f*; (*in finger*) espigón *m*.

2 *attr*: **~ group** grupo *m* disidente, facción *f*; **~ party** partido *m* nuevo formado a raíz de la escisión de otro.

3 *vt* astillar, hacer astillas.

4 *vi* astillarse, hacerse astillas; **to ~ off** separarse.

splinterbone ['splɪntəbəʊn] *n* peroné *m*.

splinterless ['splɪntəlɪs] *adj* inastillable.

splinterproof ['splɪntəpruːf] *adj*: **~ glass** cristal *m* inastillable.

split [splɪt] **1** *n* (*crack*) hendedura *f*, raja *f*, grieta *f*; (*fig*) división *f*; cisma *m*; (*Pol*) escisión *f*; (*quarrel*) ruptura *f*; **a three-way ~** una división en tres partes; **there are threats of a ~ in the progressive party** hay amenazas de escisión en el partido progresista; **to do the ~s** despatarrarse, esparrancarse.

2 *adj* partido, hendido; *party etc* escindido, dividido; **~ infinitive** *infinitivo m en el que un adverbio o una frase se intercala entre 'to' y el verbo*; **~ pea** guisante *m* majado; **~ personality** personalidad *f* desdoblada; **~ pin** (*Brit*) chaveta *f*, pasador *m*; **~ screen** pantalla *f* partida; **~-screen facility** capacidad *f* de pantalla partida; **the party was ~** el partido estaba escindido; **the party is ~ 3 ways** el partido está escindido en 3 grupos; **the votes are ~ 5-3** los votos están repartidos 5 a 3; **it was a ~ decision** la decisión no fue unánime; *V* **second 3 (a)**.

3 (*irr: pret and ptp* **split**) *vt* (*cleave*) partir, hender, rajar; dividir; repartir; **to ~ the atom** desintegrar el átomo; **to ~ the difference** partir la diferencia; **the sea had ~ the ship in two** el mar había partido el barco en dos; **the blow ~ his head open** el golpe le abrió la cabeza; **the dispute ~ the party** la disputa escindió el partido.

4 *vi* **(a)** (*also* **to ~ up**) partirse, henderse, rajarse; dividirse; (*party*) escindirse; **the ship ~ on the rocks** el buque se estrelló contra las rocas; **my head is ~ting** me duele terriblemente la cabeza.

(b) (*Brit**) soplar‡, chivatear‡ (*on sb* contra uno); **don't ~ on me** de esto no digas ni pío.

(c) (*esp US**) largarse‡, irse.

◆**split off 1** *vt* separar.

2 *vi* separarse, desprenderse, (*Pol*) escindirse.

◆**split up 1** *vt* partir, dividir; *estate* parcelar; **we'll ~ the work up among us** dividiremos el trabajo entre nosotros.

2 *vi* **(a)** = **split 4 (a)**.

(b) (*persons*) separarse; (*crowd*) dispersarse; **let's ~ up for safety** separémonos para mayor seguridad; **they were married 14 years but then they ~ up** estuvieron casados durante 14 años pero luego se separaron.

split-level ['splɪt,levl] *adj house* construido sobre dos niveles, con planta baja de dos niveles, a desnivel; **~ cooker** cocina *f* encimera.

split-off ['splɪtɒf] *n* separación *f*; (*Pol etc*) escisión *f*.

splitting ['splɪtɪŋ] **1** *adj headache* terrible, enloquecedor. **2** *n*: **~ of the atom** desintegración *f* del átomo.

split-up ['splɪtʌp] *n* ruptura *f*; separación *f*.

splodge [splɒdʒ] *n*, **splotch** [splɒtʃ] *n* mancha *f*, borrón *m*.

splurge* [splɜːdʒ] **1** *n* **(a)** (*show*) fachenda* *f*, ostentación *f*. **(b)** (*excess*) derroche *m*, exceso *m*. **2** *vi*: **to ~ on sth** derrochar dinero comprando algo.

splutter ['splʌtəʳ] **1** *n* (*of fat etc*) chisporroteo *m*; (*of speech*) farfulla *f*. **2** *vt* decir balbuceando; **'Yes', he ~ed** 'Sí', balbuceó. **3** *vi* chisporrotear; farfullar, balbucear; (*engine*) renquear.

spoil [spɔɪl] **1** *n* (*also* **~s**) despojo *m*, botín *m*; trofeo *m*; **~ system** (*US*) sistema *m* de repartirse los empleos entre los del partido victorioso; **the ~s of war** el botín de la guerra, los trofeos de la guerra.

2 (*irr: pret and ptp* **spoiled** *or* **spoilt**) *vt* **(a)** echar a perder, estropear, malograr, arruinar; deteriorar; *voting paper* invalidar; **to ~ sb's fun** aguar la fiesta a uno; **it quite ~ed our holiday** arruinó completamente nuestras vacaciones; **it would ~ my appetite** me quitaría el apetito; **the coast has been ~ed by development** la costa ha sido arruinada por la urbanización; **and there were 20 ~ed papers** y hubo 20 votos inválidos; **to get ~ed** echarse a perder, estropearse.

(b) (*pamper*) *child* mimar, consentir.

3 *vi* **(a)** echarse a perder, estropearse; arruinarse; dañarse, deteriorarse; **if we leave it here it will ~** si lo dejamos aquí se estropeará.

(b) to be ~ing for a fight querer de todos modos luchar, tener ganas de pelearse.

spoilage ['spɔɪlɪdʒ] *n* (*process*) deterioro *m*; (*thing, amount spoilt*) desperdicio *m*.

spoiled [spɔɪld] **1** *adj* (*US*) *food* pasado, malo; *milk* cortado; = **spoilt 2**. **2** = **spoilt 1**.

spoiler ['spɔɪləʳ] *n* (*Aut, Aer*) alerón *m*, spoiler *m*.

spoilsport ['spɔɪlspɔːt] *n* aguafiestas *m*; **to be a ~** aguar la fiesta.

spoilt [spɔɪlt] **1** *pret and ptp of* **spoil**. **2** *adj* **(a)** estropeado; dañado, deteriorado; *vote* nulo. **(b)** *child* consentido, muy mimado.

spoke[1] [spəʊk] *n* rayo *m*, radio *m*; **to put a ~ in sb's wheel** meter un palo en la rueda de uno.

spoke[2] [spəʊk] *pret of* **speak**.

spoken ['spəʊkən] **1** *ptp of* **speak**. **2** *adj* hablado; **the ~ language** la lengua hablada, la lengua oral.

spokeshave ['spəʊkʃeɪv] *n* raedera *f*.

spokesman ['spəʊksmən] *n*, *pl* **spokesmen** ['spəʊksmən] portavoz *m*, vocero *m* (*esp LAm*); **to act as ~ for** hablar en nombre de; **they made him ~** le eligieron para hablar en su nombre.

spokesperson ['spəʊkspɜːsn] *n* portavoz *mf*.

spokeswoman ['spəʊkswʊmən] *n*, *pl* **spokeswomen** ['spəʊkswɪmɪn] portavoz *f*.

spoliation [,spəʊlɪ'eɪʃən] *n* despojo *m*.

spondee ['spɒndiː] *n* espondeo *m*.

sponge [spʌndʒ] **1** *n* **(a)** esponja *f*; **to throw in the ~** arrojar (*or* tirar) la toalla.

(b) (*Culin*) bizcocho *m*.

2 *vt* **(a)** (*wash: also* **to ~ down**) lavar con esponja, lavar con trapo, limpiar con esponja; **to ~ a stain off** quitar una mancha con una esponja.

(b) (*) **he ~d £5 off me** me sacó 5 libras de gorra*.

3 *vi* (*) dar sablazos*, vivir de gorra*, gorrear; **to ~ on sb** vivir a costa de uno; **to ~ on sb for sth** sacar algo de gorra a uno*.

◆**sponge down** *vt* = **sponge 2 (a)**.

◆**sponge up** *vt* absorber.

spongebag ['spʌndʒbæg] *n* (*Brit*) esponjera *f*.

spongecake ['spʌndʒkeɪk] *n* bizcocho *m*.

sponge pudding [,spʌndʒ'pʊdɪŋ] *n* pudín *m* de bizcocho.

sponger* ['spʌndʒəʳ] *n* gorrón* *m*, sablista* *mf*.

sponginess ['spʌndʒɪnɪs] *n* esponjosidad *f*.

sponging* ['spʌndʒɪŋ] *n* gorronería* *f*.

spongy ['spʌndʒɪ] *adj* esponjoso.

sponsor ['spɒnsəʳ] **1** *n* patrocinador *m*, -ora *f* (*also Rad*,

Sport, TV); (*godparent*) padrino *m*, madrina *f*; (*of membership etc*) padrino *m*; (*Comm*) fiador *m*, garante *m*; (*Parl*: *of bill*) promotor *m*, -ora *f*.

2 *vt* patrocinar; (*Rad, TV*) patrocinar, costear, presentar; *idea, plan etc* fomentar, promover; (*Parl*) *bill* promover; (*as godparent, for membership etc*) apadrinar, actuar de padrino a; **~ed walk** *marcha emprendida a cambio de donaciones a una obra benéfica*.

sponsorship ['spɒnsəʃɪp] *n* patrocinio *m*, patrocinazgo *m*; **under the ~ of** patrocinado por, bajo los auspicios de.

spontaneity [ˌspɒntə'neɪɪtɪ] *n* espontaneidad *f*.

spontaneous [spɒn'teɪnɪəs] *adj* espontáneo.

spontaneously [spɒn'teɪnɪəslɪ] *adv* espontáneamente.

spoof* [spu:f] **1** *n* (*trick*) trampa *f*, truco *m*, mistificación *f*; (*Liter etc*) parodia *f* (*on* de); documento *m* (*etc*) apócrifo. **2** *adj*: **~ letter** carta *f* paródica, carta *f* apócrifa. **3** *vt* engañar, burlar, mistificar. **4** *vi* bromear.

spook* [spu:k] **1** *n* (**a**) espectro *m*. (**b**) (*US**) espía *mf*, agente *m* secreto, agente *f* secreta. **2** *vt* (*US*) asustar, pegar un susto a.

spooky* ['spu:kɪ] *adj* (*like a ghost*) fantasmal, espectral; (*mysterious*) misterioso; (*frightening*) escalofriante, horripilante.

SPOOL [spu:l] *n abbr of* **simultaneous peripherical operation on-line** operación *f* simultánea de periféricos en línea.

spool [spu:l] *n* (*Sew, Phot, Fishing*) carrete *m*; (*of sewing machine*) canilla *f*.

spoon [spu:n] **1** *n* cuchara *f*; (*Fishing*) cucharilla *f*; **to be born with a silver ~ in one's mouth** nacer en buena cuna, criarse en buenos pañales.

2 *vt* (*also* **to ~ out**) cucharear, sacar con cuchara; (*fig*) sacar como en cuchara.

3 *vi* (*) acariciarse amorosamente, besuquearse*.

◆**spoon off** *vt fat, cream etc* quitar con la cuchara.

◆**spoon out** *vt* = **spoon 2**.

◆**spoon up** *vt* recoger con cuchara.

spoonbill ['spu:nbɪl] *n* espátula *f*.

spoonerism ['spu:nərɪzəm] *n juego de palabras* (*o error divertido*) *que consiste en trastrocar los sonidos iniciales de dos o más vocablos*.

spoon-feed ['spu:nfi:d] (*irr*: *V* **feed**) *vt* dar de comer con cuchara a; (*fig*) tratar como un niño a, ayudar hasta con las cosas más sencillas a.

spoon-fed ['spu:nfed] *adj* muy mimado.

spoonful ['spu:nfʊl] *n* cucharada *f*.

spoor [spʊəʳ] *n* pista *f*, rastro *m*.

sporadic [spə'rædɪk] *adj* esporádico.

sporadically [spə'rædɪkəlɪ] *adv* esporádicamente.

spore [spɔ:ʳ] *n* espora *f*.

sporran ['spɒrən] *n* (*Scot*) sporran *m* (*escarcela que se lleva sobre la falda escocesa*).

sport [spɔ:t] **1** *n* (**a**) (*games in general*) deporte *m*; (*hunting*) caza *f*; deporte *m*; (*amusement*) juego *m*, diversión *f*; (*plaything*) víctima *f*, juguete *m*; **the ~ of kings** el deporte de los reyes (*el hipismo*); **in ~** en broma; **to have some good ~** tener éxito en la caza, lograr unas cuantas piezas hermosas; **the trout here give good ~** aquí las truchas no se rinden fácilmente; **to make ~ of sb** burlarse de uno.

(**b**) (*person*) buen chico *m*; buen perdedor *m*; **yes, ~*** (*Australia*) sí, macho*; **be a ~!** ¡como amigo!; **he's a real ~** es una persona realmente buena.

(**c**) (*Bio*) mutación *f*.

2 *attr*: deportivo; de deportes; **~s car** coche *m* deportivo, deportivo *m*, coche *m* sport; **~s centre, ~s complex, ~s hall** polideportivo *m*; **~(s) coat** (*US*) = **~s jacket**; **~s day** (*Brit*) día *m* de competiciones deportivas (de un colegio); **~s desk** sección *f* de deportes; **~s editor** jefe *mf* de la redacción deportiva; **~s facilities** instalaciones *fpl* deportivas; **~s field, ~s ground** campo *m* deportivo, campo *m* de deportes, centro *m* deportivo (*LAm*); **~s jacket** chaqueta *f* sport, americana *f* de sport; **~s page** página *f* deportiva.

3 *vt* llevar; gastar; lucir, ostentar.

4 *vi* divertirse; jugar, juguetear.

sportiness ['spɔ:tɪnɪs] *n* (*lit*) deportividad *f*; (*fig*) cursilería *f*.

sporting ['spɔ:tɪŋ] *adj* deportivo; *conduct, spirit etc* deportivo, caballeroso; *chance, offer* que da cierta posibilidad de éxito; *dog, gun* de caza; **that's very ~ of you** es una oferta (*etc*) muy caballerosa; **I'm a ~ man** me gusta hacer apuestas arriesgadas.

sportingly ['spɔ:tɪŋlɪ] *adv* de modo deportivo.

sportive ['spɔ:tɪv] *adj* juguetón.

sportscast ['spɔ:tskɑ:st] *n* (*US*) programa *m* deportivo.

sportsman ['spɔ:tsmən] *n*, *pl* **sportsmen** ['spɔ:tsmən] (*player, hunter*) deportista *m*; (*honourable person*) persona *f* honrada, caballero *m*; **the ~ of the year** el deportista del año.

sportsmanlike ['spɔ:tsmənlaɪk] *adj* deportivo; honrado, caballeroso.

sportsmanship ['spɔ:tsmənʃɪp] *n* deportividad *f*.

sportswear ['spɔ:tswɛəʳ] *n* ropa *f* de deporte.

sportswoman ['spɔ:tswʊmən] *n*, *pl* **sportswomen** ['spɔ:tswɪmɪn] deportista *f*.

sports-writer ['spɔ:tsraɪtəʳ] *n* cronista *m* deportivo, cronista *f* deportiva.

sporty ['spɔ:tɪ] *adj* (**a**) (*liking sport*) deportivo; aficionado a los deportes.

(**b**) (*fig*) alegre; guasón, jovial.

(**c**) (*US*) disipado, libertino; elegante, guapo.

spot [spɒt] **1** *n* (**a**) (*place in general*) sitio *m*, lugar *m*; **a pleasant ~** un lugar agradable; **a good ~ for trout** un buen lugar para las truchas; **high ~** punto *m* cumbre; **to be in a** (**tight**) **~** estar en un aprieto; **to have a soft ~ for sb** tener una debilidad por uno; **to know sb's weak ~s** saber de qué pie cojea uno; **to put one's finger on the weak ~** poner el dedo en la llaga.

(**b**) (*phrases with* **on**) **on this very ~** en este mismo sitio; **our man on the ~** nuestro hombre sobre el terreno; **the reporter was on the ~** el reportero estaba allí mismo; **the firemen were on the ~ in 3 minutes** los bomberos llegaron dentro de 3 minutos, acudieron los bomberos a los 3 minutos; **I always have to be on the ~** estoy de servicio siempre; **to do sth on the ~** hacer algo en el acto, hacer algo acto seguido; hacer algo sin demora; **to pay cash on the ~** (*US*) pagar al contado; **to put sb on the ~** poner a uno en la encrucijada, poner a uno en un aprieto (*or* un apuro); **now I'm really on the ~** ahora me veo de verdad entre la espada y la pared; **to run on the ~** correr en parada.

(**c**) (*Med etc*) grano *m*, lunar *m*; (*freckle*) peca *f*; (*stain*) mancha *f*; **measles ~s** manchas *fpl* de sarampión; **to break** (*or* **come**) **out in ~s** salir a uno granos en la piel; **it made a ~ on the table** hizo una mancha en la mesa.

(**d**) (*of colour*) punto *m*; pinta *f*, mancha *f*; **a cloth with blue ~s** un paño con puntos azules; **to knock ~s off sb*** dar ciento y raya a uno; **this can knock ~s off yours any time*** éste da ciento y raya al tuyo en cualquier momento; **five ~‡** (*US*) billete *m* de 5 dólares; **ten ~‡** (*US*) billete *m* de 10 dólares.

(**e**) (*esp Brit*: *small quantity*) poquito *m*, poquitín *m*; (*of rain*) gota *f*; **just a ~, thanks** un poquitín, gracias; **we had a few ~s** tuvimos algunas gotitas; **a ~ of bother** cierto disgusto, un poco de dificultad; **he had a ~ of bother with the police** se armó un lío con la policía; **we're in a ~ of trouble** tenemos cierta dificultad; **without a ~ of trouble** sin dificultad alguna.

(**f**) (*Rad, TV*) espacio *m*, cuña *f*.

(**g**) **~s** (*Comm*) géneros *mpl* vendidos al contado; géneros *mpl* para entrega inmediata.

(**h**) **night ~*** sala *f* de fiestas; lugar *m* de diversión nocturna.

(**i**) (*) = **spotlight**.

2 *attr* (**a**) **~ cash** dinero *m* contante; **~ goods** géneros *mpl* vendidos al contado; géneros *mpl* para entrega inmediata; **~ market** mercado *m* al contado; **~ price** precio *m* al contado (*or* de entrega inmediata).

(**b**) **~ check** comprobación *f* en el acto, reconocimiento *m* rápido; **~ survey** inspección *f* sorpresa; **~ test** prueba *f* superficial.

3 *vt* (**a**) (*speckle*) manchar, motear, salpicar (*with* de); **to ~ sb with mud** salpicar a uno de lodo.

(**b**) (*notice, see*) notar, observar; encontrar; descubrir; *error* reparar en; (*recognize*) reconocer; (*select*) elegir, escoger; **I ~ted him at once** le reconocí en seguida; **did you ~ the winner?** ¿has adivinado el ganador?; ¿has pronosticado el ganador?

4 *vi*: **to ~** (*with rain*) chispear.

spot-check ['spɒtˌtʃek] *vt* revisar en el acto.

spotless ['spɒtlɪs] *adj* nítido; sin manchas, inmaculado; (*clean*) perfectamente limpio, como una tacita de plata.

spotlessly ['spɒtlɪslɪ] *adv*: **~ clean** limpísimo, como una tacita.

spotlessness ['spɒtlɪsnɪs] *n* nitidez *f*; perfecta limpieza *f*.

spotlight ['spɒtlaɪt] **1** *n* (*Theat*: *lamp*) foco *m*, reflector *m*, proyector *m*, (*light*) luz *f* del foco; (*Aut*) faro *m* auxiliar; (*fig*) luz *f* concentrada; **to be in the ~** (*fig*) estar bajo la luz de la publicidad, ser el foco de la atención pública; **to**

turn the ~ on sb (*fig*) volver sobre uno la luz de la publicidad (*or* de la atención pública *etc*).
2 *vt* iluminar; destacar, subrayar.
spot-on* [ˌspɒtˈɒn] **1** *adj*: **what he said was ~** lo que dijo era muy justo. **2** *adv*: **she guessed ~** lo adivinó exactamente.
spotted [ˈspɒtɪd] *adj* manchado; moteado; **a dress ~ with blue** un vestido con puntos azules; **a dress ~ with mud** un vestido manchado de lodo.
spotter [ˈspɒtəʳ] *n* (*Aer etc*) observador *m*, -ora *f*; (*Brit Rail*) coleccionista *mf* de números de locomotoras.
spotting [ˈspɒtɪŋ] *n* punteo *m*, moteamiento *m*; **to go train/plane ~** ir a ver trenes/aviones.
spotty [ˈspɒtɪ] *adj* manchado, lleno de manchas; (*Med*) (*pimply*) con granos; (*of infection*) con manchas; **some ~ herbert*** algún criajo*; **to be all ~** estar cubierto de manchas.
spouse [spaʊs] *n* cónyuge *mf*.
spout [spaʊt] **1** *n* (*of jar*) pico *m*; (*of teapot, wine jug*) pitón *m*, pitorro *m*; (*of guttering*) canalón *m*; (*pipe*) caño *m*, conducto *m*; (*jet of water*) chorro *m*; (*column of water*) surtidor *m*; **to be up the ~*** (*Brit*: *person, in a jam*) estar en un apuro, (*pregnant*) estar en estado; **my holiday's up the ~*** (*Brit*) mis vacaciones se hicieron pedazos.
2 *vt* arrojar en chorro; levantar un surtidor de; (*fig*) declamar, recitar; soltar; **he can ~ figures about it** es capaz de soltarte una retahíla de cifras.
3 *vi* chorrear; (*fig*) recitar, perorar; **he was still ~ing when we left** seguía perorando cuando salimos.
sprain [spreɪn] **1** *n* torcedura *f*, desgarro *m* (*LAm*). **2** *vt* torcer; **to ~ one's wrist** torcerse la muñeca.
sprang [spræŋ] *pret of* **spring**.
sprat [spræt] *n* espadín *m*, sardineta *f*.
sprawl [sprɔːl] **1** *n* (*of body*) postura *f* desgarbada; (*of town etc*) extensión *f*; **an endless ~ of suburbs** una interminable extensión de barrios exteriores; **urban ~** urbanización *f* caótica.
2 *vi* arrellanarse, repanchigarse; extenderse (en postura desgarbada), tumbarse (de modo poco elegante); (*plant, town*) extenderse; **he was ~ed in a chair** estaba tumbado de modo poco elegante en un sillón; **the body was ~ed on the floor** el cadáver estaba tumbado en el suelo; **to send sb ~ing (with a blow)** derribar a uno por el suelo; **the jolt sent him ~ing** la sacudida le hizo ir rodando por el suelo.
sprawling [ˈsprɔːlɪŋ] *adj person, position* desmadejado; *handwriting* desgarbado; *city* desparramado.
spray[1] [spreɪ] *n* (*Bot*) ramita *f*, ramo *m*.
spray[2] [spreɪ] **1** *n* **(a)** (*liquid*) rociada *f*; (*of sea*) espuma *f*; (*as irrigation*) riego *m* por aspersión; (*of insecticide etc*) pulverización *f*.
(b) (*implement*) (*scent ~*) atomizador *m*; (*paint ~*) pistola *f* (rociadora) de pintura; (*Med*) rociador *m*; (*insecticide ~*) pulverizador *m*; **to paint with a ~** pintar con pistola.
2 *vt* rociar, regar (*with* de); atomizar, pulverizar; **to ~ the roses with insecticide** rociar las rosas de insecticida; **to ~ paint on to a car** pintar un coche con una pistola rociadora; **to ~ a house with bullets** rociar una casa de balas.
◆**spray out** *vi* (*liquid etc*) salir a chorro; **water ~ed out all over them** el agua les caló.
spraycan [ˈspreɪkæn] *n* espray *m*, pulverizador *m*.
sprayer [ˈspreɪəʳ] *n* = **spray**[2] **1 (b)**.
spraygun [ˈspreɪgʌn] *n* pistola *f* rociadora; pulverizador *m*.
spray-paint [ˈspreɪpeɪnt] *n* pintura *f* para pistola (*or* de espray).
spread [spred] **1** *n* **(a)** (*act*) extensión *f*; propagación *f*, diseminación *f*, difusión *f*; generalización *f*; proliferación *f*; **the ~ of education** la extensión de la educación; **the ~ of nuclear weapons** la proliferación de armas nucleares.
(b) (*of wings*) envergadura *f*; (*of figures, marks etc*) extensión *f*; abanico *m*, gama *f*, escala *f*; **middle-age ~** gordura *f* de la mediana edad.
(c) (*: *meal*) comilona* *f*, banquetazo* *m*.
(d) (*Culin*: *cheese ~ etc*) pasta *f*.
(e) (*Typ*) anuncio *m* (*or* artículo *m etc*) a doble página.
2 (*irr*: *pret and ptp* **spread**) *vt* extender, tender; *intangible things* propagar, diseminar, difundir; divulgar; generalizar; *butter etc* untar; *banner, sails, wings* desplegar; *net* tender; *table* poner; (*scatter*) esparcir, desparramar; **to ~ butter on one's bread** untar el pan con mantequilla, extender mantequilla sobre el pan; **to ~ cream on one's face** extender crema sobre el rostro; **to ~ oil on the sea** tender una capa de aceite sobre el mar; **to ~ the sea with oil** cubrir el mar con una capa de aceite; **meadows ~ with flowers** prados cubiertos de flores; **the peacock ~s its tail** el pavo real hace la rueda; **repayments will be ~ over 18 months** los pagos se efectuarán a lo largo de 18 meses; **to ~ news about** divulgar una noticia; **our resources are very thinly ~** tenemos poco margen en la distribución de nuestros recursos; **the book ~s error** el libro disemina el error.
3 *vi* extenderse; cundir; propagarse, difundirse; divulgarse; generalizarse; desplegarse; (*scatter*) esparcirse, desparramarse; **the fire ~ rapidly** el incendio se extendió rápidamente; **the strike ~ to other workers** la huelga se extendió a otros obreros; **a knowledge of this ~ widely** el conocimiento de esto se divulgó a muchas partes; **the disease ~** la enfermedad se propagó.
4 *vr*: **to ~ o.s.** **(a)** (*physically*) arrellanarse; ponerse a sus anchas, tomar una postura cómoda; **I like to ~ myself** me gusta tener mucho espacio (para trabajar cómodamente *etc*).
(b) (*: *in speech*) explayarse, hablar prolijamente.
(c) **to ~ o.s. too thin** traerse demasiadas cosas entre manos, dispersar esfuerzos en demasía.
◆**spread out** **1** *vt* separar; abrir, extender, desplegar; **to ~ a map out on a table** extender un mapa sobre una mesa.
2 *vi* (*persons*) separarse; desparramarse.
spread-eagle [ˈspredˈiːgl] *vt* extender (completamente), despatarrar.
spread-eagled [ˈspredˈiːgld] *adj* despatarrado.
spreader [ˈspredəʳ] *n* (*for butter etc*) cuchillo *m* para esparcir; (*for glue etc*) paleta *f*; (*Agr*) esparcidor *m*.
spreadsheet [ˈspredʃiːt] *n* hoja *f* electrónica, hoja *f* de cálculo.
spree [spriː] *n* juerga *f*, parranda *f*; excursión *f*; **to be (out) on a ~** estar de juerga; **to go on a ~** ir de juerga; **let's have a ~** echemos una cana al aire.
sprig [sprɪg] *n* (*Bot*) ramita *f*; (*of heather etc*) espiga *f*; (*Tech*) puntilla *f*.
sprightliness [ˈspraɪtlɪnɪs] *n* viveza *f*, energía *f*, animación *f*.
sprightly [ˈspraɪtlɪ] *adj* vivo, enérgico, animado.
spring [sprɪŋ] **1** *n* **(a)** (*of water*) fuente *f*, manantial *f*; **hot ~** fuente *f* termal; **~ water** agua *f* de manantial.
(b) (*season*) primavera *f*; **in ~, in the ~** en la primavera; **~ is in the air** se nota la llegada de la primavera.
(c) (*leap*) salto *m*, brinco *m*; **in one ~** de un salto; **to take a ~ into the air** dar un salto.
(d) (*bounciness*) elasticidad *f*; **to walk with a ~ in one's step** andar con pasos alegres, caminar alegre y confiado.
(e) (*Mech*: *of watch etc*) resorte *m*, (*of mattress, seat etc*) muelle *m*; **~s** (*Aut*) ballestas *fpl*.
2 *attr*: **~ chicken** polluelo *m*; **she's no ~ chicken*** *V* **chicken 1**; **~ onion** (*Brit*) cebollita *f*; **~ sunshine** sol *m* de primavera, sol *m* primaveral.
3 (*irr*: *pret* **sprang**, *ptp* **sprung**) *vt* **(a)** (*leap*) saltar, saltar por encima de.
(b) (*warp*) torcer, combar.
(c) *mine* volar; *trap* hacer saltar; **to ~ a leak** abrirse una vía de agua; **to ~ a piece of news on sb** comunicar una noticia imprevista a uno; **to ~ a surprise on sb** coger a uno de improviso; **to ~ an idea on sb** espetar una idea a uno, sugerir una idea a uno de buenas a primeras.
(d) (*Hunting*) *game* levantar; **to ~ a prisoner from jail*** ayudar a un preso a salir de la cárcel.
4 *vi* **(a)** (*water etc*) brotar, nacer; salir en chorro; (*Bot*) brotar; **to ~ into existence** nacer de la noche a la mañana, aparecer repentinamente; **to ~ from** (*fig*) nacer de, proceder de, provenir de; *family* ser de, nacer de; **a man sprung from the people** un hombre surgido de la plebe.
(b) (*leap*) saltar, brincar; **the lid sprang open** la tapa se abrió de golpe; **to ~ aside** hacerse de prisa a un lado; **to ~ at sb** abalanzarse sobre uno; **to ~ back** saltar para atrás; **the branch sprang back** la rama volvió a su posición como un látigo; **where on earth did you ~ from?** ¿de dónde diablos has salido?; **to ~ into the air** saltar en el aire; **to ~ into the saddle** saltar a la silla; **to ~ out of bed** saltar de la cama; **to ~ to one's feet** levantarse de un salto; **to ~ to sb's aid** acudir con toda rapidez a ayudar a uno.
(c) (*warp*) torcerse, combarse.
◆**spring up** *vi* **(a)** (*grow*) (*plant*) brotar; crecer rápidamente; (*problem*) surgir, presentarse; (*friendship etc*) nacer; **the weeds ~ up all over** las malas hierbas aparecen por todas las partes.
(b) (*person, animal*) levantarse de un salto; (*of breeze*

etc) levantarse de pronto.
spring balance ['sprɪŋ'bæləns] *n* peso *m* de muelle.
spring binder [ˌsprɪŋ'baɪndəʳ] *n* carpeta *f* de pinza.
springboard ['sprɪŋbɔːd] *n* trampolín *m*; (*fig*) plataforma *f* de lanzamiento; ~ **dive** salto *m* de trampolín.
springbok ['sprɪŋbɒk] *n* gacela *f* (*del sur de África*).
spring-bolt ['sprɪŋbəʊlt] *n* pestillo *m* de golpe.
spring-clean ['sprɪŋ'kliːn] **1** *vt* limpiar completamente. **2** *vi* limpiarlo todo, limpiar toda la casa.
spring-cleaning ['sprɪŋ'kliːnɪŋ] *n* limpieza *f* general; **to do the** ~ limpiar toda la casa.
spring fever ['sprɪŋ'fiːvəʳ] *n* desasosiego *m* primaveral, sentimiento *m* de malestar (*or* intranquilidad *etc*); deseo *m* fuerte de cambiar de estilo de vida; (*hum*) celo *m* amoroso.
spring-gun ['sprɪŋgʌn] *n* trampa *f* de alambre y escopeta.
springiness ['sprɪŋɪnɪs] *n* elasticidad *f*.
spring-like ['sprɪŋlaɪk] *adj day, weather* primaveral.
spring-lock ['sprɪŋlɒk] *n* cerradura *f* de resorte.
spring mattress ['sprɪŋ'mætrɪs] *n* colchón *m* de muelles, somier *m*.
spring-tide ['sprɪŋ'taɪd] *n* marea *f* viva.
springtime ['sprɪŋtaɪm] *n* primavera *f*.
springy ['sprɪŋɪ] *adj* elástico; *turf etc* muelle; *movement, step* ligero.
sprinkle ['sprɪŋkl] **1** *n* rociada *f*; salpicadura *f*; **a ~ of rain** unas gotitas de lluvia; **a ~ of salt** un poquito de sal.
2 *vt* salpicar, rociar (*with* de); sembrar (*with* de); (*with holy water*) asperjar; esparcir; **to ~ water on a plant, to ~ a plant with water** rociar una planta de agua; **a rose ~d with dew** una rosa cubierta de rocío; **they are ~d about here and there** están esparcidos aquí y allá.
3 *vi* (*with rain*) lloviznar.
sprinkler ['sprɪŋkləʳ] *n* (*Agr*) rociadera *f*, aparato *m* de lluvia artificial; (*for lawn*) aspersor *m*; (*of watering can etc*) regadera *f*; (*in fire-fighting*) aparato *m* de rociadura automática; (*Eccl*) hisopo *m*; (*Agr*) ~ **system** sistema *m* de regadío por aspersión.
sprinkling ['sprɪŋklɪŋ] *n* rociada *f*, salpicadura *f*; aspersión *f*; **a ~ of knowledge** unos pocos conocimientos; **there was a ~ of young people** había unos cuantos jóvenes.
sprint [sprɪnt] **1** *n* (*in race*) (e)sprint *m*; (*dash*) carrera *f*.
2 *vi* (*in race*) (e)sprintar; (*dash*) correr a todo correr, precipitarse; **he ~ed for the bus** corrió a toda prisa para coger el autobús; **we shall have to** ~ tendremos que correr.
sprinter ['sprɪntəʳ] *n* (e)sprínter *mf*, velocista *mf*.
sprit [sprɪt] *n* botavara *f*, verga *f* de abanico.
sprite [spraɪt] *n* duende *m*, trasgo *m*; hada *f*.
spritsail ['sprɪtseɪl, *Naut* 'sprɪtsl] *n* cebadera *f*, vela *f* de abanico.
sprocket ['sprɒkɪt] **1** *n* rueda *f* de espigas. **2** *attr*: ~ **feed** avance *m* por rueda de espigas.
sprocket wheel ['sprɒkɪtwiːl] *n* rueda *f* de cadena.
sprog‡ [sprɒg] *n* rorro* *m*, bebé *m*.
sprout [spraʊt] **1** *n* brote *m*, retoño *m*; **~s** coles *fpl* de Bruselas.
2 *vt* echar, hacerse; **to ~ new leaves** echar nuevas hojas; **the calf is ~ing horns** le salen los cuernos al ternero; **the town is ~ing new buildings** en la ciudad surgen nuevos edificios.
3 *vi* brotar, retoñar, echar retoños; (*shoot up*) crecer rápidamente; **skyscrapers are ~ing up** se levantan rápidamente los rascacielos.
spruce¹ [spruːs] *adj* aseado, acicalado, pulcro.
◆**spruce up** **1** *vt* arreglar, componer; **all ~d up** muy acicalado.
2 *vr*: **to ~ o.s. up** arreglarse; ataviarse; mejorar de aspecto, hacerse más elegante.
spruce² [spruːs] *n* (*Bot*: *also* ~ **tree**) picea *f*.
sprucely ['spruːslɪ] *adv*: ~ **dressed** elegantemente vestido.
spruceness ['spruːsnɪs] *n* aseo *m*, pulcritud *f*; elegancia *f*.
sprung [sprʌŋ] **1** *ptp of* **spring**. **2** *adj*: ~ **bed** cama *f* de muelles; **interior ~ mattress** somier *m*, colchón *m* de muelles; ~ **seat** asiento *m* de ballesta.
spry [spraɪ] *adj* ágil, activo.
SPUC [spʌk] *n abbr of* **Society for the Protection of Unborn Children** ≃ Federación *f* Española de Asociaciones Pro-Vida.
spud [spʌd] **1** *n* (**a**) (*Agr*) escarda *f*. (**b**) (*) patata *f*, papa *f* (*LAm*). **2** *vt* escardar.
spume [spjuːm] *n* (*liter*) espuma *f*.
spun [spʌn] **1** *pret and ptp of* **spin**. **2** *adj*: ~ **glass** lana *f* de vidrio; ~ **silk** seda *f* hilada; ~ **yarn** meollar *m*.
spunk [spʌŋk] *n* (**a**) (‡: *courage*) agallas* *fpl*; arrojo *m*, coraje *m*. (**b**) (**‡: *semen*) leche**‡ *f*. (**c**) (*esp Australia*) guaperas* *m*.
spunky‡ ['spʌŋkɪ] *adj* (**a**) valiente, arrojado. (**b**) (*esp Australia*) guaperas*.
spur [spɜːʳ] **1** *n* espuela *f*; (*Zool*) espolón *m*; (*Geog*) espolón *m*; (*fig*) estímulo *m*, aguijón *m*; (*Rail*) ramal *m* corto; **the ~ of hunger** el estímulo del hambre; **it will be a ~ to further progress** estimulará a más progresos; **on the ~ of the moment** sin reflexión, en un arranque, de improviso; **it was a ~ of the moment decision** fue una decisión tomada al instante; **to win one's ~s** distinguirse, demostrar de modo concluyente lo que vale uno.
2 *vt* (*also* **to ~ on**) espolear, picar con las espuelas; **to ~ on** (*fig*) estimular, incitar, acuciar; **to ~ sb (on) to do sth** incitar a uno a hacer algo, dar a uno un aliento para que haga algo; **this ~red him (on) to greater efforts** esto le incitó a hacer mayores esfuerzos; **~red on by greed** bajo el aguijón de la codicia, acuciado por la codicia.
3 *vi*: **to ~ on** picar el caballo con las espuelas; apretar el paso.
spurge [spɜːdʒ] *n* euforbio *m*.
spur-gear ['spɜːgɪəʳ] *n* rueda *f* dentada recta.
spurge laurel ['spɜːdʒˌlɒrəl] *n* lauréola *f*, torvisco *m*.
spurious ['spjʊərɪəs] *adj* falso, espurio.
spuriously ['spjʊərɪəslɪ] *adv* falsamente.
spuriousness ['spjʊərɪəsnɪs] *n* falsedad *f*.
spurn [spɜːn] *vt* desdeñar, rechazar.
spurt [spɜːt] **1** *n* esfuerzo *m* supremo; **final** ~ esfuerzo *m* final (para ganar una carrera); **to put in** (*or* **on**) **a** ~ hacer un esfuerzo supremo, acelerar; *V also* **spirt**.
2 *vi* hacer un esfuerzo supremo, acelerar; *V also* **spirt**.
spur-wheel ['spɜːwiːl] *n* engranaje *m* cilíndrico.
sputnik ['spʊtnɪk] *n* sputnik *m*.
sputter ['spʌtəʳ] = **splutter**.
sputum ['spjuːtəm] *n* esputo *m*.
spy [spaɪ] **1** *n* espía *mf*; ~ **plane** avión *m* espía; ~ **ring** red *f* de espionaje; ~ **satellite** satélite *m* espía; ~ **ship** buque *m* espía; ~ **story** novela *f* de espionaje.
2 *vt* divisar, columbrar; lograr ver; observar; descubrir; **finally I spied him coming** por fin pude verle viniendo.
3 *vi* espiar, ser espía: **I** ~ (*game*) veo-veo (*m*); **he spied for Slobodia** fue espía al servicio de Eslobodia; **to ~ on sb** espiar a uno, observar a uno clandestinamente; seguir los pasos a uno.
◆**spy out** *vt*: **to ~ out the land** reconocer el terreno.
spycatcher ['spaɪkætʃəʳ] *n* agente *mf* de contraespionaje.
spyglass ['spaɪglɑːs] *n* catalejo *m*.
spyhole ['spaɪhəʊl] *n* mirilla *f*.
spying ['spaɪɪŋ] *n* espionaje *m*.
spy-in-the-sky* [ˌspaɪɪnðə'skaɪ] *n* (*satellite*) satélite *m* espía.
spy-plane ['spaɪpleɪn] *n* avión *m* espía.
Sq. *abbr of* **Square** plaza *f*.
sq. (*Math*) *abbr of* **square** cuadrado.
sq.ft. *abbr of* **square foot** pie *m* cuadrado, *abbr of* **square feet** pies *mpl* cuadrados.
squab [skwɒb] *n* (**a**) (*Orn*) pichón *m*; pollito *m*, polluelo *m*; (*fig*) persona *f* regordeta. (**b**) (*cushion*) cojín *m*; (*sofa*) sofá *m*, canapé *m*.
squabble ['skwɒbl] **1** *n* riña *f*, disputa *f*. **2** *vi* reñir (*about, over* por cuestión de), disputar, pelearse.
squabbler ['skwɒbləʳ] *n* pendenciero *m* -a *f*.
squabbling ['skwɒblɪŋ] *n* riñas *fpl*, disputas *fpl*.
squad [skwɒd] *n* (*Mil*) pelotón *m*; escuadra *f*; (*of police*) brigada *f*, grupo *m*, escuadrón *m*; (*Sport*) equipo *m*.
squad-car ['skwɒdˌkɑːʳ] *n* coche-patrulla *m*.
squaddie* ['skwɒdɪ] *n* soldado *m* raso.
squadron ['skwɒdrən] *n* (*Aer, Mil*) escuadrón *m*; (*Naut*) escuadra *f*.
squadron-leader ['skwɒdrən'liːdəʳ] *n* (*Brit*) comandante *m* (de aviación).
squalid ['skwɒlɪd] *adj* (*dirty*) miserable, vil, asqueroso; *motive etc* vil; *affair* asqueroso.
squall¹ [skwɔːl] **1** *n* (*cry*) chillido *m*, grito *m*, berrido *m*. **2** *vi* chillar, gritar, berrear.
squall² [skwɔːl] *n* (*Naut*: *gust*) ráfaga *f*; (*brief storm*) chubasco *m*, turbión *m*; (*fig*) tempestad *f*; **there are ~s ahead** (*fig*) el futuro se anuncia no muy tranquilo.
squalling ['skwɔːlɪŋ] *adj child* chillón, berreador.
squally ['skwɔːlɪ] *adj wind* que viene a ráfagas; *day* de chubascos; (*fig*) turbulento, lleno de dificultades.
squalor ['skwɒləʳ] *n* miseria *f*; suciedad *f*; **to live in ~** vivir en la miseria, vivir en la sordidez.
squander ['skwɒndəʳ] *vt money* malgastar, derrochar, des-

pilfarrar; disipar (*on* en); *opportunity* desperdiciar; *time, resources* emplear mal.

square [skwɛəʳ] **1** *adj* (**a**) (*in shape*) cuadrado; *corner* en ángulo recto; *edge* escuadrado; *build* robusto, fornido; *jaw, shoulder* cuadrado.

(**b**) (*Math*) cuadrado; **~ kilometre** kilómetro *m* cuadrado; **~ measure** medida *f* cuadrada; **~ root** raíz *f* cuadrada; **2 metres ~** 2 metros en cuadro.

(**c**) (*fig*) *treatment etc* justo, equitativo; *person* honrado, formal; *refusal* rotundo; **~ deal** justicia *f*, trato *m* equitativo; **I want a ~ deal** yo pido justicia; **he didn't get a ~ deal** le trataron injustamente; **~ meal** comida *f* realmente buena; **it's 3 days since I had a ~ meal** hace 3 días que no como decentemente; **it met with a ~ refusal** fue rechazado de plano.

(**d**) (*even, balanced*) **to be ~ with sb** estar en paz con uno, no deber nada a uno; (*Sport*) ir iguales, ir empatados; **now we're all ~** ahora vamos iguales; **we can start again all ~** podemos volver a comenzar en pie de igualdad; **if you pay me a pound we'll call it ~** si me pagas una libra diremos que no hay más deuda; **to get ~ with sb** ajustar cuentas con uno, desquitarse con uno; **I'll get ~ with him yet!** ¡ya le ajustaré las cuentas!

(**e**) (*) *person* carca*; *idea etc* anticuado.

2 *adv*: **~ to, ~ with** en ángulo recto con; **it fell ~ in the middle** cayó de lleno en el centro, cayó exactamente en el centro.

3 *n* (**a**) (*shape*) cuadrado *m*; cuadro *m* (*also Mil*); (*of chessboard, graph paper*) casilla *f*; **a 6-metre ~** un cuadrado de 6 metros de lado; **we're back to ~ one** estamos de nuevo en el punto de partida; **to divide sth into ~s** dividir algo en cuadrados.

(**b**) (*of town*) plaza *f*, zócalo *m* (*Mex*); (*US*) manzana *f*, cuadra *f* (*LAm*).

(**c**) (*Math*) cuadrado *m*; **4 is the ~ of 2** 4 es el cuadrado de 2.

(**d**) (*Archit, Tech*) escuadra *f*.

(**e**) (*Univ**) birrete *m*; (*kerchief*) pañuelo *m*.

(**f**) (*) carroza* *mf*, carca* *mf*.

4 *vt* (**a**) (*make ~*) cuadrar; (*Archit, Tech*) escuadrar.

(**b**) (*arrange*) arreglar; (*reconcile*) ajustar, acomodar; *account* ajustar, pagar; (*bribe*) sobornar, comprar el silencio (*or* la ayuda *etc*) de; **can you ~ it with your conscience?** ¿lo puedes acomodar con tu conciencia?; **I'll ~ (it with) the porter*** lo arreglaré con el conserje.

(**c**) (*Math*) cuadrar.

5 *vi* cuadrar, conformarse (*with* con); **it doesn't ~ with what you said before** esto no cuadra con lo que dijiste antes; **it doesn't ~ with the facts** esto no cuadra con los hechos.

◆**square up** *vi* (**a**) **to ~ up to sb** ponerse en actitud para defenderse contra uno, mostrarse resuelto a defenderse contra uno.

(**b**) **to ~ up with sb** ajustar cuentas con uno, pagar a uno.

squarebashing* [ˈskwɛəˌbæʃɪŋ] *n* (*Brit*) instrucción *f*.

squared [skwɛəd] *adj paper* cuadriculado.

square dance [ˈskwɛəˌdɑːns] *n* baile *m* de figuras.

square-faced [ˌskwɛəˈfeɪst] *adj* de cara cuadrada.

squarely [ˈskwɛəlɪ] *adv* (**a**) en cuadro. (**b**) *refuse* rotundamente; honradamente. (**c**) de lleno, directamente; **we must face this ~** tenemos que hacer frente a esto sin pestañear; **it hit ~ in the middle** dio de lleno en el centro.

square-toed [ˌskwɛəˈtəʊd] *adj shoes* de punta cuadrada.

squarial [ˈskwɛərɪəl] *n* antena *f* cuadrada.

squash¹ [skwɒʃ] **1** *n* (**a**) (*Brit: drink*) zumo *m*, jugo *m* (*LAm*); **orange ~** naranjada *f*, zumo *m* de naranja, jugo *m* de naranja (*LAm*).

(**b**) (*crowd*) apiñamiento *m*, agolpamiento *m*; **there was such a ~ in the doorway** había tantísima gente en la puerta, se apiñaba tanto la gente en la puerta.

2 *vt* (*flatten*) aplastar; *argument* confutar; *person* apabullar, reducir a silencio.

3 *vi* (*get crushed*) aplastarse.

◆**squash in 1** *vt* apretar; apiñar; **can you ~ my shoes in?** ¿puedes hacer caber mis zapatos?; **can you ~ 2 more in the car?** ¿caben 2 más en el coche?

2 *vi* entrar (apretadamente, a pesar de la muchedumbre *etc*); **we all ~ed in** entramos todos aunque con dificultad.

◆**squash together 1** *vt* apretar; apiñar.

2 *vi* apiñarse, estar muy juntos.

◆**squash up** *vi* apretarse (más); correrse a un lado, hacer lugar.

squash² [skwɒʃ] *n*, **squash-rackets** [ˈskwɒʃˌrækɪts] *n* squash *m*.

squash³ [skwɒʃ] *n* (*US Bot*) calabacín *m*, calabacita *f*.

squashy [ˈskwɒʃɪ] *adj* blando y algo líquido, muelle y húmedo.

squat [skwɒt] **1** *adj person* rechoncho, achaparrado; *building* desproporcionadamente bajo.

2 *n* (*) comunidad *f* de '*squatters*'; vivienda *f* ocupada por '*squatters*'.

3 *vi* (**a**) (*also* **to ~ down**) agacharse, sentarse en cuclillas; (*) sentarse.

(**b**) (*on property*) establecerse sin derecho, apropiarse sin derecho.

squatter [ˈskwɒtəʳ] *n* (*Hist*) colono *m* usurpador, intruso *m*, -a *f*, persona *f* que se establece en un terreno público sin derecho; (*in house*) squátter *mf*, ocupante *mf* ilegal (de vivienda), paracaidista *mf* (*Mex*).

squatting [ˈskwɒtɪŋ] *n* ocupación *f* ilegal de una propiedad.

squaw [skwɔː] *n* india *f* norteamericana, piel roja *f*.

squawk [skwɔːk] **1** *n* graznido *m*, chillido *m*. **2** *vi* graznar, chillar.

squeak [skwiːk] **1** *n* (*of hinge, wheel etc*) chirrido *m*, rechinamiento *m*; (*of shoe*) crujido *m*; (*of mouse etc*) chillido *m*, grito *m* agudo; (*of pen*) raspear *m*; **to have a narrow ~** escaparse por un pelo; **I couldn't get a ~ out of him** no pude sacarle palabra alguna; **we don't want a ~ out of you about this** de esto no digas ni pío.

2 *vi* (**a**) chirriar, rechinar; crujir; chillar, dar chillidos, dar gritos agudos; raspear.

(**b**) **to ~ by*** pasar muy justo; arreglárselas.

squeaker [ˈskwiːkəʳ] *n* (*in toy etc*) chirriador *m*.

squeaky [ˈskwiːkɪ] *adj* chirriador; que cruje; chillón; que raspea; **~ clean** relimpio, perfectamente limpio; (*fig*) perfectamente honrado, sin sospecha alguna.

squeal [skwiːl] **1** *n* chillido *m*, grito *m* agudo; **with a ~ of pain** con un chillido de dolor; **with a ~ of brakes** con un chirriar de frenos.

2 *vt*: **'Yes', he ~ed** 'Sí', dijo chillando.

3 *vi* (**a**) chillar, dar gritos agudos; (*brakes, tyres*) chirriar.

(**b**) (*: *complain*) quejarse; **don't come ~ing to me** no vengas a quejarte a mí.

(**c**) (‡: *inform*) cantar*, chivatear‡ (*on* contra).

squeamish [ˈskwiːmɪʃ] *adj* remilgado, delicado, susceptible; aprensivo; **I'm not ~** no tengo esa delicadeza, eso me trae sin cuidado; **I'm ~ about spiders** tengo horror a las arañas; **don't be so ~** no seas tan aprensivo, quítate esos remilgos; **to feel ~** sentir náuseas.

squeamishness [ˈskwiːmɪʃnɪs] *n* remilgos *mpl*, delicadeza *f*, susceptibilidad *f*; aprensión *f*; náuseas *fpl*; **to feel a certain ~** sentir cierta repugnancia.

squeegee [ˈskwiːˈdʒiː] *n* enjugador *m* de goma, escobilla *f* de goma.

squeeze [skwiːz] **1** *n* (**a**) (*act, pressure*) estrujón *m*, estrujadura *f*; presión *f*; (*of hand*) apretón *m*; (*in bus etc*) apiñamiento *m*, apretura *f*; **a ~ of lemon** unas gotas de limón; **it was a tight ~ in the bus** íbamos muy apretados en el autobús; **it was a tight ~ to get through** había muy poco espacio para pasar; **to give sb's hand a little ~** apretar suavemente la mano a uno; **to give sth a ~** apretar algo.

(**b**) (*Econ etc*) apretón *m*; (*of credit*) restricción *f*; (*difficulty*) apuro *m*, aprieto *m*; **to put the ~ on sb*** apretar las tuercas a uno.

(**c**) (*Bridge*) tenaza *f* (*in diamonds* a diamantes).

2 *vt* (*painfully*) estrujar, apretar; *hand etc* apretar; presionar; **to ~ out** *juice* exprimir, *person* excluir; **3 were ~d to death** 3 murieron estrujados; **I ~d my finger in the door** me pillé el dedo en la puerta; **to ~ a lemon, to ~ the juice out of a lemon** exprimir el zumo (*LAm*: el jugo) de un limón; **to ~ money out of sb** sacar dinero a uno; **to ~ information out of sb** arrancar información a uno; **to ~ clothes into a case** meter ropa apretadamente en una maleta; **to ~ sb in hearts** atenazar a uno a corazones.

3 *vi*: **to ~ through a crowd** abrirse paso (a codazos) por entre una multitud; **to ~ through a hole** lograr pasar por un agujero.

◆**squeeze in 1** *vt*: **can you ~ 2 more in?** ¿caben 2 más?; ¿puedes meter a 2 más; **I'll see if we can ~ you in for Thursday** (*Theat etc*) veremos si quedan por casualidad entradas para el jueves, (*for appointment*) veremos si es posible ofrecerles hora el jueves.

2 *vi* introducirse con dificultad en, deslizarse en.

◆**squeeze past** *vi* deslizarse; lograr pasar.

◆**squeeze up** *vi* apretarse (más); correrse a un lado, hacer lugar.
squeeze-box ['skwi:zbɒks] *n* concertina *f*.
squeezer ['skwi:zəʳ] *n* exprimelimones *m*, exprimidor *m*.
squelch [skweltʃ] **1** *vt* aplastar, despachurrar; **to ~ one's way through mud** ir chapoteando por el lodo.
2 *vi* chapotear, ir chapoteando; **to ~ through the mud** ir chapoteando por el lodo.
squib [skwɪb] *n* buscapiés *m*.
squid [skwɪd] *n* calamar *m*.
squiffy* ['skwɪfɪ] *adj* (*Brit*): **to be ~** estar achispado*.
squiggle ['skwɪgl] *n* garabato *m*.
squint [skwɪnt] **1** *n* (**a**) (*Med*) estrabismo *m*; (*~ing look*) mirada *f* bizca; (*sidelong glance*) mirada *f* de soslayo, mirada *f* furtiva; **he has a terrible ~** tiene un marcado estrabismo.
(**b**) (*) vistazo *m*; **have a ~ at this** mírame esto; **let's have a ~** dame un vistazo, déjame ver.
2 *vi* (**a**) (*Med*) bizquear, ser bizco; (*look sidelong*) mirar de soslayo, torcer la vista; (*narrow eyes*) entornar (*or* entrecerrar) los ojos; cerrar casi los ojos; **to ~ at sth** mirar algo de soslayo; **he ~ed in the sunlight** entornó los ojos en el sol.
(**b**) (*) **to ~ at sth** echar un vistazo (*or* una ojeada) a algo.
squint-eyed ['skwɪnt'aɪd] *adj* bizco.
squire ['skwaɪəʳ] **1** *n* (*landowner*) propietario *m*, hacendado *m*; (*Hist*) escudero *m*; (*lady's escort*) galán *m*, acompañante *m*; **the ~** (*in relation to villagers etc*) el señor; **the ~ of Ambridge** el señor de Ambridge, el mayor terrateniente de Ambridge; **yes, ~!*** (*Brit*) ¡sí, jefe!; **which way, ~?*** ¿por dónde, caballero?
2 *vt lady* acompañar.
squirearchy ['skwaɪərɑ:kɪ] *n* aristocracia *f* rural, terratenientes *mpl*.
squirm [skwɜ:m] *vi* retorcerse, revolverse; **to ~ with embarrassment** estar violento, avergonzarse mucho; **I'll make him ~** yo le haré sufrir.
squirrel ['skwɪrəl] *n* ardilla *f*.
◆**squirrel away** *vt nuts etc* almacenar.
squirt [skwɜ:t] **1** *n* (**a**) (*jet*) chorro *m*, jeringazo *m*; (*implement*) jeringa *f*.
(**b**) (*) farolero* *m*, farsante* *m*, mequetrefe *m*.
2 *vt* arrojar un chorro de, arrojar a chorros; jeringar; **to ~ water at sb** lanzar un chorro de agua hacia uno.
3 *vi* salir a chorros, chorrear; **the water ~ed into my eye** salió un chorro de agua que me dio en los ojos.
squirter ['skwɜ:təʳ] *n* atomizador *m*.
Sr *abbr of* **Senior.**
Sri Lanka [,sri:'læŋkə] *n* Sri Lanka *m*.
Sri Lankan [,sri:'læŋkən] **1** *adj* de Sri Lanka. **2** *n* nativo *m*, -a *f* (*or* habitante *mf*) de Sri Lanka.
SRN *n* (*Brit*) *abbr of* **state registered nurse** enfermera *f* diplomada.
SRO (*US*) *abbr of* **standing room only.**
SS (**a**) *n* (*Brit*) *abbr of* **steamship** vapor *m*. (**b**) *abbr of* **Saints.**
SSA *n* (*US*) *abbr of* **Social Security Administration** ≈ Seguro *m* Social.
SSE *abbr of* **south-south-east** sudsudeste *m*, *also adj*, SSE.
SSI *n abbr of* **small-scale integration** integración *f* a pequeña escala.
SSSI *n abbr of* **site of special scientific interest.**
SST *n* (*US*) *abbr of* **supersonic transport.**
SSW *abbr of* **south-south-west** sudsudoeste *m*, *also adj*, SSO.
St (**a**) (*Rel*) *abbr of* **Saint** San, Santa, Sto., Sta., S. (**b**) (*Geog*) *abbr of* **Strait** estrecho *m*. (**c**) *abbr of* **Street** Calle *f*, C. (**d**) *abbr of* **stone** (= *14 libras = 6,348 kg*). (**e**) *abbr of* **summer time** hora *f* de verano.
St. *abbr of* **Station** estación *f*.
stab [stæb] **1** *n* (**a**) (*with knife etc*) puñalada *f*; (*wound in general*) herida *f*; (*of pain*) pinchazo *m*, punzada *f*, dolor *m* agudo; **~ in the back** (*fig*) puñalada *f* por la espalda, puñalada *f* encubierta.
(**b**) (*) tentativa *f*; **to have a ~ at sth** intentar algo, probar a hacer algo.
2 *vt* apuñalar, dar de puñaladas a; **to ~ sb with a knife** herir a uno con un cuchillo; **to ~ sb in the back** (*fig*) apuñalar a uno por la espalda, apuñalar a uno encubiertamente; **to ~ sb to death** matar a uno a puñaladas.
3 *vi*: **to ~ at sb** tratar de apuñalar a uno; **he ~bed at the picture with his finger** señaló el cuadro con un movimiento brusco del dedo.
stabbing ['stæbɪŋ] **1** *n* puñalada *f*, puñaladas *fpl*, el apuñalar; muerte *f* a puñaladas. **2** *adj*: **~ pain** dolor *m* punzante.
stability [stə'bɪlɪtɪ] *n* estabilidad *f*.
stabilization [,steɪbəlaɪ'zeɪʃən] *n* estabilización *f*.
stabilize ['steɪbəlaɪz] **1** *vt* estabilizar. **2** *vi* estabilizarse.
stabilizer ['steɪbəlaɪzəʳ] *n* (*Culin*) estabilizante *m*; (*Tech*) estabilizador *m*.
stable¹ ['steɪbl] *adj* estable, firme; (*Med*) estacionario; *job* permanente; *relationship, marriage etc* sólido, firme; *character* equilibrado.
stable² ['steɪbl] **1** *n* cuadra *f*, caballeriza *f*; (*group of racehorses*) cuadra *f*; **to shut** (*or* **close**) **the ~ door after the horse has bolted** (*or* **gone**) a buenas horas, mangas verdes.
2 *vt* poner en una cuadra, guardar en una cuadra.
stableboy ['steɪblbɔɪ] *n*, **stable-lad** ['steɪbllæd] *n* mozo *m* de cuadra.
stableman ['steɪblmən] *n*, *pl* **stablemen** ['steɪblmən] mozo *m* de cuadra.
stablemate ['steɪblmeɪt] *n* (*horse*) caballo *m* de la misma cuadra; (*fig*) camarada *m*.
stab wound ['stæbwu:nd] *n* puñalada *f*.
staccato [stə'kɑ:təʊ] **1** *adv* staccato. **2** *adj* staccato.
stack [stæk] **1** *n* (**a**) montón *m*, rimero *m*, pila *f*; (*Agr*) almiar *m*, hacina *f*; (*Mil*) pabellón *m* de fusiles; (*book ~*) estantería *f* de libros.
(**b**) (*) montón* *m*; **we have ~s, thanks** gracias, tenemos montones; **we have ~s of time** nos sobra tiempo; **I have ~s of work to do** tengo un montón de trabajo que hacer.
(**c**) (*of chimney*) cañón *m* de chimenea, fuste *m* de chimenea.
2 *vt* (**a**) amontonar, apilar; recoger en un montón, formar una pila de; (*Agr*) hacinar; (**well**) **~ed**⁑ (*US*) *woman* bien formada, muy buena*.
(**b**) **the cards are ~ed against us** (*fig*) la suerte está en contra nuestra.
stacker ['stækəʳ] *n* (*for printer*) apiladora *f*.
stadium ['steɪdɪəm] *n*, *pl* **stadia** ['steɪdɪə] *or* **stadiums** estadio *m*.
staff [stɑ:f] **1** *n* (**a**) (*pl* **staves** [steɪvz] *or* **staffs**) (*stick*) palo *m*; (*walking stick*) bastón *m*, (*pilgrim's*) bordón *m*; (*symbol of authority*) bastón *m* de mando; (*Eccl*) báculo *m*; (*of flag, lance etc*) asta *f*; (*fig*) sostén *m*, apoyo *m*.
(**b**) (*persons*: *pl* **staffs**) personal *m*; (*establishment*) plantilla *f* de personal; (*Mil*) estado *m* mayor; (*of company*) equipo *m* directivo; (*Scol, Univ*) profesorado *m*, personal *m* docente; **to be on the ~** ser de plantilla, ser de planta (*LAm*); tener un puesto (permanente); **to join the ~** entrar a formar parte del personal; **to leave the ~** dimitir; **they keep a ~ of 5** (*servants*) tienen 5 criados.
(**c**) (*Mus*: *pl* **staves**) pentagrama *m*.
2 *attr*: **~ association** asociación *f* del personal; **~ canteen** comedor *m* del personal; **~ college** escuela *f* militar superior; **~ meeting** reunión *f* del personal; **~ nurse** enfermera *f* cualificada; **~ officer** oficial *m* del Estado Mayor; **~-student ratio** proporción *f* alumnos-profesor; **~ training** formación *f* de personal.
3 *vt* proveer de personal; **to be well ~ed** tener un buen personal.
staffing ['stɑ:fɪŋ] *n* empleo *m* de personal; **~ ratio** proporción *f* alumnos-profesor.
staffroom ['stɑ:frʊm] *n* sala *f* de profesores.
stag [stæg] **1** *n* (**a**) (*Zool*) ciervo *m*, venado *m*. (**b**) (*Fin*) especulador *m* con nuevas emisiones. (**c**) (*man*) soltero *m*.
2 *adj* de hombres, para hombres; masculino; **~ party** fiesta *f* de despedida de soltero; **to go ~ to a party** (*US*) ir sin compañía a una fiesta.
stag-beetle ['stæg,bi:tl] *n* ciervo *m* volante.
stage [steɪdʒ] **1** *n* (**a**) (*platform*) plataforma *f*, estrado *m*, tablado *m*; (*of microscope*) portaobjeto *m*; (*of rocket*) escalón *m*, piso *m*; **a 4-~ rocket** un cohete de 4 pisos; **the second ~ fell away** se separó el segundo escalón.
(**b**) (*Theat*) escena *f*; (*fig*) escenario *m*, teatro *m*; **~ left** parte *f* de la escena a la izquierda del actor (que mira al público); **~ right** parte *f* de la escena a la derecha del actor (que mira al público); **I get nervous on ~** me pongo nervioso en la escena; **you're on ~ in 2 minutes** sales en 2 minutos; **to go on the ~** hacerse actor, hacerse actriz; **to put a play on the ~** poner una obra; **to put a novel on the ~** dramatizar una novela, llevar una novela a la escena; **don't put your daughter on the ~** no permita que su hija se haga actriz; **to set the ~ for** (*fig*) disponer el escenario

para; **to write for the** ~ escribir para el teatro.

(**c**) (*point, section*: *of journey*) etapa *f*, jornada *f*; (*of road, pipeline etc*) tramo *m*; (*fig*) fase *f*, etapa *f*; grado *m*; **in ~s** por etapas; **in** (*or* **by**) **easy ~s** en cortas etapas; gradualmente, poco a poco; **at this ~ in the negotiations** en esta fase de las negociaciones; **what ~ have we reached?** ¿a qué punto hemos llegado?; **to go through a difficult ~** pasar por una fase difícil; **to have a work in the final ~s** tener un trabajo ultimado; **~ race** carrera *f* por etapas.

2 *vt play* representar, poner (en escena); escenificar; (*bring about*) efectuar, lograr, llevar a cabo; *recovery* efectuar; (*arrange*) arreglar; organizar; **that was no accident, it was ~d** eso no fue accidente, fue organizado; **to ~ a comeback** restablecerse, rehabilitarse; **to ~ a demonstration** organizar una manifestación.

stage box ['steɪdʒ,bɒks] *n* palco *m* de proscenio.

stagecoach ['steɪdʒkəʊtʃ] *n* diligencia *f*.

stagecraft ['steɪdʒkrɑːft] *n* arte *m* teatral, escenotecnia *f*.

stage designer ['steɪdʒdɪ,zaɪnəʳ] *n* decorador *m*, -ora *f* de teatro, escenógrafo *m*, -a *f*.

stage direction ['steɪdʒdɪ,rekʃən] *n* acotación *f*.

stage director ['steɪdʒdɪ,rektəʳ] *n* director *m*, -ora *f* de escena.

stage door ['steɪdʒ'dɔːʳ] *n* entrada *f* de artistas.

stage fright ['steɪdʒfraɪt] *n* miedo *m* al público.

stagehand ['steɪdʒhænd] *n* tramoyista *m*, sacasillas *m*.

stage-manage ['steɪdʒ,mænɪdʒ] *vt play, production* dirigir; (*fig*) *event, confrontation etc* orquestar.

stage manager ['steɪdʒ,mænɪdʒəʳ] *n* director *m*, -ora *f* de escena; (*TV*) regidor *m*, -ora *f*.

stage name ['steɪdʒ,neɪm] *n* nombre *m* artístico.

stage-struck ['steɪdʒstrʌk] *adj* apasionado por el teatro.

stage whisper ['steɪdʒ'wɪspəʳ] *n* aparte *m*.

stagey ['steɪdʒɪ] *adj* teatral, dramático.

stagflation [stæg'fleɪʃən] *n* (e)stagflación *f*, estanflación *f*.

stagger ['stægəʳ] **1** *n* tambaleo *m*; **~s** (*Vet*) modorra *f*.

2 *vt* (**a**) (*amaze*) asombrar, consternar, sorprender; (*cause to waver*) hacer dudar, hacer vacilar; **you ~ me!** ¡me asombras!, ¡me asustas!; **I was ~ed to hear that ...** me consterné al saber que ...

(**b**) *hours, holidays, payments* escalonar; *spokes etc* alternar.

3 *vi* tambalear, titubear, hacer eses; **he ~ed to the door** fue tambaleando a la puerta; **he was ~ing about** iba tambaleando.

staggering ['stægərɪŋ] *adj* asombroso, pasmoso.

staghound ['stæghaʊnd] *n* perro *m* de caza, sabueso *m*.

staghunt ['stæghʌnt] *n* cacería *f* de venado.

staghunting ['stæg,hʌntɪŋ] *n* caza *f* de venado.

staging ['steɪdʒɪŋ] **1** *n* (**a**) (*scaffolding*) andamiaje *m*. (**b**) (*Theat*) escenificación *f*, puesta *f* en escena. (**c**) (*Space*) desprendimiento *m* (de una sección de un cohete). **2** *attr*: **~ post** (*Mil, also gen*) escala *f*.

stagnancy ['stægnənsɪ] *n* estancamiento *m*.

stagnant ['stægnənt] *adj* estancado; (*fig*) estancado, paralizado, inmóvil; *society etc* anquilosado; (*Fin*) inactivo.

stagnate [stæg'neɪt] *vi* estancarse; estar estancado, quedar estancado (*also fig*); (*fig*) estar paralizado.

stagnation [stæg'neɪʃən] *n* estancamiento *m*; (*fig*) estancamiento *m*, paralización *f*, inmovilismo *m*; anquilosamiento *m*; inactividad *f*.

stagy ['steɪdʒɪ] *adj* = **stagey**.

staid [steɪd] *adj* serio, formal.

staidness ['steɪdnɪs] *n* seriedad *f*, formalidad *f*.

stain [steɪn] **1** *n* (**a**) (*mark*) mancha *f*; (*dye*) tinte *m*, tintura *f*; (*paint*) pintura *f*.

(**b**) (*fig*) mancha *f*; **without a ~ on one's character** sin una sola mancha en la reputación.

2 *vt* manchar; (*dye*) teñir, colorar; (*paint*) pintar; **her hands were ~ed with blood** sus manos estaban manchadas de sangre; **~ed glass** vidrio *m* de color; **~ed glass window** vidriera *f* (de colores).

3 *vi* mancharse.

stainless ['steɪnlɪs] *adj* inmaculado; inmanchable; *steel* inoxidable.

stain-remover ['steɪnrɪ,muːvəʳ] *n* quitamanchas *m*.

stair [stɛəʳ] *n* peldaño *m*, escalón *m*; (*stairway*) escalera *f*; **~s** escalera *f*; **flight of ~s** tramo *m* de escalera; **life below ~s** vida *f* de los criados; **gossip below ~s** habladurías *fpl* de la servidumbre.

staircarpet ['stɛə,kɑːpɪt] *n* alfombra *f* de escalera.

staircase ['stɛəkeɪs] *n* escalera *f*; caja *f* de escalera.

stair-rod ['stɛərɒd] *n* varilla *f* (sujetadora de alfombra de escalera).

stairway ['stɛəweɪ] *n* = **staircase**.

stairwell ['stɛəwel] *n* hueco *m* de la escalera.

stake [steɪk] **1** *n* (**a**) (*post*) estaca *f*, poste *m*; (*for plant*) rodrigón *m*.

(**b**) (*for execution*) poste *m*; hoguera *f*; **to burn sb at the ~** quemar a uno en el poste; **to die at the ~** morir en la hoguera; **to be condemned to the ~** ser condenado a morir en la hoguera.

(**c**) (*bet*) puesta *f*, apuesta *f*, parada *f*; **~s** (*prize*) premio *m*, (*race*) carrera *f*; **the issue at ~** el punto en cuestión; **to be at ~** estar en juego, estar en litigio; estar en peligro; **there is a lot at ~ here** esto nos importa muchísimo, esto nos interesa muchísimo; **to have a ~ in** tener interés en; **Britain had a big ~ in Ruritania** Gran Bretaña tuvo muchos intereses en Ruritania; **X is top in the popularity ~s** en la popularidad X va en cabeza.

2 *vt* (**a**) (*also* **to ~ off, to ~ out**) estacar; cercar con estacas, señalar con estacas; *plant* rodrigar.

(**b**) (*bet*) apostar (*on* a); (*Fin*) aventurar, arriesgar; invertir (*on* en); **to ~ one's all** jugar el todo por el todo; aventurarlo todo; **to ~ one's reputation on sth** jurar como hombre honrado que algo es así; **to ~ a claim** hacer una reclamación; **to ~ one's claim to a job** afirmar su derecho a un puesto.

◆**stake off** *vt* = **stake 2** (**a**).

◆**stake out** *vt* (**a**) = **stake 2** (**a**).

(**b**) *property etc* poner bajo vigilancia.

stakeholder ['steɪk,həʊldəʳ] *n persona que guarda las apuestas*.

stake-out ['steɪkaʊt] *n* vigilancia *f*.

stalactite ['stæləktaɪt] *n* estalactita *f*.

stalagmite ['stæləgmaɪt] *n* estalagmita *f*.

stale [steɪl] *adj food* no fresco, pasado, rancio; *bread* duro; *air* viciado; *news* viejo; *joke* viejo, mohoso; *cheque* caducado; (*old-fashioned*) anticuado, pasado de moda; *person* cansado; **I'm getting ~** me estoy cansando; ya no tengo la inventiva de antes.

stalemate ['steɪlmeɪt] **1** *n* (*Chess*) tablas *fpl* (por ahogado); (*fig*) paralización *f*, estancamiento *m*; **the ~ is complete** la paralización es completa; **to reach ~** llegar a un punto muerto; **there is ~ between the two powers** las relaciones entre las dos potencias están en un punto muerto.

2 *vt* (*Chess*) ahogar, dar tablas por ahogado a; (*fig*) paralizar.

stalemated ['steɪlmeɪtɪd] *adj* (*fig*) *discussions* estancado, en un punto muerto; *project* en un punto muerto; *person* en tablas.

staleness ['steɪlnɪs] *n* rancidez *f*; dureza *f*; lo viciado; lo viejo, lo mohoso; lo anticuado; cansancio *m*, falta *f* de inventiva.

Stalin ['stɑːlɪn] *nm* Stalin.

Stalinism ['stɑːlɪnɪzəm] *n* estalinismo *m*.

Stalinist ['stɑːlɪnɪst] **1** *adj* estalinista. **2** *n* estalinista *mf*.

stalk[1] [stɔːk] **1** *vt game* cazar al acecho, acechar; *person* seguir los pasos a.

2 *vi* (*also* **to ~ along**) andar con paso majestuoso; **to ~ away, to ~ off** irse con paso airado; **to ~ out** salir ofendido, salir con paso airado.

stalk[2] [stɔːk] *n* (*Bot*) tallo *m*, caña *f*; (*cabbage* ~) troncho *m*; (*of glass*) pie *m*.

stalk-eyed ['stɔːkaɪd] *adj* (*Zool*) de ojos pedunculares.

stalking-horse ['stɔːkɪŋhɔːs] *n* pretexto *m*.

stall [stɔːl] **1** *n* (*Agr*: *stable*) establo *m*, (*part of stable*) casilla *f* de establo, (*manger*) pesebre *m*; (*in market etc*) puesto *m*, caseta *f*; (*Brit Theat*) butaca *f*, luneta *f* (*Mex*); (*Eccl*) silla *f* de coro; (*US*: *in car park*) emplazamiento *m*; **to set out one's ~** (*fig*) exponer lo que se ofrece (a la venta).

2 *vt* (**a**) (*Aut etc*) parar, cortar accidentalmente, atascar.

(**b**) **to ~ sb off** deshacerse de uno mediante algún pretexto, tener a uno a raya.

3 *vi* (**a**) (*Aut etc*) pararse, calar(se), atascarse; **we ~ed on a steep hill** quedamos parados en una cuesta abrupta, se nos atascó el motor en una cuesta abrupta; **the talks are** (*or* **have**) **~ed** las negociaciones están en un callejón sin salida.

(**b**) (*fig*) buscar evasivas, evitar contestar directamente, ir con rodeos; **stop ~ing!** ¡déjese de evasivas!; **the minister ~ed for 20 minutes** durante 20 minutos el ministro evitó contestar directamente.

stall-fed ['stɔːlfed] *adj* engordado en establo.

stallholder ['stɔːl,həʊldəʳ] *n* dueño *m*, -a *f* de un puesto (de mercado *etc*).

stallion ['stæliən] *n* caballo *m* padre, semental *m*.

stalwart ['stɔːlwət] **1** *adj* (*in build*) fornido, robusto; (*in spirit*) leal; valiente; cien por cien, incondicional; **a ~ supporter of ...** partidario incondicional de ...
2 *n* partidario *m*, -a *f* leal.

stamen ['steɪmen] *n* estambre *m*.

stamina ['stæmɪnə] *n* resistencia *f*, aguante *m*; nervio *m*, vigor *m*; **intellectual ~** vigor *m* intelectual; **has he enough ~ for the job?** ¿tiene bastante resistencia para el puesto?; **you need ~** hace falta tener nervio.

stammer ['stæməʳ] **1** *n* tartamudeo *m*, balbuceo *m*; **he has a bad ~** tartamudea terriblemente.
2 *vt* (*also* **to ~ out**) balbucir, decir tartamudeando.
3 *vi* tartamudear; balbucir.

stammerer ['stæmərəʳ] *n* tartamudo *m*, -a *f*.

stammering ['stæmərɪŋ] **1** *adj* tartamudo. **2** *n* tartamudeo *m*.

stammeringly ['stæmərɪŋlɪ] *adv*: **he said ~** dijo tartamudeando.

stamp [stæmp] **1** *n* (**a**) (*with foot*) patada *f*; **with a ~ of her foot** dando una patada.
(**b**) (*rubber ~*) estampilla *f*; (*die*) cuño *m*, troquel *m*.
(**c**) (*mark*) marca *f*, huella *f*, impresión *f*; **a man of his ~** un hombre de su temple, (*pej*) un hombre de esa calaña; **it bears the ~ of genius** lleva el sello de la genialidad; **to leave** (*or* **put**) **one's ~ on sth** poner (*or* dejar) su sello en algo.
(**d**) (*postage ~*) sello *m* (de correos), estampilla *f* (*LAm*); (*fiscal ~, revenue ~*) timbre *m*, póliza *f*; (*trading ~*) cupón *m*; (*for free food etc*) bono *m*, vale *m*.
2 *vt* (**a**) **to ~ one's foot** patear, golpear con el pie; (*in dancing*) zapatear; (*horse*) piafar.
(**b**) (*impress mark etc on*) estampar, imprimir; *coin, design* estampar; *passport* sellar; (*fig*) marcar, señalar; sellar; **paper ~ed with one's name** papel *m* con el nombre de uno impreso, papel *m* con membrete; **to ~ sth on one's memory** grabar algo en la memoria de uno; **his manners ~ him a gentleman** sus modales le señalan como caballero.
(**c**) (*mark with rubber ~*) estampillar; (*mark with fiscal ~*) timbrar; *letter* pegar un sello a, poner un sello en; franquear; **~ed addressed envelope** sobre *m* con las propias señas de uno y con sello; **the letter is insufficiently ~ed** la carta no lleva suficiente franqueo; **they ~ed my passport at the frontier** sellaron mi pasaporte en la frontera.
3 *vi* patear, golpear con los pies; pisar muy fuerte; (*disapprovingly*) patalear; (*of horse*) piafar; **he ~s about the house** anda por la casa pisando muy fuerte; **to ~ on** pisotear, hollar; **sb ~ed on my foot** alguien me pisoteó el pie.
4 *vr*: **to ~ o.s. on sth** poner (*or* dejar) su sello en algo.

◆**stamp down** *vt*: **to ~ sth down** apisonar algo, comprimir algo con los pies.

◆**stamp out** *vt* (**a**) (*extinguish*) *fire* apagar pateando; (*fig*) extirpar, acabar con, desarraigar; **we must ~ out this abuse** tenemos que acabar con esta injusticia; **the doctors ~ed out the epidemic** los médicos dominaron la epidemia.
(**b**) **they ~ed out the rhythm** marcaron el ritmo con los pies.

stamp-album ['stæmp,ælbəm] *n* álbum *m* para sellos.

stamp-book ['stæmpbʊk] *n* (*collection*) albúm *m* de sellos; (*for posting*) libro *m* de sellos.

stamp-collecting ['stæmpkə,lektɪŋ] *n* filatelia *f*.

stamp-collection ['stæmpkə,lekʃən] *n* colección *f* de sellos.

stamp-collector ['stæmpkə,lektəʳ] *n* filatelista *mf*.

stamp-dealer ['stæmp,diːləʳ] *n* comerciante *mf* en sellos (de correo).

stamp-duty ['stæmp,djuːtɪ] *n* impuesto *m* (*or* derecho *m*) del timbre.

stamped [stæmpt] *adj paper* sellado, timbrado; *envelope* con sello, que lleva sello.

stampede [stæm,piːd] **1** *n* espantada *f*, desbandada *f*, estampida *f* (*LAm*); **there was a sudden ~ for the door** de repente se precipitaron todos hacia la puerta; **the exodus turned into a ~** el éxodo se transformó en una fuga precipitada.
2 *vt* hacer huir en desorden; hacer desbandarse; infundir un terror pánico a; **to ~ sb into doing sth** infundir terror a uno para que haga algo; hacer que uno haga algo sin la debida reflexión; **let's not be ~d** no obremos precipitadamente.
3 *vi* huir en desorden, huir precipitadamente; desbandarse.

stamping-ground* ['stæmpɪŋ,graʊnd] *n* territorio *m* personal; lugar *m* predilecto; guarida *f*; **this is his private ~** éste es terreno particular suyo, éste es coto cerrado de su propiedad; **to keep off sb's ~** no invadir el territorio de uno.

stamp-machine ['stæmpmə,ʃiːn] *n* expendedor *m* automático de sellos (de correo).

Stan [stæn] *nm familiar form of* **Stanley**.

stance [stæns] *n* postura *f*; **to take up a ~** adoptar una postura.

stanch [stɑːntʃ] *vt blood* restañar.

stanchion ['stɑːnʃən] *n* puntal *m*, montante *m*.

stand [stænd] **1** *n* (**a**) (*position*) posición *f*, postura *f*; **to take up one's ~ by the door** ponerse cerca de la puerta; **to take one's ~ on a principle** aferrarse a un principio, sentar cátedra sobre un principio; **to take a firm ~** adoptar una actitud firme.
(**b**) (*Mil*) parada *f*, alto *m*; resistencia *f*; **the ~ of the Australians at Tobruk** la resistencia de los australianos en Tobruk; **they turned and made a ~** hicieron alto para resistir de nuevo; **to make a ~ against sth** oponer resistencia a algo, hacer frente a algo.
(**c**) (*for taxis*) parada *f*.
(**d**) (*Theat*) función *f*, representación *f*.
(**e**) (*support: for lamp etc*) sostén *m*; pie *m*, pedestal *m*; (*for display*) mesilla *f*; (*hall~*) perchero *m*; (*Mus*) atril *m*.
(**f**) (*in market etc*) puesto *m*; barraca *f*, caseta *f*; (*news~*) quiosco *m*; (*band~*) quiosco *m*; (*at exhibition*) stand *m*; (*Sport*) tribuna *f*; **to take the ~** (*esp US*) subir a la tribuna de los testigos, (*fig*) prestar declaración.
(**g**) (**) empalme** *m*.
(**h**) (*of trees*) línea *f*, grupo *m*, hilera *f*; plantación *f*.
2 (*irr: pret and ptp* **stood**) *vt* (**a**) (*place*) poner, colocar (de pie); **to ~ sth (up) against a wall** poner algo contra una pared; **to ~ a vase on a table** poner un florero sobre una mesa.
(**b**) **to ~ one's ground** mantenerse firme, mantenerse en sus trece.
(**c**) (*tolerate*) tolerar, aguantar, soportar; resistir (a); *test* salir muy bien de; *cost* pagar, sufragar, correr con; **it won't ~ the cold** no resiste el (*or* al) frío; **his heart couldn't ~ the shock** su corazón no resistió el (*or* al) choque; **the company will have to ~ the loss** la compañía tendrá que encargarse de las pérdidas; **I can't ~ him** no le puedo ver; **I can't ~ Debussy** no aguanto a Debussy; **I can ~ anything but that** lo aguanto todo menos eso; **I can't ~ it any longer!** ¡no aguanto más!, ¡no puedo más!; *V* **chance**.
(**d**) (*pay for*) **to ~ sb a drink** invitar a uno a beber, pagar la bebida de uno; **he stood beers all round** invitó a todos a tomar cerveza; **he stood me lunch** me pagó la comida.
3 *vi* (**a**) (*be upright*) estar de pie, estar parado (*LAm*); (*get up*) levantarse, ponerse de pie; **all ~!** ¡levántense!; **~ at ease!** en su lugar ¡descanso!; **he could hardly ~** apenas podía mantenerse de pie; **to ~ at the bar** estar junto al bar; **to ~ in the doorway** estar en la puerta; **to ~ talking** seguir hablando; quedarse a hablar; **we stood chatting for half an hour** charlamos durante media hora, pasamos media hora charlando; **he left everybody else ~ing** (*fig*) dejó a todos muy atrás, dejó a todos parados (*LAm*); superó fácilmente a los demás; *V* **end, leg** *etc*.
(**b**) (*of measurement*) medir; **the tree ~s 30 metres high** el árbol mide 30 metros, el árbol tiene 30 metros de alto; **he ~s a good 6 feet** mide 6 pies largos; **the mountain ~s 3000 metres high** la montaña tiene una altura de 3000 metros.
(**c**) (*be, be placed*) estar, estar situado, encontrarse; **it ~s beside the town hall** está junto al ayuntamiento; **to buy a house as it ~s** comprar una casa tal como está; **to let sth ~ in the sun** poner algo al sol, dejar algo al sol; **the car has been ~ing in the sun** el coche ha estado expuesto al sol; **nothing now ~s between us** ya no existe ningún estorbo entre nosotros.
(**d**) (*remain*) quedar en pie, mantenerse en vigor; (*last*) perdurar, durar; **the record ~s at 10 minutes** el record está en 10 minutos, el tiempo récord sigue siendo de 10 minutos; **the objection ~s** la objeción es válida, la objeción vale; **the contract ~s** el contrato sigue en vigor; **the theory ~s or falls by this** con esto o se confirma o se destruye la teoría; **it has stood for 600 years** ha durado 600 años ya, lleva ya 600 años de vida; *V* **fast**[1], **firm**[1] *etc*.
(**e**) (*temporary conditions*) **as things ~, as it ~s** tal como están las cosas; **how do we ~?** ¿cómo estamos?; **I like to**

know where I ~ me gusta estar enterado de mi situación (con relación a otras personas); **where do you ~ with him?** ¿cuáles son tus relaciones con él?; **to ~ well with sb** llevarse bien con uno, ser tenido en mucho por uno.

(**f**) (*remain undisturbed*) estar; sedimentar; **to allow a liquid to ~** dejar estar un líquido; **let it ~ for 3 days** dejarlo así durante 3 días; **don't let the tea ~** no dejes que se pase el té.

(**g**) (*special cases*) **to ~ as a candidate** (*Brit*) presentarse como candidato; **to ~ (as) security for sb** (*Fin*) salir fiador de uno, (*fig*) salir por uno; **the thermometer ~s at 40°** el termómetro marca 40 grados; **there is £50 ~ing to your credit** Vd tiene 50 libras en el haber; **sales ~ at 5% more than last year** las ventas han aumentado en un 5 por cien en relación con el año pasado; **we ~ to lose a lot** para nosotros supondría una pérdida importante, estamos en peligro de perder bastante; **what do we ~ to gain by it?** ¿qué posibilidades hay para nosotros de ganar algo?, ¿qué ventaja nos daría esto?; **he ~s to win £5** tiene la posibilidad de ganar 5 libras; *V* **need** *etc*.

◆**stand about, stand around** *vi* estar; esperar; seguir en un sitio sin propósito fijo; **they just ~ about all day** pasan todo el día por ahí sin hacer nada; **they kept us ~ing about for hours** nos hicieron esperar (de pie) durante horas enteras.

◆**stand aside** *vi* apartarse, quitarse de en medio, hacerse a un lado; **~ aside, please!** ¡apártense, por favor!; **we cannot ~ aside and do nothing** no podemos estar sin hacer nada; **he stood aside when he could have helped** se mantuvo aparte cuando pudo ayudar.

◆**stand back** *vi* (**a**) (*person*) retroceder, moverse hacia atrás; **~ back, please!** ¡más atrás, por favor!; *V also* **stand aside**.

(**b**) (*house etc*) estar algo apartado (*from* de).

◆**stand by 1** *vt promise* cumplir, atenerse a; *person* apoyar, defender; no abandonar; **the Minister stood by his decision** el Ministro mantuvo su decisión; **I ~ by what I said** reafirmo lo que dije, lo dicho dicho.

2 *vi* (**a**) (*as onlooker*) estar presente (sin intervenir); estar de mirón; *V also* **stand aside.**

(**b**) (*on alert*) estar alerta, mantenerse listo; estar dispuesto para el combate (*etc*); estar a la expectativa; **~ by for further news** estén listos para recibir más noticias; **the Navy is ~ing by to help** unidades de la Flota están listas para prestar ayuda; **~ by for take-off!** ¡listos para despegar!

◆**stand down** *vi* (**a**) retirarse; ceder (su puesto *etc*); renunciar a su oportunidad (*etc*); **someone has to ~ down** alguien tiene que ceder; **the candidate is ~ing down in favour of a younger person** el candidato se retira a favor de una persona más joven; **you may ~ down** (*Jur etc*) Vd puede retirarse.

(**b**) **the troops have stood down** (*Mil*) ha terminado el estado de alerta (militar).

◆**stand for** *vt* (**a**) (*represent*) representar; (*mean*) significar; **'A ~s for apple'** 'M es de manzana'; **here a dash ~s for a word** aquí una raya representa una palabra.

(**b**) *post* proponerse para, ofrecerse para, presentarse como candidato a; **he stood for Parliament in 1987** se presentó en las elecciones parlamentarias de 1987; **he stood for Castroforte** fue uno de los candidatos en Castroforte; **he stood for Labour** fue candidato laborista.

(**c**) (*support*) apoyar, defender; hablar por; creer en; afirmar su adhesión a.

(**d**) (*tolerate*) aguantar; permitir, consentir; **I'll not ~ for that** eso no lo permito, eso no se debe consentir; **I'll not ~ for your whims any longer** no aguanto tus caprichos un momento más.

◆**stand in** *vi* (**a**) **to ~ in to the shore** acercarse a la costa.

(**b**) **to ~ in for sb** suplir a uno.

(**c**) **to ~ in with sb** apoyar a uno; declararse por uno; (*financially*) compartir el gasto con uno.

◆**stand off 1** *vt workers* despedir (temporalmente, por falta de trabajo), suspender.

2 *vi* apartarse, guardar las distancias; (*Naut*) apartarse.

◆**stand out** *vi* (**a**) (*project*) salir, sobresalir; destacar (*against* contra, sobre).

(**b**) (*be outstanding*) destacarse, descollar, sobresalir; llamar la atención, impresionar.

(**c**) **to ~ out to sea** hacerse a la mar.

(**d**) (*remain firm*) mantenerse firme; **to ~ out against** oponerse (resueltamente) a; **to ~ out for** insistir en, no ceder hasta obtener.

◆**stand over 1** *vt*: **to ~ over sb to see that he works** vigilar a uno para asegurar que trabaja.

2 *vi* (*remain in suspense*) quedar en suspenso; **to let an item ~ over** dejar un asunto para la próxima vez.

◆**stand to** *vi* estar alerta, estar sobre las armas.

◆**stand up 1** *vt* (**a**) (*place*) = **stand 2** (**a**).

(**b**) (*) dar plantón a*, dejar plantado*.

2 *vi* (**a**) (*rise*) levantarse, ponerse de pie; (*be standing*) estar de pie; **a brew so strong that a spoon could ~ up in it** un brebaje en el cual se podría mantener de pie una cuchara; **we must ~ up and be counted** (*fig*) tenemos que declararnos abiertamente.

(**b**) (*argument etc*) ser sólido, ser lógico; convencer; **the case did not ~ up in court** la acusación no se mantuvo en el tribunal.

(**c**) **to ~ up for sb** defender a uno; **to ~ up for o.s.** no achantarse; defenderse a sí mismo.

(**d**) **to ~ up to sb** resistir (resueltamente) a uno, hacer frente a uno; **to ~ up to a test** salir bien de una prueba; **it ~s up to hard wear** es muy resistente; **it won't ~ up to close examination** no resiste al examen cuidadoso.

stand-alone ['stændələun] *adj*: **~ (computer) system** sistema *m* autónomo.

standard ['stændəd] **1** *n* (**a**) (*flag*) estandarte *m*, bandera *f*; **to raise the ~ of revolt** pronunciarse, sublevarse.

(**b**) (*measure etc used as norm*) patrón *m*; pauta *f*, norma *f*, estándar *m*; (*fig*) modelo *m*, regla *f*.

(**c**) (*moral*) criterio *m*; **~s** valores *mpl* morales; **double ~s** doble tabla *f* de valores; **by any ~** por cualquier criterio; **he has good ~s** tiene buen criterio; **she has no ~s** carece de valores morales; **to apply a double ~** medir a dos raseros; **to judge by that ~ ...** si lo juzgamos desde ese criterio ...

(**d**) (*degree of excellence*) nivel *m*, grado *m*; **~ of living** nivel *m* de vida; **~ of culture** nivel *m* de cultura; **at first-year university ~** al nivel del primer año universitario; **of low ~** de baja calidad; inferior; **to be below ~** estar por debajo del nivel correcto, ser inferior; **to be up to ~** estar conforme con el debido nivel; **to set a good ~** establecer un buen nivel.

(**e**) (*Bot*) árbol *m* (*etc*) de tronco derecho; (*of small lamp*) pie *m*; (*of street lamp*) poste *m*.

2 *adj* normal, corriente; estándar; uniforme, estereotipado; de serie; **5th gear now ~ on this car** 5ª velocidad ahora de serie en este coche; **~ agreement** acuerdo *m* normal; **~ costs** costos *mpl* normales; **~ deviation** desviación *f* normal; **~ English** inglés *m* normativo; **~ error** error *m* estándar; **~ gauge** vía *f* normal; **~ lamp** (*Brit*) lámpara *f* de pie; **~ mark** (*on silver*) contraste *m*; **~ measure** medida *f* tipo; **~ model** modelo *m* estándar; (*car*) coche *m* de serie; **~ nomenclature** nomenclatura *f* oficial; **~ pitch** diapasón *m* normal; **~ practice** norma *f*, práctica *f* común; **~ price** precio *m* oficial, precio *m* normal; **~ quality** calidad *f* normal; **~ rate** tipo *m* de interés vigente; **~ time** hora *f* legal; **~ unit** (*Elec, Gas*) paso *m* (de contador); **~ weight** peso *m* legal; **~ work of reference** obra *f* clásica de consulta; **that word is hardly ~** esa palabra apenas pertenece al léxico oficial; **the practice became ~ in the 1940s** la práctica llegó a ser corriente en los años 40.

standard-bearer ['stændəd,beərəʳ] *n* abanderado *m*; (*fig*) jefe *m*, adalid *m*.

standardization [,stændədaɪ'zeɪʃən] *n* normalización *f*, estandarización *f*.

standardize ['stændədaɪz] *vt* normalizar, regularizar, estandarizar, uniformar.

stand-by ['stænd*b*aɪ] **1** *n* (**a**) (*person*) persona *f* de toda confianza, persona *f* siempre dispuesta a prestar su ayuda; reserva *f*; paño *m* de lágrimas; (*thing*) recurso *m* seguro, recurso *m* favorito, artículo *m* de toda confianza; (*loan*) crédito *m* contingente, stand-by *m*.

(**b**) (*alert*) alerta *m*; aviso *m* (para partir); (*Aer*) stand-by *m*, lista *f* de espera; **to be on ~** estar sobre aviso, estar preparado, (*doctor*) estar listo para acudir; **to be on 24-hours ~** estar listo para partir dentro de 24 horas; **to put sb on 3-day ~** avisar a uno para que esté listo para partir dentro de 3 días.

2 *attr*: **~ aircraft** avión *m* de reserva; **~ air ticket** billete *m* para la lista de reserva; **~ arrangements** (*Fin*) acuerdo *m* de reserva; **~ credit** crédito *m* disponible, crédito *m* stand-by; **~ facility** stand-by *m*, lista *f* de reserva; **~ generator** generador *m* de reserva; **~ passenger** pasajero *m*, -a *f* en la lista de espera; **~ (ticket)** billete *m* stand-by.

standee* [stæn'diː] *n* (*US*) espectador *m*, -ora *f* que asiste de pie.

stand-in ['stændɪn] *n* suplente *mf* (*for* de); (*Cine*) doble *mf* (*for* de).

standing ['stændɪŋ] **1** *adj* (**a**) (*upright*) derecho; (*on foot*) de pie, en pie; *stone* derecho, vertical; *crop* que sigue creciendo, que está sin segar; *water* estancado, encharcado; ~ **start** salida *f* parada; **to leave sb** ~ dejar a uno muy atrás, (*fig*) aventajar a uno con mucho, resultar ser muy superior a uno; *V* **ovation**.

(**b**) (*permanent*) *army, committee, rule etc* permanente; *custom* arraigado; *grievance, joke* constante, eterno; ~ **order** (*Brit*: *at bank*) orden *f* bancaria, (*Comm*) pedido *m* permanente, pedido *m* regular; ~ **orders** (*of meeting*) reglamento *m*, estatuto *m*.

2 *n* (**a**) (*position*) posición *f*, situación *f*; (*repute*) reputación *f*; categoría *f*; importancia *f*; **financial** ~ solvencia *f*; **social** ~ posición *f* social; **of high** ~ de categoría; **the restaurant has a high** ~ el restaurante tiene una buena reputación; **a man of some** ~ un hombre de cierta categoría; **the relative** ~ **of these problems** la relativa importancia de estos problemas; **to be in good** ~ gozar de buen crédito; tener buena reputación; **what is his** ~ **locally?** ¿qué reputación tiene en la ciudad? (*etc*); **he has no** ~ **in this matter** no tiene voz ni voto en este asunto.

(**b**) (*duration*) duración *f*; existencia *f*; (*seniority*) antigüedad *f*; **of only 6 months'** ~ que existe desde hace 6 meses solamente; **a captain of only a month's** ~ un capitán que lleva solamente un mes en el puesto (*or* en tal graduación); **of long** ~ de mucho tiempo, existente desde hace mucho tiempo, viejo.

(**c**) (*US Aut*) **'no** ~**'** 'prohibido estacionarse'.

standing room ['stændɪŋrʊm] *n* sitio *m* para estar de pie.

stand-off ['stændɒf] *n* (**a**) (*US*: *deadlock*) punto *m* muerto; (*paralysis*) parálisis *f*; situación *f* estancada; (*stalemate*) empate *m*. (**b**) ~ **half** medio *m* de apertura.

stand-offish [,stænd'ɒfɪʃ] *adj* reservado, endiosado, que se da aires de superioridad; poco amable, frío.

stand-offishly [,stænd'ɒfɪʃlɪ] *adv* con poca amabilidad, fríamente.

stand-offishness [,stænd'ɒfɪʃnɪs] *n* reserva *f*; endiosamiento *m*, superioridad *f*; falta *f* de amabilidad, frialdad *f*.

standpat ['stæn*d*pæt] *adj* inmovilista.

standpipe ['stændpaɪp] *n* columna *f* de alimentación; (*in street*) tubo *m* vertical.

standpoint ['stæn*d*pɔɪnt] *n* punto *m* de vista; **from the** ~ **of** ... desde el punto de vista de ...

standstill ['stæn*d*stɪl] *n* parada *f*; paro *m*; alto *m*; paralización *f*; **to be at a** ~ estar parado; estar paralizado; **negotiations are at a** ~ las negociaciones están paralizadas; **to bring a car to a** ~ parar un coche; **to bring an industry to a** ~ paralizar una industria; **to bring traffic to a** ~ paralizar el tráfico, parar totalmente el tráfico; **to come to a** ~ (*persons*) pararse, hacer alto, (*vehicle*) pararse, (*industry etc*) quedar paralizado.

stand-to [,stænd'tu:] *n* alerta *m*.

stand-up ['stændʌp] *adj*: ~ **buffet** comida *f* tomada de pie; ~ **collar** cuello *m* alto; ~ **comic** cómico *m* caricato; ~ **fight** pelea *f* violenta, riña *f* a puñetazos, (*fig*) altercado *m* violento.

stank [stæŋk] *pret of* **stink**.

stanley knife ['stænlɪ,naɪf] *n*, *pl* **stanley knives** ['stænlɪ,naɪvz] cuchilla *f* para moqueta.

stannic ['stænɪk] *adj* estánnico.

stanza ['stænzə] *n* estrofa *f*, estancia *f*.

stapes ['steɪpi:z] *n*, *pl* **stapedes** [stæ'pi:di:z] (*Anat*) estribo *m*.

staphylococcus [,stæfɪlə'kɒkəs] *n*, *pl* **staphylococci** [,stæfɪlə'kɒkaɪ] estafilococo *m*.

staple[1] ['steɪpl] **1** *n* (*fastener*) grapa *f*, corchete *m* (*SC*); ~ **gun** grapadora *f*. **2** *vt* (*also* **to** ~ **together**) grapar.

staple[2] ['steɪpl] **1** *adj* principal; establecido; corriente; **their** ~ **food** (*or* **diet**) su comida corriente, su alimento de primera necesidad.

2 *n* (*chief product*) producto *m* principal; (*raw material*) materia *f* prima; (*of wool*) fibra *f* (textil); (*of conversation etc*) asunto *m* principal, elemento *m* esencial.

stapler ['steɪplə^r] *n*, **stapling machine** ['steɪplɪŋmə,ʃi:n] *n* grapadora *f*.

star [stɑ:^r] **1** *n* (**a**) (*Astron*) estrella *f*, astro *m*; (*Typ*) asterisco *m*; **S~s and Stripes** (*US*) (bandera *f* de) las barras y las estrellas, Bandera *f* Estrellada; **S~ of David** estrella *f* de David; **to be born under a lucky** ~ nacer con estrella; **to believe in one's lucky** ~ creer en su buena estrella; **you can thank your lucky** ~**s that** ... puedes dar las gracias a Dios porque ...; **to see** ~**s** (*fig*) ver las estrellas.

(**b**) (*person*) figura *f* destacada, figura *f* más brillante; (*Cine etc*) astro *m*, estrella *f*, vedette *f*; **the** ~ **of the team was X** la figura más destacada del equipo fue X.

2 *attr* principal; destacado, más brillante; **their** ~ **player** su jugador más destacado, su jugador más brillante; ~ **role** papel *m* estelar; ~ **screwdriver** destornillador *m* de estrella; ~ **show** programa *m* estelar; ~ **sign** signo *m* del Zodíaco; ~ **turn** atracción *f* especial, número *m* más destacado; **'S~ Wars'** 'Guerra *f* de las Galaxias'.

3 *vt* (**a**) (*adorn with* ~*s*) estrellar, adornar con estrellas, sembrar de estrellas; (*mark with* ~) señalar con asterisco.

(**b**) (*Cine etc*) presentar como estrella; **a film** ~**ring Greta Garbo** una película que presenta a Greta Garbo en el papel principal.

4 *vi* (*Cine etc*) ser el astro, ser la estrella; tener el papel principal; (*be outstanding*) destacar, descollar, actuar brillantemente; **the 3 films in which James Dean** ~**red** las 3 películas que protagonizó James Dean; **he didn't exactly** ~ **in that game** en ese partido no destacó que digamos.

-star [stɑ:^r] *attr ending in compounds*: *eg* **4~ hotel** hotel *m* de 4 estrellas; **4~ (petrol)** gasolina *f* extra, súper *f*.

starboard ['stɑ:bɔ:d] **1** *n* estribor *m*; **the sea to** ~ la mar a estribor; **land to** ~**!** ¡tierra a estribor!

2 *adj lights etc* de estribor; **on the** ~ **side** a estribor.

3 *vt*: **to** ~ **the helm** poner el timón a estribor, virar a estribor.

starch [stɑ:tʃ] **1** *n* almidón *m*; (*in food*) fécula *f*. **2** *vt* almidonar.

star-chamber ['stɑ:,tʃeɪmbə^r] *adj* (*fig*) secreto y arbitrario.

starched [stɑ:tʃt] *adj* almidonado.

starch-reduced ['stɑ:tʃrɪ,dju:st] *adj bread etc* de régimen, con menos fécula.

starchy ['stɑ:tʃɪ] *adj* feculento; (*fig*) estirado, entonado, etiquetero.

star-crossed ['stɑ:,krɒst] *adj* malhadado, desventurado.

stardom ['stɑ:dəm] *n* estrellato *m*; **to reach** ~ alcanzar el estrellato.

stardust ['stɑ:dʌst] *n* (*fig*) encanto *m*, embeleso *m*.

stare [stɛə^r] **1** *n* mirada *f* fija; **to give sb a** ~ mirar fijamente a uno.

2 *vt*: **to** ~ **sb out of countenance** desconcertar a uno mirándole fijamente; **it's staring you in the face** salta a la vista.

3 *vi* mirar fijamente; **don't** ~**!** ¡no mires tan fijo!; **it's rude to** ~ es de mala educación mostrar tanta curiosidad; **to** ~ **at sb** mirar fijamente a uno, clavar la vista en uno, (*in surprise*) mirar a uno con sorpresa; **to** ~ **into the distance, to** ~ **into space** estar mirando a las nubes.

starfish ['stɑ:fɪʃ] *n*, *pl invar* estrella *f* de mar.

stargaze ['stɑ:geɪz] *vi* mirar las estrellas; (*fig*) distraerse, mirar las telarañas.

stargazer ['stɑ:,geɪzə^r] *n* astrónomo *m*, -a *f*.

stargazing ['stɑ:,geɪzɪŋ] *n* estudio *m* de las estrellas; astronomía *f*; (*fig*) distracción *f*.

stargrass ['stɑ:grɑ:s] *n* azucena *f*.

staring ['stɛərɪŋ] *adj* que mira fijamente, curioso; *eyes* saltón, (*in fear*) lleno de espanto.

stark [stɑ:k] **1** *adj* (*stiff*) rígido; (*utter*) completo, puro; (*unadorned*) escueto, severo; *cliff etc* espantoso, ceñudo.

2 *adv*: ~ **staring mad,** ~ **raving mad** loco de atar; ~ **naked** en cueros, en pelota, como le parió su madre.

starkers‡ ['stɑ:kəz] *adj*: **to be** ~ (*Brit*) estar en cueros*.

starkly ['stɑ:klɪ] *adv* completamente; ~ **evident** completamente claro; **he put the choice** ~ nos ofreció la alternativa y nada más.

starkness ['stɑ:knɪs] *n* desolación *f*, severidad *f*.

starless ['stɑ:lɪs] *adj* sin estrellas.

starlet ['stɑ:lɪt] *n* estrella *f* joven, estrella *f* en ciernes, aspirante *f* a estrella.

starlight ['stɑ:laɪt] *n* luz *f* de las estrellas; **by** ~ a la luz de las estrellas.

starling ['stɑ:lɪŋ] *n* estornino *m*.

starlit ['stɑ:lɪt] *adj* iluminado por las estrellas.

star-of-Bethlehem [,stɑ:rəv'beθlɪhem] *n* (*Bot*) leche *f* de gallina, matacandiles *m*.

starry ['stɑ:rɪ] *adj* estrellado, sembrado de estrellas.

starry-eyed ['stɑ:rɪ'aɪd] *adj* inocentón, ingenuo; idealista, poco práctico; lleno de amor (*or* entusiasmo *etc*) candoroso.

star shell ['stɑ:ʃel] *n* cohete *m* luminoso, bengala *f*.

star-spangled ['stɑ:,spæŋgld] *adj* estrellado; **the S~ Banner** la Bandera Estrellada.

star-studded ['stɑː,stʌdɪd] *adj sky* estrellado; (*fig*) *play, cast* lleno de estrellas.

start [stɑːt] **1** *n* (**a**) (*fright etc*) susto *m*, sobresalto *m*; (*of horse*) respingo *m*; **to give a sudden ~** sobresaltarse; **to give sb a ~** asustar a uno, dar un susto a uno; **what a ~ you gave me!** ¡qué susto me diste!; **to wake with a ~** despertarse sobresaltado; *V* **fit²**.

(**b**) (*beginning*) principio *m*, comienzo *m*; (*departure*) salida *f*, partida *f*; (*of race*) salida *f*; (*point of starting*) punto *m* de arranque; **at the ~** al principio; **at the very ~** muy al principio, en los mismos comienzos; **at the ~ of the century** a principios del siglo; **we are at the ~ of sth big** estamos en los comienzos de algo grandioso; **for a ~** en primer lugar, para empezar; **from the ~** desde el principio; **from ~ to finish** desde el principio hasta el fin, de cabo a rabo; **to get off to a bad ~** comenzar mal; **to get off to a good ~** empezar bien, (*fig*) comenzar felizmente, entrar con buen pie; **to give sb a ~ in life** ayudar a uno a situarse en la vida; **the review gave the book a good ~** la reseña ayudó al libro a venderse bien desde el principio; **to make a ~** empezar; **to make an early ~** ponerse en camino temprano; **to make a fresh** (*or* **new**) **~ in life** hacer vida nueva, empezar de nuevo; **to make a good ~ (in life)** emprender felizmente su carrera.

(**c**) (*advantage*) ventaja *f*; **to give sb a 5 minute ~** dar a uno una ventaja de 5 minutos; **to have a ~ on sb** tener ventaja sobre uno.

2 *vt* (**a**) (*begin*) comenzar, empezar; iniciar; principiar; *discussion etc* abrir, iniciar; (*undertake*) emprender; *bottle* abrir; **to ~ negotiations** iniciar las negociaciones; **to ~ a new life** comenzar una vida nueva; **to ~ a novel** empezar a escribir (*or* leer) una novela; **to ~ a family** (empezar a) tener hijos; **don't ~ that again!** ¡no vuelvas a eso!; **now she's ~ed a baby*** ahora está encinta; **we can't ~ a baby yet*** todavía no podemos tener un niño; **to ~ to** + *infin*, **to ~** + *ger* comenzar a + *infin*, empezar a + *infin*; **~ moving!** ¡menearse!; **~ talking!** ¡desembucha!

(**b**) (*give signal for*: *also* **to ~ off**) **to ~ (off) a race** dar la señal de salida para una carrera.

(**c**) (*disturb*: *also* **to ~ up**) **to ~ a partridge** levantar una perdiz.

(**d**) (*cause*) causar, provocar; **to ~ a fire** causar un incendio; **it ~ed the collapse of the empire** dio comienzo al derrumbamiento del imperio.

(**e**) (*found*: *also* **to ~ up**) fundar, crear; **to ~ (up) an enterprise** fundar una empresa; **to ~ (up) a newspaper** fundar un periódico.

(**f**) (*Mech*: *also* **to ~ up**) poner en marcha, hacer funcionar; *car, engine* arrancar; *clock* poner en marcha.

(**g**) (*with personal object*: *also* **to ~ off**) **to ~ sb reminiscing** hacer que uno empiece a contar sus recuerdos; **once you ~ him (off) on that** en cuanto le pones a hablar de eso; **to ~ sb (off) on a career** ayudar a uno a emprender una carrera; **they ~ed her (off) in the sales department** la emplearon primero en la sección de ventas.

3 *vi* (**a**) (*in fright*) asustarse, sobresaltarse, sobrecogerse (*at* a, *with* de); **to ~ from one's chair** levantarse asustado de su silla; **to ~ out of one's sleep** despertarse sobresaltado; **his eyes were ~ing out of his head** se le saltaban los ojos de la cabeza.

(**b**) (*timber etc*) combarse, torcerse; (*rivets etc*) soltarse.

(**c**) (*begin*: *also* **to ~ off**) comenzar, empezar; principiar; iniciarse; (*on journey*) partir, ponerse en camino; (*of bus, train*) salir; (*in race*) salir; (*car, engine etc*) arrancar, ponerse en marchar; empezar a funcionar; **to ~ by** + *ger* comenzar + *ger*; **~ing from Tuesday** a partir del martes; **the route ~s from here** la ruta sale de aquí; **to ~ afresh** volver a empezar, comenzar de nuevo; **to ~ at the beginning** empezar desde el principio; **to ~ on a task** empezar un cometido; emprender una tarea; **to ~ on something new** emprender algo nuevo; **to ~ with a prayer** empezar con una oración; **what shall we ~ (off) with?** ¿con qué empezamos?; **to ~ with** (*as adv phrase*) en primer lugar, para empezar; en el principio.

(**d**) (*Mech*: *also* **to ~ up**) ponerse en marcha, empezar a funcionar; (*car, engine*) arrancar(se).

◆**start after** *vt*: **to ~ after sb** salir en busca de uno; ir en pos de uno.

◆**start back** *vi* (**a**) (*return*) emprender el viaje de regreso; **it's time we ~ed back** es hora de volvernos.

(**b**) (*recoil*) retroceder; **to ~ back in horror** retroceder horrorizado.

◆**start in** *vi* empezar; poner manos a la obra, empezar a trabajar (*etc*); **then she ~ed in** luego ella metió su cuchara.

◆**start off 1** *vt V* **start 2 (b), 2 (g)**.

2 *vi* (*begin*) comenzar, empezar; (*on journey*) partir, ponerse en camino; (*bus, train etc*) salir.

◆**start on*** *vt* (*quarrel with*) meterse con; (*scold*) regañar.

◆**start out** *vi* = **start off 2**.

◆**start over** *vi* (*US*) volver a empezar.

◆**start up 1** *vt V* **start 2 (c), 2 (e), 2 (f)**.

2 *vi* (**a**) (*begin*) comenzar, empezar; (*Mus*) empezar a tocar; (*Mech*) arrancar(se).

(**b**) (*jump etc*) incorporarse bruscamente, ponerse de pie de un salto; *V also* **start 3 (d)**.

starter ['stɑːtəʳ] *n* (**a**) (*person*) (*judge*) juez *m* de salida; (*competitor*) corredor *m*, -ora *f*; caballo *m* (*etc*). (**b**) (*Aut etc*) (*motor*) motor *m* de arranque; (*button*) botón *m* de arranque. (**c**) (*Brit Culin*) entremés *m*; **for ~s*** de entrada, para empezar.

starting-block ['stɑːtɪŋ,blɒk] *n* taco *m* de salida; **to be on the ~s** (*fig*) estar en la recámara.

starting-gate ['stɑːtɪŋgeɪt] *n* cajón *m* de salida, parrilla *f* de salida.

starting-grid ['stɑːtɪŋ,grɪd] *n* parrilla *f* de arranque.

starting-handle ['stɑːtɪŋ,hændl] *n* (*Brit*) manivela *f* de arranque.

starting-line ['stɑːtɪŋlaɪn] *n* línea *f* de salida.

starting-motor ['stɑːtɪŋ,məʊtəʳ] *n* motor *m* de arranque.

starting-point ['stɑːtɪŋpɔɪnt] *n* punto *m* de partida, punto *m* de arranque.

starting-post ['stɑːtɪŋpəʊst] *n* poste *m* de salida.

starting-price ['stɑːtɪŋpraɪs] *n* cotización *f*, puntos *mpl* de ventaja al empezar la carrera.

starting salary ['stɑːtɪŋ,sælərɪ] *n* sueldo *m* incial.

starting-switch ['stɑːtɪŋswɪtʃ] *n* botón *m* de arranque.

startle ['stɑːtl] *vt* asustar, sobrecoger; alarmar; **you quite ~d me!** ¡vaya susto que me has dado!; **it ~d him out of his serenity** le hizo perder su serenidad.

startled ['stɑːtld] *adj animal* asustado, espantado; *person* sorprendido; *expression, voice* de sobresalto, sobresaltado.

startling ['stɑːtlɪŋ] *adj* asombroso, sorprendente; alarmante; sobrecogedor; *colour etc* chillón; *dress etc* llamativo, exagerado.

start-up ['stɑːtʌp] *attr*: **~ costs** gastos *mpl* de puesta en marcha.

starvation [stɑː'veɪʃən] **1** *n* hambre *f*, (*Med*) inanición *f*; muerte *f* por hambre; (*fig*) privación *f*; **to die of ~** morir de hambre; **they are threatened with ~** les amenaza el hambre.

2 *attr*: **~ diet** régimen *m* de hambre; **~ wages** sueldo *m* de hambre.

starve [stɑːv] **1** *vt* (**a**) (*kill*) hacer morir de hambre; (*deprive of food*) privar de comida, hacer pasar hambre; **to ~ sb to death** hacer a uno morir de hambre; **to ~ a town into surrender** hacer que una ciudad se rinda por hambre.

(**b**) (*fig*) **to ~ sb of sth** privar a uno de algo; **to be ~d of affection** estar privado de cariño (paternal *etc*).

2 *vi* (**a**) (*die*) morir de hambre; (*lack food*) pasar hambre, padecer hambre; **to ~ to death** morir de hambre.

(**b**) (*fig*) morir de hambre; **I'm simply starving!** ¡estoy muerto de hambre!, ¡qué hambre tengo!

◆**starve out** *vt*: **to ~ a garrison out** hacer que una guarnición se rinda por hambre.

starving ['stɑːvɪŋ] *adj* hambriento, famélico.

stash* [stæʃ] **1** *n* escondite *m*; alijo *m*. **2** *vt*: **to ~ away** ir acumulando; ocultar para uso futuro.

stasis ['steɪsɪs] *n* estasis *f*.

state [steɪt] **1** *n* (**a**) (*condition*) estado *m*, condición *f*; **in this ~ of affairs** (estando) así las cosas, en estas circunstancias; **if this ~ of affairs continues** si las cosas siguen así; **~ of emergency** estado *m* de emergencia, estado *m* de excepción; **to declare a ~ of emergency** declarar el estado de emergencia; **~ of health** salud *f*, estado *m* físico; **~ of mind** estado *m* de ánimo; **~ of play** (*Sport*) situación *f* del juego, (*fig*) situación *f*; **~ of siege** estado *m* de sitio; **~ of war** estado *m* de guerra; **~ of weightlessness** estado *m* de ingravidez; **in a comatose ~** en estado comatoso; **races still in a savage ~** razas *fpl* todavía en estado de salvajismo; **to be in a bad ~** estar en mal estado; **to be in a good ~** estar en buenas condiciones; **he's not in a (fit) ~ to do it** no está en condiciones para hacerlo; **he arrived home in a shocking ~** llegó a casa en un estado espantoso; **she was in no ~ to talk** no estaba en condiciones para hablar.

(**b**) (*anxiety*) agitación *f*; estado *m* nervioso; **to be in a great ~** estar muy agitado, estar aturrulado; **now don't get into a ~ about it** no te pongas nervioso.

(**c**) (*rank*) rango *m*, dignidad *f*; **he attained the ~ of bishop** llegó a la dignidad de obispo.

(**d**) (*pomp*) pompa *f*, fausto *m*; ceremonia *f*; **in ~** con gran pompa; **to dine in ~** cenar con mucha ceremonia; **to live in ~** vivir lujosamente; **to travel in ~** viajar con gran pompa; **to lie in ~** estar expuesto en capilla ardiente.

(**e**) (*Pol*) estado *m*; **the S~** el Estado; **the S~s** (*US*) los Estados Unidos; **~ line** (*US*) frontera *f* de estado, frontera *f* entre dos estados; **a ~ within a ~** un estado dentro del estado; **Secretary of S~** (*US*) Ministro *m*, -a *f* de Asuntos Exteriores; **Secretary of S~ for ...** Ministro *m*, -a *f* de ...

2 *attr* (*Pol etc*) estatal, del Estado; público; **~ aid** ayuda *f* estatal; **~ apartments** apartamentos *mpl* oficiales; **~ banquet** banquete *m* de gala; **~ control** control *m* estatal, control *m* público; **S~ Department** (*US*) Ministerio *m* de Asuntos Exteriores; **~ education** (*Brit*) enseñanza *f* pública; **~ funeral** funeral *m* de Estado; **~ highway** (*US*) ≃ carretera *f* nacional; **~ papers** documentos *mpl* de Estado; **~ pension** pensión *f* estatal; **~ school** (*Brit*) escuela *f* pública; **~ secret** secreto *m* de Estado; **~ subsidy** subvención *f* estatal; **~ tax** (*US*) impuesto *m* del Estado (*p.ej. de Ohio*); **~ trooper** (*US*) policía *m* del Estado (*p.ej. de Idaho*); **~ visit** visita *f* de Estado.

3 *vt* (**a**) declarar, afirmar, decir; manifestar; consignar, hacer constar; **as ~d above** como se ha dicho arriba; **it is nowhere ~d that ...** no se dice en ninguna parte que ...; **I have seen it ~d that ...** he visto afirmarse que ...; **he is ~d to have been there** se afirma que estuvo allí; **~ your name** escriba su nombre; **cheques must ~ the amount clearly** los cheques han de consignar claramente la cantidad; **it must be ~d in the records** tiene que hacerse constar en los archivos.

(**b**) *case* exponer, explicar; *law* formular; *problem* plantear, exponer; **to ~ the case for the prosecution** explicar los hechos en que se basa la acusación.

state-controlled ['steɪtkən'trəʊld] *adj* controlado por el Estado, estatal.

statecraft ['steɪtkrɑːft] *n* arte *m* de gobernar; política *f*; diplomacia *f*.

stated ['steɪtɪd] *adj* dicho; indicado; fijo, establecido; **the sum ~** la cantidad dicha; **on the ~ date** en la fecha indicada; **within ~ limits** dentro de límites fijos.

statehood ['steɪthʊd] *n* categoría *f* de estado, dignidad *f* de estado; **when the country achieves ~** cuando el país alcance la categoría de estado.

stateless ['steɪtlɪs] *adj* desnacionalizado, apátrida, sin patria.

stateliness ['steɪtlɪnɪs] *n* majestad *f*, majestuosidad *f*.

stately ['steɪtlɪ] *adj* majestuoso; imponente; augusto; **~ home** casa *f* solariega.

statement ['steɪtmənt] *n* declaración *f*, afirmación *f*, manifestación *f*; informe *m*, relación *f*; exposición *f*; (*Fin*) estado *m* de cuenta; (*Comput*) sentencia *f*; (*Jur*) declaración *f*; **~ of account** estado *m* (*Mex*: extracto *m*) de cuenta; **official ~** informe *m* oficial, nota *f* oficial; **according to his own ~** según su propia declaración; **to make a ~** (*Jur*) prestar declaración.

state-of-the-art [ˌsteɪtəvðɪ'ɑːt] *adj* moderno, al día; de vanguardia; **it's ~** es lo más moderno (*or* reciente).

state-owned [ˌsteɪt'əʊnd] *adj* nacional, estatal.

stateroom ['steɪtrʊm] *n* camarote *m*.

stateside* ['steɪtsaɪd] *adv* (*US*) (*be*) en Estados Unidos; (*go*) a Estados Unidos, hacia Estados Unidos.

statesman ['steɪtsmən] *n*, *pl* **statesmen** ['steɪtsmən] estadista *m*, hombre *m* de estado.

statesmanlike ['steɪtsmənlaɪk] *adj* (digno) de estadista.

statesmanship ['steɪtsmənʃɪp] *n* arte *m* de gobernar; habilidad *f* de estadista; **that showed true ~** eso demostró su verdadera capacidad de estadista; **~ alone will not solve the problem** la habilidad de los estadistas no resolverá el problema por sí sola.

state-subsidized [ˌsteɪt'sʌbsɪdaɪzd] *adj* subvencionado por el Estado.

state-trading countries ['steɪtˌtreɪdɪŋ'kʌntrɪz] *npl* países *mpl* de comercio estatal.

static ['stætɪk] **1** *adj* inactivo, inmóvil, estancado; (*Phys*) estático. **2** *n* (*also* **~s**) (*Phys*) estática *f*; (*Rad*) parásitos *mpl*.

station ['steɪʃən] **1** *n* (**a**) (*place*) puesto *m*, sitio *m*; situación *f*; **Roman ~** sitio *m* ocupado por los romanos; **the only ~ for this rare plant** el único sitio donde existe esta planta tan poco frecuente; **action ~s!** ¡a sus puestos!; **from my ~ by the window** desde el sitio donde estaba junto a la ventana; **to take up one's ~** colocarse, ir a su puesto.

(**b**) (*~ in life*) posición *f* social; puesto *m* en la sociedad; **of humble ~** de baja posición social, de condición humilde; **a man of exalted ~** un hombre de rango elevado; **to marry below one's ~** casarse con un hombre (*or* una mujer) de posición social inferior; **to get ideas above one's ~** darse aires de superioridad, darse tono.

(**c**) (*specific*) estación *f*; (*Rad*) emisora *f*; (*Rail*) estación *f* (de ferrocarril); (*police ~*) comisaría *f*; **S~s of the Cross** Vía *f* Crucis.

2 *vt* colocar, situar; (*Mil*) estacionar, destinar; *missile etc* emplazar.

3 *vr*: **to ~ o.s.** colocarse, situarse.

stationary ['steɪʃənərɪ] *adj* estacionario; inmóvil; *engine etc* estacionario, fijo; **to remain ~** (*person*) quedar inmóvil, estar sin moverse.

stationer ['steɪʃənəʳ] *n* papelero *m*, -a *f*; **~'s (shop)** papelería *f*.

stationery ['steɪʃənərɪ] **1** *n* papelería *f*, papel *m* de escribir, efectos *mpl* de escritorio. **2** *attr*: **S~ Office** Imprenta *f* Nacional.

station house ['steɪʃənˌhaʊs] *n*, *pl* **station houses** ['steɪʃənˌhaʊzɪz] (*US Rail*) estación *f* de ferrocarril; (*police*) comisaría *f*.

stationmaster ['steɪʃənˌmɑːstəʳ] *n* jefe *m* de estación.

station wagon ['steɪʃənˌwægən] *n* (*US*) furgoneta *f*, rubia *f*, camioneta *f*.

statistic [stə'tɪstɪk] *n* estadística *f*, número *m*; **~s** (*as subject*) estadística *f*; (*numbers*) estadísticas *fpl*.

statistical [stə'tɪstɪkəl] *adj* estadístico; **~ package** paquete *m* estadístico.

statistically [stə'tɪstɪkəlɪ] *adv*: **to prove sth ~** probar algo por medios estadísticos; **~ that may be true** en cuanto a la estadística eso puede ser cierto.

statistician [ˌstætɪs'tɪʃən] *n* estadístico *mf*.

stative ['steɪtɪv] *adj*: **~ verb** verbo *m* de estado.

stator ['steɪtəʳ] *n* estator *m*.

statuary ['stætjʊərɪ] **1** *adj* estatuario. **2** *n* (*art*) estatuaria *f*; (*statues*) estatuas *fpl*.

statue ['stætjuː] *n* estatua *f*.

statuesque [ˌstætjʊ'esk] *adj* escultural.

statuette [ˌstætjʊ'et] *n* figurilla *f*, estatuilla *f*.

stature ['stætʃəʳ] *n* (**a**) (*lit*) estatura *f*, talla *f*; **to be of short ~** ser de estatura baja, tener poca talla.

(**b**) (*fig*) talla *f*; valor *m*, carácter *m*; **to have sufficient ~ for a post** estar a la altura de un cargo; **he lacks moral ~** le falta carácter.

status ['steɪtəs] **1** *n* posición *f*, condición *f*; (e)status *m*; rango *m*, categoría *f*; prestigio *m*; reputación *f*; (*Jur*) estado *m*; (*civil etc*) estado *m*; **social ~** posición *f* social; **the ~ of the Negro population** la posición social de la población negra; **what is his ~ in the profession?** ¿qué rango ocupa en la profesión?, ¿cómo se le considera en la profesión?; **he has not sufficient ~ for the job** no tiene categoría bastante alta para este cargo.

2 *attr*: **~ inquiry** comprobación *f* de valoración crediticia; **~ line** línea *f* de situación, línea *f* de estado; **~ report** informe *m* situacional; **~ symbol** signo *m* exterior de prestigio social.

status quo ['steɪtəs'kwəʊ] *n* statu *m* quo.

statute ['stætjuːt] **1** *n* ley *f*, estatuto *m*; **by ~** según la ley, de acuerdo con la ley. **2** *attr*: **~ law** ley *f* escrita.

statute book ['stætjuːtbʊk] *n* código *m* de leyes; **to be on the ~** ser ley.

statutory ['stætjʊtərɪ] *adj* estatutario; *holiday, right etc* legal; **~ meeting** junta *f* constitutiva.

staunch¹ [stɔːntʃ] *adj* leal, firme, incondicional.

staunch² [stɔːntʃ] *vt* = **stanch**.

staunchly ['stɔːntʃlɪ] *adv* lealmente, firmemente, incondicionalmente.

staunchness ['stɔːntʃnɪs] *n* lealtad *f*, firmeza *f*.

stave [steɪv] **1** *n* (*of barrel*) duela *f*; (*of ladder*) peldaño *m*; (*Mus*) pentagrama *m*; (*Liter*) estrofa *f*.

2 (*irr*: *pret and ptp* **stove** *or* **staved**) *vt* = **stave in, stave off**.

◆**stave in** *vt* romper, quebrar a golpes; desfondar.

◆**stave off** *vt attack* rechazar; apartar, mantener a distancia; *threat etc* evitar, conjurar; (*delay*) diferir; aplazar.

staves [steɪvz] *npl of* **staff**.

stay¹ [steɪ] **1** *n* (**a**) estancia *f*, permanencia *f*; visita *f*; **a ~**

of 10 days una estancia de 10 días; ~ **in hospital** estancia *f* hospitalaria; **our second** ~ **in Murcia** nuestra segunda visita a Murcia; **come for a longer** ~ **next year** ven a estar más tiempo el año que viene.

(**b**) (*Jur*) suspensión *f*, prórroga *f*; ~ **of execution** aplazamiento *m* de una sentencia; ~ **of proceedings** sobreseimiento *m*.

2 *vt* (**a**) (*check*) detener; controlar; poner freno a; *epidemic etc* tener a raya; *hunger* matar, engañar; **to** ~ **one's hand** contenerse, detenerse; **to** ~ **sb's hand** parar la mano a uno.

(**b**) (*Jur*) suspender, prorrogar; aplazar.

(**c**) (*last out*) *race* terminar; *distance* cubrir, cubrir toda la extensión de.

3 *vi* (**a**) (*wait*) esperar; ~**!** ¡espera!

(**b**) (*remain*) quedar, quedarse, permanecer; (*as guest etc*) hospedarse, estar, vivir; **you** ~ **right there** tú te quedas ahí, no te muevas de ahí; **to** ~ **at home** quedarse en casa; **to** ~ **in bed** guardar cama; **how long can you** ~**?** ¿hasta cuándo te puedes quedar?; **what? you** ~**ed for the Debussy?** ¿cómo? ¿os quedasteis a escuchar el Debussy?; **to** ~ **for supper, to** ~ **to supper** quedarse a cenar; **to** ~ **at an hotel** hospedarse en un hotel; **to** ~ **with friends** hospedarse con unos amigos; **where are you** ~**ing?** ¿dónde vives?; **she came for a weekend and** ~**ed 3 years** vino a pasar el fin de semana y permaneció 3 años; **it has clearly come to** ~ evidentemente tiene carácter permanente; **things can't be allowed to** ~ **like that** no podemos permitir que las cosas sigan así.

(**c**) (*remain, with adj*) **it** ~**s red** sigue tan rojo como antes; **if it** ~**s fine** si continúa el buen tiempo, si el tiempo sigue bueno; **it** ~**s motionless for hours** sigue durante horas enteras sin moverse; **he** ~**ed faithful to his wife** siguió fiel a su mujer.

(**d**) (*last out*) resistir; **the horse doesn't** ~ el caballo no resiste esa distancia, el caballo no tiene bastante resistencia; ~ **with it!*** ¡sigue adelante!, ¡no te dejes desanimar!

◆**stay away** *vi* ausentarse (*from* de), no asistir (*from* a); **you** ~ **away from my daughter!** ¡no vengas más por aquí a molestar a mi hija!; ~ **away from that machine** no te acerques a esa máquina.

◆**stay behind** *vi* quedarse; quedarse en casa, no salir; **they made him** ~ **behind after school** le hicieron quedar en la escuela después de las clases; **we told him to** ~ **behind till the last lap** dijimos que quedase atrás hasta la última vuelta.

◆**stay down** *vi* (**a**) permanecer abajo; (*bending*) permanecer doblado; (*lying down*) permanecer en el suelo; (*under water*) permanecer bajo el agua; (*Scol*) seguir en la misma clase.

(**b**) **nothing he eats will** ~ **down** no retiene nada de lo que come.

◆**stay in** *vi* (**a**) (*cork etc*) quedarse puesto.

(**b**) (*person: at home*) quedarse en casa, no salir.

◆**stay on** *vi* (**a**) (*lid etc*) quedarse puesto, seguir en su lugar.

(**b**) (*person*) quedarse; permanecer, continuar en su lugar; **he** ~**ed on as manager** siguió en su puesto de gerente, (*after change*) pasó a ser gerente (de la misma compañía); **they** ~**ed on after everyone else had left** se quedaron después de que todos los demás se habían marchado.

◆**stay out** *vi* (**a**) (*person*) quedarse fuera, no volver a casa; **she** ~**s out till midnight** no vuelve a casa hasta medianoche.

(**b**) (*striker*) mantenerse en huelga, no volver al trabajo.

(**c**) **to** ~ **out of** no tomar parte en; **you** ~ **out of this!** ¡no te metas en esto!, ¡tú fuera!

◆**stay over** *vi* pasar la noche, pernoctar; quedarse un poco.

◆**stay up** *vi* (**a**) (*remain standing etc*) mantenerse de pie; seguir en buen estado; **the team** ~**s up** el equipo sigue en la división superior.

(**b**) (*person*) velar, no acostarse, seguir sin acostarse; **to** ~ **up all night** trasnochar; **don't** ~ **up for me** no os quedéis esperándome hasta muy tarde.

stay² [steɪ] **1** *n* (**a**) (*Mech*) sostén *m*, soporte *m*, puntal *m*; (*Naut*) estay *m*; ~**s** corsé *m*.

(**b**) (*fig*) sostén *m*, apoyo *m*; **the** ~ **of one's old age** el sostén de su vejez.

2 *vt* sostener, apoyar, apuntalar; **this will** ~ **you till lunchtime** esto te ayudará a resistir hasta la comida, esto engañará el hambre hasta la comida.

stay-at-home ['steɪəthəʊm] **1** *adj* casero, hogareño. **2** *n* persona *f* casera, persona *f* hogareña.

stayer ['steɪəʳ] *n* (*horse*) caballo *m* apto para carreras de distancia; (*person*) persona *f* de carácter firme, persona *f* de mucho aguante.

staying-power ['steɪɪŋ,paʊəʳ] *n* resistencia *f*, aguante *m*.

staysail ['steɪseɪl, (*Naut*) 'steɪsl] *n* vela *f* de estay.

STD *n* (**a**) (*Brit Telec*) *abbr of* **Subscriber Trunk Dialling**; ~ **code** prefijo *m* para conferencias interurbanas (automáticas). (**b**) (*Med*) *abbr of* **sexually transmitted disease** enfermedad *f* de transmisión sexual, ETS *f*.

stead [sted] *n*: **in his** ~ en su lugar; **to stand sb in good** ~ ser útil a uno, aprovechar a uno.

steadfast ['stedfəst] *adj* firme, resuelto; constante; tenaz; *gaze* fijo; ~ **in adversity** firme en el infortunio; ~ **in danger** impertérrito; ~ **in love** constante en el amor.

steadfastly ['stedfəstlɪ] *adv* firmemente, resueltamente; con constancia; tenazmente; fijamente.

steadfastness ['stedfəstnɪs] *n* firmeza *f*, resolución *f*; constancia *f*; tenacidad *f*; fijeza *f*.

steadily ['stedɪlɪ] *adv* firmemente, fijamente; de modo estable; regularmente, constantemente, uniformemente; continuamente; sin parar, ininterrumpidamente; sensatamente; seriamente; diligentemente; tranquilamente; resueltamente; imperturbablemente; **it gets** ~ **worse** se hace cada vez peor; **the temperature goes** ~ **up** la temperatura sube constantemente, la temperatura no deja de subir; **to work** ~ trabajar ininterrumpidamente; **she looked at me** ~ me miró sin pestañear.

steadiness ['stedɪnɪs] *n* firmeza *f*, fijeza *f*; estabilidad *f*; regularidad *f*, constancia *f*, uniformidad *f*; sensatez *f*, juicio *m*; seriedad *f*, formalidad *f*; diligencia *f*; serenidad *f*, ecuanimidad *f*; sangre *f* fría; imperturbabilidad *f*.

steady ['stedɪ] **1** *adj* firme, fijo; estable; regular, constante, uniforme; continuo, ininterrumpido; (*in character*) sensato, juicioso; serio, formal; (*at work*) diligente, trabajador; aplicado; *boyfriend etc* fijo; formal; (*not nervous*) sereno, tranquilo, ecuánime; resuelto; imperturbable; ~ **demand** demanda *f* constante; ~ **job** empleo *m* seguro, empleo *m* fijo; ~ **progress** progreso *m* ininterrumpido; ~**-state theory** teoría *f* de la creación continua; ~ **temperature** temperatura *f* constante, temperatura *f* uniforme; **with a** ~ **hand** con mano firme; **at a** ~ **pace** a paso regular; **as** ~ **as a rock** firme como una roca; **the car is very** ~ **at corners** el coche es muy estable en las curvas; **there was a** ~ **downpour for 3 hours** llovió sin interrupción durante 3 horas; **we were going at a** ~ **90 kph** íbamos a una velocidad uniforme de 90 kph; **he plays a very** ~ **game** juega muy sensatamente.

2 *adv*: ~**!** ¡con calma!, ¡despacio!; **they are going** ~ **now*** son novios formales ya; **they've been going** ~ **for 6 months*** llevan 6 meses de relaciones; **is he going** ~ **with her?*** ¿es novio formal de ella?

3 *n* (*****) novio *m*, -a *f* formal.

4 *vt* (*hold*) mantener firme, sujetar en posición firme; (*stabilize*) estabilizar, hacer más estable; uniformar, regularizar; *nerves* calmar; *nervous person* (*also* **to** ~ **down, to** ~ **up**) tranquilizar, *wild person* hacer que siente la cabeza.

5 *vi* (*also* **to** ~ **down, to** ~ **up**) (*market, price etc*) estabilizarse, hacerse más estable; uniformarse, regularizarse; (*person*) calmarse; tranquilizarse; sentar la cabeza.

6 *vr*: **to** ~ **o.s.** afirmarse, recobrar el equilibrio; **to** ~ **o.s. against sth** apoyarse en algo.

steak [steɪk] *n* biftec *m*; filete *m*; (*of meat other than beef*) tajada *f*; ~ **and kidney pie** pastel *m* de biftec y riñones.

steakhouse ['steɪkhaʊs] *n*, *pl* **steakhouses** ['steɪk,haʊzɪz] parrilla *f*.

steak-knife ['steɪknaɪf] *n*, *pl* **steak-knives** ['steɪknaɪvz] cuchillo *m* para el biftec.

steal [stiːl] (*irr*: *pret* **stole**, *ptp* **stolen**) **1** *vt* robar, hurtar; (*fig*) robar; **to** ~ **a glance at sb** mirar de soslayo a uno, echar una mirada furtiva a uno.

2 *vi* (**a**) (*thieve*) robar, hurtar; **to live by** ~**ing** vivir del robo.

(**b**) **to** ~ **into a room** deslizarse en un cuarto, entrar en un cuarto a hurtadillas; **to** ~ **up on sb** acercarse a uno sin ruido.

◆**steal away, steal off** *vi* marcharse sigilosamente, escabullirse.

stealing ['stiːlɪŋ] *n* robo *m*, hurto *m*.

stealth [stelθ] *n* cautela *f*, sigilo *m*; **by** ~ a escondidas, a

hurtadillas, sigilosamente.
stealthily ['stelθɪlɪ] *adv* clandestinamente, a hurtadillas.
stealthiness ['stelθɪnɪs] *n* cautela *f*, sigilo *m*; cárácter *m* furtivo.
stealthy ['stelθɪ] *adj* cauteloso, sigiloso, furtivo; clandestino.
steam [stiːm] **1** *n* vapor *m*; vaho *m*, humo *m*; **full ~ ahead!** ¡todo avante!; **to get up ~** acumular vapor, dar presión; **to let off ~** descargar vapor, (*fig*) desahogarse; **the ship went on under its own ~** el buque siguió adelante con sus propios motores; **to come under one's own ~** venir por los propios medios; **to run out of ~** (*fig*) perder vigor, perder su fuerza; **to take the ~ out of a situation** reducir la tensión de una situación.
2 *attr* de vapor; **~ bath** baño *m* de vapor; **~ heat** calor *m* por vapor; **~ iron** plancha *f* de vapor.
3 *vt* (**a**) (*Culin*) cocer al vapor.
(**b**) *window* empañar.
(**c**) **to ~ open an envelope** abrir un sobre por medio de vapor; **to ~ a stamp off** separar un sello por medio de vapor.
4 *vi* (**a**) (*give out ~*) echar vapor; **the bowl was ~ing on the table** la cacerola humeaba en la mesa.
(**b**) (*move etc, function*) **to ~ ahead** avanzar, (*fig*) adelantarse mucho; **to ~ along** ir, avanzar (echando vapor); **we were ~ing at 12 knots** íbamos a 12 nudos, navegábamos a 12 nudos; **the ship ~ed into harbour** el buque entró al puerto; **the train ~ed out** salió el tren.
◆**steam up 1** *vt window* empañar; **the windows quickly get ~ed up** las ventanas se empañan pronto; **to get ~ed up about sth** (*fig*) excitarse por algo, exaltarse por algo; **don't get ~ed up!*** ¡no te exaltes!, ¡cálmate!
2 *vi* (*window*) empañarse.
steamboat ['stiːmbəut] *n* vapor *m*, buque *m* de vapor.
steam-driven ['stiːm,drɪvn] *adj* impulsado por vapor, a vapor.
steam-engine ['stiːm,endʒɪn] *n* máquina *f* de vapor.
steam-hammer ['stiːm'hæməʳ] *n* maza *f* a vapor, maza *f* mecánica.
steamer ['stiːməʳ] *n* (**a**) (*ship*) vapor *m*, buque *m* de vapor. (**b**) (*Culin*) vaporera *f*.
steaming ['stiːmɪŋ] **1** *adj* (**a**) *kettle, plate* humeante. (**b**) (*: *angry*) furioso. (**c**) (‡: *drunk*) ajumado‡. **2** *n* (*) *atraco en transportes públicos*.
steam-organ ['stiːm,ɔːgən] *n* órgano *m* de vapor.
steamroller ['stiːm,rəuləʳ] **1** *n* apisonadora *f*.
2 *vt* allanar con apisonadora; (*fig*) aplastar, arrollar; **to ~ a bill through parliament** hacer aprobar un proyecto de ley a rajatabla.
steamship ['stiːmʃɪp] *n* vapor *m*, buque *m* de vapor; **~ company, ~ line** compañía *f* naviera.
steam shovel ['stiːm,ʃʌvl] *n* (*US*) pala *f* mecánica de vapor, excavadora *f*.
steam turbine ['stiːm'tɜːbaɪn] *n* turbina *f* de vapor.
steamy ['stiːmɪ] *adj* (**a**) vaporoso; *room etc* lleno de vapor; *atmosphere* húmedo y de mucho calor; *window* empañado. (**b**) (*) *film etc* erótico; *relationship* apasionado.
steed [stiːd] *n* (*liter*) corcel *m*.
steel [stiːl] **1** *n* (**a**) acero *m*; **to be made of ~** (*fig*) ser de bronce; **to fight with cold ~** luchar con armas blancas.
(**b**) (*sharpener*) chaira *f*, eslabón *m*; (*for striking spark*) eslabón *m*.
2 *attr* de acero; acerado; **~ band** banda *f* de percusión del Caribe; **~ guitar** guitarra *f* de cordaje metálico; **~ helmet** casco *m* (de acero); **~ industry** industria *f* siderúrgica; **~ maker, ~ manufacturer** fabricante *m* de acero; **~ tape** cinta *f* métrica de acero; **~ wool** virutas *fpl* de acero.
3 *vt* acerar; revestir de acero; **to ~ one's heart** hacerse duro de corazón; **to ~ one's men** infundir valor a los suyos.
4 *vr*: **to ~ o.s.** fortalecerse (*against* contra); **to ~ o.s. to do sth** cobrar bastante ánimo para hacer algo, persuadirse a hacer algo.
steel-clad ['stiːlklæd] *adj* revestido de acero, acorazado.
steel-grey [,stiːl'greɪ] *adj* gris metálico.
steel mill ['stiːlmɪl] *n* acería *f*, fábrica *f* de acero; fábrica *f* siderúrgica, fundidora *f* (*LAm*).
steel-plated [,stiːl'pleɪtɪd] *adj* chapado en acero.
steelworker ['stiːl,wɜːkəʳ] *n* trabajador *m* siderúrgico.
steelworks ['stiːlwɜːks] *n, pl invar* acería *f*, fábrica *f* de acero, fábrica *f* siderúrgica.
steely ['stiːlɪ] *adj* acerado; (*fig*) inflexible, duro; *gaze* duro; **~ blue** azul metálico.
steelyard ['stiːljɑːd] *n* romana *f*, báscula *f*.
steely-eyed [,stiːlɪ'aɪd] *adj* de mirada penetrante.
steep[1] [stiːp] *adj* (**a**) (*lit*) escarpado, abrupto; *cliff etc* cortado a pico, precipitoso; *stairs etc* empinado; **a ~ slope** una fuerte pendiente; **it's too ~ for the tractor** la pendiente es demasiado fuerte para el tractor; **it's a ~ climb** es una cuesta empinada.
(**b**) (*) *price etc* exorbitante, excesivo; *story etc* difícil de creer, increíble; **that's pretty ~!** ¡eso es demasiado!, ¡no hay derecho!; **it seems a bit ~ that ...** no parece razonable que + *subj*.
steep[2] [stiːp] **1** *vt* empapar, remojar (*in* en); **~ed in** (*fig*) saturado de, impregnado de, empapado en; **a town ~ed in history** una ciudad saturada de historia.
2 *vi*: **to leave sth to ~** dejar algo en remojo.
steeple ['stiːpl] *n* aguja *f*, campanario *m*, torre *f*.
steeplechase ['stiːpl,tʃeɪs] *n* carrera *f* de obstáculos, carrera *f* de vallas.
steeplechasing ['stiːpl,tʃeɪsɪŋ] *n* deporte *m* de las carreras de obstáculos.
steeplejack ['stiːpldʒæk] *n* reparador *m* de chimeneas, torres *etc*.
steeply ['stiːplɪ] *adv*: **the mountain rises ~** la montaña está cortada a pico; **the road climbs ~** la carretera sube muy empinada; **prices have risen ~** los precios han subido muchísimo.
steepness ['stiːpnɪs] *n* lo escarpado, lo abrupto; lo precipitoso; lo fuerte.
steer[1] [stɪəʳ] **1** *vt* guiar, dirigir; *car etc* conducir, manejar (*LAm*); *ship* gobernar; **to ~ one's way through a crowd** abrirse paso por entre una multitud; **you nearly ~ed us into that rock** por poco dimos con aquella roca; **I ~ed her across to the bar** la llevé hacia el bar; **he ~ed me on to a good job*** me enchufó para un buen trabajo.
2 *vi* conducir, manejar (*LAm*); gobernar; **who's going to ~?** ¿quién manejará el volante (*or* timón *etc*)?; **can you ~?** ¿sabes gobernar el barco (*etc*)?; **to ~ for** dirigirse a, dirigirse hacia, ir con rumbo a; **to ~ clear of** evitar cualquier contacto con.
steer[2] [stɪəʳ] *n* buey *m*; novillo *m*; **to sell sb a bum ~*** (*US*) dar información falsa a uno, embaucar a uno.
steerage ['stɪərɪdʒ] *n* entrepuente *m*; **to go ~** viajar en tercera clase.
steering ['stɪərɪŋ] **1** *n* (*Aut etc*) dirección *f*, conducción *f*; (*Naut*) gobierno *m*. **2** *adj*: **~ committee** comité *m* directivo.
steering-arm ['stɪərɪŋɑːm] *n* brazo *m* de dirección.
steering-column ['stɪərɪŋ,kɒləm] *n* columna *f* de dirección.
steering-lock ['stɪərɪŋlɒk] *n* (*Aut*) (*anti-theft device*) dispositivo *m* antirrobo; cierre *m* de dirección; (*turning circle*) capacidad *f* de giro.
steering-wheel ['stɪərɪŋwiːl] *n* volante *m* (de dirección).
steersman ['stɪəzmən] *n, pl* **steersmen** ['stɪəzmən] timonero *m*.
stellar ['steləʳ] *adj* estelar.
stem[1] [stem] **1** *n* (**a**) (*of plant*) tallo *m*, (*of tree*) tronco *m*, (*of leaf etc*) pedúnculo *m*; (*of glass*) pie *m*; (*of pipe*) cañón *m*, tubo *m*; (*Mech*) vástago *m*; (*of word*) tema *m*.
(**b**) (*Naut*) roda *f*, tajamar *m*; **from ~ to stern** de proa a popa.
2 *vi*: **to ~ from** provenir de, proceder de, resultar de.
stem[2] [stem] *vt* (*check, stop*) refrenar, detener; *flood* represar; *attack* rechazar, parar; *flow of blood* restañar.
stench [stentʃ] *n* hedor *m*.
stencil ['stensl] **1** *n* (*Tech*) patrón *m* picado, estarcido *m*; (*for lettering*) plantilla *f*; (*for typing*) cliché *m*, clisé *m*.
2 *vt* estarcir; (*in typing*) hacer un cliché de.
stenographer [ste'nɒgrəfəʳ] *n* (*US*) taquígrafo *m*, -a *f*, estenógrafo *m*, -a *f*.
stenography [ste'nɒgrəfɪ] *n* (*US*) taquigrafía *f*, estenografía *f*.
stentorian [sten'tɔːrɪən] *adj* estentóreo.
STEP [step] *n abbr of* **Science and Technology for Environmental Protection** Ciencia *f* y Tecnología para la Protección del Medio Ambiente.
step [step] **1** *n* (**a**) (*pace*) paso *m*; (*sound*) paso *m*, pisada *f*; (*footprint*) huella *f*; (*of dance*) paso *m*; (*Comput*) paso *m*; **at every ~** a cada paso; **~ by ~** paso a paso, poco a poco; **it's a good ~** es bastante camino, está algo lejos; **it's quite a ~ to the village** el pueblo queda algo lejos, hay mucho camino para ir al pueblo; **to be in ~ with** llevar el paso con, (*fig*) estar conforme a, estar de acuerdo con; **to be out of ~ with** no ir al paso de, no llevar el paso con, (*fig*) estar en desacuerdo con; estar desfasado de; **to break ~** romper el paso; **to fall into ~** empezar a llevar el paso,

(*fig*) conformarse; **to follow in sb's ~s** seguir los pasos de uno; **to keep in ~** llevar el paso; **to retrace one's ~s** desandar lo andado, volver sobre los pasos; **to take a ~** dar un paso; **to turn one's ~s towards** dirigirse hacia; **to watch one's ~** ir con tiento.

(**b**) (*measure*) paso *m*; medida *f*, gestión *f*; **~s to deal with the problem** medidas *fpl* para resolver el problema; **the first ~ is to ...** la primera medida a tomar es ...; **it's a great** (*or* **big**) **~ forward** esto significa un gran avance; es un paso gigante; **it's a ~ in the right direction** es una medida plausible; **what's the next ~?** ¿qué hacemos después?; **the next ~ is to** + *infin* luego hay que + *infin*, lo que se hace luego es + *infin*; **to take ~s to** + *infin* tomar medidas para + *infin*; **one can't take a single ~ without ...** no se puede dar un solo paso sin ...

(**c**) (*stair*) peldaño *m*, escalón *m*, grada *f*; (*of vehicle*) estribo *m*.

(**d**) **~s** (*stairs*) escalera *f*; (*outside building*) escalinata *f*; **folding ~s, pair of ~s** (*Brit*) escalera *f* de tijera, escalera *f* doble.

2 *vt* (**a**) (*place at intervals*) escalonar, colocar de trecho en trecho.

(**b**) *distance* (*also* **to ~ out**) medir a pasos; **to ~ it out** apretar el paso, andar más rápidamente.

3 *vi* dar un paso; (*walk*) ir, andar, caminar; (*with care, heavily etc*) pisar; **~ this way** haga el favor de pasar por aquí; **to ~ on sth** pisar algo; **~ on it!** ¡date prisa!, ¡apúrate! (*LAm*); **to ~ on board** ir a bordo; **just ~ outside a moment** (*challenge*) pues salga un momento; **to ~ over sth** evitar pisar algo, evitar chocar con algo; **he ~ped carefully over the cable** pasó por encima del cable con cuidado.

◆**step aside** *vi* hacerse a un lado, apartarse.

◆**step back** *vi* retroceder, dar un paso hacia atrás; **we ~ back into the 18th century** volvemos al siglo XVIII.

◆**step down 1** *vt* reducir, disminuir.

2 *vi* bajar (*from* de); (*fig*) ceder su puesto; darse de baja; retirarse; renunciar a sus pretensiones; **to ~ down for someone else** retirarse en favor de otro.

◆**step forward** *vi* dar un paso (hacia adelante).

◆**step in** *vi* entrar; (*fig*) intervenir; **~ in!** ¡adelante!, ¡pasa!

◆**step inside** *vi*: **~ inside!** ¡adelante!, ¡pasa!

◆**step out 1** *vt distance* medir a pasos.

2 *vi* (*go out*) salir; (*hurry*) apretar el paso, andar más rápidamente.

◆**step up 1** *vt* aumentar, elevar; *campaign* reforzar; *production, current* aumentar.

2 *vi* subir (*on* a); **to ~ up to sb** acercarse a uno; **to ~ up to receive a prize** avanzar a recibir un premio.

stepbrother ['step,brʌðə^r] *n* hermanastro *m*.

step-by-step [,stepbaɪ'step] *adj*: **~ instructions** instrucciones *fpl* paso a paso.

stepchild ['steptʃaɪld] *n*, *pl* **stepchildren** ['step,tʃɪldrən] hijastro *m*, -a *f*, alnado *m*, -a *f*.

stepdaughter ['step,dɔːtə^r] *n* hijastra *f*.

stepfather ['step,fɑːðə^r] *n* padrastro *m*.

Stephen ['stiːvn] *nm* Esteban.

stepladder ['step,lædə^r] *n* escalera *f* de tijera, escalera *f* doble.

stepmother ['step,mʌðə^r] *n* madrastra *f*.

step-parent ['step,pɛərənt] *n* (*father*) padrastro *m*, (*mother*) madrastra *f*.

steppe [step] *n* estepa *f*.

stepping-stone ['stepɪŋstəʊn] *n* pasadera *f*; (*fig*) escalón *m* (*to* para llegar a).

stepsister ['step,sɪstə^r] *n* hermanastra *f*.

stepson ['stepsʌn] *n* hijastro *m*.

step-up ['stepʌp] *n* elevación *f*; aumento *m*; aceleración *f*; refuerzo *m*; (*promotion*) ascenso *m*.

ster. *abbr of* **sterling**.

stereo... ['sterɪəʊ] *pref* estereo...

stereo ['sterɪəʊ] *n* (**a**) *abbr of* **stereophonic**: (*all senses*) estéreo *m*; **recorded in ~** grabado en estéreo; **~ sound** sonido *m* estéreo, sonido *m* estereofónico.

(**b**) *abbr of* **stereoscope, stereotype** *etc* estéreo *m*.

stereogram ['sterɪəgræm] *n*, **stereograph** ['sterɪəgræf] *n* estereografía *f*.

stereophonic [,sterɪə'fɒnɪk] *adj* estereofónico.

stereophony [sterɪ'ɒfənɪ] *n* estereofonía *f*.

stereoscope ['sterɪəskəʊp] *n* estereoscopio *m*.

stereoscopic [,sterɪəs'kɒpɪk] *adj* estereoscópico; *film* tridimensional, en relieve.

stereotype ['sterɪətaɪp] **1** *n* clisé *m*, estereotipo *m*. **2** *vt* clisar, estereotipar; (*fig*) estereotipar.

sterile ['steraɪl] *adj* estéril.

sterility [ste'rɪlɪtɪ] *n* esterilidad *f*.

sterilization [,sterɪlaɪ,zeɪʃən] *n* esterilización *f*.

sterilize ['sterɪlaɪz] *vt* esterilizar.

sterling ['stɜːlɪŋ] **1** *adj* (**a**) (*fig*) verdadero, excelente; **a ~ character** una persona de toda confianza; **a person of ~ worth** una persona de grandes méritos.

(**b**) (*Econ*) **pound ~** libra *f* esterlina; **~ area** zona *f* de la libra esterlina; **~ balances** balances *mpl* de libras esterlinas.

(**c**) **~ silver** plata *f* de ley.

2 *n* libras *fpl* esterlinas.

stern[1] [stɜːn] *adj* severo; duro; austero; **a ~ glance** una mirada severa; **a ~ warning** un aviso terminante; **he was very ~ with me** fue muy duro conmigo; **but he was made of ~er stuff** pero él tenía más carácter.

stern[2] [stɜːn] *n* popa *f* (*also Anat*‡).

sternly ['stɜːnlɪ] *adv* severamente; duramente; austeramente; terminantemente; **she looked at me ~** me miró severamente.

sternness ['stɜːnnɪs] *n* severidad *f*; dureza *f*; austeridad *f*; lo terminante.

sternum ['stɜːnəm] *n* esternón *m*.

steroid ['stɪərɔɪd] *n* esteroide *m*.

stertorous ['stɜːtərəs] *adj* estertoroso.

stet [stet] *vi* (*Typ*) vale, deje como está.

stethoscope ['steθəskəʊp] *n* estetoscopio *m*.

Stetson ['stetsən] ® *n* sombrero *m* (de hombre) de alas anchas.

stevedore ['stiːvɪdɔː^r] *n* estibador *m*.

Steve [stiːv] *nm familiar form of* **Stephen, Steven.**

Steven ['stiːvn] *nm* Esteban.

stew [stjuː] **1** *n* cocido *m*; estofado *m*, guisado *m* (*LAm*); **to be in a ~*** pasar apuros, sudar la gota gorda; **now we're properly in the ~*** la hemos pringado de verdad*.

2 *attr*: **~ meat** (*US*) carne *f* de vaca.

3 *vt* estofar; guisar; *fruit* cocer, hacer una compota de; **~ed apples** compota *f* de manzanas.

4 *vi* (*tea*) pasarse; **to let sb ~ in his own juice** dejar a uno cocer en su propia salsa.

steward ['stjuːəd] *n* (*on estate etc*) administrador *m*; (*butler*) mayordomo *m*; (*Naut, in club etc*) camarero *m*; (*bouncer*) portero *m*, encargado *m*, -a *f* del servicio de orden y entrada; (*Aer*) auxiliar *m* de vuelo.

stewardess ['stjʊədes] *n* (*Naut*) camarera *f*; (*Aer*) auxiliar *f* de vuelo, azafata *f*, aeromoza *f* (*LAm*).

stewardship ['stjʊədʃɪp] *n* administración *f*, gobierno *m*.

stewing steak ['stjuːɪŋ,steɪk] *n* (*Brit*) carne *f* de vaca.

stewpan ['stjuːpæn] *n*, **stewpot** ['stjuːpɒt] *n* cazuela *f*, cacerola *f*, puchero *m*.

St. Ex., St. Exch. *abbr of* **Stock Exchange** Bolsa *f*.

Stg *abbr of* **sterling** esterlina, ester.

stick[1] [stɪk] **1** *n* (**a**) palo *m*, vara *f*; (*as weapon*) palo *m*, porra *f*; (*walking ~*) bastón *m*; (*Aer*) palanca *f* de mando; (*of wax, gum etc*) barra *f*; (*of bombs*) grupo *m*; (*of celery*) tallo *m*; **~s** (*for the fire*) astillas *fpl*, leña *f*; **~ of furniture** mueble *m*; **policy of the big ~** política *f* del palo grueso; **policy of the ~ and the carrot** política *f* del garrote y la zanahoria; **to be in a cleft ~** estar entre la espada y la pared; **to give sb the ~, to take the ~ to sb** dar palo a uno; **the critics gave him a lot of ~** los críticos le dieron una buena paliza; **to get** (*or* **take**) **a lot of ~** recibir una buena paliza; tener que aguantar mucho; **I got the dirty end of the ~** me tocó bailar con la más fea; **they live out in the ~s*** viven en el quinto pino.

(**b**) **old ~** (*Brit**) tío* *m*; **he's a funny old ~** es un tío raro (*or* divertido)*.

2 *attr*: **~ shift** (*US*) palanca *f* de marchas.

stick[2] [stɪk] (*irr*: *pret and ptp* **stuck**) **1** *vt* (**a**) (*gum*) pegar, encolar; **to ~ a poster on the wall** pegar un póster a la pared; **'~ no bills'** 'prohibido fijar carteles'; **he tried to ~ the crime on his brother*** trató de colgar el crimen a su hermano*.

(**b**) (*thrust*) clavar, hincar; **to ~ a knife into a table** clavar un cuchillo en una mesa.

(**c**) (*place, put*) poner, meter; **~ it on the shelf** ponlo en el estante; **~ it in your case** mételo en la maleta; **we'll ~ an advert in the paper*** pondremos un anuncio en el periódico; **they've stuck £5 on the price*** han subido el precio en 5 libras; **you know where you can ~ that!***‡ ¡que te jodas!‡

(**d**) (*pierce*) picar; **to ~ sb with a bayonet** herir a uno con bayoneta, clavar la bayoneta a uno; **a cork stuck all**

over with pins un corcho lleno de alfileres, un corcho todo cubierto de alfileres; **I've stuck the needle into my finger** me he picado el dedo con la aguja.

(**e**) (*esp Brit*: *tolerate*) resistir, aguantar; **I can't ~ him at any price** no le puedo ver de ninguna manera; **I can't ~ it any longer** no aguanto más, no resisto más.

(**f**) (*passive*: *stop*) **to get stuck in the snow** quedar sin poderse mover en la nieve; **he's stuck in France** sigue en Francia sin poder moverse; **he's stuck in a boring job** tiene un trabajo muy aburrido (y no puede buscarse otro); **the mechanism was stuck** el mecanismo estaba bloqueado; **the lift is stuck at the 9th floor** el ascensor se ha atrancado en el piso 9.

(**g**) (*fig phrases*) **let's get stuck in!*** ¡vamos!; ¡a trabajar!; **to get stuck into sth*** emprender algo en serio, dedicarse seriamente a algo; **now we're stuck*** estamos clavados; **to be stuck with sth*** tener que cargar con algo; **we got stuck with this problem*** nos quedamos con este problema; **and now we're stuck with it*** y ahora no lo podemos quitar de encima, y ahora no hay manera de deshacernos de eso; **he's never stuck for an answer** siempre tiene una contestación pronta; **I was stuck with him for 2 hours*** tuve que soportar su compañía durante 2 horas; **the problem had them all stuck*** el problema les tenía a todos perplejos; **we're stuck at No. 13*** no logramos pasar más allá del núm. 13; **to be stuck on sb‡** estar enamorado de uno.

2 *vi* (**a**) (*gum etc*) pegarse, adherirse; **this stamp won't ~** este sello no se pega; **the name stuck to him** el apodo se le pegó; **the charge seems to have stuck** la acusación no ha sido olvidada nunca; **to make an agreement ~** hacer que un acuerdo sea efectivo (*or* duradero); **to make a charge ~** hacer que una acusación tenga efecto.

(**b**) (*in mud*) atascarse, quedar atascado; (*mechanism etc*) bloquearse, trabarse, no poder moverse; pegarse; (*pin etc*) prender, estar prendido; **it stuck to the wall** quedó pegado a la pared; **to ~ fast in the mud** quedar clavado en el barro; **the door ~s in wet weather** en tiempo de lluvia la puerta se pega.

(**c**) (*remain*) pararse, quedarse parado; (*stay*) quedarse, permanecer; **I ~** (*Cards*) me planto; **here I am and here I ~** aquí estoy y aquí me quedo; **this thought stuck in my mind** esto se clavó en mi pensamiento; **to ~ at sth** (*not give up*) persistir en algo, no abandonar algo, seguir trabajando (*etc*) en algo; **to ~ by sb** (*follow*) pegarse a uno, pisar los talones a uno; (*support*) apoyar a uno, defender a uno, ser fiel a uno; **to ~ to one's principles** seguir fiel a sus principios, aferrarse a sus principios; **to ~ to a promise** cumplir una promesa; **to ~ to it** persistir, no cejar, seguir trabajando (*etc*); **~ to it!** ¡ánimo!; **let's ~ to the matter in hand** ciñámonos al asunto, no perdamos de vista el tema principal, volvamos al grano; **to ~ to sb = to ~ by sb**; **to ~ to sb like a limpet** (*or* **leech**) pegarse a uno como una lapa; **to ~ with sb = to ~ by sb**; **~ with us and you'll be all right** quédate con nosotros y todo saldrá bien; **you'll have to ~ with it** tendrás que seguir del mismo modo.

(**d**) (*balk*) plantarse; retroceder (*at* ante); **he ~s at nothing** no siente escrúpulo por nada, no se para en barras; **he wouldn't ~ at murder** hasta cometería un asesinato, no se arredraría ante el homicidio; **that's where I ~** yo de ahí no paso.

◆**stick around** *vi* esperar por ahí, quedarse.

◆**stick back** *vt* (**a**) (*replace*) volver a su lugar.

(**b**) (*gum etc*) volver a pegar.

◆**stick down** (**a**) *vt* (*gum etc*) pegar.

(**b**) (*put down*) poner, dejar; *note* apuntar (rápidamente).

◆**stick in** *vt* (**a**) (*thrust in*) clavar, hincar; meter; introducir; (*add, insert*) introducir, añadir.

(**b**) (*) **to get stuck in(to it)** poner manos a la obra, empezar a trabajar (*etc*) en serio; **get stuck in!** ¡a ello!, ¡apúrate!

◆**stick on 1** *vt* (**a**) *stamp etc* pegar.

(**b**) *hat* ponerse, calarse; *coat etc* ponerse.

(**c**) *extra cost etc* añadir; **they've stuck 10p on a litre** han subido el precio del litro en 10p.

2 *vi* adherirse, pegarse; quedar pegado.

◆**stick out 1** *vt* (**a**) *tongue* asomar, sacar; *leg etc* extender; *chest* sacar; *head* asomar.

(**b**) (*) aguantar; **to ~ it out** aguantar (hasta el final).

2 *vi* (**a**) (*project*) salir, sobresalir; asomarse.

(**b**) (*fig*) ser evidente; **it ~s out a mile** salta a los ojos, se ve a la legua; **it ~s out like a sore thumb** resalta como una mosca en la leche.

(**c**) (*insist*) **to ~ out for sth** insistir en algo, no ceder hasta obtener algo; **they're ~ing out for more money** porfían en reclamar más dinero, se empeñan en pedir más dinero.

◆**stick together 1** *vt* pegar; unir con cola (*etc*).

2 *vi* (**a**) (*adhere*) pegarse, quedar pegados.

(**b**) (*persons etc*) mantenerse unidos; no separarse; (*fig*) cerrar las filas.

◆**stick up 1** *vt* (**a**) *notice etc* fijar, pegar; *hand etc* levantar, alzar; **~ 'em up!** ¡arriba las manos!

(**b**) (‡) *person* atracar, encañonar‡; *bank etc* asaltar.

2 *vi* (**a**) (*show above*) salir, sobresalir (por encima), asomarse (por encima); (*hair etc*) estar de punta.

(**b**) **to ~ up for sb*** defender a uno, sacar la cara por uno.

sticker ['stɪkəʳ] *n* (**a**) (*person*) persona *f* aplicada, persona *f* perseverante. (**b**) (*label*) etiqueta *f* engomada; pegatina *f*, pegatín *m*.

stickiness ['stɪkɪnɪs] *n* (**a**) (*lit*) pegajosidad *f*; viscosidad *f*; bochorno *m*, humedad *f* (con calor). (**b**) (*fig*) lo difícil.

sticking-plaster ['stɪkɪŋ,plɑːstəʳ] *n* (*Brit*) esparadrapo *m*, curita *f* (*LAm*), tirita *f* (*LAm*).

sticking-point ['stɪkɪŋ,pɔɪnt] *n* punto *m* de fricción.

stick-insect ['stɪkɪnsekt] *n* insecto *m* palo.

stick-in-the-mud ['stɪkɪnðəmʌd] *n* persona *f* pesada; persona *f* rutinaria; reaccionario *m*, -a *f*, persona *f* chapada a la antigua, retrógrado *m*.

stickleback ['stɪklbæk] *n* espinoso *m*.

stickler ['stɪkləʳ] *n* rigorista *mf* (*for* en cuanto a), persona *f* etiquetera; **he's a real ~ for correct spelling** insiste terminantemente en la correcta ortografía.

stick-on ['stɪkɒn] *adj* adhesivo.

stickpin ['stɪkpɪn] *n* (*US*) alfiler *m* de corbata.

stick-up‡ ['stɪkʌp] *n* atraco *m*, asalto *m*.

sticky ['stɪkɪ] *adj* (**a**) pegajoso; viscoso; *label* engomado; *atmosphere* bochornoso, húmedo (y con calor); **~ tape** cinta *f* adhesiva; **to have ~ fingers*** ser largo de uñas. (**b**) (*) *problem, person* difícil; *situation* difícil, violento; **to come to a ~ end** tener mal fin, ir a acabar mal; **to have a ~ time** pasar un mal rato; **he was very ~ about signing it** se puso muy difícil al firmarlo.

stiff [stɪf] **1** *adj* (**a**) (*unbending*) rígido, inflexible, tieso; *door, joint* duro, tieso; *collar, shirt front* duro, (*starched*) almidonado; *brush* duro; *paste, soil* espeso, consistente; **as ~ as a poker** tieso como un ajo; **to be ~ in the legs** tener las piernas entumecidas; **to be ~ with cold** estar aterido; **you'll feel ~ tomorrow** mañana te van a doler los músculos, mañana tendrás agujetas.

(**b**) (*fig*) *breeze* fuerte; *climb, examination, task, test etc* difícil; *resistance* tenaz; *price* exorbitante, subido; *bow* frío; *person* etiquetero, ceremonioso; *manner* estirado; **she poured herself a ~ whisky** se sirvió una copa grande de whisky.

2 *adv*: **to be worried ~** estar muy preocupado.

3 *n* (‡) fiambre* *m*, cadáver *m*.

stiffen ['stɪfn] **1** *vt* hacer más rígido, atiesar; endurecer; hacer más espeso; *limb* entumecer, agarrotar; *morale, resistance etc* fortalecer.

2 *vi* hacerse más rígido, atiesarse; endurecerse; hacerse más espeso, espesarse; entumecerse; fortalecerse, robustecerse; hacerse más tenaz; **when I said this she ~ed** al decir yo esto, se volvió menos cordial; **the breeze ~ed** refrescó el viento; **resistance to the idea seems to have ~ed** parece que ha aumentado la oposición a esta idea.

stiffener ['stɪfənəʳ] *n* (*starch etc*) apresto *m*; (*plastic strip*) lengüeta *f*.

stiffly ['stɪflɪ] *adv* rígidamente, tiesamente; **to move ~** moverse con dificultad, moverse despacio con los miembros entumecidos; **she said ~** dijo fríamente, dijo estirada; **this was ~ resisted** a esto opusieron una tenaz resistencia.

stiff-necked ['stɪf'nekt] *adj* (*fig*) terco, obstinado; estirado.

stiffness ['stɪfnɪs] *n* (*V adj*) (**a**) rigidez *f*, inflexibilidad *f*, tiesura *f*; dureza *f*; espesura *f*, consistencia *f*; entumecimiento *m*. (**b**) fuerza *f*; dificultad *f*, lo difícil; tenacidad *f*; lo exorbitante; frialdad *f*, carácter *m* etiquetero, carácter *m* estirado.

stifle ['staɪfl] **1** *vt* ahogar, sofocar; (*fig*) suprimir; **to ~ a yawn** ahogar un bostezo, contener un bostezo; **to ~ opposition** suprimir la oposición.

2 *vi* ahogarse, sofocarse.

stifling ['staɪflɪŋ] *adj* sofocante (*also fig*), bochornoso; **it's ~ in here** aquí dentro hay un calor sofocante; **the atmos-**

phere in the company is ~ en la compañía hay una atmósfera sofocante.

stigma ['stɪgmə] *n, pl* **stigmas** (*Bot, Med*), *pl* **stigmata** [stɪg'mɑːtə] (*Rel*) estigma *m*; (*moral stain*) estigma *m*, tacha *f*, baldón *m*.

stigmatic [stɪg'mætɪk] (*Rel*) **1** *adj* estigmatizado. **2** *n* estigmatizado *m*, -a *f*.

stigmatize ['stɪgmətaɪz] *vt* estigmatizar; **to ~ sb as** calificar a uno de, tachar a uno de.

stile [staɪl] *n* escalera *f* para pasar una cerca.

stiletto [stɪ'letəʊ] *n* estilete *m*; (*tool*) pinzón *m*; **~ heel** (*Brit*) tacón *m* de aguja.

still[1] [stɪl] **1** *adj* (*motionless*) inmóvil; quieto; (*and quiet*) tranquilo, silencioso; *wine* no espumoso; **~ life** bodegón *m*, naturaleza *f* muerta; **~ life painter** bodegonista *mf*; **to keep ~** estar inmóvil, no moverse; **keep ~!** ¡estáte quieto!; **he fell and lay ~** cayó y permaneció inmóvil; **to sit ~** estarse quieto en su silla; **sit ~!** ¡quieto!; **to stand ~** estarse quieto; **my heart stood ~** se me paró el corazón.

2 *n* (**a**) (*liter*) silencio *m*, calma *f*; **in the ~ of the night** en el silencio de la noche.

(**b**) (*Cine*) fotograma *m*.

3 *vt* calmar, tranquilizar; aquietar; (*silence*) acallar.

still[2] [stɪl] **1** *adv* todavía, aún; **~ more** aun más, más aun; **~ better** mejor aun, aun mejor; **there are ~ 2 more** quedan 2 más; **he ~ hasn't come** no ha venido todavía; **I can ~ recall it** todavía lo recuerdo, lo recuerdo aún; **I ~ play a bit** sigo jugando un poco; **do you ~ believe that?** ¿sigues creyendo eso?; **~ and all*** (*esp US*) en resumidas cuentas, bien mirado todo.

2 *conj* sin embargo, con todo, a pesar de todo; **~, it was worth it** sin embargo, valió la pena.

still[3] [stɪl] *n* alambique *m*.

stillbirth ['stɪl,bɜːθ] *n* nacimiento *m* de un niño muerto.

stillborn ['stɪl,bɔːn] *adj* (**a**) nacido muerto, mortinato; **the child was ~** el niño nació muerto. (**b**) (*fig*) fracasado, malogrado.

stillness ['stɪlnɪs] *n* inmovilidad *f*; quietud *f*; tranquilidad *f*, silencio *m*.

stilt [stɪlt] *n* zanco *m*; (*Archit*) pilar *m*, soporte *m*; pilote *m*.

stilted ['stɪltɪd] *adj* afectado, hinchado, artificial.

stimulant ['stɪmjʊlənt] **1** *adj* estimulante. **2** *n* estimulante *m*, excitante *m*; (*drink*) bebida *f* alcohólica.

stimulate ['stɪmjʊleɪt] *vt* estimular; *growth etc* favorecer, fomentar, promover; *demand* estimular; **to ~ sb to do sth** estimular a uno a hacer algo, incitar a uno a hacer algo.

stimulating ['stɪmjʊleɪtɪŋ] *adj* (*Med etc*) estimulador, estimulante; *experience, book etc* sugestivo; alentador; inspirador.

stimulation [,stɪmjʊ'leɪʃən] *n* (*stimulus*) estímulo *m*; (*state*) excitación *f*.

stimulus ['stɪmjʊləs] *n, pl* **stimuli** ['stɪmjʊlaɪ] estímulo *m*, incentivo *m*.

stimy ['staɪmɪ] *vt* = **stymie**.

sting [stɪŋ] **1** *n* (**a**) (*Zool, Bot: organ*) aguijón *m*; **but there's a ~ in the tail** pero viene algo no tan agradable al final.

(**b**) (*act, wound*) picadura *f*; (*pain*) escozor *m*; picazón *m*; (*pain, fig*) punzada *f*; **a ~ of remorse** una punzada de remordimiento; **the ~ of the rain in one's face** el azote de la lluvia en la cara; **I felt the ~ of his irony** su ironía me hirió en lo vivo; **this will take the ~ out of it** esto lo hará más aceptable, esto servirá para dorar la píldora.

(**c**) (*esp US‡*) timo *m*.

2 (*irr: pret and ptp* **stung**) *vt* (**a**) picar; punzar; (*make smart*) picar, escocer en; (*of hot dishes*) resquemar; (*of hail etc*) azotar; **the bee stung him** la abeja le picó; **my conscience stung me** me remordió la conciencia; **the reply stung him to the quick** la respuesta le hirió en lo vivo; **he was clearly stung by this remark** era evidente que este comentario hizo mella en él.

(**b**) **to ~ sb to do sth** incitar a uno a hacer algo, provocar a uno a hacer algo.

(**c**) (*****) **they stung me for £4** me clavaron 4 libras*; **how much did they ~ you (for)?** ¿cuánto te clavaron?*

3 *vi* picar; escocer; **moths don't ~** las mariposas no pican; **my eyes ~** me pican los ojos; **that mouthful stung** ese bocado me quemó la lengua; **that blow really stung** ese golpe me dolió de verdad.

stingily ['stɪndʒɪlɪ] *adv* con tacañería.

stinginess ['stɪndʒɪnɪs] *n* tacañería *f*.

stinging ['stɪŋɪŋ] **1** *adj insect etc* que pica, que tiene aguijón; *pain* punzante; *remark etc* mordaz. **2** *n* (*sensation*) escozor *m*; picazón *m*; punzada *f*.

stinging-nettle ['stɪŋɪŋ,netl] *n* ortiga *f*.

sting-ray ['stɪŋreɪ] *n* pastinaca *f*.

stingy ['stɪndʒɪ] *adj* tacaño; **to be ~ with sth** ser tacaño con algo.

stink [stɪŋk] **1** *n* (**a**) hedor *m*, mal olor *m*; tufo *m*; **a ~ of ...** un hedor a ...; **the ~ of corruption** el olor a corrupción.

(**b**) (*****) lío *m**, follón* *m*; **there was a tremendous ~ about it** se armó un tremendo follón*; **to kick up** (*or* **make** *etc*) **a ~** armar un escándalo, armar un follón*.

2 (*irr: pret* **stank**, *ptp* **stunk**) *vt*: **to ~ out** *room* apestar, hacer oler mal; **to ~ sb out** ahuyentar a uno con un mal olor.

3 *vi* (**a**) heder, oler mal (*of* a); **it ~s in here** aquí huele que apesta.

(**b**) (*****) **the idea ~s** es una idea horrible; **I think the plan ~s** creo que es un proyecto abominable; **as a headmaster he ~s** como director es fatal*; **they are ~ing with money** son unos ricachos*, tienen tanto dinero que da asco.

stink-bomb ['stɪŋk'bɒm] *n* bomba *f* fétida.

stinker‡ ['stɪŋkəʳ] *n* (*person*) mal bicho *m*, canalla *m*; **you ~!** ¡bestia!*; **this problem is a ~** problema endiablado es éste.

stinking ['stɪŋkɪŋ] **1** *adj* (**a**) hediondo, fétido. (**b**) (*****) horrible, bestial, asqueroso. **2** *adv*: **to be ~ rich‡** ser un ricacho, tener tanto dinero que da asco.

stint [stɪnt] **1** *n* (**a**) (*amount of work*) destajo *m*; tarea *f*; **to do one's ~** hacer su parte, trabajar (*etc*) como se debe, (*fig*) cumplir con las obligaciones que uno tiene, hacer su contribución; **to finish one's ~** terminar el trabajo que le corresponde a uno.

(**b**) **without ~** libremente, generosamente; sin restricción.

2 *vt* limitar, restringir; escatimar; **he did not ~ his praises** no escatimó sus elogios, prodigó sus elogios; **to ~ sb of sth** privar a uno de algo, dar a uno menor cantidad de algo de la que pide (*or* necesita).

3 *vr*: **to ~ o.s.** estrecharse, privarse de cosas; **don't ~ yourself!** ¡no te prives de nada!, ¡sírvete (*etc*) cuanto quieras!; **to ~ o.s. of sth** privarse de algo, negarse algo, no permitirse algo.

stipend ['staɪpend] *n* estipendio *m*, sueldo *m*.

stipendiary [staɪ'pendɪərɪ] **1** *adj* estipendiario. **2** *n* estipendiario *m*.

stipple ['stɪpl] *vt* puntear; granear.

stipulate ['stɪpjʊleɪt] **1** *vt* estipular, poner como condición; especificar. **2** *vi*: **to ~ for sth** estipular algo, poner algo como condición.

stipulation [,stɪpjʊ'leɪʃən] *n* estipulación *f*, condición *f*.

stir[1] [stɜːʳ] **1** *n* (**a**) acto *m* de agitar (*etc*); hurgonada *f*; **to give one's tea a ~** remover su té; **give the fire a ~** remueve un poco la lumbre.

(**b**) (*fig*) conmoción *f*, revuelo *m*; sensación *f*; agitación *f*; **to cause a ~** causar una sensación, armar gran revuelo; provocar mucho interés; **it didn't make much of a ~** apenas despertó interés alguno; **there was a great ~ in parliament** hubo una gran conmoción en el parlamento.

2 *vt* (**a**) *liquid etc* remover, agitar, revolver, menear; *fire* atizar, hurgar; **to ~ sugar into coffee** añadir azúcar a su café removiéndolo; **'~ before using'** 'agítese antes de usar'.

(**b**) (*move*) mover, agitar; **a breeze ~red the leaves** una brisa movió las hojas; **he never ~ed a foot all day** no movió el pie en todo el día.

(**c**) (*fig*) *emotions* conmover, despertar; *imagination* estimular; **to ~ sb to do sth** incitar a uno a hacer algo; **to ~ sb to pity** provocar a uno a lástima, excitar compasión en uno; **to feel deeply ~red** conmoverse profundamente, estar muy emocionado; **we were all ~red by the speech** el discurso nos conmovió a todos.

3 *vi* (**a**) (*move*) moverse, menearse; **she hasn't ~red all day** no se ha movido en todo el día; **he never ~red from the spot** no abandonó el sitio ni un solo momento; **don't you ~ from here** no te muevas de aquí; **nobody is ~ring yet** están todavía en cama.

(**b**) (*****) acizañar, meter cizaña.

◆**stir up** *vt* (**a**) *liquid etc* remover, agitar, revolver, menear.

(**b**) (*fig*) *passions* excitar; *revolt* fomentar; *trouble* armar; **to ~ up the past** remover el pasado.

stir[2]‡ [stɜːʳ] *n* (*esp US*) chirona‡ *f*.

stir-fry ['stɜːfraɪ] **1** *vt* sofreír. **2** *n* sofrito *m* (chino).

stirring ['stɜːrɪŋ] **1** *adj speech etc* emocionante, conmovedor; inspirador; *period etc* turbulento, agitado. **2** *n*: **there were ~s of protest** la gente empezó a protestar; **I sense no ~ of interest** no creo que se esté despertando el interés.

stirrup ['stɪrəp] *n* estribo *m*.
stirrup-pump ['stɪrəppʌmp] *n* bomba *f* de mano.
stitch [stɪtʃ] **1** *n* (**a**) (*Sew*) puntada *f*, punto *m*; (*Med*: *in surgery*) punto *m* de sutura; **a ~ in time saves 9** una puntada a tiempo ahorra ciento, quien acude a la gotera acude a la casa; **she hadn't a ~ on** estaba en pelota; **he hadn't a dry ~ on him** estaba calado hasta los huesos; **to put ~es in a wound** suturar una herida.
(**b**) (*pain*) punto *m*, punzada *f*; **to have a ~** tener flato; **we were in ~es*** nos moríamos de risa*.
2 *vt* (*also* **to ~ down, to ~ together, to ~ up**) coser; (*Med*) suturar.
◆**stitch up**‡ *vt* incriminar dolosamente, vender*.
stitching ['stɪtʃɪŋ] *n* puntadas *fpl*, puntos *mpl*.
stoat [stəʊt] *n* armiño *m*.
stock [stɒk] **1** *n* (**a**) (*of tree*) tronco *m*, (*of vine*) cepa *f*, (*for grafting*) patrón *m*.
(**b**) (*Bot*: *species*) alhelí *m*.
(**c**) (*family*) estirpe *f*, linaje *m*, raza *f*; **of good ~** de buen linaje; **of good Castilian ~** de buena cepa castellana.
(**d**) (*handle*) mango *m*; (*of gun*) caja *f*, culata *f*.
(**e**) **~s** (*Hist*: *punishment*) cepo *m*.
(**f**) **~s** (*Naut*) astillero *m*, grada *f* de construcción; **to be on the ~s** (*ship*) estar en vía de construcción, (*book etc*) estar en preparación; **he has 3 plays on the ~s** tiene 3 obras entre manos.
(**g**) (*supply*) provisión *f*, (*Comm*) surtido *m*, existencias *fpl*, stock *m*; **~ of spares** stock *m* de recambios; **to be in ~** estar en existencia, estar en almacén; **to be out of ~** estar agotado; **we are out of ~ of umbrellas** no nos quedan paraguas, están agotados los paraguas; **to have sth in ~** tener algo en existencia; **to lay in a ~ of** proveerse de, hacer provisión de; **to take ~** hacer inventario (*of* de); **to take ~ of** (*fig*) asesorarse de, considerar; evaluar.
(**h**) (*Agr*) (*live ~*) ganado *m*, ganadería *f*; (*dead ~*) aperos *mpl*; *V* **rolling** *etc*.
(**i**) (*Culin*) caldo *m*.
(**j**) (*Fin*: *of company*) capital *m* (comercial); (*shares*) acciones *fpl*, valores *mpl*; **~s and shares** valores *mpl*; **his ~ is going up** su reputación crece, su crédito aumenta.
2 *attr* (*Comm*) de surtido, en existencia; *size etc* de serie, corriente, normal; (*Theat*) de repertorio; *phrase* hecho; *remark* banal, vulgar; *response etc* que se espera, acostumbrado, consagrado; **~ control** control *m* de existencias; **~ option plan** plan *m* que permite que los ejecutivos de una empresa compren acciones en ella a un precio favorable; **~ warrant** certificado *m* de derechos (para compra de acciones a precio fijo).
3 *vt* (**a**) (*also* **to ~ up**) (*supply*) surtir, proveer, abastecer (*with* de); **to ~ a pond with fish** poblar un charco de peces.
(**b**) (*keep*) tener existencias de, tener el almacén; **we don't ~ that brand** no tenemos esa marca; **do you ~ bananas?** ¿vende Vd plátanos?
◆**stock up 1** *vt* = **stock 3** (**a**).
2 *vi*: **to ~ up with** proveerse de, adquirir existencias de, (*fig*) ir acumulando.
stockade [stɒ'keɪd] *n* estacada *f*; (*US**) prisión *f* militar.
stockbreeder ['stɒk,bri:dəʳ] *n* ganadero *m*.
stockbreeding ['stɒk,bri:dɪŋ] *n* ganadería *f*.
stockbroker ['stɒk,brəʊkəʳ] *n* bolsista *mf*, agente *mf* de bolsa, corredor *m* de bolsa; **~ belt** zona *f* residencial de los bolsistas.
stockbroking ['stɒk,brəʊkɪŋ] *n* correduría *f* de bolsa.
stock car ['stɒkkɑ:ʳ] *n* (*Rail*) borreguero *m*, vagón *m* de ganado; (*Aut, Sport*) stock-car *m*.
stock-car racing ['stɒkkɑ:,reɪsɪŋ] *n* carreras *fpl* de stock-car.
stock company ['stɒk,kʌmpənɪ] *n* sociedad *f* anónima, sociedad *f* (*or* compañía *f*) de acciones.
stock-cube ['stɒkkju:b] *n* cubito *m*.
stock exchange ['stɒkɪks,tʃeɪndʒ] **1** *n* bolsa *f*; **to be on the ~** ser bolsista, ser miembro de la bolsa, dedicarse a negocios de bolsa; **prices on the ~** cotizaciones *fpl* de bolsa. **2** *attr* bursátil.
stockfish ['stɒkfɪʃ] *n* pescado *m* de seco.
stockholder ['stɒk,həʊldəʳ] *n* (*US*) accionista *mf*.
Stockholm ['stɒkhəʊm] *n* Estocolmo *m*.
stockily ['stɒkɪlɪ] *adv*: **~ built** de complexión robusta.
stockiness ['stɒkɪnɪs] *n* robustez *f*.
stockinet [,stɒkɪ'net] *n* tela *f* de punto.
stocking ['stɒkɪŋ] *n* media *f*; (*knee-length*) calceta *f*; **a pair of ~s** un par de medias; **in one's ~ed feet** sin zapatos.
stocking-filler ['stɒkɪŋ,fɪləʳ] *n* pequeño regalo *m* de Navidad (*que completa la 'media' de los regalos*).
stock-in-trade ['stɒkɪn'treɪd] *n* (*Comm*) capital *m*; existencias *fpl*, existencia *f* de mercancías; (*fig*) repertorio *m*; **that joke is part of his ~** es un chiste de su repertorio.
stockist ['stɒkɪst] *n* (*Brit*) distribuidor *m*, -ora *f*.
stockjobber ['stɒk,dʒɒbəʳ] *n* (*Brit*) agiotista *mf*.
stockjobbing ['stɒk,dʒɒbɪŋ] *n* agiotaje *m*.
stockkeeper ['stɒkki:pəʳ] *n* almacenero *m*, -a *f*.
stocklist ['stɒklɪst] *n* (*Fin*) lista *f* de valores y acciones; (*Comm*) lista *f* de existencias.
stock market ['stɒk,mɑ:kɪt] *n* = **stock exchange**.
stockpile ['stɒkpaɪl] **1** *n* reservas *fpl* (de materias primas). **2** *vt* acumular, poner en reserva, formar una reserva de.
stock raising ['stɒk,reɪzɪŋ] *n* ganadería *f*.
stockroom ['stɒkrʊm] *n* almacén *m*, depósito *m*.
stock-still ['stɒk'stɪl] *adv*: **to be** (*or* **stand**) **~** estar completamente inmóvil.
stocktaking ['stɒk,teɪkɪŋ] *n* (*Brit*) inventario *m*, balance *m*; **~ sale** venta *f* postbalance; **to do the ~** hacer el inventario.
stocky ['stɒkɪ] *adj* rechoncho, bajo pero fuerte.
stockyard ['stɒkjɑ:d] *n* corral *m* de ganado.
stodge* [stɒdʒ] *n* (*Brit*) comida *f* indigesta, cosas *fpl* indigestas.
stodgy ['stɒdʒɪ] *adj food* indigesto, pesado; *book, style etc* pesado.
stogie, stogy ['stəʊgɪ] *n* (*US*) cigarro *m*, puro *m*.
stoic ['stəʊɪk] **1** *adj* estoico. **2** *n* estoico *m*.
stoical ['stəʊɪkəl] *adj* estoico.
stoically ['stəʊɪklɪ] *adv* estoicamente, impasiblemente.
stoicism ['stəʊɪsɪzəm] *n* estoicismo *m*.
stoke [stəʊk] (*also* **to ~ up**) **1** *vt furnace* cargar, cebar; *fire* echar carbón a; (*fig*) cebar; (*hum*) atiborrarse de.
2 *vi* cebar el hogar, echar carbón a la lumbre; (*hum*) atiborrarse.
stoker ['stəʊkəʳ] *n* fogonero *m*.
stokehold ['stəʊkhəʊld] *n* cuarto *m* de calderas.
stokehole ['stəʊkhəʊl] *n* boca *f* del horno.
STOL [stɒl] *n abbr of* **short take-off and landing** despegue *m* y aterrizaje cortos.
stole[1] [stəʊl] *n* estola *f*.
stole[2] [stəʊl] *pret of* **steal**.
stolen ['stəʊlən] *ptp of* **steal**; **~ goods** géneros *mpl* robados.
stolid ['stɒlɪd] *adj* impasible, imperturbable; flemático; (*pej*) terco.
stolidity [stɒ'lɪdɪtɪ] *n* impasibilidad *f*, imperturbabilidad *f*; flema *f*; terquedad *f*.
stolidly ['stɒlɪdlɪ] *adv* impasiblemente, imperturbablemente.
stomach ['stʌmək] **1** *n* estómago *m*; vientre *m*; (*fig*) deseo *m*, apetito *m* (*for* de); **they have no ~ for the fight** no tienen valor para la pelea; **it turns my ~** me revuelve el estómago.
2 *attr* estomacal, de(l) estómago; **~ upset** trastorno *m* estomacal.
3 *vt* (*fig*) tragar, aguantar.
stomach-ache ['stʌməkeɪk] *n* dolor *m* de estómago.
stomach-pump ['stʌməkpʌmp] *n* bomba *f* estomacal.
stomp [stɒmp] **1** *vt* (*US*) = **stamp 2** (**a**). **2** *vi* pisar muy fuerte.
stone [stəʊn] **1** *n* (**a**) piedra *f*; (*commemorative*) lápida *f*; **within a ~'s throw** a tiro de piedra, a dos pasos; **to cast the first ~** lanzar la primera piedra; **which of you shall cast the first ~?** ¿cuál de vosotros se atreve a lanzar la primera piedra?; **to leave no ~ unturned** no dejar piedra por mover, revolver Roma con Santiago.
(**b**) (*of fruit*) hueso *m*.
(**c**) (*Med*) cálculo *m*, piedra *f*; (*as complaint*) mal *m* de piedra.
(**d**) (*Brit*: *weight*: *pl* **stone**) = *14 libras = 6,348 kg.*
2 *adj* de piedra; **S~ Age** Edad *f* de (la) Piedra.
3 *vt* (**a**) apedrear, lapidar; **~ me!**‡ ¡caray!*
(**b**) *fruit* deshuesar.
stone-blind ['stəʊn'blaɪnd] *adj* completamente ciego.
stone-broke* ['stəʊn'brəʊk] *adj* (*US*) = **stony-broke.**
stonechat ['stəʊntʃæt] *n* culiblanco *m*.
stone-cold [,stəʊn'kəʊld] *adj* muy frío, totalmente frío; **to be ~ sober** no estar borracho en lo más mínimo.
stonecrop ['stəʊnkrɒp] *n* uva *f* de gato.
stonecutter ['stəʊn,kʌtəʳ] *n* = **stonemason**.
stoned‡ [stəʊnd] *adj* (*drunk*) trompa‡, borracho, como una cuba*; (*Drugs*) colocado‡.
stone-dead ['stəʊn'ded] *adj* más muerto que una piedra; **it killed the idea ~** acabó completamente con la idea.
stone-deaf ['stəʊn'def] *adj* completamente sordo, más sordo

que una tapia.

stone-ground ['stəʊn,graʊnd] *adj flour* molido por piedras.

stonemason ['stəʊn'meɪsn] *n* albañil *m*; (*in quarry*) cantero *m*.

stone-pit ['stəʊnpɪt] *n*, **stone-quarry** ['stəʊn,kwɒrɪ] *n* cantera *f*.

stonewall ['stəʊn'wɔːl] *vi* emplear una táctica de cerrojo; (*fig*) negarse a contestar claramente, prolongar un asunto mediante evasivas.

stonewalling ['stəʊn'wɔːlɪŋ] *n* táctica *f* de cerrojo.

stoneware ['stəʊnwɛəʳ] **1** *n* gres *m*. **2** *adj* de gres.

stonewashed ['stəʊn,wɒʃt] *adj jeans* lavado a la piedra.

stonework ['stəʊnwɜːk] *n* cantería *f*, obra *f* de sillería; piedras *fpl*.

stonily ['stəʊnɪlɪ] *adv* (*fig*) glacialmente, fríamente.

stony ['stəʊnɪ] *adj* (**a**) *material* pétreo; como piedra, parecido a piedra; *ground* pedregoso, cubierto de piedras. (**b**) *glance* glacial, frío; *heart* empedernido; *stare* duro; *silence* sepulcral.

stony-broke* ['stəʊnɪ'brəʊk] *adj*: **to be ~** (*Brit*) no tener un céntimo, estar tronado*.

stony-faced [,stəʊnɪ'feɪst] *adj* de expresión pétrea.

stony-hearted ['stəʊnɪ'hɑːtɪd] *adj* de corazón empedernido.

stood [stʊd] *pret and ptp of* **stand**.

stooge* [stuːdʒ] **1** *n* hombre *m* de paja*; secuaz *m*, partidario *m*; paniaguado *m*; (*of comedian*) compañero *m*. **2** *vi*: **to ~ for sb** ayudar a uno; servir humildemente a uno.

◆**stooge about, stooge around** *vi* estar sin hacer nada, estar por ahí; vagabundear.

stook [stuːk] **1** *n* tresnal *m*, garbera *f*. **2** *vt* poner en tresnales.

stool [stuːl] *n* (**a**) (*seat*) taburete *m*, escabel *m*; (*folding*) silla *f* de tijera; **to fall between two ~s** quedarse sin el pan y sin la torta.

(**b**) (*Bot*) planta *f* madre.

(**c**) (*Med*) cámaras *fpl*.

stool-pigeon* ['stuːl,pɪdʒən] *n* soplón* *m*, chivato* *m*.

stoop¹ [stuːp] **1** *n* inclinación *f*; (*defect*) cargazón *f* de espaldas; **to walk with a ~** andar encorvado.

2 *vt* inclinar, bajar.

3 *vi* inclinarse, encorvarse; (*permanently, as defect*) ser cargado de espaldas, andar encorvado; **to ~ to pick sth up** inclinarse para recoger algo; **to ~ to** + *infin* (*fig*) rebajarse a + *infin*.

stoop² [stuːp] *n* (*US*) pórtico *m*, pequeña veranda *f*.

stooping ['stuːpɪŋ] *adj* inclinado, encorvado; cargado de espaldas.

stop [stɒp] **1** *n* (**a**) (*gen*) parada *f*; alto *m*; pausa *f*, interrupción *f*; **a 20-minute ~ for coffee** un alto de 20 minutos para tomar café; **to be at a ~** estar parado; quedar paralizado; **to bring to a ~** *vehicle* parar; *production, progress etc* parar, paralizar; **to come to a ~** venir a parar, pararse; **to come to a dead** (*or* **sudden**) **~** pararse en seco, detenerse repentinamente; **to come to a full ~** pararse, paralizarse, quedar detenido en un punto muerto; **to go on for 2 hours without a ~** continuar durante 2 horas sin parar (*or* sin interrupción); **to put a ~ to sth** poner fin a algo, acabar con algo.

(**b**) (*stay*) estancia *f*; **a ~ of a few days** una estancia de unos días.

(**c**) (*of bus, tram etc*) parada *f*; (*Aer, Naut*) escala *f*; **to make a ~ at Bordeaux** hacer escala en Burdeos.

(**d**) (*Typ*: *also* **full ~**) punto *m*.

(**e**) (*Mus*) (*of organ*) registro *m*; (*of guitar*) traste *m*; (*of other instrument*) llave *f*; **to pull out all the ~s** (*fig*) desplegar todos sus recursos, tocar todos los registros.

(**f**) (*Mech*) tope *m*, retén *m*.

(**g**) (*Phon*: *also* **~ consonant**) (consonante *f*) oclusiva *f*.

2 *vt* (**a**) (*block*: *also* **to ~ up**) *leak, hole etc* tapar; cegar; *road etc* cerrar, obstruir, bloquear; *tooth* empastar; *flow of blood* restañar; *cheque* anular, cancelar; **to ~ one's ears** taparse los oídos; **to ~ a gap** tapar un agujero, (*fig*) llenar un vacío.

(**b**) (*arrest progress of*) parar, detener; *ball, bullet, engine, car, charge, traffic etc* parar; *blow* rechazar, parar; *aggression* rechazar, contener; *danger, threat* evitar, estorbar; *process* terminar; *abuse* poner fin a, acabar con; (*forbid*) prohibir, poner fin a; **~ thief!** ¡al ladrón!; **and there is nothing to ~ him** y no hay nada que se lo impida; **the walls ~ some of the noise** las paredes suprimen una parte del ruido; **the curtains ~ the light** las cortinas impiden la entrada de la luz; **this should ~ any further trouble** esto habrá de evitar cualquier dificultad en el futuro; **to ~ sb** (**from**) **doing sth** (*prevent*) impedir a uno hacer algo, (*forbid*) prohibir a uno hacer algo; **to ~ sth being done** impedir que algo se haga; **to ~ sth happening** evitar que algo ocurra.

(**c**) (*cease*) terminar; **~ it!** ¡basta!, ¡basta ya!, ¡párate! (*LAm*); **~ that noise!** ¡basta ya de ruido!; **~ the nonsense!** ¡déjate de tonterías!; **to ~ work** suspender el trabajo, dejar de trabajar.

(**d**) (*suspend*) *payments etc* suspender; *supply* cortar, interrumpir; **to ~ sb's electricity** cortar la electricidad de uno; **to ~ sb's wages** suspender el pago del sueldo de uno; **to ~ a pound out of sb's wages** retener una libra del sueldo de uno; **all leave is ~ped** han sido cancelados todos los permisos; **to ~ the milk for a fortnight** cancelar la leche durante quince días.

3 *vi* (**a**) (*cease motion*) parar, pararse; detenerse; hacer alto; (*finish, run out*) terminarse, acabarse; (*supply etc*) cortarse, interrumpirse; (*process, rain etc*) cesar; **the car ~ped** se paró el coche; **where does the bus ~?** ¿dónde para el autobús?; **the clock has ~ped** el reloj se ha parado; **~!** ¡pare!, ¡alto!; **when the programme ~s** cuando termine el programa; **payments have ~ped** (*temporarily*) se han suspendido los pagos, (*permanently*) han terminado los pagos; **the rain has ~ped** la lluvia ha cesado, ha dejado de llover; **he seems not to know when to ~** parece no saber cuándo conviene hacer alto; **to ~ to do sth** detenerse a hacer algo.

(**b**) (*stay*) hospedarse, alojarse (*at* en, *with* con); quedarse; **she's ~ping with her aunt** se hospeda en casa de su tía; vive con su tía; **did you ~ till the end?** ¿te quedaste hasta el fin?

(**c**) (*with verb constructions*) **to ~ doing sth** dejar de hacer algo; **she never ~s talking** habla incansablemente, no termina de hablar; **it has ~ped raining** ha dejado de llover, ya no llueve.

4 *vr* (**a**) **I ~ped myself in time** me detuve a tiempo.

(**b**) **to ~ o.s. doing sth** abstenerse de hacer algo, guardarse de hacer algo; **I can't seem to ~ myself doing it** parece que no puedo dejar de hacerlo.

◆**stop away** *vi* ausentarse (*from* de); no asistir (*from* a); **you ~ away from my sister!** ¡no vengas más por aquí a molestar a mi hermana!

◆**stop behind** *vi* quedarse; quedarse en casa, no salir; **they made him ~ behind after school** le hicieron quedar en la escuela después de las clases.

◆**stop by** *vi* detenerse brevemente; **I'll ~ by your house** pasaré por tu casa; **I'll ~ by on the way to school** me asomaré de paso al colegio.

◆**stop in** *vi* quedarse en casa, no salir; **don't ~ in for me** no te quedes esperándome en casa.

◆**stop off** *vi* interrumpir el viaje (*at* en); hacer escala (*at* en).

◆**stop out** *vi* quedarse fuera; no volver a casa.

◆**stop over** *vi* pasar la noche, pernoctar; quedarse un poco.

◆**stop up 1** *vt V* **stop 2** (**a**).

2 *vi* (*Brit*) velar, no acostarse, seguir sin acostarse; **don't ~ up for me** no os quedéis esperándome hasta muy tarde.

stop-and-go ['stɒpən'gəʊ] *n* (*US*) = **stop-go**.

stopcock ['stɒpkɒk] *n* llave *f* de cierre.

stopgap ['stɒpgæp] **1** *n* (*thing*) recurso *m* provisional, expediente *m*; (*person*) tapagujeros *m*, sustituto *m*, tapaboquetes *m*. **2** *attr*: **~ measure** medida *f* interina.

stop-go ['stɒp'gəʊ] *n*: **period of ~** período *m* cuando una política de expansión económica alterna con otra de restricción.

stoplights ['stɒplaɪts] *npl* (*Aut*) luces *fpl* de freno; (*US*) luces *fpl* de tráfico, semáforo *m*.

stop-off ['stɒpɒf] *n*, **stopover** ['stɒpəʊvəʳ] *n* parada *f* intermedia; escala *f*; interrupción *f* de un viaje.

stoppage ['stɒpɪdʒ] *n* (**a**) parada *f*, cesación *f*, detención *f*; interrupción *f*; (*of work*) paro *m*, suspensión *f*; (*of pay*) suspensión *f*; (*from pay*) descuento *m*; (*in game*) detención *f*; (*strike*) huelga *f*. (**b**) (*blockage*) obstrucción *f*.

stopper ['stɒpəʳ] **1** *n* tapón *m*; (*Tech*) taco *m*, tarugo *m*. **2** *vt* tapar, taponar.

stopping ['stɒpɪŋ] **1** *n* (**a**) parada *f*; suspensión *f*. (**b**) (*of tooth*) empaste *m*. **2** *adj*: **~ train** tren *m* correo, tren *m* ómnibus.

stopping-place ['stɒpɪŋpleɪs] *n* paradero *m*; (*of bus etc*) parada *f*.

stop-press ['stɒp'pres] *n* (*also* **~ news**) noticias *fpl* de última hora; '**~**' (*as heading*) 'al cerrar la edición'.

stopwatch ['stɒpwɒtʃ] *n* cronógrafo *m*.

storage ['stɔːrɪdʒ] **1** *n* almacenaje *m*, depósito *m*; (*Comput*) almacenamiento *m*; **to put sth into ~** poner algo en almacén.

2 *attr*: **~ battery** acumulador *m*; **~ capacity** capacidad *f* de almacenaje; **~ charges** derechos *mpl* de almacenaje; **~ device** dispositivo *m* de almacenaje; **~ heater** acumulador *m*; **~ room** (*US*) trastero *m*; **~ space** depósito *m*; **~ tank** (*for oil etc*) tanque *m* de almacenamiento; (*for rainwater*) tanque *m* de reserva; **~ unit** (*furniture*) armario *m*.

store [stɔːʳ] **1** *n* (**a**) (*stock*) provisión *f*; (*reserve*) reserva *f*; repuesto *m*; (*Brit*: *storehouse*) almacén *m*, depósito *m*; **to be in ~** estar en almacén, estar en depósito; **what is in ~ for sb** lo que le espera a uno, lo que la suerte tiene guardado para uno; **what has the future in ~ for us?** ¿qué guarda el futuro para nosotros?; **that is a treat in ~** eso es un placer que nos guarda el futuro; **to have** (*or* **keep**) **sth in ~** tener algo en reserva; **to lay in a ~ of** hacer provisión de, proveerse de; **to put** (*or* **set**) **great ~ by sth** conceder mucha importancia a algo, estimar algo en mucho; **to set little ~ by sth** conceder poca importancia a algo, estimar algo en poco.

(**b**) (*quantity*) abundancia *f*; tesoro *m*; **a great ~ of expertise** gran pericia *f*; **he has a ~ of knowledge about ...** tiene grandes conocimientos de ...

(**c**) **~s** (*Mil etc*) (*food*) víveres *mpl*, provisiones *fpl*, (*equipment*) pertrechos *mpl*; (**war**) **~s** material *m* bélico.

(**d**) (*shop*: *esp US*) tienda *f*, almacén *m*; **Bloggs's S~s** Almacenes *mpl* Bloggs; (*US*) **~ clerk** dependiente *m*, -a *f*; **to mind the ~*** (*US*) cuidar de los asuntos; *V* **department store**.

2 *attr* (*US*: *also* **~-bought**) de confección, de serie.

3 *vt* almacenar; poner en reserva, tener en reserva, guardar; *documents* archivar; (*Comput*) almacenar.

4 *vi* conservarse (bien *etc*).

◆**store away** *vt* almacenar; poner en reserva, tener en reserva, guardar.

◆**store up** *vt* acumular, ir acumulando, amontonar; **a hatred ~d up over centuries** un odio almacenado durante siglos.

store card ['stɔːkɑːd] *n* tarjeta *f* de compra.

storefront ['stɔːfrʌnt] *n* (*US*) escaparate *m*.

storehouse ['stɔːhaʊs] *n*, *pl* **storehouses** ['stɔːˌhaʊzɪz] almacén *m*, depósito *m*; (*fig*) mina *f*, tesoro *m*.

storekeeper ['stɔːˌkiːpəʳ] *n* almacenero *m*; (*US*) tendero *m*; (*Naut*) pañolero *m*.

storeroom ['stɔːrʊm] *n* despensa *f*; depósito *m*; (*Naut*) pañol *m*.

storey, (*US*) **story²** ['stɔːrɪ] *n* piso *m*; **a 9-~ building** un edificio de 9 pisos.

storeyed, (*US*) **storied** ['stɔːrɪd] *adj ending in compounds*: **an 8-~ building** un edificio de 8 pisos.

stork [stɔːk] *n* cigüeña *f*.

storm [stɔːm] **1** *n* (**a**) (*Met*) tormenta *f*, tempestad *f*, temporal *m*; (*Naut*) borrasca *f*; (*of wind*) vendaval *m*, huracán *m*; **to brave the ~** aguantar la tempestad; **to ride out a ~** capear un temporal, hacer frente a un temporal.

(**b**) (*fig*) tempestad *f*, borrasca *f*; **a ~ in a teacup** (*Brit*) una tempestad en un vaso de agua; **~ of abuse** torrente *m* de injurias; **~ of criticism** vendaval *m* de críticas, nube *f* de críticas; **there were ~s of applause** sonaron fuertes aplausos, hubo repetidas salvas de aplausos; **there was a political ~** hubo un gran revuelo político; **it caused an international ~** levantó una polvareda internacional; **to bring a ~ about one's ears** atraer sobre sí una lluvia de protestas.

(**c**) (*Mil*) **to take a town by ~** tomar una ciudad por asalto; **the play took Paris by ~** la obra cautivó a todo París.

2 *vt* (*Mil*) asaltar, tomar por asalto.

3 *vi* rabiar, bramar; **to ~ at sb** tronar contra uno, enfurecerse con uno; **he came ~ing into my office** entró rabiando en mi oficina; **he ~ed on for an hour about the government** pasó una hora lanzando improperios contra el gobierno; **he ~ed out of the meeting** salió de la reunión como un huracán.

stormbound ['stɔːmbaʊnd] *adj* inmovilizado por el mal tiempo.

storm centre, (*US*) **storm center** ['stɔːmˌsentəʳ] *n* centro *m* de la tempestad; (*fig*) foco *m* de los disturbios, centro *m* de la agitación.

stormcloud ['stɔːmklaʊd] *n* nubarrón *m*.

storm-door ['stɔːmdɔːʳ] *n* contrapuerta *f*.

storming ['stɔːmɪŋ] *n* asalto *m* (*of* a).

stormproof ['stɔːmpruːf] *adj* a prueba de tormentas.

storm-signal ['stɔːmˌsɪgnl] *n* señal *f* de temporal.

storm-tossed ['stɔːmtɒst] *adj* sacudido por la tempestad.

storm-trooper ['stɔːmˌtruːpəʳ] *n* guardia *m* de asalto.

storm-troops ['stɔːmtruːps] *npl* tropas *fpl* de asalto.

stormwater ['stɔːmˌwɔːtəʳ] *n* agua *f* de lluvia.

stormy ['stɔːmɪ] *adj* tempestuoso, borrascoso (*also fig*); **~ petrel** (*Orn*) petrel *m* de la tempestad, (*fig*) persona *f* pendenciera, persona *f* de vida borrascosa.

story¹ ['stɔːrɪ] *n* (**a**) (*account*) historia *f*, relación *f*, relato *m*; (*Liter*) cuento *m*, historieta *f*; (*joke*) cuento *m*, chiste *m*; **the ~ of her life** la historia de su vida; **the ~ of their travels** la relación de sus viajes; **his ~ is that ...** según él dice ..., según lo que él cuenta ...; **that's another ~** eso es harina de otro costal; **that's not the whole ~** no te lo han contado en su totalidad, hay una parte que no te han contado; **it's the** (**same**) **old ~** es lo de siempre; **it's a long ~** es largo de contar; **to cut a long ~ short** para abreviar, en resumidas cuentas; **the ~ goes that ...** dice el cuento que ...; **to tell a ~** contar un cuento, narrar una historia; **the marks tell their own ~** las señales hablan por sí solas, las señales no necesitan interpretación; **the full ~ has still to be told** todavía no se ha hecho pública toda la historia; **what a ~ this house could tell!** ¡cuántas cosas nos diría esta casa!

(**b**) (*plot*) argumento *m*, trama *f*.

(**c**) (*fig*) cuento *m*, mentira *f*; embuste *m*; **a likely ~!** ¡puro cuento!, ¡qué cuento más inverosímil!; **to tell stories** contar embustes; **don't tell stories!** ¡no me vengas con tus embustes!

(**d**) (*Press, TV*) artículo *m*; reportaje *m*; noticia *f*.

story² ['stɔːrɪ] *n* (*US Archit*) = **storey**.

storyboard ['stɔːrɪˌbɔːd] *n* (*Cine*) dibujos *mpl* (*or* fotos *fpl*) secuenciales de imágenes, guión *m* gráfico.

storybook ['stɔːrɪbʊk] **1** *n* libro *m* de cuentos. **2** *attr*: **a ~ ending** una conclusión como el fin de una novela.

story-line ['stɔːrɪlaɪn] *n* argumento *m*.

storyteller ['stɔːrɪˌteləʳ] *n* cuentista *mf*; (*fibber*) cuentista *mf*, embustero *m*, -a *f*.

story-writer ['stɔːrɪˌraɪtəʳ] *n* narrador *m*, -ora *f*.

stoup [stuːp] *n* copa *f*, frasco *m*; (*Eccl*) pila *f*.

stout [staʊt] **1** *adj* (**a**) (*solid*) sólido, robusto, macizo, fuerte; *person* gordo, corpulento; (*sturdy*) fornido.

(**b**) (*fig*) (*brave*) valiente; (*resolute*) resuelto; *resistance etc* terco, tenaz; **~ fellow!** ¡muy bien!; **he's a ~ fellow** es un buen chico; **with ~ hearts** resueltamente.

2 *n* (*Brit*) *especie de cerveza negra*.

stout-hearted ['staʊt'hɑːtɪd] *adj* valiente, resuelto.

stoutly ['staʊtlɪ] *adv*: **~ built** de construcción sólida, fuerte; **to resist ~** resistir tenazmente; **he ~ maintains that ...** sostiene resueltamente que ...

stoutness ['staʊtnɪs] *n* gordura *f*, corpulencia *f*.

stove¹ [stəʊv] *n* (*for heating*) estufa *f*; (*esp US*: *for cooking*) hornillo *m*, cocina *f* (de gas *etc*), horno *m* (*LAm*), estufa *f* (*Mex*).

stove² [stəʊv] *pret and ptp of* **stave**.

stovepipe ['stəʊvpaɪp] **1** *n* tubo *m* de estufa. **2** *attr*: **~ hat** chistera *f*.

stow [stəʊ] *vt* meter, poner, colocar; (*Naut*) estibar, arrumar; (*and hide*: *also* **to ~ away**) esconder; **where can I ~ this?** ¿esto dónde lo pongo?; **~ it!‡** ¡déjate de eso!, ¡cállate!, ¡basta ya!

◆**stow away** **1** *vt*: **to ~ food away*** despachar rápidamente una comida, zamparse una comida.

2 *vi* viajar de polizón (*on a ship* en un buque), viajar sin pagar y clandestinamente.

stowage ['stəʊɪdʒ] *n* (*act*) estiba *f*, arrumaje *m*; (*place*) bodega *f*.

stowaway ['stəʊəweɪ] *n* polizón *m*, llovido *m*.

strabismus [strə'bɪzməs] *n* estrabismo *m*.

Strabo ['streɪbəʊ] *nm* Estrabón.

straddle ['strædl] *vt* esparrancarse encima de, estar con una pierna a cada lado de; *horse* montar a horcajadas; *target* horquillar.

strafe [strɑːf] *vt* bombardear, cañonear, atacar; destrozar a tiros.

strafing ['strɑːfɪŋ] *n* ametrallamiento *m*.

straggle ['strægl] *vi* (*lag*) rezagarse; (*get lost*) extraviarse; (*spread*) extenderse, estar esparcido; (*wander*) vagar, vagar en desorden, (*Bot*) lozanear; **the village ~s on for miles** el pueblo se extiende varios kilómetros (sin tener un plano fijo); **the guests ~d out into the night** los invitados salieron poco a poco y desaparecieron en la noche; **her hair ~s over her face** el pelo le cae en desorden por la cara.

◆**straggle away, straggle off** *vi* dispersarse.

straggler ['stræglər] *n* rezagado *m*, -a *f*.

straggling ['stræglɪŋ] *adj*, **straggly** ['stræglɪ] *adj* disperso; rezagado; extendido; desordenado.

straight [streɪt] **1** *adj* (**a**) (*not bent*) derecho, recto; *line* recto; *back* erguido; *hair* lacio; **he carries himself as ~ as a ramrod** se mantiene perfectamente erguido; **~ razor** (*US*) navaja *f* de barbero.

(**b**) (*honest*) honrado; *answer* franco, directo; *denial, refusal* categórico, rotundo; **as ~ as a die** (*fig*) derecho como una vela, honrado a carta cabal; **is he ~?** ¿es de fiar?; **let me be ~ with you** te digo esto con toda franqueza, no hagamos confusiones.

(**c**) (*plain, uncomplicated*) sencillo; *drink* sin mezcla, puro; (*Pol*) *fight* de dos candidatos solamente; (*Theat*) *part, play* serio; **~ man** (*Theat*) actor *m* que da pie al cómico.

(**d**) (*in order*) en orden; **it's all ~ now** todo está en regla ya; **your tie isn't ~** tu corbata no está bien; **let's get this ~** pongamos las cosas claras, digámoslo claramente; vamos a concretar; **to put things ~** arreglar cosas, poner las cosas en orden; **to put the record ~** hacer constar la verdad, explicar los hechos; **are your affairs ~ at last?** ¿por fin has arreglado tus asuntos?

(**e**) (*: *not gay*) hetero*, heterosexual, no homosexual.

2 *adv* (**a**) (*in a ~ line*) derecho, directamente, en línea recta; **to fly ~** volar en línea recta; **~ above us** directamente encima de nosotros; **it's ~ across the road from us** está exactamente enfrente de nosotros; **~ ahead, ~ on** todo seguido, todo recto, derecho (*LAm*); **keep ~ on for Toledo** vayan Vds todo seguido para Toledo; **I went ~ home** fui derecho a mi casa; **I went ~ to my room** fui derecho a mi cuarto, fui a mi cuarto sin detenerme para nada; **to look sb ~ in the eye** mirar directamente a los ojos de uno.

(**b**) (*immediately, without diversion*) directamente; inmediatamente; **~ after this** inmediatamente después de esto; luego; **~ away** en seguida, inmediatamente; **~ off** sin parar, sin interrupción; de un tirón; sin vacilar; **for 3 days ~ off** durante 3 días seguidos; **he read the whole of Proust ~ off** leyó toda la obra de Proust de un tirón; **she just went ~ off** se fue sin vacilar; **he said ~ off that ...** dijo sin vacilar que ...; **to come ~ to the point** ir directamente al grano; **to drink ~ from the bottle** beber de la misma botella.

(**c**) (*frankly*) francamente, con franqueza; (*honestly*) honradamente; **I tell you ~, I'll give it to you ~** te lo digo con toda franqueza; **~ out** francamente, sin rodeos; **he's always dealt very ~ with me** siempre se ha portado conmigo como hombre honrado, siempre me ha tratado con justicia; **~ up!*** ¡te lo juro!

(**d**) (*pure*) sin mezcla; **we drink it ~** lo bebemos sin mezcla.

(**e**) (*) **to go ~** enmendarse, hacer nueva vida, vivir dentro de la ley; **he's been going ~ for a year now** lleva un año sin tener nada que ver con el crimen.

(**f**) (*Theat*) **he played the part ~** hizo el papel de manera seria; **we'll do 'Lear' ~ this time** esta vez haremos 'Lear' sin bromas.

3 *n*: **the ~** (*Racing, Rail*) la recta; **out of** (**the**) **~** fuera de la plomada, no vertical; **to depart from the ~ and narrow** apartarse del buen camino; **to keep sb on the ~ and narrow** asegurar que uno no se aparte del buen camino.

straightaway ['streɪtə'weɪ] *adv* en seguida, inmediatamente, luego, luego (*Mex*).

straightedge ['streɪtedʒ] *n* regla *f* de borde recto.

straighten ['streɪtn] **1** *vt* (*also* **to ~ out**) enderezar, poner derecho; (*fig*) arreglar, poner en orden; *problem* resolver; *confused situation* desenmarañar.

2 *vi* (*person*) enderezarse, ponerse derecho; erguirse.

◆**straighten out** *vt* = **straighten 1**.

◆**straighten up 1** *vt room* arreglar.

2 *vi* enderezarse, ponerse derecho; erguirse.

3 *vr*: **to ~ o.s. up** = **straighten 2**.

straight-faced ['streɪt'feɪst] **1** *adj* serio, grave, solemne; **a ~ attitude** una actitud seria.

2 *adv*: **he told the joke very ~** contó el chiste con cara muy seria.

straightforward [ˌstreɪt'fɔːwəd] *adj* (*honest*) honrado; (*plain-spoken*) franco; (*simple*) sencillo; *answer* claro, franco.

straightforwardly [ˌstreɪt'fɔːwədlɪ] *adv* honradamente; francamente; sencillamente.

straightforwardness [ˌstreɪt'fɔːwədnɪs] *n* honradez *f*; franqueza *f*; sencillez *f*; claridad *f*.

straightness ['streɪtnɪs] *n* (*honesty*) sinceridad *f*, honestidad *f*; (*frankness*) franqueza *f*.

straight-out* ['streɪtaʊt] *adj answer, refusal* sincero, franco; *supporter, enthusiast, thief* cien por cien.

strain[1] [streɪn] **1** *n* (**a**) (*Mech*) tensión *f*; esfuerzo *m*; (*damage*) deformación *f*; **the ~ on a rope** la tensión de una cuerda; **to take the ~ off a beam** disminuir la presión sobre una viga; **can you take some of the ~?** ¿me puedes ayudar a sostener (*etc*) esto?

(**b**) (*fig*) tensión *f*, tirantez *f*; esfuerzo *m* (grande, excesivo); (*mental*) agotamiento *m* nervioso, postración *f* nerviosa; **the ~s of international politics** las tensiones de la política internacional; **the ~s on the economy** las presiones sobre la economía; **the ~s of modern life** las tensiones de la vida moderna; **the ~ of 6 hours at the wheel** el agotamiento nervioso que producen 6 horas al volante; **to write without ~** escribir sin esfuerzo; **to put a great ~ on sb** someter a uno a gran esfuerzo; exigir un gran esfuerzo a uno.

(**c**) (*Med*) torcedura *f*; distensión *f* (muscular).

(**d**) (*Mus*) **~s** son *m*, compases *mpl*; **the ~s of a waltz** los compases de un vals; **the bride came in to the ~s of the wedding march** la novia entró a los acordes (*or* compases) de la marcha nupcial.

(**e**) (*tenor*) tenor *m*, estilo *m*, sentido *m*; **there was a lot else in the same ~** hubo mucho más a este tenor.

2 *vt* (**a**) (*stretch*) estirar, poner tirante, tender con fuerza.

(**b**) (*Med: overtax*) deformar, dañar por esfuerzo excesivo; *back, muscle etc* torcerse; *eyes* cansar; *heart* cansar (exigiendo un esfuerzo excesivo a); *patience etc* cansar, abusar de; *meaning, word* forzar, hacer violencia a; *friendship, relationship* pedir demasiado a; crear tensiones en, crear tirantez en; **to ~ one's ears to hear** esforzarse por oír; **to ~ the law to help sb** hacer violencia a una ley para ayudar a uno.

(**c**) **to ~ sb to one's breast**†† (*liter*) abrazar a uno estrechamente, estrechar a uno entre los brazos.

(**d**) (*filter*) filtrar; (*Culin*) colar.

3 *vi*: **to ~ at sth** esforzarse tirando de algo, tirar con fuerza de algo; **don't ~ at it** no te esfuerces tanto, no te hagas daño tirando tanto; **they ~ed at the crate** manipularon el cajón con gran esfuerzo; **to ~ after sth** esforzarse por conseguir algo; **to ~ to do sth** esforzarse por hacer algo, hacer grandes esfuerzos por lograr algo.

◆**strain off** *vt*: **to ~ the water off** separar el agua, colar el agua.

strain[2] [streɪn] *n* (*breed*) raza *f*, linaje *m*; (*tendency*) tendencia *f*; **a ~ of weakness** un rasgo de debilidad; **a ~ of madness** una vena de locura.

strained [streɪnd] *adj muscle etc* torcido; *laugh, smile etc* forzado; *relations* tenso, tirante; *style* que muestra esfuerzo, afectado.

strainer ['streɪnər] *n* (*Culin*) colador *m*; (*Tech*) filtro *m*, coladero *m*.

strait [streɪt] *n* (**a**) (*Geog*: *also* **~s**) estrecho *m*; **the S~ of Gibraltar** el Estrecho de Gibraltar.

(**b**) (*fig*) **~s** estrecheces *fpl*; situación *f* apurada, apuro *m*; **to be in dire ~s** estar muy apurado; **the economic ~s we are in** el aprieto económico en que nos encontramos.

straitened ['streɪtnd] *adj*: **in ~ circumstances** en apuro, en la necesidad.

straitjacket ['streɪt,dʒækɪt] *n* camisa *f* de fuerza; (*fig*) corsé *m*.

strait-laced ['streɪt'leɪst] *adj* gazmoño; remilgado.

strand[1] [strænd] (*Naut*) **1** *n* (*liter*) playa *f*, ribera *f*.

2 *vt ship* varar, encallar; **to ~ sb without money in London** dejar a uno sin dinero ni recursos en Londres; **to be ~ed** (*person*) quedar solo, estar sin poderse ayudar, estar abandonado, (*by missing train etc*) quedarse colgado; (*car etc*) quedar inmovilizado; **to leave sb ~ed** dejar a uno desamparado, dejar a uno plantado.

3 *vi* varar, encallar.

strand[2] [strænd] *n* (*of rope*) ramal *m*; (*of thread*) hebra *f*, filamento *m*; (*of hair*) trenza *f*; (*of plant*) brizna *f*; **to tie up the loose ~s** (*fig*) atar cabos.

strange [streɪndʒ] *adj* (*unknown*) desconocido (*to* de); (*new*) nuevo (*to* para), no acostumbrado; (*odd*) extraño, raro, curioso; (*exotic*) exótico, peregrino; **how ~!** ¡qué raro!; **it is ~ that ...** es raro que + *subj*; **I find it ~ that ...** me extraña que + *subj*, para mí resulta incomprensible que +

subj; **I felt rather ~ at first** al principio no me sentí cómodo, me sentí algo molesto al principio; **I am ~ to the work** soy nuevo en el oficio, el trabajo es nuevo para mí; **~ to say** ... aunque parece mentira ...; **I never sleep well in a ~ bed** no duermo nunca bien en una cama que no sea la mía; **don't talk to any ~ men** no hables con ningún desconocido.

strangely ['streɪndʒlɪ] *adv* extrañamente; de un modo raro; **it was ~ familiar to me** me era extrañamente familiar; **she acts somewhat ~** se comporta de un modo bastante raro; **~ (enough), I never met him** aunque parezca mentira, no le conocí nunca.

strangeness ['streɪndʒnɪs] *n* novedad *f*; extrañeza *f*, rareza *f*; lo exótico.

stranger ['streɪndʒəʳ] *n* desconocido *m*, -a *f*; (*from another area etc*) forastero *m*, -a *f*; **he's a ~ to me** es un desconocido para mí; **I'm a ~ here** no soy de aquí, soy nuevo aquí; **hullo ~!** ¡cuánto tiempo sin vernos!; **you're quite a ~!** ¡apenas te dejas ver!; **he is no ~ to vice** conoce bien los vicios.

strangle ['stræŋgl] *vt* estrangular; (*fig*) *abuse, sob etc* ahogar; **a ~d cry** un grito entrecortado.

stranglehold ['stræŋglhəʊld] *n* (*Sport*) collar *m* de fuerza; (*fig*) dominio *m* completo; **to have a ~ on sth** dominar algo completamente.

strangler ['stræŋgləʳ] *n* estrangulador *m*.

strangling ['stræŋglɪŋ] *n* estrangulación *f*.

strangulated ['stræŋgjʊleɪtɪd] *adj* estrangulado; **~ hernia** hernia *f* estrangulada.

strangulation [,stræŋgjʊ'leɪʃən] *n* estrangulación *f* (*also Med*).

strap [stræp] **1** *n* correa *f*; (*Sew etc*) tira *f*, banda *f*; (*shoulder ~*) tirante *m*, hombrera *f*; **to give sb the ~** azotar a uno, darle a uno con la correa.

2 *vt* (**a**) (*tie*) atar con correa.

(**b**) **to ~ sb** (*as punishment*) azotar a uno, darle a uno con la correa.

◆**strap down** *vt*: **to ~ sb down** sujetar a uno con correa.

◆**strap in** *vt object, child* sujetar con correas; **he isn't properly ~ped in** no está bien atado.

◆**strap on** *vt object* atar con correas; *watch* ponerse.

◆**strap up** *vt* = **strap 2** (**a**).

strapped [stræpt] *adj*: **to be ~ for funds** andar mal de dinero, tener dificultades económicas.

strap-hang* ['stræphæŋ] *vi* viajar de pie (agarrado a la correa).

strap-hanger* ['stræphæŋəʳ] *n* pasajero *m*, -a *f* que va de pie (agarrado, -a a la correa).

strapless ['stræplɪs] *adj dress* sin tirantes.

strapping ['stræpɪŋ] *adj* robusto, fornido.

Strasbourg ['stræzbɜːg] *n* Estrasburgo *m*.

strata ['strɑːtə] *n, pl of* **stratum**.

stratagem ['strætɪdʒəm] *n* estratagema *f*.

strategic(al) [strə'tiːdʒɪk(əl)] *adj* estratégico.

strategist ['strætɪdʒɪst] *n* estratega *mf*.

strategy ['strætɪdʒɪ] *n* estrategia *f*.

stratification [,strætɪfɪ'keɪʃən] *n* estratificación *f*.

stratified ['strætɪfaɪd] *adj* estratificado.

stratify ['strætɪfaɪ] **1** *vt* estratificar. **2** *vi* estratificarse.

stratigraphic [,strætɪ'græfɪk] *adj* estratigráfico.

stratigraphy [strə'tɪgrəfɪ] *n* estratigrafía *f*.

stratocumulus [,streɪtəʊ'kjuːmjʊləs] *n, pl* **stratocumuli** [,streɪtəʊ'kjuːmjʊlaɪ] estratocúmulo *m*.

stratosphere ['strætəʊsfɪəʳ] *n* estratosfera *f*.

stratospheric [,strætəʊs'ferɪk] *adj* estratosférico.

stratum ['strɑːtəm] *n, pl* **strata** ['strɑːtə] estrato *m*; (*fig*) estrato *m*, capa *f*.

stratus ['streɪtəs] *n, pl* **strati** ['streɪtaɪ] estrato *m*.

straw [strɔː] **1** *n* paja *f*; (*drinking ~*) pajita *f*, popote *m* (*Mex*), pitillo *m* (*And, Carib*), sorbete *m* (*Carib, SC*); **to drink through a ~** sorber con una pajita; **it's the last ~!** ¡es el colmo!, ¡no faltaba más!; **it's a ~ in the wind** sirve de indicio; **to clutch at ~s** agarrarse a un clavo ardiendo; **to draw** (*or* **get**) **the short ~** ser elegido para hacer algo desagradable; **the ~ that breaks the camel's back** la gota que colma el vaso.

2 *attr* de paja; (*colour*) pajizo, color paja; **~ hat** sombrero *m* de paja, canotier *m*; **~ man** hombre *m* de paja; **~ poll, ~ vote** votación *f* de tanteo.

strawberry ['strɔːbərɪ] *n* (*fruit and plant*) fresa *f*, frutilla *f* (*LAm*); (*large, cultivated*) fresón *m*; **~ blonde** rubia *f* fresa; **~ mark** (*on skin*) mancha *f* de nacimiento, antojo *m*.

strawberry-bed ['strɔːbərɪbed] *n* fresal *m*.

straw-coloured, (*US*) **straw-colored** ['strɔːkʌləd] *adj* pajizo, color paja.

strawloft ['strɔːlɒft] *n* pajar *m*, pajera *f*.

stray [streɪ] **1** *adj animal etc* extraviado; mostrenco; *bullet* perdido; (*isolated*) aislado; (*scattered*) disperso; (*sporadic*) esporádico; **a ~ cat** un gato extraviado, un gato callejero; **in a few ~ cases** en algunos casos aislados; en algún que otro caso; **a few ~ thoughts** unos cuantos pensamientos inconexos.

2 *n* (**a**) (*animal*) animal *m* extraviado *m*; (*child*) niño *m* sin hogar, niño *m* desamparado, niña *f* sin hogar, niña *f* desamparada.

(**b**) **~s** (*Rad*) parásitos *mpl*.

3 *vi* (*lose o.s.*) extraviarse, perderse; (*wander*) vagar, errar; **to ~ from** apartarse de (*also fig*); **we had ~ed 2 kilometres from the path** nos habíamos desviado 2 kilómetros del camino; **they ~ed into the enemy camp** erraron el camino y se encontraron en el campamento enemigo; **if the gate is left open the cattle ~** si se deja abierta la puerta las vacas se escapan; **my thoughts ~ed to the holidays** empecé a pensar en las vacaciones.

streak [striːk] **1** *n* raya *f*, lista *f*, línea *f* delgada; (*of mineral*) veta *f*, vena *f*; (*fig: of madness etc*) vena *f*; (*of luck*) racha *f*; **~ of lightning** rayo *m* (*also fig*); **there is a ~ of Spanish blood in her** tiene una pequeña parte de sangre española; **he had a yellow ~** era un tanto cobarde; **he went past like a ~ (of lightning)** pasó como un rayo.

2 *vt* rayar (*with* de).

3 *vi* (**a**) **to ~ along** correr a gran velocidad; **to ~ past** pasar como un rayo.

(**b**) (*) correr desnudo.

streaker* ['striːkəʳ] *n* corredor *m* desnudo, corredora *f* desnuda.

streaking* ['striːkɪŋ] *n* carrera *f* desnudista.

streaky ['striːkɪ] *adj* (**a**) rayado, listado; (*Brit*) *bacon* veteado, entreverado; *rock etc* veteado. (**b**) *shot* afortunado.

stream [striːm] **1** *n* (*brook*) arroyo *m*, riachuelo *m*; (*river*) río *m*; (*current*) corriente *f*; (*jet etc*) chorro *m*, flujo *m*; (*fig*) torrente *m*; lluvia *f*, oleada *f*; (*of cars etc*) caravana *f*, riada *f*; **~s of abuse** torrente *m* de injurias; **~s of people** una multitud de gente, un sinfín de gente; **~ of consciousness** monólogo *m* interior; **an unbroken ~ of cars** una riada de coches; **the B ~** (*Brit Scol*) el grupo B; **people were coming out in ~s** la gente salía en tropel; **in one continuous ~** ininterrumpidamente; **against the ~** contra la corriente; **with the ~** con la corriente; **to come on ~** (*oilwell etc*) empezar a producir; (*Comm*) entrar en (pleno) funcionamiento.

2 *attr*: **~ feed** alimentación *f* continua.

3 *vt* (**a**) *water etc* derramar, dejar correr; *blood* manar; **his face ~ed blood** la sangre le corría por la cara.

(**b**) (*Scol*) clasificar, poner en grupos.

4 *vi* (*liquid*) correr, fluir; (*blood*) manar, correr; (*in wind etc*) ondear, flotar; **her eyes were ~ing** lloraba a mares; **the gas made my eyes ~** el gas me hizo lagrimear; **her cheeks were ~ing with tears** las lágrimas le corrían por las mejillas, tenía las mejillas bañadas en lágrimas; **to ~ out** (*liquid*) brotar, chorrear, salir a borbotones; **people came ~ing out** la gente salía en tropel; **the cars kept ~ing past** los coches pasaban ininterrumpidamente; **her hair ~ed in the wind** su pelo le ondeaba al viento.

streamer ['striːməʳ] *n* flámula *f*; (*Naut*) gallardete *m*; (*of paper, at parties etc*) serpentina *f*.

streaming ['striːmɪŋ] *n* (*Scol*) división *f* en grupos.

streamline ['striːmlaɪn] *vt* aerodinamizar; (*fig*) coordinar, perfeccionar, hacer más eficiente.

streamlined ['striːmlaɪnd] *adj* aerodinámico.

street [striːt] **1** *n* calle *f*; **it's right up my ~** (*Brit*) de eso sí sé algo; eso viene pintiparado para mí; **to be ~s ahead of sb** (*Brit*) llevar mucha ventaja a uno, haberse adelantado mucho a uno; **we are ~s ahead of them in design** les damos ciento y raya en el diseño; **they're ~s apart** les separa un abismo, no tienen color*; **they're not in the same ~ as us** (*Brit*) no están a nuestra altura, no admiten comparación con nosotros; **to be on the ~s** (*prostitute*) hacer la calle; *V* **walk 2** (**d**).

2 *attr* callejero, de la calle; **~ accident** accidente *m* de circulación; **~ arab** golfo *m*, chicuelo *m* de la calle; **~ cred(ibility)** dominio *m* de la contracultura urbana; **~ cry** pregón *m*; **~ incident** incidente *m* callejero; **at ~ level** en el nivel de la calle; **~ market** mercado *m* callejero; **~ musician** músico *m* ambulante; **~ photographer** fotógrafo *m* callejero; **~ theatre** teatro *m* de calle; **~ value** valor *m* en la calle; ~ **vendor** (*US*) vendedor *m* callejero, vendedora *f* callejera.

streetcar ['stri:tkɑ:ʳ] *n* (*US*) tranvía *m*.

street-cleaner ['stri:t,kli:nəʳ] *n* barrendero *m*, -a *f*.

street door ['stri:t'dɔ:ʳ] *n* puerta *f* principal, puerta *f* de la calle.

street-fighting ['stri:t,faɪtɪŋ] *n* luchas *fpl* en las calles.

street lamp ['stri:tlæmp] *n*, **street light** ['stri:tlaɪt] *n* farol *m*.

street-lighting ['stri:t,laɪtɪŋ] *n* alumbrado *m* público.

street-map ['stri:tmæp] *n* plano *m* (de la ciudad).

streetsmart ['stri:tsmɑ:t] *adj* (*US*) = **streetwise**.

street-sweeper ['stri:t,swi:pəʳ] *n* barrendero *m*.

street-urchin ['stri:t,ɜ:tʃɪn] *n* golfo *m*, chicuelo *m* de la calle.

streetwalker ['stri:t,wɔ:kəʳ] *n* (prostituta *f*) callejera *f*.

streetwise ['stri:twaɪz] *adj child* pícaro; muy listo, de mucha mundología; experimentado en la vida callejera.

strength [streŋθ] *n* (**a**) (*gen*) fuerza *f*; (*toughness*) resistencia *f*; (*of person*) fuerzas *fpl*, vigor *m*; (*of colour, feeling etc*) intensidad *f*; (*of drink*) fuerza *f*; **the ~ of the pound** (*exchange value*) el valor de la libra; (*high value*) la fortaleza de la libra, el vigor de la libra; **~ of character** carácter *m*, firmeza *f* de carácter; **~ of will** resolución *f*; **on the ~ of** fundándose en, confiando en; **on the ~ of that success she applied for promotion** a base de ese éxito solicitó el ascenso; **with all one's ~** con todas sus fuerzas; **his ~ failed him** se sintió desfallecer, le abandonaron sus fuerzas; **give me ~!** ¡Dios me dé paciencia!; **it goes from ~ to ~** está cada vez más fuerte; **to save** (*or* **reserve**) **one's ~** reservarse.

(**b**) (*Mil etc*) número *m*, complemento *m*; efectivos *mpl*; **to be at full ~** tener todo su complemento; **to be below** (*or* **under**) **~** no tener suficiente mano de obra (*or* suficientes efectivos *etc*); **his supporters were there in ~** asistían muchos partidarios suyos; **they came in ~** vinieron en gran número; **to be on the ~** ser miembro del regimiento (*etc*); ser de plantilla; **to take sb on to the ~** dar a uno un puesto en el regimiento (*etc*).

strengthen ['streŋθən] **1** *vt* fortalecer, reforzar, hacer más fuerte; consolidar. **2** *vi* fortalecerse, reforzarse, hacerse más fuerte; consolidarse.

strengthening ['streŋθənɪŋ] **1** *adj* (*Med etc*) fortificante, tonificante. **2** *n* fortalecimiento *m*, refuerzo *m*; consolidación *f*.

strenuous ['strenjʊəs] *adj* (*energetic*) enérgico, vigoroso; (*tough*) arduo; (*exhausting*) agotador; *opposition etc* tenaz; *exercise* fuerte; **to make ~ efforts to** + *infin* esforzarse enérgicamente por + *infin*.

strenuously ['strenjʊəslɪ] *adv* enérgicamente, vigorosamente; tenazmente; **to try ~ to** + *infin* procurar por todos los medios + *infin*.

streptococcus [,streptəʊ'kɒkəs] *n*, *pl* **streptococci** [,streptəʊ'kɒkaɪ] estreptococo *m*.

streptomycin [,streptəʊ'maɪsɪn] *n* estreptomicina *f*.

stress [stres] **1** *n* (**a**) (*constraining force*) fuerza *f*, compulsión *f*; presión *f*; **under ~ of** bajo la compulsión de, impulsado por.

(**b**) (*strain*) tensión *f*; (*Med*) estrés *m*, tensión *f* nerviosa; **the ~es and strains of modern life** las presiones y tensiones de la vida moderna; **times of ~** tiempos *mpl* difíciles; **to be under ~** sufrir una tensión nerviosa; **to subject sb to great ~** someter a uno a grandes tensiones.

(**c**) (*emphasis*) énfasis *m*; (*Ling*) acento *m* tónico; **~ mark** tilde *m*; **~ system** sistema *m* de acentos, acentuación *f*; **the ~ is on the second syllable** el acento tónico cae en la segunda sílaba, la segunda sílaba está acentuada; **to lay great ~ on sth** insistir mucho en algo, subrayar algo, recalcar la importancia de algo.

(**d**) (*Mech*) tensión *f*, carga *f*; esfuerzo *m*.

2 *vt* (**a**) (*Ling*) acentuar.

(**b**) (*emphasize*) subrayar, recalcar; poner el énfasis en; insistir en; llamar la atención sobre; **I must ~ that ...** tengo que subrayar que ...

stressed [strest] *adj* acentuado.

stressful ['stresfʊl] *adj* lleno de tensión (nerviosa); que produce tensión (nerviosa), estresante.

stretch [stretʃ] **1** *n* (**a**) (*act of ~ing*) extensión *f*; estirón *m*; **for hours at a ~** durante horas enteras; **3 days at a ~** 3 días seguidos; **he read the lot at one ~** los leyó todos de un tirón; **to be at full ~, to go at full ~** esforzarse al máximo, emplear todas sus fuerzas (físicas *etc*); **when the engine is at full ~** cuando el motor rinde su potencia máxima; **with arms at full ~** con los brazos completamente extendidos; **by a ~ of the imagination** con un esfuerzo de imaginación; **not by any ~ of the imagination** aun haciendo un gran esfuerzo de imaginación.

(**b**) (*amount of ~*) elasticidad *f*; **~ fabric** tela *f* elástica.

(**c**) (*distance*) trecho *m*; extensión *f*; (*of road etc*) tramo *m*; (*scope*) alcance *m*; (*of time*) período *m*; **in that ~ of the river** en aquella parte del río; **a splendid ~ of countryside** un magnífico paisaje; **for a long ~ it runs between ...** una extensión considerable corre entre ...; **for a long ~ of time** durante mucho tiempo.

(**d**) (‡) **a ~** una condena de un año de prisión; **a 5-year ~** una condena de 5 años; **he's doing a ~** está en chirona‡.

2 *vt* (**a**) (*also* **to ~ out**) (*pull out*) extender, estirar, alargar; (*widen*) ensanchar, dilatar; *arm* extender; *hand etc* tender, alargar; (*spread on ground etc*) extender; **to ~ one's legs** estirar las piernas, (*after stiffness*) desentumecerse las piernas, (*fig*) dar un paseíto; **the blow ~ed him** (**out**) **cold on the floor** el golpe le tumbó sin sentido en el suelo.

(**b**) *money, resources* estirar, hacer llegar; **our resources are fully ~ed** nuestros recursos están empleados a tope.

(**c**) *meaning* forzar, violentar; **that's ~ing it too far** eso va demasiado lejos; **to ~ the rules for sb** ajustar las reglas a beneficio de uno; *V* **point**.

(**d**) *athlete, student etc* exigir el máximo esfuerzo a; **the course does not ~ the students enough** el curso no exige bastante esfuerzo a los estudiantes.

3 *vi* (*also* **to ~ out**) extenderse, estirarse, alargarse; ensancharse, dilatarse; (*after sleep etc*) desperezarse, estirar los brazos (*etc*), desentumecerse las piernas; **this cloth won't ~** esta tela no se estira, esta tela no da de sí; **will it ~?** (*ie reach*) ¿llega?; **how far will it ~?** ¿hasta dónde llega?; ¿hasta dónde se extiende?; **it ~es for miles along the river** se extiende varios kilómetros a lo largo del río.

4 *vr*: **to ~ o.s.** (**a**) (*after sleep etc*) estirarse, estirarse los brazos.

(**b**) (*make effort*) esforzarse al máximo; **he doesn't ~ himself** no se esfuerza bastante, no se exige bastante esfuerzo a sí mismo.

◆**stretch out 1** *vt* = **stretch 2** (**a**).

2 *vi*: **he ~ed out on the ground** se tendió en el suelo; **to ~ out to reach sth** alargar el brazo (*etc*) para tomar algo; *V also* **stretch 3**.

◆**stretch up** *vi*: **to ~ up to reach sth** alargar el brazo (*etc*) para tomar algo.

stretcher ['stretʃəʳ] **1** *n* (*Tech*) (*for gloves etc*) ensanchador *m*; (*for canvas*) bastidor *m*; (*Archit*) soga *f*; (*Med*) camilla *f*. **2** *vt*: **to ~ sb away** (*or* **off**) llevar a uno en camilla.

stretcher-bearer ['stretʃə,bɛərəʳ] *n* camillero *m*.

stretcher-case ['stretʃəkeɪs] *n* enfermo *m*, -a *f* (*or* herido *m*, -a *f*) que tiene que ser llevado en camilla.

stretcher-party ['stretʃə,pɑ:tɪ] *n* equipo *m* de camilleros.

stretchmark ['stretʃ,mɑ:k] *n* estría *f*.

stretchy ['stretʃɪ] *adj* elástico.

strew [stru:] (*irr*: *pret* **strewed**, *ptp* **strewed** *or* **strewn**) *vt* (*scatter*) derramar, esparcir; (*cover*) cubrir, sembrar (*with* de); **to ~ one's belongings about the room** dejar sus cosas en desorden por todo el cuarto; **there were fragments ~n about everywhere** había fragmentos desparramados por todas partes; **to ~ sand on the floor** cubrir el suelo de arena, esparcir arena sobre el suelo; **the floors are ~n with rushes** los suelos están cubiertos de juncos.

striated [straɪ'eɪtɪd] *adj* estriado.

stricken ['strɪkən] *adj* (*and in some senses ptp of* **strike**) (*wounded*) herido; (*doomed*) condenado; (*suffering*) afligido; (*damaged*) destrozado; (*ill*) enfermo; **the ~ city** la ciudad condenada, la ciudad destrozada; **the ~ families** las familias afligidas; **to be ~ with** estar afligido por; **to be ~ with grief** estar agobiado por el dolor; **she was ~ with remorse** le remordió la conciencia.

-stricken ['strɪkən] *adj ending in compounds*: **drought~** aquejado de sequía, afectado por la sequía.

strict [strɪkt] *adj* (**a**) (*precise*) estricto; exacto, preciso; riguroso; **in the ~ sense of the word** en el sentido estricto de la palabra; **we need ~ accuracy here** aquí es necesario emplear la más rigurosa exactitud; **~ liability** (*Jur*) responsabilidad *f* absoluta; **~ neutrality** neutralidad *f* rigurosa; **in ~ confidence** en la más absoluta confianza (*and V* **confidence**).

(**b**) (*severe, stern*) *order, ban etc* terminante; *discipline* severo, riguroso; *person* severo, riguroso; escrupuloso; **they're terribly ~ here** aquí son terriblemente rigurosos; **to be ~ with sb** ser severo con uno, tratar a uno con severidad.

strictly ['strɪktlɪ] *adv* (*V adj*) (**a**) estrictamente; exactamente; rigurosamente; ~ **confidential** estrictamente confidencial; '~ **private**' (*notice*) 'propiedad privada', 'prohibido el paso'; ~ **speaking** en rigor; **not** ~ **true** no del todo verdad; ~ **between ourselves** ... en confianza entre los dos ...; **to be** ~ **accurate** ... para decirlo con toda precisión ...; **to remain** ~ **neutral** guardar la más rigurosa neutralidad.

(**b**) terminantemente; severamente; rigurosamente; **to treat sb very** ~ tratar a uno con mucha severidad; **she was** ~ **brought up** se la educó estrictamente; **it is** ~ **forbidden to** + *infin* queda terminantemente prohibido + *infin.*

strictness ['strɪktnɪs] *n* (*V adj*) (**a**) exactitud *f*; rigor *m.* (**b**) severidad *f*; lo terminante.

stricture ['strɪktʃəʳ] *n* (**a**) (*Med*) constricción *f.* (**b**) (*fig*) censura *f*, crítica *f*, reparo *m*; **to pass** ~**s on sb** censurar a uno, poner reparos a uno.

stridden ['strɪdn] *ptp of* **stride.**

stride [straɪd] **1** *n* zancada *f*, tranco *m*, paso *m* largo; (*in measuring*) paso *m*; **he set off with big** ~**s** partió a grandes zancadas; **to get into one's** ~, **to hit one's** ~ (*US*) alcanzar el ritmo acostumbrado, cogerle el tranquillo a la tarea; **to make great** ~**s** hacer grandes progresos; **to take it in one's** ~ sabérselo tomar bien, hacerlo sin cejar, estar a la altura de las circunstancias.

2 (*irr*: *pret* **strode,** *ptp* **stridden**) *vt horse* montar a horcajadas; poner una pierna a cada lado de; (*cross*) cruzar de un tranco.

3 *vi* (*also* **to** ~ **along**) andar a trancos, andar a pasos largos, dar zancadas.

◆**stride away, stride off** *vi* alejarse a grandes zancadas.

◆**stride up** *vi*: **to** ~ **up and down** andar de aquí para allá a pasos largos; **to** ~ **up to sb** acercarse resueltamente a uno.

stridency ['straɪdənsɪ] *n* estridencia *f*, estridor *m*; lo chillón; lo estrepitoso.

strident ['straɪdənt] *adj* estridente; *colour, person* chillón; *protest* fuerte, estrepitoso.

stridently ['straɪdəntlɪ] *adv* ruidosamente, de modo estridente; estrepitosamente.

strife [straɪf] *n* lucha *f*; (*not armed*) lucha *f*, contienda *f*; disensión *f*; **domestic** ~ riñas *fpl* domésticas; **internal** ~ disensión *f* interna; **to cease from** ~ deponer las armas.

strife-ridden ['straɪf,rɪdn] *adj* conflictivo.

strike [straɪk] **1** *n* (**a**) (*of labour*) huelga *f*, paro *m* (*esp LAm*); **to be on** ~ estar en huelga; **to come out on** ~, **to go on** ~ ponerse en huelga, declarar la huelga.

(**b**) (*discovery*) descubrimiento *m* (repentino); **a big oil** ~ un descubrimiento de petróleo en gran cantidad; **to make a** ~ hacer un descubrimiento.

(**c**) (*Sport*) golpe *m.*

(**d**) (*Mil*) ataque *m*; **air** ~ ataque *m* aéreo, bombardeo *m.*

2 *attr*: ~ **ballot,** ~ **vote** votación *f* a huelga; ~ **committee** comité *m* de huelga; ~ **force** fuerza *f* de asalto; fuerza *f* expedicionaria.

3 (*irr*: *pret* **struck,** *ptp* **struck** *and in some senses* **stricken**) *vt* (**a**) (*hit*) golpear; (*with fist etc*) pegar, dar una bofetada a; (*wound*) herir; (*Tech*) percutir; (*with bullet etc*) alcanzar; *ball* golpear; *blow* asestar (*at* a); *chord, note* tocar; *instrument* herir, pulsar; tocar; **never** ~ **a woman** no pegar nunca a una mujer; **he struck her** (**a blow**) la pegó, le dio un golpe; **to** ~ **one's fist on the table, to** ~ **the table with one's fist** golpear la mesa con el puño; **the president was struck by two bullets** el presidente fue alcanzado por dos balas; **the tower was struck by lightning** cayó un rayo en la torre; **a fisherman was struck by lightning** un pescador fue alcanzado por un rayo; **the light** ~**s the window** la luz hiere la ventana.

(**b**) (*produce, make*) *coin, medal* acuñar; *a light, match* frotar, encender; **to** ~ **sparks from sth** hacer que algo eche chispas; **to** ~ **a cutting** hacer que un esqueje arranque; **to** ~ **root** echar raíces, arraigar; **to** ~ **terror into sb** infundir terror a uno.

(**c**) (*collide with, meet*) dar con; *rocks etc* chocar contra, estrellarse contra; *mine* chocar con; *difficulty, obstacle* encontrar, topar con; **a sound struck my ear** un ruido hirió mi oído; **what** ~**s the eye is the poverty** lo que más llama la atención es la pobreza; **his head struck the beam** dio con la cabeza contra la viga.

(**d**) (*of thoughts, impressions*) **it** ~**s me that** ..., **the thought** ~**s me that** ... se me ocurre que ...; **has it ever struck you that** ...? ¿has pensado alguna vez que ...?; **it** ~**s me as being most unlikely** se me hace muy poco probable; **at least that's how it** ~**s me** por lo menos eso es lo que pienso yo; **how does she** ~ **you?** ¿qué te parece (ella)?, ¿qué impresión te hace ella?; **I was much struck by his sincerity** su sinceridad me impresionó mucho; **I'm not much struck** (**with him**) no me hace buena impresión.

(**e**) (*find*) descubrir, encontrar; **to** ~ **oil** descubrir un yacimiento de petróleo, (*fig*) encontrar una mina; **he struck it rich** descubrió un buen filón, tuvo mucha suerte.

(**f**) (*take down*) **to** ~ **camp** levantar el campamento; **to** ~ **the flag** arriar la bandera.

(**g**) **to** ~ **work** abandonar el trabajo, declarar la huelga.

(**h**) *attitude* tomar, adoptar.

(**i**) (*arrive at, attain*) **to** ~ **an average** sacar el promedio; **to** ~ **a balance** (*Comm*) hacer balance, (*fig*) establecer un equilibrio (*between* entre); **to** ~ **a bargain** cerrar un trato; **to** ~ **a deal** llegar a un acuerdo, (*Comm*) cerrar un trato.

(**j**) (*delete*) borrar, tachar.

(**k**) (*cause to become*) **to** ~ **sb blind** cegar a uno; **to** ~ **sb dead** matar a uno; **may I be struck dead if** ... que me maten si ...; **to** ~ **sb dumb** (*fig*) dejar a uno sin habla.

4 *vi* (**a**) (*attack, Mil etc*) atacar; (*snake etc*) morder, atacar; **now is the time to** ~ éste es el momento para atacar; **to** ~ **against sth** dar con algo, dar contra algo, chocar contra algo; **to** ~ **at sb** asestar un golpe a uno, tratar de golpear a uno; acometer a uno; (*Mil*) atacar a uno; **this** ~**s at our very existence** esto amenaza nuestra misma existencia; **when panic** ~**s** cuando cunde el pánico, cuando se extiende el pánico.

(**b**) (*clock*) dar la hora; **the clock has struck** ha dado la hora ya; **when one's hour** ~**s** cuando llega la hora de uno.

(**c**) (*labour*) abandonar el trabajo, declarar la huelga; estar en huelga, huelguear (*And*); **to** ~ **for higher wages** hacer una huelga para conseguir un aumento de los sueldos.

(**d**) (*match*) encenderse.

(**e**) (*Naut*: *run aground*) encallar; tocar el fondo, dar contra las rocas.

(**f**) (*esp Naut*: *surrender*) arriar la bandera.

(**g**) (*Bot*) echar raíces, arraigar.

(**h**) (*move, go*) **to** ~ **across country** ir a campo traviesa; **to** ~ **into the woods** ir por el bosque, penetrar en el bosque; **the sun** ~**s through the mist** el sol penetra por entre la niebla.

(**i**) **to** ~ (**it**) **lucky** tener suerte, estar de suerte.

◆**strike back** *vi* devolver el golpe (*at* a); tomar represalias (*at* contra).

◆**strike down** *vt* derribar; (*kill*) matar; **he was struck down by paralysis** tuvo una parálisis, le acometió una parálisis; **he was struck down in his prime** se le llevó la muerte en la flor de la vida.

◆**strike off 1** *vt* (**a**) (*cut off*) cortar; cercenar, quitar de golpe; (*from list*) borrar, tachar.

(**b**) (*deduct*) rebajar.

(**c**) (*Typ*) tirar, imprimir.

2 *vi*: **the road** ~**s off to the right** el camino tuerce a la derecha.

◆**strike on** *vt*: **to** ~ **on an idea** ocurrírsele a uno una idea.

◆**strike out 1** *vt* borrar, tachar.

2 *vi* (**a**) empezar a repartir golpes; **to** ~ **out wildly** dar golpes sin mirar a quien.

(**b**) (*set off*) **to** ~ **out for the shore** (empezar a) nadar (resueltamente) hacia la playa; **to** ~ **out for o.s., to** ~ **out on one's own** hacerse independiente, hacer rancho aparte, obrar por cuenta propia.

◆**strike through 1** *vt* tachar. **2** *vi* penetrar, pasar por.

◆**strike up 1** *vt music* iniciar, empezar a tocar; *conversation* entablar; *friendship* trabar.

2 *vi*: **the orchestra struck up** la orquesta empezó a tocar.

◆**strike upon** *vt* = **strike on.**

strike-bound ['straɪkbaʊnd] *adj* paralizado por la huelga.

strikebreaker ['straɪk,breɪkəʳ] *n* esquirol *m.*

strike fund ['straɪkfʌnd] *n* fondo *m* de huelga.

strike pay ['straɪkpeɪ] *n* subsidio *m* de huelga.

striker ['straɪkəʳ] *n* (**a**) (*worker*) huelguista *mf.* (**b**) (*Sport*) ariete *m.*

striking ['straɪkɪŋ] *adj* (**a**) notable, impresionante; chocante, sorprendente; *contrast etc* acusado; *colour etc* llamativo; **of** ~ **appearance** de aspecto impresionante; **a** ~ **woman** una mujer imponente; **it is** ~ **that** ... es chocante que ... (**b**) **the** ~ **workers** los obreros que están de huelga.

strikingly ['straɪkɪŋlɪ] *adv* notablemente; de modo sorprendente; **a** ~ **beautiful woman** una mujer de notable hermosura, una mujer extraordinariamente hermosa.

string [strɪŋ] **1** *n* (**a**) (*cord*) cuerda *f*, mecate *m* (*Carib, Mex*); (*thin*) cordel *m*, bramante *m*; guita *f*; (*of beads*) hilo *m*, sarta *f*, collar *m*; (*of onions, garlic*) ristra *f*; (*of horses etc*) reata *f*; (*of lies*) sarta *f*; (*of curses*) serie *f*, retahila *f*; (*row*) fila *f*, hilera *f*; (*of people*) hilera *f*, desfile *m*; (*of vehicles*) caravana *f*; **a whole ~ of errors** toda una serie de errores; **to have sb on a ~** dominar a uno completamente, tener a uno en un puño; **to have two ~s to one's bow** tener dos cuerdas en su arco; **to pull ~s** tocar resortes, mover palancas.

(**b**) (*Mus*) cuerda *f*; **~s** instrumentos *mpl* de cuerda.

(**c**) (*Bot*) fibra *f*, nervio *m*.

(**d**) (*fig*) condición *f*; **without ~s** sin condiciones; **there are no ~s attached** esto es sin compromiso alguno.

(**e**) (*Comput*) cadena *f*.

2 *attr*: **~ bag** bolsa *f* de red; **~ beans** habichuelas *fpl*, judías *fpl* verdes, ejotes *mpl* (*Mex*), porotos *mpl* verdes (*SC*); **~ instrument** instrumento *m* de cuerda; **~ orchestra** orquesta *f* de cuerdas; **~ quartet** cuarteto *m* de cuerdas.

3 (*irr*: *pret and ptp* **strung**) *vt* (**a**) *pearls etc* (*also* **to ~ together**) ensartar; *bow, violin* encordar; **to ~ sentences together** ir ensartando frases; **they are just stray thoughts strung together** son pensamientos aislados que se han ensartado sin propósito*.

(**b**) *beans etc* desfibrar.

◆**string along*** **1** *vt*: **to ~ sb along** embaucar a uno. **2** *vi* ir también, venir también; **to ~ along with sb** pegarse a uno, acompañar a uno.

◆**string out** *vt* espaciar, escalonar; extender; **the posts are strung out across the desert** hay una serie de puestos aislados a través del desierto; **the convoy is strung out along the road** la caravana se extiende por la carretera; **his plays are strung out over 40 years** aparecieron sus obras a intervalos durante 40 años.

◆**string up 1** *vt* (**a**) *onions etc* colgar (con cuerda); *nets* extender; (*) *victim* ahorcar, linchar. (**b**) **to be all strung up** estar muy tenso, estar muy nervioso.

2 *vr*: **to ~ o.s. up to do sth** resolverse a hacer algo, cobrar ánimo para hacer algo.

stringed [strɪŋd] *adj instrument* de cuerda(s); **4-~** de 4 cuerdas.

stringency ['strɪndʒənsɪ] *n* (*V adj*) (**a**) rigor *m*, severidad *f*. (**b**) tirantez *f*, dificultad *f*; **economic ~** situación *f* económica apurada, estrechez *f*.

stringent ['strɪndʒənt] *adj* (**a**) riguroso, severo; **~ rules** reglas *fpl* rigurosas; **we shall have to be ~ about it** tendremos que obrar con rigor.

(**b**) (*Comm etc*) tirante, difícil.

stringently ['strɪndʒəntlɪ] *adv* severamente, rigurosamente.

stringer ['strɪŋəʳ] *n* (*journalist*) corresponsal *mf* local.

string-pulling ['strɪŋ,pʊlɪŋ] *n* enchufismo* *m*.

string vest [,strɪŋ'vest] *n* camiseta *f* de malla.

stringy ['strɪŋɪ] *adj* fibroso, lleno de fibras.

strip [strɪp] **1** *n* (**a**) tira *f*; banda *f*, faja *f*; (*of land*) zona *f*, franja *f*; (*of metal*) cinta *f*, lámina *f*; (*cartoon*) tira *f*; (*Aer*: *landing ~*) pista *f*; **to tear sb off a ~*, to tear a ~ off sb*** poner a uno como un trapo*.

(**b**) (*Brit Sport*) camiseta *f*; colores *mpl*.

(**c**) (*) acto *m* de desnudarse, despelote* *m*; **~ club, ~ joint** (*US**), **~ show** (show *m* de) estriptise *f*, espectáculo *m* de desnudo; **to do a ~** desnudarse, despelotarse*.

2 *vt* (**a**) (*denude*) desnudar, quitar la ropa (*etc*) a; **to ~ sb naked** desnudar a uno completamente, dejar a uno en cueros; **to ~ sb of sth** despojar a uno de algo; **to ~ a house of its furniture** dejar una casa sin muebles; **to ~ a company of its assets** despojar a una empresa de su activo; **~ped of all the verbiage, this means ...** sin toda la palabrería, esto quiere decir ...; **to ~ sb to the skin** dejar a uno en cueros.

(**b**) (*Tech*: *also* **to ~ down**) desmontar, desmantelar; *gears* estropear.

3 *vi* desnudarse, quitarse la ropa; **to ~ to the skin** quitarse toda la ropa; **to ~ to the waist** desnudarse hasta la cintura.

◆**strip down** *vt* = **strip 2** (**b**).

◆**strip off 1** *vt paint etc* quitar; (*violently*) arrancar; **to ~ off one's clothes** quitarse (rápidamente) la ropa, despojarse de la ropa; **the wind ~ped the leaves off the trees** el viento arrancó las hojas de los árboles.

2 *vi* desnudarse; (*paint etc*) desprenderse; separarse.

strip cartoon ['strɪpkɑː'tuːn] *n* (*Brit*) historieta *f*, tira *f* cómica, banda *f* de dibujos.

stripe [straɪp] **1** *n* raya *f*, lista *f*, banda *f*; (*Mil*) galón *m*; (*lash*) azote *m*, (*weal*) cardenal *m*; **of the worst ~** de la peor calaña. **2** *vt* rayar, listar (*with* de).

striped [straɪpt] *adj* listado, rayado; *trousers etc* a rayas.

strip lighting ['strɪp,laɪtɪŋ] *n* (*Brit*) alumbrado *m* fluorescente, alumbrado *m* de tubos.

stripling ['strɪplɪŋ] *n* mozuelo *m*, joven *m* imberbe.

stripper* ['strɪpəʳ] *n* estriptista* *mf*.

strip poker [,strɪp'pəʊkəʳ] *n* strip poker *m*.

strip-search ['strɪpsɜːtʃ] **1** *n* (*also* **~ing**) registro *m* en el que la persona se ha de desnudar. **2** *vt*: **he was ~ed at the airport** se tuvo que desnudar para ser registrado en el aeropuerto.

striptease ['strɪptiːz] *n* estriptise *f*, striptease *m*.

strip-wash ['strɪpwɒʃ] **1** *n* lavado *m* por completo (de un inválido). **2** *vt* lavar por completo (a un inválido).

stripy ['straɪpɪ] *adj* listado, rayado.

strive [straɪv] (*irr*: *pret* **strove**, *ptp* **striven**) *vi* esforzarse, afanarse, luchar; **to ~ after sth, to ~ for sth** luchar por conseguir algo, afanarse por conseguir algo; **to ~ against sth** luchar contra algo; **to ~ to do sth** esforzarse por hacer algo, luchar por hacer algo.

striven ['strɪvn] *ptp of* **strive**.

striving ['straɪvɪŋ] *n* esfuerzos *mpl*, el esforzarse.

strobe [strəʊb] **1** *adj lights* estroboscópico. **2** *n* (**a**) (*also* **~ light, ~ lighting**) luces *fpl* estroboscópicas. (**b**) = **stroboscope**.

stroboscope ['strəʊbəskəʊp] *n* estroboscopio *m*.

strode [strəʊd] *pret of* **stride**.

stroke [strəʊk] **1** *n* (**a**) (*blow*) golpe *m*; **10 ~s of the lash** 10 azotes; **~ of lightning** rayo *m*; **at a ~, at one ~** de un golpe; **with one ~ of his knife** de un solo cuchillazo; **with one fell ~** de un solo golpe fatal.

(**b**) (*Sport etc*: *Cricket, Golf*) golpe *m*; jugada *f*; (*Billiards*) tacada *f*; (*Rowing*) remada *f*, golpe *m*; (*Swimming*: *movement*) brazada *f*, (*type of ~*) estilo *m*; **with a total of 281 ~s** con un total de 281 golpes; **good ~!** ¡muy bien!; **he went ahead at every ~** se adelantaba con cada brazada; **they are rowing a fast ~** reman a ritmo rápido; **to put sb off his ~** hacer que uno falle con su golpe; **he hasn't done a ~ of work** no ha hecho absolutamente nada; **he doesn't do a ~** no da golpe; **~ of diplomacy** éxito *m* diplomático; **~ of genius** rasgo *m* de ingenio, genialidad *f*; **the idea was a ~ of genius** la idea ha sido genial; **~ of luck** racha *f* de suerte; **by a ~ of luck** por suerte; **then we had a ~ of luck** luego nos favoreció la suerte; **a good ~ of business** un buen negocio; **his greatest ~ was to ...** su golpe maestro fue ...

(**c**) (*of bell, clock*) campanada *f*; **on the ~ of 12** al acabar de dar las 12, a las 12 en punto; **to arrive on the ~ (of time)** llegar a la hora justa.

(**d**) (*of piston*) carrera *f*; **two-~ engine** motor *m* de dos tiempos.

(**e**) (*Med*) ataque *m* fulminante, apoplejía *f*; **to have a ~** tener una apoplejía; *V* **heatstroke**.

(**f**) (*of pen*) trazo *m*; rasgo *m*, plumada *f*, plumazo *m*; (*of pencil*) trazo *m*; (*of brush*) pincelada *f*; (*Typ*) barra *f* oblicua; **at a ~ of the pen, with one ~ of the pen** de un plumazo; **with a thick ~ of the pen** con un trazo grueso de la pluma.

(**g**) (*Rowing*: *person*) primer remero *m*; **to row ~** ser el primer remero, remar en el primer puesto.

(**h**) (*caress*) caricia *f*; **she gave the cat a ~** acarició el gato; **with a light ~ of the hand** con un suave movimiento de la mano; con una leve caricia.

2 *vt* (**a**) (*caress*) acariciar; frotar suavemente; *chin* pasar la mano sobre, pasar la mano por.

(**b**) **to ~ a boat** ser el primer remero; **to ~ a boat to victory** ser el primero remero del bote vencedor.

stroll [strəʊl] **1** *n* paseo *m*, vuelta *f*; **to go for a ~, to have a ~, to take a ~** dar un paseo (*o* una vuelta).

2 *vi* pasear(se), dar un paseo, deambular, callejear; **to ~ up and down** pasearse de acá para allá; **to ~ up to sb** acercarse tranquilamente a uno.

stroller ['strəʊləʳ] *n* paseante *mf*; (*US*) cochecito *m*, sillita *f* de ruedas.

strong [strɒŋ] **1** *adj* fuerte; recio, robusto; enérgico; vigoroso; sólido; (*Fin*) firme; *accent* marcado; *believer* fervoroso; *candidate* que tiene buenas posibilidades, respetable; *characteristic* acusado; *coffee* fuerte, cargado; *colour* intenso; *constitution* robusto; *conviction* profundo, sincero; *drink* fuerte, alcohólico; *emotion* fuerte, intenso; *evidence* fehaciente; *feature* acusado; *flavour* fuerte; *language* fuerte, indecente; *measure* enérgico; *personality* enérgico, fuerte; *point* (*of argument*) fuerte; *protest* enérgico; *reason* convincente; *situation* dramático, lleno de emoción; *smell* fuerte, penetrante, punzante; *solution* concentrado; *suit* (*Cards*) largo; *supporter* acérrimo; *tea* fuerte, cargado; *terms* enfático; *verb* irregular; *voice* fuerte; *wind* fuerte, recio, violento; **to be as ~ as a horse** ser tan fuerte como un toro; **to be ~ in the arm** tener los brazos fuertes; **to be ~ in** (*or* **on**) **chemistry** estar fuerte en química; **we are ~ in forwards** tenemos una buena línea delantera; **the gallery is ~ in Goya** el museo es rico en obras de Goya; **he's getting ~er every day** se va reponiendo poco a poco; **when you are ~ again** cuando te hayas repuesto del todo; **a group 20 ~** un grupo de 20 (miembros *etc*); **they were 50 ~** eran 50, contaban 50.

2 *adv*: **the market closed ~** el mercado se cerró en situación firme; **to come on ~*** mostrarse demasiado severo; reaccionar demasiado; **she was coming on ~*** se veía que ella se sentía atraída por él (*etc*); **the firm is still going ~** la empresa todavía marcha bien; **she was still going ~ at 92** se encontraba todavía en forma a los 92 años; **he was still going ~ at the tape** al llegar a la cinta corría todavía con pleno vigor; **he pitches it pretty ~** exagera mucho, es un exagerado.

strong-arm ['strɒŋɑːm] *adj policy, methods* de mano dura.

strong-armed ['strɒŋ'ɑːmd] *adj* de brazos fuertes.

strongbox ['strɒŋbɒks] *n* caja *f* de caudales, caja *f* fuerte.

stronghold ['strɒŋhəʊld] *n* fortaleza *f*, plaza *f* fuerte; (*fig*) baluarte *m*, centro *m*; **the last ~ of ...** el último reducto de ...

strongly ['strɒŋlɪ] *adv* fuertemente; enérgicamente, vigorosamente; firmemente; fervorosamente; intensamente; **I ~ believe that ...** creo firmemente que ...; **he smelled ~ of beer** despedía fuerte olor a cerveza; **~ built** sólidamente construido, de construcción sólida; **~ marked** acusado, acentuado; **a ~ worded letter** una carta de tono enérgico.

strongman ['strɒŋmæn] *n, pl* **strongmen** ['strɒŋmen] (*Circus*) forzudo *m*, hércules *m*; (*Pol etc*) hombre *m* fuerte.

strong-minded ['strɒŋ'maɪndɪd] *adj* resuelto, decidido; de carácter.

strong-mindedly [ˌstrɒŋ'maɪndɪdlɪ] *adv* resueltamente.

strong-mindedness ['strɒŋ'maɪndɪdnɪs] *n* resolución *f*; carácter *m*.

strongpoint ['strɒŋpɔɪnt] *n* fuerte *m*, puesto *m* fortificado.

strongroom ['strɒŋrʊm] *n* cámara *f* acorazada.

strong-willed ['strɒŋ'wɪld] *adj* resuelto, de voluntad firme; (*pej*) obstinado.

strontium ['strɒntɪəm] *n* estroncio *m*; **~ 90** estroncio *m* 90.

strop [strɒp] **1** *n* suavizador *m*. **2** *vt* suavizar.

strophe ['strəʊfɪ] *n* estrofa *f*.

stroppy* ['strɒpɪ] *adj*: **to get ~** (*Brit*) cabrearse*, ponerse negro*, ponerse chulo*.

strove [strəʊv] *pret of* **strive**.

struck [strʌk] *pret and ptp of* **strike**.

structural ['strʌktʃərəl] *adj* estructural.

structuralism ['strʌktʃərəlɪzəm] *n* estructuralismo *m*.

structuralist ['strʌktʃərəlɪst] **1** *adj* estructuralista. **2** *n* estructuralista *mf*.

structurally ['strʌktʃərəlɪ] *adv* estructuralmente, desde el punto de vista de la estructura; **~ sound** de estructura sólida.

structure ['strʌktʃəʳ] **1** *n* estructura *f*; construcción *f*. **2** *vt* estructurar.

structured ['strʌktʃəd] *adj* estructurado; **~ activity** actividad *f* estructurada.

struggle ['strʌgl] **1** *n* lucha *f*; contienda *f*, conflicto *m*; (*effort*) esfuerzo *m*; **without a ~** sin luchar, (*bloodlessly*) sin efusión de sangre; **the ~ for survival** la lucha por la vida; **the ~ to find a flat** la lucha por encontrarse un piso.

2 *vi* luchar; esforzarse; bregar, forcejear, debatirse; **to ~ to do sth** luchar por hacer algo, esforzarse por hacer algo; **to ~ in vain** luchar en vano; **to ~ to one's feet** levantarse con esfuerzo; **he ~d up the rock** subió penosamente por la roca; **the light tries to ~ through the panes** la luz se esfuerza por penetrar por los cristales; **we ~d through the crowd** nos abrimos camino bregando por la multitud.

◆**struggle along** *vi* (*lit*) avanzar con dificultad, avanzar penosamente; (*fig*: *financially*) ir apurado.

◆**struggle back** *vi* (*return*) volver penosamente; **to ~ back to solvency** esforzarse por volver a ser solvente.

◆**struggle on** *vi* seguir luchando; seguir resistiendo; no cejar; **we ~d on another kilometre** avanzamos con dificultad un kilómetro más.

struggling ['strʌglɪŋ] *adj artist etc* poco reconocido; **a ~ novelist** un novelista que lucha por abrirse camino.

strum [strʌm] **1** *vt guitar etc* rasguear; tocar distraídamente. **2** *vi* cencerrear.

strumpet ['strʌmpɪt] *n* ramera *f*.

strung [strʌŋ] *pret and ptp of* **string**; *V* **highly**.

strut¹ [strʌt] *vi* (*also* **to ~ about, to ~ along**) pavonearse, contonearse; **to ~ into a room** entrar pavoneándose en un cuarto; **to ~ past sb** pasar delante de uno con paso majestuoso.

strut² [strʌt] *n* puntal *m*, riostra *f*, tornapunta *f*.

strychnine ['strɪkniːn] *n* estricnina *f*.

Stuart ['stjuːət] *nm* Estuardo.

stub [stʌb] **1** *n* (*of tree*) tocón *m*; (*of cigarette*) colilla *f*; (*of candle, pencil etc*) cabo *m*; (*of cheque, receipt*) resguardo *m*, talón *m*.

2 *vt*: **to ~ one's toe** dar con el dedo del pie contra algo, dar un tropezón.

◆**stub out** *vt cigarette* apagar.

◆**stub up** *vt tree trunks* desarraigar, quitar, arrancar.

stubble ['stʌbl] *n* rastrojo *m*; (*on chin*) barba *f* de tres días.

stubblefield ['stʌblfiːld] *n* rastrojera *f*.

stubbly ['stʌblɪ] *adj chin* cerdoso, con barba de tres días; *beard* de tres días.

stubborn ['stʌbən] *adj* tenaz; *refusal* resuelto; inquebrantable; (*pej*) terco, testarudo, porfiado; **as ~ as a mule** terco como una mula.

stubbornly ['stʌbənlɪ] *adv* tenazmente; tercamente, con porfía; **he ~ refused to +** *infin* se negó resueltamente a + *infin*.

stubbornness ['stʌbənnɪs] *n* tenacidad *f*; terquedad *f*, testarudez *f*, porfía *f*.

stubby ['stʌbɪ] *adj* achaparrado.

STUC *n abbr of* **Scottish Trades Union Congress**.

stucco ['stʌkəʊ] **1** *n* estuco *m*. **2** *adj* de estuco. **3** *vt* estucar.

stuck [stʌk] *pret and ptp of* **stick**.

stuck-up* ['stʌk'ʌp] *adj* engreído, presumido; **to be very ~ about sth** presumir mucho a causa de algo.

stud¹ [stʌd] **1** *n* (*boot ~*) taco *m*; (*decorative*) tachón *m*, clavo *m* (de adorno); (*collar ~, shirt ~*) botón *m* (de camisa).

2 *vt* tachonar; adornar con clavos; (*fig*) sembrar (*with* de).

stud² [stʌd] *n* (**a**) (*~ farm*) caballeriza *f*, yeguada *f*. (**b**) (‡: *man*) semental‡ *m*.

studbook ['stʌdbʊk] *n* registro *m* genealógico de caballos.

student ['stjuːdənt] **1** *n* (*pupil*) alumno *m*, -a *f*; (*Univ*) estudiante *mf*; (*researcher*) investigador *m*, -ora *f*; **French ~** (*by nationality*) estudiante *m* francés, estudiante *f* francesa, (*by subject*) estudiante *mf* de francés; **old ~s' association** asociación *f* de ex alumnos.

2 *attr* estudiantil; **~ body** alumnado *m*; **~ driver** (*US*) aprendiz *m* de conductor, aprendiza *f* de conductora; **~ grant** beca *f*; **~ nurse** estudiante *mf* de enfermera (*or* de A.T.S.); **~ teacher** (*secondary*) profesor *m*, -a *f* en prácticas; (*primary*) maestro *m*, -a *f* en prácticas; **~ union** (*club*) club *m* de estudiantes universitarios; (*trade union*) sindicato *m* estudiantil.

studentship ['stjuːdəntʃɪp] *n* beca *f*.

stud farm ['stʌdfɑːm] *n* caballeriza *f*, yeguada *f*.

studhorse ['stʌdhɔːs] *n* caballo *m* padre.

studied ['stʌdɪd] *adj calm etc* calculado, deliberado; estudiado; *insult* premeditado; *pose, style* afectado.

studio ['stjuːdɪəʊ] **1** *n* (*in most senses*) estudio *m*; (*sculptor's*) taller *m*. **2** *attr*: **~ apartment, ~ flat** estudio *m*; **~ audience** público *m* de estudio; **~ couch** sofá-cama *m*; **~ director** director *m*, -ora *f* de interiores.

studious ['stjuːdɪəs] *adj person* estudioso; aplicado, asiduo; *effort* asiduo; *politeness* calculado, esmerado.

studiously ['stjuːdɪəslɪ] *adv* con aplicación; **he ~ avoided mentioning the matter** evitó cuidadosamente aludir al asunto, se guardó de aludir al asunto.

studiousness ['stjuːdɪəsnɪs] *n* aplicación *f*.

stud mare ['stʌd,mɛəʳ] *n* yegua *f* de cría.

study ['stʌdɪ] **1** *n* (**a**) (*in most senses*) estudio *m*; **to be in a brown ~** estar absorto en la meditación, estar en Babia; **to make a ~ of sth** estudiar algo, investigar algo; **my studies show that ...** mis estudios demuestran que ...

(**b**) (*room*) despacho *m*, cuarto *m* de trabajo, estudio *m*.

2 *vt* estudiar; investigar; examinar, mirar detenidamente; escudriñar.

3 *vi* estudiar; **to ~ under sb** estudiar con uno, trabajar bajo la dirección de uno; **to ~ for an exam** prepararse para un examen; **to ~ to be an agronomist** estudiar para agrónomo.

study-group ['stʌdɪ'gruːp] *n* grupo *m* de estudio.
study-tour ['stʌdɪˌtʊə^r] *n* viaje *m* de estudio.
stuff [stʌf] **1** *n* **(a)** *(material in general)* materia *f*; material *m*, sustancia *f*; **it's strange ~** es una sustancia singular; **there is some good ~ in that book** ese libro tiene cosas buenas; **there's good ~ in him** tiene buenas cualidades; **it's poor ~** no vale para nada; **do you call this ~ beer?** ¿llamas a esto cerveza?; **I can't read his ~** no alcanzo a leer sus libros; **I can't listen to his ~** no aguanto su música; **that's the ~!** ¡muy bien!; **have you brought the ~?** ¿lo has traído?, ¿has traído aquello?; **argument is the very ~ of politics** la discusión es la misma esencia de la política; **he is of the ~ that heroes are made of** tiene madera de héroe; **show him what ~ you are made of** demuéstrale tus cualidades, muéstrale si puedes o no.
(b) *(material, cloth)* tela *f*, paño *m*.
(c) (*: *possessions*) cosas *fpl*, chismes *mpl*; **he leaves his ~ scattered about** deja sus cosas de cualquier modo; **is this your ~?** ¿es tuyo esto?
(d) (*: *nonsense*) tonterías *fpl*; **all that ~ about Cervantes** todas esas tonterías acerca de Cervantes; **~ and nonsense!** ¡ni hablar!, ¡narices!*
(e) (*) **hot ~*** cosa *f* maravillosa, persona *f* estupenda*; **she's hot ~** es cachonda, es de plan*; **he's hot ~ at chess** es un hacha para el ajedrez*.
(f) (*) **to do one's ~** actuar, trabajar *etc*; **do your ~!** ¡vamos!, ¡a ello!; **you do your ~ next** tú eres el próximo; **he doesn't do his ~** no trabaja *(etc)* como debiera; **he certainly knows his ~** conoce perfectamente su oficio, domina su especialidad.
(g) *(US Drugs‡)* polvo* *m*, droga *f*, chocolate‡ *m*.
2 *vt* **(a)** *(fill) container* llenar, hinchar, atiborrar *(with* de); *(stow) contents* meter sin orden, meter de prisa *(into* en); *hole, leak etc* tapar, atascar; *(Culin)* rellenar; *animal (for exhibition)* disecar; **he ~ed it into his pocket** lo metió de prisa en el bolsillo; **can we ~ any more in?** ¿cabe más?; **her head is ~ed with formulae** tiene la cabeza atiborrada de fórmulas; **two centuries ~ed with history** dos siglos prietos *(or* llenos) de historia. **(b)** (**‡**) joder; **get ~ed!**‡** ¡vete a la porra!*, ¡vete al carajo!**‡**; **~ the government!**‡** ¡que se joda el gobierno!**‡**; **you can ~ that idea**‡** al carajo con esa idea**‡**.
3 (*) *vi* atracarse, comer a dos carrillos.
4 *vr*: **to ~ o.s. with food** darse un atracón, atiborrarse de comida; **I have to ~ myself with sedatives** me veo obligado a embutirme de calmantes.
◆stuff away* *vt food* zampar, devorar.
◆stuff up *vt*: **to get ~ed up** *(pipe etc)* atascarse, quedar obstruido; **to be ~ed up with (a) cold*** estar fuertemente acatarrado.
stuffed [stʌft] *adj animal* disecado; **~ shirt** *(fig)* persona *f* estirada; **~ toy** *(US)* muñeco *m* de peluche.
stuffily ['stʌfɪlɪ] *adv say* en tono de desaprobación, con desaprobación.
stuffiness ['stʌfɪnɪs] *n* **(a)** *(in room)* mala ventilación *f*, falta *f* de aire. **(b)** *(fig)* estrechez *f* de miras; lo estirado; lo remilgado, pesadez *f*.
stuffing ['stʌfɪŋ] *n* *(of furniture, animal)* relleno *m*, borra *f*; *(Culin)* relleno *m*; **he's got no ~** no tiene carácter, no tiene agallas; **he had the ~ knocked out of him by the blow** el golpe le dejó sin fuerzas ni ánimo; **to knock the ~ out of sb** dar una paliza a uno.
stuffy ['stʌfɪ] *adj* **(a)** *room* mal ventilado, donde falta el aire; *atmosphere* cargado, sofocante; **it's ~ in here** aquí falta el aire, aquí huele a encerrado.
(b) *(narrow-minded)* de miras estrechas; *(stiff)* estirado; *(prudish)* remilgado; *(boring)* pesado, poco interesante.
stultify ['stʌltɪfaɪ] *vt* hacer inútil, quitar valor a, anular; hacer (parecer) ridículo.
stultifying ['stʌltɪfaɪɪŋ] *adj* que hace inútil, que hace ineficaz; agobiador, opresivo, sofocante.
stumble ['stʌmbl] **1** *n* tropezón *m*, traspié *m*.
2 *vi* tropezar, dar un traspié; **to ~ against** tropezar contra, tropezar con; **to ~ on, to go stumbling on** avanzar dando traspiés; **to ~ over** tropezar en; **to ~ through a speech** pronunciar un discurso de cualquier manera, pronunciar torpemente un discurso.
◆stumble across, stumble (up)on *vt* tropezar con, encontrar por casualidad.
stumbling-block ['stʌmblɪŋblɒk] *n* *(fig)* tropiezo *m*, piedra *f* de tropiezo, obstáculo *m*.
stump [stʌmp] **1** *n* **(a)** cabo *m*, fragmento *m*, último pedazo *m*; *(of tree etc)* tocón *m*; *(of limb)* muñón *m*; *(of tooth)* raigón *m*; *(Cricket)* poste *m*, palo *m*; *(Art)* esfumino *m*; (*: *leg*) pierna *f*; **to stir one's ~s*** menearse, moverse.
(b) **to be** *(or* **go) on the ~** *(US)* hacer (una) campaña.
(c) **to find o.s. up a ~*** *(US)* quedarse uno de piedra, estar perplejo.
2 *vt* **(a)** (*: *puzzle*) desconcertar, dejar perplejo, dejar confuso; **I'm properly ~ed** estoy totalmente perplejo; no sé qué hacer *(or* decir *etc)*; no sé qué consejo darte; **he was ~ed for an answer** no sabía qué contestar.
(b) **to ~ the country** *(US)* recorrer el país pronunciando discursos.
3 *vi*: **to ~ about, to ~ along** andar pisando muy fuerte; *(lamely)* andar cojeando.
◆stump up *(Brit)* **1** *vt*: **to ~ up £5** apoquinar 5 libras, desembolsar 5 libras *(for sth* para comprar algo, por algo).
2 *vi* apoquinar, soltar la guita *(for sth* para pagar algo).
stumpy ['stʌmpɪ] *adj person etc* achaparrado; *pencil etc* corto, reducido a casi nada, muy gastado.
stun [stʌn] *vt* **(a)** *(Med)* dejar sin sentido; aturdir de un golpe; *animal* aturdir. **(b)** *(fig)* aturdir, pasmar, dejar pasmado; **the news ~ned everybody** la noticia aturdió a todos; **this will ~ you** esto será una gran sorpresa para ti; **the family were ~ned by his death** la familia quedó anonadada a raíz de su muerte.
stung [stʌŋ] *pret and ptp of* **sting**.
stun grenade ['stʌngrə'neɪd] *n* granada *f* detonadora, granada *f* de estampida.
stunk [stʌŋk] *ptp of* **stink**.
stunned [stʌnd] *adj (lit)* aturdido, atontado; *(fig)* pasmado.
stunner* ['stʌnə^r] *n* persona *f* maravillosa, cosa *f* estupenda*; **the picture is a ~** el cuadro es maravilloso; **she's a real ~** es francamente estupenda*.
stunning ['stʌnɪŋ] *adj* **(a)** *blow* que aturde. **(b)** *news etc* pasmoso; *dress, girl etc* estupendo, maravilloso.
stunningly ['stʌnɪŋlɪ] *adv dressed etc* sensacionalmente.
stunt¹ [stʌnt] *vt* atrofiar, impedir el desarrollo de.
stunt² [stʌnt] **1** *n* *(Aer)* vuelo *m* acrobático, ejercicio *m* acrobático; *(display)* proeza *f* excepcional; maniobra *f* sensacional; *(Comm)* truco *m* publicitario, treta *f* publicitaria; **it's just a ~ to get your money** es solamente un truco para sacarte dinero; **to pull a ~** hacer algo peligroso (y tonto).
2 *attr*: **~ flier** aviador *m* acrobático, aviadora *f* acrobática.
3 *vi* hacer vuelos acrobáticos, hacer maniobras sensacionales.
stunted ['stʌntɪd] *adj* enano, achaparrado, mal desarrollado.
stuntman ['stʌntmæn] *n, pl* **stuntmen** ['stʌntmen], **stuntwoman** ['stʌntwʊmən] *n, pl* **stuntwomen** ['stʌntwɪmɪn] especialista *mf, persona que se dedica a desempeñar los papeles peligrosos en el cine y otros espectáculos.*
stupefaction [ˌstjuːpɪ'fækʃən] *n* estupefacción *f*.
stupefy ['stjuːpɪfaɪ] *vt* **(a)** *(Med)* causar estupor a, dejar sin conocimiento; **stupefied by drink** en estado de estupor después de haber bebido, *(permanently)* embrutecido por el alcohol.
(b) *(fig)* pasmar, causar estupor a, dejar estupefacto.
stupefying ['stjuːpɪfaɪɪŋ] *adj (fig)* pasmoso.
stupendous [stjuː'pendəs] *adj* estupendo, asombroso.
stupendously [stjuː'pendəslɪ] *adv* estupendamente.
stupid ['stjuːpɪd] *adj (with sleep etc)* en estado de estupor, atontado; *(silly)* estúpido; **you ~ child!** ¡bobo!; **don't be ~** no seas bobo; **don't do that, ~!** ¡no hagas eso, imbécil!; **that was ~ of you, that was a ~ thing to do** eso fue una estupidez; **I've done a ~ thing** he hecho algo tonto; **to drink o.s. ~** beber tanto que uno queda en estado de estupor.
stupidity [stjuː'pɪdɪtɪ] *n* estupidez *f*.
stupidly ['stjuːpɪdlɪ] *adv* estúpidamente.
stupidness ['stjuːpɪdnɪs] *n* = **stupidity**.
stupor ['stjuːpə^r] *n* estupor *m (also fig)*.
sturdily ['stɜːdɪlɪ] *adv* fuertemente; vigorosamente; enérgicamente; tenazmente; **~ built** de construcción sólida; *person* robusto.
sturdiness ['stɜːdɪnɪs] *n* robustez *f*, fuerza *f*; energía *f*; tenacidad *f*.
sturdy ['stɜːdɪ] *adj* robusto, fuerte; vigoroso; *opposition etc* enérgico; *resistance* tenaz; **~ independence** espíritu *m* fuerte de independencia.
sturgeon ['stɜːdʒən] *n, pl invar* esturión *m*.
stutter ['stʌtə^r] **1** *n* tartamudeo *m*; **he has a bad ~** tartamudea terriblemente; **to say sth with a ~** decir algo tartamudeando. **2** *vt* *(also* **to ~ out)** balbucir, decir

tartamudeando. **3** *vi* tartamudear; balbucir.
stutterer ['stʌtərə^r] *n* tartamudo *m*, -a *f*.
stuttering ['stʌtərɪŋ] **1** *adj* tartamudo. **2** *n* tartamudeo *m*.
stutteringly ['stʌtərɪŋlɪ] *adv*: **he said ~** dijo tartamudeando.
sty[1] [staɪ] *n* (**a**) pocilga *f*, zahurda *f*. (**b**) (‡) comisaría *f*.
sty[2], stye [staɪ] *n* (*Med*) orzuelo *m*.
Stygian ['stɪdʒɪən] *adj* estigio.
style [staɪl] **1** *n* (**a**) (*gen*) estilo *m*; (*Art, Liter etc*) estilo *m*; (*fashion*) estilo *m*; moda *f*; (*elegance*) elegancia *f*; **~ of living** estilo *m* de vida; **in the Italian ~** al estilo italiano, a la italiana; **that's the ~!** ¡bravo!, ¡muy bien!; **there's no ~ about him** no tiene elegancia en absoluto; **she has ~** tiene garbo, tiene aquél; lo hace todo con elegancia; **to cramp sb's ~** cortar los vuelos a uno; **to be in ~** estar de moda; **to do sth in ~** hacer algo con todo lujo, hacer algo como se debe; **to travel in ~** viajar con todo confort; **to live in ~** vivir en el lujo; **he won in fine ~** ganó de manera impecable, ganó limpiamente.
(**b**) (*of address*) tratamiento *m*; título *m*.
2 *vt* (**a**) *dress* cortar a la moda, estilizar; *hair* marcar.
(**b**) (*entitle*) intitular, nombrar.
3 *vr*: **to ~ o.s.** intitularse, darse el título de.
stylebook ['staɪlbʊk] *n* libro *m* de estilo.
stylesheet ['staɪl,ʃiːt] *n* hoja *f* de estilo.
styling ['staɪlɪŋ] *n* estilización *f*.
stylish ['staɪlɪʃ] *adj* elegante; a la moda; garboso, estiloso.
stylishly ['staɪlɪʃlɪ] *adv* elegantemente.
stylishness ['staɪlɪʃnɪs] *n* elegancia *f*.
stylist ['staɪlɪst] *n* estilista *mf*.
stylistic [staɪ'lɪstɪk] **1** *adj* estilístico. **2** *n*: **~s** estilística *f*.
stylistically [staɪ'lɪstɪklɪ] *adv* estilísticamente; **~ distinguished** distinguido en cuanto al estilo.
stylized ['staɪlaɪzd] *adj* estilizado.
stylus ['staɪləs] *n* (*pen*) estilo *m*; (*of record-player*) aguja *f*.
stymie* ['staɪmɪ] *vt*: **to ~ sb** bloquear a uno, poner obstáculos infranqueables delante de uno; **now we're properly ~d!** ¡la hemos pringado de verdad!*, ¡la liamos!*
styptic ['stɪptɪk] **1** *adj* estíptico; **~ pencil** lapicero *m* hemostático. **2** *n* estíptico *m*.
Styx [stɪks] *n* Estigio *m*, Laguna *f* Estigia.
suasion ['sweɪʒən] *n* (*liter*) persuasión *f*.
suave [swɑːv] *adj* afable, cortés, fino; (*pej*) zalamero.
suavely ['swɑːvlɪ] *adv* afablemente, cortésmente, con finura; (*pej*) con zalamería.
suavity ['swɑːvɪtɪ] *n* afabilidad *f*, cortesía *f*, finura *f*; (*pej*) zalamería *f*.
sub[1] [sʌb] *n and vt abbr of* **subaltern**; **sub-edit**; **sub-editor**; **submarine**; **subscription**; **substitute**.
sub[2] [sʌb] *vi*: **to ~ for sb** hacer las veces de uno.
sub[3]* [sʌb] **1** *n* (*advance on wages*) avance *m*, anticipo *m*. **2** *vt* anticipar dinero a.
sub... [sʌb] *pref* sub...
subalpine ['sʌb'ælpaɪn] *adj* subalpino.
subaltern ['sʌbltən] *n* (*Brit*) alférez *m*; subalterno *m*.
subarctic ['sʌb'ɑːktɪk] *adj* subártico.
subatomic [,sʌbə'tɒmɪk] *adj* subatómico.
sub-branch ['sʌbbrɑːntʃ] *n* subdelegación *f*.
subcommittee ['sʌbkə,mɪtɪ] *n* subcomisión *f*.
subconscious ['sʌb'kɒnʃəs] **1** *adj* subconsciente. **2** *n*: **the ~** el subconsciente, la subconsciencia; **in one's ~** en el subconsciente.
subconsciously ['sʌb'kɒnʃəslɪ] *adv* de modo subconsciente.
subcontinent ['sʌb'kɒntɪnənt] *n* subcontinente *m*.
subcontract **1** ['sʌb'kɒntrækt] *n* subcontrato *m*. **2** [,sʌbkən'trækt] *vt* subcontratar.
subcontractor ['sʌbkən'træktə^r] *n* subcontratista *mf*.
subculture ['sʌb,kʌltʃə^r] *n* subcultura *f*.
subcutaneous ['sʌbkjʊ'teɪnɪəs] *adj* subcutáneo.
subdivide ['sʌbdɪ'vaɪd] **1** *vt* subdividir. **2** *vi* subdividirse.
subdivision ['sʌbdɪ,vɪʒən] *n* subdivisión *f*.
subdue [səb'djuː] *vt* (*conquer*) sojuzgar, dominar, avasallar; *passions etc* dominar; *colour, voice etc* suavizar.
subdued [səb'djuːd] *adj emotion etc* templado, suave; *voice* bajo; *colour* suave, apagado; *light* tenue; *lighting* disminuido; *person* (*docile*) sumiso, manso, (*depressed*) deprimido; **you were very ~ last night** anoche has mostrado poca animación, anoche estabas bastante callado; **he's very ~ these days** ahora es muy serio.
sub-edit ['sʌb'edɪt] *vt* (*Brit*) *article* corregir, preparar para la prensa.
sub-editor ['sʌb'edɪtə^r] *n* (*Brit*) redactor *m*, -ora *f*.
sub-entry ['sʌbentrɪ] *n* (*Book-keeping*) subasiento *m*, subapunte *m*.
subgroup ['sʌbgruːp] *n* subgrupo *m*.
subhead(ing) ['sʌb,hed(ɪŋ)] *n* subtítulo *m*.
subhuman ['sʌb'hjuːmən] *adj* infrahumano.
subject **1** ['sʌbdʒɪkt] *adj* (**a**) *people* subyugado, esclavizado.
(**b**) **to be ~ to** (*at times*) estar propenso a, estar sujeto a; **this programme is ~ to change** este programa está sujeto a cambios; **all prices are ~ to alteration** todos los precios están sujetos a cambios.
(**c**) **to be ~ to** (*by nature*) ser propenso a; **he is very ~ to colds** es muy propenso a acatarrarse.
(**d**) (*conditional*) **~ to anything he may say** esto depende de lo que diga él; **~ to the approval of** sujeto a la aprobación de; (*liable*) **~ to change without notice** sujeto a cambio sin previo aviso; **~ to correction** bajo corrección.
2 ['sʌbdʒɪkt] *n* (**a**) (*Pol*) súbdito *m*, -a *f*; **British ~** súbdito *m* británico, súbdita *f* británica; **liberty of the ~** libertad *f* del ciudadano; libertad *f* del individuo.
(**b**) (*Gram*) sujeto *m*.
(**c**) (*theme*) tema *m*, materia *f*; asunto *m*, cuestión *f*; (*Scol, Univ*) asignatura *f*; (*Art, Liter, Mus*) tema *m*; **on the ~ of ...** a propósito de ...; **it's a delicate ~** es un asunto delicado; **to change the ~** volver la hoja, cambiar de conversación; **to keep off a ~** no aludir a un tema, no discutir una cuestión; **to raise the ~ of the war** introducir el tema de la guerra, empezar a hablar de la guerra; **this raises the whole ~ of money** esto plantea el problema general del dinero.
(**d**) (*Med etc*) caso *m*; **he's a nervous ~** es un caso nervioso; **guinea pigs make excellent ~s** los conejillos son materia excelente (para los experimentos *etc*).
3 ['sʌbdʒɪkt] *attr*: **~ heading** título *m* de materia; **~ index** (*in book*) índice *m* de materias; (*in library*) catálogo *m* de materias; **~ pronoun** pronombre *m* de sujeto.
4 [səb'dʒekt] *vt* (**a**) (*conquer*) sojuzgar, dominar.
(**b**) (*submit*) someter (*to* a); **to ~ sb to a test** poner a uno a prueba; **to ~ a book to criticism** someter un libro a la crítica; **to be ~ed to inquiry** ser sometido a la investigación; **I will not be ~ed to this questioning** no tolero esta interrogación; **she was ~ed to much indignity** tuvo que aguantar muchas afrentas.
subjection [səb'dʒekʃən] *n* sujeción *f*; sometimiento *m*; **to bring a people into ~** subyugar a un pueblo; **to hold a people in ~** tener subyugado a un pueblo; **to be in ~ to sb** estar sometido a uno; **to be in a state of complete ~** estar completamente sumiso.
subjective [səb'dʒektɪv] *adj* subjetivo.
subjectively [səb'dʒektɪvlɪ] *adv* subjetivamente.
subjectivism [səb'dʒektɪvɪzəm] *n* subjetivismo *m*.
subjectivity [,sʌbdʒek'tɪvɪtɪ] *n* subjetividad *f*.
subject-matter ['sʌbdʒɪkt,mætə^r] *n* materia *f*; tema *m*; (*of letter etc*) contenido *m*.
subjoin ['sʌb'dʒɔɪn] *vt* adjuntar.
sub judice [sʌb'djuːdɪsɪ] *adj*: **the matter is ~** el asunto está en manos del tribunal.
subjugate ['sʌbdʒʊgeɪt] *vt* subyugar.
subjugation [,sʌbdʒʊ'geɪʃən] *n* subyugación *f*; **to live in ~** vivir subyugado.
subjunctive [səb'dʒʌŋktɪv] **1** *adj* subjuntivo; **~ mood** modo *m* subjuntivo. **2** *n* subjuntivo *m*.
sublease ['sʌb'liːs] **1** *vt* realquilar, subarrendar. **2** ['sʌb,liːs] *n* subarriendo *m*.
sublessee [,sʌble'siː] *n* subarrendatario *m*, -a *f*.
sublessor [,sʌble'sɔː^r] *n* subarrendador *m*, -ora *f*.
sublet ['sʌb'let] (*irr*: *V* **let[2]**) *vt* realquilar, subarrendar.
sub-librarian ['sʌblaɪ'brɛərɪən] *n* subdirector *m*, -ora *f* de biblioteca.
sub-lieutenant ['sʌblef'tenənt] *n* (*Brit Naut*) alférez *m* de fragata; (*Mil*) subteniente *m*, alférez *m*.
sublimate **1** ['sʌblɪmɪt] *n* sublimado *m*. **2** ['sʌblɪmeɪt] *vt* (*all senses*) sublimar.
sublimation [,sʌblɪ'meɪʃən] *n* sublimación *f*.
sublime [sə'blaɪm] **1** *adj* sublime. **2** *n*: **the ~** lo sublime; **to go from the ~ to the ridiculous** pasar de lo sublime a lo ridículo.
sublimely [sə'blaɪmlɪ] *adv* sublimemente; **~ unaware of ...** completamente inconsciente de ..., demasiado exaltado para darse cuenta de ...
subliminal [sʌb'lɪmɪnl] *adj* subliminal, subliminar; **~ advertising** publicidad *f* subliminal.
subliminally [sʌb'lɪmɪnəlɪ] *adv* subliminalmente.
sublimity [sə'blɪmɪtɪ] *n* sublimidad *f*.
submachine-gun ['sʌbmə'ʃiːngʌn] *n* pistola *f* ametralladora, metralleta *f*.
submarine [,sʌbmə'riːn] **1** *adj* submarino. **2** *n* (**a**) submarino *m*. (**b**) (*US**) sándwich *m* mixto de tamaño

grande.

submarine-chaser [ˌsʌbməˈriːnˌtʃeɪsəʳ] *n* cazasubmarinos *m.*

submariner [sʌbˈmærɪnəʳ] *n* submarinista *m.*

sub-menu [ˈsʌbˌmenjuː] *n* submenú *m.*

submerge [səbˈmɜːdʒ] **1** *vt* sumergir; (*flood*) inundar, cubrir. **2** *vi* sumergirse.

submerged [səbˈmɜːdʒd] *adj* sumergido.

submergence [səbˈmɜːdʒəns] *n* sumersión *f*, sumergimiento *m*, hundimiento *m.*

submersible [səbˈmɜːsəbl] *adj* sumergible.

submersion [səbˈmɜːʃən] *n* sumersión *f.*

submicroscopic [ˈsʌbˌmaɪkrəsˈkɒpɪk] *adj* submicroscópico.

submission [səbˈmɪʃən] *n* (**a**) (*state*) sumisión *f.* (**b**) (*act*) presentación *f* (*of evidence* de datos *etc*), entrega *f.* (**c**) (*Jur etc*) argumento *m*, alegato *m*; **in my ~** de acuerdo con mi tesis, según yo creo.

submissive [səbˈmɪsɪv] *adj* sumiso.

submissively [səbˈmɪsɪvlɪ] *adv* sumisamente.

submissiveness [səbˈmɪsɪvnɪs] *n* sumisión *f.*

submit [səbˈmɪt] **1** *vt* someter; *evidence* presentar, aducir; *report* presentar; *account* rendir; **to ~ that** ... proponer que ..., sugerir que ...; **I ~ that** ... me permito decir que ...; **to ~ a play to the censor** someter una obra al censor; **to ~ a dispute to arbitration** someter una disputa a arbitraje.

2 *vi* someterse, rendirse; **to ~ to** someterse a; resignarse a, conformarse con; **he had to ~ to this indignity** tuvo que aguantar esta afrenta.

subnormal [ˈsʌbˈnɔːməl] **1** *adj* subnormal. **2** *npl*: **the ~** los subnormales.

suborbital [ˈsʌbˈɔːbɪtəl] *adj* suborbital.

subordinate 1 [səˈbɔːdnɪt] *adj* subordinado (*also Gram*); secundario, de importancia secundaria, menos importante; **A is ~ to B** A queda subordinado a B; A no tiene tanta importancia como B; A depende de B.

2 [səˈbɔːdɪnɪt] *n* subordinado *m*, -a *f.*

3 [səˈbɔːdɪneɪt] *vt* subordinar (*to* a).

subordination [səˌbɔːdɪˈneɪʃən] *n* subordinación *f.*

suborn [sʌˈbɔːn] *vt* sobornar.

subparagraph [sʌbˈpærəˌgrɑːf] *n* subpárrafo *m.*

subplot [ˈsʌbˌplɒt] *n* intriga *f* secundaria.

subpoena [səbˈpiːnə] **1** *n* comparendo *m*, citación *f* (judicial), apercibimiento *m.* **2** *vt* mandar comparecer, citar a uno (para estrados).

subpopulation [ˈsʌbˌpɒpjʊˈleɪʃən] *n* subgrupo *m* de población.

sub post-office [ˌsʌbˈpəʊstˌɒfɪs] *n* subdelegación *f* de correos.

subrogate [ˈsʌbrəgɪt] *adj* subrogado, sustituido; **~ language** lenguaje *m* subrogado.

sub rosa [ˈsʌbˈrəʊzə] **1** *adj* secreto, de confianza; **it's all very ~** todo es de lo más secreto. **2** *adv* en secreto, en confianza.

subroutine [ˌsʌbruːˈtiːn] *n* subrutina *f.*

sub-Saharan [ˈsʌbsəˈhɑːrən] *adj* subsahariano.

subscribe [səbˈskraɪb] **1** *vt* (**a**) *money* suscribir, contribuir, dar; **~d capital** capital *m* suscrito.

(**b**) *signature* poner; *document etc* firmar, poner su firma en.

2 *vi* suscribir; **to ~ for sth** contribuir dinero para algo; **to ~ to a paper** suscribirse a un periódico, abonarse a un periódico; **to ~ to an opinion** suscribir una opinión, aprobar una opinión.

subscriber [səbˈskraɪbəʳ] *n* suscriptor *m*, -ora *f*, abonado *m*, -a *f*; (*St Ex*) suscriptor *m*, -ora *f.*

subscript [ˈsʌbskrɪpt] *n* subíndice *m.*

subscription [səbˈskrɪpʃən] **1** *n* suscripción *f*, abono *m*; (*to club*) cuota *f*; (*St Ex*) suscripción *f*; **to pay one's ~** suscribirse, abonarse, (*to club*) pagar su cuota; **to take out a ~ to a journal** abonarse a una revista. **2** *attr*: **~ fee, ~ rate** tarifa *f* de suscripción; **~ form** hoja *f* de suscripción.

subsection [ˈsʌbˌsekʃən] *n* subsección *f*, subdivisión *f.*

subsequent [ˈsʌbsɪkwənt] *adj* subsiguiente; posterior, ulterior; **~ to** posterior a; **~ to this** (*as prep*) después de esto, a raíz de esto.

subsequently [ˈsʌbsɪkwəntlɪ] *adv* después, más tarde, con posterioridad.

subserve [səbˈsɜːv] *vt* ayudar, favorecer.

subservience [səbˈsɜːvɪəns] *n* subordinación *f* (*to* a); servilismo *m.*

subservient [səbˈsɜːvɪənt] *adj* (**a**) (*secondary*) subordinado (*to* a). (**b**) (*cringing*) servil.

subset [ˈsʌbˌset] *n* subconjunto *m.*

subside [səbˈsaɪd] *vi* (*water*) bajar; (*foundations, ground, pavement etc*) hundirse; (*wind*) amainar, hacerse menos violento; (*threat etc*) disminuir, alejarse; (*excitement etc*) calmarse; **to ~ into a chair** dejarse caer en una silla.

subsidence [səbˈsaɪdəns] *n* bajada *f*; hundimiento *m*, (*of pavement, road*) socavón *m*; amaine *m*; disminución *f*; apaciguamiento *m.*

subsidiary [səbˈsɪdɪərɪ] **1** *adj* subsidiario; secundario; auxiliar; (*Fin*) afiliado, filial; **~ company** empresa *f* filial.

2 *n* filial *f*, sucursal *f.*

subsidize [ˈsʌbsɪdaɪz] *vt* subvencionar; **~d** subvencionado, que tiene subvención (gubernamental *etc*).

subsidy [ˈsʌbsɪdɪ] *n* subvención *f*, subsidio *m.*

subsist [səbˈsɪst] *vi* subsistir; sustentarse (*on a food* con una comida).

subsistence [səbˈsɪstəns] **1** *n* subsistencia *f*; sustentación *f*; (*allowance*) dietas *fpl.* **2** *attr*: **~ allowance** dietas *fpl*; **~ economy** economía *f* de subsistencia; **~ farming** agricultura *f* de subsistencia; **~ wage** salario *m* de subsistencia; **to live at ~ level** vivir muy justo, poderse sustentar apenas.

subsoil [ˈsʌbsɔɪl] *n* subsuelo *m.*

subsonic [ˈsʌbˈsɒnɪk] *adj* subsónico.

subspecies [ˈsʌbˈspiːʃiːz] *n, pl invar* subespecie *f.*

substance [ˈsʌbstəns] *n* sustancia *f*; esencia *f*, parte *f*, parte *f* esencial; **in ~** en esencia, esencialmente; **an argument of ~** un argumento sólido; **man of ~** hombre *m* acaudalado; **the ~ is good but the style poor** la materia es buena pero el estilo malo.

substandard [ˈsʌbˈstændəd] *adj* inferior, inferior al nivel normal, no del todo satisfactorio.

substantial [səbˈstænʃəl] *adj* sustancial, sustancioso; *part, proportion* importante; *sum* considerable; *loss* importante; *build etc* sólido, fuerte; *person* acomodado; acaudalado; **~ damages** (*Jur*) daños *mpl* y perjuicios generales; **to be in ~ agreement** estar de acuerdo en gran parte.

substantially [səbˈstænʃəlɪ] *adv* sustancialmente; **~ built** de construcción sólida; **~ true** en gran parte verdadero; **it contributed ~ to our success** contribuyó materialmente a nuestro éxito.

substantiate [səbˈstænʃɪeɪt] *vt* establecer, comprobar, justificar.

substantiation [səbˌstænʃɪˈeɪʃən] *n* comprobación *f*, justificación *f.*

substantival [ˌsʌbstənˈtaɪvəl] *adj* sustantivo.

substantive [ˈsʌbstəntɪv] **1** *adj* sustantivo. **2** *n* sustantivo *m.*

substation [ˈsʌbˌsteɪʃən] *n* (*Elec*) subestación *f.*

substitute [ˈsʌbstɪtjuːt] **1** *n* (*person*) sustituto *m*, -a *f*, suplente *mf* (*for* de); (*Sport*) suplente *mf*; (*thing*) sustituto *m*, sucedáneo *m*; artículo *m* de reemplazo; **there is no ~ for petrol** la gasolina es insustituible; **this is a poor ~ for the real thing** esto no sustituye plenamente lo auténtico.

2 *adj* sucedáneo; de reemplazo; *person* suplente; **~ teacher** (*US*) profesor *m* suplente, profesora *f* suplente.

3 *vt* sustituir (*A for B* B por A); reemplazar (*A for B* A por B).

4 *vi*: **to ~ for sb** suplir a uno, hacer las veces de uno.

substitution [ˌsʌbstɪˈtjuːʃən] *n* sustitución *f*; reemplazo *m.*

substratum [ˈsʌbˈstrɑːtəm] *n, pl* **substrata** [ˈsʌbˈstrɑːtə] sustrato *m.*

substructure [ˈsʌbˌstrʌktʃəʳ] *n* infraestructura *f.*

subsume [səbˈsjuːm] *vt* subsumir.

subsystem [ˈsʌbˌsɪstəm] *n* subsistema *m.*

subteen* [ˌsʌbˈtiːn] *n* preadolescente *mf*, menor *mf* de trece años.

subtenancy [ˈsʌbˈtenənsɪ] *n* subarriendo *m.*

subtenant [ˈsʌbˈtenənt] *n* subarrendatario *m*, -a *f.*

subterfuge [ˈsʌbtəfjuːdʒ] *n* subterfugio *m.*

subterranean [ˌsʌbtəˈreɪnɪən] *adj* subterráneo.

subtext [ˈsʌbtekst] *n* subtexto *m.*

subtilize [ˈsʌtɪlaɪz] **1** *vt* sutilizar. **2** *vi* sutilizar.

subtitle [ˈsʌbˌtaɪtl] **1** *n* subtítulo *m.* **2** *vt* subtitular.

subtle [ˈsʌtl] *adj* sutil; fino, delicado; *charm* misterioso; *perfume* delicado, sutil, tenue; *irony etc* fino; (*crafty*) astuto; **that wasn't very ~ of you** en eso te has mostrado poco fino.

subtlety [ˈsʌtltɪ] *n* sutileza *f*; finura *f*, delicadeza *f*; lo misterioso; astucia *f.*

subtly [ˈsʌtlɪ] *adv* sutilmente; finamente, delicadamente; misteriosamente; astutamente.

subtopia [ˌsʌbˈtəʊpɪə] *n* (*hum*) (vida *f etc* de los) barrios *mpl* exteriores.

subtotal [ˈsʌbˌtəʊtl] *n* total *m* parcial.

subtract [səbˈtrækt] *vt* sustraer, restar; **to ~ 5 from 9** restar 5 a 9.

subtraction [səbˈtrækʃən] *n* sustracción *f*, resta *f.*

subtropical [ˈsʌbˈtrɒpɪkəl] *adj* subtropical.

suburb ['sʌbɜːb] *n* barrio *m*, barrio *m* exterior; colonia *f*; **new ~** barrio *m* nuevo, ensanche *m*; **a London ~** un barrio londinense, un distrito en las afueras de Londres; **the (outer) ~s** los barrios exteriores, las afueras.
suburban [sə'bɜːbən] *adj* suburbano; *train* de cercanías.
suburbanite [sə'bɜːbənaɪt] **1** *adj* surburbano. **2** *n* habitante *mf* de los barrios exteriores.
suburbia [sə'bɜːbɪə] *n* (*freq pej*) los barrios exteriores, las afueras; manera *f* de vivir de los barrios exteriores.
subvention [səb'venʃən] *n* subvención *f*.
subversion [səb'vɜːʃən] *n* subversión *f*.
subversive [səb'vɜːsɪv] **1** *adj* subversivo. **2** *n* subversor *m*; elemento *m* subversivo, persona *f* de dudosa lealtad política.
subvert [sʌb'vɜːt] *vt* subvertir, trastornar.
subway ['sʌbweɪ] **1** *n* (*esp Brit*) paso *m* subterráneo, paso *m* inferior; (*US Rail*) metro *m*. **2** *attr*: **~ station** (*US*) estación *f* de metro.
sub-zero ['sʌb'zɪərəʊ] *adj*: **in ~ temperatures** a una temperatura bajo cero.
succeed [sək'siːd] **1** *vt* suceder a; **to ~ sb in a post** suceder a uno en un puesto; **spring is ~ed by summer** a la primavera le sigue el verano.
2 *vi* **(a)** (*be successful*: *of person*) tener éxito, triunfar; (*of plan etc*) salir bien; **but he did not ~ (in this)** pero no tuvo éxito (con esto), pero no lo consiguió; **to ~ in life** triunfar en la vida; **to ~ in one's hopes** ver logradas sus esperanzas; **to ~ in one's plan** llevar a cabo su proyecto; **to ~ in doing sth** lograr hacer algo, conseguir hacer algo.
(b) (*follow*) suceder; seguir; heredar; **who ~s?** ¿quién hereda?; **to ~ to the crown** suceder a la corona, heredar la corona; **to ~ to the throne** subir al trono; **to ~ to an estate** heredar una finca.
succeeding [sək'siːdɪŋ] *adj* futuro; subsiguiente; sucesivo; **on 3 ~ Saturdays** tres sábados seguidos; **in the ~ chaos** en la confusión subsiguiente; **~ generations will do better** las generaciones futuras harán mejor; **each ~ year brought ...** cada año sucesivo trajo ...
success [sək'ses] **1** *n* éxito *m*, buen éxito *m*; triunfo *m*; prosperidad *f*; **another ~ for our team** nuevo éxito *m* para nuestro equipo; **without ~** sin éxito, sin resultado; **to be a ~** (*person*) tener éxito; (*plan etc*) ser un acierto, dar resultado; **he was a great ~** tuvo mucho éxito; **he was not a ~ as Segismundo** no estuvo bien en el papel de Segismundo; **the play was a ~ in New York** la obra obtuvo un éxito en Nueva York; **the new car is not a ~** el nuevo coche no es satisfactorio; **the plan was a ~** el proyecto salió muy bien; **she had no ~** no tuvo éxito; **to make a ~ of sth** tener éxito en algo; **to meet with ~** tener éxito; prosperar.
2 *attr*: **~ story** historia *f* de un éxito.
successful [sək'sesfʊl] *adj person* afortunado, feliz, que tiene éxito, exitoso; *attempt, plan etc* logrado, exitoso; *business etc* próspero; *effort* fructuoso; *candidate* elegido, afortunado; **to be ~** (*person*) tener éxito, triunfar; (*business etc*) prosperar; **to be entirely ~** tener un éxito completo; **to be ~ in doing sth** lograr hacer algo; **he was not ~ last time** no lo logró la última vez.
successfully [sək'sesfəlɪ] *adv* con éxito; afortunadamente; prósperamente.
succession [sək'seʃən] **1** *n* **(a)** (*series*) sucesión *f*, serie *f*; **in ~** sucesivamente; **4 times in ~** 4 veces seguidas; **in quick ~** en rápida sucesión; rápidamente uno tras otro; **after a ~ of disasters** después de una serie de catástrofes.
(b) (*to post etc*) sucesión *f* (*to* a); **in ~ to sb** sucediendo a uno; como sucesor de uno; **Princess Rebecca is 7th in ~ to the throne** la princesa Rebeca ocupa el 7° puesto en la línea de sucesión a la corona.
(c) (*descendants*) descendencia *f*.
2 *attr*: **~ duty** derechos *mpl* de sucesión.
successive [sək'sesɪv] *adj* sucesivo; consecutivo; **4 ~ days** 4 días seguidos.
successively [sək'sesɪvlɪ] *adv* sucesivamente.
successor [sək'sesəʳ] *n* sucesor *m*, -ora *f*.
succinct [sək'sɪŋkt] *adj* sucinto.
succinctly [sək'sɪŋktlɪ] *adv* sucintamente.
succinctness [sək'sɪŋktnɪs] *n* concisión *f*.
succour, (*US*) **succor** ['sʌkəʳ] **1** *n* socorro *m*. **2** *vt* socorrer.
succulence ['sʌkjʊləns] *n* suculencia *f*.
succulent ['sʌkjʊlənt] **1** *adj* suculento; carnoso. **2** *n* (*plant*) planta *f* carnosa.
succumb [sə'kʌm] *vi* sucumbir (*to* a).
such [sʌtʃ] **1** *adj* **(a)** (*of that sort*) tal; semejante; parecido; tanto; **~ a book** tal libro; **~ books** tales libros; **in ~ cases** en tales casos, en semejantes casos; **we had ~ a case last year** tuvimos un caso parecido el año pasado; **on just ~ a day in June** un día exactamente parecido de junio; **no ~ thing!** ¡no hay tal!, ¡ni hablar!; **there's no ~ thing** no hay tal cosa; **did you ever see ~ a thing?** ¿se vio jamás tal cosa?; **some ~ idea** alguna idea de este tipo, alguna idea por el estilo; **~ a plan is most unwise** un proyecto así es poco aconsejable, un proyecto de ese tipo no es aconsejable; **no ~ book exists** no existe tal libro; **X was ~ a one** X era así; **~ is life** así es la vida; **~ is not the case** esto no es así; **I am in ~ a hurry** tengo tanta prisa, estoy tan de prisa; **~ an honour!** ¡tanto honor!; **it caused ~ trouble that ...** dio lugar a tantos disgustos que ...
(b) (*gen*) **~ as** tal como; **~ a man as Ganivet** un hombre tal como Ganivet; **~ writers as Quevedo** los escritores tales como Quevedo; **~ money as I have** el dinero que tengo; **~ stories as I know** las historias que conozco; **there are no ~ things as giants** los gigantes no existen; **it is not ~ as to cause worry** no es tal que haya de causar inquietud; **it made ~ a stir as had not been known before** tuvo una repercusión como no se había conocido hasta entonces; **~ as?** ¿por ejemplo?
2 *adv* tan; **~ good food** comida *f* tan buena; **~ a clever girl** muchacha *f* tan inteligente; **it's ~ a long time ago** hace tanto tiempo ya.
3 *pron* los que, las que; **we took ~ as we wanted** tomamos los que queríamos; **I will send you ~ as I receive** te mandaré los que reciba; **and as ~ he was promoted** y como tal le ascendieron; **we know of none ~** no tenemos noticias de ninguno así; **there are no trees as ~** no hay árboles propiamente dichos, no hay árboles que digamos, no hay árboles árboles; **rabbits and hares and ~** conejos *mpl* y liebres y tal; **may all ~ perish!** ¡mueran cuantos hay como él!; **this is my car ~ as it is** tal como es, éste es mi coche; **he read the documents ~ as they were** leyó los documentos, los que había.
such-and-such ['sʌtʃənsʌtʃ] *adj*: **she lives in ~ a street** vive en tal o cual calle; **on ~ a day in May** a tantos de mayo; **I am not concerned with ~** no tengo que ver con aquello y lo otro.
suchlike ['sʌtʃlaɪk] **1** *adj* tal, semejante; **sheep and ~ animals** ovejas *fpl* y otros tales animales, ovejas *fpl* y otros animales de la misma clase.
2 *pron*: **thieves and ~** ladrones *mpl* y gente de esa calaña, ladrones *mpl* y otras tales personas; **buses and lorries and ~** autobuses *mpl* y camiones y tal.
suck [sʌk] **1** *n* chupada *f*; sorbo *m*; (*at breast*) mamada *f*; **to give ~ (to)** amamantar.
2 *vt* **(a)** chupar; sorber; *breast* mamar; **to ~ one's fingers** chuparse los dedos. **(b) we were ~ed into the controversy** fuimos involucrados en la controversia sin querer.
3 *vi* chupar; mamar; **to ~ at sth** chupar algo; **this ~s⁑** es la mierda⁑, esto apesta‡.
◆**suck down** *vt* tragar.
◆**suck in** *vt liquid* sorber; *air, dust etc* aspirar.
◆**suck out** *vt* succionar.
◆**suck up 1** *vt* aspirar; absorber.
2 *vi*: **to ~ up to sb*** dar coba a uno*, hacer la pelotilla a uno*.
sucker ['sʌkəʳ] **1** *n* **(a)** (*Zool*) ventosa *f*.
(b) (*Bot*) serpollo *m*, mamón *m*.
(c) (‡: *person*) primo* *m*, bobo *m*; **some ~** algún pobre hombre; **to be a ~ for sth** no poder resistir algo; sucumbir pronto a los encantos de algo.
2 *vt* (*US*‡) estafar, timar, embaucar; **to get ~ed out of 6 grand** ser objeto de un timo de 6.000 dólares.
sucking-pig ['sʌkɪŋpɪg] *n* lechón *m*, lechoncillo *m*, cochinillo *m*.
suckle ['sʌkl] **1** *vt* amamantar, dar el pecho a; (*fig*) criar.
2 *vi* lactar.
suckling ['sʌklɪŋ] *n* mamón *m*, -ona *f*; **~ pig** cochinillo *m*.
sucks-boo* ['sʌks'buː] *excl* ¡narices!*
sucrose ['suːkrəʊz] *n* sacarosa *f*.
suction ['sʌkʃən] *n* succión *f*.
suction pump ['sʌkʃənpʌmp] *n* bomba *f* aspirante, bomba *f* de succión.
Sudan [sʊ'dɑːn] *n* Sudán *m*.
Sudanese [ˌsuːdə'niːz] **1** *adj* sudanés. **2** *n* sudanés *m*, -esa *f*.
sudden ['sʌdn] *adj* (*rapid, hurried*) repentino, súbito; (*unexpected*) imprevisto, impensado; *change of temperature, curve etc* brusco; **~ death** (*Sport*) desempate *m* instantáneo, muerte *f* súbita; **~ infant death syndrome** síndrome *m* de la muerte infantil súbita; **all of a ~** de

repente.

suddenly ['sʌdnlɪ] *adv* de repente, de pronto; inesperadamente; bruscamente.

suddenness ['sʌdnnɪs] *n* lo repentino; lo imprevisto; brusquedad *f.*

suds [sʌdz] *npl* (**a**) (*also* **soap** ~) jabonaduras *fpl*, espuma *f* de jabón. (**b**) (*US*‡) cerveza *f.*

Sue [suː] *nf familiar form of* Susan.

sue [suː] **1** *vt*: **to ~ sb** demandar a uno (*for sth* por algo), llevar a uno ante el tribunal; **to ~ sb for damages** demandar a uno por daños y perjuicios; **to be ~d for libel** ser demandado por calumnia.

2 *vi* (**a**) (*Jur*) presentar demanda; **to ~ for divorce** presentar demanda de divorcio, solicitar el divorcio.

(**b**) **to ~ for peace** pedir la paz.

suède [sweɪd] **1** *n* suecia *f*, ante *m*, gamuza *f* (*LAm*); ~ **gloves** guantes *mpl* de ante, guantes *mpl* de cabritilla; ~ **shoes** zapatos *mpl* de ante.

suet [sʊɪt] *n* sebo *m*; ~ **pudding** pudín *m* a base de sebo.

Suetonius [swiː'təʊnɪəs] *nm* Suetonio.

suety ['sʊɪtɪ] *adj* seboso.

Suez Canal ['suːɪzkə'næl] *n* Canal *m* de Suez.

suffer ['sʌfəʳ] **1** *vt* (**a**) (*painfully*) sufrir, padecer; (*bear*) aguantar, sufrir; (*undergo*) sufrir, experimentar; **I can't ~ it a moment longer** no puedo aguantarlo un momento más; **it has ~ed a sharp decline** ha experimentado un brusco descenso; **to ~ a defeat** sufrir una derrota; **to ~ death** morir, ser muerto; **he doesn't ~ fools gladly** no tiene paciencia con los imbéciles.

(**b**) (*allow*) permitir, tolerar; **to ~ sb to do sth** permitir a uno hacer algo; autorizar a uno para que haga algo; **to ~ sth to be done** permitir que se haga algo.

2 *vi* (**a**) sufrir, padecer; **did you ~ much?** ¿sufriste mucho?; **how I ~ed!** ¡lo que sufrí!; **the army ~ed badly** el ejército tuvo pérdidas importantes; **sales have ~ed badly** las ventas han sido afectadas seriamente; **the town ~ed in the raids** la ciudad sufrió grandes daños en los bombardeos; **we will see that you do not ~ by the changes** aseguraremos que Vd no pierda nada a consecuencia de estos cambios.

(**b**) **to ~ for one's sins** sufrir las consecuencias de sus pecados; **you will ~ for it** lo pagarás después.

(**c**) (*be afflicted*) **to ~ from** sufrir, padecer (de), estar afligido por; (*fig*) adolecer de; ser la víctima de; **to ~ from boils** tener diviesos; **to ~ from rheumatism** padecer de reumatismo; **to ~ from the effects of sth** resentirse de algo, estar resentido de algo; **she ~s from her environment** es la víctima de su ambiente; **the house is ~ing from neglect** la casa padece abandono; **your style ~s from over-elaboration** su estilo adolece de una excesiva complicación.

sufferance ['sʌfərəns] *n* tolerancia *f*; **on ~** por tolerancia.

sufferer ['sʌfərəʳ] *n* (*Med*) enfermo *m*, -a *f* (*from* de); víctima *f*; **~s from diabetes** los enfermos de diabetes, los diabéticos; **the ~s from the earthquake** las víctimas del terremoto.

suffering ['sʌfərɪŋ] **1** *adj* que sufre; (*Med*) doliente, enfermo.

2 *n* sufrimiento *m*, padecimiento *m*; (*grief etc*) dolor *m*; **after months of ~** después de sufrir durante meses; **the ~s of the soldiers** los padecimientos de los soldados.

suffice [sə'faɪs] **1** *vt* satisfacer; ser bastante para. **2** *vi* bastar, ser suficiente; **~ it to say that** ... basta decir que ...

sufficiency [sə'fɪʃənsɪ] *n* (*state*) suficiencia *f*; (*quantity*) cantidad *f* suficiente; **to have a ~** estar acomodado.

sufficient [sə'fɪʃənt] *adj* suficiente, bastante; **to be ~** ser suficiente, bastar.

sufficiently [sə'fɪʃəntlɪ] *adv* suficientemente, bastante; ~ **good** bastante bueno.

suffix ['sʌfɪks] **1** *n* sufijo *m*. **2** *vt* añadir como sufijo (*to* a).

suffocate ['sʌfəkeɪt] **1** *vt* ahogar, asfixiar, sofocar. **2** *vi* ahogarse, asfixiarse, quedar asfixiado, sofocarse.

suffocating ['sʌfəkeɪtɪŋ] *adj* sofocante, asfixiante; ~ **heat** calor *m* sofocante.

suffocation [ˌsʌfə'keɪʃən] *n* sofocación *f*, asfixia *f.*

suffragan ['sʌfrəgən] **1** *adj* sufragáneo. **2** *n* obispo *m* sufragáneo.

suffrage ['sʌfrɪdʒ] *n* (**a**) (*franchise*) sufragio *m*; derecho *m* de votar; **to get the ~** obtener el derecho de votar.

(**b**) (*formal*: *vote*) voto *m*; aprobación *f.*

suffragette [ˌsʌfrə'dʒet] *n* sufragista *f.*

suffuse [sə'fjuːz] *vt* bañar, cubrir (*with* de); difundirse por; **~d with light** inundado de luz, bañado de luz; **eyes ~d with tears** ojos *mpl* bañados de lágrimas.

suffusion [sə'fjuːʒən] *n* difusión *f.*

sugar ['ʃʊgəʳ] **1** *n* (**a**) azúcar *m and f*. (**b**) (*US**) **hi, ~!** ¡oye, preciosidad!* (**c**) (*euph**) **oh ~!** ¡caracoles!*

2 *attr*: ~ **cube,** ~ **lump** terrón *m* de azúcar; ~ **plantation** cañaveral *m*, plantación *f* de caña de azúcar; ~ **refinery** refinería *f* de azúcar, trapiche *m*, ingenio *m* azucarero.

3 *vt* azucarar; echar azúcar a (*or* en), añadir azúcar a; **~ed almonds** peladillas *fpl*, almendras *fpl* garapiñadas.

sugar-basin ['ʃʊgəˌbeɪsn] *n* (*Brit*) azucarero *m.*

sugar-beet ['ʃʊgəbiːt] *n* remolacha *f* azucarera.

sugar-bowl ['ʃʊgəbəʊl] *n* azucarero *m.*

sugar-candy ['ʃʊgəˌkændɪ] *n* azúcar *m* candi.

sugar-cane ['ʃʊgəkeɪn] *n* caña *f* de azúcar.

sugar-coated ['ʃʊgə'kəʊtɪd] *adj* azucarado, garapiñado.

sugar daddy* ['ʃʊgəˌdædɪ] *n* viejo *m* adinerado amante de una joven, protector *m* (de una joven).

sugared ['ʃʊgəd] *adj* = **sugary.**

sugar-free [ˌʃʊgə'friː] *adj*, **sugarless** ['ʃʊgəlɪs] *adj* sin azúcar.

sugarloaf ['ʃʊgələʊf] *n* pan *m* de azúcar.

sugarmill ['ʃʊgəmɪl] *n* ingenio *m* azucarero.

sugarplum ['ʃʊgəplʌm] *n* confite *m.*

sugar-tongs ['ʃʊgətɒŋz] *npl* tenacillas *fpl* para azúcar.

sugary ['ʃʊgərɪ] *adj* (**a**) azucarado. (**b**) (*fig*) *style etc* meloso, almibarado; (*sentimental*) sensiblero, sentimental; romántico.

suggest [sə'dʒest] **1** *vt* sugerir; (*point to*) indicar; (*advise*) aconsejar, indicar; (*hint*) insinuar; (*evoke*) evocar, hacer pensar en; **to ~ that** ... (*of person*) sugerir que ..., proponer que ...; **this ~s that** ... esto hace pensar que ..., esto lleva a pensar que ...; **I ~ to you that** ... (*in law speeches*) ¿no es cierto que ...?; **we ~ you contact X** les aconsejamos contactar con X; **it doesn't exactly ~ a careful man** no parece indicar un hombre prudente; **the coins ~ a Roman building** las monedas indican un edificio romano; **the symptoms ~ an operation** los síntomas aconsejan una operación; **prudence ~s a retreat** la prudencia nos aconseja retirarnos; **what are you ~ing?** ¿qué es lo que insinúa Vd?, ¿qué es lo que pretende Vd?

2 *vr*: **an idea ~s itself** se me ocurre una idea; **nothing ~s itself** no se me ocurre nada.

suggestibility [səˌdʒestɪ'bɪlɪtɪ] *n* sugestionabilidad *f.*

suggestible [sə'dʒestɪbl] *adj person* sugestionable.

suggestion [sə'dʒestʃən] *n* (**a**) sugerencia *f*; indicación *f*; insinuación *f*; **~s box** buzón *m* de sugerencias; **if I may make** (*or* **offer**) **a ~** si se me permite proponer algo; **my ~ is that** ... yo propongo que ...; **that is an immoral ~** ésa es una idea inmoral; **following your ~** ... siguiendo sus indicaciones ...; **I am writing at the ~ of Z** le escribo siguiendo la indicación de Z; **there is no ~ of corruption** nada indica la corrupción, no hay indicio de corrupción.

(**b**) (*hypnotic*) sugestión *f.*

(**c**) (*trace*) sombra *f*, traza *f*; **with just a ~ of garlic** con un poquitín de ajo; **with a ~ of irony in his voice** con un punto de ironía en la voz.

suggestive [sə'dʒestɪv] *adj* sugestivo; (*pej*) indecente; ~ **of** que evoca, que hace pensar en; que trasciende a.

suggestively [sə'dʒestɪvlɪ] *adj* (*pej*) indecentemente.

suggestiveness [sə'dʒestɪvnɪs] *n* (*pej*) indecencia *f.*

suicidal [ˌsʊɪ'saɪdl] *adj* suicida; **to have a ~ tendency** tener tendencia al suicidio; **I feel ~ this morning** esta mañana estoy por desesperarme; **he drives in a ~ way** es un suicida conduciendo; **it would be ~** sería peligrosísimo.

suicide ['sʊɪsaɪd] **1** *n* (*act*) suicidio *m*; (*person*) suicida *mf*; **to commit ~** suicidarse; **it would be ~ to say so** sería peligrosísimo decirlo.

2 *attr*: ~ **attempt** tentativa *f* de suicidio; ~ **note** nota *f* en la que se explica el motivo del suicidio; ~ **pact** acuerdo *m* para suicidarse (dos personas al mismo tiempo); ~ **squad** comando *m* suicida.

suit [suːt] **1** *n* (**a**) (*garment*) (*man's*) traje *m*; terno *m* (*LAm*); (*woman's*) traje *m* de chaqueta; ~ **of armour** armadura *f*; ~ **of clothes** traje *m.*

(**b**) (*Jur*) pleito *m*, litigio *m*, proceso *m*; **to bring a ~** poner pleito; **to bring** (*or* **file**) **a ~ against sb** entablar demanda contra uno (*for sth* por algo).

(**c**) (*request*) petición *f*; **at the ~ of** a petición de.

(**d**) (*in marriage*) petición *f* de mano, oferta *f* de matrimonio; **to press one's ~** hacer una oferta de matrimonio.

(**e**) (*Cards*) palo *m*, color *m*; **long ~, strong ~** palo *m* largo; **to have nothing in that ~** tener fallo a ese palo; **to follow ~** servir del (*or* el) palo, (*fig*) hacer lo mismo,

swish [swɪʃ] **1** *n* silbido *m*; crujido *m*.
2 *adj* (*) (*smart*) elegantísimo; (*posh*) de buen tono.
3 *vt* (**a**) *cane* agitar (*or* blandir) produciendo un silbido; *tail* agitar, menear.
(**b**) (*) azotar.
4 *vi* silbar; sonar, crujir.

Swiss [swɪs] **1** *adj* suizo; ~ **roll** (*Culin*) brazo *m* de gitano. **2** *n* suizo *m*, -a *f*.

switch [swɪtʃ] **1** *n* (**a**) (*stick*) vara *f*, varilla *f*; (*whip*) látigo *m*.
(**b**) (*of hair*) trenza *f* postiza, trenza *f*, postizo *m*.
(**c**) (*Rail*: *points*) aguja *f*; (*change of line*) desviación *f*.
(**d**) (*Elec etc*) interruptor *m*, conmutador *m*, llave *f*, botón *m*.
(**e**) (*change*) cambio *m*; giro *m*; **a rapid ~ of plan** un cambio repentino de plan; **to do a ~, to make a ~** hacer un cambio.
2 *vt* (**a**) *tail* agitar, menear.
(**b**) (*Rail*) desviar, cambiar de vía; **to ~ a train to another line** cambiar un tren a otra vía.
(**c**) (*change*) *position etc* cambiar; *policy etc* cambiar de; **to ~ the conversation (to another subject)** cambiar de tema; **so we ~ed hats** así que cambiamos los sombreros.
3 *vi* (*change*) cambiar; **to ~ (over) from Y to Z** cambiar de Y a Z, dejar Y para tomar Z.

◆**switch back** *vi* volver a su posición (*or* política *etc*) original; **to ~ back to** volver a, cambiar de nuevo a.

◆**switch off** **1** *vt* (*Elec*) desconectar, quitar; *light* apagar; *engine* parar.
2 *vi* desconectar la televisión (*etc*); (*fig*) dejar de prestar atención.

◆**switch on** **1** *vt* (*Elec*) encender, conectar, poner; prender (*LAm*); (*Aut etc*) arrancar, poner en marcha; **please ~ the radio on** por favor, enciende la radio; **to leave the television ~ed on** dejar puesta la televisión.
2 *vi* encender la radio, poner la televisión (*etc*); arrancar el motor.

◆**switch over** **1** *vt*: **to ~ over A and B** cambiar A con B, invertir A y B.
2 *vi*: **to ~ over to another station** cambiar a otra emisora; **we've ~ed over altogether to gas** lo hemos cambiado todo a gas; *V also* **switch 3**.

◆**switch round** **1** *vt* cambiar, invertir; arreglar de otro modo.
2 *vi* cambiar de sitio, cambiar de idea.

switchback [ˈswɪtʃbæk] *n* (*Brit*) (*at fair etc*) montaña *f* rusa, tobogán *m*; (*road*) camino *m* de fuertes altibajos, carretera *f* llena de baches.

switchblade [ˈswɪtʃ,bleɪd] *n* (*US*) navaja *f* de muelle, navaja *f* de resorte.

switchboard [ˈswɪtʃbɔːd] *n* (*Tech*) cuadro *m* de mandos; (*Elec*) tablero *m* de conmutadores, cuadro *m* de distribución; (*Telec*: *at exchange*) cuadro *m* de conexión manual, (*in office etc*) centralita *f*, conmutador *m* (*LAm*); ~ **operator** telefonista *mf*.

switch-hit [,swɪtʃˈhɪt] (*US*) *vi* ser ambidextro en el bateo.

switch-hitter [,swɪtʃˈhɪtəʳ] *n* (*US*) (*Baseball*) bateador *m* ambidextro; (*) bisexual *m*.

switchman [ˈswɪtʃmən] *n*, *pl* **switchmen** [ˈswɪtʃmən] guardagujas *m*.

switch-over [ˈswɪtʃəʊvəʳ] *n* cambio *m* (*to* a); nuevo rumbo *m*, nuevo enfoque *m*.

switchtower [ˈswɪtʃ,taʊəʳ] *n* (*US*) garita *f* de señales.

switchyard [ˈswɪtʃjɑːd] *n* (*US*) patio *m* de maniobras, estación *f* clasificadora.

Switzerland [ˈswɪtsələnd] *n* Suiza *f*.

swivel [ˈswɪvl] **1** *n* eslabón *m* giratorio; pivote *m*.
2 *attr* giratorio, movil; ~ **seat** silla *f* giratoria.
3 *vt* (*also* **to ~ round**) girar.
4 *vi* (*also* **to ~ round**) girar; (*person*) volverse, girar sobre los talones.

◆**swivel round** **1** *vt* = **swivel 3**. **2** *vi* = **swivel 4**.

swizz* [swɪz] *n*, **swizzle*** [ˈswɪzl] *n* (*Brit*) = **swindle**.

swizzle-stick [ˈswɪzlstɪk] *n* paletilla *f* para cóctel.

swollen [ˈswəʊlən] *ptp of* **swell**.

swollen-headed [ˈswəʊlənˈhedɪd] *adj* vanidoso, engreído.

swoon [swuːn] **1** *n* desmayo *m*, desvanecimiento *m*; **to fall in a ~** desmayarse.
2 *vi* (*also* **to ~ away**) desmayarse, desvanecerse; **she ~ed at the news** al saber la noticia se desmayó.

swoop [swuːp] **1** *n* calada *f*, descenso *m* súbito; arremetida *f*; (*by police*) redada *f*; visita *f* de inspección; **at one fell ~, in one ~** de un solo golpe.
2 *vi* (*bird*: *also* **to ~ down**) calarse, abatirse; abalanzarse; precipitarse, lanzarse (*on* sobre); **the plane ~ed low over the village** el avión picó y voló muy bajo sobre el pueblo; **the police ~ed on 8 suspects** en una redada la policía detuvo a 8 sospechosos; **he ~ed on this mistake** se lanzó sobre este error.

swoosh [swʊ(ː)ʃ] = **swish**.

swop [swɒp] = **swap**.

sword [sɔːd] *n* espada *f*; **to cross ~s with sb** habérselas con uno; reñir con uno; **to put people to the ~** pasar a cuchillo a unas gentes; **those that live by the ~ die by the ~** el que a hierro mata a hierro muere.

sword dance [ˈsɔːddɑːns] *n* danza *f* de espadas.

swordfish [ˈsɔːdfɪʃ] *n* pez *m* espada, emperador *m* (*Carib*).

swordplay [ˈsɔːdpleɪ] *n* esgrima *f*; manejo *m* de la espada; **the film has 5 minutes of ~** en la película se combate a espada durante 5 minutos.

swordsman [ˈsɔːdzmən] *n*, *pl* **swordsmen** [ˈsɔːdzmən] espada *f*, espadachín *m*; (*Fencing*) esgrimidor *m*; **a good ~** una buena espada.

swordsmanship [ˈsɔːdzmənʃɪp] *n* esgrima *f*, manejo *m* de la espada.

swordstick [ˈsɔːdstɪk] *n* bastón *m* de estoque.

sword-swallower [ˈsɔːd,swɒləʊəʳ] *n* tragasables *mf*.

sword-thrust [ˈsɔːdθrʌst] *n* estocada *f*.

swore [swɔːʳ] *pret of* **swear**.

sworn [swɔːn] **1** *ptp of* **swear**. **2** *adj enemy* implacable; *evidence*, *statement* dado bajo juramento, jurado.

swot* [swɒt] (*Brit*) **1** *n* empollón* *m*, -ona *f*. **2** *vt* empollar*. **3** *vi* empollar*; **to ~ at sth** empollar algo*.

◆**swot up*** *vti*: **to ~ up (on) one's maths** empollar matemáticas*.

swotting* [ˈswɒtɪŋ] *n*: **to do some ~** empollar*; **too much ~ is a bad idea** empollar demasiado no es bueno*.

swum [swʌm] *ptp of* **swim**.

swung [swʌŋ] *pret and ptp of* **swing**.

sybarite [ˈsɪbəraɪt] *n* sibarita *mf*.

sybaritic [,sɪbəˈrɪtɪk] *adj* sibarita, sibarítico.

sycamore [ˈsɪkəmɔːʳ] *n* (*also* **~ tree**) sicomoro *m*.

sycophancy [ˈsɪkəfənsɪ] *n* adulación *f*; servilismo *m*.

sycophant [ˈsɪkəfənt] *n* sicofanta *m*, sicofante *m*, adulador *m*, -ora *f*, pelotillero *m*, -a *f*; persona *f* servil; sobón *m*.

sycophantic [,sɪkəˈfæntɪk] *adj person* servil, sobón; *speech etc* adulatorio; *manner* servil.

Sydney [ˈsɪdnɪ] *n* Sidney *m*.

syllabi [ˈsɪlə,baɪ] *npl of* **syllabus**.

syllabic [sɪˈlæbɪk] *adj* silábico.

syllabication [sɪ,læbɪˈkeɪʃən] *n*, **syllabification** [sɪ,læbɪfɪˈkeɪʃən] *n* silabeo *m*, división *f* en sílabas.

syllable [ˈsɪləbl] *n* sílaba *f*; **I will explain it in words of one ~** te lo explico como a un niño.

syllabub [ˈsɪləbʌb] *n dulce frío hecho con nata o leche, licor y zumo de limón*.

syllabus [ˈsɪləbəs] *n*, *pl* **syllabuses** *or* **syllabi** [ˈsɪlə,baɪ] programa *m* (*esp* de estudios), plan *m* de estudios.

syllogism [ˈsɪlədʒɪzəm] *n* silogismo *m*.

syllogistic [,sɪləˈdʒɪstɪk] *adj* silogístico.

syllogize [ˈsɪlədʒaɪz] *vi* silogizar.

sylph [sɪlf] *n* (*Myth*) silfo *m*, sílfide *f*; (*woman*) sílfide *f*.

sylphlike [ˈsɪlflaɪk] *adj figure etc* de sílfide.

sylvan [ˈsɪlvən] *adj* selvático, silvestre; rústico.

Sylvia [ˈsɪlvɪə] *nf* Silvia.

symbiosis [,sɪmbɪˈəʊsɪs] *n* simbiosis *f*.

symbiotic [,sɪmbɪˈɒtɪk] *adj* simbiótico.

symbol [ˈsɪmbəl] *n* símbolo *m*.

symbolic(al) [sɪmˈbɒlɪk(əl)] *adj* simbólico; **symbolic logic** lógica *f* simbólica.

symbolically [sɪmˈbɒlɪkəlɪ] *adv* simbólicamente.

symbolism [ˈsɪmbəlɪzəm] *n* simbolismo *m*.

symbolist [ˈsɪmbəlɪst] **1** *adj* simbolista. **2** *n* simbolista *mf*.

symbolize [ˈsɪmbəlaɪz] *vt* simbolizar.

symmetrical [sɪˈmetrɪkəl] *adj* simétrico.

symmetrically [sɪˈmetrɪkəlɪ] *adv* simétricamente.

symmetry [ˈsɪmɪtrɪ] *n* simetría *f*.

sympathetic [,sɪmpəˈθetɪk] *adj* (**a**) (*showing pity*) compasivo (*to* con), compadecido; (*kind*) amable, benévolo; (*understanding*) comprensivo; **we found a ~ policeman** encontramos a un policía que amablemente nos ayudó (*etc*); **they were ~ but could not help** se compadecieron de nosotros pero no podían hacer nada para ayudarnos; **they are ~ to actors** están bien dispuestos hacia los actores; **he wasn't in the least ~** no mostró compasión alguna.
(**b**) *ink*, *nerve*, *pain etc* simpático.

sympathetically [,sɪmpəˈθetɪkəlɪ] *adv* con compasión; amablemente, benévolamente; con comprensión; **she looked at**

seguir el ejemplo (de uno).

2 *vt* (**a**) (*adapt*) adaptar, ajustar, acomodar (*to* a); **to ~ one's style to one's audience** adaptar su estilo al público; **~ing the action to the word** uniendo la acción a la palabra; **the coat and hat are well ~ed** el abrigo y el sombrero van bien juntos; **they are well ~ed to each other** están hechos el uno para el otro; **he is not ~ed for** (*or* **to be**) **a doctor** no es apto para ser médico.

(**b**) (*be suitable: clothes*) sentar a, ir bien a, caer bien a; (*in general*) convenir; gustar; **the coat ~s you** el abrigo te sienta, el abrigo te va bien; **the climate does not ~ me** el clima no me sienta bien; **the job ~s me nicely** el puesto me conviene perfectamente; **does this ~ you?** ¿te gusta esto?; **come when it ~s you** ven cuando quieras, ven cuando te convenga; **I know what ~s me best** sé lo que me conviene; **I shall do it when it ~s me** lo haré cuando me dé la gana.

3 *vr*: **he ~s himself** hace lo que le da la gana, hace lo que quiere; **~ yourself!** ¡haz lo que quieras!, ¡como quieras!

suitability [ˌsuːtəˈbɪlɪtɪ] *n* conveniencia *f*; idoneidad *f* (*for* para).

suitable [ˈsuːtəbl] *adj* conveniente, apropiado; adecuado, idóneo; indicado; **the most ~ man for the job** el hombre más indicado para el puesto; **is this hat ~?** ¿me conviene este sombrero?; **the film is not ~ for children** la película no es apta para menores; **we didn't find anything at all ~** no encontramos nada a propósito, no encontramos nada que nos conviniera; **Tuesday is the most ~ day** el martes nos conviene más.

suitably [ˈsuːtəblɪ] *adv* convenientemente; apropiadamente; **~ dressed for tennis** convenientemente vestido para el tenis.

suitcase [ˈsuːtkeɪs] *n* maleta *f*, valija *f* (*LAm*), veliz *m* (*Mex*).

suite [swiːt] *n* (*of retainers*) séquito *m*, comitiva *f*; (*of furniture*) juego *m*, mobiliario *m*; (*rooms*) serie *f* de habitaciones, grupo *m* de habitaciones; (*Mus*) suite *f*; **bedroom ~** (juego *m* de muebles para) alcoba *f*; **dining-room ~** comedor *m*.

suiting [ˈsuːtɪŋ] *n* (*Comm*) tela *f* para trajes.

suitor [ˈsuːtəʳ] *n* pretendiente *m*; (*Jur*) demandante *mf*.

sulfate [ˈsʌlfeɪt] *etc* (*US*) = **sulphate** *etc*.

sulk [sʌlk] **1** *n*: **~s** mohína *f*, murria *f*, mal humor *m*; **to have the ~s** estar mohíno, estar de mal humor; **to get the ~s** amohinarse. **2** *vi* estar mohíno, estar amohinado, poner cara larga, estar de mal humor.

sulkily [ˈsʌlkɪlɪ] *adv* con mohíno; *answer etc* con mal humor, de mala gana.

sulkiness [ˈsʌlkɪnɪs] *n* mohína *f*, murria *f*, mal humor *m*.

sulky [ˈsʌlkɪ] *adj* mohíno; malhumorado; resentido; **to be ~** estar mohíno, estar de mal humor.

sullen [ˈsʌlən] *adj* hosco, malhumorado; resentido; taciturno; *countryside* triste; *sky* plomizo.

sullenly [ˈsʌlənlɪ] *adv* hoscamente; *answer* con mal humor; *look* con resentimiento.

sullenness [ˈsʌlənnɪs] *n* hosquedad *f*, mal humor *m*; resentimiento *m*; taciturnidad *f*.

sully [ˈsʌlɪ] *vt* (*liter*) manchar.

sulphate, (*US*) **sulfate** [ˈsʌlfeɪt] *n* sulfato *m*; **copper ~** sulfato *m* de cobre.

sulphide, (*US*) **sulfide** [ˈsʌlfaɪd] *n* sulfuro *m*.

sulphonamide, (*US*) **sulfonamide** [sʌlˈfɒnəmaɪd] *n* sulfamida *f*.

sulphur, (*US*) **sulfur** [ˈsʌlfəʳ] *n* azufre *m*; **~ dioxide** dióxido *m* de azufre.

sulphureous, (*US*) **sulfureous** [sʌlˈfjʊərɪəs] *adj* sulfúrico.

sulphuric, (*US*) **sulfuric** [sʌlˈfjʊərɪk] *adj* sulfúrico; **~ acid** ácido *m* sulfúrico.

sulphurous, (*US*) **sulfurous** [ˈsʌlfərəs] *adj* sulfuroso, sulfúreo.

sultan [ˈsʌltən] *n* sultán *m*.

sultana [sʌlˈtɑːnə] *n* (**a**) (*person*) sultana *f*. (**b**) (*fruit*) pasa *f* de Esmirna.

sultanate [ˈsʌltənɪt] *n* sultanato *m*.

sultriness [ˈsʌltrɪnɪs] *n* bochorno *m*; calor *m* sofocante.

sultry [ˈsʌltrɪ] *adj* (**a**) *weather* bochornoso; *heat, atmosphere* sofocante. (**b**) (*fig*) apasionado; seductor, provocativo.

sum [sʌm] *n* (*total*) suma *f*, total *m*; (*quantity*) suma *f*, cantidad *f*; (*Math*) problema *m* de aritmética; **~ total** total *m* (completo); **it is greater than the ~ of its parts** es mayor que la suma de sus partes; **the ~ total of my ambitions is ...** la meta de mis ambiciones es ..., lo único que ambiciono es ...; **in ~** en suma, en resumen; **to do ~s in one's head** hacer un cálculo mental; **I was very bad at ~s** era muy malo en aritmética.

◆**sum up 1** *vt* (*tot up*) sumar; (*review*) resumir; (*evaluate rapidly*) tomar las medidas a, evaluar (rápidamente), justipreciar; **to ~ up an argument** resumir un argumento, recapitular un argumento; **to ~ up a debate** recapitular los argumentos empleados en un debate; **she ~med me up at a glance** me tomó las medidas con una sola mirada; **he ~med up the situation quickly** se dio cuenta rápidamente de la situación.

2 *vi* recapitular, hacer un resumen; **to ~ up ...** en resumen ...

sumac(h) [ˈsuːmæk] *n* zumaque *m*.

Sumatra [sʊˈmɑːtrə] *n* Sumatra *f*.

summarily [ˈsʌmərɪlɪ] *adv* sumariamente.

summarize [ˈsʌməraɪz] *vti* resumir.

summary [ˈsʌmərɪ] **1** *adj* sumario. **2** *n* resumen *m*, sumario *m*; **in ~** en resumen.

summation [sʌˈmeɪʃən] *n* (*act*) adición *f*; recapitulación *f*, resumen *m*; (*total*) suma *f*, total *m*.

summer [ˈsʌməʳ] **1** *n* verano *m*, estío *m*; **a girl of 17 ~s** una joven de 17 abriles; **a ~'s day** un día de verano; **to spend the ~** veranear, pasar el verano.

2 *attr day, clothing, residence* de verano; *season* veraniego; *resort* de veraneo; *weather, heat* estival; **~ camp** (*US*) colonia *f* veraniega infantil; **~ holidays** vacaciones *fpl* de verano, veraneo *m*; **~ school** escuela *f* de verano; **~ time** (*with reference to change of hour*) hora *f* de verano.

3 *vi* veranear, pasar el verano.

summerhouse [ˈsʌməhaʊs] *n*, *pl* **summerhouses** [ˈsʌməˌhaʊzɪz] cenador *m*, glorieta *f*.

summertime [ˈsʌmətaɪm] *n* (*Brit: season*) verano *m*.

summery [ˈsʌmərɪ] *adj* veraniego, estival.

summing-up [ˈsʌmɪŋˈʌp] *n* resumen *m*, recapitulación *f*.

summit [ˈsʌmɪt] **1** *n* cima *f*, cumbre *f* (*also fig*). **2** *attr*: **~ conference** conferencia *f* (en la) cumbre; **~ meeting** cumbre *f*.

summitry [ˈsʌmɪtrɪ] *n* (*hum*) arte *m* de celebrar conferencias cumbre; política *f* en la cumbre.

summon [ˈsʌmən] *vt servant etc* llamar; *meeting* convocar; *aid* pedir, requerir; (*Jur*) citar, emplazar; **to be ~ed to sb's presence** ser llamado a la presencia de uno; **they ~ed me to advise them** me llamaron para que les diera consejos; **to ~ a town to surrender** hacer una llamada a una ciudad para que se rinda, intimar a una ciudad que se rinda.

◆**summon up** *vt courage* armarse de, cobrar; *memory* evocar.

summons [ˈsʌmənz] **1** *n* llamamiento *m*, llamada *f*; requerimiento *m*; (*Jur*) citación *f*; **to serve a ~ on sb** entregar una citación a uno; **to take out a ~ against sb** entablar demanda contra uno, citar a uno (para estrados).

2 *vt* citar, emplazar.

sumo [ˈsuːməʊ] *n* (*also* **~ wrestling**) sumo *m*.

sump [sʌmp] *n* (*Brit Aut etc*) cárter *m*, colector *m* de aceite; (*Min etc*) sumidero *m*; (*fig*) letrina *f*.

sumptuary [ˈsʌmptjʊərɪ] *adj* suntuario.

sumptuous [ˈsʌmptjʊəs] *adj* suntuoso.

sumptuously [ˈsʌmptjʊəslɪ] *adv* suntuosamente.

sumptuousness [ˈsʌmptjʊəsnɪs] *n* suntuosidad *f*.

sun [sʌn] **1** *n* sol *m*; **in the July ~** bajo el sol de julio; **to be out in the ~** estar al sol; **the milk stood in the ~ all day** la leche estuvo al sol todo el día; **he called me all the names under the ~** me dijo de todo; **there's nothing new under the ~** no hay nada realmente nuevo; **they stock everything under the ~** tienen de todo como en botica; **there's no reason under the ~** no hay razón alguna; **to bask in the ~** tomar el sol, estar tumbado al sol; **you've caught the ~** te ha dado el sol; **to have a place in the ~** (*fig*) tener una buena situación; **(put it) where the ~ do(es)n't shine!**‡ (*US*) ¡(métetelo) donde te quepa!‡; **the ~ is shining** hace sol, el sol brilla.

2 *attr* de sol; solar.

3 *vt* asolear.

4 *vr*: **to ~ o.s.** asolearse, tomar el sol.

Sun. [sʌn] *n abbr of* **Sunday** domingo *m*, dom.º.

sunbaked [ˈsʌnbeɪkt] *adj* endurecido al sol.

sunbath [ˈsʌnbɑːθ] *n*, *pl* **sunbaths** [ˈsʌnbɑːðz] baño *m* de sol.

sunbathe [ˈsʌnbeɪð] *vi* tomar el sol.

sunbather [ˈsʌnbeɪðəʳ] *n* persona *f* que toma el sol.

sunbathing [ˈsʌnbeɪðɪŋ] *n* baños *mpl* de sol.

sunbeam [ˈsʌnbiːm] *n* rayo *m* de sol.

sunbed [ˈsʌnbed] *n* (*in garden etc*) tumbona *f*; (*with sunray* *lamp)* cama *f* de rayos infrarrojos, cama *f* solar.

sunblind ['sʌnblaɪnd] *n* toldo *m*; store *m*.

sunblock ['sʌnblɒk] *n* filtro *m* solar.

sunbonnet ['sʌn,bɒnɪt] *n* gorro *m* de sol.

sunburn ['sʌnbɜ:n] *n* (*tan*) bronceado *m*; (*painful*) quemadura *f* del sol.

sunburned ['sʌnbɜ:nd] *adj*, **sunburnt** ['sʌnbɜ:nt] *adj* (*tanned*) tostado por el sol, bronceado; (*painfully*) quemado por el sol; **to get ~** broncearse; sufrir quemaduras del sol.

sundeck ['sʌndek] *n* cubierta *f* de sol.

sundae ['sʌndeɪ] *n helado con frutas, nueces etc.*

Sunday ['sʌndɪ] **1** *n* domingo *m*.
2 *attr* dominical, de domingo; **~ best** ropa *f* dominguera; **~ opening** = **~ trading**; **~ paper** periódico *m* del domingo; **~ school** escuela *f* dominical, catequesis *f*; **~ school teacher** profesor *m*, -ora *f* de escuela dominical; **~ supplement** suplemento *m* dominical; **~ trading** apertura *f* dominical; **~ trading laws** leyes *fpl* reguladoras de la apertura dominical.

sunder ['sʌndəʳ] *vt* (*liter*) romper, dividir, hender; separar.

sundew ['sʌndju:] *n* rocío *m* de sol.

sundial ['sʌndaɪəl] *n* reloj *m* de sol.

sundown ['sʌndaʊn] *n* puesta *f* del sol; anochecer *m*; **at ~** al anochecer; **before ~** antes del anochecer.

sundowner* ['sʌndaʊnəʳ] *n* (*Brit*) *trago de licor que se toma al anochecer.*

sun-drenched ['sʌndrentʃt] *adj* inundado de sol.

sundress ['sʌndres] vestido *m* de playa.

sun-dried ['sʌndraɪd] *adj* secado al sol.

sundry ['sʌndrɪ] **1** *adj* varios, diversos; **all and ~** todos y cada uno. **2** *npl*: **sundries** (*Comm*) géneros *mpl* diversos; (*expenses*) gastos *mpl* diversos.

sun-filled ['sʌnfɪld] *adj* soleado.

sunfish ['sʌnfɪʃ] *n* peje-sol *m*.

sunflower ['sʌn,flaʊəʳ] **1** *n* girasol *m*. **2** *attr*: **~ oil** aceite *m* de girasol; **~ seeds** pipas *fpl*.

sung [sʌŋ] *ptp of* **sing**.

sunglasses ['sʌn,glɑ:sɪz] *npl* gafas *fpl* de sol.

sun-god ['sʌngɒd] *n* dios *m* del sol, divinidad *f* solar.

sunhat ['sʌnhæt] *n* pamela *f*, sombrero *m* ancho.

sunk [sʌŋk] *ptp of* **sink**.

sunken ['sʌŋkən] *adj* hundido.

sunlamp ['sʌnlæmp] *n* lámpara *f* de sol artificial, lámpara *f* ultravioleta.

sunless ['sʌnlɪs] *adj* sin sol.

sunlight ['sʌnlaɪt] *n* sol *m*, luz *f* del sol, luz *f* solar; **in the ~** al sol; **the ~ is strong** el sol es fuerte; **hours of ~** (*Met*) horas *fpl* de insolación.

sunlit ['sʌnlɪt] *adj* iluminado por el sol.

sun-lotion ['sʌn,ləʊʃən] *n* bronceador *m*.

sun-lounge ['sʌnlaʊndʒ] *n* solana *f*.

sunlounger ['sʌn,laʊndʒəʳ] *n* tumbona *f*.

Sunni ['sʌnɪ] **1** *adj* sunita. **2** *n* sunita *mf*.

sunny ['sʌnɪ] *adj* (**a**) *place, room etc* soleado; expuesto al sol; bañado de sol, iluminado por el sol; *day* de sol; **it is ~** hace sol; **June is a ~ month** junio tiene mucho sol; **Málaga is sunnier than Manchester** Málaga tiene más sol que Manchester.
(**b**) (*fig*) *face* risueño; *smile, disposition* alegre; **to be on the ~ side of 40*** tener menos de 40 años; **eggs ~ side up** (*US*) huevos *mpl* al plato, huevos *mpl* fritos (*sin haberles dado la vuelta en la sartén*).

sun-parlour, (*US*) **sun-parlor** ['sʌnpɑ:ləʳ] *n* solana *f*.

sunray ['sʌnreɪ] *attr*: **~ lamp** lámpara *f* ultravioleta; **~ treatment** helioterapia *f*, tratamiento *m* con lámpara ultravioleta.

sunrise ['sʌnraɪz] **1** *n* salida *f* del sol; **from ~ to sunset** de sol a sol. **2** *attr*: **~ industries** industrias *fpl* del porvenir, industrias *fpl* de alta tecnología.

sunroof ['sʌnru:f] *n* (*Aut*) techo *m* corredizo, techo *m* de corredera, techo *m* solar.

sunset ['sʌnset] **1** *n* puesta *f* del sol, ocaso *m*. **2** *attr*: **~ industries** industrias *fpl* crepusculares.

sunshade ['sʌnʃeɪd] *n* (*portable*) quitasol *m*; (*over table*) sombrilla *f*; (*awning*) toldo *m*.

sunshine ['sʌnʃaɪn] **1** *n* (**a**) sol *m*, luz *f* del sol; **in the ~** al sol; **hours of ~** (*Met*) horas *fpl* de insolación; **daily average ~** insolación *f* media diaria.
(**b**) (*) **hello, ~!** (*to child*) ¡hola, nena!*; **now look here, ~** (*iro*) mira, macho*.
2 *attr*: **~ roof** techo *m* corredizo, techo *m* de corredera.

sunspot ['sʌnspɒt] *n* mancha *f* solar.

sunstroke ['sʌnstrəʊk] *n* insolación *f*, asoleada *f* (*And*); **to have ~** sufrir una insolación.

sunsuit ['sʌnsu:t] *n* traje *m* de playa.

suntan ['sʌntæn] **1** *n* bronceado *m*. **2** *attr*: **~ lotion** bronceador *m*.

suntanned ['sʌntænd] *adj* bronceado.

suntrap ['sʌntræp] *n* solana *f*, lugar *m* muy soleado.

sunup ['sʌnʌp] *n* (*US*) salida *f* del sol.

sup [sʌp] **1** *vt* (*also* **to ~ up**) sorber, beber a sorbos. **2** *vi* cenar; **to ~ off sth, to ~ on sth** cenar algo.

super ['su:pəʳ] **1** *adj* (*) estupendo*, bárbaro*, súper*; **how ~!** ¡qué bien!; **the new car is ~** el nuevo coche es estupendo*; **we had a ~ time** lo pasamos bomba*.
2 *n* (*) (*abbr Theat, Cine*) figurante *m*, -a *f*; comparsa *mf*; (*Tech*: *superintendent*) superintendente *m*, (*of police*) comisario *m*.

super... ['su:pəʳ] *pref* super..., sobre...; *eg* **~-salesman** supervendedor *m*.

superabound [,su:pərə'baʊnd] *vi* sobreabundar (*in, with* en).

superabundance [,su:pərə'bʌndəns] *n* sobreabundancia *f*, superabundancia *f*.

superabundant [,su:pərə'bʌndənt] *adj* sobreabundante, superabundante.

superannuate [,su:pə'rænjʊeɪt] *vt* jubilar.

superannuated [,su:pə'rænjʊeɪtɪd] *adj* jubilado; (*fig*) anticuado.

superannuation [,su:pə,rænjʊ'eɪʃən] **1** *n* jubilación *f*. **2** *attr*: **~ contribution** cuota *f* de jubilación.

superb [su:'pɜ:b] *adj* magnífico, espléndido.

superbly [su:'pɜ:blɪ] *adv* magníficamente; **a ~ painted picture** un cuadro de la mayor excelencia técnica; **a ~ fit man** un hombre en magnífico estado físico.

supercargo ['su:pə,kɑ:gəʊ] *n* sobrecargo *m*.

supercharged ['su:pətʃɑ:dʒd] *adj* sobrealimentado.

supercharger ['su:pətʃɑ:dʒəʳ] *n* sobrealimentador *m*.

supercilious [,su:pə'sɪlɪəs] *adj* desdeñoso, arrogante; suficiente.

superciliously [,su:pə'sɪlɪəslɪ] *adv* desdeñosamente, con desdén; con aire de suficiencia.

superciliousness [,su:pə'sɪlɪəsnɪs] *n* desdén *m*, arrogancia *f*.

superconductivity [,su:pə,kɒndʌk'tɪvɪtɪ] *n* superconductividad *f*.

superconductor [,su:pəkən'dʌktəʳ] *n* superconductor *m*.

super-duper* ['su:pə'du:pəʳ] *adj* estupendo*, magnífico, de aúpa*; **~!** ¡magnífico!

superego ['su:pər,i:gəʊ] *n* superego *m*.

supererogation [,su:pər,erə'geɪʃən] *n* supererogación *f*.

superficial [,su:pə'fɪʃəl] *adj* superficial.

superficiality [,su:pə,fɪʃɪ'ælɪtɪ] *n* superficialidad *f*.

superficially [,su:pə'fɪʃəlɪ] *adv* superficialmente; en la superficie; **~ this may be true** a primera vista esto puede ser verdad.

superfine ['su:pəfaɪn] *adj* extrafino.

superfluity [,su:pə'flʊɪtɪ] *n* superfluidad *f*; **there is a ~ of ...** hay exceso de ...

superfluous [sʊ'pɜ:flʊəs] *adj* superfluo; sobrante, que sobra, que está de más; **it is ~ to say that ...** no hace falta decir que ...

superfluously [sʊ'pɜ:flʊəslɪ] *adv* superfluamente; **he added ~** añadió fuera de propósito.

superglue ['su:pə,glu:] *n* supercola *f*.

supergrass‡ ['su:pəgrɑ:s] *n* supersoplón* *m*, -ona *f*.

superheat [,su:pə'hi:t] *vt* sobrecalentar.

superhighway ['su:pə'haɪweɪ] *n* (*US*) autopista *f* (de varios carriles).

superhuman [,su:pə'hju:mən] *adj* sobrehumano.

superimpose ['su:pərɪm'pəʊz] *vt* sobreponer (*on* en).

superinduce ['su:pərɪn'dju:s] *vt* sobreañadir, inducir por añadidura.

superintend [,su:pərɪn'tend] *vt* vigilar; supervisar, dirigir.

superintendence [,su:pərɪn'tendəns] *n* superintendencia *f*; supervisión *f*, dirección *f*.

superintendent [,su:pərɪn'tendənt] *n* superintendente *mf*; inspector *m*, -ora *f*; supervisor *m*, -ora *f*; (*in swimming pool etc*) vigilante *mf*; **~ of police** comisario *m* de policía.

superior [sʊ'pɪərɪəʳ] **1** *adj* superior (*to* a); (*smug*) desdeñoso; satisfecho, suficiente; **she thinks herself very ~** se da aires de suficiencia; **he said in that ~ tone** dijo en ese tono suficiente.
2 *n* superior *m*; (*Eccl*) superior *m*, -ora *f*; **Mother S~** (madre *f*) superiora *f*.

superiority [sʊ,pɪərɪ'ɒrɪtɪ] *n* superioridad *f* (*to* a); desdén *m*; suficiencia *f*.

superlative [sʊ'pɜ:lətɪv] **1** *adj* superlativo (*also Gram*), extremo. **2** *n* superlativo *m*.

superlatively [sʊ'pɜːlətɪvlɪ] *adv* en sumo grado, extremadamente; ~ **fit** en óptimo estado físico.
superman ['suːpəmæn] *n, pl* **supermen** ['suːpəmen] superhombre *m*.
supermarket ['suːpə,mɑːkɪt] *n* supermercado *m*.
supernatural [,suːpə'nætʃərəl] **1** *adj* sobrenatural. **2** *n*: **the** ~ lo sobrenatural.
supernormal [,suːpə'nɔːməl] *adj* superior a lo normal.
supernumerary [,suːpə'njuːmərərɪ] **1** *adj* supernumerario. **2** *n* supernumerario *m*, -a *f*; (*Theat, Cine*) figurante *m*, -a *f*, comparsa *mf*.
superphosphate [,suːpə'fɒsfeɪt] *n* superfosfato *m*.
superpose ['suːpəpəʊz] *vt* sobreponer, superponer.
superposition ['suːpəpəzɪʃən] *n* superposición *f*.
superpower ['suːpə,paʊə^r] *n* superpotencia *f*.
superscript [,suːpə'skrɪpt] *n* superíndice *m*.
superscription [,suːpə'skrɪpʃən] *n* sobrescrito *m*.
supersede [,suːpə'siːd] *vt* reemplazar, sustituir; suplantar.
supersensitive ['suːpə'sensɪtɪv] *adj* extremadamente sensible (*to* a).
supersonic ['suːpə'sɒnɪk] *adj* supersónico; ~ **bang**, ~ **boom** estampido *m* supersónico, bang *m* sónico.
supersonically ['suːpə'sɒnɪkəlɪ] *adv fly etc* a velocidad supersónica.
superstar ['suːpəstɑː^r] *n* superestrella *f*.
superstition [,suːpə'stɪʃən] *n* superstición *f*.
superstitious [,suːpə'stɪʃəs] *adj* supersticioso.
superstitiously [,suːpə'stɪʃəslɪ] *adv* supersticiosamente.
superstore ['suːpəstɔː^r] *n* (*Brit*) hipermercado *m*.
superstratum [,suːpə'strɑːtəm] *n, pl* **superstratums** *or* **superstrata** [,suːpə'strɑːtə] superstrato *m*.
superstructure ['suːpə,strʌktʃə^r] *n* superestructura *f*.
supertanker ['suːpə,tæŋkə^r] *n* superpetrolero *m*, petrolero *m* gigante.
supertax ['suːpətæks] *n* sobreimpuesto *m*; (*rate*) sobretasa *f*.
supervene [,suːpə'viːn] *vi* sobrevenir.
supervise ['suːpəvaɪz] *vt* supervisar; (*Univ*) *thesis* dirigir.
supervision [,suːpə'vɪʒən] *n* supervisión *f*: **to work under the ~ of ...** trabajar bajo la supervisión de ...
supervisor ['suːpəvaɪzə^r] *n* supervisor *m*, -ora *f*; (*Univ*) director *m*, -ora *f*.
supervisory ['suːpəvaɪzərɪ] *adj*: **in a ~ post** en un cargo de supervisor; **in his ~ capacity** en su función de supervisor.
supine ['suːpaɪn] **1** *adj* supino; (*fig*) flojo, sin carácter, débil. **2** *n* supino *m*.
supper ['sʌpə^r] *n* cena *f*; **the Last S~** la Última Cena; **to stay to ~** quedarse a cenar; **to have ~** cenar.
suppertime ['sʌpətaɪm] *n* hora *f* de cenar.
supplant [sə'plɑːnt] *vt* suplantar.
supple ['sʌpl] *adj* flexible.
supplement **1** ['sʌplɪmənt] *n* suplemento *m*; apéndice *m*; (*Press*) suplemento *m*. **2** [sʌplɪ'ment] *vt* suplir, complementar; **to ~ one's income by writing** aumentar sus ingresos escribiendo artículos (*etc*).
supplementary [,sʌplɪ'mentərɪ] *adj* suplementario; adicional; *question* (*Parl*) adicional, oral; ~ **benefit** (*Brit formerly*) beneficio *m* suplementario.
suppleness ['sʌplnɪs] *n* flexibilidad *f*.
suppliant ['sʌplɪənt] **1** *adj* suplicante. **2** *n* suplicante *mf*.
supplicant ['sʌplɪkənt] *n* suplicante *mf*.
supplicate ['sʌplɪkeɪt] *vti* suplicar.
supplication [,sʌplɪ'keɪʃən] *n* súplica *f*.
supplier [sə'plaɪə^r] *n* suministrador *m*, -ora *f*; (*Comm*) proveedor *m*, -ora *f*; distribuidor *m*, -ora *f*; **from your usual ~** de su proveedor habitual.
supply [sə'plaɪ] **1** *n* (**a**) suministro *m*, provisión *f*, abastecimiento *m*; (*stock*: *Comm*) surtido *m*, existencias *fpl*; (*Comm, Econ*) oferta *f*; **electricity ~** suministro *m* de electricidad; **the ~ of fuel to the engine** el suministro de combustible al motor; **~ and demand** oferta *f* y demanda; **new cars are in short ~** hay pocos coches nuevos, hay escasez de coches nuevos; **we need a fresh ~ of coffee** hace falta proveernos de café; **to lay in a ~ of** proveerse de, hacer provisión de.

(**b**) **supplies** (*food*) provisiones *fpl*, víveres *mpl*; (*Mil*) pertrechos *mpl*; **electrical supplies** artículos *mpl* eléctricos; **office supplies** material *m* para oficina; **supplies are running low** escasean las provisiones; se están agotando las existencias.

(**c**) (*Parl*) provisión *f* financiera; **Committee on S~** Comisión *f* del Presupuesto; **to vote supplies** votar créditos.

2 *vt* (**a**) *material etc* suministrar, facilitar, proporcionar; (*Comm*) surtir; *army, city etc* aprovisionar; **the tradesmen who ~ us** nuestros proveedores; **can you ~ this spare part?** ¿pueden facilitarme este repuesto?; **she supplied the vital clue** ella nos dio la pista esencial; **to ~ sb with sth** (*of supplies*) abastecer a uno de algo, proveer a uno de algo; **he supplied us with some facts** nos facilitó (*or* proporcionó) varios datos; **this supplied me with the chance** esto me brindó la oportunidad; **we are not supplied with a radio** no estamos provistos de radio.

(**b**) (*make good*) *want* suplir.
supply ship [sə'plaɪʃɪp] *n* buque *m* de abastecimiento.
supply-side [sə'plaɪ,saɪd] *attr*: ~ **economics** economía *f* de oferta.
supply teacher [sə'plaɪ'tiːtʃə^r] *n* maestro *m*, -a *f* suplente.
support [sə'pɔːt] **1** *n* (**a**) (*Tech*) soporte *m*, apoyo *m*; pilar *m*.

(**b**) (*fig*) apoyo *m*; (*person*) sostén *m*; **moral ~** apoyo *m* moral; **financial ~** ayuda *f* económica; **in ~ of** en apoyo de; **documents in ~ of an allegation** documentos *mpl* que confirman una alegación; **to speak in ~ of a candidate** apoyar la candidatura de uno; **I will give you every ~** te apoyaré todo lo que pueda; **the proposal got no ~** la propuesta no recibió apoyo alguno; **to lean on sb for ~** apoyarse en uno; **they depend on him for financial ~** dependen de él para mantenerse, reciben ayuda económica de él; **our ~ comes from the workers** nos apoyan los obreros, los obreros son partidarios nuestros; **liberal ~ got him elected** los votos de los liberales aseguraron su elección.

2 *attr*: ~ **buying** compra *f* proteccionista; ~ **hose**, ~ **stockings** venda *f* (*or* media *f*) elástica; ~ **price** precio *m* de apoyo.

3 *vt* (**a**) (*Tech*) apoyar, sostener; **it is ~ed on 4 columns** descansa sobre 4 columnas, está apoyado en 4 columnas.

(**b**) (*uphold*) apoyar; sostener, mantener; *campaign* apoyar, respaldar; *life* sostener; *motion* aprobar, votar por; *team* ser hincha de; (*corroborate*) confirmar; (*Comput*) apoyar; **I cannot ~ what you are doing** no apruebo lo que estás haciendo; **the liberals will ~ it** los liberales votarán en favor.

(**c**) (*financially*) mantener.

4 *vr*: **to ~ o.s.** (*physically*) apoyarse (*on* en); (*financially*) mantenerse; ganarse la vida.
supportable [sə'pɔːtəbl] *adj* soportable.
supporter [sə'pɔːtə^r] *n* (**a**) (*Tech*) soporte *m*, sostén *m*; (*Her*) tenante *m*, soporte *m*. (**b**) (*person*) defensor *m*, -ora *f*; (*Pol etc*) partidario *m*, -a *f*; (*Sport*) seguidor *m*, -ora *f*, hincha *mf*; **~s' club** peña *f* deportiva; **after the match ~s flooded on to the pitch** al terminar el partido los hinchas invadieron el campo de juego.
supporting [sə'pɔːtɪŋ] *adj film, role* secundario; ~ **feature** (*Cine*) complemento *m*.
supportive [sə'pɔːtɪv] *adj* (*esp US*) soportante; amable, compasivo; ~ **of** que apoya a; **a ~ role** un papel de apoyo, un papel fortalecedor; **I have a very ~ family** tengo una familia que me ayuda mucho.
supportiveness [sə'pɔːtɪvnɪs] *n* sustentación *f*.
support ship [sə'pɔːtʃɪp] *n* barco *m* de apoyo.
suppose [sə'pəʊz] **1** *vt* (**a**) (*assume as hypothesis*) suponer; figurarse, imaginarse; **let us ~ that X equals 3** supongamos que X vale 3; **let us ~ that ...** pongamos por caso que ..., vamos a poner que ...; **let us ~ we are living in the 8th century** figurémonos que vivimos en el siglo VIII.

(**b**) (*= 'if'*) **~ he comes, supposing (that) he comes** y ¿si viene?; **even supposing it were true** aun en el caso de que fuera verdad; **always supposing he comes** siempre y cuando venga; **~ they could see us now!** ¡si solamente pudieran vernos ahora!

(**c**) (*imperative*: *'I suggest'*) **~ we have a go** ¿probamos?; **~ we buy it?** ¿qué te parece si lo compramos?; **~ you have a wash?** ¿no crees que conviene ir a lavarte?

(**d**) (*presuppose*) suponer, presuponer; **that ~s unlimited resources** eso supone unos recursos ilimitados.

(**e**) (*take for granted, assume*) suponer, presumir; creer; **I ~ so** supongo que sí, creo que sí, (*unwillingly*) no hay más remedio, no cabe otra explicación; **it is not to be ~d that ...** no se ha de suponer que ..., no se imagine nadie que ...; **I ~ you are right** me supongo que tendrás razón, debes de tener razón; **I don't ~ he really means it** no creo que lo diga en serio; **do you ~ that ...?** ¿crees en serio que ...?; **who do you ~ was there?** ¿quiénes crees tú que estaban?; **you don't ~ he'll get lost?** ¿crees posible que se pierda?; **what's that ~d to mean?** ¿qué quieres decir con eso?; **I ~ you know that** ... me imagino que sabes que ...; **I don't ~ you could lend me a pound?, I ~ you couldn't lend me a pound?** ¿podrías por casualidad prestarme una libra?; **he is ~d to be coming** se cree que va a venir, se supone que va a venir; **and he's ~d to be an expert!** ¡y él que tiene fama de experto!; **he's ~d to be in Wales** dicen que está en Gales.

(**f**) (*of obligation*) deber; **he's the one who's ~d to do it** él es quien debe hacerlo, le toca a él hacerlo; **you're ~d to be in bed** tú deberías estar en la cama; **you're not ~d to eat those** no deberías comer aquéllos, no se te permite comer aquéllos.

2 *vi*: **just ~!** ¡imagínate!; **you'll come, I ~?** ¿me imagino que vendrás?

supposed [sə'pəʊzd] *adj* supuesto, pretendido.

supposedly [sə'pəʊzɪdlɪ] *adv* según cabe suponer; **he had ~ gone to Scotland** según lo que se creía había ido a Escocia; **the ~ brave James Bond** el James Bond que se suponía tan valiente; el supuesto valiente James Bond.

supposing [sə'pəʊzɪŋ] *as conj* si, en el caso de que; *V* **suppose** (**b**).

supposition [ˌsʌpə'zɪʃən] *n* suposición *f*, hipótesis *f*; **that is pure ~** eso es una hipótesis nada más.

suppositious [ˌsʌpə'zɪʃəs] *adj*, **supposititious** [səˌpɒzɪ'tɪʃəs] *adj* fingido, espurio, supositicio.

suppository [sə'pɒzɪtərɪ] *n* supositorio *m*.

suppress [sə'pres] *vt* (*in most senses*) suprimir; *yawn etc* ahogar; *emotion* contener; *heckler etc* reprimir, hacer callar; *scandal etc* disimular.

suppressed [sə'prest] *adj book etc* suprimido; **with ~ emotion** con emoción contenida; **a half ~ laugh** una risa mal disimulada.

suppression [sə'preʃən] *n* supresión *f*; represión *f*; disimulación *f*.

suppressor [sə'presəʳ] *n* supresor *m*.

suppurate ['sʌpjʊəreɪt] *vi* supurar.

suppuration [ˌsʌpjʊə'reɪʃən] *n* supuración *f*.

supra... ['suːprə] *pref* supra...; **~normal** supranormal; **~renal** suprarrenal.

supranational ['suːprə'næʃənl] *adj* supranacional.

suprasegmental [ˌsuːprəseg'mentl] *adj* suprasegmental.

supremacist [sʊ'preməsɪst] *n* partidario *m*, -a *f* de la supremacía (de un grupo, raza *etc*).

supremacy [sʊ'preməsɪ] *n* supremacía *f*.

supreme [sʊ'priːm] *adj* supremo; sumo, *eg* **with ~ indifference** con suma indiferencia; **S~ Being** Ser *m* Supremo; **S~ Court** Tribunal *m* Supremo, Corte *f* Suprema (*LAm*); **to reign ~** (*fig*) estar en la cumbre (de su profesión *etc*), no tener rival alguno.

supremely [sʊ'priːmlɪ] *adv* sumamente.

supremo [sʊ'priːməʊ] *n* jefe *m*.

Supt (*Brit*) *abbr of* **Superintendent** comisario *m* de policía.

sura ['sʊərə] *n* sura *m*.

surcharge 1 ['sɜːtʃɑːdʒ] *n* sobrecarga *f*, sobretasa *f*; recargo *m*. **2** [sɜː'tʃɑːdʒ] *vt* sobrecargar.

surd [sɜːd] *n* número *m* sordo.

sure [ʃʊəʳ] **1** *adj* (**a**) (*infallible, safe*) seguro; cierto; *aim etc* certero; *hand, touch* firme; **as ~ as fate, as ~ as eggs** con toda seguridad; **~ thing!** (*US*) ¡por supuesto!

(**b**) (*certain*) seguro; **to be ~!** ¡claro!; **and there he was, to be ~** y ahí estaba, efectivamente; **are you quite ~?** ¿estás seguro del todo?; **I'm perfectly ~** estoy perfectamente seguro; **to be ~ about sth** estar seguro de algo; **I'm not so ~ about that** no estoy del todo seguro, no diría yo tanto; **to be ~ of o.s.** estar seguro de sí mismo; **to be ~ that** ... estar seguro de que ...; **it is ~ that he will come** es seguro que vendrá; **I'm ~ I don't know** que me maten si lo sé; **it is ~ to rain** seguramente lloverá; **he is ~ to come** seguramente vendrá; **be ~ to turn the gas off** ten cuidado de cortar el gas; **be ~ to go and see her** no dejes de ir a verla, ve a verla sin falta.

(**c**) **I don't know for ~** no sé con seguridad, no sé a punto fijo; **that's for ~** eso es seguro; **he'll come next time for ~** vendrá la próxima vez sin falta.

(**d**) **to make ~ of** *facts* verificar, comprobar, cerciorarse de; **to make ~ of sb** asegurarse del apoyo de uno, asegurarse de poder contar con uno; **(in order) to make quite ~** para asegurarse del todo; **it's best to make ~** vale más estar seguro; **to make ~ that** ... asegurar que ..., cerciorarse de que ...

2 *adv* (**a**) **~!** (*esp US*) sí; ¡claro!; ¡naturalmente!; ¡ya lo creo!; **~ enough** efectivamente, en efecto; **he'll come ~ enough** seguramente vendrá; **it's petrol ~ enough** en efecto es gasolina.

(**b**) (*US*) **that ~ was a rich man** ése sí que era rico; **that meat was ~ tough** la carne esa fue verdaderamente dura.

sure-fire ['ʃʊə'faɪəʳ] *adj* de éxito seguro, seguro.

sure-footed ['ʃʊə'fʊtɪd] **1** *adj* de pie firme. **2** *adv* con pie firme.

surely ['ʃʊəlɪ] *adv* seguramente; ciertamente; por supuesto; **~!** (*US: gladly*) con mucho gusto; **~ not?** ¿será posible?; **~ you don't mean it?** ¿seguramente no lo dices en serio?; **~ you don't expect me to do it?** ¿no querrás que lo haga yo?; **~ you don't believe him?** ¿no irás a creerle?; **it will ~ happen** seguramente pasará; **~ he's come (hasn't he?)** ¿será posible que no haya venido?; **~ he hasn't come (has he?)** ¿será posible que haya venido?; **~ to goodness** (*or* **God**) **you know that!** ¡no es posible que ignores eso!

sureness ['ʃʊənɪs] *n* seguridad *f*; certeza *f*; lo certero; firmeza *f*.

surety ['ʃʊərətɪ] *n* (*sum*) garantía *f*; fianza *f*; (*person*) fiador *m*, -ora *f*; garante *mf*; **to go** (*or* **stand**) **~ for sb** ser fiador de uno, salir garante por uno; **in his own ~ of £500** bajo su propia fianza de 500 libras.

surf [sɜːf] **1** *n* (*foam*) espuma *f*; (*waves*) olas *fpl*, rompientes *mpl*; (*swell*) oleaje *m*. **2** *vi* hacer surf.

surface ['sɜːfɪs] **1** *n* superficie *f*; exterior *m*; (*of road*) firme *m*; **we haven't done more than scratch the ~ yet** todavía no hemos ido al fondo de este problema (*etc*); **the tension below** (*or* **beneath**) **the ~** la tirantez que no se ve, la tensión oculta; **on the ~ it seems that** ... a primera vista parece que ...; **to come** (*or* **rise**) **to the ~** salir a la superficie.

2 *attr* de la superficie; **~ area** área *f* de la superficie; **~ noise** ruido *m* de la superficie; **~ tension** tensión *f* superficial; **~ water** aguas *fpl* superficiales; **~ workers** personal *m* del exterior, personal *m* que trabaja a cielo abierto; **by ~ mail** (*land*) por vía terrestre, (*sea*) por vía marítima.

3 *vt* poner superficie a; recubrir, revestir; (*smoothe*) alisar.

4 *vi* (*submarine etc*) salir a la superficie, emerger; **he ~s in London occasionally** de vez en cuando asoma la cara en Londres.

surface-(to)-air ['sɜːfɪs(tuː)'ɛəʳ] *attr*: **~ missile** proyectil *m* tierra-aire.

surfboard ['sɜːfbɔːd] *n* plancha *f* de surf, tabla *f* de surf.

surfboarder ['sɜːfˌbɔːdəʳ] *n* surfista *mf*.

surfboarding ['sɜːfˌbɔːdɪŋ] *n* surf *m*, acuaplano *m*.

surfeit ['sɜːfɪt] **1** *n* (*satiety*) hartura *f*, saciedad *f*; (*indigestion*) empacho *m*; (*excess*) exceso *m*; superabundancia *f*; **there is a ~ of** hay exceso de; **he died of a ~ of lampreys** murió después de hartarse de lampreas.

2 *vt* hartar, saciar (*on, with* de).

3 *vr*: **to ~ o.s.** hartarse, saciarse (*on, with* de).

surfer ['sɜːfəʳ] *n* tablista *mf*.

surfing ['sɜːfɪŋ] *n*, **surfriding** ['sɜːfˌraɪdɪŋ] *n* (*Brit*) surf *m*, acuaplano *m*.

surge [sɜːdʒ] **1** *n* (**a**) (*Naut*) oleaje *m*, oleada *f*; (*fig*) oleada *f*, ola *f*; **a ~ of people** una oleada de gente; **there was a ~ of sympathy for him** hubo una oleada de compasión por él.

(**b**) (*Elec*) sobretensión *f* transitoria.

2 *vi* (*water*) agitarse, hervir; **the crowd ~d into the building** la multitud entró a tropel en el edificio; **people ~d down the street** una oleada de gente avanzó por la calle; **blood ~d into her face** se le subió la sangre a la cara; **they ~d round him** se apiñaban en torno suyo.

surgeon ['sɜːdʒən] *n* cirujano *m*, -a *f*; (*Mil, Naut*) médico *m*, oficial *m* médico; **S~ General** (*Mil*) cirujano *m* general.

surgery ['sɜːdʒərɪ] **1** *n* (**a**) (*art, operation*) cirugía *f*. (**b**) (*Brit: room*) clínica *f*, consultorio *m*, gabinete *m* de consulta. **2** *attr*: **~ hours** horas *fpl* de consulta.

surgical ['sɜːdʒɪkəl] *adj* quirúrgico; **~ dressing** vendaje *m* quirúrgico; **~ spirit** (*Brit*) alcohol *m* de 90°.

surgically ['sɜːdʒɪklɪ] *adv* quirúrgicamente; por medios quirúrgicos.

Surinam [ˌsʊərɪ'næm] *n* Surinam *m*.

Surinamese [ˌsʊərɪnæ'miːz] **1** *adj* surinamés. **2** *n* surinamés *m*, -esa *f*.

surliness ['sɜːlɪnɪs] *n* hosquedad *f*, mal humor *m*; falta *f* de educación; aspereza *f*.

surly ['sɜːlɪ] *adj* hosco, malhumorado; maleducado; **of a ~ disposition** de genio áspero; **he gave me a ~ answer** contestó malhumorado.

surmise 1 ['sɜːmaɪz] *n* conjetura *f*, suposición *f*; **my ~ is that** ... lo que yo supongo es que ... **2** [sɜː'maɪz] *vt* conjeturar, suponer; **I ~d as much** ya lo suponía; **as one could ~ from his book** según cabía entender en su libro.

surmount [sɜː'maʊnt] *vt* (**a**) *difficulty* superar, vencer. (**b**)

~ed by (*Archit etc*) coronado de.
surmountable [sɜː'maʊntəbl] *adj* superable.
surname ['sɜːneɪm] **1** *n* apellido *m.* **2** *vt* apellidar.
surpass [sɜː'pɑːs] **1** *vt* sobrepasar, superar, exceder; eclipsar; **it ~es anything we have seen before** supera a cuanto hemos visto antes.
2 *vr*: **to ~ o.s.** excederse a sí mismo.
surpassing [sɜː'pɑːsɪŋ] *adj* incomparable, sin par; **of ~ beauty** de hermosura sin par.
surplice ['sɜːpləs] *n* sobrepelliz *f.*
surplus ['sɜːpləs] **1** *n* excedente *m,* sobrante *m,* exceso *m;* (*Fin, Comm*) superávit *m;* **the 1995 wheat ~** el excedente de trigo de 1995.
2 *attr* excedente, sobrante; de sobra; **~ energy** energía *f* sobrante; **~ store** tienda *f* de excedentes; **my ~ socks** los calcetines que me sobran, los calcetines que no necesito; **American ~ wheat** el excedente de trigo norteamericano; **stocks ~ to requirements** existencias *fpl* que exceden de las necesidades; **sale of ~ stock** liquidación *f* de saldos; **have you any ~ sheets?** ¿tenéis sábanas que os sobren?
surprise [sə'praɪz] **1** *n* sorpresa *f;* asombro *m,* extrañeza *f;* **~, ~!** ¡bomba!; **much to my ~, to my great ~** con gran sorpresa mía; **with a look of ~** con un gesto de extrañeza; **it was a ~ to find that ...** fue una sorpresa encontrar que ...; **imagine my ~** imaginaos cuál sería mi asombro; **it came as a ~ to us** nos cogió de nuevas; **to give sb a ~** dar una sorpresa a uno; **to take sb by ~** sorprender a uno, coger a uno desprevenido.
2 *attr*: **~ attack** sorpresa *f,* ataque *m* por sorpresa, ataque *m* imprevisto; **~ defeat** derrota *f* sorpresa, derrota *f* sorpresiva; **~ package** sorpresa *f;* **~ party** fiesta *f* de sorpresa.
3 *vt* sorprender; asombrar, extrañar; (*Mil*) coger por sorpresa; **to ~ sb in the act** coger a uno in fraganti; **you ~ me!** ¡me asombras!; **it ~s me to learn that ...** me asombra saber que ...; **to be ~d** quedar asombrado; **to be ~d to see sb** asombrarse de ver a uno; **I should not be ~d if ...** no me sorprendería que + *subj*; **to look ~d** hacer un gesto de extrañeza.
surprising [sə'praɪzɪŋ] *adj* sorprendente, asombroso.
surprisingly [sə'praɪzɪŋlɪ] *adv* de modo sorprendente; asombrosamente; **he is ~ young** se asombra uno de descubrir que es tan joven; **and then ~ he left** y luego con asombro de todos partió; **~ enough, he agreed** cosa sorprendente, asintió.
surreal [sə'rɪəl] *adj* surreal, surrealista.
surrealism [sə'rɪəlɪzəm] *n* surrealismo *m.*
surrealist [sə'rɪəlɪst] **1** *adj* surrealista. **2** *n* surrealista *mf.*
surrealistic [sə,rɪə'lɪstɪk] *adj* surrealista.
surrender [sə'rendəʳ] **1** *n* rendición *f,* capitulación *f;* entrega *f;* renuncia *f;* cesión *f;* abandono *m;* **the ~ of Breda** la rendición de Breda; **~ of property** (*Jur*) cesión *f* de bienes; **no ~!** ¡no nos rendimos nunca!; **to make a ~ of one's principles** transigir con sus principios.
2 *attr*: **~ value** valor *m* de rescate.
3 *vt* (*Mil*) rendir, entregar; *goods* entregar; *claim, right* renunciar a; *lease, ownership* ceder; *insurance policy* rescatar; *hope* renunciar a, abandonar.
4 *vi* rendirse, entregarse; **to ~ to the police** entregarse a la policía; **I ~!** ¡me rindo!
5 *vr*: **to ~ o.s. to remorse** abandonarse al remordimiento.
surreptitious [,sʌrəp'tɪʃəs] *adj* subrepticio, clandestino.
surreptitiously [,sʌrəp'tɪʃəslɪ] *adv* subrepticiamente, clandestinamente; a hurtadillas.
surrogacy ['sʌrəgəsɪ] *n* (*in child-bearing*) subrogación *f,* alquiler *m* de madres.
surrogate ['sʌrəgeɪt] *n* sustituto *m,* suplente *m;* (*Brit Eccl*) vicario *m;* **~ coffee** sucedáneo *m* de café; **~ mother** madre *f* portadora, madre *f* alquilada, concertada *f;* **~ motherhood** alquiler *m* de úteros.
surround [sə'raʊnd] **1** *n* marco *m;* borde *m.*
2 *vt* rodear, cercar, circundar; (*Mil*) copar, cercar; sitiar; **a town ~ed by hills** una ciudad rodeada de colinas; **she was ~ed by children** estaba rodeada de niños.
surrounding [sə'raʊndɪŋ] **1** *adj* circundante; **in the ~ hills** en las colinas vecinas, en las colinas de alrededor; **in the ~ darkness** en la oscuridad que le (*etc*) envolvía.
2 *npl*: **~s** (*of place*) alrededores *mpl,* cercanías *fpl,* contornos *mpl;* (*environment*) ambiente *m.*
surtax ['sɜːtæks] *n* sobreimpuesto *m;* (*rate*) sobretasa *f.*
surtitle ['sɜːtaɪtl] *n* sobretítulo *m.*
surveil [sə'veɪl] *vt* (*US*) vigilar.
surveillance [sɜː'veɪləns] *n* vigilancia *f;* **to be under ~** estar vigilado, estar bajo vigilancia; **to keep sb under ~** vigilar a uno.
survey 1 ['sɜːveɪ] *n* inspección *f,* examen *m;* estudio *m;* reconocimiento *m;* (*of land*) apeo *m,* medición *f;* (*of building, property*) inspección *f;* (*poll*) encuesta *f;* (*general view*) vista *f* de conjunto; (*as published report, to purchaser etc*) informe *m;* **he gave a general ~ of the situation** hizo un informe general sobre la situación; **to make a ~ of housing in a town** estudiar la situación de la vivienda en una ciudad.
2 [sɜː'veɪ] *vt* (*look at*) mirar, contemplar; (*inspect*) inspeccionar, examinar; (*study*) estudiar, hacer un estudio de; *ground before battle etc* reconocer; *land* apear, medir; *town etc* levantar el plano de; (*take general view of*) pasar en revista; obtener una vista de conjunto de; **he ~ed the desolate scene** miró detenidamente la triste escena; **monarch of all he ~s** monarca *m* de todo cuanto domina con la vista; **the report ~s housing in Slobodia** el informe estudia la situación de la vivienda en Eslobodia; **the book ~s events up to 1972** el libro pasa revista de los sucesos hasta 1972.
surveying [sɜː'veɪɪŋ] *n* agrimensura *f;* planimetría *f;* topografía *f.*
surveyor [sə'veɪəʳ] *n* (*Brit*: *of land*) agrimensor *m,* -ora *f;* topógrafo *m,* -a *f;* (*of property*) inspector *m,* -ora *f.*
survival [sə'vaɪvəl] **1** *n* **(a)** (*act*) supervivencia *f;* **~ of the fittest** supervivencia *f* de los más aptos.
(b) (*relic*) supervivencia *f;* vestigio *m,* reliquia *f.*
2 *attr*: **~ bag** saco *m* de supervivencia; **~ course** curso *m* de supervivencia; **~ kit** equipo *m* de emergencia.
survive [sə'vaɪv] **1** *vt* (*all senses*) sobrevivir a; **he is ~d by his wife and 3 sons** le sobreviven su esposa y 3 hijos. **2** *vi* sobrevivir; (*remain, persist*) durar, perdurar, subsistir; **on my salary I can just ~** con mi sueldo vivo muy justo; **he ~d on nuts for several weeks** logró vivir durante varias semanas comiendo nueces.
surviving [sə'vaɪvɪŋ] *adj spouse, children etc* sobreviviente; **~ company** (*Fin: after merger*) compañía *f* resultante.
survivor [sə'vaɪvəʳ] *n* superviviente *mf.*
sus‡ [sʌs] *n* (= *suspicion*): **he was picked up on ~** la policía le detuvo por sospechoso.
Susan ['suːzn] *nf* Susana.
susceptibility [sə,septə'bɪlɪtɪ] *n* susceptibilidad *f,* sensibilidad *f* (*to* a); (*Med*) propensión *f* (*to* a); **to offend sb's susceptibilities** ofender las susceptibilidades (*or* la delicadeza) de uno.
susceptible [sə'septəbl] *adj* susceptible, sensible (*to* a); (*Med*) propenso (*to* a); (*easily moved*) impresionable; (*to women*) enamoradizo; **to be ~ of** admitir, dar lugar a.
Susie ['suːzɪ] *nf familiar form of* **Susan.**
suspect 1 ['sʌspekt] *adj* sospechoso; **they are all ~** todos están bajo sospecha; **his fitness is ~** es sospechoso de no estar en buen estado físico, su estado físico deja lugar a dudas.
2 ['sʌspekt] *n* sospechoso *m,* -a *f;* **the chief ~ is the butler** el más sospechoso es el mayordomo.
3 [səs'pekt] *vt* (*accusingly*) sospechar; (*fear*) recelar, recelarse de; (*believe*) imaginar, figurar, creer; **to ~ sb of a crime** hacer a uno sospechoso de un crimen, sospechar a uno de haber cometido un crimen; **I ~ her of having stolen it** sospecho que ella lo ha robado; **I ~ him of being the author** sospecho que él es el autor; **are you ~ed?** ¿estás tú bajo sospecha?; **he never ~ed her** él nunca sospechó de ella; **he ~s nothing** no se recela de nada; **I ~ all Slobodians** me recelo de todos los eslobodios; **I ~ it may be true** tengo la sospecha de que puede ser verdad, creo que puede ser verdad; **it's not paid for, I ~** sospecho que no está pagado; **I ~ed as much** ya me lo figuraba.
suspected [səs'pektɪd] *adj thief etc* presunto; **X went off the field with a ~ fracture** X abandonó el campo con sospecha de fractura.
suspend [səs'pend] *vt* (*all senses*) suspender; **his licence was ~ed for 6 months, he was ~ed for 6 months** le retiraron el carnet por 6 meses, le quitaron la licencia por 6 meses; **to ~ sb from work** (*or* **his post**) suspender a uno de su empleo; **~ed animation** animación *f* suspendida; **2-year ~ed sentence** libertad *f* condicional de 2 años.
suspender [səs'pendəʳ] *n* liga *f;* **~s** ligas *fpl,* (*US*) tirantes *mpl.*
suspender-belt [səs'pendəbelt] *n* (*Brit*) liguero *m,* portaligas *m.*
suspense [səs'pens] **1** *n* **(a)** (*uncertainty*) incertidumbre *f,* duda *f;* ansiedad *f;* (*Liter, Theat, Cine etc*) suspense *m;* tensión *f;* **to keep sb in ~** dejar a uno en la incertidum-

bre; **the ~ became unbearable** la tensión se hizo inaguantable; **the ~ is killing me!** ¡no puedo con tanta emoción!

(**b**) (*Jur etc*) suspensión *f*; **it is in ~** está en suspenso; **the question is in ~** la cuestión está pendiente.

2 *attr*: **~ account** cuenta *f* transitoria (*or* de orden).

suspension [səs'penʃən] **1** *n* (*gen, Tech*) suspensión *f*; **~ of payments** suspensión *f* de pagos; **~ of driving licence** privación *f* del carnet de conducir.

2 *attr*: **~ bridge** puente *m* colgante; **~ file** archivador *m* colgante; **~ points** puntos *mpl* suspensivos.

suspensory [səs'pensərı] **1** *adj* suspensorio. **2** *n* (*also* **~ bandage**) suspensorio *m*.

suspicion [səs'pıʃən] *n* (**a**) (*mistrust etc*) sospecha *f*; recelo *m*; **my ~ is that ...** sospecho que ...; **to be above ~** estar por encima de toda sospecha; **to be under ~** ser sospechoso, estar bajo sospecha; **to arouse ~** despertar recelos; **to arouse sb's ~s** despertar los recelos de uno; **to arrest sb on ~** detener a uno como sospechoso; **to cast ~s on sb's honesty** hacer que se dude de la honradez de uno; **to have one's ~s about sth** tener sospechas acerca de algo; **I had no ~ that ...** no sospechaba que ...; **to lay o.s. open to ~** hacerse sospechoso; **I was right in my ~s** resultaron ser ciertas mis sospechas; **~ fell on him** se empezó a sospechar de él.

(**b**) (*trace*) traza *f* ligera, sombra *f*, pizca *f*; (*aftertaste*) dejo *m*; **there is a ~ of corruption about it** esto tiene un dejo de corrupción, esto huele un poquito a corrupción; **there is just a ~ of a rigged game** hay cierto olorcillo a tongo.

suspicious [səs'pıʃəs] *adj* (**a**) (*feeling suspicion*) suspicaz, desconfiado, receloso; **to be ~ about sth** recelarse de algo, tener sospechas acerca de algo; **that made him ~** eso le hizo sospechar.

(**b**) (*causing suspicion*) sospechoso; **it's highly ~** es sumamente sospechoso; **it looks very ~ to me** me parece muy sospechoso.

suspiciously [səs'pıʃəslı] *adv* (**a**) *look etc* con recelo, desconfiadamente.

(**b**) *behave etc* de modo sospechoso; **it looks ~ like measles to me** para mí tiene toda la apariencia de ser sarampión.

suspiciousness [səs'pıʃəsnıs] *n* (*V adj*) (**a**) recelo *m*. (**b**) lo sospechoso, carácter *m* sospechoso.

suss* [sʌs] *vt* (*Brit*): **to ~ sth out** investigar algo, explorar algo; (tratar de) aclarar algo, (procurar) entender algo; **we couldn't ~ it out at all** no logramos sacar nada en claro; **I ~ed him out at once** le calé en seguida.

sustain [səs'teın] *vt* (**a**) (*bear weight of*) sostener, apoyar; *body, life* sustentar; (*Mus*) sostener; *part* estar al nivel de; hacer dignamente; *pretence* continuar; *effort* sostener, continuar; *assertion* sostener; *objection* (*Jur*) confirmar la validez de; *charge, theory* confirmar, corroborar.

(**b**) (*suffer*) *attack* sufrir (y rechazar); *damage* sufrir; *injury* sufrir, tener, recibir; *loss* sufrir, tener.

sustainable [səs'teınəbl] *adj* sostenible; sustentable.

sustained [səs'teınd] *adj effort etc* sostenido, ininterrumpido, continuo; *note* sostenido; *applause* prolongado.

sustaining [səs'teınıŋ] *adj food* nutritivo; **~ pedal** pedal *m* de sostenido.

sustenance ['sʌstınəns] *n* sustento *m*; **they depend for their ~ on, they get their ~ from** se sustentan de, se alimentan de.

suture ['suːtʃər] **1** *n* sutura *f*. **2** *vt* suturar, coser.

suzerain ['suːzəreın] *n* soberano *m*, -a *f*.

suzerainty ['suːzəreıntı] *n* soberanía *f*.

svelte [svelt] *adj* esbelto.

SW (**a**) *abbr of* **south-west** suroeste *m*, *also adj*, SO. (**b**) *n* (*Rad*) *abbr of* **short wave** onda *f* corta, OC.

swab [swɒb] **1** *n* (*cloth, mop*) estropajo *m*, trapo *m*, (*Naut*) lampazo *m*; (*Mil*) escobillón *m*; (*Med*) algodón *m*, torunda *f*.

2 *vt* (*also* **to ~ down**) limpiar (con estropajo *etc*), fregar.

swaddle ['swɒdl] *vt* envolver (*in* en); *baby* empañar, fajar; **he came out ~d in bandages** salió envuelto en vendas.

swaddling clothes ['swɒdlıŋkləʊðz] *npl* (*Liter*) pañales *mpl*; **to be still in ~** (*fig*) estar todavía en mantillas.

swag* [swæg] *n* botín *m*.

swagger ['swægər] **1** *n* contoneo *m*, pavoneo *m*; **to walk with a ~** andar contoneándose, andar con paso jactancioso.

2 *adj* (*Brit**) muy elegante, muy pera*.

3 *vi* (*also* **to ~ about, to ~ along**) contonearse, pavonearse, andar pavoneándose; **he ~ed over to our table** se acercó a nuestra mesa con aire fanfarrón; **with that he ~ed out** con eso salió con paso jactancioso.

swaggering ['swægərıŋ] *adj person* fanfarrón, jactancioso; *gait* importante, jactancioso.

swain [sweın] *n* (†† *or hum*) (*lad*) zagal *m*; (*suitor*) pretendiente *m*, amante *m*.

swallow[1] ['swɒləʊ] **1** *n* trago *m*; **at one ~, with one ~** de un trago.

2 *vt* (**a**) (*lit*) tragar; engullir, deglutir; *bait* tragarse; **he ~ed the lot** se lo tragó todo; **just ~ this pill** tómate esta píldora.

(**b**) (*fig*) tragar; **to ~ an insult** tragar un insulto; **to ~ one's pride** humillarse, olvidarse de su amor propio; **he ~ed the story** se tragó la bola; **to ~ one's words** desdecirse, retractarse.

3 *vi*: **to ~, to ~ hard** (*fig*) tragar saliva.

◆**swallow down** *vt* tragar.

◆**swallow up** *vt* (**a**) *food etc* tragar; acabar de comer.

(**b**) (*fig*) *savings etc* agotar, consumir; (*of the sea*) tragar; **the mist ~ed them up** la niebla les envolvió; **they were soon ~ed up in the darkness** desaparecieron pronto en la oscuridad.

swallow[2] ['swɒləʊ] *n* (*Orn*) golondrina *f*; **one ~ doesn't make a summer** una golondrina no hace verano.

swallow-dive ['swɒləʊ'daıv] *n* salto *m* de ángel.

swallowtail ['swɒləʊteıl] *n* (*butterfly*) macaón *m*.

swam [swæm] *pret of* **swim**.

swamp [swɒmp] **1** *n* pantano *m*, marisma *f*, ciénaga *f*.

2 *attr*: **~ fever** paludismo *m*.

3 *vt* (**a**) (*submerge*) sumergir, cubrir de agua (*etc*); (*flood*) inundar, llenar de agua; (*sink*) hundir.

(**b**) (*fig*) abrumar (*with* de), agobiar (*with* de); **towards the end of the game they ~ed us** hacia el fin del partido nos arrollaron completamente; **they have ~ed us with applications** nos han abrumado de solicitudes; **we are ~ed with work** estamos agobiados de trabajo, tenemos trabajo hasta encima de las cejas.

4 *vi* (*of field etc*) inundarse, quedar inundado, empantanarse.

swampland ['swɒmplænd] *n* ciénaga *f*, pantano *m*, marisma *f*.

swampy ['swɒmpı] *adj* pantanoso; **to become ~** empantanarse.

swan [swɒn] **1** *n* cisne *m*; **the S~ of Avon** el Cisne del Avon (*Shakespeare*); **~ dive** (*US*) salto *m* de ángel; **'S~ Lake'** 'El lago de los cisnes'. **2** *vi*: **to ~ around*** gandulear, vivir en el ocio; darse buena vida; **to ~ off*** irse tranquilamente, partir con la mayor serenidad.

swank* [swæŋk] **1** *n* (**a**) (*vanity, boastfulness*) fachenda* *f*; ostentación *f*; **it's just a lot of ~** no es sino fachenda*; **he does it for ~** lo hace para darse tono.

(**b**) (*person*) currutaco *m*; fachendón* *m*, -ona *f*; **he's a terrible ~** es terriblemente fachendón*.

2 *vi* darse tono, darse humos, fachendear*, fanfarronear, presumir; **to ~ about** (*adv*) pavonearse; **to ~ about sth** fachendear a causa de algo*, darse humos con motivo de algo.

swanky* ['swæŋkı] *adj person* ostentoso, fachendoso*, fachendón*; *car etc* la mar de elegante*, muy pera*.

swannery ['swɒnərı] *n* colonia *f* de cisnes.

swansdown ['swɒnzdaʊn] *n* (*feathers*) plumón *m* de cisne; (*Texas*) fustán *m*, muletón *m*.

swansong ['swɒnsɒŋ] *n* canto *m* del cisne.

swap [swɒp] **1** *n* intercambio *m*, canje *m*; **~s** (*stamps*) duplicados *mpl*; **it's a fair ~** es un trato equitativo.

2 *vt* intercambiar, canjear; **to ~ stories** (**with sb**) contarse chistes; **we sat ~ping reminiscences** estábamos contando nuestros recuerdos; **will you ~ your hat for my jacket?** ¿quieres cambiar tu sombrero por mi chaqueta?; **to ~ places with sb** cambiar de silla (*etc*) con uno.

3 *vi* hacer un intercambio; cambiar con uno; **I wouldn't ~ with anyone** no cambio con nadie; **shall we ~?** ¿cambiamos?

◆**swap (a)round, swap over** *vti* cambiar.

SWAPO ['swɑːpəʊ] *n abbr of* **South West Africa People's Organization.**

sward [swɔːd] *n* (*Liter*) césped *m*.

swarm[1] [swɔːm] **1** *n* (*of bees etc*) enjambre *m*; (*fig*) multitud *f*, muchedumbre *f*; **a ~ of mosquitoes** un enjambre de mosquitos; **a ~ of creditors** un enjambre de acreedores; **they came in ~s** vinieron en tropel; **there were ~s of women** hubo una multitud de mujeres, hubo millares de mujeres.

2 *vi* (**a**) (*bees*) enjambrar.

(b) (*other insects, people etc*) hormiguear, pulular; **to ~ with** (*of place*) hervir de, pulular de, estar plagado de; **the tourists ~ everywhere** en todas partes pululan los turistas; **Stratford ~s with Americans** Stratford hierve de americanos; **children ~ed all over the car** los niños hormigueaban por todo el coche.

swarm[2] [swɔːm] *vi*: **to ~ up a tree** trepar (rápidamente) a un árbol.

swarthiness [ˈswɔːðɪnɪs] *n* tez *f* morena, color *m* moreno; lo atezado.

swarthy [ˈswɔːðɪ] *adj* moreno, atezado.

swashbuckler [ˈswɒʃˌbʌkləʳ] *n* espadachín *m*, matón *m*.

swashbuckling [ˈswɒʃˌbʌklɪŋ] *adj* (a) (*gen*) valentón, fanfarrón. (b) (*Cine*) *hero* de película de aventuras; *film* de aventuras, de capa y espada.

swastika [ˈswɒstɪkə] *n* esvástica *f*, cruz *f* gamada.

swat [swɒt] 1 *vt fly* aplastar, matar. 2 *vi*: **to ~ at a fly** tratar de aplastar una mosca (con palmeta).

swath [swɔːθ] *n, pl* **swaths** [swɔːðs], **swathe**[1] [sweɪð] *n* guadaña *f*, ringlera *f* (de heno segado *etc*); **to cut corn in ~s** segar el trigo y dejarlo en ringleras; **to cut ~s through sth** avanzar por algo a guadañadas.

swathe[2] [sweɪð] *vt* envolver; fajar; (*with bandage*) vendar; **~d in sheets** envuelto en sábanas.

swatter [ˈswɒtəʳ] *m* palmeta *f* matamoscas.

sway [sweɪ] 1 *n* (a) (*movement*) balanceo *m*, oscilación *f*; (*violent jerk*) sacudimiento *m*; vaivén *m*.

(b) (*rule*) imperio *m*, dominio *m*; (*influence*) influencia *f*, ascendiente *m*; (*power*) poder *m*; **his ~ over the party** su influencia con el partido, su dominio del partido; **to bring a people under one's ~** sojuzgar un pueblo, hacer que un pueblo reconozca el dominio de uno; **to hold ~ over a nation** gobernar una nación, dominar una nación.

2 *vt* (a) (*move*) balancear, hacer oscilar; sacudir; hacer tambalear.

(b) (*influence*) mover, influir en; inclinar; **these factors finally ~ed me** estos factores terminaron de convencerme; **he is not ~ed by any such considerations** tales cosas no influyen en él en absoluto; **I allowed myself to be ~ed** me dejé persuadir.

3 *vi* balancearse, oscilar (*in the wind* al viento); mecerse; bambolearse; tambalearse; **she ~s as she walks** se cimbrea al andar; **he was ~ing with drink** estaba tan borracho que se tambaleaba; **the train ~ed from side to side** el tren se bamboleaba de un lado para otro.

Swazi [ˈswɑːzɪ] 1 *adj* swazilandés, suazilandés. 2 *n* swazilandés *m*, -esa *f*, suazilandés *m*, -esa *f*.

Swaziland [ˈswɑːzɪlænd] *n* Swazilandia *f*, Suazilandia *f*.

swear [swɛəʳ] (*irr*: *pret* **swore**, *ptp* **sworn**) 1 *vt* (a) *oath* prestar, jurar; *fidelity* jurar; **I ~ it!** ¡lo juro!; **I ~ (that) I did not steal it** juro que no lo robé; **I could have sworn that was Lulu** juraría que ésa fue Lulú, que me maten si aquélla no fue Lulú; **to ~ sth on the Bible** jurar algo sobre la Biblia; **to ~ to do sth** jurar hacer algo.

(b) **to ~ sb to secrecy** hacer que uno jure no revelar algo.

2 *vi* (a) (*solemnly*) jurar; **to ~ to do sth** declarar algo bajo juramento; **I could ~ to it** juraría que fue así; **I can't ~ to it** no lo sé a punto fijo, no puedo afirmarlo con entera confianza.

(b) (*with swearwords*) jurar, decir tacos, soltar palabrotas, (*blasphemously*) blasfemar; **don't ~ in front of the children** no digas palabrotas estando los pequeños delante; **to ~ like a trooper** jurar como un carretero; **he swore most horribly** soltó unos tremendos tacos; **it's enough to make a bishop ~** esto bastaría para hacer blasfemar a un obispo; **to ~ at sb** maldecir a uno, echar pestes de uno; **he was ~ing about the police** echaba pestes de la policía.

3 *n*: **to have a good ~*** desahogarse soltando palabrotas.

◆**swear by** *vt*: **to ~ by sth** jurar por algo, (*fig*) tener entera confianza en algo, creer ciegamente en algo.

◆**swear in** *vt*: **to ~ sb in** tomar juramento a uno, juramentar a uno, hacer prestar juramento a uno; **to be sworn in** prestar juramento.

◆**swear off** *vt*: **to ~ off alcohol** (jurar) renunciar al alcohol.

swearword [ˈswɛəwɜːd] *n* taco *m*, palabrota *f*; grosería *f* (*LAm*).

sweat [swet] 1 *n* (a) sudor *m*; **by the ~ of one's brow** con el sudor de su frente; **to be in a ~** estar sudando, estar todo sudoroso, (*fig*) estar en un apuro, apurarse; **to be in a ~ about sth** estar muy preocupado por algo; **to get into a ~** empezar a sudar; **to get into a ~ about sth** apurarse por algo.

(b) (*) trabajo *m* difícil, trabajo *m* pesado; **what a ~ that was!** eso ¡cómo nos hizo sudar!; **we had such a ~ to do it** nos costó hacerlo; **no ~!** ¡no hay problema!, ¡está chupado!⁑

(c) **old ~*** veterano *m*.

2 *vt* (a) sudar; **to ~ blood** (*fig*) sudar la gota gorda.

(b) *workers* explotar.

3 *vi* sudar; **to ~ a lot, to ~ like a bull** (*or* **pig** *etc*) sudar la gota gorda.

◆**sweat off** *vt*: **I ~ed off half a kilo** me quité medio kilo sudando.

◆**sweat out** *vt*: **to ~ a cold out** quitarse un resfriado sudando; **to ~ it out*** aguantarlo todo; armarse de paciencia; **they left him to ~ it out*** no hicieron nada para ayudarle.

sweatband [ˈswetbænd] *n* (*on hat*) badana *f* del forro del sombrero, tafilete *m*; (*on head*) venda *f*, banda *f*; (*on wrist*) muñequera *f*.

sweated [ˈswetɪd] *adj*: **~ labour** trabajo *m* muy mal pagado.

sweater [ˈswetəʳ] *n* suéter *m*, jersey *m*.

sweat gland [ˈswetglænd] *n* glándula *f* sudorípara.

sweating [ˈswetɪŋ] 1 *adj* sudoroso. 2 *n* transpiración *f*; (*of workers*) explotación *f*.

sweatshirt [ˈswetˈʃɜːt] *n* niki *m*, camisa *f* floja (de deporte *etc*), sudadera *f*.

sweatshop [ˈswetˈʃɒp] *n* fábrica *f* donde se explota al obrero.

sweatsuit [ˈswetsuːt] *n* chandal *m*.

sweaty [ˈswetɪ] *adj* sudoroso; cubierto de sudor, mojado de sudor; **to be all ~** estar todo sudoroso.

Swede [swiːd] *n* sueco *m*, -a *f*.

swede [swiːd] *n* (*Brit Bot*) naba *f*, nabo *m* gallego.

Sweden [ˈswiːdn] *n* Suecia *f*.

Swedish [ˈswiːdɪʃ] 1 *adj* sueco. 2 *n* (*Ling*) sueco *m*.

sweep [swiːp] 1 *n* (a) (*act of ~ing*) barredura *f*, escobada *f*; **this room could do with a ~** hace falta barrer esta habitación; **we gave it a ~** lo limpiamos, lo barrimos; **to make a clean ~** (*Sport*) ganar todos los puntos, (*Cards*) copar, ganar todas las bazas; **to make a clean ~ of** cambiar completamente, hacer tabla rasa de.

(b) (*by police etc*) redada *f*; **they made a ~ for hidden arms** hicieron una redada buscando armas clandestinas.

(c) (*movement of arm*) gesto *m*, movimiento *m*; (*of scythe*) golpe *m*, guadañada *f*; (*of net*) redada *f*; (*of bean etc*) trayectoria *f*; (*of events etc*) marcha *f*.

(d) (*person*) deshollinador *m*.

(e) (*area*) extensión *f*; (*of wings*) envergadura *f*; (*range*) alcance *m*; (*curve*) curva *f*; **the whole ~ of the Thames at Putney** toda la extensión del Támesis en Putney; **a wide ~ of country** una ancha extensión de paisaje, un paisaje extenso; **the ~ of her lines** (*Naut etc*) su línea, su perfil (aerodinámico *etc*).

(f) = **sweepstake**.

2 (*irr*: *pret and ptp* **swept**) *vt* (a) *room, surface* barrer; *chimney* deshollinar; *channel etc* dragar; **to ~ a room clean** barrer un cuarto; **to ~ a channel clear of mines** barrer las minas de un canal; **the beach was swept by great waves** la playa fue barrida (*or* azotada) por olas gigantescas; **to ~ a road with bullets** barrer una carretera con balas; **to ~ the horizon with a telescope** examinar toda la extensión del horizonte con un telescopio.

(b) *dust* barrer, quitar barriendo; *mines* rastrear, barrer; *person, obstacle etc* arrastrar, llevarse; **a wave swept him overboard** fue arrastrado por una ola y cayó al mar; **he was swept off his feet by the water** fue arrastrado por la corriente; **to ~ a girl off her feet** arrebatar a una chica; **they swept him off to lunch** se lo llevaron con toda prisa a comer.

3 *vi* (a) (*with broom*) barrer.

(b) (*extend*) extenderse (*along, down etc* por); **the river ~s away to the east** el río hace una gran curva hacia el este; **the hills ~ down to the sea** las colinas bajan (majestuosamente) hacia el mar; **the road ~s up to the house** la carretera llega hasta la casa (de modo impresionante).

(c) (*of movement*) **to ~ into a room** entrar en una sala con paso majestuoso; **she swept past me angrily** pasó enfadada delante de mí; **it swept round the corner** dobló velozmente la esquina; **they swept down the slope** se lanzaron cuesta abajo; descendieron precipitadamente por la cuesta; **to ~ down on sb** abalanzarse sobre uno.

◆**sweep along** 1 *vt* arrastrar, llevar; **the crowd swept him along** le arrastró la multitud, desapareció arrastrado por la multitud.

2 *vi*: **the car swept along** el coche avanzó a gran velocidad.

◆**sweep aside** *vt object* apartar bruscamente con la mano; *protest* desatender, no hacer caso alguno de; *suggestion* desechar bruscamente; *opposition* barrer; *difficulty* quitar de en medio.

◆**sweep away 1** *vt* barrer; (*snatch*) arrebatar, arrastrar; (*remove*) quitar, eliminar, suprimir; *vestige etc* borrar.

2 *vi* irse rápidamente; irse con paso majestuoso.

◆**sweep by** *vi* pasar rápidamente; pasar majestuosamente; (*nearly touch*) rozar.

◆**sweep down 1** *vt* arrastrar, llevar; **the current ~s logs down with it** la corriente arrastra (*or* lleva) consigo los troncos.

2 *vi V* **sweep 3** (**b**), **3** (**c**).

◆**sweep off** = **sweep away**.

◆**sweep on** *vi* seguir su avance inexorable.

◆**sweep out 1** *vt room* barrer.

2 *vi* salir (con paso majestuoso).

◆**sweep up 1** *vt* barrer, recoger.

2 *vi* (**a**) (*clean up*) **to ~ up after sb** recoger la basura que ha dejado uno; **to ~ up after a party** limpiar después de un guateque.

(**b**) (*approach*) **to ~ up to sb** acercarse indignado a uno; acercarse con paso majestuoso a uno; **the car swept up to the house** el coche llegó con toda velocidad a la casa; *V also* **sweep 3 b**.

sweepback ['swi:pbæk] *n* (*of aircraft wing etc*) ángulo *m* de flecha.

sweeper ['swi:pə^r] *n* (*person*) barrendero *m*, -a *f*; (*Ftbl*) escoba *m*; (*machine*) barredera *f*.

sweeping ['swi:pɪŋ] **1** *adj* (**a**) *gesture* dramático; *bow* profundo; *flight* majestuoso.

(**b**) *statement etc* general, tajante, terminante, dogmático; *change* radical, fundamental; **that's pretty ~** eso es mucho decir.

2 *npl*: **~s** barreduras *fpl*; (*fig, of society etc*) heces *fpl*.

sweepstake ['swi:psteɪk] *n* lotería *f* (*esp* de carreras).

sweet [swi:t] **1** *adj* (**a**) (*of taste*) dulce; azucarado; **this coffee is too ~** este café tiene demasiado azúcar; **is it ~ enough for you?** ¿te he puesto bastante azúcar?, ¿está bastante dulce?; **~ chestnut** (*fruit*) castaña *f*; (*tree*) castaño *m*; **~ oil** aceite *m* de oliva; **~ pea** guisante *m* de olor, alverjilla *f*: **~ potato** batata *f*, camote *m*, boniato *m* (*CAm*).

(**b**) (*fresh, pleasant*) *food* fresco, nuevo; *smell* fragante, agradable, bueno; *breath* sano; *land* fértil; en buen estado.

(**c**) (*of sounds*) dulce, melodioso.

(**d**) (*of person's character*) dulce, amable, simpático; **isn't he ~?** ¡es un ángel!; **that's very ~ of you** eres muy amable; **to be ~ on sb*** estar un poco enamorado de uno; **to keep sb ~*** asegurarse de la amistad de uno, asegurarse de la buena voluntad de uno (mediante un regalo, propina *etc*).

(**e**) (*generally agreeable, charming*) *memory, revenge etc* dulce; *face* lindo; *dress etc* mono, majo, precioso; **it is ~ to be able to ...** es agradable poder ...; **it's ~ of you to say that** eres muy amable al decir eso; **you look so ~ in that hat** con ese sombrero eres un encanto; **what a ~ little hat!** ¡qué sombrerito más mono!; **to go one's own ~ way, to please one's own ~ self** ir a su aire, ir a lo suyo.

(**f**) *running of car, machine etc* suave.

2 *adv*: **to smell ~** tener buen olor, oler bien; **to taste ~** tener un sabor dulce, saber a dulce.

3 *n* (*esp Brit*) (**a**) dulce *m*, caramelo *m*; **~s** dulces *mpl*, bombones *mpl*, golosinas *fpl*; **the ~s of solitude** las dulzuras de la soledad; **the ~s of office** las ventajas materiales de estar en el poder, los premios que brinda el triunfo político.

(**b**) (*Brit*: *course*) postre *m*.

(**c**) **yes, my ~** sí, mi amor.

sweet-and-sour ['swi:tən'saʊə^r] **1** *adj* agridulce. **2** *n* (*Culin*) *plato agridulce* (*especialmente en la comida china*).

sweetbreads ['swi:tbredz] *npl* lechecillas *fpl*, mollejas *fpl*.

sweetbriar, sweetbrier ['swi:tbraɪə^r] *n* eglantina *f*, escaramujo *m* oloroso.

sweetcorn ['swi:tkɔ:n] *n* maíz *m* tierno.

sweeten ['swi:tn] *vt* (**a**) endulzar (*also fig*); azucarar, poner azúcar a. (**b**) (*****) (*also* **to ~ up**) *person* (*bribe*) sobornar, (*win over*) asegurarse la buena voluntad de, captar la benevolencia de; *deal* hacer más atractivo.

sweetener ['swi:tnə^r] *n* (**a**) edulcorante *m*, dulcificante *m*. (**b**) (*****) astilla* *f*.

sweetening ['swi:tnɪŋ] *n* (*Culin*) dulcificante *m*.

sweetheart ['swi:thɑ:t] *n* novio *m*, -a *f*; **yes, ~** sí, mi amor.

sweetie* ['swi:tɪ] *n* (**a**) (*person*) chica *f*; novia *f*; **she's a ~** es un encanto, es muy mona; **isn't she a ~?** ¡qué chica más mona!; **hi, ~!** ¡oye, preciosidad!* (**b**) (*Scot*: *sweet*) dulce *m*, caramelo *m*.

sweetish ['swi:tɪʃ] *adj* algo dulce.

sweetly ['swi:tlɪ] *adv* dulcemente; amablemente; suavemente.

sweetmeats ['swi:tmi:ts] *npl* dulces *mpl*, confites *mpl*.

sweet-natured [ˌswi:t'neɪtʃəd] *adj* dulce, amable.

sweetness ['swi:tnɪs] *n* dulzura *f*; lo dulce, lo azucarado; fragancia *f*; buen olor *m*; fertilidad *f*; amabilidad *f*; suavidad *f*; **now all is ~ and light** reina ahora la más perfecta armonía; **to go around spreading ~ and light** ir por el mundo con una sonrisa amable para todos; **he was all ~ and light yesterday** ayer (contra costumbre) estuvo la mar de amable (*or* razonable *etc*).

sweet-scented ['swi:t'sentɪd] *adj* perfumado, fragante, de olor agradable.

sweetshop ['swi:tʃɒp] *n* (*Brit*) bombonería *f*, confitería *f*, dulcería *f* (*LAm*).

sweet-smelling ['swi:t'smelɪŋ] *adj* = **sweet-scented**.

sweet talk ['swi:t'tɔ:k] **1** *n* halagos *mpl*, palabras *fpl* almibaradas, engatusamiento *m*. **2 sweet-talk** *vt* engatusar, lisonjear; (*US**) enrollarse con.

sweet-tempered ['swi:t'tempəd] *adj* de carácter dulce, amable; **she's always ~** es siempre tan amable, no se altera nunca.

sweet-toothed ['swi:t'tu:θt] *adj* goloso.

sweet william ['swi:t'wɪlɪəm] *n* minutisa *f*.

swell [swel] **1** *n* (**a**) (*Naut*) mar *m* de fondo, marejada *f*, oleaje *m*.

(**b**) (*Mus*) crescendo *m*.

(**c**) (*Anat etc*) = **swelling**.

(**d**) (*†) (*stylish person*) guapo *m*, majo *m*; (*important person*) pez *m* gordo*, espadón* *m*; **the ~s** la gente bien, la gente de buen tono.

2 *adj* (*) (*in dress etc*) elegantísimo; (*fine, good*) estupendo*, bárbaro*, de órdago*; (*esp US*) **we had a ~ time** lo pasamos en grande*; **it's a ~ place** es un sitio estupendo*; **that's mighty ~ of you** eres muy amable.

3 (*irr*: *pret* **swelled**, *ptp* **swollen**) *vt* (**a**) (*physically*) hinchar; abultar; inflar; (*Med*) hinchar; **to have a swollen hand** tener la mano hinchada; **eyes swollen with tears** ojos *mpl* hinchados de lágrimas; **the rains had swollen the river** las lluvias habían hecho crecer el río; **the river is swollen** el río está crecido.

(**b**) *sound* aumentar; *numbers etc* aumentar; engrosar; **this will go to ~ the numbers of ...** esto vendrá a aumentar el número de ...

4 *vi* (**a**) (*physically*: *also* **to ~ up**) hincharse; abultarse; inflarse; (*of river etc*) crecer; **her arm ~ed up** se le hinchó el brazo; **to ~ with pride** envanecerse, (*justifiably*) sentirse lleno de orgullo.

(**b**) (*in extent, numbers*) crecer, aumentar(se); **numbers have swollen greatly** el número se ha aumentado muchísimo; **the debt had swollen to ...** la deuda había aumentado mucho hasta alcanzar la cifra de ...; **the little group soon ~ed into a crowd** el pequeño grupo se transformó pronto en multitud.

◆**swell up** *vi V* **swell 4** (**a**).

swellhead* ['swelhed] *n* (*US*) vanidoso *m*, -a *f*.

swellheaded* ['swel'hedɪd] *adj* (*US*) vanidoso, engreído.

swelling ['swelɪŋ] *n* hinchazón *f*; protuberancia *f*; (*Med*) tumefacción *f*; (*bruise*) chichón *m*, bulto *m*; (*of gland etc*) ganglio *m*.

swelter ['sweltə^r] *vi* abrasarse, sofocarse de calor; chorrear de sudor; **we ~ed in 40°** nos sofocábamos a una temperatura de 40 grados.

sweltering ['sweltərɪŋ] *adj day* de muchísimo calor; *heat* sofocante, abrasador; **it's ~ in here** está sofocante aquí.

swept [swept] *pret and ptp of* **sweep**.

sweptback ['swept'bæk] *adj wing* en flecha; *aircraft* con alas en flecha.

swerve [swɜ:v] **1** *n* (**a**) (*dodge, turn*) desvío *m* brusco, viraje *m* repentino; (*of body, in sport etc*) esguince *m*, regate *m*.

(**b**) (*spin on ball*) efecto *m*; **to put a ~ on a ball** lanzar una pelota con efecto.

2 *vt* (**a**) desviar bruscamente, torcer (a un lado).

(**b**) *ball* dar efecto a, lanzar con efecto, sesgar.

3 *vi* desviarse bruscamente; hurtar el cuerpo; (*ball*) torcerse; **to ~ to the right** torcer repentinamente a la derecha.

swift [swɪft] **1** *adj* rápido, veloz; repentino; pronto; **~ of foot** de pies ligeros; **to be ~ to anger** tener prontos enojos; **we must be ~ to act** tenemos que obrar con toda prontitud.

2 *n* vencejo *m*.

swift-flowing ['swɪft'fləʊɪŋ] *adj current* rápido; *river* de corriente rápida.

swift-footed ['swɪft'fʊtɪd] *adj* de pies ligeros, veloz.

swiftly ['swɪftlɪ] *adv* rápidamente, velozmente; repentinamente; pronto.

swiftness ['swɪftnɪs] *n* rapidez *f*, velocidad *f*; lo repentino; prontitud *f*.

swig* [swɪg] **1** *n* trago *m*, tragantada* *f*; **have a ~ of this** bébete un poco de esto; **he took a ~ at his flask** se echó un trago de la botella.

2 *vt* beber; beber a grandes tragos.

swill [swɪl] **1** *n* (**a**) bazofia *f*; (*pej*) bazofia *f*, aguachirle *f*; **how can you drink this ~?** ¿cómo te es posible beber esta basura?

(**b**) **to give sth a ~ (out)** limpiar algo con agua.

2 *vt* (**a**) (*clean*: *also* **to ~ out**) lavar, limpiar con agua.

(**b**) (*drink*) beber (a grandes tragos).

3 *vi* emborracharse.

swim [swɪm] **1** *n* (**a**) nadada *f* (*LAm*); **after a 2-kilometre ~** después de nadar 2 km; **it's a long ~ back to the shore** nos costará llegar a la playa; **that was a long ~ for a child** eso fue mucho nadar para un niño; **that was a nice ~!** ¡cuánto me gusta nadar así!; **I like a ~** me gusta nadar, me gusta la natación; **to go for a ~, to have a ~** ir a nadar.

(**b**) **to be in the ~** estar al corriente; **to keep in the ~** mantenerse al día.

2 (*irr*: *pret* **swam**, *ptp* **swum**) *vt* (**a**) *river etc* pasar a nado, cruzar a nado; **it was first swum in 1900** un hombre lo cruzó a nado por primera vez en 1900; **it has not been swum before** hasta ahora nadie lo ha cruzado a nado.

(**b**) **she can't ~ a stroke** no sabe nadar en absoluto; **before I had swum 10 strokes** antes de haber dado 10 brazadas; **he can ~ 2 lengths** puede nadar 2 largos; **can you ~ the crawl?** ¿sabes hacer el crol?

3 *vi* (**a**) nadar; **to ~ across a river** pasar un río a nado; **to ~ out to sea** alejarse nadando de la playa; **to ~ under water** nadar debajo del agua, bucear; **then we swam back** luego volvimos (nadando); **we shall have to ~ for it** tendremos que echarnos al agua, tendremos que salvarnos nadando; **to go ~ming** ir a nadar, ir a bañarse.

(**b**) **the meat was ~ming in gravy** la carne estaba inundada de salsa, la carne flotaba en salsa.

(**c**) (*head*) dar vueltas; **everything swam before my eyes** todo parecía estar girando alrededor de mí, todo parecía bailar ante mis ojos.

swimmer ['swɪməʳ] *n* nadador *m*, -ora *f*.

swimming ['swɪmɪŋ] *n* natación *f*.

swimming-bath ['swɪmɪŋbɑːθ] *n*, *pl* **swimming-baths** ['swɪmɪŋbɑːðz] (*Brit*) piscina *f*, pileta *f*.

swimming-cap ['swɪmɪŋkæp] *n* gorro *m* de baño.

swimming-costume ['swɪmɪŋ,kɒstjuːm] *n* (*Brit*) traje *m* de baño, bañador *m*.

swimming gala ['swɪmɪŋ,gɑːlə] *n* exhibición *f* de natación.

swimmingly ['swɪmɪŋlɪ] *adv*: **to go ~** ir a las mil maravillas.

swimming-pool ['swɪmɪŋpuːl] *n* piscina *f*, pileta *f*, alberca *f* (*Mex*).

swimming-trunks ['swɪmɪŋtrʌŋks] *npl* pantalón *m* de baño, bañador *m*.

swimsuit ['swɪmsuːt] *n* traje *m* de baño, bañador *m*.

swimwear ['swɪmwɛəʳ] *n* trajes *mpl* de baño.

swindle ['swɪndl] **1** *n* estafa *f*, timo *m*; **it's a ~!** ¡nos han robado!

2 *vt* estafar, timar; **to ~ sb out of sth** estafar algo a uno, quitar algo a uno por estafa.

swindler ['swɪndləʳ] *n* estafador *m*, timador *m*.

swine [swaɪn] **1** *n* (**a**) (*Zool pl*: **swine**) cerdos *mpl*, puercos *mpl*.

(**b**) (*) canalla *m*, cochino *m*; marrano* *m* (*LAm*); **you ~!** ¡canalla!; **what a ~ he is!** ¡es un canalla!; **they're a lot of ~** son unos cochinos.

2 *attr*: **~ fever** fiebre *f* porcina.

swineherd†† ['swaɪnhɜːd] *n* porquero *m*.

swing [swɪŋ] **1** *n* (**a**) (*movement*) balanceo *m*, oscilación *f*, vaivén *m*; (*of pendulum*) oscilación *f*; (*Boxing*) golpe *m* lateral, swing *m*; **it has a ~ of 2 metres** tiene un recorrido de 2 metros; **to give the starting handle a ~** girar la manivela; **to give a hammock a ~** empujar una hamaca; **to give a child a ~** empujar a un niño en un columpio; balancear a un niño colgado de los brazos (*etc*); **he took a ~ at me** me asestó un golpe; **he took a ~ at me with the axe** trató de golpearme con el hacha.

(**b**) (*Pol*: *in votes etc*) movimiento *m*, desplazamiento *m*, viraje *m*; **a sudden ~ in opinion** un viraje repentino de la opinión; **the ~ of the pendulum** el flujo y reflujo de la popularidad (de los partidos); **there was a strong ~ in the election** en las elecciones se registró un fuerte viraje; **a ~ of 5% would give the opposition the majority** un 5 por 100 de desplazamiento de los votos daría a la oposición la mayoría.

(**c**) (*seat*) columpio *m*; **what you lose on the ~s you gain on the roundabouts** lo que no va en lágrimas va en suspiros.

(**d**) (*rhythm*) ritmo *m* (fuerte, agradable); (*kind of music*) swing *m*; **~ band** orquesta *f* de swing; **a tune that goes with a ~** una melodía que tiene un ritmo marcado; **it all went with a ~** todo fue sobre ruedas; **to walk with a ~** andar rítmicamente; **to be in full ~** estar en plena marcha, estar en plena actividad; **to get into the ~ of things** irse acostumbrando; coger el tino; ponerse al corriente de las cosas (*or* la situación).

2 (*irr*: *pret and ptp* **swung**) *vt* (**a**) (*to and fro*) balancear; hacer oscilar; (*on a swing*) columpiar; (*brandish*) blandir, menear; *arms* menear; *propeller* girar; **to ~ a child** empujar a un niño en un columpio; balancear a un niño colgado de los brazos (*etc*); **he sat on the table ~ing his legs** estaba sentado sobre la mesa balanceando las piernas; **to ~ one's fist at sb** asestar un golpe (lateral) a uno con el puño; **he swung the case up on to his shoulders** haciendo un esfuerzo se echó la maleta sobre los hombros.

(**b**) (*fig*) *policy* cambiar; *outcome* determinar, decidir; influir en; *voters* hacer cambiar de opinión; **he swung the party behind him** obtuvo el apoyo del partido, logró la aprobación del partido; **eventually he managed to ~ it*** por fin lo logró.

(**c**) (*) **to ~ it** fingirse enfermo, racanear*, hacer el rácano*; **to ~ it on sb** embaucar a uno.

3 *vi* (**a**) (*to and fro*) balancearse; oscilar; (*on a swing*) columpiarse; (*hang*) colgar, pender; (*door etc*) girar; **to ~ at anchor** estar anclado; **the door ~s on its hinges** la puerta gira sobre sus goznes; **it swung open** de pronto se abrió; **it ~s in the wind** se balancea al viento; **a revolver swung from his belt** un revólver colgaba de su cinturón; **he'll ~ for it** le ahorcarán por ello.

(**b**) (*change direction*) cambiar de dirección; **the car swung into the square** el coche viró y entró en la plaza; **to ~ into action** ponerse en marcha; empezar a ponerse por obra; **the country has swung to the right** el país ha virado a la derecha.

(**c**) (*strike*) **to ~ at a ball** tratar de golpear una pelota; **he swung at me** me asestó un golpe.

4 *vr*: **to ~ o.s. into the saddle** subir a la silla con un solo movimiento enérgico.

◆**swing round 1** *vt* (*turn*) girar, hacer girar; **he swung the car round** hizo un viraje brusco; **they swung the gun barrel round** hicieron girar el cañon.

2 *vi* (*change direction*) cambiar de dirección; **he swung round** giró sobre los talones, se volvió bruscamente; **it swung right round** dio una vuelta completa.

3 *vr*: **to ~ o.s. round** girar sobre los talones.

swing bridge ['swɪŋ'brɪdʒ] *n* puente *m* giratorio.

swing door ['swɪŋ'dɔːʳ] *n* (*Brit*) puerta *f* batiente.

swingeing ['swɪndʒɪŋ] *adj majority* abrumador; *penalty etc* severísimo.

swinger* ['swɪŋəʳ] *n*: **he's a ~** (*with it*) es muy mundano, es muy moderno; (*going to parties*) es un asiduo en las fiestas; (*sexually*) no tiene inhibiciones.

swinging ['swɪŋɪŋ] *adj* (**a**) (*) city etc alegre, movido, de vida alegre, lleno de diversiones. (**b**) **~ door** (*US*) puerta *f* giratoria.

swing-wing ['swɪŋwɪŋ] *attr* de geometría variable.

swinish ['swaɪnɪʃ] *adj* (*fig*) cochino, canallesco; brutal.

swipe [swaɪp] **1** *n* golpe *m* fuerte; **to take a ~ at sb** asestar un golpe a uno.

2 *vt* (**a**) golpear fuertemente; pegar; **he ~s her** la pega.

(**b**) (‡) apandar‡, guindar‡.

3 *vi*: **to ~ at sb** asestar un golpe a uno.

swirl [swɜːl] **1** *n* remolino *m*, torbellino *m*; **it disappeared in a ~ of water** desapareció en el agua arremolinada; **the ~ of the dancers' skirts** el movimiento de las faldas de las bailadoras.

2 *vi* arremolinarse; girar, girar confusamente.

me ~ me miró compasiva.
sympathize ['sɪmpəθaɪz] *vi* (*in sorrow etc*) compadecerse, condolerse; (*understand*) comprender; **I really do ~** lo siento de verdad; **to ~ with sb** compadecerse de uno, condolerse de uno; **I ~ with what you say, but ...** comprendo el punto de vista de Vd, pero ...; **those who ~ with our demands** los que apoyan nuestras reclamaciones; **to ~ with sb in his bereavement** dar el pésame a uno por la muerte de ...; **they called to ~** vinieron a dar el pésame.
sympathizer ['sɪmpəθaɪzəʳ] *n* simpatizante *mf*, partidario *m*, -a *f* (*with* de).
sympathy ['sɪmpəθɪ] *n* (**a**) (*fellow-feeling*) simpatía *f*; solidaridad *f*; **~ strike** huelga *f* de solidaridad; **~ vote** voto *m* de consolación; **I am not in ~ with him** no comparto su criterio, no lo entiendo así; **the sympathies of the crowd were with him** la multitud estaba de lado de él, la multitud le apoyaba; **to strike in ~ with sb** declararse en huelga por solidaridad con uno.
(**b**) (*pity*) compasión *f*, condolencia *f*; sentimiento *m*; (*kindness*) amabilidad *f*, benevolencia *f*; **he has my ~** le compadezco; **my sympathies are with her family** lo siento por la familia de ella; **have you no ~?** ¿no tiene compasión?; **to express one's ~** dar el pésame (*on the death of* por la muerte de); **his ~ for the underdog** su compasión por los desvalidos.
symphonic [sɪm'fɒnɪk] *adj* sinfónico.
symphony ['sɪmfənɪ] *n* sinfonía *f*; **~ orchestra** orquesta *f* sinfónica.
symposium [sɪm'pəʊzɪəm] *n*, *pl* **symposiums** *or* **symposia** [sɪm'pəʊzɪə] simposio *m*.
symptom ['sɪmptəm] *n* síntoma *m*; indicio *m*.
symptomatic [,sɪmptə'mætɪk] *adj* sintomático (*of* de).
synagogue ['sɪnəgɒg] *n* sinagoga *f*.
sync* [sɪŋk] *n abbr of* **synchronization**: **in ~** en sincronización; **they are in ~** (*fig*) están sincronizados; **out of ~** (*fig*) desincronizado.
synchromesh ['sɪŋkrəʊ'meʃ] *n* (*also* **~ gear**) cambio *m* sincronizado de velocidades.
synchronic [sɪŋ'krɒnɪk] *adj* sincrónico.
synchronism ['sɪŋkrənɪzəm] *n* sincronismo *m*.
synchronization [,sɪŋkrənaɪ'zeɪʃən] *n* sincronización *f*.
synchronize ['sɪŋkrənaɪz] **1** *vt* sincronizar (*with* con); **~d swimming** natación *f* sincronizada. **2** *vi* sincronizarse, ser sincrónico (*with* con); coincidir (*with* con).
synchronous ['sɪŋkrənəs] *adj* sincrónico, síncrono.
synchrotron ['sɪŋkrə,trɒn] *n* sincrotrón *m*.
syncopate ['sɪŋkəpeɪt] *vt* sincopar.
syncopation [,sɪŋkə'peɪʃən] *n* síncopa *f*.
syncope ['sɪŋkəpɪ] *n* (*Med*) síncope *m*; (*Ling, Mus*) síncopa *f*.
syncretism ['sɪŋkrətɪzəm] *n* sincretismo *m*.
syndic ['sɪndɪk] *n* síndico *m*.
syndicalism ['sɪndɪkəlɪzəm] *n* sindicalismo *m*.
syndicalist ['sɪndɪkəlɪst] **1** *adj* sindicalista. **2** *n* sindicalista *mf*.
syndicate 1 ['sɪndɪkɪt] *n* (**a**) (*gen*) sindicato *m*; (*news agency*) agencia *f* de prensa; (*chain of papers*) cadena *f* de periódicos. (**b**) (*****: *criminals*) banda *f* de malhechores, cuadrilla *f* de bandidos. **2** ['sɪndɪkeɪt] *vt* sindicar; **~d loan** préstamo *m* sindicado.
syndrome ['sɪndrəʊm] *n* síndrome *m*.
synecdoche [sɪ'nekdəkɪ] *n* sinécdoque *f*.
synergy ['sɪnədʒɪ] *n* sinergia *f*.
synod ['sɪnəd] *n* sínodo *m*.
synonym ['sɪnənɪm] *n* sinónimo *m*.
synonymous [sɪ'nɒnɪməs] *adj* sinónimo (*with* con).
synonymy [sɪ'nɒnəmɪ] *n* sinonimia *f*.
synopsis [sɪ'nɒpsɪs] *n*, *pl* **synopses** [sɪ'nɒpsiːz] sinopsis *f*.
synoptic(al) [sɪ'nɒptɪk(əl)] *adj* sinóptico.
synovial [saɪ'nəʊvɪəl] *adj* sinovial.
syntactic(al) [sɪn'tæktɪk(əl)] *adj* sintáctico.
syntagm ['sɪntæm] *n*, **syntagma** [sɪn'tægmə] *n* sintagma *m*.
syntagmatic [,sɪntæg'mætɪk] *adj* sintagmático.
syntax ['sɪntæks] **1** *n* sintaxis *f*. **2** *attr*: **~ error** error *m* sintáctico.
synthesis ['sɪnθəsɪs] *n*, *pl* **syntheses** ['sɪnθəsiːz] síntesis *f*.
synthesize ['sɪnθəsaɪz] *vt* sintetizar.
synthesizer ['sɪnθəsaɪzəʳ] *n* sintetizador *m*.
synthetic [sɪn'θetɪk] **1** *adj* sintético; **~ fiber** (*US*), **~ fibre** fibra *f* sintética; **~ rubber** caucho *m* artificial. **2 ~s** *npl* fibras *fpl* sintéticas.
synthetically [sɪn'θetɪkəlɪ] *adv* sintéticamente.
syphilis ['sɪfɪlɪs] *n* sífilis *f*.
syphilitic [,sɪfɪ'lɪtɪk] **1** *adj* sifilítico. **2** *n* sifilítico *m*, -a *f*.
syphon ['saɪfən] = **siphon**.
Syracuse ['saɪərəkjuːz] *n* Siracusa *f*.
Syria ['sɪrɪə] *n* Siria *f*.
Syrian ['sɪrɪən] **1** *adj* sirio. **2** *n* sirio *m*, -a *f*.
syringe [sɪ'rɪndʒ] **1** *n* jeringa *f*, jeringuilla *f*. **2** *vt* jeringar.
syrup ['sɪrəp] *n* jarabe *m*; almíbar *m*.
syrupy ['sɪrəpɪ] *adj* (**a**) parecido a jarabe, espeso como jarabe. (**b**) (*fig*) sensiblero, sentimentaloide*, dulzarrón.
system ['sɪstəm] *n* (**a**) (*gen*) sistema *m*; método *m*; (*Med*) organismo *m*, constitución *f*; (*Elec*) circuito *m*, instalación *f*; **the S~** (*Pol*) el Sistema; **~s analysis** análisis *m* de sistemas; **~s analyst** analista *mf* de sistemas; **~ disk** disco *m* del sistema; **~s engineer** ingeniero *m* de sistemas; **~s engineering** ingeniería *f* de sistemas; **~s programmer** programador *m*, -ora *f* de sistemas; **~s software** software *m* del sistema; **a shock to the ~** una sacudida para el organismo; **to get sth out of one's ~** (*fig*) quitarse algo de encima.
(**b**) (*orderliness*) método *m*; **he lacks ~** carece de método.
systematic [,sɪstə'mætɪk] *adj* sistemático, metódico.
systematically [,sɪstə'mætɪkəlɪ] *adv* sistemáticamente, metódicamente.
systematization ['sɪstəmətaɪ'zeɪʃən] *n* sistematización *f*.
systematize ['sɪstəmətaɪz] *vt* sistematizar.

T

T, t [tiː] *n* (*letter*) T, t; **T for Tommy** T de Tarragona; **T~bar lift** *n* remolque *m* T-bar; **T-bone steak** *n* entrecote *m*; **T-intersection** (*US*), **T-junction** cruce *m* en T; **T-shaped** en forma de T; **T-shirt** camiseta *f*, niki *m*, playera *f* (*LAm*), remera *f* (*LAm*); **T-square** doble escuadra *f*, escuadra *f* T; **that's it to a T** es eso exactamente; **it fits you to a T** te sienta perfectamente; **it suits you to a T** te viene de perlas.

TA *n* (**a**) (*Brit*) *abbr of* **Territorial Army** ejército *m* de reserva. (**b**) (*US Univ*) *abbr of* **teaching assistant**.

ta* [tɑː] *interj* (*Brit*) ¡gracias!; **~ very much!** ¡muchas gracias!

tab¹ [tæb] *n* oreja *f*, lengüeta *f*; (*label*) etiqueta *f*; (*of cheque*) resguardo *m*; (*US*) cuenta *f*; **~s** (*Theat*) cortina *f* a la italiana; **to keep ~s on sb** echar un ojo sobre uno, vigilar a uno; **to keep ~s on sth** tener algo a la vista, tener cuenta de algo; **to pick up the ~** pagar la cuenta, (*fig*) asumir la responsabilidad.

tab² [tæb] **1** *n* tabulación *f*. **2** *vt* tabular.

tabard ['tæbəd] *n* tabardo *m*.

Tabasco [tə'bæskəʊ] ® *n* tabasco *m*.

tabby ['tæbɪ] **1** *adj* atigrado. **2** *n* (*also* **~ cat**) gato *m* atigrado, gata *f* atigrada.

tabernacle ['tæbənækl] *n* tabernáculo *m*.

tab key ['tæbkiː] *n* tecla *f* de tabulación.

table ['teɪbl] **1** *n* (**a**) (*furniture*) mesa *f*; (*Archit*) tablero *m*; (*of land*) meseta *f*; **~ manners** modales *mpl* de mesa; **~ salt** sal *f* de mesa; **to keep a good ~** tener buena mesa; **to clear the ~** quitar la mesa; **the whole ~ laughed** se rieron todos los comensales; **to lay the ~, to set the ~** poner la mesa; **to put a proposal on the ~** (*Brit*) ofrecer una propuesta para discutir, (*US*) aplazar la discusión de una propuesta; **to rise from the ~** levantarse de la mesa; **to sit down to ~** sentarse a (*or* en) la mesa; **to turn the ~s on sb** devolver la pelota a uno, volver las tornas a uno.

(**b**) (*Math etc*) tabla *f*; (*statistical etc*) tabla *f*, cuadro *m*; (*of prices*) lista *f*, tarifa *f*; (*league ~*) liga *f*; clasificación *f*, escalafón *m*; **~ of contents** índice *m* de materias; **we are in fourth place in the ~** ocupamos el cuarto lugar en la clasificación.

2 *vt* (**a**) (*Brit Parl etc*) *motion* presentar, poner sobre la mesa.

(**b**) (*set out*) poner en una tabla, disponer en un cuadro; ordenar sistemáticamente.

(**c**) (*US: postpone*) aplazar, archivar, posponer; *bill* dar carpetazo a, dar largas a.

tableau ['tæbləʊ] *n*, *pl* **tableaus** *or* **tableaux** ['tæbləʊz] cuadro *m* (vivo).

tablecloth ['teɪblklɒθ] *n*, *pl* **tablecloths** ['teɪblklɒθs] mantel *m*.

tablecover ['teɪbl,kʌvəʳ] *n* mantel *m*.

table d'hôte ['tɑːbl'dəʊt] *n* menú *m*.

table-football [,teɪbl'fʊtbɔːl] *n* futbolín *m*.

table-lamp ['teɪbllæmp] *n* lámpara *f* de mesa.

tableland ['teɪbllænd] *n* meseta *f*, altiplano *m* (*LAm*).

table-leg ['teɪblleg] *n* pata *f* de mesa.

table-linen ['teɪbl,lɪnɪn] *n* mantelería *f*.

tablemat ['teɪblmæt] *n* salvaplatos *m*, salvamanteles *m*.

Table Mountain ['teɪbl'maʊntɪn] *n* Monte *m* de la Mesa.

table-napkin ['teɪbl,næpkɪn] *n* servilleta *f*.

table-runner ['teɪbl,rʌnəʳ] *n* mantelillo *m*, camino *m* de mesa.

tablespoon ['teɪblspuːn] *n* (*spoon*) cuchara *f* grande, cuchara *f* para servir; (*quantity*) cucharada *f*.

tablespoonful ['teɪbl,spuːnfʊl] *n* cucharada *f*.

tablet ['tæblɪt] *n* tabla *f*; tableta *f*; (*Med*) tableta *f*, comprimido *m*; (*of soap etc*) pastilla *f*; (*stone, inscribed*) lápida *f*; (*writing ~*) bloc *m*, taco *m* (de papel).

table-talk ['teɪbltɔːk] *n* conversación *f* de sobremesa.

table-tennis ['teɪbl,tenɪs] *n* tenis *m* de mesa, ping-pong *m*; **~ player** jugador *m*, -ora *f* de ping-pong (*or* de tenis de mesa).

table-top ['teɪbltɒp] *n* superficie *f* de la mesa.

tableware ['teɪblwɛəʳ] *n* vajilla *f*, servicio *m* de mesa.

tablewater ['teɪbl,wɔːtəʳ] *n* agua *f* mineral.

table wine ['teɪblwaɪn] *n* vino *m* de mesa.

tabloid ['tæblɔɪd] *n* (*Med*) tableta *f*, comprimido *m*; (*newspaper*) tabloide *m*; **the ~s** (*pej*) la prensa amarilla.

taboo [tə'buː] **1** *adj* tabú, prohibido; **the subject is ~** el asunto es tema tabú. **2** *n* tabú *m*; **all kinds of ~s** toda clase de tabúes. **3** *vt* declarar tabú, prohibir.

tabular ['tæbjʊləʳ] *adj* tabular.

tabulate ['tæbjʊleɪt] *vt* disponer en tablas, exponer en forma de tabla; contabilizar; (*Comput*) tabular.

tabulation [,tæbjʊ'leɪʃən] *n* disposición *f* en tablas, exposición *f* en forma de tabla; contabilización *f*.

tabulator ['tæbjʊleɪtəʳ] *n* tabulador *m*.

tachograph ['tækəgrɑːf] *n* tacógrafo *m*.

tachometer [tæ'kɒmɪtəʳ] *n* tacómetro *m*.

tachycardia [,tækɪ'kɑːdɪə] *n* taquicardia *f*.

tachymeter [tæ'kɪmɪtəʳ] *n* taquímetro *m*.

tacit ['tæsɪt] *adj* tácito.

tacitly ['tæsɪtlɪ] *adv* tácitamente.

taciturn ['tæsɪtɜːn] *adj* taciturno.

taciturnity [,tæsɪ'tɜːnɪtɪ] *n* taciturnidad *f*.

Tacitus ['tæsɪtəs] *nm* Tácito.

tack [tæk] **1** *n* (**a**) (*nail*) tachuela *f*.

(**b**) (*Brit Sew*) hilván *m*.

(**c**) (*Naut: rope*) amura *f*; (*course*) virada *f*, bordada *f*; (*fig*) rumbo *m*, dirección *f*; línea *f* de conducta, política *f*; **to be on the right ~** (*fig*) ir por buen camino; **to be on the wrong ~** (*fig*) estar equivocado; **to try another ~** (*fig*) abordar un problema desde otro punto de partida; cambiar de política.

2 *vt* (**a**) (*nail*) clavar con tachuelas.

(**b**) (*Brit Sew*) hilvanar.

3 *vi* (*Naut*) virar, cambiar de bordada; **the ship ~ed this way and that** el buque daba bordadas.

◆**tack down** *vt*: **to ~ sth down** afirmar algo con tachuelas, sujetar algo con tachuelas.

◆**tack on** *vt*: **to ~ sth on to a letter** añadir algo a una carta; **somehow it got ~ed on** de algún modo u otro llegó a ser añadido a la parte principal.

tackle ['tækl] **1** *n* (**a**) (*esp Naut: pulley*) aparejo *m*; polea *f*; (*ropes*) jarcia *f*; cordaje *m*.

(**b**) (*gear, equipment*) equipo *m*, avíos *mpl*, aperos *mpl*; (*fig*) cosas *fpl*, enseres *mpl*; (*fishing ~*) aparejo *m* de pescar.

(**c**) (*Ftbl etc*) entrada *f*; (*Rugby*) placaje *m*.

2 *vt* (*grapple with*) agarrar, asir; atacar; (*Ftbl*) entrar, atajar, blocar; (*Rugby*) placar; *problem* abordar, atacar; *task* emprender; **he had to ~ 3 intruders** tuvo que hacer frente a 3 intrusos; **he ~d Greek on his own** emprendió el estudio del griego sin ayuda de nadie; **did you ever ~ Mulacén?** ¿os atrevisteis alguna vez a escalar el Mulacén?; **can you ~ another helping?** ¿puedes comerte otra porción?; **I'll ~ him about it at once** lo discutiré con él en seguida (quiera o no quiera).

tacky¹ ['tækɪ] *adj* pegajoso.

tacky²* ['tækɪ] *adj* (*shabby*) raído; (*shoddy*) de pacotilla, malísimo; (*ostentatious*) cursi, vulgar; (*eccentric*) estrafalario; *house* feo, destartalado; *problem* peliagudo.

taco ['tɑːkəʊ] *n* (*US*) (*especie de*) *tortilla rellena hecha con harina de maíz.*

tact [tækt] *n* tacto *m*, discreción *f*.

tactful ['tæktfʊl] *adj* discreto, diplomático; **be as ~ as you**

can use la mayor discreción; **that was not very ~ of you** pudieras haberlo hecho con más tacto.
tactfully ['tæktfəlɪ] *adv* discretamente, diplomáticamente.
tactfulness ['tæktfʊlnɪs] *n* tacto *m*, discreción *f*.
tactic ['tæktɪk] *n* táctica *f*; maniobra *f*; **~s** (*collectively*) táctica *f*.
tactical ['tæktɪkəl] *adj* táctico; **~ voting** votación *f* táctica.
tactically ['tæktɪkəlɪ] *adv* tácticamente.
tactician [tæk'tɪʃən] *n* táctico *m*.
tactile ['tæktaɪl] *adj* táctil.
tactless ['tæktlɪs] *adj* indiscreto, falto de tacto, poco diplomático.
tactlessly ['tæktlɪslɪ] *adv* indiscretamente, de modo poco diplomático.
tactlessness ['tæktlɪsnɪs] *n* indiscreción *f*, falta *f* de tacto.
tadpole ['tædpəʊl] *n* renacuajo *m*.
taffeta ['tæfɪtə] *n* tafetán *m*.
taffrail ['tæfreɪl] *n* coronamiento *m*, pasamano *m* de la borda.
Taffy* ['tæfɪ] *n* galés *m*.
taffy ['tæfɪ] *n* (*US*) (**a**) = **toffee**. (**b**) (*) coba* *f*.
tag¹ [tæg] **1** *n* (**a**) (*loose end*) cabo *m*, rabito *m*; (*torn piece, hanging piece*) pingajo *m*; (*metal tip*) herrete *m*; (*label*) etiqueta *f*, marbete *m*, (*for identification etc*) chapa *f*; (*for criminal*) etiqueta *f* personal de control; **~** (**question**) cláusula *f* final interrogativa.
(**b**) (*commonplace*) dicho *m*, lugar *m* común; muletilla *f*; (*quotation*) cita *f* trillada.
2 *vt* (**a**) (*follow*) seguir de cerca, pisar los talones a.
(**b**) (*label*) poner una etiqueta a, pegar una etiqueta a; *criminal* controlar electrónicamente.
◆**tag along** *vi* (*jog along*) seguir despacio su camino; proceder con calma; (*accompany*) ir también, venir después.
◆**tag on** **1** *vt*: **to ~ sth on to an article** pegar algo a un artículo; **can we ~ this on?** ¿podemos añadir esto?
2 *vi*: **to ~ on to sb** pegarse a uno.
tag² [tæg] *n* (*game*) marro *m*; **to play ~** jugar al marro.
tagmeme ['tægmiːm] *n* tagmema *m*.
tagmemics [tæg'miːmɪks] *n* tagmética *f*.
Tagus ['teɪgəs] *n* Tajo *m*.
Tahiti [tɑː'hiːtɪ] *n* Tahití *m*.
tail [teɪl] **1** *n* (**a**) (*Anat*) cola *f*, rabo *m*; (*loose end*) cabo *m*; (*of hair*) trenza *f*; (*of comet*) cabellera *f*; (*Aer*) cola *f*; (*of procession etc*) cola *f*, parte *f* final; (*of coat*) faldón *m*, faldillas *fpl*; (*of shirt*) faldón *m*; **~s** (*coat*) frac *m*; (*of coin*) cruz *f*; **with its ~ between its legs** con el rabo entre las piernas; **~s you lose** cruz y pierdes; **to turn ~** volver la espalda, huir.
(**b**) (*: *buttocks*) trasero *m*; **to work one's ~ off** sudar tinta*.
(**c**) (*US*‡: *girls*) jais‡ *fpl*; **a piece of ~‡** una jai‡, una tía*.
(**d**) (*: *person following*) sombra *f*.
2 *vt* (**a**) (*follow*) seguir (de cerca), seguir y vigilar.
(**b**) *animal* descolar; *fruit* quitar el tallo a.
3 *vi*: **to ~ after sb** seguir a uno (de mala gana).
◆**tail away** *vi* ir disminuyendo (*into* hasta, hasta no ser más que), desaparecer poco a poco; **his voice ~ed away** su voz se fue debilitando; **after that the book ~s away** después de eso el libro ya no es tan bueno, después de eso el libro no tiene tantas cosas buenas.
◆**tail back** *vi*: **the traffic ~ed back to the bridge** la cola de coches se extendía atrás hasta el puente.
◆**tail off** *vi* = **tail away**.
tailback ['teɪlbæk] *n* (*Brit Aut*) caravana *f*, cola *f*, embotellamiento *m*.
tailboard ['teɪlbɔːd] *n* escalera *f*, tablero *m* posterior.
tailcoat ['teɪlkəʊt] *n* frac *m*.
-tailed [teɪld] *adj* con rabo ..., *eg* **long~** con rabo largo, rabilargo.
tail-end ['teɪl'end] *n* cola *f*; extremo *m*; parte *f* de atrás, parte *f* posterior; (*fig*) parte *f* que queda, porción *f* inservible; **at the ~ of the summer** en los últimos días del verano.
tailgate ['teɪlgeɪt] **1** *n* portón *m*. **2** *vt* ir a rebufo de. **3** *vi* ir a rebufo.
tail-gunner ['teɪl,gʌnəʳ] *n* artillero *m* de cola.
tail-lamp ['teɪllæmp] *n* piloto *m*, luz *f* trasera.
tailless ['teɪllɪs] *adj* sin rabo.
taillight ['teɪllaɪt] *n* piloto *m*, luz *f* trasera, calavera *f* (*Mex*).
tail-off ['teɪlɒf] *n* disminución *f* (paulatina).
tailor ['teɪləʳ] **1** *n* sastre *m*; **~'s** (**shop**) sastrería *f*; **~'s chalk** jabón *m* de sastre; **~'s dummy** maniquí *m*. **2** *vt suit* hacer, confeccionar; (*fig*) adaptar.
tailored ['teɪləd] *adj*: **~ dress** vestido *m* sastre; **a well-~ suit** un traje bien hecho, un traje que entalla bien.
tailoring ['teɪlərɪŋ] *n* (*craft*) sastrería *f*; (*cut*) corte *m*, hechura *f*.
tailor-made ['teɪləmeɪd] *adj* (**a**) *garment* hecho por sastre, de sastre; **~ costume** traje *m* hechura sastre.
(**b**) **~ for you** (*fig*) especial para Vd, creado especialmente para Vd.
tailpiece ['teɪlpiːs] *n* (*Typ*) florón *m*; (*addition*) apéndice *m*, añadidura *f*.
tailpipe ['teɪlpaɪp] *n* (*US*) tubo *m* de escape.
tailplane ['teɪlpleɪn] *n* cola *f*, plano *m* de cola.
tailskid ['teɪlskɪd] *n* patín *m* de cola.
tailspin ['teɪlspɪn] *n* barrena *f* picada.
tailwheel ['teɪl'wiːl] *n* rueda *f* de cola.
tailwind ['teɪlwɪnd] *n* viento *m* de cola.
taint [teɪnt] **1** *n* infección *f*; (*fig*) mancha *f*, tacha *f*; olor *m* (*of* a); **the ~ of sin** la mancha del pecado; **not free from the ~ of corruption** no sin cierto olor a corrupción.
2 *vt meat, food* contaminar; (*fig*) manchar, tachar (*LAm*).
tainted ['teɪntɪd] *adj* viciado, corrompido; *meat etc* pasado, contaminado; **a belief ~ with heresy** una creencia no exenta de herejía; **to become ~** (*meat etc*) echarse a perder.
Taiwan [,taɪ'wɑːn] *n* Taiwán *m*.
Taiwanese [,taɪwə'niːz] **1** *adj* taiwanés. **2** *n* taiwanés *m*, -esa *f*.
take [teɪk] (*irr*: *pret* **took**, *ptp* **taken**) **1** *n* (**a**) (*Cine, Phot*) toma *f*, vista *f*.
(**b**) (*money*) ingresos *mpl*; recaudación *f*; (*US Comm*) caja *f*, ventas *fpl* (del día *etc*).
(**c**) **to be on the ~*** (*US*) estar dispuesto a dejarse sobornar.
2 *vt* (**a**) (*gen*) tomar; (*by force*) coger (*Sp*), agarrar (*esp LAm*), asir, arrebatar; (*steal*) robar; (*keep*) quedarse con; **to ~ sth from sb** tomar algo a uno; **who took my beer?** ¿quién se ha llevado mi cerveza?; **to ~ a book from a shelf** sacar un libro de un estante; **to ~ a passage from an author** tomar un pasaje de un autor; **seeing that film took me out of myself** esa película me hizo olvidar mis propios problemas; **to ~ sb's arm** tomar del brazo a uno; **to ~ sb in one's arms** abrazar a uno, rodear a uno con los brazos; **with an attitude of ~ it or leave it** con actitud de lo toma o lo deja.
(**b**) (*capture*) *city etc* tomar, conquistar; *specimen, fish etc* coger; (*Chess etc*) comer; *prisoner* hacer; *suspect, wanted man* coger, detener; **to ~ sb alive or dead** coger a uno vivo o muerto; **the devil ~ it!** ¡maldición!, ¡que se lo lleve el diablo!; **to be ~n ill** ponerse enfermo, enfermar; **we were very ~n with him** le encontramos simpatiquísimo; **I'm not at all ~n with the idea** la idea no me gusta nada, la idea no me hace gracia.
(**c**) (*win*) *prize* ganar; *trick* ganar, hacer; **to ~ one's degree** recibir un título; **to ~ a degree in** licenciarse en; **to ~ £30 a day** cobrar 30 libras al día; **last year we took £30,000** el año pasado los ingresos sumaron 30.000 libras; **El Toboso took both points** El Toboso ganó los dos puntos; **V took a point from B** V sacó un punto a B.
(**d**) (*rent*) alquilar; **we shall ~ a house for the summer** alquilaremos una casa para el verano; **we took rooms at Torquay** alquilamos un piso en Torquay.
(**e**) (*occupy*) ocupar; **is this seat ~n?** ¿está ocupado este asiento?; **please ~ your seats!** ¡siéntense, por favor!
(**f**) (*go by*) *bus, train etc* coger (*Sp*), tomar (*LAm*); *road* tomar, ir por; *fence* saltar, saltar por encima de; **~ the first on the right** vaya por la primera calle a la derecha; **we took the wrong road** nos equivocamos de camino; **we ~ the golden road to Samarkand** vamos por el camino dorado de Samarkand.
(**g**) (*ingest*) *drink, food* tomar; **to ~ a meal** comer; **he took no food for 4 days** estuvo 4 días sin comer; **how much alcohol had he ~n?** ¿cuánto alcohol había ingerido?; **'not to be ~n'** (*Med*) 'para uso externo'; **will you ~ sth before you go?** ¿quieres tomar algo antes de irte?
(**h**) (*have, make, undertake etc*) *bath, bend, breath, decision, exercise, holiday, liberty, possession* tomar; *step, walk*, dar; *photo* sacar, tomar; *ticket* sacar; *trip* hacer; *oath* prestar; *census* levantar, efectuar; *examination* presentarse para, sufrir; *opportunity* aprovechar; **~ five!*, ~ ten!*** (*US*) ¡haz una pausa!, ¡descansa un rato!
(**i**) (*receive*) recibir, tomar; *advice* seguir; *bet* aceptar, hacer; *responsibility* asumir; *lodger* recibir; *pupils* tomar;

course of study seguir, cursar; *subject* estudiar; *newspaper etc* leer, abonarse a; ~ **that!** ¡toma!; ~ **it from me!** ¡escucha lo que te digo!; **you can** ~ **it from me that ...** puedes tener la seguridad de que ...; **to** ~ **the service** (*Tennis*) restar la pelota, ser restador; **he took the ball full in the chest** el balón le dio de lleno en el pecho; **what will you** ~ **for it?** ¿cuánto pides por él?; **to** ~ **a wife** casarse, contraer matrimonio; **to** ~ **sb into partnership** tomar a uno como socio; **to** ~ **(holy) orders** ordenarse de sacerdote; *V* **badly, ill** *etc.*

(**j**) (*tolerate*) aguantar, sufrir; **we can** ~ **it** lo aguantamos todo; **he took a lot of punishment** le dieron muy duro; **London took a battering in 1941** Londres recibió una paliza en 1941, Londres sufrió terriblemente en 1941; **his arrogance is hard to** ~ su arrogancia es inaguantable; **I won't** ~ **no for an answer** no permito que digas no, no permito que me des una respuesta negativa; **I won't** ~ **that from you** no permito que digas eso; no acepto tal cosa de ti.

(**k**) (*consider*) tomar, considerar; **now** ~ **Ireland** consideren el caso de Irlanda, pongamos por caso Irlanda; **taking one thing with another ...** considerándolo todo junto ..., considerándolo en conjunto ...; **taking one year with another ...** tomando un año con otro ...

(**l**) (*contain*) tener cabida para; **a car that** ~**s 6 passengers** un coche con cabida para 6 personas, un coche donde caben 6 personas; **can you** ~ **2 more?** ¿puedes llevar 2 más?, ¿caben otros 2?; **it won't** ~ **any more** no cabe(n) más; **it** ~**s weights up to 8 tons** soporta pesos hasta de 8 toneladas.

(**m**) (*experience*) experimentar; *illness* coger (*Sp*), agarrar (*LAm*); **to** ~ **cold** coger un resfriado (*Sp*), resfriarse; **to** ~ **fright** asustarse (*at* de); **to** ~ **a dislike to sb** coger antipatía a uno; **I do not** ~ **any satisfaction from ...** no experimento satisfacción alguna de ...; *V* **liking** *etc.*

(**n**) (*suppose*) suponer; **I** ~ **it that ...** supongo que ..., me imagino que ...; **I** ~ **her to be about 30** supongo que tiene unos 30 años; **I took him for a foreigner** creí que era extranjero, le tomé por extranjero; **what do you** ~ **me for?** ¿por quién me has tomado?, ¿crees que soy un tonto?; **we took A for B** equivocamos A con B.

(**o**) (*require*) necesitar; hacer falta; **a recipe that** ~**s 10 eggs** una receta en la que hacen falta 10 huevos; **it** ~**s a lot of courage** exige gran valor; **it** ~**s a brave man to do that** hace falta que un hombre tenga mucho valor para hacer eso; **he's got what it** ~**s*** tiene lo que hace falta; **it** ~**s 4 days** es cosa de 4 días; **a letter** ~**s 4 days to get there** una carta tarda 4 días en llegar allá; **it won't** ~ **long** no lleva mucho tiempo; **however long it** ~**s** el tiempo que sea; **it took 3 policemen to hold him down** se necesitaron 3 policías para sujetarle; **that verb** ~**s the dative** ese verbo rige el dativo; *V* **size** *etc.*

(**p**) (*lead, transport*) llevar; **to** ~ **sth to sb** llevar algo a uno; **to** ~ **sb somewhere** llevar a uno a un sitio; **we took her to the doctor** la llevamos al médico; **an ambulance took him to hospital** una ambulancia le llevó al hospital; **they took me over the factory** me mostraron la fábrica, me acompañaron en una visita a la fábrica; **to** ~ **sb for a walk** llevar a uno de paseo; **it took us out of our way** nos hizo desviarnos; **whatever took you to Miami?** ¿con qué motivo fuiste a Miami?, ¿para qué fuiste a Miami?

3 *vi* (**a**) (*stick*) pegar; (*set*) cuajar; (*vaccination*) prender; (*of plant*) arraigar; (*succeed*) tener éxito; resultar ser eficaz.

(**b**) **he** ~**s well** (*Phot*) sale bien (en fotografías), es muy fotogénico.

◆**take after** *vt* (*in looks*) salir a, parecerse a; (*in conduct*) seguir el ejemplo de.

◆**take against** *vt* cobrar antipatía a, encontrar antipático.

◆**take along** *vt* llevar, traer (consigo).

◆**take apart 1** *vt* desmontar; (*****) *room etc* destrozar, *person* dar una paliza a; **I'll** ~ **him apart!*** ¡le rompo la cara!; **the police took the place** ~ la policía investigó minuciosamente el local.

2 *vi*: **it** ~**s apart easily** se desmonta fácilmente.

◆**take aside** *vt* llevar aparte.

◆**take away 1** *vt* (**a**) (*carry away, lead away*) llevarse.

(**b**) (*remove*) quitar; llevarse.

(**c**) (*Math*) restar (*from* de); **7** ~ **away 4 is 3** 7 menos 4 son 3.

2 *vi*: **that** ~**s away from its value** eso le quita valor, eso rebaja su valor.

◆**take back** *vt* (**a**) *words* retractar; *promise* desdecirse de; *husband* recibir otra vez; *object* recibir devuelto; **the company took him back** la compañía volvió a emplearle, la compañía le restituyó a su puesto.

(**b**) (*return*) devolver.

(**c**) (*Typ*) trasladar al renglón anterior.

(**d**) **the sight took me back many years** ver aquello me recordó cosas de hace muchos años; **it** ~**s you back, doesn't it?** ¡cuántos recuerdos (de los buenos tiempos)!

◆**take down** *vt* (**a**) *object* bajar; descolgar; *poster etc* despegar; *decorations* quitar; *trousers* bajar; *V* **peg.**

(**b**) (*dismantle*) desmontar, desarmar.

(**c**) (*note*) apuntar; poner por escrito.

◆**take from** *vt* = **take away from**; *V* **take away 1** (**c**).

◆**take in** *vt* (**a**) *chairs, harvest* recoger; *sail* desmontar; *work* aceptar, admitir, recibir; *food* tomar; ingerir; *lodger* recibir, acoger (en casa).

(**b**) (*Sew*) achicar.

(**c**) (*include*) incluir, abarcar.

(**d**) (*grasp*) comprender.

(**e**) (*: *cheat*) embaucar, estafar; dar gato por liebre a; **I was properly** ~**n in by the disguise** el disfraz me despistó completamente; **don't let yourself be** ~**n in by appearances** no te dejes engañar por las apariencias.

◆**take off 1** *vt* (**a**) (*remove*) *clothing* quitarse; *limb* amputar; *lid, wrapping, stain* quitar; (*unstick*) despegar; *discount* descontar, rebajar; **they took 2 names off the list** quitaron dos nombres de la lista, tacharon dos nombres de la lista; **the 5 o'clock train has been** ~**n off** han cancelado el tren de las 5.

(**b**) (*lead away*) llevarse; **they took him off to lunch** se lo llevaron a comer.

(**c**) (*imitate*) imitar; contrahacer, parodiar.

2 *vi* (**a**) (*depart*) salir (*for* para); largarse (*for* para); (*Aer*) despegar (*for* con rumbo a).

(**b**) (*succeed*) empezar a tener éxito, empezar a cuajar; **the idea never really took off** la idea no llegó a cuajar; **this style may** ~ **off** este estilo puede ponerse de moda.

◆**take on 1** *vt* (**a**) *work* aceptar; emprender; *cargo* cargar, tomar; *duty* tomar sobre sí, cargar con, encargarse de; **he's** ~**n on more than he bargained for** le está resultando peor de lo que se creía, no contaba con tener que esforzarse tanto.

(**b**) (*in contest*) jugar contra; habérselas con; **I'll** ~ **you on!** ¡acepto (el desafío)!

(**c**) *employee* contratar.

(**d**) (*assume*) asumir, tomar.

2 *vi* (**a**) (*fashion etc*) establecerse, cuajar; ponerse de moda.

(**b**) (*Brit**) apurarse, excitarse, ponerse nervioso; quejarse; **don't** ~ **on so!** ¡no te apures!, ¡cálmate!

◆**take out** *vt* (**a**) (*lead out*) llevar fuera; *child, dog* llevar de paseo; *girl* invitar; escoltar, acompañar; salir con.

(**b**) (*remove*) quitar; (*extract*) sacar, extraer; (*Mil etc*) eliminar.

(**c**) *insurance* firmar; *licence, patent* obtener.

(**d**) (*tire*) **it took it out of me** me agotó, me rindió.

(**e**) **to** ~ **it out on sb** desahogarse riñendo a uno.

◆**take over 1** *vt* (**a**) (*transport*) llevar.

(**b**) *control, responsibility* asumir; encargarse de; *leadership, office* asumir, tomar posesión de; *company* comprar; tomar el control de; **the tourists have** ~**n over the beaches** los turistas han acaparado las playas; **the army has** ~**n over power** el ejército se ha hecho cargo del poder, el ejército ha ocupado el poder.

2 *vi* (*in post*) tomar posesión; entrar en funciones; (*in relay race*) tomar el relevo, (*in lead*) tomar la delantera; (*at controls*) asumir el mando, (*Aut*) tomar el volante, (*Aer*) tomar los mandos; (*emotion*) cundir, dominar, llegar a dominar; **when the army** ~**s over** cuando el ejército se haga cargo del poder; **then panic took over** luego cundió el pánico.

◆**take to** *vt* (**a**) (*liking*) *person* coger simpatía a (*Sp*), tomar cariño a, encariñarse con (*LAm*); *thing* aficionarse a, cobrar afición a; **I didn't much** ~ **to him** no me resultó simpático; **I didn't** ~ **to the idea** la idea no me gustaba.

(**b**) **to** ~ **to** + *ger* (*start*) empezar a + *infin*; dedicarse a + *infin*; aficionarse a + *infin.*

(**c**) **to** ~ **to drink** darse a la bebida; *V* **bed, hill** *etc.*

◆**take up 1** *vt* (**a**) (*carry up*) subir.

(**b**) (*lift*) coger (*Sp*), recoger; *carpet etc* quitar; *passengers* recoger; *arms* empuñar.

(**c**) (*occupy*) *room, time* ocupar, llenar; *residence* establecer, fijar; *post* tomar posesión de.

(**d**) (*absorb*) absorber.

(**e**) *study, career* empezar, emprender; dedicarse a;

case emprender investigaciones acerca de; *story* empezar a contar, (*after break*) reanudar; *challenge* aceptar.

(**f**) **to ~ sb up on a point** censurar un punto a uno; expresar dudas acerca de algo que uno ha dicho; **I feel I must ~ you up on that** creo que es mi deber comentar lo que has dicho; **I'll ~ you up on that offer** acepto esa oferta; **I'll ~ you up on that some day** algún día recordaré lo que has dicho.

2 *vi*: **to ~ up with sb** relacionarse con uno, estrechar amistad con uno; empezar a alternar con uno; **he took up with a most unsuitable girl** entró en relaciones con una joven nada conveniente.

◆**take upon** *vt*: **to ~ sth upon o.s.** tomar algo sobre sí, encargarse de algo; **to ~ it upon o.s. to** + *infin* atreverse a + *infin*, (*pej*) tener bastante caradura como para + *infin*.

takeaway ['teɪkəweɪ] *n* (*Brit*) tienda *f* donde se venden comidas para llevar; **~ food, ~ meal** comida *f* para llevar; **a Chinese ~** una comida china para llevar.

take-home ['teɪkhəʊm] *attr*: **~ pay** sueldo *m* neto, sueldo *m* líquido.

taken ['teɪkən] *ptp of* **take.**

takeoff ['teɪkɒf] *n* (**a**) (*Aer*) despegue *m*; **short ~ aircraft** avión *m* de despegue corto. (**b**) (*imitation*) imitación *f*; parodia *f*; sátira *f*. (**c**) (*Mech*) **power ~** toma *f* de fuerza.

takeover ['teɪk,əʊvəʳ] *n* toma *f* de posesión; entrada *f* en funciones; relevo *m* (en el mando); **the ~ of company A by company Z** la adquisición (*or* compra) de la compañía A por la compañía Z; **~ bid** oferta *f* pública de adquisición (de acciones), OPA *f*.

taker ['teɪkəʳ] *n*: **~s of snuff** los que acostumbran tomar rapé; **~s of drink in moderation** los que beben con moderación; **at £5 there were no ~s** a un precio de 5 libras nadie se ofreció a comprarlo; **this challenge found no ~s** no hubo nadie que quisiera aceptar este desafío.

take-up ['teɪkʌp] *n* tasa *f* de aceptación, porcentaje *m* de personas que aceptan (*or* cobran *etc*).

taking ['teɪkɪŋ] **1** *adj* atractivo, encantador.

2 *n* (**a**) (*Mil*) toma *f*, conquista *f*.

(**b**) **~s** (*Fin*) ingresos *mpl*; (*at show etc*) taquilla *f*, entrada *f*, recaudación *f*; **this year's ~s were only half last year's** este año se ha embolsado sólo la mitad de la recaudación del año pasado.

(**c**) **it's yours for the ~** tómalo si quieres.

talc [tælk] *n* talco *m*.

talcum powder ['tælkəm,paʊdəʳ] *n* (polvos *mpl* de) talco *m*.

tale [teɪl] *n* cuento *m*; historia *f*, relación *f*; (*pej*) cuento *m*, patraña *f*; **'T~s of King Arthur'** 'Leyendas *fpl* del Rey Artús'; **old wives' ~** cuento *m* de viejas, patraña *f*; **I hear ~s about you** me cuentan cosas acerca de ti; **to tell ~s (out of school)** (*inform*) soplar, chismear; (*fib*) contar cuentos; **he told the ~ of his life** contó la historia de su vida; **he had quite a ~ to tell** tuvo bastante que contar; **sound the alarm, or we shan't live to tell the ~** toca el timbre, o no salimos vivos de esto; **it tells its own ~** habla por sí.

talebearer ['teɪl,bɛərəʳ] *n* soplón *m*, -ona *f*, chismoso *m*, -a *f*.

talent ['tælənt] *n* talento *m* (*for* para); **man of ~** hombre *m* de talento; **all the local ~** toda la gente de talento de la comarca; **there wasn't much ~ at the dance*** en el baile casi no había chicas atractivas; **he watches for ~ at away matches** busca jugadores de talento en los partidos fuera de casa.

talented ['tæləntɪd] *adj* talentoso, de talento.

talent-scout ['tælənt,skaʊt] *n*, **talent-spotter** ['tælənt,spɒtəʳ] *n* cazatalentos *mf*.

taletelling ['teɪl,telɪŋ] *n* chismorreo *m*.

talisman ['tælɪzmən] *n* talismán *m*.

talk [tɔːk] **1** *n* (*conversation*) conversación *f*, (*chat*) charla *f*, plática *f* (*Mex*); (*informal lecture*) charla *f*; (*gossip*) chismes *mpl*, habladurías *fpl*; **~s** (*negotiations*) negociaciones *fpl*; **it's just ~** son cosas que se dicen, son rumores; **with him it's all ~** con éste son palabras nada más; **she's the ~ of the town** todos hablan de ella, es la comidilla de la ciudad; **there is (some) ~ of** se habla de; **there has been some ~ of his going** se ha hablado de que va él; **to give a ~** dar una charla (*about* sobre); **to have a ~ to** (*or* **with**) **sb** hablar con uno; **we must have a ~ sometime** tenemos que citarnos un día para hablar.

2 *vt* hablar; **to ~ Arabic** hablar árabe; **~ some Arabic to me** dime algo en árabe, dime unas palabras de árabe; **to ~ business** hablar de negocios; **to ~ nonsense** no decir más que tonterías; **to ~ sense** hablar con juicio, hablar razonablemente; *V* **shop** *etc.*

3 *vi* hablar (*about, of* de; *to* con, a); charlar, platicar (*Mex*); **it's all ~ and no do** todo es hablar y no se hace nada; **'he's so untidy' ... 'you can ~!'*** 'vive en el mayor desorden' ... '¡y tú que lo dices!'; **now you're ~ing!** ¡así se habla!; **it's easy for him to ~, but ...** es natural que lo diga él, pero ...; **look who's ~ing!** ¡quién lo dice!, ¡mira quien habla!; **to keep sb ~ing** entretener a uno en conversación; **to ~ through one's hat** decir tonterías; **~ about fleas!** ¡y las pulgas!; ¡Dios mío, qué pulgas!; **what shall we ~ about?** ¿de qué vamos a hablar?; **it is much ~ed about** se habla mucho de ello; **to get o.s. ~ed about in the papers** lograr que los periódicos hablen de uno; **he knows what he's ~ing about** habla con conocimiento de causa; **he doesn't know what he's ~ing about** no tiene la menor idea; **I'm not ~ing about you** no lo digo por ti; **~ing of bats, we ...** a propósito de los murciélagos, nosotros ...; **to ~ to o.s.** hablar consigo mismo; *V* **big.**

4 *vr*: **to ~ o.s. hoarse** enronquecer a fuerza de hablar.

◆**talk away 1** *vt*: **to ~ an hour away** pasar una hora charlando.

2 *vi* hablar mucho, no parar de hablar; seguir hablando; **~ away!** ¡di lo que quieras!

◆**talk back** *vi* replicar; contestar con frescura.

◆**talk down 1** *vt* (**a**) (*silence*) **to ~ sb down** reducir a uno al silencio, hacer callar a uno.

(**b**) **to ~ a plane down** controlar el aterrizaje de un avión desde tierra.

(**c**) *idea, plan* rebajar, quitar importancia a.

2 *vi*: **to ~ down to sb** darse aires de superioridad con uno, tratar a uno como un niño.

◆**talk into** *vt*: **to ~ sb into sth** convencer a uno para que haga algo; **to ~ o.s. into sth** convencerse a sí mismo, autosugestionarse; **you've ~ed me into it!** ¡me habéis convencido!

◆**talk on** *vi* no parar de hablar.

◆**talk out** *vt* (**a**) **to ~ out a bill** prolongar la discusión de un proyecto de ley de manera que no se pueda votar.

(**b**) (*dissuade*) **to ~ sb out of sth** disuadir a uno de algo; **he ~ed himself out of the job** hizo tan mala impresión hablando que no le dieron el puesto.

(**c**) *problem* discutir, examinar, resolver discutiendo.

◆**talk over** *vt* hablar de, discutir; pasar revista a; **I must ~ it over with my boss** tengo que discutirlo con mi jefe; **let's ~ it over** examinémoslo más detenidamente.

◆**talk round** *vt* (**a**) **to ~ sb round** llegar a convencer a uno; **she knows how to ~ him round** ella sabe cómo convencerle. (**b**) **they're only ~ing round the problem** están dando vueltas al problema sin resolverlo.

◆**talk through** *vt*: **to ~ a plan through** examinar un proyecto discutiéndolo; **let's ~ it through** discutámoslo.

◆**talk up** (*US*) **1** *vt product etc* dar bombo a*, hacer campaña en favor de; sobrevalorar; *person, possibility* mejorar la imagen de.

2 *vi* (*speak frankly*) decir las cosas como son, no callarse ni una.

talkative ['tɔːkətɪv] *adj* locuaz, hablador, platicón (*Mex*).

talkativeness ['tɔːkətɪvnɪs] *n* locuacidad *f*.

talked-of ['tɔːktɒv] *adj*: **a much ~ event** un suceso muy sonado.

talker ['tɔːkəʳ] *n* hablador *m*, -ora *f*; **to be a good ~** hablar bien; tener una conversación amena; **he's just a ~** habla mucho pero no hace nada.

talkie ['tɔːkɪ] *n* película *f* sonora; **the ~s** el cine sonoro.

talking ['tɔːkɪŋ] **1** *adj* parlante; *bird* parlero; **~ book** libro *m* hablado (para ciegos); **~ film, ~ picture** película *f* sonora; **~ head** (*TV*) locutor *m*, -ora *f*, busto *m* parlante.

2 *n* conversación *f*; palabras *fpl*; **'no ~'** 'prohibido hablar'; **no ~, please,** ¡silencio, por favor!; **she does all the ~** ella es quien habla.

talking-point ['tɔːkɪŋpɔɪnt] *n* tema *m* de conversación.

talking-shop ['tɔːkɪŋ,ʃɒp] *n lugar donde se habla mucho pero no se hace nada.*

talking-to ['tɔːkɪŋtuː] *n*: **to give sb a ~** echar un rapapolvo a uno.

talk-show ['tɔːkʃəʊ] *n* programa *m* de entrevistas (informales).

tall [tɔːl] *adj* (**a**) alto; grande; **a building 30 metres ~** un edificio que tiene 30 metros de alto; **how ~ you've got!** ¡qué grande estás!; ¡cómo has crecido!; **how ~ are you?** ¿cuánto mides?; **I'm 6 feet ~** mido 6 pies; **to walk ~** andar con la cabeza alta.

(**b**) (*fig*) **~ order** exigencia *f* exagerada, cosa *f* de mucho pedir; **~ story** cuento *m* exagerado, cuento *m* chino.

tallboy ['tɔːlbɔɪ] *n* (*Brit*) cómoda *f* alta.

tallness ['tɔːlnɪs] *n* altura *f*; talla *f*.

tallow ['tæləʊ] *n* sebo *m.*
tallowy ['tæləʊɪ] *adj* seboso.
tally ['tælɪ] **1** *n* (*stick*) tarja *f*; (*account*) cuenta *f*; (*fig*) número *m*, total *m*; **to keep a ~ of** llevar la cuenta de.
2 *vi* concordar, corresponder, cuadrar (*with* con).
tally clerk ['tælɪklɑːk] *n* medidor *m*, -ora *f*.
tallyho ['tælɪ'həʊ] *interj* ¡hala! (*grito del cazador de zorras*).
Talmud ['tælmʊd] *n* Talmud *m.*
Talmudic [tæl'mʊdɪk] *adj* talmúdico.
talon ['tælən] *n* garra *f*.
tamable ['teɪməbl] *adj* domable, domesticable.
tamarind ['tæmərɪnd] *n* tamarindo *m.*
tamarisk ['tæmərɪsk] *n* tamarisco *m.*
tambour ['tæmbʊəʳ] *n* tambor *m.*
tambourine [ˌtæmbə'riːn] *n* pandereta *f*.
Tamburlaine ['tæmbəˌleɪn] *nm* Tamerlán.
tame [teɪm] **1** *adj* (**a**) (*tamed*) domesticado; (*by nature*) manso, dócil; **I'll ask my ~ psychiatrist** se lo preguntaré a mi psiquíatra de casa; **we have a ~ rabbit** tenemos un conejo doméstico (*or* casero); **the birds are growing ~** los pájaros se van domesticando.
(**b**) (*spiritless*) insípido, soso; (*boring, flat*) soso, aburrido.
2 *vt animal* domar, domesticar; amansar; *passion etc* reprimir, contener.
tamely ['teɪmlɪ] *adv* sumisamente.
tameness ['teɪmnɪs] *n* mansedumbre *f*; insipidez *f*, sosería *f*; falta *f* de temor.
tamer ['teɪməʳ] *n* domador *m*, -ora *f*.
Tamil ['tæmɪl] **1** *adj* tamil. **2** *n* tamil *mf*.
taming ['teɪmɪŋ] *n* domadura *f*; **'The T~ of the Shrew'** 'La fierecilla domada'.
tam o' shanter [ˌtæmə'ʃæntəʳ] *n* boina *f* escocesa.
tamp [tæmp] *vt* (*also* **to ~ down, to ~ in**) apisonar, afirmar; (*Min*) atacar.
tamper ['tæmpəʳ] *vi*: **to ~ with** (*mess up*) estropear, manosear, descomponer; ajar; *lock* tratar de forzar; *document* falsificar; interpolar; *witness* sobornar; (*meddle in*) entrometerse en; **my car had been ~ed with** algo se había hecho a mi coche; **they are ~ing with our plans** están estropeando nuestros planes.
tampon ['tæmpən] *n* tapón *m*; (*Med*) tampón *m.*
tan [tæn] **1** *n* (*sun*) bronceado *m*, tostado *m*; (*bark*) casca *f*; (*colour*) color *m* café claro, color *m* canela; **to acquire a ~, to get a ~** ponerse moreno, morenearse, broncearse (*LAm*).
2 *adj* color café claro, color canela, color marrón; *shoes* de color.
3 *vt* (**a**) (*of sun*) poner moreno, morenear, broncear, tostar.
(**b**) *leather* curtir, adobar; **to ~ sb*, to ~ the hide off sb*** zurrar a uno*.
4 *vi* ponerse moreno, morenearse, tostarse, broncearse (*LAm*).
tandem ['tændəm] **1** *n* tándem *m*. **2** *adj, adv* en tándem; **to do sth in ~** hacer algo conjuntamente (*with sb* con uno).
tang [tæŋ] *n* (**a**) (*of knife*) espiga *f*. (**b**) (*taste*) sabor *m*, sabor *m* fuerte y picante; **it has the ~ of the soil** tiene fuerte sabor a tierra.
tangent ['tændʒənt] *n* tangente *f*; **to fly off at a ~, to go off at a ~** salirse por la tangente.
tangential [tæn'dʒenʃəl] *adj* tangencial.
tangerine [ˌtændʒə'riːn] *n* mandarina *f*, clementina *f*.
tangibility [ˌtændʒɪ'bɪlɪtɪ] *n* tangibilidad *f*.
tangible ['tændʒəbl] *adj* tangibie; (*fig*) tangible, palpable, concreto, sensible; **~ assets** activo *m* tangible.
tangibly ['tændʒəblɪ] *adv* de modo palpable, concretamente.
Tangier(s) [tæn'dʒɪə(z)] *n* Tánger *m.*
tangle ['tæŋgl] **1** *n* nudo *m*; enredo *m*, maraña *f*; (*of streets etc*) laberinto *m*; (*fig*) enredo *m*, lío *m*; confusión *f*; **to be in a ~** estar enmarañado, haberse formado un nudo; (*fig*) estar en confusión; **I'm in a ~ with the accounts** me he hecho un lío con las cuentas; **to get into a ~** hacerse un nudo, anudarse; (*fig*) enredarse, enmarañarse; **I got into a ~ with the police** me hice un lío con la policía.
2 *vt* (*also* **to ~ up**) enredar, enmarañar.
3 *vi* (*also* **to ~ up**) enredarse, enmarañarse; **to ~ with sb** pelearse con uno, meterse con uno; habérselas con uno.
tangled ['tæŋgld] *adj* enredado, enmarañado; (*fig*) enmarañado, complicado.
tango ['tæŋgəʊ] **1** *n, pl* **tangos** tango *m*. **2** *vi* bailar el tango; **it takes two to ~*** es cosa de dos.
tangy ['tæŋɪ] *adj* fuerte y picante.
tank [tæŋk] **1** *n* (**a**) tanque *m*, depósito *m*; (*large, water*) cisterna *f*, aljibe *m*. (**b**) (*Mil*) tanque *m*, carro *m* (de combate).
2 *vt* (‡) machacar, vapulear, dar una paliza a.
◆**tank along*** *vi* ir a toda pastilla*.
◆**tank up** *vt* (*Brit*): **to be ~ed up** ir como una moto, llevar una (buena) moto; **to get ~ed up‡** emborracharse (*on beer* bebiendo cerveza).
tankard ['tæŋkəd] *n* bock *m*, pichel *m.*
tank car ['tæŋkkɑːʳ] *n* (*US*) vagón *m* cisterna.
tank-engine ['tæŋkˌendʒɪn] *n* locomotora *f* ténder.
tanker ['tæŋkəʳ] *n* (*Naut*) petrolero *m*; (*Aut*) camión-tanque *m*, camión *m* cisterna.
tankful ['tæŋkfʊl] *n* contenido *m* (*or* capacidad *f*) de un depósito (*esp* de gasolina); **to get a ~ of petrol** llenar el depósito de gasolina; **a ~ is 25 litres** la capacidad del depósito es de 25 litros.
tank wagon ['tæŋkˌwægən] *n* (*Rail*) vagón *m* cisterna; (*Aut*) camión *m* cisterna.
tanned [tænd] *adj* moreno.
tanner[1] ['tænəʳ] *n* curtidor *m.*
tanner[2]‡† ['tænəʳ] *n* (*Brit*) seis peniques *mpl*, moneda *f* de seis peniques (antiguos).
tannery ['tænərɪ] *n* curtiduría *f*, tenería *f*.
tannic ['tænɪk] *adj*: **~ acid** ácido *m* tánico.
tannin ['tænɪn] *n* tanino *m.*
tanning ['tænɪŋ] *n* (**a**) (*of leather*) curtido *m*. (**b**) (*) zurra* *f*; **to give sb a ~*** zurrar a uno*.
tannoy ['tænɔɪ] *n* sistema *m* de anuncios por altavoces.
tansy ['tænzɪ] *n* tanaceto *m*, atanasia *f*.
tantalize ['tæntəlaɪz] *vti* atormentar (mostrando *or* prometiendo lo que no se puede conseguir), tentar (con cosas imposibles).
tantalizing ['tæntəlaɪzɪŋ] *adj* atormentador, tentador; seductor; **it is ~ to think that ...** es tentador pensar que ...; **with ~ slowness** con desesperante lentitud; **a most ~ offer** una oferta de lo más tentador.
tantalizingly ['tæntəlaɪzɪŋlɪ] *adv* de modo atormentador, de modo tentador.
tantamount ['tæntəmaʊnt] *adj*: **~ to** equivalente a; **this is ~ to** esto equivale a.
tantrum* ['tæntrəm] *n* rabieta* *f*, berrinche* *m*; **to have** (*or* **throw**) **a ~** coger una rabieta*.
Tanzania [ˌtænzə'niːə] *n* Tanzania *f*.
Tanzanian [ˌtænzə'nɪən] **1** *adj* tanzano. **2** *n* tanzano *m*, -a *f*.
Taoist ['tɑːəʊɪst] **1** *adj* taoista. **2** *n* taoista *mf*.
tap[1] [tæp] **1** *n* (**a**) (*Brit*: *water~*) grifo *m*, llave *f* (*LAm*), canilla *f* (*LAm*); (*Brit*: *gas~*) llave *f*; (*Brit*: *of barrel*) espita *f*; (*tool*) macho *m* de terraja; (*Elec*) derivación *f*; **beer on ~** cerveza *f* (sacada) de barril, cerveza *f* servida al grifo; **to be on ~** (*fig*) estar a mano, estar disponible, estar listo.
(**b**) (*Elec*) derivación *f*; (*Telec*) escucha *f*, pinchazo* *m*.
2 *vt* (**a**) *barrel* espitar; *tree* sangrar; (*Med*) hacer una puntura en; *resources* explotar, utilizar; **to ~ sb for information*** tratar de sacar información de uno; **he tried to ~ me for £5*** quería que le prestase 5 libras.
(**b**) *wire* (*Elec*) hacer una derivación en; (*Telec*) intervenir, interceptar, pinchar*, escuchar clandestinamente.
3 *vi*: **to ~ into sb's supply** utilizar la provisión de otro; **to ~ into sb's ideas** aprovechar las ideas de otro, conectar con las ideas de otro.
tap[2] [tæp] **1** *n* palmadita *f*; golpecito *m*, golpe *m* ligero; (*on typewriter etc*) tecleo *m*, tic-tac *m*; **there was a ~ on the door** llamaron suavemente a la puerta; **I felt a ~ on my shoulder** sentí una palmadita en el hombro.
2 *vt* dar una palmadita a (*or* en); golpear suavemente, golpear ligeramente; *typewriter etc* pulsar; **to ~ in a nail** hacer que entre un clavo golpeándolo ligeramente.
3 *vi* dar golpecitos; (*on typewriter etc*) teclear; **to ~ at a door** llamar suavemente a una puerta; **he ~ped on the table several times** dio varios golpecitos en la mesa.
◆**tap out** *vt* (**a**) **to ~ out a message in morse** enviar un mensaje en Morse.
(**b**) **to ~ out one's pipe** vaciar la pipa golpeándola ligeramente.
tap-dance ['tæpdɑːns] **1** *n* zapateado *m*. **2** *vi* zapatear.
tap-dancer ['tæpˌdɑːnsəʳ] *n* bailarín *m*, -ina *f* de zapateado.
tap-dancing ['tæpˌdɑːnsɪŋ] *n* zapateado *m*, claqué *m.*
tape [teɪp] **1** *n* (*Sew etc*) cinta *f*; (*Sport*) cinta *f*; (*ceremonial*) cinta *f* simbólica; (*sticking ~*) cinta *f* adhesiva, (*Med*) esparadrapo *m*; (*recording ~*) cinta *f* de grabación, cinta *f* magnetofónica; (*~ measure*) cinta *f* métrica; **the Watergate ~s** las grabaciones de Watergate.

2 *vt* (**a**) (*seal*) poner una cinta a, cerrar con una cinta. (**b**) (*record*) grabar en cinta, registrar en un magnetofón.
(**c**) **I've got him ~d*** (*Brit*) le tengo calado; **we've got it all ~d*** lo tenemos todo organizado, todo funciona perfectamente.
tape deck ['teɪpdek] *n* unidad *f* de cinta.
tape drive ['teɪpdraɪv] *n* accionador *m* de cinta.
tape-measure ['teɪp,meʒəʳ] *n* cinta *f* métrica.
taper ['teɪpəʳ] **1** *n* bujía *f*, cerilla *f*; (*Eccl*) cirio *m*. **2** *vt* afilar, ahusar. **3** *vi* ahusarse, rematar en punta.
◆**taper away, taper off** *vi* ir disminuyendo.
tape-record ['teɪprɪ,kɔːd] *vt* grabar en cinta, registrar en un magnetofón.
tape-recorder ['teɪprɪ,kɔːdəʳ] *n* magnetofón *m*, magnetófono *m*, grabadora *f* de cinta (*LAm*).
tape-recording ['teɪprɪ,kɔːdɪŋ] *n* grabación *f* en cinta.
tapered ['teɪpəd] *adj*, **tapering** ['teɪpərɪŋ] *adj* ahusado, que termina en punta; (*Mech*) cónico; *finger* afilado.
tapestry ['tæpɪstrɪ] *n* (*object*) tapiz *m*; (*art*) tapicería *f*.
tape unit ['teɪpjuːnɪt] *n* unidad *f* de cinta.
tapeworm ['teɪpwɜːm] *n* tenia *f*, solitaria *f*.
tapioca [,tæpɪ'əʊkə] *n* tapioca *f*.
tapir ['teɪpəʳ] *n* tapir *m*.
tapper ['tæpəʳ] *n* (*Elec, Telec*) manipulador *m*.
tappet ['tæpɪt] *n* alzaválvulas *m*.
taproom ['tæprʊm] *n* (*Brit*) bodegón *m*.
taproot ['tæpruːt] *n* raíz *f* central.
tapwater ['tæp,wɔːtəʳ] *n* (*Brit*) agua *f* corriente, agua *f* de grifo.
tar¹ [tɑːʳ] **1** *n* alquitrán *m*, brea *f*.
2 *vt* alquitranar, embrear; **to ~ and feather sb** emplumar a uno; **a newly ~red road** una carretera recién alquitranada; **he's ~red with the same brush** él es otro que tal, son lobos de la misma camada.
tar²* [tɑːʳ] *n* (*also* **Jack T~**) marinero *m*.
tarantella [,tærən'telə] *n* tarantela *f*.
tarantula [tə'ræntjʊlə] *n* tarántula *f*.
tardily ['tɑːdɪlɪ] *adv* tardíamente; lentamente.
tardiness ['tɑːdɪnɪs] *n* tardanza *f*; lentitud *f*.
tardy ['tɑːdɪ] *adj* (*late*) tardío; (*slow*) lento.
tare¹ [tɛəʳ] *n* (*Bot: also* **~s**) arveja *f*; (*Bib*) cizaña *f*.
tare² [tɛəʳ] *n* (*Comm*) tara *f*.
target ['tɑːgɪt] **1** *n* (*Mil*) blanco *m*; (*fig*) blanco *m*, objetivo *m*; **our ~ is £100** nuestro objetivo es reunir (*etc*) 100 libras, nos proponemos reunir (*etc*) 100 libras; **the ~s for production in 2000** los objetivos previstos para la producción en 2000; **to be the ~ for criticism** ser el blanco de la crítica; **to be on ~** llevar la dirección que se había previsto, ir hacia el blanco.
2 *attr*: **~ audience** público *m* objetivo; **~ date** fecha *f* tope, fecha *f* señalada; **~ figure** cifra *f* tope; **~ group** grupo *m* objeto; **~ language** (*study*) lengua *f* objeto de estudio; (*translation*) lengua *f* de llegada; (*Comput*) lenguaje *m* objeto; **~ market** mercado *m* objetivo; **~ practice** prácticas *fpl* de tiro, tiro *m* al blanco; **~ price** precio *m* indicativo.
3 *vt* elegir como blanco; **the money should be ~ted on X** sería mejor dirigir el dinero hacia X, convendría invertir los fondos en X; **the factory is ~ted for closure** se propone cerrar la fábrica, se elige la fábrica para cerrar.
targetable ['tɑːgɪtəbl] *adj* dirigible.
tariff ['tærɪf] **1** *n* tarifa *f*, arancel *m*. **2** *attr* arancelario; **~ barrier, ~ wall** barrera *f* arancelaria; **~ reform** reforma *f* arancelaria.
tarmac ['tɑːmæk] ® *n* (*esp Brit*) alquitranado *m*; **the ~** (*Aer*) el asfaltado.
tarn [tɑːn] *n* lago *m* pequeño de montaña.
tarnation* [tɑː'neɪʃən] *n* (*US dialect*) ¡diablos!
tarnish ['tɑːnɪʃ] **1** *vt* deslustrar, quitar el brillo a; (*fig*) deslustrar, empañar. **2** *vi* deslustrarse, perder su brillo, empañarse.
tarnished ['tɑːnɪʃt] *adj* deslustrado (*also fig*), sin brillo.
tarot ['tærəʊ] *n* tarot *m*.
tarp* [tɑːp] *n* (*US*) *abbr of* **tarpaulin**.
tarpaulin [tɑː'pɔːlɪn] *n* alquitranado *m*, encerado *m*.
tarpon ['tɑːpɒn] *n* tarpón *m*.
tarragon ['tærəgən] *n* estragón *m*.
tarry¹ ['tɑːrɪ] *adj* alquitranado, embreado; cubierto (*or* manchado *etc*) de alquitrán; **to taste ~** saber a alquitrán.
tarry² ['tærɪ] *vi* (*liter*) (*stay*) quedarse; (*dally*) entretenerse, quedarse atrás; (*be late*) tardar (en venir).
tarsus ['tɑːsəs] *n*, *pl* **tarsi** ['tɑːsaɪ] tarso *m*.
tart¹ [tɑːt] *adj* ácido, agrio; (*fig*) áspero.
tart² [tɑːt] *n* (**a**) (*esp Brit Culin*) tarta *f*; (*fruit*) pastelillo *m* de fruta, (*jam*) pastelillo *m* de mermelada. (**b**) (*****) furcia* *f*, fulana* *f*.
◆**tart up*** (*Brit pej*) **1** *vt house etc* renovar, rejuvenecer, remodelar.
2 *vr*: **to ~ o.s. up** remozarse; ataviarse; (*with make-up*) pintarse, maquillarse.
tartan ['tɑːtən] *n* tartán *m*, (diseño *m* a) cuadros *mpl* escoceses; **a ~ scarf** una bufanda escocesa.
Tartar ['tɑːtəʳ] **1** *adj* tártaro. **2** *n* tártaro *m*, -a *f*; (*fig*) arpía *f*, fiera *f*; **to catch a ~** dar con la horma de su zapato.
tartar ['tɑːtəʳ] *n* (*Chem*) tártaro *m*; (*on teeth*) sarro *m*, tártaro *m*.
tartar(e) ['tɑːtəʳ] *attr*: **~ sauce** salsa *f* tártara; **~ steak** *biftec crudo, picado y condimentado con sal, pimiento, cebolla etc.*
tartaric [tɑː'tærɪk] *adj*: **~ acid** ácido *m* tartárico.
Tartary ['tɑːtərɪ] *n* Tartaria *f*.
tartly ['tɑːtlɪ] *adv* (*fig*) ásperamente.
tartness ['tɑːtnɪs] *n* acidez *f*, agrura *f*; (*fig*) aspereza *f*.
tarty* ['tɑːtɪ] *adj* putesco*.
Tarzan ['tɑːzən] *nm* Tarzán.
task [tɑːsk] **1** *n* tarea *f*, labor *f*; empresa *f*, cometido *m*, deber *m*; (*Comput*) tarea *f*; **to set sb the ~ of doing sth** encargar a uno hacer algo, dar a uno el encargo de hacer algo; **to take sb to ~** reprender a uno (*for sth* algo), llamar a uno a capítulo.
2 *vt*: **to ~ sb to do sth** encargar a uno el deber de hacer algo.
task force ['tɑːskfɔːs] *n* (*Mil*) destacamento *m* especial; (*Naut*) fuerza *f* expedicionaria.
taskmaster ['tɑːsk,mɑːstəʳ] *n* amo *m* (severo); capataz *m* (severo); **he's a hard ~** es un tirano, es muy exigente.
Tasmania [tæz'meɪnɪə] *n* Tasmania *f*.
Tasmanian [tæz'meɪnɪən] **1** *adj* tasmanio. **2** *n* tasmanio *m*, -a *f*.
tassel ['tæsəl] *n* borla *f*.
taste [teɪst] **1** *n* (**a**) (*flavour*) sabor *m* (*of* a); dejo *m* (*of* de); **it has an odd ~** tiene un sabor raro, sabe algo raro; **it has no ~** no sabe a nada, es insípido.
(**b**) (*sense of ~*) paladar *m*; **sweet to the ~** con sabor dulce.
(**c**) (*sample*) muestra *f*; (*sip*) sorbo *m*, trago *m*; **just a ~, then** pues un sorbito nada más, pues sólo un poquitín; **add a ~ of salt** añadir una pizca de sal; **may I have a ~?** ¿me permites probarlo?; **we got a ~ of what was to come** tuvimos una muestra de lo que había de venir después, se nos proporcionó un anticipo de lo que nos esperaba; **we had a ~ of his bad temper** tuvimos una muestra de su mal humor.
(**d**) (*liking*) afición *f*, inclinación *f*, gusto *m*; **one's ~s in music** los gustos musicales de uno; **to acquire** (*or* **develop**) **a ~ for** tomar gusto a, cobrar afición a; **to have a ~ for** gustar de, ser aficionado a; **with sugar to ~** con azúcar al gusto, con azúcar a discreción; **it is to my ~** me gusta; **Wagner is not to my ~** no me gusta Wagner; **~s differ, each to his own ~** entre gustos no hay disputa.
(**e**) (*good ~ etc*) **good ~** buen gusto *m*; **people of ~** gente *f* de buen gusto; **they certainly have ~** es cierto que tienen buen gusto; **to be in bad** (*or* **poor**) **~** ser de mal gusto.
2 *vt* (**a**) (*sample*) probar; probar un bocado de, tomarse un trago de; (*professionally*) catar; **just ~ this** prueba un poco de esto; **I haven't ~ed salmon for years** hace años que no como salmón; **he hadn't ~ed food for 3 days** desde hacía 3 días no comía.
(**b**) (*perceive flavour of*) percibir un sabor de; **I fancy I ~ garlic** creo notar un sabor a ajos; **I can't ~ anything when I have a cold** cuando estoy resfriado no noto sabor alguno.
(**c**) (*experience*) experimentar, conocer; **at last we ~ed happiness** por fin conocimos la felicidad; **when he first ~ed power** cuando conoció por primera vez las delicias del poder.
3 *vi*: **it doesn't ~ at all** no se nota sabor alguno; **it ~s good** es muy sabroso, está sabrosísimo, está muy rico; **it ~s all right to me** para mi gusto está bien; **to ~ of** saber a, tener sabor a; **it doesn't ~ of anything in particular** no sabe a nada en particular.
taste-bud ['teɪstbʌd] *n* papila *f* del gusto.
tasteful ['teɪstfʊl] *adj* elegante, de buen gusto.
tastefully ['teɪstfəlɪ] *adv* elegantemente, con buen gusto; **a ~ furnished flat** un piso amueblado con buen gusto, un piso con muebles elegantes.
tastefulness ['teɪstfʊlnɪs] *n* elegancia *f*, buen gusto *m*.
tasteless ['teɪstlɪs] *adj* (*flat*) insípido, soso, insulso; (*in bad*

taste) de mal gusto.

tastelessly ['teɪstlɪslɪ] *adv* insípidamente; con mal gusto.

tastelessness ['teɪstlɪsnɪs] *n* insipidez *f*; mal gusto *m*.

taster ['teɪstəʳ] *n* (**a**) (*person*) catador *m*, -ora *f*. (**b**) (*fig*) muestra *f*.

tastily ['teɪstɪlɪ] *adv* sabrosamente, apetitosamente.

tastiness ['teɪstɪnɪs] *n* sabor *m*, lo sabroso, lo apetitoso.

tasty ['teɪstɪ] *adj* sabroso, apetitoso.

tat¹ [tæt] *vi* (*Sew*) hacer encaje.

tat²* [tæt] *n* (*Brit*) ropa *f* vieja; objetos *mpl* viejos, (*fig*) basura *f*.

tata* ['tæ'tɑː] *interj* (*Brit*) adiós, adiosito*.

tattered ['tætəd] *adj person* andrajoso, harapiento; *dress, flag etc* en jirones.

tatters ['tætəz] *npl* andrajos *mpl*; jirones *mpl*; **a tramp in ~** un vagabundo andrajoso; **his jacket hung in ~** su chaqueta estaba hecha jirones.

tatting ['tætɪŋ] *n* (trabajo *m* de) encaje *m*.

tattle ['tætl] **1** *n* (*chat*) charla *f*; (*gossip*) chismes *mpl*, habladurías *fpl*. **2** *vi* (*chat*) charlar, parlotear; (*gossip*) chismear, contar chismes.

tattler ['tætləʳ] *n* charlatán *m*, -ana *f*; chismoso *m*, -a *f*.

tattletale* ['tætlteɪl] *n* (*US*) (*person*) acusica* *mf*; (*talk*) cotilleo *m*, chismes *mpl* y cuentos *mpl*.

tattoo¹ [tə'tuː] *n* (*Mil*) retreta *f*; (*Brit*: *pageant*) gran espectáculo *m* militar, exhibición *f* del arte militar; **to beat a ~ with one's fingers** tamborilear con los dedos.

tattoo² [tə'tuː] **1** *n* tatuaje *m*. **2** *vt* tatuar.

tattooist [tə'tuːɪst] *n* especialista *mf* en tatuaje, tatuador *m*, -ora *f*.

tatty* ['tætɪ] *adj* (*esp Brit*) raído, desaseado; poco elegante; en mal estado.

taught [tɔːt] *pret and ptp of* **teach**.

taunt [tɔːnt] **1** *n* mofa *f*, pulla *f*, dicterio *m*; sarcasmo *m*, dicho *m* sarcástico.

2 *vt* mofarse de; insultar, reprochar con insultos; **to ~ sb with sth** echar algo en cara a uno.

taunting ['tɔːntɪŋ] *adj* insultante, mofador, burlón.

tauntingly ['tɔːntɪŋlɪ] *adv* burlonamente, en son de burla.

tauromachy ['tɔːrəmækɪ] *n* tauromaquia *f*.

Taurus ['tɔːrəs] *n* (*Zodiac*) Tauro *m*.

taut [tɔːt] *adj* tieso, tenso, tirante; (*fig*) tirante.

tauten ['tɔːtn] **1** *vt* tensar, estirar; (*Naut*) tesar. **2** *vi* tensarse, estirarse, ponerse tieso.

tautness ['tɔːtnɪs] *n* tiesura *f*, tirantez *f*.

tautological [ˌtɔːtə'lɒdʒɪkəl] *adj* tautológico.

tautology [tɔː'tɒlədʒɪ] *n* tautología *f*.

tavern ['tævən] *n* taberna *f*.

tawdriness ['tɔːdrɪnɪs] *n* lo charro; lo cursi; lo indigno.

tawdry ['tɔːdrɪ] *adj* charro; de oropel, de relumbrón, cursi; *motive etc* indigno, vergonzoso.

tawny ['tɔːnɪ] *adj* leonado; (*wine parlance*) ámbar oscuro, tostado; **~ owl** cárabo *m*.

tax [tæks] **1** *n* (**a**) impuesto *m* (*on* sobre), contribución *f*; tributo *m*; derechos *mpl*; **free of ~** exento de contribuciones, no imponible; **profits after ~** beneficios *mpl* postimpositivos; **profits before ~** beneficios *mpl* preimpositivos; **to collect a ~** recaudar contribuciones; **to cut ~es** reducir impuestos; **to levy a ~ on sth** imponer contribución sobre algo.

(**b**) (*fig*) carga *f* (*on* sobre), esfuerzo *m* (*on* para); **it is a ~ on his energies** exige un esfuerzo de él.

2 *attr*: **~ accountant** contable *m* especializado, contable *f* especializada en asuntos tributarios; **~ allowance** desgravación *f* fiscal; **~ appraiser** tasador *m*, -ora *f* de impuestos; **the ~ authority** la Hacienda, el Fisco; **~ avoidance** evasión *f* fiscal; **~ base** base *f* imponible; **~ bracket** categoría *f* tributaria, categoría *f* fiscal; **~ burden** presión *f* fiscal; **~ code, ~ coding** código *m* impositivo; **~ disc** (*Brit*) pegatina *f* del impuesto de circulación; **~ evader** evasor *m*, -ora *f* de impuestos; **~ evasion** fraude *m* fiscal; **~ exemption** exención *f* contributiva, exención *f* de impuestos; **~ exile** persona *f* autoexiliada para evitar los impuestos; **~ form** impreso *m* de declaración de renta; **~ haven** paraíso *m* fiscal, refugio *m* fiscal; **~ incentive** incentivo *m* fiscal; **~ inspector** inspector *m*, -ora *f* de Hacienda; **~ law** derecho *m* tributario; **~ matters** asuntos *mpl* tributarios; **to declare sth for ~ purposes** declarar algo al fisco; **~ rebate** devolución *f* de impuestos, reembolso *m* fiscal; **~ reduction** reducción *f* de impuestos; **~ relief** desgravación *f* (de impuestos), desgravación *f* fiscal; **~ return** declaración *f* de renta; **~ shelter** protección *f* fiscal; **~ system** sistema *m* tributario, tributación *f*; **~ year** año *m* fiscal.

3 *vt* (**a**) (*Fin*) *person* imponer contribuciones a, *thing* imponer contribución sobre, gravar con un impuesto; **the wife is separately ~ed** la esposa paga contribuciones por separado; **they are heavily ~ed** pagan unas fuertes contribuciones; **the rich are being ~ed out of existence** los ricos pagan tantas contribuciones que dejarán pronto de existir.

(**b**) (*Jur*) *costs* tasar.

(**c**) (*fig*) cargar, abrumar (*with* de); *resources etc* exigir un esfuerzo excesivo a, someter a un esfuerzo excesivo; *patience* agotar; *tolerance* abusar de.

(**d**) (*fig*: *accuse*) acusar (*with* de); interrogar (*with* acerca de); **to ~ sb with a fault** censurar una falta a uno.

taxable ['tæksəbl] *adj* imponible, gravable, sujeto a contribución, sujeto a impuesto; **~ income** renta *f* imponible.

taxation [tæk'seɪʃən] **1** *n* (*taxes*) impuestos *mpl*, contribuciones *fpl*; (*system*) sistema *m* tributario, tributación *f*, fiscalidad *f*.

2 *attr* tributario; **~ system** sistema *m* tributario, tributación *f*.

tax-collecting ['tækskəˌlektɪŋ] *n* recaudación *f* de impuestos.

tax-collector ['tækskəˌlektəʳ] *n* recaudador *m*, -ora *f* de impuestos.

tax-deductible ['tæksdɪ'dʌktəbl] *adj* desgravable.

taxeme ['tæksiːm] *n* taxema *m*.

tax-exempt ['tæksɪg'zempt] *adj* (*US*) exento de contribuciones; exento de impuesto.

tax-free ['tæks'friː] (*Brit*) **1** *adj* exento de contribuciones, no imponible. **2** *adv*: **to live ~** vivir sin pagar contribuciones.

taxi ['tæksɪ] **1** *n* taxi *m*. **2** *vi* (**a**) (*Aut*) ir en taxi. (**b**) (*Aer*) carretear, rodar de suelo.

taxicab ['tæksɪkæb] *n* taxi *m*.

taxidermist ['tæksɪdɜːmɪst] *n* taxidermista *mf*.

taxidermy ['tæksɪdɜːmɪ] *n* taxidermia *f*.

taxi-driver ['tæksɪˌdraɪvəʳ] *n* taxista *mf*.

taxi-fare ['tæksɪˌfɛəʳ] *n* tarifa *f* de taxi.

taxi-man ['tæksɪmæn] *n*, *pl* **taxi-men** ['tæksɪmen] taxista *m*.

taximeter ['tæksɪˌmiːtəʳ] *n* taxímetro *m*, contador *m* de taxi.

taxing ['tæksɪŋ] *adj problem* dificilísimo; *journey* duro, agotador; *task* absorbente.

taxi-rank ['tæksɪræŋk] *n*, **taxi-stand** ['tæksɪstænd] *n* parada *f* de taxis.

taxiway ['tæksɪweɪ] *n* (*Aer*) pista *f* de rodaje.

taxman* ['tæksmæn] *n*, *pl* **taxmen** ['tæksmen] recaudador *m* de impuestos.

taxonomist [tæk'sɒnəmɪst] *n* taxonomista *mf*.

taxonomy [tæk'sɒnəmɪ] *n* taxonomía *f*.

taxpayer ['tæksˌpeɪəʳ] *n* contribuyente *mf*.

TB *n abbr of* **tuberculosis** tuberculosis *f*.

tbsp(s) *abbr of* **tablespoonful(s)**.

TD *n* (**a**) (*US Ftbl*) *abbr of* **touchdown**. (**b**) (*US*) *abbr of* **Treasury Department**. (**c**) (*Ireland*) *abbr of* **Teachta Dála** miembro *mf* del parlamento irlandés.

te [tiː] (*Mus*) si *m*.

tea [tiː] *n* (**a**) (*drink, plant*) té *m*; **not for all the ~ in China** por nada del mundo. (**b**) (*esp Brit*: *meal*) té *m*, merienda *f*; **to have ~** tomar el té, merendar.

teabag ['tiːbæg] *n* bolsita *f* de té.

teabreak ['tiːbreɪk] *n* (*Brit*) descanso *m* para el té; ≃ tiempo *m* del bocadillo.

tea-caddy ['tiːˌkædɪ] *n* bote *m* para té.

teacake ['tiːkeɪk] *n* (*Brit*) bollito *m*.

teach [tiːtʃ] (*irr*: *pret and ptp* **taught**) **1** *vt* enseñar; **to ~ sb how to do sth** enseñar a uno a hacer algo; **to ~ sb a language** enseñar una lengua a uno, instruir a uno en una lengua; **to ~ sb a lesson** (*fig*) hacer que uno vaya aprendiendo, escarmentar a uno; **that will ~ him!** ¡así irá aprendiendo!, ¡así escarmienta!; **he taught me a thing or two** me enseñó bastante, me enseñó cuántos son cinco; **I'll ~ you to leave the gas on!** ¡así aprenderás a no dejar encendido el gas!

2 *vi* enseñar; ser profesor(a), dedicarse a la enseñanza.

teachability [ˌtiːtʃə'bɪlɪtɪ] *n* (*esp US*) educabilidad *f*.

teachable ['tiːtʃəbl] *adj* (*esp US*) educable.

teacher ['tiːtʃəʳ] *n* (*in general*) preceptor *m*, profesor *m*, -ora *f*; (*grammar school*) profesor *m*, -ora *f* (de instituto), (*in other school*) maestro *m*, -a *f*; **our French ~** nuestro profesor de francés.

teacher-pupil ratio [ˌtiːtʃəˌpjuːpl'reɪʃɪəʊ] *n* proporción *f* profesor-alumnos.

teacher training ['tiːtʃə'treɪnɪŋ] **1** *n* (*Brit*) formación *f* pedagógica. **2** *attr*: **~ college** ≃ Instituto *m* de Ciencias de la Educación, ICE *m*.

tea-chest ['tiːtʃest] *n* caja *f* para té.

teach-in [ˈtiːtʃˌɪn] *n* reunión *f* de autoenseñanza colectiva.
teaching [ˈtiːtʃɪŋ] **1** *n* (**a**) (*act*) enseñanza *f*. (**b**) (*belief*) enseñanza *f*, doctrina *f*; **~s** enseñanzas *fpl*, doctrinas *fpl*.
2 *attr* docente; ~ **aids** ayudas *fpl* pedagógicas, ayudas *fpl* para la enseñanza; ~ **center** (*US*), ~ **centre** centro *m* docente; ~ **hospital** hospital *m* utilizado para la enseñanza de la medicina; ~ **machine** autoprofesor *m*, profesor *m* robot; ~ **materials** materiales *mpl* didácticos, materiales *mpl* pedagógicos; ~ **practice** prácticas *fpl* de enseñanza; ~ **profession** magisterio *m*; ~ **staff** personal *m* docente, profesorado *m*.
teacloth [ˈtiːklɒθ] *n* (*Brit*) paño *m* de cocina.
tea-cosy [ˈtiːkəʊzɪ] *n* (*Brit*) cubretetera *f*, guardacalor *m* de la tetera.
teacup [ˈtiːkʌp] *n* taza *f* para té.
tea-dance [ˈtiːdɑːns] *n* té *m* bailable, té-baile *m*.
tea-garden [ˈtiːgɑːdn] *n* (*café*) café *m* al aire libre; (*Agr*) plantación *f* de té.
teahouse [ˈtiːhaʊs] *n*, *pl* **teahouses** [ˈtiːhaʊzɪz] salón *m* de té.
teak [tiːk] *n* teca *f*, madera *f* de teca.
teakettle [ˈtiːketl] *n* (*US*) tetera *f*.
teal [tiːl] *n* cerceta *f*.
tealeaf [ˈtiːliːf] *n*, *pl* **tealeaves** [ˈtiːliːvz] hoja *f* de té.
team [tiːm] **1** *n* (*of persons*) equipo *m*, grupo *m*; (*Sport*) equipo *m*; (*in panel game*) jurado *m*; (*of horses*) tiro *m*; (*of oxen*) yunta *f*.
2 *attr*: ~ **championship** campeonato *m* por equipos; ~ **game** juego *m* de equipos; ~ **mate** compañero *m*, -a *f* de equipo; ~ **member** miembro *mf* del equipo; ~ **spirit** compañerismo *m*, espíritu *m* de equipo; ~ **tournament** torneo *m* por equipos.
3 *vt*: **a film which ~s A with Z** una película que asocia A con Z, una película que ofrece juntamente A y Z.
◆**team up** *vi* asociarse, formar un equipo (*with* con).
teamster [ˈtiːmstəʳ] *n* (*US*) camionero *m*, camionista *m*.
teamwork [ˈtiːmwɜːk] *n* labor *f* de equipo, trabajo *m* en equipo; cooperación *f*, colaboración *f*.
tea-party [ˈtiːpɑːtɪ] *n* té *m*.
teapot [ˈtiːpɒt] *n* tetera *f*.
tear[1] [tɛəʳ] **1** *n* rasgón *m*, desgarrón *m*; **it has a ~ in it** está roto.
2 (*irr*: *pret* **tore**, *ptp* **torn**) *vt* (**a**) (*rip*) rasgar, desgarrar; *flesh* lacerar, romper; (*to pieces*) romper, despedazar, hacer pedazos; **to ~ a hole in a cloth** rasgar un paño; **to ~ one's hair** mesarse el pelo; **to ~ a muscle** desgarrarse un músculo; **to ~ open** abrir apresuradamente, abrir violentamente.
(**b**) (*snatch*) arrancar; **to ~ sth from sb** arrancar algo a uno, quitar algo a uno violentamente.
(**c**) (*fig*) **the country was torn by civil war** el país fue desgarrado por una guerra civil; **she was torn by conflicting emotions** estaba atormentada por emociones opuestas, le desgarraban emociones opuestas; **I am very much torn** sigo sin saber a qué carta quedarme.
3 *vi* (**a**) (*cloth etc*) rasgarse, romperse; **it ~s easily** se rasga fácilmente.
(**b**) **to ~ at the earth with one's hands** tratar frenéticamente de remover la tierra con las manos; **she tore at my eyes** trató de arrancarme los ojos; **he tore at the paper wrapping** luchó violentamente por quitar la envoltura.
(**c**) (*rush*) lanzarse, precipitarse; **to ~ into a room** entrar precipitadamente en un cuarto; **the press tore into him*** la prensa le puso como un trapo*; **to ~ past** pasar como un rayo.
◆**tear along** *vi* correr precipitadamente, precipitarse; ir a máxima velocidad; **to ~ along the street** correr a todo gas por la calle.
◆**tear apart** *vt object* hacer trizas, destrozar; **he tore the theory apart** hizo la teoría pedazos; **the dispute was ~ing the company apart** la disputa dividía la empresa en bandas opuestas; **nothing could ~ them apart** nada podía separarlos; **the conflicting loyalties were ~ing her apart** las lealtades opuestas le partían el corazón.
◆**tear away 1** *vt* arrancar, quitar violentamente; **the wind tore the flag away** el viento arrancó la bandera; **eventually we tore him away from the party** por fin le arrancamos de la fiesta.
2 *vi* marcharse precipitadamente; salir disparado.
3 *vr*: **to ~ o.s. away** irse de mala gana; **I couldn't ~ myself away** no pude arrancarme de allí; **if you can ~ yourself away from that book** si puedes dejar ese libro de las manos un momento.
◆**tear down** *vt flag, hangings etc* quitar (arrancando), arrancar (de las paredes *etc*); *building* derribar, echar abajo.
◆**tear off 1** *vt* (**a**) (*remove*) arrancar.
(**b**) (*) *letter etc* escribir de prisa.
2 *vi* = ~ **away**.
◆**tear out 1** *vt* arrancar. **2** *vi* salir disparado.
◆**tear up 1** *vt paper etc* romper; *plant* desarraigar (violentamente), arrancar.
2 *vi* llegar a toda pastilla.
tear[2] [tɪəʳ] *n* lágrima *f*; **to be in ~s** estar llorando; **to burst into ~s, to dissolve** (*or* **melt**) **into ~s** deshacerse en lágrimas; **to shed bitter ~s** llorar amargamente; **nobody is going to shed a ~ over that** nadie soltará una lágrima por eso; **to wipe away one's ~s** secarse las lágrimas.
tearaway [ˈtɛərəweɪ] *n* (*Brit*) alborotador *m*, -ora *f*, gamberro *m*, -a *f*.
teardrop [ˈtɪədrɒp] *n* lágrima *f*.
tear-duct [ˈtɪədʌkt] *n* conducto *m* lacrimal.
tearful [ˈtɪəfʊl] *adj* lloroso, llorón; lacrimoso; **to say in a ~ voice** decir llorando.
tearfully [ˈtɪəfəlɪ] *adv*: **to say ~** decir lloroso, decir llorando.
teargas [ˈtɪəgæs] **1** *n* gas *m* lacrimógeno. **2** *attr*: ~ **bomb** bomba *f* lacrimógena; ~ **grenade** granada *f* lacrimógena.
3 *vt crowd etc* atacar con gas lacrimógeno.
tearing [ˈtɛərɪŋ] *adj* (**a**) **with a ~ noise** con un ruido de tela que se rasga. (**b**) (*fig*) **at a ~ speed** a una velocidad vertiginosa, a una velocidad peligrosa; **to be in a ~ hurry** estar muy de prisa.
tear-jerker* [ˈtɪəˌdʒɜːkəʳ] *n* (*song*) canción *f* lacrimógena; (*play*) obra *f* lacrimógena, dramón *m* muy sentimental*; (*film*) película *f* lacrimógena.
tear-jerking* [ˈtɪəˌdʒɜːkɪŋ] *adj* lacrimógeno, muy sentimental.
tear-off [ˈtɛərɒf] *attr* (de) trepado; ~ **calendar** calendario *m* de taco.
tearoom [ˈtiːrʊm] *n* salón *m* de té.
tea rose [ˌtiːˈrəʊz] *n* rosa *f* de té.
tearsheet [ˈtɛəʃiːt] *n* hoja *f* separable, página *f* recortable.
tear-stained [ˈtɪəsteɪnd] *adj* manchado de lágrimas.
tease [tiːz] **1** *n* (**a**) (*person*) embromador *m*, -ora *f*, guasón *m*, -ona *f*; **he's a dreadful ~** es terriblemente guasón, le gusta atormentar a las personas.
(**b**) **to do sth for a ~** hacer algo para divertirse.
2 *vt* (**a**) (*annoy*) jorobar, fastidiar, molestar; (*banter*) embromar, tomar el pelo a, guasearse con, (*cruelly*) atormentar; (*sexually*) atormentar, tentar; dar esperanzas a; **they ~ her about her hair** la molestan con chistes acerca de su pelo, la atormentan por lo de su pelo; **I don't like being ~d** no me gusta que se me tome el pelo.
(**b**) (*Tech*) cardar.
◆**tease out** *vt wool etc* desenredar, separar; *information* ir sacando (con dificultad), sonsacar.
teasel [ˈtiːzl] *n* (*Bot*) cardencha *f*; (*Tech*) carda *f*.
teaser [ˈtiːzəʳ] *n* (**a**) (*person*) = **tease 1** (**a**). (**b**) (*puzzle*) rompecabezas *m*.
tea-service [ˈtiːˌsɜːvɪs] *n*, **tea-set** [ˈtiːset] *n* servicio *m* de té.
teashop [ˈtiːʃɒp] *n* (*Brit*) café *m*, cafetería *f*, (*strictly*) salón *m* de té.
teasing [ˈtiːzɪŋ] **1** *adj* guasón, burlón. **2** *n* guasa *f*, burlas *fpl*.
teaspoon [ˈtiːspuːn] *n* (*spoon*) cucharilla *f*, cucharita *f*; (*quantity*) cucharadita *f*.
teaspoonful [ˈtiːspʊnfʊl] *n* cucharadita *f*.
tea-strainer [ˈtiːˌstreɪnəʳ] *n* colador *m* de té.
teat [tiːt] *n* (*of human*) pezón *m*; (*of animal*) teta *f*; (*Brit*: *of bottle*) chupador *m*, tetina *f*, pezón *m* de goma.
tea-table [ˈtiːˈteɪbl] *n* mesita *f* de té.
teathings [ˈtiːθɪŋz] *npl* servicio *m* del té.
teatime [ˈtiːtaɪm] *n* hora *f* del té, hora *f* de la merienda.
tea-towel [ˈtiːˌtaʊəl] *n* (*Brit*) paño *m* de cocina, trapo *m* de cocina (*LAm*).
teatray [ˈtiːtreɪ] *n* bandeja *f* (del té).
tea-trolley [ˈtiːˌtrɒlɪ] *n* (*Brit*) carrito *m* (del té).
tea-urn [ˈtiːɜːn] *n* tetera *f* grande.
tea-waggon [ˈtiːˈwægən] *n* (*US*) carrito *m* (del té).
'tec* [tek] *n* = **detective**.
tech [tek] *n* (**a**) *abbr of* **technology** tecnología *f*. (**b**) *abbr of* **technical college**.
technetium [tekˈniːʃɪəm] *n* tecnetio *m*.
technical [ˈteknɪkəl] *adj* técnico; ~ **adviser** asesor *m* técnico, asesora *f* técnica; ~ **college** (*Brit*) escuela *f* de artes y oficios, universidad *f* laboral; ~ **drawing** dibujo *m* técnico; ~ **hitch** problema *m* de carácter técnico; ~ **knockout** K.O.

m técnico; ~ **offence** delito *m* técnico.

technicality [ˌteknɪ'kælɪtɪ] *n* (**a**) (*nature*) tecnicidad *f*, carácter *m* técnico. (**b**) (*detail*) detalle *m* técnico, cosa *f* técnica; (*word*) tecnicismo *m*; **I don't understand all the technicalities** no entiendo todos los detalles técnicos; **it failed because of a** ~ fracasó debido a una dificultad técnica.

technically ['teknɪkəlɪ] *adv* técnicamente.

technician [tek'nɪʃən] *n* técnico *m*, -a *f*; (*Univ etc*) ayudante *mf* de laboratorio.

Technicolor ['teknɪˌkʌlər] ® **1** *n* tecnicolor ® *m*; **in** ~ en tecnicolor. **2** *adj* en tecnicolor; de tecnicolor.

technique [tek'niːk] *n* técnica *f*.

techno... ['teknəʊ] *pref* tecno...

technocracy [tek'nɒkrəsɪ] *n* tecnocracia *f*.

technocrat ['teknəʊkræt] *n* tecnócrata *mf*.

technocratic [ˌteknə'krætɪk] *adj* tecnocrático.

technological [ˌteknə'lɒdʒɪkəl] *adj* tecnológico.

technologist [tek'nɒlədʒɪst] *n* tecnólogo *m*, -a *f*.

technology [tek'nɒlədʒɪ] *n* tecnología *f*; técnica *f*.

techy ['tetʃɪ] *adj* = **testy**.

tectonic [tek'tɒnɪk] **1** *adj* tectónico; ~ **movement** movimiento *m* tectónico; ~ **plate** placa *f* tectónica. **2** ~**s** *npl* tectónica *f*.

Ted [ted] *nm familiar form of* **Edward**.

tedder ['tedər] *n* heneador *m*.

Teddy ['tedɪ] *nm familiar form of* **Edward**.

teddy (bear) ['tedɪ(beər)] *n* osito *m* de felpa.

teddy-boy ['tedɪbɔɪ] *n* (*Brit*) gamberro *m* (de atuendo eduardiano).

tedious ['tiːdɪəs] *adj* aburrido, pesado.

tediously ['tiːdɪəslɪ] *adv* aburridamente, de modo pesado.

tediousness ['tiːdɪəsnɪs] *n*, **tedium** ['tiːdɪəm] *n* tedio *m*, aburrimiento *m*, pesadez *f*.

tee [tiː] *n* tee *m*, soporte *m*; **third** ~ salida *f* número 3.

◆**tee off** *vi* golpear desde el tee.

◆**tee up** *vt* (*Golf*) *ball* colocar en el tee; (*Football*) preparar.

tee-hee ['tiː'hiː] **1** *n* risita *f* (tonta); ~! ¡ji!, ¡ji!, ¡ji! **2** *vi* reírse con una risita tonta, reírse un poquito.

teem [tiːm] *vi* abundar, pulular; **to** ~ **with** abundar en, hervir de; estar lleno de; **the book** ~**s with errors** el libro está plagado de errores; **to** ~ **with rain** diluviar.

teeming ['tiːmɪŋ] *adj* numerosísimo; *rain* torrencial; **the** ~ **millions** los muchos millones; **a lake** ~ **with fish** un lago que rebosa de peces; **through streets** ~ **with people** por calles atestadas de gente.

teen* [tiːn] **1** *adj* = **teenage**. **2** *n* = **teenager**.

teenage ['tiːneɪdʒ] *adj*, *attr fashion etc* de los adolescentes, de los jóvenes (de 13 a 19 años); **he has** ~ **daughters already** tiene hijas adolescentes ya.

teenager ['tiːnˌeɪdʒər] *n* adolescente *mf*, joven *mf* de 13 a 19 años; **a club for** ~**s** un club para jóvenes (*de 13 a 19 años*).

teens [tiːnz] *npl* edad *f* de adolescencia, edad *f* de 13 a 19 años; **to be in one's** ~ ser adolescente, tener de 13 a 19 años; **to be still in one's** ~ ser todavía adolescente, no haber cumplido aún los 20.

teensy(-weensy)* ['tiːnzɪ('wiːnzɪ)] *adj*, **teeny(-weeny)*** ['tiːnɪ('wiːnɪ)] *adj* chiquito, chiquitín.

teeny-bopper* ['tiːnɪ'bɒpər] *n* quinceañera *f* (apasionada de la música pop).

tee-shirt ['tiːʃɜːt] *n* = **T-shirt** (*in* **T**).

teeter ['tiːtər] *vi* balancearse, oscilar; (*US*) columpiarse; **to** ~ **on the edge of sth** balancearse en el borde de algo, (*fig*) estar sin resolverse sobre algo.

teeth [tiːθ] *npl of* **tooth**.

teethe [tiːð] *vi* endentecer, echar los dientes.

teething ['tiːðɪŋ] **1** *n* dentición *f*. **2** *attr*: ~ **troubles** (*fig*) problemas *mpl* de dentición.

teething-ring ['tiːðɪŋrɪŋ] *n* chupador *m*, mordedor *m*.

teetotal ['tiː'təʊtl] *adj* que no bebe alcohol, abstemio; *propaganda etc* antialcohólico.

teetotalism ['tiː'təʊtəlɪzəm] *n* abstinencia *f* (de bebidas alcohólicas).

teetotaller, (*US*) **teetotaler** ['tiː'təʊtlər] *n* abstemio *m*, -a *f*, persona *f* que no bebe alcohol.

TEFL ['tefəl] *n abbr of* **Teaching English as a Foreign Language**.

Teflon ['teflɒn] ® *n* teflón ® *m*.

tegument ['tegjʊmənt] *n* tegumento *m*.

Teheran, Tehran [teə'rɑːn] *n* Teherán *m*.

tel. *abbr of* **telephone** teléfono *m*, tel.

tele... ['telɪ] *pref* tele...

telecast ['telɪkɑːst] **1** *n* programa *m* de televisión. **2** *vti* transmitir por televisión.

telecommunication ['telɪkəˌmjuːnɪ'keɪʃən] *n* telecomunicación *f*.

telecommute ['telɪkəmˌjuːt] *vi* teletrabajar, trabajar a distancia.

telecommuter ['telɪkəmˌjuːtər] *n* teletrabajador *m*, -ora *f*, trabajador *m*, -ora *f* a distancia.

telecommuting ['telɪkəmˌjuːtɪŋ] *n* teletrabajo *m*, trabajo *m* a distancia.

teleconference ['telɪ'kɒnfərəns] *n* teleconferencia *f*.

telefilm ['telɪfɪlm] *n* telefilm(e) *m*.

telegenic [ˌtelɪ'dʒenɪk] *adj* televisivo, telegénico.

telegram ['telɪgræm] *n* telegrama *m*; **to send sb a** ~ poner un telegrama a uno.

telegraph ['telɪgrɑːf] **1** *n* telégrafo *m*. **2** *attr* telegráfico; ~ **pole** poste *m* telegráfico; ~ **wire** hilo *m* telegráfico. **3** *vti* telegrafiar.

telegraphese ['telɪgrɑː'fiːz] *n* estilo *m* telegráfico.

telegraphic [ˌtelɪ'græfɪk] *adj* telegráfico.

telegraphist [tɪ'legrəfɪst] *n* telegrafista *mf*.

telegraphy [tɪ'legrəfɪ] *n* telegrafía *f*.

telekinesis [ˌtelɪkɪ'niːsɪs] *n* telequinesia *f*.

telematic [ˌtelɪ'mætɪk] *adj* telemático.

telemessage ['telɪmesɪdʒ] *n* (*Brit*) telegrama *m*.

telemetry [tɪ'lemɪtrɪ] *n* telemetría *f*.

teleology [ˌtelɪ'ɒlədʒɪ] *n* teleología *f*.

teleordering ['telɪˌɔːdərɪŋ] *n* pedido *m* telefónico.

telepath ['telɪpæθ] *n* telépata *mf*.

telepathic [ˌtelɪ'pæθɪk] *adj* telepático.

telepathically [ˌtelɪ'pæθɪklɪ] *adv* telepáticamente, por telepatía.

telepathist [tɪ'lepəθɪst] *n* telepatista *mf*.

telepathy [tɪ'lepəθɪ] *n* telepatía *f*.

telephone ['telɪfəʊn] **1** *n* teléfono *m*; **to be on the** ~ (*subscriber*) tener teléfono, (*be speaking*) estar hablando por teléfono; **you're wanted on the** ~ quieren hablar con Vd por teléfono, le llaman al teléfono.

2 *attr* telefónico; ~ **answering machine** contestador *m* automático; ~ **book** guía *f* telefónica; ~ **booth** (*US*), ~ **box** (*Brit*) locutorio *m*, cabina *f* de teléfono; ~ **call** llamada *f* (telefónica); ~ **directory** guía *f* telefónica; ~ **exchange** central *f* telefónica; ~ **kiosk** (*Brit*) locutorio *m*, cabina *f* de teléfono; ~ **line** cable *m* telefónico, línea *f* telefónica; ~ **message** mensaje *m* telefónico; ~ **number** número *m* de teléfono; ~ **operator** telefonista *mf*; ~ **sales** ventas *fpl* por teléfono; ~ **salesperson** vendedor *m*, -ora *f* por teléfono; ~ **subscriber** abonado *m* telefónico, abonada *f* telefónica; ~ **tapping** intervención *f* telefónica.

3 *vti* llamar por teléfono, llamar al teléfono, telefonear.

telephonic [ˌtelɪ'fɒnɪk] *adj* telefónico.

telephonist [tɪ'lefənɪst] *n* (*esp Brit*) telefonista *mf*.

telephony [tɪ'lefənɪ] *n* telefonía *f*.

telephoto ['telɪ'fəʊtəʊ] *adj*: ~ **lens** objetivo *m* telefotográfico, teleobjetivo *m*.

teleprinter ['telɪˌprɪntər] *n* (*Brit*) teletipo *m*, teleimpresora *f*.

teleprocessing [ˌtelɪ'prəʊsesɪŋ] *n* teleproceso *m*.

teleprompter ['telɪˌprɒmptər] *n* teleprompter *m*, chuleta* *f*.

telesales ['telɪˌseɪlz] *npl* ventas *fpl* por teléfono.

telescope ['telɪskəʊp] **1** *n* telescopio *m*. **2** *vt* telescopar; enchufar; **to** ~ **sth into sth else** meter algo dentro de otra cosa. **3** *vi* telescoparse; enchufarse; **A** ~**s into B** A se mete dentro de B.

telescopic [ˌtelɪs'kɒpɪk] *adj* telescópico; enchufable, de enchufe; ~ **lens** teleobjetivo *m*; ~ **sight** mira *f* telescópica, visor *m* telescópico.

teleshopping ['telɪˌʃɒpɪŋ] *n* (*US*) compras *fpl* por teléfono.

teletext ['telɪtekst] *n* teletex(to) *m*.

telethon ['teləθɒn] *n* (*TV*) *programa televisivo especial con fines benéficos*.

Teletype ['telɪˌtaɪp] ® *n* teletipo *m*.

teletypewriter [ˌtelɪ'taɪpraɪtər] (*US*) *n* = **teleprinter**.

televangelist [ˌtelɪ'vændʒəlɪst] *n* evangelista *mf* de la tele.

televiewer ['telɪˌvjuːər] *n* televidente *mf*, telespectador *m*, -ora *f*.

televise ['telɪvaɪz] *vt* televisar.

television ['telɪˌvɪʒən] **1** *n* televisión *f*; **to be on** ~ estar en la televisión; **to watch** ~ mirar la televisión.

2 *attr* de televisión, televisivo; ~ **aerial** antena *f* de televisión; ~ **announcer** locutor *m*, -ora *f* de televisión; ~ **broadcast** emisión *f* televisiva; ~ **lounge** sala *f* de televisión; ~ **network** cadena *f* (*or* red *f*) de televisión; ~ **programme** programa *m* de televisión; ~ **room** sala *f* de televisión; ~ **screen** pantalla *f* de televisión; ~ **set** televisor *m*, aparato *m* de televisión; ~ **studio** estudio *m*

de televisión; ~ **tube** tubo *m* de rayos catódicos, cinescopio *m*.
televisual [telɪ'vɪzjʊəl] *adj* televisivo.
telex ['teleks] **1** *n* télex *m*; ~ **number** número *m* de télex; ~ **operator** operador *m*, -ora *f* de télex. **2** *vt* transmitir (*or* enviar) por télex.
tell [tel] (*irr*: *pret and ptp* **told**) **1** *vt* (**a**) (*gen*) decir; *adventure, story etc* contar; (*formally*) comunicar, informar; **to ~ a lie** mentir; **to ~ sb the news** comunicar las noticias a uno, contar novedades a uno; **to ~ the truth** decir la verdad (*V also* **truth**); **to ~ sb sth** decir algo a uno; **I have been told that** ... me han dicho que ..., se me ha dicho que ...; **I hear ~ that** ... dicen que ...; **I am glad to ~ you that** ... (*formal letter*) me es grato comunicarle que ...; **~ me all about it** cuéntame todo; **I'll ~ you all about it** te (lo) diré todo; **I told him about the missing money** le informé acerca del dinero perdido, le dije lo del dinero desaparecido; **I cannot ~ you how pleased I am** no encuentro palabras para expresar mi contento; **so much happened that I can't begin to ~ you** pasaron tantas cosas que no sé cómo empezar a contarlas; **I ~ you no!, I ~ you it isn't!** ¡te digo que no!; **I told you so!** ya lo decía yo; **didn't I ~ you so?** ¿no te lo dije ya?; **I ~ myself it can't be true** digo para mí que no puede ser verdad; **there were 3, I ~ you, 3** había 3, ¿me oyes?, 3; **you can't ~ her anything she doesn't know about cars** no se le puede decir nada sobre coches que ella no sepa.

(**b**) (*gen*: *idiomatic uses*) **~ me another!** ¡vaya!; **~ that to the marines!** ¡a otro perro con ese hueso!; **you're ~ing me!** ¡a quién se lo cuentas!; **he's no saint, let me ~ you!** ¡no es ningún santo, te lo aseguro!; **he won't like it, I can ~ you** esto seguramente no le va a caer en gracia; **I could ~ you a thing or two about him** hay cosas de él que yo me sé; **I ~ you what!** ¡se me ocurre una idea!; **it hurt more than words can ~** dolió una barbaridad, dolió lo indecible.

(**c**) (*announce*) decir, anunciar; (*of clock, dial etc*) indicar, marcar; **the sign ~s us which way to go** la señal nos dice qué ruta conviene seguir; **the clock ~s the quarter hours** el reloj da los cuartos de hora; **to ~ sb's fortune** decir a uno la buenaventura.

(**d**) (*order*) **to ~ sb to do sth** decir a uno que haga algo, mandar a uno hacer algo; **I told you not to** te dije que no lo hicieras; **do as you are told!** ¡haz lo que te digo!; **he won't be told** no acepta las órdenes de nadie; no quiere hacer caso de ningún consejo.

(**e**) (*distinguish*) distinguir; (*recognize*) conocer, reconocer; **to ~ A from B** distinguir A de B; **to ~ right from wrong** (saber) distinguir el bien del mal; **one can ~ he's a German** se conoce que es alemán; **you can ~ him in any disguise** se le reconoce bajo cualquier disfraz; **can you ~ the time?** ¿sabes decir la hora?; *V* **apart**.

(**f**) (*know*) saber; **how can I ~ what she will do?** ¿cómo voy a saber lo que ella hará?; **I couldn't ~ how it was done** no sabía cómo se hizo; **I can't ~ the difference** no veo la diferencia; **you can't ~ much from his letter** su carta nos dice bien poco, su carta apenas sirve para aclarar el asunto; **we can't ~ much from this** no es posible deducir mucho de esto.

(**g**) (*count*) contar; **to ~ one's beads** rezar el rosario; **30 pigs all told** en total 30 cerdos.

2 *vi* (**a**) (*speak*) **to ~ of** hablar de; **I hear ~ of a disaster** oigo hablar de una catástrofe, tengo noticias de una catástrofe; **I have never heard ~ of it** no he oído nunca hablar de eso; **the ruins told of a sad history** las ruinas hablaban de una triste historia.

(**b**) (**: be talebearer*) soplar*.

(**c**) (*have an effect*) tener efecto, hacer mella; **blood will ~** la sangre cuenta; **words that ~** palabras *fpl* que hacen mella, palabras *fpl* que impresionan; **every blow told** cada golpe tuvo su efecto; **it told on his health** afectó su salud, se dejó ver en su salud; **the effort was beginning to ~ (on him)** el esfuerzo empezaba a afectarle de mala manera; **everything ~s against him** todo obra en contra de él; **stamina ~s in the long run** a la larga importa más la resistencia, a la larga vale más la resistencia.

(**d**) (*know*) saber; **how can I ~?** ¿cómo lo voy a saber?, ¿yo qué sé?; **who can ~?** ¿quién sabe?; **we cannot ~** (nos) es imposible saberlo; **it's hard for anyone to ~** es difícil que nadie lo sepa; **you never can ~** nunca se sabe; podría ser tanto lo uno como lo otro.
◆**tell off** *vt* (**a**) (*order*) ordenar, mandar. (**b**) (**: reprimand*) **to ~ sb off** reñir a uno, echar un rapapolvo a uno*.
◆**tell on*** *vt*: **to ~ on sb** soplarse de uno*, chivatear contra uno*‡.
teller ['telə^r] *n* (*of story*) narrador *m*, -ora *f*; (*Parl*) escrutador *m*, -ora *f*; (*in bank*) cajero *m*, -a *f*.
telling ['telɪŋ] **1** *adj* eficaz; fuerte, enérgico; **a ~ argument** un argumento eficaz.

2 *n* narración *f*; **there is no ~** nunca se sabe, es imposible saberlo; **there is no ~ what he will do** es imposible saber qué va a hacer; **the story did not lose in the ~** el cuento no perdió en la narración.
telling-off* [ˌtelɪŋ'ɒf] *n* bronca *f*, reprimenda *f*.
telltale ['telteɪl] **1** *adj* revelador; indicador. **2** *n* soplón* *m*, -ona *f*; (*Naut*) axiómetro *m*.
tellurium [te'lʊərɪəm] *n* telurio *m*.
telly* ['telɪ] *n* (*Brit*) tele* *f*.
temblor ['temblə^r] *n* (*US*) temblor *m* de tierra.
temerity [tɪ'merɪtɪ] *n* temeridad *f*; **to have the ~ to** + *infin* atreverse a + *infin*; **and you have the ~ to say ...!** ¡y Vd se atreve a decir que ...!, ¡y Vd me dice tan fresco que ...!
temp[1] [temp] (*Brit abbr of* **temporary**) **1** *n* empleado *m* eventual, empleada *f* eventual. **2** *vi* trabajar como empleado eventual (*or* empleada eventual).
temp.[2] *abbr of* **temperature**.
temper ['tempə^r] **1** *n* (**a**) (*nature, disposition*) disposición *f*, natural *m*; humor *m*, genio *m*; (*bad*) genio *m*, mal genio *m*; **~!** ¡qué mal genio!; **bad ~, hot ~, quick ~** genio *m*, mal genio *m*, genio *m* vivo; **good ~** buen humor *m*; **to be in a good ~** estar de buen humor; **he has a ~** tiene genio; **he has a foul** (*or* **vile** *etc*) **~** es un hombre de malas pulgas; **to have a quick ~** tener genio, tener prontos de enojo; **to keep one's ~** contenerse, no alterarse; **to fly into a ~, to lose one's ~** perder la paciencia, enojarse (*with* con); **to try sb's ~** probar la paciencia de uno.

(**b**) (*of metal*) temple *m*.

2 *vt metal* templar; (*fig*) templar, moderar, mitigar; **to ~ justice with mercy** templar la justicia con la compasión.
tempera ['tempərə] *n* pintura *f* al temple.
temperament ['tempərəmənt] *n* temperamento *m*, disposición *f*; (*moodiness, difficult ~*) excitabilidad *f*, tendencia *f* a cambiar repentinamente de humor; genio *m*; **he has a ~** tiene genio, tiene sus caprichos.
temperamental [ˌtempərə'mentl] *adj* (**a**) (*relating to temperament*) complexional, relativo al temperamento. (**b**) (*moody, difficult*) excitable, caprichoso, sujeto a impulsos repentinos.
temperance ['tempərəns] **1** *n* templanza *f*; moderación *f*; abstinencia *f* (*del alcohol*).

2 *attr*: **~ hotel** hotel *m* donde no se sirven bebidas alcohólicas; **~ movement** campaña *f* antialcohólica.
temperate ['tempərɪt] *adj* templado; moderado; (*in drinking*) abstemio; *climate, zone* templado; **to be ~ in one's demands** ser moderado en sus exigencias.
temperature ['temprɪtʃə^r] *n* temperatura *f*; (*Med*: *high ~*) calentura *f*, fiebre *f*; **~ chart** gráfico *m* de temperaturas; **to have a ~, to run a ~** tener fiebre, tener calentura; **to take sb's ~** tomar la temperatura de uno.
tempered ['tempəd] *adj* templado.
-tempered ['tempəd] *adj ending in compounds*: de ... humor; *V* **bad, good** *etc*.
tempest ['tempɪst] *n* tempestad *f*.
tempestuous [tem'pestjʊəs] *adj* tempestuoso; (*fig*) tempestuoso, borrascoso.
Templar ['templə^r] *n* templario *m*.
template, (*US*) **templet** ['templɪt] *n* plantilla *f*.
temple[1] ['templ] *n* (*Rel*) templo *m*; **the T~** (*London*) el Colegio de Abogados.
temple[2] ['templ] *n* (*Anat*) sien *f*; (*US*: *of spectacles*) patilla *f*.
tempo ['tempəʊ] *n*, *pl* **tempi** ['tempiː] (*Mus*) tempo *m* (*also fig*); tiempo *m*; (*fig*) ritmo *m*.
temporal ['tempərəl] *adj* temporal.
temporarily ['tempərərɪlɪ] *adv* temporalmente.
temporary ['tempərərɪ] *adj* temporáneo, provisional; transitorio, poco duradero, de poca duración; *official* interino; (*of worker's status*) temporero; **~ injunction** interdicto *m* temporal; **~ secretary** secretaria *f* eventual; **~ surface** firme *m* provisional; **these arrangements are purely ~** este arreglo es provisional nada más; **there was a ~ improvement** hubo una mejora temporal.
temporize ['tempəraɪz] *vi* contemporizar.
tempt [tempt] *vt* (**a**) tentar; atraer; seducir; **to ~ sb to do sth** tentar a uno a hacer algo, inducir a uno a hacer algo; **to be ~ed to do sth** (*fig*) estar tentado de hacer algo; **there was a time when he was ~ed to resign** hubo un momento en que estuvo tentado de dimitir; **to allow o.s. to be ~ed** ceder a la tentación; **I am ~ed** es una oferta atractiva, es una perspectiva agradable; **I am very ~ed**

tengo muchas ganas; **doesn't the idea ~ you at all?** ¿la idea no te interesa siquiera un poquitín?; **can I ~ you to another cup?** ¿quieres otra taza?
(**b**) (†, *Bib etc*) poner a prueba; tentar; **one must not ~ fate** (*or* **providence**) no hay que tentar a la suerte.

temptation [temp'teɪʃən] *n* tentación *f*; atractivo *m*, aliciente *m*; **there is a ~ to** + *infin* es tentador + *infin*; hay tendencia a + *infin*; **to give way** (*or* **yield**) **to ~** ceder a la tentación; **to lead sb into ~** hacer que uno caiga en el pecado; **lead us not into ~** no nos dejes caer en la tentación; **to resist ~** resistir (a) la tentación (*of* + *ger* de + *infin*); **to put ~ in sb's way** exponer a uno a la tentación.

tempter ['temptəʳ] *n* tentador *m*.

tempting ['temptɪŋ] *adj* tentador; atractivo; *meal* apetitoso, rico; *theory etc* seductor; **a ~ offer** una oferta tentadora; **it is ~ to think so** estamos tentados de considerarlo así; es fácil asentir a ello.

temptingly ['temptɪŋlɪ] *adv* de modo tentador; de modo seductor; apetitosamente.

temptress ['temptrɪs] *n* tentadora *f*.

ten [ten] **1** *adj* diez; **some ~ people** una decena de personas; **~ metre line** línea *f* de diez metros. **2** *n* diez *m*; (*as round number*) decena *f*; **~s of thousands of Spaniards** decenas de miles de españoles; **~ to 1 you're right** seguro que tienes razón; **they're ~ a penny** son comunísimos; los hay baratísimos.

tenable ['tenəbl] *adj* defendible, sostenible.

tenacious [tɪ'neɪʃəs] *adj* tenaz; porfiado; **to be ~ of life** estar muy apegado a la vida, aferrarse a la vida.

tenaciously [tɪ'neɪʃəslɪ] *adv* tenazmente; porfiadamente.

tenacity [tɪ'næsɪtɪ] *n* tenacidad *f*; porfía *f*.

tenancy ['tenənsɪ] *n* tenencia *f*; (*of house*) inquilinato *m*, ocupación *f*; (*lease*) arriendo *m*.

tenant ['tenənt] **1** *adj*: **~ farmer** agricultor *m* arrendatario.
2 *n* (*inhabitant*) habitante *mf*, morador *m*, -ora *f*; (*paying rent*) inquilino *m*, -a *f*, arrendatario *m*, -a *f*.

tenantry ['tenəntrɪ] *n* inquilinos *mpl*; (*Agr*) agricultores *mpl* arrendatarios.

tench [tentʃ] *n, pl invar* tenca *f*.

tend[1] [tend] *vi* tender; **to ~ to, to ~ towards** tender a, inclinarse a, tener tendencia a; **we ~ to think that ...** nos inclinamos a pensar que ...; **it ~s to be the case that ...** suele ser que ..., en general es que ...; **I rather ~ to agree with you** casi estoy por compartir ese criterio; **anything that ~s to help solve the problem** cualquier cosa que contribuya a resolver el problema, todo lo que conduzca a resolver el problema; **it is a blue ~ing to green** es un azul que tira a verde; **these clothes ~ to shrink** estas prendas tienen tendencia a encogerse; **which way is it ~ing?** ¿hacia qué lado se inclina?

tend[2] [tend] *vt sick etc* cuidar, atender; *cattle* guardar; *machine* manejar, operar, servir; mantener.

tendency ['tendənsɪ] *n* tendencia *f*, inclinación *f*, propensión *f*; proclividad *f*; **he has a ~ to say too much** tiene tendencia a decir demasiado; **there is a ~ for the ponds to dry up** los estanques tienden a secarse; **the present ~ to the left** la actual tendencia hacia la izquierda.

tendentious [ten'denʃəs] *adj* tendencioso.

tendentiously [ten'denʃəslɪ] *adv* de modo tendencioso.

tendentiousness [ten'denʃəsnɪs] *n* tendenciosidad *f*.

tender[1] ['tendəʳ] *n* (*Rail*) ténder *m*; (*Naut*) gabarra *f*, embarcación *f* auxiliar.

tender[2] ['tendəʳ] **1** *n* (**a**) (*Comm*) oferta *f*, proposición *f*; **~ documents** pliegos *mpl* de propuesta; **call for ~** propuesta *f* para licitación de obras; **to make a ~, to put in a ~** hacer una oferta (*for* para la construcción (*etc*) de), ofertar; **to put sth out to ~** solicitar ofertas para algo.
(**b**) **legal ~** moneda *f* corriente, moneda *f* de curso legal.
2 *vt* ofrecer; *resignation etc* presentar; *thanks* dar.
3 *vi* (*Comm*) ofertar, hacer una oferta (*for* para).

tender[3] ['tendəʳ] *adj* (**a**) (*soft*) tierno, blando; *spot* delicado, sensible; (*painful*) dolorido; *age etc* tierno; *conscience* escrupuloso; *problem, subject* espinoso, delicado, difícil; **those of ~ years** los de tierna edad; **I still feel ~ there** ese sitio me duele todavía; **it is ~ to the touch** duele cuando se toca.
(**b**) (*affectionate*) tierno, afectuoso; compasivo; **I have ~ memories of her** la recuerdo con mucha ternura.

tenderfoot ['tendəfut] *n* (*esp US*) recién llegado *m*; principiante *m*, novato *m*.

tender-hearted ['tendə'hɑːtɪd] *adj* compasivo, bondadoso, tierno de corazón.

tender-heartedness ['tendə'hɑːtɪdnɪs] *n* compasión *f*, bondad *f*, ternura *f*.

tenderize ['tendəraɪz] *vt* ablandar.

tenderizer ['tendəraɪzəʳ] *n* ablandador *m*.

tenderloin ['tendəlɔɪn] *n* (**a**) (*meat*) filete *m*. (**b**) (*US**) barrio *m* de vicio y corrupción reconocidos.

tenderly ['tendəlɪ] *adv* tiernamente, con ternura.

tenderness ['tendənɪs] *n* ternura *f*; lo delicado; sensibilidad *f*.

tendon ['tendən] *n* tendón *m*.

tendril ['tendrɪl] *n* zarcillo *m*.

tenement ['tenɪmənt] *n* vivienda *f*; habitación *f*; **~ house, ~s** casa *f* de pisos, casa *f* de vecindad.

Tenerife [,tenə'riːf] *n* Tenerife *m*.

tenet ['tenət] *n* principio *m*, dogma *m*.

tenfold ['tenfəuld] **1** *adj* décuplo, diez veces mayor. **2** *adv* diez veces.

ten-gallon ['ten'gælən] *attr*: **~ hat** sombrero *m* tejano.

Tenn. (*US*) *abbr of* **Tennessee**.

tenner* ['tenəʳ] *n* (*Brit*) billete *m* de diez libras, (*US*) billete *m* de diez dólares.

tennis ['tenɪs] *n* tenis *m*; **~ elbow** sinovitis *f* del codo, codo *m* de tenista.

tennis-ball ['tenɪsbɔːl] *n* pelota *f* de tenis.

tennis-court ['tenɪskɔːt] *n* pista *f* de tenis, cancha *f* de tenis (*LAm*).

tennis-player ['tenɪs,pleɪəʳ] *n* tenista *mf*.

tennis-racquet ['tenɪs,rækɪt] *n* raqueta *f* de tenis.

tennis-shoe ['tenɪsʃuː] *n* zapatilla *f* de tenis.

tenon ['tenən] *n* espiga *f*, almilla *f*.

tenor ['tenəʳ] **1** *adj instrument, part, voice* de tenor; *aria* para tenor. **2** *n* (**a**) (*Mus*) tenor *m*. (**b**) (*purport*) tenor *m*, tendencia *f*; curso *m*.

tenpin bowling ['tenpɪn'bəulɪŋ] *n*, **tenpins** ['tenpɪnz] *npl* (*US*) bolos *mpl*, bolera *f*.

tense[1] [tens] *n* (*Gram*) tiempo *m*.

tense[2] [tens] **1** *adj* (*stretched*) tirante, estirado, tieso; (*stiff*) rígido, tieso; *moment, nerves, situation etc* tenso; **it has been a ~ day** la jornada ha sido muy tensa; **we waited with ~ expectancy** aguardamos con tensa expectación; **he looked rather ~** parecía estar algo tenso.
2 *vt* tensar, tesar; estirar.

◆tense up *vi* tensarse.

tensely ['tenslɪ] *adv* tensamente, con tensión.

tenseness ['tensnɪs] *n* tirantez *f*; tensión *f*.

tensile ['tensaɪl] *adj* tensor; extensible; de tensión, relativo a la tensión; **~ strength** resistencia *f* a la tensión.

tension ['tenʃən] *n* tirantez *f*; tensión *f*; **~ headache** dolor *m* de cabeza producido por la tensión.

tent [tent] *n* tienda *f* (de campaña), carpa *f* (*LAm*).

tentacle ['tentəkl] *n* tentáculo *m*.

tentative ['tentətɪv] *adj* provisional; experimental; de prueba, de ensayo; **these are ~ conclusions** son conclusiones provisionales; **everything is very ~ at the moment** por el momento todo es de carácter provisional; **she's a rather ~ person** es una persona bastante indecisa.

tentatively ['tentətɪvlɪ] *adv* provisionalmente; en vía de prueba, como tanteo; **'yes', he said ~** 'sí', dijo sin gran confianza.

tenterhooks ['tentəhuks] *npl*: **to be on ~** estar sobre ascuas; tener el alma en vilo; **to keep sb on ~** tener a uno sobre ascuas.

tenth [tenθ] **1** *adj* décimo. **2** *n* décimo *m*; (*part*) décima parte *f*, décima *f*.

tentpeg ['tent,peg] *n* (*Brit*) estaquilla *f*, estaca *f* (de tienda).

tentpole ['tentpəul] *n*, (*US*) **tent stake** ['tentsteɪk] mástil *m* de tienda, poste *m* de tienda.

tenuity [te'njuɪtɪ] *n* tenuidad *f*; raridad *f*.

tenuous ['tenjuəs] *adj* tenue; sutil; *connection* poco fuerte; *argument* poco sólido; *air* raro.

tenuously ['tenjuəslɪ] *adv* tenuemente, sutilmente.

tenure ['tenjuəʳ] **1** *n* (**a**) (*of land etc*) posesión *f*, tenencia *f*, ocupación *f*. (**b**) (*Univ etc*) permanencia *f*; **teacher with ~** profesor *m*, -ora *f* de número, profesor *m* numerario, profesora *f* numeraria; **teacher without ~** profesor *m* no numerario, profesora *f* no numeraria; **~ track position** (*US*) puesto *m* con posibilidad de obtener la permanencia.
2 *vt* (*US*) conceder la permanencia a.

tepee ['tiːpiː] *n* (*US*) tipi *m*.

tepid ['tepɪd] *adj* tibio.

tepidity [te'pɪdɪtɪ] *n*, **tepidness** ['tepɪdnɪs] *n* tibieza *f*.

terbium ['tɜːbɪəm] *n* terbio *m*.

tercentenary [,tɜːsen'tiːnərɪ] *n* tricentenario *m*.

tercet ['tɜːsɪt] *n* terceto *m*.

Terence ['terəns] *nm* Terencio.

term [tɜːm] **1** *n* (**a**) (*limit*) término *m*, límite *m*, fin *m*; (*Comm*) plazo *m*; **to put** (*or* **set**) **a ~ to** señalar un límite a; fijar un plazo para.

(**b**) (*period*) período *m*; duración *f*; plazo *m*; (*of president etc*) mandato *m*; **during his ~ of office** durante su mandato; **for a ~ of 6 years** durante (*or* para) un período de 6 años; **in the long ~** a la larga; **in the medium ~** a plazo medio; **in the short ~** en el futuro próximo.

(**c**) (*Scol, Univ*) trimestre *m*; **during ~, in ~** durante el curso; **out of ~** fuera del curso; **to keep ~s** residir, estar de interno, cumplir su período de residencia.

(**d**) (*Math, Logic*) término *m*; **A expressed in ~s of B** A expresado en términos de B; **in ~s of production we are doing well** por lo que se refiere a (*or* en cuanto a) la producción vamos bien; **he was talking in ~s of buying it** hablaba de la posibilidad de comprarlo; **he sees novels in ~s of sociology** considera la novela en su función sociológica, se explica la novela desde el punto de vista sociológico.

(**e**) (*word*) término *m*; vocablo *m*, voz *f*, expresión *f*; **in plain ~s, in simple ~s** en términos sencillos, en lenguaje sencillo; **in no uncertain ~s** en términos que no pueden ser más claros; **to choose one's ~s carefully** eligir sus palabras con cuidado; **she described it in glowing ~s** lo describió con mucho entusiasmo.

(**f**) **~s** (*conditions*) condiciones *fpl*; **~s of payment** condiciones *fpl* de pago; **~s of reference** puntos *mpl* de mandato, puntos *mpl* de consulta; **~s of sale** condiciones *fpl* de venta; **~s of surrender** capitulaciones *fpl*, condiciones *fpl* de la rendición; **~s of trade** términos *mpl* del intercambio; **according to the ~s of the contract** según las condiciones del contrato, conforme a lo estipulado en el contrato; **not on any ~s** bajo ningún concepto; **what are your ~s?** ¿cuáles son sus condiciones?; **to accept sb on his own ~s** aceptar a uno sabiendo lo que es, aceptar a uno sin esperar cambiar su naturaleza; **to come to ~s** llegar a un acuerdo, ponerse de acuerdo; **to come to ~s with a situation** adaptarse a una situación, conformarse con una situación; **to dictate ~s** dictar las condiciones; **you may name your own ~s** Vd puede estipular lo que quiera.

(**g**) **~s** (*Comm, Fin*) precio *m*, tarifa *f*; **our ~s for full board** nuestro precio para la pensión completa; **'inclusive ~s: £50'** '50 libras todo incluido', 'pensión completa: 50 libras'; **we bought it on advantageous ~s** lo compramos a buen precio; **we offer easy ~s** ofrecemos facilidades de pago.

(**h**) **~s** (*relationship*) relaciones *fpl*; **to be on easy** (*or* **familiar**) **~s with sb** tener confianza con uno; **to be on bad ~s with sb** llevarse mal con uno, estar en malas relaciones con uno; **to be on good ~s with sb** estar en buenas relaciones con uno; **we are on the best of ~s** somos muy amigos; **we're not on speaking ~s** no nos hablamos; **what ~s are they on?** ¿cuáles son sus relaciones?; **they were not competing on equal** (*or* **the same**) **~s** no competían en un pie de igualdad; **to fight sb on equal ~s** luchar con uno en iguales condiciones.

2 *attr*: **~ insurance** seguro *m* temporal; **~ loan** préstamo *m* a plazo fijo; **~ paper** (*US*) trabajo *m* escrito trimestral (*o* semestral).

3 *vt* llamar; nombrar, denominar; calificar de; **he ~s himself a businessman** se llama hombre de negocios; **I ~ it a disgrace** lo llamo una vergüenza, digo que es una vergüenza.

termagant ['tɜːməgənt] *n* arpía *f*, fiera *f*.

terminal ['tɜːmɪnl] **1** *adj* (**a**) terminal (*also Med*), final; **~ illness** enfermedad *f* terminal; **~ patient** enfermo *m*, -a *f* terminal.

(**b**) (*Scol, Univ*) trimestral.

2 *n* (**a**) (*Elec*) borne *m*; polo *m*; (*Comput*) terminal *f*.

(**b**) (*Aer, Naut, Rail*) terminal *f*.

terminally ['tɜːmɪnəlɪ] *adv*: **the patient is ~ ill** el enfermo está en fase terminal.

terminate ['tɜːmɪneɪt] **1** *vt* terminar; *pregnancy* interrumpir. **2** *vi* terminar(se).

termination [,tɜːmɪ'neɪʃən] *n* terminación *f* (*also Gram*); (*of pregnancy*) interrupción *f*.

termini ['tɜːmɪnaɪ] *npl of* **terminus**.

terminological [,tɜːmɪnə'lɒdʒɪkəl] *adj* terminológico.

terminology [,tɜːmɪ'nɒlədʒɪ] *n* terminología *f*.

terminus ['tɜːmɪnəs] *n, pl* **termini** ['tɜːmɪnaɪ] *or* **terminuses** término *m*; (*Rail*) estación *f* terminal, término *m*.

termite ['tɜːmaɪt] *n* termita *f*, termes *m*, comején *m*.

termtime ['tɜːmtaɪm] *n* trimestre *m*.

tern [tɜːn] *n* golondrina *f* de mar; **common ~** charrán *m* común.

ternary ['tɜːnərɪ] *adj* ternario.

Terpsichore [tɜːp'sɪkərɪ] *nf* Terpsícore.

terpsichorean [,tɜːpsɪkə'riːən] *adj* coreográfico, de Terpsícore.

Ter(r). *abbr of* **Terrace.**

terrace ['terəs] **1** *n* (*Agr*) terraza *f*; (*raised bank*) terraplén *m*; (*Brit*: *of houses*) hilera *f* de casas sin división entre sí; (*roof*) azotea *f*; **~s** (*Brit Sport*) gradas *fpl*, graderío *m*.

2 *vt* aterrazar, formar terrazas en; terraplenar.

terraced ['terəst] *adj* en terrazas; terraplenado; **~ gardens** jardines *mpl* colgantes; **~ house** *casa que forma parte de una hilera de casas sin interrupción.*

terracotta ['terə'kɒtə] **1** *n* terracota *f*. **2** *adj* terracota.

terra firma [,terə'fɜːmə] *n* tierra *f* firme.

terrain [te'reɪn] *n* terreno *m*.

terrapin ['terəpɪn] *n* tortuga *f* de agua dulce.

terrarium [te'rɛərɪəm] *n* terrario *m*.

terrazzo [te'rætsəʊ] *n* terrazo *m*.

terrestrial [tɪ'restrɪəl] *adj* terrestre.

terrible ['terəbl] *adj* terrible; horrible, malísimo, fatal; **it was just ~** fue sencillamente horrible; **I've been a ~ fool** yo he sido la mar de tonto; **his Spanish is ~** su español es fatal.

terribly ['terəblɪ] *adv* (**a**) (*very*) terriblemente, espantosamente; **it's ~ dangerous** es tremendamente peligroso; **I think he's ~ nice** para mi gusto es simpatiquísimo. (**b**) (*very badly*) horriblemente; **she plays ~** toca malísimamente.

terrier ['terɪə^r] *n* terrier *m*.

terrific [tə'rɪfɪk] *adj* tremendo; (*) bárbaro*, fabuloso*; **~!** ¡estupendo!*; **what ~ news!** ¡qué noticia más estupenda!*; **isn't he ~?** ¿es fabuloso, no?*; **we had a ~ time** lo pasamos en grande*.

terrifically [tə'rɪfɪkəlɪ] *adv* tremendamente; (*) tremendamente*, fabulosamente*.

terrify ['terɪfaɪ] *vt* aterrar, aterrorizar; **to ~ sb out of his wits** dar un susto mortal a uno.

terrifying ['terɪfaɪɪŋ] *adj* aterrador, espantoso.

terrifyingly ['terɪfaɪɪŋlɪ] *adv* espantosamente.

terrine [te'riːn] *n* terrina *f*.

territorial [,terɪ'tɔːrɪəl] **1** *adj* territorial; **T~ Army** segunda reserva *f*; **~ waters** aguas *fpl* territoriales, aguas *fpl* jurisdiccionales. **2** *n* (*Brit*) reservista *m*.

territoriality [,terɪ,tɔːrɪ'ælɪtɪ] *n* territorialidad *f*.

territory ['terɪtərɪ] *n* territorio *m*; **mandated ~** territorio *m* bajo mandato.

terror ['terə^r] *n* (**a**) (*fear*) terror *m*, espanto *m*; **~ campaign** campaña *f* de terror; **to live in ~** vivir en el terror; **to sow ~ everywhere** sembrar el terror por todas partes; **he went** (*or* **was**) **in ~ of his life** temía por su vida, temía ser asesinado; **I have a ~ of bats** tengo horror a los murciélagos; **he had a ~ of flying** le daba miedo volar; **the headmistress holds no ~s for me** la directora no me infunde miedo a mí.

(**b**) (*person*) **a little ~, a ~ of a child** un niño terrible; **he's a ~ on the roads** es terrible conduciendo; **he was the ~ of the boys** fue el terror de los más pequeños.

terrorism ['terərɪzəm] *n* terrorismo *m*.

terrorist ['terərɪst] **1** *adj* terrorista. **2** *n* terrorista *mf*.

terrorize ['terəraɪz] *vt* aterrorizar.

terror-stricken ['terə,strɪkən] *adj*, **terror-struck** ['terə,strʌk] *adj* espantado, preso de pánico.

Terry ['terɪ] *nmf familiar form of* **Terence, Theresa.**

terry (cloth) ['terɪ(,klɒθ)] *n* (*US*) felpa *f*; toalla *f*.

terse [tɜːs] *adj* breve, conciso, lacónico; brusco.

tersely ['tɜːslɪ] *adv* concisamente, lacónicamente; bruscamente.

terseness ['tɜːsnɪs] *n* brevedad *f*, concisión *f*, laconismo *m*; brusquedad *f*.

tertiary ['tɜːʃərɪ] *adj* terciario; **~ production** producción *f* terciaria.

Tertullian [tɜː'tʌlɪən] *nm* Tertuliano.

Terylene ['terəliːn] ® *n* (*Brit*) terylene ® *m*.

TESL ['tes(ə)l] *n abbr of* **Teaching (of) English as a Second Language.**

TESOL ['tesɒl] *n abbr of* **Teaching of English to Speakers of Other Languages.**

Tess [tes] *nf*, **Tessa** ['tesə] *nf familiar forms of* **Teresa.**

tessel(l)ated ['tesɪleɪtɪd] *adj* de mosaico; formado con teselas; **~ pavement** mosaico *m*.

tessel(l)ation [,tesɪ'leɪʃən] *n* mosaico *m*.

test [test] **1** *n* (**a**) prueba *f*; ensayo *m*; (*Scol, Univ etc*) examen *m*, test *m*; ejercicio *m*; (*Chem*) prueba *f*, análisis m; (*standard of judgement*) criterio *m*; **the ~ is whether ...** la piedra de toque es si ...; **to put sth to the ~** poner algo a prueba, someter algo a prueba; **to stand the ~** soportar la prueba; **it has stood the ~ of time** ha resistido el paso del tiempo.

(**b**) (*Brit Sport*) = **~-match.**

2 *attr* de prueba(s); **~ ban treaty** tratado *m* de suspensión de pruebas nucleares; **~ bore** prueba *f* de sondeo.

3 *vt* probar, poner a prueba, someter a prueba; examinar; *sight* graduar; (*Chem etc*) ensayar; *new drug etc* experimentar; **it severely ~ed our nerves** puso nuestros nervios a toda prueba; **the new weapon is being ~ed** se está sometiendo a prueba la nueva arma.

4 *vi*: **to ~ for a gas leak** hacer investigaciones para ver si hay una fuga de gas; **how do you ~ for gas?** ¿cómo se comprueba la presencia de gas?; **~ing, ~ing!** (*microphone etc*) ¡uno, dos, tres!; **he ~ed positive** (*Med*) dio positivo.

◆**test out** *vt* comprobar.

testament ['testəmənt] *n* testamento *m*; **New T~** Nuevo Testamento *m*; **Old T~** Antiguo Testamento *m*.

testamentary [,testə'mentərı] *adj* testamentario.

testator [tes'teıtəʳ] *n* testador *m*.

testatrix [tes'teıtrıks] *n* testadora *f*.

test-bed ['testbed] *n* banco *m* de pruebas.

test-bench ['testbentʃ] *n* banco *m* de pruebas.

test-card ['testkɑːd] *n* (*Brit*) carta *f* de ajuste.

test-case ['testkeıs] *n* pleito *m* de ensayo (*para determinar la interpretación de una nueva ley*).

test-data ['tes*t*,deıtə] *n* datos *mpl* de prueba.

test-drill ['tes*t*,drıl] *vi* sondear.

test-drive ['tes*t*,draıv] **1** *n* prueba *f* de carretera. **2** *vt car* someter a prueba de carretera.

tester[1] ['testəʳ] *n* (*person*) ensayador *m*, -ora *f*.

tester[2] ['testəʳ] *n* (†) baldaquín *m*.

testes ['testiːz] *npl* testes *mpl*.

test-flight ['testflaıt] *n* vuelo *m* de ensayo.

testicle ['testıkl] *n* testículo *m*.

testify ['testıfaı] **1** *vt* atestiguar, dar fe de; **to ~ that ...** testificar que ...; declarar que ...

2 *vi* (**a**) (*Jur*) prestar declaración, declarar.

(**b**) **to ~ to sth** atestiguar algo, atestar algo; (*fig*) atestiguar algo, dar fe de algo.

testily ['testılı] *adv answer etc* con enojo, malhumoradamente.

testimonial [,testı'məunıəl] *n* (**a**) certificado *m*; (*reference about person*) recomendación *f*, carta *f* de recomendación; **as a ~ to** como testimonio a, en homenaje a.

(**b**) (*gift*) regalo *m*, obsequio *m* (de jubilación *etc*).

testimony ['testımənı] *n* testimonio *m*, declaración *f*; **in ~ whereof ...** en fe de lo cual ...; **to bear ~ to sth** atestar algo.

testing ['testıŋ] **1** *adj*: **it was a ~ experience for her** fue una experiencia que la ponía a prueba; **it was a ~ time** fue un período difícil. **2** *n* pruebas *fpl*; ensayo *m*; puesta *f* a prueba; comprobación *f*.

testing-ground ['testıŋgraund] *n* zona *f* de pruebas, terreno *m* de pruebas.

testis ['testıs] *n*, *pl* **testes** ['testiːz] testículo *m*, teste *m*.

test-match ['testmætʃ] *n* (*Brit*) partido *m* internacional.

testosterone [te'stɒstərəun] *n* testosterona *f*.

test-paper ['test,peıpəʳ] *n* (**a**) (*Scol etc*) test *m*, examen *m*. (**b**) (*Chem*) papel *m* reactivo.

test-piece ['testpiːs] *n* (*Mus*) obra *f* elegida para un certamen de piano (*etc*).

test-pilot ['test,paılət] *n* piloto *mf* de pruebas.

test-run ['testrʌn] *n* prueba *f*, ensayo *m*.

test-tube ['test*t*juːb] *n* probeta *f*; **~ baby** niño *m*, -a *f* (de) probeta, bebé *mf* (de) probeta.

testy ['testı] *adj* irritable, malhumorado.

tetanus ['tetənəs] *n* tétanos *m*.

tetchily ['tetʃılı] *adv* malhumoradamente.

tetchiness ['tetʃınıs] *n* malhumor *m*.

tetchy ['tetʃı] *adj* (*Brit*) = **testy.**

tête-à-tête ['teıtɑː'teıt] *n* conversación *f* íntima.

tether ['teðəʳ] **1** *n* atadura *f*, traba *f*, cuerda *f*; *V* **end.**

2 *vt* atar, atar con una cuerda (*to* a).

tetragon ['tetrəgən] *n* tetrágono *m*.

tetrahedron ['tetrə'hiːdrən] *n* tetraedro *m*.

tetrameter [te'træmıtəʳ] *n* tetrámetro *m*.

tetrathlon [te'træθlən] *n* tetratlón *m*.

Teuton ['tjuːtən] *n* teutón *m*, -ona *f*.

Teutonic [tjʊ'tɒnık] *adj* teutónico.

Tex. (*US*) *abbr of* **Texas.**

Texan ['teksən] **1** *adj* tejano. **2** *n* tejano *m*, -a *f*.

Texas ['teksəs] *n* Tejas *m*.

Texican ['teksıkən] *n* (*hum*), **Tex-Mex** ['teks'meks] *n lengua mixta angloespañola de los estados del suroeste de EE.UU.*

text [tekst] *n* texto *m*; (*subject*) tema *m*; **to stick to one's ~** no apartarse de su tema.

textbook ['teks*t*bʊk] *n* libro *m* de texto; **a ~ case of ...** un caso clásico de ...

text editor ['tekst,edıtəʳ] *n* (*Comput*) editor *m* de texto.

textile ['tekstaıl] **1** *adj* textil; **~ industry** industria *f* textil. **2** *n* textil *m*, tejido *m*.

text processing ['tekst'prəusesıŋ] *n* proceso *m* de textos, tratamiento *m* de textos.

text processor ['tekst'prəusesəʳ] *n* procesador *m* de textos.

textual ['tekstjʊəl] *adj* textual; **~ criticism** crítica *f* textual.

textually ['tekstjʊəlı] *adv* textualmente.

texture ['tekstʃəʳ] *n* textura *f* (*also fig*).

TGIF* *abbr of* **thank God it's Friday.**

TGWU *n* (*Brit*) *abbr of* **Transport and General Workers' Union.**

Thai [taı] **1** *adj* tailandés. **2** *n* (**a**) tailandés *m*, -esa *f*. (**b**) (*Ling*) tailandés *m*.

Thailand ['taılænd] *n* Tailandia *f*.

thalassaemia [,θælə'siːmıə] *n* anemia *f* de Cooley.

thalidomide [θə'lıdəumaıd] ® *n* talidomida ® *f*.

thallium ['θælıəm] *n* talio *m*.

Thames [temz] *n* Támesis *m*; **he won't set the ~ on fire** no descubrirá la pólvora, no es ningún genio.

than [ðæn] *conj* (**a**) que; **I have more ~ you** yo tengo más que tú; **he swears less ~ her** él usa menos palabrotas que ella; **nobody is more sorry ~ I (am)** nadie lo siente más que yo; **he has more money ~ brains** tiene más dinero que inteligencia; **clothes come out whiter ~ white** sale la ropa más blanca que blanca; **it is better to phone ~ to write** más vale telefonear que escribir; **I'll do anything rather ~ that** haré cualquier cosa que no sea ésa, lo haré todo menos eso.

(**b**) (*with numerals*) de; **more ~ 90** más de 90; **~ than half** más de la mitad; **not less ~ 8** no menos de 8; **more ~ once** más de una vez; **it doesn't happen more ~ once** no ocurre más que una sola vez.

(**c**) (*with following clause*) **they have more money ~ we have** tienen más dinero del que nosotros tenemos, tienen más dinero que nosotros; **we have more chips ~ you have** nosotros tenemos más patatas fritas de las que vosotros tenéis (*or* que vosotros); **it was an even sillier play ~ we had thought** la obra fue aun más estúpida de lo que habíamos pensado; **the car went faster ~ we had expected** el coche fue más rápidamente de lo que habíamos esperado.

thank [θæŋk] **1** *vt*: **to ~ sb** dar las gracias a uno; **~ you** gracias; **~ you!** (*emphatic, reciprocating thanks*) ¡a usted!; **~ you very much** muchas gracias; **no ~ you** (no) gracias; **~ God!** ¡gracias a Dios!; **I cannot ~ you enough!** ¡cuánto te lo agradezco!; **to ~ sb for sth** agradecer algo a uno; **~ you for the present** muchas gracias por el regalo; **did you ~ him for the flowers?** ¿le diste las gracias por las flores?; **you have him to ~ for that** eso tienes que agradecérselo a él, ese favor se lo debes a él; **he has himself to ~ for that** él mismo tiene la culpa de eso; **which he could never properly ~ you for** que nunca podría agradecerte bastante; **he won't ~ you for telling her** no te agradecerá el habérselo dicho a ella; **I'll ~ you not to do it** agradecería que no lo hicieras; **I'll ~ you to be more polite!** ¡conviene hablar con más educación!; **without so much as a '~ you'** sin la menor señal de agradecimiento.

2 *npl*: **~s** gracias *fpl*; **many ~s!, ~s very much!, ~s a lot!** ¡muchas gracias!, ¡muchísimas gracias!; **my warmest ~s for your help** mis gracias más efusivas por tu ayuda; **that's all the ~s I get!** ¡como se me agradece!; **~s to the rain the game was abandoned** debido a la lluvia el partido fue anulado; **~s to you** gracias a ti; **no ~s to you** no te debo nada a ti; **it's all ~ to Brand X** todo lo debo (*etc*) a la marca X; **~ be to God** gracias a Dios; **to give ~s** dar las gracias (*for* por).

3 *attr*: **~s offering** prueba *f* de gratitud.

thankful ['θæŋkfʊl] *adj* agradecido; **to be ~ to +** *infin* alegrarse de + *infin*; **let us be ~ that ...** agradezcamos que + *subj*; **how ~ we were for that umbrella!** ¡cuánto nos ayudó ese paraguas!, ¡cómo bendecimos ese paraguas!

thankfully ['θæŋkfəlı] *adv* con gratitud, con agradecimiento; **he said ~** dijo agradecido; dijo con alivio.

thankfulness ['θæŋkfʊlnıs] *n* gratitud *f*, agradecimiento *m*.

thankless ['θæŋklıs] *adj person* ingrato; *task* ímprobo, ingrato.

thanksgiving [ˈθæŋks,gɪvɪŋ] *n* acción *f* de gracias; **T~ Day** (*Canada, US*) día *m* de Acción de Gracias.

thankyou [ˈθæŋkjʊ] *n* gracias *fpl*; **now a big ~ to John** ahora, nuestras gracias más sinceras para Juan; **it's a way of saying ~ to the nurses** es un modo de dar las gracias a las enfermeras.

that [ðæt] **1** *dem adj* (*pl* **those**) *m*: ese, (*more remote*) aquel; *f*: esa, (*more remote*) aquella; **~ book** ese libro; **~ hill over there** aquella colina; **~ one** ése, aquél; **~ lad of yours** ese chico tuyo; **what about ~ cheque?** ¿y el cheque ese?

2 *dem pron* (*pl* **those**) *m*: ése, (*more remote*) aquél; *f*: ésa, (*more remote*) aquélla; *'neuter'*: eso, aquello; **this car is new but ~ is old** este coche es nuevo pero ése es viejo; **~ is true** eso es verdad; **~ is all I can tell you** eso es todo lo que puedo decirte; **~'s what I say** eso digo yo, lo mismo digo yo; **they all say ~** todos dicen lo mismo; **what is ~?** ¿qué es?, ¿eso qué es?; **who is ~?** ¿quién es?; **~ is Joe** es Pepe; **~ is (to say)** ... esto es ...; es decir ...; **bees and wasps and (all) ~** abejas y avispas y cosas así; **~'s it, we've finished** ya está, hemos terminado; **they get their wages and ~'s it** tienen su sueldo y eso es todo; **~'s it! she can find her own gardener!** ¡se acabó! puede buscarse jardinero por su cuenta; **and ~'s ~!** ¡y eso es todo!, ¡y sanseacabó!, ¡y santas pascuas!; **you can't go and ~'s ~** no puedes ir y no hay más qué decir; **so ~ was ~** y no había más que hacer, y ahí terminó la cosa; **~'s odd!** ¡qué raro!, ¡qué cosa más rara!; **will he come? ... ~ he will!** ¿si vendrá? ... ¡ya lo creo!; **after ~** después de eso; **at ~** acto seguido, sin más; con eso, con lo cual; **and it was broken at ~** y además estaba roto; **it will cost $20, if ~** costará 20 dólares o algo menos; **do it like ~** hazlo de esa manera, hazlo de la manera que ves; **with ~** con eso; **if it comes to ~** en tal caso; si vamos a eso; **how do you like ~?** ¿qué te parece?, (*iro*) ¡vaya!

3 *rel pron* (**a**) que; **the book ~ I read** el libro que leí; **the houses ~ I painted** las casas que pinté; **all ~ I have** todo lo que tengo.

(**b**) (*with prep*) que, el cual, la cual *etc*; **the box ~ I put it in** la caja en la cual lo puse, la caja donde lo puse; **the house ~ we're speaking of** la casa de que hablamos; **not ~ I know of** no que yo sepa.

(**c**) (*expressions of time*) **the evening ~ we went to the theatre** la tarde en que fuimos al teatro; **the summer ~ it was so hot** el verano cuando hacía tanto calor.

4 *adv* tan; **~ far** tan lejos; **~ high** tan alto, así de alto; **~ many frogs** tantas ranas; **~ much money** tanto dinero; **it is ~ much better** es tanto mejor; **he can't be ~ clever** no puede ser tan inteligente como tú dices; **nobody can be ~ rich** nadie puede ser tan rico como eso; **I didn't know he was ~ ill** no sabía que estuviera tan enfermo; **he was ~ wild*** estaba tan furioso; **it was ~ cold!** ¡hacía tanto frío!

5 *conj* (**a**) que; **I believe ~ he exists** creo que existe; **~ he should behave like this!** ¡que se comporte así!; **~ he should behave like this is incredible** que se comporte así es increíble; **~ he refuses is natural** el que rehúse es natural; **oh ~ we could!** ¡ojalá pudiéramos!, ¡ojalá!; *V* **would** *etc*.

(**b**) (*in order that*) para que + *subj*, *eg* **it was done (so) ~ he might sleep** se hizo para que pudiera dormir; *V* **so**.

(**c**) **in ~** en que, por cuanto.

thatch [θætʃ] **1** *n* (*straw*) paja *f*; (*roof*) techo *m* de paja; cubierta *f* de paja. **2** *vt* poner techo de paja a.

thatched [θætʃt] *adj*: **~ cottage** casita *f* con techo de paja; **~ roof** techo *m* de paja; cubierta *f* de paja; **the roof is ~** el techo es de paja.

thatcher [ˈθætʃəʳ] *n* techador *m*.

thatching [ˈθætʃɪŋ] *n* paja *f* (para techar).

thaw [θɔː] **1** *n* deshielo *m*.

2 *vt* deshelar, derretir; (*fig*) ablandar, hacer menos severo; **to ~ out** *meat etc* deshelar.

3 *vi* deshelarse, derretirse; (*fig*) ablandarse, hacerse menos severo; (*person*) hacerse más afable, ir perdiendo su reserva; **to ~ out** deshelarse; **it is ~ing** deshiela.

the [ðiː, ðə] **1** *def art* (**a**) el, la, (*pl*) los, las (*masculine singular* a + el = al, *eg* **to the man** al hombre; *masculine singular* de + el = del, *eg* **of the cat** del gato).

(**b**) (*'neuter'*) lo; **~ good and ~ beautiful** lo bueno y lo bello; **within the realms of ~ possible** dentro de lo posible; **it is ~ unusual which counts** es lo insólito lo que importa.

(**c**) (*special uses*) **Charles ~ Fifth** Carlos Quinto; **Philip ~ Second** Felipe Segundo; **~ Browns** los Brown; **~ cheek of it!** ¡qué frescura!; **oh ~ pain!** ¡ay qué dolor!; **how's ~ leg?** ¿cómo va la pierna?; **he hasn't ~ sense to understand** no tiene bastante inteligencia para comprender; **the child has ~ measles** el niño tiene sarampión; **2 dollars ~ pound** 2 dólares la libra.

(**d**) (*emphatic*) **he's ~ man for the job** es él hombre ideal para el puesto; es él hombre más indicado para el puesto; **you don't mean ~ Professor Bloggs?** ¿quieres decir el célebre profesor Bloggs?, ¿quieres decir el profesor Bloggs de que se habla tanto?; **it was ~ colour of 1991** fue el color que estaba tan de moda en 1991.

2 *adv*: **~ more he works the more he earns** cuanto más trabaja (tanto) más gana; **~ sooner ~ better** cuanto antes mejor; **it will be all ~ better** será tanto mejor.

theatre, (*US*) **theater** [ˈθɪətəʳ] *n* teatro *m* (*also fig, Mil etc*); (*lecture ~*) aula *f*; **~ of the absurd** teatro *m* de lo absurdo; **to go to the ~** ir al teatro.

theatregoer, (*US*) **theatergoer** [ˈθɪətə,gəʊəʳ] *n* aficionado *m*, -a *f* al teatro.

theatre-in-the-round [ˈθɪətərɪnðəˈraʊnd] *n* teatro *m* de escenario central.

theatreland [ˈθɪətəlænd] *n* teatrolandia *f*.

theatrical [θɪˈætrɪkəl] **1** *adj* teatral; *company etc* de teatro; *person's manner* teatral; **~ agent** agente *mf* de teatro; **~ company** compañía *f* de teatro. **2** *npl*: **~s** funciones *fpl* teatrales; **amateur ~s** teatro *m* de aficionados.

theatricality [θɪ,ætrɪˈkælɪtɪ] *n* teatralidad *f*, lo teatral.

theatrically [θɪˈætrɪkəlɪ] *adv* teatralmente, de modo teatral; de modo exagerado.

Thebes [θiːbz] *n* Tebas *f*.

thee [ðiː] *pron* (†† *or poet*) te; (*after prep*) ti; **with ~** contigo.

theft [θeft] *n* hurto *m*, robo *m*.

their [ðɛəʳ] *poss adj* su(s).

theirs [ðɛəz] *poss pron* (el) suyo, (la) suya *etc*.

theism [ˈθiːɪzəm] *n* teísmo *m*.

theist [ˈθiːɪst] *n* teísta *mf*.

theistic [θiːˈɪstɪk] *adj* teísta.

them [ðem, ðəm] *pron* (*acc*) los, las; (*dat*) les; (*after prep*) ellos, ellas.

thematic [θɪˈmætɪk] *adj* temático.

theme [θiːm] *n* tema *m*.

theme-park [ˈθiːmpɑːk] *n* parque *m* museo.

themesong [ˈθiːmsɒŋ] *n*, **themetune** [ˈθiːmtjuːn] *n* motivo *m* principal.

themselves [ðəmˈselvz] *pron* (*subject*) ellos mismos, ellas mismas; (*acc, dat*) se; (*after prep*) sí (mismos, mismas); *V* **oneself**.

then [ðen] **1** *adv* (**a**) (*at that time*) entonces; por entonces; en ese momento; a la sazón, en aquella época; **it was ~ 8 o'clock** eran las 8, eran las 8 ya; **he was ~ a little-known writer** en aquella época era un escritor poco conocido; **~ and there** en el acto, en seguida; **before ~** antes; hasta entonces, hasta ese momento; **by ~** para entonces, antes de eso; **even ~ it didn't work** aun así, no funcionaba; **from ~ on, since ~** desde entonces, desde aquel momento, a partir de entonces; **just ~** en ese mismo momento; precisamente entonces; **until ~** hasta entonces.

(**b**) (*next, afterwards*) luego, después; **~ we went to Jaca** luego fuimos a Jaca; **first this ~ that** primero esto y luego aquello; **what ~?, and ~ what?** ¿qué pasó después?, y después ¿qué?

(**c**) (*in that case*) pues, en ese caso; **what ~?** ¿y qué?, ¿qué más?; **can't you hear me, ~?** ¿es que no me oyes?; **~ what do you want?** ¿pues que es lo que quieres?; **but ~ we shall lose money** pero en ese caso perdemos dinero; **but ~, you can't tell** pero vamos, nadie lo sabe.

(**d**) (*furthermore*) además; **and ~ again he's a red** y además es un rojo.

2 *conj* pues, en ese caso; por tanto; entonces; **what do you want me to do ~?** ¿pues qué quieres que haga yo?; **~ you don't want it?** ¿así que no lo quieres?, ¿con qué no lo quieres?; **well ~** ahora bien, pues; *V* **now 1 (d)**.

3 *adj* entonces, de entonces; **the ~ King of Slobodia** el entonces rey de Eslobodia, el rey de Eslobodia de entonces; **the ~ existing government** el gobierno que existía en esa época, el gobierno de entonces.

thence [ðens] *adv* (*liter*) (**a**) (*from that place*) de allí, desde allí. (**b**) (*therefore*) por eso, por consiguiente.

thenceforth [ˈðensˈfɔːθ] *adv*, **thenceforward** [,ðensˈfɔːwəd] *adv* (*liter*) desde entonces, de allí en adelante, a partir de entonces.

theocracy [θɪˈɒkrəsɪ] *n* teocracia *f*.

theocratic [θɪəˈkrætɪk] *adj* teocrático.

theodolite [θɪˈɒdəlaɪt] *n* teodolito *m*.

theologian [θɪəˈləʊdʒɪən] *n* teólogo *m*, -a *f*.

theological [θɪəˈlɒdʒɪkəl] *adj* teológico; **~ college** seminario *m.*

theologist [θɪ'ɒlədʒɪst] *n* teólogo *m*, -a *f*.

theology [θɪ'ɒlədʒɪ] *n* teología *f*.

theorem ['θɪərəm] *n* teorema *m*.

theoretic(al) [θɪə'retɪk(əl)] *adj* teórico.

theoretically [θɪə'retɪkəlɪ] *adv* teóricamente, en teoría.

theoretician [,θɪərə'tɪʃən] *n*, **theorist** ['θɪərɪst] *n* teórico *m*, -a *f*, teorizante *mf*.

theorize ['θɪəraɪz] *vi* teorizar.

theorizer ['θɪəraɪzər] *n* teorizante *mf*.

theory ['θɪərɪ] *n* teoría *f*; **in ~** teóricamente, en teoría.

theosophical [θɪə'sɒfɪkəl] *adj* teosófico.

theosophy [θɪ'ɒsəfɪ] *n* teosofía *f*.

therapeutic(al) [,θerə'pjuːtɪk(əl)] *adj* terapéutico.

therapeutics [,θerə'pjuːtɪks] *n* terapéutica *f*.

therapist ['θerəpɪst] *n* terapeuta *mf*.

therapy ['θerəpɪ] *n* terapia *f*, terapéutica *f*.

there [ðɛər] **1** *adv* (**a**) (*place*) allí; allá; (*~ near you*) ahí; **back ~, down ~, over ~** allá; **12 kilometres ~ and back** 12 kilómetros ida y vuelta; **it's in ~** está allí dentro; **when we left ~** cuando partimos de allí.

(**b**) (*less precisely*) ahí; **mind out ~!** ¡ojo!, ¡cuidado!; ¡cuidado ahí!; **make way ~!** ¡abran paso!, ¡atención!; **hurry up ~!** ¡despabílate!; ¡menearse!; **you ~!** ¡eh, usted!; **~ we differ** en ese punto discrepamos; **'~ you are', he said, handing the book over** 'ahí lo tienes', dijo, entregando el libro; **if the demand is ~, the product will appear** si existe la demanda, aparecerá el producto; **~ and then** en el acto, en seguida; **~ again** por otra parte; **~ you go again** vuelves a las tuyas; **it wasn't what I wanted, but ~ you go*** no era lo que buscaba, pero ¿qué le vamos a hacer?; **~ you are, what did I tell you!**, ¿ves? es lo que te dije; **~ you are wrong** en eso te equivocas; **~'s the bus** ahí está el autobús; ya viene el autobús; **~ she comes** ya viene; **~ we were, stuck** así que nos encontramos allí sin podernos mover.

(**c**) **~ is, ~ are** hay; **~ will be** habrá; **~ were 10** había 10, hubo 10; **how many are ~?** ¿cuántos hay?; **~ was laughter at this** en esto hubo risas; **~ was singing and dancing** se cantó y se bailó; **~ is a pound missing** falta una libra; **~ is no wine left** no hay vino, no queda vino; **are ~ any bananas?** ¿hay plátanos?

(**d**) (*) **he's all ~** es la mar de listo*; **he's not all ~** le falta un tornillo*.

2 *interj* ¡vaya!; **~, ~** (*comforting*) ¡cálmate!, ¡ya, ya!, ¡no es nada!, ¡no te preocupes!; **~, drink this** bebe esto; **but ~, what's the use?** pero ¡vamos!, es inútil; **I'm not going, so ~!*** pues no voy, y fastídiate*.

thereabouts ['ðɛərəbaʊts] *adv* por ahí, allí cerca; **12 or ~** 12 más o menos, alrededor de 12; **£5 or ~** 5 libras o así.

thereafter [ðɛər'ɑːftər] *adv* después, después de eso.

thereat [ðɛər'æt] *adv* (*thereupon*) con eso, acto seguido; (*for that reason*) por eso, por esa razón.

thereby ['ðɛə'baɪ] *adv* por eso, de ese modo; por esa razón; **it does not ~ become easier** no por eso se hace más fácil; **~ hangs a tale** eso tiene su cuento.

therefore ['ðɛəfɔːr] *adv* por tanto, por lo tanto, por consiguiente; por esta razón; **~ X = 4** luego X vale 4; **I think, ~ I am** pienso, luego existo.

therefrom [ðɛə'frɒm] *adv* de ahí, de allí.

therein [ðɛər'ɪn] *adv* (*inside*) allí dentro; (*in this regard*) en eso, en esto, en este respecto; **~ lies the danger** ahí está el peligro, en eso consiste el peligro.

thereof [ðɛər'ɒv] *adv* de eso, de esto; de lo mismo.

thereon [ðɛər'ɒn] *adv* = **thereupon**.

there's [ðɛəz] = **there is; there has.**

Theresa [tɪ'riːzə] *nf* Teresa.

thereto [ðɛə'tuː] *adv* a eso, a ello.

thereunder [,ðɛər'ʌndər] *adv* (*formal*) allí expuesto.

thereupon ['ðɛərə'pɒn] *adv* (*at that point*) en eso, con eso; acto seguido, en seguida; (*consequently*) por tanto; por consiguiente.

therewith [ðɛə'wɪθ] *adv* con eso, con lo mismo.

therm [θɜːm] *n* termia *f*.

thermal ['θɜːməl] **1** *adj* termal; térmico; **~ baths, ~ spring** termas *fpl*; **~ blanket** manta *f* térmica; **~ paper** papel *m* térmico; **~ printer** termoimpresora *f*; **~ reactor** reactor *m* térmico; **~ underwear** ropa *f* interior térmica.

2 *n* térmica *f*, corriente *f* térmica.

thermic ['θɜːmɪk] *adj* térmico.

thermionic [,θɜːmɪ'ɒnɪk] *adj* termiónico; **~ valve** lámpara *f* termiónica.

thermo... ['θɜːməʊ] *pref* termo...

thermocouple ['θɜːməʊ,kʌpl] *n* termopar *m*, par *m* térmico.

thermodynamic ['θɜːməʊdaɪ'næmɪk] **1** *adj* termodinámico. **2** *n*: **~s** termodinámica *f*.

thermoelectric ['θɜːməʊɪ'lektrɪk] *adj* termoeléctrico; **~ couple** par *m* termoeléctrico.

thermometer [θə'mɒmɪtər] *n* termómetro *m*.

thermonuclear ['θɜːməʊ'njuːklɪər] *adj* termonuclear.

thermopile ['θɜːməʊpaɪl] *n* termopila *f*.

thermoplastic [,θɜːməʊ'plæstɪk] *n* termoplástico *m*.

Thermopylae [θɜː'mɒpɪliː] *n* Termópilas *fpl*.

Thermos ['θɜːməs] ® *n* (*Brit*: *also* **~ bottle, ~ flask**) termos ® *m*, termo *m*.

thermosetting [,θɜːməʊ'setɪŋ] *adj*: **~ plastics** plásticos *mpl* termoestables.

thermostat ['θɜːməstæt] *n* termostato *m*.

thermostatic [,θɜːməs'tætɪk] *adj* termostático.

thesaurus [θɪ'sɔːrəs] *n* tesoro *m*; diccionario *m*; antología *f*.

these [ðiːz] (*pl of* **this**) **1** *dem adj m*: estos; *f*: estas. **2** *dem pron m*: éstos; *f*: éstas; *V also* **this**.

Theseus ['θiːsjuːs] *nm* Teseo.

thesis ['θiːsɪs] *n*, *pl* **theses** ['θiːsiːz] tesis *f*.

Thespian ['θespɪən] (*liter, hum*) **1** *adj* de Tespis; (*fig*) dramático, trágico. **2** *n* actor *m*, actriz *f*.

Thespis ['θespɪs] *nm* Tespis.

Thessalonians [,θesə'ləʊnɪənz] *npl* tesalonios *mpl*.

Thessaly ['θesəlɪ] *n* Tesalia *f*.

Thetis ['θiːtɪs] *nf* Tetis.

they [ðeɪ] *pron* ellos, ellas; **~ who** los que, quienes.

they'd [ðeɪd] = **they would; they had.**

they'll [ðeɪl] = **they will, they shall.**

they're [ðɛər] = **they are.**

they've [ðeɪv] = **they have.**

thiamine ['θaɪəmiːn] *n* tiamina *f*.

thick [θɪk] **1** *adj* (**a**) (*of solid*) espeso; *thread, stroke etc* grueso; *book, file etc* abultado; **it is 2 metres ~** tiene 2 metros de espesor; **on ice only 4 centimetres ~** sobre hielo de solamente 4 centímetros de espesor; **to give sb a ~ ear** (*Brit**) pegar a uno.

(**b**) (*dense*) *forest, vegetation etc* espeso, denso; *growth* tupido; *eyebrows, beard* poblado; **the leaves were ~ on the ground** había una capa espesa de hojas en el suelo; **bodies lay ~ on the road** había cadáveres por doquier en la carretera; **the field is ~ with strawberries** el campo abunda en fresas; **the place will be ~ with tourists** el sitio estará atestado de turistas.

(**c**) (*of liquid*) (*cloudy*) turbio, (*stiff*) viscoso; *cream, gravy etc* espeso; *fog, smoke* denso, espeso; *air* viciado; *voice* velado, apagado, poco distinto; *accent* cerrado; **the air is pretty ~ in here** la atmósfera está bastante cargada aquí, aquí huele a encerrado; **the air was ~ with insults** el aire estaba lleno de insultos.

(**d**) (*Brit**: *stupid*) torpe, lerdo; **he's as ~ as two (short) planks** es más corto que las mangas de un chaleco.

(**e**) (*: *of relationship*) íntimo; **they're very ~** son íntimos amigos, están a partir un piñón; **they're as ~ as thieves** son uña y carne; **A is ~ with B** A tiene mucha intimidad con B.

(**f**) (*: *unjust*) **it's a bit ~!** (*Brit*) ¡no hay derecho!, ¡esto es injusto!; **it's a bit ~ to have to** + *infin* es injusto tener que + *infin*.

2 *adv*: **to spread butter ~** poner mucha mantequilla; **put the paint on ~** ponga una buena capa de pintura; **they cut the bread very ~** sirven el pan en trozos muy gruesos; **the blows fell ~ and fast upon him** le llovieron los golpes encima; **to lay it on ~*** *V* **lay on 1** (**b**).

3 *n* (**a**) **in the ~ of battle** en lo más reñido de la batalla; **in the ~ of the crowd** en medio de la multitud; **he likes to be in the ~ of things** le gusta tener una vida muy activa, le gusta estar en el centro de las actividades, le gusta estar muy metido en todo.

(**b**) **to stick to sb through ~ and thin** apoyar a uno contra viento y marea, apoyar a uno incondicionalmente.

thicken ['θɪkən] **1** *vt* espesar, hacer más espeso.

2 *vi* (**a**) (*lit*) espesarse, hacerse más espeso; hacerse más denso; (*Culin*) espesarse.

(**b**) (*plot*) complicarse, enmarañarse más.

thickener ['θɪkənər] *n* espesador *m*.

thicket ['θɪkɪt] *n* matorral *m*, espesura *f*.

thickheaded* ['θɪk'hedɪd] *adj* (*Brit*) torpe, lerdo; terco.

thickheadedness* ['θɪk'hedɪdnɪs] *n* torpeza *f*; terquedad *f*.

thickie*, thicky* ['θɪkɪ] *n* bobo *m*, -a *f*.

thick-lipped ['θɪk'lɪpt] *adj* de labios gruesos, bezudo.

thickly ['θɪklɪ] *adv* espesamente; gruesamente; *speak* con voz apagada, indistintamente; **~ populated areas** regiones *fpl* densamente pobladas; **bread ~ spread with butter** pan *m* con mucha mantequilla, pan *m* con una buena capa de mantequilla; **the snow was falling ~** nevaba muchísimo.

thickness ['θɪknɪs] *n* espesura *f*; densidad *f*; grueso *m*; (*in measuring*) espesor *m*; grosor *m*; **what is the ~ of the snow?** ¿cuánta nieve hay?; **boards of the same ~** tablas *fpl* del mismo espesor.

thicko* ['θɪkəʊ] = **thickie.**

thickset ['θɪk'set] *adj* rechoncho, grueso.

thickskinned ['θɪk'skɪnd] *adj* (*fig*) insensible, duro.

thief [θiːf] *n, pl* **thieves** [θiːvz] ladrón *m*, -ona *f*; **stop ~!** ¡al ladrón!; **to set a ~ to catch a ~** poner a pillo pillo y medio.

thieve [θiːv] *vti* hurtar, robar.

thievery ['θiːvərɪ] *n* hurto *m*, robo *m*, latrocinio *m*.

thieving ['θiːvɪŋ] **1** *adj* ladrón, largo de uñas. **2** *n* hurto *m*, robo *m*, latrocinio *m*.

thievish ['θiːvɪʃ] *adj* ladrón; **to have ~ tendencies** ser largo de uñas.

thievishness ['θiːvɪʃnɪs] *n* propensión *f* a robar.

thigh [θaɪ] *n* muslo *m*.

thighbone ['θaɪbəʊn] *n* fémur *m*.

thimble ['θɪmbl] *n* (*Sew*) dedal *m*; (*Naut*) guardacabo *m*.

thimbleful ['θɪmblfʊl] *n* dedada *f*; **just a ~** unas gotas nada más.

thin [θɪn] **1** *adj* (**a**) *materials* delgado; *clothing, covering* ligero; *veil etc* transparente; diáfano; *layer* tenue, fino, delgado; *person* flaco; **with ~ legs** con piernas flacas; **to be as ~ as a rake** (*or* **lath** *or* **rail** *US*) estar en los huesos; **to get ~ner, to grow ~ner** enflaquecer.

(**b**) *hair* ralo, escaso; *crop, crowd, population* poco denso, escaso; **doctors are ~ on the ground** hay pocos médicos, escasean los médicos; **the wheat is ~ this year** este año hay poco trigo; **he's getting ~ on top** le escasea el pelo por encima, está un poco calvo.

(**c**) *liquid* poco denso; *soup, wine* aguado; que más bien parece ser agua; *scent, sound* tenue; *air, light* tenue, sutil; *voice* delgado; **in a ~ voice** con un hilo de voz; **at 20,000 metres the air is ~** a los 20.000 metros el aire está enrarecido; *V also* **air.**

(**d**) *excuse etc* poco convincente, flojo; **to have a ~ time*** pasarlo mal, pasar por un período difícil; **they gave him a ~ time of it*** hicieron sufrir al pobre, le hicieron sudar la gota gorda*; **my patience is wearing ~** se me agota la paciencia; **that excuse is wearing a bit ~** ese pretexto está resultando inaceptable; **the joke is wearing ~** el chiste ya no tiene gracia.

2 *adv*: **to spread butter ~** poner poca mantequilla; **they cut the bread very ~** sirven el pan en trozos muy delgados.

3 *vt*: **to ~ paint (down)** desleir la pintura, diluir la pintura; **to ~ soup (down)** aguar la sopa.

4 *vi* (*slim*) adelgazar(se), (*and weaken*) enflaquecer; (*crowd etc*) hacerse menos denso, aclararse; (*number etc*) reducirse; **his hair is ~ning** está perdiendo el pelo.

◆**thin down 1** *vt*: **to ~ sb down** adelgazar a uno, hacer que uno enflaquezca; *V also* **thin 3. 2** *vi* adelgazar.

◆**thin out 1** *vt plants etc* entresacar, aclarar; *crowd, number, army etc* reducir, mermar. **2** *vi*: **the forest starts to ~ out here** aquí el bosque empieza a ser menos denso.

thine [ðaɪn] *poss pron* (††) (el) tuyo, (la) tuya *etc*; **mine and ~** lo mío y lo tuyo; **for thee and ~** para ti y los tuyos; **what is mine is ~** lo que es mío es tuyo.

thing [θɪŋ] *n* (**a**) (*object*) cosa *f*; objeto *m*; artículo *m*; **~s** (*belongings*) cosas *fpl*, efectos *mpl*; (*equipment*) avíos *mpl*, equipo *m*; (*clothes*) ropa *f*, trapos *mpl*; (*luggage*) equipaje *m*; **~s of value** objetos *mpl* de valor; **a ~ of beauty** un objeto bello; **my painting ~s** mis avíos de pintar; **tea ~s** servicio *m* de té; **to wash up the tea ~s** lavar la vajilla; **where shall I put my ~s?** ¿dónde pongo mis cosas?; **to pack up one's ~s** hacer las maletas; **you must be seeing ~s** estás viendo visiones; **to take off one's ~s** desnudarse, quitarse la ropa.

(**b**) (*person*) ser *m*, criatura *f*; (*pej*) sujeto *m*; (*animal*) criatura *f*; **you poor ~!, poor old ~!** ¡pobrecito!; **he's a poor old ~ now** ahora no vale para nada; **you beastly** (*or* **horrid, rotten** *etc*) **~!** ¡canalla!; **how are you, old ~?**† ¿qué tal, hijo?

(**c**) (*matter, circumstance etc*) cosa *f*; asunto *m*; **the main ~** lo más importante, lo esencial; **above all ~s** ante todo, sobre todo; **for one ~** en primer lugar; **and for another ~** ... y además ..., y por otra parte ...; **a gentleman in all ~s** un caballero en todos los aspectos; **no such ~!** ¡no hay tal!; ¡ni hablar!; **what with one ~ and another** entre unas cosas y otras; **one ~ or the other** ... una de dos ...; **it's neither one ~ nor the other** no es ni lo uno ni lo otro; **first ~ (in the morning)** a primera hora (de la mañana); **you don't know the first ~ about it** no sabes nada en absoluto de esto; **last ~ (at night)** a última hora (de la noche); antes de acostarse; **the first ~ to do is** ... lo primero que hay que hacer es ...; **that's the last ~ we want** eso es lo que queremos menos; **the best ~ would be to** + *infin* lo mejor sería + *infin*; **the next best ~** lo mejor después de eso; **(the) next ~ I knew, he'd gone** de repente, resultó que se había ido; **it's a good ~ that** ... menos mal que ...; **the good ~ about it is that** ... lo bueno es que ...; **to be on to a good ~** haber encontrado algo bueno; ir por buen camino; **it's finished and a good ~ too** se acabó y me alegro de ello; **it was a close ~, it was a near ~** (*race*) fue una carrera muy reñida; (*accident*) por poco chocamos, casi chocamos; (*escape*) escapé (*etc*) por un pelo; **it's the real ~** es auténtico; **this is the real ~ at last** por fin lo tenemos sin trampa ni cartón; **it's the very ~!, it's just the ~!** ¡es exactamente lo que necesitábamos!; **it's one ~ to buy it, quite another to make it work** es fácil comprarlo, pero no es tan fácil hacerlo funcionar; **it's just one of those ~s** son cosas que pasan, son cosas de la vida; **that's the ~ for me** eso es lo que me hace falta; **he's got a ~ going with her*** se entiende con ella; **he's got a ~ for her*** está colado por ella*; **he had a ~ with her 2 years ago*** se lió con ella hace 2 años*; **the ~ is** ... el caso es que ..., es que ...; **the ~ is this** ... la dificultad es que ...; se trata de saber si ...; **the ~ is to sell your car first** conviene vender primero tu coche; **the only ~ is to paint it** no hay más remedio que pintarlo; **the play's the ~** lo que importa es la representación; **this is too much of a good ~** esto es demasiado; **as ~s are** tal como están las cosas; **how are ~s?** ¿qué tal?; **how are ~s with you?** ¿qué tal te va?; ¿cómo te va eso?; **~s are going badly** las cosas van mal; **that's how ~s are** así están las cosas; **with ~s as they are** tal como están las cosas; **I've done a silly ~** he hecho algo tonto; **we had hoped for better ~s** habíamos esperado algo mejor; **I don't know a ~ about cars** no sé nada en absoluto de coches; **I didn't know a ~ for that exam** para ese examen yo estaba pez; **she knows a good ~ when she sees it** sabe obrar de acuerdo con su propio interés; **he knows a ~ or two** sabe cuántos son cinco; **he makes a good ~ out of it** sabe sacar provecho de ello, con eso tiene un buen negocio; **he made a great ~ out of the accident** exageró mucho el accidente; explotó mucho las consecuencias del accidente; **don't make a ~ of it!** ¡no exageres!, ¡no es para tanto!; **to make a mess of ~s** estropearlo, hacerlo todo mal; **did you ever see such a ~?** ¿se vio jamás tal cosa?; **to try to be all ~s to all men** tratar de serlo todo para todos.

(**d**) (*fashion*) **the latest ~ in hats** la última moda del sombrero, el sombrero según la moda actual; **it's quite the ~** está muy de moda.

(**e**) (*socially acceptable* **~**) **it's not the (done) ~** eso no se hace, eso no está bien visto; **to do the right ~** obrar bien, obrar honradamente.

(**f**) (*obsession*) obsesión *f*; manía *f*; **she has a ~ about snakes** está obsesionada por las culebras, le obsesionan las culebras; **he's got a ~ about me** me tiene manía.

(**g**) (*: *activity, preference*) **his ~ is fast cars** lo suyo son los coches rápidos; **it's not my ~** no es lo mío; **you can see it's not her ~** se ve que no es lo suyo; **to do one's (own) ~** ir a su aire, ir a lo suyo.

thingumabob* ['θɪŋəmɪbɒb] *n*, **thingamajig*** ['θɪŋəmɪdʒɪg] *n*, **thingummy*** ['θɪŋəmɪ] *n*, **thingy*** ['θɪŋɪ] (*thing*) cosa *f*, chisme *m*; (*person*) fulano *m*, ése *m*, ésa *f*; **old ~ with the specs** fulano el de las gafas.

think [θɪŋk] (*irr*: *pret and ptp* **thought**) **1** *vt* (**a**) (*believe*) pensar, creer; considerar; opinar; **I ~ so** creo que sí; **I ~ not** creo que no; **I thought so, I thought as much** ya me lo figuraba; lo había previsto ya; **I shouldn't ~ so** creo que no; **I should ~ so too!** ¡haces muy bien!; ¡ya era hora!; ¡buena falta te hacía!; **and it was free, I don't ~!*** ¿gratuito? ¡ni pensarlo!; **I ~ (that) it is true** creo que es verdad; **I don't ~ it can be done** no creo que se pueda hacer, no creo que sea factible; **so you ~ that ...?** ¿así que crees que ...?; **that's what you ~!** ¡(que) te crees tú eso!; **what do you ~ I should do?** ¿qué crees (tú) que debiera hacer?, ¿qué me aconsejas hacer?; **I would have thought that** ... hubiera creído que ...; **I never thought that** ... nunca pensé que ...; **one might ~ that** ... podría creerse que ...; **anyone would ~ he was dying** cualquiera diría que se estaba muriendo; **who'd have thought it?** ¿quién lo diría?; **I ~ it very difficult** lo creo (*or* veo) muy difícil; **I don't ~ it at all likely** lo creo muy poco probable; **everyone thought**

him mad todos le tenían por loco; **they are thought to be poor** se cree que son pobres; **you must ~ me very rude** vas a creer que soy muy descortés; **he ~s himself very clever** se cree la mar de listo; **she's very pretty, don't you ~?** es muy guapa, ¿no crees?

(**b**) (*conceive, imagine*) pensar, creer; imaginar; **who do you ~ you are?** ¿quién se cree Vd que es?; **who do you ~ you are to come marching in?** y Vd ¿qué derecho cree tener para entrar aquí tan fresco?; **~ what we could do with that house!** ¡imagina lo que podríamos hacer con esa casa!; **to ~ that ...!** ¡y pensar que ...!; **to ~ she once slept here!** ¡pensar que ella durmió aquí una vez!; **I can't ~ what you mean** no llego a entender lo que quieres decir; **I can't ~ what he can want** no llego a comprender su motivo; **to ~ great thoughts** pensar cosas profundas, tener pensamientos profundos.

(**c**) (*be of opinion*) pensar; **she didn't know what to ~** no sabía a qué carta quedarse; no sabía a qué atenerse; **now I don't know what to ~** ahora estoy en duda; **what do you ~?** ¿qué te parece?; **what do you ~ about it?** ¿qué te parece (de esto)?; **see what you ~ about it and let me know** estúdialo y dime luego tu opinión; **what do you ~ of him?** ¿qué piensas de él?, ¿qué te parece él?, ¿qué concepto tienes de él?; **to ~ highly of sb** tener en mucho a uno; **to ~ little of sb** tener en poco a uno; **to ~ well of sb** tener una buena opinión de uno; **he is well thought of here** aquí se le estima mucho; **we don't ~ much of X** tenemos un concepto más bien bajo de X; **I don't ~ much of that cheese** no me gusta nada ese queso; **I told him what I thought of him** le dije la opinión que tenía de él; le dije un par de cosas.

(**d**) (*intend*) pensar; **to ~ to** + *infin* pensar + *infin*; **I came here ~ing to question you** vine aquí con la intención de hacerte unas preguntas.

(**e**) (*expect*) esperar; contar con; **I never thought to hear that from you** no esperaba nunca escuchar tales palabras de ti; **we little thought that ...** estábamos lejos de pensar que ...; **I didn't ~ to see you here** no contaba con verte aquí.

(**f**) (*remember*) **I didn't ~ to tell him** me olvidé de decírselo.

(**g**) (*of ideas occurring*) **I was ~ing that ...** se me ocurrió pensar que ...; **I didn't ~ to do it** no se me ocurrió hacerlo.

2 *vi* (**a**) (*gen*) pensar; meditar, reflexionar; discurrir, razonar; **I ~, therefore I am** pienso, luego existo; **he doesn't ~ coherently** no discurre bien; **to ~ (long and) hard** pensar mucho; **to act without ~ing** obrar sin reflexionar; **~ before you reply** reflexiona antes de contestar; **give me time to ~** dame tiempo para reflexionar; **now let me ~** déjame pensar; veamos, vamos a ver; **I'm sorry, I wasn't ~ing** lo siento, no me había fijado; **to ~ again, to ~ twice** pensar dos veces; volver a pensarlo, reflexionar; **~ again!** ¡medítalo!; **we didn't ~ twice about it** no vacilamos un instante, no había lugar a dudas; **to ~ aloud** pensar en alta voz, expresar lo que uno piensa; **to ~ about sth** pensar algo bien, considerar algo detenidamente, reflexionar sobre algo; consultar algo con la almohada; **I'll ~ about it** lo pensaré; **you just ~ about it!** ¡medítalo!; **you ~ about money too much** le das demasiada importancia al dinero; **to ~ for o.s.** pensar por sí mismo.

(**b**) (*devote thought to, remember*) **to ~ about** pensar en; **that is worth ~ing about** eso vale la pena de pensarlo; **there is much to ~ about** hay tantas cosas que tener en cuenta; **you've given us a lot to ~ about** nos has dado mucho en que pensar; **~ (about) what you have done** recapacita lo que has hecho; **to ~ of** pensar en; **I ~ of you always, I am always ~ing of you** pienso constantemente en ti; **~ of a number** piensa en un número; **~ of me tomorrow in the exam** ayúdame mañana en el examen con tus pensamientos; **one can't ~ of everything** es imposible atender a todo, es imposible preverlo todo; **(now I come) to ~ of it ...** ahora que lo pienso ..., por cierto ...; **I couldn't ~ of the right word** no pude recordar la palabra exacta; **what(ever) can you have been ~ing of?** ¿qué demonios pensabas hacer?; ¿cómo se te ocurrió hacer (*etc*) eso?; **his style makes me ~ of Baroja** su estilo me hace pensar en el de Baroja, su estilo recuerda el de Baroja.

(**c**) (*be sympathetic to, take into account*) **to ~ of** considerar, tener en cuenta; **to ~ of other people's feelings** tener en cuenta los sentimientos de los demás; **one has to ~ of the expense** hay que considerar lo que se gasta; **he ~s of nobody but himself** no piensa más que en sí mismo; **but she has children to ~ about** pero ella tiene que pensar en sus hijos.

(**d**) (*imagine*) imaginar(se); **~ of me in a bikini!** ¡imagíname en bikini!; **~ of what might have happened!** ¡piensa en lo que podía ocurrir!; **~ of the cost of it all!** ¡piensa en lo que cuesta todo esto!; **and to ~ of her going there alone!** ¡y pensar que ella fue allí sola!; **have you ever thought of going to Cuba?** ¿has pensado alguna vez en ir a Cuba?; **just ~!** ¡fíjate!, ¡imagínate!

(**e**) (*of ideas occurring*) **I was ~ing that ...** se me ocurrió pensar que ...; **I thought of learning Basque** pensaba aprender el vasco, se me ocurrió aprender el vasco; **don't you ever ~ of washing?** ¿no se te ocurre alguna vez lavarte?; **I was the one who thought of it first** fui yo quien tuve la idea primero; **what(ever) will he ~ of next?** ¿qué se le va a ocurrir en lo sucesivo?

3 *n* (*) **I'll have a ~ about it** lo pensaré; **I'll have a good ~ about it** lo pensaré mucho, lo estudiaré; **I was just having a quiet ~** meditaba tranquilamente; **you'd better have another ~** conviene volver a pensarlo, conviene reconsiderarlo; **then she's got another ~ coming** tendrá que desengañarse, le espera una sorpresa desagradable.

◆**think back** *vi* recordar; **try to ~ back** trata de recordar; **I ~ back to that moment when ...** recuerdo ese momento cuando ...

◆**think out** *vt plan etc* imaginar, idear; elaborar; *answer* meditar a fondo; descubrir (después de pensarlo mucho); *problem* estudiar, resolver (después de pensarlo mucho); **this needs ~ing out** esto hay que pensarlo mucho; **a well thought out answer** una respuesta estudiada, una contestación razonada; **he ~s things out for himself** razona por sí mismo.

◆**think over** *vt*: **to ~ sth over** considerar algo detenidamente; reflexionar sobre algo; consultar algo con la almohada; **I'll ~ it over** lo pensaré; **~ it over!** ¡medítalo!

◆**think through** *vt* considerar detalladamente, estudiar con la mayor seriedad; **this plan has not been properly thought through** este proyecto no ha sido pensado con el debido cuidado.

◆**think up** *vt* imaginar, idear; *excuse* inventar; **who thought this one up?** ¿quién ideó esto?, ¿a quién se le ocurrió esto?

thinkable [ˈθɪŋkəbl] *adj* concebible; **is it ~ that ...?** ¿es concebible que + *subj*?, ¿se concibe que + *subj*?

thinker [ˈθɪŋkəʳ] *n* pensador *m*, -ora *f*.

thinking [ˈθɪŋkɪŋ] **1** *adj* pensante, que piensa; inteligente, racional; serio; **to any ~ person** para cualquier persona racional, para el que piensa; **the ~ person's novelist** el novelista para el lector inteligente.

2 *n* pensamiento *m*; (*thoughts collectively*) pensamientos *mpl*; **good ~!** ¡muy bien!, ¡genial!; **his way of ~** su modo de pensar; **to my way of ~** a mi juicio, en mi opinión.

think-tank [ˈθɪŋktæŋk] *n* grupo *m* de expertos; gabinete *m* de estrategia.

thin-lipped [ˈθɪnˈlɪpt] *adj* de labios apretados.

thinly [ˈθɪnlɪ] *adv*: **~ disguised as ...** ligeramente disfrazado de ...; **with ~ spread butter** con una capa delgada de mantequilla.

thinner [ˈθɪnəʳ] *n* disolvente *m*, diluyente *m*.

thinness [ˈθɪnnɪs] *n* delgadez *f*; flaqueza *f*; tenuidad *f*.

thin-skinned [ˈθɪnˈskɪnd] *adj* de piel fina; (*fig*) sensible, demasiado sensible.

third [θɜːd] **1** *adj* tercero; **~ degree** (*US*) *V* **degree** (**e**); **~ estate** estado *m* llano; **~ party** tercera persona *f*, tercero *m*; **~-party insurance** seguro *m* de responsabilidad social, seguro *m* contra terceros; **~ person** tercera persona *f*; **~ time lucky!** ¡a la tercera va la vencida!; **T~ World** Tercer Mundo *m*; **~ world** *attr* tercermundista.

2 *n* (**a**) tercio *m*, tercera parte *f*; **two-~s of the votes** dos tercios de los votos; **two-~s of those present** las dos terceras partes de los asistentes.

(**b**) (*Mus*) tercera *f*.

(**c**) (*Brit Univ*) tercera clase *f*.

(**d**) (*Aut*) tercera velocidad *f*; **in ~** en tercera.

3 *adv* en tercer lugar; **to travel ~** viajar en tercera clase.

third-class [ˈθɜːdˈklɑːs] **1** *adj* de tercera clase; (*pej*) de tercera clase, de baja categoría. **2** *adv*: **to travel ~** viajar en tercera. **3** *n* (*US Post*) tarifa *f* de impreso.

thirdly [ˈθɜːdlɪ] *adv* en tercer lugar.

third-rate [ˈθɜːdˈreɪt] *adj* de baja categoría.

thirst [θɜːst] **1** *n* sed *f*; **the ~ for** (*fig*) la sed de, el ansia de, el afán de; **to quench one's ~** apagar la sed. **2** *vi*: **to ~**

for (*fig*) tener sed de, ansiar.

thirstily ['θɜːstɪlɪ] *adv*: **he drank ~** bebió como si tuviera mucha sed.

thirsty ['θɜːstɪ] *adj* sediento; *land* árido, que necesita regarse mucho; **to be ~** tener sed; **how ~ I am!** ¡qué sed tengo!; **it's ~ work** es un trabajo que da sed.

thirteen ['θɜː'tiːn] *adj* trece.

thirteenth ['θɜː'tiːnθ] *adj* decimotercio, decimotercero.

thirtieth ['θɜːtɪɪθ] *adj* trigésimo, treinta; **the ~ anniversary** el treinta aniversario.

thirty ['θɜːtɪ] *adj* treinta; **the thirties** (*eg* 1930s) los años treinta; **to be in one's thirties** tener más de treinta años.

thirtyish ['θɜːtɪɪʃ] *adj* treintañero, de unos treinta años.

thirty-second ['θɜːtɪ'sekənd] *adj*: **~ note** (*US*) fusa *f*.

this [ðɪs] (*pl* **these**) **1** *dem adj m*: este; *f*: esta; **~ evening** esta tarde; **~ coming week** esta semana que viene; **~ day last year** hoy hace un año; **~ day fortnight** hoy a quince días, de hoy en quince días.

2 *dem pron m*: éste; *f*: ésta; *'neuter'*: esto; **~ is new** esto es nuevo; **like ~** así, de este modo; **it was like ~** te contaré la cosa como pasó; te diré lo que pasó; **we talked about ~ and that** hablamos de esto y lo otro; **what with ~, that and the other** con esto, lo otro y lo demás; **what's all ~?** ¿qué pasa?; **who's ~?** ¿quién es?; **~ is Joe** (*on telephone etc*) aquí Pepe, soy Pepe; **~ is Joe Soap** (*introduction*) quiero presentarle al señor Joe Soap; **~ is Tuesday** hoy es martes; **but ~ is May** pero estamos en mayo; **'but he's nearly bald' ... '~ is it'** 'pero está casi calvo' ... 'ahí está la dificultad'.

3 *adv*: **~ far** tan lejos; **~ high** tan alto, así de alto (*and V* **that 4**).

thistle ['θɪsl] *n* cardo *m*.

thistledown ['θɪsldaʊn] *n* vilano *m* (de cardo).

thistly ['θɪslɪ] *adj* (*prickly*) espinoso; (*full of thistles*) lleno de cardos; *problem etc* espinoso, erizado de dificultades.

thither† ['ðɪðəʳ] *adv* allá.

tho'* [ðəʊ] *conj* = **though**.

thole [θəʊl] *n* escálamo *m*.

Thomas ['tɒməs] *nm* Tomás; **Saint ~** Santo Tomás; **~ More** Tomás Moro.

Thomism ['tɒmɪzəm] *n* tomismo *m*.

Thomist ['tɒmɪst] **1** *adj* tomista. **2** *n* tomista *mf*.

thong [θɒŋ] *n* correa *f*.

Thor [θɔːʳ] *n* Tor *m*.

thoracic [θɔː'ræsɪk] *adj* torácico.

thorax ['θɔːræks] *n* tórax *m*.

thorium ['θɔːrɪəm] *n* torio *m*.

thorn [θɔːn] *n* espina *f* (*also fig*); **to be a ~ in the flesh of sb** ser una espina en el costado de uno.

thornbush ['θɔːnbʊʃ] *n* espino *m*.

thornless ['θɔːnlɪs] *adj* sin espinas.

thorn-tree ['θɔːntriː] *n* espino *m*.

thorny ['θɔːnɪ] *adj* espinoso (*also fig*).

thorough ['θʌrə] *adj* (*complete*) completo, cabal; acabado; (*not superficial*) minucioso, concienzudo, meticuloso; **he's very ~** es muy cuidadoso, es muy concienzudo; **to have a ~ knowledge of a region** conocer una región a fondo; **we made a ~ search** lo registramos minuciosamente; **there will be a ~ investigation into the charges** las acusaciones serán investigadas a fondo; **I felt a ~ idiot** me sentía totalmente imbécil; **the man's a ~ rogue** es un bribón redomado.

thoroughbred ['θʌrəbred] **1** *adj* de pura sangre. **2** *n* pura sangre *mf*.

thoroughfare ['θʌrəfeəʳ] *n* vía *f* pública; carretera *f*, calle *f*; **'no ~'** 'prohibido el paso', 'paso prohibido'.

thoroughgoing ['θʌrə,gəʊɪŋ] *adj person* cien por cien, de cuerpo entero; *examination etc* minucioso, a fondo.

thoroughly ['θʌrəlɪ] *adv*: **to know sth ~** conocer algo a fondo; **to investigate sth ~** investigar algo a fondo; **he works ~** trabaja cuidadosamente, trabaja concienzudamente; **a ~ bad influence** una influencia totalmente mala; **a ~ stupid thing to do** una acción completamente estúpida.

thoroughness ['θʌrənɪs] *n* minuciosidad *f*, meticulosidad *f*; perfección *f*; **with great ~** con el mayor esmero, con todo cuidado.

those [ðəʊz] (*pl of* **that**) **1** *dem adj m*: esos, (*more remote*) aquellos; *f*; esas, (*more remote*) aquellas.

2 *dem pron m*: ésos, (*more remote*) aquéllos; *f*: ésas, (*more remote*) aquéllas; **~ of** los de, las de; **~ which** los que, las que; **~ who** los que, las que, quienes; *V also* **that.**

thou[1] [ðaʊ] *pron* (†) tú.

thou[2]* [θaʊ] *abbr of* **thousand.**

though [ðəʊ] **1** *conj* aunque; si bien; **~ it was raining at the time** aunque llovía entonces; (**even**) **~ he doesn't want to** aunque no quiera; **as ~** como si + *subj*; **~ small it's good** aunque (es) pequeño es bueno; **strange ~ it may appear** aunque parezca extraño, por extraño que parezca; **what ~ there is no money?** (*liter*) ¿qué importa que no haya dinero?

2 *adv* sin embargo; **it's not so easy, ~** sin embargo no es tan fácil; **did he ~?** ¿de veras?

thought [θɔːt] **1** *pret and ptp of* **think.**

2 *n* (**a**) (*gen*) pensamiento *m*; idea *f*, concepto *m*; reflexión *f*, meditación *f*; consideración *f*; (*thoughtfulness*) solicitud *f*; **the ~ of Sartre** el pensamiento de Sartre; **happy ~** idea *f* luminosa; **that's a ~!** eso hay que tenerlo en cuenta; **after much ~, on second ~s** después de pensarlo bien, después de mucho pensar; **my ~s were elsewhere** pensaba en otra cosa; **his one ~ is to** + *infin* su único propósito es de + *infin*; **the very ~ frightens me** sólo pensar en ello me da miedo; **to collect one's ~s** orientarse, concentrarse; **let me collect my ~s** déjame pensar; **to give ~ to sth** pensar algo, meditar algo; considerar algo detenidamente; **we must give some ~ to the others** hay que tener en cuenta a los demás, conviene tener presentes a los demás; **I didn't give it another** (*or* **a second**) **~** no volví a pensar en ello; **don't give it another ~** no vuelvas a pensar en eso; **I was too busy to give it another** (*or* **a second**) **~** estaba demasiado ocupado para volver a pensar en eso; **he hasn't a ~ in his head** no tiene nada en la cabeza; **I had no ~ of offending you** no tenía la intención de ofenderle; **I had no ~ of such a thing** no se me había ocurrido tal cosa; **I once had ~s of marrying her** hace tiempo pensaba casarme con ella; **then I had second ~s** luego tuve otra idea, mudé luego de parecer; **to be lost in ~** estar absorto en meditación; **perish the ~!** ¡ni por pensamiento!, ¡Dios me libre!; **to read sb's ~s** adivinar el pensamiento de uno; **to take ~ how to do sth** pensar cómo hacer algo; **to take no ~ for the morrow** no pensar en mañana, no preparar para el futuro.

(**b**) (*fig*) pizca *f*, poquito *m*; **it's a ~ too bright** es un poquito claro.

thoughtful ['θɔːtfʊl] *adj* (*pensive*) pensativo, meditabundo; (*in character*) serio; (*kind*) atento, solícito, considerado; (*far-sighted*) clarividente, previsor; **how ~ of you!, that's very ~ of you!** ¡qué detalle!, ¡es Vd muy amable!; **he's a ~ boy** es un chico serio.

thoughtfully ['θɔːtfəlɪ] *adv* pensativamente; seriamente; atentamente, solícitamente, con consideración; con clarividencia, con previsión; **'Yes', he said ~** 'Sí', dijo pensativo; **sb had ~ provided a cup** alguien había puesto amablemente una taza.

thoughtfulness ['θɔːtfʊlnɪs] *n* seriedad *f*; carácter *m* reflexivo; atención *f*, solicitud *f*, consideración *f*; clarividencia *f*, previsión *f*.

thoughtless ['θɔːtlɪs] *adj act* irreflexivo, descuidado; *person* inconsiderado, desconsiderado, inconsciente.

thoughtlessly ['θɔːtlɪslɪ] *adv* sin pensar, irreflexivamente; inconscientemente; impensadamente, insensatamente; **to act ~** obrar con poca consideración, obrar sin pensar.

thoughtlessness ['θɔːtlɪsnɪs] *n* irreflexión *f*, descuido *m*; inconsideración *f*, inconsciencia *f*.

thought-process ['θɔːt,prəʊses] *n* proceso *m* mental.

thought-provoking ['θɔːtprə,vəʊkɪŋ] *adj* que hace reflexionar.

thought-reader ['θɔːt,riːdəʳ] *n* lector *m*, -ora *f* (*or* adivinador *m*, -ora *f*) de pensamientos.

thought-reading ['θɔːt,riːdɪŋ] *n* adivinación *f* de pensamientos.

thought-transference ['θɔːt,trænsfərəns] *n* transmisión *f* de pensamientos.

thousand ['θaʊzənd] **1** *adj* mil; **a ~, one ~** mil; **4 ~ specimens** cuatro mil ejemplares; **I've got a ~ and one things to do** tengo la mar de cosas que hacer*.

2 *n* mil *m*; (*more loosely*) millar *m*; **they sell them by the ~** los venden a millares; **they were there in ~s** los había a millares; **I've told you ~s of times** te lo he dicho mil veces.

thousandfold ['θaʊzəndfəʊld] **1** *adj* multiplicado por mil; de mil veces. **2** *adv* mil veces.

thousandth ['θaʊzəntθ] **1** *adj* milésimo. **2** *n* milésimo *m*.

thraldom ['θrɔːldəm] *n* (*liter*) esclavitud *f*.

thrall [θrɔːl] *n* (*liter*) (*person*) esclavo *m*, -a *f*; (*state*) esclavitud *f*; **to be in ~ to** ser esclavo de; **to hold sb in ~** retener a uno en la esclavitud.

thrash [θræʃ] **1** *vt* (**a**) (*beat*) golpear; *person* apalear, (*as punishment*) azotar, zurrar; (*Sport etc*) dar una paliza a, cascar.

(**b**) *legs etc* mover violentamente, agitar mucho.

(**c**) (*Agr*) trillar.

2 *n* (*Brit*‡) guateque *m*, party *m*.

◆**thrash about** *vi* sacudirse, dar revueltas; revolcarse; debatirse; **he ~ed about with his stick** daba golpes por todos lados con su bastón; **they were ~ing about in the water** se estaban revolcando en el agua.

◆**thrash out** *vt problem, difficulty* resolver mediante larga discusión, discutir largamente.

thrashing ['θræʃɪŋ] *n* zurra *f*, paliza *f*; **to give sb a ~** zurrar a uno, dar una paliza a uno; **to give a team a ~** dar una paliza a un equipo.

thread [θred] **1** *n* (**a**) (*Sew etc*) hilo *m*; (*fibre*) hebra *f*, fibra *f*; (*of silkworm, spider etc*) hebra *f*; **to hang by a ~** pender de un hilo; **to lose the ~** (**of what one is saying**) perder el hilo (de su discurso); **to pick** (*or* **take**) **up the ~ again** coger el hilo, tomar el hilo.

(**b**) (*of screw*) filete *m*, rosca *f*.

(**c**) **~s*** (*US*) trapos* *mpl*.

2 *vt needle* enhebrar; *beads etc* ensartar; **to ~ one's way through** colarse a través de, abrirse paso por, lograr pasar por.

threadbare ['θredbeəʳ] *adj* raído, gastado; *excuse etc* flojo, poco convincente.

threadworm ['θredwɜːm] *n* lombriz *f* intestinal.

threat [θret] *n* amenaza *f*; **it is a grave ~ to ...** constituye una grave amenaza para ...

threaten ['θretn] **1** *vt* amenazar, proferir amenazas contra; acechar; **to ~ violence** amenazar con (la) violencia, amenazar con ponerse violento; **to ~ sb with sth** amenazar a uno con algo; **a species ~ed with extinction** una especie amenazada de extinción; **to ~ to +** *infin* amenazar con + *infin*; **to ~ to kill sb** amenazar con matar a uno; **it is ~ing to rain** amenaza llover.

2 *vi* amenazar.

threatening ['θretnɪŋ] *adj* amenazador, amenazante.

threateningly ['θretnɪŋlɪ] *adv* de modo amenazador; *say etc* en tono amenazador.

three [θriː] **1** *adj* tres. **2** *n* tres *m*; **~'s a crowd** tres es muchedumbre.

three-act ['θriː'ækt] *adj play* de tres actos, en tres actos.

three-colour(ed), (*US*) **three-color(ed)** ['θriː'kʌləd] *adj attr* de tres colores, tricolor.

three-cornered ['θriː'kɔːnəd] *adj* triangular; **~ hat** tricornio *m*, sombrero *m* de tres picos.

three-D ['θriː'diː] **1** *adj* tridimensional. **2** *n*: **in ~** en tres dimensiones.

three-day eventing [ˌθriːdeɪ'ventɪŋ] *n concurso hípico que dura tres días y consta de tres pruebas distintas.*

three-decker ['θriː'dekəʳ] *n* (*Naut*) barco *m* de tres cubiertas; (*Liter*) novela *f* de tres tomos; (*Culin*) sándwich *m* de tres pisos.

three-dimensional ['θriːdɪ'menʃənl] *adj* (*abbr* **3-D**) tridimensional.

threefold ['θriːfəʊld] **1** *adj* triple. **2** *adv* tres veces.

three-legged ['θriː'legɪd] *adj* de tres piernas; *race, stool* de tres patas.

threepence ['θrepəns] *n* (*Brit*) 3 peniques *mpl*.

threepenny ['θrepənɪ] *adj* (*Brit*) de 3 peniques; (*fig*) de poca monta, despreciable; **~ bit, ~ piece** moneda *f* de 3 peniques; **T~ Opera** Ópera *f* de perra gorda.

three-phase ['θriːfeɪz] *adj* (*Elec*) trifásico.

three-piece ['θriːpiːs] *adj*: **~ costume, ~ suit** terno *m*; **~ suite** tresillo *m*.

three-ply ['θriːplaɪ] *adj wood* de tres capas; *wool* triple, de tres hebras.

three-point turn [ˌθriːpɔɪnt'tɜːn] *n* cambio *m* de sentido en tres movimientos.

three-quarter [ˌθriː'kwɔːtəʳ] *adj*: **~-length sleeves** mangas *fpl* tres cuartos.

three-quarters [ˌθriː'kwɔːtəz] **1** *n* tres cuartos *mpl*, tres cuartas partes *fpl*; **in ~ of an hour** en tres cuartos de hora; **I've done ~ of the work** he hecho las tres cuartas partes del trabajo. **2** *adv*: **the tank is ~ full** quedan las tres cuartas partes en el depósito.

threescore ['θriːskɔːʳ] *n* sesenta; **~ years and ten** setenta años.

three-sided ['θriː'saɪdɪd] *adj* trilátero.

threesome ['θriːsəm] *n* grupo *m* de tres, conjunto *m* de tres.

three-way ['θriːweɪ] *adj*: **~ split** división *f* en tercios.

three-wheeler ['θriː'wiːləʳ] *n* coche *m* de tres ruedas.

threnody ['θrenədɪ] *n* lamento *m*; canto *m* fúnebre.

thresh [θreʃ] *vt* trillar.

thresher ['θreʃəʳ] *n* trilladora *f*.

threshing ['θreʃɪŋ] *n* trilla *f*.

threshing-floor ['θreʃɪŋflɔːʳ] *n* era *f*.

threshing-machine ['θreʃɪŋməˌʃiːn] *n* trilladora *f*.

threshold ['θreʃhəʊld] **1** *n* umbral *m*; **to be on the ~ of** (*fig*) estar en los umbrales de, estar en la antesala de, estar al borde de; **to cross sb's ~** traspasar el umbral de uno; **to have a low pain ~** tener poca tolerancia del dolor.

2 *attr*: **~ agreement** convenio *m* de nivel crítico; **~ price** precio *m* umbral, precio *m* mínimo.

threw [θruː] *pret of* **throw**.

thrice [θraɪs] *adv* (††) tres veces.

thrift [θrɪft] *n*, **thriftiness** ['θrɪftɪnɪs] *n* economía *f*, frugalidad *f*.

thriftless ['θrɪftlɪs] *adj* malgastador, pródigo.

thriftlessness ['θrɪftlɪsnɪs] *n* prodigalidad *f*.

thrifty ['θrɪftɪ] *adj* (**a**) (*frugal*) económico, frugal, ahorrativo. (**b**) (*US*) próspero.

thrill [θrɪl] **1** *n* emoción *f*; sensación *f*; estremecimiento *m*; **with a ~ of excitement, he ...** estremecido de emoción, él ...; **what a ~!** ¡qué emoción!; **it's the ~ of the year** es la sensación del año; **he just does it for the ~** lo hace simplemente porque le emociona; **to get a ~ out of sth** emocionarse con algo; **it gives me a ~** me emociona; me hace mucha ilusión.

2 *vt* emocionar, conmover, estremecer; hacer ilusión a; **the film ~ed me** la película me emocionó; **I was ~ed to get your letter** tu carta me hizo mucha ilusión; **we were ~ed with** (*or* **about, at**) **your news** tu noticia nos emocionó muchísimo.

3 *vi* emocionarse, conmoverse, estremecerse; **to ~ to sb's touch** estremecerse al ser tocado por uno.

thriller ['θrɪləʳ] *n* novela *f* (*or* obra *f*, película *f*) escalofriante, novela *f* de suspense, novela *f* de misterio.

thrilling ['θrɪlɪŋ] *adj* emocionante, conmovedor; apasionante; sensacional; **an absolutely ~ journey** un viaje de lo más sensacional; **a ~ play** una obra muy emocionante; **how ~!** ¡qué emoción!

thrillingly ['θrɪlɪŋlɪ] *adv* de modo emocionante; de modo sensacional.

thrive [θraɪv] (*irr*: *pret* **thrived, throve,** *ptp* **thriven**) *vi* (*do well*) prosperar, medrar; florecer; (*grow*) crecer mucho, desarrollarse bien; **he ~s on hard work** le gusta estar muy ocupado, se encuentra perfectamente bien con un trabajo agotador; **the plant ~s here** la planta crece muy bien aquí; **children ~ on milk** a los niños les aprovecha la leche.

thriven ['θrɪvn] *ptp of* **thrive.**

thriving ['θraɪvɪŋ] *adj* próspero, floreciente.

throat [θrəʊt] *n* garganta *f*; (*from exterior*) cuello *m*; **they are at each other's ~s all the time** se atacan uno a otro todo el tiempo; **to clear one's ~** carraspear, aclarar la voz; **to cut one's ~** cortarse la garganta; **he's cutting his own ~** (*fig*) está actuando en perjuicio propio, se está haciendo daño a sí mismo; **to jump down sb's ~** lanzarse a criticar a uno en el acto, criticar a uno sin esperar razones; **to moisten one's ~** remojar el gaznate; **to thrust** (*or* **ram**) **sth down sb's ~** (*fig*) hacer que uno trague algo a la fuerza, meter algo a uno por las narices.

throaty ['θrəʊtɪ] *adj* gutural; ronco.

throb [θrɒb] **1** *n* (*of heart etc*) latido *m*, pulsación *f*; palpitación *f*; (*of engine*) vibración *f*; (*of emotion*) estremecimiento *m*.

2 *vi* latir; palpitar; vibrar; estremecerse; **the crowd ~bed with excitement** la multitud se estremeció emocionada.

throbbing ['θrɒbɪŋ] **1** *adj* palpitante; vibrante; *pain* pungente; *rhythm* marcado, fuerte. **2** *n* latido *m*, pulsación *f*; palpitación *f*; vibración *f*; estremecimiento *m*.

throes [θrəʊz] *npl* (*of death*) agonía *f*; (*of childbirth etc*) dolores *mpl*; (*fig*) angustia *f*, agonía *f*; **to be in the ~ of** estar en medio de; estar sufriendo todas las molestias de.

thrombosis [θrɒm'bəʊsɪs] *n* trombosis *f*.

throne [θrəʊn] *n* trono *m*; (*freq fig*) corona *f*, poder *m* real; **to ascend the ~, to come to the ~** subir al trono.

throneroom ['θrəʊnrʊm] *n* sala *f* del trono.

throng [θrɒŋ] **1** *n* multitud *f*, tropel *m*, muchedumbre *f*; **great ~s of tourists** multitudes *fpl* de turistas; **to come in a ~** venir en tropel.

2 *vt* atestar, llenar de bote en bote; **everywhere is ~ed** todo está lleno, todo está atestado; **the streets are ~ed with tourists** las calles están atestadas de turistas.

3 *vi*: **to come ~ing** venir en tropel, venir en masa; **to ~ round sb** apiñarse en torno a uno; **to ~ to hear sb** venir en tropel a escuchar a uno; **to ~ together** reunirse en tropel.

thronging ['θrɒŋɪŋ] *adj crowd etc* grande, apretado, nutrido.

throttle ['θrɒtl] **1** *n* (*Anat*) gaznate *m*; (*Mech*) regulador *m*, válvula *f* reguladora, estrangulador *m*; (*Aut, loosely*) acelerador *m*; **to give an engine full ~** acelerar un motor al máximo.

2 *vt* ahogar, estrangular; (*Mech*) estrangular.

3 *vi* asfixiarse, ahogarse.

◆**throttle back, throttle down** (*Mech*) **1** *vt*: **to ~ back** (*or* **~ down**) **the engine** moderar la marcha.

2 *vi* moderar la marcha.

through, (*US also*) **thru** [θru:] **1** *adv* (**a**) (*of place*) de parte a parte, completamente; **the nail went right ~** el clavo penetró de parte a parte; **the wood has rotted ~** la madera se ha podrido completamente; **it's frozen** (**right**) **~** está completamente helado; **the train goes ~ to Burgos** el tren va directo a Burgos; *V* **wet 1** (**a**).

(**b**) (*of time, process*) desde el principio hasta el fin; hasta el fin; **did you stay right ~?** ¿te quedaste hasta el final?; **we're staying ~ till Tuesday** nos quedamos hasta el martes; **to sleep the whole night ~** dormir la noche entera; **he knew it right ~** lo sabía todo, lo sabía de corrido.

(**c**) (*with* **to be**) **you're ~!** (*Telec*) ¡puede hablar!, ¡hable!; **you're ~!*** (*US*) ¡queda Vd despedido!; **are you ~?** ¿has terminado?; **we'll be ~ at 7** terminaremos a las 7; **when I'm ~ with him** cuando haya terminado con él; **I'm not ~ with you yet** todavía no he terminado de decirte (*etc*) lo que tenía pensado; **are you ~ with that book?** ¿has terminado de leer ese libro?; **I'm ~ with bridge** renuncio al bridge, ya no vuelvo a jugar al bridge; **I'm ~ with her** he roto con ella; **she told him they were ~** ella le dijo que habían terminado sus relaciones.

(**d**) **a Catalan ~ and ~** catalán hasta los tuétanos, catalán por los cuatro costados; *V* **carry through, fall through** *etc*.

(**e**) **to put sb ~ to** (*Brit Telec*) poner a uno con.

2 *prep* (**a**) (*of place*) por; a través de; de un lado a otro de; **to look ~ a telescope** mirar por un telescopio; **to walk ~ the woods** dar un paseo por el bosque; **the bullet went ~ 3 layers** la bala penetró 3 capas; **it went right ~ the wall** atravesó por toda la pared; **half-way ~ the film** a la mitad de la película.

(**b**) (*of time*) hasta, hasta e incluso; (**from**) **Monday ~ Friday** (*US*) desde el lunes hasta el viernes, de lunes a viernes; **all ~ our stay** durante toda nuestra estancia; **right ~ the year** durante el año entero.

(**c**) **he's ~ the exam** ha aprobado el examen.

(**d**) (*of means*) mediante, por medio de; por, por causa de; debido a; gracias a; **~ him I found out that ...** por él supe que ...; **~ not knowing the way** por no saber el camino; **he got it ~ friends** lo consiguió por medio de sus amigos; **it was ~ you that we were late** fue por vosotros por lo que llegamos tarde; **to act ~ fear** obrar movido por el miedo.

3 *adj carriage, train* directo; *traffic* de paso.

throughout [θrʊ'aʊt] **1** *adv* (**a**) (*of place*) en todas partes, por todas partes; **the hull is welded ~** el casco está totalmente soldado; **the room has been cleaned ~** el cuarto ha sido limpiado completamente; **the house has electric light ~** la casa tiene luz eléctrica en todos los cuartos.

(**b**) (*of time, process*) todo el tiempo, desde el principio hasta el fin; **the weather was good ~** hizo buen tiempo todos los días; **it's a boring journey ~** es un viaje pesado en todo el recorrido, todo el viaje es monótono.

2 *prep* (**a**) (*of place*) por todo, por todas partes de; **~ the country** por todo el país, en todo el país.

(**b**) (*of time, process*) durante todo, en todo.

throughput ['θru:pʊt] *n* rendimiento *m* total (de procesamiento); producto *m*, productividad *f*; capacidad *f* de ejecución.

throughway ['θru:weɪ] *n* (*US*) autopista *f* de peaje.

throve [θrəʊv] *pret of* **thrive**.

throw [θrəʊ] **1** *n* echada *f*, tirada *f*, tiro *m*; (*move, at games*) jugada *f*; (*in wrestling*) derribo *m*; (*at dice*) lance *m*; **within a stone's ~** a tiro de piedra; **they're £5 a ~*** cuestan 5 libras cada uno.

2 (*irr*: *pret* **threw**, *ptp* **thrown**) *vt* (**a**) (*gen*) echar, tirar, lanzar, arrojar; *dice* echar; *glance* lanzar, dirigir; *kiss* echar, tirar; **they threw a coat over her** le echaron encima un abrigo; **to ~ a ball 200 metres** lanzar (*LAm*: echar) una pelota 200 metros; **to ~ a bridge over a river** tender (*or* construir) un puente sobre un río; **to ~ a door open** abrir una puerta de golpe, abrir una puerta de par en par; **to ~ two rooms into one** unir dos cuartos; **to ~ the blame on sb** echar la culpa a uno; **to ~ the book at sb** acusar a uno de todo lo posible; castigar a uno con todo rigor; **to ~ temptation in sb's path** exponer a uno a la tentación; **to be ~n on one's own resources** tener que depender de sí mismo, no tener más que los propios recursos.

(**b**) (*direct*) *light, shadow, slides etc* proyectar; *punch* dar, asestar (*at* a); **to ~ light on** (*fig*) aclarar, arrojar luz sobre.

(**c**) *rider* desmontar, desarzonar; *opponent* derribar; *skin* mudar, quitarse; **to be ~n** (*rider*) ser derribado.

(**d**) (*: *disconcert*) confundir, desconcertar, dejar perplejo; **this answer seemed to ~ him** esta respuesta parecía desconcertarle.

(**e**) (*Tech*) *pot* formar, dar forma a, hacer; tornear; *silk* torcer.

(**f**) (*: *phrases*) **to ~ a fight** perder deliberadamente un encuentro; **to ~ a fit** sufrir un ataque (epiléptico); sufrir una crisis nerviosa; desmayarse; (*fig*) subirse por las paredes*; **to ~ a party** dar una fiesta (*for sb* en honor de uno).

3 *vr*: **to ~ o.s. at sb's feet** echarse a los pies de uno; **to ~ o.s. at sb** (*or* **at sb's head**) asediar a uno; **to ~ o.s. backwards** echarse hacia atrás; **to ~ o.s. down from a building** arrojarse desde un edificio; **to ~ o.s. into the fray** lanzarse a la batalla; **to ~ o.s. on sb** lanzarse sobre uno, precipitarse sobre uno; **to ~ o.s. to the ground** tirarse al suelo.

◆**throw about** *vt* tirar, esparcir; **to ~ money about** derrochar dinero; **to ~ one's arms about** agitar mucho los brazos; **to ~ o.s. about** agitar mucho los brazos; **they were ~ing a ball about** jugaban con una pelota.

◆**throw around** *vt* pasarse de uno a otro.

◆**throw aside** *vt* tirar, botar (*LAm*), tirar a un lado; apartar; desechar.

◆**throw away** *vt* (**a**) tirar, echar, botar (*LAm*); desechar; *money* malgastar, derrochar; *one's life* sacrificar inútilmente; *chance* desperdiciar; **it's old and can be ~n away** es viejo y se puede tirar.

(**b**) *line, remark* dejar caer; decir al azar; (*lose effect of*) perder todo el efecto de.

◆**throw back** *vt* (**a**) *ball* devolver; *fish* devolver al agua; *offer* rechazar (con desprecio).

(**b**) *hair, head* echar hacia atrás; **to ~ o.s. back** echarse hacia atrás.

(**c**) *enemy* rechazar, arrollar; **he was ~n back on his own resources** tuvo que depender de sus propios recursos.

◆**throw down** *vt ball etc* echar a tierra; lanzar hacia abajo; *building, defences* derribar, echar abajo; *arms, tools* dejar, abandonar; *glove* (*fig*) arrojar; *challenge* lanzar; **to ~ o.s. down** echarse a tierra; **it's ~ing it down*** está lloviendo a cántaros.

◆**throw in** *vt* (**a**) (*Sport*) *ball* sacar; *remark* hacer, insertar, lanzar (de improviso); *cards* arrojar sobre la mesa (en señal de abandono).

(**b**) (*as addition*) añadir; dar de más, ofrecer de más; **with an extra meal ~n in** con una comida de más, con una comida gratis.

◆**throw off** *vt* (**a**) *burden, yoke* sacudirse, deshacerse de, quitarse de encima; *clothes* quitarse (de prisa); *disguise* abandonar; *habit* dejar, renunciar a; *pursuers* zafarse de; *infection* reponerse de; (*emit*) emitir, despedir, arrojar; **in order to ~ the dogs off the scent** para despistar a los perros; **in order to ~ the police off the trail** para despistar a la policía.

(**b**) *composition* hacer rápidamente; improvisar.

◆**throw on** *vt clothes* ponerse (de prisa); *coal etc* echar.

◆**throw out** *vt* (**a**) *rubbish* tirar; *defective article* desechar, tirar; *person* echar, expulsar; poner de patitas en la calle, correr (*Mex*); (*Parl*) *bill* rechazar; (*emit*) emitir, despedir, arrojar; **to ~ out one's chest** sacar el pecho, abultar el pecho; **it has ~n many men out of work** ha privado de trabajo a muchos hombres.

(**b**) *idea, suggestion* lanzar; hacer (de improviso); *challenge* lanzar.

(**c**) *calculation* falsear; perturbar, afectar mal; (*disconcert*) *person* desconcertar, desorientar.

◆**throw over** *vt intention etc* dejar, abandonar; *friend, lover* romper con.

◆**throw together** *vt* (**a**) (*make hastily*) hacer rápidamente; construir (*etc*) a la buena de Dios; (*assemble*) reunir de prisa, juntar de cualquier manera.

(**b**) *persons* poner juntos (por casualidad); **they were ~n together by chance** se conocieron por casualidad.

◆**throw up 1** *vt* (**a**) (*cast up*) lanzar (*LAm*: echar) al aire; lanzar (*LAm*: echar) hacia arriba; *defences* levantar rápidamente, construir de prisa; *ideas etc* provocar; ofrecer, ocasionar.

(**b**) (*vomit*) vomitar, echar, devolver.

(**c**) (*give up*) *project etc* abandonar; *claim, post* renunciar a.

2 *vi* vomitar; **it makes me ~ up** (*fig*) me da asco, me repugna.

throwaway ['θrəʊəweɪ] *adj* (**a**) **~ wrapping** envase *m* desechable, envase *m* a tirar. (**b**) **~ line** palabras *fpl* al aire, observación *f* poco importante; **in a ~ tone** como quien no dice nada.

throwback ['θrəʊbæk] *n* salto *m* atrás, tornatrás *m*, reversión *f* (*to* a); **it's like a ~ to the old days** es como una reversión a los viejos tiempos.

thrower ['θrəʊəʳ] *n* lanzador *m*, -ora *f*.

throw-in ['θrəʊɪn] *n* saque *m* (de banda).

throwing ['θrəʊɪŋ] *n* (*Sport*) lanzamiento *m*.

thrown [θrəʊn] *ptp of* **throw**.

throw-out ['θrəʊaʊt] *n* cosa *f* desechada, cosa *f* inútil.

thru [θru:] (*US*) = **through**.

thrum [θrʌm] **1** *vt piano* teclear en; *guitar* rasguear, rasguear las cuerdas de. **2** *vi* teclear; rasguear las cuerdas.

thrush[1] [θrʌʃ] *n* (*Orn*) zorzal *m*, tordo *m*.

thrush[2] [θrʌʃ] *n* (*Med*) afta *f*; (*Vet*) arestín *m*.

thrust [θrʌst] **1** *n* (**a**) (*push*) empuje *m*; (*Mil*) avance *m*, ataque *m*; (*of sword*) estocada *f*; (*of dagger*) puñalada *f*; (*of knife*) cuchillada *f*.

(**b**) (*Mech*) empuje *m*.

(**c**) (*taunt*) pulla *f*; **a shrewd ~** un golpe certero, un golpe bien dado; **that was a ~ at you** eso lo dijo por ti, esa observación iba dirigida contra ti.

(**d**) (*thrustfulness*) empuje *m*, dinamismo *m*.

(**e**) (*basic meaning*: *of speech etc*) idea *f* clave.

2 (*irr*: *pret and ptp* **thrust**) *vt* (*push*) empujar; (*drive*) impeler, impulsar; (*insert*) introducir, meter (*into* en); (*insert piercingly*) clavar, hincar (*into* en); **to ~ a dagger into sb's back** clavar un puñal en la espalda de uno; **to ~ a stick into the ground** hincar un palo en el suelo; **to ~ one's hands into one's pockets** meter las manos en los bolsillos; **to ~ sb through with a sword** atravesar a uno (de parte a parte) con una espada; **with an arrow ~ through his hat** con una flecha que le atravesaba el sombrero; **to ~ one's way to the front** abrirse paso hacia adelante, empujar hacia adelante; **to ~ back** *crowd* hacer retroceder, *enemy* arrollar, rechazar, *thought* rechazar; **to ~ sth on sb** imponer algo a uno; obligar a uno a aceptar algo; **Spain had greatness ~ upon her** España recibió su grandeza sin buscarla, se le impuso la grandeza a España sin quererlo ella.

3 *vi*: **to ~ at sb** asestar un golpe a uno; **to ~ past sb** cruzar (empujando) delante de uno; **to ~ through** abrirse paso por la fuerza.

4 *vr*: **to ~ o.s. in** introducirse a la fuerza; (*fig*) entrometerse.

◆**thrust aside** *vt person* apartar bruscamente, *plan* rechazar.

◆**thrust forward 1** *vt* empujar hacia adelante.

2 *vi* seguir adelante, proseguir su marcha (*etc*), (*Mil*) avanzar.

3 *vr*: **to ~ o.s. forward** (*fig*) ponerse delante de otros, darse importancia; ofrecerse (con poca modestia).

◆**thrust out** *vt* sacar, sacar fuera; *hand* tender; *tongue* sacar; *head* asomar; **to ~ sb out of a door** expulsar (*or* echar) a uno por una puerta.

thrustful ['θrʌstfʊl] *adj*, **thrusting** ['θrʌstɪŋ] *adj* emprendedor, vigoroso, dinámico; (*pej*) agresivo.

thrustfulness ['θrʌstfʊlnɪs] *n* empuje *m*, pujanza *f*, dinamismo *m*; (*pej*) agresividad *f*.

thruway ['θru:weɪ] *n* (*US*) autopista *f* de peaje.

Thucydides [θju:'sɪdɪdi:z] *nm* Tucídides.

thud [θʌd] **1** *n* ruido *m* sordo, golpe *m* sordo; **it fell with a ~** cayó ¡zas!

2 *vi* hacer un ruido sordo, caer (*etc*) con un ruido sordo, caer ¡zas!; **to ~ across the floor** andar con pasos pesados; **he was ~ding about upstairs all night** pasó la noche andando con pasos pesados por el piso de arriba; **a shell ~ded into the hillside** una granada estalló en el monte.

thug [θʌg] *n* asesino *m*, gángster *m*; gorila *m*; gamberro *m*; (*fig, as term of abuse etc*) bruto *m*, bestia *f*, desalmado *m*.

thuggery ['θʌgərɪ] *n* gangsterismo *m*, matonismo *m*; brutalidad *f*.

thulium ['θju:lɪəm] *n* tulio *m*.

thumb [θʌm] **1** *n* pulgar *m*; **I'm all ~s today** hoy soy un manazas, hoy estoy desmañado por completo; **to be under sb's ~** estar dominado por uno; **to twiddle one's ~s** (*fig*) estar mano sobre mano; **they gave it the ~s down** lo rechazaron, lo desaprobaron; **they gave it the ~s up** lo aprobaron; **he gave me a ~s up sign** me indicó con el pulgar que todo iba bien.

2 *vt* (**a**) *book, magazine* manosear; **a well ~ed book** un libro muy manoseado.

(**b**) (*) **to ~ a lift, to ~ a ride** hacer autostop, hacer dedo (*SC*), pedir aventón (*Mex*); **to ~ a lift to London** viajar en autostop a Londres.

(**c**) **to ~ one's nose at sb** hacer un palmo de narices a uno.

◆**thumb through** *vt*: **to ~ through a book** hojear un libro.

thumb-index ['θʌm'ɪndeks] *n* índice *m* recortado, uñero *m*.

thumbnail ['θʌmneɪl] *n* uña *f* del pulgar; **~ sketch** dibujo *m* en miniatura.

thumbprint ['θʌmprɪnt] *n* impresión *f* del pulgar.

thumbscrew ['θʌmskru:] *n* empulgueras *fpl*.

thumbstall ['θʌmstɔ:l] *n* dedil *m*.

thumbtack ['θʌmtæk] *n* (*US*) chinche *f*, chincheta *f*.

thump [θʌmp] (*Brit*) **1** *n* (*blow*) golpazo *m*, porrazo *m*; (*noise of fall etc*) ruido *m* sordo; **it came down with a ~** cayó ¡zas!

2 *vt* golpear, aporrear; (*as punishment*) dar una paliza a; **to ~ the table** golpear la mesa, dar golpes en la mesa.

3 *vi* (*of heart*) latir con golpes pesados; (*of machine*) funcionar con ruido sordo, vibrar con violencia; **it came ~ing down** cayó ¡zas!; **he ~ed across the floor** anduvo con pasos pesados.

◆**thump out** *vt*: **to ~ out a tune on the piano** tocar una melodía al piano golpeando las teclas.

thumping* ['θʌmpɪŋ] **1** *adj* enorme, enorme de grande; descomunal. **2** *adv*: **a ~ great book** un enorme libro, un librote.

thunder ['θʌndəʳ] **1** *n* trueno *m*; (*loud report*) tronido *m*; (*of passing vehicle etc*) rodar *m* pesado, estruendo *m*; (*of applause*) estruendo *m*; (*of hooves*) estampido *m*; **with a face like** (*or* **as black as**) **~** con cara de pocos amigos; **there is ~ about, there is ~ in the air** amenaza tronar; **to steal sb's ~** adelantarse a uno robándole una idea (*or* un chiste, una observación *etc*).

2 *vt*: **to ~ threats against sb** fulminar amenazas contra uno; **to ~ out an order** dar una orden en tono muy fuerte; **'yes', he ~ed** 'sí', rugió.

3 *vi* tronar; **the guns ~ed in the distance** los cañones retumbaban a lo lejos; **the train ~ed past** el tren pasó con gran estruendo.

thunderbolt ['θʌndəbəʊlt] *n* rayo *m*; (*fig*) rayo *m*, bomba *f*.

thunderclap ['θʌndəklæp] *n* tronido *m*.

thundercloud ['θʌndəklaʊd] *n* nube *f* tormentosa, nubarrón *m*.

thunderflash ['θʌndəflæʃ] *n* petardo *m*.

thundering* ['θʌndərɪŋ] **1** *adj* enorme, imponente; **it's a ~ nuisance** es una tremenda lata*; **it was a ~ success** obtuvo un tremendo éxito. **2** *adv*: **a ~ great row** un ruido de todos los demonios; **it's a ~ good film** es una película la mar de buena*.

thunderous ['θʌndərəs] *adj applause etc* atronador, ensordecedor.

thunderstorm ['θʌndəstɔ:m] *n* tormenta *f*, tronada *f*.

thunderstruck ['θʌndəstrʌk] *adj* (*fig*) atónito, pasmado, estupefacto.

thundery ['θʌndərɪ] *adj weather* tormentoso, bochornoso.

Thuringia [θjʊə'rɪndʒɪə] *n* Turingia *f*.

Thur(s). *abbr of* **Thursday** jueves *m*, juev.

Thursday ['θɜ:zdɪ] *n* jueves *m*.

thus [ðʌs] *adv* así; de este modo; **~ far** hasta aquí; **~ it is that ...** así es que ..., es por eso que ...; **~, when he got home ...** así que, cuando llegó a casa ...

thwack [θwæk] = **whack**.

thwart[1] [θwɔ:t] *vt* frustrar; impedir, estorbar; *plan etc* frustrar, desbaratar; **to be ~ed at every turn** verse frustrado en todo.

thwart[2] [θwɔ:t] *n* (*Naut*) bancada *f*.

thy†† [ðaɪ] *poss adj* tu(s).

thyme [taɪm] *n* tomillo *m*.

thymus ['θaɪməs] *n* timo *m*.

thyroid ['θaɪrɔɪd] **1** *adj* tiroideo. **2** *n* (*also* **~ gland**) tiroides *m*.

thyself†† [ðaɪ'self] *pron* (*subject*) tú mismo, tú misma; (*acc, dative*) te; (*after prep*) ti (mismo, misma).

ti [ti:] *n* (*Mus*) si *m*.

tiara [tɪˈɑːrə] *n* diadema *f*; (*pope's*) tiara *f*.

Tiber [ˈtaɪbəʳ] *n* Tíber *m*.

Tiberius [taɪˈbɪərɪəs] *nm* Tiberio.

Tibet [tɪˈbet] *n* el Tibet.

Tibetan [tɪˈbetən] **1** *adj* tibetano. **2** *n* (**a**) tibetano *m*, -a *f*. (**b**) (*Ling*) tibetano *m*.

tibia [ˈtɪbɪə] *n* tibia *f*.

tic [tɪk] *n* (*Med*) tic *m*.

tich* [tɪtʃ] *n* renacuajo* *m*.

tichy* [ˈtɪtʃɪ] *adj* pequeñito*, chiquitito*.

tick[1] [tɪk] **1** *n* (**a**) (*of clock*) tictac *m*.

(**b**) (*Brit*: *moment*) momento *m*, instante *m*; **at 6 o'clock on the ~** a las 6 en punto; **to arrive at** (*or* **on**) **the ~** llegar puntualmente; **half a ~!, just a ~!** ¡un momentito!; **I shan't be a ~** tardo dos minutos nada más, termino en seguida; **he won't take two ~s to do it** lo hará en menos de nada.

(**c**) (*mark*) señal *f*, marca *f* (de aprobación); palomita *f*; **to put a ~ against sb's name** poner una señal contra el nombre de uno.

2 *vt* (*Brit*: *also* **to ~ off**) poner una señal contra; tildar.

3 *vi* hacer tictac; **I wonder what makes him ~*** me pregunto de dónde saca tanta energía.

◆**tick away, tick by** *vi*: **time is ~ing away** *or* **by** el tiempo pasa.

◆**tick off** *vt* (**a**) = **tick[1] 2**; (*count*) contar en los dedos.

(**b**) **to ~ sb off*** (*Brit*: *reprimand*) echar una bronca a uno, regañar a uno.

(**c**) **to ~ off*** (*US*: *annoy*) fastidiar, dar la lata a*.

◆**tick over** *vi* (*Brit*) (*Aut, Mech*) marchar al ralentí; (*fig*) ir tirando, mantenerse a flote; funcionar a ritmo lento.

tick[2] [tɪk] *n* (*Zool*) garrapata *f*.

tick[3] [tɪk] *n* (*cover*) funda *f*.

tick[4]* [tɪk] *n* (*Brit*: *credit*) crédito *m*; **to buy sth on ~** comprar algo de fiado; **to live on ~** vivir de fiado.

ticker* [ˈtɪkəʳ] *n* (*watch*) reloj *m*; (*heart*) corazón *m*.

ticker-tape [ˈtɪkəteɪp] *n* cinta *f* de cotizaciones.

ticket [ˈtɪkɪt] **1** *n* (*bus ~, Rail etc*) billete *m*; boleto *m* (*LAm*); (*Cine, Theat*) entrada *f*; localidad *f*, boleto *m* (*LAm*), boleta *f* (*LAm*); (*label*) etiqueta *f*, rótulo *m*; (*counterfoil*) talón *m*; (*at dry-cleaner's etc*) resguardo *m*; (*Aut*) multa *f* (por infracción del código *etc*); (*US Pol*) lista *f* de candidatos, candidatura *f*; programa *m* político, programa *m* electoral; **that's the ~!*** ¡muy bien!, ¡eso es!; ¡así me gustas!; ¡es lo que hacía falta!

2 *vt* (**a**) (*label*) rotular, poner etiqueta a. (**b**) (*US*) *passenger* expedir un billete a; **~ed passengers** viajeros *mpl* con billete, viajeros *mpl* que tienen billete.

ticket-agency [ˈtɪkɪtˌeɪdʒənsɪ] *n* (*Rail etc*) agencia *f* de viajes; (*Theat*) agencia *f* de localidades.

ticket-barrier [ˈtɪkɪtˌbærɪəʳ] *n* (*Brit Rail*) *barrera más allá de la cual se necesita billete*.

ticket-collector [ˈtɪkɪtkəˌlektəʳ] *n*, **ticket-inspector** [ˈtɪkɪtɪnˌspektəʳ] *n* revisor *m*, -ora *f*, controlador *m*, -ora *f* de boletos (*LAm*).

ticket-holder [ˈtɪkɪtˌhəʊldəʳ] *n* poseedor *m*, -ora *f* de billete; (*season ~, at theatre etc*) abonado *m*, -a *f*; (*season ~, Ftbl*) socio *m*, -a *f*; (*of travelcard etc*) titular *mf*.

ticket-office [ˈtɪkɪtˌɒfɪs] *n* (*Rail*) despacho *m* de billetes, despacho *m* de boletos (*LAm*); (*Theat etc*) taquilla *f*, boletería *f* (*LAm*).

ticket-of-leave [ˈtɪkɪtəvˈliːv] *n* (*Brit*) cédula *f* de libertad condicional; **~ man** hombre *m* bajo libertad condicional.

ticket-tout [ˈtɪkɪtˌtaʊt] *n* revendedor *m* (de entradas).

ticket-window [ˈtɪkɪtˌwɪndəʊ] *n* ventanilla *f*; (*Rail etc*) despacho *m* de billetes; (*Theat etc*) taquilla *f*.

ticking[1] [ˈtɪkɪŋ] *n* (*material*) cutí *m*, terliz *m*.

ticking[2] [ˈtɪkɪŋ] *n* (*of clock*) tictac *m*.

ticking-off* [ˈtɪkɪŋˈɒf] *n* (*Brit*) bronca *f*; **to give sb a ~** echar una bronca a uno, regañar a uno.

tickle [ˈtɪkl] **1** *n*: **to give the cat a ~** acariciar al gato; **to have a ~ behind one's ear** sentir cosquillas detrás de la oreja; **to have a ~ in one's throat** tener picor de garganta; **he never got a ~ all day** (*Fishing*) no picó pez alguno en todo el día; **at £5 he never got a ~*** a 5 libras nadie le echó un tiento*.

2 *vt* (**a**) cosquillear, hacer cosquillas a; *cat etc* acariciar.

(**b**) (*: *amuse*) divertir; hacer gracia a; (*delight*) chiflar*; **it ~d us no end** nos divirtió mucho, nos hizo mucha gracia; **we were ~d to death about it, we were ~d pink about it** nos moríamos de risa con eso*.

3 *vi*: **my ear ~s** siento cosquillas en la oreja, siento hormiguillo en la oreja; **don't, it ~s!** ¡por Dios, que me hace cosquillas!

tickler [ˈtɪkləʳ] *n* (*Brit*) problema *m* difícil.

tickling [ˈtɪklɪŋ] *n* cosquillas *fpl*.

ticklish [ˈtɪklɪʃ] *adj*, **tickly*** [ˈtɪklɪ] *adj* (**a**) cosquilloso; **to be ~** tener cosquillas, ser cosquilloso.

(**b**) *problem etc* peliagudo, espinoso; delicado; **it's a ~ business** es un asunto delicado.

ticktack [ˈtɪktæk] *n* (*Racing*) *lenguaje de signos utilizado por los corredores de apuestas en las carreras de caballos*.

tick-tock [ˈtɪkˈtɒk] *n* tictac *m*.

tic-tac-toe [ˌtɪktækˈtəʊ] *n* (*US*) tres *m* en raya.

tidal [ˈtaɪdl] *adj* de marea; **~ basin** dique *m* de marea; **~ energy** energía *f* de las mareas; **~ wave** maremoto *m*, ola *f* de marea; (*fig*) ola *f* gigantesca; **the river is ~ up to here** la marea sube hasta aquí; **the Mediterranean is not ~** en el Mediterráneo no hay mareas.

tidbit [ˈtɪdbɪt] (*US*) = **titbit**.

tiddler* [ˈtɪdləʳ] *n* (**a**) (*Brit*) (*stickleback*) espinoso *m*; (*small fish*) pececillo *m*. (**b**) (*child*) nene *m*, -a *f*.

tiddly* [ˈtɪdlɪ] *adj* (*esp Brit*) achispado*.

tiddlywink [ˈtɪdlɪwɪŋk] *n* pulga *f*; **~s** (*game*) juego *m* de pulgas.

tide [taɪd] *n* marea *f*; (*fig*) corriente *m*; marcha *f*, progreso *m*; tendencia *f*; **high ~** pleamar *f*, (*fig*) cumbre *f*, apogeo *m*; **low ~** bajamar *f*, (*fig*) punto *m* más bajo; **the rising ~ of public indignation** la creciente indignación pública; **the ~ of battle turned** cambió la suerte de la batalla; **the ~ of events** la marcha de los sucesos; **to go against the ~** ir contra la corriente; **to go with the ~** seguir la corriente.

◆**tide over** *vt*: **to ~ sb over** ayudar a uno a salvar el bache, ayudar a uno a salir de un apuro.

tideless [ˈtaɪdlɪs] *adj* sin mareas.

tideline [ˈtaɪdlaɪn] *n*, **tidemark** [ˈtaɪdmɑːk] *n* lengua *f* del agua; (*hum*) cerco *m* (de suciedad, en bañera *etc*).

tiderace [ˈtaɪdreɪs] *n* aguaje *m*, marejada *f*.

tidewater [ˈtaɪdˌwɔːtəʳ] (*Brit*) **1** *n* agua *f* de marea. **2** *attr* drenado por las mareas, costero.

tideway [ˈtaɪdweɪ] *n* canal *m* de marea.

tidily [ˈtaɪdɪlɪ] *adv* bien, en orden; aseadamente, pulcramente; metódicamente; **to be ~ dressed** ir bien vestido; **to arrange things ~** poner las cosas en orden.

tidiness [ˈtaɪdɪnɪs] *n* buen orden *m*; limpieza *f*; aseo *m*, pulcritud *f*; carácter *m* metódico.

tidings [ˈtaɪdɪŋz] *npl* noticias *fpl*.

tidy [ˈtaɪdɪ] **1** *adj* (**a**) *objects etc* en orden, ordenado; *room, desk* limpio; bien arreglado; *appearance, dress* aseado, pulcro; *person* metódico; **to get a room ~** limpiar un cuarto, arreglar un cuarto; **to make o.s. ~** asearse, arreglarse; **he has a ~ mind** tiene una mentalidad lógica, tiene una inteligencia metódica.

(**b**) (*) *pace* bastante rápido; *sum* considerable; **it cost a ~ bit** costó bastante; **he's a pretty ~ player** es un jugador bastante estimable.

2 *vt* arreglar, poner en orden, limpiar; **to ~ one's hair** arreglarse el pelo.

◆**tidy away** *vt*: **to ~ books away** devolver los libros a su lugar; **to ~ the dishes away** quitar los platos.

◆**tidy out** *vt* ordenar, limpiar, arreglar.

◆**tidy up 1** *vt* arreglar, poner en orden, limpiar.

2 *vi* arreglar las cosas, ponerlo todo en orden.

3 *vr*: **to ~ o.s. up** asearse, arreglarse.

tidy-out [ˈtaɪdɪˈaʊt] *n*, **tidy-up** [ˈtaɪdɪˈʌp] *n*: **to have a ~** ordenar (la casa, la habitación *etc*).

tie [taɪ] **1** *n* (**a**) (*bond*) lazo *m*, vínculo *m*; **the ~s of friendship** los lazos de la amistad; **the ~s of blood** los lazos del parentesco.

(**b**) (*hindrance*) estorbo *m*; **the children are a ~ in the evenings** los pequeños son un estorbo para poder salir por las tardes; **he has no ~s here** no tiene nada que le retenga aquí, no tiene nada que le impida irse de aquí.

(**c**) (*cord etc*) atadura *f*, ligazón *f*; (*Brit*: *neck~*) corbata *f*; (*Archit*) tirante *m*; (*US Rail*) traviesa *f*; (*Mus*) ligado *m*.

(**d**) (*Sport*: *match*) encuentro *m*, partido *m*.

(**e**) (*draw*) empate *m*; **it ended in a ~ at 3-all** terminó en empate a 3; **there was a ~ in the voting** en la votación resultó un empate.

2 *vt* (**a**) atar, liar; enlazar, unir; (*Mus*) ligar; *bow, knot, necktie* hacer; (*fig, with bond*) liar, ligar, vincular; **to ~ two things together** atar dos cosas; **to ~ a dog to a post** atar un perro a un poste; **to ~ sb's hands** atar las manos a uno (*also fig*); **to ~ one on*** emborracharse; **his hands are ~d** tiene las manos atadas (*also fig*); **to be ~d hand and foot** (*fig*) verse atado de pies y manos.

(**b**) (*hinder*) estorbar; (*limit*) limitar, restringir (*to* a); **we are very ~d in the evenings** por las tardes nos vemos bastante estorbados para salir; **are we ~d to this plan?** ¿estamos restringidos a este plan?; **the house is ~d to her husband's job** la casa está ligada al puesto que tiene su marido, la casa pertenece a la compañía en que trabaja su marido.

3 *vi* (*draw*) empatar; **we ~d with them 4-all** empatamos con ellos a 4.

◆**tie back** *vt hair etc* atar, liar.

◆**tie down** *vt* (**a**) atar; sujetar, afianzar (con cuerdas *etc*); inmovilizar.

(**b**) (*restrict etc*) limitar, restringir; obligar; **to ~ sb down to a task** obligar a uno a hacer una tarea; **to ~ sb down to a contract** obligar a uno a cumplir (*or* respetar) un contrato; **we can't ~ him down to a date** no podemos conseguir que fije una fecha; **we're ~d down for months to come** no podemos aceptar otro compromiso por muchos meses; **I refuse to be ~d down** me niego a atarme, no me dejaré atar; **I don't want to ~ myself down to attending** no quiero comprometerme a asistir.

◆**tie in 1** *vt* relacionar, asociar; **I'm trying to ~ that in with what was said earlier** trato de relacionar eso con lo que se dijo antes; **can you ~ in A with B?** ¿puedes compaginar A y B?

2 *vi*: **it all ~s in** todo concuerda, todo se encaja bien; **it doesn't ~ in with what he told us** no cuadra con lo que nos dijo.

◆**tie on** *vt* atar, pegar.

◆**tie together** *vt* atar, liar; *persons etc* liar, vincular.

◆**tie up 1** *vt* (**a**) (*bind*) atar, liar; envolver; (*Naut*) atracar (*to* a); **to get (o.s.) all ~d up** (*fig*) armarse un lío.

(**b**) (*esp US*: *block, stop*) obstruir, bloquear; *programme* interrumpir; *production etc* paralizar, parar; **the fog ~d up all the shipping** la niebla inmovilizó toda la navegación.

(**c**) *capital* inmovilizar; invertir (sin poder retirar); **he has a fortune ~d up in property** tiene una fortuna inmovilizada en bienes raíces.

(**d**) (*conclude*) *business* despachar, arreglar; *deal* concluir; *problem etc* resolver; **we'll soon have it all ~d up** pronto lo arreglamos todo.

(**e**) (*: *occupy*) **he's ~d up with the manager just now** ahora está conferenciando con el jefe, de momento está tratando un asunto con el jefe; **I'm ~d up tomorrow** mañana estoy liado; **he's ~d up with a girl in Lima** tiene un lío con una chica en Lima*.

(**f**) (*link*) **it's all ~d up with the fact that ...** todo depende del hecho de que ...; **the company is ~d up with a Spanish firm** la compañía tiene relaciones con una firma española.

2 *vi* (*Naut*) atracar, amarrar; (*fig*) llegar a puerto; **to ~ up at a wharf** atracar en un muelle; **to ~ up to a post** atracar a un poste.

tie-break(er) ['taɪbreɪk(əʳ)] *n* (*Tennis*) tiebreak *m*, desempate *m* (por muerte súbita); (*in quiz*) punto *m* decisivo.

tie-clip ['taɪklɪp] *n* pinza *f* de corbata.

tied [taɪd] *adj* (*Sport*) empatado; (*Mus*) ligado.

tie-in ['taɪɪn] *n* (*fig*) unión *f*; relación *f* estrecha (*between* entre).

tieless ['taɪlɪs] *adj* sin corbata.

tie-on ['taɪɒn] *adj* para atar.

tiepin ['taɪpɪn] *n* alfiler *m* de corbata.

tier [tɪəʳ] *n* grada *f*, fila *f*; piso *m*; nivel *m*; **to arrange in ~s** disponer en gradas.

tiered ['tɪəd] *adj* con gradas, en una serie de gradas; **steeply ~** con gradas en fuerte pendiente; **a three-~ cake** un pastel de tres pisos.

tie-tack ['taɪtæk] *n* (*US*) = **tiepin**.

tie-up ['taɪʌp] *n* (*link*) enlace *m*; vinculación *f*; (*by strike etc*) paralización *f*; (*US*: *of traffic*) bloqueo *m*; embotellamiento *m*; (*US*: *stoppage*) interrupción *f*.

tiff* [tɪf] *n* riña *f*, pelea *f*.

tiffin ['tɪfɪn] *n* (*Indian*) almuerzo *m*.

tig [tɪg] *n*: **to play ~** jugar al marro.

tiger ['taɪgəʳ] *n* tigre *mf*.

tigerish ['taɪgərɪʃ] *adj* (*fig*) salvaje, feroz.

tiger lily ['taɪgə,lɪlɪ] *n* tigridia *f*.

tiger moth [,taɪgə'mɒθ] *n* mariposa *f* tigre.

tiger's eye ['taɪgəz'aɪ] *n* (*Min*) ojo *m* de gato.

tight [taɪt] **1** *adj* (**a**) (*not leaky*) impermeable; a prueba de ...; *container* estanco; *joint* hermético.

(**b**) (*taut*) tieso, tirante; (*stretched*) estirado; *nut etc* apretado; *clothing* ajustado, ceñido, (*too ~*) apretado, estrecho; *embrace* estrecho; *box* bien cerrado; *curve* cerrado; *schedule* apretado; *control* riguroso, estricto; **as ~ as a drum** muy tirante; **it's a ~ fit** me (*etc*) viene muy estrecho; **to be in a ~ corner** (*or* **situation**) estar en un aprieto; **to keep ~ hold of sth** seguir fuertemente agarrado a algo; (*fig*) controlar algo rigurosamente.

(**c**) *money* escaso; *credit* difícil.

(**d**) (*close-fisted*) agarrado, tacaño.

(**e**) (*: *drunk*) borracho; **to be ~** estar borracho; **to get ~** emborracharse (*on gin* bebiendo ginebra).

2 *adv* herméticamente; de modo tirante; apretadamente, estrechamente; **the door was shut ~** la puerta estaba bien cerrada; **shut the box ~** cierra bien la caja; **screw the nut up ~** aprieta la tuerca a fondo, apriete bien la tuerca; **to hold sth ~** agarrar algo fuertemente; **to hold sb ~** abrazar a uno estrechamente; **hold ~!** ¡agárrense bien!; **to sit ~** estarse quieto, no moverse, seguir en su lugar; seguir sin hacer nada; **sleep ~!** ¡que duermas bien!; **to squeeze sb's hand ~** apretar mucho la mano a uno.

3 *npl*: **~s** (*Brit*) panti *m*, medias *fpl* (enteras); (*Theat*) mallas *fpl*; (*US*) traje *m* de malla.

tighten ['taɪtn] **1** *vt* (*also* **to ~ up**) (**a**) (*tauten*) atiesar, estirar; estrechar; *nut etc* apretar.

(**b**) (*fig*) *regulations etc* hacer más severo; apretar; hacer observar, velar por la observancia de; *restrictions* reforzar, apretar, aplicar en forma más rigurosa.

2 *vi* atiesarse, estirarse; estrecharse; apretarse; **to ~ up on** *V* **1**.

◆**tighten up** *vti* = **tighten**.

tightening ['taɪtnɪŋ] *n* tensamiento *m*.

tight-fisted ['taɪt'fɪstɪd] *adj* agarrado, tacaño.

tight-fitting ['taɪt'fɪtɪŋ] *adj* muy ajustado, muy ceñido.

tight-knit ['taɪt'nɪt] *adj* estrechamente unidos entre sí; *family etc* muy unido.

tight-lipped ['taɪt'lɪpt] *adj* (*fig*) callado; hermético; **to maintain a ~ silence** mantener un silencio absoluto; **he's being very ~ about it** sobre eso no dice nada en absoluto.

tightly ['taɪtlɪ] *adv V* **tight 2**.

tightness ['taɪtnɪs] *n* impermeabilidad *f*; lo estanco; lo hermético; tensión *f*, tirantez *f*; lo apretado, estrechez *f*; escasez *f*; tacañería *f*; **to have a ~ in the chest** sentir opresión en el pecho.

tightrope ['taɪtrəʊp] *n* alambre *m* (de circo *etc*); **to be on a ~, to be walking a ~** (*fig*) andar a la cuerda floja, hacer equilibrios (*between A and B* entre A y B).

tightrope walker ['taɪtrəʊp,wɔːkəʳ] *n* funámbulo *m*, -a *f*, volatinero *m*, -a *f*, equilibrista *mf*.

tightwad* ['taɪtwɒd] *n* (*US*) cicatero *m*.

tigress ['taɪgrɪs] *n* tigresa *f*, tigre hembra *f*.

Tigris ['taɪgrɪs] *n* Tigris *m*.

tilde ['tɪldɪ] *n* tilde *f*.

tile [taɪl] **1** *n* (*roof ~*) teja *f*; (*floor ~*) baldosa *f*; (*wall ~, coloured, glazed*) azulejo *m*; (**) sombrero *m*; **he's got a ~ loose*** le falta un tornillo*; **to spend a night on the ~s** (*Brit*) estar fuera toda la noche, pasar la noche de juerga*.

2 *vt roof* tejar; cubrir de tejas; *floor* embaldosar; *wall* adornar con azulejos; **~d roof** techo *m* de tejas, tejado *m*.

tiling ['taɪlɪŋ] *n* tejas *fpl*, tejado *m*; baldosas *fpl*, embaldosado *m*; azulejos *mpl*.

till[1] [tɪl] *vt* (*Agr*) cultivar, labrar.

till[2] [tɪl] **1** *prep* hasta. **2** *conj* hasta que; (*for usage V* **until**).

till[3] [tɪl] *n* (*drawer*) cajón *m*; (*machine*) caja *f* registradora; **they caught him with his hand** (*or* **fingers**) **in the ~** le cogieron robando (dentro de la empresa *etc*).

tillage ['tɪlɪdʒ] *n* cultivo *m*, labranza *f*.

tiller ['tɪləʳ] *n* (*Naut*) caña *f* del timón.

tilt [tɪlt] **1** *n* (**a**) (*sloping*) inclinación *f*; ladeo *m*; **it is on the ~, it has a ~ to it** está ladeado; **to give sth a ~** inclinar algo, ladear algo.

(**b**) (*Hist*) torneo *m*, justa *f*; (**at**) **full ~** a toda velocidad; **to run full ~ into a wall** dar de lleno contra una pared; **to have a ~ at** arremeter contra.

2 *vt* inclinar, ladear; **~ it this way** inclínalo hacia este lado; **~ it back** inclínalo hacia atrás; **to ~ over a table** volcar una mesa.

3 *vi* (**a**) inclinarse, ladearse; **to ~ over** (*lean*) inclinarse, (*fall*) volcarse, caer; **lorry that ~s up** camión *m* que bascula, camión *m* basculante.

(**b**) (*Hist*) justar; **to ~ against** arremeter contra.

tilth [tɪlθ] *n* cultivo *m*, labranza *f*; condición *f* (cultivable) de la tierra.

Tim [tɪm] *nm familiar form of* **Timothy**.

timber ['tɪmbəʳ] **1** *n* (*material*) madera *f* (de construcción);

(*growing trees*) árboles *mpl*, árboles *mpl* de monte; bosque *m*; (*beam*) madero *m*, viga *f*, (*Naut*) cuaderna *f*; **~!** ¡ojo, que cae!, ¡agua va!

2 *vt* enmaderar.

timbered ['tɪmbəd] *adj house etc* enmaderado; *land* arbolado; **the land is well ~** el terreno tiene mucho bosque.

timbering ['tɪmbərɪŋ] *n* maderamen *m*.

timberland ['tɪmbəlænd] *n* (*US*) tierras *fpl* maderables.

timberline ['tɪmbəlaɪn] *n* límite *m* forestal.

timber merchant ['tɪmbəˌmɜːtʃənt] *n* (*Brit*) maderero *m*.

timber-wolf ['tɪmbəˌwʊlf] *n*, *pl* **timber-wolves** ['tɪmbəˌwʊlvz] lobo *m* gris norteamericano.

timber-yard ['tɪmbəjɑːd] *n* (*Brit*) almacén *m* de madera.

timbre [tɛ̃ːmbr] *n* timbre *m*.

timbrel ['tɪmbrəl] *n* pandereta *f*.

time [taɪm] **1** *n* (**a**) (*gen*) tiempo *m*; (**Father**) **T~** el Tiempo; **~ flies** el tiempo vuela; **~ presses** el tiempo apremia; **~ will show, ~ will tell** el tiempo lo dirá; **race against ~** carrera *f* contra (el) reloj; **for all ~** para siempre; **in (good) ~, in process of ~, as ~ goes on** andando el tiempo, con el tiempo; **all in good ~** todo a su tiempo; **all in good ~!** ¡despacio!; **one of the best of all ~** uno de los mejores de todos los tiempos; **~ and motion study** estudios *mpl* de tiempo y movimiento, estudio *m* de desplazamientos y tiempos; **~!** ¡es la hora!, ¡la hora!; **~ gentlemen please!** ¡se cierra!; **half the ~ he's drunk** la mayor parte del tiempo está borracho; **it's only a matter** (*or* **question**) **of ~ before it falls** sólo es cuestión de tiempo antes de que caiga; **my ~ is my own** dispongo libremente de mi tiempo; **to find ~ for** encontrar tiempo para; **to gain ~** ganar tiempo; **we have ~, we have plenty of ~** tenemos tiempo de sobra; **to have no ~ to read** no tener tiempo para leer; (*fig*) **I've no ~ for him** no le aguanto; **I've no ~ for sport** (*fig*) desprecio los deportes, no apruebo los deportes; **to have ~ on one's hands** estar ocioso; no saber cómo ocuparse; tener tiempo de sobra; **to kill ~** entretener el tiempo, pasar el rato, matar el tiempo; **to lose ~** atrasarse; **to lose no ~ in** + *ger* no tardar en + *infin*; **there is no ~ to lose** (*or* **to be lost**) no hay que perder tiempo; **to make ~*** (*US*) ganar tiempo, apresurarse; **he's making ~ with his secretary*** (*US*) está tratando de acostarse con su secretaria; **to make up for lost ~** recuperar el tiempo perdido; **to play for ~** tratar de ganar tiempo; **to be pressed for ~** andar escaso de tiempo; **it takes ~** requiere tiempo, lleva su tiempo; **it takes ~ to** + *infin* se tarda bastante en + *infin*; **it took him all his ~ to find it** sólo encontrarlo le ocupó bastante tiempo; **to take one's ~** hacer las cosas con calma; ir despacio, no darse prisa; **he's certainly taking his ~** es cierto que tarda bastante ya; **take your ~!** tómate el tiempo que necesites, ¡no hay prisa!; **to take ~ by the forelock** tomar la ocasión por los pelos; *V* **waste 3**.

(**b**) (*period*) período *m*, tiempo *m*; plazo *m*; **~ deposit** depósito *m* a plazo; **~ loan** préstamo *m* a plazo fijo; **a long ~** mucho tiempo; **a long ~ ago** hace mucho tiempo, hace tiempo; **a short ~** poco tiempo, un rato; **a short ~ ago** hace poco; **a short ~ after** poco tiempo después, al poco tiempo; **for a ~** durante un rato, durante una temporada; **for a long ~ to come** hasta que haya transcurrido mucho tiempo; **for some ~ past** de algún tiempo a esta parte; **for the ~ being** por ahora; **he hasn't been seen for a long ~** hace mucho tiempo que no se le ve; **in (good) ~** (*early*) a tiempo, con tiempo; **to arrive in good ~** llegar con bastante anticipación; **let me know in good ~** avíseme con anticipación; **he'll come in his own good ~** vendrá cuando le parezca conveniente; **we made good ~ on the journey** el viaje ha sido rápido; el viaje ha sido sin problemas; **in a short ~** en breve; con la mayor brevedad; **in a short ~ they were all gone** muy pronto habían desaparecido todos; **in 2 weeks' ~** en 2 semanas; al cabo de 2 semanas; **in no ~ at all** en muy poco tiempo; **within the agreed ~** dentro del plazo convenido; dentro del límite de tiempo que se había fijado; **to do ~*** cumplir una condena; **it will last our ~** durará lo que nosotros; **to serve one's ~** hacer su aprendizaje; **to take a long ~ to** + *infin* tardar mucho en + *infin*.

(**c**) (*at work*) horas *fpl* de trabajo; jornada *f*; **he did the draft in** (*or* (*US*) **on**) **his own ~** preparó el borrador fuera de (las) horas de trabajo; **to be on** (*or* **to work**) **short ~** trabajar en jornadas reducidas; **on Saturdays they pay ~ and a half** los sábados pagan lo normal más la mitad; **~ and motion study** estudio *m* de tiempos y movimientos; *V also* **full-~, short-~** *etc*.

(**d**) (*epoch, period*; *often* **~s**) época *f*, tiempos *mpl*; **a sign of the ~s** un indicio de cómo cambian los tiempos; **the good old ~s** los buenos tiempos pasados; **the ~s we live in** los tiempos en que vivimos; **these naughty ~s** estos tiempos tan escandalosos; **that was all before my ~** todo eso fue antes de mis tiempos; **in my ~(s)** en mis tiempos; **in Victoria's ~(s)** en los tiempos de Victoria, en la época victoriana, bajo el reinado de Victoria; **in our ~** en nuestra época; **in ~s past, in former** (*or* **olden, older**) **~s** en otro tiempo, antiguamente; **in ~s to come** en los siglos venideros; **~s are somewhat hard** atravesamos un período bastante difícil; **those were tough ~s** fue un período de grandes dificultades; **what ~s they were!, what ~s we had!** ¡qué tiempos aquellos!; **how ~s change!** ¡cómo cambian las cosas!; **the ~s are out of joint** los tiempos actuales estan revueltos; **one of the greatest footballers of our ~** uno de los mejores futbolistas de nuestros tiempos; **~ was when ...** hubo un tiempo en que ...; **to be behind the ~s** (*person*) ser un atrasado; estar atrasado de noticias; (*thing*) estar fuera de moda, haber quedado anticuado; **to fall on hard ~s** estar en el tiempo de las vacas flacas; **to keep abreast of** (*or* **up with**) **the ~s, to move with the ~s** ir con los tiempos, mantenerse al día.

(**e**) (*moment, point of ~*) momento *m*; **any ~** en cualquier momento; **come (at) any ~ (you like)** ven cuando quieras; **it might happen (at) any ~** podría ocurrir de un momento a otro; **at the ~, at that ~** por entonces; en aquella época, en aquel entonces; a la sazón; **at this particular ~** en este preciso momento; **at the present ~** en la actualidad, actualmente; **at one ~** en cierto momento, en cierta época; había momentos en que ...; **at one ~ ..., at another ~ ...** ora ..., ora ...; **Rodriguez, at one ~ minister of ...** Rodríguez, ministro que fue de ...; **at no ~** jamás, nunca; **at a given ~** en un momento convenido; **at a convenient ~** en un momento oportuno; **at the proper ~** en el momento oportuno; **at the same ~** al mismo tiempo; a la vez; **at ~s** a veces; **at all ~s** en todo momento, siempre; **at odd ~s** de vez en cuando; **at various ~s in the past** en determinados momentos del pasado; **between ~s** en los intervalos; **by this ~** ya, antes de esto; (**by**) **this ~ next year** para estas fechas del año que viene; **by the ~ we got there** antes de que llegásemos, antes de nuestra llegada, antes de llegar nosotros; cuando llegamos; **from ~ to ~** de vez en cuando; **from that ~ (on)** desde entonces, a partir de entonces; **until such ~ as he agrees** hasta que consienta; **now is the ~ to do it** éste es el momento en que conviene hacerlo; **now is the ~ to plant roses** ésta es la época para plantar las rosas; **the proper ~ to do it is ...** el momento más indicado para hacerlo es ...; **when the ~ comes** cuando llegue el momento; **the ~ has come to** + *infin* ha llegado el momento de + *infin*; **to choose one's ~ carefully** elegir con cuidado el momento más propicio; **her ~ was drawing near** se acercaba el momento de dar a luz; **his ~ was drawing near** se acercaba a la muerte; **this is no ~ for superstition** éste no es el momento para mostrarse supersticioso, tal momento no es para tomar en serio las supersticiones.

(**f**) (*as marked on clock*) hora *f*; **what's the ~?** ¿qué hora es?; **what ~ do you make it?, what do you make the ~?** ¿qué hora tienes?; **have you the right ~?** ¿tienes la hora exacta?; **the ~ is 2.30** son las 2 y media; **a watch that keeps good ~** un reloj muy exacto; **to look at the ~** mirar su reloj.

(**g**) (*as marked on clock*: *phrases with prep etc*) **(and) about ~ too!, (and) not before ~!** ¡ya era hora!; **it is about ~ he was there** ya era hora que estuviera allí; **to be 23 minutes ahead of ~** llevar 23 minutos de adelanto; **to arrive ahead of ~** llegar temprano; **to die before one's ~** morir temprano; **to be behind ~** atrasarse, retrasarse; **the train is 8 minutes behind ~** el tren lleva 8 minutos de retraso; **to come in (good) ~ for lunch** venir con bastante anticipación a comer; **we were just in ~ to see it** llegamos justo a tiempo para verlo; **to start in good ~** partir a tiempo, partir pronto; **to be on ~** ser puntual, llegar (*etc*) puntualmente; llegar a la hora exacta; **to be up to ~** llegar sin retraso; **at any ~ of the day or night** en cualquier momento del día o de la noche; **at this ~ of day** a esta hora; **at any one ~ there is room for 12 readers** en un momento dado hay sitio para 12 lectores; **to pass the ~ of day with sb** detenerse a charlar un rato con uno; **I wouldn't give him the ~ of day** a mi él me tiene sin cuidado, me importa un rábano; **it's ~ for tea** es la hora del té; ha llegado la hora de servir el té; **it's coffee ~** es la hora del café; **it's ~ to go** ya es hora de marcharse;

it's high ~ ya era hora; **it's high ~ that ...** ya va siendo hora de + *infin*, es hora de que + *subj*; **there's a ~ and a place for everything** todo tiene su hora y su lugar debidos; éste no es ni el momento ni el lugar indicado.

(**h**) (*as marked by calendar*) época *f*; temporada *f*; estación *f*; **~ payment** (*US*) pago *m* a plazos; **at my ~ of life** a mi edad, con los años que yo tengo; **at this ~ of year** en esta época del año; **it's a lovely ~ of year** es una estación encantadora; **my favourite ~ is autumn** mi estación predilecta es el otoño.

(**i**) (**good** ~ *etc*) **to have a good ~ (of it)** pasarlo bien; **have a good ~!** ¡que lo pases bien!; **to give sb a good ~** hacer que uno se divierta; hacer que uno lo pase bien; **she's out for a good ~** se propone divertirse; **all they want to do is have a good ~** no quieren más que divertirse; **we had a high old ~*** lo hemos pasado en grande*; **we have a lovely ~** lo pasamos la mar de bien*; **I hope you have a lovely ~!** ¡que os divirtáis!; **to have a rough** (*or* **bad, thin** *etc*) **~ of it** pasarlo mal, pasarlas negras; **what a ~ we'll have with the girls!** ¡vaya juergazo que nos vamos a correr con las chicas!*; **the big ~** (*US*) el gran mundo, la primera división; **to make it into the big ~*** abrirse paso y entrar en el gran mundo, ascender a primera división, triunfar.

(**j**) (*occasion*) vez *f*; **3 ~s** 3 veces; **this ~** esta vez; **last ~** la última vez; **next ~** la próxima vez; **the first ~ I did it** la primera vez que lo hice; **for the first ~** por primera vez; **for the last ~** por última vez; **~ after ~, ~ and again** repetidas veces; **each ~, every ~** cada vez; **each ~ that ...** cada vez que ...; **he won every ~** ganó todas las veces; **it's the best, every ~!** ¡es el mejor, no hay duda!; **give me beer every ~!** ¡para mí, siempre cerveza!; **many ~s** muchas veces; **many a ~ I saw him act, many's the ~ I saw him act** muchas veces le vi representar; **several ~s** varias veces; **the second ~ round** en la segunda vuelta; **third ~ lucky!** ¡a la tercera va la vencida!; **nine ~s out of ten, ninety-nine ~s out of a hundred** (*fig*) casi siempre; **I remember the ~ when ...** me acuerdo de cuando ...; **to bide one's ~** esperar la hora propicia; **for weeks at a ~** durante semanas enteras, durante semanas seguidas; **to do 2 things at a ~** hacer 2 cosas a la vez; hacer 2 cosas al mismo tiempo; **to eat biscuits 4 at a ~** comer 4 galletas a la vez; **he ran upstairs 3 at a ~** subió la escalera de 3 en 3 escalones.

(**k**) (*Math*) **4 ~s 3** 4 por 3; **it's 4 ~s as fast as yours** es 4 veces más rápido que el tuyo.

(**l**) (*adv phrase*) **at the same ~ you must remember that ...** de todas formas conviene recordar que ...; **at the same ~ as** (*fig*) al mismo tiempo que, al igual que, a la par que.

(**m**) (*Mus*) tiempo *m*; compás *m*; **in 3/4 ~** al compás de 3 por 4; **in ~ to the music** al compás de la música; **to beat** (*or* **keep**) **~** llevar el compás; **to get out of ~** perder el ritmo, dejar de llevar el compás; **to mark ~** (*Mil*) marcar el paso; (*fig*) esperar, hacer tiempo.

(**n**) (*Mech*) **the ignition is out of ~** el encendido está fuera de fase, el encendido funciona mal.

2 *vt* (**a**) (*reckon ~ of*) medir el tiempo de, calcular la duración de; *race* cronometrar.

(**b**) (*regulate*) *watch* regular, poner en hora; **it is ~d to go off at midnight** debe estallar a medianoche, la espoleta está graduada para que explote a medianoche; **the train is ~d for 6** el tren debe llegar a las 6.

(**c**) (*do at right ~*) hacer en el momento oportuno; **you ~d that perfectly** elegiste a la perfección el momento para hacerlo (*etc*).

time-bomb ['taɪmbɒm] *n* bomba *f* de efecto retardado.

time-capsule ['taɪm,kæpsjuːl] *n* cápsula *f* del tiempo.

time-card ['taɪm,kɑːd] *n* tarjeta *f* de registro horario.

time-clock ['taɪm'klɒk] *n* reloj *m* registrador, reloj *m* de control de asistencia.

time-consuming ['taɪmkən,sjuːmɪŋ] *adj* que exige mucho tiempo.

time-exposure ['taɪmɪk,spəʊʒər] *n* pose *f*, exposición *f*.

time-fuse ['taɪmfjuːz] *n* temporizador *m*, espoleta *f* graduada, espoleta *f* de tiempo.

time-honoured, (*US*) **time-honored** ['taɪm,ɒnəd] *adj* sacramental, consagrado, clásico.

timekeeper ['taɪm,kiːpər] *n* (*watch*) reloj *m*, cronómetro *m*; (*person*) cronometrador *m*, -ora *f*, apuntador *m*, -ora *f* del tiempo; **to be a good ~** ser puntual.

time-lag ['taɪmlæg] *n* intervalo *m*; retraso *m*, pérdida *f* de tiempo; desfase *m*.

time-lapse photography ['taɪmlæpsfə'tɒgrəfɪ] *n* fotografía *f* de lapso de tiempo.

timeless ['taɪmlɪs] *adj* eterno; atemporal; *race etc* sin limitación de tiempo.

timelessness ['taɪmlɪsnɪs] *n* atemporalidad *f*.

time-limit ['taɪm,lɪmɪt] *n* limitación *f* de tiempo; (*esp Comm*) plazo *m*; (*closing date*) fecha *f* tope; **without a ~** sin limitación de tiempo; **to fix a ~ for sth** fijar un plazo para algo, señalar un plazo a algo.

timeliness ['taɪmlɪnɪs] *n* oportunidad *f*.

time-lock ['taɪmlɒk] *n* cerradura *f* de tiempo.

timely ['taɪmlɪ] *adj* oportuno.

time machine [,taɪmmə'ʃiːn] *n* máquina *f* de transporte a través del tiempo.

time-out [,taɪm'aʊt] *n* (*US*) tiempo *m* muerto.

timepiece ['taɪmpiːs] *n* reloj *m*.

timer ['taɪmər] *n* (*Culin*) avisador *m*, reloj *m* automático; (*egg ~ etc*) reloj *m* de arena; (*Mech*) reloj *m* automático; (*Aut etc*) distribuidor *m* de encendido.

timesaver ['taɪm,seɪvər] *n* ahorrador *m* de tiempo.

time-saving ['taɪm,seɪvɪŋ] *adj* que ahorra tiempo.

time-scale ['taɪmskeɪl] *n* escala *f* de tiempo.

timeserver ['taɪm,sɜːvər] *n* contemporizador *m*.

timeshare ['taɪmʃɛər] **1** *n* (**a**) (*Comput*) tiempo *m* compartido. (**b**) = **time-sharing** (**b**). **2** *vt* (*Comput*) utilizar colectivamente, utilizar en sistema de tiempo compartido.

time-sharing ['taɪm,ʃɛərɪŋ] *n* (**a**) tiempo *m* compartido (*also Comput*). (**b**) (*for holiday etc*) multipropiedad *f*; **~ flat** piso *m* en edificio de multipropiedad.

time-sheet ['taɪmʃiːt] *n* hoja *f* de asistencia, hoja *f* de horas trabajadas.

time-signal ['taɪm,sɪgnl] *n* señal *f* horaria.

time-signature ['taɪm'sɪgnɪtʃər] *n* compás *m*, signatura *f* de compás.

time-slice ['taɪmslaɪs] *n* fracción *f* de tiempo.

time-switch ['taɪmswɪtʃ] *n* interruptor *m* horario.

timetable ['taɪm,teɪbl] **1** *n* horario *m*; (*programme of classes etc*) programa *m*; (*of negotiations*) calendario *m*; (*as booklet*) guía *f*. **2** *vt* programar.

timetabling ['taɪmteɪblɪŋ] *n* programación *f*.

time trial ['taɪmtraɪəl] *n* prueba *f* contra reloj; cronometrada *f*.

timewarp ['taɪmwɔːp] *n* salto *m* en el tiempo, túnel *m* del tiempo.

time-wasting ['taɪmweɪstɪŋ] *adj* que hace perder tiempo.

timework ['taɪmwɜːk] *n* trabajo *m* a jornal; trabajo *m* por horas.

timeworn ['taɪmwɔːn] *adj* deteriorado por el tiempo.

time zone ['taɪmzəʊn] *n* huso *m* horario.

timid ['tɪmɪd] *adj* tímido.

timidity [tɪ'mɪdɪtɪ] *n* timidez *f*.

timidly ['tɪmɪdlɪ] *adv* tímidamente.

timidness ['tɪmɪdnɪs] *n* timidez *f*.

timing ['taɪmɪŋ] **1** *n* (*reckoning of time*) medida *f* del tiempo, medida *f* de la duración; (*rhythm*) ritmo *m*, cadencia *f*, compás *m*; (*Sport etc*) cronometraje *m*; **the ~ of this is important** importa hacer esto en el momento exacto, importa elegir el momento más propicio para hacer esto.

2 *attr* (*Mech*) de distribución, de encendido; **~ device** (*of bomb*) temporizador *m*; **~ gear** engranaje *m* de distribución; **~ mechanism** dispositivo *m* para medir el tiempo.

timorous ['tɪmərəs] *adj* temeroso, tímido; *animal* huraño, asustadizo.

Timothy ['tɪməθɪ] *nm* Timoteo.

timpani ['tɪmpənɪ] *npl* tímpanos *mpl*, atabales *mpl*.

timpanist ['tɪmpənɪst] *n* timbalero *m*.

tin [tɪn] **1** *n* (**a**) (*element, metal*) estaño *m*; (*~plate*) hojalata *f*.

(**b**) (*esp Brit: container*) lata *f*, bote *m*, pote *m* (*Mex*), tarro *m* (*And, SC*); **meat in ~s** carne *f* en lata, carne *f* enlatada.

2 *attr* de estaño; de hojalata; **~ can** lata *f*, bote *m*; **~ god** héroe *m* de cartón; **he has a ~ ear** (*US Mus*) tiene mal oído; **~ hat*** casco *m* de acero; **~ lizzie*** (*Aut*) genoveva *f*, viejo trasto *m*; **~ soldier** soldado *m* de plomo.

3 *vt* (**a**) (*cover with ~*) estañar.

(**b**) (*can*) envasar en lata, conservar en lata, enlatar; *V also* **tinned.**

tincture ['tɪŋktʃər] **1** *n* tintura *f* (*also fig, Pharm*). **2** *vt* tinturar, teñir (*with* de).

tinder ['tɪndər] *n* yesca *f* (*also fig*); **to burn like ~** arder como la yesca.

tinderbox ['tɪndəbɒks] *n* yescas *fpl*; (*fig*) polvorín *m*.

tinder-dry [,tɪndə'draɪ] *adj* muy seco, reseco.

tine [taɪn] *n* (*fork*) diente *m*; (*pitchfork*) púa *f*.

tinfoil ['tɪnfɔɪl] *n* papel *m* (de) estaño, papel *m* (de) aluminio.

ting [tɪŋ] = **tinkle.**

ting-a-ling ['tɪŋə'lɪŋ] *n* tilín *m*; **to go ~** hacer tilín.

tinge [tɪndʒ] **1** *n* tinte *m*; (*fig*) dejo *m*; matiz *m*; **not without a ~ of regret** no sin cierto sentimiento.

2 *vt* teñir (*with* de); (*fig*) matizar (*with* de); **pleasure ~d with sadness** placer *m* matizado de tristeza, placer *m* no exento de tristeza.

tingle ['tɪŋgl] **1** *n* comezón *f*; hormigueo *m* (de la piel); (*thrill*) estremecimiento *m*.

2 *vi* sentir comezón, sentir hormigueo; (*ears*) zumbar; (*thrill*) estremecerse (*with* de).

tingling ['tɪŋglɪŋ] *n* hormigueo *m*.

tingly ['tɪŋglɪ] *adj*: **~ feeling** sensación *f* de hormigueo; **my arm feels ~** siento hormigueo en el brazo; **I feel ~ all over** se me estremece todo el cuerpo.

tinker ['tɪŋkəʳ] **1** *n* (**a**) (*esp Brit*) calderero *m* hojalatero; (*gipsy*) gitano *m*.

(**b**) (*) pícaro *m*, tunante *m*; **you ~!** ¡tunante!

2 *vt* (*also* **to ~ up**) remendar; (*pej*) remendar mal, remendar chapuceramente.

3 *vi*: **to ~ with** (*mend*) tratar de reparar; (*play*) jugar con, manosear; (*and damage*) estropear; **they're only ~ing with the problem** no se esfuerzan seriamente por resolver el problema; **he's been ~ing with the car all day** ha pasado todo el día tratando de reparar el coche.

tinkle ['tɪŋkl] **1** *n* (**a**) tilín *m*, retintín *m*; campanilleo *m*, cencerreo *m*.

(**b**) (*Brit Telec**) llamada *f*; **I'll give you a ~** te llamaré.

2 *vt* hacer retiñir; hacer tintinar; hacer campanillear.

3 *vi* retiñir, tintinar; campanillear.

tinkling ['tɪŋklɪŋ] **1** *adj* que hace tilín (*etc*); **a ~ sound** un tilín (*etc*); **a ~ stream** un arroyo cantarín.

2 *n* tilín *m*, retintín *m*; campanilleo *m*, cencerreo *m*.

tin-mine ['tɪnmaɪn] *n* mina *f* de estaño.

tin-miner ['tɪn,maɪnəʳ] *n* minero *m* de estaño.

tinned [tɪnd] *adj* (*Brit*) en lata, de lata; **~ tangerines** mandarinas *fpl* en conserva.

tinnitus [tɪ'naɪtəs] *n* zumbido *m*.

tinny ['tɪnɪ] *adj* (**a**) *taste* que sabe a lata; *sound* cascado, que suena a lata. (**b**) (*) inferior, de poco valor, de pacotilla; desvencijado.

tin-opener ['tɪn,əʊpnəʳ] *n* (*Brit*) abrelatas *m*.

Tin Pan Alley [,tɪnpæn'ælɪ] *n* industria *f* de la música pop.

tinplate ['tɪnpleɪt] *n* hojalata *f*.

tinpot* ['tɪnpɒt] *adj* de pacotilla, de poca monta.

tinsel ['tɪnsəl] **1** *n* oropel *m* (*also fig*); (*cloth*) lama *f* de oro (*or* de plata).

2 *adj* de oropel; (*fig*) de oropel, de relumbrón.

tinsmith ['tɪnsmɪθ] *n* hojalatero *m*.

tint [tɪnt] **1** *n* tinte *m*, matiz *m*, color *m*; media tinta *f*.

2 *vt* teñir, matizar (*blue* de azul); **it's yellow ~ed with red** es amarillo matizado de rojo; **to ~ one's hair** teñirse el pelo.

tintack ['tɪntæk] *n* (*Brit*) tachuela *f*.

tinted ['tɪntɪd] *adj glass, windscreen* tintado; *spectacles* ahumado.

tintinnabulation ['tɪntɪ,næbjʊ'leɪʃən] *n* campanilleo *m*.

tiny ['taɪnɪ] *adj* pequeñito, chiquitín, diminuto, minúsculo.

tip¹ [tɪp] **1** *n* (*end*) punta *f*, cabo *m*, extremidad *f*; (*of stick etc*) regatón *m*, casquillo *m*; (*of finger*) yema *f*, punta *f*; (*of cigarette*) boquilla *f*, embocadura *f*; **from ~ to toe** de pies a cabeza; **I had it on the ~ of my tongue** lo tenía en la punta de la lengua; **it's only the ~ of the iceberg** no es más que la punta del iceberg.

2 *vt* poner regatón a; **~ped with steel** con punta de acero.

tip² [tɪp] **1** *n* (**a**) (*gratuity*) propina *f*, gratificación *f*; **to give** (*or* **leave**) **sb a ~** dar una propina a uno.

(**b**) (*hint*) aviso *m*, advertencia *f*; consejo *m*, indicación *f*; (*to police etc*) soplo* *m*, chivatazo* *m*; (*Racing*) confidencia *f*; pronóstico *m* confidencial; **let me give you a ~** permítame darle un consejo; **if you take my ~** si sigues mi consejo; **the horse is a hot ~ for the 2.30** se pronostica con seguridad que el caballo ganará la carrera de las 2 y media.

2 *vt* (**a**) (*tap, strike*) golpear ligeramente, tocar ligeramente (al pasar), chocar ligeramente con; **to ~ one's hat to sb** tocarse el sombrero para saludar a uno.

(**b**) (*reward*) dar una propina a, dejar una propina para; **to ~ sb a pound** dar a uno una libra de propina; **to ~ sb generously** dar a uno una propina generosa.

(**c**) *winner* pronosticar, recomendar, elegir; **I ~ that horse to win** pronostico que ganará ese caballo; **he is being freely ~ped for the job** muchos creen que le darán el puesto; **he is strongly ~ped as prime minister** se pronostica con confianza que será primer ministro.

tip³ [tɪp] **1** *n* (*Brit*) (*rubbish ~*) vertedero *m*, basurero *m*, tiradero *m* (*LAm*); escombrera *f*; **this room is a ~*** este cuarto es un basurero.

2 *vt* (*incline*) inclinar, ladear; *drinking vessel* empinar; *seat* abatir, levantar; **to ~ away** *liquid* vaciar, verter, echar; **it's ~ping it down*** está lloviendo a cántaros; **to ~ sb off his seat** hacer que uno caiga de su asiento; **to ~ sb into the water** hacer caer a uno al agua (empujándole); **he ~s the scales at 100 kg** pesa 100 kg; **to ~ one's hand*** (*US*: **one's mitt‡**) delatarse a sí mismo involuntariamente.

3 *vi* (*incline*) inclinarse, ladearse; (*topple*) tambalearse; **he ~ped off into the sea** perdió el equilibrio y cayó al mar.

◆**tip back, tip backward(s) 1** *vt* inclinar hacia atrás.

2 *vi* inclinarse hacia atrás.

◆**tip forward(s) 1** *vt* inclinar hacia adelante.

2 *vi* inclinarse hacia adelante.

◆**tip off** *vt* avisar, notificar; **to ~ sb off** advertir a uno clandestinamente; **the police had beed ~ped off** la policía había recibido un soplo.

◆**tip out** *vt*: **to ~ out the contents of a box** verter el contenido de una caja, vaciar una caja; **all the passengers were ~ped out** todos los pasajeros cayeron fuera.

◆**tip over 1** *vt* volcar.

2 *vi* volcarse; caer.

◆**tip up 1** *vt* (*incline*) inclinar, ladear; *container* volcar; *person* hacer perder el equilibrio; hacer caer, volcar; derribar.

2 *vi* volcarse; (*seat*) abatirse, levantarse; (*lorry etc*) bascular.

tip-cart ['tɪpkɑːt] *n* volquete *m*.

tip-off ['tɪpɒf] *n* advertencia *f* (clandestina), aviso *m*; soplo* *m*, chivatazo* *m*.

tipped [tɪpt] *adj* (*Brit*) *cigarette* emboquillado, con filtro.

tipper ['tɪpəʳ] *n* volquete *m*.

tippet ['tɪpɪt] *n* esclavina *f*.

Tipp-Ex ['tɪpeks] ® **1** *n* Tippex ® *m*, corrector *m*. **2** *vt* (*also* **to ~ out, to ~ over**) corregir con Tippex.

tipple ['tɪpl] **1** *n* bebida *f* (alcohólica); **his ~ is Cointreau** él bebe Cointreau; **what's your ~?** ¿qué quieres tomar?

2 *vi* beber más de la cuenta; envasar, empinar el codo.

tippler ['tɪpləʳ] *n* bebedor *m*, -ora *f*.

tippy-toe ['tɪpɪtəʊ] (*US*) = **tiptoe.**

tipsily ['tɪpsɪlɪ] *adv* como borracho; **to walk ~** andar con pasos de borracho.

tipsiness ['tɪpsɪnɪs] *n* vinolencia *f*, chispa* *f*.

tipster ['tɪpstəʳ] *n* pronosticador *m*.

tipsy ['tɪpsɪ] *adj* achispado*, bebido, tomado (*LAm*).

tiptoe ['tɪptəʊ] **1** *n*: **to walk on ~** caminar de puntillas; **to stand on ~** ponerse de puntillas.

2 *vi*: **to ~ across the floor** atravesar el suelo de puntillas; **to ~ to the window** ir de puntillas a la ventana; **to ~ in** entrar de puntillas; **to ~ out** salir de puntillas.

tiptop ['tɪp'tɒp] *adj* de primera, excelente; **in ~ condition** en excelentes condiciones; **a ~ show** un espectáculo de primerísima calidad.

tip-up ['tɪpʌp] *attr lorry* basculante; *seat* abatible.

tirade [taɪ'reɪd] *n* invectiva *f*, diatriba *f*.

tire¹ ['taɪəʳ] **1** *vt* cansar, fatigar; (*bore*) aburrir.

2 *vi* cansarse, fatigarse; aburrirse; **to ~ of** cansarse de; aburrirse con; **she ~s easily** se cansa pronto.

◆**tire out** *vt*: **to ~ sb out** cansar a uno, rendir a uno de cansancio, agotar las fuerzas de uno.

tire² ['taɪəʳ] *n* (*US*) = **tyre.**

tired ['taɪəd] *adj* (**a**) *movement, voice* cansado; **in a ~ voice** con voz cansada; **the ~ old clichés** los lugares comunes de siempre, los tópicos trillados.

(**b**) *person* cansado, fatigado; **to be ~** estar cansado; **to be ~ out** estar rendido, estar agotado; **to be ~ and emotional, to be as ~ as a newt** (*euph*) estar mareado; **I'm ~ of all that** estoy harto de todo eso; **to get** (*or* **grow**) **~ of doing sth** cansarse de hacer algo; **I get ~ of telling you** estoy harto de decírtelo; **you make me ~** me fastidias.

tiredly ['taɪədlɪ] *adv walk etc* como cansado; *say* con voz cansada.

tiredness ['taɪədnɪs] *n* cansancio *m*, fatiga *f*.

tireless ['taɪəlɪs] *adj* infatigable, incansable.

tirelessly ['taɪəlɪslɪ] *adv* infatigablemente, incansablemente.

tiresome ['taɪəsəm] *adj* molesto, fastidioso; *person* pesado; **how very ~!** ¡qué lata!; **he's a ~ sort** es un pesado; **he can be ~** a veces es un pesado.

tiresomeness [ˈtaɪəsəmnɪs] *n* molestia *f*, fastidio *m*, lo fastidioso; pesadez *f*.

tiring [ˈtaɪərɪŋ] *adj* molesto, fatigoso, que cansa, agotador; **after a ~ journey** después de un viaje cansado; **it's ~ work** es un trabajo agotador.

tiro [ˈtaɪərəʊ] *n* novicio *m*, -a *f*, principiante *mf*.

tisane [tɪˈzæn] *n* tisana *f*.

tissue [ˈtɪʃuː] *n* (*cloth*) tisú *m*, lama *f*; (*handkerchief*) pañuelo *m* de papel; (*Anat etc*) tejido *m*; **a ~ of lies** una sarta de mentiras; **~ paper** papel *m* (de) seda.

tit[1] [tɪt] *n* (*Orn*) paro *m*; (*blue~*) herrerillo *m* común; (*coal~*) carbonero *m* garrapinos; (*long-tailed ~*) mito *m*.

tit[2] [tɪt] *n*: **~ for tat!** ¡donde las dan las toman!; **so that was ~ for tat** así que ajustamos cuentas, así que le pagué en la misma moneda.

tit[3]‡ [tɪt] *n* (**a**) (*Anat*) teta* *f*; pezón *m*; **~s** tetas* *fpl*; **to get on sb's ~s** sacar de quicio a uno, cabrear a uno*. (**b**) (*fool*) gilipollas‡ *m*.

Titan [ˈtaɪtən] *n* titán *m*.

titanic [taɪˈtænɪk] *adj* titánico; inmenso, gigantesco.

titanium [tɪˈteɪnɪəm] *n* titanio *m*.

titbit [ˈtɪtbɪt] *n*, (*US*) **tidbit** [ˈtɪdbɪt] *n* golosina *f* (*also fig*); (*news*) pedazo *m*.

titch* [tɪtʃ], **titchy*** [ˈtɪtʃɪ] = **tich, tichy**.

titfer‡ [ˈtɪtfəʳ] *n* (*Brit*) chapeo‡ *m*.

tithe [taɪð] *n* (*Eccl*) diezmo *m*.

Titian [ˈtɪʃɪən] *nm* Ticiano.

titillate [ˈtɪtɪleɪt] *vt* estimular, excitar, encandilar.

titillation [ˌtɪtɪˈleɪʃən] *n* estimulación *f*, excitación *f*, encandilamiento *m*.

titivate [ˈtɪtɪveɪt] **1** *vt* emperejilar, ataviar, adornar. **2** *vi* emperejilarse, ataviarse; arreglarse.

title [ˈtaɪtl] **1** *n* (**a**) (*appellation, heading*) título *m*; (*Sport*) título *m*, campeonato *m*; **noble ~, ~ of nobility** título *m* de nobleza; **what ~ are you giving the book?** ¿qué título vas a dar al libro?, ¿cómo vas a titular el libro?; **what ~ should I give him?** ¿qué tratamiento debo darle?; **George V gave him a ~** Jorge V le ennobleció.

(**b**) (*Jur*) título *m*, derecho *m*; **his ~ to the property** su derecho a la propiedad.

2 *vt* titular, intitular.

titled [ˈtaɪtld] *adj* con título de nobleza, noble.

title deed [ˈtaɪtldiːd] *n* título *m* de propiedad.

title-fight [ˈtaɪtlfaɪt] *n* combate *m* por un título.

title-holder [ˈtaɪtlˌhəʊldəʳ] *n* titular *mf*, campeón *m*, -ona *f*.

title-page [ˈtaɪtlpeɪdʒ] *n* portada *f*.

title role [ˈtaɪtlˈrəʊl] *n* papel *m* principal.

titmouse [ˈtɪtmaʊs] *n*, *pl* **titmice** [ˈtɪtmaɪs] *V* **tit**[1].

titrate [ˈtaɪtreɪt] *vt* valorar.

titration [taɪˈtreɪʃən] *n* valoración *f*.

titter [ˈtɪtəʳ] **1** *n* risa *f* disimulada. **2** *vi* reírse disimuladamente.

tittle [ˈtɪtl] *n* pizca *f*, ápice *m*; **there's not a ~ of truth in it** eso no tiene ni pizca de verdad.

tittle-tattle [ˈtɪtlˌtætl] *n* chismes *m*, chismografía *f*.

titty‡ [ˈtɪtɪ] *n* = **tit**[3]; **that's tough ~!** ¡mala suerte!

titular [ˈtɪtjʊləʳ] *adj* titular; nominal.

tiz* [tɪz] *n*, **tizzy*** [ˈtɪzɪ] *n*: **to be in a ~** estar nervioso, estar aturdido; **to get into a ~** ponerse nervioso, aturdirse.

TM *n* (**a**) *abbr of* **transcendental meditation.** (**b**) (*Comm*) *abbr of* **trademark.**

TN (*US Post*) *abbr of* **Tennessee.**

TNT *n abbr of* **trinitrotoluene** trinitrotolueno *m*.

to [tuː, tə] **1** *prep* (**a**) (*dat*) a; **to give sth ~ sb** dar algo a uno; **I gave it ~ my friend** se lo di a mi amigo; **the person I sold it ~** la persona a quien lo vendí; **it belongs ~ me** me pertenece a mí, es mío; **it's new ~ me** es nuevo para mí; **I said ~ myself** dije para mí; **what is that ~ me?** y eso ¿qué me importa?; **they were kind ~ me** fueron amables conmigo.

(**b**) (*of movement, direction*) a; hacia; **to go ~ the town** ir a la ciudad; **to go ~ school** ir a la escuela; **to go ~ Italy** ir a Italia; **to go ~ Rome** ir a Roma; **to go ~ Peru** ir al Perú; **to go ~ the doctor** ir al médico; **let's go ~ John's** vamos a casa de Juan; **from door ~ door** de puerta en puerta; **the road ~ Zaragoza** la carretera de Zaragoza; **it's 90 kilometres ~ Lima** de aquí a Lima hay 90 kilómetros; **~ the left** a la izquierda; **~ the west** al oeste, hacia el oeste.

(**c**) (*as far as, right up to*) hasta; **to count up ~ 20** contar hasta 20; **~ this day** hasta hoy, hasta el día de hoy; **I'll see you ~ the door** te acompaño hasta la puerta; **funds ~ the value of ...** fondos *mpl* por valor de ...; **~ some degree** hasta cierto punto; **it's accurate ~ a millimetre** es exacto hasta el milímetro; **to be wet ~ the skin** estar mojado hasta los huesos; **they perished ~ a man** perecieron todos (sin excepción); **everybody down ~ the youngest** todos hasta el más joven.

(**d**) (*against*) a, contra; **to stand back ~ back** estar espalda con espalda; **to talk to sb man ~ man** hablar con uno de hombre a hombre; **to turn a picture ~ the wall** volver un cuadro contra la pared; **to clasp sb ~ one's breast** estrechar a uno contra su pecho.

(**e**) (*of time*) a, hasta; **from morning ~ night** de la mañana a la noche, desde la mañana hasta la noche; **8 years ago ~ the day** hoy hace exactamente 8 años; **at 8 minutes ~ 10** a las 10 menos 8; **a quarter ~ 5** las 5 menos cuarto.

(**f**) (*of*) de; **wife ~ Mr Milton** mujer *f* del Sr Milton; **secretary ~ the manager** secretaria *f* del gerente; **ambassador ~ King Cole** embajador *m* cerca del rey Cole; **he is heir ~ the duke** es heredero del duque; **he was heir ~ a million** había de heredar un millón de libras; **he has been a good friend ~ us** ha sido buen amigo nuestro.

(**g**) (*of dedications*) a; **greetings ~ all our friends!** ¡saludos a todos los amigos!; **welcome ~ you all!** ¡bienvenida a todos!, ¡bienvenidos todos!; **'~ Sue Atkins'** (*in book*) 'para Sue Atkins'; **to build a monument ~ sb** erigir un monumento en honor de uno; **here's ~ you!** ¡vaya por ti!, ¡por ti!; **to drink ~ sb** brindar por uno, beber a la salud de uno.

(**h**) (*in comparisons*) a; **inferior ~** inferior a; **that's nothing ~ what is to come** eso no es nada en comparación con lo que está todavía por venir.

(**i**) (*of proportion*) a; **A is ~ B as C is ~ D** A es a B como C es a D; **by a majority of 12 ~ 10** por una mayoría de 12 a 10; **Slobodia won by 4 goals ~ 2** ganó Eslobodia por 4 goles a 2; **the odds are 8 ~ 1** los puntos de ventaja son de 8 a 1; **200 people ~ the square mile** 200 personas por milla cuadrada.

(**j**) (*concerning*) a; **what do you say ~ this?** ¿qué contestación me das a esto?, ¿cómo contestas a esto?; **what would you say ~ a beer?** ¿qué te parece una cerveza?; **that's all there is ~ it** no hay nada más; no hay ningún misterio; todo queda tan sencillo como ves; **'~ repairing pipes: ...'** (*bill*) 'Reparación de los tubos: ...'; **'~ services rendered: ...'** 'Por los servicios que se han prestado: ...'

(**k**) (*according to*) según; **~ all appearances** al parecer, según todos los indicios; **~ my way of thinking** según mi modo de pensar; **it is not ~ my taste** no me gusta; **to write ~ sb's dictation** escribir al dictado de uno; **~ the best of my recollection** que yo recuerde; **it is sung ~ the tune of 'Tipperary'** se canta con la melodía de 'Tipperary'; **they came out ~ the strains of the national anthem** salieron a los compases del himno nacional.

(**l**) (*of purpose, result*) **~ this end** con este propósito; **to come ~ sb's aid** acudir en ayuda de uno; **to sentence sb ~ death** condenar a uno a muerte; **~ my great surprise** con gran sorpresa mía; **~ my lasting shame I did nothing** con gran vergüenza mía no hice nada; **to put an army ~ flight** poner en fuga a un ejército; **to go ~ ruin** arruinarse, echarse a perder; **to run ~ seed** granar, dar en grana (*and V* **seed**).

2 *prep* (*before infin*) (**a**) (*with simple infin, not translated*) **~ know** saber, conocer; **'~ be or not ~ be'** 'ser o no ser'; (*following another verb a variety of constructions appears, for which see the verb in each case, eg*) **to forbid sb ~ do sth** prohibir a uno hacer algo; **to begin ~ do sth** comenzar a hacer algo, empezar a hacer algo; **to try ~ do sth** tratar de hacer algo, procurar hacer algo; **I want you ~ do it** quiero que lo hagas; **I wanted you ~ do it** quería que lo hicieras; **they asked me ~ do it** me pidieron que lo hiciera.

(**b**) (*purpose*) para; **I did it ~ help you** lo hice para ayudarte.

(**c**) (*purpose, with verbs of motion*) a, para; **I came ~ see you** vine a verte; **I came specially ~ see you** vine expresamente para verte.

(**d**) (*result*) **I have done nothing ~ deserve this** no he hecho nada que mereciera esto.

(**e**) (*equivalent to* **on** + *ger*) **~ see him now one would never think that ...** al verle (*or* viéndole) ahora no creería nadie que ...

(**f**) (*expressing subsequent fact*) para; **I arrived ~ find she had gone** llegué para descubrir que ella se había ido; **it disappeared never ~ be found again** desapareció para no volver a encontrarse jamás.

(**g**) (*with ellipsis of verb*) **I don't want ~** no quiero; **you**

ought ~ debieras hacerlo (*etc*); **I should love** ~! ¡ojalá!, ¡cuánto me gustaría hacerlo (*etc*)!; **we didn't want to sell it but we had** ~ no queríamos venderlo pero tuvimos que hacerlo, no queríamos venderlo pero no había más remedio.

(**h**) **something** ~ **eat** algo de comer; **I have things** ~ **do** tengo cosas que hacer; **there is much** ~ **be done** hay mucho que hacer; **that book is still** ~ **be written** ese libro está todavía por escribir; **there was no-one for me** ~ **consult** no había nadie a quien yo pudiese consultar; **he is not** ~ **be trusted** no hay que fiarse de él; **he's not the sort** ~ **do that** no es capaz de hacer eso, tal cosa no cabe en él; **this is the time** ~ **do it** éste es el momento de hacerlo; **and who is he** ~ **protest?** ¿y quién es él para protestar?

(**i**) (*construction after adjs etc*) **to be ready** ~ **go** estar listo para partir; **it's hard** ~ **get hold of** es difícil de obtener; **he's slow** ~ **learn** es lento en aprender, aprende lentamente; **you are foolish** ~ **try it** eres un tonto si lo emprendes; **is it good** ~ **eat?** ¿es bueno de (*or* para) comer?, ¿se puede comer?; **to be the first** ~ **do sth** ser el primero en hacer algo; **who was the last** ~ **see her?** ¿quién fue el último en verla?; **he's a big boy** ~ **be still in short trousers** es mayorcito ya para llevar todavía pantalón corto; **it's too heavy** ~ **lift** es demasiado pesado para levantar; **it's too hot** ~ **touch** no se puede tocar por el mucho calor; **he's too old** ~ **manage it** es demasiado viejo para poder hacerlo.

3 *adv*: **to come** ~ (*Naut*) fachear; (*Med*) volver en sí; **to lie** ~ ponerse a la capa; **to push the door** ~ cerrar la puerta (empujándola); *V* **fro.**

toad [təʊd] *n* sapo *m*.

toadflax ['təʊdflæks] *n* linaria *f*.

toad-in-the-hole [ˌtəʊdɪnðə'həʊl] *n* (*Brit*) empanada *f* de salchichas.

toadstool ['təʊdstuːl] *n* seta *f* (venenosa).

toady* ['təʊdɪ] **1** *n* pelotillero* *m*, lameculos‡ *m*. **2** *vi*: **to** ~ **to sb** hacer la pelotilla a uno*, dar coba a uno*.

toadying ['təʊdɪɪŋ] *n*, **toadyism** ['təʊdɪɪzəm] *n* adulación *f* servil, coba* *f*.

toast [təʊst] **1** *n* (**a**) (*Culin*) pan *m* tostado, tostada *f*; **a piece of** ~ un trozo de pan tostado.

(**b**) (*drink*) brindis *m* (*to* por); **to drink a** ~ **to sb** brindar por uno; **here's a** ~ **to all who ...** brindemos por todos los que ...; **A will propose a** ~ **to B** A pronunciará algunas palabras al brindar por B; **she was the** ~ **of the town** la celebraron mucho en toda la ciudad, en todas partes de la ciudad se brindó por ella.

2 *vt* (**a**) (*Culin*) tostar; ~**ed sandwich** sándwich *m* tostado; **to** ~ **one's toes by the fire** calentar los pies cerca del fuego.

(**b**) (*drink to*) brindar por, beber a la salud de; **we** ~**ed the victory in champagne** celebramos la victoria con champán.

toaster ['təʊstəʳ] *n* tostador *m*.

toasting-fork ['təʊstɪŋfɔːk] *n* tostadera *f*.

toast list ['təʊstlɪst] *n* lista *f* de brindis.

toastmaster ['təʊstˌmɑːstəʳ] *n* oficial *m* que anuncia a los oradores en un banquete.

toastrack ['təʊstræk] *n* portatostadas *m*.

toasty ['təʊstɪ] *n* sándwich *m* tostado.

tobacco [tə'bækəʊ] *n* tabaco *m*; ~ **industry** industria *f* tabacalera; ~ **plant** planta *f* de tabaco; ~ **plantation** tabacal *m*.

tobacco-jar [tə'bækəʊdʒɑːʳ] *n* tabaquera *f*.

tobacconist [tə'bækənɪst] *n* (*Brit*) estanquero *m*, -a *f*, tabaquero *m*, -a *f*; ~**'s** (**shop**) estanco *m*, tabaquería *f*.

tobacco-pouch [tə'bækəʊpaʊtʃ] *n* petaca *f*.

Tobago [tə'beɪgəʊ] *n* Tobago *f*.

-to-be [tə'biː] *adj ending in compounds* futuro; *V* **be 11.**

toboggan [tə'bɒgən] **1** *n* tobogán *m*, trineo *m*; ~ **run** pista *f* de tobogán. **2** *vi* ir en tobogán, deslizarse en tobogán.

toby jug ['təʊbɪdʒʌg] *n bock de cerveza en forma de hombre.*

toccata [tə'kɑːtə] *n* tocata *f*.

tocsin ['tɒksɪn] *n* campana *f* de alarma, rebato *m*; campanada *f* de alarma; (*fig*) voz *f* de alarma; **to sound the** ~ (*fig*) dar la voz de alarma, tocar a rebato.

tod‡ [tɒd] *n* (*Brit*): **on one's** ~ a solas.

today [tə'deɪ] **1** *adv* hoy; (*at the present time*) hoy día, hoy en día; ~ **week, a week** ~ de hoy en ocho días, dentro de una semana; **a fortnight** ~ de hoy en quince días; **a year ago** ~ hoy hace un año; **from** ~ desde hoy, a partir de hoy; **early** ~ hoy temprano; **all day** ~ todo hoy; **what day is it** ~? ¿qué día es hoy?, ¿a cuántos estamos?; **here** ~ **and gone tomorrow** se cambia constantemente.

2 *n* hoy *m*; ~ **is Monday** hoy es lunes; ~ **is the 4th** estamos a 4; ~**'s paper** el periódico de hoy; **the writers of** ~ los escritores de hoy.

toddle ['tɒdl] *vi* (*begin to walk*) empezar a andar, dar los primeros pasos; (*walk unsteadily*) caminar sin seguridad; (*) (*go*) ir; (*stroll*) dar un paseo; (*depart*: *also* **to** ~ **off**) irse, marcharse; **we must be toddling*** es hora de irnos; **so I** ~**d round to see him*** así que fui a visitarle.

toddler ['tɒdləʳ] *n* pequeñito *m*, -a *f* (que aprende a andar, que da sus primeros pasos).

toddy ['tɒdɪ] *n* ponche *m*.

to-do* [tə'duː] *n* lío* *m*, follón* *m*; **there was a great** ~ hubo un tremendo follón*; **what's all the** ~ **about?** ¿a qué tanto jaleo?; **she made a great** ~ armó un lío imponente*.

toe [təʊ] **1** *n* (*Anat*) dedo *m* del pie; punta *f* del pie; (*of sock*) punta *f*; (*of shoe*) puntera *f*; **big** ~ dedo *m* gordo del pie, dedo *m* grande del pie; **little** ~ dedo *m* pequeño del pie; **to keep sb on his** ~**s** mantener a uno en estado de vigilancia, hacer que uno siga estando alerta; **you have to keep on your** ~**s** hay que estar alerta, hay que mantenerse bien despierto; **to tread on sb's** ~**s** ofender a uno; **to turn up one's** ~**s*** estirar la pata*.

2 *vt* tocar con la punta del pie; *V* **line¹**.

toecap ['təʊkæp] *n* puntera *f*.

toe-clip ['təʊklɪp] *n* calapiés *m*.

-toed [təʊd] *adj ending in compounds* de ... dedos del pie, *eg* **four**~ de cuatro dedos del pie.

TOEFL ['təʊfəl] *n abbr of* **Test of English as a Foreign Language.**

toehold ['təʊhəʊld] *n* punto *m* de apoyo (para el pie).

toenail ['təʊneɪl] *n* uña *f* del dedo del pie.

toe-piece ['təʊpiːs] *n* espátula *f*, punta *f*.

toerag‡ ['təʊræg] *n* mequetrefe *m*.

toff* [tɒf] *n* (*Brit*) currutaco *m*, chuleta* *m*.

toffee ['tɒfɪ] *n* (*Brit*) caramelo *m*, melcocha *f*; **he can't do it for** ~* no tiene la menor idea de cómo hay que hacerlo.

toffee-apple ['tɒfɪˌæpl] *n* manzana *f* acaramelada.

toffee-nosed* ['tɒfɪ'nəʊzd] *adj* presumido, engreído.

tofu ['təʊˌfuː] *n* tofu *m*, tofú *m*.

tog* [tɒg] **1** *vt*: **to** ~ **sb up** ataviar a uno (*in* de), vestir a uno de modo impresionante (*or* ridículo *etc*) (*in* de); **to get** ~**ged up** ataviarse, vestirse.

2 *vr*: **to** ~ **o.s. up** ataviarse, vestirse (*in* de), emperejilarse.

3 *npl*: ~**s** ropa *f*.

toga ['təʊgə] *n* toga *f*.

together [tə'geðəʳ] **1** *adv* (**a**) (*in company*) junto, juntos; juntamente; **let's get it** ~* (*US*) organicémonos, pongamos manos a la obra; **now we're** ~ ahora estamos juntos; **they were all** ~ **in the bar** todos estaban reunidos en el bar; **we're in this** ~ en esto tenemos igual responsabilidad los dos; nos une la misma suerte; **they were both in it** ~ resultó que los dos se habían confabulado, los dos estaban metidos en el asunto; **you can't all get in** ~ no podéis entrar todos a la vez; ~ **they managed it** entre los dos lo lograron; **they belong** ~ están bien juntos, forman una pareja; **they work** ~ trabajan juntos; *V* **bring, call** *etc*.

(**b**) ~ **with** junto con; conjuntamente con; ~ **with A, B is important** junto con A es importante B.

(**c**) (*simultaneously, in concert*) juntos, a la vez, a un tiempo; **all** ~ **now!** (*singing*) ¡todos en coro!; (*pulling*) ¡todos a la vez!; ¡bien, ahora!; **we'll do parts A and B** ~ haremos juntamente las partes A y B; **don't all talk** ~ no habléis todos a la vez.

(**d**) (*continuously*) seguido; sin interrupción; **for weeks** ~ durante semanas seguidas.

2 *adj* (*esp US**) equilibrado, cabal.

togetherness [tə'geðənɪs] *n* sentimiento *m* de estar todos estrechamente unidos; compañerismo *m*; espíritu *m* de familia (*or* de grupo *etc*).

toggle ['tɒgl] **1** *n* cazonete *m* de aparejo; fiador *m*. **2** *attr*: ~ **key,** ~ **switch** conmutador *m* de palanca, tecla *f* de conmutación binaria.

Togo ['təʊgəʊ] *n* Togo *m*.

Togolese [ˌtəʊgəʊ'liːz] **1** *adj* togolés. **2** *n* togolés *m*, -esa *f*.

toil [tɔɪl] **1** *n* labor *f*, trabajo *m*; fatiga *f*; afán *m*, esfuerzo *m*; **after months of** ~ después de meses de trabajo (agotador).

2 *vi* (**a**) (*work hard*) trabajar; fatigarse; apurarse, afanarse; **to** ~ **to do sth** esforzarse por hacer algo, afanarse por hacer algo; **we** ~**ed at it for hours** trabajamos en ello durante muchas horas (sin éxito); **they** ~**ed on into the night** siguieron trabajando hasta muy entrada la noche.

(**b**) (*labour*) **to ~ along** caminar con dificultad, avanzar penosamente; **to ~ up a hill** subir penosamente una colina; **the engine is beginning to ~** el motor empieza a funcionar con dificultad.

toilet ['tɔɪlɪt] **1** *n* (**a**) (*process of dressing*) tocado *m*; atavío *m*; (*dress*) vestido *m*.
(**b**) (*lavatory*) inodoro *m*, lavabo *m*, wáter *m*, sanitario *m* (*Mex*); **'T~s'** 'Servicios', 'Baño'; **to go to the ~s** ir al wáter, ir al baño (*LAm*).
2 *attr* de tocador; **~ articles, ~ requisites** artículos *mpl* de tocador; **~ set** juego *m* de tocador.

toilet-bag ['tɔɪlɪtbæg] *n*, **toilet-case** ['tɔɪlɪtkeɪs] *n* neceser *m*, estuche *m* de aseo, bolso *m* de aseo.

toilet-bowl ['tɔɪlɪtbəʊl] *n*, **toilet-pan** ['tɔɪlɪt,pæn] *n* taza *f* (de retrete).

toilet-paper ['tɔɪlɪt,peɪpə^r] *n* papel *m* higiénico.

toiletries ['tɔɪlɪtrɪz] *npl* artículos *mpl* de tocador.

toilet-roll ['tɔɪlɪt,rəʊl] *n* (rollo *m* de) papel *m* higiénico.

toilet-seat ['tɔɪlɪtsiːt] *n* asiento *m* de retrete.

toilet-soap ['tɔɪlɪt,səʊp] *n* jabón *m* de tocador.

toilette [twɑː'let] *n* = **toilet**.

toilet-tissue ['tɔɪlɪt,tɪʃuː] *n* papel *m* higiénico.

toilet-train ['tɔɪlɪttreɪn] *vt*: **to ~ a child** acostumbrar a un niño a no ensuciarse.

toilet-training ['tɔɪlɪt,treɪnɪŋ] *n*: **~ can be difficult** acostumbrar a un niño a no ensuciarse puede resultar difícil.

toilet-water ['tɔɪlɪt'wɔːtə^r] *n* agua *f* de colonia.

toils [tɔɪlz] *npl* red *f*, lazo *m*.

toilsome ['tɔɪlsəm] *adj* penoso, laborioso, arduo.

toilworn ['tɔɪlwɔːn] *adj* completamente cansado, rendido.

to-ing ['tuːɪŋ] *n*: **~ and fro-ing** ir *m* y venir, trajín *m*.

toke‡ [təʊk] *n* (*US Drugs*) calada *f*.

token ['təʊkən] **1** *n* (**a**) (*sign, symbol*) señal *f*, muestra *f*, indicio *m*; (*remembrance*) prenda *f*, recuerdo *m*; (*of one's appreciation etc*) detalle *m*, señal *f* de agradecimiento; **as a ~ of, in ~ of** en señal de; como recuerdo de; **by the same ~** igualmente; del mismo modo; **love ~** prenda *f* de amor.
(**b**) (*disc etc*) ficha *f*, disco *m* (metálico); (*coupon*) bono *m*, vale *m*.
2 *adj* simbólico; **~ amount** cantidad *f* testimonial; **the ~ black** el negro simbólico; **~ payment** pago *m* nominal, pago *m* simbólico; **to put up a ~ resistance** oponer una resistencia simbólica, resistir por pura fórmula; **~ strike** huelga *f* simbólica; **~ woman** mujer-muestra *f*, representación *f* femenina.

tokenism ['təʊkənɪzəm] *n* programa *m* político de fachada.

Tokyo ['təʊkjəʊ] *n* Tokio *m*, Tokío *m*.

told [təʊld] *pret and ptp of* **tell**.

tolerable ['tɒlərəbl] *adj* (**a**) (*bearable*) tolerable, soportable. (**b**) (*fair*) regular, pasable.

tolerably ['tɒlərəblɪ] *adv* bastante; pasablemente; **a ~ good player** un jugador bastante bueno, un jugador pasable; **it is ~ certain that ...** es casi seguro que ...

tolerance ['tɒlərəns] *n* (**a**) tolerancia *f*; paciencia *f*, indulgencia *f*. (**b**) (*margin*) tolerancia *f*.

tolerant ['tɒlərənt] *adj* tolerante; indulgente; **to be ~ of** tolerar, ser tolerante de.

tolerantly ['tɒlərəntlɪ] *adv* con tolerancia; con indulgencia.

tolerate ['tɒləreɪt] *vt* tolerar, soportar, aguantar; **are we to ~ this?** ¿hemos de soportar esto?; **I can't ~ any more** no aguanto más; **it is not to be ~d** es intolerable, es insoportable.

toleration [,tɒlə'reɪʃən] *n* tolerancia *f*; **religious ~** tolerancia *f* religiosa; libertad *f* de cultos.

toll[1] [təʊl] *n* (**a**) (*payment*) peaje *m*, portazgo *m*; (*on bridge*) pontazgo *m*; **~ motorway** autopista *f* de peaje; **to pay ~** pagar el peaje.
(**b**) (*losses, casualties*) mortalidad *f*, número *m* de víctimas, número *m* de pérdidas; **the ~ on the roads** el número de víctimas en accidentes de circulación; **there is a heavy ~** hay muchas víctimas, son muchos los muertos; **the disease takes a heavy ~ each year** cada año la enfermedad se lleva a muchas víctimas, cada año la enfermedad causa gran número de muertes; **to take ~ of** causar bajas en, tener su efecto en; **the effort took its ~ on all of us** el esfuerzo tuvo un grave efecto en todos nosotros.

toll[2] [təʊl] **1** *vt bell* tañer, tocar, doblar (a muerto); **to ~ the hour** dar la hora.
2 *vi* doblar (a muerto); **the bells were ~ing in mourning for ...** doblaron las campanas en señal de duelo por ...; **'For whom the bell ~s'** 'Por quien doblan las campanas'.

tollbar ['təʊlbɑː^r] *n* barrera *f* de peaje.

tollbooth ['təʊlbuːð] *n* cabina *f* de peaje.

tollbridge ['təʊlbrɪdʒ] *n* puente *m* de peaje.

toll call ['təʊlkɔːl] *n* (*US*) conferencia *f*.

toll-free [,təʊl'friː] *adv* (*US*): **to call ~** llamar sin pagar.

tollgate ['təʊlgeɪt] *n* barrera *f* de peaje.

tolling ['təʊlɪŋ] *n* tañido *m*, doblar *m*.

tollkeeper ['təʊl,kiːpə^r] *n* peajero *m*, portazguero *m*.

toll road ['təʊlrəʊd] *n* carretera *f* de peaje.

tollway ['təʊlweɪ] *n* (*US*) autopista *f* de peaje.

Tom [tɒm] *nm familiar form of* **Thomas**; **~ Dick and Harry** cada quisque *m*, cualquier hijo *m* de vecino; Fulano, Mengano y Zutano; **you shan't marry any ~ Dick or Harry** no te casarás con un cualquiera; **~ Thumb** Pulgarcito.

tom [tɒm] *n* gato *m* (macho).

tomahawk ['tɒməhɔːk] *n* tomahawk *m*; **to bury the ~** (*US*) echar pelillos a la mar, envainar la espada.

tomato [tə'mɑːtəʊ, (*US*) tə'meɪtəʊ] **1** *n*, *pl* **tomatoes** [tə'mɑːtəʊz] (*fruit*) tomate *m*; (*plant*) tomatera *f*.
2 *attr*: **~ juice** jugo *m* de tomate; **~ ketchup** salsa *f* de tomate; **~ paste, ~ purée** puré *m* de tomate; **~ plant** tomatera *f*; **~ sauce** salsa *f* de tomate.

tomb [tuːm] *n* tumba *f*, sepulcro *m*.

tombola [tɒm'bəʊlə] *n* (*Brit*) tómbola *f*.

tomboy ['tɒmbɔɪ] *n* muchacha *f* hombruna, muchachota *f*, chica *f* poco femenina.

tomboyish ['tɒmbɔɪɪʃ] *adj* marimacho.

tombstone ['tuːmstəʊn] *n* lápida *f* sepulcral.

tomcat ['tɒmkæt] *n* (*cat*) gato *m* (macho); (*US‡*) mujeriego *m*, calavera *m*.

tome [təʊm] *n* (*hum*) librote *m*.

tomfool ['tɒm'fuːl] **1** *adj* tonto, estúpido. **2** *n* tonto *m*, imbécil *m*.

tomfoolery [tɒm'fuːlərɪ] *n* pataratas *fpl*, payasadas *fpl*.

Tommy ['tɒmɪ] *nm familiar form of* **Thomas**; **~ (Atkins)** (*Brit*) *el soldado raso inglés*.

tommy-gun ['tɒmɪgʌn] *n* metralleta *f*, pistola *f* ametralladora.

tommy-rot* ['tɒmɪrɒt] *n* tonterías *fpl*.

tomorrow [tə'mɒrəʊ] **1** *adv* mañana; **~ evening** mañana por la tarde; **~ morning** mañana por la mañana; **a week ~** de mañana en ocho días.
2 *n* mañana *f*; **the day after ~** pasado mañana; **~ is Sunday** mañana es domingo; **~ is another day** mañana es otro día; **he drank like there was no ~*** bebió como si fuera la última vez; **will ~ do?** ¿lo puedo dejar para mañana?; ¿te conviene mañana?; **~'s paper** el periódico de mañana.

tom-tit ['tɒmtɪt] *n* paro *m*, carbonero *m* común.

tom-tom ['tɒmtɒm] *n* tantán *m*.

ton [tʌn] *n* (**a**) (*weight*; *Brit*: = 1016 kg; *US*: *also* **short ~** = 907.18 kg) tonelada *f*; **it weighs a ~** pesa una tonelada.
(**b**) (*) **~s** montones* *mpl*; **we have ~s of it at home** en casa lo tenemos a montones*; **we have ~s of time** nos sobra tiempo, tenemos tiempo de sobra.
(**c**) (‡) velocidad *f* de 100 millas por hora; **to do a ~** ir a 100 millas por hora (en moto); **~ up boys** (*Brit*) motoristas *mpl* que hacen 100 millas por hora.

tonal ['təʊnl] *adj* tonal.

tonality [təʊ'nælɪtɪ] *n* tonalidad *f*.

tone [təʊn] **1** *n* (**a**) (*in most senses*) tono *m*; (*of colour*) tono *m*, tonalidad *f*; matiz *m*; **in low ~s** en tono bajo; **in an angry ~** en tono de enojo.
(**b**) (*class*) clase *f*; dignidad *f*; buen tono *m*, elegancia *f*; **the place has ~** el sitio tiene buen tono, es un sitio elegante; **the clientèle gives the restaurant ~** la clientela da distinción al restaurante; **he lowers the whole ~ of the occasion** rebaja toda la dignidad de la ceremonia (*etc*).
(**c**) (*tendency*) tono *m*, nota *f*; **the ~ of the market** la nota dominante del mercado, el tono del mercado.
2 *vt* (*Mus*) entonar; (*Phot*) virar.
3 *vi* armonizar, ir bien juntos.

◆**tone down** *vt* (**a**) *noise* reducir, disminuir; *radio etc* reducir el volumen de; **~ it down!** ¡menos ruido! (**b**) *colour* hacer menos brillante. (**c**) *speech etc* moderar (el tono de).

◆**tone up** *vt muscles* poner en forma, fortalecer.

tone colour, (*US*) **tone color** ['təʊn,kʌlə^r] *n* (*Mus*) timbre *m*.

tone-control ['təʊnkən,trəʊl] *n* control *m* de tonalidad.

tone-deaf ['təʊn'def] *adj* que no tiene oído musical.

tone language ['təʊn,læŋgwɪdʒ] *n* lengua *f* tonal.

toneless ['təʊnlɪs] *adj* soso, flojo; *voice* monótono; apagado, inexpresivo.

tonelessly ['təʊnlɪslɪ] *adv* monótonamente.

tone poem ['təʊn,pəʊɪm] *n* poema *m* sinfónico.

toner ['təʊnəʳ] *n* (*for photocopier*) virador *m*; (*for skin*) tonificante *m*.
ton(e)y* ['təʊnɪ] *adj* (*US*) de buen tono, elegante.
Tonga ['tɒŋə] *n* Tonga *f*.
tongs [tɒŋz] *npl* (*for coal etc*) tenazas *fpl*; (*for sweets, sugar, hair*) tenacillas *fpl*; **a pair of ~** unas tenazas, unas tenacillas.
tongue [tʌŋ] *n* (**a**) (*Anat*) lengua *f*; (*of shoe etc*) lengüeta *f*; (*of bell*) badajo *m*; (*of flame, land*) lengua *f*; **with one's ~ in one's cheek** irónicamente, burla burlando; **a ~ in cheek remark** una observación irónica; **I can't get my ~ round these Ruritanian names** estos nombres ruritanios resultan impronunciables; **so you've found your ~?** ¿así que estás dispuesto por fin a hablar?; **to give ~** empezar a ladrar; **to give a ready ~** no morderse la lengua; **to hold one's ~** callarse; **hold your ~!** ¡a callarse!; **to loosen sb's ~** hacer hablar a uno; **wine loosens the ~** el vino suelta la lengua; **have you lost your ~?** ¿estás mudo o qué?; **the formula came tripping off her ~** pronunció la fórmula con la mayor facilidad.
(**b**) (*Ling*) lengua *f*, idioma *m*; **in the Slobodian ~** en eslobodiano, en la lengua eslobodia; **to speak in ~s** hablar en lenguas desconocidas.
tongue-and-groove [,tʌŋən'gruːv] *n* machihembrado *m*.
tongue-lashing ['tʌŋ'læʃɪŋ] *n* latigazo *m*, reprensión *f*; **to give sb a ~** poner a uno como un trapo.
tongue-tied ['tʌŋtaɪd] *adj* que tiene dificultad al hablar, que tiene defecto del habla; (*fig*) tímido, premioso, confuso.
tongue-twister ['tʌŋ,twɪstəʳ] *n* trabalenguas *m*.
tonic ['tɒnɪk] **1** *adj* tónico; **~ accent** acento *m* tónico.
2 *n* (**a**) (*Mus*) tónica *f*.
(**b**) (*Med*) tónico *m*; (*as drink, with gin etc*; *also* **~ water**) (agua *f*) tónica *f*; (*fig*) tónico *m*; **this news will be a ~ for the market** esta noticia será un tónico para la bolsa.
tonicity [tɒ'nɪsɪtɪ] *n* tonicidad *f*.
tonic water ['tɒnɪk,wɔːtəʳ] *n* agua *f* tónica.
tonight [tə'naɪt] *adv* esta noche.
tonnage ['tʌnɪdʒ] *n* tonelaje *m*.
tonne [tʌn] *n* tonelada *f* (métrica) (= 1.000 kg).
-tonner ['tʌnəʳ] *n ending in compounds* de ... toneladas; **a 1,000~** un barco de 1.000 toneladas.
tonometer [təʊ'nɒmɪtəʳ] *n* tonómetro *m*.
tonsil ['tɒnsl] *n* amígdala *f*, angina *f* (*Mex*); **to have one's ~s out** sacarse las amígdalas.
tonsillectomy [,tɒnsɪ'lektəmɪ] *n* tonsilectomía *f*, amigdalotomía *f*.
tonsillitis [,tɒnsɪ'laɪtɪs] *n* amigdalitis *f*.
tonsorial [tɒn'sɔːrɪəl] *adj* (*esp hum*) barberil; relativo a la barba.
tonsure ['tɒnʃəʳ] **1** *n* tonsura *f*. **2** *vt* tonsurar.
Tony ['təʊnɪ] *nm familiar form of* **Anthony**.
too [tuː] *adv* (**a**) (*excessively*) demasiado; muy; **it's ~ hard** es demasiado duro, es muy duro; **it's ~ easy** es muy fácil, es muy sencillo; **it's ~ heavy for me to lift** es demasiado pesado para que lo levante; **~ often** con demasiada frecuencia, muy a menudo; **it's not ~ difficult** no es muy difícil; **I'm not ~ keen on the idea** la idea no me hace gracia que digamos; **it's ~ early for that** es (muy) temprano para eso; **~ right!, ~ true!** ¡muy bien dicho!, ¡y cómo!; *V* **many, much, well.**
(**b**) (*also*) también; además, por otra parte; **I went ~** yo fui también; **and it's broken ~** y además está roto; **she is, ~!** ¡y tanto que lo es!
took [tʊk] *pret of* **take.**
tool [tuːl] **1** *n* (**a**) herramienta *f*; utensilio *m*; **(set of) ~s** útiles *mpl*, utillaje *m*; **garden ~s** útiles *mpl* de jardinería; **plumber's ~s** útiles *mpl* de fontanero; **the ~s of one's trade** las cosas que uno necesita para su oficio; **to down ~s** suspender el trabajo; (*strike*) declararse en huelga; **give us the ~s and we will finish the job** dadnos las herramientas y nosotros terminaremos la obra.
(**b**) (*fig*: *person, book etc*) instrumento *m*; **the book is an essential ~** el libro es indispensable, el libro es instrumento imprescindible; **he was an unwilling ~ of the gang** sin quererlo fue un instrumento de la pandilla; **he is just the ~ of the minister** es la criatura del ministro nada más.
2 *vt* labrar con herramienta; *book* estampar en seco; filetear.
toolbag ['tuːlbæg] *n* bolsa *f* de herramientas.
toolbox ['tuːlbɒks] *n*, **tool chest** ['tuːltʃest] *n* caja *f* de herramientas.
tooled-up‡ ['tuːld'ʌp] *adj* armado.
tooling ['tuːlɪŋ] *n* estampación *f* en seco; fileteado *m*.
toolkit ['tuːlkɪt] *n* juego *m* de herramientas.
toolmaker ['tuːl,meɪkəʳ] *n* tallador *m* de herramientas.
toolmaking ['tuːl,meɪkɪŋ] *n* talladura *f* de herramientas.
toolroom ['tuːlrʊm] *n* departamento *m* de herramientas.
toolshed ['tuːlʃed] *n* cobertizo *m* para herramientas.
toot [tuːt] **1** *n* sonido *m* breve (de claxon *etc*); **he went off with a ~ on the horn** partió con un breve toque de bocina.
2 *vt* sonar, tocar.
3 *vi* sonar (la bocina *etc*); (*person*) tocar la bocina, dar un bocinazo.
tooth [tuːθ] *n*, *pl* **teeth** [tiːθ] (**a**) (*Anat*) diente *m*; (*esp molar*) muela *f*; **in the teeth of the wind** contra un viento violento; **in the teeth of great opposition** contra una resistencia de lo más terco; **to be armed to the teeth** estar armado hasta los dientes; **to cast sth in sb's teeth** echar algo en cara a uno; **to cut one's teeth** endentecer, echar los dientes; **to be fed up to the (back) teeth with** estar hasta la coronilla de; **to fight ~ and nail** luchar encarnizadamente; **to get one's teeth into** hincar el diente a (*also fig*); **the Commission must be given more teeth** hay que dar poderes efectivos a la Comisión; **to have a ~ out** hacerse sacar una muela; **she has a sweet ~** le gustan las cosas dulces; es golosa; **to lie in one's teeth** mentir descaradamente; **we've got to set our teeth and get on with it** tenemos que apretar los dientes e ir adelante; **to show one's teeth** enseñar los dientes.
(**b**) (*of saw, wheel*) diente *m*; (*of comb*) púa *f*.
toothache ['tuːθeɪk] *n* dolor *m* de muelas.
toothbrush ['tuːθbrʌʃ] *n* cepillo *m* de dientes; **~ moustache** bigote *m* de cepillo.
toothcomb ['tuːθkəʊm] *n*: **to go through sth with a fine ~** registrar algo minuciosamente.
toothed [tuːθt] *adj wheel etc* dentado; de dientes ..., *eg* **big-~** de dientes grandes.
toothless ['tuːθlɪs] *adj* desdentado, sin dientes; (*fig*) ineficaz, sin poder efectivo.
toothpaste ['tuːθpeɪst] *n* pasta *f* dentífrica, dentífrico *m*, crema *f* dental.
toothpick ['tuːθpɪk] *n* palillo *m* (mondadientes), mondadientes *m*.
tooth-powder ['tuːθ,paʊdəʳ] *n* polvos *mpl* dentífricos.
toothsome ['tuːθsəm] *adj* sabroso.
toothy ['tuθɪ] *adj* dentudo, dentón; **to give sb a ~ smile** sonreír a uno mostrando mucho los dientes.
tootle ['tuːtl] **1** *n* sonido *m* breve (de flauta, trompeta *etc*); serie *f* de notas breves; **give us a ~ on your trumpet** tócanos algo a la trompeta; *V also* **toot.**
2 *vt flute etc* tocar.
3 *vi* (**a**) tocar la flauta (*etc*); *V also* **toot.**
(**b**) (*Aut**) **we ~d down to Brighton** hicimos una escapada a Brighton, fuimos de excursión a Brighton; **we were tootling along at 60** íbamos a 60.
toots(y)* ['tuːts(ɪ)] *n* (*US*) chica *f*, gachí‡ *f*; **hey ~!** ¡oye, guapa!
top¹ [tɒp] **1** *n* (**a**) (*topmost point*) cumbre *f*, cima *f*; ápice *m*; (*of tree*) copa *f*; (*of head*) coronilla *f*; (*of building*) remate *m*; (*of wall*) coronamiento *m*; (*of wave*) cresta *f*; (*of stairs etc*) lo alto, parte *f* alta; (*of list, page, table, classification*) cabeza *f*; primer puesto *m*, primera posición *f*; (*of plant*) hojas *fpl*, parte *f* superior; (*further part*) otro extremo *m*; parte *f* más lejana; **at the ~ of the hill** en la cumbre de la colina; **at the ~ of the tree** en lo alto del árbol; **at the ~ of the list** a la cabeza de la lista, en la primera posición de la lista; **executives who are at the ~ of their careers** ejecutivos que están en la cumbre de sus carreras; **El Toboso is at the ~ of the league** El Toboso encabeza la liga, El Toboso va en primera posición de la liga; **he lives at the ~ of the house** ocupa el piso más alto de la casa; **I saw him at the ~ of the street** le vi al otro extremo de la calle; **he sits at the ~ of the table** se sienta a la cabecera de la mesa; **she's at the ~ of the bill** está en la cabecera del cartel; **from ~ to bottom** de arriba abajo, de cabo a rabo; **the system is rotten from ~ to bottom** el sistema entero está podrido; **from ~ to toe** de pies a cabeza; **I said it off the ~ of my head** lo dije sin pensar; **speaking off the ~ of my head, I would say ...** hablando así sin pensarlo, yo diría que ...; **on ~** encima; **to be on ~** estar encima; estar en la parte superior; (*fig*) llevar ventaja, estar ganando; **to come out on ~** salir ganando, salir ganancioso; **it's just one thing on ~ of another** es una cosa tras otra; **next second the lorry was on ~ of us** al instante el camión se nos echó encima; **the flat is so small we live on ~ of each other** el piso es tan pequeño que vivimos amontonados; **I'm on ~ of my work now** ahora

puedo con el trabajo; **things are getting on ~ of her** los problemas empiezan a afectarla de mala manera; **and then on ~ of all that ...** y luego por añadidura ..., y como si eso fuera poco ...; y luego para colmo de desgracias ...; **over the ~** excesivo, desmesurado; **to go over the ~** (*Mil*) lanzarse al ataque (saliendo de las trincheras); (*fig*) pasarse (de lo razonable), desbordarse; **this proposal is really over the ~** esta propuesta pasa de la raya; **he doesn't have much up ~*** no es muy listo que digamos.

(**b**) (*surface*) superficie *f*; **on ~ of** sobre, encima de; **it floats on ~ of the water** flota sobre el agua; **oil comes to the ~** el aceite sube a la superficie; **the table ~ is damaged** la superficie de la mesa está deteriorada.

(**c**) (*Naut*) cofa *f*.

(**d**) (*cap of bottle*) cápsula *f*, tapa *f*; (*of pen*) capuchón *m*; (*lid*) tapa *f*, tapadera *f*; (*of carriage*) baca *f*; (*of bus*) piso *m* superior, imperial *f*; (*US Aut*) capota *f*; **with a sliding ~, with a sunshine ~** descapotable, con techo corredizo; **to blow one's ~*** subirse por las paredes‡.

(**e**) (*maximum, best*) lo mejor; **the ~ of the flood** (*or* **tide**) la pleamar; **the ~ of the morning to you!** (*Ir*) ¡buenos días!; **'T~ of the Pops'** ≃ 'Los cuarenta principales' (*Sp*); **to be at the ~ of one's form** estar en plena forma; **to shout at the ~ of one's voice** llamar a voz en grito; **it's the ~s*** es tremendo*, es fabuloso*, es la flor de la canela; **she's ~s*** es la reoca*.

2 *adj* (*highest*) más alto, el más alto; cimero; *part* superior, más alto; *floor, stair etc* más alto, último; (*first*) primero; (*greatest*) máximo; (*highest in rank*) principal, primero; puntero; *leader* supremo, máximo; *price* máximo, tope; **~ banana*** (*US*) pez *m* gordo*; **~ brass*** jefazos* *mpl*; **~ copy** original *m*; **to pay ~ dollar for sth*** (*US*) pagar una cosa a precio de oro; **~ executive** alto ejecutivo *m*; **~ gear** (*Brit*) directa *f*; **~ leaders** máximos dirigentes *mpl*; **~ management** alta gerencia *f*; **~ people** gente *f* bien; **~ secret document** documento *m* ultrasecreto; **~ security jail** cárcel *f* de alta (*or* máxima) seguridad; **~ spin** efecto *m* de avance, lift *m*; **~ team** equipo *m* líder; **the T~ 20** (*Mus*) los 20 principales; **at ~ speed** a máxima velocidad; **the ~ men in the party** los líderes del partido, los jerarcas del partido; **he was ~ boy** se clasificó primero (entre los muchachos); **to come ~** ganar, ganar el primer puesto, clasificarse primero; **he came ~ in maths** tuvo la mejor nota en matemáticas.

3 *vt* (**a**) *tree* desmochar; *plant* descabezar; *fruit etc* quitar las hojas (*etc*) de; (‡) *person* colgar.

(**b**) (*complete upper part of*) coronar, rematar; **the wall is ~ped with stone** el muro tiene un coronamiento de piedras; **and to ~ it all ...** y por añadidura ...; y para colmo de desgracias ...

(**c**) (*exceed*) exceder, aventajar; rebasar; salir por encima de; **to ~ sb in height** ser más alto que uno; **to ~ sb by a head** sacar a uno una cabeza; **this ~s everything** esto supera a todo lo demás; **we have ~ped last year's takings by £200** hemos recaudado 200 libras más que el año pasado, los ingresos exceden a los del año pasado en 200 libras; **sales ~ped the million mark** las ventas rebasaron el millón.

(**d**) (*reach summit of*) llegar a la cumbre de; *class, list* encabezar, estar a la cabeza de; llegar a ocupar la primera posición de; **the team ~ped the league all season** el equipo iba en cabeza de la liga toda la temporada; **to ~ the bill** (*Theat*) estar en la cabecera del cartel.

◆**top off** *vt*: **to ~ off a building** terminar el piso superior de un edificio; **he ~ped this off by saying that ...** esto lo remató diciendo que ...; **he ~ped off the 8th course with a cup of coffee** para completar el octavo plato se bebió una taza de café.

◆**top up** (*Brit*) **1** *vt* completar; rellenar; redondear; (*level up*) nivelar; **to ~ up sb's glass** acabar de llenar (*or* volver a llenar) el vaso de uno; **to ~ up a battery** recargar una batería hasta el nivel indicado; **shall I ~ you up?** ¿te doy más?

2 *vi*: **to ~ up with fuel** repostar combustible; **to ~ up with oil** poner aceite; **we ~ped up with a couple of beers** como remate nos bebimos un par de cervezas.

top² [tɒp] *n* (*spinning ~*) peonza *f*, peón *m*; (*humming ~, musical ~*) trompa *f*.

topaz ['təʊpæz] *n* topacio *m*.

top boots ['tɒpbu:ts] *npl* botas *fpl* de campaña.

topcoat ['tɒpkəʊt] *n* sobretodo *m*.

top-drawer [ˌtɒp'drɔ:ʳ] *adj* de alta sociedad.

top dressing ['tɒp'dresɪŋ] *n* abono *m* (aplicado a la superficie).

tope [təʊp] *vi* beber (más de la cuenta), emborracharse.

topee ['təʊpi:] *n* salacot *m*.

toper ['təʊpəʳ] *n* borrachín *m*.

top-flight ['tɒpflaɪt] *adj* sobresaliente, de primera (clase).

topgallant [tɒp'gælənt, *Naut* tə'gælənt] *n* (*also* **~ sail**) juanete *m*.

top hat ['tɒp'hæt] *n* chistera* *f*, sombrero *m* de copa.

top-hatted ['tɒp'hætɪd] *adj* en chistera, enchisterado.

top-heaviness ['tɒp'hevɪnɪs] *n* (*fig*) macrocefalia *f*.

top-heavy ['tɒp'hevɪ] *adj* demasiado pesado por arriba; (*fig*) falto de equilibrio, mal equilibrado; macrocefálico; (*) tetuda*.

topiary ['təʊpɪərɪ] *n* arte *m* de recortar los arbustos en formas de animales *etc*.

topic ['tɒpɪk] *n* asunto *m*, tema *m*.

topical ['tɒpɪkəl] *adj* (**a**) actual, de interés actual, corriente; **~ talk** charla *f* sobre cuestiones del día, charla *f* sobre actualidades; **a highly ~ question** una cuestión de palpitante actualidad. (**b**) (*US*) local.

topicality [ˌtɒpɪ'kælɪtɪ] *n* (**a**) actualidad *f*; importancia *f* actual, interés *m* actual. (**b**) (*US*) localidad *f*.

topknot ['tɒpnɒt] *n* moño *m* (*also Orn*); (*) cabeza *f*.

topless ['tɒplɪs] **1** *adj* top-less; **~ bar** bar *m* top-less; **~ swimsuit** monoquini *m*. **2** *adv*: **to go ~** andar top-less.

top-level ['tɒp'levl] *adj* de primer nivel; **~ conference** conferencia *f* de alto nivel.

top-loader [ˌtɒp'ləʊdəʳ] *n* lavadora *f* de carga superior.

topmast ['tɒpmɑ:st] *n* mastelero *m*.

topmost ['tɒpməʊst] *adj* más alto, el más alto.

top-notch* ['tɒp'nɒtʃ] *adj* de primerísima categoría.

topographer [tə'pɒgrəfəʳ] *n* topógrafo *m*, -a *f*.

topographic(al) [ˌtɒpə'græfɪk(l)] *adj* topográfico.

topography [tə'pɒgrəfɪ] *n* topografía *f*.

topper* ['tɒpəʳ] *n* (**a**) (*hat*) chistera* *f*, sombrero *m* de copa. (**b**) **the ~ was that ...** (*US*) para colmo ..., para acabar de rematar ...*

topping* ['tɒpɪŋ] **1** *adj* (*Brit*†) bárbaro*, pistonudo*. **2** *n* (*Culin*) cubierta *f*.

topple ['tɒpl] **1** *vt* (*also* **to ~ over**) derribar, derrocar; tumbar; hacer caer; volcar.

2 *vi* (*also* **to ~ down**) caerse, venirse abajo; (*also* **to ~ over**) volcarse; (*lose balance*) perder el equilibrio; (*totter*) tambalearse; **he ~d over a cliff** cayó por un precipicio; **after the crash the bus ~d over** después del choque el autobús se volcó.

top-rank(ing) ['tɒp'ræŋk(ɪŋ)] *adj* de primera categoría; *officer* de alta graduación.

topsail ['tɒpsl] *n* gavia *f*.

top-secret ['tɒp'si:krɪt] *adj* ultrasecreto, de reserva absoluta.

top-selling ['tɒp'selɪŋ] *adj* = **best-selling**.

topside ['tɒpˌsaɪd] *n* lado *m* superior, superficie *f* superior; (*Culin*) tapa *f* y tajo redondo.

topsoil ['tɒpsɔɪl] *n* capa *f* superficial del suelo.

topsy-turvy ['tɒpsɪ'tɜ:vɪ] **1** *adv* en desorden, patas arriba; **everything is ~** todo está patas arriba. **2** *adj* confuso, desordenado.

top-up ['tɒpʌp] **1** *n*: **would you like a ~?** ¿quiere que se lo llene? **2** *attr*: **~ loan** (*Brit*) *préstamo gubernamental a estudiantes*.

tor [tɔ:ʳ] *n* colina *f* abrupta y rocosa, pico *m* pequeño (*esp en el suroeste de Inglaterra*).

torch [tɔ:tʃ] *n* (*flaming*) antorcha *f*, tea *f*, hacha *f*; (*Brit*: *electric*) linterna *f* eléctrica, lámpara *f* de bolsillo; **to carry a ~ for sb** (*fig*) seguir enamorada de uno (*esp* a pesar de no ser correspondido por él).

torchbearer ['tɔ:tʃˌbeərəʳ] *n* persona *f* que lleva una antorcha.

torchlight ['tɔ:tʃlaɪt] *n* luz *f* de antorcha; **~ procession** desfile *m* con antorchas.

tore [tɔ:ʳ] *pret of* **tear**.

toreador ['tɒrɪədɔ:ʳ] *n* torero *m*.

torment 1 ['tɔ:ment] *n* tormento *m*; angustia *f*; suplicio *m*; **the ~s of jealousy** los tormentos de los celos; **to be in ~** estar sufriendo, sufrir mucho.

2 [tɔ:'ment] *vt* atormentar, martirizar; torturar; **we were ~ed by thirst** sufrimos los tormentos de la sed; **she was ~ed by doubts** la atormentaron las dudas; **don't ~ the cat** no le des guerra al gato.

tormentor [tɔ:'mentəʳ] *n* atormentador *m*, -ora *f*.

torn [tɔ:n] *ptp of* **tear**.

tornado [tɔ:'neɪdəʊ] *n*, *pl* **tornadoes** [tɔ:'neɪdəʊz] tornado *m*.

torpedo [tɔ:'pi:dəʊ] **1** *n*, *pl* **torpedoes** [tɔ:'pi:dəʊz] torpedo *m*.

2 *vt* torpedear (*also fig*).
torpedo-boat [tɔːˈpiːdəubəut] *n* torpedero *m*, lancha *f* torpedera.
torpedo-tube [tɔːˈpiːdəutjuːb] *n* (tubo *m*) lanzatorpedos *m*.
torpid [ˈtɔːpɪd] *adj* aletargado, inactivo; (*fig*) torpe, apático; aburrido.
torpidity [tɔːˈpɪdɪtɪ] *n*, **torpor** [ˈtɔːpəʳ] *n* letargo *m*, inactividad *f*; (*fig*) torpeza *f*, apatía *f*; aburrimiento *m*.
torque [tɔːk] **1** *n* par *m* de torsión. **2** *attr*: ~ **wrench** llave *f* dinamométrica.
torrent [ˈtɒrənt] *n* torrente *m* (*also fig*); **to rain in ~s** llover a cántaros, diluviar.
torrential [tɒˈrenʃəl] *adj* torrencial.
torrid [ˈtɒrɪd] *adj* tórrido.
torsion [ˈtɔːʃən] *n* torsión *f*.
torso [ˈtɔːsəu] *n*, *pl* **torsos** [ˈtɔːsəuz] torso *m*.
tort [tɔːt] *n* agravio *m*, tuerto *m*.
tortilla [tɔːˈtiːə] *n* tortilla *f*.
tortoise [ˈtɔːtəs] *n* tortuga *f*.
tortoiseshell [ˈtɔːtəsʃel] **1** *n* (**a**) carey *m*. (**b**) (*butterfly*: *small* ~) ortiguera *f*; (*cat*) gato *m* pardo. **2** *attr*: ~ **glasses** gafas *fpl* de carey.
tortuous [ˈtɔːtjuəs] *adj* tortuoso.
torture [ˈtɔːtʃəʳ] **1** *n* tortura *f*; (*fig*) tormento *m*; **it was ~!** ¡lo que sufrí!; **to put sb to the ~** torturar a uno.
2 *attr*: ~ **chamber** cámara *f* de tortura.
3 *vt* torturar; (*fig*) atormentar; *sense etc* torcer, violentar; **to be ~d by doubts** ser atormentado por las dudas.
torturer [ˈtɔːtʃərəʳ] *n* verdugo *m*.
torturing [ˈtɔːtʃərɪŋ] *adj* torturador, atormentador.
Tory [ˈtɔːrɪ] (*Brit*) **1** *adj* conservador; **the T~ Party** el Partido Conservador. **2** *n* conservador *m*, -ora *f*.
Toryism [ˈtɔːrɪɪzəm] *n* (*Brit*) conservatismo *m*, conservadurismo *m*.
tosh* [tɒʃ] *n* música *f* celestial*; **~!** ¡tonterías!
toss [tɒs] **1** *n* (**a**) (*movement*: *of head etc*) movimiento *m* brusco; sacudida *f*, meneo *m*; (*throw*) echada *f*, tirada *f*; (*by bull*) cogida *f*; (*fall from horse*) caída *f*; **the ball came to him full ~** la pelota llegó a sus manos sin tocar la tierra; **he took a bad ~** sufrió una violenta caída; **I don't give a ~‡** me la trae floja‡.
(**b**) (*of coin*) echada *f*; sorteo *m* (para la elección de lado *etc*); **to argue the ~** andar en dimes y diretes, discutir; **to win the ~** ganar el sorteo.
2 *vt head etc* mover bruscamente, hacer un movimiento brusco de; sacudir, menear; (*throw*) echar, tirar; (*of bull*) coger (y lanzar al aire); *coin* echar a cara o cruz; **to ~ a salad** darle vueltas a una ensalada; **to ~ sb in a blanket** mantear a uno; **the horse ~ed its head** el caballo levantó airosamente la cabeza.
3 *vi* (**a**) (*also* **to ~ about, to ~ around**) agitarse, sacudirse; (*of plumes etc*) ondear; (*a boat*: *gently*) balancearse sobre las ondas, (*violently*) ser sacudido por las ondas; **to ~ (in one's sleep), to ~ and turn** revolverse (en la cama).
(**b**) (*also* **to ~ up**) jugar a cara o cruz (*for sth* algo); (*Sport*) sortear (*for sth* algo); **we'll ~ up to see who does it** jugaremos a cara o cruz para decidir quién lo hará.
◆**toss about, toss around** **1** *vt* lanzar acá y allá; **the currents ~ed the boat about** las corrientes zarandeaban la embarcación.
2 *vi V* **toss 3** (**a**).
◆**toss aside** *vt* echar a un lado, apartar bruscamente, abandonar.
◆**toss away** *vt* echar, tirar.
◆**toss off** **1** *vt poem etc* escribir rapidísimamente; **to ~ off a drink** beberse algo de un trago, beberse algo rápidamente.
2 *vi* (‡‡) hacerse una paja‡‡.
◆**toss over** *vt*: **to ~ a book over to sb** tirar un libro a uno; **~ it over!** ¡dámelo!
◆**toss up** **1** *vt coin* echar a cara o cruz.
2 *vi* = **toss 3** (**b**).
tosser‡‡ [ˈtɒsəʳ] *n* (*Brit*) mamón‡ *m*, gilipollas* *m*.
toss-up [ˈtɒsʌp] *n*: **it's a ~** tanto puede ser lo uno como lo otro; **it's a ~ whether I go or stay** no me decido si irme o quedarme; **it was a ~ between X and Y** había iguales posibilidades para X e Y.
tot[1] [tɒt] *n* (**a**) (*esp Brit*: *drink*) trago *m*, copita *f*; **just a ~** unas gotitas nada más; **let's go in here for a ~** entremos aquí a tomar algo. (**b**) (*child*) nene *m*, -a *f*.
tot[2] [tɒt] (*esp Brit*) **1** *vt*: **to ~ up** sumar. **2** *vi*: **it ~s up to £5** suma 5 libras, viene a ser 5 libras; **what does it ~ up to?** ¿cuánto suma?
total [ˈtəutl] **1** *adj* (*Math etc*) total; (*complete, utter*) total, completo, entero; **the ~ losses amount to ...** las pérdidas suman un total de ...; **what is the ~ amount?** ¿cuánto es el importe total?; **~ assets** activo *m* total; **~ failure** fracaso *m* completo, fracaso *m* rotundo; **~ liabilities** pasivo *m* total; **~ loss** (*Comm*) pérdida *f* total; **~ output** producción *f* total; **~ war** guerra *f* total; **we were in ~ ignorance** lo ignorábamos por completo; **the disagreement is ~** el desacuerdo es total; *V* **abstainer**.
2 *n* total *m*; suma *f*; cantidad *f* global; **it comes to a ~ of ...** suma en total ..., asciende a ...; **the sum ~ of all this was that ...** el resultado de todo esto fue que ...
3 *vt* (**a**) (*add up*: *also* **to ~ up**) sumar.
(**b**) (*amount to*) ascender a, sumar, totalizar.
(**c**) (*US‡*) *car* dejar hecho chatarra, destrozar, desguazar.
totalitarian [ˌtəutælɪˈtɛərɪən] *adj* totalitario.
totalitarianism [ˌtəutælɪˈtɛərɪənɪzəm] *n* totalitarismo *m*.
totality [təuˈtælɪtɪ] *n* totalidad *f*.
totalizator [ˈtəutəlaɪzeɪtəʳ] *n* totalizador *m*.
totalize [ˈtəutəlaɪz] *vt* totalizar.
totally [ˈtəutəlɪ] *adv* totalmente, completamente.
tote[1]* [təut] *n* totalizador *m*.
tote[2]* [təut] *vt* acarrear, llevar (con dificultad); **I ~d it around all day** cargué con él todo el día; (*also in compounds*): **gun-toting policemen** policías *mpl* pistoleros.
totem [ˈtəutəm] *n* tótem *m*.
totemic [təuˈtemɪk] *adj* totémico.
totemism [ˈtəutəmɪzəm] *n* totemismo *m*.
totem-pole [ˈtəutəmpəul] *n* tótem *m*.
totter [ˈtɒtəʳ] *vi* (*stagger*) bambolearse, tambalearse; (*be about to fall*) tambalearse, estar para desplomarse.
tottering [ˈtɒtərɪŋ] *adj*, **tottery** [ˈtɒtərɪ] *adj* tambaleante; nada seguro; ruinoso; **he's getting tottery** empieza a andar con poca seguridad; **with tottering steps** con pasos inseguros, con pasos vacilantes.
toucan [ˈtuːkən] *n* tucán *m*.
touch [tʌtʃ] **1** *n* (**a**) (*sense of ~*) tacto *m*; **it feels rough to the ~** es áspero al tacto.
(**b**) (*act of ~ing*) toque *m*; contacto *m*; (*light brushing*) roce *m*; (*Mus, of typist*) pulsación *f*; (*Art*) pincelada *f*, toque *m*; **~ therapy** terapia *f* táctil; **final ~, finishing ~** última mano *f*, último toque *m*; **to give sth a finishing ~, to put the finishing ~ to sth** dar el último toque a algo; **common ~, human ~, personal ~** (*in person's character*) don *m* de gentes, (*in contacts etc*) nota *f* personal, nota *f* humana; **the master's ~** la mano del maestro; **it has the ~ of genius** lleva el sello de la genialidad; **it's the Nelson ~** es el estilo de Nelson; **the cold ~ of a dead fish** el contacto helado con un pez muerto; **at a ~ of her hand, I ...** al tocarme la mano de ella, yo ...; **with the barest ~ of a finger** con una ligerísima presión del dedo; **by ~** a tiento, tentándolo; **I felt a ~ on my neck** sentí que alguien me tocaba el cuello; **to give sb a ~ on the arm** tocar el brazo de uno.
(**c**) (*contact*) contacto *m*; **to be in ~ with sb** estar en contacto (*or* comunicación) con uno; **I'll be in ~** (*writing*) te escribiré, (*phoning*) te llamaré; **to be in ~ with new inventions** estar al tanto de los inventos, mantenerse al corriente de los inventos; **to be out of ~ with sb** haber perdido contacto con uno; **he's completely out of ~** sus ideas están completamente postergadas, está quedando anticuado; **we're very much out of ~ here** aquí casi no recibimos noticias de lo que pasa; **to get in ~ with sb** contactar a uno, ponerse en contacto con uno; **you can get into ~ with me at No. 7** puede contactarme en el número 7; **you ought to get in ~ with the police** conviene informar a la policía; **to keep in ~ with sb** mantener relaciones con uno; **well, keep in ~!** ¡bueno, no pierdas contacto!; **to lose ~ with sb** perder contacto con uno; **to put sb into ~ with another person** ayudar a uno a establecer contacto con otra persona.
(**d**) (*) **he's an easy** (*or* **soft**) **~** es la mar de generoso*; **he's good for a ~** seguramente nos dará (*or* prestará) algo; **to make a ~** lograr sacar dinero de uno, lograr dar un sablazo a uno*.
(**e**) (*small quantity*) pizca *f*; poquito *m*; (*Med*) ataque *m* leve; **a ~ of the sun** una insolación; **with a ~ of irony** con un dejo de ironía, con un punto de ironía; **to add a ~ of salt** agregar un poquitín de sal; **to have a ~ of 'flu** tener un ataque leve de gripe.
(**f**) (*Sport*) touche *f*, parte *f* fuera de juego; **to be in ~** estar fuera de juego; **to kick for ~, to kick the ball into ~**

poner el balón fuera de juego.

(**g**) (*as adv*) **it's a ~ expensive** es un poquito caro.

2 *vt* (**a**) (*come into contact with*) tocar; (*and explore*) palpar; (*brush against*) rozar; (*reach*) alcanzar; **~ and move!** ¡pieza tocada, pieza jugada!; **to ~ sth with one's finger** tocar algo con el dedo; **sb ~ed me on the arm** alguien me tocó el brazo; **don't ~!** ¡no tocar!, ¡fuera las manos!; **his property ~es ours** su propiedad linda con la nuestra, su finca es contigua a la nuestra; **and the police can't ~ him** y la policía no puede tocarle; **I never ~ed her!** ¡no la toqué siquiera!; **I wouldn't ~ it (with a barge pole)** no lo quiero ver ni de lejos; **to ~ ground** tocar tierra, tomar tierra; **~ wood!** ¡toco madera!

(**b**) (*eat, drink*) tomar, probar; **I haven't ~ed a mouthful** no he probado bocado; **I never ~ onion** no como cebolla; **I never ~ gin** no bebo nunca ginebra.

(**c**) (*equal*) compararse con, igualar; **there's no violinist to ~ him, no one can ~ him as a violinist** no hay violinista que se le iguale, no hay violinista que pueda compararse con él.

(**d**) (*make an impression on*) hacer efecto en, hacer mella en; **this saw won't ~ it** esta sierra no le hace mella, esta sierra es inútil para esto; **I couldn't ~ the third question** no pude tocar siquiera la tercera pregunta.

(**e**) (*move*) conmover, enternecer; **I was deeply ~ed** me conmoví mucho, me emocioné profundamente; **it ~ed our hearts** enterneció nuestros corazones; **no one can see it without being ~ed** nadie lo ve sin conmoverse.

(**f**) (*concern*) afectar, tocar; **it ~es us all closely** nos toca de cerca a todos; **if it ~es the national interest** si afecta al interés nacional.

(**g**) (*****) **to ~ sb for a loan** dar un sablazo a uno*, lograr sacar dinero de uno; **to ~ sb for £5** lograr que uno preste 5 libras.

3 *vi* (*come into contact*) tocarse; encontrarse; tocar al pasar, pasar rozando; (*collide*) chocar ligeramente; (*be adjacent*) lindar, estar contiguo; **our hands ~ed** se encontraron nuestras manos; **the subjects ~ at several points** los temas tienen varios aspectos en común.

◆touch at *vi* tocar en, hacer escala en.

◆touch down 1 *vt* (*Sport*) poner en tierra.

2 *vi* (**a**) (*Aer*) tocar tierra, aterrizar, (*loosely*) llegar; (*on sea*) amerizar, amarar.

(**b**) (*Sport*) tocar en tierra.

◆touch off *vt explosive* explotar, hacer estallar; *revolt* provocar, hacer estallar; *idea* dar origen a; *argument* causar, provocar.

◆touch on *vt* mencionar (de paso), referirse (brevemente) a.

◆touch up *vt* (**a**) (*Art, Phot etc*) retocar.

(**b**) (‡) meter mano a, manosear.

touch-and-go ['tʌtʃən'gəʊ] **1** *adj decision* difícil, dudoso. **2** *n*: **it's ~ whether ...** está en vilo si ..., es difícil decidir si ...; **3 hours of ~** 3 horas de tira y afloja.

touchdown ['tʌtʃdaʊn] *n* (*Aer*) aterrizaje *m*, (*loosely*) llegada *f*; (*on sea*) amerizaje *m*, amaraje *m*; (*Sport*) ensayo *m*, tanto *m*.

touché [tuː'ʃeɪ] *excl* ¡es verdad!; ¡dices bien!

touched* [tʌtʃt] *adj* chiflado*, tocado.

touchiness ['tʌtʃɪnɪs] *n* susceptibilidad *f*.

touching ['tʌtʃɪŋ] **1** *adj* conmovedor, patético. **2** *prep* tocante a.

touchingly ['tʌtʃɪŋlɪ] *adv* de modo conmovedor, patéticamente.

touch judge ['tʌtʃdʒʌdʒ] *n* juez *m* lateral.

touchline ['tʌtʃlaɪn] *n* (*Soccer etc*) línea *f* de banda; (*Rugby*) línea *f* de toque, línea *f* lateral.

touchpaper ['tʌtʃpeɪpə^r] *n* mecha *f*.

touch-sensitive ['tʌtʃ'sensɪtɪv] *adj* sensible al tacto.

touchstone ['tʌtʃstəʊn] *n* piedra *f* de toque (*also fig*).

touch-type ['tʌtʃtaɪp] *vi* mecanografiar al tacto.

touch-typing ['tʌtʃˌtaɪpɪŋ] *n* mecanografía *f* al tacto.

touch-typist ['tʌtʃˌtaɪpɪst] *n* mecanógrafo *m*, -a *f* al tacto.

touchy ['tʌtʃɪ] *adj* susceptible, quisquilloso; **to be ~** ofenderse por poca cosa, tener prontos enojos; **he's ~ about his weight** no le hacen gracia las referencias a su gordura, no le gusta que se le tome el pelo con motivo de su gordura.

tough [tʌf] **1** *adj* (**a**) *materials* duro, fuerte, resistente; *meat* duro, estropajoso; (*leathery*) correoso; **it's as ~ as old boots** es duro como una suela.

(**b**) (*hardy*) resistente, fuerte, vigoroso; **~ guy*** machote* *m*; **the ~ sports** los deportes violentos; **he's pretty ~** tiene mucha resistencia.

(**c**) (*unyielding, stubborn*) tenaz, terco; *policy* duro, de mano dura; *person* (*pej*) duro, malvado; **we can expect ~ resistance** podemos contar con una resistencia tensa.

(**d**) (*difficult*) difícil, penoso; *problem* espinoso; *journey, work* arduo; **there's a ~ road ahead** el camino a recorrer es arduo; **to have a ~ time of it** pasar las de Caín.

(**e**) (*of luck etc*) malo; **~!, ~ luck!** ¡mala suerte!; **that's pretty ~** eso me parece muy injusto; **but it was ~ on the others** pero perjudicó a los demás, pero fue muy desagradable para los demás.

2 *n* (*****) machote* *m*; (*pej*) gorila* *m*, forzudo *m*.

3 *vt*: **to ~ it out*** (*hold out*) no cejar, no ceder; mantenerse firme; (*rough it*) pasar estrecheces, vivir sin comodidades.

toughen ['tʌfn] (*also fig*) **1** *vt* endurecer, fortalecer. **2** *vi* endurecerse.

◆toughen up = toughen.

toughened ['tʌfnd] *adj* endurecido, fortalecido.

toughly ['tʌflɪ] *adv* vigorosamente; tenazmente, tercamente.

tough-minded ['tʌf'maɪndɪd] *adj* duro, severo; nada sentimental.

toughness ['tʌfnɪs] *n* dureza *f*, resistencia *f*; (*strictness*) inflexibilidad; lo correoso; vigor *m*; tenacidad *f*, terquedad *f*; lo difícil, lo penoso; lo arduo; **the job needs a certain ~** el trabajo exige cierta resistencia.

Toulon [tuː'lɔ̃ːŋ] *n* Tolón *m*.

Toulouse [tuː'luːz] *n* Tolosa *f* (de Francia).

toupée ['tuːpeɪ] *n* casquete *m*, peluca *f*.

tour ['tʊə^r] **1** *n* (*journey*) viaje *m* (largo), excursión *f* (larga); (*by team, actors, musicians etc*) gira *f*; (*of building, exhibition*) visita *f*; inspección *f*; **~ of duty** período *m* de servicio; **~ of inspection** visita *f*; recorrido *m* de inspección; **the Australian ~ of 1972** la gira australiana de 1972; **the ~ includes a week in Venice** el programa del viaje incluye una semana en Venecia; **to be on ~** estar de viaje; (*team etc*) estar de gira; **to go on ~** partir de viaje, (*team etc*) partir de gira; **to take a company on ~** llevar a una compañía de gira; **to take a play on ~** llevar una obra a una serie de teatros (de provincia *etc*).

2 *attr*: **~ guide** guía *m* turístico, guía *f* turística; **~ operator** (*Brit*) touroperador *m*, -ora *f*, operador *m* turístico, operadora *f* turística.

3 *vt country etc* viajar por, recorrer (como turista); *building, exhibition* visitar, recorrer.

4 *vi* viajar; estar de viaje, hacer viaje de turista; **we're just ~ing around** hacemos visitas de turismo aquí y allá.

Touraine [tʊ'reɪn] *n* Turena *f*.

tour de force ['tʊədə'fɔːs] *n* proeza *f*, hazaña *f*.

tourer ['tʊərə^r] *n* (coche *m* de) turismo *m*.

touring ['tʊərɪŋ] **1** *n* turismo *m*; viajes *mpl* turísticos.

2 *attr*: **~ company** compañía *f* ambulante; **~ team** equipo *m* en gira; equipo *m* visitante.

tourism ['tʊərɪzəm] *n* turismo *m*.

tourist ['tʊərɪst] **1** *n* turista *mf*.

2 *attr* turista, turístico; para turistas; de viajes; **of ~ interest** de interés turístico; **~ agency** agencia *f* de viajes; **~ bureau, ~ office** oficina *f* de viajes; **~ class** clase *f* turística; **~ industry, ~ trade** industria *f* del turismo; **~ information centre** = oficina *f* de información y turismo; **~ season** temporada *f* del turismo; **~ trap** trampa *f* de turistas, lugar *m* cazaturistas; **~ visa** visado *m* turístico, visa *f* turística (*LAm*).

touristy* ['tʊərɪstɪ] *adj* (demasiado) turístico, turistizado.

tournament ['tʊənəmənt] *n* torneo *m*; concurso *m*, certamen *m*.

tourney ['tʊənɪ] *n* torneo *m*.

tourniquet ['tʊənɪkeɪ] *n* torniquete *m*.

touse* [taʊz] *vt* dar una paliza a (*also fig*).

tousing* ['taʊzɪŋ] *n* paliza *f* (*also fig*).

tousle ['taʊzl] *vt* ajar, desarreglar; *hair* despeinar.

tousled ['taʊzld] *adj* ajado, desarreglado, en desorden; *hair* despeinado.

tout [taʊt] **1** *n* (*seller*) pregonero *m*; (*agent*) gancho *m*; (*ticket ~*) reventa* *m*, revendedor *m*; (*Racing*) pronosticador *m*.

2 *vt wares* ofrecer, pregonar; *tickets* revender.

3 *vi*: **to ~ for custom** solicitar clientes; tratar de hacer un negocio.

tout court ['tuː'kʊə^r] *adv*: **his name is Rodríguez ~** se llama Rodríguez a secas.

tow[1] [təʊ] **1** (*act*) remolque *m*; (*rope*) remolque *m*, cable *m* de remolque; (*thing towed*) vehículo *m* (*etc*) remolcado; **to be on** (*or* (*US*) **in**) **~** ser remolcado, ir de remolque; **to**

have a car in ~ llevar un coche de remolque; **he had 3 girls in** ~ iba acompañado de 3 chicas, (*fig*) andaba en relaciones con 3 chicas, tenía 3 chicas al retortero; **to take in** ~ dar remolque a.

2 *attr*: ~ **car** (*US*) grúa *f*, coche *m* de remolque.

3 *vt* remolcar, llevar a remolque; (*Naut*) atoar, toar; **to** ~ **sth about** (*fig*) llevar algo consigo.

◆**tow away** *vt* remolcar, quitar remolcando.

tow² [təʊ] *n* estopa *f*.

towage ['təʊɪdʒ] *n* (*act*) remolque *m*; (*fee*) derechos *mpl* de remolque.

toward(s) [tə'wɔːd(z)] *prep* (*of direction*) hacia; (*of time*) hacia, cerca de; (*of attitude*) con, para con; **his feelings** ~ **the church** sus sentimientos para con la iglesia; ~ **noon** hacia mediodía; ~ **6 o'clock** hacia las 6; **we're saving** ~ **our holiday** ahorramos dinero para nuestras vacaciones; **it helps** ~ **a solution** contribuye a la solución, ayuda en el esfuerzo por encontrar una solución.

towaway zone ['təʊəweɪ,zəʊn] *n* (*US Aut*) *zona de aparcamiento prohibido donde la grúa procede a retirar los vehículos.*

towbar ['təʊbɑːʳ] *n* barra *f* de remolque.

towboat ['təʊbəʊt] *n* (*US*) remolcador *m*.

towel ['taʊəl] **1** *n* toalla *f*; **to throw in the** ~ tirar la toalla.
2 *vt* secar con toalla; frotar con toalla.

towelling, (*US*) **toweling** ['taʊəlɪŋ] *n* género *m* para toallas, felpa *f*.

towel-rack ['taʊəlræk] *n*, **towel-rail** ['taʊəlreɪl] *n* toallero *m*.

tower ['taʊəʳ] **1** *n* torre *f*; (*bell*~) campanario *m*; ~ **of strength** baluarte *m*, bastión *m*.

2 *attr*: ~ **block** (*Brit*) torre *f* (de viviendas).

3 *vi* (*also* **to** ~ **up**) elevarse; encumbrarse; **to** ~ **above, to** ~ **over** dominar, destacarse sobre, (*fig*) descollar entre; **it** ~**s to over 300 metres** se eleva a más de 300 metros; **he** ~**s above his contemporaries** descuella fuertemente entre sus coetáneos.

towering ['taʊərɪŋ] *adj mountain* encumbrado; elevado, elevadísimo; *building* muy alto, imponente por su altura; *figure* destacado, dominante; *rage* muy violento.

tow-headed [,təʊ'hedɪd] *adj* rubio, rubiacho.

towline ['təʊlaɪn] *n* (*Naut*) sirga *f*; (*Aut*) cable *m* de remolque.

town [taʊn] **1** *n* ciudad *f*; (*smaller, country* ~) pueblo *m*, población *f*; ~ **and gown** ciudadanos *mpl* y universitarios, ciudad *f* y universidad; **to be on the** ~* estar en plan de juerga*; **to go (out) on the** ~* salir de juerga*; **to live in** ~ vivir en la capital (*esp* Londres); **Jake's back in** ~! ¡ha vuelto Jake!; **to go up to** ~ ir a la capital (nacional *or* local); **to go to** ~ ir a la ciudad; **to go to** ~ **on*** dedicarse con entusiasmo a, entregarse de lleno a; **he certainly went to** ~ **on that mistake** de verdad sacó partido de ese error; **he's out of** ~ está fuera, está de viaje; **he's from out of** ~ (*US*) es forastero, no es de aquí; **to paint the** ~ **red** echar una cana al aire.

2 *attr* urbano; urbanístico; de (la) ciudad, municipal; ~ **centre** centro *m* urbano; ~ **clerk** secretario *m*, -a *f* del Ayuntamiento; ~ **council** (*Brit*) concejo *m* municipal, ayuntamiento *m*; ~ **councillor** (*Brit*) concejal *m*, -ala *f*; ~ **crier** pregonero *m* público; ~**-dweller** ciudadano *m*, -a *f*; ~ **hall** (*Brit*) ayuntamiento *m*; ~ **house** casa *f* adosada; (*not country*) residencia *f* urbana; ~ **plan** plan *m* de desarrollo urbano; ~ **planner** (*Brit*) urbanista *mf*; ~ **planning** (*Brit*) urbanismo *m*.

townee [taʊ'niː] *n*, (*US*) **townie** ['taʊnɪ] *n* habitante *mf* de la ciudad; hombre *m* (*or* mujer *f etc*) de la ciudad.

townsfolk ['taʊnzfəʊk] *npl* ciudadanos *mpl*.

township ['taʊnʃɪp] *n* municipio *m*, término *m* municipal; pueblo *m*.

townsman ['taʊnzmən] *n*, *pl* **townsmen** ['taʊnzmən] ciudadano *m*; (*as opposed to countryman*) hombre *m* de la ciudad, habitante *m* de la ciudad.

townspeople ['taʊnz,piːpl] *npl* ciudadanos *mpl*.

townswoman ['taʊnzwʊmən] *n*, *pl* **townswomen** ['taʊnzwɪmɪn] ciudadana *f*; (*as opposed to countrywoman*) habitante *f* de la ciudad.

towpath ['təʊpɑːθ] *n* camino *m* de sirga.

towrope ['təʊrəʊp] *n* remolque *m*, cable *m* de remolque; (*on canal*) sirga *f*.

tow truck ['təʊtrʌk] *n* (*US*) (camión *m*) grúa *f*, coche *m* de remolque.

toxaemia, (*US*) **toxemia** [tɒk'siːmɪə] *n* toximia *f*.

toxic ['tɒksɪk] **1** *adj* tóxico; ~ **alga** alga *f* tóxica; ~ **substance** sustancia *f* tóxica; ~ **waste** desechos *mpl* tóxicos, residuos *mpl* tóxicos. **2** *n* tóxico *m*.

toxicity [,tɒk'sɪsɪtɪ] *n* toxicidad *f*.

toxicological [,tɒksɪkə'lɒdʒɪkəl] *adj* toxicológico.

toxicologist [,tɒksɪ'kɒlədʒɪst] *n* toxicólogo *m*, -a *f*.

toxicology [,tɒksɪ'kɒlədʒɪ] *n* toxicología *f*.

toxin ['tɒksɪn] *n* toxina *f*.

toy [tɔɪ] **1** *n* juguete *m*; (*pej, iro*) juguete *m*, chuchería *f*.

2 *attr railway etc* de juguete, de jugar; ~ **car** coche *m* de juguete; ~ **dog** (*small*) perrito *m*, perro *m* faldero; ~ **soldier** soldadito *m* de plomo; ~ **theatre** teatro *m* de títeres; ~ **train** tren *m* de juguete.

3 *vi*: **to** ~ **with** *object* jugar con, divertirse jugando con; *food* comiscar; *idea* dar vueltas a, acariciar; *sb's affections* divertirse con.

toybox ['tɔɪbɒks] *n* caja *f* de juguetes.

toyboy ['tɔɪbɔɪ] *n* amante *m* (de una mujer más vieja).

toy-maker ['tɔɪ,meɪkəʳ] *n* fabricante *mf* de juguetes.

toyshop ['tɔɪʃɒp] *n* juguetería *f*.

toytown ['tɔɪtaʊn] *adj* (**a**) = **Mickey Mouse.** (**b**) **he's a** ~ **revolutionary** es un aspirante a revolucionario.

trace¹ [treɪs] **1** *n* rastro *m*, huella *f*; vestigio *m*; señal *f*, indicio *m*; (*small amount*) pequeñísima cantidad *f*, pizca *f*; (*Chem, Med*) indicio *m*; (*remaining taste etc*) dejo *m*; **without a** ~ **of ill feeling** sin asomo de rencor; **sunk without** ~ desaparecido sin dejar el menor indicio; **to vanish without** ~ desaparecer sin dejar rastro; **there is no** ~ **of it now** no queda vestigio alguno de ello ahora; **we looked all over but couldn't find a single** ~ buscamos por todas partes pero sin encontrar el menor indicio.

2 *vt* (**a**) *curve, line etc* trazar; (*with tracing paper*) calcar. (**b**) (*follow trail of*) seguir, seguir la pista de; rastrear; (*find, locate*) encontrar; localizar, averiguar el paradero de; **I cannot** ~ **any reference to it** no he logrado encontrar ninguna referencia a ello; **she was finally** ~**d to a house in Soho** por fin la encontraron en una casa del Soho; **to** ~ **an idea for sb** exponer una idea a uno.

◆**trace back** *vt*: **to** ~ **one's ancestry back to Ferdinand III** hacer remontar su ascendencia hasta Fernando III; **to** ~ **a rumour back to its source** averiguar dónde se originó un rumor, seguir la pista de un rumor hasta llegar a su punto de partida.

trace² [treɪs] *n* tirante *m*, correa *f*; **to kick over the** ~**s** sacar los pies del plato, mostrar las herraduras.

traceable ['treɪsəbl] *adj*: **a person not now** ~ una persona cuyo paradero actual es imposible de encontrar; **an easily** ~ **reference** una referencia fácil de encontrar.

trace element ['treɪs,elɪmənt] *n* oligoelemento *m*.

tracer ['treɪsəʳ] **1** *n* (*Chem, Med*) indicador *m*, trazador *m*.

2 *attr*: ~ **bullet** bala *f* trazadora; ~ **element** elemento *m* trazador.

tracery ['treɪsərɪ] *n* tracería *f*.

trachea [trə'kɪə] *n* tráquea *f*.

tracheotomy [,trækɪ'ɒtəmɪ] *n* traqueotomía *f*.

trachoma [træ'kəʊmə] *n* tracoma *m*.

tracing ['treɪsɪŋ] *n* calco *m*.

tracing-paper ['treɪsɪŋ,peɪpəʳ] *n* papel *m* de calco.

track [træk] **1** *n* (**a**) (*mark: of animal*) huella *f*; pista *f*, rastro *m*; (*of person*) pista *f*; (*of vehicle*) huella *f*; (*of wheel*) rodada *f*; (*of boat*) estela *f*; (*of hurricane*) rastro *m*, marcha *f*; (*of bullet, rocket etc*) trayectoria *f*; **to be on sb's** ~(**s**) seguir la pista de uno; **he had the police on his** ~ le buscaba la policía, le estaba cazando la policía; **they got on to his** ~ **very quickly** se pusieron sobre la pista muy pronto; **to cover up one's** ~**s** borrar sus huellas, procurar no dejar rastro de sí; **to follow in sb's** ~ seguir el camino que ha marcado uno; **to keep** ~ **of sb** no perder de vista a uno; seguir la suerte a uno; **to keep** ~ **of new inventions** mantenerse al tanto de los nuevos inventos; **to lose** ~ **of sb** perder a uno de vista; **to lose** ~ **of what sb is saying** perder el hilo de lo que está diciendo uno; **to make** ~**s*** irse, largarse; **we must be making** ~**s*** tenemos que marcharnos; **to stop (dead) in one's** ~**s** pararse en seco; **to stop sb (dead) in his** ~**s** parar a uno en seco; **to throw sb off the** ~ despistar a uno.

(**b**) (*path*) senda *f*, camino *m*; **to be on the right** ~ ir por buen camino; **to be on the wrong** ~ (*fig*) haberse equivocado, estar equivocado; **to be way off the** ~ estar totalmente despistado; **to put sb on the right** ~ mostrar a uno el camino que le conviene seguir.

(**c**) (*Sport*) pista *f*; (*lane*) carril *m*; **to be on the fast** (*or* **inside**) ~ (*fig*) ser ambicioso, tener ganas de ascender.

(**d**) (*Rail*) vía *f*; **to cross the** ~**s** cruzar la vía; **to live on the wrong side of the** ~**s** (*esp US*) vivir en los barrios pobres; **to jump the** ~(**s**), **to run off the** ~(**s**) descarrilar.

(**e**) (*Mech*: *also* **caterpillar** ~**s**) oruga *f*.

(**f**) (*on tape*) banda *f*, canal *m*; (*Comput*) pista *f*.

2 *attr*: ~ **activities,** ~ **athletics** (*US*) atletismo *m*; ~ **event** prueba *f* atlética en pista; ~ **record** (*Sport*) récord *m*; (*fig*) historial *m*, hoja *f* de servicios.

3 *vt animal* rastrear, seguir la pista de; *satellite etc* rastrear, seguir la trayectoria de.

4 *vi*: **to** ~ **along** avanzar por, ir por, seguir.

◆**track down** *vt* localizar, averiguar el paradero (*or* origen) de, buscar y encontrar; **finally we ~ed it down in the library** por fin lo encontramos en la biblioteca.

tracked [trækt] *adj*: ~ **vehicle** vehículo *m* con orugas.

tracker ['trækəʳ] *n* rastreador *m*.

tracker-dog ['trækədɒg] *n* perro *m* rastreador.

tracking ['trækɪŋ] *n* rastreo *m*; ~ **device** dispositivo *m* de localización.

tracking-station ['trækɪŋ,steɪʃən] *n* centro *m* de seguimiento, estación *f* de rastreo.

trackless ['træklɪs] *adj* sin caminos, impenetrable.

trackman ['trækmən] *n*, *pl* **trackmen** ['trækmən] (*US*) obrero *m* de ferrocarril.

track meet ['træk'mi:t] *n* (*US*) concurso *m* de carreras y saltos.

track-race ['trækreɪs] *n* carrera *f* en pista.

track-racing ['træk,reɪsɪŋ] *n* carreras *fpl* en pista, ciclismo *m* (*etc*) en pista.

trackshoes ['trækʃu:z] *npl* zapatillas *fpl* para pista de atletismo (claveteadas).

tracksuit ['træksu:t] *n* chandal *m*.

tract¹ [trækt] *n* región *f*, zona *f*; extensión *f*; (*Anat*) región *f*.

tract² [trækt] *n* (*pamphlet*) folleto *m*; (*treatise*) tratado *m*.

tractable ['træktəbl] *adj person* tratable, dócil; *problem* soluble; *material* dúctil, maleable.

traction ['trækʃən] **1** *n* tracción *f*. **2** *attr*: ~ **engine** locomóvil *m*, máquina *f* de tracción.

tractive ['træktɪv] *adj* tractivo.

tractor ['træktəʳ] *n* tractor *m*.

tractor-drawn ['træktədrɔ:n] *adj* arrastrado por tractor.

tractor drive ['træktə,draɪv] *n* tractor *m*.

tractor-driver ['træktə,draɪvəʳ] *n* tractorista *mf*.

tractor feed ['træktə,fi:d] *n* arrastre *m* de papel por tracción.

trad* [træd] *adj abbr of* **traditional.**

trade [treɪd] **1** *n* (**a**) (*commerce*) comercio *m*; negocio *m*; tráfico *m* (*in* en); industria *f*; **the wool** ~ la industria lanera; **the** ~ **in drugs, the drug** ~ el tráfico en narcóticos, el comercio de narcóticos; **to be in** ~ ser comerciante, tener un negocio, (*esp*) tener una tienda; **to do a good** (*or* **brisk, roaring**) ~ hacer un buen negocio (*in* con); *V* **retail** *etc*.

(**b**) (*calling*) oficio *m*, profesión *f*; ramo *m*; empleo *m*; oficio *m* manual; **a butcher by** ~ de oficio carnicero; **a lawyer by** ~ (*hum*) de profesión abogado; **to carry on a** ~ ejercer un oficio; **to put sb to a** ~ hacer que uno aprenda un oficio; **known in the** ~ **as** ... conocido por los que son del ramo como ...

(**c**) ~**s** (*Geog*) vientos *mpl* alisios.

2 *attr* de comercio, comercial; mercantil; ~ **agreement** acuerdo *m* comercial; ~ **allowance,** ~ **discount** descuento *m* comercial; ~ **association** asociación *f* mercantil; ~ **barriers** barreras *fpl* arancelarias; ~ **cycle** ciclo *m* mercantil; ~ **deficit** déficit *m* comercial; **T**~ **Descriptions Act** (*Brit*) *ley sobre descripciones comerciales*; ~ **directory** guía *f* mercantil; ~ **discount** descuento *m* para el comercio; ~ **fair,** ~ **show** feria *f* de muestras, feria *f* comercial; ~ **figures** estadísticas *fpl* comerciales; ~ **gap** déficit *m* del balance comercial; ~ **journal** periódico *m* gremial; ~ **mission** misión *f* comercial; ~ **paper** revista *f* comercial; ~ **press** prensa *f* especializada; ~ **price** precio *m* al comerciante, precio *m* al por mayor, precio *m* al detallista; ~ **reference** referencia *f* comercial; ~ **restrictions** restricciones *fpl* comerciales; ~ **route** ruta *f* comercial; ~ **sanctions** sanciones *fpl* comerciales; ~ **secret** secreto *m* de fábrica, secreto *m* profesional; **on** ~ **terms** con descuento para el comercio; ~ **war** guerra *f* comercial.

3 *vt* (*fig*) vender; **to** ~ **A for B** cambiar A por B, trocar A por B.

4 *vi* comerciar (*in* en, *with* con); **we do not** ~ **with Ruritania** no tenemos relaciones comerciales con Ruritania; **to cease trading** dejar de existir, dejar de comerciar; **to** ~ **on an advantage** aprovecharse de una ventaja, explotar una ventaja.

◆**trade in** *vt*: **to** ~ **a car in** ofrecer un coche como parte del pago, devolver un coche usado al comprar otro nuevo.

◆**trade off** *vt*: **to** ~ **off one thing for another** renunciar a algo a cambio de otra cosa.

trade-in ['treɪdɪn] *attr*: ~ **arrangements** sistema *m* de devolver un artículo usado al comprar otro nuevo; ~ **price,** ~ **value** valor *m* de un artículo usado que se descuenta del precio de otro nuevo.

trademark ['treɪdmɑ:k] *n* marca *f* registrada, marca *f* de fábrica; (*fig*) marca *f*, sello *m*.

tradename ['treɪdneɪm] *n* nombre *m* comercial, nombre *m* de fábrica; marca *f*.

trade-off ['treɪdɒf] *n* intercambio *m*, canje *m*; concesiones *fpl* mutuas; compensación *f*.

trader ['treɪdəʳ] *n* comerciante *m*; traficante *m*; (*street* ~) vendedor *m* ambulante; (*Hist*) mercader *m*.

tradescantia [,trædəs'kæntɪə] *n* tradescantia *f*.

tradesman ['treɪdzmən] *n*, *pl* **tradesmen** ['treɪdzmən] (*shopkeeper*) tendero *m*; (*roundsman*) repartidor *m*, proveedor *m*; (*artisan*) artesano *m*; ~**'s entrance** entrada *f* de servicio, puerta *f* de servicio.

tradespeople ['treɪdz,pi:pl] *npl* tenderos *mpl*.

trade(s) union ['treɪd(z)'ju:njən] **1** *n* sindicato *m*, gremio *m* (obrero); **to form a** ~ formar un sindicato, agremiarse.

2 *attr* sindical, gremial; ~ **labour** mano *f* de obra agremiada; ~ **movement** movimiento *m* sindical; ~ **shop** taller *m* donde todos los obreros son miembros de un sindicato.

trade unionism ['treɪd'ju:njənɪzəm] *n* sindicalismo *m*, sistema *m* de sindicatos.

trade unionist ['treɪd'ju:njənɪst] *n* sindicalista *mf*, miembro *mf* de un sindicato.

trade winds ['treɪdwɪndz] *npl* vientos *mpl* alisios.

trading ['treɪdɪŋ] **1** *attr* comercial, mercantil; ~ **account** cuenta *f* comercial, cuenta *f* de compraventa; ~ **estate** (*Brit*) zona *f* comercial; ~ **floor** parqué *m*; ~ **loss** pérdidas *fpl*; ~ **nation** nación *f* con importante comercio exterior; ~ **partner** socio *m*, -a *f* comercial; ~ **port** puerto *m* comercial; ~ **post** factoría *f*; ~ **profits for 1995** beneficios *mpl* obtenidos en el ejercicio de 1995; ~ **results** balance *m* comercial; ~ **stamp** cupón *m*, sello *m* de prima.

2 *n* (**a**) (*Comm*) comercio *m*; tráfico *m*; **to stop** ~**, to suspend** ~ dejar de comerciar. (**b**) (*St Ex*) operaciones *fpl* bursátiles.

tradition [trə'dɪʃən] *n* tradición *f*.

traditional [trə'dɪʃənl] *adj* tradicional; clásico, consagrado; **it is** ~ **for them to sing** por tradición cantan, cantan de acuerdo con la tradición.

traditionalism [trə'dɪʃnəlɪzəm] *n* tradicionalismo *m*.

traditionalist [trə'dɪʃnəlɪst] **1** *adj* tradicionalista. **2** *n* tradicionalista *mf*.

traditionality [trə,dɪʃə'nælətɪ] *n* tradicionalidad *f*.

traditionally [trə'dɪʃnəlɪ] *adv* tradicionalmente; según tradición, de acuerdo con la tradición.

traduce [trə'dju:s] *vt* calumniar, denigrar.

traffic ['træfɪk] **1** *n* (**a**) (*Aut etc*) circulación *f*, tráfico *m*, tránsito *m* (*LAm*); movimiento *m*; **the** ~ **is heavy this morning** hay mucho tráfico esta mañana; ~ **was quite light** había poco tráfico; ~ **was blocked for some hours** la circulación quedó interrumpida durante varias horas.

(**b**) (*trade*) tráfico *m*, comercio *m* (*in* en); (*pej*) trata *f* (*in* de); **the drug** ~ el tráfico en narcóticos.

2 *attr* de la circulación, del tráfico, del tránsito (*LAm*); ~ **accident** accidente *m* de circulación; ~ **circle** (*US*) cruce *m* giratorio, glorieta *f*, redondel *m*; ~ **cone** cono *m* señalizador; ~ **control** (*act*) control *m* del tráfico; (*lights*) semáforo *m*; **to be on** ~ **duty** estar en tráfico; ~ **flow** flujo *m* de tráfico; ~ **island** (*Brit*) refugio *m*; ~ **offence** (*Brit*), ~ **violation** infracción *f* de tránsito; ~ **police** policía *f* de tráfico; ~ **warden** (*Brit*) controlador *m*, -ora *f* de estacionamiento.

3 *vi* traficar, comerciar (*in* en); (*pej*) tratar (*in* en).

trafficator ['træfɪkeɪtəʳ] *n* (*Brit*) indicador *m* de dirección, flecha *f* de dirección.

traffic-jam ['træfɪkdʒæm] *n* embotellamiento *m*, atasco *m*, aglomeración *f*; **a 5-mile** ~ una cola de coches que se extiende hasta 5 millas; **there are always** ~**s here** aquí siempre se embotella el tráfico, aquí siempre hay atasco.

trafficker ['træfɪkəʳ] *n* traficante *m* (*in* en), tratante *m* (*in* en).

traffic-lights ['træfɪklaɪts] *npl* semáforo *m*, luces *fpl* (de tráfico), señales *fpl* (de tráfico).

traffic-sign ['træfɪksaɪn] *n* señal *f* de tráfico.

tragedian [trə'dʒi:dɪən] *n* trágico *m*.

tragedienne [trədʒi:dɪ'en] *n* trágica *f*, actriz *f* trágica.

tragedy ['trædʒɪdɪ] *n* tragedia *f*; **it is a** ~ **that** ... es trágico que ...; **what a** ~! ¡qué trágico!; **the** ~ **of it is that** ... lo trágico es que ...

tragic [ˈtrædʒɪk] *adj* trágico.

tragically [ˈtrædʒɪkəlɪ] *adv* trágicamente; **don't take it too ~** no seas tan pesimista.

tragicomedy [ˈtrædʒɪˈkɒmɪdɪ] *n* tragicomedia *f.*

tragicomic [ˈtrædʒɪˈkɒmɪk] *adj* tragicómico.

trail [treɪl] **1** *n* (**a**) (*wake*) estela *f*; (*of comet, rocket*) cola *f*; **~ of fire** estela *f* de fuego; **the speech left a long ~ of comments** el discurso ha dejado larga estela de comentarios; **the hurricane left a ~ of destruction** el huracán dejó una estela de estragos.

(**b**) (*track of animal*) rastro *m*, pista *f*; **false ~** pista *f* falsa; **to be on the ~ of, to follow the ~ of** seguir la pista de; **to pick up the ~** encontrar la pista.

(**c**) (*path, road*) camino *m*, sendero *m*; (*Pol*: *of campaign*) recorrido *m*.

2 *vt* (**a**) (*drag*) arrastrar; *arms* bajar.

(**b**) (*track*) rastrear, seguir la pista de; seguir de cerca; (*of detective etc*) vigilar; **have that man ~ed** que vigilen (*or* sigan) a ese hombre.

(**c**) (*Cine*) poner un tráiler (*or* avance) de.

3 *vi* (**a**) (*be drawn along*) arrastrarse; **he walked with his coat ~ing on the ground** andaba arrastrando su abrigo por los suelos; **with a small boat ~ing behind** con un bote remolcado.

(**b**) (*of person*) **to ~ along** arrastrarse; caminar penosamente, ir con aire desanimado; **to ~ far behind** quedar muy a la zaga, rezagarse mucho; **El Toboso is ~ing at the foot of the league** El Toboso va en última posición de la liga; **the children ~ed home in the rain** los niños se fueron muy tristes a su casa bajo la lluvia.

(**c**) (*plant*) arrastrarse; trepar.

◆trail away, trail off *vi* esfumarse, ir desapareciendo (hasta perderse completamente), desvanecerse poco a poco.

trailblazer [ˈtreɪlbleɪzəʳ] *n* pionero *m*, -a *f*.

trailblazing [ˈtreɪlbleɪzɪŋ] **1** *adj* pionero. **2** *n* trabajo *m* (*or* viaje *etc*) pionero.

trailer [ˈtreɪləʳ] **1** *n* (**a**) (*Aut etc*) remolque *m*; (*caravan*) caravana *f*. (**b**) (*Cine*) tráiler *m*, avance *m*. **2** *attr*: **~ park** (*US*) cámping *m* para remolques, cámping *m* para caravanas.

trailing [ˈtreɪlɪŋ] *adj* colgado; *plant* rastrero, trepador; **~ edge** borde *m* de salida, borde *m* posterior.

trail truck [ˈtreɪltrʌk] *n US*) tráiler *m*.

train [treɪn] **1** *n* (**a**) (*Rail*) tren *m*; **by ~** (*go*) en tren, (*send*) por ferrocarril; **to catch a ~** coger un tren (*Sp*), tomar un tren; **to change ~s** cambiar de tren, hacer transbordo.

(**b**) (*Mech*) tren *m*; **~ of gears** tren *m* de engranajes.

(**c**) (*series*) serie *f*, sucesión *f*; **a ~ of cars** una serie de coches; **~ of powder** reguero *m* de pólvora; **~ of events** serie *f* de sucesos; **~ of thought** hilo *m* del pensamiento; **he began another ~ of thought** dejó discurrir el pensamiento en otra cosa, dirigió el pensamiento a otra cosa; **in an unbroken ~** en una serie ininterrumpida; sin solución de continuidad; **it is in ~** está en preparación; **to set sth in ~** poner algo en movimiento, empezar a poner algo en obra.

(**d**) (*of dress*) cola *f*; **to carry sb's ~** llevar la cola del vestido de una.

(**e**) (*entourage*) séquito *m*, comitiva *f*; (*of mules*) recua *f*, reata *f*; **it brought ruin in its ~** acarreó la ruina, trajo consigo la ruina.

2 *attr*: **~ attendant** (*US*) empleado *m*, -a *f* de coches-cama; **~ service** servicio *m* de trenes; **~ set** ferrocarril *m* de juguete; **~ station** estación *f* de ferrocarril.

3 *vt* (**a**) (*instruct etc*) adiestrar; preparar, formar; (*Mil*) adiestrar, ejercitar; disciplinar; (*in new technique*) capacitar; *child* enseñar; (*Sport*) entrenar, preparar; *animal* amaestrar; *horse* entrenar; *voice* educar; **they ~ boys for the Navy** preparan a los muchachos para la Marina; **to ~ sb in firearms** enseñar a uno el manejo de las armas de fuego; **where were you ~ed?** ¿dónde cursó Vd sus estudios?; **he was ~ed at Salamanca** tuvo su formación profesional en Salamanca; **to ~ sb to do sth** enseñar a uno a hacer algo, enseñar a uno el arte (*or* la técnica *etc*) de hacer algo; habituar a uno a hacer algo, acostumbrar a uno a hacer algo.

(**b**) (*direct*) *gun* apuntar (*on* a); *camera, telescope* enfocar (*on* a); *plant* guiar (*up, along* por).

4 *vi* (**a**) (*instruct o.s.*) adiestrarse; prepararse, formarse; educarse; (*Mil*) adiestrarse, ejercitarse; (*Sport etc*) entrenarse; **I ~ for 6 hours a day** me entreno 6 horas diarias, hago prácticas durante 6 horas cada día; **to ~ as a teacher, to ~ to become a teacher** estudiar para profesor; **we're ~ing for the cup game** nos entrenamos para el partido de copa; **where did you ~?** ¿dónde cursó Vd sus estudios?, ¿dónde se formó Vd?

(**b**) (*Rail*) ir en tren; **then we ~ed to Seville** luego fuimos en tren a Sevilla.

5 *vr*: **to ~ o.s. in a craft** enseñarse un arte, adiestrarse en un arte; **to ~ o.s. to do sth** enseñarse a hacer algo; habituarse a hacer algo, formarse la costumbre de hacer algo.

◆train up *vt*: **to ~ sb up** preparar a uno, formar a uno.

trained [treɪnd] *adj teacher etc* graduado, diplomado; *worker* cualificado, capacitado, especializado; *animal* amaestrado; **a well-~ child** un niño (bien) educado, un niño bien enseñado; **a well-~ horse** un caballo bien preparado; **a well-~ army** un ejército disciplinado; **a fully-~ nurse** una enfermera diplomada.

trainee [treɪˈniː] **1** *n* aprendiz *m* (profesional), aprendiza *f* (profesional); (*US Mil*) recluta *mf* en período de aprendizaje. **2** *attr*: **~ manager** aprendiz *m*, -iza *f* de administración.

trainer [ˈtreɪnəʳ] *n* (**a**) (*Sport*: *person*) entrenador *m*, -ora *f*, preparador *m* físico, preparadora *f* física; (*of horses*) entrenador *m*, -ora *f*; (*of circus animals*) domador *m*, -ora *f*.

(**b**) (*plane*) entrenador *m*.

(**c**) **~s** (*shoes*) zapatillas *fpl* de deporte.

training [ˈtreɪnɪŋ] **1** *n* adiestramiento *m*; preparación *f*, formación *f* (profesional); orientación *f*; instrucción *f*; (*Mil*) instrucción *f*, ejercicios *mpl*; (*Sport*) entrenamiento *m*, preparación *f* (física); (*of staff for new job*) capacitación *f*; **to be in ~** estar entrenado, estar en forma; **to be out of ~** estar desentrenado.

2 *attr*: **~ camp** campamento *m* de instrucción; **~ center** (*US*), **~ centre** centro *m* de instrucción; centro *m* de formación laboral; **~ course** curso *m* de entrenamiento; **~ manual** manual *m* de instrucción; **~ plane** entrenador *m*; **~ scheme** plan *m* de formación profesional; **~ shoes** zapatillas *fpl* de deporte.

training college [ˈtreɪnɪŋˌkɒlɪdʒ] *n* escuela *f* normal.

training-ship [ˈtreɪnɪŋʃɪp] *n* buque-escuela *m*.

trainman [ˈtreɪnmæn] *n, pl* **trainmen** [ˈtreɪnmen] (*US*) ferroviario *m*; guardafrenos *m*.

train-spotter [ˈtreɪnspɒtəʳ] *n* aficionado *m*, -a *f* a locomotoras.

train-spotting [ˈtreɪnspɒtɪŋ] *n*: **~ is very popular in Britain** el ir a ver trenes es muy popular en Gran Bretaña.

traipse* [treɪps] *vi* ir (a desgana), andar (penosamente); andar sin propósito fijo; **we ~d about all morning** pasamos toda la mañana yendo de acá para allá; **I had to ~ over to see him** tuve que tomarme la molestia de ir a verle.

trait [treɪt] *n* rasgo *m*.

traitor [ˈtreɪtəʳ] *n* traidor *m*, -ora *f*; **to be a ~ to one's country** traicionar a la patria; **to turn ~** volverse traidor, volver la casaca.

traitorous [ˈtreɪtərəs] *adj* traidor; traicionero.

traitorously [ˈtreɪtərəslɪ] *adv* traidoramente, con traición.

traitress [ˈtreɪtrɪs] *n* traidora *f*.

Trajan [ˈtreɪdʒən] *nm* Trajano.

trajectory [trəˈdʒektərɪ] *n* trayectoria *f*.

tram [træm] *n*, **tramcar** (*Brit*) [ˈtræmkɑːʳ] *n* tranvía *m*, tren *m* (*Mex*).

tramlines [ˈtræmlaɪnz] *npl* (*Brit*) carriles *mpl* de tranvía; (*Sport*) líneas *fpl* laterales.

trammel [ˈtræməl] **1** *vt* poner trabas a, trabar, impedir. **2** *npl*: **~s** trabas *fpl*.

tramp [træmp] **1** *n* (**a**) (*sound of feet*) marcha *f* pesada, pasos *mpl* pesados.

(**b**) (*hike*) paseo *m* largo, caminata *f*, excursión *f* a pie; **to go for a ~ in the hills** hacer una excursión a pie por la montaña; **after a ~ of many miles** después de recorrer muchos kilómetros a pie; **it's a long ~** es mucho camino.

(**c**) (*person*: *man*) vago *m*, vagabundo *m*; (*woman*: *US**) puta *f*, fulana *f*; **you (little) ~!** ¡lagarta!

(**d**) (*Naut*: *also* **~ steamer**) vapor *m* volandero.

2 *vt* (*stamp on*) pisar con fuerza; (*walk across*) recorrer a pie, hacer una excursión por; **to ~ the streets** andar (penosamente) por las calles, recorrer (de muy mala gana) las calles; **they had to ~ it** tuvieron que ir a pie.

3 *vi* marchar pesadamente, andar con pasos pesados; ir a pie; **sb ~ed up to the door** alguien se acercó con pasos pesados a la puerta; **to ~ along** caminar (con pasos pesados); **to ~ up and down** andar de acá para allá.

trample [ˈtræmpl] **1** *vt* (*also* **to ~ underfoot**) pisar, pisotear, hollar.

2 *vi* (*also* **to ~ about, to ~ along**) pisar fuerte, andar con pasos pesados; **to ~ on sth** pisar algo, pisotear algo, hollar algo; **to ~ on sb** (*fig*) tratar a uno sin miramientos; **to ~ on sb's feelings** (*fig*) herir los sentimientos de uno.
trampoline ['træmpəlɪn] *n* trampolín *m*, cama *f* elástica.
tramway ['træmweɪ] *n* (*Brit*) tranvía *m*.
trance [trɑːns] *n* rapto *m*, arrobamiento *m*, éxtasis *m*; (*Med*) catalepsia *f*; (*spiritualistic*) trance *m*; estado *m* hipnótico; **to go into a ~** entrar en un estado hipnótico, (*fig*) extasiarse.
tranche [trɑːnʃ] *n* parte *f*, tajada *f*.
tranny* ['trænɪ] *n* = **transistor.**
tranquil ['træŋkwɪl] *adj* tranquilo.
tranquillity, (*US*) **tranquility** [træŋ'kwɪlɪtɪ] *n* tranquilidad *f*.
tranquillize, (*US*) **tranquilize** ['træŋkwɪlaɪz] *vt* tranquilizar.
tranquillizer, (*US*) **tranquilizer** ['træŋkwɪlaɪzəʳ] *n* tranquilizante *m*.
trans... [trænz] *pref* trans..., tras...
trans. (**a**) *abbr of* **translation** traducción *f*. (**b**) *abbr of* **translated** traducido, trad. (**c**) *abbr of* **transferred.**
transact [træn'zækt] *vt* hacer, despachar; tramitar.
transaction [træn'zækʃən] *n* (*deal*) negocio *m*, transacción *f*, operación *f*; (*act*) negociación *f*, tramitación *f*; **~s** (*of society*) actas *fpl*, memorias *fpl*.
transatlantic ['trænzət'læntɪk] *adj* transatlántico.
transceiver [træn'siːvəʳ] *n* transceptor *m*, transmisor-receptor *m*.
transcend [træn'send] *vt* exceder, superar, rebasar.
transcendence [træn'sendəns] *n*, **transcendency** [træn'sendənsɪ] *n* superioridad *f*; lo sobresaliente; (*Philos*) trascendencia *f*.
transcendent [træn'sendənt] *adj* superior; sobresaliente.
transcendental [ˌtrænsen'dentl] *adj* trascendental; **~ meditation** meditación *f* trascendental.
transcontinental ['trænzˌkɒntɪ'nentl] *adj* transcontinental.
transcribe [træn'skraɪb] *vt* transcribir, copiar.
transcript ['trænskrɪpt] *n* trasunto *m*, copia *f*; transcripción *f*; (*US Scol etc*) expediente *m*.
transcription [træn'skrɪpʃən] *n* (*act*) transcripción *f*; (*copy*) transcripción *f*, trasunto *m*, copia *f*; **phonetic ~** pronunciación *f* fonética.
transculturation [ˌtrænzkʌltʃʊ'reɪʃən] *n* transculturación *f*.
transducer [trænz'djuːsəʳ] *n* transductor *m*.
transect [træn'sekt] *n* transecto *m*.
transept ['trænsept] *n* crucero *m*.
transfer 1 ['trænsfəʳ] *n* (**a**) (*act*) transferencia *f*, traspaso *m*; (*Jur*) transferencia *f*, cesión *f*; enajenación *f*; transbordo *m*; (*Sport*) traspaso *m*; traslado *m*; **~ of ownership** cesión *f* de propiedad.
(**b**) (*picture*) cromo *m*, calcomanía *f*.
2 ['trænsfəʳ] *attr*: **~ desk** mostrador *m* de transbordo; **~ fee** traspaso *m*; **~ list** lista *f* de traspasos; **~ lounge** sala *f* de tránsito; **~ rate, ~ speed** velocidad *f* de transferencia.
3 [træns'fɜːʳ] *vt property etc* transferir, traspasar, pasar (*to* a); (*Jur*) transferir, ceder; enajenar; *passenger etc* transbordar; (*Sport*) traspasar; (*to new post, place etc*) trasladar; (*in banking, accounting etc*) transferir; **to ~ one's affections to another** dar su amor a otro; **~red charge call** (*Brit*) conferencia *f* a cobro revertido, conferencia *f* por cobrar (*LAm*).
4 [træns'fɜːʳ] *vi* (*to a post etc*) trasladarse (*to* a); (*Rail etc*) cambiar, hacer transbordo (*to* a); **to ~ to a new course** cambiar a otra asignatura; **the firm is ~ring to Quito** la compañía se traslada a Quito.
transferable [træns'fɜːrəbl] *adj* transferible; **not ~** intransferible.
transference ['trænsfərəns] *n* transferencia *f*; traspaso *m*; traslado *m*.
transfiguration [ˌtrænsfɪgə'reɪʃən] *n* transfiguración *f*.
transfigure [træns'fɪgəʳ] *vt* transfigurar, transformar (*into* en).
transfix [træns'fɪks] *vt* traspasar, pasar de parte a parte; **to be ~ed, to stand ~ed** (*fig*) estar totalmente pasmado (*with* de), estar completamente paralizado (*with* de).
transform [træns'fɔːm] *vt* transformar (*into* en), convertir; metamorfosear (*into* en).
transformation [ˌtrænsfə'meɪʃən] *n* transformación *f*, conversión *f*; metamorfosis *f*.
transformational [ˌtrænsfə'meɪʃənl] *adj* transformacional.
transformer [træns'fɔːməʳ] **1** *n* transformador *m*. **2** *attr*: **~ station** estación *f* transformadora.
transfuse [træns'fjuːz] *vt* transfundir; *blood* hacer una transfusión de.
transfusion [træns'fjuːʒən] *n* transfusión *f*; **to give sb a blood ~** hacer a uno una transfusión de sangre.
transgress [træns'gres] **1** *vt* (*go beyond*) traspasar, exceder, ir más allá de; (*violate*) violar, infringir; (*sin against*) pecar contra.
2 *vi* pecar, cometer una transgresión.
transgression [træns'greʃən] *n* pecado *m*, transgresión *f*; infracción *f*.
transgressor [træns'gresəʳ] *n* transgresor *m*, -ora *f*; pecador *m*, -ora *f*; infractor *m*, -ora *f*.
tranship [træn'ʃɪp] *vt* tra(n)sbordar.
transhipment [træn'ʃɪpmənt] *n* tra(n)sbordo *m*.
transience ['trænzɪəns] *n* lo pasajero, transitoriedad *f*, fugacidad *f*.
transient ['trænzɪənt] **1** *adj* pasajero, transitorio, fugaz. **2** *n* (*US*) transeúnte *mf*.
transistor [træn'zɪstəʳ] *n* (*also* **~ set**) transistor *m*.
transistorized [træn'zɪstəraɪzd] *adj* transistorizado.
transit ['trænzɪt] **1** *n* tránsito *m*, paso *m*; **in ~** de tránsito, de paso. **2** *attr*: **~ camp** campamento *m* de tránsito; **~ lounge** (*Brit*) sala *f* de tránsito; **~ visa** visado *m* de tránsito, visa *f* de tránsito (*LAm*).
transition [træn'zɪʃən] **1** *n* transición *f*, paso *m* (*from* de, *to* a); transformación *f*, evolución *f* (*to* en). **2** *attr*: **~ period** período *m* de transición.
transitional [træn'zɪʃənəl] *adj* transicional, de transición.
transitive ['trænzɪtɪv] *adj* transitivo; **~ verb** verbo *m* transitivo.
transitively ['trænzɪtɪvlɪ] *adv* transitivamente.
transitory ['trænzɪtərɪ] *adj* transitorio.
translatable [trænz'leɪtəbl] *adj* traducible.
translate [trænz'leɪt] *vt* (**a**) (*Ling*) traducir (*from* de, *into* a); (*fig*) interpretar; **to ~ words into deeds** convertir palabras en acción; **to ~ centigrade into Fahrenheit** convertir grados centígrados en Fahrenheit; **how do you ~ 'posh'?** ¿cómo se traduce 'posh'?
(**b**) (*change post of*: *esp Rel*) trasladar (*from* de, *to* a).
translation [trænz'leɪʃən] *n* (**a**) traducción *f*; versión *f*. (**b**) traslado *m*.
translator [trænz'leɪtəʳ] *n* traductor *m*, -ora *f*.
transliterate [trænz'lɪtəreɪt] *vt* transcribir.
transliteration [ˌtrænzlɪtə'reɪʃən] *n* transliteración *f*, transcripción *f*.
translucence [trænz'luːsns] *n* translucidez *f*.
translucent [trænz'luːsnt] *adj* translúcido.
transmigrate ['trænzmaɪ'greɪt] *vi* transmigrar.
transmigration [ˌtrænzmaɪ'greɪʃən] *n* transmigración *f*.
transmissible [trænz'mɪsəbl] *adj* transmisible.
transmission [trænz'mɪʃən] **1** *n* (*all senses*) transmisión *f*. **2** *attr*: **~ shaft** árbol *m* de transmisión.
transmit [trænz'mɪt] *vt* (*all senses*) transmitir (*to* a).
transmitter [trænz'mɪtəʳ] *n* (*apparatus*) transmisor *m*; (*station*) estación *f* transmisora, emisora *f*.
transmogrify [trænz'mɒgrɪfaɪ] *vt* transformar (como por encanto; *into* en), metamorfosear (extrañamente; *into* en).
transmutable [trænz'mjuːtəbl] *adj* transmutable.
transmutation [ˌtrænzmjuː'teɪʃən] *n* transmutación *f*.
transmute [trænz'mjuːt] *vt* transmutar (*into* en).
transnational [trænz'næʃənəl] **1** *adj* transnacional. **2** *n* transnacional *f*.
transom ['trænsəm] *n* (*Archit*) travesaño *m*; (*US*) (montante *m* de) abanico *m*.
transparency [træns'pærənsɪ] *n* (**a**) (*quality*) transparencia *f*. (**b**) (*Brit Phot*) diapositiva *f*, filmina *f*, proyección *f*.
transparent [træns'pærənt] *adj* transparente, diáfano; (*fig*) claro, limpio; *excuse etc* transparente, clarísimo.
transparently [træns'pærəntlɪ] *adv* de modo transparente; **~ clear** meridianamente claro; **~ false** a todas luces falso, obviamente falso.
transpiration [ˌtrænspɪ'reɪʃən] *n* transpiración *f*.
transpire [træns'paɪəʳ] **1** *vt* transpirar.
2 *vi* (**a**) (*of fluid, odour*) transpirar.
(**b**) (*become known*) revelarse, divulgarse, saberse; **finally it ~d that ...** por fin se supo que ..., por fin se desprendió que ...
(**c**) (*happen*) tener lugar, pasar, ocurrir; **his report on what ~d** su informe acerca de lo que pasó.
transplant 1 ['trænsplɑːnt] *n* trasplante *m*. **2** [træns'plɑːnt] *vt* trasplantar (*also Med*).
transplantation [ˌtrænsplɑːn'teɪʃən] *n* trasplante *m* (*also Med*).
transponder [træn'spɒndəʳ] *n* transpondedor *m*.
transport 1 ['trænspɔːt] *n* (**a**) (*gen*) transporte *m*; acarreo *m*; **Ministry of T~** (*Brit*) Ministerio *m* de Transportes.
(**b**) (*ship*) navío *m* de transporte; (*Aer*) avión *m* de

transporte.

(**c**) (*fig*) transporte *m*, éxtasis *m*; **to be in a ~ of delight** estar extasiado, extasiarse; **to be in a ~ of rage** estar fuera de sí (de rabia).

2 ['trænspɔːt] *attr*: **~ café** (*Brit*) restaurante *m* de carretera; **~ costs** gastos *mpl* de transporte, gastos *mpl* de acarreo.

3 [træns'pɔːt] *vt* (**a**) (*lit*) transportar; llevar, acarrear; (*Hist*) *convict* deportar.

(**b**) (*fig*) transportar, embelesar; **to be ~ed with joy** estar extasiado, extasiarse.

transportable [træns'pɔːtəbl] *adj* transportable.

transportation [ˌtrænspɔː'teɪʃən] *n* transporte *m*, transportación *f*; transportes *mpl*; (*Hist*: *Jur*) deportación *f*; **the ~ system** el sistema de transportes.

transporter [træns'pɔːtəʳ] *n* transportista *m*, transportador *m*.

transpose [træns'pəʊz] *vt* transponer, cambiar (*into* a); (*Mus*) transportar.

transposition [ˌtrænspə'zɪʃən] *n* transposición *f*; (*Mus*) transporte *m*.

trans-Pyrenean [trænz,pɪrə'niːən] *adj* transpirenaico.

transsexual [trænz'seksjʊəl] **1** *adj* transexual. **2** *n* transexual *mf*.

transship [træns'ʃɪp] *vt* tra(n)sbordar.

transshipment [træns'ʃɪpmənt] *n* tra(n)sbordo *m*.

trans-Siberian [trænzsaɪ'bɪərɪən] *adj* transiberiano.

transubstantiate [ˌtrænsəb'stænʃɪeɪt] *vt* transubstanciar.

transubstantiation ['trænsəb,stænʃɪ'eɪʃən] *n* transubstanciación *f*.

transversal [trænz'vɜːsəl] *adj* transversal.

transverse ['trænzvɜːs] *adj* transverso, trasversal.

transversely [trænz'vɜːslɪ] *adv* transversalmente.

transvestism ['trænz,vestɪzəm] *n* travestismo *m*.

transvestite [trænz'vestaɪt] **1** *adj* travestido. **2** *n* travestido *m*, -a *f*, travestí *mf*.

trap [træp] **1** *n* (**a**) (*gen*) trampa *f*; (*fig*) trampa *f*, lazo *m*; **it's a ~** aquí hay trampa; **to catch an animal in a ~** coger (*LAm*: agarrar) un animal con una trampa; **he was caught in his own ~** cayó en su propia trampa; **we were caught like rats in a ~** estábamos como ratas en ratonera; **to lure sb into a ~** hacer que uno caiga en una trampa; **to set a ~ for sb** tender un lazo a uno.

(**b**) (‡) boca *f*; **to keep one's ~ shut** cerrar el buzón‡; **you keep your ~ shut about this** de esto no digas ni pío; **shut your ~!** ¡callarse!

(**c**) (*Tech*) sifón *m*; bombillo *m*.

(**d**) (*~door*) escotilla *f*, trampa *f*; (*Theat*) escotillón *m*.

(**e**) (*carriage*) tartana *f*, coche *m* ligero de dos ruedas.

2 *vt* (**a**) *animal* coger (*LAm*: agarrar) en una trampa, entrampar, atrapar; coger con trampas.

(**b**) *person* atrapar, aprisionar; *vehicle, ship etc* aprisionar, bloquear; **the miners are ~ped** los mineros están aprisionados, los mineros están atrapados; **we were ~ped in the snow** estábamos aprisionados por la nieve; **the climbers were ~ped** los alpinistas estaban inmovilizados.

(**c**) **to ~ a ball** parar el balón (con los pies); **to ~ one's foot in the door** cogerse (*LAm*: atraparse) el pie en la puerta.

(**d**) (*fig*) hacer caer en el lazo, entrampar; **to ~ sb into an admission** lograr mediante un ardid que uno haga una confesión; **she ~ped him into marriage** logró mañosamente que se casara con ella; **to ~ sb into saying sth** lograr mañosamente que uno diga algo.

trapdoor ['træpdɔːʳ] *n* escotilla *f*, trampa *f*; (*Theat*) escotillón *m*.

trapes [treɪps] *vi* = **traipse**.

trapeze [trə'piːz] **1** *n* trapecio *m* (de circo, de gimnasia). **2** *attr*: **~ artist** trapecista *mf*.

trapezium [trə'piːzɪəm] *n* (*Math*) trapecio *m*.

trapezoid ['træpɪzɔɪd] *n* trapezoide *m*.

trapper ['træpəʳ] *n* cazador *m* (*esp* de animales de piel), trampero *m*.

trappings ['træpɪŋz] *npl* arreos *mpl*; jaeces *mpl*; (*fig*) adornos *mpl*, galas *fpl*; **shorn of all its ~** sin ninguno de sus adornos, desprovisto de adorno; **that statement, shorn of its ~** ... esa declaración, en términos escuetos ...; **with all the ~ of kingship** con todo el boato de la monarquía.

trappist ['træpɪst] **1** *adj* trapense. **2** *n* trapense *m*.

trash [træʃ] **1** *n* pacotilla *f*, hojarasca *f*; trastos *mpl* viejos; (*esp US*) basura *f*; **the book is ~** el libro es una basura, el libro no vale para nada; **he talks a lot of ~** no dice más que tonterías; (**human**) **~** gente *f* inútil, gentuza *f*; **~!** ¡tonterías!

2 *vt* (*US*) (**a**) (*wreck*) hacer polvo, destrozar. (**b**) (*rubbish*) condenar como inútil, criticar duramente.

trash-can ['træʃ'kæn] *n* (*US*) cubo *m* de la basura, balde *m* de la basura (*LAm*).

trash-heap ['træʃhiːp] *n* basurero *m*.

trashy ['træʃɪ] *adj* inútil, baladí.

trauma ['trɔːmə] *n* trauma *m*.

traumatic [trɔː'mætɪk] *adj* traumático.

traumatism ['trɔːmætɪzəm] *n* traumatismo *m*.

traumatize ['trɔːmətaɪz] *vt* traumatizar.

travail ['træveɪl] *n* (†† *or hum*) esfuerzo *m* penoso; (*Med*) dolores *mpl* del parto; **to be in ~** afanarse, azacanarse; (*Med*) estar de parto.

travel ['trævl] **1** *n* (**a**) viajes *mpl*, el viajar; **~s** viajes *mpl*; **to be on one's ~s** estar de viaje.

(**b**) (*Mech*) recorrido *m*.

2 *attr* de viajes, de turismo; **~ agency** agencia *f* de viajes; **~ agent** agente *mf* de viajes; **~ brochure** prospecto *m* de viaje; **~ bureau** oficina *f* de información (para turistas); **~ expenses** gastos *mpl* de viaje; **~ goods** artículos *mpl* de viaje; **~ insurance** seguro *m* de viaje.

3 *vt* (**a**) *country etc* viajar por (todas partes de), recorrer.

(**b**) *distance* recorrer, hacer, cubrir; **we ~led 50 miles that day** ese día cubrimos 50 millas.

4 *vi* (**a**) (*make a journey*) viajar; **to ~ by car** viajar en coche, ir en coche; **he ~s into the centre to work** se desplaza al centro a trabajar; **they have ~led a lot** han viajado mucho, han visto mucho mundo; **to ~ round the world** dar la vuelta al mundo; **to ~ over** viajar por, recorrer.

(**b**) (*go at a speed etc*) ir; **it ~s at 600 mph** tiene una velocidad de 600 mph; **we were ~ling at 30 mph** íbamos a 30 mph; **you were ~ling too fast** ibas a velocidad excesiva, ibas demasiado de prisa; **he was certainly ~ling** es cierto que iba a buen tren; **light ~s at a speed of ...** la luz viaja a una velocidad de ...; **news ~s fast** las noticias viajan rápido.

(**c**) (*move, pass*) correr; moverse, desplazarse; **it ~s along this wire** corre por este hilo; **it doesn't ~ freely on its rod** no corre lisamente por la varilla; **it ~s 3 centimetres** (*Mech*) tiene un recorrido de 3 centímetros; **his eye ~led slowly over the scene** examinó detenidamente la escena.

(**d**) (*reach*) llegar, extenderse; **will it ~ that far?** ¿llega hasta allí?, ¿se puede estirar hasta allí?

(**e**) (*of wine etc*) poderse transportar; **it's a nice wine but it won't ~** es un buen vino pero no viaja.

(**f**) (*Comm*) ser viajante; **he ~s for Pérez** es viajante de la compañía Pérez; **he ~s in underwear** es viajante de una compañía que fabrica ropa interior; **he ~s in soap** es viajante en jabones.

travelator ['trævəleɪtəʳ] *n* (*US*) cinta *f* transbordadora, pasillo *m* móvil.

travelled, (*US*) **traveled** ['trævld] *adj* que ha viajado; **much ~, widely ~** que ha viajado mucho, que ha visto mucho mundo.

traveller, (*US*) **traveler** ['trævləʳ] *n* viajero *m*, -a *f*; (*Comm*: *also* **commercial ~**) viajante *m*; **a ~ in soap** un viajante en jabones; **~'s check** (*US*), **~'s cheque** cheque *m* de viaje; **~'s joy** (*Bot*) clemátide *f*.

travelling, (*US*) **traveling** ['trævlɪŋ] **1** *adj*, *attr salesman, exhibition etc* ambulante; *expenses* de viaje; *crane etc* corredero, corredizo; *bag, clock, rug* de viaje; **~ folk, ~ people** gitanos *mpl*.

2 *n* el viajar, viajes *mpl*.

travelogue, (*US*) **travelog** ['trævəlɒg] *n* película *f* de viajes; documental *m* de interés turístico.

travel-sick ['trævəlsɪk] *adj* mareado; **to get ~** marearse.

travel-sickness ['trævl,sɪknɪs] *n* mareo *m*.

travel-worn ['trævlwɔːn] *adj* fatigado por el viaje, rendido después de tanto viajar.

traverse ['trævəs] **1** *n* (*Tech*) travesaño *m*; (*Mil*) través *m*; (*Mountaineering*) escalada *f* oblicua, camino *m* oblicuo.

2 *vt* atravesar, cruzar; recorrer; pasar por; **we are traversing a difficult period** atravesamos un período difícil.

3 *vi* (*Mountaineering*) hacer una escalada oblicua.

travesty ['trævɪstɪ] **1** *n* parodia *f* (*also fig*). **2** *vt* parodiar.

trawl [trɔːl] **1** *n* (**a**) (*net*) red *f* barredera. (**b**) (*act*) rastreo *m*; **a ~ through police files** un rastreo de los archivos policiales.

2 *vt* rastrear; dragar; **to ~ up** pescar, sacar a la superficie.

3 *vi* (**a**) pescar al arrastre, rastrear. (**b**) **to ~ through the files** rastrear los archivos; **to ~ for evidence** rastrear buscando pruebas.
trawler ['trɔːləʳ] *n* arrastrero *m*, barco *m* rastreador.
trawling ['trɔːlɪŋ] *n* pesca *f* a la rastra.
tray [treɪ] *n* bandeja *f*, charola *f* (*Mex*); (*of balance*) platillo *m*; (*drawer*) cajón *m*, batea *f*; (*Phot, Tech*) cubeta *f*.
traycloth ['treɪklɒθ] *n* cubrebandeja *m*.
treacherous ['tretʃərəs] *adj* traidor, traicionero; falso; (*fig*) engañoso, incierto, nada seguro; *memory* infiel; *ground* movedizo; *ice etc* peligroso, poco firme.
treacherously ['tretʃərəslɪ] *adv* traidoramente, a traición; falsamente; engañosamente; peligrosamente.
treachery ['tretʃərɪ] *n* traición *f*, perfidia *f*; falsedad *f*; **an act of ~** una traición.
treacle ['triːkl] (*Brit*) **1** *n* melaza *f*. **2** *attr*: **~ tart** tarta *f* de melaza.
treacly ['triːklɪ] *adj* parecido a melaza; cubierto de melaza.
tread [tred] **1** *n* (**a**) (*step*) paso *m*, pisada *f*; (*gait*) andar *m*, modo *m* de andar; **with heavy ~** con pasos pesados, pisando fuertemente; **with measured ~** con pasos rítmicos.
(**b**) (*of stair*) huella *f*; (*of shoe*) suela *f*; (*of tyre*) banda *f* de rodaje.
2 (*irr*: *pret* **trod,** *ptp* **trodden**) *vt* (*also* **to ~ down, to ~ underfoot**) pisar, pisotear, hollar; *path* batir; ir por, caminar por; (*fig*) abrir; *grapes* pisar; *dance* bailar; **to ~ water** pedalear en agua; **a place never trodden by human feet** un sitio no hollado por pie humano; **he trod his cigarette end into the mud** apagó la colilla pisándola en el lodo.
3 *vi* pisar; poner el pie; **to ~ on** pisar; **to ~ on sb's heels** pisar los talones a uno; **careful you don't ~ on it!** ¡ojo, que lo vas a pisar!; **to ~ carefully, to ~ warily** (*fig*) andar con pies de plomo; **we must ~ very carefully in this matter** en este asunto conviene andar con pies de plomo; **to ~ softly** pisar dulcemente, no hacer ruido al andar.
◆**tread down** *vt* pisar; *V also* **tread 2**.
◆**tread in** *vt root, seedling* asegurar pisando la tierra alrededor.
treadle ['tredl] *n* pedal *m*.
treadmill ['tredmɪl] *n* rueda *f* de andar; (*fig*) rutina *f*, monotonía *f*; tráfago *m*; **back to the ~!** ¡volvamos al trabajo!
Treas. *abbr of* **Treasurer.**
treason ['triːzn] *n* traición *f*; **high ~** alta traición *f*.
treasonable ['triːzənəbl] *adj* traidor, desleal.
treasure ['treʒəʳ] **1** *n* tesoro *m*; (*fig*) tesoro *m*; joya *f*, preciosidad *f*; **yes, my ~** sí, mi tesoro; **~s of Spanish art** joyas *fpl* del arte español; **our charlady is a real ~** nuestra asistenta es una verdadera joya.
2 *vt* (**a**) **to ~ up** (*keep carefully*) atesorar; guardar, acumular.
(**b**) (*fig*) guardar como un tesoro; apreciar muchísimo; *memory etc* guardar.
treasured ['treʒəd] *adj memory etc* entrañable; *possession* valioso, precioso.
treasure-house ['treʒəhaʊs] *n*, *pl* **treasure-houses** ['treʒə,haʊzɪz] tesoro *m* (*also fig*).
treasure-hunt ['treʒəhʌnt] *n* caza *f* al tesoro.
treasurer ['treʒərəʳ] *n* tesorero *m*, -a *f*.
treasure-trove ['treʒətrəʊv] *n* tesoro *m* hallado; (*fig*) tesoro *m* (escondido).
treasury ['treʒərɪ] **1** *n* (**a**) tesoro *m*, tesorería *f*, fisco *m*, erario *m*, hacienda *f*; **T~**, (*US*) **T~ Department** Ministerio *m* de Hacienda.
(**b**) (*anthology*) tesoro *m*, antología *f*, florilegio *m*.
2 *attr*: **T~ Bench** (*Brit*) banco *m* azul, banco *m* del gobierno; **~ bill** (*US*), **~ bond** (*US*) pagaré *m* (*or* bono *m*) del Tesoro; **T~ promissory note** pagaré *m* del Tesoro; **T~ stock** (*Brit*) bonos *mpl* del Tesoro; (*US*) acciones *fpl* rescatadas; **~ warrant** autorización *f* para pago de fondos públicos.
treat [triːt] **1** *n* (**a**) (*entertainment*) convite *m*; (*present*) regalo *m*; (*outing*) visita *f*; **it's my ~** invito yo; **to have a Dutch ~** pagar cada uno su cuota, ir a escote; **to stand sb a ~** invitar a uno.
(**b**) (*pleasure*) placer *m*, gusto *m*; recompensa *f* (especial); **a ~ in store** un placer futuro, un placer guardado para el futuro; **it is a ~ to hear you** da gusto escucharte, es un placer escucharte; **it's no sort of ~ for me** para mí no es ningún placer; **just to give them all a ~** sólo para darles placer a todos; **to give o.s. a ~** permitirse un lujo, permitirse hacer algo no acostumbrado.
(**c**) **it suited us a ~*** (*Brit*) nos convenía a las mil maravillas.
2 *vt* (**a**) (*behave towards*) tratar; **to ~ sb well** tratar bien a uno; **to ~ sb as if he were a child** tratar a uno como a un niño; **to ~ sth as a joke** tomar algo en broma, tomar algo en chunga.
(**b**) (*invite*) invitar, convidar (*to* a); **I'm ~ing you** invito yo; **they ~ed him to a dinner** le obsequiaron con un banquete; **let me ~ you to a drink** permíteme invitarte a tomar algo.
(**c**) (*Med*) tratar, curar; atender, asistir; **to ~ sb for a broken leg** curar la pierna rota de uno; **to ~ sb with X-rays** dar a uno un tratamiento de rayos X; **which doctor is ~ing you?** ¿qué médico te atiende?
(**d**) (*Tech*) tratar; **to ~ a substance with acid** tratar una sustancia con ácido.
(**e**) *subject, theme* tratar, discutir; **he ~s the subject objectively** trata el asunto con objetividad.
3 *vi* (**a**) (*negotiate*) **to ~ for peace** pedir la paz; **to ~ with sb** tratar con uno, negociar con uno.
(**b**) (*discuss*) **to ~ of** tratar de, discutir; versar sobre.
4 *vr*: **to ~ o.s. to sth** permitirse el lujo, permitirse algo no acostumbrado.
treatise ['triːtɪz] *n* tratado *m*.
treatment ['triːtmənt] *n* tratamiento *m*; (*Med*) tratamiento *m*, cura *f*, medicación *f*; **good ~** buen tratamiento *m*, buenos tratos *mpl*; **his ~ of his parents** su conducta con sus padres; **our ~ of foreigners** el trato que damos a los extranjeros; **to give sb the ~*** hacer sufrir a uno; **to respond to ~** responder al tratamiento.
treaty ['triːtɪ] *n* tratado *m*; **T~ of Accession** (*to EC*) Tratado *m* de Adhesión; **T~ of Rome** Tratado *m* de Roma; **T~ of Utrecht** Tratado *m* de Utrecht.
treble ['trebl] **1** *adj* (**a**) triple.
(**b**) (*Mus*) de tiple; **~ clef** clave *f* de sol.
2 *n* (**a**) (*Mus*) tiple *mf*; voz *f* de tiple. (**b**) (*drink*) triple *m*.
3 *vt* triplicar.
4 *vi* triplicarse.
trebly ['treblɪ] *adv* tres veces; **it is ~ dangerous to ...** es tres veces más peligroso ...
tree [triː] **1** *n* (**a**) árbol *m*; **~ structure** estructura *f* arbórea; **~ of knowledge** árbol *m* de la ciencia; **to be at the top of the ~** estar en la cumbre de su profesión; **to be up a ~*** estar en un aprieto; **to be barking up the wrong ~** tomar el rábano por las hojas.
(**b**) (*for shoes*) horma *f*; (*of saddle*) arzón *m*.
2 *vt animal etc* ahuyentar por un árbol, hacer refugiarse en un árbol.
tree-covered ['triː,kʌvəd] *adj* arbolado.
tree-creeper ['triː,kriːpəʳ] *n* trepatroncos *m*.
tree-frog ['triːfrɒg] *n* rana *f* de San Antonio, rana *f* arbórea.
tree-house ['triːhaʊs] *n*, *pl* **tree-houses** ['triː,haʊzɪz] cabaña *f* (de niños) sobre un árbol.
treeless ['triːlɪs] *adj* pelado, sin árboles.
treeline ['triːlaɪn] *n* límite *m* forestal.
tree-lined ['triːlaɪnd] *adj* arbolado.
tree-planting ['triːplɑːntɪŋ] *n* plantación *f* de árboles; repoblación *f* forestal.
tree-surgeon ['triː,sɜːdʒən] *n* arboricultor *m*, -ora *f* (que se ocupa de las enfermedades de los árboles).
treetop ['triːtɒp] *n* copa *f*, cima *f* de árbol.
treetrunk ['triːtrʌŋk] *n* tronco *m* de árbol.
trefoil ['trefɔɪl] *n* trébol *m*.
trek [trek] **1** *n* migración *f*; (*day's march*) jornada *f*; (*) viaje *m* largo y difícil; caminata *f*; excursión *f*; **it's quite a ~ to the shops*** las tiendas quedan muy lejos.
2 *vi* emigrar; viajar; (*) ir (de mala gana), caminar (penosamente); **we ~ked for days on end** caminamos día tras día; **I had to ~ up to the top floor** tuve que subir hasta el último piso.
trekking ['trekɪŋ] *n* trekking *m*.
trellis ['trelɪs] *n* enrejado *m*; (*Bot*) espaldera *f*, espaldar *m*.
trelliswork ['trelɪswɜːk] *n* enrejado *m*.
tremble ['trembl] **1** *n* temblor *m*, estremecimiento *m*; **to be all of a ~** estar todo tembloroso; **she said with a ~ in her voice** dijo temblando.
2 *vi* temblar, estremecerse (*at* ante, *with* de); vibrar; agitarse; **to ~ all over** estar todo tembloroso; **to ~ like a leaf** temblar como un azogado.
trembling ['tremblɪŋ] **1** *adj* tembloroso. **2** *n* temblar *m*, temblor *m*, estremecimiento *m*; vibración *f*; agitación *f*.
tremendous [trə'mendəs] *adj* tremendo, inmenso, formidable; (*) tremendo*, estupendo*; **that's ~!** ¡qué estupendo*!; **there was a ~ crowd** había una inmensa

multitud.
tremendously [trəˈmendəslɪ] *adv* tremendamente; **~ good** tremendamente bueno.
tremolo [ˈtreməlәʊ] *n* trémolo *m.*
tremor [ˈtreməʳ] *n* temblor *m*; estremecimiento *m*; vibración *f*; **earth ~** temblor *m* de tierra; **he said without a ~** dijo sin inmutarse; **it sent ~s through the system** sacudió el sistema.
tremulous [ˈtremjʊləs] *adj* trémulo, tembloroso; tímido.
tremulously [ˈtremjʊləslɪ] *adv* trémulamente; tímidamente.
trench [trentʃ] **1** *n* zanja *f*, foso *m*; (*Mil*) trinchera *f*.
2 *attr*: **~ warfare** guerra *f* de trincheras.
3 *vt* hacer zanjas (*or* fosos) en; (*Mil*) hacer trincheras en, atrincherar; (*Agr*) excavar.
trenchant [ˈtrentʃənt] *adj* mordaz, incisivo.
trenchantly [ˈtrentʃəntlɪ] *adv* mordazmente.
trenchcoat [ˈtrentʃkəʊt] *n* trinchera *f*, guerrera *f*.
trencher [ˈtrentʃəʳ] *n* tajadero *m.*
trencherman [ˈtrentʃəmæn] *n*, *pl* **trenchermen** [ˈtrentʃəmən]: **to be a good ~** comer bien, tener siempre buen apetito.
trend [trend] **1** *n* tendencia *f*; curso *m*, dirección *f*, marcha *f*; (*fashion*) boga *f*, moda *f*; **now there is a ~ towards ...** ahora hay tendencia hacia ...; **~s in popular music** tendencias *fpl* de la música popular.
2 *vi* tender.
trendiness [ˈtrendɪnɪs] *n* ultramodernismo *m*; tendencia *f* ultramodernista; afán *m* de estar al día.
trendsetter [ˈtrend,setəʳ] *n* persona *f* que inicia la moda.
trendy [ˈtrendɪ] **1** *adj* según la última moda, muy al día; de acuerdo con las tendencias actuales, modernísimo, marchoso*. **2** *n* persona *f* de tendencias ultramodernas, marchoso* *m*, -a *f*.
Trent [trent] *n* Trento *m.*
trepan [trɪˈpæn] *vt* trepanar.
trephine [treˈfiːn] **1** *n* trépano *m.* **2** *vt* trepanar.
trepidation [,trepɪˈdeɪʃən] *n* turbación *f*, agitación *f*; **in some ~** algo turbado, agitado.
trespass [ˈtrespəs] **1** *n* (**a**) (*illegal entry*) intrusión *f*, entrada *f* ilegal; entrada *f* sin derecho, penetración *f* en finca ajena. (**b**) (*transgression*) infracción *f*, violación *f*, ofensa *f*; (*Eccl*) pecado *m*; **forgive us our ~es** perdónanos nuestras deudas.
2 *vi* (**a**) entrar sin derecho (*on* en), entrar ilegalmente (*on* en); penetración *f* en finca ajena; **to ~ against** infringir, violar; **to ~ upon** (*fig*) abusar de; **to ~ upon sb's privacy** invadir la vida íntima de uno; **may I ~ upon your kindness to ask that ...** permítame molestarle pidiendo que ...; perdone Vd que le moleste pidiendo que ...
(**b**) (*Eccl*) pecar (*against* contra).
trespasser [ˈtrespəsəʳ] *n* intruso *m*, -a *f*; **'T~s will be prosecuted'** 'se procederá contra los intrusos', (*loosely*) 'Prohibida la entrada'.
tress [tres] *n* trenza *f*; **~es** cabellera *f*, pelo *m.*
trestle [ˈtresl] **1** *n* caballete *m.* **2** *attr*: **~ bridge** puente *m* de caballetes; **~ table** mesa *f* de caballete.
trews [truːz] *npl* (*Scot*) pantalón *m* de tartán.
tri... [traɪ] *pref* tri...
triad [ˈtraɪəd] *n* tríada *f*.
trial [ˈtraɪəl] **1** *n* (**a**) (*Jur*) proceso *m*, juicio *m*, vista *f* de una causa; **~ by jury** juicio *m* por jurado; **detention without ~** detención *f* sin procesamiento; **new ~** revisión *f*; **to be on ~** estar en juicio; **to be on ~ for one's part in a crime** ser procesado por su complicidad en un crimen; **to be on ~ for one's life** ser acusado de un crimen capital; **to bring sb to ~** procesar a uno; **to commit sb for ~** remitir a uno al tribunal; **to go on ~, to stand one's ~** ser procesado.
(**b**) (*test*) prueba *f*, ensayo *m*; tentativa *f*; (*of sheepdogs etc*) concurso *m*; **~s** (*Sport, Tech*) pruebas *fpl*; **~ of strength** prueba *f* de fuerza; **by a system of ~ and error** por un sistema de tanteo, por un procedimiento empírico; **to be on ~** estar a prueba; **to give sb a ~** poner a uno a prueba.
(**c**) (*hardship*) aflicción *f*, adversidad *f*; desgracia *f*; (*nuisance*) molestia *f*; **~s and tribulations** aflicciones *fpl*; **the ~s of old age** las aflicciones de la vejez; **the child is a great ~ to them** el niño les amarga la vida.
2 *attr* (**a**) (*Jur*) procesal; relativo al proceso.
(**b**) (*test, practice*) de prueba, de ensayo; **~ balance** balance *m* de comprobación; **~ balloon** (*US*) globo *m* sonda; **on a ~ basis** a prueba; **~ flight** vuelo *m* de prueba; **~ run, ~ trip** viaje *m* de ensayo.
triangle [ˈtraɪæŋgl] *n* triángulo *m* (*also Mus*).
triangular [traɪˈæŋgjʊləʳ] *adj* triangular.
triangulate [traɪˈæŋgjʊleɪt] *vt* triangular.
triangulation [traɪ,æŋgjʊˈleɪʃən] *n* triangulación *f*.
triathlon [traɪˈæθlən] *n* triatlón *m.*
tribal [ˈtraɪbəl] *adj* tribal.
tribalism [ˈtraɪbəlɪzəm] *n* tribalismo *m.*
tribe [traɪb] *n* tribu *f* (*also Zool*); (*fig*) tropel *f*, masa *f*; ralea *f*.
tribesman [ˈtraɪbzmən] *n*, *pl* **tribesmen** [ˈtraɪbzmən] miembro *m* de una tribu; **to stir up the tribesmen** sublevar las tribus; **the tribesmen are friendly** las tribus son amistosas.
tribulation [,trɪbjʊˈleɪʃən] *n* tribulación *f*; **~s** aflicciones *fpl*, dificultades *fpl*, sufrimientos *mpl*.
tribunal [traɪˈbjuːnl] *n* tribunal *m.*
tribune [ˈtrɪbjuːn] *n* (*stand*) tribuna *f*; (*person*) tribuno *m.*
tributary [ˈtrɪbjʊtərɪ] **1** *adj* tributario. **2** *n* (*person*) tributario *m*; (*Geog*) afluente *m.*
tribute [ˈtrɪbjuːt] *n* (*payment, tax*) tributo *m*; (*fig*) homenaje *m*; elogio *m*; (*in flowers etc*) ofrenda *f*; **that is a ~ to his loyalty** eso acredita su lealtad, eso hace honor a su lealtad; **to pay ~ to** rendir homenaje a, elogiar, pronunciar elogios de.
trice [traɪs] *n*: **in a ~** en un santiamén.
tricentenary [,traɪsenˈtiːnərɪ] **1** *adj* (de) tricentenario; **~ celebrations** celebraciones *fpl* de(l) tricentenario. **2** *n* tricentenario *m.*
triceps [ˈtraɪseps] *n* tríceps *m.*
trick [trɪk] **1** *n* (**a**) (*deceit*) engaño *m*, truco *m*; (*swindle*) estafa *f*; (*ruse*) trampa *f*, ardid *f*, estratagema *f*; (*harmless deception*) travesura *f*; (*hoax*) trastada *f*, primada *f*, burla *f*; **dirty ~, low ~, shabby ~** mala pasada *f*, faena *f*; **~s of the trade** trucos *mpl* del oficio, triquiñuelas *fpl* del oficio; **there must be a ~ in it** aquí debe haber trampa; **he's up to all the ~s, he knows a ~ or two** se lo sabe todo; **he's up to his old ~s again** ha vuelto a hacer de las suyas; **how's ~s?*** ¿cómo te va?, ¿cómo van las cosas?; **I know a ~ worth two of that** yo me sé algo mucho mejor; **to play a ~ on sb** hacer una mala pasada a uno, hacer una faena a uno; (*practical joke*) gastar una broma a uno; **his memory played him a ~** le falló la memoria; **unless my eyes are playing me ~s** a menos que me engañen mis ojos; **they tried every ~ in the book** emplearon todos los trucos.
(**b**) (*peculiarity*) peculiaridad *f* (personal); (*custom*) hábito *m*, manía *f*; **certain ~s of style** ciertas peculiaridades estilísticas, ciertos rasgos del estilo; **it's just a ~ he has** es una manía suya; **it's a ~ of the light** es una ilusión de la luz; **history has a ~ of repeating itself** la historia tiene tendencia a repetirse.
(**c**) (*card ~*) juego *m* de naipes, truco *m* de naipes; (*conjuring ~*) juego *m* de manos; (*in circus*) número *m*; **the whole bag of ~s*** todo el rollo*; **that should do the ~** eso es lo que hace falta.
(**d**) (*Cards*) baza *f*; **to take all the ~s** ganar (*or* hacer) todas las bazas; **he doesn't miss a ~** (*fig*) no pierde ripio.
(**e**) (*knack*) tino *m*, truco *m*; **to get the ~ of it** coger el tino, aprender el modo de hacer algo.
(**f**) (‡: *of prostitute*) cliente *m*; **to turn a ~** ligar un cliente*.
2 *attr*: **~ photography** trucaje *m*; **~ question** pregunta *f* de pega; **~ riding** acrobacia *f* ecuestre.
3 *vt* (*deceive*) engañar; trampear; burlar; (*swindle*) estafar, timar; **we were ~d** nos engañaron, nos dejamos engañar; **to ~ sb into doing sth** lograr mañosamente que uno haga algo, inducir fraudulentamente a uno a hacer algo; **to ~ sb out of sth** quitar mañosamente algo a uno, estafar algo a uno.
◆**trick out, trick up** *vt* (*decorate*) ataviar (*with* de).
trick-cyclist [ˈtrɪkˈsaɪklɪst] *n* ciclista *mf* acróbata.
trickery [ˈtrɪkərɪ] *n* astucia *f*, superchería *f*, mañas *fpl*; (*Jur*) fraude *m*; **to obtain sth by ~** obtener algo fraudulentamente.
trickle [ˈtrɪkl] **1** *n* hilo *m*, chorro *m* delgado, goteo *m*; (*fig*) pequeña cantidad *f*; **a ~ of people** unas pocas personas; **we received a ~ of news** nos llegaba alguna que otra noticia; **what was a ~ is now a flood** lo que era un goteo es ya un torrente.
2 *vt* dejar caer gota a gota, dejar salir en un chorro delgado; **you're trickling blood** estás sangrando un poco.
3 *vi* (**a**) (*liquid*) gotear, salir gota a gota, salir en un chorro delgado; (*fig*) salir poco a poco; **blood ~d down his cheek** la sangre le corría gota a gota por la mejilla.
(**b**) (*of persons*) salir (*etc*) poco a poco; **people kept trickling in** iban llegando unas cuantas personas; **shall we ~ over to the café?*** ¿nos trasladamos al café?

◆**trickle away** *vi*: **our money is trickling away** nuestro dinero se consume poco a poco.

trickle-charger ['trɪkl,tʃɑːdʒəʳ] *n* cargador *m* de batería.

trickster ['trɪkstəʳ] *n* estafador *m*, -ora *f*, embustero *m*.

tricksy ['trɪksɪ] *adj* (*playful*) juguetón; guasón; (*crafty*) astuto, mañoso.

tricky ['trɪkɪ] *adj person* astuto; mañoso, tramposo; *situation etc* delicado, difícil; *problem* espinoso; **it's all rather ~** es un poco complicado, es un tanto difícil.

tricolour, (*US*) **tricolor** ['trɪkələʳ] *n* tricolor *f*, bandera *f* tricolor.

tricorn ['traɪkɔːn] **1** *adj* tricornio. **2** *n* tricornio *m*.

tricycle ['traɪsɪkl] *n* triciclo *m*.

trident ['traɪdənt] *n* tridente *m*.

Tridentine [traɪ'dentaɪn] *adj* tridentino.

tried [traɪd] *adj* probado, de toda garantía.

triennial [traɪ'enɪəl] *adj* trienal.

triennially [traɪ'enɪəlɪ] *adv* trienalmente, cada tres años.

trier ['traɪəʳ] *n* persona *f* que se esfuerza mucho.

trifle ['traɪfl] **1** *n* (**a**) (*unimportant thing*) friolera *f*, bagatela *f*, fruslería *f*; **£5 is a mere ~** 5 libras son una bagatela; **he worries about ~s** se preocupa por pequeñeces (*or* nimiedades); **any ~ can distract her** le distrae cualquier tontería; **you could have bought it for a ~** hubieras podido comprarlo por una tontería.

(**b**) **a ~** (*as adv*) un poquito, un poquitín; algo; **it's a ~ difficult** es un tantico difícil; **it's a ~ too much** es un poquito demasiado; **we were a ~ put out** quedamos algo desconcertados.

(**c**) (*Culin*) dulce *m* de bizcocho borracho.

2 *vi*: **to ~ with one's food** comer melindrosamente, hacer melindres al comer; **to ~ with sb** jugar con uno, tratar a uno con poca seriedad; **he's not a person to be ~d with** es persona que hay que tratar con la mayor seriedad; **to ~ with a girl's affections** jugar con el amor de una joven.

◆**trifle away** *vt* malgastar, desperdiciar.

trifler ['traɪfləʳ] *n* persona *f* frívola, persona *f* informal.

trifling ['traɪflɪŋ] *adj* insignificante, sin importancia, de poca monta.

triforium [traɪ'fɔːrɪəm] *n* triforio *m*.

trigger ['trɪgəʳ] **1** *n* (*Mil*) gatillo *m*; (*Tech*) disparador *m*, tirador *m*.

2 *vt*: **to ~ (off)** hacer estallar; (*Mech*) hacer funcionar, poner en movimiento; (*fig*) provocar, hacer estallar, desencadenar.

trigger finger ['trɪgə,fɪŋgəʳ] *n* índice *m* de la mano derecha (empleado para apretar el gatillo).

trigger-happy ['trɪgə,hæpɪ] *adj* pronto a disparar.

trigonometric(al) ['trɪgənə'metrɪk(əl)] *adj* trigonométrico.

trigonometry [,trɪgə'nɒmɪtrɪ] *n* trigonometría *f*.

trijet ['traɪdʒet] *n* trirreactor *m*.

trike* [traɪk] *n* triciclo *m*.

trilateral ['traɪ'lætərəl] *adj* trilátero.

trilby ['trɪlbɪ] *n* (*Brit*: *also* **~ hat**) (sombrero *m*) flexible *m*, sombrero *m* tirolés.

trilingual ['traɪ'lɪŋgwəl] *adj* trilingüe.

trill [trɪl] **1** *n* (*of bird*) trino *m*, gorjeo *m*; (*Mus*) trino *m*, quiebro *m*; (*of R*) vibración *f*. **2** *vt* pronunciar con vibración. **3** *vi* trinar, gorjear.

trillion ['trɪlɪən] *n* (*Brit*) trillón *m*; (*US*) billón *m*.

trilogy ['trɪlədʒɪ] *n* trilogía *f*.

trim [trɪm] **1** *adj* aseado, arreglado; elegante; en buen estado; **she has a ~ figure** tiene buen tipo.

2 *n* (**a**) (*condition*) estado *m*, condición *f*; buen estado *m*; (*of boat*) asiento *m*; (*of sails*) orientación *f*; **in good ~** en buen estado, en buenas condiciones, *person* en forma; **in fighting ~** listo para el combate, listo para entrar en acción; **to get things into ~** arreglar las cosas; hacer sus preparativos.

(**b**) (*cut*) recorte *m*; **to give one's hair a ~** recortarse el pelo.

(**c**) (*edging*) borde *m*, guarnición *f*.

3 *vt* (**a**) (*tidy*) arreglar, ordenar; disponer; ajustar, componer; *boat* equilibrar; *sails* orientar.

(**b**) (*Sewing*) *dress* adornar, guarnecer (*with* de); **sleeves ~med with lace** mangas *fpl* guarnecidas de encaje.

(**c**) (*cut*) cortar; *hair, hedge* recortar; *bush etc* podar; *lamp, wick* despabilar; *wood* desbastar, alisar.

◆**trim away** *vt* cortar, quitar.

◆**trim down** *vt* recortar.

◆**trim off** *vt* = **trim away**.

◆**trim up 1** *vt* arreglar, componer.

2 *vr*: **to ~ o.s. up** arreglarse.

trimaran ['traɪməræn] *n* trimarán *m*.

trimester [trɪ'mestəʳ] *n* trimestre *m*.

trimming ['trɪmɪŋ] *n* adorno *m*, guarnición *f*; orla *f*; **~s** (*cuttings*) recortes *mpl*; (*adornments*) adornos *mpl*; accesorios *mpl*; (*pej*) arrequives *mpl*; **without all the ~s** sin todos aquellos adornos.

trimness ['trɪmnɪs] *n* aseo *m*; elegancia *f*; buen estado *m*.

trimphone ['trɪmfəʊn] *n* ≈ teléfono *m* góndola.

Trinidad ['trɪnɪdæd] *n* Trinidad *f*.

Trinidadian [,trɪnɪ'dædɪən] **1** *adj* de Trinidad. **2** *n* nativo *m*, -a *f* (*or* habitante *mf*) de Trinidad.

trinitrotoluene [traɪ'naɪtrəʊ'tɒljuːiːn] *n* trinitrotolueno *m*.

Trinity ['trɪnɪtɪ] **1** *n* Trinidad *f*. **2** *attr*: **~ Sunday** Domingo *m* de la Santísima Trinidad; **~ term** trimestre *m* de verano.

trinket ['trɪŋkɪt] *n* dije *m*, chuchería *f*; **~s** (*pej*) baratijas *fpl*, chucherías *fpl*.

trinomial [traɪ'nəʊmɪəl] **1** *adj* trinomio. **2** *n* trinomio *m*.

trio ['trɪəʊ] *n* trío *m*.

trip [trɪp] **1** *n* (**a**) (*journey*) viaje *m*; (*excursion*) excursión *f*; **he's away on a ~** está de viaje; **to take a ~** hacer un viaje; salir de excursión; **I must take a ~ into town** tengo que ir a la ciudad.

(**b**) (*stumble*) tropezón *m*, traspié *m*; (*in wrestling etc*) zancadilla *f*; (*fig*) desliz *m*, tropiezo *m*.

(**c**) (*Mech*) trinquete *m*, disparo *m*.

(**d**) (‡: *on drug*) viaje‡ *m*.

2 *vt* (*also* **to ~ up**) hacer tropezar, hacer caer, (*deliberately*) echar la zancadilla a; **to ~ sb up** (*fig*) coger a uno en una falta, hundir a uno; **the fourth question ~ped him up** la cuarta pregunta le confundió, la cuarta pregunta le desconcertó.

3 *vi* (**a**) **to ~ along, to go ~ping along** andar (*or* ir, correr *etc*) con paso ligero, andar airosamente.

(**b**) (*stumble*: *also* **to ~ up**) tropezar (*against, on, over* en), caer, dar un tropezón; (*fig*) tropezar, equivocarse.

(**c**) (‡: *on drug*) ir de viaje‡.

◆**trip over** *vi* tropezar, caer, dar un tropezón.

◆**trip up 1** *vi* = **trip 3** (**b**).

2 *vt* = **trip 2**.

tripartite ['traɪ'pɑːtaɪt] *adj* tripartito.

tripe [traɪp] *n* (**a**) (*Culin*) callos *mpl*; guata *f* (*Mex*), mondongo *m* (*SC*); **~s** (*Anat, hum*) tripas *fpl*.

(**b**) (*esp Brit**) tonterías *fpl*, bobadas *fpl*; **what utter ~!** ¡tonterías!; **he talks a lot of ~** no habla más que bobadas.

triphase ['traɪfeɪz] *adj* trifásico.

triphthong ['trɪfθɒŋ] *n* triptongo *m*.

triple ['trɪpl] **1** *adj* triple; **~ glazing** triple acristalamiento *m*; **~ jump** triple salto *m*; **~ the sum** el triple; **T~ Alliance** Triple Alianza *f*.

2 *n* triple *m*.

3 *vt* triplicar.

4 *vi* triplicarse.

triplet ['trɪplɪt] *n* (*Mus*) tresillo *m*; (*Poet*) terceto *m*; **~s** (*persons*) trillizos *mpl*, -as *fpl*.

triplicate 1 ['trɪplɪkɪt] *adj* triplicado. **2** ['trɪplɪkɪt] *n*: **in ~** por triplicado. **3** ['trɪplɪkeɪt] *vt* triplicar.

triply ['trɪplɪ] *adv* tres veces; **~ dangerous** tres veces más peligroso.

tripod ['traɪpɒd] *n* trípode *m*.

Tripoli ['trɪpəlɪ] *n* Trípoli *m*.

tripper ['trɪpəʳ] *n* (*Brit*) excursionista *mf*; (*day ~*) turista *mf* (que hace una visita de un día).

tripping ['trɪpɪŋ] *adj* ligero, airoso.

triptych ['trɪptɪk] *n* tríptico *m*.

tripwire ['trɪpwaɪəʳ] *n* cable *m* trampa.

trireme ['traɪriːm] *n* trirreme *m*.

trisect [traɪ'sekt] *vt* trisecar.

Tristan ['trɪstən] *nm*, **Tristram** ['trɪstrəm] *nm* Tristán.

trisyllabic ['traɪsɪ'læbɪk] *adj* trisilábico.

trisyllable ['traɪ'sɪləbl] *n* trisílabo *m*.

trite [traɪt] *adj* vulgar, trivial; gastado, trillado y llevado.

tritely ['traɪtlɪ] *adv* vulgarmente, trivialmente.

triteness ['traɪtnɪs] *n* vulgaridad *f*, trivialidad *f*; lo gastado.

Triton ['traɪtn] *nm* Tritón.

tritone ['traɪtəʊn] *n* tritono *m*.

triturate ['trɪtʃəreɪt] *vt* triturar.

trituration [,trɪtʃə'reɪʃən] *n* trituración *f*.

triumph ['traɪʌmf] **1** *n* triunfo *m*; éxito *m*; **a new ~ for Slobodian industry** nuevo éxito de la industria eslobodia; **to achieve a great ~** obtener un gran éxito; **it is a ~ of man over nature** en esto el hombre triunfa de la naturaleza; **to come home in ~** volver a casa triunfalmente.

2 *vi* triunfar; **to ~ over a difficulty** triunfar de una dificultad; **to ~ over the enemy** triunfar sobre el enemigo.

triumphal [traɪˈʌmfəl] *adj* triunfal; **~ arch** arco *m* triunfal.

triumphalism [traɪˈʌmfəlɪzəm] *n* triunfalismo *m*.

triumphant [traɪˈʌmfənt] *adj* triunfante; victorioso; **he was ~** estaba jubiloso, estaba lleno de júbilo.

triumphantly [traɪˈʌmfəntlɪ] *adv* triunfalmente, de modo triunfal; **he said ~** dijo en tono triunfal.

triumvirate [traɪˈʌmvɪrɪt] *n* triunvirato *m*.

triune [ˈtraɪjuːn] *adj* trino.

trivet [ˈtrɪvɪt] *n* (*US*) salvamanteles *m*.

trivia [ˈtrɪvɪə] *npl* trivialidades *fpl*.

trivial [ˈtrɪvɪəl] *adj* trivial, insignificante; banal; superficial; *excuse, pretext etc* frívolo, poco serio.

triviality [ˌtrɪvɪˈælɪtɪ] *n* (**a**) (*V adj*) trivialidad *f*, insignificancia *f*; banalidad *f*; superficialidad *f*; frivolidad *f*, falta *f* de seriedad; trivialidades *fpl*. (**b**) **a ~** una nimiedad; **to worry about trivialities** preocuparse por nimiedades.

trivialization [ˌtrɪvɪəlaɪˈzeɪʃən] *n* trivialización *f*, banalización *f*.

trivialize [ˈtrɪvɪəlaɪz] *vt* trivializar, banalizar.

trivially [ˈtrɪvɪəlɪ] *adv* trivialmente, banalmente.

trochaic [trɒˈkeɪɪk] *adj* trocaico.

trochee [ˈtrɒkiː] *n* troqueo *m*.

trod [trɒd] *pret of* **tread.**

trodden [ˈtrɒdn] *ptp of* **tread.**

troglodyte [ˈtrɒglədaɪt] *n* troglodita *m*.

troika [ˈtrɔɪkə] *n* troica *f*.

Trojan [ˈtrəʊdʒən] **1** *adj* troyano; **~ horse** caballo *m* de Troya; **~ War** Guerra *f* de Troya. **2** *n* troyano *m*, -a *f*.

troll [trəʊl] *n* gnomo *m*, duende *m*.

trolley [ˈtrɒlɪ] *n* (**a**) (*esp Brit*) (*hand ~*) carretilla *f*; (*of supermarket*) carrito *m*; (*tea ~*) mesita *f* de ruedas; (*Med*) camilla *f* de ruedas; (*child's*) carretón *m*. (**b**) (*Tech*) corredera *f* elevada; (*Elec*) trole *m*, arco *m* de trole; **to be off one's ~*** (*US*) estar chiflado*. (**c**) (*US*) tranvía *m*.

trolleybus [ˈtrɒlɪbʌs] *n* trolebús *m*.

trolleycar [ˈtrɒlɪkɑːʳ] *n* (*US*) tranvía *m*.

trolley-pole [ˈtrɒlɪpəʊl] *n* trole *m*.

trollop [ˈtrɒləp] *n* marrana *f*; puta *f*.

trombone [trɒmˈbəʊn] *n* trombón *m*.

trombonist [trɒmˈbəʊnɪst] *n* (*orchestral*) trombón *mf*; (*jazz etc*) trombonista *mf*.

troop [truːp] **1** *n* (**a**) banda *f*, grupo *m*, compañía *f*; (*Mil*) tropa *f*, (*of cavalry*) escuadrón *m*; (*Theat*) *V* **troupe; ~s** (*Mil*) tropas *fpl*; **to come in a ~** venir en tropel, venir en masa.

(**b**) **the steady ~ of feet** el ruido rítmico de pasos.

2 *vt*: **to ~ the colour** (*Brit*) presentar la bandera, desfilar con la bandera.

3 *vi*: **to ~ along** marchar (todos juntos); **to ~ away, to ~ off** marcharse en tropel; **to ~ out** salir todos juntos, salir en masa; **to ~ past** desfilar (ante); **to ~ together** reunirse en masa.

troop-carrier [ˈtruːpˌkærɪəʳ] *n* transporte *m* de tropas; camión *m* blindado.

trooper [ˈtruːpəʳ] *n* soldado *m* de caballería; (*US*) soldado *m* de reserva.

troopship [ˈtruːpʃɪp] *n* transporte *m*.

troop train [ˈtruːptreɪn] *n* tren *m* militar.

trope [trəʊp] *n* tropo *m*.

trophy [ˈtrəʊfɪ] *n* trofeo *m*.

tropic [ˈtrɒpɪk] *n* trópico *m*; **~s** trópicos *mpl*, zona *f* tropical; **T~ of Cancer** trópico *m* de Cáncer; **T~ of Capricorn** trópico *m* de Capricornio.

tropic(al) [ˈtrɒpɪk(əl)] *adj* tropical.

troposphere [ˈtrɒpəsfɪəʳ] *n* troposfera *f*.

Trot* [trɒt] *n abbr of* **Trotskyist.**

trot[1] [trɒt] **1** *n* (**a**) (*pace*) trote *m*; **at an easy ~, at a slow ~** a trote corto; **to break into a ~** echar a trotar; **for 5 days on the ~** durante 5 días seguidos; **Barataria won 5 times on the ~** Barataria ganó 5 veces de carrerilla; **to be always on the ~** no parar nunca, tener una vida ajetreada; **to keep sb on the ~** no dejar a uno descansar.

(**b**) **to have the ~s‡** tener el vientre descompuesto, tener cagueruelas‡ *fpl*.

2 *vt horse* hacer trotar.

3 *vi* (**a**) trotar, ir al trote.

(**b**) (*) ir; irse, marcharse; **we must be ~ting** es hora de marcharnos.

◆**trot along** *vi* (**a**) = **trot over.**

(**b**) = **trot away.**

◆**trot away, trot off** *vi* irse, marcharse; **we must be ~ting off** es hora de marcharnos.

◆**trot out** *vt excuses etc* ensartar; *arguments* sacar a relucir, presentar otra vez; *erudition* hacer alarde de.

◆**trot over, trot round** *vi*: **he ~s round to the shop** sale a la tienda en una carrera.

trot[2] [trɒt] *n* (*US*) chuleta *f*.

troth [trəʊθ] *n* (†† *or hum*) *V* **plight.**

Trotskyism [ˈtrɒtskɪɪzəm] *n* trotskismo *m*.

Trotskyist [ˈtrɒtskɪɪst] **1** *adj* trotskista. **2** *n* trotskista *mf*.

trotter [ˈtrɒtəʳ] *n* (**a**) (*horse*) trotón *m*, caballo *m* trotón. (**b**) (*Culin*) pie *m* de cerdo, manita *f* de cerdo.

trotting [ˈtrɒtɪŋ] *n* (*Sport*) trote *m*.

troubadour [ˈtruːbədɔːʳ] *n* trovador *m*.

trouble [ˈtrʌbl] **1** *n* (**a**) (*grief, affliction*) aflicción *f*; pena *f*, angustia *f*; (*misfortune*) desgracia *f*, desventura *f*; (*worry*) inquietud *f*, preocupación *f*; (*difficult situation*) apuro *m*, aprieto *m*; **my ~ and strife‡** la parienta; **to be in ~** estar en un apuro; **to be in great ~** estar muy apurado; **now your ~s are over** ya no tendrás de que preocuparte, se acabaron las preocupaciones; **life is full of ~s** la vida está llena de aflicciones; **then this ~ came upon them** luego sufrieron esta aflicción; **to drown one's ~s** beber para olvidar sus aflicciones; **to lay up ~ for o.s.** hacer algo que causará pena en el futuro; **to tell sb one's ~s** contar sus desventuras a uno.

(**b**) (*difficulty*) dificultad *f*; disgusto *m*; (*hindrance*) estorbo *m*, inconveniente *m*; **family ~s** dificultades *fpl* domésticas; **money ~s** dificultades *fpl* económicas; **the ~ is that ...** la dificultad es que ..., lo malo es que ..., el inconveniente es que ...; **what's the ~?, what seems to be the ~?** ¿pasa algo?; **that's just the ~** ahí está (la madre del cordero); **their aunt is a great ~ to them** su tía constituye un gran estorbo para ellos; **it's just asking for ~** eso es buscarse complicaciones; **she never gave us any ~** nunca nos dio un disgusto; **to get into ~** meterse en un lío; **Peter got into ~ for saying that** Pedro se mereció una bronca diciendo eso; **he got into ~ with the police** tuvo una dificultad con la policía; **to get sb into ~** comprometer a uno, crear un lío a uno; **to get a girl into ~** dejar encinta a una joven; **to get out of ~** salir del apuro; **to get sb out of ~** ayudar a uno a salir del apuro; echar un cable a uno; **you'll have ~ with it** tendrás dificultades con eso; **did you have any ~?** ¿tuviste alguna dificultad?; **to make ~ for sb** crear un lío a uno; amargar la vida a uno.

(**c**) (*bother*) molestia *f*; dificultad *f*; (*effort*) esfuerzo *m*; **with no little ~** con bastante dificultad, con no poca dificultad; **it's no ~** no es molestia; **it's no ~ to do it properly** no cuesta nada hacerlo bien; **it's more ~ than it's worth, it's not worth the ~** no vale la pena; **nothing is too much ~ for her** para ella todo es poco; **to give sb ~** causar molestia a uno; **to go to the ~ of + *ger*** darse la molestia de + *infin*; **we had ~ getting here in time** nos costó trabajo llegar aquí a tiempo; **we had all our ~ for nothing** todo aquello fue trabajo perdido; **to put sb to the ~ of doing sth** molestar a uno pidiéndole que haga algo; **I fear I am putting you to a lot of ~** me temo que esto te vaya a molestar bastante; **to save o.s. the ~** ahorrarse el trabajo; **to spare no ~ in order to + *infin*** no regatear medio para + *infin*; **to take the ~ to + *infin*** tomarse la molestia de + *infin*; **he didn't even take the ~ to say thank you** ni se dignó siquiera darme las gracias; **to take a lot of ~** esmerarse, trabajar (*etc*) con el mayor cuidado.

(**d**) (*Med: upset*) enfermedad *f*, mal *m*; **heart ~** enfermedad *f* cardíaca; **it's my old ~** ha vuelto lo de antes.

(**e**) (*Mech: upset*) avería *f*; fallo *m*; **engine ~** avería *f* del motor; **a mechanic put the ~ right** un mecánico reparó las piezas averiadas; **we drove 5,000 miles without ~ of any kind** cubrimos 5.000 millas sin la menor avería.

(**f**) (*upset: between persons*) disgusto *m*, desavenencia *f*, sinsabor *m*; **the Parnell ~** el caso Parnell; **there is constant ~ between them** riñen constantemente; **X caused ~ between Y and Z** X provocó un disgusto entre Y y Z.

(**g**) (*unrest, Pol etc*) conflicto *m*; trastorno *m*, disturbio *m*; **the Irish ~s** los conflictos de los irlandeses; **labour ~s** conflictos *mpl* laborales; **there's ~ at t'mill** hay un disturbio en la fábrica, hay huelga en la fábrica; **there's ~ brewing** soplan vientos de fronda; **to stir up ~** meter cizaña, revolver el ajo.

2 *vt* (**a**) (*afflict, grieve*) afligir; (*worry*) inquietar, preocupar; (*disturb*) agitar, turbar; **the thought ~d him** el pensamiento le afligió; **the heat ~d us** nos molestó el calor; **his eyes ~ him** le duelen los ojos; **I am deeply ~d**

estoy sumamente preocupado; **it's not that that ~s me** no me inquieto por eso, eso me trae sin cuidado.

(**b**) (*bother*) molestar, incomodar; (*badger*) importunar; **I'm sorry to ~ you** lamento tener que molestarle; **may I ~ you for a match?** ¿tienes fuego por favor?, ¿me haces el favor de darme fuego?; **may I ~ you to hold this?** ¿te molestaría tener esto?; **does it ~ you if I smoke?** ¿te molesta que fume?; **I shan't ~ you with all the details** no te molesto citando todos los detalles; **maths never ~d me at all** las matemáticas no me costaron trabajo en absoluto.

3 *vi* preocuparse, molestarse; **please don't ~!** ¡no te molestes!, ¡no te preocupes!; **don't ~ to write** no te molestes en escribir; **he didn't ~ to shut the door** no se tomó la molestia de cerrar la puerta; **if you had ~d to find out** si te hubieras tomado la molestia de averiguarlo.

4 *vr*: **to ~ o.s. about sth** preocuparse por algo; **to ~ o.s. to do sth** tomarse la molestia de hacer algo; **don't ~ yourself!** ¡no te molestes!, ¡no te preocupes!

troubled ['trʌbld] *adj person* inquieto, preocupado; *expression* preocupado; *period* turbulento, agitado; *life, story* accidentado; *waters* revuelto, turbio; **to look ~** parecer estar preocupado.

trouble-free ['trʌblfriː] *adj* libre de inquietudes, totalmente tranquilo; (*Pol etc*) libre de disturbios; (*Aut, Mech*) exento de averías; **a thousand ~ miles** mil millas sin avería alguna.

troublemaker ['trʌbl,meɪkəʳ] *n* alborotador *m*, -ora *f*, buscarruidos *m*, elemento *m* perturbador.

troublemaking ['trʌbl,meɪkɪŋ] *adj* alborotador, perturbador.

trouble-shooter ['trʌbl,ʃuːtəʳ] *n* apagafuegos *mf*, bombero *m*.

troublesome ['trʌblsəm] *adj* molesto, fastidioso; importuno; dificultoso; **it's very ~** es terriblemente molesto; **now don't be ~** no seas difícil, no te pongas así.

trouble-spot ['trʌblspɒt] *n* centro *m* de fricción, lugar *m* turbulento, punto *m* conflictivo.

troublous ['trʌbləs] *adj* (*liter*) *times* turbulento, agitado, revuelto.

trough [trɒf] *n* (**a**) (*depression*) depresión *f*, hoyo *m*; (*between waves*) seno *m*; (*channel*) canal *m*; (*Met*) mínimo *m* de presión; (*fig*) parte *f* baja, punto *m* más bajo.

(**b**) (*drinking ~*) abrevadero *m*; (*feeding ~*) pesebre *m*, comedero *m*; (*kneading ~*) artesa *f*; (*of stone*) pila *f*.

trounce [traʊns] *vt* (*thrash*) pegar, zurrar, dar una paliza a; (*defeat*) derrotar, cascar; (*castigate*) fustigar.

troupe [truːp] *n* (*Theat etc*) compañía *f*, grupo *m*, conjunto *m*.

trouper ['truːpəʳ] *n* (*Theat*) miembro *mf* de una compañía de actores; **old ~** actor *m* veterano, actriz *f* veterana.

trouser ['traʊzəʳ] **1** *npl*: **~s** (*esp Brit*) pantalones *mpl*, pantalón *m*; **a pair of ~s** un pantalón, unos pantalones; **to wear the ~s** (*fig*) llevar los pantalones.

2 *attr*: **~ leg** pierna *f* de pantalón; **~ pocket** bolsillo *m* del pantalón; **~ suit** (*Brit*) traje-pantalón *m*.

trouser-press ['traʊzəpres] *n* prensa *f* para pantalones.

trousseau ['truːsəʊ] *n*, *pl* **trousseaus** *or* **trousseaux** ['truːsəʊz] ajuar *m*, equipo *m* (de novia).

trout [traʊt] *n*, *pl invar* trucha *f*; **old ~*** arpía *f*, bruja* *f*.

trout-fishing ['traʊt,fɪʃɪŋ] *n* pesca *f* de truchas.

trove [trəʊv] *n* V **treasure-trove**.

trowel ['traʊəl] *n* (*Agr*) desplantador *m*, transplantador *m*; (*builder's*) paleta *f*, llana *f*.

Troy [trɔɪ] *n* Troya *f*.

troy (weight) ['trɔɪ('weɪt)] *n* peso *m* troy.

truancy ['truənsɪ] *n* ausencia *f* sin permiso.

truant ['truənt] **1** *adj* (*slack*) gandul, haragán, vago; (*absent*) ausente, desparecido.

2 *n* (*slacker*) gandul *m*, vago *m*; (*absentee*) novillero *m*, -a *f*; **to play ~** ausentarse, (*Scol*) hacer novillos.

3 *vi* (*US*) ausentarse (*from* de); (*Scol*) hacer novillos.

truce [truːs] *n* (*Mil*) tregua *f*; (*fig*) suspensión *f*, cesación *f*; **to call a ~ to sth** suspender algo.

truck¹ [trʌk] **1** *n*: **to have no ~ with sb** no tratar con uno, no tener relaciones con uno; **we want no ~ with that** no queremos tener nada que ver con eso.

2 *attr*: **~ system** (*Hist*) pago *m* de salarios en especie.

truck² [trʌk] **1** *n* (*esp US*: *waggon*) carro *m*; (*hand~*) carretilla *f*; (*Rail*) vagón *m* (de mercancías); (*lorry*) camión *m*. **2** *vt* (*US*) llevar, transportar.

truckage ['trʌkɪdʒ] *n* (*US*) acarreo *m*.

truck-driver ['trʌk,draɪvəʳ] *n* (*esp US*) camionero *m*, camionista *m*, conductor *m* de camión.

trucker ['trʌkəʳ] *n* (*US*) camionero *m*, camionista *m*.

truck farm ['trʌk'fɑːm] *n* (*US*), **truck garden** ['trʌk'gɑːdn] *n* (*US*) huerto *m* de hortalizas.

truck farmer ['trʌk,fɑːməʳ] *n* (*US*) hortelano *m*, -a *f*.

truck farming ['trʌk,fɑːmɪŋ] *n* (*US*) horticultura *f*.

trucking ['trʌkɪŋ] (*US*) **1** *n* acarreo *m*, transporte *m*. **2** *attr*: **~ company** compañía *f* de transporte por carretera.

truckle ['trʌkl] *vi*: **to ~ to sb** someterse servilmente a uno.

trucklebed ['trʌkl'bed] *n* carriola *f*.

truckload ['trʌkləʊd] *n* carretada *f*; vagón *m* (lleno); **~s of soldiers** camiones *mpl* llenos de soldados; **by the ~** (*fig*) a carretadas, a montones.

truckman ['trʌkmən] *n*, *pl* **truckmen** ['trʌkmən] (*US*) camionero *m*, camionista *m*.

truckstop ['trʌkstɒp] *n* (*US*) restaurante *m* de carretera.

truculence ['trʌkjʊləns] *n* agresividad *f*; mal humor *m*, aspereza *f*.

truculent ['trʌkjʊlənt] *adj* agresivo; malhumorado, áspero.

truculently ['trʌkjʊləntlɪ] *adv behave* de modo agresivo; *answer* malhumorado, ásperamente.

trudge [trʌdʒ] **1** *n* caminata *f* (difícil, larga, penosa).

2 *vt* recorrer a pie (penosamente); **we ~d the streets looking for him** nos cansamos buscándole por las calles.

3 *vi* (*also* **to ~ along**) caminar penosamente, andar con dificultad.

true [truː] **1** *adj* (**a**) (*not false*) verdadero; **~!, too ~!** ¡es verdad!; **how (very) ~!** ¡es mucha verdad!; **it is ~ that ...** es verdad que ...; **can this be ~?** ¿es cierto esto?; **so ~ is this that ...** tan(to) es así que ...; **to come ~** realizarse, cumplirse, verificarse; **to hold sth to be ~** creer que algo es verdad; **it holds ~ of ...** también es cierto por lo que se refiere a ...

(**b**) (*genuine*) auténtico, verdadero, genuino; *account* verídico; *copy* fiel, exacto; **~ to life** realista, verista, conforme con la realidad; **~ to type** conforme con el tipo; **what is the ~ situation?** ¿cuál es la verdadera situación?; **it is not a ~ account of what happened** no es un informe verdadero de lo que pasó; **in a ~ spirit of service** en un auténtico espíritu de servicio; **like a ~ Englishman** como un inglés auténtico.

(**c**) *measures etc* exacto; *surface, join* uniforme, a nivel; *upright* a plomo; *wheel* centrado; *voice* justo, afinado; **the walls are not ~** las paredes no están a plomo.

(**d**) (*faithful*) fiel, leal; **a ~ friend** un fiel amigo; **all good men and ~** todos los buenos y leales; **to be ~ to sb** ser fiel a uno; **to be ~ to one's word** cumplir su promesa, cumplir lo prometido.

2 *adv*: **to aim ~** apuntar bien, acertar en la puntería; **to breed ~** reproducirse conforme con el tipo; **to run ~ to type** estar conforme con el tipo; **now tell me ~** dime la verdad.

3 *n*: **to be out of ~** (*things joining*) no estar a nivel, estar mal alineado, estar desalineado; (*things vertical*) no estar a plomo; (*wheel*) estar descentrado.

true-blue ['truː'bluː] **1** *adj* rancio, de lo más rancio. **2** *n* partidario *m*, -a *f* de lo más leal, partidario *m* acérrimo, partidaria *f* acérrima.

true-born ['truː'bɔːn] *adj* auténtico, verdadero.

true-bred ['truː'bred] *adj* de casta legítima, de pura sangre.

true-life ['truːlaɪf] *adj* verdadero, conforme con la realidad.

truelove ['truːlʌv] *n* novio *m*, -a *f*, amor *m*, fiel amante *mf*.

truffle ['trʌfl] *n* trufa *f*.

trug [trʌg] *n* (*Brit*) cesto *m* de flores.

truism ['truːɪzəm] *n* perogrullada *f*, tópico *m*; **it is a ~ to say that ...** es un tópico decir que ...

truly ['truːlɪ] *adv* verdaderamente; auténticamente; exactamente; fielmente; **and ~ it was tough** y efectivamente fue difícil; **a ~ great painting** un cuadro verdaderamente grande; **really and ~?** ¿de veras?; **yours ~** le saluda atentamente; **yours ~*** (*ie, myself*) este cura*, servidor, menda*; **nobody knows it better than yours ~** nadie lo sabe mejor que este servidor.

trump [trʌmp] **1** *n* (*also* **~ card**) triunfo *m*; **hearts are ~s** triunfan corazones, pintan corazones; **what's ~s?** ¿a qué pinta?; **he always turns up ~s** (*Brit*) no nos falla nunca, es persona de la mayor confianza.

2 *vt* (*Cards*) fallar.

3 *vi* triunfar, poner un triunfo.

◆**trump up** *vt charge* forjar, falsificar, inventar.

trumped-up ['trʌmpt'ʌp] *adj accusation etc* forjado, inventado.

trumpery ['trʌmpərɪ] **1** *adj* frívolo; (*valueless*) inútil, sin valor; (*insignificant*) sin importancia; (*trashy*) de relumbrón. **2** *n* oropel *m*.

trumpet ['trʌmpɪt] **1** *n* trompeta *f*; **to blow one's own ~** (*fig*) hacer autobombo, autobombearse. **2** *attr*: **~ blast, ~**

call trompetazo *m*; (*fig*) clarinazo *m*. **3** *vt* trompetear; (*fig*: *also* **to ~ forth**) pregonar, anunciar (a son de trompeta). **4** *vi* (*elephant*) barritar.

trumpeter ['trʌmpɪtəʳ] *n* (*orchestral*) trompetero *m*, trompeta *mf*; (*jazz etc*) trompetista *mf*.

trumpeting ['trʌmpɪtɪŋ] *n* bramido *m*.

truncate [trʌŋ'keɪt] *vt* truncar.

truncated [trʌŋ'keɪtɪd] *adj* truncado, trunco.

truncating [trʌŋ'keɪtɪŋ] *n* (*Comput*) truncamiento *m*.

truncation [trʌŋ'keɪʃən] *n* truncamiento *m*.

truncheon ['trʌntʃən] *n* porra *f*.

trundle ['trʌndl] **1** *vt* hacer rodar, hacer correr (sobre ruedas); (*fig*) llevar, arrastrar (con dificultad). **2** *vi* rodar (con mucho ruido, pesadamente).

◆**trundle on** *vi* avanzar (con mucho ruido, pesadamente).

trunk [trʌŋk] **1** *n* (*Anat, Bot*) tronco *m*; (*case*) baúl *m*; (*US Aut*) maletero *m*, portaequipaje *m*, baúl *m* (*LAm*); maletera *f* (*LAm*); (*elephant's*) trompa *f*.

2 *attr*: **~ call** (*Brit*) conferencia *f* (interurbana); **~ line** (*Rail*) línea *f* troncal; (*Telec*) línea *f* principal; **~ road** (*Brit*) carretera *f* nacional.

3 *npl*: **~s** traje *m* de baño, bañador *m*.

trunnion ['trʌnɪən] *n* muñón *m*.

truss [trʌs] **1** *n* (*bundle*) lío *m*, paquete *m*; (*of hay etc*) haz *m*, lío *m*; (*of fruit*) racimo *m*; (*Archit*) entramado *m*; (*Med*) braguero *m*.

2 *vt* (*tie*) liar, atar; *fowl* espetar; (*Archit*) apuntalar, apoyar con entramado.

◆**truss up** *vt*: **to ~ sb up** atar a uno con cuerdas (*etc*).

trust [trʌst] **1** *n* (**a**) (*belief, faith*) confianza *f* (*in* en); **to put one's ~ in** confiar en; **to take sth on ~** aceptar algo a ojos cerrados, creer algo sin tener (*or* pedir) pruebas de ello.

(**b**) (*Comm*) **to supply goods on ~** suministrar artículos al fiado, proveer artículos a crédito.

(**c**) (*charge*) cargo *m*, deber *m*, obligación *f*; responsabilidad *f*; **our sacred ~** nuestra sagrada obligación; **position of ~** puesto *m* de responsabilidad, puesto *m* de confianza; **to commit sth to sb's ~** confiar algo a uno; **to desert one's ~** faltar a su deber.

(**d**) (*Jur*) fideicomiso *m*; **to hold money in ~ for sb** tener dinero en administración a nombre de uno.

(**e**) (*Comm, Fin*) trust *m*; (*pej*) monopolio *m*, cartel *m*.

2 *attr*: **~ account** cuenta *f* fiduciaria; **~ company** banco *m* fideicomisario; **~ fund** fondo *m* de fideicomiso; **~ territory** mandato *m*.

3 *vt* (**a**) (*believe in, rely on*) confiar en, fiarse de; tener confianza en; creer; **don't you ~ me?** ¿no te fías de mí?; **she is not to be ~ed** ella no es de fiar; **you can't ~ a word he says** es imposible creer ninguna palabra suya; **to ~ sb with sth** confiar algo a uno; **to ~ sb with a task** confiar un cometido a uno; **will you ~ me with your bike?** ¿me permites usar tu bicicleta?; **to ~ sb to do sth** confiar en que uno haga algo; **~ you!** ¡siempre igual!, ¡lo mismo que siempre!; **~ him to make a mess of it** no es sorprendente que lo haya hecho mal; **mother wouldn't ~ us out of her sight** mamá no permitía que nos alejásemos de ella, mamá nos tenía cosidos a sus faldas.

(**b**) (*Comm*) dar al fiado.

(**c**) (*hope*) esperar; **I ~ not** espero que no; **I ~ that all will go well** espero que todo vaya bien.

4 *vi* confiar; esperar; **to ~ in God** confiar en Dios; **to ~ to chance, to ~ to luck** confiar en tener suerte; hacer algo a la ventura.

trusted ['trʌstɪd] *adj* leal, de confianza.

trustee [trʌs'tiː] *n* (*in bankruptcy*) síndico *m*; (*holder of property for another*) fideicomisario *m*, -a *f*, depositario *m*, -a *f*, administrador *m*, -ora *f*; (*of college*) regente *m*, -a *f*.

trusteeship [trʌs'tiːʃɪp] *n* cargo *m* de síndico, cargo *m* de fideicomisario (*etc*); administración *f* fiduciaria.

trustful ['trʌstfʊl] *adj*, **trusting** ['trʌstɪŋ] *adj* confiado.

trustingly ['trʌstɪŋlɪ] *adv* confiadamente.

trustworthiness ['trʌst,wɜːðɪnɪs] *n* formalidad *f*, honradez *f*, confiabilidad *f*; carácter *m* fidedigno; exactitud *f*.

trustworthy ['trʌst,wɜːðɪ] *adj person* formal, honrado, confiable, de confianza; *news, source etc* fidedigno; *statistics etc* exacto.

trusty ['trʌstɪ] **1** *adj servant etc* fiel, leal; *weapon* seguro, bueno. **2** *n* recluso *m*, -a *f* de confianza.

truth [truːθ] **1** *n*, *pl* **truths** [truːðz] verdad *f*; realidad *f*; verosimilitud *f*; **the plain ~** la pura verdad, la verdad lisa y llana; **the whole ~** toda la verdad; **the ~ of the matter is that ..., ~ to tell ..., to tell you the ~ ...** la verdad del caso es que ..., a decir verdad ...; **there is some ~ in this** hay una parte de verdad en esto; **~ will out** no hay mentira que no salga; **to tell the ~** decir la verdad; **to tell sb a few home ~s** decir a uno cuatro verdades; **in ~** en verdad, a la verdad.

2 *attr*: **~ drug** suero *m* de la verdad.

truthful ['truːθfʊl] *adj account* verídico, exacto; *person* veraz; **are you being ~?** ¿es esto la verdad?

truthfully ['truːθfəlɪ] *adv* con verdad; **now tell me ~** ahora bien, dime la verdad.

truthfulness ['truːθfʊlnɪs] *n* veracidad *f*; verdad *f*, exactitud *f*.

try [traɪ] **1** *n* (**a**) (*attempt*) tentativa *f*; **to have a ~** hacer una tentativa, probar suerte; **to have a ~ for a job** presentarse como candidato a un puesto, solicitar un puesto; **have another ~!** ¡a probar otra vez!; **it's worth a ~** vale la pena probarlo; **he did it (at the) first ~** lo hizo la primera vez.

(**b**) (*Rugby*) ensayo *m*; **to score a ~** marcar un ensayo.

2 *vt* (**a**) (*attempt*) intentar, probar; **shall we ~ it?** ¿lo probamos?; **you tried only 3 questions** has intentado 3 preguntas nada más.

(**b**) (*test*) probar, poner a prueba, ensayar; **to ~ one's strength** ensayar sus fuerzas; **to ~ one's strength against sb** ensayarse para determinar cuál de los dos es más fuerte; **we tried 3 hotels but they had no room** preguntamos en 3 hoteles pero no tenían habitación; **~ this door** a ver si esta puerta se abre; **he kept on ~ing the handle** siguió tirando del puño; **he was tried and found wanting** fue sometido a prueba y resultó ser deficiente.

(**c**) (*expose to suffering*) hacer sufrir; afligir; **his much-tried relations** sus familiares que tanto habían sufrido; **they have been sorely tried** han sufrido mucho.

(**d**) (*tire*) *eyes* cansar; *person* irritar; **to ~ one's eyes by reading too much** cansarse los ojos leyendo demasiado; **you ~ my patience** me haces perder la paciencia.

(**e**) (*taste, sample*) probar; **have you tried these olives?** ¿has probado estas aceitunas?

(**f**) (*Jur*) *case* ver; *person* procesar (*for* por), juzgar; **to be tried for murder** ser procesado por asesino; **to be tried by one's peers** ser juzgado por sus iguales.

3 *vi* probar; esforzarse; **to ~ one's best, to ~ one's hardest** esforzarse mucho, poner todo su esfuerzo; **~ as he would ...** por más que se esforzase ...; **to ~ again** volver a probar; **you had better not ~** más vale no probarlo; le aconsejo no hacerlo; **to ~ for sth** tratar de obtener algo; **to ~ for a post** presentarse como candidato a un puesto, solicitar un puesto; **to ~ to do sth, to ~ and do sth** tratar de hacer algo, intentar hacer algo; procurar hacer algo; querer hacer algo; **he tried to get in but couldn't** quiso entrar pero no pudo; **it's ~ing to rain** empieza a llover, quiere llover; **~ not to cough** procura no toser, procura contener la tos; **do ~ to understand** trata de comprender; **it's no use ~ing to persuade him** no vale la pena tratar de convencerle.

◆**try on** *vt* (**a**) *dress* probarse, medirse (*Mex*).

(**b**) (*) **to ~ it on with sb** tratar de embaucar a uno; **he's just ~ing it on** lo hace nada más para ver si tragamos el anzuelo; **don't ~ anything on with me!** ¡no lo vayas a intentar conmigo!

◆**try out** *vt* probar, poner a prueba, someter a prueba, ensayar; **~ it out on the dog first** dáselo primero al perro (para ver qué pasa), pruebalo dándosele de comer al perro.

◆**try over** *vt* (*Mus etc*) ensayar.

trying ['traɪɪŋ] *adj* molesto; cansado; difícil.

try-on* ['traɪɒn] *n* trampa *f*, tentativa *f* de engañar, farol *m*.

try-out ['traɪaʊt] *n* prueba *f*; **to give a car a ~** someter un coche a prueba.

tryst [trɪst] *n* (*liter, hum*) cita *f*; lugar *m* de una cita.

tsar [zɑːʳ] *n* zar *m*.

tsarina [zɑː'riːnə] *n* zarina *f*.

tsetse fly ['tsetsɪflaɪ] *n* (mosca *f*) tsetsé *f*.

T-shirt ['tiːʃɜːt] *n V* **T**.

tsp(s) *abbr of* **teaspoonful(s)**.

TT (**a**) *abbr of* **teetotal**; **teetotaller.** (**b**) *n* (*Aut*) *abbr of* **Tourist Trophy.** (**c**) (*Agr*) *abbr of* **tuberculin-tested** a prueba de tuberculinas. (**d**) (*US Post*) *abbr of* **Trust Territory.** (**e**) *n* (*Fin*) *abbr of* **telegraphic transfer** transferencia *f* telegráfica.

TU *n abbr of* **trade(s) union.**

tub [tʌb] **1** *n* tina *f*; cubo *m*, cuba *f*, balde *m* (*LAm*); artesón *m*; (*bath~*) baño *m*, bañera *f*, tina *f* (*LAm*); (*of washing-machine*) tambor *m*; (*Naut**) carcamán *m*; **to have a ~*** (*Brit*) tomar un baño.

2 *vi* tomar un baño.

tuba ['tju:bə] *n* tuba *f.*
tubby* ['tʌbɪ] *adj* rechoncho.
tube [tju:b] *n* (**a**) (*gen*) tubo *m*; (*TV*) tubo *m*; (*US Rad*) lámpara *f*; (*Aut*) cámara *f* de aire; (*Anat*) trompa *f*; **the ~*** la tele*; **it's all gone down the ~*** todo se ha perdido, todo se ha echado a perder. (**b**) (*Brit Rail*) metro *m*; **to go by ~** ir en el metro, viajar por metro.
tubeless ['tju:blɪs] *adj tyre* sin cámara.
tuber ['tju:bəʳ] *n* tubérculo *m.*
tubercle ['tju:bəkl] *n* (*all senses*) tubérculo *m.*
tubercular [tjʊ'bɜ:kjʊləʳ] *adj* tubercular; (*Med*) tuberculoso.
tuberculin [tjʊ'bɜ:kjʊlɪn] *n* tuberculina *f.*
tuberculosis [tjʊ,bɜ:kjʊ'ləʊsɪs] *n* tuberculosis *f.*
tuberculous [tjʊ'bɜ:kjʊləs] *adj* tuberculoso.
tube-station ['tju:b,steɪʃən] *n* (*Brit*) estación *f* de metro.
tubing ['tju:bɪŋ] *n* tubería *f*, cañería *f* (*LAm*); tubos *mpl*; **a piece of ~** un trozo de tubo.
tub-thumper ['tʌb,θʌmpəʳ] *n* (*Brit*) orador *m* demagógico.
tub-thumping ['tʌb,θʌmpɪŋ] (*Brit*) **1** *adj* demagógico. **2** *n* oratoria *f* demagógica.
tubular ['tju:bjʊləʳ] *adj* tubular, en forma de tubo; *furniture* de tubo.
TUC *n* (*Brit*) *abbr of* **Trades Union Congress.**
tuck [tʌk] **1** *n* (**a**) (*Sew*) alforza *f*; pliegue *m*; **to take a ~ in a dress** hacer una alforza en un vestido.
(**b**) (*Brit**) (*food*) provisiones *fpl*, comestibles *mpl*; (*sweets*) dulces *fpl*, golosinas *fpl.*
2 *vt* (*Sew*) alforzar; plegar.
3 *vi*: **to ~ into sth*** comer algo vorazmente, zamparse algo.
◆**tuck away** *vt* (**a**) (*hide*) ocultar, esconder; **~ it away out of sight** ocúltalo para que no se vea; **the village is ~ed away among the woods** la aldea se esconde en el bosque; **he ~ed it away in his pocket** lo guardó en el bolsillo.
(**b**) (*: *eat*) devorar, zampar; **he can certainly ~ it away** ése sí sabe comer; **I can't think where he ~s it all away** no llego a comprender dónde lo almacena.
◆**tuck in 1** *vt*: **to ~ in a flap** meter una solapa para dentro; **to ~ bedclothes in** remeter la ropa de la cama.
2 *vi* (*) comer con apetito, comer vorazmente; **~ in!** ¡a comer!, ¡a ello!
◆**tuck under** *vt*: **to ~ A under B** poner A debajo de B; esconder A debajo de B.
◆**tuck up** *vt skirt, sleeves* arremangar; **to ~ sb up in bed** arropar a uno en la cama; (*fig*) acostar a uno; **you'll soon be nicely ~ed up** pronto te verás metido cómodamente en la cama.
tucker* ['tʌkəʳ] *vt* (*US*: *also* **to ~ out**) cansar, agotar.
tuck-in* ['tʌk'ɪn] *n* banquetazo* *m*, comilona* *f*; **to have a good ~** darse un atracón*.
tuck-shop ['tʌkʃɒp] *n* (*Brit Scol*) bombonería *f*, confitería *f.*
Tudor ['tju:dəʳ] *adj* Tudor; **the ~ period** la época de los Tudor.
Tue(s). *abbr of* **Tuesday** martes, mart.
Tuesday ['tju:zdɪ] *n* martes *m.*
tufa ['tju:fə] *n* toba *f.*
tuft [tʌft] *n* (*of hair*) copete *m*; (*of hairs, wool*) mechón *m*; (*of feathers*) cresta *f*, copete *m*; (*on helmet etc*) penacho *m*; (*of plant*) mata *f.*
tufted ['tʌftɪd] *adj* copetudo.
tug [tʌg] **1** *n* (**a**) (*action*) tirón *m*; estirón *m*; **to give sth a ~** tirar de algo, dar un estirón a algo.
(**b**) (*Naut*) remolcador *m.*
2 *vt* (**a**) (*pull*) tirar de; dar un estirón a; **to ~ sth along** arrastrar algo, llevar algo arrastrándolo.
(**b**) (*Naut*) remolcar; **eventually they ~ged the boat clear** por fin sacaron el barco a flote.
3 *vi*: **to ~ at sth** tirar de algo; **somebody was ~ging at my sleeve** alguien me tiraba de la manga; **they ~ged their hardest** se esforzaron muchísimo tirando de él.
tugboat ['tʌgbəʊt] *n* remolcador *m.*
tug-of-love* [,tʌgəv'lʌv] *n* litigio *m* entre padres por la custodia de los hijos (después de un divorcio *etc*).
tug-of-war ['tʌgə(v)'wɔ:ʳ] *n* lucha *f* de la cuerda; (*fig*) lucha *f*; tira *m* y afloja; **then comes the ~** luego es el momento crítico, luego se inicia la lucha decisiva.
tuition [tjʊ'ɪʃən] **1** *n* enseñanza *f*, instrucción *f*; (*US*) matrícula *f*; **private ~** clases *fpl* particulares (*in* de). **2** *attr*: **~ fee** tasa *f* (de instrucción).
tulip ['tju:lɪp] *n* tulipán *m.*
tulip-tree ['tju:lɪptri:] *n* tulipanero *m*, tulipero *m.*
tulle [tju:l] *n* tul *m.*
tumble ['tʌmbl] **1** *n* caída *f*; (*somersault*) voltereta *f*; **to have a ~, to take a ~** caerse; **to have a ~ in the hay** retozar, hacer el amor (en el pajar); **to take a ~** (*fig*) bajar de golpe, dar un bajón.
2 *vt* (*knock down*) derribar, abatir, tumbar; (*fig*) derrocar; (*upset*) derramar, hacer caer; (*disarrange*) desarreglar; **to ~ sb in the hay** tumbar a una (en el pajar).
3 *vi* (**a**) (*fall*) caer; (*stumble*) tropezar; **to toss and ~** (*in bed*) agitarse, revolverse mucho; **to ~ in, to ~ into bed** acostarse; acostarse del modo que sea.
(**b**) **to ~ to sth*** (*Brit*) caer en la cuenta de algo, comprender algo.
◆**tumble down** *vi* caer; desplomarse, hundirse, venirse abajo.
◆**tumble out 1** *vt* echar en desorden.
2 *vi* salir en desorden; **to ~ out of a car** caerse de un coche; **to ~ out of bed** levantarse de prisa.
◆**tumble over 1** *vt* derramar, hacer caer.
2 *vi*: **to go tumbling over and over** ir rodando, ir dando tumbas.
tumbledown ['tʌmbldaʊn] *adj* destartalado, ruinoso.
tumbledryer ['tʌmbl,draɪəʳ] *n* secadora *f.*
tumbler ['tʌmbləʳ] *n* (**a**) (*glass*) vaso *m.* (**b**) (*of lock*) seguro *m*, fiador *m*; **~ switch** interruptor *m* de resorte. (**c**) (*person*) volteador *m*, -ora *f*; (*Orn*) pichón *m* volteador.
tumbleweed ['tʌmblwi:d] *n* (*US*) planta *f* rodadora.
tumbrel ['tʌmbrəl], **tumbril** ['tʌmbrɪl] *n* chirrión *m*, carreta *f.*
tumefaction [,tju:mɪ'fækʃən] *n* tumefacción *f.*
tumescent [tju:'mesnt] *adj* tumescente.
tumid ['tju:mɪd] *adj* túmido.
tummy* ['tʌmɪ] *n* barriguita* *f*, tripas* *fpl*; **~ tuck** cirugía *f* plástica anti-michelines*.
tummy-ache* ['tʌmɪeɪk] *n* dolor *m* de tripas*.
tumour, (*US*) **tumor** ['tju:məʳ] *n* tumor *m.*
tumult ['tju:mʌlt] *n* tumulto *m*, alboroto *m.*
tumultuous [tju:'mʌltjʊəs] *adj* tumultuoso.
tumultuously [tju:'mʌltjʊəslɪ] *adv* tumultuosamente.
tumulus ['tju:mjʊləs] *n*, *pl* **tumuli** ['tju:mjʊlaɪ] túmulo *m.*
tun [tʌn] *n* tonel *m.*
tuna ['tju:nə] *n*, (*US*) **tuna fish** ['tju:nəfɪʃ] *n* atún *m.*
tundra ['tʌndrə] *n* tundra *f.*
tune [tju:n] **1** *n* (**a**) (*melody*) aire *m*, melodía *f*, tonada *f*; (*fig*) tono *m*; **she calls the ~ in their house** ella lleva la voz cantante en su casa; **to change one's ~, to sing another ~** cambiar de disco*, mudar de tono; **it goes to the ~ of 'Greensleeves'** se canta con la melodía de 'Greensleeves'; **to the ~ of £500** por la bonita suma de 500 libras.
(**b**) **to be in ~** (*Mus*) estar templado, estar afinado; **to sing in ~** cantar afinadamente, cantar bien; **to be in ~ with** (*fig*) armonizar con, concordar con; **to be out of ~** (*Mus*) estar destemplado, estar desafinado; **to sing out of ~** desafinar, cantar mal; **to be out of ~ with** (*fig*) desentonar con, estar en desacuerdo con; **to go out of ~** desafinar.
2 *vt* afinar, acordar, templar.
◆**tune in 1** *vt*: **to be ~d in*** estar en la onda*; estar al tanto (*to* de).
2 *vi* sintonizar; **to ~ in to a station** sintonizar una emisora.
◆**tune out** *vi* (*US*) desconectar la televisión (*etc*).
◆**tune up 1** *vt* (*Mus*) afinar, acordar, templar; (*Aut*) poner a punto, reglar, afinar.
2 *vi* (*Mus*) afinar el instrumento, acordar el instrumento; **we're still just tuning up** (*fig*) estamos todavía en la fase preliminar.
tuneful ['tju:nfʊl] *adj* melodioso, armonioso.
tunefully ['tju:nfəlɪ] *adv* melodiosamente, armoniosamente.
tunefulness ['tju:nfʊlnɪs] *n* lo melodioso, lo armonioso.
tuneless ['tju:nlɪs] *adj* disonante, discordante.
tunelessly ['tju:nlɪslɪ] *adv* de modo disonante.
tuner ['tju:nəʳ] *n* (**a**) (*person*) afinador *m.* (**b**) (*Rad, TV*: *knob*) botón *m* sintonizador.
tune-up ['tju:nʌp] *n* (*Mus*) afinación *f*; (*Aut*) puesta *f* a punto, reglaje *m.*
tungsten ['tʌŋstən] *n* tungsteno *m.*
tunic ['tju:nɪk] *n* túnica *f*; (*Brit Mil*) guerrera *f*, blusa *f.*
tuning ['tju:nɪŋ] *n* (*Mus*) afinación *f*; (*Rad*) sintonización *f*; (*Aut*) afinación *f*, reglaje *m.*
tuning-coil ['tju:nɪŋkɔɪl] *n* bobina *f* sintonizadora.
tuning-fork ['tju:nɪŋfɔ:k] *n* diapasón *m.*
tuning-knob ['tju:nɪŋnɒb] *n* botón *m* sintonizador.
Tunis ['tju:nɪs] *n* Túnez *m* (*ciudad*).
Tunisia [tju:'nɪzɪə] *n* Túnez *m* (*país*).
Tunisian [tju:'nɪzɪən] **1** *adj* tunecino. **2** *n* tunecino *m*, -a *f.*
tunnel ['tʌnl] **1** *n* túnel *m*; (*Min*) galería *f.*

2 *vt* construir un túnel bajo, construir un túnel a través de; **a mound ~led by rabbits** un montículo lleno de madrigueras de conejo; **wood ~led by beetles** madera *f* carcomida, madera *f* agujereada por coleópteros; **shelters ~led out in the hillsides** refugios *mpl* horadados en las colinas.

3 *vi* construir un túnel (*or* galería); (*animal*) excavar una madriguera; **they ~ into the hill** construyen un túnel bajo la colina; **to ~ down into the earth** perforar un túnel en la tierra; **the rabbits ~ under the fence** los conejos hacen madrigueras que pasan debajo de la valla; **they ~led their way out** escaparon excavando un túnel.

tunnel vision ['tʌnl'vɪʒən] *n* visión *f* de túnel; (*fig*) estrechez *f* de miras.

tunny ['tʌnɪ] *n* atún *m*; **striped ~** bonito *m*.

tuppence ['tʌpəns] *n* = **twopence.**

tuppenny ['tʌpənɪ] *adj* = **twopenny.**

turban ['tɜːbən] *n* turbante *m*.

turbid ['tɜːbɪd] *adj* túrbido.

turbine ['tɜːbaɪn] *n* turbina *f*.

turbo ['tɜːbəʊ] *n* (*fan*) turbosoplador *m*; (*in cars*) turbo(compresor) *m*.

turbo... ['tɜːbəʊ] *pref* turbo...

turbocharged ['tɜːbəʊtʃɑːdʒd] *adj* turbocargado, turboalimentado.

turbocharger ['tɜːbəʊ,tʃɑːdʒəʳ] *n* turbocompresor *m*, turbo *m*.

turbofan ['tɜːbəʊfæn] *n* turboventilador *m*.

turbogenerator ['tɜːbəʊ'dʒenəreɪtəʳ] *n* turbogenerador *m*.

turbojet ['tɜːbəʊ'dʒet] **1** *n* turborreactor *m*. **2** *attr* turborreactor.

turboprop ['tɜːbəʊ'prɒp] **1** *n* turbohélice *m*. **2** *attr* turbohélice.

turbot ['tɜːbət] *n* rodaballo *m*.

turbulence ['tɜːbjʊləns] *n* turbulencia *f*; desorden *m*, disturbios *mpl*; (*Met*) turbulencia *f*.

turbulent ['tɜːbjʊlənt] *adj* turbulento; revoltoso.

turd** [tɜːd] *n* (**a**) cagada** *f*, zurullo** *m*. (**b**) (*person*) mierda** *mf*.

tureen [tə'riːn] *n* sopera *f*.

turf [tɜːf] **1** *n*, *pl* **turfs** *or* **turves** [tɜːvz] (**a**) (*sward*) césped *m*; (*clod*) tepe *m*, césped *m*; (*in turfing*) pan *m* de hierba; (*peat*) turba *f*; **the T~** el turf, las carreras de caballos.

(**b**) (*US**) territorio *m* propio de uno.

2 *attr*: **~ accountant** (*Brit*) corredor *m* de apuestas.

3 *vt* (*also* **to ~ over**) encespedar, cubrir con céspedes.

♦turf out* *vt*: **to ~ sb out** (*Brit*) echar a uno, expulsar a uno.

turgid ['tɜːdʒɪd] *adj* turgente; (*fig*) hinchado; pesado, indigesto.

turgidity [tɜː'dʒɪdɪtɪ] *n* turgencia *f*; (*fig*) hinchazón *f*; pesadez *f*.

Turin [tjʊ'rɪn] *n* Turín *m*.

Turk [tɜːk] *n* turco *m*, -a *f*; (*fig*) persona *f* incontrolable, elemento *m* alborotador; **little ~, young ~** tunante *m*.

Turkey ['tɜːkɪ] *n* Turquía *f*.

turkey ['tɜːkɪ] *n* (**a**) (*Orn*) pavo *m*, -a *f*, guajolote *m* (*Mex*), chompipe *m* (*CAm*); **to talk ~*** (*US*) hablar en serio. (**b**) (*US***) patoso *m*, -a *f*, pato *m* mareado*. (**c**) (*Theat**) fracaso *m*.

turkeycock ['tɜːkɪkɒk] *n* pavo *m* (*also fig*).

Turkish ['tɜːkɪʃ] **1** *adj* turco; **~ bath** baño *m* turco; **~ coffee** café *m* turco; **~ delight** rahat *m* lokum; **~ towel** (*US*) toalla *f*. **2** *n* turco *m*.

Turkish-Cypriot ['tɜːkɪʃ'sɪprɪət] **1** *adj* turcochipriota. **2** *n* turcochipriota *mf*.

turmeric ['tɜːmərɪk] *n* cúrcuma *f*.

turmoil ['tɜːmɔɪl] *n* confusión *f*, desorden *m*; alboroto *m*; tumulto *m*; (*mental*) trastorno *m*; **everything is in (a) ~** todo es confusión, todo está revuelto; **we had complete ~ for a week** durante una semana reinó la confusión.

turn [tɜːn] **1** *n* (**a**) (*revolution*) vuelta *f*, revolución *f*; (*of spiral*) espira *f*; **with a quick ~ of the hand** con un movimiento rápido de la mano; **he never does a hand's ~** no da golpe; **the meat is done to a ~** la carne está en su punto; **to give a screw another ~** apretar un tornillo una vuelta más.

(**b**) (*change of direction*) cambio *m* de dirección; (*Aut: by vehicle*) giro *m*, vuelta *f*; (*Aut: turning off*) salida *f*; (*Naut*) viraje *m*; (*Swimming*) vuelta *f*; (*in road*) curva *f*, vuelta *f*; recodo *m*; **'no left ~'** (*Aut*) 'prohibido girar a la izquierda'; **~ of the tide** cambio *m* de la marea, vuelta *f* de la marea (*also fig*); **at every ~** a cada paso, a cada momento; **at the ~ of the century** al final del siglo; **the tide is on the ~** la marea está cambiando; **the milk is on the ~** la leche está cortándose; **to make a ~ to the left** girar a la izquierda; **to make a ~ to port** virar a babor; **I think we missed our ~ back there** creo que allí atrás nos hemos pasado de la salida; **things took a new ~** las cosas cambiaron de aspecto; **events took a tragic ~** los acontecimientos tomaron un cariz trágico; **events are taking a sensational ~** los acontecimientos vienen tomando un rumbo sensacional; **then things took a ~ for the better** luego las cosas empezaron a mejorar.

(**c**) (*Med: fainting fit etc*) vahido *m*, desmayo *m*; (*crisis*) crisis *f*, ataque *m*; (*fright*) susto *m*; **it gave me quite a ~** me dio todo un susto; **he had another ~ last night** anoche le dio otro ataque.

(**d**) (*short walk*) vuelta *f*; **to take a ~ in the park** dar una vuelta por el parque.

(**e**) (*successive opportunity*) turno *m*, vez *f*; oportunidad *f*; **~ and ~ about** cada uno por turno; ahora esto y luego aquello; **by ~s, in ~** por turnos, sucesivamente; **I felt hot and cold by ~s** tuve calor y luego frío en momentos sucesivos; **it's my ~** me toca a mí; **then it was my ~ to protest** luego protesté a mi vez; **it's her ~ next** le toca a ella después, ella es la primera en turno; **your ~ will come** tendrás tu oportunidad; **to give up one's ~** ceder la vez; **to go out of ~** jugar (*etc*) fuera de orden; **to miss one's ~** perder la vez; perder la ocasión; **the player shall miss two ~s** el jugador deberá perder dos jugadas; **to take one's ~** esperar su turno; turnar, alternar; **to take ~s at the controls** alternar a los mandos; **to take a ~ at the wheel** conducir por su turno; **to take ~s at doing sth, to take it in ~s to do sth** hacer algo por turnos, turnar para hacer algo.

(**f**) (*esp Brit Theat etc*) número *m*; **he came on and did a funny ~** salió a escena y presentó un número cómico.

(**g**) (*service*) **bad ~** mala jugada *f*, mala pasada *f*; **good ~** favor *m*, servicio *m*; **to do sb a bad ~** hacer una mala pasada a uno; **a scout does a good ~ each day** el explorador hace una buena acción cada día; **one good ~ deserves another** amor con amor se paga; **it will serve my ~** servirá para lo que yo quiero.

(**h**) (*inclination*) propensión *f* (*to* a); (*of mind*) disposición *f*, sesgo *m*; (*talent*) talento *m*, aptitud *f*; **to have a ~ for business** tener aptitud para los negocios; **it showed an odd ~ of mind** demostró una disposición de ánimo algo rara.

(**i**) (*form*) forma *f*; **the ~ of her arm** la configuración de su brazo, el contorno de su brazo; **~ of phrase** giro *m*, expresión *f*; **that's a French ~ of phrase** eso es un modismo francés; **the car has a good ~ of speed** el coche tiene buena aceleración.

2 *vt* (**a**) (*revolve*) girar, hacer girar; *handle* dar vueltas a, torcer; *key* dar vuelta a; *screw* atornillar, destornillar; **the belt ~s the wheel** la correa hace girar la rueda; **~ it to the left** dale una vuelta hacia la izquierda; **you can ~ it through 90°** se puede girarlo hasta 90 grados.

(**b**) (*~ to the other side*) volver; *ankle* torcer; *brain* trastornar; *pages of book* pasar, volver; *stomach, soil etc* revolver; *hay etc* volver al revés; **to ~ a page** volver una hoja; **to ~ a dress inside out** volver un vestido del revés; **the plough ~s the soil** el arado revuelve la tierra.

(**c**) (*direct*) volver; dirigir; *blow* desviar; **to ~ one's head** volver la cabeza; **to ~ one's steps homeward** dirigirse a casa, volver los pasos hacia casa; **to ~ one's eyes in sb's direction** volver la mirada hacia donde está uno; **to ~ a gun on sb** apuntar un revólver a uno; **we managed to ~ his argument against him** pudimos volver su argumento contra él mismo; **to ~ A against B** predisponer a A en contra de B; **they ~ed him against his parents** le enemistaron con sus padres; **to ~ sb from doing sth** disuadir a uno de hacer algo; **we must ~ our thoughts to ...** hemos de concentrar nuestro pensamiento en ...; **if you will ~ your attention to ...** tengan la bondad de fijar la atención en ...

(**d**) (*pass*) *corner* doblar; **he has ~ed 50** ha cumplido los 50, ya tiene lo menos 50 años; **it's ~ed 11 o'clock** son las 11 dadas, ya dieron las 11.

(**e**) (*transform*) cambiar, mudar (*into, to* en); convertir, transformar (*into, to* en); *milk* agriar, volver agrio; **to ~ iron into gold** transformar el hierro en oro; **his admiration was ~ed to scorn** su admiración se transformó en desprecio; **to ~ verse into prose** verter verso en prosa; **to ~ a play into a film** hacer una versión cinematográfica de una obra dramática; **to ~ English into Spanish** traducir el inglés al español, verter el inglés en español; **to ~ colour** cambiar de color; **the heat ~ed the walls black** el calor volvió negras las paredes, el calor ennegreció las paredes.

(**f**) (*Tech*) tornear; **to ~ wood on a lathe** labrar la madera en un torno; **a well ~ed leg** una pierna bien formada, una pierna bien torneada; **a well ~ed sentence** una frase elegante.

3 *vi* (**a**) (*revolve*) girar, dar vueltas; (*of person*) volverse; girar sobre los talones; **my head is ~ing** mi cabeza está dando vueltas; **to toss and ~ in bed** revolverse en la cama; **everything ~s on whether ...** todo depende de si ...; **the conversation ~ed on newts** la conversación versaba sobre los tritones, el tema de la conversación era los tritones.

(**b**) (*change direction*) volver, volverse; (*Aer, Naut*) virar; (*Aut*) girar, torcer; (*tide*) repuntar; (*weather etc*) cambiar; **to ~ left** torcer a la izquierda; **right ~!** (*Mil*) derecha ... ¡ar!; **to ~ into a road** entrar en una calle; **to ~ to port** virar a babor; **to ~ for home** volver hacia casa; **please ~ to page 34** vamos a la página 34, por favor la página 34; **the wind has ~ed** el viento ha cambiado de dirección; **to wait for the weather to ~** esperar a que cambie el tiempo; **then our luck ~ed** luego mejoramos de suerte; **he ~ed to me and smiled** se volvió hacia mí y sonrió; **to ~ to sb for help** acudir a uno a pedir ayuda; **he ~ed to politics** se volvió a la política; **he ~ed to mysticism** recurrió al misticismo; empezó a estudiar el misticismo; **farmers are ~ing from cows to pigs** los granjeros cambian de vacas a cerdos; **our thoughts ~ to those who ...** pensamos ahora en los que ...; **I don't know which way to ~** estoy para volverme loco; **I don't know where to ~ for money** no sé en qué parte ir a buscar dinero; **to ~ against sb, to ~ on sb** volverse contra uno; **to ~ against sth** coger aversión a algo.

(**c**) (*change*) cambiar, cambiarse; convertirse, transformarse (*into, to* en); (+ *adj*) ponerse, volverse; (+ *n*) hacerse; (*leaves*) descolorarse; dorarse; (*milk*) agriarse, cortarse; **it ~s red** se pone colorado; **matters are ~ing serious** las cosas se ponen graves; **then he began to ~ awkward** luego empezó a ponerse difícil; **the princess ~ed into a toad** la princesa se transformó en sapo, la princesa quedó transformada en sapo; **it ~ed to stone** se convirtió en piedra; **to ~ soldier** hacerse soldado; **to ~ communist** hacerse comunista.

◆**turn about, turn around 1** *vt V* **~ round. 2** *vi* dar una vuelta completa; (*Pol*) cambiar completamente de política; **about ~!** (*Mil*) media vuelta ... ¡ar!

◆**turn aside 1** *vt* desviar, apartar.

2 *vi* desviarse (*from* de); apartarse del camino; **I ~ed aside in disgust** me aparté lleno de asco.

◆**turn away 1** *vt* despedir; rechazar, no aceptar.

2 *vi* volver la cara.

◆**turn back 1** *vt* (**a**) (*fold*) doblar.

(**b**) *clock* retrasar.

(**c**) *person* hacer volver; hacer retroceder; **they were ~ed back at the frontier** en la frontera les hicieron volver.

2 *vi* volverse (atrás); retroceder; volverse sobre sus pasos; **there can be no ~ing back now** ahora no vale volverse atrás.

◆**turn down** *vt* (**a**) (*bend, fold*) doblar, tornar; *case, glass etc* poner boca abajo; *thumb* volver hacia abajo.

(**b**) *gas, radio etc* bajar.

(**c**) *offer* rechazar; *candidate, suitor* no aceptar; **he was ~ed down for the job** no le dieron el puesto.

◆**turn in 1** *vt* (**a**) (*fold*) doblar hacia adentro.

(**b**) *essay, report* entregar, presentar; *wanted man* entregar (a la policía).

2 *vi* (**a**) (*fold*) doblarse hacia adentro; apuntar hacia adentro.

(**b**) (*: *go to bed*) acostarse, ir a la cama.

◆**turn off 1** *vt* (**a**) *light* apagar; (*Elec*) desconectar, quitar; cortar; *engine* parar; *tap* cerrar; *gas* cortar, cerrar la llave de.

(**b**) **it quite ~s me off*** me repugna, me deja frío.

2 *vi* desviarse (*from the path* del camino).

◆**turn on** *vt* (**a**) (*Elec*) encender, conectar, poner, prender (*LAm*); *tap* abrir; *gas* abrir la llave de; (*) *charm* desplegar, poner en juego; **to leave the radio ~ed on** dejar la radio encendida.

(**b**) (*: *excite*) emocionar; enrollar*; encandilar, chiflar*; **he doesn't ~ me on** no me chifla*; **whatever ~s you on** lo que te guste, lo que quieras; **to be ~ed on (with drugs)**‡ estar iluminado‡.

◆**turn out 1** *vt* (**a**) *light* apagar; *gas* cortar, cerrar la llave de.

(**b**) *person etc* echar, expulsar; poner en la calle; *rubbish* tirar, botar, vaciar.

(**c**) *pocket etc* vaciar; *room* limpiar, despejar.

(**d**) *product* hacer, producir, fabricar; **the college ~s out good secretaries** el colegio produce buenas secretarias.

(**e**) **to ~ out the guard** formar la guardia.

(**f**) **to be well ~ed out** ir bien vestido, estar bien trajeado.

2 *vi* (**a**) (*from bed*) levantarse, abandonar la cama; (*from house*) salir de casa, salir a la calle; (*guard*) formarse, presentarse para servicio.

(**b**) (*transpire*) **how are things ~ing out?** ¿cómo van tus cosas?; **it all ~ed out well** todo salió bien; **it ~s out to be harder than we thought** resulta más difícil de lo que pensábamos; **it ~s out that he's a vegetarian** resulta que es vegetariano; **as it ~s out** por fin; **as it ~ed out nobody went** por fin no fue nadie.

◆**turn over 1** *vt* (**a**) *page etc* volver; *container, vehicle* volcar; (*upside down*) volver, poner al revés; **the thieves ~ed the place over*** los ladrones saquearon el local.

(**b**) (*Mech*) *engine* hacer girar; *matter in mind* revolver, meditar.

(**c**) (*hand over*) entregar, ceder, traspasar (*to* a).

(**d**) (*Comm*) *sum* mover, facturar; **they ~ over a million a year** su volumen de ventas (*or* producción *etc*) es de un millón al año.

2 *vi* (**a**) revolverse; (*Aut etc*) capotar, dar una vuelta de campana; **it ~ed over and over** fue dando tumbos; **my stomach ~ed over** se me revolvió el estómago.

(**b**) **please ~ over** véase al dorso.

◆**turn round 1** *vt* (**a**) *object etc* volver, girar. (**b**) (*change*) cambiar; reformar; **it is time to ~ the economy round** es el momento de dar una nueva dirección a la economía.

2 *vi* (*revolve*) girar; dar vueltas; (*person*) volverse, girar sobre los talones; **I could hardly ~ round** apenas podía revolverme; **as soon as I ~ed round they were quarrelling again** en cuanto les volví la espalda se pusieron otra vez a reñir; **the government has ~ed right round** el gobierno ha cambiado completamente de rumbo; **to ~ round and round** seguir dando vueltas.

◆**turn to** *vi* empezar; empezar a trabajar (*etc*); **everyone had to ~ to and help** todos tuvieron que ayudar; **we must all ~ to** todos tenemos que poner manos a la obra.

◆**turn up 1** *vt* (**a**) (*bend*) doblar hacia arriba; (*shorten*) acortar, hacer más corto.

(**b**) *gas* abrir (más); *radio etc* poner más fuerte.

(**c**) *earth* revolver; *buried object* desenterrar, hacer salir a la superficie.

(**d**) (*find*) encontrar; tropezar con; *reference* buscar, consultar.

(**e**) **~ it up!**‡ ¡por favor!

2 *vi* (**a**) (*print upwards*) doblarse hacia arriba, apuntar hacia arriba.

(**b**) (*appear*) aparecer, surgir; (*card etc*) salir; (*arrive, show up*) llegar, acudir; presentarse; asomar la cara; (*be found again*) volver a aparecer; **we'll see if anyone ~s up** veremos si viene alguien; **he ~ed up 2 hours late** llegó con 2 horas de retraso; **he never ~s up at class** no asiste nunca a la clase; **sth is sure to ~ up** es seguro que surgirá alguna solución.

turnabout ['tɜːnəbaʊt] *n*, **turnaround** ['tɜːnəraʊnd] *n* (**a**) (*change*) cambio *m* completo, giro *m* en redondo, giro *m* total. (**b**) (*of ship etc*) tiempo *m* de descarga y carga, tiempo *m* en puerto (*etc*).

turncoat ['tɜːnkəʊt] *n* renegado *m*, -a *f*; **to become a ~** volver la chaqueta.

turned-down ['tɜːnd'daʊn] *adj* doblado hacia abajo.

turned-up ['tɜːnd'ʌp] *adj* doblado hacia arriba; *nose* respingona.

turner ['tɜːnəʳ] *n* tornero *m*.

turnery ['tɜːnərɪ] *n* tornería *f*.

turning ['tɜːnɪŋ] *n* vuelta *f*; ángulo *m*; recodo *m*; **the first ~ on the left** la primera bocacalle a la izquierda; **we parked in a side ~** aparcamos el coche en una calle que salía de la carretera.

turning-circle ['tɜːnɪŋ,sɜːkl] *n* (*Aut*) círculo *m* de viraje, diámetro *m* de giro.

turning-lathe ['tɜːnɪŋleɪð] *n* torno *m*.

turning-point ['tɜːnɪŋpɔɪnt] *n* (*fig*) punto *m* decisivo, coyuntura *f* crítica; **that was the ~** eso fue la vuelta de la marea, eso marcó el cambio decisivo.

turnip ['tɜːnɪp] *n* nabo *m*.

turnkey ['tɜːnkiː] **1** *n* (**a**) (*Hist*) llavero *m* (de una cárcel), carcelero *m*. (**b**) (*Comput*) llave *f* de seguridad. **2** *attr*: ~

system sistema *m* de seguridad.
turn-off ['tɜːnɒf] *n* (**a**) (*Aut*) salida *f* (de una carretera *etc*). (**b**) (*) **he's a real** ~ ése me cae gordo*; **the film was a complete** ~ la película fue asquerosa; **his breath is a big** ~ su aliento me repugna.
turn-on* ['tɜːnɒn] *n* (*girl*) tía *f* buena*.
turnout ['tɜːnaʊt] *n* (**a**) (*attendance*) concurrencia *f*; número *m* de asistentes; (*paying spectators*) entrada *f*, público *m*; (*at election*) número *m* de votantes; **there was a poor** ~ había poca gente, asistieron pocos; **we hope for a good** ~ **at the dance** esperamos que el baile sea muy concurrido.
(**b**) (*output*) producción *f*.
(**c**) (*dress*) atuendo *m*.
(**d**) (*cleaning*) limpieza *f* (general).
turnover ['tɜːn,əʊvəʳ] *n* (**a**) (*Comm*) volumen *m* de negocios, volumen *m* de ventas, facturación *f*; número *m* de transacciones; movimiento *m* de mercancías; rotación *f* de existencias; **there is a rapid** ~ **in staff** hay mucho movimiento de personal.
(**b**) (*Culin*) empanada *f*.
turnpike ['tɜːnpaɪk] *n* (*Hist*) barrera *f* de portazgo; (*US Aut*) autopista *f* de peaje.
turn-round ['tɜːnraʊnd] *n* = **turnabout, turnaround.**
turn signal ['tɜːn,sɪgnl] *n* (*US*) indicador *m* (de dirección).
turnspit ['tɜːnspɪt] *n* mecanismo *m* que da vueltas al asador.
turnstile ['tɜːnstaɪl] *n* torniquete *m*.
turntable ['tɜːn,teɪbl] **1** *n* (*Rail*) placa *f* giratoria; (*of gramophone*) plato *m* giratorio, giradiscos *m*. **2** *attr*: ~ **ladder** escalera *f* de bomberos.
turn-up ['tɜːnʌp] *n* (**a**) (*Brit*: *of trousers*) vuelta *f*. (**b**) **that was a** ~ **for him** en eso tuvo mucha suerte; **what a** ~ **for the book!** ¡qué sorpresa más agradable!
turpentine ['tɜːpəntaɪn] *n* aguarrás *m*, trementina *f*.
turpitude ['tɜːpɪtjuːd] *n* (*liter*) infamia *f*, vileza *f*; **to be dismissed for gross moral** ~ ser despedido por inmoralidad manifiesta, ser expulsado por conducta infame.
turps* [tɜːps] *n abbr of* **turpentine.**
turquoise ['tɜːkwɔɪz] *n* turquesa *f*.
turret ['tʌrɪt] *n* (*Archit*) torreón *m*; (*Mil, Hist*) torre *f*, torrecilla *f*; (*of tank, warship, aircraft*) torreta *f*; (*US Tech*) cabrestante *m*.
turtle ['tɜːtl] *n* tortuga *f* marina; **to turn** ~ volverse patas arriba, (*Naut*) zozobrar, (*Aut etc*) volcarse, dar una vuelta de campana.
turtledove ['tɜːtldʌv] *n* tórtola *f*.
turtleneck ['tɜːtlnek] *n* (*US*: *also* ~ **sweater**) (jersey *m* de) cuello *m* de cisne.
Tuscan ['tʌskən] **1** *adj* toscano. **2** *n* (**a**) toscano *m*, -a *f*. (**b**) (*Ling*) toscano *m*.
Tuscany ['tʌskənɪ] *n* la Toscana.
tush [tʌʃ] *excl*: ~! ¡bah!
tusk [tʌsk] *n* colmillo *m*.
tussle ['tʌsl] **1** *n* (*struggle*) lucha *f* (*for* por); (*scuffle*) pelea *f*, agarrada *f*.
2 *vi* luchar (*with* con); pelearse, reñir (*about, over* por causa de); **they** ~**d with the police** se pelearon con la policía.
tussock ['tʌsək] *n* montecillo *m* de hierba.
tut [tʌt] (*also* **tut-tut**) **1** *interj* ¡vamos!, ¡eso no!; ¡pche!; ¡qué horror! **2** *vi* hacer un gesto de desaprobación.
tutelage ['tjuːtɪlɪdʒ] *n* tutela *f*; **under the** ~ **of** bajo la tutela de.
tutelary ['tjuːtɪlərɪ] *adj* tutelar.
tutor ['tjuːtəʳ] **1** *n* (*Hist*) ayo *m*; (*private teacher*) preceptor *m*, -ora *f*; profesor *m*, -ora *f* particular; (*Brit Univ, approx*) profesor *m*, -ora *f* que tiene a su cargo un pequeño grupo de estudiantes; (*teaching assistant*) profesor *m*, -ora *f* auxiliar; (*moral* ~) profesor *m* consejero, profesora *f* consejera; (*eg for OU, UNED*) tutor *m*, -ora *f*; (*Jur*) tutor *m*.
2 *attr*: ~ **group** (*Brit*) grupo *m* de tutoría.
3 *vt* enseñar, instruir; dar clase particular a; **to** ~ **a boy in French** dar a un muchacho clases particulares de francés.
tutorial [tjuː'tɔːrɪəl] **1** *adj* preceptoral; tutorial; (*Jur*) tutelar. **2** *n* (*Univ*) clase *f* particular, clase *f* que consiste en un grupo pequeño de estudiantes; (*eg for OU, UNED*) tutoría *f*.
tutti-frutti [,tʊtɪ'frʊtɪ] *n* tutti-frutti *m*.
tutu ['tuːtuː] *n* tutú *m*.
tuwhit-tuwhoo [tʊ'wɪttə'wuː] *n* ulular *m*.
tuxedo [tʌk'siːdəʊ] *n* (*US*) smoking *m*, esmoquin *m*.
TV *n abbr of* **television** televisión *f*, TV.
TVA *n* (*US*) *abbr of* **Tennessee Valley Authority.**
TVEI *n* (*Brit*) *abbr of* **technical and vocational educational initiative.**
TVP *n abbr of* **texturized vegetable protein.**
twaddle ['twɒdl] *n* tonterías *fpl*, bobadas *fpl*.
twain [tweɪn] (††) *n*: **the** ~ los dos; **to split sth in** ~ partir algo en dos; **and ne'er the** ~ **shall meet** sin que el uno se acerque al otro jamás.
twang [twæŋ] **1** *n* (*Mus etc*) tañido *m*, punteado *m*; (*of bow etc*) ruido *m*, sonido *m* (de cuerda que se estira y se suelta); (*nasal* ~) gangueo *m*, timbre *m* nasal; **with an American** ~ con voz gangosa americana.
2 *vt* (*Mus*) puntear; *bowstring* estirar y soltar repentinamente.
3 *vi* producir un sonido agudo; (*in speaking*) hablar con timbre nasal.
twangy ['twæŋɪ] *adj string etc* elástico, muy estirado; *accent* nasal, gangoso.
'twas [twɒz] (††) = **it was.**
twat** [twæt] *n* (**a**) (*Anat*) coño** *m*. (**b**) (*person*) gilipollas* *mf*.
tweak [twiːk] **1** *n* pellizco *m*; **to give sb a** ~ dar un pellizco a uno. **2** *vt* pellizcar (retorciendo); **to** ~ **sth off** quitar algo pellizcándolo.
twee* [twiː] *adj* (*Brit*) *person* afectado, repipi*; *style etc* amanerado; dulzón, sensiblero.
tweed [twiːd] *n* tweed *m*, mezcla *f* de lana; ~**s** (*suit*) traje *m* de tweed.
tweedy ['twiːdɪ] *adj* con traje de tweed, vestido de tweed; (*fig*) aristocrático (y rural).
'tween [twiːn] *prep* (*liter*) = **between.**
tweet [twiːt] *n* pío pío *m*. **2** *vi* piar.
tweeter ['twiːtəʳ] *n* altavoz *m* para altas audiofrecuencias.
tweezers ['twiːzəz] *npl* bruselas *fpl*, pinzas *fpl*; **a pair of** ~ unas bruselas, unas pinzas.
twelfth [twelfθ] **1** *adj* duodécimo; **T**~ **Night** Noche *f* de Reyes, Epifanía *f*. **2** *n* duodécimo *m*; doceavo *m*, duodécima parte *f*.
twelve [twelv] **1** *adj* doce; **a** ~ **inch** (*Mus*) un maxisingle. **2** *n* doce *m*.
twelvemonth†† ['twelvmʌnθ] *n* año *m*; **this day** ~ de hoy en un año; **we've not seen him for a** ~ hace un año que no le vemos.
twelve-tone ['twelvtəʊn] *adj* dodecafónico.
twentieth ['twentɪɪθ] **1** *adj* vigésimo. **2** *n* vigésimo *m*, vigésima parte *f*.
twenty ['twentɪ] **1** *adj* veinte; ~**-two metre line** (*Rugby*) línea *f* de veintidós metros; ~**-**~ **vision** visión *f* normal. **2** *n* veinte *m*; **the twenties** (*eg 1920s*) los años veinte; **to be in one's twenties** tener más de veinte años.
twenty-first ['twentɪfɜːst] *n* (*birthday*) cumpleaños *m* veintiuno; (*party*) fiesta *f* del cumpleaños veintiuno.
twentyfold ['twentɪfəʊld] **1** *adv* veinte veces. **2** *adj* veinte veces mayor.
twenty-four ['twentɪ'fɔːʳ] *attr*: '~ **hour service**' '24 horas de servicio', 'abierto 24 horas'.
twentyish ['twentɪɪʃ] *adj* de unos veinte años.
twerp* [twɜːp] *n* berzotas* *mf*; **you** ~! ¡imbécil!
twice [twaɪs] *adv* dos veces; ~ **as much** dos veces más; **A is** ~ **as big as B** A es dos veces más grande que B; **I am** ~ **as old as you are** tengo dos veces la edad de Vd, tengo el doble de la edad de Vd; ~ **the sum,** ~ **the quantity** el doble; **at a speed** ~ **that of sound** a una velocidad dos veces superior a la del sonido; **he said 'she's** ~ **the woman you are'** dijo 'como mujer ella vale dos veces lo que tú'; **since the operation he is** ~ **the man he was** después de la operación vale dos veces lo de antes; **to do sth** ~ **over** hacer algo dos veces, volver a hacer algo; **to go to a meeting** ~ **weekly** ir a una reunión dos veces por semana; **he didn't have to be asked** ~ no se hizo de rogar.
twiddle ['twɪdl] **1** *n* vuelta *f* (ligera); **to give a knob a** ~ girar un botón.
2 *vt* girar, hacer girar; jugar con; revolver ociosamente.
3 *vi*: **to** ~ **round** dar vueltas, girar; **to** ~ **with sth** jugar con algo (entre los dedos).
twig¹ [twɪg] *n* ramita *f*; ~**s** (*for fire*) leña *f* menuda.
twig²* [twɪg] (*Brit*) **1** *vt* comprender, caer en la cuenta de. **2** *vi* comprender, caer en la cuenta.
twilight ['twaɪlaɪt] **1** *n* crepúsculo *m*; (*fig*) crepúsculo *m*, ocaso *m*; **at** ~ al anochecer; **in the** ~ en el crepúsculo; **in the** ~ **of his room** en la media luz de su habitación.
2 *adj* crepuscular; ~ **area,** ~ **zone** zona *f* gris; ~ **sleep** sueño *m* crepuscular; **a** ~ **world** un mundo crepuscular.
twilit ['twaɪlɪt] *adj*: **in the** ~ **woods** en el bosque con luz

crepuscular; **in some ~ area of the mind** en alguna zona crepuscular de la mente.

twill [twɪl] *n* tela *f* cruzada.

'twill [twɪl] = **it will.**

twin [twɪn] **1** *adj* gemelo; **~ beds** camas *fpl* gemelas; **~ brother** hermano *m* gemelo; **~ sister** hermana *f* gemela; **~ town** (*Brit*) ciudad *f* gemela.

2 *n* gemelo *m*, -a *f*; **John and his ~** Juan y su hermano gemelo.

3 *vt*: **the town with which Wigan is ~ned** la ciudad que tiene a Wigan como gemela.

twin-bedded ['twɪn'bedɪd] *adj room* con camas gemelas.

twin-cylinder ['twɪn'sɪlɪndə^{r}] **1** *adj* de dos cilindros, bicilíndrico. **2** *n* bicilindro *m*.

twine [twaɪn] **1** *n* guita *f*, hilo *m*, bramante *m*.

2 *vt* (*weave*) tejer; (*encircle*) ceñir, rodear; (*roll up*) enrollar; **she ~d the string round her finger** enrolló la cuerda sobre el dedo; **she ~d her arms about his neck** le rodeó el cuello con los brazos.

3 *vi* (*of spiral movement*) enroscarse; (*plant*) trepar, entrelazarse; (*road*) serpentear.

twin-engined ['twɪn'endʒɪnd] *adj* bimotor.

twinge [twɪndʒ] *n* punzada *f*, dolor *m* agudo; (*fig*) remordimiento *m*; **I've been having ~s of conscience** me ha estado remordiendo la conciencia.

twining ['twaɪnɪŋ] *adj plant* sarmentoso, trepador.

twin-jet ['twɪn'dʒet] **1** *adj* birreactor. **2** *n* birreactor *m*.

twinkle ['twɪŋkl] **1** *n* centelleo *m*, parpadeo *m*; **in a ~** en un instante; **'No', he said with a ~** 'No', dijo maliciosamente, 'No' dijo medio riendo; **he had a ~ in his eye** se le reían los ojos; **when you were only a ~ in your father's eye** cuando tú no eras más que una vida en potencia.

2 *vi* (*of light*) centellear, parpadear, titilar; (*of eyes*) brillar; (*of feet*) moverse rápidamente.

twinkling ['twɪŋklɪŋ] **1** *adj light* centelleante, titilante; *eye* brillante, risueño; *feet* rápido, ligero.

2 *n* centelleo *m*, parpadeo *m*; **in the ~ of an eye** en un abrir y cerrar de ojos.

twinning ['twɪnɪŋ] *n* (*Brit*) hermanación *f* de dos ciudades.

twinset ['twɪnset] *n* (*Brit*) conjunto *m*.

twin-tub ['twɪn'tʌb] *n* lavadora *f* de dos tambores.

twirl [twɜːl] **1** *n* vuelta *f* (rápida), giro *m*; (*of pen etc*) rasgo *m*; (*of body*) pirueta *f*.

2 *vt* girar rápidamente, dar vueltas rápidas a; voltear; (*twist*) torcer.

3 *vi* girar rápidamente, dar vueltas rápidas; piruetear.

twirp* [twɜːp] *n* = **twerp.**

twist [twɪst] **1** *n* (**a**) (*of yarn*) torzal *m*; (*of hair*) mecha *f*; trenza *f*; (*of tobacco*) rollo *m*; (*of paper*) cucurucho *m*; (*coil*) vuelta *f*; (*spiral shape*) enroscadura *f*; (*in road etc*) vuelta *f*, recodo *m*; **~s and turns** vueltas *fpl*; **to take a ~ round a post with a rope** atar una cuerda alrededor de un poste; **the plot has an unexpected ~** la trama tiene un lance inesperado, la trama tiene un giro imprevisto; **he gave a new ~ to the old story** introdujo un nuevo giro en la vieja historia; **to be round the ~*** estar chiflado*.

(**b**) (*twisting action*) torsión *f*, torcimiento *m*; (*Med*) torcedura *f*; (*on ball*) efecto *m*; **to give one's ankle a ~** torcerse el tobillo; **to give a knob a ~** girar un botón; **with a quick ~ of the hand** torciendo rápidamente la mano.

(**c**) (*of mind*) rasgo *m* peculiar, sesgo *m*, peculiaridad *f*.

(**d**) (*Mus*) twist *m*.

(**e**) (*) estafa *f*, trampa *f*; **it's a ~!** ¡aquí hay trampa!; ¡me han robado!

2 *vt* (**a**) (*wrench out of shape*) torcer, retorcer; *ball* dar efecto a, lanzar con efecto; (*turn*) dar vueltas a, girar; (*give spiral form to*) enroscar, formar en espiral; (*interweave*) trenzar, entrelazar; (*fig*) *sense, argument* forzar, retorcer, torcer; **to ~ sb's arm** torcer el brazo a uno (*and V* **arm[1]** (**a**)); **to ~ one's arm** torcerse el brazo; **to ~ sth out of shape** deformar algo torciéndolo.

(**b**) (*) estafar, robar; **I've been ~ed!** ¡me han robado!

3 *vi* (**a**) torcerse, retorcerse; (*coil up*) enroscarse, ensortijarse; (*of road etc*) serpentear, dar vueltas; (*writhe*) retorcerse, revolcarse.

(**b**) (*dance*) bailar el twist.

◆**twist off** *vt*: **to ~ a piece off** separar un trozo torciéndolo; **you ~ the top off like this** se quita la tapa dándole vueltas así.

◆**twist round** *vt* dar vueltas a, girar.

◆**twist up** *vt*: **to ~ paper up into a ball** retorcer un papel en forma de pelota.

twisted ['twɪstɪd] *adj idea, person* estrafalario, raro; pervertido.

twister ['twɪstə^{r}] *n* (**a**) (*Brit*) tramposo *m*, estafador *m*. (**b**) (*US*) huracán *m*.

twisting ['twɪstɪŋ] *n* retorcimiento *m*.

twit[1]* [twɪt] *n* (*Brit*) imbécil *mf*, tonto *m*, -a *f*.

twit[2] [twɪt] *vt* embromar, tomar el pelo a, guasearse con; **to ~ sb about sth** tomar el pelo a uno con motivo de algo.

twitch [twɪtʃ] **1** *n* sacudida *f* repentina, tirón *m*; (*nervous*) tic *m*, contracción *f* nerviosa; movimiento *m* espasmódico.

2 *vt* tirar bruscamente de, tirar ligeramente de; *hands* crispar, retorcer; *ears, nose etc* mover nerviosamente; **to ~ sth away from sb** quitar algo a uno con un movimiento rápido.

3 *vi* crisparse; moverse nerviosamente.

twitchy ['twɪtʃɪ] *adj* nervioso; **to get ~** ponerse nervioso, inquietarse.

twitter ['twɪtə^{r}] **1** *n* (*bird*) gorjeo *m*; (*) agitación *f*, inquietud *f*, nerviosismo *m*; **to be all of a ~, to be in a ~** estar nerviosísimo, estar muy agitado.

2 *vi* gorjear; (*) agitarse, estar inquieto, estar nervioso.

'twixt [twɪkst] *prep* (*liter*) = **betwixt**; *V* **between.**

two [tuː] **1** *adj* dos.

2 *n* dos *m*; **~ by ~, in ~s** de dos en dos; **to break sth in ~** romper algo en dos, partir algo por la mitad; **they're ~ of a kind** son tal para cual; **to put ~ and ~ together** atar cabos.

two-bit* ['tuːbɪt] *adj* (*US*) de poca monta, de tres al cuarto.

two-chamber ['tuː'tʃeɪmbə^{r}] *adj parliament* bicamaral, de dos cámaras.

two-colour ['tuː'kʌlə^{r}] *adj* bicolor, de dos colores.

two-cycle ['tuː'saɪkl] *adj engine* de dos tiempos.

two-cylinder ['tuː'sɪlɪndə^{r}] *adj* bicilíndrico, de dos cilindros.

two-decker ['tuː'dekə^{r}] *n* autobús *m* de dos pisos.

two-dimensional ['tudaɪ'menʃənl] *adj* bidimensional.

two-door ['tuː'dɔː^{r}] *adj car* de dos puertas.

two-edged ['tuː'edʒd] *adj* de doble filo.

two-engined ['tuː'endʒɪnd] *adj* bimotor.

two-faced ['tuː'feɪst] *adj* (*fig*) doble, falso.

two-fisted* [ˌtuː'fɪstɪd] *adj* (*US*) fortachón*, chicarrón.

twofold ['tuːfəʊld] **1** *adv* dos veces. **2** *adj* doble.

two-handed ['tuː'hændɪd] *adj* de dos manos; *tool etc* para dos manos.

two-legged ['tuː'legɪd] *adj* de dos piernas, bípedo.

two-masted ['tuː'mɑːstɪd] *adj* de dos palos.

two-party ['tuː'pɑːtɪ] *adj state etc* de dos partidos.

twopence ['tʌpəns] *npl* (*Brit*) 2 peniques *mpl*; *V* **care.**

twopenny ['tʌpənɪ] *adj* (*Brit*) de 2 peniques, que vale 2 peniques; (*fig*) insignificante, miserable, despreciable.

twopenny-halfpenny ['tʌpnɪ'heɪpnɪ] *adj* (*Brit fig*) insignificante, despreciable.

two-phase ['tuː'feɪz] *adj* bifásico.

two-piece ['tuː'piːs] **1** *adj* de dos piezas. **2** *n* dos piezas *m*, conjunto *m*.

two-ply ['tuː'plaɪ] *adj wood* de dos capas; *wool* doble.

two-seater ['tuː'siːtə^{r}] **1** *attr* biplaza, de dos plazas. **2** *n* coche *m* (*or* avión *m etc*) biplaza.

twosome ['tuːsəm] *n* pareja *f*; grupo *m* de dos, partido *m* de dos.

two-star (petrol) ['tuːstɑː('petrəl)] *n* (*Brit*) gasolina *f* normal.

two-storey ['tuː'stɔːrɪ] *adj house* de dos pisos.

two-stroke ['tuː'strəʊk] **1** *adj engine* de dos tiempos. **2** *n* (*also*: **~ oil**) aceite *m* para motores de dos tiempos.

two-time* ['tuː'taɪm] *vt* (*US*) (*gen*) hacer una mala jugada a, traicionar; *lover* poner los cuernos a, engañar.

two-timer [ˌtuː'taɪmə^{r}] *n* (*US*) (**a**) (*gen*: *traitor*) traidor *m*, -ora *f*, traicionero *m*. (**b**) (*in marriage*) marido *m* (*or* mujer *f*) infiel.

two-tone ['tuː'təʊn] *adj car* bicolor, de dos colores.

'twould [twʊd] = **it would.**

two-way ['tuː'weɪ] *adj*: **~ radio** transmisor-receptor *m*; **~ street** calle *f* de doble sentido; **~ switch** conmutador *m* de dos direcciones; **~ traffic** circulación *f* en ambas direcciones.

two-wheeler ['tuː'wiːlə^{r}] *n* bicicleta *f*.

TX (*US Post*) *abbr of* **Texas.**

Tx *abbr of* **telex.**

tycoon [taɪ'kuːn] *n* magnate *m*.

tyke [taɪk] *n* (**a**) (*) (*dog*) perro *m* de la calle; (*child*) chiquillo *m*; **you little ~!** ¡tunante! (**b**) (*pej**: *also* **Yorkshire ~**) hombre *m* de Yorkshire.

tympani ['tɪmpənɪ] *npl* (*Mus*) = **timpani.**

tympanum ['tɪmpənəm] *n* (*Anat, Archit*) tímpano *m*.

type [taɪp] **1** *n* (**a**) (*characteristic specimen*) tipo *m*; **to deviate from the ~** apartarse del tipo; **to revert to ~** saltar atrás en la cadena natural; **she was the very ~ of Spanish beauty** era el tipo exacto de la belleza española.

(**b**) (*: *person*) tipo* *m*, sujeto* *m*; **he's an odd ~** es un tipo raro.

(**c**) (*class*) tipo *m*, género *m*; **people of that ~** la gente de ese tipo; **he's not my ~** ese tipo de hombre no me gusta, no me gustan los hombres así; **what ~ of car is it?** ¿qué modelo de coche es?

(**d**) (*Typ*) tipo *m* (de letra), letra *f*, carácter *m*; (*collectively*) tipos *mpl*.

2 *vt* (*also* **to ~ out, to ~ up**) escribir a máquina, hacer a máquina, mecanografiar.

3 *vi* escribir a máquina; **'secretary ... must be able to ~'** 'secretaria ... sabiendo mecanografía'.

typecast ['taɪpkɑːst] (*irr*: *V* **cast**) **1** *vt actor* encasillar. **2** *adj actor* encasillado.

typeface ['taɪpfeɪs] *n* = **type 1** (**d**); área *f* de texto impreso, (*loosely*) tipografía *f*.

typescript ['taɪpskrɪpt] **1** *adj* mecanografiado. **2** *n* mecanografiado *m*.

typeset ['taɪpset] *vt* componer.

typesetter ['taɪp,setəʳ] *n* (*person*) cajista *m*; (*machine*) máquina *f* de componer.

typesetting ['taɪp,setɪŋ] *n* composición *f* (tipográfica).

typewrite ['taɪpraɪt] (*irr*: *V* **write**) *vt* = **type 2**.

typewriter ['taɪp,raɪtəʳ] **1** *n* máquina *f* de escribir. **2** *attr*: **~ ribbon** cinta *f* para máquina de escribir.

typewriting ['taɪp,raɪtɪŋ] *n* mecanografía *f*.

typewritten ['taɪp,rɪtn] *adj* mecanografiado, escrito a máquina.

typhoid ['taɪfɔɪd] *n* tifoidea *f*, fiebre *f* tifoidea.

typhoon [taɪ'fuːn] *n* tifón *m*.

typhus ['taɪfəs] *n* tifus *m*.

typical ['tɪpɪkəl] *adj* típico; característico; clásico; **the ~ Spaniard** el español típico; **wearing the ~ beret** con la clásica boina; **it is ~ of him that ...** es característico de él que ...; **isn't that just ~!** ¡eso es muy de él!

typically ['tɪpɪkəlɪ] *adv* típicamente; **all that is ~ Spanish** todo lo que es típico de España; **a ~ smug person** una persona típicamente satisfecha.

typify ['tɪpɪfaɪ] *vt* tipificar; simbolizar; representar, ser ejemplo de.

typing ['taɪpɪŋ] **1** *n* mecanografía *f*. **2** *attr*: **~ agency** agencia *f* mecanográfica; **~ error** error *m* mecanográfico; **~ paper** papel *m* para máquina de escribir; **~ pool** sala *f* de mecanógrafas; servicio *m* de mecanógrafas; **~ speed** palabras *fpl* por minuto (mecanografiadas).

typist ['taɪpɪst] *n* mecanógrafo *m*, -a *f*.

typo* ['taɪpəʊ] *n* errata *f*.

typographer [taɪ'pɒgrəfəʳ] *n* tipógrafo *m*, -a *f*.

typographic(al) [,taɪpə'græfɪk(əl)] *adj* tipográfico.

typography [taɪ'pɒgrəfɪ] *n* tipografía *f*.

typology [taɪ'pɒlədʒɪ] *n* tipología *f*.

tyrannic(al) [tɪ'rænɪk(əl)] *adj* tiránico.

tyrannically [tɪ'rænɪkəlɪ] *adv* tiránicamente.

tyrannicide [tɪ'rænɪsaɪd] *n* (*act*) tiranicidio *m*; (*person*) tiranicida *mf*.

tyrannize ['tɪrənaɪz] **1** *vt* tiranizar. **2** *vi*: **to ~ over a people** tiranizar un pueblo.

tyranny ['tɪrənɪ] *n* tiranía *f*.

tyrant ['taɪrənt] *n* tirano *m*, -a *f*.

Tyre ['taɪəʳ] *n* Tiro *m*.

tyre ['taɪəʳ] **1** *n* (*Aut etc*) neumático *m*, llanta *f* (*LAm*); (*outer cover*) cubierta *f*; (*inner tube*) cámara *f* (de aire); (*of cart*) llanta *f*, calce *m*; (*of pram etc*) rueda *f* de goma.

2 *attr*: **~ pressure** presión *f* de los neumáticos.

tyre-burst ['taɪəbɜːst] *n* pinchazo *m*, reventón *m*.

tyre valve ['taɪəvælv] *n* válvula *m* de neumático.

tyro ['taɪərəʊ] *n* = **tiro**.

Tyrol [tɪ'rəʊl] *n* el Tirol.

Tyrolean [,tɪrə'lɪ(ː)ən], **Tyrolese** [,tɪrə'liːz] **1** *adj* tirolés. **2** *n* tirolés *m*, -esa *f*.

Tyrrhenian [tɪ'riːnɪən] *adj* tirrénico.

tzar [zɑːʳ] *n* zar *m*.

tzarina [zɑː'riːnə] *n* zarina *f*.

U

U[1], u [juː] *n* (*letter*) U, u *f*; **U for Uncle** U de Uruguay; **U-bend** (*Brit*) codo *m*, curva *f* en U; **U-boat** submarino *m* (alemán); **U-shaped** en forma de U; **U-turn** viraje *m* en U, giro *m* de 180 grados (*also fig*).
U[2] *adj* (**a**) (*Brit*) *abbr of* **upper-class.** (**b**) (*Cine*) *abbr of* **universal** todos los públicos.
UAE *npl abbr of* **United Arab Emirates** Emiratos *mpl* Árabes Unidos, EAU *mpl*.
ubiquitous [juː'bɪkwɪtəs] *adj* ubicuo, omnipresente, que se encuentra en todas partes; **it is ~ in Spain** se encuentra en toda España; **the secretary has to be ~** el secretario tiene que estar constantemente en todas partes.
ubiquity [juː'bɪkwɪtɪ] *n* ubicuidad *f*, omnipresencia *f*.
UCCA ['ʌkə] *n* (*Brit*) *abbr of* **Universities Central Council on Admissions.**
UDA *n* (*Brit*) *abbr of* **Ulster Defence Association** *organización paramilitar protestante en Irlanda del Norte*.
UDC *n* (*Brit*) *abbr of* **Urban District Council.**
udder ['ʌdəʳ] *n* ubre *f*.
UDF *n* (*Brit*) *abbr of* **Ulster Defence Force** *organización paramilitar protestante en Irlanda del Norte*.
UDI *n* (*Brit*) *abbr of* **unilateral declaration of independence.**
UDR *n* (*Brit*) *abbr of* **Ulster Defence Regiment** *fuerza de seguridad de Irlanda del Norte*.
UEFA [jʊ'eɪfə] *npl abbr of* **Union of European Football Associations.**
UFC *n* (*Brit*) *abbr of* **Universities' Funding Council** *entidad que controla las finanzas de las universidades*.
UFO *n abbr of* **unidentified flying object** objeto *m* volante (*or* volador) no identificado, OVNI *m*.
ufologist [,juː'fɒlədʒɪst] *n* ufólogo *m*, -a *f*.
ufology [,juː'fɒlədʒɪ] *n* ufología *f*.
Uganda [juː'gændə] *n* Uganda *f*.
Ugandan [juː'gændən] **1** *adj* ugandés. **2** *n* ugandés *m*, -esa *f*.
ugh [ɜːh] *interj* ¡puf!
uglify ['ʌglɪfaɪ] *vt* afear.
ugliness ['ʌglɪnɪs] *n* fealdad *f*, lo feo; lo peligroso; lo repugnante.
ugly ['ʌglɪ] *adj appearance, person* feo; *custom, vice etc* feo, repugnante, asqueroso; *situation, wound* peligroso; *rumour etc* nada grato, inquietante; *mood* peligroso, violento; **~ duckling** patito *m* feo (*also fig*); **to be as ~ as sin** ser más feo que Picio; **to turn ~*** ponerse violento, amenazar violencia.
UHF *n abbr of* **ultra high frequency** frecuencia *f* ultraelevada, UHF *f*.
uh-huh ['ʌ,hʌ] *excl* (*agreeing*) a-ha.
UHT *adj abbr of* **ultra heat-treated** uperizado.
UK *n abbr of* **United Kingdom** Reino *m* Unido, R.U. *m*.
Ukraine [juː'kreɪn] *n* Ucrania *f*.
Ukrainian [juː'kreɪnɪən] **1** *adj* ucranio. **2** *n* ucranio *m*, -a *f*.
ukulele [,juːkə'leɪlɪ] *n* ukulele *m*.
ulcer ['ʌlsəʳ] *n* úlcera *f*; (*fig*) llaga *f*.
ulcerate ['ʌlsəreɪt] **1** *vt* ulcerar. **2** *vi* ulcerarse.
ulceration [,ʌlsə'reɪʃən] *n* ulceración *f*.
ulcerous ['ʌlsərəs] *adj* ulceroso.
ullage ['ʌlɪdʒ] *n* (*loss*) merma *f*; (*amount remaining*) atestadura *f*.
ulna ['ʌlnə] *n*, *pl* **ulnae** ['ʌlniː] cúbito *m*.
ULSI *n abbr of* **ultra-large-scale integration** integración *f* a ultra gran escala.
Ulster ['ʌlstəʳ] *n* Ulster *m*.
Ulsterman ['ʌlstəmən] *n*, *pl* **Ulstermen** ['ʌlstəmən] nativo *m* (*or* habitante *m*) de Ulster.
ult. [ʌlt] *adv* (*Comm*) *abbr of* **ultimo**; **the 5th ~** el 5 del mes pasado.
ulterior [ʌl'tɪərɪəʳ] *adj* ulterior; **~ motive** motivo *m* oculto, segunda intención *f*.
ultimate ['ʌltɪmɪt] *adj* (*furthest*) más remoto, extremo; (*final*) último, final; *destination etc* definitivo; *purpose, reason, truth etc* fundamental, esencial; **it's the ~ in hair-styling** es el último grito del peinado.
ultimately ['ʌltɪmɪtlɪ] *adv* (*in the end*) por último, al final; (*in the long run*) a la larga; (*fundamentally*) en el fondo, fundamentalmente.
ultimatum [,ʌltɪ'meɪtəm] *n*, *pl* **ultimata** [,ʌltɪ'meɪtə] *or* **ultimatums** ultimátum *m*.
ultimo ['ʌltɪməʊ] *adv* = **ult.**
ultra... ['ʌltrə] *pref* ultra...
ultra-fashionable ['ʌltrə'fæʃnəbl] *adj* muy de moda, elegantísimo.
ultrafine [,ʌltrə'faɪn] *adj* ultrafino.
ultramarine [,ʌltrəmə'riːn] **1** *adj* ultramarino. **2** *n* azul *m* ultramarino, azul *m* de ultramar.
ultramodern ['ʌltrə'mɒdən] *adj* ultramoderno.
ultra-red [,ʌltrə'red] *adj* ultrarrojo, infrarrojo.
ultrasensitive ['ʌltrə'sensɪtɪv] *adj* ultrasensitivo.
ultra-short wave ['ʌltrə,ʃɔːt'weɪv] **1** *n* onda *f* ultracorta. **2** *attr* de onda ultracorta.
ultrasonic ['ʌltrə'sɒnɪk] *adj* ultrasónico.
ultrasound ['ʌltrəsaʊnd] *n* ultrasonido *m*.
ultraviolet ['ʌltrə'vaɪəlɪt] *adj* ultravioleta; **~ light** luz *f* ultravioleta; **~ radiation** radiación *f* ultravioleta; **~ rays** rayos *mpl* ultravioleta; **~ treatment** tratamiento *m* de onda ultravioleta.
ululate ['juːljʊleɪt] *vi* ulular.
ululation [,juːljʊ'leɪʃən] *n* ululato *m*.
Ulysses [juː'lɪsiːz] *nm* Ulises.
um [ʌm] *interj* pues, es decir, esto ...; **to ~ and err** vacilar.
umber ['ʌmbəʳ] **1** *n* tierra *f* de sombra. **2** *adj* color ocre oscuro, pardo oscuro.
umbilical [,ʌmbɪ'laɪkəl] *adj* umbilical; **~ cord** cordón *m* umbilical.
umbilicus [,ʌmbɪ'laɪkəs] *n* ombligo *m*.
umbrage ['ʌmbrɪdʒ] *n* resentimiento *m*; **to take ~** ofenderse (*at* por), resentirse (*at* de).
umbrella [ʌm'brelə] *n* paraguas *m*; (*on beach etc*) quitasol *m*; (*Mil: of fire*) cortina *f* de fuego antiaéreo; (*of aircraft*) sombrilla *f* protectora; **~ organization** organización *f* paraguas.
umbrella stand [ʌm'breləstænd] *n* paragüero *m*.
umlaut ['ʊmlaʊt] *n* (*phenomenon*) metafonía *f*; (*symbol*) diéresis *f*.
umpire ['ʌmpaɪəʳ] **1** *n* árbitro *mf*. **2** *vti* arbitrar.
umpteen* ['ʌmptiːn] *adj* tantísimos, muchísimos.
umpteenth* ['ʌmptiːnθ] *adj* enésimo; **for the ~ time** por enésima vez.
UMW *n* (*US*) *abbr of* **United Mineworkers of America.**
un... [ʌn] *pref* in...; des...; no ...; nada ...; poco ...; sin ...; anti...
UN *npl abbr of* **United Nations** Naciones *fpl* Unidas, NN.UU.
unabashed ['ʌnə'bæʃt] *adj* descarado, desvergonzado; desenfadado; **'Yes', he said quite ~** 'Sí', dijo sin alterarse.
unabated ['ʌnə'beɪtɪd] *adj* sin disminución, no disminuido.
unabbreviated ['ʌnə'briːvɪeɪtɪd] *adj* íntegro, completo.
unable ['ʌn'eɪbl] *adj*: **to be ~ to do sth** no poder hacer algo, estar sin poder hacer algo; ser incapaz de hacer algo; verse imposibilitado de hacer algo; **I am ~ to see why** no veo por qué, no comprendo cómo; **those ~ to go** los que no pueden ir.
unabridged ['ʌnə'brɪdʒd] *adj* íntegro, integral.
unaccented ['ʌnæk'sentɪd] *adj* inacentuado, átono.
unacceptable ['ʌnək'septəbl] *adj* inaceptable.
unacceptably ['ʌnək'septəblɪ] *adv* inaceptablemente.
unaccommodating ['ʌnə'kɒmədeɪtɪŋ] *adj* poco amable, poco servicial, poco acomodaticio.

unaccompanied ['ʌnə'kʌmpənɪd] *adj* (*Mus*) sin acompañamiento, no acompañado; **to go somewhere ~** ir a un sitio sin compañía, ir solo a un sitio.
unaccomplished ['ʌnə'kʌmplɪʃt] *adj* (**a**) *task* incompleto, sin acabar. (**b**) *person* sin talento.
unaccountable ['ʌnə'kaʊntəbl] *adj* inexplicable.
unaccountably ['ʌnə'kaʊntəblɪ] *adv* inexplicablemente; **~ annoyed** extrañamente enfadado, enfadado sin motivo.
unaccounted ['ʌnə'kaʊntɪd] *adj*: **two passengers are ~ for** no hay noticias de dos de los pasajeros, se ignora la suerte de dos de los pasajeros; **two books are ~ for** faltan dos libros.
unaccustomed ['ʌnə'kʌstəmd] *adj* (**a**) **to be ~ to sth** no estar acostumbrado a algo; **to be ~ to doing sth** no acostumbrar hacer algo, no tener la costumbre de hacer algo; **~ as I am to public speaking** aunque no tengo experiencia de hablar en público.
(**b**) **with ~ zeal** con un entusiasmo insólito.
unacknowledged ['ʌnək'nɒlɪdʒd] *adj* no reconocido; *letter etc* no contestado, sin contestar.
unacquainted ['ʌnə'kweɪntɪd] *adj*: **to be ~ with sth** desconocer algo, ignorar algo.
unadaptable ['ʌnə'dæptəbl] *adj* inadaptable.
unadapted ['ʌnə'dæptɪd] *adj* inadaptado.
unaddressed ['ʌnə'drest] *adj letter* sin señas.
unadopted ['ʌnə'dɒptɪd] *adj* (*Brit*) *road* no oficial (*siendo de los vecinos la responsabilidad de su mantenimiento*).
unadorned ['ʌnə'dɔːnd] *adj* sin adorno, sencillo; **beauty ~** la hermosura sin adorno; **the ~ truth** la verdad lisa y llana.
unadulterated ['ʌnə'dʌltəreɪtɪd] *adj* sin mezcla, puro.
unadventurous ['ʌnəd'ventʃərəs] *adj* poco atrevido.
unadvisable ['ʌnəd'vaɪzəbl] *adj* poco aconsejable; **it is ~ to** + *infin* es poco aconsejable + *infin.*
unaesthetic, (*US*) **unesthetic** [ˌʌniːs'θetɪk] *adj* antiestético.
unaffected ['ʌnə'fektɪd] *adj* (**a**) *person etc* sin afectación. (**b**) **to be ~ by** no ser afectado por.
unaffectedly ['ʌnə'fektɪdlɪ] *adv* sin afectación; sinceramente, hondamente.
unaffiliated [ˌʌnə'fɪlɪˌeɪtɪd] *adj* no afiliado.
unafraid ['ʌnə'freɪd] *adj* sin temor, impertérrito.
unaided ['ʌn'eɪdɪd] **1** *adv* sin ayuda, por sí solo. **2** *adj*: **by his own ~ efforts** por sí solo, sin ayuda de nadie.
unalike [ˌʌnə'laɪk] *adj* no parecido.
unalloyed ['ʌnə'lɔɪd] *adj* sin mezcla, puro.
unalterable [ʌn'ɒltərəbl] *adj* inalterable.
unalterably [ʌn'ɒltərəblɪ] *adv* de modo inalterable; **we are ~ opposed to it** nos oponemos rotundamente a ello.
unaltered ['ʌn'ɒltəd] *adj* inalterado, sin cambiar, sin alteración.
unambiguous ['ʌnæm'bɪgjʊəs] *adj* inequívoco.
unambiguously ['ʌnæm'bɪgjʊəslɪ] *adv* de modo inequívoco.
unambitious ['ʌnæm'bɪʃəs] *adj* poco ambicioso, poco emprendedor.
un-American ['ʌnə'merɪkən] *adj* antiamericano, poco americano.
unamiable ['ʌn'eɪmɪəbl] *adj* poco simpático.
unanimity [ˌjuːnə'nɪmɪtɪ] *n* unanimidad *f.*
unanimous [juː'nænɪməs] *adj* unánime.
unanimously [juː'nænɪməslɪ] *adv* unánimamente; por unanimidad; **the motion was passed ~** la moción fue aprobada por unanimidad.
unannounced ['ʌnə'naʊnst] *adj*: **to arrive ~** llegar sin dar aviso.
unanswerable [ʌn'ɑːnsərəbl] *adj question* incontestable; (*attack etc*) irrebatible, irrefutable.
unanswered ['ʌn'ɑːnsəd] *adj question* incontestado, sin contestar; *letter* no contestado, sin contestar.
unappealable ['ʌnə'piːləbl] *adj* inapelable.
unappealing ['ʌnə'piːlɪŋ] *adj* poco atractivo.
unappetizing ['ʌn'æpɪtaɪzɪŋ] *adj* poco apetitoso, poco apetecible; (*fig*) repugnante, nada atractivo.
unappreciative ['ʌnə'priːʃɪətɪv] *adj* desagradecido; **to be ~ of sth** no apreciar algo.
unapproachable ['ʌnə'prəʊtʃəbl] *adj* inaccesible; *person* intratable, inabordable.
unappropriated [ˌʌnə'prəʊprɪeɪtɪd] *adj balance etc* no asignado, sin asignar.
unarguable [ʌn'ɑːgjʊəbəl] *adj* indiscutible, incuestionable.
unarguably [ʌn'ɑːgjʊəblɪ] *adv* indiscutiblemente; **it is ~ true that ...** es una verdad incuestionable que ...
unarmed ['ʌn'ɑːmd] *adj* que no lleva armas, desarmado; (*defenceless*) inerme; **~ combat** combate *m* sin armas.
unashamed ['ʌnə'ʃeɪmd] *adj* desvergonzado, descarado; **he was quite ~ about it** no tuvo remordimiento alguno por esto, no sintió el menor remordimiento.
unashamedly ['ʌnə'ʃeɪmɪdlɪ] *adv* desvergonzadamente; **to be ~ proud of sth** enorgullecerse sin remordimiento de algo.
unasked ['ʌn'ɑːskt] *adj*: **to do sth ~** hacer algo motu proprio; **they came to the party ~** vinieron al guateque sin ser invitados.
unassailable [ˌʌnə'seɪləbl] *adj fortress* inexpugnable; *position* inatacable; *argument* irrebatible; **he is quite ~ on that score** no se le puede atacar por ese lado.
unassisted ['ʌnə'sɪstɪd] *adj* sin ayuda, por sí solo.
unassuming ['ʌnə'sjuːmɪŋ] *adj* modesto, sin pretensiones.
unassumingly ['ʌnə'sjuːmɪŋlɪ] *adv* modestamente.
unattached ['ʌnə'tætʃt] *adj part etc* suelto, separable; disponible; *person* libre, no prometido, soltero; (*Mil*) de reemplazo; (*Jur*) no embargado.
unattainable ['ʌnə'teɪnəbl] *adj* inasequible; *record etc* inalcanzable.
unattended ['ʌnə'tendɪd] *adj* descuidado; sin guardia, sin personal; **to leave sth ~** dejar algo sin vigilar.
unattractive ['ʌnə'træktɪv] *adj* poco atractivo.
unattractiveness ['ʌnə'træktɪvnɪs] *n* falta *f* de atractivo.
unattributable ['ʌnə'trɪbjʊtəbl] *adj news* de fuente que no se puede revelar.
unauthorized ['ʌn'ɔːθəraɪzd] *adj* no autorizado.
unavailable ['ʌnə'veɪləbl] *adj* indisponible, inasequible; (*Comm*) agotado; *person* que no puede atender a uno, que no está libre.
unavailing ['ʌnə'veɪlɪŋ] *adj* inútil, vano, infructuoso.
unavailingly ['ʌnə'veɪlɪŋlɪ] *adv* inútilmente, en vano.
unavoidable [ˌʌnə'vɔɪdəbl] *adj* inevitable, ineludible; **it is ~ that ...** es inevitable que ...
unavoidably [ˌʌnə'vɔɪdəblɪ] *adv* inevitablemente; **he is ~ detained** tiene un retraso inevitable.
unaware ['ʌnə'wɛəʳ] *adj* inconsciente; **to be ~ that ...** ignorar que ...; **I am not ~ that ...** no ignoro que ...; **to be ~ of sth** ignorar algo, no darse cuenta de algo.
unawareness ['ʌnə'wɛənɪs] *n* inconsciencia *f* (*of* de).
unawares ['ʌnə'wɛəz] *adv* de improviso, inopinadamente; **to catch sb ~** coger a uno desprevenido.
unbacked ['ʌn'bækt] *adj* sin respaldo; (*Fin*) al descubierto.
unbalance ['ʌn'bæləns] *n* desequilibrio *m.*
unbalanced ['ʌn'bælənst] *adj* desequilibrado; (*mentally*) trastornado, desequilibrado; (*Fin*) que no está en equilibrio.
unban ['ʌn'bæn] *vt* levantar la prohibición de; despenalizar.
unbandage ['ʌn'bændɪdʒ] *vt* desvendar, quitar las vendas a.
unbaptized ['ʌnbæp'taɪzd] *adj* sin bautizar.
unbar ['ʌn'bɑːʳ] *vt door etc* desatrancar; (*fig*) abrir, franquear.
unbearable [ʌn'bɛərəbl] *adj* inaguantable, insufrible, insoportable.
unbearably [ʌn'bɛərəblɪ] *adv* insoportablemente; **it is ~ hot** hace un calor inaguantable; **she is ~ vain** es vanidosa en un grado inaguantable.
unbeatable ['ʌn'biːtəbl] *adj* insuperable; *team etc* imbatible; *price, offer* inmejorable.
unbeaten ['ʌn'biːtn] *adj team* imbatido; *army* invicto; *price* no mejorado.
unbecoming ['ʌnbɪ'kʌmɪŋ] *adj* indecoroso, impropio; *dress etc* que sienta mal a uno; **it is ~ to** + *infin* no es elegante + *infin.*
unbeknownst ['ʌnbɪ'nəʊnst] *adv*: **~ to me** sin saberlo yo.
unbelief ['ʌnbɪ'liːf] *n* (*Rel*: *in general*) descreimiento *m,* (*of person*) falta *f* de fe; escepticismo *m*; (*astonishment*) incredulidad *f.*
unbelievable [ˌʌnbɪ'liːvəbl] *adj* increíble; **it is ~ that ...** es increíble que + *subj.*
unbelievably [ˌʌnbɪ'liːvəblɪ] *adv* increíblemente.
unbeliever ['ʌnbɪ'liːvəʳ] *n* no creyente *mf,* descreído *m,* -a *f.*
unbelieving ['ʌnbɪ'liːvɪŋ] *adj* incrédulo.
unbend ['ʌn'bend] (*irr*: *V* **bend**) **1** *vt* desencorvar, enderezar. **2** *vi* (*fig*) suavizarse; (*person*) hacerse más afable.
unbending ['ʌn'bendɪŋ] *adj* inflexible, rígido; *person* inflexible; poco afable.
unbias(s)ed ['ʌn'baɪəst] *adj* imparcial.
unbidden ['ʌn'bɪdn] *adj*: **to do sth ~** hacer algo espontáneamente; **they came to the party ~** vinieron al guateque sin ser invitados.
unbind ['ʌn'baɪnd] (*irr*: *V* **bind**) *vt* desatar; (*unbandage*) desvendar.
unbleached ['ʌn'bliːtʃt] *adj* sin blanquear.
unblemished [ʌn'blemɪʃt] *adj* sin tacha, intachable, sin

mancha.

unblinking [ʌn'blɪŋkɪŋ] *adj* imperturbable; (*pej*) desvergonzado.

unblock ['ʌn'blɒk] *vt pipe etc* desatascar, desobstruir; *road etc* desbloquear, abrir, franquear.

unblushing [ʌn'blʌʃɪŋ] *adj* desvergonzado, fresco.

unblushingly [ʌn'blʌʃɪŋlɪ] *adv* desvergonzadamente; **he said ~** dijo tan fresco.

unbolt ['ʌn'bəʊlt] *vt* desatrancar.

unborn ['ʌn'bɔːn] *adj* no nacido aún, nonato; **generations yet ~** generaciones *fpl* que están todavía por nacer (*or* que están por venir).

unbosom [ʌn'bʊzəm] *vr*: **to ~ o.s. of sth** desahogarse de algo, confesar algo espontáneamente; **to ~ o.s. to sb** abrir su pecho a uno, desahogarse con uno.

unbound ['ʌn'baʊnd] *adj* sin encuadernar, en rústica.

unbounded [ʌn'baʊndɪd] *adj* ilimitado, infinito.

unbowed ['ʌn'baʊd] *adj*: **with head ~** con la cabeza erguida; orgullosamente.

unbreakable ['ʌn'breɪkəbl] *adj* irrompible, inquebrantable.

unbribable ['ʌn'braɪbəbl] *adj* insobornable.

unbridgeable [ʌn'brɪdʒəbl] *adj gap etc* abismal, infranqueable.

unbridled [ʌn'braɪdld] *adj* (*fig*) desenfrenado.

unbroken ['ʌn'brəʊkən] *adj crockery etc* entero, intacto; *seal* intacto; *time, silence* no interrumpido; *series* continuo, sin solución de continuidad; *sheet of ice etc* continuo; *soil* sin labrar; *record* imbatido; *horse* no domado; *spirit* indómito.

unbuckle ['ʌn'bʌkl] *vt* deshebillar.

unbudgeted [ʌn'bʌdʒɪtɪd] *adj* no presupuestado.

unburden [ʌn'bɜːdn] **1** *vt person* aliviar; **to ~ sb of a load** aliviar a uno quitándole un peso; **to ~ one's heart** abrir su pecho.

2 *vr*: **to ~ o.s.** abrir su pecho (*to sb* a uno); **to ~ o.s. of sth** desahogarse de algo, confesar algo abiertamente.

unburied ['ʌn'berɪd] *adj* insepulto.

unbusinesslike [ʌn'bɪznɪslaɪk] *adj* poco práctico, poco metódico; informal; que carece de instinto comercial.

unbutton ['ʌn'bʌtn] **1** *vt* desabotonar, desabrochar. **2** *vi* (*) hacerse más afable.

uncalled-for [ʌn'kɔːldfɔːʳ] *adj* gratuito, inmerecido; fuera de lugar; impertinente.

uncannily [ʌn'kænɪlɪ] *adv* misteriosamente; **it is ~ like the other one** tiene un extraño parecido con el otro, se parece extraordinariamente al otro.

uncanny [ʌn'kænɪ] *adj* misterioso, extraño, extraordinario; **it's quite ~** es extraordinario; **it's ~ how he does it** no llego a comprender cómo lo hace.

uncap ['ʌn'kæp] *vt* destapar.

uncared-for ['ʌn'kɛədfɔːʳ] *adj* descuidado; *person* abandonado, desamparado; *appearance* desaseado, de abandono; *building etc* abandonado.

uncaring ['ʌnkɛərɪŋ] *adj* poco compasivo; **he went on all ~** siguió sin hacer caso.

uncarpeted ['ʌn'kɑːpɪtɪd] *adj* no enmoquetado.

uncashed ['ʌn'kæʃt] *adj cheque* no cobrado, sin cobrar.

uncatalogued ['ʌn'kætəlɒgd] *adj* no catalogado.

unceasing [ʌn'siːsɪŋ] *adj* incesante.

unceasingly [ʌn'siːsɪŋlɪ] *adv* incesantemente, sin cesar.

uncensored ['ʌn'sensəd] *adj* no censurado.

unceremonious ['ʌn,serɪ'məʊnɪəs] *adj* descortés, brusco, poco formal.

unceremoniously ['ʌn,serɪ'məʊnɪəslɪ] *adv* sin miramientos.

uncertain [ʌn'sɜːtn] *adj* incierto, dudoso; *person* (*of character*) indeciso, vacilante; *temper* vivo; **to be ~ of** no estar seguro de; **I am ~ whether ...** no estoy seguro si ...

uncertainly [ʌn'sɜːtnlɪ] *adv* inciertamente; **he said ~** dijo indeciso.

uncertainty [ʌn'sɜːtntɪ] *n* incertidumbre *f*, duda *f*; indecisión *f*, irresolución *f*; **in view of this ~ ...** teniendo en cuenta estas dudas ...; **in order to remove any ~** para disipar cualquier duda.

uncertificated ['ʌnsə'tɪfɪkeɪtɪd] *adj teacher etc* sin título.

unchain ['ʌn'tʃeɪn] *vt* desencadenar.

unchallengeable ['ʌn'tʃælɪndʒəbl] *adj* incontestable, incuestionable.

unchallenged ['ʌn'tʃælɪndʒd] *adj* incontestado; **we cannot let that go ~** eso no lo podemos dejar pasar sin protesta.

unchangeable [ʌn'tʃeɪndʒəbl] *adj* inalterable, inmutable.

unchanged ['ʌn'tʃeɪndʒd] *adj* sin alterar; **everything is still ~** todo sigue igual.

unchanging [ʌn'tʃeɪndʒɪŋ] *adj* inalterable, inmutable.

uncharacteristic [,ʌnkærəktə'rɪstɪk] *adj* poco característico, nada típico.

uncharitable [ʌn'tʃærɪtəbl] *adj* poco caritativo, duro.

uncharted ['ʌn'tʃɑːtɪd] *adj* inexplorado, desconocido.

unchaste ['ʌn'tʃeɪst] *adj* impúdico; *spouse* infiel.

unchecked ['ʌn'tʃekt] **1** *adv continue etc* libremente, sin estorbo, sin restricción. **2** *adj abuse etc* desenfrenado; *fact etc* no comprobado.

unchivalrous ['ʌn'ʃɪvəlrəs] *adj* poco caballeroso, poco caballeresco.

unchristian ['ʌn'krɪstɪən] *adj* poco cristiano, indigno de un cristiano.

uncial ['ʌnsɪəl] **1** *adj* uncial. **2** *n* uncial *f*.

uncircumcised ['ʌn'sɜːkəmsaɪzd] *adj* incircunciso.

uncivil ['ʌn'sɪvɪl] *adj* descortés, grosero, incivil; **to be ~ to sb** ser grosero con uno.

uncivilized ['ʌn'sɪvɪlaɪzd] *adj* incivilizado, inculto.

unclad ['ʌn'klæd] *adj* desnudo.

unclaimed ['ʌn'kleɪmd] *adj* sin reclamar, sin dueño.

unclasp ['ʌn'klɑːsp] *vt dress etc* desabrochar; *hands* soltar, separar.

unclassified ['ʌn'klæsɪfaɪd] *adj* sin clasificar.

uncle ['ʌŋkl] *n* (**a**) tío *m*; **my ~ and aunt** mis tíos; **U~ Sam** el tío Sam (*personificación de EE.UU.*); **U~ Tom** negro *m* que trata de congraciarse con los blancos; **to cry** (*or* **say**) **~*** (*US*) rendirse, darse por vencido. (**b**) (‡) perista* *m*.

unclean ['ʌn'kliːn] *adj* sucio, inmundo; (*fig*) deshonesto; (*ritually*) impuro.

uncleanliness ['ʌn'klenlɪnɪs] *n* suciedad *f*; (*fig*) deshonestidad *f*.

unclear [,ʌn'klɪəʳ] *adj* poco claro, nada claro; **to be ~ about** no estar seguro de.

unclench ['ʌn'klen*t*ʃ] *vt* desapretar, soltar, aflojar.

unclimbed ['ʌn'klaɪmd] *adj* no escalado.

unclog ['ʌn'klɒg] *vt* desobstruir, desatrancar.

unclothe ['ʌn'kləʊð] *vt* desnudar.

unclothed ['ʌn'kləʊðd] *adj* desnudo.

unclouded ['ʌn'klaʊdɪd] *adj* despejado, sin nubes.

uncoil ['ʌn'kɔɪl] **1** *vt* desenrollar. **2** *vi* desenrollarse; desovillarse; (*snake*) desanillarse.

uncollected [,ʌnkə'lektɪd] *adj goods, luggage* sin recoger; *tax* no recaudado, sin cobrar.

uncoloured, (*US*) uncolored ['ʌn'kʌləd] *adj* sin color, incoloro; *account etc* objetivo.

uncombed ['ʌn'kəʊmd] *adj* despeinado, sin peinar.

uncomely ['ʌn'kʌmlɪ] *adj* desgarbado.

uncomfortable [ʌn'kʌmfətəbl] *adj* (*physically*) incómodo; *feeling* molesto; **to be ~** (*chair etc*) ser incómodo; (*person*) estar inquieto, sentirse molesto; **I feel ~ about the change** el cambio me trae preocupado; **we had an ~ few minutes** pasamos un mal rato; **to make life ~ for sb** amargar la vida a uno, crear dificultades a uno.

uncomfortably [ʌn'kʌmfətəblɪ] *adv* incómodamente; **he thought ~** pensaba con cierto remordimiento, pensaba algo inquieto; **the shell fell ~ close** cayó el proyectil inquietantemente cerca.

uncommitted ['ʌnkə'mɪtɪd] *adj* no comprometido; *nation* no alineado.

uncommon [ʌn'kɒmən] **1** *adj* poco común, nada frecuente; fuera de lo común; extraño, insólito. **2** *adv* (*) sumamente, extraordinariamente.

uncommonly [ʌn'kɒmənlɪ] *adv* raramente, rara vez; extraordinariamente; **that's ~ kind of you** ha sido Vd amabilísimo; **not ~** con cierta frecuencia.

uncommunicative ['ʌnkə'mjuːnɪkətɪv] *adj* poco comunicativo, reservado.

uncomplaining ['ʌnkəm'pleɪnɪŋ] *adj* resignado, sumiso.

uncomplainingly ['ʌnkəm'pleɪnɪŋlɪ] *adv* con resignación, sumisamente.

uncompleted ['ʌnkəm'pliːtɪd] *adj* incompleto, inacabado.

uncomplicated [ʌn'kɒmplɪkeɪtɪd] *adj person etc* sin complicaciones, sencillo.

uncomplimentary ['ʌn,kɒmplɪ'mentərɪ] *adj* nada lisonjero, poco halagüeño.

uncomprehending ['ʌn,kɒmprɪ'hendɪŋ] *adj* incomprensivo.

uncompromising [ʌn'kɒmprəmaɪzɪŋ] *adj* intransigente, inflexible.

uncompromisingly [ʌn'kɒmprəmaɪzɪŋlɪ] *adv* inflexiblemente, intransigentemente.

unconcealed ['ʌnkən'siːld] *adj* abierto, no disimulado; **with ~ glee** con abierta satisfacción.

unconcern ['ʌnkən'sɜːn] *n* (*calm*) calma *f*, tranquilidad *f*, (*in face of danger*) sangre *f* fría; (*lack of interest*) indiferencia *f*, despreocupación *f*.

unconcerned ['ʌnkən'sɜːnd] *adj* tranquilo; indiferente, despreocupado; **he went on speaking ~** siguió hablando sin

inmutarse; **to be ~ about sth** no inquietarse por algo.
unconcernedly [ˈʌnkənˈsɜːnɪdlɪ] *adv* con calma, tranquilamente; con sangre fría; con indiferencia; sin preocuparse, sin inquietarse.
unconditional [ˈʌnkənˈdɪʃənl] *adj* incondicional, sin condiciones; **~ surrender** rendición *f* sin condiciones.
unconditionally [ˈʌnkənˈdɪʃnəlɪ] *adv* incondicionalmente.
unconfessed [ˈʌnkənˈfest] *adj sin* no confesado; *die* sin confesar.
unconfined [ˈʌnkənˈfaɪnd] *adj* ilimitado, no restringido, libre; **let joy be ~** que se regocijen todos, que la alegría no tenga límite.
unconfirmed [ˈʌnkənˈfɜːmd] *adj* no confirmado, inconfirmado.
uncongenial [ˈʌnkənˈdʒiːnɪəl] *adj* antipático; desagradable.
unconnected [ˈʌnkəˈnektɪd] *adj* inconexo; **~ with** no relacionado con.
unconquerable [ʌnˈkɒŋkərəbl] *adj* inconquistable, invencible.
unconquered [ʌnˈkɒŋkəd] *adj* invicto.
unconscionable [ʌnˈkɒnʃnəbl] *adj* desmedido, desrazonable.
unconscious [ʌnˈkɒnʃəs] **1** *adj* (**a**) (*unaware*) inconsciente, no intencional; **to be ~ of** estar inconsciente de, ignorar, no darse cuenta de; **to remain blissfully ~ of the danger** continuar tan tranquilo sin darse cuenta del peligro.
(**b**) (*Med*) sin sentido, desmayado, inconsciente; **to be ~** estar sin sentido, estar desmayado; **to be ~ for 3 hours** pasar 3 horas sin sentido; **to become ~** perder el sentido, perder el conocimiento, desmayarse; **to fall ~** caer sin sentido; **they found him ~** le encontraron inconsciente.
2 *n*: **the ~** el inconsciente.
unconsciously [ʌnˈkɒnʃəslɪ] *adv* inconscientemente; **~ funny** cómico sin querer.
unconsciousness [ʌnˈkɒnʃəsnɪs] *n* inconsciencia *f*; (*Med*) insensibilidad *f*, pérdida *f* de conocimiento, falta *f* de sentido.
unconsidered [ˈʌnkənˈsɪdəd] *adj* desatendido; irreflexivo; **~ trifles** pequeñeces *fpl* de ninguna importancia.
unconstitutional [ˈʌn,kɒnstɪˈtjuːʃənl] *adj* inconstitucional, anticonstitucional.
unconstitutionally [ʌn,kɒnstɪˈtjuːʃnəlɪ] *adv* inconstitucionalmente, anticonstitucionalmente.
unconstrained [ˈʌnkənˈstreɪnd] *adj* libre, espontáneo, franco.
unconsummated [ʌnˈkɒnsəmeɪtɪd] *adj marriage* no consumado.
uncontested [ˈʌnkənˈtestɪd] *adj* incontestado; (*Parl*) *seat* ganado sin oposición, no disputado.
uncontrollable [ˈʌnkənˈtrəʊləbl] *adj* incontrolable; *temper* ingobernable; *laughter* incontenible; *terror etc* irrefrenable.
uncontrollably [ˈʌnkənˈtrəʊləblɪ] *adv* incontrolablemente; ingobernablemente; inconteniblemente; irrefrenablemente.
uncontrolled [ˈʌnkənˈtrəʊld] *adj* incontrolado, libre, desenfrenado.
uncontroversial [ˈʌn,kɒntrəˈvɜːʃəl] *adj* no controvertido, nada conflictivo.
unconventional [ˈʌnkənˈvenʃənl] *adj* poco convencional; *person* poco formalista, original, despreocupado.
unconventionality [ˈʌnkən,venʃəˈnælɪtɪ] *n* originalidad *f*.
unconversant [ˈʌnkənˈvɜːsənt] *adj*: **to be ~ with** no estar al tanto de, estar poco versado en.
unconverted [ˈʌnkənˈvɜːtɪd] *adj* no convertido (*also Fin*).
unconvertible [,ʌnkənˈvɜːtɪbl] *adj currency* inconvertible.
unconvinced [ˈʌnkənˈvɪnst] *adj*: **to remain ~** seguir siendo escéptico, seguir sin convencerse.
unconvincing [ˈʌnkənˈvɪnsɪŋ] *adj* poco convincente.
unconvincingly [ˈʌnkənˈvɪnsɪŋlɪ] *adv argue etc* sin convencer a nadie.
uncooked [ˈʌnˈkʊkt] *adj* sin cocer, crudo.
uncool* [ʌnˈkuːl] *adj* (**a**) (*unsophisticated*) nada sofisticado; (*unfashionable*) fuera de moda, anticuado. (**b**) (*excitable*) excitable, emocionado; (*tense*) nervioso.
uncooperative [ˈʌnkəʊˈɒpərətɪv] *adj* poco dispuesto a ayudar, nada servicial.
uncoordinated [ˈʌnkəʊˈɔːdɪneɪtɪd] *adj* no coordinado, incoordinado.
uncork [ˈʌnˈkɔːk] *vt* descorchar, destapar.
uncorrected [ˈʌnkəˈrektɪd] *adj* sin corregir.
uncorroborated [ˈʌnkəˈrɒbəreɪtɪd] *adj* no confirmado, sin corroborar.
uncorrupted [ˈʌnkəˈrʌptɪd] *adj* incorrupto; **~ by** no corrompido por.
uncount [ˈʌnˈkaʊnt] *adj*: **~ noun** sustantivo *m* no contable.
uncountable [ˈʌnˈkaʊntəbl] *adj* incontable.
uncounted [ˈʌnˈkaʊntɪd] *adj* sin cuenta.
uncouple [ˈʌnˈkʌpl] *vt* desacoplar, desenganchar.
uncouth [ʌnˈkuːθ] *adj* grosero, ineducado, inculto.
uncover [ʌnˈkʌvəʳ] *vt* descubrir; (*remove lid of*) destapar; (*remove coverings of*) dejar al descubierto; (*disclose*) descubrir, dejar al descubierto, dejar patente.
uncovered [ʌnˈkʌvəd] *adj* descubierto, sin cubierta; destapado; (*Fin*) *loan* en descubierto; *person* sin seguro, no asegurado.
uncritical [ˈʌnˈkrɪtɪkəl] *adj* falto de sentido crítico.
uncritically [ˈʌnˈkrɪtɪkəlɪ] *adv* sin sentido crítico.
uncross [ˈʌnˈkrɒs] *vt legs* descruzar.
uncrossed [ˈʌnˈkrɒst] *adj cheque* sin cruzar.
uncrowned [ˈʌnˈkraʊnd] *adj* sin corona; **the ~ king of Slobodia** el rey sin corona de Eslobodia.
UNCTAD [ˈʌŋktæd] *n abbr of* **United Nations Conference on Trade and Development.**
unction [ˈʌŋkʃən] *n* (*unguent*) unción *f*, ungüento *m*; (*fig*) unción *f*; celo *m*, fervor *m*; (*pej*) efusión *f*, celo *m* fingido, fervor *m* afectado; zalamería *f*; **extreme ~** (*Eccl*) extremaunción *f*; **he said with ~** dijo efusivo.
unctuous [ˈʌŋktjʊəs] *adj* (*fig*) afectadamente fervoroso; sobón, zalamero; **in an ~ voice** en tono efusivo, en tono meloso.
unctuously [ˈʌŋktjʊəslɪ] *adv* efusivamente, melosamente, zalameramente.
unctuousness [ˈʌŋktjʊəsnɪs] *n* (*fig*) efusión *f*, celo *m* fingido, fervor *m* afectado; zalamería *f*.
uncultivable [ˈʌnˈkʌltɪvəbl] *adj* incultivable.
uncultivated [ˈʌnˈkʌltɪveɪtɪd] *adj* inculto (*also fig*).
uncultured [ˈʌnˈkʌltʃəd] *adj* inculto, iletrado.
uncurl [ˈʌnˈkɜːl] **1** *vt* desrizar, desenrollar, abrir. **2** *vi* desrizarse, desenrollarse, abrirse; desovillarse.
uncut [ˈʌnˈkʌt] *adj* sin cortar; *stone* sin labrar; *diamond* en bruto, sin tallar; *book* sin abrir; *film, text* integral, sin cortes.
undamaged [ʌnˈdæmɪdʒd] *adj* indemne, intacto; sin sufrir desperfectos.
undamped [ˈʌnˈdæmpt] *adj enthusiasm etc* no disminuido.
undated [ˈʌnˈdeɪtɪd] *adj* sin fecha.
undaunted [ˈʌnˈdɔːntɪd] *adj* impávido, impertérrito; **he carried on quite ~** siguió sin inmutarse; **with ~ bravery** con valor indomable; **to be ~ by** no dejarse desanimar por.
undeceive [ˈʌndɪˈsiːv] *vt* desengañar, desilusionar.
undecided [ˈʌndɪˈsaɪdɪd] *adj question* pendiente, no resuelto; *person's character* indeciso; **we are still ~ whether to** + *infin* no hemos decidido todavía si + *infin*; **that is still ~** eso queda por resolver.
undecipherable [ˈʌndɪˈsaɪfərəbl] *adj* indescifrable.
undeclinable [ˈʌndɪˈklaɪnəbl] *adj* indeclinable.
undefeated [ˈʌndɪˈfiːtɪd] *adj* invicto, imbatido; **he was ~ at the end** siguió invicto al final.
undefended [ˈʌndɪˈfendɪd] *adj* indefenso; (*Jur*) *suit* ganado por incomparecencia del demandado.
undefiled [ˈʌndɪˈfaɪld] *adj* puro, inmaculado; **~ by any contact with ...** no corrompido por contacto alguno con ...
undefined [,ʌndɪˈfaɪnd] *adj* indefinido, indeterminado.
undelivered [,ʌndɪˈlɪvəd] *adj goods, letters* sin entregar, no entregado.
undemanding [,ʌndɪˈmɑːndɪŋ] *adj person* poco exigente; *job* que exige poco esfuerzo.
undemocratic [,ʌndeməˈkrætɪk] *adj* antidemocrático.
undemonstrative [ˈʌndɪˈmɒnstrətɪv] *adj* reservado, cohibido, poco expresivo.
undeniable [,ʌndɪˈnaɪəbl] *adj* innegable; **it is ~ that ...** es innegable que ...
undeniably [,ʌndɪˈnaɪəblɪ] *adv* indudablemente; **it is ~ true that ...** es innegable que ...; **an ~ successful trip** un viaje de éxito innegable.
undenominational [ˈʌndɪ,nɒmɪˈneɪʃənl] *adj* no sectario.
undependable [ˈʌndɪˈpendəbl] *adj* poco formal, poco confiable.
under [ˈʌndəʳ] **1** *adv* (**a**) debajo; abajo; *V* **down** *etc.* (**b**) **he was ~ for several hours*** estuvo sin conocimiento durante varias horas.
2 *prep* (**a**) (*place: precise*) debajo de, *eg* **~ the table** debajo de la mesa; (*less precise*) bajo, *eg* **~ the sky** bajo el cielo, **~ the water** bajo el agua.
(**b**) (*place, fig*) **~ the Romans** bajo los romanos; **~ Ferdinand VII** bajo Fernando VII, durante el reinado de Fernando VII; **~ the command of** bajo el mando de; **~ lock and key** bajo llave; **~ oath** bajo juramento; **~ full sail**

a todo trapo, a vela llena; a toda vela; **the field is ~ wheat** el campo está sembrado de trigo.

(**c**) (*number etc*) **~ 50** menos de 50; **any number ~ 90** cualquier número inferior a 90; **in ~ 2 hours** en menos de 2 horas; **aged ~ 21** que tiene menos de 21 años; **it sells at ~ £5** se vende a menos de 5 libras.

(**d**) (*according to, by*) con arreglo a, de acuerdo con, conforme a, según; **~ Article 25 of the Code** conforme al Artículo 25 del Código; **his rights ~ the contract** sus derechos según el contrato.

under- [ˈʌndəʳ] *pref* (**a**) (*insufficiently*) insuficientemente; *eg* **~prepared** insuficientemente preparado.

(**b**) (*less than*) **an ~15** un joven de menos de 15 años, una persona que tiene menos de 15 años; **the Spanish ~21 team** la selección española sub-21.

(**c**) *part etc* bajo, inferior; *clothing* inferior; (*in rank*) subalterno, segundo; **the ~cook** la segunda cocinera; **the ~gardener** el mozo de huerto.

under-achieve [ˌʌndərəˈtʃiːv] *vi* no desarrollar su potencial, no rendir (como se debe).

under-achievement [ˌʌndərəˈtʃiːvmənt] *n* bajo rendimiento *m.*

under-achiever [ˌʌndərəˈtʃiːvəʳ] *n* (*Brit*) persona *f* que no desarrolla su potencial, persona *f* que no rinde (como se debe).

underact [ˈʌndərˈækt] *vi* no dar de sí, hacer un papel sin el debido brío.

under-age [ˌʌndərˈeɪdʒ] *adj* menor de edad.

underarm [ˈʌndərɑːm] **1** *n* sobaco *m,* axila *f.*

2 *attr* (*Anat*) sobacal, del sobaco; *service etc* hecho con la mano debajo del hombro; **~ deodorant** desodorante *m.*

3 *adv*: **to serve ~** sacar con la mano debajo del hombro.

underbelly [ˈʌndəˌbelɪ] *n* panza *f*; (*fig*) parte *f* indefensa, parte *f* más expuesta al ataque.

underbid [ˈʌndəˈbɪd] (*irr*: *V* **bid**) **1** *vt* ofrecer precio más bajo que. **2** *vi* (*Bridge*) declarar menos de lo que tiene uno.

underbody [ˈʌndəbɒdɪ] *n* (*Aut*) bajos *mpl* del chasis.

underbrush [ˈʌndəbrʌʃ] *n* (*US*) maleza *f,* monte *m* bajo.

undercapitalized [ˈʌndəˈkæpɪtəlaɪzd] *adj* subcapitalizado, descapitalizado.

undercarriage [ˈʌndəˌkærɪdʒ] *n,* **undercart*** [ˈʌndəkɑːt] *n* tren *m* de aterrizaje.

undercharge [ˈʌndəˈtʃɑːdʒ] *vt* cobrar menos del precio justo a.

underclass [ˈʌndəklɑːs] *n* clase *f* inferior.

underclothes [ˈʌndəkləʊðz] *npl,* **underclothing** [ˈʌndəˌkləʊðɪŋ] *n* ropa *f* interior, ropa *f* íntima (*LAm*); **to be in one's ~** estar en paños menores.

undercoat [ˈʌndəkəʊt] **1** *n* primera capa *f*; (*paint itself*) pintura *f* preparatoria.

2 *vt* poner una primera capa a; (*US Aut*) proteger contra la corrosión.

undercooked [ˈʌndəˈkʊkt] *adj* medio crudo.

undercover [ˈʌndəˌkʌvəʳ] *adj* secreto, clandestino.

undercurrent [ˈʌndəˌkʌrənt] *n* corriente *f* submarina, contracorriente *f*; (*fig*) nota *f* callada; tendencia *f* oculta; **an ~ of criticism** una serie de críticas calladas.

undercut [ˈʌndəkʌt] (*irr*: *V* **cut**) *vt competitor* vender más barato que.

underdeveloped [ˈʌndədɪˈveləpt] *adj* infradesarrollado, subdesarrollado; (*Phot*) insuficientemente revelado.

underdevelopment [ˈʌndədɪˈveləpmənt] *n* infradesarrollo *m,* subdesarrollo *m.*

underdog [ˈʌndədɒg] *n* (*socially*) desvalido *m*; (*in game*) perdidoso *m,* el que está perdiendo; **the ~s** los de abajo, los débiles, los desamparados.

underdone [ˈʌndəˈdʌn] *adj* poco hecho.

underdrawers [ˈʌndəˈdrɔːəz] *npl* (*US*) calzoncillos *mpl.*

underdress [ˈʌndəˈdres] *vi* vestirse sin la debida elegancia, no vestirse de forma apropiada.

underemphasize [ˌʌndərˈemfəsaɪz] *vt* subenfatizar.

underemployed [ˈʌndərɪmˈplɔɪd] *adj* subempleado.

underemployment [ˌʌndərɪmˈplɔɪmənt] *n* subempleo *m.*

underestimate 1 [ˈʌndərˈestɪmɪt] *n* estimación *f* demasiado baja; infraestimación *f,* infravaloración *f.* **2** [ˈʌndərˈestɪmeɪt] *vt* subestimar; infraestimar, infravalorar.

under-expose [ˈʌndərɪksˈpəʊz] *vt* subexponer, exponer insuficientemente.

under-exposed [ˈʌndərɪksˈpəʊzd] *adj* subexpuesto.

under-exposure [ˈʌnderɪksˈpəʊʒəʳ] *n* subexposición *f.*

underfed [ˈʌndəˈfed] *adj* subalimentado, desnutrido.

underfeed [ˈʌndəˈfiːd] (*irr*: *V* **feed**) *vt* alimentar insuficientemente.

underfeeding [ˈʌndəˈfiːdɪŋ] *n* subalimentación *f,* desnutrición *f.*

underfelt [ˈʌndəfelt] *n* arpillera *f.*

underfinanced [ˌʌndəfaɪˈnænst] *adj* insuficientemente financiado.

underfloor [ˈʌndəflɔːʳ] *adj* de debajo del suelo.

underfoot [ˈʌndəˈfʊt] *adv* debajo de los pies; **it's very wet ~** el suelo está mojado.

underfund [ˌʌndəˈfʌnd] *vt* infradotar.

underfunded [ˌʌndəˈfʌndɪd] *adj* infradotado.

underfunding [ˌʌndəˈfʌndɪŋ] *n* infradotación *f.*

undergarment [ˈʌndəˌgɑːmənt] *n* prenda *f* de ropa interior (*LAm*: íntima); **~s** ropa *f* interior, ropa *f* íntima (*LAm*).

undergo [ˈʌndəˈgəʊ] (*irr*: *V* **go**) *vt* sufrir, experimentar; *operation* someterse a; *treatment* recibir; **to ~ repairs** ser reparado.

undergraduate [ˈʌndəˈgrædjʊɪt] **1** *n* estudiante *mf* (*no licenciado*).

2 *attr student* no licenciado; *study* de licenciatura, para estudiantes no licenciados; **~ humour** humor *m* estudiantil; **70 ~ rooms** 70 habitaciones para estudiantes.

underground [ˈʌndəgraʊnd] **1** *adj* (**a**) (*lit*) subterráneo; **~ railway** ferrocarril *m* subterráneo.

(**b**) (*fig*) clandestino, secreto; **~ cinema** cine *m* underground.

2 *adv* (**a**) (*lit*) bajo tierra; **it's 6 feet ~** está a 6 pies bajo tierra.

(**b**) (*Pol etc*) clandestinamente, en la clandestinidad; **this may drive the party ~** esto puede obligar al partido a pasar a la clandestinidad.

3 *n* (**a**) (*Brit Rail*) metro *m.*

(**b**) (*Mil, Pol*) resistencia *f*; movimiento *m* clandestino.

undergrowth [ˈʌndəgrəʊθ] *n* maleza *f,* monte *m* bajo.

underhand [ˈʌndəhænd] **1** *adj* (*Sport*) *service etc* hecho con la mano debajo del hombro; (*fig*) *method* turbio, poco limpio; *trick* malo; *attack* solapado.

2 *adv*: **to serve ~** sacar con la mano debajo del hombro.

underhandedly [ˌʌndəˈhændɪdlɪ] *adv* bajo mano.

underinvestment [ˌʌndərɪnˈvesmənt] *n* infrainversión *f.*

underlay [ˈʌndəleɪ] *n* (*for carpet*) refuerzo *m* (de alfombra).

underlie [ˌʌndəˈlaɪ] (*irr*: *V* **lie²**) *vt* estar debajo de, extenderse debajo de; servir de base a; (*fig*) subyacer a, estar a la base de, ser la razón fundamental de.

underline [ˌʌndəˈlaɪn] *vt* subrayar (*also fig*).

underling [ˈʌndəlɪŋ] *n* subordinado *m,* inferior *m.*

underlining [ˈʌndəˈlaɪnɪŋ] *n* subrayado *m.*

underlip [ˈʌndəlɪp] *n* labio *m* inferior.

underlying [ˈʌndəˈlaɪɪŋ] *adj* subyacente; (*fig*) fundamental, esencial; **the ~ problem is that ...** el problema de fondo es que ...

undermanned [ˈʌndəˈmænd] *adj*: **to be ~** estar sin la debida plantilla, no tener el debido personal.

undermanning [ˌʌndəˈmænɪŋ] *n* escasez *f* de mano de obra, falta *f* de personal.

undermentioned [ˈʌndəˈmenʃənd] *adj* abajo citado.

undermine [ˌʌndəˈmaɪn] *vt* socavar, minar (*also fig*); **his health is being ~d by overwork** el exceso de trabajo le está arruinando la salud.

undermost [ˈʌndəməʊst] *adj* (el) más bajo.

underneath [ˈʌndəˈniːθ] **1** *adv* debajo, por debajo. **2** *prep* bajo, debajo de, por debajo de. **3** *adj* inferior, de abajo; **the ~ one** el de abajo. **4** *n* superficie *f* inferior.

undernourished [ˈʌndəˈnʌrɪʃt] *adj* desnutrido.

undernourishment [ˈʌndəˈnʌrɪʃmənt] *n* desnutrición *f.*

underpaid [ˈʌndəˈpeɪd] *adj* insuficientemente retribuido, mal pagado.

underpants [ˈʌndəpænts] *npl* calzoncillos *mpl,* calzones *mpl* (*LAm*).

underpart [ˈʌndəpɑːt] *n* parte *f* inferior.

underpass [ˈʌndəpɑːs] *n* paso *m* inferior.

underpay [ˈʌndəˈpeɪ] (*irr*: *V* **pay**) *vt* pagar mal, pagar un sueldo insuficiente a.

underpin [ˌʌndəˈpɪn] *vt* (*Archit*) apuntalar; (*fig*) *argument, case* secundar, sostener.

underpinning [ˌʌndəˈpɪnɪŋ] *n* apuntalamiento *m.*

underplay [ˈʌndəˈpleɪ] **1** *vt*: **to ~ a part** hacer flojamente un papel.

2 *vi* (*Theat*) hacer flojamente su papel, estar muy flojo en su papel.

underpopulated [ˈʌndəˈpɒpjʊleɪtɪd] *adj* poco poblado, con baja densidad de población.

underprice [ˈʌndəˈpraɪs] *vt* señalar un precio demasiado bajo a; **at 5 dollars it is ~d** el precio de 5 dólares es más bien bajo.

underpricing ['ʌndə'praɪsɪŋ] *n* asignación *f* de precios demasiado bajos.

underprivileged ['ʌndə'prɪvɪlɪdʒd] *adj* desvalido, desfavorecido, desamparado.

underproduction ['ʌndəprə'dʌkʃən] *n* producción *f* insuficiente.

underrate [ˌʌndə'reɪt] *vt* subestimar.

underrated [ˌʌndə'reɪtɪd] *adj* subestimado; infravalorado.

underripe ['ʌndə'raɪp] *adj* poco maduro, verde.

underscore [ˌʌndə'skɔːʳ] *vt* subrayar, recalcar.

undersea ['ʌndəsiː] **1** *adj* submarino. **2** *adv* bajo la superficie del mar.

underseal ['ʌndəsiːl] *vt* (*Brit*) impermeabilizar (por debajo), proteger contra la corrosión.

undersealing ['ʌndəsiːlɪŋ] *n* (*Brit*) impermeabilización *f* de los bajos.

undersecretary ['ʌndə'sekrətərɪ] *n* subsecretario *m*, -a *f*.

undersecretaryship ['ʌndə'sekrətərɪʃɪp] *n* subsecretaría *f*.

undersell ['ʌndə'sel] (*irr*: *V* **sell**) *vt person* vender a precio más bajo que; *article* malvender; **Burnley has been undersold as a tourist centre** no se ha hecho la debida publicidad de Burnley como centro turístico.

undersexed [ˌʌndə'sekst] *adj* de libido floja.

undershirt ['ʌndəʃɜːt] *n* (*US*) camiseta *f*.

undershoot [ˌʌndə'ʃuːt] (*irr*: *V* **shoot**) **1** *vt target* (*fig*) no alcanzar, no llegar a. **2** *vi* no alcanzar el blanco; **we have undershot by £80** nos faltan 80 libras para alcanzar el objetivo.

undershorts ['ʌndəˌʃɔːts] *npl* (*US*) calzoncillos *mpl*.

underside ['ʌndəsaɪd] *n* superficie *f* inferior; (*of small object*) envés *m*, cara *f* inferior.

undersigned ['ʌndəsaɪnd] *adj*: **the ~** el abajofirmante, el infraescrito, (*pl*) los abajofirmantes, los infraescritos.

undersized ['ʌndə'saɪzd] *adj* pequeño, no bastante grande, de tamaño insuficiente; *person* sietemesino.

underskirt ['ʌndəskɜːt] *n* (*Brit*) enaguas *fpl*.

underslung ['ʌndəslʌŋ] *adj* (*Aut*) colgante.

understaffed ['ʌndə'stɑːft] *adj*: **to be ~** estar falto de personal, no tener el debido personal.

understand [ˌʌndə'stænd] (*irr*: *V* **stand**) **1** *vt* (**a**) (*grasp*) comprender, entender; **I don't ~ Arabic** no entiendo el árabe; **I don't ~ you** no te entiendo; **I don't ~ why** no entiendo por qué; **we ~ each other** nos entendemos, nos comprendemos; **as I ~ it** según tengo entendido.

(**b**) (*assume*) sobreentender; **one has to ~ 3 words here** aquí se sobreentienden 3 palabras; *V also* **understood**.

(**c**) (*believe*) entender; **I ~ that ...** (*formal declarations*) quedo informado de que ...; **I ~ (that) you have been absent** tengo entendido que has estado ausente; **to give sb to ~ that ...** dar a uno a entender que ...; **I was given to ~ that ...** me dieron a entender que ..., me hicieron creer que ...

2 *vi* comprender, entender; **I ~** lo comprendo; **I quite ~** lo comprendo perfectamente; **do you ~?** ¿me entiendes?, ¿comprendes?

understandable [ˌʌndə'stændəbl] *adj* comprensible; **it is ~ that ...** se comprende que ...; **it is very ~ that ...** se comprende perfectamente que ...

understandably [ˌʌndə'stændəblɪ] *adv* naturalmente; (*lit*) comprensiblemente; **he ~ refused** naturalmente se negó, se comprende que rehusara.

understanding [ˌʌndə'stændɪŋ] **1** *adj* comprensivo, compasivo; **they were very ~ about it** se mostraron muy comprensivos; **he gave me an ~ look** me miró compasivo.

2 *n* (**a**) (*intelligence*) entendimiento *m*, inteligencia *f*; (*grasp*) comprensión *f*; **he has good ~** tiene una inteligencia fina; **his ~ of these problems** su comprensión de estos problemas, su capacidad para comprender estos problemas.

(**b**) (*agreement*) acuerdo *m*, arreglo *m*; **to come to an ~ with sb** ponerse de acuerdo con uno, llegar a un acuerdo con uno; **to have an ~ with sb** tener un acuerdo (*esp* verbal) con uno; **I have an ~ with the milkman** tengo un arreglo con el lechero, nos entendemos el lechero y yo; **on the ~ that ...** con tal que + *subj*, bien entendido que + *subj*.

(**c**) (*sympathy*) comprensión *f* mutua, inteligencia *f*; simpatía *f*; **this will encourage good ~ between peoples** esto ha de fomentar la buena inteligencia entre los pueblos.

understandingly [ˌʌndə'stændɪŋlɪ] *adv* con comprensión, compasivamente; **he looked at me ~** me miró compasivamente.

understate ['ʌndə'steɪt] *vt* minimizar; *situation* describir quitándole importancia; *gravity* atenuar; *needs* subestimar; (*Gram*) atenuar.

understated [ˌʌndə'steɪtɪd] *adj* comedido.

understatement ['ʌndəˌsteɪtmənt] *n* atenuación *f*; descripción *f* insuficiente; (*Gram*) atenuación *f*; (*quality*) moderación *f*, modestia *f* excesiva; **the ~ of the year** el eufemismo del año.

understood [ˌʌndə'stʊd] *adj and ptp* (**a**) **~?** ¿comprendido?; **it is ~ that ...** (*believed*) se cree que ..., tenemos entendido que ...; (*understandable*) se comprende que ...; **that is ~** eso se entiende; **it being ~ that ...** con tal que + *subj*; **I wish it to be ~ that ...** entiéndase que ..., quiero decir bien claro que ...; **to make o.s. ~** hacerse entender.

(**b**) (*assumed*) **with 3 words ~** con 3 palabras que se sobreentienden; **it is an ~ thing that ...** se entiende que ..., se acepta el que ...

understorey ['ʌndəˌstɔːrɪ] *n* monte *m* bajo.

understudy ['ʌndəˌstʌdɪ] **1** *n* suplente *mf*, sobresaliente *mf*. **2** *vt* doblar a, aprender un papel para poder suplir a.

undertake [ˌʌndə'teɪk] (*irr*: *V* **take**) *vt task etc* emprender; acometer; *duty etc* encargarse de; **to ~ to do sth** comprometerse a hacer algo, prometer hacer algo; **to ~ that ...** comprometerse a que ..., prometer que ...

undertaker ['ʌndəˌteɪkəʳ] *n* director *m* de pompas fúnebres; **~'s** funeraria *f*.

undertaking [ˌʌndə'teɪkɪŋ] *n* (**a**) (*Comm*) empresa *f*; (*task*) empresa *f*, tarea *f*. (**b**) (*pledge*) garantía *f*, compromiso *m*, promesa *f*; **to give an ~ that ...** prometer que ..., asegurar que ...; **I can give no such ~** no puedo comprometerme a eso, no puedo dar esa promesa.

under-the-counter* [ˌʌndəðə'kaʊntəʳ] *adj goods etc* adquirido por la trastienda*.

undertone ['ʌndətəʊn] *n* (*sound*) voz *f* baja, sonido *m* suave; (*Art*) matiz *m* suave; (*of criticism etc*) nota *f* callada, trasfondo *m*, corriente *f* oculta, sentimiento *m* no expresado; **in an ~** en voz baja; **there are ~s of protest here** aquí hay notas calladas de protesta.

undertow ['ʌndətəʊ] *n* resaca *f*.

under-use 1 [ˌʌndə'juːs] *n* infrautilización *f*. **2** [ˌʌndə'juːz] *vt* infrautilizar.

under-utilization [ˌʌndə'juːtəlaɪzeɪʃən] *n* infrautilización *f*.

under-utilized [ˌʌndə'juːtəlaɪzd] *adj* infrautilizado.

undervalue ['ʌndə'væljuː] *vt* subvalorar, minusvalorar, valorizar incompletamente, apreciar en menos de su justo valor; (*fig*) subestimar; menospreciar; **he has been ~d as a writer** como escritor no se le ha apreciado debidamente.

underwater ['ʌndə'wɔːtəʳ] *adj* submarino; **~ archaeology** arqueología *f* submarina; **~ diver** submarinista *mf*; **~ exploration** exploración *f* submarina; **~ fisherman** submarinista *mf*; **~ fishing** pesca *f* submarina.

underwear ['ʌndəwɛəʳ] *n* ropa *f* interior, ropa *f* íntima (*LAm*).

underweight [ˌʌndə'weɪt] *adj* de peso insuficiente; **to be ~** (*person*) no pesar bastante, estar flaco.

underwhelm ['ʌndə'welm] *vt* (*hum*) impresionar muy poco; **this left us somewhat ~ed** esto apenas nos impresionó.

underworld ['ʌndəwɜːld] **1** *adj* (**a**) (*of hell*) infernal. (**b**) (*criminal*) criminal, del hampa. **2** *n* (**a**) (*hell*) infierno *m*; (*of spirits*) inframundo *m*. (**b**) (*criminal*) hampa *f*, mundo *m* del hampa, bajos fondos *mpl*.

underwrite ['ʌndəraɪt] (*irr*: *V* **write**) *vt* asegurar, asegurar contra riesgos; (*on 2nd insurance*) reasegurar; (*fig*) apoyar, respaldar, aprobar, garantizar.

underwriter ['ʌndəˌraɪtəʳ] *n* asegurador *m*, -ora *f*, reasegurador *m*, -ora *f*.

undeserved ['ʌndɪ'zɜːvd] *adj* inmerecido.

undeservedly ['ʌndɪ'zɜːvɪdlɪ] *adv* inmerecidamente.

undeserving ['ʌndɪ'zɜːvɪŋ] *adj* indigno, de poco mérito.

undesirable ['ʌndɪ'zaɪərəbl] **1** *adj* indeseable; **it is ~ that ...** no es recomendable que + *subj*, es poco aconsejable que + *subj*. **2** *n* indeseable *mf*.

undetected ['ʌndɪ'tektɪd] *adj* no descubierto; **to go ~** pasar inadvertido.

undetermined ['ʌndɪ'tɜːmɪnd] *adj* (*unknown*) indeterminado; (*uncertain*) incierto.

undeterred ['ʌndɪ'tɜːd] *adj*: **he was ~ by ...** no se dejó intimidar por ...; **he carried on ~** siguió sin inmutarse.

undeveloped ['ʌndɪ'veləpt] *adj* subdesarrollado; *fruit etc* verde, inmaturo; *film* sin revelar; *land* sin cultivar; *resources* sin explotar.

undeviating [ʌn'diːvɪeɪtɪŋ] *adj* directo, constante; **to follow an ~ path** seguir un curso recto.

undeviatingly [ʌn'diːvɪeɪtɪŋlɪ] *adv* directamente, constantemente; **to hold ~ to one's course** seguir su curso sin apartarse para nada de él.

undiagnosed [ʌn'daɪəg,nəʊzd] *adj* sin diagnosticar.

undies* ['ʌndɪz] *npl* paños *mpl* menores.

undigested ['ʌndaɪ'dʒestɪd] *adj* indigesto.

undignified [ʌn'dɪgnɪfaɪd] *adj act, position etc* indecoroso; *person* sin dignidad, informal, poco serio.

undiluted ['ʌndaɪ'lu:tɪd] *adj* sin diluir, puro; (*fig*) puro.

undiminished ['ʌndɪ'mɪnɪʃt] *adj* no disminuido.

undimmed ['ʌn'dɪmd] *adj* (*fig*) no empañado.

undiplomatic ['ʌn,dɪplə'mætɪk] *adj* poco diplomático, indiscreto.

undiscernible ['ʌndɪ'sɜ:nəbl] *adj* imperceptible.

undiscerning ['ʌndɪ'sɜ:nɪŋ] *adj* sin discernimiento, poco discernidor.

undischarged ['ʌndɪs'tʃɑ:dʒd] *adj debt* impagado, por pagar; *promise* no cumplido; ~ **bankrupt** quebrado *m* no rehabilitado, persona *f* que sigue en estado de quiebra.

undisciplined [ʌn'dɪsɪplɪnd] *adj* indisciplinado.

undisclosed ['ʌndɪs'kləʊzd] *adj* no revelado, sin revelar.

undiscovered ['ʌndɪs'kʌvəd] *adj* no descubierto; **he remained ~ for 3 days** siguió durante 3 días sin descubrir.

undiscriminating ['ʌndɪs'krɪmɪneɪtɪŋ] *adj* sin discernimiento, poco discernidor.

undisguised ['ʌndɪs'gaɪzd] *adj* sin disfraz; (*fig*) franco, abierto; **with ~ satisfaction** con abierta satisfacción.

undismayed ['ʌndɪs'meɪd] *adj* impávido; **he was ~ by this** no se dejó desanimar por esto; **he said ~** dijo sin inmutarse.

undisposed-of ['ʌndɪs'pəʊzdɒv] *adj* (*Comm*) no vendido.

undisputed ['ʌndɪs'pju:tɪd] *adj* incontestable, indiscutible.

undistinguished ['ʌndɪs'tɪŋgwɪʃt] *adj* más bien mediocre.

undistributed [,ʌndɪs'trɪbjʊtɪd] *adj*: ~ **profit** beneficios *mpl* no distribuidos.

undisturbed ['ʌndɪs'tɜ:bd] *adj* tranquilo, sin molestar; **to leave things ~** dejar las cosas como están, dejar las cosas sin tocar; **he was ~ by this** no se perturbó con esto; **to go on with one's work ~** continuar su trabajo en paz; **he likes to be left ~** no quiere que le interrumpan las visitas (*or* llamadas *etc*).

undivided ['ʌndɪ'vaɪdɪd] *adj* indiviso, íntegro, entero; **I want your ~ attention** quiero que me presten toda su atención.

undo ['ʌn'du:] (*irr*: *V* **do**) *vt arrangement etc* anular; *work* deshacer; *knot* desatar; *clasp* desabrochar; *packet* abrir; *mischief* reparar; *command* cancelar; *V also* **undone**.

undoing ['ʌn'du:ɪŋ] *n* ruina *f*, perdición *f*; **that was his ~** aquello fue su ruina.

undomesticated ['ʌndə'mestɪkeɪtɪd] *adj* indomado, no domesticado.

undone ['ʌn'dʌn] *adj*: **I am ~!** (*liter*) ¡estoy perdido!, ¡es mi ruina!; **to come ~** *knot etc* desatarse; **to leave sth ~** *task* dejar algo sin hacer.

undoubted [ʌn'daʊtɪd] *adj* indudable.

undoubtedly [ʌn'daʊtɪdlɪ] *adv* indudablemente, sin duda.

undreamt-of [ʌn'dremtɒv] *adj* no soñado, inimaginable, nunca pensado.

undress ['ʌn'dres] **1** *n* traje *m* de casa, desabillé *m*; (*Mil*) uniforme *m* (de diario); **in a state of ~** desnudo. **2** *vt* desnudar. **3** *vi* desnudarse.

undressed [ʌn'drest] *adj hide* sin adobar, sin curtir; *salad etc* sin salsa; **to get ~** desnudarse, quitarse los vestidos.

undrinkable ['ʌn'drɪŋkəbl] *adj* no potable, imbebible.

undue ['ʌn'dju:] *adj* indebido, excesivo.

undulate ['ʌndjʊleɪt] *vi* ondular, ondear.

undulating ['ʌndjʊleɪtɪŋ] *adj* ondulante, ondeante; *land* ondulado.

undulation [,ʌndjʊ'leɪʃən] *n* ondulación *f*.

undulatory ['ʌndjʊlətərɪ] *adj* ondulatorio.

unduly ['ʌn'dju:lɪ] *adv* indebidamente, excesivamente, con exceso; **we are not ~ worried** no estamos mayormente preocupados.

undying [ʌn'daɪɪŋ] *adj* (*fig*) imperecedero, inmarcesible.

unearned ['ʌn'ɜ:nd] *adj* no ganado; ~ **income** renta *f* (no salarial), rentas *fpl*; ~ **increment** plusvalía *f*.

unearth ['ʌn'ɜ:θ] *vt* desenterrar; (*fig*) desenterrar, descubrir.

unearthly [ʌn'ɜ:θlɪ] *adj* sobrenatural; *light etc* misterioso, fantástico; *hour etc* intempestivo, inverosímil.

unease [ʌn'i:z] *n* malestar *m*.

uneasily [ʌn'i:zɪlɪ] *adv* inquietamente, con inquietud; **I noted ~ that** ... me inquieté al observar que ...

uneasiness [ʌn'i:zɪnɪs] *n* inquietud *f*; desasosiego *m*, intranquilidad *f*.

uneasy [ʌn'i:zɪ] *adj calm, peace, etc* inseguro; *sleep* poco tranquilo; *conscience* desasosegado, intranquilo; **to be ~** estar inquieto (*about* por), sentirse mal a gusto; **to become ~** empezar a inquietarse (*about* por); **I have an ~ feeling that** ... me inquieta la posibilidad de que + *subj*; **to make sb ~** intranquilizar a uno, turbar a uno.

uneatable ['ʌn'i:təbl] *adj* incomible, que no se puede comer.

uneaten ['ʌn'i:tn] *adj* no comido, sin comer.

uneconomic(al) ['ʌn,i:kə'nɒmɪk(əl)] *adj* antieconómico.

unedifying ['ʌn'edɪfaɪɪŋ] *adj* indecoroso, poco edificante.

unedited [ʌn'edɪtɪd] *adj* inédito.

uneducated ['ʌn'edjʊkeɪtɪd] *adj* inculto, ignorante.

unemotional ['ʌnɪ'məʊʃənl] *adj character* impasible, reservado; *person* que no se deja emocionar; *account etc* objetivo.

unemotionally ['ʌnɪ'məʊʃnəlɪ] *adv*: **to look on ~** mirar impasible, mirar sin dejarse emocionar.

unemployable ['ʌnɪm'plɔɪəbl] *adj* inútil para el trabajo.

unemployed ['ʌnɪm'plɔɪd] **1** *adj person* parado, sin empleo, desempleado; *capital etc* sin utilizar, no utilizado. **2** *n*: **the ~** los parados, los sin trabajo, los desempleados.

unemployment ['ʌnɪm'plɔɪmənt] **1** *n* paro *m* (forzoso), desempleo *m*, desocupación *f*. **2** *attr*: ~ **benefit** (*Brit*) subsidio *m* de paro; ~ **figures** cifras *fpl* del paro.

unencumbered ['ʌnɪn'kʌmbəd] *adj* suelto, sin trabas; (*estate etc*) libre de gravamen; ~ **by** no impedido por, sin el estorbo de.

unending [ʌn'endɪŋ] *adj* interminable, sin fin.

unendurable ['ʌnɪn'djʊərəbl] *adj* inaguantable, insufrible.

unengaged ['ʌnɪn'geɪdʒd] *adj* libre; sin compromiso.

un-English ['ʌn'ɪŋglɪʃ] *adj* poco inglés, indigno de un inglés.

unenlightened ['ʌnɪn'laɪtnd] *adj person, age* ignorante, poco instruido; *policy etc* poco ilustrado.

unenterprising ['ʌn'entəpraɪzɪŋ] *adj person* falto de iniciativa, poco emprendedor; *policy etc* tímido.

unenthusiastic ['ʌnɪn,θu:zɪ'æstɪk] *adj* poco entusiasta; **everybody seemed rather ~ about it** nadie se mostró mayormente entusiasmado con la idea.

unenthusiastically ['ʌnɪn,θu:zɪ'æstɪkəlɪ] *adv* sin entusiasmo.

unenviable ['ʌn'envɪəbl] *adj* poco envidiable.

unequal ['ʌn'i:kwəl] *adj* desigual; desproporcionado; **to be ~ to a task** no estar a la altura de una tarea, no tener fuerzas para una tarea.

unequalled, (*US*) **unequaled** ['ʌn'i:kwəld] *adj* inigualado, sin par; **a record ~ by anybody** un historial mejor que el de nadie.

unequally ['ʌn'i:kwəlɪ] *adv* desigualmente; desproporcionadamente.

unequivocal ['ʌnɪ'kwɪvəkəl] *adj* inequívoco.

unequivocally ['ʌnɪ'kwɪvəkəlɪ] *adv* de modo inequívoco, sin dejar lugar a dudas.

unerring ['ʌn'ɜ:rɪŋ] *adj* infalible.

UNESCO [ju:'neskəʊ] *n abbr of* **United Nations Educational, Scientific and Cultural Organization** Organización *f* de las Naciones Unidas para la Educación, la Ciencia y la Cultura, UNESCO *f*.

unescorted [,ʌnɪs'kɔ:tɪd] *adj* sin escolta; sin compañía, sin compañero.

unessential ['ʌnɪ'senʃəl] **1** *adj* no esencial. **2** *npl*: **the ~s** las cosas (*or* los aspectos *etc*) no esenciales.

unesthetic [,ʌni:s'θetɪk] *adj* (*US*) antiestético.

unethical ['ʌn'eθɪkəl] *adj* inmoral; poco honrado.

uneven ['ʌn'i:vən] *adj* desigual; *road etc* quebrado, ondulado, lleno de baches; *land* accidentado, escabroso.

unevenly ['ʌn'i:vənlɪ] *adv* desigualmente.

unevenness ['ʌn'i:vənnɪs] *n* desigualdad *f*; escabrosidad *f*.

uneventful ['ʌnɪ'ventfʊl] *adj* sin incidentes notables, sin accidentes, tranquilo.

uneventfully ['ʌnɪ'ventfʊlɪ] *adv* tranquilamente.

unexampled ['ʌnɪg'zɑ:mpld] *adj* sin igual, sin precedente.

unexceptionable [,ʌnɪk'sepʃnəbl] *adj* intachable, impecable.

unexceptional [,ʌnɪk'sepʃənl] *adj* usual, corriente, normal.

unexciting ['ʌnɪk'saɪtɪŋ] *adj* poco emocionante, de poco interés.

unexpected ['ʌnɪks'pektɪd] *adj* inesperado, inopinado.

unexpectedly ['ʌnɪks'pektɪdlɪ] *adv* inesperadamente, inopinadamente.

unexpended ['ʌnɪks'pendɪd] *adj* no gastado.

unexpired ['ʌnɪks'paɪəd] *adj bill* no vencido; *lease, ticket* no caducado.

unexplained ['ʌnɪks'pleɪnd] *adj* inexplicado.

unexploded ['ʌnɪks'pləʊdɪd] *adj* sin explotar.

unexploited ['ʌnɪks'plɔɪtɪd] *adj* inexplotado, sin explotar.

unexplored ['ʌnɪks'plɔ:d] *adj* inexplorado.

unexposed ['ʌnɪks'pəʊzd] *adj* no descubierto; (*Phot*) inexpuesto.

unexpressed ['ʌnɪks'prest] *adj* no expresado; tácito.

unexpressive [ˈʌnɪksˈpresɪv] *adj* inexpresivo.
unexpurgated [ˈʌnˈekspɜːgeɪtɪd] *adj* sin expurgar, íntegro.
unfading [ʌnˈfeɪdɪŋ] *adj* (*fig*) inmarcesible, imperecedero.
unfailing [ʌnˈfeɪlɪŋ] *adj* indefectible; *zeal* infalible; *supply* inagotable.
unfailingly [ʌnˈfeɪlɪŋlɪ] *adv* indefectiblemente; infaliblemente; inagotablemente; **to be ~ courteous** ser siempre cortés, no faltar en ningún momento a la cortesía.
unfair [ˈʌnˈfɛəʳ] *adj comment, practice etc* injusto, no equitativo; *dismissal* improcedente; *competition* desleal; *play* sucio; *tactics* no aprobado, no permitido por las reglas; **that's very ~** eso es muy injusto; **how ~!** ¡no hay derecho!; **it was ~ of him to** + *infin* era injusto que él + *subj*.
unfairly [ˈʌnˈfɛəlɪ] *adv* injustamente; deslealmente; de modo contrario a las reglas; **he was ~ condemned** se le condenó injustamente.
unfairness [ˈʌnˈfɛənɪs] *n* injusticia *f*; deslealtad *f*; suciedad *f*.
unfaithful [ˈʌnˈfeɪθfʊl] *adj* infiel (*to* a).
unfaithfulness [ˈʌnˈfeɪθfʊlnɪs] *n* infidelidad *f*.
unfaltering [ʌnˈfɔːltərɪŋ] *adj* resuelto, firme.
unfalteringly [ʌnˈfɔːltərɪŋlɪ] *adv* resueltamente, decididamente, firmemente.
unfamiliar [ˈʌnfəˈmɪlɪəʳ] *adj subject etc* desconocido, nuevo; **to be ~ with** desconocer, ignorar.
unfamiliarity [ˈʌnfəˌmɪlɪˈærɪtɪ] *n* no familiaridad *f*, desconocimiento *m*.
unfashionable [ˈʌnˈfæʃnəbl] *adj* pasado de moda, fuera de moda; poco elegante; **it is now ~ to talk of ...** no está de moda ahora hablar de ...
unfasten [ˈʌnˈfɑːsn] *vt* (*untie*) desatar; *dress* desabrochar; *door* abrir; (*get free*) soltar; (*loosen*) aflojar.
unfathomable [ʌnˈfæðəməbl] *adj* insondable.
unfathomed [ˈʌnˈfæðəmd] *adj* no sondado.
unfavourable, (*US*) **unfavorable** [ˈʌnˈfeɪvərəbl] *adj* desfavorable, adverso; *outlook etc* poco propicio; *weather* malo.
unfavourably, (*US*) **unfavorably** [ˈʌnˈfeɪvərəblɪ] *adv* desfavorablemente; **to be ~ impressed** formarse una impresión desfavorable.
unfeeling [ʌnˈfiːlɪŋ] *adj* insensible.
unfeelingly [ʌnˈfiːlɪŋlɪ] *adv* insensiblemente.
unfeigned [ʌnˈfeɪnd] *adj* sincero, no fingido, verdadero.
unfeignedly [ʌnˈfeɪnɪdlɪ] *adv* sin fingimiento, verdaderamente.
unfeminine [ʌnˈfemɪnɪn] *adj* poco femenino.
unfermented [ˈʌnfəˈmentɪd] *adj* no fermentado.
unfettered [ˈʌnˈfetəd] *adj* sin trabas.
unfilled [ˈʌnˈfɪld] *adj*: **~ orders** pedidos *mpl* pendientes.
unfinished [ˈʌnˈfɪnɪʃt] *adj* incompleto, inacabado, inconcluso, sin terminar; **I have 3 ~ letters** tengo 3 cartas por terminar; **we have ~ business** tenemos asuntos pendientes.
unfit 1 [ˈʌnˈfɪt] *adj* (*incompetent*) incapaz, incompetente; (*unsuitable*) no apto (*for* para); (*useless*) inservible, inadecuado (*for* para); (*unworthy*) indigno (*to* de); (*ill*) enfermo, indispuesto, (*injured*) lesionado; **~ to eat** impropio para el consumo humano; **~ for publication** indigno de publicarse, no apto para publicar; **~ for military service** no apto para el servicio militar; **he is quite ~ to hold office** es totalmente incapaz de ocupar ningún cargo; **the road is ~ for lorries** el camino es intransitable para los camiones.
2 [ʌnˈfɪt] *vt*: **to ~ sb for sth** inhabilitar a uno para algo, incapacitar a uno para algo; **he is ~ted for such a career** no es apto para tal carrera.
unfitness [ˈʌnˈfɪtnɪs] *n* incapacidad *f*, incompetencia *f*; falta *f* de aptitud; inadecuación *f*; (*Med*) mala salud *f*, falta *f* de salud.
unfitting [ʌnˈfɪtɪŋ] *adj* impropio.
unflagging [ʌnˈflægɪŋ] *adj* incansable.
unflaggingly [ʌnˈflægɪŋlɪ] *adv* incansablemente.
unflappability* [ˌʌnflæpəˈbɪlɪtɪ] *n* imperturbabilidad *f*.
unflappable* [ˈʌnˈflæpəbl] *adj* imperturbable.
unflattering [ˈʌnˈflætərɪŋ] *adj* poco lisonjero, poco grato.
unflatteringly [ˈʌnˈflætərɪŋlɪ] *adv* de modo poco lisonjero.
unfledged [ˈʌnˈfledʒd] *adj* implume.
unflinching [ˈʌnˈflɪntʃɪŋ] *adj* impávido, resuelto.
unflinchingly [ˈʌnˈflɪntʃɪŋlɪ] *adv* impávidamente, resueltamente.
unfocus(s)ed [ˈʌnˈfəʊkəst] *adj eyes* desenfocado; *desires* sin objetivo concreto, nada concreto; *energies* que carece de dirección.
unfold [ʌnˈfəʊld] **1** *vt* desplegar, desdoblar, abrir; *idea, plan* exponer; *secret* revelar; **to ~ a map on a table** extender un mapa sobre una mesa.
2 *vi* desplegarse, desdoblarse, abrirse; (*view etc*) revelarse, extenderse.
unforced [ʌnˈfɔːst] *adj style etc* natural, sin artificialidad; *error* no forzado.
unforeseeable [ˈʌnfɔːˈsiːəbl] *adj* imprevisible.
unforeseen [ˈʌnfɔːˈsiːn] *adj* imprevisto.
unforgettable [ˈʌnfəˈgetəbl] *adj* inolvidable.
unforgettably [ˈʌnfəˈgetəblɪ] *adv* de manera inolvidable; **~ beautiful** tan hermoso que resulta inolvidable.
unforgivable [ˈʌnfəˈgɪvəbl] *adj* imperdonable, indisculpable.
unforgiving [ˈʌnfəˈgɪvɪŋ] *adj* implacable.
unforgotten [ˈʌnfəˈgɒtn] *adj* no olvidado.
unformatted [ˈʌnˈfɔːmætɪd] *adj* no formateado, sin formatear.
unformed [ˈʌnˈfɔːmd] *adj* informe, sin formar aún.
unforthcoming [ˈʌnfɔːθˈkʌmɪŋ] *adj* poco comunicativo.
unfortified [ˈʌnˈfɔːtɪfaɪd] *adj* no fortificado; *town* abierto.
unfortunate [ʌnˈfɔːtʃnɪt] **1** *adj person* desgraciado, desdichado, desventurado; *event* funesto, desgraciado; *manner, remark* infeliz, inoportuno; **how very ~!** ¡qué mala suerte!, ¡qué desgracia!; **it is most ~ that ...** es muy de lamentar que + *subj*; **you have been most ~** has tenido muy mala suerte.
2 *n* desgraciado *m*, -a *f*.
unfortunately [ʌnˈfɔːtʃnɪtlɪ] *adv* por desgracia, desgraciadamente, desafortunadamente; **it is ~ true that ...** desgraciadamente es verdad que ...; **an ~ phrased statement** una declaración expresada en términos infelices.
unfounded [ˈʌnˈfaʊndɪd] *adj* infundado, que carece de fundamento.
unframed [ˈʌnˈfreɪmd] *adj* sin marco.
unfreeze [ˈʌnˈfriːz] **1** *vt* descongelar. **2** *vi* descongelarse.
unfrequented [ˈʌnfrɪˈkwentɪd] *adj* poco frecuentado.
unfriendliness [ˈʌnˈfrendlɪnɪs] *n* hostilidad *f*.
unfriendly [ˈʌnˈfrendlɪ] *adj* poco amistoso.
unfrock [ˈʌnˈfrɒk] *vt* degradar, expulsar; *priest* secularizar, exclaustrar.
unfruitful [ˈʌnˈfruːtfʊl] *adj* infructuoso.
unfulfilled [ˈʌnfʊlˈfɪld] *adj* incumplido.
unfunny* [ˈʌnˈfʌnɪ] *adj* nada divertido.
unfurl [ʌnˈfɜːl] *vt* desplegar.
unfurnished [ˈʌnˈfɜːnɪʃt] *adj* desamueblado, sin muebles.
ungainliness [ʌnˈgeɪnlɪnɪs] *n* desgarbo *m*, torpeza *f*.
ungainly [ʌnˈgeɪnlɪ] *adj* desgarbado, torpe.
ungallant [ˈʌnˈgælənt] *adj* falto de cortesía, descortés.
ungenerous [ˈʌnˈdʒenərəs] *adj* poco generoso.
ungentlemanly [ʌnˈdʒentlmənlɪ] *adj* poco caballeroso, indigno de un caballero.
un-get-at-able* [ˈʌngetˈætəbl] *adj* inaccesible.
ungird [ˈʌnˈgɜːd] (*irr*: *V* **gird**) *vt* desceñir.
unglazed [ˈʌnˈgleɪzd] *adj* no vidriado; *window* sin cristales.
ungodliness [ʌnˈgɒdlɪnɪs] *n* impiedad *f*.
ungodly [ʌnˈgɒdlɪ] *adj* impío, irreligioso; (*) atroz; **at this ~ hour** a hora tan inverosímil, a hora tan poco católica*.
ungovernable [ʌnˈgʌvənəbl] *adj* ingobernable; *temper* incontrolable, irrefrenable.
ungracious [ˈʌnˈgreɪʃəs] *adj* descortés, grosero; **it would be ~ to refuse** sería descortés no aceptarlo.
ungraciously [ˈʌnˈgreɪʃəslɪ] *adv* descortésmente.
ungrammatical [ˈʌngrəˈmætɪkəl] *adj* incorrecto, agramatical, antigramatical.
ungrammatically [ˈʌngrəˈmætɪkəlɪ] *adv* incorrectamente; **to talk Spanish ~** hablar español con poca corrección.
ungrateful [ʌnˈgreɪtfʊl] *adj* desagradecido, ingrato.
ungratefully [ʌnˈgreɪtfəlɪ] *adv* desagradecidamente.
ungrudging [ˈʌnˈgrʌdʒɪŋ] *adj* liberal, generoso; sin escatimar; *support etc* incondicional.
ungrudgingly [ʌnˈgrʌdʒɪŋlɪ] *adv* liberalmente, generosamente; de buena gana, incondicionalmente.
unguarded [ˈʌnˈgɑːdɪd] *adj* (*Mil*) indefenso, no defendido, sin protección; *remark etc* imprudente; **in an ~ moment** en un momento de descuido.
unguent [ˈʌŋgwənt] *n* ungüento *m*.
ungulate [ˈʌŋgjʊleɪt] **1** *adj* ungulado. **2** *n* ungulado *m*.
unhampered [ˈʌnˈhæmpəd] *adj* libre, sin estorbos; **~ by** no estorbado por.
unhand [ʌnˈhænd] *vt* soltar; **~ me, sir!** ¡suélteme, señor!
unhandy [ʌnˈhændɪ] *adj person* desmañado; *thing* incómodo; **to be ~ with sth** ser desmañado en el manejo de algo.
unhappily [ʌnˈhæpɪlɪ] *adv* (*miserably*) infelizmente; (*unfortunately*) desgraciadamente.

unhappiness [ʌnˈhæpɪnɪs] *n* desdicha *f*, tristeza *f*; desgracia *f*.

unhappy [ʌnˈhæpɪ] *adj person* infeliz, desdichado; *childhood etc* desgraciado; (*ill-fated*) malhadado, infausto; *remark etc* infeliz, inoportuno; **that ~ time** aquella triste época; **to be ~ about sth** inquietarse por algo, no aceptar algo de buena gana; **we are ~ about the decision** no nos gusta la decisión; **to make sb ~** poner triste a uno, amargar la vida a uno; **she was ~ in her marriage** era desgraciada en su matrimonio.

unharmed [ˈʌnˈhɑːmd] *adj person* ileso, incólume; *thing* indemne; **to escape ~** salir ileso.

unharness [ˈʌnˈhɑːnɪs] *vt* desguarnecer.

UNHCR *n abbr of* **United Nations High Commission for Refugees** Alta Comisión *f* de las Naciones Unidas para los Refugiados.

unhealthy [ʌnˈhelθɪ] *adj person* enfermizo; *place* malsano, insalubre; *complexion* de aspecto poco sano; *curiosity* morboso.

unheard [ˈʌnˈhɜːd] *adj*: **to condemn sb ~** condenar a uno sin oírle.

unheard-of [ʌnˈhɜːdɒv] *adj* inaudito.

unheated [ˈʌnˈhiːtɪd] *adj* sin calentar; sin calefacción.

unheeded [ˈʌnˈhiːdɪd] *adj* desatendido; **the warning went ~** nadie prestó atención a la advertencia, nadie hizo caso de la advertencia.

unheeding [ˈʌnˈhiːdɪŋ] *adj* desatento, sordo; **they passed by ~** pasaron sin prestar atención.

unhelpful [ˈʌnˈhelpfʊl] *adj person* poco servicial; nada simpático; *advice etc* inútil.

unhelpfully [ˈʌnˈhelpfʊlɪ] *adv* poco servicialmente.

unhelpfulness [ˈʌnˈhelpfʊlnɪs] *n* falta *f* de espíritu servicial; falta *f* de simpatía; inutilidad *f*.

unheralded [ˈʌnˈherəldɪd] *adj*: **to arrive ~** llegar sin dar aviso.

unhesitating [ʌnˈhezɪteɪtɪŋ] *adj person etc* resuelto; *reply etc* pronto.

unhesitatingly [ʌnˈhezɪteɪtɪŋlɪ] *adv*: **he said ~** dijo sin vacilar, dijo decidido.

unhindered [ˈʌnˈhɪndəd] *adj* libre, sin estorbos; **~ by** no estorbado por.

unhinge [ʌnˈhɪndʒ] *vt* desquiciar; (*fig*) *mind* trastornar; *person* trastornar el juicio de.

unhinged [ˈʌnˈhɪndʒd] *adj* (*mad*) loco.

unhistorical [ˈʌnhɪsˈtɒrɪkəl] *adj* antihistórico, que no tiene nada de histórico.

unhitch [ˈʌnˈhɪtʃ] *vt* desenganchar.

unholy [ʌnˈhəʊlɪ] *adj* impío; (*) atroz.

unhook [ˈʌnˈhʊk] *vt* desenganchar; (*from wall etc*) descolgar; *dress* desabrochar.

unhoped-for [ʌnˈhəʊptfɔːʳ] *adj* inesperado.

unhopeful [ʌnˈhəʊpfʊl] *adj prospect* poco alentador, poco prometedor; *person* pesimista.

unhorse [ˈʌnˈhɔːs] *vt* desarzonar.

unhurried [ˈʌnˈhʌrɪd] *adj* lento, pausado, parsimonioso.

unhurriedly [ˈʌnˈhʌrɪdlɪ] *adv* lentamente, pausadamente, con parsimonia.

unhurt [ˈʌnˈhɜːt] *adj* ileso, incólume; **to escape ~** salir ileso.

unhygienic [ˈʌnhaɪˈdʒiːnɪk] *adj* antihigiénico.

uni... [ˈjuːnɪ] *pref* uni...

unicameral [ˈjuːnɪˈkæmərəl] *adj* unicameral.

UNICEF [ˈjuːnɪsef] *n abbr of* **United Nations International Children's Emergency Fund** Fondo *m* Internacional de las Naciones Unidas de Socorro a la Infancia, UNICEF *m*.

unicellular [ˈjuːnɪˈseljʊləʳ] *adj* unicelular.

unicorn [ˈjuːnɪkɔːn] *n* unicornio *m*.

unicycle [ˈjuːnɪˌsaɪkl] *n* monociclo *m*.

unidentifiable [ˈʌnaɪˌdentɪˈfaɪəbl] *adj* no identificable.

unidentified [ˈʌnaɪˈdentɪfaɪd] *adj* sin identificar, no identificado aún.

unification [ˌjuːnɪfɪˈkeɪʃən] *n* unificación *f*.

uniform [ˈjuːnɪfɔːm] **1** *adj* uniforme; igual, constante; **to make sth ~** hacer algo uniforme, uniformar algo.

2 *n* uniforme *m*; **in ~** (*fig*) en filas; **in full ~** de gran uniforme.

uniformed [ˈjuːnɪfɔːmd] *adj* uniformado.

uniformity [ˌjuːnɪˈfɔːmɪtɪ] *n* uniformidad *f*.

uniformly [ˈjuːnɪfɔːmlɪ] *adv* uniformemente, de modo uniforme.

unify [ˈjuːnɪfaɪ] *vt* unificar, unir.

unifying [ˈjuːnɪfaɪɪŋ] *adj factor etc* unificador.

unilateral [ˈjuːnɪˈlætərəl] *adj* unilateral; **~ disarmament** desarme *m* unilateral.

unilateralism [ˈjuːnɪˈlætərəlɪzəm] *n* opinión *f* (*or* campaña *f etc*) a favor del desarme unilateral.

unilateralist [ˈjuːnɪˈlætərəlɪst] *n* persona *f* que está a favor del desarme unilateral.

unilaterally [ˈjuːnɪˈlætərəlɪ] *adv* unilateralmente.

unilingual [ˌjuːnɪˈlɪŋgwəl] *adj* monolingüe.

unimaginable [ˌʌnɪˈmædʒɪnəbl] *adj* inconcebible, inimaginable.

unimaginably [ˌʌnɪˈmædʒɪnəblɪ] *adv* inimaginablemente, inconcebiblemente.

unimaginative [ˈʌnɪˈmædʒɪnətɪv] *adj* poco imaginativo.

unimaginatively [ˈʌnɪˈmædʒɪnətɪvlɪ] *adv* poco imaginativamente.

unimpaired [ˈʌnɪmˈpɛəd] *adj* no disminuido; no afectado; intacto, entero.

unimpeachable [ˌʌnɪmˈpiːtʃəbl] *adj* irrecusable, intachable; **from an ~ source** de fuente fidedigna.

unimpeded [ˈʌnɪmˈpiːdɪd] *adj* sin estorbo.

unimportant [ˈʌnɪmˈpɔːtənt] *adj* sin importancia, insignificante.

unimpressed [ˈʌnɪmˈprest] *adj* no impresionado; **he remained ~** no se convenció; **I remain ~ by the new building** el nuevo edificio no me impresiona.

unimpressive [ˈʌnɪmˈpresɪv] *adj* poco impresionante, poco convincente; *person* soso, insignificante.

unimproved [ˌʌnɪmˈpruːvd] *adj land* (*not drained*) sin drenar; (*not treated*) sin abonar.

uninfluenced [ˈʌnˈɪnflʊənst] *adj*: **~ by any argument** no afectado por ningún argumento; **a style ~ by any other** un estilo no influido por ningún otro.

uninformative [ˈʌnɪnˈfɔːmətɪv] *adj* poco informativo.

uninformed [ˈʌnɪnˈfɔːmd] *adj character* desinformado, poco instruido, ignorante; **to be ~ about sth** no estar enterado de algo, desconocer algo.

uninhabitable [ˈʌnɪnˈhæbɪtəbl] *adj* inhabitable.

uninhabited [ˈʌnɪnˈhæbɪtɪd] *adj* deshabitado, inhabitado; desierto.

uninhibited [ˈʌnɪnˈhɪbɪtɪd] *adj* nada cohibido, desinhibido, totalmente libre.

uninitiated [ˈʌnɪˈnɪʃɪeɪtɪd] **1** *adj* no iniciado. **2** *n*: **the ~** los no iniciados.

uninjured [ˈʌnˈɪndʒəd] *adj* ileso; **to escape ~** salir ileso.

uninspired [ˈʌnɪnˈspaɪəd] *adj* sin inspiración, soso, mediocre.

uninspiring [ˈʌnɪnˈspaɪərɪŋ] *adj* nada inspirador.

uninsured [ˈʌnɪnˈʃʊəd] *adj* no asegurado.

unintelligent [ˈʌnɪnˈtelɪdʒənt] *adj* ininteligente, poco inteligente.

unintelligibility [ˈʌnɪnˌtelɪdʒəˈbɪlɪtɪ] *n* ininteligibilidad *f*, incomprensibilidad *f*.

unintelligible [ˈʌnɪnˈtelɪdʒəbl] *adj* ininteligible, incomprensible.

unintelligibly [ˈʌnɪnˈtelɪdʒəblɪ] *adv* de modo ininteligible, de modo incomprensible.

unintended [ˈʌnɪnˈtendɪd] *adj*, **unintentional** [ˈʌnɪnˈtenʃənl] *adj* involuntario, no intencional; **it was ~** fue sin querer.

unintentionally [ˈʌnɪnˈtenʃnəlɪ] *adv* sin querer.

uninterested [ʌnˈɪntrɪstɪd] *adj* sin interés; **to be ~ in a subject** no tener interés en un asunto.

uninteresting [ˈʌnˈɪntrɪstɪŋ] *adj* poco interesante, falto de interés.

uninterrupted [ˈʌnˌɪntəˈrʌptɪd] *adj* ininterrumpido, sin interrupción.

uninterruptedly [ˈʌnˌɪntəˈrʌptɪdlɪ] *adv* ininterrumpidamente.

uninvited [ˈʌnɪnˈvaɪtɪd] *adj guest* no invitado; *comment* gratuito; **to do sth ~** hacer algo sin ser rogado; **they came to the party ~** vinieron al guateque sin ser invitados.

uninviting [ˈʌnɪnˈvaɪtɪŋ] *adj* poco atractivo.

union [ˈjuːnjən] **1** *n* unión *f*; (*marriage*) enlace *m*; (*Pol*) sindicato *m*, gremio *m* obrero; (*Mech*) unión *f*, manguito *m* de unión; **the U~** (*USA*) la Unión.

2 *attr* sindical, de los sindicatos, gremial; **~ catalog(ue)** catálogo *m* colectivo, catálogo *m* conjunto; **~ member** miembro *mf* del sindicato, sindicalista *mf*; **~ membership** sindicalización *f*; **~ shop** (*US*) taller *m* de obreros agremiados, taller *m* de afiliación (sindical) obligatoria; **~ suit** (*US*) prenda *f* interior de cuerpo entero.

unionism [ˈjuːnjənɪzəm] *n* (**a**) *V* **trade(s) unionism.** (**b**) **U~** (*Brit Pol*) unionismo *m*.

unionist [ˈjuːnjənɪst] **1** *n* (**a**) *V* **trade(s) unionist.** (**b**) **U~** (*Brit Pol*) unionista *mf*. **2** *adj* (*Brit Pol*) unionista.

unionize [ˈjuːnjənaɪz] **1** *vt* sindicar, agremiar. **2** *vi* sindicarse, agremiarse.

Union Jack [ˈjuːnjənˈdʒæk] *n* (*Brit*) *bandera del Reino Unido.*

Union of South Africa [ˈjuːnjənəvˌsaʊθˈæfrɪkə] *n* Unión *f* Sudafricana.

Union of Soviet Socialist Republics ['ju:njənəv'səuvıət'səuʃəlıstrı'pʌblıks] *n* Unión *f* de Repúblicas Socialistas Soviéticas.
unique [ju:'ni:k] *adj* único.
uniquely [ju:'ni:klı] *adv* especialmente.
uniqueness [ju:'ni:knıs] *n* unicidad *f*.
unisex ['ju:nıseks] *adj* unisex(o).
unison ['ju:nızn] *n* armonía *f*; (*Mus*) unisonancia *f*; **to sing in ~** cantar al unísono; **to act in ~ with sb** obrar de acuerdo con uno.
unissued ['ʌn'ıʃu:d] *adj*: **~ capital** capital *m* no emitido.
unit ['ju:nıt] **1** *n* unidad *f* (*also Math, Mil*); (*Elec*: *measurement*) unidad *f*; (*Mech, Elec*) grupo *m*; (*Univ*) unidad *f* de valor; **~ of account** unidad *f* de cuenta.
2 *attr*: **~ charge, ~ cost** costo *m* por unidad; costo *m* unitario; **~ furniture** muebles *mpl* de elementos adicionables, muebles *mpl* combinados; **~ price** precio *m* unitario; **~ trust** (*Brit*) fondo *m* de inversión mobiliaria.
Unitarian [,ju:nı'tɛərıən] **1** *adj* unitario. **2** *n* unitario *m*, -a *f*.
Unitarianism [,ju:nı'tɛərıənızəm] *n* unitarismo *m*.
unitary ['ju:nıtərı] *adj* unitario; **~ labour costs** costes *mpl* laborales unitarios.
unite [ju:'naıt] **1** *vt* unir, juntar; (*marry*) casar; *parts of country* unificar.
2 *vi* unirse, juntarse; **to ~ against sb** unirse para hacer frente a uno; **to ~ in doing sth** unirse para hacer algo, concertarse para hacer algo.
united [ju:'naıtıd] *adj* unido.
United Arab Emirates [ju:'naıtıd'ærəbe'mıərıts] *npl* Emiratos *mpl* Árabes Unidos.
United Arab Republic [ju:'naıtıd'ærəbrı'pʌblık] *n* República *f* Árabe Unida.
United Kingdom [ju:'naıtıd'kıŋdəm] *n* Reino *m* Unido (*Inglaterra, Gales, Escocia, Irlanda del Norte*).
United Nations [ju:'naıtıd'neıʃənz] *npl* Naciones *fpl* Unidas.
United States (of America) [ju:'naıtıd'steıts(əvə'merıkə)] *npl* (Los) Estados *mpl* Unidos (de América).
unity ['ju:nıtı] *n* unidad *f*; unión *f*; armonía *f*; **~ of place** unidad *f* de lugar; **~ of time** unidad *f* de tiempo.
Univ. *abbr of* **University**.
univalent ['ju:nı'veılənt] *adj* univalente.
univalve ['ju:nıvælv] **1** *adj* univalvo. **2** *n* molusco *m* univalvo.
universal [,ju:nı'vɜ:səl] **1** *adj* universal; **~ heir** heredero *m* único; **~ joint** junta *f* cardán, junta *f* universal; **U~ Postal Union** Unión *f* Postal Universal; **~ product code** (*US*) código *m* de barras; **~ suffrage** sufragio *m* universal; **its use has been ~ since 1900** desde 1900 tiene un empleo general; **soap is now ~** el jabón se emplea ahora en todas partes; **to become ~** universalizarse, generalizarse; **to make ~** universalizar, generalizar. **2** *n* universal *m*.
universality [,ju:nıvɜ:'sælıtı] *n* universalidad *f*.
universalize [,ju:nı'vɜ:səlaız] *vt* universalizar.
universally [,ju:nı'vɜ:səlı] *adv* universalmente; generalmente, comúnmente; **~ known** mundialmente conocido.
universe ['ju:nıvɜ:s] *n* universo *m*.
university [,ju:nı'vɜ:sıtı] **1** *n* universidad *f*; **to be at ~** estar en la universidad; **to go to ~** ir a la universidad.
2 *attr degree, library, year etc* universitario; *professor, student* de universidad; **~ entrance** acceso *m* a la universidad; **~ town** ciudad *f* que tiene universidad.
unjust ['ʌn'dʒʌst] *adj* injusto.
unjustifiable [ʌn'dʒʌstıfaıəbl] *adj* injustificable.
unjustifiably [ʌn'dʒʌstıfaıəblı] *adv* injustificadamente.
unjustified ['ʌn'dʒʌstıfaıd] *adj* injustificado; *text* no alineado, no justificado.
unjustly ['ʌn'dʒʌstlı] *adv* injustamente.
unkempt ['ʌn'kempt] *adj appearance* desaseado, descuidado; *hair* despeinado.
unkind [ʌn'kaınd] *adj* (*of person etc*) poco amable, nada amistoso; poco compasivo; cruel, despiadado; *remark, word, blow* cruel; *climate* riguroso; **that was very ~ of him** en eso no se mostró nada amable; **he was ~ enough to** + *infin* fue lo bastante cruel como para + *infin*.
unkindly [ʌn'kaındlı] *adv* cruelmente; **don't take it ~ if ...** no lo tome a mal si ...
unkindness [ʌn'kaındnıs] *n* (**a**) (*quality*) falta *f* de amabilidad; crueldad *f*, rigor *m*, severidad *f*. (**b**) (*act*) acto *m* de crueldad.
unknowable ['ʌn'nəuəbl] *adj* inconocible; insondable, impenetrable; **the ~** lo inconocible.
unknowing ['ʌn'nəuıŋ] *adj* inconsciente.
unknowingly ['ʌn'nəuıŋlı] *adv* sin querer; sin saberlo; **he did it all ~** lo hizo sin darse cuenta.
unknown ['ʌn'nəun] **1** *adj* desconocido, ignorado; ignoto; incógnito; **the ~ soldier** el soldado desconocido; **towards ~ regions** hacia regiones desconocidas; **a substance ~ to science** una sustancia ignorada por la ciencia; **~ quantity** (*Math, fig*) incógnita *f*.
2 *adv*: **~ to me** sin saberlo yo.
3 *n* (*person*) desconocido *m*, -a *f*; (*Math, also fig*) incógnita *f*; **the ~** lo desconocido; **to go out into the ~** salir a explorar tierras incógnitas.
unlace ['ʌn'leıs] *vt* desenlazar; *shoes* desatar los cordones de.
unladen ['ʌn'leıdn] *adj* vacío, sin cargamento.
unladylike ['ʌn'leıdılaık] *adj* vulgar, ordinario, impropio de una señora.
unlamented ['ʌnlə'mentıd] *adj* no llorado, no lamentado.
unlatch ['ʌn'lætʃ] *vt door* abrir, alzar el pestillo de, abrir levantando el picaporte de.
unlawful ['ʌn'lɔ:fʊl] *adj* ilegal, ilícito.
unlawfully ['ʌn'lɔ:fəlı] *adv* ilegalmente, ilícitamente.
unleaded [,ʌn'ledıd] **1** *adj petrol* sin plomo. **2** *n* gasolina *f* sin plomo.
unlearn ['ʌn'lɜ:n] *vt* desaprender, olvidar.
unlearned ['ʌn'lɜ:nıd] *adj* indocto, ignorante.
unleash ['ʌn'li:ʃ] *vt dog* desatraillar, soltar; (*fig*) desencadenar, desatar.
unleavened ['ʌn'levnd] *adj* ázimo, sin levadura; **~ bread** pan *m* ázimo, pan *m* cenceño.
unless [ən'les] *conj* a menos que + *subj*; a no ser que + *subj*; **~ you can find another one** a menos que puedas encontrar otro; **~ I am mistaken** si no me equivoco; **~ I hear to the contrary** a menos que me digan lo contrario.
unlettered ['ʌn'letəd] *adj* indocto.
unlicensed ['ʌn'laısənst] *adj* sin permiso, sin licencia, no autorizado.
unlike ['ʌn'laık] **1** *adj* desemejante, distinto; (*Math*) de signo contrario; **they are quite ~** son muy distintos, no se parecen en nada.
2 *prep* a diferencia de; **it's quite ~ him** no es nada característico de él; **the photo is quite ~ him** la foto no le representa en absoluto; **I, ~ others, ...** yo, a diferencia de otros ...
unlikeable ['ʌn'laıkəbl] *adj* antipático.
unlikelihood [ʌn'laıklıhʊd] *n*, **unlikeliness** [ʌn'laıklınıs] *n* improbabilidad *f*.
unlikely [ʌn'laıklı] *adj* improbable, poco probable; difícil; (*odd*) inverosímil; **it is most ~** no es nada probable; **I think it very ~** lo creo muy poco probable; **it is ~ that he will come, he is ~ to come** no es probable que venga; **wearing a most ~ hat** con un sombrero inverosímil.
unlimited [ʌn'lımıtıd] *adj* ilimitado, sin límite; **~ company** compañía *f* ilimitada; **~ liability** (*Comm*) responsabilidad *f* ilimitada.
unlined ['ʌn'laınd] *adj coat* sin forro; *face* sin arrugas; *paper* sin rayar.
unlisted ['ʌn'lıstıd] *adj*: **~ company** sociedad *f* sin cotización oficial, compañía *f* no cotizable; **~ number** (*US*) número *m* que no figura en la guía telefónica; **~ securities** valores *mpl* no inscritos en bolsa.
unlit ['ʌn'lıt] *adj* oscuro, sin luz; *street* sin alumbrado, sin faroles.
unload ['ʌn'ləud] **1** *vt* descargar; (*get rid of*) deshacerse de.
2 *vi* descargar.
unloading ['ʌn'ləudıŋ] *n* descarga *f*.
unlock ['ʌn'lɒk] *vt* abrir (con llave); *mystery etc* resolver.
unlooked-for [ʌn'lʊktfɔ:ʳ] *adj* inesperado, inopinado.
unloose ['ʌn'lu:s], **unloosen** [ʌn'lu:sn] *vt* aflojar, desatar, soltar.
unlovable ['ʌn'lʌvəbl] *adj* antipático, poco amable.
unloved ['ʌn'lʌvd] *adj* no amado; **to feel ~** sentirse rechazado.
unlovely ['ʌn'lʌvlı] *adj* feo, desgarbado, sin atractivo.
unloving ['ʌn'lʌvıŋ] *adj* nada cariñoso.
unluckily [ʌn'lʌkılı] *adv*: **~ I couldn't go** desgraciadamente no pude ir; **it was ~ left at the station** por desgracia quedó olvidado en la estación.
unluckiness [ʌn'lʌkınıs] *n* mala suerte *f*; lo nefasto.
unlucky [ʌn'lʌkı] *adj person, stroke etc* desgraciado; (*ill-omened*) funesto, nefasto; **a very ~ day** un día de los menos propicios; **to be ~** (*person*) tener mala suerte; **I've been ~ all my life** toda la vida he sido desgraciado; **how very ~!** ¡qué mala suerte!; **it's ~ to go under ladders** pasar por debajo de las escaleras trae mala suerte.
unmade ['ʌn'meıd] *adj bed* deshecho; *road* sin alquitranar.
unmake ['ʌn'meık] (*irr*: *V* **make**) *vt* deshacer.

unman ['ʌn'mæn] *vt* (**a**) (*cow*) acobardar. (**b**) *post etc* desguarnecer.
unmanageable [ʌn'mænɪdʒəbl] *adj* (*unwieldy*) inmanejable, difícil de manejar; *person* indócil, ingobernable.
unmanly ['ʌn'mænlɪ] *adj* afeminado; cobarde.
unmanned ['ʌn'mænd] *adj* no tripulado.
unmannerly [ʌn'mænəlɪ] *adj* descortés, mal educado.
unmarked ['ʌn'mɑːkt] *adj* sin marcar; *police-car* camuflado; (*uninjured*) ileso; (*Sport*) desmarcado.
unmarketable ['ʌn'mɑːkɪtəbl] *adj* invendible.
unmarriageable ['ʌn'mærɪdʒəbl] *adj* incasable.
unmarried ['ʌn'mærɪd] *adj* soltero; **~ mother** madre *f* soltera; **the ~ state** el estado de soltero, el celibato.
unmask ['ʌn'mɑːsk] **1** *vt* desenmascarar (*also fig*). **2** *vi* quitarse la máscara, descubrirse.
unmast ['ʌn'mɑːst] *vt* desarbolar.
unmatched ['ʌn'mætʃt] *adj* incomparable, sin par.
unmemorable ['ʌn'memərəbəl] *adj* nada memorable, indigno de ser recordado.
unmentionable [ʌn'menʃnəbl] **1** *adj* que no se puede mencionar; indescriptible, indecible. **2** *npl*: **~s** (*hum*) prendas *fpl* íntimas, pantalones *mpl*.
unmerciful [ʌn'mɜːsɪfʊl] *adj* despiadado.
unmercifully [ʌn'mɜːsɪfəlɪ] *adv* despiadadamente.
unmerited ['ʌn'merɪtɪd] *adj* inmerecido.
unmethodical ['ʌnmɪ'θɒdɪkəl] *adj* poco metódico, desordenado.
unmindful [ʌn'maɪndfʊl] *adj*: **to be ~ of** no pensar en; **~ of the danger, he** ... él, sin pensar en el peligro ...
unmistak(e)able ['ʌnmɪs'teɪkəbl] *adj* inconfundible, inequívoco.
unmistak(e)ably ['ʌnmɪs'teɪkəblɪ] *adv* de modo inconfundible; **it is ~ mine** sin duda alguna es mío.
unmitigated [ʌn'mɪtɪgeɪtɪd] *adj* no mitigado, absoluto; *dislike etc* implacable; *rogue etc* redomado; **it was an ~ disaster** fue un desastre total.
unmixed ['ʌn'mɪkst] *adj* sin mezcla, puro.
unmolested ['ʌnmə'lestɪd] *adj* tranquilo, seguro; sin ser abordado; **to do sth ~** hacer algo sin ser molestado por otros.
unmotivated ['ʌn'məʊtɪveɪtɪd] *adj* inmotivado, sin motivo.
unmounted ['ʌn'maʊntɪd] *adj* *rider* desmontado; *stone* sin engastar; *photo, stamp* sin pegar.
unmourned ['ʌn'mɔːnd] *adj* no llorado.
unmoved ['ʌn'muːvd] *adj* impasible; **to remain ~ by** no dejarse conmover por, seguir siendo insensible a; **it leaves me ~** me trae sin cuidado.
unmoving ['ʌn'muːvɪŋ] *adj* inmóvil.
unmusical ['ʌn'mjuːzɪkəl] *adj* (*Mus*) inarmónico; *person* poco aficionado a la música; sin oído para la música.
unmuzzle [ˌʌn'mʌzl] *vt* *dog* quitar el bozal a; (*fig*) *press etc* quitar la mordaza a; **~d** sin bozal; (*fig*) libre, sin mordaza.
unnamed ['ʌn'neɪmd] *adj* sin nombre, innominado.
unnatural [ʌn'nætʃrəl] *adj* antinatural, no natural, contrario a la naturaleza; anormal; *habit, vice* perverso; *person's manner* afectado.
unnaturally [ʌn'nætʃrəlɪ] *adv* de manera poco natural; anormalmente; perversamente; **not ~ he was cross** era lógico que se enfadara, lógicamente se enfadó.
unnavigable ['ʌn'nævɪgəbl] *adj* innavegable.
unnecessarily [ʌn'nesɪsərɪlɪ] *adv* innecesariamente, sin necesidad.
unnecessary [ʌn'nesɪsərɪ] *adj* innecesario, inútil; **it is ~ to add that** ... huelga añadir que ...
unneighbourly, (*US*) **unneighborly** ['ʌn'neɪbəlɪ] *adj* poco amistoso, impropio de un buen vecino.
unnerve ['ʌn'nɜːv] *vt* acobardar, amilanar.
unnerved ['ʌn'nɜːvd] *adj* acobardado, desanimado.
unnerving ['ʌn'nɜːvɪŋ] *adj* desconcertante.
unnoticed ['ʌn'nəʊtɪst] *adj* inadvertido, desapercibido; **to go ~, to pass ~** pasar inadvertido.
unnumbered ['ʌn'nʌmbəd] *adj* sin numerar; (*countless*) innumerable.
UNO *n abbr of* **United Nations Organization** Organización *f* de las Naciones Unidas, ONU *f*.
unobjectionable ['ʌnəb'dʒekʃnəbl] *adj* intachable, impecable; aceptable; *person etc* inofensivo.
unobservant ['ʌnəb'zɜːvənt] *adj* poco observador; distraído, que no se fija.
unobserved ['ʌnəb'zɜːvd] *adj* desapercibido; **to get away ~** lograr escapar inadvertido.
unobstructed ['ʌnəb'strʌktɪd] *adj* libre, sin obstáculos, despejado.
unobtainable ['ʌnəb'teɪnəbl] *adj* (*Comm etc*) agotado, que no se puede conseguir.
unobtrusive ['ʌnəb'truːsɪv] *adj* discreto, modesto.
unobtrusively ['ʌnəb'truːsɪvlɪ] *adv* discretamente, modestamente.
unoccupied ['ʌn'ɒkjʊpaɪd] *adj* *house* deshabitado; *territory* despoblado, sin habitantes, (*Pol*) libre, sin colonizar; *seat, place* libre; *post* vacante; *person* desocupado, ocioso.
unofficial ['ʌnə'fɪʃəl] *adj* extraoficial, no oficial, oficioso; **~ strike** huelga *f* no oficial; **from an ~ source** de fuente oficiosa.
unofficially ['ʌnə'fɪʃəlɪ] *adv* de modo extraoficial.
unopened ['ʌn'əʊpənd] *adj* sin abrir.
unopposed ['ʌnə'pəʊzd] *adj* sin oposición; sin contrincante; (*Mil*) sin encontrar resistencia; **to be returned ~** (*Parl*) ganar un escaño por ser el único candidato que se presenta.
unorganized ['ʌn'ɔːgənaɪzd] *adj* no organizado.
unoriginal ['ʌnə'rɪdʒɪnəl] *adj* poco original.
unorthodox ['ʌn'ɔːθədɒks] *adj* poco ortodoxo, nada convencional; (*Eccl*) heterodoxo.
unostentatious ['ʌnˌɒsten'teɪʃəs] *adj* modesto, sin ostentación.
unpack ['ʌn'pæk] **1** *vt* desembalar, desempaquetar, desempacar (*LAm*); *suitcase* vaciar, deshacer. **2** *vi* deshacer las maletas, desempacar (*LAm*).
unpacking ['ʌn'pækɪŋ] *n* desembalaje *m*; desempaquetado *m*.
unpaid ['ʌn'peɪd] *adj* *bill* por pagar, no pagado; *debt* no liquidado; *work, person* no retribuido.
unpalatable [ʌn'pælɪtəbl] *adj* *food* incomible, de mal sabor; (*fig*) desagradable, intragable, nada grato; **the ~ truth** la verdad lisa y llana.
unparalleled [ʌn'pærəleld] *adj* sin paralelo, incomparable, sin par; sin precedentes; **this is ~ in our history** esto no tiene precedentes en nuestra historia.
unpardonable [ʌn'pɑːdnəbl] *adj* imperdonable, indisculpable.
unpardonably [ʌn'pɑːdnəblɪ] *adv* imperdonablemente.
unparliamentary ['ʌnˌpɑːlə'mentərɪ] *adj* antiparlamentario.
unpatented ['ʌnˌpeɪtntɪd] *adj* sin patentar.
unpatriotic ['ʌnˌpætrɪ'ɒtɪk] *adj* antipatriótico.
unpatriotically ['ʌnˌpætrɪ'ɒtɪkəlɪ] *adv* de modo antipatriótico.
unpaved ['ʌn'peɪvd] *adj* sin pavimentar.
unperceived ['ʌnpə'siːvd] *adj* inadvertido, desapercibido.
unperturbed ['ʌnpɜː'tɜːbd] *adj* impertérrito; **he carried on ~** continuó sin alterarse, siguió sin inmutarse; **~ by this disaster** ... sin dejarse desanimar por esta catástrofe ...
unpick ['ʌn'pɪk] *vt* *seam* descoser.
unpin ['ʌn'pɪn] *vt* desprender; quitar los alfileres de.
unplaced ['ʌn'pleɪst] *adj* (*Sport*) no colocado.
unplanned ['ʌn'plænd] *adj* sin planear; imprevisto.
unplayable ['ʌn'pleɪəbl] *adj* *pitch* en condiciones tan malas que está inservible.
unpleasant [ʌn'pleznt] *adj* desagradable; repugnante; *person* (*by character*) antipático, (*in words etc*) grosero, mal educado; **he was ~ to her** se portó groseramente con ella; **he had some very ~ things to say** hizo unas observaciones de las más desagradables; **it was a most ~ hour** fue una hora muy desagradable.
unpleasantly [ʌn'plezntlɪ] *adv* desagradablemente; **'No', he said ~** 'No', dijo en tono nada amistoso; **the bomb fell ~ close** cayó la bomba lo bastante cerca como para inquietarnos.
unpleasantness [ʌn'plezntnɪs] *n* lo desagradable; lo repugnante; antipatía *f*; (*quarrel*) desavenencia *f*, disgusto *m*; **that ~ with the conductor** aquel disgusto con el cobrador; **there has been a lot of ~** ha habido muchos disgustos.
unpleasing [ʌn'pliːzɪŋ] *adj* poco atractivo, antiestético; poco grato (*to* a).
unplug ['ʌn'plʌg] *vt* desenchufar, desconectar.
unplumbed ['ʌn'plʌmd] *adj* no sondado, insondable.
unpoetic(al) ['ʌnpəʊ'etɪk(əl)] *adj* poco poético.
unpolished ['ʌn'pɒlɪʃt] *adj* sin pulir; *diamond* en bruto; (*fig*) grosero, tosco, inculto.
unpolluted ['ʌnpə'luːtɪd] *adj* impoluto; no contaminado.
unpopular ['ʌn'pɒpjʊlə'] *adj* impopular, poco popular; **it is ~ with the miners** los mineros no lo quieren; **the decision is ~** la decisión no es popular; **to make o.s. ~** hacerse detestar; **you will be very ~ with me** no te lo agradeceré.
unpopularity ['ʌnˌpɒpjʊ'lærɪtɪ] *n* impopularidad *f*.
unpopulated ['ʌn'pɒpjʊleɪtɪd] *adj* deshabitado, desierto.

unpractical ['ʌn'præktɪkəl] *adj* falto de sentido práctico, poco práctico, desmañado.
unpractised, (*US*) **unpracticed** [ʌn'præktɪst] *adj* inexperto.
unprecedented [ʌn'presɪdəntɪd] *adj* sin precedentes, inaudito.
unpredictability ['ʌnprɪˌdɪktə'bɪlɪtɪ] *n* imprevisibilidad *f*, incertidumbre *f*; carácter *m* caprichoso, volubilidad *f*.
unpredictable ['ʌnprɪ'dɪktəbl] *adj thing* imprevisible, incierto; *person* caprichoso, voluble, de reacciones imprevisibles, desconcertante.
unpredictably ['ʌnprɪ'dɪktəblɪ] *adv* de manera imprevisible; caprichosamente, de manera voluble; de manera desconcertante.
unprejudiced [ʌn'predʒʊdɪst] *adj* imparcial.
unpremeditated ['ʌnprɪ'medɪteɪtɪd] *adj* impremeditado.
unprepared ['ʌnprɪ'pɛəd] *adj* no preparado; *speech etc* improvisado; **to be ~ for sth** no contar con algo, no esperar algo; **to catch sb ~** coger (*LAm*: agarrar) a uno desprevenido.
unpreparedness ['ʌnprɪ'pɛərɪdnɪs] *n* desapercibimiento *m*, desprevención *f*.
unprepossessing ['ʌnˌpriːpə'zesɪŋ] *adj* poco atractivo.
unpresentable ['ʌnprɪ'zentəbl] *adj* mal apersonado.
unpretentious ['ʌnprɪ'tenʃəs] *adj* modesto, nada pretencioso, sin pretensiones.
unpriced ['ʌn'praɪst] *adj* sin precio.
unprincipled [ʌn'prɪnsɪpld] *adj* poco escrupuloso, cínico, sin conciencia.
unprintable ['ʌn'prɪntəbl] *adj* intranscribible, indecente.
unproductive ['ʌnprə'dʌktɪv] *adj capital, soil etc* improductivo; *meeting etc* infructuoso.
unprofessional ['ʌnprə'feʃənl] *adj* (*ethically*) indigno de su profesión; contrario a la ética profesional; (*unskilled*) inexperto.
unprofitable [ʌn'prɒfɪtəbl] *adj enterprise* improductivo; *meeting etc* infructuoso; (*useless*) inútil; (*financially*) antieconómico, poco provechoso, nada lucrativo.
unpromising ['ʌn'prɒmɪsɪŋ] *adj* poco prometedor; **it looks ~** no promete mucho.
unprompted ['ʌn'prɒmptɪd] *adj* espontáneo.
unpronounceable ['ʌnprə'naʊnsəbl] *adj* impronunciable.
unpropitious ['ʌnprə'pɪʃəs] *adj* impropicio, poco propicio.
unprotected ['ʌnprə'tektɪd] *adj* sin protección, desprotegido, indefenso.
unproved ['ʌn'pruːvd] *adj* no probado.
unprovided ['ʌnprə'vaɪdɪd] *adj*: **~ for** (*unforeseen*) imprevisto; (*person*) desamparado, desvalido; **~ with** desprovisto de.
unprovoked ['ʌnprə'vəʊkt] *adj* no provocado, sin provocación.
unpublished ['ʌn'pʌblɪʃt] *adj* inédito, sin publicar.
unpunctual ['ʌn'pʌŋktjʊəl] *adj* poco puntual; **this train is always ~** este tren siempre llega con retraso.
unpunctuality ['ʌnˌpʌŋktjʊ'ælɪtɪ] *n* falta *f* de puntualidad; atraso *m*.
unpunished ['ʌn'pʌnɪʃt] *adj* impune; **to go ~** (*crime*) quedar sin castigo; (*person*) escapar sin castigo, salir impune.
unputdownable ['ʌnpʊt'daʊnəbl] *adj* que no se puede dejar de la mano, absorbente.
unqualified ['ʌn'kwɒlɪfaɪd] *adj person* incompetente; sin título; *workman* no cualificado; *success, assertion* incondicional; *praise* grande; **to be ~ to do sth** no reunir las condiciones para hacer algo.
unquenchable [ʌn'kwentʃəbl] *adj* (*fig*) inextinguible; *thirst* inapagable; *desire etc* insaciable.
unquestionable [ʌn'kwestʃənəbl] *adj* incuestionable, indiscutible.
unquestionably [ʌn'kwestʃənəblɪ] *adv* indudablemente.
unquestioned [ʌn'kwestʃənd] *adj* indiscutido, incontestable.
unquestioning [ʌn'kwestʃənɪŋ] *adj* incondicional; *faith etc* ciego.
unquestioningly [ʌn'kwestʃənɪŋlɪ] *adv* incondicionalmente; ciegamente.
unquiet ['ʌn'kwaɪət] *adj* inquieto.
unquote ['ʌn'kwəʊt] *n*: **'~'** 'fin *m* de la cita'.
unquoted ['ʌn'kwəʊtɪd] *adj share etc* no cotizado, sin cotización oficial.
unravel [ʌn'rævəl] *vt* desenmarañar; (*fig*) desenmarañar, desembrollar.
unread ['ʌn'red] *adj* no leído; **to leave sth ~** dejar algo sin leer.
unreadable ['ʌn'riːdəbl] *adj* ilegible; (*fig*) imposible de leer, de lectura muy pesada; **I found the book ~** el libro me resultó pesadísimo.
unreadiness ['ʌn'redɪnɪs] *n* desapercibimiento *m*; desprevención *f*.
unready ['ʌn'redɪ] *adj* desapercibido, desprevenido.
unreal ['ʌn'rɪəl] *adj* (**a**) irreal; imaginario, ilusorio. (**b**) (*esp US**) (*extraordinary*) increíble; (*difficult*) dificilísimo.
unrealistic ['ʌnrɪə'lɪstɪk] *adj* ilusorio, fantástico; irrealista; *estimate etc* no basado en los hechos, disparatado; *scheme* impracticable; *person* poco realista.
unrealistically ['ʌnrɪə'lɪstɪkəlɪ] *adv* ilusoriamente; impracticablemente; poco realistamente.
unreality ['ʌnrɪ'ælɪtɪ] *n* irrealidad *f*.
unrealizable ['ʌnrɪə'laɪzəbl] *adj* irrealizable.
unrealized ['ʌn'rɪːəlaɪzd] *adj* no realizado, que ha quedado sin realizar; *objective* no logrado.
unreason ['ʌn'riːzn] *n* insensatez *f*.
unreasonable [ʌn'riːznəbl] *adj* irrazonable, poco razonable; *demand etc* excesivo; **he was most ~ about it** se negó a considerarlo razonablemente; **don't be so ~!** ¡no seas tan porfiado!; ¡no te pongas así!
unreasonableness [ʌn'riːznəblnɪs] *n* irracionalidad *f*; exorbitancia *f*, lo excesivo; (*of person*) porfía *f*.
unreasonably [ʌn'riːznəblɪ] *adv*: **to be ~ difficult about sth** porfiar estúpidamente en algo.
unreasoning [ʌn'riːznɪŋ] *adj* irracional.
unreceptive ['ʌnrɪ'septɪv] *adj* poco receptivo.
unreclaimed ['ʌnrɪ'kleɪmd] *adj land* no rescatado, no utilizado.
unrecognizable ['ʌn'rekəgnaɪzəbl] *adj* irreconocible, desconocido.
unrecognized ['ʌn'rekəgnaɪzd] *adj* no reconocido; **he went ~ through the market** atravesó el mercado sin que nadie le conociese.
unreconstructed [ˌʌnriːkəns'trʌktɪd] *adj* (*fig*) no reformado, sin reformar; tradicional.
unrecorded ['ʌnrɪ'kɔːdɪd] *adj* no registrado, de que no hay constancia.
unredeemed ['ʌnrɪ'diːmd] *adj* no redimido; *promise* sin cumplir, incumplido; *pledge* no desempeñado; *bill* sin redimir; *debt* sin amortizar; **~ by** no compensado por.
unreel [ʌn'rɪəl] *vt* desenrollar.
unrefined ['ʌnrɪ'faɪnd] *adj material* no refinado; (*fig*) inculto.
unreflecting ['ʌnrɪ'flektɪŋ] *adj* irreflexivo.
unreformed ['ʌnrɪ'fɔːmd] *adj* no reformado.
unregarded ['ʌnrɪ'gɑːdɪd] *adj* desatendido, no estimado; **those ~ aspects** aquellos aspectos de los que nadie hace caso.
unregenerate ['ʌnrɪ'dʒenərɪt] *adj* empedernido.
unregistered ['ʌn'redʒɪstəd] *adj* no registrado; *letter* sin certificar.
unregretted ['ʌnrɪ'gretɪd] *adj* no llorado, no lamentado.
unrehearsed ['ʌnrɪ'hɜːst] *adj speech etc* improvisado; *incident* imprevisto.
unrelated ['ʌnrɪ'leɪtɪd] *adj* inconexo.
unrelenting ['ʌnrɪ'lentɪŋ] *adj* inexorable, implacable.
unreliability ['ʌnrɪˌlaɪə'bɪlɪtɪ] *n* falta *f* de fiabilidad.
unreliable ['ʌnrɪ'laɪəbl] *adj person* informal, de poca confianza; *news* nada fidedigno; *machine etc* que no es de fiar.
unrelieved ['ʌnrɪ'liːvd] *adj* absoluto, monótono, total; **~ by** no aliviado por, no mitigado por; **3 hours of ~ boredom** 3 horas de aburrimiento total.
unremarkable ['ʌnrɪ'mɑːkəbl] *adj* ordinario, corriente.
unremarked ['ʌnrɪ'mɑːkt] *adj* inadvertido.
unremitting ['ʌnrɪ'mɪtɪŋ] *adj* infatigable, incansable; cansante, incesante.
unremittingly ['ʌnrɪ'mɪtɪŋlɪ] *adv* incansablemente.
unremunerative ['ʌnrɪ'mjuːnərətɪv] *adj* poco remunerador, poco lucrativo.
unrepealed ['ʌnrɪ'piːld] *adj* no revocado.
unrepeatable ['ʌnrɪ'piːtəbl] *adj* que no puede repetirse; **what he said is quite ~** no me atrevo a repetir lo que me dijo.
unrepentant ['ʌnrɪ'pentənt] *adj* impenitente.
unreported [ˌʌnrɪ'pɔːtɪd] *adj crime* no denunciado, sin denunciar; **the news went ~** la noticia no fue comunicada.
unrepresentative ['ʌnˌreprɪ'zentətɪv] *adj assembly etc* poco representativo; (*untypical*) poco típico, nada característico.
unrepresented ['ʌnˌreprɪ'zentɪd] *adj* sin representación; **they are ~ in the House** no tienen representación en la Cámara.
unrequited ['ʌnrɪ'kwaɪtɪd] *adj* no correspondido.
unreserved ['ʌnrɪ'zɜːvd] *adj* no reservado, libre.

unreservedly [ˈʌnrɪˈzɜːvɪdlɪ] *adv* sin reserva, incondicionalmente.

unresisting [ˈʌnrɪˈzɪstɪŋ] *adj* sumiso.

unresolved [ˈʌnrɪˈzɒlvd] *adj problem* no resuelto, pendiente.

unresponsive [ˈʌnrɪsˈpɒnsɪv] *adj* insensible, sordo (*to* a).

unrest [ʌnˈrest] *n* malestar *m*, inquietud *f*; (*Pol*) conflictividad *f*, desasosiego *m*, (*active*) desorden *m*; **the ~ in the Congo** los disturbios del Congo.

unrestrained [ˈʌnrɪˈstreɪnd] *adj* desenfrenado, desembarazado (de trabas); *language, remarks* libre.

unrestrainedly [ˈʌnrɪˈstreɪnɪdlɪ] *adv* desenfrenadamente, con desenfreno; sin trabas; libremente.

unrestricted [ˈʌnrɪˈstrɪktɪd] *adj* sin restricción, libre.

unrevealed [ˈʌnrɪˈviːld] *adj* no revelado.

unrewarded [ˈʌnrɪˈwɔːdɪd] *adj* sin recompensa, sin premio; **his work went ~** su labor quedó sin recompensa.

unrewarding [ˈʌnrɪˈwɔːdɪŋ] *adj* sin provecho, infructuoso, inútil.

unrighteous [ʌnˈraɪtʃəs] **1** *adj* malo, perverso. **2** *npl*: **the ~** los malos, los perversos.

unripe [ˈʌnˈraɪp] *adj* verde, inmaturo.

unrivalled, (*US*) **unrivaled** [ʌnˈraɪvəld] *adj* sin par, incomparable; **Bilbao is ~ for food** la cocina bilbaína es incomparable.

unroadworthy [ˈʌnˈrəʊd,wɜːðɪ] *adj* en condiciones no aptas para circular.

unrobe [ˈʌnˈrəʊb] **1** *vi* desvestirse, desnudarse. **2** *vt* (*frm*) desvestir, desnudar.

unroll [ˈʌnˈrəʊl] **1** *vt* desenrollar. **2** *vi* desenrollarse.

unromantic [ˈʌnrəˈmæntɪk] *adj* poco romántico.

unroof [ˈʌnˈruːf] *vt* destechar, quitar el techo de.

unrope [ˈʌnˈrəʊp] **1** *vt* desatar. **2** *vi* desatarse.

unruffled [ˈʌnˈrʌfld] *adj person* imperturbable, ecuánime; *hair, surface* liso; **he carried on quite ~** siguió sin inmutarse.

unruled [ˈʌnˈruːld] *adj paper* sin rayar.

unruly [ʌnˈruːlɪ] *adj* revoltoso, ingobernable; *hair* despeinado.

UNRWA [ˈʌnrə] *n abbr of* **United Nations Relief and Works Agency.**

unsaddle [ˈʌnˈsædl] *vt rider* desarzonar; *horse* desensillar, quitar la silla a.

unsafe [ˈʌnˈseɪf] *adj machine, car etc* inseguro; *policy, journey* peligroso, arriesgado; **~ to eat** malo para comer; **~ to drink** malo para beber; **it is ~ to rely on it** no se puede contar con eso; **it is ~ to let him have a gun** es peligroso permitirle llevar escopeta.

unsaid [ˈʌnˈsed] *adj* sin decir, sin expresar; **to leave sth ~** callar algo, dejar de decir algo; **to leave nothing ~** no dejar nada en el tintero; **much was left ~** se dejaron de decir muchas cosas.

unsalaried [ˈʌnˈsælərɪd] *adj* sin sueldo, no remunerado.

unsal(e)able [ˈʌnˈseɪləbl] *adj* invendible.

unsalted [ˌʌnˈsɒltɪd] *adj* sin sal.

unsanitary [ˌʌnˈsænɪtərɪ] *adj* insalubre, antihigiénico.

unsatisfactory [ˈʌn,sætɪsˈfæktərɪ] *adj* insatisfactorio.

unsatisfied [ˈʌnˈsætɪsfaɪd] *adj* insatisfecho.

unsatisfying [ˈʌnˈsætɪsfaɪɪŋ] *adj* que no satisface, insuficiente.

unsaturated [ˈʌnˈsætʃəreɪtɪd] *adj* no saturado, insaturado.

unsavoury, (*US*) **unsavory** [ˈʌnˈseɪvərɪ] *adj* desagradable, repugnante; *person* indeseable.

unsay [ˈʌnˈseɪ] (*irr*: *V* **say**) *vt* desdecirse de.

unscathed [ˈʌnˈskeɪðd] *adj* ileso; **to get out ~** salir ileso.

unscheduled [ˈʌnˈʃedjuːld] *adj* no programado; no previsto.

unscholarly [ˈʌnˈskɒləlɪ] *adj person* nada erudito; poco metódico; *work* indigno de un erudito.

unschooled [ˈʌnˈskuːld] *adj* indocto; no instruido, sin instrucción; **to be ~ in a technique** no haber aprendido nada de una técnica.

unscientific [ˈʌn,saɪənˈtɪfɪk] *adj* poco científico.

unscramble [ˈʌnˈskræmbl] *vt message* descifrar; (*TV*) descodificar.

unscrew [ˈʌnˈskruː] *vt* destornillar.

unscripted [ˈʌnˈskrɪptɪd] *adj* improvisado; sin guión.

unscrupulous [ʌnˈskruːpjʊləs] *adj* poco escrupuloso, sin escrúpulos, desaprensivo.

unscrupulously [ʌnˈskruːpjʊləslɪ] *adv* de modo poco escrupuloso.

unscrupulousness [ʌnˈskruːpjʊləsnɪs] *n* falta *f* de escrúpulos, desaprensión *f*.

unseal [ˈʌnˈsiːl] *vt* desellar, abrir.

unseasonable [ʌnˈsiːznəbl] *adj* intempestivo; fuera de estación.

unseasonably [ʌnˈsiːznəblɪ] *adv* inoportunamente.

unseasoned [ˈʌnˈsiːznd] *adj* no sazonado.

unseat [ˈʌnˈsiːt] *vt rider* desarzonar; *passenger etc* echar de su asiento; (*Parl*) hacer perder su escaño.

unseaworthy [ˈʌnˈsiː,wɜːðɪ] *adj* innavegable.

unsecured [ˈʌnsɪˈkjʊəd] *adj* (*Fin*) no respaldado, sin aval; **~ creditor** acreedor *m* común; **~ debt** deuda *f* sin respaldo.

unseeded [ˈʌnˈsiːdɪd] *adj player* no preseleccionado.

unseeing [ˈʌnˈsiːɪŋ] *adj* (*fig*) ciego.

unseemliness [ʌnˈsiːmlɪnɪs] *n* lo indecoroso, falta *f* de decoro, impropiedad *f*.

unseemly [ʌnˈsiːmlɪ] *adj* indecoroso, impropio.

unseen [ˈʌnˈsiːn] **1** *adj* invisible; secreto, oculto; inadvertido; *translation* hecho a primera vista; **he managed to get through ~** logró pasar inadvertido.

2 *n* (**a**) (*esp Brit*) traducción *f* hecha a primera vista. (**b**) **the ~** lo invisible, lo oculto.

unsegregated [ˈʌnˈsegrɪgeɪtɪd] *adj* no segregado, sin segregación (racial *etc*).

unselfconscious [ˈʌn,selfˈkɒnʃəs] *adj* natural.

unselfconsciously [ˈʌn,selfˈkɒnʃəslɪ] *adv* de manera desenfadada.

unselfish [ˈʌnˈselfɪʃ] *adj* desinteresado; abnegado; altruista.

unselfishly [ˈʌnˈselfɪʃlɪ] *adv* desinteresadamente; abnegadamente; de modo altruista, con altruismo.

unselfishness [ˈʌnˈselfɪʃnɪs] *n* desinterés *m*; abnegación *f*; altruismo *m*.

unsentimental [ˈʌnsentɪˈmentəl] *adj* nada sentimental.

unserviceable [ˈʌnˈsɜːvɪsəbl] *adj* inservible, inútil.

unsettle [ˈʌnˈsetl] *vt* perturbar, agitar, inquietar.

unsettled [ˈʌnˈsetld] *adj person* inquieto, intranquilo; *weather* variable; *state, market* inestable; *land* inhabitado, despoblado, no colonizado, sin poblar; *question* pendiente; *account* por pagar; **he's feeling ~ in his job** no está del todo contento en su puesto, se siente algo molesto en su puesto.

unsettling [ˈʌnˈsetlɪŋ] *adj influence etc* perturbador, inquietante.

unsex [ˈʌnˈseks] *vt* privar de la sexualidad, suprimir el instinto sexual de.

unshackle [ˈʌnˈʃækl] *vt* desencadenar, quitar los grillos a.

unshaded [ˈʌnˈʃeɪdɪd] *adj place* sin sombra; con luz directa; *bulb* sin pantalla.

unshak(e)able [ˈʌnˈʃeɪkəbl] *adj resolve* inquebrantable; **he was ~ in his resolve** se mostró totalmente resuelto; **after 3 hours he was still ~** después de 3 horas siguió tan resuelto como antes.

unshaken [ˈʌnˈʃeɪkən] *adj* impertérrito; **he was ~ by what had happened** no se dejó amedrentar por lo que había pasado.

unshaven [ˈʌnˈʃeɪvn] *adj* sin afeitar.

unsheathe [ˈʌnˈʃiːð] *vt* desenvainar.

unship [ˈʌnˈʃɪp] *vt goods* desembarcar; *rudder, mast etc* desmontar.

unshockable [ˈʌnˈʃɒkəbl] *adj*: **she's ~** no se escandaliza por nada, no es fácil que se asombre.

unshod [ˈʌnˈʃɒd] *adj* descalzo; *horse* desherrado.

unshrinkable [ˈʌnˈʃrɪŋkəbl] *adj* inencogible.

unshrinking [ʌnˈʃrɪŋkɪŋ] *adj* impávido.

unsighted [ˈʌnˈsaɪtɪd] *adj*: **I was ~ for a moment** por un momento no pude ver, por un momento tuve la vista impedida.

unsightliness [ʌnˈsaɪtlɪnɪs] *n* fealdad *f*.

unsightly [ʌnˈsaɪtlɪ] *adj* feo, repugnante.

unsigned [ˈʌnˈsaɪnd] *adj* sin firmar.

unsinkable [ˈʌnˈsɪŋkəbl] *adj* insumergible.

unskilled [ˈʌnˈskɪld] *adj worker* no cualificado; *work* no especializado.

unskil(l)ful [ˈʌnˈskɪlfʊl] *adj* inexperto, desmañado.

unskimmed [ˈʌnˈskɪmd] *adj* sin desnatar.

unsmiling [ˈʌnˈsmaɪlɪŋ] *adj* sin sonrisa.

unsmilingly [ˈʌnˈsmaɪlɪŋlɪ] *adv* sin sonreír; con gesto severo.

unsociability [ˈʌn,səʊʃəˈbɪlɪtɪ] *n* insociabilidad *f*.

unsociable [ʌnˈsəʊʃəbl] *adj* insociable; *person* poco sociable, huraño.

unsocial [ʌnˈsəʊʃəl] *adj*: **to work ~ hours** trabajar fuera de las horas normales.

unsold [ˈʌnˈsəʊld] *adj* sin vender; **to remain ~** quedar sin vender.

unsoldierly [ˈʌnˈsəʊldʒəlɪ] *adj* indigno de un militar, impropio de un militar.

unsolicited [ˈʌnsəˈlɪsɪtɪd] *adj* no solicitado.

unsolvable [ˈʌnˈsɒlvəbl] *adj* irresoluble, insoluble.

unsolved [ˈʌnˈsɒlvd] *adj* no resuelto; **~ crime** crimen *m* que sigue sin resolver.

unsophisticated ['ʌnsə'fɪstɪkeɪtɪd] *adj* sencillo, cándido, ingenuo.
unsought ['ʌn'sɔːt] *adj* no solicitado; no buscado; **the offer came quite ~** se hizo la oferta sin que se hubiera pedido nada.
unsound ['ʌn'saʊnd] *adj* (*in construction*) defectuoso; *fruit* podrido; *argument, opinion* falso, erróneo; **of ~ mind** mentalmente incapacitado; **the book is ~ on some points** no hay que fiarse del libro en ciertos aspectos, el libro tiene algunas cosas erróneas.
unsoundness ['ʌn'saʊndnɪs] *n* lo defectuoso; falsedad *f*, lo erróneo.
unsparing [ʌn'spɛərɪŋ] *adj* (*generous*) generoso, pródigo; *effort* incansable; (*cruel*) despiadado; **to be ~ of praises** no escatimar las alabanzas; **to be ~ in one's efforts to** + *infin* no regatear esfuerzo por + *infin*.
unsparingly [ʌn'spɛərɪŋlɪ] *adv* generosamente, pródigamente; incansablemente.
unspeakable [ʌn'spiːkəbl] *adj* indecible; (*very bad*) incalificable.
unspeakably [ʌn'spiːkəblɪ] *adv*: **to suffer ~** sufrir lo indecible; **it was ~ bad** fue horroroso.
unspecified ['ʌn'spesɪfaɪd] *adj* no especificado.
unspectacular [ˌʌnspek'tækjʊləʳ] *adj* poco aparatoso; nada llamativo.
unspent ['ʌn'spent] *adj* no gastado.
unsplinterable ['ʌn'splɪntərəbl] *adj* inastillable.
unspoiled ['ʌn'spɔɪld] *adj*, **unspoilt** ['ʌn'spɔɪlt] *adj* intacto; no estropeado; *child* natural, no mimado; *countryside* que conserva sus encantos, que sigue en su estado natural.
unspoken ['ʌn'spəʊkən] *adj* no expresado, tácito.
unsporting ['ʌn'spɔːtɪŋ] *adj*, **unsportsmanlike** ['ʌn'spɔːtsmənlaɪk] *adj* antideportivo.
unstable ['ʌn'steɪbl] *adj* inestable.
unstamped ['ʌn'stæmpt] *adj* sin sello, sin franquear.
unstated [ʌn'steɪtɪd] *adj wish etc* no expresado; *understanding* tácito.
unstatesmanlike ['ʌn'steɪtsmənlaɪk] *adj* indigno (*or* impropio) de un estadista.
unsteadily ['ʌn'stedɪlɪ] *adv* inestablemente, inseguramente; inconstantemente.
unsteadiness ['ʌn'stedɪnɪs] *n* inestabilidad *f*, inseguridad *f*; inconstancia *f*; lo movedizo, falta *f* de firmeza.
unsteady ['ʌn'stedɪ] *adj* inestable, inseguro; inconstante; (*shaky*) movedizo, poco firme; **to be ~ on one's feet** no poder estar de pie sin tambalearse, titubear.
unstick ['ʌn'stɪk] *vt* despegar.
unstinted [ʌn'stɪntɪd] *adj praise etc* generoso; *effort* incansable.
unstinting [ʌn'stɪntɪŋ] *adj*: **to be ~ in one's praise** ser pródigo de alabanzas, no escatimar sus alabanzas; **to be ~ in one's efforts to** + *infin* no regatear esfuerzo por + *infin*.
unstitch ['ʌn'stɪtʃ] *vt* descoser; **to come ~ed** descoserse.
unstop ['ʌn'stɒp] *vt* desobstruir, desatascar.
unstoppable ['ʌn'stɒpəbl] *adj* incontenible, irrefrenable; (*Sport*) *shot etc* imparable.
unstrap [ʌn'stræp] *vt* quitar la correa de; soltar.
unstressed ['ʌn'strest] *adj* átono, inacentuado.
unstring ['ʌn'strɪŋ] (*irr*: *V* **string**) *vt* (*Mus*) desencordar; *nerves* trastornar; *pearls* desensartar.
unstructured ['ʌn'strʌktʃəd] *adj* sin estructura, no estructurado.
unstuck ['ʌn'stʌk] *adj*: **to come ~** despegarse, desprenderse, soltarse; (*fig*) fracasar; sufrir un revés; **where he comes ~ is ...** a él lo que le pierde es ...
unstudied ['ʌn'stʌdɪd] *adj* natural, sin afectación.
unsubdued ['ʌnsəb'djuːd] *adj* indomado.
unsubmissive ['ʌnsəb'mɪsɪv] *adj* insumiso.
unsubstantial ['ʌnsəb'stænʃəl] *adj* insustancial.
unsubstantiated ['ʌnsəb'stænʃɪeɪtɪd] *adj* no probado, no corroborado.
unsuccessful ['ʌnsək'sesfʊl] *adj person, negotiation etc* fracasado; *effort etc* infructuoso, inútil, ineficaz; infeliz; **to be ~** fracasar, malograrse, no tener éxito; no poder; **to be ~ in doing sth** no lograr hacer algo, fracasar en sus esfuerzos por hacer algo, no poder hacer algo.
unsuccessfully ['ʌnsək'sesfəlɪ] *adv* en vano, sin éxito, inútilmente.
unsuitability ['ʌn,suːtə'bɪlɪtɪ] *n* impropiedad *f*; inconveniencia *f*; lo inadecuado; lo inoportuno; incompetencia *f*; ineptitud *f*.
unsuitable ['ʌn'suːtəbl] *adj* inapropiado; inconveniente; inadecuado; inoportuno; (*in a post etc*) inepto, no apto; **a most ~ word** una palabra sumamente impropia; **he married a most ~ girl** se casó con una chica nada conveniente; **the film is ~ for children** la película no es apta para menores.
unsuitably ['ʌn'suːtəblɪ] *adv* inapropiadamente; **~ dressed** vestido de manera inapropiada.
unsuited ['ʌn'suːtɪd] *adj*: **~ for** inepto para, no apto para; **~ to do sth** inepto para hacer algo; **they are ~ to each other** son incompatibles (el uno con el otro).
unsullied ['ʌn'sʌlɪd] *adj* inmaculado, no corrompido; **~ by** no corrompido por.
unsung ['ʌn'sʌŋ] *adj* desconocido, no celebrado.
unsupported ['ʌnsə'pɔːtɪd] *adj statement etc* que carece de base firme, no apoyado por datos; *candidate* sin apoyo, no respaldado por nadie.
unsure ['ʌn'ʃʊəʳ] *adj* inseguro, poco seguro; **he seemed very ~ about it** no parecía estar muy seguro de ello.
unsurmountable ['ʌnsə'maʊntəbl] *adj* insuperable.
unsurpassable ['ʌnsə'pɑːsəbl] *adj* inmejorable, insuperable.
unsurpassed ['ʌnsə'pɑːst] *adj* insuperado, sin par; **~ in quality** de calidad inmejorable; **~ by anybody** no superado por nadie.
unsurprising ['ʌnsə'praɪzɪŋ] *adj* nada sorprendente.
unsurprisingly ['ʌnsə'praɪzɪŋlɪ] *adv*: **the news was received, ~, in silence** la noticia fue recibida, naturalmente, en silencio.
unsuspected ['ʌnsəs'pektɪd] *adj* insospechado.
unsuspecting ['ʌnsəs'pektɪŋ] *adj* nada suspicaz, sin recelo, confiado, desprevenido.
unsweetened ['ʌn'swiːtnd] *adj* sin azucarar.
unswerving [ʌn'swɜːvɪŋ] *adv resolve* inquebrantable; *loyalty* inquebrantable, firme; *course* sin vacilar.
unswervingly [ʌn'swɜːvɪŋlɪ] *adv*: **to be ~ loyal to sb** seguir totalmente leal a uno; **to hold ~ to one's course** seguir sin vacilar.
unsympathetic ['ʌn,sɪmpə'θetɪk] *adj* incompasivo, poco compasivo; falto de comprensión; indiferente; **he was totally ~** no mostró la más mínima comprensión; **they were ~ to my plea** no hicieron caso de mi ruego; **I am not ~ to your request** no veo con malos ojos su petición.
unsystematic ['ʌn,sɪstɪ'mætɪk] *adj* poco sistemático, poco metódico.
unsystematically ['ʌn,sɪstɪ'mætɪkəlɪ] *adv* de modo poco metódico.
untainted ['ʌn'teɪntɪd] *adj* inmaculado, no corrompido; *food* no contaminado; **~ by** no corrompido por.
untam(e)able ['ʌn'teɪməbl] *adj* indomable.
untamed ['ʌn'teɪmd] *adj* indomado.
untangle ['ʌn'tæŋgl] *vt* desenmarañar.
untanned ['ʌn'tænd] *adj* sin curtir.
untapped ['ʌn'tæpt] *adj resources* sin explotar.
untarnished ['ʌn'tɑːnɪʃt] *adj reputation etc* sin tacha.
untasted ['ʌn'teɪstɪd] *adj* sin probar.
untaught ['ʌn'tɔːt] *adj* no enseñado; (*ignorant*) sin instrucción.
untaxed ['ʌn'tækst] *adj* libre de impuestos, no sujeto a contribuciones.
unteachable ['ʌn'tiːtʃəbl] *adj* incapaz de aprender.
untempered ['ʌn'tempəd] *adj steel etc* sin templar.
untenable ['ʌn'tenəbl] *adj* insostenible.
untenanted ['ʌn'tenəntɪd] *adj* desocupado, vacío.
untended [ʌn'tendɪd] *adj* no atendido, no vigilado; **he left the car ~** dejó el coche sin vigilar.
untested ['ʌn'testɪd] *adj* no probado.
unthinkable [ʌn'θɪŋkəbl] **1** *adj* inconcebible, impensable; **it is ~ that ...** es inconcebible que + *subj*. **2** *n*: **the ~** lo inconcebible.
unthinking ['ʌn'θɪŋkɪŋ] *adj* irreflexivo.
unthinkingly ['ʌn'θɪŋkɪŋlɪ] *adv* irreflexivamente, sin pensar.
unthought-of [ʌn'θɔːtɒv] *adj* inimaginable, inconcebible.
unthread ['ʌn'θred] *vt cloth* deshebrar, descoser; *needle* desenhebrar; *pearls* desensartar.
unthrifty ['ʌn'θrɪftɪ] *adj* manirroto; impróvido.
untidily [ʌn'taɪdɪlɪ] *adv* desaliñadamente; sin método; en desorden; **she does everything ~** todo lo hace de cualquier modo.
untidiness [ʌn'taɪdɪnɪs] *n* desaliño *m*; falta *f* de método; desorden *m*.
untidy [ʌn'taɪdɪ] *adj* (*in dress, appearance*) desaliñado, desaseado; *work* poco metódico; *room* en desorden, desordenado; **she's a very ~ person** es una persona que vive sin método, es una persona que hace las cosas (*or* deja sus cosas) de cualquier modo, es una persona desordenada.

untie [ˈʌnˈtaɪ] *vt* desatar.
until [ənˈtɪl] **1** *prep* (*also* **up** ~) hasta; ~ **10** hasta las 10; ~ **his arrival** hasta su llegada.
2 *conj* (**a**) (*of future time*) hasta que + *subj*, *eg* **wait** ~ **I get back** espera hasta que yo vuelva.
(**b**) (*of past time*) hasta que + *indic*, *eg* **he did nothing** ~ **I told him** no hizo nada hasta que yo se lo dije.
untilled [ˈʌnˈtɪld] *adj* sin cultivar.
untimely .[ʌnˈtaɪmlɪ] *adj* intempestivo, inoportuno; prematuro.
untiring [ʌnˈtaɪərɪŋ] *adj* incansable.
untiringly [ʌnˈtaɪərɪŋlɪ] *adv* incansablemente.
unto [ˈʌntʊ] *prep* (††) *V* **to; towards.**
untold [ˈʌnˈtəʊld] *adj story* nunca contado, inédito; *secret* nunca revelado; *loss, wealth etc* incalculable, fabuloso; *suffering* indecible.
untouchable [ʌnˈtʌtʃəbl] (*India*) **1** *adj* intocable. **2** *n* intocable *mf*.
untouched [ˈʌnˈtʌtʃt] *adj* intacto; (*safe*) incólume, indemne; **a product** ~ **by human hand** un producto que ninguna mano humana ha tocado; **he is** ~ **by any plea** es insensible a todas las súplicas; **to leave one's food** ~ dejar su comida sin probar; **those peoples** ~ **by civilization** esos pueblos no alcanzados por la civilización.
untoward [ˌʌntəˈwɔːd] *adj* desfavorable; adverso; *event etc* fatal, funesto.
untrained [ˈʌnˈtreɪnd] *adj person* inexperto; (*unskilled*) no cualificado; *teacher etc* sin título, que no tiene título; (*Sport*) no entrenado; *soldier* desentrenado; *animal* sin amaestrar, no adiestrado.
untrammelled, (*US*) **untrameled** [ʌnˈtræməld] *adj* ilimitado.
untransferable [ˈʌntrænsˈfɜːrəbl] *adj* intransferible.
untranslatable [ˈʌntrænzˈleɪtəbl] *adj* intraducible.
untravelled, (*US*) **untraveled** [ˈʌnˈtrævld] *adj place* inexplorado; *road etc* no trillado, poco frecuentado; *person* que no ha viajado.
untreated [ʌnˈtriːtɪd] *adj injury* no tratado, no curado; *effluent* no tratado, sin tratar.
untried [ˈʌnˈtraɪd] *adj* (**a**) *method etc* no probado; *person* novicio, no puesto a prueba; *soldier* bisoño. (**b**) (*Jur*) *person* no procesado, *case* no visto.
untrimmed [ˈʌnˈtrɪmd] *adj hedge* sin recortar, sin podar; *wood* sin desbastar; *dress* sin guarnición.
untrodden [ˈʌnˈtrɒdn] *adj* no trillado, sin pisar.
untroubled [ˈʌnˈtrʌbld] *adj* tranquilo; ~ **by thoughts of her** sin pensar en ella para nada, no afectado por ningún recuerdo de ella.
untrue [ˈʌnˈtruː] *adj statement* falso; *world etc* ficticio, imaginario; *person* infiel, desleal; **that is wholly** ~ eso es completamente falso.
untrustworthy [ˈʌnˈtrʌstˌwɜːðɪ] *adj person* informal, indigno de confianza; *source etc* no fidedigno; *book etc* de dudosa autoridad; *machine, car* inseguro.
untruth [ˈʌnˈtruːθ] *n, pl* **untruths** [ˈʌnˈtruːðz] mentira *f*.
untruthful [ˈʌnˈtruːθfʊl] *adj* mentiroso, falso.
untruthfully [ˈʌnˈtruːθfəlɪ] *adv* falsamente.
untruthfulness [ˈʌnˈtruːθfʊlnɪs] *n* falsedad *f*.
untutored [ˈʌnˈtjuːtəd] *adj* indocto, poco instruido; *mind, taste* no formado.
untwine [ˈʌnˈtwaɪn] *vt,* **untwist** [ˈʌnˈtwɪst] *vt* destorcer.
untypical [ˈʌnˈtɪpɪkəl] *adj* atípico.
unusable [ˈʌnˈjuːzəbl] *adj* inservible, inútil.
unused *adj* (**a**) [ˈʌnˈjuːzd] *stamp etc* nuevo, sin usar; sin estrenar. (**b**) [ˈʌnˈjuːst] **to be** ~ **to** no estar acostumbrado a.
unusual [ʌnˈjuːʒʊəl] *adj* insólito, poco común, inusual; inusitado.
unusually [ʌnˈjuːʒʊəlɪ] *adv*: **an** ~ **awkward matter** un asunto extraordinariamente difícil; **an** ~ **gifted man** un hombre de talentos poco comunes; **he arrived** ~ **late** llegó más tarde que de costumbre.
unutterable [ʌnˈʌtərəbl] *adj* indecible.
unutterably [ʌnˈʌtərəblɪ] *adv* indeciblemente.
unvaried [ʌnˈvɛərɪd] *adj* sin variación, constante; (*pej*) monótono.
unvarnished [ˈʌnˈvɑːnɪʃt] *adj* sin barnizar; (*fig*) sencillo, llano, sin adornos; **the** ~ **truth** la verdad lisa y llana.
unvarying [ʌnˈvɛərɪɪŋ] *adj* invariable, constante.
unveil [ʌnˈveɪl] *vt* quitar el velo a; *statue etc* descubrir.
unveiling [ʌnˈveɪlɪŋ] *n* descubrimiento *m* (de una estatua); (*ceremony*) inauguración *f*.
unventilated [ˈʌnˈventɪleɪtɪd] *adj* sin ventilación, sin aire.
unverifiable [ˈʌnˈverɪfaɪəbl] *adj* no comprobable, que no puede verificarse.
unverified [ˈʌnˈverɪfaɪd] *adj* sin verificar.
unversed [ˈʌnˈvɜːst] *adj*: ~ **in** poco ducho en.
unvisited [ˈʌnˈvɪzɪtɪd] *adj* no visitado, no frecuentado.
unvoiced [ˈʌnˈvɔɪst] *adj* no expresado; (*Gram*) sordo.
unwaged [ʌnˈweɪdʒd] **1** *adj* sin sueldo. **2** *n*: **the** ~ los que no reciben sueldo.
unwanted [ˈʌnˈwɒntɪd] *adj* superfluo; *child* no deseado; *pregnancy* no deseado, involuntario.
unwarily [ʌnˈwɛərɪlɪ] *adv* imprudentemente, incautamente.
unwariness [ʌnˈwɛərɪnɪs] *n* imprudencia *f*.
unwarlike [ˈʌnˈwɔːlaɪk] *adj* pacífico, poco belicoso.
unwarranted [ʌnˈwɒrəntɪd] *adj* injustificado.
unwary [ʌnˈwɛərɪ] *adj* imprudente, incauto.
unwashed [ˈʌnˈwɒʃt] **1** *adj* sin lavar, sucio. **2** *npl*: **the Great U**~ (*hum*) la plebe.
unwavering [ʌnˈweɪvərɪŋ] *adj loyalty, resolve* inquebrantable, firme; *course* constante; *gaze* fijo.
unwaveringly [ʌnˈweɪvərɪŋlɪ] *adv* firmemente; constantemente; **to hold** ~ **to one's course** seguir su curso sin apartarse para nada de él.
unwearying [ʌnˈwɪərɪɪŋ] *adj* incansable.
unwed [ˈʌnˈwed] *adj* soltero.
unwelcome [ʌnˈwelkəm] *adj* importuno, molesto, inoportuno; desagradable; **a most** ~ **piece of news** una noticia excepcionalmente desagradable (*to* para); **the change is not** ~ el cambio no es del todo molesto para nosotros.
unwelcoming [ʌnˈwelkəmɪŋ] *adj person* nada simpático, poco cordial; *place* poco acogedor.
unwell [ˈʌnˈwel] *adj*: **to be** ~ estar indispuesto; **to feel** ~ sentirse mal; **I felt** ~ **on the ship** me mareé en el barco.
unwholesome [ˈʌnˈhəʊlsəm] *adj* insalubre, nocivo; (*morally*) indeseable.
unwieldy [ʌnˈwiːldɪ] *adj* pesado, abultado, difícil de manejar.
unwilling [ˈʌnˈwɪlɪŋ] *adj* desinclinado; no querer; **to be** ~ **to do sth** no querer hacer algo, estar poco dispuesto a hacer algo; **to be** ~ **for sb to do sth** no querer que uno haga algo, estar poco dispuesto a permitir que uno haga algo.
unwillingly [ˈʌnˈwɪlɪŋlɪ] *adv* de mala gana.
unwillingness [ˈʌnˈwɪlɪŋnɪs] *n* falta *f* de inclinación, desgana *f*; **his** ~ **to help us** su desgana para ayudarnos, su resistencia para ayudarnos.
unwind [ˈʌnˈwaɪnd] (*irr*: *V* **wind²**) **1** *vt* desenvolver; *thread* desovillar. **2** *vi* desenvolverse; desovillarse; (*fig*: *relax*) esparcirse, relajarse.
unwisdom [ˈʌnˈwɪzdəm] *n* imprudencia *f*.
unwise [ˈʌnˈwaɪz] *adj* imprudente; poco aconsejable, desaconsejado; **it would be** ~ **to** + *infin* sería poco aconsejable + *infin*; **that was most** ~ **of you** en eso has sido muy imprudente.
unwisely [ˈʌnˈwaɪzlɪ] *adv* imprudentemente.
unwitting [ʌnˈwɪtɪŋ] *adj* inconsciente.
unwittingly [ʌnˈwɪtɪŋlɪ] *adv* inconscientemente; sin saber, sin darse cuentar.
unwomanly [ʌnˈwʊmənlɪ] *adj* poco femenino.
unwonted [ʌnˈwəʊntɪd] *adj* insólito, inusitado.
unworkable [ˈʌnˈwɜːkəbl] *adj* impracticable; (*Min*) inexplotable.
unworldly [ˈʌnˈwɜːldlɪ] *adj* poco mundano, poco realista.
unworn [ˈʌnˈwɔːn] *adj* nuevo, sin estrenar.
unworthiness [ʌnˈwɜːðɪnɪs] *n* indignidad *f*, falta *f* de mérito.
unworthy [ʌnˈwɜːðɪ] *adj* indigno (*of* de); **to be** ~ **to do sth** ser indigno de hacer algo; **it is** ~ **of attention** no merece atención.
unwounded [ˈʌnˈwuːndɪd] *adj* ileso.
unwrap [ˈʌnˈræp] *vt* desenvolver; *parcel* deshacer, desempaquetar.
unwritten [ˈʌnˈrɪtn] *adj* no escrito.
unyielding [ʌnˈjiːldɪŋ] *adj* inflexible.
unyoke [ˈʌnˈjəʊk] *vt* desuncir.
unzip [ˈʌnˈzɪp] *vt* abrir la cremallera (*LAm*: el cierre) de.
up [ʌp] **1** *adv* (**a**) (*gen*) hacia arriba; arriba, para arriba; en el aire, en lo alto; ~! ¡arriba!, (*from bed*) ¡levántate!; ~ **(with) the revolution!** ¡viva la revolución!; **all the way** ~ durante toda la subida, en todo el recorrido; en toda su extensión; **halfway** ~ a mitad de camino; **'this side** ~**'** 'este lado hacia arriba'; **'road** ~**'** 'cerrado por obras'; ~ **above** allí arriba; **to be** ~ **above sth** estar por encima de algo; ~ **in London** allá en Londres; **my office is 5 floors** ~ mi oficina está en el quinto piso; **we're** ~ **for the day** hemos venido a pasar el día; **when I was** ~ (*Univ*) cuando yo estaba en la universidad, cuando yo era estudiante; **to**

throw sth ~ (in the air) lanzar algo al aire, lanzar algo por alto; **to walk ~ and down** pasearse, andar de un lado para otro, andar de acá para allá.

(**b**) (*out of bed*) **to be ~** estar levantado; **we were ~ at 7** nos levantamos a las 7; **to be ~ and about again** estar levantado ya; estar mucho mejor; **to be ~ and doing** ser activo; **to be ~ all night** no acostarse en toda la noche; **we were still ~ at midnight** a medianoche seguíamos sin acostarnos.

(**c**) (*fig*) **when the sun is ~** después de la salida del sol; cuando brilla el sol; **the river is ~** el río ha subido; **the tide is ~** la marea está alta.

(**d**) (*of price, quantity etc*) **potatoes are ~** han subido las patatas; **the thermometer is ~ 2 degrees** ha subido el termómetro 2 grados; **Ceuta were 3 goals ~** Ceuta tenía 3 goles de ventaja; **we were 20 points ~ on them** les llevábamos una ventaja de 20 puntos.

(**e**) (*upwards*) **from £2 ~** de 2 libras para arriba; **from the age of 13 ~** desde los 13 años para arriba; a partir de los 13 años.

(**f**) (*on a level*) **put it ~ beside the other one** ponlo junto al otro; **to be ~ with sb** estar a la altura de uno, haber alcanzado el nivel de uno; **is he ~ to advanced work?** ¿tiene capacidad para estudios superiores?; **to be ~ to a task** estar a la altura de un cometido; **I don't feel ~ to it** no me siento con fuerzas para ello; **it's not ~ to much** no vale gran cosa; **to be well ~ in maths** ser fuerte en matemáticas.

(**g**) **to be ~ against difficulties** tener dificultades, haber tropezado con dificultades; **to be ~ against it** estar en un aprieto; **now we're really ~ against it!** ¡con la iglesia hemos topado!; **to be ~ against sb** tener que habérselas con uno; *V* **hard** *etc*.

(**h**) (*: *wrong*) **what's ~?** ¿qué pasa?; **what's ~ with John?** ¿qué le pasa a Juan?; **there's sth ~** pasa algo malo, (*of a plot*) están tramando algo.

(**i**) (*finished*) **time is ~** se ha terminado el tiempo permitido, es la hora; se ha agotado el tiempo; **when the period is ~** cuando termine el plazo; **his holiday is ~** han terminado ya sus vacaciones; **our time here is ~** no podemos estar más tiempo aquí, se ha acabado nuestra estancia aquí; *V* **all**.

(**j**) (*as far as*) **~ to** hasta; **~ to now** hasta ahora; **~ to here** hasta aquí; **~ to this week** hasta esta semana; **~ to £10** hasta 10 libras; **to count ~ to 100** contar hasta 100; **they advanced ~ to the wood** avanzaron hasta el bosque.

(**k**) (*busy doing*) **they're ~ to sth** están tramando algo; **what are you ~ to?** ¿qué haces ahí?; **what are you ~ to with that knife?** ¿qué haces con ese cuchillo?; **what does he think he's ~ to?** ¿qué diablos piensa hacer?; **I see what you're ~ to** te veo venir.

(**l**) (*incumbent on*) **it is ~ to you to decide** te toca a ti decidir; **I feel it is ~ to me to tell him** creo que me incumbe a mí decírselo; **if it was ~ to me** si yo tuviera que decidirlo.

(**m**) (*US**) **a bourbon (straight) ~** un bourbon sin hielo; **two fried eggs, ~** un par de huevos fritos boca arriba.

(**n**) **to be ~ and running** estar en funcionamiento; **to get sth ~ and running** poner algo en funcionamiento.

2 *prep* (**a**) en lo alto de; encima de; **~ a tree** en lo alto de un árbol; **halfway ~ the stairs** a mitad de la escalera; **halfway ~ the mountain** a mitad de la subida del monte; **they live further ~ the road** viven en esta calle pero más arriba; **he went off ~ the road** se fue calle arriba; **~ (the) river** río arriba.

(**b**) **~ yours!**‡ ¡vete a hacer puñetas!‡, ¡vete a hacer morcillas!‡

3 *adj* (**a**) **the ~ train** (*Brit*) el tren ascendente.

(**b**) **to be ~*** (*elated*) estar en plena forma.

4 *n* (**a**) **~s and downs** vicisitudes *fpl*, alternativas *fpl*, altibajos *mpl*, peripecias *fpl*; **after many ~s and downs** después de mil peripecias; **the ~s and downs that every politician has** las alternativas a que está sometido todo político.

(**b**) **it's on the ~ and ~** (*Brit*) va cada vez mejor; (*US*) eso está en regla, eso es legítimo.

5 *vt price* subir, aumentar; **to ~ an offer** aumentar una oferta, ofrecer más.

6 *vi* (*) **to ~ and** + *inf* ponerse de repente a + *infin*; **he ~ped and hit her** sin más la pegó; **he ~ped and offed** sin más se largó*; **she ~ped and left** se levantó y se marchó.

up-and-coming [ˈʌpəndˈkʌmɪŋ] *adj* joven y prometedor, nuevo y emprendedor.

up-and-down [ˈʌpənˈdaʊn] *adj movement* vertical, perpendicular; *business, progress etc* poco uniforme, variable; (*eventful*) accidentado, con altibajos.

up-and-under [ˌʌpənˈʌndəʳ] *n* (*Rugby*) patada *f* a seguir.

upbeat [ˈʌpˈbiːt] **1** *adj* (*) optimista, animado, alegre. **2** *n* (*Mus*) tiempo *m* débil, tiempo *m* no acentuado; (*fig: in prosperity*) aumento *m*.

up-bow [ˈʌpbəʊ] *n* (*Mus*) movimiento *m* ascendente del arco.

upbraid [ʌpˈbreɪd] *vt* reprender, censurar; **to ~ sb with sth** censurar algo a uno.

upbringing [ˈʌpˌbrɪŋɪŋ] *n* educación *f*, crianza *f*.

upcast [ˈʌpkɑːst] *n* (*Min; also* **~ shaft**) pozo *m* de ventilación.

upchuck‡ [ˈuptʃʌk] *vi* (*US*) echar los hígados por la boca‡, vomitar.

upcoming [ˈʌpkʌmɪŋ] *adj* (*US*) venidero, futuro; que se acerca.

upcountry [ˈʌpˈkʌntrɪ] **1** *adv*: **to be ~** estar tierra adentro, estar en el interior; **to go ~** ir hacia el interior, penetrar en el interior. **2** *adj* del interior.

up-current [ˈʌpˈkʌrənt] *n* (*Aer*) viento *m* ascendente.

update **1** [ˈʌpdeɪt] *n* puesta *f* al día; actualización *f*; últimas noticias *fpl*; (*~d version*) versión *f* actualizada; **he gave me an ~ on ...** me puso al día con respecto a ... **2** [ʌpˈdeɪt] *vt* modernizar, actualizar; **to ~ sb on a matter** poner a uno al tanto de un asunto, dar a uno los últimos detalles de un asunto.

updating [ʌpˈdeɪtɪŋ] *n* puesta *f* al día; actualización *f*.

upend [ʌpˈend] *vt* poner vertical; volver de arriba abajo, poner al revés; *person* volcar.

up-front* [ʌpˈfrʌnt] **1** *adj* (**a**) (*esp US: frank*) abierto, franco, sincero. (**b**) (*US: important*) importante. (**c**) (*paid in advance*) pagado por adelantado. **2** *adv* (**a**) **to pay ~ for sth** pagar algo por adelantado. (**b**) (*esp US: frankly*) sinceramente, abiertamente.

upgrade **1** [ˈʌpgreɪd] *n* (**a**) (*slope*) cuesta *f*, pendiente *f*; **to be on the ~** ir cuesta arriba, prosperar, estar en auge; (*Med*) estar mejor, estar reponiéndose. (**b**) (*of system etc*) mejoramiento *m*, reforma *f*; (*Comput*) modernización *f*, potenciamiento *m*. **2** [ʌpˈgreɪd] *vt person* ascender; *job* asignar a un grado más alto; valorar en más; *system etc* mejorar, reformar; (*Comput*) modernizar, potenciar, mejorar las prestaciones de.

upgrad(e)able [ʌpˈgreɪdəbl] *adj* mejorable, modernizable.

upheaval [ʌpˈhiːvəl] *n* (*Geol*) solevantamiento *m*; (*fig*) cataclismo *m*, sacudida *f*, convulsión *f*.

uphill [ˈʌpˈhɪl] **1** *adv* cuesta arriba; **to go ~** ir cuesta arriba; **the road goes ~ for 2 miles** la carretera sube durante 2 millas.

2 *adj*: **it's an ~ task** es una labor ardua, es un trabajo ímprobo.

uphold [ʌpˈhəʊld] (*irr: V* **hold**) *vt* (*hold up*) sostener, apoyar; (*maintain*) sostener, defender; (*Jur*) confirmar.

upholder [ʌpˈhəʊldəʳ] *n* defensor *m*, -ora *f*.

upholster [ʌpˈhəʊlstəʳ] *vt* tapizar, entapizar (*with* de); **well ~ed*** atocinado*.

upholsterer [ʌpˈhəʊlstərəʳ] *n* tapicero *m*, -a *f*.

upholstery [ʌpˈhəʊlstərɪ] *n* tapicería *f*, tapizado *m*; (*cushioning etc*) almohadillado *m*; (*Aut etc*) guarnecido *m*, tapizado *m*.

UPI *n* (*US*) *abbr of* **United Press International.**

upkeep [ˈʌpkiːp] *n* conservación *f*; (*of car, house etc*) mantenimiento *m*; (*cost*) gastos *mpl* de mantenimiento.

upland [ˈʌplənd] **1** *n* tierra *f* alta, meseta *f*; **~s** tierras *fpl* altas. **2** *adj* de la meseta.

uplift **1** [ˈʌplɪft] *n* sustentación *f*; (*fig*) inspiración *f*, edificación *f*; **moral ~** edificación *f*. **2** [ʌpˈlɪft] *vt* (*fig*) inspirar, edificar.

uplifted [ʌpˈlɪftɪd] *adj face* vuelto hacia arriba; **with ~ arms** con los brazos en alto.

uplifting [ʌpˈlɪftɪŋ] *adj* inspirador, ennoblecedor, edificante.

up-market [ʌpˈmɑːkɪt] **1** *adj product* superior, para la sección superior del mercado (*or* de la clientela). **2** *adv*: **to go ~** buscar clientela en la sección superior.

upon [əˈpɒn] *prep V* **on.**

upper [ˈʌpəʳ] **1** *adj* superior, más alto; de arriba; *class* alto; *deck, floor etc* superior, de arriba; (*in Geog names*) alto; **~ atmosphere** atmósfera *f* superior; **~ chamber** (*Parl*) cámara *f* alta; **the ~ circle** (*Brit Theat*) la galería superior; **~ class** clase *f* alta; **~ crust*** flor *f* y nata, clase *f* alta; **U~ Egypt** Alto Egipto *m*; **U~ House** (*Parl*) Cámara *f* Alta; **~ lip** labio *m* superior; **~ school** cursos *mpl* superiores.

2 *n* (**a**) (*of shoe*) pala *f*; **to be on one's ~s*** no tener un céntimo.

(**b**) (‡: *drug*) estimulante *m.*

(**c**) (*: *US Rail*) litera *f* de arriba.

upper-case ['ʌpə'keɪs] *attr* mayúsculo, de letra mayúscula.

upper-class ['ʌpə'klɑːs] *adj* de la clase alta.

upper-crust* ['ʌpə'krʌst] *adj* de categoría (social) superior, de buen tono.

uppercut ['ʌpəkʌt] *n* uppercut *m*, gancho *m* a la cara.

uppermost ['ʌpəməʊst] **1** *adj* (**a**) (*highest*) (el) más alto; **to put sth face ~** poner algo cara arriba.

(**b**) (*fig*) principal, predominante; **what is ~ in sb's mind** lo que ocupa el primer lugar en el pensamiento de uno; **it was ~ in my mind** pensé en eso antes que en otra cosa.

2 *adv* encima.

Upper Volta [ˌʌpə'vɒltə] *n* Alto Volta *m.*

uppish* ['ʌpɪʃ] *adj*, **uppity*** ['ʌpɪtɪ] *adj* (*Brit*) engreído; fresco; **to get ~** engreírse.

upraise [ʌp'reɪz] *vt* levantar; **with arm ~d** con el brazo levantado.

upright ['ʌpraɪt] **1** *adj* vertical; derecho; *piano* vertical, recto; (*fig*) honrado, recto, probo.

2 *adv*: **to hold o.s. ~** mantenerse erguido; **to sit bolt ~** (*state*) estar muy derecho en su silla.

3 *n* montante *m*; (*goalpost*) poste *m.*

uprightly ['ʌpˌraɪtlɪ] *adv* (*fig*) honradamente, rectamente.

uprightness ['ʌpˌraɪtnɪs] *n* (*fig*) honradez *f*, rectitud *f.*

uprising ['ʌpraɪzɪŋ] *n* alzamiento *m*, sublevación *f.*

up-river ['ʌp'rɪvə^r] *adv* = **upstream.**

uproar ['ʌprɔː^r] *n* alboroto *m*, tumulto *m*; escándalo *m*; **at this there was ~** en esto estallaron ruidosas las protestas, en esto se armó un escándalo; **the whole place was in ~** la sala estaba alborotada.

uproarious [ʌp'rɔːrɪəs] *adj* tumultuoso, estrepitoso; *laughter* tumultuoso, escandaloso; *joke etc* divertidísimo; *success* clamoroso.

uproariously [ʌp'rɔːrɪəslɪ] *adv* tumultuosamente, con estrépito; **to laugh ~** estar para morirse de risa.

uproot [ʌp'ruːt] *vt* desarraigar, arrancar; (*destroy*) eliminar, extirpar; **whole families have been ~ed** se han desplazado familias enteras.

upsa-daisy ['ʌpsəˌdeɪzɪ] *excl* ¡aúpa!

upset **1** ['ʌpset] *n* (*accident*) vuelco *m*; (*in plans etc*) revés *m*, contratiempo *m*; (*Med*) trastorno *m*, desarreglo *m*; **to have a stomach ~** tener un trastorno estomacal, tener el estómago trastornado.

2 [ʌp'set] (*irr*: *V* **set**) *vt* (*overturn*) volcar, trastornar; (*spill*) derramar; *stomach* trastornar, hacer daño a; *plans etc* dar al traste con; *person* (*emotionally*) desconcertar, alterar, perturbar; **garlic ~s me** el ajo no me sienta bien; **the news ~ her a lot** la noticia le causó gran pesar; **I didn't intend to ~ her** no tenía la intención de alterarla.

3 [ʌp'set] *vr*: **to ~ o.s.** acongojarse, apurarse; preocuparse; **don't ~ yourself!** ¡no te acongojes!, ¡no te preocupes!

4 [ʌp'set] *adj*: **to be ~** estar perturbado, estar acongojado, estar preocupado; sentirse molesto; **to get ~** alterarse, perturbarse; **she looked terribly ~** parecía estar apuradísima; **she is easily ~** se apura por cualquier cosa; **what are you so ~ about?** ¿qué te preocupa tanto?, ¿a qué se debe tanto sentimiento?; **I have an ~ stomach** tengo el estómago trastornado.

5 ['ʌpset] *attr*: **~ price** (*esp Scot, US*) precio *m* mínimo, precio *m* de salida.

upsetting [ʌp'setɪŋ] *adj* inquietante, desconcertante.

upshot ['ʌpʃɒt] *n* resultado *m*; **in the ~** al fin y al cabo; **the ~ of it all was ...** resultó por fin que ...

upside-down ['ʌpsaɪd'daʊn] **1** *adv* al revés; **to turn a box ~** volver una caja al revés, invertir una caja; **to turn a room ~** introducir el desorden en un cuarto; **we turned everything ~ looking for it** al buscarlo lo revolvimos todo, en la búsqueda lo registramos todo de arriba abajo.

2 *adj* al revés; **to be ~** estar al revés, tener lo de arriba abajo; **the room was ~** reinaba la mayor confusión en el cuarto, en el cuarto todo estaba patas arriba.

upstage ['ʌp'steɪdʒ] **1** *adv*: **to be ~** estar en el fondo de la escena; **to go ~** ir hacia el fondo de la escena.

2 *adj* (*) engreído.

3 *vt*: **to ~ sb** lograr captar la atención del público a costa de otro; (*fig*) eclipsar a uno.

upstairs ['ʌp'stɛəz] **1** *adv* arriba; **to go ~** ir arriba, subir al piso superior; **to walk slowly ~** subir lentamente la escalera.

2 *adj* de arriba; **we looked out of an ~ window** nos asomamos a una ventana del piso superior.

3 *n*: **the ~** el piso superior, la parte de arriba.

upstanding [ʌp'stændɪŋ] *adj* (**a**) **a fine ~ young man** un buen mozo gallardo. (**b**) **be ~!** (*Jur etc*) ¡levántense!; ¡de pie, por favor!

upstart ['ʌpstɑːt] **1** *adj* arribista; advenedizo; **some ~ youth** algún joven presuntuoso. **2** *n* arribista *mf*; advenedizo *m*, -a *f*; insolente *mf.*

upstate ['ʌp'steɪt] *adj* (*US, esp of New York*) interior, septentrional.

upstream ['ʌp'striːm] *adv* aguas arriba, río arriba (*from* de); **to go ~** ir río arriba; **to swim ~** nadar contra la corriente; **a town ~ from Windsor** una ciudad más arriba de Windsor; **about 3 miles ~ from Seville** unas 3 millas más arriba de Sevilla.

upstretched ['ʌpstretʃt] *adj* extendido hacia arriba.

upstroke ['ʌpstrəʊk] *n* (*with pen*) trazo *m* ascendente; (*Mech*) carrera *f* ascendente.

upsurge ['ʌpsɜːdʒ] *n* acceso *m*, aumento *m* grande; **a great ~ of interest in Góngora** un gran renacimiento del interés por Góngora; **there has been an ~ of feeling about this question** ha aumentado de pronto la preocupación por esta cuestión.

upswept ['ʌpswept] *adj* *wing* elevado, inclinado hacia arriba; **with ~ hair** con peinado alto.

upswing ['ʌpswɪŋ] *n* movimiento *m* hacia arriba; (*fig*) alza *f*, auge *m*, curva *f* ascensional, mejora *f* notable (*in, of* de).

uptake ['ʌpteɪk] *n* (**a**) (*acceptance*) recepción *f*, aceptación *f*; (*intake*) consumo *m*; admisión *f*, cantidad *f* admitida. (**b**) **to be quick on the ~** verlas venir, cogerlas al vuelo; **to be a bit slow on the ~** ser algo torpe.

upthrust ['ʌp'θrʌst] **1** *adj* empujado hacia arriba, dirigido hacia arriba; (*Geol*) solevantado. **2** *n* empuje *m* hacia arriba; (*Geol*) solevantamiento *m.*

uptight* [ʌp'taɪt] *adj* tenso, nervioso; **to get ~ about sth** ponerse nervioso por algo.

uptime ['ʌptaɪm] *n* tiempo *m* de operación.

up-to-date ['ʌptə'deɪt] *adj* moderno, actual; al día; *V also* **date.**

up-to-the-minute ['ʌptəðə'mɪnɪt] *adj* de última hora.

uptown ['ʌp'taʊn] (*US*) **1** *adv* hacia las afueras, hacia los barrios exteriores. **2** *adj* exterior, de las afueras.

upturn **1** ['ʌptɜːn] *n* mejora *f*, aumento *m* (*in* de); (*Econ etc*) repunte *m.* **2** [ʌp'tɜːn] *vt* volver hacia arriba; (*overturn*) volcar.

upturned ['ʌptɜːnd] *adj* vuelto hacia arriba; *nose* respingón.

UPU *n abbr of* **Universal Post Union** Unión *f* Postal Universal, UPU.

upward ['ʌpwəd] *adj* *curve, movement etc* ascendente, ascensional; *slope* en pendiente; *tendency* al alza; **~ mobility** (posibilidades *fpl* de) ascenso *m* social.

upwardly ['ʌpwədlɪ] *adv*: **~ mobile** emprendedor, dinámico, que va en alza.

upward(s) ['ʌpwəd(z)] *adv* hacia arriba; **to lay sth face ~** poner algo con la cara hacia arriba; **to look ~** mirar hacia arriba; **£50 and ~** de 50 libras para arriba; **from the age of 13 ~** desde los 13 años para arriba; a partir de los 13 años; **~ of 200** más de 200.

upwind ['ʌp'wɪnd] *adv*: **to stay ~** quedarse en la parte de donde sopla el viento.

URA *n* (*US*) *abbr of* **Urban Renewal Administration.**

Urals ['jʊərəlz] *npl* Urales *mpl*, Montes *mpl* Urales.

uranalysis [jʊərə'nælɪsɪs] *n* = **urinalysis.**

uranium [jʊə'reɪnɪəm] *n* uranio *m.*

Uranus [jʊə'reɪnəs] *n* Urano *m.*

urban ['ɜːbən] *adj* urbano; **~ area** zona *f* urbana; **~ flight** éxodo *m* rural; **~ guerrilla** guerrillero *m* urbano, guerrillera *f* urbana; **~ renewal** renovación *f* urbana; **~ sprawl** extensión *f* urbana.

urbane [ɜː'beɪn] *adj* urbano, cortés, fino.

urbanity [ɜː'bænɪtɪ] *n* urbanidad *f*, cortesía *f*, fineza *f.*

urbanization ['ɜːbənaɪ'zeɪʃən] *n* urbanización *f.*

urbanize ['ɜːbənaɪz] *vt* urbanizar.

urchin ['ɜːtʃɪn] *n* galopín *m*, pilluelo *m*, golfillo *m.*

Urdu ['ʊəduː] *n* urdu *m.*

urea ['jʊərɪə] *n* urea *f.*

ureter [jʊə'riːtə^r] *n* uréter *m.*

urethra [jʊə'riːθrə] *n* uretra *f.*

urge [ɜːdʒ] **1** *n* impulso *m*; instinto *m*, deseo *m*; ansia *f*; ambición *f*; **the ~ to win** el afán de victoria; **the ~ to write** el deseo apremiante de escribir, la ambición de hacerse escritor; **to feel an ~ to do sth** ansiar hacer algo, sentirse impulsado a hacer algo; **to get the ~, to have the ~** entrarle a uno ganas (*to +infin* de *+infin*).

2 *vt* (**a**) **to ~ sb to do sth** instar a uno a hacer algo, incitar a uno a hacer algo, recomendar a uno encarecidamente que haga algo; **to ~ that sth should be done** recomendar encarecidamente que se haga algo.

(**b**) **to ~ sth on sb** incitar a uno a algo, recomendar encarecidamente algo a uno; **to ~ a policy on the government** hacer presión en el gobierno para que adopte una política.

◆**urge on** *vt*: **to ~ sb on** animar a uno, instar a uno a ir adelante.

urgency [ˈɜːdʒənsɪ] *n* urgencia *f*; **with a note of ~ in his voice** en tono algo perentorio, con una nota de perentoriedad; **is there much ~ about this?** ¿corre prisa esto?; **it is a matter of ~** es un asunto urgente.

urgent [ˈɜːdʒənt] *adj* urgente; *tone etc* apremiante, perentorio; *entreaty etc* insistente, apremiante; **it is ~ that ...** urge que + *subj*; **is this ~?** ¿corre prisa esto?

urgently [ˈɜːdʒəntlɪ] *adv* urgentemente; de modo apremiante, con insistencia.

uric [ˈjʊərɪk] *adj* úrico; **~ acid** ácido *m* úrico.

urinal [jʊəˈraɪnl] *n* (*building*) urinario *m*; (*vessel*) orinal *m*.

urinalysis [jʊərəˈnælɪsɪs] *n* análisis *m* de orina.

urinary [ˈjʊərɪnərɪ] *adj* urinario.

urinate [ˈjʊərɪneɪt] **1** *vt* orinar. **2** *vi* orinar(se).

urine [ˈjʊərɪn] *n* orina *f*, orines *mpl*.

urn [ɜːn] *n* urna *f*; (*for tea*) tetera *f* (grande).

urogenital [ˌjʊərəʊˈdʒenɪtl] *adj* urogenital.

urological [ˌjʊərəʊˈlɒdʒɪkl] *adj* urológico.

urologist [jʊəˈrɒlədʒɪst] *n* urólogo *m*, -a *f*.

urology [jʊəˈrɒlədʒɪ] *n* urología *f*.

Ursa Major [ˈɜːsəˈmeɪdʒəʳ] *n* Osa *f* Mayor.

Ursa Minor [ˈɜːsəˈmaɪnəʳ] *n* Osa *f* Menor.

urticaria [ˌɜːtɪˈkɛərɪə] *n* urticaria *f*.

Uruguay [ˈjʊərəgwaɪ] *n* el Uruguay.

Uruguayan [ˌjʊərəˈgwaɪən] **1** *adj* uruguayo. **2** *n* uruguayo *m*, -a *f*.

US *n abbr of* **United States** Estados *mpl* Unidos, EE.UU.

us [ʌs] *pron* nos; (*after prep*) nosotros, nosotras.

USA *n* (**a**) *abbr of* **United States of America** Estados *mpl* de América, EE.UU. (**b**) *abbr of* **United States Army.**

usable, useable [ˈjuːzəbl] *adj* utilizable, aprovechable; **~ space** espacio *m* útil; **it is no longer ~** ya no sirve.

USAF *n abbr of* **United States Air Force.**

usage [ˈjuːzɪdʒ] *n* (**a**) (*custom*) uso *m*, costumbre *f*; **in the ~ of railwaymen** en el lenguaje de los ferroviarios, en el uso ferroviario; **an ancient ~ of the Celts** una antigua usanza de los celtas.

(**b**) (*treatment*) tratamiento *m*; trato *m*, tratos *mpl*; (*handling*) manejo *m*; **kind ~** buenos tratos *mpl*, buen tratamiento *m*; **it's had some rough ~** ha sido manejado con bastante dureza.

USCG *n* (*US*) *abbr of* **United States Coast Guard.**

USDA *n abbr of* **United States Department of Agriculture.**

USDAW [ˈʌzdɔː] *n abbr of* **Union of Shop, Distributive and Allied Workers** *sindicato de empleados de comercio.*

USDI *n abbr of* **United States Department of the Interior.**

use 1 [juːs] *n* (**a**) (*employment*) uso *m*, empleo *m*; manejo *m*; **a new ~ for old tyres** nuevo método *m* para utilizar los neumáticos viejos; **'directions for ~'** 'modo *m* de empleo'; **for the ~ of the blind** para uso de los ciegos, para los ciegos; **fit for ~** servible, en buen estado; **ready for ~** listo para usar; **care in the ~ of guns** cuidado *m* en el manejo de las armas de fuego; **word in ~** palabra *f* en uso, palabra *f* que se usa; **it is not now in ~** ya no se usa; **it has not been in ~ for 5 years** hace 5 años que no se usa; **an article in everyday ~** un artículo de uso diario; **it is now out of ~** ya no se usa; eso ha quedado anticuado, eso está fuera de moda ya; **to find a ~ for sth** utilizar algo, aprovechar algo; **it improves with ~** mejora con el uso; **to make ~ of** servirse de; utilizar, aprovechar; explotar; (*right etc*) valerse de, ejercer; **to make good ~ of** aprovecharse debidamente de; **to put sth to good ~** servirse de algo, sacar partido de algo; hacer que algo trabaje (*or* rinda *etc*); **to put sth into ~** poner algo en servicio.

(**b**) (*usage*) **'the carpark is for the ~ of customers only'** 'sólo para clientes'; **to have the ~ of a garage** poder usar un garaje; **I have the ~ of it on Sundays** me permiten usarlo los domingos; **I should like to have the ~ of it** quisiera poderlo usar; **he lost the ~ of his arm** se le quedó inútil el brazo.

(**c**) (*usefulness*) utilidad *f*; **to be of ~** servir (*for* para); **to be of no ~** no servir; **can I be of any ~?** ¿puedo ayudar?; **it's (of) no ~** es inútil; **it's no ~ your protesting** de nada sirve quejarse, es inútil quejarse; **it's no ~ discussing it further** no vale la pena discutirlo más; **he's no ~** no vale para nada; **he's no ~ as a goalkeeper** no sirve como portero; **what's the ~ of all this?** ¿de qué sirve todo esto?, ¿qué utilidad tiene todo esto?, ¿qué finalidad tiene todo esto?; **to have no ~ for sth** no tener uso para algo, no poder usar algo; **to have no ~ for sb** despreciar a uno; **I've no ~ for those who ...** detesto a los que ...; **to have no further ~ for sth** no poder usar algo más; **it has its ~s** tiene sus aspectos útiles; de algo nos sirve.

(**d**) (*custom*) uso *m*, costumbre *f*.

2 [juːz] *vt* (**a**) (*employ*) *object, tool etc* usar, emplear; servirse de, utilizar; manejar; **he ~d a knife** empleó un cuchillo; **are you using this book?** ¿te hace falta este libro?, ¿estás trabajando con este libro?; **which book did you ~?** ¿qué libro consultaste?; **I could ~ a drink!*** ¡no me vendría mal un trago!; **this room could ~ some paint*** no le vendría mal a este cuarto una mano de pintura; **careful how you ~ that razor!** ¡cuidado con la navaja esa!; **have you ~d a gun before?** ¿has manejado alguna vez una escopeta?; **the money is ~d for the poor** el dinero se dedica a los pobres, el dinero se emplea en los pobres; **the word is no longer ~d** la palabra ya no se usa; **may I ~ your name?** ¿puedo dar su nombre?; **to ~ sth as a hammer** emplear algo como martillo; **to ~ sth for a purpose** servirse de algo con un propósito.

(**b**) (*employ*) *abstract things* emplear; **to ~ force** emplear la fuerza; **to ~ every means** emplear todos los medios; no perdonar esfuerzo (*to* + *infin* por + *infin*); **to ~ one's influence** ejercer su influencia.

(**c**) (*treat*) tratar; **to ~ sb well** tratar bien a uno; **to ~ sb roughly** tratar a uno brutalmente; **she had been cruelly ~d by ...** había sido tratada con crueldad por ...

3 [juːz] *vi* (*Drugs*⁑) drogarse.

4 [juːs] *v/aux*: **I ~d to go** iba, solía ir, acostumbraba ir, tenía la costumbre de ir; **but I ~d not to** pero antes no; **things aren't what they ~d to be** las cosas ya no son lo que eran.

◆**use up** *vt*: **to ~ sth up** consumir algo, agotar algo; **it's all ~d up** todo está agotado; **when we've ~d up all our money** cuando hayamos gastado todo nuestro dinero; **please ~ up all the coffee** que no quede café sin beber.

useable [ˈjuːzəbl] = **usable.**

used *adj* (**a**) [juːzd] usado; gastado, viejo; *stamp* usado; **~ car** coche *m* de ocasión; **~ literature** (*US*) libros *mpl* de segunda mano.

(**b**) [juːst] (*accustomed*) **to be ~ to** estar acostumbrado a; **to be ~ to** + *ger* estar acostumbrado a + *infin*; **to get ~ to** acostumbrarse a; **I still haven't got ~ to the lifts** todavía no me he acostumbrado a los ascensores.

useful [ˈjuːsfʊl] *adj* útil; provechoso; **a ~ player** un buen jugador, un jugador que vale; **~ capacity** capacidad *f* útil; **it is very ~ to be able to ...** es muy útil poder ...; **he's ~ with his fists** sabe defenderse con los puños; **he's ~ with a gun** sabe manejar un fusil; **would it be ~ to buy two?** ¿sería bueno comprar dos?; **to come in ~** servir, ser útil; venir a propósito; **to make o.s. ~** ayudar, trabajar (*etc*); **come on, make yourself ~!** ¡vamos, a trabajar!; **we had a ~ time in Spain** nuestra estancia en España fue muy provechosa.

usefully [ˈjuːsfəlɪ] *adv* útilmente; provechosamente, con provecho; **there was nothing that could ~ be said** no había nada provechoso que se pudiese decir.

usefulness [ˈjuːsfʊlnɪs] *n* utilidad *f*; valor *m*; provecho *m*; **it has outlived its ~** ha dejado de tener utilidad.

useless [ˈjuːslɪs] *adj* inútil; inservible; inoperante; *person* inepto, incompetente; **he's ~** no vale para nada; **he's ~ as a forward** no vale como delantero; **it is ~ to shout** de nada sirve gritar, es inútil gritar; **to make** (*or* **render**) **sth ~** inutilizar algo.

uselessly [ˈjuːslɪslɪ] *adv* inútilmente, en vano.

uselessness [ˈjuːslɪsnɪs] *n* inutilidad *f*.

user [ˈjuːzəʳ] *n* usuario *m*, -a *f*; (*Drugs*) drogadicto *m*, -a *f*; **heroin ~** heroinómano *m*, -a *f*; **~ identification** identificación *f* del usuario; **~ language** lenguaje *m* del usuario.

user-definable [ˌjuːzədɪˈfaɪnəbl] *adj*, **user-defined** [ˌjuːzədɪˈfaɪnd] *adj* definido por el usuario.

user-friendliness [ˌjuːzəˈfrendlɪnɪs] *n* facilidad *f* de uso, facilidad *f* de manejo.

user-friendly [ˌjuːzəˈfrendlɪ] *adj* amistoso, fácil de utilizar, fácil para el usuario.

user software [ˈjuːzəˈsɒftwɛəʳ] *n* software *m* del usuario.

USES *n abbr of* **United States Employment Service.**

USGS *n abbr of* **United States Geological Survey.**

usher ['ʌʃəʳ] **1** *n* ujier *m*, portero *m*; (*Theat*) acomodador *m*; (*at public meeting etc*) guardia *m* de sala, encargado *m* del orden.

2 *vt* **to ~ sb into a room** hacer pasar a uno a un cuarto, hacer entrar a uno en un cuarto; **to ~ sb out** acompañar a uno a la puerta.

◆**usher in** *vt*: **to ~ sb in** (*Theat etc*) acomodar a uno; **I was ~ed in by the butler** el mayordomo me hizo pasar; **it ~ed in a new reign** anunció un nuevo reinado, marcó el comienzo del reinado nuevo; **summer was ~ed in by storms** el verano empezó con tormentas.

usherette [,ʌʃə'ret] *n* acomodadora *f*.

USIA *n abbr of* **United States Information Agency**.

USM *n* (**a**) *abbr of* **United States Mail**. (**b**) (*Fin*) *abbr of* **unlisted securities market** mercado *m* de valores no cotizados en la Bolsa. (**c**) *abbr of* **United States Mint**.

USN *n abbr of* **United States Navy**.

USP *n abbr of* **unique sales** (*or* **selling**) **proposition**.

USPHS *n abbr of* **United States Public Health Service**.

USPS *n abbr of* **United States Postal Service**.

USS *n abbr of* **United States Ship** (*or* **Steamer**).

USSR *n abbr of* **Union of Soviet Socialist Republics** Unión *f* de Repúblicas Socialistas Soviéticas, URSS *f*.

usu. (**a**) *abbr of* **usual**. (**b**) *abbr of* **usually**.

usual ['juːʒʊəl] **1** *adj* usual; acostumbrado, habitual; corriente; normal; **as ~** como de costumbre, como siempre; **as per ~!*** ¡lo de siempre!; **more than ~** más que de costumbre, más que lo normal; **his ~ restaurant** su restaurante habitual; **to come earlier than ~** venir antes de la hora (*or* fecha *etc*) acostumbrada; **it's not ~** no es normal; **it's not ~ for people to leave so soon** no es normal marcharse tan pronto.

2 *n*: **my ~ please!*** ¡lo de siempre!, ¡como de costumbre!

usually ['juːʒʊəlɪ] *adv* por lo general, por regla general; **we ~ wash it ourselves** acostumbramos lavarlo nosotros mismos; **what do you do ~?** ¿qué hacen Vds normalmente?; **we have to be more than ~ careful** tenemos que tomar más cuidado que de costumbre; **not ~** por lo general no.

usufruct ['juːzjʊfrʌkt] *n* usufructo *m*.

usufructuary [,juːzjʊ'frʌktjʊərɪ] *n* usufructuario *m*, -a *f*.

usurer ['juːʒərəʳ] *n* usurero *m*.

usurious [juː'zjʊərɪəs] *adj* usurario.

usurp [juː'zɜːp] *vt* usurpar.

usurpation [,juːzɜː'peɪʃən] *n* usurpación *f*.

usurper [juː'zɜːpəʳ] *n* usurpador *m*, -ora *f*.

usurping [juː'zɜːpɪŋ] *adj* usurpador.

usury ['juːʒʊrɪ] *n* usura *f*.

UT (*US Post*) *abbr of* **Utah**.

utensil [juː'tensl] *n* utensilio *m*; **kitchen ~s** utensilios *mpl* de cocina, (*set*) batería *f* de cocina.

uterine ['juːtəraɪn] *adj* uterino.

uterus ['juːtərəs] *n* útero *m*.

utilitarian [,juːtɪlɪ'tɛərɪən] **1** *adj* utilitario. **2** *n* utilitarista *mf*.

utilitarianism [,juːtɪlɪ'tɛərɪənɪzəm] *n* utilitarismo *m*.

utility [juː'tɪlɪtɪ] **1** *n* (**a**) utilidad *f*. (**b**) **public ~** (empresa *f* de) servicio *m* público. **2** *attr car, clothing etc* utilitario; **~ room** office *m*; trascocina *f*; **~ vehicle** furgoneta *f*, camioneta *f*.

utilization [,juːtɪlaɪ'zeɪʃən] *n* utilización *f*.

utilize ['juːtɪlaɪz] *vt* utilizar.

utmost ['ʌtməʊst] **1** *adj* mayor; supremo; **of the ~ importance** de primerísima importancia; **with the ~ ease** con suma facilidad.

2 *n*: **the ~ that one can do** todo lo que puede hacer uno; **to do one's ~** hacer todo lo posible (*to* + *infin* por + *infin*); **200 at the ~** 200 a lo más, 200 a lo sumo; **to the ~** al máximo, hasta más no poder; **to the ~ of one's ability** lo mejor que sepa uno.

Utopia [juː'təʊpɪə] *n* Utopía *f*.

Utopian [juː'təʊpɪən] **1** *adj dream etc* utópico; *person* utopista. **2** *n* utopista *mf*.

utricle ['juːtrɪkl] *n* utrículo *m*.

utter[1] ['ʌtəʳ] *adj* completo, total, absoluto; *fool, madness etc* puro; **~ nonsense!** ¡tonterías!; **it was an ~ disaster** fue un desastre total; **he was in a state of ~ depression** estaba completamente abatido.

utter[2] ['ʌtəʳ] *vt* (**a**) *words* pronunciar; *cry etc* dar; *threat, insult etc* proferir; *libel* publicar; **she never ~ed a word** no dijo nada, no dijo ni pío; **don't ~ a word about it** de esto no digas ni pío.

(**b**) *counterfeit money* poner en circulación, expender.

utterance ['ʌtərəns] *n* (**a**) (*remark*) palabras *fpl*, declaración *f*. (**b**) (*expression*) expresión *f*; **to give ~ to** expresar, manifestar, declarar. (**c**) (*style*) pronunciación *f*; articulación *f*.

utterly ['ʌtəlɪ] *adv* completamente, totalmente, del todo.

uttermost ['ʌtəməʊst] *adj* más remoto, más lejano; extremo; *V* **utmost**.

UV *adj abbr of* **ultraviolet** ultravioleta, UV.

uvula ['juːvjələ] *n* úvula *f*.

uvular ['juːvjələʳ] *adj* uvular.

uxorious [ʌk'sɔːrɪəs] *adj* muy enamorado de su mujer, enamorado con exceso (*or* con ostentación) de su mujer.

V

V, v [viː] *n* (*letter*) V, v *f*; **V for Victor** V de Valencia; **V for victory** V de la victoria; **V-neck** cuello *m* en V; escote *m* en V; **V-necked** con cuello en V; con escote en V; **V-shaped** en forma de V; **V-sign** V *f* de la victoria; (*obscene*) corte *m* de mangas; **to give sb the V-sign** hacer un corte de mangas a uno; **V1** (*flying bomb*) bomba *f* volante (*1944-45*); **V2** (*rocket*) cohete *m* (*1944-45*).

v. (**a**) (*Liter*) *abbr of* **verse** estrofa *f*.
(**b**) (*Bible*) *abbr of* **verse** versículo *m*, vers.º.
(**c**) *prep* (*Sport, Jur etc*) *abbr of* **versus, against** contra, versus, v.
(**d**) (*Elec*) *abbr of* **volt(s)** voltío(s) *m(pl)*.
(**e**) *abbr of* **vide, see** véase, vid., vide, v.
(**f**) *abbr of* **very**.
(**g**) *abbr of* **volume**.

V&A *n* (*Brit*) *abbr of* **Victoria and Albert Museum**.

VA (*US Post*) *abbr of* **Virginia**.

vac* [væk] *n* (*Brit*) (**a**) = **vacation**. (**b**) = **vacuum**.

vacancy [ˈveɪkənsɪ] *n* (**a**) (*emptiness*) lo vacío; (*of mind etc*) vaciedad *f*, vacuidad *f*.
(**b**) (*in boarding-house etc*) cuarto *m* vacante; **have you any vacancies?** ¿hay algún cuarto libre?, ¿tiene algo disponible?; **we have no vacancies for August** para agosto no hay nada disponible, en agosto todo está lleno.
(**c**) (*in post*) vacante *f*; **'vacancies'** 'se ofrece trabajo', 'se necesita mano de obra'; **'~ for keen young man'** 'búscase joven enérgico'; **to fill a ~** proveer una vacante.

vacant [ˈveɪkənt] *adj* (**a**) *seat, room etc* libre, desocupado; disponible; *space* vacío, desocupado; **~ lot** (*US*) solar *m*; **~ post** vacante *f*; **is this seat ~?** ¿está libre este asiento?; **have you a room ~?** ¿tienen algo disponible?; **to become ~, to fall ~** (*post*) vacar.
(**b**) *look etc* distraído, vago, (*stupid*) de bobo.

vacantly [ˈveɪkəntlɪ] *adv look etc* distraídamente, vagamente, (*stupidly*) sin comprender, boquiabierto.

vacate [vəˈkeɪt] *vt house* desocupar; *post* dejar, dejar vacante, salir de; *throne etc* renunciar a.

vacation [vəˈkeɪʃən] **1** *n* (**a**) (*esp Brit*) (*Jur*) vacaciones *fpl*; **long ~** (*Univ*) vacación *f* de verano.
(**b**) (*US*) vacaciones *fpl*; **to be on ~** estar de vacaciones.
2 *attr*: **~ course** curso *m* de vacaciones, (*esp*) curso *m* de verano; **~ job** empleo *m* de verano; **~ pay** paga *f* de las vacaciones; **~ resort** centro *m* turístico; **~ season** temporada *f* de las vacaciones.
3 *vi* (*US*) estar de vacaciones; tomarse unas vacaciones; pasar las vacaciones; *V also* **holiday**.

vacationer [vəˈkeɪʃənəʳ] *n*, **vacationist** [vəˈkeɪʃənɪst] *n* (*US*) veraneante *mf*.

vaccinate [ˈvæksɪneɪt] *vt* vacunar.

vaccination [ˌvæksɪˈneɪʃən] *n* vacunación *f*.

vaccine [ˈvæksiːn] *n* vacuna *f*.

vacillate [ˈvæsɪleɪt] *vi* (*sway, vary*) oscilar (*between* entre); (*hesitate*) vacilar, dudar; **to ~ about a course of action** no resolverse a seguir una política determinada.

vacillating [ˈvæsɪleɪtɪŋ] *adj* vacilante, irresoluto.

vacillation [ˌvæsɪˈleɪʃən] *n* vacilación *f*.

vacuity [væˈkjuːɪtɪ] *n* (**a**) vacuidad *f*. (**b**) (*silly remarks*) **vacuities** vaciedades *fpl*.

vacuous [ˈvækjʊəs] *adj* bobo, necio.

vacuum [ˈvækjʊm] **1** *n* (**a**) vacío *m*; **it can't exist in a ~** no puede existir en el vacío. (**b**) (*) **to give a room a ~** limpiar un cuarto con aspiradora. **2** *attr* de vacío; al vacío. **3** *vt* (*) pasar la aspiradora por.

vacuum bottle [ˈvækjʊmˌbɒtl] *n* (*US*) termo(s) *m*.

vacuum-cleaner [ˈvækjʊmˌkliːnəʳ] *n* aspiradora *f*.

vacuum-flask [ˈvækjʊmflɑːsk] *n* (*Brit*) termo(s) *m*.

vacuum-packed [ˈvækjʊmˈpækt] *adj* empaquetado al vacío, envasado al vacío.

vacuum-pump [ˈvækjʊmˈpʌmp] *n* bomba *f* al vacío.

vade mecum [ˈvɑːdɪˈmeɪkʊm] *n* vademécum *m*.

vagabond [ˈvægəbɒnd] **1** *adj* vagabundo. **2** *n* vagabundo *m*, -a *f*.

vagary [ˈveɪgərɪ] *n* (*whim*) capricho *m*, extravagancia *f*; (*of thermometer etc*) irregularidad *f*, variación *f*; (*of the mind*) divagación *f*; **the vagaries of taste** lo caprichoso del gusto, la inconstancia de la moda.

vagina [vəˈdʒaɪnə] *n* vagina *f*.

vaginal [vəˈdʒaɪnəl] *adj* vaginal; **~ smear** frotis *m* vaginal.

vagrancy [ˈveɪgrənsɪ] *n* vagancia *f*, vagabundaje *m*; **~ in 16th century Spain** los vagabundos (*or* el vagabundeo) en España en el siglo XVI.

vagrant [ˈveɪgrənt] **1** *adj* vagabundo, vagante; (*fig*) errante. **2** *n* vagabundo *m*, -a *f*.

vague [veɪg] *n* (**a**) (*unclear*) vago; indistinto, borroso; incierto; impreciso; **the ~ outline of a ship** el perfil indistinto de un buque; **the outlook is somewhat ~** la perspectiva es algo incierta; **it is a ~ concept** es un concepto impreciso; **he made some ~ promises** hizo varias promesas imprecisas; **I haven't the ~st** no tengo la más remota idea.
(**b**) (*of person*: *in giving details etc*) impreciso, equívoco; (*by nature*) de ideas poco precisas; de actitud poco concreta; (*absent-minded*) despistado, distraído: **he was ~ about the date** no quiso precisar la fecha, no dijo concretamente cuál era la fecha; **he's terribly ~** tiene un tremendo despiste, es un despistado; **you mustn't be so ~** hay que decir las cosas con claridad, hay que concretar; **I am ~ on the subject of ants** sé muy poca cosa en concreto de las hormigas; **then he went all ~** luego comenzó a hablar vagamente; **to look ~** tener aire distraído.

vaguely [ˈveɪglɪ] *adv* vagamente; indistintamente; imprecisamente; distraídamente; **a picture ~ resembling another** un cuadro que tiene cierto parecido vago con otro; **he talks very ~** habla en términos muy vagos; **she looked at me ~** me miró distraída, me miró sin comprender.

vagueness [ˈveɪgnɪs] *n* (*V adj*) (**a**) vaguedad *f*; lo indistinto, lo borroso. (**b**) incertidumbre *f*, imprecisión *f*; despiste *m*, distracción *f*.

vain [veɪn] *adj* (**a**) (*useless*) vano, inútil; **in ~** en vano; **it is ~ to try** es inútil intentarlo; **all our efforts were in ~** todos nuestros esfuerzos resultaron ser infructuosos; **to take sb's name in ~** hablar con poco respeto de uno.
(**b**) (*conceited*) vanidoso; presumido, engreído; **she is very ~ about her hair** es muy orgullosa de su cabello, se enorgullece de su cabello.

vainglorious [veɪnˈglɔːrɪəs] *adj* vanaglorioso.

vainglory [veɪnˈglɔːrɪ] *n* vanagloria *f*.

vainly [ˈveɪnlɪ] *adv* (**a**) vanamente, inútilmente; infructuosamente; sin éxito. (**b**) vanidosamente.

valance [ˈvæləns] *n* cenefa *f*, doselera *f*.

vale [veɪl] *n* valle *m*; **~ of tears** valle *m* de lágrimas.

valediction [ˌvælɪˈdɪkʃən] *n* despedida *f*.

valedictory [ˌvælɪˈdɪktərɪ] **1** *adj address etc* de despedida. **2** *n* (*US*) oración *f* de despedida.

valence [ˈveɪləns] *n* valencia *f*.

Valencian [vəˈlensɪən] **1** *adj* valenciano. **2** (**a**) *n* valenciano *m*, -a *f*. (**b**) (*Ling*) valenciano *m*.

valency [ˈveɪlənsɪ] *n* valencia *f*.

valentine [ˈvæləntaɪn] *n* (**a**) **St V~'s Day** día *m* de San Valentín, día *m* de los enamorados (*14 febrero*).
(**b**) (*also* **~ card**) tarjeta *f* del día de San Valentín (*enviada por jóvenes, sin firmar, de tono amoroso o jocoso*).
(**c**) (*person*) novio *m*, -a *f* (*escogido el día de San Valentín*).

valerian [vəˈlɪərɪən] *n* valeriana *f*.

valet ['vælɪ] *n* ayuda *m* de cámara; '~ **parking**' (*US*) 'con servicio de aparcamiento a cargo del hotel'; ~**ing service** servicio *m* de planchado.
valetudinarian ['vælɪ,tju:dɪ'nɛərɪən] **1** *adj* valetudinario. **2** *n* valetudinario *m*, -a *f*.
Valhalla [væl'hælə] *n* Valhala *m*.
valiant ['vælɪənt] *adj* (*liter*) esforzado, denodado.
valiantly ['vælɪəntlɪ] *adv* esforzadamente, denodadamente, con denuedo.
valid ['vælɪd] *adj* válido; *ticket etc* valedero; *law* vigente; **a ticket ~ for 3 months** un billete valedero para 3 meses; **that ticket is no longer ~** ese billete ya no vale, ese billete ha caducado ya; **that argument is not ~** ese argumento no vale, ese argumento no es válido.
validate ['vælɪdeɪt] *vt* convalidar.
validation [,vælɪ'deɪʃən] *n* convalidación *f*.
validity [və'lɪdɪtɪ] *n* validez *f*; vigencia *f*.
valise [və'li:z] *n* valija *f*, maleta *f*.
Valium ['vælɪəm] ® *n* valium ® *m*.
Valkyrie ['vælkɪrɪ] *n* Valquiria *f*.
valley ['vælɪ] *n* valle *m*.
valorous ['vælərəs] *adj* (*liter*) esforzado, denodado.
valour, (*US*) **valor** ['vælə^r] *n* valor *m*, valentía *f*.
valuable ['væljuəbl] **1** *adj* valioso; estimable; costoso; **a ~ contribution** una valiosa aportación; **is it ~?** ¿vale mucho?
2 ~**s** *npl* objetos *mpl* de valor, valores *mpl*.
valuation [,vælju'eɪʃən] *n* valuación *f*, valorización *f*; tasación *f*; **to make a ~ of sth** valorar algo, valorizar algo; **to take sb at his own ~** aceptar todo lo que dice uno acerca de sí mismo.
valuator ['væljʊ,eɪtə^r] *n* valuador *m*, -ora *f*, tasador *m*, -ora *f*.
value ['vælju:] **1** *n* (**a**) (*gen*) valor *m*; estimación *f*; importancia *f*; (*Gram, Mus etc*) valor *m*; **~ of money** valor *m* del dinero; **things of ~** cosas *fpl* de valor; **of great ~** de gran valor, muy valioso (*to* para); **of no ~** sin valor; **to be of ~ to sb** ser de valor para uno, ser útil a uno; **to be of little ~ to sb** ser de poco valor para uno, servir poco a uno; **of what ~ is Greek nowadays?** ¿qué valor tiene el griego hoy?, ¿qué utilidad tiene el griego hoy?; **to the ~ of** por valor de; **this dress is good ~ (for the money)** este vestido bien vale lo que pagué por él; **to get good ~ for one's money** gastar su dinero bien; sacar jugo al dinero; **to set a ~ of £200 on sth** tasar algo en 200 libras; **to set a high ~ on sb** estimar a uno en mucho, tener un concepto muy bueno de uno; **to attach no ~ to** no conceder importancia a.
(**b**) (*moral*) ~**s** valores *mpl* morales, principios *mpl*; **sense of ~s** sentido *m* de los valores morales; **~ judgement** juicio *m* de valor.
2 *vt* (*financially*) valorar, valorizar, tasar (*at* en); (*morally etc*) estimar, apreciar; (~ *highly*) tener en mucho, tener un buen concepto de, apreciar; **it is ~d at £8** está valorado en 8 libras; **I ~ my leisure** para mí son muy importantes mis ratos de ocio; **he doesn't ~ his life** desprecia su vida, no hace estimación de su vida; **she sent her jewellery to be ~d** envió sus joyas para que se las tasaran.
value-added ['vælju:'ædɪd] *adj*: **~ tax** (*Brit*) impuesto *m* sobre el valor añadido.
valued ['vælju:d] *adj* estimado, apreciado; **my ~ colleague** mi estimado colega.
valueless ['væljʊlɪs] *adj* sin valor.
valuer ['valjʊə^r] *n* tasador *m*, -ora *f*.
valve [vælv] *n* (*Anat, Mech*) válvula *f*; (*Rad*) lámpara *f*, válvula *f*; (*Bot, Zool*) valva *f*.
valve-tester ['vælv,testə^r] *n* comprobador *m* de válvulas.
vamoose‡ [və'mu:s] *vi* largarse*; desaparecer.
vamp¹ [væmp] **1** *n* (*of shoe*) empella *f*, pala *f*; (*patch*) remiendo *m*.
2 *vt shoe* poner empella a; remendar; (*Mus*) improvisar, improvisar un acompañamiento para; **to ~ up an engine** (*repair*) componer un motor, (*supercharge*) sobrealimentar un motor.
3 *vi* (*Mus*) improvisar (un acompañamiento).
vamp²* [væmp] **1** *n* vampiresa *f*, vampi* *f*.
2 *vt* coquetear con, flirtear con; **to ~ sb into doing sth** engatusar a uno para que haga algo.
vampire ['væmpaɪə^r] *n* (**a**) (*Zool*) vampiro *m*. (**b**) (*fig*) vampiro *m*; (*woman*) vampiresa *f*.
van¹ [væn] *n* (*Mil, fig*) vanguardia *f*; **to be in the ~** ir a la vanguardia; **to be in the ~ of progress** estar en la vanguardia del progreso.
van² [væn] *n* (*Brit Aut*) camioneta *f*, furgoneta *f*; (*for removals*) camión *m* de mudanzas; (*Brit Rail*) furgón *m*.
vanadium [və'neɪdɪəm] *n* vanadio *m*.
Vandal ['vændəl] **1** *adj* vándalo, vandálico. **2** *n* (**a**) (*Hist*) vándalo *m*, -a *f*. (**b**) **v~** gamberro *m*, vándalo *m*, -a *f*.
Vandalic [væn'dælɪk] *adj* vándalo, vandálico.
vandalism ['vændəlɪzəm] *n* vandalismo *m*, gamberrismo *m*; **piece of ~** acto *m* de vandalismo.
vandalize ['vændəlaɪz] *vt* destruir, estropear, arruinar.
van-driver ['væn'draɪvə^r] *n* conductor *m*, -ora *f* de camioneta.
vane [veɪn] *n* (*weathercock*) veleta *f*; (*of mill*) aspa *f*; (*of propeller*) paleta *f*; (*of feather*) barbas *fpl*.
vanguard ['vængɑ:d] *n* vanguardia *f*; **to be in the ~** ir a la vanguardia; **to be in the ~ of progress** estar en la vanguardia del progreso.
vanilla [və'nɪlə] *n* vainilla *f*.
vanish ['vænɪʃ] *vi* desaparecer, desvanecerse; **to ~ without trace** desaparecer sin dejar rastro.
vanishing-cream ['vænɪʃɪŋ,kri:m] *n* crema *f* de día.
vanishing-point ['vænɪʃɪŋ,pɔɪnt] *n* punto *m* de fuga.
vanity ['vænɪtɪ] *n* vanidad *f*; **all is ~** todo es vanidad; **to do sth out of ~** hacer algo por vanidad.
vanity-case ['vænɪtɪ,keɪs] *n* neceser *m* de belleza, polvera *f* (de bolsillo).
vanity unit ['vænɪtɪ'ju:nɪt] *n* lavabo *m* empotrado.
vanpool ['vænpu:l] *n* (*US*) furgonetas *fpl* de uso compartido.
vanquish ['væŋkwɪʃ] *vt* (*liter*) vencer, derrotar.
vantage ['vɑ:ntɪdʒ] *n* ventaja *f*.
vantage-point ['vɑ:ntɪdʒ,pɔɪnt] *n* posición *f* ventajosa, lugar *m* estratégico; (*for views*) punto *m* panorámico; **from our modern ~ we can see that ...** desde nuestra atalaya moderna vemos que ...
vapid ['væpɪd] *adj* insípido, soso.
vapidity [væ'pɪdɪtɪ] *n* insipidez *f*, sosería *f*.
vaporization [,veɪpəraɪ'zeɪʃən] *n* vaporización *f*.
vaporize ['veɪpəraɪz] **1** *vt* vaporizar, volatilizar. **2** *vi* vaporizarse, volatilizarse.
vaporous ['veɪpərəs] *adj* vaporoso.
vapour, (*US*) **vapor** ['veɪpə^r] **1** *n* vapor *m*; vaho *m*, exhalación *f*; **the ~s** (*Med*†) los vapores.
2 *attr*: **~ trail** estela *f* de humo.
3 *vi* (*US*) fanfarronear; **to ~ about** decir disparates de.
variability [,vɛərɪə'bɪlɪtɪ] *n* variabilidad *f*.
variable ['vɛərɪəbl] **1** *adj* variable; **~ costs** costes *mpl* variables; **~ yield securities** valores *mpl* de renta variable. **2** *n* variable *f*.
variance ['vɛərɪəns] *n*: **to be at ~** estar en desacuerdo (*with* con), desentonar (*with* con), estar reñidos (*with* con).
variant ['vɛərɪənt] **1** *adj* variante. **2** *n* variante *f*.
variation [,vɛərɪ'eɪʃən] *n* variación *f* (*also Mus*); (*variant form*) variedad *f*.
varicoloured, (*US*) **varicolored** ['værɪ'kʌləd] *adj* abigarrado, multicolor.
varicose ['værɪkəʊs] *adj* varicoso; **~ veins** varices *fpl*.
varied ['vɛərɪd] *adj* variado.
variegated ['vɛərɪgeɪtɪd] *adj* abigarrado; jaspeado.
variegation [,vɛərɪ'geɪʃən] *n* abigarramiento *m*.
variety [və'raɪətɪ] **1** *n* variedad *f* (*also Bio*); diversidad *f*; (*Comm*: *of stock*) surtido *m*; **in a ~ of colours** en varios colores, de diversos colores, (*Comm*) en diversos colores; **in a ~ of ways** de diversas maneras; **a ~ of opinions was expressed** se expresaron diversas opiniones; **for ~** por variar; **to lend ~ to sth** servir para variar algo, dar diversidad a algo; **~ is the spice of life** en la variedad está el gusto.
2 *attr*: **~ artist(e)** artista *mf* de variedades; **~ show** revista *f*, show *m*; **~ store** (*US*) tienda *f* barata que vende de todo, bazar *m*; **~ theatre** teatro *m* de variedades.
variola [və'raɪələ] *n* viruela *f*.
various ['vɛərɪəs] *adj* vario, diverso; **for ~ reasons** por diversas razones; **in ~ ways** de diversos modos; **at ~ times in the past** en determinados momentos del pasado.
variously ['vɛərɪəslɪ] *adv* diversamente, de diversos modos; **she stated her age ~** declaraba su edad de diversos modos.
varmint ['vɑ:mɪnt] *n* (*Hunting*) bicho *m*; (*) golfo *m*, bribón *m*.
varnish ['vɑ:nɪʃ] **1** *n* barniz *m*; (*for nails*) esmalte *m* para las uñas, laca *f* para las uñas; (*fig*) barniz *m*, capa *f*, apariencia *f*.
2 *vt* barnizar; *nails* laquear, esmaltar; (*fig*: *also* **to ~ over**) colorear, encubrir, disimular, paliar; **~ed wood** madera *f* barnizada, madera *f* con barniz.
varsity ['vɑ:sɪtɪ] **1** *n* (*Brit**) universidad *f*. **2** *attr*: **V~ Match** partido *m* entre las Universidades de Oxford y Cambridge.
vary ['vɛərɪ] **1** *vt* variar; *decision etc* cambiar, modificar.

2 *vi* variar; (*disagree*) estar en desacuerdo; discrepar (*from* de); (*deviate*) desviarse (*from* de); **it varies** depende; **it varies from 2 to 10** varía de 2 a 10; **it varies a lot from the norm** se desvía mucho de la norma; **authors ~ about the date** los autores discrepan acerca de la fecha; **it varies in price** varía de precio; **they ~ in price** los hay de diversos precios; **it varies inversely with ...** varía en razón inversa según ...

varying ['vɛərɪɪŋ] *adj* cambiante; diverso; **with ~ results** con resultados diversos.

vascular ['væskjʊlər] *adj* vascular.

vase [vɑːz] *n* florero *m*, jarrón *m*.

vasectomy [væ'sektəmɪ] *n* vasectomía *f*.

Vaseline ['væsɪliːn] ® *n* vaselina ® *f*.

vasoconstrictor [ˌveɪzəʊkən'strɪktər] *n* vasoconstrictor *m*.

vasodilator [ˌveɪzəʊdaɪ'leɪtər] *n* vasodilatador *m*.

vassal ['væsəl] *n* vasallo *m*.

vassalage ['væsəlɪdʒ] *n* vasallaje *m*.

vast [vɑːst] *adj* vasto; inmenso, enorme; dilatado; *majority* abrumador.

vastly ['vɑːstlɪ] *adv* enormemente; **~ improved** muy mejorado; **~ superior to** con mucho superior a; **we were ~ amused** nos reímos muchísimo con eso; **~ different** muy distinto.

vastness ['vɑːstnɪs] *n* inmensidad *f*.

VAT [viːeɪ'tiː, væt] *n* (*Brit*) *abbr of* **value-added tax** impuesto *m* sobre el valor añadido, IVA *m*; **~-registered company** compañía *f* declarante del IVA.

vat [væt] *n* tina *f*, tinaja *f*, cuba *f*.

Vatican ['vætɪkən] **1** *n* Vaticano *m*. **2** *adj* vaticano, del Vaticano; **~ City** Ciudad *f* del Vaticano.

vatman* ['vætmæn] *n*, *pl* **vatmen** ['vætmen] recaudador *m* del impuesto de valor añadido.

vaudeville ['vəʊdəvɪl] *n* (*esp US*) vodevil *m*, vaudeville *m*.

vault[1] [vɔːlt] **1** *n* (*Archit*) bóveda *f*; (*for wine*) bodega *f*; (*of bank*) sótano *m*, cámara *f* acorazada; (*tomb*) tumba *f*; (*of church*) cripta *f*; **family ~** panteón *m* familiar; **~ of heaven** bóveda *f* celeste.

2 *vt* abovedar.

vault[2] [vɔːlt] **1** *n* salto *m*; **at one ~, with one ~** de un solo salto.

2 *vi* saltar; **to ~ into the saddle** colocarse de un salto en la silla; **to ~ over a stream** cruzar un arroyo de un salto.

3 *vt* saltar.

vaulted ['vɔːltɪd] *adj* abovedado.

vaulting ['vɔːltɪŋ] *n* abovedado *m*; (*Sport*) salto *m* con pértiga.

vaulting-horse ['vɔːltɪŋ,hɔːs] *n* potro *m* (de madera).

vaunt [vɔːnt] **1** *vt* jactarse de, hacer alarde de; lucir, ostentar. **2** *vi* jactarse.

vaunted ['vɔːntɪd] *adj* cacareado, alardeado; **much ~** tan cacareado.

vaunting ['vɔːntɪŋ] **1** *adj* jactancioso. **2** *n* jactancia *f*.

VC *n* (**a**) (*Brit Mil*) *abbr of* **Victoria Cross** *condecoración británica*. (**b**) (*Univ*) *abbr of* **Vice-Chancellor.** (**c**) *abbr of* **vice-chairman.**

VCR *n abbr of* **video-cassette recorder.**

VD *n abbr of* **venereal disease** enfermedad *f* venérea.

VDT *n* (*esp US*) *abbr of* **visual display terminal.**

VDU *n abbr of* **visual display unit** unidad *f* de despliegue visual, UDV *f*, unidad *f* de presentación visual, UPV *f*; **~ operator** operador *m*, -ora *f* de UDV.

veal [viːl] *n* ternera *f*.

vector ['vektər] *n* vector *m*.

Veda ['veɪdə] *n* Veda *m*.

V-E Day [ˌviː'iːdeɪ] *n abbr of* **Victory in Europe Day** día *m* de la victoria en Europa, *8 mayo 1945*.

Vedic ['veɪdɪk] *adj* védico.

veep* [viːp] *n* (*US*) vicepresidente *m*, -a *f*.

veer [vɪər] *vi* (*also* **to ~ round**) (*ship, also fig*) virar; (*wind*) girar, cambiar; **the country has ~ed to the left** el país ha virado hacia la izquierda; **it ~s from one extreme to the other** oscila desde un extremo al otro; **people are ~ing round to our point of view** la gente está empezando a aceptar nuestro criterio.

veg* [vedʒ] *n abbr of* **vegetable**(**s**) verdura *f*, vegetales *mpl*.

◆**veg out*** *vi* (*US*) relajarse, descansar; tumbarse.

vegan ['viːgən] *n* vegeteriano *m* estricto, vegetariana *f* estricta.

vegeburger* ['vedʒɪ,bɜːgər] *n* = **veggie burger**.

vegetable ['vedʒɪtəbl] **1** *n* (**a**) (*Bot*) vegetal *f*; (*edible plant*) legumbre *f*, hortaliza *f*; **~s** (*on sale as food, as item of diet*) legumbres *fpl*, hortalizas *fpl*, (*cooked, greens*) verduras *fpl*.

(**b**) (*human ~*) vegetal *mf*.

2 *attr*: **~ dish** plato *m* de legumbres, (*vessel*) fuente *f* de legumbres; **~ fat** grasa *f* vegetal; **~ garden** huerto *m* (de hortalizas); **~ kingdom** reino *m* vegetal; **~ marrow** (*esp Brit*) calabacín *m*; **~ matter** materia *f* vegetal; **~ oil** aceite *m* vegetal; **~ patch** huerto *m*, huertecito *m*; **~ salad** ensalada *f* verde; macedonia *f* de verduras con mayonesa, ensaladilla *f* rusa; **~ soup** sopa *f* de hortelano.

vegetarian [ˌvedʒɪ'tɛərɪən] **1** *adj* vegetariano. **2** *n* vegetariano *m*, -a *f*.

vegetarianism [ˌvedʒɪ'tɛərɪənɪzəm] *n* vegetarianismo *m*.

vegetate ['vedʒɪteɪt] **1** *vt*: **the land is sparsely ~d** la tierra tiene escasa vegetación. **2** *vi* vegetar (*also fig*).

vegetation [ˌvedʒɪ'teɪʃən] *n* vegetación *f*.

vegetative ['vedʒɪtətɪv] *adj* vegetativo.

veggie* ['vedʒɪ] **1** *adj* vegetariano; **~ burger** hamburguesa *f* vegetal, hamburguesa *f* vegetariana. **2** *n* vegetariano *m*, -a *f*.

vehemence ['viːɪməns] *n* vehemencia *f*; violencia *f*, pasión *f*.

vehement ['viːɪmənt] *adj* vehemente; violento, apasionado; **a ~ speech** un discurso apasionado; **there was ~ opposition** hubo una resistencia violenta.

vehemently ['viːɪməntlɪ] *adv* con vehemencia; violentamente, apasionadamente; **we are ~ opposed to it** nos oponemos totalmente a ello, estamos cien por cien en contra.

vehicle ['viːɪkl] *n* vehículo *m*; (*means*) vehículo *m*, medio *m*, instrumento *m* (*for* de).

vehicular [vɪ'hɪkjʊlər] *adj road etc* de vehículos, para coches; **~ traffic** circulación *f* rodada.

veil [veɪl] **1** *n* velo *m* (*also Phot and fig*); **under a ~ of secrecy** en el mayor secreto; **to draw a ~ over sth** correr un velo sobre algo, encubrir algo; **we had better draw a ~ over that** es mejor no hablar de eso; **to take the ~** tomar el hábito, meterse monja.

2 *vt* velar (*also fig*); **eyes ~ed by tears** ojos *mpl* empañados por lágrimas; **the town was ~ed by mist** la ciudad estaba cubierta por un velo de niebla.

veiled [veɪld] *adj* velado; encubierto; **with ~ irony** con velada ironía; **that was a ~ reference to the bishop** fue una referencia velada al obispo.

veiling ['veɪlɪŋ] *n* (*Phot*) velo *m*.

vein [veɪn] *n* (*Anat, Bot*) vena *f*; (*Min: of ore etc*) filón *m*, veta *f*; (*in stone*) vena *f*; (*in wood*) fibra *f*; hebra *f*, veta *f*; (*fig*) vena *f*, rasgo *m*; **a ~ of madness** una vena de loco, un rasgo de locura; **to be in ~** estar en vena; **to be in the ~ for** estar de humor para.

veined [veɪnd] *adj* veteado, jaspeado.

veining ['veɪnɪŋ] *n* (*Anat etc*) venas *fpl*; (*Min*) vetas *fpl*, veteado *m*.

velar ['viːlər] *adj* velar.

Velasquez, Velazquez [vɪ'læskwɪz] *nm* Velázquez.

Velcro ['velkrəʊ] ® *n* velcro ® *m*.

veld(t) [velt] *n* sabana *f*.

vellum ['veləm] **1** *n* vitela *f*. **2** *attr*: **~ paper** papel *m* vitela.

velocipede†† [və'lɒsɪpiːd] *n* velocípedo†† *m*.

velocity [vɪ'lɒsɪtɪ] *n* velocidad *f*.

velodrome ['viːlə,drəʊm] *n* velódromo *m*.

velour(s) [və'lʊər] *n* terciopelo *m*.

velum ['viːləm] *n* velo *m* del paladar.

velvet ['velvɪt] **1** *n* terciopelo *m*; (*on antlers*) piel *f* velluda, vello *m*; **to be on ~*** estar en situación muy ventajosa, vivir en Jauja; **a skin like ~** una piel aterciopelada.

2 *adj*, *attr* (*velvety*) aterciopelado; (*of ~*) de terciopelo.

velveteen ['velvɪtiːn] *n* pana *f*.

velvety ['velvɪtɪ] *adj* aterciopelado; (*fig*) *voice etc* de terciopelo.

venal ['viːnl] *adj* venal.

venality [viː'nælɪtɪ] *n* venalidad *f*.

vend [vend] *n* vender.

vendee [ven'diː] *n* comprador *m*, -ora *f*.

vendetta [ven'detə] *n* enemistad *f* mortal, odio *m* de sangre; disputa *f*; **to carry on a ~ against sb** hacer una campaña contra uno; hostigar a uno, perseguir a uno.

vending ['vendɪŋ] *n* venta *f*, distribución *f*.

vending-machine ['vendɪŋmə,ʃiːn] *n* vendedora *f* automática.

vendor ['vendɔːr] *n* vendedor *m*, -ora *f*; (*pedlar*) buhonero *m*.

veneer [və'nɪər] **1** *n* chapa *f*, enchapado *m*; (*fig*) barniz *m*, apariencia *f*; **with a ~ of culture** con un barniz de cultura; **it's just a ~** es un barniz superficial nada más.

2 *vt* chapear.

venerable ['venərəbl] *adj* venerable.

venerate ['venəreɪt] *vt* venerar, reverenciar.

veneration [ˌvenəˈreɪʃən] *n* veneración *f*; **his ~ for ...** la veneración que sentía por ...; **to hold sb in ~** reverenciar a uno.
venereal [vɪˈnɪərɪəl] *adj* venéreo; **~ disease** enfermedad *f* venérea.
Venetian [vɪˈniːʃən] **1** *adj* veneciano; **~ blind** persiana *f*. **2** *n* veneciano *m*, -a *f*.
Venezuela [ˌveneˈzweɪlə] *n* Venezuela *f*.
Venezuelan [ˌveneˈzweɪlən] **1** *adj* venezolano. **2** *n* venezolano *m*, -a *f*.
vengeance [ˈvendʒəns] *n* venganza *f*; **with a ~** con creces; de verdad; **it's raining with a ~** está lloviendo de verdad; **to take ~ on sb** vengarse de (*or* en) uno.
vengeful [ˈvendʒfʊl] *adj* (*liter*) vengativo.
venial [ˈviːnɪəl] *adj* venial.
veniality [ˌviːnɪˈælɪtɪ] *n* venialidad *f*.
Venice [ˈvenɪs] *n* Venecia *f*.
venison [ˈvenɪzn] *n* carne *f* de venado.
venom [ˈvenəm] *n* veneno *m*; (*fig*) virulencia *f*, malignidad *f*; **he spoke with real ~ in his voice** habló en tono de verdadero odio.
venomous [ˈvenəməs] *adj* venenoso; (*fig*) virulento, maligno; *tongue* viperino.
venomously [ˈvenəməslɪ] *adv* (*fig*) con malignidad, con odio.
venous [ˈviːnəs] *adj* (*Med*) venoso.
vent [vent] **1** *n* (*opening*) abertura *f*; válvula *f*; (*Mech*) válvula *f* de purga, orificio *m*, lumbrera *f*; (*airhole*) respiradero *m*; (*in pipe*) ventosa *f*; (*Zool*) cloaca *f*; **to give ~ to** dar salida a, desahogar, expresar; **to give ~ to one's feelings** desahogarse; **to give ~ to a sigh** exhalar un suspiro.
2 *vt* (*Mech*) purgar; (*discharge*) descargar, emitir, dejar escapar; (*pierce*) agujerear; *feelings etc* desahogar, descargar; **to ~ one's anger** desahogar su cólera, desahogarse; **to ~ one's spleen** descargar la bilis (*on* contra).
ventilate [ventɪleɪt] *vt* ventilar (*also fig*).
ventilation [ˌventɪˈleɪʃən] **1** *n* ventilación *f*. **2** *attr*: **~ shaft** pozo *m* de ventilación.
ventilator [ˈventɪleɪtəʳ] *n* ventilador *m*.
ventral [ˈventrəl] *adj* ventral.
ventricle [ˈventrɪkl] *n* ventrículo *m*.
ventriloquism [venˈtrɪləkwɪzəm] *n* ventriloquia *f*.
ventriloquist [venˈtrɪləkwɪst] *n* ventrílocuo *m*, -a *f*.
venture [ˈventʃəʳ] **1** *n* aventura *f*, empresa *f* (arriesgada); **at a ~** a la ventura; **his ~ into business** su aventura en el mundo de los negocios; **it seemed a stupid ~ at the time** en aquel momento parecía ser una empresa descabellada; **a new ~ in publishing** un nuevo rumbo en la edición de libros, una nueva empresa editorial.
2 *attr*: **~ capital** capital-riesgo *m*.
3 *vt* aventurar; (*stake*) jugar; *opinion etc* osar expresar; **they ~d everything** lo jugaron todo; **if I may ~ an opinion** si me permite expresar mi opinión; **may I ~ a guess?** ¿puedo hacer una conjetura?; **he ~d to remark that ...** se permitió observar que ...; **nothing ~ nothing gain** quien no se arriesga no pasa la mar.
4 *vi* (**a**) **to ~ on sth** arriesgarse en algo, osar emprender algo, lanzarse a algo; **when we ~d on this** cuando emprendimos esto; **to ~ into a wood** (osar) penetrar en un bosque; **to ~ out of doors** osar salir fuera, arriesgarse fuera.
(**b**) **to ~ to** + *infin* osar + *infin*, atreverse a + *infin*; permitirse + *infin*; **I ~ to add that ...** me permito agregar que ...; **I ~ to write to you** me tomo la libertad de dirigirme a Vd; **but he did not ~ to speak** pero no osó hablar.
◆**venture forth** *vi* (*liter*) aventurarse a salir.
venturesome [ˈventʃəsəm] *adj person* atrevido, audaz; *enterprise* arriesgado, azaroso.
venue [ˈvenjuː] *n* punto *m* de reunión, lugar *m* de reunión; **the ~ for the next match** el campo para el próximo partido; **change of ~** (*Jur*) cambio *m* de jurisdicción; **the ~ has been changed** se ha cambiado de lugar.
Venus [ˈviːnəs] *n* (*Myth*) Venus *f*; (*Astron*) Venus *m*.
veracious [vəˈreɪʃəs] *adj* veraz.
veracity [vəˈræsɪtɪ] *n* veracidad *f*.
veranda(h) [vəˈrændə] *n* veranda *f*, terraza *f*, galería *f*.
verb [vɜːb] *n* verbo *m*.
verbal [ˈvɜːbəl] *adj* verbal.
verbalize [ˈvɜːbəlaɪz] **1** *vt* expresar en palabras; exteriorizar hablando. **2** *vi* expresarse en palabras; **he does not ~ easily** no se expresa con facilidad.
verbally [ˈvɜːbəlɪ] *adv* verbalmente; de palabra, por boca.
verbatim [vɜːˈbeɪtɪm] **1** *adj* palabra por palabra, literal. **2** *adv* palabra por palabra, literalmente.
verbena [vɜːˈbiːnə] *n* verbena *f*.
verbiage [ˈvɜːbɪɪdʒ] *n* verbosidad *f*, palabrería *f*.
verbose [vɜːˈbəʊs] *adj* verboso, prolijo.
verbosely [vɜːˈbəʊslɪ] *adv* prolijamente.
verbosity [vɜːˈbɒsɪtɪ] *n* verbosidad *f*.
verdant [ˈvɜːdənt] *adj* verde.
verdict [ˈvɜːdɪkt] *n* (*Jur*) veredicto *m*, fallo *m*, sentencia *f*, juicio *m*; (*fig*) opinión *f*, juicio *m*; **a ~ of guilty** una sentencia de culpabilidad; **open ~** juicio *m* en el que se determina el crimen sin designar el culpable; **what's your ~?** ¿qué opinas de esto?, ¿qué juicio te has formado sobre esto?; **his ~ on the wine was unfavourable** hizo un juicio desfavorable acerca del vino; **to bring in a ~, to return a ~** pronunciar una sentencia, fallar, dar un fallo; **to bring in a ~ of guilty** pronunciar una sentencia de culpabilidad.
verdigris [ˈvɜːdɪgriːs] *n* verdete *m*, cardenillo *m*.
verdure [vɜːdjʊəʳ] *n* verdor *m*.
verge [vɜːdʒ] *n* borde *m*, margen *m*; **to be on the ~ of disaster** estar a dos dedos del desastre, estar en el mismo borde de la catástrofe; **to be on the ~ of a nervous breakdown** estar al borde de una crisis nerviosa; **to be on the ~ of a great discovery** estar en la antesala de un gran descubrimiento; **we are on the ~ of war** estamos al borde de la guerra; **she was on the ~ of tears** estaba para deshacerse en lágrimas; **to be on the ~ of** + *ger* estar a punto de + *infin*.
◆**verge on** *vi* acercarse a, rayar en; estar a un paso mínimo de; **a state verging on madness** un estado que raya en la locura.
verger [ˈvɜːdʒəʳ] *n* sacristán *m*.
Vergil [ˈvɜːdʒɪl] *nm* Virgilio.
Vergilian [vəˈdʒɪlɪən] *adj* virgiliano.
verifiable [ˈverɪfaɪəbl] *adj* comprobable, verificable.
verification [ˌverɪfɪˈkeɪʃən] *n* comprobación *f*, verificación *f*.
verifier [ˈverɪfaɪəʳ] *n* (*Comput*) verificador *m*.
verify [ˈverɪfaɪ] *vt* comprobar, verificar; (*Comput*) verificar.
verisimilitude [ˌverɪsɪˈmɪlɪtjuːd] *n* verosimilitud *f*.
veritable [ˈverɪtəbl] *adj* verdadero; **a ~ monster** un verdadero monstruo.
veritably [ˈverɪtəblɪ] *adv* verdaderamente.
verity [ˈverɪtɪ] *n* verdad *f*; **the eternal verities** las verdades eternas.
vermicelli [ˌvɜːmɪˈselɪ] *n* fideos *mpl*.
vermicide [ˈvɜːmɪsaɪd] *n* vermicida *m*.
vermifuge [ˈvɜːmɪfjuːdʒ] *n* vermífugo *m*.
vermilion [vəˈmɪlɪən] **1** *n* bermellón *m*. **2** *adj* bermejo.
vermin [ˈvɜːmɪn] *n* (*insects etc*) bichos *mpl*, sabandijas *fpl*; parásitos *mpl*; (*mammals*) alimañas *fpl*; (*fig*) sabandijas *pl*; (*persons*) chusma *f*.
verminous [ˈvɜːmɪnəs] *adj* verminoso, piojoso; (*fig*) vil.
vermouth [ˈvɜːməθ] *n* vermú *m*, vermut *m*.
vernacular [vəˈnækjʊləʳ] **1** *adj* (**a**) (*Ling*) vernáculo, vulgar; **in ~ Persian** en persa vulgar, en la lengua vernácula de Persia. (**b**) *architecture etc* típico; local, regional; doméstico.
2 *n* lengua *f* vernácula; (*fig*) lenguaje *m* corriente, lenguaje *m* vulgar.
vernal [ˈvɜːnl] *adj equinox* de invierno; (*liter*) *flowers* de primavera.
Veronica [vəˈrɒnɪkə] *nf* Verónica.
veronica [vəˈrɒnɪkə] *n* (*Bot*) verónica *f*.
verruca [vəˈruːkə] *n* verruga *f*.
Versailles [vεəˈsaɪ] *n* Versalles *m*.
versatile [ˈvɜːsətaɪl] *adj* versátil.
versatility [ˌvɜːsəˈtɪlɪtɪ] *n* versatilidad *f*.
verse [vɜːs] **1** *n* (**a**) (*stanza*) estrofa *f*; (*of Bible*) versículo *m*; **'The Satanic V~s'** 'Los versículos satánicos'. (**b**) (*genre*) verso *m*; (*poetry*) poesías *fpl*, versos *mpl*; **is it in ~?** ¿está en verso?
2 *attr*: **~ drama** teatro *m* en verso, drama *m* poético; **a ~ version of the 'Celestina'** una versión en verso de la 'Celestina'.
versed [vɜːst] *adj*: **to be well ~ in** estar versado en, conocer, ser conocedor de.
versification [ˌvɜːsɪfɪˈkeɪʃən] *n* versificación *f*.
versifier [ˈvɜːsɪfaɪəʳ] *n* versificador *m*, -ora *f*, versista *mf*.
versify [ˈvɜːsɪfaɪ] **1** *vt* versificar. **2** *vi* versificar, escribir versos.
version [ˈvɜːʃən] *n* versión *f*; **in Lope's ~ of the story** en la versión que hizo Lope de la historia; **my ~ of events is as follows ...** yo veo los sucesos del siguiente modo ..., así es como yo veo los hechos; **according to his ~** según su interpretación; **that's a different ~ again** ése es otro modo distinto de contarlo.

verso ['vɜːsəʊ] *n* verso *m*.
versus ['vɜːsəs] *prep* contra.
vertebra ['vɜːtɪbrə] *n, pl* **vertebrae** ['vɜːtɪbriː] vértebra *f*.
vertebral [vɜːtɪbrəl] *adj* vertebral.
vertebrate ['vɜːtɪbrɪt] **1** *adj* vertebrado. **2** *n* vertebrado *m*.
vertex [vɜːteks] *n, pl* **vertices** [vɜːtɪsiːz] vértice *m*.
vertical ['vɜːtɪkəl] **1** *adj* vertical; ~ **integration** integración *f* vertical; ~ **section** sección *f* vertical, corte *m* vertical. **2** *n* vertical *f*.
vertically ['vɜːtɪkəlɪ] *adv* verticalmente.
vertiginous [vɜː'tɪdʒɪnəs] *adj* vertiginoso.
vertigo ['vɜːtɪgəʊ] *n* vértigo *m*.
verve [vɜːv] *n* energía *f*, empuje *m*; brío *m*; entusiasmo *m*.
very ['verɪ] **1** *adv* (**a**) (*extremely*) muy; ~ **good** muy bueno; **'That will be all' — 'V~ good, sir'** 'Nada más' — 'Muy bien, señor'; ~ **well** muy bien; **he couldn't ~ well refuse** no pudo muy bien negarse a hacerlo; ~ **much** mucho, muchísimo; **'Did you enjoy it?' — 'V~ much so'** '¿Te ha gustado?' — 'Sí, mucho'; **she felt ~ much better** se encontró muchísimo mejor; **I was ~ (much) surprised** me sorprendió mucho, para mí era una gran sorpresa; **it's not so ~ difficult** no es tan difícil, la dificultad no es tan grande; **that's ~ kind of you** eres muy amable; **you're not being ~ helpful** realmente no nos ayudas nada; **it is ~ cold** (*object*) está muy frío, (*weather*) hace mucho frío.
(**b**) (*absolutely*) **the ~ first** el primero, el primero de todos; **the ~ best** el mejor, el mejor que haya; **we did our ~ best** hicimos todo lo que pudimos; **try your ~ hardest** esfuércese al máximo; **at the ~ most** a lo más, a lo sumo, todo lo más; **the ~ most we can offer** el límite de lo que podemos ofrecer; **the ~ next day** precisamente el día siguiente; **the ~ same hat** el idéntico sombrero, el mismísimo sombrero.
(**c**) (*alone, in reply to question*) mucho; **are you tired? — ~** ¿estás cansado? — mucho.
(**d**) (*emotional use*) **they are so ~ poor** son pobrísimos; **it is a ~ good wine** es un vino rebueno, es un vino requetebueno.
2 *adj* (**a**) (*precise, exact*) mismo; **in this ~ house** en esta misma casa; **at that ~ moment** en ese mismo momento; **to the ~ bone** hasta el mismo hueso; **he's the ~ man we want** es precisamente el hombre que buscamos; **it's the ~ thing!** ¡es exactamente lo que necesitamos!; **at the ~ beginning** ya en los comienzos; **the ~ bishop himself was there** el mismísimo obispo estaba allí, hasta el propio obispo estaba allí; **the ~ idea!** ¡ni hablar!, ¡qué cosas dices!; **the ~ thought frightens me** sólo pensar en ello me da miedo.
(**b**) (*liter*) **the veriest rascal** el mayor bribón; **the veriest simpleton** el más bobo.
vesicle ['vesɪkl] *n* vesícula *f*.
vespers ['vespəz] *npl* vísperas *fpl*.
vessel ['vesl] *n* (**a**) (*Anat, Bot*) vaso *m*; (*receptacle*) vasija *f*, recipiente *m*; **he's a weak ~** es una persona sin carácter.
(**b**) (*Naut*) buque *m*, barco *m*.
vest[1] [vest] *n* (*Brit*) camiseta *f*; (*US*) chaleco *m*.
vest[2] [vest] *vt* (*frm*) (**a**) **to ~ sb with sth** investir a uno de algo.
(**b**) **to ~ rights in sb** conferir derechos a uno, conceder derechos a uno, revestir a uno de derechos; **by the authority ~ed in me** en virtud de la autoridad que se me ha concedido; **to ~ property in sb** ceder una propiedad a uno, hacer a uno titular de una propiedad.
vesta ['vestə] *n* cerilla *f*.
vestal ['vestl] **1** *adj* vestal. **2** *n* vestal *f*.
vested ['vestɪd] *adj right* inalienable; ~ **interest** interés *m* personal; ~ **interests** intereses *mpl* creados.
vestibule ['vestɪbjuːl] *n* vestíbulo *m*; (*hall of house*) zaguán *m*; (*anteroom*) antecámara *f*.
vestige ['vestɪdʒ] *n* vestigio *m*, rastro *m*; (*Bio*) rudimento *m*; **not a ~ of it remains** no queda rastro de ello, de ello no queda ni el menor vestigio; **without a ~ of decency** sin la menor decencia; **if there is a ~ of doubt** si hay una sombra de duda.
vestigial [ves'tɪdʒɪəl] *adj* vestigial; rudimentario.
vestment ['vestmənt] *n* vestidura *f*.
vest-pocket [vest'pɒkɪt] *adj* (*US*) de bolsillo.
vestry ['vestrɪ] *n* sacristía *f*.
vesture ['vestʃəʳ] *n* (*liter*) vestidura *f*.
Vesuvius [vɪ'suːvɪəs] *n* Vesubio *m*.
vet [vet] **1** *n* (**a**) *abbr of* **veterinary surgeon, veterinarian** veterinario *mf* (*also* -a *f*).
(**b**) (*US**) *abbr of* **veteran** ex combatiente *m*.
2 *vt* repasar, revisar; examinar, investigar; aprobar; (*give clearance to*) acreditar; **he's ~ting the proofs** está corrigiendo las pruebas; **we'll have it ~ted by the boss** haremos que el jefe lo revise; **he was ~ted by Security** fue investigado por la Seguridad, (*and cleared*) fue acreditado por la Seguridad.
vetch [vetʃ] *n* arveja *f*.
veteran ['vetərən] **1** *adj* veterano. **2** *n* veterano *m*; (*esp US*) ex combatiente *m*.
veterinarian [,vetərɪ'nɛərɪən] *n* (*US*) veterinario *mf* (*also* -a *f*).
veterinary ['vetərɪnərɪ] *adj* veterinario; ~ **medicine,** ~ **science** medicina *f* veterinaria, veterinaria *f*; ~ **school** escuela *f* de veterinaria; ~ **surgeon** (*esp Brit*) veterinario *mf* (*also* -a *f*).
veto ['viːtəʊ] **1** *n, pl* **vetoes** ['viːtəʊz] veto *m*; **to have a ~** tener veto; **to put a ~ on sth** poner su veto a algo.
2 *vt* vedar, vetar, prohibir; **he ~ed it** lo prohibió, lo vedó; **the president ~ed it** el presidente le puso su veto.
vetting ['vetɪŋ] *n* (*check*) examen *m* previo; investigación *f*; (*clearance*) acreditación *f*; (*test of loyalty*) prueba *f* de lealtad.
vex [veks] *vt* (*anger*) fastidiar, irritar, contrariar; (*make impatient*) impacientar, sacar de quicio; (*afflict*) afligir; **the problems that are ~ing the country** los problemas que afligen el país, los problemas que alteran el país.
vexation [vek'seɪʃən] *n* irritación *f*, contrariedad *f*; impaciencia *f*; aflicción *f*; **he had to put up with numerous ~s** tuvo que soportar muchos disgustos.
vexatious [vek'seɪʃəs] *adj* fastidioso, molesto, engorroso.
vexed [vekst] *adj* (**a**) (*annoyed*) **to be ~ about sth** estar enfadado de (*or* por) algo, estar enojado por algo (*LAm*); **to be ~ with sb** estar enfadado con uno; **to be very ~** estar muy enfadado; **to get ~** enfadarse, impacientarse; **in a ~ tone** en tono ofendido, en tono de enojo. (**b**) ~ **question** cuestión *f* batallona.
vexing ['veksɪŋ] *adj* fastidioso, molesto, engorroso; **it's very ~** es una lata.
VFD *n* (*US*) *abbr of* **voluntary fire department.**
v.g. *abbr of* **very good** muy bueno, sobresaliente, S.
VHF *n abbr of* **very high frequency** frecuencia *f* muy alta, VHF.
VHS *n abbr of* **video home system.**
VI (*US Post*) *abbr of* **Virgin Islands.**
via ['vaɪə] *prep* por, por vía de; **we came ~ London** pasamos por Londres.
viability [,vaɪə'bɪlɪtɪ] *n* viabilidad *f*.
viable ['vaɪəbl] *adj* viable.
viaduct ['vaɪədʌkt] *n* viaducto *m*.
vial ['vaɪəl] *n* frasquito *m*.
viands ['vaɪəndz] *npl* (*liter*) manjares *mpl* (exquisitos).
viaticum [vaɪ'ætɪkəm] *n* viático *m*.
vibes* [vaɪbz] *npl* (**a**) (*abbr of* **vibrations**) (*from band, singer*) vibraciones *fpl*, ambiente *m*; **I got good ~ from her** me cayó muy bien. (**b**) (*Mus: abbr of* **vibraphone**) vibráfono *m*.
vibrancy ['vaɪbrənsɪ] *n* energía *f*, dinamismo *m*; vitalidad *f*.
vibrant ['vaɪbrənt] **1** *adj* vibrante (*also fig; with* de). **2** *n* vibrante *f*.
vibraphone ['vaɪbrə,fəʊn] *n* vibráfono *m*.
vibrate [vaɪ'breɪt] *vti* vibrar.
vibration [vaɪ'breɪʃən] *n* vibración *f*.
vibrato [vɪ'brɑːtəʊ] *n* vibrato *m*.
vibrator [vaɪ'breɪtəʳ] *n* vibrador *m*.
vibratory ['vaɪbrətərɪ] *adj* vibratorio.
viburnum [vaɪ'bɜːnəm] *n* viburno *m*.
Vic [vɪk] (**a**) *nm familiar form of* **Victor.** (**b**) *nf abbr of* **Victoria.**
vicar ['vɪkəʳ] *n* vicario *m*; (*Anglican*) párroco *m*, cura *m*.
vicarage ['vɪkərɪdʒ] *n* casa *f* del párroco.
vicar-general ['vɪkə'dʒenərəl] *n* vicario *m* general.
vicarious [vɪ'kɛərɪəs] *adj* experimentado por otro; indirecto; *responsibility* delegado; **to get ~ pleasure out of sth** sentir placer por lo que está haciendo otro; **I got a ~ thrill** me emocioné mucho sin tener nada que ver con lo que pasaba.
vicariously [vɪ'kɛərɪəslɪ] *adv*: **to feel excitement ~** emocionarse por lo que está haciendo otro, emocionarse a través de la emoción de otro.
vice[1] [vaɪs] **1** *n* vicio *m*. **2** *attr*: ~ **squad** brigada *f* contra el vicio.
vice[2], (*US*) **vise** [vaɪs] *n* (*Mech*) torno *m* de banco, tornillo *m* de banco.
vice[3] ['vaɪsɪ] *prep* en lugar de, sustituyendo a.
vice... [vaɪs] *pref* vice...
vice-admiral ['vaɪs'ædmərəl] *n* vicealmirante *m*.

vice-chairman ['vaɪs'tʃɛəmən] *n, pl* **vice-chairmen** ['vaɪs'tʃɛəmən] vicepresidente *m.*
vice-chairmanship ['vaɪs,tʃɛəmənʃɪp] *n* vicepresidencia *f.*
vice-chancellor ['vaɪs'tʃɑːnsələʳ] *n* (*Univ*) ≃ rector *m.*
vice-consul ['vaɪs'kɒnsəl] *n* vicecónsul *mf.*
vice-presidency ['vaɪs'prezɪdənsɪ] *n* vicepresidencia *f.*
vice-president ['vaɪs'prezɪdənt] *n* vicepresidente *m,* -a *f.*
vice-principal ['vaɪs'prɪnsɪpəl] *n* (*US Scol*) subdirector *m,* -ora *f.*
viceroy ['vaɪsrɔɪ] *n* virrey *m.*
viceroyalty ['vaɪs'rɔɪəltɪ] *n* virreinato *m.*
vice versa ['vaɪsɪ'vɜːsə] *adv* viceversa, a la inversa; **and ~** y viceversa, y a la inversa.
vicinity [vɪ'sɪnɪtɪ] *n* (**a**) (*area*) vecindad *f,* región *f*; **and other towns in the ~** y otras ciudades de la región, y otras ciudades cercanas; **we are in the ~ of Wigan** estamos en la región de Wigan, estamos cerca de Wigan; **in the ~ of 90** unos 90, alrededor de 90.
(**b**) (*nearness*) proximidad *f* (*to* de).
vicious ['vɪʃəs] *adj* (*related to vice*) vicioso; *person* depravado, perverso; cruel; *dog* bravo; *horse* resabiado, arisco; *blow* cruel, sañudo; *crime* atroz; *criticism* virulento, cruel, rencoroso; **~ circle** círculo *m* vicioso; **with ~ intent** con mala intención, con intención criminal.
viciously ['vɪʃəslɪ] *adv* viciosamente; perversamente, cruelmente; con virulencia, con rencor, rencorosamente.
viciousness ['vɪʃəsnɪs] *n* viciosidad *f*; perversidad *f,* crueldad *f*; bravura *f,* resabios *mpl*; atrocidad *f*; virulencia *f,* rencor *m.*
vicissitudes [vɪ'sɪsɪtjuːdz] *npl* vicisitudes *fpl*; altibajos *mpl,* peripecias *fpl.*
vicissitudinous [vɪ,sɪsɪ'tjuːdɪnəs] *adj* agitado, accidentado.
Vicky ['vɪkɪ] *nf familiar form of* **Victoria.**
victim ['vɪktɪm] *n* víctima *f*; **the ~s** (*suffering survivors*) los damnificados; **to be the ~ of an accident** ser víctima de un accidente, morir (*etc*) en un accidente; **to be the ~ of a swindle** ser víctima de una estafa; **to fall a ~ to flu** enfermar con la gripe; **to fall a ~ to sb's charms** rendirse (*or* sucumbir) a los encantos de uno.
victimization [,vɪktɪmaɪ'zeɪʃən] *n* sacrificio *m*; persecución *f*; (*of striker etc*) castigo *m,* represalias *fpl.*
victimize ['vɪktɪmaɪz] *vt* victimizar; escoger y castigar, tomar represalias contra; **the strikers should not be ~d** no hay por qué castigar a los huelguistas; **she feels she has been ~d** ella cree que ha sido escogida como víctima.
victimless ['vɪktɪmlɪs] *adj* sin víctimas.
Victor ['vɪktəʳ] *nm* Victor.
victor ['vɪktəʳ] *n* vencedor *m,* -ora *f.*
Victoria [vɪk'tɔːrɪə] *nf* Victoria.
Victoria Falls [vɪk'tɔːrɪə'fɔːlz] *npl* Cataratas *fpl* de Victoria.
Victorian [vɪk'tɔːrɪən] **1** *adj* victoriano. **2** *n* victoriano *m,* -a *f.*
Victoriana [vɪk,tɔːrɪ'ɑːnə] *npl* objetos *mpl* victorianos, antigüedades *fpl* victorianas.
victorious [vɪk'tɔːrɪəs] *adj* victorioso; **the ~ team** el equipo vencedor, los vencedores; **to be ~** triunfar (*over* sobre), salir victorioso, vencer.
victoriously [vɪk'tɔːrɪəslɪ] *adv* victoriosamente, triunfalmente.
victory ['vɪktərɪ] *n* victoria *f*; triunfo *m*; **~ V** V *f* de la victoria; **to win a famous ~** obtener un triunfo señalado.
victual ['vɪtl] **1** *vt* abastecer, avituallar. **2** *vi* abastecerse, avituallarse, tomar provisiones. **3** *npl*: **~s** víveres *mpl,* provisiones *fpl.*
victualler ['vɪtləʳ] *n*: *V* **license[2] 1.**
vicuña [vɪ'kjuːnə] *n* vicuña *f.*
vide ['vɪdeɪ] *vt* vea, véase.
videlicet [vɪ'diːlɪset] *adv* a saber.
video ['vɪdɪəʊ] **1** *n* vídeo *m.*
2 *attr* vídeo, de vídeo; **~ camera** videocámara *f*; **~ cassette** casete *m* de vídeo, videocasete *m*; **~ cassette recorder** videograbadora *f*; **~ club** videoclub *m*; **~ disc,** (*US*) **~ disk** videodisco *m*; **~ film** película *f* de vídeo, videofilm *m*; **~ frequency** videofrecuencia *f*; **~ game** videojuego *m*; **~ library** videoteca *f*; **~ magazine** videorrevista *f*; **~ nasty*** videofilm *m* de horror; videofilm *m* porno*; **~ piracy** videopiratería *f*; **~ projector** videoproyector *m*; **~ recorder** vídeo *m,* videograbadora *f*; **~ recording** (*act*) videograbación *f,* (*object*) videograma *m*; **~ shop** tienda *f* de vídeo; **~ terminal** terminal *m* de vídeo, videoterminal *m.*
3 *vt* hacer un vídeo de.
video... ['vɪdɪəʊ] *pref* vídeo...
videophone ['vɪdɪəʊ,fəʊn] *n* videófono *m,* videoteléfono *m.*
videotape ['vɪdɪəʊ,teɪp] **1** *n* cinta *f* de vídeo, videocinta *f.* **2** *attr*: **~ library** videoteca *f*; **~ recorder** videograbadora *f.* **3** *vt* grabar en (cinta de) vídeo.
videotaping ['vɪdɪəʊ,teɪpɪŋ] *n* videograbación *f.*
videotex ['vɪdɪəʊ,teks] *n* vídeotex *m.*
videotext ['vɪdɪəʊ,tekst] *n* videotexto *m.*
vie [vaɪ] *vi* competir, ser rivales; **to ~ for sth** disputarse algo; **to ~ with sb for sth** disputar algo a alguien, luchar contra uno para conseguir algo; **to ~ with sb** competir con uno, rivalizar con uno.
Vienna [vɪ'enə] *n* Viena *f.*
Viennese [,vɪə'niːz] **1** *adj* vienés. **2** *n* vienés *m,* -esa *f.*
Vietcong [,vjet'kɒŋ] **1** *adj* del Vietcong. **2** *n* vietcong *mf.*
Vietnam ['vjet'næm] *n* Vietnam *m.*
Vietnamese [,vjetnə'miːz] **1** *adj* vietnamita. **2** *n* (**a**) vietnamita *mf.* (**b**) (*Ling*) vietnamita *m.*
vieux jeu ['vɪɜː'ʒɜː] *adj* anticuado, fuera de moda.
view [vjuː] **1** *n* (**a**) (*gen*) vista *f*; panorama *m*; perspectiva *f*; (*Art, Phot*) panorama *m*; (*landscape*) paisaje *m*; **it's a beautiful ~** es un bello panorama; **there is a fine ~ from the top** desde la cumbre se ofrece un magnífico panorama; **50 ~s of Venice** 50 vistas de Venecia; **a ~ of Toledo from the north** Toledo en su aspecto norte, Toledo visto desde el norte; **to be in ~** ser visible; **to be in full ~** ser totalmente visible; **he did it in full ~ of hundreds of people** lo hizo estando delante centenares de personas, lo hizo a plena vista de centenares de personas; **to have** (*or* **keep**) **sb in ~** no perder a uno de vista; **to be on ~** estar expuesto; **to come into ~** aparecer, presentarse; **the house will be on ~ to the public on Saturdays** la casa estará abierta al público los sábados.
(**b**) (*opinion etc*) opinión *f,* parecer *m*; criterio *m*; actitud *f*; **in my ~** en mi opinión; **in ~ of this** en vista de esto; **with a ~ to doing sth** con miras a hacer algo, con el propósito de hacer algo; **our ~ of the problem** nuestro modo de enfocar el problema; **what is the government's ~?** ¿cuál es el parecer del gobierno?; **it is not easy to form a ~** no es fácil llegar a una conclusión; **to have** (*or* **keep**) **sth in ~** tener algo en cuenta, tener algo presente; **I do not share that ~** no comparto ese criterio; **to take the ~ that ...** opinar que ...; **to take the long ~** considerar un asunto a largo plazo; **we take a different ~** nosotros pensamos de otro modo; **to take a dim** (*or* **poor**) **~ of sb** tener un concepto desfavorable de uno, ver a uno con malos ojos; **I should take a dim ~ if ...** no me agradaría que + *subj.*
2 *vt* (**a**) (*see, examine*) mirar; ver, contemplar; examinar, inspeccionar; **we went to ~ the house** fuimos a ver la casa; **Cadiz ~ed from the sea** Cádiz visto desde el mar.
(**b**) (*TV*) ver, mirar.
(**c**) (*consider*) considerar; ver, mirar; **we ~ it with some alarm** para nosotros es motivo de cierta alarma; **how does the government ~ it?** ¿cuál es el parecer del gobierno?
3 *vi* (*TV*): **were you ~ing last night?** ¿estabas viendo la televisión anoche?; **do you spend much time ~ing?** ¿pasas mucho tiempo viendo televisión?
viewdata ['vjuː,deɪtə] *npl* vídeodatos *mpl.*
viewer ['vjuːəʳ] *n* (**a**) (*onlooker*) espectador *m,* -ora *f*; (*TV*) televidente *mf,* telespectador *m,* -ora *f.* (**b**) (*apparatus*) visionador *m,* visionadora *f.*
viewfinder ['vjuː,faɪndəʳ] *n* visor *m* (de imagen).
viewing ['vjuːɪŋ] **1** *adj*: **~ habits** hábitos *mpl* de los telespectadores; **the ~ public** los telespectadores, la audiencia televisiva; **TV ~ figures** cifras *fpl* de audiencia televisiva; *V* **peak 2.**
2 *n* (**a**) (*gen*) visita *f,* inspección *f.*
(**b**) (*TV*: *act*) ver *m* la televisión; (*programmes*) programas *mpl,* programación *f*; **your ~ for the weekend** sus programas para el fin de semana; **late-night ~** programas *mpl* para las altas horas; **tennis makes good ~** el tenis va bien en televisión, el tenis es muy televisivo.
viewpoint ['vjuːpɔɪnt] *n* (**a**) (*Geog*) mirador *m,* punto *m* panorámico.
(**b**) (*fig*) punto *m* de vista; criterio *m*; **from the ~ of the economy** desde el punto de vista de la economía.
vigil ['vɪdʒɪl] *n* vigilia *f*; **to keep ~** velar.
vigilance ['vɪdʒɪləns] **1** *n* vigilancia *f*; **to escape sb's ~** burlar la vigilancia de uno. **2** *attr*: **~ committee** (*US*) comité *m* de autodefensa.
vigilant ['vɪdʒɪlənt] *adj* vigilante; desvelado, alerta.
vigilante ['vɪdʒɪ'læntɪ] *n* vigilante *m.*
vigilantly ['vɪdʒɪləntlɪ] *adv* vigilantemente.
vignette [vɪ'njet] *n* (*Phot, Typ*) viñeta *f*; (*character sketch*

etc) esbozo *m* en miniatura, esbocito *m*; estampa *f*.

vigorous ['vɪgərəs] *adj* vigoroso, enérgico, pujante.

vigorously ['vɪgərəslɪ] *adv* vigorosamente, con vigor, enérgicamente.

vigour, (*US*) **vigor** ['vɪgəʳ] *n* vigor *m*, energía *f*, pujanza *f*; **in the full ~ of manhood** en la flor de la edad viril.

Viking ['vaɪkɪŋ] *n* vikingo *m*.

vile [vaɪl] *adj* vil; infame, detestable; (*very bad*) horrible, asqueroso; **the weather was ~** el tiempo fue horrible; **it's a ~ play** es una obra malísima; **he has a ~ temper** tiene un genio de perro, es un hombre de malas pulgas; **that was a ~ thing to say** eso fue infame.

vilely ['vaɪllɪ] *adv* vilmente; de modo infame, de modo detestable; malísimamente, horriblemente; **he treated her ~** la trató de modo infame.

vileness ['vaɪlnɪs] *n* vileza *f*, infamia *f*; lo horrible, lo asqueroso; **the ~ of the weather** el tiempo tan horrible que hace.

vilification [,vɪlɪfɪ'keɪʃən] *n* vilipendio *m*.

vilify ['vɪlɪfaɪ] *vt* vilipendiar.

villa ['vɪlə] *n* (*Roman etc*) villa *f*; (*seaside*) chalet *m*; (*country house*) casa *f* de campo, quinta *f*.

village ['vɪlɪdʒ] **1** *n* (*small*) aldea *f*, pueblecito *m*; lugar *m*; (*large*) pueblo *m*.

2 *attr* aldeano; pueblerino; de aldea, de la aldea; **~ cricket** criquet *m* pueblerino; **~ green** césped *m* comunal; **~ hall** sala *f* del pueblo; **~ idiot** tonto *m* del lugar; **~ store** tienda *f* del pueblo.

villager ['vɪlɪdʒəʳ] *n* aldeano *m*, -a *f*.

villain ['vɪlən] *n* malvado *m*; (*Liter*) malo *m*, traidor *m*; (*criminal*) ladrón *m*, criminal *m*; (*hum*) tunante *m*, bribón *m*; **you ~!** ¡ladrón!; **the ~ of the piece is X** el que debiera cargar con la culpa de esto es X, el verdadero responsable es X.

villainous ['vɪlənəs] *adj* malvado, vil, infame; (*very bad*) malísimo, horrible; **and other ~ characters** y otros personajes infames.

villainously ['vɪlənəslɪ] *adv* vilmente; **~ ugly** feísimo.

villainy ['vɪlənɪ] *n* maldad *f*, vileza *f*.

villein ['vɪlɪn] *n* (*Hist*) villano *m*, -a *f*.

vim [vɪm] *n* energía *f*, empuje *m*, vigor *m*.

VIN *n abbr of* **vehicle identification number.**

vinaigrette [,vɪneɪ'gret] *n* vinagreta *f*.

Vincent ['vɪnsənt] *nm* Vicente.

vindicate ['vɪndɪkeɪt] **1** *vt* vindicar, justificar. **2** *vr*: **to ~ o.s.** justificarse.

vindication [,vɪndɪ'keɪʃən] *n* vindicación *f*, justificación *f*.

vindictive [vɪn'dɪktɪv] *adj* vengativo; rencoroso; **to feel ~ about sth** guardar rencor por algo; **to feel ~ towards sb** guardar rencor a uno.

vindictively [vɪn'dɪktɪvlɪ] *adv* rencorosamente, con rencor.

vindictiveness [vɪn'dɪktɪvnɪs] *n* deseo *m* de venganza, espíritu *m* de venganza; rencor *m*.

vine [vaɪn] *n* vid *f*; (*climbing, trained*) parra *f*.

vine arbour, (*US*) **vine arbor** ['vaɪn,ɑːbəʳ] *n* emparrado *m*.

vinegar ['vɪnɪgəʳ] *n* vinagre *m*.

vinegary ['vɪnɪgərɪ] *adj* vinagroso.

vinegrower ['vaɪn,grəʊəʳ] *n* viticultor *m*, -ora *f*, viñador *m*, -ora *f*.

vinegrowing ['vaɪn,grəʊɪŋ] *n* viticultura *f*.

vineleaf ['vaɪnliːf] *n*, *pl* **vineleaves** ['vaɪnliːvz] hoja *f* de parra, hoja *f* de vid, pámpana *f*.

vineyard ['vɪnjəd] *n* viña *f*, viñedo *m*.

vino* ['viːnəʊ] *n* vino *m*, tintorro* *m*, purrela *f*.

vinous ['vaɪnəs] *adj* vinoso.

vintage ['vɪntɪdʒ] **1** *n* (*season, harvest*) vendimia *f*; (*with reference to quality or year*) cosecha *f*; **the 1990 ~** la cosecha de 1990; **it will be a good ~** la cosecha promete ser buena.

2 *adj* clásico; **~ wine** vino *m* añejo, vino *m* de calidad; vino *m* de crianza; **~ car** coche *m* de época, coche *m* antiguo, coche *m* clásico; **it was a ~ year** fue un año famoso, fue un año clásico; **it has been a ~ year for plays** en el teatro ha sido una temporada excelente.

vintner ['vɪntnəʳ] *n* vinatero *m*.

vinyl ['vaɪnl] **1** *n* vinilo *m*; **~ acetate** acetato *m* de vinilo. **2** *adj* vinílico.

viol ['vaɪəl] *n* viola *f*.

viola^1 ['vaɪələ] *n* (*Bot*) viola *f*, violeta *f*.

viola^2 [vɪ'əʊlə] **1** *n* (*Mus*) viola *f*; **~ da gamba** viola *f* de gamba; **~ d'amore** viola *f* de amor. **2** *attr*: **~ player** viola *mf*.

violate ['vaɪəleɪt] *vt* (*rape*) violar; (*Jur*) violar, quebrantar, infringir; *privacy* invadir.

violation [,vaɪə'leɪʃən] *n* violación *f*; **in ~ of a law** violando así una ley; **in ~ of sb's privacy** invadiendo la vida privada de uno.

violator ['vaɪəleɪtəʳ] *n* violador *m*, -ora *f*; (*of law*) infractor *m*, -ora *f*.

violence ['vaɪələns] *n* violencia *f*; **there was ~** se recurrió a la fuerza; **there has been ~ on the streets** ha habido violencia en las calles; **to die by ~** morir violentamente; **to do sb a ~** agredir a uno, herir a uno; **to do ~ to** violentar; **to do ~ to a theory** torcer una teoría; **to offer ~** mostrarse violento; **to resort to ~** recurrir a la fuerza, venirse a las manos; tomar medidas violentas; **to rob sb with ~** robar algo a uno a mano airada.

violent ['vaɪələnt] *adj* violento; *feeling etc* intenso, acerbo; *pain* intenso; *colour* chillón; **to become ~** mostrarse violento; apelar a la fuerza; **to lay ~ hands on sb** agredir a uno; **to take a ~ dislike to sb** tomar un odio intenso a uno.

violently ['vaɪələntlɪ] *adv* violentamente, con violencia; **to die ~** morir violentamente; **to fall ~ in love with sb** enamorarse perdidamente de uno; **he expresses himself rather ~** se expresa en términos algo violentos.

violet ['vaɪəlɪt] **1** *n* (*Bot*) violeta *f*; (*colour*) violado *m*, violeta *f*. **2** *adj* violado, violeta; **~ color** (*US*), **~ colour** color *m* violeta.

violin [,vaɪə'lɪn] **1** *n* violín *m*. **2** *attr*: **~ case** maletín *m* de violín.

violinist [,vaɪə'lɪnɪst] *n* violinista *mf*.

violoncellist [,vaɪələn'tʃelɪst] *n* violonchelista *mf*.

violoncello [,vaɪələn'tʃeləʊ] *n* violonchelo *m*.

VIP *n* (*freq hum*) *abbr of* **very important person** personaje *m*, figura *f*, VIP *m*; **to give sb the ~ treatment** tratar a uno como VIP.

viper ['vaɪpəʳ] *n* víbora *f*.

viperish ['vaɪpərɪʃ] *adj* (*fig*) viperino.

virago [vɪ'rɑːgəʊ] *n* fiera *f*, arpía *f*.

viral ['vaɪərəl] *adj* vírico.

Virgil ['vɜːdʒɪl] *nm* Virgilio.

Virgilian [vɜː'dʒɪlɪən] *adj* virgiliano.

virgin ['vɜːdʒɪn] **1** *adj* virgen; *cork, forest, soil etc* virgen. **2** *n* virgen *f*; **the V~** la Virgen; **the Blessed V~** la Santísima Virgen.

virginal ['vɜːdʒɪnl] **1** *adj* virginal. **2 ~s** *npl* (*Mus*) espineta *f*.

Virginian [və'dʒɪnɪən] **1** *adj* virginiano. **2** *n* **(a)** virginiano *m*, -a *f*. **(b)** (*also* **~ tobacco**) tobaco *m* rubio.

Virgin Isles ['vɜːdʒɪn,aɪlz] *npl* Islas *fpl* Vírgenes.

virginity [vɜː'dʒɪnɪtɪ] *n* virginidad *f*.

Virgo ['vɜːgəʊ] *n* (*Zodiac*) Virgo *f*.

virgule ['vɜːgjuːl] (*US Typ*) barra *f* oblicua.

virile ['vɪraɪl] *adj* viril.

virility [vɪ'rɪlɪtɪ] *n* virilidad *f*.

virologist [,vaɪə'rɒlədʒɪst] *n* virólogo *m*, -a *f*.

virology [,vaɪə'rɒlədʒɪ] *n* virología *f*.

virtual ['vɜːtjʊəl] *adj* virtual; **~ memory, ~ storage** memoria *f* virtual; **the ~ dictator of the country** el que es en efecto el dictador del país; **it was a ~ defeat** era prácticamente una derrota; **he made a ~ admission of guilt** en efecto se confesó culpable.

virtually ['veːtjʊəlɪ] *adv* virtualmente; prácticamente; **it is ~ impossible to do anything** es prácticamente imposible hacer nada, es casi imposible hacer nada; **it ~ destroyed the building** destruyó virtualmente el edificio.

virtue ['vɜːtjuː] *n* virtud *f*; (*of woman*) honra *f*; **a woman of easy ~** una mujer de vida alegre, una mujer de moralidad laxa; **by ~ of, in ~ of** en virtud de; **he had designs on her ~** iba a tratar de seducirla; **her ~ was in no danger** su honra no estaba en peligro; **to make a ~ of necessity** hacer de la necesidad (una) virtud; **I see no ~ in that** no encuentro ninguna ventaja en eso; **I see no ~s in trams** no comprendo el porqué de los tranvías.

virtuosity [,vɜːtjʊ'ɒsɪtɪ] *n* virtuosismo *m*.

virtuoso [,vɜːtjʊ'əʊzəʊ] *n*, *pl* **virtuosos** *or* **virtuosi** [,vɜːtjʊ'əʊzɪ] virtuoso *m*.

virtuous ['vɜːtjʊəs] *adj* virtuoso.

virtuously ['vɜːtjʊəslɪ] *adv* virtuosamente.

virulence ['vɪrʊləns] *n* virulencia *f*.

virulent ['vɪrʊlənt] *adj* virulento.

virulently ['vɪrʊləntlɪ] *adj* con virulencia.

virus ['vaɪərəs] **1** *n* virus *m* (*also Comput*). **2** *attr*: **~ disease** enfermedad *f* vírica.

visa ['viːzə] **1** *n* visado *m*, visa *m*, visa *f* (*LAm*). **2** *vt* visar.

visage ['vɪzɪdʒ] *n* (*liter*) semblante *m*.

vis-à-vis ['viːzəviː] *prep* respecto de, con relación a; para con; frente a.

viscera ['vɪsərə] *npl* vísceras *fpl*.

visceral ['vɪsərəl] *adj* visceral.
viscid ['vɪsɪd] *adj* viscoso.
viscose ['vɪskəʊs] **1** *adj* viscoso. **2** *n* viscosa *f*.
viscosity [vɪs'kɒsɪtɪ] *n* viscosidad *f*.
viscount ['vaɪkaʊnt] *n* vizconde *m*.
viscountcy ['vaɪkaʊntsɪ] *n* vizcondado *m*.
viscountess ['vaɪkaʊntɪs] *n* vizcondesa *f*.
viscous ['vɪskəs] *adj* viscoso.
vise [vaɪs] *n* (*US*) = **vice²**.
visibility [,vɪzɪ'bɪlɪtɪ] *n* visibilidad *f* (*also Aer etc*); **in good ~** en buenas condiciones de visibilidad; **there was a ~ of 500 metres** la visibilidad era de 500 metros; **~ is down to nil** la visibilidad queda reducida a cero.
visible ['vɪzəbl] *adj* visible; **~ exports** exportaciones *fpl* visibles; **~ imports** importaciones *fpl* visibles; **~ reserve** reserva *f* visible.
visibly ['vɪzəblɪ] *adv* visiblemente; **he had got ~ thinner** había adelgazado visiblemente; **she was ~ moved** patentizó su emoción, acusó una fuerte conmoción.
Visigoth ['vɪzɪgɒθ] *n* visigodo *m*, -a *f*.
Visigothic [,vɪzɪ'gɒθɪk] *adj* visigodo, visigótico.
vision ['vɪʒən] *n* (**a**) visión *f* (*also Eccl*); (*eyesight*) vista *f*; **to have normal ~** tener la vista normal.
(**b**) (*farsightedness*) clarividencia *f*; **a man of ~** un hombre clarividente; **he had the ~ to see that ...** era lo bastante clarividente como para ver que ...
(**c**) (*dream*) sueño *m*; **my ~ of the future** mi sueño del porvenir, mi manera de imaginar el futuro; **to have ~s of wealth** soñar con ser rico; **I had ~s of getting lost** me veía ya perdido.
visionary ['vɪʒənərɪ] **1** *adj* visionario. **2** *n* visionario *m*, -a *f*.
vision-mixer ['vɪʒən,mɪksəʳ] *n* (*TV*) mezclador *m*, -ora *f* de imágenes.
visit ['vɪzɪt] **1** *n* visita *f*; **on an official ~** en visita oficial; **on a private ~** en visita privada; **to be on a ~ to ...** estar de visita en ...; **to pay sb a ~** hacer una visita a uno; **to return a ~** devolver una visita.
2 *vt* (**a**) (*go and see*) visitar, hacer una visita a; ir a; conocer; **when we first ~ed the town** cuando conocimos la ciudad por primera vez; **to ~ the sick** visitar a los enfermos.
(**b**) (†: *inflict, afflict*) **to ~ a punishment on sb** castigar a uno con algo, mandar un castigo a uno; **they were ~ed with the plague** sufrieron el azote de la peste.
3 *vi* (*also* **to go ~ing**) hacer visitas; **to ~ with sb** (*US*) visitar a uno; charlar con uno.
visitation [,vɪzɪ'teɪʃən] *n* (**a**) (*Eccl*) visitación *f*; (*inspection*) inspección *f*; (*) visitón* *m*. (**b**) (*punishment*) castigo *m*.
visiting ['vɪzɪtɪŋ] *adj* de visita; **~ card** (*Brit*) tarjeta *f* de visita; **~ hours, ~ time** horas *fpl* de visita; **~ nurse** (*US*) enfermera *f* que visita a domicilio; **~ professor** profesor *m*, -ora *f* visitante; **~ team** equipo *m* visitante; **we're on ~ terms** nos visitamos.
visitor ['vɪzɪtəʳ] *n* visitante *mf*; (*to one's home*) visita *f*; (*tourist*) turista *mf*, visitante *mf*; (*tripper*) excursionista *mf*; (*stranger*) forastero *m*, -a *f*; **~'s book** libro *m* de visitas, libro *m* de honor; **~ center** (*US*), **~ centre** centro *m* de información; **the museum had 900 ~s** el museo recibió a 900 visitantes; **we can't invite you because we have ~s** no podemos invitarte pues tenemos visita; **sorry, we're just ~s here** lo siento, estamos aquí de visita nada más; **the summer ~s bring a lot of money** los veraneantes aportan mucho dinero.
visor ['vaɪzəʳ] *n* visera *f*.
VISTA ['vɪstə] *n* (*US*) *abbr of* **Volunteers in Service to America** programa *m* de ayuda voluntaria a los necesitados.
vista ['vɪstə] *n* vista *f*, panorama *m*; (*fig*) perspectiva *f*; **there are new ~s** hay perspectivas nuevas; **it opened up ~s of wealth** ofreció perspectivas de riqueza.
visual ['vɪzjʊəl] *adj* visual; **~ aid** ayuda *f* visual; **~ display unit** unidad *f* de despliegue visual; **~ effects** efectos *mpl* visuales.
visualize ['vɪzjʊəlaɪz] *vt* (**a**) (*form a picture of*) representarse (en la mente), imaginarse.
(**b**) (*foresee*) prever; **the government ~s that ...** el gobierno prevé que ...; **we do not ~ any great change** no prevemos ningún cambio de importancia; **that is not how we ~d it** eso no corresponde a lo que nosotros preveíamos.
visually ['vɪzjʊəlɪ] *adv* visualmente; **~ handicapped person** invidente *mf*.
vital ['vaɪtl] **1** *adj* (**a**) (*essential*) esencial; imprescindible; de suma importancia, trascendental; **of ~ importance** de primerísima importancia, de importancia primordial (*to* para); **the book is ~** el libro es esencial; **it is ~ that ...** es esencial que + *subj*, importa muchísimo que + *subj*.
(**b**) (*critical*) decisivo, crítico; **at the ~ moment** en el momento decisivo.
(**c**) *person* (*of character*) enérgico, vivo, lleno de vida; **she's a very ~ person** es una persona que rebosa de energía.
(**d**) (*relating to life*) vital; **~ parts** partes *fpl* vitales; **~ statistics** estadísticas *fpl* demográficas, bioestadística *f*; (*hum*) medidas *fpl* vitales, mensuraciones *fpl*.
2: **~s** *npl* partes *fpl* vitales.
vitality [vaɪ'tælɪtɪ] *n* vitalidad *f*, energía *f*.
vitalize ['vaɪtəlaɪz] *vt* vitalizar, vivificar, infundir nueva vida a.
vitally ['vaɪtəlɪ] *adv*: **~ important** de primerísima importancia; **it is ~ important that ...** es esencial que + *subj*.
vitamin ['vɪtəmɪn] **1** *n* vitamina *f*. **2** *attr content etc* vitamínico; **~ deficiency** avitaminosis *f*; **~-enriched** enriquecido con vitaminas; **~ tablet** pastilla *f* de vitaminas.
vitaminize ['vɪtəmɪnaɪz] *vt* vitaminar.
vitaminized ['vɪtəmɪnaɪzd] *adj* vitamin(iz)ado, reforzado con vitaminas.
vitiate ['vɪʃɪeɪt] *vt* viciar (*also Jur*); estropear, destruir; quitar valor a.
viticulture ['vɪtɪkʌltʃəʳ] *n* viticultura *f*.
vitreous ['vɪtrɪəs] *adj* vítreo.
vitrifaction [,vɪtrɪ'fækʃən] *n* vitrificación *f*.
vitrify ['vɪtrɪfaɪ] **1** *vt* vitrificar. **2** *vi* vitrificarse.
vitriol ['vɪtrɪəl] *n* vitriolo *m*.
vitriolic [,vɪtrɪ'ɒlɪk] *adj* (*fig*) mordaz, vitriólico.
vitro ['vɪtrəʊ] *V* **in vitro**.
vituperate [vɪ'tju:pəreɪt] *vt* vituperar, llenar de injurias.
vituperation [vɪ,tju:pə'reɪʃən] *n* vituperio *m*, injurias *fpl*.
vituperative [vɪ'tju:pərətɪv] *adj* vituperioso, injurioso.
viva¹ ['vaɪvə] *n* (*Brit*) examen *m* oral.
viva² ['vi:və] *interj*: **~ Diana!** ¡viva Diana!
vivacious [vɪ'veɪʃəs] *adj* animado, vivaz, alegre, lleno de vida.
vivaciously [vɪ'veɪʃəslɪ] *adj* animadamente, alegremente.
vivacity [vɪ'væsɪtɪ] *n* animación *f*, vivacidad *f*, vida *f*, alegría *f*.
vivarium [vɪ'vɛərɪəm] *n* vivero *m*.
viva voce ['vaɪvə'vəʊsɪ] **1** *adv* de viva voz. **2** *adj exam* oral. **3** *n* (*Brit*) examen *m* oral.
vivid ['vɪvɪd] *adj* vivo; *colour, light* intenso; *flash* súbito; *impression, memory etc* vivo; *description* gráfico, enérgico, pintoresco.
vividly ['vɪvɪdlɪ] *adv* intensamente; súbitamente; vivamente; enérgicamente, con rasgos enérgicos, de modo pintoresco.
vividness ['vɪvɪdnɪs] *n* viveza *f*; intensidad *f*; vivacidad *f*; energía *f*.
vivify ['vɪvɪfaɪ] *vt* vivificar.
viviparous [vɪ'vɪpərəs] *adj* vivíparo.
vivisection [,vɪvɪ'sekʃən] *n* vivisección *f*.
vivisectionist [,vɪvɪ'sekʃənɪst] *n* vivisector *m*, -ora *f*.
vixen ['vɪksn] *n* zorra *f*, raposa *f*; (*woman*) arpía *f*.
viz. [vɪz] *adv abbr of* **videlicet, namely** verbigracia, v.gr.
vizier [vɪ'zɪəʳ] *n* visir *m*; **grand ~** gran visir *m*.
V-J Day [,vi:'dʒeɪ,deɪ] *n abbr of* **Victory over Japan Day** *Brit*: *15 agosto 1945*; *US*: *2 septiembre 1945*.
VLF *n abbr of* **very low frequency**.
VLSI *n abbr of* **very large-scale integration** integración *f* a muy gran escala.
VOA *n abbr of* **Voice of America** Voz *f* de América.
vocable ['vəʊkəbl] *n* vocablo *m*.
vocabulary [vəʊ'kæbjʊlərɪ] *n* vocabulario *m*, léxico *m*.
vocal ['vəʊkəl] **1** *adj* (**a**) (*Anat*) vocal; **~ cords** cuerdas *fpl* vocales; **~ organs** órganos *mpl* vocales, órganos *mpl* de la voz.
(**b**) (*Mus*) vocal; **~ score** partitura *f* vocal.
(**c**) (*noisy*) ruidoso; chillón, gritón; **they're getting rather ~ about it** están empezando a protestar; **there was some ~ opposition** hubo alguna oposición ruidosa.
2 **~s** *npl* voz *f*, canto *m*; **backing ~s** voz *f* auxiliar; **lead ~s** voz *f* principal.
vocalic [vəʊ'kælɪk] *adj* vocálico.
vocalist ['vəʊkəlɪst] *n* cantante *mf*; (*in cabaret etc*) vocalista *mf*.
vocalize ['vəʊkəlaɪz] **1** *vt* vocalizar. **2** *vi* vocalizarse.
vocally ['vəʊkəlɪ] *adv* vocalmente; ruidosamente.
vocation [vəʊ'keɪʃən] *n* vocación *f*; **to have a ~ for art** tener vocación por el arte; **he has missed his ~** se ha equivocado de carrera.

vocational [vəʊ'keɪʃənl] *adj* vocacional, profesional; ~ **guidance** guía *f* vocacional, orientación *f* profesional; ~ **training** formación *f* vocacional (*or* profesional).

vocative ['vɒkətɪv] **1** *adj* vocativo; ~ **case** = **2**. **2** *n* vocativo *m*.

vociferate [vəʊ'sɪfəreɪt] *vti* vociferar, gritar.

vociferation [vəʊ,sɪfə'reɪʃən] *n* vociferación *f*.

vociferous [vəʊ'sɪfərəs] *adj* vocinglero, clamoroso; vociferante; ruidoso; **there were ~ protests** hubo protestas ruidosas, se protestó ruidosamente.

vociferously [vəʊ'sɪfərəslɪ] *adv* a gritos, clamorosamente; ruidosamente.

vodka ['vɒdkə] *n* vodka *m*.

vogue [vəʊg] **1** *n* boga *f*, moda *f*; **the ~ for short skirts** la moda de la falda corta; **to be in ~** estar de moda, estar en boga. **2** *attr*: ~ **word** palabra *f* que está de moda.

voice [vɔɪs] **1** *n* (**a**) (*gen*) voz *f*; **in a gentle ~** en tono dulce; **in a loud ~** en voz alta; **in a low ~** en voz baja; **with one ~** a una voz, al unísono; **to be in (good) ~** estar en voz; **to find one's ~** volver a poder hablar; **to give ~ to** expresar, hacerse eco de; **to have no ~ in a matter** no tener voz en capítulo; **to keep one's ~ down** seguir hablando en tono bajo; **to lower one's ~** bajar el tono; **to raise one's ~** levantar el tono, (*protest*) protestar.

(**b**) (*Ling, Gram*) voz *f*; **active ~** voz *f* activa; **passive ~** voz *f* pasiva.

2 *attr*: ~ **box** caja *f* laríngea; ~ **parts** melodía *f*; ~ **recognition** reconocimiento *m* de la voz; ~ **synthesis** síntesis *f* de la voz; ~ **synthesizer** sintetizador *m* de la voz humana; ~ **training** educación *f* de la voz.

3 *vt* (**a**) (*express*) expresar, hacerse eco de.

(**b**) (*Ling*) sonorizar.

voice-activated ['vɔɪs'æktɪveɪtəd] *adj* activado por sonido.

voiced [vɔɪst] *adj* sonoro.

voiceless ['vɔɪslɪs] *adj* sordo.

voice-over ['vɔɪs,əʊvə^r] *n* voz *f* en off.

voiceprint ['vɔɪs,prɪnt] *n* impresión *f* vocal.

void [vɔɪd] **1** *adj* (*empty*) vacío; desocupado; *post* vacante; (*Jur*) nulo, inválido; **to be ~ of** estar falto de, estar desprovisto de; **to make a contract ~** anular un contrato, invalidar un contrato; **to make sb's efforts ~** hacer inútiles los esfuerzos de uno; *V* **null**.

2 *n* (**a**) (*lit, fig*) vacío *m*; hueco *m*, espacio *m*; **the ~** la nada; **to fill the ~** llenar el hueco; **to have an aching ~** tener mucha hambre.

(**b**) (*Cards*) fallo *m*; **to have a ~ in hearts** tener fallo a corazones.

3 *vt* (**a**) evacuar, vaciar.

(**b**) (*Jur*) anular, invalidar.

voile [vɔɪl] *n* gasa *f*.

vol., vols *abbr of* **volume(s)** tomo(s) *m(pl)*, t.

volatile ['vɒlətaɪl] *adj* volátil (*also fig*); ~ **memory** memoria *f* no permanente.

volatility [,vɒlə'tɪlɪtɪ] *n* volatilidad *f* (*also fig*).

volatilize [vɒ'lætəlaɪz] **1** *vt* volatilizar. **2** *vi* volatilizarse.

vol-au-vent ['vɒləʊvɑ̃] *n* volován *m*.

volcanic [vɒl'kænɪk] *adj* volcánico.

volcano [vɒl'keɪnəʊ] *n, pl* **volcanoes** [vɒl'keɪnəʊz] volcán *m*.

vole [vəʊl] *n* campañol *m*.

volition [və'lɪʃən] *n* volición *f*; **of one's own ~** por voluntad propia, espontáneamente, motu propio.

volley ['vɒlɪ] **1** *n* (**a**) (*of shots*) descarga *f*, descarga *f* cerrada; (*of stones etc*) lluvia *f*; (*of applause*) salva *f*; (*of abuse etc*) torrente *m*, retahíla *f*.

(**b**) (*Tennis*) voleo *m*.

2 *vt* (**a**) (*Tennis*) volear.

(**b**) *abuse etc* dirigir (*at* a).

3 *vi* (*Mil*) lanzar una descarga.

volleyball ['vɒlɪbɔːl] *n* vol(e)ibol *m*, balonvolea *m*.

volleyer ['vɒlɪə^r] *n* especialista *mf* en voleas.

volt [vəʊlt] *n* voltio *m*.

voltage ['vəʊltɪdʒ] *n* voltaje *m*.

voltaic [vɒl'teɪɪk] *adj* voltaico.

volte-face ['vɒlt'fɑːs] *n* viraje *m*, cambio *m* súbito de opinión.

voltmeter ['vəʊlt,miːtə^r] *n* voltímetro *m*.

volubility [,vɒljʊ'bɪlɪtɪ] *n* locuacidad *f*.

voluble ['vɒljʊbl] *adj person* locuaz, hablador; **in ~ French** en francés suelto y rápido; **a ~ protest** una protesta larga y enérgica.

volubly ['vɒljʊblɪ] *adv* de modo locuaz, con locuacidad; con soltura, rápidamente; larga y enérgicamente.

volume ['vɒljuːm] **1** *n* (**a**) (*book*) volumen *m*; (*number in series*) tomo *m*; **in the third ~** en el tercer tomo; **an edition in 4 ~s** una edición en 4 tomos; **it speaks ~s** es sumamente significativo; **it speaks ~s for it** lo evidencia de modo inconfundible; **it speaks ~s for him** es un testimonio muy significativo acerca de él.

(**b**) (*size*) volumen *m*; **production ~** cantidad *f* de producción.

(**c**) (*sound*) volumen *m* (sonoro); **to turn the ~ up** aumentar el sonido.

(**d**) (*large amount*) cantidad *f*, masa *f*; (*of water*) cantidad *f* de agua; caudal *m* (de un río *etc*).

2 *attr*: ~ **business** empresa *f* que comercia sólo en grandes cantidades; ~ **control** control *m* de volumen; ~ **discount** descuento *m* por volumen de compras; ~ **sales** ventas *fpl* a granel.

volumetric [,vɒljʊ'metrɪk] *adj* volumétrico.

voluminous [və'luːmɪnəs] *adj* voluminoso.

voluntarily ['vɒləntərɪlɪ] *adv* voluntariamente, espontáneamente, sin ser forzado.

voluntary ['vɒləntərɪ] **1** *adj* voluntario; espontáneo; libre; ~ **controls** controles *mpl* voluntarios; ~ **liquidation** liquidación *f* voluntaria; ~ **redundancy,** ~ **severance** baja *f* incentivada, baja *f* por incentiva; ~ **worker** trabajador *m* voluntario, trabajadora *f* voluntaria. **2** *n* solo *m* de órgano; **trumpet ~** solo *m* de trompeta.

volunteer [,vɒlən'tɪə^r] **1** *n* voluntario *m*.

2 *adj, attr force etc* de voluntarios.

3 *vt* (**a**) *information, services* ofrecer; *remark* hacer.

(**b**) (*) **they ~ed him for the job** le señalaron contra su voluntad para el puesto.

4 *vi* ofrecerse (voluntario); (*Mil*) alistarse voluntario; **to ~ for service overseas** ofrecerse para servir en ultramar; **to ~ to do a job** ofrecerse a hacer un trabajo; **he wasn't forced to, he ~ed** nadie le obligó a ello, se ofreció libremente.

voluptuary [və'lʌptjʊərɪ] *n* voluptuoso *m*, -a *f*.

voluptuous [və'lʌptjʊəs] *adj* voluptuoso.

voluptuously [və'lʌptjʊəslɪ] *adj* voluptuosamente.

voluptuousness [və'lʌptjʊəsnɪs] *n* voluptuosidad *f*.

vomit ['vɒmɪt] **1** *n* vómito *m*. **2** *vt* vomitar, arrojar. **3** *vi* vomitar, tener vómitos.

vomiting ['vɒmɪtɪŋ] *n* vómito *m*.

voodoo ['vuːduː] *n* vudú *m*.

voracious [və'reɪʃəs] *adj* voraz.

voraciously [və'reɪʃəslɪ] *adv* vorazmente.

voracity [vɒ'ræsɪtɪ] *n* voracidad *f*.

vortex ['vɔːteks] *n, pl* **vortices** ['vɔːtɪsiːz] vórtice *m*.

Vosges [vəʊʒ] *npl* Vosgos *mpl*.

votary ['vəʊtərɪ] *n* (*Rel*) devoto *m*, -a *f*; (*fig*) partidario *m*, -a *f*.

vote [vəʊt] **1** *n* (**a**) (*gen*) voto *m*; sufragio *m*; **to cast one's ~, to give one's ~** dar su voto (*for, to* a); **how many ~s did he get?** ¿cuántos votos obtuvo?; **he won by 89 ~s** ganó por 89 votos.

(**b**) (*voting*) votación *f*; (*election*) elección *f*, elecciones *fpl*; ~ **of censure** voto *m* de censura; ~ **of confidence** voto *m* de confianza; ~ **of no confidence** voto *m* de censura; ~ **of thanks** palabras *fpl* de agradecimiento; **by popular ~** por votación popular, (*fig*) en la opinión de muchos; **by secret ~** por votación secreta; **to allow a free ~** dejar libertad de voto; **as the 1931 ~ showed** según demostraron las elecciones de 1931; **to put a motion to the ~, to take a ~ on a motion** someter una moción a votación; **let's take a ~ on it** ¡votémoslo!

(**c**) (*right to ~*) derecho *m* de votar, sufragio *m*; **when women got the ~** cuando se concedió a las mujeres el derecho de votar; **to have the ~** tener el derecho de votar.

2 *vt*: **to ~ a sum for defence** votar una cantidad para la defensa; **she was ~d Miss Granada 1995** fue elegida como Miss Granada 1995; **we ~d it a failure** opinamos que fue un fracaso; **the team ~d it a hit** el equipo pronosticó que tendría éxito; **to ~ that ...** resolver por votación que ...; **I ~ that ...*** propongo que ..., sugiero que ...; **to ~ sb into office** elegir a uno para ocupar un puesto.

3 *vi* votar; (*go to polls*) ir a votar, acudir a las urnas; **to ~ for sb** votar por uno; **to ~ Socialist** votar socialista, votar por los socialistas; **to ~ with one's feet** expresar su opinión no acudiendo (*or* abandonando la organización *etc*).

◆**vote down** *vt*: **to ~ a proposal down** rechazar una propuesta por votación; **we ~d that idea down** rechazamos esa idea.

◆**vote in** *vt*: **to ~ a government in** elegir un gobierno.

◆**vote out** *vt* rechazar (por votación, en elecciones).

◆**vote through** *vt* aprobar (por votación).

vote-catching ['vəʊtkætʃɪŋ] **1** *adj* electoralista. **2** *n* electoralismo *m.*

voter ['vəʊtəʳ] *n* votante *mf.*

voting ['vəʊtɪŋ] **1** *n* votación *f.* **2** *attr*: ~ **booth** cabina *f* de votación; ~ **machine** (*US*) máquina *f* de votar; ~ **paper** papeleta *f* (de votación); ~ **pattern** tendencia *f* de la votación; ~ **power** potencia *f* electoral; ~ **register** registro *m* electoral; ~ **right** derecho *m* a voto; ~ **share** acción *f* con derecho a voto.

votive ['vəʊtɪv] *adj* votivo.

vouch [vaʊtʃ] **1** *vt* garantizar, atestiguar; confirmar; **to ~ that ...** afirmar que ..., asegurar que ...

2 *vi*: **to ~ for sth** garantizar algo; confirmar algo; responder de algo; **I cannot ~ for its authenticity** no puedo responder de su autenticidad; **to ~ for sb** responder por uno.

voucher ['vaʊtʃəʳ] *n* documento *m* justificativo; (*Comm*) comprobante *m*; vale *m*, cupón *m.*

vouchsafe [vaʊtʃ'seɪf] *vt* conceder, otorgar; *reply etc* servirse hacer, dignarse hacer; **to ~ to** + *infin* dignarse + *infin.*

vow [vaʊ] **1** *n* voto *m* (*also Eccl*); promesa *f* solemne; **lovers' ~s** promesas *fpl* solemnes de los amantes; **the ~ of poverty** el voto de pobreza; **to be under a ~ to do sth** haber hecho voto de hacer algo, haber prometido solemnemente hacer algo; **to take a ~ to** + *infin* hacer voto de + *infin*, jurar + *infin*; **to take ~s** profesar.

2 *vt*: **to ~ vengeance against sb** jurar vengarse (de uno); **to ~ that ...** jurar que ..., prometer solemnemente que ...; **to ~ to** + *infin* hacer voto de + *infin*, jurar + *infin.*

vowel [vaʊəl] **1** *n* vocal *f.* **2** *attr* vocálico; ~ **shift** cambio *m* vocálico; ~ **sound** sonido *m* vocálico; ~ **system** sistema *m* vocálico.

voyage ['vɔɪɪdʒ] **1** *n* viaje *m* (por mar, en barco); (*crossing*) travesía *f*; **the ~ out** el viaje de ida; **the ~ home** el viaje de regreso.

2 *vi* viajar (por mar); navegar; **to ~ across unknown seas** viajar por mares desconocidos.

voyager ['vɔɪədʒəʳ] *n* viajero *m*, -a *f* (por mar).

voyeur [vwɑː'jɜːʳ] *n* voyer *m*, mirón *m.*

voyeurism [vwɑː'jɜːrɪzəm] *n* voyerismo *m*, mironismo *m.*

V.P. *n abbr of* **Vice-President** Vicepresidente *mf*, V.P.

vs *abbr of* **versus** contra, versus, vs.

VSO *n* (*Brit*) *abbr of* **Voluntary Service Overseas.**

VSOP *abbr of* **very special** (*or* **superior**) **old pale.**

VT (*US Post*) *abbr of* **Vermont.**

VTOL ['viːtɒl] *n abbr of* **vertical take-off and landing** (*aircraft*) avión *m* de despegue y aterrizaje cortos, ADAC.

VTR *n abbr of* **videotape recorder.**

Vulcan ['vʌlkən] *nm* Vulcano.

vulcanite ['vʌlkənaɪt] *n* vulcanita *f*, ebonita *f.*

vulcanization [,vʌlkənaɪ'zeɪʃən] *n* vulcanización *f.*

vulcanize ['vʌlkənaɪz] *vt* vulcanizar.

vulcanologist [,vʌlkən'ɒlədʒɪst] *n* vulcanólogo *m*, -a *f.*

vulcanology [,vʌlkə'nɒlədʒɪ] *n* vulcanología *f.*

vulgar ['vʌlgəʳ] **1** *adj* (**a**) (*of the people*) vulgar; **V~ Latin** latín *m* vulgar; **in the ~ tongue** en la lengua vulgar, en la lengua vernácula; **that is a ~ error** eso es un error vulgar.

(**b**) (*indecent*) ordinario, grosero; (*in bad taste*) de mal gusto, cursi; *joke, song* verde, colorado (*LAm*); *person* ordinario. **2** *npl*: **the ~** el vulgo.

vulgarian [vʌl'gɛərɪən] *n* persona *f* ordinaria; (*wealthy*) ricacho *m*, -a *f.*

vulgarism ['vʌlgərɪzəm] *n* vulgarismo *m.*

vulgarity [vʌl'gærɪtɪ] *n* (*V* **vulgar**) vulgaridad *f*; ordinariez *f*, grosería *f*; mal gusto *m*, cursilería *f*; lo verde, indecencia *f*; **such ~!** ¡qué ordinario!, ¡qué indecente!; **no ~, please** por favor, nada de indecencias.

vulgarize ['vʌlgəraɪz] *vt* vulgarizar.

vulgarly ['vʌlgəlɪ] *adv* vulgarmente; de modo ordinario; groseramente; con mal gusto, de modo cursi; indecentemente; **X, ~ known as Y** X, vulgarmente llamado Y.

Vulgate ['vʌlgɪt] *n* Vulgata *f.*

vulnerability [,vʌlnərə'bɪlɪtɪ] *n* vulnerabilidad *f.*

vulnerable ['vʌlnərəbl] *adj* vulnerable (*to* a).

vulpine ['vʌlpaɪn] *adj* vulpino (*also fig*).

vulture ['vʌltʃəʳ] *n* buitre *m* (*also fig*).

vulva ['vʌlvə] *n* vulva *f.*

vv. *abbr of* **verses**; *V* **v.** (**a**), (**b**).

v.v. *abbr of* **vice versa.**

vying ['vaɪɪŋ] *ger of* **vie.**

W

W, w ['dʌbljʊ] *n* (*letter*) W, w *f*; **W for William** W de Washington.

W *abbr of* **west** oeste *m*, O; *also adj*.

w. *abbr of* **watt(s)** vatio(s) *m(pl)*, v.

WA (*US Post*) *abbr of* **Washington** (*estado*).

wacky* ['wækɪ] *adj* (*US*) *person* chiflado*; *thing* absurdo.

wad [wɒd] **1** *n* (*stuffing*) taco *m*, tapón *m*; (*in gun, cartridge*) taco *m*; (*of cotton wool etc*) bolita *f* de algodón; (*of papers*) lío *m*; (*of banknotes*: *US*) fajo *m*.

2 *vt* (*stuff*) rellenar; (*Sew*) acolchar.

wadding ['wɒdɪŋ] *n* (*wad*) taco *m*, tapón *m*; relleno *m*; (*lining*) entretela *f*, forro *m*; (*Med*) algodón *m* hidrófilo.

waddle ['wɒdl] **1** *n* anadeo *m*; **to walk with a ~** andar como pato, anadear. **2** *vi* anadear; **she ~d over to the window** fue anadeando a la ventana.

wade [weɪd] **1** *vt* vadear.

2 *vi* (*also* **to ~ along**) caminar por el agua (*or* nieve, lodo *etc*), (*waist-deep etc*) caminar con el agua hasta la cintura (*etc*); **we shall have to ~** tendremos que meternos en el agua; **to ~ across a river** vadear un río; **to ~ ashore** llegar a tierra vadeando; **to ~ into sb** (*fig*) emprenderla con uno, arremeter contra uno; **to ~ into a meal** echarse sobre una comida; **to ~ through the water** caminar por el agua; **to ~ through a book** leerse un libro a pesar de lo aburrido (*or* lo difícil *etc*); **it took me an hour to ~ through your essay** tardé una hora en leer tu ensayo.

◆wade in *vi* entrar en el agua; (*fig*) entrar pisando fuerte.

wader ['weɪdəʳ] *n* (**a**) (*Orn*) ave *f* zancuda. (**b**) **~s** botas *fpl* altas de goma.

wadge [wɒdʒ] *n* = **wodge**.

wadi ['wɒdɪ] *n cauce de río en el norte de África*.

wading bird ['weɪdɪŋ,bɜːd] *n* ave *f* zancuda.

wading pool ['weɪdɪŋ,puːl] *n* (*US*) estanque *m* para chapotear, estanque *m* (*or* piscina *f*) para niños.

wafer ['weɪfəʳ] *n* (**a**) (*biscuit*) galleta *f*; (*with ice cream*) barquillo *m*; (*for sealing*) oblea *f*; (*Eccl*) hostia *f*. (**b**) (*Comput*) oblea *f*, microplaqueta *f*.

wafer-thin ['weɪfə'θɪn] *adj* delgadísimo, finísimo.

wafery ['weɪfərɪ] *adj* delgado, ligero.

waffle ['wɒfl] **1** *n* (**a**) (*Culin*) gofre *m*; **~ iron** molde *m* para hacer gofres.

(**b**) (*Brit**) palabras *fpl* inútiles, palabrería *f*; (*in essay etc*) paja *f*.

2 *vi* (*Brit**: *also* **to ~ on**) dar el rollo*, ser muy charlatán, parlotear; (*in essay etc*) poner mucha paja.

waft [wɑːft] **1** *n* soplo *m*, ráfaga *f* de olor.

2 *vt* llevar por el aire; hacer flotar; (*stir*) mecer, mover.

3 *vi* moverse (de un sitio a otro); ser llevado por el aire; flotar.

wag¹ [wæg] **1** *n* meneo *m*, movimiento *m*; (*of tail*) coleada *f*.

2 *vt* mover, menear, agitar; **the dog ~ged its tail** el perro meneó la cola.

3 *vi* moverse, menearse, agitarse; **tongues were ~ging about their relationship** las malas lenguas se ocupaban de sus relaciones; **this will make the tongues ~** esto dará en qué hablar.

wag² [wæg] *n* (*joker*) bromista *m*, zumbón *m*.

wage [weɪdʒ] **1** *n* (*also* **~s**) salario *m*; (*esp day* **~**) jornal *m*; (*fig*) pago *m*; premio *m*.

2 *attr* salarial; **~s bill** gastos *mpl* de nómina; **~ claim** (*Brit*) reivindicación *f* salarial; **~ differential** diferencia *f* salarial; **~ freeze** congelación *f* de los salarios; **~ increase** aumento *m* salarial; **~ packet** sobre *m* de pago; **~-price spiral** espiral *f* de precios y salarios; **~ rates** escala *f* salarial; **~ restraint** restricción *f* salarial, moderación *f* salarial; **~ rise** aumento *m* salarial; **~ scale** escala *f* salarial; **~ settlement** acuerdo *m* salarial; **~s slip** hoja *f* salarial, papeleta *f* de salario.

3 *vt war* hacer; *battle* librar, dar; *campaign* proseguir.

wage-earner ['weɪdʒ,ɜːnəʳ] *n* asalariado *m*, -a *f*.

wager ['weɪdʒəʳ] **1** *n* apuesta *f*; **to lay a ~** hacer una apuesta; **to lay a ~ on a horse** apostar dinero a un caballo.

2 *vt* apostar; **to ~ £20 on a horse** apostar 20 libras a un caballo; **to ~ that ...** apostar a que ...; **he won't do it, I ~ !** ¡a que no lo hace!

wages ['weɪdʒɪz] *npl V* **wage**.

wage-worker ['weɪdʒ,wɜːkəʳ] *n* (*US*) asalariado *m*, -a *f*.

waggish ['wægɪʃ] *adj* zumbón, bromista.

waggishly ['wægɪʃlɪ] *adv*: **he said ~** dijo zumbón.

waggle ['wægl] = **wag¹**.

wag(g)on ['wægən] *n* carro *m*; (*Brit Rail*) vagón *m*; (*US*: *also* **station ~**) furgoneta *f*, rubia *f*, camioneta *f*; (*US*: *police van*) furgón *m* policial; **to be on the (water) ~*** no beber; **to go on the (water) wagon*** resolverse a no beber; **to hitch one's ~ to a star** picar muy alto.

wag(g)onage ['wægənɪdʒ] *n* acarreo *m*; transporte *m* en vagones (*etc*).

wag(g)onload ['wægənləʊd] *n* carretada *f*, carga *f* de un carro (*etc*); **50 ~s of coal** 50 vagones de carbón.

Wagnerian [vɑːg'nɪərɪən] *adj* wagneriano.

wagtail ['wægteɪl] *n* lavandera *f*.

waif [weɪf] *n* niño *m* abandonado, niña *f* abandonada; **~s and strays** niños *mpl* desamparados.

wail [weɪl] **1** *n* (*cry*) lamento *m*, gemido *m*; (*baby's first cry*) vagido *m*; (*complaint*) queja *f*, protesta *f*; **a great ~ went up** pusieron el grito en el cielo.

2 *vi* lamentarse, gemir; (*child*) gimotear; llorar; (*complain*) quejarse, protestar.

wailing ['weɪlɪŋ] *n* lamentación *f*, lamentaciones *fpl*, gemidos *mpl*; vagidos *mpl*; quejas *fpl*, protestas *fpl*; **W~ Wall** Muro *m* de las Lamentaciones.

wain [weɪn] *n* carro *m*; **the W~** (*Astron*) el Carro.

wainscot ['weɪnskət] *n* friso *m*; entablado *m*, revestimiento *m* (de la pared).

wainscotting ['weɪnskətɪŋ] *n* revestimiento *m*.

waist [weɪst] *n* (*Anat etc*) cintura *f*, talle *m*; (*fig, narrow part*) cuello *m*; (*Naut*) combés *m*.

waistband ['weɪsɪbænd] *n* pretina *f*, cinturón *m*.

waistcoat ['weɪskəʊt] *n* (*Brit*) chaleco *m*.

waist-deep ['weɪsɪ'diːp] *adv* hasta la cintura.

-waisted ['weɪstɪd] *adj* de cintura ..., de talle ..., *eg* **slim-~** de cintura delgada.

waist-high ['weɪst'haɪ] **1** *adv* hasta la cintura; al nivel de la cintura. **2** *adj*: **~ vegetation** vegetación *f* que crece hasta la altura de la cintura.

waistline ['weɪstlaɪn] *n* talle *m*, cintura *f*.

wait [weɪt] **1** *n* (**a**) espera *f*; (*pause*) pausa *f*, intervalo *m*; **there was a ~ of 10 minutes** tuvimos que esperar 10 minutos; **to have a long ~** tener que esperar mucho tiempo; **to be** (*or* **lie**) **in ~** acechar (*for sb* a uno).

(**b**) **~s** (*Brit*) murga *f* (de Nochebuena).

2 *vt* esperar; aplazar; guardar para después; **to ~ one's chance** esperar su ocasión; **we'll ~ dinner for you** no empezaremos a cenar hasta que vengas.

3 *vi* (**a**) esperar; aguardar; **~ a moment!** ¡un momento!, ¡momentito! (*LAm*); (*fig, querying*) ¡oiga!; **~ and see!** espera y verás; **there's a parcel ~ing to be collected** hay un paquete que recoger; **the dishes can ~** no hay prisa con los platos; **all that can ~ till tomorrow** todo eso lo podemos dejar para mañana; **'repairs while you ~'** 'reparaciones en el acto', 'reparaciones instantáneas'; **just you ~!** ¡me las pagarás!; **just you ~ till your father finds out!** ¡a ver qué pasa cuando se entere tu padre!; **I can't ~**

estoy impaciente (*to* + *infin* por + *infin*); **~ till you're asked** espera hasta que te inviten; **~ till you're older** eso es para cuando seas algo mayor; **to keep sb ~ing** hacer esperar a uno; **to ~ for sb** esperar a uno, (*in ambush*) acechar a uno; **to ~ for sb to do sth** esperar hasta que uno haga algo; **we are ~ing for you to decide** estamos pendientes de la decisión de Vd; **what are you ~ing for?** (*hurry up*) ¡vamos ya!, ¡date prisa!; **~ for it!** (*guess what*) ¡a ver si lo adivinas!; (*not yet*) ¡todavía no!

(**b**) (*as servant etc*) servir; **to ~ at table** servir a la mesa.

◆**wait about, wait around** *vi* esperar, perder el tiempo.

◆**wait behind** *vi* quedarse; **to ~ behind for sb** quedarse para esperar a uno.

◆**wait in** *vi*: **to ~ in for sb** estar en casa (*etc*) esperando a uno.

◆**wait on** *vt* (**a**) **to ~ on sb** servir a uno; **to ~ on sb hand and foot** desvivirse por uno, mimar a uno.

(**b**) (*frm*) = **wait upon** (**a**).

◆**wait out** *vt* quedarse hasta el final de; **to ~ sb out** esperar más que uno.

◆**wait up** *vi* velar, no acostarse, seguir sin acostarse; **don't ~ up for me!** ¡idos (*LAm*: váyanse) a la cama sin esperarme!

◆**wait upon** *vt* (**a**) **to ~ upon sb** (*frm*) cumplimentar a uno, presentar sus respetos a uno.

(**b**) = **wait on** (**a**).

waiter ['weɪtəʳ] *n* camarero *m*, mesero *m* (*LAm*).

waiting ['weɪtɪŋ] **1** *adj*: **~ time** tiempo *m* de espera; **to play a ~ game** dejar pasar el tiempo. **2** *n* (**a**) espera *f*; **all this ~!** ¡tanto esperar! (**b**) (*frm*) servicio *m*; **to be in ~ on sb** estar de servicio con uno, servir a uno.

waiting-list ['weɪtɪŋ'lɪst] *n* lista *f* de espera.

waiting-room ['weɪtɪŋrʊm] *n* sala *f* de espera.

waitress ['weɪtrɪs] *n* camarera *f*, mesera *f* (*LAm*); **~!** ¡señorita!

waive [weɪv] *vt* renunciar a; prescindir de.

waiver ['weɪvəʳ] *n* renuncia *f*.

wake¹ [weɪk] *n* (*Naut*) estela *f*; **in the ~ of** (*fig*) como consecuencia de, tras, después de, a raíz de; **wars bring misery in their ~** las guerras acarrean la miseria; **they came in the ~ of the invaders** siguieron a los invasores.

wake² [weɪk] **1** *n* (*over corpse*) vela *f*, velatorio *m*, velorio *m* (*esp LAm*).

2 (*irr*: *pret* **woke**, *ptp* **woken, waked**) *vt* (*also* **to ~ up**) despertar; *corpse* velar; **a noise which would ~ the dead** un ruido que despertaría a un muerto.

3 *vi* (*also* **to ~ up**) despertar, despertarse; **~ up!** ¡despierta!; **she woke up with a start** despertó sobresaltada; **he woke up (to find himself) in prison** amaneció en la cárcel; **he woke up to find himself rich** a la mañana siguiente amaneció rico; **to ~ up to reality** despertar a la realidad; **to ~ up to the truth** darse cuenta de la verdad.

wakeful ['weɪkfʊl] *adj* (*awake*) despierto; (*alert*) vigilante; desvelado; (*unable to sleep*) insomne; **to have a ~ night** pasar la noche sin dormir, pasar la noche en blanco.

wakefulness ['weɪkfʊlnɪs] *n* vigilancia *f*, desvelo *m*; insomnia *f*.

waken ['weɪkən] **1** *vt* despertar. **2** *vi* despertar, despertarse.

wakey-wakey* ['weɪkɪ'weɪkɪ] *excl* ¡arriba!

waking ['weɪkɪŋ] **1** *adj*: **in one's ~ hours** en las horas en que uno está despierto. **2** *n* despertar *m*; **on ~** al despertar.

Wales [weɪlz] *n* Gales *f*.

walk [wɔːk] **1** *n* (**a**) (*spell of ~ing: stroll*) paseo *m*; (*hike*) caminata *f*, excursión *f* a pie; (*Sport*) marcha *f*; **it's only a 10-minute ~ from here** ir desde aquí a pie es sólo cosa de 10 minutos; **from there you have a short ~ to his house** desde allí a su casa se va a pie en muy poco tiempo; **to go for** (*or* **have, take**) **a ~** dar un paseo, dar una vuelta; **to take sb for a ~** llevar a uno de paseo; **take a ~!*** ¡lárgate*!

(**b**) (*gait*) andar *m*, paso *m*; **he has an odd sort of ~** tiene un modo de andar algo raro; **to know sb by** (*or* **from**) **his ~** conocer a uno por su modo de andar; **he went at a quick ~** caminó a un paso rápido.

(**c**) (*route*) **there's a nice ~ by the river** se pasea muy bien a lo largo del río, es encantador pasearse a lo largo del río; **this is my favourite ~** éste es mi paseo favorito.

(**d**) (*fig*) **~ of life** profesión *f*; esfera *f*; clase *f* social; **people from every ~ of life** gente *f* de toda condición.

(**e**) (*avenue*) paseo *m*, alameda *f*.

2 *vt* (**a**) *person* llevar a paseo, pasear; **to ~ sb off his legs** dejar a uno rendido caminando; **to ~ a girl home** acompañar a una joven a su casa; **I'll ~ you to the station** te acompaño a la estación; **she ~s the dog every day** lleva al perro de paseo todos los días.

(**b**) **to ~ a horse** llevar un caballo al paso.

(**c**) (*distance*) cubrir, recorrer a pie, andar; **we ~ed 40 kilometres yesterday** ayer anduvimos 40 kilómetros.

(**d**) **to ~ the streets** andar por las calles, callejear, (*aimlessly*) vagar por las calles; (*prostitute*) hacer la carrera; (*be homeless*) no tener hogar, estar sin techo; **to ~ the boards** salir a escena; **to ~ the wards** hacer prácticas de clínica.

(**e**) (*****) **don't worry, you'll ~ it** no te preocupes, será facilísimo.

3 *vi* (**a**) (*gen*) andar, caminar (*LAm*); **'W~'** (*US Aut*) 'Cruzar'; **'Don't W~'** (*US Aut*) 'No cruzar'; **can the boy ~ yet?** ¿sabe andar el niño ya?; **~ a little with me** ven a acompañarme un poco; **to ~ in one's sleep** ser sonámbulo, pasearse dormido; **to ~ downstairs** bajar la escalera; **to ~ upstairs** subir la escalera; **to ~ slowly** andar despacio.

(**b**) (*not ride*) andar, ir a pie; (*stroll*) pasearse; **we had to ~** tuvimos que ir andando; **to ~ home** ir andando hasta casa; **you can ~ there in 5 minutes** en 5 minutos se va allá andando; **we were out ~ing** nos estábamos paseando.

(**c**) (*ghost*) andar, aparecer.

(**d**) (***: *disappear*) volar*.

◆**walk about** *vi* pasearse; ir y venir.

◆**walk across** *vi* cruzar.

◆**walk around** *vi* dar una vuelta, pasearse.

◆**walk away** *vi* (**a**) (*lit*) irse; alejarse (*from sb* de uno); **to ~ away from a problem** negarse a afrontar un problema; **you can't just ~ away from it!** ¡no puedes irte como si no hubiera nada!

(**b**) **to ~ away with** *prize* llevarse, copar, largarse con; (*steal*) robar.

◆**walk back** *vi* volver a pie, regresar andando.

◆**walk down** *vi* bajar (a pie).

◆**walk in** *vi* entrar; **'please ~ in'** 'entren sin llamar'; **who should ~ in but Joe** y ¡bomba! entra Pepe; **to ~ in on sb** interrumpir a uno.

◆**walk into** *vt* (**a**) **to ~ into a room** entrar en un cuarto; **to ~ into an ambush** caer en una trampa; **you really ~ed into that one!*** ¡te has dejado embaucar por las buenas!

(**b**) (*collide with*) chocar con, dar con, dar contra; (***: *meet*) topar, tropezar con.

(**c**) (*****) *food* devorar, zampar.

(**d**) **to ~ into sb*** (*attack*) atacar a uno, arremeter contra uno.

(**e**) (*****) **to ~ into a job** conseguir fácilmente un puesto.

◆**walk off 1** *vt*: **to ~ off a headache** quitarse un dolor de cabeza dando un paseo, dar una vuelta para quitarse un dolor de cabeza; **to ~ off one's lunch** bajar la comida dando un paseo.

2 *vi* (**a**) irse; alejarse; **he ~ed off angrily** se fue enfadado.

(**b**) **to ~ off with** *prize* llevarse, copar, largarse con; (*steal*) robar.

◆**walk on** *vi* (**a**) (*continue*) seguir andando (*or* caminando (*LAm*)).

(**b**) (*Theat*) salir de figurante.

◆**walk out** *vi* (**a**) salir; (*from meeting*) salir, retirarse; (*on strike*) declararse en huelga; **you can't ~ out now!** ¡no puedes marcharte ahora!

(**b**) **to ~ out on sb** abandonar a uno; **to ~ out on a girl** dejar plantada a una chica, plantar a una chica.

◆**walk over 1** *vt* (*treat badly*) **to ~ all over sb** atropellar a uno, tratar a uno a coces; **they ~ed all over us in the second half** nos cascaron en el segundo tiempo.

2 *vi* (*Sport*) ganar; ganar la carrera por ser el único caballo (*etc*) que participa.

◆**walk through** *vt* (*Theat*) ensayar (por primera vez).

◆**walk up** *vi* subir (a pie); **~ up!, ~ up!** ¡vengan!, ¡acérquense!; **to ~ up to sb** acercarse a uno, abordar a uno; **to ~ up and down** pasearse (de acá para allá).

walkabout ['wɔːkəbaʊt] *n* paseo *m* entre el público; **to go ~** pasearse entre el público.

walkaway ['wɔːkəweɪ] *n* (*US*) victoria *f* fácil.

walker ['wɔːkəʳ] *n* (**a**) (*stroller*) paseante *mf*; (*not rider*) peatón *m*; (*Sport*) marchador *m*, -ora *f*; (*hiker*) andarín *m*, -ina *f*; **to be a great ~** ser gran andarín; ser aficionado a las excursiones a pie.

(**b**) (*apparatus*) pollera *f*, andador *m*.

walker-on ['wɔːkər'ɒn] *n* (*Theat*) figurante *m*, -a *f*, comparsa *mf*; (*Cine*) extra *mf*.

walkies* ['wɔːkɪz] *n sing* paseo *m*; **to take the dog ~** llevar al perro de paseo.

walkie-talkie ['wɔːkɪ'tɔːkɪ] *n* transmisor-receptor *m* portátil, walki-talki *m*.

walk-in ['wɔːkɪn] **1** *adj* (**a**) *furniture* empotrado; **~ cupboard** alacena *f* ropera. (**b**) **in ~ condition** en condiciones de habitabilidad, habitable. **2** *n* (*US*) (**a**) = **~ cupboard**. (**b**) (*victory*) victoria *f* fácil.

walking ['wɔːkɪŋ] **1** *adj* ambulante; **~ delegate** (*US*) delegado *m*, -a *f* sindical; **~ pace** paso *m* de andar; **~ papers*** (*US*) pasaporte* *m*, aviso *m* de despido; **~ race** carrera *f* pedestre; **~ shoes** zapatos *mpl* para caminar; **~ tour** viaje *m* a pie, excursión *f* a pie; **the ~ wounded** los heridos que pueden ir de pie; **it's within ~ distance** se puede ir allí andando; **he's a ~ encyclopaedia** es una enciclopedia ambulante.

2 *n* paseo *m*, pasearse *m*; (*as exercise*) marcha *f*; (*Sport*) marcha *f* (atlética).

walking-on [,wɔːkɪŋ'ɒn] *adj*: = **walk-on**.

walking-stick ['wɔːkɪŋstɪk] *n* bastón *m*.

Walkman ['wɔːkmən] ® *n*, *pl* **Walkmans** ['wɔːkmənz] Walkman ® *m*.

walk-on ['wɔːkɒn] *adj*: **~ part** (*Theat*) papel *m* de figurante, papel *m* de comparsa; (*Cine*) papel *m* de extra.

walkout ['wɔːkaʊt] *n* (*from conference*) salida *f*, retirada *f*; (*strike*) huelga *f*; **to stage a ~** (*leave*) salir, retirarse, (*strike*) declarar la huelga, salir del trabajo.

walkover ['wɔːk,əʊvəʳ] *n* (*Sport*) walkover *m*; (*fig*) triunfo *m* fácil, pan *m* comido; **it won't be a ~** no va a ser un paseo.

walk-through ['wɔːkθruː] *n* ensayo *m*.

walk-up ['wɔːkʌp] *n* (*US*) pisos *mpl* sin ascensor.

walkway ['wɔːkweɪ] *n* pasarela *f*.

wall [wɔːl] **1** *n* muro *m*; (*interior, Anat etc*) pared *f*; (*city ~*) muralla *f*; (*garden ~*) tapia *f*; (*fig*) barrera *f*; (*Sport*: *of players*) barrera *f*; **the Great W~ of China** la Gran Muralla China; **the north ~ of the Eiger** la pared norte del Eiger; **to break the ~ of silence** romper el muro del silencio; **to climb the ~*, to go up the ~*** subirse por las paredes*; **to come up against a blank** (*or* **brick**) **~** (*fig*) tener por delante una barrera infranqueable; **to do sth off the ~*** (*US*) hacer algo espontáneamente, hacer algo de improviso; **it drives** (*or* **sends**) **me up the ~*** me vuelve loco, me hace subir por las paredes*; **to go to the ~** ser desechado por inútil, (*Comm*) quebrar, ir a la bancarrota; **to push sb to the ~** poner a uno en una situación muy difícil; **~s have ears** las paredes oyen.

2 *attr map etc* de pared, mural.

3 *vt* murar; cerrar con muro; *city* amurallar; *garden* tapiar, cercar con tapia.

◆**wall in** *vt* cerrar con muro; *garden* tapiar, cercar con tapia.

◆**wall off** *vt* amurallar; separar con un muro.

◆**wall up** *vt person* emparedar; *opening* cerrar con muro, tabicar.

wallaby ['wɒləbɪ] *n* ualabí *m*.

wallah* ['wɒlə] *n* hombre *m*; (*pej*) tío* *m*, sujeto* *m*; **the ice-cream ~** el hombre de los helados; **the ~ with the beard** él de la barba.

wallbars ['wɔːlbɑːz] *npl* espalderas *fpl*.

wallboard ['wɔːlbɔːd] *n* (*US*) cartón *m* de yeso; fibra *f* prensada (para paredes).

wall-clock ['wɔːlklɒk] *n* reloj *m* de pared.

wall-covering ['wɔːl,kʌvərɪŋ] *n* material *m* de decoración de paredes.

walled [wɔːld] *adj city* amurallado; *garden* con tapia.

wallet ['wɒlɪt] *n* cartera *f*, billetera *f* (*LAm*).

wall-eyed ['wɔːl'aɪd] *adj* de ojos incoloros; estrábico.

wallflower ['wɔːl,flaʊəʳ] *n* alhelí *m*; **to be a ~** (*fig*) ser la fea del baile, comer pavo.

wall-map ['wɔːlmæp] *n* mapa *m* mural.

Walloon [wɒ'luːn] **1** *adj* valón. **2** *n* (**a**) valón *m*, -ona *f*. (**b**) (*Ling*) valón *m*.

wallop* ['wɒləp] **1** *n* (**a**) (*blow*) golpe *m*, golpazo *m*; **~!** ¡zas!; **to give sb a ~** pegar a uno; **it packs a ~*** (*US*) es muy fuerte, tiene mucho efecto.

(**b**) (*speed*) velocidad *f*; **to go at a fair ~** correr rápidamente.

(**c**) (*Brit*: *beer*) cerveza *f*.

2 *vt* golpear fuertemente; (*punish*) zurrar*.

walloping* ['wɒləpɪŋ] **1** *adj* colosal, grandote. **2** *n* zurra* *f*, paliza *f*; **to give sb a ~** dar una paliza a uno (*also fig*).

wallow ['wɒləʊ] **1** *n*: **I had a good ~ in the bath** descansé bañándome largamente. **2** *vi* revolcarse (*in* en); **to ~ in** (*fig*) revolcarse en, sumirse en; **to ~ in money** nadar en la opulencia; **to ~ in vices** revolcarse en los vicios.

wall-painting ['wɔːl,peɪntɪŋ] *n* pintura *f* mural.

wallpaper ['wɔːl,peɪpəʳ] **1** *n* papel *m* pintado, papel *m* de paredes. **2** *vt* empapelar.

wall-socket ['wɔːl,sɒkɪt] *n* enchufe *m* de pared.

Wall Street ['wɔːlstriːt] *n* (*US*) *calle de la Bolsa y de muchos bancos en Nueva York*; (*fig*) mundo *m* bursátil, mundo *m* financiero; **shares rose sharply on ~** las acciones subieron bruscamente en la Bolsa (de Nueva York).

wall-to-wall ['wɔːltə'wɔːl] *adj*: **~ carpet** moqueta *f* de pared a pared.

wally* ['wɒlɪ] *n* gili* *mf*, criajo* *m*.

walnut ['wɔːlnʌt] *n* (*nut*) nuez *f*; (*tree, wood*) nogal *m*.

walnut-tree ['wɔːlnʌttriː] *n* nogal *m*.

walrus ['wɔːlrəs] **1** *n* morsa *f*. **2** *attr*: **~ moustache** bigotes *mpl* de foca.

Walter ['wɔːltəʳ] *nm* Gualterio.

waltz [wɔːlts] **1** *n* vals *m*; **it was a ~!*** (*US*) ¡fue tirado!*, ¡fue coser y cantar! **2** *vi* valsar; **to ~ in*** entrar tan fresco*; **to ~ out*** salir tan fresco*.

wan [wɒn] *adj* pálido, macilento; (*sad*) triste.

wand [wɒnd] *n* (*of office*) vara *f*; **magic ~** varilla *f* de virtudes.

wander ['wɒndəʳ] **1** *vt* vagar por, recorrer; **to ~ the streets** vagar por las calles, pasearse por las calles, callejear; **to ~ the world** vagar por el mundo.

2 *vi* vagar, pasearse sin propósito fijo, deambular; ir a la deriva, viajar al azar; andar perdido; (*get lost*) extraviarse; **to ~ aimlessly** deambular; **to ~** (**in one's mind**) divagar, delirar; **to ~ from the path** desviarse camino, descaminarse; **to ~ from the point** salirse del tema; **to ~ off** irse (distraído); **the children ~ed off into the woods** los niños se alejaron sin rumbo y entraron en el bosque; **his speech ~ed on and on** continuó incansable su discurso tan confuso; **to ~ round a shop** curiosear en una tienda; **to let one's mind ~** dejar que la imaginación fantasee.

3 *n* paseo *m*; **to take** (*or* **go for**) **a ~** pasearse, dar un paseo.

◆**wander about, wander around** *vi* deambular.

wanderer ['wɒndərəʳ] *n* hombre *m* errante, mujer *f* errante; (*traveller*) viajero *m*, -a *f*; (*pej*) vagabundo *m*, -a *f*; (*tribesman etc*) nómada *mf*; **I've always been a ~** nunca he querido establecerme de fijo en un sitio.

wandering ['wɒndərɪŋ] **1** *adj* errante, errabundo; *stream* sinuoso; *salesman etc* ambulante; *tribesman* nómada; *mind, thoughts* distraído. **2** *npl*: **~s** viajes *mpl*; errabundeo *m*; andanzas *fpl*; (*pej*) vagabundeo *m*; (*Med*) delirio *m*.

wanderlust ['wɒndəlʌst] *n* pasión *f* de viajar, ansia *f* de ver mundo.

wane [weɪn] **1** *n*: **to be on the ~** menguar, estar menguando; (*fig*) decaer, menguar, disminuir; declinar, estar en decadencia. **2** *vi* = **to be on the ~**.

wangle* ['wæŋgl] **1** *n* chanchullo* *m*, trampa *f*, truco *m*; **it's a ~** aquí hay trampa; **he got in by a ~** se las arregló para ser admitido.

2 *vt* (**a**) *job etc* mamarse*, agenciarse, conseguir; **he ~d his way in** logró entrar gracias a un truco; **he'll ~ it for you** te lo procurará por el sistema que él se sabe; **can you ~ me a free ticket?** ¿puedes procurarme una entrada de favor?

(**b**) *accounts etc* amañar.

wangler* ['wæŋgləʳ] *n* chanchullero* *m*, trapisondista *mf*.

wangling* ['wæŋglɪŋ] *n* chanchullos* *mpl*, trampas *fpl*; **there's a lot of ~ goes on** hay muchas trampas.

waning ['weɪnɪŋ] **1** *adj moon* menguante; (*fig*) decadente. **2** *n* (*of moon*) menguante *f*; (*fig*) mengua *f*; disminución *f*; decadencia *f*.

wank** [wæŋk] (*Brit*) **1** *n*: **to have a ~** = **2**. **2** *vi* hacerse una paja**.

wanker** ['wæŋkəʳ] *n* (*fig*) tío *m* tonto*.

wanly ['wɒnlɪ] *adv* pálidamente; (*sadly*) tristemente.

wanness ['wɒnnɪs] *n* palidez *f*.

want [wɒnt] **1** *n* (**a**) (*lack*) falta *f*; ausencia *f*; (*shortage*) carencia *f*, escasez *f*; **~ of judgement** falta *f* de juicio; **for ~ of** por falta de; **for ~ of anything better** por falta de algo mejor; **for ~ of sth to do** por no tener nada que hacer; **to feel the ~ of** sentir la falta de.

(**b**) (*poverty*) miseria *f*, pobreza *f*, indigencia *f*; **to be in ~** estar necesitado.

(**c**) (*need*) necesidad *f*; **my ~s are few** necesito poco; **to be in ~ of** necesitar; **to attend to sb's ~s** atender a las necesidades de uno; **it fills a long-felt ~** viene a llenar un vacío hace tiempo sentido; **~ ad*** (*US*) anuncio *m* clasificado.

2 *vt* (**a**) (*Brit*: *need*: *of person*) necesitar; **all I ~ is sleep** lo único que necesito es dormir; **children ~ lots of sleep** los niños necesitan dormir mucho; **we have all we ~** tenemos todo lo que necesitamos; **you ~ to be careful*** hay que tener mucho ojo; **what you ~ is a good hiding*** no te vendría mal una paliza de las buenas; **those ~ing a job** los que buscan trabajo; **'~ed'** (*police notice*) 'se busca'; **the ~ed man** el hombre buscado; **the most ~ed man** el hombre más buscado; **'~ed: general maid'** (*advert*) 'necesítase criada para todo'; **he is ~ed for murder** se le busca por asesino.

(**b**) (*need*: *of thing*) exigir, requerir; **it ~s some doing** no es nada fácil hacerlo; **that work ~s a lot of time** ese trabajo exige mucho tiempo; **does my hair ~ cutting?** ¿me hace falta cortar el pelo?; **the house will ~ painting next year** el año que viene será necesario pintar la casa.

(**c**) (*wish*) querer, desear; **she knows what she ~s** ella se sabe lo que quiere; **I ~ to see the manager!** ¡quiero ver al gerente!; **to ~ sb to do sth** querer que uno haga algo; **I ~ him sent away at once** quiero que se le despida en seguida; **I was ~ing to leave** estaba deseando marcharme; **what does he ~ with me?** ¿qué quiere de mí?, ¿qué tiene que ver conmigo?; **he ~s £200 for the picture** pide 200 libras por el cuadro; **you don't ~ much!** (*iro*) ¡eso no es mucho pedir!; **you're ~ed on the 'phone** te llaman al teléfono.

(**d**) (*lack*) carecer de; **he ~s talent** carece de talento; **he ~s enterprise** le falta iniciativa; **the contract ~s only his signature** sólo hace falta que firme el contrato; **it ~s 2 for a complete set** faltan 2 para hacer una serie completa; **it ~ed only this last step to** + *infin* sólo hacía falta este último paso para + *infin*.

3 *vi* (**a**) (*lack*) **to ~ for** necesitar, carecer de; **they ~ for nothing** no carecen de nada, lo tienen todo.

(**b**) **he ~s out*** quiere dejarlo, quiere terminar con eso.

wanting ['wɒntɪŋ] *adj* defectuoso; deficiente (*in* en), falto (*in* de); **charity is ~ in the novel** a la novela le falta caridad, la novela es deficiente en caridad; **there is sth ~** falta algo; **he is ~ing in enterprise** le falta iniciativa, está falto de iniciativa; **he was tried and found ~** se le sometió a la prueba y resultó que le faltaban las cualidades indispensables.

wanton ['wɒntən] *adj* (**a**) (*playful*) juguetón; (*wayward*) travieso; caprichoso; (*unrestrained*) desenfrenado; (*licentious*) lascivo.

(**b**) (*motiveless*) sin motivo, inmotivado; *destruction* sin propósito, sin sentido; *cruelty* gratuito.

wantonly ['wɒntənlɪ] *adv* (*V adj*) (**a**) caprichosamente; desenfrenadamente; lascivamente. (**b**) sin motivo; sin propósito; gratuitamente.

wantonness ['wɒntənnɪs] *n* (*V adj*) (**a**) lo caprichoso; desenfreno *m*; lascivia *f*. (**b**) falta *f* de motivo; lo gratuito.

war [wɔːʳ] **1** *n* guerra *f*; **~ of nerves** guerra *f* de nervios; **~ of words** guerra *f* de propaganda; **~ to the knife** guerra *f* a muerte; **Great W~** (*1914-18*) Primera Guerra *f* Mundial; **Second World W~** (*1939-45*) Segunda Guerra *f* Mundial; **the period between the ~s** (*1918-39*) el período de entreguerras; **to be at ~** estar en guerra (*with* con); **you've been in the ~s!** (*to child*) ¡vuelve el guerrero herido!; **to declare ~** declarar la guerra (*on* a); **to go to ~** emprender la guerra; hacer la guerra; **we shall not go to ~ over the Slobodian question** no emprenderemos la guerra por la cuestión de Eslobodia; **they went to ~ singing** fueron a la guerra cantando; **to make ~** hacer la guerra (*on* a).

2 *attr* (*in most senses*) de guerra; **~ clouds** nubes *fpl* de guerra; **~ correspondent** corresponsal *mf* de guerra; **~ crime** crimen *m* de guerra; **~ criminal** criminal *mf* de guerra; **~ dead** muertos *mpl* en campaña; **~ debt** deuda *f* de guerra; **~ effort** esfuerzo *m* bélico; **on a ~ footing** en pie de guerra; **~ material** material *m* bélico; **~ memorial** monumento *m* a los caídos; **W~ Office** (†) Ministerio *m* de Guerra; **~ widow** viuda *f* de guerra.

3 *vi* (*liter*) guerrear (*on* con).

warble ['wɔːbl] **1** *n* trino *m*, gorjeo *m*. **2** *vt song etc* cantar trinando, cantar con trinos. **3** *vi* trinar, gorjear.

warbler ['wɔːbləʳ] *n* mosquitero *m*, curruca *f*.

warbling ['wɔːblɪŋ] *n* gorjeo *m*.

warcry ['wɔːkraɪ] *n* grito *m* de guerra.

ward [wɔːd] **1** *n* (**a**) (*~ship*) tutela *f*, custodia *f*; **in ~** bajo tutela.

(**b**) (*person*) pupilo *m*, -a *f*; **~ of court** persona *f* bajo la protección del tribunal.

(**c**) (*Brit Pol*) distrito *m* electoral.

(**d**) (*of hospital*) sala *f*, crujía *f*; **'W~ 7'** 'Sala 7'; **to walk the ~s** hacer prácticas de clínica.

(**e**) (*of key*) guarda *f*.

2 *attr*: **~ round** (*Med*) visita *f* de salas.

◆**ward off** *vt blow* desviar, parar; *danger* evitar; *attack* rechazar, defenderse contra; *cold* protegerse de.

-ward(s) [wəd(z)] *suf* hacia; **townward(s)** hacia la ciudad; **pubward(s)** hacia la taberna.

war-dance ['wɔːdɑːns] *n* danza *f* guerrera.

warden ['wɔːdn] *n* guardián *m*; vigilante *mf*; (*Univ etc*) director *m*, -ora *f*; (*Aut*) controlador *m*, -ora *f* de estacionamiento; (*of castle etc*) alcaide *m*.

warder ['wɔːdəʳ] *n* (*esp Brit*) celador *m*, -ora *f*.

ward heeler ['wɔːd'hiːləʳ] *n* (*US Pol*) muñidor *m*.

wardress ['wɔːdrɪs] *n* celadora *f*.

wardrobe ['wɔːdrəʊb] **1** *n* (*clothes*) vestidos *mpl*, trajes *mpl*; (*Theat*) vestuario *m*; (*cupboard*) guardarropa *m*, armario *m* (ropero); ropero *m* (*LAm*); (*in hall*) gabanero *m*.

2 *attr*: **~ dealer** ropavejero *m*; **~ mistress** guardarropa *f*; **~ trunk** baúl *m* ropero.

wardroom ['wɔːdrʊm] *n* (*Naut*) cámara *f* de oficiales.

wardship ['wɔːdʃɪp] *n* tutela *f*.

warehouse 1 ['wɛəhaʊs] *n*, *pl* **warehouses** ['wɛə,haʊzɪz] almacén *m*, depósito *m*. **2** *attr*: **~ keeper** almacenista *m*; **~ loan** préstamo *m* de almacén; **~ manager** gerente *m* de almacén; **~ price** precio *m* en almacén; **~ receipt** recibo *m* de almacén; **~ warrant** duplicado *m* del certificado de almacén. **3** ['wɛəhaʊz] *vt* almacenar.

warehouseman ['wɛəhaʊsmən] *n*, *pl* **warehousemen** ['wɛəhaʊsmən] almacenista *m*.

warehousing ['wɛəhaʊzɪŋ] *n* almacenamiento *m*.

wares [wɛəz] *npl* mercancías *fpl*; **to cry one's ~** pregonar sus mercancías.

warfare ['wɔːfɛəʳ] *n* guerra *f*; (*as study*) arte *m* militar, arte *m* de la guerra.

war-fever ['wɔː,fiːvəʳ] *n* psicosis *f* de guerra.

war-game ['wɔːgeɪm] *n* simulacro *m* de guerra; juego *m* de guerra.

warhead ['wɔːhed] *n* (*of torpedo*) punta *f* de combate; (*of rocket*) cabeza *f* de guerra; **nuclear ~** cabeza *f* nuclear.

warhorse ['wɔːhɔːs] *n* caballo *m* de guerra; (*fig*) veterano *m*.

warily ['wɛərɪlɪ] *adj* con cautela, cautelosamente; **to tread ~** (*also fig*) andar con pies de plomo.

wariness ['wɛərɪnɪs] *n* cautela *f*, precaución *f*; recelo *m*.

warlike ['wɔːlaɪk] *adj* guerrero, belicoso.

war-loan ['wɔːləʊn] *n* empréstito *m* de guerra.

warlock ['wɔːlɒk] *n* brujo *m*, hechicero *m*.

warlord ['wɔːlɔːd] *n* señor *m* de la guerra; jefe *m* militar.

warm [wɔːm] **1** *adj* (**a**) caliente (*pero no con exceso*); (*not too hot*) templado, tibio; *climate* cálido; *day, summer* caluroso, de calor; *blanket, clothing etc* cálido; **~ front** frente *m* caliente; **to be ~** (*person*) tener calor, (*thing*) estar caliente, (*weather*) hacer calor; **to be very ~** (*person*) tener mucho calor, (*thing*) estar muy caliente, (*weather*) hacer mucho calor; **to get ~** (*thing*) calentarse, (*weather*) empezar a hacer calor; **to get ~** (*person*) entrar en calor; **I still haven't got ~** todavía no he entrado en calor; **you're getting ~!** (*in games*) ¡te quemas!; **to keep o.s. ~** mantener el calor del cuerpo; **to keep sth ~** tener algo caliente, mantener el calor de algo; **to be as ~ as toast** estar muy bien de caliente.

(**b**) (*fig*) *scent* fresco; *tint* cálido; *thanks* efusivo; *heart, temperament* afectuoso; *dispute* acalorado; *greeting, welcome* caluroso; *hope* ardiente, sincero; *applause* cálido, entusiasta; *supporter* entusiasta; **it's ~ work** es un trabajo que hace sudar.

2 *n*: **to be in the ~** estar al calor, estar donde hay un calor agradable; **come and have a ~ by the fire** ven a calentarte junto a la lumbre.

3 *vt* calentar; *heart etc* alegrar, regocijar; (*) zurrar*.

4 *vi* **I** (*or* **my heart**) **~ed to him** le fui cobrando simpatía; **to ~ to one's subject** entusiasmarse con su tema.

5 *vr*: **to ~ o.s. at the fire** calentarse junto a la lumbre.

◆**warm up 1** *vt food* recalentar; *engine* calentar; *atmosphere etc* avivar, reanimar.

2 *vi* precalentarse (*also Sport*); (*argument*) acalorarse; **things are ~ing up** hay más actividad, hay más animación; **the game is ~ing up** el partido se está animando.

warm-blooded ['wɔːm'blʌdɪd] *adj* de sangre caliente; (*fig*) ardiente, apasionado.

warmed-up ['wɔːmd'ʌp] *adj* recalentado.

warm-hearted ['wɔːm'hɑːtɪd] *adj* bondadoso, afectuoso.

warming ['wɔːmɪŋ] *n* (**a**) recalentamiento *m.* (**b**) (*) zurra* *f.*
warming-pan ['wɔːmɪŋpæn] *n* calentador *m* (de cama).
warmly ['wɔːmlɪ] *adv* (**a**) **the sun shone** ~ brillaba el sol y hacía calor; **to dress** ~ arroparse, ir bien abrigado; **the flat was very** ~ **heated** el piso tenía buena calefacción.
(**b**) (*fig*) efusivamente, con efusión; afectuosamente; calurosamente; con entusiasmo; **he thanked me most** ~ me dio las más efusivas gracias; **he shook my hand** ~ me estrechó la mano afectuosamente; **we** ~ **welcome it** nosotros lo acogemos con entusiasmo.
warmonger ['wɔːˌmʌŋgəʳ] *n* belicista *m.*
warmongering ['wɔːˌmʌŋgərɪŋ] **1** *adj* belicista. **2** *n* belicismo *m.*
warmth [wɔːmθ] *n* (**a**) calor *m*; lo cálido, lo caluroso.
(**b**) (*fig*) efusión *f*; afecto *m*; lo caluroso; entusiasmo *m*; **the** ~ **of their greeting** su acogida calurosa; **he replied with some** ~ contestó bastante indignado.
warm-up ['wɔːmʌp] **1** *n* (*Sport*) precalentamiento *m*, calentamiento *m* previo; actividad *f* preliminar, preparativos *mpl*. **2** *attr*: ~ **suit** (*US*) chandal *m.*
warn [wɔːn] *vt* avisar, advertir; amonestar; prevenir; **to** ~ **the police** avisar a la policía; **the bell is to** ~ **the workmen** el timbre es para dar aviso a los obreros; ~ **me before you blow it up** avísame antes de volarlo; **you have been** ~**ed!** ¡está Vd prevenido!; **to** ~ **sb not to do sth** advertir a uno que no haga algo; **to** ~ **sb about sth** amonestar a uno acerca de algo; **to** ~ **sb against sb else** prevenir a uno contra otra persona; **to** ~ **sb of a danger** prevenir a uno contra un peligro; **to** ~ **sb off** expulsar a uno; **to** ~ **sb off a subject** advertir a uno que no se meta en un asunto; **I** ~**ed him off Espronceda** le dije que no le convenía estudiar a Espronceda.
warning ['wɔːnɪŋ] **1** *n* aviso *m*, advertencia *f*; **without** ~ sin dar aviso, sin previo aviso; **it fell without** ~ cayó de repente, cayó inesperadamente; **they came without** ~ vinieron sin avisar; **let this be a** ~ **to you** que esto te sirva de escarmiento; **thank you for the** ~ gracias por la advertencia; **the bell gives** ~ el timbre da la alarma; **to give sb a week's** ~ avisar a uno con ocho días de anticipación; **to give sb due** ~ avisar a uno con mucha antelación; **you were given due** ~ te avisamos debidamente; **I give you due** ~ **that** ... le advierto en serio que ...; **to send a** ~ **to the police** avisar a la policía; **to sound a** ~ dar un aviso; dar la voz de alarma; **to take** ~ **from** aprender la lección de, escarmentar en.
2 *adj*: ~ **device** dispositivo *m* de alarma; ~ **light** luz *f* de advertencia; ~ **notice** aviso *m*; ~ **shot** cañonazo *m* de advertencia, disparo *m* de advertencia; ~ **sign** señal *f* de peligro; **in a** ~ **tone** en tono amonestador; ~ **triangle** (*Aut*) triángulo *m* señalizador; ~ **voices** voces *fpl* admonitorias.
warp [wɔːp] **1** *n* (**a**) (*in weaving*) urdimbre *f.* (**b**) (*of wood*) deformación *f*, alabeo *m*, comba *f*; (*fig*) sesgo *m.*
2 *vt wood* deformar, alabear, torcer; *mind* pervertir, torcer, afectar.
3 *vi* deformarse, alabearse, torcerse.
war-paint ['wɔːpeɪnt] *n* pintura *f* de guerra.
warpath ['wɔːpɑːθ] *n*: **to be on the** ~ estar en pie de guerra, estar preparado para la guerra; (*fig*) estar dispuesto a armar un lío; estar buscando pendencia.
warped [wɔːpt] *adj wood* deformado, torcido; *character, sense of humour etc* pervertido.
warping ['wɔːpɪŋ] *n* (*of wood*) deformación *f*, alabeo *m*; (*Aer*) torsión *f.*
warplane ['wɔːpleɪn] *n* avión *m* militar.
warrant ['wɒrənt] **1** *n* (**a**) (*justification*) autorización *f*, justificación *f.*
(**b**) (*certificate*) cédula *f*, certificado *m*; (*Comm*) garantía *f*; (*Jur*) mandamiento *m* judicial; mandato *m*, orden *f*; ~ **of arrest** orden *f* de prisión; ~ **issue** emisión *f* de cédula; **there is a** ~ **out for his arrest** se ha ordenado su detención.
2 *vt* (**a**) (*justify*) autorizar, justificar; **nothing** ~**s such an assumption** no hay nada que justifique tal suposición; **this order** ~**s your immediate attention** esta orden exige que Vd le preste atención en seguida; **the facts do not** ~ **it** los hechos no lo justifican.
(**b**) (*Comm etc*) garantizar, certificar; **I** ~ (**you**) te lo aseguro.
warrantable ['wɒrəntəbl] *adj* justificable.
warranted ['wɒrəntɪd] *adj* (**a**) (*justified*) justificado. (**b**) (*guaranteed*) garantizado; ~ **18 carat gold** certificado de oro de 18 quilates.
warrant officer ['wɒrəntˌɒfɪsəʳ] *n* (*Mil*) brigada *m*; (*Naut*) contramaestre *m.*
warrantor ['wɒrəntɔːʳ] *n* garante *mf.*
warranty ['wɒrəntɪ] *n* garantía *f*; **without** ~ sin garantía.
warren ['wɒrən] *n* madriguera *f* (de conejos); (*fig*) (*house etc*) conejera *f*, casa *f* con muchísimos inquilinos; casa *f* laberíntica; (*area of town*) barrio *m* densamente poblado; **it is a** ~ **of little streets** es un laberinto de callejuelas.
warring ['wɔːrɪŋ] *adj interests, nations etc* opuestos, reñidos entre sí, en lucha abierta entre sí.
warrior ['wɒrɪəʳ] *n* guerrero *m*; **the Unknown W**~ el Soldado Desconocido.
Warsaw ['wɔːsɔː] **1** *n* Varsovia *f.* **2** *attr*: ~ **Pact** Pacto *m* de Varsovia.
warship [wɔːʃɪp] *n* buque *m* de guerra, barco *m* de guerra.
wart [wɔːt] *n* (*Med, Bot*) verruga *f*; ~**s and all** con todas sus imperfecciones.
wart-hog ['wɔːthɒg] *n* jabalí *m* verrugoso, facochero *m.*
wartime ['wɔːtaɪm] **1** *n* tiempo *m* de guerra; **in** ~ en tiempos de guerra, en la guerra. **2** *attr* de tiempos de guerra, de guerra.
war-torn ['wɔːˌtɔːn] *adj* destrozado por la guerra.
warty ['wɔːtɪ] *adj* verrugoso.
war-weary ['wɔːˌwɪərɪ] *adj* cansado de la guerra.
war-wounded ['wɔːˌwuːndɪd] *npl*: **the** ~ los heridos de guerra.
wary ['wɛərɪ] *adj* cauteloso, cauto; **it's best to be** ~ **here** aquí conviene andar con pies de plomo; **I was** ~ **about it** tuve mis dudas acerca de ello, me recelé, desconfié de ello; **to keep a** ~ **eye on sb** vigilar a uno con recelo, tener cuidado con uno.
war-zone ['wɔːzəʊn] *n* zona *f* de guerra.
was [wɒz, wəz] *V* **be.**
wash [wɒʃ] **1** *n* (**a**) (*act of* ~*ing*) lavado *m*; baño *m*; **to give sth a** ~ lavar algo; **to have a** ~ lavarse; **to have a** ~ **and brush-up** lavarse y arreglarse; **my shirt is at** (*or* **in**) **the** ~ mi camisa se está lavando, mi camisa está en la lavandería; **to send sheets to the** ~ mandar sábanas a la lavandería; **it will all come out in the** ~ todo saldrá en la colada.
(**b**) (*clothes: dirty*) ropa *f* sucia, ropa *f* para lavar; (*hung to dry*) tendido *m*, colada *f*; **the Monday** ~ la ropa para lavar el lunes.
(**c**) (*of ship*) remolinos *mpl*; (*Aer*) disturbio *m* aerodinámico; **the** ~ **of the water** (*sound*) el movimiento del agua, el chapoteo del agua.
(**d**) (*liquid: hair*~) champú *m*; (*mouth*~) enjuague *m*; (*of distemper, paint*) capa *f*; pintura *f*; (*of insecticide etc*) baño *m*; (*liquid remains*) lavazas *fpl*, despojos *mpl* líquidos; (*pej*) aguachirle *f*; **a coat of blue** ~ una capa de pintura azul.
2 *vt* (**a**) (*clean with water etc*) lavar; *dishes* fregar; *clothes* lavar; **to** ~ **one's hair** lavarse el pelo; **to** ~ **one's hands** lavarse las manos; **to** ~ **sth clean** limpiar algo lavándolo, lavar algo hasta dejarlo limpio; **the sea** ~**ed it clean of oil** el mar le quitó todo el aceite.
(**b**) **to** ~ **the walls with distemper** dar una capa de pintura (al temple) a las paredes; **to** ~ **a metal with gold** dar una capa de oro a un metal, bañar un metal en oro.
(**c**) **an island** ~**ed by a blue sea** una isla bañada por el mar azul.
(**d**) (*of river, sea: carry*) llevar, llevarse; **the house was** ~**ed downstream** la casa fue llevada aguas abajo; **the sea** ~**ed it ashore** el mar lo echó a la playa; **he was** ~**ed overboard** fue arrastrado por las olas.
3 *vi* (**a**) (*have a* ~) lavarse; (*do the* ~*ing*) lavar la ropa.
(**b**) **a cloth that** ~**es well** una tela que puede lavarse; **it's nice but it won't** ~ es atractivo pero no se puede lavar; **that excuse won't** ~**!*** (*Brit*) ¡esa excusa no cuela!
(**c**) (*of sea etc*) moverse; chapotear; **the river was** ~**ing against the top of the bridge** el río estaba a la altura de la parte alta del puente; **the sea** ~**ed over the promenade** el mar inundó el paseo marítimo.
◆**wash away** *vt* (**a**) *dirt* quitar (lavando).
(**b**) **the boat was** ~**ed away** el bote fue arrastrado por la corriente; **the river** ~**ed away part of the bank** el río se llevó una parte de la orilla.
◆**wash down** *vt* (**a**) *car, wall* lavar.
(**b**) **to** ~ **one's dinner down with wine** regar la cena con vino.
(**c**) (*by flood etc*) llevar, arrastrar.
◆**wash off** **1** *vt* quitar (lavando), hacer desaparecer (lavando).
2 *vi*: **it** ~**es off easily** se quita fácilmente (lavándolo); **it won't** ~ **off** no se quita, no sale.
◆**wash out** **1** *vt* (**a**) *vessel* lavar, enjuagar; *stain* lavar.

(**b**) **to feel ~ed out** no estar bien de salud; estar muy cansado; **to look ~ed out** estar ojeroso.

(**c**) (*ruin*) arruinar, acabar con; **the game was ~ed out** el partido fue cancelado debido a la lluvia; **it ~ed out our last chance** acabó con nuestra última posibilidad; **let's ~ it all out** abandonémoslo todo, renunciemos a la empresa.

2 *vi*: **the colour ~es out** el color se destiñe.

◆**wash through** *vt clothes* lavar rápidamente.

◆**wash up 1** *vt* (**a**) (*Brit*) *dishes* fregar, lavar.

(**b**) **the sea ~ed it up** el mar lo echó, el mar lo arrojó (a la playa).

(**c**) (*) **that's all ~ed up** eso es un fracaso total, eso ya se acabó; **he's all ~ed up** está hecho una calamidad.

2 *vi* (**a**) (*Brit*) fregar los platos.

(**b**) (*US*) lavarse, lavarse las manos.

Wash. (*US*) *abbr of* **Washington**.

washable [ˈwɒʃəbl] *adj* lavable.

wash-and-wear [ˈwɒʃənˈwɛəʳ] *adj clothing* de no planchar, de lava y pon.

wash bag [ˈwɒʃbæg] *n* (*US*) esponjera *f*.

washbasin [ˈwɒʃˌbeɪsn] *n* (*Brit*), **washbowl** [ˈwɒʃbəʊl] *n* palangana *f*, jofaina *f*.

washboard [ˈwɒʃbɔːd] *n* tabla *f* de lavar; (*US*) rodapié *m*, zócalo *m*.

washcloth [ˈwɒʃklɒθ] *n*, *pl* **washcloths** [ˈwɒʃklɒθs, ˈwɒʃklɒðz] (*US*) paño *m* para lavarse, manopla *f*.

washday [ˈwɒʃdeɪ] *n* día *m* de colada.

washed-out [ˈwɒʃtaʊt] *adj* deslavazado.

washer [ˈwɒʃəʳ] *n* (**a**) (*Tech*) arandela *f*; (*on tap*) arandela *f*, zapatilla *f*. (**b**) (*washing-machine*) lavadora *f*.

washerwoman [ˈwɒʃəˌwʊmən] *n*, *pl* **washerwomen** [ˈwɒʃəˌwɪmɪn] lavandera *f*.

wash-house [ˈwɒʃhaʊs] *n*, *pl* **washhouses** [ˈwɒʃˌhaʊzɪz] lavadero *m*.

washing [ˈwɒʃɪŋ] *n* (**a**) (*act*) lavado *m*, el lavar. (**b**) (*clothes: dirty*) ropa *f* sucia, ropa *f* para lavar; (*hung to dry*) tendido *m*, colada *f*; **to take in ~** ser lavandera.

washing-day [ˈwɒʃɪŋdeɪ] *n* día *m* de colada.

washing-line [ˈwɒʃɪŋˈlaɪn] *n* cuerda *f* de tender la ropa.

washing-machine [ˈwɒʃɪŋməˌʃiːn] *n* lavadora *f*.

washing-powder [ˈwɒʃɪŋˌpaʊdəʳ] *n* (*Brit*) jabón *m* en polvo.

washing-soda [ˈwɒʃɪŋˌsəʊdə] *n* sosa *f*, carbonato *m* sódico.

Washington [ˈwɒʃɪŋtən] *n* Washington *m*.

washing-up [ˈwɒʃɪŋˈʌp] *n* (*Brit*) (*act*) fregado *m*, el fregar (los platos); (*dishes: to be washed*) platos *mpl* para lavar; (*washed*) platos *mpl* lavados; **~ liquid** detergente *m* líquido, lavavajillas *m*; **he did all the ~** fregó todos los platos.

wash-leather [ˈwɒʃˌleðəʳ] *n* (*Brit*) gamuza *f*.

wash-out* [ˈwɒʃaʊt] *n* desastre *m*, fracaso *m*; **it was a ~** fue un fracaso total; **he's a ~** es una calamidad*.

washrag [ˈwɒʃræg] *n* (*US*) paño *m* de cocina; = **washcloth**.

washroom [ˈwɒʃrʊm] *n* lavabo *m*, aseos *mpl*, sanitarios *mpl* (*LAm*), baño *m* (*LAm*).

wash sale [ˈwɒʃseɪl] *n* (*US*) venta *f* ficticia.

washstand [ˈwɒʃstænd] *n* lavabo *m*, lavamanos *m*.

washtub [ˈwɒʃtʌb] *n* tina *f* de lavar; (*bath*) bañera *f*.

washy [ˈwɒʃɪ] *adj* aguado, diluido; débil; (*fig*) flojo, soso.

wasn't [ˈwɒznt] = **was not**.

WASP* [wɒsp] *n* (*US*) *abbr for* **White Anglo-Saxon Protestant**.

wasp [wɒsp] *n* avispa *f*; **~s' nest** avispero *m* (*also fig*).

waspish [ˈwɒspɪʃ] *adj character* irascible; *person* de prontos enojos, fácil de enojar; *comment* mordaz, punzante.

waspishly [ˈwɒspɪʃlɪ] *adv* mordazmente.

wasp waist [ˈwɒspˈweɪst] *n* (*fig*) talle *m* de avispa.

wasp-waisted [ˈwɒspˈweɪstɪd] *adj* (*fig*) con talle de avispa.

wassail†† [ˈwɒseɪl] **1** *n* (*drink*) cerveza *f* especiada; (*festivity*) juerga *f*, fiesta *f* de borrachos. **2** *vi* beber mucho.

wastage [ˈweɪstɪdʒ] *n* desgaste *m*, desperdicio *m*; pérdida *f*; (*from container*) merma *f*; **the ~ of our resources** el desperdicio de nuestros recursos; **the ~ rate among students** la proporción de estudiantes que no terminan su licenciatura (*etc*); **the ~ rate among entrants to the profession** el porcentaje de los que abandonan la profesión poco tiempo después de ingresar en ella.

waste [weɪst] **1** *adj* (*rejected*) desechado, de desecho; (*left over*) sobrante, superfluo; (*useless*) inútil; *land* baldío; yermo; **~ disposal unit** triturador *m* de basuras; **~ material** material *m* de desecho; **~ paper** papel *m* viejo, papel *m* de desecho, papeles *mpl* usados; **~ products** (*Bio*) desperdicios *mpl*, (*of industry*) residuos *mpl*; **~ steam** vapor *m* de escape; **'The W~ Land'** 'Tierra *f* baldía'; **to lay ~** asolar, devastar; **to lie ~** quedar sin cultivar; quedar sin utilizar.

2 *n* (**a**) (*act*) despilfarro *m*, derroche *m*; (*of time etc*) pérdida *f*; (*wastage*) desgaste *m*, desperdicio *m*; merma *f*; **it's a ~ of time** es tiempo perdido; **it's a ~ of effort** es un esfuerzo inútil; **there's a lot of ~ here** hay mucho desperdicio aquí; **to go to ~**, **to run to ~** echarse a perder, perderse.

(**b**) (**~** *material*) desperdicios *mpl*, desechos *mpl*; (*rubbish*) basura *f*; (*industrial*) residuos *mpl*, vertidos *mpl*.

(**c**) (*land*) yermo *m*, tierra *f* baldía; desierto *m*; **lost in the ~s of Siberia** perdido en la inmensidad de Siberia; **to plough the ~s of Siberia** cultivar la tierra baldía de Siberia.

3 *vt* (**a**) (*squander*) despilfarrar, derrochar; malgastar; *time etc* perder; (*not use*) desperdiciar; *opportunity etc* desaprovechar, desperdiciar; (*use up*) agotar, consumir; **a ~d life** una vida desperdiciada; **nothing is ~d** no queda nada sin aprovechar; **we ~d 3 litres of petrol** perdimos 3 litros de gasolina; **to ~ no time in doing sth** hacer algo cuanto antes; **we must ~ no time** no hay que perder tiempo; **you're wasting your time talking to him** es tiempo perdido hablar con él; **don't ~ your efforts on him** no te canses tratando de hacer cosas por él.

(**b**) *body etc* consumir, gastar, debilitar.

(**c**) (*US*‡: *kill*) mandar al otro mundo*, cargarse*.

4 *vi* (**a**) **~ not, want not** la economía protege de la necesidad. (**b**) (**~** *away*) gastarse, perderse.

◆**waste away** *vi* consumirse, mermar; (*person*) consumirse; **you're not exactly wasting away** (*iro*) no pareces haber enflaquecido de modo peligroso que digamos.

wastebasket [ˈweɪstˌbɑːskɪt] *n* (*US*) cesto *m* de los papeles, papelera *f*.

wastebin [ˈweɪstˈbɪn] *n* (*Brit*) cubo *m* de la basura.

wasted [ˈweɪstɪd] *adj opportunity* desaprovechado; *effort* inútil, vano; *person* (*thin*) demacrado; *limb* atrofiado; (*: *from drugs*) destrozado.

wasteful [ˈweɪstfʊl] *adj person etc* pródigo, despilfarrado, derrochador; *process* antieconómico, dispendioso; *expenditure* pródigo, excesivo; **it is ~ of effort** no utiliza debidamente el esfuerzo.

wastefully [ˈweɪstfəlɪ] *adv* pródigamente; antieconómicamente; excesivamente.

wastefulness [ˈweɪstfʊlnɪs] *n* prodigalidad *f*, despilfarro *m*; falta *f* de economía, lo antieconómico; lo excesivo.

wasteland [ˈweɪstlænd] *n* tierra *f* baldía, yermo *m*, erial *m*.

wastepaper-basket [weɪstˈpeɪpəˌbɑːskɪt] *n* cesto *m* de los papeles, papelera *f*.

waste-pipe [ˈweɪstpaɪp] *n* tubo *m* de desagüe.

waster [ˈweɪstəʳ] *n* (*person*) derrochador *m*, perdido *m*.

wasting [ˈweɪstɪŋ] *adj disease* debilitante; *asset* agotable.

wastrel [ˈweɪstrəl] *n* derrochador *m*, perdido *m*.

watch [wɒtʃ] **1** *n* (**a**) (*vigilance*) vigilancia *f*; (*act of ~ing*) vigilia *f*, vela *f*; **to be on the ~** estar a la mira (*for* de), estar al acecho, vigilar; **they're on the ~ for smugglers** están alerta por si hay contrabandistas, están al acecho de los contrabandistas; **we have the place under ~** estamos vigilando el local; **to keep ~** estar de guardia; **to keep ~ all night** velar toda la noche; **to keep a close ~ on sth** vigilar algo con mucho cuidado; **to keep ~ over** *person* velar, vigilar; *thing* velar por; **to set a ~ on sb** poner a uno bajo vigilancia.

(**b**) (*period of duty*) guardia *f*; **to have a 4-hour ~** estar de guardia durante 4 horas.

(**c**) (*persons: Hist*) ronda *f*; (*Mil: persons*) guardia *f*, (*1 man*) guardia *m*, centinela *m*; (*Naut: persons*) guardia *f*, vigía *f*, (*1 man*) vigía *m*; **officer of the ~** oficial *m* de guardia.

(**d**) (*timepiece*) reloj *m* (de bolsillo, de pulsera); **what does your ~ say?** ¿qué hora tienes?

2 *vt* (**a**) (*guard*) guardar, vigilar; proteger.

(**b**) (*observe*) observar, mirar; (*at length*) contemplar; (*spy on*) espiar, acechar; (*TV etc*) ver; **did you ~ the programme?** ¿viste el programa?; **to ~ sb doing sth** ver a uno hacer algo, observar mientras uno hace algo, observar a uno hacer algo; **now ~ this closely** ahora observen esto detenidamente; **we are being ~ed** nos están observando; **have you ever ~ed an operation?** ¿has visto alguna vez una operación?; **Big Brother is ~ing you** el Gran Hermano te vigila.

(**c**) (*be careful with*) ser cuidadoso con, prestar atención a, tener ojo a; **~ it!** ¡ojo!, ¡cuidado!, ¡abusado! (*Mex*); **you'd better ~ it** conviene tener más cuidado; mejor será que tengas cuidado; (*Aut: slogan*) **~ your speed!** ¡atención a la velocidad!; ~ **your language!** ¡cuida tu vocabulario!; **we shall have to ~ the expenses** tendremos que estudiar detalladamente los gastos; convendrá tener ojo con los gastos; ~ **how you go!** ¡anda con cuidado!; *V* **step** *etc.*

(**d**) *chance etc* esperar, aguardar; **he ~ed his chance and slipped out** esperó el momento propicio y se escabulló.

3 *vi* ver, mirar; observar; (*watchfully*) vigilar; **you ~!** (*wait and see*) ¡espera y verás!; (*see this*) ¡mira esto!, ¡a ver esto!; **to ~ for sb** esperar a uno, aguardar a uno; **to ~ for sth to happen** esperar a que pase algo; **to ~ over sb** velar a uno; **to ~ over the safety of the country** velar por la seguridad de la patria; **to ~ over a property** vigilar una propiedad.

◆**watch out** *vi* tener ojo, tener cuidado; estar alerta; ~ **out!** ¡ojo!, ¡abusado! (*Mex*); ~ **out for thieves!** ¡cuidado con los ladrones!; **to ~ out for trouble** estar alerta por si hay problemas, estar al acecho por si hay disturbios; **then you'd better ~ out!** ¡pues aténgase a las consecuencias!

watchband ['wɒtʃbænd] *n* (*US*) pulsera *f* de reloj, correa *f* de reloj.

watchcase ['wɒtʃkeɪs] *n* caja *f* de reloj.

watchdog ['wɒtʃdɒg] **1** *n* perro *m* guardián; (*fig*) perro *m* vigilante, guardián *m*, -ana *f*. **2** *attr*: ~ **committee** comisión *f* de vigilancia, comisión *f* de seguimiento.

watcher ['wɒtʃəʳ] *n* observador *m*, -ora *f*; espectador *m*, -ora *f*; (*pej*) mirón *m*, -ona *f*.

-watcher ['wɒtʃəʳ] *n ending in compounds, eg* **China-~** especialista *mf* en asuntos chinos, sinólogo *m*, -a *f*; *V* **bird-~** *etc.*

watchful ['wɒtʃfʊl] *adj* vigilante; observador; (*esp fig*) desvelado; **under the ~ gaze of ...** bajo la vigilante mirada de ...

watchfully ['wɒtʃfəlɪ] *adv* vigilantemente.

watchfulness ['wɒtʃfʊlnɪs] *n* vigilancia *f*; desvelo *m*.

watchglass ['wɒtʃglɑːs] *n* cristal *m* de reloj.

watchmaker ['wɒtʃ,meɪkəʳ] *n* relojero *m*; **~'s (shop)** relojería *f*.

watchman ['wɒtʃmən] *n*, *pl* **watchmen** ['wɒtʃmən] guardián *m*; (*night ~*) (*in street, flats*) sereno *m*, (*in factory etc*) vigilante *m* nocturno.

watch night service ['wɒtʃ'naɪt'sɜːvɪs] *n* (*Rel*) servicio *m* de fin de año.

watchstem ['wɒtʃstəm] *n* (*US*) cuerda *f*.

watchstrap ['wɒtʃstræp] *n* pulsera *f* de reloj, correa *f* de reloj.

watchtower ['wɒtʃ,taʊəʳ] *n* atalaya *f*, vigía *f*, torre *f* de vigilancia.

watchword ['wɒtʃwɜːd] *n* (*Mil etc*) santo *m* y seña; (*motto*) lema *m*, consigna *f*.

water ['wɔːtəʳ] **1** *n* (**a**) agua *f*; **like ~** (*fig*) como agua, pródigamente, en abundancia; **like ~ off a duck's back** como si nada; **the square is under ~** la plaza está inundada; **a lot of ~ has flowed** (*or* **passed**) **under the bridge** (*fig*) ya ha llovido desde entonces; **that's all ~ under the bridge now** todo eso queda ya a la espalda; **to be in hot ~*** estar metido en un lío*; **to get into hot ~*** cargársela* (*for, over* en el asunto de); meterse en un lío*; **to hold ~** retener el agua, (*fig*) estar bien fundado, ser lógico; **that excuse won't hold ~** esa excusa no vale; **to pour cold ~ on an idea** echar un jarro de agua fría a una idea; **to spend money like ~** derrochar dinero; **to swim under ~** nadar bajo el agua; **to test the ~(s)** (*fig*) probar la temperatura del agua; **to turn on the ~** hacer correr el agua; (*from tap*) abrir el grifo; **still ~s run deep** la procesión va por dentro; no te fíes del agua mansa.

(**b**) (*urine*) orina *f*, orines *mpl*; **to make** (*or* **pass**) ~ hacer aguas, mear.

(**c**) (*Med*) **~s** aguas *fpl*; **to drink** (*or* **take**) **the ~s at Harrogate** tomar las aguas en Harrogate.

(**d**) (*of sea etc*) agua *f*; **the ~s of the Ebro** las aguas del Ebro; **by ~** por mar; **on land and ~** por tierra y por mar; **to back ~** ciar; **to fish in troubled ~s** pescar en río revuelto; **to get into deep ~(s)** meterse en honduras; **low ~** *etc V* **tide**.

(**e**) (*Med*) **~ on the brain** hidrocefalía *f*; **~ on the knee** derrame *m* sinovial.

(**f**) **of the first ~** de lo mejor, de primerísima calidad.

2 *attr* acuático; de agua; para agua; **~ biscuit** galleta *f* de soda; **~ blister** ampolla *f*; **~ buffalo** búfalo *m* de agua, carabao *m*; **~ chestnut** castaña *f* de agua; **~ cooler** enfriadora *f* de agua; **~ plants** plantas *fpl* acuáticas; **~ purification plant** estación *f* depuradora de aguas residuales; **~ supply** abastecimiento *m* de agua.

3 *vt garden, plant* regar; *horses* abrevar; *wine* aguar; diluir; (*moisten*) mojar, humedecer; **to ~ a plant with an insecticide** regar (*or* rociar) una planta con insecticida; **the river ~s the provinces of ...** el río riega las provincias de ...; **to ~ capital** emitir un número excesivo de acciones; **to ~ down** aguar; diluir; (*fig*) mitigar; suavizar; **I should ~ the abuse down a bit** conviene suavizar un poco las injurias.

4 *vi* (*of eyes*) hacerse agua, lagrimear, llorar; **my mouth ~ed** se me hizo la boca agua; **it's enough to make your mouth ~** se hace la boca agua.

waterage ['wɔːtərɪdʒ] *n* transporte *m* por barco.

waterbed ['wɔːtə'bed] *n* cama *f* de agua.

water bird ['wɔːtəbɜːd] *n* ave *f* acuática.

waterborne ['wɔːtəbɔːn] *adj* llevado por barco (*etc*); **~ traffic** tráfico *m* fluvial, tráfico *m* marítimo.

waterbottle ['wɔːtə,bɒtl] *n* cantimplora *f*.

water-butt ['wɔːtə'bʌt] *n* tina *f* para agua.

water-cannon ['wɔːtə'kænən] *n* cañón *m* de agua.

water-carrier ['wɔːtə,kærɪəʳ] *n* aguador *m*.

water-cart ['wɔːtəkɑːt] *n* cuba *f* de riego, carro *m* aljibe; (*motorized*) camión *m* de agua.

water-closet ['wɔːtə,klɒzɪt] *n* (*freq abbr WC*) wáter *m*, inodoro *m*.

watercolour, (*US*) **watercolor** ['wɔːtə,kʌləʳ] *n* acuarela *f*.

watercolourist, (*US*) **watercolorist** ['wɔːtə,kʌlərɪst] *n* acuarelista *mf*.

water-cooled ['wɔːtəkuːld] *adj* refrigerado por agua.

water-cooling ['wɔːtəkuːlɪŋ] *n* refrigeración *f* por agua.

watercourse ['wɔːtəkɔːs] *n* (*stream*) arroyo *m*; (*canal*) canal *m*; (*bed*) lecho *m*, cauce *m*.

watercress ['wɔːtəkres] *n* berro *m*, mastuerzo *m*.

water-diviner ['wɔːtədɪ,vaɪnəʳ] *n* zahorí *m*.

water-divining ['wɔːtədɪ,vaɪnɪŋ] *n* arte *m* del zahorí.

watered ['wɔːtəd] *adj* aguado; **~ stock** acciones *fpl* diluidas.

watered-down ['wɔːtəd'daʊn] *adj wine etc* aguado, bautizado; (*fig*) *account, version* saneado.

waterfall ['wɔːtəfɔːl] *n* cascada *f*, salto *m* de agua, catarata *f*.

waterfowl ['wɔːtəfaʊl] *npl* aves *fpl* acuáticas.

waterfront ['wɔːtəfrʌnt] *n* (*esp US*) terreno *m* ribereño; (*harbour area*) puerto *m*, muelles *mpl*, dársenas *fpl*.

water-heater ['wɔːtə'hiːtəʳ] *n* calentador *m* de agua.

waterhole ['wɔːtəhəʊl] *n* charco *m*; abrevadero *m*.

water-ice ['wɔːtəraɪs] *n* (*Brit*) sorbete *m*, helado *m*.

watering ['wɔːtərɪŋ] *n* riego *m*; **frequent ~ is needed** hay que regar con frecuencia.

watering-can ['wɔːtərɪŋkæn] *n* regadera *f*.

watering-hole ['wɔːtərɪŋ'həʊl] *n* (*for animals*) abrevadero *m*; (*) pub *m*.

watering-place ['wɔːtərɪŋpleɪs] *n* (*spa*) balneario *m*; (*seaside resort*) playa *f*, ciudad *f* marítima de veraneo; (*Agr*) abrevadero *m*.

water-jacket ['wɔːtə,dʒækɪt] *n* camisa *f* de agua.

water-jump ['wɔːtə'dʒʌmp] *n* foso *m* (de agua).

waterless ['wɔːtəlɪs] *adj* sin agua, árido.

water-level ['wɔːtə,levl] *n* nivel *m* del agua; (*Naut*) línea *f* de agua.

water-lily ['wɔːtə,lɪlɪ] *n* nenúfar *m*.

waterline ['wɔːtəlaɪn] *n* línea *f* de flotación.

waterlogged ['wɔːtəlɒgd] *adj ground etc* anegado, inundado; *wood etc* empapado; **to get ~** anegarse; empaparse.

Waterloo [,wɔːtə'luː] *n* Waterloo *m* (*1815*); **he met his ~** se le llegó su San Martín.

water main ['wɔːtə'meɪn] *n* cañería *f* principal.

waterman ['wɔːtəmən] *n*, *pl* **watermen** ['wɔːtəmən] barquero *m*.

watermark ['wɔːtəmɑːk] *n* filigrana *f*.

water-meadow ['wɔːtə,medəʊ] *n* prado *m* (junto al río *or* sujeto a inundaciones).

watermelon ['wɔːtə,melən] *n* sandía *f*.

watermeter ['wɔːtə,miːtəʳ] *n* contador *m* de agua.

watermill ['wɔːtəmɪl] *n* molino *m* de agua.

waterpark ['wɔːtəpɑːk] *n* parque *m* acuático.

waterpipe ['wɔːtəpaɪp] *n* caño *m* de agua.

water-pistol ['wɔːtə'pɪstl] *n* pistola *f* de agua.

water-polo ['wɔːtə'pəʊləʊ] *n* polo *m* acuático, water-polo *m*.

water power ['wɔːtə,paʊəʳ] *n* fuerza *f* hidráulica.

waterproof ['wɔːtəpruːf] **1** *adj* impermeable. **2** *n* impermeable *m*. **3** *vt* impermeabilizar.

waterproofing ['wɔːtə'pruːfɪŋ] *n* (*process*) impermeabilización *f*; (*material*) impermeabilizante *m*.

water-pump ['wɔːtəpʌmp] *n* bomba *f* de agua.

water-rat ['wɔːtəræt] *n* rata *f* de agua.

water rate ['wɔːtəreɪt] *n* (*Brit*) tarifa *f* de agua; impuesto *m*

sobre el agua.
water-repellent ['wɔːtərɪ'pelənt] **1** *adj* hidrófugo. **2** *n* hidrófugo *m.*
water-resistant ['wɔːtərɪ'zɪstənt] *adj* a prueba de agua; *ink* indeleble; *material* impermeable.
watershed ['wɔːtəʃed] *n* (*Geog*) línea *f* divisoria de las aguas, parteaguas *m*; cuenca *f*; (*fig*) división *f,* línea *f* divisoria; **the ~ of the Duero** la cuenca del Duero.
waterside ['wɔːtəsaɪd] **1** *n* orilla *f* del agua, ribera *f.* **2** *attr* ribereño; situado en la orilla.
water-ski ['wɔːtəskiː] *vi* esquiar en el agua.
water-skier ['wɔːtə,skiːər] *n* esquiador *m* acuático, esquiadora *f* acuática.
water-skiing ['wɔːtə,skiːɪŋ] *n* esquí *m* acuático.
water-snake ['wɔːtə'sneɪk] *n* culebra *f* de agua.
water-softener ['wɔːtə'sɒfnər] *n* ablandador *m* de agua.
water-soluble ['wɔːtə'sɒljʊbl] *adj* soluble en agua, hidrosoluble.
watersports ['wɔːtəspɔːts] *npl* deportes *mpl* acuáticos.
waterspout ['wɔːtəspaʊt] *n* tromba *f* marina.
water-table ['wɔːtə,teɪbl] *n* capa *f* freática, nivel *m* de agua freática.
water-tank ['wɔːtətæŋk] *n* cisterna *f,* depósito *m* de agua; aljibe *m.*
watertight ['wɔːtətaɪt] *adj compartment etc* estanco; hermético; (*fig*) irrecusable, completamente lógico.
water-tower ['wɔːtə,taʊər] *n* arca *f* de agua, alcubilla *f.*
water-vapour, (*US*) **water-vapor** ['wɔːtə,veɪpər] *n* vapor *m* de agua.
water-vole ['wɔːtəvəʊl] *n* rata *f* de agua.
water-waggon ['wɔːtə'wægən] *n* (*US*) vagón-cisterna *m.*
waterway ['wɔːtəweɪ] *n* vía *f* fluvial; (*inland* ~) canal *m,* canal *m* navegable.
waterweed ['wɔːtə'wiːd] *n* planta *f* acuática.
waterwheel ['wɔːtəwiːl] *n* rueda *f* hidráulica; (*Agr*) noria *f.*
water-wings ['wɔːtəwɪŋz] *npl* nadaderas *fpl,* flotadores *mpl.*
waterworks ['wɔːtəwɜːks] *n* (**a**) central *f* depuradora; (*loosely*) (sistema *m* de) abastecimiento *m* de agua. (**b**) (‡) (*Anat*) vías *fpl* urinarias. (**c**) (*) **to turn on the ~** echar a llorar.
watery ['wɔːtərɪ] *adj substance* acuoso; (*wet*) húmedo, mojado; *eye* lagrimoso; *sky* que amenaza lluvia, lluvioso; *soup, wine* débil, flojo.
WATS ['wɒts] *n* (*US*) *abbr of* **Wide Area Telecommunications Service.**
watt [wɒt] *n* vatio *m.*
wattage ['wɒtɪdʒ] *n* vataje *m.*
wattle[1] ['wɒtl] *n* zarzo *m*; ~ **and daub** zarzos *mpl* y barro.
wattle[2] ['wɒtl] *n* (*Orn*) barba *f.*
wave [weɪv] **1** *n* (**a**) (*of water*) ola *f*; ~ **energy** energía *f* de las ondas; **to make ~s** (*fig*: *rock the boat*) hacer olas, (*play up*) dar guerra, (*make a fuss*) armar un lío.
(**b**) (*Phys, Rad*) onda *f*; **long ~** onda *f* larga; **medium ~** onda *f* media; **short ~** onda *f* corta.
(**c**) (*in hair, on surface*) ondulación *f.*
(**d**) (*fig*) oleada *f*; **~ of enthusiasm** oleada *f* de entusiasmo; **~ of panic** oleada *f* de pánico; **~ of strikes** oleada *f* de huelgas; **cold ~** oleada *f* de frío; **the first ~ of the attack** la primera oleada de asalto; **the attackers came in ~s** las tropas atacaron en oleadas.
(**e**) (*movement of hand*) movimiento *m,* ademán *m* (de la mano), señal *f* (hecha con la mano); **with a ~ of his hand** con un movimiento de la mano, haciendo una señal con la mano; **with a ~ he was gone** hizo una señal con la mano y desapareció.
(**f**) (*Liter etc*) **new ~** nueva ola *f.*
2 *vt* (**a**) (*brandish*) agitar, (*threateningly*) blandir; *flag etc* ondear, agitar; **don't ~ it about!** ¡no lo agites!; **he ~d the ticket under my nose** agitó el billete en mis narices; **to ~ one's hand to sb** hacer una señal a uno con la mano; **to ~ one's arms about** agitar mucho los brazos; **to ~ sb goodbye** decir adiós a uno con la mano; **to ~ a handkerchief to sb** agitar el pañuelo para dar una señal a uno; **he ~d a greeting to the crowd** saludó a la multitud con un movimiento de la mano.
(**b**) *hair etc* ondular; **to have one's hair ~d** hacerse ondular el pelo, hacerse una permanente.
3 *vi* (**a**) (*person*) hacer señales con la mano, agitar el brazo; **to ~ to sb** hacer señales con la mano a uno; **we ~d as the train drew out** cuando partió el tren nos dijimos adiós con la mano.
(**b**) (*flag etc*) ondear; flotar; (*arm etc*) agitarse.
◆**wave aside, wave away** *vt offer etc* rechazar; **to ~ sb aside** hacer una señal a uno para que se aparte; **he ~d my help aside** indicó con un movimiento de la mano que no necesitaba mi ayuda.
◆**wave down** *vt*: **to ~ a car down** hacer señales a un coche para que pare.
◆**wave off** *vt*: **to ~ sb off** decir adiós a uno con la mano.
◆**wave on** *vt*: **to ~ sb on** hacer señales a uno para que avance.
waveband ['weɪvbænd] *n* banda *f* de ondas; **long ~** banda *f* de onda larga.
wavelength ['weɪvleŋθ] *n* longitud *f* de onda; **we are not on the same ~** (*fig*) no estamos en la misma onda.
wavelet ['weɪvlɪt] *n* pequeña ola *f,* olita *f,* rizo *m.*
waver ['weɪvər] *vi* (*oscillate*) oscilar (*between* entre); (*hesitate*) dudar, vacilar; (*weaken*) flaquear; **I ~ed for some days** durante varios días no me resolví; **he's beginning to ~** está empezando a vacilar.
wave range ['weɪvreɪndʒ] *n* (*Rad*) gama *f* de ondas.
waverer ['weɪvərər] *n* indeciso *m,* -a *f,* irresoluto *m,* -a *f.*
wavering ['weɪvərɪŋ] **1** *adj* indeciso, irresoluto, vacilante. **2** *n* oscilación *f*; vacilación *f,* irresolución *f.*
wavy ['weɪvɪ] *adj hair, surface* ondulado; *motion* ondulante.
wavy-haired ['weɪvɪ'hɛəd] *adj* de pelo ondulado.
wax[1] [wæks] **1** *n* cera *f*; (*in ear*) cera *f* de los oídos, cerumen *m,* cerilla *f.* **2** *adj* de cera; ~ **paper** papel *m* encerado; ~ **seal** sello *m* de lacre. **3** *vt* encerar.
wax[2] [wæks] *vi* (*moon*) crecer; (*with adj*) ponerse, hacerse; **to ~ enthusiastic** entusiasmarse; **to ~ talkative** empezar a hablar mucho; **to ~ and wane** crecer y descrecer.
waxed [wækst] *adj paper etc* encerado; *jacket* impermeabilizado.
waxen ['wæksən] *adj* (*of wax*) de cera; (*like wax*) ceroso, parecido a cera; como cera; de color de cera.
waxing ['wæksɪŋ] **1** *adj moon* creciente. **2** *n* crecimiento *m.*
waxwork ['wækswɜːk] *n* figura *f* de cera; **~s** museo *m* de (figuras de) cera.
waxy ['wæksɪ] *adj* = **waxen.**
way [weɪ] **1** *n* (**a**) (*road*) camino *m,* vía *f*; carretera *f*; calle *f*; **W~ of the Cross** Vía *f* Crucis, viacrucis *f*; **permanent ~** vía *f*; **the public ~** la vía pública; **across the ~, over the ~** enfrente (*from* de); **by ~ of** vía, por vía de; pasando por.
(**b**) (*route*) camino *m,* ruta *f* (*to* de); **the ~ to the station** el camino de la estación; **which is the ~ to the station, please?** por favor, ¿qué camino tomo para ir a la estación?, ¿cómo se llega a la estación? (*LAm*); **this isn't the ~ to Lugo!** ¡por aquí no se va a Lugo!; **the ~ is hard** el camino es duro; **the ~ of virtue** el camino de la virtud; **to go the shortest ~** ir por el camino más corto; **to go the ~ of all good things** desaparecer como todo lo bueno; **to go the ~ of all flesh** fenecer como todo ser humano; **to lead the ~** ir primero, (*fig*) dar el ejemplo, mostrar el camino; **to prepare the ~** preparar el terreno (*for* a, para); **on the ~** en el camino; durante el viaje; **on the ~ here** mientras veníamos aquí; **on the ~ to Aranjuez** camino de Aranjuez; **it's on the ~ to Murcia** está en la carretera de Murcia; **they have another child on the ~** tienen otro niño en camino; **you pass it on your ~ home** cae de camino para tu casa; **your house is on my ~** tu casa me viene de camino; **the place is very out of the ~** el lugar es muy remoto, el sitio es bastante aislado; **the subject is rather out of the ~** el tema es algo insólito; **her painting is nothing out of the ~** su pintura no tiene nada de particular; **to go out of one's ~** desviarse del camino; **to go out of one's ~ to** + *infin* (*fig*) tomarse la molestia de + *infin*; desvivirse por + *infin.*
(**c**) (*route, with adv*) **~ down** bajada *f,* ruta *f* para bajar; **~ in** entrada *f*; **'~ in'** 'entrada'; **Spain's ~ into the United Nations** el camino que siguió España para ingresar en las Naciones Unidas; **to find a ~ in** encontrar un modo de entrar; **~ out** salida *f*; **'~ out'** 'salida'; **you'll find it on the ~ out** lo encontrarás cerca de la salida; **it's on its ~ out** está en camino de desaparecer, ya está pasando de moda; **there's no ~ out** (*fig*) no hay salida, no hay solución, esto no tiene solución; **there's no other ~ out** (*fig*) no hay más remedio; **~ through** paso *m*; **'no ~ through'** 'cerrado el paso'; **~ up** subida *f,* ruta *f* para subir.
(**d**) (*route, with personal associations*) **he is well on his ~ to finishing it** lo tiene casi terminado; **to ask the ~** preguntar cómo se llega a un lugar, preguntar una dirección; **if the chance comes my ~** si se presenta la oportunidad; **to feel one's ~** andar a tientas, (*fig*) proceder con tiento; **to find one's ~ into a building** encontrarse un modo de entrar en un edificio; **the cat found the ~ into the pantry** el gato

logró introducirse en la despensa; **can you find your ~ home?** ¿sabes por dónde ir a tu casa?; **to go the wrong ~** equivocarse de camino; **to go one's own ~** (*fig*) ir a la suya; hacer rancho aparte; **I know my ~ about town** conozco el plano de la ciudad; **she knows her ~ about** (*fig*) tiene bastante experiencia; no es que sea una inocente; **to lose one's ~** extraviarse, errar el camino; **to make one's ~ to** dirigirse a; **to make one's ~ home** ir a casa, volver a casa; **to make one's ~ through a crowd** abrirse camino por la gente; **to make one's ~ in the world** hacer progresos en su profesión, hacerse (una) carrera; valerse por sí mismo; **he had to make his own ~ in the art world** tuvo que abrirse camino por sus propios medios en el mundo del arte; **to pay one's ~** (*in restaurant*) pagar su parte; (*Fin*) ser solvente; **the company isn't paying its ~** la compañía tiene un saldo negativo; **the department pays its ~** la sección tiene beneficios suficientes; **Britain must pay her ~** Gran Bretaña tiene que lograr la solvencia; **to see one's ~ (clear) to** + *ger or infin* ver la forma de + *infin*; **could you possibly see your ~ to** + *infin*? ¿tendrías la amabilidad de + *infin*?; **we're on our ~!** ¡vamos para allá!; (*Sport etc*) **we're on our ~ up** estamos en fase ascendente; **to start on one's ~** ponerse en camino; **to work one's ~ up a rock** escalar a duras penas una roca, escalar poco a poco una roca; **to work one's ~ to the front** abrirse camino hacia la primera fila (*etc*); **he worked his ~ up in the company** a fuerza de trabajar llegó a ocupar un alto puesto en la sociedad; logró ser ascendido en la sociedad gracias a sus esfuerzos personales; **he worked his ~ up from nothing** empezó sin nada y fue muy lejos por sus méritos personales.

(**e**) (*path*) camino *m*, vía *f*; **the middle ~** el camino de en medio; **to be in sb's ~** estorbar a uno; **am I in the ~?** ¿estorbo?; **to get in the ~** estorbar; **to get in one another's ~** estorbarse uno a otro; **to put difficulties in sb's ~** crear dificultades a uno; **to stand in sb's ~** estorbar; **now nothing stands in our ~** ahora no hay obstáculo alguno; **his age stands in his ~** su edad es una desventaja para él; **to stand in the ~ of progress** estorbar el progreso, ser un estorbo para el progreso; **out of my ~!** ¡quítese de delante!; **it's out of the ~ of the wind** está al abrigo del viento; **to get out of the ~** quitarse de en medio; **to get sth out of the ~** quitar algo de en medio; **to get sb out of the ~** quitar a uno de en medio; **as soon as I've got my exams out of the ~** en cuanto esté libre de exámenes; **one should keep matches out of the ~ of children** no se debe dejar las cerillas al alcance de los niños; **I kept well out of the ~** me mantuve muy lejos; **I try to keep out of his ~** procuro evitar cualquier contacto con él; **he wants his wife out of the ~** quiere deshacerse de su mujer; **to bar the ~, to block the ~** cerrar el paso; **to clear a ~ for** abrir camino para; **to clear the ~** despejar el camino; **to fight one's ~ out** lograr salir luchando; **to fight one's ~ to the sea** abrirse paso luchando hacia el mar; **to force one's ~ through** abrirse paso luchando; **to force one's ~ in** introducirse a la fuerza; **to hack one's ~ through sth** abrirse paso por algo a fuerza de tajos; **to leave the ~ open for further talks** dejar la vía libre para otra conferencia; **to leave the ~ open to abuse** dejar vía libre al desafuero; **make ~!** ¡calle!; **to make ~** hacer sitio (*for* para); **to take the easy ~ out** optar por la solución más fácil.

(**f**) (*distance*) distancia *f*; trayecto *m*, recorrido *m*; **there are flowers all the ~** por todo el recorrido hay flores; **it rained all the ~ there** durante todo el viaje llovió; **I was sick part of the ~** me mareé durante una parte del viaje; **a little ~ away, a little ~ off** no muy lejos, a poca distancia; **a long ~ away, a long ~ off** muy lejos, a gran distancia; a lo lejos; **spring is a long ~ off** la primavera queda muy lejos; **it's a long** (*or* **good**) **~** es mucho camino; **it's a long ~ from here** está muy lejos de aquí; **you're a long ~ out** Vd se ha extraviado bastante, (*fig*) Vd está muy errado; **we've come a long ~ since then** hemos hecho muchos progresos desde entonces; **to go the long ~ round** ir por rodeos; **he'll go a long ~** irá lejos; **we have a long ~ to go** tenemos mucho camino por delante; **it should go a long** (*or* **some**) **~ towards** + *ger* ha de contribuir mucho a + *infin*; **a little help goes a long ~** una pequeña ayuda puede ser muy valiosa; **that's a long ~ from the truth** eso queda muy lejos de la verdad, dista mucho de ser verdad; **better by a long ~** mucho mejor, mejor pero con mucho; **not by a long ~** ni con mucho; **a short ~ off** no muy lejos, a poca distancia; **I can swim quite a ~ now** ahora puedo nadar bastante bien.

(**g**) (*direction*) dirección *f*, sentido *m*; **this ~** por aquí; **'this ~ for the lions'** 'a los leones'; **this ~ and that** por aquí y por allá, en todas direcciones; **down our ~** en nuestro barrio; en nuestra región; allí donde vivimos nosotros; **it's out Windsor ~** está en la región de Windsor, está cerca de Windsor; **which ~ are you going?** ¿por dónde vas?; **which ~ did it go?** ¿hacia dónde fue?; **which ~ do we go from here?** ¿por dónde vamos desde aquí?; **which ~ is the wind blowing?** ¿de dónde sopla el viento?; **she didn't know which ~ to look** no sabía adónde poner los ojos; **to look the other ~** (*fig*) hacer la vista gorda; no darse por aludido; **it doesn't matter to me one ~ or the other** me es igual, me da lo mismo; **it doesn't often come my ~** no se me ofrece muy a menudo; **if the chance comes your ~** si tienes la oportunidad; **are you going my ~?** ¿vas por donde voy yo?

(**h**) (*of position*) **turn it the other ~ round** vuélvelo al revés; **it was you who invited her, not the other ~ round** eres tú quien la invitaste, no al revés; **it's the wrong ~ up** está al revés, lo de abajo está arriba; **put it right ~ up** ponlo bien, enderézalo; **to rub an animal up the wrong ~** frotar a un animal a contrapelo; **to rub sb up the wrong ~** irritar a uno, sacar a uno de quicio; **they seem to rub each other up the wrong ~** parecen irritarse mutuamente; **we'll split it 3 ~s** lo dividiremos en 3 partes iguales.

(**i**) (*means*) medio *m*; **~s and means** medios *mpl*; **Committee on W~s and Means** Comité *m* del Presupuesto; **W~s and Means Committee** (*US*) Comité *m* de Medios y Arbitrios; **that's not the right ~** no es ése el método correcto; **we'll find a ~ of doing it** buscaremos el modo de hacerlo; **love will find a ~** el amor encontrará el camino; **no ~!*** ¡ni hablar!; **no ~ was that a goal*!** ¡imposible que fuera eso un gol!; **there is no ~ I am going to agree** no hay posibilidad de que yo consienta.

(**j**) (*manner*) manera *f*, modo *m*; forma *f*; método *m*, sistema *m*; **~ of life** estilo *m* de vida; **each ~** (*Racing*) (a) ganador y colocado; **this ~, in this ~** de este modo; **it doesn't matter one ~ or the other** no importa ni para esto ni para aquello; **one ~ or another I'm going back** de algún modo u otro voy a volver; **a week one ~ or the other won't matter** no importa que sea una semana más o una semana menos; **you can't have it both ~s** tienes que optar por lo uno o lo otro; **an odd ~ of talking** un extraño modo de hablar; **the only ~ of doing it** la única forma de hacerlo; **there are many ~s of ...** hay muchas maneras de ...; **her ~ of looking at things** su modo de ver las cosas; **my ~ is to** + *infin* mi sistema consiste en + *infin*; **he has his own ~ of doing it** tiene su sistema particular para hacerlo; **that's the ~!** ¡así!; ¡eso es!; **that's the ~ money goes** así se gasta el dinero; **the ~ things are** tal como están las cosas; **to leave things the ~ they are** dejar las cosas como están; **the ~ things are going we shall have nothing left** si esto continúa así nos vamos a quedar sin nada; **it was this ~ ...** lo que pasó fue esto ...; **that ~ it won't disturb anybody** si lo hacemos (*etc*) así, no molestará a nadie; **it looks that ~** así parece; **she's clever that ~** para esas cosas es muy lista; **that's always the ~ with him** siempre le pasa igual; **there are no two ~s about it** no cabe otra posibilidad, no le encuentro otra posibilidad; yo lo veo perfectamente claro.

(**k**) (*manner*: *phrases with* in) **in a ~** hasta cierto punto; en cierto modo; **in this ~** de este modo; **in one ~ or another** de algún modo; **in the same ~** del mismo modo; **in more ~s than one** de más de una manera; **he had little in the ~ of education** tuvo poca educación formal, hizo pocos estudios; **in a general ~ this is true** en general esto es verdad; **without in any ~ wishing to** + *infin* sin querer en lo más mínimo + *infin*, sin tener intención alguna de + *infin*; **I'll do it in my own ~** lo haré según mi método particular; **he's a good sort in his ~** tiene sus rarezas pero es buena persona; a pesar de todo es buena persona; **they interpret it each in his own ~** lo interpretan cada uno a su modo; **he said in his rough ~** dijo en ese tono suyo un poco brusco; **to go on in the same old ~** continuar como siempre, seguir empleando los viejos métodos; **to be in a small ~ of business** tener un negocio modesto.

(**l**) (*custom*) costumbre *f*; **the ~s of the Spaniards** las costumbres de los españoles; **the ~s of good society** los modales de la buena sociedad; la etiqueta de la buena sociedad; **that is our ~ with traitors** así tratamos a los traidores; **he has a ~ with him** tiene atractivo personal, es simpático; tiene dotes de persuasión; **he has his little ~s** tiene sus manías, tiene sus rarezas; **he has a ~ with children** sabe captarse a los niños, los niños le encuentran muy simpático; **he has a ~ with people** tiene don de gentes; **he had his wicked** (*or evil*) ~ **with her** se la llevó al huerto, la sedujo; **the child has some pretty ~s** el niño hace cosas que encantan; **to mend one's ~s** enmendarse, reformarse; **to be out of the ~ of** + *ger* haber perdido la costumbre de + *infin*; **to get out of the ~ of** + *ger* perder la costumbre de + *infin*; **to get into the ~ of** + *ger* (*by habit*) adquirir la costumbre de + *infin*, (*by learning*) aprender el modo de + *infin*.

(**m**) (*of will*) **to get one's** (**own**) ~ salirse con la suya; **they had it all their own ~ in the second half** en el segundo tiempo hicieron lo que les dio la gana; **have it your own ~!** ¡como quieras!; ¡tú te lo has buscado!; **they didn't have things all their own** ~ no dominaron el partido (*etc*) completamente, su dominio no fue completo; **he wants his own ~ all the time** todo el tiempo insiste en su punto de vista, siempre quiere salirse con la suya.

(**n**) (*respect*) respecto *m*; **in a** ~ en cierto modo, hasta cierto punto; **in no** ~ de ningún modo; **in every possible** ~ en todos los respectos; desde todos los puntos de vista; **I will help in every possible** ~ ayudaré por todos los medios a mi disposición; **in many ~s** en muchos respectos, por muchas cosas; **in some ~s** en ciertos modos; **in a big ~*** en grande*, en gran escala; **we lost in a really big ~*** perdimos de modo realmente espectacular; **in a small** ~ en pequeña escala; **we help in a small** ~ ayudamos un poco, prestamos una modesta ayuda; **he's not a plumber in the ordinary** ~ no es de esos fontaneros corrientes; no es un fontanero de profesión; **in the ordinary ~ we go out once a week** en general salimos una vez por semana.

(**o**) (*Naut etc*) **to be under** ~ estar en marcha, (*fig*) avanzar, estar en curso; **to gather** ~ empezar a moverse; acelerar, ir más rápidamente; **to get under** ~ (*Naut*) zarpar, hacerse a la vela; (*Aut etc*) ponerse en marcha; (*person*) partir, ponerse en camino; **things are getting under ~ at last** por fin las cosas están haciendo progresos; **to get a ship under** ~ hacer navegar un barco; **to give** ~ (*break*) hundirse, ceder, romperse; (*Brit Aut etc*) ceder el paso; **'give ~'** 'ceda el paso'; **to give ~ to the left** ceder el paso a la izquierda; **the radio gave ~ to a television set** la radio cedió el paso a un televisor; **you gave ~ too easily** abandonaste demasiado pronto, te dejaste vencer demasiado fácilmente; **she gave ~ to tears** se deshizo en lágrimas; **he never gives ~ to despair** nunca se abandona a la desesperación.

(**p**) (*state*) estado *m*; **things are in a bad** ~ las cosas van mal; **the car is in a bad** ~ el coche está en mal estado; **he's in a very bad** ~ (*Med*) está grave, está de cuidado; **he's in a fair ~ to succeed** tiene buenas posibilidades de lograrlo.

(**q**) (*with* by) **by the** ~ a propósito; por cierto; entre paréntesis, de paso; **by the ~!** ¡eh!; ¡oiga!; **oh, and by the ~** ... hay otra cosa ..., antes que se me olvide ...; **all this is by the** ~ todo esto está un poco al margen, todo esto está entre paréntesis; **by ~ of** como, a modo de; **by ~ of an answer** a título de respuesta; **by ~ of a warning** a modo de advertencia; **he's by ~ of being a painter** tiene algo de pintor, tiene sus ribetes de pintor.

2 *adv*: ~ **back in 1900** allá en 1900; **that was ~ back** eso fue hace mucho tiempo ya; ~ **down** (**below**) muy abajo; ~ **out to sea** mar afuera; **you're ~ out in your sum** te has equivocado mucho en el cálculo; ~ **up in the sky** muy alto en el cielo.

-way [weɪ] *in compounds, eg* **a five-~ split** una división en cinco partes.

waybill [ˈweɪbɪl] *n* hoja *f* de ruta.

wayfarer [ˈweɪˌfɛərəʳ] *n* caminante *mf*; viajero *m*, -a *f*.

wayfaring tree [ˈweɪfɛərɪŋˌtriː] *n* viburno *m*.

waylay [weɪˈleɪ] (*irr*: *V* **lay**) *vt* acechar; salir al paso a; detener; **they were waylaid by thieves** les atacaron unos ladrones; **I was waylaid by the manager** me detuvo el gerente.

way-out* [ˈweɪˈaʊt] *adj* ultramoderno, revolucionario, nueva ola.

wayside [ˈweɪsaɪd] **1** *n* borde *m* del camino, borde *m* de la carretera; **by the** ~ al borde de la carretera; **to fall by the** ~ caer en el camino.

2 *attr* del borde del camino; *inn etc* de camino, de carretera; *flower* silvestre.

way station [ˈweɪˌsteɪʃən] *n* (*US*) apeadero *m*; (*fig*) paso *m* intermedio.

wayward [ˈweɪwəd] *adj* (*self-willed*) voluntarioso; (*naughty*) travieso; rebelde; (*capricious*) caprichoso; (*freakish*) caprichoso, variable, inexplicable.

waywardness [ˈweɪwədnɪs] *n* voluntariedad *f*; travesura *f*; rebeldía *f*; lo caprichoso; variabilidad *f*.

W/B *n abbr of* **waybill**.

WBA *n abbr of* **World Boxing Association**.

WC *n* (*Brit*) *abbr of* **water closet** wáter *m*, WC.

WCC *n abbr of* **World Council of Churches**.

wdv *abbr of* **written-down value** valor *m* amortizado.

we [wiː] *pron* nosotros, nosotras.

w/e *abbr of* **week ending** semana *f* que termina el día ...

WEA *n* (*Brit*) *abbr of* **Workers' Educational Association**.

weak [wiːk] **1** *adj* débil; flojo; *argument etc* flojo, poco convincente; *market etc* flojo; *sound* débil, tenue; *character*, *currency* débil; *tea etc* claro, no muy cargado; **to grow** ~ debilitarse; **to have ~ eyes** ser corto de vista; **to have a ~ stomach** tener el estómago delicado; **her maths is ~, she is ~ at maths** es floja en matemáticas.

2: **the** ~ *npl* los débiles.

weaken [ˈwiːkən] **1** *vt* debilitar; (*lessen*) disminuir, reducir; (*mitigate*) atenuar, mitigar; **this fact ~s your case** este dato quita fuerza a su argumento; **his resignation ~ed the party** su dimisión debilitó el partido.

2 *vi* debilitarse; flaquear, desfallecer; (*give way*) ceder, abandonar; **his influence is ~ing** su influencia flaquea; **we must not ~ now** ahora tenemos que mantenernos firmes; **prices have ~ed** las cotizaciones han aflojado.

weak-kneed [ˈwiːkˈniːd] *adj* (*fig*) sin resolución, sin carácter, débil.

weakling [ˈwiːklɪŋ] *n* ser *m* delicado, persona *f* débil; cobarde *m*; (*of litter etc*) redrojo *m*; (*in health*) persona *f* enfermiza; **he's no** ~ no es ningún debilucho.

weakly [ˈwiːklɪ] **1** *adj* enclenque, achacoso, enfermizo. **2** *adv* débilmente; flojamente; tenuemente.

weak-minded [ˈwiːkˈmaɪndɪd] *adj* mentecato, imbécil; (*irresolute*) vacilante, sin carácter.

weakness [ˈwiːknɪs] *n* (*quality*) debilidad *f*; flojedad *f*; tenuidad *f*; (*weak point*) flaco *m*, lado *m* débil; desventaja *f*; (*of character*) falta *f* de voluntad; falta *f* de carácter; **to have a ~ for** tener gusto por, ser muy aficionado a; **to make allowances for human** ~ tener en cuenta la flaqueza humana.

weak-willed [ˈwiːkˈwɪld] *adj* de voluntad débil, indeciso.

weal¹ [wiːl] *n* (††) bienestar *m*; **the common** ~ el bien público.

weal² [wiːl] *n* (*Med*) verdugón *m*.

wealth [welθ] **1** *n* riqueza *f*; abundancia *f*; **for all his** ~ a pesar de su riqueza; por rico que sea; **with a ~ of details** con abundantes detalles, con acopio de datos.

2 *attr*: ~ **tax** impuesto *m* sobre el patrimonio.

wealthy [ˈwelθɪ] **1** *adj* rico; acaudalado, pudiente. **2** *npl*: **the** ~ los ricos.

wean [wiːn] *vt* destetar; **to ~ sb from sth** (*fig*) ir apartando a uno de algo, desacostumbrar a uno de algo.

weaning [ˈwiːnɪŋ] *n* destete *m*, ablactación *f*.

weapon [ˈwepən] *n* arma *f*.

weaponry [ˈwepənrɪ] *n* armas *fpl*.

wear [wɛəʳ] **1** *n* (**a**) (*use*) uso *m*; **for evening** ~ para la noche, para llevar de noche; **for everyday** ~ para uso diario, para todos los días, para todo trote; **for hard** ~ resistente, duradero; **he got 4 years' ~ out of it** la prenda le duró 4 años; **you will get plenty of ~ out of this** esto le ha de durar muchos años, esto tiene gran durabilidad.

(**b**) (~ *and tear*) deterioro *m*, desgaste *m*, uso *m*; **the ~ on the engine** el desgaste del motor; **one has to allow for ~ and tear** hay que tener en cuenta el desgaste natural; **to look the worse for ~, to show signs of** ~ mostrarse deteriorado, dar indicios de deterioro; **she looks the worse for ~*** parece algo desmejorada.

(**c**) (*clothing*) ropa *f*; prenda *f*; **children's** ~ ropa *f* para niños; **summer** ~ ropa *f* de verano; **light ~ for hot countries** ropa *f* ligera para países cálidos; **it is compulsory ~ for schoolboys** la prenda es obligatoria para los colegiales.

2 (*irr*: *pret* **wore**, *ptp* **worn**) *vt* (**a**) *objects in general* llevar, usar, gastar; *clothing* llevar; traer, traer puesto; vestir; *shoes* calzar; *look, smile etc* tener; (*put on*) ponerse; **she wore her blue dress** llevaba el vestido azul; **she wore blue** se vestía de azul, vestía un vestido azul; **what shall I ~?** ¿qué me pongo?; **I have nothing to ~ to the dinner** no tengo qué ponerme para ir a la cena; **I haven't worn that for ages** hace siglos que no me pongo eso; **were you ~ing a watch?** ¿llevabas reloj?; **my uncle wore a beard** mi tío llevaba barba; **Eskimos don't ~ bikinis** los esquimales no usan bikini; **what size do you ~?** ¿qué número tiene Vd?; **to ~ one's hair long** llevar el pelo largo, dejarse el pelo largo; **he wore a big smile** sonreía alegremente; **he wore a serious look** parecía grave, tenía el gesto grave.

(b) (~ *out*) desgastar, deteriorar; **to ~ sth into holes, to ~ holes in sth** hacer agujeros en algo (rayéndolo *etc*); **to ~ sth to a threadbare state** dejar algo raído.

(c) (*Brit**) aguantar; consentir, permitir; **he won't ~ that** eso no lo permitirá; **we'll see if he'll ~ it** veremos si consiente en ello.

3 *vi* (a) (*last*) durar; **they will ~ for years** le durarán muchos años; **that dress has worn well** ese vestido ha durado mucho; **she's worn well*** se ha conservado muy bien, no representa su edad; **the theory has worn well** la teoría ha resistido muy bien, la teoría ha sido muy duradera.

(b) (*rub etc thin*) **the cloth has worn into holes** al paño le han salido agujeros con el uso; **the rock has worn smooth** la roca se ha alisado.

4 *vr*: **to ~ o.s. to death** matarse (trabajando *etc*).

◆**wear away 1** *vt* gastar, desgastar; raer; consumir; **he's worn away to a shadow** está hecho una sombra.

2 *vi* gastarse, desgastarse; consumirse.

◆**wear down 1** *vt material* gastar, desgastar; *resistance* agotar; rendir; *patience* agotar, cansar; *enemy* cansar hasta rendir.

2 *vi* (*material*) gastarse, desgastarse.

◆**wear off** *vi* quitarse; pasar, desaparecer; **the pain is ~ing off** está desapareciendo el dolor, ya duele menos; **it soon wore off** pronto desapareció; **when the novelty ~s off** cuando la novedad deje de serlo.

◆**wear on** *vi* (*time*) pasar, ir pasando, transcurrir; **the year is ~ing on** están pasando los meses; **as the evening wore on** a medida que avanzaba la noche.

◆**wear out 1** *vt clothes etc* usar, desgastar; romper con el uso; **you can ~ them out next winter** los acabarás de gastar el invierno que viene.

2 *vi* usarse, romperse con el uso, quedar inservible; consumirse.

3 *vr*: **to ~ o.s. out** agotarse, matarse.

◆**wear through 1** *vt* gastar.

2 *vi* (*clothing etc*) gastarse, desgastarse.

wearable ['wɛərəbl] *adj* que se puede llevar; **it's still ~** todavía se puede llevar.

wearer ['wɛərəʳ] *n* el (*or* la) que lleva puesto algo; **~s of bowler hats** los que llevan hongo; **straight from maker to ~** directamente del fabricante al cliente.

wearily ['wɪərɪlɪ] *adv* cansadamente, fatigadamente; **he said ~** dijo cansado, dijo en tono de hastío.

weariness ['wɪərɪnɪs] *n* cansancio *m*, fatiga *f*; abatimiento *m*, hastío *m*; aburrimiento *m*.

wearing ['wɛərɪŋ] *adj* cansado, pesado, molesto.

wearisome ['wɪərɪsəm] *adj* cansado, pesado; fatigoso, agotador.

weary ['wɪərɪ] **1** *adj* (*tired*) cansado, fatigado; (*dispirited*) abatido, hastiado; (*tiring*) aburrido, pesado; (*annoying*) fastidioso; **to be ~ of** estar cansado de, estar harto de; **to grow ~ of** cansarse de; **three ~ hours** tres horas aburridas; **five ~ miles** cinco millas pesadas.

2 *vt* cansar, fatigar; aburrir.

3 *vi* cansarse, fatigarse; **to ~ of** cansarse de; aburrirse de; **to ~ of** + *ger* cansarse de + *infin*.

weasel ['wiːzl] **1** *n* comadreja *f*. **2** *attr*: **~ words** ambages *mpl*, palabras *fpl* equívocas.

weather ['weðəʳ] **1** *n* tiempo *m*; (*harsh ~*) intemperie *f*; **~ permitting** si el tiempo no lo impide; **in the hot ~** cuando hace calor; **in this ~** con el tiempo que hace; **it is fine ~** hace buen tiempo, el tiempo es bueno; **what's the ~ like?** ¿qué tiempo hace?; **he has to go out in all ~s** tiene que salir en todo tiempo; **it gets left outside in all ~s** está fuera a la intemperie; **to be under the ~** (*Med*) estar mal, estar indispuesto, (*with drink*) estar con la turca*; **to make heavy ~ of sth** encontrar algo difícil; crearse dificultades al tratar de hacer algo.

2 *attr* meteorológico, del tiempo; (*Naut*) de barlovento; **~ balloon** globo *m* meteorológico; **~ bureau** (*US*) oficina *f* meteorológica; **~ conditions** estado *m* del tiempo; **to keep a ~ eye on sth** observar algo con atención; **~ forecast** pronóstico *m* del tiempo, boletín *m* meteorológico; **~ forecaster** meteorólogo *m*, -a *f*; **~ map** mapa *m* meteorológico; **~ report** boletín *m* meteorológico; **~ side** costado *m* de barlovento.

3 *vt* (a) *storm etc* (*also* **to ~ out**) aguantar, hacer frente a; superar, sobrevivir a; **the government has ~ed many storms** el gobierno ha aguantado muchas tempestades.

(b) (*Naut*) *cape* doblar; pasar a barlovento.

(c) (*Geol etc*) desgastar; *wood* curar; *skin* curtir.

4 *vi* (*Geol*) desgastarse; (*skin etc*) curtirse a la intemperie.

weather-beaten ['weðə,biːtn] *adj* deteriorado por la intemperie; *skin* curtido.

weatherboard ['weðəbɔːd] *n* (*Brit*) tabla *f* de chilla; **~ house** (*US*) casa *f* de madera.

weather-bound ['weðəbaʊnd] *adj* bloqueado por el mal tiempo.

weathercock ['weðəkɒk] *n* veleta *f*.

weathered ['weðəd] *adj oak etc* maduro, curado.

weatherman ['weðəmæn] *n*, *pl* **weathermen** ['weðəmen] hombre *m* del tiempo, meteorólogo *m*.

weatherproof ['weðəpruːf] *adj* a prueba de la intemperie; *clothing* impermeable, impermeabilizado.

weathership ['weðəʃɪp] *n* barco *m* del servicio meteorológico.

weather-station ['weðə,steɪʃən] *n* estación *f* meteorológica.

weather-strip ['weðəstrɪp] *n* burlete *m*.

weather-vane ['weðəveɪn] *n* veleta *f*.

weave [wiːv] **1** *n* tejido *m*; textura *f*.

2 (*irr*: *pret* **wove**, *ptp* **woven**) *vt* (a) tejer; trenzar; entretejer, entrelazar; (*fig*) *plot* urdir, tramar; **to ~ details into a story** entretejer detalles en un cuento; **to ~ episodes into a plot** ir entretejiendo episodios para formar un argumento.

(b) **to ~ one's way through** abrirse paso (por entre).

3 *vi* (a) tejer.

(b) **to ~ in and out** (*boxer etc*) evadirse torciendo rápidamente a derecha e izquierda; **the plane was weaving in and out among the clouds** el avión serpenteaba (*or* zigzagueaba) entre las nubes; **to ~ in and out among traffic** serpentear por entre el tráfico (para adelantarse a toda prisa); **the road ~s about a lot** el camino serpentea mucho; **let's get weaving!*** ¡vamos!

weaver ['wiːvəʳ] *n* tejedor *m*, -ora *f*.

weaving ['wiːvɪŋ] **1** *n* tejeduría *f*. **2** *attr* de tejer, para tejer; de tejidos.

weaving-machine ['wiːvɪŋmə,ʃiːn] *n* telar *m*.

weaving-mill ['wiːvɪŋmɪl] *n* tejeduría *f*.

web [web] *n* (*fabric*) tela *f*, tejido *m*; (*spider's*) telaraña *f*; (*membrane*) membrana *f*; (*fig*) red *f*; **a ~ of intrigue** un tejido de intrigas; **a ~ of spies** una red de espías.

webbed [webd] *adj foot* palmeado.

webbing ['webɪŋ] *n* cincha *f*, (*Tech*) pretina *f* de reps.

web-footed ['web'fʊtɪd] *adj* palmípedo.

wed [wed] **1** *vt* casarse con; (*of priest etc, also fig*) casar. **2** *vi* casarse.

we'd [wiːd] = **we would; we had.**

wedded ['wedɪd] *adj* (a) (*person*) casado; *bliss, life etc* conyugal; **his ~ wife** su legítima esposa.

(b) **to be ~ to** estar casado con; (*fig: connected*) estar relacionado con, estar unido a; **to be ~ to an opinion** aferrarse a una opinión, estar aferrado a una opinión; **to be ~ to a pursuit** ser aficionado a una actividad, ser entusiasta de un pasatiempo.

wedding ['wedɪŋ] **1** *n* boda *f*; casamiento *m*; bodas *fpl*; (*fig*) unión *f*, enlace *m*; **civil ~** matrimonio *m* civil; **to have a civil ~** casarse por lo civil; **to have a church ~** casarse por la iglesia; **to have a quiet ~** casarse en la intimidad, casarse en privado.

2 *attr* de boda, de bodas; nupcial.

wedding anniversary ['wedɪŋ,ænɪ'vɜːsərɪ] *n* aniversario *m* de bodas.

wedding band ['wedɪŋ'bænd] *n* = **wedding-ring.**

wedding breakfast ['wedɪŋ'brekfəst] *n* banquete *m* de boda.

wedding-cake ['wedɪŋkeɪk] *n* tarta *f* de boda, pastel *m* de boda.

wedding-day ['wedɪŋdeɪ] *n* día *m* de (la) boda.

wedding-dress ['wedɪŋdres] *n* traje *m* de novia.

wedding-march ['wedɪŋmɑːtʃ] *n* marcha *f* nupcial.

wedding-night ['wedɪŋnaɪt] *n* noche *f* de (la) boda, noche *f* de bodas.

wedding-present ['wedɪŋ,preznt] *n* regalo *m* de boda.

wedding-ring ['wedɪŋrɪŋ] *n* anillo *m* de boda, alianza *f*.

wedge [wedʒ] **1** *n* cuña *f*; calce *m*, calza *f*; (*of cake etc*) porción *f*, pedazo *m* (grande); (*Golf*) wedge *m*, cucharilla *f*; **it's the thin end of the ~** por ahí empieza, esto puede ser el principio de muchos males; **to drive a ~ between two people** romper el vínculo que une a dos personas, enemistar a dos personas, separar a dos personas.

2 *vt* acuñar, calzar; **to ~ a door open** mantener abierta una puerta con calza; **it's ~d** está sin poderse mover, se ha agarrado; **I was ~d between two bishops** me encontré apretado entre dos obispos, estuve inmovilizado entre dos obispos.

◆**wedge in 1** *vt*: **can we ~ a few more in?** ¿podemos introducir algunos más (por apretados que estén)?

2 *vr*: **to ~ o.s. in** introducirse con dificultad.

wedge-heeled [ˌwedʒ'hi:ld] *adj*: **~ shoes** topolinos *mpl*.

wedge-shaped ['wedʒʃeɪpt] *adj* de forma de cuña.

wedlock ['wedlɒk] *n* matrimonio *m*; **to be born out of ~** nacer fuera del matrimonio.

Wednesday ['wenzdeɪ] *n* miércoles *m*.

Wed(s). *abbr of* **Wednesday** miércoles *m*, miérc.

wee[1] [wi:] *adj* (*Scot**) pequeñito, diminuto; **a ~ bit** un poquitín, un poquito; **I'm a ~ bit worried** estoy un poco inquieto.

wee[2]‡ [wi:] *n*, *vi*: **to (have a) ~** hacer pipí‡.

weed [wi:d] **1** *n* (**a**) (*Bot*) mala hierba *f*; **the ~** (*hum*) el tabaco; **~s** malas hierbas *fpl*, hierbajos *mpl*.

(**b**) (*: *person*) madeja *mf*.

2 *vt ground* escardar, desherbar, sachar; **to ~ out** *plant* arrancar; (*fig*) suprimir, quitar, eliminar.

weeding [wi:dɪŋ] *n* escarda *f*.

weed-killer ['wi:dˌkɪlə^r] *n* herbicida *m*.

weeds [wi:dz] *npl*: **widow's ~** ropa *f* de luto.

weedy ['wi:dɪ] *adj* (**a**) *ground* lleno de malas hierbas. (**b**) (*) *person* flaco, desmirriado; **~ youth** mozalbete *m*.

week [wi:k] *n* semana *f*; **~ in, ~ out** semana tras semana; **twice a ~** dos veces a la semana; **this day ~, a ~ today** de hoy en ocho días, dentro de ocho días; **tomorrow ~, a ~ from tomorrow** (*US*) de mañana en ocho días; **Tuesday ~** del martes en ocho días; **in a ~ or so** dentro de unos ocho días; **in the middle of the ~** a mitad de semana; **it changes from ~ to ~** esto cambia cada semana; **I haven't seen her for** (*or* **in**) **~s** hace tiempo que no la veo; **allow 4 ~s for delivery** dejar 4 semanas para entrega; **to knock sb into the middle of next ~*** dar una tremenda paliza a uno.

weekday ['wi:kdeɪ] *n* día *m* laborable; **on a ~** entre semana.

weekend ['wi:k'end] **1** *n* fin *m* de semana, weekend *m*; **a ~ trip** una excursión de fin de semana; **~ case** maletín *m* de viaje; **~ cottage** casita *f* de fin de semana; **to stay over the ~** pasar el fin de semana; **to take a long ~** hacer puente.

2 *as adv*: **they are away ~s** están fuera los fines de semana.

3 *vi* pasar el fin de semana.

weekender ['wi:k'endə^r] *n* persona *f* que va a pasar solamente el fin de semana (en una casa de campo *etc*).

weekly ['wi:klɪ] **1** *adj* semanal; de cada semana; **~ paper** semanario *m*; **~ report** informe *m* semanal; **~ statement** (*Fin*) balance *m* semanal, estado *m* de cuenta semanal. **2** *adv* semanalmente, cada semana; **£15 ~** 15 libras por semana. **3** *n* semanario *m*.

weenie ['wi:nɪ] *n* (*US Culin*) salchicha *f* de Frankfurt.

weeny* ['wi:nɪ] *adj* chiquitito*, minúsculo.

weeny-bopper* ['wi:nɪ'bɒpə^r] *n* doceañera *f* (aficionada de la música pop).

weep [wi:p] (*irr*: *pret and ptp* **wept**) **1** *vt tears* llorar, derramar; **to ~ one's eyes out** llorar a mares.

2 *vi* llorar; **I could have wept** era para desesperarse; **to ~ for sb** llorar a uno; **to ~ for joy** llorar de alegría; **to ~ for one's sins** llorar sus pecados; **to ~ for what has happened** llorar por lo que ha pasado; **to ~ to see sth** llorar al ver algo.

3 *n*: **to have a good ~** aliviarse llorando.

weeping ['wi:pɪŋ] **1** *adj* lloroso; **~ willow** sauce *m* llorón. **2** *n* llanto *m*, lágrimas *fpl*.

weepy ['wi:pɪ] **1** *adj* llorón, que llora por poca cosa; (*) *film etc* lacrimógeno. **2** *n* (*) (*Brit*) película *f* (*etc*) lacrimógena.

weever ['wi:və^r] *n* peje *m* araña.

weevil ['wi:vl] *n* gorgojo *m*.

weewee‡ ['wi:wi:] **1** *n* pipí‡ *m*. **2** *vi* hacer pipí‡.

w.e.f. *abbr of* **with effect from.**

weft [weft] *n* trama *f*; (*fig*) red *f*.

weigh [weɪ] **1** *vt* (**a**) (*lit*) pesar; **to ~ sth in one's hand** pesar algo en la mano.

(**b**) (*fig*) pesar, ponderar; **to ~ sth in one's mind** ponderar algo, meditar algo; **to ~ A against B** contraponer A y B, considerar A con relación a B; **to ~ the pros and cons** pesar las ventajas y las desventajas; **to ~ one's words** medir las palabras.

(**c**) **to ~ anchor** levar anclas.

2 *vi* (**a**) (*lit*) pesar; **it ~s 4 kilos** pesa 4 kilos; **how much does it ~?** ¿cuánto pesa?; **it ~s heavy** pesa mucho.

(**b**) **it ~s on his mind** pesa sobre su mente, le preocupa, le inquieta; **her absence began to ~ (up)on me** su ausencia empezaba a inquietarme; **these factors do not ~ with him** estos factores no tienen importancia para él, estos factores no influyen en él.

◆**weigh down** *vt* sobrecargar; (*fig*) abrumar, agobiar (*with* de); **she was ~ed down with parcels** iba muy cargada de paquetes; **a branch ~ed down with fruit** una rama doblada bajo el peso del fruto; **to be ~ed down with sorrow** estar agobiado de dolor.

◆**weigh in** *vi* (**a**) (*jockey*) pesarse; **to ~ in at 65 kilos** pesar 65 kilos.

(**b**) (*pej*) entrar pisando fuerte; intervenir (sin ser llamado); **to ~ in with an argument** intervenir afirmando que ...

◆**weigh out** *vt* pesar.

◆**weigh up** *vt* (**a**) (*lit*) = **weigh 1**(**a**).

(**b**) (*fig*) = **weigh 1**(**b**); **to ~ sb up** formar un juicio sobre uno.

weighbridge ['weɪbrɪdʒ] *n* báscula-puente *f*, báscula *f* de puente.

weigh-in ['weɪɪn] *n* peso *m*, pesaje *m*.

weighing-machine ['weɪɪŋməˌʃi:n] *n* báscula *f*.

weight [weɪt] **1** *n* (**a**) peso *m*; (*heaviness*) peso *m*, pesadez *f*; **~ note** certificado *m* de peso; **3 kilos in ~** que pesa 3 kilos, de 3 kilos; **it is worth its ~ in gold** vale su peso en oro; **to feel the ~ of, to test** (*or* **try**) **the ~ of sth** sopesar algo; **he carries too much ~** pesa demasiado; **to gain ~, to put on ~** engordar, hacerse más gordo; **to lose ~** adelgazar; **sold by ~** vendido a peso; **to take the ~ off one's feet** sentarse y descansar, dejar descansar los pies.

(**b**) (*of clock*; *disc etc used on scales*) pesa *f*; **system of ~s and measures** sistema *m* de pesos y medidas; **to put the ~** lanzar el peso; **putting the ~** lanzamiento *m* del peso.

(**c**) (*fig*: *of worries etc*) peso *m*, carga *f*; (*of blow*) fuerza *f*; (*importance*) peso *m*, autoridad *f*, importancia *f*; **the ~ of the years** la carga de los años; **a blow without much ~ behind it** un golpe de poca fuerza; **a person of no ~** una persona de poca monta, una persona de escasa importancia; **these are arguments of some ~** son argumentos de cierto peso; **that's a ~ off my mind** es un gran alivio para mí; **he carries no ~** no tiene autoridad; **those arguments carry great ~ with the minister** esos argumentos influyen poderosamente en el ministro; **to chuck*** (*or* **throw**) **one's ~ about** darse importancia; hablar (*etc*) en tono autoritario; **to give due ~ to an argument** conceder la debida importancia a un argumento; **he doesn't pull his ~ in the section** no trabaja en la sección tanto como debiera; **to throw one's ~ behind sb** apoyar a uno con toda su fuerza.

2 *vt* cargar (*with* de), añadir peso a; (*hold down*) sujetar con un peso; (*statistically*) ponderar; **this is ~ed in your favour** esto se inclina del lado de Vd, esto le favorece a Vd.

◆**weight down** *vt* sujetar con un peso (*or* una piedra *etc*).

weighted [weɪtɪd] *adj* compensado, ponderado; **~ average** media *f* ponderada; **~ index** índice *m* compensado.

weightiness ['weɪtɪnɪs] *n* peso *m*; (*fig*) peso *m*, importancia *f*; influencia *f*.

weighting ['weɪtɪŋ] *n* (*on salary*) aumento *m* por coste de vida; (*Scol*) factor *m* de valoración; (*Statistics*) ponderación *f*; **London ~** subsidio *m* por residir en Londres.

weightless ['weɪtlɪs] *adj* ingrávido.

weightlessness ['weɪtlɪsnɪs] *n* ingravidez *f*.

weightlifter ['weɪtˌlɪftə^r] *n* levantador *m* de pesas, halterófilo *m*, haltera *m*.

weightlifting ['weɪtˌlɪftɪŋ] *n* levantamiento *m* de pesas, halterofilia *f*.

weight-training ['weɪtˌtreɪnɪŋ] *n* entrenamiento *m* con pesas.

weight-watcher ['weɪtˌwɒtʃə^r] *n* persona *f* que quiere evitar engordar.

weight-watching ['weɪtˌwɒtʃɪŋ] *n* conciencia *f* de la necesidad de no engordar; campaña *f* pro adelgazamiento, régimen *m* para adelgazar.

weighty ['weɪtɪ] *adj* pesado; (*fig*) importante, de peso, influyente.

weir [wɪə^r] *n* vertedero *m*, vertedor *m*; cañal *m*, encañizada *f*; (*fish-trap*) presa *f*, pesquera *f*.

weird [wɪəd] *adj* misterioso, fantástico, sobrenatural; (*odd*) raro, extraño; **how ~!** ¡qué raro!

weirdly ['wɪədlɪ] *adv* misteriosamente, fantásticamente; extrañamente; **~ dressed** vestido de un modo raro.

weirdness ['wɪədnɪs] *n* misterio *m*, lo fantástico, lo sobrenatural; rareza *f*.

weirdo* ['wɪədəʊ] *n*, **weirdy*** ['wɪədɪ] *n* bicho *m* raro.

welch* [welʃ] *vi* = **welsh.**

welcome ['welkəm] **1** *adj* (**a**) bienvenido; **~!** ¡bienvenido!; **~ on board!** ¡bienvenidos a bordo!; **~ to Spain!** ¡bienvenido a España!; **to make sb ~** recibir a uno afectuosamente, dar una buena acogida a uno; **I didn't feel very ~ there** no creía que mi presencia allí les fuera muy grata; **to put out the ~ mat for sb** recibir a uno con todos los honores.

(**b**) (*pleasing*) grato, agradable; **that is ~ news** es una noticia grata; **it's a ~ change** es un cambio muy aceptable; **a glass of sherry is always ~** siempre se agradece una copita de jerez, una copita de jerez siempre viene bien.

(**c**) **you're ~!** (*answer to thanks*) ¡de nada!, ¡no hay de qué!; (*iro*) ¡buen provecho te haga!; **you are ~ to it** está a tu disposición; **you are ~ to try** eres muy dueño de probarlo, tienes permiso para probarlo; **you will always be ~ here** estás en tu casa.

2 *n* bienvenida *f*; (buena) acogida *f*, recepción *f*; **to bid sb ~** dar la bienvenida a uno; **to give sb a hearty ~** acoger a uno con entusiasmo; **the crowd gave him an enthusiastic ~** el público le dispensó una calurosa acogida; **to meet with a cold ~** ser recibido fríamente; **what sort of a ~ will this product get?** ¿qué aceptación tendrá este artículo?

3 *vt* dar la bienvenida a; acoger, recibir; aprobar; **they went to the airport to ~ him** fueron a recibirle al aeropuerto; **to ~ sb with open arms** recibir a uno con los brazos abiertos; **we should ~ this tendency** deberíamos dar la bienvenida a esta tendencia; **we ~ this step** aprobamos esta medida; **I'd ~ a cup of coffee** no me vendría mal una taza de café.

◆**welcome back** *vt*: **to ~ sb back** dar una buena acogida a uno cuando regresa.

welcoming ['welkəmɪŋ] *adj* acogedor, cordial.

weld [weld] **1** *vt* (**a**) (*Tech*) soldar; **to ~ parts together** soldar unas piezas; **the hull is ~ed throughout** el casco es totalmente soldado.

(**b**) (*fig*) **to ~ together** soldar, unir, unificar; **we must ~ them together into a new body** hemos de soldarlos para formar un nuevo organismo.

2 *vi* soldarse.

welder ['weldəʳ] *n* soldador *m*.

welding ['weldɪŋ] **1** *n* soldadura *f*. **2** *attr* de soldar, de soldadura, soldador; **~ torch** soplete *m* soldador.

welfare ['welfɛəʳ] **1** *n* (**a**) (*well-being*) bienestar *m*, bien *m*; prosperidad *f*; **child ~** bienestar *m* de los niños; **to work for the nation's ~** trabajar en bien de la nación.

(**b**) (*social aid etc*) asistencia *f* social, beneficencia *f* social; **to be on ~, to live on ~** vivir a cargo de la asistencia social.

2 *attr*: **~ centre** centro *m* de asistencia social; **~ state** estado *m* de bienestar, estado *m* asistencial, estado *m* benefactor; **~ work** trabajos *mpl* de asistencia social; **~ worker** asistente *mf* social.

Welfarism ['welfɛərɪzəm] *n* (*US*) *teoría y práctica de la protección de la salud y del bienestar públicos.*

well¹ [wel] **1** *n* pozo *m*; (*fig*) fuente *f*, manantial *m*; (*of stairs*) hueco *m*, caja *f*; **to sink a ~** perforar un pozo.

2 *vi* (*also* **to ~ out, to ~ up**) brotar, manar.

well² [wel] **1** *adv* (**a**) bien; **~ and good** muy bien; **the child speaks ~** el niño habla bien; **it's ~ painted** está bien pintado; **you would do ~ to think seriously about our offer** le convendría considerar seriamente nuestra oferta; *V* **speak, think** *etc*.

(**b**) (*intensive*) **we got ~ and truly wet** nos mojamos de verdad; **~ over a thousand** mucho más de mil; **they may ~ be lying** es muy posible que mientan; **it was ~ worth the trouble** realmente valió la pena; **we were ~ beaten** nos derrotaron fácilmente; **you may ~ ask** con razón preguntas.

(**c**) (*with qualifying adv*) **very ~** muy bien; **very ~, I'll do it** bueno, lo haré; **that's all very ~, but ...** todo eso está muy bien, pero ...; **all too ~, only too ~** de sobra, sobradamente.

(**d**) **as ~** también; **it's just as ~ you've come** menos mal que has venido; **she cried, as ~ she might** lloró, y con razón; **it is as ~ to remember that ...** conviene recordar que ...; **in cars as ~ as on bikes** en coches así como en bicicletas; **she swims as ~ as she walks** nada tan bien como anda; **you might as ~ tell me the truth** más valdría decirme la verdad; **A as ~ as B** A además de B, tanto A como B.

(**e**) (*concessive*) pues; **~ now** ahora bien; **~, it was like this** bueno, te lo diré; bueno, pasó lo siguiente; **~?** ¿y entonces?; **~ then** pues bien; **~ then?** ¿y qué?

2 *excl*: **~!** ¡vaya!, ¡caramba!; **~, ~!** ¡vaya, vaya!; **~, that's that!** ¡bueno, asunto concluido!

3 *adj* bien, bien de salud; **are you ~?** ¿qué tal estás?; **I'm very ~, thanks** estoy muy bien, gracias; **I'm fairly ~** estoy regular; **she's not been ~ lately** recientemente ha estado algo indispuesta; **I don't feel at all ~** no me siento nada bien; **to get ~** reponerse (*after* de); **to make sb ~** curar a uno, devolver la salud a uno.

4 *n*: **to leave ~ alone** no tocar, dejar las cosas como están; **to speak ~ of sb** hablar de uno en términos elogiosos; **to think ~ of sb** tener un buen concepto de uno; **to wish sb ~** desear todo lo mejor a uno.

well- [wel] *adv in compounds*: bien ..., *eg* **~-preserved** bien conservado.

we'll [wi:l] = **we will, we shall.**

well-adjusted ['weləˈdʒʌstɪd] *adj* equilibrado.

well-aimed ['welˈeɪmd] *adj* certero.

well-appointed ['weləˈpɔɪntɪd] *adj* bien amueblado.

well-argued ['welˈɑ:gju:d] *adj* razonado.

well-attended ['weləˈtendɪd] *adj* muy concurrido.

well-balanced ['welˈbælənsd] *adj* bien equilibrado.

well-behaved ['welbɪˈheɪvd] *adj* bien educado, formal; *animal* manso.

wellbeing ['wel,bi:ɪŋ] *n* bienestar *m*.

wellborn ['welˈbɔ:n] *adj* bien nacido.

well-bred ['welˈbred] *adj* bien educado, culto, cortés; *accent etc* culto; *animal* de raza, pura sangre.

well-brought-up ['welˈbrɔ:tʌp] *adj child* educado.

well-built ['welˈbɪlt] *adj* sólidamente construido, de construcción sólida; *person* fornido.

well-chosen ['welˈtʃəʊzn] *adj* elegido con cuidado; *remarks, words etc* acertado.

well-cooked ['welˈkʊkt] *adj* (*tasty*) bien preparado; (*cooked long*) muy hecho.

well-defined ['weldɪˈfaɪnd] *adj* bien definido.

well-deserved ['weldɪˈzɜ:vd] *adj* merecido.

well-developed ['weldɪˈveləpt] *adj arm, muscle etc* bien desarrollado; *sense* agudo, fino.

well-disposed ['weldɪsˈpəʊzd] *adj* favorable, benévolo; bienintencionado; **to be ~ towards sth** estar bien dispuesto hacia algo.

well-documented ['welˈdɒkjʊ,mentɪd] *adj* documentado.

well-dressed ['welˈdrest] *adj* bien vestido.

well-earned ['welˈɜ:nd] *adj* merecido.

well-educated ['welˈedjʊkeɪtɪd] *adj* instruido, culto.

well-equipped ['welɪˈkwɪpt] *adj* bien equipado.

well-established ['welɪˈstæblɪʃt] *adj* sólidamente establecido; *custom* muy arraigado; *firm* sólido, de buena reputación.

well-favoured, (*US*) **well-favored** ['welˈfeɪvəd] *adj* bien parecido.

well-fed ['welˈfed] *adj* bien alimentado, que come bien; (*in appearance*) regordete.

well-fixed* ['welˈfɪkst] *adj* (*US*): **to be ~** nadar en la abundancia, estar boyante; **we're ~ for food** tenemos comida de sobra.

well-formed ['welˈfɔ:md] *adj* (*Ling*) gramatical.

well-formedness ['welˈfɔ:mdnɪs] *n* gramaticalidad *f*.

well-founded ['welˈfaʊndɪd] *adj* (bien) fundado.

well-groomed ['welˈgru:md] *adj* acicalado.

well-grown ['welˈgrəʊn] *adj* grande, maduro, adulto.

wellhead ['welhed] *n* fuente *f*, manantial *m*.

well-heeled* ['welˈhi:ld] *adj* ricacho*.

wellies* ['welɪz] *npl* (*Brit*) = **wellingtons.**

well-informed ['welɪnˈfɔ:md] *adj* (*in general*) enterado, instruido; **to be ~ about sth** estar muy enterado de algo, estar al corriente de algo.

Wellington ['welɪŋtən] *n* Wellington *m*.

wellingtons ['welɪŋtənz] *npl*, **wellington boots** ['welɪŋtənˈbu:ts] *npl* (*Brit*) botas *fpl* de goma.

well-intentioned ['welɪnˈtenʃnd] *adj* bienintencionado; *lie* piadoso.

well-judged ['welˈdʒʌdʒd] *adj* bien calculado.

well-kept ['welˈkept] *adj* (muy) cuidado, bien conservado, en buen orden; **a ~ secret** un secreto bien guardado.

well-knit ['welˈnɪt] *adj body* robusto, fornido; *scheme etc* lógico, bien razonado; *speech etc* bien pensado, de estructura lógica.

well-known ['welˈnəʊn] *adj* (muy) conocido.

well-liked ['welˈlaɪkt] *adj* querido, apreciado.

well-loved ['welˈlʌvd] *adj* muy querido, amado.

well-made ['wel'meɪd] *adj* bien hecho, fuerte.
well-managed ['wel'mænɪdʒd] *adj* bien administrado; bien dirigido.
well-mannered ['wel'mænəd] *adj* educado, culto, cortés.
well-marked ['wel'mɑːkt] *adj* bien marcado.
well-matched ['wel'mætʃt] *adj* muy iguales.
well-meaning ['wel'miːnɪŋ] *adj* bienintencionado.
well-meant ['wel'ment] *adj* bienintencionado.
well-nigh ['welnaɪ] *adv* casi; punto menos que; **it's ~ finished** está casi terminado; **this is ~ impossible** esto es punto menos que imposible.
well-nourished ['wel'nʌrɪʃt] *adj* bien alimentado.
well-off ['wel'ɒf] *adj* (**a**) (*financially*) acomodado; pudiente; adinerado; **the less ~** las gentes menos pudientes; **he spoke with a ~ accent** habló con acento culto, (*pej*) habló con acento afectado.
(**b**) (*in circumstances*) **she's ~ without him** está mejor sin él; **you don't know when you're ~** no sabes los muchos beneficios que tienes.
well-oiled* ['wel'ɔɪld] *adj* hecho una cuba*.
well-padded* ['wel'pædɪd] *adj* gordo.
well-paid ['wel'peɪd] *adj* bien pagado, bien retribuido.
well-preserved ['welprɪ'zɜːvd] *adj* = **well-kept**; *person* bien conservado.
well-proportioned ['welprə'pɔːʃnd] *adj* bien proporcionado, de forma elegante; *person* de talle elegante.
well-read ['wel'red] *adj* leído, instruido; culto; **to be ~ in history** haber leído mucha historia, estar muy documentado en historia.
well-respected ['welrɪ'spektɪd] *adj* respetado, estimado.
well-rounded ['wel'raʊndɪd] *adj* redondeado, acabado.
well-spent ['wel'spent] *adj* bien empleado, fructuoso.
well-spoken ['wel'spəukən] *adj* bienhablado, con acento culto.
well-stacked* ['wel'stækt] *adj* de buen tipo, curvilínea.
well-stocked ['wel'stɒkt] *adj* bien provisto, bien surtido; **~ shelves** estantes *mpl* llenos.
well-thought-of ['wel'θɔːtɒv] *adj* bien reputado, de buena reputación.
well-thought-out ['wel,θɔːt'aʊt] *adj* bien planeado.
well-timed ['wel'taɪmd] *adj* oportuno.
well-to-do ['weltə'duː] *adj* acomodado, pudiente; **the ~** la gente pudiente, (*also pej*) la gente bien.
well-travelled, (*US*) **well-traveled** ['wel'trævld] *adj person* que ha viajado mucho, que ha visto mucho mundo; *path* trillado.
well-tried ['wel'traɪd] *adj method* comprobado.
well-trodden ['wel'trɒdn] *adj* trillado.
well-turned ['wel'tɜːnd] *adj* elegante.
well-wisher ['wel,wɪʃəʳ] *n* partidario *m*, -a *f*.
well-worn ['wel'wɔːn] *adj garment* raído; *path* trillado; *cliché* traído y llevado, trillado, manoseado.
well-written ['wel'rɪtn] *adj* bien escrito.
Welsh [welʃ] **1** *adj* galés, de Gales; **~ rabbit, ~ rarebit** pan *m* con queso tostado.
2 *n* (**a**) **the ~** *pl* los galeses.
(**b**) (*Ling*) galés *m*.
welsh* [welʃ] *vi* (*bookmaker*) largarse sin pagar*; dejar de cumplir una obligación (*on sb* contraída con uno).
Welshman ['welʃmən] *n, pl* **Welshmen** ['welʃmən] galés *m*.
Welshwoman ['welʃ,wʊmən] *n, pl* **Welshwomen** ['welʃ,wɪmɪn] galesa *f*.
welt [welt] **1** *n* (**a**) (*of shoe*) vira *f*; (**b**) (*weal*) verdugón *m*. **2** *vt* (**a**) poner vira a. (**b**) pegar, zurrar, hacer verdugones a.
welter ['weltəʳ] **1** *n* confusión *f*, mezcla *f* confusa, mescolanza *f*, revoltijo *m*; **in a ~ of blood** en un mar de sangre. **2** *vi* revolcarse; **to ~ in** estar bañado en, bañarse en.
welterweight ['weltəweɪt] *n* wélter *m*; **light ~** wélter *m* ligero.
wen [wen] *n* lobanillo *m*, quiste *m* sebáceo; **the Great W~** el gran tumor (*Londres*).
wench [wentʃ] **1** *n* mozuela *f*, muchacha *f*; (*pej*) moza *f*; (*whore*) puta *f*. **2** *vi* (*also* **to go ~ing**) ir de fulanas, putañear.
wend† [wend] *vt*: **to ~ one's way to** enderezar sus pasos a.
Wendy house ['wendɪ,haʊs] *n, pl* **Wendy houses** ['wendɪ,haʊzɪz] (*Brit*) casa *f* de muñecas (suficientemente grande para entrar).
went [went] *pret of* **go.**
wept [wept] *pret and ptp of* **weep.**
were [wɜːʳ] *pret of* **be.**
we're [wɪəʳ] = **we are.**
weren't [wɜːnt] = **were not.**
werewolf ['wɪəwʊlf] *n, pl* **werewolves** ['wɪəwʊlvz] hombrelobo *m*.
wert†† [wɜːt] *V* **be.**
Wesleyan ['wezlɪən] **1** *adj* metodista. **2** *n* metodista *mf*.
Wesleyanism ['wezlɪənɪzəm] *n* metodismo *m*.
west [west] **1** *n* oeste *m*, occidente *m*; **the W~** el Oeste, el Occidente; **tales of the American W~** cuentos *mpl* del Oeste americano.
2 *adj* del oeste, occidental; *wind* del oeste; **W~ Africa** África *f* Occidental; **W~ Bank** (*Middle East*) Cisjordania *f*; **W~ Berlin** (*Hist*) Berlín *m* Oeste; **W~ German** (*Hist*: *n*) alemán *m*, -ana *f* occidental, (*adj*) germanooccidental; **W~ Germany** (*Hist*) Alemania *f* Occidental; **to go ~*** (*object, machine*) romperse, estropearse; (*plan etc*) fracasar; (*person*) estirar la pata*.
westbound ['westbaʊnd] *adj traffic* que va hacia el oeste; *carriageway* dirección oeste.
westerly ['westəlɪ] *adj* oeste; *wind* del oeste.
western ['westən] **1** *adj* occidental, del oeste. **2** *n* western *m*.
westerner ['westənəʳ] *n* habitante *mf* del Oeste; (*Pol etc*) occidental *mf*.
westernization ['westənaɪ'zeɪʃən] *n* occidentalización *f*.
westernize ['westənaɪz] *vt* occidentalizar.
westernized ['westənaɪzd] *adj* occidentalizado, influido por el Occidente; **to become ~** occidentalizarse.
westernmost ['westənməʊst] *adj* (el) más occidental, situado más al oeste.
west-facing ['west'feɪsɪŋ] *adj* con cara al oeste, orientado hacia el oeste; **~ slope** vertiente *f* oeste.
West Indian ['west'ɪndɪən] **1** *adj* antillano. **2** *n* antillano *m*, -a *f*.
West Indies ['west'ɪndiːz] *npl* Antillas *fpl*.
westward ['westwəd] **1** *adj advance etc* hacia el oeste, en dirección oeste. **2** *adv* (*also* **~s**) hacia el oeste, en dirección oeste.
wet [wet] **1** *adj* (**a**) (*naturally*) húmedo; (*accidentally, temporarily*) mojado; *paint etc* fresco; **~ blanket*** aguafiestas *mf*; **~ dream** polución *f* nocturna; **~ fish** pescado *m* fresco; (*) tío *m* tonto*; **the ~ look** acabado *m* con aparencia de mojado; **in ~ clothes** en ropa mojada; **cheeks ~ with tears** mejillas *fpl* bañadas de lágrimas; **to be ~ through, to be ~ to the skin** estar mojado hasta los huesos; **the ink is still ~** la tinta no se ha secado todavía; **the baby's ~** el bebé se ha meado; **to be ~ behind the ears*** estar con la leche en los labios; **to get ~** mojarse; **to get one's feet ~** mojarse los pies; **it grows in ~ places** se encuentra en lugares húmedos.
(**b**) (*weather*) lluvioso; **a ~ day** un día de lluvia; **a ~ climate** un clima lluvioso; **the ~ season** la estación de las lluvias; **in ~ weather** cuando llueve; **it was ~ in the night** llovió durante la noche; **it was too ~ for us to go out** llovió tanto que no pudimos salir.
(**c**) (*Brit**: *stupid*) soso, bobo; **don't be so ~**! ¡no seas bobo!
(**d**) (*Brit Pol**) derechista moderado, de la derecha moderada.
(**e**) (*US**) antiprohibicionista.
(**f**) **you're all ~*** (*US*) estás totalmente equivocado, estás metiendo la pata a fondo*.
2 *n* (**a**) humedad *f*; (*rain*) lluvia *f*; **it's out in the ~** está fuera a la intemperie.
(**b**) (*US**) = **wetback.**
(**c**) (*Brit Pol**) político *mf* de la derecha moderada.
3 *vt* mojar, humedecer; *tea* hacer; echar agua hirviente a; (*) *bargain* cerrar con un brindis; **to ~ the bed** orinarse en la cama; **to ~ one's pants** orinarse en las bragas.
4 *vr*: **to ~ o.s.** mearse.
wetback ['wetbæk] *n* (*US*) inmigrante *m* (mejicano) ilegal; bracero *m*.
wether ['weðəʳ] *n* carnero *m* castrado.
wetland ['wetlənd] *n* pantano *m*, zona *f* húmeda, zona *f* acuosa; **~s** pantanos *mpl*, tierras *fpl* pantanosas.
wetness ['wetnɪs] *n* humedad *f*; (*raininess*) lo lluvioso.
wet-nurse ['wetnɜːs] *n* nodriza *f*, ama *f* de cría.
wetsuit ['wetsuːt] *n* vestido *m* isotérmico.
wetting ['wetɪŋ] *n* mojada *f*; **to get a ~** mojarse; **to give sb a ~** mojar a uno.
WEU *n abbr of* **Western European Union.**
we've [wiːv] = **we have.**
WFTU *n abbr of* **World Federation of Trade Unions** Federación *f* Sindical Mundial, FSM *f*.
whack [wæk] **1** *n* (**a**) (*blow*) golpe *m* grande, golpe *m*

ruidoso; porrazo *m*; **to give sb a ~** darle a uno ¡zas!; **to give sth a ~** golpear algo ruidosamente.

(**b**) (*: *attempt*) tentativa *f*; **to have a ~ at sth** intentar algo, probar algo; **let's have a ~** probemos, vamos a ver.

(**c**) (*Brit**: *share*) parte *f*, porción *f*; **you should get your ~** seguramente recibirás lo tuyo; **top ~** salario *m* máximo.

(**d**) **out of ~*** (*US*) estropiciado*, fastidiado.

2 *vt* (**a**) (*beat*) golpear, aporrear; (*defeat*) dar una paliza a.

(**b**) (*fig*) **the problem has me ~ed** todavía el problema me trae perplejo; **we've got the problem ~ed at last** por fin hemos resuelto el problema.

whacked* ['wækt] *adj* (*Brit*): **to be ~** estar agotado, estar hecho polvo*.

whacking ['wækıŋ] **1** *adj* (*esp Brit*) grandote, enorme, imponente.

2 *adv* (*: *esp Brit*): **a ~ big book** un libro enorme de grande, un tomazo*.

3 *n* zurra *f*; **to give sb a ~** zurrar a uno, pegar a uno.

whacky* ['wækı] *adj* (*US*) = **wacky**.

whale [weıl] *n* ballena *f*; **a ~ of a difference*** una enorme diferencia; **to have a ~ of a time*** divertirse en grande*, pasarlo bomba*.

whalebone ['weılbəʊn] *n* ballena *f*, barba *f* de ballena.

whale-oil ['weılɔıl] *n* aceite *m* de ballena.

whaler ['weılə^r] *n* (*person, ship*) ballenero *m*.

whaling ['weılıŋ] *n* pesca *f* de ballenas.

whaling-ship ['weılıŋʃıp] *n* ballenero *m*.

whaling-station ['weılıŋ,steıʃən] *n* estación *f* ballenera.

wham [wæm] (**a**) = **whang**. (**b**) *interj*: **~!** ¡zas!

whammy* ['wæmı] *n* (*US*) mala sombra *f*, mala suerte *f*, mala pata *f*.

whang [wæŋ] **1** *n* golpe *m* resonante.

2 *vt* golpear de modo resonante.

3 *vi*: **to ~ against sth, to ~ into sth** chocar ruidosamente con algo.

wharf [wɔːf] *n, pl* **wharfs** *or* **wharves** [wɔːvz] muelle *m*; **ex ~** franco en el muelle; **price ex ~** precio *m* franco de muelle.

wharfage ['wɔːfıdʒ] *n* muellaje *m*.

what [wɒt] **1** *adj* (**a**) (*rel*) el ... que, la ... que, lo ... que *etc*; **~ little I had** lo poco que tenía; **with ~ money I have** con el dinero que tengo; **buy ~ food you like** compra los comestibles que quieras.

(**b**) (*interrog*) qué; cuál de ...; **~ book do you want?** ¿qué libro quieres?, ¿cuál de los libros quieres?; **~ news did he bring?** ¿qué noticias trajo?

(**c**) (*interj*) qué; **~ a man!** ¡qué hombre!; **~ luck!** ¡qué suerte!; **~ a fool I've been!** ¡qué tonto he sido!; **~ an ugly dog!** ¡qué perro más (*or* tan) feo!

(**d**) (*interj, iro*) lindo, valiente, bueno; **~ a general!** ¡valiente general!; **~ an excuse!** ¡buen pretexto!

2 *pron* (**a**) (*rel*, = *that which*) el que, la que, lo que (*etc*); **~ I like is tea** lo que me gusta de verdad es el té; **that is not ~ I asked for** eso no es lo que pedí; **~ is done is done** lo que está hecho no se puede cambiar; **and ~ not, and ~ have you, and I don't know ~** y qué sé yo qué más; **and ~ is more ...** y además ...; **~ with the weather and the crisis** entre el mal tiempo y la crisis; **~ with one thing and another** entre una cosa y otra; **come ~ may** venga lo que viniere; **say ~ he will** diga lo que diga; **business is not ~ it was** los negocios no son lo que eran; **not a day but ~ it rains** no hay día que no llueva; **to give sb ~ for*** cargarse a uno*.

(**b**) (*interrog*) ¿qué?; (*please repeat*) ¿cómo?; **~ is it?** ¿qué es?; **~'s that?** ¿y eso qué es?; **~ is that to you?** y eso ¿qué te importa?; **'I'm going to be an actress' — 'You ~?'*** 'Voy a hacerme actriz' — ¿Qué dices?'; **do you want it or ~?** ¿lo quieres o qué?; **~ is the reason?** ¿cuál es la razón?; **~ is the formula for ...?** ¿cuál es la fórmula de ...?; **~ is this called?** ¿cómo se llama esto?; **~ can we do?** ¿qué podemos hacer?; **~ do 4 and 3 make?** ¿cuánto suman 4 y 3?; **so ~?** ¿y qué?; **so ~ if it does rain?** y si llueve, ¿qué?; **so ~ if he is gay?** y ¿nos importa que sea gay?; **~ if ...?** ¿y si ...?, ¿qué será si ...?; **~ of it?, ~ of that?** y eso ¿qué importa?; (**do**) **you know ~, I think he's drunk** creo que está borracho, ¿sabes?; **I know ~, let's ring her up** se me ocurre una idea: llamémosla al teléfono; **I know ~ you're after** sé lo que buscas; **I don't know ~ to do** no sé qué hacer; **I'll tell you ~** se me ocurre una idea, tengo una idea; **he knows ~'s ~** sabe cuántas son cinco; **rats and mice and God knows ~** ratas y ratones y Dios sabe qué más; *V* **about, for** *etc*.

(**c**) (*interj*) ¡cómo!; **~! you sold it!** ¡cómo! ¡lo has vendido!; **~! a man in your room?** ¡qué horror! ¿un hombre en tu cuarto?; **shameful, ~?** (*esp Brit*) vergonzoso, ¿no?

what-d'ye-call-him* ['wɒtdʒʊ,kɔːlım] *pron* fulano; **old ~ with the red nose** ése que tiene la nariz tan coloradota.

what-d'ye-call-it* ['wɒtdʒʊ,kɔːlıt] *pron* cosa *f*, chisme *m*; **he does it with the ~** lo hace con el chisme ese; **that green ~ on the front** esa cosa verde en la parte delantera.

whatever [wɒt'evə^r] **1** *pron* lo que; todo lo que; **~ you like** lo que quieras; **~ you find** cualquier cosa que encuentres; **~ I have is yours** todo lo que tengo es tuyo; **~ it may be** sea lo que sea; **~ he says** diga lo que diga; **~ you say** (*acquiescing*) lo que quieras; **~ happens** pase lo que pase; **or ~ they're called** o como quiera que se llamen; **~ do you mean?** pero ¿qué diablos quieres decir?; **or ~** o lo que sea; **~ did you do?** ¿pues qué hiciste?

2 *adj* (**a**) **~ book you choose** qualquier libro que elijas; **~ books you choose** cualquier libro de los que elijas; **every book of ~ size** todo libro tamaño que sea; **~ time is it?** ¿qué hora podrá ser?

(**b**) (*negative*) **no man ~** ningún hombre sea quien sea; **nothing ~** nada en absoluto; **he said nothing ~ of interest** no dijo nada en absoluto que tuviera interés; **it's of no use ~** no sirve para nada en absoluto.

what-ho* ['wɒt'həʊ] *interj* (*surprise*) ¡caramba!, ¡vaya!; (*greeting*) ¡hola!, ¡oye!

whatnot ['wɒtnɒt] **1** *n* (**a**) (*furniture*) juguetero *m*. (**b**) (*) (*whatsit*) chisme *m*. **2** *pron*: **and ~*** y qué sé yo, y un largo etcétera.

what's-his-name* ['wɒtsız,neım] *pron* fulano; **old ~ with the limp** fulano el cojo.

whatsit* ['wɒtsıt] *n* chisme *m*.

whatsoever [,wɒtsəʊ'evə^r] *pron, adj* = **whatever**.

wheat [wiːt] **1** *n* trigo *m*; **to separate the ~ from the chaff** (*fig*) separar la cizaña del buen grano. **2** *attr* de trigo, trigueño; **~ loaf** pan *m* de trigo.

wheatear ['wiːtıə^r] *n* (*Orn*) collalba *f*.

wheaten ['wiːtn] *adj* de trigo, trigueño; de color de trigo.

wheatfield ['wiːtfiːld] *n* trigal *m*.

wheatgerm ['wiːtdʒɜːm] *n* germen *m* de trigo.

wheatmeal ['wiːtmiːl] *n* harina *f* de trigo.

wheatsheaf ['wiːtʃiːf] *n* gavilla *f* de trigo.

wheedle ['wiːdl] *vt* engatusar; **to ~ sb into doing sth** engatusar a uno para que haga (*or* para hacer) algo, conseguir por medio de halagos que uno haga algo; **to ~ sth out of sb** sonsacar algo a alguien.

wheedling ['wiːdlıŋ] **1** *adj* mimoso. **2** *n* mimos *mpl*, halagos *mpl*.

wheel [wiːl] **1** *n* (**a**) rueda *f*; (*steering ~*) volante *m*; (*potter's*) torno *m*; (*Naut*) timón *m*; **~ of fortune** rueda *f* de fortuna; **the ~s of government** el mecanismo del gobierno; **big ~** (*at fair*) noria *f*, (*: *person*) personaje *m*, pez *m* gordo*; **to be at** (*or* **behind**) **the ~** estar al volante, estar conduciendo; **there are ~s within ~s** esto es más complicado de lo que parece, esto tiene su miga; **a basket on ~s** una cesta con ruedas; **are you on ~s?*** (*US*) ¿tienes coche?, ¿estás motorizado?*; **to oil the ~s** (*fig*) lubricar el mecanismo; **to take the ~** tomar el volante.

(**b**) (*Mil*) vuelta *f*, conversión *f*; **a ~ to the right** una vuelta hacia la derecha.

2 *attr* (*Aut*) **four ~ drive** tracción *f* a las cuatro ruedas; **front ~ drive** tracción *f* delantera; **rear ~ drive** tracción *f* trasera.

3 *vt* (*turn*) hacer girar; hacer rodar; *bicycle, pram* empujar; *child* pasear en cochecito; **we ~ed it over to the window** lo empujamos hasta la ventana; **when it broke down I had to ~ it** cuando se averió tuve que empujarlo.

4 *vi* (*turn*) girar; rodar; dar vueltas; (*birds*) revolotear; (*Mil*) dar una vuelta, cambiar de frente; **to ~ left** dar una vuelta hacia la izquierda; **to ~ round** (*person*) girar sobre los talones; (*fig*) cambiar de rumbo, cambiar de opinión.

wheelbarrow ['wiːl,bærəʊ] *n* carretilla *f*.

wheelbase ['wiːlbeıs] *n* batalla *f*, distancia *f* entre ejes.

wheelbrace ['wiːlbreıs] *n* llave *f* de ruedas en cruz.

wheelchair ['wiːltʃɛə^r] *n* silla *f* de ruedas.

wheel-clamp ['wiːlklæmp] **1** *n* cepo *m*. **2** *vt* poner cepo a, inmovilizar con el cepo; **I found I was ~ed** me encontré inmovilizado con el cepo.

wheeled [wiːld] *adj*: **~ traffic** tránsito *m* rodado; **~ transport** transporte *m* rodado.

-wheeled [wiːld] *adj ending in compounds*: *eg* **four~** de cuatro ruedas.

wheeler-dealer* ['wiːlə,diːlə^r] *n* comerciante *m* poco es-

crupuloso.
wheel horse* ['wi:lhɔ:s] *n* (*US*) trabajador *m*, -ora *f* infatigable, mula *f* de carga.
wheelhouse ['wi:lhaʊs] *n*, *pl* **wheelhouses** ['wi:l,haʊzɪz] timonera *f*, cámara *f* del timonel.
wheeling ['wi:lɪŋ] *n*: ~ **and dealing*** negocios *mpl* sucios, intrigas *fpl*.
wheelwright ['wi:lraɪt] *n* ruedero *m*, carretero *m*.
wheeze [wi:z] **1** *n* (**a**) resuello *m* (ruidoso), resuello *m* asmático; respiración *f* sibilante.
(**b**) (*Brit**) truco *m*, treta *f*; idea *f*; **that's a good** ~ es buena idea; **to think up a** ~ idear una treta.
2 *vt*: **'Yes,' he ~d** 'Sí', dijo en voz asmática.
3 *vi* resollar (con ruido), jadear; respirar con silbido.
wheezing ['wi:zɪŋ] *adj*, **wheezy** ['wi:zɪ] *adj breath* ruidoso, difícil; *pronunciation* sibilante.
whelk [welk] *n* buccino *m*.
whelp [welp] **1** *n* cachorro *m*. **2** *vi* parir (*la perra etc*).
when [wen] **1** *adv* cuándo; ~ **did it happen?** ¿cuándo ocurrió?; **I know ~ it happened** yo sé cuándo ocurrió; ~ **is the interview?** ¿cuándo es la entrevista?; **say** ~ (*in pouring drink*) dime cuándo; **since ~?** ¿desde cuándo?; **since ~ do you have a car?** ¿de cuándo acá tienes tú coche?; **till ~?** ¿hasta cuándo?
2 *conj* (**a**) cuando; ~ **I came in** cuando yo entré; al entrar (yo); ~ **I was young** cuando era joven; en mi juventud; **you can go ~ I have finished** puedes irte en cuanto yo termine; ~ **the bridge is built** cuando se construya el puente; **he's only happy ~ drunk** es feliz únicamente cuando está borracho; **he did it ~ a child** lo hizo de niño, lo hizo siendo niño.
(**b**) (*rel*) cuando; **this is ~ it always rains** esto es cuando llueve siempre; **at the very moment ~** ... en el mismo momento en que (*or* cuando) ...; **one day ~ the tide is out** un día cuando la marea esté baja.
whence [wens] *adv* (*liter*) (**a**) (*of place*) ¿de dónde?; ~ **comes it that** ...? ¿cómo es que ...?
(**b**) (*fig*) por lo cual, y por consiguiente; ~ **I conclude that** ... por lo cual concluyo que ...
whenever [wen'evəʳ] **1** *conj* siempre que, cuandoquiera que; cuando, todas las veces que; **come ~ you like** ven cuando quieras; **I go ~ I can** voy todas las veces que puedo; ~ **you see one of those, stop** siempre que veas uno de ésos, para; **we will help ~ possible** ayudaremos siempre cuando sea posible.
2 *adv*: ~ **can he have done it?** ¿cuándo demonios ha podido hacerlo?; ~ **do I have the time for such things?** ¿cuándo crees que tengo tiempo para estas cosas?; **Monday, Tuesday, or ~** el lunes o el martes o cuando sea, el lunes o el martes o algún día de éstos.
where [wɛəʳ] *adv* (**a**) (*interrog*) ¿dónde?; ~ **am I?** ¿dónde estoy?; **I know ~ he is** yo sé dónde está; ~ **are you going?** ¿adónde vas?; ~ **are you from?** ¿de dónde eres?; ~ **should we be if** ...? ¿dónde estaríamos nosotros si ...?; ~ **is the sense of it?** ¿qué sentido tiene?
(**b**) (*rel*) donde; ~ **possible** donde sea posible; **go ~ you like** ve donde quieras; **this is ~ we got to** éste es el punto al que habíamos llegado; **this is ~ we got out** nos apeamos aquí, aquí es donde nos apeamos; **we are at the stage ~ we have to be careful** estamos en el punto en que tenemos que andar con cuidado; **the house ~ I was born** la casa donde nací, la casa en la que nací; **from ~ I'm sitting** desde aquí, desde donde estoy sentado; **that's just ~ you're wrong** en eso te equivocas; **that's ~ I disagree with you** en eso no estoy de acuerdo contigo; ~ **this book is dangerous is in suggesting that** ... el aspecto peligroso de este libro es la sugerencia de que ...; ~ **husband and wife both work, benefits are** ... en el caso de que los dos esposos trabajan, los beneficios son ...
whereabouts 1 ['wɛərə'baʊts] *adv* ¿dónde? **2** ['wɛərəbaʊts] *n* paradero *m*; **nobody knows his ~** se desconoce su paradero actual.
whereas [wɛər'æz] *conj* visto que, por cuanto, mientras; (*in legal parlance*) considerando que.
whereat [wɛər'æt] *adv* (*liter*) con lo cual.
whereby [wɛə'baɪ] *adv* (*frm*) por lo cual, por donde; **the rule ~ it is not allowed to** + *infin* la regla según (*or* mediante) la cual no se permite + *infin* .
wherefore†† ['wɛəfɔ:ʳ] **1** *adv* (*why*) por qué; (*and for this reason*) y por tanto, por lo cual.
2 *n*: **the whys and ~s** las razones, el por qué; los detalles, la explicación detallada.
wherein†† [wɛər'ɪn] *adv* en donde.
whereof†† [wɛər'ɒv] *adv* de que.
whereon [wɛər'ɒn] *adv* (*liter*) en que.
wheresoever [,wɛəsəʊ'evəʳ] *adv* (*liter*) dondequiera que.
whereto [,wɛə'tu:] *adv* (*frm*, ††) adonde.
whereupon ['wɛərəpɒn] *adv* con lo cual, después de lo cual.
wherever [wɛər'evəʳ] **1** *conj* dondequiera que; ~ **you go I'll go too** dondequiera que vayas yo te acompañaré; ~ **I am** (esté) donde esté; ~ **possible** donde sea posible; **he follows me ~ I go** me sigue por donde vaya; ~ **they went they were cheered** por dondequiera que fueron se les aplaudió; **sit ~ you like** siéntate donde te parezca bien; **I'll buy them ~ they come from** los compraré no importa su procedencia, los compraré vengan de donde vengan.
2 *adv*: ~ **did you put it?** ¿dónde demonios lo pusiste?; ~ **can they have got to?** ¿dónde diablos se habrán metido?; **in Madrid or Barcelona or ~** en Madrid o Barcelona o donde sea.
wherewith [wɛə'wɪθ] *adv* con lo cual.
wherewithal ['wɛɒwɪðɔ:l] *n* medios *mpl*, recursos *mpl*, cónquibus *m* (*hum*); **they haven't got the ~** no tienen los medios.
wherry ['werɪ] *n* chalana *f*.
whet [wet] *vt tool* afilar, amolar; *appetite*, *curiosity* estimular, despertar, aguzar.
whether ['weðəʳ] *conj* si; **I do not know ~** ... no sé si ...; **I doubt ~** ... dudo que + *subj*; ~ **he is here or in Madrid** que esté aquí o en Madrid; ~ **she sings or dances** que cante o baile; ~ **they come or not** vengan o no (vengan).
whetstone ['wetstəʊn] *n* piedra *f* de amolar, afiladera *f*.
whew [hwju:] *interj* ¡vaya!, ¡caramba!
whey [weɪ] *n* suero *m*.
whey-faced ['weɪ'feɪst] *adj* pálido.
whf *abbr of* **wharf**.
which [wɪtʃ] **1** *adj* (**a**) (*interrog*) ¿qué?; ¿cuál?; ~ **picture do you prefer?** ¿qué cuadro prefieres?, ¿cuál de los cuadros prefieres?; **I don't know ~ tie he wants** no sé qué corbata quiere; ~ **way did she go?** ¿por dónde se fue?; ~ **one?** ¿cuál?; ~ **one of us?** ¿cuál de nosotros?; ~ **house do you live in?** ¿en qué casa vives?, ¿qué casa es la tuya?
(**b**) (*rel*) **he used 'peradventure', ~ word is now archaic** dijo 'peradventure', palabra que ha quedado anticuada; **look ~ way you will** ... miren por donde miren ...
2 *pron* (**a**) (*interrog*) ¿cuál?; ~ **do you want?** ¿cuál quieres?; ~ **of you did it?** ¿cuál de vosotros lo hizo?; **I don't mind ~** no me importa cuál; **I can't tell ~ is ~** no sé cuál es cuál.
(**b**) (*rel*) que; lo que; **the bear ~ I saw** el oso que vi; **two forms ~ are to be filled in** dos formularios que deberán llenarse; **the meeting ~ we attended** la reunión a que asistimos; **it rained hard ~ upset her** llovió mucho, lo que la desconcertó; ... ~ **God forbid** ... lo que Dios no quiera.
(**c**) (*rel governed by prep*) el que (*etc*), el cual (*etc*); lo cual; **the hotel at ~ we stayed** el hotel en el que nos hospedamos; **the cities to ~ we are going** las ciudades a las que vamos; **the bull ~ I'm talking about** el toro del que hablo; **at ~** con lo cual, sobre lo cual; **from ~ we deduce that** ... de lo cual deducimos que ...; **after ~ we went to bed** después de lo cual nos acostamos.
whichever [wɪtʃ'evəʳ] **1** *adj* cualquier; ~ **possibility you choose** cualquier posibilidad que elijas; ~ **way you look at it** se mire como se mire; **you can choose ~ system you want** puedes elegir el sistema que quieras; ~ **system you have there are difficulties** hay dificultades no importa el sistema que tengas.
2 *pron* cualquiera; el que, la que; **choose ~ is easiest** elige el que sea más fácil; ~ **of the methods you choose** cualquiera de los métodos que elijas, no importa el método que elijas; ~ **can he mean?** ¿cuál demonios querrá decir?
whiff [wɪf] **1** *n* soplo *m*, soplo *m* fugaz; vaharada *f*; bocanada *f*; (*smell*) olorcillo *m*; **a ~ of grapeshot** un poco de metralla; **not a ~ of wind** ni el menor soplo de viento; **to catch a ~ of sth** percibir un olorcillo de algo, oler algo brevemente; **to go out for a ~ of air** salir a tomar el fresco; **what a ~!** ¡qué olor!
2 *vi* (*) oler (mal); **to ~ of** oler a.
Whig [wɪg] (*Pol Hist*) **1** *n político liberal de los siglos XVII y XVIII*. **2** *adj* liberal.
while [waɪl] **1** *n* (**a**) rato *m*, tiempo *m*; **after a ~** poco tiempo después, al poco tiempo; **for a ~** durante algún tiempo; **a good ~, a great ~, a long ~** largo rato, mucho tiempo; **a long ~ ago** hace mucho; **it will be a good ~ before he gets here** tardará bastante en llegar; **it will be a good ~ before they finish** tardarán bastante en terminar; **a**

little ~ ago hace poco; **it takes quite a ~** es cosa de bastante tiempo, exige mucho tiempo; **in a short ~** dentro de poco; **stay a ~ with us** quédate un rato con nosotros.

(**b**) **the ~** entretanto, mientras tanto; **all the ~** todo el tiempo; **he looked at me the ~** mientras tanto me estaba mirando.

(**c**) **it is worth ~ to ask whether ...** vale la pena preguntar si ...; **it's not worth my ~** desde mi punto de vista no vale la pena; **we'll make it worth your ~** le pagaremos bien, le compensaremos.

2 *conj* (**a**) (*time*) mientras; **~ this was happening** mientras pasaba esto; **~ you are away** mientras estés fuera; **she fell asleep ~ reading** se durmió leyendo; **to drink ~ on duty** beber estando de servicio.

(**b**) (*concessive*) aunque, bien que; **~ I admit it is awkward** aunque confieso que es difícil.

(**c**) (*whereas*) mientras; **I have a blue car ~ you have a red one** yo tengo un coche azul y el tuyo es rojo.

(**d**) (*contrast*) si bien; **~ this used to be true, it is no longer so** si bien esto era verdad, ya no es así.

◆**while away** *vt*: **to ~ away the time** pasar el rato, entretener el tiempo.

whilst [waɪlst] *conj* = **while.**

whim [wɪm] *n* capricho *m*, antojo *m*, manía *f*; **a passing ~** un capricho; **her every ~** todos sus antojos y fantasías; **it's just a ~ of hers** es un capricho suyo; **as the ~ takes me** según se me antoja.

whimbrel ['wɪmbrəl] *n* zarapito *m*.

whimper ['wɪmpəʳ] **1** *n* quejido *m*, gemido *m*; **without a ~** sin quejarse. **2** *vt*: **'Yes', she ~ed** 'Sí', dijo lloriqueando. **3** *vi* lloriquear; quejarse, gemir.

whimpering ['wɪmpərɪŋ] **1** *adj* que lloriquea. **2** *n* lloriqueo *m*, gimoteo *m*.

whimsical ['wɪmzɪkəl] *adj person* caprichoso; antojadizo; *idea* caprichoso, fantástico; **to be in a ~ mood** estar de humor para dejar volar la fantasía.

whimsicality [wɪmzɪ'kælɪtɪ] *n* capricho *m*, fantasía *f*; **a novel of a pleasing ~** una novela de agradable fantasía.

whimsically ['wɪmzɪkəlɪ] *adv* caprichosamente; fantásticamente.

whimsy ['wɪmzɪ] *n* (*whim*) capricho *m*, antojo *m*; (*whimsicality*) fantasía *f*, extravagancia *f*.

whin [wɪn] *n* tojo *m*.

whine [waɪn] **1** *n* (*complaining cry*) quejido *m*, gimoteo *m*, (*of dog*) gañido *m*; (*of bullet*) silbido *m*.

2 *vt*: **'Yes', he ~d** 'Sí', dijo gimoteando.

3 *vi* quejarse, gimotear; gañir; silbar; (*fig*) quejarse; **don't come whining to me about it** no venga a mí a quejarse; **the dog was whining to be let in** el perro estaba gañendo para que le abrieran.

whinge* [wɪndʒ] *vi* (**a**) (*complain*) quejarse. (**b**) = **whine 2.**

whining ['waɪnɪŋ] **1** *adj* quejumbroso; que gimotea. **2** *n* quejidos *mpl*, gimoteo *m*; el silbar.

whinny ['wɪnɪ] **1** *n* relincho *m*. **2** *vi* relinchar.

whip [wɪp] **1** *n* (**a**) (*riding ~*) látigo *m*; (*used in punishment*) azote *m*, zurriago *m*.

(**b**) (*Brit Parl*: *call*) llamada *f*; **three-line ~** llamada *f* apremiante (para que un diputado acuda a votar en un debate importante).

(**c**) (*Parl*: *person*) oficial *m* disciplinario de partido.

(**d**) (*Culin*) postre *m* de nata y huevos batidos.

2 *vt* (**a**) azotar; dar con un látigo; (*Culin*) batir; (*defeat*) batir, cascar; (*criticize etc*) fustigar.

(**b**) *rope* ligar, envolver con cuerda; (*Sew*) sobrecoser.

(**c**) (*Brit**) birlar*.

(**d**) **to ~ sb off to a meeting** llevar a uno con toda prisa a una reunión.

(**e**) **he was ~ping the crowd into a frenzy** provocaba el frenesí en la multitud.

3 *vi* moverse rápidamente; ir con toda prisa; **the car ~ped past** el coche pasó como un rayo.

◆**whip away 1** *vt*: **to ~ sth away from sb** arrebatar algo a uno.

2 *vi*: = **whip 3.**

◆**whip back** *vi* (*return*) volverse de golpe; (*bounce back*) rebotar de repente hacia atrás.

◆**whip in** *vt* (*Hunting*) *hounds* llamar, reunir; (*Parl*) *member* llamar para que vote; *electors* hacer que acudan a las urnas.

◆**whip off** *vt lid etc* quitar con un movimiento brusco; *dress* quitarse bruscamente.

◆**whip on** *vt lid etc* poner con un movimiento brusco; *dress* ponerse bruscamente.

◆**whip out** *vt* sacar de repente.

◆**whip round** *vi* (**a**) (*turn*) volverse de repente.

(**b**) (*) **I'll ~ round to the shop** voy corriendo a la tienda; **the car ~ped round the corner** el coche dobló la esquina a gran velocidad.

(**c**) **to ~ round for sb*** hacer una colecta para uno.

◆**whip through** *vt book* leer rápidamente; *task, homework* realizar de un tirón.

◆**whip up** *vt* (**a**) *feeling* avivar, estimular; *support* procurar.

(**b**) (*Culin*) *cream etc* batir.

(**c**) (*pick up*) coger de repente; arrebatar.

whipcord ['wɪpkɔːd] *n* tralla *f*.

whip-hand ['wɪp'hænd] *n*: **to have the ~** llevar la ventaja (*over sb* a uno); llevar la batuta, mandar.

whiplash ['wɪplæʃ] **1** *n* tralla *f*, latigazo *m*. **2** *attr*: **~ injury** desnucamiento *m*, latigazo *m*.

whipped [wɪpt] *adj cream etc* batido.

whipper-in ['wɪpər'ɪn] *n* (*Hunting*) montero *m* que cuida los perros de caza.

whippersnapper ['wɪpə,snæpəʳ] *n* (*also* **young ~**) mequetrefe *m*.

whippet ['wɪpɪt] *n* lebrel *m*.

whipping ['wɪpɪŋ] *n* azotamiento *m*; flagelación *f*; (*defeat*) derrota *f*; (*criticism etc*) paliza *f*; **to give sb a ~** azotar a uno, (*fig*) dar una paliza a uno.

whipping-boy ['wɪpɪŋbɔɪ] *n* cabeza *f* de turco.

whipping-top ['wɪpɪŋtɒp] *n* peonza *f*, trompo *m*.

whip-round* ['wɪpraʊnd] *n* (*Brit*) colecta *f*; **to have a ~ for sb** hacer una colecta para uno.

whipsaw ['wɪpsɔː] *n* sierra *f* cabrilla.

whirl [wɜːl] **1** *n* (**a**) (*turn*) giro *m*, vuelta *f*; (*turning*) rotación *f*; el girar; (*of dust, water etc*) remolino *m*; **a ~ of pleasures** un torbellino de placeres; **my head is in a ~** mi cabeza está dando vueltas; **he disappeared in a ~ of dust** desapareció en una polvareda. (**b**) (*) **let's give it a ~** vamos a probarlo.

2 *vt* (*make turn*) hacer girar, hacer dar vueltas, dar vueltas a; (*wave, shake*) agitar; (*transport*) llevar con toda rapidez; **he ~ed his hat round his head** agitaba el sombrero alrededor de la cabeza; **he ~ed her off to the dance** la llevó con toda rapidez al baile; **the train ~ed us off to Paris** el tren nos llevó muy rápidamente a París.

3 *vi* (*spin*) girar rápidamente, dar vueltas; (*of dust, water*) arremolinarse; **my head ~s** mi cabeza está dando vueltas; **they ~ed past us in the dance** pasaron delante de nosotros girando alegremente en el baile.

◆**whirl round** *vi* girar rápidamente, dar vueltas; (*dust, water*) arremolinarse.

whirligig ['wɜːlɪgɪg] *n* (*toy*) molinete *m*; (*roundabout*) tiovivo *m*; (*Ent*) girino *m*; (*fig*) vicisitudes *fpl*; movimiento *m* confuso.

whirlpool ['wɜːlpuːl] *n* torbellino *m*, remolino *m*; (*fig*) vorágine *f*.

whirlwind ['wɜːlwɪnd] **1** *n* torbellino *m*, manga *f* de viento; **like a ~** como un torbellino, como una tromba; **to reap the ~** segar lo que se ha sembrado, padecer las consecuencias. **2** *attr* rapidísimo; **a ~ courtship** un noviazgo brevísimo; **they took us on a ~ tour** nos llevaron en una gira relámpago.

whirlybird* ['wɜːlɪbɜːd] *n* (*US*) helicóptero *m*.

whirr [wɜːʳ] **1** *n* (*of bird's wings*) ruido *m*, aleteo *m*, batir *m*, (*of insect's wings*) zumbido *m*; (*of machine*: *quiet*) zumbido *m*, runrún *m*, (*louder*) rechino *m*.

2 *vi* hacer ruido, batir; zumbar, runrunear; rechinar; **the cameras ~ed** runruneaban las cámaras.

whisk [wɪsk] **1** *n* (*brush*) escobilla *f*; (*fly ~*) mosqueador *m*; (*Culin*) espumadera *f*, batidor *m*, (*electric etc*) batidora *f*.

2 *vt* (**a**) (*Brit Culin*) batir.

(**b**) (*fig*) **they ~ed him off to a meeting** le llevaron con toda prisa a una reunión; **we were ~ed up in the lift to the 9th floor** el ascensor nos llevó con toda rapidez al piso 9.

3 *vi* moverse rápidamente.

◆**whisk away 1** *vt* (**a**) *dust etc* quitar con un movimiento brusco; **the horse ~ed the flies away with its tail** el caballo ahuyentó las moscas con un movimiento brusco de la cola.

(**b**) **she ~ed it away from me** me lo arrebató; me lo quitó de repente; **the waiter ~ed the dishes away** el camarero quitó los platos en un periquete.

2 *vi* desaparecer de repente.

◆**whisk off** *vt dust etc* quitar con un movimiento brusco.

◆**whisk up** *vt* (*Culin*) batir.

whisker ['wɪskəʳ] *n* pelo *m* (de la barba); **~s** barbas *fpl*; (*moustache*) bigotes *mpl*; (*side ~s*) patillas *fpl*; (*Zool*) bigotes *mpl*; **by a ~** por un pelo; **he was within a ~ of ...**

estaba a dos dedos de ...

whiskered ['wɪskəd] *adj* bigotudo.

whisky, (*Ireland, US*) **whiskey** ['wɪskɪ] *n* whisk(e)y *m*, güisqui *m*; ~ **and soda** whisky *m* con sifón, whisky *m* con soda.

whisper ['wɪspəʳ] **1** *n* (**a**) (*low tone*) cuchicheo *m*; (*of leaves*) susurro *m*; **to say sth in a** ~ decir algo en tono muy bajo; **to speak in a** ~ hablar muy bajo; **her voice scarcely rose above a** ~ apenas pudo hablar sino en tono muy bajo.

(**b**) (*rumour*) rumor *m*, voz *f*; **at the least** ~ **of scandal** al menor indicio del escándalo; **there is a** ~ **that** ... corre la voz de que ..., se rumorea que ...

2 *vt* (**a**) decir en tono muy bajo; **to** ~ **sth to sb, to** ~ **a word in sb's ear** decir algo al oído de uno.

(**b**) (*fig*) **it is** ~**ed that** ... corre la voz de que..., se rumorea que ...

3 *vi* cuchichear, hablar muy bajo; (*leaves*) susurrar; **to** ~ **to sb** cuchichear a uno, decir algo al oído de uno; **just** ~ **to me** dímelo al oído; **stop** ~**ing!** ¡silencio!; **it's rude to** ~ **in company** es de mala educación cuchichear en compañía.

whispering ['wɪspərɪŋ] **1** *n* (**a**) cuchicheo *m*; (*of leaves*) susurro *m*.

(**b**) (*gossip*) chismes *mpl*, chismografía *f*; (*rumours*) rumores *mpl*.

2 *attr*: ~ **campaign** campaña *f* de rumores; campaña *f* de difamación; ~ **gallery** galería *f* con eco.

whist [wɪst] *n* (*Brit*) whist *m*.

whist-drive ['wɪstdraɪv] *n* certamen *m* de whist.

whistle ['wɪsl] **1** *n* (**a**) (*sound*) silbido *m*, silbo *m*, pitido *m*; **final** ~ pitido *m* final.

(**b**) (*instrument*) silbato *m*, pito *m*; **blast on the** ~ pitido *m*; **the referee blew his** ~ el árbitro pitó; **to blow the** ~ **on sb*** llamar a uno al orden; delatar a uno; poner fin a las actividades de uno; **to wet one's** ~* remojar el gaznate*, beber un trago.

2 *vt* silbar; **to** ~ **a tune** silbar una melodía.

3 *vi* silbar; (*Sport etc*) pitar; **it** ~**d past my ear** pasó (silbando) muy cerca de mi oreja, me rozó casi la oreja al pasar; **the car** ~**d past us** el coche pasó como una bala; **the boys** ~ **at the girls** los chicos silban a las chicas; **the crowd** ~**d at the referee** el público silbó al árbitro; **he** ~**d for a taxi** llamó un taxi con un silbido; **the referee** ~**d for a foul** el árbitro pitó falta; **he can** ~ **for it*** lo pedirá en vano, que espere sentado.

◆**whistle up** *vt* (**a**) **to** ~ **up one's dog** llamar a su perro con un silbido.

(**b**) (*fig*) (*find*) encontrar, hacer aparecer; *meal* preparar, servir; *people* reunir.

whistle-stop ['wɪslstɒp] **1** *n* (*US*) población *f* pequeña. **2** *attr*: ~ **tour** gira *f* electoral muy rápida.

Whit [wɪt] **1** *n* Pentecostés *m*. **2** *attr* de Pentecostés; ~ **Sunday** domingo *m* de Pentecostés; ~ **week** semana *f* de Pentecostés.

whit [wɪt] *n*: **never a** ~, **not a** ~ ni pizca; **without a** ~ **of** sin pizca de; **every** ~ **as good as** de ningún modo inferior a.

white [waɪt] **1** *adj* blanco; *hair, meat, wine etc* blanco; *face* (*of complexion*) blanco, (*with fear*) pálido; (*fig*) honorable, decente; ~ **blood-cell** célula *f* sanguínea blanca; ~ **bread** pan *m* blanco, pan *m* candeal; ~ **Christmas** Navidad *f* nevada; ~ **coffee** (*Brit*) café *m* con leche; **to show the** ~ **feather** mostrarse cobarde; ~ **flag** bandera *f* blanca; ~ **flour** harina *f* blanca; ~ **goods** (*linens*) ropa *f* blanca; (*US: domestic appliances*) (aparatos *mpl*) electrodomésticos *mpl*; ~ **heat** candencia *f*; ~ **hope** esperanza *f* dorada; ~ **horses** (*waves*) palomas *fpl*; **W**~ **House** (*US*) Casa *f* Blanca; ~ **lead** albayalde *m*; ~ **lie** mentirilla *f*, mentira *f* piadosa (*or* caritativa); ~ **magic** magia *f* blanca; ~ **meat** carne *f* blanca; ~ **noise** sonido *m* blanco, sonido *m* uniforme; ~ **paper** (*Parl*) libro *m* blanco; ~ **pepper** pimienta *f* blanca; ~ **slave trade** trata *f* de blancas; ~ **tie** corbatín *m* blanco; ~ **water** aguas *fpl* bravas; ~ **wedding** boda *f* de iglesia (en la que la novia viste de blanco); **to be as** ~ **as a sheet** estar pálido como la muerte; **to go** ~, **to turn** ~ (*thing*) blanquear, (*person*) palidecer, ponerse pálido.

2 *n* (**a**) (*colour*) blanco *m*, color *m* blanco; (*whiteness*) blancura *f*; (*of egg*) clara *f* del huevo, blanquillo *m* (*LAm*); **the** ~ **of the eye** el blanco del ojo.

(**b**) (*person*) blanco *m*, -a *f*.

(**c**) ~**s** *pl* traje *m* blanco de deporte.

whitebait ['waɪtbeɪt] *n* (*gen pl*) espadines *mpl*, chanquetes *mpl*.

whitebeam ['waɪtbiːm] *n* mojera *f*.

white-collar ['waɪt,kɒləʳ] *adj worker* de cuello blanco; *crime* de guante blanco.

white elephant ['waɪt'elɪfənt] *n* maula *f*, cosa *f* dispendiosa e inútil.

white-faced ['waɪt'feɪst] *adj* blanco (como papel).

whitefish ['waɪtfɪʃ] *n* (*species*) corégono *m*; (*collectively*) pescado *m* magro, pescado *m* blanco.

whitefly ['waɪt,flaɪ] *n* mosca *f* blanca.

white-haired ['waɪt'hɛəd] *adj*, **white-headed** ['waɪt'hedɪd] *adj* de cabeza blanca, de pelo blanco; ~ **boy*** favorito *m*, protegido *m*.

Whitehall [,waɪt'hɔːl] *n calle de Londres en la cual hay muchos ministerios*; (*fig*) el gobierno de Gran Bretaña.

white-hot ['waɪt'hɒt] *adj* candente, calentado al blanco.

whiten ['waɪtn] **1** *vt* blanquear. **2** *vi* blanquear; (*person*) palidecer, ponerse pálido.

whitener ['waɪtnəʳ] *n* blanqueador *m*.

whiteness ['waɪtnɪs] *n* blancura *f*.

whitening ['waɪtnɪŋ] *n* (*chalk etc*) tiza *f*; (*for shoes*) blanco *m* para zapatos; (*whitewash*) jalbegue *m*.

whiteout ['waɪtaʊt] *n* (*Met*) resplandor *m* sin sombras; (*block*) bloqueo *m* total causado por la nieve; (*fig*) masa *f* confusa.

white sauce ['waɪt'sɔːs] *n* salsa *f* bechamel.

white spirit ['waɪt'spɪrɪt] *n* (*Brit*) trementina *f*.

whitethorn ['waɪtθɔːn] *n* espino *m*.

whitethroat ['waɪtθrəʊt] *n* curruca *f* zarcera.

whitewash ['waɪtwɒʃ] **1** *n* (**a**) jalbegue *m*.

(**b**) (*fig*) blanqueo *m*.

2 *vt* (**a**) enjalbegar, encalar, blanquear.

(**b**) (*fig*) blanquear.

(**c**) (*Sport**) dejar en blanco, dar un baño a*.

whither ['wɪðəʳ] *adv* (*liter*) ¿adónde?

whiting¹ ['waɪtɪŋ] *n* (*colouring*) tiza *f*, blanco *m* de España; blanco *m* para zapatos.

whiting² ['waɪtɪŋ] *n, pl invar* (*Fish*) pescadilla *f*.

whitish ['waɪtɪʃ] *adj* blanquecino, blancuzco.

whitlow ['wɪtləʊ] *n* panadizo *m*.

Whitsun ['wɪtsn] **1** *n* Pentecostés *m*. **2** *attr* de Pentecostés.

Whitsuntide ['wɪtsntaɪd] **1** *n* Pentecostés *m*. **2** *attr* de Pentecostés.

whittle ['wɪtl] *vt* cortar pedazos a (con un cuchillo), tallar.

◆**whittle away, whittle down** *vt* reducir poco a poco, rebajar gradualmente.

whiz(z)* [wɪz] *n* as* *m*; **he's a** ~ **at tennis** es un as del tenis.

whizz [wɪz] **1** *n* silbido *m*, zumbido *m*.

2 *vi* silbar, zumbar; (*arrow*) rehilar; **to** ~ **along, to go** ~**ing along** ir como una bala; **it** ~**ed past my head** pasó (silbando) muy cerca de mi cabeza; me rozó casi la cabeza al pasar; **the sledge** ~**ed down the slope** el trineo bajó la cuesta a gran velocidad.

whizzkid* ['wɪzkɪd] *n* chico *m* prodigio.

WHO *n abbr of* **World Health Organization** Organización *f* Mundial de la Salud, OMS *f*.

who [huː] *pron* (**a**) (*interrog*) quién; ~ **is it ?** ¿quién es?; ~ **are they ?** ¿quiénes son?; **I know** ~ **it was** yo sé quién fue; ~ **do you think you are?** ¿quién se cree Vd que es?; ~ **does she think she is?** ¿qué derecho se cree tener para hacer (*etc*) eso?; **'W~'s W~'** 'Quién es Quién'; **you'll soon get to know** ~**'s** ~ **in the office** pronto sabrás quién es quién en la oficina; ~ **should it be but Jaimito?** y henos aquí a Jaimito, y como por milagro aparece Jaimito.

(**b**) (= *whom*) ~ **are you looking for?** ¿a quién buscas?

(**c**) (*rel*) que; el (*etc*) que, quien; **my cousin** ~ **plays the accordion** mi primo que toca el acordeón; **he** ~ **wishes to** ... el que quiera ...; **those** ~ **swim** los que nadan; **deny it** ~ **may** niéguelo quien quiera, aunque habrá quien lo niegue.

whoa [wəʊ] *interj* ¡so!

who'd [huːd] = **who had; who would.**

whodun(n)it* [huː'dʌnɪt] *n* novela *f* policíaca.

whoever [huː'evəʳ] *pron* (**a**) (*rel*) quienquiera que, cualquiera que; ~ **finds it can keep it** quienquiera que lo encuentre puede quedarse con él; **I'll talk to** ~ **it is** hablaré con quien sea; ~ **said that was an idiot** el que dijo eso fue un imbécil; **ask** ~ **you like** pregúntaselo a cualquiera, pregúntaselo a quien te parezca bien; **I was told as much by Count A or Baron B or** ~ me lo dijo el conde A o el barón B o el que fuera.

(**b**) (*interrog*) ¿quién?; ~ **can have told you that?** ¿quién diablos te dijo eso?

whole [həʊl] **1** *adj* (**a**) (*entire*) todo, entero; total; íntegro; ~ **milk** leche *f* sin desnatar; ~ **note** (*US*) semibreve *f*; ~

number número *m* entero; **the ~ world** el mundo entero; **she swallowed it ~** se lo tragó entero; **a pig roasted ~** un cerdo asado entero; **along its ~ length** por todo el largo; **is that the ~ truth?** ¿me has contado toda la verdad?; **but the ~ man eludes us** pero el hombre en su totalidad se nos escapa; **but the ~ purpose was to ...** pero la única finalidad era de ...; **a ~ lot of people will be glad** muchísimas personas se alegrarán.

(**b**) (*unbroken*) sano; ileso, intacto; **not a cup was left ~ after the party** después de la fiesta no quedó copa sana; **to our surprise he came back ~** con gran sorpresa nuestra volvió ileso.

2 *n* todo *m*; total *m*; conjunto *m*, totalidad *f*; **nearly the ~ of our production** casi toda nuestra producción; **the ~ of Madrid** todo Madrid; **the ~ of his works** todas sus obras, la totalidad de sus obras; **the ~ and its parts** el todo y sus partes; **as a ~** en su totalidad, en conjunto; **on the ~** en general, por regla general.

wholefood(s) ['həʊlfuːd(z)] **1** *n* comida *f* naturista, alimentos *mpl* integrales. **2** *attr*: **~ restaurant** restaurante *m* naturista.

wholehearted ['həʊl'hɑːtɪd] *adj* entusiasta, incondicional, cien por cien.

wholeheartedly ['həʊl'hɑːtɪdlɪ] *adv* con entusiasmo, incondicionalmente, cien por cien.

wholeheartedness ['həʊl'hɑːtɪdnɪs] *n* entusiasmo *m*.

wholemeal ['həʊlmiːl] (*Brit*) *adj* integral; **~ bread** pan *m* integral; **~ flour** harina *f* integral.

wholeness ['həʊlnɪs] *n* totalidad *f*; integridad *f*.

wholesale ['həʊlseɪl] **1** *n* venta *f* al por mayor.

2 *attr* (**a**) **~ dealer**, **~ trader** comerciante *mf* al por mayor, mayorista *mf*; **~ price** precio *m* al por mayor; **~ price index** índice *m* de precios al por mayor; **~ trade** comercio *m* al por mayor.

(**b**) (*fig*) en masa; general; **~ destruction** destrucción *f* general.

3 *adv* (**a**) **to buy ~** comprar al por mayor; **to sell sth ~** vender algo al por mayor.

(**b**) (*fig*) masivo, en masa; sin hacer distinción de personas (*etc*); **the books were burnt ~** los libros fueron quemados en masa.

wholesaler ['həʊl,seɪləʳ] *n* comerciante *mf* al por mayor, mayorista *mf*.

wholesome ['həʊlsəm] *adj* sano, saludable.

wholesomeness ['həʊlsəmnɪs] *n* lo sano, lo saludable.

whole-wheat ['həʊlwiːt] *adj* de trigo integral, hecho con trigo entero.

who'll [huːl] = **who will; who shall.**

wholly ['həʊlɪ] *adv* enteramente, completamente.

whom [huːm] *pron* (**a**) (*interrog*) a quién; **~ did you see?** ¿a quién viste?; **of ~ are you talking?** ¿de quién hablas?; **I know of ~ you are talking** sé de quién hablas; **from ~ did you receive it?** ¿de quién lo recibiste?

(**b**) (*rel*) que, a quien; **the lady ~ I saw** la señora a quien vi; **the lady with ~ I was talking** la señora con quien hablaba; **three policemen, all of ~ were drunk** tres policías, todos borrachos; **three policemen, none of ~ wore a helmet** tres policías, ninguno de los cuales llevaba casco.

whomever [huːm'evəʳ] *pron V* **whoever.**

whoop [huːp] **1** *n* alarido *m*, grito *m*; **with a ~ of joy** con un grito de alegría.

2 *vt*: **to ~ it up*** divertirse ruidosamente; echar una cana al aire.

3 *vi* gritar, dar alaridos.

whoopee [wʊ'piː] **1** *excl* ¡estupendo! **2** *n* juerga *f*, guateque *m*; **to make ~*** divertirse una barbaridad*; **~ cushion** *artículo de broma* (cojín *m* de ventosidades).

whooping-cough ['huːpɪŋ,kɒf] *n* tos *f* ferina, coqueluche *f*.

whoops [wuːps] *excl* ¡epa!, ¡lep!

whoosh [wʊ(ː)ʃ] *n ruido del agua etc que sale bajo presión, o del viento fuerte*; **it came out with a ~** salió con mucho ruido; salió de repente.

whop‡ [wɒp] *vt* pegar.

whopper* ['wɒpəʳ] *n* (*big thing*) cosa *f* muy grande; (*lie*) mentirón *m*, embuste *m*; **that fish is a ~** ese pez es enorme; **what a ~!** ¡qué enorme!

whopping* ['wɒpɪŋ] *adj* enorme, muy grande, grandísimo.

whore ['hɔːʳ] **1** *n* puta *f*. **2** *vi* (*also* **to go whoring**) putañear, putear.

who're [huːəʳ] = **who are.**

whorehouse ['hɔːhaʊs] *n*, *pl* **whorehouses** ['hɔː,haʊzɪz] (*US*) casa *f* de putas.

whorl [wɜːl] *n* (*of shell*) espira *f*; (*Bot*) verticilo *m*; (*Tech*) espiral *f*.

whortleberry ['wɜːtl,bərɪ] *n* arándano *m*.

who's [huːz] = **who is; who has.**

whose [huːz] **1** *pron* (*interrog*) ¿de quién; **~ is this?** ¿de quién es esto?, ¿a quién pertenece esto?; **I know ~ it was** sé de quién era.

2 *adj* (**a**) (*interrog*) ¿de quién?; **~ car did you go in?** ¿en qué coche fuiste?; **~ fault was it?** ¿quién tuvo la culpa?; **~ umbrella did you take?** ¿de quién es el paraguas que tomaste?

(**b**) (*rel*) cuyo; **the man ~ hat I took** el hombre cuyo sombrero tomé; **the man ~ seat I sat in** el hombre en cuya silla me senté; **those ~ passports I have** aquellas personas cuyos pasaportes tengo.

whosis ['huːzɪs] *n* (*US*) (**a**) (*thing*) cosa *f*, chisme *m*, chifurrio* *m*. (**b**) (*person*) fulano *m*, -a *f*, cómo-se-llame *m*.

whosoever [,huːsəʊ'evəʳ] = **whoever.**

who've [huːv] = **who have.**

whozis ['huːzɪs] *n* (*US*) = **whosis.**

whse *abbr of* **warehouse.**

why [waɪ] **1** *adv* ¿por qué?, ¿para qué?; ¿por qué razón?; ¿con qué objeto?; **~ not?** ¿por qué no?, ¿cómo no?; **~ did you do it?** ¿por qué lo hiciste?; **~ on earth didn't you tell me?** ¿por qué demonios no me lo dijiste?; **I know ~ you did it** sé por qué lo hiciste; **~ he did it we shall never know** no sabremos nunca por qué razón lo hizo; **that's ~ I couldn't come** por eso no pude venir, ésa es la razón por la que no pude venir; **which is ~ I am here** razón por la cual estoy aquí.

2 *interj* ¡cómo!, ¡toma!; **~, what's the matter?** bueno, ¿qué pasa?; **~, it's you!** ¡toma, eres tú!; **~, there are 8 of us!** ¡si somos 8!; **~, it's easy!** ¡vamos, es muy fácil!

3 *n* por qué *m*, porqué *m*; causa *f*, razón *f*.

whyever ['waɪ'evəʳ] *adv*: **~ did you do it?** ¿por qué demonios lo hiciste?

WI (**a**) *abbr of* **West Indies** Antillas *fpl*. (**b**) *n* (*Brit*) *abbr of* **Women's Institute.** (**c**) (*US Post*) *abbr of* **Wisconsin.**

wick [wɪk] *n* mecha *f*; **he gets on my ~‡** me hace subir por las paredes*; **to dip one's ~*‡** echar un polvo*‡.

wicked ['wɪkɪd] *adj* (**a**) (*iniquitous*) malo, malvado; perverso; inicuo; **you're a ~ man** (*hum*) eres muy malo; **that was a ~ thing to do** eso fue inicuo.

(**b**) (*fig*) *satire etc* muy mordaz, cruel; *temper* muy vivo; (*very bad*) horroroso, horrible, malísimo; **a ~ waste** un despilfarro escandaloso; **it's ~ weather** hace un tiempo horrible; **it's a ~ car to start** este coche es horrible para arrancar.

(**c**) (‡) de puta madre‡.

wickedly ['wɪkɪdlɪ] *adv* mal; perversamente; inicuamente; cruelmente; horriblemente.

wickedness ['wɪkɪdnɪs] *n* maldad *f*; perversidad *f*; iniquidad *f*; crueldad *f*; **all manner of ~** toda clase de maldades.

wicker ['wɪkəʳ] **1** *n* mimbre *m or f*. **2** *attr* de mimbre.

wickerwork ['wɪkəwɜːk] **1** *n* artículos *mpl* de mimbre; cestería *f*; (*of chair etc*) rejilla *f*. **2** *attr* de mimbre.

wicket ['wɪkɪt] *n* (*gate*) postigo *m*, portillo *m*; (*Cricket: stumps*) rastrillo *m*, palos *mpl*, (*pitch*) terreno *m*; **to be on a sticky ~** estar en una situación difícil.

wide [waɪd] **1** *adj* (**a**) ancho; extenso, vasto; *gap* grande, muy abierto; *difference* grande, considerable; *understanding etc* amplio; **it is 3 metres ~** tiene 3 metros de ancho; **how ~ is it?** ¿cuánto tiene de ancho?; **eyes ~ with fear** ojos muy abiertos de miedo; **the ~ plains of Castile** las extensas llanuras de Castilla; **the ~ world** el ancho mundo; **his ~ knowledge of the subject** sus amplios conocimientos del tema.

(**b**) **~ boy*** (*Brit*) astuto *m*, taimado *m*.

2 *adv* lejos; extensamente; **far and ~** por todas partes; **to be ~ open** estar muy abierto, (*door etc*) estar abierto de par en par; **to be ~ open to criticism** estar expuesto a ser criticado de todos lados; **to open one's eyes ~** abrir mucho los ojos; **to fling the door ~** abrir la puerta de par en par; **they are set ~ apart** están puestos muy lejos uno de otro, están muy apartados; **the shot went ~** el tiro no dio en el blanco.

-wide [waɪd] *adj ending in compounds*: **nation-~** por toda la nación, a escala nacional; de toda la nación; **a country-~ inquiry** una investigación a escala nacional.

wide-angle ['waɪd,æŋgl] *adj lens etc* granangular.

wide-awake ['waɪdə'weɪk] *adj* completamente despierto; (*fig*) despabilado; vigilante, alerta.

wide-bodied ['waɪd'bɒdɪd] *adj* (*Aer*) de fuselaje ancho.

wide-eyed ['waɪd'aɪd] *adj* con los ojos desorbitados, con los ojos desmesuradamente abiertos; (*fig*) inocente, cándido.

widely ['waɪdlɪ] *adv* extensamente; generalmente; **to travel ~** viajar extensamente; viajar por muchos países (*etc*); **it is ~ believed that ...** por todas partes se cree que ...; **the opinion is ~ held** es una creencia general; **a ~-known author** un autor generalmente conocido; **a ~-read student** un estudiante que ha leído mucho.

widen ['waɪdn] **1** *vt* ensanchar; ampliar, extender. **2** *vi* (*also* **to ~ out**) ensancharse; **the passage ~s out into a cave** el pasillo se ensancha para formar una caverna.

wideness ['waɪdnɪs] *n* anchura *f*; extensión *f*, amplitud *f*.

wide-ranging ['waɪd,reɪndʒɪŋ] *adj survey etc* de gran alcance, de amplia extensión; *interests* múltiples, muy diversos.

wide-screen ['waɪdskriːn] *adj film* para pantalla ancha.

widespread ['waɪdspred] *adj* (**a**) extendido; **with arms ~** con los brazos extendidos, con los brazos abiertos.

(**b**) (*fig*) extenso, amplio; muy difundido, general; **to become ~** extenderse, generalizarse; **there is ~ fear that ...** muchos temen que ...; **knowledge of this is now ~** el conocimiento de esto está muy difundido ahora.

widgeon ['wɪdʒən] *n* ánade *m* silbón.

widow ['wɪdəʊ] **1** *n* viuda *f*; **~'s pension** viudedad *f*; **W~ Twankey** la viuda de Twankey; **I'm a golf ~** paso mucho tiempo sola mientras mi marido juega al golf; **all the cricket ~s got together for tea** las mujeres cuyos maridos estaban jugando al críquet se reunieron para tomar el té; **to be left a ~** enviudar, quedar viuda.

2 *vt* dejar viuda (*or* viudo); **she was twice ~ed** quedó viuda dos veces; **his ~ed mother** su madre viuda; **she has been ~ed for 5 years** enviudó hace 5 años, lleva 5 años de viuda.

widowed ['wɪdəʊd] *adj* viudo.

widower ['wɪdəʊəʳ] *n* viudo *m*.

widowhood ['wɪdəʊhʊd] *n* viudez *f*.

width [wɪdθ] *n* anchura *f*; extensión *f*, amplitud *f*; (*of cloth*) ancho *m*; **to be 6 centimetres in ~** tener 6 centímetros de ancho; **to swim a ~** hacer un ancho (de la piscina).

widthways ['wɪdθweɪz] *adv*, **widthwise** ['wɪdθwaɪz] *adv* de canto.

wield [wiːld] *vt pen, sword etc* manejar; *sceptre* empuñar; *power* ejercer, poseer; **to ~ a pen in the service of ...** menear cálamo al servicio de ...

wiener schnitzel ['viːnə'ʃnɪtsəl] *n* escalope *m* de ternera con guarnición.

wienie ['wiːnɪ] *n* (*US Culin*) = **weenie.**

wife [waɪf] *n, pl* **wives** [waɪvz] mujer *f*, esposa *f*; **the ~*** la parienta*; **'The Merry Wives of Windsor'** 'Las alegres comadres de Windsor'; **~'s earned income** ingresos *mpl* de la mujer; **this is my ~** ésta es mi mujer; **my boss and his ~** mi jefe y su esposa; **to take a ~** casarse; **to take sb to ~** casarse con una, contraer matrimonio con una.

wifely ['waɪflɪ] *adj* de esposa, de mujer casada.

wife-swapping ['waɪf,swɒpɪŋ] *n* cambio *m* de pareja.

wig [wɪg] *n* peluca *f*.

wigeon ['wɪdʒən] *n* ánade *m* silbón.

wigging* ['wɪgɪŋ] *n* (*Brit*) peluca* *f*, rapapolvo* *m*, bronca *f*; **to give sb a ~** echar una peluca a uno*.

wiggle ['wɪgl] **1** *n* meneo *m*; (*in walking*) contoneo *m*; **to walk with a ~** contonearse, caminar contoneándose.

2 *vt* menear; *hips etc* mover mucho.

3 *vi* menearse rápidamente; moverse mucho; (*in walking*) contonearse, caminar contoneándose.

wiggly ['wɪglɪ] *adj* que se menea, que se mueve mucho; *line* ondulado.

wight [waɪt] *n* (†† *or hum*) criatura *f*; (*luckless ~, sorry ~*) pobre hombre *m*.

wigmaker ['wɪg,meɪkəʳ] *n* peluquero *m*.

wigwam ['wɪgwæm] *n* wigwam *m*, tipi *m*.

wilco [,wɪl'kəʊ] *adv* (*Telec*) ¡procedo!

wild [waɪld] **1** *adj* (**a**) (*not domesticated*) *animal, man* salvaje; *flower, plant* silvestre; campestre, de los campos; *country* agreste, difícil, bravo; **~ beast** fiera *f*; **~ beast show** espectáculo *m* de fieras; **~ card** comodín *m* (*also Comput*); **~ character** carácter *m* comodín; **~ oat** avena *f* silvestre; **to sow one's ~ oats** (*fig*) correrla, pasar las mocedades; **~ rabbit** conejo *m* de monte; **~ and woolly** rústico, tosco; **to grow ~** crecer libre, crecer sin cultivo; **to run ~** (*plant*) volver al estado silvestre.

(**b**) (*of cruel disposition*) feroz, fiero, bravo; *horse* sin domar, cerril.

(**c**) (*rough*) *wind etc* furioso, violento; *weather* tormentoso; *sea* bravo; **it was a ~ night** fue una noche de tormenta.

(**d**) (*unrestrained, disordered*) *child* desmandado, desgobernado; *laughter, party, enthusiasm etc* loco; **W~ West** el oeste norteamericano (*bajo su aspecto heroico*); **he was ~ in his youth, he had a ~ youth** tuvo una juventud desordenada; **to lead a ~ life** vivir desenfrenadamente; **the room was in ~ disorder** el cuarto estaba en el mayor desorden; **they were ~ times** fue un período turbulento, fueron años alborotados; **to run ~** (*children*) vivir como salvajes; **that dog is running ~** ese perro está sin controlar.

(**e**) *person* loco, insensato; frenético; **to be ~ about sb** andar loco por uno; **to be ~ with joy** estar loco de alegría; **to be ~ with sb** estar furioso contra uno; **it drives me ~, it makes me ~** me saca de quicio, me hace rabiar; **it drives them ~ with desire** las pone muy cachondas; **to get ~** ponerse furioso, ponerse negro; **he has ~ eyes** tiene ojos de loco; **the crowd went ~** la multitud se puso loca (*with excitement* de emoción); **I'm not exactly ~ about it*** la idea no me llena de entusiasmo que digamos.

(**f**) (*rash, ill-judged*) extravagante, estrafalario; disparatado, descabellado; fantástico; **there was some ~ talk** se propusieron unas ideas estrafalarias, se dijeron cosas insensatas; **it's a ~ exaggeration** es una enorme exageración; **to make a ~ guess** hacer una conjetura extravagante; **he had some ~ scheme for ...** tuvo algún proyecto disparatado de ...

2 *n* tierra *f* virgen, tierra *f* poco poblada (*or* poco conocida); soledad *f*, yermo *m*; **the call of the ~** la atracción de la soledad, el encanto de las tierras vírgenes; **it's a pet and couldn't live in the ~** es un animal doméstico que no podría vivir en la naturaleza; **when do they breed in the ~?** ¿cuándo se reproducen en estado natural?; **to go out into the ~s** ir a vivir en tierras poco conocidas; **they live out in the ~s of Berkshire** viven en lo más remoto de Berkshire.

wildcat ['waɪld'kæt] **1** *n* (**a**) (*Zool*) gato *m* montés. (**b**) (*for oil*) perforación *f* de sondaje en tierra virgen.

2 *attr*: **~ strike** huelga *f* salvaje; **~ scheme** proyecto *m* descabellado, proyecto *m* arriesgado; **~ venture** proyecto *m* arriesgado.

3 *vi* (*US*) hacer perforaciones para extraer petróleo.

wildebeest ['wɪldɪbiːst] *n* ñu *m*.

wilderness ['wɪldənɪs] *n* desierto *m*, yermo *m*, soledad *f*; (*virgin land*) tierra *f* virgen; **a ~ of ruins** un desierto de ruinas, una infinidad de ruinas; **he spent 4 years in the ~ before returning to power** pasó 4 años en el desierto antes de volver al poder.

wild-eyed ['waɪld'aɪd] *adj* de mirada salvaje.

wildfire ['waɪld,faɪəʳ] *n*: **to spread like ~** propagarse como la pólvora, correr como un reguero de pólvora.

wildfowl ['waɪldfaʊl] *npl* aves *fpl* de caza, (*esp*) ánades *mpl*.

wildfowler ['waɪld,faʊləʳ] *n* cazador *m* de ánades.

wildfowling ['waɪld,faʊlɪŋ] *n* caza *f* de ánades.

wild-goose chase [,waɪld'guːstʃeɪs] *n* empresa *f* desatinada, búsqueda *f* inútil.

wildlife ['waɪldlaɪf] *n* fauna *f* (y flora *f*); **~ park, ~ reserve** reserva *f* natural; **~ trust** asociación *f* protectora de la naturaleza.

wildly ['waɪldlɪ] *adv blow etc* (*of wind*) furiosamente, violentamente; *live* desordenadamente, de modo alborotado; *behave* de modo indisciplinado; (*madly*) locamente, insensatamente; frenéticamente; *act* sin reflexión; **to be ~ happy** estar loco de contento; **to shoot ~** disparar sin apuntar; **to hit out ~** repartir golpes a tontas y a locas; **to talk ~** (*loosely*) hablar sin ton ni son, hablar incoherentenmente, (*extravagantly*) hablar como un loco; **she looked ~ from one to another** miró con ojos espantados a uno y a otro; **you're guessing ~** haces conjeturas sin pensar; **to clap ~** aplaudir frenéticamente; **to dash about ~** correr como un loco de aquí para allá.

wildness ['waɪldnɪs] *n* (*V adj*) (**a**) estado *m* salvaje, lo salvaje; estado *m* silvestre; lo agreste, lo difícil; braveza *f*.

(**b**) ferocidad *f*, fiereza *f*.

(**c**) furia *f*, violencia *f*.

(**d**) desgobierno *m*, desenfreno *m*; turbulencia *f*, lo alborotado.

(**e**) locura *f*, insensatez *f*; frenesí *m*.

(**f**) extravagancia *f*, lo estrafalario; lo disparatado; lo fantástico.

wiles [waɪlz] *npl* engaños *mpl*, tretas *fpl*, ardides *mpl*.

wilful, (*US*) **willful** ['wɪlfʊl] *adj person* voluntarioso; testarudo; *child* travieso; *act* intencionado, deliberado; *murder etc* premeditado; **you have been ~ about it** has sido testarudo en esto.

wilfully, (*US*) **willfully** ['wɪlfəlɪ] *adv* voluntariosamente; intencionadamente; deliberadamente; con premeditación; **you have ~ ignored** ... te has obstinado en no hacer caso de ...

wilfulness, (*US*) **willfulness** ['wɪlfʊlnɪs] *n* voluntariedad *f*; testarudez *f*; lo travieso; lo intencionado; lo premeditado.

wiliness ['waɪlɪnɪs] *n* astucia *f*.

Will [wɪl] *nm familiar form of* **William.**

will[1] [wɪl] *v aux* (**a**) (*forming future tense*) **he ~ come** vendrá; **you won't lose it, ~ you?** ¿no lo vas a perder, eh?; **you ~ come to see us, won't you?** ¿vendrás a vernos, no?

(**b**) (*future emphatic*) **I ~ do it!** ¡sí lo haré!; **no he won't!** ¡no lo hará!; **I ~** (*marriage service*) sí quiero.

(**c**) (*wish*) querer; **no, he won't** no, no quiere; **come when you ~** ven cuando quieras; **do as you ~** haz lo que quieras, haz lo que te parezca bien; **look where you ~** mires donde mires.

(**d**) (*conjecture*) **that ~ be the postman** será el cartero; **she'll be about 50** tendrá como 50 años.

(**e**) (*consent*) **the engine won't start** el motor no arranca, el motor no quiere arrancar; **a man who ~ do that ~ do anything** un hombre que es capaz de eso es capaz de todo; **despite the doctor she ~ smoke** a pesar del médico, se empeña en fumar; **wait a moment, ~ you?** espera un momento, ¿quieres?; **won't you sit down?** ¿quiere sentarse?, siéntese, por favor; **I ~ not have it!** ¡no lo permito!; **he ~ have none of it** no lo aprueba de ningún modo, no quiere ni siquiera pensarlo; **I ~ not have it that** ... no permito que se diga que + *subj*; *V also* **have 1** (**i**).

(**f**) (*habit, potentiality*) **the car ~ do up to 220 kph** el coche hará hasta 220 kph; **accidents ~ happen** siempre pueden ocurrir accidentes, ocurren inevitablemente accidentes; **boys ~ be boys** así son los chicos; juventud no conoce virtud.

will[2] [wɪl] **1** *n* (**a**) (*faculty*) voluntad *f*; (*free ~*) albedrío *m*; (*wish*) voluntad *f*, placer *m*, deseo *m*; **iron ~, ~ of iron** voluntad *f* de hierro; **the ~ to win** el afán de triunfar, la voluntad de ganar; **the ~ of God** la voluntad de Dios; **against one's ~** contra su voluntad; mal de su grado; a pesar suyo, a desgana; **at ~** a voluntad; **of one's own free ~** por voluntad propia; **it is my ~ that you should do it** quiero que lo hagas; **where there's a ~ there's a way** querer es poder; **to do sb's ~** hacer la voluntad de uno; **Thy ~ be done** hágase tu voluntad; **she has a ~ of her own** tiene voluntad propia; **to set to work with a ~** empezar a trabajar con ilusión (*or* con entusiasmo), emprender resueltamente una tarea.

(**b**) *V* **good ~, ill ~.**

(**c**) (*testament*) testamento *m*; **the last ~ and testament of** ... la última voluntad de ...; **to make one's ~** hacer su testamento, otorgar testamento.

2 *vt* (*pret, ptp* **willed**) (**a**) (*dispose*) querer; ordenar, disponer; **God has so ~ed it** Dios lo ha ordenado así; **if God ~s** si lo quiere Dios; **having ~ed the end we must ~ the means** quien desea el fin ordena los medios.

(**b**) (*urge by willpower*) lograr por fuerza de voluntad; sugestionar; **to ~ sb to do sth** sugestionar a uno para que haga algo; **I was ~ing you to win** estaba deseando mucho que ganaras, te estaba ayudando a ganar con la fuerza de mi voluntad.

(**c**) (*by testament*) legar, dejar en testamento; **he ~ed his pictures to the nation** legó sus cuadros a la nación.

willful ['wɪlfʊl] *adj* (*US*) *etc* = **wilful** *etc.*

William ['wɪljəm] *nm* Guillermo; **~ the Conqueror** Guillermo el Conquistador.

willie‡ [wɪlɪ] *n* (*Brit*) = **willy.**

willies* ['wɪlɪz] *npl*: **to get the ~** pegarse un susto*, pasar horrores*; **I get the ~ whenever I think about it** me horroriza pensar en ello; **it gives me the ~** me da horror.

willing ['wɪlɪŋ] **1** *adj* (**a**) (*helpful*) servicial; complaciente; de buena voluntad, de buen corazón; (*voluntary*) espontáneo; **a ~ boy** un chico de buen corazón, un chico que trabaja (*etc*) de buena gana; **we need ~ helpers** necesitamos personas dispuestas a ayudarnos; **there were plenty of ~ hands** hubo muchos que nos ayudaron espontáneamente.

(**b**) **to be ~** querer, querer hacerlo (*etc*); **are you ~ ?** ¿quieres?; **God ~** si Dios quiere; **I asked her and she was quite ~** se lo pedí y ella asintió gustosa; **to be ~ to do sth** estar dispuesto a hacer algo, consentir en hacer algo; **he was ~ for me to take it** me permitió llevarlo, consintió en que me lo llevase; **to be ~ that** ... consentir en que + *subj*, permitir que + *subj*.

2 *n*: **to show ~*** demostrar su buena voluntad.

willingly ['wɪlɪŋlɪ] *adv* de buena gana, con gusto; **they ~ helped us** nos ayudaron de buena gana; **did he come ~ or by force?** ¿vino libremente o a la fuerza?; **yes, ~** sí, con mucho gusto.

willingness ['wɪlɪŋnɪs] *n* buena voluntad *f*, complacencia *f*; deseo *m* de servir (*or* ayudar *etc*); consentimiento *m*; **in spite of his ~ to buy it** a pesar de que estaba dispuesto a comprarlo.

will-o'-the-wisp ['wɪləðə'wɪsp] *n* fuego *m* fatuo; (*fig*) quimera *f*, ilusión *f*, sueño *m* imposible.

willow ['wɪləʊ] *n* (*also* **~-tree**) sauce *m*.

willowherb ['wɪləʊhɜːb] *n* adelfa *f*.

willow-pattern ['wɪləʊ,pætən] *adj*: **~ plate** plato *m* de estilo chino.

willow-warbler ['wɪləʊ,wɔːbləʳ] *n* mosquitero *m* musical.

willowy ['wɪləʊɪ] *adj* (*fig*) esbelto, cimbreño.

willpower ['wɪlpaʊəʳ] *n* fuerza *f* de voluntad.

Willy ['wɪlɪ] *nm familiar form of* **William.**

willy‡ ['wɪlɪ] *n* colita‡ *f*.

willy-nilly ['wɪlɪ'nɪlɪ] *adv* de grado o por fuerza, quiera o no quiera.

wilt[1]†† [wɪlt] *V* **will**[1].

wilt[2] [wɪlt] **1** *vt* marchitar; (*fig*) debilitar, hacer decaer.

2 *vi* marchitarse; (*fig*) debilitarse, decaer; (*lose courage*) perder el ánimo, desanimarse; (*of effort etc*) languidecer.

Wilts [wɪlts] *n abbr of* **Wiltshire.**

wily ['waɪlɪ] *adj* astuto, mañoso.

WIMP* [wɪmp] *n abbr of* **windows, icons, menus** (*or* **mice**), **pointers.**

wimp* [wɪmp] *n* pobre hombre *m*, burro *m*; endeble *mf*, enclenque *mf*.

wimpish* ['wɪmpɪʃ] *adj* endeble, débil.

wimpishness* ['wɪmpɪʃnɪs] *n* lo endeble, debilidad *f*.

wimple ['wɪmpl] *n* griñon *m*.

win [wɪn] **1** *n* victoria *f*, triunfo *m*; éxito *m*; **another ~ for Castroforte** nueva victoria del Castroforte; **their fifth ~ in a row** su quinta victoria consecutiva; **to back a horse for a ~** apostar dinero a un caballo para el primer puesto; **to have a ~** ganar, vencer; **to play for a ~** jugar para ganar.

2 (*irr*: *pret and ptp* **won**) *vt* (**a**) *race, cup, prize etc* ganar; *victory* llevarse; **it won him the first prize** le valió el primer premio.

(**b**) (*obtain*) lograr, conseguir; *sympathy, support* atraerse, captar; **how to ~ friends and influence people** cómo ganar amigos e influenciar a las personas; **to ~ sb's esteem** llegar a ser estimado por uno; **to ~ sb's favour** alcanzar el favor de uno; **to ~ sb's love** enamorar a uno; **to ~ glory** laurearse; **to ~ a reputation for honesty** granjearse una reputación de honrado.

(**c**) *metal* extraer (*from* de); arrancar (*from* a).

(**d**) **he won his way to the top** alcanzó la cumbre, llegó (a duras penas) a la cumbre.

3 *vi* ganar; triunfar; tener éxito; **to ~ by a head** ganar por una cabeza; **if you're up against the minister you can't ~** si tienes el ministro en contra no hay manera de salir ganando; **OK, you ~** muy bien, tú ganas.

◆**win back** *vt land etc* reconquistar, volver a conquistar; *gambling loss etc* recobrar; *support etc* volver a ganar.

◆**win out** *vi* ganar, tener éxito.

◆**win over, win round** *vt supporters etc* atraerse, conquistar; (*to an opinion*) convencer; **eventually we won him round to our point of view** por fin le persuadimos a adoptar nuestro punto de vista.

◆**win through** *vi* triunfar por fin, tener al fin el éxito deseado; **to ~ through to a place** alcanzar un sitio, llegar por fin a un sitio.

wince [wɪns] **1** *n* mueca *f* de dolor; **he said with a ~** dijo con una mueca de dolor.

2 *vi* hacer una mueca de dolor, estremecerse; (*flinch*) retroceder, asustarse; **without wincing** sin pestañear.

winch [wɪntʃ] **1** *n* cabrestante *m*, torno *m*. **2** *vt*: **to ~ up** levantar con un torno (*etc*).

Winchester disk ['wɪntʃɪstə'dɪsk] ® *n* disco *m* Winchester ®.

wind[1] [wɪnd] **1** *n* (**a**) (*gen*) viento *m*; **high ~** viento *m* fuerte; **west ~** viento *m* del oeste; **~s of change** aires *mpl* de cambio, vientos *mpl* nuevos; **that's all a lot of ~** todo eso son chorradas*; **where is the ~?, which way is the ~?** ¿de dónde sopla el viento?; **it's an ill ~ that blows nobody any good** no hay mal que por bien no venga; a río revuelto, ganancia de pescadores; **to be in the ~** (*fig*) estar en el aire, estar en preparación; **there's sth in the ~** algo flota en el aire; están tramando algo; **to get ~ of sth**

llegar a saber algo, husmear algo; **to get** (*or* **have**) **the ~ up*** (*Brit*) encogérsele a uno el ombligo*; **to put the ~ up sb*** (*Brit*) meter a uno el ombligo para dentro; **it properly put the ~ up me*** (*Brit*) me dio un susto de los buenos; **to raise the ~*** conseguir fondos; **to see which way the ~ blows** esperar para ver por dónde van los tiros.

(**b**) (*Naut*) viento *m*; **between ~ and water** cerca de la línea de flotación; **in the teeth of the ~** contra el viento; **to run before the ~** navegar viento en popa; **to sail close to the ~** (*fig*) decir (*etc*) cosas algo peligrosas, correr riesgo de provocar un escándalo; **to take the ~ out of sb's sails** bajar los humos a uno.

(**c**) (*Med*) flato *m*, flatulencia *f*; (*from bowel*) pedo *m*, (*from stomach*) eructo *m*; **to break ~** ventosear, soltar un pedo; **to bring up ~** eructar.

(**d**) (*breath*) aliento *m*, resuello *m*; **to be short of ~** respirar con dificultad, estar corto de aliento; **to get one's second ~** volver a respirar normalmente, cobrar el aliento; (*fig*) renovar fuerzas.

(**e**) (*Mus*) **the ~** los instrumentos de viento.

2 *attr*: **~ energy, ~ power** energía *f* del viento, energía *f* eólica; **~ farm** parque *m* eólico; **~ instrument** instrumento *m* de viento; **~ machine** máquina *f* de viento; **~ turbine** aerogenerador *m*.

3 *vt*: **to ~ sb** dejar a uno sin aliento; **to be ~ed by a ball** quedar sin aliento después de ser golpeado por un balón; **to be ~ed after a race** quedar sin aliento después de una carrera.

wind² [waɪnd] (*irr*: *pret and ptp* **wound²**) **1** *n* (**a**) (*bend*) curva *f*, recodo *m*.

(**b**) **to give one's watch a ~** dar cuerda al reloj; **give the handle another ~** dale otra vuelta a la manivela.

2 *vt* (**a**) (*wrap etc*) enrollar, envolver; *wool etc* devanar, ovillar; **to ~ one's arms round sb** rodear a uno con los brazos, abrazar a uno estrechamente; **to ~ in a fishing line** ir cobrando sedal; **to ~ wool into a ball** ovillar lana, hacer un ovillo de lana; **~ this round your head** envuélvete la cabeza con esto, líate esto a la cabeza; **with a rope wound tightly round his waist** con una cuerda que le ceñía estrechamente la cintura.

(**b**) *handle* (*also* **to ~ round, to ~ up**) dar vueltas a, girar; *clock, watch, clockwork toy etc* dar cuerda a, remontar.

(**c**) **the road ~s its way through the valley** la carretera serpentea por el valle.

3 *vi* (*also* **to ~ along, to ~ round**) (*road etc*) serpentear; **the road ~s up the valley** el camino serpentea por el valle; **to ~ round** (*snake etc*) enroscarse; **the procession wound round the town** el desfile serpenteaba por la ciudad; **the car wound slowly up the hill** el coche subió lentamente la colina culebreando.

◆**wind back** *vt tape etc* girar hacia atrás, rebobinar.

◆**wind down 1** *vi* (*lit*) (*clock*) pararse; (*: *relax*) relajarse; desconectar; (*fig*: *activity, event*) tocar a su fin.

2 *vt* (**a**) *car window* bajar. (**b**) (*fig*) *company, department etc* reducir las actividades de (antes de cerrar); *operation* limitar progresivamente.

◆**wind forward** *vt tape etc* girar hacia adelante.

◆**wind off** *vt* devanar; desenrollar.

◆**wind on** = **wind forward**.

◆**wind up 1** *vt* (**a**) **to ~ sth up with a winch** levantar algo con cabrestante.

(**b**) *handle etc V* **wind² 2** (**b**).

(**c**) (*fig*: *nervously*) agitar, emocionar con exceso; **she's dreadfully wound up** está muy tensa; **it gets me all wound up (inside)** con esto me pongo nervioso, esto me emociona terriblemente.

(**d**) (*: *pull sb's leg*) tomar el pelo a*.

(**e**) (*end*) terminar, concluir; (*Comm*) liquidar; **he wound up his speech by saying that ...** terminó su discurso diciendo que; **the company was ordered to be wound up** se ordenó la liquidación de la sociedad.

2 *vi* (**a**) *V* **wind² 3**.

(**b**) (*close*) terminar, acabar; **how does the play ~ up?** ¿cómo termina la obra?; **we wound up in Santander** fuimos a parar en Santander; **he ~s up for the government** cierra el debate por el gobierno.

windbag ['wɪndbæg] *n* saco *m* de aire; (*person*) charlatán *m*, -ana *f*.

windblown ['wɪndbləʊn] *adj leaf etc* llevado por el viento, arrancado por el viento; *hair* despeinado por el viento.

windborne ['wɪndbɔːn] *adj* llevado por el viento.

windbreak ['wɪndbreɪk] *n* abrigada *f*; protección *f* contra el viento, barrera *f* rompevientos, cortavientos *m*.

windbreaker ['wɪnd,breɪkəʳ] *n* (*US*) cazadora *f*.

windburn ['wɪnd,bɜːn] *n*: **to get ~** curtirse al viento.

windcheater ['wɪnd'tʃiːtəʳ] *n* cazadora *f*.

windchill ['wɪndtʃɪl] *attr*: **the ~ factor** el efecto enfriador del viento.

wind-chimes ['wɪndtʃaɪmz] *npl* móvil *m* de campanillas.

windcone ['wɪndkəʊn] *n* manga *f*, indicador *m* cónico de la dirección del viento.

winder ['waɪndəʳ] *n* devanadera *f*; carrete *m*, bobina *f*.

windfall ['wɪndfɔːl] **1** *n* fruta *f* caída; (*fig*) ganancia *f* inesperada, golpe *m* de suerte inesperado, cosa *f* llovida del cielo. **2** *attr*: **~ profits** beneficios *mpl* imprevistos; **~ tax** impuesto *m* sobre los beneficios extraordinarios.

windgauge ['wɪndgeɪdʒ] *n* anemómetro *m*.

winding ['waɪndɪŋ] **1** *adj* tortuoso, sinuoso, serpentino; **~ staircase** escalera *f* de caracol.

2 *n* (*of watch*) cuerda *f*; (*of road*) tortuosidad *f*; (*Elec*) bobinado *m*, devanado *m*; **the ~s of a river** las vueltas de un río, los meandros de un río.

winding-gear ['waɪndɪŋgɪəʳ] *n* manubrio *m*, cabrestante *m*.

winding-sheet ['waɪndɪŋʃiːt] *n* mortaja *f*.

winding-up ['waɪndɪŋ'ʌp] *n* conclusión *f*; (*Comm*) liquidación *f*.

windjammer ['wɪnd,dʒæməʳ] *n* buque *m* de vela (grande y veloz).

windlass ['wɪndləs] *n* torno *m*, maquinilla *f*; cabrestante *m*.

windless ['wɪndlɪs] *adj* sin viento.

windmill ['wɪndmɪl] *n* molino *m* (de viento); (*toy*) molinete *m*.

window ['wɪndəʊ] **1** *n* ventana *f*; (*shop ~*) escaparate *m*, vidriera *f* (*LAm*); (*of booking office etc, of envelope*) ventanilla *f*; (*of train*) ventanilla *f*; (*of car*) ventanilla *f*, cristal *m*, luna *f*, luneta *f*; (*Comput*) ventana *f*; **good sense flies out of the ~** se desvanece el buen sentido; **to lean out of the ~** asomarse a la ventana; **to look out of the ~** mirar por la ventana.

2 *attr*: **~ envelope** sobre *m* de ventanilla.

windowbox ['wɪndəʊbɒks] *n* jardinera *f* de ventana.

window-cleaner ['wɪndəʊ,kliːnəʳ] *n* limpiacristales *m*.

window-dresser ['wɪndəʊ,dresəʳ] *n* escaparatista *mf*, decorador *m*, -ora *f* de escaparates.

window-dressing ['wɪndəʊ,dresɪŋ] *n* decoración *f* de escaparates, escaparatismo *m*; (*fig*) camuflaje *m*; fachada *f*; (esfuerzo *m* por salvar las) apariencias *fpl*; (*in accounts etc*) presentación *f* de información especiosa.

window-frame ['wɪndəʊfreɪm] *n* marco *m* de ventana.

window-ledge ['wɪndəʊledʒ] *n* antepecho *m*, alféizar *m*, repisa *f* (*LAm*).

windowpane ['wɪndəʊpeɪn] *n* cristal *m*, vidrio *m* (*LAm*).

window-seat ['wɪndəʊsiːt] *n* asiento *m* junto a una ventana, (*Rail etc*) asiento *m* junto a una ventanilla.

window-shop ['wɪndəʊʃɒp] *vi* ir de escaparates.

window-shopping ['wɪndəʊ,ʃɒpɪŋ] *n*: **I like ~** me gusta ir de escaparates.

windowsill ['wɪndəʊsɪl] *n* alféizar *m*, antepecho *m*.

windpipe ['wɪndpaɪp] *n* tráquea *f*.

wind-powered ['wɪnd,paʊəd] *adj* impulsado por el viento, que funciona con energía eólica.

windproof ['wɪndpruːf] *adj* a prueba de viento.

windscreen ['wɪndskriːn] *n*, (*US*) **windshield** ['wɪndʃiːld] *n* parabrisas *m*.

windscreen-washer ['wɪndskriːn'wɒʃəʳ] *n*, (*US*) **windshield washer** ['wɪndʃiːld'wɒʃəʳ] *n* lavaparabrisas *m*.

windscreen-wiper ['wɪndskriːn,waɪpəʳ] *n*, (*US*) **windshield wiper** ['wɪndʃiːld,waɪpəʳ] *n* limpiaparabrisas *m*, escobilla *f*.

windsleeve ['wɪndsliːv] *n*, **windsock** ['wɪndsɒk] *n* manga *f* (de viento).

windstorm ['wɪndstɔːm] *n* ventarrón *m*, huracán *m*.

windsurf ['wɪndsɜːf] *vi* practicar el windsurf.

windsurfer ['wɪndsɜːfəʳ] *n* tablista *mf*, surfista *mf*.

windsurfing ['wɪndsɜːfɪŋ] *n* windsurf *m*, surf *m* a vela; **to go ~** hacer windsurf.

windswept ['wɪndswept] *adj* azotado por el viento, barrido por el viento; *person* despeinado.

wind-tunnel ['wɪnd,tʌnl] *n* túnel *m* aerodinámico, túnel *m* de pruebas aerodinámicas.

wind-up ['waɪndʌp] *n* (**a**) (*: *joke*) tomadura* *f* de pelo. (**b**) = **winding up**.

windward ['wɪndwəd] **1** *adj* de barlovento. **2** *n* barlovento *m*; **to ~** a barlovento.

Windward Isles ['wɪndwəd,aɪlz] *npl* Islas *fpl* de Barlovento.

windy ['wɪndɪ] *adj* (**a**) ventoso; *day* de mucho viento; *place* expuesto al viento; **it is ~ today** hoy hace viento; **it's ~ out here** aquí fuera el viento sopla fuerte, aquí fuera hay mucho viento.

(**b**) *speech, style etc* pomposo, hinchado.

(**c**) (*Brit**) **to be ~** pasar miedo; **to get ~** encogérsele a uno el ombligo*; **are you ~?** ¿tienes mieditis?*

wine [waɪn] **1** *n* vino *m*; **good ~ needs no bush** el buen paño en el arca se vende.

2 *attr* (*colour*) color vino.

3 *vt*: **to ~ and dine sb** dar a uno muy bien de comer y de beber, hacer grandes agasajos a uno.

wine-bar ['waɪnbɑːʳ] *n* bar *m* especializado en servir vinos.

winebibber ['waɪn,bɪbəʳ] *n* bebedor *m*, -ora *f*.

wine-bottle ['waɪn,bɒtl] *n* botella *f* de vino.

wine-cask ['waɪnkɑːsk] *n* tonel *m* de vino, barril *m* de vino.

winecellar ['waɪn,seləʳ] *n* bodega *f*.

wineglass ['waɪnglɑːs] *n* copa *f* (para vino), vaso *m* (para vino).

wine-grower ['waɪn,grəʊəʳ] *n* viñador *m*, -ora *f*, vinicultor *m*, -ora *f*.

wine-growing ['waɪn,grəʊɪŋ] **1** *adj* vinícola. **2** *n* vinicultura *f*.

winelist ['waɪnlɪst] *n* lista *f* de vinos.

winemanship ['waɪnmən'ʃɪp] *n* pericia *f* en vinos, oenofilia *f*.

wine-merchant ['waɪn,mɜːtʃənt] *n* (*Brit*) vinatero *m*, -a *f*.

winepress ['waɪnpres] *n* prensa *f* de uvas, lagar *m*.

winery ['waɪnərɪ] *n* (*US*) lagar *m*.

wineskin ['waɪnskɪn] *n* pellejo *m*, odre *m*.

wine-taster ['waɪn,teɪstəʳ] *n* catavinos *mf*, probador *m*, -ora *f* de vinos, catador *m*, -ora *f* de vinos.

wine-tasting ['waɪn,teɪstɪŋ] *n* cata *f* de vinos.

wine vinegar [,waɪn'vɪnɪgəʳ] *n* vinagre *m* de vino.

winewaiter ['waɪn,weɪtəʳ] *n* escanciador *m*, sumiller *m*.

wing [wɪŋ] **1** *n* ala *f*; (*Archit*) ala *f*; (*Brit Aut*) aleta *f*, guardabarros *m*; (*of chair*) cabecera *f*, oreja *f*; (*Sport*: *position*) ala *f*, exterior *m*, (*player*) extremo *m*, -a *f*; (*Aer*: *section*) escuadrilla *f*; **~s** (*Theat*) bastidores *mpl*; **left ~** (*Pol*) ala *f* izquierda; **right ~** (*Pol*) ala *f* derecha; **on the ~s of fantasy** en alas de la fantasía; **to be on the ~** estar volando; **to be on the left ~, to belong to the left ~** (*Pol*) ser de izquierdas; **to clip sb's ~s** cortar las alas a uno; **to shoot a bird on the ~** matar un pájaro al vuelo; **to stretch** (*or* **spread**) **one's ~s** (*fig*) empezar a volar; **to take ~** irse volando, alzar el vuelo; **to take sb under one's ~** tomar a uno bajo su protección; **to be waiting in the ~s** (*fig*) esperar entre bastidores.

2 *vt* (**a**) *bird* tocar, herir en el ala; *person* herir en el brazo.

(**b**) **to ~ one's way** volar, ir volando.

3 *vi* volar.

wingcase ['wɪŋkeɪs] *n* (*Zool*) élitro *m*.

wingchair ['wɪŋtʃɛəʳ] *n* butaca *f* de orejas, butaca *f* orejera.

wing-collar ['wɪŋ,kɒləʳ] *n* cuello *m* de puntas.

wing commander ['wɪŋkə,mɑːndəʳ] *n* teniente *m* coronel de aviación.

wingding‡ ['wɪŋ,dɪŋ] *n* (*US*) fiesta *f* animada, guateque *m* divertido.

winged [wɪŋd] *adj* (*Zool*) alado; *seed* con alas.

-winged [wɪŋd] *adj ending in compounds* de alas; **brown-~** de alas pardas; **four-~** de cuatro alas.

winger ['wɪŋəʳ] *n* extremo *m*, -a *f*, ala *mf*.

wingless ['wɪŋlɪs] *adj* sin alas.

wing-mirror ['wɪŋ,mɪrəʳ] *n* (*Brit*) retrovisor *m*.

wingnut ['wɪŋnʌt] *n* tuerca *f* mariposa.

wingspan ['wɪŋspæn] *n*, **wingspread** ['wɪŋspred] *n* envergadura *f* (de alas).

wingtip ['wɪŋtɪp] *n* punta *f* del ala.

wink [wɪŋk] **1** *n* (*blink*) pestañeo *m*; (*meaningful*) guiño *m*; **I didn't get a ~ of sleep** no pegué ojo; **to give sb a ~** guiñar el ojo a uno; **to have 40 ~s** descabezar un sueño, echarse una siestecita; **he said with a ~** dijo guiñándome el ojo; **I didn't sleep a ~** no pegué ojo; **to tip sb the ~*** avisar a uno clandestinamente.

2 *vt eye* guiñar.

3 *vi* (*blink*) pestañear; (*meaningfully*) guiñar el ojo; (*of light, star etc*) titilar, parpadear; **to ~ at sb** guiñar el ojo a uno; **to ~ at sth** (*fig*) hacer la vista gorda a algo, fingir no ver algo.

winker ['wɪŋkəʳ] *n* (*Brit Aut*) intermitente *m*.

winking ['wɪŋkɪŋ] **1** *n* pestañeo *m*; **it was as easy as ~** era facilísimo. **2** *adj* pestañeante.

winkle ['wɪŋkl] **1** *n* (*Brit*) bígaro *m*, bigarro *m*.

2 *vt*: **to ~ sb out** hacer salir a uno; **to ~ a secret out of sb** sonsacar un secreto a uno; **to ~ sth out of a crevice** sacar algo con dificultad de una grieta.

winner ['wɪnəʳ] *n* (*person, horse etc*) ganador *m*, -ora *f*, vencedor *m*, -ora *f*; (*book, entry etc*) obra *f* premiada; (*Tennis: ball*) pelota *f* imposible de restar; **this disc is a ~!** ¡este disco es fabuloso!; **the tune is bound to be a ~** la melodía obtendrá seguramente un éxito; **he knew he was on** (**to**) **a ~** sabía que con ese producto (*etc*) tenía asegurado el triunfo.

winning ['wɪnɪŋ] **1** *adj* (**a**) *person, horse, team etc* vencedor, victorioso; *book, entry etc* premiado; *hit, shot* decisivo.

(**b**) *smile, ways etc* atractivo, encantador.

2 *npl*: **~s** ganancias *fpl*.

winning-post ['wɪnɪŋpəʊst] *n* poste *m* de llegada, meta *f*.

winnow ['wɪnəʊ] *vt* aventar.

winnower ['wɪnəʊəʳ] *n*, **winnowing machine** ['wɪnəʊɪŋmə,ʃiːn] *n* aventadora *f*.

wino‡ ['waɪnəʊ] *n* alcohólico *m*, -a *f*.

winsome ['wɪnsəm] *adj* atractivo, encantador.

winter ['wɪntəʳ] **1** *n* invierno *m*.

2 *attr* de invierno, invernal; **~ clothes** ropa *f* de invierno; **~ Olympics** Olimpíada *f* de invierno; **~ quarters** cuarteles *mpl* de invierno; **~ solstice** solsticio *m* invernal; **~ sports** deportes *mpl* de invierno; **~ sports centre** (*or* **resort**) estación *f* invernal; **~ time** (*hour*) hora *f* de invierno.

3 *vi* invernar.

wintergreen ['wɪntəgriːn] *n* aceite *m* de gualteria.

winterize ['wɪntəraɪz] *vt* (*US*) adaptar para el invierno.

winterkill ['wɪntə'kɪl] (*US*) **1** *vt* matar de frío.

2 *vi* perecer a causa del frío.

wintertime ['wɪntətaɪm] *n* invierno *m*.

wintry ['wɪntrɪ] *adj* de invierno, invernal; frío, glacial; (*fig*) glacial.

wipe [waɪp] **1** *n* (**a**) limpión *m*, limpiadura *f*; **to give sth a ~** (**down** *etc*) limpiar algo, pasar un trapo (*etc*) sobre algo.

(**b**) (‡) cate* *m*, lapo* *m*.

2 *vt* limpiar; enjugar; *dishes* secar; **to ~ a table dry** secar una mesa con un trapo, enjugar una mesa; **to ~ one's brow** enjugarse la frente; **to ~ one's eyes** enjugarse las lágrimas; **to ~ a child's eyes** enjugar las lágrimas a un niño; **to ~ one's nose** sonarse (las narices).

3 *vi* secar los platos.

◆**wipe away, wipe off** *vt* quitar con un trapo, quitar frotando.

◆**wipe down** *vt* limpiar.

◆**wipe out** *vt* (*erase*) borrar; (*suppress*) borrar, cancelar; suprimir; *debt* liquidar; *memory* borrar; (*destroy*) destruir, extirpar; (*kill off completely*) aniquilar.

◆**wipe up** *vt* limpiar; **to ~ up the dishes** secar los platos.

wipe-out ['waɪpaʊt] *n* (**a**) (*destruction*) aniquilación *f*, destrucción *f*. (**b**) (*windsurfing*) caída *f*.

wiper ['waɪpəʳ] *n* (**a**) (*cloth*) paño *m*, trapo *m*. (**b**) (*Brit Aut*) limpiaparabrisas *m*, escobilla *f*.

wire ['waɪəʳ] **1** *n* (**a**) alambre *m*; **down to the ~*** (*US*) hasta el final, hasta la última; **to come** (*or* **get**) **in** (**just**) **under the ~*** (*US*) llegar justo a tiempo; **to get one's ~s crossed** (*fig*) sufrir un malentendido; **to pull ~s*** tocar resortes; **he can pull ~s*** tiene muchos enchufes*, tiene buenas agarraderas*.

(**b**) (*Telec*) telegrama *m*; **to send sb a ~** poner un telegrama a uno.

2 *vt* (**a**) *house* instalar el alambrado de; *fence* alambrar; **it's ~d for sound** tiene el alambrado para el sonido; **it's ~d to the alarm** está conectado a la alarma; **~d, ~ up*** (*US*) tenso, malhumorado, de mal genio.

(**b**) **to ~ sb** poner un telegrama a uno; **to ~ information to sb** enviar información a uno por telegrama.

3 *vi* poner un telegrama (*for sth* pidiendo algo, *to sb* a uno).

◆**wire up** *vt* instalar el alambrado de, cablear, alambrar; **it's all ~d up for television** se ha completado la instalación eléctrica para la televisión; *V* **wire 2**.

wire brush ['waɪə'brʌʃ] *n* cepillo *m* de alambre.

wirecutters ['waɪə,kʌtəz] *npl* cizalla *f*, cizallas *fpl*, cortaalambres *m*.

wire-haired ['waɪəhɛəd] *adj dog* de pelo áspero.

wireless ['waɪəlɪs] (*esp Brit*) **1** *n* (**a**) (*as science etc*) radio *f*, radiofonía *f*. (**b**) (†: *set*) radio *f*, receptor *m* de radio, radiorreceptor *m*; **by ~, on the ~, over the ~** por radio; **to talk on the ~** hablar por radio.

2 *attr* de radio, radiofónica; **~ message** radiograma *m*.

3 *vt* radiar, transmitir por radio.

4 *vi*: **to ~ to sb** enviar un mensaje a uno por radio.

wireless cabin ['waɪəlɪs,kæbɪn] *n* cabina *f* de radio.

wireless operator ['waɪəlɪs,ɒpəreɪtəʳ] *n* radiotelegrafista *mf*, radio *mf*.

wireless set ['waɪəlɪsset] *n* radio *f*, receptor *m* de radio, radiorreceptor *m*.

wireless station ['waɪəlɪs,steɪʃən] *n* emisora *f*.

wire netting ['waɪə'netɪŋ] *n* red *f* de alambre, alambrada *f*, tela *f* metálica.

wirepuller* ['waɪə,pʊləʳ] *n* enchufista* *mf*.

wirepulling* ['waɪə,pʊlɪŋ] *n* empleo *m* de resortes, enchufismo* *m*.

wiretap ['waɪətæp] *vi* intervenir las conexiones telefónicas, practicar escuchas telefónicas.

wiretapping ['waɪə'tæpɪŋ] *n* intervención *f* de las conexiones telefónicas.

wire wool ['waɪə'wʊl] *n* lana *f* de alambre.

wireworm ['waɪəwɜːm] *n* gusano *m* de elatérido.

wiring ['waɪərɪŋ] **1** *n* alambrado *m*, cableado *m*, instalación *f* eléctrica. **2** *attr*: ~ **diagram** esquema *m* del alambrado.

wiry ['waɪərɪ] *adj person, build* delgado pero fuerte; *hand* nervudo, nervioso.

Wis., Wisc. (*US*) *abbr of* **Wisconsin**.

wisdom ['wɪzdəm] **1** *n* sabiduría *f*; saber *m*; prudencia *f*, juicio *m*; lo acertado, acierto *m*; **doubts were expressed about the ~ of the visit** se dudaba si era prudente hacer esta visita; **in her ~ she decided not to go** muy prudentemente decidió no ir. **2** *attr*: ~ **tooth** muela *f* del juicio.

wise¹ [waɪz] *adj* **(a)** (*learned*) sabio; (*prudent*) prudente, juicioso; *move, step etc* acertado; **a ~ man** un sabio; ~ **guy*** sabelotodo* *m*, vivo *m*; ~ **guy, huh?*** ¿Vd se lo sabe todo, eh?; **the (Three) W~ Men (of the East)** los Reyes Magos; **it does not seem ~ to** + *infin* no parece aconsejable + *infin*; **you would be ~ to ask him first** sería aconsejable preguntarle primero; **the ~st thing to do is ...** lo más prudente es ...; **I'm none the ~r** sigo sin entenderlo, ahora lo entiendo menos que antes; **nobody will be any the ~r** nadie sabrá de esto, nadie se dará cuenta; **that wasn't very ~ of you** en eso no has sido muy prudente.

(b) (*) **to be ~ to sb** conocer el juego de uno, calar a uno; **to get ~ to sth** caer en la cuenta de algo; **to put sb ~ to sth** poner a uno al tanto de algo, informar a uno acerca de algo.

◆**wise up*** *vi* (*esp US*) informarse, enterarse (*to* de); ponerse al tanto (*to* de); caer en la cuenta (*to* de).

wise² [waɪz] *n* (††) guisa *f*, modo *m*; **in this ~** de esta guisa; **in no ~** de ningún modo.

-wise [waɪz] *suffix* con respecto a, en cuanto a, relativo a, por lo que se refiere a; **profitwise** en cuanto a las ganancias; **how are you off money-wise?** ¿cómo estás en cuanto a dinero?

wiseacre ['waɪz,eɪkəʳ] *n* sabihondo *m*.

wisecrack ['waɪzkræk] **1** *n* cuchufleta *f*, chiste *m*, salida *f*. **2** *vi* cuchufletear; **'you weigh a ton', he ~ed** 'pesas más que un burro en brazos' dijo bromeando.

wisely ['waɪzlɪ] *adv* sabiamente; prudentemente, con prudencia; acertadamente.

wish [wɪʃ] **1** *n* **(a)** (*desire, will*) deseo *m* (*for* de); ruego *m*; **according to one's ~es** según los deseos de uno; **her ~ to do it** su deseo de hacerlo; **your ~ is my command** sus deseos son órdenes para mí; **it has long been my ~ to** + *infin* desde hace mucho tiempo vengo deseando + *infin*, desde hace mucho tengo la intención de + *infin*; **to go against sb's ~es** oponerse a los deseos de uno; **the fairy granted her 3 ~es** el hada le concedió 3 deseos; **you shall have your ~** se hará lo que pides, se cumplirá tu deseo; **I have no great ~ to go** me apetece poco ir, realmente no tengo ganas de ir; **to make a ~** pensar un deseo, formular un deseo.

(b) with best ~es (*in letter*) saludos de tu amigo ..., un abrazo de ...; **with best ~es for the future** con mis augurios para el porvenir; **I went to give him my best ~es** fui a darle la enhorabuena; **please give him my best ~es** por favor dale recuerdos míos, salúdale de mi parte; **we sent a message of good ~es on Slobodian independence day** enviamos un mensaje de buenos augurios el día de independencia de Eslobodia.

2 *vt* **(a)** (*desire*) desear, querer; **I do not ~ it** no lo quiero, no quiero que se haga.

(b) to ~ sb good luck, to ~ sb well desear a uno mucha suerte; **I ~ you all possible happiness** os deseo la más completa felicidad; **I don't ~ her ill, I don't ~ her any harm** no le deseo ningún mal; **to ~ sb good morning** dar los buenos días a uno; **to ~ sb goodbye** despedirse de uno; **to ~ sb a happy Christmas** desear a uno unas Pascuas muy felices, felicitarle a uno las Pascuas.

(c) (*with verb complement*) **to ~ to do sth** querer hacer algo, desear hacer algo; **to ~ sb to do sth** querer que uno haga algo; **what do you ~ me to do?** ¿qué quieres que haga?; **I do ~ you'd let me help** me gustaría muchísimo que me dejaras ayudar; **I ~ she'd come** estoy deseando que venga; **I ~ed after that I had stayed till the end** después de eso sentí no haberme quedado hasta el fin; **I ~ I could!** ¡ojalá!, ¡ojalá pudiera!; **I ~ it were not so** ojalá no fuera así; **I ~ I could be there!** ¡ojalá estuviera allí!

(d) (*) **to ~ sth on sb** lograr que uno acepte algo que no desea; **the job was ~ed on me** me dieron el cometido sin quererlo yo, me impusieron el trabajo; **she was ~ed on us as a guest** nos impusieron que la invitáramos; **I wouldn't ~ that on anybody** eso no lo desearía para nadie.

3 *vi* hacer un voto; **to ~ for sth** desear algo, anhelar algo; **what more could you ~ for?** ¿qué más podría desear?; **she has everything she could ~ for** tiene todo cuanto podría desear.

wishbone ['wɪʃbəʊn] *n* espoleta *f*.

wishful ['wɪʃfʊl] *adj* deseoso (*to* + *infin* de + *infin*); ilusionado; ~ **thinking** ilusiones *fpl*, ilusionismo *m*, espejismo *m*.

wish-fulfilment ['wɪʃfʊl'fɪlmənt] *n* ilusiones *fpl*, ilusionismo *m*, espejismo *m*.

wishing-bone ['wɪʃɪŋbəʊn] *n* espoleta *f*.

wish-wash* ['wɪʃwɒʃ] *n* aguachirle *f*.

wishy-washy* ['wɪʃɪ,wɒʃɪ] *adj* soso, flojo, insípido.

wisp [wɪsp] *n* (*fragment*) trozo *m* ligero, pedazo *m* menudo; (*trace*) vestigio *m*; (*of grass*) manojito *m*; brizna *f*; (*of hair*) mechón *m*; (*of cloud*) jirón *m*; ~ **of smoke** columna *f* delgada, espiral *f* ligera.

wispy ['wɪspɪ] *adj* delgado, sutil, tenue.

wisteria [wɪs'tɪərɪə] *n* vistaria *f*, glicina *f*.

wistful ['wɪstfʊl] *adj* triste, melancólico; pensativo.

wistfully ['wɪstfəlɪ] *adv* tristemente, con melancolía; pensativamente; **she looked at me ~** me miró pensativa.

wistfulness ['wɪstfʊlnɪs] *n* tristeza *f*, melancolía *f*; lo pensativo.

wit¹ [wɪt] *n*: **to ~** (*Jur or hum*) a saber, esto es.

wit² [wɪt] *n* **(a)** (*understanding*) inteligencia *f*, entendimiento *m*, juicio *m*; talento *m*; **a battle of ~s** una contienda entre dos inteligencias; **to be at one's ~'s end** estar para volverse loco (*wondering what to do* pensando qué hacer); **to be out of one's ~s** estar fuera de sí; **to collect** (*or* **gather**) **one's ~s** reconcentrarse; **to frighten sb out of his ~s** dar a uno un susto mortal; **to have** (*or* **keep**) **one's ~s about one** tener mucho ojo; conservar su presencia de ánimo; **he hadn't the ~ to see that ...** no tenía bastante inteligencia para comprender que ...; **to live by one's ~s** vivir del cuento, ser caballero de industria; **to sharpen one's ~s** aguzar el ingenio, despabilarse; **to use one's ~s** usar su sentido común; valerse de su ingenio.

(b) (*humour, wittiness*) ingenio *m*, agudeza *f*; sal *f*; gracia *f*; **the ~ and wisdom of Joe Soap** las agudezas y sabiduría de Joe Soap; **to have a ready** (*or* **pretty**) **~** ser ingenioso, tener chispa; **there's a lot of ~ in the book** el libro tiene mucha sal; **a story told without ~** un cuento narrado sin gracia; **in a flash of ~ he said ...** con un rasgo de ingenio dijo ...

(c) (*person*) chistoso *m*, -a *f*, persona *f* de mucha sal; (*Hist*) ingenio *m*; **an Elizabethan ~** un ingenio de la época isabelina.

witch [wɪtʃ] *n* bruja *f*, hechicera *f*; **~es' sabbath** aquelarre *m*.

witchcraft ['wɪtʃkrɑːft] *n* brujería *f*.

witchdoctor ['wɪtʃ,dɒktəʳ] *n* hechicero *m*.

witchery ['wɪtʃərɪ] *n* brujería *f*; (*fig*) encanto *m*, magia *f*.

witch-hazel ['wɪtʃ,heɪzl] *n* olmo *m* escocés.

witch-hunt ['wɪtʃhʌnt] *n* caza *f* de brujas, cacería *f* de brujas.

witching ['wɪtʃɪŋ] *attr*: ~ **hour** (*hum*) hora *f* de las brujas.

with [wɪð, wɪθ] *prep* **(a)** (*gen*) con; en compañía de; **I was ~ him** yo estaba con él; **she stayed with friends** se hospedó con unos amigos; **I'll be ~ you in a moment** un momento y estoy con vosotros; **to leave sth ~ sb** dejar algo en manos de uno; **to leave a child ~ sb** dejar a un niño al cuidado de uno; **that problem is always ~ us** ese problema sigue afectándonos, ese problema no se resuelve; **the fashion ended ~ the century** la moda terminó al terminar el siglo, la moda terminó cuando el siglo; **~ the Alcántara it is the biggest ship of its class** junto con el Alcántara es el mayor buque de su tipo; **she's good ~ children** sabe manejar a los niños, es muy buena con los niños; **I am ~ you there** en eso estoy de acuerdo contigo; **he took it away ~ him** se lo llevó consigo; ~ **no** sin, *eg* ~ **no trouble at all** sin dificultad alguna; **I'm sorry, I'm not** ~ **you*** lo siento, pero te he perdido*; **are you** ~ **me?*** ¿me entendéis?

(**b**) (*descriptive*) de, con; **a house** ~ **big windows** una casa con grandes ventanas; **the fellow** ~ **the big beard** él de la barba grande; **you can't speak to the queen** ~ **your hat on** no se puede hablar con la reina llevando puesto el sombrero.

(**c**) (*in spite of*) con; ~ **all his faults** con todos sus defectos.

(**d**) (*according to*) según, de acuerdo con; **it varies** ~ **the season** varía según la estación.

(**e**) (*manner*) con; ~ **all his might** con todas sus fuerzas; ~ **all speed** a toda prisa; ~ **one blow** de un solo golpe; **to cut wood** ~ **a knife** cortar madera con un cuchillo; **to welcome sb** ~ **open arms** recibir a uno con los brazos abiertos; **to walk** ~ **a stick** andar con un bastón.

(**f**) (*cause*) de; **to jump** ~ **joy** saltar de alegría; **to shake** ~ **fear** temblar de miedo; **to shiver** ~ **cold** tiritar de frío; **the hills are white** ~ **snow** las colinas están cubiertas de nieve; **to be ill** ~ **measles** tener sarampión; **it's pouring** ~ **rain** está lloviendo a cántaros; **to fill a glass** ~ **wine** llenar un vaso de vino.

(**g**) (*construction with certain words*) **the trouble** ~ **Harry** la dificultad con Enrique; el disgusto que hubo con Enrique; **it's a habit** ~ **him** es una costumbre que tiene, es cosa de él; **be honest** ~ **me** cuéntamelo con toda franqueza; **be honest** ~ **yourself** no te forjes ilusiones; **you must be patient** ~ **her** hay que tener paciencia con ella; **we agree** ~ **you** estamos de acuerdo contigo; **to fill sb** ~ **fear** infundir miedo a uno; llenar a uno de miedo.

(**h**) (*) **to be** ~ **it** estar al tanto, estar al día; tener ideas modernas; comprender el mundo actual, estar de acuerdo con las tendencias actuales; (*of dress etc*) estar de moda; **to get** ~ **it** ponerse al día, (*in dress etc*) ponerse a la moda.

withal†† [wɪ'ðɔːl] *adv* además, también; por añadidura.

withdraw [wɪθ'drɔː] (*irr*: *V* **draw**) **1** *vt object* retirar, sacar, quitar (*from* de); *troops, money, stamps, ambassador etc* retirar (*from* de); *words* retractar; (*Jur*) *charge* apartar.

2 *vi* (*Mil etc*) retirarse (*from* de, *to* a), replegarse; (*Sport*) abandonar; (*move away*) apartarse, alejarse, irse; (*before orgasm*) dar marcha atrás; **he withdrew a few paces** se retiró unos pasos, se apartó un poco; **then they all withdrew** luego se retiraron todos; **to** ~ **from business** retirarse de los negocios; **to** ~ **from a contest** abandonar, renunciar a tomar parte en una contienda; **to** ~ **in favour of sb else** renunciar en favor de otro; **to** ~ **into o.s.** ensimismarse; **you can't** ~ **now** no puedes abandonar ahora.

withdrawal [wɪθ'drɔːəl] **1** *n* retirada *f*; retiro *m*; abandono *m*; retractación *f*; renuncia *f*; (*before orgasm*) marcha *f* atrás; **to make a** ~ **of funds from a bank** efectuar una retirada de fondos de un banco; **they made a rapid** ~ se retiraron rápidamente.

2 *attr*: ~ **notice** (*Fin*) aviso *m* de retirada de fondos; ~ **symptoms** síndrome *m* de la abstinencia.

withdrawn [wɪθ'drɔːn] **1** *ptp of* **withdraw**. **2** *adj* reservado, encerrado en sí mismo, introvertido.

withe [wɪθ] *n* mimbre *m or f*.

wither ['wɪðəʳ] **1** *vt* marchitar, secar; (*fig*) aplastar; **to** ~ **sb with a look** aplastar (*or* fulminar) a uno con la mirada.

2 *vi* marchitarse, secarse.

◆**wither away** *vi* extinguirse.

withered ['wɪðəd] *adj* marchito, seco.

withering ['wɪðərɪŋ] *adj heat* abrasador; *gunfire etc* arrollador; *look, tone* fulminante; *criticism* mordaz.

witheringly ['wɪðərɪŋlɪ] *adv say, look* desdeñosamente.

withers ['wɪðəz] *npl* cruz *f* (de caballo).

withhold [wɪθ'həʊld] (*irr*: *V* **hold**) *vt* (*keep back*) retener; (*refuse*) negar; (*refuse to reveal*) ocultar; no revelar; **to** ~ **a pound of sb's pay** retener una libra del pago a uno; **to** ~ **one's help** negarse a ayudar a uno; **to** ~ **the truth from sb** no revelar la verdad a uno.

within [wɪð'ɪn] **1** *adv* dentro; **from** ~ desde dentro, desde el interior.

2 *prep* (*inside*) dentro de; (~ *range of*) al alcance de; **here** ~ **the town** aquí dentro de la ciudad; ~ **a radius of 10 kilometres** en un radio de 10 kilómetros; **we were** ~ **100 metres of the summit** estábamos a menos de 100 metros de la cumbre, nos faltaban sólo 100 metros para llegar a la cumbre; **the village is** ~ **a mile of the river** el pueblo dista poco menos de una milla del pueblo; **to be** ~ **an inch of** estar a dos dedos de; **to be** ~ **call** estar al alcance de la voz; ~ **the week** antes de terminar la semana; ~ **a year of her death** menos de un año después de su muerte; ~ **the stipulated time** dentro del plazo señalado; **to keep** ~ **the law** obrar dentro de la ley; **to live** ~ **one's income** vivir con arreglo a los ingresos; **a voice** ~ **me said** ... una voz interior me dijo ...

with-it* ['wɪðɪt] *adj*: **a** ~ **dress** un vestido a la moda.

without [wɪð'aʊt] **1** *adv* (*liter*) fuera; por fuera; **from** ~ desde fuera.

2 *prep* sin; a falta de, en ausencia de; ~ **a tie** sin corbata; **3 days** ~ **food** 3 días sin comer; ~ **speaking** sin hablar, sin decir nada; ~ **my noticing it** sin verlo yo, sin que yo lo notase; **not** ~ **some difficulty** no sin alguna dificultad.

with-profits ['wɪθ'prɒfɪts] *adj*: ~ **endowment assurance** seguro *m* dotal con beneficios.

withstand [wɪθstænd] (*irr*: *V* **stand**) *vt* resistir a; oponerse a; aguantar.

withy ['wɪðɪ] *n* mimbre *m or f*.

witless ['wɪtlɪs] *adj* estúpido, tonto; **to scare sb** ~ dar un susto mortal a uno.

witness ['wɪtnɪs] **1** *n* (**a**) (*evidence*) testimonio *m*; **in** ~ **of** en fe de; **in** ~ **whereof** en fe de lo cual; **to bear** ~ **to** dar fe de, atestiguar.

(**b**) (*person*) testigo *mf* (*also Jur*); espectador *m*, -ora *f*; ~ **for the defence** testigo *mf* de descargo; ~ **for the prosecution** testigo *mf* de cargo; **there were no** ~**es** no hubo testigos; **we want no** ~**es to this** no queremos que nadie vea esto, no queremos que haya testigos; **I was** (**a**) ~ **to this event** yo presencié este suceso; **to call sb as** ~ citar a uno como testigo.

2 *vt* (**a**) (*see*) asistir a, presenciar, ser espectador de; ver; **the accident was** ~**ed by two people** hay dos testigos del accidente, dos personas vieron el accidente; **I have never** ~**ed such scenes before** no he visto nunca tales escenas; **this period** ~**ed important changes** este período fue testigo de cambios importantes; **to** ~ **sb doing sth** ver a uno que hace algo, ver cómo uno hace algo.

(**b**) ~ **what happened when** ... ved lo que pasó cuando ..., consideren lo que pasó cuando ...; ~ **the case of X** según quedó demostrado en el caso de X; ~ **my hand** en fe de lo cual firmo.

(**c**) **to** ~ **a document** firmar un documento como testigo.

3 *vi*: **to** ~ **to sth** dar testimonio de algo.

witness-box ['wɪtnɪsbɒks] *n*, (*US*) **witness stand** ['wɪtnɪsstænd] *n* barra *f* de los testigos, puesto *m* de los testigos, tribuna *f* de los testigos.

witter* ['wɪtəʳ] *vi* (*Brit*) parlotear; **to** ~ **on about sth** hablar de algo sin cesar; **stop** ~**ing** (**on**)! ¿quieres callarte de una vez?

witticism ['wɪtɪsɪzəm] *n* agudeza *f*, chiste *m*, ocurrencia *f*, dicho *m* gracioso.

wittily ['wɪtɪlɪ] *adv* ingeniosamente; con gracia, de modo divertido.

wittiness ['wɪtɪnɪs] *n* agudeza *f*, viveza *f* de ingenio; gracia *f*, lo divertido.

wittingly ['wɪtɪŋlɪ] *adv* a sabiendas.

witty ['wɪtɪ] *adj person* ingenioso, chistoso, salado; *remark, speech etc* gracioso, divertido, ocurrente; **he's very** ~ tiene mucha gracia, es un tipo muy salado.

wives [waɪvz] *npl of* **wife**.

wizard ['wɪzəd] **1** *n* (**a**) (*magician*) hechicero *m*, brujo *m*, mago *m*. (**b**) (*: *expert*) as* *m*, genio *m*; experto *m*. **2** *adj* (*esp Brit**) estupendo*, maravilloso.

wizardry ['wɪzədrɪ] *n* hechicería *f*, brujería *f*.

wizened ['wɪznd] *adj* seco, marchito; *person, skin etc* arrugado, apergaminado.

wk *abbr of* **week** semana *f*, sem.

W/L *abbr of* **wavelength** longitud *f* de onda.

Wm *abbr of* **William**.

WMO *n abbr of* **World Meteorological Organization** Organización *f* Meteorológica Mundial, OMM *f*.

WNW *abbr of* **west-north-west** oesnoroeste, ONO.

WO *n* (*Mil*) *abbr of* **Warrant Officer**.

wo [wəʊ] *interj*, **woa** [wəʊ] *interj* = **whoa**.

woad [wəʊd] *n* hierba *f* pastel, glasto *m*.

wobble ['wɒbl] **1** *n* bamboleo *m*, tambaleo *m*; **to walk with a** ~ tambalearse al andar, andar tambaleándose; **this chair has a** ~ esta silla está coja, esta silla cojea.

2 *vi* (**a**) bambolear, tambalearse; vacilar, oscilar; (*rock*) balancearse; (*of chair etc*) cojear, ser poco firme.

(**b**) (*be indecisive*) vacilar.

wobbly ['wɒblɪ] **1** *adj* inseguro, poco firme, cojo. **2** *n*: **to throw a** ~* ponerse histérico.

wodge* [wɒdʒ] *n* trozo *m*.
woe [wəʊ] *n* (*liter*) aflicción *f*, dolor *m*; mal *m*, infortunio *m*; **~ is me!** ¡ay de mí!; **~ betide him who ...!** ¡ay del que ...!; **to tell sb one's ~s** contar a uno sus males; **it was such a tale of ~** fue una historia tan triste, fue una historia tan llena de desgracias.
woebegone ['wəʊbɪ,gɒn] *adj* desconsolado, angustiado.
woeful ['wəʊfʊl] *adj person etc* triste, afligido, desconsolado; *sight, story etc* triste, lamentable.
woefully ['wəʊfəlɪ] *adv* tristemente; lamentablemente.
Wog‡ [wɒg] *n* (*Brit pej*) negro *m*, -a *f*.
wok [wɒk] *n cazuela china de base redonda*.
woke [wəʊk] *pret of* **wake²**.
woken ['wəʊkn] *ptp of* **wake²**.
wold [wəʊld] *n* (*approx*) rasa *f* ondulada.
wolf [wʊlf] **1** *n*, *pl* **wolves** [wʊlvz] lobo *m*, a *f*; (*) tenorio *m*; **lone ~** (*fig*) solitario *m*; **~ in sheep's clothing** lobo *m* en piel de cordero; **to cry ~** gritar al lobo; **to keep the ~ from the door** guardarse del hambre, evitar caer en la miseria; **to throw sb to the wolves** arrojar a uno a los lobos.
2 *vt* (*also* **to ~ down**) *food* zamparse, comer vorazmente.
wolfcub ['wʊlfkʌb] *n* lobato *m*, lobezno *m*.
wolfhound ['wʊlfhaʊnd] *n* perro *m* lobo.
wolfish ['wʊlfɪʃ] *adj* lobuno.
wolfpack ['wʊlfpæk] *n* manada *f* de lobos.
wolfram ['wʊlfrəm] *n* volframio *m*, wolfram *m*.
wolf-whistle ['wʊlf,wɪsl] *n* silbido *m* de admiración.
wolverine ['wʊlvəri:n] *n* carcayú *m*, glotón *m*.
wolves [wʊlvz] *npl of* **wolf**.
woman ['wʊmən] **1** *n*, *pl* **women** ['wɪmɪn] mujer *f*; (*servant*) criada *f*; **as one ~** unánimemente; como una sola mujer, todas a una; **my good ~** buena mujer; **I'm not a drinking ~** no bebo, no soy de las que beben; **~ to ~** de mujer a mujer; **she's her own ~** es una mujer muy fiel a sí misma; **young ~** joven *f*; **old ~** vieja *f*; **my old ~*** la parienta*, mi media naranja; **he's rather an old ~** es una persona bastante sosa; se queja por poca cosa; se inquieta sin motivo; **~ of the town** prostituta *f*; **~ of the world** mujer *f* mundana; **women's football** fútbol *m* para mujeres, fútbol *m* femenino; **women's group** grupo *m* femenino; **women's movement** movimiento *m* feminista; **his ~** (*lover*) su querida, su amante; **X and all his women** X y todas sus queridas; **Z and his kept ~** Z y su querida; **to make an honest ~ of sb** casarse con una (a causa de haberla dejado encinta); **he runs after women** se dedica a la caza de mujeres.
2 *attr*: **~ doctor** médica *f*; **~ driver** conductora *f*; **~ pilot** piloto *f*; **~ priest** mujer *f* sacerdote; **~ writer** escritora *f*.
woman-hater ['wʊmən,heɪtəʳ] *n* misógino *m*.
womanhood ['wʊmənhʊd] *n* (**a**) (*women in general*) mujeres *fpl*, sexo *m* femenino. (**b**) (*age*) edad *f* adulta (de mujer); **to reach ~** llegar a la edad adulta (de mujer). (**c**) (*womanliness*) feminidad *f*.
womanish ['wʊmənɪʃ] *adj* mujeril, propio de mujer; *man* afeminado.
womanize ['wʊmənaɪz] *vi* ser mujeriego, dedicarse a la caza de mujeres.
womanizer ['wʊmənaɪzəʳ] *n* mujeriego *m*.
womanizing ['wʊmənaɪzɪŋ] *n* el ser mujeriego; caza *f* de mujeres.
womankind ['wʊmən'kaɪnd] *n* mujeres *fpl*, sexo *m* femenino.
womanlike ['wʊmənlaɪk] *adj* mujeril.
womanliness ['wʊmənlɪnɪs] *n* feminidad *f*.
womanly ['wʊmənlɪ] *adj* femenino.
womb [wu:m] *n* matriz *f*, útero *m*; (*fig*) seno *m*.
wombat ['wɒmbæt] *n* wombat *m*.
women ['wɪmɪn] *npl of* **woman**; **~'s doubles** dobles *mpl* femeninos, dobles *mpl* de damas; **w~'s libber*** liberacionista *f*, feminista *f*; **~'s page** sección *f* para la mujer; **~'s rights** derechos *mpl* de la mujer; **~'s team** equipo *m* femenino.
womenfolk ['wɪmɪnfəʊk] *npl* las mujeres.
won [wʌn] *pret and ptp of* **win**.
wonder ['wʌndəʳ] **1** *n* (**a**) (*object*) maravilla *f*; prodigio *m*; portento *m*, milagro *m*; **the ~ of electricity** el milagro de la electricidad; **~s of science** maravillas *fpl* de la ciencia; **the 7 ~s of the world** las 7 maravillas del mundo; **a nine-days' ~** un prodigio que deja pronto de serlo; **no ~!** ¡no me extraña!; **and no ~** y con razón, como era lógico, como era de esperar; **he paid cash, for a ~** pagó al contado, por milagro; **~s never cease!** ¡todavía hay milagros!; **the ~ of it was that ...** lo asombroso fue que ...; **it is a ~ that ...** es un milagro que ...; **it is no** (*or* **little, small**) **~ that ...** no es sorprendente que + *subj*, no es mucho que + *subj*; **to do ~s with sth** hacer maravillas con algo; **it did ~s for her health** tuvo efectos milagrosos en su salud; **he promised ~s** prometió el oro y el moro; **to work ~s** hacer milagros.
(**b**) (*sense of ~*) admiración *f*, asombro *m*; **to be lost in ~** quedar asombrado.
2 *attr*: **~ boy** joven *m* prodigio; **~ drug** remedio *m* milagroso.
3 *vt* desear saber, preguntarse; **I ~ what he'll do now** me pregunto qué hará ahora; **I ~ if she'll come** me pregunto si viene, ¿si vendrá?; **I ~ who first said that** ¿quién habrá dicho eso por primera vez?; **I ~ if you really love me** a veces me pregunto si me quieres de verdad; **I ~ whether the milkman's been** a ver si el lechero habrá venido; **she ~ed whether to go on** no sabía si seguir adelante; **if you're ~ing how to do it** si no sabes cómo hacerlo.
4 *vi* (**a**) (*reflect*) **I ~!** ¡quizá!, ¡quién sabe!; **I often ~** me lo pregunto mucho; **it set me ~ing** me hizo pensar; **I ~ed about that for a long time** le di muchas vueltas a eso; **I'm ~ing about buying some** pienso en la conveniencia de comprar algunos.
(**b**) (*marvel*) admirarse, asombrarse, maravillarse (*at* de); **I ~ at your rashness** me admiro de tu temeridad, me asombra tu temeridad; **that's hardly to be ~ed at** eso no tiene nada de extraño, no hay que asombrarse de eso; **I shouldn't ~!** ¡sería lógico!; **I shouldn't ~ if ...** no me sorprendería que + *subj*; **she's married by now, I shouldn't ~** se habrá casado ya como sería lógico, cabe presumir que está casada ya; **can you ~?** ¿natural, no?
wonderful ['wʌndəfʊl] *adj* maravilloso; estupendo; **~!** ¡estupendo!
wonderfully ['wʌndəfəlɪ] *adv* maravillosamente.
wondering ['wʌndərɪŋ] *adj tone, look etc* perplejo, sorprendido.
wonderingly ['wʌndərɪŋlɪ] *adv*: **to look ~ at sb** mirar a uno perplejo, mirar a uno sorprendido.
wonderland ['wʌndəlænd] *n* país *m* de las maravillas, mundo *m* maravilloso.
wonderment ['wʌndəmənt] *n* = **wonder 1** (**b**).
wonderstruck ['wʌndəstrʌk] *adj* asombrado, pasmado.
wonder-worker ['wʌndə,wɜ:kəʳ] *n* (*Med etc*) droga *f* (*etc*) milagrosa.
wondrous ['wʌndrəs] **1** *adj* (*liter*) maravilloso. **2** *adv* (*liter*, ††) = **wondrously**.
wondrously ['wʌndrəslɪ] *adv* (*liter*) maravillosamente; **~ beautiful** extraordinariamente hermoso, hermoso en extremo.
wonky* ['wɒŋkɪ] *adj* (*Brit*) (*unsteady*) poco firme, poco seguro; flojo; (*broken down*) descompuesto.
wont [wəʊnt] **1** *adj*: **to be ~ to** + *infin* soler + *infin*, acostumbrar + *infin*; **as he was ~ (to)** como solía (hacer).
2 *n* costumbre *f*; **it is his ~ to** + *infin* suele + *infin*, acostumbra + *infin*.
won't [wəʊnt] = **will not**.
wonted ['wəʊntɪd] *adj* (*liter*) acostumbrado.
woo [wu:] *vt* (*liter*) pretender, cortejar; (*fig*) procurar ganarse la amistad de, solicitar el apoyo de; *fame etc* buscar, procurar.
wood [wʊd] **1** *n* (**a**) (*forest*) bosque *m*; **~s** bosque *m*, bosques *mpl*, monte *m*; **we're not out of the ~ yet** todavía está la pelota en el tejado; **he can't see the ~ for the trees** los árboles no le están dejando ver el bosque; **to take to the ~s** echarse al monte.
(**b**) (*material*) madera *f*; (*fire ~*) leña *f*; **dead ~** ramas *fpl* muertas; leña *f* seca; (*fig*) material *m* inútil, personas *fpl* inútiles; **to knock on ~** (*US*), **to touch ~** tocar madera; **we shall manage it, touch ~** lo lograremos si Dios quiere (*or* Dios mediante).
(**c**) (*in winemaking etc*) barril *m*; **drawn from the ~** de barril.
(**d**) (*Mus*) instrumentos *mpl* de viento de madera.
(**e**) (*Bowls*) bola *f*.
2 *attr* (**a**) (*of forest*) de los bosques, selvático.
(**b**) (*of material*) de madera; **~ alcohol, ~ spirit** alcohol *m* metálico.
wood anemone ['wʊdən'emənɪ] *n* anémona *f* de los bosques.
woodbine ['wʊdbaɪn] *n* madreselva *f*.
wood-block ['wʊdblɒk] *n* bloque *m* de madera; (*in paving*) adoquín *m* de madera, tarugo *m*.
wood-carving ['wʊd,kɑ:vɪŋ] *n* escultura *f* en madera, talla *f*

(en madera).

woodchuck ['wʊdtʃʌk] *n* marmota *f* de América.

woodcock ['wʊdkɒk] *n* becada *f*, chocha *f*, chochaperdiz *f*.

woodcraft ['wʊdkrɑːft] *n* conocimiento *m* de la vida del bosque.

woodcut ['wʊdkʌt] *n* grabado *m* en madera, xilografía *f*.

woodcutter ['wʊd,kʌtəʳ] *n* leñador *m*.

wooded ['wʊdɪd] *adj* arbolado, enselvado.

wooden ['wʊdn] *adj* (**a**) de madera; de palo; ~ **nickel*** (*US*) baratija *f*, objeto *m* sin valor; **to try to sell sb ~ nickels*** (*US*) intentar darle a uno gato por liebre, tratar de engañar a uno; ~ **spoon** cuchara *f* de palo; (*fig*) premio *m* para el peor, premio *m* para el último.

(**b**) (*fig*) *face etc* sin expresión, inexpresivo; de estatua; *personality* soso, poco imaginativo, sin animación; *response etc* inflexible.

wood engraving ['wʊdɪn'greɪvɪŋ] *n* grabado *m* en madera.

wooden-headed ['wʊdn'hedɪd] *adj* cabezahueca.

woodenly ['wʊdnlɪ] *adv say etc* sin expresión, inexpresivamente.

woodland ['wʊdlənd] **1** *n* bosque *m*, monte *m*, arbolado *m*. **2** *attr* de los bosques, selvático.

woodlark ['wʊdlɑːk] *n* totovía *f*, cogujada *f*.

woodlouse ['wʊdlaʊs] *n*, *pl* **woodlice** ['wʊdlaɪs] cochinilla *f*.

woodman ['wʊdmən] *n*, *pl* **woodmen** ['wʊdmən] leñador *m*; trabajador *m* forestal.

woodpecker ['wʊd,pekəʳ] *n* pájaro *m* carpintero, pito *m*, pico *m*; **green ~** pito *m* real; **lesser spotted ~** pico *m* menor.

woodpigeon ['wʊd,pɪdʒən] *n* paloma *f* torcaz.

woodpile ['wʊdpaɪl] *n* montón *m* de leña.

wood-pulp ['wʊdpʌlp] *n* pulpa *f* de madera, lignocelulosa *f*, pasta *f* celulosa.

wood shavings ['wʊd,ʃeɪvɪŋz] *npl* virutas *fpl*.

woodshed ['wʊdʃed] *n* leñera *f*.

woodsy ['wʊdzɪ] *adj* (*US*) selvático.

woodwind ['wʊdwɪnd] *n* (*also* ~ **instruments**) instrumentos *mpl* de viento de madera.

woodwork ['wʊdwɜːk] *n* (**a**) (*wood*) maderaje *m*; molduras *fpl*; (*of goal*) madera *f*; **they come crawling out of the ~** (*fig*) salen de la madera como carcomas. (**b**) (*craft*) carpintería *f*, ebanistería *f*, artesanía *f* en madera.

woodworm ['wʊdwɜːm] *n* carcoma *f*; **the table has ~** la mesa está carcomida.

woody ['wʊdɪ] *adj tissue etc* leñoso.

woof[1] [wuːf] *n* trama *f*.

woof[2] [wʊf] **1** *n* (*bark*) ladrido *m*. **2** *vi* ladrar.

woofer ['wuːfəʳ] *n* altavoz *m* para sonidos graves.

wooing ['wuːɪŋ] *n* galanteo *m*.

wool [wʊl] **1** *n* lana *f*; (*) pelo *m*; **a dyed in the ~ supporter** un partidario fanático, un partidario acérrimo; **to pull the ~ over sb's eyes** dar a uno gato por liebre; **all ~ and a yard wide** (*US*) de lo bueno lo mejor, auténtico, sin trampa ni cartón.

2 *attr* de lana; lanar; ~ **trade** comercio *m* de lana.

wool-gathering ['wʊl,gæðərɪŋ] *n*: **to go ~** estar en la luna, estar en Babia.

woollen, (*US*) **woolen** ['wʊlən] **1** *adj* de lana; lanar, lanero; ~ **industry** industria *f* de la lana.

2 *npl*: **~s** ropa *f* (*esp* interior) de lana; (*Comm*) géneros *mpl* de lana.

woolliness, (*US*) **wooliness** ['wʊlɪnɪs] *n* lanosidad *f*; (*fig*) lo borroso; confusión *f*.

woolly, (*US*) **wooly** ['wʊlɪ] **1** *adj* lanudo, lanoso; de lana; *outline etc* borroso; *idea, thinking* confuso. **2** *npl*: **woollies,** (*US*) **woolies** ropa *f* (*esp* interior) de lana.

woolly-minded ['wʊlɪ'maɪndɪd] *adj* confuso.

woolman ['wʊlmæn] *n*, *pl* **woolmen** ['wʊlmen] (*trader*) comerciante *m* en lanas; (*manufacturer*) dueño *m* de una fábrica textil, lanero *m*.

wool-merchant ['wʊl,mɜːtʃənt] *n* comerciante *m* en lanas, lanero *m*.

woolsack ['wʊlsæk] *n*: **the W~** (*Brit Parl*) saco *m* de lana (*silla del Gran Canciller en la Cámara de los Lores*).

woozy* ['wuːzɪ] *adj* aturdido, confuso; (*Med*) ligeramente indispuesto, mareado.

Wop‡ [wɒp] *n* italiano *m*, -a *f*.

Worcs. *abbr of* **Worcestershire.**

word [wɜːd] **1** *n* (**a**) (*gen*) palabra *f*; vocablo *m*; voz *f*, término *m*; **~s** (*of song*) letra *f*; **~ for ~** palabra por palabra; **~ of honour** palabra *f*, palabra *f* de honor; **high ~s** palabras *fpl* airadas, palabras *fpl* mayores; **fine ~s** palabras *fpl* elocuentes (pero quizá poco sinceras); **a man of few ~s** un hombre nada locuaz; **never a ~** ni una palabra; **by ~ of mouth** de palabra; **too funny for ~s** tremendamente divertido; **too stupid for ~s** de lo más estúpido; **in a ~** en una palabra; **in other ~s** en otros términos; es decir ..., esto es; **in the ~s of Calderón** con palabras de Calderón, como dice Calderón; **in his own ~s** con sus propias palabras; **without a ~** sin decir palabra; **a ~ to the wise is sufficient** al buen entendedor pocas palabras le bastan; **that's not the ~ I would have chosen** yo no me hubiera expresado así; **the ~ is going round that ...** se dice que ..., corre la voz de que ...; **his ~ is law** su palabra es ley; **it's his ~ against mine** es su palabra contra la mía; **it's the last ~ in luxury** es el último grito del lujo; **rough isn't the ~ for it** brutal no basta, brutal es poco; **there is no other ~ for it** no se puede llamar de otro modo; **~s fail me** no encuentro palabras para expresarme; **~s failed me** me quedé de una pieza; **~s passed between them** cambiaron algunas palabras injuriosas; **not to breathe a ~** no decir palabra, no decir ni pío; **to eat one's ~s** tragarse lo dicho, desdecirse, retractarse; **I can't get a ~ out of him** no logro sacarle una palabra; **not to let sb get a ~ in edgeways** no dejar a uno meter baza; **to have a ~ with sb** cambiar unas palabras con uno; **I'll have a ~ with him about it** hablaré con él, lo discutiré con él, se lo mencionaré; **could I have a (short) ~ with you?** ¿me permite una palabra?; **to have ~s with sb** tener palabras con uno, reñir con uno; **the referee had ~s with him** el árbitro le dijo cuatro palabras; **I had a few ~s with him yesterday** cambié algunas palabras con él ayer; **to have the last ~ in an argument** decir la última palabra en una discusión; **I won't hear a ~ against him** no permito que se le critique; **not to mince one's ~s** no tener pelos en la lengua, no morderse la lengua; **to put in a (good) ~ for sb** defender a uno, hablar por uno; **you're putting ~s into my mouth** te refieres a cosas que yo no he dicho; **she didn't say so in so many ~s** no lo dijo exactamente así, no lo dijo así concretamente; **he never said a ~** no dijo una sola palabra; **don't say a ~ about this** de esto no digas ni pío; **nobody had a good ~ to say for him** nadie quería defenderle, nadie habló en su favor; **I now call on Mr X to say a few ~s** ahora le cedo la palabra al Señor X, ahora le invito al Sr X a hacer uso de la palabra; **many a true ~ is spoken in jest** las bromas a veces pueden ser veras; **you took the ~s right out of my mouth** me quitaste la palabra de la boca; **to weigh one's ~s** medir las palabras.

(**b**) (*message*) aviso *m*, recado *m*; noticia *f*; **~ came that ...** llegó noticia de que ..., se supo que ...; **to bring ~ of sth to sb** dar a uno la noticia de algo; **to leave ~** dejar recado; **to leave ~ that ...** dejar dicho que ...; **pass the ~ that it's time to go** diles que es hora de marcharnos; **to send ~** mandar recado; **to send sb ~ of sth** avisar a uno de algo; **to spread the ~** propagar la noticia.

(**c**) (*promise*) palabra *f*; (**upon**) **my ~!** ¡caramba!; **he is a man of his ~** es hombre de entera confianza; **his ~ is as good as his bond** su palabra merece entera confianza; **to be as good as one's ~** cumplir lo prometido; **to break one's ~** faltar a la palabra; **to give sb one's ~ that ...** prometer que ...; **to go back on one's ~** faltar a la palabra; **to hold** (*or* **keep**) **sb to his word** coger a uno la palabra; **to keep one's ~** cumplir su promesa, cumplir lo prometido; **take my ~ for it** te lo aseguro; **I take your ~ for it** acepto lo que me dices, lo creo; **to take sb at his ~** aceptar lo que uno dice.

(**d**) (*order*) orden *f*; (*pass~*) santo *m* y seña; **~ of command** voz *f* de mando; **the ~ has gone round that ...** se ha transmitido la orden de que ...; **to give the ~** dar la orden; **you have only to say the ~** solamente hace falta que des la orden.

(**e**) (*Rel*) Verbo *m*; **the W~ of God** el Verbo de Dios.

2 *vt* redactar; expresar; **a simply ~ed refusal** una negativa sencilla; **it is not very clearly ~ed** los términos no son muy claros; **a well-~ed declaration** una declaración bien expresada; **how shall we ~ it?** ¿cómo lo expresamos?

wordage ['wɜːdɪdʒ] *n* número *m* de palabras, recuento *m* de palabras.

word-blind ['wɜːd,blaɪnd] *adj* aléxico.

word-blindness ['wɜːd,blaɪndnɪs] *n* alexia *f*.

wordbook ['wɜːdbʊk] *n* vocabulario *m*.

word-class ['wɜːdklɑːs] *n* categoría *f* gramatical (de las palabras).

word-count ['wɜːdkaʊnt] *n* recuento *m* de vocabulario.

word-formation ['wɜːdfɔː,meɪʃən] *n* formación *f* de palabras.

word-game ['wɜːdgeɪm] *n* juego *m* de formación (*or* adivinación *etc*) de palabras.

wordiness ['wɜ:dɪnɪs] *n* verbosidad *f*, prolijidad *f*.
wording ['wɜ:dɪŋ] *n* fraseología *f*, estilo *m*; términos *mpl*.
wordless ['wɜ:dlɪs] *adj* sin palabras; silencioso.
wordlist ['wɜ:dlɪst] *n* lista *f* de palabras, vocabulario *m*.
word-of-mouth ['wɜ:dəv'maʊθ] *adj* verbal, oral; *V also* **word 1 (a)**.
word-order ['wɜ:d,ɔ:dəʳ] *n* orden *m* de palabras.
word-perfect ['wɜ:d'pɜ:fɪkt] *adj*: **to be ~** saber perfectamente su papel.
word-picture ['wɜ:d,pɪktʃəʳ] *n* descripción *f*.
wordplay ['wɜ:dpleɪ] *n* juego *m* de palabras.
word-process ['wɜ:d'prəʊses] *vt* procesar.
word-processing ['wɜ:d'prəʊsesɪŋ] *n* proceso *m* de textos, tratamiento *m* de textos.
word-processor ['wɜ:d'prəʊsesəʳ] *n* procesador *m* de textos, procesador *m* de palabras.
wordsmith ['wɜ:dsmɪθ] *n* (*hum*) artífice *mf* de la palabra, (*esp*) poeta *mf*.
wordwrap ['wɜ:dræp] *n* salto *m* de línea automático.
wordy ['wɜ:dɪ] *adj* verboso, prolijo.
wore [wɔ:ʳ] *pret of* **wear**.
work [wɜ:k] **1** *n* **(a)** (*gen*) trabajo *m*; empleo *m*, ocupación *f*; **to be at ~** estar trabajando; estar en la fábrica, estar en la oficina (*etc*); tener trabajo; **there are forces at ~** hay fuerzas en movimiento; **to be in ~** tener trabajo, tener un empleo; **to be out of ~** estar desempleado; estar parado, no tener trabajo; **to put** (*or* **throw**) **sb out of ~** privar a uno de trabajo; **to make short ~ of sth** despachar algo rápidamente, (*fig*) zamparse algo; **to go the right way to ~** empezar correctamente; **to set to ~** ponerse a trabajar, (*fig*) poner manos a la obra; **to set sb to ~** poner a uno a trabajar.

(b) (*task, ~ to be done*) trabajo *m*; labor *f*; **a piece of ~** un trabajo, una labor; **the dictator and all his ~s** el dictador y todo lo suyo; **day's ~** jornal *m*; **it's all in a day's ~** estamos acostumbrados a eso; **it was grim ~** (*fig*) fue una cosa repugnante; **it's nice ~ if you can get it** es muy agradable para los que tienen esa suerte; **~ in progress** trabajo *m* en curso; **~ has begun on the new dam** se han comenzado las obras del nuevo embalse; **it's closed for ~ on the steeple** está cerrado debido a las obras del campanario; **I have my ~ cut out as it is** ya tengo trabajo hasta por encima de las cejas; **I had my ~ cut out to stop it** me costó detenerlo; **you'll have your ~ cut out trying to stop him** te costará muchísimo trabajo impedirle; **to do one's ~** hacer su trabajo; **the medicine had done its ~** la medicina había tenido efecto.

(c) (*product*: *Art, Liter etc*) obra *f*; **the ~s of God** las obras de Dios; **good ~s** buenas obras *fpl*; **a literary ~** una obra literaria; **~ of art** obra *f* de arte; **the ~s of Cervantes** las obras de Cervantes; **~ of reference** libro *m* de consulta.

(d) ~s (*Mil*) obras *fpl*, fortificaciones *fpl*; (*public*) obras *fpl*; **Ministry of W~s** Ministerio *m* de Obras Públicas.

(e) ~s (*Mech*) mecanismo *m*; motor *m*; **to bung** (*or* **gum**) **up the ~s** paralizar el motor.

(f) ~s (*Brit*: *factory*) fábrica *f*; taller *m*; **gas~s** fábrica *f* de gas.

(g) (*) **the ~s** todo, la totalidad; **they gave him the ~s** le hicieron sufrir, le sometieron a un severo interrogatorio (*etc*); **let's give it the ~s** vamos a probarlo, probemos.

(h) ~s (‡: *syringe*) chuta‡ *f*.

2 *attr*: **~ camp** campamento *m* laboral; **~s council** consejo *m* de obreros, comité *m* de empresa; **~ experience** experiencia *f* laboral; **~ factor** factor *m* laboral; **~s manager** gerente *m* de fábrica; **~s outing** excursión *f* del personal; **~ relief** trabajo *m* para asistencia a los parados; **~ study** estudio *m* del trabajo, (*US Scol*) práctica *f* estudiantil; **~ week** (*US*) semana *f* laboral.

3 *vt* **(a)** (*cause to ~*) *men* hacer trabajar; **they ~ed us from 8 till 6** nos hicieron trabajar de 8 a 6.

(b) (*Mech etc*) *machine* hacer funcionar; manejar, operar; *brake* accionar; *moving part* mover; **it is ~ed by electricity** funciona con electricidad, es accionado por electricidad; **can you ~ it?** ¿sabes manejarlo?; **can we ~ that scheme again?** ¿podemos volver a emplear ese sistema?; **he ~ed the lever up and down** movió la palanca hacia arriba y hacia abajo.

(c) (*bring about*) *change* producir, motivar; *miracle, cure etc* hacer, efectuar, operar; *mischief* hacer; **to ~ it*** lograrlo, conseguirlo, manejar las cosas; **they ~ed it so that she could come*** se las arreglaron para que ella pudiese venir; **they ~ed his promotion*** agenciaron su ascenso, hicieron diligencias para asegurar su ascenso.

(d) (*Sew*) bordar; **~ed with blue thread** bordado de hilo azul.

(e) *wood etc* tallar; *metal* trabajar; **~ed flint** piedra *f* tallada.

(f) *mine* explotar; *land* cultivar; **he ~s the eastern part of the province** trabaja en la parte este de la provincia; se dedica a cubrir la parte este de la provincia; **we ~ed the river bank looking for the plant** recorrimos la orilla del río buscando la planta; **this land has not been ~ed for many years** estas tierras hace mucho tiempo que no se cultivan.

(g) to ~ one's passage on a boat costear el viaje trabajando.

(h) (*manoeuvre etc*) *ship* maniobrar; **to ~ an incident into a book** introducir un episodio en un libro; **we'll try to ~ in a reference somewhere** trataremos de insinuar una referencia en alguna parte; **can't you ~ me into your plans?** ¿no sería posible dejarme entrar a formar parte de tus proyectos?; **to ~ one's hands free** lograr soltar las manos; **to ~ one's way to the top of the company** llegar a ocupar un alto puesto en la sociedad a fuerza de trabajar; **to ~ one's way up a cliff** escalar a duras penas un precipicio, escalar poco a poco un precipicio (*and V* **way (d)**).

4 *vi* **(a)** (*gen*) trabajar (*at, on* en); (*be in a job*) tener trabajo, tener un empleo; **to ~ hard** trabajar mucho; **to ~ like a slave** (*or* **Trojan** *etc*) trabajar como un demonio; **what are you ~ing at** (*or* **on**) **now?** ¿en qué trabajas ahora?, (*more generally*) ¿a qué te dedicas ahora?; **they're ~ing on the car now** están trabajando en el coche ahora; **they will get ~ing on it at once** empezarán la reparación (*etc*) en seguida; **the police are ~ing on it** la policía lo está investigando; **have you any clue to ~ on?** ¿tienes alguna pista que seguir?; **there are few facts to ~ on** apenas hay datos en que basarse; **we ~ on the principle that ...** nos atenemos al principio de que ..., nos guiamos por el principio de que ...; **we'll ~ on him*** trataremos de convencerle.

(b) (*Mech etc*) funcionar, marchar; **it won't ~** no funciona; **'not ~ing'** (*lift etc*) 'no funciona'; **to get sth ~ing** hacer funcionar algo; reparar algo para que funcione; **it ~s off the mains** funciona con electricidad de la red, se conecta con la red; **the motor ~s with gas** el motor funciona con gas; **it's ~ing as planned** funciona de acuerdo con el plan.

(c) (*medicine etc*) ser eficaz, surtir efecto, obrar; **how long does it take to ~?** ¿cuánto tiempo hace falta para que empiece a surtir efecto?; **this can ~ both ways** esto puede ser un arma de doble filo, esto puede ser contraproducente; **the scheme won't ~** el proyecto no es práctico, esto no será factible, el proyecto no tendrá resultados útiles; **it won't ~, I tell you!** ¡te digo que no se puede (hacer)!

(d) (*yeast*) fermentar.

(e) (*mouth, face*) torcerse, moverse.

(f) to ~ loose *V* **loose**.

5 *vr*: **to ~ o.s. to death** matarse trabajando, matarse con exceso de trabajo; **to ~ o.s. into a frenzy** excitarse hasta el frenesí, exaltarse en grado extremo.

◆**work away** *vi* seguir trabajando, trabajar sin parar.
◆**work in 1** *vt screw etc* introducir poco a poco; meter con esfuerzo; *quotation etc* deslizar.

2 *vi* **(a)** (*substance*) penetrar poco a poco, calarse; introducirse.

(b) it ~s in quite well with our plans esto se ajusta bastante bien a nuestros planes, esto cuadra bastante bien con nuestros planes.

◆**work off 1** *vt* **(a)** *debt etc* pagar con su trabajo.

(b) to ~ off one's feelings desahogarse, aliviarse; **to ~ off surplus fat** quitarse las grasas excesivas trabajando; **don't ~ your bad temper off on me!** ¡no te desahogues riñendo conmigo!

2 *vi* (*part*) separarse, soltarse (con el uso); (*pain*) ir desapareciendo.

◆**work on** *vi* seguir trabajando.
◆**work out 1** *vt* **(a)** *problem* resolver; *sum* calcular, hacer; *idea* desarrollar, elaborar; *plan* trazar, elaborar; **to ~ out one's own solution** determinar su propia suerte.

(b) *mine* agotar.

(c) to ~ out one's time servir el aprendizaje; (*in prison*) cumplir su condena.

2 *vi* **(a)** resultar; resolverse; **it doesn't ~ out** (*sum*) no sale; **it ~s out at £8** llega a 8 libras, asciende a 8 libras, viene a sumar 8 libras; **how much does it ~ out at?** ¿cuánto suma?; **everything ~ed out well** todo resultó perfecto, la cosa salió bien; **how did it ~ out?** ¿qué tal salió?

(b) (*athlete*) entrenarse, prepararse.

◆**work over*** *vt* (*beat up*) dar una paliza a, apalizar.

◆**work round** *vi*: **eventually he ~ed round to the price** por fin llegó a mencionar el precio; **what are you ~ing round to?** ¿adónde va a parar todo esto?

◆**work up 1** *vt* (**a**) *business* desarrollar; fomentar; *theme* elaborar; **together they ~ed the business up from nothing** entre los dos crearon el negocio de la nada; **you could ~ this story up into a film** podrías elaborar este cuento para hacer una película.

(**b**) *feelings* excitar; *crowd etc* emocionar, encandilar; **it gets me properly ~ed up** (*moved*) me emociona mucho, con esto me emociono mucho; (*with anger*) me saca de quicio; **now don't get ~ed up!** ¡no te pongas nervioso!, ¡cálmate!; **the speaker was ~ing them up into a frenzy** el orador excitaba los ánimos hasta el frenesí.

2 *vi*: **what are you ~ing up to?** ¿adónde va a parar todo esto?, ¿qué propósito tiene todo esto?; **I thought he was ~ing up to a proposal** creía que estaba preparando el terreno para hacerme una declaración.

3 *vr*: **to ~ o.s. up** exaltarse, sofocarse; emocionarse mucho; ponerse nervioso.

workable ['wɜːkəbl] *adj* práctico, factible.

workaday ['wɜːkədeɪ] *adj* de cada día; (*fig*) rutinario, prosaico.

workaholic [ˌwɜːkə'hɒlɪk] *n* trabajador *m* obsesivo, trabajadora *f* obsesiva, curroadicto* *m*, -a *f*.

workbasket ['wɜːkˌbɑːskɪt] *n* neceser *m* de costura.

workbench ['wɜːkbenʧ] *n* obrador *m*, banco *m* de trabajo.

workbook ['wɜːkbʊk] *n* libro *m* de trabajo; (*Scol*) cuaderno *m*.

workbox ['wɜːkbɒks] *n* neceser *m* de costura.

workday ['wɜːkdeɪ] *n* (*US*) día *m* laborable.

work ethic ['wɜːkˌeθɪk] *n* ética *f* del trabajo.

worker ['wɜːkəʳ] *n* trabajador *m*, -ora *f*; obrero *m*, -a *f* (*also Pol*); operario *m*, -a *f*; (*ant, bee*) obrera *f*; **all the ~s in the industry** todos los trabajadores de la industria; **what about the ~s?** ¿y los obreros?, ¡justicia para los obreros!; **he's a fast ~** trabaja con toda prisa; (*fig*) trabaja rápido.

worker-ant ['wɜːkərænt] *n* hormiga *f* obrera.

worker-bee ['wɜːkəbiː] *n* abeja *f* obrera.

worker-priest ['wɜːkəpriːst] *n* sacerdote *m* obrero.

work file ['wɜːkfaɪl] *n* fichero *m* de trabajo.

workflow ['wɜːkfləʊ] *n* volumen *m* de trabajo.

workforce ['wɜːkfɔːs] *n* mano *f* de obra, personal *m*.

workhorse ['wɜːkˌhɔːs] *n* caballo *m* de tiro; (*fig*) persona *f* muy trabajadora.

workhouse ['wɜːkhaʊs] *n*, *pl* **workhouses** ['wɜːkˌhaʊzɪz] (*Brit Hist*) asilo *m* de pobres; asilo *m* de ancianos; asilo *m* para desamparados.

work-in ['wɜːkɪn] *n* ocupación *f* laboral (de una fábrica *etc*), encierro *m*.

working ['wɜːkɪŋ] **1** *adj*: **~ assets** activo *m* circulante; **~ capital** capital *m* de explotación; **the ~ class** la clase obrera; **~ clothes** ropa *f* de trabajo; **~ conditions** condiciones *fpl* de trabajo; **~ control** control *m* efectivo; **~ day** (*Brit*) (*weekday*) día *m* laborable, (*time*) jornada *f*; **~ environment** ambiente *m* laboral; **~ expenses** gastos *mpl* de explotación; **~ face** cara *f* de trabajo; **~ hypothesis** hipótesis *f* de guía; **~ lunch** almuerzo *m* de trabajo; **~ majority** mayoría *f* suficiente; **~ man** obrero *m*; **~ model** modelo *m* que funciona; **~ mother** madre *f* trabajadora; **~ paper** documento *m* de trabajo; **~ partner** socio *m* activo; **~ party** (*Brit*) grupo *m* de trabajo; **~ population** población *f* ocupada, población *f* activa; **~ week** semana *f* laborable; **~ woman** mujer *f* trabajadora.

2 *n* (**a**) trabajo *m*, el trabajar; funcionamiento *m*; explotación *f*; manejo *m*, operación *f*; labra *f*, laboreo *m*.

(**b**) **~s** (*Min etc*) labores *fpl* .

working-class ['wɜːkɪŋklɑːs] *adj* de la clase obrera.

workload ['wɜːkləʊd] *n* cantidad *f* de trabajo.

workman ['wɜːkmən] *n*, *pl* **workmen** ['wɜːkmən] obrero *m*; trabajador *m*; **workmen's compensation insurance** seguro *m* de compensación por accidentes laborales; **to be a good ~** ser buen trabajador, trabajar bien.

workmanlike ['wɜːkmənlaɪk] *adj* competente, concienzudo.

workmanship ['wɜːkmənʃɪp] *n* hechura *f*; arte *m*, artificio *m*; destreza *f*, habilidad *f*; **of fine ~** esmerado, exquisito.

workmate ['wɜːkmeɪt] *n* compañero *m*, -a *f* de trabajo.

workout ['wɜːkaʊt] *n* (período *m* de) entrenamiento *m*, ejercicios *mpl*.

workpeople ['wɜːkˌpiːpl] *n* obreros *mpl*; personal *m*, mano *f* de obra.

work-permit ['wɜːkˌpɜːmɪt] *n* permiso *m* de trabajo.

workplace ['wɜːkˌpleɪs] *n* lugar *m* de trabajo.

workroom ['wɜːkrʊm] *n* taller *m*, sala *f* de trabajo.

work-sharing ['wɜːkˌʃɛərɪŋ] *n* repartimiento *m* del trabajo.

worksheet ['wɜːkʃiːt] *n* hoja *f* de trabajo.

workshop ['wɜːkʃɒp] *n* taller *m*; (*at congress etc*) taller *m* de trabajo.

workshy ['wɜːkʃaɪ] *adj* gandul, holgazán, vago.

workstation ['wɜːkˌsteɪʃən] *n* puesto *m* de trabajo, estación *f* de trabajo.

worktable ['wɜːkˌteɪbl] *n* mesa *f* de trabajo.

work therapy ['wɜːkˌθerəpɪ] *n* laborterapia *f*, terapia *f* laboral.

worktop ['wɜːktɒp] *n* encimera *f*.

work-to-rule ['wɜːktə'ruːl] *n* (*Brit*) huelga *f* de celo, paro *m* técnico.

work-worn ['wɜːkwɔːn] *adj* agotado (por el trabajo).

world [wɜːld] **1** *n* (**a**) (*gen, Geog*) mundo *m*, tierra *f*; **all the ~ over** en todas partes del mundo; **are there ~s other than ours?** ¿existen otros mundos aparte de éste nuestro?; **it's a small ~** el mundo es un pañuelo; **to feel on top of the ~** estar como un reloj; **to go round the ~** dar la vuelta al mundo; **to knock about the ~, to see the ~** ver mundo; **he lives in a ~ of his own** habita un pequeño mundo suyo, queda absorto en sus cosas sin prestar atención a otros; **the ~ and his wife** todos, todo quisque; **the Joe Soaps of this ~ always lose out** los Rodríguez de este mundo siempre salen perdiendo.

(**b**) **New W~** Nuevo Mundo *m*; **Old W~** Viejo Mundo *m*.

(**c**) (*realm*) mundo *m*; **the ~ of sport, the sporting ~** el mundo deportivo, el mundo de los deportes; **the business ~** el mundo comercial, los negocios; **the animal ~** el reino animal; **the Roman ~** el mundo romano; **the ~ of dreams** el mundo de la fantasía, el mundo de los sueños.

(**d**) (*society*) **man of the ~** hombre *m* de mundo; **to come down in the ~** venir a menos; **to go up in the ~** prosperar, hacer progresos en su carrera, ser ascendido; **to have the ~ at one's feet** triunfar, estar en la cumbre de la fama (*etc*); **to take the ~ as it is** adaptarse a la realidad, aceptar la vida como es.

(**e**) (*this life, Rel etc*) mundo *m*; siglo *m*; **the other ~, the next ~, the ~ to come** el otro mundo; **~ without end** por los siglos de los siglos; **in the ~** (*Eccl*) en el siglo; **in this ~** en esta vida; **it's out of this ~** es tremendo, es increíble; **he's not long for this ~** le queda poco tiempo de vida; **to bring into the ~** echar al mundo; **to come into the ~** nacer.

(**f**) (*emphatic idioms etc*) **not for all the ~** por nada del mundo; **nothing in the ~ would make me do it, I wouldn't do it for the ~** no lo haría por nada del mundo; **what in the ~ can I do about it?** ¿qué demonios puedo hacer?; **it's what she most wants in the ~** es lo que ella más desea sobre todas las cosas; **to be alone in the ~** estar totalmente solo, estar completamente desamparado; **it was for all the ~ as if ...** fue exactamente como si + *subj*; **I'm the ~'s worst cook** soy el peor cocinero del mundo; **she's** (*or* **she means**) **all the ~ to me** para mí ella es el mundo entero; **their views are ~s apart** sus opiniones están totalmente opuestas; **they're ~s apart politically** en política los separa un abismo; **there is a ~ of difference between A and X** A y X son totalmente distintos; **there is a ~ of difference between buying one and using one** de comprarlo a usarlo hay gran trecho; **since the ~ began** desde que el mundo es mundo; **to be dead to the ~** (*asleep*) estar profundamente dormido, (*drunk*) estar completamente borracho; **it did him the ~ of good** le hizo la mar de bien; le fue muy provechoso; **he'll never set the ~ on fire** nunca hará nada extraordinario; **to think the ~ of sb** tener un altísimo concepto de uno.

2 *attr* mundial; universal; **W~ Bank** Banco *m* Mundial; **~ champion** campeón *m*, -ona *f* mundial; **~ championship** campeonato *m* mundial; **W~ Cup** Copa *f* Mundial; **~ dealer network** red *f* de tratantes mundiales; **~ fair** feria *f* mundial; **~ language** lengua *f* universal; **~ market** mercado *m* mundial; **~ market price** precio *m* de mercado mundial; **~ power** potencia *f* mundial; **on a ~ scale** a escala mundial; **W~ Series** (*US*) campeonato *m* nacional de béisbol; **W~ title** título *m* mundial; **~ war** guerra *f* mundial; **W~ War One** la Primera Guerra Mundial; **W~ War Two** la Segunda Guerra Mundial.

world-beater ['wɜːldˌbiːtəʳ] *n* campeón *m*, -ona *f* mundial.

world-class ['wɜːldklɑːs] *adj* de calidad mundial.

world-famous ['wɜːld'feɪməs] *adj* mundialmente conocido, famosísimo.

worldliness ['wɜːldlɪnɪs] *n* mundanería *f*.

worldly ['wɜːldlɪ] *adj* mundano; **all my ~ goods** todo lo que tengo, todo lo mío.

worldly-wisdom ['wɜːldlɪ'wɪzdəm] *m* mundología *f*; astucia *f*.

worldly-wise ['wɜːldlɪ'waɪz] *adj* que tiene mucho mundo; astuto.

world-shaking ['wɜːld,ʃeɪkɪŋ] *adj*, **world-shattering** ['wɜːld,ʃætərɪŋ] *adj* pasmoso.

world view ['wɜːld'vjuː] *n* cosmovisión *f*.

world-weariness ['wɜːld'wɪərɪnɪs] *n* hastío *m*.

world-weary ['wɜːld'wɪərɪ] *adj* hastiado, cansado de la vida.

world-wide ['wɜːld'waɪd] **1** *adv* mundialmente, en (*or* por) todo el mundo. **2** *adj* mundial, universal.

WORM [wɔːm] *abbr of* **write once read many times**.

worm [wɜːm] **1** *n* (**a**) (*grub*) gusano *m*; (*earth~*) lombriz *f*; (*person*) canalla *m*, persona *f* de lo más vil; **~s** (*Med*) lombrices *fpl*; **to have ~s** (*animal*) tener lombrices; **the ~ will turn** la paciencia tiene límite.

(**b**) (*Mech*) tornillo *m* sin fin.

2 *vt* (**a**) **to ~ one's way along** serpentear, avanzar serpenteando; **to ~ one's way into a group** insinuarse en un grupo, introducirse astutamente en un grupo; **to ~ a secret out of sb** sonsacar un secreto a uno.

(**b**) *animal* quitar las lombrices a.

3 *vr*: **to ~ o.s. along** arrastrarse como un gusano; **to ~ o.s. through sth** atravesar algo serpenteando.

worm-eaten ['wɜːm,iːtn] *adj wood* carcomido; *cloth* apolillado.

wormhole ['wɜːmhəʊl] *n* agujero *m* de gusano, picadura *f* de polilla.

worm(ing) powder ['wɜːm(ɪŋ),paʊdəʳ] *n* polvos *mpl* antigusanos.

wormwood ['wɜːmwʊd] *n* ajenjo *m*; (*fig*) hiel *f*, amargura *f*.

wormy ['wɜːmɪ] *adj* gusanoso, agusanado, lleno de gusanos; carcomido; apolillado.

worn [wɔːn] **1** *ptp of* **wear**. **2** *adj carpet etc* gastado, deteriorado; *face, person* cansado; **he's looking very ~** tiene aspecto de muy cansado.

worn-out ['wɔːn'aʊt] *adj* gastado; estropeado; inservible; inútil; anticuado; **to be ~** (*person*) estar rendido.

worried ['wʌrɪd] *adj tone, look etc* inquieto, preocupado; **to be ~ about sth** inquietarse por algo, estar preocupado por algo; **I'm not ~ either way** me es igual con cualquiera; **that's got them ~** eso les ha dado en qué pensar; **you had me ~ for a moment** empezabas a preocuparme; **to look ~** tener aire preocupado, parecer estar inquieto.

worrier ['wʌrɪəʳ] *n* aprensivo *m*, -a *f*; **he's a terrible ~** es muy aprensivo, se inquieta por cualquier cosa.

worrisome ['wʌrɪsəm] *adj* inquietante, preocupante; aprensivo.

worry ['wʌrɪ] **1** *n* inquietud *f*, preocupación *f*; cuidado *m*; problema *m*; **~ line** arruga *f* de preocupación; **financial worries** preocupaciones *fpl* financieras; **he had business worries** tenía problemas con sus negocios; **it's a great ~ to us all** nos trae a todos muy preocupados; **what's your ~?** ¿qué mosca te ha picado?, ¿qué problema es éste?; **the ~ of having to +** *infin* el problema de tener que + *infin*; **to settle sb's worries** resolver los problemas de uno.

2 *vt* (**a**) (*make anxious*) inquietar, intranquilizar, preocupar; molestar; **that photo worries me** esa foto me inquieta; no estoy satisfecho con esa foto; **what worries me is not that at all** no es eso lo que me preocupa; **it worries me terribly** me tiene preocupadísimo; **that doesn't ~ me in the least** eso me tiene absolutamente sin cuidado.

(**b**) (*dog etc*) *prey* pillar, sacudir y morder, morder sacudiendo; **that dog worries sheep** el perro ese ataca las ovejas; **is this man ~ing you, madam?** ¿le molesta este hombre, señora?

3 *vi* inquietarse, preocuparse (*about, over* por); apurarse; molestarse; **he worries a lot** se apura por cualquier cosa; **not to ~*!** ¡no hay problema!; ¡todos tranquilos!; **don't ~!** ¡no te preocupes!; ¡descuida!; **it's all right, don't ~** está bien, no te molestes; **don't ~ about me** no te preocupes por mí; **that's nothing to ~ about** no hay que preocuparse por eso; **I've got quite enough to ~ about without that** tengo bastante problema sin preocuparme de eso; **I should ~!** y a mí ¿qué?

◆**worry at** *vt bone etc V* **2** (**b**); *problem V* **worry out**.

◆**worry out** *vt*: **to ~ out a problem** esforzarse por resolver un problema, devanarse los sesos para resolver un problema; **finally we worried it out** por fin lo resolvimos a costa de mucho trabajo.

worrying ['wʌrɪɪŋ] *adj* inquietante, preocupante.

worse [wɜːs] **1** *adj comp of* **bad**; peor; inferior; **A is ~ than B** A es peor que B, A es inferior a B; **~ and ~!** ¡peor todavía!; **it gets ~ and ~** va de mal en peor; **it's ~ than ever** es peor que nunca; **it could have been ~!** ¡menos mal!; **it would have been ~ if ...** hubiera sido más grave si ...; **it will be the ~ for you** será peor para ti; **so much the ~ for him** tanto peor para él; **to be the ~ for drink** estar algo borracho, estar tomado (*LAm*); **to be the ~ for wear** estar deteriorado (*and V* **wear**); **he is none the ~ for it** no se ha hecho daño; la experiencia no le ha hecho mal (*V also* **none**); **to get ~, to grow ~** empeorar, hacerse peor, (*Med*) ponerse peor, empeorar; **to make a situation ~** agravar una situación, hacer una situación más difícil; **to make matters ~** para colmo de desgracias; **I don't think any the ~ of you** esto no afecta la opinión que tengo de ti.

2 *adv comp of* **badly**; **it hurts ~** me duele más; **she behaves ~ than ever** se comporta peor que nunca; **you might do ~** hay cosas peores; **you might do ~ than to +** *infin* sería quizá posible + *infin*, quizá sea aconsejable + *infin*; **he is now ~ off than before** ahora está peor que antes; **we are ~ off than them for books** en cuanto a libros nosotros estamos peores que ellos.

3 *n* el peor, lo peor; **there is ~ to come** hay más, todavía no te he dicho (*etc*) lo peor; **it's changed for the ~** ha empeorado.

worsen ['wɜːsn] **1** *vt* agravar, hacer peor; hacer más difícil.

2 *vi* empeorar, hacerse peor; agravarse; hacerse más difícil; (*Med*) ponerse peor, empeorar.

worsening ['wɜːsnɪŋ] **1** *adj situation* que empeora, que va de mal en peor. **2** *n* empeoramiento *m*.

worship ['wɜːʃɪp] **1** *n* (**a**) (*adoration*) adoración *f*, veneración *f*; (*organized ~*) culto *m* (*of* a); (*church service*) culto *m*, oficio *m*; **with a look of ~** con una mirada llena de adoración; **place of ~** edificio *m* de culto.

(**b**) (*esp Brit*: *in titles*) **His W~ the Mayor of X** el señor alcalde de X; **Your W~** (*to judge*) señor juez, (*to mayor*) señor alcalde; **if your w~ wishes** (*iro*) si el caballero lo desea, si su señoría quiere.

2 *vt* adorar (*also fig*), venerar.

3 *vi* asistir al culto, ir a misa (*etc*); **to ~ at the shrine of ...** rezar en el santuario de ...

worshipful ['wɜːʃɪpfʊl] *adj* (*esp Brit*: *in titles*) excelentísimo.

worshipper, (*US*) **worshiper** ['wɜːʃɪpəʳ] *n* adorador *m*, -ora *f*, devoto *m*, -a *f*; **~s** (*collectively*) fieles *mpl*.

worst [wɜːst] **1** *adj superl of* **bad**; (el) peor; **the ~ film of the three** la peor película de las tres; **~ case analysis** análisis *m* del peor de los casos.

2 *adv superl of* **badly**; peor; **I did it ~** yo lo hice peor.

3 *n* lo peor; **in the ~ of the winter** en lo peor del invierno; **in the ~ of the storm** en el peor momento de la tormenta; **when the crisis was at its ~** en el momento más grave de la crisis; **at (the) ~** en el peor de los casos; **that's the ~ of it** ésa es la peor parte; **the ~ of it is that ...** lo peor del caso es que ...; **if the ~ comes to the ~** si pasa lo peor; **do your ~!** ¡haga todo lo que quiera!; **to get the ~ of it** salir perdiendo, llevar la peor parte, sufrir más que su contrincante; **to give sb the ~ of it** derrotar a uno; **we're over (***or* **past) the ~ of it now** lo peor ha pasado, hemos vencido la cuesta ya; **once you get the ~ over** en cuanto salves el bache; **to think the ~ of sb** pensar lo peor de uno; tener una opinión bajísima de uno.

4 *vt* vencer, derrotar; salir superior a, quedar por encima de.

worsted ['wʊstɪd] *n* estambre *m*.

worth [wɜːθ] **1** *adj* (**a**) (*in monetary senses*) equivalente a, que vale, del valor de; **it's ~ £5** vale 5 libras; **what's this ~?** ¿cuánto vale esto?; **it's not ~ much** no vale mucho; apenas tiene valor; **he was ~ a million when he died** murió millonario, murió dejando una fortuna de un millón; **what's the old man ~?** ¿cuánto dinero tiene el viejo?; **one Ruritanian is ~ 3 Slobodians** un ruritano vale por (*or* equivale a) 3 eslobodios; **I tell you this for what it's ~** te digo esto sin poder afirmar que sea cierto, te digo esto por si acaso el dato te interesa; **it's more than my job's ~ to tell you** me costaría mi empleo decirte eso; **to run for all one is ~** correr a todo correr; **to sing for all one is ~** cantar con toda el alma.

(**b**) (*deserving*) digno de, que merece; **it's not ~ it, it's not ~ the trouble** no vale la pena; **a thing ~ having** una cosa digna de ser poseída, una cosa que vale la pena adquirir; **is the book ~ buying?** ¿me vale la pena comprar el libro? **it's ~ thinking about** merece que se considere, merece consideración; *V* **while**.

2 *n* (*monetary*) valor *m*; (*fig*) valía *f*, mérito *m*; **£30's ~**

of books libros *mpl* por valor de 30 libras; **50 pesetas' ~ of sweets** 50 pesetas de bombones; **he had no chance to show his true ~** no tuvo ocasión de demostrar su verdadero valía; **his moral ~ is not in question** no se trata de su valor moral; **what's the ~ of this table?** ¿cuánto vale esta mesa?; *V* **money's-worth**.

worthily ['wɜːðɪlɪ] *adv* dignamente; **to respond ~ to an occasion** estar a la altura de las circunstancias.

worthiness ['wɜːðɪnɪs] *n* mérito *m*, merecimiento *m*.

worthless ['wɜːθlɪs] *adj* sin valor; inútil, que no vale para nada; **~ cheque** cheque *m* sin fondos; **a ~ individual** una persona despreciable; **he's not completely ~** no es que carezca absolutamente de buenas cualidades.

worthlessness ['wɜːθlɪsnɪs] *n* falta *f* de valor; inutilidad *f*; lo despreciable.

worthwhile ['wɜːθ'waɪl] *adj* valioso, útil; digno de consideración; que vale la pena; **a ~ film** una película seria, una película que merece atención; *V also* **while**.

worthy ['wɜːðɪ] **1** *adj* **(a)** (*meritorious*) meritorio; benemérito; respetable; loable, plausible; *motive etc* honesto, honrado; **a ~ person** una persona respetable; **your ~ newspaper** (*letter to editor*) su estimado periódico.

(b) (*deserving*) **~ of** digno de; **~ of remark** notable, digno de notar; **~ of respect** digno de respeto, respetable; **to be ~ of sth** ser digno de algo, merecer algo; **it is ~ of note that ...** vale observar que ...; es notable que ...; **that comment was not ~ of you** esa observación fue indigna de Vd; **the car is ~ of a better driver** el coche merece tener mejor conductor.

2 *n* (*freq hum*) personaje *m*; dignatario *m*.

wossname* ['wɒsneɪm] *pron* fulano; **old ~ with the glasses** fulano el de las gafas.

wot‡ [wɒt] *pron interrog* = **what 2 (b)**.

wotcher‡ ['wɒtʃəʳ] *excl* (*Brit*) ¡hola!

would [wʊd] *v aux* **1 (a)** (*used to form conditional tense*) **she ~ come** vendría; **if you asked him he ~ do it** si se lo pidieras lo haría; **if you had asked him he ~ have done it** si se lo hubieras pedido lo habría hecho (*or* lo hubiera hecho); **I thought you ~ want to know** se me figuraba que desearías saber; **I ~ have a word with him (if I were you)** sería aconsejable discutirlo con él; **I ~n't worry too much if I were you** yo en tu lugar no me preocuparía mucho de eso; **you'd never know she was not a native Spanish speaker** nadie diría que el español no es su lengua materna.

(b) (*conditional, emphatic*) **you ~ be the one to forget** desde luego eres tú el que se olvida; **it ~ be you!** ¡tú tenías que ser!; **well he ~, ~n't he?** es lógico que dijera (*etc*) eso.

(c) (*conditional, probability*) **it ~ seem so** así parece ser; **it ~ be about 8 o'clock** serían las 8.

(d) (*conjecture*) **what ~ this be?** ¿qué será esto?

2 (a) (*wish*) querer; **what ~ you have me do?** ¿qué quieres que haga?; **try as he ~** por mucho que se esforzara, por más que intentase; **the place where I ~ be** el lugar donde me gustaría estar; **~ (that) it were not so!** (*liter*) ¡ojalá no fuera así!; **~ to God!, ~ to heaven!** (*liter*) ¡ojalá!

(b) (*consent*) querer; **~ you care for some tea?** ¿quieres una taza de té?; **~ you tell me your name?** ¿me hace el favor de darme su nombre?; **he ~ not do it** no quería hacerlo, se negó a hacerlo; **he ~n't say if it was true** no quiso decir si era verdad.

(c) (*habit*) **he ~ paint it each year** solía pintarlo cada año, lo pintaba cada año.

would-be ['wʊdbiː] *adj*: **a ~ poet** un aspirante a poeta, uno que presume de poeta, uno que quiere ser poeta.

wouldn't ['wʊdnt] = **would not**.

would've ['wʊdəv] = **would have**.

wound¹ [wuːnd] **1** *n* herida *f*; **to lick one's ~s** lamer sus heridas; **to open up old ~s** renovar la herida.

2 *vt* herir (*also fig*); **to ~ sb's feelings** herir los sentimientos de uno.

wound² [waʊnd] *pret and ptp of* **wind²**.

wounded ['wuːndɪd] **1** *adj* herido (*also fig*). **2** *npl*: **the ~** los heridos.

wounding ['wuːndɪŋ] *adj remark, tone* hiriente, mordaz.

wove [wəʊv] *pret of* **weave**.

woven ['wəʊvən] *ptp of* **weave**.

wow* [waʊ] **1** *excl* ¡caramba!, ¡caray*! **2** *vt* chiflar*, cautivar. **3** *n* (*Acoustics*) lloro *m*, bajón *m* del volumen.

WP (a) *n abbr of* **word processing, word processor**. **(b)** *abbr of* **weather permitting** si lo permite el tiempo.

WPC *n abbr of* **Woman Police Constable**.

WPI *n abbr of* **wholesale price index**.

wpm *abbr of* **words per minute** palabras *fpl* por minuto, p.p.m.

WRAC *n* (*Brit*) *abbr of* **Women's Royal Army Corps**.

wrack¹ [ræk] *n* (*Bot*) fuco *m*, alga *f*.

wrack² [ræk] = **rack¹** *and* **rack²**.

WRAF *n* (*Brit*) *abbr of* **Women's Royal Air Force**.

wraith [reɪθ] *n* fantasma *m*.

wrangle ['ræŋgl] **1** *n* altercado *m*, riña *f* (indecorosa), pelea *f* (*LAm*). **2** *vi* reñir (indecorosamente), pelear (*LAm*) (*about, over* a causa de, *with* con); (*in bargaining*) regatear.

wrangling ['ræŋglɪŋ] *n* riña *f*, discusión *f*.

wrap [ræp] **1** *n* (*indoor*) bata *f*, (*outdoor*) abrigo *m*; **to keep sth under ~s** (*fig*) guardar algo secreto, no revelar algo.

2 *vt* (*also* **to ~ up**) envolver; (*for warmth*) arropar; (*cover*) cubrir; **shall I ~ it (up) for you?** ¿se lo envuelvo?; **he does so ~ it up** (*fig*) lo dice con tal exceso de palabras, lo expone de manera tan enmarañada; **to be ~ped up in** estar envuelto en; (*fig*) estar absorto en, estar completamente dedicado a; **he is ~ped up in her** no quiere pensar en nada sino en ella, está absorto en ella; **they are ~ped in each other** están absortos el uno en el otro.

◆wrap up 1 *vt* = **wrap 2**.

2 *vi* arroparse, arrebujarse; **~ up!*** ¡cállate!; **see that you ~ up warm** cuida de arroparte bien.

wraparound ['ræpəˌraʊnd] *n* reciclado *m*, bucle *m*.

wrapper ['ræpəʳ] *n* (*of packet etc*) envoltura *f*, envase *m*; (*of book*) sobrecubierta *f*, camisa *f*; (*postal*) faja *f*.

wrapping ['ræpɪŋ] *n* envoltura *f*, envase *m*.

wrapping-paper ['ræpɪŋˌpeɪpəʳ] *n* papel *m* de envolver.

wrath [rɒθ] *n* (*lit*) cólera *f*, ira *f*; (*fig, of storm etc*) ira *f*, furia *f*.

wrathful ['rɒθfʊl] *adj* (*liter*) colérico, iracundo.

wrathfully ['rɒθfəlɪ] *adv* coléricamente, airadamente.

wreak [riːk] *vt* (*liter*) ejecutar; *destruction etc* hacer, causar; *vengeance* tomar (*on* en); *anger* descargar (*on* en); *punishment* infligir (*on* en); **to ~ havoc** hacer (*or* causar) estragos.

wreath [riːθ] *n, pl* **wreaths** [riːðz] (*of flowers etc*) guirnalda *f*, (*funeral ~*) corona *f* (mortuoria); (*of smoke*) espiral *f*; **laurel ~** corona *f* de laurel.

wreathe [riːð] **1** *vt* (*encircle*) ceñir, rodear (*with* de); (*plait*) trenzar; entrelazar; (*garland*) enguirnaldar (*with* con); **to ~ flowers into one's hair** ponerse flores en el pelo; **a face ~d in smiles** una cara envuelta en sonrisas, una cara muy risueña; **trees ~d in mist** árboles *mpl* envueltos en niebla.

2 *vi* (*of smoke etc*; *also* **to ~ upwards**) enroscarse, formar espirales, elevarse en espirales.

wreck [rek] **1** *n* **(a)** (*Naut: act*) naufragio *m*; (*ship*) buque *m* naufragado, buque *m* hundido; **the ship was a total ~** el buque se consideró como totalmente perdido.

(b) (*Rail etc*) colisión *f*, accidente *m*.

(c) (*fig*) ruina *f*, destrucción *f*; **the ~ of one's hopes** la ruina de las esperanzas de uno; **he's a (***or* **an old) ~** es un carcamal; **I'm a ~, I feel a ~** estoy hecho polvo; **she's a nervous ~** tiene los nervios destrozados; **I'm a nervous ~** tengo los nervios de punta; **if this goes on I shall be a nervous ~** si las cosas siguen así acabaré con los nervios destrozados; **she looks a ~** está hecha una pena.

2 *vt* **(a)** *ship* hacer naufragar, hundir, destruir; *train* descarrilar; *car, plane, mechanism etc* estropear, destrozar; **you've ~ed my gears** has estropeado la caja de cambios; **to be ~ed** (*Naut*) naufragar, irse a pique, ser hundido; **the ship was ~ed on those rocks** el buque naufragó en aquellas rocas.

(b) (*fig*) *hopes etc* arruinar, destruir, acabar con.

wreckage ['rekɪdʒ] *n* **(a)** (*act*) naufragio *m*; (*fig*) naufragio *m*, ruina *f*, destrucción *f*.

(b) (*remains*: *Naut*) pecios *mpl*, restos *mpl* de un buque naufragado; (*of car etc*) restos *mpl*; (*of house etc*) escombros *mpl*, ruinas *fpl*.

wrecked [rekt] *adj ship* naufragado, hundido; *car etc* estropeado, averiado; (‡) colocado‡.

wrecker ['rekəʳ] *n* (*gen*) destructor *m*, -ora *f*; (*Hist: of ships*) provocador *m* de naufragios; (*esp US: person*) demoledor *m*; (*US: tow truck*) camión-grúa *m*.

wrecking ball ['rekɪŋˌbɔːl] *n* martillo *m* de demolición.

wren [ren] *n* **(a)** (*Orn*) troglodito *m*. **(b) W~** (*Brit Navy*) *miembro de la sección femenina de la marina británica.*

wrench [rentʃ] **1** *n* **(a)** (*tug*) arranque *m*, tirón *m*; (*Med*) torcedura *f*; **to give sth a ~** tirar violentamente de algo, torcer algo violentamente; **to give one's arm a ~** torcerse el brazo.

(**b**) (*tool*) llave *f* inglesa.

(**c**) (*fig*) dolor *m*; sacudida *f*; choque *m*; **the ~ of parting** el dolor de la separación, la angustia de la separación; **it was a ~ to have to leave** fue angustioso tener que partir.

2 *vt* arrancar, tirar violentamente de; **to ~ one's arm** torcerse el brazo, dislocarse el brazo; **to ~ sth (away) from sb** arrebatar algo a uno; **to ~ sth off** arrancar algo; **to ~ a door open** abrir una puerta con un tirón (violento); **to ~ a bulb out** arrancar una bombilla.

3 *vi and vr*: **he ~ed (himself) free** haciendo un gran esfuerzo se soltó.

wrest [rest] **1** *vt*: **to ~ sth from sb** arrebatar (*or* arrancar) algo a uno, arrancar algo a uno; **to ~ gold from the rocks** extraer a duras penas oro de las rocas; **to ~ a living from the soil** vivir penosamente cultivando la tierra.

2 *vr*: **to ~ o.s. free** (lograr) libertarse tras grandes esfuerzos; **try to ~ yourself free** procura soltarte haciendo un esfuerzo.

wrestle ['resl] **1** *n* lucha *f*; partido *m* de lucha; **to have a ~ with sb** luchar con uno.

2 *vt* luchar con, luchar contra; **to ~ sb to the ground** tumbar a uno, derribar a uno.

3 *vi* luchar (*with* con, contra); **to ~ with** (*fig*) luchar con; **we are wrestling with the problem** estamos luchando con el problema, nos esforzamos por resolver el problema; **the pilot ~d with the controls** el piloto luchaba con los mandos.

wrestler ['reslə^r] *n* luchador *m*, -ora *f*.

wrestling ['reslɪŋ] **1** *n* lucha *f*; (*freestyle* ~) lucha *f* libre. **2** *attr*: **~ match** partido *m* de lucha.

wretch [retʃ] *n* desgraciado *m*, -a *f*, infeliz *mf*; **little ~** (*often hum*) tunante *m*, pícaro *m*, -a *f*; **some poor ~** algún desgraciado, algún pobre diablo; **you ~!** (*hum*) ¡canalla!, ¡granuja!

wretched ['retʃɪd] *adj* (*unfortunate*) desgraciado, desdichado; (*contemptible*) miserable, despreciable; pobre, lamentable; (*very bad*) horrible; (*ill*) malo, enfermo; **that ~ dog** ese maldito perro; **where's that ~ stick?** ¿dónde está el condenado bastón ese?; **it's ~ weather** hace un tiempo de perros; **what ~ luck!** ¡qué perra suerte!; **I'm a ~ player** juego malísimamente; **to feel ~** (*Med*) sentirse muy mal; (*depressed*) estar deprimido, estar abatido; **I felt ~ about it** me daba grandes remordimientos.

wretchedly ['retʃɪdlɪ] *adv* lamentablemente; horriblemente; muy mal; **to be ~ unlucky** tener malísima suerte; **she plays ~** toca horriblemente mal; **they treated her ~** la trataron de modo infame.

wretchedness ['retʃɪdnɪs] *n* desgracia *f*, desdicha *f*; lo despreciable; lo lamentable; lo horrible; infamia *f*; depresión *f*, abatimiento *m*.

wrick [rɪk] **1** *n* torcedura *f*. **2** *vt* (*Brit*) torcer; **to ~ one's neck** darse un tortícolis.

wriggle ['rɪgl] **1** *n* meneo *m*; serpenteo *m*, culebreo *m*.

2 *vt* menear; *ears, hips etc* mover; **to ~ one's way into** deslizarse en, introducirse (con dificultad) en; **to ~ one's way through** lograr pasar (con dificultad) por.

3 *vi* menearse; (*also* **to ~ along**) culebrear, moverse culebreando, avanzar serpenteando; **to ~ away** escaparse culebreando; **to ~ out of a difficulty** escaparse mañosamente de un apuro; **to ~ through a hole** pasar (culebreando, con dificultad) por un agujero; **to ~ with pain** retorcerse de dolor.

◆**wriggle about, wriggle around** *vi* culebrear, serpentear; (*snake, worm*) culebrear; (*fish*) colear; (*person*) moverse mucho.

wriggly ['rɪglɪ] *adj* sinuoso, tortuoso.

wring [rɪŋ] (*irr*: *pret and ptp* **wrung**) **1** *vt* (**a**) (*squeeze, twist*) torcer, retorcer; *clothes* escurrir; *hands* retorcer; *animal's neck* torcer; **to ~ clothes out** escurrir la ropa; **to ~ water out of clothes** exprimir el agua de la ropa.

(**b**) (*fig*) *heart etc* acongojar, apenar; **to ~ money out of sb** sacar dinero a uno; **to ~ a concession out of sb** arrancar una concesión a uno; **eventually we wrung the truth out of them** por fin pudimos arrancarles la verdad.

2 *n*: **to give clothes a ~** exprimir el agua de la ropa.

◆**wring out** *vt* = **wring 1 (a)**, **1 (b)**.

wringer ['rɪŋə^r] *n* escurridor *m*, máquina *f* de exprimir; **to put sb through the ~*** hacer sufrir a uno.

wringing ['rɪŋɪŋ] *adj*: **to be ~ (wet)** estar empapado, (*person*) estar calado hasta los huesos.

wrinkle ['rɪŋkl] **1** *n* (**a**) arruga *f*; pliegue *m*. (**b**) (*) (*idea*) idea *f*, noción *f*; (*tip*) indicación *f*; (*dodge*) truco *m*. **2** *vt* (*also* **to ~ up**) *fabric etc* arrugar; *brow* fruncir. **3** *vi* (*also* **to ~ up**) arrugarse; plegarse, ajarse; fruncirse.

wrinkled ['rɪŋkld] *adj*, **wrinkly** ['rɪŋklɪ] *adj* arrugado, lleno de arrugas.

wrinklies* ['rɪŋklɪz] *npl* viejos *mpl*.

wrist [rɪst] *n* muñeca *f*.

wristband ['rɪstbænd] *n* (*of shirt*) puño *m*; (*of watch*) pulsera *f*; (*Sport*) muñequera *f*.

wrist joint ['rɪst,dʒɔɪnt] *n* articulación *f* de la muñeca.

wristlet ['rɪstlɪt] **1** *n* pulsera *f*, muñequera *f*, brazalete *m*. **2** *attr*: **~ watch** reloj *m* de pulsera.

wristwatch ['rɪstwɒtʃ] *n* reloj *m* de pulsera.

writ [rɪt] **1** *n* escritura *f*; (*Jur*) orden *f*, mandato *m*, decreto *m* judicial; requisitoria *f*, citación *f*; (*fig*) autoridad *f*; **~ for an election** autorización *f* para celebrar elecciones; **~ of attachment** orden *f* de embargo; **~ of execution** auto *m* de ejecución; **~ of restraint** inhibitoria *f*; **to issue a ~** dar orden, hacer un decreto judicial; **to issue a ~ against sb** demandar a uno en juicio; **to issue a ~ for slander against sb** demandar a uno por calumnia; **to serve a ~ on sb** entregar una orden (*etc*) a uno; **his ~ does not run here** aquí él no tiene autoridad, su autoridad no se extiende hasta aquí.

2 (†) *ptp*: **it's just the old policy ~ large** es solamente la vieja política con adornos; es la misma política en forma exagerada; **guilt was ~ large on his face** se hacía patente la culpa en su cara.

write [raɪt] (*irr*: *pret* **wrote**, *ptp* **written**) **1** *vt* (**a**) (*gen*) escribir; redactar; poner por escrito; **did I ~ that?** ¿lo escribí yo así?; ¿fui capaz de escribir eso?; **how is that written?** ¿cómo se escribe eso?; **she ~s a good hand** tiene buena letra; **his guilt was written all over his face** tenía aspecto de culpable, delataba su culpabilidad; **he had 'policeman' written all over him** llevaba 'policía' escrito por todas partes.

(**b**) (*compose*) escribir; componer.

2 *vi* (**a**) (*gen*) escribir; **as I ~** mientras escribo estas líneas; **we ~ to each other** nos escribimos, nos carteamos; **will you ~ to me?** ¿me escribirás?; **I wrote to him to come** le escribí diciéndole que viniera; **that's nothing to ~ home about** eso no tiene nada de particular, no es nada del otro mundo; **I'll ~ for it at once** lo pediré por escrito en seguida, escribiré para pedirlo en seguida.

(**b**) (*as profession*) escribir, ser escritor; **he ~s for a living** se gana la vida escribiendo, es escritor de profesión; **he ~s as a hobby** escribe como distracción; **to ~ for a paper** colaborar en un periódico, escribir en un periódico.

◆**write away** *vi* = **write off 2**.

◆**write back** *vi* contestar.

◆**write down** *vt* (**a**) (*note*) apuntar, anotar; (*put in writing*) poner por escrito; (*record*) registrar, hacer constar; **we wrote him down as useless** decidimos que era inútil; **written-down value** valor *m* rebajado, valor *m* amortizado.

(**b**) (*Comm*) rebajar, bajar el precio de; reducir el valor nominal de.

◆**write in 1** *vt* escribir, insertar; (*US Pol*) *candidate* añadir a la lista oficial.

2 *vi* escribir (*for sth* solicitando algo).

◆**write into** *vt* incluir en, hacer constar en; **the details will be written into the contract** se harán constar los detalles en el contrato.

◆**write off 1** *vt* (**a**) (*write quickly*) escribir rápidamente, escribir en seguida.

(**b**) (*Comm, fig*) *debt etc* borrar, cancelar, anular; **to ~ sth off as a total loss** considerar algo como totalmente perdido; **the car had to be written off** el coche se consideró como sin valor alguno; **to ~ £1000 off for depreciation** quitar 1000 libras al valor nominal por depreciación; **he had been written off as a failure** se le había considerado como un fracasado.

2 *vi* escribir (con prontitud) (*for sth* solicitando algo).

◆**write out** *vt* (**a**) escribir; *cheque* escribir, extender; (*transcribe*) copiar, transcribir; (*in full*) escribir en su forma completa, escribir sin abreviar.

(**b**) **he was written out of the series** suprimieron el papel que tenía en la telenovela (*etc*).

◆**write up** *vt* (**a**) *report* escribir; *event* escribir una crónica de, hacer un reportaje de; *diary, ledger* poner al día.

(**b**) (*) **to ~ sb up (in a big way)** dar bombo a uno*, describir a uno en términos elogiosos; **to ~ sth up (in a big way)** describir algo exageradamente.

write-off ['raɪtɒf] *n* (*Comm*) depreciación *f*; (*of debt*) cancelación *f*; (*fig*) pérdida *f* total; (*person*) fracasado *m*, -a *f*, caso *m* desahuciado; **the car is a complete ~** el coche no sirve para nada.

write-protect ['raɪtprə'tekt] *vt* proteger contra escritura.

writer ['raɪtəʳ] *n* escritor *m*, -ora *f*; autor *m*, -ora *f*; **the (present) ~** el que esto escribe; **~ to the signet** (*Scot*) notario *m*; **a ~ of detective stories** un autor de novelas policíacas; **~'s cramp** calambre *m* de los escribientes; **to be a poor ~** (*in handwriting*) tener mala letra.

write-up ['raɪtʌp] *n* (*report*) crónica *f*, reportaje *m*; (*pej*) bombo *m*, descripción *f* exagerada, descripción *f* muy elogiosa.

writhe [raɪð] *vi* retorcerse, contorcerse; debatirse; **to ~ with pain, to ~ in pain** retorcerse de dolor; **to make sb ~** (*painfully*) hacer sufrir a uno, atormentar a uno, (*with disgust*) dar asco a uno; **it made me ~ with embarrassment** con eso me sentí terriblemente molesto.

◆writhe about, writhe around *vi* retorcerse.

writing ['raɪtɪŋ] **1** *n* (**a**) (*art in general*) el escribir, escritura *f*; **in ~** por escrito; **evidence in ~** declaración *f* escrita, testimonio *m* por escrito; **at the time of ~** en el momento de escribir esto; **to commit sth to ~, to put sth in ~** poner algo por escrito.

(**b**) (*hand~*) escritura *f*, letra *f*; **in one's own ~** de su propia letra, de su puño y letra; **in Góngora's own ~** de puño y letra de Góngora; **~ on the wall** advertencias *fpl* graves, profecías *fpl* terribles; **the ~ is on the wall for them** es una advertencia muy clara para ellos; **he had seen the ~ on the wall** se había dado cuenta de que era un aviso del cielo.

(**c**) (*thing written*) escrito *m*; obra *f*; **the ~s of Cela** las obras de Cela.

(**d**) (*profession*) profesión *f* de autor; trabajo *m* literario; **he earns a bit from his ~** gana algo con su trabajo literario.

2 *attr* de escribir; **~ materials** artículos *mpl* de escritorio.

writing-case ['raɪtɪŋkeɪs] *n* (*Brit*) recado *m* de escribir.

writing-desk ['raɪtɪŋdesk] *n* escritorio *m*.

writing-pad ['raɪtɪŋpæd] *n* taco *m* de papel, bloc *m*.

writing-paper ['raɪtɪŋ,peɪpəʳ] *n* papel *m* de escribir.

written ['rɪtn] **1** *ptp of* **write**. **2** *adj* escrito; **~ offer** oferta *f* por escrito; **~ statement** declaración *f* escrita; **the ~ word** la palabra escrita.

WRNS [renz] *n* (*Brit*) *abbr of* **Women's Royal Naval Service.**

wrong [rɒŋ] **1** *adj* (**a**) (*morally: wicked*) malo, inicuo; (*unfair*) injusto; **it's ~ to steal** malo es robar; **that was very ~ of you** en eso has hecho muy mal; **you were ~ to** + *infin* hiciste mal en + *infin*; **what's ~ with a drink now and again?** ¿será pecado tomar algo de vez en cuando?; **what's ~ in cuddling?** ¿qué tiene de malo abrazarse?, ¿es que es un pecado abrazarse?

(**b**) (*incorrect*) erróneo, incorrecto, inexacto, equivocado; **the ~ use of drugs** el uso impropio de las drogas; **to be ~** (*person*) no tener razón; equivocarse, estar equivocado; **that is ~** eso no es exacto, eso no es cierto; **the answer is ~** la respuesta es inexacta; **is that still ~?** ¿eso está mal todavía?; **that clock is ~** ese reloj anda mal, ese reloj no marcha bien.

(**c**) (*improper, not sought, not wanted*) impropio, inoportuno; **it's the ~ one** no es el que buscaba (*or* quería), no es el que hacía falta; **~ side** (*of cloth etc*) revés *m*, envés *m*; **to be ~ side out** estar al revés; **he was driving on the ~ side (of the road)** conducía por el lado prohibido (de la carretera); **at the ~ time** inoportunamente; **it's in the ~ place** está mal situado, está mal colocado; **I'm in the ~ job** tengo un puesto que no me conviene, soy miembro de una profesión que no me conviene; me he equivocado de profesión; **we were on the ~ train** nos habíamos equivocado de tren; **is this the ~ road?** ¿nos habremos equivocado de camino?; **to play a ~ note** tocar una nota falsa; **to say the ~ thing** decir algo inoportuno; **you have the ~ number** (*Telec*) Vd se ha equivocado de número; *V* **way** etc.

(**d**) (*amiss*) **sth is ~** hay algo que no está bien; **is anything ~?, is sth ~?** ¿pasa algo?; **what's ~ with you?** ¿qué te pasa?; **I hope there's nothing ~ at home** espero que no pase nada en casa; **sth's ~ with my watch** le pasa algo a mi reloj, mi reloj no anda bien; **there is sth ~ with my lights** los faros tienen una avería, pasa algo a los faros.

2 *adv* mal; sin razón; injustamente; incorrectamente, equivocadamente; al revés; **to answer ~** contestar mal, contestar incorrectamente; **you did ~** hiciste mal; **you're doing it all ~** no se hace así, no comprendes el modo de hacerlo; **to get it ~** (*misunderstand*) comprender mal; no acertar; (*Math etc*) calcular mal, equivocarse (en el cálculo); **don't get me ~** entiéndame bien; **to go ~** (*on route*) equivocarse de camino; extraviarse; (*in calculation*) equivocarse; (*morally*) extraviarse, caer en el vicio; (*of affair*) ir mal, salir mal; (*Mech*) fallar; estropearse, averiarse; dejar de funcionar; **sth went ~ with the gears** pasó algo a la caja de cambios, se averió la caja de cambios; **sth went ~ with their plans** algo falló en sus planes, fracasaron sus planes; **sth is seriously ~** pasa algo grave; **you can't go ~!** ¡no tiene pérdida!

3 *n* (**a**) (*evil*) mal *m*; **to know right from ~** saber distinguir el bien del mal; **two ~s do not make a right** no se subsana un error cometiendo otro.

(**b**) (*injustice*) injusticia *f*; agravio *m*, entuerto *m*; **to do sb a great ~** ser muy injusto con uno, agraviar seriamente a uno; **to labour under a sense of ~** sentirse agraviado; **to right a ~** deshacer un agravio, acabar con un abuso.

(**c**) **to be in the ~** no tener razón, estar equivocado; tener la culpa; **to put sb in the ~** hacer quedar mal a uno, echar la culpa a uno.

4 *vt* agraviar; ser injusto con; **you ~ me** eso no es justo; **to feel that one has been ~ed** sentirse agraviado.

wrongdoer ['rɒŋ,du:əʳ] *n* malhechor *m*, -ora *f*; pecador *m*, -ora *f*.

wrongdoing ['rɒŋ,du:ɪŋ] *n* maldad *f*; pecado(s) *m(pl)*; perversidad *f*; crimen *m*, crímenes *mpl*.

wrong-foot ['rɒŋ'fʊt] *vt* poner en situación violenta (*or* desfavorable); **that left us ~ed** eso nos dejó en una situación violenta.

wrongful ['rɒŋfʊl] *adj* injusto; ilegal; **~ arrest** detención *f* ilegal; **~ dismissal** despido *m* arbitrario, despido *m* improcedente.

wrongfully ['rɒŋfəlɪ] *adv* injustamente; ilegalmente.

wrong-headed ['rɒŋ'hedɪd] *adj* obstinado, terco, perversamente equivocado; **to be ~ about sth** obstinarse perversamente en sostener (*etc*) algo.

wrong-headedly ['rɒŋ'hedɪdlɪ] *adv* obstinadamente, perversamente.

wrong-headedness ['rɒŋ'hedɪdnɪs] *n* obstinación *f*, terquedad *f*; error *m* perverso.

wrongly ['rɒŋlɪ] *adv* mal; injustamente; incorrectamente; equivocadamente; al revés; **he ~ maintains that ...** sostiene equivocadamente que ...; **to put a screw in ~** poner un tornillo mal; **she had been very ~ treated** la habían tratado muy injustamente.

wrongness ['rɒŋnɪs] *n* iniquidad *f*; injusticia *f*; inexactitud *f*, error *m*, falsedad *f*; impropiedad *f*, inoportunidad *f*.

wrote [rəʊt] *pret of* **write**.

wrought [rɔ:t] **1** (††) *pret and ptp of* **work**; **he ~ valiantly** (*liter*) luchó denodadamente, trabajó con esfuerzo; **great changes have been ~** se han efectuado grandes cambios; **destruction ~ by the floods** daños *mpl* causados por las inundaciones. **2** *adj* (**a**) **~ iron** hierro *m* forjado, hierro *m* batido. (**b**) **to be ~ (up)** (*person*) estar muy agitado, estar muy nervioso.

wrought-up ['rɔ:t'ʌp] *adj* agitado, nervioso.

wrung [rʌŋ] *pret and ptp of* **wring**.

WRVS *n* (*Brit*) *abbr of* **Women's Royal Voluntary Service.**

wry [raɪ] *adj* torcido; *sense of humour, joke etc* pervertido, raro; *speech etc* irónico, lleno de ironía; **to make a ~ face** hacer una mueca, torcer el gesto.

wryly ['raɪlɪ] *adv* irónicamente, con ironía.

wryneck ['raɪnek] *n* torcecuello *m*.

WSW *abbr of* **west-south-west** oessudoeste, OSO.

wt *abbr of* **weight** peso *m*.

W/T *abbr of* **wireless telegraphy** radiotelegrafía *f*.

WV (*US Post*) *abbr of* **West Virginia.**

W. Va. (*US*) *abbr of* **West Virginia.**

WWI *n abbr of* **World War One.**

WW2 *n abbr of* **World War Two.**

WWF *n abbr of* **World Wildlife Fund** Fundación *f* Mundial para la Naturaleza.

WY (*US Post*) *abbr of* **Wyoming.**

wych-elm ['wɪtʃ'elm] *n* olmo *m* escocés, olmo *m* de montaña.

Wyo. (*US*) *abbr of* **Wyoming.**

WYSIWYG ['wɪzɪ,wɪg] *abbr of* **what you see is what you get.**

X

X, x [eks] *n* (*letter*) X, x *f*; (*Math, fig*) x *f*; incógnita *f*; **X for Xmas** X de Xiquena; **X marks the spot** el sitio está señalado con una X; **if you have X pesetas a year** si tienes equis pesetas al año; **for X number of years** por equis años; ~ **chromosome** cromosoma *m* X; **X-rated** (*US*) para mayores de 18 años.
Xavier ['zeɪvɪə^r] *nm* Javier.
xenon ['zenɒn] *n* xenón *m*.
xenophobe ['zenəfəʊb] *n* xenófobo *m*, -a *f*.
xenophobia [ˌzenə'fəʊbɪə] *n* xenofobia *f*.
xenophobic [ˌzenə'fəʊbɪk] *adj* xenófobo.
Xenophon ['zenəfən] *nm* Jenofonte.
Xerox ['zɪərɒks] ® **1** *n* (*machine*) fotocopiadora *f*; (*copy*) fotocopia *f*. **2** *vt* fotocopiar.
Xerxes ['zɜːksiːz] *nm* Jerjes.
Xmas ['eksməs] *n abbr of* **Christmas.**
X-ray ['eks'reɪ] **1** *n* radiografía *f*; **~s** rayos *mpl* X. **2** *attr* radiográfico; ~ **examination** examen *m* con rayos X; ~ **photograph** radiografía *f*; ~ **treatment** tratamiento *m* de rayos X. **3** *vt* radiografiar.
xylograph ['zaɪləgrɑːf] *n* xilografía *f*, grabado *m* en madera.
xylographic [zaɪlə'græfɪk] *adj* xilográfico.
xylography [zaɪ'lɒgrəfɪ] *n* xilografía *f*.
xylophone ['zaɪləfəʊn] *n* xilófono *m*.
xylophonist [zaɪ'lɒfənɪst] *n* xilofonista *mf*.

Y

Y, y [waɪ] *n* (*letter*) Y, y *f*; **Y for Yellow, Y for Yoke** (*US*) Y de Yegua; ~ **chromosome** cromosoma *m* Y.

yacht [jɒt] **1** *n* (*esp large, seagoing*) yate *m*, velero *m*, balandra *f*; (*small, model*) balandro *m*.

2 *vi* pasear en yate, navegar en yate; tomar parte en regatas de balandros; dedicarse al balandrismo.

yacht club [ˈjɒtklʌb] *n* club *m* náutico.

yachting [ˈjɒtɪŋ] **1** *n* deporte *m* de la vela, balandrismo *m*; pasear *m* en yate, navegar *m* en yate; regatas *fpl* de balandros.

2 *attr* de yates, de balandros; de balandristas; **in ~ circles** entre los aficionados al deporte de la vela, entre balandristas; **it's not a ~ coast** en esa costa no se practica el deporte de la vela.

yacht race [ˈjɒtreɪs] *n* regata *f* de yates, regata *f* de balandros.

yachtsman [ˈjɒtsmən] *n*, *pl* **yachtsmen** [ˈjɒtsmən] deportista *m* náutico; yatista *m*, balandrista *m*.

yachtsmanship [ˈjɒtsmənʃɪp] *n* arte *m* de navegar en yate (*or* balandro).

yachtswoman [ˈjɒtswʊmən] *n*, *pl* **yachtswomen** [ˈjɒtswɪmɪn] deportista *f* náutica; yatista *f*, balandrista *f*.

yack* [jæk] *n*, **yackety-yak*** [ˈjækɪtɪˈjæk] **1** *n* (*chatter*) palabreo *m*, cháchara *f*; (*argument*) dimes *mpl* y diretes; (*insistence*) machaqueo *m*. **2** *vi* (*pej*) hablar como una cotorra.

yah [jɑː] *interj* ¡bah!

yahoo [jɑːˈhuː] *n* patán *m*.

yak [jæk] *n* yac *m*, yak *m*.

Yale [jeɪl] ® *attr*: ~ **lock** cerradura *f* de cilindro.

yam [jæm] *n* batata *f*, ñame *m*, camote *m*.

yammer* [ˈjæməʳ] *vi* quejarse, gimotear.

Yank* [jæŋk] *n* yanqui *mf*.

yank [jæŋk] **1** *n* tirón *m*; **to give a rope a ~** tirar de una cuerda. **2** *vt* tirar de.

◆**yank off*** *vt* (**a**) (*detach*) quitar de un tirón.

(**b**) **to ~ sb off to jail** coger y meter a uno en la cárcel.

◆**yank out*** *vt*: **to ~ a nail out** sacar un clavo de un tirón.

Yankee [ˈjæŋkɪ] **1** *adj* yanqui. **2** *n* yanqui *mf*.

yap [jæp] **1** *n* ladrido *m* agudo. **2** *vi* dar ladridos agudos; (*: *chat*) charlar; (*: *protest*) quejarse, protestar (sin razón).

yapping [ˈjæpɪŋ] *n* ladridos *mpl* agudos.

yard[1] [jɑːd] *n* (**a**) yarda *f* (= *91,44 cm*); **an essay ~s long** un ensayo kilométrico; **he pulled out ~s of handkerchief** sacó un enorme pañuelo; **with a face a ~ long** con una cara muy larga; **a few ~s off** a unos metros, a poca distancia.

(**b**) (*Naut*) verga *f*.

yard[2] [jɑːd] *n* (*of house*) patio *m*; (*of farm etc*) corral *m*; (*Scol*) patio *m* de recreo; (*US*) jardincito *m*; **the Y~, Scotland Y~** (*Brit*) *oficina central de la policía de Londres*.

yardage [ˈjɑːdɪdʒ] *n* ≃ metraje *m*.

yardarm [ˈjɑːdɑːm] *n* verga *f*, penol *m*.

yardstick [ˈjɑːdstɪk] *n* (*fig*) criterio *m*, norma *f*.

yarn [jɑːn] **1** *n* (**a**) (*thread etc*) hilo *m*, hilaza *f*.

(**b**) (*tale*) cuento *m*, historia *f*; **to spin a ~** contar una historia; contar cosas inverosímiles; **to spin sb a ~** disculparse con un pretexto inverosímil.

2 *vi* contar historias; contar cosas inverosímiles; contar chistes.

yarrow [ˈjærəʊ] *n* milenrama *f*.

yashmak [ˈjæʃmæk] *n* velo *m* (de musulmana).

yaw [jɔː] (*Naut*) **1** *n* guiñada *f*. **2** *vi* guiñar, hacer una guiñada.

yawl [jɔːl] *n* yol *m*, yola *f*.

yawn [jɔːn] **1** *n* bostezo *m*; **it was a ~ from start to finish*** fue aburridísimo; **to say sth with a ~** decir algo bostezando.

2 *vt* (*also* **to ~ out**) decir bostezando; **to ~ one's head off** bostezar mucho; bostezar abriendo muchísimo la boca.

3 *vi* bostezar; (*fig*) abrirse.

yawning [ˈjɔːnɪŋ] *adj gap etc* muy abierto, grande.

yd *abbr of* **yard** yarda *f*, yda.

ye[1] [jiː] *pron* (††, *liter, dial*) vosotros, vosotras.

ye[2] [jiː] *def art* (††) = **the**.

yea†† [jeɪ] **1** *adv* (*yes*) sí; (*indeed*) sin duda, ciertamente; (*moreover*) además. **2** *n* sí *m*; **the ~s and the nays** los votos a favor y los votos en contra.

yeah* [jɛə] *adv* = **yes**.

year [ˈjɪəʳ] *n* (**a**) año *m*; ~ **of grace** año *m* de gracia; ~ **end** final *m* del año; **in the ~ of our Lord ...** en el año del Señor ...; **all the ~ round** durante todo el año; ~ **in, ~ out** año tras año; todos los años sin falta; **3 times a ~** 3 veces al año; **100 dollars a ~** 100 dólares al año; **to reckon by the ~** calcular por años; **in after ~s** en los años siguientes, años después; **in the ~ dot** en el año de la nana; **since the ~ dot** desde el año de la nana, desde siempre; **not from one year's end to the other** nunca jamás; **of late ~s** en estos últimos años; **last ~** el año pasado; **the ~ before last** el año antepasado; **next ~** (*looking to future*) el año que viene, (*in past time*) el año siguiente; **he got 10 ~s** le condenaron a 10 años de prisión; **it takes ~s** es cosa de años y años, se tarda años y años; **we waited ~s** esperamos una eternidad.

(**b**) (*~s of person*) **in my early ~s** en mi infancia, en mi juventud; **in his late ~s** en sus últimos años; **he died in his 89th ~** murió en el año 89 de su vida; **she's very spry for a woman of her ~s** para una mujer de su edad es muy ágil; **he looks old for his ~s** aparenta más años de los que tiene; **he's getting on in ~s** va para viejo, es bastante viejo; **the work has put ~s on him** el trabajo le ha hecho envejecer bastante; **that hairdo takes ~s off you** ese peinado te quita muchos años; **to reach ~s of discretion** llegar a la edad adulta.

(**c**) (*Scol, Univ*) año *m*, curso *m*; **he's in (the) second ~** está en el segundo curso; **the fellows in my ~** los chicos de mi curso; **he's in fourth ~ Law** estudia cuarto de Derecho.

yearbook [ˈjɪəbʊk] *n* anuario *m*.

yearling [ˈjɪəlɪŋ] **1** *adj* primal. **2** *n* primal *m*, -ala *f*.

yearlong [ˈjɪəˈlɒŋ] *adj* que dura un año (entero).

yearly [ˈjɪəlɪ] **1** *adj* anual; ~ **payment** anualidad *f*. **2** *adv* anualmente, cada año; (**once**) ~ una vez al año.

yearn [jɜːn] *vi* suspirar; **to ~ for** anhelar, añorar, ansiar, suspirar por; *person* suspirar por; **to ~ to** + *infin* anhelar + *infin*, suspirar por + *infin*.

yearning [ˈjɜːnɪŋ] **1** *adj* ansioso, anhelante; *look, tone etc* tierno, amoroso. **2** *n* ansia *f*, anhelo *m*, añoranza *f* (*for* de).

yearningly [ˈjɜːnɪŋlɪ] *adv* ansiosamente, con ansia; tiernamente, amorosamente.

year-round [ˈjɪəˈraʊnd] *adj* que dura todo el año, de todo un año.

yeast [jiːst] *n* levadura *f*.

yeasty [ˈjiːstɪ] *adj* (**a**) *smell, taste* a levadura. (**b**) (*fig*) frívolo, superficial.

yell [jel] **1** *n* grito *m*, alarido *m*, chillido *m*; **to give a ~, to let out a ~** dar un alarido. **2** *vt* (*also* **to ~ out**) gritar, decir a gritos, vociferar. **3** *vi* (*also* **to ~ out**) gritar, dar un alarido.

yelling [ˈjelɪŋ] *n* gritos *mpl*, alaridos *mpl*, chillidos *mpl*.

yellow [ˈjeləʊ] **1** *adj* (**a**) amarillo; *hair* rubio; ~ **fever** fiebre *f* amarilla; ~ **jersey** jersey *m* (*or* maillot *m*) amarillo; ~ **journalism** (*US*) amarillismo *m*; ~ **line** línea *f* amarilla (de estacionamiento limitado); ~ **pages** (*Telec*) páginas *fpl* amarillas; ~ **press** prensa *f* sensacional; **Y~ Sea** Mar *m* Amarillo; **to go ~, to turn ~** amarillear, amarillecer.

(**b**) (*cowardly*) cobarde.
2 *n* amarillo *m*.
3 *vt* volver amarillo.
4 *vi* amarillecer, amarillear, ponerse amarillo.

yellow belly‡ [ˈjeləʊˌbelɪ] *n* cagueta‡ *mf*.

yellow card [ˈjeləʊˈkɑːd] *n* tarjeta *f* amarilla.

yellowhammer [ˈjeləʊˌhæməʳ] *n* ave *f* tonta, verderón *m*.

yellowish [ˈjeləʊɪʃ] *adj* amarillento.

yellowness [ˈjeləʊnɪs] *n* amarillez *f*.

yellow peril [ˈjeləʊˈperɪl] *n* peligro *m* amarillo.

yellowy [ˈjeləʊɪ] *adj* amarillento, que tira a amarillo.

yelp [jelp] **1** *n* gañido *m*. **2** *vi* gañir; (*person*) gritar, dar un grito.

yelping [ˈjelpɪŋ] *n* gañidos *mpl*.

Yemen [ˈjemən] *n* Yemen *m*.

Yemeni [ˈjemənɪ] **1** *adj* yemenita. **2** *n* yemenita *mf*.

yen[1] [jen] *n* (*coin*) yen *m*.

yen[2]* [jen] *n* deseo *m* vivo; **to have a ~ to** + *infin* desear vivamente + *infin*, anhelar + *infin*.

yeoman [ˈjəʊmən] **1** *n*, *pl* **yeomen** [ˈjəʊmən] (*Brit Hist*) (**a**) (*also* **~ farmer**) labrador *m* rico, pequeño propietario *m* rural, pequeño terrateniente *m*.
(**b**) (*Mil*) soldado *m* (voluntario) de caballería; **~ of the guard** (*Brit*) alabardero *m* de la Casa Real.
2 *attr*: **to give ~ service** (*fig*) prestar grandes servicios.

yeomanry [ˈjəʊmənrɪ] *n* (**a**) clase *f* de los labradores ricos, pequeños propietarios *mpl* rurales. (**b**) (*Brit Mil*) caballería *f* voluntaria.

yep* [jep] *adv* (*esp US*) sí.

yes [jes] **1** *adv* sí; **~?** (*doubtfully*) ¿es cierto eso?, ¿ah sí?; **~?** (*awaiting further reply*) ¿y qué más?; **~?** (*answering knock at door*) ¿quién es?, ¡adelante!; **~ and no** (*sort of*) un poco sí y un poco no; **to say ~** decir que sí, (*to marriage proposal*) dar el sí; **he says ~ to everything** se allana a todo, se conforma con cualquier cosa.
2 *n* sí *m*; **he gave a reluctant ~** asintió pero de mala gana.

yes man* [ˈjesmæn] *n*, *pl* **yes men** [ˈjesmen] pelotillero* *m*.

yes-no question [ˌjesˈnəʊˌkwestʃən] *n* pregunta *f* de sí o no.

yesterday [ˈjestədeɪ] **1** *adv* ayer; **~ afternoon** ayer por la tarde; **~ morning** ayer por la mañana; **late ~** ayer a última hora; **no later than ~** ayer mismo, ayer precisamente; **he wasn't born ~** no es ningún niño.
2 *n* ayer *m*; **the day before ~** anteayer; **~ was Monday** ayer era lunes; **all our ~s** todos nuestros ayeres.

yesteryear [ˈjestəˈjɪəʳ] *adv* (*poet*) antaño.

yet [jet] **1** *adv* (**a**) todavía, aún; **as ~** hasta ahora, todavía; **not ~, not just ~** todavía no; **I hear it ~** lo oigo todavía; **need you go ~?** ¿tienes que irte ya?; **I don't have to go ~** me puedo quedar todavía un poco; **it is ~ to be settled** eso queda por resolver; **half is ~ to be built** la mitad queda todavía por construir; **it hasn't happened ~** todavía no ha ocurrido; no ha ocurrido aún; **it's not time ~** todavía no es hora.
(**b**) (*emphatic*) todavía; **~ again** otra vez (más); **~ more** todavía más, más todavía, más aun.
2 *conj* con todo, a pesar de todo; **and ~** y sin embargo, pero con todo; **we'll do it ~** a pesar de todo lo lograremos.

yeti [ˈjetɪ] *n* yeti *m*.

yew [juː] *n* (*also* **~-tree**) tejo *m*.

YHA *n* (*Brit*) *abbr of* **Youth Hostels Association.**

Yid‡ [jɪd] *n* (*pej*) judío *m*, -a *f*.

Yiddish [ˈjɪdɪʃ] **1** *adj* judío. **2** *n* (y)iddish *m*, yíd(d)ish *m*, judeo-alemán *m*.

yield [jiːld] **1** *n* producción *f*; productividad *f*; (*Agr*) cosecha *f*; (*Fin, Comm*) rendimiento *m*, renta *f*, (*on capital*) rédito *m*; **net ~** rédito *m* neto; **a ~ of 5%** un rédito de 5 por cien; **what is the ~ on the shares?** ¿cuánto rinden las acciones?
2 *vt* (**a**) *crop, result* producir, dar; *profit* rendir; *opportunity etc* ofrecer, dar, deparar; **the shares ~ 5%** las acciones rinden el 5 por cien, las acciones dan un rédito de 5 por cien.
(**b**) (*give up*: *also* **to ~ up**) entregar, ceder.
3 *vi* (*submit*) rendirse, someterse; (*give way*) ceder; (*US Aut*) ceder el paso; **to ~ to a plea** ceder a un ruego; **to ~ to temptation** ceder a la tentación; **I ~ to nobody in my admiration for ...** admiro como todos a ..., no me quedo corto en mi admiración por ...; **finally the door ~ed** por fin cedió la puerta; **the ice began to ~** el hielo empezó a ceder; el hielo empezó a romperse; **we shall never ~** no nos rendiremos nunca.

yielding [ˈjiːldɪŋ] *adj* flexible, blando; (*fig*) dócil, complaciente; tierno, amoroso.

yippee* [jɪˈpiː] *interj* ¡estupendo!*

YMCA *n abbr of* **Young Men's Christian Association.**

yob* [ˈjɒb] *n*, **yobbo*** [ˈjɒbəʊ] *n* (*Brit*) gamberro *m*.

yod [jɒd] *n* yod *f*.

yodel, yodle [ˈjəʊdl] **1** *n* canto *m* a la tirolesa. **2** *vt* cantar a la tirolesa. **3** *vi* = **2**.

yoga [ˈjəʊgə] *n* yoga *m*.

yoghourt, yog(h)urt [ˈjəʊgət] *n* yogur *m*.

yogi [ˈjəʊgɪ] *n* yogui *m*.

yo-heave-ho [jəʊˈhiːvˈhəʊ] *interj* = **heave-ho.**

yoke [jəʊk] **1** *n* (*of oxen*) yunta *f*; (*carried on shoulder*) balancín *m*, percha *f*; (*Mech*) horquilla *f*; (*Sew*) canesú *m*; (*fig*) yugo *m*; **under the ~ of the Nazis** bajo el yugo de los nazis, bajo la férula de los nazis; **to throw off the ~** sacudir el yugo.
2 *vt* (*also* **to ~ together**) uncir, acoplar; (*fig*) unir.

yokel [ˈjəʊkəl] *n* palurdo *m*, patán *m*.

yolk [jəʊk] *n* yema *f* (de huevo).

yomp [jɒmp] *vi* caminar penosamente (a través del campo).

yon [jɒn] *adv* (†† *or prov*) aquel.

yonder†† [ˈjɒndəʳ] **1** *adj* aquel. **2** *adv* allá, a lo lejos.

yonks* [jɒŋks] *n*: **for ~** hace siglos; **I haven't seen you for ~** hace siglos que no te veo.

yoo-hoo* [ˈjuːˈhuː] *excl* ¡yu-hu!*

yore†† [jɔːʳ] *n*: **of ~** (*liter*) de antaño, de otro tiempo, de hace siglos.

Yorks [jɔːks] *n abbr of* **Yorkshire.**

you [juː] *pron* **1** *in familiar use, with second person verb*: (*subject*: *sing*) tú, (*pl*) vosotros, vosotras, ustedes (*LAm*); (*acc, dat*: *sing*) te, (*pl*) os, les (*LAm*); (*after prep*: *sing*) ti, (*pl*) vosotros, vosotras, ustedes (*LAm*); **with ~** (*sing, reflexive*) contigo, (*pl, reflexive*) con vosotros, con vosotras, con ustedes (*LAm*).
2 *in formal use, with third person verb*: (*subject*: *sing*) usted, (*pl*) ustedes; (*acc, dat*: *sing*) le, la, (*pl*) les; (*after prep*: *sing*) usted, (*pl*) ustedes; **with ~** (*sing and pl, reflexive*) consigo.
3 *when impersonal or general, often translated by* (**a**) *reflexive*: **~ can't do that** eso no se hace, eso no se permite; **~ can't smoke here** no se puede fumar aquí, no se permite fumar aquí, se prohibe fumar aquí; **when ~ need one it's not here** cuando se necesita uno, no está aquí.
(**b**) uno: **~ never know whether ...** uno nunca sabe si ...
(**c**) *impersonal constructions*: **~ need to check it every day** hay que comprobarlo cada día, conviene comprobarlo cada día; **~ must paint it** hace falta pintarlo.
4 *phrases and special uses*: **~ rogue!** ¡canalla!; **~ there!** ¡eh! ¡usted!; **~ doctors** vosotros los médicos; **~ Spaniards** vosotros los españoles; **poor ~!, poor old ~!, ~ poor old thing!** ¡pobrecito!; **away with ~!** ¡vete!, ¡fuera de aquí!; **between ~ and me** entre tú y yo; **if I were ~** yo que tú, yo en tu lugar; **there's a pretty girl for ~!** ¡mira que chica más guapa!

you'd [juːd] = **you would; you had.**

you-know-who* [ˌjuːnəʊˈhuː] *n* tú ya sabes quien, fulano.

you'll [juːl] = **you will, you shall.**

young [jʌŋ] **1** *adj* joven; nuevo, reciente; *brother etc* menor; **a ~ man** un joven; **a ~ woman** una joven; **'Portrait of the Artist as a Y~ Man'** 'Retrato del artista adolescente'; **~ offender** (*Brit*) delincuente *mf* juvenil; **the ~er son** el hijo menor; **Pitt the Y~er** Pitt el Joven, Pitt hijo; **the ~ idea, Y~ England** las nuevas generaciones, la juventud de hoy; **~ Turk** (*Pol etc*) joven turco *m*; **in my ~ days** en mi juventud; **if I were 10 years ~er** si tuviera 10 años menos; **you're only ~ once** no se es joven más que una vez en la vida, hay que aprovechar la juventud mientras dure; **I'm not so ~ as I was** empiezo a notar los efectos de la edad, ya no soy lo que fui en mis veinte; **the night is ~** la noche es joven; **the pile is like a ~ mountain** el montón se parece a una montaña menor de edad; **to marry ~** casarse joven.
2 *npl* (**a**) **the ~** los jóvenes, la juventud; **old and ~** grandes y pequeños. (**b**) (*Zool*) cría *f*, hijuelos *mpl*.

youngish [ˈjʌŋɪʃ] *adj* bastante joven, más bien joven.

young-looking [ˈjʌŋˌlʊkɪŋ] *adj* de aspecto joven.

youngster [ˈjʌŋstəʳ] *n* joven *mf*, jovencito *m*, -a *f*.

your [ˈjʊəʳ] *poss adj* **1** *in familiar use, second person*: tu(s); vuestro(s), vuestra(s). **2** *in formal use, third person*: su(s).

you're [ˈjʊəʳ] = **you are.**

yours [ˈjʊəz] *poss pron* **1** *in familiar use, second person*: (*sing*) (el) tuyo, (la) tuya *etc*; (*pl*) (el) vuestro, (la) vuestra *etc*, el de ustedes, la de ustedes (*LAm*).
2 *in formal use, third person*: el suyo, (la) suya *etc*; **you**

and ~ Vd y los suyos.

3 *in ending letters*: ~ **faithfully** le saluda atentamente; *V* **sincerely** *etc*.

yourself [jə'self] *pron* **1** *in familiar use, second person*: (*subject*) tú mismo, tú misma; (*acc, dat*) te; (*after prep*) ti (mismo, misma). **2** *in formal use, third person*: (*subject*) usted mismo, usted misma; (*acc, dat*) se; (*after prep*) sí (mismo, misma); *V* **oneself.**

yourselves [jə'selvz] *pron pl* **1** *in familiar use, second person*: (*subject*) vosotros mismos, vosotras mismas, ustedes mismos, ustedes mismas (*LAm*); (*acc, dat*) os, se (*LAm*); (*after prep*) vosotros (mismos), vosotras (mismas), ustedes mismos, ustedes mismas (*LAm*).

2 *in formal use, third person*: (*subject*) ustedes mismos, ustedes mismas; (*acc, dat*) se; (*after prep*) sí (mismos, mismas); *V* **oneself.**

youth [ju:θ] **1** *n, pl* **youths** [ju:ðz] (**a**) (*gen*) juventud *f*. (**b**) (*person*) joven *m*. (**c**) (*persons collectively*) jóvenes *mpl*, juventud *f*; **present-day British** ~ la juventud actual inglesa; **Hitler Y**~ Juventudes *fpl* Hitlerianas.

2 *attr*: ~ **club** club *m* juvenil, casal *m* de jóvenes; ~ **employment scheme** plan *m* de empleo juvenil.

youthful ['ju:θfʊl] *adj* juvenil; joven; **to look** ~ tener aspecto joven, parecer joven.

youthfulness ['ju:θfʊlnɪs] *n* juventud *f*.

youth hostel ['ju:θ,hɒstl] *n* albergue *m* para jóvenes.

youth hostelling ['ju:θ,hɒstəlɪŋ] *n*: **to go** ~ pasar las vacaciones en albergues para jóvenes.

you've [ju:v] = **you have**.

yowl [jaʊl] **1** *n* aullido *m*, alarido *m*. **2** *vi* aullar, dar alaridos.

yo-yo ['jəʊjəʊ] ® *n* (**a**) yoyó ® *m*. (**b**) (*US*‡) bobo *m*, -a *f*, imbécil *mf*.

yr (**a**) *abbr of* **year** año *m*, a. (**b**) *abbr of* **your** su *etc*.

yrs (**a**) *abbr of* **years** años *mpl*. (**b**) *abbr of* **yours** suyo *etc*.

YT (*Canada*) *abbr of* **Yukon Territory**.

YTS *n* (*Brit*) *abbr of* **Youth Training Scheme** *plan de promoción de empleo para jóvenes*.

ytterbium [ɪ'tɜ:bɪəm] *n* iterbio *m*, yterbio *m*.

yttrium ['ɪtrɪəm] *n* itrio *m*.

yucca ['jʌkə] *n* yuca *f*.

yuck* [jʌk] *excl* ¡puaj!*, ¡puaf!*

yucky* ['jʌkɪ] *adj* asqueroso.

Yugoslav ['ju:gəʊ'slɑ:v] **1** *adj* yugo(e)slavo. **2** *n* yugo(e)slavo *m*, yugo(e)slava *f*.

Yugoslavia ['ju:gəʊ'slɑ:vɪə] *n* Yugo(e)slavia *f*.

Yugoslavian ['ju:gəʊ'slɑ:vɪən] *adj* yugo(e)slavo.

yuk* [jʌk] *excl* = **yuck**.

Yule(tide) ['ju:l(taɪd)] *n* (*liter*) Navidad *f*; **at** ~ por Navidades; ~ **log** leño *m* de Navidad.

yum* [jʌm] *interj*: ~-~! ¡ñam, ñam, ñam!*

yummy* ['jʌmɪ] *adj* de rechupete*.

yup* [jʌp] *adv* (*US*) sss*, sí.

yuppie* ['jʌpɪ] *n abbr of* **young upwardly mobile professional** yuppie *mf*; ~ **disease,** ~ **flu** síndrome *m* vírico.

YWCA *n abbr of* **Young Women's Christian Association.**

Z

Z, z [zed, (*US*) ziː] *n* (letter) Z, z *f*; **Z for Zebra** Z de Zaragoza.
zaftig* [ˈzæftɪg] *adj* (*US*) *woman* regordeta y mona.
Zaire [zɑːˈiːəʳ] *n* Zaire *m*.
Zairean [zɑːˈiːərɪən] **1** *adj* zaireño. **2** *n* zaireño *m*, -a *f*.
Zambesi [zæmˈbiːzɪ] *n* Zambeze *m*.
Zambia [ˈzæmbɪə] *n* Zambia *f*.
Zambian [ˈzæmbɪən] **1** *adj* zambiano. **2** *n* zambiano *m*, -a *f*.
zany [ˈzeɪnɪ] *adj* tonto; *humour etc* estrafalario, surrealista.
Zanzibar [ˈzænzɪbɑːʳ] *n* Zanzíbar *m*.
zap* [zæp] **1** *excl* ¡zas! **2** *vt person* cargarse*; (*Comput*) borrar, suprimir. **3** *vi* ir corriendo.
◆**zap along*** *vi* ir a toda pastilla*.
zappy* [ˈzæpɪ] *adj car* alegre, respondón; *computer* veloz; *prose, style* ágil; *approach* vivaz.
zeal [ziːl] *n* celo *m*, entusiasmo *m* (*for* por), ardor *m*.
zealot [ˈzelət] *n* fanático *m*, -a *f*.
zealotry [ˈzelətrɪ] *n* fanatismo *m*.
zealous [ˈzeləs] *adj* celoso (*for* de), entusiasta (*for* de); apasionado (*for* por).
zealously [ˈzeləslɪ] *adv* con entusiasmo.
zebra [ˈziːbrə] **1** *n* cebra *f*. **2** *attr*: ~ **crossing** (*Brit*) paso *m* de cebra.
zebu [ˈziːbuː] *n* cebú *m*.
zed [zed] *n*, (*US*) **zee** [ziː] *n* zeta *f*.
Zen [zen] **1** *n* Zen *m*. **2** *attr*: ~ **Buddhism** budismo *m* Zen; ~ **Buddhist** budista *mf* Zen.
zenana [zeˈnɑːnə] *n* harén *m* indio.
zenith [ˈzenɪθ] *n* cenit *m*; (*fig*) cenit *m*, apogeo *m*, punto *m* culminante; **to be at the ~ of one's power** estar en el apogeo de su poder.
Zeno [ˈzɪːnəʊ] *n* Zenón *m*.
Zephaniah [ˌzefəˈnaɪə] *n* Sofonías *m*.
zephyr [ˈzefəʳ] *n* céfiro *m*.
zeppelin [ˈzeplɪn] *n* zepelín *m*.
zero [ˈzɪərəʊ] **1** *adj* cero, nulo; ~ **gravity** gravedad *f* nula; ~ **growth** crecimiento *m* cero; ~ **hour** hora *f* H; ~ **option** opción *f* cero; **to be ~-rated for VAT** tener tipo cero del IVA; ~ **rating** tasa *f* cero. **2** *n* cero *m*; **absolute** ~ cero *m* absoluto; **it is 5° below** ~ hace cinco grados bajo cero.
◆**zero in** *vi*: **to ~ in on** (*move in on*) dirigirse de cabeza a; (*fig: identify*) identificar; (*concentrate on*) dirigir todos sus esfuerzos a; **he ~ed in on those who ...** (*fig*) reservó sus críticas más acérrimas para los que ...
zest [zest] *n* gusto *m*, entusiasmo *m*; **to do sth with ~** hacer algo con entusiasmo; **to eat with ~** comer con gusto.
zestful [ˈzestfʊl] *adj* entusiasta.
zestfully [ˈzestfəlɪ] *adv* con entusiasmo.
Zeus [zjuːs] *nm* Zeus.
zigzag [ˈzɪgzæg] **1** *n* zigzag *m*. **2** *adj* en zigzag. **3** *vi* zigzaguear, moverse en zigzag; (*person*) hacer eses.
zilch‡ [zɪltʃ] *n* (*US*) nada de nada, cero; **he's a real ~** es un cero a la izquierda.
zillion* [ˈzɪljən] (*US*) **1** *adj*: **a ~ dollars** tropecientos dólares*; **a ~ problems** tropecientos problemas*, problemas a montones*. **2** *n*: **~s of dollars** tropecientos dólares*.
Zimbabwe [zɪmˈbɑːbwɪ] *n* Zimbabue *m*.
Zimbabwean [zɪmˈbɑːbwɪən] **1** *adj* zimbabuo. **2** *n* zimbabuo *m*, -a *f*.
zinc [zɪŋk] **1** *n* cinc *m*. **2** *attr*: ~ **ointment** pomada *f* de zinc; ~ **oxide** óxido *m* de zinc.
zing [zɪŋ] **1** *n* silbido *m*; (*) gusto *m*, entusiasmo. **2** *vi* (*bullet, arrow*) silbar; **the bullet ~ed past his ear** la bala le pasó silbando cerca de la oreja; **the cars ~ed past** los coches pasaron estruendosamente.
zinnia [ˈzɪnɪə] *n* rascamoño *m*, zinnia *f*.
Zion [ˈzaɪən] *n* Sión *m*.
Zionism [ˈzaɪənɪzəm] *n* sionismo *m*.
Zionist [ˈzaɪənɪst] **1** *adj* sionista. **2** *n* sionista *mf*.
zip [zɪp] **1** *n* (**a**) (*sound*) silbido *m*, zumbido *m*.
(**b**) (*Brit*: *also* **~-fastener**) cremallera *f*, cierre *m* (de cremallera).
(**c**) (*) energía *f*, vigor *m*.
2 *vt* (**a**) **to ~ open** abrir (la cremallera *or* el cierre de).
(**b**) (*close*: *also* **to ~ up**) cerrar (la cremallera *or* el cierre de).
3 *vi*: **to ~ past** pasar silbando; (*fig*) pasar como un rayo.
◆**zip up 1** *vt* = **zip 2. 2** *vi* cerrar.
zipcode [ˈzɪpkəʊd] *n* (*US Post*) código *m* postal.
zip-fastener [ˈzɪpˌfɑːsnəʳ] *n* cremallera *f*, cierre *m* (de cremallera).
zipgun [ˈzɪpgʌn] *n* (*US*) arma *f* de fuego de fabricación casera.
zipper [ˈzɪpəʳ] *n* (*esp US*) = **zip-fastener**.
zippy* [ˈzɪpɪ] *adj* enérgico, vigoroso; pronto, rápido.
zircon [ˈzɜːkən] *n* circón *m*.
zirconium [zɜːˈkəʊnɪəm] *n* circonio *m*.
zit* [zɪt] *n* grano *m*.
zither [ˈzɪðəʳ] *n* cítara *f*.
zodiac [ˈzəʊdɪæk] *n* zodíaco *m*.
zombie [ˈzɒmbɪ] *n* zombi *m* (*also fig*).
zonal [ˈzəʊnl] *adj* zonal.
zone [zəʊn] **1** *n* zona *f*. **2** *vt* dividir por zonas, distribuir en zonas.
zoning [ˈzəʊnɪŋ] *n* división *f* por zonas, distribución *f* en zonas.
zonked‡ [zɒŋkt] *adj* (*on drink, drugs*) colocado‡; (*exhausted*) hecho polvo*.
zoo [zuː] *n* zoo *m*, jardín *m* zoológico, parque *m* zoológico; (*small, private*) colección *f* de fieras.
zoological [ˌzəʊəˈlɒdʒɪkəl] *adj* zoológico; ~ **gardens** *V* **zoo**.
zoologist [zəʊˈɒlədʒɪst] *n* zoólogo *m*, -a *f*.
zoology [zəʊˈɒlədʒɪ] *n* zoología *f*.
zoom [zuːm] **1** *n* (**a**) (*sound*) zumbido *m*. (**b**) (*Aer*) empinadura *f*. **2** *vi* (**a**) zumbar; **it ~ed past my ear** pasó zumbando cerca de mi oído. (**b**) (*Aer*) empinarse.
◆**zoom in** *vi* (*Cine*) dar un golpe de zoom (*on* para captar).
zoom-lens [ˈzuːmˈlenz] *n* zoom *m*, teleobjetivo *m*.
zoomorph [ˈzəʊəʊmɒːf] *n* zoomorfo *m*.
zoomorphic [ˌzəʊəʊˈmɒːfɪk] *adj* zoomórfico.
zooplankton [ˌzəʊəʊˈplæŋktən] *n* zooplancton *m*.
zoot-suit* [ˈzuːtsuːt] *n traje de espaldas anchas y de pantalones anchos de los años 40.*
Zoroaster [ˌzɒrəʊˈæstəʳ] *nm* Zoroastro.
zucchini [zuːˈkiːnɪ] *n*, *pl invar* (*US*) calabacín *m*, calabacines *mpl*, calabacita *f* (*LAm*).
Zulu [ˈzuːluː] **1** *adj* zulú. **2** *n* zulú *mf*.
Zululand [ˈzuːluːlænd] *n* Zululandia *f*.
zygote [ˈzaɪgəʊt] *n* cigoto *m*, zigoto *m*.

APPENDICES
APÉNDICES

THE SPANISH VERB

Each verb entry in the Spanish-English section of the Dictionary includes a reference by number and letter to the tables below, in which the simple tenses and parts of the three conjugátions and of irregular verbs are set out. For verbs having only a slight irregularity the indication of it is given in the main text of the dictionary (*eg* **escribir** [3a; *ptp* **escrito**]) and is not repeated here. Certain other verbs have been marked in the main text as *defective* and in some cases indications of usage have been given there, but for further information it is best to consult a full grammar of the language.

Certain general points may be summarized here:

The **imperfect** is regular for all verbs except *ser* (*era* etc) and *ir* (*iba* etc).

The **conditional** is formed by adding to the stem of the future tense (in most cases the infinitive) the endings of the imperfect tense of *haber*: *contaría etc*. If the stem of the future tense is irregular, the conditional will have the same irregularity: *decir – diré, diría*; *poder – podré, podría*.

Compound tenses are formed with the auxiliary *haber* and the past participle:

perfect	he cantado (*subj*: haya cantado)
pluperfect	había cantado (*subj*: hubiera cantado, hubiese cantado)
future perfect	habré cantado
conditional perfect	habría cantado
perfect infinitive	haber cantado
perfect gerund	habiendo cantado

The **imperfect subjunctives** I and II can be seen as being formed from the 3rd person plural of the preterite, using as a stem what remains after removing the final *-ron* syllable and adding to it *-ra* (I) or *-se* (II), *eg*:

cantar: canta/ron – cantara, cantase
perder: perdie/ron – perdiera, perdiese
reducir: reduje/ron – redujera, redujese

The form of the **imperative** depends not only on number but also on whether the person(s) addressed is (are) treated in familiar or in formal terms. The 'true' imperative is used only in familiar address in the affirmative:

cantar: canta (tú), cantad (vosotros)
vender: vende (tú), vended (vosotros)
partir: parte (tú), partid (vosotros)

(There are a few irregular imperatives in the singular – *salir – sal, hacer – haz*, etc, but all the plurals are regular.) The imperative affirmative in formal address requires the subjunctive: *envíemelo, háganlo, conduzca Vd con más cuidado, ¡oiga!* The imperative negative in both familiar and formal address also requires the subjunctive: *no me digas, no os preocupéis, no grite tanto Vd, no se desanimen Vds.*

Continuous tenses are formed with *estar* and the gerund: *está leyendo, estaba lloviendo, estábamos hablando de eso*. Other auxiliary verbs may occasionally replace *estar* in certain senses: *según voy viendo, va mejorando, iba cogiendo flores, lo venía estudiando desde hacía muchos años*. Usage of the continuous tenses does not exactly coincide with that of English.

The **passive** is formed with tenses of *ser* and the past participle, which agrees in number and gender with the subject: *las casas fueron construidas, será firmado mañana el tratado, después de haber sido vencido*. The passive is much less used in Spanish than in English, its function often being taken over by a reflexive construction, by *uno*, etc.

SPANISH VERB CONJUGATIONS

INFINITIVE	PRESENT INDICATIVE	PRESENT SUBJUNCTIVE	PRETERITE
[1a] **cantar** (regular: see table at end of list)			
Gerund: *cantando*			
[1b] **cambiar**	cambio	cambie	cambié
i of the stem is not stressed and the	cambias	cambies	cambiaste
verb is regular	cambia	cambie	cambió
Gerund: *cambiando*	cambiamos	cambiemos	cambiaron
	cambiáis	cambiéis	cambiasteis
	cambian	cambien	cambiaron
[1c] **enviar**	env**í**o	env**í**e	envié
i of the stem stressed in parts of the	env**í**as	env**í**es	enviaste
present tenses	env**í**a	env**í**e	envió
Gerund: *enviando*	enviamos	enviemos	enviamos
	enviáis	enviéis	enviasteis
	env**í**an	env**í**en	enviaron
[1d] **evacuar**	evacuo	evacue	evacué
u of the stem is not stressed and the	evacuas	evacues	evacuaste
verb is regular	evacua	evacue	evacuó
Gerund: *evacuando*	evacuamos	evacuemos	evacuamos
	evacuáis	evacuéis	evacuasteis
	evacuan	evacuen	evacuaron
[1e] **situar**	sit**ú**o	sit**ú**e	situé
u of the stem stressed in parts of the	sit**ú**as	sit**ú**es	situaste
present tenses	sit**ú**a	sit**ú**e	situó
Gerund: *situando*	situamos	situemos	situamos
	situáis	situéis	situasteis
	sit**ú**an	sit**ú**en	situaron
[1f] **cruzar**	cruzo	cru**c**e	cru**c**é
Stem consonant **z** written **c** before **e**	cruzas	cru**c**es	cruzaste
Gerund: *cruzando*	cruza	cru**c**e	cruzó
	cruzamos	cru**c**emos	cruzamos
	cruzáis	cru**c**éis	cruzasteis
	cruzan	cru**c**en	cruzaron
[1g] **picar**	pico	pi**qu**e	pi**qu**é
Stem consonant **c** written **qu** before **e**	picas	pi**qu**es	picaste
Gerund: *picando*	pica	pi**qu**e	picó
	picamos	pi**qu**emos	picamos
	picáis	pi**qu**éis	picasteis
	pican	pi**qu**en	picaron
[1h] **pagar**	pago	pa**gu**e	pa**gu**é
Stem consonant **g** written **gu** (with **u**	pagas	pa**gu**es	pagaste
silent) before **e**	paga	pa**gu**e	pagó
Gerund: *pagando*	pagamos	pa**gu**emos	pagamos
	pagáis	pa**gu**éis	pagasteis
	pagan	pa**gu**en	pagaron

INFINITIVE	PRESENT INDICATIVE	PRESENT SUBJUNCTIVE	PRETERITE
[1i] **averiguar**	averiguo	averi**gü**e	averi**gü**é
u of the stem written **ü** (so that it is pronounced) before **e**	averiguas	averi**gü**es	averiguaste
Gerund: *averiguando*	averigua	averi**gü**e	averiguó
	averiguamos	averi**gü**emos	averiguamos
	averiguáis	averi**gü**éis	averiguasteis
	averiguan	averi**gü**en	averiguaron
[1j] **cerrar**	c**ie**rro	c**ie**rre	cerré
Stem vowel **e** becomes **ie** when stressed	c**ie**rras	c**ie**rres	cerraste
Gerund: *cerrando*	c**ie**rra	c**ie**rre	cerró
	cerramos	cerremos	cerramos
	cerráis	cerréis	cerrasteis
	c**ie**rran	c**ie**rren	cerraron
[1k] **errar**	**ye**rro	**ye**rre	erré
As [1j], but diphthong written **ye-** at the start of the word	**ye**rras	**ye**rres	erraste
Gerund: *errando*	**ye**rra	**ye**rre	erró
	erramos	erremos	erramos
	erráis	erréis	errasteis
	yerran	**ye**rren	erraron
[1l] **contar**	c**ue**nto	c**ue**nte	conté
Stem vowel **o** becomes **ue** when stressed	c**ue**ntas	c**ue**ntes	contaste
Gerund: *contando*	c**ue**nta	c**ue**nte	contó
	contamos	contemos	contamos
	contáis	contéis	contasteis
	c**ue**ntan	c**ue**nten	contaron
[1m] **agorar**	ag**üe**ro	ag**üe**re	agoré
As [1l], but diphthong written **üe** (so that the **u** is pronounced)	ag**üe**ras	ag**üe**res	agoraste
Gerund: *agorando*	ag**üe**ra	ag**üe**re	agoró
	agoramos	agoremos	agoramos
	agoráis	agoréis	agorasteis
	ag**üe**ran	ag**üe**ren	agoraron
[1n] **jugar**	j**ue**go	j**uegu**e	ju**gu**é
Stem vowel **u** becomes **ue** when stressed; stem consonant **g** written **gu** (with **u** silent) before **e**	j**ue**gas	j**uegu**es	jugaste
Gerund: *jugando*	j**ue**ga	j**uegu**e	jugó
	jugamos	ju**gu**emos	jugamos
	jugáis	ju**gu**éis	jugasteis
	j**ue**gan	j**uegu**en	jugaron
[1o] **estar**	estoy	esté	estuve
Irregular.	estás	estés	estuviste
Imperative: *está* (*tú*)	está	esté	estuvo
Gerund: *estando*	estamos	estemos	estuvimos
	estáis	estéis	estuvisteis
	están	estén	estuvieron
[1p] **andar**	ando	ande	anduve
Irregular.	andas	andes	anduviste
Gerund: *andando*	anda	ande	anduvo
	andamos	andemos	anduvimos
	andáis	andéis	anduvisteis
	andan	anden	anduvieron

INFINITIVE	PRESENT INDICATIVE	PRESENT SUBJUNCTIVE	PRETERITE
[1q] **dar** Irregular. Gerund: *dando*	doy das da damos dais dan	dé des dé demos deis den	di diste dio dimos disteis dieron
[2a] **temer** (regular: see table at end of list)			
[2b] **vencer** Stem consonant **c** written **z** before **a** and **o** Gerund: *venciendo*	ven**z**o vences vence vencemos vencéis vencen	ven**z**a ven**z**as ven**z**a ven**z**amos ven**z**áis ven**z**an	vencí venciste venció vencimos vencisteis vencieron
[2c] **coger** Stem consonant **g** written **j** before **a** and **o** Gerund: *cogiendo*	co**j**o coges coge cogemos cogéis cogen	co**j**a co**j**as co**j**a co**j**amos co**j**áis co**j**an	cogí cogiste cogió cogimos cogisteis cogieron
[2d] **conocer** Stem consonant **c** becomes **zc** before **a** and **o** Gerund: *conociendo*	cono**zc**o conoces conoce conocemos conocéis conocen	cono**zc**a cono**zc**as cono**zc**a cono**zc**amos cono**zc**áis cono**zc**an	conocí conociste conoció conocimos conocisteis conocieron
[2e] **leer** Unstressed **i** between vowels is written **y**. Past Participle: *leído* Gerund: *leyendo*	leo lees lee leemos leéis leen	lea leas lea leamos leáis lean	leí leíste le**y**ó leímos leísteis le**y**eron
[2f] **tañer** Unstressed **i** after **ñ** (and also after **ll**) is omitted Gerund: *tañendo*	taño tañes tañe tañemos tañéis tañen	taña tañas taña tañamos tañáis tañan	tañí tañiste ta**ñó** tañimos tañisteis ta**ñ**eron
[2g] **perder** Stem vowel **e** becomes **ie** when stressed Gerund: *perdiendo*	p**ie**rdo p**ie**rdes p**ie**rde perdemos perdéis p**ie**rden	p**ie**rda p**ie**rdas p**ie**rda perdamos perdáis p**ie**rdan	perdí perdiste perdió perdimos perdisteis perdieron
[2h] **mover** Stem vowel **o** becomes **ue** when stressed Gerund: *moviendo*	m**ue**vo m**ue**ves m**ue**ve movemos movéis m**ue**ven	m**ue**va m**ue**vas m**ue**va movamos mováis m**ue**van	moví moviste movió movimos movisteis movieron

INFINITIVE	PRESENT INDICATIVE	PRESENT SUBJUNCTIVE	PRETERITE
[2i] **oler**	**hue**lo	**hue**la	olí
As [2h], but diphthong is written **hue-**	**hue**les	**hue**las	oliste
at the start of the word	**hue**le	**hue**la	olió
Gerund: *oliendo*	olemos	olamos	olimos
	oléis	oláis	olisteis
	huelen	**hue**lan	olieron
[2j] **haber** (see table at end of list)			
[2k] **tener**	tengo	tenga	tuve
Irregular.	tienes	tengas	tuviste
Future: *tendré*	tiene	tenga	tuvo
Imperative: *ten* (*tú*)	tenemos	tengamos	tuvimos
Gerund: *teniendo*	tenéis	tengáis	tuvisteis
	tienen	tengan	tuvieron
[2l] **caber**	quepo	quepa	cupe
Irregular.	cabes	quepas	cupiste
Future: *cabré*	cabe	quepa	cupo
Gerund: *cabiendo*	cabemos	quepamos	cupimos
	cabéis	quepáis	cupisteis
	caben	quepan	cupieron
[2m] **saber**	sé	sepa	supe
Irregular.	sabes	sepas	supiste
Future: *sabré*	sabe	sepa	supo
Gerund: *sabiendo*	sabemos	sepamos	supimos
	sabéis	sepáis	supisteis
	saben	sepan	supieron
[2n] **caer**	caigo	caiga	caí
Unstressed **i** between vowels written	caes	caigas	caíste
y, as [2e].	cae	caiga	ca**y**ó
Past Participle: *caído*	caemos	caigamos	caímos
Gerund: *cayendo*	caéis	caigáis	caísteis
	caen	caigan	ca**y**eron
[2o] **traer**	traigo	traiga	traje
Irregular.	traes	traigas	trajiste
Past Participle: *traído*	trae	traiga	trajo
Gerund: *trayendo*	traemos	traigamos	trajimos
	traéis	traigáis	trajisteis
	traen	traigan	trajeron
[2p] **valer**	valgo	valga	valí
Irregular.	vales	valgas	valiste
Future: *valdré*	vale	valga	valió
Gerund: *valiendo*	valemos	valgamos	valimos
	valéis	valgáis	valisteis
	valen	valgan	valieron
[2q] **poner**	pongo	ponga	puse
Irregular.	pones	pongas	pusiste
Future: *pondré*	pone	ponga	puso
Past Participle: *puesto*	ponemos	pongamos	pusimos
Imperative: *pon* (*tú*)	ponéis	pongáis	pusisteis
Gerund: *poniendo*	ponen	pongan	pusieron

INFINITIVE	PRESENT INDICATIVE	PRESENT SUBJUNCTIVE	PRETERITE
[2r] **hacer**	hago	haga	hice
Irregular.	haces	hagas	hiciste
Future: *haré*	hace	haga	hizo
Past Participle: *hecho*	hacemos	hagamos	hicimos
Imperative: *haz* (*tú*)	hacéis	hagáis	hicisteis
Gerund: *haciendo*	hacen	hagan	hicieron
[2s] **poder**	puedo	pueda	pude
Irregular.	puedes	puedas	pudiste
In present tenses like [2h].	puede	pueda	pudo
Future: *podré*	podemos	podamos	pudimos
Gerund: *pudiendo*	podéis	podáis	pudisteis
	pueden	puedan	pudieron
[2t] **querer**	quiero	quiera	quise
Irregular.	quieres	quieras	quisiste
In present tenses like [2g].	quiere	quiera	quiso
Future: *querré*	queremos	queramos	quisimos
Gerund: *queriendo*	queréis	queráis	quisisteis
	quieren	quieran	quisieron
[2u] **ver**	veo	vea	vi
Irregular.	ves	veas	viste
Imperfect: *veía*	ve	vea	vio
Past Participle: *visto*	vemos	veamos	vimos
Gerund: *viendo*	veis	veáis	visteis
	ven	vean	vieron

[2v] **ser** (see table at end of list)

[2w] **placer.** Exclusively 3rd person singular. Irregular forms: Present subj. *plazca* (less commonly *plega* or *plegue*); Preterite *plació* (less commonly *plugo*); Imperfect subj. I *placiera*, II *placiese* (less commonly *plugiera*, *plugiese*).

[2x] **yacer.** Archaic. Irregular forms: Present indic. *yazco* (less commonly *yazgo* or *yago*), *yaces* etc; Present subj. *yazca* (less commonly *yazga* or *yaga*), *yazcas* etc; Imperative *yace* (*tú*) (less commonly *yaz*).

[2y] **raer.** Present indic. usually *raigo*, *raes* etc (like *caer* [2n]), but *rayo* occasionally found; Present subj. usually *raiga*, *raigas* etc (also like *caer*), but *raya*, *rayas* etc occasionally found.

[2z] **roer.** Alternative forms in present tenses: Indicative, *roo, roigo* or *royo*; *roes, roe* etc. Subjunctive, *roa, roiga* or *roya*. First persons usually avoided because of the uncertainty. The gerund is *royendo*.

[3a] **partir** (regular: see tables at end of list)

INFINITIVE	PRESENT INDICATIVE	PRESENT SUBJUNCTIVE	PRETERITE
[3b] **esparcir**	espar**z**o	espar**z**a	esparcí
Stem consonant **c** written **z** before **a**	esparces	espar**z**as	esparciste
and **o**	esparce	espar**z**a	esparció
Gerund: *esparciendo*	esparcimos	espar**z**amos	esparcimos
	esparcís	espar**z**áis	esparcisteis
	esparcen	espar**z**an	esparcieron
[3c] **dirigir**	diri**j**o	diri**j**a	dirigí
Stem consonant **g** written **j** before **a**	diriges	diri**j**as	dirigiste
and **o**	dirige	diri**j**a	dirigió
Gerund: *dirigiendo*	dirigimos	diri**j**amos	dirigimos
	dirigís	diri**j**áis	dirigisteis
	dirigen	diri**j**an	dirigieron

INFINITIVE	PRESENT INDICATIVE	PRESENT SUBJUNCTIVE	PRETERITE
[3d] **distinguir**	distingo	distinga	distinguí
u after the stem consonant **g** omitted	distingues	distingas	distinguiste
before **a** and **o**	distingue	distinga	distinguió
Gerund: *distinguendo*	distinguimos	distingamos	distinguimos
	distinguís	distingáis	distinguisteis
	distinguen	distingan	distinguieron
[3e] **delinquir**	delinco	delinca	delinquí
Stem consonant **qu** written **c** before **a**	delinques	delincas	delinquiste
and **o**	delinque	delinca	delinquió
Gerund: *delinquiendo*	delinquimos	delincamos	delinquimos
	delinquís	delincáis	delinquisteis
	delinquen	delincan	delinquieron
[3f] **lucir**	luzco	luzca	lucí
Stem consonant **c** becomes **zc** before **a**	luces	luzcas	luciste
and **o**	luce	luzca	lució
Gerund: *luciendo*	lucimos	luzcamos	lucimos
	lucís	luzcáis	lucisteis
	lucen	luzcan	lucieron
[3g] **huir**	huyo	huya	huí
A **y** is inserted before endings not be-	huyes	huyas	huiste
ginning with **i**.	huye	huya	huyó
Gerund: *huyendo*	huimos	huyamos	huimos
	huís	huyáis	huisteis
	huyen	huyan	huyeron
[3h] **gruñir**	gruño	gruña	gruñí
Unstressed **i** after **ñ** (and also after **ch**	gruñes	gruñas	gruñiste
and **ll**) omitted	gruñe	gruña	gruñó
Gerund: *gruñendo*	gruñimos	gruñamos	gruñimos
	gruñís	gruñáis	gruñisteis
	gruñen	gruñan	gruñeron
[3i] **sentir**	siento	sienta	sentí
The stem vowel **e** becomes **ie** when	sientes	sientas	sentiste
stressed; **e** becomes **i** in 3rd persons of	siente	sienta	sintió
Preterite, 1st and 2nd persons pl. of	sentimos	sintamos	sentimos
Present Subjunctive.	sentís	sintáis	sentisteis
Gerund: *sintiendo*	sienten	sientan	sintieron
In *adquirir* the stem vowel **i** becomes **ie** when stressed			
[3j] **dormir**	duermo	duerma	dormí
The stem vowel **o** becomes **ue** when	duermes	duermas	dormiste
stressed; **o** becomes **u** in 3rd persons	duerme	duerma	durmió
of Preterite, 1st and 2nd persons pl. of	dormimos	durmamos	dormimos
Present Subjunctive.	dormís	durmáis	dormisteis
Gerund: *durmiendo*	duermen	duerman	durmieron
[3k] **pedir**	pido	pida	pedí
The stem vowel **e** becomes **i** when	pides	pidas	pediste
stressed, and in 3rd persons of Preter-	pide	pida	pidió
ite, 1st and 2nd persons pl. of Present	pedimos	pidamos	pedimos
Subjunctive.	pedís	pidáis	pedisteis
Gerund: *pidiendo*	piden	pidan	pidieron

INFINITIVE	PRESENT INDICATIVE	PRESENT SUBJUNCTIVE	PRETERITE
[3l] **reír**	río	ría	reí
Irregular.	ríes	rías	reíste
Past Participle: *reído*	ríe	ría	rió
Gerund: *riendo*	reímos	riamos	reímos
Imperative: *ríe* (*tú*)	reís	riáis	reísteis
	ríen	rían	rieron
[3m] **erguir**	yergo	yerga	erguí
Irregular.	yergues	yergas	erguiste
Gerund: *irguiendo*	yergue	yerga	irguió
Imperative: *yergue* (*tú*) and less	erguimos	yergamos	erguimos
commonly *irgue* (*tú*)	erguís	yergáis	erguisteis
	yerguen	yergan	irguieron
[3n] **reducir**	redu**zc**o	redu**zc**a	red**uj**e
The stem consonant **c** becomes **zc** be-	reduces	redu**zc**as	red**uj**iste
fore **a** and **o** as [3f]; irregular preter-	reduce	redu**zc**a	red**uj**o
ite in **-uj-**	reducimos	redu**zc**amos	red**uj**imos
Gerund: *reduciendo*	reducís	redu**zc**áis	red**uj**isteis
	reducen	redu**zc**an	red**uj**eron
[3o] **decir**	digo	diga	dije
Irregular.	dices	digas	dijiste
Future: *diré*	dice	diga	dijo
Past Participle: *dicho*	decimos	digamos	dijimos
Gerund: *diciendo*	decís	digáis	dijisteis
Imperative: *di* (*tú*)	dicen	digan	dijeron
[3p] **oír**	oigo	oiga	oí
Irregular.	o**y**es	oigas	oíste
Unstressed **i** between vowels becomes	o**y**e	oiga	o**y**ó
y	oímos	oigamos	oímos
Past Participle: *oído*	oís	oigáis	oísteis
Gerund: *oyendo*	o**y**en	oigan	o**y**eron
[3q] **salir**	salgo	salga	salí
Irregular.	sales	salgas	saliste
Future: *saldré*	sale	salga	salió
Imperative: *sal* (*tú*)	salimos	salgamos	salimos
Gerund: *saliendo*	salís	salgáis	salisteis
	salen	salgan	salieron
[3r] **venir**	vengo	venga	vine
Irregular.	vienes	vengas	viniste
Future: *vendré*	viene	venga	vino
Gerund: *viniendo*	venimos	vengamos	vinimos
Imperative: *ven* (*tú*)	venís	vengáis	vinisteis
	vienen	vengan	vinieron
[3s] **ir**	voy	vaya	fui
Irregular.	vas	vayas	fuiste
Imperfect: *iba*	va	vaya	fue
Gerund: *yendo*	vamos	vayamos	fuimos
Imperative: *ve* (*tú*), *id* (*vosotros*)	vais	vayáis	fuisteis
	van	vayan	fueron

[1a] **cantar** (regular verb)

INDICATIVE

Present
canto
cantas
canta
cantamos
cantáis
cantan

Imperfect
cantaba
cantabas
cantaba
cantábamos
cantabais
cantaban

Preterite
canté
cantaste
cantó
cantamos
cantasteis
cantaron

Future
cantaré
cantarás
cantará
cantaremos
cantaréis
cantarán

Gerund
cantando

CONDITIONAL
cantaría
cantarías
cantaría
cantaríamos
cantaríais
cantarían

Imperative
canta (tú)
cantad (vosotros)

Past Participle
cantado

SUBJUNCTIVE

Present
cante
cantes
cante
cantemos
cantéis
canten

Imperfect
cantara/-ase
cantaras/-ases
cantara/-ase
cantáramos/-ásemos
cantarais/-aseis
cantaran/-asen

[2a] **temer** (regular verb)

INDICATIVE

Present
temo
temes
teme
tememos
teméis
temen

Imperfect
temía
temías
temía
temíamos
temíais
temían

Future
temeré
temerás
temerá
temeremos
temeréis
temerán

Preterite
temí
temiste
temió
temimos
temisteis
temieron

Gerund
temiendo

CONDITIONAL
temería
temerías
temería
temeríamos
temeríais
temerían

Imperative
teme (tú)
temed (vosotros)

Past Participle
temido

SUBJUNCTIVE

Present
tema
temas
tema
temamos
temáis
teman

Imperfect
temiera/-iese
temieras/-ieses
temiera/-iese
temiéramos/-iésemos
temierais/-ieseis
temieran/-iesen

[3a] **partir** (regular verb)

INDICATIVE

Present
parto
partes
parte
partimos
partís
parten

Imperfect
partía
partías
partía
partíamos
partíais
partían

Preterite
partí
partiste
partió
partimos
partisteis
partieron

Future
partiré
partirás
partirá
partiremos
partiréis
partirán

Gerund
partiendo

CONDITIONAL
partiría
partirías
partiría
partiríamos
partiríais
partirían

Imperative
parte (tú)
partid (vosotros)

Past Participle
partido

SUBJUNCTIVE

Present
parta
partas
parta
partamos
partáis
partan

Imperfect
partiera/-iese
partieras/-ieses
partiera/-iese
partiéramos/-iésemos
partierais/-ieseis
partieran/-iesen

[2j] **haber**

INDICATIVE

Present
he
has
ha
hemos
habéis
han

Imperfect
había
habías
había
habíamos
habíais
habían

Preterite
hube
hubiste
hubo
hubimos
hubisteis
hubieron

Future
habré
habrás
habrá
habremos
habréis
habrán

Gerund
habiendo

Past Participle
habido

CONDITIONAL
habría
habrías
habría
habríamos
habríais
habrían

SUBJUNCTIVE

Present
haya
hayas
haya
hayamos
hayáis
hayan

Imperfect
hubiera/-iese
hubieras/-ieses
hubiera/-iese
hubiéramos/-iésemos
hubierais/-ieseis
hubieran/-iesen

[2v] **ser**

INDICATIVE

Present
soy
eres
es
somos
sois
son

Imperfect
era
eras
era
éramos
erais
eran

Preterite
fui
fuiste
fue
fuimos
fuisteis
fueron

Future
seré
serás
será
seremos
seréis
serán

Gerund
siendo

Past Participle
sido

CONDITIONAL
sería
serías
sería
seríamos
seríais
serían

Imperative
sé (tú)
sed (vosotros)

SUBJUNCTIVE

Present
sea
seas
sea
seamos
seáis
sean

Imperfect
fuera/-ese
fueras/-eses
fuera/-ese
fuéramos/-ésemos
fuerais/-eseis
fueran/-esen

EL VERBO INGLÉS

El verbo inglés es bastante más sencillo que el español, a lo menos en cuanto a su forma. Hay muchos verbos fuertes o irregulares (damos una lista de ellos a continuación) y varias clases de irregularidad ortográfica (véanse las notas al final); pero hay una sola conjugación, y dentro de cada tiempo no hay variación para las seis personas excepto en el presente (tercera persona de singular). Por tanto, no es necesario ofrecer para el verbo inglés los cuadros y paradigmas con que se suele explicar el verbo español; la estructura general y las formas del verbo inglés se resumen en las siguientes notas.

Indicativo

(a) **Presente**: tiene la misma forma que el infinitivo en todas las personas menos la tercera del singular; en ésta, se añade una **-s** al infinitivo, p.ej. **he sells,** o se añade **-es** si el infinitivo termina en sibilante (los sonidos [s], [z], [ʃ] y [tʃ]; en la escritura **-ss, -zz, -sh** y **-ch,** etc). Esta **-s** añadida tiene dos pronunciaciones: tras consonante sorda se pronuncia sorda [s], p.ej. **scoffs** [skɒfs], **likes** [laɪks], **taps** [tæps], **waits** [weɪts], **baths** [bɑːθs]; tras consonante sonora se pronuncia sonora, p.ej. **robs** [rɒbz], **bends** [bendz], **seems** [siːmz], **gives** [gɪvz], **bathes** [ˈbeɪðz]; **-es** se pronuncia también sonora tras sibilante o consonante sonora, o letra final del infinitivo, p.ej. **races** [ˈreɪsɪz], **urges** [ˈɜːdʒɪz], **lashes** [ˈlæʃɪz], **passes** [ˈpɑːsɪz].

Los verbos que terminan en **-y** la cambian en **-ies** en la tercera persona del singular, p.ej. **tries, pities, satisfies**; pero son regulares los verbos que en el infinitivo tienen una vocal delante de la **-y,** p.ej. **pray – he prays, annoy – she annoys.**

El verbo **be** es irregular en todas las personas:

I am	we are
you are	you are
he is	they are

Cuatro verbos más tienen forma irregular en la tercera persona del singular:

do – he does [dʌz]	go – he goes [gəʊz]
have – he has [hæz]	say – he says [sez]

(b) **Pretérito** (o **pasado simple**) **y participio de pasado**: tienen la misma forma en inglés; se forman añadiendo **-ed** al infinitivo, p.ej. **paint – I painted – painted,** o bien añadiendo **-d** a los infinitivos terminados en **-e** muda, p.ej. **bare – I bared – bared, move – I moved – moved, revise – I revised – revised.** (Para los muchos verbos irregulares, véase la lista abajo.) Esta **-d** o **-ed** se pronuncia por lo general [t]: **raced** [reɪst], **passed** [pɑːst]; pero cuando se añade a un infinitivo terminado en consonante sonora o en **r,** se pronuncia [d], p.ej. **bared** [bɛəd], **moved** [muːvd], **seemed** [siːmd], **buzzed** [bʌzd]. Si el infinitivo termina en **-d** o **-t,** la desinencia **-ed** se pronuncia como una sílaba más, [ɪd], p.ej. **raided** [ˈreɪdɪd], **dented** [ˈdentɪd]. Para los verbos cuyo infinitivo termina en **-y,** véase **Verbos débiles** (e) abajo.

(c) **Tiempos compuestos del pasado**: se forman como en español con el verbo auxiliar **to have** y el participio de pasado: perfecto **I have painted,** pluscuamperfecto **I had painted.**

(d) **Futuro y condicional** (o **potencial**): se forma el futuro con el auxiliar **will** o **shall** y el infinitivo, p.ej. **I will do it, they shall not pass**; se forma el condicional (o potencial) con el auxiliar **would** o **should** y el infinitivo, p.ej. **I would go, if she should come.** Como en español y de igual formación existen los tiempos compuestos llamados futuro perfecto, p.ej. **I shall have finished,** y potencial compuesto, p.ej. **I would have paid.**

(e) Para cada tiempo del indicativo existe una forma continua que se forma con el tiempo apropiado del verbo **to be** (equivalente en este caso al español **estar**) y el participio de presente (véase abajo): **I am waiting, we were hoping, they will be buying it, they would have been waiting still, I had been painting all day.** Conviene subrayar que el modo de emplear estas formas continuas no corresponde siempre al sistema español.

Subjuntivo

Este modo tiene muy poco uso en inglés. En el presente tiene la misma forma que el infinitivo en todas las personas, (**that**) **I go,** (**that**) **she go** etc. En el pasado simple el único verbo que tiene forma especial es **to be,** que es **were** en todas las personas, (**that**) **I were,** (**that**) **we were** etc. En los demás casos donde la lógica de los tiempos en español pudiera parecer exigir una forma de subjuntivo en pasado, el inglés emplea el presente, p.ej. **he had urged that we do it at once.** El subjuntivo se emplea obligatoriamente en inglés en **if I were you, if he were to do it, were I to attempt it** (el indicativo **was** es tenido por vulgar en estas frases y análogas); se encuentra también en la frase fosilizada **so be it,** y en el lenguaje oficial de las actas, etc, p.ej. **it is agreed that nothing be done, it was resolved that the pier be painted** (pero son igualmente correctos **should be done, should be painted**).

Gerundio y participio de presente

Tienen la misma forma en inglés; se añade al infinitivo la desinencia **-ing,** p.ej. **washing, sending, passing.** Para las muchas irregularidades ortográficas de esta desinencia, véase la sección **Verbos débiles** abajo.

Voz pasiva

Se forma exactamente como en español, con el tiempo apropiado del verbo **to be** (equivalente en este caso a **ser**) y el participio de pasado: **we are forced to, he was killed, they had been injured, the company will be taken over, it ought to have been rebuilt, were it to be agreed.**

Imperativo

Hay solamente una forma, que es la del infinitivo: **tell me, come here, don't do that.**

VERBOS FUERTES (O IRREGULARES)

INFINITIVO	PRETÉRITO	PARTICIPIO DE PASADO
abide	abode *or* abided	abode *or* abided
arise	arose	arisen
awake	awoke	awaked
be	was, were	been
bear	bore	(*llevado*) borne, (*nacido*) born
beat	beat	beaten
become	became	become
beget	begot, (††) begat	begotten
begin	began	begun
bend	bent	bent
beseech	besought	besought
bet	bet *or* betted	bet *or* betted
bid (*ordenar*)	bade	bidden
(*licitar etc*)	bid	bid
bind	bound	bound
bite	bit	bitten
bleed	bled	bled
blow	blew	blown
break	broke	broken
breed	bred	bred
bring	brought	brought
build	built	built
burn	burned *or* burnt	burned *or* burnt
burst	burst	burst
buy	bought	bought
can	could	–
cast	cast	cast
catch	caught	caught
choose	chose	chosen
cleave[1] (*vt*)	clove *or* cleft	cloven *or* cleft
cleave[2] (*vi*)	cleaved, (††) clave	cleaved
cling	clung	clung
come	came	come
cost (*vt*)	costed	costed
(*vi*)	cost	cost
creep	crept	crept
cut	cut	cut
deal	dealt	dealt
dig	dug	dug
do	did	done
draw	drew	drawn
dream	dreamed *or* dreamt	dreamed *or* dreamt
drink	drank	drunk
drive	drove	driven
dwell	dwelt	dwelt
eat	ate	eaten
fall	fell	fallen
feed	fed	fed
feel	felt	felt
fight	fought	fought
find	found	found
flee	fled	fled
fling	flung	flung
fly	flew	flown
forbid	forbad(e)	forbidden
forget	forgot	forgotten
forsake	forsook	forsaken
freeze	froze	frozen
get	got	got, (*US*) gotten
gild	gilded	gilded *or* gilt
gird	girded *or* girt	girded *or* girt
give	gave	given
go	went	gone
grind	ground	ground
grow	grew	grown
hang	hung, (*Law*) hanged	hung, (*Law*) hanged
have	had	had
hear	heard	heard
heave	heaved, (*Naut*) hove	heaved, (*Naut*) hove
hew	hewed	hewed *or* hewn
hide	hid	hidden
hit	hit	hit
hold	held	held
hurt	hurt	hurt
keep	kept	kept
kneel	knelt	knelt
know	knew	known
lade	laded	laden
lay	laid	laid
lead	led	led
lean	leaned *or* leant	leaned *or* leant
leap	leaped *or* leapt	leaped *or* leapt
learn	learned *or* learnt	learned *or* learnt
leave	left	left
lend	lent	lent
let	let	let
lie	lay	lain
light	lit *or* lighted	lit *or* lighted
lose	lost	lost
make	made	made
may	might	–
mean	meant	meant
meet	met	met
mow	mowed	mown *or* mowed
pay	paid	paid
put	put	put
quit	quit *or* quitted	quit *or* quitted
read [riːd]	read [red]	read [red]
rend	rent	rent
rid	rid	rid
ride	rode	ridden
ring	rang	rung
rise	rose	risen
run	ran	run
saw	sawed	sawed *or* sawn
say	said	said
see	saw	seen
seek	sought	sought
sell	sold	sold
send	sent	sent
set	set	set
sew	sewed	sewn
shake	shook	shaken
shave	shaved	shaved *or* shaven
shear	sheared	sheared *or* shorn
shed	shed	shed
shine	shone	shone

INFINITIVO	PRETÉRITO	PARTICIPIO DE PASADO
shoe	shod	shod
shoot	shot	shot
show	showed	shown *or* showed
shrink	shrank	shrunk
shut	shut	shut
sing	sang	sung
sink	sank	sunk
sit	sat	sat
slay	slew	slain
sleep	slept	slept
slide	slid	slid
sling	slung	slung
slink	slunk	slunk
slit	slit	slit
smell	smelled *or* smelt	smelled *or* smelt
smite	smote	smitten
sow	sowed	sowed *or* sown
speak	spoke	spoken
speed (*vt*)	speeded	speeded
(*vi*)	sped	sped
spell	spelled *or* spelt	spelled *or* spelt
spend	spent	spent
spill	spilled *or* spilt	spilled *or* spilt
spin	spun, (††) span	spun
spit	spat	spat
split	split	split
spoil	spoiled *or* spoilt	spoiled *or* spoilt
spread	spread	spread
spring	sprang	sprung
stand	stood	stood
stave	stove *or* staved	stove *or* staved
steal	stole	stolen
stick	stuck	stuck
sting	stung	stung
stink	stank	stunk
strew	strewed	strewed *or* strewn
stride	strode	stridden
strike	struck	struck
string	strung	strung
strive	strove	striven
swear	swore	sworn
sweep	swept	swept
swell	swelled	swollen
swim	swam	swum
swing	swung	swung
take	took	taken
teach	taught	taught
tear	tore	torn
tell	told	told
think	thought	thought
thrive	throve *or* thrived	thriven *or* thrived
throw	threw	thrown
thrust	thrust	thrust
tread	trod	trodden
wake	woke *or* waked	woken *or* waked
wear	wore	worn
weave	wove	woven
weep	wept	wept
win	won	won
wind	wound	wound
wring	wrung	wrung
write	wrote	written

N.B. – No constan en esta lista los verbos compuestos con prefijo etc; para ellos véase el verbo básico, p.ej. para **forbear** véase **bear**, para **understand** véase **stand**.

VERBOS DÉBILES CON IRREGULARIDAD ORTOGRÁFICA

(**a**) Hay muchos verbos cuya ortografía varía ligeramente en el participio de pasado y en el gerundio. Son los que terminan en consonante simple precedida de vocal simple acentuada; antes de añadirles la desinencia **-ed** o **-ing,** se dobla la consonante:

Infinitivo	*Participio de pasado*	*Gerundio*
sob	sobbed	sobbing
wed	wedded	wedding
lag	lagged	lagging
control	controlled	controlling
dim	dimmed	dimming
tan	tanned	tanning
tap	tapped	tapping
prefer	preferred	preferring
pat	patted	patting

(pero **cook-cooked-cooking, fear-feared-fearing, roar-roared-roaring,** donde la vocal no es simple y por tanto no se dobla la consonante).

(**b**) Los verbos que terminan en **-c** la cambian en **-ck** al añadirse las desinencias **-ed, -ing**:

frolic	frolicked	frolicking
traffic	trafficked	trafficking

(**c**) Los verbos terminados en **-l, -p,** aunque precedida de vocal átona, tienen doblada la consonante en el participio de pasado y en el gerundio en el inglés británico, pero simple en el de Estados Unidos:

grovel	(*Brit*) grovelled	(*Brit*) grovelling
	(*US*) groveled	(*US*) groveling
travel	(*Brit*) travelled	(*Brit*) travelling
	(*US*) traveled	(*US*) traveling
worship	(*Brit*) worshipped	(*Brit*) worshipping
	(*US*) worshiped	(*US*) worshiping

Nota – existe la misma diferencia en los sustantivos formados sobre tales verbos: (*Brit*) traveller = (*US*) traveler, (*Brit*) worshipper = (*US*) worshiper.

(**d**) Si el verbo termina en **-e** muda, se suprime ésta al añadir las desinencias **-ed, -ing**:

rake	raked	raking
care	cared	caring
smile	smiled	smiling
move	moved	moving
invite	invited	inviting

(Pero se conserva esta **-e** muda delante de **-ing** en los verbos **dye, singe** y otros, y en los pocos que terminan en **-oe**: **dyeing, singeing, hoeing.**)

(**e**) Si el verbo termina en **-y** (con las dos pronunciaciones de [ɪ] y [aɪ]) se cambia ésta en **-ied** (con las pronunciaciones respectivas de [ɪd] y [aɪd]) para formar el pretérito y el participio de pasado: **worry-worried-worried**; **pity-pitied-pitied**; **falsify-falsified-falsified**; **try-tried-tried.** El gerundio de tales verbos es regular: **worrying, trying** etc. Pero el gerundio de los verbos monosílabos **die, lie, vie** se escribe **dying, lying, vying.**

ASPECTS OF WORD FORMATION IN SPANISH

Processes of word formation in Spanish are in some respects far richer and more complex than those of English, and users of the dictionary may find the following notes of interest as guides which both draw together and extend information conveyed in the main alphabetic list.

1 Prefixes and prefixed elements

These very largely correspond to those of English when drawn, as so many are, from the common Graeco-Latin stock: **contra-**, **des-**, **dis-**, **ex-**, **hiper-**, **hipo-**, **para-**, **re-**, **ultra-** and so on, with **auto-** representing both English **auto-** and **self-**. There is normally total correspondence also in the immense range of scientific elements, allowance being made for phonetic and orthographic adjustments such as **lympho-/linfo-**. Elements may build up in blinding-with-science advertisements such as that for **electrofisiohidroterapias**. There are a few traditional Spanish intensifying prefixes which have no corresponding English forms: see **re-**, **requete-**, **recontra-**, also **archi-** which is much more used than **arch-** in English. These may be combined for exceptional emphasis: **archirrequetedicho** 'oft-repeated'.

2 Formation by suffix

(a) In both languages many suffixes of Latin origin correspond perfectly and will not be discussed here: **-al/-al**, **-ific(al)/-ífico**, **-ity/-idad**, **-ous/-oso**, **-tion/-ción**, and others. It is probable but not wholly predictable that in both languages on any one base the full range of forms can be built: for example **-izar**, **-izado**, **-izante**, **-izaje**, **-ización**, **-izacionar**, **-izacionismo**, though Spanish with its greater degree of latinity may much exceed English in this regard (**tecnocratizarse** 'to become technocratic'; 'to become dominated by technocrats'; **desgubernamentalización**, **destrascendentalización**). See further remarks below on **-able**, **-abilidad**.

(b) For other suffixes, hundreds of items have been listed in the main body of the dictionary because they are sufficiently common to warrant this. They are of two types. In the first group are those words which have become fully 'lexicalized' and need separate treatment, such as **casita**, **españolito**, **lentillas**, **librote**, **mujeraza**, **mujerzuela**, **palabrota**. In the second group, an occasional series has been included in the main dictionary as an illustration of the process here under discussion: see for example **amigacho-amigazo-amiguete-amigote-amiguito**. In any case, the notion of what may be considered 'lexicalized' is very unsure.

(c) Identification of the base word is easy in most cases. Normally, but far from always, the suffixed form retains the gender of the original noun. Certain changes of what is or becomes with suffix a medial consonant need to be borne in mind: **lazo-lacito**, **voz-vocecita**, **barco-barquito**, **loco-loquillo**. Sometimes two or even more suffixes are built on a base: **facilonería** consists of **fácil** + **-ón** + **-ería**, **hombrachón** consists of **hombre** + **-acho** + **-ón**, **tristoncete** consists of **triste** + **-ón** + **ete**, **gentucilla** consists of **gente** + **-uza** + **-illa**, while real complexities are offered by **es una marisabidilla** and **hay peces pero son chiquititecillos**. The need for a compounding consonant is seen in some formations: **hombre** will not make ***hombrito** or ***hombrillo**, but **hombrecito**, **hombrecillo**.

(d) Nearly all the suffixes to be listed below are nouns and adjectives. There is little one can say about the formation of verbs except to note that it is less free than in English (in which one can all too readily say 'the troops will be helicoptered in', 'the match was weathered off', 'please have this text word-processed and the data accessed'). New verbs almost always belong to the first **-ar** conjugation (including **-ear**, **-ificar**, **-izar**) and may themselves be built on noun or adjectival suffixes or related to them (eg **mariconear** supposing noun suffix **-eo**).

(e) Few adverbs are listed below; they are readily formed in the standard way from the feminine form of the adjective + **-mente**. Speakers and writers of Spanish in ordinary colloquial registers tend to avoid these forms (this does not refer to such ordinary forms as eg **rápidamente**), preferring less pretentious circumlocutions ('de una manera ...', etc), but the **-mente** forms appear powerfully in literary and journalistic writing and are often much more expressive than the English adverbial form in **-ly**. Thus we find **obrar maquiavélicamente** 'to act in a Machiavellian fashion', **pintar goyescamente** 'to paint in the manner of Goya', **una fruta gustativamente superior** 'a fruit which is superior in terms of flavour', **generacionalmente hablando** 'speaking in terms of generations', **solicitar improrrogablemente** 'apply with no possible extension of the deadline', **una republiquilla mafiosamente organizada** 'a potty republic organized on Mafia lines', and even – as an imaginative nonce-word – **huyó gacelamente** 'she fled with the grace of a gazelle' (there being no base adjective ***gacelo**).

(f) The usage discussed below is that of Spain. Latin-American Spanish offers notable differences from this: some suffixes of Spain are hardly used in Latin America, while **-ito** is used far more and often without any perceptible diminutive or emotive function (eg **Con permiso** 'May I come in?' in Spain may be **Con permisito** in Venezuela). See eg **ahorita**, **lueguito**.

(g) While some of the suffixes listed below present no semantic problem, being wholly objective or neutral (when designating largeness or smallness), some of these and many others may carry an emotive charge (intensifying, belittling, self-deprecatory, ironical, admiring ...) for the speaker or writer and this is often a subtle one. It follows that to give an English translation or even an impression in a few words is difficult: the reader should try to form his own sense by inspecting a wide range of examples of the same suffix, including some which are cross-referenced to the main dictionary. The expressive wealth of formation by suffix can be illustrated by the following collection of forms all based on **rojo** in its political sense and gathered from the press in recent years: **rojamen, rojazo, rojeras, rojería, rojerío. rojete, rojillo, rojismo, rojista, rojoide**. For English readers the best study is that of Anthony Gooch, **Diminutive, Augmentative and Pejorative Suffixes in Modern Spanish** (Oxford etc, Pergamon Press, 1967, 2nd ed. 1970), with thousands of examples and English versions which are both sensitive and lively. What follows is a selection only, of common and current items, and is in no way to be taken as a comprehensive survey.

-able, -abilidad (*also* -ible, -ibilidad)

This suffix often expresses more than the corresponding English **-able, -ability** (or English does not tolerate the corresponding forms). Examples are **idolatrable** 'that can be idolatrized', **indeglutible** 'that cannot be swallowed, unswallowable', **jubilable** 'of pensionable age', **tanques largables** 'tanks that can be jettisoned'. The latinate nature of Spanish permits such formations as **inasequibilidad, inconsultabilidad, la indescarrilabilidad del nuevo tren**.

-aco, -aca

Pejorative noun suffix: **hombraco** 'contemptible fellow, horrible chap', **tiparraco** 'odious individual, creep'. Compare in the dictionary **libraco, pajarraco**.

-acho, -acha

Pejorative noun suffix: **vulgacho** 'the common herd'. Compare in the dictionary **hombracho, populacho, ricacho**.

-ada

(i) A noun suffix expressing 'an act by or typical of': **carlistada** 'Carlist uprising', **escocesada** 'typically Scottish thing to do', 'just what one might expect of a Scot'; compare in the dictionary **bobada, perrada, puñalada**.

(ii) A noun suffix implying some notion of collectivity, as in **extranjerada** 'group of foreigners', **parrafada** 'good long chat', and compare in the dictionary **camada, hornada, indiada, muslada**. Beyond these one finds also an intensifying function, as in **gozada, liada, riada**, with which perhaps belong **panzada, tripada** 'bellyful'.

-ado, -aje

These noun suffixes of similar function are enjoying some popularity at the moment in new formations which express a process (often rendered by English **-ing**): **blanqueado** and **lavado (del dinero)** 'laundering (of money)', **lastrado** 'ballasting', **clonaje, gemelaje** 'cloning', **matonaje** 'bully-boy behaviour', **reciclaje**. A particular function of **-ado** is to express a collectivity, in English 'the body of ...': see in the dictionary **alumnado, campesinado, estudiantado, profesorado**.

-ajo, -aja

Strongly pejorative noun suffix: **muñecajo** 'rotten old doll', **papelajo** 'dirty old bit of paper'; see further in the dictionary **pintarrajo**. Among adjectives one finds **pequeñajo** 'wretchedly small'.

-amen

A humorous augmentative: **barrigamen** 'grossly fat belly', **labiamen** 'great red gash of a made-up mouth', **papelamen** 'lots of paper'. Compare in the dictionary **caderamen, culamen, muslamen, tetamen**, whose tone is warmly appreciative. In **ladrillamen** 'brickwork' and **maderamen** 'woodwork' there is a collective connotation.

-ante

A neutral adjectival suffix which generally corresponds to English **-ing**. Self-explanatory are eg **destripante, gimoteante, lastrante, masificante, mistificante, mitificante**: less transparent are the **crónicas masacrantes** 'vicious reports' which a journalist wrote about an event. Compare in the dictionary **golfante, hilarante, pimpante, preocupante**, and see also **-izante**.

-ata

See in the dictionary the group **bocata, drogata, fumata, tocata**, colloquial variations created by young people.

-azo, -aza

(i) Augmentative of more or less neutral tone: **animalazo** 'huge creature, whacking great brute', **generalazo** 'important general', **golpazo** 'heavy blow', **jovenazo** 'big lad, strapping youth'.

(ii) Augmentative of favourable tone: **hembraza** 'magnificent figure of a woman', **soy madrileñazo** 'I'm from Madrid and proud of it', **morenazo** 'man with dark good looks'; 'man with a lovely tan', **talentazo** 'immense talent'.

(iii) Augmentative of unfavourable tone: **cochinaza** 'dirty sow of a woman', **locaza** 'outrageous old queen', **melenaza** 'great mop of long hair'; **¡ostiazo!** (see **hostia (d)**).

(iv) The suffix may signify 'a blow with ...': **ladrillazo** 'blow with a brick', **misilazo** 'missile strike'; compare in the dictionary **aldabonazo**, **codazo**, etc. **Cristazo** 'blow with a crucifix' is rumoured to exist, and one can readily imagine a **diccionariazo**.

(v) The suffix may signify 'a sound made with ...': **cornetazo** 'bugle-call, blast on the bugle'; compare in the dictionary **telefonazo** and (with probable sounds) **frenazo**.

(vi) The (attempted) blow may be a military one, a coup or attack: in the past a **gibraltarazo** may have been contemplated, and there was certainly a **malvinazo**. See in the dictionary **cuartelazo**, **tejerazo**.

-e

This is increasingly used as a noun suffix to refer to a process: **manduque** 'eating', **tueste** 'roasting' (of coffee). Compare in the dictionary **cuelgue, derrame, desfase, desmadre**.

-ejo, -eja

Mostly a pejorative suffix: **discursejo** 'rotten speech', **grupejo** 'insignificant little group', **nos costó un milloncejo** 'it cost us all of a million', **todo por unas cuantas pesetejas** 'all for a few measly pesetas'. See in the dictionary **animalejo**, **caballejo**, **palabreja**. Sometimes the sense is simply diminutive, eg **gracejo**, **rinconcejo**.

-eo

This like **-e** refers to a process or continuing act, and is much commoner: **guitarreo** 'strumming on the guitar', **ligoteo** 'chatting-up', **mariposeo** 'flirting', **marisqueo** 'gathering shellfish'. See in the dictionary **cachondeo**, **gimoteo**, **musiqueo**, **papeleo**.

-eras

A strongly intensifying masculine singular suffix: **guarreras** 'filthy person', **macheras** 'over-the-top macho man'. Compare **boceras, golferas, guaperas**.

-ería

Among a very wide variety of applications of this common suffix one may distinguish a general notion of quality inherent in the base noun or adjective: **marchosería, matonería, mitinería, milagrería, pelmacería** (compare in the dictionary **chiquillería, nadería, patriotería, tontería**). The suffix may also indicate 'place where', as in **floristería, frutería**; a recent invention is **liguería**, 'pick-up joint'.

-ero

The wide application of this mainly adjectival suffix may be gauged from eg **cafetero, carero, etiquetero**, **faldero**, **futbolero**, **patriotero**, **pesetero** in the dictionary. A **barco atunero/bacaladero/camaronero/marisquero** will fish for tunny, cod, shrimps, and shellfish respectively.

-esco

English **-esque** is only a pale equivalent of this adjectival suffix. Self-explanatory are **chaplinesco**, **tarzanesco**, and in the dictionary **goyesco**, **mitinesco**, **oficinesco**. One notes **con lentitud notariesca** 'with all a lawyer's dreary deliberation', **Madrid se va poniendo pulpesco** (Gooch) 'Madrid is extending its tentacles in all directions', and of London, **el ambiente minifaldesco de los años 60** 'the swinging '60s scene'.

-ete, -eta

Mildly diminutive noun and adjectival suffix: **alegrete** 'a bit merry', **guapete** 'quite handsome'; **unos duretes** 'a few measly pesetas', **tartaleta** 'small cake'. Compare in the dictionary **galancete, palacete, pobrete**.

-ez

A noun suffix which can often be translated by the English abstract **-ness**: **grisez**, **majez**, **menudez**, **modernez**, **muchachez**, and in the dictionary eg **gelidez**, **morenez**, **testarudez**.

-iano

A common adjectival suffix which English **-ian** might but usually cannot represent when attached to personal names: not only, in the dictionary, native **calderoniano**, **galdosiano**, **lorquiano**, but also **galbraithiano**, **goethiano**, **grouchiano**, **joyciano** (and **joyceano**), **una novela lampedusiana**. Some forms may puzzle foreign learners: eg **la poesía juanramoniana** refers to the work of the Spanish poet Juan Ramón Jiménez.

-ico, -ica

As an adjective, this is a regional (Aragon and Navarre, Granada, Murcia) variant of **-ito**: **me duele un tantico, ¿te han dejado solico?** As a noun it is a contemptuous diminutive: **cobardica, llorica, miedica, mierdica, sólo me pidió medio milloncico**. Compare in the dictionary **acusica**, **roñica**.

-il

An adjectival suffix which is not specially pejorative but conveys a mildly ironical tone. Senses are transparent: **caciquil**, **curanderil**, **una dieta garbancil**, **machil** 'a bit too macho', **ministeril**, **ratonil**. Very expressive are **urraquil**, which depends on the word **urraca**, 'magpie', with its thievish propensities, and **sus encantos cleopatriles** 'her *femme fatale* (-like) charms'.

-illo, -illa

A noun and adjectival suffix, gently diminutive and often implying a degree of good-humoured condescension. For adjectives, consider **un vino ligerillo** 'a pleasantly light wine', **una sevillana**

guapilla 'a pretty and provocative Sevillian girl', **es dificilillo** 'it's a wee bit tricky'. For nouns, **un lugarcillo** 'a nice little place', **jefecillo** 'local boss, petty boss', **jequecillo** 'petty sheik', **un olorcillo a corrupción** 'a slight smell of corruption'. More plainly pejorative are **empleadillo**, **ministrillo**, **personajillo**.

-ín, -ina

A mildly approving suffix for nouns and adjectives, quite widely used but specially attached to Asturias and Granada: **guapín**, **guapina**, **jovencina**, **monín**, **pequeñín**; **cafetín** is in part demeaning but also affectionate, and **tontín** to a child will not cause alarm.

-ísimo

This suffix is not one of the degrees of comparison but implies 'very' with various nuances:

(i) 'Very', neutral in tone: **un asunto importantísimo** 'a very important matter, a most important matter'; **una cuestión discutidísima** 'a highly controversial question'; **un desarrolladísimo sentido de orgullo** 'a very highly developed sense of pride'; **es dificilísimo** 'it is extremely difficult'.

(ii) More emotionally: **es simpatiquísimo** 'he's terribly nice, he's awfully kind'; **es guapísima** 'she really is pretty'.

(iii) Exaggerating somewhat in order to impress: **un libro grandísimo** 'an enormous great book, a megatome'; **una comida costosísima**. There may be humour or irony, depending on context: **la superfinísima actriz**, **esta cursilísima costumbre**.

(iv) Passionately patriotic: **aquel españolísimo plato** 'that most Spanish of all dishes'; **la madrileñísima plaza de Santa Ana** St Anne's Square which is so (endearingly) typical of Madrid'.

(v) Exceptionally, one finds this suffix attached to a noun: **aquí ella es la jefísima** 'she's the only real boss round here'.

(vi) Adverbs may be formed in the usual way on some of these forms, eg **brillantísimamente**, **riquísimamente**.

-ismo

In hundreds of simple cases, Spanish words in **-ismo** naturally correspond to English **-ism**. But Spanish uses the suffix much more and in creations which English has to express in a circumlocutory way: while **japonesismo** might just be 'Japanese-ness', and **ilegalismo** is hardly more than **ilegalidad** 'illegality', **el guitarrismo moderno** has to be 'modern guitar-playing' and **gorilismo** 'rule by bully-boys'. **El felipismo** sums up criticism of the Spanish Prime Minister Felipe González. Real complications start with such examples as **gaudinismo** 'style and practices of the architect Gaudí', **gubernamentalismo** 'government interventionism, tendency for the government to intervene in everything', **el paragüismo de los gallegos** 'devotion of the Galicians to their umbrellas', **importanadismo** and in America **quemimportismo** 'couldn't-care-less attitude', while **el lolitismo** has to be left to the imagination of the reader.

-ista

This forms nouns of common gender and adjectives also. Simple cases such as **comunista** again correspond precisely to English, but many do not: an **independista** supports an independence movement, that is **un movimiento independentista**; a **madridista** is a supporter of Real Madrid football club, and many Spanish teams acquire similarly-designated supporters; a **maximarquista** and a **plusmarquista** are record-holders, a **pluriempleísta** is a moonlighter having two or more jobs, and a **mariposista** specializes in the butterfly stroke. Compare in the dictionary **congresista**, **juerguista**, **ordenancista**.

-itis

A few formations on this adopt the suffix of eg **bronquitis** and humourously imply a medical condition: **barriguitis** 'tendency to get a paunch, paunchiness', **concursitis** 'obsessive wish to enter competitions', **empatitis** 'tendency to draw games', **mudancitis** 'disease which leads one to move house perpetually'. See in the dictionary **gandulitis**, **holgazanitis**.

-ito, -ita

This suffix is the commonest of all. One can discern at least three categories:

(i) The purely diminutive: **Juanito** 'Johnny', **su hijito** 'her small son, her baby', **es más bien bajita** 'she's rather on the short side'. Among adverbs one finds **salimos tempranito, pues hazlo prontito**.

(ii) Diminutive with added affective (usually kindly) nuance: **jugosito** 'nice and juicy', **limpito** 'clean as a new pin', **un golito** 'a nice little goal', **iban cogiditos de la mano, ¡pobrecito!** 'poor old chap!', 'poor little fellow!', etc. One may be self-deprecating: **te traigo un regalito**, **ofrecemos una fiestecita en casa**, or one may need to apologize for troubling others: **¿me echas una firmita aquí?** 'could you please sign here?' To small children it is natural to say **hay que ser educaditos** 'we must be on our best behaviour'.

(iii) Other uses express a kind of superlative: **ahora mismito** 'this very instant', **estaba solito** 'he was all on his own', **están calentitos** 'they're piping hot', **lo mejorcito que haya** 'the very best there is'.

-izante

This adjectival and noun suffix may correspond to English **-izing**, as in **medida liberalizante, tendencia modernizante**, but sometimes goes beyond this: **idiotizante** 'stupefying', **colores mimetizantes, hormona masculinizante.** Compare **teorizante** and others in the dictionary.

-izo

This adjectival suffix expresses the 'quality' of the base word: see in the dictionary eg **acomodadizo, huidizo, quebradizo, rollizo.**

-ocracia

Spanish **meritocracia** = English 'meritocracy', but Spanish seems to have a greater capacity for rather bitterly humorous formations with this suffix: **gorilocracia** 'reign of the strong-arm men', **mojigatocracia** 'rule by hypocritical establishment circles'. See further in the dictionary **dedocracia, falocracia, yernocracia.**

-oide

This adjectival and noun suffix implies 'somewhat, rather', and is always pejorative: **extranjeroide** 'somewhat foreign', **locoide** and **tontoide, estas tramas fascistoides** 'these quasi-fascist schemes', while a **liberaloide** is a 'pseudo-liberal' who might well indulge in **sentimentaloidería.**

-ón, -ona

This very frequent noun and adjectival suffix has several differing connotations:

(i) purely augmentative: **muchachón, generalón** 'really important general', **pistolón, liberalón, lingotón** 'big shot of whisky' (etc), **doncellona** 'unmarried lady of a certain age'; among adjectives, **grandón** 'tall and solidly built', **gastón** 'free-spending', **docilón** 'extremely placid'.

(ii) augmentative with a strongly approving tone: **mimosón, simpaticón, guapetón** (see **guapetona** in the dictionary: a word so rich that it has formed the subject of a learned article).

(iii) augmentative with unpleasant or strongly ironic nuances: **britanicón** 'overbearing Brit of the old school', **hombrón** 'hulking great brute', **milagrón** 'great miracle', **movidón** (see **movida** in the dictionary).

-osis

Like **-itis**, this is for jocular formations which echo the common suffix of medical terms. Recently noted: **ligosis** 'obsessive womanizing'.

-ote, -ota

An adjectival and noun augmentative, with varying nuances. Among adjectives, **gordote, guapote, liberalote, mansote** (of a bull) carry little extra charge, as is the case also with nouns **aldeota, drogota, muchachote, pasota**. Stronger feelings emerge with **presumidote** 'impossibly vain', **militarote** 'overblown braggart soldier', **britanicote** 'Colonel-Blimpish Brit'. One man who stole a glance at an attractive girl took a longer look, explaining that his **miradita** became a **miradota.**

-uco, -uca

This is a diminutive suffix, not common except perhaps in Santander province (**niñuco** 'very small boy'), and more especially a pejorative one: **frailuco** 'contemptible little priest', **mujeruca** 'very odd little woman'.

-ucho, -ucha

Much like the preceding, and commoner: **debilucho** 'weakish', **delicaducho** 'rather delicate', **delgaducho** 'terribly thin, scrawny', **morenucho** 'extremely swarthy'; a **hotelucho** would be classed as minus two stars. See in the dictionary **cuartucho, novelucha.**

-udo, -uda

This adjectival suffix expresses the notion of 'possessing (the base quality) in abundance': **mostachudo, patilludo, talentudo; una caligrafía garrapatuda** 'nasty scrawled writing', Compare in the dictionary **concienzudo, huesudo, linajudo, melenudo, suertudo.**

-uelo, -uela

A diminutive and sometimes affectionate suffix: **gordezuelo, pequeñuelo; muchachuelo, tontuela.**

-ujo, -uja

A strongly pejorative suffix for adjective and noun: **papelujo** 'wretched bit of paper'; **estrechujo, pequeñujo.**

-uzo, -uza

A very strongly pejorative suffix for adjective and noun: **marranuzo** 'filthy, stinking'; **carnuza** 'rotten awful meat'.

3 Designations of women in the professions etc.

(a) In recent decades the entry of women into many professions previously more or less closed to them has caused developments and problems for Spanish with its consistent gender-marking of nouns (in contrast to English with its very restricted perception of gender in such usages as 'she will dock tomorrow' and 'she's been a very good car', together, naturally, with the full range of biological pairs 'fox/vixen', 'bull/cow' and so on). What follows is an attempt to outline aspects of usage and problems in Spanish, without recommendations which it would be perilous to offer in a time of rapid change. Alternative possibilities have been offered in many entries in the main text of the dictionary. The remarks relate to Peninsular Spanish; usage in Latin America, especially in countries with strongly conservative social structures, is very varied and often different from that of Spain.

(b) There is generally no problem about the morphology (forms) of the feminine. A noun whose masculine ends in **-o** has a feminine in **-a**; **la médica, la ministra, la bióloga, la bioquímica**. The same is true of **-or -ora**: **la instructora, la lectora, la embajadora, la conductora**, and of other pairs such as **alcalde/alcaldesa, coronel/coronela, capitán/capitana, presidente/presidenta, jefe/jefa**, while all nouns in **-ista** are of common gender anyway, **el/la periodista** etc. (note however the special case of **el modisto**). There is doubt as between **la juez** and **la jueza**.

(c) Usage, however, often invalidates any automatic application of forms mentioned above. On the one hand, some women in the professions may feel that they have attained full status and equality with men colleagues only when the established standard word is applied to them: one may expect **la abogada** and this will often be correct, but sometimes a woman prefers to be **la abogado** and equally **la médico, la arquitecto, la dramaturgo**. It was noticeable that for a time the Spanish press referred to **la primer ministro** in several countries and then passed to **la primera ministra**. There seems to be resistance to the adoption of **la soldada**.

(d) There is a special problem when a feminine form already exists in a pejorative sense which may for a time preclude, for some speakers and writers, its use about a woman with a newly-attained professional or other status: such words as **jefa** and **socia** are concerned here. It was noticed that the woman circulation manager of a Spanish newspaper sent out subscription forms for some years signing her name over the words **Jefe de Márketing** and then changing the first to **Jefa**. The women members of a society will more likely be **las miembros** but one notes a tendency for them to be **las socias**, showing that the old pejorative sense is no longer a bar to this. There is also a group of words for sciences whose existence may in some contexts cause doubt: because **la física** is 'physics' there may be uncertainty about whether a woman physicist should be **una física** or **una físico**. A few special cases cause difficulties of other kinds: since **la policía** is established as 'the police force', it is not readily applicable to a policewoman in case confusion should arise, and informants specify that while they will refer to **una policía** 'a policewoman' and **unas policías** 'several policewomen', they would avoid such usage with the definite article and say **la mujer policía** 'the policewoman' or possibly take refuge in the safely bi-gender **la agente**. If there is doubt a woman should naturally be asked which designation she herself prefers. It may also be the case that organizations have their house-rules too, though these may be very haphazardly applied: thus **El País** of 9 May 1990 headlines a report **Sanción ratificada contra una médica**, but in the body of the article the woman concerned is twice referred to as **la médico**.

(e) In the category of military and similar ranks older senses have been relegated as archaisms: **la coronela** was 'the colonel's lady' but is now '(woman) colonel', **la embajadora** is not 'the ambassador's wife' but '(woman) ambassador', and **la alcaldesa** is '(woman) mayor'. In other walks of life a woman poet is **una poeta**, since **poetisa** is as unthinkable as English 'poetess', and a woman writer is **una autora**, to be translated as 'author' rather than 'authoress'. A woman minister in a nonconformist church may safely be called **la pastora**, but it is wholly unsure by what term women priests in the Anglican Church are or will be known.

4 Attributive use of nouns

(a) Examples of such formations as **el patrón oro** go back to the 17th century, but remained rare until recent times when there has been an explosion of the attributive use of nouns (defined as the use of a noun in a qualifying or adjectival function but without concord of number or gender). Much of this is owed to the influence of English, but some formations now go well beyond any possible pattern existing in English. **Buque fantasma** translates English 'ghost ship' and **gobierno fantasma** was once formed as a calque on English 'shadow cabinet', but the usage then develops a momentum of its own in Spanish and we find **empresa fantasma, gol fantasma** and other expressive formations.

(b) Well-established usages are covered in many cases by entries in the dictionary. Such are **cuestión clave, programa coloquio, reunión cumbre, fecha límite, cárcel modelo, mitín monstruo, emisión pirata, planta piloto, peso pluma, niña prodigio, país satélite, coches sport, precio tope**. There is a range of attributives which may go with eg **efecto**: **efecto avalancha/ boomerang/ dominó/ Doppler/embudo/escoba/pistón/túnel**), and **efecto invernadero** seems to have displaced earlier **efecto de invernadero**. Formations such as **faros antiniebla, manifestaciones antihuelga, medidas antipolución** are now standard, as are many others in the domains of fashion (**falda pantalón, falda tubo**) and cuisine, etc. These correspond closely to English models. Statements about colour in attributive form are also standard usage, eg **un vestido color (de) lila, uniformes verde oliva, cortinas verde oscuro** (but naturally **cortinas verdes** with concord). The same is true of phrases with **modelo, tipo**, and similar words: **un coche modelo Tiburón 1500, aviones tipo Concorde, el factor Rhesus, un sombrero estilo Bogart**, and also of biological definitions such as **el pájaro hembra, las musarañas macho**.

(c) Creativity in this aspect in journalistic Spanish has now gone well beyond any possible English model, however: examples are **un jugador promesa, horas punta, tecnología punta,**

tránsito punta, el grupo revelación de 1992, una teoría puente. Abbreviations may figure too in a kind of journalistic shorthand: **tres aviones USA, dos agentes CIA**.

(d) While the principle of non-concord is the soundest one, as above, speakers may occasionally treat the attributive element as an adjective and assign it concord for number (but never for gender): **hay dos palabras claves, pedimos pagos extras**. One finds both **hombres rana** and **hombres ranas**. In the press those who compose headlines may not always agree with those who write articles: **Cambio 16** on 11 August 1986 carried the headline **Matilde Fernández explica por qué no ha habido mujeres ministro en el nuevo gobierno**, while the body of the report below included the words **no se han conseguido mujeres ministros**.

(e) Confusion reigns in the use or absence of the hyphen in such combinations: **hombre rana, hombre-rana**. If the combination is brief there is a tendency to use the hyphen: **granja-escuela, grúa-puente, dos grúas-puente**. The Academy appears to rule against the hyphen but has hardly put its mind as yet to this relatively new and rapidly-developing usage.

Note: * preceding a word denotes an invented form.

NUMERALS — LOS NÚMEROS

CARDINAL NUMBERS — NÚMEROS CARDINALES

nought, zero	**0**	cero
one	**1**	(*m*) uno, (*f*) una
two	**2**	dos
three	**3**	tres
four	**4**	cuatro
five	**5**	cinco
six	**6**	seis
seven	**7**	siete
eight	**8**	ocho
nine	**9**	nueve
ten	**10**	diez
eleven	**11**	once
twelve	**12**	doce
thirteen	**13**	trece
fourteen	**14**	catorce
fifteen	**15**	quince
sixteen	**16**	dieciséis
seventeen	**17**	diecisiete
eighteen	**18**	dieciocho
nineteen	**19**	diecinueve
twenty	**20**	veinte
twenty-one	**21**	veintiuno (*see note* **b**)
twenty-two	**22**	veintidós
twenty-three	**23**	veintitrés
thirty	**30**	treinta
thirty-one	**31**	treinta y uno
thirty-two	**32**	treinta y dos
forty	**40**	cuarenta
fifty	**50**	cincuenta
sixty	**60**	sesenta
seventy	**70**	setenta
eighty	**80**	ochenta
ninety	**90**	noventa
ninety-nine	**99**	noventa y nueve
a (*or* one) hundred	**100**	cien, ciento (*see note* **c**)
a hundred and one	**101**	ciento uno
a hundred and two	**102**	ciento dos
a hundred and ten	**110**	ciento diez
a hundred and eighty-two	**182**	ciento ochenta y dos
two hundred	**200**	(*m*) doscientos, (*f*) –as
three hundred	**300**	(*m*) trescientos, (*f*) –as
four hundred	**400**	(*m*) cuatrocientos, (*f*) –as
five hundred	**500**	(*m*) quinientos, (*f*) –as
six hundred	**600**	(*m*) seiscientos, (*f*) –as
seven hundred	**700**	(*m*) setecientos, (*f*) –as
eight hundred	**800**	(*m*) ochocientos, (*f*) –as
nine hundred	**900**	(*m*) novecientos, (*f*) –as
a (*or* one) thousand	**1000**	mil
a thousand and two	**1002**	mil dos
two thousand	**2000**	dos mil
ten thousand	**10000**	diez mil
a (*or* one) hundred thousand	**100000**	cien mil
a (*or* one) million	**1000000**	un millón (*see note* **d**)
two million	**2000000**	dos millones (*see note* **d**)

Notes on usage of the cardinal numbers

(**a**) **One,** and the other numbers ending in one, agree in Spanish with the noun (stated or implied): *una casa, un coche, si se trata de pagar en libras ello viene a sumar treinta y una, había ciento una personas.*

(**b**) **21**: In Spanish there is some uncertainty when the number is accompanied by a feminine noun. In the spoken language both *veintiuna peseta* and *veintiuna pesetas* are heard; in 'correct' literary language only *veintiuna pesetas* is found. With a masculine noun the numeral is shortened in the usual way: *veintiún perros rabiosos*. These remarks apply also to 31, 41 *etc*.

(**c**) **100**: When the number is spoken alone or in counting a series of numbers both *cien* and *ciento* are heard. When there is an accompanying noun the form is always *cien: cien hombres, cien chicas.* In the compound numbers note 101 = *ciento uno,* 110 = *ciento diez,* but 100000 = *cien mil.*

(**d**) **1000000**: In Spanish the word *millón* is a noun, so the numeral takes *de* when there is a following noun: *un millón de fichas, tres millones de árboles quemados.*

(**e**) In Spanish the cardinal numbers may be used as nouns, as in English; they are always masculine: *jugó el siete de corazones, el once nacional de Ruritania, éste es el trece y nosotros buscamos el quince.*

(**f**) To divide the larger numbers clearly a point is used in Spanish where English places a comma: English 1,000 = Spanish 1.000, English 2,304,770 = Spanish 2.304.770. (This does not apply to dates: see below.)

ORDINAL NUMBERS — NÚMEROS ORDINALES

first	**1**	primero (*see note* **b**)
second	**2**	segundo
third	**3**	tercero (*see note* **b**)
fourth	**4**	cuarto
fifth	**5**	quinto
sixth	**6**	sexto
seventh	**7**	séptimo
eighth	**8**	octavo
ninth	**9**	noveno, nono
tenth	**10**	décimo
eleventh	**11**	undécimo
twelfth	**12**	duodécimo
thirteenth	**13**	decimotercio, decimotercero
fourteenth	**14**	decimocuarto
fifteenth	**15**	decimoquinto
sixteenth	**16**	decimosexto
seventeenth	**17**	decimoséptimo
eighteenth	**18**	decimoctavo
nineteenth	**19**	decimonoveno, decimonono
twentieth	**20**	vigésimo
twenty-first	**21**	vigésimo primero, vigésimo primo
twenty-second	**22**	vigésimo segundo
thirtieth	**30**	trigésimo
thirty-first	**31**	trigésimo primero, trigésimo primo
fortieth	**40**	cuadragésimo
fiftieth	**50**	quincuagésimo
sixtieth	**60**	sexagésimo

seventieth	**70**	septuagésimo
eightieth	**80**	octogésimo
ninetieth	**90**	nonagésimo
hundredth	**100**	centésimo
hundred and first	**101**	centésimo primero
hundred and tenth	**110**	centésimo décimo
two hundredth	**200**	ducentésimo
three hundredth	**300**	trecentésimo
four hundredth	**400**	cuadringentésimo
five hundredth	**500**	quingentésimo
six hundredth	**600**	sexcentésimo
seven hundredth	**700**	septingentésimo
eight hundredth	**800**	octingentésimo
nine hundredth	**900**	noningentésimo
thousandth	**1000**	milésimo
two thousandth	**2000**	dos milésimo
millionth	**1000000**	millonésimo
two millionth	**2000000**	dos millonésimo

Notes on usage of the ordinal numbers

(**a**) All these numbers are adjectives in *-o*, and therefore agree with the noun in number and gender: *la quinta vez, en segundas nupcias, en octavo lugar*.

(**b**) *primero* and *tercero* are shortened to *primer, tercer* when they directly precede a masculine singular noun: *en el primer capítulo, el tercer hombre* (but *los primeros coches en llegar, el primero y más importante hecho*).

(**c**) In Spanish the ordinal numbers from 1 to 10 are commonly used; from 11 to 20 rather less; above 21 they are rarely written and almost never heard in speech (except for *milésimo*, which is frequent). The custom is to replace the forms for 21 and above by the cardinal number: *en el capítulo treinta y seis, celebran el setenta aniversario* (or *el aniversario setenta*), *en el poste ciento cinco contando desde la esquina*.

(**d**) **Kings, popes and centuries**. The ordinal numbers from 1 to 9 are employed for these in Spanish as in English: *en el siglo cuarto, Eduardo octavo, Pío nono, Enrique primero*. For 10 either the cardinal or the ordinal may be used: *siglo diez* or *siglo décimo, Alfonso diez* or *Alfonso décimo*. For 11 and above it is now customary to use only the cardinal number: *Alfonso once* (but *onceno* in the Middle Ages), *Juan veintitrés, en el siglo dieciocho*.

(**e**) **Abbreviations.** English 1st, 2nd, 3rd, 4th, 5th *etc* = Spanish 1° *or* 1er, 2°, 3° *or* 3er, 4°, 5° and so on (*f*: 1^{era}, 2^{a}).

(**f**) See also the notes on Dates, below.

DECIMALS — LAS DECIMALES

In Spanish a comma is written where English writes a point: English 3·56 (three point five six) = Spanish 3,56 (*tres coma cinco seis*); English ·07 (point zero seven) = Spanish ,07 (*coma cero siete*). The recurring decimal 3·3333 may be written in English as 3·3 and in Spanish as 3,3.

FRACTIONS — NÚMEROS QUEBRADOS

one half, a half	**½**	(m) *medio*, (f) *media*
one and a half *helpings*	**1½**	(*una*) *porción y media*
two and a half kilos	**2½**	*dos kilos y medio*
one third, a third	**⅓**	*un tercio, la tercera parte*
two thirds	**⅔**	*dos tercios, las dos terceras partes*
one quarter, a quarter	**¼**	*un cuarto, la cuarta parte*
three quarters	**¾**	*tres cuartos, las tres cuartas partes*
one sixth, a sixth	**⅙**	*un sexto, la sexta parte*
five and five sixths	**5⅚**	*cinco y cinco sextos*
one twelfth, a twelfth	**1/12**	*un duodécimo; un dozavo, la duodécima parte*
seven twelfths	**7/12**	*siete dozavos*
one hundredth, a hundredth	**1/100**	*un centésimo, una centésima parte*
one thousandth, a thousandth	**1/1000**	*un milésimo*

UNITS — NOMENCLATURA

3,684 is a four-digit number	*3.684 es un número de cuatro dígitos* (or *guarismos*)
It contains 4 units, 8 tens, 6 hundreds and 3 thousands	*Contiene 4 unidades, 8 decenas, 6 centenas y 3 unidades de millar*
The decimal ·234 contains 2 tenths, 3 hundredths and 4 thousandths	*la fracción decimal ,234 contiene 2 décimas, 3 centésimas y 4 milésimas*

PERCENTAGES — LOS PORCENTAJES

2½% two and a half per cent	*2½ por 100*, (less frequently) *2½%*; *dos y medio por cien, dos y medio por ciento* (in spoken usage and among the authorities there is disagreement about *cien/ciento* here).
18% of the people here are over 65	*el dieciocho por cien de la gente aquí tienen más de 65 años.*
Production has risen by 8%	*la producción ha aumentado en un 8 por 100.*
(*See also* per, hundred *in the main text.*)	(*Vése también* por, cien/ciento *en el diccionario*)

CALCULATIONS

8 + 6 = 14 eight and (*or* plus) six are (*or* make) fourteen
15 – 3 = 12 fifteen take away three are (*or* equals) twelve, three from fifteen leaves twelve
3 × 3 = 9 three threes are nine, three times three is nine
32 ÷ 8 = 4 thirty-two divided by eight is (*or* equals) four
3^2 = 9 three squared is nine
2^5 = 32 two to the fifth (*or* to the power of five) is (*or* equals) thirty-two
$\sqrt{16}$ = 4 the square root of sixteen is four

SIGNS

+ addition sign
+ plus sign (*eg* + 7 = plus seven)
– subtraction sign
– minus sign (*eg* – 3 = minus three)
× multiplication sign
÷ division sign
$\sqrt{}$ square root sign
∞ infinity
≡ sign of identity, is exactly equal to
= sign of equality, equals
≃ is approximately equal to
≠ sign of inequality, is not equal to
$>$ is greater than
$<$ is less than

EL CÁLCULO

8 + 6 = 14 *ocho y* (or *más*) *seis son catorce*
15 – 3 = 12 *quince menos tres resta doce, de tres a quince van doce*
3 × 3 = 9 *tres por tres son nueve*
32 ÷ 8 = 4 *treinta y dos dividido por ocho es cuatro*
3^2 = 9 *tres al cuadrado son nueve*
2^5 = 32 *dos a la quinta potencia son treinta y dos*
$\sqrt{16}$ = 4 *la raíz cuadrada de dieciséis es cuatro.*

LOS SIGNOS

+ signo de adición
+ signo de más (*p.ej.* + 7 = 7 de más)
– signo de sustracción
– signo de menos (*p.ej.* – 3 = 3 de menos)
× signo de multiplicación
: signo de división
$\sqrt{}$ signo de raíz cuadrada
∞ infinito
≡ signo de identidad, es exactamente igual a
= signo de igualdad, es igual a
≈ es aproximadamente igual a
≠ signo de no identidad, no es igual a
$>$ es mayor que
$<$ es menor que

WEIGHTS AND MEASURES PESOS Y MEDIDAS

METRIC SYSTEM – SISTEMA MÉTRICO

Measures formed with the following prefixes are mostly omitted:

Se omiten la mayor parte de las medidas formadas con los siguientes prefijos:

deca-	10 times	10 veces	*deca-*
hecto-	100 times	100 veces	*hecto-*
kilo-	1000 times	1000 veces	*kilo-*
deci-	one tenth	una décima	*deci-*
centi-	one hundredth	una centésima	*centi-*
mil(l)i-	one thousandth	una milésima	*mili-*

Linear measures – medidas de longitud

1 millimetre (milímetro)	=	0·03937 inch (pulgada)
1 centimetre (centímetro)	=	0·3937 inch (pulgada)
1 metre (metro)	=	39·37 inches (pulgadas)
	=	1·094 yards (yardas)
1 kilometre (kilómetro)	=	0·6214 mile (milla) *or* almost exactly five-eighths of a mile

Square measures – medidas cuadradas o de superficie

1 square centimetre (centímetro cuadrado)	=	0·155 square inch (pulgada cuadrada)
1 square metre (metro cuadrado)	=	10·764 square feet (pies cuadrados)
	=	1·196 square yards (yardas cuadradas)
1 square kilometre (kilómetro cuadrado)	=	0·3861 square mile (milla cuadrada)
	=	247·1 acres (acres)
1 are = 100 square metres (área)	=	119·6 square yards (yardas cuadradas)
1 hectare = 100 ares (hectárea)	=	2·471 acres (acres)

Cubic measures – medidas cúbicas

1 cubic centimetre (centímetro cúbico)	=	0·061 cubic inch (pulgada cúbica)
1 cubic metre (metro cúbico)	=	35·315 cubic feet (pies cúbicos)
	=	1·308 cubic yards (yardas cúbicas)

Measures of capacity – medidas de capacidad

1 litre (litro) = 1000 cubic centimetres	=	1·76 pints (pintas)
	=	0·22 gallon (galón)

Weights – pesos

1 gramme (gramo)	=	15·4 grains (granos)
1 kilogramme (kilogramo)	=	2·2046 pounds (libras)
1 quintal (quintal métrico) = 100 kilogrammes	=	220·46 pounds (libras)
1 metric ton (tonelada métrica) = 1000 kilogrammes	=	0·9842 ton (tonelada)

BRITISH SYSTEM – SISTEMA BRITÁNICO

Linear measures – medidas de longitud

1 inch (pulgada)	=	2,54 centímetros
1 foot (pie) = 12 inches	=	30,48 centímetros
1 yard (yarda) = 3 feet	=	91,44 centímetros
1 furlong (estadio) = 220 yards	=	201,17 metros
1 mile (milla) = 1760 yards	=	1.609,33 metros
	=	1.609 kilómetros

Surveyors' measures – medidas de agrimensura

1 link = 7·92 inches	=	20,12 centímetros
1 rod (*or* pole, perch) = 25 links	=	5,029 metros
1 chain = 22 yards = 4 rods	=	20,12 metros

Square measures – medidas cuadradas o de superficie

1 square inch (pulgada cuadrada)	=	6,45 cm^2
1 square foot (pie cuadrado) = 144 square inches	=	929,03 cm^2
1 square yard (yarda cuadrada) = 9 square feet	=	0,836 m^2
1 square rod = 30·25 square yards	=	25,29 m^2
1 acre = 4840 square yards	=	40,47 áreas
1 square mile (milla cuadrada) = 640 acres	=	2,59 km^2

Cubic measures – medidas cúbicas

1 cubic inch (pulgada cúbica)	=	16,387 cm^3
1 cubic foot (pie cúbico) = 1728 cubic inches	=	0,028 m^3
1 cubic yard (yarda cúbica) = 27 cubic feet	=	0,765 m^3
1 register ton (tonelada de registro) = 100 cubic feet	=	2,832 m^3

Measures of capacity – medidas de capacidad

(a) Liquid—para líquidos

1 gill	=	0,142 litro
1 pint (pinta) = 4 gills	=	0,57 litro
1 quart = 2 pints	=	1,136 litros
1 gallon (galón) = 4 quarts	=	4,546 litros

(b) Dry—para áridos

1 peck = 2 gallons	=	9,087 litros
1 bushel = 4 pecks	=	36,36 litros
1 quarter = 8 bushels	=	290,94 litros

Weights – pesos (Avoirdupois system – sistema avoirdupois)

1 grain (grano)	=	0,0648 gramo
1 drachm *or* dram = 27,34 grains	=	1,77 gramos
1 ounce (onza) = 16 dra(ch)ms	=	28,35 gramos
1 pound (libra) = 16 ounces	=	453,6 gramos
	=	0,453 kilogramo
1 stone = 14 pounds	=	6,348 kilogramos
1 quarter = 28 pounds	=	12,7 kilogramos
1 hundredweight = 112 pounds	=	50,8 kilogramos
1 ton (tonelada) = 2240 pounds= 20 hundredweight	=	1.016 kilogramos

US MEASURES – MEDIDAS NORTEAMERICANAS

In the US the same system as that which applies in Great Britain is used for the most part; the main differences are mentioned below.

En EE.UU. se emplea en general el mismo sistema que en Gran Bretaña; las principales diferencias son las siguientes:

Measures of capacity – medidas de capacidad

(a) Liquid—para líquidos

1 US liquid gill	=	0,118 litro
1 US liquid pint = 4 gills	=	0,473 litro
1 US liquid quart = 2 pints	=	0,946 litro
1 US gallon = 4 quarts	=	3,785 litros

(b) Dry—para áridos

1 US dry pint	=	0,550 litro
1 US dry quart = 2 dry pints	=	1,1 litros
1 US peck = 8 dry quarts	=	8,81 litros
1 US bushel = 4 pecks	=	35,24 litros

Weights – pesos

1 hundredweight (*or* short hundredweight) = 100 pounds	=	45,36 kilogramos
1 ton (*or* short ton) = 2000 pounds = 20 short hundredweights	=	907, 18 kilogramos

TRADITIONAL SPANISH WEIGHTS AND MEASURES – PESOS Y MEDIDAS ESPAÑOLES TRADICIONALES

These are the measures which were standard until the introduction of the metric system in Spain in 1871, and they are still in use in some provinces and in agriculture.

Son éstas las medidas que se emplearon hasta la introducción del sistema métrico en España en 1871. Se emplean todavía en algunas provincias y en la agricultura

Linear measures – medidas de longitud

1 vara	=	0·836 metre
1 braza	=	1·67 metres
1 milla	=	1·852 kilometres
1 legua	=	5·5727 kilometres

Square measure – medida cuadrada o de superficie

1 fanega = 6460 square metres = 1·59 acres

Measures of capacity – medidas de capacidad

(a) Liquid—para líquidos

1 cuartillo	=	0·504 litre
1 azumbre = 4 cuartillos	=	2·016 litres
1 cántara = 8 azumbres	=	16·128 litres

(b) Dry – para áridos

1 celemín	=	4·625 litres
1 fanega = 12 celemines	=	55·5 litres = 1·58 bushels

Weights – pesos

1 onza	=	28·7 grammes
1 libra = 16 onzas	=	460 grammes
1 arroba = 25 libras	=	11·502 kilogrammes = 25 pounds
1 quintal = 4 arrobas	=	46 kilogrammes

TIME / LA HORA

TIME	LA HORA
2 hours 33 minutes and 14 seconds	*2 horas 33 minutos y 14 segundos*
half an hour	*media hora*
a quarter of an hour	*un cuarto de hora*
three quarters of an hour	*tres cuartos de hora*
what's the time?	*¿qué hora es?*
what do you make the time?	*¿qué hora tienes?*
have you the right time?	*¿tiene Vd la hora exacta?*
I make it 2.20	*yo tengo las dos veinte*
my watch says 3.37	*mi reloj marca las tres treinta y siete*
it's 1 o'clock	*es la una*
it's 2 o'clock	*son las dos*
it's 5 past 4	*son las cuatro y cinco*
it's 10 to 6	*son las seis menos diez*
it's half-past 8	*son las ocho y media*
it's a quarter past 9	*son las nueve y cuarto*
it's a quarter to 2	*son las dos menos cuarto*
at 10 a.m.	*a las diez de la mañana*
at 4 p.m.	*a las cuatro de la tarde*
at 11 p.m.	*a las once de la noche*
at exactly 3 o'clock, at 3 sharp, at 3 on the dot	*a las tres en punto*
the train leaves at 19.32	*el tren sale a las diecinueve treinta y dos*
(at) what time does it start?	*¿a qué hora comienza?*
it is just after 3	*son un poco más de las tres*
it is nearly 9	*son casi las nueve*
about 8 o'clock	*cerca de las ocho, hacia las ocho, a eso de las ocho*
at (*or* by) 6 o'clock at the latest	*a las seis a más tardar*
have it ready for 5 o'clock	*téngalo listo para las cinco*
it is full each night from 7 to 9	*está lleno todas las noches de siete a nueve*
'closed from 1.30 to 4.30'	*'cerrado de 1.30 a 4.30'*
until 8 o'clock	*hasta las ocho*
it would be about 11	*serán las once*
it would have been about 10	*serían las diez*
at midnight	*a medianoche*
before midday, before noon	*antes del mediodía*

DATES / LAS FECHAS

N.B. The days of the week and the months are written with small letters in Spanish: *lunes, martes, febrero, mayo.*

DATES	LAS FECHAS
the 1st of July, July 1st	*el 1º de julio, el primero de julio*
the 2nd of May, May 2nd	*el 2 de mayo, el dos de mayo* (the cardinal numbers are used in Spanish for dates from 2nd to 31st)
on the 21st (of) June	*el 21 de junio, el día veintiuno de junio*
on Monday	*el lunes*
he comes on Mondays	*viene los lunes*
'closed on Fridays'	*'cerrado los viernes'*
he lends it to me from Monday to Friday	*me lo presta de lunes a viernes*
from the 14th to the 18th	*desde el 14 hasta el 18, desde el catorce hasta el dieciocho*
what's the date?, what date is it today?	*¿qué día es hoy?*
today's the 12th	*hoy es el doce, estamos a doce*
one Thursday in October	*un jueves en octubre*
about the 4th of July	*hacia el cuatro de julio*
Heading of letters: 19th May 1984	*19 de mayo de 1984*
1975, nineteen (hundred and) seventy-five	*mil novecientos setenta y cinco*
4 B.C., B.C. 4	*4 a. de J.C.* (see main text)
70 A.D., A.D. 70	*70 d. de J.C.* (see main text)
in the 13th Century	*en el siglo XIII, en el siglo trece*
in (*or* during) the 1930s	*en el decenio de 1930 a 40, durante los años treinta*
in 1940 something	*en el año 1940 y tantos*

(*See also in the main text of the dictionary* **week, year** *etc.*)

LANGUAGE IN USE
LENGUA Y USO

Beryl T. Atkins
with
Hélène M.A. Lewis

One need which cannot be supplied within the word-based format of the conventional bilingual dictionary is that experienced by people trying to set down their own thoughts in a foreign language. They may not know even in their own language exactly how these thoughts might best be expressed, and indeed many language teachers rightly object to the framing of the thought in the native language before the expression process begins, maintaining that this leads to a distortion both of the thought itself and of its eventual expression in the other language. Non-native speakers, even the most competent, often have difficulty in expressing their thoughts in a sufficiently sensitive, varied and sophisticated way. It is to meet the needs of these people that we have designed this new section in our bilingual dictionary.

This section contains thousands of phrases and expressions grouped according to the **function** that is being performed when they are used in communication. A glance at the Contents on p. 908 will show the themes that have been included. Some of the most notorious areas of difficulty are addressed in this section, for example the concepts of possibility, obligation and so on, often expressed in English by modal verbs, where the difficulty for the non-native speaker is as much syntactical as lexical.

Each function presents an individual set of problems and challenges for the user. For example, the needs of someone attempting to express tactful advice or contradiction are quite different from those of someone drawing up a job application, and these varied needs are met in correspondingly varied ways within this secton.

The **design** of this section is entirely different from that of the dictionary proper, in that the approach is monolingual rather than bilingual. There is no question of any attempt to make the parallel columns into sets of equivalents, but simply to construct useful bridges across the language barrier.

Like the rest of this dictionary, this section has been designed as a **tool** for non-native speakers: it will serve particularly those skilled in the other language and able to recognise what they are looking for when they see it. It is not, and could not be, a comprehensive listing of the immense riches that each language offers in any area of thought. It is, rather, a selection – we hope a useful one – made to provide a channel between the user's passive and active knowledge of the foreign language. In controlled situations, such as the classroom, this section of the dictionary will also, we trust, provide a valuable teaching aid in language learning.

See CONTENTS page 908

Francisco Ariza

Una de las necesidades a las que no se puede atender con el formato basado en la palabra individual del diccionario bilingüe convencional es la que sienten las personas que tratan de expresar sus propias ideas en una lengua extranjera. Es posible que ni siquiera en su propio idioma sepan exactamente cuál es la mejor forma de expresar estos pensamientos: ciertamente, muchos profesores de idiomas se oponen a que la idea se formule en la lengua nativa antes de comenzar el proceso de expresión, afirmando que esto lleva a una deformación tanto de la idea misma como de su expresión final en la segunda lengua. Los usuarios de idiomas de los que no son hablantes nativos, incluso los más competentes, muchas veces tienen dificultades en expresar sus pensamientos de manera suficientemente rica, precisa y elegante. Para atender a las necesidades de estas personas hemos preparado esta nueva sección de nuestro diccionario bilingüe.

Estas páginas contienen miles de frases y locuciones agrupadas según la **función** que desempeñan cuando se usan en la comunicación hablada o escrita. Basta con echar una ojeada al índice de la pág. 908 para ver los temas que se han incluido. En esta sección se encontrarán algunas de las conocidas zonas lingüísticas que tradicionalmente se han considerado de especial dificultad: por ejemplo, los conceptos de posibilidad, obligación, etc., que en inglés se suelen expresar por medio de verbos modales, puntos en los que la dificultad para el hablante no nativo es de índole sintáctica y léxica a la vez.

Cada función presenta al usuario de la lengua un tipo particular de problemas y desafíos. Así, las necesidades de alguien que quiere dar consejos o expresar su desacuerdo de manera socialmente aceptable son totalmente distintas de las de quien prepara por escrito su candidatura para un puesto de trabajo. La presentación de las diferentes soluciones lingüísticas, dentro de esta sección, varía según las diversas necesidades de que se trate.

El **diseño** de esta sección es completamente distinto del empleado en el resto del diccionario, puesto que aquí el enfoque es monolingüe en vez de bilingüe. No hemos tratado, pues, de presentar columnas paralelas con expresiones o elementos léxicos equivalentes, sino que simplemente hemos intentado tender posibles puentes por encima de las barreras lingüísticas.

Igual que el resto del diccionario, esta sección se ha concebido como una **herramienta de trabajo** para los hablantes no nativos: será de máxima utilidad a quienes posean un elevado nivel de competencia en la segunda lengua, que por tanto serán capaces de reconocer lo que buscan cuando lo vean. No se trata, ni podría tratarse, de un catálogo completo de las enormes riquezas que ofrece cada lengua en cualquier parcela del pensamiento, sino más bien de una selección, esperamos que útil, destinada a permitir que el usario del idioma relacione su conocimiento pasivo de la lengua con su conocimiento activo. En las situaciones en que se puede ejercer mayor control lingüístico, como por ejemplo en el aula, es nuestra esperanza que esta sección del diccionario sirva como una valiosa ayuda didáctica en el aprendizaje de la lengua extranjera.

Véase ÍNDICE de MATERIAS página 908

SUGGESTIONS

GIVING SUGGESTIONS

Le sugiero que lo haga cuanto antes.	*I suggest that*
Yo propongo que se tome una decisión inmediata.	*I suggest that*
No se olvide de avisarme en cuanto llegue.	*don't forget to ...*
En vez de volver a salir, **podríamos** cenar en casa.	*we could*
¿Qué le parecería que fuésemos mañana?	*what (would you say) if*
Yo sugeriría que le escribieran con una respuesta concreta.	*I would like to suggest that*
Si me permite una sugerencia: podríamos recibirle el martes por la tarde.	*I'll make a suggestion, if I may*
Lo mejor sería que nos avisasen antes.	*it would be best if*
Creo que convendría sacarlo de aquí.	*I think it would be a good idea to ...*
Quizás sería conveniente llamar antes por teléfono.	*it might be a good idea to ...*
Sería buena idea mandar un télex.	*it would be a good idea to ...*
Lo que sugiero es lo siguiente *or* **Mi sugerencia es la siguiente**: por ahora no cambiemos de planes.	*what I suggest is that*
¿Le parece a usted bien que vayamos esta tarde?	*may we*
Lo que podríamos hacer es hablar con él antes de que se marche a Italia.	*what we could do is to ...*
¿Les importaría que fuésemos antes al hotel?	*would you mind if*
¿Qué les parecería encargárselo a Comercial Hispana?	*what about*
¿Le parecería bien *or* **¿Estaría de acuerdo en** volver a este mismo lugar el año que viene?	*would you agree to ...*
Si le parece bien, llegaremos el día 5 a Madrid.	*if you agree, we shall ...*
Quizás habría que ser un poco más firmes con ellos.	*we might have to ...*
¿Por qué no se lo dice usted directamente?	*why don't you*
¿No le atrae la idea de ser libre?	*doesn't the idea of ... attract you?*
Debía usted comprar más.	*you should*
Si yo estuviera en su lugar *or* **Yo, en su lugar,** *or* **De estar en su lugar** no lo dudaría.	*if I were you*
Yo que tú no haría nada por ahora.	*if I were you*
¿Le puedo hacer una propuesta que quizás le parezca interesante?	*may I make a suggestion?*
¿Le puedo proponer algo?	*may I make a suggestion?*
No sería mala idea ampliarlo todo.	*it mightn't be a bad idea to ...*
Convendría salir cuanto antes.	*we should*
Permítame usted recordarle que el plazo vence mañana.	*may I remind you that*
Sería preferible llamarle por teléfono.	*it would be better to ...*
Quizás lo mejor sería comunicárselo por escrito.	*perhaps it would be best to ...*
Quizás lo que debíamos hacer es no preocuparnos demasiado de los demás.	*perhaps we shouldn't*
¿Le importaría a usted explicármelo todo otra vez?	*would you mind*

ASKING FOR SUGGESTIONS

¿Qué (le parece que) se puede hacer?	*what (do you think) can be done?*
¿Quizás se le ocurre algo mejor?	*perhaps you have a better suggestion?*
¿Qué sugiere usted que haga?	*what do you suggest I do?*
¿Tiene usted alguna sugerencia?	*do you have any suggestions?*
¿Se les ocurre a ustedes algo sobre el asunto?	*do you have any ideas on*
¿Qué piensa usted que debería decir?	*what do you suggest I should ...*

AND, ACCORDING TO CONTEXT:

si no le parece mal/tenga cuidado de no/le recomiendo que/haga lo que haga, no/¿qué le parece?/le agradecería que hiciera/podría redundar en su propio beneficio/se me ha ocurrido que/espero que no se ofenda si/conociendo la situación, yo me atrevería a decir que/podría tener algo que ver con/si desea saber mi opinión, creo que sería mejor que usted/sin duda sería aconsejable

ADVICE

ASKING FOR ADVICE

¿Le podría pedir consejo? // ¿Me permite usted que le pida un consejo?	*may I ask you for some advice?*
¿Les puedo pedir que me aconsejen lo que debo hacer en mi situación actual?	*may I ask you to advise me about*
¿Me podría usted dar un consejo?	*could you give me a piece of advice?*
Necesito que me aconseje sobre la política de esta compañía.	*I need you to advise me about*
¿Qué haría usted en mi lugar?	*what would you do in my place?*
Le agradecería que me asesorase usted sobre este asunto.	*I should be grateful for your advice about*
¿Me podrían ustedes dar su opinión sobre la compra de un coche?	*I'd like your opinion about*

GIVING ADVICE

Te aconsejo que lo tomes con calma.	*I advise you to ...*
Yo creo *or* **pienso** *or* **opino que debería** tomar este asunto más en serio.	*I think you should*
Me parece que no se debería actuar de esa manera.	*I think that one should not ...*
Quizás habría que preparar unos planes más detallados.	*we might have to ...*
En mi opinión, la única salida posible es ésta.	*in my opinion*
Mi consejo es que se dirijan ustedes al Ministerio.	*my advice is to ...*
Yo le aconsejaría que no se preocupara demasiado.	*I would advise you not to ...*
Yo le aconsejaría dejarlo en paz.	*I would advise you to ...*
No debería usted mandárselo sin avisarle antes.	*you shouldn't*
Yo no le aconsejaría viajar en barco.	*I wouldn't advise you to ...*
Más vale que no digamos *or* **Más valdría que** no dijésemos nada por ahora.	*we'd better*
A mi modo de ver, esa manera de actuar es improcedente.	*the way I look at it*
A mi parecer, no sería conveniente tomar ese tipo de medidas.	*in my view it wouldn't be suitable to ...*
Si me permite usted darle *or* **que le dé** *or* **ofrecerle** *or* **que le ofrezca un consejo,** lo que debe hacer es pedir un aumento de sueldo.	*if you'll let me give/offer you a piece of advice*
Yo, personalmente, creo que lo que deben hacer es esperar.	*personally, I think that what you should do is to ...*
Sería prudente llamar antes por teléfono, por si acaso está fuera.	*it would be wise to ...*
No sería mala idea enviarlo todo exprés.	*it wouldn't be a bad idea to ...*
Quizás podrían hacerlo sin mi ayuda.	*perhaps you could*
Debía usted hacerlo cuanto antes, porque si no les va a molestar.	*you should*
¿Se le ha ocurrido a usted la posibilidad de encargárselo a otro?	*have you considered the possibility of*
Sería totalmente desaconsejable intervenir ahora.	*it is highly inadvisable to ...*
Permítanme ustedes que insista en la necesidad de presionar a la compañía.	*I would urge you to ...*
Les aconsejo encarecidamente que tomen este asunto muy en serio.	*I strongly advise you to ...*
Haga lo que haga, *or* **Pase lo que pase, no deje usted de** cumplir con los requisitos legales.	*do not fail to ...*
Lo mejor que puede hacer es dirigirse a la oficina central.	*the best thing you can do is to ...*

WARNINGS

Le advierto a usted que esto lo hace contra mi voluntad.	*I warn you that*
Es absolutamente indispensable *or* **Es de absoluta necesidad que** lleguen los pedidos la semana que viene.	*it is vital that ...*
Un consejo: esa agencia no es de fiar.	*a word of warning:*
Tómelo como una advertencia *or* **Que sirva de advertencia**: sería una medida que podría tener consecuencias nefastas.	*take it as a warning:*
Sería una locura publicarlo ahora.	*it would be madness to ...*
Corren ustedes el riesgo de que se enteren.	*you are running the risk that*
De no hacerlo así, las consecuencias podrían ser graves.	*unless you ...*
Debo advertirle que ese tipo de transacción es ilegal en este país.	*I should warn you that*

OFFERS

Me tiene a su entera disposición para todo lo que necesite.	*I am completely at your disposal*
¿Quiere usted que vuelva mañana?	*would you like me to ...*
¿Le **podría** hacer una visita?	*may I*
Si usted quiere, le **podría** llevar en coche.	*I could ... if you like*
¿Me permite usted darle un consejo?	*would you allow me to ...*
Permítame usted por lo menos acompañarle hasta la estación.	*at least allow me to ...*
¿Quiere usted que se lo arreglemos nosotros?	*would you like us to ...*
¿Le gustaría que viniésemos a verle otra vez mañana?	*would you like us to ...*
No duden ustedes en pedirme ayuda siempre que la necesiten.	*don't hesitate to ...*
Yo me encargaré de darles todas las facilidades posibles.	*I'll take care of*
Estoy (plenamente) dispuesto a hacer todo lo que usted me diga.	*I am (fully) prepared to ...*
Sería un placer poder servirle en todo lo que le haga falta.	*it would be a pleasure to ...*
Quizás podríamos escribir a los editores y explicar el problema.	*perhaps we could*
¿Le atrae la idea de que viajemos juntos?	*does the idea of ... appeal to you?*

REQUESTS

Por favor, no se olvide de hablar con Juan cuando esté usted en Madrid.	*please don't forget to ...*
Les ruego que me devuelvan los documentos.	*I'd like to ask you to ...*
¿Podría usted enviarme un ejemplar?	*could you*
¿Le puedo pedir que conteste por escrito a este cliente?	*could I ask you to ...*
¿Quiere darse prisa, **si no le importa?**	*would you mind*
Le ruego que no se quede usted con las llaves.	*please don't*
Perdone, pero **debo insistir en que** se dirija al Director.	*I must insist that*
Preferiría que no lo utilizara a partir de las ocho.	*I would prefer you not to ...*

(more indirectly)

¿Le importaría *or* **¿Le molestaría** prestarme un ejemplar?	*would you mind*
Le agradecería que me ayudara usted a resolver este problema.	*I would be grateful for your help in*
Si no le molesta *or* **Si no es mucha molestia, ¿me podría** atender ahora?	*if it's not too much trouble, could you*
Nos vendría bien saberlo mañana, antes de la reunión.	*it would be extremely useful for us to*
Contamos con que usted les avise con tiempo.	*we are relying on you to ...*

(more formally)

¿Sería tan amable de enseñármelo usted mismo?	*would you be so kind as to ...*
Se ruega que ocupen los asientos antes de las diez.	*kindly*
Tengan a bien comunicarnos la respuesta por télex.	*we would be very grateful if*
Nos permitimos rogarles que permanezcan aquí hasta que se les avise.	*you are kindly requested to ...*
Esperamos que les sea posible ampliar la producción.	*we hope that you will be able to*
Confío en que no les ocasionará demasiada molestia atender mi petición.	*I trust that*
Desearíamos pedirles que se ocupasen ustedes mismos de este asunto.	*we would like to ask you to ...*
Le agradecería enormemente que tuviese la amabilidad de contestar a mi carta del mes pasado.	*I would be very grateful if you would kindly*
Les quedaríamos muy agradecidos si pudiesen enviarnos la información necesaria a la mayor brevedad.	*we would be exceedingly grateful if*

AND, ACCORDING TO CONTEXT:

le ruego que me disculpe por molestarle con esta petición/espero no robarle demasiado tiempo con/si no es demasiada molestia/espero que no le importe atender este asunto/no olvide/por lo que más quiera, no/si me lo permite, quisiera recordarle que/quedamos a la espera de recibir de usted

COMPARISONS

En comparación con Inglaterra, España tiene un clima más soleado.	*in comparison with*
Esta casa **no tiene comparación con** aquélla.	*there is no comparison between ... and ...*
Si compara el nivel de vida de Inglaterra **con** el de Portugal, salen ganando los ingleses.	*if you compare ... with ...*
Ese coche es **relativamente** barato, para lo que es.	*relatively*
Los informes de este año son **(mucho) más interesantes que** los del año pasado.	*(much) more interesting than*
Es **cada vez más** difícil encontrar un piso en el casco antiguo//Es **cada vez menos** frecuente encontrar a gente que fuma.	*more and more// less and less*
Es como el que tenía mi abuela, **pero más grande.**	*it's like ... but bigger*
Es parecido al que utilizaba el año pasado, pero mucho mejor.	*it's similar to*
Esta casa tiene poca luz, **mientras que** la otra tiene mucha.	*whereas*
Se parecen mucho, y sin embargo se llevan muy mal.	*they are very similar, yet*
Lo que distingue *or* **diferencia a** esta compañía **de** la otra es la fama tan buena que tiene.	*what distinguishes ... from*

(comparing favourably)

Este vino **es muy superior al** otro.	*is far superior to*
En esto **no hay comparación posible**: prefiero el sur.	*they bear no comparison*
Aquí no cabe comparación: este aparato funciona mucho mejor que ése.	*there is no possible comparison here*
Este diseño **es muchísimo mejor que** ese otro.	*is far better than*

(comparing unfavourably)

No hay comparación posible: esta calculadora es muy inferior.	*they bear no comparison*
Esta traducción **es muy inferior a** la que hicieron la última vez.	*is far inferior to ...*
La película **es mucho menos** interesante **que** el libro.	*is much less ... than*
Estos dos informes **no tienen comparación.**	*do not bear comparison*
Estas cámaras fotográficas **son mucho peores que** las que se fabrican en Japón.	*are much worse than*

(great similarity)

Estos dos niños **se parecen muchísimo**; ¿serán gemelos?	*look just like one another*
Esto **equivale a** veinte horas de trabajo.	*is the equivalent of*
Lo mismo se podría decir de esa otra propuesta.	*the same is true of*
Estos dos cuadros **valen lo mismo** *or* **tienen el mismo valor.**	*are worth the same*
Estos dos pianos **no se diferencian en nada.**	*there is no difference between*

(great difference)

No se parece en nada a su padre.	*doesn't look anything like ...*
La diferencia entre ellos es muy grande//Hay una gran diferencia entre ellos.	*there is a great difference between them*
No se pueden comparar: son totalmente distintos.	*there can be no possible comparison*
No veo parecido alguno entre los dos modelos.	*I cannot see any resemblance whatsoever between*
Como deportista, Juan **no le llega ni a la suela de los zapatos.**	*has nothing on*
Los resultados de este año **no tienen ni punto de comparación** con los de los años anteriores.	*there is no comparison between ... and...*

OPINIONS

ASKING FOR SOMEBODY'S OPINION

¿Qué opina usted *or* **¿Qué piensa usted** del mercado libre?	*what is your opinion of/what do you think of*
En su opinión, ¿debemos firmar el contrato?	*in your opinion, should we*
¿Qué cree usted que debían hacer los sindicatos?	*what do you think ... should ...*
¿Me podría dar su opinión acerca de los resultados del experimento?	*would you tell me what you think about*
Me interesaría *or* **Me gustaría saber su opinión acerca del** último informe.	*I would be interested to know what you think about*
¿Me podría decir lo que opina sobre las reformas?	*could you tell me what you think about*
¿Qué le parece a usted esta posibilidad?	*what do you think of*
¿Cree usted que la situación actual puede empeorar?	*do you think that*
¿Cree usted en el principio de la autodeterminación de los pueblos?	*do you believe in*

EXPRESSING YOUR OPINION

Yo creo que *or* **Yo considero que** cada cual debe cumplir sus obligaciones.	*I think that*
Para mí personalmente la Agencia Sánchez es aceptable.	*personally, I find*
Por mí *or* **En lo que a mí respecta** *or* **En cuanto a mí,** pueden ustedes hacer lo que mejor les parezca.	*as far as I am concerned*
Lo que es yo, no lo considero necesario.	*I, personally, do not*
Supongo que *or* **Me imagino que** habrá que vigilarlo todo.	*I suppose/I imagine that*
Lo que yo creo es que ha sido todo demasiado fácil.	*what I think is that*
En mi opinión, fue un error no haberle contratado cuando se ofreció para colaborar con nosotros.	*in my opinion*
Según mi criterio, la situación no está como para abrir una nueva sucursal.	*in my view*
A mi modo de ver, todos tenemos algún talento.	*the way I look at it*
No creo que sea conveniente que les dejemos plantados.	*I do not think it is right to*
A mi parecer, no hay otra salida posible.	*to my mind*
Parece que no va a resultar.	*it doesn't look as if*
Me de la impresión de que podría ser muy peligroso.	*I have the impression that it could*
Estoy convencida de que no cuentan con fondos suficientes.	*I am convinced that*
Pensándolo bien, creo que sería posible entregarlos a primeros de mes.	*on further consideration, I think that*
Si reflexionamos, podríamos llegar a la conclusión de que sería mejor aceptar.	*on second thoughts*
Si quiere que le diga lo que pienso, no me gusta nada que actúe usted de esa forma.	*if you want my opinion, ...*
Debo reconocer que *or* **Debo admitir que** tenía usted toda la razón.	*I must admit that*
Estoy totalmente segura de que nos lo van a devolver.	*I am quite sure that*
Tengo que decir que no me gusta nada.	*I feel I should say that*
Si desea mi opinión, se la puedo expresar con toda claridad.	*if you would like my opinion, ...*
Si quiere mi sincera opinión en lo que se refiere a sus propuestas, no me convencen.	*if you want my honest opinion, ...*
No puedo menos de pensar que aquí hay algo raro.	*I cannot help thinking that*
Tengo la sensación de que no va a dar resultado.	*I have a feeling that*
Con el debido respeto, debo decirle que eso no es así.	*with all due respect, I feel I should tell you that*

REPLYING WITHOUT GIVING AN OPINION

Es difícil prever qué necesidades puede haber sin conocer las circunstancias.	*it is difficult to tell ...*
Me resulta difícil emitir una opinión definitiva sobre el tema.	*it is difficult for me to give a final opinion on*
Todo dependerá de lo que usted quiera decir con 'trabajo equilibrado'.	*it all depends on what you mean by ...*
No deseo comprometer a la compañía **a** terminar el encargo para el 15 de enero.	*I don't want to commit ... to ...*
No soy yo quien puede pronunciarse sobre ese tema.	*I'm not in a position to ...*
No puedo inclinarme ni por un lado ni por el otro.	*I cannot say one way or the other*

LIKES, DISLIKES AND PREFERENCES

ASKING ABOUT THESE

¿Le gusta su trabajo?	*do you like*
¿Le gustaría jugar al tenis?	*would you like to ...*
¿Le gusta vivir en esta ciudad?	*do you like*
De los que han mandado, **¿cuál prefiere usted?** *or* **¿cuál le gusta más?**	*which do you prefer*
Me gustaría saber lo que opina sobre la selección que hemos hecho.	*I would like to know your opinion of*
Les gusta comer más temprano, **¿verdad?**	*you like to ... don't you?*

SAYING WHAT YOU LIKE

Me ha gustado mucho el regalo que me han enviado.	*I liked ... very much*
Nos gusta que los amigos nos visiten con frecuencia.	*we like it when*
Me encanta *or* **Me gusta muchísimo** la comida española, sobre todo la paella.	*I love*
Disfruto mucho de la vida madrileña en todas las épocas del año.	*I really enjoy*
Salir al campo **es uno de mis grandes placeres.**	*one of the things I most enjoy is*
Lo que más me gusta es observar a la gente.	*I like ... better than anything else*
No me desagrada salir de paseo aunque haga mucho frío.	*I quite like*
Me cae muy bien Juana, y nos llevamos estupendamente.	*I like Juana very much*

SAYING WHAT YOU DISLIKE

No me gusta que fumen los niños.	*I don't like*
No aguanto que me hagan esperar.	*I cannot stand*
Lo que más me molesta es la lluvia.	*what I dislike most is*
No puedo soportar que la gente no cumpla lo prometido.	*I can't bear it when*
Me horrorizan *or* **Me dan horror** *or* **Aborrezco** las corridas de toros.	*I really hate*
No encuentro ningún placer en revisar informes mal escritos.	*I get no pleasure at all from*
No aguanto el pescado frito: me molesta el olor.	*I can't stand*
Sus canciones **no tienen nada de especial.**	*are nothing special*
No me gusta nada *or* **en absoluto que** ellos hablen mal de nosotros por detrás.	*I do not like it at all when*
Le he cogido manía a ese chico.	*I have taken a dislike to*
No me cae nada simpática *or* **Me cae muy mal ...**	*I don't like ... at all*

SAYING WHAT YOU PREFER

Prefiero las novelas **a** la televisión.	*I prefer X to Y*
Prefiero que llegues tarde **a que** no vengas.	*I prefer you to ... rather than ...*
Si no le incomoda *or* **importa, preferiría** empezar a las nueve.	*if it doesn't put you out, I'd prefer to ...*
Preferiría que me lo enseñase antes de firmarlo.	*I would prefer you to ...*
Más vale dejar el deporte hasta que mejore el tiempo.	we (I, you, etc) *had better*
Sería mejor hacerlo de otra manera.	*it would be better to ...*
Tenemos gran preferencia por la exportación.	*we have a marked preference for*
Nos vendría mucho mejor recibirles la semana que viene.	*it would suit us much better to*
Ese tipo de contrato **nos conviene mucho más.**	*suits us much better*
Me convendría más que viniesen ustedes el lunes.	*it would be better for me if*

EXPRESSING INDIFFERENCE

Me es *or* **da igual** *or* **Me es** *or* **da lo mismo** hacerlo así **o** de la otra forma.	*it is all the same to me whether ... or ...*
Me da igual que vengan ustedes hoy **o** mañana.	*it is equally suitable for you to ... or ...*
Me es totalmente indiferente que ellos lo acepten o lo rechacen.	*it makes absolutely no difference to me whether*
No tengo preferencia especial.	*I do not mind one way or the other*
Casi prefiero que lo dejemos para otro día.	*I'd as soon*
Como quiera usted, podemos salir ahora o dejarlo para más tarde.	*as you wish*
No tiene la más mínima importancia que llegue el miércoles o el jueves.	*it is absolutely immaterial whether*

INTENTIONS AND DESIRES

ASKING WHAT SOMEONE INTENDS OR WANTS

¿Qué piensa hacer? — *what are you going to do?*

¿Qué planes tienen ustedes? // ¿Qué intenciones tienen? — *what are your plans?*

¿Qué es lo que ustedes desean *or* **esperan** conseguir? — *what are you hoping to ...*

Sería útil saber lo que piensa hacer en cuanto a este asunto. — *it would be useful (*for me etc*) to know what you are thinking of ...*

Quisiera saber cómo piensa actuar en lo referente a este negocio. — *I should like to know ...*

Quisiéramos saber lo que sus clientes esperan conseguir. — *we should like to know what your clients expect to ...*

SAYING WHAT YOU INTEND

Voy a salir en avión el jueves que viene//**Pienso** salir en avión el jueves que viene. — *I am going to // I intend to*

Saldremos de Inglaterra el día 5 a primera hora. — *we shall*

Está previsto que lleguen ustedes a Madrid por la tarde. — *the plan is that*

Tenía planeado que fuésemos de excursión a la sierra. — *I had planned for us to ...*

Me propongo hablar con el Director General. — *I intend to ...*

Teníamos pensado visitar el Museo Romántico. — *we had planned to ...*

Pienso quedarme en casa todo el fin de semana. — *my intention is to ...*

He estado pensando en la posibilidad de cambiar de trabajo. — *I have been considering the possibility of*

Iba a *or* **Tenía pensado** *or* **Tenía la intención de** hablar con él del asunto, pero no he tenido tiempo de hacerlo. — *I was going to ... // I had thought of ... // I intended to ...*

No tengo la más mínima intención de volver a hacerlo. — *I have absolutely no intention of*

No pienso hablar de su dimisión. — *I do not intend to ...*

Lo que quería era que se diese prisa. — *what I wanted was for you to ...*

Hemos decidido abrir una sucursal en Sevilla **a fin de** ampliar el negocio. — *with a view to*

Para conseguir aumentar las ventas hay que invertir más capital. — *in order to*

SAYING WHAT YOU WOULD LIKE

Me gustaría reservar una habitación para el 10 de agosto. — *I would like to ...*

Quisiera comer fuera los fines de semana. — *I should like to ...*

Me habría *or* **Me hubiera gustado** ir a recibirle, pero a última hora surgió un imprevisto. — *I should have liked to ...*

Sí que me hubiese agradado poder ir a Valencia, pero tuve que dejarlo para cumplir con otras obligaciones. — *I certainly would have liked to be able to ...*

Ojalá pudiésemos ayudarle a solucionar el problema. — *I only wish we could*

Ojalá lleguen esta semana. — *I very much hope that*

Es de esperar que sea verdad//**Sólo podemos confiar en que** sea verdad. — *we can but hope that*

Nuestro sincero deseo es que todo salga bien. — *we sincerely hope that*

Mi único deseo sería complacerles a ustedes. — *my only wish would be to ...*

Esperemos que todo se haga según nuestros planes. — *let us hope that*

Lo que de verdad me gustaría es que viniesen ustedes a vernos a Madrid para que pudiésemos tratar en persona. — *what I would really like is for you to ...*

SAYING WHAT YOU WANT TO DO OR NOT TO DO

Quiero salir el lunes 2 de noviembre por la mañana temprano. — *I want to ...*

Quisiera emplear ese dinero de otra manera. — *I would like to ...*

No quiero que vayan a pensar otra cosa. — *I do not want ... to ...*

Querría ir al teatro Lope de Vega a ver la obra de Lorca. — *I should like to ...*

No desearíamos causarle molestias. — *we would not wish to ...*

Me gustaría mucho más que ellos fuesen conscientes de sus responsabilidades. — *I would much rather they ...*

No se trata de hablar otra vez con ellos, sino de que acepten lo que hemos propuesto ya varias veces. — *it is not a question of*

Estamos decididos: hay que publicar el informe. — *we have made up our minds: ...*

Está resuelta a no dejarlo hasta que acabe. — *she is determined not to ...*

Estoy totalmente a favor de / en contra de contratar nuevo personal. — *I am totally in favour of / against*

PERMISSION

ASKING FOR PERMISSION

¿Puedo trasladarme a otra habitación?	*may I*
¿Podría cambiar a otro horario, a fin de terminar más pronto?	*could I*
Espero que no le incomode que cambie de hotel.	*I hope it doesn't put you out if*
¿Me permitiría usar su carro mientras esté en Quito?	*would you allow me to ...*
¿Tendrían la amabilidad de enseñarme las otras muestras?	*would you be so kind as to ...*
¿Me permitiría consultar el diccionario grande de la Real Academia?	*would you allow me to ...*
¿Se puede cambiar el modelo dentro de un plazo razonable?	*can I*
¿Sería posible recibirlos sin tardanza?	*would it be possible to ...*
¿Tendrían inconveniente en que nos quedásemos un rato más?	*would you mind if*
¿Está permitido usar diccionario en el examen?	*is it permissible to ...*
Si no les molesta, quisiera usar el télex.	*if you don't mind, I would like to ...*
Espero que no les importe que hagamos uso de esta información.	*I hope you do not mind if*

GIVING PERMISSION

Puede escoger otro modelo, si le conviene más.	*you can*
Le ruego que haga todas las preguntas que quiera.	*please do not hesitate to ...*
Naturalmente, pueden redactarlo como mejor les parezca.	*by all means, you may*
Estoy plenamente de acuerdo en que se lleven a cabo todos los planes previstos.	*I fully agree that*
Le autorizo *or* **Tiene usted mi autorización para** firmar en nuestro nombre.	*I authorise you to ...*
Tiene autorización oficial para instalar aquí su casa central.	*you have official permission to ...*

REFUSING PERMISSION

Siento mucho no poder aceptar sus propuestas.	*I am sorry I cannot accept*
No puede hacer los dos cursos a la vez; tendrá que escoger uno u otro.	*you cannot*
No puedo permitir que trabaje los fines de semana.	*I cannot allow you to ...*
Lo siento mucho, pero me es imposible darle permiso.	*I am very sorry but I cannot*
Me opongo a que se les permita acudir a la reunión.	*I am opposed to allowing*
Me niego a aprobar esos planes.	*I refuse to ...*
Le prohíbo categóricamente que se comunique con los testigos.	*I absolutely forbid you to ...*
Aun lamentándolo mucho, debemos rehusar su petición.	*regrettably, we must*

HAVING PERMISSION OR NOT HAVING IT

Me está prohibido *or* **Se me ha prohibido** *or* **No me está permitido** hablar del tema con usted.	*I am not allowed to ...*
El médico me ha prohibido fumar.	*the doctor has forbidden me to ...*
Tengo totalmente prohibido el alcohol, a causa de mi enfermedad de hígado.	*I am not allowed*
Se opone totalmente a que solicitemos una entrevista.	*she is totally against our ...*
Se me ha permitido *or* **Tengo permiso para** quedarme hasta las once.	*I am allowed to ...*
Me dijo que podría venir cuando quisiera.	*she said I could ...*
No tenemos ninguna obligación de consultarle.	*we are not under any obligation to ...*
Le permiten *or* **Le dejan** acostarse a la hora que quiera.	*they allow her to ...*
Está totalmente *or* **Está terminantemente prohibido** circular en dirección contraria.	*is absolutely forbidden*
Han dicho que nos dejan salir los domingos si queremos.	*they have said that they will let us*
Tengo autorización para firmar en nombre del Consejo de Administración.	*I have been authorized to ...*
Usted no tiene por qué intervenir en el asunto.	*you are not supposed to ...*
En este tipo de transacción **está permitido** contar con un pequeño margen de error.	*is allowable*

OBLIGATION

SAYING WHAT SOMEONE MUST DO

Tienes que *or* **Debes tratar de** convencerles.	*you must try to ...*
No debíamos actuar de esta manera.	*we should not ...*
Me veo obligado a *or* **Me veo en la necesidad de** salir antes de las cinco.	*I absolutely must*
Es absolutamente necesario entregar *or* **que entregue** la mercancía antes del día 9.	*it is essential that you ...*
Es preciso que se presenten ustedes aquí cuanto antes.	*it is necessary for you to ...*
En Madrid **no se puede** aparcar en casi ningún sitio.	*you are not allowed to ...*
Las circunstancias **me obligan a** regresar a mi país.	*force me to ...*
Se vio obligada a quedarse dos semanas más de lo previsto.	*she found it necessary to ...*
Es obligatorio pagar las tasas **antes de** matricularse.	*you must ... before you ...*
No me queda más remedio que informar a las autoridades.	*I have no alternative but to ...*
Es absolutamente imprescindible *or* **esencial** *or* **indispensable** que pueda contar con el apoyo del director en este asunto.	*it is absolutely essential*
Se me ha encargado que realice esta inspección.	*I have been given the job of*
Me han encargado que revise la nueva edición.	*I have been given the task of*
Cuando hay un accidente **se exige a** los testigos **que** informen *or* **se requiere que** los testigos informen a la policía.	*are required to ...*
Para solicitar ese trabajo **es requisito indispensable** haber cumplido los 21 años.	*in order to ... it is an essential requirement*
Para obtener el certificado **hay que** ir a la ventanilla número 8.	*in order to ... you have to ...*
Las aduanas **estipulan lo que** los viajeros pueden pasar sin pagar impuestos.	*... is laid down*
Hay que presentar el carnet de identidad en la entrada.	*you will have to ...*

(enquiring if one is obliged to do something)

¿Estoy obligada a *or* **¿Tengo obligación de** atenerme a estas normas?.	*do I have to ...*
¿De verdad tengo que pagar?	*do I really have to ...*
¿Se necesita carnet de conducir?	*do I need*

SAYING WHAT SOMEONE IS NOT OBLIGED TO DO

No necesita traer fotografías.	*you don't need to ...*
No hace falta que tomen ustedes las comidas en el hotel **si no quieren.**	*you needn't ... if you don't want to*
No tiene que *or* **No está obligada a** contestar **si no quiere.**	*you do not have to ... if you don't want to*
No es obligatorio llevar el pasaporte.	*it is not compulsory to ...*
No es necesario hacer trasbordo, **puede** ir directamente.	*you won't have to ..., you can ...*
No tiene usted obligación de hacerlo así **si no quiere.**	*you are not under any obligation*
No tiene sentido que vaya usted a esa oficina.	*it makes no sense for you to ...*
No vale *or* **No merece la pena** preocuparse por traducirlo todo.	*it is not worth*
No quiero obligarle a hablarme del accidente si usted no quiere.	*I don't want to force you to ...*
Usted no tiene que seguir **las mismas** normas **que** los socios permanentes.	*you needn't ... the same ... as ...*
No tenemos por qué aceptar su última oferta.	*there is no reason why we should ...*
No es indispensable que lleguemos antes de las ocho.	*it is not absolutely necessary for us to ...*

SAYING WHAT SOMEONE MUST NOT DO

No le permito que me hable usted de ese modo// **No tiene usted derecho a** hablarme de ese modo.	*you have no right to ...*
Está prohibido *or* **Se prohíbe** pisar el césped.	*it is forbidden to ...*
No se puede solicitar permiso de trabajo **hasta que** no se consiga trabajo.	*you cannot ... until you have ...*
No debemos suponer que podemos aplicar los mismos criterios.	*we should not suppose that we can*
No le puedo permitir que hable de esta manera de su compañía.	*I cannot allow you to ...*
Le prohíbo nombrar al Director para nada.	*I forbid you to ...*
Haga lo que haga, no me hable más del tema.	*whatever you do, don't ...*

AGREEMENT

AGREEING WITH A STATEMENT

Estamos de acuerdo con ustedes.	*we agree with you*
Compartimos el mismo punto de vista que ustedes // Somos del mismo parecer que ustedes.	*we are of the same view*
Estoy de acuerdo en que es muy difícil encontrarle en casa, **pero** hay que seguir intentándolo.	*I accept that ... but ...*
Estoy totalmente de acuerdo con todo lo que ha dicho mi estimado amigo.	*I fully agree with*
Yo, como usted, creo que este asunto se podría tratar más detenidamente.	*I agree with you that*
Tiene usted toda la razón en prohibir el uso de términos imprecisos.	*you are quite right to ...*
Reconozco que volvemos al mismo tema que antes, pero lo creo necesario.	*I realize that*
Es cierto que es un tema que nunca se ha tratado en serio.	*it is true that*
Comprendo muy bien que hay que insistir.	*I fully understand that*
Le doy toda la razón.	*you are quite right*
Es probable que tenga razón cuando dice que lo hemos dejado demasiado tarde.	*you are probably right in saying that*
Admito ese punto, y también su argumento sobre la disponibilidad de las mercancías.	*I grant you that point, and also your argument about*
Admito que estaba equivocado.	*I admit that*
Acepto que ustedes trataron de avisarnos con tiempo.	*I accept that*

AGREEING TO A PROPOSAL

Estoy de acuerdo en que debía hablar con ustedes directamente.	*I agree that I should ...*
Accedemos a enviar los productos sin previo pago.	*we agree to ...*
No tengo ningún inconveniente en aceptar sus propuestas.	*I have nothing against*
En líneas generales, estamos de acuerdo con sus propuestas en lo relativo a la compra de la casa.	*in general, we accept your proposals regarding*
Mis clientes **están conformes con** el precio que usted pide.	*agree with*
Estoy de acuerdo en que venga a vernos su representante.	*I agree that*
Acepto que debemos cumplir el contrato.	*I accept that we should ...*
Tengo mucho gusto en apoyar la propuesta.	*I am very pleased to be able to ...*
Sin duda apoyaremos todo lo que ustedes propongan.	*of course we will ...*
A primera vista, su propuesta parece cubrir todas nuestras necesidades.	*at first sight, your offer appears to ...*

AGREEING TO A REQUEST

Acepto con mucho gusto su invitación a visitarle en México.	*I am very pleased to accept*
Llegaré el sábado a las tres, **tal como me ha pedido** que haga.	*I will ..., as you asked me to*
Seguiré sus instrucciones al pie de la letra.	*I will follow your instructions to the letter*
Tendré en cuenta sus consejos en lo que respecta a las ventas.	*I will bear in mind your advice about*
Tenemos sumo gusto en aceptar los términos del contrato.	*we are delighted to accept*
Tomamos nota de lo que nos comunican acerca del cambio de fechas para la reservación de habitación.	*we have taken note of what you have told us about*
Tendré presentes sus observaciones en lo referente al programa.	*I will bear in mind your remarks about*
Trataremos de satisfacer sus deseos en cuanto a la presentación del producto.	*we will try to meet your wishes about*
Encuentro la relación de fechas **totalmente satisfactoria.**	*is perfectly satisfactory*
Las fechas y horas que propone para las diversas reuniones **me vienen bien.**	*suit me well*

AND, ACCORDING TO CONTEXT:

yo pienso lo mismo que usted/como usted ha señalado, con toda la razón/estoy dispuesto a dar luz verde a/ciertamente, estoy a favor de/no veo motivo para oponerme a/esto es completamente satisfactorio/estoy plenamente dispuesto a/aprobaremos el uso de/no cabe duda sobre/no puedo poner en tela de juicio los hechos presentados/no se puede negar que/me apresuro a comunicarle mi total aprobación de/esto es exactamente lo que yo había esperado/quisiera instarle a que lo hiciese/he asumido este asunto, y/me parece una postura totalmente razonable/esto queda justificado por

DISAGREEMENT

DISAGREEING WITH WHAT SOMEONE HAS SAID

Estoy totalmente en contra de que se espere hasta el año que viene.	*I am totally opposed to*
Se equivoca usted al decir que el plazo vence el día treinta.	*you are wrong to ...*
Siento decirle que no tiene razón.	*I am sorry to say*
Yo creo que hace mal en rechazar su propuesta.	*I think it's a mistake to ...*
Está usted equivocado si piensa que han cumplido sus obligaciones.	*you are wrong to think that*
No estoy de acuerdo con usted en este punto.	*I do not agree with you on this matter*
Me parece que aquí ha habido un error, pues las cifras no coinciden.	*I think that there has been a mistake here, because*
No comparto sus opiniones sobre la dirección de nuestros planes.	*I do not agree with what you say about*
Considero que un retraso así **no tiene justificación.**	*I do not accept that there is any justification for*
Niego categóricamente que sean de mala calidad.	*I absolutely deny that*
No entiendo *or* **No llego a entender cómo hemos podido** llegar a esta situación.	*I do not understand how we can have*
Yo no lo veo así.	*I don't see it that way*
Siento tener que contradecirle, pero creo que los hechos me dan la razón.	*I am sorry to have to contradict you, but I think that*
Lamento tener que llevarle la contraria, pero por experiencia propia sé que la situación va a empeorar si no tomamos medidas adecuadas.	*I am sorry I have to disagree with you, but*
No es cierto que lo hayan enviado a tiempo.	*it is not true that*
Mi planteamiento es diferente.	*the way I see it is different*
No se trata de que esta vez haya cometido un error **sino de que** siempre lo hace todo mal.	*it is not a question of ..., but ...*

DISAGREEING WITH WHAT SOMEONE PROPOSES

Me temo que no me será posible aceptar su proyecto.	*I am afraid I shall not be able to ...*
Lamentablemente, me es imposible acudir a la cita.	*regrettably, I cannot ...*
No creo que debamos tomarlo demasiado en serio.	*I do not think we should ...*
Nos oponemos categóricamente a este tipo de interferencias.	*we are completely against*
Me niego a permitirle *or* **dejarle** perder el tiempo de esta manera.	*I refuse to allow you to ...*
Siento no poder aceptar lo que usted dice // **Lo siento, pero no puedo aceptar** lo que usted sugiere.	*I am sorry I cannot accept*
Me es imposible apoyar su solicitud.	*I cannot give you my support for*
Nos veremos obligados a vetar la propuesta.	*we shall be obliged to ...*
Lo sentimos mucho, pero nuestro deber es oponernos a lo que ustedes proponen.	*regrettably, our duty is to ...*

REFUSING A REQUEST

Aun sintiéndolo mucho, tengo que negarme a hacer lo que nos piden.	*I am very sorry, but I must refuse to ...*
Debo comunicarle que su petición ha sido denegada.	*I must tell you that your request has been turned down*
Por desgracia *or* **Desgraciadamente, su demanda no puede ser atendida.**	*unfortunately, your request cannot be granted*
No accederemos jamás a introducir la jornada de 35 horas.	*we shall never agree to ...*
Lo siento mucho, pero no estoy en condiciones de aceptar su propuesta en este momento.	*I am very sorry, but I am not in a position to ...*
No podemos de ninguna manera concederles lo que nos piden.	*we cannot under any circumstances ...*
Me es difícil dar curso a su solicitud.	*I am having difficulties in ...*
Lamentamos no poder hacer lo que ustedes desean.	*we are very sorry, but we cannot ...*
Es totalmente imposible reducir el personal de la empresa.	*... is totally out of the question*
Me niego por completo a tomar una medida de carácter dudosamente legal.	*I absolutely refuse to ...*
Sencillamente, debe usted rehusar una demanda que carece de sentido.	*you must simply say no to*

APPROVAL

Me parece muy bien que la reunión se celebre en Barcelona.	*I approve of*
Nos parece una idea excelente que haya decidido usted encargarse del departamento de traducción.	*we thoroughly approve of your decision to …*
Nos parece estupendo todo lo que ustedes proponen.	*we approve highly of*
¡Qué idea tan buena! // ¡Qué buena idea!	*what a good idea!*
Tendré un gran placer en *or* **Será un placer** colaborar con ellos.	*I will be delighted to …*
Hizo usted bien en llamarme.	*you did the right thing to …*
Tiene toda la razón en reclamar sus derechos.	*you are quite right to …*
Estamos a favor de que se mejoren las comunicaciones.	*we are in favour of*
Estoy conforme con la decisión del otro juez.	*I agree with*

(more formally)

Le agradezco su amabilidad en ofrecernos los servicios de su compañía, **los cuales tengo mucho gusto en aceptar.**	*I am grateful for your kind offer of …, which I am delighted to accept*
Nos complace aceptar su propuesta.	*we are pleased to …*
Celebramos la aparición de su nuevo libro sobre la España actual.	*is very welcome*
Acogeremos con mucho gusto todo lo que ustedes deseen sugerirnos.	*we welcome wholeheartedly*
Cualquier contribución por su parte **será bien recibida.**	*will be welcome*
Nos alegramos de haber recibido el informe, que nos ha tranquilizado mucho.	*we were very pleased to …*
Nos han causado una impresión muy favorable sus esfuerzos.	*we have been very favourably impressed by*
Aceptamos con sumo gusto que nos visiten en Caracas en el mes de mayo.	*we are happy to agree to your visiting us*

DISAPPROVAL

No me parece bien la lista que mi secretaria acaba de mostrarme.	*I disapprove of*
Para mí es inconcebible que no hayan previsto los inconvenientes.	*I think it is inconceivable that*
Me parece muy mal que muestren una actitud tan intransigente.	*I disapprove of (the fact that)*
La forma como se llevó la negociación **no fue de su agrado.**	*did not meet with his approval*
Deberíamos haber recibido una notificación sobre la fecha de la conferencia.	*we ought to have had notice of*
Ellos no debían haberlo hecho de esa forma.	*they should not have …*
La culpa es de ellos por no haber conseguido un mayor número de alumnos: **debían haber** hecho más propaganda.	*it is their fault if …: they should have …*
No deseo culpar a nadie, pero ya les advertí que debían prestar más atención a los detalles.	*I don't want to blame anyone, but I warned you that*
No tendremos más remedio que *or* **Nos veremos obligados a** exigir responsabilidades.	*we shall be forced to …*
Es imposible tolerar esta situación un día más.	*we cannot put up with*
Habrían hecho mejor en decírnoslo antes.	*it would have been better if*
Creo que hizo usted mal *or* **cometió un error en** marcharse dejándonos el problema sin resolver.	*I think you were wrong to …*
Me decepcionó bastante su actitud.	*I was rather disappointed by*
No estoy nada contento con lo que ellos nos dicen.	*I am not happy about*
No estoy nada satisfecha con lo que ha sucedido últimamente.	*I am rather unhappy about*
Es una verdadera lástima que se comporten así.	*it is a terrible shame that*
Me veo obligado a expresar mi desaprobación por la actuación del representante de la Empresa Casas.	*I feel obliged to …*
No entiendo cómo pueden ustedes hacer eso.	*I don't understand how you can*
Me opongo totalmente a que se vuelva a discutir el tema.	*I am totally opposed to*
Deseamos protestar contra la severidad de la pena impuesta por el juez.	*we would like to protest about*
¿Con qué derecho creen que pueden detener a la gente?	*what right do they think they have to …*
Me disgusta profundamente el que hayan rescindido ustedes el contrato.	*I am profoundly unhappy that*
Me parece deplorable que no se cumpla lo prometido.	*I find it deplorable that*
Es lamentable que la policía mantuviese una actitud de indiferencia.	*it is regrettable that*
Mis superiores **condenan totalmente** sus acciones **y desean desentenderse por completo de** las posibles consecuencias.	*… totally condemn … and wish to dissociate themselves*

CERTAINTY, POSSIBILITY AND CAPABILITY

EXPRESSING CERTAINTY

Estoy segura *or* **Estoy convencida de** haber pagado la cuenta del teléfono.	*I am sure*
Estamos convencidos de que todo saldrá bien.	*we are convinced that*
Sé con seguridad que han tratado de escribirnos.	*I am quite sure that*
Sin lugar a dudas *or* **No cabe duda de que** actuó precipitadamente.	*there is no doubt that*
Está claro que *or* **Es evidente que** él no sabe lo que hace.	*it is obvious that*
Tengo la certeza de haberle visto la semana pasada.	*I am certain that*
Es innegable que los resultados de las elecciones son muy poco alentadores para nuestro partido.	*it is undeniable that*
Por supuesto que terminarán el trabajo antes de la fecha tope.	*of course they will ...*
Es seguro que llegan mañana.	*it's certain that*
Ni que decir tiene que pueden venir.	*it goes without saying that*
He investigado el tema, y **todo indica** *or* **parece indicar que** se trata de un error.	*everything seems to indicate that*
Nadie puede negar que vale mucho como trabajador.	*no one can deny that*
No dejaré de comunicarle el resultado // **Sin falta** le comunicaré el resultado.	*I will not fail to ...*
Hay que admitir que las ventajas pueden ser grandes.	*one must admit that*

EXPRESSING PROBABILITY

Seguramente no les quedan *or* no les quedarán fondos.	*they have probably ...*
Es probable que necesite ayuda para establecerse en esta ciudad.	*will probably ...*
Probablemente no lo sabía.	*probably*
Creo que debe andar por los cincuenta años.	*I think he must ...*
No me extrañaría que se hubiese trasladado a otra universidad.	*I wouldn't be surprised if*
La comisión se formará **con toda probabilidad** el mes que viene.	*in all probability*
Debe (de) haberlo sabido ayer.	*she probably*
Sin duda ha recibido nuevas instrucciones.	*doubtless*
Parece haber tenido problemas con la compra de la casa.	*seems to have ...*
Le **tienen que haber** informado sus colegas.	*must have ...*
Parece muy probable que esto se resuelva en la próxima reunión.	*it seems most likely that*
Me parece muy posible que la idea fracase.	*I think it very possible that*
Existe una probabilidad bastante grande de que decidan otra cosa // **Hay un buen chance de que** decidan otra cosa (*LAm*).	*there is a good chance that*
Parece ser que no les gustó.	*it seems that*
Estimamos que debe haberles costado unos diez millones.	*we estimate that it must have*

EXPRESSING POSSIBILITY

Podría haber retraso.	*there could be*
Tal vez se trate de un nuevo contrato.	*perhaps it is about*
Quizá(s) haga falta una investigación.	*maybe ... will be necessary*
Puede que no venga otra vez hasta el año que viene.	*she may not*
Puede ser que no haya tenido todavía tiempo de hacerlo.	*it may be that*
¿Se puede marcar directamente desde mi habitación un número de Inglaterra?	*can one*
A lo mejor lo podré hacer pasado mañana.	*maybe*
También **cabe la posibilidad de que** nos toque la lotería.	*there is also the possibility that*
Acaso se arrepientan de lo que han hecho.	*perhaps*
¿Se trata, **tal vez**, de un desconocido?	*perhaps*
¿Es posible que haya mentido?	*is it possible that*
¿Y **no cabe pensar que** se han equivocado?	*is there no chance that*
Es muy posible que se nieguen.	*it is quite possible that*
No hay que descartar la posibilidad de que la policía logre detener al ladrón.	*there is a chance that*
Si actúan ustedes de ese modo, **podrían correr el riesgo de** perder dinero.	*you may be running the risk of ...*
Yo creo que **es posible** impugnar la decisión.	*... can be ...*
Puede que los inspectores **hayan** terminado **ya** su informe.	*may have already*
Parece (ser) que *or* **Según parece** no fue él quien lo hizo.	*it looks as if*
Por lo que parece *or* **Por lo visto** han realizado grandes avances.	*as far as one can tell*

EXPRESSING DOUBT

No es seguro que vengan el mes que viene.	*it is not certain that*
No estoy seguro de poder terminarlo a tiempo.	*I am not sure that*
No sé si será posible recibirles a ustedes el lunes.	*I don't know if*
Dudo que pueda llegar antes de las tres.	*I doubt whether*
Es dudoso que sea tan fácil como a usted le parece.	*it is unlikely to ...*
Dudamos que jamás haya hecho tal propuesta.	*we doubt whether*
Todavía cabe duda acerca de la mejor manera de llevarlo a cabo.	*there is still doubt about*
No estoy segura de que vayan a aceptar sus condiciones.	*I am not sure that they are going to ...*
No tengo muy claro que esto sea lo que más nos convenga.	*I am not very sure that*
No tiene necesariamente que gastar más dinero.	*you don't necessarily have to ...*
No hay ninguna seguridad de que ellos vayan a cumplir su promesa.	*we cannot be certain that*
Me extrañaría *or* **Me sorprendería mucho que** cambiara de planes.	*I would be most surprised if*
No se sabe con seguridad quién era el responsable del depósito de joyas.	*it is not known for certain*
Ya veremos si es conveniente o no meterse en ese tipo de aventuras.	*we will see whether*
Me pregunto si será verdad que piensan abrir una nueva oficina.	*I wonder whether it is true that*
No existe indicación alguna de que ellos hayan actuado ilegalmente.	*there is no indication that*

EXPRESSING IMPROBABILITY

Me parece poco probable que encuentren ustedes una solución mejor.	*I think you are unlikely to ...*
Es muy improbable que lleguen a un acuerdo.	*it is very unlikely that*
No parece que se encuentre muy enfermo.	*he is unlikely to ...*
Me sorprendería mucho que viniera tan pronto.	*I would be very surprised if*
Es muy dudoso que lo haga sin consultarnos.	*it is most doubtful that he will ...*
Dudo mucho que jamás tengamos que repetirlo.	*I doubt very much that we will ever ...*
Tienen poca probabilidad de terminarlo a tiempo.	*they are unlikely to ...*
Dudo muchísimo que llegue a pasar eso.	*I think it most unlikely that*

EXPRESSING IMPOSSIBILITY

No es posible *or* **Es imposible** salvarle de la ruina.	*it is impossible to ...*
Es completamente imposible concederle a usted un nuevo plazo para pagar.	*it is totally impossible to ...*
Es imposible *or* **No es posible que** se trate de la misma persona.	*we cannot be*
Lo siento: **me es completamente imposible** ceder en este asunto.	*it is impossible for me to ...*
No existe ni la más mínima posibilidad de que se publique este año.	*there is not the slightest chance of*
No hay ninguna posibilidad de que llegue el autobús antes de las 8.	*there is no chance that*
No cabe posibilidad alguna de que se publique este año.	*there's no possibility at all that*

EXPRESSING WHAT SOMEONE IS ABLE OR UNABLE TO DO

Mi amigo Gabriel **es (in)capaz de** traducir del italiano al ruso.	*is (un)able to ...*
¿Sabe usted escribir a máquina?	*do you know how to ...*
Sabe tocar muy bien el piano.	*she can ...*
Entiende el español, pero no lo habla.	*she can understand*
Tiene **conocimientos básicos de** informática.	*some basic knowledge of*
Desde aquí **veo** la playa muy bien.	*I can see*
Es totalmente incapaz de aceptar consejos.	*he is completely unable to ...*
No sé cómo decírselo: he recibido malas noticias.	*I don't know how to tell you: ...*
Este chico **no sirve para** este trabajo.	*is no good at*
Le puedo dejar que utilice mi despacho.	*I can let you*
Me es imposible llamarle hasta mañana.	*I cannot ...*
Puedo prestarle cinco mil pesetas.	*I am able to ...*

EXPLANATIONS

PREPOSITIONS

El asunto se ha retrasado **a causa de** mi enfermedad.	*because of*
Hoy lo he solucionado todo, **gracias a** su ayuda.	*thanks to*
No pudo continuar, **por falta de** tiempo.	*for lack of*
El vuelo llegó con retraso **debido a** la tormenta.	*owing to*
Por razones de salud, tiene que veranear en la sierra.	*for ... reasons*
A *or* **Como consecuencia de** la subida del petróleo, la vida está mucho más cara.	*as a result of*
Están dispuestos a hacerlo, **a cambio de** nuestra colaboración en la otra empresa.	*in return for*
A pesar de todo, no creo que se pueda aceptar su explicación.	*in spite of everything*

CONJUNCTIONS

Le han aceptado **porque** tenía muchas recomendaciones.	*because*
Tendrá éxito, **pues** es muy inteligente.	*for*
En vista de que no había trenes, se fue en avión.	*as*
Como estaba lloviendo, me quedé en casa.	*since*
En este momento no puedo hacerlo; **por (lo) tanto,** se lo encargaré a mi colega.	*therefore*
Me es imposible recibirle el sábado, **puesto que** *or* **ya que** estaré fuera.	*since*
No salió, **por miedo a** perderse.	*for fear that*
Con el pretexto de que estaba enormemente ocupada, no quiso hacerlo.	*with the excuse that*
En vista de que ha cambiado la situación, me siento en la obligación de consultar con mi jefa.	*in view of the fact that*
Mientras ellos sigan en contacto, nosotros no podremos quejarnos.	*so long as*
Con tal que nos escriban, estaremos conformes.	*providing*

OTHER USEFUL VOCABULARY

Eso quiere decir que la explicación es falsa.	*that means that*
Se trata de que necesitamos que nos comuniquen en seguida su decisión.	*the point is that*
Ha tenido muy mala suerte, **por eso** le tengo tanta lástima.	*that is why*
Habían salido ya, **de modo que** cuando él llegó encontró la casa vacía.	*so that*
Ya no hay tiempo para hacerlo hoy, **así es que** tendremos que esperar hasta mañana.	*so*
Es que a mí no me gusta esa manera de actuar.	*the thing is ...*
El descenso en los beneficios **se debe a** *or* **es debido a que** han invertido mucho capital en nueva maquinaria.	*is due to the fact that*
Las pérdidas **se deben a** falta de planificación.	*are due to*
De hecho, ella está sin trabajo desde hace un año.	*in fact*
Prometió hacerlo, **y en efecto** *or* **efectivamente** lo hizo.	*and indeed*
La recesión mundial **ha causado** un aumento en el desempleo.	*has caused*
Lo que usted dice **está relacionado y** *or* **tiene que ver con** un aspecto distinto del tema.	*is related to*
Las causas de la situación actual **se remontan al** siglo pasado.	*go back to*
Resultó que el experimento fracasó por completo.	*it so happened that*
No desean decir nada, **o sea**, que ellos se niegan a colaborar.	*that is to say*
En ese caso *or* **Entonces**, debemos tratar de encontrar nuevos clientes.	*in that case*
Las razones por las que me ausenté de Madrid fueron de índole personal.	*the reasons why*
Fue por ese motivo por lo que se negaron a apoyarnos.	*that's why*
Yo personalmente **lo atribuyo a** un error por parte del conductor.	*I attribute it to*
Por lo que se ha podido saber, los fondos eran insuficientes.	*it transpires that*
Sus problemas **arrancan de** una primera decisión equivocada.	*... arise from*

AND, ACCORDING TO CONTEXT:

está claro por qué/para ser exactos, nosotros/quisiera señalar que/se basa en/esto ocasionó/esto tiene que ver con/como consecuencia

APOLOGIES

MAKING AN APOLOGY

Siento tener que interrumpir esta reunión.	*I am sorry I have to ...*
Siento mucho no haberles comunicado a ustedes antes la noticia.	*I am very sorry I didn't*
Discúlpeme por haberle molestado.	*excuse me for ...*
Lamento *or* **Siento mucho que haya tenido que** esperar.	*I am sorry that you have had to ...*
Lamentamos enormemente *or* **Sentimos mucho** el error.	*we are very sorry for*
Perdone usted que no le haya avisado a tiempo.	*do forgive me for not ...*
No tengo perdón *or* **No me puedo perdonar por haberme** olvidado de avisarle antes.	*it is unforgivable of me to have*
Desde luego, **ha sido una lástima que** no pudiésemos asistir al concierto.	*it was a pity that*
De verdad es una pena no poder hacer nada.	*it is indeed a pity that I cannot*
Por desgracia, no me es posible llegar a la hora indicada.	*unfortunately, I shall not be able to ...*
Fue culpa mía que mi secretaria no se ocupase antes de su asunto.	*it was my fault that*

(more formally)

Les rogamos que acepten nuestras sinceras disculpas por este lamentable retraso.	*we beg you to accept our sincere apologies for*
Sentimos muchísimo haberles causado tantas molestias.	*we are very sorry to have*
Lamentamos *or* **Sentimos no poder** facilitarles más información.	*we regret that we cannot*
Deseamos pedir perdón *or* **disculpas** (*esp LAm*) **por** todo lo sucedido.	*we wish to apologise for*
Aun sintiéndolo mucho, tenemos que anunciar un descenso en las ganancias.	*we regret to ...*
Le ruego a usted que me dispense (*Sp*) *or* **disculpe** (*esp LAm*) por el retraso.	*I beg you to excuse*

(more tentatively, or suggesting explanation)

Ahora me doy cuenta de que no debía haberlo autorizado.	*I realize now that*
Reconozco que me equivoqué al recomendar que se aceptase el encargo.	*I admit that*
¡Ojalá no lo hubiese olvidado!	*if only*
Se debió a un error por nuestra parte, por el que les pedimos que nos disculpen.	*it happened because of a mistake on our part, for which we apologise*
Espero que comprenda usted lo difícil de nuestra situación.	*I hope that you appreciate*
En vista de lo sucedido, **no me queda más remedio que pedirles perdón** *or* **disculpas** (*esp LAm*) **por** haber fracasado.	*in view of ... I can only apologise for*
Desgraciadamente *or* **Lamentablemente, no ha salido tal como** lo habíamos proyectado.	*unfortunately, it didn't work out the way*
Me responsabilizo de todos los errores que se han encontrado en el informe.	*I accept full responsibility for*
Admito que me equivoqué.	*I accept that I made a mistake*
No era mi intención causarle problemas, **pero me vi obligado a** actuar sin consultarle.	*I didn't mean to ..., but I had to ...*
Pensé que hacía bien en dirigirme a ellos directamente.	*I thought I was doing the right thing in ...*
No había otra salida posible: fue necesario confesarlo todo.	*there was no alternative: ...*
Fui yo el responsable del malentendido.	*I was responsible for the misunderstanding*
Teníamos entendido que ellos estaban de acuerdo.	*we understood that*
Estamos haciendo todo lo posible para mejorar la situación.	*we are doing our best to ...*

ANSWERING AN APOLOGY

No importa que no pudiesen ustedes enviar a tiempo los libros que les encargamos.	*it does not matter that*
No se preocupe usted por no haber podido venir la semana pasada.	*don't worry about*
No ha sido en realidad ninguna molestia cambiar la fecha de la entrevista.	*it was really no bother to ...*
El retraso **no tiene ninguna importancia.**	*... is of no consequence*
Aceptamos de buen grado sus disculpas.	*we willingly accept your apologies*

Francisco Romero García
Reyes Católicos, 25 -2.º izquierda
Antequera (Málaga)

Antequera, 24 de noviembre de 1993

Sr. Director Gerente
Manufacturas Metálicas Madrileñas
Gran Vía, 22
Madrid

Muy señor mío:

Con referencia al puesto recientemente anunciado en El País de Director de Ventas para el sur de España, me dirijo a usted ahora para comunicarle que he decidido presentar mi candidatura. Adjunto toda la documentación necesaria, incluidos los certificados que me pedían en su carta, así como un Curriculum Vitae detallado.

Como ya mencioné anteriormente, en vista de la distancia les rogaría que, si desean que acuda a Madrid para asistir a una entrevista, me lo avisen con tiempo suficiente.

Quedo, pues, a la espera de sus gratas noticias

Les saluda atentamente,

FRG.

CURRICULUM VITAE

APELLIDOS	RODRÍGUEZ RAMIRO
NOMBRE	José María
LUGAR DE NACIMIENTO	Lugo.
FECHA DE NACIMIENTO	2 de julio de 1955.
NACIONALIDAD	Española de origen.
ESTADO CIVIL	Casado.
D.N.I.	27 658 765.
DIRECCIÓN	Calle Antonio de Nebrija, 8, Cuenca.
TELÉFONO	966 54 67 09.
ESTUDIOS[1]	Bachillerato y COU en el Instituto Nacional de Enseñanza Media de Cuenca; Licenciado en Económicas por la Universidad Complutense, 1980.
INFORMACIÓN COMPLEMENTARIA QUE ESTIME DE INTERÉS	Miembro colegiado de la Asociación Nacional de Empleados de Banco; Certificado Superior en Inglés, Escuela Central de Idiomas, Madrid, 1982; Carnet de conducir, desde 1976.
CARGOS QUE HA EJERCIDO	Empleado (categoría B) del Banco de Vizcaya, Cuenca, de 1980 a 1982.
OCUPACIÓN ACTUAL	Jefe del departamento de contabilidad, Banco de Vizcaya, Cuenca, desde 1982.

[1] People with British, American or other qualifications applying for jobs in Spanish-speaking countries might use some form of wording to explain their qualifications, such as "equivalente al bachillerato superior español/mejicano" etc. (3 A-levels), "equivalente a una licenciatura en Letras/Ciencias" etc. (B.A., B.Sc. etc). Alternatively, "Licenciado en Lenguas Clásicas" etc. might be used.

USEFUL VOCABULARY

En contestación a su anuncio aparecido en *La Vanguardia* con fecha de ayer, les agradecería que me enviasen todos los datos relativos a las plazas vacantes (*Sp*) *or* vacantes (*LAm*) junto con los impresos necesarios para hacer la solicitud.

In reply to your advertisement in yesterday's 'Vanguardia', I should be grateful if you could send me all the necessary information about the jobs advertised and an application form.

Soy estudiante de 1.° de Idiomas Modernos, y desearía trabajar en España durante el próximo verano. Les agradecería que me mandasen el folleto explicativo *Campos de trabajo para estudiantes* que he visto anunciado en la oficina del sindicato estudiantil.

I am a first-year Modern Languages student and I would like to work in Spain next summer. I would be grateful if you could send me the information brochure 'Campos de trabajo para estudiantes' which I have seen advertised in the Students' Union.

Deseo trabajar en España a fin de mejorar mis conocimientos del español y para obtener experiencia del trabajo de hostelería.

I wish to work in Spain in order to improve my Spanish and to gain experience of hotel work.

He visto el anuncio de plazas vacantes (*Sp*) *or* vacantes (*LAm*) para profesores de inglés para extranjeros en su Academia de Idiomas, y les ruego tengan la bondad de enviarme toda la información que consideren necesaria para solicitar una de estas plazas vacantes *or* vacantes.

I have seen the advertisement about jobs in your Language School for teachers of English as a Foreign Language, and I would be grateful if you would send me all the information I need in order to apply.

Soy licenciado en Ciencias de la Información (*Sp*) *or* Computación (*LAm*) y llevo seis meses trabajando en la redacción y administración de un periódico local, donde estoy a cargo de todo lo relativo a los ordenadores de que disponemos.

I have a degree in Information Science, and for the last six months I have been working in the editorial and administrative department of a local newspaper where I am in charge of all aspects of computer use.

Aunque no tengo experiencia previa de este tipo de trabajo, he desempeñado otros trabajos eventuales durante las vacaciones de verano, y les puedo dar los nombres de las entidades que me han empleado, si los desea.

Although I have not got any previous experience of this kind of work, I have had other holiday jobs, and can supply references from my employers if you would like them.

Mi sueldo actual es de ... anuales y tengo cinco semanas de vacaciones pagadas al año.

My current salary is ... per annum, and I have five weeks paid holiday per year.

Además del inglés, mi lengua materna, poseo buenos conocimientos del español y hablo algo de francés y alemán.

As well as speaking English, I have a good knowledge of Spanish, and speak some French and German.

Estaría disponible para comenzar el trabajo después del final de abril.

I shall be available from the end of April.

He recibido su amable carta del 2 del corriente, en la que me ofrece una entrevista para el próximo día 10. Deseo confirmar que acudiré a su oficina central a las 11.30 de la mañana para asistir a la misma.

Thank you for your letter of the 2nd, inviting me to attend for interview on the 10th. I would like to confirm that I shall be at your head office at 11.30.

Al presentar mi solicitud para este puesto tengo que mencionar a dos personas que estén dispuestas a facilitar un informe confidencial sobre mí, y por tanto me dirijo a usted para preguntarle si tendría la amabilidad de permitirme que diese su nombre para este fin.

I have to give the names of two referees with my application for this job, and I am writing to ask if you would be kind enough to allow me to put your name forward.

El señor (don: *Sp*) Jaime Toribio Lerma ha solicitado la plaza (*Sp*) *or* vacante (*LAm*) de recepcionista en este hotel y ha citado su nombre como el de la persona que puede enviarnos un informe confidencial acerca de su aptitud para este tipo de trabajo. Le agradeceríamos mucho que nos dijera si, en su opinión, este señor es una persona idónea para este tipo de trabajo.

Mr Jaime Toribio Lerma has applied for the job of hotel receptionist with us and has given your name as a referee. We would be grateful if you would kindly let us know whether in your opinion he is suitable for this post.

Su respuesta será tratada con la mayor reserva y discreción.

Your answer will be treated in strict confidence.

Le agradeceríamos que en su respuesta nos informara sobre cuánto tiempo hace que conoce al candidato, en qué capacidad le ha tratado, su idoneidad para este puesto y las cualidades personales, académicas y profesionales por las que le recomienda.

Would you be kind enough in your reply to mention how long and in what capacity you have known the applicant, his suitability for this job, and the personal qualities and academic and professional qualifications which lead you to recommend him.

Me es muy grato recomendarles a la señora (doña: *Sp*) Juana Pacheco de Díaz para el puesto de funcionaria encargada de los asuntos relativos a la vivienda. Hace más de diez años que conozco a esta señora, y siempre me ha parecido una persona de carácter agradable y buena voluntad, así como digna de toda confianza.

I am very pleased to be able to recommend Mrs Juana Pacheco de Díaz for the post of housing officer; I have known her for over ten years, during which time I have found her to be cheerful and helpful at all times, and completely reliable.

LIBRERÍA ESTUDIO S.A.

EDITORES • REPRESENTANTES • DISTRIBUIDORES
CASA FUNDADA EN 1942

CERTIFICADA

Mesón de la Estrella, 144
Apartado 52.345
41005 Sevilla

Señores de
West Distribution Services Ltd
14 St David's Place
Glasgow G4 7MF

Sevilla, 12 de octubre de 1992

Muy señores nuestros:

Recibimos oportunamente su atenta carta de fecha 20 de septiembre, en la que se interesan por la posibilidad de que nos visite en Sevilla su representante el Sr John Kirk aprovechando su próximo viaje por España, con el objeto de tratar de establecer una relación más estrecha entre nuestras respectivas Casas. Tendremos, naturalmente, mucho gusto en recibirle, y le sugerimos la fecha de lunes 26 de octubre, a las 10 de la mañana, en esta oficina para nuestro primer contacto.

Sin otro particular, quedamos a la espera de sus gratas noticias,

Atentamente,

J. J. Rodríguez

Juan José Rodríguez

Director Comercial

Calzados la Zaragozana

Fabricación de zapatos y botas de alta calidad

Carretera de Aragón, s/n
28034 MADRID
Teléfono (91) 47.28.95

Madrid, 2 de octubre de 1993

Señores A B Peterson & Co
(A la atención de la Sra. Green)
114 Potter's Bar Road
London NW3 5TW

Su ref. IFA/ABP/05-1
Nuestra ref. HP/54

Estimados señores:

Por la presente damos respuesta a su carta del 17-9-93, referente a un saldo pendiente de 34.000 pesetas.

Al respecto les informamos que este saldo viene del pago de su factura Núm. 86-109876, efectuado el 19-5-93, de cuyo importe se descontaron las notas de crédito número 12-03145 de £400 y la número 11-24567 de £700, abonándoseles el importe neto de £1000, información que les brindamos oportunamente.

Esperamos que se sirvan revisar esta operación con el fin de aclarar nuestra cuenta con ustedes.

Sin otro particular, les saludamos muy atentamente

Andrés Carbonell

(Firmado) Andrés Carbonell
Jefe de Ventas

Adj.

ENQUIRIES

Según hemos comprobado en la última edición de su catálogo general, tienen una oferta especial de muebles de oficina.

We see from your latest catalogue that there is a special offer for office furniture

Les agradeceríamos que nos enviasen la información necesaria sobre esta oferta, incluyendo precios, descuentos por pedidos al por mayor, forma de pago y fechas de entrega.

We would be grateful if you could send us full details of this offer, including prices, wholesale discounts, payment terms and delivery times.

... AND REPLIES

Les agradecemos su carta del 12 del corriente, y nos complace poder decirles que todos los productos que ustedes mencionan son parte de nuestra producción actual, por lo que confiamos en poder servirles. Tengan la bondad de darnos detalles completos de lo que necesitan.	*Thank you for your letter of the 12th. We are pleased to inform you that all the products you mention are part of our current range, and so we are sure we can assist you. Please send us full details of what you require.*
En contestación a su carta de fecha 5 de agosto, nos complacemos en enviarles nuestra lista completa de precios, condiciones de compra, envío de los productos, formas de pago y el tipo de garantías que ofrecemos.	*In answer to your letter of 5 August we are pleased to send you a complete price list, and details of purchase terms, despatch, methods of payment and the guarantees we offer.*

ORDERS

Les rogamos nos envíen cuanto antes, a ser posible por correo aéreo, los artículos siguientes:	*Please send the following items as soon as possible, preferably by airmail:*
Este pedido se basa en la información contenida en el catálogo general de sus productos, que ustedes nos enviaron el mes pasado.	*This order is based on the information in the general catalogue you sent us last month.*

... AND REPLIES

Les agradecemos su pedido de fecha 11 de marzo, que ejecutaremos a la mayor brevedad.	*Thank you for your order of 11 March, which we will deal with as soon as possible.*
Hemos recibido el encargo que nos hacen de nueva maquinaria, cuya producción iniciaremos en breve.	*We have received the order for new machinery which we will very shortly put into production.*
Lamentamos no poder atender inmediatamente el envío de los pedidos que nos hacen en su atenta carta, pero confiamos en poder mandárselos todos a principios del próximo mes.	*Unfortunately we cannot attend to your order immediately, but we are confident that we will be able to send you everything at the beginning of next month.*

DELIVERIES

Estamos a la espera de sus instrucciones en lo que respecta a la entrega de las mercancías.	*We await your instructions with regard to delivery of the goods.*
Su pedido se ejecutó el día 4 del presente y los productos fueron enviados por correo aéreo el lunes de la semana pasada.	*Your order was dealt with on the 4th and the goods were sent airmail on Monday last week.*
Deseamos comunicarles que todavía no hemos recibido los artículos que pedimos en nuestra carta con fecha 4 de julio.	*Please note that we have not yet received the items we asked for in our letter of 4 July.*
Acusamos recibo de la remesa que Vds despacharon el día 9 de septiembre.	*We acknowledge receipt of the consignment you sent on 9 September.*
Les ruego que tengan a bien acusar recibo de	*Please acknowledge receipt of ...*
Lo sentimos mucho, pero no nos es posible aceptar responsabilidad alguna por los daños sufridos por las mercancías.	*We regret that we are unable to accept any responsibility for the damage to the goods.*

PAYMENT

Tenemos mucho gusto en adjuntar nuestra factura número 87961.	*Please find enclosed our invoice no. 87961.*
El valor de los productos enviados asciende a	*The total value of the goods we have sent is ....*
Les agradeceríamos que nos enviasen la liquidación lo antes posible.	*We would be grateful if you would settle this account as soon as possible.*
Nos complace adjuntar el talón bancario *or* cheque núm. 873451 por valor de ... en liquidación de la factura recibida oportunamente, núm. 50702.	*We have pleasure in enclosing cheque no. 873451 for ... in settlement of your invoice no. 50702.*
Nos permitimos señalar un error que hemos detectado en la cantidad que nos han girado en pago de la factura núm. ..., y les agradeceríamos que tuvieran la amabilidad de enviar el saldo correspondiente.	*We would like to draw your attention to an error we have found in the amount you sent us in settlement of invoice no. ..., and we would be grateful if you could send us the balance.*
La equivocación se debió a un error de contabilidad. Les pedimos que nos disculpen.	*The mistake was due to a book-keeping error. Please accept our apologies.*
Les agradecemos el pago realizado a través de la transferencia bancaria recibida hoy, en liquidación de nuestra factura. Tendremos mucho gusto en continuar nuestras relaciones comerciales con su compañía.	*Thank you for the banker's order in settlement of our invoice which we received today. We look forward to doing business with you again.*

Alicante, 10 de marzo de 1993

Mi querido amigo y colega:

Recibí oportunamente tu carta, escrita durante las vacaciones de verano. Perdona que no haya contestado hasta ahora, aunque esto no quiere decir que no nos hayamos acordado de ti. Tanto María como yo tenemos recuerdos muy agradables de la temporada que pasamos en tu casa. En realidad, el objeto principal de esta carta es preguntar si te gustaría venir a estar un par de semanas con nosotros a finales de la primavera o principio del verano. Nos convendría especialmente la última semana de mayo y la primera de junio, si es que esas fechas te vienen bien a ti.

Un saludo muy afectuoso de María, y un abrazo de

José

Passeig de Sant Joan, 201 2.[1], 3.[a]
08037 Barcelona

Casa Pepe
Productos de Artesanía y
Objetos de Regalo
Avenida de las Palmeras, 19
Granada

Barcelona, 23 de noviembre de 1993

Apreciados señores:

Me dirijo a ustedes para pedirles que tengan la amabilidad de enviarme el catálogo completo de sus productos, junto con la última lista de precios. Me interesa especialmente todo lo relacionado con la artesanía regional española y los objetos de decoración.

Quedando a la espera de sus noticias, me es grato saludarles atentamente.

M. Ramírez Goyos

María Ramírez Goyos

STANDARD OPENING AND CLOSING FORMULAE

Used when the recipient is not personally known to you		
Muy señor mío: (*esp Sp*)	Le saluda(n)[1] atentamente	[1] *if the signatory is more than one person*
Distinguido(a) señor(a): (*Sp*)	Reciba un atento saludo de	
Distinguida señorita: (*Sp*)	Reciba un respetuoso saludo de	
Estimado(a) señor(a): (*LAm*)		
Estimada señorita: (*LAm*)		

TO ACQUAINTANCES AND FRIENDS

When the person is known to you, but you would use 'Usted'		
Estimado señor (García):[2] Estimada señora (Pérez): Estimada señorita (González): Estimado colega: Estimado José:	Reciba un cordial saludo de	[2] *the forms Sr., Sra., Srta. can be used before the surname*
Fairly informal: 'Tú' or 'Usted' could be used		
Mi querido amigo: Mi querida amiga: Mi apreciado amigo: Mi apreciada amiga:	Un afectuoso saludo de	

TO CLOSE FRIENDS AND FAMILY

Querido Juan: Querida María: Mi querido Pepe: Mis queridos primos:	Recibe un fuerte abrazo de Muchos besos y abrazos de Afectuosamente Tu amigo que no te olvida Con mucho cariño	

WRITING TO A FIRM OR INSTITUTION (see also page 856)

Muy señor mío:[1] (*esp Sp*)	Le saluda(n)[2] atentamente	[1] *if the addressee's job title etc. is given*
Muy señores nuestros:[3] (*esp Sp*)	Les saluda(n) atentamente	[2] *if the signatory is more than one person*
Estimados señores:[3] (*LAm*)		
De nuestra consideracíon:[3] (*LAm*)		[3] *if not naming individual addressee*

TO A PERSON IN AN IMPORTANT POSITION

Señor Director: Señor Secretario General:	Respetuosamente le saluda	

STARTING A LETTER

Formal (use of usted):	
Acusamos recibo de la carta dirigida al Director Gerente de esta empresa.	*We acknowledge receipt of your letter to the Managing Director.*
Ayer tuve el gusto de recibir su carta con fecha ... de ...	*Thank you very much for your letter of ...*
Tengo el gusto de dirigirme a usted para solicitar información sobre ...	*I am writing to you to ask for information about ...*
Me dirijo a ustedes para preguntar si les sería posible conseguirme los siguientes libros:	*I am writing to ask if you could obtain the following books for me:*
Probablemente recordará usted que mi familia y yo pasamos dos días en el hotel de su digna dirección la semana pasada. Me dirijo a Vd para preguntar si han encontrado el abrigo que mi hija dejó olvidado en su habitación.	*You will probably remember that my family and I stayed at your hotel for two days last week. I am writing to ask if you have found the coat my daughter left in her room.*
Informal (use of tú):	
Me he alegrado mucho de recibir tu carta de la semana pasada.	*I was delighted to get your letter last week.*
Por fin tuve la agradable sorpresa de tener noticias tuyas, después de tanto tiempo.	*It was a nice surprise to hear from you after all this time.*
Perdona que haya tardado tanto en contestar a tu carta del 12 de abril, pero es que he estado ocupadísima.	*I'm sorry to have taken so long to answer your letter of April 12, but I've been very very busy.*
Supongo que será una sorpresa para ti recibir esta carta después de un silencio tan largo.	*You may be surprised to get this letter after such a long silence.*
Después de mucho pensarlo, me he decidido a escribir esta carta, lo que no me va a resultar nada fácil.	*After mulling it over I have decided to write this letter, which is not going to be at all easy.*

ENDING A LETTER

Muchos recuerdos de Juan y de los niños, y un saludo muy afectuoso para ti de (+ *signature*)	*Best wishes from Juan and the children, yours ...*
Quedo a la espera de tus noticias.	*Looking forward to hearing from you.*
Un cordial saludo para tu madre, y un afectuoso abrazo de (+ *signature*)	*Warmest regards to your mother and best wishes from me,*
María dice que te mande un abrazo de su parte. Hasta cuando gustes venir a vernos, que ojalá sea pronto.	*María sends you her warmest regards. Hoping to see you soon, ...*
Te deseamos mucha suerte en tus planes, y nos despedimos con un cariñoso saludo para ti y los tuyos.	*We wish you the very best luck with your plans. Kindest regards to you all.*
Que disfrutes mucho de las vacaciones. Un abrazo de (+ *signature*)	*Hoping you enjoy your holidays, yours ...*
Dale recuerdos a tu familia de nuestra parte. Hasta siempre, (+ *signature*).	*Remember us to your family. Yours ...*
Ya sabes que estoy para lo que mandes.	*You know that if you want anything all you have to do is let me know.*
Hasta pronto. No dejes de escribir en cuanto puedas.	*Hoping to hear from you soon. Do write when you can.*
Esperamos tener muy pronto noticias tuyas.	*We look forward to hearing from you very soon.*
Tu amigo que no te olvida, (+ *signature*).	*Affectionately ...*

TRAVEL PLANS

Les agradecería que me enviaran su lista de precios.	*I would be grateful if you could send me your price list.*
Quisiera reservar una habitación en su hotel para la noche del 3 de julio próximo, por una noche solamente.	*I would like to book a room for the night of 3 July for one night only.*
Les quedaría muy agradecido si pudiesen confirmar a vuelta de correo la reserva (*Sp*) *or* reservación (*LAm*) que hice en mi carta anterior de dos habitaciones dobles, con ducha y pensión completa, para la semana del 7 al 14 de septiembre.	*Please would you confirm by return the reservation I made in my earlier letter for two double rooms, with shower, and full board, for the week of 7 to 14 September.*
Les ruego tengan la bondad de decirme si es necesario pagar un depósito al confirmar la reserva (*Sp*) *or* reservación (*LAm*).	*Please let me know if I have to pay a deposit in order to confirm the booking.*

THANKS AND BEST WISHES

EXPRESSING THANKS

Escribo para darte las gracias por el gran favor que nos has hecho.	*I am writing to thank you for ...*
Te estoy muy agradecida por lo que has hecho por mí.	*I am very grateful to you for ...*
Por favor, dale las gracias de mi parte a tu marido por el interés que se ha tomado en ayudarme a resolver el problema del cambio de casa.	*please thank your husband from me for ...*
Les agradezco sinceramente todas sus atenciones durante mi estadía con su familia.	*thank you very much indeed for ...*
Me dirijo a ustedes en nombre de nuestro Gerente General **para expresarles su agradecimiento por** la hospitalidad con que le acogieron durante su visita.	*on behalf of ... I would like to thank you for ...*
Le ruego que transmita a sus colegas nuestro reconocimiento **por** el interés que mostraron en nuestras propuestas.	*please give our warmest thanks to your colleagues for ...*

BEST WISHES

Con los mejores deseos de (+ *signature*)	*Card: with best wishes from ...*
Con un atento saludo de (+ *signature*)	*with all good wishes from*
Un cordial saludo de (+ *signature*)	*Best wishes from ...*
Le deseamos todo lo mejor durante su estancia en	*wishing you a happy stay in ...*

(season's greetings)

¡Feliz Navidad! (+ *signature*)	*Merry Christmas from ...*
Felices Pascuas y Próspero Año Nuevo (+ *signature*)	*Merry Christmas and a Happy New Year from ...*
Le deseamos felices Navidades y un feliz año 1992	*Season's greetings from ...*
Nuestros mejores deseos para el Nuevo Año	*Our very best wishes for the New Year.*

(birthday and saint's day greetings)

(*NB: In Spanish-speaking countries it is more common to celebrate one's saint's day than one's birthday*)

¡Felicidades! (+ *signature*)	*Happy Birthday*
Muchas felicidades en tu cumpleaños, y que cumplas muchos más.	*Many happy returns of the day.*
(*On saint's day*) Felicidades en el día de tu santo y un saludo muy afectuoso de (+ *signature*)	*Best wishes on your saint's day from ...*
Te deseo todo tipo de felicidad en el día de tu santo/cumpleaños.	*Wishing you every happiness on your saint's day/birthday.*
¡Feliz cumpleaños! // ¡Feliz aniversario! (*CAm*) // ¡Feliz onomástico! (*CAm*)	*Happy Birthday! // Happy Birthday // Best wishes on your saint's day.*

(get well wishes)

Me he enterado de que estás enferma y quiero desearte que te pongas bien cuanto antes.	*I heard that you were ill and wish you a speedy recovery.*
Esperamos que te recuperes cuanto antes de tu enfermedad.	*We hope you get over your illness soon.*

(wishing someone success)

Te deseo que tengas éxito en los exámenes.	*I wish you every success in your exams.*
Te deseamos el mayor de los exítos en tu nuevo trabajo.	*We wish you every success in your new job.*
Esperamos que te acompañe el éxito en tu nueva carrera.	*We hope that you will be successful in your new career.*
Unas líneas solamente, para desearte que todo vaya muy bien y que tengas éxito el próximo sábado.	*Just a couple of lines to wish you every success for next Saturday.*

(sending congratulations)

Enhorabuena (*Sp*) *or* felicitaciones por tu éxito en los exámenes/ por haber aprobado el examen de conducir.	*Congratulations on your success in the exams / on passing your driving test.*
Me alegro mucho de que todo haya ido bien, y te doy la enhorabuena (*Sp*) *or* te felicito.	*I am very pleased that everything went well and I would like to congragulate you.*

ANNOUNCEMENTS, INVITATIONS AND RESPONSES

ANNOUNCEMENTS

(announcing a birth)

(*NB: It is not common to announce births in the way they are announced in English-speaking countries*)

Carmen García Goyos y Juan Antonio Rodríguez Arenas tienen el gusto de anunciar el nacimiento de su hija María Cristina el 3 de abril pasado. Tanto la madre como la recién nacida se encuentran en perfecto estado de salud. — *Card or formal letter: 'are happy to announce the birth of'*

Unas líneas muy rápidas para comunicarte que el domingo pasado Lola dio a luz a un niño precioso, al que llamaremos Luis Alberto. Por suerte, no hubo complicaciones de ningún tipo, y mi mujer y el niño salieron de la clinica sólo tres días después del parto. — *Letter to friend: 'just to let you know that we have had a son'*

(... and responding)

Les felicitamos sinceramente por la feliz llegada al mundo de su hija, y deseamos a la familia entera todo lo mejor. — *Formal letter: 'we send you our congratulations on'*

Nos hemos alegrado mucho de saber que Juana ha tenido una niña, y de que todo haya ido bien. Un saludo muy afectuoso para los felices padres y nuestros deseos de una vida larga y dichosa para la recién nacida. — *Formal letter: 'we were delighted to hear that Juana has had a baby'*

(announcing an engagement)

Los señores de Ramírez López y de Ortega de los Ríos se complacen en anunciar el compromiso matrimonial de sus hijos Roberta y José María. — *Announcement: 'are happy to announce the engagement of'*

Deseamos participarte que Ana y Manolo se han prometido. No han decidido todavía la fecha de la boda, pero será en la primavera. Como es natural, todos nos alegramos mucho de que hayan tomado esta decisión y compartimos su felicidad. — *Letter to a friend: 'we would like to let you know that ... have got engaged ... we are all very happy for them'*

(... and responding)

Hemos sabido que se ha anunciado su compromiso matrimonial con la Srta. Gil de la Casa, y aprovechamos esta ocasión para darles la enhorabuena (*Sp*) *or* felicitarles a los dos en tal feliz ocasión. — *Formal: 'send you both our very best wishes on this happy occasion'*

Me he enterado de que se ha formalizado el compromiso de boda. Nos alegramos mucho y les deseamos a los novios todo lo mejor. — *Card: 'glad to hear of ... send them our best wishes'*

(announcing a marriage)

Jacinta Pérez Cantillosa y Antonio Fayos de la Cuadra tienen el gusto de invitarles a la ceremonia de la boda de su hija María de los Ángeles con don Pedro Carbonell i Trueta, que se celebrará el próximo día 25 de abril a las 10 de la mañana en la Parroquia de Santa María la Grande, y a lá recepción que tendrá lugar a continuación en la Sala Redonda del Restaurante Casa Pepe. — *Formal invitation: 'request the pleasure of your company at the wedding of ... and at the reception afterwards at ...'*

Tenemos mucho gusto en comunicarles que nuestra boda se celebró el pasado día 4 en el Juzgado Municipal (*Sp*) *or* Registro Civil (*LAm*) de esta localidad. Nuestra nueva dirección es: — *Informal letter: 'we got married here on the 4th'*

(... and responding)

Hemos recibido su amable invitación a la boda de sus hijos, que tenemos sumo gusto en aceptar. Aprovechamos la ocasión para felicitar sinceramente a los novios. — *Formal reply to invitation: 'and have much pleasure in accepting'*

Hemos recibido la participación del próximo enlace de Inés con don Alfredo Muñiz, junto con la invitación a la ceremonia de la boda, pero lamentamos no poder asistir ya que .. — *Formal reply to invitation: 'regret we are unable to attend because ...'*

Muchas felicidades y un cordial saludo (+ *signature*) — *Card with gift: 'with congratulations and best wishes'*

(announcing a change of address)

Deseamos comunicarles nuestra nueva dirección a partir del 1 de marzo: Fernández de la Hoz, 25 – 2.° derecha, 28010 Madrid. Teléfono 543-43-43. — *Formal private or business letter*

(announcing a death)

La familia Gómez de Barquero se duele en participar el fallecimiento de D. Juan Gómez de Barquero y Torres, a la edad de 76 años, en la Clínica de la Milagrosa, el 23 del mes corriente. La ceremonia religiosa, que tendrá carácter estrictamente privado, tendrá lugar el viernes 25, a las 6 de la tarde, en la Capilla de Santo Tomás de la Santa Catedral.

Formal announcement: 'announce with deep sorrow and regret the death of ... the funeral service will be held at ... on ...'

Con gran dolor anunciamos que nuestro querido padre, Don Carlos de la Fuente Delgado, ha fallecido en la madrugada del 10 de agosto. Rogamos una oración por su alma.

Formal letter: 'it is with deepest sorrow that we have to inform you'

(... and responding)

Nuestro más sincero pésame por tan dolorosa pérdida.// Nuestro más sentido pésame por tan sensible pérdida.

Generally suitable formula: 'our deepest sympathy with you in your loss'

Nos hemos enterado, con el mayor pesar, del reciente fallecimiento de su querida madre, y deseamos expresar nuestras más sinceras condolencias por tan triste pérdida: de veras les acompañamos en el sentimiento, y hacemos votos para que todos ustedes tengan la entereza de espíritu necesaria para hacer frente a estos momentos de dolor.

Formal letter: 'it was with the greatest sorrow that we learnt of the death of'

He sabido hoy mismo que ha muerto Javier como consecuencia de un accidente. Te aseguro que tengo una pena muy grande y que no he dejado de pensar en ti. De verdad lo siento en el alma. Comprendo que las palabras no te darán ningún consuelo, pero quiero que sepas que puedes contar conmigo para cualquier cosa que necesites.

Informal letter: 'I was terribly upset to hear of the death of'

INVITATIONS

(formal invitations)

See p.862, **'announcing a marriage ... and responding'**.

María Luisa Gómez y Roberto Sánchez tienen el gusto de invitarles al bautizo de su hija Luisita, que se celebrará el domingo día 3, a las 11 de la mañana, en la Iglesia de San Marcos de esta localidad, y a la recepción que se ofrecerá a continuación en la casa de los abuelos maternos, situada en Corredera de San Juan, 24.

Card: 'request the pleasure of your company at the christening of'

El Director del Ateneo se complace en invitarles a tomar una copa de vino el viernes 30 a las 8 de la tarde, con ocasión del homenaje que se ofrecerá al distinguido escritor ...

'have plesure in inviting you to ...'

Tenemos el gusto de invitarle a cenar con nosotros el próximo sábado 14, aprovechando su paso por esta ciudad.

'request the pleasure of your company at dinner on ...'

(... and replies)

See p.862, **'announcing a marriage ... and responding'**.

Agradecemos su amable invitación, que aceptamos con mucho gusto.

'we accept your kind invitation with the greatest pleasure'

Hemos recibido su invitación, pero lamentamos no poder asistir, como hubiera sido nuestro deseo, por tener un compromiso previo.

'we regret that we are unable to come owing to'

(informal invitations)

Vamos a reunirnos unos cuantos amigos en casa el sábado por la tarde para tomar unas copas y picar algo, y nos encantaría que pudieras venir tú también, sola o acompañada, como prefieras.

'we're getting together with some friends ... delighted if you could join us'

Deseamos corresponder a tu amabilidad al tenernos en tu casa el verano pasado, y hemos pensado que podrías pasar con nosotros las vacaciones de Semana Santa, si te viene bien.

'we would like to repay your kindness in ... you would be welcome to spend ... with us'

Pascual y yo normalmente pasamos el mes de agosto completo en el apartamento de Gandía, pero en junio y julio lo tienes a tu disposición. No tienes más que avisar si quieres pasar allí una temporada.

'if you would like to ... you need only let us know'

(... and replies)

Te damos las gracias por tu amable invitación.

'thank you for your kind invitation'

Te agradezco enormemente tu amabilidad al invitarme a pasar con vosotros este verano. Ya estoy deseando que llegue el momento de ponerme en camino.

'very kind of you to invite me to ... looking forward very much to ...'

ESSAY AND REPORT WRITING

THE BROAD OUTLINE OF THE ESSAY

Introductory remarks

En el presente escrito **vamos a enfrentarnos con la cuestión de** la influencia que puede haber tenido el turismo en el desarrollo de la España contemporánea.	*we are going to tackle the question of*
Este informe trata de la relación existente entre la publicidad y la ampliación de los mercados nacionales en la década de los setenta.	*this report deals with*
En este ensayo pretendemos dar respuesta a una cuestión de importancia crucial: ¿a qué se deben las fluctuaciones en el saldo de la balanza de pagos?	*the aim of this essay is to answer a crucial question*
El punto de partida de nuestro estudio podría ser la presentación de un bosquejo rápido de cómo se ha desarrollado la inversión extranjera en nuestro país desde la llegada de la democracia.	*a useful starting point for this study is*
Un problema que se debate con frecuencia hoy día es el de los cambios en la estructura de la familia.	*a problem that is often debated nowadays is that of*
Sería ingenuo suponer que ésta es la primera, o la más importante, contribución al estudio de este tema.	*it would be naïve to suppose that*
Para entrar en la cuestión que tenemos planteada **tenemos que hacer referencia en primer lugar a** sus antecedentes históricos.	*we must first refer to*
Hoy día todo el mundo está de acuerdo en que nuestro nivel de vida va en aumento. **Sin embargo, cabe preguntarse si** esta mejora afecta de igual modo a todas las capas sociales.	*nowadays everyone agrees that ... however, it is open to question whether*
Una vez más, **se ha planteado el tema del** papel de la mujer en el mundo empresarial.	*the issue of ... has been raised*
Se suele decir que la televisión influye mucho en la actitud de los jóvenes. **Convendría examinar esta afirmación a la luz de** los actuales planes del gobierno de dar la luz verde a la televisión privada.	*it is often said that ... this statement needs to be examined in the light of*
Existe una gran divergencia de opiniones sobre las recientes reformas educativas en España.	*there is a wide variety of opinions about*
Uno de los problemas en que se piensa más a menudo en la actualidad **es el de** la seguridad ciudadana.	*one of the problems ... is that of*
El meollo de la cuestión, en el que debemos concentrar la atención, es el conflicto entre las tendencias económicas y las medidas gubernamentales.	*what we are mainly concerned with here is*
Vivimos en un mundo en el que el turismo ya no es un lujo.	*we live in a world in which*
La historia nos ofrece una fuente inagotable de ejemplos de la ambición y la tiranía de las naciones dominantes.	*history provides numerous examples of*
'Hoy las ciencas adelantan que es una barbaridad': así dice la conocida frase de una zarzuela tradicional española.	*'science is making enormous strides today', according to*
Una actitud muy extendida hoy día es la de considerar que nada tiene valor permanente.	*there is a widespread attitude nowadays that*
Este ensayo **es un intento de** presentar de manera sencilla el tema de la evolución de la prensa local durante los últimos diez años.	*... is an attempt to*

Developing the argument

A manera de introducción, podemos decir que el paro es la lacra más grave del mundo contemporáneo.	*by way of introduction, we can say that*
En primer lugar, **se va a tratar el tema del** tráfico por carretera en general, **haciendo hincapié en** las normas generales, **para después considerar** algunos aspectos parciales de la cuestión.	*the issue of ... will be dealt with, emphasizing ... and then ... will be considered*
Debe quedar bien sentado desde un principio que no trataremos de inmiscuirnos en el campo de las decisiones políticas.	*what should be established at the very outset is that*
Empecemos por considerar las ventajas y los inconvenientes de la vida en el campo.	*let's start by considering*
En primer lugar, tratemos de entender bien cuáles son los objetivos que se ha fijado el autor.	*let's begin by trying to understand thoroughly*
Incluso una consideración somera de la cuestión revela ya cierto número de problemas fundamentales que han sido desatendidos en el pasado inmediato.	*even a superficial look at this issue reveals*
Cuando nos referimos a la cultura, **pensamos** principalmente **en** un concepto antropológico.	*when we talk of ... we think of*
Lo primero que hay que decir sobre el tema que nos ocupa es que la sociedad de consumo tiene sus propias características.	*the first thing to be said about the topic under consideration is that*
Para comenzar, consideremos la información de que se dispone en cuanto a la importancia y extensión del problema.	*to start with, let's consider*

The other side of the argument

Comencemos con un esfuerzo consciente por comprender los antecedentes del problema y las razones por las que aún no se ha encontrado una solución universalmente aceptada.	*let's begin by making a conscious effort to*
Conviene ahora tratar de un aspecto distinto del tema, pero que está relacionado con lo dicho anteriormente.	*it is now time to discuss*
Pasemos ahora a considerar otro aspecto del tema.	*let's now go on to consider*
El tema que nos ocupa **se puede enfocar de otra manera, es decir, considerando** primero los antecedentes históricos.	*another way of looking at this question is to*
En contrapartida, según cifras oficiales, en España más de la tercera parte de la fuerza laboral es femenina.	*the other side of the coin is that*
Sin embargo, debemos plantear la cuestión de los beneficios económicos de la inversión del capital.	*finally, we must raise the question of*
Debemos ocuparnos ahora de un aspecto diferente del tema que estamos tratando.	*we must now consider a different facet of*
Los argumentos en contra de la propuesta **parecen tener gran peso.**	*the arguments against ... seem very cogent*
No sería demasiado difícil aducir razones convincentes a favor de lo que propone el ejecutivo.	*it would not be too difficult to make out a convincing case for*
En contra de estos argumentos se podría objetar que hasta ahora nuestra compañía nunca ha actuado sin consultar primero a todos los interesados.	*the objection to these arguments could be that*

The balanced view

Si sopesamos cuidadosamente los pros y los contras del problema, comprobaremos que la decisión es sumamente difícil.	*if one weighs the pros and cons*
Se podría abordar el tema de las ventas por correspondencia **desde otro punto de vista.**	*the issue of ... could be approached from another angle*
A fin de cuentas, debemos reconocer que hay que atenerse a los deseos del público.	*at the end of the day, it must be acknowledged that*
Sin duda se trata de un problema de poca importancia, si se compara con las pérdidas que hemos venido soportando últimamente.	*this is a relatively minor problem, when compared to*
Habría que asumir otros factores que probablemente han contribuido de igual manera.	*other factors that ... should be taken into account*
Sin duda resultará interesante comprobar si aparece el mismo fenómeno en otras partes del mundo.	*it will be interesting to see whether*
Sin embargo, cabe apuntar que no todos podrán beneficiarse de las nuevas leyes sobre la gratuidad de la enseñanza.	*however, it should be pointed out that*

In conclusion

La cuestión de que nos hemos venido ocupando **se reduce, en lo esencial, al** análisis de la psicología del personaje principal.	*boils down to*
El problema que estamos tratando se puede resumir de esta manera: no estamos satisfechos con la actuación de nuestros representantes en el extranjero.	*the issue under consideration can be summed up thus:*
Ha llegado el momento de preguntarnos **cuáles son las conclusiones válidas que se pueden sacar de** nuestro análisis.	*what conclusions can be drawn from*
Todo lo precedente puede servir de ilustración de un hecho indiscutible: que es necesario respetar los derechos de las minorías lingüísticas.	*everything that has been said illustrates*
Vemos, pues, que el problema no tiene fácil solución.	*we can see, then, that*
En definitiva, por tanto, sólo el gobierno tiene capacidad y competencia para actuar en este terreno.	*ultimately, then*
La mejor forma de resumir los argumentos presentados en este estudio **sería** afirmar que nos enfrentamos con un dilema: o renovarse o decaer.	*the best way of summing up is to*
Todos los argumentos mencionados **apuntan a la misma conclusión**: **que** la culpa del accidente fue del conductor del camión.	*point to the same conclusion: that*
En conclusión/Para concluir/Para terminar, debemos enfrentarnos con un problema que hasta ahora no se ha tratado en profundidad.	*in conclusion/to conclude*
Las distintas facetas del tema que hemos tratado admiten una única explicación; **por tanto, la conclusión obligada es que** esta empresa debe declarar la bancarrota.	*the inevitable conclusion, therefore, is that*
Para llevar a término el presente análisis **sólo falta añadir que** los expertos de la Compañía Naviera del Mediterráneo llegaron independientemente a la misma conclusión.	*to conclude ... it only remains to add that*

CONSTRUCTING A PARAGRAPH

Ordering various elements within it

Habría que distinguir diversos aspectos en relación con las tendencias literarias de la época que estamos tratando de analizar.	*we must distinguish between several different aspects of*
La segunda razón por la que sería justificable cambiar de política a este respecto **es que**, al acercarse las elecciones, los ciudadanos deben ver claramente la dinámica de la actuación del gobierno.	*the second reason why it would be ... is that*
El punto de partida será el estudio de las corrientes literarias previas a este movimiento. **En segundo lugar,** examinaremos el momento histórico, teniendo en cuenta toda una serie de factores ambientales además de sociológicos, **a fin de** poder situar al autor en su época. **Y, por último**, analizaremos cada una de las obras.	*our starting point is ... then we will ... so as to ... and finally*
Si se parte del principio de que la reglamentación es obsoleta, se podrá comprender mejor que los directivos gocen de amplias facultades.	*if one starts from the principle that*
Varios factores han contribuido al éxito del congreso: en primer lugar la buena organización; **en segundo lugar**, la publicidad; **en tercer lugar**, la eficacia de nuestros colaboradores; **y finalmente**, el entusiasmo de los participantes.	*several factors have contributed to ... first ... second ... third ... and finally ...*
Para entender lo que está ocurriendo **resulta esencial** relacionar la subida de los precios con una política económica transitoria.	*in order to understand ... it is essential to ...*
De la misma forma que es posible cambiar de actitud, **también** se puede renovar el entusiasmo cuando se fijan metas distintas.	*just as ... so ...*
En conexión con este tema, podríamos añadir que las medidas que se tomaron en 1984 no se podían haber previsto dos años antes.	*in this connection, we could also point out that*
En una palabra, fue un desastre total.	*in a word*
Más adelante se presentará un análisis pormenorizado.	*later on a detailed analysis will be presented*
Este aspecto del tema está íntimamente relacionado con la cuestión tratada en el capítulo anterior.	*this aspect of the issue is closely linked to*
Pero volvamos de nuevo al asunto que nos ocupa.	*but let's return to*
Ni los partidos de izquierda **ni** las centrales sindicales parecen estar ahora muy seguros de qué camino tomar.	*neither ... nor*

Adding, enumerating etc

Podemos plantearnos también una cuestión que tiene mucho que ver con nuestro tema central.	*a question that ... can also be raised*
Antes sería conveniente dirigir la atención por un momento a otro aspecto del problema.	*we should first turn our attention for a moment to*
A propósito, las leyes tampoco aclaran hasta dónde llegan las competencias de cada Comunidad Autónoma.	*incidentally*
Conviene hacer una breve referencia al hecho de que los presupuestos comunitarios deben ser sometidos a la aprobación del pleno de la Asamblea General.	*it should be mentioned in passing that*
A la luz de estos hechos se puede, y se debe, ser más tolerante con la infracción de la ley.	*in the light of*
Otro hecho importante es que los dos jefes de Estado han aprobado un comunicado conjunto.	*another important fact is that*
Por añadidura, la afirmación que aparece al final es totalmente gratuita.	*added to that*
Se podría mencionar, **en apoyo de nuestra tesis,** el trabajo de los investigadores precedentes.	*in support of our argument*
Es más, el gobierno ni siquiera ha protestado.	*moreover*
Se debe recordar, además, que en 1975 se adoptó una resolución que todavía tiene validez.	*besides, it must be remembered that*
Se examinan aquí los orígenes del problema, **además de** algunas de las soluciones propuestas.	*as well as*
Empleados, funcionarios, altos cargos, **incluso** los Directores Generales: **todos** amenazan con declararse en huelga.	*even ... all (of them) ...*

One's own point of view

El argumento básico que puede servir para revalidar nuestro enfoque es que, simplemente, se trata de un caso de absoluta necesidad.	*the fundamental argument for our approach is that*
Nuestra visión del problema tiene justificaciones históricas.	*our way of looking at the problem*
Podría afirmarse que se va a plantear un debate político en la derecha española.	*it could be claimed that*
Mi opinión personal sobre el asunto es que ya hemos sufrido bastantes pérdidas, y que por tanto es hora de introducir medidas proteccionistas.	*my personal opinion on the matter is that*
Mi punto de vista es que no tenemos derecho a aprovecharnos de la ignorancia de nuestros inversores.	*my own point of view is that*
Mi parecer ya lo he expresado en repetidas ocasiones: creo en la lealtad profesional por encima de todo.	*my viewpoint*
Hablando desde un punto de vista puramente subjetivo, debo decir que no veo la lógica en que se basa la propuesta, a pesar de todas las estadísticas que se aducen para apoyarla.	*speaking purely personally*
Mi criterio es, simplemente, **que** hablando se entiende la gente; debemos, por lo tanto, proseguir con las negociaciones.	*it seems to me that*
Estoy total y absolutamente convencido de que todo tipo de patriotismo está fuera de lugar.	*I feel most strongly that*
Me podría atrever a decir que el primer ministro está perdiendo influencia en el seno de su propio partido.	*I would even go as far as to say that*

Someone else's point of view

Según el autor del informe, **es cierto que** se sufragaron todos los gastos haciendo uso de fondos legítimos.	*according to ... it is the case that*
Existe un segundo argumento a favor de la mejora de las vías férreas **que no se puede dejar de lado.**	*there's an additional argument in favour of ... that cannot be ignored*
Los argumentos en contra de la propuesta **parecen tener gran peso.**	*the arguments against ... seem very cogent*
A juzgar por lo que dice el informe, hay pocas esperanzas por ahora.	*to judge by*
El autor asegura/mantiene/afirma/defiende la tesis de que lo que importa es lo que se aprende sobre la base de la experiencia, y que los condicionamientos con que nacemos carecen de importancia en la adquisición del idioma.	*the author asserts/maintains/states/holds that*
Los autores del informe **dan a entender que** sería inútil buscar responsabilidades más allá de sus propios hallazgos.	*give us to understand that*
El autor **llama la atención del lector hacia** la posibilidad de que la crisis actual se prolongue más allá de lo previsto.	*draws the attention of the reader to*
Lo que quiere decir en realidad es que está en desacuerdo con todo tipo de creencia religiosa.	*what he really means is that*
Si no he entendido mal, la tesis que defiende es que a la mayoría de la gente le trae totalmente sin cuidado la política.	*if I understand him correctly, what he is claiming is that*

Introducing an example

La situación que estamos tratando **se puede ilustrar con un ejemplo**:	*... can be illustrated with an example:*
Bastaría con poner un ejemplo para demostrar nuestra teoría.	*one example is enough to*
Uno de los ejemplos más sorprendentes se encuentra en el tercer capítulo.	*one of the most striking examples*

Introducing a quotation or source

Según el refrán español, 'más vale tarde que nunca'.	*according to*
'Las apariencias engañan', **concluye/declara/observa** Galdós.	*concludes/states/observes*
Como señala el nuevo Código de la Circulación, las autopistas de peaje siempre proporcionan una alternativa mejor a la red viaria existente de antemano.	*as pointed out in*
El arte es imitación de la vida, y no al revés, **tal como habían sostenido los realistas.**	*just as ... maintained*
Dice la tradición que el Apóstol Santiago se apareció en la Batalla de Covadonga.	*tradition has it that*
Para decirlo con las palabras de Cervantes, 'los dos somos para en uno', es decir, estamos hechos el uno para el otro.	*in the words of Cervantes*
En una cita atribuida al Padre Mariana este autor declaró la legitimidad de la violencia por razones de estado.	*in a quotation attributed to*

THE MECHANICS OF THE ARGUMENT

Introducing a fact

Podemos asegurar que las medidas adoptadas pondrán más dinero en circulación.	*we are sure that*
No se pueden perder de vista los hechos reales.	*we must not lose sight of the (hard) facts.*
Se sabe, por ejemplo, cuáles son los puntos más peligrosos.	*we know*
Pongamos sobre el tapete los datos con que ya contamos: el informe de la policía y la declaración del único testigo presencial.	*let's put the available information on the table:*
Es curioso observar que en nuestra época los principales problemas sociales siguen sin resolverse.	*it is a curious fact that*
Conforme *or* **A medida que se avanza** en la lectura de esta obra, **se abren nuevas perspectivas.**	*as the reader progresses, new perspectives open up*
Ninguna de las partes ignora que éste **es un hecho incontrovertible.**	*... is a fact that cannot be ignored*

Indicating a supposition

No resulta del todo aventurado afirmar que la causa principal de los cambios sociales y demográficos en este país ha sido el llamado éxodo rural.	*it is not an overstatement to say that*
Puede que todo esto sea verdad, pero va a ser difícil convencer a nuestros accionistas.	*all this may well be true, but*
Casi podría decirse que sólo ha llamado la atención por los rasgos chocantes de su personalidad.	*it could almost be said that*
No sería de extrañar que algún día los hechos le dieran la razón.	*it would not be surprising if*
Existe la posibilidad de que su trabajo dé fruto alguna vez.	*there is a chance that*
Se puede suponer/imaginar/conjeturar que persistirán en su actitud.	*one may suppose/imagine/ conjecture that*
Supongamos *or* **Imaginemos que** sea cierto.	*let's suppose that*
Se ha mencionado la posibilidad de nuevas negociaciones.	*the possibility of ... has been mentioned*

Expressing a certainty

No se puede negar que los accidentes de tráfico aéreo son, aunque no muy frecuentes, preocupantes.	*it cannot be denied that*
Lo cierto es que se trata de un argumento muy pobre.	*the truth is that*
En efecto, se puede demostrar que los libros de cuentas fueron falsificados.	*it can indeed be proved that*
Parece evidente que las cifras publicadas no responden a la realidad.	*it seems clear that*
Está claro que se encuentran en apuros económicos.	*it is evident that*
Es cierto/verdad/seguro/indisputable/innegable/obvio que las nuevas propuestas son un paso positivo; pero esto no quiere decir que tengan que aceptarse en su forma actual.	*it is true/certain/indisputable/ undeniable/obvious that*
Es indudable que *or* **No cabe duda (alguna) de que** la vigilancia de los agentes de tráfico suele ser irreprochable.	*there cannot be any doubt that*
Todo lleva *or* **conduce a la misma conclusión**: **que** existe un defecto de fabricación.	*everything leads to the same conclusion: that*
Todos coinciden en que se trata de una innovación importante.	*everyone agrees that*
No hay duda de que la actuación de la Guardia Civil en ambas ocasiones fue correcta.	*there is no doubt that*
Ha quedado demostrado, por consiguiente, que los argumentos de nuestros rivales respecto a este tema carecen de fundamento.	*it has been proved, therefore, that*

Indicating doubt or uncertainty

Sería arriesgado pensar que se trata de una situación provisional.	*it would be dangerous to think that*
Está por ver si la nueva vacuna puede servir para prevenir este tipo de enfermedad.	*it remains to be seen whether*
Es poco probable que la respuesta del gobernador satisfaga a todo el mundo.	*it is unlikely that*
Los cálculos están mal hechos, **lo cual introduce un elemento de duda en cuanto a** la validez de los experimentos.	*... which casts doubt on*
Resulta difícil creer que estos resultados puedan ser posibles.	*it is difficult to believe that*
Hay que preguntarse si tales afirmaciones podrían estar justificadas.	*one wonders whether*
Valdría la pena, con todo, recordar que la política de becas no se ajusta todavía a las necesidades de la sociedad.	*it is as well to remind ourselves that*

Conceding a point

El primer argumento de peso con que debemos enfrentarnos es que los problemas de la siderurgia y de la construcción naval son imposibles de resolver satisfactoriamente para todos en las circunstancias actuales. — *the first major argument we must confront*

La desventaja de este argumento es que puede resultar excesivamente novedoso y atrevido para las mentalidades más tradicionales. — *the snag about this argument is that*

Se podría llegar a admitir que tienen razón en lo que dicen, **pero nuestras objeciones siguen en pie.** — *we may agree that ... yet our objections still stand*

Hay que aceptar/admitir que es un proyecto largamente deseado por muchos países europeos. — *it must be granted/admitted that*

Lo menos que se puede decir de estas medidas **es que** no pueden hacer daño a nadie. — *the least that can be said is that*

Llama la atención, **no obstante** *or* **sin embargo,** la insistencia especial en descubrir los motivos de sus acciones. — *however*

A pesar de todo, los españoles percibieron siempre su presencia militar como una imposición. — *nevertheless*

Hasta cierto punto tienen razón, pero no les conviene insistir. — *to a certain extent*

Estoy de acuerdo con ellos en casi todo lo que dicen, **pero no** comparto su punto de vista en lo referente a las ventas a plazos. — *I agree with them on ... but not on ...*

No se puede negar que la diplomacia española ha desplegado estos últimos días una gran actividad. — *it cannot be denied that*

No olvidemos que la peseta ha llegado al mismo tipo de cambio frente al dólar que tenía en 1982. — *let's not forget that*

En definitiva, un tratado de cooperación tiene que ser el fruto de una voluntad de entendimiento que ese país, hoy por hoy, no practica. — *in the final analysis*

Emphasizing particular points

No sería exagerado decir que la juventud de hoy mantiene una actitud hacia la sociedad que es totalmente nueva y sin precedentes. — *it would not be an exaggeration to say that*

Una de las características más importantes del problema de que nos ocupamos **es que** no es exclusivo de ningún país, sino que se encuentran situaciones parecidas en todas partes del mundo. — *one of the main features of the problem is that*

Convendría, a estas alturas, dar cuenta de los factores que han contribuido a facilitar la exportación española de automóviles. — *it might be a good idea, at this stage, to describe*

Sería conveniente pasar ahora a examinar las razones por las que nuestra compañía lleva dos años con saldo negativo en sus ventas en el norte del país. — *it is necessary at this point to consider why*

Con esto llegamos a la parte central y más importante del informe recibido. — *we now come to the core of*

Examinemos con más detalle el argumento central que se nos presenta. — *let's examine in greater detail*

Es interesante observar cómo han sido las mujeres quienes han estado siempre en la vanguardia de la reforma legislativa. — *it is interesting to note how*

Por encima de todas estas consideraciones, sigue siendo verdad que debemos aprender de nuestros propios errores. — *over and above all these considerations, it remains true that*

No sólo se ha creado la expectativa de nuevos contactos, **sino que también** parece que se podría incluir a los países árabes en las negociaciones. — *not only have ... but also*

No solamente se trata de una medida necesaria y elogiable, **sino que además** si se aplaza para el futuro puede que no llegue nunca a introducirse. — *not only ... but in addition*

No es que se trate de una crueldad hacer experimentos con animales vivos, **sino que** es absolutamente inmoral. — *the point is not that ... but rather that*

Lo malo no es que el gobierno mismo cometa desmanes, **sino que** la prensa no lo denuncie. — *the trouble is not that ... but rather that*

El SIDA es una enfermedad incurable, **y, lo que es aun más importante,** parece haber tomado desprevenidas a las autoridades de muchos países. — *... and, what is even more important,*

Indicating agreement

Estamos en completo acuerdo con lo que proponen.	*we fully agree with*
Estos datos **son totalmente exactos,** tanto en conjunto como en los detalles.	*are totally accurate*
Creemos que su explicación **es totalmente convincente.**	*is totally convincing*
Lo único que podemos hacer es aceptar sus conclusiones.	*the only thing we can do is to accept their conclusions*
Todo parecía indicar que se trataba de un accidente muy grave.	*everything suggested that*
Es evidente que las centrales sindicales han dado prueba de sentido común.	*it is evident that*

Indicating disagreement

Es imposible aceptar el punto de vista del autor sobre este tema.	*it is impossible to accept*
La primera parte del informe **no merece que se le preste atención.**	*is not worthy of our attention*
La solución que se pretende dar **resulta más que discutible.**	*is of very doubtful validity*
Queremos **expresar nuestra reserva // presentar ciertas objeciones.**	*to make some reservations / raise some objections*
El periódico, en su edición de hoy, **refuta el argumento de que** la crisis estructural se debe a la actual política del gobierno.	*refutes the claim that*
Me parece que esta versión de lo que sucedió **se puede poner en tela de juicio.**	*is questionable*
Aunque tenga razón el autor en lo que dice, sus argumentos no están bien concatenados.	*even if the author is right*
Lo que dice el informe sobre la tragedia acaecida en Filipinas **queda muy lejos de la verdad.**	*is very far from the truth*
No se puede pasar por alto, sin comentar, una falsedad **tan** notoria.	*one cannot let pass without comment such a*
Sería demasiado ingenuo descartar la posibilidad de corrupción.	*it would be naïve to*
En realidad, no se pueden demostrar las afirmaciones contenidas en el informe, que en su mayoría son estimaciones subjetivas sin fundamento real.	*in fact, ... cannot be proved*
Parece *or* **Resulta difícil admitir la posibilidad de que** sea cierto.	*it is difficult to see how*
Sus argumentos **carecen de base firme** en la investigación.	*have no firm basis*

Approval

Debe parecernos bien lo que han hecho.	*we must approve of*
Afortunadamente, no hubo víctimas en el atentado	*fortunately,*
La decisión del Presidente Ortega de aceptar la negociación **ha sido el suceso más alentador** de esta semana.	*has been the most encouraging event*
Es fácil comprender que se sientan satisfechos con el acuerdo.	*one can well understand that*
La mejor solución sería sin duda referir el asunto al comité de investigación.	*the best solution would no doubt be*
Basta comenzar a leer esta obra **para sentirse** transportado al siglo pasado.	*you only have to ... to feel ...*
La delegación del gobierno **hizo bien en** prohibir las manifestaciones en determinadas calles de la capital.	*was right to*
Ciertamente, ya era hora de que se formulase una política oficial de museos.	*it was certainly time that*
Por fin sale a la luz una obra que de veras se enfrenta con una cuestión muchas veces evitada.	*at last a work is published that*
Las dificultades siguen siendo enormes, pero los pasos que se han dado pueden servir para despejar el horizonte, **y por tanto merecen nuestra aprobación.**	*and therefore deserve our approval*

Disapproval

No puede parecernos bien la manera de actuar de las fuerzas armadas en esta ocación.	*we cannot approve of*
Es lamentable que el sistema financiero español no se haya repuesto todavía de la sacudida que sufrió hace unos meses.	*it is regrettable that*
Es una verdadera lástima que no se pueda llegar a un acuerdo sobre desarme nuclear total.	*it is a pity that*
Por desgracia, la violencia obligó a suspender las elecciones.	*unfortunately,*
Sería sorprendente que la opinión pública permaneciera indiferente.	*it would be surprising if*
Resulta difícil comprender cómo se puede llegar a tales conclusiones.	*it is difficult to see how*

Making a correction

En realidad *or* **De hecho,** las indicaciones son que se echará tierra sobre el asunto.	*in (actual) fact*
Se trata más bien de un problema de presentación.	*it is rather a question of*
Lo que dice el autor **no se basa en hechos comprobados.**	*is not based on verified facts*
Pasemos revista a los hechos que conocemos.	*let's review the facts*

Indicating the reason for something

Se ha perdido una excelente oportunidad, **lo que se ha debido a que** nadie ha sido suficientemente perspicaz.	*and the reason for it was that*
Las cifras no son fiables, **puesto que** *or* **dado que** se basan en cálculos erróneos.	*given that*
Si se llegan a aceptar las propuestas del ayuntamiento, **será sin duda porque** se habrá hecho presión a los concejales.	*it will certainly be due to*
La devaluación de la peseta **explicaría** el descenso en las ventas durante la segunda mitad del año.	*would explain*
La única explicación que cabe es que ha habido un malentendido.	*the only possible explanation is that*
Los costes han mantenido una progresión moderada, **lo cual explica** la postura actual del ministro de economía.	*which explains*

Setting out the consequences of something

Esta decisión **tuvo consecuencias felices / nefastas.**	*had happy / fatal consequences*
Su nombramiento como jefe del departamento **tuvo el efecto de** unir a todos en la oposición.	*had the effect of*
Lo único que se puede deducir de todo esto es que no están dispuestos a ayudarnos.	*the only conclusion to be drawn from all this is that*
La conclusión a que nos lleva este análisis es que se asegura la continuidad de la actual política económica.	*the conclusion to which this analysis leads is that*
Estaba muy descontento, y **ésa es la causa de que** haya dimitido.	*that is why*
El resultado de la propaganda **será que** mucha gente se abstendrá de votar en el País Vasco.	*the result of ... will be that ...*
Las aerolíneas van a reducir sus tarifas, **lo que llevará a** un aumento en los viajes por avión.	*which will lead to*
Se va a reorganizar la oficina, **lo que significa que** el número de empleados disminuirá.	*which means that*
De este razonamiento se sigue que los guerrilleros han accedido a un alto el fuego solamente en las zonas que les conviene.	*it follows from this reasoning that*
Se han negado a hacer ningún tipo de declaración, **lo que parece confirmar** que actúan según un plan preestablecido.	*which seems to confirm that*
Así pues, el papel de los países democráticos no puede ser otro que ayudar al pueblo nicaragüense.	*thus*

Contrasting or comparing

No hay incompatibilidad entre los dos enfoques.	*... are not incompatible*
Estos puntos de vista son divergentes, pero no se excluyen.	*these points of view, while different, are not mutually exclusive*
Parece que contamos con amplia posibilidad de escoger; **pero en realidad** toda elección está condicionada por factores fácilmente previsibles, que la publicidad puede por tanto tratar de controlar.	*it seems to be the case that ... yet in point of fact*
No se puede decir que haya sido una medida innovativa; **en cambio, sí es cierto que** la propuesta fue compartida por amplios sectores.	*it certainly cannot be claimed that ...; in contrast, it is quite true that ...*
Hay una diferencia fundamental entre los que ... **y** los que ...	*there is a basic difference between ... and ...*
La diferencia estriba únicamente en (el hecho de) que el nuevo modelo funciona a más velocidad.	*the only difference is that*
Hay quienes dicen que la decisión final se tomará en otoño próximo, **mientras que otros afirman que** lo que se desea es dar largas al asunto.	*there are those who say that ... whereas others claim that*
Por un lado *or* **Por una parte,** el número de coches sigue aumentado; **por otro / por otra,** las carreteras están cada vez más deterioradas.	*on the one hand ...; on the other*
En contraste con *or* **En contraposición con** la falta de interés que ha mostrado el ayuntamiento, la Diputación apoya y estimula la continuación de las protestas de los empresarios.	*in contrast with*

EL TELÉFONO / THE TELEPHONE

PARA HACER UNA LLAMADA	GETTING A NUMBER
Could you get me Newhaven 465786 please. (four-six-five-seven-eight-six)	*Por favor, ¿me puede dar el 043 65 27 82? (cero cuarenta y tres, sesenta y cinco, veintisiete, ochenta y dos)*
You'll have to look up the number in the directory.	*Tendrá usted que consultar la guía (telefónica).*
You should get the number from International Directory Enquiries.	*Le podrán dar el número si llama a Información Internacional.*
Would you give me Directory Enquiries please.	*¿Me da Información (Urbana/Interurbana), por favor?*
Can you give me the number of the Decapex company, of 54 Broad Street, Newham.	*¿Me puede decir el número de la compañía Decapex? La dirección es Plaza Mayor, 34, Carmona, provincia de Sevilla.*
It's not in the book.	*No está en la guía.*
They're ex-directory (*Brit*).//They're unlisted (*US*).	*Es un número privado.*
What is the code for Exeter?	*¿Cuál es el prefijo para León?*
Can I dial direct to Colombia?	*¿Puedo llamar a Colombia marcando directamente?*
You omit the '0' when dialling England from Spain.	*No marque el cero del prefijo cuando llame a Londres desde España.*
How do I make an outside call?//What do I dial for an outside line?	*¿Qué hay que hacer para obtener línea?*

DIFERENTES TIPOS DE LLAMADAS	DIFFERENT TYPES OF TELEPHONE CALL
It's a local call.	*Es una llamada local* or *urbana.*
This is a long-distance call from Worthing.	*Es una llamada interurbana desde Barcelona.*
I want to make an international call.	*Deseo llamar al extranjero.*
I want to make a reverse charge call *o* a transferred charge call to a London number (*Brit*).//I want to call a London number collect (*US*).	*Quisiera hacer una llamada a cobro revertido* or *a cargo revertido a un número de Londres.*
I'd like to make a personal call (*Brit*) *o* a person-to-person call (*US*) to Joseph Broadway on Jamestown 123456.	*Quiero hacer una conferencia personal a don Juan Crespo, el número es el 25-46-79.*
I want an ADC call to Bournemouth.	*Deseo llamar a Valencia y que me digan lo que ha costado la llamada.*
I'd like an alarm call for 7.30 tomorrow morning.	*Por favor, ¿me podrían avisar por teléfono mañana por la mañana a las siete y media?*

HABLA EL TELEFONISTA	THE OPERATOR SPEAKS
Number, please.	*¿Dígame? ¿Qué número desea?*
What number do you want?//What number are you calling?//What number are you dialling?	*¿Con qué número desea comunicar?*
Where are you calling from?	*¿Desde dónde llama usted?*
You can dial the number direct.	*Puede marcar el número directamente.*
Replace the receiver and dial again.	*Cuelgue y vuelva a marcar.*
There's a Mr Sandy Campbell calling you from Canberra and wishes you to pay for the call. Will you accept it?	*Hay una llamada para usted del señor López Guerra, que telefonea desde Bilbao y desea hacerlo a cargo revertido. ¿Acepta usted la llamada?*
Can Mr Williams take a personal call (*Brit*)?//Can Mr Williams take a person-to-person call (*US*)?	*¿Se puede pasar aviso de llamada al señor Williams?*
Go ahead, caller.	*Ya puede hablar, señor/señora/señorita.*
(*Directory Enquiries*) There's no listing under that name.	(Información*) Ese nombre no viene en la guía.*
There's no reply from 45 77 57 84.	*El 945 77 57 84 no contesta.*
I'll try to reconnect you.	*Voy a intentar otra vez comunicar con este número.*
Hold the line, caller.	*No se retire, señor/señora/señorita.*
All lines to Bristol are engaged – please try later.	*Las líneas están saturadas; llame más tarde, por favor.*
I'm trying it for you now.	*Le voy a poner ahora (Sp)// Le estoy conectando (LAm).*
It's ringing.//Ringing for you now.	*Está sonando* or *llamando.*
The line is engaged (*Brit*).//The line is busy (*US*).	*Está comunicando.*

CUANDO EL ABONADO CONTESTA	WHEN YOUR NUMBER ANSWERS
Could I have extension 516?//Can you give me extension 516?	*¿Me da la extensión* or *interno (SC)* 516?
Is that Mr Lambert's phone?	*¿Es éste el número del señor Lambert?*
Could I speak to Mr Swinton please?//I'd like to speak to Mr Swinton, please.//Is Mr Swinton there?	*Por favor, ¿podría hablar con el señor García?// Quisiera hablar con el señor García, por favor.// ¿Está el Sr. García?*
Could you put me through to Dr Henderson, please?	*¿Me pone (Sp)* or *conecta (LAm) con el doctor Rodríguez, por favor?*
Who's speaking?	*¿Me puede decir quién habla?//¿De parte de quién?*
I'll try again later.	*Volveré a llamar más tarde.*
I'll call back in half an hour.	*Llamaré otra vez dentro de media hora.*
Could I leave my number for her to call me back?	*¿Podría darle mi número y decirle que haga el favor de llamarme?*
I'm ringing from a callbox (*Brit*).//I'm calling from a pay station (*US*).	*Llamo desde una cabina (telefónica).*
I'm phoning from England.	*Llamo desde Inglaterra.*
Would you ask him to ring me when he gets back?	*¿Quiere pedirle que me llame cuando vuelva?*
Could you ring that number for me?	*¿Me puede conseguir ese número?*

CONTESTA LA CENTRALITA/EL CONMUTADOR	THE SWITCHBOARD OPERATOR SPEAKS
Queen's Hotel, can I help you?	*Hotel Castellana, ¿dígame?*
Who is calling, please?	*¿Me puede decir quién habla?*
Who shall I say is calling?	*¿De parte de quién?*
Do you know his extension number?	*¿Sabe usted qué extensión* or *interno (SC) es?*
I am connecting you now.//I'm putting you through now.	*Le pongo (Sp).// Le conecto (LAm).*
I'm putting you through now to Mrs Thomas.	*Le pongo (Sp)* or *conecto (LAm) con la señora de Martínez.*
I have a call from Tokyo for Mrs Thomas.	*Hay una llamada de Tokio para la señora de Martínez.*
I've got Miss Martin on the line for you.	*La señorita Martín quiere hablar con usted.*
Miss Paxton is calling you from Paris.	*La Srta. Pérez le llama desde París.*
Dr Craig is talking on the other line.	*El doctor Rodríguez está hablando por el otro teléfono.*
Sorry to keep you waiting.	*Perdone la demora, pero no se retire.*
There's no reply.	*No contesta.*
You're through to Mr Walsh.	*Ahora le paso con el señor Arias.*

PARA CONTESTAR	ANSWERING THE TELEPHONE
Hullo, this is Anne speaking.	*Sí, soy Ana, dígame.*
(*Is that Anne?*) Speaking.	(¿Es Ana?) *Al aparato// Sí, soy yo// Sí, aquí Ana.*
Would you like to leave a message?	*¿Quiere dejar (algún) recado?*
Can I take a message for him?	*¿Quiere que le pase un recado?*
Don't hang up yet.	*No cuelgue.// No se retire.*
Put the phone down and I'll call you back.	*Cuelgue y espere que le llame.*
Please speak after the tone.	*Deje su mensaje después de la señal.*

EN CASO DE DIFICULTAD	WHEN IN TROUBLE
I can't get through (at all).	*No consigo comunicar.*
The number is not ringing.	*El teléfono no suena.*
I'm getting 'number unobtainable'.//I'm getting the 'number unobtainable' signal.	*Me sale la señal de línea desconectada.*
Their phone is out of order.	*Ese teléfono tiene una avería.*
We were cut off.	*Nos han cortado (la comunicación).*
I must have dialled the wrong number.	*Debo haberme equivocado de número.*
We've got a crossed line.	*Hay un cruce de líneas.*
I've called them several times with no reply.	*He llamado varias veces y no contestan.*
You gave me a wrong number.	*No me han dado el número que pedí.*
I got the wrong extension.	*Me han dado una extensión que no era la que yo quería.*
This is a very bad line.	*Se oye muy mal.// La línea está muy mal.*

SUGERENCIAS

We could stop off in Barcelona for a day or two, if you would like to.	*podríamos*
How do you fancy a couple of days at the sea?	*te gustaría*
What would you say to a morning on the Grand Canal?	*qué le parecería*
Would you like to visit the castle while you are here?	*le gustaría*
I suggest *o* **I would suggest** *o* **I'd like to suggest that** we offer him the job.	*sugiero que*
What if we were to arrange a meeting for the end of May?	*y si quedamos en*
Perhaps we should ask him if he would like to come with us?	*quizás debíamos*
Why not go round to see him yourself?	*por qué no*
Suppose *o* **Supposing** you were to rent a house in Sicily?	*qué te parece la idea de*
Perhaps you might care to add your name to this list?	*no quisiera usted*
You could *o* **You might** buy the tickets for both of us, if you agree.	*podría usted*
In your place *o* **If I were you,** I'd be very careful.	*yo en su lugar*
What do you think about trying to set up such a meeting?	*qué le parece a usted la posibilidad de*
Have you ever thought of applying for the job?	*ha pensado usted alguna vez en*
I've got an idea – let's invite him over here.	*tengo una idea: invitémosle ...*
If I may make a suggestion, why not discuss it with him?	*si me permite(n) una sugerencia*
If I might be permitted to suggest something: would you take her on in your department for a while?	*si me permite(n) una sugerencia*
We propose that half the fee be paid in advance, and half on completion of the contract.	*proponemos que*

(con cierta duda)

It is quite important that you should wait till he returns.	*es importante que*
I am convinced that this would be a dangerous step to take.	*estoy convencido de que*
I was thinking of going there next month – how about it?	*pensaba en*
There would be a lot to be said for acting at once.	*sería muy conveniente*
Might I be allowed to offer a little advice? – talk it over with your parents first.	*¿me permite(n) que le(s) dé un consejo?*
If you want my advice, I'd steer well clear of them.	*en mi opinión, haría(n) bien en*
In these circumstances, **it might be better to** wait.	*sería mejor*
It might be a good thing *o* **It might be a good idea** to warn her about this.	*sería buena idea*
If you were to give me the negative, **I could** get copies made.	*si usted me diese ... yo podría*
Would it matter if you didn't hand in the essay on time?	*importaría mucho que*
Say you were to change the date of your holiday?	*y si cambia*
Some people might prefer to wait until they are sure of the money before acting.	*puede que algunos prefieran*
Perhaps it might be as well to ask her permission first?	*quizás sería preferible*
I'd be very careful not to commit myself.	*yo tendría mucho cuidado con*

PARA PEDIR SUGERENCIAS

What would you do in my place? // What would you do if you were me?	*¿qué haría usted en mi lugar?*
Have you any idea what the best way to go about it is?	*tiene usted alguna idea sobre*
I wonder if you have any suggestion to offer on where we might go for a few days?	*no sé si podría usted sugerir algo*
I'm a bit doubtful about where to start.	*no estoy muy seguro de*

Y, SEGÚN EL CONTEXTO:

if you don't object/I'd like to ask you a favour/I would advise you to .../take care not to .../I would recommend/whatever you do, don't .../perhaps you would kindly/I cannot put it too strongly/my idea was to .../how do you feel about this?/I should be grateful if you would/it could be in your interest to .../it occurred to me that/I would be delighted to .../I hope you will not be offended if/if I were to make an informed guess, I'd say/it might have something to do with/if you ask me, you'd better/it would certainly be advisable to ...

CONSEJOS

PARA PEDIR CONSEJO

I'd like your advice about *o* **I'd appreciate your advice about** where to go in Italy.	*quisiera pedirle consejo sobre*
What would you advise me to do in the circumstances?	*¿usted qué me aconsejaría hacer?*
Would you advise me to do as they ask?	*me aconsejaría que*
How would you go about it, in my place? // **What would you do,** if you were me?	*qué haría usted*
Do you think I ought to sell it to him?	*cree usted que debería …*
What would you recommend in these circumstances?	*qué me recomienda*

PARA ACONSEJAR

If you want my advice, I'd steer well clear of them.	*si quiere que le dé un consejo, haría usted bien en*
Take my advice and don't rush into anything.	*siga mi consejo y*
My advice would be to have nothing to do with this affair.	*yo le aconsejaría que*
I would strongly advise you to reconsider this decision.	*le aconsejo encarecidamente que*
I would advise you against doing that.	*le aconsejaría que no*
It would certainly be advisable *o* **You would be well advised** to get his permission before going any further in this matter.	*sin duda sería aconsejable …*
In your place I would *o* **If I were you I would** clear it with her headmaster first.	*en su lugar yo …*
I think you should *o* **I think you ought to** send it by express post, as time is so important.	*yo creo que debería usted*
Why don't you explain to her exactly what happened?	*por qué no*
If you want my opinion, I'd go by air to save time.	*si quiere que le dé mi opinión, yo …*
You'd be as well to think it over carefully, before taking any decision.	*haría usted bien en*
Would you allow me to suggest something? You could go there direct from London.	*¿me permite que le haga una sugerencia?*
If you ask me, you'd better find another travel agency.	*si quiere usted mi opinión, más vale que*
Do be sure you read the small print before you sign anything.	*asegúrese de*
Try to avoid a quarrel with him, for my sake.	*procure*
Whatever you do, don't drink the local brandy.	*haga lo que haga*
We believe that **you would be ill-advised to** have any dealings with this firm.	*haría mal en*

(más tentativamente)

It might be wise *o* **It might be a good thing to** go and see your doctor about this.	*tal vez sería prudente que/ quizás sería preferible*
In view of the present situation, **it might be better to** think it over for a while before acting.	*probablemente sería mejor*
I'd be very careful not to commit myself.	*yo tendría mucho cuidado de no*
You might like *o* **You might care to** write to him and explain what happened.	*acaso podrías*
There would be something to be said for acting at once.	*no sería mala idea*
I wonder if it might be as well to wait for another few days?	*me pregunto si no sería conveniente*

PARA HACER UNA ADVERTENCIA

Take care not to spend too much money.	*procure no*
Be careful not to believe everything they tell you.	*tenga cuidado de no*
Make sure you don't *o* **Mind you don't** sign anything.	*vaya con cuidado de no*
I'd think twice about going on holiday with her.	*yo me lo pensaría dos veces antes de*
It would be sensible to consult someone who knows the country before making detailed plans.	*sería más prudente*
It would be sheer madness to marry him when you feel that way about him.	*sería una locura*
You're risking a long delay in Cairo, if you decide to come back by that route.	*se expone usted a*

OFERTAS

May I show you the city when you are here?	*me permite*
Would you like me to find out more about it for you?	*quiere usted que yo*
Is there anything I can do about your accommodation?	*hay algo que pueda hacer*
We would like to offer you the post of assistant manager.	*quisiéramos ofrecerle*
I might perhaps *o* **I could perhaps** give you a hand with the painting?	*quizás yo podría*
Shall I collect the documents for you on my way there?	*quiere que*
How about letting me find some help for you in the house?	*qué tal si*

(más indirectamente)

Say I were to lend you the money till your bursary comes through?	*supongamos que yo*
Would you allow me to contribute towards the cost?	*me permitiría*
I would be delighted to help, if I may.	*tendría mucho gusto en*
I hope you will not be offended if I offer a contribution towards the expense you are incurring.	*espero que no le ofenda que*
It would give me great pleasure to welcome you to my home.	*tendría mucho gusto en*
I'd like to pay my share, **if it's all the same to you.**	*si no le molesta*
If you don't mind, I'll buy my own tickets.	*si no le importa*
Do let me know if I can help you on anything else.	*no deje de avisarme si*
If I can be of any assistance, please **do not hesitate to** write to me.	*no dude en*
What if I were to call for you in the car?	*y si yo*
It occurred to me that I might go with you as far as the border at least?	*se me ha ocurrido que podría*

PETICIONES

Would you please *o* **Will you please** call in and see her if you have time when you are in Rome.	*tendría usted la gentileza de ...*
Would you please *o* **Would you kindly** reserve one single room for those nights.	*tendría usted la amabilidad de ...*
Could you *o* **Would it be possible for you to** arrange for a car to come to the airport for me?	*podría usted*
Would you mind letting me have a copy of your letter to him?	*le importaría*
Might I ask you to *o* **Could I ask you to** let me have a note of his address some time?	*quisiera pedirle que*

(de manera más protocolaria)

I should be grateful if you would let me know which you have in stock.	*le agradecería que me avisase*
I would ask you / I must ask you not to use the telephone for long-distance calls.	*quisiera pedirle que / debo rogarle que*
We should be glad to receive your cheque for this amount by return of post.	*le agradeceríamos que nos mandaran*
You are requested to return the books to us at once.	*le rogamos que*
Kindly inform us when your account will be in credit.	*tenga la bondad de*

(más indirectamente)

I would rather you didn't tell him what I said.	*preferiría que no*
It would be very helpful if *o* **It would be very useful if you** could find me a room there.	*sería de gran utilidad que usted*
I was hoping that you might find time to go and see her.	*yo esperaba que*
I wonder whether you might not ask her for it?	*me pregunto si no podría*
I would appreciate it if you could let me have copies of the best photographs.	*le agradecería que*

COMPARACIONES

This year's sales figures are very high **in comparison with** *o* **compared with** *o* **when compared with** those of our competitors.	*en comparación con*
By comparison, this one is much more expensive.	*en comparación*
If you compare New York and Washington, you realise how pleasant the latter is to live in.	*si se compara*
If we set the overall cost **against** our estimate, we can see how inaccurate it was.	*si comparamos ... con*
This house has a lovely garden, **whereas** *o* **whilst** the other has only a small yard.	*mientras que*
The quality of the painting is very disappointing **beside** that of the sculpture section in the exhibition.	*si se compara con*
In contrast to Joan's, Anne's career has flourished since she left university.	*en contraste con*
As opposed to *o* **Unlike** John's, Peter's work is careful and thorough.	*a diferencia de*
This is **nowhere near as** large **as** the other one.	*no es ni mucho menos tan ... como ...*
There is no comparison between them *o* **You cannot compare them at all** *o* **They are simply not comparable** – the first scheme is clearly much more ambitious than the second.	*no se pueden (ni) comparar*
The former looks good, but **the latter** is more effective.	*aquél ... éste*
There is some resemblance between the two photographs.//**There is some similarity between** them.	*hay cierto parecido entre*
There is some difference between them.	*hay cierta diferencia entre*
It's swings and roundabouts – what you gain on one, you lose on the other.	*viene a ser lo mismo*
It is something like a television screen, **but** much smaller.	*es algo así como ... sólo que*
He's like his brother, **only** fairer.	*se parece a ... pero es*
What differentiates him from similar writers is his grasp of social truths.	*lo que le distingue de*

(comparaciones favorables)

It is greatly superior to that restaurant we went to last time we were in Rome.	*es muy superior a*
The imported version just **can't compete with** the one we make ourselves.	*no puede competir con*
I think James **has the edge over** Paul in maths.	*es ligeramente superior a*
The little chest of drawers **is really in a class of its own.**	*es único en su género*

(comparaciones desfavorables)

It is **much inferior to** the sample they sent us.	*es muy inferior a*
His book **is not worthy of comparison with** *o* **does not bear comparison with** the writings of the experts in the field.	*no tiene punto de comparación con*
I'm afraid her work simply **does not measure up to** that of her classmates.	*no está a la altura de*
The English forwards **were no match for** the French, who scored three goals in the first half.	*eran muy inferiores a*
As far as brains go, **he is not in the same class as** *o* **he is not a patch on** his father.	*no le llega a la suela de los zapatos*

(gran parecido)

It is really much the same as the other.//**There's not much difference between** them.//**There's not much to choose between** them.	*no hay gran diferencia entre*
These rings **are** about **equal in** value.//They **are of equal** value.	*son del mismo valor*
The value of this house **is equivalent to** *o* **corresponds to** that of the one you own.	*es equivalente a*
It has been likened to *o* **It has been compared to** one of Wordsworth's later poems.	*se ha comparado con*
His exam results **are on a par with** those of his brother.	*están al mismo nivel que*

(gran diferencia)

They are simply not comparable *o* **You just can't compare them at all** – they are so different in their approach.	*sencillamente, no son comparables*
There is little correlation between one set of results and the other.	*apenas hay correlación entre*
They have so little in common that it is a waste of time trying to assess their respective merits.	*tienen tan poco en común*

OPINIONES

PARA PEDIR A ALGUIEN SU OPINIÓN

What do you think of / What is your opinion on the way he has behaved over this?	*qué piensa / opina usted de*
If I may ask your opinion, **how do you see** the traffic developing in this part of the town?	*cómo cree usted que*
I'd be interested to know what your reaction is to the latest report on food additives.	*me interesaría saber qué le parece*
Can you tell me **what your own feelings are about** the way the house was sold?	*qué es lo que usted piensa de*
What are your thoughts on the subject of how to earn more money?	*qué opina usted sobre el tema de*
I have been asked to find out **what your attitude is to** this problem.	*su actitud hacia*
Have you come to any conclusions about how we should plan the next stage?	*ha llegado usted a alguna conclusión sobre*

PARA EXPRESAR LA PROPIA OPINIÓN

In my opinion *o* **As I see it,** that was the best thing that could have happened to them.	*a mi parecer*
I feel children shouldn't be ordered around too much.	*yo pienso que*
Personally, I believe her sister should have invited her to stay.	*personalmente, yo creo que*
When I think about it, **it seems to me that** there are too many people chasing too few jobs.	*me parece que*
I have the impression that there has been enough money spent on this project already.	*tengo la impresión de que*
I have an idea *o* **a hunch** he might be coming back before the end of the summer.	*tengo la corazonada de que*
I daresay he'll apologise if you give him time.	*me imagino que*
To my mind, he's the wrong man for the job.	*a mi ver*
From my point of view *o* **As far as I am concerned,** television is a complete waste of time.	*desde mi punto de vista*
My own view of the matter is that the government will have to act quickly.	*yo por mi parte opino que*
My own point of view is that *o* **It's my belief that** people are best left to sort out their own lives.	*yo creo personalmente que*
It's my opinion that *o* **I am of the opinion that** such people should not be allowed to get access to public funds.	*yo soy de la opinión de que*
I am convinced that they did it in order to make things difficult for us.	*estoy convencido de que*
From where I stand, it looks as though the school will have to close.	*desde mi punto de vista parece que*
If you ask me *o* **If you want to know what I think** *o* **If you want my opinion,** he should have been sent to hospital right away.	*si quiere que le dé mi opinión*

PARA RESPONDER SIN DAR UNA OPINIÓN

I should prefer not to comment on that statement at the moment.	*preferiría no hacer ningún comentario sobre*
I would rather not commit myself at this stage.	*prefiero no pronunciarme*
I don't know what to think about *o* **I don't know what to say about** the new scheme to brighten up the town.	*no sé qué pensar sobre*
This is not something I have given a lot of thought to.	*no he reflexionado lo suficiente sobre el tema*
I have no particular views on this subject. // **I haven't any strong feelings about** it.	*no tengo opinión formada sobre*
I am not in a position to say much about what is going on at these talks, as I have been abroad for some time.	*no me encuentro en situación de poder decir*
I haven't any idea *o* **I haven't the slightest notion** what we ought to do now.	*no tengo ni la más mínima noción de*
I'm afraid **I am totally ignorant about** *o* **I know nothing at all about** the internal combustion engine.	*no sé absolutamente nada de*
It all depends on what you mean by ...	*todo depende de lo que usted entienda por*
It depends on your point of view.	*depende de cuál sea su punto de vista*
It is difficult to say who is right about this.	*es difícil decidir*
It doesn't much matter to me, whether or not he decides to go.	*a mí me da igual*

GUSTOS Y PREFERENCIAS

PARA PREGUNTAR LO QUE GUSTA O SE PREFIERE

Would you like to visit the castle, while you are here?	*le gustaría*
How do you feel about going to a cricket match when you're in England?	*le apetecería*
What do you like doing best, when you are on holiday?	*qué prefiere hacer*
What's your favourite way to spend an evening?	*cómo prefiere usted …*
Which of the two do you prefer?	*¿cuál de los dos prefiere usted?*

PARA EXPRESAR EL GUSTO

I'm very keen on gardening.	*me entusiasma*
As for seaside towns, **I'm very fond of** Brighton.	*tengo una predilección especial por*
What I like better than anything else is *o* **There's nothing I like more than** a quiet evening by the fire with a book.	*no hay nada que me guste más que*
For me, there's nothing to compare with the Italian Renaissance painters.	*para mí, no hay nada que pueda compararse con*
I must admit to a certain affection for *o* **fondness for** *o* **weakness for** Victorian houses.	*tengo cierta debilidad por*
I have a soft spot for labradors.	*tengo debilidad por*
I like people to be on time for their appointments.	*me gusta que la gente sea*

PARA DECIR LO QUE A UNO NO LE GUSTA

I very much dislike that sort of holiday.	*no me gusta nada*
I can't stand *o* **I can't bear** books that other people have written on.	*no puedo soportar*
I'm not too keen on seaside holidays.	*no me hacen mucha gracia*
I can't say writing essays **appeals to me very much.**	*no puedo decir que … me atraiga demasiado*
It's not my kind of book (*o* film *o* place *etc*).	*no es el tipo de … que más me atrae*
I'm fed up with snooker on television.	*estoy harto de*
Cowboy films **aren't my favourite** form of entertainment.	*no son … que más me gusta*
I'm not too wild about *o* **I can't get up any enthusiasm for** hill-walking.	*no me inspira gran entusiasmo*
Politics **isn't really my thing,** I'm afraid.	*no es realmente mi tema favorito*
I've gone off the idea of cycling round Holland.	*se me han quitado las ganas de*
There's nothing I like less *o* **There's nothing I dislike more** than having to get up at dawn.	*no hay nada que más aborrezca*
I don't much like the fact that he is always late on Monday mornings.	*no me hace mucha gracia que*
I took a dislike to him the moment I saw him.	*le tomé manía*
What I hate most is waiting in queues for buses.	*lo que más aborrezco*
I find it intolerable that there should be no public transport here on Sundays.	*me parece intolerable que*
I don't mind most insects but **I have a horror of** flies.	*le(s) tengo horror a*

PARA DECIR LO QUE UNO PREFIERE

I should prefer to *o* **I would rather** wait until we have enough money to go by air.	*preferiría*
I'd prefer not to *o* **I'd rather not** go and see her until I have found the book she lent me.	*preferiría no*
I'd prefer you not to *o* **I'd rather you didn't** invite him.	*prefiero que no*
I like the blue curtains **better than** the red ones.//**I prefer** the blue curtains **to** the red ones.	*me gustan más … que*

PARA EXPRESAR INDIFERENCIA

I have no particular preference.	*no tengo preferencia especial*
I don't mind at all – let's do whichever is easiest.	*me da exactamente lo mismo*
I really don't care what you tell her.	*me trae sin cuidado*
I don't feel strongly about what sort of transport we choose – why don't you make that decision?	*no tengo preferencia especial en cuanto a*
It makes no odds, one way or the other.	*(me) da igual una cosa que otra*

INTENCIONES Y DESEOS

PARA PREGUNTAR LO QUE ALGUIEN DESEA O PIENSA HACER

Will you take the job?//**Do you intend to** *o* **Do you mean to** take the job?	*tiene usted intención de*
What flight **do you mean** *o* **do you intend to** take to New York?	*... piensa usted*
What do you propose to do with the money you have inherited?	*qué se propone hacer*
It would be useful to know **what your intentions are** *o* **what you intend to do.**	*cuáles son sus intenciones/lo que piensa hacer*
What had you in mind for the rest of the programme?	*qué es lo que tenía pensado*
Did you mean to tell him how much you had paid for the house, or did the figure just slip out?	*lo hizo a propósito cuando ...*

PARA EXPRESAR LAS INTENCIONES

I am going *o* **I intend** *o* **I mean** *o* **My intention is** to sell the car as soon as I can.	*voy a*
They intended him to go to university, but he did not pass his exams.	*querían que él ...*
I have made up my mind *o* **I have decided** to go to university.	*he decidido*
I am thinking of going to live in the country when I retire.	*estoy pensando en*
I am hoping to go and see her when I am in the States.	*espero*
They have every intention of returning next year.	*tienen verdadera intención de*
I went to London, **intending to** visit her *o* **with the intention of** visiting her, but she was away on business.	*con la intención de*
What I have in mind is to start a small hardware business.	*lo que tengo pensado es*
I aim to reach Africa in three months.	*pretendo*
He resolved to *o* **He made a resolution to** devote his life to the welfare of the underprivileged.	*decidió*
Our aim *o* **Our object** in buying the company is to provide work for the people of the village.	*nuestro objetivo*
My whole point in complaining **was to** get something done about the state of the roads.	*lo que yo quería conseguir al ... era*
We plan to move *o* **We are planning on** moving into the European market next year.	*proyectamos*
They bought the land **in order to** farm it *o* **for the purpose of** farming it.	*con el propósito de*
He studied history, **with a view to** becoming a politician when he left college.	*con vistas a*

PARA DECIR LO QUE UNO NO QUIERE HACER

I didn't mean *o* **I didn't intend** to offend her, but she made me very angry.	*no era mi intención*
I intend not to *o* **I don't intend to** pay unless he completes the work.	*no tengo intención de*
His parents **didn't intend him to be** a miner, but it was the only work he could find.	*no querían que él fuese*
He had no intention of accepting the post even if it were offered to him.	*no tenía ninguna intención de*
We are not thinking of advertising this post at the moment.	*no tenemos previsto*

PARA EXPRESAR LO QUE SE DESEA HACER

I should like to see the Sistine Chapel.	*quisiera*
Her father **wanted her to be** a teacher.	*quería que ella fuese*
Robert **wished** to work abroad but could not get a work permit.	*deseaba*
I am very keen to see more students take up engineering.	*vería con mucho agrado que*
I'm longing to *o* **I'm dying to** go to Australia, but I can't afford it yet.	*estoy deseando*
I insist that you inform me as soon as you hear from them.	*insisto en que*

PARA EXPRESAR LO QUE NO SE DESEA HACER

I don't want *o* **I have no wish** *o* **I haven't any desire to** take the credit for something I did not do.	*no tengo ninguna intención de*
I wouldn't want you to change your plans for my sake.	*no quisiera que*
I refuse to tell you where I put the documents.	*me niego a*
I should prefer you not to speak to her about this.	*preferiría que no*

PERMISO

PARA PEDIR PERMISO

May I *o* **Might I** *o* **Can I** *o* **Could I** tell her about this? — *puedo*

Would you let me *o* **Would you allow me to** be present at the interview? — *me permitiría usted*

Would it be possible for us to leave the car in your garage for a week? — *podríamos*

Is there any chance of borrowing your boat while we are at the lake? — *habría alguna posibilidad de*

Do you mind if I come to the meeting next week? — *le importa que*

Would it be all right if I arrived on Monday instead of Tuesday? — *le parece bien que*

Would it bother you if I invited him? // **Would you have anything against** my inviting him? — *tendría usted inconveniente en que*

Would you have any objection *o* **Would there be any objection to** my bringing a friend with me? — *le parecería bien que*

Would you be kind enough to allow me *o* **I should be grateful if you would allow me to** travel with your group as far as the border. — *sería usted tan amable de permitirme*

May I be permitted *o* **May I be allowed to** leave early on these three days? — *me estaría permitido*

Are we allowed *o* **Are we permitted** *o* **Is it allowed** *o* **Is it permitted to** visit the Cathedral? // Is visiting the Cathedral **permitted?** — *está permitido*

Is it permissible to take photographs inside the gallery? — *permiten que*

PARA DAR PERMISO

You can *o* **You may** have the car if you promise to drive carefully. — *puede*

Of course you must borrow our boat – we are always glad when friends use it. // **By all means,** borrow our boat ... — *no faltaría más, claro que puede*

I should be delighted if you gave my name as a reference for this job. — *tendré mucho gusto en que*

It's all right by me *o* **I'm quite happy if** you want to skip the Cathedral visit. — *me parece muy bien que*

Of course I don't mind if you prefer to stay in Italy for another week. — *naturalmente que no me importa*

I have no objection at all to your quoting me in your article. // **I have nothing against** your quoting me. — *no tengo nada en contra de que*

You have my permission to be absent for that week. — *cuente usted con mi permiso para*

We should be happy to allow you to inspect the papers here. — *nos complace permitirle*

You are allowed to visit the Museum, as long as you apply in writing to the Curator first. — *se le permite*

We have been given permission *o* **We have been authorised to** hold the meeting in the town hall. — *nos han autorizado para*

The manager **is quite agreeable to** *o* **has agreed to** our using his premises. — *ha accedido a que*

PARA NEGAR PERMISO

You can't *o* **You mustn't** go anywhere near the research lab. — *no debe*

I should prefer you not to *o* **I wouldn't want you to** *o* **I'd rather you didn't** give them my name. — *preferiría que no*

We regret that it is not possible for you to visit the castle at the moment, owing to the building works. — *desgraciadamente, no le va a ser posible*

I cannot allow this *o* **I cannot permit this** for the time being. — *no puedo permitirlo*

I couldn't possibly allow you to show the photographs to a publisher. — *no puedo permitirle bajo ningún concepto que*

I'm not allowed to visit such places alone. — *no me dejan*

I forbid you to approach him on my behalf. // **You must not** approach him. — *le prohíbo que*

You must not *o* **You are forbidden to** enter the premises without authority from the owners. — *se prohíbe*

I've been forbidden to swim for the moment. — *tengo prohibido*

My doctor **forbids me** any alcohol. // **I've been forbidden** alcohol by my doctor. — *me ha prohibido*

It is strictly forbidden to carry weapons in this country. // Carrying weapons **is strictly prohibited.** — *está terminantemente prohibido*

OBLIGACIÓN

PARA EXPRESAR LO QUE UNO ESTÁ OBLIGADO A HACER

You must *o* **You have got to** *o* **You have to** be back before midnight.	*tiene que*
You must not fail to pay the amount owing, or you will become liable to prosecution.	*tiene obligación de*
You will go directly to the headmaster's office, and wait for me there.	*vaya*
They could not get into the country **without** a visa.//**They had to have** a visa **to** get into the country.	*no pudieron ... sin*
She was obliged to give up her room in the hostel.	*ella se vio obligada a*
He was **forced to** *o* **obliged to** ask his family for a loan.//He was **driven to** asking his family for a loan.	*él se vio obligado a*
You need to *o* **You must** *o* **You have to** have an address in Rome before you can apply for the job.	*usted debe*
Three passport photos **are required.**	*hacen falta ...*
It is essential *o* **It is of the utmost importance** to know what the career options are like, before choosing a course of study.	*es imprescindible*
Go and see Pompeii – **it's a must!**	*no deje de*
You really must *o* **You really should** *o* **You really ought to** be more careful with your things.	*realmente debería usted*
You certainly ought to visit the Colosseum.	*sin duda debe*
A clean driving licence is **indispensable** *o* **necessary** *o* **essential** *o* **compulsory** for the job.//It is **a requirement of** the job.	*es indispensable*
I must now offer my resignation: in the circumstances, **I cannot do otherwise** *o* **I have no alternative.**	*no puedo hacer otra cosa*
You have to come with me – **there's no two ways about it,** since I don't speak the language at all.	*no tiene más remedio que*

(para preguntar si uno está obligado a hacer algo)

Do I need to *o* **Must I** *o* **Do I have to** *o* **Have I got to** have a work permit?	*es necesario*
Ought I to *o* **Should I** take some reading matter?	*debía*
Is it necessary to *o* **Must one** *o* **Does one need to** *o* **Does one have to** *o* **Has one got to** own a pair of skis?	*se tiene que*
Am I meant *o* **Am I expected** *o* **Am I supposed to** fill in this bit of the form too?	*estoy obligado a*

PARA EXPRESAR LO QUE UNO NO ESTÁ OBLIGADO A HACER

You needn't *o* **You don't have to** *o* **You haven't got to** go there if you don't want to.	*no hace falta que*
I haven't got to apply before September, but I'd like to do so before I leave on holiday.	*no tengo que*
It is not necessary *o* **There's no need** *o* **It is not compulsory** *o* **It is not obligatory to** have a letter of acceptance in advance, but it does help.	*no es obligatorio*
You are not obliged *o* **You are under no obligation to** invite him, but it would be a kindness to do so.	*no tiene obligación de*
Surely I needn't *o* **Surely I haven't got to** give him all the details immediately?	*supongo que no tengo que*

PARA EXPRESAR LO QUE ALGUIEN NO DEBE HACER

You must not *o* **You are not allowed to** sit the exam more than three times.	*no le está permitido*
You must not *o* **On no account must you** show this document to any unauthorised person.	*no debe de ninguna manera*
It is forbidden *o* **It is not allowed to** bring cameras into the gallery without prior permission from the owners.	*está prohibido*
I forbid you to return there.//**You are forbidden to** return there.	*le prohíbo que*
Smoking **is forbidden** *o* **is prohibited** in the dining room.//Smoking **is not allowed** *o* **is not permitted** in the dining room.	*se prohíbe*
You're not supposed to *o* **You're not meant to** use this room unless you are a club member.	*en principio no puede*
You cannot be out of the country for longer than three months **without** losing your right to this grant.	*usted no puede ... sin*

ACUERDO

PARA EXPRESAR ACUERDO CON LO QUE SE DICE

I fully agree with you *o* **I totally agree with you** on this point.//**We are in complete agreement** on this.	*estoy totalmente de acuerdo con usted*
You're quite right *o* **You are quite correct** when you say the fault lies with the government policy here.	*tiene toda la razón*
I share your opinion that this was extremely badly arranged.//**I share** your concern about this matter.//**I share** your views about this.	*comparto*
I think **we see eye to eye** on the question of who should pay for these.	*estamos totalmente de acuerdo*
We are of the same mind, certainly, **when it comes to** allocating responsibility within the department.	*somos del mismo parecer en lo que se refiere a*
We have been thinking along the same lines, that is quite clear.	*nuestros pensamientos han coincidido*
We are broadly in agreement with you on the way to approach this problem.	*convenimos con usted en lo principal en cuanto a*
There are several **points of contact** between us.	*coincidimos en muchos puntos*
My own experience certainly **bears out** *o* **confirms** what you say.	*confirma*
Our conclusions **are entirely consistent with** your findings.	*se corresponden por completo con*
My own independent statistics **corroborate** those of your researcher.	*corroboran*
We must endorse, with some hesitation, your conclusions on this matter.	*nos adherimos a*
Our opinion coincides with yours on all the important points.	*coincidimos con ustedes en*
We applaud the group's decision to stand firm on this point.	*celebramos*
I take your point about the increased transport costs.	*admito que tiene razón en cuanto a*
I am prepared to concede that a trip to Australia is justified.	*estoy dispuesto a conceder*
It's true that you had the original idea, **but** many other people worked on it.	*es cierto que ... pero*
I have no objection to this being done.//**I do not object to** your doing this.	*no tengo inconveniente en que*

PARA EXPRESAR ACUERDO CON LO PROPUESTO

This solution is most **acceptable to** us.	*aceptable*
We will readily fall in with these proposals.	*aceptaremos de buen grado*
I like the sound of what you say about *o* **I do like your idea of** limiting sightseeing to mornings only.	*me parece bien su idea de*
This certainly **seems the right way to go about it.**	*parece la forma correcta de proceder*
As for the idea of your speaking to him about it, **I should certainly welcome this.**	*estoy totalmente conforme con ello*
The proposed scheme **meets with our approval.**	*tiene nuestra aprobación*
This is a proposal which **deserves our wholehearted support.**	*merece nuestro apoyo total*
I will certainly **give my backing to** such a scheme.	*apoyaré*

PARA EXPRESAR ACUERDO CON LO PEDIDO

Of course **I shall be happy to** get the tickets.	*tendré mucho gusto en*
I'll do as you suggest and send him the documents.	*seguiré su consejo*
There is no problem about getting tickets for him, and I shall do it at the end of the week.	*no hay problema en cuanto a*
We should be delighted to cooperate with you in this enterprise.	*estaremos encantados de*
We shall comply with your request at once.	*accederemos a su petición*

Y, SEGÚN EL CONTEXTO:

I think the same as you do/as you have quite rightly pointed out/I'll go along with that/it makes sense to do this/I am fully in accord with/I am prepared to give the go-ahead to/I am certainly in favour of/I can see no reason to oppose this/this is quite satisfactory/I am quite ready to .../we shall sanction the use of/if you insist, I shall .../there can be no doubt about/I cannot dispute the facts given in/there's no denying that/I hasten to agree with/this is just what I had hoped for/after thinking this over/I hoped you would say this

DESACUERDO

PARA EXPRESAR DESACUERDO CON LO QUE DICE ALGUIEN

I cannot agree with what you say about this.//**I absolutely disagree** *o* **I totally disagree** with you on this.	*no estoy de acuerdo en absoluto*
You are quite wrong when you suggest that it was his fault.	*se equivoca usted por completo*
There must be some mistake – the ferry could not cost as much as that.	*debe haber un error*
This cannot be the case.//I am obliged to point out that **this is not the case.**	*esto no puede ser*
You are wrong *o* **You are mistaken** in believing that my son was involved.	*está usted equivocado*
This is your view of the events: **it is certainly not mine.**	*yo no lo veo así*
Surely you cannot believe all this?	*supongo que usted no se creerá*
I can't share your point of view on this.//This is your opinion: I am afraid **I cannot share** it.//**I cannot share** your concern for this section of the group.	*no comparto*
I cannot accept this interpretation of the events.	*no puedo aceptar*
I entirely reject all you say about this.	*rechazo totalmente*
We explicitly reject the implication in your letter.	*rechazamos categóricamente*
We must agree to differ on this one.	*tendremos que aceptar que no estamos de acuerdo*
I cannot support you on this matter.	*no puedo apoyarle*
I am afraid that **I'm not altogether with you** on this.	*no coincido del todo con usted*
I can't go along with all you say about them.	*no estoy de acuerdo con*
I have discussed this matter with my colleagues, and **we cannot accept your version of the events.**	*no podemos aceptar su versión de lo sucedido*
The facts do not bear out this assertion.	*los hechos se contradicen con*
This report **diverges from the facts** as I know them.	*no se corresponde con los hechos*
I am afraid I think the whole thing **sounds rather unlikely.**	*parece poco probable*
I take great exception to this statement.	*me ofende mucho*

PARA EXPRESAR DESACUERDO CON LO PROPUESTO

I am not too keen on this idea.//**I don't think much of this idea.**	*no creo que sea buena idea*
I am afraid it seems to me to be **the wrong sort of approach to** such a problem.	*un enfoque erróneo de*
This does not seem to be the right way of dealing with the problem.	*no parece la forma correcta de*
While we are grateful for the suggestion, **we are unfortunately unable to** implement this change.	*por desgracia nos es imposible*
It is not feasible to change the schedule at this late stage.	*no es factible*
This is **not a viable alternative.**	*no es una alternativa viable*
I'm dead against this idea.	*me opongo categóricamente a*
I will not hear of such a thing.	*no quiero ni oír hablar de*
I regret that I am not in a position to accept your kind offer, but it is much appreciated nonetheless.	*lo siento, pero no estoy en situación de aceptar*

PARA DENEGAR UNA PETICIÓN

I won't agree *o* **I can't agree** to do that.	*me niego a*
I cannot in all conscience do what you request.	*mi conciencia no me permite acceder a*
I hope you are not too upset, but **I just can't manage it.**	*está fuera de mis posibilidades*
I cannot possibly comply with this request.	*me es completamente imposible acceder a*
I wouldn't dream of doing a thing like that.	*ni siquiera se me pasaría por la imaginación*
I refuse point blank to have anything to do with this affair.	*me niego en redondo*
It would not be possible for me to do this.	*me sería imposible*
This is quite **out of the question** for the time being.	*totalmente imposible*
It is unfortunately impracticable for us to commit ourselves at this stage.	*por desgracia, nos resultaría muy difícil*
In view of the proposed timescale, **I must reluctantly decline to** take part.	*sintiéndolo mucho, tengo que negarme a*

APROBACIÓN

You are quite right to wait before making such an important decision.	*tiene usted toda la razón en*
I entirely approve of the idea of meeting you all in Geneva.	*me parece muy bien*
I have a very high opinion of *o* **I have a very high regard for** *o* **I think very highly of** the school, and of its headmistress.	*tengo muy buena opinión de*
We are all very enthusiastic about *o* **We are all very keen on** his proposals for a new sports centre here.	*estamos todos muy entusiasmados con*
It's just the sort of arrangement **I wanted.**	*es exactamente el tipo de ... que yo quería*
I certainly go along with that!	*¡completamente de acuerdo!*
I am very much in favour of that sort of thing.	*estoy totalmente a favor de*
This project **is worthy of our admiration,** in that it attempts to alleviate poverty and hunger.	*merece nuestra admiración*
I certainly admire his courage in attempting such a daunting task.	*admiro enormemente*
I applaud your honesty in admitting all that.	*aplaudo*
I shall certainly give it my backing, as it seems the best hope the company has of surviving this very difficult period.	*sin duda lo respaldaré*
Thank you for sending the draft programme: **I like the look of it very much indeed.**	*me ha causado muy buena impresión*
I must congratulate you on the careful way you approached this problem.	*le felicito por*
There are considerable advantages in such a method, not only from the point of view of cost effectiveness, but also ...	*presenta ventajas considerables*
I can thoroughly recommend this plan of action, which has clearly been carefully thought out.	*le recomiendo encarecidamente*
This plan **deserves our total support** *o* **deserves our wholehearted approval.**	*merece nuestro apoyo total*
We are pleased to recognise the merits of this scheme.	*tenemos mucho gusto en reconocer los méritos de*
We view this proposal **favourably,** not least because it is based on a clear perception of the needs of the situation.	*consideramos ... favorablemente*
We endorse completely all that is proposed for this region.	*apoyamos totalmente*

DESAPROBACIÓN

I strongly disapprove of *o* **I heartily disapprove of** such behaviour.	*estoy totalmente en contra de*
I cannot support *o* **I cannot approve of** any sort of testing of the drug on live animals.	*no puedo apoyar*
We are opposed to *o* **We condemn** all forms of professional malpractice.	*estamos en contra de*
I write to complain of what is being done in the name of progress.	*le escribo para presentar una queja por*
I must object to this attempt to damage our hospital service.	*deseo presentar objeciones en contra de*
I can't say I'm pleased about what has happened.	*no se puede decir que esté muy contento con*
I don't think much of what this government has done so far.	*me parece mal*
I take a dim view of *o* **I take a poor view of** students who do not do enough work.	*me parece inaceptable que*
I have a poor opinion of *o* **I have a low opinion of** people like him.	*me merecen muy baja opinión*
I'm fed up with having to wait so long for a passport.	*estoy harto de*
I've had about enough of this sort of insinuation.	*ya me estoy cansando de*
I can't bear *o* **I can't stand** people who smoke between courses in a restaurant.	*no aguanto que*
I am very unhappy about your idea of going off to Turkey on your own.	*estoy en contra de*
He was quite wrong to tell her what I said about her.	*hizo muy mal en*
They should not have refused to give her the money.	*no deberían haberse*
How dare he say that such people do not matter!	*cómo se atreve a ...*

Y, SEGÚN EL CONTEXTO:

it is really necessary to .../this does not seem to be the right way of going about it/it seems to be the wrong approach/I greatly dislike/I write to protest against/this is a dreadful nuisance/with considerable dissatisfaction/I reproach him with/I am sorry to learn that/it is a disgrace/it is a scandal

CERTEZA, POSIBILIDAD Y CAPACIDAD

PARA EXPRESAR CERTEZA

I am sure *o* **I am certain** *o* **I am positive** *o* **I am convinced that** he will keep his word to us.	*estoy seguro de que*
We now know for certain *o* **We now know for sure** that the exam papers were seen by several students before the day of the exam.	*ahora sabemos con seguridad*
It is certain *o* **It is indisputable** *o* **It is undeniable that** the two men met last Friday in London.	*es indudable que*
There is no doubt *o* **There can be no doubt that** the goods arrived in Liverpool on May 9th.	*no cabe duda de que*
It has been established beyond all possible doubt *o* **It has been established once and for all** that he was working for a foreign power during the time he was in Cairo.	*ha quedado demostrado de una vez para siempre*
From all the evidence it is clear that they were planning to gain control of the company.	*todo parece indicar que*
It is beyond all doubt *o* **It is beyond dispute** *o* **It is beyond question that** their country is rich enough to support such research.	*es innegable que*
No one can deny that the weather there is better for skiing.	*nadie puede negar que*
We shall not fail to let you have the papers as soon as we have processed them.	*no dejaremos de*
It is inevitable that they will get to know of our meeting.	*es inevitable que*
You have my absolute assurance that this is the case.	*le doy garantía absoluta de que*
Make no mistake about it – I shall return when I have proof of your involvement.	*puede usted estar seguro de que*
I can assure you that I have had nothing to do with any dishonest trading.	*le aseguro que*
She was bound to discover that you and I had talked.	*era inevitable que ella ...*
I made sure that *o* **I made certain that** no one was listening to our conversation.	*me aseguré de que*

PARA EXPRESAR PROBABILIDAD

It is highly probable *o* **quite likely that** they will come to the airport to meet you.//They will **very probably** come to meet you.	*es muy probable que*
He **must** know what we want of him.	*debe de*
The cheque **should** reach you in Saturday's post.	*debía*
It wouldn't surprise me to learn that he was working for the Americans.	*no me sorprendería descubrir que*
There is a strong chance that *o* **It seems highly likely that** they will agree to the deal.	*hay bastante probabilidad de que*
The probability is *o* **The likelihood is that** we shall have to pay more for it if we buy it from them.//**In all probability** *o* **In all likelihood** we shall have to pay more.	*lo probable es que*
It is reasonable to think that he will agree to join us.	*hay razones para pensar que*
It would appear *o* **It would seem that** he knew James Joyce in Ireland.	*según parece*
The chances are that *o* **The odds are that** *o* **There is a good chance that** you are right.	*lo más probable es que*
It stands to reason that he had seen the book before.	*es lógico pensar que*

PARA EXPRESAR POSIBILIDAD

The situation **could** *o* **might** change from day to day.	*podría*
Perhaps he has already arrived.	*quizá(s)*
It would appear *o* **It would seem that** the grey car had been in an accident.	*según parece*
It is possible that *o* **It is conceivable that** they had met before.	*es posible que*
It may be that I shall come to the States in the autumn.	*podría ser que*
It is within the bounds of possibility that he will know the man you speak of.	*está dentro de lo posible que*
There is reason to believe that the books were stolen from the library.	*hay razón para suponer que*
There are grounds for believing *o* **There are grounds for the belief that** they knew what we were doing as early as 1970.	*existen motivos para suponer que*
I venture to suggest that he could be the man we need.	*me atrevería a sugerir que*
There is the outside chance that the hotel isn't yet full.	*hay una remota posibilidad de que*

PARA EXPRESAR DUDA O INCERTIDUMBRE

I doubt if he knows where it came from.//**It is doubtful whether** he knows where it came from.	*dudo que*
It isn't certain *o* **It isn't known for sure** where she is.	*no se sabe con seguridad*
It is not necessarily the case.	*no es necesariamente así*
I am not sure *o* **I am not certain** *o* **I am not convinced** *o* **I cannot say definitely that** these goods will sell.	*no estoy seguro de que*
We are still in the dark about where the letter came from.	*seguimos sin saber*
I am wondering if I should offer to help them out?	*estoy dudando si debía*
There is no proof what he says is correct.	*no existen pruebas de que*
It is touch-and-go whether they can save the company.	*es difícil saber si será posible*
It's all still up in the air – we shan't know for certain until the end of next week.	*está todavía por decidir*
It is debatable whether there is any value in interviewing him so long after the event.	*no está claro que*
It's anyone's guess who will be chosen.	*no se puede prever*
I have my doubts about the value of the experiment.	*tengo mis dudas en lo que respecta a*

PARA EXPRESAR IMPROBABILIDAD

It is highly improbable that there could be any saving in the original budget.	*es poco probable que*
You probably have not yet seen the document I am referring to.	*probablemente todavía no ha*
In the unlikely event that she should get in touch with you, please let me know immediately.	*en el caso improbable de que*
There is but a small chance that anyone survived such a horrendous accident.	*apenas existe una pequeña posibilidad de que*
It is scarcely to be expected that the university will contribute towards the cost.	*no se puede esperar que*

PARA EXPRESAR IMPOSIBILIDAD

Such a thing **cannot** happen.	*no puede*
It cannot be the case that they want to return to the East.	*no puede ser que*
It is quite impossible that *o* **It is out of the question that** *o* **It is unthinkable that** such a thing should happen.	*es inconcebible que*
They **couldn't possibly have** arrived already.	*no es posible que hayan*
This rules out any possibility of their working with us again.	*esto descarta cualquier posibilidad de que*
There is not (even) the remotest chance that *o* **There is absolutely no chance that** he will succeed.	*no hay ni la más remota posibilidad de que*
There is no question of our giving them a contribution to this fund.	*está descartada la posibilidad de que*
There can be no return to earlier standards.	*no cabe*

PARA EXPRESAR LO QUE ALGUIEN ES CAPAZ O INCAPAZ DE HACER

I can drive a car.//**I am able to** drive a car.//**I know how to** drive a car.	*sé*
I can't drive a car, I'm afraid.//**I don't know how to** drive a car.	*no sé*
Applicants **must be able to** use a word processor.	*deben ser capaces de*
Can you speak Spanish?//**Do you speak** Spanish?	*¿habla usted español?*
I can *o* **I am able to** lend him the money.	*puedo*
He is quite incapable of telling a lie.//**He is quite unable to** tell a lie.//**He cannot** tell a lie.	*es completamente incapaz de*
He was quite **incapable of** passing that examination.//He was quite **unable to** pass it.	*fue incapaz de*
It is quite impossible for me to be in Paris next week.//**I cannot** be in Paris next week.	*me es completamente imposible//no puedo*
We are not in a position to give any sort of decision yet.	*no estamos en situación de*
He has been ill, and is still **not up to** *o* **equal to** any heavy work.	*le es imposible*
I'm quite hopeless at *o* **I am no good at** decorating and practical things.	*no sirvo para*
I'm afraid the task proved quite **beyond his powers** *o* **beyond his capabilities** *o* **beyond his abilities.**//It proved quite **beyond him.**	*él no estuvo/estaba a la altura de*
He simply **could not cope with** the stresses of family life.	*no pudo hacer frente a*
He **is qualified to** teach physics.	*está capacitado para*

EXPLICACIONES

PREPOSICIONES

He had to refuse promotion, **because of** *o* **on account of** his wife's health.	*a causa de*
He behaved like that **out of** *o* **through** *o* **from** sheer embarrassment.	*por*
Owing to lack of time, we have been unable to complete the job.	*por*
We have been forced to reduce our staff **as a result of** the economic crisis.	*como consecuencia de*
I have succeeded in proving my innocence, **thanks to** your timely help.	*gracias a*
By virtue of his connection with the family, he was allowed to enter the building.	*en virtud de*
The government financed this **by means of** massive tax increases.	*por medio de*
In exchange for *o* **In return for** financial aid, we gave them a lot of publicity.	*a cambio de*
Following this incident, all trade between the two countries was stopped.	*a raíz de*
We gave them the contract **on the strength of** these promises.	*sobre la base de*
In view of their poor production record, we have decided not to renew their contract.	*en vista de*
In the light of what has happened so far, we have decided not to renew their licence.	*en vista de*
The Government extended police powers **in the face of** the renewed outbursts of violence.	*ante*
He hid the wallet, **for fear of** being accused of having stolen it.	*por miedo a*
We cannot do this **for lack of** *o* **for want of** funds.	*por falta de*
With so many people there, it was difficult to find him.	*con*

CONJUNCIONES

They won't come, **because** they can't afford it.	*porque*
They won't come, **for the simple reason that** they can't afford it.	*por la sencilla razón de que*
As we have none in stock at the moment, we are forced to delay this shipment.	*como*
Given that inflation is still rising, house prices are unlikely to remain stable.	*dado que*
Since for the moment these are out of stock, we cannot dispatch your order.	*puesto que*
Seeing that *o* **In view of the fact that** there is no money left, we cannot do what we planned.	*en vista de que*
This will have no immediate effect, **for** some delay is inevitable.	*pues*
They can't afford it, **so** they won't come.	*así (es) que*
We have to re-order the parts: **therefore** there will be a delay of several weeks.	*por (lo) tanto*
He refused, **on the grounds that** he had so little time at his disposal.	*con el pretexto de que*
Now (that) beef is so expensive, more people are buying pork.	*ahora que*

VOCABULARIO DE POSIBLE UTILIDAD

I attribute this to lack of foresight on the part of the committee.	*lo atribuyo a*
The change in his attitude was **caused by** *o* **brought about by** their rejection of his proposals.	*se produjo a consecuencia de*
The situation **goes back to** *o* **dates from** his decision not to contest the seat.	*se remonta a*
This situation is **due to** an unfortunate miscalculation on our part.	*se debe a*
He was retired early, **on** health **grounds** *o* **for** health **reasons.**	*por razones de*
It was like this: she had been ill for several weeks and hadn't heard the news.	*lo que pasó fue que*
This alteration to the programme **gave rise to** *o* **provoked** *o* **produced** a lot of comment.	*dio lugar a*
The reason that they withdrew was that the scheme cost too much.	*la razón por la cual*
It was her stupidity that **led to** *o* **caused** the accident.	*causó*
The thing is that her French isn't good enough.	*es que*

DISCULPAS

I'm really very sorry – I can't come on Sunday after all, as I have to go and visit my sister.	*lo siento muchísimo*
I'm sorry to disturb you.//**I'm sorry that** you have been troubled.	*perdone/perdone que*
I can't tell you how sorry I am about this unfortunate incident.	*no sé como decirte cuánto lo siento*
Please forgive me for not asking your permission before approaching him.	*le ruego que me disculpe por*
Do forgive me – I should have checked with your office first.	*perdone*
I must apologise for all the inconvenience you have been caused.	*discúlpenme por*
I am sorry to have to tell you that your application arrived too late.	*siento tener que decirle que*

(de manera más protocolaria)

I would ask you to excuse this misunderstanding on our part.	*le ruego que me dispense*
I can only apologise once again, on behalf of the Committee, for the disturbances at your lecture.	*una vez más le pido disculpas por*
I am writing to ask you to forgive our apparent rudeness in not replying to your original letter.	*me dirijo a ustedes para rogarles que nos disculpen*
We send you our most sincere apologies for all the difficulties that have occurred in this matter.	*lamentamos sinceramente lo ocurrido y le pedimos disculpas por*

(para decir que se lamenta lo sucedido)

I am very upset about the whole affair, which should never have happened.	*estoy muy disgustado (Sp)* or *apenado (LAm) por*
I am really ashamed of what happened last week.	*me siento realmente avergonzado por*
I wish I hadn't mentioned it at all, although at the time it didn't seem important.	*ojalá no lo hubiera mencionado nunca*
I should never have said a thing like that.	*nunca debí haber*
To my great regret, we have been unable to dissuade him.	*muy a pesar mío*
Unfortunately, it is not possible for me to do any more to help you in this matter.	*por desgracia no puedo*
I am entirely to blame for all this – I should have phoned the travel agency myself.	*la culpa es toda mía*
It is my fault that this misunderstanding happened, and I have written to the head of department explaining the circumstances.	*yo tengo la culpa de que*
I have absolutely no excuse for this error on my part.	*el error que cometí no tiene justificación alguna*
I am afraid I quite forgot about it until the office had closed.	*me temo que*
I admit I gave him the papers, and should not have done so.	*admito que*
It was an accident – I can assure you **I didn't mean to** break the clock.	*fue un accidente ... lo hice sin querer*
I really didn't do it on purpose – I had not realised that the handle had already been damaged.	*de veras no lo hice a propósito*
It is exceedingly unfortunate that the tickets were mislaid.	*es muy de lamentar que*
We regret to inform you that *o* **We must regretfully inform you that** this title is now out of print.	*lamento tener que informarle que*
We very much regret that we cannot publish this work.	*lo sentimos mucho, pero no podemos*

(para sugerir una explicación)

I was simply trying to give you less work.	*yo sólo quería*
You may find this difficult to believe, but **I thought I was doing the right thing.**	*yo lo hice con toda mi buena intención*
There has obviously been an error in our accounting procedure, possibly owing to our recent change in computing facilities.	*está claro que ha habido un error*
I was anxious not to upset him any more, as he was clearly very worried by what happened.	*quería evitar la posibilidad de*
We were obliged to accept their conditions.	*nos vimos obligados a*
We were under the impression that these figures had been passed by the Accounts Office.	*teníamos entendido que*
We had unfortunately no choice in the matter.	*por desgracia, no tuvimos otra alternativa*
I can assure you that **I had nothing to do with** the arrangements.	*yo no tuve nada que ver con*
We had no alternative but to terminate his contract at once.	*no pudimos hacer otra cosa que*

11 North Street
Barnton,
BN7 2BT

19th February, 1993

The Personnel Director,
Messrs. J.M. Kenyon Ltd.,
Firebrick House,
Clifton, MC45 6RB

Dear Sir or Madam,[1]

With reference to your advertisement in today's Guardian, I wish to apply for the post of systems analyst.

I enclose my curriculum vitae. Please do not hesitate to contact me if you require any further details.

Yours faithfully,

CURRICULUM VITAE

NAME	Rosalind Anna WILLIAMSON
ADDRESS	11 North Street, Barnton, BN7 2BT, England
TELEPHONE	Barnton (0294) 476230
DATE OF BIRTH	6.5.1963
MARITAL STATUS	Single
NATIONALITY	British
QUALIFICATIONS[2]	B.A. 2nd class Honours degree in Italian with French, University of Newby, England (June 1985) A-levels: Italian (A), French (B), English (D) (1981) O-Levels in 9 subjects. (1979)
PRESENT POST	Assistant Personnel Officer, Metal Company plc, Barnton (since January 1987)
PREVIOUS EMPLOYMENT	Nov. 1985 - Jan. 1986: Personnel trainee, Metal Company plc. Oct. 1981 - June 1985: Student, University of Newby.

SKILLS, INTERESTS AND EXPERIENCE: fluent Italian & French; adequate German; some Russian; car owner and driver (clean licence); riding & sailing.

THE FOLLOWING HAVE AGREED TO PROVIDE REFERENCES:

Ms. Alice Bluegown, Personnel Manager, Metal Company plc, Barnton, NB4 3KL

Dr. I.O. Sono, Department of Italian, University of Newby, Newby, SR13 2RR

[1] Cuando no se sabe si el destinatario es hombre o mujer, se debe usar esta fórmula. Por otra parte, si se conoce la identidad del destinatario se puede utilizar una de estas formas al escribir el nombre y dirección:

Mr Derek Balder,
Mrs Una Claridge,
Ms Nicola Stokes,
O
Personnel Director
Messrs. J.M. Kenyon Ltd. etc.

En el encabezamiento de la carta, las fórmulas correspondientes serían: "Dear Mr Balder", "Dear Mrs Claridge" etc, "Dear Sir/Madam" (según corresponda, si se sabe si es hombre o mujer), "Dear Sir or Madam" (si no se sabe).

Las cartas que comienzan con el nombre de la persona en el encabezamiento (e.g. "Dear Mr Balder") pueden terminar con la fórmula de despedida "Yours sincerely"; las que empiezan con "Dear Sir/Madam" normalmente acaban con "Yours faithfully", seguido de la firma. Véanse más detalles en las páginas 892 y 894.

[2] Si se solicita un puesto en el extranjero se puede emplear una frase que explique el título académico que se posee, p.ej. "Spanish/Mexican etc. equivalent of A-Levels (bachillerato superior)", "equivalent to a degree in Modern Languages etc. (licenciatura en Filología Moderna etc)".

EXPRESIONES ÚTILES

In reply to your advertisement for a trainee manager in today's *Daily News*, I should be grateful if you would please send me further details of this post, together with an application form.

En contestación a su anuncio aparecido en el 'Daily News' de hoy, le agradecería que me enviase más información sobre este puesto, junto con los impresos necesarios para hacer la solicitud.

I am a first-year Modern Languages student and I would like to work in Spain next summer. I would be grateful if you could send me the information brochure '*Campos de trabajo para estudiantes*' which I have seen advertised in the Students' Union.

Soy estudiante de 1.° de Idiomas Modernos, y desearía trabajar en España durante el próximo verano. Les agradecería que me mandasen el folleto explicativo 'Campos de trabajo para estudiantes' que he visto anunciado en la oficina del sindicato estudiantil.

I have three years' experience of office work, and have used a word-processor.

Tengo tres años de experiencia de trabajo de oficina, y sé utilizar el ordenador de textos.

Although I have not got any previous experience of this type of work, I have had other holiday jobs, and can supply references from my employers, if you would like them.

Aunque no tengo experiencia previa de este tipo de trabajo, he desempeñado otros trabajos eventuales de vacaciones y le puedo dar los nombres de las entidades con las que he estado empleado, si los desea.

My present salary is ... per annum, and I have four weeks holiday per year with pay.

Mi sueldo anual es ..., y tengo cuatro semanas de vacaciones pagadas al año.

I am particularly interested in this job, as I am very anxious to work in publishing.

Tengo especial interés en este puesto, pues tengo grandes deseos de trabajar en una casa editorial.

I wish to work in England in order to improve my English and to gain experience of hotel work.

Deseo trabajar en Inglaterra a fin de mejorar mis conocimientos del inglés y para obtener experiencia del trabajo de hostelería.

As well as speaking Spanish, I have a good knowledge of English, and speak some French and German.

Además del español, mi lengua materna, poseo buenos conocimientos del inglés y hablo algo de francés y alemán.

I shall be available from the end of April.

Estaría disponible para comenzar el trabajo después del final de abril.

I enclose a stamped addressed envelope for your reply.

Adjunto un sobre franqueado y con la dirección, para su respuesta.

Thank you for your letter of 19th March. I shall be pleased to attend for interview at your offices in Park Lane on Thursday, 24th March, at 10.30 a.m.

He recibido su amable carta del 19 de marzo. Tendré mucho gusto en asistir a la entrevista, en sus oficinas de Park Lane, el jueves 24 de marzo, a las 10.30.

I have to give names of two referees with my application for this job, and I am writing to ask if you would be kind enough to allow me to put your name forward.

Al presentar mi solicitud para este puesto tengo que mencionar a dos personas que estén dispuestas a facilitar un informe confidencial sobre mí, y por tanto me dirijo a usted para preguntarle si tendría la amabilidad de permitirme que diese su nombre para este fin.

I have applied for a job in the Beaufort Hotel in Furness and they have asked me to provide the names of two people in companies where I have worked to date who will give references. I would be very grateful if you would be one of my referees. If you are prepared to provide a reference, they will contact you directly.

He solicitado un puesto de trabajo en el hotel Beaufort de Furness, el cual me ha comunicado que precisa, como referencias, los nombres de dos directivos de compañías en las que haya trabajado hasta ahora. Le agradecería mucho que fuese usted una de esas personas. Si tiene la amabilidad de aceptar, el hotel se dirigirá a usted directamente.

Mr James Henderson has applied for the job of hotel receptionist with us and has given your name as a referee. We would be grateful if you would kindly let us know whether in your opinion he is suitable for this post.

El señor James Henderson ha solicitado la plaza (Sp) or vacante (LAm) de recepcionista en este hotel y ha citado su nombre como el de la persona que puede enviarnos un informe confidencial acerca de su aptitud para este tipo de trabajo. Le agradeceríamos mucho que nos dijera si, en su opinión, este señor es una persona idónea para este tipo de trabajo.

Your answer will be treated in confidence.

Su respuesta será tratada con la mayor reserva y discreción.

Would you be kind enough to mention in your reply how long you have known Miss Jones, in what capacity, and whether you can recommend her for this type of employment.

Le rogamos que en su respuesta mencione cuánto tiempo hace que conoce a la señorita Jones y en qué capacidad, y si se siente capaz de recomendarla para este tipo de empleo.

It is with pleasure that I write to recommend Mrs Amy Whitehead for the post of housing officer: I have known her for over ten years, during which time I have found her to be cheerful and helpful at all times, and completely reliable.

Me es muy grato recomendarles a la señora Amy Whitehead para el puesto de funcionaria encargada de los asuntos relativos a la vivienda. Hace más de diez años que conozco a esta señora, y siempre me ha parecido una persona de carácter agradable y buena voluntad, así como digna de toda confianza.

James & Hedgehopper Limited

MASTER CUTLERS
Railway Arcade, Harley SG16 4BD

Tel: Harley (0123) 99876

29th January, 1993

Dr. T. Armitage,
65 Middlewich Street,
Addenborough,
AG3 9LL

Dear Sir,

Thank you for your letter of 23rd January. We still stock the type of knife that you are looking for, and are pleased to enclose our catalogue and price list. We would draw your attention to the discount prices which are operative until 15th March on this range of goods.

Yours faithfully,
for JAMES & HEDGEHOPPER LTD

William Osgood

William Osgood
Managing Director

SMITH, JONES & ROBINSON LIMITED

Rainwear Manufacturers
Block 39, Newtown Industrial Estate,
Newtown SV7 3QS

Tel: 0965 477366

8th August, 1993

Our ref: SAL/35/IM
Your ref: JCB/JO

Messrs. Kidsfunwear Ltd.,
3 High Street,
Barnton, BN17 2EJ

For the attention of Mr. J. Brown

Dear Sir,

Thank you for your enquiry about our children's rainwear. We have pleasure in enclosing our latest catalogue and current price list, and would draw your attention particularly to our SUNFLOWER range. We are prepared to offer the usual discount on these items, and we look forward to receiving your order.

Yours faithfully,

Ian MacIntosh

Ian MacIntosh

Sales Department

PETICIÓN DE INFORMACIÓN

We see from your latest catalogue that there is a special offer for office furniture.

Según hemos comprobado en la última edición de su catálogo general, tienen una oferta especial de muebles de oficina.

We would be grateful if you could send us full details of this offer, including prices, wholesale discounts, payment terms and delivery times.

Les agradeceríamos que nos enviasen la información necesaria sobre esta oferta, incluyendo precios, descuentos por pedidos al por mayor, forma de pago y fechas de entrega.

... Y RESPUESTAS

Thank you for your letter of the 12th. We are pleased to inform you that all the products you mention are part of our current range, and so we are sure we can assist you. Please send us full details of what you require.

Les agradecemos su carta del 12 del corriente, y nos complace poder decirles que todos los productos que ustedes mencionan son parte de nuestra producción actual, por lo que confiamos en poder servirles. Tengan la bondad de darnos detalles completos de lo que necesitan.

In answer to your letter of 5 August we are pleased to send you a complete price list, and details of purchase terms, despatch, methods of payment and the guarantees we offer.

En contestación a su carta de fecha 5 de agosto, nos complacemos en enviarles nuestra lista completa de precios, condiciones de compra, envío de los productos, formas de pago y el tipo de garantías que ofrecemos.

PEDIDOS

Please send the following items as soon as possible, preferably by airmail:

Les rogamos nos envíen cuanto antes, a ser posible por correo aéreo, los artículos siguientes:

This order is based on the information in the general catalogue you sent us last month.

Este pedido se basa en la información contenida en el catálogo general de sus productos, que ustedes nos enviaron el mes pasado.

... Y RESPUESTAS

Thank you for your order of 11 March, which we will deal with as soon as possible.

Les agradecemos su pedido de fecha 11 de marzo, que ejecutaremos a la mayor brevedad.

We have received the order for new machinery which we will very shortly put into production.

Hemos recibido el encargo que nos hacen de nueva maquinaria, cuya producción iniciaremos en breve.

Unfortunately we cannot attend to your order immediately, but we are confident that we will be able to send you everything at the beginning of next month.

Lamentamos no poder atender inmediatamente el envío de los pedidos que nos hacen en su atenta carta, pero confiamos en poder mandárselos todos a principios del próximo mes.

ENTREGAS

We await your instructions with regard to delivery of the goods.

Estamos a la espera de sus instrucciones en lo que respecta a la entrega de las mercancías.

Your order was dealt with on the 4th and the goods were sent airmail on Monday last week.

Su pedido se ejecutó el día 4 del presente y los productos fueron enviados por correo aéreo el lunes de la semana pasada.

Please note that we have not yet received the items we asked for in our letter of 4 July.

Deseamos comunicarles que todavía no hemos recibido los artículos que pedimos en nuestra carta con fecha 4 de julio.

We acknowledge receipt of the consignment you sent on 9 September.

Acusamos recibo de la remesa que Vds despacharon el día 9 de septiembre.

We wish to draw your attention to an error in the last consignment of goods we received.

Con la presente queremos informarles que ha habido un error en el envío de la última remesa de productos que hemos recibido.

We regret that we are unable to accept any responsibility for the damage to the goods.

Lo sentimos mucho, pero no nos es posible aceptar responsabilidad alguna por los daños sufridos por las mercancías.

PAGOS

Please find enclosed our invoice no. 87961.

Tenemos mucho gusto en adjuntar nuestra factura número 87961.

The total value of the goods we have sent is ....

El valor de los productos enviados asciende a ....

We would be grateful if you would settle this account as soon as possible.

Les agradeceríamos que nos enviasen la liquidación lo antes posible.

We have pleasure in enclosing cheque no. 873451 for ... in settlement of your invoice no. 50702.

Nos complace adjuntar el talón bancario or *cheque núm. 873451 por valor de ... en liquidación de la factura recibida oportunamente, núm. 50702.*

We would like to draw your attention to an error we have found in the amount you sent us in settlement of invoice no. ..., and we would be grateful if you could send us the balance.

Nos permitimos señalar un error que hemos detectado en la cantidad que nos han girado en pago de la factura núm. ..., y les agradeceríamos que tuvieran la amabilidad de enviar el saldo correspondiente.

The mistake was due to a book-keeping error. Please accept our apologies. We have pleasure in enclosing a cheque for the difference between the amount of the invoice and payment made so far.

La equivocación se debió a un error de contabilidad. Les pedimos que nos disculpen, y tenemos sumo gusto en adjuntar un cheque por la diferencia entre el pago efectuado y el valor de su factura.

11 South Street
BARCOMBE
BN7 2BT

14th November, 1993

Dear Betty,

It seems such a long time since we last met and caught up with each other's news. However, I'm writing to say that Peter and I plan to take our holiday this summer in the Lake District, and we'll be driving past Preston on the M6 some time during the morning of Friday, July 23rd. Will you be at home then? Perhaps we could call in? It would be lovely to see you and Alan again and to get news of Janie and Mark. Do let me know whether Friday, 23rd is convenient. We would expect to arrive at your place at around 11 a.m. or so, and hope very much to see you then.

With love from

Susan

---

65 Middlewich Street,
ADDENBOROUGH.
AG3 9LL

23rd January, 1993

Mr. J. Hedgehopper,
Hedgehopper's Knives Ltd.,
Railway Arcade,
HARLEY

Dear Mr Hedgehopper,

Some years ago I bought a SHARPCUTTER knife from you, and, as you know, it has been invaluable to me. Unfortunately, however, I have now lost it, and wonder if you still stock this range? If so, I should be grateful if you would let me have details of the various types of knife you make, and of their prices.

Yours sincerely,

Thomas Armitage

Thomas Armitage

A ALGUIEN CONOCIDO PERSONALMENTE

Dear Mr. Brown, Dear Mrs. Drake, Dear Mr. & Mrs. Charlton, Dear Miss Baker, Dear Ms. Black, Dear Dr. Armstrong, Dear Professor Lyons, Dear Sir Gerald, Dear Lady McLeod, Dear Andrew, Dear Margaret,	Yours sincerely With all good wishes, Yours sincerely With kindest regards, Yours sincerely	*tratamiento más cordial*

A UN(A) AMIGO(A), A UN PARIENTE

Dear Victoria,	With love from	
My dear Albert,	Love from	
Dear Aunt Eleanor,		
Dear Granny and Grandad,	Love to all	
Dear Mum and Dad,	Love from us all	
My dear Elizabeth,	Yours	*tratamiento familiar*
Dearest Norman,	All the best	
My dearest Mother,		
My dearest Dorinda,	With much love from	
My darling Augustus,	Lots of love from	*tratamiento afectuoso*
	Much love, as always	
	All my love	

CARTAS COMERCIALES (véase también pág. 892)

Dear Sirs,[1]		
Dear Sir,[2]		[2] *para dirigirse a un hombre*
Dear Madam,[3]	Yours faithfully	[3] *para dirigirse a una mujer*
Dear Sir or Madam,[4]		[4] *cuando no se sabe si se dirige uno a un hombre o una mujer*

A UN CONOCIDO O UN(A) AMIGO(A)

Dear Alison,	Yours sincerely	
Dear Annie and George,		
Dear Uncle Eric,	With best wishes, Yours sincerely	
Dear Mrs. Newman,		
Dear Mr. and Mrs. Jones,	With kindest regards, Yours sincerely	*tratamiento más cordial*
My dear Miss Armitage,	All good wishes, Yours sincerely	
	With best wishes, *(etc)* Yours ever	
	Kindest regards, Best wishes	*tratamiento familiar*
	With best wishes, As always	

PARA EMPEZAR UNA CARTA

I was delighted to get your letter last week.	*Me he alegrado mucho de recibir tu carta de la semana pasada.*
It was a nice surprise to hear from you after all this time.	*Por fin tuve la agradable sorpresa de tener noticias tuyas, después de tanto tiempo.*
I'm sorry to have taken so long to answer your letter of April 12, but I've been very, very busy.	*Perdona que haya tardado tanto en contestar a tu carta del 12 de abril, pero es que he estado ocupadísima.*
You may be surprised to get this letter after such a long silence.	*Supongo que será una sorpresa para ti recibir esta carta después de un silencio tan largo.*
After mulling it over I have decided to write this letter, which is not going to be at all easy.	*Después de mucho pensarlo, me he decidido a escribir esta carta, lo que no me va a resultar nada fácil.*
It was good to hear from you.	*Nos alegramos de tener noticias de usted(es).*
Thank you very much for your letter of ...	*Formal: ayer tuve el gusto de recibir su carta con fecha de*
I am writing to you to ask for information about	*Tengo el gusto de dirigirme a usted para solicitar información sobre ...*
I am writing to ask if you could obtain the following books for me:	*Me dirijo a ustedes para preguntar si les sería posible conseguirme los siguientes libros:*
Would you please send me ... I enclose my cheque for £35.50.	*Les ruego que me envíen ... adjunto cheque por valor de £35.50.*
You will probably remember that my family and I stayed at your hotel for two days last week. I am writing to ask if you have found the coat my daughter left in her room.	*Probablemente recordará usted que mi familia y yo pasamos dos días en el hotel de su digna dirección la semana pasada. Me dirijo a Vd para preguntar si han encontrado el abrigo que mi hija dejó olvidado en su habitación.*

PARA TERMINAR UNA CARTA

Best wishes from Juan and the children, yours (+ *firma*).	*Muchos recuerdos de Juan y de los niños, y un saludo muy afectuoso para ti de ...*
Looking forward to hearing from you.	*Quedo a la espera de tus noticias.*
Best regards to your mother and best wishes from me, (+ *firma*).	*Un cordial saludo para tu madre, y un afectuoso abrazo de ...*
María sends you her warmest regards. Hoping to see you soon (+ *firma*).	*María dice que te mande un abrazo de su parte. Hasta cuando gustes venir a vernos, que ojalá sea pronto.*
We wish you the very best luck with your plans. Kindest regards to you all.	*Te deseamos mucha suerte en tus planes, y nos despedimos con un cariñoso saludo para ti y los tuyos.*
Hoping you enjoy your holidays, yours (+ *firma*).	*Que disfrutes mucho de las vacaciones. Un abrazo de ...*
Remember us to your family. Yours (+ *firma*).	*Dale recuerdos a tu familia de nuestra parte. Hasta siempre, ...*
You know that if you want anything all you have to do is let me know.	*Ya sabes que estoy para lo que mandes.*
Hoping to hear from you soon. Do write when you can.	*Hasta pronto. No dejes de escribir en cuanto puedas.*
We look forward to hearing from you very soon.	*Esperamos tener muy pronto noticias tuyas.*
Affectionately, (+ *firma*).	*Tu amigo que no te olvida, ...*

PREPARATIVOS DE VIAJES

I would be grateful if you could send me your price list.	*Les agradecería que me enviaran su lista de precios.*
I would like to book a room for the night of 3 July for one night only.	*Quisiera reservar una habitación en su hotel para la noche del 3 de julio próximo, por una noche solamente.*
Please would you confirm by return the reservation I made in my earlier letter for two double rooms, with shower, and full board, for the week of 7 to 14 September.	*Les quedaría muy agradecido si pudiesen confirmar a vuelta de correo la reserva* (*Sp*) *or reservación* (*LAm*) *que hice en mi carta anterior de dos habitaciones dobles, con ducha y pensión completa, para la semana del 7 al 14 de septiembre.*
Please let me know if I have to pay a deposit in order to confirm the booking.	*Les ruego tengan la bondad de decirme si es necesario pagar un depósito al confirmar la reserva.*
Please keep our room for us on September 3, even though we may be late in arriving.	*Quisiera rogarles que mantengan la reserva* (*Sp*) *or reservación* (*LAm*) *de la habitación para el 3 de septiembre, aunque nos retrasemos en llegar.*

AGRADECIMIENTOS Y SALUDOS

AGRADECIMIENTOS

I am writing to thank you for the favour you did us.	*escribo para darte las gracias por*
I am very grateful to you for what you did for me.	*te estoy muy agradecida por*
Please thank your husband from me for his help in arranging everything.	*por favor, dale las gracias de mi parte a tu marido por*
Thank you very much indeed for all your kindness during my stay with your family.	*les agradezco sinceramente todas sus atenciones*
I would like to thank you on behalf of the Sales Manager **for** your help in making the conference such a success.	*me dirijo a ustedes en nombre de ... para expresarles su agradecimiento por*
Please give our warmest thanks to your colleagues for their contribution.	*le ruego que transmita a sus colegas nuestro reconocimiento por*

SALUDOS

NB: *En esta sección* [...] *representa 'a Merry Christmas and a Happy New Year', 'a happy birthday', 'a speedy recovery' etc.*

With all good wishes for [...] from (+ *signature*).	*(fórmula que se suele emplear en una tarjeta, que puede acompañar un regalo) con un cordial saludo de ...*
With love and best wishes for [...].	*con un afectuoso saludo y recuerdos de*
Do give my best wishes to your mother for [...].	*le ruego que le dé recuerdos a su madre, a quien deseo ...*
Roger joins me in sending you all our very best wishes for [...].	*Roger y yo les enviamos un cordial saludo y les deseamos ...*

(por Navidad o Año Nuevo)

With Season's greetings, and very best wishes from (+ *signature*).	*les deseamos que pasen bien las fiestas de fin de año*
Mary and I send you all our very best wishes for 1993.	*Mary y yo les deseamos que el año nuevo les traiga todo tipo de suerte y felicidad*

(en el cumpleaños)

I am writing to wish you many happy returns of the day.	*muchas felicidades en tu cumpleaños*
This is to send you our fondest love and very best wishes on your eighteenth birthday – Many Happy Returns from us all.	*aquí va un abrazo muy fuerte de todos nosotros y el deseo de que pases muy bien el día de tu cumpleaños*
I'd like to wish you a happy birthday for next Saturday.	*te deseo que el sábado tengas un cumpleaños muy feliz*

(para desear restablecimiento de la salud)

I was very sorry to hear that you were not well, and send you my best wishes for a speedy recovery.	*siento mucho que no te encuentres bien, y te deseo que te repongas cuanto antes*

(para desear suerte en algo)

NB: En esta sección [...] *representa 'interview', 'driving test', 'exam', 'new job' etc.*

I am writing to send you best wishes for your [...].	*le escribo para desearle todo lo mejor en*
Good luck for your [...] – I hope things go well for you on Friday.	*le deseo buena suerte en*

(para felicitar a alguien por algo)

This is to send you our warmest congratulations and best wishes on [...].	*nuestra más sincera enhorabuena* (Sp) or *felicitaciones y mejores deseos en la ocasión de*
Allow me to offer you my heartiest congratulations on [...].	*permítame que le ofrezca mi enhorabuena más sincera por*
We all send you our love and congratulations on such an excellent result.	*te felicitamos todos por ... y te mandamos un abrazo muy fuerte*

ANUNCIOS, INVITACIONES Y RESPUESTAS

ANUNCIO DE NATALIDAD

Mr. and Mrs. Jonathan Ridge are happy to announce the birth of their daughter Emma, in Glasgow, on 20 June 1992.

'los señores de Ridge tienen sumo gusto en anunciar'

I am very glad to say that Hamish and Stephanie had a son, William Rupert, on 22 August, and that mother and child are both well.

Carta a un amigo o conocido: 'me es muy grato comunicarle que Hamish y Stephanie han tenido un hijo, al que han puesto el nombre de ...'

... Y RESPUESTAS

With warmest congratulations to you both on the birth of your son, and best wishes to Alexander for good health and happiness throughout his life.

Tarjeta: 'nuestra sincera enhorabuena a los dos por el nacimiento de ...'

We were delighted to learn of the birth of Diana and send our most sincere congratulations to you both, and our very best wishes to the baby for health, happiness and prosperity throughout her life.

Tarjeta: 'nos hemos alegrado mucho de enterarnos del nacimiento de la pequeña Diana y les damos nuestra sincera enhorabuena a los padres'

PARA ANUNCIAR UN COMPROMISO DE BODA

Mr. and Mrs. Robert Jamieson are pleased to announce the engagement of their daughter Fiona to Mr. Joseph Bloggs.

Anuncio: 'se complacen en anunciar el compromiso de boda de'

Polly and Richard have got engaged – you can imagine how delighted we all are about this.

Carta a un amigo o conocido: 'se han prometido: puedes imaginar lo contentos que estamos todos'

... Y RESPUESTAS

Fiona and Joseph: with our warmest congratulations on your engagement, and our best wishes for a long and happy life together.

Tarjeta que acompaña un regalo: 'Nuestras más sinceras felicitaciones por vuestro compromiso de boda'

I was very glad to learn of your engagement to Richard, and send you both my congratulations and very best wishes for your future happiness.

Carta a un amigo o conocido: 'Me he alegrado mucho de enterarme de que te has prometido a Richard'

ANUNCIO DE BODA

Mr. and Mrs. William Morris are happy to announce the marriage of their daughter Sarah to Mr. Jack Bond, in St. Francis Church, Newtown, on 11 September 1992.

Anuncio: 'se complacen en anunciar la boda de'

Stephen and Amanda were married here, in the registry office, last Saturday.

Carta a un amigo o conocido: 'Stephen y Amanda se casaron ... el sábado pasado'

... Y RESPUESTAS

With congratulations on your marriage and all good wishes to you both for your future happiness.

Tarjeta que acompaña un regalo: 'felicitaciones por vuestra boda; os deseamos un futuro muy feliz'

We were delighted to learn of your daughter's marriage to Jack Bond, and send you our best wishes on this happy occasion.

Carta a un conocido: 'Nos hemos alegrado mucho de saber que'

I was so glad to hear that you and Robin were getting married, and send you both my most sincere congratulations and best wishes for your future happiness.

Carta a un amigo: 'Me he alegrado mucho de saber que'

PARA ANUNCIAR UN FALLECIMIENTO

Mrs. Mary Smith announces with deep sorrow the death of her husband, John R. Smith, at Sheffield, on 8th August 1992, after a long illness. The funeral took place privately.

Anuncio: 'se duele en participar el fallecimiento de': En caso de que se anuncie 'No letters, please', es mejor no escribir

It is with the deepest sorrow that I have to tell you that Joe's father passed away three weeks ago.

Carta a un conocido: 'Con gran dolor, tenemos que participarle que'

I lost my dear wife a little over a month ago.

Carta a un amigo: '... perdí a mi querida esposa'

... Y RESPUESTAS

My husband and I were greatly saddened to learn of the passing of Dr. Smith, and send you and your family our most sincere condolences in your very sad loss. *Carta a un conocido: 'deseamos expresar a usted y a su familia nuestro más sentido pésame'*

I was terribly upset to hear of Jim's death, and I am writing to send you all my warmest love and deepest sympathy in your tragic loss. *Carta a un amigo: 'Me ha llegado la triste noticia de la muerte ... y te escribo para decirte que lo siento enormemente.'*

INVITACIONES OFICIALES

Mr. and Mrs. Mark Green request the pleasure of the company of Mr. James Brown at the marriage of their daughter Annabel to Mr. Paul Piper, in St. Peter's Church, Newtown, on Saturday, 19th February 1993 at 3 p.m., and afterwards at the Grand Hotel, Newtown. *'solicitan el placer de la compañia del Sr. James Brown en la ocasión de la boda de'*

The Chairman and Governors of Trentbury College request the pleasure of the company of Miss Charlotte Young at a dinner to mark the fiftieth anniversary of the founding of the college. *'solicitan el placer de la compañia de'*

Peter and Susan Atkins request the pleasure of your company at a reception (*o* dinner *etc*) to celebrate their Silver Wedding, on Saturday, 10 July 1994, at 8 p.m. at the Bows Hotel. *'tienen el placer de invitarle a la recepción'*

... Y RESPUESTAS

Mr. James Brown thanks Mr. and Mrs. Green for their kind invitation to the marriage of their daughter Annabel on 19th February, and accepts with pleasure/but regrets that he is unable to accept. *'agradece su amable invitación ... que le es muy grato aceptar/ que lamenta no poder aceptar'*

Miss Charlotte Young wishes to thank the Chairman and Governors of Trentbury College for thir kind invitation to dinner and has much pleasure in accepting/but regrets that she is unable to accept. *'agradece su amable invitación ... que tiene mucho gusto en aceptar/que lamenta tener que declinar'*

INVITACIONES PARA AMIGOS Y CONOCIDOS

We are celebrating Rosemary's engagement to David by holding a dinner and dance at the Central Hotel on Friday, 21st March, and very much hope that you will be able to join us then. *'vamos a celebrar el compromiso de boda ... y están ustedes invitados'*

We are giving a small dinner party on Saturday next for Lorna and Ian, who are home from Canada for a few weeks, and hope you will be able to come. *'vamos a dar una cena en honor de ... y nos encantaria que ustedes pudiesen asistir'*

We should be very pleased if you and Letitia could dine with us on the Sunday evening, if you have arrived in town by then. *'nos sería muy grato que ... cenasen con nosotros'*

Our Managing Director, James Glasgow, will be in Edinburgh on Friday 16 November, and we are holding a small dinner party for him on that day at 8 p.m. here. We hope that you and Margery will be able to join us then. *'daremos aquí una pequeña cena en su honor ... a la que nos gustaría mucho que asistiesen ustedes'*

Would you be free for lunch one day next week? *'podríamos almorzar juntos'*

We are planning a trip to Norway, probably in June for two weeks, and wonder if you would like to join us. *'hemos pensado que a lo mejor podrías venir con nosotros'*

Would you be interested in coming with us to the Lake District? *'¿te interesaría venir con nosotros?'*

Why don't you come over for a weekend and let us show you Sussex? *'¿por qué no te vienes a pasar un fin de semana?'*

... Y RESPUESTAS

It was so kind of you to invite me to meet James Glasgow and I shall be happy to come to dinner that evening/but I am afraid that I cannot accept your invitation to dinner. *'le agradezco mucho su amabilidad al (+ infin) ... tendré mucho gusto en asistir/lo siento, pero no me es posible aceptar la invitación'*

Thank you for inviting me – I accept with the greatest of pleasure. *'gracias por la invitación, que acepto con gran placer'*

It is very kind of you to invite me, and I shall be very pleased to come. *'son ustedes muy amables; me será muy grato aceptar su invitación'*

Thank you so much for your kind invitation to dinner on Saturday – unfortunately George and I will be out of town that weekend, and so I am afraid we have to refuse. *'muchas gracias por ... Por desgracia estaremos fuera ... aun sintiéndolo mucho, no nos será posible asistir'*

I am terribly sorry, but I shan't be able to come on Saturday. *'lo siento muchísimo, pero no podré ir el sábado'*

REDACCIÓN

LÍNEAS GENERALES DEL ARGUMENTO

Para presentar el tema

It is often said *o* **It is often asserted** *o* **It is often claimed that** the youth of today doesn't care for anything but pleasure.	*se suele decir que*
It would be universally acknowledged that unemployment is the greatest scourge of our days.	*todo el mundo reconoce que*
It is a truism *o* **It is a commonplace that** nothing of value is achieved without dedication.	*es un tópico decir que*
It is undeniably true that war springs from greed.	*es innegable que*
It is a well-known fact that children up to the age of three have no concept of extension in time.	*es un hecho conocido que*
For the great majority of people, literature is a subject that is studied in school but which has no relevance to life as they know it.	*para la inmensa mayoría de la gente*
It is sometimes forgotten that investment is essential for economic growth.	*a veces se olvida que*
It would be naïve to suppose that all politicians act in the public interest all of the time.	*sería ingenuo suponer que*
It would hardly be an exaggeration to say that carelessness is the reason for all road accidents.	*no sería exagerado decir que*
There are several aspects to the problem of understanding Shakespearean comedy.	*hay diversas facetas en el problema de*
A problem that is often debated nowadays is that of world famine and how to deal with it.	*un problema que se discute a menudo hoy día es el de*
The question of whether Hamlet was really mad has occupied critics for generations.	*el tema de ...*
The concept of existentialism **is not an easy one to grasp.**	*no es fácil captar lo que es ...*
The idea of getting rich without too much effort **has universal appeal.**	*una idea que atrae a todo el mundo es la de*
We live in a world in which capitalism seems triumphant.	*vivimos en un mundo en el que ...*
One of the most striking features of this problem (*o* **issue** *o* **topic** *o* **question**) is the way it arouses strong emotions. // **One of the most striking aspects of ...**	*una de las características más interesantes del problema* (or *del asunto* or *del tema* or *de la cuestión)*
A number of key issues arise from this statement.	*... plantea cierto número de cuestiones fundamentales*
History provides numerous instances of misguided national heroes who eventually did more harm than good.	*la historia nos presenta numerosos ejemplos de*
It is hard to open a newspaper nowadays without being faced (*o* **confronted**) **with** some new example of mindless violence.	*es difícil hoy día abrir un periódico sin encontrar noticias de*
What this question boils down to is: was Eliot at heart more of a philosopher than a poet?	*esta cuestión se reduce esencialmente a lo siguiente:*
What can we make of a somewhat sweeping assertion like this? It would be dangerous to reject it in its entirety without ...	*¿cómo se puede entender una generalización de este tipo?*
First of all, let us try to understand what the writer really means.	*en primer lugar, tratemos de entender ...*
It is easy enough to make broad generalisations about the evils of alcohol, **but in reality the issue is an extremely complex one.**	*es relativamente fácil hablar en términos generales de ..., pero en realidad este tema es muy complejo*
This statement **merits closer examination.** We might ask ourselves why ...	*merece ser analizado con cuidado*
The public in general tends to believe that all education is a good thing, without regard to the quality of that education.	*el público en general se inclina a creer que*
What we are mainly concerned with here is the confict between what the hero says and what he does.	*el tema principal que nos ocupa en esta ocasión es el de ...*
It is often the case that truth is stranger than fiction, and never more so than in this instance.	*suele suceder que*
By way of introduction, let us give a brief review of the background to this question.	*a manera de introducción*
We commonly think of people **as** isolated individuals, but in fact few of us ever spend more than an hour or two of our waking hours alone.	*se suele pensar en ... en términos de*
It is surprising that faith survives at all, far less that it should flourish, **in an industrialised society like ours.**	*en una sociedad industrializada como la nuestra*

Para comenzar el desarrollo de los argumentos o presentar una tesis

The first thing that needs to be said is that the author is presenting a one-sided, even bigoted, view.	*lo primero que hace falta decir es que*
What should be established at the very outset is that we are dealing here with a practical rather than a philosophical issue.	*debe quedar bien sentado desde el principio que*
First of all, let us consider the advantages of urban life.	*en primer lugar, consideremos*
Let us begin with *o* **I propose to consider first** the social aspects of this question.	*comencemos por // voy a considerar en primer lugar*
Let us see if there is any real substance in this claim (*o* **assertion** *o* **statement**).	*veamos si hay fundamento en esta afirmación*
Was Othello a naïve man or not? This is a question **at which we must take a careful** (*o* **close**) **look**, before we ...	*... que debemos examinar con atención*
An argument in support of this approach is that it does in fact produce practical results.	*en apoyo de este enfoque se puede decir que*
We are often faced in daily life with the choice between our sense of duty and our own personal inclinations.	*en la vida real nos vemos muchas veces ante la necesidad de escoger entre*
Even the most superficial look at this issue raises fundamental questions about the nature and purpose of human existence.	*incluso una primera consideración del tema suscita ya cuestiones fundamentales acerca de*
We must distinguish carefully between the two possible interpretations of this statement.	*debemos distinguir cuidadosamente entre*
This brings us to the question of whether the language used is appropriate to the task the author sets himself.	*esto nos lleva a la consideración de si*
It is interesting to consider how far this is true of other nations.	*es interesante considerar*
One might mention, **in support of the above thesis,** the striking speech of Frederick in Act III.	*en apoyo de la tesis ya mencionada*
The second reason for advocating this course of action is that it benefits the community at large.	*la segunda razón a favor de*
Another telling argument in support of this viewpoint **is that** it makes sense economically.	*otro argumento de peso es el de que*
An important aspect of Milton's imagery **is** the play of light and shade.	*un aspecto importante de ... es ...*
It would be reasonable to assume that the writer is sincere in his praise of such behaviour.	*sería razonable suponer que*
The fundamental reason for believing this assumption to be true is that subsequent events seem to prove it.	*la razón fundamental por la que se debe pensar que esta tesis es correcta es que*
We need not concern ourselves here with the author's intentions in disclosing these facts so early in the book.	*no es necesario que, al tratar este tema, nos preocupemos por*
It is now time to discuss the character of Sir James, and how this develops during the course of the first act.	*pasemos ahora a ocuparnos de*
When we speak of culture, **we have in mind** the development of the human spirit and its expression in various ways.	*cuando hablamos de ... pensamos en ...*
I will confine myself to a brief outline of the problem, looking more particularly at how it affects the poorer countries of Africa.	*me conformaré con presentar esquemáticamente*
I am not here concerned with the undoubted difficulties and pitfalls inherent in the introduction of a new form of examination in secondary education.	*no entra en mi propósito examinar ahora*
It is worth stating at this point that the position is exactly the same in most other countries.	*al llegar a este punto se hace necesario afirmar que*
Finally, there is the related problem of how to explain the concept of original sin.	*finalmente, debemos mencionar el problema, que está relacionado con el anterior, de*

Para presentar un punto de vista diferente, o una antítesis

On the other hand, it is observable that people do not normally behave like this in practice.	*por otra parte, se puede observar que*
It may be asserted, however, that this is a superficial point of view.	*se puede afirmar, sin embargo, que*
The other side of the coin is, however, that free enterprise may create economic chaos in certain circumstances.	*la otra cara de la moneda, no obstante, es que*
Another way of looking at this question is to consider its social implications.	*otra manera de enfocar el tema sería*
The snag about this argument is that it undermines the principles of free speech.	*el problema que plantea este argumento es que*
The author says it is style that matters. **The very opposite may be true.**	*es posible que la verdad sea totalmente diferente.*
The claim she makes **has much to recommend it, but** it goes too far.	*... tiene su valor, pero ...*
It is difficult to share the writer's belief (*o* **view** *o* **opinion**) **that** with a little goodwill everything comes right in the end.	*es difícil compartir la opinión del autor de que*
To say that Parker's death was fortuitous **is,** however, **a totally unjustified assumption.**	*... constituye un supuesto que está totalmente sin justificar*
In actual fact it would be more accurate to say that the fault lies in the monetary system itself.	*en realidad sería más exacto decir que*
All this may well be true enough, but we should not forget the victim herself.	*es muy posible que todo esto sea cierto, pero*
If you consider the author's real intentions, **this argument is an extremely weak one.**	*... este argumento carece de solidez*
Hackneyed arguments of this kind are scarcely convincing even in the popular press, far less in a work which claims to have been seriously researched.	*los argumentos manidos, como éste,*
Paradoxical though it may seem, we must look for good in evil itself, for without that evil, how may good be identified?	*aunque resulte paradójico*
It will be objected that punctuality, or at least a semblance of it, is necessary for civilised life.	*se objetará que*
The difficulty about supporting this statement **is that** the facts appear to contradict it.	*es difícil ... porque ...*

Para sugerir la solución o presentar una síntesis

The fact of the matter is surely that *o* **The truth of the matter is surely that** television presentation does influence voting patterns.	*lo cierto, sin duda alguna, es que*
We have now established certain principles, but when all is said and done **it must be acknowledged that** a purely theoretical approach to social issues is sterile.	*hay que reconocer que*
How can we reconcile these two apparently contradictory viewpoints?	*cómo se pueden reconciliar*
Of all these attempts to explain the playwright's intentions, **the last seems to offer the most convincing explanation.**	*... este último parece ofrecer la explicación más convincente*
There is much to be said on both sides of this question. On balance (*o* **On reflection**), **however,** the arguments for the local rather than the national approach **have most to recommend them.**	*los dos lados de la cuestión cuentan con puntos a favor. Sin embargo, en última instancia parece que ... presentan más puntos positivos que negativos*
If one weighs the pros and cons (of the case), the argument for freedom of speech in these circumstances is hard to sustain.	*si se sopesan los pros y los contras*
One might be tempted to think that better technology is the solution, but **in actual fact** human attitudes are the vital element.	*... en realidad ...*
It is easy to believe that this could never happen in a civilized society, **but the truth is that** it happens everywhere, and it happens more and more often.	*... pero la verdad es que*
From all this it follows that these claims are false.	*de todo lo cual se sigue que*
The key to this whole problem must surely be the development of heavy industries in that part of the country.	*la clave del problema está sin duda en*
The social and economic **consequences of the facts we have mentioned above** are too important to ignore.	*las consecuencias ... de los hechos que hemos mencionado anteriormente*
These two points of view, **while distinct, are not mutually exclusive.**	*... aunque son diferentes, no se excluyen el uno al otro*
In the final analysis, the themes of the novel are confused.	*en última instancia*
To recap *o* **To sum up,** the cost of raw materials is falling faster than was ever expected in the early 1980s.	*para resumir: ...*

La conclusión

What conclusions can be drawn from all this?	*qué conclusiones se pueden sacar de*
The most sensible (*o* **satisfactory** *o* **convincing) conclusion we can come to** is that the author has not succeeded in putting his message across.	*la conclusión más satisfactoria a que se puede llegar es decir que*
All this goes to show that it is unwise to make generalisations about human beings.	*todo lo cual sirve para demostrar que*
Surely the lesson to be learned from what has happened in Europe is that minorities should be respected.	*sin duda, la consecuencia que se puede sacar de*
The inescapable conclusion which emerges from what I have said is that health is too important to leave to the doctors.	*la conclusión inevitable que se deduce de todo lo dicho es que*
The problem we have considered **clearly does not admit of an easy solution, but** it is to be hoped that governments will take steps to ameliorate its worst effects.	*está claro que el problema que hemos analizado no tiene fácil solución, pero ...*
This brief account of the origin of the play is necessarily limited in scope.	*esta breve exposición de*
The relations between the hero and heroine appear complex, but **to put the whole matter in a nutshell**, they are both more interested in power than in love.	*... para decirlo en una palabra*
Ultimately, then, these two approaches are impossible to reconcile.	*en última instancia, pues, ...*
All in all, we must acknowledge that the main interest of the book lies in its treatment of jealousy.	*en conjunto*
The play no doubt has an important message: nevertheless, **at the end of the day, it must be acknowledged that** it is a very bad play.	*... al final hay que reconocer que*
The best way of summing up the arguments I have put forward for equality of opportunity is that human rights have precedence over social inhibitions.	*la mejor forma de resumir*
It would appear, then, that in a sane society nobody would be a social outcast.	*según parece, pues, ...*
I have demonstrated that Cox's claims are based on a false assumption.	*según he demostrado, ...*
To sum up, I believe that urgent action is needed.	*en resumen*

LA ESTRUCTURA DEL PÁRRAFO

Secuencia de ideas dentro del párrafo

This brings us to the question of whether we can believe in a benevolent deity.	*esto nos lleva a enfrentarnos con el tema de si*
On the one hand, wealth corrupts: **on the other,** it can achieve great things.	*por una parte ...; por otra ...*
As for the theory of value, it counts for nothing in this connection.	*en cuanto a*
Compared with the heroine, Alison is an insipid character.	*en comparación con*
In the first (*o* **second** *o* **third** *etc*) **place**, let us consider the style of the novel.	*en primer* (etc) *lugar*
First of all, I will outline the benefits of the system: **next,** I propose to examine its disadvantages: **finally,** we will consider the views of the recipients.	*comenzaré por ...; luego, ...; y finalmente, ...*
The arguments in favour of this theory **fall into two groups: first,** those which rely on statistics, and **secondly,** those based on principle.	*pertenecen a dos categorías diferentes: primero ...; y segundo, ...*
Incidentally, we must not forget the contribution of Horatio to this scene.	*por cierto que no debemos olvidar*
As far as the character of Tyson **is concerned,** we can only admire his persistence.	*en lo que se refiere a*
Over and above all these considerations, there is the question of whether the country can afford such luxuries.	*por encima de todas estas consideraciones está*
Added to that, there is his remarkable sense of detail.	*por añadidura,*
Similarly, a good historian will never be obsessed with dates.	*de forma parecida*
There is a fundamental difference between people who act from the heart and those who act from the head.	*hay una diferencia fundamental entre*
There are important differences between these two approaches – differences which we ignore at our peril.	*existen diferencias importantes entre*
In the field of education it is clear that we have not learned by our mistakes.	*en el campo de la pedagogía,*
From the earliest days of nuclear development, it was plain that the potential danger of the process was perhaps the most important single aspect.	*desde los albores de*
Once, **many decades ago,** a foreign observer commented that English people were incapable of discussing principles.	*... hace decenas de años*
The alternative is to accept the world as it is, and concentrate one's efforts on one's own spiritual development.	*la alternativa es*
A further complication is that the characters on stage at this point include the music master himself.	*una complicación adicional es que*
He considers the effect of this on the lives of the people, **as well as** on the economy of the country.	*... además de*
Also, there is the question of how this may be validated.	*además, está*
The book has considerable depth: **equally,** it has style.	*... en igual medida*
As regards *o* **As for** the habits of foreigners, **one may observe that** they are very like our own.	*en cuanto a ... se observa que*
In order to clear the ground, I will give a brief account of Mason's theory.	*para despejar el terreno*
The problem is how to explain why people behave as they do.	*el problema está en explicar*

Para presentar un punto de vista personal

My own view of this is that the writer is quite wrong in this assertion.	*lo que pienso sobre el tema es que*
That is the popular viewpoint, but **speaking personally** I cannot see its logic.	*desde mi punto de vista personal, ...*
Jennings is, **it seems to me,** over-optimistic in his claim that no one is ever hurt by such wheeling and dealing.	*a mí me parece que*
My personal opinion of this argument is that it lacks depth.	*mi opinión personal sobre ... es que*
The author argues for patriotism, but **I feel strongly that** this is a delusion.	*estoy firmemente convencido de que*
In my opinion, nearly everybody overestimates the size of the problem.	*en mi opinión*
For my part, I cannot discount what their spokesman said.	*por mi parte*
I maintain that no one has the right to deprive these people of their home.	*yo soy partidario de la tesis de que*

Para presentar el punto de vista de otra persona

The writer **asserts** (*o* **claims** *o* **maintains** *o* **states) that** intelligence is conditioned by upbringing.	*el autor afirma que*
They would have us believe that the market is fair.	*desean convencernos de que*
The official view is that this cannot affect the population adversely.	*el punto de vista oficial es que*
The author **gives us to understand that** his main aim is merely to please.	*el autor nos da a entender que*
The position was put, with commendable clarity, by James Armitage, in a classic essay on this subject some years ago.	*el tema quedó explicado con toda claridad por*
When one considers the man's achievements, **the portrait of him painted in this volume** amounts to little more than a calumny.	*la imagen de él que se presenta en este libro*
The writer **puts the case for** restrictions on the freedom of speech very persuasively.	*presenta los argumentos a favor de*
The House of Commons, **it has been said,** is like an elephant's trunk: it can fell an oak or pick up a pin.	*según se ha dicho*
This line of thinking leads the author into the dangerous territory of feminist polemics.	*esta manera de pensar*
The animals are perhaps more attractive – **which brings us to another side of the question**: can the human race survive?	*lo cual nos lleva a otro aspecto del tema:*
The writer here **is clearly concerned to** convey her conviction that life is seldom worth living, and never worth living to the full.	*está claro que lo que desea es*
The author **draws our attention to the fact that** nowhere in the world is the soil so poor.	*trata de dirigir nuestra atención al hecho de que*
What this character **is really saying is that** he disagrees with the foundations of religious belief.	*lo que dice en realidad ... es que*
According to the writer, these figures are inaccurate.	*según el autor*
The speaker is claiming, **if I understand her rightly,** that people do not really care about politics.	*si no me equivoco en la interpretación*

Para poner un ejemplo o aducir una cita

We should consider, **for example** *o* **for instance,** the problems faced by tourists in a strange land.	*por ejemplo*
Take the case of Heathcote in 'Lost Masters'.	*consideremos el caso de*
To illustrate the truth of this, one has only to mention the tragic death of Ophelia.	*para ilustrar esto*
A single, but striking, example of this tendency is the way people dress for parties.	*uno de los ejemplos, interesante por cierto, de*
One instance is enough to show how powerful a device this is.	*basta citar un solo ejemplo para mostrar*
As Chesterton **remarked,** there is a purpose to everything.	*como hizo notar ...*
A recent newspaper article claimed that inflation was now beaten.	*según aseguraba recientemente un artículo periodístico*
Wordsworth **observed with much truth** that daffodils are impressive in large numbers.	*observó, y no le faltaba razón, que*
According to the Prime Minister, our foreign policy is benevolent.	*según*
The writer **makes this point graphically,** by instancing the plight of those whose beliefs clash with the society they belong to.	*ilustra gráficamente este punto*
Writing in 1932, Professor Armour-Jenkins said **that** unemployment had destroyed the minds of one generation, and the bodies of the next.	*en 1932 escribía ... que*
This passage **serves to illustrate** the way in which the writer, more than any other Irish writer of his time, looks sympathetically at the problems of the English middle classes.	*sirve para ilustrar*
Take another example: many thousands of people have been and still are condemned to a life of sickness and pain because the hospital service cannot cope with the demand for its services.	*pongamos otro ejemplo: ...*

DESARROLLO DE LA ARGUMENTACIÓN

Para apoyar un argumento

It is obvious to everyone that Freud is right.	*es evidente para todos que*
What is quite certain is that justice will triumph.	*no hay ninguna duda de que*
The writer **clearly** does not understand the issue.	*está claro que*
The fact of the matter is that nuclear waste is and always will be harmful.	*lo cierto es que*
It is easy to concentrate on this aspect of the problem, but **the real question at issue** is different.	*en realidad aquí se trata de*
The facts speak for themselves: James is guilty.	*los hechos hablan por sí mismos: ...*
Politicians make much of educational aims, but **what we are concerned with here is** the financial resources to achieve these.	*lo que nos preocupa ahora es*
It should be stressed that this is only a preliminary assumption.	*hace falta insistir en que*
It would be ridiculous to assert that any one political doctrine holds the answer to our quest for Utopia.	*sería ridículo pretender que*
Few will dispute the claim that the microchip has changed our lives, although many will wish to take issue with the statement that it has changed them for the better.	*pocas personas negarán que*
It is undoubtedly true that time is money.	*sin lugar a dudas, ...*

Para atenuar un argumento

The new law **could have far-reaching implications for** patterns of crime.	*... podría tener consecuencias importantes en cuanto a*
There might well be an explanation which we have overlooked.	*es posible que haya*
Such a response **suggests that** *o* **might be taken to mean that** the group lacked enthusiasm for the project.	*... sugiere que*
Let us assume (*o* **suppose** *o* **conjecture**) **that** Mary does love Worthington.	*vamos a suponer que*
There is a strong possibility that *o* **There is strong probability that** Worthington loves Mary.	*es muy probable que*
One might reasonably suppose *o* **One might justifiably assume that** such behaviour would be frowned upon in any civilised society.	*no faltaría razón para suponer que*

Para expresar dudas

It is questionable whether the author intended this.	*no es seguro que*
The government's present attitude **raises the whole question of** whether local government can survive in its present form.	*... plantea el tema de*
This line of reasoning **sets a serious question mark against** the future of education.	*... suscita graves dudas sobre*
It remains to be seen (however) whether new techniques can be found in time.	*está por ver (sin embargo) si*
It is to be doubted whether the book is intended to convey a real message.	*se debe dudar que*
It may well be that Johnson is serious in this, but his motives are certainly **questionable.**	*es posible que ..., pero caben muchas dudas sobre ...*
Few people would deny the benefits of such a scheme. **But, it may be urged**, few people would identify the need for it in the first place.	*pero se podría contestar que*
It is certainly true that moral factors are important in this area, **but I wonder whether** the economic background is not more crucial.	*sin duda es cierto que ..., pero yo pienso que quizás*
We can believe the author **up to a point, but** it is hard to be sure that he is right all the time.	*... hasta cierto punto, pero*
In spite of the known facts, there must be serious doubts about the validity of this approach.	*a pesar de la información que tenemos, cabe dudar de ...*
It is certainly possible that *o* **It cannot be ruled out that** the author wished us to believe this.	*bien puede que*
It may be conceded that in this play Hector is a type rather than a person.	*se puede admitir que*
Of course, one could reduce the number of accidents by such a method, **but** we must ask ourselves whether the price is not too high.	*desde luego ..., pero*
Undoubtedly this has improved life for a large section of our society, **but** we must consider carefully the implications of this fact.	*indudablemente ..., pero*
It cannot be denied that the buildings are unusual, **but** whether they are beautiful is quite another matter.	*no se puede negar que ..., pero*

Para expresar acuerdo

Nothing could be more true than this portrayal of the pangs of youthful love.	*nada podría ser más cierto que*
We must acknowledge the validity of the point made by Bevin.	*debemos reconocer*
In a minor sense, however, one is forced to admit that **these criticisms have some validity.**	*hay algo de razón en estas críticas*
It is, **as the writer says,** a totally unexpected event.	*como dice el autor*
Their opponents **are to be congratulated on** the accuracy of their predictions.	*hay que felicitar ... por*
He says, **rightly in my view**, that there is no meaning in this statement.	*en mi opinión con toda la razón*
In Act II, the hero makes **an extremely perspicacious remark** about John's intentions.	*una observación muy perspicaz*

Para expresar desacuerdo

It is hard to agree with the popular view that religious belief is out-of-date.	*es difícil estar de acuerdo con*
This statement **is totally inaccurate** *o* **is very far from the truth** in many respects.	*es absolutamente falso*
Unfortunately, **there is not the slightest evidence to justify such a claim.**	*esta afirmación carece totalmente de justificación*
This argument **offers no solution to** the problems which have beset the artist from time immemorial.	*... no presenta ninguna solución para*
This is clearly a false view of the poet's intentions.	*es evidente que se trata de una deformación de*
The pessimistic view of life **should not go unchallenged.**	*debemos tratar de rebatir ...*
This simplistic notion of Shakespeare's aim **is quite unconvincing.**	*este interpretación simplista de ... no puede convencer a nadie*
I find it impossible to accept the philosophical argument for this.	*me parece imposible aceptar*

Para recalcar algún punto concreto

Let us be clear that the essential question is not one of money.	*hay que dejar bien claro que*
It should never be forgotten that the writer belongs to his own times.	*no se debe olvidar nunca que*
It is hard to overemphasize the importance of keeping an open mind.	*no se puede insistir demasiado en la importancia de*
This disaster **underlines the importance of** good safety measures.	*... demuestra la importancia de*
Most important of all, we must understand the feelings of the victims.	*lo que importa más que nada es que*
The reasoning behind this conclusion **deserves especial consideration.**	*... merece consideración especial*
Not only does this passage enlighten us, **but it also** inspires us.	*no sólo ... sino que también ...*
It is well worth noting the background to this argument.	*merece la pena fijarse en*
It is essential to realise that the problem will not be solved by more spending.	*es esencial que nos demos cuenta de que*
This scene is a difficult one, **especially in view of** the unlikely background events.	*sobre todo si se tiene en cuenta*
Next **I wish to focus our attention on** the use of dramatic irony.	*deseo concentrarme en ...*
What is more, the argument lacks conviction.	*lo que es más*
It is no coincidence that law comes before order in the popular mind.	*no es simple coincidencia que*
Another argument supports this thesis: without the contribution which the working married woman makes to the economy, taxes would rise immediately.	*hay otro argumento que podría servir para reforzar la tesis:*
The chief feature of this scheme is its emphasis on equality of opportunity rather than material goods.	*la característica principal*
Let us remember that any chain is only as strong as its weakest link.	*recordemos que*
Moreover, it was significant that the Conference rejected the call for peace at any price.	*es más, lo significativo fue que*
Virginia Woolf's attitude to this, as to many things, **is particularly interesting in that** it reflects the artist's sense of isolation.	*... lo que tiene especial interés es que*

CONTENTS

(Spanish-English section)

ÍNDICE DE MATERIAS

(sección inglés-español)